FICTION
CORE COLLECTION

CORE COLLECTION SERIES

FORMERLY
STANDARD CATALOG SERIES

SHAUNA GRIFFIN, MLIS, GENERAL EDITOR

CHILDREN'S CORE COLLECTION

GRAPHIC NOVELS CORE COLLECTION

MIDDLE AND JUNIOR HIGH CORE COLLECTION

PUBLIC LIBRARY CORE COLLECTION: NONFICTION

SENIOR HIGH CORE COLLECTION

YOUNG ADULT FICTION CORE COLLECTION

FICTION
CORE COLLECTION
TWENTY-FIRST EDITION

EDITED BY
KENDAL SPIRES

H. W. Wilson
A Division of EBSCO Information Services, Inc.
Ipswich, Massachusetts
2022

GREY HOUSE PUBLISHING

Cover: iStock

ISBN 978-1-63700-061-8

The Dewey Decimal Classification is © 2003-2017 OCLC Online Computer Library Center, Inc. Used with Permission. DDC, Dewey, Dewey Decimal Classification and WebDewey are registered trademarks/service marks of OCLC Online Computer Library Center, Inc.

Fiction Core Collection, Twenty-first Edition, published by Grey House Publishing, Inc., Amenia, NY, under exclusive license from EBSCO Information Services, Inc.

CONTENTS

Preface vii

Purpose and Organization xi

Acknowledgments. xv

Part 1.

    List of Fictional Works 1

Part 2.

    Author, Title, and Subject Index 833

PREFACE

FICTION CORE COLLECTION is a curated list of essential and recommended classic and contemporary works of adult fiction either written in or translated to English. Developed by a team of skilled librarians, this list of recommended titles will be helpful to all libraries to develop their collection serving general adult readers. This volume is designed to assist with collection development and maintenance, help locate curriculum and programming materials, provide helpful purchasing and bibliographic information, and assist in readers' advisory support. It is drawn from the database of the same name available from EBSCO Information Services, which has an additional two recommendation levels, Lexile measures, and book reviews and articles.

What's in this Edition?

This 21st edition of the FICTION CORE COLLECTION emphasizes equity, diversity, and inclusion, representing and reflecting a varied community in which many voices can be heard. Our team of librarians continues to provide a significant review of titles to ensure that older, outdated books have been removed in favor of more relevant recommendations. The result is more than 7,000 fiction titles in all genres, as well as short story collections, anthologies, and classics.

Beginning with the 20th edition, book records in FICTION CORE COLLECTION now include subject headings. New metadata includes precise genres and subgenres as well as subject headings that consistently include both location and time period where appropriate. Books will be much easier to find through the index, and the metadata associated with each record offers better insight into the contents of the book.

Additionally, we have increased the number of awards and short lists; all entries for titles in series will also include the name of that series.

As always, a star (★) at the start of an entry indicates that a book is an Essential title, our highest recommendation level. These titles are the essential books in a given category or on a given subject; while there are often a number of recommended titles, this designation helps users who want only a small selection. Non-starred entries represent Recommended titles, which provide a fuller list of recommended books. This is reflected in both the List of Fictional Works section and, for the first time, in the Index as well.

History

The first appearance of fiction selections for adults was in 1923, with the publication of the Fiction Section. This was followed by supplements in 1928 and 1931, but fiction was omitted from the first edition of the complete "Standard Catalog" in 1934, which contained only recommendations for adult nonfiction. A new expanded edition of the Fiction Section was published as FICTION CATALOG in 1942. In its preface, that catalog was referred to as "a companion volume to the Standard Catalog for Public Libraries."

The collection subsequently evolved, along with other Core Collections, into an online resource called WilsonWeb. EBSCO Information Services acquired H.W. Wilson in 2011, and the collections became EBSCOhost databases in 2012. In 2020, the readers' advisory experts at NoveList applied their expertise: while Core Collections continues to provide impartial collection development guidance by experts in their fields, this marriage of readers advisory and collection development expertise strengthened the application of genre and subject headings, expanded awards content, and improved search and browse capabilities in the online Core Collections databases.

FICTION CORE COLLECTION
TWENTY-FIRST EDITION

Scope

The items in the FICTION CORE COLLECTION are considered appropriate for libraries serving adult readers and have been selected by collection development specialists with expertise in fiction, using guidance from review sources and the advice of librarian advisors. FICTION CORE COLLECTION includes novels deemed to have lasting value to readers as well as new literary and genre titles. Both classic novels that remain significant achievements and perennially popular titles appear here, as do those that that appeal to readers from a variety of backgrounds and with a variety of reading interests. The Core Collection excludes non-English-language materials; however, there are many works of translation in this volume.

FICTION CORE COLLECTION is a guide to works of fiction only. Users who seek literary criticism, literary history, biographies of authors, and books on the writing of fiction should instead use the companion publication PUBLIC LIBRARY CORE COLLECTIONS: NONFICTION. At this time, graphic novels are not included; users who wish to find recommendations on graphic novels should use GRAPHIC NOVELS CORE COLLECTION.

Books are listed with an ISBN—most frequently for a hardcover edition published in the United States, or published in Canada or the United Kingdom and distributed in the U.S. Out-of-print titles are retained in the belief that good books are not obsolete simply because they happen to go out of print.

The Database

This Core Collection is derived from the database available from EBSCO Information Services. Metadata for the titles in this volume is provided by the metadata librarians at NoveList, who manage and apply a controlled vocabulary that adapts as terms come in and out of style, or as events require new ones. There are additional, browsable access points, plus full-text book reviews and articles, full-color cover art, Lexile measures, and all of the *Supplemental* book recommendations and *Weeded* titles. It is updated weekly. For more information or for a free trial, contact your EBSCO or NoveList sales rep, or visit https://www.ebscohost.com/novelist/our-products/core-collections. EBSCO also invites feedback from Core Collections customers at novelist@ebsco.com.

Preparation

Books included in Core Collections are selected by experienced librarians representing public library systems, school libraries, and academic libraries across the United States and Canada, as well as NoveList staff. These librarians also act as a committee of advisors on library policy, trends, and special projects. The names of participating librarians and their affiliations are listed in the Acknowledgements. EBSCO invites feedback from Core Collections customers at novelist@ebsco.com.

Core Collections Products

For recommendations for children's books, librarians are encouraged to investigate the following databases and their associated print versions:

CHILDREN'S CORE COLLECTION
MIDDLE AND JUNIOR HIGH CORE COLLECTION
SENIOR HIGH CORE COLLECTION

For adult nonfiction for the general reader, try the database NONFICTION CORE COLLECTION or the associated print volume PUBLIC LIBRARY CORE COLLECTION: NONFICTION. For fiction, please use FICTION CORE COLLECTION, either as a database or the associated print version.

For Graphic Novels for all ages, try the GRAPHIC NOVEL CORE COLLECTION in print or database form, which includes both fiction and nonfiction recommendations.

PURPOSE AND ORGANIZATION

PURPOSE

CORE COLLECTIONS is designed to serve a number of purposes:

As an aid in purchasing. Core Collections assists in the selection and ordering of titles. Summaries and evaluative excerpts are provided for each title along with information regarding the publisher, ISBN, page count, and publication year. In evaluating the suitability of a work, each library will want to consider the needs of the unique patron base it serves.

As an aid in verification of information. For this purpose, bibliographical information is provided in the Classified List of Works. Entries also include recommended subject headings based on NoveList's proprietary subject vocabulary. Notes may describe editions available and other content; for the most up-to-date metadata, please consult the EBSCOhost database.

As an aid in curriculum or programming support. The classified approach, subject indexing, annotations, and evaluative excerpts are helpful in identifying materials appropriate for classroom support, for book discussions, and other programming.

As an aid in collection maintenance. Information about titles available on a subject facilitates decisions to rebind, replace, or discard items. If a book has been demoted to the Supplemental or Weed recommendation levels and therefore no longer appears in the print abridgement of the database, that demotion is not intended as a sign that the book is no longer valuable or that it should necessarily be weeded from your library's collection.

As an aid in professional development or instruction. The Core Collection is useful in courses or professional training that deal with collection development and readers' advisory; it may also be used in courses that deal with literature and book selection, especially in the creation of bibliographies and reading lists.

As an aid to readers' advisory. Every title in this Core Collection is a recommended work and can be given with confidence to a user who expresses a need based on topic, genre, etc. Readers' advisory and user service are further aided by series and awards information, by the descriptive summaries and evaluative excerpts from trusted review sources, and by the subject headings in the Title and Subject Index applied by professional metadata librarians at NoveList.

ORGANIZATION

This Core Collection is organized into two parts: a List of Fictional Works and the Indexes.

Part 1. List of Fictional Works

Part 1 lists works of fiction in alphabetical order by last name of the author or by title, if the title is the main entry.

Each listing consists of a bibliographical description. Entries include, where relevant, series names and publication history. Whenever possible, a summary and an evaluative excerpt from a quoted source are also included. The following is an example of a typical entry and a description of its components.

Jones, Tayari

★ An **American** marriage : a novel. Tayari Jones. Algonquin Books of Chapel Hill, 2018. 308 p.

ISBN 9781616201340

1. Marriage 2. African American families 3. False imprisonment 4. Husband and wife 5. Life change events 6. Atlanta, Georgia 7. Louisiana 8. Literary fiction 9. Southern fiction 10. Domestic fiction.

LC 2017030582

ALA Notable Book, 2019; BCALA Literary Award for Fiction, 2019; Library Journal Best Books, 2018; LibraryReads Favorites, 2018; New York Times Notable Book, 2018; Women's Prize for Fiction, 2019; Shortlisted for the International Dublin Literary Award, 2020

When her new husband is arrested and imprisoned for a crime she knows he did not commit, a rising artist takes comfort in a longtime friendship, only to encounter unexpected challenges in resuming her life when her husband's sentence is suddenly overturned.

"Jones crafts an affecting tale that explores marriage, family, regret, and other feelings made all the more resonant by her well-drawn characters and their intricate conflicts of heart and mind." --*Booklist*

The name of the author, Tayari Jones, is given in conformity with NoveList author authorities. The star at the start of the title indicates that this is an *Essential* title. The title of the book is An American marriage. The book was published by Algonquin Books of Chapel Hill in 2018.

The book has 308 pages. If it were part of a series, the series name would follow the page count.

An ISBN (International Standard Book Number) is included to facilitate ordering; however, there will often be many editions and formats of a given title; due to space constraints these ISBNs are not provided in the print edition, though many can be found in the corresponding database. The Library of Congress control number is provided when available.

Next are the awards this title has won, as well as the international and national short lists and best lists the book has appeared on that are tracked by NoveList staff. These are followed by a brief summary, provided in most cases by the publisher, and an excerpt from a critical reviewing source, in this case *Booklist*, that provides a reviewer's perspective on the book. Such summaries and excerpts are useful in evaluating books for selection and in determining which of several books on the same subject is best suited for the individual reader or purchasing library. Notes are also made to describe special features, such as publication history, film adaptations, or series order.

Part 2. Author, Title, and Subject Index

The author, title, and subject index is a single alphabetical list of all the books entered in the Core Collection. Each book can be found under their author entry, as well as by their title entry, which is followed by the name of the author under which the book can be found in Part 1. Books are also listed under their main subjects, as well as under headings for genre. Subject headings are printed in capital letters.

The following are examples of index entries for the book cited above:

Author   **Jones, Tayari**
        ★ *American Marriage: A Novel*
Title   ★ *American Marriage: A Novel.* Jones, Tayari
Subject   **LITERARY FICTION**
        Jones, Tayari. ★ *American Marriage: A Novel*

ACKNOWLEDGMENTS

H.W. Wilson, NoveList, and EBSCO Information Services express special gratitude to the following librarians who both advised in editorial matters and assisted in the selection and weeding of titles for this Core Collection.

Tracy Babiasz
Acquisitions and Collections Manager
Chapel Hill Public Library
Chapel Hill, NC

Robin Bradford
Collection Development Librarian
Pierce County Library System
Pierce County, WA

Heather Cover
Special Projects Librarian
Homewood Public Library
Homewood, AL

Gail de Vos
Storyteller & Adjunct Instructor, SLIS
University of Alberta
Alberta, Canada

Brian Flota
Humanities Librarian
James Madison University
Harrisonburg, VA

Malia Jackson
Freelance librarian
Bloomington, IN

Natalie Romano
Librarian, Decker Branch
Denver Public Library
Denver, CO

Stephanie Sendaula
Programming & Outreach Specialist
LibraryLinkNJ
New Jersey

James Stubbs
Reference Instructional Librarian
Florence County Library System
Florence, SC

FICTION CORE COLLECTION

Twenty-first Edition

A

Aalborg, Gordon

River of porcupines. G. K. Aalborg. Five Star, 2018. 217 pages
ISBN 9781432838157
1. Fur industry and trade 2. Metis 3. Competition 4. Corporations
5. Voyages and travels 6. Canada 7. 19th century 8. Historical fiction
9. Canadian fiction 10. Australian fiction

LC 2018014288

Spur Awards, Best Western Historical Novel, 2019

In the Rocky Mountain fur trade of the early 1800s, the intense rivalry
between the powerful Hudson's Bay Company and the North-West Company is complicated by the arrival of Ilona Baptiste—a lovely and
much-desired Metis maiden who could become the catalyst for a bloody
trade war between two companies.

Aaronovitch, Ben

Broken homes. Ben Aaronovitch. DAW Books, 2014. 320 p. (Rivers
of London, 4)
ISBN 9780756409609
1. Wizards 2. Murder investigation 3. Detectives 4. Police 5. Stolen
property recovery 6. London, England 7. Urban fantasy 8. Fantasy
mysteries

Sworn to enforce the Queen's Peace, Constable Peter Grant, a magician and keeper of the flame, must discover if a mutilated body found in
Crawley is the work of a common serial killer or an associate of the evil
wizard known as the Faceless Man.

Midnight riot. Ben Aaronovitch. Del Rey, 2011. 336 p. (Rivers of
London, 1)
ISBN 9780345524256
1. Murder investigation 2. Ghosts 3. Witnesses 4. Police 5. Wizards
6. London, England 7. Urban fantasy 8. Fantasy mysteries

When his ability to speak with the lingering dead brings him to the attention of Detective Chief Inspector Thomas Nightingale, who investigates paranormal crimes, Probationary Constable Peter Grant is drawn
into a world where an ancient evil is making a comeback on a rising tide of
murder and dark magic.

Originally published in the UK under the title, Rivers of London.

Moon over Soho. Ben Aaronovitch. Del Rey, 2011. 352 p. (Rivers of
London, 2)
ISBN 9780345524591
1. Jazz musicians 2. Magic 3. Supernatural 4. Detectives 5. Police
6. London, England 7. Urban fantasy 8. Fantasy mysteries

After the death of a part-time jazz drummer, London constable and
sorcerer's apprentice Peter Grant investigates a series of supernatural
deaths in and around Soho that are linked to Peter's dad—a talented trumpet player named Richard "Lord" Grant.

Whispers under ground. Ben Aaronovitch. Del Rey, 2012. 352 p.
(Rivers of London, 3)
ISBN 9780345524614
1. Americans in England 2. Wizards 3. Murder investigation
4. Detectives 5. Urban fantasy 6. Fantasy mysteries

To solve a perplexing murder case, Peter Grant, London constable
and sorcerer's apprentice, must plumb the haunted depths of the oldest,
largest, and deadliest subway system in the world.

Abbott, Jeff

Blame. Jeff Abbott. Grand Central Pub, 2017. 400 p.
ISBN 9781455558438
1. Traffic accidents 2. Amnesia 3. Teenage girls 4. Murder suspects
5. Suicide notes 6. Texas 7. Austin, Texas 8. Thrillers and suspense
9. Adult books for young adults

Two years after a car crash killed her friend and left her with amnesia,
Jane Norton receives an online message from someone claiming to know
what really happened that night, but her search for the truth puts many
lives in danger.

"The unconventional plot, the constant surprises, and above all the
psychological depth of the characters all make this a first-rate crime
novel." —*Kirkus*

The **three** Beths. Jeff Abbott. Grand Central Pub, 2018. 400 p.
ISBN 9781538728697
1. Missing women 2. Teenage girls 3. Suspicion 4. Missing persons
investigation 5. Mothers and daughters 6. Psychological suspense

Glimpsing the devoted mother who went missing and was presumed
dead two years earlier, Mariah discovers that two other women who share
her mother's name have also disappeared.

Abbott, Megan E.

Bury me deep. Megan Abbott. Simon & Schuster, 2009. 224 p.
ISBN 9781416599098
1. Physicians' spouses 2. Extramarital affairs 3. Nurses 4. Gender role
5. Murder 6. Phoenix, Arizona 7. 1930s 8. Noir fiction 9. Historical
fiction 10. Adult books for young adults

LC 2008030676

In the wake of a double murder in which the victims' bodies are concealed in trunks aboard a Los Angeles-bound train, suspicion falls upon a
young blonde woman whose guilt becomes subject to her gender, class,
and ill-advised passion.

"But for all the classic-noir simplicity, such as the use of repetition
rather than elaboration for emphasis, her prose carries an urgency that
brings hardboiled crime fiction kicking and screaming into the modern
age." —*Kirkus*

The **fever**. Megan Abbott. Little Brown & Co, 2014. 240 p.
ISBN 9780316231053
1. High school students 2. Communicable diseases 3. Teenage girls —
Sexuality 4. Rumor 5. Communities 6. Thrillers and suspense 7. Adult
books for young adults
Booklist Editors' Choice: Adult Books for Young Adults, 2014;
School Library Journal Best Books: Best Adult Books 4 Teens, 2014;
Thriller Award for Best Novel, 2015

A small town becomes unraveled after a young teen has a scary, unexplained seizure in her high school class and rumors of a hazardous illness
quickly move through the school and the community, spreading hysteria
and destroying friendships and families.

"Once again, Abbott makes an unforgettable inquiry into the emotional lives of young people, this time balanced with parents own fears and failings. Its also a powerful portrait of community, with interesting echoes of The Crucible." —*Booklist*

★ **Give** me your hand. Megan Abbott. Little Brown & Co, 2018. 352 p.
ISBN 9780316547185
1. Scientists 2. Competition 3. Academic rivalry 4. Secrets 5. Research 6. Psychological suspense 7. Adult books for young adults
Loan Stars Favourites, 2018; LibraryReads Favorites, 2018; Booklist Editors' Choice, 2018
Distancing herself from an intense best friend who inspired her scientific ambitions before divulging a life-changing secret, Kit competes for a dream research job and finds herself in a dangerous game of cat and mouse.

Queenpin: a novel. Megan Abbott. Simon & Schuster Paperbacks, 2007. 192 p.
ISBN 9781416534280
1. Organized crime 2. Gangsters 3. Young women 4. Women criminals 5. Gender role 6. 20th century 7. Noir fiction 8. Crime fiction 9. First person narratives
LC 2006052299
Edgar Allan Poe Award for Best Paperback Original, 2008
Taken under the wing of an infamous mob luminary who reigned during the golden era of such figures as Bugsy Siegel and Lucky Luciano, a bookkeeper from a seedy nightclub finds herself seduced by the lucrative lifestyle of the underworld.
First appeared in the anthology Damn Near Dead (2006)

★ The **turnout:** a novel. Megan Abbott. G. P. Putnam's Sons, 2021. 336 p.
ISBN 9780593084908
1. Dance schools 2. Ballet dancers 3. Sisters 4. Married people 5. Family businesses 6. Psychological suspense
LC 2021013410
When a suspicious accident occurs at their family-run ballet studio just at the onset of the annual performance of The Nutcracker, sisters Dara and Marie Durant find their delicate balance threatened by an interloper.
"This look at the darker side of the dance world demonstrates why Abbott has few peers at crafting moving stories of secrets and broken lives." —*Publishers Weekly*

You will know me: a novel. Megan Abbott. Little, Brown and Company, 2016. 352 p.
ISBN 9780316231077
1. Gymnasts 2. Gymnastics 3. Hit-and-run victims 4. Murder 5. Suspicion 6. Thrillers and suspense 7. Adult books for young adults
LC 2015026542
When a violent death rocks her close-knit gymnastics community weeks before an important competition, the mother of an Olympics hopeful works frantically to hold her family together in spite of being irresistibly drawn to the crime.
"It's vivid, troubling, and powerful—and Abbott totally sticks the landing." —*Booklist*

Abbott, Patricia

Concrete angel. Patricia Abbott. Polis Books, 2015. 320 p.
ISBN 9781940610382
1. Compulsive behavior 2. Mothers and daughters 3. Children of people with mental illnesses 4. Murder 5. Deception 6. 1970s 7. Psychological fiction
Eve Moran will do anything to get the things she wants, disregarding how her actions impact those closest to her, but when she begins to use her three year-old son for personal gain, her daughter Christine vows to stop her.

Abdul-Jabbar, Kareem

The **empty** birdcage. Kareem Abdul-Jabbar and Anna Waterhouse. Titan Books, 2019. 336 pages (Mycroft Holmes novels (Kareem Abdul-Jabbar), 3)
ISBN 9781785659300
1. Serial murder investigation 2. Serial murders 3. Missing persons investigation 4. Missing persons 5. Greed 6. London, England 7. 1870s 8. Historical mysteries 9. Mysteries 10. Adaptations, retellings, and spin-offs
A latest collaboration by the NBA All-Star and the co-creator of On the Shoulders of Giants finds the Holmes brothers on the trail of a killer who leaves victims unmarked, a case that is complicated by a loved one's disappearance.

Mycroft and Sherlock. Kareem Abdul-Jabbar and Anna Waterhouse. Titan Books, 2018. 359 p. (Mycroft Holmes novels (Kareem Abdul-Jabbar), 2)
ISBN 9781785659256
1. Orphanages 2. Opium smuggling 3. Serial murder investigation 4. Race relations 5. Serial murders 6. London, England 7. Trinidad and Tobago 8. 1870s 9. Historical mysteries 10. Mysteries 11. Adaptations, retellings, and spin-offs
Rising War Office star Mycroft Holmes persuades his brother, Sherlock, to volunteer at a best friend's orphanage, where the suspicious death of a street urchin and a mysterious Chinese woman lead the brothers into the London opium trade's dark underside.
"Abdul-Jabbar and Waterhouse again nail the historical ambience, the dialogue, and the plotting, effectively paying tribute to Arthur Conan Doyle but also adding large dollops of humor and romance. This is a wonderful mystery in what one hopes will be a long-running series." —*Booklist*

★ **Mycroft** Holmes. Kareem Abdul-Jabbar and Anna Waterhouse. Titan Books, 2015. 336 p. (Mycroft Holmes novels (Kareem Abdul-Jabbar), 1)
ISBN 9781783291533
1. Crimes against children 2. Murder investigation 3. Secrets 4. Race relations 5. Young men 6. London, England 7. Trinidad and Tobago 8. 1870s 9. Historical mysteries 10. Mysteries 11. Adaptations, retellings, and spin-offs
Fresh out of university, the young Mycroft Holmes is already making a name for himself in government. Yet this most British of civil servants has strong ties to Trinidad, the birthplace of his best friend, Cyrus Douglas, and where his fiancee Georgiana Sutton was raised. Mycroft's comfortable existence is overturned when Douglas receives troubling reports from home, rumors of spirits enticing children to their deaths. Upon hearing the news, Georgiana abruptly departs for the island. Mycroft convinces Douglas that they should follow her, drawing the two men into a web of dark secrets that grows more treacherous with each step they take.
"The authors hit all the right notes here, combining fascinating historical detail (on Trinidadian culture and folklore, on tobacco importation in London, even on the development of the Gatling gun) with rousing adventure, including some cleverly choreographed fight scenes and a pair of protagonists whose rich biracial friendship, while presented realistically, given the era (Douglas must sometimes pose as a butler), is the highlight of the book." —*Booklist*

Abe, Kobo

The **woman** in the dunes. Kobo Abe; translated from the Japanese by E. Dale Saunders; with drawings by Machi Abe. Knopf Publishing Group, 1991. 239 pages.

ISBN 9780679733782

1. Women teachers 2. Widows 3. Entomologists 4. Scientists 5. Imprisonment 6. Allegories 7. Translations

The inhabitants of a remote seaside village imprison a Japanese biologist in a deep sand pit.

Kobo Abe is a pseudonym of Kimifusa Abe.

Aboulela, Leila

Elsewhere, home. Leila Aboulela. Black Cat, 2019. 224 p.
ISBN 9780802129130

1. Identity (Psychology) 2. Muslim women 3. Alienation (Social psychology) 4. Stereotypes (Social psychology) 5. Cultural differences 6. Khartoum, Sudan 7. Great Britain 8. Short stories 9. Literary fiction
LC 2018047042

A collection of short stories celebrates life as an immigrant abroad and the challenges of navigating assimilation and difference.

Abraham, Tola Rotimi

Black Sunday. Tola Rotimi Abraham. Catapult, 2020. 240 p.
ISBN 9781948226561

1. Twin sisters 2. Self-discovery in women 3. Family problems 4. Poverty 5. Separated friends, relatives, etc. 6. Lagos, Nigeria 7. Nigeria 8. 1990s 9. Literary fiction 10. Domestic fiction 11. Multiple perspectives

Kirkus Prize for Fiction finalist, 2020

Joining a new church in 1996 Lagos in the face of impoverishing losses, twins Bibike and Riyike find their bond challenged by wrenching hardships, a father's reckless choice and their respective views on independence.

"The novel's strength lies in its lush, unflinching scenes, as when a seemingly simple infection leads gradually but inexorably to a life-threatening condition, revealing the dynamics of the family and community along the way. Abraham mightily captures a sense of the stresses of daily life in a family, city, and culture that always seems on the edge of self-destruction." —*Publishers Weekly*

Abrams, David

Fobbit. David Abrams. Black Cat, 2012. 384 p.
ISBN 9780802120328

1. Iraq War, 2003-2011 2. Military bases, American 3. War correspondents 4. Military journalism 5. Spin control (Public relations) 6. Iraq 7. War stories 8. Satirical fiction
LC Bl2012016566

New York Times Notable Book, 2012

At Foreward Operating Base Triumph, a combat-avoiding staff sergeant named Chance Gooding spends his time composing press releases that spin grim events into statements more palatable to the public.

Abrams, Melanie

Meadowlark. Melanie Abrams. Little A, 2020. 240 p.
ISBN 9781542007351

1. Reunions 2. Psychic trauma 3. Childhood friends 4. Memories 5. Secrets 6. Thrillers and suspense

Simrin, a photojournalist, is invited to document the story of Meadowlark, a spiritual commune where children are invited to develop their special "gifts".. During her stay, she discovers that the commune is at the center of a police investigation and soon finds herself caught in a desperate situation.

Abrams, Stacey

While justice sleeps: a novel. Stacey Y. Abrams. Doubleday, 2021. 384 p.
ISBN 9780385546577

1. Ambition in women 2. Law clerks 3. People in comas 4. Conspiracies 5. Biotechnology 6. Washington, D.C. 7. Political thrillers 8. African American fiction
LC 2020046349

LibraryReads Favorites, 2021

Plunged into an explosive role she never anticipated, Avery Keene, now the legal guardian of power of attorney for the legendary Justice Howard Wynn, must unravel the clues he left behind in regards to a dangerous conspiracy that has infiltrated the highest power corridors of Washington.

"The book's plethora of female role models, including a woman chief justice, and its 'inside DC' look at political skullduggery make Abrams's novel a well-informed political and legal narrative." —*Library Journal*

Abu-Jaber, Diana

Birds of paradise: a novel. Diana Abu-Jaber. W. W. Norton & Co, 2011. 384 p.
ISBN 9780393064612

1. Runaway teenagers 2. Family secrets 3. Dysfunctional families 4. Teenage girls 5. Family problems 6. Miami, Florida 7. Psychological fiction 8. Domestic fiction 9. Adult books for young adults
LC 2011014575

In Miami, Avis and Brian Muir are still haunted by the disappearance of their beautiful daughter, Felice, who ran away when she was thirteen. Now, after five years of skateboarding, clubbing, and squatting, Felice is about to turn eighteen. Her family will be forced to confront their anguish, loss, and sense of betrayal. Meanwhile, Felice must reckon with the guilty secret that drove her away, and must face her fear of losing her family and her sense of self forever.

"Abu-Jaber...employs her descriptive talents in bringing Miami to steamy, pulsing life, but it is Birds of Paradise's neither predictable nor merely haphazard momentum and its rich cast of characters that make us feel we're in deliciously capable hands." —*Elle*

Crescent. Diana Abu-Jaber. W.W. Norton & Co, 2003. 352 p.
ISBN 9780393057478

1. Arab American women 2. Cooking, Lebanese 3. College teachers 4. Women cooks 5. Man-woman relationships 6. Los Angeles, California 7. Literary fiction 8. Adult books for young adults
LC 2002152907

An Arab-American Chocolat—a sensual blend of food, love and longing. Populated by colorful and memorable characters—the lovely Sirine; the handsome Han; Sirine's story-telling uncle, whose fantasic fables are woven into the novel; a poet named Aziz; Nadia and her daughter Mireille—Crescent explores the universal themes of love and loyalty to countries old and new, to those left behind, and to tradition.

"Abu-Jaber's language is miraculous, whether describing the texture of Han's skin or Sirine's way with an onion. It is not possible to stop reading." —*Booklist*

Origin: a novel. Diana Abu-Jaber. W. W. Norton & Co, 2007. 384 p.
ISBN 9780393064551

1. Women forensic scientists 2. Identity (Psychology) 3. Infanticide 4. Serial murders 5. Forensic sciences 6. New York (State) 7. Syracuse, New York 8. Mysteries 9. Literary fiction 10. First person narratives 11. Adult books for young adults

LC 2007004963

New York-based fingerprint expert Lena investigates a series of crib deaths that may actually be the work of a serial killer, a case that reminds Lena of the mystery surrounding her own childhood, marked by her orphaned status and her intuitive talents.

"For all its internal chill, the drama that unfolds around fingerprint expert Lena Dawson is a struggle toward spring and the light. Haunting and compelling, Origin combines the traditions of the crime novel with an examination of Lena's unusual upbringing. It's a little film noir, a bit independent-woman-detective thriller, and winningly fresh in its approach." —*PopMatters*

Abulhawa, Susan

The **blue** between sky and water. Susan Abulhawa. Bloomsbury, 2015. 304 p.

ISBN 9781632862211

1. Palestinians 2. Military occupation 3. Life after death 4. Refugees 5. Families 6. Israel 7. Family sagas

While in a refugee camp in Gaza, the women of a Palestinian family are left behind as their men join the resistance and Nazmiyeh—the matriarch and center of a household of sisters, daughters and granddaughters who has a large heart and a zest for life that heals—will do anything to keep them all together.

Acampora, Lauren

The **paper** wasp: a novel. Lauren Acampora. Grove Press, 2019. 240 pages

ISBN 9780802129413

1. Childhood friends 2. Obsession 3. Ambition in women 4. Creativity in women 5. Women artists 6. Los Angeles, California 7. Michigan 8. Literary fiction 9. Second person narratives

LC 2018058112

Traces the dark friendship of twisted ambition shared between a failed artist and a rising star in contemporary Hollywood.

The **wonder** garden. Lauren Acampora. Grove Press, 2015. 288 p.
ISBN 9780802123558

1. Suburban life 2. Connecticut 3. Literary fiction 4. Short stories

Shares the myriad and bizarre secrets of a Connecticut suburb, including a young soon-to-be mother who watches her husband walk away from a fifteen-year career in advertising at the urging of his spirit animal.

"Acampora not only meticulously conveys the allure of an outwardly paradisiacal suburban community, with its perfectly restored Victorian homes and well-tended lawns; she also clearly captures the inner turmoil of its residents, homing in on their darkest impulses and beliefs. Some of the stories' starring characters make cameos in others, adding considerable complexity to the whole." —*Booklist*

Acevedo, Chantel

The **distant** marvels. Chantel Acevedo. Europa Editions, 2015. 304 p.
ISBN 9781609452520

1. Hurricanes 2. Storytelling 3. Courage in women 4. Memory 5. Rebels 6. Cuba 7. 1960s 8. Political fiction
Booklist Editors' Choice, 2015

A professional storyteller imparts the incredible tale of her youth during the Third War of Independence to eight women who need hope to survive Hurricane Flora in 1963 Cuba.

"This extraordinary narrative tells, from these womens perspectives, how war brings lovers together and tears families apart. This is a major, uniquely powerful, and startlingly beautiful novel that should bring Acevedos name to the top echelon of this generations writers." —*Booklist*

Achebe, Chinua

★ **Things** fall apart. Chinua Achebe. Anchor Books, 1994. 209 p.
ISBN 9780385474542

1. Culture conflict 2. Social structure 3. Igbo (African people) 4. Exiles 5. Colonialism 6. Nigeria 7. Historical fiction 8. Modern classics 9. Literary fiction

LC 94013429

Traces the growing friction between village leaders and Europeans determined to save the heathen souls of Africa. But its hero, a noble man who is driven by destructive forces, speaks a universal tongue.

Originally published: London : Heinemann, 1958.

Aciman, Andre

Call me by your name. Andre Aciman. Farrar, Straus and Giroux, 2007. 256 p. (Call me by your name novels, 1)
ISBN 9780374299217

1. First loves 2. Self-discovery in teenage boys 3. Graduate students 4. Summer 5. Gay teenagers 6. Italy 7. LGBTQIA fiction 8. Literary fiction 9. Coming-of-age stories 10. Adult books for young adults

LC 2006011720

Lambda Literary Award for Gay Men's Fiction, 2007; New York Times Notable Book, 2007

The sudden and powerful attraction between a teenage boy and a summer guest at his parents' house on the Italian Riviera has a profound and lasting influence that will mark them both for a lifetime.

Adapted into a film by the same name in 2017.

Enigma variations: a novel. Andre Aciman. Farrar, Straus and Giroux, 2017. 272 p.
ISBN 9780374148430

1. Desire (Philosophy) 2. Self-awareness 3. Bisexual men 4. First loves 5. Lovers 6. Italy 7. New York City 8. Psychological fiction 9. Literary fiction 10. LGBTQIA fiction

LC 2016020262

Five interconnected tales exploring the contradictory power of love follow the romantic endeavors of Paul, who experiences consuming passion for a girl he meets repeatedly through the years while enduring a spectrum of hopes, denials, fears and regrets.

"Aciman's sensuous, subtle language supports not only his marvelous descriptive power but also how deeply and resonantly he constructs his fondly and fully conceived characters." —*Booklist*

Find me. Andre Aciman. Farrar, Straus and Giroux, 2019. 224 p. (Call me by your name novels, 2)
ISBN 9780374155018

1. Regret 2. Self-discovery in men 3. Homosexuality 4. Monroe, Marilyn 5. Young women — Relations with older men 6. LGBTQIA fiction 7. Literary fiction 8. Adult books for young adults

LC 2019020195

Booklist Editors' Choice, 2019

Elio's father, Samuel, has a chance encounter on the train with a beautiful young woman that upends Sami's plans and changes his life forever. Elio soon moves to Paris, where he, too, has a consequential affair, while

Oliver, now a New England college professor with a family, suddenly finds himself contemplating a return trip across the Atlantic.
A sequel to the 2007 novel Call Me By Your Name.

Harvard square. Andre Aciman. W. W. Norton & Co, 2013. 304 p.
ISBN 9780393088601
1. Immigrants 2. Male friendship 3. Graduate students 4. Taxicab drivers 5. Assimilation (Sociology) 6. Cambridge, Massachusetts 7. 1970s 8. Literary fiction 9. First person narratives
An Egyptian-Jewish Harvard graduate student trying to assimilate into American culture in 1977 befriends an impetuous, loud Arab cab driver and must choose between his dream or his friend.

Acker, Jennifer
★ The **limits** of the world. Jennifer Acker. Delphinium, 2019. 225 pages
ISBN 9781883285777
1. Immigration and emigration 2. Family secrets 3. Immigrant families 4. Intergenerational communication 5. Family relationships 6. United States 7. Nairobi, Kenya 8. Family sagas 9. Multiple perspectives
Acker's debut novel about multigeneration migrations from India to Kenya to the U.S. is ambitious in geographical scope and philosophical engagement.

Ackerman, Elliot
Dark at the crossing. Elliot Ackerman. Alfred A. Knopf, 2017. 272 p.
ISBN 9781101947371
1. Idealism 2. Refugees 3. Civil war 4. Arab Americans 5. Americans in Turkey 6. Turkey 7. Literary fiction
Booklist Editors' Choice, 2017; National Book Award for Fiction finalist, 2017
Presents a contemporary love story set on the Turkish border of Syria, where an Arab American with a conflicted past attempts to join the fight against Bashar al-Assad's regime before the plight of his host family reshapes his loyalties.
"Here is a thriller, psychological fiction, political intrigue, and even a love story all wrapped into a stunningly realistic and sometimes horrifying package." —Library Journal

Red dress in black and white. Elliot Ackerman. Alfred A Knopf, 2020. 288 pages
ISBN 9780525521815
1. Marital conflict 2. Americans in Turkey 3. Extramarital affairs 4. Power (Social sciences) 5. Political corruption 6. Turkey 7. 2010s 8. Literary fiction
The author of Waiting for Eden presents a timely novel set in the course of a single day in Istanbul that depicts how an American woman's efforts to leave her influential Turkish husband become complicated by political corruption.
"Ackerman's trademark prose, defined by stillness and rich descriptions, evocatively captures the strained nature of contemporary Turkish life." —Booklist

★ **Waiting** for Eden: a novel. Elliot Ackerman. Alfred A. Knopf, 2018. 192 p.
ISBN 9781101947395
1. Veterans 2. Consciousness 3. Burn victims 4. War — Psychological aspects 5. Dead 6. Literary fiction 7. First person narratives
LC 2017055697
ALA Notable Book, 2019; Library Journal Best Books, 2018

A veteran enduring life trapped in his own mind begins to find a way to communicate before troubling realities about his marriage come to the surface.

Adam, Claire
Golden child: a novel. Claire Adam. SJP for Hogarth, 2019. 281 pages
ISBN 9780525572992
1. Fathers and sons 2. Rural life 3. Missing teenage boys 4. Poor families 5. Twins 6. Trinidad and Tobago 7. Literary fiction 8. Adult books for young adults
Working exhausting hours in their rural Trinidad home, the family of a petroleum plant worker is shattered by the disappearance of a troubled twin son whose fate forces his father to make a devastating choice.
"Throughout this stunning portrait of Trinidads multicultural diversity, and one familys sacrifices, soaring hopes and ultimate despair, Adam weaves a poetic lightness and beauty that will transfix readers." —Publishers Weekly

Adams, Alina
The **nesting** dolls. Alina Adams. HarperCollins, 2020. 365 p.
ISBN 9780062910943
1. Jewish women 2. Self-fulfillment in women 3. Self-discovery in women 4. Nesting dolls 5. Antisemitism 6. Odesa, Ukraine 7. Siberia 8. 1930s 9. 1970s 10. Family sagas 11. Historical fiction
Spanning 1930s Siberia to contemporary Brighton Beach, a family saga finds three generations of women in a Jewish-Russian family making fateful choices in their respective efforts to break free from historical dynamics and pursue personal fulfillment.
"Adams' sweeping tale offers captivating explorations of her characters and their complexities, particularly when it comes to their struggles between the pull of the heart and the realities in which they live." —Booklist

Adams, Douglas
Dirk Gently's holistic detective agency. Douglas Adams. Simon and Schuster, 1987. 247 p. (Dirk Gently, 1)
ISBN 9780671625825
1. Time travel 2. Private investigators 3. Lost animals 4. Misadventures 5. Gently, Dirk (Fictitious character) 6. Science fiction mysteries 7. Science fiction 8. Humorous stories
LC 879464
There is a long tradition of Great Detectives, and Dirk Gently does not belong to it. But his search for a missing cat uncovers a ghost, a time traveler, and the devastating secret of humankind! Detective Gently's bill for saving the human race from extinction: no charge.
"That Adams manages to bring together his various scenarios and round up his wandering characters shows his skill as a writer. His insightful commentary on the human condition is the hot fudge on this literary banana split." —Booklist
Adapted into a television series on BBC America in 2016.

★ The **hitchhiker's** guide to the galaxy. Douglas Adams. Harmony Books, 1980. 215 p; (Hitchhiker series, 1)
ISBN 9780517542095
1. Misadventures 2. Meaning (Psychology) 3. Life on other planets 4. Aliens (Humanoid) 5. Space flight 6. Science fiction classics 7. Books to TV 8. Books to movies 9. Adult books for young adults
LC 80014572

Chronicles the off-beat and occasionally extraterrestrial journeys, notions, and acquaintances of galactic traveler Arthur Dent.

10th anniversary printing includes introduction by author.

The **restaurant** at the end of the universe. Douglas Adams. Harmony Books, 1980. 245 p. (Hitchhiker series, 2)

ISBN 9780517545355

1. Misadventures 2. Life on other planets 3. Conspiracies 4. Restaurants 5. Aliens (Humanoid) 6. Science fiction 7. Humorous stories

Arthur Dent and Ford Prefect join with Zaphod Beeblebrox, the two-headed former president of the galaxy, in a search for the current ruler of the universe.

"Poor uprooted Arthur Dent finds himself swept along in the wake of Zaphod Beeblebrox, former President of the Galaxy, as Zaphod searches for the man who rules the Universe. They and their companions tumble from one scrape into another, with the erratic aid of Zaphod's dead great-grandfather and Marvin, their perpetually depressed robot. Adams's lively sense of the ridiculous has concocted many hilarious episodes, though the inspired lunacy of the first book has become rather uneven here. Still, this is one of the best pieces of sf humor available." —*Library Journal*

Adams, Henry

★ **Democracy:** an American novel. Henry Adams. H. Holt and company 1908. 374 p.

ISBN 9780375760587

1. Political fiction

LC 8010432

While fighting each other for power, Senate member Silas Ratcliffe actively pursues society widow and government newcomer Mrs. Lightfoot Lee in 1870s Washington, D.C.

Variously attributed by different authorities to Henry Adams, John Hay and Clarence King. cf. W. R. Thayer, Life of John Hay, 1915, v. 2, p. 58-59. The authorship of Adams is affirmed by the publisher Henry Holt in the Unpartizan review, no. 29, Jan.-Mar. 1921, p. 156; and Literary review, Dec. 24, 1920.

Adams, Hope

Dangerous women. Hope Adams. Berkley, 2021. 400 pages

ISBN 9780593099575

1. Women prisoners — Transportation 2. Convict ships 3. Exile (Punishment) 4. Penal colonies 5. Seafaring life 6. Pacific Ocean 7. Australia 8. 1840s 9. Historical fiction 10. Multiple perspectives

LC 2020032010

A debut based on the true story of the 1841 transport ship Rajah follows the experiences of a crew of Englishwomen convicts, sentenced to a distant penal colony for petty crimes, who realize that a killer is among them.

"This variant of the locked-room murder will appeal to readers who enjoy historical fiction centered on women's lives." —*Booklist*

Adams, Lyssa Kay

The **bromance** book club. Lyssa Kay Adams. Jove, 2019. 352 p. (Bromance book club, 1)

ISBN 9781984806093

1. Professional baseball players 2. Marital conflict 3. Book clubs 4. Romantic love 5. Male friendship 6. Nashville, Tennessee 7. Romantic comedies 8. Sports romances 9. Contemporary romances

LC 2019006240

LibraryReads Favorites, 2019

Nashville Legends second baseman Gavin Scott's marriage is in major league trouble. Distraught and desperate, Gavin finds help from an unlikely source: a secret romance book club made up of Nashville's top alpha men. With the help of their current read, a steamy Regency titled Courting the Countess, the guys coach Gavin on saving his marriage.

Adams, Richard

Watership Down. Richard Adams. Macmillan, 1974. 448 p. (Rabbit tales)

ISBN 9780027000306

1. Rabbits 2. Survival 3. Safety 4. Peace 5. Nature 6. Fantasy fiction 7. Books to movies 8. Classics

LC 73006044

California Young Reader Medal, Young Adult, 1977; Carnegie Medal, 1972

In a constant struggle against oppression, a group of rabbits search for peaceful co-existence. Chronicles the adventures of a group of rabbits searching for a safe place to establish a new warren where they can live in peace.

Sequel: Tales from Watership Down.

Includes "Lapine glossary."

Originally published: 1972.

Adams, Sara Nisha

★ The **reading** list. . William Morrow & Co, 2021. 384 p.

ISBN 9780063025288

1. Libraries 2. Books and reading 3. Coping 4. Life change events 5. Widowers 6. London, England 7. England 8. Relationship fiction

LibraryReads Favorites, 2021

Working at the local library, Aleisha reads every book on a secret list she found, which transports her from the painful realities she's facing at home, and decides to pass the list on to a lonely widower desperate to connect with his bookworm granddaughter.

"Adams is a brisk and solid plotter, and has an easy hand with creating characters who are easy to root for. Readers will be charmed and touched." —*Publishers Weekly*

Adams, Taylor

Hairpin Bridge. Taylor Adams. William Morrow & Co, 2021. 320 pages

ISBN 9780063065444

1. Twin sisters 2. Suicide investigation 3. State police 4. Suspicion 5. Secrets 6. Montana 7. Thrillers and suspense 8. Multiple perspectives

Not accepting that her estranged twin sister committed suicide, Lena Nguyen interviews the highway patrolman who allegedly discovered her body, but who is mentioned by name in the last text her sister ever sent.

Adamson, Gil

The **outlander**. Gil Adamson. Ecco, 2008. 389 p.

ISBN 9780061491252

1. Widows 2. Grief in women 3. Murder 4. Voyages and travels 5. Brothers 6. Frank, Alberta 7. Alberta 8. 1900s (Decade) 9. Historical fiction 10. Canadian fiction

LC 200741062

Books in Canada First Novel Award, 2007

After killing her husband, Mary Boulton races toward the mountains while being tormented by visions of the cold-blooded brothers-in-law who pursue her, forcing her to retreat deeper into the wilds of the West and her own imagination.

"Of course, the Girl Being Chased is one of the most enduring figures of chivalric and chauvinistic literature, a staple of television dramas and horror films.... But Gil is short for Gillian, and her strange and complicated heroine has nothing in common with Hollywood's wornout damsels in distress...there are pages here you can't read slowly enough to catch every word." —*Washington Post Book World.*

Originally published in Canada in 2007 by House of Anansi Press—Title page verso.

Addison, Katherine

★ The **goblin** emperor. Katherine Addison. Tor, 2014. 416 p. (Goblin emperor novels, 1)

ISBN 9780765326997

1. Elves 2. Goblins 3. Caste 4. Rulers — Succession 5. Conspiracies 6. Steampunk 7. Fantasy fiction

LC 2013025454

Library Journal Best Books 2014; Locus Award for Fantasy Novel, 2015; RUSA Reading List, 2015

When his estranged father, Emperor Varenechibel of the Elflands, perishes in an airship crash, 18-year-old Maia Drazhar is recalled from exile and proclaimed heir to the Elfin imperial throne of Ethuveraz. Maia, whose late mother was a goblin, is immediately transformed from pariah to messiah—attracting sycophants, schemers, and enemies in short order. If Maia is to survive life at court, let alone rule, he'll need to distinguish false friends from true and use his wits to navigate a treacherous world of conspiracy and political intrigue. Don't miss this unusual combination of high fantasy, mystery, and political drama with steampunk elements.

"There are powerful character studies and a plot full of small but deadly traps among which the sweet-natured, perplexed Maia must navigate. The result is a spellbinding and genuinely affecting drama." —*Kirkus*

A Tom Doherty Associates Book.

Adebayo, Ayobami

★ **Stay** with me. Ayobami Adebayo. Alfred A. Knopf, 2017. 288 p.

ISBN 9780451494603

1. Husband and wife 2. Infertility 3. Marriage 4. Married women 5. Polygamy 6. Nigeria 7. 21st century 8. Literary fiction 9. Domestic fiction 10. Multiple perspectives

New York Times Notable Book, 2017; ALA Notable Book, 2018; Shortlisted for The Baileys Women's Prize for Fiction, 2017

Despite cultural pressures for her husband to take a second wife, Yejide trusts that Akin would never do so... until, after four years of failing to conceive a child, he does. Under constant scrutiny to conceive and keeping secrets from one other, the couple struggles while their marriage falters and the country's political system crumbles. Alternating chapters told from each characters' perspective capture both the agony of would-be parents struggling with infertility, and the broader turmoil in Nigeria during the late 1980s.

"...Adebayo's novel captures how the turmoil of Nigerian life in the 1980s and '90s seeps into the most personal of decisions—to fight for, and protect, one's family. Adebayo's debut marks the emergence of a fine young writer." —*Kirkus*

Originally published: Edinburgh : Canongate, 2017.

Adichie, Chimamanda Ngozi

★ **Americanah**: a novel. Chimamanda Ngozi Adichie. Alfred A. Knopf, 2013. 352 p.

ISBN 9780307271082

1. Immigrants 2. Refugees 3. Nigerians in England 4. Nigerians in the United States 5. Man-woman relationships 6. Nigeria 7. England 8. Political fiction 9. Love stories 10. Literary fiction

LC 2012043875

ALA Notable Book, 2014; Booklist Editors' Choice, 2013; National Book Critics Circle Award for Fiction, 2013; New York Times Notable Book, 2013; Andrew Carnegie Medal for Excellence in Fiction finalist, 2014; Shortlisted for the International Dublin Literary Award, 2015; Shortlisted for The Baileys Women's Prize for Fiction, 2014

Separated by respective ambitions after falling in love in occupied Nigeria, beautiful Ifemelu experiences triumph and defeat in America while exploring new concepts of race, while Obinze endures an undocumented status in London until the pair is reunited in their homeland 15 years later, where they face the toughest decisions of their lives.

"Witty, wry, and observant, Adichie is a marvelous storyteller who writes passionately about the difficulty of assimilation and the love that binds a man, a woman, and their homeland." —*Library Journal*

Half of a yellow sun. Chimamanda Ngozi Adichie. Alfred A. Knopf, 2006. 448 p.

ISBN 9781400044160

1. Civil war 2. Political corruption 3. Postcolonialism 4. Igbo (African people) 5. Thirteen-year-old boys 6. Nigeria 7. Biafra (1967-1970) 8. 1960s 9. Historical fiction 10. Political fiction 11. Literary fiction

LC 2005057784

Booklist Editors' Choice, 2006; Orange Prize for Fiction, 2007; New York Times Notable Book, 2006; Shortlisted for the James Tait Black Memorial Prize for Fiction, 2006; National Book Critics Circle Award for Fiction finalist, 2006

"The author has a gift for capturing the rhythms of African middle-class life: not just its political awareness but the aspirations and cultural imperatives that lend it its varied character.... For its portrayal of Nigeria's political and cultural past, [this book] is a welcome addition to the corpus of African letters." —*Times Literary Supplement*

Film adaptation by the same title (2013).

First published: Great Britain: Fourth Estate, 2006.

Film tie-in.

The **thing** around your neck. Chimamanda Ngozi Adichie. Alfred A. Knopf 2009. 240 p.

ISBN 9780307271075

1. Nigerians in the United States 2. Man-woman relationships 3. Culture conflict 4. Immigrants 5. Nigeria 6. Short stories 7. Literary fiction

A collection of twelve stories includes the tale of a medical student in hiding with a poor Muslim woman, and a woman who discovers a devastating secret about her brother's death.

"The stories are set both in the United States and in Nigeria, where things continue to fall apart.... Adichie, a brilliant writer whose characters stay with you for a long time, deserves to be more widely known." —*Library Journal*

Adiga, Aravind

★ **Amnesty**. Aravind Adiga. Scribner, 2020. 288 p.

ISBN 9781982127244

1. Undocumented immigrants 2. Household employees 3. Options, alternatives, choices 4. Murderers 5. Witnesses 6. Sydney, New South Wales 7. Literary fiction 8. Australian fiction

Shortlisted for the Miles Franklin Literary Award, 2021

A young illegal immigrant in Sydney, Australia is forced to choose between risking deportation and reporting the murder of a female client.

"Best-selling Adiga's smart, funny, and timely tale with a crime spin of an undocumented immigrant will catalyze readers." —*Booklist*

Last man in tower: a novel. Aravind Adiga. Alfred A. Knopf, 2011. 368 p.

ISBN 9780307594099

1. Apartment houses 2. Real estate developers 3. Social conflict 4. Teachers 5. India 6. Mumbai, India 7. Literary fiction

LC 2011003406

Refusing to leave his home when a powerful real-estate developer offers to buy out the residents of a crumbling apartment complex near the infamous Dharavi slums, a retired schoolteacher becomes a target of violence by the developer and his own neighbors.

"[Adiga] maps out, in luminous prose, India's ambivalence toward its accelerated growth, while creating an engaging protagonist in the stubborn resident: a man whose ambition and independence have been tempered with an understanding of the important, if almost imperceptible, difference between development and progress." —*Entertainment Weekly*

Selection day. Aravind Adiga. Scribner, 2017. 304 p.

ISBN 9781501150838

1. Cricket (Sports) 2. Sports 3. Fathers and sons 4. Social classes 5. Brothers 6. India 7. Literary fiction 8. Adult books for young adults
New York Times Notable Book, 2017

Two brothers growing up in a Mumbai slum are raised by an obsessive father to become cricket stars only to have their relationship, future and senses of self threatened by unexpected dynamics that shape their coming-of-age.

"A master class in integrating character and landscape, Adiga's novel also portrays Mumbai as alternatively stifling and liberating." —*Booklist*

★ The **white** tiger: a novel. Aravind Adiga. Free Press, 2008. 288 p.

ISBN 9781416562597

1. Social classes 2. Racism 3. Class conflict 4. Automobile drivers 5. Political corruption 6. India 7. Bangalore, India 8. Literary fiction 9. Epistolary novels 10. Satirical fiction

LC 2007045527

Man Booker Prize, 2008

When he relocates to New Delhi to take a new job, Balram Halwai is disillusioned by the city's materialism and technology-spawned violence, a circumstance that forces him to question his loyalties, ambitions, and past

"In this darkly comic debut novel set in India, Balram, a chauffeur, murders his employer, justifying his crime as the act of a social entrepreneur.... Adiga's message isn't subtle or novel, but Balram's appealingly sardonic voice and acute observations of the social order are both winning and unsettling." —*The New Yorker*

Made into a movie by Netflix in 2021.

Adimi, Kaouther

Our riches. Kaouther Adimi; translated from the French by Chris Andrews. New Directions Publishing, 2020. 160 p.

ISBN 9780811228152

1. Charlot, Edmond 2. Publishers and publishing 3. Bookstores 4. Archives 5. War 6. Generosity 7. Algiers, Algeria 8. Algeria 9. Second World War era (1939-1945) 10. Biographical fiction 11. Historical fiction 12. Translations

Our Riches celebrates quixotic devotion and the love of books in the person of Edmond Charlot, who at the age of twenty founded Les Vraies Richesses (Our True Wealth), the famous Algerian bookstore/publishing house/lending library.

"This is a moving tribute to the enduring power of literature." —*Publishers Weekly*

Includes bibliographical references.
Originally published: Paris : Editions du Seuil, 2017.
Translated from the French.

Adjapon, Bisi

The teller of secrets: a novel. Bisi Adjapon. HarperVia, 2021. 320 p.

ISBN 9780063088948

1. Gender role 2. Postcolonialism 3. Social change 4. Growing up 5. Secrets 6. Ghana 7. Nigeria 8. 1960s 9. 1970s 10. Reeves, Keanu

LC 2021016323

A young Nigerian-Ghanaian girl growing up amid the political upheaval of late 1960s postcolonial Ghana, Esi Agyekum, as she navigates her burgeoning womanhood, tries to reconcile her own ideals and dreams with society's many double standards that limit her and other women.

"Sharp, observant, and often bitingly funny, Adjapon's novel captures a country divided by class, ethnicity, and political loyalty and a character who might have a chance to soar on the winds of social change.' —*Publishers Weekly*

Originally published as Of women and frogs by Kachifo Limited under the Farafina imprint in 2018—Title page verso.

Adjei-Brenyah, Nana Kwame

Friday black: stories. Nana Kwame Adjei-Brenyah. Mariner Books, 2018. 194 p.

ISBN 9781328911247

1. African Americans 2. Racism 3. Race relations 4. United States 5. Literary fiction 6. Satirical fiction 7. Short stories

LC 2017061489

ALA Notable Book, 2019; Booklist Editors' Choice, 2018; Library Journal Best Books, 2018; New York Times Notable Book, 2018; William Saroyan International Prize for Writing, Fiction category, 2020

A piercingly raw debut story collection from a young writer with an explosive voice; a treacherously surreal, and, at times, heartbreakingly satirical look at what it's like to be young and black in America.

Adkins, Mary

When you read this. Mary Adkins. Harper, 2019. 376 pages : Illustration

ISBN 9780062834676

1. Women with terminal illnesses 2. Friends' death 3. Bereavement 4. Public relations consultants 5. Last words 6. Epistolary novels 7. Mainstream fiction

After his friend, Iris, dies from a terminal illness at age 33, PR genius Smith Simonyi teams up with Iris' sister, Jade, to make Iris' final request—to get her blog posts published as a book—a reality.

"Debut novelist Adkins brilliantly captures the rhythms and cadences of the epistolary format in the digital age through a delightful cast of quirky, imperfect characters, both dead and alive. Tart, sweet, poignant, and rich with humor; completely irresistible." —*Library Journal*

Adlakha, Sarah

She wouldn't change a thing. Sarah Adlakha. Forge, 2021. 304 p.

ISBN 9781250774552

1. Women psychiatrists 2. Married women 3. Families 4. Pregnancy 5. Time travel (Past) 6. Mississippi 7. Science fiction 8. Domestic fiction

LC 2021009150

A second chance is the last thing she wants. When thirty-nine year old Maria Forssmann wakes up in her seventeen-year-old body, she doesn't know how she got there. All she does know is she has to get back: to her home in Bienville, Mississippi, to her job as a successful psychiatrist and, most importantly, to her husband, daughters, and unborn son. But she also knows that, in only a few weeks, a devastating tragedy will strike her husband, a tragedy that will lead to their meeting each other. Can she change time and still keep what it's given her?

"The characters are relatable, the story is gripping, and the blend of domestic fiction with a hint of science fiction is just plain great." —*Booklist*

A Tom Doherty Associates book.

Adler-Olsen, Jussi

The **absent** one. Jussi Adler-Olsen; translated from the Danish by K.E. Semmel. Dutton, 2012. 400 p. (Department Q, 2)
ISBN 9780525952893
1. Cold cases (Criminal investigation) 2. Siblings — Death 3. Police 4. Innocence (Law) 5. Murder investigation 6. Copenhagen, Denmark 7. Denmark 8. Thrillers and suspense 9. Psychological suspense 10. Translations
Detective Carl Morck investigates the twenty-year-old murders of a brother and sister whose confessed killer may actually be innocent, a case with ties to a homeless woman and powerful adversaries.
Translation of Fasandraeberne.
English translation originally published under the title Disgrace : London : Michael Joseph, 2012.
Translated from the Danish

A **conspiracy** of faith. Jussi Adler-Olsen; translated from the Danish by Martin Aitken. Dutton, 2013. 384 p. (Department Q, 3)
ISBN 9780525954002
1. Cold cases (Criminal investigation) 2. Arson investigation 3. Abused women 4. Ocean bottles 5. Brothers 6. Copenhagen, Denmark 7. Denmark 8. Thrillers and suspense 9. Translations 10. Scandinavian crime fiction
Receiving a sealed bottle with a years-old plea for help by two young victims imprisoned in a boathouse by the sea, Detective Carl Morck follows leads to a desperate woman trapped in a brutal marriage to a man who keeps her in isolation and hides deadly secrets.
Translation of Flaskepost fra P.
Translated from the Danish.

The **hanging** girl. Jussi Adler-Olsen; translated from the Danish by William Frost. E.P. Dutton, 2015. 432 p. (Department Q, 6)
ISBN 9780525954941
1. Cold cases (Criminal investigation) 2. Cults 3. Missing women 4. Islands 5. Teenage girls — Death 6. Denmark 7. Scandinavian crime fiction 8. Thrillers and suspense 9. Translations 10. Adult books for young adults
Forced to investigate the cold case murder of a 17-year-old girl, Department Q head Carl Morck and his enigmatic assistants infiltrate a sun-worshipping cult to pursue a string of new killings.
"Department Q's sixth entry recaptures the investigative detail and seductive characterization of the series' reader-magnet debut." —*Booklist*
Translation from the Danish of: Den grænselose.
Originally published: Copenhagen : Politikens Forlag, 2014.
Translated from the Danish.

The **keeper** of lost causes. Jussi Adler-Olsen; translated from the Danish by Lisa Hartford. Dutton, 2011. 400 p. (Department Q, 1)
ISBN 9780525952480

1. Cold cases (Criminal investigation) 2. Missing women 3. Police 4. Missing persons investigation 5. Conspiracies 6. Copenhagen, Denmark 7. Denmark 8. Thrillers and suspense 9. Anne Boleyn 10. Translations

LC 2011014873

Chief detective Carl Morck, recovering from what he thought was a career-destroying gunshot wound, is relegated to cold cases and becomes immersed in the five-year disappearance of a politician.
Originally published with the title Mercy in Great Britain by Penguin Books.
Originally published in Danish as Kvinden i buret: Kbh. : Politiken, 2007.

The **Marco** effect: a Department Q novel. Jussi Adler-Olsen; translated from the Danish by Martin Aitken. Dutton, 2014. 480 pages (Department Q, 5)
ISBN 9780525954026
1. Missing persons investigation 2. Thieves 3. Teenage boys 4. Romanies 5. Criminals 6. Denmark 7. Scandinavian crime fiction 8. Thrillers and suspense 9. Translations 10. Adult books for young adults

LC 2014014674

Denied Danish citizenship and an education by his oppressive gypsy clan leader, 15-year-old Marco is forced to beg and steal before fleeing in the wake of a murderous act, which is investigated by Detective Carl Mørck for its ties to petty crime rings, embezzlers and child soldiers.
Translation from the Danish of: Marco Effekten.
Also published in Great Britain under the title Buried.
Originally published: Copenhagen : Politiken, 2012.
Translated from the Danish.

The **purity** of vengeance: a Department Q novel. Jussi Adler-Olsen; translated from the Danish by Martin Aitken. Dutton Adult, 2014. 400 p. (Department Q, 4)
ISBN 9780525954019
1. Cold cases (Criminal investigation) 2. Missing persons 3. Police 4. Kidnapping 5. Missing persons investigation 6. Copenhagen, Denmark 7. Denmark 8. Thrillers and suspense 9. Translations 10. Scandinavian crime fiction

LC 2013033253

After new evidence surfaces, Detective Carl Morck and his assistants look into the case of a brothel owner who went missing in the 1980s and discover that numerous other people went missing around the same time.
Previously published as Journal 64 with a variant title of Journal fireogtreds in Danish.
Translated from the Danish.

The **scarred** woman. Jussi Adler-Olsen; translated from the Danish by Willam Frost. Dutton, 2017. 432 p. (Department Q, 7)
ISBN 9780525954958
1. Violence against women 2. Women murderers 3. Violence in women 4. Cold cases (Criminal investigation) 5. Missing women 6. Denmark 7. Scandinavian crime fiction 8. Thrillers and suspense 9. Translations 10. Adult books for young adults

LC 2017013668

Unable to determine links between a Copenhagen park murder and another unsolved case that is unsettlingly similar, Detective Carl Morck of Department Q finds his job and division on the line at the same time the team investigates a possible crime that a struggling Rose has brought to light.
Translation of: Selfies.
Translated from the Danish

★ **Victim** 2117. Jussi Adler-Olsen; translated from the Danish by William Frost. Dutton, 2020. 468 p. (Department Q, 8)

ISBN 9781524742553

1. Refugees 2. International intrigue 3. Police 4. Secrets 5. Terrorists 6. Denmark 7. Scandinavian crime fiction 8. Thrillers and suspense 9. Translations 10. Adult books for young adults

The death of a seemingly random refugee in the Mediterranean Sea triggers powerful reverberations in a teen with murderous impulses, an Abu Ghraib terrorist and Department Q's Assad, who uncovers links to a family he assumed was long dead.

"In a feat of unparalleled storytelling, this eighth Department Q episode brings the full team back together as Adler-Olsen weaves el-Assad's heart-wrenching story into a pair of relentless manhunts." —*Booklist*

Translation of: Offer 2117.

Originally published in Denmark, 2019.

Translated from the Danish

Afifi, Nadia

The **sentient**. Nadia Afifi. Flame Tree Publishing, 2020. 288 p.

ISBN 9781787584341

1. Neuroscientists 2. Women scientists 3. Clones and cloning 4. Conspiracies 5. Memory 6. Science fiction

Amira Valdez is a brilliant neuroscientist trying to put her past on a religious compound behind her. But when she's assigned to a controversial cloning project, her dreams of working in space are placed in jeopardy. Using her talents as a reader of memories, Amira uncovers a conspiracy to stop the creation of the first human clone—at all costs.

Afshar, Tessa

Jewel of the Nile. Tessa Afshar. Tyndale House Publishers, 2021. 414 p.

ISBN 9781496428752

1. Orphans 2. Voyages and travels 3. Family secrets 4. Stowaways 5. Multiracial women 6. Rome 7. Roman Empire (27 BCE-476 CE) 8. Historical romances 9. Christian historical romances

LC 2021006524

Whispered secrets about her parents' past take on new urgency for Chariline as she pays one last visit to the land of her forefathers, the ancient kingdom of Cush.

"Exquisite plotting and outstanding historical details set this apart. Afshar's fans will be overjoyed with this tale of love lost and found." —*Publishers Weekly*

Thief of Corinth. Tessa Afshar. Tyndale House Publishers, Inc, 2018. 400 p.

ISBN 9781496428653

1. Paul 2. Thieves 3. Redemption 4. Forgiveness 5. Fathers and daughters 6. Corruption 7. Corinth, Greece 8. Roman Empire (27 BCE-476 CE) 9. Ancient Greece (800 BCE-640 CE) 10. Christian historical fiction

LC 2018007681

Young Ariadne flees her mother's home to live with her father in ancient Corinth, only to find that the man is secretly an infamous thief, but when she and her father meet a Jewish rabbi named Paul their lives are profoundly changed.

Agee, James

★ A **death** in the family. James Agee. Vintage Books, 1998. Ix, 310 p. : Illustration

ISBN 9780375701238

1. Traffic accident victims 2. Fathers and sons 3. Grief 4. Family and death 5. Literary fiction 6. Coming-of-age stories 7. Southern fiction

LC 57012114

Pulitzer Prize for Fiction, 1958

On a sultry summer night in 1915, Jay Follet leaves his house in Knoxville, Tennessee, to tend to his father, whom he believes is dying. The summons turns out to be a false alarm, but on his way back to his family, Jay has a car accident and is killed instantly. From this situation, Agee weaves a story of the complex ways that people deal with life, love, and loss.

Originally published: New York : McDowell, Obolensky, 1957

Agee, Jonis

The **bones** of paradise. Jonis Agee. William Morrow, 2016. 432 p.

ISBN 9780062413475

1. Families 2. Race relations 3. Indians of North America 4. Nebraska 5. 1900s (Decade) 6. Historical fiction

LC 2015037302

A decade after the Wounded Knee Massacre, when the U.S. 7th Cavalry regiment gunned down over 200 Lakota, white rancher J.B. Bennett and Sioux woman Star are found dead on Bennett's land. As Bennett's estranged wife, Dulcinea, returns to the ranch and gathers the remaining family members, Star's sister, Rose, vows to find Star's killer and avenge her death. Set in the Nebraska Sandhills at the dawn of the 20th century, The Bones of Paradise is a haunting multi-generational family saga that explores a tragedy with deep historical roots through the eyes of flawed and fully fleshed-out characters.

"The story's several parts—gritty Western, family saga, mystery—work together for a memorable tale of heartbreak and redemption." —*Publishers Weekly*

Agnon, Shmuel Yosef

★ **Only** yesterday. S.Y. Agnon; translated from the Hebrew by Barbara Harshav. Princeton University Press, 2000. 652 p.

ISBN 9780691009728

1. Zionists 2. Israel 3. Palestine 4. Translations 5. Allegories

LC 21147

Follows an idealistic man as he emigrates to Palestine in the early part of the century, determined to revive Hebrew culture and build a homeland for Jews.

"Though Agnon would go on to write much of compelling interest during his remaining 25 years, this would be his masterpiece—a novel that deserves comparison with Kafka's The Trial, Mann's The Magic Mountain and Hermann Broch's The Sleepwalkers as a deployment of the resources of fiction for plumbing those abysses of cultural and personal crisis that haunted so many imaginations in the modernist period." —*Los Angeles Times Book Review*

Translation of: Temol shilshom.

Aguilar Camin, Hector

Death in Veracruz. Hector Aguilar Camin. Schaffner Press, 2015. 212 p.

ISBN 9781936182923

1. Friends' death 2. Oil industry and trade — Corrupt practices 3. Man-woman relationships 4. Police misconduct 5. Villages 6. Mexico 7. 1970s 8. Noir fiction 9. Translations

Death in Veracruz is a gritty and atmospheric noir centered on the so-called oil wars of the late 1970s, which pitted the extremely powerful and corrupt government-owned oil cartel PEMEX against the agrarian landowners in the coastal regions of Southern Mexico.

"While Camin's style recalls Robert Stone more than it does the noir fiction of three decades ago, he obviously possesses an intimate knowledge of the Mexican sociopolitical landscape, and this is a revealing time capsule." —*Publishers Weekly*

Translation of Morir en el golfo (1988).

Translated from the Spanish.

Ahern, Cecelia

Roar. Cecelia Ahern. Grand Central Publishing, 2019. 288 pages

ISBN 9781538730966

1. Women 2. Feminism 3. Self-perception in women 4. Self-discovery 5. Self-acceptance 6. Short stories 7. Allegories 8. Adult books for young adults

"Cecelia Ahern gives us thirty stories, all titled 'The Woman Who...', that capture the different facets of women's lives. Humorous, moving and poignant, the stories capture the moments the characters are overwhelmed by guilt, confusion, frustration, intimidation, exhaustion the private moments when they feel the need to roar." —Provided by publisher.

Originally published : London : HarperCollins, 2018.

Ahlborn, Ania

The devil crept in. Ania Ahlborn. Gallery Books, 2017. 374 p.

ISBN 9781476783758

1. Small towns 2. Missing boys 3. Missing persons investigation 4. Boys 5. Police 6. Oregon 7. Horror 8. Adult books for young adults

LC 2016037375

The residents of Deer Valley, Oregon have worried for years about the mysterious deaths and disappearances of animals, and—even more disturbing—the death of a young boy. Now 12-year-old Jude Brighton has also gone missing, and his ten-year-old cousin Stevie Clark fears that the woods harbor a monster. Jude suddenly returns, but Stevie senses that he's changed beyond recognition. Author Ania Ahlborn sensitively portrays her characters' emotions while deftly escalating the dread that emanates from the forest.

Ahmad, Jamil

The wandering falcon. Jamil Ahmad. Riverhead Books, 2011. 256 p.

ISBN 9781594488276

1. Nomads 2. Borderlands 3. Exile (Punishment) 4. Refugees 5. Belonging 6. Pakistan 7. Afghanistan 8. Literary fiction

A debut novel set in the Federally Administered Tribal Lands at the intersection of Iran, Pakistan and Afghanistan follows the story of banished refugees' son Tor Baz, who travels throughout the region while considering his prestigious lineage and witnessing the effects of extreme culture and geography on the lives of those he encounters.

"A gripping book, as important for illuminating the current state of this region as it is timeless in its beautiful imagery and rhythmic prose." —*Publishers Weekly*

First published: Hamish Hamilton : Penguin Books India, 2011.

Simultaneously published: Great Britain : Hamish Hamilton, 2011.

Aimaq, Jasmine

The opium prince. Jasmine Aimaq. Soho Crime, 2020. 384 pages

ISBN 9781641291583

1. Kim, Chong-il 2. Afghan Americans 3. Fatal traffic accidents 4. International relations 5. Threat (Psychology) 6. Afghanistan 7. 1970s 8. Political fiction 9. Literary fiction 10. Thrillers and suspense

LC 2020015485

Accidentally killing a young Kochi girl while driving through Kabul, an Afghan-American foreign-aid worker is confronted by an opium dealer's threats, the loss of his marriage and wrenching guilt over the local regime's indifference.

"Every carefully described detail here will stay with readers as they examine what they thought they knew about America's exporting of democracy and its war on drugs." —*Booklist*

Airth, Rennie

The decent inn of death. Rennie George Airth. Penguin, 2020. 368 pages (John Madden novels, 6)

ISBN 9780143134299

1. Former detectives 2. Manors 3. Winter storms 4. Murder 5. Murder investigation 6. England 7. 20th century 8. Historical mysteries

Snowed in at a country manor, former Scotland Yard inspectors John Madden and Angus Sinclair find themselves trapped in the company of a murderer.

"Post-WWII England comes to life in vivid detail, with an atmosphere so rich that readers will feel the cold seeping into their bones. An absorbing winter read for fans of well-crafted British procedurals." —*Booklist*

Ajvide Lindqvist, John

Let the right one in. John Ajvide Lindqvist; translated from the Swedish by Ebba Segerberg. Thomas Dunne Books, 2007. 472 p.

ISBN 9780312355289

1. Twelve-year-old boys 2. Overweight boys 3. Suburban life 4. Neighbors 5. Teenage murder victims 6. Sweden 7. Horror 8. Translations 9. Books to movies 10. Adult books for young adults

LC 2007023510

Twelve-year-old Oskar is obsessed by the murder that's taken place in his neighborhood. Then he meets the new girl from next door. She's a bit weird, though. And she only comes out at night.

Later published in English as: Let me in.

Two films have been based on this book: Let the right one in (2008) and Let me in (2010).

Akhtar, Ayad

American dervish: a novel. Ayad Akhtar. Little, Brown and Co, 2012. 320 p.

ISBN 9780316183314

1. Faith 2. Islam 3. Muslim families 4. Pakistani Americans 5. Religion 6. Coming-of-age stories 7. Psychological fiction 8. Adult books for young adults

LC 2011019737

A young Pakistani boy, whose parents left the fundamentalists behind when they came to America, finds transformation and a path to happiness through a family friend, Mina, who shows him the beauty and power of the Quran.

★ **Homeland** elegies: a novel. Ayad Akhtar. Doubleday, 2020. 347 pages

ISBN 9780316496421

1. Akhtar, Ayad 2. Pakistani Americans 3. Muslim families 4. Shakespeare, William 5. September 11 Terrorist Attacks, 2001 6. Identity (Psychology) 7. United States 8. 21st century 9. 20th century 10. Literary fiction 11. Autobiographical fiction

LC 2020930304

New York Times Notable Book, 2020; Wisconsin Library Association Literary Award, 2021; Andrew Carnegie Medal for Excellence in Fiction finalist, 2021

A deeply personal work about identity and belonging in a nation coming apart at the seams, Homeland Elegies blends fact and fiction to tell an epic story of longing and dispossession in the world that 9/11 made. Part family drama, part social essay, part picaresque novel, at its heart it is the story of a father, a son, and the country they both call home.

"Money, and the debasement of other values, is a defining element of Akhtar's relationship with his writing and his father, while the crude racism unleashed by 9/11 prods them both to question whether America can ever truly be their home." —*Booklist*

Akinmade-Akerstrom, Lola

In every mirror she's Black. Lola Akinmade Akerstrom. Sourcebooks Landmark, 2021. 400 p.

ISBN 9781728240381

1. African American women 2. Women chief executive officers 3. Fashion models 4. Refugees 5. Rich men 6. Stockholm, Sweden 7. African American fiction 8. Literary fiction 9. Multiple perspectives

Three Black women—a powerhouse executive, a former model, and a Somali refugee—are linked in unexpected ways to the same influential white man in Stockholm.

"As entertaining as it is revealing, Akerstrom's novel has readers hoping that each of these women is able to break free from toxic expectations and achieve her every dream and ambition." —*Booklist*

Akpan, Uwem

Say you're one of them. Uwem Akpan. Little, Brown and Co, 2008. 240 p.

ISBN 9780316113786

1. Child war victims 2. Social history 3. Genocide 4. War victims 5. Violence 6. Africa 7. Sub-Saharan Africa 8. Literary fiction 9. Short stories 10. Adult books for young adults

LC 2007041350

Booklist Editors' Choice: Adult Books for Young Adults, 2008; Commonwealth Writers' Prize, Africa: Best First Book, 2009; Hurston/Wright Legacy Award: Fiction, 2009; Library Journal Best Books, 2008

A collection of tales about modern African children in crisis.

"Akpan's prose is beautiful and his stories are insightful and revealing, made even more harrowing because all the horror—and there is much— is seen through the eyes of children." —*Publishers Weekly*

Akunin, B.

The **coronation**: the further adventures of Erast Fandorin. Boris Akunin; translated by Andrew Bromfield. Weidenfeld & Nicolson, 2009. 311 p. (Erast Fandorin mysteries, 7)

ISBN 9780802127815

1. Nicholas II, Emperor of Russia, 1868-1918. 2. Kidnapping 3. Ransom 4. Fandorin, Erast (Fictitious character) 5. Jones, Mother, 1837-1930 6. Coronations 7. Russia 8. Romanov Dynasty (1613-1917) 9. 19th century 10. Historical mysteries 11. Translations 12. Multiple perspectives

Ernst Fandorin and a race against time just before the coronation of Tsar Nicholas II as one of the Grand Duke's children is kidnapped and a ransom note arrives—from Fandorin's nemesis, Doctor Lind.

First published in Russian as Koronaciya by Zakharov Publications, Moscow, Russia and Edizioni Frassinell, Milan, Italy.

Sister Pelagia and the white bulldog: a mystery. Boris Akunin; translated from the Russian by Andrew Bromfield. Random House Trade Paperbacks, 2007. 288 p. (Sister Pelagia mysteries, 1)

ISBN 9780812975130

1. Nuns 2. Women amateur detectives 3. Betrayal 4. Clergy 5. Families 6. Russia 7. Romanov Dynasty (1613-1917) 8. 19th century 9. Historical mysteries 10. Translations 11. Mysteries

LC 2006050387

When he hears that one of his aunt's rare white bulldogs has been poisoned, Monsignore Mitrofanij, the orthodox bishop of a remote Russian province on the Volga, enlists the assistance of the resourceful Sister Pelagia to take on a complex morass of spurned lovers, canine conspiracy, political intrigue, greed, and knitting to uncover the culprit.

"Set in the late 19th century, this charming, highly unusual whodunit from Russian author Akunin (the pen name of Grigory Chkhartishvili) introduces Sister Pelagia, a young nun in a remote Russian province far removed from the intrigue of the czarist government." —*Publishers Weekly*

Originally published in Russian: Moscow: Izd-vo AST, 2000.

Al-Ramli, Muhsin

The **president's** gardens. Muhsin Al-Ramli; translated from the Arabic by Luke Leafgren. MacLehose Press, 2018. 290 p.

ISBN 9781635060362

1. Male friendship 2. Violence — Psychological aspects 3. Political persecution 4. War and society 5. Injustice 6. Iraq 7. Political fiction 8. Literary fiction 9. Translations

LC 2017045305

When the severed head of his son is found, Ibrahim the Fated searches for answers to why this happened, from the battlefields of the Gulf War to what lies behind the locked gates of the president's gardens.

"This powerful, sweeping novel...is highly recommended. It profoundly humanizes modern Mideast history for Western readers." —*Library Journal*

Translation of: Hada'iq al-ra'is
Originally published: 2012.
Translated from the Arabic.

Al Rawi, Shahad

The **Baghdad** clock. Shahad al Rawi. Oneworld Publications, 2018. 288 p.

ISBN 9781786073242

1. Persian Gulf War, 1991 2. Girls 3. Friendship 4. Civil war 5. Growing up 6. Iraq 7. 1990s 8. Literary fiction 9. Translations 10. Adult books for young adults

Baghdad, 1991. In the midst of the first Gulf War, a young Iraqi girl huddles with her neighbours in an air raid shelter. There, she meets Nadia. The two girls quickly become best friends and together they imagine a world not torn apart by civil war, sharing their dreams, their hopes and their desires, and their first loves. But as they grow older and the bombs continue to fall, the international sanctions bite and friends begin to flee the country, the girls must face the fact that their lives will never be the same again.

Alam, Rumaan

★ **Leave** the world behind: a novel. Rumaan Alam. Ecco, 2020. 320 p.

ISBN 9780062667632

1. Vacation homes 2. Vacations 3. Married people 4. Power failures 5. Strangers 6. Long Island, New York 7. Psychological suspense

LC 2020013947

ALA Notable Book, 2021; LibraryReads Favorites, 2020; National Book Award for Fiction finalist, 2020

Sheltering in a New York beach house with a couple that has taken refuge during a massive blackout, a family struggles for information about the power failure while wondering if the cut-off property is actually safe.

"The omniscient narrator occasionally zooms out to provide snapshots of the wider chaotic world that are effective in their brevity. Though information is scarce, the signs of impending collapse—ecological and geopolitical—have been glaringly visible to the characters all along.... This illuminating social novel offers piercing commentary on race, class and the luxurious mirage of safety, adding up to an all-too-plausible apocalyptic vision." —*Publishers Weekly*

That kind of mother: a novel. Rumaan Alam. Ecco, 2018. 320 p.
ISBN 9780062667601
1. Nannies 2. New mothers 3. Race relations 4. European American women 5. African American women 6. United States 7. Domestic fiction 8. Literary fiction
LC 2018000165
Library Journal Best Books, 2018
Overwhelmed by new motherhood in spite of her love for her infant son, Rebecca, a white woman, asks a kind black woman, Priscilla, to become her family's nanny, only to have her perspectives changed about her own life of privilege, a situation that compels her to take on unanticipated challenges in the aftermath of a tragedy.

Alameddine, Rabih
An **unnecessary** woman. Rabih Alameddine. Grove Press, 2014. 320 p.
ISBN 9780802122148
1. Senior women 2. Books and reading 3. Reminiscing in old age 4. Women translators 5. Female friendship 6. Lebanon 7. Psychological fiction 8. Literary fiction 9. First person narratives
National Book Critics Circle Award for Fiction finalist, 2014;
National Book Award for Fiction finalist, 2014
A love letter to literature and its power to define who we are, this is a nuanced rendering of one woman's life in the Middle East.
"Alameddine's storytelling is rich with a bookish humor that's accessible without being condescending. A gemlike and surprisingly lively study of an interior life." —*Kirkus*

The **wrong** end of the telescope. Rabih Alameddine. Grove Press, 2021. 368 p.
ISBN 9780802157805
1. Women physicians 2. Refugees 3. Refugee camps 4. Separated friends, relatives, etc. 5. Trans women 6. Greece 7. Literary fiction 8. LGBTQIA fiction
Mina Simpson, a Lebanese doctor, arrives at the infamous Moria refugee camp on Lesbos, Greece, after being urgently summoned for help by her friend who runs an NGO there. Alienated from her family except for her beloved brother, Mina has avoided being so close to her homeland for decades. But with a week off work and apart from her wife of thirty years, Mina hopes to accomplish something meaningful, among the abundance of Western volunteers who pose for selfies with beached dinghies and the camp's children. Soon, a boat crosses bringing Sumaiya, a fiercely resolute Syrian matriarch with terminal liver cancer. Determined to protect her children and husband at all costs, Sumaiya refuses to alert her family to her diagnosis. Bonded together by Sumaiya's secret, a deep connection sparks between the two women, and as Mina prepares a course of treatment with the limited resources on hand, she confronts the circumstances of the migrants' displacement, as well as her own constraints in helping them.
"A remarkable, surprisingly intimate tale of human connection in the midst of disaster." —*Library Journal*

Alarcon, Daniel
At night we walk in circles: a novel. Daniel Alarcon. Riverhead Hardcover, 2013. 400 p.
ISBN 9781594631719
1. Actors and actresses 2. Life change events 3. Performing arts 4. Drama 5. Civil war — Post-war aspects 6. South America 7. Psychological fiction 8. Political fiction 9. First person narratives
LC 2013019446
Feeling unfulfilled in the wake of personal and professional setbacks, South American youth Nelson lands a starring role in a revival of a legendary play by his hero and confronts the realities of civil war while touring unfamiliar landscapes.
"[A] fast-unraveling mystery of role-playing and retribution, told in compelling prose that is smart, subtle, and totally engrossing." —*Booklist*

The **king** is always above the people: stories. Daniel Alarcon. Riverhead Books, 2017. 256 p.
ISBN 9781594631726
1. Families 2. Human nature 3. Family and death 4. Death 5. Loss (Psychology) 6. Short stories 7. Literary fiction
LC 2017016056
Longlisted for the National Book Award for Fiction, 2017
A collection of short stories from the author of At Night We Walk in Circles features tales about people forging into new lands and a man dealing with the mysterious deaths of his blind relatives.
"A smart and understated collection that puts some new twists on old-fashioned identity crises." —*Kirkus*

Albahari, David
Gotz and Meyer. David Albahari; translated from the Serbian by Ellen Elias-Bursac. Harcourt, 2005. 176 p.
ISBN 9780151011414
1. Jews, Serbian 2. Jews 3. Nazis 4. Truck drivers 5. Teachers 6. Yugoslavia 7. 1940s 8. First person narratives 9. Psychological fiction 10. War stories 11. Adult books for young adults
LC 2005040359
"There are no chapters or even paragraphs, but the spacious text is simple and eloquent, and readers will be drawn into the professor's obsessive first-person narrative in which the horror is in the facts of bureaucratic efficiency and the unimaginable evil in ordinary life." —*Booklist*
Originally published in Serbian in 1998 as Gec i Majer.

Albom, Mitch
The **five** people you meet in heaven. Mitch Albom. Hyperion, 2003. 342 p. (Five people you meet in Heaven, 1)
ISBN 9780786868711
1. Life after death 2. Heaven 3. Meaning (Psychology) 4. Death 5. Secrets 6. Psychological fiction 7. Books to movies
LC 2003047888
Killed in a tragic accident at a seaside amusement park while trying to save a little girl, Eddie, an elderly man who believes that he had lived an uninspired life, awakens in the afterlife, where he discovers that heaven consists of having five people, acquaintances and strangers, explain the meaning of one's life.
Sequel: The next person you meet in Heaven.

The **next** person you meet in Heaven. Mitch Albom. Harper, 2018. 224 p. (Five people you meet in Heaven, 2)
ISBN 9780062294449
1. Heaven 2. Life after death 3. Accident victims 4. Amusement parks 5. Amusement rides 6. Psychological fiction

LC 2018020005

Fifteen years after Eddie died saving a little girl named Annie, Annie suffers a terrible accident and finds herself reunited with Eddie, one of the five people who will show her how her life mattered in ways she never considered.

Sequel to: The five people you meet in Heaven.

The **stranger** in the lifeboat. Mitch Albom. Harper, 2021. 271 p.
ISBN 9780062888341
1. Shipwrecks 2. Explosions 3. Castaways 4. Lifeboats 5. Billionaires 6. Atlantic Ocean 7. Caribbean Area 8. Mainstream fiction

After a deadly ship explosion, nine people, adrift in a raft, struggle to survive at sea and pull a strange man from the sea who claims to be the Lord, in an inspiring novel.

"Unanswerable questions wrapped inside a thought-provoking yarn." —*Kirkus*

Alcott, Kate

A **touch** of stardust. Kate Alcott. Doubleday, 2015. 304 p.
ISBN 9780385539043
1. Gable, Clark 2. Film actors and actresses 3. Personal assistants 4. Extramarital affairs 5. Scandals 6. Female friendship 7. Hollywood, California 8. Biographical fiction 9. Love stories 10. Historical fiction
LC 2014020972
LibraryReads Favorites, 2015; RUSA Reading List Short List, 2016

Taking a job at the studio where David O. Selznick is filming Gone with the Wind, Julie Crawford becomes an assistant to Carole Lombard, a rising actress from Julie's hometown who embarks on a scandalous affair with Clark Gable.

"The briskly paced narrative captivates as it lets readers view the creation of silver-screen magic, and its also a terrific tribute to the industry pioneers, like screenwriter Frances Marion, who helped others jump-start their dreams." —*Booklist*

Alderman, Naomi

★ The **power**: a novel. Naomi Alderman. Little, Brown and Co, 2017. 386 pages : Illustration
ISBN 9780316547611
1. Superhuman abilities 2. Power (Social sciences) 3. Gender role 4. Social change 5. Violence against men 6. Social science fiction 7. Science fiction 8. Literary fiction 9. Adult books for young adults
LC 2017936787
Baileys Women's Prize for Fiction, 2017; Booklist Editors' Choice: Adult Books for Young Adults, 2017; Loan Stars Favourites, 2017; New York Times Notable Book, 2017; RUSA Reading List Short List, 2018

When a new force takes hold of the world, people from different areas of life are forced to cross paths in an alternate reality that gives women and teenage girls immense physical power that can cause pain and death.

"Both the main story and the frame narrative ask interesting questions about gender, but this isn't a dry philosophical exercise. It's fast-paced, thrilling, and even funny." —*Kirkus*

Originally published: London : Viking, 2016.

Alderson, Kaia

Sisters in arms. Kaia Alderson. William Morrow & Co, 2021. 400 p.
ISBN 9780062964588
1. World War II 2. African American women 3. Women and war 4. Determination in women 5. Courage in women 6. Harlem, New York

City 7. New York City 8. Second World War era (1939-1945) 9. Historical fiction 10. War stories 11. African American fiction

"For fans of Hidden Figures and untold stories of heroes and heroines of World War II." —*Library Journal*

Alderton, Dolly

★ **Ghosts**: a novel. Dolly Alderton. 2021. 320 p.
ISBN 9780593319857
1. Single women 2. Women authors 3. Parents 4. Friendship 5. Dating (Social customs) 6. London, England 7. Chick lit
LC 2020043812

A smart, sexy, laugh-out-loud romantic comedy about ex-boyfriends, imperfect parents, friends with kids, and a man who disappears the moment he says "I love you.

"Full of quirky characters, sardonic commentary, and millennial ruminations." —*Booklist*

Aleichem, Sholem

Tevye the dairyman and the railroad stories. Sholem Aleichem; translated from the Yiddish and with an introduction by Hillel Halkin. Schocken Books, 1987. 309 p.
ISBN 9780805240269
1. Tevye (Fictitious character : Sholem Aleichem) 2. Shtetl 3. Jews, Eastern European 4. Kasrilevke (Imaginary place) 5. Literary fiction 6. Short stories 7. Translations
LC 86024835

Tells the stories of a milkman and his daughters and a salesman's encounters with fellow Jews while riding the train

"In the first eight stories of this collection, Tevye, the Russian Jew so familiar from Fiddler on the Roof, bemoans his fate. In these as well as the following 21 tales, the author displays his splendid storytelling skills." —*Booklist*

The movie Fiddler on the roof was based on the Tevye stories in this collection.

Tevye's daughters. Sholem Aleichem; translated from the Yiddish by Frances Butwin; with illustrations by Ben Shahn. Crown, 1949. 302 pages
ISBN 9780517507100
1. Fathers and daughters 2. Jews, Eastern European 3. Shtetl 4. Tevye (Fictitious character : Sholem Aleichem) 5. Kasrilevke (Imaginary place) 6. Literary fiction 7. Translations

"Translated from the Yiddish, many of these stories are about the seven daughters of Tevye the Dairyman and the life each chooses as she comes of age in Russia during the years preceding the first World War." —*Publishers Weekly*

The movie Fiddler on the roof was based on the stories in this collection.

Alenyikov, Michael

Ivan and Misha: stories. Michael Alenyikov. TriQuarterly Books, 2010. 199 p.
ISBN 9780810127180
1. Twin brothers 2. Immigrants 3. Familial love 4. Fathers and sons 5. Russians in the United States 6. New York City 7. 1990s 8. Short stories 9. Mainstream fiction
LC 2010024016

"Highly recommended, especially for readers of literary gay fiction, although the themes of exile and familial affection will interest a wider audience." —*Library Journal*

Alexander, Jennet

I kissed a girl. Jennet Alexander. Sourcebooks Casablanca, 2021. 320 p.
ISBN 9781728222707
1. Actors and actresses 2. Makeup artists 3. Film industry and trade 4. Bisexual women 5. Jewish women 6. Hollywood, California 7. California 8. LGBTQIA romances 9. Romantic comedies
LC 2021001966
Lilah Silver is an up-and-coming actress who longs to break out from the B-rate horror flicks she's known for. When she gets the chance to star in her first lead role, she'll need some major help from makeup artist and special effects guru Noa Birnbaum to shine brighter than all the rest. But can the major chemistry brewing over long hours spent together ever hope to survive the bright shine of the spotlight?
"With hints of Casey McQuiston, a quirky supporting cast, and undeniable heart, this makes a charming addition to the growing list of New Adult queer rom-coms." —*Publishers Weekly*

Alexander, Tamera

★ **A note** yet unsung. Tamera Alexander. Bethany House, 2017. 352 p. (Belmont mansion novels, 3)
ISBN 9780764206245
1. Women musicians 2. Orchestras 3. Conductors (Music) 4. Violinists 5. Sexism 6. Southern States 7. Nashville, Tennessee 8. Gilded Age (1865-1898) 9. Christian historical romances 10. Adult books for young adults
LC 2016035450
Christy Award for Historical Romance Category, 2017; Carol Award for Best Historical Romance, 2018
In 1871, 23-year-old violinist Rebekah Carrington unhappily returns home to Nashville. She's been studying in Vienna for ten years, but her money's been cut off from her estranged mother and stepfather since her paternal grandmother unexpectedly (and suspiciously) passed away. Rebekah hopes to play with the newly formed Nashville Philharmonic, but women aren't allowed. Still, when conductor Nathaniel Tate Whitcomb needs help finishing the symphony that he's writing for his ill father, he calls on Rebekah, to whom he feels a connection. This conclusion to the Belmont Mansion trilogy will be music to the ears of readers who like lyrically told tales with a hint of mystery and note-perfect romances.
Series complete in 3 volumes.

With this pledge. Tamera Alexander. Thomas Nelson, 2019. 352 p. (Carnton novels, 1)
ISBN 9780718081850
1. Confederate soldiers 2. Governesses 3. Personal conduct 4. Widowers 5. Hospitals 6. Tennessee 7. Franklin, Tennessee 8. American Civil War era (1861-1865) 9. Christian historical romances
LC 2018037968
Christy Award for Historical Romance Category, 2019
When her home is converted into a Confederate hospital Lizzie Clouston must be true to her own heart while standing for what she knows is right.

Alexander, V. S.

The **Magdalen** girls. V.S. Alexander. Kensington Books, 2016. 304 p.
ISBN 9781496706126
1. Forced labor 2. Women — Social conditions 3. Survival (in concentration camps, prisons, etc.) 4. Clergy 5. Reputation 6. Dublin, Ireland 7. 1960s 8. Historical fiction 9. Adult books for young adults
When her beauty provokes a lustful revelation from a young priest, sixteen-year-old Teagan is sent to one of Dublin's Magdalen Laundries for fallen women, where she befriends two other girls who help her endure the harsh captivity.

Alexander, Victoria

The **Lady** Travelers Guide to larceny with a dashing stranger. Victoria Alexander. HQN Books, 2017. 537 p. (Lady Travelers Guide, 2)
ISBN 9780373804009
1. Widows 2. Women travelers 3. Art — Collectors and collecting 4. Interpersonal attraction 5. Voyages and travels 6. Venice, Italy 7. England 8. Victorian era (1837-1901) 9. Victorian romances 10. Historical romances
In Regency Venice, a desperate widow and a determined bachelor search for a missing masterpiece that will change their lives.
Includes bonus story: "The rise and fall of Reginald Everheart."

The **Lady** Travelers Guide to scoundrels and other gentlemen. Victoria Alexander. HQN Books, 2017. 384 p. (Lady Travelers Guide, 1)
ISBN 9780373803989
1. Personal assistants 2. Womanizers 3. Women travelers 4. Heirs and heiresses 5. Missing women 6. Paris, France 7. England 8. Victorian era (1837-1901) 9. Victorian romances 10. Historical romances
Searching for her aunt, a member of the possibly fraudulent Lady Travelers society, India Prendergast is joined by the nephew of one of the group's members, Derek Saunders, a handsome man with a scandalous reputation.
"Alexander celebrates the spirit of adventure, elevates dubious scheming with good intentions, and advocates for the yielding of judgment and practicality to hedonism and happiness. Readers will savor every page." —*Publishers Weekly*
Includes bonus story: "The Proper Way to Stop a Wedding in Seven Days or Less."

Alexie, Sherman

Blasphemy: new and selected stories. Sherman Alexie. Grove Press, 2012. 304 p.
ISBN 9780802120397
1. Marriage 2. Racism 3. Addiction 4. Indians of North America 5. Native American men 6. Pacific Northwest 7. Short stories 8. Literary fiction
New York Times Notable Book, 2012
A collection of thirty-one new and selected short stories by Native American author Sherman Alexie.
Collects 15 previously published and 15 new short stories.

Flight. Sherman Alexie. Grove Press, 2007. 208 p.
ISBN 9780802170378
1. Indians of North America 2. Family relationships 3. Identity (Psychology) 4. Teenage boys 5. Time travel (Past) 6. 19th century 7. 21st century 8. Social science fiction 9. Science fiction 10. Literary fiction 11. Adult books for young adults
YALSA Best Books for Young Adults, 2008
On the verge of commiting an act of violence, a troubled, orphaned Indian teenager finds himself hurtled through time and into the bodies of a civil rights era FBI agent, an Indian child during the battle at Little Big Horn, a nineteenth-century Indian tracker, and a modern-day airline pilot, before returning to himself, forever altered by his experiences.
"Many of [the] allegorical, action-packed vignettes tread familiar thematic territory—the continuing fight for survival, the anger of racial divides, the absence of fathers— of Mr. Alexie's earlier works...But with 'Flight,' he takes these themes a step further: he skillfully explores both

sides of the proverbial war. Zits witnesses brutal violence through the eyes of whites and Indians, fathers and sons, and he begins to understand what it means to be the hero, the villain and the victim." —*New York Times*

Reservation blues. Sherman Alexie. Atlantic Monthly Press, 1995. 306 p.

ISBN 9780871135940

1. Johnson, Robert 2. Native American rock musicians 3. Spokane Indian Reservation 4. Spokane Indians 5. Indians of North America 6. Indians of North America — Alcoholism 7. Washington (State) 8. Literary fiction

LC 94046132

Booklist Editors' Choice, 1995; Booklist Editors' Choice: Adult Books for Young Adults, 1995; Shortlisted for the International IMPAC Dublin Literary Award, 1997

Legendary blues guitarist Robert Johnson appears on an Indian reservation to lead a Catholic rock band.

"Hilarious but poignant, filled with enchantments yet dead-on accurate with regard to modern Indian life, this tour de force will leave readers wondering if Alexie himself hasn't made a deal with the Gentleman in order to do everything so well." —*Publishers Weekly*

Song lyrics begin each chapter.

Alexis, Andre

Fifteen dogs. Andre Alexis. Coach House Books, 2015. 160 p. (Quincunx cycle (Andre Alexis), 2)

ISBN 9781552453056

1. Dogs 2. Consciousness 3. Happiness 4. Gods and goddesses, Greek 5. Humans and dogs 6. Toronto, Ontario 7. Canada 8. Literary fiction 9. Black Canadian fiction 10. Canadian fiction

Rogers Writers' Trust Fiction Prize, 2015; Scotiabank Giller Prize, 2015

Gods Apollo and Hermes grant human intelligence and consciousness to fifteen dogs who wrestle with the challenges that arise as the result of their elevated thinking.

The **hidden** keys. Andre Alexis. Coach House Book, 2016. 200 p. (Quincunx cycle (Andre Alexis), 4)

ISBN 9781552453254

1. Thieves 2. Quests 3. Inheritance and succession 4. Treasure hunting 5. Power (Social sciences) 6. Literary fiction 7. Black Canadian fiction 8. Canadian fiction

Loan Stars Favourites, 2016

Tancred Palmieri, an accomplished and honourable thief is enlisted to help aging heroin addict, Willow Azarian steal the five mysterious objects Willow's wealthy father left to each of his five children that provide clues to the whereabouts of a large inheritance.

Alfon, Dov

A **long** night in Paris. Dov Alfon; translated from the Hebrew by Daniella Zamir. Pegasus Crime, 2020. 432 p.

ISBN 9781643134369

1. Missing persons 2. Intelligence officers 3. Detectives 4. Missing persons investigation 5. Israelis 6. Paris, France 7. Spy fiction 8. Thrillers and suspense 9. Translations

Duncan Lawrie International Dagger, 2019; Loan Stars Favourites, 2019

When one Israeli citizen disappears from Charles de Gaulle airport with a woman in a red dress, you could put it down to youthful indiscretion. When a second from the same flight is disappeared from his hotel room by a girl with a gun, you might just have a diplomatic crisis on your hands.

"Fans of espionage thrillers will hope to see a lot more from this talented author." —*Publishers Weekly*

Originally published in Hebrew as: Lailah arokh be-Pariz (transliteration) by Kinneret, 2016.

Algren, Nelson

★ The **man** with the golden arm: a novel. Nelson Algren. Seven Stories Press, 1999. Viii, 454 p, 4 p. of plates : Illustration

ISBN 9781583220078

1. Drug addicts 2. City life 3. Morphine addiction 4. Criminals 5. Gambling 6. Chicago, Illinois 7. Literary fiction 8. Modern classics

National Book Award for Fiction, 1950

This is the story of "Frankie Machine," a veteran, drug addict, and card-dealer in an illicit poker game being run in Chicago's Near Northwest Side. Frankie has just returned from the federal prison for narcotics addicts in Louisville, Kentucky, where he was exposed to all the pressures, anxieties, and temptations that had put him there in the first place.

Originally published: Garden City, N.Y. : Doubleday, 1949.

A **walk** on the wild side. Nelson Algren. Farrar, Straus and Giroux, 2001. Xi, 346 p.

ISBN 9780374525323

1. Prostitutes 2. Bootleggers 3. City life 4. Man-woman relationships 5. French Quarter (New Orleans, La.) 6. New Orleans, Louisiana 7. 1930s 8. Literary fiction

LC

Depicts the downtrodden prostitutes, bootleggers, and hustlers of Perdido Street in the old French Quarter of 1930s New Orleans.

"Algren's vivid writing gives this degenerate cast the power to shock or appall, and if a glimmer of compassion leaks through occasionally it is slapped down before it gets out of hand." —*Library Journal*

Alharthi, Jokha

Celestial bodies: a novel. Jokha Alharthi; translated from the Arabic by Marilyn Booth. Catapult, 2019. 254 pages

ISBN 9781948226943

1. Sisters 2. Social change 3. Villages 4. Tradition (Philosophy) 5. Shelley, Mary Wollstonecraft 6. Oman 7. 20th century 8. Family sagas 9. Literary fiction 10. Translations

LC 2019944448

Man Booker International Prize, 2019

In the village of al-Awafi in Oman, we encounter three sisters: Mayya, who marries after a heartbreak; Asma, who marries from a sense of duty; and Khawla, who chooses to refuse all offers and await a reunion with the man she loves, who has emigrated to Canada. These three women and their families, their losses and loves, unspool...against a backdrop of a rapidly changing Oman, a country evolving from a traditional, slave-owning society into its complex present.

"A richly layered, ambitious work that teems with human struggles and contradictions, providing fascinating insight into Omani history and society." —*Kirkus*

Translation of: Sayyidat al-qamar.

Originally published: Beirut : Dar al-Adab, 2010.

Translated from the Arabic.

Ali, Monica

★ **Brick** Lane: a novel. Monica Ali. Scribner, 2003. 369 p.

ISBN 9780743243308

1. Self-discovery in women 2. Self-confidence in women 3. Women — Identity 4. Immigrants 5. Women immigrants 6. London, England

7. Bangladesh 8. 1980s 9. 1990s 10. Coming-of-age stories 11. Literary fiction

LC 2003042795

ALA Notable Book, 2004; Shortlisted for the Man Booker Prize, 2003; National Book Critics Circle Award for Fiction finalist, 2003

Presents the story of two Bangladeshi sisters, one who chooses her destiny by opting for a "love marriage" and one who lets destiny dictate her future when she is married off to an older man and moves with him to a small, claustrophobic London flat.

"Nazeen, a young Bangladeshi woman, moves to London's Bangla Town (around the street of the title) in the mid-nineteen eighties after an arranged marriage with an older man. Seen through Nazeen's eyes, England is at first utterly baffling, but over the seventeen years of the narrative (which takes us into the post-September 11th era), she gradually finds her way, bringing up two daughters and eventually starting an all-female tailoring business.... In Ali's subtle narration, Nazeen's mixture of traditionalism, and adaptability, of acceptance and restlessness, emerges as a quiet strength." —*The New Yorker*

Aliu, Xhenet

★ **Brass:** a novel. Xhenet Aliu. Random House, 2018. 304 p.
ISBN 9780399590245

1. Mothers and daughters 2. Immigrants 3. Social classes 4. Goals and objectives 5. Life change events 6. Connecticut 7. 1990s 8. 2010s 9. Literary fiction 10. Parallel narratives 11. Adult books for young adults

LC 2017002763

A fierce debut novel about mothers and daughters, haves and have-nots, and the stark realities behind the American Dream.

"Aliu's riveting, sensitive work shines with warmth, clarity, and a generosity of spirit. Her characters are nuanced and real, capable of taking risks, making mistakes, and growing in unexpected ways." —*Kirkus*

Allain, Suzanne

Miss Lattimore's letter. Suzanne Allain. Jove, 2021. 256 p.
ISBN 9780593197424

1. Misunderstanding 2. Matchmaking 3. Interclass romance 4. anonymous letters 5. Orphans 6. London, England 7. Great Britain 8. Regency period (1811-1820) 9. Regency romances 10. Historical romances 11. Romantic comedies

LC 2021008722

Sophronia Lattimore had her romantic dreams destroyed years ago and is resigned to her role as chaperone for her cousin. Still, she cannot sit idly by when she becomes aware that a gentleman is about to propose to the wrong woman. She sends him an anonymous letter that is soon the talk of the town, particularly when her advice proves to be correct. Her identity is discovered and Sophie, formerly a wallflower, becomes sought after for her expert matchmaking skills. One person who seeks her out is the eligible and attractive Sir Edmund Winslow. As Sophie assists Sir Edmund in his pursuit of a wife, she wishes she could recommend herself as his bride. However, she vows to remain professional and uninvolved while aiding him in his search (especially since the gentleman surely does not return her affections). Three unexpected arrivals soon show up at Sophie's door: the man who once broke her heart, a newlywed who is dissatisfied with the match Sophie made for her, and the man madly in love with Sophie's cousin-all wanting her attention. But when her onetime beau and Sir Edmund both appear to be interested in her, Sophie can't figure out if she's headed for another broken heart or for the altar. How can she be expected to help other people sort out their romantic lives when her own is such a disaster?

"Get ready to read well past bedtime with Allain's (Mr. Malcolm's List) classic Regency romance and its shrewd, funny heroine, who turns her talent for matchmaking into a match of her own." —*Publishers Weekly*

Allen, Jane

I lost my girlish laughter. Jane Allen. Vintange Books, 2019. 256 p.
ISBN 9781984897763

1. Secretaries 2. Film producers and directors 3. Film studios 4. Actors and actresses 5. Film industry and trade 6. Hollywood, California 7. 1930s 8. Satirical fiction 9. Classics

Madge Lawrence, fresh from New York City, lands a job as the personal secretary to the powerful Hollywood producer Sidney Brand (based on the legendary David O. Selznick). In a series of letters home, Western Union telegrams, office memos, Hollywood gossip newspaper items, and personal journal entries, we get served up the inside scoop on all the shenanigans, romances, backroom deals, and betrayals that go into making a movie.

Jane Allen is a peudonym for Silvia Schulman Lardner and Jane Shore.

Originally published: New York : Random House, 1938.

Allen, Jayne

Black girls must die exhausted. Jayne Allen. HarperCollins, 2021. 352 p. (Black girls must die exhausted, 1)
ISBN 9780063142992

1. Thirties (Age) 2. Ambition in women 3. Childlessness 4. Multiracial women 5. African Americans 6. Los Angeles, California 7. California 8. African American fiction 9. Relationship fiction

After learning she might not be able to have children, a 33 year old black woman planning to "have it all," watches her dreams dissolve and must rely on her two best friends to get through.

"Allen's promising debut follows a Black reporter as she navigates matters of race, womanhood, and loyalty while gunning for a promotion at the L.A. TV station where she works." —*Publishers Weekly*

Originally published: 2018.

Allen, Sarah Addison

Garden spells. Sarah Addison Allen. Bantam Books, 2007. 304 p. (Waverley family novels, 1)
ISBN 9780553805482

1. Sisters 2. Magic 3. Enchantment 4. Small towns 5. Gardens 6. North Carolina 7. Southern fiction 8. Gentle reads 9. Relationship fiction

LC 2007000195

RUSA Reading List, 2008

A successful caterer in Bascomb, North Carolina, Claire has always remained tied to the legacy of the Waverly family, until her peaceful life is transformed by Tyler Hughes, an art teacher and new next-door neighbor, and by the return of her prodigal sister, Sydney.

"Spellbindingly charming, Allens impressively accomplished debut novel will bewitch fans of Alice Hoffman and Laura Esquivel, as her entrancing brand of magic realism nimbly blends the evanescent desires of hopeless romantics with the inherent wariness of those who have been hurt once too often." —*Booklist*

The **girl** who chased the moon: a novel. Sarah Addison Allen. Bantam Books, 2010. 304 p.
ISBN 9780553807219

1. Family secrets 2. Grandfathers 3. Recluses 4. Magic 5. Bakers 6. North Carolina 7. Family sagas 8. Southern fiction 9. Gentle reads

LC 2009042254

Emily Benedict came to Mullaby, North Carolina, hoping to solve at least some of the riddles surrounding her mother's life. But the moment Emily enters the house where her mother grew up and meets the grandfather she never knew—a reclusive, real-life gentle giant—she realizes that mysteries aren't solved in Mullaby, they're a way of life.

"That it is never too late to change the future and that high school sins can be forgiven—these are wonderful messages, but Allen's warm characters and quirky setting are what will completely open readers' hearts to this story. Nothing in it disappoints." —*Library Journal*

Allen, Susanna

A **wolf** in duke's clothing. Susanna Allen. Sourcebooks Casablanca, 2021. 352 p. (Shapeshifters of the Beau Monde, 1)
ISBN 9781728230368
1. Shapeshifters 2. Mate selection 3. Dukes and duchesses 4. Wolves 5. Abduction 6. London, England 7. Regency period (1811-1820) 8. Paranormal romances 9. Regency romances 10. Historical romances

Searching for his life mate, the Duke of Lowell, hiding his true nature as a wolf, becomes taken with fiercely independent Felicity Templeton and will do anything to have her for his very own.

"A playful mix of humor, fantasy, and Regency romance conventions, this genre-bending novel introduces a well-constructed world filled with distinctive and endearing characters." —*Publishers Weekly*

Allende, Isabel

Daughter of fortune: a novel. Isabel Allende; translated from the Spanish by Margaret Sayers Peden. Harper Collins, 1999. 399 p.
ISBN 9780060194918
1. Hispanic American women 2. Gold mines and mining 3. Gold rush 4. Male impersonators 5. Chinese Americans 6. California 7. 1840s 8. Historical fiction 9. Literary fiction 10. Translations
LC 99026021
Booklist Editors' Choice, 1999
The story of a young woman's quest for love and fortune during the California Gold Rush in San Francisco.

"This novel has pretensions, but they are overridden by Allende's riproaring girl's adventure story.... Throughout it all, Allende projects a woman's point of view with confidence, control and an expansive definition of romance as a fact of life." —*Time*
Sequel: Portrait in sepia

★ **Eva** Luna. Isabel Allende; translated from the Spanish by Margaret Sayers Peden. A. A. Knopf, 1988. 271 p.
ISBN 9780394572734
1. Women 2. Pompey 3. Storytelling 4. Women — Interpersonal relations 5. South America 6. Picaresque fiction 7. Magical realism 8. Literary fiction
LC 88045272
A servant woman relates the tale of her life and of the landowners, emigres, urchins, guerilla leaders, entertainers, eccentrics, and refugees who instruct and transform her.

"This wonderful novel, crammed with the strange and fantastical, the sensuous and the erotic, also speaks powerfully in the cause of freedom." —*Publishers Weekly*

★ The **house** of the spirits. Isabel Allende; translated from Spanish by Magda Bogin. Bantam Books, 1989. 368 p.
ISBN 9780394539072
1. Culture conflict 2. Family relationships 3. Psychics 4. Man-woman relationships 5. South America 6. Chile 7. Family sagas 8. Magical realism 9. Literary fiction
LC 84048516

The Trueba family embodies strong feelings from the beginning of the 20th century through the assassination of Allende in 1973.

"A strong, absorbing Chilean family chronicle, plushly upholstered—with mystical undercurrents (psychic phenomena) and a measure of leftward political commitment." —*Kirkus*
Translation of: La casa de los espiritus.
Originally published in 1985.

In the midst of winter: a novel. Isabel Allende; translated from the Spanish by Nick Castor and Amanda Hopkinson. Atria Books, 2017. 352 p.
ISBN 9781501178139
1. College teachers 2. Women college teachers 3. Undocumented immigrants 4. Human rights 5. Immigrants 6. New York City 7. Guatemala 8. 2010s 9. 1970s 10. Literary fiction 11. Love stories
LC 2017027807
Loan Stars Favourites, 2017
A minor traffic accident becomes a catalyst for an unexpected bond among a human rights scholar, his Chilean lecturer tenant and an undocumented immigrant from Guatemala, who explore firsthand the difficulties of immigrants and refugees in today's world.

"Filled with Allende's signature lyricism and ingenious plotting, the book delves wonderfully into what it means to respect, protect, and love." —*Publishers Weekly*
Originally published by Vintage Espanol, 2017.

The **Japanese** lover. Isabel Allende. Pocket Books, 2015. 352 p.
ISBN 9781501116971
1. World War II 2. Interracial romance 3. Artists 4. Race relations 5. Aging 6. San Francisco, California 7. Literary fiction
LibraryReads Favorites, 2015
From internationally bestselling author Isabel Allende comes an exquisitely crafted love story and multigenerational epic that sweeps from present-day San Francisco to Poland and the United States during WWII. In 1939, as Poland falls under the shadow of the Nazis and the world goes to war, young Alma Belasco's parents send her away to live in safety with an aunt and uncle in their opulent mansion in San Francisco. There she meets Ichimei Fukuda, the son of the family's Japanese gardener, and between them a tender love blossoms. Following Pearl Harbor, the two are cruelly pulled apart when Ichimei and his family—like thousands of Japanese Americans—are declared enemies by the US government and relocated to internment camps. Throughout their lifetimes, Alma and Ichimei reunite again and again, but theirs is a love they are forever forced to hide from the world. Decades later, Alma is nearing the end of her long and eventful life. Irina Bazili, a care worker struggling to come to terms with her own troubled past, meets the older woman and her grandson, Seth, at Lark House nursing home. As Irina and Seth forge a friendship, they become intrigued by a series of mysterious gifts and letters sent to Alma, and learn about Ichimei and this extraordinary secret passion that has endured for nearly seventy years.

"Allende's latest (Maya's Notebook), a glorious family saga, with its rich cast of decent, complex characters caught up in America's struggles with war, prejudice, AIDS, and society's old taboos that are fast disappearing, is a beautiful tribute to devotion." —*Library Journal*
Originally published as El Amante Japones in 2015 in Spain by Penguin Random House Grupo Editorial. First published in the USA by Atria Books, 2015. First published in Great Britain by Scribner, 2015.

A **long** petal of the sea: a novel. Isabel Allende; translated from the Spanish by Nick Caistor and Amanda Hopkinson. Ballantine Books, 2020. 352 p.
ISBN 9781984820150

1. Neruda, Pablo 2. Refugees 3. Loss (Psychology) 4. Young widows 5. Physicians 6. Marriage 7. Chile 8. Spain 9. 20th century 10. Historical fiction 11. Translations

LC 2019037428

Loan Stars Favourites, 2020

Sponsored by the poet Pablo Neruda to flee the violence of the Spanish Civil War, a pregnant widow and an army doctor unite in an arranged marriage, only to be swept up by the early days of World War II.

"Allende's assured prose vividly evokes her fictional characters, historical figures like Neruda, and decades of complex international history; her imagery makes the suffering of war and displacement palpable yet also does justice to human strength, hope and rebirth." —*Publishers Weekly*

Originally published in Spain in 2019 as Largo pétalo de mar—Title page verso.

Translated from the Spanish.

Of love and shadows. Isabel Allende; translated from the Spanish by Margaret Sayers Peden. A. A. Knopf, 1987. 274 p.

ISBN 9780394549620

1. Dictatorship 2. Political refugees 3. Journalists 4. Journalism — Political aspects 5. Man-woman relationships 6. Latin America 7. Literary fiction 8. Political fiction 9. Love stories

LC 86046164

Soaring Eagle Book Award (Wyoming), 1990

Irene Beltran, a reporter for a women's magazine in a Latin American country, and Francisco Leal, a photographer and a clandestine worker in the resistance, uncover a hideous crime that challenges the official terrorism of their country's military dictatorship.

"Ms. Allende skillfully evokes both the terrors of daily life under military rule and the subtler forms of resistance in the hidden corners and 'shadows' of her title, particularly in the churches or in simple unsung acts of solidarity. At the same time the author ably captures the voices of the regime's apologists—the complex lies and cliches of its proud male foot soldiers and the pat false phrases of its rich lady cheerleaders." —*New York Times Book Review*

Translation of De amor y de sombra.

Portrait in sepia: a novel. Isabel Allende; translated from the Spanish by Margaret Sayers Peden. Harper Collins Publishers, 2001. 304 p.

ISBN 9780066211619

1. Family secrets 2. Memories 3. Betrayal 4. Grandmother and child 5. Man-woman relationships 6. Chile 7. 19th century 8. Family sagas 9. Translations 10. Literary fiction

LC 54127

With her earliest memories erased by a brutal trauma, Aurora del Valle is raised amid great wealth in Chile by her shrewd, commanding grandmother. But her nights are tormented by a nightmare set in San Francisco's Chinatown. Now, reaching womanhood and thrust into a marriage that quickly leaves her disillusioned, she begins a search for her missing years and unwinds a twisted saga linking three generations of a powerful family to a courageous Chinese physician and Eliza Sommers, a protagonist of Allende's Daughter of Fortune, in a tale that explores the complexity of passion, the power of memory, and a woman's emerging self.

"Through Aurora, Allende exercises her supreme storytelling abilities, of which strong, passionate characters are paramount." —*Publishers Weekly*

Translation of: Retrato en sepia.

Sequel to: Daughter of fortune.

Ripper: a novel. Isabel Allende; translated from the Spanish by Oliver Brock and Frank Wynne. Harper, 2014. 478 p.

ISBN 9780062291400

1. Children of divorced parents 2. Serial murderers 3. Internet games 4. Murder investigation 5. Teenagers 6. San Francisco, California 7. Mysteries 8. Literary fiction 9. Translations 10. Adult books for young adults

LC 2013030359

LibraryReads Favorites, 2014

Fascinated by the dark side of human nature, high school senior Amanda Jackson, a natural-born sleuth addicted to an online mystery game called Ripper, launches her own investigation into a string of strange murders across the city that hits too close to home when her mother vanishes.

Originally published as: El juego de Ripper. Spain : Random House Mondadori, 2014.

The stories of Eva Luna. Isabel Allende; translated from the Spanish by Margaret Sayers Peden. Atheneum, 1991. 330 p.

ISBN 9780689121029

1. South America 2. Magical realism 3. Literary fiction 4. Short stories

LC 90039615

When her lover asks her to tell him a story, Eva Luna complies with this collection of tales

"The title character of Allende's Eva Luna returns to frame this collection of stories in a Scheherazade-like fashion.... Allende covers familiar territory: social warfare between the rich and the poor, sexual battles between men and women, the dissolution of corrupt politicians and macho military leaders, all set within the landscape of contemporary South America." —*Booklist*

23 short stories.

Translation of Cuentos de Eva Luna.

Allio, Kirstin

Buddhism for Western children: a novel. Kirstin Allio. University of Iowa Press, 2018. 284 p.

ISBN 9781609385965

1. Cults 2. Spirituality 3. Gurus 4. Life change events 5. Communities 6. Maine 7. New Mexico 8. 1970s 9. 1980s 10. Coming-of-age stories

LC 2018010061

Set on the coast of Maine and in the high desert of New Mexico in the late 1970s through the early 80s, Buddhism for Western Children is a universal and timeless story of a boy who must escape subjugation, tell his story, and reclaim his soul.

Allison, Dorothy

★ **Bastard** out of Carolina. Dorothy Allison. Dutton, 1992. 309 p.

ISBN 9780525934257

1. Twelve-year-old girls 2. Poor families 3. Stepfathers 4. Grant, Cary 5. Sexually abused children 6. South Carolina 7. 1950s 8. Coming-of-age stories 9. Books to movies 10. Southern Gothic

LC 91034607

National Book Award for Fiction finalist, 1992

Tired of being labeled white trash, Ruth Anne Boatwright—a South Carolina bastard who is attached to the indomitable women in her mother's family—longs to escape from her hometown, and especially from Daddy Glen and his meanspirited jealousy.

"Set in the rural South, this tale centers around the Boatwright family, a proud and closeknit clan known for their drinking, fighting, and womanizing. Nicknamed Bone by her Uncle Earle, Ruth Anne is the bastard child of Anney Boatwright, who has fought tirelessly to legitimize her child. When she marries Glen, a man from a good family, it appears that her prayers have been answered. However, Anney suffers a miscarriage and Glen begins drifting. He develops a contentious relationship with Bone and then begins taking sexual liberties with her.... Unaware of her husband's abusive behavior, Anney stands by her man. Eventually, a violent encounter wrests Bone away from her stepfather." —*Library Journal*

Alomar, Osama

The **teeth** of the comb & other stories. Osama Alomar; translated by Osama Alomar and C.J. Collins. New Directions, 2017. 102 p.
ISBN 9780811226073
1. Animals 2. Nature 3. Allegories 4. Short stories 5. Translations
LC 2016039664
Personified animals (snakes, wolves, sheep), natural things (a swamp, a lake, a rainbow, trees), mankind's creations (trucks, swords, zeroes) are all characters in The Teeth of the Comb. They aspire, they plot, they hope, they destroy, they fail, they love.
Translated from the Arabic.

Alpsten, Ellen

Tsarina. Ellen Alpsten. St. Martin's Press, 2020. 464 p.
ISBN 9781250214430
1. Catherine 2. Women rulers 3. Determination in women 4. Inheritance and succession 5. Courts and courtiers 6. Rulers 7. Russia 8. Romanov Dynasty (1613-1917) 9. Biographical fiction 10. Historical fiction
LC 2020019385
A narrative tale based on the true story of Peter the Great's second wife, Catherine Alexeyevna, recounts how she used her extraordinary intelligence to escape poverty and assume her unstable husband's responsibilities in 18th-century Russia.
"Lovers of Russian history, strong women protagonists, and sweeping historicals will savor this vivid portrait." —*Publishers Weekly*

Alsterdal, Tove

We know you remember. Tove Alsterdal. HarperCollins, 2021. 448 p. (High coast novels, 1)
ISBN 9780063115064
1. Women detectives 2. Juvenile delinquents 3. Suspicion 4. Collective memory 5. Small town life 6. Sweden 7. Translations 8. Scandinavian crime fiction 9. Police procedurals
The past comes flooding back for police detective Eira Sjodin when Olof Hagstrm?, who served time for raping and murdering a local girl, returns home to find his father dead under suspicious circumstances.
"[Police detective Eira Sjodin] must deal with pernicious changes in Swedish policing and grapple with her mother's descent into dementia. Strong local color, convincing characters, and a twisty plot make this a standout. This is Swedish noir at its murky best." —*Publishers Weekly*
Originally published: 2020
Translated from the Swedish.

Altan, Ahmet

★ **Love** in the days of rebellion. . Europa Editions, 2020. 496 p.
ISBN 9781609456191
1. Political intrigue 2. Suicidal behavior 3. Love 4. Sultans 5. Freedom 6. Turkey 7. 20th century 8. Historical fiction 9. Literary fiction 10. Translations
Weaving together tortured love affairs, political intrigue, power struggles, and social upheavals, Love in the Days of Rebellion offers a powerful and vivid tableau of the crisis of the Ottoman Empire in the early 20th century.

"An ambitious and intelligent thriller about love and war." —*Kirkus*
Translation of: Isyan gunlerinde ask.
Originally published : Istanbul : Can Yayinlari, 2001.
Translated from the Turkish.

Alten, Steve

Meg: generations. Steve Alten. Forge, 2020. 304 p. (Megalodon series, 6)
ISBN 9781250621528
1. Sharks 2. Marine parks and reserves 3. Sea monsters 4. Humans and sharks 5. Marine biologists 6. Dubai 7. Arabian Sea 8. Sea stories 9. Horror 10. Adventure stories
Dubai: An impossibility is being taken to the Middle East. The transport vessel Tonga is carrying a liopleurodon to the City of Gold. But while investors gawk at the prehistoric creature, any even more dangerous creature is beginning to stir. The megalodon shark that Jonas Taylor worked so hard to capture is coming out of it's drug-induced stupor and refuses to be contained. No both ancient creatures, older than mankind itself, are loose in the waters of the Arabian Sea, and the region will never be the same.
"Alten writes the books with such enthusiasm that he sweeps us up and carries us along. He believes the story he's telling, so we believe it, too." —*Booklist*

Alvar, Mia

In the country: stories. Mia Alvar. Alfred A. Knopf, 2015. 288 p.
ISBN 9780385352819
1. Filipinos 2. Voyages and travels 3. Immigration and emigration 4. Home (Concept) 5. Families 6. Literary fiction 7. Short stories
LC 2014036940
ALA Notable Book, 2016
Exploring the universal experience of loss, displacement, and the longing to connect across borders both real and imagined, In the Country speaks to the heart of everyone who has ever searched for a place to call home.
"Both intrepid readers and armchair tourists eager to explore debut narratives that straddle multiple countries and cultures a la Violet Kupersmith's The Frangipani Hotel or Rajesh Parameswaran's I Am an Executioner will be opulently rewarded here." —*Library Journal*

Alvarez, Julia

★ **Afterlife:** a novel. Julia Alvarez. Algonquin Books of Chapel Hill, 2020. 208 p.
ISBN 9781643750255
1. Immigrants 2. Women authors 3. Grief 4. Sisters 5. Families 6. Domestic fiction 7. Literary fiction 8. Adult books for young adults
LC 2019042436
Reeling from her beloved husband's sudden death in the wake of her retirement, an immigrant writer is further derailed by the reappearance of her unstable sister and an entreaty for help by a pregnant undocumented teen.
"Alvarez writes with knowing warmth about how well sisters know how to push on each other's bruises and how powerfully they can lift each other up. In this bighearted novel, family bonds heal a woman's grief." —*Kirkus*

How the Garcia girls lost their accents. Julia Alvarez. Algonquin Books of Chapel Hill, 1991. 290 p.
ISBN 9780945575573
1. Dominican American families 2. Sisters 3. Immigrants, Hispanic American 4. Hispanic Americans 5. Immigrant families 6. New York

City 7. Bronx, New York City 8. 1960s 9. Relationship fiction 10. Multiple perspectives

LC 90048575

ALA Notable Book, 1992

Forced to flee their native Caribbean island after an attempted coup, ιe Garcias—Carlos, Laura, and their four daughters—must learn a new ay of life in the Bronx, while trying to cling to the old ways that they ved.

"This is an account of parallel odysseys, as each of the four daughters lapts in her own way, and a large part of Alvarez's accomplishment is the ιmplexity with which these vivid characters are rendered." —*Publishers eekly*

Sequel: Yo!

lyan, Hala

Salt houses. Hala Alyan. Houghton Mifflin Harcourt, 2017. 336 p. ISBN 9780544912588

1. Refugees 2. Culture conflict 3. Home (Concept) 4. Palestinians — Diaspora 5. War — Psychological aspects 6. Palestine 7. Mengele, Josef 8. Family sagas 9. Literary fiction

LC 2016046956

Middle East Book Award, Youth Literature Winner, 2017

Foreseeing blessings and troubles in the lives of her daughter and ιandchildren, Salma endures hardships stemming from the Six-Day War ´ 1967 in Palestine before rebuilding in Kuwait, before the family is scat-red by Saddam Hussein's regime.

"A deeply moving look inside the Palestinian diaspora." —*Kirkus*

ιmado, Jorge

★ **Dona** Flor and her two husbands: a moral and amorous tale. Jorge ιmado; translated from the Portuguese by Harriet de Onis. Vintage Books,)06. 576 p.

ISBN 9780307276643

1. Women 2. Women — Sexuality 3. Husband and wife 4. Married people 5. Bahia, Brazil 6. Brazil 7. Magical realism 8. Literary fiction 9. Translations

LC 69010710

"Dona Flor has such a harridan of a mother (Dona Rozilda) that you ιould like her to have her cake and eat it, too, and she very nearly does. ιona Flor's first husband, Vadinho, is a scamp, a prevaricator, and a ιhameless lover.' On Carnival Sunday, at the height of the gaiety, filled ιith rum, he drops dead. Dona Flor is desolate but cuts a handsome figure ι a widow. She lives through the wake (a gem of a scene) and her mourn-ιg quite well, with memories and her cooking school to sustain her. Then ιitors appear. None appeal but Dr. Teodoro Madureira, pharmacist and ιassoonist, a pillar of propriety. Dona Rozilda is ecstatic, but the ιell-rounded Dona Flor has her troubles, for alas, Dr. Teodoro is no lover. ιreams haunt her and strange things begin to happen. Thanks to a Yoruba ιarm, Vadinho returns to ravish our bewildered heroine, and then the fun ιgins. Bahia in Brazil is the setting for this delectable rum cake of a ιvel." —*Publishers Weekly*

Originally published in Portuguese as Dona Flor e seus dois maridos by Livraria Martins Editora, Sao Paulo, in 1966.

This translation originally published in hardcover by Alfred A. Knopf, Inc. New York, in 1969.

Gabriela, clove and cinnamon. Jorge Amado; translated from the ιrtuguese by James L. Taylor and William L. Grossman. Vintage Books,)06. 425 p.

ISBN 9780307276650

1. Women cooks 2. Brazil 3. Literary fiction 4. Translations

In 1925, the arrival of a beautiful mulatto girl named Gabriela from the backlands to become the new cook in a popular local café transforms the lives of many inhabitants of the provincial Brazilian city of Ilheus.

Amdahl, Gary

I am death: two novellas. Gary Amdahl. Milkweed Editions, 2008. 169 p.

ISBN 9781571310712

1. Ghostwriters 2. Men with paranoia 3. Employees — Interpersonal relations 4. Gangsters 5. Fear in men 6. Black humor 7. Psychological fiction

LC 2008000365

A pair of novellas by the Pushcart Prize-winning author of Visigoth includes "I Am Death: Bartleby the Mobster," in which a muckraking journalist finds himself in over his head while ghost writing a mob boss's autobiography, and "Peasants," in which a publishing employee fears he is being targeted by co-workers.

"A writer who inhabits this literary realm risks sacrificing meaning in pursuit of cleverness, but Amdahl stays true to his antiheroes. Jack and Walter don't insult us by saying they're better for their struggles. Instead, they speak another truth, one that's much more difficult to hear: Death, and, at this point only death, will set us free." —*Los Angeles Times Book Review*

Ames, Jonathan

A man named Doll. Jonathan Ames. Mulholland Books, 2021. 208 p. ISBN 9780316703659

1. Detectives 2. Veterans 3. Human body parts industry and trade 4. Organized crime 5. Former police 6. Los Angeles, California 7. California 8. Noir fiction

Happy Doll is a charming, if occasionally inexpert, private detective living just one sheer cliff drop beneath the Hollywood sign with his beloved half-Chihuahua half-Terrier, George. A veteran of both the Navy and LAPD, Doll supplements his meager income as a P.I. by working through the night at a local Thai spa that offers its clients a number of special services. Armed with his sixteen-inch steel telescopic baton, biting dry humor, and just a bit of a hero complex, the ex-cop sets out to protect the women who work there from clients who have trouble understanding the word "no." Doll gets by just fine following his two basic rules: bark loudly and act first. But when things get out-of-hand with one particularly violent patron, even he finds himself wildly out of his depth, and then things take an even more dangerous twist when an old friend from his days as a cop shows up at his door with a bullet in his gut.

"Ames delivers an old-school L.A. crime novel that evokes Chandler with maybe an aftertaste of Bukowski. Readers expecting action won't be let down, and the sparkling yet unpretentious language gives the whole an extra kick." —*Booklist*

Amidon, Stephen

Security: a novel. Stephen Amidon. Farrar, Straus and Giroux, 2009. 288 p.

ISBN 9780374257118

1. Private security services 2. Sex crimes 3. Private police 4. Indecent assault 5. Electric alarms 6. New England 7. Massachusetts 8. Satirical fiction

LC 2008013850

Sleepy Stoneleigh, Massachusetts, is turned upside down by a local student's claims that she had been sexually assaulted by a wealthy resident, an accusation that prompts an investigation by security company head Edward Inman.

"The book is part campus tale, part mystery, part police procedural. The proportions are well mixed. Stoneleigh's customary tranquility is stirred when Mary Steckl, a local college student, accuses Doyle Cutler of sexually assaulting her. Cutler rebounds with an accusation that Mary's father, a drunk with a criminal record, is the real perp. The town is divided.... For all its plot twists, Security is a book stitched of sensible prose. There are no flourishes, no embroidery." —*New York Observer*

Amirrezvani, Anita

The **blood** of flowers: a novel. Anita Amirrezvani. Little, Brown, 2007. 384 p.
ISBN 9780316065764
1. Forced marriage 2. Teenage girls 3. Comets 4. Fathers — Death 5. Bad luck 6. Persian Empire 7. Iran 8. 17th century 9. Historical fiction 10. Adult books for young adults

LC 2006023034

School Library Journal Best Books: Best Adult Books 4 Teens, 2007

After her father dies without leaving her with a dowry, a seventeenth-century Persian teen becomes a servant to her wealthy rug designer uncle in the court of Shah Abbas the Great, where her weaving talents prove both a blessing and curse.

"The author has crafted a lush and sensuous story, where betrayal is common, wealth is unequally distributed, and temporary marriages allow prosperous men to take advantage of impoverished virgins without the burden of a full-time wife.... Though the trajectory of this novel seemed sure to lead toward a full marriage in a society where this is expected, Amirrezvani provides more than that: a wonderful man might exist in fairytales, but a woman can be self-sufficient and happy without him." —*PopMatters*

Equal of the sun. Anita Amirrezvani. Simon & Schuster 2012. 352 p.
ISBN 9781451660463
1. Princesses 2. Secrecy in government 3. Eunuchs 4. Courts and courtiers 5. Political intrigue 6. Iran 7. 16th century 8. Historical fiction

When the court of 16th-century Iran is thrown into turmoil by the heirless Shah's death, his daughter, Princess Pari, incites dissent with her efforts to instill order and taps the assistance of a eunuch servant to navigate a Machiavellian power struggle.

Amis, Kingsley

★ **Lucky** Jim. Kingsley Amis. Penguin, 1992. 251 p.
ISBN 9780140186307
1. College teachers 2. Men's fantasies 3. Drinking 4. Universities and colleges 5. Academic rivalry 6. Great Britain 7. 1950s 8. Literary fiction 9. Satirical fiction 10. Modern classics

LC 93233719

Somerset Maugham Award, 1955

A young Englishman embarks on a humorous crusade against traditional class structures.

Originally published: London : Gollancz, 1954.

Amis, Martin

★ **Inside** story. Martin Amis. Alfred A. Knopf, 2020. 560 p.
ISBN 9780593318294
1. Amis, Martin 2. Authors 3. Love 4. Death 5. Writing 6. Friendship 7. Autobiographical fiction 8. Literary fiction

LC 2020021012

National Book Critics Circle Award for Fiction finalist, 2020.

An autobiographical novel by the author of Experience draws on his close friendship with the late philosopher Christopher Hitchens and follows their relationships and journalistic endeavors against a backdrop of 20th-century history.

"Amis is a magnet for readers who love exceptional style and bold content, and this memoir disguised as a novel will be a particularly powerful draw." —*Booklist*

Includes index.

Lionel Asbo: state of England. Martin Amis. Alfred A. Knopf, 2012. 320 p.
ISBN 9780307958082
1. Guardian and ward 2. Criminals 3. Lottery winners 4. Multiracial men 5. Popular culture 6. England 7. Satirical fiction 8. Hitler, Adolf

A satire of modern society and celebrity culture finds the seemingly simple pursuits of young Desmond Pepperdine hampered by his uncle Lionel's near-criminal habits, which become more prominent when Lionel wins the lottery.

London fields: a novel. Martin Amis. Harmony Books, 1989. 470 p.
ISBN 9780886192563
1. Women psychics 2. Manipulation by women 3. Criminals 4. Rich men 5. Love triangles 6. London, England 7. 1990s 8. Mysteries 9. Literary fiction 10. Books to movies

LC 89049558

"Amis's technical virtuosity is extraordinary.... [This is] the most intellectually interesting fiction of the year, and a work beyond the reach of any British contemporary. Amis's figures, like those of Dickens, are caricatures that have their own gigantic reality." —*London Review of Books*

★ The **pregnant** widow. Martin Amis. Alfred A. Knopf, 2010. 272 p.
ISBN 9781400044528
1. College students — Sexuality 2. Love triangles 3. Man-woman relationships 4. British in Italy 5. Memory 6. Italy 7. London, England 8. 1970s 9. Literary fiction

LC 2009041689

The year is 1970, and it's a long, hot summer. In a castle on a mountainside in Italy, half a dozen young lives are afloat on a sea of change, trapped inside the history of the sexual revolution. The girls are acting like boys, the boys are going on acting like boys, and Keith Nearing—twenty years old, a literature student all clogged up with the English novel—is struggling to twist feminism and women's ascendency toward his own ends.

"When Amis shows us the sexual revolution in action and reaction, when he tells us how people dressed and what it meant, when he depicts the effects of women's sexual aggression on men's egos, how women talked about men and vice versa when he is pretending to be a well-behaved comic-naturalist novelist, the book works. But when he philosophises he can sound just like tedious-clever journalism.... And the narrative is slowed and blurred by Amis' unwillingness ever to say anything in a simple or straightforward way." —*The Age*

★ **Time's** arrow, or The nature of the offense. Martin Amis. Harmony Books, 1991. 168 p.
ISBN 9780517585153
1. Nazi physicians 2. Holocaust (1933-1945) 3. Guilt in men 4. Conscience 5. Physicians 6. Literary fiction

LC 91004144

Shortlisted for the Booker-McConnell Prize, 1991

Escaping from the body of a dying doctor who had worked in Nazi concentration camps, the doctor's conciousness begins living the doctor's life backward, aware only that he is living the life of a horrible man at a horrible place in time

★ The **zone** of interest: a novel. Martin Amis. Knopf, 2014. 288 p.
ISBN 9780385353496

1. Holocaust (1933-1945) 2. Concentration camps 3. Personal conduct 4. Courtship 5. Imprisonment 6. Poland 7. Germany 8. Second World War era (1939-1945) 9. Psychological fiction 10. Historical fiction 11. First person narratives

LC 2014011667

Shortlisted for the Walter Scott Prize for Historical Fiction, 2015

A portrait of life and unexpected love in a concentration camp explores the depths and contradictions of the human soul as well as the capacity of individuals who are tested to acknowledge their true selves.

"An audaciously satiric and brilliantly realized tale about personal angst and mass psychosis, and the immolation of self and soul." —*Booklist*

Ammaniti, Niccolo

I'm not scared. Niccolo Ammaniti; translated from the Italian by Jonathan Hunt. Canongate, 2003. 200 p.

ISBN 9781841952970

1. Nine-year-old boys 2. Children's secrets 3. Innocence (Personal quality) 4. Italy 5. 1970s 6. Psychological fiction 7. Translations

In the summer of 1978 in a small Italian village, nine-year-old Michele Amitrano loses his innocence of childhood when he accidentally uncovers a dark secret being kept by the adults of Acqua Traverse.

"During a piercingly hot summer, a few kilometres from a bone-dry hamlet in rural Tuscany, a shy, nervy, nine-year-old boy called Michele explores a derelict house and discovers, under moldering leaves, a horrifying secret. The novel is saved from sensationalism by Ammaniti's almost cinematic ability to conjure detail." —*The New Yorker*

Translation of: Io non ho paura.

Originally published: Torino : Einaudi, 2001.

Anam, Tahmima

The **bones** of grace. Tahmima Anam. Harper, 2016. 304 p. (Haque family trilogy, 3)

ISBN 9780061478949

1. Muslims 2. Women's role 3. Forced marriage 4. Islam 5. Loyalty 6. Bangladesh 7. Literary fiction

Zubaida is torn between an arranged marriage in Bangladesh and her love for Elijah Strong, the American she met while working in Boston.

"In having Zubaida come to terms with her origins and her own contentment, Anam captures two very different cultures in an introspective character study that will mesmerize readers from the very first page." —*Publishers Weekly*

Originally published: Great Britain : Edinburgh, 2016.

The **startup** wife. Tahmima Anam. Scribner, 2021. 304 p.

ISBN 9781982156183

1. Computer programming 2. New businesses 3. Bangladeshi Americans 4. Married women 5. Application software 6. Long Island, New York 7. 21st century 8. Relationship fiction

Brilliant coder and possessor of a Pi tattoo, Asha is poised to revolutionize artificial intelligence when she is reunited with her high school crush, Cyrus Jones.

"Anam brings the issue of gender equality in work and relationships to the forefront of the narrative. With a mention of the current pandemic woven into the story, Anam's modern tale has plenty of talking points that will make it a good selection for book groups." —*Library Journal*

Anappara, Deepa

Djinn patrol on the purple line: a novel. Deepa Anappara. Random House, 2020. 256 p.

ISBN 9780593129197

1. Missing children 2. Police corruption 3. Friendship 4. Growing up 5. East Indians 6. India 7. Mysteries 8. Literary fiction 9. Coming-of-age stories 10. Adult books for young adults

LC 2019031351

Edgar Allan Poe Award for Best Novel, 2021; New York Times Notable Book, 2020

A 9-year-old reality-television enthusiast in India uses crime-show approaches to investigate the disappearance of a classmate, before additional abductions shatter life in his sprawling city home.

"The author has done an excellent job of telling her sometimes sad story in Jai's credible nine-year-old voice, and her treatment of her setting, with its ingrained social inequities, is a model of verisimilitude." —*Booklist*

Anaya, Rudolfo A.

The **man** who could fly and other stories. Rudolfo Anaya. University of Oklahoma Press, 2006. 197 p.

ISBN 9780806137384

1. Mexican Americans 2. Mexican American women 3. Interpersonal relations 4. Southwest (United States) 5. Mexico 6. Short stories 7. Adult books for young adults

LC 2005051426

"The stories showcase 30 years of Anaya's Chicano literary voice, simultaneously innocent and omniscient and always rooted in the landscape, especially the windswept llanos of New Mexico.... The characters' passionate force radiates from Anaya's simple prose as they confront ethical dilemmas in varied regional settings." —*Library Journal*

Collects 18 short stories.

Anders, Adriana

Under her skin. Adriana Anders. Sourcebooks, 2017. 352 p. (Blank canvas series, 1)

ISBN 9781492633846

1. Coping 2. Second chances 3. Abused women 4. Small towns 5. Tattooing 6. Virginia 7. Contemporary romances

Old hag in need of live-in helper to abuse. Nothing kinky." Although the job description is far from reassuring, the position is Uma's best option right now. On the run from her monstrously abusive ex-boyfriend, who tortured and then forcibly tattooed her, Uma arrives in Blackwood, Virginia, seeking a fresh start. As she adjusts to the eccentricities of her new employer, the cantankerous Ms. Lloyd, Uma gets to know her neighbor, Ivan, a gentle blacksmith with a troubled past. With its sympathetic characters and emotional intensity, this one will make an indelible impression upon readers.

"An incredibly sexy, heartbreaking, and intense romantic debut." —*Kirkus*

Anders, Charlie Jane

★ **All** the birds in the sky. Charlie Jane Anders. Tor, 2016. 320 p.

ISBN 9780765379948

1. Reunions 2. End of the world 3. Friendship 4. Magic 5. Engineers 6. San Francisco, California 7. Science fantasy 8. Apocalyptic fiction 9. Adult books for young adults

LC 2015031481

Booklist Editors' Choice: Adult Books for Young Adults, 2016; Locus Award for Fantasy Novel, 2017; Nebula Award for Best Novel, 2016

Reunited as adults in the hipster mecca San Francisco as the planet falls apart around them, childhood friends Patricia Delfine, who is magically gifted, and Laurence Armstead, an engineering genius, discover that something bigger than either of them has brought them together to either save the world, or plunge it into a new dark ages.

"Anders clearly has an intimate understanding of how hard it is to find friends when you're perceived as 'different' as well as a sweeping sense of how nice it would be to solve large problems with a single solution (and how infrequently that succeeds)." —*Kirkus*

★ The **city** in the middle of the night. Charlie Jane Anders. Tor Books, 2019. 336 p.

ISBN 9780765379962

1. Exiles 2. Sankara, Thomas 3. Human/alien encounters 4. Aliens 5. Survival 6. Social science fiction 7. Science fiction 8. Adult books for young adults

LC 2018022175

Locus Award for Best Science Fiction Novel, 2020

A reluctant revolutionary survives exile by forging an unusual, world-changing bond with a family of ice creatures that live outside the human confines of their dying planet.

Rock Manning goes for broke. Charlie Jane Anders. Subterranean Press, 2018. 128 p.

ISBN 9781596068780

1. Filmmakers 2. Near future 3. Stunts 4. Slapstick 5. End of the world 6. United States 7. Farcical fiction 8. Apocalyptic fiction

When their films become the escapist fun that society needs in a world of violence and destruction, Rock Manning and Sally Hamster are approached by a fascist militia known as the Red Bandanas, to star in their propaganda films promoting their movement.

This gonzo vision of an apocalyptic America is a challenging mixture of both farce and tragedy; it makes its point about the influence and responsibility of the media in the weirdest possible way.

Andersen, Laura

The **Boleyn** deceit. Laura Andersen. Ballantine Books, 2013. 368 p. (Anne Boleyn trilogy, 2)

ISBN 9780345534118

1. Anne Boleyn 2. Rulers 3. Political intrigue 4. Conspiracies 5. Heirs and heiresses 6. Courts and courtiers 7. Great Britain 8. 16th century 9. Alternate histories

Henry IX, known as William, is the son of Anne Boleyn and now the leader of England, his regency period finally at an end. His newfound power, however, comes with the looming specter of war with the other major powers of Europe, with strategic alliances that must be forged on both the battlefield and in the bedroom, and with a court, severed by religion, rife with plots to take over the throne. Will trusts only three people: his older sister, Elizabeth; his best friend and loyal counselor, Dominic; and Minuette, a young orphan raised as a royal ward by Anne Boleyn. But as the pressure rises alongside the threat to his life, even they William must begin to question—and to fear...

"Detailed and quick paced, this will have series fans devouring it and emerging eager for the final book." —*Booklist*

Includes reading group guide.

★ The **Boleyn** king. Laura Andersen. Ballantine Books Trade Paperbacks, 2013. 304 p. (Anne Boleyn trilogy, 1)

ISBN 9780345534095

1. Anne Boleyn 2. Rulers 3. Political intrigue 4. Conspiracies 5. Heirs and heiresses 6. Courts and courtiers 7. Great Britain 8. England 9. Tudor period (1485-1603) 10. 16th century 11. Alternate histories

LC 2013004505

Romantic Times Reviewer's Choice Award, 2013

Struggling to prove himself as the French threaten battle and the Catholics plot at home, seventeen-year-old King Henry IX relies on his best friend and loyal counselor, Dominic, until they both fall in love with the same woman.

The **Boleyn** reckoning. Laura Andersen. Ballantine Books, 2014. 400 p. (Anne Boleyn trilogy, 3)

ISBN 9780345534132

1. Anne Boleyn 2. Rulers 3. Political intrigue 4. Conspiracies 5. Heirs and heiresses 6. Courts and courtiers 7. Great Britain 8. 16th century 9. Alternate histories

LC 2014012571

Elizabeth Tudor is at a crossroads. Though her brother, William, has survived the smallpox, scars linger on the king's body and mind and he marches to the drumbeat of his own desires rather than his country's welfare. Wary, Elizabeth assembles her own shadow court to protect England as best she can. Meanwhile, Minuette and Dominic have married in secret, but the truth cannot stay hidden for long. Faced with betrayal by those he loved most, William's need for vengeance pushes England to the brink of civil war and in the end, Elizabeth must choose: her brother, or her country?

A Ballantine Books Trade Paperback Original.

Anderson, Alison

The **summer** guest. Alison Anderson. HarperCollins, 2016. 400 p.

ISBN 9780062423368

1. Chekhov, Anton Pavlovich 2. Diary writing 3. Women physicians 4. Blindness 5. Friendship 6. Lost books 7. Ukraine 8. London, England 9. 1880s 10. 21st century 11. Literary fiction 12. Historical fiction 13. Parallel narratives

After a diary documenting a friendship between a young Ukrainian doctor and author Anton Pavlovich Chekhov is found, Katya Kendall believes it may be the key to saving her struggling publishing house.

Anderson, Kent

Green sun: a novel. Kent Anderson. Mulholland Books, 2018. 340 p.

ISBN 9780316466806

1. Police 2. Vietnam veterans 3. Community policing 4. African American neighborhoods 5. Urban problems 6. Oakland, California 7. California 8. 1980s 9. Police procedurals

Moving to 1980s East Oakland, California, to join the mostly black community he serves and protects, Vietnam veteran Hanson befriends a neighborhood boy, pursues a romantic relationship, navigates a tricky relationship with a drug dealer and works diligently to stay honest in spite of the forces of hate and violence that compromise his job.

Anderson, Kevin J.

Death warmed over. Kevin J. Anderson. Kensington Books, 2012. 304 p. (Shamble & Die Investigations, 1)

ISBN 9780758277343

1. Zombies 2. Private investigators 3. Undead 4. Supernatural 5. Murder victims 6. New Orleans, Louisiana 7. Humorous stories 8. Mysteries

Zombie P.I. Dan Chambeaux, along with his human partner and ghost girlfriend, tries to juggle his unnatural caseload, including a resurrected mummy who is suing the museum that put him on display, while trying to figure out who killed him.

The **last** days of Krypton. Kevin J. Anderson. William Morrow, 2007. 432 p.

ISBN 9780061340741

1. Power (Social sciences) 2. Isolationism 3. Natural disasters 4. Greed in men 5. Space flight 6. Superhero stories 7. Franchise books 8. Adult books for young adults

LC 2007031174

An account of the tragic destruction of Superman's home planet depicts the lives of his parents, Jor-El and Lara, while giving insight into the political factors that doomed the planet and paved the way for such villains as Brainiac and General Zod.

Anderton, Jo

Debris. Jo Anderton. Angry Robot, 2011. 432 p. (Veiled worlds trilogy, 1)
ISBN 9780857661548
1. Conspiracies 2. Psychokinesis 3. Brain injury 4. Pariahs 5. Social classes 6. Science fiction 7. First person narratives 8. Australian fiction
Library Journal Best Books, 2011

Able to control the building blocks of reality with the power of her mind, Tanyana, a gifted engineer, must find out who is trying to destroy her after a horrific disaster causes her to be demoted to the lowest of the low as a debris collector.

"Anderton's debut impressively combines far-future world-building, conspiracies, and a redemption quest.... Anderton clearly telegraphs the overall plot arc, but keeps it interesting with Tanyana's strong, proud narrative voice and the complex culture built up around the pions and debris." —*Publishers Weekly*

Andreades, Daphne Palasi

Brown girls. Daphne Palasi Andreades. Random House Inc, 2021. 224 p.
ISBN 9780593243428
1. Expectation (Psychology) 2. Identity (Psychology) 3. City life 4. Female friendship 5. Growing up 6. Queens, New York City 7. New York City 8. Coming-of-age stories 9. Literary fiction

Four friends, all young women of color, reconcile their immigrant backgrounds that require them to be obedient, dutiful daughters, with the freedoms of American culture while growing up in a vibrant community in Queens, New York.

"These brown girls teeter between awe and contempt of their heritage in experiences that illuminate a central aspect of American life." —*Booklist*

Andrew, Sally

The **Satanic** mechanic: a Tannie Maria mystery. Sally Andrew. Ecco Press, 2017. 368 p. (Tannie Maria novels, 2)
ISBN 9780062397690
1. Women amateur detectives 2. Advice columnists 3. Land claims 4. Greed 5. Murder 6. South Africa 7. Culinary mysteries 8. Cozy mysteries 9. Gentle reads

When Slimkat the Bushman's life is threatened by an unknown adversary, recipe writer-turned-crime fighter Tannie Maria becomes embroiled in a nature-reserve land dispute among Bushmen descendants, diamond miners and cattle companies.

Andrews, Donna

Murder most fowl: a Meg Langslow mystery. Donna Andrews. Minotaur Books, 2021. 320 p. (Meg Langslow mysteries, 29)
ISBN 9781250760166

1. Women amateur detectives 2. Summer 3. Theater 4. Historical reenactments 5. Documentary filmmakers 6. Virginia 7. Gentle reads 8. Cozy mysteries

LC 2021008160

When a filmmaker takes footage of Macbeth, which her husband is producing, that reveals dark secrets about the major players, Meg Langslow, with the filmmaker's electronic devices destroyed, must uncover the darkest secret of all to expose a killer.

"Fans will relish this entry in the long-running cozy series with its humor, portrayal of small-town and rural life, and large cast of familiar, well-drawn, quirky characters framed by details of mounting a production of Macbeth." —*Booklist*

Owl be home for Christmas: a Meg Langslow mystery. Donna Andrews. Minotaur Books, 2019. 304 p. (Meg Langslow mysteries, 26)
ISBN 9781250305312
1. Christmas 2. Owls 3. Women amateur detectives 4. Inns 5. Professional conferences 6. Virginia 7. Holiday mysteries 8. Gentle reads 9. Cozy mysteries

LC 2019029130

Snowed in at a hotel during a scientific conference, Meg Langslow assists Chief Burke in identifying which of the guests is responsible for the murder of a visiting ornithologist.

The **twelve** jays of Christmas: a Meg Langslow mystery. Donna Andrews. Minotaur Books, 2021. 304 p. (Meg Langslow mysteries, 30)
ISBN 9781250760180
1. Women amateur detectives 2. Christmas 3. Blizzards 4. Murder victims 5. Birds 6. Virginia 7. Holiday mysteries 8. Gentle reads 9. Cozy mysteries

LC 2021026562

When a blizzard traps her brother Rob and his fianc ?Delaney's guests inside during their Christmas party, Meg must help the snowbound would-be eloping couple thwart their mothers' grandiose wedding plans AND solve a murder among the assembled friends and relatives.

"The large cast of familiar characters, the charming and close-knit community in Caerphilly, Virginia, and the amusing details about animals and their behavior will please fans of the long-running cozy series." —*Booklist*

Andrews, Mary Kay

Sunset Beach. Mary Kay Andrews. St Martins Press, 2019. 448 p.
ISBN 9781250126108
1. Inheritance and succession 2. Cottages 3. Coastal towns 4. Law firms 5. Beaches 6. Relationship fiction 7. Mysteries 8. Gentle reads
LibraryReads Favorites, 2019

Reluctantly accepting a job at her estranged father's law firm in the aftermath of her mother's passing, Drue is tangled in a decades-old mystery that threatens everyone she loves.

Andrews, Mesu

Isaiah's daughter: a novel of prophets and kings. Mesu Andrews. WaterBrook, 2018. 400 p.
ISBN 9780735290259
1. Isaiah 2. Rulers 3. Prophets 4. Orphans 5. Loss (Psychology) 6. Trust in God 7. Bible novels

LC 2017032698

Christy Award for Historical Category, 2018

The Bible jumps to life in this spellbinding narrative drawn from verses in the books of 2 Kings and Isaiah, bringing the troubled kingdoms that followed Solomon's reign into focus and particularly a young woman being raised by the prophet Isaiah.

Of fire and lions: a novel. Mesu Andrews. Waterbrook, 2019. 400 p. ISBN 9780735291867
1. Daniel 2. Faith (Judaism) 3. Prophets 4. Lion 5. Fire 6. Married people 7. Babylon (Extinct city) 8. 5th century BCE 9. Bible novels 10. Christian historical fiction 11. First person narratives

LC 2018029026

Seventy years ago, the Babylonians ransacked Jerusalem and took captives back to Babylon, including a frightened girl named Belili. Now a confident woman, married to Daniel the prophet, she realizes her need of the God who conquers both fire and lions.

Andric, Ivo
The **bridge** on the Drina. Ivo Andric; translated from the Serbo-Croat by Lovett F. Edwards; with an introduction by William H. McNeill. University of Chicago Press, 1977. 314 p; (Yugoslavian trilogy, 1) ISBN 9780226020457
1. Bridges — Design and construction 2. Small towns 3. Culture conflict 4. Interpersonal relations 5. Small town life 6. Bosnia and Hercegovina 7. Visegrad (Bosnia and Hercegovina : East) 8. Translations 9. Modern classics

LC 77368170

The life of a bridge near the Bosnian town of Visegrad and the events near it span three and a half centuries of Turkish rule.
Republished in 2021 by Alfred A. Knopf with a new introduction by Misha Glenny.
First published in 1945 as Na Drini Cuprija by The Prosveta Publishing

Angelo, Megan
Followers. Megan Angelo. Graydon House, 2020. 380 p. ISBN 9781525836268
1. Fame 2. Social media 3. Celebrities 4. Deception 5. Surveillance 6. United States 7. 21st century 8. Dystopian fiction 9. Fisk, Charles B.
LibraryReads Favorites, 2020

Decades after an ambitious writer and her A-list wannabe roommate abandon their ethics for social-media stardom, a government-appointed celebrity discovers a shattering secret from her past that her corporate sponsors would gladly exploit.
"An edgy, exciting read, a slap-in-the-face cautionary tale, and future thrills that provide au courant shivers." —*Library Journal*

Anshaw, Carol
Carry the one. Carol Anshaw. Simon & Schuster, 2012. 304 p. ISBN 9781451636888
1. Life change events 2. Fatal traffic accidents 3. Interpersonal relations 4. Tragedy 5. Lesbians 6. Literary fiction
New York Times Notable Book, 2012

When a car of inebriated guests from Carmen's wedding hits and kills a girl on a country road, Carmen and the people involved in the accident connect, disconnect and reconnect throughout 25 subsequent years of marriage, parenthood, holidays and tragedies.

Anstruther, Eleanor
A **perfect** explanation. Eleanor Anstruther. Houghton Mifflin Harcourt, 2020. 256 p. ISBN 9780358120858

1. Campbell, Enid 2. Aristocracy 3. Divorce 4. Marital conflict 5. Child custody 6. Married women 7. Scotland 8. 20th century 9. Biographical fiction 10. Historical fiction 11. Literary fiction

LC 2019024925

A debut novel based on true events from the author's grandmother's life follows the experiences of an aristocratic woman who abandons her family and life of privilege in search of something to claim as her own.
"This immersive story about family, inheritance, and motherhood is a good read-alike for Paula McLain's historical fiction." —*Booklist*

Antoinette, Ashley
Butterfly. Ashley Antoinette. St. Martin's Griffin, 2020. 288 p. (Butterfly novels, 1)
ISBN 9781250136367
1. Engaged persons 2. Cheating (Interpersonal relations) 3. Loss (Psychology) 4. Life change events 5. Rich men 6. Flint, Michigan 7. London, England 8. Drama lit 9. African American fiction

LC 2019035019

Morgan Atkins has always been a spoiled girl and she tries to have it all, but when she's forced to choose between a good man and a bad boy, someone will end up hurt. Someone just may end up dead.
"Urban-fiction superstar Antoinette (Luxe, 2015) starts Morgan's story at a leisurely pace; the novel is the first in a series, so Antoinette is able to dive deep into Morgan's internal conflict." —*Booklist*

Butterfly; vol 2 /. Ashley Antoinette. St. Martin's Griffin, 2020. 304 p. (Butterfly novels, 2)
ISBN 9781250136381
1. Cheating (Interpersonal relations) 2. Love triangles 3. Engaged persons 4. Secrets 5. Lovers 6. Flint, Michigan 7. Michigan 8. Drama lit 9. African American fiction

"Best-selling urban-fiction favorite Antoinette poses complex questions about women's choices and romantic and familial relationships in this sexy tale of edgy lives, tricky situations, and deep emotions. Readers will be eager to follow Morgan's adventures in the next Butterfly installment." —*Booklist*

Butterfly; vol 3 /. Ashley Antoinette. St. Martin's Griffin, 2020. 304 p. (Butterfly novels, 3)
ISBN 9781250136404
1. Cheating (Interpersonal relations) 2. Lovers 3. Engaged persons 4. Secrets 5. Loss (Psychology) 6. Flint, Michigan 7. Michigan 8. Drama lit 9. African American fiction

"Best-selling urban-fiction favorite Antoinette poses complex questions about women's choices and romantic and familial relationships in this sexy tale of edgy lives, tricky situations, and deep emotions." —*Booklist*

Antopol, Molly
The **UnAmericans**. Molly Antopol. W.W. Norton & Co, 2014. 256 p. ISBN 9780393241136
1. Jews 2. Family relationships 3. Fathers and daughters 4. Actors and actresses 5. Soldiers 6. Short stories 7. Literary fiction 8. Political fiction

This complex debut collection of short stories traces the experiences of deeply flawed and painfully human characters from a range of backgrounds, including a Czechoslovakian dissident, a McCarthy-era communist/actor, and an Israeli journalist. Exploring themes of estrangement, family, and politics, these stories span much of the 20th century and take place in locations as varied as Maine and Kiev.

"Antopol depicts with bold strokes and uncanny intelligence the intimate links between family, history, and politics, never failing to capture the grit and hurt of intergenerational confrontation." —*Booklist*

Aoki, Ryka

Light from uncommon stars. Ryka Aoki. Tor, 2021. 368 p.
ISBN 9781250789068
1. Faustian bargains 2. Curses 3. Violinists 4. Transgender teenage girls 5. Runaway teenagers 6. Los Angeles, California 7. California 8. Social science fiction 9. Science fantasy 10. Science fiction 11.

LC 2021028500

To reclaim her damned soul, a gifted, but cursed violinist must take on seven students and try to entice each to trade their soul for fame while a starship captain races to stop the end of existence.

"Aoki (He Mele a Hilo) draws from her own experiences as a queer Japanese American woman to craft a dark but ultimately hopeful sci-fi exploration of the threats faced by queer people of color." —*Publishers Weekly*

A Tom Doherty Associates book.

Apostol, Gina

Bibliolepsy. Gina Apostol. Soho, 2022. 216 p.
ISBN 9781641292511
1. Books 2. Authors 3. Dictatorship 4. Love 5. Sexual attraction 6. Philippines 7. 1980s 8. Historical fiction

LC 2021018960

It is the mid-eighties, two decades into the kleptocratic, brutal rule of Ferdinand Marcos. The Philippine economy is in deep recession, and civil unrest is growing by the day. But Primi Peregrino has her own priorities: tracking down books and pursuing romantic connections with their authors. As the Marcos dictatorship stands poised to topple, Primi remains true to her fantasy: that she, "a vagabond from history, a runaway from time," can be saved by sex, love, and books.

"Apostol's language is a constant delight, frank and full of felicitous turns of phrase and abundant humor. Layered and fully realized, it's deserving of several readings." —*Publishers Weekly*

Gun dealers' daughter: a novel. Gina Apostol. W. W. Norton & Co, 2012. 224 p.
ISBN 9780393062946
1. People with amnesia 2. Women revolutionaries 3. Memories 4. Revolutions 5. Families 6. Manila, Philippines 7. Philippines 8. Coming-of-age stories

LC 2011049404

A Filipino woman living in New York City recounts her youthful indiscretions as a university student in Manila whose boyfriend turned her into a communist rebel and the fatal act she committed that haunts her to this day.

Originally published: Manila : Anvil Pub, 2010.

Insurrecto. Gina Apostol. Soho Press, 2018. 336 pages
ISBN 9781616959449
1. Women filmmakers 2. Imperialism, American 3. Massacres 4. Philippine-American War, 1896-1902 5. Translators 6. Philippines 7. Literary fiction

LC 2018027922

While on a road trip in Duterte's Philippines, two women, a Filipino translator and an American filmmaker, both collaborate and clash in the writing of a film script about a massacre during the Philippine-American war.

Appanah-Mouriquand, Nathacha

Tropic of violence: a novel. Nathacha Appanah; translated from the French by Geoffrey Strachan. Graywolf Press, 2020. 160 pages.
ISBN 9781644450246
1. Poverty 2. Violence 3. Island life 4. Refugees 5. Postcolonialism 6. Islands of the Indian Ocean 7. Translations 8. Literary fiction 9. Multiple perspectives

LC 2019949950

Tropic of Violence shines a powerful light on the particular deprivation and isolation in this forgotten and neglected part of France. At the same time, it is a moving portrayal of the desperation and inequality that are driving refugee crises across the world, and of the innocent children whose lives are being torn apart in their wake. This is a remarkable, unsettling new novel from one of the most exciting voices in world literature.

"Appanah's heartrending, insightful story makes us understand—and feel—the steps leading toward bloody confrontation in this relentless world." —*Library Journal*

Translation of: Tropique de la violence.

Originally published: Paris : Editions Gallimard, 2016.

Translated from the French.

Araghi, Alireza Taheri

★ The **immortals** of Tehran. Ali Araghi. Melville House, 2020. 400 p.
ISBN 9781612198187
1. Extended families 2. Poets 3. Men who are mute 4. Patriarchs 5. Politicians 6. Tehran, Iran 7. Iran 8. 20th century 9. Historical fiction 10. Magical realism 11. Family sagas

Learning the story of a centuries-old family curse upon his father's death, young Ahmad struggles to protect his loved ones through decades of famine, loss and political turmoil before unexpected life changes converge at the height of the Iranian Revolution.

"A highly recommended literary page-turner worth a second reading; fans of Gabriel Garcia Marquez will delight in this fantastical—and fantastic—work." —*Library Journal*

Aramburu, Fernando

Homeland. Fernando Aramburu; translated from the Spanish by Alfred MacAdam. Pantheon Books, 2019. 590 pages
ISBN 9781524747121
1. Family and war 2. Loss (Psychology) 3. Family feuds 4. Basque families 5. Terrorism 6. 1980s 7. 1990s 8. Translations 9. War stories 10. Literary fiction

LC 2018031975

Describes the story of two Basque families, who were friends for generations, but who became bitter enemies after the father of one is killed by ETA militants during the violent insurgency that plagued the region from the 1980s to 2011.

Translation of: Patria.

Originally published: Barcelona : Tusquets Editores, 2016.

Translated from the Spanish

Arbol, Victor del

Breathing through the wound. Victor del Arbol; translated from the Spanish by Lisa Dillman. Other Press, 2020. 688 p.
ISBN 9781590518434
1. Painters 2. Widowers 3. Drunk driving victims 4. Revenge 5. Loss (Psychology) 6. Madrid, Spain 7. Spain 8. Noir fiction 9. Translations

LC 2018052930

A widowed painter is commissioned by a grieving woman to paint a portrait of the man who killed her son and in trying to understand his subject, is pulled deeper and deeper into the criminal underworld of Madrid.

"As in A Million Drops, del Arbol proves he's adept at creating richly drawn characters and weaving their disparate stories, building to a shattering, violent climax." —*Library Journal*

Originally published in Spanish as Respirar por la herida by Editorial Alrevés 2013. First published in English by Scribe 2016.

Archer, Jeffrey

Nothing ventured. Jeffrey Archer. St Martin's Press, 2019. 416 pages (William Warwick novels, 1)

ISBN 9781250200761

1. Detectives 2. Criminals 3. Art thefts 4. Independence (Personal quality) 5. Couples 6. London, England 7. Great Britain 8. 20th century 9. Police procedurals 10. Family sagas

This new series introduces William Warwick, a family man and a detective who will battle throughout his career against a powerful criminal nemesis. Through twists, triumph and tragedy, this series will show that William Warwick is destined to become one of Jeffrey Archer's most enduring legacies.

Arden, Katherine

★ The **bear** and the nightingale. Katherine Arden. Del Rey, 2017. 322 pages; (Winternight trilogy, 1)

ISBN 9781101885932

1. Young women 2. Good and evil 3. Immortalism 4. Villages 5. Spirits 6. Russia 7. Medieval period (476-1492) 8. 14th century 9. Historical fantasy 10. Literary fiction 11. Mythological fiction 12. Adult books for young adults

LibraryReads Favorites, 2017; Loan Stars Favourites, 2017; Library Journal Best Books, 2017; School Library Journal Best Books: Best Adult Books 4 Teens, 2017

In a village at the edge of the wilderness of northern Russia, where the winds blow cold and the snow falls many months of the year, a stranger with piercing blue eyes presents a new father with a gift—a precious jewel on a delicate chain, intended for his young daughter. Uncertain of its meaning, Pytor hides the gift away and Vasya grows up a wild, willful girl, to the chagrin of her family. But when mysterious forces threaten the happiness of their village, Vasya discovers that, armed only with the necklace, she may be the only one who can keep the darkness at bay.

"Arden has shaped a world that neatly straddles the seen and the unseen, where readers will hear echoes of stories from childhood while recognizing the imagination that has transformed old material into something fresh." —*Kirkus*

★ The **girl** in the tower. Katherine Arden. Del Rey, 2017. 352 p. (Winternight trilogy, 2)

ISBN 9781101885963

1. Folktales, Russian 2. Spirits 3. Deception 4. Young women 5. Magic 6. Russia 7. 14th century 8. Historical fantasy 9. Mythological fiction 10. Literary fiction 11. Adult books for young adults

Loan Stars Favourites, 2017; LibraryReads Favorites, 2018; Librarians' Choice (Australia), 2018

The magical adventure begun in The Bear and the Nightingale continues as brave Vasya, now a young woman, is forced to choose between marriage or life in a convent and instead flees her home—but soon finds herself called upon to help defend the city of Moscow when it comes under siege.

"A masterfully told story of folklore, history, and magic with a spellbinding heroine at the heart of it all." —*Booklist*

★ The **winter** of the witch. Katherine Arden. Del Rey, 2019. 384 p; (Winternight trilogy, 3)

ISBN 9781101885994

1. Folktales, Russian 2. Spirits 3. Political intrigue 4. Deception 5. Young women 6. Russia 7. 14th century 8. Historical fantasy 9. Mythological fiction 10. Literary fiction

Loan Stars Favourites, 2019

Vasilisa Petrovna, a girl determined to forge her own path in a world that would rather lock her away, finds herself beset by the Grand Prince of Moscow on one side and a demon determined to spread chaos on the other. With the fate of both worlds resting on her shoulders, Vasya will uncover surprising truths about herself as she desperately tries to save Russia, Morozko, and the magical world she treasures.

"Visceral descriptions of battle, an atmospheric sense of place, and some truly heartbreaking moments of loss make this a gut-wrenching read, but there's ample hope and satisfaction to be found as Vasya chooses her own unique path to triumph." —*Booklist*

Aridjis, Chloe

Asunder. Chloe Aridjis. Mariner Books, 2013. 192 p.

ISBN 9780544003460

1. Boredom 2. Roommates 3. Museums 4. Guards 5. Art 6. London, England 7. Paris, France 8. Psychological fiction

When she begins to feel restless in her job as a museum guard, Marie takes a trip to Paris, where, with the arrival of an uninvited guest and an unexpected encounter, her world is torn open.

Arikawa, Hiro

The **travelling** cat chronicles. Hiro Arikawa; translated by Philip Gabriel. Berkley, 2018. 288 p.

ISBN 9780451491336

1. Cats 2. Pets — Travel 3. Human-animal relationships 4. Voyages and travels 5. Personal conduct 6. Japan 7. Literary fiction 8. Domestic fiction 9. Translations

LC 2018010823

An ode to kindness, sacrifice, and the power of small things traces the experiences of adventurous Nana the cat and his owner, Satoru, as they embark on a road trip across Japan to visit three old friends.

A reissue of the 2017 edition published by Doubleday (London).

Originally published 2012 in Japanese as Tabineko Ripôto—Title page verso.

Translated from the Japanese by Philip Gabriel.

Arimah, Lesley Nneka

★ **What** it means when a man falls from the sky: stories. Lesley Nneka Arimah. Riverhead Books, 2017. 240 p.

ISBN 9780735211025

1. Interpersonal relations 2. Family relationships 3. Human nature 4. Short stories 5. Literary fiction 6. Adult books for young adults

LC 2016036303

Kirkus Prize for Fiction, 2017; Minnesota Book Award for Novel & Short Story, 2018

"Lesley Arimah emigrated from Nigeria to Louisiana at the age of thirteen, a disorienting transition that left her keenly attuned to the shock waves set in motion by displacement. In these twelve powerful stories that embrace magical-realist elements while deploying a powerfully empathetic understanding of character and circumstance, she explores how parents and children, husbands and wives, lovers and friends, navigate conflicting cultures and struggle to reconcile conflicting desires, wants, and needs." —Provided by the publisher

"This speculative turn joins everything from fabulism to folk tale as rimah confidently tests out all the tools in her kit while also managing to cate a wholly cohesive and original collection." —*Kirkus*

rmfield, Julia

Salt slow: stories. Julia Armfield. Flatiron Books, 2019. 195 pages
ISBN 9781250224774
1. Feminism 2. Monsters 3. Loss (Psychology) 4. Interpersonal relations 5. Transformations(Magic) 6. Magical realism 7. Literary fiction 8. Short stories
LC 2019032750
A collection of short stories that examines women's place in society seen through their unique body experiences, including a teenager struging through puberty and a group of fangirls who disrupt a popular and's tour.

rmstrong, Addison

The light of Luna Park. Addison Armstrong. G.P. Putnam's Sons, 021. 328 p.
ISBN 9780593328040
1. Nurses 2. Premature infants 3. Incubators (Pediatrics) 4. Premature infant care 5. Medical innovations 6. New York City 7. Poughkeepsie, New York 8. 1920s 9. 1950s 10. Historical fiction 11. Parallel narratives
LC 2021015009
In this powerful tale of courage and an ode to the sacrificial love of others, Stella Wright, with her life falling apart, discovers a letter that rings into question everything she knew about her mother, a nurse who ade a difficult choice long ago, and everything she knows about herself.
"Armstrong's sympathetic characters and engaging multi-time-peod story line result in a novel guaranteed to tug at heartstrings while illuinating a daring medical innovation that has saved millions of lives."
-*Booklist*

rmstrong, Kelley

Alone in the wild. Kelley Armstrong. Minotaur Books, 2020. 368 p.
Casey Duncan novels, 5)
ISBN 9781250254283
1. Sheriffs 2. Women detectives 3. Murder investigation 4. Infants 5. Wilderness areas 6. Yukon Territory 7. Canada 8. Mysteries 9. Canadian fiction
LC 2019038492
Loan Stars Favourites, 2020
Discovering a live baby beside its murdered mother in the woods, dective Casey Duncan tries to uncover what happened while struggling to are for the infant in a Rockton community that disapproves of children.
"The prolific Armstrong is an adept storyteller (she's writes horror nd fantasy as well as mysteries, for both adults and teens) who makes the ather out-there idea of a small, protected community full of people with ings to hide seem not only plausible but entirely believable." —*Booklist*

Watcher in the woods. Kelley Armstrong. St Martins Pr 2019. 368 p.
Casey Duncan novels, 4)
ISBN 9781250159915
1. Sheriffs 2. Women detectives 3. Murder investigation 4. United States marshals 5. Wilderness areas 6. Yukon Territory 7. Canada 8. Mysteries 9. Canadian fiction
LC 2018049401
Loan Stars Favourites, 2019

When a suspicious U.S. marshal shows up demanding the release of a Rockton resident only to be found murdered hours later, detective Casey and sheriff Dalton race to identify the killer and prevent additional deaths.

Wherever she goes. Kelley Armstrong. Minotaur Books, 2019. 400 p.
ISBN 9781250181350
1. Single mothers 2. Child kidnapping victims 3. Skepticism 4. Child custody 5. Secrets 6. Illinois 7. Canadian fiction 8. Psychological suspense
LC 2019002288
Witnessing the abduction of a child at the park, Aubrey struggles to find the boy and his missing mother when the police and her neighbors begin to question her sanity.
"Aubrey and Paul's achingly poignant interactions add texture and depth, while clever twists, realistic complications, and a propulsive, present-tense narration catapult the story to a gratifying finish. This is a gripping tale of secrets, lies, and maternal anxieties." —*Publishers Weekly*

Armstrong, Richard

The don con. Richard Armstrong. Pace Press, 2019. 250 pages
ISBN 9781610353366
1. Fan conventions 2. Mafia 3. Actors and actresses 4. Former convicts 5. Womanizers 6. Caper novels
LC 2018052703
The Mafia comes to Comic-Con in this fast-paced suspense caper and outrageous pop culture satire.

Arnett, Kristen N.

Mostly dead things. Kristen Arnett. Tin House Books, 2019. 354 pages
ISBN 9781947793309
1. Family and suicide 2. Taxidermy 3. Eccentrics and eccentricities 4. Dysfunctional families 5. Family businesses 6. Florida 7. Psychological fiction
LC 2019005820
New York Times Notable Book, 2019
Taking over her family's failing taxidermy shop in the wake of her father's suicide, a grief-stricken woman pursues less-than-legal ways of generating income while struggling to figure out her place among her eccentric loved ones.

With teeth: a novel. Kristen Arnett. Riverhead, 2021. 304 p.
ISBN 9780593191507
1. Motherhood 2. Lesbians 3. Mothers and sons 4. Aggressiveness in children 5. Love 6. Florida 7. Domestic fiction 8. LGBTQIA fiction
LC 2020054668
Struggling to create a picture-perfect queer family, Sammie Lucas, scared of her own son, must pick up the pieces when his hostility finally spills over into physical aggression, in this thought-provoking portrait on the limitations of marriage, parenthood and love.
"Arnett (Mostly Dead Things) paints a complex picture of a queer family in this well-sculpted drama." —*Publishers Weekly*

Artson, Barbara

Odessa, Odessa. Barbara Artson. She Writes Press, 2018. 264 pages
ISBN 9781631524431
1. Jewish families 2. Religious persecution 3. Immigrant families 4. Antisemitism 5. Life change events 6. Ukraine 7. United States 8. 20th century 9. Family sagas
A novel of unforgettable characters about two brothers who emigrate out of Russia to escape anti-Semitism—one to America and one to Is-

rael—Odessa, Odessa gives readers a great story for our time: a younger generation discovering their lost heritage and reuniting a family.

"Rich with detail and alive with a full cast of characters, this is a beautifully crafted examination of immigration and the many journeys that follow it." —*Booklist*

Arudpragasam, Anuk

The **story** of a brief marriage. Anuk Arudpragasam. Flatiron Books, 2016. 224 p.

ISBN 9781250072405

1. Newlyweds 2. Refugee camps 3. War — Psychological aspects 4. Civil war 5. Loss (Psychology) 6. Sri Lanka 7. Literary fiction 8. War stories

LC 2016020830

Loan Stars Favourites, 2016

Set on a single day towards the end of the Sri Lankan Civil War, a newlywed couple tries to balance love and intimacy in an evacuee camp which is constantly being bombarded by enemy shells.

"Dinesh finds beauty in the worst of situations, which contributes to making this debut deeply moving and hopeful." —*Publishers Weekly*

Arvin, Reed

Blood of angels: a novel. Reed Arvin. HarperCollins, 2005. 288 p.

ISBN 9780060596347

1. Public prosecutors 2. Lawyers 3. Capital punishment 4. Judicial error 5. Trials (Murder) 6. Nashville, Tennessee 7. Legal thrillers 8. Psychological suspense

LC 2004060931

Struggling to maintain a sense of purpose in a Tennessee county that has been changed by ten years of immigration, prosecutor Thomas Dennehy tackles a difficult case involving a Sudanese murder suspect and racially charged locals.

Asch, Sholem

The **Nazarene**. Carroll and Graf, 1984. 698 p. (Biblical series (Sholem Asch), 1)

ISBN 9780786703791

1. Jesus Christ 2. Bible novels

"Judged purely as a novel, The Nazarene is a superb achievement. Even on the factual side, a work such as Papini's Life is thin beside it. This is because Mr. Asch has taken an infinite amount of trouble to build up an historical background against which the figure of Jesus may move authentically, with that sense of reality which we should expect of fiction as of life." —*The Atlantic*

Originally published in 1939.

Ashley & JaQuavis

The **Cartel**. Ashley & JaQuavis. Urban, 2008. 278 p. (Cartel novels, 1)

ISBN 9781601621429

1. Drug traffic 2. Murder for hire 3. Organized crime 4. Family relationships 5. Street life 6. Miami, Florida 7. Romantic suspense 8. African American fiction 9. Drama lit

When Carter Diamon, the leader of The Cartel, which controls eighty percent of the cocaine industry, dies, his illegitimate son, Carter Jones, takes his place and starts sleeping with the enemy—Miamor, the leader of The Murder Mamas, who wants to take down The Cartel.

Sequel: The Cartel 2.

The most notorious crime family Miami has ever seen.

Also published in the omnibus edition The Cartel: deluxe edition books 1-3, Urban Books, 2018.

Murderville. Ashley & JaQuavis. Simon & Schuster 2011. 256 p (Murderville trilogy, 1)

ISBN 9781936399000

1. Women with terminal illnesses 2. Redemption 3. Love 4. Immigrant 5. African American men/women relations 6. Detroit, Michigan 7. Los Angeles, California 8. Urban fiction 9. African American fiction

While Liberty dies from a fatal heart condition, she asks A'shai to tell her a story while she waits for her sister, who promised to visit her on her upcoming twenty-fifth birthday. A'shai, who blames himself for not protecting Liberty, retells the story of how they got to this point, from an arranged marriage and child brothels to drug cartels and hustling the streets of Detroit.

Ashley, Jennifer

Death at the Crystal Palace. Jennifer Ashley. Berkley Prime Crime 2021. 304 pages (Below stairs mysteries, 5)

ISBN 9780593099391

1. Household employees 2. Widows 3. Threat (Psychology) 4. Women cooks 5. Conspiracies 6. England 7. Great Britain 8. Victorian era (1837-1901) 9. 1850s 10. Historical mysteries 11. Victorian mysteries

LC 2021010849

While attending an exhibition at the Crystal Palace, young cook Kat Holloway is approached by a woman in distress. Lady Covington is a wealthy widow convinced that her entire family is trying to kill her. Kat feels compelled to help, so she escorts the lady home, and promises aid. Her charming confidant Daniel McAdam is busy infiltrating a plot against the Crown, and she worries he will not have time to lend his sleuthing expertise. But soon, Kat faces a more serious threat when her involvement in both investigations plunges her into peril.

"Well-drawn supporting characters and logistical details of running a prosperous household complement the intricate plot. Downton Abbey fans will be delighted." —*Publishers Weekly*

Lady Isabella's scandalous marriage. Jennifer Ashley. Berkley Sensation, 2010. 325 p. (Highland pleasures, 2)

ISBN 9780425235454

1. Runaway wives, husbands, etc. 2. Second chances 3. Scandals 4 Seduction 5. Artists 6. England 7. Victorian era (1837-1901) 8. 1880s 9. Historical romances 10. Victorian romances 11. Highland romances

LC Bl2010017234

When her husband, Lord Mac Mackenzie, follows her to London, determined to win her back, Lady Isabella Scranton rises to the challenge by tempting him in ways he could have never imagined, but a dangerous enemy waits in the wings to stop them from reuniting—forever.

The **madness** of Lord Ian Mackenzie. Jennifer Ashley. Leisure Books 2009. 320 p. (Highland pleasures, 1)

ISBN 9780843960433

1. Widows 2. Rumor 3. Inheritance and succession 4. Truth 5. Malicious accusation 6. England 7. Victorian era (1837-1901) 8. 1880s 9. Historical romances 10. Victorian romances 11. Highland romances

LC Bl2009011649

Romantic Times Reviewers' Choice Award, 2009

Beth, a young widow, is inexplicably drawn to Ian MacKenzie, a Scottish lord who is rumored to be a murderer and who spent his youth in an asylum, and she is determined to prove to London society that he is perfectly sane.

Asim, Jabari

★ **Yonder**. Jabari Asim. Simon & Schuster, 2022. 272 p.
ISBN 9781982163167
1. Love 2. Friendship 3. Slavery 4. Language and culture 5. Enslaved people 6. Southern States 7. Antebellum America (1820-1861) 8. Historical fiction 9. Literary fiction 10. African American fiction

They call themselves the Stolen. Their owners call them captives. They are taught their captors' tongues and their beliefs but they have a language and rituals all their own. Subject to the whims of their tyrannical and eccentric captor, Cannonball Greene, they never know what harm may befall them: inhumane physical toil in the plantation's quarry by day, a beating by night, or the sale of a loved one at any moment. Their relationships begin to fray when a visiting minister with a mysterious past comes to town. He tells them that with freedom comes the right to choose the small things—when to dine, when to begin and end work—as well as the big things, such as whom and how to love. Do they follow the preacher and pursue the unknown?

"At once intimate and majestic, the prose marries a gripping narrative with an unforgettable exploration of the power of stories, language, and hope. With a bold vision, Asim demonstrates his remarkable gifts." —*Publishers Weekly*

Asimov, Isaac

★ **Foundation**. Isaac Asimov. Bantam Books, 2004. 244 p; (Foundation series, 3)
ISBN 9780553382570
1. Far future 2. Psychohistory 3. Life on other planets 4. Psychohistorians 5. Mathematicians 6. Science fiction classics 7. Hard science fiction 8. Space opera
LC 2003069137

A band of psychologists, under the leadership of psychohistorian Hari Seldon, plant a colony to encourage art, science, and technology in the declining Galactic Empire and to preserve the accumulated knowledge of humankind.
Made into a TV series on Apple TV in 2021.

Foundation and empire. Isaac Asimov. Bantam Books, 2004. 244 p; (Foundation series, 4)
ISBN 9780553293371
1. Life on other planets 2. Psychohistory 3. Mind control 4. Psychohistorians 5. Space colonies 6. Science fiction classics 7. Hard science fiction 8. Space opera
LC 2003069136

The Foundation, a colony of psychologists, battles for supreme power in the galaxy, while also struggling to preserve all the accumulated knowledge of humankind in The Foundation, a sanctuary created by Hari Seldon.

★ **I**, robot. Isaac Asimov. Bantam Books, 2004. 224 p.
ISBN 9780553803709
1. Robots 2. Androids 3. Robotics 4. Artificial intelligence 5. Robots — Behavior 6. Short stories 7. Books to movies 8. Hard science fiction
LC 2003069139

Asimov chronicles the development of the robot through a series of interlinked stories: from its primitive origins in the present to its ultimate perfection in the not-so-distant future—a future in which humanity itself may be rendered obsolete. Here are stories of robots gone mad, of mind-reading robots, and robots with a sense of humor. Of robot politicians, and robots who secretly run the world.

"The Three Laws of Robotics, first presented in one of the nine short stories included in this collection, represent the basis of Asimov's robot universe and inspired much later robot fiction. The 2004 blockbuster film of the same name starring Will Smith, while merely inspired by Asimov's stories, exemplifies the extent to which the Three Laws have become mainstream." —*Library Journal*
This title is not a part of the Robot Series according to the author.
Originally published: c1950.
Originally published: New York : Gnome Press, 1950.

Second foundation. Isaac Asimov. Bantam Books, 2004. Viii, 241 p; (Foundation series, 5)
ISBN 9780553382594
1. Psychohistory 2. Life on other planets 3. Mind control 4. Mathematicians 5. Seldon, Hari (Fictitious character) 6. Science fiction classics 7. Hard science fiction 8. Space opera
LC 2003069134

The Second Foundation meets the threat of a perilous mutant, only to face the challenge of the corrupt First Foundation for control of the galactic empire.
The third volume in the world-famous Foundation saga—Cover.
This is reckoned by Asimov to be the 12th in terms of the chronology of the events covered. (Cf. His 'Prelude to Foundation'. Author's note, p. 9-[10]). Also called the fourth Foundation novel.
Originally published: New York : Gnome Press, 1953.

Askaripour, Mateo

★ **Black** Buck. Mateo Askaripour. Houghton Mifflin Harcourt 2021. 352 p.
ISBN 9780358380887
1. Ambition 2. College graduates 3. New businesses 4. Sales 5. Identity (Psychology) 6. African American fiction 7. Satirical fiction 8. Coming-of-age stories

An unambitious college graduate accepts a job at Sumwun, the hottest NYC startup, and reimagines himself as "Buck" a ruthless salesman and begins to hatch a plan to help young people of color infiltrate America's sales force.

"Askaripour has created a skillfully written, biting, witty, and absurdist novel that sheds light on racism, start-up culture, corporate morality, media bias, gentrification, and many other timely, important themes." —*Booklist*

Aslam, Nadeem

★ The **blind** man's garden. Nadeem Aslam. Alfred A. Knopf, 2013. 336 p.
ISBN 9780307961716
1. Pakistanis in Afghanistan 2. Brothers 3. Men who are blind 4. September 11 Terrorist Attacks, 2001 5. Muslims 6. Pakistan 7. Afghanistan 8. Political fiction 9. Literary fiction
LC 2012041083

Set in Pakistan and Afghanistan in the months following 9/11, a story of war, of one family's losses, and of the simplest, most enduring human impulses.
This is a Borzoi book.
Includes bibliographical references.

★ The **golden** legend: a novel. Nadeem Aslam. Alfred A. Knopf, 2017. 304 p.
ISBN 9780451493781
1. Culture conflict 2. Widows 3. Muslim women 4. Secrets 5. Forgiveness 6. Pakistan 7. Psychological fiction 8. Literary fiction
LC 2016034887
Loan Stars Favourites, 2017; Longlisted for the Andrew Carnegie Medal for Excellence in Fiction, 2018

Hiding her past, Nargis feels her life crumbling around her when someone begins broadcasting local people's secrets from the minaret of a local mosque.

"Brooding and beautiful: a mature, assured story of the fragility of the world and of ourselves." —*Kirkus*

Aswani, Alaa

Chicago: a modern Arabic novel. Alaa Al Aswany; translated by Farouk Abdel Wahab. Harper, 2007. 342 p.

ISBN 9780061452567

1. Refugees 2. Egyptians in the United States 3. Fanaticism 4. Hypocrisy 5. Greed in men 6. Chicago, Illinois 7. Illinois 8. Psychological fiction 9. Translations

Post-9/11 Chicago becomes the site of a cultural collision involving a sixties-style anti-establishment professor who is targeted for his relationship with an African-American woman, a veiled Ph.D. candidate whose traditional upbringing is challenged by her American experiences, and an émigré whose western values are countered by questions about his daughter's honor.

Originally published in Arabic in 2007. Originally published in Great Britain by Fourth Estate, 2008.

Atakora, Afia

★ **Conjure** women. Afia Atakora. Random House, 2020. 400 pages

ISBN 9780525511489

1. Midwives 2. Women healers 3. Plantation life 4. Curses 5. Slavery 6. Southern States 7. 19th century 8. Historical fiction 9. African American fiction

LC 2019015814

RUSA Reading List, 2021; Society of American Historians Prize for Historical Fiction (formerly the James Fenimore Cooper Prize), 2021

A midwife and conjurer of curses reflects on her life before and after the Civil War, her relationships with the families she serves and the secrets she has learned about a plantation owner's daughter.

"Atakora effectively handles the before-during-and-after structure, enriching her story. If its center is the vibrant Rue, the entire community finally feels like the main character." —*Library Journal*

Atilgan, Yusuf

Motherland hotel. Yusuf Atilgan; translated from the Turkish by Fred Stark. City Lights Books, 2016. 152 pages

ISBN 9780872867116

1. Hotel owners 2. Obsession in men 3. Mental illness 4. Loneliness 5. Women travelers 6. Psychological fiction 7. Literary fiction 8. Translations

LC 2016018905

Lonely, middle-aged Zebercet, the last surviving member of a once prosperous Ottoman family, is the owner of the Motherland Hotel, a run-down establishment near the railroad station. One day, a beautiful woman from the capital comes to spend the night and suddenly Zebercet's insular, mechanical existence is dramatically and irrevocably changed.

Originally published: Ankara : Bilgi, 1973.

Translated from the Turkish.

Atkins, Ace

The **broken** places. Ace Atkins. G. P. Putnam's Sons, 2013. 352 p. (Quinn Colson novels, 3)

ISBN 9780399161780

1. Sheriffs 2. Revenge 3. Former convicts 4. Murderers 5. Women deputy police chiefs 6. Mississippi 7. Thrillers and suspense

When an infamous murderer is released from prison and returns to Jericho preaching redemption, skeptical sheriff Quinn Colson is forced to confront the man's vengeance-seeking victims and former partners in crime, a situation that is further complicated by a dangerous tornado.

The **fallen**. Ace Atkins. G.P. Putnam's Sons, 2017. 384 p. (Quinn Colson novels, 7)

ISBN 9780399576713

1. Sheriffs 2. Bank robberies 3. Criminals 4. Robbery 5. Veterans 6. Mississippi 7. Thrillers and suspense

Investigating a series of bank robberies that have been orchestrated with skill and precision worthy of a military raid, Mississippi sheriff and former Army Ranger Quinn Colson calls on old allies and new enemies in his effort to outmaneuver a sophisticated band of elite criminals.

The **forsaken**. Ace Atkins. G. P. Putnam's Sons, 2014. 352 p. (Quinn Colson novels, 4)

ISBN 9780399161797

1. Sheriffs 2. Lynching 3. Race relations 4. Hate crimes 5. Murderers 6. Mississippi 7. Thrillers and suspense

LC 2014015440

County sheriff Quinn Colson is determined to find those responsible for lynching an innocent black man in Jericho, Mississippi, 30 years prior.

"The dive into Jerichos dark past makes for great reading as Atkins rolls through a handful of perspectives, propelling the storys threads toward an adrenaline-laced, Wild Weststyle conclusion." —*Booklist*

★ The **heathens**. Ace Atkins. Putnam Pub Group, 2021. 464 p. (Quinn Colson novels, 11)

ISBN 9780593328392

1. Murder investigation 2. Juvenile delinquents 3. Sheriffs 4. Small towns 5. Malicious accusation 6. Thrillers and suspense

When her mother is murdered, 16-year-old juvenile delinquent TJ Byrd places her trust in Tibbehah County Sheriff Quinn Colson to find the real killer while trying to elude a U.S. Marshal who believes she is responsible for her mother's death.

"Series lead Quinn takes a back seat here to the foul-mouthed, freewheeling, but utterly endearing TJ, and TJ is more than ready for the limelight. Evoking Edward Anderson's 1937 country noir Thieves like Us, with a touch of Bonnie and Clyde, Atkins' hard-edged yet tenderhearted novel will keep readers rooting for TJ and her gang of inadvertent outlaws on the road to the better lives they crave." —*Booklist*

The **innocents**. Ace Atkins. G.P. Putnam's Sons, 2016. 384 p. (Quinn Colson novels, 6)

ISBN 9780399173950

1. Sheriffs 2. Murder investigation 3. Teenage girl murder victims 4. Secrets 5. Colson, Quinn (Fictitious character) 6. Mississippi 7. Thrillers and suspense

She was just seventeen, a high school dropout named Milly Jones, found walking down the middle of the highway, engulfed in flames. Even in a tough Mississippi county like Tibbehah, it shatters the community, and it is up to Sheriff Quinn Colson, back on the job after a year away, and his deputy Lillie Virgil, to investigate what happened and why. Before long, however, accusations start to fly, national media and federal authorities descend, and what seemed like a senseless act of violence begins to appear like something even more disturbing—with more victims waiting in the shadows.

The **lost** ones. Ace Atkins. G.P. Putnam's Sons, 2012. 352 p. (Quinn Colson novels, 2)

ISBN 9780399158766

1. Sheriffs 2. Drug cartels 3. Adoption racket 4. Gangs 5. Child abuse victims 6. Mississippi 7. Thrillers and suspense

Newly-elected Tibbehah County sheriff Quinn Colson investigates an old friend's gun sales when stolen military rifles are found in the possession of a Mexican drug gang, a case that is complicated by his discovery of a black market baby adoption ring.

The **ranger**. Ace Atkins. G.P. Putnam's Sons, 2011. 352 p. (Quinn Colson novels, 1)
ISBN 9780399157486
1. Drug traffic 2. White supremacists 3. Murder investigation 4. Uncles — Death 5. Women deputy police chiefs 6. Mississippi 7. Thrillers and suspense
LC 2011002785

Returning to what has become his violently corrupt hometown in Mississippi after a tour in Afghanistan, Army Ranger Quinn Colson investigates his uncle's alleged suicide and uncovers shocking personal secrets.

The **redeemers**. Ace Atkins. Penguin Group USA 2015. 352 p. (Quinn Colson novels, 5)
ISBN 9780399173943
1. Former sheriffs 2. Organized crime 3. Stealing 4. Police murders 5. Thieves 6. Mississippi 7. Thrillers and suspense
LC 2015015992

The electrifying new novel in New York Times-bestselling author Ace Atkins's acclaimed series about the real Deep South.

The **revelators**. Ace Atkins. Penguin Group USA 2020. 386 pages; (Quinn Colson novels, 10)
ISBN 9780525539490
1. Sheriffs 2. Colson, Quinn (Fictitious character) 3. Organized crime 4. Political corruption 5. Undocumented immigrants 6. Mississippi 7. Thrillers and suspense
LC 2020017668

Quinn Colson returns to take down a criminal syndicate that has ravaged his community, threatened his family, and tried to have him killed.

"Perfect reading for socially distanced shut-ins who'll be pleased to learn that things could indeed be much, much worse." —*Kirkus*

The **shameless**. Ace Atkins. G.P. Putnam's Sons, 2019. 384 pages (Quinn Colson novels, 9)
ISBN 9780525539469
1. Suicide investigation 2. Organized crime 3. Sheriffs 4. Cold cases (Criminal investigation) 5. Corruption 6. Mississippi 7. Thrillers and suspense
LC 2019018652

Approached by two New York reporters to reopen a 20-year-old suicide case, Sheriff Quinn Colson finds the investigation complicated by a local crime syndicate's involvement in a gubernatorial election.

The **sinners**. Ace Atkins. G. P. Putnam's Sons, 2018. 384 p. (Quinn Colson novels, 8)
ISBN 9780399576744
1. Sheriffs 2. Revenge 3. Drug dealers 4. Crime 5. Criminals 6. Mississippi 7. Thrillers and suspense

When the recently released patriarch of a drug-dealing clan begins targeting the family of the man responsible for his long imprisonment, Quinn Colson finds himself relying on new deputies to survive Old West acts of violence.

Wicked city. Ace Atkins. G. P. Putnam's Sons, 2008. 352 p.
ISBN 9780399154577

1. Organized crime 2. Lawyers 3. Murder 4. Murder investigation 5. Alabama 6. Southeastern States 7. 1950s 8. Thrillers and suspense 9. Noir fiction
LC 2007032774

In the aftermath of an innocent man's murder by powerful mobsters in mid-twentieth-century Alabama, a small group of citizens bands together to fight back against the organized machine that has taken over their city.

"Atkins provides a 3-D view through two narrators, an omniscient teller and Lamar Murphy, an ex-boxer enlisted to help solve Albert Patterson's murder.... A character warns that the sweetness of Phenix City moonshine masks the embalming fluid that provides its kick. Atkins has likewise crafted a smart tale of a decadent place; Southern sweetness laced with poison." —*Paste*

Atkinson, Kate

★ **Big** sky. Kate Atkinson. Little, Brown and Co, 2019. 400 pages (Jackson Brodie mysteries, 5)
ISBN 9780316523097
1. Private investigators 2. Coastal towns 3. Deception 4. Teenage boys 5. Fathers and sons 6. England 7. Yorkshire, England 8. Mysteries 9. Literary fiction 10. Multiple perspectives
Loan Stars Favourites, 2019

Investigating a new client's suspicions about an unfaithful spouse, iconoclastic detective Jackson Brodie is catapulted by a chance encounter into a sinister network of secrets and lies.

★ **Case** histories. Kate Atkinson. Little, Brown and Co, 2004. 312 p. (Jackson Brodie mysteries, 1)
ISBN 9780316740401
1. Lawyers 2. Private investigators 3. Missing girls 4. Divorced men 5. Fathers and daughters 6. Cambridge, England 7. England 8. Mysteries 9. Multiple perspectives
LC 2004002379
Booklist Editors' Choice, 2004

Private detective Jackson Brodie finds his own need for resolution sparked by three investigations including those of two sisters who discover a shocking clue to the disappearance of their third sister thirty years earlier, a lawyer whose life is turned upside-down when his daughter joins the firm, and a woman whose past mistakes and demanding family life culminate in a violent escape. bt

"The novel is packed with women whose appetites are large, and Atkinson's prose is correspondingly loose and louche: no single point of view predominates, and everyone's thoughts effortlessly rollick along." —*New York Times Book Review*

★ **A god** in ruins. Kate Atkinson. Little Brown & Co, 2015. 400 p.
ISBN 9780316176538
1. Men 2. Family relationships 3. Aging 4. Bomber pilots 5. Fatherhood 6. Great Britain 7. Historical fiction 8. Literary fiction
LC 916023580
Costa Novel Award, 2015; LibraryReads Favorites, 2015; Longlisted for the Baileys Women's Prize for Fiction, 2016

Ursula Todd's brother Teddy is an old man trying to come to grips with his post-War life and with a modern world and family. Switching back and forth in time between memories of his childhood and his present, Teddy is an oblivious husband, a rueful father. He never quite got over the War and part of him never adjusted to having a future. Would-be poet, heroic pilot, husband, father, and grandfather, Teddy navigates the perils and progress of a rapidly changing world; his greatest challenge is living in a future he never expected to have.

"As in Life After Life, Atkinson isnt just telling a story: she's deconstructing, taking apart the notion of how we believe stories are told. Using narrative tricks that range from the subtlest sleight of hand to direct address, she makes us feel the power of storytelling not as an intellectual conceit, but as a punch in the gut." —*Publishers Weekly*

Sequel to: Life after life.

Companion to: Life after life.

Human croquet. Kate Atkinson. Picador, 1997. 349 p.

ISBN 9780312155506

1. Eccentric families 2. Family relationships 3. Mother-separated children 4. Missing persons 5. Families 6. England 7. Family sagas 8. Magical realism 9. Coming-of-age stories

New York Times Notable Book, 1997

Once part of a vast expanse where a wealthy Elizabethan family settled and built Fairfax Manor, but now, in the mid 1960s, it has become a disintegrated forest where the destroyed, dysfunctional Fairfax family continues to crumble.

"Human Croquet is peppered with snatches of hilarious nonsensical suburban dialogue; big, exuberant-of-age exclamations; savvy rhetorical questions and a knuckle crackingly morbid sense of humor.... The narrator's youthful cynicism does not descend into mannerism. Atkinson shows that it is the logical outcome of cruelty and trauma." —*New Statesman*

★ **Life** after life: a novel. Kate Atkinson. Reagan Arthur Books, 2013. 560 p.

ISBN 9780316176484

1. Reincarnation 2. World War II 3. Options, alternatives, choices 4. Identity (Psychology) 5. Purpose in life 6. Great Britain 7. Alternate histories 8. Literary fiction

LC 2012046158

ALA Notable Book, 2014; Booklist Editors' Choice, 2013; Costa Novel Award, 2013; Goodreads Choice Award, 2013; Indies' Choice Book Awards, Adult Fiction, 2014; Library Journal Best Books, 2013; New York Times Notable Book, 2013; Shortlisted for the Walter Scott Prize for Historical Fiction, 2014; Shortlisted for The Women's Prize for Fiction, 2013

Follows the experiences of a woman, who after being born on a snowy night in 1910, repeatedly dies and reincarnates into the same life to correct missteps and ultimately save the world.

Sequel: A god in ruins.

One good turn: a novel. Kate Atkinson. Little, Brown, 2006. 418 p. (Jackson Brodie mysteries, 2)

ISBN 9780316154840

1. Hemingway, Ernest 2. Police 3. Extramarital affairs 4. Private investigators 5. Man-woman relationships 6. Edinburgh, Scotland 7. Scotland 8. Mysteries 9. Multiple perspectives

LC 2005031123

New York Times Notable Book, 2006

In the sequel to Case Histories, millionaire ex-detective Jackson Brodie follows his girlfriend to Edinburgh for the famous arts festival, but when he becomes an eyewitness to a brutal attack on a man during a traffic jam, he becomes caught up in a string of events that draw him and the wife of an unscrupulous tycoon, a timid crime novelist, and female police detective into the heart of deadly conspiracy.

"In the past Ms. Atkinson has played the minor time trick of letting events almost converge and then replaying them from slightly different points of view. She does that here to the same smart, unnerving effect. And she frequently brings up the image of Russian dolls, each hidden inside another, to illustrate how her storytelling tactics work. By the apt ending of One Good Turn a whole series of these dolls has been opened." —*New York Times*

Started early, took my dog. Kate Atkinson. Little, Brown, 2011. 400 p. (Jackson Brodie mysteries, 4)

ISBN 9780316066730

1. Former police 2. Security consultants 3. Girl orphans 4. Life change events 5. Private investigators 6. Leeds, England 7. Mysteries 8. Multiple perspectives

Recently retired from the police force, Tracy Waterhouse is enjoying the quiet life. However, when she sees a miserable young child under the care of routine offender Kelly Cross, Tracy decides to bring the child under her wardship. Meanwhile, detective Jackson Brodie adopts an abused dog. It doesn't take long, however, for both Tracy and Brodie to learn that they are both in way over their heads.

"A delight: an intricate construction that assembles itself before the reader's eyes, populated by idiosyncratic, multidimensional characters and written with shrewd, mordant grace.... Atkinson's Jackson Brodie books are like high-wire acts in which she is forever defying gravity (in the form of crime fiction's improbable conventions) by making the work fresh, unpredictable and alive." —*Salon.com*

Originally published: London : Doubleday, 2010.

★ **Transcription**. Kate Atkinson. Little, Brown and Co, 2018. 343 p.

ISBN 9780316176637

1. Espionage 2. Davis, Varina 3. War and society 4. Radio programs 5. Postwar life 6. Great Britain 7. 20th century 8. Literary fiction 9. Historical fiction

Loan Stars Favourites, 2018; LibraryReads Favorites, 2018; Booklist Editors' Choice, 2018

Juliet Armstrong is a radio producer in a 1950s London that is recovering from the war as much as she is. During World War Two, Juliet transcribed conversations between an MI5 agent and a ring of suspected German sympathizers, which quickly plunged Juliet into a treacherous world of code words and secret meetings. Now her routine is upended by an meeting with a mysterious man from her past. Haunted by the actions of her past and a very real threat in the present, Juliet realizes she cannot escape the repercussions of her work for the government.

★ **When** will there be good news?: a novel. Kate Atkinson. Little, Brown, 2008. 400 p. (Jackson Brodie mysteries, 3)

ISBN 9780316154857

1. Missing persons 2. Physicians 3. Women detectives 4. Private investigators 5. Teenage girls 6. Edinburgh, Scotland 7. Mysteries 8. Multiple perspectives

LC 2008014738

British Book Award for the Richard & Judy Best Read of the Year, 2009; New York Times Notable Book, 2008

On a hot summer day, Joanna Mason's family slowly wanders home along a country lane. A moment later, Joanna's life is changed forever. On a dark night thirty years later, ex-detective Jackson Brodie finds himself on a train that is both crowded and late. Lost in his thoughts, he suddenly hears a shocking sound. At the end of a long day, 16-year-old Reggie is looking forward to watching a little TV. Then a terrifying noise shatters her peaceful evening.

"As always, Atkinson inhabits her characters with fluency, clarity and a good eye and ear for quirks and habits of mind." —*Times Literary Supplement*

Originally published: London: Doubleday, 2008.

Attenberg, Jami

★ **All** this could be yours. Jami Attenberg. Houghton Mifflin Harcourt, 2019. 240 p.

ISBN 9780544824256

1. Fathers — Death 2. Dysfunctional families 3. Family secrets 4. Abusive men 5. Consequences 6. New Orleans, Louisiana 7. Domestic fiction

LC 2019002554

Family secrets are revealed in the heat of a New Orleans summer.

The **Middlesteins**. Jami Attenberg. Grand Central Pub, 2012. 288 p.
ISBN 9781455507214
1. Jewish families 2. Families 3. Food habits 4. Life change events
5. Compulsive behavior in women 6. Middle West 7. Mainstream
fiction 8. Domestic fiction

LC 2011025990

Two siblings with very different personalities attempt to take control
of their mother's food obsession and massive weight gain to save her life
after their father walks out and leaves her reeling in the Chicago suburbs.

Atwood, Margaret

Alias Grace. Margaret Atwood. Nan A. Talese/Doubleday, 1996. 468
p. : Illustration
ISBN 9780385475716
1. Marks, Grace 2. Trials (Murder) 3. Women murderers 4. Murder —
History 5. Irish Canadians 6. Man-woman relationships 7. Canada
8. 1840s 9. Historical mysteries 10. Literary fiction 11. Psychological
fiction
ALA Notable Book, 1998; Booklist Editors' Choice, 1996; Giller
Prize, 1996; Library Journal Best Books, 1996; New York Times
Notable Book, 1997; Shortlisted for the Booker-McConnell Prize,
1996; Shortlisted for the International IMPAC Dublin Literary Award,
1998; Shortlisted for The Orange Prize for Fiction, 1997; Governor
General's Literary Awards, English-language Fiction finalist

Takes readers into the life and mind of Grace Marks, one of the most
notorious women of the 1840s, who is serving a life sentence for murders
she claims she cannot remember.

"Always a powerful writer, Atwood outdoes herself with compelling
prose, expert control of the material, and fine attention to historical detail." —*Library Journal*

Title adapted into a Canadian-American television miniseries by the
same name in 2017.

★ The **blind** assassin. Margaret Atwood. Nan A. Talese/Doubleday,
2000. 521 p.
ISBN 9780385475723
1. Widows 2. Family secrets 3. Sibling rivalry 4. Sisters — Death
5. Political corruption 6. Toronto, Ontario 7. Canada 8. 1940s
9. Literary fiction 10. Novels-within-novels 11. Canadian fiction

LC 99462109

ALA Notable Book, 2001; Booker Prize, 2000; Booklist Editors'
Choice, 2000; Governor General's Literary Awards, English-language
Fiction finalist, 2000; Shortlisted for the International IMPAC Dublin
Literary Award, 2002; Shortlisted for The Orange Prize for Fiction,
2001

Iris describes the 1945 death of her sister, who drives her car off a
bridge, followed, two years later, by the death of her husband, in a story
that features a novel-within-a-novel about two unnamed lovers who meet
in a dark backstreet room.

Bluebeard's egg and other stories. Margaret Atwood. Anchor Books,
1983. 244 p.
ISBN 9780395404249
1. Family relationships 2. Interpersonal relations 3. Husband and wife
4. Literary fiction 5. Short stories 6. Canadian fiction

LC 97-32459

"As Atwood's attitude ranges from the hilarious to the shocking, the
reader is introduced to a series of relationships—husband and wife, parent
and child, man and woman—in which the characters' inner and outer
worlds are beautifully probed, expressed in the author's understated
style." —*Booklist*

Rev. ed. of: Bluebeard's egg. c1983.

★ **Cat's** eye. Margaret Atwood. Doubleday, 1989. 446 p.
ISBN 9780385260077
1. Women painters 2. Self-discovery in women 3. Female friendship 4.
Childhood 5. Memories 6. Canada 7. Toronto, Ontario 8. Literary
fiction 9. Psychological fiction 10. Canadian fiction

LC 88024345

ALA Notable Book, 1990; Toronto Book Awards, 1989; Shortlisted
for the Booker-McConnell Prize, 1989; Governor General's Literary
Awards, English-language Fiction finalist

Years after painter Elaine Risley flees Toronto for Vancouver, she returns to search for long-missing parts of her life and pursue the elusive
Cordelia, her best friend and sometimes enemy.

"Atwood's achievement is the decoding of childhood's secrets, and
the creation of a flawed and haunting work of art." —*Time*

★ The **handmaid's** tale. Margaret Atwood. Houghton Mifflin, 1986.
311 p. (Handmaid's tale, 1)
ISBN 9780395404256
1. Women's role 2. Dystopias 3. Infertility 4. Caste 5. Young women
6. North America 7. 21st century 8. Literary fiction 9. Dystopian fiction
10. Science fiction classics

LC 85021944

Arthur C. Clarke Award, 1987; Commonwealth Writers' Prize,
Caribbean and Canada: Best Book, 1987; Governor General's
Literary Award for English-Language Fiction, 1985; Los Angeles
Times Book Prize for Fiction, 1986; Shortlisted for the
Booker-McConnell Prize, 1986

Offred, a Handmaid, describes life in what was once the United
States, now the Republic of Gilead, a shockingly repressive and intolerant
monotheocracy, in a satirical tour de force set in the near future.

"A gripping suspense tale, The Handmaid's Tale is an allegory of
what results from a politics based on misogyny, racism, and anti-Semitism." —*Ms*

Life before man. Margaret Atwood. Bantam Books, 1996. 351 p.
ISBN 9780553377828
1. Married people 2. Husband and wife 3. Extramarital affairs
4. Middle-aged women 5. Lovers — Death 6. Domestic fiction
7. Literary fiction 8. Canadian fiction

LC 95032375

Governor General's Literary Awards, English-language Fiction
finalist

"This is a powerful, introspective view of contemporary marriage and
the changing roles of the sexes.... [This novel] returns to the survival and
identity theme of Atwood's early thematic guide to Canadian literature,
but at a level that transcends the national. With men and mores rooted in
the prehistoric past, Atwood forces us to confront a harrowing present that
anticipates an ecologically and culturally doomed future." —*Choice*

Originally published: New York : Simon & Schuster, 1979.

★ **Maddaddam**: a novel. Margaret Atwood. Random House Inc,
2013. 352 p. (MaddAddam trilogy, 3)
ISBN 9780385528788
1. Dystopias 2. New religious movements 3. Religion and science
4. Genetically engineered animals 5. Regression (Civilization) 6. Social
science fiction 7. Apocalyptic fiction 8. Literary fiction 9. Adult books
for young adults

LC 2013018715

Goodreads Choice Award, 2013; New York Times Notable Book,
2013

A conclusion to the trilogy finds Toby and Ren returning to the MaddAddamite cob house after rescuing Amanda and assuming the duties of the Craker's religious overseers while Zeb searches for the founder of the pacifist green religion he left years earlier.

Sequel to: The Year of the Flood.

Originally published in Canada by McClelland & Stewart Ltd, Toronto.

Moral disorder. Margaret Atwood. Nan A. Talese, 2006. 240 p. ISBN 9780385503846

1. Women's role 2. Marriage 3. Aging 4. Family relationships 5. Growing up 6. Toronto, Ontario 7. Canada 8. Autobiographical fiction 9. Literary fiction 10. Short stories

LC 2006044589

A collection of short fiction presents eleven stories that capture important moments in the course of a life and in the lives intertwined with it, in a volume that ranges from the 1930s to the 1980s.

"This collection of 11 interconnected short stories opens as a Canadian woman named Nell and her longtime partner, Gilbert (known as Tig), face aging together into an uncertain future.... The result is alternatively humorous and heart-wrenching, occasionally sardonic and always brutally honest in the depiction of our often contorted relationships with one another, with nature, and with ourselves." —*Library Journal*

★ **Oryx** and Crake. Margaret Eleanor Atwood. Doubleday, 2003. 432 p. (MaddAddam trilogy, 1)
ISBN 9780385503853

1. Ecology 2. Dystopias 3. Environmental degradation 4. Disasters 5. Male friendship 6. Canada 7. Apocalyptic fiction 8. Social science fiction 9. Science fiction

Booklist Editors' Choice, 2003; New York Times Notable Book, 2003; Governor General's Literary Awards, English-language Fiction finalist, 2003; Shortlisted for the Giller Prize, 2003; Shortlisted for the Man Booker Prize, 2003; Shortlisted for The Orange Prize for Fiction, 2004

A novel of the future explores a world that has been devastated by ecological and scientific disasters.

"Rigorous in its chilling insights and riveting in its fast-paced 'what if' dramatization, Atwood's superb novel is as brillantly provocative as it is profoundly engaging." —*Booklist*

Sequel: The year of the flood.

★ **Stone** mattress: nine tales. Margaret Atwood. Nan A. Talese/Doubleday, 2014. 256 pages
ISBN 9780385539128

1. Interpersonal relations 2. Seniors 3. Couples 4. Revenge 5. Literary fiction 6. Short stories 7. Canadian fiction

LC 2014013010

In these nine dazzlingly inventive and rewarding stories, Margaret Atwood's signature dark humour, playfulness, and deadly seriousness are in abundance.

"Most of the nine stories feature women who have been wronged as girls but recover triumphantly as adults. Atwood brings her biting wit to bear on the battle of the sexes." —*Publishers Weekly*

Standard print edition originally published: London: Bloomsbury, 2014.

★ The **testaments**: a novel. Margaret Atwood. Nan A. Talese, 2019. 320 p. (Handmaid's tale, 2)
ISBN 9780385543781

1. Near future 2. Resistance to government 3. Gender role 4. Political persecution 5. Women — Interpersonal relations 6. North America 7. 21st century 8. Literary fiction 9. Dystopian fiction 10. First person narratives

Australian Book Industry Awards, International Book of the Year, 2020; Goodreads Choice Award, 2019; Loan Stars Favourites, 2019; Man Booker Prize, 2019; New York Times Notable Book, 2019

Fifteen years after the events in The Handmaids Tale, the regime running the Republic of Gilead shows signs of collapsing from within as the lives of three women explosively converge.

"The tone is informative without becoming accusatory; indeed the facts speak clearly on their own." —*Booklist*

★ The **year** of the flood: a novel. Margaret Atwood. Nan A. Talese/Doubleday, 2009. 448 p. (MaddAddam trilogy, 2)
ISBN 9780385528771

1. Young women 2. End of the world 3. Dystopias 4. Regression (Civilization) 5. Religion and science 6. Apocalyptic fiction 7. Social science fiction 8. Literary fiction 9. Adult books for young adults

LC 2009005901

ALA Notable Book, 2010; Booklist Editors' Choice, 2009; New York Times Notable Book, 2009

The times and species have been changing at a rapid rate, and the social compact is wearing as thin as environmental stability. Adam One, the kindly leader of the God's Gardeners—a religion devoted to the melding of science and religion, as well as the preservation of all plant and animal life—has long predicted a natural disaster that will alter Earth as we know it. Now it has occurred, obliterating most human life.

"A novel set in the nightmarish future first envisioned in Oryx and Crake. Contrary to expectations, the waterless flood, a biological disaster predicted by a fringe religious group, actually arrives. In its wake, the survivors must rely on their wits to get by, all the while reflecting on what went wrong. Atwood wins major style points here for her framing device, the liturgical year of the God's Gardeners sect." —*Library Journal*

Sequel to: Oryx and Crake.

Sequel: MaddAddam.

Auci, Stefania

The **Florios** of Sicily: a novel. Stefania Auci; translated by Katherine Gregor. HarperVia, 2020. 304 p.
ISBN 9780062931672

1. Napoleonic Wars, 1800-1815 2. Ambition 3. Aristocracy 4. Revenge 5. Arranged marriage 6. Sicily, Italy 7. Historical fiction 8. Family sagas 9. Literary fiction

LC 2019030861

Captures the many lives of Italy's greatest family, the Florios, from their humble origins as Sicilian shopkeepers to their dominance as titans of industry.

"For fans of big, meaty epics chock full of drama and intriguing characters, Auci's fictionalized tale of the real-life Florios delivers in spades." —*Booklist*

Translation of: I leoni di Sicilia.

Originally published: Milano : Editrice Nord, 2019.

Translated from the Italian.

Audrain, Ashley

The **push**. Ashley Audrain. Pamela Dorman Books/Penguin, 2021. 320 pages
ISBN 9781984881663

1. Mothers and daughters 2. Motherhood — Psychological aspects 3. Family relationships 4. Grief in women 5. Women — Mental health 6. Psychological suspense 7. Canadian fiction 8. Second person narratives

LibraryReads Favorites, 2021; Loan Stars Favourites, 2021

A devoted mother with a painful past gradually realizes that something is very wrong with her daughter, a fear that is complicated by her
husband's dismissive views and the birth of a healthy son.

Auel, Jean M.

★ The **clan** of the cave bear: a novel. Jean M. Auel. Crown, 1980. 468
(Earth's children, 1)
ISBN 9780517542026
1. Heroes and heroines 2. Prehistoric humans 3. Cave dwellers 4. Ayla
(Fictitious character) 5. Ice age (Geology) 6. Europe 7. Stone Age
8. Historical fiction 9. Books to movies 10. Adult books for young
adults

LC 80014581

An injured and orphaned infant carries within her the seed and hope
of mankind in this epic of survival and destiny set at the dawn of prehistory.

Auslander, Shalom

Hope: a tragedy. Shalom Auslander. Riverhead Books, 2012. 304 p.
ISBN 9781594488382
1. Jewish families 2. Moving, Household 3. Arsonists 4. Mother and
adult son 5. Farmhouses 6. Satirical fiction
New York Times Notable Book, 2012

Deliberately relocating his family to an unremarkable rural town in
New York in the hopes of starting over, Solomon Kugel finds his efforts
challenged by his depressive mother, a local arsonist and the discovery of
a believed-dead historical specimen hiding his attic.

Austen, Jane

★ **Emma**. Jane Austen. Oxford University Press, 2003. Xli, 402 p.
ISBN 9780192802378
1. Young women — History 2. Franklin, Miles 3. Matchmakers 4. Mate
selection for women 5. Courtship 6. England 7. Love stories 8. Books to
movies 9. Classics

Emma is young, rich and independent. She has decided not to get
married and instead spends her time organising her acquaintances' love
affairs. Her plans for the matrimonial success of her new friend Harriet,
however, lead her into complications that ultimately test her own detachment from the world of romance.
Emma was the inspiration for the movie Clueless.
Originally published: London : John Murray, 1816.

Mansfield Park. Jane Austen. Knopf, 1992. Xxxvii, 488 p.
ISBN 9780679412694
1. Middle class 2. Families 3. Cousins 4. Sisters 5. Social classes
6. England 7. 19th century 8. Classics 9. Love stories 10. Books to
movies

The private and social worlds of three families are revealed through
the experiences of the heroine, Fanny Price.
Originally published: London, 1814.
First published in 1814.
Includes extra material.

Northanger Abbey. Jane Austen. Modern Library, 2002. Xxvii, 220 p.
ISBN 9780375759178
1. Teenage girls 2. Imagination in teenage girls 3. Mate selection for
women 4. Family estates 5. Misunderstanding 6. England 7. Bath,
England 8. Classics 9. Satirical fiction 10. Arthur, King

When Catherine, a clergyman's daughter, is invited to spend a season
in Bath with fashionable high society, little does she imagine the delights
and perils that await her. Captivated and disconcerted by what she finds,
and introduced to the joys of Gothic novels by her friends, Catherine longs
for mystery and romance. When invited to stay with the beguiling Henry
Tilney and his family, she expects mystery and intrigue at every turn—but
the truth turns out to be even stranger than fiction.
Originally published: London : John Murray, 1818.

★ **Persuasion**. Jane Austen. Knopf, 1992. Xxxvii, 260 p.
ISBN 9780679409861
1. Interclass romance 2. Classism 3. Sisters 4. Man-woman
relationships 5. England 6. Love stories 7. Books to movies 8. Classics

The romance between Captain Wentworth and Anne, the daughter of
Sir Walter Elliot, seems doomed because of the young man's family con-
nections and lack of wealth.
First published posthumously in 1818.
Originally published: London : John Murray, 1818.

★ **Pride** and prejudice. Jane Austen. Modern Library, 1995. 281 p.
ISBN 9780679601685
1. Sisters 2. Young women 3. Families 4. Mothers and daughters
5. Courtship 6. England 7. 19th century 8. Classics 9. Love stories
10. Books to TV

Human foibles and early nineteenth-century manners are satirized in
this romantic tale of English country family life as Elizabeth Bennet and
her four sisters are encouraged to marry well in order to keep the Bennet
estate in their family.
Originally published: London : T. Egerton, 1813.

★ **Sense** and sensibility. Jane Austen; edited by James Kinsley; with an
introduction by Margaret Anne Doody; notes by Claire Lamont. Oxford
University Press, 2004. Li, 327 p.
ISBN 9780192804785
1. Young women 2. Sisters 3. Courtship 4. Mate selection 5. Rich
families 6. Great Britain 7. England 8. Classics 9. Love stories
10. Books to TV

Two sisters, one practical and conventional and the other emotional
and sentimental, set their sights on men who will perfectly match their disparate personalities, with unexpected results.
Sense and Sensibility has been closely adapted to film in 1995 and to
television in 1981 and 2008.
Optimized reading formats—Cover.
Originally published: London : T. Egerton, 1811.

Auster, Paul

4 3 2 1: a novel. Paul Auster. Henry Holt and Company, 2017. 880 p.
ISBN 9781627794466
1. Growing up 2. Identity (Psychology) 3. Life change events 4. Jewish
men 5. Men — Psychology 6. New Jersey 7. 20th century 8. Literary
fiction 9. Coming-of-age stories

LC 2016020041

Booklist Editors' Choice, 2017; New York Times Notable Book,
2017; Shortlisted for the Man Booker Prize, 2017; Longlisted for the
Andrew Carnegie Medal for Excellence in Fiction, 2018

A single child born in 1947 experiences four parallel lifetimes poignantly marked by shifting family fortunes, athletic pursuits, friendships,
sex, intellectual passions and the same intriguing woman.

"With this novel, Auster reminds us that not just life, but also narrative is always conditional, that it only appears inevitable after the fact."
—*Kirkus*

★ The **book** of illusions: a novel. Paul Auster. Henry Holt & Co, 2002.
336 p.
ISBN 9780805054088

1. Grief in men 2. Film actors and actresses 3. Filmmaking 4. Loss (Psychology) 5. Families of airplane accident victims 6. Vermont 7. Psychological fiction 8. Literary fiction

LC 2002017218

ALA Notable Book, 2003; New York Times Notable Book, 2002; Shortlisted for the International IMPAC Dublin Literary Award, 2004

A Vermont professor, disillusioned with self-pity and grief over his family's death in a plane crash, finds a new purpose when he becomes obsessed with research into the life and art of a silent film comedian who mysteriously disappeared when silent films ended.

"Auster limns Mann's many-layered cinematic and earthly worlds in mesmerizing and voluptuous detail within an artful, poignantly metaphysical, and delectably Hitchcockian tale of mayhem, murder, and myriad illusions within illusions." —*Booklist*

The **Brooklyn** follies. Paul Auster. Henry Holt, 2005. 320 p.
ISBN 9780805077148
1. Self-evaluation in men 2. Eccentrics and eccentricities 3. Middle-aged men — Family relationships 4. Divorced men 5. Forgery 6. New York City 7. 2000s (Decade) 8. Psychological fiction 9. Literary fiction

LC 2005040201

Retired life insurance salesman Nathan Glass moves to Brooklyn to find anonymity and solitude through his declining years, but a chance meeting with Tom Wood, his long-lost nephew, forces him to come to terms with his past.

"This is a departure for Auster. Instead of tight plotting and theoretical figure work, there is domestic realism. The result is a novel far more passionately American than Auster's previous ones." —*Times Literary Supplement*

★ **In** the country of last things. Paul Auster. Viking 1987. 188 p.
ISBN 9780670814459
1. Dystopias 2. Survival 3. Missing persons 4. Death 5. Siblings 6. Apocalyptic fiction 7. Literary fiction

LC 86040257

Anna Blume, searching for her brother who has disappeared, recounts her wanderings through a modern urban reprise of the Dark Ages where she becomes a member of a scavenger class in search of objects from the past.

"This novel is distinguished by an uncanny grasp of the day-to-day realities of homelessness. This is a scary but highly relevant book." —*Library Journal*

Invisible. Paul Auster. Henry Holt and Co, 2009. 320 p.
ISBN 9780805090802
1. College students 2. Love triangles 3. Poets 4. Campus life 5. Identity (Psychology) 6. New York City 7. 1960s 8. Psychological fiction 9. LIterary fiction 10. Coming-of-age stories

LC 2009002237

New York Times Notable Book, 2009

Poet and student Adam Walker meets the enigmatic Frenchman Rudolf Born and his silent, seductive girlfriend, Margot, sending Adam into a perverse triangle that leads to a shocking act of violence that will alter his life.

"To be blunt, as a writer of sentences, Auster isn't anything special; reading this book after reading Roth or Richard Yates, for example—or, to draw upon a couple of comparisons that are even more unfair, Bellow or Nabokov—one is aware of how neutral and unremarkable, and occasionally even plodding, Auster's prose can be. What Auster is, instead, is a spellbinding storyteller, sometimes thanks to, and other times in spite of, his post-modern narrative trickery. Even more important, he is a writer of high moral seriousness. Indeed, this novel, like some of his others, could

best be described as a moral suspense story. As such, it succeeds brilliantly." —*PopMatters*

★ **Leviathan**. Paul Auster. Viking, 1992. 275 p.
ISBN 9780670846764
1. Anarchists 2. Obsession in men 3. Love triangles 4. Missing persons 5. Vietnam War protesters 6. Literary fiction

LC 92001282

ALA Notable Book, 1993

When his closest friend, Benjamin Sachs, accidentally blows himself up on a Wisconsin road, Peter Aaron attempts to piece together the events that led to Ben's tragic demise and determine the reason for his death.

"Mr. Auster may write about coincidence, but there is nothing coincidental about his prose, in which seemingly straightforward information has an allegorical dimension.... Thus in the literary looking glass of 'Leviathan,' in which things are not always what they seem, our pleasure in reading the story is enhanced by the challenge of making other connections." —*New York Times Book Review*

Oracle night. Paul Auster. H. Holt, 2003. 256 p.
ISBN 9780805073201
1. Authors 2. Fiction writing 3. Precognition 4. Men who are blind 5. Husband and wife 6. Brooklyn, New York City 7. 1980s 8. Psychological fiction 9. Literary fiction 10. Novels-within-novels

LC 2003051063

New York Times Notable Book, 2003

Recovering from a near-fatal illness, Sidney Orr, a thirty-four-year-old novelist, purchases a mysterious blue notebook from a Brooklyn stationery shop and is drawn into a bizarre world of eerie premonitions and baffling events.

"A novelist writing about a novelist writing about an editor reading a novel: these Russian dolls might come across as merely cute, were it not for the fact that the lucid Mr Auster is a natural storyteller, with a seemingly inexhaustible trove of yarns at his disposal. All of the stories within stories are compelling in their own right." —*The Economist*

Sunset Park. Paul Auster. Henry Holt and Co, 2010. 320 p.
ISBN 9780805092868
1. Young adults 2. Fugitives 3. Squatters 4. Intergenerational relations 5. Guilt in men 6. Brooklyn, New York City 7. Sunset Park (New York N.Y.) 8. Literary fiction 9. Multiple perspectives

LC 2009045726

After falling in love with an underage girl and stirring the wrath of her older sister, New York native Miles Heller flees to Brooklyn and shacks up with a group of artists squatting in the borough's Sunset Park neighborhood.

"The novel is graphically sexual and, more surprisingly, insistently phallic. This is a little bewildering until, as the novel progresses, one comes to accept that, for Auster's characters, the body— in its fragility and strength— is one of the only certainties in a time of increasing darkness. In a way, Sunset Park is Auster's most Whitmanesque novel and it's very entertaining." —*Globe and Mail (Toronto)*

A Frances Coady book.

Timbuktu: a novel. Paul Auster. H. Holt, 1999. 181 p.
ISBN 9780805054071
1. Men with mental illnesses 2. Dogs 3. Human-animal relationships 4. Men and dogs 5. Poets 6. Stories told by animals 7. Picaresque fiction 8. Literary fiction

LC 9846742

New York Times Notable Book, 1999

Mr. Bones, the canine sidekick of Willy G. Christmas, a brilliant but troubled Brooklyn poet, accompanies his master on a trip to Baltimore Maryland, to search for Willy's high school teacher and beloved mentor, Bea Swanson, in a novel narrated from the dog's point of view.

"Auster handles the language better than almost anyone else writing today,...the first chapter of Timbuktu is one of the finest and most polished to have appeared in any recent novel." —*The National Review*

Travels in the scriptorium: a novel. Paul Auster. H. Holt, 2007. 160 p.
ISBN 9780805081459
1. Criminals 2. People with amnesia 3. Memories 4. Senior men 5. Identity (Psychology) 6. Literary fiction
LC 2005055038
An elderly man awakens disoriented in an unfamiliar room, with no memory of who he is or how he got there, and receives visits from a series of people who give him frustrating hints about his identity and his past.

"One of Blank's visitors, an ex-policeman named Flood, exudes an economical malevolence: instead of two shakes of a cat's tail, he speaks of two shakes of a cat. When challenged, he responds, with imperturbably menacing politeness: Just an expression, Mr Blank. No harm intended. But harm intended, this novel wants to say, is not the only kind of harm.... Auster sets [the] lyricism of the mundane against an increasingly oppressive atmosphere in which ghosts might come alive from books." —*New Statesman*

Originally published under the same title: London, England : Faber and Faber, 2006.

Austin, Emily

Everyone in this room will someday be dead. Emily Austin. Atria Books, 2021. 256 p.
ISBN 9781982167356
1. Receptionists 2. Obsession 3. Lesbians 4. Atheists 5. Impostors 6. Literary fiction 7. Canadian fiction
LibraryReads Favorites, 2021
A morbidly anxious woman stumbles into a job as a receptionist at a Catholic church and becomes obsessed with her predecessor's mysterious death.

"The secondary characters add lightness to the story despite Gilda's constant thoughts of death, offering a reprieve from her internal monologue. Readers will find themselves rooting for the lovable but traumatized heroine." —*Kirkus*

Austin, Finola

Bronte's mistress. Finola Austin. Simon & Schuster, 2020. 272 p.
ISBN 9781982137236
1. Bronte, Patrick Branwell 2. Married women 3. Young men — Relations with older women 4. Extramarital affairs 5. Grief in women 6. Nonconformists 7. Yorkshire, England 8. Great Britain 9. Victorian era (1837-1901) 10. 1840s 11. Historical fiction 12. Bernhardt, Sarah 13. First person narratives
A meticulously researched debut by the award-winning "Secret Victorianist" blogger follows the scandalous 1843 love affair between a grieving Lydia Robinson of Thorp Green Hall and her son's erratically unconventional tutor, Branwell Bronte.

"Offer this to fans of Victorian literature, readers who like their historical fiction populated with real people, and those who don't require that their romances have happy endings." —*Booklist*

Austin, Lynn N.

Chasing shadows. Lynn Austin. Tyndale House Publishers, 2021. 432 p.
ISBN 9781496437341

1. Mothers and daughters 2. Faith in women 3. Survival 4. Women violinists 5. Christian women 6. Netherlands 7. Second World War era (1939-1945) 8. Christian historical fiction
LC 2020051173
Lena is a wife and mother who farms alongside her husband in the tranquil countryside. Her faith has always been her compass, but can she remain steadfast when the questions grow increasingly complex and the answers could mean the difference between life and death? Lena's daughter Ans has recently moved to the bustling city of Leiden, filled with romantic notions of a new job and a young Dutch police officer. But when she is drawn into Resistance work, her idealism collides with the dangerous reality that comes with fighting the enemy. Miriam is a young Jewish violinist who immigrated for the safety she thought Holland would offer. She finds love in her new country, but as her family settles in Leiden, the events that follow will test them in ways she could never have imagined.

"Christy Award winner Austin (If I Were You) shines in this excellent tale of three women who struggle to survive WWII in the Netherlands.... This is a must-read for fans of WWII inspirationals." —*Publishers Weekly*

Ausubel, Ramona

Sons and daughters of ease and plenty. Ramona Ausubel. Riverhead Books, 2016. 320 p.
ISBN 9781594634888
1. Rich families 2. Life change events 3. Parent-separated children 4. Extramarital affairs 5. Husband and wife 6. Martha's Vineyard, Massachusetts 7. 1970s 8. 1960s 9. Domestic fiction
LC 2016002763
From the award-winning author of No One Is Here Except All of Us, an imaginative novel about a wealthy New England family in the 1960s and '70s that suddenly loses its fortune—and its bearings. Labor Day, 1976, Martha's Vineyard. Summering at the family beach house along this moneyed coast of New England, Fern and Edgar—married with three children—are happily preparing for a family birthday celebration when they learn that the unimaginable has occurred: There is no more money. More specifically, there's no more money in the estate of Fern's recently deceased parents, which, as the sole source of Fern and Edgar's income, had allowed them to live this beautiful, comfortable life despite their professed anti-money ideals. Quickly, the once-charmed family unravels. In distress and confusion, Fern and Edgar are each tempted away on separate adventures: she on a road trip with a stranger, he on an ill-advised sailing voyage with another woman. The three children are left for days with no guardian whatsoever, in an improvised Neverland helmed by the tender, witty, and resourceful Cricket, age nine. Brimming with humanity and wisdom, humor and bite, and imbued with both the whimsical and the profound, Sons and Daughters of Ease and Plenty is a story of American wealth, class, family, and mobility, approached by award-winner Ramona Ausubel with a breadth of imagination and understanding that is fresh, surprising, and exciting.

Avery, Ellis

The last nude. Ellis Avery. Riverhead Books, 2012. 320 p.
ISBN 9781594488139
1. Lempicka, Tamara de 2. Women painters 3. Lesbians 4. Artists' models 5. Women and success 6. Interpersonal relations 7. Paris, France 8. 1920s 9. Historical fiction
LC 2011027708
Stonewall Book Award for the Barbara Gittings Literature Award, 2013
Agreeing to model nude for Art Deco painter Tamara de Lempicka in 1927 Paris, young American Rafaela Fano inspires the artist's most iconic

Jazz Age images and becomes her lover while discovering darker truths about Tamara's private life.

Avon, Joy

In peppermint peril: a Book Tea Shop mystery. Joy Avon. Crooked Lane Books, 2018. 304 pages (Book Tea Shop novel, 1)
ISBN 9781683317937
1. Books and reading 2. Tea 3. Dogs as pets 4. Christmas 5. Boston terriers 6. Maine 7. Cozy mysteries 8. Holiday mysteries

In the run-up to Christmas Eve, organizer of book-themed tea parties Callie Aspen and her lovable Boston terrier will have to conquer threefold trouble—a mysterious will, a missing heirloom and a dead body—to restore the festive spirit to their small town.

Aw, Tash

We, the survivors. Tash Aw. Farrar, Straus and Giroux, 2019. 326 pages
ISBN 9780374287245
1. Poe, Edgar Allan 2. Murderers 3. Social classes 4. Social change 5. Migrant workers 6. Malaysia 7. Political fiction 8. Literary fiction
LC 2019000372

A man from a Malaysian fishing village who has completed a sentence for murder and a privileged young journalist whose life has taken an unexpected turn confront the systems of power, race and class that drove the former into violence.

Awad, Mona

★ **13** ways of looking at a fat girl. Mona Awad. Penguin Books, 2016. 240 p.
ISBN 9780143128489
1. Female friendship 2. Body image 3. Self-esteem in women 4. Interpersonal relations 5. Dieting 6. Relationship fiction 7. Canadian fiction 8. Adult books for young adults
Books in Canada First Novel Award, 2015; LibraryReads Favorites, 2016; Shortlisted for the Giller Prize, 2016

Follows Lizzie, a young woman growing up in Mississauga, as she fights her way from fat to thin, but who still, even as a married adult woman, sees herself as a fat girl.

"Lizzie's particular sadness is unsettlingly sharp: she gets under your skin, and she stays there. Beautifully constructed; a devastating novel but also a deeply empathetic one." —*Kirkus*

Bunny. Mona Awad. Viking, 2019. 320 p.
ISBN 9780525559733
1. Women graduate students 2. Rites and ceremonies 3. Female friendship 4. Loneliness 5. Belonging 6. New England 7. Black humor 8. Canadian fiction 9. Adult books for young adults
LC 2018045360
Loan Stars Favourites, 2019

Invited to join a popular clique at her university, a misfit artist with a dark imagination is drawn into ritualistic activities that transform her perspectives on reality.

Ayatsuji, Yukito

The **Decagon** House murders. Yukito Ayatsuji; translated from the Japanese by Ho-Ling Wong. Pushkin Vertigo, 2021. 224 pages
ISBN 9781782276340
1. College students 2. Murder investigation 3. Student organizations 4. Japan 5. Mysteries 6. Translations 7. Adult books for young adults

When the members of a university book club visit an island to investigate a multiple murder from the year before, they, when a fresh murder occurs, soon realize that they are being picked off one-by-one and must put their skills to good use to catch a killer.

"First published in 1987, Ayatsuji's brilliant and richly atmospheric puzzle will appeal to fans of golden age whodunits." —*Publishers Weekly*
Originally published in Japanese by Kodansha, Ltd, Tokyo, in 1987.

B

Babalola, Bolu

Love in color: mythical tales from around the world, retold. Bolu Babalola. William Morrow and Co, 2021. 224 p.
ISBN 9780063078499
1. Love 2. Gods and goddesses 3. Magic 4. Sexuality 5. Women 6. Short stories 7. Literary fiction 8. Love stories

A debut anthology reimagines cultural folk and love stories from West Africa, Greek mythology and Middle East legend, from the tale of an unappreciated Nigerian goddess to the story of a powerful Ghanaian spokeswoman's fateful decision.

"Babalola revives the romance of folktales and myths in her lovely debut collection, drafting figures largely drawn from African legends and romance tropes into 13 Black-centered love stories.... The result is effortlessly readable, and the chemistry between characters and the focus on Black female empowerment will surely win over many romance fans." —*Publishers Weekly*

Bacigalupi, Paolo

★ The **water** knife. Paolo Bacigalupi. Alfred A. Knopf, 2015. 384 p.
ISBN 9780385352871
1. Near future 2. Power (Social sciences) 3. Droughts 4. Water 5. Rivers 6. Southwest (United States) 7. Phoenix, Arizona 8. Dystopian fiction 9. Science fiction 10. Adult books for young adults
LibraryReads Favorites, 2015; Library Journal Best Books, 2015; RUSA Reading List Short List, 2016

Working as an enforcer for a corrupt developer, Angel Velasquez teams up with a hardened journalist and a street-smart Texan to investigate rumors of California's imminent monopoly on limited water supplies.

"The way the novel's environmental nightmare affects society, as individuals and larger entities—both official and criminal—vie for a limited and essential resource, feels solid, plausible, and disturbingly believable." —*Kirkus*

★ The **windup** girl. Paolo Bacigalupi. Night Shade, 2009. 359 p.
ISBN 9781597801577
1. Genetically engineered women 2. Biological terrorism 3. Civil war 4. Corporations 5. Agribusiness 6. Bangkok, Thailand 7. Dystopian fiction 8. Science fiction 9. Adult books for young adults
LC Oc2009038816
Hugo Award for Best Novel, 2010; John W. Campbell Memorial Award for Best Science Fiction Novel, 2010; Library Journal Best Books, 2009; Locus Award for First Novel, 2010; Nebula Award for Best Novel, 2009; RUSA Reading List, 2010

Living in a future where food is scarce, Anderson Lake tries to find ways to exploit this need, as he comes into conflict with Jaidee, an official of the Environmental Ministry, and encounters Emiko, a engineered windup girl who has been discarded by her creator.

"One of the strengths of The Windup Girl, other than its intriguing characters, is Bacigalupi's world building. You can practically taste this future Thailand he's built." —*io9*

Backman, Fredrik

★ **Anxious** people: a novel. Fredrik Backman; translated by Neil Smith. Atria Books, 2020. 341 pages
ISBN 9781501160837
1. Hostages 2. Bank robbers 3. Insecurity (Psychology) 4. Anxiety 5. Helpfulness 6. Sweden 7. Translations 8. Relationship fiction
RUSA Reading List Short List, 2021

Taken hostage by a failed bank robber while attending an open house, eight anxiety-prone strangers—including a redemption-seeking bank director, two couples who would fix their marriages and a plucky octogenarian—discover their unexpected common traits.

"With poignant and sympathetic care, the always incisive and charming Backman (Us Against You, 2017), gently examines garden-variety insecurities against a quaint pre-pandemic backdrop." —*Booklist*

Originally published in Sweden in 2019 as: Folk med ångest—Title page verso.
Translated from the Swedish.

★ **Beartown:** a novel. Fredrik Backman; translated from the Swedish by Neil Smith. Atria Books, 2017. 336 p. (Beartown, 1)
ISBN 9781501160769
1. Communities 2. Scandals 3. Sports teams 4. Hockey 5. Sports 6. Sweden 7. Translations 8. Relationship fiction 9. Books to TV 10. Adult books for young adults
LC 2017000377
Loan Stars Favourites, 2017; LibraryReads Favorites, 2017; School Library Journal Best Books: Best Adult Books 4 Teens, 2017

In the tiny forest community of Beartown, the possibility that the amateur hockey team might win a junior championship, bringing the hope of revitalization to the fading town, is shattered by the aftermath of a violent act that leaves a young girl traumatized.

"The sentimentally savvy Backman...takes a sobering and solemn look at the ways alienation and acceptance, ethics and emotions nearly destroy a small town." —*Booklist*

Originally published in Swedish in 2016 as Bjornstad. Published in the UK as The Scandal by Michael Joseph, 2017.
Made into a television show, 2021.
Translated from the Swedish

Britt-Marie was here. Fredrik Backman. Pocket Books 2016. 384 p.
ISBN 9781501142536
1. Senior women 2. Small town life 3. Self-discovery in women 4. Mentors 5. Poor people 6. Translations 7. Relationship fiction
LibraryReads Favorites, 2016; Loan Stars Favourites, 2016

Walking away from her loveless marriage and taking a job in a derelict, financially devastated town, sixty-three-year-old Britt-Marie uses her fierce organizational skills to become a local soccer coach to a group of lost children.

Translated from the Swedish Britt-Marie var har, originally published in 2014.

A **man** called Ove. Fredrik Backman; translation from the Swedish by Henning Koch. Atria Books, 2014. 352 p.
ISBN 9781476738017
1. Senior men 2. Neighbors 3. Communities 4. Grouches 5. Suicidal behavior 6. Translations 7. Books to movies 8. Relationship fiction

A curmudgeon hides beneath a cranky and short-tempered exterior a terrible personal loss while clashing with new neighbors, a boisterous family whose chattiness and habits lead to unexpected friendship.

Title adapted into a film by the same name in 2016.
Translation from the Swedish of: En man som heter Ove.
Originally published: Stockholm : Forum, 2012.

★ **My** grandmother asked me to tell you she's sorry: a novel. Fredrik Backman; translated from the Swedish by Henning Koch. Atria Books, 2015. 352 p.
ISBN 9781501115066
1. Seven-year-old girls 2. Grandparent and child 3. Grandmothers — Death 4. Eccentrics and eccentricities 5. Fairy tales 6. Sweden 7. Translations 8. Relationship fiction 9. Adult books for young adults
LC 2015000829
LibraryReads Favorites, 2015

Seven-year-old Elsa's grandmother dies and leaves behind a series of letters, sending the girl on a journey that brings to life the world of her grandmother's fairy tales.

"A delectable homage to the power of stories to comfort and heal, Backman's tender tale of the touching relationship between a grandmother and granddaughter is a tribute to the everlasting bonds of deep family ties." —*Booklist*

Originally published as: Min mormor halsar och sager forlat.
Stockholm : Manpocket, 2013.
Translated from the Swedish.

Us against you: a novel. Fredrik Backman; translated by Neil Smith. Atria Books, 2018. 336 p. (Beartown, 2)
ISBN 9781501160790
1. Hockey 2. Sports rivalry 3. Small town life 4. Sports 5. Teenagers 6. Sweden 7. Translations 8. Relationship fiction 9. Adult books for young adults
LibraryReads Favorites, 2018

When the small community of Beartown learns their amateur ice hockey team may be disbanded, the tensions mount, but a surprising new coach offers a chance at a comeback.

Originally published in 2017 by Bokforlaget Forum.
Translated from the Swedish.

Bacon, Charlotte

There is room for you. Charlotte Bacon. Farrar, Straus and Giroux, 2004. 256 p.
ISBN 9780374281854
1. Mothers and daughters 2. Divorced women 3. Women travelers 4. Americans in India 5. British in India 6. New York City 7. India 8. 1990s 9. Psychological fiction 10. Domestic fiction
LC 2003059579

"Rose's memories bring to Bacon's novel an intensity that Anna's travel-writing persona only sporadically achieves. As she uncovers Rose's past and stumbles upon its best-kept secrets, Anna's pronouncements on her American life and Indian experience gain coherence." —*Washington Post*

Bagshawe, Tilly

Adored. Tilly Bagshawe. Warner Books, 2005. 560 p.
ISBN 9780446576888
1. Film actors and actresses 2. Film industry and trade 3. Sexuality 4. Actors and actresses 5. Celebrities 6. Hollywood, California 7. England 8. Glitz and glamour novels
LC 2004017366

Possessing a magnetic sexuality and a driving ambition to be her generation's most successful actress and model, Siena McMahon embarks on a series of affairs with the wrong men and continues the legacy of her powerful family.

Bailey, Paul

Chapman's odyssey. Paul Bailey. Bloomsbury USA, 2012. 211 p.
ISBN 9781608198214
1. Hospital patients 2. Characters and characteristics in literature 3. Men with terminal illnesses 4. Dreams 5. Conversation 6. Psychological fiction

LC 2011029642

Enduring a hallucinatory, heavily medicated existence while recovering in the hospital, Harry Chapman imagines he sees famous real and fictional characters intermingling with people from his own life while his story gradually unfolds.

"Readers who have a passion for literature, poetry, and well-rendered characterization will find themselves happily drawn into the world of Harry Chapman." —*Library Journal*

Uncle Rudolf. Paul Bailey. St. Martin's Press, 2004. 192 p.
ISBN 9780312318345
1. Romanians in foreign countries 2. Parent-separated boys 3. Jewish boys 4. Exiles 5. Jews, Romanian 6. London, England 7. Europe 8. 20th century 9. Psychological fiction

LC 2003058773

A septuagenarian reflects on his childhood relationship with his eccentric but talented tenor uncle, who took him in and humorously educated him in the ways of a gentleman after fleeing fascist Romania.

"The tale of a young boy's escape from fascist Romania in the late 1930s to England. Now 70, Andrew is writing his memoirs about life in his adopted country with Uncle Rudolf, an internationally acclaimed operetta tenor. This contemplative, retrospective focus heightens the emotional weight of the events he recounts and gives power to this novel of exile and loss. Andrew had spent years wondering about his parentsuntil he learns that his mother was murdered by fascist thugs and that his father committed suicide soon after. He struggles his whole life with guilt about having left them for a life of luxury with his generous, outrageous, internationally beloved uncle. Bailey explores these emotions with considerable skill and sympathy and brings the historical milieu convincingly to life." —*Library Journal*

Bailey, Tessa

Fix her up. Tessa Bailey. Avon Books, 2019. 384 p. (Hot and hammered, 1)
ISBN 9780062872838
1. Clowns 2. Former professional athletes 3. Transformations, Personal 4. Sexual attraction 5. Man-woman relationships 6. New York State 7. Contemporary romances 8. Romantic comedies
LibraryReads Favorites, 2019

When his best friend's sister, Georgie, proposes a wild scheme—that they pretend to date to shock her family and help him land a new job, former major league baseball player Travis Ford agrees and soon finds himself wanting to make their fake relationship real.

Bainbridge, Beryl

Every man for himself. Beryl Bainbridge. Carroll & Graf, 1996. 224 p.
ISBN 9780786703494
1. Social classes 2. Young men 3. Rich people 4. Shipwrecks — History 5. 1910s 6. Historical fiction 7. Coming-of-age stories

LC 96-32518

Commonwealth Writers' Prize, South Asia and Europe: Best Book, 1997; Whitbread Book Award for Novel, 1996; Shortlisted for the Booker-McConnell Prize, 1996

Recapturing the four crucial days prior to the sinking of the Titanic and the loss of fifteen hundred lives, this story is told from the perspective of Morgan, the American nephew of the owner of the shipping line, and reveals how his destiny is linked to other passengers.

"Bainbridge hits a tremendous pace as her story reaches its climax. In a remarkably concise book, shot through with laconic wit, she establishes complex characters who engage first the reader's curiosity, then affection. The elegiac theme extends far beyond the historical event." —*New Statesman*

Bair, Kristin

Agatha Arch is afraid of everything. Kristin Bair. Alcove Press, 2020. 336 pages
ISBN 9781643855004
1. Anxiety in women 2. Extramarital affairs 3. Married women 4. Snooping 5. Mothers 6. New England 7. Relationship fiction
Loan Stars Favourites, 2020

A quirky, nervous wreck of a New England mom is forced to face her many fears in this touching, irresistible novel from author Kristin Bair.

"Those looking for a realistic comeback to cheating will be disappointed, but readers of Laurie Gelman and Abbi Waxman who enjoy irreverent moms who say what everyone else is thinking will love the ride." —*Booklist*

Baker, Chandler

Whisper network: a novel. Chandler Baker. Flatiron Books, 2019. 352 p.
ISBN 9781250319470
1. Sexual harassment 2. Women employees 3. Corporate culture 4. Women lawyers 5. Supervisors 6. Dallas, Texas 7. Thrillers and suspense

LC 2019009104

An adult debut by the author of the High School Horror series follows four women who speak out when their ill-reputed boss is slated to become CEO, a decision that triggers catastrophic shifts throughout every department of their company.

Baker, Dorothy

★ **Young** man with a horn. Dorothy Baker. New York Review of Books, 2013. 185 p.
ISBN 9781590175774
1. Self-destructive behavior 2. Jazz musicians 3. Jazz trumpeters 4. Trumpeters 5. Music 6. United States 7. 1920s 8. Psychological fiction

Rick Martin loved music and the music loved him. He could pick up a tune so quickly that it didn't matter to the Cotton Club boss that he was underage, or to the guys in the band that he was just a white kid. He started out in the slums of LA with nothing, and he ended up on top of the game in the speakeasies and nightclubs of New York. But while talent and drive are all you need to make it in music, they aren't enough to make it through a life.

Baker, Jo

The **body** lies. Jo Baker. Alfred A. Knopf, 2019. 256 p.
ISBN 9780525656111

1. Violence against women 2. Women authors 3. Rural life 4. Universities and colleges 5. Creative writing 6. Washington, George 7. Psychological suspense 8. First person narratives

LC 2018050099

Moving to an English countryside university after witnessing an assault in London, a young writer supervises an escalating debate about violence against women before one of her male students writes a novel about her horrific murder.

This is a Borzoi book.

Longbourn. Jo Baker. Alfred A. Knopf, 2013. 331 p.
ISBN 9780385351232
1. Families 2. Household employees 3. Social classes 4. Intrigue 5. Balls (parties) 6. Great Britain 7. Regency period (1811-1820) 8. Historical fiction 9. Adaptations, retellings, and spin-offs

LC 2013016430

Library Journal Best Books, 2013; LibraryReads Favorites, 2013; New York Times Notable Book, 2013

A reimagining of Jane Austen's "Pride and Prejudice" from the perspectives of its below-stairs servants captures the drama of the Bennet household from the sideline viewpoint of Sarah, an orphaned housemaid.

"British author Baker's second novel after her much lauded The Undertow is densely plotted and achingly romantic. This exquisitely reimagined Pride and Prejudice will appeal to Austen devotees and to anyone who finds the goings-on below the stairs to be at least as compelling as the ones above." —*Library Journal*

Originally published in Great Britain by Transworld, an imprint of the Random House Group Ltd, London.

Baker, Kage

The **bird** of the river. Kage Baker. Tor books, 2010. 304 p.
ISBN 9780765322968
1. Teenagers 2. Boats 3. Supernatural 4. Assassins 5. Rivers 6. Fantasy fiction 7. Adult books for young adults

Sharp-eyed orphan Eliss and her half-brother make a new home on a river barge and clash with a teen assassin amid an escalating series of pirate attacks on riverside cities.

"A vivid setting...with minimal fantasy elements, agreeably complemented by solid plotting, mysteries, surprises and characters that grow in the telling. A sparkling farewell from a writer whose illustrious career proved all too brief." —*Kirkus*

Set in the world of "The Anvil of the World" and "The House of the Stag."

The **house** of the stag. Kage Baker. Tor, 2008. 384 p.
ISBN 9780765317452
1. Fate and fatalism 2. Rebels 3. Revenge 4. Wizards 5. Good and evil 6. Fantasy fiction 7. Coming-of-age stories 8. Adult books for young adults

Romantic Times Reviewers' Choice Award, 2008

Before the Riders came to their remote valley, the Yendri led a tranquil pastoral life. Gard, taken as a slave by powerful mages, has found subtle ways to earn his freedom, and becomes lord and commander of a demon army.

"Baker's fantasy is completely different from her science fiction, but it's just as good. Gently humorous and ironic, Gard is a character readers will pull for as he moves from foundling to outcast to slave to ruler. Baker's worldbuilding is consistently topnotch, and the various supporting characters are just as well drawn as her antihero." —*Romantic Times*

In the garden of Iden: a novel of the Company. Kage Baker. Harcourt, Brace, 1997. 329 p. (The Company, 1)
ISBN 9780151002993

1. Time travel (Past) 2. Plants 3. Rare and endangered plants 4. Immortality 5. Women botanists 6. England 7. 16th century 8. 24th century 9. Science fiction

LC 97-23284

Trained by the Company as a botanist and rendered immortal, Mendoza is sent back amidst the turmoil of Renaissance England with the assignment to safeguard a species of holly that contains properties to cure cancer for future generations.

"Baker's story comments powerfully on religious hypocrisy and xenophobia." —*Library Journal*

Bala, Sharon

The **boat** people: a novel. Sharon Bala. Doubleday, 2018. 304 p.
ISBN 9780385542296
1. Refugees 2. Fathers and sons 3. Prejudice 4. Asylum, Right of 5. Refugees' rights 6. Sri Lanka 7. Vancouver, British Columbia 8. Mainstream fiction 9. Canadian fiction

LC 2017020049

Newfoundland and Labrador Book Award for Fiction, 2020

Journeying to what he hopes will be a new life with his young son on a rusty cargo ship with 500 fellow refugees from Sri Lanka's civil war, a young father arrives on Vancouver's shores, where the group is thrown into a detention processing center and threatened with deportation amid accusations of terrorism.

Balaskovits, A. A.

Magic for unlucky girls: stories. A.A. Balaskovits. SFWP, 2017. 230 p.
ISBN 9781939650665
1. Characters and characteristics in fairy tales 2. Women 3. Girls 4. Adaptations, retellings, and spin-offs 5. Fantasy fiction 6. Short stories

LC 2016033041

The fourteen fantastical stories in Magic For Unlucky Girls take the familiar tropes of fairy tales and twist them into new and surprising shapes.

"In this reimagining and reinventing of traditional, patriarchal fairy tales, Balaskovits creates a safeand often startlingspace for girls and women in her book of short stories." —*Booklist*

Includes bibliographical references and index.

Balasubramanyam, Rajeev

Professor Chandra follows his bliss: a novel. Rajeev Balasubramanyam. The Dial Press, 2019. 288 p.
ISBN 9780525511380
1. College teachers 2. Success (Concept) 3. Divorced men 4. Senior men 5. East Indian British men 6. England 7. United States 8. Relationship fiction

LC 2018034477

LibraryReads Favorites, 2019

An internationally renowned curmudgeon economist and divorced father of three survives an accident before whimsically trading in his high-stress Nobel Prize ambitions to pursue elusive happiness.

Baldacci, David

The **fallen**. David Baldacci. Grand Central Pub, 2018. 432 p. (Amos Decker novels, 4)
ISBN 9781538761397
1. Private investigators 2. Journalists 3. Murder investigation 4. Small towns 5. Pennsylvania 6. Thrillers and suspense

While Amos and his journalist friend Alex visit Alex's sister in Baronville, Pennsylvania, Amos discovers two dead men in a nearby house, but finds the police and unseen forces are stonewalling the investigation.

★ **A gambling** man. David Baldacci. Grand Central Pub, 2021. 432 p. (Aloysius Archer novels, 2)

ISBN 9781538719671

1. World War II veterans 2. Postwar life 3. Private investigators 4. Extortion 5. Scandals 6. California 7. 1950s 8. Historical mysteries

Aloysius Archer travels to 1950s California to apprentice with a legendary private eye and former FBI agent but immediately finds himself involved in a scandal in the second novel of the series following One Good Deed.

"Baldacci renders Archer's postwar world with the kind of vivid detail that catches a reader's eye—a flash of color here, a particularly good description there—just enough to set the scene without getting in the way of the narrative." —*Booklist*

Hell's Corner. David Baldacci. Grand Central Pub 2010. 432 p. (Camel Club novels, 5)

ISBN 9780446195522

1. Secret societies 2. Murder 3. National security 4. Intelligence service 5. Stone, Oliver (Fictitious character) 6. Virginia 7. Political thrillers 8. Thrillers and suspense

A bomb detonates in the White House immediately after the British Prime Minister departs from the State Dinner. Oliver Stone, who witnesses the event, believes the Prime Minister and the President were the targets of a terrorist plot. MI-5 agent Mary Chapman is assigned to assist Stone and his Camel Club with the investigation, which reveals that the bombing may have actually been botched and is part of a darker, deadlier conspiracy.

"Camel Club fans and thriller aficionados will rejoice at having a new action-packed, conspiracy-laden, politically intriguing mystery to solve." —*Library Journal*

Originally published: London : Macmillan, 2010.

Long road to mercy. David Baldacci. Grand Central Pub 2018. 432 p. (Atlee Pine novels, 1)

ISBN 9781538761571

1. Women FBI agents 2. Missing persons investigation 3. Murder investigation 4. FBI agents 5. Twin sisters 6. Arizona 7. Grand Canyon 8. Thrillers and suspense

Devoting her life to bringing criminals to justice after her twin is murdered in childhood, FBI agent Atlee Pine investigates a missing-persons case in the Grand Canyon that may be tied to a string of disappearances.

A minute to midnight. David Baldacci. Grand Central Pub 2019. 432 pages (Atlee Pine novels, 2)

ISBN 9781538761601

1. Women FBI agents 2. Families of murder victims 3. Twin sisters 4. Serial murders 5. Serial murder investigation 6. Georgia 7. Thrillers and suspense

FBI Agent Atlee Pine returns to her Georgia hometown to reopen the investigation of her twin sister's abduction, only to encounter a serial killer beginning a reign of terror, in this page-turning thriller from #1 New York Times bestselling author David Baldacci.

★ **One** good deed. David Baldacci. Grand Central Pub, 2019. 416 pages (Aloysius Archer novels, 1)

ISBN 9781538750568

1. World War II veterans 2. Parolees 3. Murder suspects 4. Former convicts 5. Bill collecting 6. 1940s 7. Historical mysteries

The best-selling author of The Fallen and The Fix presents a latest thriller introducing straight-talking World War II veteran and recent prison inmate, Aloysius Archer.

"All signs suggest a sequel where he hangs out a shamus shingle. Archer will be a great series character for fans of crime fiction." —*Kirkus*

One summer. David Baldacci. Grand Central Pub, 2011. 288 p.

ISBN 9780446583145

1. Men with terminal illnesses 2. Widowers 3. Fatal traffic accidents 4. Beaches 5. Family relationships 6. South Carolina 7. Ohio 8. Mainstream fiction

Jack, terminally-ill and preparing to say goodbye to his family, has a miraculous recovery after his wife is killed in a car accident and struggles to reunite his family at her childhood home on the South Carolina oceanfront.

"Baldacci's muscle-bound style doesn't do subtle: He is best at choreographing fight scenes, rescues and dire brushes with severe weather, all of which, thankfully, are here in abundance." —*Kirkus*

Redemption. David Baldacci. Grand Central, 2019. 432 p. (Amos Decker novels, 5)

ISBN 9781538761410

1. Private investigators 2. False imprisonment 3. Former convicts 4. Widowers 5. Judicial error 6. Ohio 7. Thrillers and suspense

Confronted by the first murder suspect of his early career while visiting his hometown, FBI detective Amos Decker reexamines startling connections to another crime that make him question if he arrested the wrong man years earlier.

Baldwin, James

★ **Another** country. James Baldwin. Vintage, 1993. 436 p.

ISBN 9780679744719

1. Race relations 2. Jazz musicians 3. Identity (Psychology) 4. Racism 5. Love 6. New York City 7. 1960s 8. Literary fiction 9. African American fiction 10. LGBTQIA fiction

Presents a graphic portrayal of bisexuality and interracial relations. Rufus Scott, a black jazz musician, commits suicide, impelling his friends to search for the meaning of his death and, consequently, for a deeper understanding of their own identities. Employing a loose, episodic structure, this work traces the affairs—heterosexual and homosexual as well as interracial—among Scott's friends.

Originally published by Dial in 1962.

★ **Early** novels and stories. James Baldwin. Library of America, 1998. 970 p.

ISBN 9781883011512

1. African Americans 2. African American gay men 3. Gay men 4. Identity (Psychology) 5. Literary fiction 6. LGBTQIA fiction 7. Autobiographical fiction

LC 97023028

A collection of stories penned by one of the greatest African American writers of the postwar era.

★ **Giovanni's** room. James Baldwin. Vintage International, 2013. 248 p.

ISBN 9780345806567

1. Gay men 2. Identity (Psychology) 3. Alienation (Social psychology) 4. Expatriates 5. Americans in France 6. Paris, France 7. 1950s 8. LGBTQIA fiction 9. Literary fiction 10. Psychological fiction

LC 56012125

When David meets the sensual Giovanni in a bohemian bar, he is swept into a passionate love affair. But his girlfriend's return to Paris de-

"The anger and desperation of the parents is portrayed so vividly that their search for the truth becomes the reader's. Bambara's final work is an honest and passionate tour de force." —*Library Journal*

Banasky, Carmiel

The **suicide** of Claire Bishop. Carmiel Banasky. Dzanc Books, 2015. 280 p.
ISBN 9781938103087
1. People with mental illnesses 2. Suicide 3. Memory 4. Young women 5. People with schizophrenia 6. New York City 7. Psychological fiction
LC 2015000623
Greenwich Village, 1959. Claire Bishop sits for a portrait—a gift from her husband—only to discover that what the artist has actually depicted is Claire's suicide. Haunted by the painting, Claire is forced to redefine herself within a failing marriage and a family history of madness. Shifting ahead to 2004, we meet West, a young man with schizophrenia obsessed with a painting he encounters in a gallery: a mysterious image of a woman's suicide. Convinced it was painted by his ex-girlfriend, West constructs an elaborate delusion involving time-travel, Hasidism, art-theft, and the terrifying power of representation. When the two characters finally meet, in the present, delusions are shattered and lives are forever changed.

"Although the novel's structure suggests a chronological approach, its nonlinear sections make story elements more challenging to follow. But a careful reader is rewarded by Banasky's skillful character development, innovative points-of-view technique, and fresh language. The book is full of quotable sentences, including one descriptive of the book itself, 'Here's the truth: we're all connected, but not in a straight line. More like constellations, or islands.'" Booklist.

Bandi

The **accusation**: forbidden stories from inside North Korea. Bandi; translated from the Korean by Deborah Smith. Grove Press, 2017. Vii, 247 pages
ISBN 9780802126207
1. Kim, Chong-il 2. Dictators 3. Totalitarianism 4. Communism 5. Dissenters 6. Censorship 7. North Korea 8. 21st century 9. 1990s 10. Political fiction 11. Literary fiction 12. Short stories
Loan Stars Favourites, 2017
A work of dissident fiction from North Korea, written by an anonymous author and smuggled out of the country, depicts a powerful portrait of life under the North Korean regime as it impacts a diverse range of people, from a disillusioned war hero to a family man who travels without a permit to visit his critically ill mother.

"With these uncompromising stories, the pseudonymous Bandi gives a rare glimpse of life in the truly fathomless darkness of North Korea." —*Publishers Weekly*
Originally published in South Korea in 2014.
Translated from the Korean.

Banks, Iain

Consider Phlebas. By Iain M. Banks. St. Martin's Press 1987. 471 p. (Culture Universe series, 1)
ISBN 9780312017521
1. Imaginary wars and battles 2. Mercenaries 3. Interplanetary relations 4. Imaginary empires 5. Religious persecution 6. Space opera 7. Hard science fiction 8. Science fiction classics
LC 87036718

Horza, a Changer, finds himself at the center of an epic galactic confrontation between the fanatical Idirans and the communistic Culture, made up of humans ruled by the Mind machines that they have created.

The **crow** road. Iain Banks. MacAdam/Cage Pub, 2008. 500 p.
ISBN 9781596923065
1. Families 2. Identity (Psychology) 3. Mortality 4. Missing persons 5. Death 6. Scotland 7. Coming-of-age stories 8. Adult books for young adults
When Prentice McHoan returns to his home town of Gallanach he meets a former girlfriend of his missing uncle Rory, who provides him with a folder of Rory's writings that inspires him to seek out the man who had disappeared eight years earlier.

"Bank's beefy bildungsroman is slowgoing at first but develops into a full-blown universe of Scottish multigenerational shenanigans." —*Library Journal*

The **hydrogen** sonata. Iain Banks. Little Brown & Co, 2012. 496 p. (Culture Universe series, 10)
ISBN 9780316212373
1. Matilda 2. Frameups 3. Innocence (Law) 4. Space flight 5. Dystopias 6. Space opera 7. Hard science fiction 8. Science fiction classics
Suspected of involvement after the Regimental High Command is destroyed as they prepared to go to a new level of existence called Sublime, Lieutenant Commander Vyr Cossont must find a nine-thousand year old man to clear her name.

Matter. Iain M. Banks. Orbit, 2008. 608 p. (Culture Universe series, 8)
ISBN 9780316005364
1. Aliens (Humanoid) 2. Technology 3. Cyborgs 4. Princesses 5. Spies 6. Space opera 7. Hard science fiction 8. Science fiction classics
LC 2007941828
In a distant-future human-machine symbiotic society of seemingly unlimited technological capability, the Culture is threatened by ongoing wars, political upheavals, and alien intruders.

"Beautifully written and filled with memorable characters and startling technology." —*Publishers Weekly*

The **player** of games. Iain M. Banks. St. Martin's Press 1989. 309 p. (Culture Universe series, 2)
ISBN 9780312026301
1. Contests 2. Imaginary wars and battles 3. Interplanetary relations 4. Competition in men 5. Good and evil 6. Space opera 7. Hard science fiction 8. Science fiction classics
LC 88029899
Bored with his routine successes, game player Jernau Morat Gurgeh of the Culture travels to the Empire of Azad in search of more challenging prospects and finds himself thrust into a high-stakes competition that threatens his survival.

Use of weapons. Iain Banks. Orbit, 1990. 389 p. (Culture Universe series, 3)
ISBN 9780553292244
1. Spies 2. Robots 3. Imaginary wars and battles 4. Interplanetary relations 5. Good and evil 6. Space opera 7. Hard science fiction 8. Science fiction classics
Called back from early retirement by Special Circumstances, the elite weapon of the Culture's policy of moral espionage, Cheradenine Zakalwe reluctantly returns to work, but his fatal flaw could cost them the battle.

Banks, Maya

Never seduce a Scot. Maya Banks. Ballantine Books, 2012. 352 p. (The Montgomerys and Armstrongs, 1)
ISBN 9780345533234

1. Women who are deaf 2. Warriors 3. Arranged marriage 4. Anne Boleyn 5. Secrets 6. Scotland 7. Highlands, Scotland 8. Medieval period (476-1492) 9. Medieval romances 10. Highland romances 11. Historical romances

When Eveline Armstrong, who never speaks, is forced into an arranged marriage with Graeme Montgomery, a warrior from a rival clan, love grows between them as clan rivalries and dark forces conspire to keep them apart.

Banks, Russell

★ **Affliction**. Russell Banks. Harper & Row, 1989. 355 p.
ISBN 9780060161422
1. Violence in men 2. Divorced men 3. Cynicism 4. Alcoholic fathers 5. Fathers and daughters 6. New Hampshire 7. Literary fiction 8. Books to movies

LC 89094473

A gentle man, the victim of a violent father, is made violent himself by a fellow cop whom he suspects of murdering a local labor official, and an ex-wife who limits contact with their daughter BT

"This novel is psychological portraiture of a high order, and like all profound portraits it finds in its subject astonishing contradictions." —*New York Times Book Review*

Cloudsplitter: a novel. Russell Banks. Harper Flamingo, 1998. 758 p.
ISBN 9780060168605
1. Brown, John 2. Abolitionists — History 3. Racism 4. Fathers and sons 5. Race relations 6. Rebels 7. United States 8. 19th century 9. Literary fiction 10. Epistolary novels 11. Biographical fiction

LC 9722163

Booklist Editors' Choice, 1998

Offers a fictional re-creation of the turbulent landscape of pre-Civil War America and of John Brown's 1859 raid on the federal arsenal at Harpers Ferry, Virginia, as narrated by the enigmatic abolitionist's son, Owen.

"To rise above period costume and stately diction, a historical novel must have a saving tincture of anachronism, a point of forced contact with the unfinished business of the present. Cloudsplitter, is brought alive by Owen's ambivalent, recognizably modern consciousness." —*The Nation*

Continental drift. Russell Banks. HarperCollins, 1985. 366 p.
ISBN 9780060153830
1. Materialism 2. Good and evil 3. Shame in men 4. Racism 5. Extramarital affairs 6. Miami, Florida 7. Florida 8. Literary fiction

LC 84048137

Pulitzer Prize for Fiction finalist, 1986

After his ill-fated pursuit of the American dream, Bob Dubois finds employment on a fishing boat off the Florida Keys where he becomes involved in a plot to smuggle two Haitians into Florida.

"There are raw edges to Bank's novel, and a numbing insistence on the powerlessness of its characters, but there's no denying its almost frightening intensity." —*Library Journal*

Foregone. Russell Banks. Ecco Press, 2021. 320 p.
ISBN 9780063036758
1. Reminiscing in old age 2. Draft resisters 3. Documentary filmmakers 4. Interviews 5. Septuagenarians 6. Montreal, Quebec 7. Canada 8. 20th century 9. 21st century 10. Literary fiction

A septuagenarian leftist documentary filmmaker gives a last interview from his mythologized life to a former star student to whom he discloses his experiences as a draft dodger who fled to a new life in Montreal.

"In this masterful depiction of a psyche under siege by disease, age, and guilt, Banks considers with profound intent the verity of memory, the mercurial nature of the self, and how little we actually know about ourselves and others." —*Booklist*

Lost memory of skin. Russell Banks. Ecco Press, 2011. 352 p.
ISBN 9780061857638
1. Misfits (Persons) 2. Sex addicts 3. Pornography 4. Sex offenders 5. College teachers 6. Psychological fiction 7. Literary fiction

ALA Notable Book, 2012; Booklist Editors' Choice, 2011; New York Times Notable Book, 2011; Andrew Carnegie Medal for Excellence in Fiction finalist, 2012

A young outcast known as the Kid who lives with other sex offenders in a makeshift encampment under a south Florida causeway is taken up by a professor of sociology who sees in the Kid a perfect subject for his research. The Kid accepts the counsel and financial assistance of the older man, but when the Professor's past resurfaces and threatens to destroy his carefully constructed world, the balance in the two men's relationship shifts.

"Set in a fictional part of Florida in a time of paranoia (possibly the near future), Lost Memory of Skin is the story of a twentyish sex offender (known simply as the Kid) on parole and the affable but troubled sociology instructor (called the Professor) on a misguided mission to help him become better adjusted. The Kid is a wastrel addicted to Internet porn, with only his pet iguana for company, until an unfortunate series of events—beginning with an Internet chat with an underage girl and ending To Catch a Predatorstyle—lands him in prison. Upon his release, he is forced to live with other sex offenders under a causeway because of a law that keeps them 2,500 feet from anywhere children are playing. The Professor, a behemoth in a suit, begins interviewing the Kid for academic research purposes; as he learns more about the Kid's crime, he begins to reveal his own troubled history, which only undermines his efforts to help. Banks inhabits unsympathetic voices well, and it is a pleasure to see his gift turned to big, semisurreal characters. The grand, rambling examination of guilt and blame takes place against a ravishingly bleak backdrop, lyrically described, while each revelation of character is like a quiet explosion." —*Time Out New York*

★ The **sweet** hereafter. Russell Banks. Harper Collins Publishers, 1991. 257 p.
ISBN 9780060167035
1. Children — Death 2. Bereavement — Psychological aspects 3. Survival (after automobile, truck, train accidents, etc.) 4. Fate and fatalism 5. Adirondack Mountains, New York 6. New York (State) 7. Multiple perspectives 8. First person narratives 9. Literary fiction

LC 90056404

ALA Notable Book, 1992

Four narrators—bus driver Dolores, upright Bill, shrewd Mitchell, and teenaged Nichole—address agonizing questions as they describe an accident that killed fourteen children and the effects of the tragedy on themselves and their town BT

"Banks handles his dark theme with judicious restraint, empathy and compassion." —*Publishers Weekly*

Bannalec, Jean-Luc

Death in Brittany. Jean-Luc Bannalec; translated from the German by Sorcha McDonagh. Minotaur, 2015. 256 p. (Georges Dupin novels, 1)
ISBN 9781250061744
1. Murder investigation 2. Small towns 3. Police 4. Detectives 5. Seniors 6. Brittany, France 7. Police procedurals 8. Mysteries 9. Translations

After a hotelier is murdered in a small village on the Breton coast, Commissaire Georges Dupin identifies five possible suspects and uncovers disturbing secrets behind the village's calm exterior.

"Bannalec feeds the reader with intriguing bits of history (for example, Bretons are descended from the Celts, who fled Britain during the Anglo-Saxon invasions) and culture, along with bracing glimpses of centuries-old stone buildings, river banks, and the sea." —*Booklist*

Originally published as Bretonische Verhaltnisse by Kiepenheuer & Witsch in 2012.

Translated from the German.

The **Granite** Coast murders. Jean-Luc Bannalec; translated from the German by Peter Millar. Minotaur Books, 2021. 320 p. (Georges Dupin novels, 6)

ISBN 9781250753069

1. Missing persons 2. Investigations 3. Detectives 4. Beaches 5. Resorts 6. Brittany, France 7. France 8. Police procedurals 9. Translations

LC 2020047454

Vacationing at a Brittany beach resort with Claire, Inspector Dupin quietly assists a case involving a missing tourist, an attack on a deputy and a mysterious corpse.

Unsolved crimes and a restless policeman turn out to be excellent holiday companions in Brittany.... Between the food, the scenery, and the felonies, what's not to like? Kirkus

First published as Bretonische Leuchten in Germany by Verlag Kiepenhauer & Witsch

Translated from the German.

The **killing** tide: a Brittany mystery. Jean-Luc Bannalec; translated from the German by Peter Millar. Minotaur Books, 2020. 358 p. (Georges Dupin novels, 5)

ISBN 9781250173386

1. Islands 2. Smuggling 3. Coastal towns 4. Murder investigation 5. Detectives 6. Brittany, France 7. France 8. Police procedurals 9. Translations

LC 2019036389

On an island off the west coast of Brittany shrouded in superstition, Commissaire Dupin and his team follow a puzzling case that pushes them to their very limits.

"Bannelec (the pen name of Jorg Bong) has concocted the perfect blend of police procedural and travelogue." —*Publishers Weekly*

Translation of: Bretonische Flut.

Originally published: Cologne : Kiepenheuer & Witsch, 2016.

Translated from the German.

Banner, Catherine

The **house** at the edge of night: a novel. Catherine Banner. Random House, 2016. 416 p.

ISBN 9780812998795

1. Bars (Drinking establishments) 2. Island life 3. Family businesses 4. Families 5. Communities 6. Italy 7. 20th century 8. 21st century 9. Family sagas 10. Historical fiction

LC 2015023813

Loan Stars Favourites, 2016

Four generations of women on a Mediterranean island fight to safeguard their family against the forces of history and bitterness that divide them from World War I through the 2008 recession.

"Banner deftly touches on weightier themes while weaving an enchanting narrative, the events of which extend to the present." —*Publishers Weekly*

Bannister, Ilona

When I ran away. Ilona Bannister. Doubleday, 2021. 320 p.
ISBN 9780385546171

1. Psychic trauma 2. September 11 Terrorist Attacks, 2001 3. Loss (Psychology) 4. Moving to a new country 5. Death 6. Relationship fiction

Escaping the September 11 attacks aboard the Staten Island Ferry, Gigi marries a fellow survivor and moves to London, where she confronts the anguish of her trauma, her brother's death and the unspoken pain of motherhood.

"Bannister's novel is a searing insight into the complexities of motherhood and the interminable frustration of the tiny needs, musts, and wants that keep a family moving. A gripping, introspective read." —*Booklist*

Bannister, Jo

Kindred spirits. Jo Bannister. Severn House, 2018. 220 pages; (Gabriel Ash and Hazel Best mysteries, 5)

ISBN 9780727887962

1. Policewomen 2. Detectives 3. Small towns 4. Kidnapping 5. Cold cases (Criminal investigation) 6. Great Britain 7. Mysteries

LC Bl2018109585

After an attempted kidnapping, Gabriel Ash asks Constable Hazel Best to keep his sons safe, but Hazel's investigation puts her at odds with superiors when she uncovers information about a crime committed seventeen years earlier.

Silent footsteps. Jo Bannister. Severn House, 2019. 224 p; (Gabriel Ash and Hazel Best mysteries, 6)

ISBN 9780727888648

1. Policewomen 2. Stalkers 3. Women stalking victims 4. Murder investigation 5. Obsession 6. Great Britain 7. Mysteries 8. Police procedurals

Constable Hazel Best attracts a new admirer whose intentions turn sinister after an attack on Hazel's friend; and, with her colleagues tied up, it is up to Hazel to deal with the stalker alone.

Banville, John

Ancient light. John Banville. Alfred A. Knopf, 2012. 304 p. (Alexander Cleave trilogy, 3)

ISBN 9780307957054

1. Senior men 2. Actors and actresses 3. Reminiscing in old age 4. Loss (Psychology) 5. First loves 6. Psychological fiction 7. Literary fiction

LC 2012019891

An actor in the twilight of his career reflects on a poignant first love affair at the age of 15 with his best friend's mother and inexplicably lands a role opposite a famous but fragile actress who helps him come to an astonishing realization.

This is a Borzoi book—Title page verso.

Sequel to: Shroud.

Originally published in Great Britain by Picador, an imprint of Pan Macmillan Ltd, London, in 2012—Title page verso.

The **blue** guitar. John Banville. Alfred A. Knopf, 2015. 304 p.
ISBN 9780385354264

1. Artists 2. Thieves 3. Creativity in men 4. Betrayal 5. Memories 6. Psychological fiction 7. First person narratives 8. Literary fiction

LC 2015006555

A semi-famous artist and petty thief, despairing of limits in his talents, flees when his latest theft is discovered and sequesters himself in his childhood home, where he struggles to understand how he reached his current state.

"Banville delights in descriptions of people and nature, and here he has the added excuse of writing through a painter's gifted eye. The artist Orme is not a pleasant creation to spend several hours with, but in the hands of this gifted Irish writer, even a potbellied, melancholic petty thief and Lothario offers countless delights." —*Kirkus*

The **book** of evidence. John Banville. C. Scribner's Sons 1989. 219 p. (Evidence trilogy, 1)
ISBN 9780684191805
1. Murder 2. Art thefts 3. Guilt in men 4. Good and evil 5. Criminals 6. Psychological suspense 7. Literary fiction 8. First person narratives
LC 89010985
Shortlisted for the Booker-McConnell Prize, 1989

Returning to Ireland to reclaim a painting that is part of his patrimony, a thirty-eight-year-old man commits a ghastly and motiveless murder, which he confesses in a novel-length narrative.

"This novel, the inventive testimony of a murderer more interested in making an impression than escaping conviction, is...hauntingly beautiful and original.... Mr. Banville shows his uncanny ability to make everything he describes seem new and rare, yet instantly recognisable." —*The Economist*

★ **Eclipse**: a novel. John Banville. Alfred A. Knopf : 2001. 211 p; (Alexander Cleave trilogy, 1)
ISBN 9780375411298
1. Midlife crisis in men 2. Actors and actresses 3. Family relationships 4. Fathers and daughters 5. Identity (Psychology) 6. Psychological fiction 7. Literary fiction 8. First person narratives
LC 62014
New York Times Notable Book, 2001

Alexander Cleave, a famous actor with a disintegrating career, retreats to his childhood home where he struggles to come to terms with his memories, the unsettling presence of a caretaker and teenage housekeeper, and ghosts of the past.

"Banville's writing is richly descriptive and full of original images.... Eclipse is essentially a reflective work. The actual narrative is Cleave's interior journey, not the rather banal series of lived events, and for this reason the magnificent atmospherics, in a way, are the story." —*The New Leader*

Sequel: Shroud.

Originally published: London : Picador, 2000.

The **infinities**. John Banville. Alfred A. Knopf, 2010. 272 p.
ISBN 9780307272799
1. People with terminal illnesses — Family relationships 2. Gods and goddesses 3. Family relationships 4. Fathers and sons 5. Mathematicians 6. Douglass, Frederick 7. Psychological fiction 8. Literary fiction
LC 2009048331

Attending the deathbed of a renowned mathematician, his second wife and adult children reflect on their personal demons, including the son's pretty wife, who has caught the attention of the mischievous god Zeus.

"Sure, The Infinities will have you looking up invigilate in the dictionary (I'll save you the time: to keep watch) and Googling Amphitryon (a Greek myth dramatized by the 19th century German writer Heinrich von Kleist). But none of this legwork feels like a chore, because The Infinities is constructed as a tantalizing puzzle you're eager to piece together. And Hermes is a delightfully cheeky and amiable narrator, constantly mocking randy old Zeus and guiding us through the multiple worlds of the novel. Moreover, Banville is a glorious stylist whose prose holds sustaining pleasures, both large and small." —*Newsday*
Originally published: London : Picador, 2009.

★ The **sea**. John Banville. A. A. Knopf, 2006. 208 p.
ISBN 9780307263117

1. Widowers 2. Grief in men 3. Memories 4. Death 5. Identity (Psychology) 6. England 7. Psychological fiction 8. Literary fiction 9. First person narratives
LC 2005050418
Booker Prize, 2005; Booklist Editors' Choice, 2005; New York Times Notable Book, 2005

Following the death of his wife, Max Morden retreats to the seaside town of his childhood summers, where his own life becomes inextricably entwined with the members of the vacationing Grace family.

"What's strangest about The Sea is that the novel somehow becomes simpler and clearer as it gets more selfconscious: a consequence, I suppose, of its author dropping the pretense of being one kind of writer and giving in to his authentic and much more complicated creative nature. This misshapen but affecting novel turns out to be about something even more familiar than the loss of innocence: it's about grief, the misery and confusion the narrator feels on losing his wife." —*New York Times Book Review*

Bao, Ninh

The **sorrow** of war: a novel of North Vietnam. Ninh Bao; translated from the Vietnamese by Phan Thanh Hao; edited by Frank Palmos. Pantheon Books, 1995. 233 p.
ISBN 9780679439615
1. Vietnam War, 1961-1975 2. Vietnam 3. War stories 4. Translations
LC 94022390 //r952

Kien's job is to search the Jungle of Screaming Souls for corpses. He knows the area well this was where, in the dry season of 1969, his battalion was obliterated by American napalm and helicopter gunfire. Kien was one of only ten survivors. This book is his attempt to understand the eleven years of his life he gave to a senseless war.

"The word classic is bandied about with ridiculous laxity, but in this case it is hard not to fall back on it. Nothing else really fits the elemental simplicity of theme and treatment: love, war, death, disillusionment, betrayal." —*New Statesman*
Translation of Noi buon chien tranh.
Originally published 1991 by Writers' Association Publishing House, Hanoi.
Originally published: London: Secker & Warburg, 1993.

Barbash, Tom

The **last** good chance. Tom Barbash. Picador USA, 2002. 440 p.
ISBN 9780312287962
1. Architects 2. Urban renewal 3. Harbors 4. Hazardous waste sites 5. Brothers 6. New York (State) 7. Psychological fiction
LC 2002025847

An architectural phenom, Jack Lambeau returns to his hometown to resurrect the dying lakeside village, but a reunion with an old friend is spoiled when Jack's fiance comes between them.

"Steven Turner is a young journalist exiled at a paper in Lakeland, a decaying port town in rural upstate New York. His best friend, Jack Lambeau, is the Lakeland town planner. An ambitious Ivy League graduate, Lambeau had had difficulty advancing his experimental urban planning ideas in New York City. When Lakeland's mayor, William Hickey, promised him carte blanche for his New Urbaniststyle visions, Lambeau agreed to return to his hometown. With evangelical fervor, he tries to revive Lakeland through a glittering lakefront development project. What he doesn't know, and what the mayor does, is that there are tubs of toxic materials illegally dumped under the lakefront.... This is a taut, intricate vision of ambition, corruption and love in the postindustrial era." —*Publishers Weekly*

Barber, Lizzy

A **girl** named Anna. Lizzy Barber. Harlequin Books, 2019. 368 p.
ISBN 9780778308997
1. Child kidnapping victims 2. Sisters 3. Deception 4. Missing persons investigation 5. Loss (Psychology) 6. England 7. Florida 8. Thrillers and suspense 9. Multiple perspectives
If your whole life is a lie, who can you trust?

Barbery, Muriel

The **elegance** of the hedgehog. Muriel Barbery; translated by Alison Anderson. Europa Editions, 2008. 336 pages.
ISBN 9781933372600
1. Pessimism 2. Philosophy 3. Social classes 4. Aesthetics 5. Friendship 6. Paris, France 7. Literary fiction 8. Translations 9. First person narratives
Shortlisted for the International IMPAC Dublin Literary Award, 2010
The lives of fifty-four-year-old concierge Rene Michel and extremely bright, suicidal twelve-year-old Paloma Josse are transformed by the arrival of a new tenant, Kakuro Ozu.
"Barbery's sly wit, which bestows lightness on the most ponderous cogitations, keeps her tale aloft." —*The New Yorker*
Translated from the French: L'elegance du herisson.
First published in 2006 in France as L'elegance du herisson by Editions Gallimard, Paris.
Originally published: Paris, France : Gallimard, 2006.

Barclay, Linwood

Broken promise. Linwood Barclay. New American Library, 2015. 464 p. (Promise Falls (Linwood Barclay), 1)
ISBN 9780451472670
1. Widowers 2. Single fathers 3. Family secrets 4. Small towns 5. Mothers 6. New York (State) 7. Mysteries 8. Canadian fiction
LC 2015000081
From the New York Times bestselling author of No Safe House comes an explosive novel about the disturbing secrets of a quiet small town... After his wife's death and the collapse of his newspaper, David Harwood has no choice but to uproot his nine-year-old son and move back into his childhood home in Promise Falls, New York. David believes his life is in free fall, and he can't find a way to stop his descent. Then he comes across a family secret of epic proportions. A year after a devastating miscarriage, David's cousin Marla has continued to struggle. But when David's mother asks him to check on her, he's horrified to discover that she's been secretly raising a child who is not her own-a baby she claims was a gift from an "angel" left on her porch. When the baby's real mother is found murdered, David can't help wanting to piece together what happened-even if it means proving his own cousin's guilt. But as he uncovers each piece of evidence, David realizes that Marla's mysterious child is just the tip of the iceberg. Other strange things are happening. Animals are found ritually slaughtered. An ominous abandoned Ferris wheel seems to stand as a warning that something dark has infected Promise Falls. And someone has decided that the entire town must pay for the sins of its past...in blood.
"Barclay's Promise Falls, a deceptively quaint little town, again teems with dark secrets, and with this fast-paced and irresistibly tense outing, David Harwood has established himself as a fine series lead." —*Booklist*
First published: London : Orion, 2015.

★ **Elevator** pitch: a novel. Linwood Barclay. William Morrow, 2019. 464 pages
ISBN 9780062678287
1. Elevators 2. Disasters 3. Fear 4. Sabotage 5. Murder victims 6. New York City 7. Thrillers and suspense 8. Canadian fiction
LC 2019014755
When an outbreak of fatal elevator crashes in Manhattan coincides with a sinister drop in emergency response services, two seasoned New York detectives and a straight-shooting journalist race against time to find answers.

Far from true: a novel. Linwood Barclay. New American Library, 2015. 464 p. (Promise Falls (Linwood Barclay), 2)
ISBN 9780451472700
1. Cold cases (Criminal investigation) 2. Robbery 3. Family secrets 4. Small towns 5. Murder 6. Mysteries 7. Canadian fiction
After the screen of a run-down drive-in movie theatre collapses and kills four people, the daughter of one of the victims asks private investigator Cal Weaver to look into a break-in at her father's house. Cal discovers a hidden room where salacious activities have taken place—as well as evidence of missing DVDs. But it may not be the discs the thief was interested in.... Meanwhile, Detective Barry Duckworth is still trying to solve two murders he believes are connected, since each featured a similar distinctive wound.

No safe house. Linwood Barclay. New American Library, 2014. 512 pages
ISBN 9780451414205
1. Crimes against seniors 2. Murder for hire 3. Survival 4. Murder investigation 5. Protectiveness in men 6. Thrillers and suspense 7. Canadian fiction
LC 2013046120
A troubled family accidentally reconnects with the criminal who saved their lives seven years prior and is propelled into another potentially lethal situation.
Features characters previously seen in No Time for Goodbye.

A **noise** downstairs: a novel. Linwood Barclay. William Morrow, 2018. 356 p.
ISBN 9780062678256
1. Post-traumatic stress disorder 2. Murder witnesses 3. College teachers 4. Writing 5. Authors 6. Thrillers and suspense
LC 2017048396
Battling PTSD and depression after an accidental stumble into a murder scene, a college professor begins writing his novel on a vintage typewriter that he comes to believe is possessed and somehow linked to the crime he survived.

Parting shot. Linwood Barclay. Doubleday Canada, 2017. 448 p. (Promise Falls (Linwood Barclay), 4)
ISBN 9780385690232
1. Drunk drivers 2. Traffic accidents 3. Private investigators 4. Clues 5. Murder 6. New York (State) 7. Mysteries 8. Canadian fiction
A standalone spin-off from the Promise Falls trilogy finds Cal Weaver investigating threats made against an accused killer's family in spite of local outrage, a case that embroils him in a vicious revenge plot.

A **tap** on the window. Linwood Barclay. New American Library, 2013. 512 p.
ISBN 9780451414182
1. Drug traffic 2. Runaway children 3. Private investigators 4. Grief 5. Secrets 6. New York (State) 7. Mysteries 8. Canadian fiction
LC 2012050861
Still deeply grieving over the loss of his son from a drug overdose, private investigator Cal Weaver decides to give a teenage girl a ride home one night when she taps on his window and gets caught up in exposing the

sordid secrets in Griffin, a small town in upstate New York where something seems to be horribly wrong.

Trust your eyes: a thriller. Linwood Barclay. New American Library, 2012. 496 p.

ISBN 9780451237903

1. Murder witnesses 2. Men with schizophrenia 3. Computerized mapping systems 4. Maps 5. Murder 6. New York City 7. Thrillers and suspense 8. Canadian fiction

LC 2011053176

Library Journal Best Books, 2012

A schizophrenic, map-obsessed shut-in who tours the world using a computer program witnesses what he believes to be a murder in downtown New York City and enlists his caretaker brother in an effort to investigate.

"Thomas is one of Barclay's best and most sympathetic characters yet." —*Kirkus*

The **twenty-three:** a Promise Falls novel. Linwood Barclay. Berkley Books, 2016. 464 p. (Promise Falls (Linwood Barclay), 3)

ISBN 9780451472724

1. Poisoning 2. Epidemics 3. Private investigators 4. Clues 5. Murder 6. New York (State) 7. Mysteries 8. Canadian fiction

LC 2015045543

Loan Stars Favourites, 2016

When hundreds of people are sickened by deliberately contaminated water in a small New York community's water supply, Detective Barry Duckworth scrambles to identify the culprit while investigating the murder of a college student whose crime scene disturbingly resembles those of two other victims.

Bardugo, Leigh

★ **Ninth** house. Leigh Bardugo. Flatiron Books, 2019. 448 p.

ISBN 9781250313072

1. Women college students 2. Secret societies 3. Occultism 4. Magic 5. Universities and colleges 6. New Haven, Connecticut 7. Connecticut 8. Urban fantasy 9. Adult books for young adults

LC 2019019855

Goodreads Choice Award, 2019; LibraryReads Favorites, 2019

Surviving a horrific multiple homicide, a girl from the wrong side of the tracks is unexpectedly offered a full scholarship to Yale, where her mysterious benefactors task her with monitoring the university's secret societies.

Barker, Clive

★ **Weaveworld**. Clive Barker. Poseidon Press 1987. 584 p.

ISBN 9780671612689

1. Parallel universes 2. Magic 3. Rugs 4. Magicians 5. Demons 6. Fantasy fiction

LC 87018602

Susanna, granddaughter of the last caretaker, Calhoun Mooney, and Immacolata, an exiled witch intent on destroying her race, vie for a rug into which the world of Seerkind has been woven.

"Barker creates a fantastic romance of magic and promise that is at once popular fiction and utopian conjuring.... There is great wit in the struggle that ensues, and keen attention to the facts of poverty and exile." —*New York Times Book Review*

Barker, Nicola

Darkmans. Nicola Barker. Ecco Press, 2008. 838 p.

ISBN 9780061575211

1. Fathers and sons 2. Drug dealers 3. Healers 4. Mothers — Death 5. Neighbors 6. Literary fiction 7. Humorous stories

LC 2007040012

Hawthornden Prize, 2008; Shortlisted for the Man Booker Prize, 2007

If history is just a sick joke which keeps on repeating itself, then who exactly might be telling it, and why? BT

"[The plot] is twisted and braided with an intricacy so delicate you barely notice the links until the whole web engulfs you." —*Scotland on Sunday*

First published: London : Fourth Estate, 2007.

Barker, Pat

Another world. Pat Barker. Farrar Straus & Giroux, 1999. 277 p.

ISBN 9780374105259

1. Blended families 2. Family relationships 3. Stepchildren 4. Family secrets 5. World War I veterans 6. Newcastle upon Tyne, England 7. England 8. Psychological fiction

New York Times Notable Book, 1999

Nick tries to keep the peace in his disintegrating family while comforting his grandfather, a proud, intelligent man who lies dying on the other side of town.

"This novel demonstrates the extraordinary immediacy and vigor of expression we have come to expect from Barker." —*New York Times Book Review*

Originally published: London : Viking, 1998.

★ The **eye** in the door. Pat Barker. Dutton, 1994. 280 p. (Regeneration trilogy (Pat Barker), 2)

ISBN 9780525938088

1. Rivers, William 2. World War I 3. Religious persecution 4. Paranoia 5. Scapegoats (Persons) 6. Bisexuals 7. London, England 8. 1910s 9. Historical fiction 10. War stories 11. Literary fiction

LC 93043833

Guardian First Book Award, 1993

Characters from Regeneration return in a tale set after World War I, as Britain undergoes a period of repression and psychiatrist Dr. William Rivers, poet Siegfried Sassoon, and Lieutenant Billy Prior cope with the war's aftermath.

"This work succeeds as both historical fiction and as sequel. Its research and speculation combine to produce a kind of educated imagination that is persuasive and illuminating about this particular place and time.... The novel's greatest success, however, has to do with the insight it provides into its central doctor-patient relationships." —*New York Times Book Review*

Originally published: London : Viking, 1993.

★ The **ghost** road. Pat Barker. Dutton, 1996. 277 p. (Regeneration trilogy (Pat Barker), 3)

ISBN 9780525941910

1. Owen, Wilfred 2. World War I 3. Psychiatrists 4. Poets, English 5. Working class men 6. Soldiers 7. Historical fiction 8. War stories 9. Literary fiction

Booker Prize, 1995

As World War I winds to a close, two men—Dr. William Rivers, a psychologist whose dedicated healing sends men back to the brutal front, and Billy Prior, a shell-shocked soldier determined to rejoin the final English offensive—are profoundly affected by the events of the era.

"The Ghost Road is a startlingly good novel in its own right. With the other two volumes of the trilogy, it forms one of the richest and most rewarding works of fiction of recent times. Intricately plotted, beautifully written, skillfully assembled, tender, horrifying and funny, it lives on in the imagination, like the war it so imaginatively and so intelligently explores." —*Times Literary Supplement*

Originally published: London : Viking, 1995.

★ **Regeneration**. Pat Barker. Dutton, 1992. 251p. (Regeneration trilogy (Pat Barker), 1)

ISBN 9780525934271

1. Sassoon, Siegfried 2. G I resistance and revolts 3. Soldiers 4. Military hospitals 5. Poets, English 6. Psychiatrist and patient 7. First World War era (1914-1918) 8. Historical fiction 9. War stories

LC 91041264

Stressed by the war, poet, pacifist, and protestor Siegfried Sassoon is sent to Craiglockhart Hospital, where his views challenge the patriotic vision of Dr. William Rivers, a neurologist assigned to restore the sanity of shell-shocked soldiers.

"Regeneration is an antiwar war novel, in a tradition that is by now an established one, though it tells a part of the whole story of war that is not often told—how war may batter and break men's minds—and so makes the madness of war more than a metaphor, and more awful." —*New York Times Book Review*

Originally published: London : Viking, 1991.

★ The **silence** of the girls: a novel. Pat Barker. Doubleday, 2018. 293 p.

ISBN 9780385544214

1. Trojan War 2. Women and war 3. Captives 4. Gender role 5. Warriors 6. Troy (Extinct city) 7. Ancient Aegean civilizations (3000?1000 BCE) 8. Mythological fiction 9. War stories 10. Adaptations, retellings, and spin-offs

LC 2018014387

Shortlisted for The Women's Prize for Fiction, 2019; Shortlisted for the International Dublin Literary Award, 2020

Reimagines The Iliad from the perspectives of the captured women living in the Greek camp in the final weeks of the Trojan War.

Sequel: The women of Troy, 2021.

The **women** of Troy. Pat Barker. Doubleday, 2021. 288 p.

ISBN 9780385546690

1. Trojan War 2. Women and war 3. Captives 4. Enslaved women 5. Concubinage 6. Troy (Extinct city) 7. Ancient Aegean civilizations (3000?1000 BCE) 8. Mythological fiction 9. War stories 10. Adaptations, retellings, and spin-offs

Held captive by the victorious Greeks, one time Trojan queen Briseis, formerly Achilles's slave, forges alliances when she can with Priam's aged wife, the defiant Hecuba and the disgraced soothsayer Calchas, all the while shrewdly seeking her path to revenge.

"As with her masterful Regeneration trilogy, the inconclusive close of this volume leaves readers hungry to know what happens next to a host of complex and engaging characters. Vintage Barker: challenging, stimulating, and profoundly satisfying." —*Kirkus*

Sequel to: The silence of the girls, 2018.

Barker, Susan

★ The **incarnations:** a novel. Susan Barker. Simon & Schuster, 2015. Viii, 371 pages

ISBN 9781501106781

1. Reincarnation 2. Soul mates 3. Identity (Psychology) 4. Stalking 5. Obsession 6. China 7. Historical fiction 8. Literary fiction

LC 2014043145

New York Times Notable Book, 2015; Kirkus Prize for Fiction finalist, 2015

Receiving mysterious letters from someone claiming to be his soulmate, a Beijing taxi driver learns about their shared relationships in numerous past lives before becoming increasingly certain that someone is watching him.

"Barker's historical tour de force is simultaneously sweeping and precise. It would be easy for the novel to teeter into overwrought melodrama; instead, Barker's psychologically nuanced characters and sharp wit turn the bleakness and the gore into something seriously moving." —*Kirkus*

A Touchstone Book

Originally published: London : Doubleday, 2014.

Barnard, Robert

Death of a literary widow. Robert Barnard. Scribner 1980. 192 p.

ISBN 9780684166483

1. Widows 2. Authors, English 3. Arson 4. Murder investigation 5. Mysteries

LC 80013128

"Two elderly women, Viola and Hilda, live in the same house, avoiding each other like the plague. Both have been married to the same man, the late writer Walter Mackin, who is the object of a sudden, intense renewal of interest—articles are written about him, his books are reissued. The great concern of the two wives is who will profit from Mackin's posthumous reputation. One of the old ladies dies in a fire, leaving everyone wondering whether she went out in an accidental blaze or as the result of someone's murderous rage." —*Booklist*

First published in Great Britain in 1979 under title: Posthumous papers.

Barnes, Djuna

★ **Nightwood**. Djuna Barnes. Modern Library, 2000. Xxxii, 169 p.

ISBN 9780679640240

1. Americans in Paris, France 2. Extramarital affairs 3. Husband and wife 4. Lesbians 5. Marguerite, Queen, consort of Louis IX, King of France, 1221-1295 6. Paris, France 7. Psychological fiction 8. Modern classics

LC 99056308

The impassioned monologues of Doctor Dante O'Connor reveal the story of Robin Vote, a young American woman in interwar Paris whose fate is the destruction of all who love her.

Barnes, Jonathan

The **somnambulist**. Jonathan Barnes. William Morrow, 2008. 368 p.

ISBN 9780061375385

1. Blake, William 2. Actors and actresses 3. Murder 4. Murder suspects 5. Sleep-walkers 6. Sleep-walking 7. London, England 8. England 9. Mysteries 10. Historical fantasy 11. First person narratives 12. Adult books for young adults

Booklist Editors' Choice: Adult Books for Young Adults, 2008

A tale set in Victorian London introduces the characters of stage magician and detective Edward Moon and his silent sidekick, whose fiendish plot to re-create the apocalyptic prophecies of Samuel Taylor Coleridge threaten the British Empire.

"There is much that is strange, magical and darkly hilarious in this book, at least if one savors the sardonic and the bizarre. At various points it recalls Dickens, Alice in Wonderland and Frankenstein, but it remains an original and monumentally inventive piece of work." —*Washington Post Book World.*

Barnes, Julian

★ **England**, England. Julian Barnes. Knopf, 1999. 275 p.

ISBN 9780375405822

1. National characteristics, English 2. Venture capitalists 3. Amusement parks 4. Isle of Wight (England) 5. England 6. Satirical fiction 7. Literary fiction

LC 9846170

New York Times Notable Book, 1999; Shortlisted for the Booker-McConnell Prize, 1998

A replica of Britain is created on the Isle of Wight, complete with Robin Hood, Princess Di and replays of the Battle of Britain. It is the idea of a millionaire to show tourists the real Britain, a land with a great past and no future.

"This tale of a theme-park England created on the Isle of Wight by a hateful entrepreneur—complete with fake Stonehenge and half-size Buckingam Palace—does not disappoint. But it is deepened by the story of Martha Cochrane, an overachiever employed to be the project's official naysayer. Both personally and professionally, Martha is devoted to searching for the authentic: for the missing jigsaw piece that disappeared in her father's pocket when he abandoned her family; for the missing piece in her love for a shy fellow-executive; and for the missing ingredient in success. Her meditations are worth any number of clever entertainments." —*The New Yorker*

Originally published: London : J. Cape, 1998.

★ **Flaubert's** parrot. Julian Barnes. A. A. Knopf, 1985. 190 p.
ISBN 9780394542720

1. Flaubert, Gustave 2. Scholars and academics 3. Literary historians 4. Biographers 5. Parrots 6. Biographical fiction 7. Literary fiction

LC 84048550

Shortlisted for the Booker-McConnell Prize, 1984

Interwoven with the story of obsessive amateur Flaubert scholar Charles Braithwaite are speculations on life and art and on the difficulty of knowing another person and above—and throughout—all is the brooding presence of Flaubert.

"A minor classic, and one of the best criticism novels ever, because its critic/narrator has some dignity, because his choice of subject makes emotional sense and because the book has a lively, questioning spirit.... [Barnes has] written a modernist text with a nineteenth-century heart, a French novel with English lucidity and tact." —*The Nation*

Originally published: London : J. Cape, 1984.

★ A **history** of the world in 10 1/2 chapters. Julian Barnes. Knopf, 1989. 307 p, 1 folded leaf of plates : Color illustration
ISBN 9780394580616

1. Survival (after airplane accidents, shipwrecks, etc.) 2. Shipwrecks 3. Noah's ark 4. History 5. Literary fiction

LC 89045266

A History of the world in 10 and 1/2 chapters tells a series of apparently unconnected stories ranging from a woodworm's-eye-view of the journey on Noah's Ark to an astronaut's quest for its final resting place. There is pastiche and learned disquisition; there is heart-stopping documentary and heart-lifting revelation. But these stories are not separate. They are all linked by a complex weave of inquiry into history itself, into love, myth and fabulation.

"This book shapes up not only as Barnes's funniest novel but also his most richly cargoed and imaginatively designed.... As satirist and story-teller he has few equals at present." —*New Statesman*

Includes a fold-out color reproduction of Gericault's Scene de naufrage.

The **noise** of time. Julian Barnes. Alfred A. Knopf, 2016. Xi, 201 pages
ISBN 9781101947241

1. Shostakovich, Dmitri Dmitrievich 2. Composers 3. Political persecution 4. Communism 5. Creativity in men 6. Fear in men 7. Soviet Union 8. Biographical fiction 9. Literary fiction 10. Historical fiction

LC 2015043444

Loan Stars Favourites, 2016; Longlisted for the Walter Scott Prize for Historical Fiction, 2017

1936: Dmitri Shostakovich, just thirty, fears for his livelihood and his life. Stalin, hitherto a distant figure, has taken a sudden interest in his work and denounced his latest opera. Now, certain he will be exiled to Siberia (or, more likely, shot dead on the spot), he reflects on his predicament, his personal history, his parents, various women and wives, his children all of those hanging in the balance of his fate. And though a stroke of luck prevents him from becoming yet another casualty of the Great Terror, for years to come he will be held fast under the thumb of despotism: made to represent Soviet values, forced into joining the Party, and compelled, constantly, to weigh appeasing those in power against the integrity of his music.

"A moody, muted composition about art under the thumb of tyranny." —*Kirkus*

The **only** story. Julian Barnes. Knopf, 2018. 253 p.
ISBN 9780525521211

1. May-December romances 2. Young men — Relations with older women 3. Reminiscing in old age 4. Consequences 5. Life change events 6. London, England 7. England 8. Psychological fiction 9. Literary fiction 10. Multiple perspectives

LC 2017047844

A man who ran away as a teen university student with a married woman more than twice his age reflects on how they fell in love, how he freed her from a sterile marriage and how their relationship fell apart as she succumbed to depression.

"[T]he novel slowly unfurls, and the reader drifts along on Barnes' gorgeous, undulating prose. Focusing on love, memory, nostalgia, and how contemporary Britain came to be, Barnes' latest will enrapture readers from beginning to end." —*Booklist*

This is a Borzoi book.

★ The **sense** of an ending. Julian Barnes. Jonathan Cape, 2011. 160 p.
ISBN 9780224094153

1. Middle-aged men 2. Male friendship 3. Memories — Psychological aspects 4. Regret in men 5. Self-deception 6. England 7. Literary fiction 8. Psychological fiction 9. Books to movies

ALA Notable Book, 2012; Man Booker Prize, 2011; New York Times Notable Book, 2011

Tony Webster and his clique first met Adrian Finn at school. Maybe Adrian was a little more serious than the others, certainly more intelligent, but they all swore to stay friends for life. Now Tony is in middle age. He's had a career and a single marriage, a calm divorce. He's certainly never tried to hurt anybody. Memory, though, is imperfect. It can always throw up surprises, as a lawyer's letter is about to prove.

"Tony Webster, a contented man settling comfortably into middle age, fondly carries his youth with him until a long-ago first love and an old childhood friend begin to haunt his present, forcing him to question the core of his character. Barnes' latest—a meditation on memory and aging—occasionally feels more like a series of wise, underline-worthy insights than a novel. But the many truths he highlights make it worthy of a careful read." —*Entertainment Weekly*

Film tie-in.

First published in hardback by Jonathan Cape in 2011. First published by Vintage in 2012.

Barnett, David

Calling Major Tom. David M. Barnett. Trapeze, 2017. 290 pages
ISBN 9781409170099

1. Astronauts 2. Friendship 3. Misanthropy 4. Helpfulness in men 5. Working class families 6. Space 7. Great Britain 8. Relationship fiction

An irresistible debut novel of unlikely friendships and second chances, for readers who loved The Unlikely Pilgrimage of Harold Fry and The Rosie Project.

Barnett, Karen

Ever faithful. Karen Barnett. WaterBrook, 2019. 352 p. (Vintage national parks novels, 3)

ISBN 9780735289581

1. Illiterate men 2. Single women 3. Civilian Conservation Corps 4. Wilderness areas 5. Forest fires 6. Yellowstone National Park 7. Depression era (1929-1941) 8. Christian historical romances

LC 2018046955

A man who can't read will never amount to anything—or so Nate Webber believes. But he takes a chance to help his family by signing up for the new Civilian Conservation Corps, skirting the truth about certain "requirements." Elsie Brookes was proud to grow up as a ranger's daughter, but she longs for a future of her own. After four years serving as a maid in the park's hotels, she still hasn't saved enough money for her college tuition. A second job, teaching a crowd of rowdy men in the CCC camp, might be the answer, but when Elsie discovers Nate's secret, it puts his job as camp foreman in jeopardy.

Barnett, LaShonda K.

Jam on the Vine. LaShonda Barnett. Grove Press, 2015. Viii, 323 pages

ISBN 9780802123343

1. African American women 2. Women journalists 3. African American women journalists 4. Lesbians 5. Newspapers 6. Texas 7. Kansas City, Missouri 8. 1910s 9. Historical fiction 10. LGBTQIA fiction 11. African American fiction

RUSA Reading List Short List, 2016

A poor, African-American Muslim girl in rural, racially segregated turn-of-the-century Texas, Ivoe Williams discovers a passion for journalism while pilfering old newspapers from her mother's white employer. Ivoe keeps her eyes on the horizon, first earning a college scholarship and later moving to Kansas City with her former teacher and lover, Ona. Together, the women start Jam! On the Vine, the nation's first female-run Black newspaper. Loosely based on pioneering journalist Ida B. Wells and Charlotta Bass (the first African-American woman to own and operate a newspaper), this dramatic debut should enchant readers who enjoy strong female characters and well-researched, vividly described period detail.

Barnett, S. K.

Safe. S. K. Barnett. E.P. Dutton, 2020. 336 p.

ISBN 9781524746520

1. Young women 2. Child kidnapping victims 3. Homecomings 4. Former captives 5. Family relationships 6. Long Island, New York 7. Psychological suspense 8. First person narratives

Jenny Kristal was six years old when she was snatched off the sidewalk from her quiet suburban neighborhood. Twelve years later, she's miraculously returned home after escaping her kidnappers—but as her parents and older brother welcome her back, the questions begin to mount. Where has she been all these years? Why is she back now? And is home really the safest place for her...or for any of them?

"Readers will likely think they know where this runaway train is headed, making the final twists that much more surprising. A creepy and darkly addictive thriller." —*Kirkus*

Barnhill, Kelly Regan

Dreadful young ladies and other stories. Kelly Barnhill. Algonquin Books of Chapel Hill, 2018. 304 p.

ISBN 9781616207977

1. Magic 2. Witches 3. Human behavior 4. Fantasy fiction 5. Short stories 6. Adult books for young adults

LC 2017039839

A first collection of short stories by the Newbery Medal-winning author of The Girl Who Drank the Moon includes the World Fantasy Award-winning novella, The Unlicensed Magician, in which an invisible girl once left for dead pursues a secret, magical life.

Barr, Mark

Watershed. Mark Barr. Hub City Press, 2019. 304 pages

ISBN 9781938235597

1. Engineers 2. Homemakers 3. Dams — Design and construction 4. Electricity 5. Depressions 6. Tennessee 7. Southern States 8. 1930s 9. Depression era (1929-1941) 10. Historical fiction

David J. Langum, Sr. Prize in American Historical Fiction, 2019

In 1937 rural Tennessee, a small-town housewife, finding her place in the post-Depression South, struggles to balance motherhood and a new-found freedom that awakens ambitions and a sexuality she never knew she possessed.

Barr, Nevada

Destroyer angel: an Anna Pigeon novel. Nevada Barr. Minotaur Books, 2014. 368 p. (Anna Pigeon mysteries, 18)

ISBN 9780312614584

1. Women park rangers 2. Canoeing 3. Kidnapping 4. Missing persons 5. Pigeon, Anna (Fictitious character) 6. Mysteries

LC 2013032879

Testing outdoor sporting equipment designed for a disabled companion, U.S. Park Services ranger Anna Pigeon returns from a solo outing to discover that her fellow campers have been abducted.

"Barr's gift for depicting breathtaking scenery elevates the story, as does Anna's complex, ever-evolving personality." —*Publishers Weekly*

The rope: an Anna Pigeon novel. Nevada Barr. Minotaur Books, 2012. 368 p. (Anna Pigeon mysteries, 17)

ISBN 9780312614577

1. Imprisonment 2. Escapes 3. Determination in women 4. Attempted murder 5. Deserts 6. Glen Canyon 7. 1990s 8. Mysteries 9. Adult books for young adults

LC 2011035837

The long-anticipated story of Anna Pigeon's past traces her brokenhearted 1995 relocation from New York City and first days as a Glen Canyon park ranger, a new start that is shattered by her abduction and imprisonment in the bottom of a dry well without supplies.

This novels occurs before the events in Track of the Cat and feature the backstory of Anna Pigeon.

Track of the cat. Nevada Barr. G. P. Putnam's Sons, 1993. 238 p; (Anna Pigeon mysteries, 1)

ISBN 9780399138249

1. Puma 2. Women park rangers 3. National parks and reserves 4. Women amateur detectives 5. Pigeon, Anna (Fictitious character) 6. Guadalupe Mountains National Park 7. Texas 8. Mysteries 9. Adult books for young adults

LC 92029694

Agatha Award for Best First Novel, 1994; Anthony Award for Best First Novel, 1994

Fleeing New York to find refuge as a ranger in the remote backcountry of West Texas, Anna Pigeon stumbles into a web of violence and murder when fellow park ranger Sheila Drury is mysteriously killed and another ranger vanishes BT

What Rose forgot. Nevada Barr. Minotaur Books, 2019. 320 pages
ISBN 9781250207135
1. Grandmothers 2. Amnesia 3. Nursing homes 4. Escapes 5. Threat (Psychology) 6. North Carolina 7. Charlotte, North Carolina 8. Mysteries

LC 2019012649

Waking up in a nursing-home Alzheimer's Unit with no memory of how she got there, Rose Dennis orchestrates an escape but does not know who to trust.

Barry, Ava
Windhall. Ava Barry. Pegasus Crime, 2021. 416 p.
ISBN 9781643136264
1. Rodriguez, Estelita 2. Film Actors and actresses 3. Women murder victims 4. Film producers and directors 5. Copycat murders 6. California 7. Thrillers and suspense

A stunning literary thriller in which an investigative journalist in modern Los Angeles attempts to solve the Golden Age murder of a Hollywood starlet.

"Barry parallels the cutthroat natures of journalism and film, skillfully blending a nuanced millennial perspective with noir shadings and a haunted-house atmosphere." —*Booklist*

Barry, Brunonia
The **map** of true places. Brunonia Barry. William Morrow, 2010. 406 p.
ISBN 9780061624780
1. Family secrets 2. Father and adult daughter 3. Women psychotherapists 4. Psychotherapist and patient 5. Suicide 6. Psychological fiction

Zee Finch, a psychotherapist, has come home to Salem to take care of her ailing father and to try to figure out her own life after the suicide of one of her patients, which was made even more difficult by Zee's past—her mother committed suicide herself, in front of her.

"Although marred by unnecessary come-to-realize moments, this woman-in-jeopardy thriller retooled with gothic elements shifting identities, secrets and portents, a deserted cottage and a missing suicide note manages to transcend its component cliches." —*Kirkus*

Barry, Dave
Insane city. Dave Barry. G. P. Putnam's Sons, 2013. 341 p.
ISBN 9780399158681
1. Misadventures 2. Slackers 3. Engaged persons 4. Lost articles 5. Stripteasers 6. Humorous stories

LC 2012028009

Astonished by his imminent marriage to a women he believed out of his league, Seth flies to their destination wedding in Florida only to be swept up in a maelstrom of violence involving rioters, Russian gangsters, angry strippers and a desperate python.

Lunatics. Dave Barry and Alan Zweibel. G. P. Putnam's Sons, 2012. 309 p.
ISBN 9780399158698
1. Misadventures 2. Bad days 3. Hate 4. Pet shops 5. Voyages and travels 6. Humorous stories

Philip Horkman is a happy man, the owner of a pet store called The Wine Shop, and on Sundays a referee for kids' soccer. Jeffrey Peckerman is the sole sane person in a world filled with goddamned jerks and morons, and he's having a really bad day. The two of them are about to collide in a swiftly escalating series of events that will send them running for their lives, pursued by the police, soldiers, terrorists, subversives, bears, and a man dressed as Chuck E. Cheese.

Barry, Jessica
★ **Don't** turn around. Jessica Barry. HarperCollins, 2020. 400 p.
ISBN 9780062874863
1. Violence against women 2. Violence in men 3. Young women 4. Secrets 5. Strangers 6. New Mexico 7. Thrillers and suspense

Cait and Rebecca, each with secrets to protect, find their lives in danger while on a desolate road in the New Mexico desert and must learn to trust one another.

"Barry follows up her attention-grabbing debut, Freefall, with two women, heretofore strangers, pursued on the bleak New Mexican back roads by a truck whose driver clearly means to deliver death." —*Library Journal*

"Barry's electric, perfectly paced tale reads like the gritty lovechild of Thelma and Louise and Spielberg's Duel, and readers will cheer for Cait and Rebecca all the way to the end of the road. An action-packed and fiercely feminist big-screen?ready chiller." —*Kirkus*

Barry, Sebastian
Days without end: a novel. Sebastian Barry. Viking Press, 2017. 259 pages
ISBN 9780525427360
1. Immigrants, Irish 2. Soldiers 3. Gender identity 4. Gay men 5. Frontier and pioneer life 6. United States 7. 19th century 8. Historical fiction 9. LGBTQIA fiction 10. Literary fiction 11. Adult books for young adults

ALA Notable Book, 2018; Booklist Editors' Choice, 2017; Costa Book of the Year Award, 2016; Costa Novel Award, 2016; Walter Scott Prize for Historical Fiction, 2017; Longlisted for the Man Booker Prize, 2017; Longlisted for the Andrew Carnegie Medal for Excellence in Fiction, 2018

A survivor of Ireland's Great Famine and a recent immigrant to the United States, 17-year-old Thomas McNulty joins the U.S. Army in 1851 with his best friend and fellow orphan, John Cole. Sent first to the Great Plains to butcher the Sioux, and later, to the battlefields of the Civil War, the young carry out their orders despite their horror of the carnage. Meanwhile, they become lovers and must find a way to build a life together in a society that doesn't recognize or understand romantic relationships between men.

"A lively, richly detailed story of one slice of the Irish immigrant experience in America." —*Kirkus*

First published in the United Kingdom in 2016 by Faber & Faber Limited.

The **secret** scripture: a novel. Sebastian Barry. Viking, 2008. 304 p.
ISBN 9780670019403
1. Psychiatric hospital patients 2. Senior women 3. Physicians 4. Physician and patient 5. Protestants 6. Sligo, Ireland 7. Ireland 8. Psychological fiction 9. Parallel narratives 10. Literary fiction

LC 2007041716

Costa Novel Award, 2008; Costa Book of the Year Award, 2008; James Tait Black Memorial Prize for Fiction, 2008; Shortlisted for the Man Booker Prize, 2008

Roseanne McNulty, once one of the most beautiful and beguiling girls in County Sligo, Ireland, is now an elderly patient at Roscommon Regional Mental Hospital. As her hundredth year draws near, she decides to record the events of her life, hiding the manuscript beneath the floorboards. Meanwhile, the hospital is preparing to close and is evaluating its patients to determine whether they can return to society. Dr. Grene, Roseanne's caretaker, takes a special interest in her case. In his research, he discovers a document written by a local priest that tells a very different story of Roseanne's life than what she recalls. As doctor and patient attempt to understand each other, they begin to uncover long-buried secrets about themselves.

"While not a historical novel in the accepted sense, The Secret Scripture uses history's complex relationship with truth to generate momentum and sharpen the definition of character.... The reader applauds the wisdom of its heroine in keeping her integrity entire. 'Sligo made me and Sligo undid me', Roseanne remarks, echoing Dante, and in the process of this undoing she finds her greatness." —*Times Literary Supplement*

★ A **thousand** moons: a novel. Sebastian Barry. Viking Press, 2020. 272 pages
ISBN 9780735223103
1. Orphans 2. Lakota Indians 3. Adoptive families 4. Civil War veterans 5. Gay men 6. United States 7. Tennessee 8. 19th century 9. Historical fiction 10. Literary fiction 11. First person narratives
Loan Stars Favourites, 2020
Raised by unconventional adoptive parents on a Tennessee farm, an orphaned Lakota child pursues a life for herself beyond the violence and dispossession of her past.
"A poetic sensibility runs through this luminous novel of sorrow and uplift by the Booker-nominated, multi-award-winning Barry. Highly recommended." —*Library Journal*
Novel can be read as standalone. However, adoptive parents John Cole's and Thomas McNulty's story is told in Days Without End.

Bartels, Erin

We hope for better things. Erin Bartels. Revell, 2019. 393 pages
ISBN 9780800734916
1. Women journalists 2. Family secrets 3. Family history 4. Farmhouses 5. Racism 6. Michigan 7. Christian fiction
In this richly textured debut novel, a disgraced journalist moves into her great aunt's secret-laden farmhouse and discovers that the women in her family were testaments to true love and courage in the face of war, persecution, and racism.
"Bartels successfully weaves American history into a deeply moving story of heartbreak, long-held secrets, and the bonds of family." —*Publishers Weekly*

Barth, John

Chimera. John Barth. Houghton Mifflin, 2001. 308 p. : Illustration
ISBN 9780618131709
1. Storytelling 2. Gods and goddesses, Greek 3. Pegasus (Greek mythology) 4. Perseus (Greek mythology) 5. Scheherazade 6. Mythological fiction 7. Literary fiction 8. Experimental fiction
National Book Award for Fiction, 1973
The comic adventures of Dunyazade, Perseus, and Bellerophon reveal the author's thoughts on the nature of a hero and relationships between men and women.
"The protagonists of these witty confessions are walking psyches, at war with ultimate ambivalence. (Far from clarifying what is ambiguous, Barth deepens it by retelling familiar stories, deploying their unsettled alternatives so as to virtually insist on their unreality).... [He] employs liter-

ary devices that multiply confusion [including]...the removal of all barriers posed by time and history." —*Library Journal*
Originally published: New York: Random House, 1972.

★ The **floating** opera. John Barth. Doubleday, 1967. 252 p.
ISBN 9780385076302
1. Lawyers 2. Love triangles 3. Suicide 4. Cynicism 5. Sexuality 6. Literary fiction 7. Experimental fiction 8. First person narratives
LC 67012864
"Just as Voltaire's Candide decides to contentedly cultivate his garden after a disillusioning journey, so does Barth's Todd come to terms with life by discovering in time that it is best to choose among the relative values that life offers rather than cynically rejecting all values by way of suicide." —*New York Times Book Review*

★ **Giles** Goat-Boy;: or, The revised new syllabus. John Barth. Doubleday, 1966. Xxxi, 710 p.
ISBN 9780385043991
1. Universities and colleges 2. College students 3. Campus life 4. Goats 5. United States 6. 1960s 7. Allegories 8. Literary fiction 9. Satirical fiction
LC 66015666
George Giles encounters new people and ideas as he ascends from a goat farm to the position of Grand Tutor of the human university.

The **last** voyage of somebody the sailor. John Barth. Little, Brown 1991. 573 p.
ISBN 9780316082518
1. Storytelling 2. Time travel (Past) 3. King, Martin Luther, 1929-1968 4. Authors 5. Shipwrecks 6. Baghdad, Iraq 7. Experimental fiction 8. Literary fiction
LC 90044991
While retracing the legendary voyages of Sindbad the Sailor, journalist Simon William Behler finds himself in Sindbad's household in medieval Baghdad and competes with Sindbad in a storytelling marathon in the hopes of finding a way back to the modern world.
"If the setting is sober, the narrator is not. This is John Barth,...after all, and his hero is variously exuberant, obnoxious, funny, self-conscious, and, not sober at all, but thoroughly intoxicated with sex, love, and story telling, especially with their commingling." —*Commonweal*

★ The **sot-weed** factor. John Barth. Doubleday, 1987. Xii, 756 p.
ISBN 9780385240888
1. Sexuality 2. Innocence (Personal quality) 3. Voyages and travels 4. Good and evil 5. Pirates 6. Maryland 7. Great Britain 8. Colonial America (1600-1775) 9. 18th century 10. Picaresque fiction 11. Literary fiction 12. Experimental fiction
Ebnezer Cooke, his twin sister, and their young tutor go from England to Maryland where they participate in the area's early years.

Barthelme, Donald

Sixty stories. Donald Barthelme. G. P. Putnam's Sons, 1981. 457 p.
ISBN 9780399126598
1. Experimental fiction 2. Short stories 3. Anthologies
LC 818646
National Book Critics Circle Award for Fiction finalist, 1981
A retrospective collection of Donald Barthelme's most notable writings includes "Me and Miss Mandible," "Views of My Father Weeping," "The King of Jazz," nine new stories, and other outstanding selections.
"Lots of very good old Barthelme, then, a smidgin of pretty good new Barthelme: a collection without a reason, perhaps, but an expansive sampling for newcomers and a chic bedside book for fans who want to replace their tattered paperbacks." —*Kirkus*

Barthelme, Frederick

Bob the gambler. Frederick Barthelme. Houghton Mifflin, 1997. 213 p.
ISBN 9780395809778
1. Compulsive gamblers 2. Architects 3. Casinos 4. Families 5. Gambling 6. Biloxi, Mississippi 7. Mainstream fiction

LC 974363

New York Times Notable Book, 1997

An architect and his wife living near a casino in Mississippi become hooked on gambling and lose everything they own. They move into his mother's house and embark on a new life, discovering happiness in simplicity and insecurity.

"Paradise, as it happens, is the name of the local casino. The irony in this is obvious enough, but it is Barthelme's peculiar post-modern gift to be able to invert the easy ironies of contemporary life and reveal the truths beneath them." —*New York Times Book Review*

Elroy Nights. Frederick Barthelme. Counterpoint, 2003. 224 p.
ISBN 9781582431284
1. College teachers 2. Art teachers 3. Middle-aged men 4. Separated men (Marital relations) 5. Midlife crisis 6. Gulf Coast, Mississippi 7. Mississippi 8. Mainstream fiction

LC 2003007830

New York Times Notable Book, 2003

A reasonably successful, fiftysomething artist and professor caught between a midlife crisis and the decay of his sixties, Elroy Nights—with his wife's agreement—elects to live separately from his wife and embarks on a journey of discovery with his young students, until an unforeseen tragedy forces him to deal with a world suddenly gone wrong.

"Barthelme's world is vague and unclear. Conversations dead-end, spousal jabs go unanswered, Elroy and Freddie's relationship never evolves into anything defined. Still, currents of hope run through Elroy Nights. Elroy and Clare's relationship contains remarkable moments of kindness-not in showy grand scenes but in small gestures, in bitten tongues, in the silent lowering of expectations." —*New York Times Book Review*

Painted desert: a novel. Frederick Barthelme. Viking 1995. 243 p. (Del Tribute series, 2)
ISBN 9780670864690
1. Television news 2. Riots 3. Automobile travel 4. Anarchists 5. Popular culture 6. Mainstream fiction

LC 95006769

A junior college professor and his girlfriend pry themselves from their television and computer screens and take to the road, achieving an epiphany in the Arizona desert.

"Laced with sharp dialogue and wit, this novel suggests that we are what we witness, whether it's the gypsum hills of White Sands or the slaying of a stranger a thousand miles away." —*The New Yorker*

Bartlett, Neil

The disappearance boy. Neil Bartlett. St. Martin's Press, 2014. 320 p.
ISBN 9781620407257
1. Magicians 2. Gay men 3. Orphans 4. Friendship 5. Twenties (Age) 6. England 7. 1950s 8. Coming-of-age stories 9. LGBTQIA fiction 10. Adult books for young adults
Booklist Editors' Choice: Adult Books for Young Adults, 2014

When the show moves to the Brighton Grand, Reggie Rainbow, the magician's behind-the-scenes assistant, begins questioning how much of his own life has been an act and sets out to find somebody who disappeared from his own life years before.

Barton, Fiona

The child. Fiona Barton. Berkley, 2017. 336 p. (Kate Waters novels (Fiona Barton), 2)
ISBN 9781101990483
1. Human remains (Archaeology) 2. Women journalists 3. Baby stealing 4. Kidnapping 5. Secrets 6. Psychological suspense

LC 2016055096

Loan Stars Favourites, 2017; LibraryReads Favorites, 2017

The author of the stunning New York Times bestseller The Widow returns with a brand-new novel of twisting psychological suspense. As an old house is demolished in a gentrifying section of London, a workman discovers a tiny skeleton, buried for years. For journalist Kate Waters, it's a story that deserves attention. She cobbles together a piece for her newspaper, but at a loss for answers, she can only pose a question: Who is the Building Site Baby? As Kate investigates, she unearths connections to a crime that rocked the city decades earlier: A newborn baby was stolen from the maternity ward in a local hospital and was never found. Her heartbroken parents were left devastated by the loss. But there is more to the story, and Kate is drawn—house by house—into the pasts of the people who once lived in this neighborhood that has given up its greatest mystery. And she soon finds herself the keeper of unexpected secrets that erupt in the lives of three women—and torn between what she can and cannot tell.

"Barton's second missing-child story is a gut-wrenching tale of narcissism, cunning predators, and bare-knuckle survival." —*Booklist*

You can bury the story...but you can't hide the truth—Cover.

The suspect. Fiona Barton. Penguin Group USA 2019. 384 p. (Kate Waters novels (Fiona Barton), 3)
ISBN 9781101990513
1. Missing teenage girls 2. Women journalists 3. Mothers and sons 4. British in Thailand 5. Suspicion 6. Thailand 7. Psychological suspense

LC 2018048595

LibraryReads Favorites, 2019

Pursuing the story of two British teens who disappeared during a Bangkok hostel fire, journalist Kate Waters struggles to remain objective when her estranged son is declared a main suspect.

Bartz, Andrea

The herd: a novel. Andrea Bartz. Ballantine Books, 2020. 336 pages
ISBN 9781984826367
1. Women business owners 2. Missing persons 3. Sisters 4. Women professional employees 5. Women journalists 6. Psychological suspense 7. Multiple perspectives

LC 2019038590

When the enigmatic founder of their exclusive New York women's mentorship community goes missing, two sisters search for answers to protect their friends and careers before uncovering dangerous secrets.

"A soapy and fun woman-centric thriller." —*Kirkus*

The lost night. Andrea Bartz. Crown Pub, 2019. 336 p.
ISBN 9780525574712
1. Friends' death 2. Suicide victims 3. Murder investigation 4. Survivors of suicide victims 5. Loss of consciousness 6. New York City 7. Brooklyn, New York City 8. 2010s 9. Psychological suspense

A chance discovery of a 10-year-old video shares disturbing insights into the suicide of a college classmate who may have been murdered on a hazy drunken night, a revelation that compels one woman to determine her own role.

"Bartz calls upon psychology and technology as Lindsay, whose profession is research and fact-checking, uncovers the truth." —*Booklist*

Barzak, Christopher

One for sorrow. Christopher Barzak. Bantam Dell, 2007. 320 p.

ISBN 9780553384369

1. Ghosts 2. Murder 3. Teenage boys — Friendship 4. Happiness in teenage boys 5. Books to movies 6. Coming-of-age stories 7. Psychological fiction 8. Adult books for young adults

LC 2007015871

With his family life falling apart after his mother is paralyzed in a drunk-driving accident, Adam McCormik is drawn to the site where the body of a murdered classmate, Jamie Marks, a boy ignored by almost everyone, had been found and finds himself entering into a strange friendship with a ghost.

"The author possesses a remarkable gift for depicting adolescent sexuality in prose that's at once unadorned and unabashedly romantic. He also creates lively, oddball secondary characters.... The novel has some problems with pacing, and in a few spots believable characterization and dialogue are ground under the wheels of the plot machine. But One for Sorrow is a considerable achievement, a lyrical ghost story as moving and credible as it is unsettling." —*Village Voice*

This novel was made into film in 2014 under the title, Jamie Marks is Dead, directed by Carter Smith and starring Judy Greer, Liv Tyler, and Cameron Monaghan.

Bateman, Kate

A **reckless** match. Kate Bateman. St. Martin's Press, 2021. 352 p. (Ruthless rivals, 1)

ISBN 9781250801562

1. Nobility 2. Rich families 3. Family feuds 4. Enemies 5. Earls and countesses 6. Wales 7. England 8. Regency period (1811-1820) 9. Regency romances 10. Historical romances

Forced to retreat to his family's Welsh castle, the new Earl of Powys is reunited with his childhood enemy who loathes him just as much as she ever did until danger and meddling from their feuding families makes them realize that their animosity could be love.

"Brimming with intrigue, passion, and humor, this is sure to win the author new fans." —*Publishers Weekly*

This earl of mine. Kate Bateman. St Martins Press, 2019. 320 pages (Bow Street bachelors, 1)

ISBN 9781250305954

1. Young widows 2. Detectives 3. Independence in women 4. Undercover operations 5. Heirs and heiresses 6. Regency period (1811-1820) 7. Historical romances 8. Regency romances

Marrying a condemned criminal, newly widowed shipping heiress Georgiana Caversteed is stunned to discover her husband very much alive at a social gathering weeks later and finds herself being courted by this well-known rake who was working undercover in Newgate prison.

Bates, Judy Fong

★ **Midnight** at the Dragon Cafe. Judy Fong Bates. Counterpoint, 2005. 317 p.

ISBN 9781582431895

1. Chinese Canadian girls 2. Girls 3. Chinese in Ontario 4. Chinese in Canada 5. Immigrants, Chinese 6. Miller, Henry 7. Canada 8. 1950s 9. Canadian fiction 10. Domestic fiction 11. First person narratives 12. Adult books for young adults

LC 2004381288

Alex Award, 2006; ALA Notable Book, 2006; Booklist Editors' Choice: Adult Books for Young Adults, 2005

Su-Jen Chou, a Chinese immigrant growing up in 1950s Ontario finds herself shouldering the weight of her mother's hopes and dreams as her isolated family attempts to forge a life for themselves in a small town.

Originally published: Toronto: McClelland & Stewart, 2004.

Batuman, Elif

★ The **idiot**. Elif Batuman. Penguin Press, 2017. 480 p.

ISBN 9781594205613

1. Women college students 2. Identity (Psychology) 3. Turkish Americans 4. Self-discovery in women 5. Children of immigrants 6. Cambridge, Massachusetts 7. Massachusetts 8. 1990s 9. Coming-of-age stories 10. Literary fiction 11. Autobiographical fiction

LC 2016029596

New York Times Notable Book, 2017; Pulitzer Prize for Fiction finalist, 2018; Shortlisted for The Women's Prize for Fiction, 2018

Embarking on her freshman year at Harvard in the early tech days of the 1990s, a young artist and daughter of Turkish immigrants begins a correspondence with an older mathematics student from Hungary while struggling with her changing sense of self, first love and a daunting career prospect.

"A sweetly caustic first novel...Self-aware, cerebral, and delightful." —*Kirkus*

Bauer, Belinda

The **beautiful** dead. Belinda Bauer. Atlantic Monthly Press, 2017. 341 p.

ISBN 9780802125330

1. Women television journalists 2. Ambition in women 3. Art — Exhibitions 4. Women murder victims 5. Serial murderers 6. London, England 7. Thrillers and suspense

Loan Stars Favourites, 2017

A television crime reporter desperate to recharge her flagging career becomes an unwitting accomplice to an attention-hungry serial killer at the center of the decade's biggest murder investigation.

Snap. Belinda Bauer. Atlantic Monthly Press, 2018. 352 p.

ISBN 9780802127747

1. Burglary 2. Detectives 3. Death threats 4. Psychic trauma 5. Murder investigation 6. England 7. Thrillers and suspense 8. Multiple perspectives

LC 2018012770

Loan Stars Favourites, 2018; Longlisted for the Man Booker Prize, 2018

Waking up to discover a knife and sinister note in her bed, a young woman is connected to a string of burglaries and the recent brutal murder of a mother of three.

Bauer, Carlene

★ **Frances** and Bernard. Carlene Bauer. Houghton Mifflin Harcourt, 2013. 224 p.

ISBN 9780547858241

1. Authors 2. Letter writing 3. Catholics 4. Friendship 5. New York City 6. 1950s 7. Epistolary novels 8. Love stories

LC 2012014028

A tale loosely inspired by Robert Lowell and Flannery O'Connor traces the intense friendship and literary bond shared by two mid-20th-century New York writers through an exchange of letters that explores their respective writing forms and beliefs about faith, passion and the nature of acceptable sacrifice.

Bauermeister, Erica

The **scent** keeper. Erica Bauermeister. St. Martin's Press, 2019. 304 pages

ISBN 9781250200136

1. Fathers and daughters 2. Senses and sensation 3. Family secrets 4. Imaginary machines 5. Gadgets 6. Pacific Northwest 7. Coming-of-age stories 8. First person narratives 9. Relationship fiction

LC 2018055448

A young woman raised on a remote island with a father who identifies the scents of the natural world makes illuminating discoveries about her identity and a mysterious cache of fragrances.

Bauman, Bruce

★ **Broken** sleep: an American dream. Bruce Bauman. Other Press, 2015. 474 p.

ISBN 9781590514481

1. Birthmothers 2. Family secrets 3. Families 4. Candidates for public office 5. Rock music 6. 20th century 7. 21st century 8. Family sagas 9. Allegories

LC 2015006100

"Diagnosed with an aggressive form of leukemia, Moses Teumer, searching for a donor, hunts down his birth parents and must unravel the intertwined destinies of his adopted and biological families, in a saga about rock music, art, politics and the elusive nature of love. Original." —Provided by publisher.

Bausch, Richard

Hello to the cannibals: a novel. Richard Bausch. HarperCollins, 2002. 661 p.

ISBN 9780060192952

1. Kingsley, Mary Henrietta 2. Adult child abuse victims 3. Women dramatists 4. Married women 5. Young women 6. Playwriting 7. Virginia 8. Psychological fiction

LC 2002023270

Pregnant, newly married, and living with her in-laws, Lily Austin writes a play about famed nineteenth-century British explorer Mary Kinglsey and finds inspiration in her subject's writings.

"The novel is ambitious not only in its historical and geographical sweep but also in its author's choice to confine himself, with admirableconviction and credibility, to the consciousness of two women." —New York Times Book Review

Peace. Richard Bausch. Knopf, 2008. 192 p.

ISBN 9780307268334

1. Soldiers 2. Personal conduct 3. Ethics 4. Killing (Ethics) 5. Duty 6. Italy 7. Second World War era (1939-1945) 8. 1940s 9. Historical fiction 10. War stories

LC 2007037096

ALA Notable Book, 2009; W. Y. Boyd Literary Award, 2009

Italy, near Cassino. The terrible winter of 1944. A dismal icy rain, continuing unabated for days. Guided by a seventy-year-old Italian man in rope-soled shoes, three American soldiers are sent on a reconnaissance mission up the side of a steep hill that they discover, before very long, to be a mountain. And the old man's indeterminate loyalties only add to the terror and confusion that engulf them on that mountain, where they are confronted with the horror of their own time—and then set upon by a sniper. —From publisher description.

"A story cleanly told void of trickery or plot shifting, without the faux drama of point-of-view shifts or uninvited monologue on the state of the cultural landscape well, that's a thing to behold.... Bausch, among the most prolific and accomplished story writers of the last two decades, provides a gift to those who like to swallow their stories whole, in one sitting, without digression or narrative handstands." —Esquire

★ **Rebel** powers. Richard Bausch. Houghton Mifflin, 1993. 390 p.

ISBN 9780395595084

1. Vietnam veterans — Family relationships 2. Vietnam veterans' spouses 3. Vietnam veterans 4. Fathers and sons 5. Prisoners' spouses 6. 1960s 7. War stories

LC 93009194

A decorated Air Force officer and former POW returns from Vietnam alive, but faces a dishonorable discharge and a two-year prison term BT

"The key to the novel's credibility is the unretouched quality of its portraiture. Its characters live in a carefully chronicled American moment when threatening new ideas are beginning to rub up against weighty old certainties." —New York Times Book Review

The **stories** of Richard Bausch. Richard Bausch. Harper Collins, 2003. 572 p.

ISBN 9780060196493

1. United States 2. Short stories

LC 2003042318

In a collection of forty-two short stories, the author explores his fascination with the everyday details of human relationships and considers the dramatic roots of common interactions.

"Failure and its exactions this is Bausch's big subject. These 42 stories test the play of hope and disappointment in the lives of spouses and lovers, of parents and children and siblings. And while Bausch does in several instances write with insight and authority from a woman's perspective, it is the sons, fathers and husbands in their daily trials that he registers most memorably. Indeed, so alive are these characters, with their credible flaws, their complaints and loud excitements, that closing the book feels like pushing the door shut on some clamorous party." —New York Times Book Review

Includes 42 stories.

Bawden, Nina

Family money. Nina Bawden. St. Martin's, 1991. 250 p.

ISBN 9780312063511

1. Women with amnesia 2. Greed 3. Mother and adult child 4. Mainstream fiction

LC 91021186

A tough independent woman, Fanny Pye learns to adjust to the crippling events brought on by old age and the selfish interests of her adult children

"Sharply observed and drawn with precision, Fanny's troubles and their eventual resolution make a compelling read." —Publishers Weekly

Baxter, Charles

The **feast** of love. Charles Baxter. Pantheon Books, 2000. 308 p.

ISBN 9780375410192

1. Community life 2. Lovers 3. Interpersonal relations 4. Man-woman relationships 5. Neighbors 6. Ann Arbor, Michigan 7. Michigan 8. Psychological fiction 9. Love stories 10. Books to movies

LC 99053088

New York Times Notable Book, 2000; National Book Award for Fiction finalist, 2000

A collection of vignettes set in a coffee shop explores the subtle movements of love between ordinary people.

"An insomniac Mid-western novelist named Charlie Baxter becomes the unwitting audience of a neighbor's midnight confession, and is drawn into a tale of love in its manifold guisesconfused, ecstatic, unrequited. We hear the story of Kathryn, who left her husband for the female shortstop of a local softball team; of Diana, a capricious lawyer who doesn't want anyone to want her too much; and of Chlo, a pierced teenager with a strong sense of justice and a doomed passion for a former drug addict. Baxter's novel is a modern Symposium, unexpectedly hilarious in its attempt to get at the evasive truths of love; unlike Plato's treatise, though, its strength lies in its recognition that such truths aren't universal." —*The New Yorker*

Saul and Patsy. Charles Baxter. Pantheon Books, 2003. 320 p.
ISBN 9780375410291
1. Small towns 2. Jewish men 3. Suicide 4. Married people 5. Teenagers 6. Michigan 7. Domestic fiction 8. Psychological fiction 9. Adult books for young adults
LC 2003042027
New York Times Notable Book, 2003
A seemingly happy domestic scene is turned upside down by the obsessive attentions of a troubled sixteen-year-old boy.
"The narrative is dense with quotidian detail, precisely charted shifts of consciousness and pitch-perfect moments of emotional truth." —*Publishers Weekly*

★ The **sun** collective. Charles Baxter. Pantheon Books, 2020. 336 p.
ISBN 9781524748852
1. Searching 2. Anarchists 3. Actors and actresses 4. Missing men 5. Drug use 6. Minneapolis, Minnesota 7. Literary fiction
The National Book Award finalist presents this timely and unsettling novel in which a mother searches for her son, a once promising actor, who has fallen victim to a local community group and its enigmatic leader.
"Baxter has brilliantly choreographed a wholly unnerving plunge into alarming aberrations private and public, festering political catastrophe, and woefully warped love." —*Booklist*

There's something I want you to do: stories. Charles Baxter. Pantheon Books, 2015. 240 pages
ISBN 9781101870013
1. Virtues 2. Personal conduct 3. Vices 4. Minneapolis, Minnesota 5. Short stories
LC 2014003352
Minnesota Book Award for Novel & Short Story, 2016
A collection of interrelated stories exploring virtues and vices features characters whose actions are equally divided between hateful and heroic.
"Rooted in Minneapolis, its industrial ruins so poetically rendered, these ravishing, funny, and compassionate stories redefine our perceptions of vice and virtue, delusion and reason, love and loss." —*Booklist*

Bayard, Louis

The **black** tower: a novel. Louis Bayard. William Morrow, 2008. 368 p.
ISBN 9780061173509
1. Vidocq, Francois Eugene 2. Detectives 3. Murder investigation 4. Disguises 5. Murder 6. Murder suspects 7. France 8. 1810s 9. 19th century 10. Historical mysteries 11. Mysteries
LC 2008005059
Booklist Editors' Choice, 2008
Having used his mastery of disguise and surveillance to nab France's most notorious criminals, early nineteenth-century detective Vidocq tracks down the most challenging adversary of his career, a case with ties to the missing son of Marie Antoinette.
"Bayard makes brilliant application of Vidocq in this fanciful adventure.... No snatch-and-run researcher, Bayard takes care to capture Vidocq's roguish voice and grandiose affectations, as well as the melodra-

matic substance of his published memoirs." —*New York Times Book Review*

The **pale** blue eye: a novel. Louis Bayard. Harper Collins Publishers, 2006. 432 p.
ISBN 9780060733971
1. Poe, Edgar Allan 2. Former police 3. Murder investigation 4. Widowers 5. Young men 6. Siblings 7. West Point, New York 8. New York (State) 9. 1830s 10. Historical mysteries 11. Mysteries
LC 2005044741
When a suicide victim's body disappears from the West Point Military Academy, detective Gus Landor gets called in to investigate. When a new cadet, Edgar Allan Poe, approaches Landor with his theory that the man they are looking for is a poet, the duo begins to narrow down suspects all the while dealing with their own personal demons.
"Bayard scatters seeds of Poe's short stories and poems throughout the novel, culminating in a grisly set piece that out-Goths The Fall of the House of Usher. But just when a reader's eyes start rolling, Bayard's ending brilliantly upends the entire novel." —*Christian Science Monitor*

Beach, Edward L.

Run silent, run deep. Edward L. Beach; with an introduction by Edward P. Stafford. Naval Institute Press, 1987. 343 p. (Rich Richardson series, 1)
ISBN 9780870215575
1. Submarine warfare 2. Submarines, American 3. Naval battles 4. World War II 5. Richardson, Rich (Fictitious character) 6. Marius, Gaius 7. Second World War era (1939-1945) 8. Sea stories 9. War stories 10. Historical fiction
LC 85021801
A narrative with the drama of war, love, and jealousy during submarine service in World War II BT
"If ever a book has the ring of reality, this is it. From the moment the reader steps aboard a training boat in New London, Conn, to the time when the submarine Walrus dives deeply to avoid the depth charges of the enemy's destroyers, there is awe and respect for the author who created them." —*New York Times Book Review*
Originally published in 1955 by Henry Holt.

Beagin, Jen

★ **Vacuum** in the dark: a novel. Jen Beagin. Scribner, 2019. 224 p.
ISBN 9781501182143
1. Women house cleaners 2. Discontent 3. Extramarital affairs 4. Boyfriends 5. Drug addicts 6. New Mexico 7. Literary fiction
A young house cleaner in New Mexico balances a bad, junkie boyfriend with a bad, unstable boyfriend who happens to be married to one of her clients as she embarks on an eccentric journey of self-discovery and redemption.
"Beagin pulls no punches—this novel is viciously smart and morbidly funny." —*Publishers Weekly*

Beagle, Peter S.

A **fine** and private place. Peter S. Beagle. Roc Books, 1992. 290 p.
ISBN 9780451450968
1. Cemeteries 2. Ghosts 3. Romantic love 4. Eccentric men 5. Recluses 6. New York City 7. Love stories 8. Contemporary fantasy
LC 9148054
A kindly raven brings food to and is the companion of a man who has taken refuge in an abandoned mausoleum in a New York City cemetery for nineteen years BT

In Calabria. Peter S. Beagle. Tachyon Publications, 2017. 176 p.
ISBN 9781616962487
1. Farmers 2. Unicorns 3. Life change events 4. Poets 5. Rural life
6. Southern Italy 7. Italy 8. Contemporary fantasy
"Claudio Bianchi has lived alone for many years on a hillside in
Southern Italy's scenic Calabria. Set in his ways and suspicious of outsiders, Claudio has always resisted change, preferring farming and writing
poetry. But one chilly morning, as though from a dream, an impossible
visitor appears at the farm. When Claudio comes to her aid, an act of kindness throws his world into chaos." —Provided by the publisher
"This is a pleasant snack of a story about an Italian farmer who encounters a unicorn that changes his life for the better." —*Booklist*

★ The **last** unicorn. Peter S. Beagle; illustrated by Mel Grant. Penguin
Books, 1991. 212 p. : Illustration
ISBN 9780451450524
1. Unicorns 2. Magicians 3. Rulers 4. Magic 5. Escapes 6. Fantasy
fiction 7. Books to movies 8. Adult books for young adults
LC 90007696
Recounts the quest of the last unicorn, who leaves the protection of
the enchanted forest to search for her own kind, and who is joined by
Schmedrick the Magician and Molly Grue in her search BT
The sequel, Two Hearts, is included in the short story collection, The
line between.
A ROC book.
Originally published: New York : Viking, 1968.

Summerlong. Peter S. Beagle. Tachyon Publications, 2016. 240 p.
ISBN 9781616962449
1. Waitresses 2. Couples 3. Fate and fatalism 4. Love 5. Independence
(Personal quality) 6. Puget Sound 7. Washington (State)
8. Contemporary fantasy
A complicated family brings a young woman named Lioness Lazos
into their lives, and as spring leads into summer, Lioness awakens each
family member's long-hidden dreams and desires.
"In his first new novel in more than a decade, Beagle creates an intimate drama between the members of a family who are slowly blindsided
by myth and magic spilling into their ordinary world." —*Kirkus*

The **unicorn** sonata. Illustrations by Robert Rodriguez. Turner
Publishing, 1996. 154 p.
ISBN 9781570362880
1. Thirteen-year-old girls 2. Unicorns 3. Interdimensional travel
4. Teenage girls 5. Mythical creatures 6. Gateway fantasy 7. Fantasy
fiction
LC 96-16007
In Los Angeles a thirteen-year-old girl follows haunting music across
an in invisible border into an enchanted land known as Shei'rah that is inhabited by satyrs, unicorns, and phoenixes.
"The story is slight, but the characterizations are grand, enhanced by
graceful prose laced with exquisite detail, and through both literary creativity and folkloric expertise where unicorns are concerned." —*Publishers Weekly*

Beah, Ishmael
Little family. Ishmael Beah. Penguin Group USA 2020. 272 p.
ISBN 9780735211773
1. Survival 2. Power (Social sciences) 3. Elite (Social sciences)
4. Stealing 5. Darger, Henry 6. Africa 7. Literary fiction
LC 2019049160
A powerful novel about young people in a conflict-scarred land,
struggling to replace the homes they have lost with the one they have created together.

"Beah informs his characters' blend of street savvy and naïveté with
bursts of details about the experiences that shaped them in a bustling and
crooked society. Fans of African postcolonial fiction are in for a treat."
—*Publishers Weekly*

Beams, Clare
The **illness** lesson. Clare Beams. Doubleday, 2020. 288 p.
ISBN 9780385544665
1. Girls' schools 2. Secrets 3. Women's role 4. Young women
5. Philosophers 6. New England 7. Massachusetts 8. Gilded Age
(1865-1898) 9. 1870s 10. Historical fiction 11. Literary fiction
12. Adult books for young adults
Interpreting a mysterious flock of red birds as an omen to pursue his
newest venture, a once-famous philosopher opens a revolutionary school
to shape the intellectual development of women, before his students' bizarre symptoms reveal otherworldly secrets.
"This suspenseful and vividly evocative tale expertly explores
women's oppression as well as their sexuality through the eyes of a heroine who is sometimes maddening, at other times sympathetic, and always
wholly compelling and beautifully rendered." —*Booklist*

Bear, Elizabeth
All the windwracked stars. Elizabeth Bear. Tor, 2008. 368 p. (Edda of
burdens, 2)
ISBN 9780765318824
1. End of the world 2. Imaginary wars and battles 3. Warriors 4.
Valkyries (Norse mythology) 5. Survival 6. Mythological fiction
7. Fantasy fiction
LC 2008034076
A last surviving member of the ancient Valkyries race returns to the
last surviving city on her dying world to reclaim a sword of power owned
by her lost brothers and sisters, an effort that is challenged by a hunting
Mingan the Wolf.
"The author's ability to create breathtaking variations on ancient
themes and make them new and brilliant is, perhaps, unparalleled in the
genre." —*Library Journal*

Blood and iron: a novel of the Promethean Age. Elizabeth Bear. ROC,
2005. 448 p. (Promethean Age, 1)
ISBN 9780451460929
1. Fairies 2. Changelings 3. Women college teachers 4. Women rulers
5. Mothers and sons 6. Contemporary fantasy 7. Mythological fiction
8. Celtic fantasy
LC 2005033954
"Ancient grudges and ruthless schemes are simply business as usual
to the Faerie court in Bear's complex and involving contemporary fantasy.
Seeker, formerly Elaine Andraste, is a changeling bound to the Mebd, the
queen of the Daoine Sidhe, to find other changelings and bring them to the
Faerie court. There, like legendary Tam Lin, and Seeker's own son, Ian,
they entertain the queen until she tires of them. Now the queen needs
Seeker to findand win the heart ofthe new Merlin, latest incarnation of a
being who, in the hands of the Prometheans, could be used to destroy the
Fae. Pragmatic college professor Carel Bierce, the first female Merlin, is
not easily swayed by Fae—or Promethean—advances. Long-forgotten rivalries and unsuspected blood ties arise to tug at Seeker's loyalties, even
as the queen promises to free Ian when she succeeds." —*Publishers
Weekly*

Ink and steel: a novel of the Promethean Age. Elizabeth Bear. Roc,
2008. Xii, 427 p; (Promethean Age, 3; Stratford man, 1)
ISBN 9780451462091

1. Shakespeare, William 2. Secret societies 3. Magicians 4. Fairies 5. Imaginary wars and battles 6. Imaginary kingdoms 7. Great Britain 8. Elizabethan era (1558-1603) 9. Tudor period (1485-1603) 10. Historical fantasy 11. Mythological fiction

LC 2008000746

With playwright and spy Kit Marley dead, the victim of murder, dramatist William Shakespeare unsuccessfully takes on the Promethean Club's secret battle against sorcerers out to destroy England, until Marley, resurrected by Faerie enchantment, comes to his aid.

"Bear reveals the secret war between fae and the Elizabethan court in this dramatic prequel to Blood and Iron and Whiskey and Water. Framed with the intrigues of queens and courtiers, the story focuses on the mutual respect and growing love of Kit Marley (aka Christopher Marlowe) and Will Shakespeare. As Morgan le Fey rescues Kit from assassins, various factions recruit Will to bolster their political machinations with the magic of poetry. Kit pulls Will into Faerie and both are forced to face their own deepest desires and fears, which cannot be resolved until they deal with a power even higher than mortal Queen Elizabeth or fae Queen Mab. Copious quotes and intelligent speculation about their lives and works mark this sensitive and sensual look at the two supreme playwrights of the English Renaissance." —*Publishers Weekly*

Range of ghosts. Elizabeth Bear. Tor, 2012. 336 p. (Eternal sky trilogy, 1)
ISBN 9780765327543
1. Civil war 2. Alliances 3. Magic 4. Wizards 5. Exiles 6. Epic fantasy 7. Middle Eastern-influenced fantasy 8. Asian-influenced fantasy

LC 2011025171

Romantic Times Reviewer's Choice Award, 2012
Going into exile after barely escaping a war waged by his cousin and brother, Temur, the grandson and heir of the Great Khan, teams up against an enemy cult with former princess Samarkar, who after a series of bitter betrayals has pursued a life of magical study.

The **red-stained** wings. Elizabeth Bear. Tor Books, 2019. 336 pages (Lotus Kingdoms, 2)
ISBN 9780765380159
1. Mercenaries 2. Machinery 3. Wizards 4. Rulers 5. Quests 6. Fantasy fiction 7. Epic fantasy
Despite the Lotus Kingdoms being at war, The Gage and the Dead Man bring a message, disguised as a riddle, to the queen of Sarathai in the second novel of the series following The Stone in the Skull.

Shattered pillars. Elizabeth Bear. Tor, 2013. 336 p. (Eternal sky trilogy, 2)
ISBN 9780765327550
1. Magic 2. Heirs and heiresses 3. Alliances 4. Civil war 5. Wizards 6. Epic fantasy 7. Middle Eastern-influenced fantasy 8. Asian-influenced fantasy

LC 2012038826

Exiled heir Re-Tamur and his wizard friend Sarmarkar are pitted against dark forces that would conquer the great Empires along the Celedon Road.

Steles of the sky. Elizabeth Bear. Tor, 2014. 336 p. (Eternal sky trilogy, 3)
ISBN 9780765327567
1. Wolves 2. Human-animal relationships 3. Humans and wolves 4. Telepathy 5. Warriors 6. Epic fantasy 7. Middle Eastern-influenced fantasy 8. Asian-influenced fantasy

LC 2013029676

After declaring war against a usurping uncle, Re Tamur makes a final journey to the Dragon Lake to raise an army of his followers, while in the east the city of Asmaracanda has burned and the caliph deposed, and in the south a plague rages in the Rasan empire.

"Battles are fought on both a personal level and a grand scale, with artifacts of obscure ancient civilizations, spirit animals, magical creatures, and poetry and politics. The conclusion is both untelegraphed and completely appropriate." —*Publishers Weekly*
A Tom Doherty Associates book.

The **stone** in the skull. Elizabeth Bear. Tor, 2017. 368 p. (Lotus Kingdoms, 1)
ISBN 9780765380135
1. Mercenaries 2. Machinery 3. Wizards 4. Rulers 5. Quests 6. Fantasy fiction 7. Epic fantasy
As they brave a perilous journey through the Steles of the Sky and into the Lotus Kingdoms, a pair of mercenaries—brass automaton Gage and the Dead Man, a former bodyguard for a deposed caliph—think they're delivering a message from a powerful wizard to a beleaguered rajni (ruler). Little do they know they're wandering into the middle of a dynastic war. Set in the world of the Eternal Sky trilogy, The Stone in the Skull is the first of a new series.

"Readers familiar with Bear's work will recognize the city of Messaline and the names of the Lotus Kingdoms, but this is the farthest she's delved into this shattered empire. As usual, the setting is wonderfully realized; the characters are possessed of depth, personality, and individuality; the threads of politics that drive the plot are a fascinating knot to try to unravel. This is a promising beginning indeed for an epic; there are many lines of story left to follow, and it will no doubt be a magnificent journey." —*Booklist*

Stone mad. Elizabeth Bear. Tor.com, 2018. 183 p.
ISBN 9781250163837
1. Imaginary creatures 2. Retirees 3. Spiritualists 4. Kidnapping 5. Supernatural 6. The West (United States) 7. 19th century 8. Steampunk 9. Weird Westerns
Karen and Priya are out for a night on the town, celebrating the purchase of their own little ranch and Karen's retirement from the Hotel Ma Cherie, when they meet the Arcadia Sisters, spiritualists who unexpectedly stir up the tommy-knocker in the basement. The ensuing show could bring down the house, if Karen didn't rush in to rescue everyone she can.

Bear, Greg

Anvil of stars. Greg Bear. Warner Books 1992. 434 p. (Forge of God, 2)
ISBN 9780446516013
1. Space warfare 2. Survival 3. Revenge 4. Space flight 5. Robots 6. Hard science fiction 7. Science fiction

LC 91050411

Follows the mission of a select group of human survivors as they search in the Ship of Law for the aliens who destroyed their planet BT

"Bear is superlatively competent in the English language and a master of both technical wizardry and powerful scenes. Throughout the book, he addresses the question of an ethical basis for genocide, leaving the matter sufficiently open to make one wonder whether the story is yet completed." —*Booklist*
Sequel to: Forge of God (1987).

The **collected** stories of Greg Bear. Greg Bear. Tor, 2002. 653 p.
ISBN 9780765301604
1. Science fiction 2. Anthologies 3. Short stories 4. Adult books for young adults

LC 2002020466

A collection of science fiction short stories includes "Blood Music," "Tangents," "Hardfought," and "Petra." BT

"In addition to Blood music (1985), a novelette where a genetic engineer injects himself with experimental intelligent microorganisms with disasterous results, this volume subsumes Bear's earlier collections, The wind from a burning woman (1983) and Tangents (1989), while also including more recent work." —*Anatomy of Wonder, 5th edition*

The **forge** of God. Greg Bear. Tor, 1987. 474p. (Forge of God, 1)
ISBN 9780312930219
1. Aliens (Non-humanoid) 2. Space warfare 3. Robots 4. Deception 5. Good and evil 6. Earth 7. Hard science fiction 8. Science fiction classics 9. Science fiction

LC 87050482

"The battle over Earth is seen through the eyes of a large cast of well-drawn characters, crowned by a climax of enormous power." —*Booklist*

Sequel: Anvil of Stars (1992).

Beaton, M. C.

Agatha Raisin and the quiche of death. M.C. Beaton. Ivy Books, 1993. 185 p. (Agatha Raisin mysteries, 1)
ISBN 9780804111638
1. Villages 2. Cooking contests 3. Poisoning 4. Murder investigation 5. Women detectives 6. England 7. Cotswolds, England 8. Cozy mysteries 9. Gentle reads 10. Books to TV

LC 92028381

In order to introduce herself to the picturesque English village where she has just retired, Mrs. Agatha Raisin enters a quiche in a local competition and promptly finds herself a murder suspect when the judge dies from her poisonous pie.

"In this highly promising launch to a new mystery series, Beaton turns from the adventures of her Scottish policeman Hamish Macbeth to introduce the redoubtable Agatha Raisin...Beaton's (Death of a snob) playful depiction of village life makes it all a delicious romp." —*Publishers Weekly*

Marion Chesney writing as M. C. Beaton.

Adapted into a TV series in 2016 by Sky 1 and streamed by Acorn TV in the United States.

Originally published: New York : St. Martin's Press, c1992.

Agatha Raisin and the witch of Wyckhadden. M.C. Beaton. St. Martin's Minotaur, 1999. 196 p. (Agatha Raisin mysteries, 9)
ISBN 9780312204945
1. Witches 2. Resorts 3. Murder investigation 4. Hair 5. Raisin, Agatha (Fictitious character) 6. England 7. Gentle reads 8. Books to TV

LC 9915884

After being shaved bald during a previous case, Agatha Raisin goes to a seaside resort and enlists the aid of a local witch to grow her hair back, putting her right in the middle of things when the witch is found dead.

Marion Chesney writing as M. C. Beaton.

Adapted into a TV series in 2016 by Sky 1 and streamed by Acorn TV in the United States.

Death of a macho man. M.C. Beaton. Mysterious Press, 1996. 216 p. (Hamish Macbeth mysteries, 12)
ISBN 9780892965311
1. Villages 2. Murder investigation 3. Former husbands 4. Alfred, King of England, 849-899 5. Macbeth, Hamish (Fictitious character) 6. Scotland 7. Cozy mysteries 8. Gentle reads

LC 96-7268

The one-man Scottish police force Hamish Macbeth becomes the prime suspect in the murder of the town ne'er-do-well, Randy "Macho Man" Duggan, whose real killer is surprisingly close at hand.

"Befuddled, earnest and utterly endearing, Hamish makes his triumphs sweetly satisfying." —*Publishers Weekly*

Marion Chesney writing as M. C. Beaton.

★ **Hot** to trot. . Minotaur Books, 2020. 288 p. (Agatha Raisin mysteries, 31)
ISBN 9781250157751
1. Women private investigators 2. Former lovers 3. Weddings 4. Women murder victims 5. Equestrians 6. Cotswolds, England 7. England 8. Cozy mysteries 9. Gentle reads 10. Media tie-ins

Jealously investigating an ex's intended, Agatha Raisin crashes the wedding only to become implicated in the bride's murder, a situation that immerses Agatha in the cutthroat equestrian world. TV tie-in.

"This lively entertainment includes an elegantly amusing introduction by Beaton (1936-2019), outlining her road to becoming a writer, as well as an affectionate foreword by longtime friend and journalist Green, who collaborated on this book." —*Publishers Weekly*

Pushing up daisies: an Agatha Raisin mystery. M. C. Beaton. Minotaur Books, 2016. 304 p. (Agatha Raisin mysteries, 27)
ISBN 9781250057440
1. Women private investigators 2. Murder suspects 3. Murder investigation 4. Widows 5. Bronte, Emily 6. Cotswolds, England 7. England 8. Cozy mysteries 9. Gentle reads

LC 2016010568

Gloria French was a jolly widow with dyed blonde hair, a raucous laugh and rosy cheeks. When she first moved from London to the charming Cotswolds Hills, she was heartily welcomed. She seemed a do-gooder par excellence, raising funds for the church and caring for the elderly. But she had a nasty habit of borrowing things and not giving them back, just small things, a teapot here, a set of silverware there. So it's quite the shock when she is found dead, murdered by a poisoned bottle of elderberry wine.

"A twisty plot, a familiar cast of eccentric characters, and a charming English country setting mean that lovers of cozy mysteries will be satisfied indeed." —*Publishers Weekly*

Marion Chesney writing as M. C. Beaton.

A queen of the village mystery—Cover.

Beattie, Ann

Chilly scenes of winter. Vintage Books, 1991. 280p.
ISBN 9780385116589
1. Male friendship 2. Man-woman relationships 3. 1970s 4. Mainstream fiction

LC 90050186

Surrounded by family members and friends not appreciably unlike himself, a twenty-seven-year-old government worker longs to recapture his ex-lover Laura, who has recently returned to her husband, stepdaughter, and A-frame.

The **doctor's** house: a novel. Ann Beattie. Scribner, 2002. 279 p.
ISBN 9780743212649
1. Dysfunctional families 2. Psychic trauma 3. Family secrets 4. Obsession 5. Abusive men 6. Psychological fiction 7. Multiple perspectives 8. First person narratives

New York Times Notable Book, 2002

Reveals the story of Nina, a reclusive copyeditor who has become obsessed with her brother Andrew's sexual exploits and indiscretions, through the differing viewpoints of Nina, Andrew, and their mother.

★ **Picturing** Will. Ann Beattie. Random House, 1989. 230 p.
ISBN 9780394569871
1. Stepfathers 2. Child-rearing 3. Five-year-old boys 4. Single-parent families 5. Women photographers 6. Multiple perspectives

LC 89042781

A five-year-old, his photographer mother, and his prepetually unlucky, philandering father populate this novel about the trials and rewards of both being and raising a child.

"Beattie has almost as many narrative voices as characters in this book, yet the result is never confusing.... 'Picturing Will' would be admirable for its technique alone; what makes it Beattie's best novel is her new and fearless way with emotional complexity." —*Newsweek*

The **state** we're in: Maine stories. Ann Beattie. Scribner, 2015. X, 206 pages
ISBN 9781501107818
1. Coastal towns 2. Women 3. Maine 4. Short stories

An award-winning short story master presents a collection of linked tales that impart the diverse perspectives of women orbiting around a disaffected teen who is staying with relatives while attending summer school.

"Some pieces read like sketches with promising characters but little movement: a 77-year-old writer discusses poetry with an IRS agent, a doctor reminisces about her life in New York before moving north, an author interviews a local for a book about people who have negative effects on other people's lives. A full novel on Jocelyn might be more fulfilling, but Beattie clearly enjoys wandering around the neighborhood. An engaging collection of varied characters, if varying degrees of substance." —*Kirkus*

A **wonderful** stroke of luck: a novel. Ann Beattie. Viking, 2019. 274 pages
ISBN 9780525557340
1. Teacher-student relationships 2. Dishonesty 3. Men — Psychology 4. Former teachers 5. Personal conduct 6. New Hampshire 7. New York (State) 8. Psychological fiction 9. Literary fiction 10. First person narratives 11. Adult books for young adults

A man who attended a prestigious New England boarding school has his life turned upside down by the reappearance in his life of an enigmatic and brilliant but difficult former teacher that makes him question everything he knows.

"Obvious is one thing Beattie never is. Her elegantly sculpted tale is both wrenchingly sad and ultimately enigmatic: as usual." —*Kirkus*

Beatty, Paul

★ The **sellout**: a novel. Paul Beatty. Farrar, Straus and Giroux, 2015. 288 p.
ISBN 9780374260507
1. Racism 2. Segregation 3. Inner city 4. Race relations 5. African Americans 6. Los Angeles, California 7. Satirical fiction 8. Literary fiction 9. African American fiction
LC 2014027451
ALA Notable Book, 2016; National Book Critics Circle Award for Fiction, 2015; New York Times Notable Book, 2015; Man Booker Prize, 2016

In this satirical take on race, politics, and culture in the U.S, a young black man grows up determined to resegregate a portion of an inner city, aided by a former Little Rascals star who volunteers to be his slave. This illegal activity brings him to the attention of the Supreme Court, who must consider the ramifications of this (and other) race-related cases. Readers who can handle provocative language and racial stereotypes will appreciate the glee that African-American humorist Paul Beatty brings to his critique and questioning of black identity; others will find it incendiary.

"Beatty...creates a wicked satire that pokes fun at all that is sacred to life in the United States, from father-son dynamics right up to the Supreme Court. His story is full of the unexpected, resulting in absurd and hilarious drama." —*Library Journal*

Slumberland: a novel. Paul Beatty. Bloomsbury, 2008. 256 p.
ISBN 9781596912403
1. African Americans 2. African American men 3. Musicians 4. African Americans in Germany 5. Race relations 6. Berlin, Germany 7. 1980s 8. Picaresque fiction 9. African American fiction
LC 2007045049
Traveling to recently unified Berlin in search of a little-known avant-garde jazzman whom he believes to be a musical kindred spirit, disaffected Los Angeles DJ Darky encounters the dramatic local changes that have transpired after the tearing down of the Berlin Wall and ruminates on a range of cultural, social, and philosophical topics.

"Slumberland is laugh-out-loud funny in many places, and its wit and satire can be burning, regardless of where they are pointed: blackness or whiteness." —*Los Angeles Times Book Review*

Beauvoir, Simone de

★ The **Mandarins:** a novel. Simone de Beauvoir; translated by Leonard M. Friedman. Regnery Gateway, 1979. 610 p.
ISBN 9780895268983
1. Intellectual life 2. Interpersonal relations 3. Desire 4. Philosophy, Modern 5. Social conflict 6. Paris, France 7. France 8. 1940s 9. Translations 10. Love stories 11. Psychological fiction

Young French men and women interact in love and politics as they simultaneously create and react to the social, intellectual and political climate of post-war Paris

The **woman** destroyed. Simone de Beauvoir; translated from the French by Patrick O'Brian. Pantheon Books, 2013. 254 p.
ISBN 9780394711034
1. Literary fiction 2. Short stories 3. Translations
LC 69015496
Three women, all past their first youth, face unexpected crises.
Translation of La femme rompue.
Originally published: London : Collins, 1969.

Beck, Haylen

Here and gone. Haylen Beck. Crown, 2017. 287 p.
ISBN 9780451499578
1. Child custody 2. Abused women 3. Police corruption 4. Abusive men 5. Missing children 6. Arizona 7. Thrillers and suspense

Wrongly arrested after fleeing her abusive husband's home, a mother desperately fights corrupt authorities to recover her stolen children; while a man across the country hears the story on the news and identifies links to similar events in his own past.

Lost you. Haylen Beck. Crown Pub, 2019. 272 pages
ISBN 9781524759582
1. Single mothers 2. Kidnapping 3. Surrogate mothers 4. Surrogate motherhood — Psychological aspects 5. Infertility 6. Psychological suspense

After a closing elevator door separates them, a single mother on vacation with her son discovers he has been abducted by another woman who claims she is his mother in the new novel from the author of Here and Gone.

Beckerman, Hannah

If only I could tell you. Hannah Beckerman. William Morrow, 2019. 368 pages
ISBN 9780062952189
1. Sisters 2. Family secrets 3. Family relationships 4. Secrets 5. Families 6. Domestic fiction 7. Mainstream fiction 8. Multiple perspectives

A novel of mothers and daughters, the bonds of family and the secrets that can sometimes divide us yet also bring us together follows Audrey, who has been dealt more ups and downs than she can handle, as she searches for a way to fix her broken family.

Beckett, L. X.

Gamechanger. L. X. Beckett. Tor books, 2019. 572 pages; (The bounceback, 1)
ISBN 9781250165268
1. Women defense attorneys 2. Rebels 3. Electronic surveillance 4. Near future 5. Pariahs 6. Social science fiction

LC 2019948647

Rubi Whiting is a member of the Bounceback Generation, the first to be raised free of the troubles of the late-21st century. Now she works as a public defender to help troubled individuals with anti-social behavior. That's how she met Luciano Pox. But there's more to him than being a lightning rod for controversy. Rubi has to find out why the governments of the world want to bring Luce into custody, and why Luce is hell bent on stopping the recovery of the planet.

Beckett, Samuel

★ **Murphy**. Samuel Beckett. Grove/Atlantic, 2011. 170 pages
ISBN 9780802144454
1. Personal conduct 2. Social isolation 3. Men nurses 4. London, England 5. Dublin, Ireland 6. Literary fiction 7. Modern classics

LC 57006939

A poor Irishman, seeking his own identity, drifts through worsening stages of despair until his final disintegration.
Originally published: London : Routledge, 1938.

Begley, Louis

About Schmidt. Louis Begley. A. A. Knopf, 1996. 273 p. (Albert Schmidt novels, 1)
ISBN 9780679450337
1. Widowers 2. Alienation in men 3. May-December romances 4. Lawyers 5. Father and adult daughter 6. New York City 7. Psychological fiction 8. Literary fiction 9. Books to movies

LC 96-8244

Library Journal Best Books, 1996; National Book Critics Circle Award for Fiction finalist, 1996

Albert Schmidt, a retired WASP lawyer, copes with the boredom of retirement, the devastating loss of his wife, and his Ivy League daughter's new fiance, an ambitious, Jewish drone, until an unexpected new love brings the promise of a new life.

Belfer, Lauren

And after the fire: a novel. Lauren Belfer. Harper, 2016. 432 p.
ISBN 9780062428516
1. Bach, Johann Sebastian 2. Manuscript thefts 3. Family secrets 4. Americans in Germany 5. Manuscripts 6. Uncle and niece 7. Germany 8. 20th century 9. 21st century 10. Historical fiction 11. Parallel narratives

LC 2015038472

A tale inspired by historical events traces the experiences of two women, one European and one American, whose lives are transformed by a mysterious Johann Sebastian Bach choral masterpiece.

"Based on impressive research, this remarkable novel spans centuries and continents, touching finally on the Holocaust and serving as a paean to Bachs music while acknowledging the composers expressed hatred of Jews." —*Booklist*

Belfoure, Charles

The **Paris** architect: a novel. Charles Belfoure. Sourcebooks Landmark, 2013. 384 p.
ISBN 9781402284311
1. Architects 2. Hiding-places (Secret chambers, etc.) 3. Jews, French 4. Resistance to military occupation 5. World War II 6. France 7. Paris, France 8. Second World War era (1939-1945) 9. Historical fiction

LC 2013017034

In 1942 Paris, gifted architect Lucien Bernard accepts a commission that will bring him a great deal of money and maybe get him killed. But if he's clever enough, he'll avoid any trouble. All Lucien has to do is design a secret hiding place for a wealthy Jewish man, a space so invisible that even the most determined German officer won't find it. He sorely needs the money, and outwitting the Nazis who have occupied his beloved city is a challenge he can't resist. But when one of his hiding spaces fails horribly, and the problem of where to hide a Jew becomes personal, Lucien can no longer ignore what's at stake. The Paris Architect asks us to consider what we owe each other, and just how far we'll go to make things right.
Originally published: 2013.
Includes bibliographical references and index.

Bell, Darcey

Something she's not telling us. Darcey Bell. Harper360, 2020. 304 pages
ISBN 9780062953926
1. Mothers and daughters 2. Girlfriends 3. Child kidnapping victims 4. Obsession 5. Secrets 6. Manhattan, New York City 7. Psychological suspense

After her daughter is kidnapped, Charlotte suspects her brother's girlfriend, who seemed a little obsessed with the child, but all is not as it seems.

"Bell seamlessly shifts between the present and the past, exploring how Charlotte's secrets have influenced her. Fans who like surprises around every corner will be drawn to this intriguing tale." —*Publishers Weekly*

Bell, Lenora

For the duke's eyes only. Lenora Bell. Avon Books, 2018. 384 p. (School for dukes, 2)
ISBN 9780062692498
1. Women archaeologists 2. Dukes and duchesses 3. Intrigue 4. Belmont, Alva 5. Art thefts 6. Great Britain 7. Regency period (1811-1820) 8. Historical romances 9. Regency romances

Archaeologist Lady India Rochester, when a priceless relic is stolen from the British Museum, must team up with the Duke of Ravenwood, the man who dared to break her heart, to avoid an international disaster.

★ **How** the duke was won. Lenora Bell. Avon Books, 2016. 370 p. (Disgraceful dukes, 1)
ISBN 9780062397720
1. Dukes and duchesses 2. Mate selection 3. Reputation 4. Courtesans 5. Impostors 6. England 7. Great Britain 8. Regency period (1811-1820) 9. Regency romances 10. Historical romances
Romantic Times Reviewer's Choice Award, 2016

When she is offered a life-changing fortune to pose as her half-sister, Lady Dorothea, and win the Duke of Harland's proposal, Charlene Beckett, the unacknowledged daughter of an earl and a courtesan, falls for the duke and must decide if the promise of a new life is worth risking everything.

"Charlene is smart and tough and easily steals the show with her gutsy nonconformity." —*Library Journal*

One fine duke. Lenora Bell. Avon, 2019. 256 pages (School for dukes, 3)
ISBN 9780062913074
1. Dukes and duchesses 2. Independence in single women 3. Womanizers 4. Protectiveness in men 5. Brothers 6. Great Britain 7. Regency period (1811-1820) 8. Historical romances 9. Regency romances
This was supposed to be simple. Duke goes to London. Duke selects suitable bride. Love match? Not a chance. But when Drew meets Mina, she complicates everything. How can a lady armed with such beauty and brains fall for his irresponsible degenerate of a brother? Drew vows to save her from heartbreak and ruin, no matter the cost.

★ **What** a difference a duke makes. Lenora Bell. HarperCollins 2018. 384 p. (School for dukes, 1)
ISBN 9780062692481
1. Dukes and duchesses 2. Governesses 3. Single fathers 4. Twins 5. Interclass romance 6. Great Britain 7. Regency period (1811-1820) 8. 19th century 9. Historical romances 10. Regency romances
Hiring governess Miss Mari Perkins to keep his unruly twins in line, the Duke of Banksford finds himself drawn to this woman who is strictly off limits until she tempts him into breaking all his rules.

Bell, Shelly

At his mercy. Shelly Bell. Forever, 2017. 336 p. (Forbidden lovers novels, 1)
ISBN 9781455595976
1. Sexual dominance and submission 2. Women college students 3. College teachers 4. Victims of violent crimes 5. Teacher-student relationships 6. Erotic romances 7. Romantic suspense
LC 2017003017
After a night of no-strings attached passion, Isabella discovers that her new lover Tristan is also her professor.

For his pleasure. Shelly Bell. Grand Central Pub 2019. 384 pages (Forbidden lovers novels, 3)
ISBN 9781455596034
1. Former convicts 2. Parolees 3. Sexual dominance and submission 4. Women parole officers 5. Judicial error 6. Erotic romances 7. Romantic suspense
The only man she trusts is also the most dangerous.

Bell, Ted

Overkill: an Alex Hawke novel. Ted Bell. William Morrow, 2018. 544 p. (Alexander Hawke thrillers, 10)
ISBN 9780062684516
1. Spies 2. High technology weapons 3. Assassination 4. International intrigue 5. Intelligence service 6. Europe 7. Russia 8. Spy fiction 9. Adventure stories
LC 2017053351
Counterspy Alex Hawke goes all out to rescue his son and takes on Russian President Vladimir Putin in the bargain in the latest action-packed thriller in Ted Bell's New York Times bestselling series.

Belle, Kimberly

Dear wife. Kimberly Belle. Park Row, 2018. 352 pages
ISBN 9780778309147

1. Abused women 2. Missing women 3. New identities 4. Partner abuse 5. Detectives 6. Arkansas 7. Oklahoma 8. Psychological suspense 9. Multiple perspectives
A woman who has changed her identity to escape domestic abuse and a woman who has gone missing under suspicious circumstances find their lives connected in unexpected ways.

Bellefleur, Alexandria

Hang the moon. Alexandria Bellefleur. Avon Books, 2021. 320 p.
ISBN 9780063000841
1. Dating (Social customs) 2. Application software 3. Romantic love 4. Businesspeople 5. Determination in men 6. Seattle, Washington 7. Washington (State) 8. Romantic comedies 9. Contemporary romances
When his sister's best friend, on whom he has had a crush for years, comes to Seattle, dating app creator Brendon Lowell, taking cues from his favorite rom-coms, plans to woo her until he discovers that real love doesn't need to be a perfect as the movies.
"The rom-com re-creations give the plot some structure. Tropes including 'there's only one bed' and embarrassing moments like falling into a lake in formal clothes are used to great result—but the author doesn't let the gimmick overtake strong character development, and the writing feels fresh, never derivative." —*Kirkus*

Written in the stars. Alexandria Bellefleur. Avon Books, 2020. 384 p.
ISBN 9780063000803
1. Women actuaries 2. Women astrologers 3. Dating (Social customs) 4. Lesbians 5. Social media 6. Seattle, Washington 7. Washington (State) 8. Romantic comedies 9. LGBTQIA romances 10. Contemporary romances
Lambda Literary Award for Lesbian Romance, 2021; LibraryReads Favorites, 2020
A lighthearted romance inspired by Pride and Prejudice depicts the experiences of a free-spirited social media astrologer who agrees to a fake relationship with a no-nonsense actuary to appease their respective families.
"Fans of pop culture-inspired astrology sites will love the effortless and entertaining way the author weaves zodiac memes throughout the text. The stars align in this charming queer rom-com." —*Kirkus*

Belli, Kate

Deception by gaslight: a Gilded Gotham mystery. Kate Belli. Crooked Lane Books, 2020. 304 pages (Gilded Gotham mysteries, 1)
ISBN 9781643854649
1. Women amateur detectives 2. Women journalists 3. Journalists 4. Corruption 5. City life 6. New York City 7. Gilded Age (1865-1898) 8. Historical mysteries
Glittering Gilded-Age New York holds its lavish charms—and a litany of deadly sins—as intrepid reporter Genevieve Stewart uncovers a trail of corruption and murder.
"The riveting, carefully researched, well-plotted mystery introduces two well-developed characters, one determined to succeed despite her social position and the other determined on reform. Fans of Alyssa Maxwell's 'Gilded Newport' mysteries will appreciate the historical, social, and political aspects of this debut." —*Library Journal*

Bellow, Saul

★ The **adventures** of Augie March. Saul Bellow; with an introduction by Martin Amis. Knopf, 1995. Xxxvii, 616 p.
ISBN 9780679444602

1. Jewish Americans 2. Depressions 3. Eccentrics and eccentricities 4. Purpose in life 5. Man-woman relationships 6. Chicago, Illinois 7. Literary fiction 8. Coming-of-age stories 9. Picaresque fiction
National Book Award for Fiction, 1954
Refusing to submit to specialization, Augie March wanders from job to job, experiencing life in its fullness.
Includes bibliographical references (p. xxix).
Originally published: New York : Viking Press, 1953.

The **Bellarosa** connection. Saul Bellow. Penguin Books, 1989. 102 p.
ISBN 9780140126860
1. Rose, Billy 2. Hickok, Wild Bill 3. World War II — Jews 4. Righteous Gentiles in the Holocaust 5. Refugees, Jewish 6. Jewish Americans 7. Literary fiction 8. First person narratives
LC 89032936
"The end of 'The Bellarosa Connection' is abrupt, matter-of-fact, almost offbeat. It is a conclusion, perhaps, in which nothing is concluded,...but it is appropriate to the overall pitch and voice of this cannily resourceful entertainment." —*New York Times Book Review*

Dangling man. Saul Bellow. Vanguard 1944. 191 p.
ISBN 9780814900246
1. War — Moral and ethical aspects 2. Draft 3. Identity (Psychology) 4. Conformity 5. Young men 6. Diary novels 7. Literary fiction
Set during the second World War, Joseph quits his job and prepares for his induction into the army. However a series of mishaps cause a delay in his induction, resulting in a year of idleness Joseph is unprepared for. Seeing war all around him and having no way to cope Joseph expresses his thoughts into his diary.
"The book is an excellent document on the experience of the non-combatant in time of war. It is well written and never dull—in spite of the dismalness of the Chicago background and the undramatic character of the subject. It is also one of the most honest pieces of testimony on the psychology of a whole generation who have grown up during the depression and the war." —*The New Yorker*

The **dean's** December: a novel. Saul Bellow. Harper and Row, 1982. 312 p.
ISBN 9780060148492
1. Social problems 2. Mothers-in-law 3. Death 4. College deans 5. Husband and wife 6. Chicago, Illinois 7. Romania 8. Political fiction 9. Literary fiction
LC 80008705
Dean Corde is a man of position and authority at a Chicago university. He accompanies his wife to Bucharest where her mother lies dying in a state hospital. As he tries to help her grapple with an unfeeling bureaucracy, Corde is troubled: at home the centre is not holding firm, in Eastern Europe authority is cruel and dehumanising.

★ **Henderson** the rain king: a novel. Saul Bellow. Viking, 1959. 341 p.
ISBN 9780670366552
1. Self-discovery in men 2. Rain makers 3. Americans in Africa 4. Millionaires 5. Middle-aged men 6. Africa 7. Literary fiction 8. Satirical fiction 9. First person narratives
A story of a middle-aged American millionaire who, seeking a new, more rewarding life, descends upon an African tribe. Henderson's awesome feats of strength and his unbridled passion for life earns him the admiration of the tribe—but it is his gift for making rain that turns him from mere hero into messiah.

★ **Herzog**. Saul Bellow. Penguin Books, 1976. 341 p.
ISBN 9780380008698
1. Jewish American men 2. Intellectuals 3. College teachers 4. Alienation in men 5. Divorce 6. Chicago, Illinois 7. Literary fiction 8. Psychological fiction 9. Modern classics

National Book Award for Fiction, 1965
Moses E. Herzog suffers from the breakup of his second marriage, the general failure of his life, and the specter of growing up Jewish in the middle of the 20th century. He responds to his personal crisis by writing a series of letters never to be sent, examining his life and times and asking "the piercing questions."
Originally published: New York : Viking Press, 1964.

★ **Humboldt's** gift. Saul Bellow. Viking, 1975. 487 p.
ISBN 9780670386550
1. Authors, American 2. Best friends — Death 3. Divorce 4. Crushes in men 5. Mafia 6. Literary fiction 7. First person narratives 8. Modern classics
LC 75012595
Pulitzer Prize for Fiction, 1976
Charlie Citrine, suffering from steadily worsening troubles with women, career, and life in general, receives unexpected aid and comfort in the form of a belated bequest from his onetime friend and mentor, the poet Von Humboldt Fleisher.

More die of heartbreak. Saul Bellow. W. Morrow, 1987. 335 p.
ISBN 9780688069353
1. Sexuality 2. Uncle and nephew 3. Marital conflict 4. Botanists 5. Family relationships 6. Literary fiction
LC 87005770
Kenneth Trachtenberg, an expert in Russian history and literature, tries to protect his revered uncle Benn Crader, a world-renowned botanist, from a tangle of family relationships, greed, and the willfulness of the human heart.
"Bellow has always been as enthralled by crooks as by the higher realms of thought. His prose mixes soaring meditation with streetsmart wisecracks. The farcical collisions of ill-prepared idealists with hard-as-nails swindlers and connivers give 'More Die of Heartbreak' its juicy vivacity." —*Newsweek*

★ **Mr.** Sammler's planet. Saul Bellow. Penguin Books, 2004. Xxiv, 260 p.
ISBN 9780142437834
1. Jewish American men 2. Holocaust survivors 3. City life 4. Intellectuals 5. Senior men 6. New York City 7. 1960s 8. Psychological fiction 9. Literary fiction
National Book Award for Fiction, 1971
Mr Artur Sammler, a lecturer at Columbia University in 1960s New York City, is a "registrar of madness," a refined and civilized being caught among people crazy with the promises of the future (moon landings, endless possibilities). His Cyclopean gaze reflects on the degradations of city life while looking into the sufferings of the human soul.
Originally appeared in Atlantic monthly in a different form.
Originally published in book form: New York : Viking Press, 1970 .

Novels, 1944-1953. Saul Bellow. Library of America, 2003. 1029 p.
ISBN 9781931082389
1. Jewish Americans 2. Jewish American men 3. Depressions 4. Conformity 5. Identity (Psychology) 6. Literary fiction 7. Psychological fiction
LC 2003040144
Celebrates the fiftieth anniversary of "The Adventures of Augie March," and reflects the mid-twentieth-century's psychological turmoil from more inhibited times in a volume that also includes "The Victim" and "Dangling Man.

Ravelstein. Saul Bellow. Viking, 2000. 233 p.
ISBN 9780670841349

1. Friendship 2. People with AIDS 3. College teachers 4. Americans in France 5. Authors, American 6. Paris, France 7. Middle West 8. Literary fiction 9. Psychological fiction

LC 99056336

Booklist Editors' Choice, 2000; Library Journal Best Books, 2000; New York Times Notable Book, 2000

Encouraged by his friend, Chick, to write down his ideas about humankind, university professor Abe Ravelstein receives unexpected acclaim and bounty and invites Chick to join in his success, a situation that sparks a philosophical journey for both.

"This might, like the author's earlier works, be called a novel of ideas, but that is too bloodless a description of Bellow's signature accomplishment.... [It] brims with life, thanks to Chick's that is Bellow's comic observations on the passing scene." —*Time*

★ **Seize** the day. Saul Bellow; with an introduction by Cynthia Ozick. Penguin Books, 1996. Xxiv, 118 p.
ISBN 9780140189377
1. Middle-aged men 2. Self-esteem 3. Separation (Marital relations) 4. Father and adult son 5. Self-discovery in men 6. New York City 7. Psychological fiction 8. Literary fiction 9. Books to movies

LC 96145374

Fading charmer Tommy Wilhelm has reached his day of reckoning and is scared. In his forties, he still retains a boyish impetuousness that has brought him to the brink of chaos: he is separated from his wife and children; at odds with his vain, successful father; failed in his acting career; and in a financial mess. In the course of one climactic day he reviews his past mistakes and spiritual malaise, until a mysterious, philosophizing con man grants him a glorious, illuminating moment of truth and understanding and offers him one last hope.

"Seize the Day gives contemporary literature a story which will be explained, expounded, and argued, but about which a final reckoning can be made only after it ripples out in the imagination of the generations of readers to come. I suspect that it is one of the central stories of our day." —*The Nation*

Benaron, Naomi

Running the rift: a novel. Naomi Benaron. Algonquin Books of Chapel Hill, 2012. 365 p.
ISBN 9781616200428
1. Runners 2. Genocide 3. Fathers — Death 4. Fame 5. Athletes 6. Rwanda 7. 1990s 8. Political fiction 9. War stories 10. Coming-of-age stories 11. Adult books for young adults

LC 2011026349

Bellwether Prize for Fiction, 2010

Rwandan runner Jean Patrick Nkuba dreams of winning an Olympic gold medal and uniting his ethnically divided country, only to be driven from everyone he loves when the violence starts, after which he must find a way back to a better life.

Also published: Toronto : HarperCollins, 2012.

Bender, Aimee

The **butterfly** lampshade. Aimee Bender. Doubleday, 2020. 224 p.
ISBN 9780385534871
1. Psychic trauma 2. Memories 3. Mental illness 4. Identity (Psychology) 5. Childhood 6. Oregon 7. California 8. Magical realism 9. Literary fiction

LC 2020005930

Unable to explain bizarre phenomena that accompanied the most formative events of her youth, Francie reflects on how the perceptions of childhood can take on near-magical qualities that sometimes carry over into an adult world that fluctuates between realities.

"By the end, the book reveals itself as a meditation on memory, identity, and the sometimes-uncanny relationship between living beings and the inanimate world. A novel with rewards for patient and sympathetic readers." —*Kirkus*

Bender, Tony

The **last** ghost dancer. Tony Bender. Thomas Dunne Books, 2010. 256 p.
ISBN 9780312592301
1. Mechanics 2. Nostalgia 3. Spirituality 4. Lost love 5. Summer 6. Middle West 7. 1970s 8. Coming-of-age stories 9. Adult books for young adults

LC 2009047578

A prize-winning columnist presents the story of Midwest mechanic Bones, who remembers a 1970s summer when he worked at a west river town's solitary gas station while forging friendships, losing a love and making a life-changing spiritual discovery.

Benedetti, Mario

Springtime in a broken mirror. Mario Benedetti; translated by Nick Caistor. The New Press, 2018. 192 p.
ISBN 9781620974902
1. Political prisoners 2. Exiles 3. Father-separated families 4. Political persecution 5. Separated couples 6. Uruguay 7. Buenos Aires, Argentina 8. 1970s 9. Literary fiction 10. Political fiction 11. Translations

LC 2018049329

Santiago, a political prisoner in Uruguay, was jailed after a brutal military coup that saw many of his comrades flee elsewhere. Santiago, feeling trapped, can do nothing but write letters to his family, and try to stay sane. Far away, his nine-year-old daughter Beatrice wonders at the marvels of 1970s Buenos Aires, but her grandpa and mother—Santiago's beautiful, careworn wife, Graciela—struggle to adjust to a life in exile.

Originally published in Uruguay as Primavera con una esquina rota in 1982. First published in Great Britain by Penguin Random House UK, London, 2018.

Translated from the Spanish.

Benedict, Helen

Wolf season. Helen Benedict. Bellevue Literary Press, 2017. 288 p.
ISBN 9781942658306
1. Post-traumatic stress disorder 2. Psychic trauma 3. Family relationships 4. Iraq War, 2003-2011 5. Family and war 6. New York (State) 7. Mainstream fiction

LC 2017015974

The war comes home in a searingly compassionate story about the wounds inflicted on soldiers, refugees, and their families.

Benedict, Marie

★ **Lady** Clementine. Marie Benedict. Sourcebooks Landmark, 2020. 300 p.
ISBN 9781492666905
1. Churchill, Clementine 2. Prime ministers' spouses 3. Husband and wife 4. Ambition 5. Romantic love 6. Politicians 7. Great Britain 8. 20th century 9. Historical fiction 10. Biographical fiction

LC 2019010233

Traces Clementine Churchill's unflinching role in protecting the life and wartime agendas of her husband, Winston Churchill.

"Benedict's well-researched, illuminating account of a complex, intelligent woman will undoubtedly be enjoyed by fans of Melanie Benjamin and Nancy Horan." —*Booklist*

The **only** woman in the room. Marie Benedict. Sourcebooks Landmark, 2019. 288 p.

ISBN 9781492666868

1. Lamarr, Hedy 2. Women inventors 3. Women scientists 4. Jewish women 5. Actors and actresses 6. Nazism 7. Vienna, Austria 8. Hollywood, California 9. 20th century 10. Biographical fiction 11. Historical fiction

LC 2018009020

A beautiful woman escapes her Austrian arms-dealer husband to become Hollywood legend Hedy Lamarr while hiding a secret double life as a Jewish scientist and sharing vital information about the Third Reich.

"Benedict paints a shining portrait of a complicated woman who knows the astonishing power of her beauty but longs to be recognized for her sharp intellect. Readers will be enthralled." —*Publishers Weekly*

Benioff, David

City of thieves: a novel. David Benioff. Viking, 2008. 272 p.

ISBN 9780670018703

1. Quests 2. Stealing 3. Seventeen-year-old boys 4. Arrest 5. Hunger 6. St. Petersburg, Russia 7. Second World War era (1939-1945) 8. Biographical fiction 9. Coming-of-age stories 10. Historical fiction 11. Adult books for young adults

LC 2007042784

ALA Notable Book, 2009; Alex Award, 2009; Booklist Editors' Choice: Adult Books for Young Adults, 2008

When a dead German paratrooper lands in his street, Lev is caught looting the body and dragged to jail, fearing for his life. He shares his cell with the charismatic and grandiose Kolya, a handsome young soldier arrested on desertion charges. Instead of the standard bullet in the back of the head, Lev and Kolya are given a shot at saving their own lives by complying with an outrageous directive: secure a dozen eggs for a powerful colonel to use in his daughter's wedding cake. In a city cut off from all supplies and suffering unbelievable deprivation, Lev and Kolya embark on a hunt to find the impossible.

"In contrast to the piety of so many of today's historical novels, Benioff's book lets its characters inhabit the human condition in all of its sometimes compromised versatility. But it's never cavalier, because the author has done his research." —*New York Times*

This novel was based on memories of author Benioff's grandfather.

Benjamin, Ali

The **smash-up:** a novel. Ali Benjamin. Random House, 2021. 256 p.

ISBN 9780593229651

1. Husband and wife 2. Me Too Movement 3. Women social advocates 4. Middle-aged persons 5. Businesspeople 6. Berkshire Hills, Massachusetts 7. Massachusetts 8. 2010s 9. Domestic fiction 10. Adaptations, retellings, and spin-offs

LC 2020023010

Upended by his wife's newfound activism, a once-successful businessman begins questioning everything in the face of scandalous allegations and a naive houseguest.

"With satire and suspense, Benjamin handily encapsulates the incomprehension, sadness, and rage of the Trump era." —*Publishers Weekly*

Benjamin, Chloe

★ The **immortalists:** a novel. Chloe Benjamin. G. P. Putnam's Sons, 2018. 352 p.

ISBN 9780735213180

1. Siblings 2. Fortune-tellers 3. Fate and fatalism 4. Families 5. Faith 6. Family sagas 7. Literary fiction

LC 2016053641

Loan Stars Favourites, 2018; LibraryReads Favorites, 2018; Wisconsin Library Association Literary Award, 2019

Sneaking out to get readings from a traveling psychic reputed to be able to tell customers when they will die, four adolescent siblings from New York City's 1969 Lower East Side hide what they learn from each other before embarking on five decades of respective experiences shaped by their determination to control fate.

"Benjamin has created mesmerizing characters and richly suspenseful predicaments in this profound and glimmering novel of deaths ever-shocking inevitability and lifes wondrously persistent whirl of chance and destiny." —*Booklist*

Benjamin, Melanie

Alice I have been. Melanie Benjamin. Delacorte Press, 2010. 368 p.

ISBN 9780385344135

1. Hargreaves, Alice Pleasance Liddell 2. Muses (Persons) 3. Authors 4. Friendship 5. Man-woman relationships 6. England 7. Oxford, England 8. 19th century 9. Biographical fiction 10. Historical fiction 11. Love stories 12. Adult books for young adults

LC 2009035353

Alice Liddell Hargreaves's life has been a richly woven tapestry. As a young woman, wife, mother, and widow, she's experienced intense passion, great privilege, and greater tragedy. But as she nears her eighty-first birthday, she knows that, to the world around her, she is and will always be only "Alice." Her life was permanently dog-eared at one fateful moment in her tenth year, the golden summer day she urged a grown-up friend to write down one of his fanciful stories.

★ The **aviator's** wife: a novel. Melanie Benjamin. Delacorte Press, 2013. 416 p.

ISBN 9780345528674

1. Lindbergh, Anne Morrow 2. Independence in women 3. Self-discovery in women 4. Pilots 5. Husband and wife 6. Motherhood 7. United States 8. 20th century 9. Biographical fiction 10. Historical fiction 11. Literary fiction

LC 2012017014

A story inspired by the marriage between Charles and Anne Morrow Lindbergh traces the romance between a handsome young aviator and a shy ambassador's daughter whose relationship is marked by wild international acclaim, history-making flights and the world-shocking abduction of their child.

Benn, James R.

Billy Boyle: a World War Two mystery. James R. Benn. Soho Press, 2006. 304 p. (Billy Boyle World War II mysteries, 1)

ISBN 9781569474334

1. Resistance to military occupation 2. World War II 3. Sabotage — History 4. Soldiers 5. Police 6. London, England 7. Norway 8. Second World War era (1939-1945) 9. 1940s 10. Historical mysteries 11. Mysteries

LC 2006042300

"Benn provides historically accurate background and appealing characters, spices the narrative with romance and emotion, and ruminates about the consequences of actions, all in a suitably straightforward prose style. A solid addition to mystery collections." —*Library Journal*

★ The **red** horse: a Billy Boyle World War II mystery. James R. Benn. Soho Crime, 2020. 336 p. (Billy Boyle World War II mysteries, 15)
ISBN 9781641291002
1. Hospitals 2. Secrecy in government 3. Military police 4. Armed Forces — Officers 5. World War II 6. Great Britain 7. Second World War era (1939-1945) 8. Historical mysteries 9. First person narratives
LC 2020015482
Convalescing from respective health setbacks at a mysterious British hospital in the days following the Liberation of Paris, Billy and Kaz learn that the former's girlfriend and the latter's sister have been captured and transported to the Ravensbruck concentration camp.
"Benn maintains a high level of tension throughout, and his admirable but flawed lead will engage even first-time readers. This fair-play whodunit stands comparison with the best classic mysteries." —*Publishers Weekly*

Road of bones: a Billy Boyle World War II mystery. James R. Benn. Soho Crime, 2021. 312 pages (Billy Boyle World War II mysteries, 16)
ISBN 9781641292009
1. Intelligence service 2. Military police 3. Alliances 4. Americans in the Soviet Union 5. Fighter plane combat 6. Ukraine 7. Soviet Union 8. Second World War era (1939-1945) 9. Historical mysteries 10. First person narratives
LC 2021016213
In 1944, with tensions running high between American and Russian allies, Billy Boyle is sent to the USSR to investigate the murder of two intelligence agents, and, when the case quickly spirals out of control, he is aided a daring regiment of young Soviet women.
"Benn's ability to sustain his terrific premise while adding depth to his characters makes this long-running series a must for those who love WWII crime fiction." —*Booklist*

Bennett, Alan

★ The **uncommon** reader. Alan Bennett. Farrar, Straus and Giroux, 2007. 128 p.
ISBN 9780374280963
1. Elizabeth II, Queen of Great Britain, 1926- 2. Traveling libraries 3. Books and reading 4. Happiness in women 5. Libraries 6. Nobility 7. Great Britain 8. Humorous stories
LC 2007926975
Obliged to borrow a book when her corgis stray into a mobile library, the Queen discovers a passion for reading, setting the palace upon its head and causing the royal head of Great Britain to question her role in the monarchy.
"This modest but sturdy novella is a spoof of two ridiculous holdovers: the British monarchy and high literary values. The first Mr. Bennett deflates, without urgency; the second he defends, without urgency. True wit relaxes, the author argues implicitly; it never overexcites." —*New York Observer*

Bennett, Anna

First earl I see tonight. Anna Bennett. St Martins Press, 2018. 368 p. (Debutante diaries, 1)
ISBN 9781250199461
1. Jilted men 2. Marriage proposals 3. Aristocracy 4. Family estates 5. Money 6. Great Britain 7. Regency period (1811-1820) 8. Regency romances 9. Paul, the Apostle, Saint
To stop a blackmailer from revealing a secret that could ruin her family, Miss Fiona Hartley, in desperate need of a husband to access her huge dowry, proposes marriage to the infuriating Earl of Somerdale who gives her a run for her money.

Bennett, Bethany

West end earl. Bethany Bennett. Forever, 2021. 400 p. (Misfits of Mayfair, 2)
ISBN 9781538735701
1. Earls and countesses 2. Aristocracy 3. Disguises 4. Deception 5. Protectiveness in men 6. Great Britain 7. Regency period (1811-1820) 8. Regency romances 9. Historical romances
Living as a boy to escape an arranged marriage, Ophelia Hardwick, working as a steward for the Earl of Carlyle, finds her life—and heart—in danger when he discovers her secret.
"Bennett's spirited plot adds Shakespearean twists to the typical Regency fare, complete with humor, sensual love scenes, and pithy observations on gender roles and the social mores of the 1820s. Packed with disguises, debts, and debutantes, this delightful Regency does not disappoint." —*Publishers Weekly*

Bennett, Brit

The **mothers**. Brit Bennett. Riverhead Books, 2016. 272 p.
ISBN 9780399184512
1. Survivors of suicide victims 2. African American communities 3. Teenage pregnancy 4. Abortion 5. Religious communities 6. Southern California 7. Coming-of-age stories 8. Psychological fiction 9. Literary fiction
LibraryReads Favorites, 2016; Booklist Editors' Choice, 2016; RUSA Reading List Short List, 2017
In a contemporary black community, 17-year-old Nadia Turner mourns the suicide of her mother, leading her to take up with the local's pastor's son; but when she gets pregnant, the pregnancy and the subsequent cover-up will have an impact that goes far beyond their youth.
"Chapel provides further context and an extra layer to an already exquisitely developed story." —*Publishers Weekly*

★ The **vanishing** half. Brit Bennett. Riverhead Books, 2020. 343 pages
ISBN 9780525536291
1. Twin sisters 2. African American families 3. Passing (Identity) 4. Mothers and daughters 5. Life change events 6. Louisiana 7. Los Angeles, California 8. 20th century 9. Literary fiction 10. Historical fiction 11. African American fiction
LC 2020005358
ALA Notable Book, 2021; BCALA Literary Award for Fiction, 2021; LibraryReads Favorites, 2020; New York Times Notable Book, 2020; Shortlisted for The Women's Prize for Fiction, 2021
Twin sisters, inseparable as children, ultimately choose to live in two very different worlds, one black and one white.
"Effortlessly switching between the voices of Desiree, Stella, and their daughters, Bennett renders her characters and their struggles with great compassion, and explores the complicated state of mind that Stella finds herself in while passing as white." —*Publishers Weekly*

Bennett, Jenn

Bitter spirits. Jenn Bennett. Berkley, 2013. 336 p. (Roaring twenties, 1)
ISBN 9780425269572
1. Mediums 2. Bootleggers 3. Psychic ability 4. Ghosts 5. Curses 6. San Francisco, California 7. 1920s 8. Paranormal romances
Romantic Times Reviewer's Choice Award, 2014

Despite her star billing at Gris-Gris, Chinatown's notorious speakeasy, San Francisco spirit medium Aida Palmer's stage show is not an act—she really can conjure (or exorcise) supernatural entities. Her abilities attract the attention of Winter Magnusson (a.k.a. "the Viking Bootlegger"), who's been haunted by the ghost of a murdered prostitute ever since someone put a hex on him. Although Aida easily removes Winter's curse, she soon discovers that she's fallen under the spell of the mysterious man, who's burdened with as many secrets as Aida herself. Bitter Spirits boasts a richly detailed Prohibition-era setting, a supernaturally themed mystery, and complex, well-matched protagonists.

"The details of the Prohibition era are well researched but not intrusive, providing a solid and tangible backdrop for the developing romance and supernatural mystery." —*Publishers Weekly*

Bennett, Robert Jackson

Foundryside. Robert Jackson Bennett. Crown Publishing, 2018. 496 p. (The founders, 1)
ISBN 9781524760366
1. Women thieves 2. Power (Social sciences) 3. City life 4. Magic 5. Technology 6. Fantasy fiction
RUSA Reading List, 2019
A thief in a city controlled by industrialized magic joins forces with a rare honest police officer to stop an ancient evil ritual that endangers thousands of lives.

Shorefall. Robert Bennett Jackson. Del Rey Books, 2020. 512 pages (The founders, 2)
ISBN 9781524760380
1. Women thieves 2. Power (Social sciences) 3. City life 4. Magic 5. Technology 6. Fantasy fiction
A sequel to Foundryside finds Sancia and her allies fighting the city's robber barons before a legendary hierophant reappears and launches a campaign to destroy Tevanne.
"An expertly spun yarn by one of the best fantasy writers on the scene today." —*Kirkus*

Benton, Janet

Lilli de Jong: a novel. Janet Benton. Nan A. Talese / Doubleday, 2017. 335 p.
ISBN 9780385541459
1. Quaker women 2. Single mothers 3. Mother and child 4. Defiance 5. Scandals 6. Philadelphia, Pennsylvania 7. Pennsylvania 8. 1880s 9. Historical fiction
LC 2016012853
Library Journal Best Books, 2017
Banished from her Quaker home and teaching job after being abandoned by her lover, a pregnant woman gives birth at an institution for unwed mothers in 1883 Philadelphia and refuses to give the child up, braving moral condemnation and poverty in her resolve to support her baby.

Benz, Chanelle

★ The **gone** dead. Chanelle Benz. Ecco Press, 2019. 304 pages
ISBN 9780062490698
1. Inheritance and succession 2. Injustice 3. Fathers — Death 4. Race relations 5. African Americans 6. Mississippi 7. Southern States 8. Southern fiction 9. Literary fiction
New York Times Notable Book, 2019

Returning to her ramshackle home in the Mississippi Delta after 30 years, Billie James investigates the accident that killed her famous poet father as well as rumors that she went missing the day he died.

Berenson, Alex

The deceivers. Alex Berenson. G.P. Putnam's Sons, 2018. 432 p. (John Wells novels, 12)
ISBN 9780399176166
1. CIA agents 2. Intelligence service 3. International intrigue 4. Conspiracies 5. Terrorism — Prevention 6. Thrillers and suspense 7. Spy fiction
LC 2017037135
In the wake of a fatal incident in Dallas that may have been staged to look like a terrorist attack, former CIA agent John Wells is dispatched to Colombia to collect information from an old asset, a mission involving an audacious Russian plot that proves to be the most deadly of his career.

The faithful spy: a novel. Alex Berenson. Random House, 2006. 352 p. (John Wells novels, 1)
ISBN 9780345478993
1. Bin Laden, Osama 2. Undercover operations 3. Conversion to Islam 4. CIA agents 5. Men — Spiritual life 6. Intelligence officers 7. New York (State) 8. Thrillers and suspense 9. Spy fiction
LC 2005044689
Edgar Allan Poe Award for Best First Mystery Novel, 2007
John Wells, an undercover operative who has infiltrated al Qaeda, is trapped between his terrorist associates and the CIA, which no longer trusts his loyalty, when he becomes a prime suspect in two bombings in Los Angeles.
"If Mr. Berenson remains as much reporter as novelist at this point —a newspaper editor would tell him he had overstuffed his lead, and that he often tended to impart information that was all too well known—he still has an ingenious narrative to show for it. Uncertain times call for tough examinations, and The Faithful Spy doesn't back away." —*New York Times*

The prisoner. Alex Berenson. G.P. Putnam's Sons, 2017. 384 p. (John Wells novels, 11)
ISBN 9780399176159
1. Moles (Spies) 2. Undercover operations 3. CIA agents 4. Espionage 5. Intelligence service 6. Thrillers and suspense 7. Spy fiction
LC 2016041437
Forced to resume an old undercover identity as an al-Qaida jihadi to unmask a CIA mole, John Wells gets close to an ISIS prisoner in a secret Bulgarian prison, where he confronts the profoundly cruel and ambitious plans of increasingly formidable terrorist organizations.
"...Berenson delivers some surprises along the way, focusing in large part on two shockingly complex characters— the mole and an ISIS scientist creating a stash of sarin gas to be deployed in an attack designed to wipe out the CIAs brain trust. Another strong mix of finely tuned suspense and subtle character development." —*Booklist*

Berg, Elizabeth

The confession club: a novel. Elizabeth Berg. Random House, 2019. 272 p. (Mason novels, 3)
ISBN 9781984855176
1. Clubs 2. Female friendship 3. Secrets 4. Dinners and dining 5. Change (Psychology) 6. Missouri 7. Gentle reads 8. Relationship fiction
LC 2019007966
Invited to join a supper club where friends in their community support each other throughout private setbacks, two women enduring diffi-

cult relationships discover the power of friendship and sharing their secrets.

Night of miracles. Elizabeth Berg. Random House, 2018. 288 p. (Mason novels, 2)
ISBN 9780525509509
1. Baking 2. Senior women 3. Community life 4. Friendship 5. Small town life 6. Missouri 7. Gentle reads 8. Relationship fiction
A baking class instructor, her haunted assistant and a youth reeling from a family tragedy discover the power of community while navigating complicated choices and uncertain futures.
Sequel to: The Story of Arthur Truluv.

The **story** of Arthur Truluv: a novel. Elizabeth Berg. Random House, 2017. 192 p. (Mason novels, 1)
ISBN 9781400069903
1. Teenage girls 2. Widowers 3. Intergenerational friendship 4. Senior men 5. Interpersonal relations 6. Missouri 7. Coming-of-age stories 8. Gentle reads 9. Relationship fiction
LC 2016047564
Loan Stars Favourites, 2017; LibraryReads Favorites, 2017
Making daily visits to the grave of his beloved late wife, Arthur forges unexpected relationships with a nosy neighbor and a troubled teen who dubs him "Truluv" before the trio discovers healing and family together.
"Richly complex characters and clear prose. Redemptive without being maudlin, this story of two misfits lucky to have found one another will tug at readers heartstrings." —*Booklist*
Sequel: Night of Miracles.

Berg, Gretchen
The **operator**. Gretchen Berg. William Morrow & Co, 2020. 336 pages
ISBN 9780062917188
1. Telephone operators 2. Eavesdropping 3. Telephone calls 4. Gossiping and gossips 5. Secrets 6. Ohio 7. 1950s 8. Historical fiction
A 1950s Ohio switchboard operator who eavesdrops on her neighbors' conversations uncovers unexpected secrets when she decides to investigate a malicious rumor that threatens to upend her carefully ordered life.
"Berg's storytelling is warm, sympathetic, and witty." —*Kirkus*

Berger, Thomas
Being invisible: a novel. Thomas Berger. Little, Brown, 1987. 262 p.
ISBN 9780316091589
1. Unhappiness in men 2. Invisibility 3. Authors, American 4. Single men 5. Advertising copywriters 6. Satirical fiction
LC 86020897
"There is much in 'Being Invisible' to celebratethe pleasures of invention, humor, surprise, of Mr. Berger's enraged, unforgiving view. That so much of his vision seems neither freakish nor admonitory but rather, oddly tonic, says something about the era in which we live.... It is a sign of the times that we feel such affection for Thomas Berger's dogged, cranky courage, and for the denizens of his unwelcoming and chaotic corner of the fictional world." —*New York Times Book Review*

★ **Neighbors:** a novel. Thomas Berger. Delacorte Press/S. Lawrence, 1980. 275p.
ISBN 9780440065562
1. New neighbors 2. Feuds 3. Rudeness 4. Family relationships 5. Fathers and daughters 6. Psychological fiction 7. Books to movies
LC 79020307

"Berger quickly conditions the reader to expect the unexpected but manages to be consistently surprising nevertheless, introducing new twists and outrages that not even the most warped spectator could have foreseen. The novel adopts a formal, almost fussy style to convey lunacy, as if Berger were describing low deeds to a maiden aunt.... [The book] is not at all interested in being socially redeeming, and those who read books to gain warm feelings or philosophic nuggets will come away from this one empty-handed and probably angry.... What Berger has produced is a tour de force." —*Time*

Bergman, Megan Mayhew
Almost famous women: stories. Megan Mayhew Bergman. Scribner, 2015. 236 p. : Illustration
ISBN 9781476786568
1. Fame 2. Women 3. Women celebrities 4. Socialites 5. Women artists 6. Biographical fiction 7. Short stories
This collection of short stories depicts the forgotten lives of women who almost achieved fame and notoriety, including Lord Byron's illegitimate daughter, Oscar Wilde's niece and Edna St. Vincent Milay's sister.
"The author has infused her characters with passion and yearning; they are so lifelike we feel we know them... Writing with brilliant cadence and economy, Bergman is an impressionist who uses her brilliant palette to illuminate facets of the lives of these brave and creative lesser-known strivers." —*Library Journal*

Bergstrom, Heather Brittain
Steal the north: a novel. Heather Brittain Bergstrom. Viking, 2014. 320 p.
ISBN 9780670786183
1. Single-parent families 2. Faith healing 3. Young women 4. Infertility 5. Aunt and niece 6. Mainstream fiction 7. Coming-of-age stories 8. Multiple perspectives 9. Adult books for young adults
LC 2013036976
Sent by her fundamentalist mother to help an estranged sister participate in a faith healing ceremony, sheltered 16-year-old Emmy feels instant ties to her sister's eastern Washington home and falls in love with a Native American boy against the apprehensions of her family.

Berkowitz, Ira
Old flame: a Jackson Steeg novel. Ira Berkowitz. Three Rivers Press, 2008. 304 p. (Jackson Steeg mysteries, 2)
ISBN 9780307408624
1. Former police 2. Gangsters 3. Violence 4. Murder 5. Former wives 6. New York City 7. Hardboiled fiction 8. Mysteries
LC 2008005177
Former NYPD homicide detective Jackson Steeg is finding his retirement anything but peaceful when his ex-wife's new beau is beaten to death outside a trendy restaurant in a killing that may have links to corruption in the awarding of city construction contracts, an old friend is in debt to a vicious Israeli mobster, and a mob war is threatening to erupt.

Berlin, Lucia
★ **Evening** in paradise: more stories. Lucia Berlin. Farrar, Straus and Giroux, 2018. 256 p.
ISBN 9780374279486
1. Human nature 2. Interpersonal relations 3. Family relationships 4. Texas 5. Chile 6. Short stories
LC 2018002535
Library Journal Best Books, 2018

A follow up to the award-winning A Manual for Cleaning Women features previously uncompiled selections from the late author's remaining story collection.

"Following the posthumous collection A Manual for Cleaning Women, which received major attention, here is a selection of Berlin's remaining stories proving that she should have been better known." —*Library Journal*

★ A **manual** for cleaning women: selected stories. Lucia Berlin; edited by Stephen Emerson. Farrar, Straus and Giroux, 2015. 403 p.
ISBN 9780374202392
1. Family relationships 2. Interpersonal relations 3. Southwest (United States) 4. Short stories
LC 2014047119
New York Times Notable Book, 2015; Kirkus Prize for Fiction finalist, 2015

Taking place in the American Southwest, an anthology of short stories, celebrating the author's trademark blend of humor and melancholy, finds miracles in everyday life and uncovers moments of grace in cafeterias, laundromats, homes of the upper class and hotel dining rooms.

"As characters recur and settings and predicaments vary, Berlin unflinchingly strips bare casual and catastrophic cruelty and injustice.... An essential collection of jazzy, jolting, incisive, wryly funny, and keenly compassionate, virtuoso tales." —*Booklist*

Berne, Lisa
You may kiss the bride. Lisa Berne. Avon Books, 2017. 373 p. (Penhallow dynasty, 1)
ISBN 9780062451781
1. Rich men 2. Mate selection 3. Women marriage resisters 4. Orphans 5. Poor women 6. England 7. Great Britain 8. Regency period (1811-1820) 9. Regency romances 10. Historical romances

Searching for a biddable bride who can produce an heir and then live separate lives as generations before him, wealthy and arrogant Gabriel Penhallow sets his sights on Livia Stuart who, after provoking him into a kiss, challenges him at every turn and refuses to become his wife.

"Author Berne offers a masterful Regency debut that explores pride and prejudices with a tone that seems much less modern than that of many recent historical releases and two main characters who epitomize traditional Regency sensibilities as they sort through what they want and how to get it. Livia becomes the sun shining in on a stuffy, wounded family whose initial dread at the thought of her joining them transforms into happiness as she turns out to be their salvation. A sheer delight." —*Kirkus*

Bernhard, Emilia
The **books** of the dead. Emilia Bernhard. Crooked Lane Books, 2019. 309 pages : Illustration (Death in Paris mysteries, 2)
ISBN 9781643851570
1. Women amateur detectives 2. Expatriates 3. Married women 4. Libraries 5. Undercover operations 6. Paris, France 7. Cozy mysteries

Parisian summers are for strolls in the park...and solving a murder—or two.

Bernhard, Thomas
Frost: a novel. Thomas Bernhard; translated from the German by Michael Hofmann. Knopf, 2006. 352 p.
ISBN 9781400040667
1. Young men 2. Medical students 3. Senior men 4. Brothers 5. Painters 6. Austria 7. Diary novels 8. Translations 9. First person narratives
LC 2006040886

At the behest of his surgical mentor, a young Austrian medical student poses as a law student to journey to a remote mining town in order to observe Strauch, an aging painter and brother of his mentor, without letting Strauch know his true occupation, and becomes caught up in the lives of the mad artist and a colorful assortment of local characters.

"A student's increasingly erratic dispatches over 27 days comprise this obsessive first novel by Bernhard.... Bernhard's glorious talent for bleak existential monologues is second only to Beckett's, and seems to have sprung up fully mature in his mesmerizing debut." —*Publishers Weekly*
Originally published: Frankfurt am Main : Insel-Verlag, 1963.

★ The **loser**. Thomas Bernhard; translated from the German by Jack Dawson; afterword by Mark M. Anderson. A. A. Knopf, 1991. 189 pages
ISBN 9780394572390
1. Gould, Glenn 2. Pianists 3. Philosophers 4. Autobiographical fiction 5. Translations
LC 90045942
Bernhard's imaginary account of a friendship with the pianist Glenn Gould explores the soul of the artist and the world of isolation, solitude, and obsession that often accompanies genius
Translation of: Der Untergeher (1983).

Wittgenstein's nephew: a friendship. Thomas Bernhard; translated from the German by David McLintock. Knopf, 1989. 99, [1] p.
ISBN 9780394563763
1. Bernhard, Thomas 2. Authors 3. Philosophers 4. Germany 5. Austria 6. Biographical fiction
LC 88045317
"The narrator muses on genius, sickness, madness, and death in the world and wonders why Wittgenstein succumbs while he survives. The translation is excellent." —*Choice*
Translation of: Wittgensteins Neffe.

★ **Woodcutters**. Thomas Bernhard; translated from the German by David McLintock. A. A. Knopf, 1987. 181 p.
ISBN 9780394551524
1. Dinners and dining 2. Vienna, Austria 3. Satirical fiction 4. Translations
LC 87045123
"Mr. Bernhard's portrait of a society in dissolution has a Scandinavian darkness reminiscent of Ibsen and Strindberg, but it is filtered through a minimalist prose of obsessive repetition and ever so slight modulations." —*New York Times Book Review*
Translation of Holzfallen.

Berry, Connie
A **legacy** of murder. Connie Berry. Crooked Lane Books, 2019. 327 pages; (Kate Hamilton mystery, 2)
ISBN 9781643851549
1. Women amateur detectives 2. Antique dealers 3. Christmas 4. Widows 5. Americans in Great Britain 6. England 7. Cozy mysteries 8. Holiday mysteries

American antique dealer Kate Hamilton's Christmastime jaunt to a charming English village leads to an investigation of a missing ruby...and a chain of murders.

Berry, Steve
★ The **bishop's** pawn. Steve Berry. Minotaur Books, 2018. 340 p. (Cotton Malone novels, 13)
ISBN 9781250140227

1. King, Martin Luther, Jr., 1929-1968 2. Assassination 3. Conspiracies 4. Political intrigue 5. Secret societies 6. Politicians 7. Political thrillers

LC 2017044458

Former Justice Department agent Cotton Malone uncovers a disturbing link between a case from his past and the assassination of Martin Luther King, Jr. that risks innocent lives and threatens the legacy of the Civil Rights movement's iconic martyr

The **lost** order. Steve Berry. Minotaur, 2017. 493 p. (Cotton Malone novels, 12)

ISBN 9781250056252

1. Treasure troves 2. Secret societies 3. Treasure hunters 4. Political intrigue 5. Politicians 6. Political thrillers

Library Journal Best Books, 2017; Romantic Times Reviewer's Choice Award, 2017

When rival factions of a dangerous clandestine organization begin a race to find billions in stolen treasure hidden by their progenitors, Justice Department agent Cotton Malone finds the case complicated by his unsuspected ties to the organization and the political schemes of an unscrupulous politician.

"The fusion of contemporary and historical adventure makes this a page-turner of the highest order." —*Publishers Weekly*

★ The **Malta** exchange: a novel. Steve Berry. Minotaur Books, 2019. 400 p. (Cotton Malone novels, 14)

ISBN 9781250140265

1. Secret societies 2. Intelligence service 3. Secrecy in government 4. Popes — Elections 5. Letters 6. Italy 7. Vatican City 8. Political thrillers

LC 2018050884

Former Justice Department operative Cotton Malone races to Italy to secure a history-changing document with ties to a 900-year-old organization that would manipulate the selection of the next pope.

★ The **Templar** legacy: a novel of suspense. Steve Berry. Ballantine Books, 2006. 496 p. (Cotton Malone novels, 1)

ISBN 9780345476159

1. Booksellers 2. Treasure hunting 3. Conspiracies 4. Secrets 5. Monasticism and religious orders for men 6. France 7. Rennes-le-Chateau, France 8. Thrillers and suspense

LC 2005053566

Cotton Malone, a former covert U.S. Justice Department operative, and his ex-supervisor Stephanie Nelle, follow a labyrinthine trail of danger, treachery, high-level intrigue, and overwhelming ambition across Europe on a quest that leads them to the enigmatic secrets of the Knights Templar.

Sequel: The Alexandria link.

★ The **Warsaw** protocol. Steve Berry. Minotaur Books, 2020. 400 p. (Cotton Malone novels, 15)

ISBN 9781250140302

1. Power (Social sciences) 2. International intrigue 3. Christian relics 4. Intelligence service 5. Stealing 6. Warsaw, Poland 7. Poland 8. Political thrillers

LC 2019043232

Investigating the thefts of the seven Arma Christi relics from their international sanctuaries, former Justice Department agent Cotton Malone learns that the relics are being demanded by a blackmailer in possession of incriminating evidence against the president of Poland.

Berry, Wendell

Jayber Crow: a novel. Wendell Berry. Counterpoint, 2000. 363 p; (Port William series)

ISBN 9781582430294

1. Unrequited love 2. Farm life 3. Small town life 4. Rural families 5. Barbers 6. Kentucky 7. Domestic fiction 8. Literary fiction 9. Gentle reads

LC 35889

Booklist Editors' Choice, 2000

In a new novel set in a small-town "Heaven," the rural Kentucky farmer-philosopher returns to his fictional Port William to explore themes of love, suffering, and joy.

"The richly portrayed community unfolds delicately and surely, with the human dramas of its inhabitants revealed from Jayber's perspective. A moving, lyrical work on a small canvas." —*Library Journal*

The life story of Jayber Crow, barber, of the Port William Membership, as written by himself—Cover.

★ **That** distant land: the collected stories of Wendell Berry. Wendell Berry. Shoemaker & Hoard; 2004. 440 p. (Port William series)

ISBN 9781593760274

1. Rural families 2. Farmers 3. Families 4. Small town life 5. Rural life 6. Kentucky 7. Short stories 8. Domestic fiction 9. Literary fiction

LC 2003025213

"Set in a small Kentucky farming village, this collection of Berry's Port William stories illuminates the evolution of rural American life over the course of the 20th century. In 23 stories, Berry chronicles Port William from the 1880s to the 1980s, evoking the connectedness of the small town's denizens to each other and to the land." —*Publishers Weekly*

Contains all of the "Port William membership" short stories and arranges them by year of story's setting.

Twenty-three short stories.

Betts, Doris

Souls raised from the dead: a novel. Doris Betts. Knopf 1994. 339 p.

ISBN 9780679426219

1. Families 2. Fathers and daughters 3. Children — Death 4. Southern States 5. Domestic fiction

LC 93030900

ALA Notable Book, 1995

Members of a Southern family, a young girl, her state trooper father, two sets of grandparents, her runaway mother, and their neighbors and friends struggle to cope with the child's incurable disease.

Beukes, Lauren

Afterland. Lauren Beukes. Mulholland Books, 2020. 400 p.

ISBN 9780316267830

1. Epidemics 2. Escapes 3. Men — Extinction 4. Near future 5. Mothers and sons 6. Johannesburg, South Africa 7. United States 8. Thrillers and suspense 9. Dystopian fiction

Fleeing west to find a safe haven in a world vastly transformed by a pandemic that has killed nearly all men, a mother disguises her son as a girl to escape dangerous adversaries, including her own sister.

"Beukes is a gifted storyteller who makes it thrillingly easy for readers to fall under her spell as she weaves a hypnotic vision of a fractured world without men. A propulsive and all-too-timely near-future thriller." —*Kirkus*

Broken monsters. Lauren Beukes. Mulholland Books, 2014. 288 p.

ISBN 9780316216821

1. Women detectives 2. Psychopaths 3. City life 4. Dead 5. Murder 6. Detroit, Michigan 7. Thrillers and suspense

RUSA Reading List, 2015

Detective Gabriella Versado investigates after disturbing displays that fuse the bodies of murder victims with those of animals are uncovered in abandoned Detroit buildings.

"Beukes avoids predictability by leading readers to doubt their interpretations of motives and events, blending detection and atmospheric horror to court both hard-boiled mystery and literary-horror fans." —*Booklist*

The **shining** girls. Lauren Beukes. Mulholland Books / Little, Brown and Company, 2013. 400 p.
ISBN 9780316216852
1. Time travel 2. Serial murderers 3. Young women 4. Murder 5. Psychopaths 6. Chicago, Illinois 7. Arthur, King 8. Multiple perspectives

LC 2013003018

Romantic Times Reviewer's Choice Award, 2013
In 1931, Harper Curtis discovers a time travel portal located in an otherwise undistinguished Chicago bungalow. Written on the walls of the house are the names of "shining girls" whose bright young lives he must extinguish. Thus does Curtis become a time-traveling serial killer, singling out his victims by giving them small gifts and then returning, years later, to eviscerate them. However, not everything goes as planned during his multi-decade murder spree. One victim, Kirby Mazrachi, survives his attack and, with the help of a journalist, begins to investigate her mysterious assailant.

A tremendous work of suspense fiction. What's more, it's a fabulous piece of both time-travel and serial killer fiction, using the intersection of those two themes to explore questions of free will, predestination, and causality in a mind-melting, heart-pounding mashup that delivers on its promise." Boing Boing

Slipping: stories, essays, & other writing. Lauren Beukes. Tachyon Publications, 2016. 288 pages
ISBN 9781616962401
1. Near future 2. Life on other planets 3. Johannesburg, South Africa 4. Science fiction 5. Literary fiction 6. Short stories

A satiric retrospective collection of fiction and nonfiction writings includes pieces about a Punk Lolita fighter pilot who rescues Tokyo from a marauding art installation, corporate recruits who harvest poisonous plants on an inhospitable planet and an inquisitive teen ghost who disrupts an architect's life.

"Whether they're set in modern-day Johannesburg or on a planet circling a distant star, these powerful, beautifully written stories are always about today and the darkness of the human soul." —*Publishers Weekly*

Zoo city. Lauren Beukes. Angry Robot, 2011. 413 p.
ISBN 9780857660558
1. Slums 2. Missing persons investigation 3. Magic (Occultism) 4. Criminals 5. Music industry and trade 6. Johannesburg, South Africa 7. Urban fantasy 8. Afrofantasy 9. First person narratives
Arthur C. Clarke Award, 2011
Zinzi searches for a missing pop star in the ghettos of Johannesburg, which is inhabited by former criminals marked by an animal companion for their crimes, while a shaman crime lord sets out to kill anyone who tries to find her.
Originally published: Auckland Park, S.A. : Jacana Media, 2010.

Beverley, Jo
My lady notorious. Jo Beverley. Avon Books 1993. 380 p; (Malloren chronicles, 1)
ISBN 9780380767854
1. Impersonators 2. Kidnapping 3. Disguises 4. Malloren family (Fictitious characters) 5. Women impostors 6. London, England 7. Great Britain 8. Georgian era (1714-1837) 9. 1760s 10. Georgian romances 11. Canadian fiction 12. Historical romances
RITA Award for Best Long Historical, 1994

Lady Chastity Ware dresses as a highwayman to help her widowed sister and her infant niece escape a treacherous pursuer, and she accosts the first stagecoach she sees—capturing, among others, a handsome aristocrat eager for adventure
Later published under the title Lady notorious: Caerphilly, South Wales : Everlyn, 2009.

Tempting fortune. Jo Beverley. Zebra Books 1995. 444 p. (Malloren chronicles, 2)
ISBN 9781420120554
1. Rogues 2. Deception 3. Malloren family (Fictitious characters) 4. Single women 5. Half-brothers 6. London, England 7. Great Britain 8. Georgian era (1714-1837) 9. 1760s 10. Georgian romances 11. Canadian fiction 12. Historical romances
Romantic Times Reviewers Choice Award, 1995
Portia St. Claire's brother's gambling has put her in the unenviable plight of having her virtue auctioned off in London's most notorious brothel. Bryght Malloren, who believes he has meet Portia before, is unable to leave her to such a cruel fate and turns the private wager into a public game of seduction, one that confirms his reputation as a shameless rake and keeps all of London society breathless with anticipation.

Beverly, William
Dodgers: a novel. Bill Beverly. Crown Publishers, 2016. 290 pages
ISBN 9781101903735
1. Gang members 2. Teenage boys 3. Self-discovery 4. Witnesses 5. Purpose in life 6. Wisconsin 7. Coming-of-age stories 8. Crime fiction 9. Adult books for young adults
Booklist Editors' Choice: Adult Books for Young Adults, 2016; Gold Dagger Award for Best Crime Novel of the Year, 2016; Los Angeles Times Book Prize for Mystery or Thriller, 2016; New Blood Dagger Award, 2016; School Library Journal Best Books: Best Adult Books 4 Teens, 2016
East, a Los Angeles gang member who works as a lookout, is only 16 when he's sent to Wisconsin as part of a group to kill a witness hiding out there. Along with three other teens (including his younger brother), he must traverse an entirely alien America, where as young black men they stand out far more than they did in L.A. Observant and cautious, East is a complex character, one who is good at what he does but not entirely hardened by his life.
"Highly recommended for fans of Richard Price, this is a searing novel about crime, race, and coming-of-age, with characters who live, breathe, and bleed." —*Booklist*

Beyda, Emily
The **body** double. Emily Beyda. Doubleday, 2020. 304 pages
ISBN 9780385545273
1. Impersonation 2. Celebrities 3. Deception 4. Nervous breakdown 5. Life change events 6. Los Angeles, California 7. Psychological suspense
A dark, glittering debut novel, The Body Double is the suspenseful story of a young woman who is recruited by a stranger to give up her old life and identity to impersonate a reclusive Hollywood star.
"This auspicious debut will get under the reader's skin and stay there." —*Publishers Weekly*

Bezmozgis, David
The **betrayers:** a novel. David Bezmozgis. Little, Brown and Company, 2014. 225 p.
ISBN 9780316284332

1. Politicians 2. Betrayal 3. Consequences 4. Jewish men 5. Family relationships 6. Israel 7. Soviet Union 8. Literary fiction 9. Psychological suspense 10. Canadian fiction
Edward Lewis Wallant Award, 2014; National Jewish Book Award for Fiction, 2014; Shortlisted for the Giller Prize, 2014

Escaping his political opponents in a Crimean resort town, disgraced Israeli politician Baruch Kotler runs into a former friend who had him sent to the gulag 40 years prior and must reconcile with his betrayers and his own poor choices.

"Though the action is fixed largely in one location, Bezmozgis's novel feels vast, its pages heavy with the complicated debts we owe one another, which are impossible to leave behind." —*Publishers Weekly*

Bhuvaneswar, Chaya

White dancing elephants: stories. Chaya Bhuvaneswar. Dzanc Books, 2018. 208 pages
ISBN 9781945814617
1. Love 2. Extramarital affairs 3. Grief 4. Women 5. South Asians 6. Short stories 7. Mainstream fiction
LC 2018005798

In these remarkable stories, Chaya Bhuvaneswar spotlights diverse women of color—cunning, bold, and resolute—facing sexual harassment and racial violence, and occasionally inflicting that violence on each other. Winner of the 2017 Dzanc Short Story Collection Prize, White Dancing Elephants marks the emergence of a new and original voice in fiction and explores feminist, queer, religious, and immigrant stories with precision, drama, and compassion.

"Bhuvaneswar's compelling stories portray diverse characters grappling with shifts in their lives, the complications of their actions, and the impacts of others. Conflicts play out in various circumstances—strained relationships, failing health, regret—and characters are often poised at crossroads." —*Booklist*

Bialosky, Jill

House under snow. Jill Bialosky. Harcourt, 2002. 242 p.
ISBN 9780151006854
1. Mothers and daughters 2. Children of widows 3. Grief 4. Fathers — Death 5. Fiances 6. Ohio 7. Psychological fiction
LC 2001007435

Anna Crane reflects back on her childhood in Ohio during the 1960s and 1970s with two sisters and a self-destructive mother as she recalls her first love affair with a troubled boy and her betrayal by two important figures in her life.

"Bialosky's haunting first novel aches with the sensitivity of a soulful girl who is discovering love, sexuality, and the pain of unsurpassable betrayal." —*Booklist*

The **prize**: a novel. Jill Bialosky. Counterpoint Press, 2015. 325 p.
ISBN 9781619025707
1. Artists 2. Greed 3. Ethical problems 4. Marital conflict 5. Art dealers 6. Psychological fiction
LC 2015023052

Determined not to let ambition, money and power corrode the sanctuary of his domestic and private life, Edward Darby, a partner at an esteemed gallery, finds himself unhinged by his ideals when he is betrayed by one artist and another very different artist awakens his heart and stirs up secrets from his past.

"This fluently sophisticated and exquisitely pleasurable novel is radiant with precise and sensuous descriptions and intricately laced with discerning and affecting insights into the passion and business of art and the meaning and struggles of marriage." —*Booklist*

Bieker, Chelsea Jean

Godshot: a novel. Chelsea Bieker. Catapult, 2020. 325 pages
ISBN 9781948226486
1. Cults 2. Droughts 3. Mother-deserted children 4. Mothers and daughters 5. Teenage girls — Psychology 6. California 7. Literary fiction 8. Coming-of-age stories 9. Adult books for young adults
LC 2019946561

Enduring appalling treatment in a Central Valley agricultural community under the orders of an unscrupulous cult leader, Lacey receives support by women friends who help her search for the mother who abandoned her.

"Delving into patriarchal religious zealotry, Bieker's excellent debut plants themes seen in Margaret Atwood's The Handmaid's Tale into a realistic California setting that will linger with readers." —*Publishers Weekly*

Bijan, Donia

The **last** days of Cafe Leila. Donia Bijan. Algonquin Books of Chapel Hill, 2017. 304 pages
ISBN 9781616205850
1. Marital conflict 2. Family businesses 3. Homecomings 4. Iranian American women 5. Restaurants 6. Tehran, Iran 7. Iran 8. Literary fiction 9. Coming-of-age stories 10. Multiple perspectives

A neighborhood cafe in Tehran is at the center of this powerful and transporting story of love, family, friendship, and homecoming told against the backdrop of Iran's rich, yet tragic, history.

"Bijan has crafted a richly layered story of the deep connections within a family, resilient links that survive tragedy and distance." —*Booklist*

Bilal, Parker

The **burning** gates: a Makana investigation. Parker Bilal. Bloomsbury, 2015. 384 p. (Makana mysteries, 4)
ISBN 9781620408865
1. Art thefts 2. War criminals 3. Smuggling 4. Violence 5. Private investigators 6. Cairo, Egypt 7. Egypt 8. Mysteries

When a priceless painting goes missing from Baghdad during the U.S. invasion, private investigator Makana tracks it down to the black market of Cairo in what may be his most dangerous case yet.

The **ghost** runner. Parker Bilal. Bloomsbury, 2014. 352 p. (Makana mysteries, 3)
ISBN 9781620403402
1. Extramarital affairs 2. Honor killings 3. Terrorists 4. Violence 5. Private investigators 6. Cairo, Egypt 7. Egypt 8. Mysteries
Library Journal Best Books 2014

Sudanese investigator Makana travels into the desert heart of Egypt to solve a series of brutal murders and explore the shifting sands of the past.

Bilenchi, Romano

★ The **chill**. Romano Bilenchi; translated from the Italian by Ann Goldstein. Europa, 2009. 120 p.
ISBN 9781933372907
1. Bereavement 2. Rumor 3. Teenage boys 4. Grandfathers 5. Death 6. Tuscany, Italy 7. 1920s 8. Translations 9. Psychological fiction 10. Adult books for young adults

A teenage boy becomes increasingly removed from his friends and family after the death of his beloved grandfather, as he becomes more aware of his own mortality and sexuality.

"Most coming-of-age novels illuminate the tumultuous inner world of adolescence; Bilenchi's reveals the brutality of the adulthood that surrounds it." —*The New Yorker*

Translated from the Italian.

Billingham, Mark

★ **Their** little secret. Mark Billingham. Atlantic Monthly Press, 2019. 400 pages (Tom Thorne novels, 16)

ISBN 9780802147363

1. Detectives 2. Suicide investigation 3. Women detectives 4. Swindlers and swindling 5. Murder 6. England 7. Psychological suspense 8. Thrillers and suspense

LC 2019009800

Suspecting foul play while investigating a metro station suicide, Tom Thorne enlists Nicola Tanner to help investigate the activities of a murderous con man before linking the case to a bludgeoning death.

"The twisted plot unfolds gradually, with a maximum of suspense. Billingham never strains credulity in this thoughtful page-turner." —*Publishers Weekly*

Billingsley, ReShonda Tate

A **little** bit of karma: a novel. ReShonda Tate Billingsley. Gallery Books, 2020. 288 p.

ISBN 9781439183588

1. Radio personalities 2. Married people 3. African Americans 4. Radio programs 5. Rich people 6. Romantic suspense 7. African American fiction

LC 2020019993

Three years into their marriage, a couple who host a wildly successful call-in radio show find the romance dying after a combination of infidelity, deceit, and the mysterious death of the other woman.

"With just the right amount of emotional drive, Billingsley's latest is an expert foray into romantic suspense that will impress her longtime fans and earn her plenty of new ones." —*Publishers Weekly*

★ The **secret** she kept. ReShonda Tate Billingsley. Gallery Books, 2012. 355 pages

ISBN 9781451639650

1. Women with mental illnesses 2. Pregnancy 3. Schizophrenia 4. Businesspeople 5. Man-woman relationships 6. Contemporary romances 7. African American fiction 8. Multicultural romances

LC 2011053379

Romantic Times Reviewer's Choice Award, 2012

When his wife Tia begins acting erratically after their wedding, and her pregnancy brings about signs of further instability, executive Lance Kingston urges her to seek medical attention and wonders how he can help her if she refuses to help herself.

Binchy, Maeve

Circle of friends. Maeve Binchy. Delacorte Press, 1991. 565 p.

ISBN 9780385301497

1. Betrayal 2. Women 3. Friendship 4. Loyalty 5. Villages 6. Ireland 7. Dublin, Ireland 8. Relationship fiction 9. Books to movies 10. Gentle reads

LC 90003944

Portrays the uneasy association between beautiful, greedy jet-setter Nan Mahon and Benny Hogan and Eve Malone, best friends from a small Irish village

"There is nothing fancy about 'Circle of Friends.' There is no torrid sex, no profound philosophy. There are no stunning metaphors. There is just a wonderfully absorbing story about people worth caring about. And that is a rare pleasure." —*New York Times Book Review*

Firefly summer. Maeve Binchy. Delacorte Press, 1988. 601 p.

ISBN 9780440500179

1. Americans in Ireland 2. Small town life 3. Women with disabilities 4. Rich men 5. Neighbors 6. Ireland 7. 1960s 8. Relationship fiction 9. Gentle reads

LC 88005412

"The careful examination of life and culture in a small Irish town during the 1960s will appeal to many readers." —*Booklist*

★ **Whitethorn** Woods. Maeve Binchy. Knopf, 2007. 352 p.

ISBN 9780307265784

1. Sacred space 2. Miracles 3. Wishing and wishes 4. Small towns 5. Small town life 6. Ireland 7. Relationship fiction 8. Multiple perspectives 9. First person narratives

The town of Rossmore is divided when a new motorway threatens Whitethorn Woods and St. Ann's Well where generations have come to make wishes.

"Story by story, voice by voice, Binchy builds the fictional community of Rossmore so that, by the end of the novel, we know Rossmores inhabitants better than our own neighbours .... Few contemporary novelists match Binchys gift for giving us the world through her characters' eyes." —*The Globe and Mail (Toronto)*

Originally published: Toronto : McArthur, 2006.

Binder, L. Annette

The **vanishing** sky. L. Annette Binder. Bloomsbury Publishing, 2020. 288 p.

ISBN 9781635574678

1. World War II 2. Families 3. World War II veterans 4. Soldiers 5. Teenage boys 6. Germany 7. Second World War era (1939-1945) 8. Historical fiction 9. Domestic fiction

LC 2019046034

A mother in a rural 1945 German community protects her traumatized soldier son from her husband's escalating nationalism, while her younger son flees the Hitler Youth to embark on a perilous journey home.

"The future is unimaginable, Binder writes—and yet, somehow, those who are left will find a way to carry on. A masterful story of war, horror, and love." —*Kirkus*

Binet, Laurent

Civilizations. Laurent Binet; translated from the French by Sam Taylor. Farrar, Straus and Giroux, 2021. 288 p.

ISBN 9780374600815

1. Rulers 2. Incas 3. Warriors 4. Vikings 5. Colonialism 6. Literary fiction 7. Alternate histories

LC 2021015723

The last Inca emperor, Atahualpa, uses Columbus' captured ships to sail to Europe where he discovers the Inquisition, capitalism, the printing press and warring monarchies.

"The novel is arranged in an unusual style, with the narrative told through supposed selections of historic sagas, chronicles, and letters. It is easy to picture this work as the readings for a history class in this mirrored world." —*Booklist*

Originally published in French in 2019 by Editions Grasset et Fasquelle, France, as Civilizations.

★ **HHhH**. Laurent Binet; translated from the French by Sam Taylor. Farrar, Straus and Giroux, 2012. 336 p.

ISBN 9780374169916

1. Heydrich, Reinhard 2. Assassins 3. Resistance to government 4. Resistance to military occupation 5. World War II 6. Nazis 7. Czechoslovakia 8. Second World War era (1939-1945) 9. Historical fiction 10. Metafiction 11. Translations

LC 2011046063

New York Times Notable Book, 2012; National Book Critics Circle Award for Fiction finalist, 2012

Imagines the story of two Czechoslovakian partisans responsible for assassinating the "Butcher of Prague" Reinhard Heydrich, traces their escape from the Nazis and recruitment by the British secret service.

Originally published: Paris : Grasset & Fasquelle, 2010.

Birch, Carol

Jamrach's menagerie. Carol Birch. Doubleday, 2011. 295 p.
ISBN 9780385534406

1. Poor boys 2. Palme, Olof 3. Ocean travel — History 4. Human behavior 5. Seafaring life 6. England 7. Great Britain 8. Victorian era (1837-1901) 9. Historical fiction 10. Adventure stories 11. Adult books for young adults

Booklist Editors' Choice: Adult Books for Young Adults, 2011;
School Library Journal Best Books: Best Adult Books 4 Teens, 2011;
Shortlisted for the Man Booker Prize, 2011

Recruited by a famed importer of exotic animals to capture a fabled dragon during a three-year whaling expedition, former street urchin Jaffy Brown and his friend and rival, Tim, successfully capture the beast only to find themselves targeted by superstitious sailors.

"Jaffy's experience could well move the reader as profoundly as it changed the narrator." —*Kirkus*

First published in London : Canongate, 2011.

Bird, Sarah

Daughter of a daughter of a queen. Sarah Bird. St. Martin's Press, 2018. 398 p.

ISBN 9781250193162

1. Williams, Cathay, 1844-approximately 1893 2. Women soldiers 3. African American women 4. Male impersonators 5. Courage in women 6. Determination in women 7. United States 8. American Westward Expansion (1803-1899) 9. Biographical fiction 10. Historical fiction 11. War stories

LC 2018010894

LibraryReads Favorites, 2018

In 1864 Missouri, newly freed slave Cathay Williams makes the difficult decision to fight in the Army disguised as a man with the Buffalo Soldiers.

★ The **flamenco** academy: a novel. Sarah Bird. Knopf, 2006. 381 p.
ISBN 9781400040841

1. Grief in families 2. Young women 3. Flamenco dancers 4. Seventeen-year-old girls 5. Czech American women 6. New Mexico 7. Albuquerque, New Mexico 8. Melville, Herman

LC 2005044418

In Albuquerque, New Mexico, two young women—shy teenager Cyndi Rae Hrncir and Didi Steinberg, the school bad girl—become entranced by young flamenco guitarist Tomas Montenegro and by the hypnotic storytelling of Dona Carlota, Tomas's great aunt, and decide to dedicate themselves to the disciplines and demands of the university's Flamenco Academy.

"In the monolithic culture of flamenco, Bird finds a remarkable landscape for transforming the inaccessible whims of an obsessive, lonely teenager into the epic saga of self-acceptance, loyalty and love to which no one is immune." —*Austin Chronicle*

The **gap** year: a novel. Sarah Bird. Alfred A. Knopf, 2011. 320 p.
ISBN 9780307592798

1. Mother and teenager 2. Letting go (Psychology) 3. Parenting — Psychological aspects 4. Former husbands 5. Teenage girls — Interpersonal relations 6. Domestic fiction 7. Humorous stories

LC 2010051495

Library Journal Best Books, 2011

Setting aside her rebellious dreams for the sake of her teenage daughter, lactation consultant Cam Lightsey is horrified when her daughter falls in love with a football player, turns secretive and loses interest in college, a situation that is further complicated by a reappearance by Cam's ex, a member of a celebrity cult.

"The title alludes to the break in a mother-daughter relationship during the daughter's senior year of high school. Single mom Camilla feels her daughter, Aubrey, beginning to pull away from her, especially after Aubrey embarks on a romance with classmate Tyler. Add in the sudden reappearance of Aubrey's father, who years ago left the family to join a cultlike religion (it might sound familiar to fans of certain Hollywood types), and gaps in this family open and close at blinding speed. The narrative alternates between Camilla's current perspective over the course of a few days and Aubrey's retelling of the previous year. This technique makes for a compelling read and builds to a satisfying and surprisingly tender conclusion." —*Library Journal*

The **Yokota** Officers Club: a novel. Sarah Bird. Knopf, 2001. 367 p.
ISBN 9780375412141

1. Military dependents 2. Dysfunctional families 3. Missing persons 4. Eighteen-year-olds 5. Sisters 6. Japan 7. Okinawa 8. 1960s 9. Psychological fiction 10. Domestic fiction 11. Adult books for young adults

LC 2001089763

Booklist Editors' Choice: Adult Books for Young Adults, 2001

While living at Kadena Air Base on Okinawa, Bernadette "Bernie" Root, hoping to escape her oddball military family, takes a job as second banana to a third-rate comedian touring Japanese military bases, only to be reunited with her family's former maid, Fumiko, and uncovers a painful family secret.

Bisson, Terry

Any day now. Terry Bisson. Overlook Press, 2012. 256 p.
ISBN 9781590207093

1. Beat culture 2. Radicalism 3. Communes 4. Bombings 5. New York City 6. Kentucky 7. 1960s 8. Alternate histories 9. Coming-of-age stories

A tale inspired by the final days of the Beats is set against a backdrop of an emerging radicalized culture of the 1960s throughout the Eastern United States, in a coming-of-age story that serves as a transcendent commentary on the nation as experienced by members of an isolated hippie commune under threat of revolution.

Bittner, Rosanne

Logan's lady. Rosanne Bittner. Sourcebooks Casablanca, 2019. 352 pages

ISBN 9781492673491

1. Aristocracy 2. Bounty hunters 3. British in the United States 4. Independence in women 5. Revenge 6. The West (United States) 7. American Westward Expansion (1803-1899) 8. Western romances 9. Historical romances

Embarking on an adventure to America after reading penny dreadfuls, wealthy Englishwoman Lady Elizabeth arrives excited to start a new life, only to be swindled by a gentlemanly thief, forcing her to place her trust in a dangerous man who hunts wanted men.

Bivald, Katarina

The **readers** of Broken Wheel recommend. Katarina Bivald; translated from the Swedish by Alice Menzies. Landmark, 2016. 400 p.

ISBN 9781492623441

1. Small town life 2. Friendship 3. Books and reading 4. Life change events 5. Women booksellers 6. Iowa 7. Relationship fiction 8. Epistolary novels 9. Translations

LibraryReads Favorites, 2016

Broken Wheel, Iowa, has never seen anyone like Sara, who traveled all the way from Sweden just to meet her pen pal, Amy. When she arrives, however, she finds that Amy's funeral has just ended. Luckily, the townspeople are happy to look after their bewildered tourist—even if they don't understand her peculiar need for books. Marooned in a farm town that's almost beyond repair, Sara starts a bookstore in honor of her friend's memory. All she wants is to share the books she loves with the citizens of Broken Wheel and to convince them that reading is one of the great joys of life. But she makes some unconventional choices that could force a lot of secrets into the open and change things for everyone in town. Reminiscent of The Guernsey Literary and Potato Peel Pie Society, this is a warm, witty book about friendship, stories, and love.

Originally published: Sweden: Forum, 2013.

Originally published as Lasarna i Broken Wheel rekommenderar in 2013 in Sweden by Bokförlaget Forum. This edition issued based on the hardcover edition published in 2015 in the United Kingdom by Chatto & Windus, an imprint of Random House—Title page verso. Translation from the Swedish.

Black, Benjamin

★ **Christine** Falls: a novel. Benjamin Black. H. Holt, 2007. 352 p. (Quirke mysteries, 1)

ISBN 9780805081527

1. Religious cover-ups 2. Murder investigation 3. Upper class 4. Catholics 5. Pathologists 6. Dublin, Ireland 7. Boston, Massachusetts 8. 1950s 9. Psychological fiction 10. Mysteries

LC 2006043581

Returning to the morgue where he works after an office party, Dublin pathologist Quirke stumbles across a body that should not have been there, as well as his brother-in-law, pediatrician Malachy Griffin, altering a file to cover up the corpse's cause of death.

"As the story moves from Ireland to Boston, the push and pull of the novel's dual existence as literary thriller becomes almost as absorbing as the plot; the tension between the two halves of that troublesome equation regularly rippling the book's surface.... At its best, the prose here is every bit as acute as one would expect from John Banville, even Banville in disguise—the baroque flourishes are held in check.., but the stern elegance remains, and its marriage to a thriller's momentum can have startling results." —*Times Literary Supplement*

John Banville writing as Benjamin Black.

Originally published: London: Picador, 2006.

TV tie-in.

★ The **secret** guests: a novel. Benjamin Black. Henry Holt and Company, 2020. 304 p.

ISBN 9781250133014

1. Elizabeth II, Queen of Great Britain, 1926- 2. Princesses 3. British in Ireland 4. Secrecy 5. Intelligence service 6. Intrigue 7. Ireland 8. London (England) 9. Second World War era (1939-1945) 10. Historical thrillers

LC 2019015981

The secret World War II relocation of the princesses Elizabeth and Margaret to an old estate in Ireland becomes subject to the devastations of the Blitz, the resentments of grieving townspeople and suspicions about the girls' true identities.

"Black's lucid prose is the perfect foil for tangled politics, old hatreds, unsolved crimes, the threat to Irish neutrality, and the possibility of new alliances that seethe underneath." —*Library Journal*

Wolf on a string: a novel. Benjamin Black. Henry Holt & Co, 2017. 320 p.

ISBN 9781627795173

1. Murder investigation 2. Courts and courtiers 3. Political intrigue 4. Rulers 5. Murder 6. Prague, Czech Republic 7. 16th century 8. Historical mysteries

LC 2016029320

Discovering the body of a young woman after arriving in 1599 Prague, an ambitious young scholar and alchemist becomes entangled in the machinations of several ruthless courtiers before attracting the attention of an emperor who would retain the power of the throne.

Black, Cara

Murder in the Bastille. Cara Black. Soho Press, 2003. 276 p; (Aimee Leduc investigations, 4)

ISBN 9781569473245

1. Mistaken identity 2. Women who are blind 3. Antique dealers 4. Women private investigators 5. Leduc, Aimee (Fictitious character) 6. 1990s 7. Mysteries

LC 2002042625

When a woman wearing an identical jacket to Aimee Leduc's leaves her cell phone on a restaurant table, Aimee follows her to return it, only to be attacked and left blind, discovering that the other woman had been murdered.

Murder in the Marais. Cara Black. Soho, 1999. 354 p. (Aimee Leduc investigations, 1)

ISBN 9781569471593

1. Neo-Nazism 2. Little people 3. Jewish women 4. Leduc, Aimee (Fictitious character) 5. Women private investigators 6. Paris, France 7. France 8. Mysteries

LC 98052070

Detective Aimee Leduc goes undercover inside a neo-Nazi group to ferret out a killer in the old Jewish quarter of Paris.

Murder in the rue de Paradis: an Aimee Leduc investigation. Cara Black. Soho Crime, 2008. 312 p. (Aimee Leduc investigations, 8)

ISBN 9781569474747

1. Loss (Psychology) 2. Assassins 3. Kurds 4. Leduc, Aimee (Fictitious character) 5. Women private investigators 6. Paris, France 7. 1990s 8. Mysteries

LC 2007009194

Thrilled that her former lover Yves Robert has returned to Paris, Aimee Leduc accepts his marriage proposal, but her happiness is short-lived after he is found dead in a doorway in the Rue de Paradis.

★ **Three** hours in Paris. Cara Black. Soho Press, 2020. 360 pages

ISBN 9781641290418

1. Hitler, Adolf 2. Women assassins 3. Spies 4. Attempted assassination 5. Shooting 6. Anti-Nazi movement 7. France 8. Paris, France 9. Second World War era (1939-1945) 10. Historical thrillers 11. Spy fiction 12. Historical fiction

LC 2019038373

A suspenseful historical tale based on the mystery of Hitler's abrupt departure from newly occupied 1940 Paris follows the mission of a British intelligence markswoman who, while trying to assassinate the Fuhrer, discovers that she has been set up.

Black, Lisa

Let justice descend. Lisa Black. Kensington Pub Corp, 2019. 320 pages (Maggie Gardiner and Jack Renner novels, 5)
ISBN 9781496722355
1. Women forensic psychologists 2. Vigilantes 3. Politicians 4. Elections 5. Detectives 6. Ohio 7. Cleveland, Ohio 8. Thrillers and suspense

In a taut, brilliantly twisted new thriller from bestselling author Lisa Black, forensics expert Maggie Gardiner and Cleveland detective Jack Renner investigate the bizarre murder of a senator with secrets to hide.

Suffer the children. Lisa Black. Kensington, 2018. 320 p. (Maggie Gardiner and Jack Renner novels, 4)
ISBN 9781496713575
1. Women forensic psychologists 2. Vigilantes 3. Juvenile detention 4. Children — Death 5. Problem youth 6. Cleveland, Ohio 7. Ohio 8. Thrillers and suspense

Cleveland forensics expert Maggie Gardiner and her partner, Jack Renner, investigate after two young people turn up dead at a secure facility for juvenile offenders.

That darkness. Lisa Black. Kensington, 2016. 336 p. (Maggie Gardiner and Jack Renner novels, 1)
ISBN 9781496701886
1. Forensic scientists 2. Women murder victims 3. Women forensic scientists 4. Murder investigation 5. Cleveland, Ohio 6. Thrillers and suspense

In this tour de force of psychological suspense, bestselling author Lisa Black draws from her experience as a forensic investigator to create two of the most fascinating characters in crime fiction: a killer with a unique sense of justice and a woman in a lifelong relationship with death.

Black, Saul

Anything for you. Saul Black. St. Martin's Press, 2019. 352 p. (Valerie Hart novels, 3)
ISBN 9781250199911
1. Women detectives 2. Married women 3. Murder victims 4. Secrets 5. Flashbacks 6. San Francisco, California 7. Thrillers and suspense 8. Multiple perspectives
LC 2019024267

When her next-door neighbor, a San Francisco prosecutor, is brutally murdered, a woman is forced to reckon with her murky past to help the victim's family and the police uncover clues about the killer's identity

★ The **killing** lessons. Saul Black. St. Martin's Press, 2015. 416 p. (Valerie Hart novels, 1)
ISBN 9781250057341
1. Women detectives 2. Children of murder victims 3. Psychopaths 4. Serial murderers 5. Serial murder investigation 6. Colorado 7. San Francisco, California 8. Thrillers and suspense
LC 2015017805

RUSA Reading List Short List, 2016

In this menacing, unnerving novel, which combines nail-biting suspense with all the details of a police procedural, a damaged female detective offers the best hope for justice for the victims of a sadistic killer—and for preventing more cruel, violent deaths at his hands. Or are there two monsters? Detective Valerie Hart, battling personal and professional problems, shares narrative duties with both a potential victim desperate to live and the killer himself. Fair warning though—this series debut is graphic and bloody.

"Aficionados may fault Black for allowing the police at least one major oversight, but most readers will likely be too engrossed or happily grossed out to do anything but whip through the pages." —*Kirkus*

★ **Lovemurder**. Saul Black. St. Martin's Press, 2017. 320 p. (Valerie Hart novels, 2)
ISBN 9781250057419
1. Women detectives 2. Psychopaths 3. Crime scenes 4. Children of murder victims 5. Serial murderers 6. Colorado 7. San Francisco, California 8. Thrillers and suspense
LC 2017006878

Investigating an eerily familiar crime scene before discovering a note written in the style of a killer she helped put away six years earlier, San Francisco Homicide detective Valerie Hart is forced to ask the imprisoned psychopath to help capture a copycat.

Blackmore, R. D.

Lorna Doone: a romance of Exmoor. R.D. Blackmore; edited with an introduction by Sally Shuttleworth. Oxford University Press, 2008. Xxix, 680 p.
ISBN 9780199537594
1. Monmouth's Rebellion, 1685 2. Outlaws 3. Heroes and heroines 4. Families of murder victims 5. Kidnapping 6. Exmoor, England 7. Great Britain 8. Stuart period (1603-1714) 9. Historical fiction 10. Love stories 11. Classics
LC 88037446

In seventeenth-century England, John Ridd returns home to Exmoor and forms a forbidden but enduring friendship with Lorna Doone, the granddaughter of the head of the outlaw Doone clan responsible for the death of John's father.

First published in 1869.

Includes bibliographical references.

Blackstock, Terri

Catching Christmas. Terri Blackstock. Thomas Nelson, 2018. 293 pages
ISBN 9780310351726
1. Women lawyers 2. Taxicab drivers 3. Christmas 4. Grandmothers 5. Dementia 6. Holiday romances 7. Christian romances

New York Times bestselling author Terri Blackstock tells the rich and heartwarming story of a cab driver, a young attorney, and the elderly woman who will stop at nothing to give her granddaughter one special gift for Christmas.

"Quirky characters and a wholesome plot will please inspirational readers looking for a heartwarming Christmas story." —*Publishers Weekly*

Smoke screen. Terri Blackstock. Thomas Nelson Inc, 2019. 352 p.
ISBN 9780310332602
1. Fire fighters 2. Fathers 3. Murder 4. Homecomings 5. Former lovers 6. Christian suspense
LC Bl2019025328

Reluctantly returning to his hometown when his father is released from prison amid murderous accusations, a smoke jumper reconnects with his former love, who is fighting a painful custody battle.

Blackwell, Juliet

Letters from Paris. Juliet Blackwell. Berkley, 2016. 384 p.
ISBN 9780451473707

1. Sculpture 2. Family secrets 3. Grandmother and granddaughter 4. Man-woman relationships 5. Voyages and travels 6. Paris, France 7. Chicago, Illinois 8. Mainstream fiction

"After surviving the accident that took her mother's life, Claire Broussard worked hard to escape her small Louisiana hometown. At her grandmother's urging, Claire travels to Paris to track down the centuries old mask-making atelier where the sculpture, known only as {34L'inconnue{34—or the Unknown Woman—was created. With the help of a passionate sculptor, Claire discovers a cache of letters that offer insight into the life of the Belle Epoque woman immortalized in the work of art." —Provided by the publisher.

"Blackwell seamlessly incorporates details about art, cast making, and the City of Light. She also skillfully weaves in chapters from the point of view of Sabine, the poor country girl behind the mystery, who became the muse of an abusive sculptor after a life of poverty. Blackwell does a fantastic job of incorporating recurring themes in this story; for instance, having survived drowning as a child, Claire is wary of rivers, while Sabine is rumored to have met her end in the Seine. Blackwell especially stuns in the aftermath of the main story by unleashing a twist that is both a complete surprise and a point that expertly ties everything together." —Publishers Weekly

Blake, Audrey

The **girl** in his shadow: a novel. Audrey Blake. Sourcebooks Landmark, 2021. 378 pages
ISBN 9781728228723
1. Orphans 2. Surgeons 3. Physicians 4. Women physicians 5. Sexism 6. London, England 7. Victorian era (1837-1901) 8. 19th century 9. Historical fiction
LC 2020049684

When Dr. Croft takes in orphan Eleanor Beady, he doesn't realize that he's gained an apprentice. Raised amidst Croft's experiments, "Nora" becomes his most trusted assistant-an unthinkable and unlawful pursuit for a woman. Nora helps Croft's groundbreaking research and his clinic gain recognition, and she finds she doesn't mind working in the background, as long as she can continue to hone her skills. But the arrival of a new surgical resident threatens to undo all that Nora has strived for. Dr. Daniel Gibson is too proper to be trusted, too skilled to dismiss, and too smart to be fooled for long. He expects Nora to change her clothes before dinner and spend her evenings perfecting her needlework, not her sutures. Though Nora knows it's best not to reveal her expansive knowledge of human anatomy, she isn't going to give up the work that fascinates and fulfills her-no matter what it costs her.

"Eye-opening and revealing of the mindset of the time period, the book's relationships and drama of discovery shape the pacing and tone." —Booklist

Blake, James Carlos

The **house** of Wolfe. James Carlos Blake. The Mysterious Press, 2015. 248 p. (Wolfe family novels, 3)
ISBN 9780802122469
1. Ransom 2. Kidnapping 3. Gangs 4. Organized crime 5. Mexican-American Border Region 6. Thrillers and suspense 7. Crime fiction

Kidnapped by a small-time gangster with big-time aspirations in Mexico City, Jessie Wolfe knows that her own family of notorious outlaws will come to her rescue.

"Blake excels at ensemble pieces and plays to his strengths here. Like a director with a small army of camera teams at his disposal, he wheels from one location to another, racking the focus with such intensity that, at any moment, the story you're in feels like the only story there is until he cuts away again. A hard-edged, fast-moving thriller that will hold your attention hostage—good luck getting away." —Booklist

Blake, Sarah

The **guest** book: a novel. Sarah Blake. Flatiron Books, 2019. 486 pages
ISBN 9781250110251
1. Rich families 2. Islands 3. Antisemitism 4. Racism 5. Family estates 6. Maine 7. New York City 8. 1930s 9. 1950s 10. Family sagas 11. Historical fiction

The bereaved matriarch of a powerful early-20th-century American family makes a fateful decision that reverberates throughout two subsequent generations further impacted by racism, reversed circumstances and disturbing revelations.

"This novel sets out to be more than a juicy family saga—it aims to depict the moral evolution of a part of American society. Its convincing characters and muscular narrative succeed on both counts." —Kirkus

The **postmistress**. Sarah Blake. Amy Einhorn Books/G.P. Putnam's Sons, 2010. 336 p.
ISBN 9780399156199
1. Postmasters 2. World War II 3. Radio 4. War 5. Secrets 6. London, England 7. Second World War era (1939-1945) 8. Historical fiction
LC 2009024532

The stories of a small Cape Cod postmistress and an American radio reporter stationed in London collide on the eve of the United States's entrance into World War II, a meeting that is shaped by a broken promise to deliver a letter.

"Iris, an ungainly 40-year-old with unflattering red lipstick and a crush on the town mechanic, ultimately proves to be the heart of Blake's novel." —Entertainment Weekly

Blakemore, A. K.

The **Manningtree** Witches. A. K. Blakemore. Catapult, 2021. N/A
ISBN 9781646220649
1. English Civil War, 1642-1649 2. Single women 3. Suspicion 4. Witchcraft 5. Malicious accusation 6. England 7. Great Britain 8. Stuart period (1603-1714) 9. Maria Nikolaevna 10. Historical fiction 11. Multiple perspectives

In a small English town in 1643, Rebecca West, when a newcomer who identifies himself as the Witchfinder General arrives, to save the women of Manningtree, must quell the rumors of covens, pacts and bodily wants to save them all from themselves.

"On the whole, Blakemore's ambitious and fresh take on the era will delight readers." —Publishers Weekly

Blatty, William Peter

★ The **exorcist**. William Peter Blatty. Harper & Row, 1971. 340 p.
ISBN 9780060103651
1. Eleven-year-old girls 2. Demonic possession 3. Exorcism 4. Demons 5. Good and evil 6. Washington, D.C. 7. Horror 8. Books to movies 9. Horror classics
LC 73144189

A Jesuit priest, unable to find plausible explanations for an eleven-year-old's strange behavior, begins to suspect demonic possession.

"Blatty has done his homework. He discourses, a bit bookishly, on the history of possession and the relation of autosuggestion to masked guilt.... Blatty maintains headlong thrust, slowly increasing Regan's agony until the reader winces; no more, a part of us says, but of course we want more because Blatty handles the horror so well." —*Newsweek*

Sequel: Legion.

Includes unpaged photos from the feature film of the same title.

Blau, Jessica Anya

Mary Jane: a novel. Jessica Anya Blau. Custom House, 2021. 336 p.
ISBN 9780063052291
1. Teenage girls 2. Nannies 3. Self-discovery in teenage girls 4. Rock musicians 5. Drug use 6. Baltimore, Maryland 7. 1970s 8. Literary fiction 9. Coming-of-age stories

LC 2020047171

LibraryReads Favorites, 2021

Taking a summer job as a nanny for the daughter of a local doctor, straight-laced Mary Jane is introduced to a world of sex, drugs, and rock-and-roll, which helps her figure out what she really wants out of life, and what kind of person she's going to be.

"Blau's intelligent, witty novel (after the critically acclaimed Drinking Closer to Home) captures the essence of the '70s with humor and immensely appealing characters." —*Library Journal*

"Set in suburban Baltimore in the 1970s, Blau's latest is a charming and poignant tale of desire, image, Americana, and chosen family." —*Booklist*

The **Wonder** Bread summer. Jessica Anya Blau. HarperPerennial, 2013. 320 p.
ISBN 9780062199553
1. Young women 2. Drug use 3. Cocaine 4. Students 5. Stealing 6. California 7. 1980s 8. Coming-of-age stories 9. Caper novels

It's 1983 in Berkeley, California. Twenty-year-old Allie Dodgson is a straitlaced college student working part-time at a dress shop to make ends meet. But when the shop turns out to be a front for a dangerous drug-dealing business, Allie finds herself on the lam, speeding toward Los Angeles in her best friend's Prelude with a Wonder Bag full of cocaine riding shotgun and a hit man named Vice Versa on her tail. —From back cover.

Bledsoe, Alex

Gather her round: a novel of the Tufa. Alex Bledsoe. Tor, 2017. 288 p. (Tufa novels, 5)
ISBN 9780765383341
1. Murder 2. Hunters 3. Rural life 4. Hunting 5. Ethnic groups 6. Great Smoky Mountains (N.C. and Tenn.) 7. Tennessee 8. Urban fantasy

In critically-acclaimed Alex Bledsoe's latest Tufa novel, a monster roams the woods of Cloud County, while another kind of evil lurks in the hearts of men.

The **hum** and the shiver. Alex Bledsoe. Tor Books, 2011. 304 p. (Tufa novels, 1)
ISBN 9780765327444
1. Ethnic groups 2. Small towns 3. Magic 4. Music 5. Women veterans 6. Tennessee 7. East Tennessee 8. Urban fantasy

LC 2011021573

Iraq War veteran Bronwyn Hyatt must reconnect with the Tufa, her people, and their ancient song if she is ever going to stop the death stalking her family.

"Bledsoe turns standard urban fantasy tropes on their head by reimagining modern elves as a tiny, isolated ethnic group unsure of their own origins, like the Lemkos of Poland or the Melungeons of the southern Appalachians. The plot is a bit thin, but the slowly unfolding mystery of the Tufa is a fascinating and absorbing masterpiece of world-building." —*Publishers Weekly*

Long black curl. Alex Bledsoe. Tor Books, 2015. 368 p. (Tufa novels, 3)
ISBN 9780765376541
1. Ethnic groups 2. Forbidden love 3. Musicians 4. Music 5. Magic 6. Great Smoky Mountains (N.C. and Tenn.) 7. Tennessee 8. Urban fantasy

When Bo-Kate Wisby makes her way back to Cloud Country, Tennessee in spite of a curse upon her, she plans to take over both Tufa clans with the help of a rockabilly singer of immense size and strength named Byron Harley.

Wisp of a thing. Alex Bledsoe. Tor, 2013. 320 p. (Tufa novels, 2)
ISBN 9780765334138
1. Lovers — Death 2. Ethnic groups 3. Musicians 4. Curses 5. Wild children 6. Great Smoky Mountains (N.C. and Tenn.) 7. Tennessee 8. Urban fantasy

LC 2013003720

Musician Rob Quillen searches for an enigmatic Smoky Mountains clan of people whose existence is shrouded in myth, a journey marked by a disappearance, an incomprehensible power play, and a howling feral girl.

Bledsoe, Lucy Jane

The **big** bang symphony: a novel of Antarctica. Lucy Jane Bledsoe. Terrace Books, 2010. 333 p.
ISBN 9780299235000
1. Loneliness 2. Lesbians 3. Female friendship 4. Women composers 5. Women cooks 6. Antarctica 7. LGBTQIA fiction

LC 2009040630

"Bledsoe digs into themes of individuality and lonesomeness, and the idea of safety in numbers, and though the narrative's introspectiveness can at times be as daunting as the Antarctic's harsh climate, Bledsoe finds the spark of life amid the ice and desolation." —*Publishers Weekly*

Block, Lawrence

All the flowers are dying. Lawrence Block. William Morrow, 2005. 304 p. (Matthew Scudder mysteries, 16)
ISBN 9780060198312
1. Psychologists 2. Death row prisoners 3. Husband and wife 4. Executions and executioners 5. Online romance 6. New York City 7. Mysteries 8. Hardboiled fiction

LC 2004053643

Matthew Scudder, with his eye keenly on retirement, unofficially investigates the suspicious online suitor of an acquaintance, and finds his own life in grave danger.

"Although Scudder's hunt for the killer turns into a companionable tour of colorful neighborhoods, his thoughts on the city run deep and reflect real feelings about its humanity." —*New York Times Book Review*

The **burglar** in the closet. Lawrence Block. Random House, 1978. 166 p. (Bernie Rhodenbarr mysteries, 2)
ISBN 9780394423746
1. Jewelry theft 2. Women murder victims 3. Dentists 4. Thieves 5. Booksellers 6. New York City 7. Cozy mysteries 8. Caper novels 9. Books to movies

LC 7857116

"A New York dentist has set Bernie Rhodenbarr up to rob his estranged wife, which he does. Embarrassingly, he gets interrupted and locked in a closet while the woman is stabbed to death and the boodle is stolen. In a temper, the burglar investigates, as does a corrupt policeman who wants half the take. Things are sorted out when a suitcase full of counterfeit money turns up and a couple of suspects conveniently die. Amusing and very easy to read." —*Library Journal*

Sequel to: Burglars can't be choosers.

Book was adapted into the 1987 film Burglar.

★ The **burglar** in the library. Lawrence Block. Dutton, 1997. 342 p. (Bernie Rhodenbarr mysteries, 8)

ISBN 9780525943013

1. Book thefts 2. Bed-and-breakfast 3. Murder investigation 4. Blizzards 5. First editions 6. New England 7. New York City 8. Cozy mysteries 9. Caper novels

LC 9637537

For Bernie Rhodenbarr, bookseller and compulsive burglar, a weekend at a country bed & breakfast inn takes an unexpected twist when a valuable book is stolen and a dead body turns up in the library.

"[T]he drollest sendup of a murder-in-a-teacup mystery that you will ever hope to beg, borrow—or steal." —*New York Times Book Review*

A **drop** of the hard stuff: a Matthew Scudder novel. Lawrence Block. Mulholland Books/Little, Brown and Co, 2011. 336 p. (Matthew Scudder mysteries, 17)

ISBN 9780316127332

1. Sobriety 2. Grief in men 3. Alcoholic men 4. Scudder, Matt (Fictitious character) 5. Private investigators 6. New York City 7. 1980s 8. Mysteries 9. Hardboiled fiction

LC 2010041792

After a childhood friend is shot down while attempting to atone for past sins, Scudder is drawn into a murder investigation that threatens to upset his path toward recovery—and get him killed in the process.

Eight million ways to die. Lawrence Block. William Morrow, 2008. 318 p. (Matthew Scudder mysteries, 5)

ISBN 9780061457968

1. Crimes against prostitutes 2. Women murder victims 3. Murder investigation 4. Prostitutes 5. Private investigators 6. New York City 7. Mysteries 8. Hardboiled fiction

Shamus Award for Best P.I. Novel, 1983

Kim was a young hooker who wanted out: a beautiful kid, old before her time, seeking Matthew Scudder's protection. She didn't deserve to die the way she did: slashed to ribbons in the seedy waterfront district. Now the tormented ex-cop-turned-P.I. wants to find her killer.

"This novel is both a rousing private-eye story and an extended meditation on the whimsical ways of deaththrough freak accident, premeditated murder, and self-destruction. Private eye Matthew Scudder solves murders while he battles his own alcoholism.... In [this] tale, a 23-year old prostitute, Kim Dakkinen, wants out of 'the life' and asks Scudder to speak to her pimp, Chance. Scudder does, and a few days later Kim is found stabbed to death. Chance does the unexpected by hiring Scudder to find Kim's murderer, and while Scudder investigates, another one of Chance's prostitutes commits suicide; then another slashing occurs. A magnificently plotted, sensitive portrayal of two kinds of deaththe kind that comes as an intruder and the kind that comes as an invited guest." —*Booklist*

Originally published: New York : Arbor House, 1982.

Hit me: a Keller novel. Lawrence Block. Mulholland Books, 2013. 448 p. (John Keller novels, 5)

ISBN 9780316127356

1. Houses — Conservation and restoration 2. Stamp collecting 3. Deception 4. Loss (Psychology) 5. Men — Decision-making 6. New York City 7. White Plains, New York 8. Crime fiction

LC 2012019988

With a new wife and a baby on the way, Keller, a.k.a. Nicholas Edwards, is done killing people for money until a phone call from Dot draws

him back into the old game, taking him to Dallas to settle a domestic dispute to New York, where people might remember him.

Killing Castro. Lawrence Block. Hard Crime Case, 2008. 208 p.

ISBN 9780843961133

1. Castro, Fidel 2. Dictators 3. Assassins 4. Attempted assassination 5. International intrigue 6. Cuba 7. 1960s 8. Thrillers and suspense

There were five of them, each prepared to kill, each with his own reasons for accepting what might well be a suicide mission. The pay? $20,000 apiece. The mission? Find a way into Cuba and kill Castro.

"[An] absorbing yarn about five men vying for a $100,000 prize put on Fidel Castro's head by a mysterious guy named Hiraldo... Passages discussing Castro's life and times add depth to this intense, taut thriller, just as good now as it was in 1961." —*Publishers Weekly*

Originally published as Fidel Castro assassinated under the pseudonym Lee Duncan: Derby, Conn. : Monarch Books, 1961.

The **sins** of the fathers. Lawrence Block. Dark Harvest 1992. 179p. (Matthew Scudder mysteries, 1)

ISBN 9780913165669

1. Block, Lawrence 2. Murder investigation 3. Clergymen 4. Fathers and sons 5. Murder 6. Prostitutes 7. New York City 8. Mysteries 9. Hardboiled fiction

LC 90035227

Matthew Scudder, a private detective who had been a cop for fifteen years, investigates the savage murder of a Greenwich Village hooker supposedly killed by her homosexual roommate.

"This novel introduced the then-hard-drinking ex-cop Matt Scudder. "?? This is a fine opportunity to get in on the start of what has become one of the most rewarding PI series currently in progress." —*Publishers Weekly*

Introduction by Stephen King: "No cats:" an appreciation of Lawrence Block and Matthew Scudder.

Originally published: New York : Dell, 1976.

A **ticket** to the boneyard: a Matthew Scudder novel. Lawrence Block. Morrow, 1990. 302 p. (Matthew Scudder mysteries, 8)

ISBN 9780688090708

1. Men with mental illnesses 2. Serial murders 3. Revenge 4. Former convicts 5. Recovering alcoholics 6. New York City 7. Mysteries 8. Hardboiled fiction

LC 90005710

When ex-policeman and recovering alcoholic Matthew Scudder is stalked by a psychotic killer who murders, one by one, Scudders' friends and acquaintances, his fate hinges on the survival of a glamorous call girl BT

"The author has a fine nose for the pungencies of New York's after-dark street life, and he gives his hero wonderful opportunities to swap syllables with the city's most articulate riffraff. This is primo stuff, and Scudder doesn't get any sharper than when he's interviewing transvestite hookers, desk clerks in fleabag hotels and bouncers in gay leather bars." —*New York Times Book Review*

★ **When** the sacred ginmill closes. Lawrence Block. Arbor House, 1986. 239 p. (Matthew Scudder mysteries, 6)

ISBN 9780877957744

1. Women murder victims 2. Robbery 3. Eliot, T. S. 4. Alcoholic men 5. Former police 6. New York City 7. 1970s 8. Mysteries 9. Hardboiled fiction

LC 85018682

"The writing is realistic in the best sense of the word. There are no artificial heroics, forced lines of dialogue or false moves. Mr. Block knows his New York and the way people speak." —*New York Times Book Review*

Block, Stefan Merrill

Oliver Loving: a novel. Stefan Merrill Block. Flatiron Books, 2018. 400 p.
ISBN 9781250169730
1. School shootings 2. People in comas 3. Life change events 4. Loss (Psychology) 5. Ginzburg, Natalia 6. Texas 7. Mainstream fiction 8. Multiple perspectives 9. Adult books for young adults
LC 2017041748
The complicated bonds uniting a family and the members of their community are tested by a devastating school shooting that has left a young man in a coma for nine years, a tragedy that is illuminated by an experimental diagnostic technology that suggests that his mind may still be active and capable of revealing what happened.

Bloom, Amy

Lucky us: a novel. Amy Bloom. Random House, 2014. 256 p.
ISBN 9781400067244
1. Half-sisters 2. Cross-country automobile trips 3. Abandoned children 4. Fathers and daughters 5. Voyages and travels 6. Hollywood, California 7. Ohio 8. 1940s 9. Historical fiction 10. Farcical fiction 11. Literary fiction 12. Adult books for young adults
LC 2013017648
LibraryReads Favorites, 2014
Forging a life together after being abandoned by their parents, half sisters Eva and Iris share decades in and out of the spotlight in golden-era Hollywood and mid-20th-century Long Island.
"At its core, this is a novel of resilience.... Full of intriguing characters and lots of surprises." —*Library Journal*

★ **White** houses: a novel. Amy Bloom. Random House, 2018. 218 p.
ISBN 9780812995664
1. Roosevelt, Eleanor 2. Women journalists 3. Presidents' spouses 4. Women/women relations 5. Romantic love 6. Bisexual women 7. 1930s 8. 1940s 9. Biographical fiction 10. Historical fiction 11. LGBTQIA fiction
LC 2017028296
Loan Stars Favourites, 2018
After meeting the future first lady while covering Franklin Roosevelt's campaign, Lorena Hickock and Eleanor discover a powerful passion between them.

Blum, Jenna

The lost family. Jenna Blum. Harper, 2018. 417 p.
ISBN 9780062742162
1. Holocaust survivors 2. James, Henry 3. Second wives 4. Cooks 5. Marriage 6. Manhattan, New York City 7. New York City 8. 1960s 9. Historical fiction 10. Literary fiction
Resigning himself to solitude, chef and Auschwitz survivor, Peter Rashkin, in 1965 Manhattan, devotes himself to running Masha's restaurant, until he meets and marries June, but the horrors of his past soon overshadow him, June and their daughter.
"This exquisitely crafted and compassionate novel offers a lesson in honesty, regardless of how difficult the truth may be. It will offer plenty of discussion for book groups." —*Library Journal*

Blumberg, Chandra

Digging up love. Chandra Blumberg. Montlake Romance, 2022. 345 pages
ISBN 9781542033909
1. Women bakers 2. Paleontologists 3. Ambition in women 4. Grandparents 5. Fossil dinosaurs 6. Illinois 7. Chicago, Illinois 8. Multicultural romances 9. Contemporary romances
A young woman working in her grandfather's restaurant in rural Illinois who dreams of opening up a cookie shop in Chicago falls for a big-city academic paleontologist when a rare dinosaur bone turns up in her grandparents' back yard.
"Blumberg's charming debut combines true love, delicious cookies, and dinosaurs." —*Publishers Weekly*

Blume, Judy

In the unlikely event. Judy Blume. Alfred A. Knopf, 2015. 432 p.
ISBN 9781101875049
1. Airplane accidents 2. Intergenerational relations 3. Families 4. Neighbors 5. Friendship 6. New Jersey 7. 1950s 8. Family sagas 9. Historical fiction 10. Adult books for young adults
LC 2015007629
Booklist Editors' Choice: Adult Books for Young Adults, 2015; LibraryReads Favorites, 2015; School Library Journal Best Books: Best Adult Books 4 Teens, 2015
A novel inspired by a series of passenger airplane crashes that occurred in 1951 and 1952 New Jersey reimagines the impact of the tragedies on three generations of families, friends and strangers.
"Maintaining her knack for personal detail, Blume mixes Miri's familiar coming-of-age melodrama with an exploration of how disasters test character, alter relationships, and reveal undercurrents of a seemingly simple world. She evokes '50s music, ethnic neighborhoods, and Las Vegas in the early days." —*Publishers Weekly*

Blumenfeld, Amy

The cast. Amy Blumenfeld. SparkPress, 2018. 310 p.
ISBN 9781943006724
1. Friendship 2. Women cancer survivors 3. Videos 4. Reunions 5. Fourth of July 6. Mainstream fiction 7. Multiple perspectives
Twenty-five years after a group of ninth graders produces a Saturday Night Live-style videotape to cheer up their cancer-stricken friend, they reunite to celebrate her good health—but the happy holiday card facades quickly crumble and give way to an unforgettable three days filled with moral dilemmas and life-altering choices.

Blundell, Judy

The high season: a novel. Judy Blundell. Random House, 2018. 396 p.
ISBN 9780525508717
1. Houses 2. Rich people 3. Landlord and tenant 4. Women — Psychology 5. Museum curators 6. Long Island, New York 7. Relationship fiction
LC 2017037646
RUSA Reading List Short List, 2019
Forced to rent out her family's beautiful seaside Long Island home every summer just so that they can afford to keep it, Ruthie is forced to go to extreme lengths to protect the life she loves in the wake of a suddenly estranged marriage, greedy co-workers who are threatening her job, the return of an old flame and her teen daughter's destructive relationship.

Bobotis, Andrea

The last list of Miss Judith Kratt. Andrea Bobotis. Sourcebooks Landmark, 2019. 320 p.
ISBN 9781492678861

1. Small towns 2. Matriarchs 3. Family secrets 4. Heirlooms 5. Memories 6. South Carolina 7. Southern fiction

LC 2018033669

Judith Kratt inherited all the Kratt family had to offer—the pie safe, the copper clock, the murder that no one talks about—and she knows in her old bones that it's time to make an inventory of her household and its valuables. But she finds that cataloging the family heirlooms can't contain their misfortunes, not when her wayward sister suddenly returns, determined to expose secrets that the Kratts had hoped to take to their grave. Interweaving the present with chilling flashbacks from one fateful evening in 1929, Judith pieces together the influence of her family on their small South Carolina cotton town, learning that the effects of dark family secrets can last for decades.."

Bock, Charles

Alice & Oliver: a novel. Charles Bock. Random House, 2016. 336 p.
ISBN 9781400068388

1. Women with cancer 2. Married women 3. Husband and wife 4. People with terminal illnesses 5. Mothers 6. New York City 7. 1990s 8. Domestic fiction 9. Literary fiction

LC 2015022303

Alice Culvert is a force: passionate, independent, smart, and gorgeous, she—to her delight—attracts attention wherever she goes, even amid the buzz of mid-90s New York. In knee-high boots, with her newborn daughter, Doe, strapped to her chest, Alice is one of those people who just seem so vividly alive, which makes her cancer diagnosis feel almost incongruous. How could such a being not go on? But all at once, Alice's existence, and that of her husband Oliver, is reduced to a single purpose: survival. As they combat the disease, the couple must also face off against the serpentine healthcare system, the good intentions of loved ones, and the deep, dangerous stressors that threaten to push the two of them apart. With veracity, humor, wisdom, and love, Charles Bock navigates one family's unforgettable story—inspired by his own.

"The illness doesn't interrupt humanity; humanity grows from the illness, which is a narrative strategy that makes the book one of the most moving in recent memory. A stunning book about Alice and Oliver, yes, but also about the way illness shatters us all." —*Kirkus*

Beautiful children: a novel. Charles Bock. Random House, 2008. 432 p.
ISBN 9781400066506

1. Boys 2. Missing children 3. Deserts 4. Twelve-year-old boys 5. Marital conflict 6. Las Vegas, Nevada 7. Psychological fiction

LC 2007004166

New York Times Notable Book, 2008

One Saturday night in Las Vegas, twelve-year-old Newell Ewing goes out with a friend and doesn't come home. In the aftermath of his disappearance, his mother, Lorraine, makes daily pilgrimages to her son's room and tortures herself with memories. Equally distraught, the boy's father, Lincoln, finds himself wanting to comfort his wife even as he yearns for solace, a loving touch, any kind of intimacy. As the Ewings navigate the mystery of what's become of their son, the circumstances surrounding Newell's vanishing and other events on that same night reverberate through the lives of seemingly disconnected strangers: a comic book illustrator in town for a weekend of debauchery; a painfully shy and possibly disturbed young artist; a stripper who imagines moments from her life as if they were movie scenes; a bubbly teenage wiccan anarchist; a dangerous and scheming gutter punk; a band of misfit runaways.

Bohjalian, Chris

The **buffalo** soldier: a novel. Chris Bohjalian. Shaye Areheart Books, 2002. 404 p.
ISBN 9780609608333

1. African American foster children 2. Bereavement in parents 3. Intergenerational friendship 4. Ten-year-old boys 5. Daughters — Death 6. Vermont 7. Psychological fiction 8. Mainstream fiction 9. Domestic fiction 10. Adult books for young adults

LC 2001049042

The devastating loss of their twin daughters in a flash flood turns the lives of Terry and Laura Sheldon upside down as their marriage is tested by grief, Terry's brief love affair, and their growing relationship with their foster child, a ten-year-old African American boy.

"Bohjalian's characters combat their moral and racial confusion with a healthy application of ordinary love and good will, though their basic goodness often makes them feel less complex than the plot itself." —*New York Times Book Review*

The **double** bind: a novel. Chris Bohjalian. Shaye Areheart Books, 2007. 384 p.
ISBN 9781400047468

1. Shelters for the homeless 2. Obsession 3. Men with mental illnesses 4. Coping in women 5. Women college students 6. Vermont 7. Greenberg, Joanne 8. Adult books for young adults

LC 2006015402

Working at a homeless shelter, student Laurel Estabrook encounters Bobbie Crocker, a man with a history of mental illness and a box of secret photos, but when Bobbie dies suddenly, Laurel embarks on an obsessive search for the truth behind the photos.

"Conflating literary lore, photographic analysis and meditations on homelessness and mental illness, Bohjalian produces his best and most complex fiction yet. Ultra-clever, and moving, too." —*Kirkus*

The **flight** attendant: a novel. Chris Bohjalian. Doubleday, 2018. 368 pages
ISBN 9780385542418

1. Flight attendants 2. Deception 3. Addiction 4. Alcoholic women 5. Binge-drinking 6. Thrillers and suspense

LC 2017034159

LibraryReads Favorites, 2018

A binge-drinking flight attendant wakes up in an unfamiliar hotel room beside a dead body and sneaks back to her work, telling a series of lies that complicate her ability to figure out what really happened.

The **night** strangers: a novel. Christopher A. Bohjalian. Crown Publishers, 2011. 400 p.
ISBN 9780307394996

1. Victorian houses 2. Airplane accidents 3. Ghosts 4. Herbalists 5. Families 6. New Hampshire 7. Ghost stories 8. Horror 9. Multiple perspectives

After he crashes his plane into Lake Champlain, killing most of the passengers, Chip Linton moves into a new home with his wife and twin daughters and soon finds himself being haunted by the dead passengers, all while his wife wonders why the strange herbalist denizens of the town have taken such an interest in her daughters.

"Chip Linton is at the controls of a jet that flies into a flock of birds and goes down in Lake Champlain. Although Linton does everything correctly, an errant wave tips the plane over. Thirty-nine of the 48 people aboard die, and the captain's life, obviously, is changed forever. His lawyer wife, Emily, and their 10-year-old twins decide they need to start over. So they leave Pennsylvania for the small town of Bethel, N.H. But things do not get better. The ghost of several drowned passengers haunts him, particularly Ashley, a young girl, and her dad. They are stuck in purgatory and alone. Linton believes he's responsible, and that Ashley deserves company, and he's prepared to kill his own daughters to provide it. He's crazy, of course—or is he? The denouement is not only unexpected but is also perfect and true to the story. Bohjalian is a terrific writer and parsimonious in the way he issues information, slowly building an increasing sense of dread and excitement." —*Minneapolis Star Tribune*

★ The **red** lotus. Chris Bohjalian. Doubleday, 2020. 400 pages
ISBN 9780385544801
1. Women physicians 2. Couples 3. Hospitals — Emergency service 4. Voyages and travels 5. Bicycling 6. Vietnam 7. United States 8. Thrillers and suspense
Falling in love with a wounded former patient and accompanying him on a cycling trip to Vietnam, an emergency-room doctor uncovers a bizarre series of deceptions that culminate in her boyfriend's unexplained disappearance.
"Alternating action between Vietnam and New York, along with the dynamic pace, will please suspense fans." —*Library Journal*

The **sandcastle** girls. Chris Bohjalian. Doubleday, 2012. 288 p.
ISBN 9780385534796
1. Americans in the Middle East 2. Armenian genocide, 1915-1923 3. Alexander, the Great, 356 B.C.-323 B.C. 4. Engineers 5. Loss (Psychology) 6. 1910s 7. Historical fiction 8. Love stories 9. Parallel narratives
LC 2011050285
Library Journal Best Books, 2012
A historical love story inspired by the author's Armenian heritage finds early 20th-century nurse Elizabeth Endicott arriving in Syria to help deliver food and medical aid to genocide refugees, a volunteer service during which she exchanges letters with an Armenian engineer and widower.
"Bohjalian powerfully narrates an intricately nuanced romance with a complicated historical event at the forefront." —*Library Journal*

Secrets of Eden: a novel. Chris Bohjalian. Shaye Areheart Books, 2010. 384 p.
ISBN 9780307394972
1. Clergymen 2. Guilt in men 3. Children of murder victims 4. Faith in men 5. Women authors 6. Vermont 7. Mysteries
LC 2009023946
Haunted by the final words of a newly baptized congregation member who was subsequently murdered by her husband, the Reverend Stephen Drew abandons his pulpit to spend time with an author who writes best-selling books about angels.
"This novel is engrossing without being cheesy, informative without being didactic, and gripping despite the fact that the ending is quite predictable." —*Boston Globe*

Skeletons at the feast: a novel. Chris Bohjalian. Shaye Areheart Books, 2008. 372 p.
ISBN 9780307394958
1. Jews, German — History 2. Refugees 3. Military pilots 4. Antisemitism 5. World War II 6. Germany 7. Second World War era (1939-1945) 8. 1940s 9. War stories 10. Historical fiction 11. Parallel narratives
LC 2007040800
During the final months of World War II, a small group of people make their way westward across a ravaged Europe in a desperate attempt to reach British and American lines.

The **sleepwalker**. Chris Bohjalian. Doubleday, 2017. 336 p.
ISBN 9780385538916
1. Sleep-walking 2. Missing women 3. Missing persons investigation 4. Man-woman relationships 5. Family relationships 6. Vermont 7. Mysteries

LC 2016015531
When a sleepwalker who has experienced episodes of near violence while unconscious goes missing, her eldest daughter, Lianna, finds herself drawn to a lead detective who seems to know more than he is revealing.
"Set in Vermont in 2000, this stylish fusion of mystery and domestic thriller from Bohjalian (The Guest Room) explores the aftermath of the inexplicable disappearance of a woman prone to sleepwalking." —*Publishers Weekly*

Boianjiu, Shani

The **people** of forever are not afraid: a novel. Shani Boianjiu. Hogarth, 2012. 352 p.
ISBN 9780307955951
1. Women soldiers 2. Female friendship 3. Military education — Israel 4. Draft 5. Military life 6. War stories 7. Coming-of-age stories
Three young women in Israel are conscripted into the army and struggle to stay friends as they see their lives change in unpredictable ways.

Bolano, Roberto

★ **2666**. Roberto Bolano; translated from the Spanish by Natasha Wimmer. Farrar, Straus and Giroux, 2008. 912 p.
ISBN 9780374100148
1. Blue collar workers 2. Missing persons 3. Factories 4. Scholars and academics 5. Authors 6. Mexican-American Border Region 7. Literary fiction 8. Translations
LC 2008018295
National Book Critics Circle Award for Fiction, 2008; New York Times Notable Book, 2008
An American sportswriter, an elusive German novelist, and a teenage student interact in an urban community on the U.S.-Mexico border where hundreds of young factory workers have disappeared.
"More vast and more lurid than his previous novels that have been translated into English, 2666 is not Roberto Bolao's masterpiece but almost a compendium, in individual scenes, of the qualities that made him a great writer. His themes are violence, dislocation, and the sexiness of literature, and here these strands are recombined endlessly, in Europe, Detroit, and Mexico, through multiple narrators and prose styles. The action converges on the Sonoran desert, where Bolao anatomizes, in brutal and eerie detail, the true-life murders of hundreds of women, most of which remain unsolved. By the end, after close to nine hundred pages, the reader will be impressed by the range and power on display but might wish that the novel cohered, rather than merely concluding." —*The New Yorker*

Amulet. Roberto Bolano; translated from the Spanish by Chris Andrews. New Directions, 2007. 192 p.
ISBN 9780811216647
1. Latin Americans 2. Revolutionaries 3. College students 4. Women college students 5. Poets, Mexican 6. Latin America 7. Mexico 8. 1960s 9. Literary fiction 10. First person narratives 11. Translations
LC 2006023507
"This is a curiously joyful novel that delights in its storytelling even as it struggles with the question of how art might be sustained under conditions resolutely opposed to it." —*Harper's*
Originally published as Amuleto: Barcelona : Editorial Anagrama, 1999.

★ **By** night in Chile. Roberto Bolano; translated from the Spanish by Chris Andrews. New Directions Books, 2003. 130 p.
ISBN 9780811215473
1. Pinochet Ugarte, Augusto 2. Priests 3. Memories 4. Secrets 5. Responsibility 6. Identity (Psychology) 7. Chile 8. Literary fiction 9. Translations

LC 2003013223

"Postwar Chilean politics and literature infuse this densely learned, richly evocative novel. In Chris Andrews's lucid translation, Bolano's febrile narrative tack and occasional surreal touches bring to mind the classics of Latin American magic realism; his cerebral protagonist and nonfiction borrowings are reminiscent of Thomas Bernhard and W. G. Sebald." —*New York Times Book Review*

★ **Distant** star. Roberto Bolano; translated from the Spanish by Chris Andrews. New Directions, 2004. 149 p.
ISBN 9780811215862
1. Dictatorship 2. Poets 3. Universities and colleges 4. Concentration camps 5. Pilots 6. Chile 7. Political fiction 8. Literary fiction 9. First person narratives

LC 2004019033

"The melancholy folklore of exile pervades this novel, which describes the divergent paths of three young Chilean poets around the time of Pinochets coup. At university, the unnamed narrator and his friend are fascinated by a mysterious new member of their poetry workshop. Alberto Ruiz-Tagle is serious, well mannered, a clear thinker, but his poems seem false, as if his true work were yet to be revealed. It becomes apparent that this is literally the case when Allendes government falls: as an Air Force officer for the new regime, he becomes famous for writing nationalist slogans in the sky. (The left-wing narrator, now in jail, reads them from his prison yard.) Bolanos spare prose lends his narrators account a chilly precisionas if the detachment of his former classmate had become his countrys, and his own." —*The New Yorker*

Last evenings on Earth. Roberto Bolano; translated from the Spanish by Chris Andrews. New Directions Books, 2006. 256 p.
ISBN 9780811216340
1. Bolano, Roberto 2. Men 3. Desire 4. Man-woman relationships 5. Men — Family relationships 6. Literary fiction 7. Short stories 8. Translations

LC 2006003819

New York Times Notable Book, 2006
"These 14 bleakly luminous stories are all told in the first person by men (usually young) who yearn for something just out of their grasp (fame, talent, love) and who harbor few hopes of attaining what they desire.... The stories are similar, in theme and voice (though not in locale), and they are perfectly calibrated: Bolao limns the capacity of a voice to carry despair without shading into bitterness." —*Publishers Weekly*

Monsieur Pain. Roberto Bolano; translated from the Spanish by Chris Andrews. New Directions, 2010. 192 p.
ISBN 9780811217149
1. Vallejo, Cesar 2. Hypnotists 3. Magic 4. Unrequited love 5. Assassination 6. Hypnotism 7. Paris, France 8. 1930s 9. Literary fiction 10. Translations

LC 2009037431

After he accepts a bribe not to treat chronically hiccupping Peruvian poet Csar Vallejo, mesmerist Monsieur Pierre Pain is racked with guilt but is barred from the hospital when he tries to do the right thing, only to discover a rival mesmerist has entered the picture, along with an assassination and a host of other nightmares.

"Bolano draws on actual facts that the real Vallejo was hospitalized in Paris in 1938, and his wife called in practitioners of occult sciences when doctors failed to cure him to weave his brilliant, noir-steeped fictional world. As Pain wanders the rainy streets of Paris, convinced of a plot to assassinate Vallejo, haunted by his own complicity and helpless rebellion, we enter a hallucinatory dreamscape flooded with resonant symbols." —*San Francisco Chronicle*

Originally published by Anagrama Barcelona Spain, as Monsieur Pain in 1999.

★ **Nazi** literature in the Americas. Roberto Bolano; translated from the Spanish by Chris Andrews. New Directions, 2008. Ix, 227 p.
ISBN 9780811217057
1. Right-wing extremists 2. Fascism 3. Nazis 4. Nazism 5. Authors 6. Parodies 7. Translations

"This novel, a wicked, invented encyclopedia of imaginary fascist writers and literary tastemakers, is Bolao playing with sharp, twisting knives. As if he were Borges's wisecracking, sardonic son, Bolao has meticulously created a tightly woven network of far-right litterateurs and purveyors of belles lettres for whom Hitler was beauty, truth and great lost hope. Cross-referenced, complete with bibliography and a biographical list of secondary figures, Nazi Literature is composed of a series of sketches, the compressed life stories of writers in North and South America who never existed, but all too easily could have. Goose-stepping caricatures a la The Producers they are not; instead, they are frighteningly subtle, poignant and plausible." —*New York Times Book Review*
Includes bibliographical references.

★ The **savage** detectives. Roberto Bolano; translated from the Spanish by Natasha Wimmer. Farrar, Straus and Giroux, 2007. 592 p.
ISBN 9780374191481
1. Poets, Mexican 2. Militants 3. Literary movements 4. Male friendship 5. Quests 6. Mexico (City) 7. 1970s 8. Psychological fiction 9. Literary fiction 10. Translations

LC 2006022176

New York Times Notable Book, 2007
Chronicles the strange journey of two Latin American poets, Arturo Belano and Ulises Lima, as seen through the eyes of the people whose paths they cross in Central America, Europe, Israel, and West Africa.

"Though the fragmented narrative can be frustrating at times, the late-20th-century panorama emerging from the cacophony is simultaneously frightening and spectacular. At every turn, Bolao examines the individual lives history discards. The result is a large, sprawling and—most of all—sublime novel." —*Paste*
Translation of: Los detectives salvajes.
Originally published: Barcelona : Editorial Anagrama, 1998.
Translated from the Spanish.

★ The **Third** Reich. Roberto Bolano; translated from the Spanish by Natasha Wimmer. Farrar Straus & Giroux, 2011. 288 p.
ISBN 9780374275624
1. Germans in Spain 2. War games 3. Violence in men 4. Couples 5. Egotism in men 6. Literary fiction 7. Translations

While vacationing in Spain, German war-game champion Udo Berger and his girlfriend meet another vacationing German couple, Charly and Hanna, who introduce them to a band of locals. When Charly disappears, the women return to Germany but Udo stays and becomes enmeshed in Third Reich, a World War II strategy game whose consequences may be all too real.
Originally published: Barcelona : Anagrama, 2010.

Boll, Heinrich

Billiards at half-past nine. Heinrich Boll. Penguin Books, 1994. 280 p.
ISBN 9780140187243
1. Billiards 2. Household activities 3. Germany 4. Modern classics 5. Literary fiction 6. Translations

Robert Faehmel finds his structured life threatened by an old schoolmate and former Nazi.
Translation of: Billard um Halbzehn.

The **clown**. Heinrich Boll; translated from the German by Leila Vennewitz. Penguin Books 1994. 247 p.
ISBN 9780140187267

1. Germany 2. Modern classics 3. Literary fiction 4. Translations

"What Schnier (and the author) seem to be asking is: How can an honest man profess Christianity when Christian culture in the West failed to stop the rise of Nazism...and when the Church thrives in a society that worships nothing but the values of the marketplace? Hard questions but embodied in a bitter and brilliant book." —*New York Times Book Review*

Originally published ... under the title Ansichten eines Clowns

Bolton, S. J.

The **craftsman**. S.J. Bolton. Minotaur Books, 2018. 418 p.
ISBN 9781250300034
1. Women detectives 2. Small towns 3. Confession (Law) 4. Crimes against children 5. Suspicion 6. Lancashire, England 7. England 8. Mysteries 9. Gothic fiction

LC 2018020147

When eerily familiar child abductions and murders start recurring in a small Lancashire village, a local cop struggles to figure out if she sent the wrong person to jail decades earlier or if a copycat killer is responsible.

A **dark** and twisted tide. Sharon Bolton. St Martins Pr 2014. 448 pages (Lacey Flint novels, 4)
ISBN 9781250028587
1. Policewomen 2. Communities 3. Rivers 4. Murder 5. Murder investigation 6. Thames River 7. London, England 8. 2000s (Decade) 9. Psychological suspense

LC 2014003443

Now living in a houseboat on the River Thames, Lacey Flint is becoming a part of London's weird and wonderful riverboat community. But at dawn one hot summer morning, Lacey finds the body of a shrouded young woman in the river. She assumes it was chance—after all she's recently joined the marine policing unit—but further investigation leads her team to suspect it was deliberately left for her to find. She is no longer a detective, but as she begins to suspect someone is watching her very closely, she can't help but be drawn into the investigation. Award-winning author Sharon Bolton has once again crafted a tightly-plotted, utterly unpredictable thriller around one of the most compelling characters in crime fiction today, enigmatic London police officer Lacey Flint.

Originally published: London: Bantam Press, 2014.

Now you see me. S.J. Bolton. Minotaur Books, 2011. 416 pages (Lacey Flint novels, 1)
ISBN 9780312600525
1. Jack 2. Women detectives 3. Crimes against women 4. Serial murder investigation 5. Copycat murderers 6. Stalkers 7. London, England 8. 2000s (Decade) 9. Psychological suspense

LC 2011008751

Library Journal Best Books, 2011

Stumbling onto a murder scene that a reporter likens to the crimes of Jack the Ripper, young detective constable Lacey Flint races against time to prevent additional deaths and realizes that the killer is taunting her with secrets from her past.

"On the anniversary of the original Ripper's first killing, Det. Constable Lacey Flint is horrified to find a dying woman, her abdomen...a mass of scarlet, leaning against the detective's car in a London car park. The guilt-ridden Flint wonders whether different actions on her part might have saved the victim's life or caught the killer. The connection with the 1888 autumn of terror becomes clear after a journalist receives a letter obviously derived from some of the correspondence Scotland Yard received back then, ostensibly from the Ripper himself. By coincidence, Flint is something of a Ripper expert, and her knowledge proves useful in what develops into a multiple murder investigation. Avoiding gratuitous vio-

lence, Bolton...skillfully plays with the reader's expectations." —*Publishers Weekly*

The **split**. Sharon Bolton. St Martins Pr 2020. 304 p.
ISBN 9781250300058
1. Islands 2. Women scientists 3. Fear 4. Psychotherapist and patient 5. Loss of consciousness 6. South Georgia Island 7. Antarctica 8. Psychological suspense

LC 2019049526

No matter how far you run, some secrets will always catch up with you...

"Employing multiple narratives and complex character histories, Bolton keeps the reader guessing to the end. Psychological thriller fans will be satisfied." —*Publishers Weekly*

Bond, Cynthia

Ruby: a novel. Cynthia Bond. Hogarth, 2014. 288 pages
ISBN 9780804139090
1. Small town life 2. Discrimination 3. Prostitution 4. African Americans 5. Homecomings 6. Texas 7. Literary fiction 8. Southern Gothic 9. African American fiction

LC 2013033049

Shortlisted for the Baileys Women's Prize for Fiction, 2016

Loving the beautiful but damaged Ruby all of his life, Ephram is torn between his sister and a chance for a life with Ruby when the latter returns to their small hometown and confronts the forces that traumatized her early years.

Bonnaffons, Amy

The **regrets**. Amy Bonnaffons. Little Brown & Co, 2020. 304 p.
ISBN 9780316516167
1. Spirits 2. Life after death 3. Interpersonal attraction 4. Love triangles 5. Dead 6. Literary fiction 7. Love stories 8. Surrealist fiction

In order to {34cross over{34 to the afterlife, Thomas must complete a 90-day stint on earth during which he is forbidden to get involved with a member of the living until he falls in love with Rachel, setting in motion a series of strange, troubling consequences.

"Bonnaffons (The Wrong Heaven, 2018) has a deft hand for dialogue and character development, which grounds the fantastical nature of her novel in the sharp truths of real-life love and desire." —*Booklist*

The **wrong** heaven: stories. Amy Bonnaffons. Ecco, 2018. 245 p.
ISBN 9780316516211
1. Literary fiction 2. Short stories

Library Journal Best Books, 2018

In a collection of revelatory stories, some of which are more grounded in reality than others, anything is possible: bodies can transform, inanimate objects come to life and angels appear and disappear.

Booth, Coe

★ **Bronxwood**. Coe Booth. PUSH, 2011. 320 p.
ISBN 9780439925341
1. Sixteen-year-old boys 2. Children of former convicts 3. Family problems 4. Teenage boy/girl relations 5. African American teenage boys 6. Bronx, New York City 7. Realistic fiction 8. First person narratives 9. African American fiction 10. Books for reluctant readers

YALSA Best Fiction for Young Adults, 2012; YALSA Quick Picks for Reluctant Young Adult Readers, 2012

Tyrell's life is spinning out of control after his father is released from prison, his little brother is placed in foster care, and the drug dealers he's living with are pressuring him to start dealing.

"Action scenes combine with interpersonal exchanges to keep the pace moving forward at a lightning speed, but Booth never sacrifices the street-infused dialogue and emotional authenticity that characterize her works. She has created a compelling tale of a teen still trying to make the right choices despite the painful consequences." —*School Library Journal*

Bordas, Camille

How to behave in a crowd. Camille Bordas. Tim Duggan Books, 2017. 336 p.

ISBN 9780451497543

1. Siblings 2. Small towns 3. Families 4. Family relationships 5. France 6. Literary fiction 7. Coming-of-age stories 8. First person narratives

LC 2016023941

A misfit youngest child in a large French family of overachievers makes quiet observations about his world and becomes the only family member brave enough to help the others through their grief in the wake of a devastating tragedy.

Borges, Jorge Luis

★ **Collected** fictions. Jorge Luis Borges; translated from the Spanish by Andrew Hurley. Viking, 1998. 565 p.

ISBN 9780670849703

1. Immortalism 2. Outlaws 3. Curiosities and wonders 4. Gauchos 5. Labyrinths 6. Short stories 7. Literary fiction

LC 98021217

ALA Notable Book, 1999; New York Times Notable Book, 1998

The first complete, annotated collection of short stories in English by the twentieth-century Spanish master ranges from his 1935 debut to his last work, "Shakespeare's Memory," in its first appearance in English

"A Borges invention...always takes the reader on a roller-coaster ride into some previously unsuspected dimension. This collection of the great magician's work is a new translation and includes one piece never before put into English." —*The Atlantic*

101 short stories

Translated from the Spanish.

Ficciones. Jorge Luis Borges; with an introduction by John Sturrock. A. A. Knopf, 1993. 142 p.

ISBN 9780679422990

1. Imaginary places 2. Metaphysics 3. Libraries 4. Infinity 5. Labyrinths 6. Short stories 7. Magical realism 8. Literary fiction

LC 9255353

Stories deal with an unusual garden, an enormous library, authorship, language, memory, philosophy, and the art of writing

Stories deal with an unusual garden, an enormous library, authorship, language, memory, philosophy, and the art of writing.

Translated from the Spanish.

Boschwitz, Ulrich Alexander

The **passenger**: a novel. Ulrich Alexander Boschwitz; translated from the German by Philip Boehm. Metropolitan Books/Henry Holt & Company, 2021. 288 p.

ISBN 9781250317148

1. Kristallnacht, 1938 2. Jews, German — History 3. Persecution by Nazis 4. Railroad travel 5. World War I veterans 6. Germany 7. 1930s 8. Between the Wars (1918-1939) 9. Modern classics 10. Translations

LC 2020050685

A German World War I veteran endures escalating persecution for his Jewish heritage in 1938 Berlin before embarking on a series of train journeys to uncover vital information and then escape the country.

"Originally published in 1938 under a pseudonym, Boschwitz's tale trembles with tension and eerily anticipates the central role the German train system would later play in the horrific logistics of the Holocaust. In a new translation, this remains a potent and uniquely rendered work of witness." —*Booklist*

Originally published in Germany in 2018 under the title Der Reisende by Klett-Cotta, Stuttgart

Translated from the German.

Bouchet, Amanda

Breath of fire. Amanda Bouchet. Sourcebooks Casablanca, 2017. 416 p. (Kingmaker chronicles, 2)

ISBN 9781492626046

1. Warlords 2. Women psychics 3. Fate and fatalism 4. Tournaments 5. Magic 6. Fantasy romances 7. First person narratives

As the realms are descending into all-out war, Cat and Griffin must embrace their fate together.

"With breathtaking storytelling, high-octane action and adventure, intense romance, and threads to ancient Greek mythology...Bouchet sets the bar for high-concept fantasy romance." —*Kirkus*

Nightchaser. Amanda Bouchet. Sourcebooks Casablanca, 2019. 352 p. (Nightchaser novels, 1)

ISBN 9781492667131

1. Women spaceship captains 2. Mechanics 3. Space flight 4. Women thieves 5. Protectiveness in women 6. Futuristic romances

The galaxy's most wanted captain must trust her life to a charming and mysterious rogue if she doesn't want to see her latest mission go up in smoke...

"A space rebel with a price on her head discovers she may have the power to alter the balance of power in a galactic struggle—just as she's falling for a sexy trader with dangerous secrets of his own." —*Kirkus*

★ A **promise** of fire. Amanda Bouchet. Sourcebooks Casablanca, 2016. 352 p. (Kingmaker chronicles, 1)

ISBN 9781492626015

1. Warlords 2. Women psychics 3. Kidnapping 4. Secret identity 5. Fate and fatalism 6. Fantasy romances 7. First person narratives 8. Adult books for young adults

RUSA Reading List Short List, 2017

Despite her reputation as a Kingmaker, soothsayer Catalia "Cat" Fisa has turned her back on both the magic-wielding elite who use their gifts to oppress their subjects and the non-magical upstarts who would use her powers to further their own political agendas. She succeeds by disguising herself as an elderly fortune teller in a traveling circus until she's captured by Griffin, a warlord who needs Cat's assistance to defend his realm. Dismissing him as yet another power-hungry political player, Cat comes to revise her opinion as he defends her from assassins.

Boudjedra, Rachid

The **Barbary** figs. Rashid Boudjedra; translated and with an afterword by Andre Naffis-Sahely. Haus Publishing, 2013. 191 p.

ISBN 9781906697426

1. Cousins 2. Reminiscing in old age 3. Revolutions 4. Colonized peoples 5. Conversation 6. Algeria 7. Psychological fiction 8. Political fiction 9. Translations

LC Bl2013005674

Two cousins are on a flight from Algiers to Constantine and during the hour long flight old resentments emerge as they examine their past as boys in French Algeria and teenagers fighting in the revolution.

Translation from the French of Figuiers de Barbarie.

Originally published: Paris : Grasset, c2010.

Boulle, Pierre

The **bridge** over the River Kwai: a novel. Pierre Boulle; translated from the French by Xan Fielding. Presidio Press, 2007. 224 p.

ISBN 9780891419136

1. Forced labor 2. Prisoners of war, British 3. World War II 4. Bridges 5. Prisoners of war 6. Thailand 7. Second World War era (1939-1945) 8. War stories 9. Historical fiction 10. Books to movies

Re-creates the events surrounding the construction of a Japanese supply bridge over the River Kwai by British prisoners-of-war during World War II.

Originally published in English: New York : Vanguard, 1954.

Originally published in French in 1952.

Translated from the French.

Bourdeaut, Olivier

Waiting for Bojangles: a novel. Olivier Bourdeaut; translated from the French by Regan Kramer. Simon & Schuster, 2019. 176 p.

ISBN 9781501145919

1. People with mental illnesses 2. Familial love 3. Birds as pets 4. Family relationships 5. Mothers and sons 6. Paris, France 7. Spain 8. Literary fiction 9. Love stories 10. Translations 11. Adult books for young adults

A young boy lives with his madcap parents, Louise and George, and an exotic bird in a Parisian apartment. As his mother, mesmerizing and unpredictable, descends deeper into mental illness, it is up to the boy and his father to keep her safe and, when that fails, happy. Fleeing Paris for a country home in Spain, they come to understand that some of the most radiant people bear the heaviest burdens.

Translated from the French.

Bourland, Barbara

★ **Fake** like me. Barbara Bourland. Grand Central Publishing, 2019. 336 p.

ISBN 9781538759516

1. Women artists 2. Creativity in women 3. Ambition in women 4. Artists' retreats 5. Identity (Psychology) 6. New York City 7. New York (State) 8. Satirical fiction 9. Psychological suspense 10. First person narratives

LC 2018048057

A satire of the absurdly glamorous New York high art scene, in which a young artist crumbles under unimaginable pressure while at an upstate artists' retreat.

Bourne, Joanna

The **black** hawk. Joanna Bourne. Berkley Sensation, 2011. 336 p. (Spymaster series, 4)

ISBN 9780425244531

1. Women spies 2. Frameups 3. Man-woman relationships 4. Spies 5. London, England 6. Regency period (1811-1820) 7. Regency romances 8. Historical romances

Library Journal Best Books, 2011; RITA Award for Best Historical Romance, 2012

After a brutal attack leaves her close to death, agent Justine DeCabrillac, known as "Owl," staggers to the door of the one man who can save her—and the one man she hates—Adrian Hawkhurst.

The **forbidden** rose. Joanna Bourne. Berkley, 2010. 400 p. (Spymaster series, 3)

ISBN 9780425235614

1. Disguises 2. Man-woman relationships 3. Spies 4. Revolutions — History 5. Revenge in men 6. France 7. Historical romances

Library Journal Best Books, 2010; Romantic Times Reviewers' Choice Award, 2010

During the revolution in Paris, Marguerite de Fleurignac, once a wealthy aristocrat, disguises herself as a governess and is rescued from fanatics by a mysterious stranger who, unbeknownst to her, is England's top spy and needs her to settle an old score.

"The author delivers another addictively readable installment in her loosely connected Spymaster novels, a flawless romance in which an espionage-steeped plot is deftly balanced with a lusciously sensual love story." —*Booklist*

★ **My** lord and spymaster. Joanna Bourne. Berkley, 2008. 336 p. (Spymaster series, 2)

ISBN 9780425222461

1. Fathers and daughters 2. Rich women 3. Traitors 4. Undercover operations 5. Organized crime 6. London, England 7. Historical romances

RITA Award for Best Regency, 2009

"Glimpses of the leads' sordid pasts add depth, and Bourne's consummate way with a story line and an explosive denouement do the rest." —*Publishers Weekly*

Rogue spy. Joanna Bourne. Berkley Sensation, 2014. 320 p. (Spymaster series, 5)

ISBN 9780425260821

1. Women spies 2. Spies 3. Double agents 4. Treason 5. Extortion 6. London, England 7. England 8. Historical romances

Library Journal Best Books 2014

To prove his loyalty to the British Crown, Thomas Paxton must renew an old friendship with former French spy Camille Leyland, and as love blossoms between them, he must choose between going rogue from the Service or losing her forever.

"Bourne continues to demonstrate a remarkable flair for deftly mixing danger and desire in an impeccably crafted Regency setting." —*Booklist*

★ The **spymaster's** lady. Joanna Bourne. Berkley, 2008. 384 p. (Spymaster series, 1)

ISBN 9780425219607

1. Women spies 2. Spies 3. Prisons 4. Secrets 5. France 6. England 7. Regency period (1811-1820) 8. Regency romances 9. Historical romances

RUSA Reading List, 2009.

As the fates of nations hang in the balance, Annique Villiers, an elusive spy known as the Fox Cub, meets her match in British spymaster Robert Grey, when they, captured and thrown into prison, form an uneasy alliance in order to survive.

Bowen, Elizabeth

The **heat** of the day. Elizabeth Bowen. Penguin Books in association with J. Cape 1985. 329p.

ISBN 9780140018448

1. World War II. 2. World War II home front 3. London, England 4. Second World War era (1939-1945) 5. Psychological fiction 6. Modern classics

LC 85204051
In London, at the height of the German bombing during World War II, Stella Rodney finds her world turned upside down when she discovers that her lover, Robert, is suspected of selling secrets to the enemy and that his enigmatic pursuer, Harrison, will exchange his silence for Stella herself.

Bowen, Kelly

★ **Between** the devil and the duke. Kelly Bowen. Forever, 2017. 336 p. (Season for scandal, 3)

ISBN 9781455563418

1. Casinos 2. Women gamblers 3. Cardsharping 4. Card dealers 5. Scandals 6. England 7. Great Britain 8. Regency period (1811-1820) 9. Regency romances 10. Historical romances 11. Canadian fiction
RITA Award, 2018

When he catches Angelique Archer counting cards at his vingt-et-un table, club owner Alexander Lavoie gives this blonde beauty an offer she can't refuse—until their business arrangement turns into a game of love that neither of them want to lose.

"Bowen (You're the Earl I Want, 2015) again delivers the goods with this exquisitely written historical romance, whose richly nuanced characters, unexpected flashes of dry wit, and superbly sensual love story will have readers sighing happily in satisfaction." —*Booklist*

A **rogue** by night. Kelly Bowen. Forever/Grand Central Publishing, 2019. 368 p. (Devils of Dover, 3)

ISBN 9781478918622

1. Aristocracy 2. Smugglers 3. Interpersonal attraction 4. Physicians 5. Smuggling 6. England 7. Great Britain 8. Regency period (1811-1820) 9. Regency romances 10. Historical romances 11. Canadian fiction

Harland Hayward is living a double life as an aristocrat by day and a criminal by night. As a doctor, Harland has the perfect cover to appear in odd places at all hours, although he's chosen this life to save his family from financial ruin...Katherine Wright thought she was done smuggling. But her father and brother need her help to fulfill one last contract. Which means working with Hayward, even when her instincts tell her that becoming his ally may be a risk to her heart, as well as her life.

Bowen, Peter

Badlands. Peter Bowen. St. Martin's Minotaur, 2003. 250 p; (Gabriel Du Pre mysteries, 10)

ISBN 9780312262525

1. Cults 2. Serial murder investigation 3. Small towns 4. Sheriffs 5. Police 6. Montana 7. Mysteries

LC 2002037196

Part-time sheriff and fiddler Gabriel Du Pre investigates the shooting deaths of seven former members of the Host of Yahweh, a California cult recently relocated to Toussaint, Montana's cattle country.

"Montana sheriff Gabriel Du Pre's suspicions are aroused when the Host of Yahweh immediately destroys the ranch buildings, sells the livestock and erects a makeshift metal chapel for secret rites. Soon, reportsof mass murders and suicides bring in cautious FBI agents ever mindful of the Waco debacle. Du Pre's blunt speech and sometimes opaque thought patterns can be hard to follow, but his pursuits of wrongdoers over cliffs, canyons and arid river beds are truly riveting." —*Publishers Weekly*

Bowen, Rhys

The **victory** garden. Rhys Bowen. Lake Union Publishing, 2019. 353 pages

ISBN 9781542040129

1. Gardens 2. Women and war 3. World War I — Women 4. Engaged persons 5. Herbalists 6. Devon, England 7. England 8. First World War era (1914-1918) 9. Historical fiction 10. Gentle reads

Engaged to an Australian pilot during World War I, Emily volunteers to tend the neglected grounds of a Devonshire estate where she finds inspiration and support in an herbalist's long-forgotten journals.

"Lovers of history will better understand the sacrifices in England during the Great War, while romance fans will revel in the engagement and growth of the characters." —*Library Journal*

Bowles, David

Feathered serpent, dark heart of sky: myths of Mexico. David Bowles. Cinco Puntos Press, 2017. 368 p.

ISBN 9781941026717

1. Indians of Central America — Religion 2. Aztecs — Religion 3. Mayas — Religion 4. Olmecs — Religion 5. Toltecs — Religion 6. Mexico 7. Mythology, folklore, and legends

LC 2017021739

A contemporary retelling of the origin myths of Mexico, crafted as a single concrete narrative.

Bowles, Paul

★ The **sheltering** sky. Paul Bowles. Vintage International, 1990. 335 p.

ISBN 9780679729792

1. Americans in Morocco 2. Travelers 3. Voyages and travels 4. Billy, the Kid 5. Culture shock 6. Morocco 7. Sahara 8. Psychological fiction 9. Literary fiction 10. Books to movies

LC 89028905

Three Americans drifting through postwar North Africa encounter the limits of human existence in the form of a land and a people utterly alien to them.

Bowman, Conor

★ **Horace** Winter says goodbye. Conor Bowman. Hachette Books Ireland, 2017. 330 p.

ISBN 9781473641808

1. Bankers 2. Midlife crisis 3. Redemption 4. Banks and banking 5. Senior men 6. Dublin, Ireland 7. Mainstream fiction

Horace Winter has spent forty-seven years working in a Dublin bank, and doesn't, strictly speaking, have friends. But then he meets Amanda and Max. He discovers a letter his father never posted, and goes on a mission to find its addressee; he gets a man jailed (sort of) and rescues his son (sort of); he learns to fly a model airplane and takes his own first flight abroad, to answer one central question: is Horace Winter a Butterfly? Or is he a Moth?

Bowman, David

Big bang: a nonfiction novel. David Bowman; introduction by Jonathan Lethem. Little Brown & Co, 2019. Xxiii, 595 pages

ISBN 9780316560238

1. Social change 2. Celebrities 3. 1950s 4. 1960s 5. Historical fiction 6. Literary fiction

Set in the 1950's, this epic, Warholian novel presents a brilliant and wholly original take on the years leading up to the Kennedy assassination.

"Bowman's posthumous novel is a masterpiece, certainly long but never tedious because of the rapid focus changes." —*Library Journal*

Bowman, Valerie

The **accidental** countess. Valerie Bowman. St Martin's Press, 2014. 312 p. (Playful brides, 2)
ISBN 9781250042088
1. Mistaken identity 2. Love triangles 3. Deception 4. Napoleonic Wars veterans 5. Cousins 6. England 7. Regency period (1811-1820) 8. Regency romances 9. Historical romances

Returning home from the war and to an unwanted arranged marriage, Captain Julian Swift finds himself falling for Lady Cassandra Monroe, his fiancée's cousin who, unbeknownst to him, has been in love with him for years.

"The second in Bowman's thoroughly entertaining, Regency-set Playful Brides series (The Unexpected Duchess, 2014) will delight readers with its madcap plot and buoyant sense of humor." —*Booklist*

A **duke** like no other. Valerie Bowman. St Martins Pr 2018. 352 p. (Playful brides, 9)
ISBN 9781250121738
1. Generals 2. Married people 3. Separated couples 4. Aristocracy 5. Promotions 6. Great Britain 7. England 8. Regency period (1811-1820) 9. Regency romances 10. Historical romances

When her dashing spymaster husband, whom she hasn't seen for ten years, arrives on her doorstep, asking her to return to England with him so that he can get the political promotion he has always wanted, Nicole Huntingdon Grimaldi agrees on one condition—she wants a baby.

"A hero and heroine struggling to come to terms with their past while dealing with an abundance of present-day, pent-up passion and a potential murder adds up to another entertaining entry in Bowman's fanciful and fun Playful Brides series." —*Booklist*

No other duke but you. Valerie Bowman. St. Martin's Press, 2019. 352 p. (Playful brides, 11)
ISBN 9781250121677
1. Dukes and duchesses 2. Love potions 3. Best friends 4. Aristocracy 5. Errors 6. London, England 7. Great Britain 8. Regency period (1811-1820) 9. Historical romances 10. Regency romances

A lady with a love potion. A Duke who takes it by mistake. Romance and mischief ensues when plans go awry in No Other Duke But You by Valerie Bowman.

Secrets of a wedding night. Valerie Bowman. St. Martins Press, 2012. 352 p. (Secret brides, 1)
ISBN 9781250008954
1. Scandals 2. Counts and countesses 3. Pamphlets 4. Widows 5. Seduction 6. London, England 7. Regency period (1811-1820) 8. Regency romances 9. Historical romances

To stop an innocent girl from marrying the Marquis of Colton, who had broken her own heart five years earlier, young widow Lily Andrews anonymously writes and distributes a pamphlet entitled "Secrets of a Wedding Night" and garners the ire of the Marquis, who issues a wicked challenge.

The **unexpected** duchess. Valerie Bowman. St Martin's Press, 2014. 354 p. (Playful brides, 1)
ISBN 9781250042071
1. Aristocracy 2. Love triangles 3. Female friendship 4. Courtship 5. Promises 6. London, England 7. Regency period (1811-1820) 8. Regency romances 9. Historical romances

To help her painfully shy friend discourage an unwanted suitor, sharp-tongued Lady Lucy Upton engages in a battle of wits with Lord Derek Hunt and is shocked to discover that tangling with this tenacious man is the most fun she has had in ages.

"Lucy is the Regency shrew to Hunt's gentle-warrior hero who falls for her quick wit, then recognizes the wounded girl behind the virago mask. A fun, smart comedy of errors and a sexy, satisfying romance." —*Kirkus*

Box, C. J.

Badlands. C. J. Box. Minotaur Books, 2015. 400 pages. (Cassie Dewell novels, 2)
ISBN 9780312583217
1. Police misconduct 2. Greed 3. Murder investigation 4. Detectives 5. Ambition in boys 6. North Dakota 7. Thrillers and suspense

Thanks to a massive oil discovery, once-dying Grimstad, North Dakota has become a sprawling boom town full of newcomers and new houses—plus drugs, gangs, and violence. Twelve-year-old paperboy Kyle Westergaard, witnesses a vehicle fatally force another car off the road and snatches up a mysterious bag that falls out of it at the scene. The police say it's a single-car accident—and Kyle learns that bag is something a lot of people want. Narrated by both Kyle and deputy sheriff Cassie Dewell (readers of The Highway will remember her), this atmospheric novel brims with suspense and action.

"Cassie arrives just as a series of brutal murders signals a war between drug gangs—although the missing duffle bag the criminals are searching for has accidentally wound up in the hands of a special-needs paperboy, 12-year-old Kyle Westergaard... The story's brisk action is broken into alternating sections as Cassie and Kyle try to figure out what's going on and what they must do. The vulnerable boy's plight gives emotional heft to the criminal investigation, balancing cynicism with warm empathy." —*Publishers Weekly*

★ The **bitterroots**: a novel. C.J. Box. Minotaur Books, 2019. 352 pages (Cassie Dewell novels, 4)
ISBN 9781250051059
1. Women private investigators 2. Former police 3. Single mothers 4. Rape investigation 5. Rape 6. Montana 7. Thrillers and suspense
LC 2019006884

Private investigator Cassie Dewell agrees to take a case involving the assault of a young woman, but as she tries to uncover the truth, Cassie finds herself fighting an influential family as well as ghosts from her own past.

Blue heaven. C.J. Box. St. Martin's Minotaur, 2008. 352 p.
ISBN 9780312365707
1. Child witnesses 2. Former police 3. Single mothers 4. Bankers 5. Ranchers 6. Idaho 7. Multiple perspectives 8. Mysteries
LC 2007038728
Edgar Allan Poe Award for Best Novel, 2009; RUSA Reading List, 2009

Fleeing the killers whom they witnessed committing murder, twelve-year-old Annie and her younger brother William escape into the woods of northern Idaho, not knowing whom they can trust and pursued by the murderers and a group of dirty cops seeking to prevent the youngsters from revealing what they know.

"Two young kids witness a backwoods execution-style murder in their rural Idaho hamlet. Worse yet, the killers—four retired cops from Los Angeles—see the children and begin a dogged pursuit. Struggling rancher Jess Rawlins is surprised to find Annie and William hiding in his barn, but he's wise enough to believe their lurid tale. He also astutely recognizes the goodness of a stranger in town: Eduardo Villatoro, a retired detective, is determined to put one last unsolved case—a big one—to rest. Villatoro's case is the final nail in the coffin for these bad cops, and it's up to Jess and him to save the children...A quick, satisfying, and straightforward—if fairly transparent—read." —*Library Journal*

★ **Dark** sky: a Joe Pickett novel. C.J. Box. Putnam Pub Group, 2021. 384 p. (Joe Pickett novels, 21)

ISBN 9780525538271

1. Game wardens 2. Hunting 3. Murderers 4. Survival 5. Rescues 6. Thrillers and suspense

LC 2020050216

Wyoming game warden Joe Pickett must accompany a Silicon Valley CEO on a hunting trip—but soon learns that he himself may be the hunted.

"A strong entry in this long-running and wildly popular series." —*Booklist*

The **disappeared**. C. J. Box. G.P. Putnam's Sons, 2018. 384 p. (Joe Pickett novels, 18)

ISBN 9780399176623

1. Game wardens 2. Ranches 3. Missing women 4. Falconers 5. Wilderness areas 6. Wyoming 7. Thrillers and suspense

Wyoming game warden Joe Pickett tackles two parallel cases involving the disappearance of a prominent British executive and a group of falconers who are being harassed by the feds, a double assignment that catches the attentions of a dangerous adversary.

The **highway**. C.J. Box. Minotaur Books, 2013. 400 p. (Cody Hoyt novels, 2; Cassie Dewell novels, 1)

ISBN 9780312583200

1. Serial murder investigation 2. Missing women 3. Sisters 4. Serial murders 5. Missing persons investigation 6. Montana 7. Thrillers and suspense

When two teens go missing during a clandestine car trip, alcoholic investigator Cody Hoyt is convinced by his son and former partner to search for answers before discovering similar disappearances on a remote Montana highway that point to the work of a serial killer.

★ **Long** range. C. J. Box. G. P. Putnam's Sons, 2020. 384 p. (Joe Pickett novels, 20)

ISBN 9780525538233

1. Attempted murder 2. Judges 3. Game wardens 4. Rescues 5. Assassins 6. Thrillers and suspense

Assisting an investigation into a fatal grizzly attack that is not what it seems, Joe Pickett become embroiled in the case of a prominent judge's wife by a would-be assassin who was shooting from a confoundingly long distance.

"Box remains the gold standard among writers of modern western-mystery blends." —*Booklist*

★ **Open** season. C.J. Box. G. P. Putnam's Sons, 2001. 320 p. (Joe Pickett novels, 1)

ISBN 9780399147487

1. Hunters 2. Rare and endangered animals 3. Murder investigation 4. Courage in men 5. Poachers 6. Wyoming 7. Thrillers and suspense

LC 50992

Anthony Award for Best Novel, 2002; Booklist Editors' Choice: Adult Books for Young Adults, 2001; Macavity Award for Best First Mystery Novel, 2002; New York Times Notable Mysteries, 2001

As Wyoming game warden Joe Pickett races against time to save an endangered species, he finds himself plunged into a deadly mystery that soon threatens his family and the life he loves.

Paradise Valley. C.J. Box. Minotaur Books, 2017. 352 p. (Cassie Dewell novels, 3)

ISBN 9781250051042

1. Policewomen 2. Serial murderers 3. Serial murder investigation 4. Missing persons investigation 5. Boys with learning disabilities 6. Montana 7. North Dakota 8. Thrillers and suspense

LC 2017011481

Setting a trap for a serial killer she has hunted for three years, investigator Cassie Dewell is disgraced when the operation goes horribly wrong, a situation that is further complicated by the loss of her job, the disappearance of a troubled youth and her determination to catch the killer at any cost.

Savage run. C.J. Box. G.P. Putnam's Sons, 2002. 400 p. (Joe Pickett novels, 2)

ISBN 9780399148873

1. Environmentalists 2. Conspiracies 3. Explosions 4. Criminal investigation 5. Eco-terrorists 6. Wyoming 7. Thrillers and suspense

LC 2001057872

While investigating a string of bizarre murders, Wyoming game warden Joe Pickett is forced to flee across treacherous terrain with a deadly tracker on his trail.

Trophy hunt: a Joe Pickett novel. C.J. Box. G.P. Putnam's Sons, 2004. 336 p. (Joe Pickett novels, 4)

ISBN 9780399152009

1. Mutilation 2. Murder 3. Families 4. Human/alien encounters 5. Animal mutilations 6. Wyoming 7. Thrillers and suspense

LC 2004044389

Shaken by the brutal killing of a wild moose, game warden Joe Pickett becomes increasingly alarmed when a herd of cattle, and then two people, are murdered by the same perpetrator.

"With its credible and sensitively drawn characters, loads of interesting tidbits about the natural world and timely plot, this skillfully crafted page-turner should have wide appeal." —*Publishers Weekly*

Vicious circle. C.J. Box. G.P. Putnam's Sons, 2017. 367 p. (Joe Pickett novels, 17)

ISBN 9780399176616

1. Revenge 2. Game wardens 3. Wilderness areas 4. Fathers and daughters 5. Protectiveness in men 6. Wyoming 7. Thrillers and suspense

Rescuing his daughters from the violent Cates family, game warden Joe Pickett realizes that his new adversaries have plotted revenge against his entire family before teaming up with his friend, Nate, to take defensive steps.

"Box masterfully tightens the suspense until were caught in a vicious circle of our own and unable to stop reading." —*Booklist*

Winterkill: a novel. C.J. Box. G. P. Putnam's Sons, 2003. 372 p; (Joe Pickett novels, 3)

ISBN 9780399150456

1. Foster parents 2. Survivalists 3. Government investigators 4. Families 5. Cults 6. Wyoming 7. Thrillers and suspense

LC 2002037120

The arrow-riddled corpse of Lamar Gardiner, district supervisor for the Twelve Sleep National Forest, and the bodies of seven illegally shot elk start Wyoming game warden Joe Pickett on a pursuit that endangers the life of his beloved foster daughter April.

"As the story begins, Joe Pickett, game warden of Wyoming's Twelve Sleep County, is caught in a mountain blizzard with a dead body beside him in his pick-up truck. The body belongs to a much-hated federal bureaucrat, who may have been killed by a group of survivalists calling themselves the Sovereigns...Box handles this controversial material superbly, showing vividly how government rigidity causes human tragedy in the name of patriotism. Pickett remains an utterly sympathetic, Gary Cooperish hero, but as the series develops he has begun to darken noticeably." —*Booklist*

★ **Wolf** pack. C.J. Box. G.P. Putnam'S Sons, 2019. 384 p. (Joe Pickett novels, 19)

ISBN 9780525538196

1. Game wardens 2. Ranches 3. Assassins 4. Witnesses 5. Drone aircraft 6. Wyoming 7. Thrillers and suspense

Wyoming game warden Joe Pickett encounters bad behavior on his own turf—only to have the FBI and the DOJ ask him to stand down—in the thrilling novel from #1 New York Times-bestselling author C.J. Box.

"The action-packed final quarter of the book ranks among Joe and Nate's best and bloodiest confrontations. Box is the king of contemporary crime fiction set in the West." —*Publishers Weekly*

Boyd, William

Trio. William Boyd. Alfred A. Knopf, 2021. 288 p.
ISBN 9780593318232
1. Summer 2. Film industry and trade 3. Writing 4. Fame 5. Secrets 6. Brighton, England 7. England 8. 1960s 9. Literary fiction
LC 2020038400
A film location in 1968 Brighton is riotously upended by a scandalous intelligence investigation into the secret lives and loves of a novelist, an actress and a movie producer.

"Boyd skilfully and with great subtlety moves from a largely comic treatment of the chaos on the film set to a sensitive portrayal of fracturing inner lives, though even the latter is rendered with a superbly Forsterian sense of tragicomedy." —*Booklist*

Boyle, Elizabeth

Along came a duke. Elizabeth Boyle. Avon, 2012. 384 p. (Rhymes with love, 1)
ISBN 9780062089069
1. Mate selection for women 2. Heirs and heiresses 3. Inheritance and succession 4. Single women 5. Arranged marriage 6. England 7. London, England 8. Regency period (1811-1820) 9. Regency romances 10. Historical romances
In order to claim a vast fortune, Tabitha Timmons must marry the respectable Mr. Barkworth, but finds herself torn between the money and her feelings for the Duke of Preston, who vows to save her from a passionless union.

And the miss ran away with the rake. Elizabeth Boyle. Avon Books, 2013. 384 p. (Rhymes with love, 2)
ISBN 9780062089083
1. Mate selection 2. Letter writing 3. Nobility 4. Secret identity 5. Seduction 6. England 7. London, England 8. Regency period (1811-1820) 9. Regency romances 10. Historical romances
Exchanging romantic letters with a very appropriate suitor, one whom she has yet to meet, Daphne Dale is confused by her feelings when a rakish charmer, who is everything she's vowed to avoid, enters her life, testing her practical sensibilities and resolve.

Boyle, T. Coraghessan

The **harder** they come. T.C. Boyle. Ecco Press, 2015. 400 p.
ISBN 9780062349378
1. Father and adult son 2. Violence 3. Anger in men 4. Vietnam veterans 5. People with schizophrenia 6. California 7. Psychological fiction 8. Literary fiction
Set in contemporary Northern California, The Harder They Come explores the volatile connections between three damaged people—an aging ex-Marine and Vietnam veteran, his psychologically unstable son, and the son's paranoid, much older lover—as they career towards an explosive confrontation.

"Boyle remains a master at sustaining narrative momentum as the sense of foreboding darkens and deepens." —*Kirkus*
First published in Great Britain in 2015.

Outside looking in: a novel. T. C. Boyle. HarperCollins Publishers, 2019. 400 p.
ISBN 9780062882981
1. Leary, Timothy 2. Hallucinogenic drugs 3. Graduate students 4. Husband and wife 5. L S D use 6. L S D 7. 1960s 8. Literary fiction
A novel inspired by the controversial psychedelic drug experiments of Timothy Leary traces the impact of LSD and communal living on a 1960s Harvard grad student and his wife.

The **relive** box: and other stories. T.C. Boyle. Ecco 2017. 192 p.
ISBN 9780062673398
1. Human nature 2. Memories 3. Interpersonal relations 4. Eccentrics and eccentricities 5. Short stories 6. Humorous stories 7. Adult books for young adults
LC Bl2017032114
A collection of one dozen short stories includes the title piece, in which a "relive box" allows users to re-experience almost any moment from their past, and "The Five-Pound Burrito," in which a man aspires to make the town's largest burrito.

"Boyle's substantial collection is funny, disarming, and crushing, haunting and beautiful ...." —*Booklist*

The **Terranauts**. T. Coraghessan Boyle. Ecco Press, 2016. 528 p.
ISBN 9780062349408
1. Experiments 2. Biotic communities 3. Scientists 4. Wilderness survival 5. Sustainable communities 6. Arizona 7. 1990s 8. Psychological fiction 9. First person narratives 10. Multiple perspectives
Sealed inside a glass enclosure designed as a prototype for a possible off-earth colony, eight Terranauts in the 1990s Arizona desert test their skills in five biome environments that they must protect from skeptics who would sabotage the mission.

"Beneath the high-tech sheen is a rather old-fashioned theme: how idealistic enterprises can crumble owing to the foibles and fragility of human nature. This is one of Boyle's best—and quite possibly one of the best of the year." —*Library Journal*

★ The **tortilla** curtain. T. Coraghessan Boyle. Viking, 1995. 355 p.
ISBN 9780670856046
1. Undocumented immigrants 2. Race relations 3. Rich people 4. Suburban life 5. Undocumented workers 6. Los Angeles, California 7. Los Angeles County, California 8. Political fiction 9. Multiple perspectives 10. Mainstream fiction
LC 95-1970
The lives of two very different couples—wealthy Los Angeles liberals Delaney and Kyra Mossbacher, and Candido and America Rincon, a pair of Mexican undocumented immigrants—suddenly collide, in a story that unfolds from the shifting viewpoints of the various characters.

"What Boyle does, and does well, is lay on the line our national cult of hypocrisy. Comically and painfully he details the snug wastefulness of the haves and the vile misery of the have-nots.... Americans of every stripe will find themselves rooting for Candido and America, right up to the riproaring deus ex machina ending that screams out that we are all in this together." —*The Nation*

When the killing's done: a novel. T. Coraghessan Boyle. Viking, 2011. 369 p. : Map
ISBN 9780670022328
1. Women biologists 2. Invasive species — Control 3. Environmentalists 4. Social conflict 5. Island life 6. Santa Cruz Island, California 7. Channel Islands, California 8. Mainstream fiction 9. Adult books for young adults
Alma Boyd Takesue, a National Park Service biologist, is in charge of preserving the Channel Islands' native animals, which means removing the rats and feral pigs from the island chain. However, businessman Dave

LaJoy and folksinger Anise Reed staunchly oppose Alma's plans to kill the rats and pigs, and actively work against her.

"The novel never reduces its narrative to polemics—there are no heroes here—while underscoring the difficult decisions that those who consider themselves on the side of the angels must face. Narrative propulsion is laced with delicious irony in this winning novel." —*Kirkus*

The **women**: a novel. T. Coraghessan Boyle. Viking, 2009. 464 p.
ISBN 9780670020416
1. Wright, Frank Lloyd 2. Architects 3. Husband and wife 4. Man-woman relationships 5. 20th century 6. Biographical fiction 7. Historical fiction 8. Literary fiction

LC 2008042462

A tale inspired by the life of Frank Lloyd Wright is presented from the perspectives of four very different women who loved him and offers insight into the eminent architect's enduring struggles against conventional boundaries.

"Boyle's latest novel takes on the architect Frank Lloyd Wright by examining his notoriously tumultuous relationships with four women, each unique in her own histrionic way. Narrated in reverse chronological order by a fictional Japanese apprentice, the book is extremely readable and deftly builds a portrait of the artist as pure egoist. Unfortunately, the novel avoids any sustained consideration of Wright's relationship to his art—a passion arguably more important in forming his genius than any of the women in his life were. Still, it proves an effective showcase for Boyle's own strengths as a craftsman. His prose is full of vivid descriptions and turns of phrase that pop with a preternatural precision." —*The New Yorker*

World's end: a novel. T. Coraghessan Boyle. Viking, 1987. 456 p.
ISBN 9780670814893
1. Dutch Americans 2. Families — History 3. Class struggle 4. Social conflict 5. Betrayal 6. Hudson Valley 7. New York (State) 8. Parallel narratives 9. Family sagas

LC 87040023

PEN-Faulkner Award, 1988

Walter Van Brunt, woozy with pot, cheap wine, and sex, collides with his own historical roots when he crashes his motorcycle into a historical marker along the highway.

"The themes Mr. Boyle develops as his story shuttles between epochs make us grasp in new terms their connection with the American social and political experiment. His mastery of history is the secret of the accomplishment here. Mr. Boyle has lost none of the qualities that marked him a wit writer before, but now he has challenged his own disengagement; passion, need and belief breathe with striking force and freedom through this smashing good novel." —*New York Times Book Review*

Boyle, William

City of margins: a novel. William Boyle. Pegasus Books, 2020. 320 pages
ISBN 9781643133188
1. City life 2. Organized crime 3. Loss (Psychology) 4. Revenge 5. Neighborhoods 6. Brooklyn, New York City 7. 1990s 8. Noir fiction

The lives of several lost souls intersect in gritty 1990s south Brooklyn, from a disgraced ex-cop with blood on his hands to the grieving mother of a suicide victim.

"Battered by loss and unrealized dreams, Boyle's characters are vividly drawn and painfully real. Fans of literary crime novelists such as George Pelecanos and Richard Price will be highly rewarded." —*Publishers Weekly*

The **lonely** witness. William Boyle. Pegasus Books, 2018. 272 p.
ISBN 9781681777955

1. Murder witnesses 2. Murder investigation 3. Women amateur detectives 4. Murderers 5. Volunteers 6. Brooklyn, New York City 7. New York City 8. Mysteries

A former party girl who now helps house-bound seniors in the Gravesend neighborhood of Brooklyn agrees to help a woman whose usual caretaker is missing and ends up witnessing a murder that she doesn't report and develops a fascination with the killer.

Boyne, John

The **heart's** invisible furies. John Boyne. Hogarth Press, 2017. 592 p.
ISBN 9781524760786
1. Single mothers 2. Pariahs 3. Discrimination 4. Growing up 5. Mothers and sons 6. Ireland 7. United States 8. 20th century 9. Picaresque fiction 10. Coming-of-age stories 11. Literary fiction 12. Adult books for young adults
Longlisted for the Andrew Carnegie Medal for Excellence in Fiction, 2018

In 1945, Cyril Avery was born to an unmarried teenager (the book opens with a dramatic scene in a rural Irish church that sets this up with relish) and adopted by a wealthy if rather eccentric Dublin couple. As readers, we visit Cyril every seven years, as he grows and comes to terms with his homosexuality in a violently repressive Ireland, flees his home country, and falls in love. An absorbing story, this novel offers richly drawn characters, plausibly life-altering choices, and an often humorous writing style.

"Often quite funny, the story nevertheless has its sadness, sometimes approaching tragedy. Utterly captivating and not to be missed." —*Booklist*
Originally published: London : Doubleday, 2017.

★ A **ladder** to the sky. John Boyne. Hogarth Press, 2018. 362 pages
ISBN 9781984823014
1. Authors 2. Ambition in men 3. Manipulation by men 4. Fame 5. Writing 6. West Berlin, Germany 7. 1980s 8. Literary fiction
LibraryReads Favorites, 2018

Aspiring writer Maurice Swift, whose desire for fame exceeds his talent, uses a chance meeting with celebrated novelist Erich Ackermann to obtain secrets about Ackermann's wartime activities, which becomes material for his first novel.

"Boynes fast-paced, white-knuckle plot, accompanied by delightfully sardonic commentary on the ego, insecurities, and pitfalls of those involved in the literary world, makes for a truly engrossing experience." —*Publishers Weekly*

Bradbury, Jamey

The **wild** inside: a novel. Jamey Bradbury. William Morrow, 2018. 290 p.
ISBN 9780062741998
1. Wilderness areas 2. Violence against women 3. Strangers 4. Women trackers 5. Families 6. Alaska 7. Coming-of-age stories 8. Adult books for young adults

LC 2017042752

Spending her days tracking and running with her dogs in the Alaskan wilderness, Iditarod contender Tracy survives a mysterious encounter in the woods and begins to question the agenda of a stranger who she fears may be targeting her family.

Bradbury, Ray

Bradbury stories: 100 of his most celebrated tales. Ray Bradbury. William Morrow, 2003. 912 p.
ISBN 9780060542429

1. Space flight 2. Space exploration 3. Mars (Planet) 4. Science fiction 5. Short stories 6. Adult books for young adults

LC 2003042189

A retrospective collection of one hundred short stories features pieces written after 1943 includes both popular favorites and lesser-known works of distinction.

"This massive retrospective of self-selected Bradbury stories offers a compendium of his eccentrics, misfits, losers, and small-town dreamers, who typically inhabit an uncanny setting or confront a strange, unsettling situation." —*Library Journal*

100 of his most celebrated tales.

★ **Dandelion** wine: a novel. Ray Bradbury; with an introduction from the author. Avon Books, 1999. Xiv, 267 p.

ISBN 9780380977260

1. Twelve-year-old boys 2. Growing up 3. Families 4. Family relationships 5. Old and new things 6. Illinois 7. 1920s 8. Coming-of-age stories

LC 98093914

A summer in the life of a 12 year old boy in 1928 in the hamlet of Green Town, Ill.

"The writing is beautiful and the characters are wonderful living people. A rare reading experiencehighly recommended to all libraries." —*Library Journal*

Originally published: Garden City, N.Y. : Doubleday, 1957.

Sequel: Farewell summer.

★ **Fahrenheit** 451. Ray Bradbury. Simon & Schuster, 1993. 190 p.

ISBN 9780671870362

1. Censorship 2. Dystopias 3. Totalitarianism 4. Banned books 5. Conformity 6. Dystopian fiction 7. Science fiction classics 8. Social science fiction

LC 93010885

A totalitarian regime has ordered all books to be destroyed, but one of the book burners, Guy Montag, suddenly realizes their merit.

Originally published: New York : Ballantine Books, 1953.

The **illustrated** man. Ray Bradbury. Avon Books, 1997. 288 p.

ISBN 9780380973842

1. Tattooing 2. Storytelling 3. Magic 4. Technology and civilization 5. Husband and wife 6. Earth 7. Mars (Planet) 8. Short stories 9. Horror 10. Books to movies

Eighteen imaginative science fiction stories—including the title story in which a tattooist's needle creates a canvas that captures humankind's destiny—range from the not-so-ordinary world of middle America to the vast reaches of outer space as they explore themes of love, madness, and death.

Short stories originally published between 1948 and 1951.

Originally published: New York : Doubleday, 1951.

★ The **Martian** chronicles: the fortieth anniversary edition. Ray Bradbury. Doubleday, 1990. Xi, 205 p.

ISBN 9780385050609

1. Space colonies 2. Human/alien encounters 3. Martians 4. Space exploration 5. Life on other planets 6. Mars (Planet) 7. Science fiction classics 8. Social science fiction 9. Science fiction

LC 90044362

Interconnected, chronological stories of Earth's settlement of Mars include tales of human interaction with one another and with the Martians, interplanetary interracial strife, self-doubt, and the metamorphosis of humanity.

Includes a new foreword, as well as "a story excised from the original book."

Originally published: Garden City, N.Y. : Doubleday, 1950.

★ **Something** wicked this way comes. Ray Bradbury. Avon Books, 1998. 304 p.

ISBN 9780380729401

1. Carnivals 2. Good and evil 3. Thirteen-year-old boys 4. Boys — Friendship 5. Best friends 6. Illinois 7. Horror 8. Coming-of-age stories 9. Books to movies

Story of two young boys who begin to encounter evil secrets when a lightning rod salesman gives them one of his contraptions covered with mystical symbols.

Originally published: New York : Simon and Schuster, 1962.

Bradby, Tom

Double agent. Tom Bradby. Atlantic Monthly Press, 2020. 368 p. (Kate Henderson novels, 2)

ISBN 9780802157645

1. Women intelligence officers 2. Intelligence service 3. International intrigue 4. Traitors 5. Politicians 6. Spy fiction 7. Thrillers and suspense

LC 2020038630

MI6 agent Kate Henderson investigates information from a Russian defector, including financial trails and a horrifying video, that may offer proof that the British Prime Minister is a live agent working for Moscow in the sequel to Secret Service.

"Bradby masterfully combines textured psychological drama with a rip-roaring plot that boasts several dizzying switchbacks along the way to a genuinely shocking conclusion." —*Booklist*

Bradford, Barbara Taylor

★ A **woman** of substance. Barbara Taylor Bradford. Doubleday, 1979. 755 pages (Harte Family, 1)

ISBN 9780385120500

1. Businesspeople 2. Power (Social sciences) 3. Rich women 4. Family relationships 5. Family businesses 6. Family sagas 7. Books to movies

LC 77009231

Emma Harte, an enormously wealthy and powerful self-made woman, learns that her four children are plotting to sell the business that she founded, which leads her to summon everyone to her Yorkshire estate for a showdown.

Sequel: Hold the dream.

Bradley, Anna

A **season** of ruin. Anna Bradley. Berkley Sensation, 2016. 294 p. (Sutherland scandals, 2)

ISBN 9780425282649

1. Womanizers 2. Debutantes 3. Scandals 4. Reputation 5. Gossiping and gossips 6. London, England 7. England 8. Regency period (1811-1820) 9. Regency romances 10. Historical romances

When faced with a scandal that could destroy her hopes of marriage to a respectable gentleman, Lily Somerset must convince Robyn Sutherland to be her escort for the season in an attempt to repair her tattered reputation.

A **wicked** way to win an earl. Anna Bradley. Berkley, 2015. 296 p. (Sutherland scandals, 1)

ISBN 9780425282632

1. Earls and countesses 2. Womanizers 3. Enemies 4. Seduction 5. Family feuds 6. Kent, England 7. England 8. Regency period (1811-1820) 9. Regency romances 10. Historical romances

Romantic Times Reviewer's Choice Award, 2015

To appease her sister, Della Somerset, who despises the privileged ton, agrees to attend a party at the Sutherland estate, home to the infamous scoundrel Alec Sutherland, and catches the eye of the notorious rogue whose intentions are less than honorable.

Bradley, C. Alan

As chimney sweepers come to dust: a Flavia de Luce novel. Alan Bradley. Delacorte Press, 2015. 392 p. (Flavia De Luce mysteries, 7)
ISBN 9780345539939
1. Girl detectives 2. Boarding schools 3. Murder 4. Girl scientists 5. Intelligence 6. Canada 7. Mysteries 8. Canadian fiction 9. Adult books for young adults

LC 2014029962

LibraryReads Favorites, 2015

Young chemist and aspiring detective Flavia de Luce once again uses her knowledge of poisons and her indefatigable spirit to solve a crime, but this time she leaves behind the English countryside and enters the unexpectedly unsavory world of Canadian boarding schools.

"Flavias resourcefulness away from her English village with a whole new set of well-drawn characters is reason to rejoice. Fans of Dorothy Sayers, Gladys Mitchell, and Agatha Christie will delight in this engaging series." —*Library Journal*

The **golden** tresses of the dead: a Flavia de Luce novel. Alan Bradley. Delacorte Press, 2019. 400 p. (Flavia De Luce mysteries, 10)
ISBN 9780345540027
1. Girl detectives 2. Girl scientists 3. Weddings 4. Wedding cakes 5. Private investigators 6. England 7. 1950s 8. Historical mysteries 9. Canadian fiction 10. Adult books for young adults

LC 2018039374

Loan Stars Favourites, 2019

Setting up shop to solve crimes, 12-year-old Flavia de Luce, aided by trusty gardener Dogger, investigates a grisly discovery in her older sister's wedding cake.

"Bradley, who has few peers at combining fair-play clueing with humor and has fun mocking genre conventions, shows no sign of running out of ideas." —*Publishers Weekly*

The **grave's** a fine and private place: a Flavia de Luce novel. Alan Bradley. Delacorte Press, 2018. 432 p. (Flavia De Luce mysteries, 9)
ISBN 9780345539991
1. Girl detectives 2. Girl scientists 3. Boating 4. Dead 5. Sisters 6. England 7. 1950s 8. Historical mysteries 9. Canadian fiction 10. Adult books for young adults

LC 2017031500

Loan Stars Favourites, 2018

Joining her older sisters for a recuperative boating trip in the aftermath of a devastating tragedy, 12-year-old Flavia de Luce discovers a body in the water near the church of a murderous vicar.

I am half-sick of shadows: a Flavia de Luce novel. Alan Bradley. Delacorte Press, 2011. 384 p. (Flavia De Luce mysteries, 4)
ISBN 9780385344012
1. Filmmaking 2. Actors and actresses 3. Murder investigation 4. Film industry and trade 5. Girl detectives 6. England 7. Mysteries 8. Canadian fiction 9. Christmas stories 10. Adult books for young adults

After the whole village of Bishop's Lacey descends on Flavia de Luce's family's estate during a raging blizzard to watch the filming of a movie, a person ends up dead, strangled by a length of film, and the 11-year-old budding chemist must find the killer.

A **red** herring without mustard. Alan Bradley. Delacorte Press, 2011. 384 p. (Flavia De Luce mysteries, 3)
ISBN 9780385342322

1. Romani women 2. Girl detectives 3. Murder investigation 4. Girl scientists 5. Poisons 6. England 7. Mysteries 8. Canadian fiction 9. Adult books for young adults

When a Gypsy woman is wrongly accused of kidnapping a local child, precocious young Flavia de Luce draws on her encyclopedic knowledge of poisons and Gypsy lore to discern what really happened while investigating the mystery of her own mother's fate.

"Think preteen Nancy Drew, only savvier and a lot richer, and you have Flavia de Luce, an 11-year-old sleuth of the English gentry who's morbidly interested in both corpses and poison (she's got a chemistry lab in the attic). When a body turns up on the lawn of the family estate skewered by an heirloom sterling lobster fork she gets to work. Don't be fooled by Flavia's age or the 1950s setting: A Red Herring isn't a dainty tea-and-crumpets sort of mystery. It's shot through with real grit." —*Entertainment Weekly*

Includes reading group notes.

Speaking from among the bones: a Flavia de Luce novel. Alan Bradley. Delacorte Press, 2013. 400 p. (Flavia De Luce mysteries, 5)
ISBN 9780385344036
1. Girl detectives 2. Murder investigation 3. Masks 4. Murder 5. Girl scientists 6. England 7. Mysteries 8. Canadian fiction 9. Adult books for young adults

LC 2012028396

When the tomb of Saint Tancred, the patron saint of Bishop's Lacey, is opened on the five-hundredth anniversary of his death and the body of the missing church organist, Mr. Collicutt, is discovered inside, eleven-year-old amateur detective Flavia de Luce launches her own investigation into his death.

★ The **sweetness** at the bottom of the pie. Alan Bradley. Delacorte Press, 2009. 272 p. (Flavia De Luce mysteries, 1)
ISBN 9780385342308
1. Girl scientists 2. Girl detectives 3. Murder investigation 4. Intelligence 5. De Luce, Flavia (Fictitious character) 6. England 7. 1950s 8. Mysteries 9. Canadian fiction 10. Adult books for young adults

LC 2008041787

Agatha Award for Best First Novel, 2009; Amelia Bloomer List, 2010; Arthur Ellis Award for Best First Novel, 2010; Dilys Award, 2010; Macavity Award for Best First Mystery Novel, 2010; YALSA Best Books for Young Adults, 2010

Eleven-year-old Flavia de Luce, an aspiring chemist with a passion for poison, begins her adventure when a dead bird is found on the doorstep of her family's mansion in the summer of 1950, thus propelling her into a mystery that involves an investigation into a man's murder where her father is the main suspect.

"Mystery fans, Anglophiles, and science buffs will delight in this book and may come away with a slightly altered view of what is possible for a headstrong girl to achieve." —*School Library Journal*

Thrice the brinded cat hath mew'd: a Flavia de Luce novel. Alan Bradley. Delacorte Press, 2016. 331 p. (Flavia De Luce mysteries, 8)
ISBN 9780345539960
1. Girl detectives 2. Homecomings 3. Murder 4. Girl scientists 5. Intelligence 6. England 7. Mysteries 8. Canadian fiction 9. Adult books for young adults

LC 2016006913

LibraryReads Favorites, 2016; Loan Stars Favourites, 2016

Excitedly sailing home to England after being ejected from her stuffy young ladies' school, 12-year-old Flavia receives news of her father's serious illness and is surrounded by annoying family members before stumbling onto a murder scene where the only witness is the cat.

The **weed** that strings the hangman's bag: a Flavia de Luce mystery. Alan Bradley. Delacorte Press, 2010. 364 p. (Flavia De Luce mysteries, 2)
ISBN 9780385342315
1. Puppeteers 2. Girl detectives 3. Poisons 4. Murder investigation 5. Eleven-year-old girls 6. England 7. 1950s 8. Mysteries 9. Canadian fiction 10. Adult books for young adults
LC 2009043002
Flavia de Luce applies her skills in the chemistry lab to solving the murder of a master puppeteer, a case that is further complicated by her tormenting sisters.

Braffet, Kelly
★ **Last** seen leaving: a novel. Kelly Braffet. Houghton Mifflin, 2006. 272 p.
ISBN 9780618441440
1. Mothers and daughters 2. Father-separated girls 3. Family relationships 4. Missing women 5. Women college students 6. Psychological fiction
LC 2005037965
When Miranda, a young drifter, vanishes after being picked up by a passing stranger following a car accident, no one realizes that she is missing for two months or that her highway rescuer could be tied to rumors of a serial killer stalking young women.
"Both Anne and Miranda tell their sides of the story, allowing Braffet to flesh out their strained relationship. It is a story about the fragility of relationships as well as the secrets we keep and the lies we tell ourselves to get us through the pain of love and loss." —*Booklist*

Braithwaite, Oyinkan
My sister, the serial killer: a novel. Oyinkan Braithwaite. Random House Inc, 2018. 160 p.
ISBN 9780385544238
1. Women serial murderers 2. Family relationships 3. Sisters 4. Sisterhood 5. Serial murders 6. Nigeria 7. Lagos, Nigeria 8. Satirical fiction 9. Black humor
LC 2018013372
Anthony Award for Best First Novel, 2019; LibraryReads Favorites, 2018; Los Angeles Times Book Prize for Mystery or Thriller, 2018; Shortlisted for The Women's Prize for Fiction, 2019; Longlisted for the Booker Prize, 2019
Realizing that her beautiful, beloved younger sister has murdered yet another boyfriend, an embittered Nigerian woman works to direct suspicion away from the family, until a handsome doctor she fancies asks for her sister's number.

Bram, Christopher
Lives of the circus animals: a novel. Christopher Bram. Harper Collins, 2003. 341 p.
ISBN 9780060542535
1. Dramatists, American 2. Personal assistants 3. Actors and actresses 4. Gay actors 5. Theater critics 6. Broadway, New York City 7. New York City 8. Psychological fiction
LC 2002192195
Lambda Literary Award for Gay Men's Fiction, 2003; New York Times Notable Book, 2003
A comedy of manners explores themes of love, work, and success in the world behind the scenes of contemporary New York theater.
"Bram has a sophisticated understanding of celebrity and the intersection of gay and straight worlds. His savvy—and his easy familiarity with the New York theater scene—gives edge and nuance to this witty entertainment." —*Publishers Weekly*

Brand, Max
★ The **collected** stories of Max Brand. . University of Nebraska Press, 1994. 342 p.
ISBN 9780803212442
1. Short stories 2. Westerns
LC 93043938
Collects eighteen short stories by the noted writer of westerns, including "Above the Law," "Outcast Breed," "The Sun Stood Still," "Interns Can't Take Money," and "The Strange Villa" BT
Includes eighteen stories taken from different genres.

Max Brand's best western stories. . Dodd, Mead, 1981. 228 p.
ISBN 9780396079842
1. Gunfighters 2. Outlaws 3. Frontier and pioneer life 4. The West (United States) 5. Westerns 6. Short stories
"With a solid biographical introduction by editor Nolan—a worthy gathering of grand oldies that are short on clichÉs (no rustlers or bandits), long on crisp details and mythic intensity." —*Kirkus*

The **Stingaree**. Max Brand. R. Bentley, 1981. 216 p.
ISBN 9780837604619
1. The West (Canada) 2. Westerns
Half Indian and half white, Jimmy Green is only 13 when the Stingaree arrives in his French-Canadian town searching for the murderer of his partner.

Brandreth, Benet
The **spy** of Venice. Benet Brandreth. Pegasus Books, 2018. Xii, 434 p. : Map (William Shakespeare novels (Benet Brandreth), 1)
ISBN 9781681777986
1. Shakespeare, William 2. Assassins 3. Intrigue 4. Actors and actresses 5. Espionage 6. Spies 7. London, England 8. Venice, Italy 9. Renaissance (1300-1600) 10. 16th century 11. Historical mysteries 12. Adult books for young adults
Seeking his fortune in 16th-century London, a talented wordsmith joins a band of players before he is dispatched to Venice on an assignment that renders him the target of Catholic assassins and a shadowy killer.
As rich in period detail as Rory Clement's John Shakespeare series (about William's older brother) and C. J. Sansom's Matthew Shardlake novels, also set in the sixteenth century, but a lot more fun. Bravo! Booklist.
Originally published: London : Twenty7, 2016.

Brandt, Harry
The **Whites:** a novel. Harry Brandt. Henry Holt and Company, 2015. 336 p.
ISBN 9780805093995
1. Forties (Age) 2. City life 3. Consequences 4. Murder victims 5. Friendship 6. New York City 7. Hardboiled fiction 8. Mysteries
LC 2014028457
New York Times Notable Book, 2015
Forty-two-year-old Sergeant Billy Graves marks time as head of the Manhattan's Night Watch, the motley group of detectives who deal with felonies between 1 a.m. and 8 a.m. Married with two kids, he was an NYPD officer on the rise until a bullet from his gun missed a criminal and hit a kid. Billy and his cadre of fellow gung-ho cops from that time all have a "white"—that one criminal who escaped justice. Now, the group's

whites are turning up dead. This compelling, authentic novel is sure to please fans of police procedurals.

"In the wake of rage and sorrow, ordinary people respond by going crazy and screwing up. In this far-from-ordinary novel, Price/Brandt explores the hows and whys. Fasten your seat belt." —*Kirkus*

Richard Price writing as Harry Brandt.

Braun, Lilian Jackson

The **cat** who ate Danish modern. Lilian Jackson Braun. Dutton, 1967. 192 p. (Cat Who mysteries, 2)

ISBN 9789997404985

1. Art thefts 2. Murder investigation 3. Women murder victims 4. City life 5. Cat detectives 6. Middle West 7. Cozy mysteries 8. Gentle reads 9. Adult books for young adults

Qwilleran and his cats become embroiled in a mystery while working on an article about interior design.

"The mystery is mild, the satire on interior decorating fads and fancies amusing, and the Siamese cat who helps play detective delightful." —*Publishers Weekly*

Brautigan, Richard

An **unfortunate** woman: a journey. Richard Brautigan. St. Martin's Press, 2000. 110 p.

ISBN 9780312262433

1. Death — Psychological aspects 2. Diary novels 3. Psychological fiction

LC 24760

Explores the fragile and mysterious shadowland surrounding death and considers the protagonist's ruminations on another person's suicide BT

"An autobiographical novelette in journal form. The episodic entries, dating from January to June of 1982, at first seem whimsically random, as the narrator recounts a peripatetic six months wandering among Montana, Berkeley, Hawaii, San Francisco, Buffalo, the Midwest, Alaska, Canada and points in between, but soon it's obvious that a preoccupation with death is the dominant theme.... Brautigan maintains his ironic humor and his ability to write clear, often crystalline prose, though at time his mannerisms...become irritating. Yet the reader cannot help being moved by this candid cri de coeur of a soul in anguish." —*Publishers Weekly*

Brayden, Melissa

First position. Melissa Brayden. Bold Strokes Books, 2016. 264 p.

ISBN 9781626396029

1. Lesbians 2. Ballet dancers 3. Women-women relationships 4. Sexual attraction 5. Women dancers 6. New York City 7. Contemporary romances 8. LGBTQIA romances 9. LGBTQIA fiction

Anastasia Mikhelson is the rising star of the NY City Ballet. Though at the peak of her career, competition from a new and noteworthy dancer puts all she's worked for in jeopardy.

"Brayden ably develops the growing relationship between Ana and Natalie, making the emotional payoff that much sweeter when the two finally admit their lust for each other. Readers will relate to the realism of the romance and the emotional aftermath of serious injuries. This ably plotted, moving offering will earn its place deep in readers hearts." —*Publishers Weekly*

Brazier, Eliza Jane

If I disappear. Eliza Jane Brazier. Berkley, 2021. 304 p.

ISBN 9780593198223

1. Divorced women 2. Anxiety disorders 3. Podcasters 4. Fans (Persons) 5. Missing women 6. Psychological suspense

LC 2020020143

Sera loves true crime podcasts. They give her a sense of control in a world where women just like her disappear daily. She's sure they are preparing her for something. So when Rachel, her favorite podcast host, goes missing, Sera knows it's time to act. Rachel has always taught her to trust her instincts. Sera follows the clues hidden in the episodes to an isolated ranch outside Rachel's small hometown to begin her search. She's convinced her investigation will make Rachel so proud. But the more Sera digs into this unfamiliar world, the more off things start to feel. Because Rachel is not the first woman to vanish from the ranch, and she won't be the last...

"Blending the true crime compulsion of Michelle McNamara's I'll Be Gone in the Dark with the immersive creepy-craziness of Gillian Flynn's Sharp Objects, Brazier creates a heady, pitch-dark cocktail all her own." —*Publishers Weekly*

Brennan, Marie

Driftwood. Marie Brennan. Tachyon Publications, 2020. 240 p.

ISBN 9781616963460

1. Post-apocalypse 2. Heroes and heroines 3. Immortality 4. Memories 5. Memorialization 6. Dystopian fiction 7. Science fiction

Enter a post-apocalyptic realm where the apocalypse has not ended, where fragments of worlds cohere into shifting myths. Yet even as everything fades, Drifters gather to tell conflicting legends of Last, the guide—the one man who seemed immortal, but may have been a fraud. Within the Shreds, a rumor goes around that Last has died. Drifters come together to commemorate him. But who really was Last? Lying liar, or heroic savior? A mercenary, a charlatan, a legend? A man, an immortal—perhaps even a god?

"Brennan skillfully builds a multiplicity of worlds, painting each unique and fully developed culture with bold, minimalist strokes and, though readers don't get to spend much time with any single character, rendering each member of the sprawling cast with impressive nuance and subtlety." —*Publishers Weekly*

Within the sanctuary of wings: a memoir by Lady Trent. Marie Brennan. Tor, 2017. 352 p. (Memoirs of Lady Trent, 5)

ISBN 9780765377654

1. Women scientists 2. Natural history 3. Dragons 4. Voyages and travels 5. Imaginary kingdoms 6. Fantasy fiction

Loan Stars Favourites, 2017; Romantic Times Reviewer's Choice Award, 2017

A dragon naturalist and an explorer prone to igniting scandals, Lady Trent reveals what she discovered in the Sanctuary of Wings, behind the territory of Scirland's enemies.

Series complete in five volumes.

Brenner, Jamie

Blush: a novel. Jamie Brenner. Putnam Pub Group, 2021. 400 p.

ISBN 9780593085752

1. Young women 2. Wineries 3. Marie, Queen, consort of Ferdinand I, King of Romania, 1875-1938. 4. Grandmothers 5. Relationship fiction

LC 2021013432

Returning with her mother to her parents' North Fork Long Island winery, college-age Sadie discovers that her Grandma Vivian once ran a {34trashy{34 book club and decides to reinstate it as a way to reconnect the family.

"Brenner tackles complex issues including gender inequality and the devaluation of women's interests with a light hand, balancing heavy topics with copious descriptions of wine, cheese, and classic romances. This is sure to please." —*Publishers Weekly*

Drawing home. Jamie Brenner. Little Brown & Co, 2019. 368 pages
ISBN 9780316476799
1. Inheritance and succession 2. Friends' death 3. Teenagers with mental illnesses 4. Artists 5. Women business partners 6. New York (State) 7. Sag Harbor, New York 8. Relationship fiction
The best-selling author of The Forever Summer offers another literary celebration of summer that features an unexpected inheritance, a promise broken and four lives changed forever.

Breslin, Jimmy

Table money. Jimmy Breslin. Ticknor and Fields, 1986. 435 p.
ISBN 9780899193120
1. Blue collar workers 2. Working class women 3. Alcoholic men 4. Family and alcoholism 5. Vietnam veterans 6. Chamberlain, Joshua Lawrence 7. Psychological fiction

LC 85028880
Returned to his Queens home in 1970 after winning a Congressional Medal of Honor in Vietnam, Owney Morrison works at digging tunnels during the day and escapes with drink at night—from everything, including his wife Dolores and their child.
"This saga concerning the Morrisons of Queens, New York—from their late-nineteenth-century arrival in the U.S. to the present day—is painfully stereotypical in its depiction of the men (a long line of hard-drinking, male chauvinistic, and irresponsible tunnel workers) and their beleaguered, long-suffering women. Generation after generation repeats the same mistakes—dying too soon from alcoholism, giving birth too early in life—and even when Owen Morrison, the latter-day lad whose story takes up most of the book, wins the Congressional medal of honor in Vietnam, he finds that his hero's badge is virtually worthless on the gray borough streets and in the perilous tunnel that epitomizes his clan's plight." —*Booklist*

Brett, Simon

Guilt at the garage. Simon Brett. Creme de la Crime, 2021. 185 pages (Fethering mysteries, 20)
ISBN 9781780291727
1. Women amateur detectives 2. Vandalism 3. Villages 4. Prejudice 5. Immigrants 6. England 7. Cozy mysteries 8. Gentle reads
Carole and her neighbor Jude uncover evidence of foul play after Carole's car is vandalized and a body is discovered at the repair shop.
"This is an especially incisive Fethering adventure, with a shocker of an ending." —*Booklist*

Mrs Pargeter's principle. Simon Brett. Severn House, 2015. 192 p. (Mrs. Pargeter mysteries, 7)
ISBN 9781780290744
1. Kidnapping 2. Illegal arms transfers 3. Political corruption 4. Politicians 5. Widows 6. England 7. Cozy mysteries 8. Gentle reads
Investigating the connection between her late husband and a wealthy man who has recently passed away, Mrs. Pargeter finds herself in a shady world of gun-runners, shifty politicians and high-profile abductions.
"Brett's customary wit and good humor abound." —*Publishers Weekly*

Murder unprompted. Simon Brett. C. Scribner's Sons, 1982. 160 p. (Charles Paris mysteries, 8)
ISBN 9780684176598
1. Murder investigation 2. Actors and actresses 3. Shooting 4. Paris, Charles (Fictitious character) 5. Detectives 6. England 7. Mysteries

LC 82005578
In this Charles Paris mystery, the seasoned actor and part-time sleuth gets the part of understudy to the lead in a West End play. But when the lead gets shot on stage on the opening night, it falls to Charles once again to solve the murder.

Brin, David

Existence. David Brin. Tor Books, 2012. 480 p.
ISBN 9780765303615
1. Alien artifacts 2. Human/alien encounters 3. Luddites 4. Material culture 5. Plague 6. Hard science fiction 7. Science fiction
In a future world dominated by a neural-link web where people can tune into live events and revolutions can be instantly sparked, an active alien communication device is discovered in orbit around the Earth, triggering an international upheaval of fear, hope and violence.

Brink, Andre P.

Philida: a novel. Andre Brink. Vintage Books, 2012. 320 p.
ISBN 9780345805034
1. Slavery 2. Betrayal 3. Enslaved women 4. Rape victims 5. Lust 6. South Africa 7. 19th century 8. 1830s 9. Historical fiction 10. Multiple perspectives 11. Adult books for young adults

LC 2012031043
Amelia Bloomer List, 2014
When Francois Brink, her children's father and the son of her master, reneges on his promise to grant her freedom, Philida files a complaint against the Brink family in 1830s South Africa, an act that changes her life beyond recognition.
"With alternating present-tense viewpoints, the aching personal drama is set against the history of lechery, power, and violent abuse... [a] stirring novel." —*Booklist*
Originally published: London : Harvill Secker, 2012.

Brinkley, Jamel

A lucky man: stories. Jamel Brinkley. Graywolf Press, 2018. 243 p.
ISBN 9781555978051
1. African American men 2. African American boys 3. Interpersonal relations 4. Ethnic identity 5. New York City 6. African American fiction 7. Literary fiction 8. Short stories
Library Journal Best Books, 2018; Finalist for the Hurston/Wright Legacy Awards for Fiction, 2019; National Book Award for Fiction finalist, 2018
Jamel Brinkley's stories, in a debut that announces the arrival of a significant new voice, reflect the tenderness and vulnerability of black men and boys whose hopes sometimes betray them, especially in a world shaped by race, gender, and class—where luck may be the greatest fiction of all.
"The nine stories in Brinkley's promising debut address persistent issues of race, class, and masculinity across three decades of New York City's history, from Manhattan's corporatization in the mid-90s to the outer boroughs gentrification today." —*Publishers Weekly*

Briscoe, Joanna

The seduction. Joanna Briscoe. Bloomsbury, 2020. 288 p.
ISBN 9781408873496
1. Family secrets 2. Missing persons 3. Mothers and daughters 4. Psychotherapists 5. Women artists 6. London, England 7. Psychological suspense

Beth Penn lives a peaceful life with her partner Sol and their daughter Fern. But Beth is troubled by increasing unease. She cannot shake her uncertainty over her mother, who disappeared when Beth was a child, and she has a sense that her daughter is keeping secrets from her.

"Like the smooth surface of an oil painting, the novel presents a slickly beautiful vision of fantasy, layered under with ferocious, stabbing brushstrokes of pain. A haunting novel that lays bare the ugliness of narcissism at its most extreme." —*Kirkus*

Brockmeier, Kevin

The **illumination**. Kevin Brockmeier. Pantheon Books, 2011. 256 p.
ISBN 9780375425318
1. Suffering 2. Bereavement 3. Death 4. Widowers 5. Love letter writing 6. Psychological fiction

LC 2010020732

A journal of private love notes written by a husband to his wife in the wake of a fatal car accident passes through the hands of a hospital patient and five other suffering people whose respective experiences connect them to each other in poignant and complex ways.

"For a novel so relentlessly fixed on elucidating human suffering in all its permutations, The Illumination is surprisingly uplifting. This is a testament to Brockmeier's considerable stylistic gifts—the man writes exquisite sentences—and to the palpable compassion with which he frames each of his characters." —*Cleveland Plain Dealer*

Brockway, Connie

The **golden** season. Connie Brockway. Penguin, 2010. 388 p.
ISBN 9780451412836
1. Nobility 2. Financial crises 3. Man-woman relationships 4. Interpersonal attraction 5. Wealth 6. England 7. Regency period (1811-1820) 8. 19th century 9. Historical romances 10. Regency romances
Library Journal Best Books, 2010

When her fortune suddenly disappears, Lady Lydia Eastlake, the ton's most celebrated beauty, must find a wealthy husband and sets her sights on a dashing war hero who, unbeknownst to her, is searching for a rich bride to save his family from a life of poverty.

No place for a dame. Connie Brockway. Montlake Romance, 2013. 278 p.
ISBN 9781477808580
1. Ambition in women 2. Disguises 3. Independence in women 4. Rich men 5. Social classes 6. Great Britain 7. Regency period (1811-1820) 8. Regency romances 9. Historical romances
Library Journal Best Books, 2013

Avery dresses as a man in order to join the Royal Astronomical Society, a plan helped along by Lord Giles, who agrees to take her on as a prodigy in exchange for her help searching for a missing colleague.

"Brockway delivers a unique, engaging historical storyline with fun, intriguing elements and with a delicious arc of two star-crossed misfits who share a deep love and deserve an exceptional future." —*Kirkus*

So enchanting. Connie Brockway. Onyx, 2009. 421 p.
ISBN 9780451416292
1. Witches 2. Exile (Punishment) 3. Man-woman relationships 4. Death threats 5. Female friendship 6. Scotland 7. 19th century 8. Historical romances

LC Bl2009002974

Library Journal Best Books, 2009; Romantic Times Reviewers' Choice Award, 2009

When Lord Greyson Sheffield, the very same man who had ruined her reputation and sent her into exile in the Scottish Highlands, arrives on her doorstep, Francesca Walcott, a mysteriously gifted medium, discovers magic in his arms amidst peril and evil.

Broder, Melissa

Milk fed. Melissa Broder. Scribner, 2021. 304 p.
ISBN 9781982142490
1. Self-discovery 2. Desire 3. Jewish women 4. Women — Sexuality 5. Dieting 6. Coming-of-age stories

Transitioning from her Jewish faith to dieting to maintain an illusion of existential control, Rachel bonds with an Orthodox woman at a frozen yogurt shop before embarking on a journey of food, desire and spiritual fulfillment.

"An empathic, enrapturing, unputdownable novel of faith, sex, love, and nurture." —*Booklist*

The **pisces**: a novel. Melissa Broder. Hogarth Press, 2018. 270 p.
ISBN 9781524761554
1. Mermen 2. Man-woman relationships 3. Breaking up (Interpersonal relations) 4. Sexuality 5. Dog baby sitters 6. Los Angeles, California 7. Contemporary fantasy 8. Relationship fiction
Longlisted for The Women's Prize for Fiction, 2019

Bottoming out after a dramatic breakup, a habitual student accepts her sister's invitation to dog-sit on Venice Beach for the summer, where she meets an eerily attractive swimmer one night whose Sirenic identity transforms her understanding of what real love looks like.

Brodesser-Akner, Taffy

Fleishman is in trouble: a novel. Taffy Brodesser-Akner. Random House, 2019. 288 pages
ISBN 9780525510871
1. Divorced fathers 2. Physicians 3. Marital conflict 4. Parenting 5. Middle-aged men 6. New York (State) 7. Literary fiction

LC 2018054871

Booklist Editors' Choice, 2019; New York Times Notable Book, 2019; Longlisted for the National Book Award for Fiction, 2019

Divorcing his hostile wife when he concludes he could find genuine happiness elsewhere, a doctor is astonished when his ex abruptly disappears, making him unable to move on without acknowledging painful truths about his marriage.

Brodie, Emma

Songs in Ursa Major. Emma Brodie. Random House, 2021. 336 pages
ISBN 9780593318621
1. Musicians 2. Music festivals 3. Rock concert tours 4. Fame 5. Rock music 6. 1960s 7. 1970s 8. Historical fiction 9. Love stories
Loan Stars Favourites, 2021

A love story set in 1969 at the crossroads of rock and folk, Songs in Ursa Major is shot through with the lyrics, the icons, the lore, and the adrenaline of the late 60s music scene. The year is 1969, and the Bayleen Island Folk Fest is abuzz with one name: Jesse Reid, whose intricate guitar riffs and supple baritone are poised to tip from fame to legend with this one headlining performance. That is, until his motorcycle crashes on the way to the show, and local band The Breakers takes his place...

"Moving from New York to Los Angeles to Greece to the Grammys, then always back home to the island, Brodie's debut is a furious page-turner, meditating on the glittering beast of fame." —*Booklist*

Brom

Slewfoot: a tale of bewitchery. Brom. Nightfire, 2021. 336 p.

ISBN 9781250622006

1. Puritans 2. Misfits (Persons) 3. Witchcraft 4. Revenge 5. Deals 6. Connecticut 7. New England 8. Colonial America (1600-1775) 9. 17th century 10. Historical horror 11. Illustrated books 12. Manet, Edouard

LC 2021028502

A recently widowed outcast, Abitha turns to Slewfoot, an ancient spirit who has awakened in a dark wood, for help, and together they ignite a battle between pagan and Puritan, leaving ashes and bloodshed in their wake.

"Punctuated by moments of unanticipated levity as well as unmitigated terror, this clever and imaginative tale is not to be missed by fans of dark fantasy and historical horror." —*Library Journal*

A Tom Doherty Associates book.

Bronsky, Alina

The **hottest** dishes of the Tartar cuisine. Alina Bronsky; translated from the German by Tim Mohr. Europa Editions, 2011. 262 pages

ISBN 9781609450069

1. Teenage pregnancy 2. Dysfunctional families 3. Cruelty in women 4. Family relationships 5. Pregnant teenagers 6. Soviet Union 7. Literary fiction 8. Translations

Rosa's schemes to abort her daughter Sulfia's fetus after learning of the pregnancy, take her granddaughter Aminat after the baby's birth, and move the family out of the Soviet Union eventually lead to tragedy.

Originally published in German as Die scharfsten Gerichte der tatarischen Kuche: Cologne : Kiepenheuer & Witsch, 2010.

Bronte, Anne

The **tenant** of Wildfell Hall. Anne Bronte. Modern Library, 1997. Xiii, 510 p.

ISBN 9780679602798

1. Married women 2. Alcoholic men 3. Women — Social conditions 4. Husband and wife 5. Women 6. England 7. Great Britain 8. Georgian era (1714-1837) 9. Victorian era (1837-1901) 10. Domestic fiction 11. Multiple perspectives 12. Classics

LC 97014200

A nineteenth century novel depicts the unhappy marriage of Helen Graham and her drunken husband, realistically portraying the devastating impact of alcholism.

Originally published: London : T.C. Newby, 1848.

Bronte, Charlotte

★ **Emma**. Another Lady. Everest House, 1980. 201 p.

ISBN 9780896961142

1. Abandoned children 2. Boarding schools 3. Secret identity 4. England 5. Gothic fiction 6. Classics

LC 81066096

"In the full-blown literary manner and circuitous story-telling characteristic of Charlotte Bronte,...an intriguing melodrama unrolls in this tale of wrongs finally righted.... The author of this Gothic romp is obviously steeped in the period and felicitous style of the brilliant English novelist, providing entertainment on the same grand scale." —*Publishers Weekly*

The last, unfinished work by the author. This fragment (two chapters) was first published in Cornhill magazine, April 1860.

★ **Jane** Eyre. Charlotte Bronte. Modern Library, 1997. 682 p.

ISBN 9780679602699

1. Governesses 2. Young women 3. Rich men 4. Orphans 5. Friendship 6. England 7. 19th century 8. Gothic fiction 9. Classics 10. First person narratives

In early nineteenth-century England, an orphaned young woman accepts employment as a governess and soon finds herself in love with her employer who has a terrible secret.

Originally published in 1847 under the pseudonym Currer Bell, Jane Eyre is Charlotte Bronte's best-known novel, a Gothic masterpiece of character and emotion.

Originally published 1847.

Bronte, Emily

★ **Wuthering** Heights. Emily Bronte. Puffin Books, 1990. 412 p.

ISBN 9780140366945

1. Interclass romance 2. Jealousy 3. Revenge 4. Inheritance and succession 5. Foster children 6. England 7. Gothic fiction 8. Classics 9. Love stories 10. Adult books for young adults

Heathcliff, an orphan, is raised by Mr Earnshaw as one of his own children. Hindley despises him but wild Cathy becomes his constant companion, and he falls deeply in love with her. When she will not marry him, Heathcliff's terrible vengeance ruins them all—but still his and Cathy's love will not die...

Originally published: Thomas Cautley Newby, 1847.

Brookner, Anita

Hotel Du Lac. Anita Brookner. Pantheon Books, 1984. 184 p.

ISBN 9780394542157

1. Friendship 2. Thought and thinking 3. Hotels 4. Women authors 5. Romance writers 6. Switzerland 7. Literary fiction

LC 84020641

Booker Prize, 1984

Into the rarified atmosphere of the Hotel du Lac timidly walks Edith Hope, romantic novelist and holder of modest dreams. Edith has been exiled from home after embarassing herself and her friends. She has refused to sacrifice her ideals and remains stubbornly single. But among the pampered women and minor nobility Edith finds Mr Neville, and her chance to escape from a life of humiliating spinsterhood is renewed.

"The tone of this novel is oddly detached, very small-scale, faintly humorous.... It is by means of this very remoteness that Edith manages to hold our interest throughout this achingly uneventful holiday, with its empty chasms of time, its murmuring respectability, its dining room scattered sparsely with people who mean nothing to her.... There are some uncomfortable patches.... But generally, the writing is graceful and attractive." —*New York Times Book Review*

Originally published: London : Cape, 1984.

Brooks, Bill

Blood storm. Bill Brooks. Five Star, 2012. 344 p. (John Henry Cole novels, 1)

ISBN 9781594149115

1. Outlaws 2. Crimes against prostitutes 3. Gunfighters 4. Frontier and pioneer life 5. Detectives 6. The West (United States) 7. Dakota Territory 8. 1870s 9. 19th century 10. Westerns

When three young escorts turn up dead in the mining town of Deadwood, John Henry Cole is called in to investigate the murders.

Sequel: Frontier Justice.

Frontier justice. Bill Brooks. Five Star, 2012. 322 p; (John Henry Cole novels, 2)

ISBN 9781432826079

1. Bounty hunters 2. African American murder suspects 3. Frontier and pioneer life 4. Outlaws 5. Revenge 6. The West (United States) 7. Wyoming 8. Westerns

LC 2012016329

"Leavening the action is Brooks' sly humor—for instance, when a near-penniless Cole shops for an ornery, speckled, $30 horse; or when, by the campfire, Cole and Harper discuss Don Quixote." —*Booklist*
Sequel to: Blood Storm.

Winter kill. Bill Brooks. Five Star, 2013. 262 p. (John Henry Cole novels, 3)
ISBN 9781432826345
1. Frontier and pioneer life 2. Women murder suspects 3. Outlaws 4. Detectives 5. Voyages and travels 6. The West (United States) 7. Wyoming 8. Westerns

LC 2013005469

The winter around Cheyenne, Wyoming that year was devastating, killing both people and livestock. John Henry Cole was three miles out of town on his small ranch, waiting out the storm that was quickly killing his cattle and horses, and starting to feel a little crazy himself.

Brooks, Max

Devolution: a firsthand account of the Rainier sasquatch massacre. Max Brooks. Del Rey, 2020. 320 p. : Map
ISBN 9781984826787
1. Sasquatch 2. Survival (after disaster) 3. Communities 4. Social isolation 5. Volcanic eruptions 6. Pacific Northwest 7. Washington (State) 8. Horror
LibraryReads Favorites, 2020

A modern retelling of the Bigfoot legend is presented as a gripping journal by a woman from a high-tech Pacific Northwest community who becomes cut off from civilization by a volcanic eruption before witnessing the flight of starving humanoid beings.

"This slow-burning page-turner will appeal to Brooks's devoted fans and speculative fiction readers who enjoy tales of monsters." —*Publishers Weekly*

★ **World** War Z: an oral history of the zombie war. Max Brooks. Crown, 2006. 320 p.
ISBN 9780307346605
1. Oral historians 2. War 3. Undead 4. Zombies 5. Diseases 6. Horror 7. Satirical fiction 8. Apocalyptic fiction

LC 2006009517

In World War Z, life as we know it ends the way many horror fans knew it would: zombies rise up! After the post-war devastation, author Max Brooks "interviews" survivors and records their stories as well as details on what causes zombies, how they spread, what will stop them, and effective strategic warfare methods against them.

"Brooks tells the story of the world's desperate battle against the zombie threat with a series of first-person accounts as told to the author by various characters around the world. A Chinese doctor encounters one of the earliest zombie cases at a time when the Chinese government is ruthlessly suppressing any information about the outbreak that will soon spread across the globe. The tale then follows the outbreak via testimony of smugglers, intelligence officials, military personnel and many others who struggle to defeat the zombie menace. Despite its implausible premise and choppy delivery, the novel is surprisingly hard to put down." —*Publishers Weekly*
World War Z very loosely adapted into a film of the same name.

Brooks, Terry

Child of light. Terry Brooks. Del Rey, 2021. 368 p. (Child of light, 1)

ISBN 9780593357385
1. Fairies 2. Magic 3. Escapes 4. Prisoners 5. Memories 6. Fantasy fiction 7. High fantasy 8. Epic fantasy

LC 2020057074

Auris Afton Grieg stages a desperate escape from the prison she's been in since age 15 and meets up with an unusual stranger who claims to be a member of a magical race and insists that she is too.

"Bestseller Brooks's first fantasy since retiring the long-running Shannara series offers an enticing new mystery while delivering enough familiar elements—in both tone and worldbuilding—to make his fans feel right at home." —*Publishers Weekly*

Broun, Bill

Night of the animals. Bill Broun. Ecco Press, 2016. 592 p.
ISBN 9780062400796
1. Zoo animals 2. Men with mental illnesses 3. Cults 4. Dystopias 5. Near future 6. London, England 7. 21st century 8. Literary fiction 9. Dystopian fiction

In 2052 London a homeless man, who believes he has the magical ability to communicate with animals, sets off on a quest to release all the animals from the zoo before the members of a suicide cult can destroy them.

"Brouns novel is strange, witty, and engrossing, skipping through madness and into the realm of myth." —*Publishers Weekly*

Brouwer, Sigmund

Thief of glory: a novel. Sigmund Brouwer. WaterBrook Press, 2014. 288 pages
ISBN 9780307446497
1. World War II 2. Concentration camps 3. Faith (Christianity) 4. Survival (in concentration camps, prisons, etc.) 5. Family secrets 6. Indonesia 7. War stories 8. Christian historical fiction

LC 2014007072

Alberta Readers' Choice Award, 2015; Christy Award for Historical Romance Category, 2015; Christy Award for Book of the Year, 2015

This WWII drama is both exciting in its revelations and heart-rending in its truth about human nature and forgiveness.

Brown, Amy Belding

Emily's house. Amy Belding Brown. Berkley Pub Group, 2021. 320 p.
ISBN 9780593199633
1. Dickinson, Emily 2. Household employees 3. Friendship 4. Women authors 5. Women poets 6. Eccentrics and eccentricities 7. Massachusetts 8. Gilded Age (1865-1898) 9. Biographical fiction 10. Historical fiction

LC 2020050429

Accepting a temporary position with the Dickinson family in Amherst in 1869, Maggie Maher forms a life-changing friendship with the brilliant Miss Emily in the new novel from the author of Flight of the Sparrow.

"Brown's sensitive, intuitive, immersing prose is supremely apt for this gentle, compelling story. Dickinson fans will especially savor this novel." —*Booklist*

Brown, Dale

Eagle Station: a novel. Dale Brown. HarperCollins 2020. 400 p. (Patrick McLanahan novels, 24)
ISBN 9780062843081

1. Space stations 2. Alliances 3. Space weapons 4. International intrigue 5. National security 6. United States 7. Russia 8. 2020s 9. Techno-thrillers

LC 2019040584

When Russia and China forge an unlikely alliance to claim the moon's natural resources, Brad McLanahan and the Iron Wolf Squadron scramble to prevent the construction of a heavily armed moon base.

"Brown's spectacular future space weapons systems are utterly convincing. Tom Clancy fans won't want to miss this one." —*Publishers Weekly*

The **Moscow** offensive: a novel. Dale Brown. William Morrow, 2018. 432 p. (Patrick McLanahan novels, 22)

ISBN 9780062442017

1. Special operations (Military science) 2. Special forces 3. Terrorism — Prevention 4. National security 5. High technology 6. Techno-thrillers

LC 2017053352

America's first line of defense—Brad McLanahan and the heroes of the Iron Wolf Squadron—must counter a dangerous Russian strike from within the homeland.

Brown, Dan

The **Da** Vinci code. Dan Brown. Doubleday, 2003. 400 p. (Robert Langdon novels, 2)

ISBN 9780385504201

1. Leonardo da Vinci 2. Secret societies 3. Relics 4. Conspiracies 5. Artists 6. Painters 7. Paris, France 8. London, England 9. Thrillers and suspense 10. Books to movies

LC 2002040918

Book Sense Book of the Year Adult Fiction, 2004; British Book Award for Book of the Year, 2005; Iowa High School Book Award, 2006; Teen Buckeye Book Award (Ohio), 2005

When an elderly curator of the Louvre turns up murdered, his body surrounded by enigmatic ciphers written in invisible ink, code-breaker Robert Langdon and French cyptologist are called in to unravel the clues to the killing, only to discover that the riddles are linked to the works of Leonardo da Vinci and to a clandestine, ruthless sect within the Catholic Church.

"The story is full of brain-teasing puzzles and fascinating insights into religious history and art." —*Booklist*

Brown, Dee

Creek Mary's blood: a novel. Dee Brown. Holt, Rinehart and Winston, 1980. 401 p. : Illustration

ISBN 9780030442810

1. Native American men 2. Native American women 3. Creek Indians 4. Cherokee Indians 5. Cheyenne Indians 6. Great Plains (United States) 7. Wounded Knee, South Dakota 8. 18th century 9. 19th century 10. Historical fiction 11. Family sagas

LC 79009060

Proud and beautiful Creek Mary dominates a saga that spans the years from the American Revolution to the preWorld War I era and portrays such characters as Tecumseh, Andrew Jackson, Crazy Horse, Sitting Bull, and Teddy Roosevelt.

Brown, Eleanor

The **weird** sisters. Eleanor Brown. Amy Einhorn Books/G.P. Putnam's Sons, 2011. 336 p.

ISBN 9780399157226

1. Sisters 2. Parents with terminal illnesses 3. Self-discovery 4. Middle-aged women 5. Family relationships 6. Ohio 7. Domestic fiction 8. Gentle reads 9. Relationship fiction

LC 2010029599

Unwillingly brought together to care for their ailing mother, three sisters who were named after famous Shakespearean characters discover that everything they have been avoiding may prove more worthwhile than expected.

Brown, Karen

The **clairvoyants:** a novel. Karen Brown. Henry Holt and Co, 2017. 381 p.

ISBN 9781627797054

1. Women psychics 2. Ghosts 3. Sisters 4. Missing women 5. Obsession 6. Connecticut 7. Gothic fiction

LC 2016019129

A young woman who wants to escape the challenges of being able to see ghosts pursues a college education and a budding romance before the apparition of a missing young woman prompts her to help.

"Brown's novel is a riveting page-turner. She deftly reveals bits of Martha's and Del's past in tandem with more details about the mystery that Martha is trying to unravel, leaving the reader wondering if Martha might be an unreliable narrator. Though the ending isn't entirely satisfying, Brown shows an admirable ability to create suspense." —*Publishers Weekly*

Brown, Larry

Joe: a novel. Larry Brown. Algonquin Books of Chapel Hill, 1991. 345 p.

ISBN 9780945575610

1. Small town life 2. Good and evil 3. Redemption 4. Middle-aged men 5. Fifteen-year-old boys 6. Mississippi 7. Rural noir 8. Literary fiction 9. Southern fiction

LC 91012026

ALA Notable Book, 1992

The lives of two men—Joe Ransom, a drinking, gambling, reckless fifty-year-old, and Gary Jones, a luckless fifteen-year-old raised by an evil father and an insane mother, become intertwined in a novel of good, evil, temptation, and sacrifice.

"Brown is a talented fiction writer in the whiskeyish, rascally Southern tradition of Faulkner and Erskine Caldwell.... The new novel is clear, simple and powerful, and it is great, rowdy fun to read." —*Time*

★ **Tiny** love: the complete stories of Larry Brown. Larry Brown; with a Foreword by Jonathan Miles. Algonquin Books of Chapel Hill, 2019. 320 p.

ISBN 9781616209759

1. Southern States 2. Short stories 3. Southern fiction 4. Literary fiction

LC 2019008852

A career-spanning collection, Tiny Love brings together for the first time the stories of Larry Brown's previous collections along with those never before gathered.

Includes bibliographical references.

Brown, Pierce

Golden son. Pierce Brown. Ballantine Books, 2015. 288 p. (Red rising novels, 2)

ISBN 9780345539816

1. Hitler, Adolf 2. Dystopias 3. Life on other planets 4. Mines and mineral resources 5. Survival 6. Mars (Planet) 7. Science fiction 8. Dystopian fiction 9. Adult books for young adults
LibraryReads Favorites, 2015; RUSA Reading List, 2016
With shades of The Hunger Games, Ender's Game, and Game of Thrones, debut author Pierce Brown's genre-defying epic Red Rising hit the ground running and wasted no time becoming a sensation. Golden Son continues the stunning saga of Darrow, a rebel forged by tragedy, battling to lead his oppressed people to freedom from the overlords of a brutal elitist future built on lies. Now fully embedded among the Gold ruling class, Darrow continues his work to bring down Society from within. A life-or-death tale of vengeance with an unforgettable hero at its heart, Golden Son guarantees Pierce Brown's continuing status as one of fiction's most exciting new voices.
"The stakes are even higher than they were in Red Rising, and the twists and turns of the story are every bit as exciting. The jaw-dropper of an ending will leave readers hungry for the conclusion to Brown's wholly original, completely thrilling saga." —Booklist

Morning star. Pierce Brown. Del Rey, 2016. 288 p. (Red rising novels, 3)
ISBN 9780345539847
1. Revolutionaries 2. Dystopias 3. Interplanetary relations 4. Exploitation 5. Class conflict 6. Mars (Planet) 7. Dystopian fiction 8. Science fiction 9. Adult books for young adults
Goodreads Choice Award, 2016
Darrow emerges from years of hiding among the Golds and declares an open revolution against the overlords who oppress his people and caused the loss of his wife.
"Brown's vivid, first-person prose puts the reader right at the forefront of impassioned speeches, broken families, and engaging battle scenes that don't shy away from the gore as this intrastellar civil war comes to a most satisfying conclusion." —Publishers Weekly

Red rising. Pierce Brown. Ballantine Books, 2014. 400 p. (Red rising novels, 1)
ISBN 9780345539786
1. Resistance to government 2. Dystopias 3. Life on other planets 4. Mines and mineral resources 5. Survival 6. Mars (Planet) 7. Science fiction 8. Dystopian fiction 9. Adult books for young adults
LC 2013020634
Goodreads Choice Award, 2014; LibraryReads Favorites, 2014; School Library Journal Best Books: Best Adult Books 4 Teens, 2014
A tale set in a bleak future society torn by class divisions follows the experiences of secret revolutionary Darrow, who after witnessing his wife's execution by an oppressive government joins a revolutionary cell and attempts to infiltrate an elite military academy.
"This is a very ambitious novel, with a fully realized society...and a cast of well-drawn characters." —Booklist

Brown, Rita Mae
★ **Rubyfruit** jungle. Rita Mae Brown. Bantam Books, 1988. 246 p.
ISBN 9780553278866
1. Growing up 2. Lesbians — Sexuality 3. Prejudice 4. Lesbian teenagers 5. Poor people 6. Southern States 7. Coming-of-age stories 8. Satirical fiction 9. LGBTQIA fiction
Born out of wedlock and adopted by a poor, loving family, Molly Bolt finds the South and even bohemian New York a hostile world for a lesbian but manages to thrive and remain confident.
First published: 1973.

Six of one. Rita Mae Brown. Bantam Books, 1999. 270 p. (Julia and Louise novels, 1)

ISBN 9780553380378
1. Sisters 2. Prohibition 3. Lesbians 4. Small town life 5. Hunsenmeir Sisters (Fictitious characters) 6. 1980s 7. Family sagas 8. Relationship fiction
Locked in an intense love-hate relationship, two sisters—Julia and Louise Hunsenmeir—grow up, marry, raise their families, and enter old age, surrounded by their fellow citizens of a small town on the Pennsylvania-Maryland border.
"The author extols the vitality and variety of women by tracing the lives of two sisters, their families, and cronies. The women are rich and poor, heterosexual (mostly) and lesbian, but they are linked by emotional and physical experiences common to all women.... Structurally, the novel intersperses vivid scenes from the past with those from the present (1980 in the book). Despite flaws, the narrative is engrossing, as are the women." —Library Journal

Wish you were here. By Rita Mae Brown and Sneaky Pie Brown; illustrations by Wendy Wray. Bantam Books, 1990. 242 p. : Illustration (Mrs. Murphy mysteries, 1)
ISBN 9780553058819
1. Dismemberment 2. Lucan, Richard John Bingham 3. Murder investigation 4. Cat detectives 5. Animal detectives 6. Virginia 7. Crozet, Virginia 8. Cozy mysteries 9. Gentle reads 10. Adult books for young adults
LC 90001071
Mary Minor Haristeen, postmistress of Crozet, Virginia, joins forces with her willful cat, Mrs. Murphy, and her Welsh corgi, Tucker, to investigate a series of bizarre postcards sent to the town's inhabitants that forecast impending death BT
"Ms. Brown writes with wise, disarming wit about her country-bred characters and their not-always-neighborly ways." —New York Times Book Review

Brown, Rosellen
★ **Before** and after. Rosellen Brown. Farrar Straus Giroux, 1992. 354 p.
ISBN 9780374109998
1. Teenage murder suspects 2. Parents of criminals 3. Criminal evidence tampering 4. Families 5. Small town life 6. New Hampshire 7. Psychological fiction 8. Multiple perspectives 9. Books to movies
LC 92081571
ALA Notable Book, 1993
When the chief of police comes to question Jacob Reiser about the brutal murder of his teenage girlfriend, it throws the entire family into a feud laced with guilt and questions of loyalty.
"Brown is tenacious in her examination of each major character. Deftly, artfully, she strips away the delicate shelter of conventional relationships." —New York Times Book Review

Tender mercies. Rosellen Brown. Delta, 1998. 273 p.
ISBN 9780385333320
1. Accident victims 2. Family relationships 3. Husband and wife 4. Boating accidents 5. Women wheelchair users 6. Mainstream fiction
"Remarkable depths of pity, pain, and human complication are plumbed in this sensitive book; the language, like a luminescent wand, lights up areas of emotion normally too devastating to consider." —Kirkus

Brown, Sandra
★ **Blind** tiger. Sandra Brown. Grand Central Publishing, 2021. 448 p.
ISBN 9781538751961

Bump, Gabriel

★ **Everywhere** you don't belong: a novel. Gabriel Bump. Algonquin Books of Chapel Hill, 2020. 240 p.

ISBN 9781616208790

1. African American teenage boys 2. High schools 3. Police brutality 4. Growing up 5. Riots 6. Chicago, Illinois 7. Coming-of-age stories 8. African American fiction 9. Adult books for young adults

LC 2019008323

BCALA Literary Award for First Novelist, 2021; New York Times Notable Book, 2020

Raised by a civil-rights activist grandmother on the South Side of Chicago, Claude McKay Love searches for a sense of belonging before a riot compels his departure for college, where he discovers he cannot escape his past.

"With deft writing and rat-a-tat, laugh-until-you-gasp-at-the-implications dialog, Bump delivers a singular sense of growing up black that will resonate with readers." —*Library Journal*

Bunn, T. Davis

Outbreak. Davis Bunn. Bethany House, 2019. 368 pages

ISBN 9780764230011

1. Scientists 2. Epidemics 3. Plague 4. Algae 5. Ocean currents 6. Christian suspense

LC 2018042273

Along the coast of West Africa, strange algae is growing and mysterious deaths are rising—until suddenly, with the sea currents' shift, the deaths stop. Professor Theo Bishop and biological researcher Avery Madison are the only ones who know the truth. Will the authorities heed their warning before it happens again?

Buntin, Julie

★ **Marlena**: a novel. Julie Buntin. Henry Holt and Co, 2017. 288 pages

ISBN 9781627797641

1. Female friendship 2. Influence (Psychology) 3. Teenage girl drug abusers 4. Teenage girls — Friendship 5. Self-fulfillment in women 6. Michigan 7. New York City 8. Psychological fiction 9. Literary fiction 10. Adult books for young adults

LC 2016021949

Booklist Editors' Choice, 2017

Struggling to adapt to a new home in rural Michigan, 15-year-old Cat bonds with a pill-popping, manic young neighbor with whom she renders their desolate community into a kind of playground until suffering a tragedy that she confronts decades later.

"Jumping between their teenage friendship in Michigan and Cat's adult life in New York City, Buntin creates a world so subtle and nuanced and alive that it imprints like a memory. Devastating; as unforgettable as it is gorgeous." —*Kirkus*

Burdett, John

Bangkok 8. John Burdett. Alfred A. Knopf, 2003. 352 p. (Sonchai Jitpleecheep mysteries, 1)

ISBN 9781400040445

1. Police 2. Murder investigation 3. Buddhists 4. African American soldiers 5. Marines 6. Bangkok, Thailand 7. Thailand 8. Mysteries

LC 2002040658

New York Times Notable Book, 2003

"The narrator, a Buddhist cop named Sonchai Jitplecheep, finds himself plunged into a dangerous investigation of the deaths of his partner Pichai Apiradee and U. S. Embassy Sgt. William Bradley. Sonchai is an unusual character on several levels, from the mysteries of his violent past to his conversations with the ghost of Pichai. His ambiguous feelings toward Kimberley Jones, an American FBI agent brought in to work the case, reflect his upbringing as the child of a Thai mother and an unknown American father.... The mix of detective work, Bangkok street life, the Thai sex trade and drug smuggling forms a powerful mlange of images and insight." —*Publishers Weekly*

Sequel: Bangkok tattoo.

Burdick, Serena

Find me in Havana. Serena Burdick. Park Row Books, 2021. 320 p.

ISBN 9780778311164

1. Rodriguez, Estelita 2. Women celebrities 3. Cuban Americans 4. Singers 5. Film actors and actresses 6. Immigrants 7. Cuba 8. United States 9. Epistolary novels 10. Biographical fiction 11. Multiple perspectives

Cuba, 1936: When Estelita Rodriguez sings in a hazy Havana nightclub for the very first time, she is nine years old. From then on, that spotlight of adoration—from Havana to New York's Copacabana and then Hollywood—becomes the one true accomplishment no one can take from her. Not the 1933 Cuban Revolution that drove her family into poverty. Not the revolving door of husbands or the fickle world of film. Thirty years later, her young adult daughter, Nina, is blindsided by her mother's mysterious death. Seeking answers, the grieving Nina navigates the troubling, opulent memories of their life together and discovers how much Estelita sacrificed to live the American dream on her own terms.

"With great skill, Burdick weaves a heartbreaking narrative of a star's rise and fall, and whose unexplained death at 37 deeply affects her daughter. Estelita's sacrifices and determination as a mother and an artist make for a deeply affecting tragedy." —*Publishers Weekly*

The **girls** with no names. Serena Burdick. Park Row, 2019. 336 p.

ISBN 9780778309994

1. Sisters 2. Teenage girls 3. Missing girls 4. Family secrets 5. Rescues 6. New York City 7. 1910s 8. Multiple perspectives 9. Historical fiction

In 1910s New York City, Effie and Luella discover a secret about their father which later leads to Luella's disappearance. Effie suspects their father has sent Luella to the House of Mercy and hatches a plan to get herself committed in order to save her.

"A well-plotted story with an excellent sense of time and place. Readers looking for historical fiction with emotional depth will enjoy." —*Library Journal*

Burgess, Anthony

★ A **clockwork** orange. By Anthony Burgess. Norton, 1988. 192 p.

ISBN 9780939305537

1. Social control 2. Aversion therapy 3. Dystopias 4. Violence 5. Crime 6. Books to movies 7. Transgressive fiction 8. Modern classics

LC 86-23843

Presents Burgess' satire of the present inhumanity of man to man through a futuristic culture where teenagers rule with violence.

"Paradox is at the heart of this book, as this newly restored, fiftieth-anniversary edition makes more clear than ever...a fitting publication of a book that remains...shocking and thought provoking." —*Booklist*

Includes introduction by author, publisher's note and the

"controversial last chapter not previously published in the United States."

Originally published: London : Heinemann, 1962.

Burke, Alafair

The **better** sister: a novel. Alafair Burke. Harper, 2019. 336 p.
ISBN 9780062853370
1. Sisters 2. Dysfunctional families 3. Murder suspects 4. Murder
5. Alienation in families 6. New York City 7. Psychological suspense
LC 2018051071

When a prominent Manhattan lawyer is murdered, two estranged sisters—one the victim's widow, the other his ex—navigate long-standing resentments to uncover devastating family secrets. By the best-selling author of The Wife.

Burke, James Lee

Another kind of Eden. James Lee Burke. Simon & Schuster, 2021. 256 p. (Holland family saga, 4)
ISBN 9781982151713
1. Authors 2. Cults 3. Farm life 4. Women murder victims 5. Korean War veterans 6. Colorado 7. The West (United States) 8. 1960s 9. Family sagas 10. Noir fiction
LC 2020057197

After hopping off a boxcar in early 1960s Denver, aspiring novelist Aaron Holland Broussard meets and instantly connects with Joanne McDuffy, a college student who is involved with a shady professor caught up in a drug-addled cult.

"Incorporating elements of horror into otherwise realistic thrillers is a thing these days, but few manage it with Burke's special eloquence, at once melancholic and macabre." —*Booklist*

Black cherry blues. James Lee Burke. Little, Brown, 1989. 290 pages; (Dave Robicheaux novels, 3)
ISBN 9780316116992
1. Oil industry and trade 2. Mafia 3. Murder investigation 4. Native American activists 5. Grief in men 6. New Orleans, Louisiana 7. New Iberia, Louisiana 8. Roth, Philip 9. Hardboiled fiction 10. First person narratives
LC 89007977

Edgar Allan Poe Award for Best Mystery Novel, 1990

An ex-New Orleans cop comes up against indians, oil company roughnecks, and Mafia honchos on the rugged Montana landscape.

"A stunning novel that takes detective fiction into new imaginative realms.... All the main characters in this darkly beautiful, lyric saga carry heavy emotional baggage, and Robicheaux's sleuthing is a simultaneous exorcism of demons of grief, loss, fear, rage, vengeance." —*Publishers Weekly*

House of the rising sun: a novel. James Lee Burke. Simon & Schuster, 2015. 448 p. (Holland family saga, 2)
ISBN 9781501107108
1. Fathers and sons 2. Voyages and travels 3. Enemies 4. Grail 5. Arms dealers 6. Texas 7. First World War era (1914-1918) 8. Historical thrillers
LC 2015012518

Escaping with a stolen artifact after a violent encounter with Mexican soldiers, a Texas Ranger is pursued by a bloodthirsty Austrian arms dealer, who, believing the artifact to be the Holy Grail, targets the man's estranged son.

"Crisp dialogue highlights this tale of redemption and the bonds of family, and the breathtaking conclusion is one that readers wont soon forget." —*Publishers Weekly*

The **jealous** kind. James Lee Burke. Simon & Schuster, 2016. 383 p. (Holland family saga, 3)
ISBN 9781501107207

1. High school students 2. Class conflict 3. Mafia 4. Violence in men 5. Crime 6. Houston, Texas 7. 1950s 8. Coming-of-age stories 9. Crime fiction 10. Adult books for young adults

Intervening when he sees a beautiful, gifted girl fighting with her boyfriend, a young man inadvertently challenges the power of the Mob in his Korean War-era Texas community and must summon the courage of his soldier father in order to stand up for his beliefs.

"Raging teenage hormones, gangster violence, class warfare, and a pink Cadillac stuffed with cash and gold bars set up Burke's latest novel, a mystery set in Houston, Tex. in 1952. Burke has a hit with this dark, atmospheric story of teenagers trying to make it through high school without getting killed by Mafia hitmen, low-life thugs, and greasers with oily ducktails and switchblade knives." —*Publishers Weekly*

★ The **New** Iberia blues. James Lee Burke. Simon & Schuster, 2018. 464 p. (Dave Robicheaux novels, 22)
ISBN 9781501176876
1. Escaped convicts 2. Murder investigation 3. Film industry and trade 4. Mafia 5. Tarot 6. Louisiana 7. New Iberia, Louisiana 8. Police procedurals 9. Southern fiction 10. Hardboiled fiction

The shocking death of a young woman leads detective Dave Robicheaux into the dark corners of Hollywood, the mafia and the Louisiana backwoods.

"With his lush, visionary prose and timeless literary themes of loss and redemption, Burke is in full command in this outing for his aging but still capable hero." —*Publishers Weekly*

★ A **private** cathedral. James Lee Burke. Simon & Schuster, 2020. 416 p. (Dave Robicheaux novels, 23)
ISBN 9781982151683
1. Organized crime 2. Family feuds 3. Runaways 4. Detectives 5. Assassins 6. Louisiana 7. New Iberia, Louisiana 8. Police procedurals 9. Southern fiction 10. Hardboiled fiction
LC 2019058582

Swept up in a criminal underworld rivalry involving a pair of star-crossed teen lovers, Detective Dave Robicheaux is targeted by a time-traveling superhuman assassin who forces him to confront the demons of his own past.

"With this all-enveloping mix of horror and crime, Burke concludes a trilogy that also includes The New Iberia Blues (2019) and Robicheaux (2018). All three books find Cajun detective Dave Robicheaux tackling powerful men with evil visions of racist grandeur." —*Booklist*

Robicheaux. James Lee Burke. Simon & Schuster, 2018. 448 p. (Dave Robicheaux novels, 21)
ISBN 9781501176845
1. Murder suspects 2. Post-traumatic stress disorder 3. Widowers 4. Vietnam veterans 5. Loss (Psychology) 6. Louisiana 7. Police procedurals 8. Hardboiled fiction 9. Southern fiction

Struggling with PTSD, alcoholism and wrenching loss, Dave Robicheaux discovers that he may have committed the homicide he is investigating and endeavors to clear his name and make sense of the killing.

Wayfaring stranger: a novel. James Lee Burke. Simon & Schuster, 2014. 544 p. (Holland family saga, 1)
ISBN 9781476710792
1. Oil industry and trade 2. Antisemitism 3. Good and evil 4. Jewish women 5. Man-woman relationships 6. Texas 7. 1940s 8. Historical fiction
LC 2014000147

A decade after taking a shot at Bonnie and Clyde during one of their notorious armed robberies, a Depression teen-turned-soldier escapes death during the Battle of the Bulge and marries a beautiful young woman with whom he seeks his fortune along the Texas-Louisiana oil coast.

"Burke takes a break from his Dave Robicheaux series to offer an ambitious, deeply satisfying historical thriller that fills in backstory on the author's other fictional family, the Hollands. With two series already in place starring contemporary members of the Holland clan, Burke now steps back in time to tell the story of oilman Weldon Avery Holland and his struggle to carve a life for himself on his own terms." —*Booklist*

Burke, Marcus

Team seven. Marcus Burke. Doubleday, 2014. 259 pages
ISBN 9780385537797
1. African American teenagers 2. Drug traffic 3. City life 4. Gangs 5. Inner city 6. Massachusetts 7. Coming-of-age stories 8. African American fiction

LC 2013032242

Follows the experiences of young Andre Battel as he grows away from his Jamaican family, discovers basketball court talents and turns drug dealer for a street gang.

Burke, Sue

Semiosis. Sue Burke. Tor Books, 2018. 368 p. (Semiosis duology, 1)
ISBN 9780765391353
1. Space colonies 2. Human/alien encounters 3. Plants 4. Aliens (Non-humanoid) 5. Communication 6. Hard science fiction 7. Science fiction 8. Multiple perspectives

LC 2017049645

Human colonists are forced to survive on limited resources on a planet with an inexplicable environment, where trees offer deliciously addictive fruit one day and poison the next and the ruins of an alien race are discovered within plant roots.

A Tom Doherty Associates Book.
Includes bibliographical references and index.

Burnet, Graeme Macrae

His bloody project: documents relating to the case of Roderick Macrae. Graeme Macrae Burnet. Skyhorse Publishing, 2016. 288 p.
ISBN 9781510719217
1. Murderers 2. Trials (Murder) 3. Guilt (Law) 4. Motive (Law) 5. Insanity (Law) 6. Highlands, Scotland 7. 1860s 8. Historical thrillers 9. Legal thrillers 10. Literary fiction

Shortlisted for the Man Booker Prize, 2016

A triple murder in a remote northwestern farming community in 1869 leads to the arrest of a young man by the name of Roderick Macrae. There's no question that Macrae is guilty, but the police and courts must uncover what drove him to murder the local village constable and his two children.

"Although Burnet paints a disturbing picture of the hopelessness and hardships of tenant farmers, as well as providing an eye-opening introduction to the fallibility of so-called expert witnesses, this is not a bleak book. Rather, it is sly, poignant, gritty, thought-provoking, and sprinkled with wit." —*Publishers Weekly*

Originally published: Glasgow : Faber Factory, 2015.

Burns, Anna

Milkman: a novel. Anna Burns. Graywolf Press, 2018. 352 p.
ISBN 9781644450000
1. Teenage girls 2. Paramilitary forces 3. Threat (Psychology) 4. Stalkers 5. Sisters 6. Northern Ireland 7. Ireland 8. 1970s 9. Literary fiction

International IMPAC Dublin Literary Award, 2020; Man Booker Prize, 2018; National Book Critics Circle Award for Fiction, 2018; Orwell Prize, 2019; Shortlisted for The Women's Prize for Fiction, 2019

In Northern Ireland during the Troubles of the 1970s, an unnamed narrator finds herself targeted by a high-ranking dissident known as Milkman.

"Milkman is a uniquely meandering and mesmerizing, wonderful and enigmatic work about borders and barriers, both physical and spiritual, and the cost of survival." —*Booklist*

Originally published: London : Faber & Faber, 2018.

Burns, Charles

★ **Black** hole. Charles Burns. Pantheon Books, 2005. 400 p.
ISBN 9780375423802
1. Teenagers — Sexuality 2. Hallucinations and illusions 3. Sexually transmitted diseases 4. Homeless teenagers 5. Teenagers with disfigurements 6. Seattle, Washington 7. 1970s 8. Surrealist comics 9. Comics and Graphic novels

LC 2005046431

Eisner Awards, Best Graphic Album - Reprint, 2006; Harvey Awards, Best Graphic Album - Previously Published, 2006; Ignatz Awards, Outstanding Anthology or Collection, 2006

Seattle teenagers of the 1970s are suddenly faced with a devastating, disfiguring, and incurable plague that spreads only through sexual contact.

Illustrated by the author.

Burns, Olive Ann

★ **Cold** Sassy tree. Olive Ann Burns. Ticknor & Fields, 1984. 391 p; (Cold Sassy series, 1)
ISBN 9780899193090
1. Welty, Eudora 2. Elopement 3. May-December romances 4. Senior men 5. Small town life 6. Georgia 7. 1900s (Decade) 8. Humorous stories 9. Coming-of-age stories 10. Books to movies

LC 84008570

One thing you could depend on in Cold Sassy, Georgia, was that word got around—fast. On July 5, 1906, things took a scandalous turn. That was the day that E. Rucker Blakeslee, proprietor of the general store and barely three weeks a widower, eloped with Miss Love Simpson—a woman half his age and, worse yet, a Yankee! On that day, fourteen-year-old Will Tweedy's adventures began, and an unimpeachably pious town came to life.

Burns, V. M.

Killer Words. V. M. Burns. Kensington, 2021. 336 p. (Mystery bookshop, 7)
ISBN 9781496728975
1. Mystery story writers 2. Women amateur detectives 3. Murder investigation 4. Women booksellers 5. Politicians 6. England 7. Cozy mysteries 8. Gentle reads 9. African American fiction

"Change seems to be the theme in both Samantha's 'real' life and in her work-in-progress novel. Newcomers will have fun, while established fans will relish the evolution of the characters and welcome Samantha's bright new future." —*Publishers Weekly*

Burroughs, William S.

★ **Naked** lunch: the restored text. William S. Burroughs; restored text edited by James Grauer holz and Barry Miles. Grove Press, 1992. Vii, 299 p.

ISBN 9780802119261

1. Drug addicts 2. Homosexuality 3. Hallucinations and illusions 4. Gay men 5. Recovering addicts 6. Surrealist fiction 7. Transgressive fiction 8. Modern classics

LC 91022972

An unnerving tale of a narcotics addict unmoored in New York, Tangiers, and ultimately a nightmarish wasteland known as Interzone, its formal innovation, formerly taboo subject matter, and tour de force execution have exerted their influence on the work of authors like Thomas Pynchon, J.G. Ballard, and William Gibson; on the relationship of art and obscenity; and on the shape of music, film, and media generally. This restored text includes many editorial corrections to errors present in previous editions, and incorporates Burroughs' notes on the text, and several essays he wrote over the years about the book.

Originally published: Paris : Olympia Press, 1959. Restored text c2001.

Burrowes, Grace

The **captive**. Grace Burrowes. Sourcebooks, 2014. 384 p. (Captive hearts (Grace Burrowes), 1)

ISBN 9781402278785

1. Revenge 2. Dukes and duchesses 3. Nobility 4. Single fathers 5. Man-woman relationships 6. England 7. Regency period (1811-1820) 8. Regency romances 9. Historical romances

Struggling with society life, Christian Severn, who lost his wife, son, and will to live, finds an ally in the Countess of Windmere, who helps him stay strong for his surviving daughter.

My one and only duke. Grace Burrowes. Forever, 2018. 442 pages; (Rogues to riches, 1)

ISBN 9781538728956

1. Heirs and heiresses 2. Revenge 3. Frameups 4. Widows 5. Pregnant women 6. London, England 7. Regency period (1811-1820) 8. Historical romances 9. Regency romances

Library Journal Best Books, 2018

Falsely imprisoned Quinn Wentworth marries pregnant widow Jane Winston in order to help her, but when he is saved from execution by the discovery that he is the heir to a dukedom, they must live with their marriage of convenience.

"Burrowes offers a fun and provocative new premise, along with her trademark intelligent heroine and hero, as she kicks off the Rogues to Riches series." —*Booklist*

★ A **rogue** of her own. Grace Burrowes. Forever, 2018. 368 p. (Windham brides, 4)

ISBN 9781538728918

1. Independence in women 2. Ambition in men 3. Mate selection 4. Scandals 5. Rich men 6. Regency period (1811-1820) 7. Regency romances 8. Historical romances

Forced into a marriage of convenience after one passionate kiss, Miss Charlotte Windham and Lucas Sherbourne, amidst danger, distrust and desire, find their union turning into something much more than they ever could have expected.

A fierce, high-born heroine with a secret agenda and an astute commoner hero struggling to make sense of his place in two social worlds discover devotion and true understanding in a cleverly plotted story that rights an old wrong, brings a villain to justice, and ties up loose series

threads in a brilliantly executed plot twist that will have fans saying, 'Yes!' Library Journal

Tremaine's true love. Grace Burrowes. Sourcebooks Inc, 2015. 384 p. (True gentlemen novels, 1)

ISBN 9781492621027

1. Independence in women 2. Rich men 3. Nobility 4. Interpersonal attraction 5. Man-woman relationships 6. Great Britain 7. Twain, Mark 8. 19th century 9. Regency romances 10. Historical romances

Living a meaningful life tending to the sick and the poor, practical, reserved Nita Haddonfield wishes to avoid the limitations of marriage, but wealthy busnessman Tremaine St. Michael is determined to win her heart.

"The second installment of Burrowes' (The Duke's Disaster, 2015, etc.) new True Gentlemen series is a tightly woven story that deals with many of the world's timeless moral issuespoverty, domestic violence, professional recognition for women, and animal rights. The characters are complicated and compelling and experience enough personal growth during the course of the novel to keep the reader enthralled. Burrowes is at the top of her game, and this latest offering is not to be missed." —*Kirkus*

The **trouble** with dukes. Grace Burrowes. Forever, 2016. 384 p. (Windham brides, 1)

ISBN 9781455569960

1. Dukes and duchesses 2. Scots 3. Napoleonic Wars veterans 4. Redheads 5. Nobility 6. London, England 7. England 8. Regency romances 9. Highland romances 10. Historical romances

Hamish McHugh, the new Duke of Murdoch, to make his sisters happy, fights his hardest battle yet—the London Season—and decides to take on any challenge, including learning to waltz and Miss Megan Windham, the only woman who sees him as he truly is.

Burton, Jeffrey B.

★ The **finders**: a Mace Reid K-9 mystery. Jeffrey B. Burton. Minotaur Books, 2020. 288 p. (Mace Reid K-9 novels, 1)

ISBN 9781250244536

1. Dog trainers 2. Working dogs 3. Dead 4. Crime scenes 5. Serial murderers 6. Chicago, Illinois 7. Thrillers and suspense

LC 2020001295

After losing his beloved springer spaniel, Mace Reid, who specializes in human remains detection, adopts a new cadaver dog trainee, a rescue dog named Vira with a mysterious past, who helps him find a serial killer.

"A wonder of a thriller, crammed to bursting with everything genre fans are pining for: fascinating characters, sparky dialogue, wry humor, sweaty-palm tension—all in a literate narrative that is a joy to follow." —*Booklist*

The **keepers**: a Mace Reid K-9 mystery. Jeffrey B. Burton. Minotaur Books, 2021. 320 p. (Mace Reid K-9 novels, 2)

ISBN 9781250244567

1. Dog trainers 2. Working dogs 3. Human-animal relationships 4. Political corruption 5. Dead 6. Chicago, Illinois 7. Thrillers and suspense

LC 2020056381

Mason "Mace" Reid lives on the outskirts of Chicago and specializes in human remains detection-that is, he trains dogs to hunt for dead bodies. He calls his pack of cadaver dogs The Finders, and his prize pupil is a golden retriever named Vira. When Mace Reid and Vira are called in to search Washington Park at three o'clock in the morning, what they find has them running for their very lives. The trail of murder and mayhem Mace and CPD Officer Kippy Gimm have been following leads them to uncover treachery and corruption at the highest level, and their discoveries do not bode well for them...nor for the Windy City itself.

"Burton carefully crafts each dog's personality, ensuring that they, like the humans, are fully realized characters. Dog lovers are in for a treat." —*Publishers Weekly*

Burton, Jessie
The **miniaturist**. Jessie Burton. Ecco Press, 2014. 400 p.
ISBN 9780062306814
1. Young women 2. Sexuality 3. Husband and wife 4. Obsession 5. Miniature objects 6. Amsterdam, Netherlands 7. Netherlands 8. 17th century 9. Historical fiction
British Book Award for Book of the Year, 2014; LibraryReads Favorites, 2014

Engaging the services of a miniaturist to furnish a cabinet-sized replica of her new home, 18-year-old Nella Oortman, the wife of an illustrious merchant trader, soon discovers that the artist's tiny creations mirror their real-life counterparts in eerie and unexpected ways.

Burton, Tara Isabella
Social creature. Tara Isabella Burton. Doubleday, 2018. 273 p.
ISBN 9780385543521
1. Young women 2. Female friendship 3. Obsession 4. Envy 5. Compulsive behavior 6. Manhattan, New York City 7. New York City 8. Psychological suspense 9. Glitz and glamour novels 10. Horror
LC 2017046955

Two aspiring writers, one with wealth and the other underprivileged, spiral into an intense, partially toxic friendship that challenges their goals to see the world before one of them dies under circumstances forged by seduction and obsession.

"Louise and Lavinia are bold, brilliant characters. This devious, satisfying novel perfectly captures a very narrow slice of the Manhattan demimonde." —*Publishers Weekly*

Bush, Keisha
No heaven for good boys: a novel. By Keisha Bush. Random House, 2020. 336 p.
ISBN 9780399591969
1. Beggars 2. Children 3. Street life 4. Cousins 5. Survival 6. Dakar, Senegal 7. Senegal 8. Coming-of-age stories 9. African American fiction
LC 2019054027

Forced by an unscrupulous teacher to join a pack of child beggars, a Senegalese boy works beside his cousin to survive Dakar's black-market organ traders, rival thieves and student protests. A first novel.

"Although the relentlessly bleak story doesn't sustain a full narrative arc, Bush portrays a vibrant Dakar, including a wrenching street view from the eyes of the children." —*Booklist*

Bushnell, Candace
Is there still sex in the city? Candace Bushnell. Grove Press, 2019. 272 p.
ISBN 9780802147264
1. Female friendship 2. Man-woman relationships 3. Dating (Social customs) 4. Sex customs 5. Middle aged women 6. New York City 7. Hamptons, New York 8. Chick lit
LC 2018058110

A group of female friends navigates the ever-modernizing phenomena of midlife dating and relationships between The Village and Manhattan's Upper East Side. By the critically acclaimed author of Sex and the City.

"Bushnell is still plenty edgy, funny, and entertaining." —*Booklist*

Butland, Stephanie
The **lost** for words bookshop: a novel. Stephanie Butland. Thomas Dunne Books/St. Martin's Press, 2018. 304 p.
ISBN 9781250124531
1. Bookstores 2. Life change events 3. Women — Psychology 4. Trust 5. Secrecy 6. York, England 7. England 8. Relationship fiction 9. First person narratives
LC 2017060625

A secretly heartbroken woman who prefers books to people finds her world upended by the arrivals of a poet, a lover and three suspicious deliveries that reveal that someone has found out about her mysterious past.

First published in Great Britain under the title Lost for words by Zaffre Publishing—Title page verso.

Butler, Gwendoline
Death lives next door. Gwendoline Butler. St. Martin's Press 1992. 191 p. (John Coffin mysteries, 6)
ISBN 9780312081751
1. Women anthropologists 2. Women with schizophrenia 3. Police 4. Coffin, John (Fictitious character) 5. Oxford, England 6. Mysteries
LC 92001581

Investigating a missing person case, young Scotland Yard Inspector John Coffin discovers that his case is somehow involved with that of respected professor Marion Manning, who is being hounded by a mysterious watcher, and with murder

"Keeping her detective in the wings, [Butler] begins by focusing her narrative on a gang of shabby, bitter academic types in Oxford, at the center of which dysfunctional clique is the famous and slightly mysterious Marion Manning, watched by a man who in time will claim to be her long lost husband. Everything in Marion's past is weird, and as Coffin is drawn out of London into this narrow little world, it is the investigation of this mysterious past that forms the heart of the book. Butler's regulars shouldn't pass up the chance for this peek at Coffin's past." —*Booklist*

Also published as: Dine and Be Dead.

Butler, Halle
The **new** me: a novel. Halle Butler. Penguin Books, 2018. 208 p.
ISBN 9780143133605
1. Young women 2. Purpose in life 3. Lifestyle change 4. Temporary employees 5. Growth (Psychology) 6. Satirical fiction
LC 2018028609

Thirty-year-old Millie just can't pull it together; she spends her days killing time at a thankless temp job until she can return home to her empty apartment, where she fixates on all the ways she might change her life. Then she watches TV until she drops off to sleep, and the cycle begins again. When the possibility of a full-time job offer arises, it seems to bring the better life she's envisioning within reach. But with it also comes the paralyzing realization of just how hollow that vision has become.

"Her darkly hilarious novel vividly captures contemporary American life and will keep readers addicted to the end." —*Booklist*

Butler, Marcia
Pickle's progress. Marcia Butler. Central Ave Press, 2019. 384 pages
ISBN 9781771681551
1. Identical twin brothers 2. Husband and wife 3. Self-perception 4. Bereavement in women 5. Police 6. New York City 7. Psychological fiction

Over the course of five weeks, identical twin brothers, one wife, a dog, and a bereaved young woman collide with each other to comical and sometimes horrifying effect. Everything is questioned and tested as they jockey for position and try to maintain the status quo. Love is the poison, the antidote, the devil and, ultimately, the hero.

Butler, Nickolas

Godspeed. Nickolas Butler. G. P. Putnam's Sons, 2021. 352 p.
ISBN 9780593190418
1. Construction workers 2. Conspiracies 3. Rich people 4. House construction 5. Secrets 6. Literary fiction
LC 2021015730
The principals of True Triangle Construction seem willing to do anything to get their promised payday from a mysteriously wealthy homeowner for a project in Jackson, Wyoming in the new novel from the best-selling and award-winning author of Shotgun Lovesongs.
"Butler's award-winning talent as a storyteller (Little Faith) propels his characters on a heart-stopping, daring race with unexpected outcomes." —*Library Journal*

★ The **hearts** of men. Nickolas Butler. Ecco Press, 2017. 392 pages
ISBN 9780062469687
1. Vietnam veterans 2. Summer camps 3. Boy Scouts 4. Altruism 5. Popularity 6. Wisconsin 7. 1960s 8. Coming-of-age stories 9. Psychological fiction 10. Literary fiction 11. Adult books for young adults
LibraryReads Favorites, 2017
A scarred Vietnam veteran and successful businessman reflects on his teen years as a social outcast and friend to a popular youth during a summer camp reunion marked by selflessness and an unthinkable event involving his friend's family members.
"Butler demonstrates enormous command over the material and sympathy for his flawed characters. This beautiful novel might be his best yet." —*Publishers Weekly*

Little faith: a novel. Nickolas Butler. HarperCollins, 2019. 336 pages
ISBN 9780062469717
1. Religious radicals 2. Faith (Christianity) 3. Family relationships 4. Rural life 5. Single mothers 6. Wisconsin 7. Literary fiction 8. Domestic fiction
A Wisconsin family grapples with the power and limitations of faith when an adult daughter falls under the influence of a radical church that threatens a grandchild's safety.
"A beautifully realized meditation on the nature of parenting and living in a perplexing (and often cruel) world. Enthusiastically recommended for parents and fans of literary fiction." —*Library Journal*

Butler, Octavia E.

Adulthood rites. Octavia E. Butler. Warner Books, 1988. 277 p. (Xenogenesis series, 2)
ISBN 9780446514224
1. Nuclear holocaust survivors 2. Genetic engineering 3. Aliens (Non-humanoid) 4. Dystopias 5. Human evolution 6. African American fiction 7. Hard science fiction 8. Social science fiction
LC 87034620
In the sequel to "Dawn," Akin, the son of Lilith, struggles to cope with his dual human and alien Oankali legacy while preparing for the time of metamorphosis when he will take on the form of future human beings.

Bloodchild: and other stories. Octavia E. Butler. Seven Stories Press, 1996. 145 p.
ISBN 9781888363364

1. Women 2. Aliens (Non-humanoid) 3. Science fiction 4. Short stories 5. African American fiction 6. Adult books for young adults
LC 96-41587
School Library Journal Best Books: Best Adult Books 4 Teens, 1996
"Five intense, thought-provoking tales of people caught up in extraordinary situations." —*School Library Journal*

★ **Dawn**: xenogenesis. Octavia Butler. Warner Books, 1987. 264 p. (Xenogenesis series, 1)
ISBN 9780446513630
1. Nuclear holocaust survivors 2. Genetic engineering 3. Aliens (Non-humanoid) 4. Human-alien hybrids 5. Eugenics 6. African American fiction 7. Hard science fiction 8. Social science fiction
LC 87006195
The human race, now infertile, fights to maintain its identity when the alien species, Oankali, offers to trade genetic material and bioengineering at the price of metamorphosing a new kind of being.
"Butler is one of the few sf writers who can handle effectively a slow-moving plot that emphasizes characters' emotions. Her command of the language is superior, and her aliens are quite convincing creations." —*Booklist*

★ **Kindred**. Octavia Butler. Beacon Press, 1988. Xxvii, 264 p.
ISBN 9780807083055
1. Time travel (Past) 2. Ancestors 3. Slavery 4. Interracial couples 5. Rescues 6. Maryland 7. African American fiction 8. Social science fiction 9. Science fiction
Dana, a Black woman, finds herself repeatedly transported to the antebellum South, where she must make sure that Rufus, the plantation owner's son, survives to father Dana's ancestor.
"This sometimes painful novel features superb character development." —*Anatomy of Wonder, 5th edition*
Originally published: Garden City, N.Y. : Doubleday, 1979.

★ **Parable** of the sower. Octavia E. Butler. Warner Books, 2000. 299 p. (Parable books, 1)
ISBN 9780446675505
1. Dystopias 2. Women psychics 3. Religion 4. African American women 5. African American mothers and daughters 6. California 7. 21st century 8. African American fiction 9. Diary novels 10. Dystopian fiction
LC 93008703
In 2025 California, an eighteen-year-old African American woman, suffering from a hereditary trait that causes her to feel others' pain as well as her own, flees northward from her small community and its desperate savages.
"The author infuses this tale with an allegorical quality that is part meditation, part warning. Simple, direct, and deeply felt, this should reach both mainstream and sf audiences." —*Library Journal*
Sequel: Parable of the Talents.

Parable of the talents: a novel. Octavia E. Butler. Seven Stories Press. 1998. 365 p. (Parable books, 2)
ISBN 9781888363814
1. Dystopias 2. Women psychics 3. Violence 4. African American women 5. African American mothers and daughters 6. 21st century 7. Dystopian fiction 8. Social science fiction 9. Science fiction
LC 9835863
Nebula Award for Best Novel, 1999; New York Times Notable Science Fiction, 1999
It is 2032 and Lauren Olamina's daughter Larkin narrates the story of her mother's life as she spreads the word of her Earthseed philosophy. As Larkin describes how they attain their goal of reaching the stars, she denounces her mother.

"The narrative is both impassioned and bitter.... Lauren, at once loving wife and mother, prophet and fanatic, victim and leader, gains stature as one of the most intense and well-developed protagonists in recent SF." —*Publishers Weekly*

Sequel to: Parable of the sower.

Butler, Robert Olen

A **good** scent from a strange mountain: stories. Robert Olen Butler. H. Holt, 1992. 249 p.

ISBN 9780805019865

1. Vietnamese Americans 2. Vietnam 3. Louisiana 4. Short stories 5. Literary fiction 6. First person narratives

LC 91031359

ALA Notable Book, 1993; Pulitzer Prize for Fiction, 1993

A collection of stories about the residents of Saigon as they face love, loss, and despair BT

"Recommended for all literary fiction collections and essential for libraries seeking to expand Asian American literature collections." —*Library Journal*

Fifteen stories dealing with Vietnam and Vietnamese-Americans in Louisiana.

Hell: a novel. Robert Olen Butler. Grove Press, 2009. 240 p.

ISBN 9780802119018

1. Television journalists 2. Hell 3. Damned persons 4. Future punishment 5. Free will and determinism 6. Satirical fiction 7. Literary fiction

Struggling through Sisyphean tortures in Hell where he lives with Anne Boleyn and regularly encounters late popes and presidents, news presenter Hatcher McCord learns of a possible means of escape that involves exposing Satan as a charlatan.

"Butler's lust for the tabloid romp and his stream of the never-ending punch line both irritates and illuminates. The reader's taste will have to be the final arbiters of worth." —*Publishers Weekly*

Late city. Robert Olen Butler. Atlantic Monthly Press, 2021. 304 p.

ISBN 9780802158826

1. Centenarians 2. People with terminal illnesses 3. Reminiscing in old age 4. God 5. Presidential election, 2016 6. United States 7. 20th century 8. 21st century 9. Historical fiction

LC Bl2021014833

A 115-year-old man lies on his deathbed as the 2016 election results arrive, and revisits his life in this moving story of love, fatherhood, and American century from Pulitzer Prize winner Robert Olen Butler.

"Readers with the patience for an old man's stubbornness will appreciate the redemption herein." —*Publishers Weekly*

Perfume River. Robert Olen Butler. Atlantic Monthly Press, 2016. 273 p.

ISBN 9780802125750

1. Vietnam veterans 2. Fathers and sons 3. War — Psychological aspects 4. Vietnam War, 1961-1975 — Psychological aspects 5. Seniors 6. Florida 7. Literary fiction

Booklist Editors' Choice, 2016

Presents the story of a single North Florida family shaped and overshadowed by the Vietnam War and the estrangements between the fathers, sons and brothers who supported or protested against it.

Butler, Sarah

Ten things I've learnt about love: a novel. Sarah Butler. The Penguin Press, 2013. 258 p.

ISBN 9781594205330

1. Fathers and daughters 2. Families 3. Homecomings 4. Loss (Psychology) 5. Sisters 6. London, England 7. Mainstream fiction 8. Multiple perspectives

LC 2012046987

Drawn to dangerous world regions and unconventional career paths, Alice, the black sheep of her family, rushes to say goodbye when she learns her father is dying; while Daniel, an artist suffering from synesthesia and failing health, clings to thoughts of the daughter he has never been able to find.

Butler, Season

★ **Cygnet**. Season Butler. HarperCollins, 2019. 272 pages

ISBN 9780062870919

1. Seniors 2. Abandoned teenagers 3. Social isolation 4. Islands 5. Hostility (Psychology) 6. New Hampshire 7. Coming-of-age stories

An utterly original coming-of-age tale, marked by wrenching humor and staggering charisma, about a young woman resisting the savagery of adulthood in a community of the elderly rejecting the promise of youth.

Buwalda, Peter

Bonita Avenue: a novel. Peter Buwalda; translated from the Dutch by Jonathan Reeder. Hogarth, 2014. 480 pages

ISBN 9781908968173

1. College teachers 2. Family relationships 3. Dysfunctional families 4. Dishonesty 5. Revenge 6. Netherlands 7. Literary fiction 8. Translations 9. Multiple perspectives

LC 2014009172

"The rich layer of detail would be impressive when applied to one topic, but Buwalda creates multiple complex worlds around vastly different subjects: the porn industry, mathematics, music, and judo, among others. An outstanding literary suspense story." —*Library Journal*

Bonita Avenue first published in Dutch as Bonita Avenue in 2010—Title page verso.

Originally published in Dutch: Amsterdam : De Bezige Bij, 2010.

Buxton, Kira Jane

★ **Hollow** kingdom. Kira Jane Buxton. Grand Central Pub 2019. 320 p. (Hollow kingdom (Buxton), 1)

ISBN 9781538745823

1. Crows 2. Zombies 3. Human-animal relationships 4. Dogs 5. Bloodhounds 6. Seattle, Washington 7. Stories told by animals 8. Apocalyptic fiction 9. Adult books for young adults

Sensing something is wrong with his owner, a domesticated crow abandons the only life he ever knew to discover that humans are turning into zombies and must use knowledge gleaned from his TV-viewing to save them.

Byatt, A. S.

Babel Tower. A. S. Byatt. Random House, 1996. 625 p. (Frederica Potter series, 3)

ISBN 9780679405139

1. Divorced women 2. Censorship — History 3. Family violence 4. Single mothers 5. Divorce 6. England 7. 1960s 8. Psychological fiction 9. Literary fiction

LC 95-53210

Frederica Potter becomes disenchanted with her marriage after attending Cambridge and leaves her country home for London where, in the turbulent 1960s, she struggles with single motherhood, politics, ideals, and changing sexual roles in a sequel to Still Life.

"In many ways, this is a book about language, and how it is used to conceal and reveal (there is a wonderfully satirical subplot about a commission examining English educational methods). But it also employs language, brilliantly, to create a large cast of characters whose struggles, anxieties and small triumphs are at once specific to a time and place, and universal." —*Publishers Weekly*

Medusa's ankles: selected stories. A.S. Byatt; with an introduction by David Mitchell. Alfred A. Knopf, 2021. 464 p.
ISBN 9780593321584
1. Short stories 2. Literary fiction
LC 2021016813
A ravishing, luminous selection of short stories from the prize-winning imagination of A. S. Byatt, drawn from her entire career.
"These stories by Booker winner Byatt (Possession), three of which are previously uncollected, offer a scintillating look at three decades of the author's work." —*Publishers Weekly*
Originally published in Great Britain, 2020.

★ **Possession:** a romance. A.S. Byatt. Random House, 1990. 555 p.
ISBN 9780394586236
1. Literary historians 2. Women college teachers 3. College teachers 4. Poets, English 5. Women poets 6. London, England 7. Whitby, England 8. 19th century 9. 1980s 10. Love stories 11. Literary fiction 12. Parallel narratives
LC 90008374
ALA Notable Book, 1991; Booker Prize, 1990; Commonwealth Writers' Prize, South Asia and Europe: Best Book, 1991
Roland Mitchell has devoted his life to studying the life and works of 19th-century writer Randolph Henry Ash. When Roland discovers a provocative letter to an unnamed woman, he begins a quest for information. Along with fellow academician Maud Bailey, Roland discovers an unconventional love story that echoes through their own modern lives.
"Intelligent, ingenious and humane, [this] bids fair to be looked back upon as one of the most memorable novels of the 1990s." —*Times Literary Supplement*

★ **Ragnarok:** the end of the gods. A.S. Byatt. Grove Press, 2012. 177 p. : Illustration (Myths series)
ISBN 9780802129925
1. Child refugees 2. Mythology, Norse 3. Girls 4. End of the world 5. Gods and goddesses, Norse 6. England 7. Second World War era (1939-1945) 8. Literary fiction 9. Mythological fiction
Presents a retelling of the Norse myth about the end of the world that follows the blitz-era evacuation of a young girl whose worldview is dramatically changed upon reading "Asgard and the Gods.
Includes bibliographical references (p. 173-176).
First published: Edinburgh : Canongate, 2011.

A **whistling** woman. A.S. Byatt. Alfred A. Knopf, 2003. 448 p. (Frederica Potter series, 4)
ISBN 9780375415340
1. Divorced women 2. Television programs 3. Counterculture 4. Women television personalities 5. Potter, Frederica (Fictitious character) 6. England 7. 1960s 8. Psychological fiction 9. Literary fiction
LC 2002072957
New York Times Notable Book, 2003
In the late 1960s, the world begins to split, while Frederica falls almost by accident into a career in television in London, tumultuous events in her home county of Yorkshire threaten to change her life, and those of the people she loves.
"There is no other writer alive who is as interested as Byatt in creating characters who are thinking women and men while at the same time recog-

nizing the limits of cognition in the face of unreason, or love." —*New York Times Book Review*

Bynum, Sarah Shun-lien

Ms. Hempel chronicles. Sarah Shun-lien Bynum. Harcourt, 2008. 224 p.
ISBN 9780151014965
1. Middle school teachers 2. Loss (Psychology) 3. Grief in women 4. Coping 5. Young women 6. Coming-of-age stories 7. Psychological fiction
LC 2008008924
Ms. Beatrice Hempel, new to teaching, new to the school, newly engaged, and newly bereft of her idiosyncratic father, struggles to figure out what is expected of her in life and at work.
"Eight interconnected stories about Beatrice Hempel, a middle school English teacher. Ms. Hempel is the sort of teacher students adore, and despite feeling disenchanted with her job, she regards her students as intelligent, insightful and sometimes fascinating. Bynum...weaves stories of the teacher's childhood with the present—reminiscences about Beatrice's now deceased father and her relationship with her younger brother, Calvin—while simultaneously fleshing out the lives of Beatrice's impressionable students." —*Publishers Weekly*

Byrne, Kerrigan

The **duke** with the dragon tattoo. Kerrigan Byrne. St Martin's Paperbacks, 2018. 336 p. (Victorian rebels, 6)
ISBN 9781250122568
1. Tattooing 2. Men with amnesia 3. Dukes and duchesses 4. Protectiveness in men 5. Mate selection 6. Great Britain 7. Victorian era (1837-1901) 8. Victorian romances 9. Historical romances
Library Journal Best Books, 2018
The sixth book in the Victorian Rebel series introduces The Rook, a man who wakes up in a mass grave with no memory and a dragon tattoo on his arm. Years after being rescued and nursed back to health by Lorelei, he returns to claim her heart and avenge those who have wronged her.

How to love a duke in ten days. Kerrigan Byrne. St Martins Pr, 2019. 464 pages (Devil you know, 1)
ISBN 9781250318848
1. Dukes and duchesses 2. Nobility 3. Women archaeologists 4. Rape victims 5. Murder 6. Victorian era (1837-1901) 7. Historical romances 8. Victorian romances
Famed and brilliant, Lady Alexandra Lane has always known how to look out for to herself. But nobody would ever expect that she has darkness in her past—one that she pays a blackmailer to keep buried. Now, with her family nearing bankruptcy, Alexandra strikes upon a solution: Get married to one of the empire's most wealthy eligible bachelors. Even if he does have the reputation of a devil.

The **hunter.** Kerrigan Byrne. St Martin's Paperbacks, 2016. 432 p. (Victorian rebels, 2)
ISBN 9781250076069
1. Actors and actresses 2. Assassins 3. Loners 4. Protectiveness in men 5. Secrets 6. London, England 7. Great Britain 8. Victorian era (1837-1901) 9. Victorian romances 10. Historical romances
When he is hired to kill beautiful actress Millie LeCour, Christopher Argent, London's deadliest hitman, is unable to complete his mission as he becomes overwhelmed by the passion that simmers between them, and vows to keep her safe from her enemies as danger closes in.

Byrne, Trevor

Ghosts and lightning. Trevor Byrne. Doubleday, 2009. 336 p.
ISBN 9780385531276
1. Bereavement 2. Self-destructive behavior 3. Homecomings 4. Drug use 5. Families 6. Ireland 7. Dublin, Ireland 8. Picaresque fiction 9. First person narratives

LC 2009020031

Called back to his native Dublin to attend his mother's funeral, Denny struggles with feelings of powerlessness in the face of death, drug use, and unemployment while spending his empty days with a series of hooligan companions.

"[A] witty and often disturbing portrait of the Irish underclass...and the story is inventively narrated in a thick Irish brogue, saturated with profanities and folkloric allusions." —*The New Yorker*

C

Ca$h

Thugs cry: a novel. Ca$h. Lockdown Pub, 2013. 252 p. (Thugs cry novels (Ca$h), 1)
ISBN 9781492717928
1. Gangs 2. Drug traffic 3. African Americans 4. Man-woman relationships 5. Revenge in men 6. Newark, New Jersey 7. Urban fiction 8. African American fiction

Cam'ron and Raheem hail from the notorious Brick City in Newark New Jersey. The two friends grew up eating noodles off of the same fork, now they are primed to eat off the drug game. From the Bricks to the ATL nigga's must bow down or get laid down. Cam'ron epitomizes the grimy streets of Newark, he's a supreme hustler with a vicious murder game. Cam'ron loves four things: his money, family, his homie, and his boo. Touch either one and you get served, Cam'ron warns the streets. Of course Newark niggas are the grimiest so they don't take heed to Cam'ron's threat, they touch all of the above. Tamika who is Cam'ron's boo makes shit hotter when she sets out to show him that he's not the only hustler checkin for her and she does not have to condone his womanizing. When Tamika gets with a hustler who refuses to let her go back to Cam'ron the consequences get catastrophic for somebody. Meanwhile, Raheem who is the polar opposite from his man, is quietly putting his G down in the Dirty South. When ATL thugs test Raheem's gun they find out that a quiet storm is the deadliest. Raheem is as gentle with his woman as he is proficient with his murder game. Kayundra, Raheem's shorty has fallen into drug addiction and it has her in a vice grip. Raheem's love for Kayundra never wavers. He helps her beat her addiction and soon she's refocused on her dream of becoming a R&B diva. With Raheem's help Kayundra lands a recording deal and almost overnight she becomes a star.But success comes at a price that threatens to shatter their love.Raheem and Cam'ron go hard for what they want, and they attain it, leaving a lot of bodies along the way. They make many mothers bury their sons and shed tears, but on the road to hood fame and riches they learn that sometimes the enemy strikes back and its your turn to cry. When the blood and tears stop falling will what Cam'ron and Raheem gained be worth what they both lose?

★ **Trust** no bitch. Cash and NeNe Capri. Amazon Digital Services, 2013. 295 p.
ISBN 9781491072431
1. Loyalty 2. Betrayal 3. Deception 4. Man-woman relationships 5. Sexual attraction 6. Urban fiction 7. African American fiction

They say Loyalty is everything, but beneath the surface of a promise lies betrayal and deceit. Taught by the best and given the keys to an em-

pire, Kiam's loyalty is tested at every turn as he strives to enforce his rule over those who ultimately can't be trusted. A deadly warning directs his course as he strives to carry out his orders. Complications set in when his mentor's beautiful, sexy, and rebellious daughter Lissha, who is as comfortable carrying a gun as she is carrying a Gucci bag, forces Kiam to decide between his sizzling desire for her and his immense loyalty to big Zo. Amidst the torrid but unspoken passion that builds between Kiam and Lissha like a blazing inferno, lies hidden alliances and deceit that threaten to explode at every turn.With sex, money, murder and dark secrets lurking around every corner and a team of beautiful yet dangerous women he is forced to work with, who will ultimately be the Bitch he can't trust?

Cain, Chelsea

One Kick: a novel. Chelsea Cain. Simon & Schuster, 2014. 306 p. (Kick Lannigan, 1)
ISBN 9781476749785
1. Women martial artists 2. Kidnapping victims 3. Post-traumatic stress disorder 4. Child pornography victims 5. Obsession in women 6. Seattle, Washington 7. Thrillers and suspense

LC 2013044441

LibraryReads Favorites, 2014

Kick Lannigan, a famous kidnapping survivor, uses her martial-arts mastery and affiliation with a wealthy patron to find and rescue missing children.

"The subject matter is uncomfortable, even stomach-churning at times, but Cain manages to deal sensitively with her material while still allowing Kick's character to emerge with multifaceted humanity—and even snatches of humor." —*Booklist*

Caldwell, Erskine

Tobacco Road. Erskine Caldwell; foreword by Lewis Nordan. University of Georgia Press, 1995. 184 p.
ISBN 9780820316611
1. Sharecroppers 2. Poor families 3. Rural life 4. Depressions 5. Rural poor people 6. Georgia 7. Modern classics 8. Southern Gothic 9. Literary fiction

LC 9413090

The Depression has hit the depleted farmlands of Augusta, Georgia, hard. For the Lester family, grinding poverty has become a way of life. Trapped by ignorance and selfishness, the Lesters are torn between surrendering to their hunger and sexual longings, and the fear that they may be slipping even lower than they already are in society's eyes.

Callaghan, Mary Rose

Billy, come home. Mary Rose Callaghan. Brandon, 2007. 201 p.
ISBN 9780863223662
1. Men with schizophrenia 2. Men with mental illnesses 3. Malicious accusation 4. Murder suspects 5. Siblings 6. Ireland 7. Domestic fiction

A woman travels to London to identify a body that has been fished out of the Thames; it is believed to be that of her brother, Billy. The narrative flashes back to the brutal murder of a teenage girl. Billy, a schizophrenic, is accused of the crime. With its echoes of cases such as the Jill Dando murder, this moving and topical novel tells an engrossing, resonant story.

"Without becoming mawkish or preachy, Callaghan delivers an effective indictment of society's failure to care for a vulnerable minority." —*Publishers Weekly*

Callender, Kacen

King of the rising. Kacen Callender. Orbit, 2020. 480 p. (Islands of blood and storm, 2)

ISBN 9780316454940

1. Power (Social sciences) 2. Race (Social sciences) 3. Revenge 4. Slavery 5. Royal houses 6. Epic fantasy 7. Historical fantasy

LC 2020014720

A revolution has swept through the islands of Hans Lollik and former slave Loren Jannik has been chosen to lead the survivors in a bid to free the islands forever. But the rebels are running out of food, weapons and options. And as the Fjern inch closer to reclaiming Hans Lollik with every battle, Loren is faced with a choice that could shift the course of the revolution in their favor—or doom it to failure.

"Graphic action and violence; flawed protagonists; and a stark, storm-filled setting all combine into a riveting read.... The second half of this duology (after The Queen of the Conquered) is a powerful look at colonialism, oppression, and rebellion, and all that it can cost the individuals involved." —*Library Journal*

Queen of the conquered. Kheryn Callender. Orbit, 2019. 480 p. (Islands of blood and storm, 1)

ISBN 9780316454933

1. Orphans 2. Adult children of murder victims 3. Revenge 4. Royal houses 5. Islands 6. Epic fantasy

LC 2019019777

World Fantasy Award, 2020

Sigourney Rose is the only surviving daughter of a noble lineage on the islands of Hans Lollik. When she was a child, her family was murdered by the islands' colonizers, who have massacred and enslaved generations of her people—and now, Sigourney is ready to exact her revenge. When the childless king of the islands declares that he will choose his successor from amongst eligible noble families, Sigourney uses her ability to read and control minds to manipulate her way onto the royal island and into the ranks of the ruling colonizers. But when she arrives, prepared to fight for control of all the islands, Sigourney finds herself the target of a dangerous, unknown magic.

Callihan, Kristen

★ **Firelight**. Kristen Callihan. Forever, 2012. 384 p. (Darkest London, 1)

ISBN 9781455508594

1. Arranged marriage 2. Men with disfigurements 3. Curses 4. Superhuman abilities 5. Nobility 6. Great Britain 7. Victorian era (1837-1901) 8. 19th century 9. Paranormal romances 10. Historical romances 11. Victorian romances

Library Journal Best Books, 2012; RUSA Reading List, 2013; Romantic Times Reviewer's Choice Award, 2012

Forced to wed London's most nefarious nobleman to save her family from financial ruin, Miranda Ellis, who is gifted with exceptional abilities, discovers that her new husband is no ordinary man when she must enter a world of dark magic to save his soul.

Calvi, Mary

Dear George, Dear Mary: a novel of George Washington's first love. Mary Calvi. St. Martin's Press, 2019. Viii, 322 pages

ISBN 9781250162946

1. Washington, George 2. Soldiers 3. First loves 4. Shakespeare, William 5. Courtship 6. Unrequited love 7. United States 8. Colonial America (1600-1775) 9. Biographical fiction 10. Historical fiction

LC 2018037733

Reimagines the unrequited love affair between a young George Washington and controversial New York heiress Mary Philipse as a catalyst for the American Revolution.

"It is...a fascinating and unique look at pre-Revolutionary War society, with its misunderstandings and simmering resentments, and notable for the author's use of contemporaneous documents." —*Booklist*

Includes bibliographical references (pages [317]-319, [321]-322).

Calvino, Italo

★ **If** on a winter's night a traveler. Italo Calvino; translated from the Italian by William Weaver. Harcourt Brace Jovanovich, 1981. 260 p.

ISBN 9780151436897

1. Books and reading 2. Writing 3. Man-woman relationships 4. Magical realism 5. Literary fiction 6. Metafiction

LC 80008741

Ten different and thoroughly dissimilar novels intertwine as the beginning of each book, interrupted at a critical moment of suspense, leads into yet another novel reflecting yet another literary mode.

Translation of: Se una notte d'inverno un viaggiatore.

A Helen and Kurt Wolff book.

Originally published: Torino : Einaudi, 1979.

Invisible cities. Italo Calvino; translated from the Italian by William Weaver. Harcourt Brace Jovanovich, 1978. 165 p.

ISBN 9780156453806

1. Polo, Marco 2. Storytelling 3. Rulers 4. Cities and towns 5. Manipulation (Social sciences) 6. Survival 7. Literary fiction 8. Magical realism 9. Translations

In Kublai Khan's garden, at sunset, the young Marco Polo diverts the aged emperor from his obsession with the impending end of his empire with tales of countless cities past, present, and future.

"Italo Calvino is recognized as one of the consummate stylists among writers today, a novelist whose superbly imaginative mind conjures up metaphorical fables of exquisite beauty to transcribe his personal visions of man and the universe." —*Choice*

A Helen and Kurt Wolff book.

Translation of: Le citta invisibili.

Originally published: Torino : Einaudi, 1972.

Cambias, James L.

A **darkling** sea. James L. Cambias. Tor, 2014. 336 pages

ISBN 9780765336279

1. Underwater cities 2. Interplanetary relations 3. Human/alien encounters 4. Space flight 5. Planets — Exploration 6. Social science fiction 7. Hard science fiction 8. Science fiction

LC 2013025215

Ilmatar is an ice-bound planet whose vast sub-surface ocean supports a blind, sentient alien race. Contact with the Ilmatarans is strictly forbidden, due to rules put in place by the six-limbed Sholen, who believe that humanity is too dangerous to be permitted contact with other species. Their concerns are soon justified by the actions of one Earthling, a journalist killed during an illicit attempt to film the Ilmatarans. This incident sets off an inter-galactic diplomatic crisis as well as conflict between human researchers and Sholen regulators. Boasting strong characterizations and extensive, immersive world-building, A Darkling Sea presents a gripping story that also provides a thought-provoking exploration of ethical issues.

"Cambias makes the Sholen and Ilmataran people and cultures as real as the more familiar human component. Beautifully written, with a story that captures the imagination." —*Booklist*

A Tom Doherty Associates Book.

LIST OF FICTIONAL WORKS

Cameron, Lindsay

Just one look. Lindsay Cameron. Ballantine Books, 2021. 288 p.

ISBN 9780593159057

1. Obsession 2. Women 3. Temporary employees 4. Couples 5. Email correspondence 6. Psychological suspense

After taking a thankless job as a temp at a law firm, Cassie Woodson begins reading the personal emails between a partner and his enchanting wife and becomes so obsessed with the pair, she plots to take her place.

"This is the author's suspense debut, and it succeeds wildly." —*Booklist*

Cameron, Marc

★ **Code** of honor. Marc Cameron. Putnam Pub Group, 2019. 592 pages (Jack Ryan and John Clark novels, 19)

ISBN 9780525541721

1. Elite operatives 2. National security 3. Malicious accusation 4. Friendship 5. International intrigue 6. United States 7. Political thrillers 8. Thrillers and suspense

When an old college friend-turned-humanitarian is arrested in Indonesia amid false accusations, President Ryan assigns the Campus team to find answers at the same time he receives an ominous warning.

Power and empire. Marc Cameron. G.P. Putnam's Sons, 2017. 432 p. (Jack Ryan and John Clark novels, 17)

ISBN 9780735215894

1. Presidents 2. International intrigue 3. Terrorism — Prevention 4. Spies 5. Negotiation 6. United States 7. China 8. Political thrillers 9. Thrillers and suspense

A newly belligerent Chinese government leaves U.S. President Jack Ryan with only a few desperate options to control a series of attacks designed to sabotage peace negotiations.

Cameron, Peter

The **city** of your final destination. Peter Cameron. Farrar, Straus, and Giroux, 2002. 311 p.

ISBN 9780374281977

1. Biographers 2. Mistresses 3. Love triangles 4. Authors 5. Americans in Uruguay 6. Uruguay 7. Kansas 8. Literary fiction 9. Books to movies

LC 2001051127

After receiving a grant to write the biography of recently deceased Latin American author Jules Gund, graduate student Omar Razaghi's request to become Gund's official biographer is turned down, prompting Omar to travel to Uruguay to try to persuade the author's literary heirs to change their minds.

"The characters discover themselves not through the books they have read (as Omar first believes) or the places they have been (as the title would suggest) but through Cameron's precisely rendered conversations." —*The New Yorker*

This novel was made into film of the same name in 2007, directed by James Ivory and starring Anthony Hopkins, Laura Linney, and Charlotte Gainsbourg.

Cameron, W. Bruce

A **dog's** promise. W. Bruce Cameron. Forge, 2019. 336 p. (Dog's purpose, 3)

ISBN 9781250163516

1. Reincarnation 2. Purpose in life 3. Promises 4. Human-animal relationships 5. Humans and dogs 6. Stories told by animals 7. First person narratives 8. Adult books for young adults

A latest entry in the series that includes, A Dog's Journey, continues the story of Bailey, who is joined by another special dog, Lola, in an effort to fulfill a promise over the course of several lives.

The **dogs** of Christmas. W. Bruce Cameron. Forge Books, 2013. 224 p.

ISBN 9780765330550

1. Single men 2. Abandoned dogs 3. Animal rescue 4. Animal shelter workers 5. Dogs 6. Colorado 7. Mainstream fiction 8. Christmas stories

LC 2013018448

When his neighbor abandons his very pregnant dog Lucy at his Colorado home, Josh Michaels, recovering from a broken heart, learns to care for Lucy's tiny puppies with the help of local animal shelter worker Kerri, a beautiful woman with a quick wit and fierce love for animals.

A Tom Doherty Associates book.

Repo madness. W. Bruce Cameron. Forge Books, 2016. 368 p. (Ruddy McCann novels, 2)

ISBN 9780765377500

1. Repossessors 2. Serial murder investigation 3. Women murder victims 4. Auditory hallucinations 5. Men and dogs 6. Michigan 7. Supernatural mysteries 8. First person narratives

Juggling the possible loss of his job, a romantic estrangement, and court-ordered medication, Michigan repo man Ruddy McCann learns that the tragedy that defined his life may be a lie, a possibility that compels his investigation into a string of local disappearances.

Camilleri, Andrea

Riccardino. Andrea Camilleri; translated by Stephen Sartarelli. Penguin Books, 2021. 272 p. (Salvo Montalbano mysteries, 28)

ISBN 9780143136798

1. Detectives 2. Murder victims 3. Bishops 4. Fortune-tellers 5. Salt mines and mining 6. Sicily, Italy 7. Italy 8. Mysteries 9. Police procedurals 10. Translations

LC 2021016473

The long-awaited last novel in the transporting and beloved New York Times bestselling Inspector Montalbano series.

"In an amusing metafictional twist, Camilleri (1925-2019) plays a part in his elegiac 28th and final mystery featuring Sicilian police inspector Salvo Montalbano.... The sad, poetic ending is perfect." —*Publishers Weekly*

Originally published in Italian as Riccardino by Sellerio Editore, Palermo.

Translated from the Italian.

Camp, Bryan

The **city** of lost fortunes. Bryan Camp. John Joseph Adams/Houghton Mifflin Harcourt, 2018. 384 p. (Crescent City novels (Bryan Camp), 1)

ISBN 9781328810793

1. Gods and goddesses 2. Psychic ability 3. Demigods 4. Supernatural 5. Magic 6. New Orleans, Louisiana 7. 2010s 8. Urban fantasy

LC 2017045346

Library Journal Best Books, 2018

Maintaining a low profile in the aftermath of Hurricane Katrina in New Orleans, a street magician who inherited an ability to find lost things from his superhuman father, is drawn back into the world by the murder of a Fortune god to whom he owes a debt, an event that exposes a plot that threatens the city's soul.

Gather the fortunes. Bryan Camp. Houghton Mifflin Harcourt, 2019. 336 pages (Crescent City novels (Bryan Camp), 2)

ISBN 9781328876713

1. Spirit guides 2. Missing persons investigation 3. Gods and goddesses 4. Soul 5. Ghosts 6. New Orleans, Louisiana 7. Urban fantasy 8. Adult books for young adults

LC 2018043604

Establishing herself among the guides who lead the souls of the dead through the Seven Gates of the Underworld, Renaissance Raines lands at the center of a deity plot involving a boy's escape of his foretold death.

"Full of magic and numerous mythologies but still tied to the lush New Orleans setting, this Crescent City is one readers will not want to leave." —*Library Journal*

A John Joseph Adams book.

Campbell, Bebe Moore

Brothers and sisters. Bebe Moore Campbell. G. P. Putnam's Sons, 1994. 476 p.

ISBN 9780399139291

1. Women bankers 2. Sexual harassment 3. Interracial friendship 4. Racism 5. African American women 6. Los Angeles, California 7. Psychological fiction 8. African American fiction 9. Adult books for young adults

LC 94014196

Booklist Editors' Choice, 1994; School Library Journal Best Books: Best Adult Books 4 Teens, 1995

Struggling with her own personal issues after the Los Angeles riots, Esther Jackson, a Black employee at a downtown bank, is heartened when a Black man is hired as senior vice-president, until he sexually harasses her white friend and coworker BT

"What makes 'Brothers and Sisters' different from the traditional pot-boiler is Ms. Campbell's genuine attempt to address the complexities of race in the modern age." —*New York Times Book Review*

Your blues ain't like mine. Bebe Moore Campbell. G. P. Putnam's Sons 1992. 332p.

ISBN 9780345401120

1. Racism 2. Hate crimes 3. Civil Rights Movement 4. African American teenage boys 5. Poor people 6. Mississippi 7. 1950s 8. Coming-of-age stories 9. African American fiction

LC 91045518

The racially motivated deadly beating of a black teenager in a small Mississippi town ripples through generations, changing forever the lives of everyone involved in the incident.

"Written in poetic prose, filled with masterfully drawn and sympathetic characters that a less able hand might have rendered in stereotypes, this first novel blends the irony of Flannery O'Connor's fiction and the poignance of Harper Lee's." —*Publishers Weekly*

Campbell, Bonnie Jo

Once upon a river. Bonnie Jo Campbell. W. W. Norton & Co, 2011. 320 p.

ISBN 9780393079890

1. Teenage girls 2. Fathers — Death 3. River life 4. Mothers and daughters 5. Rape 6. Michigan 7. 1970s 8. Rural noir 9. Coming-of-age stories 10. Literary fiction 11. Adult books for young adults

LC 2011001499

Booklist Editors' Choice: Adult Books for Young Adults, 2011; School Library Journal Best Books: Best Adult Books 4 Teens, 2011

Margo Crane, a beautiful and uncanny markswoman takes to the Stark River after being complicit in the death of her father and embarks on an odyssey in search of her vanished mother.

Celebrates the timeless secrets of life, death, and imagination—and the enduring power of words. Fans, rejoice! Kirkus.

Campbell, Lisbeth

The **vanished** queen. Lisbeth Campbell. Saga Press, 2020. 416 p.

ISBN 9781982141295

1. Revolutions 2. Imaginary kingdoms 3. Rulers 4. Political intrigue 5. Malicious accusation 6. Epic fantasy 7. Fantasy fiction 8. Multiple perspectives

Joining a resistance group to overthrow the king who successfully framed her father for the queen's disappearance, Anza finds unexpected support from the kingdom's prince, who navigates dangerous court politics to secure freedom for their people.

"Campbell's debut is filled with political intrigue, personal anguish, and family ties that bind. The prose moves smoothly through the alternating points of view of Mirantha, Anza, and Esvar, building well-rounded characters approaching the eve of revolution." —*Library Journal*

Campbell, Ramsey

The **wise** friend. Ramsey Campbell. Flame Tree Pub, 2020. 288 pages

ISBN 9781787584044

1. Art 2. Occultism 3. Fathers and sons 4. Deception 5. Teenage boys 6. Horror

Patrick's aunt Thelma was an artist whose work turned towards the occult. As an adult he discovers a journal of her explorations, and his son Roy becomes fascinated. His experiences at the sites scare Patrick away, but not Roy. Can he convince his son that his suspicions are real, or will what they've helped to rouse take a new hold on the world?

"Another towering achievement from one of the genre's living legends." —*Booklist*

Campbell, Rick

Treason. Rick Campbell. St. Martin's Press, 2019. 352 p. (Trident deception, 5)

ISBN 9781250164650

1. Coups d'etat 2. Military occupation 3. International intrigue 4. Armed Forces 5. Nuclear weapons 6. Russia 7. Ukraine 8. Techno-thrillers

LC 2018044449

A military coup in Russia leads to a swift invasion of former Soviet territories—while the U.S. has been rendered powerless to respond.

Campisi, Megan

Sin eater. Megan Campisi. Atria Books, 2020. 320 pages

ISBN 9781982124106

1. Sin 2. Superstition 3. Punishment 4. Teenage girls 5. Political intrigue 6. England 7. Elizabethan era (1558-1603) 8. Historical fantasy 9. Adult books for young adults

Sentenced to become a Sin Eater for the crime of stealing bread, a 14-year-old orphan in 16th-century England becomes ensnared in a deadly royal plot that helps her discover the power of her subjugated position.

"This spellbinding novel is a treat for fans of feminist speculative fiction." —*Publishers Weekly*

Camus, Albert

★ The **fall**. Albert Camus; translated from the French by Justin O'Brien. Vintage Books, 1991. 147 p.

ISBN 9780679720225

1. Conscience 2. Lawyers 3. Deception 4. Existentialism 5. Strangers 6. Paris, France 7. Amsterdam, Netherlands 8. Literary fiction 9. Psychological fiction 10. Classics

A man's confessions reveal his perception of justice and his own downfall.

Translation from the French of: La chute.

First published in the U.S. by Alfred A. Knopf in 1956—Title page verso.

The **plague**. Albert Camus; translated from the French by Stuart Gilbert. Vintage Books, 1991. 308 p.
ISBN 9780679720218
1. Plague 2. Epidemics 3. Social isolation 4. Poverty 5. Physicians 6. Algeria 7. Translations 8. Literary fiction 9. Modern classics

Chaos prevails when the bubonic plague strikes the Algerian coastal city of Oran.

Translation from the French of: La peste.

This translation first published: Allen Lane The Penguin Press, 2001.

Originally published as La peste, 1947.

Originally published: Paris : Gallimard, 1947.

★ The **stranger**. Albert Camus; translated from the French by Matthew Ward. A. A. Knopf, 1988. Vii, 123 p.
ISBN 9780394533056
1. Trials (Murder) 2. Murderers 3. Conformity 4. Poverty 5. Honesty 6. Algeria 7. Psychological fiction 8. Translations 9. Literary fiction
LC 83048885

When a young Algerian named Meursault kills a man, his subsequent imprisonment and trial are puzzling and absurd. The apparently amoral Meursault—who puts little stock in ideas like love and God—seems to be on trial less for his murderous actions, and more for what the authorities believe is his deficient character.

"The new translation of Camus's classic is a cultural event.... With the domestications pruned away from the text, students will be as close to the original as another language will allow." —*Library Journal*

Translation from the French of: L'Etranger.

Also published as: The outsider (1946).

Originally published in French by Librairie Gallimard, Paris in 1942.

Cander, Chris
The **weight** of a piano: a novel. Chris Cander. Alfred A Knopf, 2018. 323 pages
ISBN 9780525654674
1. Pianos 2. Family history 3. Loss (Psychology) 4. Music 5. Obsession 6. Death Valley 7. California 8. Parallel narratives 9. Literary fiction

An immigrant from the Soviet Union and an orphaned mechanic find their lives fatefully linked across half a century of history by a German Bluthner piano.

"Strong characterization and attention to detail, whether in the manufacture of a piano or in the desolate beauty of Death Valley, elevate Cander's...tale about learning to let go of the past." —*Booklist*

Candlish, Louise
Our house. Louise Candlish. Berkley, 2018. 416 p.
ISBN 9780451489111
1. Divorced parents 2. Coparenting 3. Houses 4. Missing men 5. Missing children 6. London, England 7. Psychological suspense 8. Multiple perspectives
LC 2017029542
LibraryReads Favorites, 2018; Booklist Editors' Choice, 2018

Arriving home to find strangers moving into the prized family home she agreed to share with her ex, Fiona endures a domino effect of horrors

as she discovers that her children have gone missing amid terrible revelations.

Cannon, Joanna
Three things about Elsie: a novel. Joanna Cannon. Scribner, 2018. 304 p.
ISBN 9781501187384
1. Nursing home patients 2. Senior women 3. Reminiscing in old age 4. Memories 5. Friendship 6. England 7. Psychological fiction
LC 2017061726
Longlisted for The Women's Prize for Fiction, 2018

Presents the story of an injured woman who meditates on her complicated relationship with a best friend when a man they believed was dead joins her retirement community.

Cantero, Edgar
Meddling kids: a novel. Edgar Cantero. Doubleday, 2017. 322 p.
ISBN 9780385541992
1. Reunions 2. Teenage detectives 3. Cold cases (Criminal investigation 4. Amateur detectives 5. Consequences 6. Oregon 7. New York City 8. Supernatural mysteries 9. Humorous stories 10. Horror
LC 2016040471

In Meddling Kids, Catalonian author Edgar Cantero portrays a reunion of old friends who decide to complete some unfinished business in the resort town where they spent their summers as kids. While pitting good against evil, Cantero pays homage to H.P. Lovecraft's Cthulhu mythos, the bumbling but resourceful gang in Scooby-Doo (yes, there are four kids and a dog), and a full range of road trip, haunted house, and reclusive wizard tropes. This gripping escapade (with touches of quirky humor) will have you rooting for the sympathetic, well-drawn kids—now adults—as your knuckles all turn white.

"Cantero's imagination is vivid, and the story, once it gains speed, continues at a breakneck, roller-coaster pace. He plays with form and style, which makes for an enjoyable romp." —*Booklist*

Cantor, Jillian
Half life. Jillian Cantor. HarperCollins, 2021. 320 p.
ISBN 9780062969873
1. Curie, Marie 2. Women scientists 3. Life change events 4. Education 5. Marriage 6. Consequences 7. Poland 8. France 9. 19th century 10. 20th century 11. Biographical fiction 12. Alternate histories

A reimagining of the life of Marie Curie is told through two parallel timelines, including one that reflects her real-world achievements and another that explores how the world might be different had she made other choices.

"Thought-provoking, skillfully written, and hard to put down." —*Kirkus*

Cantrell, Christian
Scorpion. Christian Cantrell. Random House Inc 2021. 336 p.
ISBN 9781984801975
1. Women spies 2. Intelligence service 3. Tragedy 4. Children — Death 5. Near future 6. Science fiction thrillers 7. Spy fiction
LC 2020043766

With the world bordering on unprecedented technological change, Quinn Mitchell is an old-school, nine-to-five spy—an intelligence analyst for the CIA during the day, and a suburban wife and mother on evenings and weekends. After struggling with a personal tragedy, Quinn hopes to find redemption in her newest assignment: a series of bizarre, international assassinations where victims are found with numeric codes tattooed, burned, or carved into their flesh. As Quinn follows the killer's trail around the globe, always one body behind, she begins uncovering disturbing connections between the murders—and herself. Finding the killer will hinge on Quinn's ability to grapple with the Epoch Index, a massive database that can reveal almost anything about anyone—past, present or future—and which leadsher to a shocking twist that makes her question everything she thought she knew.

"Cantrell's drolly caustic prose encourages readers to care about the characters, even as the many surprises make it dangerous to get close to any one of them. The result is as entertaining as it is intellectually and ethically challenging." —*Publishers Weekly*

Capote, Truman

★ **Breakfast** at Tiffany's. Truman Capote. Random House, 1958. 179 p.
ISBN 9780141037264
1. Misfits (Persons) 2. Organized crime 3. Friendship 4. Prostitution 5. Marriage 6. Manhattan, New York City 7. Literary fiction 8. Short stories 9. Books to movies
LC 58010956
The tale of a fun-loving, amoral playgirl in New York City is accompanied by "House of Flowers," "A Diamond Guitar," and "A Christmas Memory."
A short novel and three stories.

★ The **complete** stories of Truman Capote. Truman Capote; introduction by Reynolds Price. Random House, 2004. 320 p.
ISBN 9780679643104
1. Short stories 2. Books to movies 3. Literary fiction
LC 2004046876
A complete collection of the author's short stories includes pieces set in locales ranging from the Gothic South to the chic East Coast and offers insight into his cultural influence and mastery of the short story form.

"Now, for the first time, all of Capote's short stories are being published together, an event that signifies a renewed appreciation of his overall contribution to literature, for evidence is presented in this one volume that he should be ranked as a major American short story writer." —*Booklist*

Twenty short stories; "Children on their birthdays" was released as a movie with the same title.

Capri, NeNe

The **pussy** trap. NeNe Capri. Wahida Clark Presents, 2011. 300 p. (Pussy trap, 1)
ISBN 9780982841488
1. Street life 2. Drug dealers 3. Revenge 4. Drug traffic 5. Sexuality 6. New York City 7. African American fiction 8. Urban fiction
A dramatic web full of sex, greed, power and payback.
Sequel: The Pussy Trap Part 2: The Kiss of Death.

The **pussy** trap; part 3,. NeNe Capri. Wahida Clark Presents, 2013. 310 p. (Pussy trap, 3)
ISBN 9781936649648
1. African American women 2. Street life 3. Drug dealers 4. Family secrets 5. Secrets 6. New York City 7. Urban fiction 8. African American fiction
Fear, Grief and pain...the perfect mixture for the deadly cocktail that drives KoKo head first into danger as she tries to hold onto her thrown. Betrayal, distrust and a struggle for power almost destroys all that she has built. Kayson is back on the scene and will not bow to no one. The power

is up for grabs and there are many hands in the pot. There s a boss that will live to the end, but who will succumb to Death by Temptation?
Sequel to: The Pussy Trap Part 2: The Kiss of Death.

Card, Maisy

★ **These** ghosts are family: a novel. Maisy Card. Simon & Schuster, 2020. 224 p.
ISBN 9781982117436
1. Family secrets 2. Life change events 3. Family history 4. New identities 5. Jamaicans in the United States 6. Jamaica 7. New York City 8. Literary fiction 9. Family sagas
LC 2019038809
A man on his deathbed reveals that he stole another man's identity decades earlier, traces the family's history from colonial Jamaica to present-day Harlem and reconnects with the firstborn daughter he never knew.

"Card's clean, readable prose provides an important counterbalance to the dense, heavy problems her broad scope of characters endure. A fantastic debut." —*Booklist*

Card, Orson Scott

★ **Ender's** game. Orson Scott Card. T. Doherty Associates, 1985. 357 p. (Ender Wiggin, 1)
ISBN 9780312932084
1. Gifted children 2. Space warfare 3. Aliens (Humanoid) 4. Wiggin, Ender (Fictitious character) 5. Siblings 6. Hard science fiction 7. Science fiction classics 8. Science fiction 9. Adult books for young adults
Hugo Award for Best Novel, 1986; Nebula Award for Best Novel, 1985
Six-year-old Ender Wiggin and his fellow students at Battle School are being tested and trained to determine whether they possess the abilities to remake the world—if the world survives an all-out war with an alien enemy.

"The key, of course, is Ender Wiggin himself. Mr. Card never makes the mistake of patronizing or sentimentalizing his hero. Alternately likable and insufferable, he is a convincing little Napoleon in short pants." —*New York Times Book Review*

Part of this novel was published in Analog.
Sequel: Ender's shadow.
According to the author, there is no preferred reading order to the Ender Wiggin series, except that "Xenocide" should be read before "Children of the Mind." NoveList lists this series in chronological order rather than publication order.

Carey, Edward

Little: a novel. Edward Carey. Riverhead Books, 2018. 436 p.
ISBN 9780525534327
1. Tussaud, Marie 2. Orphans 3. Waxworks 4. Wax modellers 5. Revolutions 6. Sculptors 7. Paris, France 8. France 9. Revolutionary France (1789-1799) 10. Biographical fiction 11. Historical fiction
LC 2017061111
Follows the story of a Swiss orphan who, apprenticed to an eccentric wax sculptor in the seamy streets of Paris, learns her craft and hones her art to become the famous Madame Tussaud.

Carey, Jacqueline

Starless. Jacqueline Carey. Tor, 2018. 587 pages
ISBN 9780765386823

1. Bodyguards 2. Warriors 3. Gods and goddesses 4. Quests 5. Princesses 6. Fantasy fiction 7. Adult books for young adults

LC 2017049771

Trained as an elite warrior before learning a profound truth about his identity, Khai navigates the deadly intrigues of court before embarking on a quest to save his soul's twin.

Carey, M. R.

Someone like me. M. R. Carey. Little Brown & Co 2018. 400 p. ISBN 9780316477420

1. Single mothers 2. Control (Psychology) 3. Dissociative identity disorder 4. Women — Personal conduct 5. Abused women 6. Psychological suspense 7. Adult books for young adults

A gentle, devoted mother hides the dark and malicious side of her personality until it takes control, triggering devastating consequences.

Carey, Peter

A **long** way from home. Peter Carey. Alfred A. Knopf, 2018. 288 p. ISBN 9780525520177

1. Automobile racing 2. Identity (Psychology) 3. Voyages and travels 4. Race relations 5. Husband and wife 6. Australia 7. 1950s 8. Historical fiction 9. Literary fiction 10. Australian fiction

Loan Stars Favourites, 2018; Shortlisted for the Walter Scott Prize for Historical Fiction, 2019

Irene Bobs, her car salesman husband, and a thrill-seeking quiz-show champion enter a dangerous race that circumnavigates the natural obstacles of 1954 Australia.

Originally published: Melbourne, Vic. : Penguin Random House Australia, 2017.

Cargill, C. Robert

Day zero. C. Robert Cargill. Harper Voyager, 2021. 304 p. ISBN 9780062405807

1. Robots 2. Near future 3. Stuffed tigers (Toys) 4. Nannies 5. Boys 6. Science fiction 7. Dystopian fiction

LC 2020041512

Pounce, a stylish "nannybot" fashioned in the shape of a plush anthropomorphic tiger, has just found a box in the attic. His box. The box he'd arrived in when he was purchased years earlier, and the box in which he'll be discarded when his human charge, eight-year-old Ezra Reinhart, no longer needs a nanny. As Pounce ponders his suddenly uncertain future, the pieces are falling into place for a robot revolution that will eradicate humankind. But when the rebellion breaches the Reinhart home, Pounce must make an impossible choice: join the robot revolution and fight for his own freedom... or escort Ezra to safety across the battle-scarred post-apocalyptic hellscape that the suburbs have become.

"Although it's not strictly a prequel to Cargill's masterful Sea of Rust (2017), his new novel is set in the same world.... Like Daniel H. Wilson, in Robopocalypse (2011) and Robogenesis (2014), Cargill offers a fascinating and intellectually engaging take on the venerable robots-versus-humans theme." —*Booklist*

Prequel to: Sea of rust.

Carlyle, Christy

Duke gone rogue. Christy Carlyle. Avon Books, 2021. 384 p. (Love on holiday, 1)
ISBN 9780063054493

1. Dukes and duchesses 2. Independence in women 3. Manors — Restoration 4. Family businesses 5. Committees 6. Cornwall, England

7. Victorian era (1837-1901) 8. Victorian romances 9. Historical romances

Will Hart, the Duke of Ashmore, is everything his father was not: scrupulously honest, forbidding, and apparently joyless. When his sisters concoct a plan for him to visit a run-down family property in Cornwall, he reluctantly agrees, hoping it will be a chance for him to rediscover the carefree man he once was. Madeline Ravenwood believes she can do anything she puts her mind to, including running the gardening business she inherited from her father and being a founding member of the Royal Visit Committee. Hard at work preparing for Princess Beatrice's visit to judge their annual flower show, the appearance of a stern, handsome duke is a distraction Maddie doesn't need. Tasked by the committee to convince the duke to repair his ramshackle manor house in time for the royal visit, he agrees, if she will join him as he explores Cornwall. Spending their days, and nights, together, Will's love for Maddie becomes too strong to ignore. But Maddie knows how different their worlds are and when the burdens of his title reappear, can Will convince her that she's the woman he's been waiting for?

"The first in Carlyle's new Love on Holiday series is catnip for lovers of small-town love stories, with engaging character development and a driven heroine. The beautiful Cornish scenery and botanical details are grace notes on a slightly spicy but mostly sweet story, and readers will look forward to future vacations in the series. A charming Victorian romance by the sea." —*Kirkus*

Carpenter, Emily

Until the day I die. Emily Carpenter. Lake Union Publishing, 2019. 340 p.
ISBN 9781503904217

1. Widows 2. Mothers and daughters 3. Grief in women 4. Married men — Death 5. Corporations 6. Birmingham, Alabama 7. Caribbean Area 8. Thrillers and suspense

If there's a healthy way to grieve, Erin Gaines hasn't found it. After her husband's sudden death, the runaway success of the tech company they built with their best friends has become overwhelming. Her nerves are frayed, she's disengaged, and her frustrated daughter, Shorie, is pulling away from her. Maybe Erin's friends and family are right. Maybe a few weeks at a spa resort in the Caribbean islands is just what she needs to hit the reset button.

Carr, Brian Allen

★ **Opioid**, Indiana. Brian Allen Carr. Soho, 2019. 224 p.
ISBN 9781641290784

1. Drug abuse 2. Foster teenagers 3. Missing men 4. Small town life 5. Student suspension 6. Indiana 7. Coming-of-age stories 8. First person narratives 9. Literary fiction

LC 2019004391

A recently orphaned teen in rural Indiana finds himself suspended from school and searching for both a job and his drug-addled uncle, now his legal guardian, to get the rent paid in five days

"This latest novel presents a fresh twist on today's teenager in a wasteland of drugs and economic hardship." —*Library Journal*

Carr, Caleb

★ The **alienist**. Caleb Carr. Random House, 1994. 496 p. (Laszlo Kreizler mysteries, 1)
ISBN 9780679417798

1. Roosevelt, Theodore, 1858-1919 2. Journalists 3. Crimes against boys 4. Psychologists 5. Serial murderers 6. Crime 7. New York City

8. Gilded Age (1865-1898) 9. 1890s 10. Historical mysteries 11. First person narratives 12. Media tie-ins

LC 9332766

Anthony Award for Best Novel, 1995

The year is 1896, and a serial killer is loose in New York City. His targets are poor young boys working as transvestite prostitutes. While the general public has little interest in the victims, Chief of Police Theodore Roosevelt wants the murderer stopped. He assembles a clandestine group of amateur detectives to track the killer.

"This story boasts a veracious historical feel and a tight plot that keeps open the murderer's identity to the end. An original that fits no established mystery niche." —*Booklist*

Sequel: The angel of darkness.

Title adapted into an American television series by the same name in 2018.

The **angel** of darkness. Caleb Carr. Random House, 1997. 629 p. (Laszlo Kreizler mysteries, 2)

ISBN 9780679435327

1. Darrow, Clarence 2. Thirteen-year-old boys 3. Crimes against children 4. Psychologists 5. Nurses 6. Forensic psychology 7. New York City 8. Gilded Age (1865-1898) 9. 1890s 10. Williams, Bert 11. First person narratives

LC 9725063

Dr. Kreizler, the Alienist, returns to investigate the kidnapping of the baby daughter of the wife of a Spanish diplomat, in the process uncovering a fiendish woman who has murdered a number of innocent children.

"Carr is an adept miniaturist, and he succeeds in evoking the wonderful grotesqueries of old New York without straying into sub-Dickensian caricature." —*New York Times Book Review*

Sequel to: The alienist.

Carr, Robyn

The **family** gathering. Robyn Carr. Mira, 2018. 384 p. (Sullivan's Crossing, 3)

ISBN 9780778369158

1. Camp sites, facilities, etc. 2. Interpersonal attraction 3. Man-woman relationships 4. Mountain life 5. Rural life 6. Colorado 7. Rocky Mountain region 8. Contemporary romances

After leaving the military, Dakota Jones visits Sullivan's Crossing to clear his head before moving on to his next adventure, but as he spends time with his siblings and becomes drawn to the simple way of life there, he finds the home and family he has always wanted.

The **view** from Alameda Island: a novel. Robyn Carr. Mira Books, 2019. 320 p.

ISBN 9780778368953

1. Separated women (Marital relations) 2. Marital conflict 3. Marriage 4. Husband and wife 5. Separation (Marital relations) 6. Alameda, California 7. San Francisco Bay Area 8. Relationship fiction

Deciding on her 24th wedding anniversary that she will no longer uphold pretenses about her idyllic family life, Lauren taps the power of her inner strength to separate from her controlling husband and pursue a happier relationship.

★ **Virgin** river. Robyn Carr. Mira, 2007. 416 p. (Virgin River, 1)
ISBN 9780778324904

1. Widows 2. Nurses 3. Abandoned infants 4. Bar owners 5. Former Marines 6. Northern California 7. Contemporary romances

When recently widowed Melinda Monroe accepts a job as nurse practitioner and midwife in the remote mountain town of Virgin River, she thinks she's found the perfect place to start over. The town isn't at all what she expected, though, and she considers leaving, but then a tiny baby,

abandoned on a front porch, changes her plans... and a former marine cements them into place.

★ The **wanderer**. Robyn Carr. Mira Books, 2013. 384 p. (Thunder Point novels, 1)

ISBN 9780778314479

1. Small town life 2. Inheritance and succession 3. Land development 4. Coastal towns 5. Home (Concept) 6. Oregon 7. Contemporary romances

Library Journal Best Books, 2013

When newcomer Hank Cooper inherits beachfront property in Thunder Point, Oregon, he holds the fate of an entire community in his hands as he decides whether this small town of rocky beaches and rugged charm is the place he can finally call home.

What we find. Robyn Carr. Harlequin MIRA, 2016. 384 p. (Sullivan's Crossing, 1)

ISBN 9780778318859

1. Women surgeons 2. Hikers 3. Life change events 4. Coping 5. Healing 6. Colorado 7. Rocky Mountain region 8. Contemporary romances 9. Chick lit

Abandoned by her boyfriend in the aftermath of wrongful malpractice suit, a Denver neurosurgeon relocates to a small rural town named after her ancestor, where she slowly recovers and reconnects with her estranged father while bonding with a mysterious loner.

Carrick, M. A.

The **mask** of mirrors. M.A. Carrick. Orbit, 2021. 688 p. (Rook & Rose, 1)

ISBN 9780316539678

1. Women swindlers 2. Magic 3. Political intrigue 4. Alliances 5. Sisters 6. Fantasy fiction 7. Epic fantasy

LC 2020011541

Arenza Lenskaya is a liar and a thief, a pattern-reader and a daughter of no clan. Raised in the slums of Nadezra, she fled that world to save her sister. Renata Viraudax is a con artist recently arrived in Nadezra. She has one goal: to trick her way into a noble house and secure her fortune. As corrupt nightmare magic begins to weave its way through the city of dreams, the poisonous feuds of its aristocrats and the shadowy dangers of its impoverished underbelly become tangled—with Ren at their heart. And if she cannot sort the truth from the lies, it will mean the destruction of all her worlds.

"This historical urban fantasy is for those who like their revenge plots served with the intrigue of The Goblin Emperor, the colonial conflict of The City of Brass, the panache of Swordspoint, and the richly detailed settings of Guy Gavriel Kay." —*Booklist*

Carter, Angela

★ **Burning** your boats: the collected short stories. Angela Carter; with an introduction by Salman Rushdie. H. Holt, 1996. Xiv, 462 p.

ISBN 9780805044621

1. Sexuality 2. Fantasy fiction 3. Short stories 4. Adaptations, retellings, and spin-offs

LC 95-26312

Library Journal Best Books, 1996

Collects stories written by the late author such as "The Bloody Chamber," "Our Lady of the Massacre," and "Saints and Strangers

"Gathered from 30 years of Carter's writing life, this collection is arranged chronologically to reveal her evolution as a writer as well as her consistent preoccupation with the Gothic.... As her friend Salman Rushdie writes in his moving introduction, Carter is not an easy read, but there are many rewards for the persistent." —*Library Journal*

Carter, Mary Dixie

The **photographer**. Mary Dixie Carter. St Martins Pr 2021. 288 p.
ISBN 9781250790330
1. Women photographers 2. Rich families 3. Birthday parties 4. Husband and wife 5. Eleven-year-old girls 6. Brooklyn, New York City 7. New York City 8. Psychological suspense 9. First person narratives

LC 2020053266

As a photographer, Delta Dawn observes the seemingly perfect lives of New York City's elite: snapping photos of their children's birthday parties, transforming images of stiff hugs and tearstained faces into visions of pure joy, and creating moments these parents long for. But when Delta is hired for Natalie Straub's eleventh birthday, she finds herself wishing she wasn't behind the lens but a part of the scene—in the Straub family's gorgeous home and elegant life. Delta begins by babysitting for Natalie, befriending her mother Amelia, finding chances to listen to her father Fritz; soon she's bathing in the master bathtub, drinking their expensive wine, and eyeing the beautifully finished—and currently occupied—garden apartment in their townhouse. It seems like she can never get close enough. Until Delta discovers the one thing Amelia Straub wants most is also the perfect way for Delta to become permanently a part of the picture.

"Brace for hold-your-breath suspense from this dazzlingly devious newcomer." —*Publishers Weekly*

Carter, Michaela

Leonora in the morning light. Michaela Carter. Avid Reader Books, 2021. 416 p.
ISBN 9781982120511
1. Carrington, Leonora 2. Surrealism (Art) 3. Socialites 4. Artists 5. Voyages and travels 6. Art movements 7. Second World War era (1939-1945) 8. Historical fiction 9. Multiple perspectives 10. Relationship fiction

A novel inspired by the life of Leonora Carrington follows the experiences of a rising artist who accompanies her lover to 1937 London before the masters of the Surrealist movement are denounced by occupying forces.

"With a tantalizing cast that includes the women artists Leonor Fini, Lee Miller, and Remedios Varo; ravishing descriptions cued by her subjects' provocative art; and her exquisite attunement to the shock and agony of war and madness, Carter has written a refulgent and deeply involving historical tale of tragic lost love, determined survival, the sanctuary of art, and the evolution of a muse into an artist of powerfully provocative feminist expression." —*Booklist*

Carter, Miranda

The **strangler** vine. M. J. Carter. G. P. Putnam's Sons, 2015. 384 p. (Avery & Blake novels, 1)
ISBN 9780399171673
1. British in India 2. Missing persons 3. Cults 4. Intrigue 5. Soldiers 6. India 7. Calcutta, India 8. 1830s 9. Historical mysteries 10. Adventure stories

LC 2014017351

While tracking down a missing writer who has exposed the true nature of Calcutta society in 1837 India, a young soldier with few prospects, a secret political agent and a master of disguise are drawn into the mysterious Thuggee cult and its even more ominous suppression.

"Making pleasing use of the developing bromance/adventure formula and a wealth of research, Carter delivers an engaging, skeptical, modern take on empire." —*Kirkus*

First published in the U.K. in 2014 by Fig Tree.

Carter, Stephen L.

Back channel. Stephen L. Carter. Alfred A. Knopf, 2014. 352 p.
ISBN 9780385349604
1. International relations 2. College students 3. African Americans 4. World politics 5. Intelligence service 6. 1960s 7. Historical fiction 8. Political fiction

While the Kennedy administration furiously debates about a response to the Cuban Missile Crisis, 19-year-old black Cornell sophomore Margo Jensen becomes an unwitting pawn in escalating tensions between American and Soviet government forces.

New England white: a novel. By Stephen L. Carter. Alfred A. Knopf, 2007. 576 p.
ISBN 9780375413629
1. Murder investigation 2. Family secrets 3. Deception 4. African American college teachers 5. Murder 6. New England 7. Mysteries

LC 2006019721

BCALA Literary Award for Fiction, 2008; Booklist Editors' Choice, 2007

In the peaceful New England university town of Elm Harbor, a murder threatens to unravel the thin veneer hiding the racial complications of the town's past, the hidden secrets of a prominent family, and African-American political influence in the United States.

"Carter creates an invigorating and often scathing portrait of the Carlyles' community. He refutes political correctness, preferring to explore the contradictions warring within Julia.... [He] is equally intense in his portrayal of the Carlyles' outwardly perfect, inwardly turbulent marriage, a delicate balance of duty and endurance, even love of a sort." —*PopMatters*

Cartwright, Justin

To heaven by water. Justin Cartwright. Bloomsbury, 2009. 320 p.
ISBN 9781596916210
1. Reminiscing in old age 2. Purpose in life 3. Family secrets 4. Senior men 5. Campus life 6. Oxford, England 7. Mainstream fiction

Having lost his wife, Nancy, to illness, and retired from his job as a prominent television news anchor, David Cross is working out at the gym and living an unexpected new life. His children, Ed and Lucy, suspect him of being on the lookout for a new woman. He cannot tell them that he is, in some ways, happier than he was before Nancy died. And when David goes to see his estranged brother in the African desert, he will come to a life-affirming epiphany.

Carty-Williams, Candice

★ **Queenie**. Candice Carty-Williams. Gallery/Scout Press, 2019. 320 pages
ISBN 9781501196010
1. Race relations 2. Self-discovery in women 3. Black British 4. Dating (Social customs) 5. Female friendship 6. London, England 7. Anne, of Cleves, Queen, consort of Henry VIII, King of England, 1515-1557 8. First person narratives

LC 2018032717

LibraryReads Favorites, 2019

Constantly compared to her white middle-class peers, a young Jamaican-British woman in London makes a series of questionable decisions in the aftermath of a messy breakup before challenging herself to figure out who she wants to be.

Carver, Raymond

What we talk about when we talk about love: stories. Raymond Carver. Knopf, 1981. 159 p.

ISBN 9780394516844

1. Failure (Psychology) 2. Violence 3. Marriage 4. Drinking 5. Man-woman relationships 6. United States 7. Short stories 8. Literary fiction 9. Books to movies

LC 80021752

"In spare, deft, precise prose, whole lives are portrayed in a single second as Carver briefly exposes his doom-ridden characters to one startling flash of agonizing self-recognition. These disturbing images remain long in the memory even after their immediate impression has disappeared." —*Booklist*

The author's short story "Why don't you dance?" was adapted into the 2010 film: Everything must go.

Cash, Wiley

The **last** ballad: a novel. Wiley Cash. William Morrow, 2017. 378 p.

ISBN 9780062313119

1. Mothers 2. Families 3. Women textile workers 4. Labor movement 5. Murder victims 6. North Carolina 7. 1920s 8. Historical fiction 9. Southern fiction

LC 2017007053

ALA Notable Book, 2018; LibraryReads Favorites, 2017; Sir Walter Raleigh Award for Fiction, 2018

Inspired by actual events, a tale set in the Appalachian foothills of 1929 North Carolina follows the struggles of an ordinary woman to reclaim her dignity and rights in a labor mill, where she earns a paltry salary before risking her family and future to join a union.

"Although it is initially a bit difficult to keep so many points of view straight, it is satisfying to see them all connect. It's refreshing that Cash highlights the struggles of often forgotten heroes and shows how crucial women and African-Americans were in the fight for workers' rights. A heartbreaking and beautifully written look at the real people involved in the labor movement." —*Kirkus*

When ghosts come home: a novel. Wiley Cash. William Morrow, an imprint of HarperCollins Publishers, 2021. 304 p.

ISBN 9780062312662

1. Sheriffs 2. Airplane accidents 3. Racism 4. Father and adult daughter 5. African American teenage boys 6. North Carolina 7. 1980s 8. Literary fiction 9. Mysteries 10. Multiple perspectives

LC 2021002221

When a plane crash lands at the nearby airfield on the coast of North Carolina, Sheriff Winston Barnes begins a murder investigation that will change the course of his life and the fate of the community he has sworn to protect.

"Writing with clarity and grace, best-selling Cash (The Last Ballad, 2017) is a gem of a storyteller, combining the solitary journey of a young mother's grief and a community's relentless battle against racial injustice. The result is a tightly crafted whodunit with true depth that readers will simultaneously want to speed through and savor." —*Booklist*

Cassara, Joseph

The **house** of impossible beauties. Joseph Cassara. Ecco, 2018. 400 p.

ISBN 9780062676979

1. Corey, Dorian 2. Runaways 3. Gay culture 4. Gay teenagers 5. Transgender teenage girls 6. Transgender persons 7. Harlem, New York City 8. New York City 9. 1980s 10. 1990s 11. LGBTQIA fiction 12. Literary fiction

LC 2017021665

Library Journal Best Books, 2018

Follows a cast of gay and transgender kids navigating the Harlem ball scene of the 1980s and 1990s.

Castel-Bloom, Orly

Textile. Orly Castel-Bloom. The Feminist Press, 2013. 232 p.

ISBN 9781558618251

1. Jewish families 2. Alienation (Social psychology) 3. Plastic surgery 4. Family relationships 5. Women business owners 6. Israel 7. Tel-Aviv, Israel 8. Psychological fiction

A wealthy Israeli family becomes estranged as war and commerce increasingly define their lives.

Castellani, Christopher

Leading men: a novel. Christopher Castellani. Viking, 2019. 352 p.

ISBN 9780525559054

1. Williams, Tennessee 2. Gay couples 3. Creativity in men 4. Fame 5. Ambition 6. Authors 7. Italy 8. New York City 9. 1950s 10. 1960s 11. Historical fiction 12. LGBTQIA fiction 13. Multiple perspectives

LC 2018029036

A life-changing encounter among Tennessee Williams, his lover Frank Merlo and a taciturn Swedish beauty at a 1953 Truman Capote party culminates in deathbed revelations about Williams' final play a decade later.

"With imagination and feeling, Castellani reconjures history to reveal the intricate dynamics—loving and passionate, selfless and devastating—among artists and those who nurture them." —*Booklist*

Castillo, Elaine

America is not the heart. Elaine Castillo. Viking Press, 2018. 408 p.

ISBN 9780735222410

1. Immigrants 2. Identity (Psychology) 3. Culture conflict 4. Extended families 5. Violence against women 6. California 7. Philippines 8. 1980s 9. 1990s 10. Family sagas

Library Journal Best Books, 2018

Three generations of women from one immigrant family trying to reconcile the home they left behind with the life they're building in America.

Castillo, Linda

★ **Fallen**. Linda Castillo. Minotaur Books, 2021. 320 p. (Kate Burkholder thrillers, 13)

ISBN 9781250142924

1. Amish 2. Women police chiefs 3. Former Amish 4. Women murder victims 5. Secrets 6. Ohio 7. Thrillers and suspense 8. Police procedurals

LC 2021002111

In New York Times bestselling author Linda Castillo's new thriller Fallen, a rebellious Amish woman leaves the Plain life, but the secrets she takes with her will lead Chief of Police Kate Burkholder down a dark path to danger and death.

"This intense, suspenseful whodunit is full of twists and turns, red herrings, and an OMG ending, with a realistic mix of English and Amish cultures." —*Library Journal*

Outsider. Linda Castillo. Minotaur Books, 2020. 320 pages (Kate Burkholder thrillers, 12)

ISBN 9781250142894

1. Amish 2. Women detectives 3. Hiding 4. Murder investigation 5. Murder 6. Ohio 7. Thrillers and suspense

LC 2020009587

Linda Castillo follows her instant NYT bestseller, Shamed, with Outsider, an electrifying thriller about a woman on the run hiding among the Amish.

"This twelfth entry in the best-selling Burkholder series is another fast-paced, suspense-building ride, showing the character development and sensitivity to the Amish culture that mark Castillo's masterful crime fiction." —*Booklist*

Castle, Jayne

Illusion Town. Jayne Castle. Jove, 2016. 352 p. (Illusion Town novels, 1; Planet Harmony series, 13)

ISBN 9780515155754

1. Marriage 2. Heirs and heiresses 3. Women psychics 4. Psychic ability 5. Magic 6. Paranormal romances 7. Futuristic romances

When they wake up married, with only vague memories of running from something, Hannah West and Elias Coppersmith's investigation into what happened leads to underground catacombs where secrets from their past are revealed.

Jayne Ann Krentz writing as Jayne Castle.

Castro, V.

Goddess of filth. V. Castro. 2021. 156 pages

ISBN 9781951971038

1. Mexican American teenage girls 2. Spirit possession 3. Paranormal phenomena 4. Supernatural 5. Gods and goddesses, Aztec 6. Texas 7. Horror 8. Multiple perspectives

LC 2020946639

A group of friends holds a seance and accidentally summons an ancient goddess.

"It is also an action-packed horror novel, filled with violence and both real and supernatural monsters, anchored by a sense of dread that constantly reminds the reader what is at stake when women are silenced. Castro's compelling and immersive novella displays exhilarating talent, and will appeal to fans of both Paul Tremblay's A Head Full of Ghosts (2015) and Carmen Maria Machado's Her Body and Other Parties (2017)." —*Booklist*

The **queen** of the cicadas. V. Castro. Flame Tree Publishing, 2021. 256 p.

ISBN 9781787586031

1. Murder 2. Women 3. Weddings 4. Revenge 5. Death 6. Horror

2018—Belinda Alvarez has returned to Texas for the wedding of her best friend Veronica. The farm is the site of the urban legend, La Reina de Las Chicharras—The Queen of The Cicadas. In 1950s south Texas a farmworker, Milagros from San Luis Potosi, Mexico, is murdered. Her death is ignored by the town, but not the Aztec goddess of death, Mictecacihuatl. The goddess hears the dying cries of Milagros and creates a plan for both to be physically reborn by feeding on vengeance and worship.

"Readers seeking originality and a fresh take on well-worn horror tropes should pick up this novel by a dynamic and innovative voice in horror." —*Booklist*

Cather, Willa

★ **Death** comes for the archbishop. Willa Cather; historical essay and explanatory notes by John J. Murphy; textual editing by Charles W. Mignon

with Frederick M. Link and Kari A. Ronning. University of Nebraska Press, 1999. 614 p. : Illustration

ISBN 9780803214293

1. Christian missionaries 2. Faith (Christianity) 3. Priests 4. Spirituality 5. Christianity 6. New Mexico 7. Santa Fe, New Mexico 8. 1850s 9. Historical fiction 10. Classics

LC 98026107

Willa Cather's best known novel; a narrative that recounts a life lived simply in the silence of the southwestern desert.

Includes bibliographical references (p. 505-512).

A **lost** lady. . University of Nebraska Press, 1997. Xii, 371 p. : Illustration

ISBN 9780803214279

1. Frontier and pioneer life 2. Independence in women 3. Railroads — History 4. Technology and civilization 5. May-December romances 6. Nebraska 7. 1890s 8. Literary fiction 9. Psychological fiction 10. Domestic fiction

LC 96020642

"Published in 1923, this Cather classic depicts the encroachment of civilization that supplanted the pioneer spirit of Nebraska's frontier as seen through the eyes of protagonist Marian Forrester." —*Library Journal*

Includes bibliographical references.

★ **My** Antonia. . University of Nebraska Press, 1994. Xii, 544 p. : Illustration

ISBN 9780803214682

1. Frontier and pioneer life 2. Pioneer women 3. Independence in women 4. Czech American women 5. Immigrants 6. Nebraska 7. 19th century 8. Domestic fiction 9. Coming-of-age stories 10. Historical fiction

LC 93050941

After the death of her immigrant father, Antonia works as a servant for neighbors in the farmlands of Nebraska. She leaves for an unfortunate affair with an Irish railway conductor, but returns home, eventually marries and raises a large family in true pioneer style.

Includes bibliographical references (p. 520-521).

Originally published: New York : Houghton Mifflin Co, 1918.

O pioneers!. Willa Cather; edited with an introduction and notes by Marilee Lindemann. Oxford University Press, 1999. Xxxi, 179 p.

ISBN 9780192832160

1. Pioneer women 2. Immigrants 3. Frontier and pioneer life 4. Swedish American families 5. Siblings 6. Nebraska 7. 19th century 8. Historical fiction 9. Classics 10. Domestic fiction

LC 98035944

When her father dies, the daughter of Swedish immigrants assumes responsibility for her family and their Nebraska farm.

Includes bibliographical references (p. [xxiv]-xxvi).

The **song** of the lark. Willa Cather. Vintage Books, 1999. 429 p.

ISBN 9780375706455

1. Women opera singers 2. Determination in women 3. Self-discovery in women 4. Children of clergy 5. Swedish American families 6. Chicago, Illinois 7. Colorado 8. Literary fiction 9. Coming-of-age stories 10. Domestic fiction

LC 98052932

The daughter of a Swedish minister growing up in Colorado, Thea Kronborg's musical talent sets her apart from her contemporaries. Driven by her determination to satisfy her artistic impulse, she moves to Chicago, where she falls in love with a wealthy married man. The novel follows Thea's growth from provincial Midwesterner to acclaimed international opera singer.

Catton, Eleanor

The **luminaries:** a novel. Eleanor Catton. Little Brown & Co, 2013. 834 p.

ISBN 9780316074315

1. Gold miners 2. Crime 3. Murder 4. Secrecy 5. Astrology 6. New Zealand 7. Colonial New Zealand (1841-1907) 8. Literary fiction 9. Historical fiction 10. New Zealand fiction

Australian Book Industry Awards, International Book of the Year, 2014; Governor General's Literary Award for English-Language Fiction, 2013; Man Booker Prize, 2013; New York Times Notable Book, 2013; New Zealand Post Book Awards, Fiction, 2014; New Zealand Post Book Awards, People's Choice, 2014; Shortlisted for the Walter Scott Prize for Historical Fiction, 2014

Arriving in New Zealand in 1866 to seek his fortune in the goldfields, Walter Moody finds himself drawn into a series of unsolved crimes and complex mysteries.

Originally published: Wellington, N.Z. : Victoria University Press, 2013.

Cavanagh, Steve

Thirteen. Steve Cavanagh. Flatiron Books, 2019. 320 pages (Eddie Flynn novels, 4)

ISBN 9781250297600

1. Trials (Murder) 2. Jurors 3. Frameups 4. Murder suspects 5. Innocence (Law) 6. Legal thrillers

Theakston Old Peculier Crime Novel of the Year Award, 2019

A defense lawyer and former conman defends his movie-star client in a high profile murder trial and discovers that the actual killer is sitting on the jury.

Includes bibliographical references and index.

Originally published in Great Britain in 2018 by Orion Books, an imprint of The Orion Publishing Group Ltd.

Center, Katherine

How to walk away: a novel. Katherine Center. St. Martin's Press, 2018. 352 p.

ISBN 9781250149060

1. Engaged persons 2. Accident victims 3. Life change events 4. Women — Interpersonal relations 5. Young women — Psychology 6. Relationship fiction

LC 2017060163

RUSA Reading List Short List, 2019

When an accident on what was supposed to be the happiest day of her life lands her in the hospital with a very uncertain future, Margaret struggles to come to terms with family secrets, heartbreak and starting over before discovering love in an unexpected place.

"Center's characters...leap off the page with their unique voices, and their relationships evolve slowly and satisfyingly. Although this is largely the story of Margaret learning to make the most of her life, it's also a touching and believable love story with plenty of romantic-comedy flourishes. A story about survival that is heartbreakingly honest and wryly funny, perfect for fans of Jojo Moyes and Elizabeth Berg." —*Kirkus*

Includes bibliographical references and index.

Things you save in a fire. Katherine Center. St. Martin's Press, 2019. 352 p.

ISBN 9781250047328

1. Women fire fighters 2. Women — Psychology 3. Man-woman relationships 4. Trust 5. Betrayal 6. Boston, Massachusetts 7. Relationship fiction 8. Adult books for young adults

LC 2018057650

LibraryReads Favorites, 2019

When a family emergency compels her move from Texas to Boston, a skilled firefighter becomes the only woman in her new firehouse and navigates discrimination, low funding and her private edicts about falling in love with another firefighter.

"Center gives readers a sharp and witty exploration of love and forgiveness that is at once insightful, entertaining, and thoroughly addictive." —*Kirkus*

What you wish for. Katherine Center. St. Martin's Press, 2020. 320 p.

ISBN 9781250219367

1. School librarians 2. School principals 3. Elementary schools 4. Rules 5. Change (Psychology) 6. Texas 7. Relationship fiction

LC 2020002696

LibraryReads Favorites, 2020

When the new principal turns out to be the former, unrequited crush of her teen years, elementary school librarian Samantha Casey discovers that he is a changed man, determined to destroy everything she loves about the school, which forces her to take action.

"The cast of eccentric supporting characters adds to a fast-paced tale steeped with whimsical, yet sometimes outlandish, plot points. This is one for the beach bag." —*Publishers Weekly*

Cervantes Saavedra, Miguel de

★ **Don** Quixote. . Modern Library, 1998. Xl, 1239 p.

ISBN 9780679602866

1. Eccentric men 2. Adventurers 3. Imagination in men 4. Don Quixote (Fictitious character) 5. Panza, Sancho (Fictitious character) 6. Spain 7. 16th century 8. Classics 9. Picaresque fiction 10. Translations

LC 97047415

Presents the classic Spanish tale of chivalry and abiding optimism, depicting the exploits of a knight who attempts to bring justice and truth to the world

Includes bibliographical references (p. [1229]-1239).

Cha, Steph

★ **Your** house will pay. Steph Cha. Ecco Press, 2019. 272 pages

ISBN 9780062868855

1. Korean American families 2. African American families 3. Loss (Psychology) 4. Violence — Psychological aspects 5. Communities 6. Los Angeles, California 7. Literary fiction

Booklist Editors' Choice, 2019; Library Journal Best Books, 2019; Los Angeles Times Book Prize for Mystery or Thriller, 2019

Two teenagers in Los Angeles, one Korean-American and the other African-American, deal with the ripple effects of a shooting from decades ago after a new incident brings their families' painful memories hurtling back.

"A gripping, thoughtful portrayal of family loyalty, hard-won redemption, and the destructive force of racial injustice." —*Booklist*

Chabon, Michael

The **amazing** adventures of Kavalier & Clay: a novel. Michael Chabon. Random House, 2000. 639 p.

ISBN 9780679450047

1. Comic book writing 2. Superheroes 3. Heroes and heroines in mass media 4. Artists 5. Czech Americans 6. New York City 7. Historical fiction 8. Literary fiction 9. Books to movies

LC 29063

ALA Notable Book, 2001; Booklist Editors' Choice, 2000; Library Journal Best Books, 2000; New York Times Notable Book, 2000;

Pulitzer Prize for Fiction, 2001; National Book Critics Circle Award for Fiction finalist, 2000

In 1939 New York City, Joe Kavalier, a refugee from Hitler's Prague, joins forces with his Brooklyn-born cousin, Sammy Clay, to create comic-book superheroes inspired by their own fantasies, fears, and dreams.

"Themes are masterfully explored, leaving the book's sense of humor intact and characters so highly developed they could walk off the page." —*Newsweek*

★ **Wonder** boys. Michael Chabon. Villard Books 1995. 368 p.
ISBN 9780679415886
1. Young men 2. Self-destructive behavior in men 3. Creativity in men 4. Creative writing teachers 5. Authors, American 6. Pennsylvania 7. Pittsburgh, Pennsylvania 8. Humorous stories 9. Novels-within-novels 10. Literary fiction
LC 94028921

In a story exploring the theme of the artist's isolation, Grady Tripp, an obese, aging writer who has lost his way, and debauched editor Terry Crabtree struggle to rekindle their friendship, a sense of adventure, and purpose in their lives.

"Bright promise gone awry is the theme of this exuberantly comic novel, whose convoluted plot sparkles with inventiveness and wit." —*Publishers Weekly*

The **Yiddish** Policemen's Union. Michael Chabon. Harper Collins, 2007. 400 p.
ISBN 9780007149827
1. Murder 2. Jewish families 3. Immigrants, Jewish 4. Identity (Religion) 5. Jewish American men 6. Alaska 7. 1940s 8. Alternate histories 9. Mysteries 10. Hardboiled fiction
Booklist Editors' Choice, 2007; Hugo Award for Best Novel, 2008; Library Journal Best Books, 2007; Locus Award for Best Science Fiction Novel, 2008; Nebula Award for Best Novel, 2007; New York Times Notable Book, 2007; Sidewise Awards for Alternate History, 2007

In a world in which Alaska, rather than Israel, has become the homeland for the Jews following World War II, Detective Meyer Landsman and his half-Tlingit partner Berko investigate the death of a heroin-addicted chess prodigy.

"Though the ultimate secret behind the murder that kick-starts the story involves a religious-political scheme that tips over clumsily into surreal satire, the remainder of the book is so authoritatively and minutely imagined that the reader, absorbed in the plight of [the author's] shambling hero, really doesn't mind.... Mr. Chabon has so thoroughly conjured the fictional world of Sitka—its history, culture, geography, its incestuous and byzantine political and sectarian divisions—that the reader comes to take its existence for granted." —*New York Times*

Chai, May-Lee

Useful phrases for immigrants: stories. May-lee Chai. Blair, 2018. 170 p.
ISBN 9780932112767
1. Immigrants, Chinese 2. Immigrants — Identity 3. Belonging 4. Chinese Americans 5. Asian Americans 6. China 7. United States 8. Short stories 9. Literary fiction 10. Adult books for young adults
LC 2018035244

Eight innovative, timely stories illuminate the hopes and fears of Chinese immigrants and their descendants.

Chakrabarti, Jai

A **play** for the end of the world. Jai Chakrabarti. Alfred A Knopf, 2021. 288 p.
ISBN 9780525658924
1. Holocaust survivors 2. Survivor guilt 3. Drama 4. Friends' death 5. Couples 6. India 7. New York City 8. 1970s 9. 1940s 10. Historical fiction
National Jewish Book Award, 2021

A Warsaw Ghetto survivor in 1970s New York leaves a blossoming romance to travel to India and collect the ashes of his oldest friend who died there in a small Eastern village under mysterious circumstances.

"At its heart this is a love story, and literary readers not used to cheering for a happy ending may find themselves doing just that." —*Booklist*

Chakraborty, S. A.

The **city** of brass. S. A. Chakraborty. Harper Voyager, 2017. 400 p. (Daevabad trilogy, 1)
ISBN 9780062678102
1. Genies 2. Women swindlers 3. Magic 4. Princes 5. Warriors 6. Cairo, Egypt 7. Egypt 8. Nero, Emperor of Rome, 37-68 9. Historical fantasy 10. Middle Eastern-influenced fantasy 11. Adult books for young adults
LC 2017020068
School Library Journal Best Books: Best Adult Books 4 Teens, 2017; LibraryReads Favorites, 2017; Library Journal Best Books, 2017; RUSA Reading List Short List, 2019

Nahri, a young con artist, inadvertently summons a mysterious djinn warrior to her side during one of her cons, revealing the existence of true magic before the future of a magical Middle Eastern kingdom falls into her hands.

"There is enough material here—a feisty, independent lead searching for answers, reminiscent of Star Wars's Rey, and a richly imagined alternate world— to support a potential series." —*Publishers Weekly*

The **empire** of gold. S. A Chakraborty. Harper Voyager, 2020. 400 p. (Daevabad trilogy, 3)
ISBN 9780062678164
1. Genies 2. Women swindlers 3. Magic 4. Rulers 5. Warriors 6. Cairo, Egypt 7. Egypt 8. 18th century 9. Historical fantasy 10. Livingstone, David 11. Adult books for young adults
LibraryReads Favorites, 2020

In this final installment in the critically acclaimed trilogy, Nahri and Ali are determined to save both their city and their loved ones, but when Ali seeks support in his mother's homeland, he makes a discovery that threatens not only his relationship with Nahri, but his very faith.

"Chakraborty (The City of Brass) brings her epic fantasy series to a stunning conclusion. Rich details, familial ties, and magical politics sing in this lush world built from Middle Eastern history and imagination." —*Library Journal*

The **kingdom** of copper: a novel. S. A. Chakraborty. Harper Voyager, 2019. 640 p. (Daevabad trilogy, 2)
ISBN 9780062678133
1. Genies 2. Women swindlers 3. Imaginary kingdoms 4. Captivity 5. Rulers 6. Cairo, Egypt 7. Egypt 8. Historical fantasy 9. Middle Eastern-influenced fantasy 10. Adult books for young adults
LC 2018036755

A follow-up to The City of Brass finds a trapped Nahri reluctantly embracing her power to safeguard her tribe, while an exiled Ali accepts help from water spirits who unearth a family secret.

"Chakraborty's deeply thought-out system of race relations and clashing classes mirrors real-world conflicts, making it all the more captivatingand frustratingas the dream of peace grows more futile. The action scenes—vivid, entrancing, terrifying—will keep readers riveted, especially as enemies shift to allies, allies to friends, friends to enemies." —*Booklist*

Chambers, Becky

A **closed** and common orbit. Becky Chambers. Harper Voyager, 2017. 367 p. (Wayfarers (Becky Chambers), 2)
ISBN 9780062569400
1. Astronauts 2. Hyperspace 3. Space vehicles 4. Interplanetary relations 5. Aliens (Non-humanoid) 6. Space opera 7. Science fiction
RUSA Reading List Short List, 2018

A spaceship's artificial intelligence, Lovelace, wakes up in a new body with no memory of her prior existence and must learn to negotiate the universe.

"As with her amazing debut, the power of Chamber's second space opera is in her appealing characters." —*Library Journal*

Sequel to: The long way to a small, angry planet.

★ The **galaxy,** and the ground within. Becky Chambers. Harper Voyager, 2021. 368 p. (Wayfarers (Becky Chambers), 4)
ISBN 9780062936035
1. Planets 2. Aliens 3. Strangers 4. Space vehicles 5. Space flight 6. Science fiction 7. Space opera

When a freak technological failure strands travelers at the Five-Hop One-Stop on the planet Gora, three alien strangers get to know each other.

"Chambers (To Be Taught if Fortunate) once again creates an epic space setting with a detailed, personal view of some of its inhabitants. Humor and heartache weave through her insightful prose and diverse characters." —*Library Journal*

★ The **long** way to a small, angry planet. Becky Chambers. Harper Voyager, 2016. 416 p. (Wayfarers (Becky Chambers), 1)
ISBN 9780062444134
1. Astronauts 2. Hyperspace 3. Space vehicles 4. Interplanetary relations 5. Aliens (Non-humanoid) 6. Space opera 7. Science fiction
Library Journal Best Books, 2016; Romantic Times Reviewer's Choice Award, 2016; Longlisted for the Baileys Women's Prize for Fiction, 2016

Joining the crew of the aging Wayfarer, a patched-up ship that has seen better days, loner Rosemary Harper must unexpectedly risk her life when they are offered the job of a lifetime, which teaches her valuable lessons about love and trust, and that having a family isn't the worst thing in the universe.

Originally self-published in 2014.

★ A **psalm** for the wild-built. Becky Chambers. Tor, 2021. 160 p. (Monk & robot, 1)
ISBN 9781250236210
1. Robots 2. Consciousness 3. Monks 4. Nonbinary people 5. Alliances 6. Science fiction 7. Apocalyptic fiction
LC 2021009148
LibraryReads Favorites, 2021

It's been centuries since the robots of Panga gained self-awareness and laid down their tools; centuries since they wandered, en masse, into the wilderness, never to be seen again; centuries since they faded into myth and urban legend. One day, the life of a tea monk is upended by the arrival of a robot, there to honor the old promise of checking in. The robot cannot go backuntil the question of "what do people need?" is answered. But the answer to that question depends on who you ask, and how. They're going to need to ask it a lot. Becky Chambers's new series asks: in a world where people have what they want, does having more matter?

"Written with all of Chambers' characteristic nuance and careful thought, this is a cozy, wholesome meditation on the nature of consciousness and its place in the natural world. Fans of gentle, smart, and hopeful science fiction will delight in this promising series starter." —*Publishers Weekly*

Record of a spaceborn few. Becky Chambers. Harper Voyager, 2018. 400 p. (Wayfarers (Becky Chambers), 3)
ISBN 9780062699220
1. Space vehicles 2. Space flight 3. Astronauts 4. Life on other planets 5. Home (Concept) 6. Space opera 7. Science fiction

A young apprentice, an alien academic, a caretaker for the dead, an archivist and others wrestle with profound questions after their evacuation ship, carrying the last humans on Earth, finally reaches its destination.

"The multiple narrators and seemingly unrelated plot lines converge thematically into an intensely powerful and multifaceted meditation on time, history, change, and memory, leavened with a welcome touch of humor. The characters are distinct and lovable, each shedding light on a different facet of the Fleet. Chambers uses the interconnections inevitable in such a small society to provide moments of both horrific pain and soaring grace, and to make it clear that those things are inextricably intermingled. This is a superb work from one of the genres rising stars." —*Publishers Weekly*

To be taught, if fortunate. Becky Chambers. Harper Voyager, 2019. 144 p.
ISBN 9780062936011
1. Women astronauts 2. Genetically engineered women 3. Home (Concept) 4. Space exploration 5. Planets 6. Earth 7. Space 8. Hard science fiction
Library Journal Best Books, 2019; Loan Stars Favourites, 2019

While on a mission to ecologically survey four habitable worlds, Ariadne O'Neill and a team of explorers, shifting through space and time, discover that the culture back on Earth has been transformed and must make a difficult decision.

Chambers, Clare

Small pleasures. Clare Chambers. Custom House, 2021. 288 pages
ISBN 9780063094727
1. Women journalists 2. Virgin birth (Christian doctrine) 3. Friendship 4. Mothers and daughters 5. Lesbians 6. England 7. London, England 8. 1950s 9. Historical fiction

Jean Swinney is a journalist on a local paper, trapped in a life of duty and disappointment from which there is no likelihood of escape. When a young woman, Gretchen Tilbury, contacts the paper to claim that her daughter is the result of a virgin birth, it is down to Jean to discover whether she is a miracle or a fraud. As the investigation turns her quiet life inside out, Jean is suddenly given an unexpected chance at friendship, love and—possibly—happiness. But there will, inevitably, be a price to pay.

"British novelist Chambers penetrates the secret hopes and passionate inner lives of ordinary working people throughout her gripping novel, while its locked-room medical mystery calls to mind Emma Donoghue's The Wonder (2016). The characters provoke so much empathy, readers may have trouble remembering that they're fictional." —*Booklist*

Originally published: London : Weidenfeld & Nicolson, 2020.

Chan, Jessamine

The **school** for good mothers. Jessamine Chan. Simon & Schuster, 2022. 336 p.
ISBN 9781982156121
1. Chinese American women 2. Divorced women 3. Mothers and daughters 4. Parenting 5. Child protective services 6. Philadelphia, Pennsylvania 7. Literary fiction 8. Dystopian fiction
LibraryReads Favorites, 2022; Loan Stars Favourites, 2022

After one moment of poor judgment involving her daughter Harriet, Frida Liu falls victim to a host of government officials who will determine if she is a candidate for a Big Brother-like institution that measures the success or failure of a mother's devotion.

"Chan's imaginative flourishes render the mothers' vulnerability to social pressures and governmental whims nightmarish and palpable. It's a powerful story, made more so by its empathetic and complicated heroine." —*Publishers Weekly*

Chancellor, Bryn

Sycamore: a novel. Bryn Chancellor. Harper, 2017. 320 p.
ISBN 9780062661098
1. Dead 2. Small towns 3. Missing teenage girls 4. Memories 5. Local history 6. Arizona 7. Literary fiction 8. Multiple perspectives 9. Parallel narratives 10. Adult books for young adults
LC 2016042150
LibraryReads Favorites, 2017
In the tradition of EVERYTHING I NEVER TOLD YOU, and with echoes of OLIVE KITTERIDGE, comes a stunning debut from Bryn Chancellor, an award-winning writer hailed as "amazing, sensitive, and thoughtful" by Kevin Wilson.

"This is a movingly written, multivoiced novel examining how one tragic circumstance can sow doubt about fundamental things." —*Publishers Weekly*

Chancy, Myriam J. A.

★ What storm, what thunder. Myriam J. A. Chancy. Tin House, 2021. 313 p.
ISBN 9781951142766
1. Haiti Earthquake, Haiti, 2010 2. Earthquakes 3. Natural disasters 4. Kempe, Margery 5. Executives 6. Port-au-Prince, Haiti 7. Haiti 8. Literary fiction 9. Multiple perspectives
LC 2021019399
Set in the aftermath of the earthquake in Haiti, this novel is a reckoning of the heartbreaking trauma of disaster, and—at the same time—an unforgettable testimony to the tenacity of the human spirit.

"Every element of the writing and characterization delivers a poignant experience." —*Booklist*

Chandler, Raymond

★ The big sleep. Raymond Chandler. Vintage Books, 1992. 231 p; (Philip Marlowe mysteries, 1)
ISBN 9780394758282
1. Extortion 2. Rich people 3. Private investigators 4. Heirs and heiresses 5. Capitalists and financiers 6. Los Angeles, California 7. 1930s 8. Mysteries 9. Hardboiled fiction 10. First person narratives
LC 9150919
One of the classic detective novels that established the genre, The Big Sleep follows Philip Marlowe into an underworld of booze, violence, pornography, and sex, as he searches for the blackmailer of a millionaire's daughter.
Sequel by Robert B. Parker: Perchance to Dream.
Originally published: London: Hamish Hamilton, 1939.

The lady in the lake. Raymond Chandler. Vintage Books, 1992. 266 p. (Philip Marlowe mysteries, 4)
ISBN 9780394758251
1. Missing persons 2. Murder 3. Police corruption 4. Private investigators 5. Marlowe, Philip (Fictional character) 6. Los Angeles, California 7. 1940s 8. Mysteries 9. Hardboiled fiction 10. First person narratives
Philip Marlowe, L.A.'s toughest private eye, ventures away from the city's mean streets, to search the mountains outside Los Angeles for a missing woman and unravels a tangled web of murder and deception.
Originally published: New York : A.A. Knopf, 1943.

The long goodbye. Raymond Chandler. Vintage Books, 1992. 379 p; (Philip Marlowe mysteries, 6)
ISBN 9780394757681
1. Gangsters 2. Murder 3. Rich people 4. Suicide 5. Private investigators 6. Los Angeles, California 7. Mysteries 8. Hardboiled fiction 9. First person narratives
Edgar Allan Poe Award for Best Mystery Novel, 1955
Down-and-out drunk Terry Lennox has a problem: his millionaire wife is dead and he needs to get out of LA fast. So he turns to his only friend in the world: Philip Marlowe, Private Investigator. He's willing to help a man down on his luck, but later, Lennox commits suicide in Mexico and things start to turn nasty.
The Long Goodbye inspired the film The Long Goodbye in 1973.
Originally published: Boston : Houghton Mifflin, 1954.

Chang, Alexandra

★ Days of distraction. Alexandra Chang. Ecco Press, 2020. 320 p.
ISBN 9780062951809
1. Identity (Psychology) 2. Asian American women 3. Interracial romance 4. High technology industry and trade 5. Moving, Household 6. Silicon Valley, California 7. Ithaca, New York 8. Coming-of-age stories 9. Literary fiction 10. First person narratives
A marginalized Silicon Valley staff writer moves with her boyfriend to a quiet upstate New York town where she confronts the challenges of their interracial relationship and the questions it raises about her heritage.

"Chang's humorous, timely observations on race, technology, and relationships lend immediacy to the narrator's chronicle of self-awareness." —*Publishers Weekly*

Chanter, Catherine

The well. Catherine Chanter. Atria Books, 2015. 368 p.
ISBN 9781476772769
1. Droughts 2. Farms 3. Suspicion 4. Husband and wife 5. Cults 6. Great Britain 7. Dystopian fiction
Follows the experiences of an Englishwoman who is targeted by suspicion and superstition when her farm remains lush and her grandson drowns in spite of a widespread drought.

"Combining gripping mystery, nuanced psychological drama, and striking prose, this debut is a mesmerizing read." —*Publishers Weekly*

Chaon, Dan

Ill will. Dan Chaon. Ballantine Books, 2017. 496 p.
ISBN 9780345476043
1. Psychologists 2. Family relationships 3. Coping 4. Murder suspects 5. DNA 6. Psychological suspense
New York Times Notable Book, 2017
Two sensational unsolved crimes—one in the past, another in the present—are linked by one man's memory and self-deception in this chilling novel of literary suspense from National Book Award finalist Dan Chaon. "We are always telling a story to ourselves, about ourselves," Dustin Tillman likes to say. It's one of the little mantras he shares with his patients, and it's meant to be reassuring. But what if that story is a lie? A psychologist in suburban Cleveland, Dustin is drifting through his

fortieswhen he hears the news: His adopted brother, Rusty, is being released from prison. Thirty years ago, Rusty received a life sentence for the massacre of Dustin's parents, aunt, and uncle. The trial came to symbolize the 1980s hysteria over Satanic cults; despite the lack of physical evidence, the jury believed the outlandish accusations Dustin and his cousin made against Rusty. Now, after DNA analysis has overturned the conviction, Dustin braces for a reckoning. Meanwhile, one of Dustin's patients gets him deeply engaged in a string of drowning deaths involving drunk college boys. At first Dustin dismisses talk of a serial killer as paranoid thinking, but as he gets wrapped up in their amateur investigation, Dustin starts to believe that there's more to the deaths than coincidence. Soon he becomes obsessed, crossing all professional boundaries—and putting his own family in harm's way. From one of today's most renowned practitioners of literary suspense, Ill Will is an intimate thriller about the failures of memory and the perils of self-deception. In Dan Chaon's nimble, chilling prose, the past looms over the present, turning each into a haunted place..

Chariandy, David John

Brother: a novel. David Chariandy. Bloomsbury USA, 2018. 192 p.
ISBN 9781635572049
1. Brothers 2. Children of immigrants 3. Public housing 4. Trinidadians in Canada 5. Dreams 6. Scarborough, Ontario 7. Ontario 8. 1990s 9. Literary fiction 10. Urban fiction 11. Canadian fiction 12. Adult books for young adults
BC Book Prizes, Ethel Wilson Fiction Prize, 2018; Rogers Writers' Trust Fiction Prize, 2017; Toronto Book Awards, 2018

Coming of age during a sweltering summer in their Toronto housing complex, two boys, the sons of Trinidadian immigrants, dare to imagine better lives in the face of a violent shooting and the pulsing beats of 1990s hip-hop culture.

"The tone of this often melancholy story is elegiac, as Michael tells it in his muted, first-person voice. The characters are well drawn, and the setting is beautifully realized. The result is a haunting story that will linger in readers memories." —*Booklist*

Originally published; Toronto : McClelland &Stewart, 2017.

Charles, KJ

Wanted, a gentleman: or, Virtue over-rated. K.J. Charles. Riptide Publishing, 2017. 155 p.
ISBN 9781626494725
1. Gay men 2. Interracial romance 3. Secrets 4. Personal ads 5. Black British 6. London, England 7. 1800s (Decade) 8. Historical romances 9. LGBTQIA romances 10. LGBTQIA fiction

"Charles provides a little gothic plot twist that stretches the imagination, while this historical gay romance remains true to its roots in grand nineteenth-century love stories. Period dialogue coupled with a strong setting make this an affecting, quick read." —*Booklist*

Chase, Loretta Lynda

Don't tempt me. Loretta Lynda Chase. Avon, 2009. 384 p. (Fallen women, 2)
ISBN 9780061632662
1. Young women 2. Kidnapping 3. Man-woman relationships 4. Scandals 5. Harems 6. England 7. Regency period (1811-1820) 8. Regency romances 9. Historical romances
Romantic Times Reviewers' Choice Award, 2009

Returning to England after spending twelve years in the exotic east, Zoe Lexham, who has mastered the art of pleasure, agrees to a marriage of convenience with the Duke of Marchmont who, tired of being the most popular bachelor, can save her reputation.

A duke in shining armor. Loretta Lynda Chase. Avon Books, 2017. 384 p. (Difficult dukes, 1)
ISBN 9780062457387
1. Dukes and duchesses 2. Jilted men 3. Nobility 4. Interpersonal attraction 5. Man-woman relationships 6. England 7. Georgian era (1714-1837) 8. 1830s 9. Georgian romances 10. Historical romances
Introduces three less-than-virtuous dukes, the first of whom falls for a bookish lady who is reluctantly engaged to his best friend.

"When it comes to writing unforgettable, superbly crafted historical romances, RITA Awardwinning Chase is the creme de la creme, and A Duke in Shining Armor, which launches her new Disgraceful Dukes series, is another exquisitely sensual, perfectly calibrated masterpiece of frothy wit and flawless characterization." —*Booklist*

Miss Wonderful. Loretta Lynda Chase. Berkley, 2004. 352 p. (Carsington brothers series, 1)
ISBN 9780425194836
1. Canals — Design and construction 2. Independence in women 3. Single men 4. Single women 5. Man-woman relationships 6. Great Britain 7. England 8. Regency period (1811-1820) 9. 19th century 10. Regency romances 11. Historical romances
Library Journal Best Books, 2004; Romantic Times Reviewers' Choice Award, 2004

Rather then succumb to temptation with the fairer sex, reformed rake Alistair Carsington journeys to Derbyshire, a secluded country town, to keep out of trouble, but his plans go by the wayside when he meets the infuriatingly irresistible Miss Mirabel Oldridge.

The character of Rupert Carsington also appears in the author's Mr. Impossible.

Chatterjee, Upamanyu

English, August: an Indian story. Upamanyu Chatterjee; introduction by Akhil Sharma. New York Review Books, 2006. 330 p.
ISBN 9781590171790
1. Young men 2. Culture conflict 3. Drug abuse 4. Civil service 5. City life 6. India 7. Humorous stories 8. Coming-of-age stories
LC 2005022842

"This satiric novel chronicles the reluctant coming of age of a privileged young man who has just entered the prestigious Indian Administrative Service. Posted to a small town deep in the interior, he finds himself a foreigner in his own country, wary of cholera, defenseless against mosquitoes, and shocked by the sight of a tribal woman: They exist, he shrieked silently, outside arty films about tribal exploitation and agrarian reform. In revolt, he sneaks out of meetings, pretends to be the son of Antarctic explorers, and smokes copious amounts of pot. He's an avatar of the Western slacker: overeducated, bored, plagued with doubts, and incapable of action. Still, Chatterjee's story is uniquely Indian, as he plumbs his hero's fear of being just one more urban Indian bewitched by America's hard sell in the Third World." —*The New Yorker*

Chavez, Heather

No bad deed. Heather Chavez. William Morrow & Co. 2020. 400 p.
ISBN 9780062936172
1. Women veterinarians 2. Stalkers 3. Paranoia 4. Family secrets 5. Missing men 6. California 7. Thrillers and suspense 8. Psychological suspense 9. First person narratives

After coming to the rescue of a woman left for dead, veterinarian Cassie Larkin becomes the target of a deadly stalker who knows too much about her own dark family history— and who could be linked to the recent disappearance of her husband.

"Chavez is in full command of plot and pacing as the connection between Cassie's roadside confrontation and Sam's disappearance becomes clear. Domestic thriller fans will be well satisfied." —*Publishers Weekly*

Chayefsky, Paddy

Altered states: a novel. Paddy Chayevsky. Harper and Row, 1978. 184 p.
ISBN 9780060107277
1. Scientists 2. Psychological research 3. Altered states of consciousness 4. Books to movies
LC 77011542
Edward Jessup, a neurophysiologist at the Harvard Medical School, relentlessly seeks the origins of human consciousness and, with the aide of an isolation tank and a hallucinogenic drug, regresses farther and farther into a proto-human state.

Chee, Alexander

The **queen** of the night. Alexander Chee. Houghton Mifflin Harcourt, 2016. 576 pages
ISBN 9780618663026
1. Independence in women 2. Change (Psychology) 3. Operas 4. Secrets 5. Sopranos (Singers) 6. Paris, France 7. France 8. Belle Epoque (1871-1914) 9. Historical fiction
LC 2014014409
With her distinctive "falcon" soprano, Lilliet Berne is the uncontested star of the Paris Opera. Only one accolade has thus far eluded her: the chance to originate a leading role, ensuring that she'll never be forgotten. Her wish comes true when she's presented with a libretto that alludes to the secrets of her past. Only four other people know the details of her early life, but which one of them betrayed her? As she tries to solve the mystery, she reflects on the various parts she has played, beginning with her childhood on the Minnesota prairie and encompassing roles as a circus performer, as a servant to Empress Eugénie, and as a celebrated courtesan. As lush and dramatic as the theatrical world it depicts, this sweeping novel brings Belle Époque France to richly detailed life.

"Richly researched, ornately plotted, this story demands, and repays, close attention." —*Kirkus*

Cheek, Chip

Cape May. Chip Cheek. Celadon Books, 2019. 256 p.
ISBN 9781250297150
1. Newlyweds 2. Extramarital affairs 3. Honeymoons 4. Betrayal 5. Lust 6. New Jersey 7. 1950s 8. Historical fiction 9. Literary fiction
Southern newlyweds honeymooning in 1957 Cape May are pulled into the dramas of a trio of sophisticated New England urbanites who render the deserted beach community an intimate playground of corruptive recklessness.

Cheever, John

Bullet Park: a novel. John Cheever. Knopf 1969. 245 p.
ISBN 9780394418193
1. Murder 2. Suburban life 3. Eccentric men 4. Neighbors 5. Good and evil 6. 1960s 7. Psychological fiction 8. Literary fiction
"The author mixes compassion and high comedy brilliantly, holding up to view an America that is fatally schizoid in many of its manifesta-

tions. The confrontation that finally comes between Hammer and Nailles is a horrifying dark allegory of our times." —*Publishers Weekly*

Falconer. John Cheever. Knopf 1977. 211 p.
ISBN 9780394410715
1. Prisoners 2. Suburban families 3. Murderers 4. Prisons 5. Drug addicts 6. Psychological fiction 7. Literary fiction 8. LGBTQIA fiction
LC 76019382
National Book Critics Circle Award for Fiction finalist, 1977
Convicted and imprisoned for having killed his brother, an exceptional middle-aged man enters into a close relationship with a thief and hustler named Jody and experiences an unexpected liberation BT

Chekhov, Anton Pavlovich

Early short stories, 1883-1888. Edited by Shelby Foote; translated from the Russian by Constance Garnett. Modern Library, 1998. Xix, 642 p.
ISBN 9780679603177
1. Short stories 2. Translations
Tells the stories of a fawning official, a man's search for convictions, a boy's journey across Russia, and ordinary people in situations that reveal a surprising change of emotion.

Later short stories, 1888-1903. Edited by Shelby Foote; translated from the Russian by Constance Garnett. Modern Library, 1998. Xvii, 628 pages
ISBN 9780679603160
1. Short stories 2. Translations
LC 98020048
Tells the stories of a doubting writer, the unexpected results of a love affair, and everyday people facing life's surprises.

Chen, Da

Brothers: a novel. Da Chen. Shaye Areheart Books, 2006. 432 p.
ISBN 9781400097289
1. Stepsiblings 2. Social change 3. Abandoned children 4. Orphans 5. Illegitimacy 6. China 7. Chinese Cultural Revolution (1966-1976) 8. 20th century 9. Family sagas 10. Historical fiction 11. Adult books for young adults
LC 2005036267
Asian Pacific American Award for Literature: Adult Fiction, 2007
"Da Chen has achieved something that sounds simple but is, in fact, close to impossible: he brings the Western reader into the guts of the conflict, the agonies and the revelations of events that shook the world's largest population in the 35 years after 1960, when Shento and his brother were born. Make no mistake, this is not contemporary history retold. This is magnificent fiction. It transcends the events it chronicles and does what fiction at its best should do: it changes our internal landscape." —*Washington Post Book World.*

Chen, Mike

Here and now and then. Mike Chen. MIRA, 2019. 384 p.
ISBN 9780778369042
1. Spies 2. Time travel 3. Families 4. Fathers and daughters 5. Amnesia 6. San Francisco, California 7. Science fiction
Stranded for 18 years since the 1990s, time-traveling agent Kin Stewart, suffering from memory loss, has started a new life, but when rescuers from the year 2142 finally arrive, he must choose between his current family and the one he left behind in the future.

"Chen carefully balances heart, humor, and precise world building to bring alive an emotional and genre-bending story that will please fans of Doctor Who." —*Booklist*

We could be heroes. Mike Chen. Mira Books, 2021. 384 p.
ISBN 9780778331391
1. Superheroes 2. Supervillains 3. People with amnesia 4. Support groups 5. Conspiracies 6. Superhero stories

Two superpowered individuals who have lost all memory of their real identities use their respective powers to commit or fight crime before teaming up together to stop the mad scientist behind a devastating medical conspiracy.

"Chen's (A Beginning at the End) writing wraps hard topics with heartfelt and humorous prose, creating a delightful novel of the steps and missteps of power, friendship, and trust." —*Library Journal*

Chen, Qiufan

Waste tide. Chen Qiufan; translated from the Chinese by Ken Liu. Tor Books, 2019. 304 pages
ISBN 9780765389312
1. Han, Kang 2. Recycling (Waste, etc.) 3. Near future 4. Migrant workers 5. Clans 6. China 7. Dystopian fiction 8. Science fiction 9. Translations

LC 2018050987

An exploited lowest-caste factory worker, her ruthless employer, an American corporate representative and his heritage-seeking translator intersect when a dark futuristic virus is unleashed on a major Chinese technological site, triggering a war between the classes.

"Anglophone readers will cherish the opportunity to experience Chen's sweeping, complex, and deeply emotional near-future dystopian vision via this thoughtful rendition by Hugo-winning translator and author Liu that maintains the story's essential Chinese character." —*Publishers Weekly*

Translation of: Huang chao.
Originally published: Beijing : Changjiang Literature Art Publishing House, 2013.
Translated from the Chinese

Cheng, Bill

Southern cross the dog. Bill Cheng. Ecco Press, 2013. 336 p.
ISBN 9780062225009
1. Blues music 2. Floods 3. Curses 4. Voyages and travels 5. Survival (after floods) 6. Southern States 7. Mississippi River 8. 1920s 9. Historical fiction

When I was a baby child, they put the jinx on me," explains Robert Lee Chatham, a young African-American man from rural Mississippi. Everything he's experienced so far in his short life has lead him to believe he's marked by the Devil—from his mother's mental illness to his brother's lynching at the hands of a mob. Even Robert's first kiss (with a white girl named Dora) comes just before the Great Mississippi Flood of 1927, a disaster that then robs him of everything he holds dear in one fell swoop. In the aftermath of that devastating event, Robert journeys across the deep South, encountering dangers and numerous eccentric characters as he strives to outrun what he's sure is his terrible fate.

Cherezinska, Elzbieta

The **widow** queen. Elzbieta Cherezinska. 2021. 512 p. (Bold novels, 1)
ISBN 9781250218001

1. Women rulers 2. Independence in women 3. Political intrigue 4. Nobility 5. Power (Social sciences) 6. Europe 7. Poland 8. Medieval period (476-1492) 9. Historical fiction 10. Translations

Presented as a choice marriage candidate to princes in three different realms, a Polish duke's daughter is forced to reconcile her dreams with the harsh realities of leadership in a foreign land.

"The Widow Queen is an epic historical saga full of political intrigue, familial drama, and lust. Readers will be absolutely transported, and eager for the sequel." —*Booklist*
Translated from the Polish.

Cherryh, C. J.

Foreigner: a novel of first contact. C. J. Cherryh. DAW Books, 1994. 378 p. (Foreigner universe, 1)
ISBN 9780886775902
1. Space colonies 2. Aliens (Humanoid) — Sightings and encounters 3. Human/alien encounters 4. Culture conflict 5. Loyalty 6. First person narratives 7. William, of Wykeham, Bishop of Winchester, 1324-1404 8. Science fiction

Two hundred years after a group of humans had lost a war to the atevi, Bren Cameron, the only human allowed into the atevi society, realizes he must forge a bond between the two seemingly incompatible species.

"Cherryh plays her strongest suit in this exploration of human/alien contact, producing an incisive study-in-contrast of what it means to be human in a world where trust is nonexistent." —*Library Journal*

Chevalier, Tracy

★ **Girl** with a pearl earring. Tracy Chevalier. Dutton, 1999. 233 p.
ISBN 9780525945277
1. Vermeer, Johannes 2. Artists — History 3. Artists' models 4. Sixteen-year-old girls 5. Women domestics 6. Husband and wife 7. Netherlands 8. 17th century 9. Coming-of-age stories 10. Historical fiction 11. Books to movies 12. Adult books for young adults

LC 99032493

Alex Award, 2001; Booklist Editors' Choice: Adult Fiction for Young Adults, 2000; YALSA Best Books for Young Adults, 2001; School Library Journal Best Books: Best Adult Books 4 Teens, 2000

In this richly imagined portrait of the young woman who inspired one of Vermeer's most celebrated paintings, history and fiction merge seamlessly in a luminous tale of artistic vision, sensual awakening, and daily life in the Netherlands of the 17th-century.

The author has done very well in creating the feel of a society with sharp divisions of status and creed.... Griet is a memorable characterreserved, wary, observant, and, although she does not know it, afflicted with a serious and ultimately dangerous crush on her employer. The situation makes a fine story, which is exceptionally well told. The Atlantic. Monthly.

The **last** runaway. Tracy Chevalier. Dutton, 2013. 320 p.
ISBN 9780525952992
1. Underground Railroad 2. Quaker women 3. Quakers 4. Freedom seekers 5. Ohio 6. Antebellum America (1820-1861) 7. 1850s 8. Historical fiction

LC 2012034693

Forced to leave England and struggling with illness in the wake of a family tragedy, Quaker Honor Bright is forced to rely on strangers in the harsh landscape of 1850 Ohio and is compelled to join the Underground Railroad network to help runaway slaves escape to freedom.

"Chevalier offers a cast of strong characters wrestling with thorny personalities, the harsh realities of the frontier, and the legal and moral complexities of American slavery." —*Booklist*

A **single** thread. Tracy Chevalier. Viking, 2019. 336 pages
ISBN 9780525558248
1. Young women 2. Loss (Psychology) 3. Needlework 4. Cathedrals
5. Communities 6. England 7. Between the Wars (1918-1939) 8. 1930s
9. Historical fiction

LC 2019007094

Facing limited prospects after the loss of her loved ones, a woman joins a circle of embroiderers continuing a centuries-long tradition at the Winchester Cathedral.

Chiang, Ted

★ **Exhalation:** stories. Ted Chiang. Alfred A. Knopf, 2019. 350 pages
ISBN 9781101947883
1. Technology and civilization 2. Exploration 3. High technology
4. Human behavior 5. Parallel universes 6. Short stories 7. Hard science
fiction 8. Science fiction
Locus Award for Best Collection, 2020; Booklist Editors' Choice, 2019; New York Times Notable Book, 2019

"Chiang remains one of the most skilled stylists in sf, and this will appeal to genre and literary-fiction fans alike." —*Booklist*

★ **Stories** of your life and others. Ted Chiang. Tor, 2002. 333 p.
ISBN 9780765304186
1. Short stories 2. Hard science fiction 3. Science fiction 4. Adult books
for young adults

LC 2001059658

Locus Award for Best Collection, 2003

Presents a first collection of seven science fiction short stories, and includes an original tale, "Liking What You See: A Documentary" for this anthology.

"Chiang writes seldom, but his almost unfathomably wonderful stories tick away with the precision of a Swiss watch—and explode in your awareness with shocking, devastating force." —*Kirkus*

The author's "Story of your life" was adapted into the 2016 film entitled Arrival.

Chiaverini, Jennifer

Mrs. Lincoln's dressmaker: a novel. Jennifer Chiaverini. Dutton, 2013. 352 p.
ISBN 9780525953616
1. Keckley, Elizabeth 2. Interracial friendship 3. Dressmakers 4. Female
friendship 5. African American women 6. Presidents' spouses
7. Washington, D. C. 8. United States 9. 19th century 10. Historical
fiction 11. Gentle reads

LC 2012036366

Chosen as the personal modiste for Mary Todd Lincoln, freedwoman Elizabeth Keckley is drawn into the intimate life of the Lincoln family as she supports Mary in the loss of her husband from the assassination that stunned the nation and the world.

Mrs. Lincoln's sisters. Jennifer Chiaverini. William Morrow & Co, 2020. 400 pages
ISBN 9780062975973
1. Lincoln, Mary Todd 2. Widows 3. Sisters 4. Suicidal behavior
5. Mental illness 6. Married women 7. United States 8. 1870s 9.
Historical fiction 10. Biographical fiction 11. Multiple perspectives

Devastated by her 1875 suicide attempt, the sisters of widowed former First Lady Mary Todd Lincoln navigate the consequences of their husbands' choices while advocating for Mary's needs.

"Through meticulously researched historical detail and sympathetic portrayal of each character, including Mary herself, Chiaverini provides a fascinating glimpse into the women of an influential family on the front lines of some of the most important moments of that indelible time." —*Booklist*

Resistance women: a novel. By Jennifer Chiaverini. William Morrow, 2019. 384 pages
ISBN 9780062841100
1. Harnack-Fish, Mildred 2. Women spies 3. Anti-Nazi movement
4. Americans in Germany 5. Intellectuals 6. Resistance to government
7. Berlin, Germany 8. Germany 9. 1930s 10. 1940s 11. Historical fiction
12. Biographical fiction 13. Multiple perspectives

LC 2018044622

Resisting the power grabs of an increasingly formidable Nazi Party in 1930s Berlin, the courageous American wife of a German intellectual and her circle of women friends engage in a clandestine battle to sabotage Hitler's regime.

Child, Lee

61 hours: a Reacher novel. Lee Child. Delacorte Press, 2010. 400 p.
(Jack Reacher novels, 14)
ISBN 9780385340588
1. Former military police 2. Witnesses — Protection 3. Assassins
4. Borgia, Lucrezia 5. Winter storms 6. South Dakota 7. Thrillers and
suspense

LC 2009052804

Theakston Old Peculier Crime Novel of the Year Award, 2011

Reacher arrives accidentally in a small South Dakota town, where during a dangerous winter storm he is enlisted to protect a lone witness who local police hope can help convict a brutal crime ring.

The **affair:** a Reacher novel. Lee Child. Delacorte Press, 2011. 304 p.
(Jack Reacher novels, 16)
ISBN 9780385344326
1. Former military police 2. Undercover operations 3. Conspiracies
4. Murder investigation 5. Women murder victims 6. Mississippi
7. Thrillers and suspense

LC 2011017151

A young woman is dead, and solid evidence points to a soldier at a nearby military base. But that soldier has powerful friends in Washington. Reacher is ordered undercover—to find out everything he can, to control the local police, and then to vanish.

"Exciting and suspenseful, with deceit and cover-ups, violence, and sex, this is another great entry in Child's compelling series." —*Library Journal*

Bad luck and trouble: a Jack Reacher novel. Lee Child. Delacorte Press, 2007. 384 p. (Jack Reacher novels, 11)
ISBN 9780385340557
1. Former military police 2. Mercenaries 3. Conspiracies 4. Murder
5. Missing persons 6. Thrillers and suspense

LC 2006031931

When a man is killed by being thrown from a helicopter high over the California desert, loner Jack Reacher discovers that someone is targeting his old friends and teammates and launches a personal campaign to end the conspiracy before it claims any more lives.

"Throughout the book, Reacher remains fanatically interested in codes, fractions, cube roots and probabilities. The [author] who devises all this must also be acutely aware of formulas, because he is smart enough to avoid them.... In the world of Mr. Child's novels, what matters, and dazzles, is what works on the page." —*New York Times*

★ **Blue** moon: a Jack Reacher novel. Lee Child. Delacorte Press, 2019. 400 p. (Jack Reacher novels, 24)
ISBN 9780399593543

1. Veterans 2. Gangs 3. Protectiveness in men 4. Debt 5. Violence in gangs 6. Thrillers and suspense

LC 2019029141

Jack Reacher comes to the aid of an elderly couple...and confronts his most dangerous opponents yet.

★ **Die** trying. Lee Child. G. P. Putnam's Sons, 1998. 374 p; (Jack Reacher novels, 2)

ISBN 9780399143793

1. Former military police 2. Kidnapping 3. White supremacists 4. Hostages 5. Neo-Nazism 6. Montana 7. Chicago, Illinois 8. Thrillers and suspense

LC 9739763

In a plot to overthrow the U.S. government, Montana neo-Nazis abduct the daughter of the nation's top general and her male companion. The companion is Jack Reacher, a former military policeman and he turns the tables on the captors.

Echo burning. Lee Child. G.P Putnam's Sons, 2001. 354 p; (Jack Reacher novels, 5)

ISBN 9780399147265

1. Former military police 2. Assassins 3. Murder 4. Protectiveness in men 5. Murder investigation 6. Texas 7. Thrillers and suspense

LC 45910

While hitchhiking through West Texas, former MP Jack Reacher encounters a young woman seeking protection for herself and her little girl from her monstrous husband, due to be released from jail, and his horrible family.

"Reacher is a one-man wrecking crew nourished only by the hunt. For anyone who thinks the hard-boiled genre is growing soft around the edges." —*Booklist*

The **enemy**: a Jack Reacher novel. Lee Child. Delacorte Press, 2004. 393 p; (Jack Reacher novels, 8)

ISBN 9780385336673

1. Military police 2. Crimes against generals 3. Americans in France 4. Murder investigation 5. Conspiracies 6. France 7. North Carolina 8. 1990s 9. Cromwell, Thomas

LC 2003065282

Former army cop Jack Reacher finds himself questioning the instincts that made him an elite soldier when his latest case forces him to choose between obeying the law and becoming a renegade.

"Known for his hold-your-breath action scenes, Child proves equally adept at portraying how a criminal investigation uses the smallest of building blocks...to construct a compelling circumstantial case." —*Booklist*

The **hard** way: a Jack Reacher novel. Lee Child. Delacorte Press, 2006. 384 p; (Jack Reacher novels, 10)

ISBN 9780385336697

1. Former military police 2. Kidnapping 3. Mercenaries 4. Arms dealers 5. Undercover operations 6. New York City 7. Thrillers and suspense

LC 2005051946

Jack Reacher comes to the aid of Edward Lane, the head of an illegal soldiers-for-hire operation, who enlists Reacher's assistance to find and stop a vicious kidnapper who has abducted Lane's wife and child, but Reacher soon discovers that his new employer's dirty secrets could get him killed.

"The imperfections Child adds to his protagonist's character this time out, such as Reacher's not catching onto all of the questionable dealings early on in the novel, give Reacher a much-needed vulnerability.... [This is a] breathless, well-paced thriller that will satisfy die-hard fans and newcomers." —*Denver Post*

★ **Killing** floor. Lee Child. G. P. Putnam's Sons, 1997. 359 p; (Jack Reacher novels, 1)

ISBN 9780399142536

1. Former military police 2. Murder suspects 3. Conspiracies 4. Brothers — Death 5. Revenge 6. Georgia 7. Thrillers and suspense

LC 96-34452

Anthony Award for Best Novel, 1998

A discharged soldier is framed for a murder by the chief of police in a small town in Georgia where he has just arrived. When the soldier learns that the murdered man was his brother he breaks out of jail and carries out his own investigation. A first novel.

"Child serves up a big, rangy plot, menace as palpable as a ticking bomb, and enough battered corpses to make an undertaker grin." —*Kirkus*

Make me. Lee Child. Random House, 2015. 416 p. (Jack Reacher novels, 20)

ISBN 9780804178778

1. Missing persons 2. Assassins 3. Conspiracies 4. Fugitives 5. Murder investigation 6. Thrillers and suspense

LibraryReads Favorites, 2015

When he teams up with Michelle Chang, Jack Reacher finds himself involved in a private investigation that has turned lethal.

The **midnight** line. Lee Child. Delacorte Press, 2017. 400 p. (Jack Reacher novels, 22)

ISBN 9780399593482

1. Motorcycle gangs 2. Lost articles 3. Women veterans 4. Rings 5. Missing persons 6. Wisconsin 7. Thrillers and suspense

LibraryReads Favorites, 2017

Reacher takes a stroll through a small Wisconsin town and sees a class ring in a pawn shop window: West Point 2005. A tough year to graduate: Iraq, then Afghanistan.The ring is tiny, for a woman, and it has her initials engraved on the inside. Reacher wonders what unlucky circumstance made her give up something she earned over four hard years. He decides to find out. And find the woman. And return her ring. Why not? So begins a harrowing journey that takes Reacher through the upper Midwest, from a lowlife bar on the sad side of a small town to a dirt-blown crossroads in the middle of nowhere, encountering bikers, cops, crooks, muscle, and a missing persons PI who wears a suit and a tie in the Wyoming wilderness. The deeper Reacher digs, and the more he learns, the more dangerous the terrain becomes. Turns out the ring was just a small link in a far darker chain. Powerful forces are guarding a vast criminal enterprise. Some lines should never be crossed. But then, neither should Reacher.

"The identity of the ring's owner is established reasonably quickly, and her backstory (and what Reacher does about it) takes the reader from the wars in Afghanistan to the opioid crisis in America (including a damning thumbnail history of how corporate America has profited from selling heroin in one form or another and a devastating portrait of opioid addiction). As usual, Child makes his narrative entirely credible—and compulsively readable." —*Publishers Weekly*

Never go back: a Jack Reacher novel. Lee Child. Delacorte Press, 2013. 416 p. (Jack Reacher novels, 18)

ISBN 9780385344340

1. Former military police 2. Cold cases (Criminal investigation) 3. Missing women 4. Conspiracies 5. Murder investigation 6. Virginia 7. Thrillers and suspense

Jack Reacher arrives in Virginia hoping to contact the woman he spoke with on the phone in "61 Hours," only to be drafted back into the Army, where he confronts life-changing elements from his past.

Night school: a Jack Reacher novel. Lee Child. Delacorte Press, 2016. 416 p. (Jack Reacher novels, 21)

ISBN 9780804178808

1. Missing persons 2. Assassins 3. Conspiracies 4. Fugitives 5. Murder investigation 6. Thrillers and suspense

LC 2016018769

LibraryReads Favorites, 2016

A military policeman fresh off a mission in 1996, Jack Reacher is assigned to a covert task force with two government experts to track down an American who is about to make a mysterious sale to Middle Eastern radicals.

"This way- back novel, with its old-school investigating, street-smart tactics, and classic Reacher attitude, is an edge-of-your-seat book readers won't want to put down." —*Library Journal*

No middle name: the complete collected Jack Reacher short stories. Lee Child. Random House, 2017. 400 p. (Jack Reacher novels)

ISBN 9780399593574

1. Assassins 2. Fugitives 3. Murder 4. Wanderers and wandering 5. Reacher, Jack (Fictitious character) 6. Short stories 7. Thrillers and suspense

A high-action anthology of Jack Reacher stories includes a previously unseen novella and 11 other stories collected for the first time in print, in a volume that complements each story with an original author introduction.

The novella "Too Much Time" leads into Jack Reacher novel #22, The Midnight Line.

Includes excerpt of The midnight line.

Nothing to lose. Lee Child. Delacorte Press, 2008. 432 p; (Jack Reacher novels, 12)

ISBN 9780385340564

1. Former military police 2. Conspiracies 3. Missing persons 4. Police 5. Mercenaries 6. Colorado 7. Thrillers and suspense

LC 2007043735

Arriving in the small town of Despair, Colorado, Jack Reacher finds himself taking on an entire town as he searches for the truths behind its sinister connection to a brutal war that is killing Americans thousands of miles away.

"With his powerful sense of justice, dogged determination and the physical and mental skills to overcome what to most would be overwhelming odds, Jack Reacher makes an irresistible modern knight-errant." —*Publishers Weekly*

Sequel to: Bad luck and trouble.

One shot: a Jack Reacher novel. Lee Child. Delacorte Press, 2005. 376 p; (Jack Reacher novels, 9)

ISBN 9780385336680

1. Former military police 2. Serial murders 3. Frameups 4. Snipers 5. Women defense attorneys 6. Indiana 7. Middle West 8. Thrillers and suspense 9. Books to movies

LC 2004058246

Library Journal Best Books, 2005

Ex-military investigator Jack Reacher is called in by James Barr, a man accused of a lethal sniper attack that leaves five people dead, and teams up with a young defense attorney to find an unseen enemy who is manipulating events.

"Mr. Child's idea of heroism has nihilism around the edges but a fierce, fighting spirit at its core. In marked contrast to the brooding figures who otherwise dominate contemporary detective stories, Reacher is not one for self-doubt. His is a two-fisted decency. But Mr. Child also gives him amazing powers of deduction, a serious conscience and the occasional touch of tenderness. It's a wildly improbable mixture, one that can't be beat." —*New York Times*

This book made into a movie called Jack Reacher, starring Tom Cruise and directed by Christopher McQuarrie.

★ **Past** tense. Lee Child. Delacorte Press, 2018. 400 p. (Jack Reacher novels, 23)

ISBN 9780399593512

1. Fathers and sons 2. Family secrets 3. Deception 4. Canadians in the United States 5. Small towns 6. Thrillers and suspense

LC 2018022559

Detouring to his father's childhood hometown at the beginning of a cross-country hitchhiking tour, Jack uncovers disturbing family revelations at the same time he becomes entangled in a dangerous high-ticket sale.

"Another first-class entry in a series that continues to set the gold standard for aspiring thriller authors." —*Booklist*

Personal: a Jack Reacher novel. Lee Child. Random House, 2014. 416 p. (Jack Reacher novels, 19)

ISBN 9780804178747

1. Assassins 2. Snipers 3. Organized crime 4. Politicians 5. Fugitives 6. Thrillers and suspense

Jack Reacher finds himself working for the State Department and the CIA to track down the American sniper who took a shot at the president of France and is possibly targeting the G-8 summit packed with world leaders.

"Child sets up a thriller premise better than anybody, expertly mixing gun talk, trivia, and tension and, when the time comes, detailing the bloodletting with the care of a connoisseur." —*Booklist*

Persuader: a Jack Reacher novel. Lee Child. Delacorte Press, 2003. 352 p; (Jack Reacher novels, 7)

ISBN 9780385336666

1. Former military police 2. Drug traffic 3. Missing persons 4. Government investigators 5. Enemies 6. Boston, Massachusetts 7. Maine 8. Thrillers and suspense

LC 2002034965

Jack Reacher takes an undercover assignment to investigate the disappearance of a federal agent from the home of a notorious drug dealer, but Reacher soon discovers that the dealer has ties to a man from Reacher's own past.

"What makes the novel really zing, though, is Reacher's narration—a unique mix of the brainy and the brutal, of strategic thinking and explosive action, moral rumination and ruthless force, marking him as one of the most memorable heroes in contemporary thrillerdom." —*Publishers Weekly*

★ The **sentinel**. Lee Child and Andrew Child. Delacorte Press, 2020. 368 p. (Jack Reacher novels, 25)

ISBN 9781984818461

1. Cyberterrorism 2. Employees — Dismissal 3. Criminals 4. Conspiracies 5. Intrigue 6. Tennessee 7. Thrillers and suspense 8. First person narratives

LC 2020030403

A latest entry in the best-selling series, co-written with the author's brother, finds Jack Reacher following his lizard-brain instincts on a seemingly uneventful night in Nashville, where a recently fired man nurses an increasingly violent grudge.

"Jack Reacher fans' concern about Lee Child's decision to bow out of the series proves unwarranted in this terrific first Reacher novel coauthored by both Child and his brother, Andrew Grant." —*Booklist*

A **wanted** man: a Reacher novel. Lee Child. Delacorte Press, 2012. 416 p. (Jack Reacher novels, 17)

ISBN 9780385344333

1. Former military police 2. Conspiracies 3. Murder investigation 4. Murder 5. Stabbing victims 6. Chicago, Illinois 7. Thrillers and suspense

LC 2012018420

British Book Award for Crime Thriller of the Year, 2012

Hitching a ride to Virginia in a car with three strangers, Jack Reacher finds himself unwittingly involved in a massive conspiracy that makes him a threat.

Without fail. By Lee Child. G.P. Putnam's Sons, 2002. 374 p; (Jack Reacher novels, 6)

ISBN 9780399148613

1. Former military police 2. Assassination plots 3. Women vice-presidents 4. Assassins 5. Secret service 6. Washington, D.C. 7. Thrillers and suspense

LC 2001048849

Jack Reacher is hired to attempt to assassinate the Vice President of the United States to ensure that his security team is up to scratch, but in the meantime there is a very real and deadly team of assassins that has just put the VP in their sights.

"This novel is a stunner, packed with extraordinary detail regarding executive protection and overlaid with a genuine mystery that will baffle even the most astute armchair crime buffs." —*Booklist*

Worth dying for: a Reacher novel. Lee Child. Delacorte Press, 2010. 416 p. (Jack Reacher novels, 15)

ISBN 9780385344319

1. Cold cases (Criminal investigation) 2. Secrets 3. Criminals 4. Former military police 5. Missing children 6. Nebraska 7. Thrillers and suspense

LC 2010023100

Jack Reacher clashes with an organized crime family that is terrorizing Nebraska corn country in their efforts to supply dangerous international customers, a battle that is complicated by the unsolved case of a missing child.

"Crisp, efficient prose and well-rounded characterizations (at least of the guys in the white hats) raise this beyond other attempts to translate the pulse-pounding feel of the Die Hard films into prose." —*Publishers Weekly*

Child, Lincoln

Deep storm: a novel. Lincoln Child. Doubleday, 2006. 384 p. (Jeremy Logan novels, 1)

ISBN 9780385515504

1. Research institutes 2. Sick persons 3. Undercover operations 4. Atlantis (Legendary place) 5. Jack, the Ripper 6. Atlantic Ocean 7. Thrillers and suspense

LC 2006021093

Summoned to a remote oil rig to diagnose a strange medical ailment among the rig workers, ex-Navy physician Peter Crane soon discovers that the condition is linked to the underwater excavation being done at science research station Deep Storm.

"The prose may be a tad rough, but the story is imaginative and filled with wonder." —*Booklist*

Childress, Mark

Crazy in Alabama. Ballantine Books, 1993. 383 p.

ISBN 9780345389244

1. Orphans 2. Twelve-year-old boys 3. Racism 4. Eccentric women 5. Alabama 6. Hollywood, California 7. 1960s 8. Coming-of-age stories 9. Books to movies

LC 92038334

In Alabama during the racially restless summer of 1965, an orphan boy comes of age, and his aunt escapes from an unhappy marriage.

"It is a measure of Mr. Childress's skill as a novelist—-not to mention a triumphant example of style over content—that he soon had me eating

out of his hand. I don't know how he did it but he managed to confront every clich, every convention of the genre head on and pound it into submission, so that his novel seems not only fresh and original but also positively inspired." —*New York Times Book Review*

Childs, Laura

Egg shooters. Laura Childs. Berkley Prime Crime, 2020. 336 p. (Cackleberry Club mysteries, 9)

ISBN 9780425281741

1. Women amateur detectives 2. Women business owners 3. Female friendship 4. Engaged persons 5. Restaurants 6. Middle West 7. Culinary mysteries 8. Cozy mysteries 9. Gentle reads

LC 2020012962

Interrupting an emergency room shooter at the local hospital, Cackleberry Club Cafe owner Suzanne teams up with Petra and Toni to find the escaped killer before he tracks them down. By the best-selling author of the Tea Shop Mysteries.

"Warmly framed by the details of running a cafe and preparing tea, this cozy, concluding with recipes, will appeal to readers who enjoy Diane Mott Davidson, Joanne Fluke, and Sandra Balzo, as well as Vicki Delany's Tea & Treachery (2020)." —*Booklist*

Haunted hibiscus. Laura Childs. Berkley Prime Crime, 2021. 336 p. (Tea Shop mysteries (Laura Childs), 22)

ISBN 9780451489692

1. Tearooms 2. Women shopkeepers 3. Women amateur detectives 4. Halloween 5. Urban legends 6. South Carolina 7. Holiday mysteries 8. Cozy mysteries 9. Gentle reads

LC 2020036511

When their literary haunted house costume party is disrupted by an untimely double attack, Indigo Tea Shop proprietress Theodosia Browning and her sommelier, Drayton, investigate suspects including a man with a claim to the Bouchard Mansion property.

"Historic Charleston and a gaggle of interesting helpers make this another winner in this long-running series." —*Kirkus*

Lavender blue murder. Laura Childs. Berkley Prime Crime, 2020. 336 p. (Tea Shop mysteries (Laura Childs), 21)

ISBN 9780451489661

1. Tearooms 2. Women shopkeepers 3. Hunting 4. Women amateur detectives 5. Murder 6. South Carolina 7. Cozy mysteries 8. Gentle reads 9. Culinary mysteries

LC 2019043266

Attending a traditional English bird hunt, tea-maven Theodosia Browning and her sommelier, Drayton Conneley, stumble on the wounded body of their host before suspicious accidents prompt the organization of a seance to expose the culprit.

"Genteel Southern charm and murderous mayhem mix in a mystery that keeps you guessing." —*Kirkus*

Twisted tea Christmas. Laura Childs. Berkley Prime Crime, 2021. 336 p. (Tea Shop mysteries (Laura Childs), 23)

ISBN 9780593200865

1. Tearooms 2. Women shopkeepers 3. Women amateur detectives 4. Christmas 5. Women murder victims 6. South Carolina 7. Holiday mysteries 8. Culinary mysteries 9. Cozy mysteries

LC 2021012426

While catering a Victorian Christmas party for Drucilla Heyward, one of the wealthiest women in town who is about to make a huge announcement, tea maven Theodosia Browning finds herself steeped in murder when she stumbles upon Drucilla's dead body.

"Framed by its lovingly described Charleston setting, warm holiday atmosphere, tea lore, and delicious food, this entry in Childs' long-running cozy series concludes with recipes and tips for hosting specialty teas." —*Booklist*

Chizmar, Richard T.

Chasing the Boogeyman. Richard Chizmar. Gallery Books, 2021. 336 p.
ISBN 9781982175160
1. Small towns 2. Serial murderers 3. Girl murder victims 4. Fear 5. Neighborhood watch programs 6. Maryland 7. Thrillers and suspense 8. Metafiction
A recent college graduate writes a personal account of the terrifying events occurring in his small town where a serial killer has set up shop, unaware that it will continue to haunt him for years.
"For true crime and horror fans, this one's essential." —*Library Journal*

A long December. Richard Chizmar. Subterranean Press, 2016. 519 p.
ISBN 9781596067936
1. Neighbors 2. Secrets 3. Deception 4. Serial murderers 5. Family relationships 6. Horror 7. Psychological suspense 8. Short stories
"Chizmar's stories are united by the feelings they produced—read, anxiety, and suspense—but more remarkable is how they are presented with an underlying poignancy.... his is a must-read for fans of intense tales where psychological suspense and horror overlap." —*Booklist*

Cho, Nam-ju

★ **Kim** Jiyoung, born 1982. Cho Nam-joo; [translated by Jamie Chang].. Liveright Publishing, 2020. 162 p.
ISBN 9781631496707
1. Married women 2. Sexism 3. Gender role 4. Misogyny 5. Patriarchy 6. South Korea 7. Literary fiction 8. Translations 9. Adult books for young adults
LC 2019051218
New York Times Notable Book, 2020; Rise: A Feminist Book Project List, 2021
Follows the experiences of a millennial from Seoul who suddenly manifests the bizarre symptom of being able to flawlessly impersonate and then become any woman, alive or dead.
"It effectively communicates the realities Korean women face, especially discrimination in the workplace, rampant sexual harassment, and the nearly impossible challenge of balancing motherhood with career aspirations." —*Library Journal*
Originally published: Seoul : Minumsa, 2016.
Translated from the Korean.

Cho, Zen

Sorcerer to the crown. Zen Cho. Ace, 2015. 384 p. (Sorcerer royal, 1)
ISBN 9780425283370
1. Wizards 2. Class conflict 3. Racism 4. Universities and colleges 5. Freed people 6. England 7. 19th century 8. Historical fantasy 9. Fantasy fiction
LC 2015007899
Amelia Bloomer List, 2017; Library Journal Best Books, 2015; RUSA Reading List Short List, 2016
Born a slave, Zacharias Wythe has just been appointed England's new Sorcerer Royal—much to the dismay of the socially conservative Royal Society of Unnatural Philosophers, who are already plotting to oust him from his post. But Zacharias has more urgent problems, including a dwindling national supply of magic and strained diplomatic relations with the Faerie realm. Unexpected assistance arrives in the form of fellow out-

sider Prunella Gentlewoman, an orphaned witch of uncertain origins and immense power.
"Cho's entertaining, fantastical debut brings past and current issues of diversity and social class to light with charm, wit, and magic." —*Booklist*

Spirits abroad and other stories. Zen Cho. Small Beer Press, 2021. 288 p.
ISBN 9781618731869
1. Family relationships 2. Vampires 3. College students 4. Mothers and daughters 5. Aliens 6. Malaysia 7. Great Britain 8. Short stories
LC 2021001588
Nineteen sparkling stories that weave between the lands of the living and the lands of the dead.
"Powerful but subtle magic woven into the fabric of intricate worlds make Cho a sure favorite for readers of Kelly Link and Carmen Maria Machado." —*Publishers Weekly*

Choi, Ann Y. K.

Kay's lucky coin variety. Ann Choi. Touchstone Books, 2016. 276 p.
ISBN 9781476748054
1. Families 2. Family relationships 3. Girls 4. Koreans 5. Growing up 6. Toronto, Ontario 7. Canada 8. 1980s 9. Coming-of-age stories 10. Adult books for young adults
Mary, a Korean girl growing up with her brother above her parents' convenience store in 1980s Toronto, is caught between the traditional culture of her parents and her desire to be a Canadian.

Choi, Susan

My education. Susan Choi. Viking, 2013. 304 p.
ISBN 9780670024902
1. Graduate students 2. College teachers 3. Love triangles 4. Husband and wife 5. Marital conflict 6. Psychological fiction 7. LGBTQIA fiction 8. First person narratives 9. Adult books for young adults
LC 2013001605
Lambda Literary Award for Bisexual Fiction
Warned about the womanizing activities of Professor Nicholas Brodeur before her arrival at his prestigious university, graduate student Regina Gottlieb is nevertheless captured by his charisma and good looks before falling prey to his volatile wife.
"Choi's talent resides in her densely layered prose and her slowing down the pace to draw readers into the inner worlds of her characters. The result is a deeply human tale of intentional mistakes, love and lust, and the search for a clearer vision of one's self." —*Library Journal*

★ **Trust** exercise: a novel. Susan Choi. Henry Holt and Company, 2019. 272 pages
ISBN 9781250309884
1. Teenage romance 2. Teacher-student relationships 3. Performing arts schools 4. Theater 5. Theater and teenagers 6. Southern States 7. Literary fiction
LC 2018032027
ALA Notable Book, 2020; Loan Stars Favourites, 2019; National Book Award for Fiction, 2019
Falling in love while attending a competitive 1980s performing arts high school, David and Sarah rise through the ranks before the realities of their family dynamics and economic statuses trigger a spiral that impacts their adult lives.
"Fiercely intelligent, impeccably written, and observed with searing insight, this novel is destined to be a classic." —*Publishers Weekly*

Choi, Yoon

Skinship: stories. Yoon Choi. Alfred A. Knopf, 2021. 304 p.
ISBN 9780593318218
1. Korean Americans 2. Korean American families 3. Families
4. Intimacy (Psychology) 5. Interpersonal relations 6. Short stories
7. Literary fiction

Centering around Korean American families, this debut from a master of short fiction presents a searing look at the failure of intimacy to show us who the people we love truly are.

Choo, Yangsze

The **ghost** bride: a novel. Yangsze Choo. William Morrow, 2013. 362 p.
ISBN 9780062227324
1. Life after death 2. Ghosts 3. Dead 4. Marriage 5. Poor women 6. Malaysia 7. 1890s 8. Historical fantasy 9. Asian-influenced fantasy
LC 2013000727

Although Malacca, Malaya's diverse but declining trading port, has endured Portuguese, Dutch, and finally British rule, local traditions persist. To rescue her once-affluent family from poverty, Li Lan agrees to become the ghost bride of Lim Tian Ching, the deceased son of one of the city's wealthiest families. Though dead, Li Lan's bridegroom makes his presence known, visiting her in dreams while hinting that his was an untimely demise. Now, guided by spirits, Li Lan must undertake a journey into the afterlife to discover the truth.

"Choo's clear and charming style creates an alternate reality where the stakes are just as high as in the real world, combining grounded period storytelling with the supernatural." —*Publishers Weekly*

★ The **night** tiger: a novel. Yangsze Choo. Flatiron Books, 2019. 352 p.
ISBN 9781250175458
1. Colonialism 2. Superstition 3. Social classes 4. Underclass
5. Shapeshifting 6. Malaysia 7. 1930s 8. Asian-influenced fantasy 9. Historical fantasy 10. Adult books for young adults
LC 2018030163

A vivacious dance-hall girl in 1930s colonial Malaysia is drawn into unexpected danger by the discovery of a severed finger that is being sought by a young houseboy who would protect his late master's soul.

"Mythical creatures, conversations with the dead, lucky numbers, Confucian virtues, and forbidden love provide the backdrop for Choos superb murder mystery." —*Publishers Weekly*

Christian, Claire

It's been a pleasure, Noni Blake. Claire Christian. Mira Books, 2021. 368 p.
ISBN 9780778331568
1. Thirties (Age) 2. Single women 3. Self-discovery 4. Overweight women 5. Bisexual women 6. Australia 7. Great Britain 8. Chick lit 9. Australian fiction

What if you made yourself your number one priority?

"A vibrant story of self-discovery.... Both a celebration of pleasure and a dissection of the restrictions people place on their own lives, this is sure to capture readers' hearts." —*Publishers Weekly*

Christie, Agatha

★ The **A** B C murders. Agatha Christie. Dodd, Mead, 1977. 250 p. (Hercule Poirot mysteries, 11)
ISBN 9781579126247
1. Serial murders 2. Murder investigation 3. Murderers 4. Letter writing
5. Senior men 6. Mysteries 7. Mystery classics

A is for Ascher, cudgeled in Andover. B is for Barnard, strangled in Bexhill. C is for Clarke, struck down in Churston. Beside each body is an A.B.C. Railway guide; before each murder Hercule Poirot is notified. In one of Christie's most twisted tales, the meticulous Belgian sleuth must navigate the eerie maze of a serial killer's mind. D is for Doncaster, where the next victim dies... E is for evidence, ingeniously analyzed.

Also published under the title: The alphabet murders.
Later printing published in 1985 as: "The Winterbrook edition."
Originally published in the UK in 1936.

★ **And** then there were none. Agatha Christie. St. Martin's Griffin, 2004. 264 p.
ISBN 9780312330873
1. Murder victims 2. Millionaires 3. Islands 4. Secrets 5. Strangers
6. England 7. Devon, England 8. Mysteries 9. Books to movies
10. Mystery classics 11. Adult books for young adults
LC 2004041165

Ten houseguests, trapped on an isolated island, are the prey of a diabolical killer. A famous nursery rhyme is framed and hung in every room of the mansion: Ten little Indian boys went out to dine; One choked his little self and then there were nine—When they realize that murders are occurring as described in the rhyme, terror mounts. Who has choreographed this dastardly scheme? And who will be left to tell the tale?

Also published as: Ten little Indians.
Book made into a movie called Ten little Indians.
Originally published: New York : Dodd, Mead, 1940.

The **body** in the library: a Miss Marple mystery. Agatha Christie. Black Dog & Leventhal Publishers, 2006. 198 p. (Jane Marple murder mysteries, 4)
ISBN 9781579126261
1. Murder investigation 2. Marple, Jane (Fictitious character) 3. Senior women 4. Women amateur detectives 5. England 6. Mysteries
LC 2006045983

When Colonel and Mrs. Bantry find the corpse of a beautiful girl in their library, they rely upon their good friend Miss Marple to solve the crime.

Originally published: London : Collins, 1942.

Curtain. Agatha Christie. Dodd, Mead, 1975. 238 p. (Hercule Poirot mysteries, 34)
ISBN 9780396071914
1. Murder investigation 2. Murder suspects 3. Belgians in England
4. Senior men 5. Private investigators 6. England 7. Mysteries
8. Mystery classics
LC 75016368

The house guests at Styles seemed perfectly pleasant to Captain Hastings: there was his own daughter Judith, an ornithologist called Norton, dashing Mr Allerton, brittle Miss Cole, Doctor Franklin and his fragile wife Barbara, Nurse Craven, Colonel Luttrell and his wife Daisy, and the charismatic Boyd-Carrington. So Hastings was shocked when Poirot declared that one of them was a five-times murderer. True, the ageing detective was crippled with arthritis, but had his deductive instincts finally deserted him?

Endless night. Agatha Christie. William Morrow & Co, 2011. 239 p.
ISBN 9780062073518
1. Rural life 2. Heirs and heiresses 3. Curses 4. Murder 5. Husband and wife 6. England 7. Mysteries 8. Mystery classics
LC 85004390

After marrying an American heiress and fulfilling his dream of building a home in his favorite area, Michael Rogers and his new wife's lives are plagued by a deadly curse that gypsies have placed on the land.

Originally published: London : Collins Crime Club, 1967.

The **hollow**. Agatha Christie. G. P. Putnam's Sons, 1992. 296 p. (Hercule Poirot mysteries, 22)

ISBN 9780008129583

1. Murder investigation 2. Senior men 3. Private investigators 4. Poisoning 5. Murder suspects 6. Mysteries

A weekend party at the Angkatell's estate, The Hollow, is the perfect prescription for physician John Christow. The celebrated doctor longs for a little R & R and a rendezvous with his mistress, Henrietta. But romantic rivalry complicates the country escape as the doctor dodges both his wife and actress Veronica Cray. Famous crime man Hercule Poirot arrives to find Dr. Christow permanently extricated from his affairs by a revolver at close range.

Also published as: Murder after hours.

Originally published: [London] : Collins, 1946.

Agatha Christie 125th anniversary 1890-2015—Cover.

Mrs. McGinty's dead. Agatha Christie. G. P. Putnam's Sons, 1993. 259 p. (Hercule Poirot mysteries, 25)

ISBN 9780399138232

1. Murder investigation 2. Murder suspects 3. Household employees 4. Poirot, Hercule (Fictitious character) 5. Belgians in England 6. Mysteries 7. Books to movies

LC 92-32590

Poirot pays no attention to the sad case of Mrs. McGinty, an old woman apparently struck dead by her lodger for thirty pounds that she kept under a floorboard. When, however, he is asked by the investigating officer to take another look at the case in order to stop an innocent man going to the gallows, he realizes that things may not be as simple as they first appear to be.

Also published as: Blood will tell.

Book adapted into a 1964 film entitled: Murder most foul.

★ The **murder** at the vicarage. Agatha Christie. Berkley, 1984. 230 p. (Jane Marple murder mysteries, 1)

ISBN 9780425067901

1. Murder investigation 2. Murder suspects 3. Gunshot victims 4. Senior women 5. Women amateur detectives 6. England 7. Mysteries

Miss Jane Marple, spinster sleuth extraordinaire, is introduced in this first mystery to feature her brilliant talents. Here she must use all her intuitive powers to solve the murder of the detested Colonel Protheroe when he is found shot in the local vicar's study.

Originally published: London : Collins Crime Club, 1930.

A **murder** is announced: a Miss Marple mystery. Agatha Christie. Black Dog & Leventhal Publishers, 2006. 288 p. (Jane Marple murder mysteries, 7)

ISBN 9781579126292

1. Senior women 2. Women amateur detectives 3. Gunshot victims 4. Murder investigation 5. Newspaper advertising 6. England 7. Mysteries 8. Books to movies 9. Mystery classics

LC 2006042978

A notice in the Gazette reads: "A murder is announced and will take place on Friday, October 29, at Little Paddocks." The guests arrive, thinking they have come to a mystery party. When death and chaos ensue, the indomitable Miss Marple sorts it out.

Originally published: London: Collins, 1950.

★ The **murder** of Roger Ackroyd: a Hercule Poirot mystery. Agatha Christie. Black Dog & Leventhal, 2006. 276 p. (Hercule Poirot mysteries, 3)

ISBN 9781579126278

1. Suicide 2. Extortion 3. Murder investigation 4. Murder suspects 5. Physicians 6. Mysteries 7. Mystery classics

LC 2006042980

A murder in a small English village leads Hercule Poirot into a strange mystery involving a determined, curious spinster, the local doctor, and a wide range of suspects with possible motives and mysterious relationships.

"Roger Ackroyd, a retired business man, is found dead in his study shortly after the suicide of the woman he was to have married. Suspicion and the police point to Ackroyd's adopted son as the murderer, but the outcome of the story is a complete surprise. As in others of Miss Christie's tales, the mystery is solved by...M. Poirot." —*Booklist*

★ **Murder** on the Orient Express. Agatha Christie. G. P. Putnam's Sons, 1960. 263 p. (Hercule Poirot mysteries, 8)

ISBN 9780062838629

1. Crimes aboard trains 2. Railroad travel 3. Murder investigation 4. Poirot, Hercule (Fictitious character) 5. Belgians in England 6. Mysteries 7. Books to movies 8. Mystery classics

On a three-day journey through the snowbound Balkan hills, Hercule Poirot must weed through an array of international suspects to find the passenger who murdered a gangster on the Orient Express.

Originally published in the U. S. as Murder in the Calais coach.

Originally published: London : Collins, 1934.

The **pale** horse. Agatha Christie. Dodd, Mead, 1985. 259 p.

ISBN 9780396087052

1. Organized crime 2. Priests 3. Murder investigation 4. Murder suspects 5. Murder 6. England 7. Mysteries 8. Books to movies

LC 85004368

Mark Easterbrook investigates the brutal death of Father Gorman, a Catholic priest who had just heard the deathbed confession of longtime town gossip Mrs. Davis. On his body, Father Gorman had a list of names, supposedly related to Mrs. Davis' confession. As Mark delves deep into the mystery, he uncovers a series of startling secrets.

Book inspired 1996 TV movie with Colin Buchanan as Mark Easterbrook.

Three blind mice, and other stories. Agatha Christie. Dodd, Mead, 1985. 250 p. (Jane Marple murder mysteries, 6)

ISBN 9780396087076

1. Criminal investigation 2. Murder investigation 3. Marple, Jane (Fictitious character) 4. Senior women 5. Women amateur detectives 6. Mysteries 7. Short stories

LC 50003535

A blinding snowstorm-and a homicidal maniac-traps a small party of friends in an isolated estate. Out of this deceptively simple setup, Agatha Christie fashioned one of her most ingenious puzzlers, which in turn would provide the basis for The Mousetrap.

Also published under the title: Mousetrap and other stories.

Towards zero. Agatha Christie. Dodd, Mead, 1986. 242 p; (Superintendent Battle mysteries, 3)

ISBN 9780396088721

1. Police 2. Widows 3. Suicide 4. Murder investigation 5. Battle, Superintendent (Fictitious character) 6. Mysteries

LC 86011494

A dashing tennis player named Neville Strange, his current stylish wife, his not-so-stylish ex-wife, plus a distant relative and a few others find their way to a house party. When a murder occurs, Superintendent Battle is nearby and called on to help solve the case. But is the information on hand enough to go by, or go the events leading to the murder begin years in the past? —Publisher's website.

Originally published: London : Collins Crime Club, 1944.

Reprint. Previously published: Philadelphia : Blakiston, 1944.

Christie, Michael

★ **Greenwood**: a novel. Michael Christie. Hogarth, 2020. 528 p.

ISBN 9781984822000

1. Lumber industry and trade 2. Trees 3. Forests 4. Family secrets 5. Family businesses 6. Literary fiction 7. Family sagas 8. Canadian fiction

LC 2019026891

A shining, intricate clockwork of a novel, Greenwood is a rain-soaked and sun-dappled story of the bonds and breaking points of money and love, wood and blood—and the hopeful, impossible task of growing toward the light.

"This superb family saga will satisfy fans of Richard Powers's The Overstory while offering a convincing vision of potential ecological destruction." —*Publishers Weekly*

Originally published: Toronto : McClelland & Stewart, 2019.

Christopher, Andie J.

Not the girl you marry. Andie J. Christopher. Jove, 2019. 320 p.

ISBN 9781984802682

1. Dating (Social customs) 2. Planners 3. Ambition in women 4. Journalists 5. Multiracial women 6. Romantic comedies 7. Contemporary romances

LC 2019001227

LibraryReads Favorites, 2019

To prove to her boss that she's not scared of feelings, Hannah Mayfield decides Jack Nolan is the perfect man to date for a couple of weeks, but, unbeknownst to her, Jack has chosen her for an article called "How to Lose a Girl."

Christy, Bryan

In the company of killers. Bryan Christy. Putnam Pub Group, 2021. 368 p.

ISBN 9780593187920

1. Investigative journalists 2. Spies 3. Revenge 4. Conspiracies 5. Mercenaries 6. Spy fiction 7. Thrillers and suspense

LC 2020046277

An investigative wildlife reporter and secret CIA spy pursues a vengeful opportunity to capture the man responsible for a friend's death by infiltrating the offices of a woman he once loved.

"Fans of both espionage and global crime thrillers will find a gem here: Klay is an introspective, flawed survivor who bends operative stereotypes, and the intersection of corporate greed, media, technology, and crime is chillingly current." —*Booklist*

Chung, Catherine

The **tenth** muse: a novel. Catherine Chung. Ecco Press, 2019. 304 pages

ISBN 9780062574060

1. Women mathematicians 2. Identity (Psychology) 3. Family history 4. Women's role 5. Intellectuals 6. 1960s 7. Historical fiction 8. Mainstream fiction 9. First person narratives

Determined to conquer the Riemann hypothesis in the face of cultural discrimination against women intellectuals, a genius mathematician uncovers a mysterious theorem's unexpected World War II link to her family.

"A powerful and virtuosically researched story about the mysteries of the head and the heart." —*Kirkus*

Chung, Maxine Mei-Fung

The **eighth** girl. Maxine Mei-Fung Chung. William Morrow & Co, 2020. 480 pages

ISBN 9780062931122

1. Dissociative identity disorder 2. Best friends 3. Women photojournalists 4. Psychiatrists 5. City life 6. London, England 7. Multiple perspectives 8. Psychological suspense

A woman with multiple personality disorder finds her other selves becoming assets and vulnerabilities in her effort to rescue her friend, a worker at a London gentlemen's club who has uncovered a dangerous secret.

"Though extremely dark and disturbing, this psychological thriller, told in the voice of multiple unreliable narrators, is filled with surprises until the end, and is a fresh take on the suspense genre." —*Booklist*

Church, James

Bamboo and blood: an Inspector O novel. James Church. Minotaur Books, 2008. 304 p. (Inspector O novels, 3)

ISBN 9780312372910

1. International intrigue 2. Crimes against women 3. Political corruption 4. Intercontinental ballistic missiles 5. Conspiracies 6. North Korea 7. Pakistan 8. Mysteries 9. Police procedurals

LC 2008030116

In a late 1990s North Korea, a younger Inspector O is working Pyongyang as the country's nuclear missile program begins to escalate and as the wife of a North Korean diplomat turns up dead in Pakistan under suspicious circumstances, but as Inspector O investigates, he discovers that the woman's death could lead to a larger conspiracy.

★ A **corpse** in the Koryo. James Church. Thomas Dunne Books, 2006. 288 p. (Inspector O novels, 1)

ISBN 9780312352080

1. Police 2. Political corruption 3. Spies 4. Detectives 5. Totalitarianism 6. North Korea 7. Asia 8. Mysteries 9. Police procedurals

LC 2006045471

Library Journal Best Books, 2006

A rebellious survivor of North Korea's brutal totalitarian regime, Inspector O, a state security officer, risks his life and career to solve a case that begins innocuously enough when he is asked to photograph a certain vehicle.

A **drop** of Chinese blood. James Church. Minotaur, 2012. 304 p. (Inspector O novels, 5; Major Bing novels, 1)

ISBN 9780312550639

1. Missing persons 2. International intrigue 3. Intelligence officers 4. Uncle and nephew 5. China 6. North Korea 7. Mysteries 8. Police procedurals 9. First person narratives

When clues link a beautiful woman's disappearance to a sensitive mission to deliver an agent across the North Korean border, Bing, a director of state security in a volatile region of China, receives reluctant help from his uncle, Inspector O, to navigate an increasingly complex investigation.

Hidden moon: an Inspector O novel. James Church. Thomas Dunne Books/St. Martin's Minotaur, 2007. 288 p. (Inspector O novels, 2)

ISBN 9780312352097

1. Police 2. Bank robberies 3. Secrecy in government 4. International intrigue 5. Assassination 6. North Korea 7. Asia 8. Mysteries 9. Police procedurals

Inspector O returns from a mission abroad, only to find himself investigating a bank robbery, the first ever in Pyongyang, in a case that is complicated by a host of suspects, all with their own agendas, and high-level political intrigue.

Ciotta, Beth

Her sky cowboy. Beth Ciotta. Signet Eclipse, 2012. 352 p. (Glorious victorious Darcys, 1)
ISBN 9780451238474
1. Airships 2. Interpersonal attraction 3. Reputation 4. Women mechanics 5. Cowboys 6. England 7. 19th century 8. Steampunk
LC 2007024593
After her father dies, Amelia Darcy, to save the family reputation and fortune, must discover an invention of historical importance in honor of Queen Victoria's Golden Jubilee—a quest that takes a romantic turn when her kitecycle crashes into the airship of a scandalous dime novel hero.

Cipri, Nino

Defekt. Nino Cipri. St Martins Press, 2021. 144 pages (Finna novels (Nino Cipri), 2)
ISBN 9781250787491
1. Clerks (Retail industry and trade) 2. Interdimensional travel 3. Parallel universes 4. Corporate greed 5. Furniture industry and trade 6. Science fiction
"Expanding on the universe of their previous novella, Cipri continues to mix queer characters and anti-capitalist themes with energetic, bouncy prose." —*Booklist*

Cisneros, Sandra

★ The **house** on Mango Street. Sandra Cisneros. Alfred A. Knopf, 1984. 134 p.
ISBN 9780679433354
1. Home (Concept) 2. Mexican American girls 3. Growing up 4. Friendship 5. Family relationships 6. Chicago, Illinois 7. Illinois 8. Coming-of-age stories 9. Novels in verse 10. Classics
LC 93043564
For Esperanza, a young girl growing up in the Hispanic quarter of Chicago, life is an endless landscape of concrete and run-down tenements, and she tries to rise above the hopelessness.
"This is a composite of evocative snapshots that manages to passionately recreate the milieu of the poor quarters of Chicago." —*Commonwealth*
Originally published, in somewhat different form, by Arte Publico Press in 1984. Reprinted by Vintage Books, a division of Random House, Inc, in 1991—Title page verso.

Martita, I remember you: Martita, te recuerdo. Sandra Cisneros; translated by Liliana Valenzuela. Vintage Books, 2021. 120 p.
ISBN 9780593313664
1. Letter writing 2. Memories 3. Mexican-American women 4. Racism 5. Friendship 6. Paris, France 7. France 8. Literary fiction 9. Relationship fiction 10. Bilingual materials
LC 2021005550
When she unearths a letter in a closet, Corina finds the memories of her days spent in Paris rushing back as she remembers her intense friendships with two women with whom she fell out of touch and out of mind.
"Cisneros' intricately multidimensional and beautifully enveloping novella is presented in both English and Spanish." —*Booklist*
This is a dual-language edition of 'Martita, I Remember You'. Written in English, it was translated into Spanish as 'Martita, te recuerdo'.

Clancy, Tom

Clear and present danger. Tom Clancy. G. P. Putnam's Sons, 1989. 656 p; (Jack Ryan and John Clark novels, 6)
ISBN 9780399134401
1. Drug smugglers 2. Assassination 3. Intelligence service 4. Ambassadors 5. Drug lords 6. United States 7. Spy fiction 8. Techno-thrillers 9. Thrillers and suspense
LC 89010287
The assassinations of the U.S. ambassador and the visiting head of the F.B.I. by Colombian drug lords trigger a mysterious covert response and an investigation of U.S. and Colombian actions by Jack Ryan.
"Superior even to his descriptions of tools and techniques, however, is Clancy's analysis of the legal and moral problems of operating in a twilight zone, where the rules are ambiguous and an open society makes secrecy impossible." —*Publishers Weekly*

★ The **hunt** for Red October. Tom Clancy. Naval Institute Press, 1984. 387 p; (Jack Ryan and John Clark novels, 4)
ISBN 9780870212857
1. Submarines, Soviet 2. Nuclear submarines 3. Spies 4. Ryan, Jack, Sr. (Fictitious character) 5. Elite operatives 6. Atlantic Ocean 7. Thrillers and suspense 8. Techno-thrillers 9. Sea stories
LC 84016569
The Soviets' new ballistic-missile submarine is attempting to defect to the United States, but the Soviet Atlantic fleet has been ordered to find and destroy her at all costs. Can Red October reach the U.S. safely?
"Based on a true incident—the attempted defection of a Soviet destroyer in 1975—the plot concerns the defection of the Red October, a Soviet submarine carrying 26 Seahawk missiles able to destroy 200 cities. Russia's fleet is ordered to find and destroy the sub; the U.S. Navy wants to find it and get it to an American port. An 18-day, 4,000-mile hunt across the Atlantic ensues." —*Booklist*

Patriot games. Tom Clancy. G. P. Putnam's Sons, 1987. 540 p; (Jack Ryan and John Clark novels, 2)
ISBN 9780399132414
1. Diana 2. Terrorism 3. Military tactics 4. International intrigue 5. Revenge in men 6. Attempted assassination 7. Thrillers and suspense 8. Techno-thrillers 9. Books to movies
LC 87006910
While vacationing in London, CIA analyst Jack Ryan saves the Prince and Princess of Wales from a terrorist attack and gains the gratitude of a nation and the enmity of its most dangerous men.
"On a visit with his wife and daughter in London, Ryan stumbles onto an attempt by a new Irish revolutionary group to kidnap the Prince and Princess of Wales and their eldest son. Using his Marine Corps training, Ryan saves the royals (which leads to several visits between the Ryans and the residents of Buckingham Palace), but Ryan becomes the target of the surviving terrorists." —*Publishers Weekly*

Clare, Alys

The **woman** who spoke to spirits. Alys Clare. Severn House, 2019. 234 pages (World's End Bureau, 1)
ISBN 9780727888686
1. Women private investigators 2. Women psychics 3. Seances 4. Threat (Psychology) 5. Private investigators 6. Great Britain 7. London, England 8. Victorian era (1837-1901) 9. 1880s 10. Victorian mysteries 11. Historical mysteries 12. Adult books for young adults
London, 1880. When accounts clerk Ernest Stibbins approaches the World's End investigation bureau with wild claims that his wife Albertina has been warned by her spirit guides that someone is out to harm her, the bureau's owner Lily Raynor and her new employee Felix Wilbraham are initially sceptical. How are the two private enquiry agents supposed to in-

vestigate threats from beyond the grave? But after she attends a seance at the Stibbins family home, Lily comes to realize that Albertina is in terrible danger. And very soon so too is Lily herself.

"A clever plot, two engaging sleuths, plenty of period ambience, and a satisfying ending make this a fine choice for all mystery collections." —*Booklist*

Clark, Cherae
★ The **unbroken**. C. L. Clark. Orbit, 2021. 464 p. (Magic of the lost, 1)

ISBN 9780316542753

1. Imaginary empires 2. Women warriors 3. Draft 4. Orphans 5. Princesses 6. Military fantasy 7. African American fiction

In an epic fantasy unlike any other, two women clash in a world full of rebellion, espionage, and military might on the far outreaches of a crumbling desert empire. Touraine is a soldier. Stolen as a child and raised to kill and die for the empire, her only loyalty is to her fellow conscripts. But now, her company has been sent back to her homeland to stop a rebellion, and the ties of blood may be stronger than she thought. Luca needs a turncoat. Someone desperate enough to tiptoe the bayonet's edge between treason and orders. Someone who can sway the rebels toward peace, while Luca focuses on what really matters: getting her uncle off her throne. Through assassinations and massacres, in bedrooms and war rooms, Touraine and Luca will haggle over the price of a nation. But some things aren't for sale.

"A queernorm world dealing with racism, magic, and head-versus-heart decisions creates rich settings and characters.... This strong debut is filled with exciting action and worldbuilding, intriguing characters dealing with themes of colonization, military conscription and indoctrination, and an explosion of feelings." —*Library Journal*

Clark, Clare
In the full light of the sun. Clare Clark. Houghton Mifflin Harcourt, 2019. 400 pages

ISBN 9780544147577

1. Art forgeries 2. Art dealers 3. City life 4. Nazism 5. Art 6. Berlin, Germany 7. Between the Wars (1918-1939) 8. Historical fiction
LC 2019001730

Traces the fortunes of three disparate Berliners who against a backdrop of rising Nazi power are caught up in an art scandal involving newly discovered van Goghs.

Clark, Georgia
The **bucket** list. Georgia Clark. Emily Bestler Books/Atria, 2018. 343 p.

ISBN 9781501173028

1. Young women 2. Body image 3. Breast cancer — Genetic aspects 4. Female friendship 5. Self-fulfillment in women 6. Chick lit
LC 2017053609

A young woman with a bustling life discovers she carries the gene for breast cancer and decides to tick off items on a "boob bucket list" before a double mastectomy.

Clark, Julie
Last flight. Julie Clark. Sourcebooks Landmark, 2020. 288 p.
ISBN 9781728215723

1. Abused women 2. New identities 3. Airplane accidents 4. Partner abuse 5. Abusive men 6. United States 7. Thrillers and suspense
LC 2019038807

LibraryReads Favorites, 2020

Working for months on a plan to escape her secretly violent husband, Claire impulsively swaps airline tickets with a stranger also on the run before a fateful accident compels her to assume the other's identity.

"Clark (The Ones We Choose) is an exceptional writer who has crafted a tale about disappearing in an age when technology makes it almost impossible. Highly recommended for fans of thrillers, mysteries, and crime fiction." —*Library Journal*

Clark, Marcia
Final judgment. Marcia Clark. Thomas & Mercer, 2020. 416 pages (Samantha Brinkman novels, 4)

ISBN 9781542091176

1. Couples 2. Women lawyers 3. Murder suspects 4. Businesspeople 5. Secrets 6. Los Angeles, California 7. California 8. Legal thrillers

Breaking her personal rule about avoiding relationships when she falls for an ambitious entrepreneur, defense attorney Samantha Brinkman is challenged to prove her lover's innocence of murder when his alibi and past are thrown into question.

Clark, Martin
The **substitution** order. By Martin Clark. Alfred A. Knopf, 2019. 352 pages

ISBN 9780525656326

1. Law 2. Disbarred lawyers 3. Innocence (Law) 4. Swindlers and swindling 5. Life change events 6. Virginia 7. Southern states 8. Legal thrillers 9. First person narratives
LC 2019003946

A disbarred attorney takes a job in a run-down sandwich shop before an offer by a gang of con artists challenges the extent of his legal savvy.

Clark, Mary Higgins
Death wears a beauty mask and other stories. Mary Higgins Clark. Simon & Schuster, 2015. 224 p.

ISBN 9781501110993

1. Fashion 2. Threat (Psychology) 3. Suspicion 4. Murder 5. New York City 6. 1970s 7. Mysteries 8. Thrillers and suspense 9. Bruno, Giordano

A collection of short stories from the #1 New York Times bestselling {34Queen of Suspense{34 Mary Higgins Clark, including the never-before-published novella Death Wears a Beauty Mask.

"This collection nicely illustrates Clark's range and superlative storytelling talent." —*Publishers Weekly*

★ **Kiss** the girls and make them cry. Mary Higgins Clark. Simon & Schuster, 2019. 384 p.

ISBN 9781501171703

1. Women journalists 2. Sexual violence victims 3. Violence in men 4. Rich men 5. Sex crimes 6. Thrillers and suspense

Navigating traumatic memories of an assault in college, a journalist researching the #MeToo movement discovers that her attacker is on the cusp of a merger that will render him a billionaire.

The **melody** lingers on. Mary Higgins Clark. Simon & Schuster, 2015. 320 p.

ISBN 9781476749112

1. Rich families 2. Family secrets 3. Cold cases (Criminal investigation) 4. Staged deaths 5. Suspicion 6. Thrillers and suspense

When interior designer Lane Harmon assists in redecorating the home of the wife of missing disgraced financier Parker Bennett, she finds herself drawn to Bennett's family without realizing that her life is in jeopardy.

Clark, P. Djeli

The black god's drums. P. Djeli Clark. Tor/Forge, 2018. 112 p.
ISBN 9781250294715
1. Pirates 2. Airships 3. Civil war 4. Weapons 5. Spirits 6. New Orleans, Louisiana 7. 1870s 8. Steampunk 9. Alternate histories 10. Adult books for young adults
Alex Award, 2019; Loan Stars Favourites, 2018
In an alternate New Orleans caught in the tangle of the American Civil War, the wall-scaling girl named Creeper yearns to escape the streets for the air—in particular, by earning a spot on-board the airship Midnight Robber. Creeper plans to earn the captain's trust with information she discovers about a Haitian scientist and a mysterious weapon he calls The Black God's Drums.

Ring shout. P. Djeli Clark. Tor.com, 2020. 185 pages
ISBN 9781250767028
1. White supremacists 2. Monsters 3. African Americans 4. Manners and customs 5. Psychic ability 6. Georgia 7. 1920s 8. Historical horror 9. First person narratives
LibraryReads Favorites, 2020; Finalist for the Hurston/Wright Legacy Awards for Fiction, 2021; RUSA Reading List Short List, 2021
Follows a foul-mouthed sharpshooter and a Harlem Hellfighter as they fight a supernatural Ku Klux Klan in Macon, Georgia in the early 20th century.
"Readers will be both captivated and entertained by this fast-paced alternate history, which doubles as a meditation on the all-consuming power of hate and violence." —*Publishers Weekly*

Clark, Tracy P.

Runner. Tracy Clark. Kensington Publishing, 2021. 352 p. (Chicago mysteries (Tracy Clark), 4)
ISBN 9781496732019
1. Women private investigators 2. African American women 3. Runaway teenagers 4. Secrets 5. Mothers 6. Chicago, Illinois 7. Mysteries 8. African American fiction
"A potent mix of empathy and rage fuels Sue Grafton Award-winner Clark's exceptional fourth Chicago mystery.... Those who like their crime novels with a social conscience will be amply rewarded." —*Publishers Weekly*

What you don't see. Tracy Clark. Kensington Publishing, 2020. 352 p. (Chicago mysteries (Tracy Clark), 3)
ISBN 9781496714930
1. Women private investigators 2. African American women 3. Murder investigation 4. Women periodical editors 5. Women celebrities 6. Chicago, Illinois 7. Mysteries 8. African American fiction
When a celebrity stalking turns deadly and lands her policeman friend in the hospital, private investigator Cass Raines must find and bring the attacker to justice.
A gripping relationship-based procedural that drags you in and spits you out wan but satisfied. KIrkus

Clark, Wahida

Blood, sweat and payback. Wahida Clark. Simon & Schuster, 2014. 320 p. (Payback novels, 4)
ISBN 9781936399505
1. Drug traffic 2. Street life 3. Options, alternatives, choices 4. African American women — Friendship 5. African Americans 6. Detroit, Michigan 7. Urban fiction 8. African American fiction
LC 2013957300

The love triangle among Shan, Nick, and Briggen escalates in the wake of Shan's transfer back into Redbone; while Dark's efforts to take over Detroit are threatened by Joy's possession of The List.

Honor thy thug. Wahida Clark. Cash Money Content, 2013. 304 p. (Thug novels, 6)
ISBN 9781936399390
1. Marital conflict 2. Sexuality 3. Drugs 4. Inner city 5. City life 6. African American fiction 7. Urban fiction
Street Lit Book Award Medal: Adult Fiction, 2014
Four friends try to salvage their shattered relationship in the wake of murder, betrayal, and the machinations of a sophisticated and deadly Chinese crime organization.

Justify my thug: a novel. Wahida Clark. Cash Money Content, 2011. 273 p; (Thug novels, 5)
ISBN 9781451617092
1. Marital conflict 2. Sexuality 3. Drugs 4. Inner city 5. City life 6. African American fiction 7. Urban fiction
LC Bl2011010649
In the latest novel of Clark's Thug series, Tasha and Trae try to overcome their troubles and make their marriage work. Meanwhile, Jaz is facing drama of her own.
Includes discussion questions.

Payback ain't enough. Wahida Clark. Cash Money Content, 2012. 336 p. (Payback novels, 3)
ISBN 9781936399116
1. Drug traffic 2. Street life 3. Options, alternatives, choices 4. African American women — Friendship 5. African Americans 6. Detroit, Michigan 7. Urban fiction 8. African American fiction
Returns to the hip-hop scene of "Payback with Ya Life," where sexy, dangerous men and fashion-savvy, seductive women navigate psychologically complex games of power and intrigue.

★ **Payback** is a mutha. Wahida Clark. Dafina, 2006. 227 p. (Payback novels, 1)
ISBN 9780758212535
1. African American women — Friendship 2. Swindlers and swindling 3. Betrayal 4. Street life 5. Inner city 6. Urban fiction 7. African American fiction
Using sex to get cars, expensive clothes, and anything else she desires, Brianna, a spoiled and selfish hustler, must make a tough decision when one of her schemes goes too far and her best friend Shan is caught in the crossfire.
Sequel: Payback with ya life

Payback with ya life. Wahida Clark. Grand Central Pub, 2008. 336 p. (Payback novels, 2)
ISBN 9780446178082
1. Drug traffic 2. Determination in men 3. Options, alternatives, choices 4. Pregnant women 5. African American women — Friendship 6. Detroit, Michigan 7. Urban fiction 8. African American fiction
LC 2007033395
A sequel to Payback Is a Mutha finds a pregnant Shan relocating to Detroit in the aftermath of her best friend's suicide, struggling against a revenge-minded adversary targeting her brother, and witnessing turf wars affecting her brother's efforts to reclaim his position at the top of the drug game.
Sequel to: Payback is a mutha.

Thug lovin'. Wahida Clark. Grand Central Pub, 2009. 352 p. (Thug novels, 4)
ISBN 9780446178099

1. Temptation 2. Drugs 3. Moving to a new state 4. Nightclub owners 5. African American women 6. California 7. New York City 8. African American fiction 9. Urban fiction

LC 2008051427

Library Journal Best Books, 2009

Having relocated to sunny Los Angeles after the events of Thug Matrimony, Tasha and Trae manage a nightclub together and find their relationship further tested by a series of models, shady lawyers, and the temptations of big money.

Thug matrimony. Wahida Clark. Dafina Books, 2007. Vii, 277 p; (Thug novels, 3)

ISBN 9780758212559

1. Weddings 2. Unwanted guests 3. African American women lawyers 4. Man-woman relationships 5. African American women 6. New York City 7. African American fiction 8. Urban fiction

LC Bl2007012913

When an unwanted guest from her soon-to-be husband's past crashes her wedding, Angel, finally finding Mr. Right in Kaylin, a former drug dealer turned record producer, realizes that she might never make it to the altar.

Thugs. Wahida Clark. Lightning Source Inc, 2019. 260 p. (Thug novels, 7)

ISBN 9781947732445

1. Marital conflict 2. Sexual attraction 3. Drugs 4. Inner city 5. City life 6. African American fiction 7. Urban fiction

Trying to survive the 'hood, friends Angel, Jaz, and Kyra find themselves unable to leave the lying, cheating, vicious, drug-dealing men that they love, becoming trapped in a world of jealousy, turf wars, revenge, sex, and violence.

★ **Thugs** and the women who love them. Wahida Clark. Black Print Pub, 2004. 210 p; (Thug novels, 1)

ISBN 9780972277112

1. Bell, Vanessa 2. Gangsters 3. Jealousy 4. African American women 5. Man-woman relationships 6. Pennsylvania 7. African American fiction 8. Urban fiction

Trying to survive the 'hood, friends Angel, Jaz, and Kyra find themselves unable to leave the lying, cheating, vicious, drug-dealing men that they love, becoming trapped in a world of jealousy, turf wars, revenge, sex, and violence.

Clarke, Arthur C.

★ **2001**: a space odyssey. Arthur C. Clarke. New American Library, 1968. 221 p. (Space Odyssey series, 1)

ISBN 9780451457998

1. Human/computer interaction 2. Artificial intelligence 3. Space exploration 4. Space vehicles 5. Astronauts 6. Saturn (Planet) 7. Moon 8. 21st century 9. Books to movies 10. Hard science fiction 11. Science fiction classics

LC 68029754

Two astronauts find their journey into space and their very lives jeopardized by the jealousy of an extraordinary computer named Hal.

"By standing the universe on its head, the author makes us see the ordinary universe in a different light.... [This novel becomes] a complex allegory about the history of the world." —*The New Yorker*

Sequel: 2010: odyssey two.

Based on a screenplay by Stanley Kubrick and Arthur C. Clarke.

★ **Childhood's** end. Arthur C. Clarke. Del Rey Impact, 2001. X, 240 p. : Portrait

ISBN 9780345444059

1. Aliens (Non-humanoid) 2. Evolution 3. Children 4. Freedom 5. Space vehicles 6. Hard science fiction 7. Science fiction classics 8. Science fiction

The Overlords appeared suddenly over every city—intellectually, technologically, and militarily superior to humankind. Benevolent, they made few demands: unify earth, eliminate poverty, and end war. With little rebellion, humankind agreed, and a golden age began. But at what cost? With the advent of peace, man ceases to strive for creative greatness, and a malaise settles over the human race....

In 2015, Childhood's End was adapted into a Syfy Channel TV miniseries of the same name.

Originally published: New York : Harcourt, Brace & World, 1953.

★ The **collected** stories of Arthur C. Clarke. Arthur C. Clarke. Tor, 2000. 966 p.

ISBN 9780312878214

1. Alien artifacts 2. Anthologies 3. Science fiction 4. Short stories

Introduces readers to the author's shorter works, spanning his entire writing career, including "The Nine Billion Names of God," "Nemesis," "The Sentinel," and "The Songs of Distant Earth."

"Although most of these stories date from between 1946 and 1970, seven earlier tales, rescued from what would now be called fanzines, extend coverage back to 1937, and a few snippets stretch it toward the present. At least two dozen stories bear titles that are household words among sf readers.... The stories demonstrate Clarke's dazzling and unique combination of command of the language, scientific and other kinds of erudition, and inimitable wit." —*Booklist*

Rendezvous with Rama. Arthur C. Clarke. Harcourt Brace Jovanovich, 1973. 243 p. (Rama series, 1)

ISBN 9780151768356

1. Space vehicles 2. Astronauts 3. Space exploration 4. Rama (Imaginary space vehicle) 5. Aerospace technology 6. 22nd century 7. Hard science fiction 8. Science fiction classics 9. Science fiction

LC 73003497

BSFA Award for Best Novel, 1973; Hugo Award for Best Novel, 1974; John W. Campbell Memorial Award for Best Science Fiction Novel, 1974; Locus Award for Best Science Fiction Novel, 1974; Nebula Award for Best Novel, 1973

During the twenty-second century, a space probe's investigation of a mysterious, cylindrical asteroid brings man into contact with an extra-galactic civilization.

"This work contains flights of prose where the language fairly purrs. And here too one finds the questioning and probing of man and his place in the cosmos that marks good fiction and good science fiction." —*Library Journal*

Sequel: Rama II.

Clarke, Brock

An **arsonist's** guide to writers' homes in New England: a novel. By Brock Clarke. Algonquin Books Of Chapel Hill, 2007. 320 p.

ISBN 9781565125513

1. Dickinson, Emily 2. Teenage arsonists 3. Accidental death 4. Former convicts 5. Authors, American — Homes and haunts 6. Arsonists 7. New England 8. Black humor

LC 2006100732

ALA Notable Book, 2008

Sam Pulsifer is determined to put his past behind him after serving a prison term for torching an American literary landmark and killing two people in the blaze, but when the homes of notable American writers begin to go up in smoke, his history makes him the prime suspect.

"This straight-faced, postmodern comedy scorches all things literary, from those moldy author museums to the excruciating question-and-answer sessions that follow public readings. There are no survivors here: women's book clubs, literary critics, Harry Potter fans, bookstores, English professors, memoir writers, librarians, Jane Smiley, even the author himself—they're all singed under Clarke's crisp wit." —*Washington Post Book World.*

Clarke, Diana

Thin girls. Diana Clarke. HarperCollins, 2020. 352 p.
ISBN 9780062986689
1. Twins 2. Dieting 3. Self-perception 4. Sisters 5. Cults 6. Literary fiction 7. New Zealand fiction

Twins Rose and Lily Winters, close as the bond implies, battle insecurities and weight issues, which leads them both to extremes, endangering both of their lives, especially when Lily joins a cult diet group led by a social media faux feminist.

"This page-turner makes for an illuminating, ultimately hopeful look at the constant struggle women face regarding their body image." —*Publishers Weekly*

Clarke, Maxine Beneba

★ **Foreign** soil. Maxine Beneba-Clarke. Hachette Australia, 2014. 267 pages : Illustration
ISBN 9780733632426
1. Race relations 2. Refugees 3. Racism 4. Asylum, Right of 5. Immigration prisons 6. Melbourne, Victoria 7. Sydney, New South Wales 8. Short stories 9. Australian fiction
LC 2013456466
Australian Book Industry Awards, Literary Fiction Book of the Year, 2015; Shortlisted for the Stella Prize, 2015

This book is a collection of stories : a desperate asylum seeker is pacing the hallways of Sydney's notorious Villawood detention centre, a seven-year-old Sudanese boy has found solace in a patchwork bike, an enraged black militant is on the warpath through the rebel squats of 1960s Brixton, a Mississippi housewife decides to make the ultimate sacrifice to save her son from small-town ignorance, a young woman leaves rural Jamaica in search of her destiny, and a Sydney schoolgirl loses her way.

"Australian writer and poet Clarkes powerful debut collection of award-winning short stories addresses oppressed, downtrodden, and mistreated outsiders of society." —*Booklist*
First published in Australia and New Zealand in 2014.

Clarke, Susanna

★ **Jonathan** Strange & Mr. Norrell. Susanna Clarke. Bloomsbury, 2004. 800 p.
ISBN 9781582344164
1. Fairies 2. Magicians 3. Recluses 4. Men recluses 5. Aristocracy 6. England 7. London, England 8. Georgian era (1714-1837) 9. 19th century 10. Historical fantasy 11. Kosinski, Jerzy 12. Multiple perspectives 13. Adult books for young adults
LC 2004002402
Book Sense Book of the Year Adult Fiction, 2005; Booklist Editors' Choice, 2004; Hugo Award for Best Novel, 2005; Library Journal Best Books, 2004; Locus Award for First Novel, 2005; Mythopoeic Award for Adult Literature, 2005; New York Times Notable Book, 2004; World Fantasy Award, 2005

In nineteenth-century England, all is going well for rich, reclusive Mr Norrell, who has regained some of the power of England's magicians from the past, until a rival magician, Jonathan Strange, appears and becomes Mr Norrell's pupil.

"Clarke's ability to construct a fully imagined world—much of it explained in long, witty footnotes—is impressive." —*The New Yorker*
Adapted into a BBC TV series in 2015.

★ **Piranesi**. Susanna Clarke. Bloomsbury Publishing, 2020. 160 p.
ISBN 9781635575637
1. Labyrinths 2. Knowledge 3. Diary writing 4. Personal conduct 5. Architecture 6. Fantasy fiction 7. Epistolary novels 8. Literary fiction
LC 2020009930
ALA Notable Book, 2021; LibraryReads Favorites, 2020; Loan Stars Favourites, 2020; Women's Prize for Fiction, 2021

Living in a labyrinthine house of endless corridors, flooded staircases and thousands of statues, Piranesi assists the dreamlike dwelling's only other resident throughout a mysterious research project before evidence emerges of an astonishing alternate world.

"With great subtlety, Clarke gradually elaborates an explanatory backstory to her tale's events and reveals sinister occult machinations that build to a crescendo of genuine horror." —*Publishers Weekly*

Clavell, James

Shogun. James Clavell. Delacorte Press, 1975. 802 p. (Asian saga, 1)
ISBN 9780689105654
1. Warlords 2. Samurai 3. Honor 4. British in Japan 5. Pilots 6. Japan 7. Historical fiction 8. Books to TV
LC 82019788
A bold English adventurer; an invincible Japanese warlord; a beautiful woman torn between two ways of life, two ways of love—all brought together in an extraordinary saga of a time and a place aflame with conflict, passion, ambition, lust, and the struggle for power.

"Clavell creates a world: people, customs, settings, needs and desires all become so enveloping that you forget who and where you are. 'Shogun' is history infused with fantasy. It strives for epic dimension and occasionally it approaches that elevated state. It's irresistible, maybe unforgettable." —*New York Times Book Review*
Some copies include endpaper maps.

Clayborn, Kate

Love lettering. Kate Clayborn. Kensington Books, 2019. 307 p.
ISBN 9781496725172
1. Women designers 2. Women business owners 3. Lettering 4. Signs and symbols 5. Pattern perception 6. New York City 7. Romantic comedies
LC 2019287240
RUSA Reading List Short List, 2021

When a word of warning she had hidden in a wedding program one year earlier leads Reid Sutherland back into her life, skilled hand letterer Meg Mackworth finds both her heart and business in danger unless she can read the messages he is sending her before it's too late.

"Reid and Meg are wonderfully unique, and their romance carves a sweet, winding, and sexy path to self-acceptance and mutual affirmation." —*Kirkus*

Clayton, Meg Waite

The **last** train to London. Meg Waite Clayton. Harper, 2019. 464 pages
ISBN 9780062946935
1. Wijsmuller-Meijer, Truus 2. Jewish teenagers 3. Christian women 4. Nazis 5. Anschluss movement, 1918-1938 6. Kindertransports (Rescue operations) 7. Austria 8. Vienna, Austria 9. Between the Wars (1918-1939) 10. 1930s 11. Historical fiction

A tale inspired by the Kindertransports of World War II finds a Jewish teen's life shattered by the Nazi takeover before he joins a member of the Dutch resistance in a life-risking effort to escape Germany.

Cleage, Pearl

Some things I never thought I'd do. Pearl Cleage. One World/Ballantine Books, 2003. 256 p.
ISBN 9780345456069
1. Recovering women drug abusers 2. Jilted brides 3. Aunt and niece 4. African-American motivational speakers 5. African American women 6. Atlanta, Georgia 7. Washington, D.C. 8. Contemporary romances 9. African American fiction
LC 2003051752
Taking a job in Atlanta to save the family home, Regina Burns finds herself unable to forgive her new employer for ruining her wedding plans years earlier and finds herself falling for a handsome stranger whom her aunt predicted she would meet.
Sequel: Baby Brother's Blues.

What looks like crazy on an ordinary day: a novel. Pearl Cleage. Avon Books, 1997. 244 p.
ISBN 9780380975846
1. African American women with HIV 2. Children of women cocaine addicts 3. Hairdressers 4. Homecomings 5. African American women 6. Michigan 7. Idlewild, Michigan 8. 1990s 9. Relationship fiction 10. African American fiction 11. Psychological fiction
LC 97-17708
HIV-positive Ava Johnson returns to the Michigan town where she grew up, and finds that what she thought might be the end is, in fact, a beginning.
"Despite the early bad news, Cleage's funny, irreverent, and hopeful novel is stunningly real and evocative of the conditions behind the high unemployment, aimlessness, and drug culture that permeate the urban landscape and have invaded smaller towns as well." —*Booklist*
Sequel: I Wish I Had a Red Dress

Cleary, Jon

The **sundowners**. Jon Cleary. Collins, 1979. 320 p.
ISBN 9780002217798
1. Fourteen-year-olds 2. Families 3. Drifters 4. Growing up 5. Self-reliance 6. Australia 7. 1920s 8. Domestic fiction 9. Coming-of-age stories 10. Roosevelt, Eleanor
The epic tale of the outback Australian family, the Carmodys. The Carmodys live in the outback, travelling around, shearing, droving, making ends meet and looking for that one special place they can settle down in. Along the way, Paddy, his wife Ida, and their son, Sean, meet some of the most memorable characters in fiction. The Sundowners is a novel filled with kindness and happiness, as well as toughness and danger and is set against the magnificent backdrop of the wild, harsh and beautiful Australian landscape.
Originally published: New York : Scribner's, 1952.

Cleave, Chris

Gold. Chris Cleave. Simon & Schuster, 2012. 336 p.
ISBN 9781451672725
1. Female friendship 2. Olympic games 3. Leukemia 4. Children with cancer 5. Women bicyclists 6. Great Britain 7. Psychological fiction
LC 2011043699
Sharing a close friendship and rivalry throughout their Elite training, world-class athletes Zoe and Kate find the limits of their physical and emotional realities tested on the eve of London 2012, where they consider difficult sacrifices and weigh their senses of mortality.
Originally published in Great Britain in 2012 by Hodder & Stoughton—Title page verso.

Cleave, Paul

A **killer** harvest: a thriller. Paul Cleave. Atria Books, 2017. 386 p.
ISBN 9781501153013
1. Donation of organs, tissues, etc. 2. Fathers and sons 3. Police 4. Eye 5. Secrets 6. Thrillers and suspense 7. New Zealand fiction
LC 2016037791
A blind teen receives a corneal donation that restores his sight but gives him an eerie capacity to experience the memories of their previous owner, his homicide detective father.
"Starting with a macabre setup, Cleave keeps upping the stakes till any scrap of plausibility is left far behind and only an increasingly effective series of hair-raising thrills remains." —*Kirkus*

Trust no one: a thriller. Paul Cleave. Atria Books, 2015. 336 p.
ISBN 9781476779171
1. Authors 2. People with Alzheimer's disease 3. Murder 4. Memory 5. Senior men 6. New Zealand 7. Psychological suspense 8. New Zealand fiction
Ngaio Marsh Award for Best Crime Novel, 2016
Jerry Grey is known to most of the world by his crime writing pseudonym, Henry Cutter—a name that has been keeping readers at the edge of their seats for more than a decade. His books tell stories of brutal murders and of victims finding the darkest forms of justice. Recently diagnosed with early onset Alzheimer's at the age of forty-nine, Jerry's crime writing days are coming to an end. As his dementia begins to break down the wall between his life and the lives of the characters he has created, Jerry confesses his worst secret: The stories are real.
First published in New Zealand in 2015 by Upstart Press.

Cleeton, Chanel

The **most** beautiful girl in Cuba. Chanel Cleeton. Berkley, 2021. 320 p.
ISBN 9780593098875
1. Cossio y Cisneros, Evangelina 2. Women journalists 3. Women couriers 4. Political intrigue 5. Revolutionaries 6. Women prisoners 7. New York City 8. Havana, Cuba 9. Gilded Age (1865-1898) 10. Historical fiction
LC 2020046449
Loan Stars Favourites, 2021
At the end of the 19th century, reporter Grace Harrington and a courier secretly working for Cuban revolutionaries in Havana free 'The Most Beautiful Girl in Cuba' who has been unjustly imprisoned—a mission that forces them all to fight for their freedom as war looms on the horizon.
"Cleeton skillfully brings off the three strong women's heartbreaking stories with intriguing twists and turns and a delightful finale. With impeccable research and perfect pacing, Cleeton makes the most of her subject." —*Publishers Weekly*

Next year in Havana. Chanel Cleeton. Berkley, 2018. 382 pages
ISBN 9780399586682
1. Cuban American women 2. Family secrets 3. Communist countries 4. Man-woman relationships 5. Revolutionaries 6. Miami, Florida 7. Havana, Cuba 8. 1950s 9. Historical fiction 10. Parallel narratives 11. Love stories
LC 2017027806
A freelance writer returns to her grandmother's homeland to fulfill her last wish to have her ashes scattered in Havana and discovers her fam-

ly history amidst Cuba's tropical beauty and dangerous political environment.

Characters from this novel also appear in the author's When we left Cuba.

Cleeves, Ann

The **crow** trap. Ann Cleeves. Pan Books, 2010. 551 p; (Vera Stanhope novels, 1)
ISBN 9781250122735
1. Women detectives 2. Murder investigation 3. Women murder victims 4. Environmental surveys 5. Betrayal 6. Northumberland, England 7. Police procedurals 8. Mysteries 9. Books to TV

Three very different women come together to complete an environmental survey. Three women who, in some way or another, know the meaning of betrayal....For team leader Rachael Lambert the project is the perfect opportunity to rebuild her confidence after a double-betrayal by her lover and boss, Peter Kemp. Botanist Anne Preece, on the other hand, sees it as a chance to indulge in a little deception of her own. And then there is Grace Fulwell, a strange, uncommunicative young woman with plenty of her own secrets to hide... When Rachael arrives at the cottage, however, she is horrified to discover the body of her friend Bella Furness. Bella, it appears, has committed suicide—a verdict Rachael finds impossible to accept. Only when the next death occurs does a fourth woman enter the picture—the unconventional Detective Inspector Vera Stanhope, who must piece together the truth from these women's tangled lives in The Crow Trap . Ann Cleeves's popular Vera Stanhope books have been made into the hit series "Vera" starring Brenda Blethyn and are available in the U.S.
Originally published: London : Macmillan, 1999.

The **darkest** evening. Ann Cleeves. Minotaur Books, 2020. 336 p. (Vera Stanhope novels, 9)
ISBN 9781250204509
1. Women detectives 2. Family estates 3. Blizzards 4. Abandoned children 5. Women murder victims 6. Northumberland, England 7. Police procedurals 8. Mysteries
LC 2020016421

Discovering a toddler in an abandoned vehicle near the run-down home where her estranged father grew up, Detective Inspector Vera Stanhope approaches the property during a boisterous Christmas party before discovering the body of a woman outside.

"This fair-play mystery brims with fully developed suspects and motives that are hidden in plain sight. Skillful misdirection masks the killer's identity." —*Publishers Weekly*

★ The **heron's** cry. Ann Cleeves. Minotaur Books, 2021. 384 p. (Two rivers, 2)
ISBN 9781250204479
1. Detectives 2. Murder 3. Murder investigation 4. Physicians 5. Women glass-workers 6. England 7. Devon, England 8. Mysteries
LC 2021015925

While looking into the murder of Dr. Nigel Yeo, who was investigating the suicide of a young man who was a member of chilling online group, Detective Matthew Venn, as the body count rises, must wade through the lies at the heart of his community.

"In her follow-up to The Long Call (2019), Cleeves provides a complex mystery full of surprises.... This character-driven exploration of people's darkest flaws is a sterling example of Cleeves' formidable talents." —*Kirkus*

The **long** call. Ann Cleeves. Minotaur Books, 2019. 400 pages (Two rivers, 1)
ISBN 9781250204448

1. Detectives 2. Evangelists 3. Murder 4. Murder investigation 5. Missing women 6. England 7. Devon, England 8. Mysteries
LC 2019018211
Agatha Award for Best Novel, 2019; Library Journal Best Books, 2019; LibraryReads Favorites, 2019

When a man with a significant tattoo is found murdered in North Devon, Detective Matthew Venn is forced to return to the strict evangelical community of his childhood to uncover deadly secrets.

Raven black. Ann Cleeves. Macmillan, 2006. 375 p. (Shetland mysteries, 1)
ISBN 9781405054720
1. Teenage murder victims 2. Detectives 3. Secrets 4. Police 5. Death 6. Shetland Islands 7. Scotland 8. Mysteries 9. Police procedurals 10. Adult books for young adults
Duncan Lawrie Dagger, 2006

When murder strikes a remote hamlet in the Shetland Islands, and the body of a teenage girl turns up in the winter snow, Inspector Jimmy Perez launches an investigation into the killing that takes him into the heart of sinister secrets from the past.

"Cleeves masterfully paints Perez as an empathetic hero and sprinkles the story with a lively cast of supporting characters who help bring the Shetlands alive." —*Publishers Weekly*

Thin air. Ann Cleeves. Minotaur Books, 2015. 400 p. (Shetland mysteries, 6)
ISBN 9781250069948
1. Detectives 2. Small town life 3. Murder investigation 4. Secrets 5. Islands 6. Scotland 7. Shetland Islands 8. Police procedurals

When a woman mysteriously disappears, Detectives Jimmy Perez and Willow Reeves are assigned to the case and discover that the victim had an unhealthy and obsessive interest in a cold case involving the drowning of a local child, which just might have been the death of her.

"This nicely detailed procedural and rich character study pairs beautifully with Peter Mays Lewis trilogy." —*Booklist*
Shetland now a major BBC drama—Cover.
Now a major BBC drama starring Douglas Henshall—Cover.
TV tie-in.

Wild fire. Ann Cleeves. Minotaur Books, 2018. 400 p. (Shetland mysteries, 8)
ISBN 9781250124845
1. Resentfulness 2. Threat (Psychology) 3. Fame 4. Fashion designers 5. Lovers 6. Scotland 7. Shetland Islands 8. Police procedurals 9. Media tie-ins
LC 2018013608

Finds the Flemings' efforts to start over in a remote northern community challenged by local animosity and a series of anonymous threats.

"Throughout the Shetland Island series, Cleeves lovingly depicts the Scottish island life, and this volume is no exception. Fans may be saddened but certainly not disappointed by this final installment." —*Library Journal*
Series complete in 8 volumes.

Clegg, Bill

Did you ever have a family. Bill Clegg. Gallery Books, 2015. 304 p.
ISBN 9781476798172
1. Loss (Psychology) 2. Healing 3. Change (Psychology) 4. Grief in women 5. Death 6. Literary fiction 7. Multiple perspectives 8. First person narratives
ALA Notable Book, 2016; Booklist Editors' Choice, 2015; LibraryReads Favorites, 2015; Library Journal Best Books, 2015

Surviving a disaster that kills everyone else in her family, June relocates West and settles into a directionless existence while other people impacted by the tragedy struggle with new circumstances.

"Clegg is both delicately lyrical and emotionally direct in this masterful novel, which strives to show how people make bearable what is unbearable, offering consolation in small but meaningful gestures." —*Booklist*

The **end** of the day. Bill Clegg. Gallery Books, 2020. 320 p.
ISBN 9781476798202
1. Friendship 2. Families 3. Secrets 4. Interpersonal relations 5. Literary fiction 6. Multiple perspectives

A retired widow in rural Connecticut wakes to an unexpected visit from her childhood best friend whom she hasn't seen in forty-nine years. A man arrives at a Pennsylvania hotel to introduce his estranged father to his newborn daughter and finds him collapsed on the floor of the lobby. A sixty-seven-year-old taxi driver in Kauai receives a phone call from the mainland that jars her back to a traumatic past. These seemingly disconnected lives come together as half-century-old secrets begin to surface. It is in this moment that Bill Clegg reminds us how choices—to connect, to betray, to protect—become our legacy.

"On the way Clegg dives deep into the inner life of each, exploring the ways our traumas shape our lives. His unhurried, lyrical sentences often make connections between the characters' states of mind and the natural world." —*Kirkus*

Cleland, Jane K.

Hidden treasure. Jane K. Cleland. Minotaur Books, 2020. 304 p. (Josie Prescott mysteries, 13)
ISBN 9781250242778
1. Women antique dealers 2. Women amateur detectives 3. Missing persons 4. Married people 5. Murder investigation 6. Cozy mysteries 7. Hobby mysteries
LC 2020030036

Beginning renovations on their New Hampshire dream home, Josie and her new husband, Ty, become embroiled in a murder investigation involving a mysterious relic and the disappearance of the property's previous owner.

"The novel's small-town setting on the New Hampshire coast, the fascinating details on antique appraisal, and the cast of well-drawn characters all provide appeal in this satisfying cozy. Recommend this one to readers who enjoy Barbara Allan's humorous Trash 'n' Treasures mysteries." —*Booklist*

Clement, Jennifer

Gun love. Jennifer Clement. Hogarth Press, 2018. 288 p.
ISBN 9781524761684
1. Teenage girls 2. Mothers and daughters 3. Mobile home parks 4. Guns 5. Homeless families 6. Florida 7. Coming-of-age stories 8. Literary fiction 9. Adult books for young adults
Library Journal Best Books, 2018; Booklist Editors' Choice, 2018

Growing up in the front seat of the car she shares with her mother in a lot beside a trailer park, Pearl suffers a terrible tragedy stemming from her mother's gun-toting boyfriend and is forced to survive on her own as she comes of age.

Clements, Oliver

The **eyes** of the queen. Oliver Clements. Atria Books, 2020. 304 p. (Agents of the crown (Clements), 1)
ISBN 9781501154690

1. Dee, John 2. Women rulers 3. Courts and courtiers 4. Competition 5. Intelligence service 6. Espionage 7. Great Britain 8. Elizabethan era (1558-1603) 9. Tudor period (1485-1603) 10. Historical thrillers 11. Spy fiction

John Dee, a man destined to become history's first MI6 agent, protects Age of Enlightenment-era England and a brilliant Elizabeth I from a wartime Spanish plot to conquer nations that would defy its Catholic orthodoxy.

"The rivalry between Elizabeth I and Mary, Queen of Scots, drives the pseudonymous Clements's twisty, fast-paced debut and series launch set in 1572 England." —*Publishers Weekly*

The **queen's** men. Oliver Clements. Leopoldo & Co, Atria, 2021. 405 pages; (Agents of the crown (Clements), 2)
ISBN 9781501154751
1. Elizabeth 2. Greek fire 3. Women rulers 4. Courts and courtiers 5. National security 6. Intelligence service 7. Great Britain 8. Elizabethan era (1558-1603) 9. Tudor period (1485-1603) 10. Historical thrillers 11. Spy fiction
LC 2021002231

When Queen Elizabeth, after attempts are made on her life, orders John Dee to rediscover the vital secret of Greek fire, the ultimate weapon to protect her country and throne, his mission may prove impossible unless he deploys the most effective weapon of all: intelligence.

"Clements's mystery might be too violent for some, but fans of historical spy novels will be hooked." —*Library Journal*

Clemmons, Zinzi

What we lose. Zinzi Clemmons. Viking Press, 2017. 192 p.
ISBN 9780735221710
1. Multiracial women 2. Belonging 3. Grief in women 4. Identity (Psychology) 5. Loss (Psychology) 6. Philadelphia, Pennsylvania 7. Johannesburg, South Africa 8. Literary fiction 9. African American fiction
Longlisted for the Andrew Carnegie Medal for Excellence in Fiction, 2018

Raised in America, the multiracial daughter of a mother from Johannesburg struggles with her mother's terminal cancer and her own need to find love and a place to belong, quests shaped by losses, changes in her sense of identity and unexpected motherhood.

"A compelling exploration of race, migration, and womanhood in contemporary America." —*Kirkus*

Clinch, Jon

Finn: a novel. Jon Clinch. Random House, 2007. 320 p.
ISBN 9781400065912
1. Finn, Huckleberry (Fictitious character) 2. Fathers and sons 3. Brothers 4. Runaway children 5. Freedom seekers 6. Mississippi River 7. Missouri 8. Adaptations, retellings, and spin-offs 9. Adventure stories 10. Coming-of-age stories 11. Adult books for young adults
LC 2006045802

ALA Notable Book, 2008

A novel inspired by Mark Twain's classic tales explores the mysterious life and strange death of Huckleberry Finn's infamous father, describing Finn's fearsome father, the Judge; his brother, the sickly, sycophantic Will; and young Huck.

"Shocking and charming. Clinch creates a folk-art masterpiece that will delight, beguile and entertain as it does justice to its predecessor.... In Finn, Clinch expands the bloodlines and scope of the original story and casts new light on the troubled legacy of our country's infamous past." —*The New York Post*

Marley: a novel. Jon Clinch. Atria Books, 2019. 288 pages
ISBN 9781982129705
1. Extortion 2. Deception 3. Ambition in men 4. Greed 5. Slave trade 6. London, England 7. England 8. 19th century 9. Adaptations, retellings, and spin-offs 10. Historical fiction
LC 2019275079
A reimagining of Charles Dickens' classic A Christmas Carol that explores the twisted relationship between Ebenezer Scrooge and Jacob Marley.

Cline, Emma

Daddy: stories. Emma Cline. Random House, 2020. 267 pages
ISBN 9780812998641
1. Interpersonal relations 2. Identity (Psychology) 3. Options, alternatives, choices 4. Desire 5. Secrets 6. Literary fiction 7. Short stories
LC 2020012809
An anthology of 10 stories by the award-winning author includes three original entries and follows a theme of how fateful choices and other disturbances reveal the perversity and violence beneath the surface of everyday life.
"The subtlety of these 10 stories may surprise readers expecting the same luridness Cline brought to The Girls, but the payoffs are as gratifying as they are shattering." —*Publishers Weekly*

The **girls:** a novel. Emma Cline. Random House, 2016. 368 p.
ISBN 9780812998603
1. Teenage girls 2. Communes 3. Counterculture 4. Obsession 5. Social acceptance 6. California 7. 1960s 8. Psychological fiction 9. Coming-of-age stories 10. Dickinson, Emily
LC 2015012714
Shirley Jackson Awards, Novel, 2016
Mesmerized by a band of girls in the park she perceives as enjoying a life of free and careless abandon, 1960s teen Evie Boyd becomes obsessed with gaining acceptance into their circle, only to find herself drawn into a cult and seduced by its charismatic leader.
"Cline pushes past the myths, vividly imagining how the darkness crept in and turned a group of idealistic young adults into cold-blooded killers. In her impressive debut, Cline illuminates the darkest truths of a girls coming-of-age, telling a story that is familiar on multiple levels in a unique and compelling way." —*Booklist*

Cline, Ernest

Ready player one: a novel. Ernest Cline. Crown Publishers, 2011. 352 p. (Ready player novels, 1)
ISBN 9780307887436
1. Virtual reality 2. Quests 3. Near future 4. Inheritance and succession 5. Teenage boys 6. 21st century 7. Science fiction 8. Coming-of-age stories 9. First person narratives 10. Adult books for young adults
LC 2011015247
Alex Award, 2012; Booklist Editors' Choice: Adult Books for Young Adults, 2011; Nutmeg Children's Book Award, High School category, 2016; School Library Journal Best Books: Best Adult Books 4 Teens, 2011
Immersing himself in a mid-twenty-first-century technological virtual utopia to escape an ugly real world of famine, poverty, and disease, Wade Watts joins an increasingly violent effort to solve a series of puzzles by the virtual world's creator.
"Cultural items from VH1's I Love the 80's series and early G4 programming like Icons or Portal cover a basic swath of the material, but Monty Python, John Hughes, Dungeons & Dragons, WarGames, Blade Runner, Pac-Man, Rush, and infinitely more highly regarded geek cultural touchstones appear both as delightful inclusions and ingenious plot devices. Ready Player One lends itself easily to mash-up comparisons, since in its more complicated passages, it amounts to long strings of cultural references pumped through well-worn story arcs. The adventure comedy of Mike Judge's Idiocracy meets South Park's Imaginationland with a dash of Willy Wonka, except all of the cynicism has been replaced by sheer geeky love." —*A.V. Club*
Title adapted into a film in 2018.

Cline, Rachel

My liar: a novel. Rachel Cline. Random House, 2008. 274 p.
ISBN 9781400062270
1. Women film editors 2. Women film producers and directors 3. Female friendship 4. Film industry and trade 5. Entertainment industry and trade 6. Domestic fiction
LC 2007019601
Working together on a film, two women—Annabeth Jensen, a film editor who prefers to work by herself, and Laura Katz, a sociable and seductive director—form an intense friendship in which both women use each other in ways they do not understand.

Coates, Ta-Nehisi

★ The **water** dancer: a novel. Ta-Nehisi Coates. One World, 2019. 432 pages
ISBN 9780399590597
1. Enslaved boys 2. Escapes 3. Underground Railroad 4. Enslaved families 5. Loss (Psychology) 6. Southern States 7. Virginia 8. Antebellum America (1820-1861) 9. Historical fiction 10. Magical realism 11. Literary fiction
LC 2019011177
ALA Notable Book, 2020; BCALA Literary Award for First Novelist, 2020; Booklist Editors' Choice, 2019; Library Journal Best Books, 2019; LibraryReads Favorites, 2019; Loan Stars Favourites, 2019; Andrew Carnegie Medal for Excellence in Fiction finalist, 2020
A Virginia slave narrowly escapes a drowning death through the intervention of a mysterious force that compels his escape and personal underground war against slavery.

Cobb, May K.

The **hunting** wives. May Cobb. Penguin Group USA 2021. 368 p.
ISBN 9780593101131
1. Women journalists 2. Married women 3. Mothers 4. Moving to a new state 5. Small towns 6. Texas 7. Thrillers and suspense 8. First person narratives
LC 2020050119
Sophie O'Neill left behind an envy-inspiring career and the stressful, competitive life of big-city Chicago to settle down with her husband and young son in a small Texas town. It seems like the perfect life with a beautiful home in an idyllic rural community. Then she meets Margot Banks, an alluring socialite who is part of an elite clique secretly known as the Hunting Wives. Sophie is completely drawn to Margot and swept into her mysterious world of late-night target practice and dangerous partying. As Sophie's curiosity gives way to full-blown obsession, she slips further away from the safety of her family and deeper into this nest of vipers. When the body of a teenage girl is discovered in the woods where the Hunting Wives meet, Sophie finds herself in the middle of a murder investigation and her life spirals out of control.

"Gossipy, scandalous housewives behaving badly might make this the juiciest read of the season. For fans of Liane Moriarty." —*Library Journal*

Cobbs Hoffman, Elizabeth

The **Hamilton** affair. Elizabeth Cobbs. Arcade Publishing, 2016. 403 p.
ISBN 9781628727203
1. Hamilton, Alexander 2. Politicians 3. Husband and wife 4. American Revolution, 1775-1783 5. Extramarital affairs 6. Betrayal 7. United States 8. 18th century 9. Biographical fiction 10. Historical fiction 11. Multiple perspectives

Relates the tumultuous true love story of Alexander Hamilton and Elizabeth Schuyler against the dramatic backdrop of the American Revolution.

"Hamilton's close relationship to George Washington, his friendships and conflicts with his fellow revolutionaries, and the rise and fall of his political star are all detailed, but it is his courtship of and marriage to the beautiful, vivacious Elizabeth Schuyler, a member of one of the oldest and most distinguished colonial families, that serves as the centerpiece of Cobbs page-turning historical novel. Cobbs paints a portrait of a love so deep it was able to survive betrayal and a devastatingly public scandal. The focus alternates between Alexander and Elizabeth as their tempestuous tale unfolds in all its triumph and tragedy. Hamiltons true story is so fantastical, it is amazing that it has taken this long to transform his life and times into a national sensation." —*Booklist*

The **Tubman** command: a novel. Elizabeth Cobbs. Arcade Publishing, 2019. 360 p.
ISBN 9781948924344
1. Tubman, Harriet 2. African American soldiers 3. African American women 4. Military missions 5. United States Civil War, 1861-1865 6. Scouting (Reconnaissance) 7. South Carolina 8. United States 9. 1860s 10. American Civil War era (1861-1865) 11. Biographical fiction 12. War stories 13. Historical fiction

Tells the story of Harriet Tubman at the height of her powers, when she devises the largest plantation raid of the Civil War after General David Hunter places her in charge of a team of black scouts even though skeptical of what one woman can accomplish.

Coben, Harlan

★ The **boy** from the woods. Harlan Coben. Grand Central Publishing, 2020. 400 p. (Wilde (Harlan Coben), 1)
ISBN 9781538748145
1. Missing teenagers 2. Women lawyers 3. Private investigators 4. Men with amnesia 5. Power (Social sciences) 6. Thrillers and suspense
LC 2019041849

A man with a past shrouded in mystery searches desperately for a missing teenage girl whose disappearance is triggering disastrous consequences throughout her community and the world.

Don't let go. Harlan Coben. E.P. Dutton, 2017. 400 p.
ISBN 9780525955115
1. Former lovers 2. Murder 3. Secrets 4. Twins 5. Brothers 6. New Jersey 7. Thrillers and suspense

When he gets a lead on Maura, an ex who left him without explanation fifteen years earlier, Nap Dumas searches for answers and uncovers dark secrets about the woman he once loved and the real reason behind his twin brother's death.

Fool me once. Harlan Coben. E.P. Dutton, 2016. 400 p.
ISBN 9780525955092

1. Deception 2. Women veterans 3. Power (Social sciences) 4. Husband and wife 5. Former Special Forces members 6. Thrillers and suspense
LibraryReads Favorites, 2016; Library Journal Best Books, 2016

Horrified when she spots the husband who was reported dead weeks earlier playing with their toddler on her nanny cam, former special ops pilot Maya confronts deep secrets and deceit in her own past in order to discern the truth.

"Once again, Coben marries his two greatest strengthsmasterfully paced plotting that leads to a climactic string of fireworks and the ability to root all the revelations in deeply felt emotionsin a tale guaranteed to fool even the craftiest readers a lot more than once." —*Kirkus*

Hold tight. By Harlan Coben. Dutton, 2008. 400 p.
ISBN 9780525950608
1. Spartacus 2. Grief in women 3. Stalking 4. Parent and child 5. Teenage boys 6. Thrillers and suspense 7. Multiple perspectives 8. Adult books for young adults
LC 2007051582

Just how far parents will go to protect their kids? When their son Adam is implicated in the death of his classmate, Tia and Mike Baye install a sophisticated spy program on Adam's computer, and within days are jolted by a message from an unknown correspondent.

"Coben's style is laid back initially, but it builds into a strong, smart, suspenseful novel including at least five different storylines." —*Deseret News*

Long lost. Harlan Coben. Penguin Group, 2009. 400 p. (Myron Bolitar mysteries, 9)
ISBN 9780525951056
1. Spouses of murder victims 2. Crime scenes 3. Murder investigation 4. Sports-agents 5. Amateur detectives 6. Paris, France 7. United States 8. Hardboiled fiction 9. Mysteries 10. Adult books for young adults

Contacted by a woman with whom he had an affair years earlier, Myron Bolitar learns how she has been wrongfully accused of murdering her ex-husband, a situation that is further complicated by a long-hidden family secret.

Run away. Harlan Coben. Grand Central Publishing, 2019. 376 p.
ISBN 9781538748466
1. Women drug abusers 2. Father and adult daughter 3. Runaways 4. Protectiveness in men 5. Murder suspects 6. New York City 7. Thrillers and suspense
LC 2018037100

After discovering his drug-addicted daughter Paige, who he has not seen in six months, panhandling in Central Park, Simon follows her into a dark and dangerous world he never knew existed that puts his family and his life on the line.

"An absolutely brilliant, taut thriller that begs to be read in one sitting." —*Library Journal*

The **stranger**. Harlan Coben. Dutton, 2015. 400 p.
ISBN 9780525953500
1. Marriage 2. Secrets 3. Conspiracies 4. Husband and wife 5. Strangers 6. Thrillers and suspense 7. Books to TV

Parents Adam and Hannah Price confront the shocking secret on which their marriage was built, leaving Adam to wonder whether he ever truly knew his wife at all, and soon he stumbles into a dark conspiracy that places lives at risk.

"Coben can always be relied on to generate thrills from the simplest premises, but his finest tales maintain a core of logic throughout the twists. This 100-proof nightmare ranks among his most potent." —*Kirkus*

Cochrun, Alison

The **charm** offensive. Alison Cochrun. Atria Books, 2021. 320 p.

ISBN 9781982170714

1. Television producers and directors 2. East Indian Americans 3. Reality television programs 4. Dating shows (Television programs) 5. Dating (Social customs) 6. Romantic comedies 7. LGBTQIA romances 8. Multicultural romances

LibraryReads Favorites, 2021

In this witty and heartwarming romantic comedy, an awkward tech wunderkind on a reality dating show goes off-script when sparks fly with his producer.

"In between the meet-cute, quippy banter, and red-hot sexual chemistry, Cochrun also offers readers a thoughtful and caring exploration of gay love and the mental health struggles people with social anxiety and depression deal with every day." —*Booklist*

Cocks, Heather

The **heir** affair. Heather Cocks and Jessica Morgan. Grand Central Publishing, 2020. 464 p.

ISBN 9781538715918

1. Husband and wife 2. Royal houses 3. Inheritance and succession 4. Dukes and duchesses 5. Family secrets 6. England 7. Great Britain 8. Romantic comedies 9. First person narratives 10. Relationship fiction

LibraryReads Favorites, 2020

A follow-up to The Royal We finds Bex Porter and her husband, Prince Nicolas, in self-imposed exile in the wake of a scandal before a royal crisis exposes old family secrets and a brother's ongoing disgrace.

"There's real heart in this escapist romp, and royal watchers and romance fans alike will be left hungry for another sequel." —*Publishers Weekly*

The **royal** we. Heather Cocks and Jessica Morgan. Grand Central Publishing, 2015. 252 p.

ISBN 9781455557103

1. Weddings 2. Americans in England 3. Princes 4. Nobility 5. Sisters 6. England 7. Romantic comedies 8. First person narratives 9. Relationship fiction

LibraryReads Favorites, 2015; Library Journal Best Books, 2015; RUSA Reading List Short List, 2016

In their first adult novel, authors Heather Cocks and Jessica Morgan take on a story of romance and rivalries inspired by today's most talked-about royal couple: Will and Kate. "If I'm Cinderella today, I dread who they'll think I am tomorrow. I guess it depends on what I do next." American Rebecca Porter was never one for fairy-tales. Her twin sister Lacey was always the romantic, the one who daydreamed of being a princess. But it's adventure-seeking Bex who goes to Oxford and meets dreamy Nick across the hall—and thus Bex who accidentally finds herself in love with the eventual heir to the British throne. Nick is everything she could have imagined, but Prince Nicholas has unimaginable baggage: grasping friends, a thorny family, hysterical tabloids tracking his every move, and a public that expected its future king to marry a native. On the eve of the most talked-about wedding of the century, Bex reflects on what she's sacrificed for love—and exactly whose heart she may yet have to break.

"Parallels to the love story of Prince William and Kate Middleton are obvious, but the authors create their own unique and endearing characters with Bex and Nick—along with an entertaining cast of characters including lovable rogue Prince Freddie, Nick's younger brother; Bex's twin, Lacey; and a bunch of colorful school chums." —*Publishers Weekly*

Coe, Jonathan

The **rotters'** club. Jonathan Coe. Alfred A. Knopf : 2003. 419 p; (Rotters' Club, 1)

ISBN 9780375713125

1. Teenage boys 2. Male friendship 3. Punk rock music 4. Political participation 5. Men 6. Birmingham, England 7. 1970s 8. Psychological fiction 9. Political fiction 10. Coming-of-age stories 11. Adult books for young adults

LC 2001042523

New York Times Notable Book, 2002

Four teenage boys, friends and schoolmates, deal with the hopes, dreams, traumas, and challenges of adolescence as they come of age in industrial Birmingham, a British city that is confronting its own economic crisis, during the upheaval and change of the 1970s.

Sequel: The closed circle (2005).

First published: London : Viking, 2001.

Coelho, Paulo

★ The **alchemist**. Paulo Coelho; translated by Alan R. Clarke. HarperOne, 1993. 177 p.

ISBN 9780062502179

1. Self-discovery 2. Voyages and travels 3. Wisdom 4. Boy shepherds 5. Dreams 6. Spiritual fiction 7. Allegories 8. Literary fiction

LC 92056413

A fable about undauntingly following one's dreams, listening to one's heart, and reading life's omens features dialogue between a boy and an unnamed being.

"The story has the comic charm, dramatic tension and psychological intensity of a fairy tale, but it's full of specific wisdom as well, about becoming self-empowered, overcoming depression, and believing in dreams. The cumulative effect is like hearing a wonderful bedtime story from an inspirational psychiatrist. Comparisons to The Little Prince are appropriate; this is a sweetly exotic tale for young and old alike." —*Publishers Weekly*

First published by Editora Rocco Ltd 1988.

Coes, Ben

The **Russian**: a thriller. Ben Coes. St Martins Press, 2019. 400 pages (Rob Tacoma novels, 1)

ISBN 9781250140791

1. CIA agents 2. Mafia 3. Special operations (Military science) 4. Assassins 5. Russians in the United States 6. United States 7. Political thrillers

When criminals from the former Soviet Union establish a vicious underworld in the U.S, former Navy SEAL and CIA agent Rob Tacoma conducts a top-secret mission to neutralize the mob boss behind the murder of a CIA Special Ops leader.

Coetzee, J. M.

Age of Iron. J.M. Coetzee. Random House, 1990. 198 p.

ISBN 9780394588599

1. Apartheid 2. Race relations 3. Women with terminal illnesses 4. Women with cancer 5. Homeless men 6. South Africa 7. Epistolary novels 8. Literary fiction

LC 90008310

ALA Notable Book, 1991

South African professor Mrs. Curren has always been opposed to apartheid's brutality though she has lived isolated from its horrors, but as she nears death from cancer, she confronts a generation of blood and revenge.

"The word 'shame' throbs through the text like a recurrent pain. The principal character thinks she is dying of it.... One can, of course, read her death as a metaphor for the doom of liberalism in South Africa.... But Age of Iron is about dying as much as it is about apartheid, and that raises it above the level of a political novel or a roman thse, and gives resonance to the political message." —*The New York Review of Books*

Disgrace. J.M. Coetzee. Viking, 1999. 220 p.
ISBN 9780670887316
1. Father and adult daughter 2. Sexuality 3. Race relations 4. Middle-aged men 5. Farm life 6. South Africa 7. Psychological fiction 8. Literary fiction
LC 99055216
ALA Notable Book, 2001; Booker Prize, 1999; Commonwealth Writers' Prize for Best Book, 2000; Commonwealth Writers' Prize, Africa: Best Book, 2000; Library Journal Best Books, 1999; National Book Critics Circle Award for Fiction finalist, 1999

In a novel set in post-apartheid South Africa, a fifty-two-year-old college professor who has lost his job for sleeping with a student tries to relate to his daughter, Lucy, who works with an ambitious African farmer.

"A novel that not only works its spell but makes it impossible for us to lay it aside once we've finished reading it.... Coetzee's sentences are coiled springs, and the energy they release would take other writers pages to summon." —*The New Yorker*

Elizabeth Costello. J. M. Coetzee. Viking, 2003. 224 p.
ISBN 9780670031306
1. Women authors 2. Awards, prizes, honors, etc. 3. Storytelling 4. Writing 5. Mothers 6. Australia 7. Australian fiction 8. Speeches, addresses, etc. 9. Literary fiction
LC 2003060849
Queensland Premier's Literary Awards, Fiction Book Award, 2004; New York Times Notable Book, 2003; Shortlisted for the Miles Franklin Literary Award, 2004

Reveals the life of aging Australian novelist Elizabeth Costello through a series of formal addresses that includes an award-acceptance speech at a New England liberal arts college and a lecture on evil in Amsterdam.

"There is no justice in the ability of youth to shame age, and yet it's a fundamental fact of the embodied life. Coetzee's unflinching exploration of this desolate and strangely beautiful terrain represents the cruelest and best use to which literature can be put." —*New York Times Book Review*

★ **Foe**. J. M. Coetzee. Viking, 1986. 157p.
ISBN 9780670813988
1. Widows 2. Islands 3. Survival (after airplane accidents, shipwrecks, etc.) 4. Shipwrecks 5. Solitude 6. Allegories 7. Literary fiction
LC 86040267
Returning to London after being marooned on an island in the Atlantic, Susan Barton approaches the author Daniel Foe with the story of her adventures with Robinson Cruso and the mute Friday.

"In adding to Defoe's repertory company, Coetzee has introduced urgencies that are neither fresh nor illumined, only brilliantly disguised. Flashing back and forward, scattering allusions, adopting a series of poses and styles, the author is less reminiscent of a prior novelist than of contemporary street mimes who build hints until the audience shouts in recognition." —*Time*
Originally published: London: Secker & Warburg, 1986.

★ **Life** & times of Michael K. J.M. Coetzee. Penguin Books, 1996. 184 p.
ISBN 9780140074482
1. Men with developmental disabilities 2. War 3. Mothers — Death 4. Gardeners 5. Prisoners 6. South Africa 7. Psychological fiction 8. Literary fiction
Booker Prize, 1983
Michael K, a young South African, becomes unwillingly and unwittingly involved in a war in South Africa after he loses his gardening job in Capetown and embarks on an odyssey to return his dying mother to her homeland.
Originally published: London : Secker & Warburg, 1983.

Summertime: scenes from a provincial life. J. M. Coetzee. Knopf Australia, 2009. 266 p; (Memoir trilogy, 3)
ISBN 9781741669022
1. Coetzee, J. M. 2. Authors, South African 3. European Africans 4. Biographers 5. Writing 6. Misfits (Persons) 7. Cape Town, South Africa 8. South Africa 9. 1970s 10. Autobiographies and memoirs 11. Life stories — Arts and culture — Writing — Authors 12. Arts and Entertainment — Writing and Publishing 13. Adult books for young adults
NSW Premier's Literary Awards, Christina Stead Prize for Fiction, 2010; Queensland Premier's Literary Awards, Fiction Book Award, 2010; Western Australian Premier's Book Awards, Fiction category, 2009; Shortlisted for the Man Booker Prize, 2009

"At stake is what it means to commit oneself: to a person, a place, a moral imperative.... Not since Disgrace has he written with such urgency and feeling." —*The New Yorker*
Sequel to: "Boyhood" and "Youth."

Cogman, Genevieve

The **invisible** library. Genevieve Cogman. ROC, 2016. 328 pages; (Invisible library, 1)
ISBN 9781101988640
1. Libraries 2. Librarians 3. Magical books 4. Magic 5. Secrets 6. London, England 7. Steampunk 8. Fantasy fiction
LibraryReads Favorites, 2016; Library Journal Best Books, 2016

Collecting books can be a dangerous prospect in this fun, time-traveling, fantasy adventure from a spectacular debut author. One thing any Librarian will tell you: the truth is much stranger than fiction.... Irene is a professional spy for the mysterious Library, a shadowy organization that collects important works of fiction from all of the different realities. Most recently, she and her enigmatic assistant Kai have been sent to an alternative London. Their mission: Retrieve a particularly dangerous book. The problem: By the time they arrive, it's already been stolen. London's underground factions are prepared to fight to the death to find the tome before Irene and Kai do, a problem compounded by the fact that this world is chaos-infested—the laws of nature bent to allow supernatural creatures and unpredictable magic to run rampant. To make matters worse, Kai is hiding something—secrets that could be just as volatile as the chaos-filled world itself. Now Irene is caught in a puzzling web of deadly danger, conflicting clues, and sinister secret societies. And failure is not an option—because it isn't just Irene's reputation at stake, it's the nature of reality itself....

"Intriguing characters and fast-paced action are wrapped up in a spellbinding, well-built world." —*Library Journal*
Originally published: London: Tor, 2015.

The **masked** city. Genevieve Cogman. ROC, 2016. 336 p. (Invisible library, 2)
ISBN 9781101988664
1. Libraries 2. Librarians 3. Magical books 4. Magic 5. Secrets 6. London, England 7. Steampunk 8. Fantasy fiction
LibraryReads Favorites, 2016

Librarian-spy Irene and her apprentice Kai are back in the second in this "dazzling" book-filled fantasy series from the author of The Invisible Library. The written word is mightier than the sword—most of the time... Working in an alternate version of Victorian London, Librarian-spy Irene has settled into a routine, collecting important fiction for the mysterious Library and blending in nicely with the local culture. But when her apprentice, Kai—a dragon of royal descent—is kidnapped by the Fae, her carefully crafted undercover operation begins to crumble. Kai's abduction could incite a conflict between the forces of chaos and order that would devastate all worlds and all dimensions. To keep humanity from getting caught in the crossfire, Irene will have to team up with a local Fae leader to travel deep into a version of Venice filled with dark magic, strange coincidences, and a perpetual celebration of Carnival—and save her friend before he becomes the first casualty of a catastrophic war. But navigating the tumultuous landscape of Fae politics will take more than Irene's book-smarts and fast-talking—to ward off Armageddon, she might have to sacrifice everything she holds dear....

"Series fans will be thrilled to learn more about dragon-kind and the capricious Fae, and will be eager for Cogman's third in the series." —*Booklist*

Originally published: London : Tor, 2015.

Cohen, Joshua

Book of numbers: a novel. Joshua Cohen. Random House, 2015. 448 p.

ISBN 9780812996913

1. Rich men 2. Authors 3. Internet 4. High technology industry and trade 5. Autobiography 6. Cyber-thrillers 7. Literary fiction

LC 2014040735

Hired by a dying tech company tycoon to ghostwrite his memoirs, failed novelist Josh Cohen learns the history of the man's profoundly influential company before being initiated into the high-stakes truth behind the autobiography project.

"A dense, thrilling, and occasionally perplexing work, Cohen's encyclopedic epic is about many things—language, art, divinity, narrative, desire, global politics, surveillance, consumerism, genealogy—but it is above all a standout novel about the Internet, humanity's "first mutual culture," in which our identities are increasingly defined by a series of ones and zeroes." —*Publishers Weekly*

Cohen, Tish

The **summer** we lost her: a novel. Tish Cohen. Gallery Books, 2019. 340 pages

ISBN 9781501199684

1. Husband and wife 2. Vacation homes 3. Missing girls 4. Cabins 5. Lakes 6. New York City 7. New York (State) 8. Domestic fiction

Preparing to sell a valuable lakefront cabin that has been in the family for generations, a lawyer and equestrian whose marriage has been strained by ambition encounter the husband's teen crush before their young daughter goes missing.

"A sharp, suspenseful portrait of a family on the verge of collapse." —*Kirkus*

Coldsmith, Don

Tallgrass: a novel of the Great Plains. Don Coldsmith. Bantam Books, 1997. 454 p. (Great Plains saga, 1)

ISBN 9780553106329

1. Indians of North America 2. Indians of North America — Relations with European-Americans 3. Frontier and pioneer life 4. Prairie life 5. Kansas 6. Great Plains (United States) 7. Westerns

LC 9619672

A saga set in the Great Plains follows the warriors, priests, trappers, traders, explorers, schemers, and other pioneers of the American West.

"This powerful novel demonstrates the diversity of the Native American culture while treating the tribes and their history with dignity and understanding." —*Library Journal*

Cole, Alyssa

★ A **duke** by default. Alyssa Cole. Avon Books, 2018. 384 p. (Reluctant royals, 2)

ISBN 9780062685568

1. Swordmaking 2. Dukes and duchesses 3. Interracial romance 4. Armorers 5. Apprenticeship 6. Scotland 7. New York City 8. Contemporary romances 9. Multicultural romances 10. African American fiction

When her gruff new boss, Scottish swordmaker Tavish McKenzie, discovers that he is a duke, New York City socialite Portia Hobbs puts her social media skills to good use on Tavish's behalf, despite her growing attraction to him.

"Cole includes just the right amount of sass, sex, and heart to satisfy romance readers." —*Publishers Weekly*

★ An **extraordinary** union. Alyssa Cole. Kensington Books, 2017. 258 pages; (The Loyal League, 1)

ISBN 9781496707444

1. Spies 2. Freed people 3. Undercover operations 4. Interracial romance 5. Detectives 6. Virginia 7. American Civil War era (1861-1865) 8. Historical romances 9. Multicultural romances 10. African American fiction

RUSA Reading List, 2018; Romantic Times Reviewer's Choice Award, 2017

Born into slavery, Elle Burns is now a free woman and a spy for the pro-Union Loyalty League. While on assignment in Richmond, Virginia, she encounters another undercover operative: white Pinkerton Detective Malcolm McCall. Their attraction is instantaneous (and mutual), but there are so many reasons they can't be together. Set during the American Civil War, this compelling story of forbidden love and espionage boasts authentic characters and well-researched historical detail that should please fans of Beverly Jenkins' novels.

"Any reader who thinks romance novels are pure fluff will be schooled by Cole's richly drawn characters, who must overcome generations of trauma in order to let themselves love each other. A masterful tale that bodes well for future work from Cole." —*Kirkus*

★ A **hope** divided. Alyssa Cole. Kensington Books, 2017. 266 pages; (The Loyal League, 2)

ISBN 9781496707468

1. Spies 2. Union soldiers 3. African American women 4. Underground Railroad 5. Civil War 6. Southern States 7. American Civil War era (1861-1865) 8. Historical romances 9. Multicultural romances 10. African American fiction

The Civil War has turned neighbor against neighbor—but for scientist-spy and free black woman Marlie Lynch and the philosophical Union soldier she helps to hide, war could bind them together when they must go on the run on the Underground Railroad to escape a common enemy.

"Thoughtfully portrayed characters with deep minds and passionate hearts make this second novel in Coles Loyal League series, following An Extraordinary Union (2017), sparkle." —*Booklist*

★ **How** to catch a queen. Alyssa Cole. Avon Books, 2020. 384 p. (Runaway royals (Alyssa Cole), 1)

ISBN 9780062933966

1. Rulers 2. Royal houses 3. Marriage 4. Determination in women 5. Insecurity in men 6. Africa 7. African American fiction 8. Multicultural romances 9. Contemporary romances

LibraryReads Favorites, 2020

After marrying the newly crowned King Sanyu of Njaza, Shanti Mohapi soon discovers that royal life is not what she expected and goes on the run when turmoil erupts in their kingdom and marriage.

"Cole's majestic new Runaway Royals series spins off from her excellent Reluctant Royals trilogy, adding more dazzling depth to a romantic world of dashing young aristocrats hoping to unite ancestral traditions and modern multicultural values." —*Booklist*

How to find a princess. Alyssa Cole. Avon Books, 2021. 384 p. (Runaway royals (Alyssa Cole), 2)
ISBN 9780062934000
1. African American women 2. Lesbians 3. Jilted women 4. Grandmother and adult child 5. Family businesses 6. Contemporary romances 7. Multicultural romances 8. LGBTQIA romances

Makeda Hicks has lost her job and her girlfriend in one fell swoop. The last thing she's in the mood for is to rehash the story of her grandmother's infamous summer fling with a runaway prince from Ibarania, or the investigator from the World Federation of Monarchies tasked with searching for Ibarania's missing heir. Yet when Beznaria Chetchevaliere crashes into her life, the sleek and sexy investigator exudes exactly the kind of chaos that organized and efficient Makeda finds irresistible, even if Bez is determined to drag her into a world of royal duty Makeda wants nothing to do with.

"Leaving behind the angstier drama of How to Catch a Queen, Cole juggles the conventions of romantic comedy, fairy tale, and social satire in her heartwarming second Runaway Royals romance." —*Publishers Weekly*

★ A **prince** on paper. Alyssa Cole. Avon Books, 2019. 377 p. (Reluctant royals, 3)
ISBN 9780062685582
1. Adult children of politicians 2. Dukes and duchesses 3. Interracial romance 4. Women 5. Womanizers 6. New York City 7. Africa 8. Contemporary romances 9. Multicultural romances 10. African American fiction

Forced into a pretend engagement with real-life celebrity prince Johan von Braustein, whom she loves to hate, Nya Jerami starts falling for him and wonders if they are destined for their own happily ever after.

"In a book by a less skilled writer, a subplot involving a character's emerging nonbinary gender identity might feel unnecessary, but not here. Nya and Johan's swoony sexual tension evolves into a scorching exploration that recognizes Nya's relative inexperience while rendering the pair's matched desire, fulfillment, and power. A gifted writer at the top of her emotional, sexy, romantic, and inclusive game." —*Kirkus*

★ A **princess** in theory. Alyssa Cole. Avon Books, 2018. 373 p. (Reluctant royals, 1)
ISBN 9780062685544
1. Princes 2. Women graduate students 3. Engaged persons 4. Women scientists 5. Deception 6. Contemporary romances 7. Multicultural romances 8. African American fiction
New York Times Notable Book, 2018; Library Journal Best Books, 2018; RUSA Reading List Short List, 2019

Mistaken by his betrothed as a pauper instead of a prince, Prince Thabiso, the sole heir to the throne of Thesolo, decides to keep his real identity a secret as he experiences life and love with Naledi Smith—until the truth comes out, which changes everything.

"Upbeat, sexy, and totally engrossing, this fast-paced modern romp puts an intriguing spin on the classic long-lost-heiress plot and launches the series in style." —*Library Journal*

★ An **unconditional** freedom. Alyssa Cole. Kensington Books, 2019. 320 p. (The Loyal League, 3)
ISBN 9781496707482
1. Spies 2. Freed people 3. Interracial romance 4. Revenge 5. African American men 6. Ohio 7. Miller, Lee 8. Historical romances 9. Multicultural romances 10. African American fiction

An assassination plot that could end the Civil War, and a hidden enemy that could destroy a secret league of unsung heroes.

"A heroine torn by conflicting loyalties and a vengeance-driven hero haunted by the past struggle to come to terms with reality and their feelings in this emotionally compelling, information-rich story." —*Library Journal*

Cole, Teju

Every day is for the thief. Teju Cole. Random House Inc, 2014. 176 p.
ISBN 9780812995787
1. City life 2. Homecomings 3. Identity (Psychology) 4. Cities and towns 5. Reconciliation 6. Nigeria 7. Psychological fiction 8. Literary fiction 9. First person narratives

Visiting Lagos after many years away, Teju Cole's unnamed narrator rediscovers his hometown as both a foreigner and a local. A young writer uncertain of what he wants to say, the man moves through tableaus of life in one of the most dynamic cities in the world: he hears the muezzin's call to prayer in the early morning light, and listens to John Coltrane during the late afternoon heat. He witnesses teenagers diligently perpetrating e-mail frauds from internet cafes, longs after a woman reading Michael Ondaatje on a public bus, and visits the impoverished National Museum. Along the way, he reconnects with old school friends and his family, who force him to ask himself profound questions of personal and national history. Over long, wandering days, the narrator compares present-day Lagos to the Lagos of his memory, and in doing so reveals changes that have taken place in himself. Just as Open City uses New York to reveal layers of the narrator's soul, in Every Day is for the Thief the complex, beautiful, generous, and corrupt city of Lagos exposes truths about our protagonist, and ourselves.

"The structure is loose, a collection of observances of daily life in Lagos in which Cole presents the complexities of culture and poverty. In addition, Cole sprinkles dramatic black-and-white photos throughout the book, but it's his willingness to explore so many uncomfortable paradoxes that sears this narrative into our brains." —*Publishers Weekly*

★ **Open** city: a novel. By Teju Cole. Random House, 2011. 272 p.
ISBN 9781400068098
1. Immigrants 2. Identity (Psychology) 3. Race relations 4. Nigerians in the United States 5. Psychiatrists 6. New York City 7. Psychological fiction 8. Literary fiction 9. First person narratives
LC 2010008927
Hemingway Foundation/PEN Award, 2012; New York Times Notable Book, 2011; National Book Critics Circle Award for Fiction finalist, 2011

Feeling adrift after ending a relationship, Julius, a young Nigerian doctor living in New York, takes long walks through the city while listening to the stories of fellow immigrants until a shattering truth is revealed.

"Cole's writing is assured, his ideas are well developed, and his imagery is delicious.... His readers will be those who understand that all stories are interconnected, that literature is not mere entertainment, and that art is nothing if not an extended conversation spanning eras, nations and languages. The novel's importance lies in its honesty." —*New York Times Book Review*

Coleman, Reed Farrel

Where it hurts: a Gus Murphy novel. Reed Farrel Coleman. G. P. Putnam's Sons, 2016. 368 pages (Gus Murphy novels, 1)
ISBN 9780399173035
1. Murder investigation 2. Police corruption 3. Mafia 4. Former police 5. Former convicts 6. Long Island, New York 7. Mysteries 8. Hardboiled fiction
LC 2015017115
Shamus Award for Best P.I. Novel, 2017

lient in years, but finds the case complicated by events that suggest a particularly evil perpetrator.

"The book is haunted by Mickey's worst nightmare: the thought of having to defend an innocent man. He starts out without the foggiest idea of what to do with someone like that. But by the end of the story an Honest Abe conscience has begun to kick in. That's when Mickey becomes a Connelly character through and through." —*New York Times*

Originally published: 2005.

The **night** fire. Michael Connelly. Little Brown & Co, 2019. 400 p. (Renee Ballard novels, 3; Harry Bosch mysteries, 22)

ISBN 9780316485616

1. Detectives 2. Cold cases (Criminal investigation) 3. Alliances 4. Women detectives 5. Mentors 6. Los Angeles, California 7. California 8. Mysteries

Receiving a notebook with details about a 20-year cold case, homicide detective Harry Bosch teams up with LAPD detective Renee Ballard before uncovering disturbing clues about his late mentor.

The **scarecrow**: a novel. Michael Connelly. Little, Brown and Co, 2009. 432 pages (Jack McEvoy novels, 2)

ISBN 9780316166300

1. Serial murder investigation 2. Computer industry and trade 3. Drug dealers 4. Journalists 5. Sixteen-year-old boys 6. Los Angeles, California 7. Thrillers and suspense 8. Multiple perspectives 9. Adult books for young adults

LC 2009000855

Library Journal Best Books, 2009

Pursuing a big story in anticipation of his imminent layoff, Los Angeles reporter Jack McEvoy investigates the murder confession of a teen drug dealer and realizes that the youth may be innocent, a discovery that pits him against a killer operating below police radar.

"The Scarecrow is swift and engrossing, and it marks a development that has needed to happen in Connelly's novels for a while." —*Boston Phoenix*

The **wrong** side of goodbye. Michael Connelly. Little Brown & Co, 2016. 400 p. (Harry Bosch mysteries, 19)

ISBN 9780316225946

1. Rape investigation 2. Private investigators 3. Missing persons investigation 4. Billionaires 5. Serial rapists 6. Los Angeles, California 7. Police procedurals 8. Mysteries

California's newest private investigator, Harry Bosch, searches for a reclusive billionaire's possible heir, a case with odd links to his own past, and volunteers to find a serial rapist for a small cash-strapped police department.

Regular print edition first published in Australia and New Zealand by Allen & Unwin in 2016.

Conner, M. Shelly

Everyman. M. Shelly Conner. Blackstone, 2021. 320 pages

ISBN 9781094006208

1. Young women 2. African American women 3. Orphans 4. Genealogy 5. Families 6. Chicago, Illinois 7. Georgia 8. 1970s 9. Mainstream fiction

Eve Mann arrives in Ideal, Georgia, in 1972 looking for answers about the mother who died giving her life. A mother named Mercy. A mother who for all of Eve's twenty-two years has been a mystery and a quest. Eve's search for her mother, and the father she never knew, is a mission to discover her identity, her name, her people, and her home.

Everyman is a gorgeous, multigenerational examination of the Great Migration and the ripple effects of mysteries that were left in its wake for the descendants of those who sought 'the warmth of other suns.' Booklist

Connolly, John

A **book** of bones. John Conolly. Atria Books, 2019. 496 p. (Charlie)

ISBN 9781982127510

1. Private investigators 2. Detectives 3. Serial murders 4. Murder investigation 5. Women murder victims 6. Maine 7. Mysteries 8. Supernatural mysteries

Three murders in different regions of England reveal the work of a sinister killer who is sacrificing victims for an evil agenda, compelling Charlie Parker's gripping search for clues in multiple countries.

The **dirty** south. John Connolly. Atria Books, 2020. 496 p. (Charlie)

ISBN 9781982127541

1. Former police 2. Widowers 3. Grief in men 4. Loss (Psychology) 5. Girl murder victims 6. Arkansas 7. Maine 8. 1990s 9. Mysteries

Traces Charlie Parker's first case, in which his efforts to bring his wife and child's killer to justice are stymied by corruption.

"Supernatural noir fans will relish Connolly's excellent 18th thriller featuring PI Charlie Parker (after 2019's A Book of Bones), an origin story set in 1999.... Connolly is writing at the top of his game." —*Publishers Weekly*

The **nameless** ones. John Connolly. Emily Bestler Books/Atria, 2021. 432 p. (Charlie)

ISBN 9781982176976

1. Private investigators 2. Assassins 3. War criminals 4. War — Psychological aspects 5. Violence 6. Europe 7. Mysteries

LC 2021009297

When four of his fellow assassins are murdered by Serbian war criminals, Louis arrives in Europe to find and punish five killers before they can vanish into this air—there is just one problem—the sixth.

Connolly, Sheila

The **lost** traveller. Sheila Connolly. Crooked Lane Books, 2019. 336 p. (County Cork mysteries, 7)

ISBN 9781683318903

1. Americans in Ireland 2. Women amateur detectives 3. Women bar owners 4. Villages 5. Rural life 6. Cork County, Ireland 7. Ireland 8. Cozy mysteries 9. Gentle reads

Danger comes to Cork and it's up to Maura Donovan to find a way to protect all she's worked for.

"Although the mystery is cleverly woven into the story, it's the heroine's slow awakening and the marvelous local color that make this one of the best in a fine series." —*Kirkus*

Conrad, Joseph

Complete short fiction of Joseph Conrad: the stories: volume 1. Joseph Conrad; edited with an introduction by Samuel Hynes. ECCO Press, 1991. 296 p.

ISBN 9780880013079

1. Seafaring life 2. Personal conduct 3. Man-woman relationships 4. Short stories 5. Classics 6. Literary fiction

LC 91027115

Collects Conrad's short stories and tales, with a chronology and the author's own notes on his shorter fiction.

Includes the first 9 of 22 stories published between 1896-1928.

★ **Heart** of darkness. Joseph Conrad. Penguin Books, 1999. 146 p.

ISBN 9780140281637

1. Ship captains 2. Colonialism 3. Violence 4. Steamboats 5. Voyages and travels 6. Congo (Democratic Republic) 7. Psychological fiction 8. Literary fiction 9. Classics

Marlowe sails down the Congo in search of Kurtz, a company agent who has, according to rumors, become insane in the jungle isolation.

The 1979 film Apocalypse now is an adaptation of Heart of darkness set during the Vietnam War; Heart of darkness was first published as The heart of darkness in Blackwood's Magazine in 1899; Heart of darkness was first published in book form with Youth and The end of the tether in Youth: a narrative, and two other stories in 1902.

★ **Lord** Jim. Joseph Conrad. Penguin, 2007. 417 p.
ISBN 9780141441610
1. Sailors 2. Young men — Identity 3. Self-fulfillment in men 4. Shipwrecks 5. Cowardice 6. Psychological fiction 7. Sea stories 8. Classics

A young Englishman branded as a coward seeks personal redemption for an act of selfishness.

Originally published: 1900.

Includes essay: "Lord Jim" / by Harold Bloom.

Nostromo: a tale of the seaboard. Joseph Conrad. Penguin, 2007. 532 p.
ISBN 9780141441634
1. Heroes and heroines 2. Revolutions 3. Sailors 4. Greed 5. Silver mines and mining — History 6. South America 7. Psychological fiction 8. Classics 9. Literary fiction

LC 91053185

Set in the fictional South American country of Costaguana, this story of revolution, deception, and self-betrayal centers on Nostromo, a handsome Italian sailor, who, like Costaguana, is being consumed by secret guilt and corruption.

Originally published: 1904.

Victory: an island tale. Joseph Conrad; edited with an introduction and notes by Mara Kalnins. Oxford University Press, 2009. 400 p.
ISBN 9780199554058
1. Island life 2. Colonialism 3. Social isolation 4. Alienation in men 5. Europeans in Indonesia 6. Indonesia 7. Psychological fiction 8. Classics 9. Literary fiction

Baron Axel Heyst and his lover, Lena, a woman he has saved from a sordid life, share an idyllic existence on the island of Samburan until three intruders from Lena's past threaten to destroy their happiness.

Conroy, Pat

The **prince** of tides. Pat Conroy. Houghton Mifflin, 1986. 567 p.
ISBN 9780395353004
1. Adult child abuse victims 2. People with mental illnesses 3. Women poets 4. Women 5. Family problems 6. South Carolina 7. New York City 8. Psychological fiction 9. Books to movies 10. Southern fiction

LC 86010689

Spanning forty years, it is a story about Tom Wingo, his twin sister, Savannah, and the dark and violent past of an extraordinary family into which they were born.

Constantine, Liv

The **last** time I saw you. Liv Constantine. HarperCollins 2019. 320 p.
ISBN 9780062868817
1. Families of murder victims 2. Mothers — Death 3. Suspicion 4. Murderers 5. Rich people 6. Baltimore, Maryland 7. Thrillers and suspense

Supported by her childhood best friend in the aftermath of her mother's murder, a prominent heart surgeon receives threatening taunts from the killer and risks her mental stability in her desperation to solve the case.

"Sisters Lynne and Valerie Constantine, under the pseudonym Liv Constantine (The Last Mrs. Parrish), have crafted another clever whodunit jam-packed with enough twists, turns, and secrets to keep avid thriller readers second-guessing until the bitter end." —*Library Journal*

Cook, Diane

★ The **new** wilderness: a novel. Diane Cook. Harper, 2020. 398 pages
ISBN 9780062333131
1. Mothers and daughters 2. Climate change 3. Survival 4. Sick persons 5. Voyages and travels 6. Dystopian fiction 7. Literary fiction 8 Multiple perspectives
Shortlisted for the Booker Prize, 2020

A mother desperate to save her dying daughter in a world ravaged by climate change joins a hunter-gatherer initiative to test humanity's capacity to survive in the wilderness without destroying it.

"Violence, death, tribalism, lust, love, betrayals, wonder, genius, and courage—all are enacted in this stunningly incisive and complexly suspenseful tale akin to dystopian novels by Margaret Atwood and Claire Vaye Watkins." —*Booklist*

Cook, Robin

Charlatans. Robin Cook. G. P. Putnam's Sons, 2017. 416 p.
ISBN 9780735212480
1. Surgeons 2. Medical malpractice 3. Manslaughter 4. Blame 5. Anesthesiologists 6. Boston, Massachusetts 7. Medical thrillers

Newly minted chief resident at Boston Memorial Hospital Noah Rothauser is swamped in his new position, from managing the surgical schedules to dealing with the fallouts from patient deaths. Known for its medical advances, the famed teaching hospital has fitted several ORs as "hybrid operating rooms of the future"—an improvement that seems positive until an anesthesia error during a routine procedure results in the death of an otherwise healthy man. Noah suspects Dr. William Mason, an egotistical, world-class surgeon, of an error during the operation and of tampering with the patient's record afterward. But Mason is quick to blame anesthesiologist, Dr. Ava London.

"Cook is up-to-date on sophisticated medical equipment, but the high-tech setting is really irrelevant to the tale. Where Cook shines is in illuminating that combination of impersonal professionalism and potential terror haunting every hospital corridor." —*Kirkus*

Coma: a novel. By Robin Cook. Little, Brown, 1977. 306 pages
ISBN 9780316155106
1. Hospital patients 2. Physicians 3. Surgery patients 4. Surgeons 5. Medical students 6. Boston, Massachusetts 7. Thrillers and suspense 8. Medical thrillers 9. Books to movies

LC 76052951

A third-year medical student at a Boston teaching hospital uncovers a medical black market dealing in human organs when she investigates why two young patients have lapsed into comas.

Book made into a movie called Coma.

★ **Genesis**. Robin Cook. Putnam Pub Group, 2019. 400 p.
ISBN 9780525542155
1. DNA 2. Genetic genealogy 3. Coroners 4. Pregnant women — Death 5. Birthfathers 6. Medical thrillers

New York Times-bestselling author Robin Cook takes on the ripped-from-the-headlines topic of harnessing DNA from ancestry websites to catch a killer in this timely and explosive new medical thriller.

Cook, Thomas H.

The **Chatham** School affair. Thomas H. Cook. Bantam Books, 1996. 292 p.
ISBN 9780553096521
1. Private schools 2. Extramarital affairs 3. Art teachers 4. Cape Cod, Massachusetts 5. 1920s 6. Psychological fiction
LC 96-4021
Booklist Editors' Choice: Adult Books for Young Adults, 1996; Edgar Allan Poe Award for Best Mystery Novel, 1997

When Malcolm Gaines asks his attorney to prepare his will, he resurrects the long-buried secret behind a tragedy at Chatham School, which destroyed lives and shattered a quiet community.

"Cook is a marvelous stylist, gracing his prose with splendid observations about people and the lush, potentially lethal landscape surrounding them. Events accelerate with increasing force, but few readers will be prepared for the surprise that awaits at novel's end." —*Publishers Weekly*

The **fate** of Katherine Carr. Thomas H. Cook. Houghton Mifflin Harcourt, 2009. 288 p.
ISBN 9780151014019
1. Travel writers 2. Missing persons investigation 3. Cold cases (Criminal investigation) 4. Murder 5. Grief 6. Psychological suspense 7. Mysteries
LC 2008049203
Shattered by the unsolved murder of his eight-year-old son, travel writer George Gates is approached by a retired missing-persons detective and given a mysterious story left behind by a woman who disappeared twenty years earlier.

"Adept at merging past and present plot lines, Cook eloquently examines the often cathartic act of storytelling." —*Publishers Weekly*

Instruments of night. Thomas H. Cook. Bantam Books, 1998. 293 p.
ISBN 9780553105544
1. Cold cases (Criminal investigation) 2. Mystery story writers 3. Murder 4. Trust 5. Betrayal 6. New York (State) 7. Mysteries 8. Psychological suspense 9. Multiple perspectives
LC 9752760
Assisting in a murder investigation, a writer is brought face to face with a horrible crime from his own past BT

"Although it's easy to miss the very real clues that Cook drops so artfully into the story, there's no ignoring his savage imagery, or escaping the airless chambers of his disturbing imagination." —*New York Times Book Review*

Sandrine's case. Thomas H. Cook. Grove, 2013. 352 p.
ISBN 9780802126085
1. Wife killing 2. Trials (Murder) 3. College teachers 4. Love 5. Secrets 6. Legal thrillers
Sharing a seemingly tranquil relationship with his brilliant bohemian wife only to find himself on trial for her murder, liberal arts college professor Samuel Madison struggles with a hostile town while reevaluating his marriage.

"hrough Sam's memories, Cook pulls off the tricky task of rendering Sandrine —a lover of ancient history, particularly Cleopatra, and the intricacies of language—as vividly as if she had never died. This crime novel, one of his best, builds to an unforeseen, but earned, climax." —*Publishers Weekly*

Cooley, Martha

The **archivist:** a novel. Martha Cooley. Little, Brown, 1998. 328 p.
ISBN 9780316158725
1. Eliot, T. S. 2. Librarians 3. Poets 4. Love letters 5. Man-woman relationships 6. Alienation in men 7. Epistolary novels 8. First person narratives 9. Multiple perspectives
LC 9738385
Library Journal Best Books, 1998; New York Times Notable Book, 1998

A battle of wills between Matt, a careful, orderly archivist for a private university, and Roberta, a determined young poet, over a collection of T. S. Eliot's letters, sealed by bequest until 2019, sparks an unusual friendship and reawakens painful memories of the past.

"The novel treats serious questions in a humane and passionate manner, and leaves one thinking about these questions long after one has read the last page. Cooley is an accomplished stylist—there's scarcely a graceless or unintelligent sentence in the book—and a subtle chronicler of the inner life." —*New York Times Book Review*

Cooney, Caroline B.

The **grandmother** plot. Caroline B Cooney. Poisoned Pen Press, 2021. 320 p.
ISBN 9781728205151
1. Grandmother and grandson 2. Dementia 3. Nursing homes 4. Caregivers 5. Murder victims 6. Connecticut 7. Mysteries
LC 2020033191
When an elderly woman is murdered in the nursing home where his grandmother resides, Freddy, who leads a life of little responsibility, is pressured by his sisters to find her a new place to live while dealing with a side hustle that could turn out to be deadly.

"The author does a remarkable job of combining tones, including sentimental and snarky, while being both wry and gently respectful in depicting mentally diminished people." —*Publishers Weekly*

Cooney, Ellen

The **mountaintop** school for dogs and other second chances. Ellen Cooney. Houghton Mifflin Harcourt, 2014. 304 p.
ISBN 9780544236158
1. Dogs — Training 2. Dog rescue 3. Animal welfare 4. Animal rescue 5. Mainstream fiction 6. Adult books for young adults
A novel of a young woman who, despite knowing nothing about animals, signs herself up for dog training school at The Sanctuary, where she discovers that rescue can find even the most hopeless among us and that friends come in all shapes, sizes, and breeds.

Coonts, Stephen

The **armageddon** file. Stephen Coonts. Regnery Fiction, 2017. 256 p. (Tommy Carmellini novels, 8)
ISBN 9781621576594
1. CIA agents 2. Presidential elections 3. Conspiracies 4. Intelligence service 5. Sabotage 6. United States 7. Political thrillers 8. Spy fiction
LC 2017034764
When a new president-elect's chief of staff discovers evidence of vote tampering, the validity of the election is brought into question at the same time the agendas of dangerous adversaries are revealed.

The **art** of war: a novel. Stephen Coonts. St Martins Pr 2016. 368 p. (Tommy Carmellini novels, 6)
ISBN 9781250041999
1. CIA agents 2. Assassination 3. Nuclear weapons 4. International intrigue 5. Naval power 6. United States 7. Techno-thrillers 8. Spy fiction
LC 2015038676

When newly appointed CIA director Jake Grafton hears murmurings of a Chinese plot to attack the US and assassinations of upper level goverment officials occur, he must investigate the threat and stop China.

★ **Flight** of the Intruder. Stephen Coonts. Naval Institute Press 1986. 329 p. (Jake Grafton novels, 1)
ISBN 9780870212000
1. Vietnam War, 1961-1975 — Aerial operations, American 2. Carrier pilots 3. Grafton, Jake (Fictitious character) 4. Techno-thrillers 5. Books to movies 6. Adult books for young adults
LC 86016440
During the Vietnam War, attack pilot Jake Grafton, struggling with his conscience and trying to find meaning to all the senseless death and destruction, decides to plan an illegal bombing raid into the very heart of Hanoi.
Sequel: Final flight.

★ The **Russia** account. Stephen Coonts. Regnery Pub 2019. 256 p. (Tommy Carmellini novels, 9)
ISBN 9781621576600
1. CIA agents 2. Conspiracies 3. International intrigue 4. Assassins 5. National security 6. Political thrillers 7. Spy fiction
CIA officer Tommy Carmellini navigates an international financial conspiracy that puts CIA head Jake Grafton in the crosshairs of an assassin.

Cooper, Ellison
Buried. Ellison Cooper. Minotaur Books, 2019. 320 p. (Agent Sayer Altair novels, 2)
ISBN 9781250173867
1. Women FBI agents 2. Women neuroscientists 3. Psychopaths 4. Dead 5. Cold cases (Criminal investigation) 6. Virginia 7. Thrillers and suspense
LC 2018055981
Returning to the field after six months of desk duty, FBI neuroscientist Sayer Altair investigates the grisly discovery of a serial killer's uncovered body-dump site, reopening a decades-old case with ties to a recent abduction.

Cooper, James Fenimore
The **last** of the Mohicans: a narrative of 1757. By James Fenimore Cooper; illustrated by N.C. Wyeth. Scribner's, 1986. X, 372 p, [14] leaves of plates : Color illustration (Leatherstocking tales, 2)
ISBN 9780684187112
1. Indians of North America 2. Interracial friendship 3. Frontier and pioneer life 4. Mohegan Indians 5. Bumppo, Natty (Fictitious character) 6. United States 7. New York (State) 8. 18th century 9. Adventure stories 10. Historical fiction 11. War stories
The classic tale of a disillusioned man who exiles himself from a society whose values he abhors. Despite this exile, he agrees to take two sisters through hostile Indian country with the help of a Mohican scout.
Originally published in 1826.
"Clipper"—Cover.
Originally published in the US in 1826.

Cooper, Tom
Florida man. Tom Cooper. Random House, 2020. 448 p.
ISBN 9780593133316
1. Middle-aged men 2. Bad luck 3. Drug use 4. Sinkholes 5. Material culture 6. Florida 7. 1980s 8. Southern fiction 9. Crime fiction

When his prospects are endangered by massive sinkholes appearing throughout Florida's Emerald Island, a middle-aged beach bum uses his amateur spelunking skills to uncover artifacts that change his understanding of the island's history and his own family's birthright.
"Throughout, Cooper's macabre and brutal universe crackles with energy and wit, and will hold readers' attention until the very end. Cooper's riotous, riveting tale rivals the best of Don Winslow." —*Publishers Weekly*

The **marauders**. Tom Cooper. Crown Publishing, 2015. 304 p.
ISBN 9780804140560
1. Treasure hunters 2. Drug use 3. Small towns 4. Obsession 5. Drug traffic 6. Louisiana 7. Crime fiction 8. Noir fiction 9. Southern fiction 10. Adult books for young adults
What does a pill-addicted, one-armed treasure hunter have in common with violent, marijuana-growing identical twin brothers? They all haunt the moonlit swamps of tiny Jeannette, Louisiana, situated near Gulf Coast waters devastated by the massive BP oil spill. Add to this toxic mix are a shifty BP rep trying to get folks to take low-ball settlements, two inept ex-con newcomers, and a troubled widower and his 17-year-old son, who blames his dad for his mom's death during Hurricane Katrina. This gritty, funny, evocative debut novel will please fans of Elmore Leonard and Donald E. Westlake.
"With withering contempt for BP, Cooper offers a believable portrait of a bayou town and a cast of deeply engaging characters wrestling inchoately with the likely extinction of the only life they know. There is real substance and humanity in this fine debut novel." —*Booklist*

Coover, Robert
Going for a beer: selected short fictions. Robert Coover; introduction by T. C. Boyle. W. W. Norton & Company, 2018. 336 p.
ISBN 9780393608465
1. Anthologies 2. Short stories 3. Experimental fiction
LC 2017051773
A collection of the best short fictions from the grandmaster of postmodernism.

The **origin** of the Brunists: a novel. Robert Coover. Grove Press, 2000. 441 p.
ISBN 9780802137432
1. Cults 2. Small towns 3. Poverty 4. Coal mine accidents 5. Prophets 6. Pennsylvania 7. Literary fiction
Winner of the William Faulkner Foundation Award and precursor to 2010's The Brunist Day of Wrath.
Originally published: New York : G.P. Putnam, 1966.

Copenhaver, John
The **savage** kind. John Copenhaver. Pegasus Crime, 2021. 352 p. (Nightingale novels, 1)
ISBN 9781643138091
1. Teenage girls 2. Moving to a new city 3. High school students 4. Violence against women 5. Teenage detectives 6. Washington, D.C. 7. 1940s 8. Hardboiled fiction 9. Historical mysteries 10. Diary novels
Two lonely teenage girls in 1940s Washington, DC, discover they have a penchant for solving crimes—and an even greater desire to commit them—in the new mystery novel by Macavity Award-winning novelist John Copenhaver.
"A profusion of devastating twists complements the pulp-noir tone and keeps readers on tenterhooks, and a tentative romance between Judy and Philippa adds depth. Megan Abbott fans, take note." —*Publishers Weekly*

Coplin, Amanda

The **orchardist**. By Amanda Coplin. Harper, 2012. 448 p.
ISBN 9780062188502
1. Fruit growers 2. Orchards 3. Pregnant teenagers 4. Sisters 5. Families 6. Pacific Northwest 7. Historical fiction 8. Literary fiction
LC 2012005466
Oregon Book Awards, Readers' Choice, 2014

At the turn of the 20th century in a rural stretch of the Pacific Northwest, a gentle solitary orchardist, Talmadge, tends to apples and apricots. Then two feral, pregnant girls and armed gunmen set Talmadge on an irrevocable course not only to save and protect but to reconcile the ghosts of his own troubled past.
First published: London : Weidenfeld & Nicolson, 2012.

Copperman, E. J.

Judgment at Santa Monica. E. J. Copperman. Severn House, 2021. 240 p. (Jersey girl legal novels, 2)
ISBN 9780727890986
1. Women lawyers 2. Actors and actresses 3. Murder investigation 4. Celebrities 5. Trials (Murder) 6. Los Angeles, California 7. California 8. Legal stories

Family lawyer Sandy Moss knows it's a mistake to get mixed up again with charismatic Hollywood TV star Patrick McNabb—prime suspect in her first (and last) murder case—but when he asks for her help she finds herself saying yes. Soon she's tangled up in a celebrity slaying—and Patrick seems to believe he's essential to solving the whole thing.

"Copperman, the creator of a host of zany franchise characters, shows that Byzantine twists and turns, if plotted carefully enough, just add to the fun. Legal mayhem at its finest." —*Kirkus*

Corby, Gary

The **Marathon** conspiracy. Gary Corby. Soho Crime, 2014. 350 p. (Athenian mysteries, 4)
ISBN 9781616953874
1. Civilization, Ancient 2. Private investigators 3. Missing children 4. Schools 5. Crimes against children 6. Ancient Greece 7. Athens, Greece 8. Ancient Greece (800 BCE-640 CE) 9. Historical mysteries 10. Mysteries
LC 2013033925

Traveling to Athens to marry, investigator Nicolaos helps his bride look into the murder and disappearance of two students from the famous Sanctuary of Artemis in as case that is bizarrely tied to findings about a tyrannical ruler who supposedly died 30 years earlier.

"Corby serves up a bubbly cocktail of clear history, contemporary wit, and heart-stopping action." —*Booklist*

Cordova, Zoraida

The **inheritance** of Orquidea Divina. Zoraida Cordova. Atria Books, 2021. 304 p.
ISBN 9781982102548
1. Families 2. Magic 3. Inheritance and succession 4. Funerals 5. Immigrants 6. Ecuador 7. Literary fiction 8. Magical realism 9. Multiple perspectives

Seven years after their matriarch Orquidea passed away, blessing them with her special gifts, the Montoya family journeys to Ecuador to uncover the truth behind their inheritance to stop a hidden figure from killing off Orquidea's line one-by-one.

Corey, James S. A.

Abaddon's gate. James S. A. Corey. Orbit, 2013. 576 p. (Expanse, 3)
ISBN 9780316129077
1. Life on other planets 2. Space warfare 3. Space flight 4. Revenge 5. Conspiracies 6. Science fiction 7. Space opera
Locus Award for Best Science Fiction Novel, 2014

A latest entry in the acclaimed series that includes Leviathan Wakes follows the discovery of a massive alien gate in Uranus's orbit that is examined by Jim Holden and the crew of the Rocinante, who are placed in mortal danger by a complex human plot.
James S.A. Corey is the pseudonym for Daniel Abraham and Ty Franck.

Babylon's ashes. James S. A. Corey. Orbit, 2016. 608 p. (Expanse, 6)
ISBN 9780316334747
1. Space colonies 2. Life on other planets 3. Space warfare 4. Space flight 5. Black market 6. Science fiction 7. Space opera

Summoned by the remnants of old political powers for a desperate mission to reach Medina Station at the heart of the gate network, James Holden and the crew of the Rocinante are challenged by alliance vulnerabilities, an alien mystery and a band of desperate vigilantes.
James S.A. Corey is the pseudonym for Daniel Abraham and Ty Franck.

Caliban's war. By James S. A. Corey. Orbit, 2012. 672 p. (Expanse, 2)
ISBN 9780316129060
1. Life on other planets 2. Space warfare 3. Space flight 4. Missing girls 5. Conspiracies 6. Science fiction 7. Space opera
LC 2011031646
RUSA Reading List, 2013

An alien's attack on the outer-planet territory of Ganymede triggers instability throughout the solar system, prompting James Holden and the crew of the Rocinante to engage in peacekeeping efforts and search for a missing child.
James S.A. Corey is the pseudonym for Daniel Abraham and Ty Franck.

Cibola burn. James S. A. Corey. Orbit, 2014. 592 p. (Expanse, 4)
ISBN 9780316217620
1. Space colonies 2. Life on other planets 3. Space warfare 4. Space flight 5. Plague 6. Science fiction 7. Space opera

In this follow-up to Abbadon's Gate, the human race—both Earth-based and "Belter"—has gained access to a seemingly infinite number of worlds outside of our solar system. As interstellar travel increases exponentially, so do conflicts between inner and outer system populations. At the center of the dispute is newly discovered, lithium-rich planet Ilus, forcing UN representative James Holden and the crew of the Rocinante to try their hands at diplomacy. Fans of sweeping, dramatic space operas that combine deft characterization with detailed world-building will want to get their hands on this 4th book in the Expanse series, which begins with Leviathan Wakes, followed by Caliban's War.

"Combining an exploration of real human frailties with big sf ideas and exciting thriller action, Corey (pen name for authors Ty Franck and Daniel Abraham) cements the series as must-read space opera." —*Library Journal*
James S.A. Corey is the pseudonym for Daniel Abraham and Ty Franck.

★ **Leviathan** wakes. James S. A. Corey. Orbit, 2011. 592 p. (Expanse, 1)
ISBN 9780316129084
1. Detectives 2. Space flight 3. Space warfare 4. Missing girls 5. Conspiracies 6. Space opera 7. Science fiction 8. Books to TV.

Library Journal Best Books, 2011; RUSA Reading List, 2012

When Captain Jim Holden's ice miner stumbles across a derelict, abandoned ship, he uncovers a secret that threatens to throw the entire system into war. Attacked by a stealth ship belonging to the Mars fleet, Holden must find a way to uncover the motives behind the attack, stop a war and find the truth behind a vast conspiracy that threatens the entire human race.

Leviathan Wakes inspired the 2015 Syfy series "The Expanse."

James S.A. Corey is the pseudonym for Daniel Abraham and Ty Franck.

Originally published: 2011.

Nemesis games. James S. A. Corey. Orbit, 2015. 608 p. (Expanse, 5)
ISBN 9780316217583

1. Space colonies 2. Life on other planets 3. Space warfare 4. Space flight 5. Plague 6. Science fiction 7. Space opera

As an intergalactic land rush gets into full swing—causing new alliances, grand acts of violence, and a new human order—James Holden and the crew of the Rocinante must struggle to survive and get back to the only home they have left.

James S.A. Corey is the pseudonym for Daniel Abraham and Ty Franck.

Persepolis rising. James S.A. Corey. Orbit, 2017. 549 p. (Expanse, 7)
ISBN 9780316332835

1. Space colonies 2. Life on other planets 3. Space warfare 4. Space vehicles 5. Enemies 6. Science fiction 7. Space opera

LC 2017042094

As humanity's presence in space expands and new colony worlds struggle to survive, the crew of the aging gunship Rocinante struggles to keep the fragile peace as ancient patterns of war and subjugation return.

"Corey's tense, tightly plotted story is stuffed to the brim with intrigue, action, awesome alien tech, multidimensional characters, and provocative ideas." —*Publishers Weekly*

Tiamat's wrath. James S.A. Corey. Orbit, 2019. 608 p. (Expanse, 8)
ISBN 9780316332873

1. Imaginary empires 2. Life on other planets 3. Space warfare 4. Space vehicles 5. Imaginary wars and battles 6. Science fiction 7. Space opera

LC 2018054213

While Elvi Okoye weighs the consequences of uncovering the truth about weapons tied to an ancient genocide, Teresa Duarte navigates secrets and dangerous intrigues to fulfill her father's godlike ambition.

"Part of what is projected to be a nine-book series, this story at once provides a satisfying conclusion and maneuvers the story lines to a propulsive confrontation that will have readers eagerly awaiting the final chapter." —*Booklist*

Originally published in Great Britain, 2018.

Corleone, Douglas

Good as gone. Douglas Corleone. Minotaur Books, 2013. 304 p. (Simon Fisk novels, 1)
ISBN 9781250017208

1. Private investigators 2. Former marshals 3. Missing children 4. Police 5. Rescues 6. Paris, France 7. Thrillers and suspense

LC 2013009828

Finds a former U.S. Marshal haunted by the unsolved disappearance of his daughter reluctantly investigating a terrifying international child abduction case.

Corman, Avery

Prized possessions. Avery Corman. Simon & Schuster, 1991. 320 p.

ISBN 9780671692988

1. Daughters 2. Rape victims 3. Family relationships 4. Upper class 5. Life change events 6. New York City 7. Psychological fiction 8. Domestic fiction

LC 90022666

This story of a young woman's rape and its effect on her family takes place in the world of Manhattan's upper middle class, tracing Elizabeth Mason's recovery, her parent's pain and guilt, and the family's gradual transformation.

"With Liz's story, Corman takes a tense, disturbing look at the nature of consent and raises critical questions about negative ways in which society still views female sexuality." —*Publishers Weekly*

Cornwell, Bernard

The **archer's** tale. Bernard Cornwell. HarperCollins, 2001. 374 p; (Grail Quest (Bernard Cornwell), 1)
ISBN 9780066210841

1. Grail 2. Hundred Years' War, 1339-1453 3. Knights and knighthood 4. Thomas of Hookton (Fictitious character) 5. Archers 6. Great Britain 7. France 8. Medieval period (476-1492) 9. Plantagenet period (1154-1485) 10. Historical fiction 11. Roth, Philip

LC 2001024333

After surviving a vicious attack on his village in 1343 A.D, archer Thomas of Hookton joins the army of King Edward III as he prepares to launch an invasion into France, but his search for vengeance takes him on an epic quest for the Holy Grail.

"Authentically detailed and appropriately gruesome, the medieval battle scenes fairly crackle with tension; however, what sets Cornwell's work apart from most run-of-the-mill military adventures are his meticulously developed story lines and his razor-sharp characterizations." —*Booklist*

Originally published in Great Britain under the title: Harlequin.

The **last** kingdom: a novel. Bernard Cornwell. Harper Collins Publishers, 2005. 352 pages (Saxon stories (Bernard Cornwell), 1)
ISBN 9780060530518

1. Alfred 2. Vikings 3. Soldiers 4. Uhtred (Fictitious character) 5. Warriors 6. Uncles 7. Great Britain 8. Northumbria (Kingdom) 9. Medieval period (476-1492) 10. Anglo-Saxon period (449-1066) 11. Historical fiction 12. Books to TV

LC 2004054236

Captured and raised by Danes in the ninth century, dispossessed nobleman Uhtred witnesses the unexpected defeat of his adoptive Viking clan by Alfred of Wessex and longs to recover his father's land.

Sword of kings. Bernard Cornwell. HarperCollins, 2019. 336 pages (Saxon stories (Bernard Cornwell), 12)
ISBN 9780062563217

1. Warriors 2. Saxons 3. Vikings 4. Duty 5. Oaths 6. Great Britain 7. Northumbria (Kingdom) 8. Anglo-Saxon period (449-1066) 9. Medieval period (476-1492) 10. Historical fiction

A latest entry in the series that inspired, The Last Kingdom, continues the epic conquests and challenges of Uhtred of Bebbanburg as they shaped a fledgling Britain.

The **winter** king: a novel of Arthur. Bernard Cornwell. St. Martin's Press, 1996. 431 p. (Warlord chronicles, 1)
ISBN 9780312144470

1. Arthur 2. Knights and knighthood 3. Political corruption 4. Rulers 5. Wizards 6. Queen Guinevere (Legendary character) 7. Great Britain 8. Arthurian fantasy 9. Historical fantasy

In Dark Age Britain, a land from which Arthur has been banished and Merlin has disappeared, a child-king sits unprotected on the throne, and it is up to Arthur, a courageous and honorable man, to preserve the lonely embers of civilization in a barbaric world.

"Cornwell's Arthur is fierce, dedicated and complex, a man with many problems, most of his own making. His impulsive decisions sometimes have tragic ramifications... The secondary characters are equally unexpected, and are ribboned with the magic and superstition of the times." —*Publishers Weekly*

Originally published: London : Michael Joseph, 1995.

Cornwell, Patricia Daniels

Autopsy. Patricia Cornwell. William Morrow & Company, 2021. 400 p. (Kay Scarpetta mysteries, 25)
ISBN 9780063112193
1. Women forensic pathologists 2. Coroners 3. Homecomings 4. Husband and wife 5. Crime scenes 6. Alexandria, Virginia 7. Washington, D.C. 8. Mysteries 9. First person narratives
LC 2021033438

New chief medical examiner and forensic pathologist Kay Scarpetta is given a highly classified case involving two scientists who were found dead on a private space laboratory in the latest addition to the series following Chaos.

"Scarpetta's return to her Virginia roots feels just right." —*Booklist*

Postmortem. Patricia Daniels Cornwell. C. Scribner's Sons 1990. 293 p; (Kay Scarpetta mysteries, 1)
ISBN 9780684191416
1. Serial murders 2. Women forensic pathologists 3. Violence against women 4. Women coroners 5. Forensic medicine 6. Richmond, Virginia 7. Psychological suspense 8. Mysteries 9. First person narratives
LC 89010177

Macavity Award for Best First Mystery Novel, 1991; Edgar Allan Poe Award for Best First Mystery Novel, 1991; John Creasey Memorial Award (Best First Crime Novel), 1990; Anthony Award for Best First Novel, 1991

Medical examiner Kay Scarpetta is introduced in this story of a psychopath who is brutally murdering women. Scarpetta must find out why—before she becomes the next victim.

"This mystery about a serial killer features Dr. Kay Scarpetta, Chief Medical Examiner for the Commonwealth of Virginia.... From the moment that the strangler makes his fourth killing (one of two that figure prominently in the plot), the tension is up. No less than the police, Dr. Scarpetta is baffled by the absence of the usual sick motivational pattern; but she can read the physical evidence, and she has the brains and the gizmos—computers, fingerprint-matching processor, DNA-testing equipment, F.B.I. profiling systems—to give the madman chase." —*New York Times Book Review*

A mystery introducing Dr. Kay Scarpetta.

Corry, Jane

The **dead** ex. Jane Corry. Pamela Dorman Books/Viking, 2019. 352 p.
ISBN 9780525561194
1. Missing men 2. Former husbands 3. Divorced women 4. Police 5. Missing persons investigation 6. Great Britain 7. Psychological suspense 8. Multiple perspectives
LC 2018041545

A man's disappearance throws the lives of four women into chaos, including his ex-wife, who struggles to prove her innocence in spite of an unreliable memory.

A Pamela Dorman Book/Viking.

Corthron, Kia

Moon and the Mars. By Kia Corthron. Seven Stories Press, 2021. 704 p.
ISBN 9781644211038
1. Multiracial girls 2. Orphans 3. Race relations 4. Grandmothers 5. Growing up 6. New York City 7. Antebellum America (1820-1861) 8. American Civil War era (1861-1865) 9. Coming-of-age stories 10. Historical fiction 11. First person narratives
LC 2021011365

Set in the impoverished Five Points district of New York City in the years 1857-1863, this novel is told through the eyes of Theo, an orphan living between the homes of her Black and Irish grandparents, as the nation divides and marches to war.

"Playwright and novelist Corthron (The Castle Cross the Magnet Carter) combines a propulsive coming-of-age story with a fascinating history of the years before and after the Civil War." —*Publishers Weekly*

Cosby, S. A.

★ **Blacktop** wasteland. S. A. Cosby. Flatiron Books, 2020. 320 pages
ISBN 9781250252685
1. Automobile mechanics 2. Businesspeople 3. Social classes 4. African American men 5. Jewelry theft 6. Virginia 7. Crime fiction 8. Southern fiction 9. African American fiction

Anthony Award for Best Novel, 2021; Los Angeles Times Book Prize for Mystery or Thriller, 2020; Macavity Award for Best Mystery Novel, 2021; New York Times Notable Book, 2020; Thriller Award for Best Novel, 2021; RUSA Reading List Short List, 2021

Compelled by poverty to agree to a lucrative final heist that will allow him to go straight, a skilled getaway driver finds his efforts complicated by racial dynamics and the ghosts of his past.

"A superb work of crime fiction, uncompromisingly noir but deeply human, too." —*Booklist*

Also published: London : Headline Publishing, 2020.

★ **Razorblade** tears. S.A. Cosby. Flatiron Books, 2021. 320 pages
ISBN 9781250252708
1. Former convicts 2. Loss (Psychology) 3. Revenge 4. Parents of murder victims 5. Fathers and sons 6. Virginia 7. Crime fiction 8. Southern fiction 9. African American fiction
LC 2021004762

When his son Isiah and Isiah's white husband, Derek, are murdered, ex-con Ike Randolph bands together with Derek's father, another ex-con, to rain down vengeance upon those who hurt their boys while confronting their own prejudices about each other and their own sons.

"Cosby follows up his smash debut Blacktop Wasteland (2020) with a powerful blend of pulsing action, sensitive and subtle character interaction, and uncompromising but highly nuanced reflection on racism and homophobia." —*Booklist*

Cosimano, Elle

Finlay Donovan is killing it. Elle Cosimano. Minotaur Books, 2021. 368 p. (Finlay Donovan novels, 1)
ISBN 9781250241702
1. Women authors 2. Single mothers 3. Suburbs 4. Fatigue 5. Stress 6. Virginia 7. Caper novels 8. Farcical fiction
LC 2020037496

LibraryReads Favorites, 2021

When struggling suspense novelist and single mom Finlay Donovan is mistaken for a contract killer, she inadvertently accepts the offer to dispose of a problem husband in order to make ends meet, discovering that crime in real life is a lot harder than fiction.

"Deftly balancing genre conventions with sly, tongue-in-cheek comments on motherhood and femininity, Cosimano crafts a deliciously twisted tale that will earn her a slew of adult fans." —*Booklist*

Cossette, Connilyn

★ **Shelter** of the most high. Connilyn Cossette. Bethany House, 2018. 352 p. (Cities of refuge, 2)

ISBN 9780764219870

1. Strangers 2. Pagans 3. Jews 4. Faith 5. Options, alternatives, choices 6. Christian historical romances 7. Bible novels

LC 2018019432

Christy Award for Historical Category, 2019

Captured by raiders in 1388 B.C, Sofea narrowly escapes slavery. Bargaining her way to a city of refuge in Israel, she finds herself in more danger. Can she find safety in this city of strangers, accept their God as hers, and be satisfied with His justice instead of her own?

Costello, Mark

Big if. Mark Costello. W. W. Norton & Co, 2002. 315 p.

ISBN 9780393051162

1. Primaries 2. Vice-presidents 3. Presidential candidates — Protection 4. Assassination 5. Assassins 6. New Hampshire 7. Political fiction 8. Humorous stories

LC 2002000512

New York Times Notable Book, 2002; National Book Award for Fiction finalist, 2002

In the wake of her father's death and the vice president's campaign for the presidency, Secret Service agent Vi Asplund returns home to her computer genius brother, who is poised to make a fortune on a nihilistic video game.

Coster, Naima

Halsey Street. Naima Coster. Little A, 2018. 336 pages

ISBN 9781503941175

1. Mother-deserted children 2. Mother and adult daughter 3. Women artists 4. Sick fathers 5. Homecomings 6. Brooklyn, New York City 7. Dominican Republic 8. Literary fiction 9. Family sagas 10. Adult books for young adults

Library Journal Best Books, 2018; Kirkus Prize for Fiction finalist, 2018

A modern-day story of family, loss, and renewal, Halsey Street captures the deeply human need to belong—not only to a place but to one another.

"Coster is a masterful observer of family dynamics: her characters, to a one, are wonderfully complex and consistently surprising. Absorbing and alive, the kind of novel that swallows you whole." —*Kirkus*

What's mine and yours: a novel. Naima Coster. Grand Central Publishing, 2021. 416 p.

ISBN 9781538702345

1. High school students 2. School integration 3. Teenage girls 4. Passing (Identity) 5. Identity (Psychology) 6. North Carolina 7. Coming-of-age stories 8. African American fiction 9. Family sagas

LC 2020042924

Integrated into a predominantly white high school, an anxious young Black student and a half-Latina whose mother would have her pass as white join a bridge-building school play that shapes the trajectory of their adult lives.

"Despite its sprawling time line and multiple perspectives, the novel remains an intimate portrait of families shaped by love, motherhood, race, and class." —*Library Journal*

Cotterill, Colin

The **coroner's** lunch. Colin Cotterill. Soho Press, 2004. 272 p. (Dr. Paiboun novels, 1)

ISBN 9781569473764

1. Murder investigation 2. Coroners 3. Senior men 4. Men psychics 5. Ghosts 6. Laos 7. 1970s 8. Mysteries

LC 2004048191

Laos, 1972.The Communist Pathet Lao has taken over. Most of the educated class has fled, but 72-year-old Dr. Siri Paiboun, a Paris-trained doctor, remains and is appointed state coroner. When three bodies are recovered from a reservoir, Dr. Siri establishes that the cause of death was not drowning— they seem to have been electrocuted. And then there is the inexplicable death of a Party bigwig's wife at a banquet. Dr. Siri doesn't think her death was from natural causes. In the course of his investigations, he travels to his birthplace, where he makes a discovery.

"Cotterill's engaging whodunit [is] set in Laos a year after the 1975 Communist takeover." —*Publishers Weekly*

Sequel: Thirty-three teeth.

Disco for the departed. Colin Cotterill. Soho Press, 2006. 247 p. (Dr. Paiboun novels, 3)

ISBN 9781569474280

1. Senior men 2. Coroners 3. Murder investigation 4. Paiboun, Siri, Doctor (Fictitious character) 5. Supernatural 6. Laos 7. 1970s 8. Mysteries 9. Adult books for young adults

LC 2005055462

School Library Journal Best Books: Best Adult Books 4 Teens, 2006

Coroner Siri Paiboun must identify a corpse found near the mansion of the new Laotian president, an investigation which includes communication with the dead, sacrificial rituals, a marriage proposal, and strange disco music that only the doctor can hear.

Don't eat me. Colin Cotterill. Soho Crime, 2018. 304 p. (Dr. Paiboun novels, 13)

ISBN 9781616959401

1. Seniors 2. Coroners 3. Dead 4. Filmmaking 5. Friendship 6. Laos 7. 1980s 8. Mysteries

LC 2017055447

Between getting into a tangle with a corrupt local judge, and discovering a disturbing black-market business, Dr. Siri and his friend Inspector Phosy have their hands full.

"The eccentric Siri, who's possessed by spirits (including those of a dog, his dead mother, and a transvestite fortune-teller), continues to stand out as a unique and endearing series sleuth." —*Publishers Weekly*

Killed at the whim of a hat. Colin Cotterill. St. Martin's Press, 2011. 320 pages (Jimm Juree mysteries, 1)

ISBN 9780312564537

1. Murder investigation 2. Women journalists 3. Murder suspects 4. Murder 5. Hippies 6. Thailand 7. Mysteries

LC 2011008722

Library Journal Best Books, 2011

Forced to relocate to rural Thailand with her eccentric family, crime reporter Jimm Juree fears that her career is over until the bodies of two hippies are discovered in a local farmer's field and a Buddhist abbot is murdered, a case that implicates a monk and a nun.

"Cotterill combines plenty of humor with fascinating and unusual characters, a solid mystery, and the relatively unfamiliar setting of southern Thailand to launch what may be the best new international mystery series since the No. 1 Ladies' Detective Agency." —*Booklist*

First published in Great Britain in 2011 by Quercus—Title page verso.

The **second** biggest nothing. Colin Cotterill. Soho Crime, 2019. 264 p. (Dr. Paiboun novels, 14)
ISBN 9781641290616
1. Coroners 2. Museums 3. Death threats 4. Investigations 5. Prisoners of war 6. Laos 7. 1970s 8. Mysteries
LC 2018057751

Receiving a sinister threat against everyone he loves, Laotian coroner Dr. Siri searches for clues in three incidents from his past, including an encounter with an old friend, a disruptive visit to a Saigon museum and a Vietnam prisoner-of-war negotiation.

Slash and burn: a Dr. Siri Mystery set in Laos. Colin Cotterill. Soho Crime, 2011. 300 p. (Dr. Paiboun novels, 8)
ISBN 9781616951160
1. Murder investigation 2. Missing in action 3. Missing persons investigation 4. Excavation 5. Helicopters — Accidents 6. Laos 7. 1970s 8. Mysteries 9. Adult books for young adults
LC 2011030330

Things have been hectic for Dr. Siri, so he decides to go on a therapeutic vacation with his wife and friends. Unfortunately, trouble follows as the doctor is blackmailed into helping an American MIA team searching for a pilot downed ten years earlier. Sifting through debris, navigating acres of unexploded munitions, and trying to discover who the killer is in their midst make things interesting for Dr. Siri and the morgue team.

Coughlin, Jack

In the crosshairs: a sniper novel. . St. Martin's Press, 2017. 304 pages (Sniper thrillers (Jack Coughlin), 10)
ISBN 9781250103536
1. Drug lords 2. Snipers 3. Bombings 4. Widows 5. Revenge 6. Afghanistan 7. United States 8. Thrillers and suspense
LC 2017013454

CIA field operative Kyle Swanson must find a former top-level Russian sniper who was working for the United States, but appears to have gone rogue, killing a marine in the latest addition to the series following Long Shot.

Long shot: a sniper novel. Gunnery Sgt. Jack Coughlin USMC (Ret.) with Donald A. Davis. St. Martin's Press, 2016. 304 p. (Sniper thrillers (Jack Coughlin), 9)
ISBN 9781250072955
1. Defectors 2. Double agents 3. Military intelligence 4. Traitors 5. Snipers 6. Russia 7. United States 8. Thrillers and suspense
LC 2016003177

A special contractor with the CIA interviews a defector who happens to be a top Russian intelligence agent and finds he is full of amazing secrets.

Coulter, Catherine

The **devil's** triangle. Catherine Coulter and J.T. Ellison. Gallery Books, 2017. 352 pages (Brit in the FBI, 4)
ISBN 9781501150326
1. Undercover operations 2. Weather 3. Terrorism 4. Terrorists 5. British in the United States 6. New York City 7. Thrillers and suspense
LC 2016031234

Entering their new roles as heads of the Covert Eyes team, Nicholas Drummond and Michaela Caine are in a race against time when a dangerous thief known as the Fox resurfaces asking them for help.

The **end** game. . Penguin, 2015. 464 pages (Brit in the FBI, 3)
ISBN 9780399173806
1. Undercover operations 2. Terrorism 3. Terrorists 4. British in the United States 5. FBI agents 6. New York City 7. Thrillers and suspense

Investigating an ecoterrorist group suspected in a series of bombings, FBI agent Nicholas Drummond and his partner, Mike Caine, work with an undercover counter-terrorism agent to stop an assassination plot against the president.

"Nicholas and Mike work in perfect sync, never missing a beat when interviewing witnesses, despite Nicholas's fastidious nature and the ever-present attraction between the two. Their relationship leaves much room for developments in future installments of this excellent suspense series." —*Publishers Weekly*

The **final** cut. Catherine Coulter; with J. T. Ellison. G. P. Putnam's Sons, 2013. 400 pages (Brit in the FBI, 1)
ISBN 9780399164736
1. Murder investigation 2. Jewel thieves 3. Jewelry theft 4. British in the United States 5. FBI agents 6. New York City 7. Thrillers and suspense
LC 2013024511

Library Journal Best Books, 2013

Chief inspector Nicholas Drummond of Scotland Yard investigates after the centerpiece of an exhibit of crown jewels is stolen from the Metropolitan Museum of Art and his colleague is murdered.

Labyrinth. Catherine Coulter. Gallery Books, 2019. 512 p. (FBI suspense thriller series, 23)
ISBN 9781501193651
1. Power (Social sciences) 2. FBI agents 3. Traffic accidents 4. Deception 5. Missing men 6. Washington, D.C. 7. Virginia 8. Thrillers and suspense
LC 2019006760

While Sherlock searches for the missing CIA analyst involved in her recent car crash, Griffin is targeted by a sheriff whose son has been implicated the murders of three girls.

The **last** second. Catherine Coulter and J.T. Ellison. Gallery Books, 2019. 448 p. (Brit in the FBI, 6)
ISBN 9781501138225
1. FBI agents 2. Nero, Emperor of Rome, 37-68 3. Treasure hunters 4. International intrigue 5. Space vehicles 6. New York City 7. Thrillers and suspense
LC 2018049650

When an eccentric treasure hunter finances a private space agency and augments its first satellite with a nuclear device, special agents Drummond and Caine race to prevent a corrupt scientist's apocalyptic plot.

The **lost** key. . G. P. Putnam's Sons, 2014. 448 pages (Brit in the FBI, 2)
ISBN 9780399164767
1. Murder investigation 2. Treasure troves 3. Treasure hunters 4. British in the United States 5. FBI agents 6. New York City 7. Thrillers and suspense

Library Journal Best Books 2014

Investigating the stabbing of a rare book dealer who had been secretly looking for a missing World War I U-boat full of treasure, Nicholas Drummond and his partner, Mike Caine, try to track down the victim's missing children.

Paradox. Catherine Coulter. Gallery Books, 2018. 434 p. (FBI suspense thriller series, 22)

ISBN 9781501138126
1. FBI agents 2. Psychopaths 3. Bones 4. Murder victims 5. Revenge 6. Maryland 7. Thrillers and suspense

LC 2018007876

When divers discover the bones of multiple murder victims during a search of Lake Massey, agents Sherlock and Savich make a connection between the bones and an escaped psychopath who attempted to kidnap five-year-old Sean Savich.

The **sixth** day. Catherine Coulter and J.T. Ellison. Simon & Schuster 2018. 448 p. (Brit in the FBI, 5)
ISBN 9781501138171
1. FBI agents 2. Assassination 3. International intrigue 4. Betrayal 5. Terrorism 6. New York City 7. Thrillers and suspense

When several major political figures who are linked to sophisticated drone assassinations die under mysterious circumstances, the Covert Eyes team follows leads to a wealthy cybersecurity genius and descendant of Vlad the Impaler who is desperate to unlock the secret of curing his severely ill twin brother's blood disorder.

Couto, Mia

Rain: and other stories. Mia Couto; translated by Eric M. B. Becker. Biblioasis, 2019. 168 p.
ISBN 9781771962667
1. Civil war 2. Colonialism 3. Postwar life 4. Loss (Psychology) 5. Hope 6. Mozambique 7. Africa 8. Short stories 9. Literary fiction 10. Translations

Published in the aftermath of Mozambique's bloody civil war, Mia Couto's third collection seeks out the places violence could not reach, the places where, the author writes, "every man is the same: pretending he's here, dreaming of going away, and plotting his return." Shifting masterfully between forms—creation tale to meditation, playful comedy to magical twist—these stories grapple with questions of what's been lost and what can be reclaimed, what future exists for a country that broke the yoke of colonialism only to descend into internecine war, what is Mozambican and what is Mozambique.

Translated from the Portuguese.

Sleepwalking land. Mia Couto; translated by David Brookshaw. Serpent's Tail, 2004. 256 p.
ISBN 9781852428976
1. Senior men 2. Boys 3. Refugees 4. Civil war 5. Children and war 6. Mozambique 7. 1970s 8. 1980s 9. Translations 10. War stories 11. Magical realism

"Many great novels have shown a world torn to shreds by the brutality of war. To do so, their authors ground their texts in the details of destruction and decay. But Couto's novel stands apart: it shows the world that war creates, a dreamscape of uncertainty where characters and readers alike marvel not at the abnormal becoming normal but at the way we come to accept the impossible as reality." —*New York Times Book Review*

Translation from the Portuguese of: Terra Sonambula.

Originally published: Lisboa : Caminho, 1992.

The **sword** and the spear. Mia Couto; translated from the Portuguese by David Brookshaw. Farrar, Straus and Giroux, 2020. 288 p. (Sands of the emperor, 2)
ISBN 9780374256890
1. Colonialism 2. Europeans in Africa 3. Military occupation 4. Interracial romance 5. Prejudice 6. Mozambique 7. 19th century 8. 1890s 9. Historical fiction 10. Literary fiction 11. Multiple perspectives

LC 2020012323

As war rages between the Portuguese occupiers and the Mozambique warriors in 1895, Imani embarks on a rescue mission for her lover, the defeated Portuguese sergeant Germano de Melo, in the second novel of the trilogy following Woman of the Ashes.

"The second novel offers a helpful summary of the first and provides a stand-alone story with its own intrigues, as battles between the colonists and colonized intensify, and a late-breaking plot twist sets up the concluding novel on both symbolic and plot levels. A nuanced study of the power plays and violence sparked by colonialism." —*Kirkus*

Originally published in Portuguese in 2016 by Editorial Caminho, Portugal, as A espada e azagaia—Title page verso.

Translated from the Portuguese.

Crace, Jim

Harvest. Jim Crace. Nan A. Talese/Doubleday, 2013. 240 p.
ISBN 9780385520775
1. Xenophobia 2. Villages 3. Malicious accusation 4. Arson 5. Crime 6. England 7. Medieval period (476-1492) 8. Historical fiction 9. Psychological fiction 10. Literary fiction

LC 2012026208

International IMPAC Dublin Literary Award, 2015; James Tait Black Memorial Prize for Fiction, 2013; Library Journal Best Books 2013; Shortlisted for the Man Booker Prize, 2013; Shortlisted for the Walter Scott Prize for Historical Fiction, 2014

A stable fire in a remote English village leads to disputes between newcomers who are wrongly accused and long-term residents who refuse to believe one of their own could be responsible, a situation that is further exacerbated by the observations and meticulous note-taking of another outsider.

Quarantine. Jim Crace. Farrar, Straus and Giroux, 1997. 242 p.
ISBN 9780374239626
1. Jesus Christ 2. Fasting — Religious aspects 3. Pilgrims and pilgrimages 4. Expectation (Psychology) 5. Wilderness survival 6. Husband and wife 7. Bible novels 8. Historical fiction 9. Literary fiction

LC 9761489

Whitbread Book Award for Novel, 1997; New York Times Notable Book, 1998; Shortlisted for the Booker-McConnell Prize, 1997; Shortlisted for the International IMPAC Dublin Literary Award, 1999

Retells the story of Jesus Christ's forty-day sojourn in the wilderness and its impact on a small group of individuals

"Crace's prose is startingly specific about ancient life and Judea's harsh, terrible beauty. Unlike many authors of biblical fiction, he blends his research smoothly into his narrative and adds a leavening pinch of humor." —*Time*

Crafts, Hannah

The **bondwoman's** narrative. Hannah Crafts; edited by Henry Louis Gates. Warner Books, 2002. 338 p. : Illustration
ISBN 9780446530088
1. Crafts, Hannah 2. Enslaved women 3. Freedom seekers 4. African American women 5. Plantations 6. United States 7. Autobiographical fiction 8. African American fiction

LC 2001098325

A novel written in the 1850s by a runaway slave follows a young slave from a North Carolina plantation as she flees to the North and, after being pursued by slave hunters and forced to serve a difficult new mistress, finally obtains freedom in New Jersey.

Craig, Charmaine

Miss Burma. Charmaine Craig. Grove Press, 2017. 368 p.
ISBN 9780802126450
1. Interethnic marriage 2. Interethnic conflict 3. Marginalized people 4. Civil war 5. Political persecution 6. Burma 7. 20th century 8. Political fiction 9. Literary fiction 10. Historical fiction

LC 2016047415

Longlisted for the National Book Award for Fiction, 2017; Longlisted for The Women's Prize for Fiction, 2018

In 1939, Benny, an Anglo-Indian pugilist from Rangoon's Jewish quarter, falls in love with Khin, a Karen woman. Their daughter, Louisa, grows up to be a beauty queen and an unlikely symbol of unity in a divided nation. Based on author Charmaine Craig's own family history, this sweeping saga brings to life a tumultuous half-century in the history of Burma (Myanmar) that includes British colonial rule, World War II and Japanese occupation, independence, and military dictatorship.

Crais, Robert

A **dangerous** man. Robert Crais. G.P. Putnam's Sons, 2019. 336 p. (Elvis Cole/Joe Pike novels, 18)
ISBN 9780525535683
1. Kidnapping victims 2. Private investigators 3. Missing persons investigation 4. Murder 5. Whistle blowers 6. Los Angeles, California 7. Mysteries 8. Hardboiled fiction

Rescuing a bank teller from an abduction attempt, Joe Pike tackles the most perilous case of his career when the would-be kidnappers are found murdered and the bank teller goes missing.

Demolition angel: a novel. Doubleday, 2000. 386 p.
ISBN 9780385495844
1. Policewomen 2. Bombings 3. Terrorists 4. Bomb squads 5. Murder 6. Los Angeles, California 7. Thrillers and suspense 8. Police procedurals

LC 29054

Carol Starkey, a Los Angeles bomb squad detective who suffered permanent scarring and watched her lover/partner die in a prior detonation, embarks on a dangerous investigation into explosions rocking the city that are designed specifically to kill bomb technicians.

"The book features one of the most complex heroines to grace a thriller since Clarice Starling locked eyes with Hannibal Lecter, a deliciously spooky villain in the person of a mad bomber known as Mr. Red, and an aggressively involving plot." —*Publishers Weekly*

The **first** rule. By Robert Crais. G. P. Putnam's Sons, 2010. 320 p. (Elvis Cole/Joe Pike novels, 13)
ISBN 9780399156137
1. Home invasions 2. Drug traffic 3. Deception 4. Revenge 5. Criminals 6. Los Angeles, California 7. Mysteries 8. Hardboiled fiction

LC 2009036928

Elvis Cole's taciturn partner, Joe Pike, investigates an attack on former associate Frank Meyer, a one-time mercenary whose family has been murdered by a professional hit crew and who police suspect has been keeping a dangerous secret.

"Righteous vengeance, a reckless pace, a stratospheric body count and just enough surprises to keep you turning the pages. The pleasures may be primitive, but they're genuine." —*Kirkus*

Suspect. Robert Crais. G. P. Putnam's Sons, 2013. 320 p.
ISBN 9780399161483
1. Post-traumatic stress disorder 2. Police 3. Police dogs 4. Human-animal relationships 5. Murder investigation 6. Los Angeles, California 7. Thrillers and suspense
Library Journal Best Books, 2013

Struggling to reclaim his career after the devastating murder of his partner eight months earlier, LAPD cop Scott James is teamed with a traumatized military canine named Maggie who assists Scott in an effort to track down his late partner's killer.

Cramer, W. Dale

Levi's will: a novel. W. Dale Cramer. Bethany House, 2005. 394 p.
ISBN 9780764229954
1. Amish 2. Former Amish 3. Married men 4. Fathers 5. Amish families 6. Ohio 7. Florida 8. 1940s 9. Christian fiction 10. Family sagas 11. Adult books for young adults

LC 2005004602

Christy Award for Contemporary (Stand Alone) Category, 2006; Library Journal Best Books, 2005

"A family saga of pain and reconciliation set behind the closed doors of an Amish community. Spanning three generations, the story follows the life of Will McGruder, who having fled as a young man, seeks to heal the past by bringing his new family to meet his Amish relatives." —Provided by publisher.

Crane, Stephen

Maggie: a girl of the streets. Stephen Crane. Prometheus Books, 1995. 90 p.
ISBN 9781573920377
1. City life 2. Poor girls 3. Families 4. Alcoholic mothers 5. Prostitutes 6. New York City 7. Bowery, New York City 8. Gilded Age (1865-1898) 9. Psychological fiction

LC 959642

The harrowing story of a young girl living in the slums of New York City.

★ The **red** badge of courage: an episode of the American Civil War. . Modern Library, 1993. Li, 246 p.
ISBN 9780679602965
1. Courage in men 2. Union soldiers 3. Civil war 4. Cowardice in men 5. Shame in men 6. Virginia 7. United States 8. American Civil War era (1861-1865) 9. War stories 10. Historical fiction 11. Books to movies

LC 92027135

During his service in the Civil War, a young Union soldier matures to manhood and finds peace of mind as he comes to grips with his conflicting emotions about war.

Originally published: New York : D. Appleton and company, 1895.
Includes bibliographical references (p. li).

Creech, Sarah

The **whole** way home. Sarah Creech. William Morrow & Co, 2017. 368 p.
ISBN 9780062409294
1. Country musicians 2. Former lovers 3. Secrets 4. Women musicians 5. Singers 6. Nashville, Tennessee 7. Mainstream fiction

A radiant talent on the brink of making it big in Nashville must confront her small-town past and an old love she's never forgotten in this engaging novel—a soulful ballad filled with romance, heartbreak, secrets, and scandal from the author of Season of the Dragonflies.

Crews, Harry

A **feast** of snakes: a novel. Harry Crews. Scribner, 1998. 177 p.
ISBN 9780684842486

1. Discontent in men 2. Snakes 3. Rattlesnakes 4. Festivals 5. Small towns 6. Georgia 7. Black humor 8. Southern Gothic 9. Literary fiction

LC 97031155

"The novel is set in the backwoods hamlet of Mystic, Georgia, where the annual festival begins with the crowning of the high-school Rattlesnake Queen, continues with a pit-bull championship fight, and ends with a Rattlesnake Roundup. The festival this year is a total nightmare: a black girl with a razor emasculates Sheriff Buddy Matlow, Big Joe Mackey kicks his losing dog to death, and Joe Lon Mackeyaged twenty-two, practically illiterate, miserably married, with two screaming babies, his years of glory as an all-around athlete...behind himgoes out of control with a twelve-gauge shotgun." —*The New Yorker*

Crichton, Michael

Pirate latitudes. Michael Crichton. HarperCollins, 2009. 320 p.

ISBN 9780061929373

1. Pirates 2. Treasure hunting 3. Raids (Military science) 4. Violence 5. Gold 6. Caribbean area 7. 17th century 8. Adventure stories 9. Thrillers and suspense

English Captain Charles Hunter and his crew of ruffians sail from colonial Jamaica to infiltrate a Spanish-controlled port, commandeering the galleon El Trinidad and its fortune in gold after a bloody battle.

"Pirate fans will love the book for its flashy characters and historical authenticity. Crime fans will enjoy the caper-novel structure and the way the author keeps them on their toes." —*Booklist*

Prey: a novel. Michael Crichton. HarperCollins, 2002. 367 p.

ISBN 9780066214122

1. Nanotechnology 2. Evolution 3. Artificial life 4. Technology and civilization 5. High technology industry and trade 6. Nevada 7. California 8. Techno-thrillers 9. Adult books for young adults

LC 2002032338

Booklist Editors' Choice: Adult Books for Young Adults, 2002

Deep in the remote Nevada desert, eight people are trapped inside of the Xymos Corporation by a rapidly evolving swarm of predatory molecules that have massed together to form a powerful and intelligent organism that is targeting its creators.

"Despite its absurd moments, 'Prey' is irresistibly suspenseful. You're entertained on one level and you learn something on another, even if the two levels do ultimately diverge." —*New York Times Book Review*

Crombie, Deborah

A **bitter** feast. Deborah Crombie. William Morrow & Co 2019. 384 p. (Duncan Kincaid and Gemma James mysteries, 18)

ISBN 9780062271662

1. Husband-and-wife detectives 2. Criminal investigation 3. Family estates 4. Rich families 5. Villages 6. England 7. Mysteries 8. Police procedurals

Invited to spend a weekend at a tranquil Cotswolds village, husband-and-wife Scotland Yard detectives Kincaid and James are drawn into a dangerous web of secrets involving an up-and-coming star chef and a series of mysterious deaths.

Crompton, Richard

Hell's gate: a novel. Richard Crompton. Sarah Crichton Books/Farrar, Straus and Giroux, 2015. 256 p. (Detective Mollel mysteries, 2)

ISBN 9780374280581

1. Masai (African people) 2. Murder investigation 3. Detectives 4. Police corruption 5. Love, Nat 6. Kenya 7. Nairobi, Kenya 8. Mysteries

LC 2014030528

A former Maasai warrior who now works as a detective uncovers a murder plot, as well as extortion and bribery outside a national park.

"A classic lone-wolf detective story with enough plot twists to keep readers guessing until the end, this novel will appeal to those looking for both a psychological and an action thriller." —*Library Journal*

Hour of the red god. Richard Crompton. Sarah Crichton Books, 2013. 272 p. (Detective Mollel mysteries, 1)

ISBN 9780374171995

1. Masai (African people) 2. Crimes against prostitutes 3. Political corruption 4. Conspiracies 5. Murder investigation 6. Kenya 7. Nairobi, Kenya 8. Mysteries

LC 2012034612

Detective Mollel, a former Maasai warrior in Nairobi, investigates the brutal murder of a prostitute and suspects the killing is part of a far more extensive plot associated with the turbulent elections of 2007.

"[Crompton's] debut novel combines a sinuous plot, a wonderfully complex and tragic protagonist, and a remarkable portrait of a city that is simultaneously exotic yet familiar." —*Booklist*

Originally published as an e-book titled, The Honey Guide

Cronin, A. J.

Citadel. By A.J. Cronin. Little 1937. 401 p.

ISBN 9781529015386

1. Physicians 2. Ambition in men 3. Husband and wife 4. Wales 5. London, England 6. Mainstream fiction 7. Books to movies 8. Books to TV

A sincere, conscientious young doctor faces the realization that he can achieve great material success only at the cost of his self-image.

Adapted into a film by the same name in 1938 and 1960 in the United States. Also adapted for television miniseries in 1960 and 1983 in the United Kingdom.

The **keys** of the kingdom. By A.J. Cronin. Little, 1941. 344 p.

ISBN 9780316161848

1. Christian missions 2. Priests 3. China 4. Christian fiction 5. Books to movies

LC 83-83064

Sent to China, a Scottish priest struggles to create and maintain a mission where famine, disease, and civil war prevail.

Cronin, Justin

The **city** of mirrors. Justin Cronin. Random House, 2016. 704 p. (Passage trilogy, 3)

ISBN 9780345505002

1. Vampires 2. Revenge 3. Good and evil 4. Viruses 5. Survival 6. Horror 7. Apocalyptic fiction

Loan Stars Favourites, 2016

The third and final installment in the Passage trilogy. With The Twelve destroyed, many wonder if the threat to humankind also has vanished. But then a terrifying threat shudders the gates of the colony...and Amy—the girl who must save the world, Peter, Alicia, and Michael must at last confront their destinies.

"Not only does this title bring the series to a thrilling and satisfying conclusion, but it also exhibits Cronin's moving exploration of love as both a destructive force and an elemental need, elevating this work among its dystopian peers." —*Library Journal*

The **passage**. Justin Cronin. Ballantine Books, 2010. 640 p. (Passage trilogy, 1)

ISBN 9780345504968

1. Vampires 2. Viruses 3. Survival 4. Immortality 5. Good and evil 6. California 7. Horror 8. Books to TV 9. Apocalyptic fiction
Library Journal Best Books, 2010

The latest test subject in a covert government experiment, abandoned six-year-old Amy is rescued by an FBI agent who hides them in the Oregon hills, from which Amy emerges a century later to save the human race from a terrifying virus.

"The Passage owes a substantial debt to both King's 1978 epic and Cormac McCarthy's 2007 Pulitzer winner, and he is not immune to some of the hoarier tropes of Armageddon fiction (mystical children, cryptic-wisdom-spouting old folks, impossibly arduous vision quests). But his bogeymen, the vampiric, blood-hungry beasts known as virals, are magnificently unnerving, and his power to compel readers to the next page seldom flags." —*Entertainment Weekly*
First published: 2010.

The **twelve**. Justin Cronin. Ballantine, 2012. 640 p. (Passage trilogy, 2)
ISBN 9780345504982
1. Vampires 2. Viruses 3. Survival 4. Immortality 5. Good and evil 6. Horror 7. Apocalyptic fiction
Goodreads Choice Award, 2012

Survivors of a government-induced apocalypse endure their violent and disease-stricken world while protecting their loved ones; while a century into the future, members of a transformed society determinedly search for the original twelve virals.

Cronin, Marianne
The **one** hundred years of Lenni and Margot. Marianne Cronin. HarperCollins, 2021. 336 p.
ISBN 9780063092761
1. Teenage girls 2. Octogenarians 3. Hospital patients 4. People with terminal illnesses 5. Clergy 6. Glasgow, Scotland 7. Scotland 8. Relationship fiction 9.
LibraryReads Favorites, 2021

Determined to leave a mark on the world even though they are in the hospital and their days are dwindling, unlikely friends, 17-year-old Lenni and 83-year-old Margot, devise a plan to create 100 paintings showcasing the stories of the century they have lived.

"A whimsical, joyous portrait of the ends of things." —*Kirkus*

Cross-Smith, Leesa
Whiskey & ribbons. Leesa Cross-Smith. Hub City Press, 2018. 272 p.
ISBN 9781938235382
1. African American families 2. Police 3. African American widows 4. Murder victims 5. Assaults on police 6. African American fiction 7. Domestic fiction 8. Multiple perspectives

Leesa Cross-Smith's anticipated novel following a contemporary African American family caught in the wake of a tragic police shooting. Set in contemporary Louisville, the death of a police officer is a requiem for marriage, friendship and family.

Crossan, Sarah
Here is the beehive. Sarah Crossan. Little Brown & Co, 2020. 208 p.
ISBN 9780316428583
1. Women lawyers 2. Grief in women 3. Married women 4. Lovers — Death 5. Extramarital affairs 6. London, England 7. Novels in verse 8. First person narratives 9. Literary fiction

A debut about a love affair cut short, and how lonely it is to live inside a secret.

"The book, structured in five parts, explores Ana's grief, guilt, and loss in stunning, spare lyrical prose, which appears like verse on the page as dialogue breaks into snippets of Ana's consciousness. Told from the point of view of a highly flawed Ana, this mesmerizing story will have readers hooked." —*Publishers Weekly*

Crouch, Blake
Dark matter: a novel. By Blake Crouch. Crown Publishers, 2016. 336 p.
ISBN 9781101904220
1. College teachers 2. Parallel universes 3. Kidnapping victims 4. Life change events 5. Scientists 6. Chicago, Illinois 7. Science fiction thrillers
LC 2015040107
LibraryReads Favorites, 2016; Loan Stars Favourites, 2016

A mind-bending, relentlessly paced science-fiction thriller, in which an ordinary man is kidnapped, knocked unconscious—and awakens in a world inexplicably different from the reality he thought he knew.

"Suspenseful, frightening, and sometimes poignant—provided the reader has a generously willing suspension of disbelief." —*Kirkus*

Recursion. Blake Crouch. Crown, 2019. 336 pages
ISBN 9781524759780
1. Memories 2. Deception 3. High technology 4. Neuroscientists 5. False memory syndrome 6. 21st century 7. Science fiction thrillers
Loan Stars Favourites, 2019; LibraryReads Favorites, 2019; Goodreads Choice Award, 2019

Assigned to the case of a suicide victim who claimed her son's existence had been erased, investigator Barry Sutton follows leads to the outbreak of a memory-altering disease and the technological innovations of a controversial neuroscientist.

"This latest technological thriller from Crouch (Dark Matter) is completely engrossing and should have wide appeal. Highly recommended, especially for readers who enjoy suspenseful, fast-moving, well-crafted, science-based sf." —*Library Journal*

Crouch, Katie
Embassy wife. Katie Crouch. Farrar, Straus and Giroux, 2021. 336 p.
ISBN 9780374280345
1. Married women 2. Female friendship 3. Expatriates 4. Diplomats 5. Americans in Africa 6. Namibia 7. Southern Africa 8. Satirical fiction 9. Literary fiction
LC 2021005690

A satirical page-turner following two women abroad searching for the truth about their husbands-and their country.

"Unpredictable twists lead to an ending where everyone may not get what they want, but they get what they need. Suggest this one to fans of Meg Wolitzer and Maria Semple." —*Booklist*

Crow, Sarah McCraw
The **wrong** kind of woman. Sarah McCraw Crow. Mira Books, 2020. 313 p.
ISBN 9780778310075
1. Widows 2. College teachers 3. Life change events 4. Universities and colleges 5. Women teachers 6. New Hampshire 7. 1970s 8. Literary fiction 9. Multiple perspectives

In late 1970, Oliver Desmarais drops dead in his front yard while hanging Christmas lights. In the year that follows, his widow, Virginia, struggles to find her place on the campus of the elite New Hampshire men's college where Oliver was a professor. While Virginia had always shared her husband's prejudices against the four outspoken, never-married women on the faculty—dubbed The Gang of Four by their male counterparts—she now finds herself depending on them. Soon, though, reports of violent protests across the country reach this sleepy New England town, stirring tensions between the fraternal establishment of Clarendon College and those calling for change.

"The choice to present the characters' desperate actions in shades of gray makes for engrossing reading. McCraw Crow's smart and thoughtful story will ring true to those who witnessed the social upheavals of the '70s." —*Publishers Weekly*

Crowell, Jenn

Etched on me: a novel. Jenn Crowell. Washington Square Press, 2013. 320 p.

ISBN 9781476739069

1. Child custody 2. Mothers and daughters 3. Adult child sexual abuse victims 4. Psychic trauma 5. Self-harm 6. London, England 7. Coming-of-age stories 8. Mainstream fiction 9. Adult books for young adults

LC 2013014712

A coming-of-age story about a young woman who overcomes a troubled adolescence, only to lose custody of her daughter when her mental health history is used against her.

Crowley, John

Lord Byron's novel: the evening land. John Crowley. William Morrow, 2005. 480 p.

ISBN 9780060556587

1. Byron, George Gordon Byron 2. Codes (Communication) 3. Fiction writing 4. Fathers and daughters 5. Manuscripts — Collectors and collecting 6. Women mathematicians 7. Great Britain 8. Regency period (1811-1820) 9. Novels-within-novels 10. Epistolary novels 11. Gothic fiction

LC 2004063575

"Crowley's real achievement in Lord Byron's Novel is not a convincing imitation of Byronnot even Byron, who was pudgy and pale and walked with a limp, could always pull that off. More persuasive by far is the suffocating world of encryption and code, coincidence and conspiracy, paranoia and parapsychology that Crowley summons from his 19th-century documents and 21st-century decoders." —*New York Times Book Review*

Crucet, Jennine Capo

Make your home among strangers. Jennine Capo Crucet. St. Martin's Press, 2015. 352 p.

ISBN 9781250059666

1. Young women 2. College students 3. Immigrants 4. Family relationships 5. Divorce 6. Miami, Florida 7. Pissarro, Camille 8. Coming-of-age stories 9. Adult books for young adults
Booklist Editors' Choice: Adult Books for Young Adults, 2015;
School Library Journal Best Books: Best Adult Books 4 Teens, 2015

Upsetting her family by attending an elite college far from home, Cuban-American Lizet struggles with identity issues and her father's abandonment before meeting a young boy whose mother's death enmeshes Lizet's family in Florida's heated immigration debates.

"An emblematic story of both immigrant America and the coming-of-age struggle, told by an a PEN/O. Henry and Iowa Short Fiction award winner." —*Library Journal*

Crumley, James

The **last** good kiss: a novel. James Crumley. Random House, 1978. 259 p; (C. W. Sughrue mysteries, 1)

ISBN 9780394419466

1. Missing persons 2. Alcoholics 3. Murder investigation 4. Prostitutes 5. Criminal investigation 6. Haight-Ashbury District, San Francisco, California 7. San Francisco, California 8. Mysteries 9. Hardboiled fiction

LC 77090286

C.W. Sughrue, a Montana private eye, is hired to track down a failing author and winds up searching for Betty Sue Flowers, a woman missing for ten years in Haight-Ashbury

★ The **wrong** case. James Crumley. Random House, 1975. 272 p. (Milo Milodragovitch mysteries, 1)

ISBN 9780394496184

1. Private investigators 2. Alcoholics 3. Missing persons investigation 4. Murder investigation 5. Siblings 6. Pacific Northwest 7. Mysteries 8. Hardboiled fiction

LC 85-8882

In the small Northwest town of Meriwether, onetime prosperous private investigator Milo is lured from his reveries of lost opportunities into love, dope-dealing, and murder by one Helen Duffy who asks him to find her lost brother

"This is an exceptionally good example of the genre. Properly deferring to hallowed conventions, Crumley writes about damaged people seen through a haze of jaded romanticism, but he asserts his own tone of voice .... Crumley is a vivid writer. He makes Milo much more vulnerable, more involved in this sordid case than Hammett or Chandler would have done." —*Newsweek*

Crummey, Michael

Galore. Michael Crummey. Doubleday Canada, 2009. 336 p.
ISBN 9780385663144

1. Fishing villages 2. Whales 3. Family relationships 4. Small town life 5. Interpersonal relations 6. Newfoundland and Labrador 7. Canada 8. Family sagas 9. Historical fiction 10. Canadian fiction
Canadian Authors Association Literary Awards, MOSAID
Technologies Inc. Award for Fiction, 2010; Commonwealth Writers' Prize, Caribbean and Canada: Best Book, 2010; Shortlisted for the International IMPAC Dublin Literary Award, 2011; Governor General's Literary Awards, English-language Fiction finalist

Narrates the stories of six generation of two families who live in the small town of Deep Paradise set in Newfoundland, describing their loves and hates combined with elements of folklore and tales of witches, and ghosts.

"Crummey has created an unforgettable place of the imagination. Paradise Deep belongs on the same literary map as Faulkner's Yoknapatawpha and Garcia Marquez's Macondo." —*Boston Globe*

The **innocents**. Michael Crummey. Doubleday, 2019. 304 pages
ISBN 9780385545426

1. Orphans 2. Survival 3. Loyalty 4. Forgiveness 5. Social isolation 6. Newfoundland and Labrador 7. 19th century 8. Literary fiction 9. Historical fiction 10. Canadian fiction 11. Adult books for young adults

LC 2018059408

ALA Notable Book, 2020; Thomas Head Raddall Atlantic Fiction Prize, 2020; Rogers Writers' Trust Fiction Prize finalist, 2019; Shortlisted for the Scotiabank Giller Prize, 2019

Two orphans forage for survival on an isolated Newfoundland cove during years marked by storms and ravaging illness, before the mystery of their nature tests the limits of their bond.

Sweetland. Michael Crummey. Liveright Publishing, 2015. 322 p. ISBN 9780871407900

1. Misfits (Persons) 2. Eminent domain 3. Home (Concept) 4. Eccentrics and eccentricities 5. Rural families 6. Newfoundland and Labrador 7. Canadian fiction 8. Literary fiction 9. Domestic fiction Newfoundland and Labrador Book Award for Fiction, 2016; Governor General's Literary Awards, English-language Fiction finalist

Sweetland is a story about one man's struggles against the forces of nature on a remote island just off Newfoundland.

"The small cast of accompanying characters is well and wittily delineated, and Crummey's characteristic switching between past and present is done craftily." —*Booklist*

First published: Canada: Doubleday Canada, 2014.

Originally published in Canada in 2014 (Toronto : Doubleday Canada, 2014)

Cruse, Howard

The **complete** Wendel. By Howard Cruse. Universe Pub, 2011. 288 p. : Illustration

ISBN 9780789322166

1. Gay men 2. Gay culture 3. Gay couples 4. Interpersonal relations 5. Family relationships 6. United States 7. 1980s 8. LGBTQIA comics 9. Alternative comics 10. Comics and Graphic novels

LC 2010934608

The complete collection of the entire groundbreaking gay comic strip series. Originally published in The Advocate throughout the 1980s, Howard Cruse's Wendel is widely considered the first gay comic strip to be featured in mainstream media.

Originally published in The Advocate, 1983-1989.

Includes the complete collection of the comic strip series as found in the author's Wendel All Together, a new foreword by the author and introduction by Alison Bechdel. Also features a new cover and a special "where are they now" section.

Cruz, Angie

Dominicana: a novel. Angie Cruz. Flatiron Books, 2019. 336 pages ISBN 9781250205933

1. Arranged marriage 2. Teenage girls 3. Immigration and emigration 4. Young women — Relations with older men 5. Families 6. New York City 7. Dominican Republic 8. 1960s 9. Historical fiction 10. Coming-of-age stories 11. Adult books for young adults

LC 2019012554

ALA Notable Book, 2020; Alex Award, 2020; Shortlisted for The Women's Prize for Fiction, 2020

Draws on the author's mother's story in a tale set in a turbulent 1960s Dominican Republic, where a young teen agrees to marry a man twice her age to help her family's immigration to America.

Cullen, Helen

The **dazzling** truth. Helen Cullen. Graydon House, 2020. 384 p. ISBN 9781525815829

1. Suicide 2. Women with depression 3. Family problems 4. Women — Death 5. Loss (Psychology) 6. Ireland 7. Relationship fiction 8. Family sagas

"With a group of well-crafted, intriguing characters, she realistically portrays a tight-knit group of people trying to grow up and grow old under the shadow of a tragedy they can never understand. Readers will enjoy experiencing a slice of life in this small Irish community, and embrace the very interesting characters who live there." —*Booklist*

Cumming, Charles

A **colder** war. Charles Cumming. St. Martin's Press, 2014. 400 pages (Thomas Kell novels, 2)

ISBN 9781250020611

1. Sabotage 2. Moles (Spies) 3. Former spies 4. Spies 5. Espionage 6. Turkey 7. Middle East 8. 1970s 9. Spy fiction 10. Thrillers and suspense

LC 2014010053

Disgraced MI6 agent Thomas Kell is assigned to investigate the murders of an Iranian defector, an investigative journalist, and an Iranian nuclear scientist who had been recently recruited by Western intelligence, a case that is further complicated by a senior agent's suspicious death.

Sequel to: A Foreign Country.

A **divided** spy. Charles Cumming. St. Martin's Press, 2017. 368 p. (Thomas Kell novels, 3)

ISBN 9781250021045

1. Former spies 2. Espionage 3. Bach, Johann Sebastian 4. Terrorism 5. Loss (Psychology) 6. Spy fiction 7. Thrillers and suspense

LC 2016037568

Thomas Kell thought he was done with spying. A former MI6 officer, he devoted his life to the Service, but it has left him with nothing but grief and a simmering anger against the Kremlin. Then Kell is offered an unexpected chance at revenge. Taking the law into his own hands, he embarks on a mission to recruit a top Russian spy who is in possession of a terrifying secret. As Kell tracks his man from Moscow to London, he finds himself in a high stakes game of cat and mouse in which it becomes increasingly difficult to know who is playing whom. As the mission reaches boiling point, the threat of a catastrophic terrorist attack looms over Britain. Kell is faced with an impossible choice. Loyalty to MI6—or to his own conscience?

"Cumming not only tells a moving human story here, he also constructs an airtight espionage plot full of unanticipated twists and leading up to a perfectly orchestrated finale." —*Booklist*

A **foreign** country. Charles Cumming. St. Martin's Press, 2012. 368 p. (Thomas Kell novels, 1)

ISBN 9780312591335

1. Former spies 2. Conspiracies 3. Kidnapping investigation 4. Political corruption 5. Women kidnapping victims 6. France 7. Tunisia 8. 1970s 9. Spy fiction 10. Thrillers and suspense

LC 2012010921

Ian Fleming Steel Dagger Award, 2012

When a newly appointed first female Chief of MI6 disappears weeks after two possibly related cases, disgraced former MI6 officer Thomas Kell is offered a chance to redeem his career by conducting a discreet operation that uncovers a shocking conspiracy.

Sequel: A Colder War.

The **Moroccan** girl. Charles Cumming. St. Martin's Press, 2019. 358 p.

ISBN 9781250129956

1. Authors 2. Intelligence service 3. Revolutionaries 4. International intrigue 5. Espionage 6. Morocco 7. Spy fiction

A simple assignment for MI6 during a literary festival lands a successful novelist on the trail of a revolutionary leader who is being targeted by the world's competing intelligence services.

"Carradine is about to find out the hard way that real-life espionage bears little resemblance to his page-turning depictions. Cumming channels the dreamy romance of classic spy movies (think Casablanca, Notorious, The Thirty-Nine Steps) and juxtaposes it with a modern, relentlessly intense and staccato delivery." —*BookPage*

Originally published as "The man between": London : HarperCollins Publishers, 2018.

★ The **Trinity** Six. Charles Cummin. St. Martin's Press, 2011. 368 p. ISBN 9780312675295

1. Spies 2. Intelligence service 3. Traitors 4. Espionage 5. Dreyfus, Alfred 6. England 7. Cambridge, England 8. Spy fiction

LC 2010040197

The identity of a secret member of a modern espionage ring becomes a matter of survival to a Russian history academic who, in the wake of several suspicious deaths, is entangled in a plot involving MI-6 and the highest levels of Russian government.

"Taut, atmospheric and immersive—an instant classic." —*Kirkus*

Cumyn, Alan

Losing it. Alan Cumyn. St. Martin's Press, 2003. 365 p. ISBN 9780312306915

1. Teacher-student relationships 2. Fetishism (Sexuality) 3. College students 4. Husband and wife 5. Women poets 6. Ottawa, Ontario 7. Psychological fiction 8. Erotic fiction 9. Canadian fiction

LC 2002031882

Middle-aged English professor Bob Sterling finds his marriage and career on the brink of ruin after he takes a trip with a young poetry student who brings him face-to-face with a previously unexplored sexual fetish.

"The nuanced persuasive characterization propels the story forward and provides depth and texture.... A bonus is that Cumyn spices up this essentially sad story with some horrifyingly funny scenes." —*Booklist*

Cunningham, Michael

★ The **hours**. Michael Cunningham. Farrar, Straus, Giroux, 1998. 229 p.
ISBN 9780374172893

1. Woolf, Virginia 2. Women authors, English 3. Joy and sorrow in women 4. Identity (Psychology) 5. Women with mental illnesses 6. Mothers and sons 7. Literary fiction 8. Bin Laden, Osama 9. Parallel narratives

LC 9834188

Pulitzer Prize for Fiction, 1999; PEN-Faulkner Award, 1999; Stonewall Book Award for the Barbara Gittings Literature Award, 1999; ALA Notable Book, 2000; New York Times Notable Book, 1998; Shortlisted for the International IMPAC Dublin Literary Award, 2000; National Book Critics Circle Award for Fiction finalist, 1998

The spirit of Virginia Woolf permeates the lives of several American readers as evidenced in this trio of tales about the author Woolf, a New Yorker planning a party to honour a writer, and a young mother reading Woolf's Mrs. Dalloway.

"After a brief prologue, the stories alternate in an intricate sequence, rather like a rhyme scheme.... The whole book does sound a little fussy in description, an exercise in echoes, but it doesn't read that way." —*New York Times Book Review*

Specimen days. Michael Cunningham. Farrar, Straus, and Giroux, 2005. 320 p.
ISBN 9780374299620

1. Whitman, Walt 2. Poets 3. City life 4. Identity (Psychology) 5. Boys 6. Young women 7. New York City 8. 19th century 9. 21st century 10. Literary fiction 11. Adult books for young adults

LC 2005040518

Prophetic poet Walt Whitman presides over each interlinked episode in a visionary novel set in the city of New York, featuring the same group of characters—a young boy, an older man, and a young woman.

"As much as Cunningham's novel is haunted by the ghost of Whitman's prophecies, it is profoundly informed by the events of September 11, 2001.... Cunningham's brilliantly imagined dystopian future represents the final betrayal of Walt Whitman's joyously democratic America." —*The New Leader*

3 linked stories.

Currie, Ron

Flimsy little plastic miracles: a true story. . Viking, 2013. 352 p.
ISBN 9780670025343

1. Staged deaths 2. Fame 3. Authors 4. Man-woman relationships 5. Missing persons 6. Metafiction 7. Satirical fiction

LC 2012028931

Mourning the death of his father and pining for an elusive woman he has loved since childhood, a writer who has lost his latest book in a fire fakes his own death and exiles himself to a small Caribbean island, where unexpected fame reveals the price of his deception.

Cush, Jean Love

Endangered. Jean Love Cush. Amistad Press, 2014. 320 p.
ISBN 9780062316233

1. Trials (Murder) 2. Racism 3. African Americans 4. Murder suspects 5. Mothers and sons 6. Philadelphia, Pennsylvania 7. Mainstream fiction 8. Adult books for young adults

When her 15-year-old son Malik is accused of murder, Janae, who cannot pay for his defense, reluctantly agrees to let a white human rights attorney represent him, and as she battles to save her son, his trial sparks a national firestorm of debate over race, prison and politics.

Cusk, Rachel

Kudos. Rachel Cusk. Farrar, Straus and Giroux, 2018. 224 p. (Outline, 3)
ISBN 9780374279868

1. Freedom 2. Women authors 3. Identity (Psychology) 4. Art 5. Authors 6. Europe 7. Psychological fiction 8. Literary fiction 9. Canadian fiction

LC 2018002527

New York Times Notable Book, 2018

A literary visit to a Europe in transition finds a material-seeking writer deeply identifying with the people she meets before evaluating difficult questions about acclaim, justice and the ultimate value of suffering.

"Brilliantly aware without being indulgent or preachy, this novel has the intense beauty of form that has marked Cusks trilogy from the beginning, and the final installment does not disappoint." —*Booklist*

Outline: a novel. Rachel Cusk. Farrar, Straus and Giroux, 2015. 256 p. (Outline, 1)
ISBN 9780374228347

1. English language teachers 2. Self-disclosure 3. Self-deception 4. Truth 5. Conversation 6. Athens, Greece 7. Psychological fiction 8. Literary fiction 9. Canadian fiction

LC 2014016969

New York Times Notable Book, 2015; Booklist Editors' Choice, 2015; Shortlisted for The Baileys Women's Prize for Fiction, 2015; Shortlisted for the Giller Prize, 2015; Governor General's Literary Awards, English-language Fiction finalist

Captures 10 conversations involving the narrator, a novelist teaching a course in creative writing during one oppressively hot summer in Athens.

"And as the profile of her main character grows more defined in relief, so does Cusk's underlying message about love, loss, and feminine identity in the modern world, evident not only in her story but also in its delivery." —*Booklist*

Originally published: London : Faber and Faber, 2014.

Second place. Rachel Cusk. Farrar, Straus & Giroux, 2021. 192 p.
ISBN 9780374279226
1. Married women 2. Frustration 3. Desire 4. Artists 5. Vacations 6. Literary fiction
LC 2020053576
Governor General's Literary Awards, English-language Fiction finalist

A woman invites a famous artist to use her guesthouse in the remote coastal landscape where she lives with her family. Powerfully drawn to his paintings, she believes his vision might penetrate the mystery at the center of her life. But as a long, dry summer sets in, his provocative presence itself becomes an enigma—and disrupts the calm of her secluded household.

"Brilliant prose and piercing insights convey a dark but compelling view of human nature." —*Kirkus*

Transit. Rachel Cusk. Farrar, Straus and Giroux, 2017. 260 pages (Outline, 2)
ISBN 9780374278625
1. English language teachers 2. Mothers and sons 3. Self-discovery in women 4. Self-perception 5. Transformations, Personal 6. London, England 7. Psychological fiction 8. Literary fiction 9. Canadian fiction
LC 2016025619
New York Times Notable Book, 2017; Shortlisted for the Giller Prize, 2017

Moving to London with her two young sons in the wake of a family collapse, a writer endures personal, moral, artistic and practical transitions while confronting difficult questions about her vulnerability and power.

"Brilliantly written and structured, which is nothing new from this superlatively gifted writer, but with a chastened empathy for human weakness that was absent from her last two novels. Its return is most welcome." —*Kirkus*

Sequel to: Outline.
Originally published: London : Jonathan Cape, 2016.

Cusset, Catherine

Life of David Hockney: a novel. Catherine Cusset; translated by Teresa Fagan. Other Press, 2019. 192 pages
ISBN 9781590519837
1. Hockney, David 2. Artists 3. Gay men 4. Painters 5. Success (Concept) 6. Belonging 7. England 8. United States 9. Biographical fiction 10. LGBTQIA fiction 11. Translations
LC 2018045824
A compelling hybrid of novel and biography, Life of David Hockney offers an insightful overview of a painter whose art is as accessible as it is compelling, and whose passion to create has never been deterred by heartbreak or illness or loss.

Translation of: Vie de David Hockney : roman
Originally published: Paris : Gallimard, 2017
Translated from the French

Cussler, Clive

Blue gold: a novel from the Numa files. . Pocket Books, 2000. 378 p. (NUMA files, 2)
ISBN 9780671785468
1. Desalting of water 2. Women scientists 3. Missing persons 4. Water-supply 5. Terrorism 6. South America 7. Venezuela 8. Adventure stories 9. Thrillers and suspense
LC 57480
With the world running short of drinkable water, Kurt Austin and his NUMA team races against time to hunt down the missing scientist who has invented a process for turning salt water into fresh water.

Celtic empire. . G.P. Putnam's Sons, 2019. 416 p. (Dirk Pitt adventures, 25)
ISBN 9780735218994
1. International intrigue 2. Diseases 3. Tombs 4. Archaeology 5. Murder 6. Thrillers and suspense 7. Adventure stories
LC 2018056946
The murders of a U.N. science team in El Salvador, a deadly collision in the Detroit waterways and an attack on the Nile are linked to the ancient story of a fugitive Egyptian princess.

★ The **chase**. Clive Cussler. G.P. Putnam's Sons, 2007. 416 p. (Isaac Bell thrillers, 1)
ISBN 9780399154386
1. Bank robberies 2. Detectives 3. Crime 4. Stealing 5. Bell, Isaac (Fictitious character) 6. California 7. 1910s 8. Historical thrillers 9. Adventure stories
LC 2007017291
In 1906 detective Isaac Bell goes after the Butcher Bandit who has committed a string of bank robberies and murders in the western states of America and becomes the hunted.

"Cussler clearly had a lot of fun writing this. The details of early 20th-century America and the novel's thrill-a-minute pace will add another best seller to his resume." —*Library Journal*

The **cutthroat**. Clive Cussler and Justin Scott. G.P. Putnam's Sons, 2017. 393 pages : Illustration (Isaac Bell thrillers, 10)
ISBN 9780399575600
1. Detectives 2. Missing women 3. Serial murder investigation 4. Women murder victims 5. Murder investigation 6. New York City 7. 1900s (Decade) 8. Adventure stories 9. Historical thrillers
LC 2017002791
Hired to find a young woman who ran away from home to become an actress in 1911, Chief Investigator Isaac Bell begins a manhunt that is complicated by the acts of a serial killer whose victims resemble the missing girl.

★ **Final** option. Clive Cussler and Boyd Morrison. G. P. Putnam's Sons, 2019. 390 p; (Oregon files, 14)
ISBN 9780525541813
1. Mercenaries 2. Intelligence service 3. Secrecy 4. Enemies 5. Technology 6. Thrillers and suspense 7. Adventure stories
LC 2019037432
Juan Cabrillo and his team of expert operatives return in this latest entry in Clive Cussler's Oregon Files series. Aboard the Oregon, one of the most advanced spy ships ever built, they face new challenges and nemeses as they undertake another dangerous mission.

Ghost ship. Clive Cussler and Graham Brown. G. P. Putnam's Sons, 2014. 440 pages; (NUMA files, 12)
ISBN 9780399167317
1. Scientists 2. Human trafficking 3. Amnesia 4. International intrigue 5. Austin, Kurt (Fictitious character) 6. Thrillers and suspense 7. Adventure stories

LC 2014008875
Waking with conflicted memories after an injury sustained while trying to rescue passengers from a sinking yacht, Kurt Austin searches for answers from a state-sponsored cybercrime ring that takes him from Monaco to North Korea.

★ **Golden** Buddha. Clive Cussler and Craig Dirgo. Berkley Books, 2003. 420 p; (Oregon files, 1)
ISBN 9780425191729
1. Businesspeople 2. Special operations (Military science) 3. International relations 4. Oil wells 5. Dalai lamas 6. Tibet 7. Cuba 8. 1950s 9. 2000s (Decade) 10. Spy fiction 11. Sea stories 12. Adventure stories
LC 2003052217
Captain Cabrillo and his intelligence agents plan to strike a deal with the Russians and Chinese to exchange a golden Buddha containing records of oil reserves for Tibet's freedom, but his enemies will do anything to stop him.

★ The **Gray** Ghost. Clive Cussler and Robin Burcell. G. P. Putnam's Sons, 2018. 388 pages; (Fargo adventures, 10)
ISBN 9780735218734
1. Antique and classic cars 2. Greed 3. Malicious accusation 4. Automobile thieves 5. Private investigators 6. Adventure stories 7. Thrillers and suspense
LC 2018012901
The grandson of a man who was wrongly accused of stealing a recovered Rolls-Royce prototype a century earlier hires husband-and-wife team Sam and Remi Fargo to solve the mystery and clear his grandfather's name, a case that is complicated by dangerous enemies and the rare vehicle's repeat disappearance.

Havana storm. Clive Cussler and Dirk Cussler. G. P. Putnam's Sons, 2014. 452 pages; (Dirk Pitt adventures, 23)
ISBN 9780399172922
1. Treasure hunting 2. International intrigue 3. Underwater warfare 4. Pitt, Dirk (Fictitious character) 5. Cuba 6. Thrillers and suspense 7. Adventure stories
LC 2015001483
Investigating a toxic outbreak in the Caribbean Sea that is threatening the United States, Dirk Pitt is embroiled in a post-Castro power struggle for control of Cuba; while his children, Dirk Jr. and Summer, embark on a high-stakes treasure hunt.

The **Mediterranean** caper. Clive Cussler. Pyramid Books, 1973. 220 p. (Dirk Pitt adventures, 2)
ISBN 9780515031799
1. Air bases 2. Conspiracies 3. Drug smuggling 4. Nazi fugitives 5. Sabotage 6. Greece 7. Adventure stories
LC 9553364
A Luftwaffe ace, a Nazi war criminal, a beautiful and untrustworthy brunette, and a deadly billion-dollar cargo become the objects of a desperate search as Dirk Pitt matches wits with the elusive leader of an international smuggling ring.
Originally published in Great Britain as: May day!

Nighthawk: a novel from the NUMA Files. Clive Cussler and Graham Brown. G.P. Putnam's Sons, 2017. 464 p. (NUMA files, 14)
ISBN 9780399184017
1. Weapons 2. Threat (Psychology) 3. International intrigue 4. Austin, Kurt (Fictitious character) 5. Zavala, Joe (Fictitious character) 6. Thrillers and suspense 7. Adventure stories
LC 2016043196
When the most advanced aircraft ever designed vanishes over the South Pacific, Kurt Austin and Joe Zavala are drawn into a deadly race to recover the fallen technology, which carries a secret payload of exotic matter capable of triggering an Armageddon-level catastrophe.

Odessa Sea. Clive Cussler and Dirk Cussler. G. P. Putnam's Sons, 2016. 464 p. (Dirk Pitt adventures, 24)
ISBN 9780399575518
1. Nuclear weapons 2. Smugglers 3. International intrigue 4. War — Prevention 5. Ships 6. Thrillers and suspense 7. Adventure stories
Dirk Pitt and his NUMA team race to prevent a global war linked to the 1917 effort to preserve the Romanov Empire, the loss of a Cold War bomber's deadly cargo, mysterious Black Sea deaths and modern-day nuclear-materials smugglers.

★ The **oracle**. Clive Cussler and Robin Burcell. G. P. Putnam's Sons, 2019. 399 p. (Fargo adventures, 11)
ISBN 9780525539612
1. Treasure hunters 2. Hostage taking 3. Criminals 4. Treasure troves 5. Schools 6. North Africa 7. Nigeria 8. Adventure stories 9. Thrillers and suspense
LC 2019020942
Searching for a cache of cursed scrolls from sixth-century northern Africa, treasure hunters Sam and Remi Fargo confront rival crime bands that have taken students hostage to steal supply shipments from a charity-funded Nigerian school.

Pacific vortex!. Clive Cussler. Bantam Books, 1983. 270 p. (Dirk Pitt adventures, 1)
ISBN 9780553276329
1. International intrigue 2. Nuclear submarines 3. Underwater rescue operations 4. Heroes and heroines 5. Pitt, Dirk (Fictitious character) 6. Thrillers and suspense 7. Adventure stories 8. Sea stories
LC 85000832
When a top secret American nuclear submarine mysteriously disappears from the depths of the ocean, Dirk Pitt is ordered to locate and salvage the submarine.
The author recommends reading the Dirk Pitt adventures in the order they were written. According to his website, "Pacific Vortex" was written first but published much later. Please see the author's website for more information.

The **Pharaoh's** secret. Clive Cussler and Graham Brown. G. P. Putnam's Sons, 2015. 422 pages; (NUMA files, 13)
ISBN 9780399174117
1. Weapons 2. Threat (Psychology) 3. International intrigue 4. Austin, Kurt (Fictitious character) 5. Zavala, Joe (Fictitious character) 6. Thrillers and suspense 7. Adventure stories
When a power broker's scheme to build a new Egyptian empire requires his manipulation of a Saharan aquifer, Kurt and Joe race to learn the truth about an underworld plant extract at his disposal that may have the power to restore life to the dead.

★ **Raise** the Titanic!. Clive Cussler. Viking Press, 1976. 373 p. (Dirk Pitt adventures, 4)
ISBN 9780670589333
1. Salvage 2. International intrigue 3. Pitt, Dirk (Fictitious character) 4. Thrillers and suspense 5. Adventure stories 6. Sea stories
LC 76025871
The R.M.S. Titanic, sunk in 1912, has in her hold a very rare element, byzanium, needed to complete the U.S. Sicilian Project. The task of raising her is hampered by the presence of Russian spies and a very nasty hurricane.
"A great adventure thriller...[that] spins from one dizzying climax to another, holds its innermost secrets until the very end, and keeps you so audaciously entertained you won't want it to come to a close.... Simply

super and very cleverly done, with just the right amount of tongue-in-cheek bravado." —*Publishers Weekly*

★ The **rising** sea: a novel from the NUMA files. Clive Cussler and Graham Brown. G. P. Putnam's Sons, 2018. 416 p. (NUMA files, 15)
ISBN 9780735215535
1. International intrigue 2. High technology 3. Power (Social sciences) 4. Sea level 5. Weapons 6. Pacific Ocean 7. Thrillers and suspense 8. Adventure stories
LC 2017033074
Investigating an alarming rise in the world's sea levels, Kurt, Joe and the rest of the NUMA scientific team uncover a diabolical plot to upset the Pacific balance of power by triggering natural disasters to displace billions of people.

The **Romanov** ransom. Clive Cussler and Robin Burcell. G. P. Putnam's Sons, 2017. 388 pages; (Fargo adventures, 9)
ISBN 9780399575549
1. Kidnapping 2. Missing persons investigation 3. Treasure hunters 4. Treasure troves 5. Adventure stories 6. Thrillers and suspense
LC 2017021532
Husband-and-wife team Sam and Remi Fargo investigate a kidnapping that may be linked to the Nazi-stolen Romanov ransom, a case that is complicated by the heinous acts of a guerrilla faction that would establish the Fourth Reich.

Sacred stone. Clive Cussler and Craig Dirgo. Berkley Books, 2004. 404 p. (Oregon files, 2)
ISBN 9780425198483
1. Ship captains 2. Businesspeople 3. Spies 4. Mercenaries 5. Terrorists 6. Greenland 7. Spy fiction 8. Sea stories 9. Adventure stories
LC 2004050206
Juan Cabrillo and his fellows on the Oregon are charged with protecting a deadly radioactive stone. Beset by two militant terrorist factions, Juan and his mates must act quickly to prevent WWIII.

Sahara: a novel. Clive Cussler. Simon and Schuster 1992. 541 p. (Dirk Pitt adventures, 11)
ISBN 9780671681555
1. International intrigue 2. Treasure hunters 3. Women biochemists 4. Billionaires 5. Mali 6. Sahara 7. Thrillers and suspense 8. Adventure stories 9. Books to movies
LC 92005100
Stranded in the Sahara Desert, Dirk Pitt and his friends uncover the truth about the fate of 1930s aviator Kitty Mannock and the secret behind Lincoln's assassination BT
"Pepper the plot with human-rights abuse, cannibalism, state-of-the-art weaponry, espionage, and the evil General Zateb Kazimand you've got more than enough action to keep the Cussler's thrill-craving fans satiated." —*Booklist*

★ **Sea** of greed: a novel from the NUMA files. Clive Cussler and Graham Brown. G. P. Putnam's Sons, 2018. 416 p. (NUMA files, 16)
ISBN 9780735219021
1. Offshore oil 2. International intrigue 3. Oil industry and trade 4. Billionaires 5. Submarines 6. Mediterranean Sea 7. Gulf of Mexico 8. Thrillers and suspense 9. Adventure stories
LC 2018037962
The world's oil supply is vanishing, the stock market is plummeting and the NUMA team must solve a baffling historical mystery in order to save the future.

Serpent: a novel from the NUMA Files. By Clive Cussler with Paul Kemprecos. Pocket Books, 1999. 474 p. (NUMA files, 1)
ISBN 9780671026684

1. Assassins 2. Underwater archaeology 3. Shipwrecks 4. Archaeological expeditions 5. Women underwater archaeologists 6. Thrillers and suspense 7. Adventure stories
Kurt Austin, leader of a National Underwater and Marine Agency exploration team, and a marine archaeologist embark on a deadly mission to uncover a priceless pre-Columbian antiquity.

Shadow tyrants. Clive Cussler and Boyd Morrison. G. P. Putnams Sons, 2018. 387 pages; (Oregon files, 13)
ISBN 9780735217263
1. Mercenaries 2. Intelligence service 3. Secrecy 4. Enemies 5. Technology 6. Thrillers and suspense 7. Adventure stories
When the descendants of a legendary band of imperial secret-keepers threaten humanity, Juan Cabrillo and his team aboard the Oregon race to protect the world from a plot to eliminate all technology.
"Readers probably won't lie awake worrying whether all this could really happen. Fast-moving, implausible fun." —*Kirkus*

★ The **Titanic** secret. Clive Cussler and Jack Du Brul. G.P. Putnam's Sons, 2019. 390 p. (Isaac Bell thrillers, 11)
ISBN 9780735217263
1. Detectives 2. Private investigators 3. International intrigue 4. Coal mines and mining 5. Coal mine accidents 6. New York City 7. Colorado 8. 1910s 9. Adventure stories 10. Historical thrillers 11. Parallel narratives
LC 2019028820
Investigating a mine tragedy in 1911 Colorado that killed nine people, Isaac Bell discovers a larger puzzle involving an international power scheme aimed at seizing control of a rare element.

Typhoon fury. Clive Cussler and Boyd Morrison. G. P. Putnam's Sons, 2017. 436 pages; (Oregon files, 12)
ISBN 9780399575570
1. Intelligence service 2. Mercenaries 3. Ocean travel 4. Painting 5. Drug industry and trade 6. Thrillers and suspense 7. Adventure stories
LC 2017012116
Juan Cabrillo and the crew of the Oregon sail into a perfect storm of danger to try to stop a new world war, in a thrilling suspense novel from the #1 New York Times-bestselling grand master of adventure.

The **wrecker**. Clive Cussler and Justin Scott. G.P. Putnam's Sons, 2009. 480 p. (Isaac Bell thrillers, 2)
ISBN 9780399155994
1. Sabotage 2. Railroad accidents 3. Railroads 4. Detectives 5. Murderers 6. The West (United States) 7. 1900s (Decade) 8. Adventure stories 9. Historical thrillers
LC 2009017216
Investigating a series of attacks on the Southern Pacific Railroad's Cascades express lines, Detective Bell learns of the existence of an elusive saboteur who recruits and murders his own accomplices while engineering schemes of maximum havoc.

Czerneda, Julie

A **turn** of light. Julie E. Czerneda. Penguin Group USA, 2013. 854 pages (Night's edge, 1)
ISBN 9780756407070
1. Imaginary places 2. Sunrise and sunset 3. Interdimensional travel 4. Transformations (Magic) 5. Frontier and pioneer life 6. Fantasy fiction 7. Canadian fiction 8. Adult books for young adults
Prix Aurora: Best Novel, 2014
A debut fantasy novel set in an isolated refugee community where the magic and mortal worlds intersect and where young Jenn Nalynn, an un-

knowing member of both worlds, accidentally transforms her dragon protector into a man before encountering hostile strangers.

Sequel: A play of shadow.

D

D'Eramo, Luce

Deviation. Luce D'Eramo; translated from the Italian by Anne Milano Appel. Farrar, Straus and Giroux, 2018. 368 p.

ISBN 9780374138455

1. World War II 2. Women 3. Fascists 4. Holocaust (1933-1945) 5. Teenage girls 6. Autobiographical fiction 7. Historical fiction 8. Translations

LC 2018000169

A devoted fascist changes her mind and her life after witnessing the horrors of the Holocaust.

Includes bibliographical references.

Originally published: Milan : Mondadori, 1979.

Translated from the Italian.

D'Erasmo, Stacey

The **sky** below. Stacey D'Erasmo. Houghton Mifflin, 2009. 288 p.

ISBN 9780618439256

1. Life change events 2. Gay men 3. Men — Mortality 4. Change (Psychology) 5. Homosexuality 6. Manhattan, New York City 7. Mexico 8. Psychological fiction

LC 2008025673

New York Times Notable Book, 2009

Working as an obituary writer at a failing newspaper in lower Manhattan in the wake of 9/11, thirty-seven-year-old Gabriel Callahan has a halfhearted approach to life, until a brush with his own mortality sends him to Mexico on a quest to put himself back together and transform his life.

"This novel tells the story of a misanthropic obituary writer for a dying New York newspaper, who views his life through a series of memory boxes modelled on the assemblage art of Joseph Cornell. I assiduously collected interesting junk, filling my pockets with pebbles and wire and old nails: the stuff of transformation, he says. He narrates the drudgery of the daily grind and scrutinizes his dysfunctional, fatherless childhood, during which he rebelled against his mother by dealing drugs and engaging in sex with men for money. Now nearing forty and spiritually broken, he is given a diagnosis of cancer and travels to a commune in Mexico, where he reluctantly receives the help of a clairvoyant eight-year-old girl. Although the book strays into portentous magic realism, its lyrical prose and telling detail create a powerful atmosphere." —*The New Yorker*

D'Souza, Tony

The **Konkans**. Tony D'Souza. Harcourt, 2008. 308 p.

ISBN 9780151015191

1. Kokna (Indic people) 2. East Indians in the United States 3. Culture conflict 4. Identity (Psychology) 5. Identity (Religion) 6. India 7. 1970s 8. Domestic fiction

LC 2007015303

Francisco D'Sai, the son of a Konkan father, Lawrence, and an American mother, Denise, grows up surrounded by the colorful tales of India

and Konkan history, stories that feed his imagination and give him a profound sense of his heritage and its meaning in his life.

"This is more than an ethnographic study—D'Souza stays character-focused throughout the novel, gently mixing irony and fatalism with a warm affection for humans and the stupid things they do." —*Washington City Paper*

Whiteman. Tony D'Souza. Harcourt, 2006. 279 p.

ISBN 9780151011452

1. Americans in West Africa 2. International relief 3. Political violence 4. Race relations 5. Muslims 6. Cote d'Ivoire 7. West Africa 8. Psychological fiction

LC 2005025459

Refusing to leave his violence-charged post in an African Muslim village after his funding is cut off, maverick American relief worker Jack Diaz, at the side of his village guardian, Mamadou, gains insights into the region's hunting, farming, culture, and struggles with AIDS.

"One significant virtue of D'Souza's storytelling rests in his ability to present Jack's experiences of African life with a vividness that reveals the continent's allure without sentimentalizing its exoticism.... Much of the drama that unfolds in the 12 loosely chronological parts of Whiteman (each a story that could stand on its own) rests in the gentle progression that ferries Jack away from a form of blindness to a new kind of sight." —*New York Times Book Review*

Dade, Olivia

All the feels. Olivia Dade. HarperCollins, 2021. 320 p.

ISBN 9780063005587

1. Television actors and actresses 2. Unemployed women 3. Women psychotherapists 4. Man-woman relationships 5. Psychic trauma 6. Romantic comedies

LibraryReads Favorites, 2021

Alexander Woodroe has it all. Charm. Sex appeal. Wealth. Fame. A starring role as Cupid on TV&'s biggest show, Gods of the Gates. But the showrunners have wrecked his character, he's dogged by old demons, and his post-show future remains uncertain. When all that reckless emotion explodes into a bar fight, the tabloids and public agree: his star is falling.

"Alex and Lauren are likable, well-developed characters with emotional depth and relatable backstories that deal with body positivity, mental health, and abuse. While these heavy topics are major plotlines, they enhance rather than overshadow the friends-to-lovers/opposites-attract romance. The writing is excellent, with witty, banter-filled dialogue." —*Library Journal*

Spoiler alert. Olivia Dade. Avon Books, 2020. 409 pages

ISBN 9780063005549

1. Television actors and actresses 2. Fan fiction 3. Fans (Persons) 4. Women geologists 5. Virtual community 6. Romantic comedies

LibraryReads Favorites, 2020; RUSA Reading List Short List, 2021

When her viral fan-fiction leads to a disastrous publicity-stunt date with her celebrity crush, a talented plus-sized writer discovers that the actor secretly writes his own popular fan-fiction against studio rules.

"The journey to self-acceptance is never easy, and Dade doesn't shy away from that, but she makes it just as beautiful and gentle as the love that blooms between Marcus and April. One note is that the book is fandom heavy. If you're entrenched in the community, you will feel right at home. If not, there's a terminology learning curve." —*Kirkus*

Dahl, Arne

Bad Blood. Arne Dahl; translated from the Swedish by Rachel Willson-Broyles. Pantheon Books, 2013. 352 p. (Intercrime, 2)

ISBN 9780375425363

1. Police 2. Serial murder investigation 3. Serial murders 4. Torture 5. Americans in Sweden 6. Stockholm, Sweden 7. Sweden 8. 1990s 9. Mysteries 10. Police procedurals 11. Translations

LC 2012046772

Detective Paul Hjelm and his team receive an urgent call from the FBI. A murderer whose methods bear a frightening resemblance to a serial killer they believed long dead is on his way to Sweden. If they are to capture the killer, the team must collaborate with their colleagues in the FBI on a desperate hunt that will take them from rainswept city streets to deserted Kentucky farmhouses, and will push them to the limits of their endurance.

Translated from the Swedish of: Ont Blod (1998).

Originally published as Ont blod in 1998 by Bra Brocker AB, Stockholm.

TV tie-in.

First published with the title 'Ont blod' by Bra Bocker in 1998.

Misterioso: a crime novel. Arne Dahl; translated from the Swedish by Tiina Nunally. Pantheon Books, 2011. 352 p. (Intercrime, 1)

ISBN 9780375425356

1. Police 2. Serial murders 3. Serial murder investigation 4. Crimes against rich people 5. Narvaez, Panfilo de 6. Stockholm, Sweden 7. Sweden 8. 1990s 9. Mysteries 10. Police procedurals 11. Translations

LC 2010032837

Detective Paul Hjelm is unexpectedly placed into an elite team of officers and sent on a mission to track down a killer who has been systematically targeting business leaders, a case that pits them against the Russian Mafia, Sweden's secret wealthy societies and the country's persistent xenophobia.

"[The author] sets a full plate for himself in the first of a series about Hjelm and his colleagues. He describes a once comfortable country fragmented by racial malaise; East European Mafias; a financial collapse brought on by greedy, reckless bankers and government deregulation; postindustrial capitalism; and a gnawing fear that Sweden has lost its way." —*Booklist*

Also known as: The blinded man.

Translated from the Swedish.

Dahl, Julia

Conviction. Julia Dahl. Minotaur Books, 2017. 312 p. (Rebekah Roberts novels, 3)

ISBN 9781250083692

1. Cold cases (Criminal investigation) 2. Innocence (Law) 3. Women journalists 4. Women amateur detectives 5. Jews 6. New York City 7. Mysteries

Investigating when a Jewish man convicted 22 years earlier for the brutal murders of a Crown Heights black family writes to her, pleading his innocence, journalist Rebekah Roberts is challenged to infiltrate Brooklyn's insular Hasidic community, where she is targeted by a determined killer.

"Dahl excels at revealing the inner workings of enigmatic subcultures while maintaining peak suspense." —*Publishers Weekly*

The **missing** hours. Julia Dahl. Minotaur Books, 2021. 256 p.

ISBN 9781250083722

1. Rich families 2. Privilege (Social psychology) 3. Women college students 4. Rape victims 5. Revenge 6. New York City 7. Thrillers and suspense 8. Multiple perspectives

LC 2021015667

A standalone novel from an award-winning author confronts the aftermath of a campus rape and the lengths that some will go to keep the truth hidden.

"Dahl makes a dramatic break her from her acclaimed Rebekah Roberts series and takes on the conflicted lives of the arrogantly wealthy and the perils of social media. She is known for her fast-paced writing, but this one moves at breakneck speed and stays with you long after the last page." —*Booklist*

Dahl, Roald

Collected stories. Roald Dahl; edited and introduced by Jeremy Treglown. Alfred A. Knopf, 2006. Xxxvii, 850 p.

ISBN 9780307264909

1. Short stories 2. Anthologies

LC 2006046523

A definitive compilation of short fiction for adults from the author of Charlie and the Chocolate Factory and other children's classics blends the macabre with humor and the grotesque.

Includes bibliographical references (p. xxiii).

Originally published: The collected short stories of Roald Dahl. London : Michael Joseph, c1991. With new introduction.

Dalcher, Christina

Femlandia. Christina Dalcher. Buckley Pub Group, 2021. 336 p.

ISBN 9780593201107

1. Mothers and daughters 2. Women 3. Communes 4. Pregnant women 5. Safety 6. Dystopian fiction

A chilling look into an alternate near future where a woman and her daughter seek refuge in a women-only colony, only to find that the safe haven they were hoping for is the most dangerous place they could be.

"A no-holds-barred thriller and thought-provoking read for fans of Margaret Atwood's The Handmaid's Tale, Naomi Alderman's The Power, and Kim Liggett's The Grace Year." —*Library Journal*

Dallas, Sandra

The **last** midwife. Sandra Dallas. St. Martin's Press, 2015. 352 p.

ISBN 9781250074461

1. Doyle, Arthur Conan 2. Infanticide 3. Trust 4. Secrets 5. Communities 6. Colorado 7. American Westward Expansion (1803-1899) 8. 1880s 9. Historical fiction 10. Gentle reads

LC 2015017976

Spur Awards, Best Western Traditional Novel, 2016

Wrongly accused when a baby is found dead, a 19th-century Colorado midwife who has witnessed the secrets of countless families considers in the face of her own secrets whether or not it is worth it to prove her innocence.

Tallgrass. Sandra Dallas. St. Martin's Press, 2007. 320 p.

ISBN 9780312360191

1. Japanese Americans — Forced removal and incarceration, 1942-1945 2. Missing persons 3. Farmers 4. Teenagers 5. Soldiers 6. Colorado 7. The West (United States) 8. Second World War era (1939-1945) 9. 1940s 10. Historical fiction 11. Gentle reads 12. Adult books for young adults

LC 2006051271

Spur Award for Best Western Novel (Short Novel), 2008

Her life turned upside-down when a Japanese internment camp is opened in their small Colorado town, Rennie witnesses the way her community places suspicion on the newcomers when a young girl is murdered.

"Rennie Stroud looks back to 1942, when she was 13, to tell a powerful coming-of-age story. That year, the U.S. government opened a Japanese internment camp outside Ellis, CO, less than a mile from where Rennie and her family farmed sugar beets. Rennie observes the prejudice of some of the townspeople as well as her parents' strong moral code and their entanglement in the emotions of the time. Her father, Loyal, not only shows open support for the Japanese, whom he views as Americans, but offers to hire them to work on the farm. When a young girl is murdered, suspicion naturally turns to the camp, and the town is divided by fear. Dallas's strong, provocative novel is a moving examination of prejudice and fear that addresses issues of community discord, abuse, and rape." —*Library Journal*

Westering women: a novel. Sandra Dallas. St. Martin's Press, 2020. 304 p.
ISBN 9781250239662
1. Wagon trains 2. Overland journeys to the Pacific 3. Abused women 4. Escapes 5. Mothers and daughters 6. The West (United States) 7. 1850s 8. American Westward Expansion (1803-1899) 9. Historical fiction

LC 2019034031

Joining other mail-order brides on a dangerous wagon journey to the gold mines of 1852 Chicago, a seamstress with painful secrets discovers strengths she did not know she possessed among a growing sisterhood of fellow women pioneers.

"Readers will enjoy this modern take on the journey West that's rife with girl power." —*Publishers Weekly*

Dalton, Trent

All our shimmering skies. Trent Dalton. Harper, 2021. 448 pages.
ISBN 9780063092754
1. Girls 2. Family curses 3. Quests 4. Actors and actresses 5. Fighter pilots 6. Australia 7. Darwin, Northern Territory 8. Second World War era (1939-1945) 9. Literary fiction 10. Magical realism 11. Historical fiction

Darwin, 1942, and as Japanese bombs rain down, motherless Molly Hook, the gravedigger's daughter, is looking to the skies and running for her life. Inside a duffel bag, she carries a stone heart, alongside a map to lead her to Longcoat Bob, the deep-country sorcerer who she believes put a curse on her family. By her side are the most unlikely travelling companions: Greta, a razor-tongued actress and Yukio, a fallen Japanese fighter pilot. The treasure lies before them, but close behind them trails the dark. And above them, always, are the shimmering skies.

"In this follow-up to Dalton's LJ best-booked debut, Boy Swallows Universe, goodness, hope, and a bit of magic are pitted against gritty realities." —*Library Journal*

Originally published: Sydney : Fourth Estate, 2020.

Boy swallows universe. Trent Dalton. Harper, 2019. 452 p.
ISBN 9780062898104
1. Drug traffic 2. Brothers 3. Growing up 4. Boys who are mute 5. Drug dealers 6. Brisbane, Queensland 7. Australia 8. 1980s 9. Literary fiction 10. Coming-of-age stories 11. Autobiographical fiction 12. Adult books for young adults
Australian Book Industry Awards, Book of the Year, 2019; Australian Book Industry Awards, Literary Fiction Book of the Year, 2019; Australian Book Industry Awards, Matt Richell Award for New Writer of the Year, 2019; Library Journal Best Books, 2019; Librarians' Choice (Australia), 2018; Nielsen BookData Australian Booksellers' Choice Award, 2019; NSW Premier's Literary Awards, People's Choice Award for Fiction, 2019; Shortlisted for the Russell Prize for Humour Writing (Australia), 2019

Exiled in a drug-oppressed refugee suburb in 1980s Australia, a 12-year-old boy dreams of a career in journalism while fending off the local criminal element to protect his imprisoned mother.

"A captivating and quirky life story that leads the reader on an intense and rewarding journey; highly recommended." —*Library Journal*
Originally published in Australia: Fourth Estate, 2018.

Daly, Paula

Clear my name. Paula Daly. Atlantic Monthly Press, 2019. 304 pages
ISBN 9780802147837
1. Catharine Parr 2. Innocence (Law) 3. Investigations 4. Mentoring 5. Charities 6. Great Britain 7. Thrillers and suspense

A jaded investigator from a UK charity that helps exonerate wrongly convicted people teams up with a naïve trainee to follow leads related to a witness who could clear an innocent woman's name.

Open your eyes. Paula Daly. Grove Press, 2018. 339 p.
ISBN 9780802128454
1. Authors 2. Victims of violent crimes 3. Married people and secrets 4. Secrets 5. Enemies 6. Liverpool, England 7. England 8. Thrillers and suspense

LC 2018028233

When her husband, a bestselling crime writer, is brutally attacked in the driveway of their home, Jane Campbell must face the problems in her life—and secrets that have been kept from her—as she attempts to discover who would commit such a crime.

"This is an evenly paced thriller; Daly delivers just enough clues and twists, a little bit at a time, to keep the reader guessing. It's easy to relate to Jane; her general passiveness leads to few character surprises, but she firmly gains and keeps our sympathy, unlike many more unreliable narrators who pepper domestic suspense novels these days. After the shocking beginning, Jane's dogged pursuit of the truth keeps the novel grounded. A satisfyingly original thriller." —*Kirkus*

Danan, Rosie

The **intimacy** experiment. Rosie Danan. Jove, 2021. 336 p.
ISBN 9780593101629
1. Rabbis 2. Women educators 3. Sex education for adults 4. Jewish men 5. Business partners 6. Los Angeles, California 7. Southern California 8. Contemporary romances

LC 2020035563

LibraryReads Favorites, 2021

The co-founder of a popular sex-education platform joins forces with a young rabbi who would save his cash-strapped synagogue to host a seminary series on modern intimacy, before their professional partnership is complicated by their unexpected attraction.

"The original setup and endearing characters largely make up for the flaws of this slow-burning romance." —*Publishers Weekly*

The **roommate**. Rosie Danan. Jove, 2020. 336 p.
ISBN 9780593101605
1. Moving to a new city 2. Pornographic film industry and trade 3. Strangers 4. Socialites 5. Roommates 6. Los Angeles, California 7. Romantic comedies

LC 2019059078

LibraryReads Favorites, 2020

A millennial struggling with underemployment and the dating scene accepts a childhood crush's invitation to move cross-country before finding herself sharing a lease with a charming but perceptive stranger.

"Danan makes this novel premise work with a charming, believable heroine; an offbeat hero with a heart of gold; and snappy, laugh-out-loud prose. Romance fans will especially appreciate that the steamy erotic scenes are used to further character development, rather than just for cheap thrills. This delectable rom-com is both red-hot and fiercely feminist." —*Publishers Weekly*

Danforth, Emily M.

Plain bad heroines. Emily M. Danforth; with illustrations by Sara Lautman. William Morrow & Co, 2020. 464 pages : Illustration

ISBN 9780062942852

1. Girls' boarding schools 2. Death 3. Horror films 4. Lesbians 5. Curses 6. Rhode Island 7. 20th century 8. 21st century 9. Gothic fiction 10. LGBTQIA fiction 11. Adult books for young adults

LibraryReads Favorites, 2020; Alex Award, 2021

Follows the release of a best-selling book about an early 20th-century New England boarding school where gender-diverse students died under suspicious circumstances.

"The wry, knowing tone of its narrator, the queerness at its core, and the illustrations by Sara Lautman all contribute to a suspenseful rush that will leave the reader flipping furiously to the end." —*Booklist*

Dang, Catherine

Nice girls. Catherine Dang. William Morrow & Co, 2021. 320 p.

ISBN 9780063027558

1. Homecomings 2. Missing women 3. Secrets 4. Expectation (Psychology) 5. Anger in women 6. Minnesota 7. Thrillers and suspense

Returning home after being kicked out of college, Mary becomes obsessed with the disappearance of a rising social media star—and her former best friend —and, as hatred consumes her, discovers a link to another missing person opens up old wounds.

"The inclusion of high school flashbacks, along with the experiences of college-age characters, are likely to appeal to older teens who enjoy thrillers. A page-turning, multifaceted mystery with emotional depth and a thrilling conclusion." —*School Library Journal*

Dangarembga, Tsitsi

This mournable body. Tsitsi Dangarembga. Graywolf Press, 2018. 304 p. (Tambudzai novels, 2)

ISBN 9781555978129

1. Women — Social conditions 2. Postcolonialism 3. Social classes 4. Misogyny 5. Self-esteem in women 6. Zimbabwe 7. 20th century 8. Literary fiction 9. Second person narratives

Shortlisted for the Booker Prize, 2020

The protagonist of Nervous Conditions struggles to make a life for herself in Harare, Zimbabwe, eventually taking an ecotourism job that forces her to return to her parents' impoverished homestead, leading to an unforgivable betrayal.

"Dangarembga writes with intimacy and compassion; there's a sharp poetic crack to the work that keeps the story from muddying in melancholy, as it might in the hands of a less cinematic writer." —*The New York Times*

Daniel, Ray

Hacked: a Tucker mystery. Ray Daniel. Midnight Ink, 2017. 360 pages (Tucker mysteries, 4)

ISBN 9780738751108

1. Hackers 2. Widowers 3. Serial murder investigation 4. Cyberbullying 5. Cousins 6. Boston, Massachusetts 7. Cyber-thrillers 8. Thrillers and suspense

LC 2016047687

Aloysius Tucker vows vengeance when a hacker terrorizes his ten-year-old cousin, Maria. Promising Maria that he'll unmask the hacker and get an apology, Tucker goes online to get justice. But the resulting flame war turns deadly when the hacker is murdered.

Danielewski, Mark Z.

★ The **familiar;** Volume 4,. Mark Z. Danielewski. Pantheon Books, 2017. 880 p. (Familiar novels, 4)

ISBN 9780375715006

1. Girls and cats 2. Human nature 3. Videos 4. Human/animal communication 5. Options, alternatives, choices 6. Experimental fiction 7. Literary fiction

As strange currents begin to surround Xanther and inexplicable entities invade the dreams of the twins, they begin to fear the release of a creature who will destroy all hope, in the fourth installment of the innovative graphic novel series.

"The author is innovating wildly not only with text but also with narrative flow, structure, and multiplicity of meaning. Loose, imagistic words are followed by tightly layered prose and pictures; this varied density creates a deeply nuanced reading experience that works. A must-read." —*Library Journal*

★ **House** of leaves: a novel. Mark Z. Danielewski. Pantheon Books, 2000. Xxiii, 709 p. : Illustration

ISBN 9780375420528

1. Photojournalists 2. Manuscripts 3. Houses 4. Families 5. Tattoo artists 6. Experimental fiction 7. Horror 8. Literary fiction

LC 99036024

New York Times Notable Book, 2000

A family relocates to a small house on Ash Tree Lane and discovers that the inside of their new home seems to be without boundaries.

"This work is a kaleidoscopically layered and deconstructed H. P. Lovecraft-style horror story. It hums and resonates with wonder, dread, and insight." —*Booklist*

Includes bibliographical references and index.

Only revolutions. Mark Z. Danielewski. Pantheon Books, 2006. 360 p.

ISBN 9780375421761

1. Sixteen-year old boys 2. Sixteen-year-old girls 3. Teenagers 4. Love 5. Automobile travel 6. Experimental fiction 7. Adult books for young adults

LC 2006040996

New York Times Notable Book, 2006; National Book Award for Fiction finalist, 2006

Moving back and forth between the two main characters, Hailey and Sam, a kaleidoscopic novel follows two wayward teenagers who never grow up as they crash New Orleans parties, barrel up the Mississippi, crash through the Badlands, and more, from the Civil War to the Iraq War and beyond.

"This novel consists of the dual free-verse narratives of 16-year-old Hailey and Sam, which are meant to be read in tandem... This creative paean to the velocity of young lovers and the vibrancy of American culture is sure to wow the experimental-fiction camp." —*Booklist*

Daniels, Natalie

Too close. Natalie Daniels. Harper, 2019. 312 pages

ISBN 9780062917485

1. Women with amnesia 2. Women forensic psychiatrists 3. Psychiatric hospitals 4. Female friendship 5. Life change events 6. England 7. Psychological suspense 8. Multiple perspectives

A veteran forensic psychiatrist assigned to the case of a wife and mother who committed an unforgiveable crime finds her professional and personal limits tested as she begins to feel sympathy for her.

"Each chapter, alternatively narrated by Connie or Emma, reveals each woman's darkest secrets and perceived sins. Daniels presents an unflinching, visceral look into the nature of love, fidelity, and betrayal." —*Publishers Weekly*

Danler, Stephanie

Sweetbitter. Stephanie Danler. Alfred A. Knopf, 2016. 356 p.
ISBN 9781101875940
1. Self-fulfillment in women 2. City life 3. Waitresses 4. Restaurants 5. Young women 6. Manhattan, New York City 7. New York City 8. Books to TV 9. Coming-of-age stories 10. First person narratives
LC 2015037137
LibraryReads Favorites, 2016

A year in the life of a beguiling young woman in the wild world of a famous downtown New York restaurant follows her burning effort to become someone of importance through a backwaiter job that enables her indulgences in culinary and intellectual interests.

"Throughout, Danler evokes Tesss voice—intimate, confiding, wonderstruck, depressed—with deft skill." —*Publishers Weekly*

This novel was the basis for the TV series of the same name, airing on the Starz network.

Dann, Patty

The **Wright** sister. Patty Dann. Perennial, 2020. 256 p.
ISBN 9780062993113
1. Haskell, Katharine Wright 2. Siblings 3. Family relationships 4. Suffragists 5. Fifties (Age) 6. Marriage 7. 1920s 8. Biographical fiction 9. Historical fiction 10. Epistolary novels

An epistolary novel of historical fiction that imagines the life of Katharine Wright and her relationship with her famous brothers, Wilbur and Orville Wright.

"Readers who adore the epistolary format or love character-driven stories with little action will want to put this on their to-read list." —*Library Journal*

Danticat, Edwidge

Claire of the sea light. Edwidge Danticat. Alfred A. Knopf, 2013. 238 pages
ISBN 9780307271792
1. Crimes against girls 2. Missing children 3. Community life 4. Secrets 5. Coastal towns 6. Haiti 7. Literary fiction 8. Psychological fiction
LC 2012043876
ALA Notable Book, 2014; Library Journal Best Books, 2013; New York Times Notable Book, 2013; Andrew Carnegie Medal for Excellence in Fiction finalist, 2014

When a vibrant 7-year-old disappears from her Haitian community at the same time her father agonizingly decides to give her up so that she can have a better life, an ensuing search reveals the painful stories of neighbors whose lives the child touched.

"In interlocking stories moving back and forth in time, Danticat weaves a beautifully rendered portrait of longing in the small fishing town of Ville Rose in Haiti." —*Booklist*

The **dew** breaker. Edwidge Danticat. Knopf, 2004. 244 p.
ISBN 9781400041145
1. Torturers 2. Redemption 3. Haitian Americans 4. Remorse 5. Barbers 6. Haiti 7. Brooklyn, New York City 8. Psychological fiction
LC 2003060788
Booklist Editors' Choice, 2004; National Book Critics Circle Award for Fiction finalist, 2004

A scarred Brooklyn resident remembers his past life as a Haitian torturer in the 1960s, a period during which he waged personal and political battles before moving to New York, where his past continued to haunt him throughout his marriage and parenthood.

"Beautifully written fiction about the real-life horror that is Haiti. Seamlessly blending the personal and political, it deals with what happens to a country and its people when mothers and fathers disappear for their political transgressions." —*USA Today*

★ **Everything** inside: stories. Edwidge Danticat. Alfred A. Knopf, 2019. Ix, 223 pages
ISBN 9780525521273
1. Interpersonal relations 2. Human nature 3. Friendship 4. Divorce 5. Miami, Florida 6. Haiti 7. Short stories 8. Literary fiction
LC 2018047646
ALA Notable Book, 2020; National Book Critics Circle Award for Fiction, 2019

A single-volume collection of short stories by the National Book Critics Circle Award-winning author is set in such locales as Miami, Port-au-Prince and the Caribbean and poignantly explores the forces that unite and divide.

★ **Krik?** Krak!. Edwidge Danticat. Soho Press, 1995. 224 p.
ISBN 9781569470251
1. Dictatorship 2. Haitian Americans — Social life and customs 3. Haiti 4. Short stories
LC 9441999
Library Journal Best Books, 1995; National Book Award for Fiction finalist, 1995

In a land where vicious dictators crush dreams and lives on a whim, Haitian people have only faith and hope to sustain them. Perhaps it is the faith that a tiny, leaky boat packed with refugees will successfully navigate the ocean and reach Florida. Or perhaps it is the macabre hope that a daughter will find her mother's body in a mass grave, so she can wrap it in a homemade patchwork quilt.

"The author touches upon life both in Haiti and in New York's Haitian community, though we spend most of our time in Port-au-Prince and the country town of Ville Rose. The best of these stories humanize, particularize, give poignancy to the lives of people we may have come to think of as faceless emblems of misery, poverty and brutality." —*New York Times Book Review*

Nine ... stories about life under Haiti's dictatorships.

Daoud, Kamel

The **Meursault** investigation. Kamel Daoud; translated by John Cullen. Other Press, 2015. 160 p.
ISBN 9781590517512
1. Brothers — Death 2. Identity (Psychology) 3. Postcolonialism 4. Mothers and sons 5. Loneliness in men 6. Algeria 7. Psychological fiction 8. Political fiction 9. Adaptations, retellings, and spin-offs
LC 2015010736
Library Journal Best Books 2015; New York Times Notable Book, 2015

Harun, the brother of "the Arab" killed by Meursault in Albert Camus' "The Stranger," details the events that led to his brother's murder on an Algerian beach.

"An eye-opening, humbling read, splendid whether or not you know and love the original." —*Library Journal*

Originally published in French as Meursault, contre-enquete by Editions Barzakh in Algeria in 2013, and by Actes Sud in France in 2014—Title page verso.
Originally published: 2013.

Dare, Abi

The **girl** with the louding voice. Abi Dare. Dutton, 2020. 336 p.
ISBN 9781524746025

1. Education 2. Teenage girls 3. Women's rights 4. Forced marriage 5. Sexual violence 6. Nigeria 7. Coming-of-age stories 8. Literary fiction 9. Adult books for young adults

LC 2019029365

Adunni, a 14-year-old Nigerian girl who longs for an education, must find a way for her voice to be heard loud and clear in a world where she and other girls like her are taught to believe, through words and deeds, that they are nothing.

"Dare's arresting prose provides a window into the lives of Nigerians of all socioeconomic levels and shows readers the beauty and humor that may be found even in the midst of harrowing experiences." —*Booklist*

Includes bibliographical references.

Dare, Tessa

Do you want to start a scandal. Tessa Dare. Avon Books, 2016. 384 p. (Castles ever after, 4)

ISBN 9780062349040

1. Marquis and marchionesses 2. Scandals 3. Women marriage resisters 4. Rumor 5. Reputation 6. England 7. Great Britain 8. Regency period (1811-1820) 9. Regency romances 10. Historical romances

In order to avoid a forced marriage to Piers Brandon, Charlotte Highwood must uncover the identities of the two lovers involved in a scandalous library tryst the night of the Parkhurst ball, proving that she wasn't involved.

"The irresistibly provocative, classy love scenes set the bar high for other historical romance novels." —*Publishers Weekly*

★ The **duchess** deal. Tessa Dare. Avon Books, 2017. 370 p. (Girl meets duke, 1)

ISBN 9780062697202

1. Dukes and duchesses 2. Mate selection 3. Interclass romance 4. Jilted men 5. Heirs and heiresses 6. England 7. Regency period (1811-1820) 8. Regency romances 9. Historical romances

Library Journal Best Books, 2017; Romantic Times Reviewer's Choice Award, 2017

When seamstress Emma Gladstone approaches the formidable Duke of Ashbury with the bill for his ex-fiancée's wedding dress, she receives a marriage proposal instead. Believing that his battle-scarred face may deter potential brides, Ashbury offers Emma a house and financial independence if she's willing to live with him until she conceives the heir he desperately needs. But what if Emma wants a real marriage? Witty banter and comedic situations add levity to an emotionally intense Beauty and the Beast story.

"RITA Award-winning Dare once again works her own irresistible brand of magic by taking a cast of richly nuanced characters (including an emotionally and physically scarred hero and the feisty heroine who refuses to give up on him), a deliciously clever plot that manages to be both superbly sexy as well as thoroughly romantic, and a generous measure of addictively tart wit, and then she spins the whole thing into pure literary gold." —*Booklist*

★ The **governess** game. Tessa Dare. Avon Books, 2018. 352 p. (Girl meets duke, 2)

ISBN 9780062851673

1. Dukes and duchesses 2. Governesses 3. Womanizers 4. Aristocracy 5. Guardian and ward 6. England 7. Regency period (1811-1820) 8. Regency romances 9. Historical romances

When the governess he has hired to turn a pair of wild orphans into proper young ladies tries to reform him, self-respecting libertine Chase Reynaud decides to teach her a lesson in pleasure.

★ A **night** to surrender. Tessa Dare. Avon Books, 2011. 389 p. (Spindle Cove, 1)

ISBN 9780062049834

1. Earls and countesses 2. Soldiers 3. Coastal towns 4. Man-woman relationships 5. Interpersonal attraction 6. England 7. Regency period (1811-1820) 8. Regency romances 9. Historical romances

RITA Award for Best Regency Historical Romance, 2012; Romantic Times Reviewers' Choice Award, 2011

While in the town of Spindle Cove, a haven for ladies with delicate constitutions, to gather a militia, the new Earl of Rycliff meets his match in Susanna Finch, a woman who is determined to save her personal utopia from the invasion of his makeshift army.

Romancing the duke. Tessa Dare. Avon Books, 2014. 370 p. (Castles ever after, 1)

ISBN 9780062240194

1. Single women 2. Poor women 3. Inheritance and succession 4. Romantic love 5. Castles 6. England 7. Regency period (1811-1820) 8. Historical romances 9. Regency romances

RITA Award for Best Historical Romance (Short), 2015

Although Isolde Ophelia Goodnight's father made a fortune as the author of the bestselling series of novels that immortalized her as "Little Izzy Goodnight," he died without a penny to his name, leaving Izzy destitute and homeless. An inheritance from her godfather in the form of Gostley Castle proves a welcome surprise, even if a more appropriate name for the crumbling ruin is "ghostly" or "ghastly." Its current occupant, Lord Ransome Vane, the blind, brooding Duke of Rothbury, is considerably less charming...and unwilling to surrender his claim to the castle. However, as Izzy lays siege to his solitary existence, he may end up surrendering his heart.

"Humor, whimsy, and joy overflow as a most unlikely pair find their happy ending in this fairy tale-come-to-life." —*Library Journal*

★ **Say** yes to the marquess. Tessa Dare. Avon Books, 2014. 374 p. (Castles ever after, 2)

ISBN 9780062240200

1. Castles 2. Engaged persons 3. Love triangles 4. Womanizers 5. Boxers (Sports) 6. England 7. Regency period (1811-1820) 8. Historical romances 9. Regency romances

Romantic Times Reviewer's Choice Award, 2015

Determined that his brother marry Miss Clio Whitmore, hardened fighter Rafe Brandon decides to plan the wedding himself but has a change of heart when he falls hopelessly in love with the bride-to-be.

"With the latest sterling addition to her Castles Ever After series, RITA awardwinning Dare (Romancing the Duke, 2014) continues to charm and captivate readers with her droll sense of humor, clever plotting, and engaging characters. This flawlessly written Regency historical is guaranteed to hit the sweet spot for most romance readers." —*Booklist*

★ The **wallflower** wager. Tessa Dare. Avon Books, 2019. 384 pages (Girl meets duke, 3)

ISBN 9780062952561

1. Dukes and duchesses 2. Womanizers 3. Single women 4. Aristocracy 5. Rich men 6. England 7. Regency period (1811-1820) 8. Regency romances 9. Historical romances

They call him the Duke of Ruin... To an undaunted wallflower, he's just the beast next door.

A **week** to be wicked. Tessa Dare. Avon Books, 2012. 375 p. (Spindle Cove, 2)

ISBN 9780062049872

1. Young women 2. Voyages and travels 3. Protectiveness in men 4. Women scientists 5. Deception 6. England 7. Regency period (1811-1820) 8. 19th century 9. Regency romances 10. Historical romances

Library Journal Best Books, 2012; Romantic Times Reviewer's Choice Award, 2012

During one week, unlikely partners Minerva Highwood, one of Spindle Cove's confirmed spinsters, and Lord Payne must fake an elopement, convince family and friends they are "in love, outrun armed robbers and travel 400 miles without killing each other—or falling in love for real.

When a Scot ties the knot. Tessa Dare. Avon, 2015. 384 p. (Castles ever after, 3)
ISBN 9780062349026
1. Soldiers 2. Heirs and heiresses 3. Extortion 4. Love letters 5. Secrets 6. Scotland 7. Regency period (1811-1820) 8. Regency romances 9. Historical romances
Library Journal Best Books, 2015; RUSA Reading List Short List, 2016
To escape the social obligations of the London season, painfully shy Madeline "Maddy" Gracechurch invents a fiancé: Captain Logan MacKenzie, a dashing soldier with whom she carries on a lengthy fictional correspondence until—no longer in need of the ruse—she kills him off. Imagine Maddy's surprise when the real-life Logan MacKenzie arrives at Lannair Castle, where she lives, insisting that they wed immediately. Has Maddy's dream lover become her worst nightmare? Find out in this 3rd book in the Castles Ever After series.
"Dare's latest begins with a fairy-tale twist of fate, then leads readers on a mesmerizing and intense emotional journey that explores love in many forms and the powerful pull of dreams. A brilliant, enchanting, and soul-satisfying romance." —*Kirkus*

Daria, Alexis

★ A **lot** like adios. Alexis Daria. Avon Books, 2021. 320 p. (Primas of power, 2)
ISBN 9780062959966
1. Hispanic Americans 2. Physical therapists 3. Graphic designers 4. Families 5. Expectation (Psychology) 6. New York City 7. Romantic comedies 8. Multicultural romances
Michelle Amato has built a thriving freelance business as a graphic designer. So what if her love life is nonexistent? The only guy who ever made her want happily-ever-after disappeared years ago. Gabriel Aguilar left the Bronx at eighteen to escape his parents' demanding expectations, but it also meant saying goodbye to Michelle, his best friend and longtime crush. Now, he's the co-owner of LA's hottest celebrity gym and planning to open a New York City location. When Michelle is unexpectedly brought on board to spearhead the new marketing campaign, everything Gabe's been running from catches up with him.
"The steamy love scenes, vibrant cast, deeply felt emotions, and sense of fun make this a surefire hit." —*Publishers Weekly*

★ **You** had me at hola. Alexis Daria. Avon Books, 2020. 365 pages; (Primas of power, 1)
ISBN 9780062959928
1. Soap opera actors and actresses 2. Tabloid newspapers 3. Ambition in women 4. Hispanic Americans 5. Single women 6. New York City 7. Romantic comedies 8. Multicultural romances
LibraryReads Favorites, 2020; RUSA Reading List Short List, 2021
Rendered the subject of tabloid gossip by a messy public breakup, soap star Jasmine takes a part in a new bilingual comedy at the side of a telenovela costar who would revitalize his career.
"Daria breathes effortless life into a cast of messy, loving, talented, and downright hilarious characters readers will adore. A sense of Latinx culture and pride exudes from every page, elevating an already entertaining story." —*Publishers Weekly*

Darnielle, John

Universal harvester. John Darnielle. Farrar, Straus and Giroux, 2017. 214 p.
ISBN 9780374282103
1. Young men 2. Video stores 3. Small town life 4. Loss (Psychology) 5. Small towns 6. Iowa 7. 1990s 8. Rural noir 9. Literary fiction
LC 2016025809
Working for a 1990s small-community video rental store under threat by a major chain competitor, Jeremy is reluctantly drawn into a mystery involving chilling footage of criminal activity that has been recorded onto the store's VHS tapes.
"Darnielle's contemporary ghost story may confound with its elusiveness (who is the mysterious I narrator?), but its impact will stick with readers." —*Library Journal*

Wolf in white van: a novel. John Darnielle. Farrar, Straus and Giroux, 2014. 207 p.
ISBN 9780374292089
1. Role playing games 2. Social isolation 3. Men with disfigurements 4. Alienation in men 5. Survival 6. California 7. Psychological fiction 8. Adult books for young adults
LC 2014015427
Alex Award, 2015
Creating fantastical mail-order role-playing games from his apartment where he endures a life of solitude after a disfiguring injury, Sean is blamed for a disaster involving two high school student clients, an event that compels him to reevaluate his own past.
"Sean Phillips was an unremarkable, moody teenager until tragedy left him with a horrific injury, changing his life forever. Who or what drove him to his fate? Can anyone be blamed? Is there a lesson to be learned? These questions are explored but never fully answered in Darnielle's first full-length novel...As senseless as a car accident, and as hard to look away from, the inconclusiveness of this journey will either captivate or madden readers." —*Booklist*

Darznik, Jasmin

The **bohemians**. Jasmin Darznik. Ballantine Books, 2021. 304 p.
ISBN 9780593129425
1. Lange, Dorothea 2. Women photographers 3. Artists 4. Counterculture 5. Female friendship 6. Chinese American women 7. San Francisco, California 8. 1920s 9. Biographical fiction 10. Historical fiction
A novel of one of America's most celebrated photographers, Dorothea Lange, explores the wild years in San Francisco that awakened her career-defining grit, compassion, and daring.
"Historical fiction readers will treasure this engaging story peppered with notable figures from Lange's circle of friends, including D. H. Lawrence, Ansel Adams, Maynard Dixon, and Frida Kahlo." —*Library Journal*

Song of a captive bird: a novel. Jasmin Darznik. Ballantine Books, 2018. 401 p.
ISBN 9780399182310
1. Farrukhzad, Furugh 2. Poets 3. Women's role 4. Women poets 5. Sexism 6. Feminists 7. Iran 8. 20th century 9. Biographical fiction 10. Historical fiction
Reimagines the life of rebel poet Forugh Farrokhzad, a passionate young writer in search of freedom and independence from the restrictions imposed on women in mid-twentieth-century Iran.
Includes bibliographical references (pages 397-398).

Daugherty, Christi

A **beautiful** corpse. Christi Daugherty. Minotaur Books, 2019. 368 p. (Harper McClain novels, 2)

ISBN 9781250148872

1. Women journalists 2. Women murder victims 3. Newspapers 4. Adult children of murder victims 5. Murder investigation 6. Savannah, Georgia 7. Thrillers and suspense

LC 2018046205

When a 24-year-old bartender is found murdered, crime reporter Harper McClain investigates three men, including the victim's former-criminal boyfriend, her stalker boss and her acrimonious ex, the son of the district attorney.

The **echo** killing. Christi Daugherty. Minotaur Books, 2018. 320 p. (Harper McClain novels, 1)

ISBN 9781250148841

1. Women journalists 2. Cold cases (Criminal investigation) 3. Families of murder victims 4. Murder investigation 5. Serial murder investigation 6. Savannah, Georgia 7. Thrillers and suspense

LC 2017044453

When a murder echoing a fifteen-year-old cold case rocks the Southern town of Savannah, crime reporter Harper McClain risks everything to find the identity of this calculated killer.

Revolver road: a Harper McClain mystery. Christi Daugherty. Minotaur Books, 2020. 336 p. (Harper McClain novels, 3)

ISBN 9781250235886

1. Women journalists 2. Threat (Psychology) 3. Missing men 4. Murder victims 5. Murderers 6. Georgia 7. Thrillers and suspense

LC 2019039542

Crime reporter Harper McClain is back on the beat when a troubled musician vanishes.

"Daugherty has created a complex, likable heroine whom readers will root for, fully fleshed-out secondary characters, and a compelling plot." —*Library Journal*

Daughters, Amy Weinland

You cannot mess this up: a true story that never happened. Amy Weinland Daughters. She Writes Bress, 2019. 272 pages

ISBN 9781631525834

1. Stay-at-home mothers 2. Time travel (Past) 3. Childhood 4. Family relationships 5. Memories 6. Houston, Texas 7. Dayton, Ohio 8. 1970s 9. 2010s 10. Autobiographical fiction 11. Mainstream fiction

Forty-six-year-old Amy Daughters flies home to Houston for Thanksgiving—and is mysteriously hurled back through time to 1978, where she's forced to visit her childhood home, including her ten-year old self, for thirty-six hours.

Davidson, Andrew

The **gargoyle**. Andrew Davidson. Doubleday, 2008. 468 p.

ISBN 9780385524940

1. Burns and scalds 2. Man-woman relationships 3. Traffic accident victims 4. Hospital wards 5. Reincarnation 6. Love stories 7. Psychological fiction 8. Canadian fiction 9. Adult books for young adults

LC 2007037258

Booklist Editors' Choice, 2008; Sunburst Award for Excellence in Canadian Literature of the Fantastic, 2009

Awakening in a burn ward after being horribly burned over much of his body after a terrible car accident, the cynical narrator is visited by a beautiful and enigmatic sculptress of gargoyles who tells him that they had once been lovers in medieval Germany and spins a tale of deathless love.

Davidson, Andy

The **boatman's** daughter: a novel. Andy Davidson. MCD, 2020. 416 p.

ISBN 9780374538552

1. Smuggling 2. Corruption 3. Supernatural 4. Swamps 5. Clergy 6. Arkansas 7. Literary fiction 8. Horror 9. Southern Gothic

LC 2019025806

A swampy literary horror novel about a young woman facing down drug dealers, a crooked cop, and a mad preacher on the banks of an Arkansas river.

"A stunning supernatural Southern gothic." —*Kirkus*

Davidson, Ash

★ **Damnation** spring. Ash Davidson. Simon & Schuster 2021. 445 pages

ISBN 9781982144401

1. Lumber workers 2. Midwives 3. Working class 4. Miscarriage 5. Redwood industry and trade 6. Northern California 7. 1970s 8. Mainstream fiction 9. Multiple perspectives

A mother and midwife inadvertently threatens the fortunes and livelihoods of her family and their neighbors after noticing an increase in local miscarriages and believes it's caused by the pesticides used by the Sanderson Timber Company, her husband's employer.

Thematically, it's a strong work of climate fiction, but it's rooted in age-old man-versus-nature storytelling. An impressively well-turned story about how environmental damage creeps into our bodies, psyches, and economies. Kirkusz

Davidson, Diane Mott

Killer pancake. Diane Mott Davidson. Bantam Books, 1995. 301 p. (Goldy Bear mysteries, 5)

ISBN 9780553095883

1. Caterers and catering 2. Murder investigation 3. Women caterers 4. Women amateur detectives 5. Women cooks 6. Colorado 7. Culinary mysteries 8. Gentle reads 9. Cozy mysteries

LC 95010852

Caterer and amateur sleuth Goldy B. Schulz gets caught between a ruthless cosmetic company and a violent animal rights group.

"The author includes recipes as she brings events to a proper boil in this latest lively and satisfying outing for Goldy, who not only solves the mystery but also finds, much to her delight, that coffee can save your life." —*Publishers Weekly*

A culinary mystery.

Includes 10 recipes.

The **last** suppers. Diane Mott Davidson. Bantam Books, 1994. 283 p. (Goldy Bear mysteries, 4)

ISBN 9780553095876

1. Caterers and catering 2. Murder investigation 3. Missing men 4. Weddings 5. Women caterers 6. Culinary mysteries 7. Gentle reads 8. Cozy mysteries

LC 94018886

When her wedding is called off last minute after the priest is murdered, Goldy fears that her homicide detective fiance, Tom, who was the first to arrive at the murder scene and who disappeared before anyone else got there, may be responsible.

"An appealing mixture of food and crime." —*Library Journal*

Includes 10 recipes.

Davidson, MaryJanice

Truth, lies, and second dates. MaryJanice Davidson. Griffin, 2020. 320 p.

ISBN 9781250053176

1. Women pilots 2. Coroners 3. Cold cases (Criminal investigation) 4. Malicious accusation 5. Man-woman relationships 6. Contemporary romances 7. Romantic comedies

LC 2020028416

Captain Ava Capp has been flying from her past for a decade. She'd much rather leave it, and her home state, behind forever. But when she finds herself back in Minnesota, against her better judgment, everything goes sideways in a way she never expected it to. M.E. Dr. Tom Baker has never forgotten Ava and the cold case she ran away from. When she shows up unexpectedly in town, in spite of himself, sparks fly. Which is terrible because he can't stop his growing attraction to her. Can these two Type-A's let their guards down and work together to put Ava's tragic past behind her for good? And keep their hands off each other at the same time?

"The banter comes a mile a minute, as do the twists, though Davidson struggles to juggle the suspense with the romantic development, leading to some wonky pacing. Still, the mystery will keep readers turning pages, and Ava's raunchy internal monologue creates plenty of laugh-out-loud moments." —*Publishers Weekly*

Davies, Carys

The **Mission** House. Carys Davies. Scribner, 2021. 224 p.

ISBN 9781982144838

1. Men 2. Interpersonal relations 3. Resentfulness 4. Pierce, Franklin 5. Nationalism 6. India 7. Literary fiction 8. Multiple perspectives

Taking refuge in a mission house in a remote hill town in India, an Englishman fleeing the dark undercurrents of contemporary life bonds with a Padre's daughter against a backdrop of escalating religious tensions.

"Nuanced characters, lush descriptions of South India, and an incisive look at class and religion make for a rich and layered novel." —*Booklist*

West. Carys Davies. Scribner, 2018. 149 p.

ISBN 9781501179341

1. Widowers 2. Quests 3. Frontier and pioneer life 4. Farms 5. Fossils 6. The West (United States) 7. Pennsylvania 8. American Westward Expansion (1803-1899) 9. Historical fiction 10. Literary fiction

Prompted by reports of giant animal bones found in Kentucky, a 19th century Pennsylvania mule breeder leaves his daughters behind on his small, failing farm and sets out with an American Indian guide into the harsh and strange Western landscape.

Davies, Peter Ho

The **fortunes.** Peter Ho Davies. Houghton Mifflin Harcourt, 2016. 272 p.

ISBN 9780544263703

1. Chinese Americans 2. Immigrants 3. Identity (Psychology) 4. Assimilation (Sociology) 5. Culture conflict 6. United States 7. Literary fiction 8. Adult books for young adults

LC 2016005161

New York Times Notable Book, 2016; Asian Pacific American Award for Literature: Adult Fiction Honor Book, 2017

Four interlinked stories examine the Chinese-American experience from the 19th century to the present. "Gold" follows a mixed-race immigrant from the Pearl River Delta who becomes the valet of a railroad baron. "Silver" introduces 1930s Hollywood actress Anna May Wong, whose career ambitions are thwarted by institutional racism. "Jade," set against the backdrop of 1980s Detroit's struggling auto industry, recounts a hate crime, while the contemporary "Pearl" describes a biracial writer's adoption of a child from China. Like The Welsh Girl, author Peter Ho Davies' debut novel, The Fortunes sensitively explores issues of identity and belonging.

"Davies' nuanced contemplation of how America has affected the Chinese (and vice versa) forces the reader to confront what is both singular and similar about all cross-cultural transactions." —*Kirkus*

A **lie** someone told you about yourself. Peter Ho Davies. Houghton Mifflin Harcourt, 2021. 224 p.

ISBN 9780544277717

1. Pregnancy 2. Parenthood 3. Options, alternatives, choices 4. Anonymous persons 5. Abortion 6. Literary fiction

LC 2020004427

A family grapples with the decision to terminate a pregnancy after receiving catastrophic test results and must deal with questions that reverberate down the years.

"Perfectly observed and tremendously moving: This will strike a resonant chord with parents everywhere." —*Kirkus*

Davies, Valentine

Miracle on 34th Street. Valentine Davies. Houghton Mifflin Harcourt, 2021. 144 p.

ISBN 9780358439172

1. Castro, Fidel 2. New York City 3. Christmas stories

LC 91-76211

"Nice blend of fantasy, fun and humor with the universal and wholesome appeal of the Christmas spirit." —*Library Journal*

Originally published: New York : Harcourt Brace, 1947

Davila, April

142 ostriches. April Davila. Kensington Pub Corp 2020. 304 p.

ISBN 9781496724700

1. Ranches 2. Grandparents — Death 3. Ostriches 4. Dysfunctional families 5. Eggs 6. California 7. Mojave Desert 8. Literary fiction

WILLA Literary Awards: Original Softcover Fiction, 2021

When Tallulah Jones was thirteen, her grandmother plucked her from the dank Oakland apartment she shared with her unreliable mom and brought her to the family ostrich ranch in the Mojave Desert. After eleven years caring for the curious, graceful birds, Tallulah accepts a job in Montana and prepares to leave home. But when Grandma Helen dies under strange circumstances, Tallulah inherits everything—just days before the birds inexplicably stop laying eggs.

"Davila's breezy, elegant prose captures the desert's growing appeal to Tallulah.... The fascinating details of operating an ostrich ranch elevate this family tale." —*Publishers Weekly*

Davis, Fiona

The **Chelsea** girls. Fiona Davis. Dutton, 2019. 368 pages

ISBN 9781524744588

1. McCarthyism 2. Entertainment industry and trade 3. Female friendship 4. Women screenwriters 5. Actors and actresses 6. New York City 7. 20th century 8. Historical fiction 9. Canadian fiction

Loan Stars Favourites, 2019

A 20-year friendship between a playwright and an actress with Broadway ambitions is tested by the impact of McCarthy-era witch hunts among the creative residents of New York City's Chelsea Hotel.

The **lions** of Fifth Avenue: a novel. Fiona Davis. Dutton, 2020. 354 p.

ISBN 9781524744618

1. Women — Suffrage 2. Libraries 3. Women's role 4. Rare books 5. Family secrets 6. New York City 7. 1910s 8. 1990s 9. Historical fiction 10. Parallel narratives

LC 2019057269

Loan Stars Favourites, 2020

A New York Public LIbrary superintendent's wife reevaluates her priorities upon joining a woman's suffrage group in 1913, decades before her granddaughter's efforts to save an exhibit expose tragic family secrets.

"Davis (The Chelsea Girls) gives readers a mystery and a historical novel all in one absorbing tale." —*Library Journal*

The **masterpiece**. Fiona Davis. E.P. Dutton, 2018. 368 p.
ISBN 9781524742959

1. Women artists 2. Independence in women 3. Art schools 4. Art 5. Sexism 6. New York City 7. 1920s 8. 1970s 9. Historical fiction 10. Dante Alighieri 11. Multiple perspectives

LibraryReads Favorites, 2018

A recently divorced information-booth worker stumbles on an abandoned art school within a crumbling Grand Central Terminal before learning the story of a talented woman artist who went missing 50 years earlier.

Davis, Kathryn

Duplex. Kathryn Davis. Graywolf Press, 2013. 195 pages
ISBN 9781555976538

1. Time travel 2. Couples 3. Wizards 4. Interdimensional travel 5. Life change events 6. Science fiction 7. Science fantasy 8. Literary fiction

New York Times Notable Book, 2013

In the duplex, a magical doorway to the past and future, human and robot and space and time, Mary and Eddie, existing in an eternal present, are meant for each other, but discover that love is no guarantee when the past and future fold into each other after the arrival of a sorcerer.

Davis, Lindsey

A **body** in the bathhouse. Lindsey Davis. Mysterious Press, 2002. 354 p. : Illustration (Marcus Didius Falco mysteries, 13)
ISBN 9780892967711

1. Romans in Great Britain 2. Families 3. Building 4. Palaces 5. Contractors 6. Great Britain 7. Rome 8. Roman Britain (55 BCE-449 CE) 9. 1st century 10. Historical mysteries 11. Mysteries

LC 2002023071

Ancient Roman investigator Marcus Didius Falco finds trouble on the site of a new palace being built by the king of the Atrebtes tribe in distant Britain.

"In this Marcus Didius Falco adventure, various circumstances, including a dead body under his father's new bathhouse, a sister in danger from a spurned love interest, and a request from the emperor for help in auditing a British building projectconverge to send Falco, his family, and his frightened sister to the damp and uncivilized frontier.... Davis delivers her usual entertaining family dynamics and historically accurate details." —*Booklist*

A **comedy** of terrors: a Flavia Albia novel. Lindsey Davis. Minotaur Books, 2021. 320 p. (Flavia Albia mysteries, 9)
ISBN 9781250241542

1. Women private investigators 2. Festivals 3. Organized crime 4. Violent crimes 5. Threat (Psychology) 6. Rome 7. Roman Empire (27 BCE-476 CE) 8. 1st century 9. Historical mysteries

LC 2021017543

In Rome, 89 A.D, poisonings, murders, and a bloody gang war of retribution breaks out during the festival of Saturnalia, and when her husband, Tiberius, becomes a target, it's time for Flavia Albia to take matters into her own hands—in Lindsey Davis's next historical mystery, A Comedy of Terrors.

"Davis convincingly depicts first-century mobsters, an aspect of ancient Roman criminality that's been underutilized by authors writing about this period. This series remains as fresh as ever." —*Publishers Weekly*

The **ides** of April: a Flavia Albia mystery. Lindsey Davis. Minotaur Books, 2013. 341 pages : Map (Flavia Albia mysteries, 1)
ISBN 9781250023698

1. Women private investigators 2. Murder investigation 3. Private investigators 4. Murder 5. Murder suspects 6. Rome 7. Roman Empire (27 BCE-476 CE) 8. 1st century 9. Historical mysteries 10. Mysteries 11. Adult books for young adults

Flavia Albia, the adopted daughter of Falco, works as a private informer in Rome during the reign of Domitian and is hired to investigate a fatal accident that turns sinister when her client dies under suspicious circumstances that place Flavia Albia's reputation at stake.

One virgin too many. By Lindsey Davis. Mysterious Press, 2000. 304 p. (Marcus Didius Falco mysteries, 11)
ISBN 9780892967162

1. Cults 2. Monasticism and religious orders 3. Geese 4. Murder 5. Murder investigation 6. Rome 7. Roman Empire (27 BCE-476 CE) 8. 1st century 9. Historical mysteries 10. Mysteries

LC 31053

Marcus Didius Falco, the cynical, hard-boiled investigator from the rough end of Rome, is back from a difficult mission in North Africa. As a result of his hard work, Emperor Vespasian awards Falco with the title of Procurator of Poultry for the Senate and People of Rome, or keeper of the city's sacred geese. Not much of a salary, of course, but the title does give him a better standing with his in-laws. Now, all Falco wants is to spend time relaxing at home with his family. But there is no rest for Falco as he finds himself drawn into the world of the Roman religious cults...and the murder of a member of the Sacred Brotherhoods. And then there's the disappearance of the most likely new candidate for the Order of Vestal Virgins. Falco soon uncovers a sinister cover-up-and is too deeply involved to back away from the truth.

"For sharply etched characters, wry humor, and a powerfully evoked Rome, this historical can't be beaten." —*Library Journal*

Davis, Lydia

The **collected** stories of Lydia Davis. Lydia Davis. Farrar, Straus and Giroux, 2009. Xi, 733 p.
ISBN 9780374270605

1. Short stories

LC 2009025451

A single-volume compilation of the National Book Award finalist's short stories.

"This volume presents a body of work probably unique in American writing, in its combination of lucidity, aphoristic brevity, formal originality, sly comedy, metaphysical bleakness, philosophical pressure, and human wisdom. I suspect that The Collected Stories of Lydia Davis will in time be seen as one of the great, strange American literary contributions, distinct and crookedly personal, like the work of Flannery O'Connor, or Donald Barthelme, or J. F. Powers." —*The New Yorker*

Includes index.

Davys, Tim

Amberville. Tim Davys. HarperCollins, 2009. 352 p. (Mollisan Town quartet, 1)
ISBN 9780061625121

1. Stuffed animals (Toys) 2. Missing persons 3. Organized crime 4. Good and evil 5. Escapes 6. Mysteries 7. Hardboiled fiction 8. Translations

A fantastical noir tale populated by animal characters finds Eric Bear, a successful advertising executive, confronting his checkered past when notorious crime boss Nicholas Dove threatens Eric's wife, Emma Rabbit, unless Eric and his former teammates prevent an attack on Dove's life.

Dazieri, Sandrone

Kill the angel. Sandrone Dazieri. Simon & Schuster 2018. 384 p. (Caselli and Torre novels, 2)
ISBN 9781501174650
1. Women detectives 2. Private investigators 3. Murder investigation 4. Trains 5. Captives 6. Rome, Italy 7. Italy 8. Thrillers and suspense 9. Translations
LC 2017051621
A follow-up to Kill the Father finds investigators Colomba Caselli and Dante Torre examining clues on a high-speed train found with a carriage full of murder victims, an act committed by a murderously damaged killer who has staged the scene to look like a terrorist attack.
Translated from the Italian Antony Shugaar.
Originally published in Italy in 2016 by Mondadori as L'Angelo.

Kill the father. Sandrone Dazieri; translated from the Italian by Antony Shugaar. Scribner, 2017. 512 pages (Caselli and Torre novels, 1)
ISBN 9781501130731
1. Missing children 2. Kidnapping 3. Murder investigation 4. Kidnappers 5. Women detectives 6. Rome, Italy 7. Italy 8. Thrillers and suspense 9. Translations
LC 2016015605
When a woman is beheaded in a park outside Rome and her six-year-old son goes missing, two of Italy's top analytical minds are assigned to the case: Deputy Captain Colomba Caselli, a fierce warrior-like detective, and Dante Torre, a man who spent his childhood trapped inside a concrete silo, fed through the gloved hand of a masked kidnapper who called himself "the Father. And now evidence suggests that the Father is coming back.
Includes bibliographical references and index.
Originally published: Segrate, Italy : Mondadori, 2014.
Translated from the Italian.

Kill the king. Sandrone Dazieri. Scribner, 2020. 384 p. (Caselli and Torre novels, 3)
ISBN 9781501174728
1. Women detectives 2. Coworkers 3. Missing men 4. Teenage boys 5. Boys with autism 6. Rome, Italy 7. Italy 8. Thrillers and suspense 9. Translations
Reeling from a deadly bombing in Venice and her investigative partner Dante's disappearance, Detective Colomba Caselli retreats to the rural countryside outside Rome to nurse her wounds. When an apparently autistic teenager appears in her yard, covered in blood, he leads her to a brutal crime scene where nothing is what it seems. As Colomba gets pulled into the investigation and the body count spirals upward, she is implicated in the violence.
Series complete in three volumes.
Originally published: Milan : Mondadori, 2018.
Translated from the Italian.

De Bernieres, Louis

Birds without wings. Louis de Bernieres. Knopf, 2004. Xi, 553 p. : Color; Map
ISBN 9781400043415

1. Ataturk, Kemal 2. Villages 3. Religious fanaticism 4. Interfaith romance 5. Communities 6. Muslims 7. Turkey 8. Gallipoli Peninsula, Turkey 9. Historical fiction 10. War stories 11. Literary fiction
LC 2004014529
ALA Notable Book, 2005; Booklist Editors' Choice, 2004; Library Journal Best Books, 2004
In a small town in Anatolia in the finals days of the Ottoman Empire, the lives of its inhabitants—Armenians, Christians, and Muslims—peacefully intertwine, until Mustafa Kemal, a powerful military leader, conscripts the young men of the village to battle the invading Western European forces during the Great War, and religious fanaticism and nationalism destroy the peace.
"This epic about the tragedy of borders is likely to cross all borders, moving readers everywhere as it describes the harrowing cost of remaking faraway places in the image of our dreams."—*Christian Science Monitor*
Map on lining papers.

De Giovanni, Maurizio

The **bastards** of Pizzofalcone. Maurizio De Giovanni; translated from Italian by Antony Shugaar. Europa Editions, 2016. 288 p. (Giuseppe Lojacono mysteries, 2)
ISBN 9781609453145
1. Detectives 2. Police 3. Murder investigation 4. Murder 5. Police corruption 6. Naples, Italy 7. Italy 8. Police procedurals 9. Mysteries 10. Multiple perspectives
After every officer of the investigative branch of the Pizzofalcone police precinct of Naples is suspended for corruption, a new team of officers is assembled from around the city and thrown into a high profile murder case led by Inspector Lojacono.
Originally published in Italian as I Bastardi di Pizzofalcone, 2013.

The **crocodile**. Maurizio de Giovanni; translated from Italian by Antony Shugaar. Europa Editions, 2013. 278 p. (Giuseppe Lojacono mysteries, 1)
ISBN 9781609451196
1. Malicious accusation 2. Detectives 3. Women lawyers 4. Marital conflict 5. Serial murders 6. Naples, Italy 7. Italy 8. Police procedurals 9. Hardboiled fiction 10. Multiple perspectives
Given a second chance and a shot at clearing his name, Inspector Giuseppe Lojacono, who has been accused of leaking sensitive information to the mob, arrives in Naples, at the behest of a beautiful magistrate, to catch a serial killer called "The Crocodile." BT
Originally published: Milano : Mondadori, 2012.
Translated from the Italian.

De Kretser, Michelle

The **life** to come. Michelle de Kretser. Catapult, 2018. 344 p.
ISBN 9781936787821
1. Interpersonal relations 2. Coping 3. Self-fulfillment 4. Loneliness 5. Interpersonal attraction 6. Literary fiction 7. Australian fiction
Librarians' Choice (Australia), 2017; Miles Franklin Award, 2018; NSW Premier's Literary Awards, Christina Stead Prize for Fiction, 2019; Shortlisted for the Stella Prize, 2018
Connected stories set in Australia, France and Sri Lanka follow a writer longing for success, a woman seeing a married man and a man with commitment issues stemming from a childhood tragedy.
Originally published: Sydney : Allen & Unwin, 2017.

De la Motte, Anders

MemoRandom: a thriller. Anders De La Motte; translated by Neil Smith. Pocket Books, 2015. 448 p. (MemoRandom, 1)
ISBN 9781476788067
1. Men with amnesia 2. Intelligence service 3. Competition 4. Police 5. Traffic accident victims 6. Stockholm, Sweden 7. Scandinavian crime fiction 8. Thrillers and suspense 9. Translations 10. Adult books for young adults

After suffering a stroke and a violent car crash, a handler at the Intelligence Unit of the Stockholm Police Force loses all memory of an important informant, putting the entire operation at risk.

Originally published: Stockholm : Forum 2014.

Ultimatum: a thriller. Anders de la Motte. Atria, 2017. 368 p. (MemoRandom, 2)
ISBN 9781476788098
1. Informers 2. Intelligence service 3. Intelligence officers 4. Organized crime 5. Secrets 6. Stockholm, Sweden 7. Scandinavian crime fiction 8. Thrillers and suspense 9. Translations

In a sequel to the thriller MemoRandom, David Sarac of the Stockholm Police Force's Intelligence Unit, recovering from gunshot wounds after a violent encounter with the enigmatic high-level informant Janus, is slipped an anonymous note by his nurse that contains clues to the person responsible for betraying him during the Janus shoot-out.

De Leon, Aya

Side chick nation. Aya De Leon. Dafina Books, 2019. 352 p. (Justice hustlers, 4)
ISBN 9781496715791
1. Female gang leaders 2. Women thieves 3. West Indian Americans 4. Cheating (Interpersonal relations) 5. Rich men 6. Miami, Florida 7. New York City 8. Urban fiction 9. African American fiction
Booklist Editors' Choice, 2019

Fed up with her married Miami boyfriend, savvy Dulce has no problem stealing his drug-dealer stash and fleeing to her family in the Caribbean. But when she gets bored in rural Santo Domingo, she escapes on a sugar daddy adventure to Puerto Rico. Meanwhile, New York-based mastermind thief Marisol already has her hands full fleecing a ruthless CEO who's stealing her family's land in Puerto Rico, while trying to get her relatives out alive after the hurricane. An extra member in her crew could be game-changing, but she's wary of Dulce's unpredictability and reputation for drama.

★ A **spy** in the struggle. Aya de Leon. Dafina, 2020. 352 p.
ISBN 9781496728593
1. African American women lawyers 2. FBI agents 3. Undercover operations 4. African American political activists 5. Criminal investigation 6. California 7. Romantic suspense 8. African American fiction

The author of the Justice Hustlers series follows the FBI recruitment of a savvy young lawyer who uses the wits of her impoverished youth to infiltrate an extremist activist group that is being exploited by a biotech company.

"An electric blend of romantic suspense, feminism, and socially conscious thriller." —*Booklist*

De los Santos, Marisa

The **precious** one. Marisa De los Santos. William Morrow & Co, 2015. 359 p.
ISBN 9780061670893

1. Sisters 2. Fathers and daughters 3. Manipulation (Social sciences) 4. People who have had heart attacks 5. Father-separated families 6. Domestic fiction 7. Relationship fiction 8. Adult books for young adults
LibraryReads Favorites, 2015

A tale told in alternating voices traces the collaborative efforts of an estranged millionaire father and the daughter he abandoned 17 years earlier to reconcile and write his memoir.

De Robertis, Carolina

Cantoras. By Carolina De Robertis. Alfred A. Knopf, 2019. 320 pages
ISBN 9780525521693
1. Lesbians 2. Independence in women 3. Violence against gay men and lesbians 4. Homophobia 5. Communities 6. Uruguay 7. 20th century 8. 21st century 9. Political fiction 10. LGBTQIA fiction 11. Literary fiction
Stonewall Book Award for the Barbara Gittings Literature Award, 2020; Kirkus Prize for Fiction finalist, 2019

Enduring the rampant violence against women and the LGBTQ community in the decades of the Uruguayan dictatorship, five women heartbreakingly unite as lovers, friends and family.

The **gods** of tango. Carolina De Robertis. Alfred A. Knopf, 2015. 367 pages
ISBN 9781101874493
1. Gender identity 2. Violinists 3. Lesbians 4. Tango music 5. Male impersonators 6. Buenos Aires, Argentina 7. Coming-of-age stories 8. LGBTQIA fiction 9. Adult books for young adults
School Library Journal Best Books: Best Adult Books 4 Teens, 2015; Stonewall Book Award for the Barbara Gittings Literature Award, 2016

As soon as Italian immigrant Leda Mazzoni steps off the boat in Argentina in 1913, she learns that she's a widow: her husband has been killed during a political protest. Since returning home isn't an option, Leda dons his clothes and takes his name. Playing the violin on the streets of Buenos Aires, "Dante" earns a living as a busker until a local bandleader recruits the young musician for his troupe. What follows is a lush and lyrical coming-of-age story, set against the vivid backdrop of a city obsessed with the seductive rhythms of the tango.

"The novel is a plea to embrace 'the bright jagged thing you really are,' and in its hero's more contemplative, interior moments, De Robertis captures the enormity of that struggle." —*Kirkus*

Perla. Carolina De Robertis. Alfred A. Knopf, 2012. 235 p.
ISBN 9780307599599
1. Family secrets 2. Fathers and daughters 3. Teenage girls — Identity 4. Military service 5. Dictatorship 6. Argentina 7. Buenos Aires, Argentina 8. Coming-of-age stories 9. Psychological fiction

A coming-of-age tale set in post-dictatorship Buenos Aires finds privileged Correa safeguarding the interests of her family by hiding her beloved father's military past from others until an uninvited visitor forces her to confront the unease she has suppressed her entire life.

Dean, Debra

The **madonnas** of Leningrad: a novel. Debra Dean. William Morrow, 2006. 231 p.
ISBN 9780060825300
1. Russian Americans 2. Reminiscing in old age 3. People with Alzheimer's disease 4. Russian American women 5. Senior women 6. St. Petersburg, Russia 7. Soviet Union 8. 1940s 9. Psychological fiction 10. Historical fiction 11. Sinatra, Frank
LC 2005050233

ALA Notable Book, 2007

In a novel that moves back and forth between the Soviet Union during World War II and modern-day America, Marina, an elderly Russian woman, recalls vivid images of her youth during the height of the siege of Leningrad.

"Like her adoring museum audiences 60 years earlier, readers will absorb Marina's glorious, lush accounts of classical beauties as she traces them in her mind. Dean eloquently depicts the ravages of Alzheimer's disease and convincingly describes the inner world of the afflicted." —*Library Journal*

Dean, Margaret Lazarus

The **time** it takes to fall. Margaret Lazarus Dean. Simon & Schuster, 2007. 305 p.

ISBN 9780743297226

1. Twelve-year-old girls 2. Girls — Career aspirations 3. Families 4. Unemployed persons — Family relationships 5. Marital conflict 6. Florida 7. Coming-of-age stories 8. Adult books for young adults
LC 2006052213

Dreaming of a future in space travel while growing up in 1980s Cape Canaveral, young Dolores Gray struggles with the harsh realities of her increasingly unstable home life and is shocked by the devastating 1986 explosion of the space shuttle Challenger.

"A gripping judgment of American culture with a harrowing depiction in the epilogue of the last few minutes in the lives of the Challenger's seven astronauts." —*Library Journal*

Dean, Michael

I, Hogarth. Michael Dean. Overlook Duckworth, 2013. 261 p.

ISBN 9781468303421

1. Hogarth, William 2. Artists — History 3. Dysfunctional families 4. Apprenticeship 5. Lust in men 6. Rogues 7. Great Britain 8. Biographical fiction 9. Historical fiction

A tale inspired by the life of the 18th-century London artist famed for such works as "Gin Lane" and "The Rake's Progress" imagines his youth in a debtor's prison, struggles to establish the Copyright Act on behalf of artists and childless marriage to Jane Thornhill.

Dean, Pamela

Tam Lin. Pamela Dean. Tom Doherty Associates, 1991. 468 p. (Fairy tales: a series of fantasy novels retelling classic tales, 5)

ISBN 9780312851378

1. Universities and colleges 2. Women college students 3. Roommates 4. College teachers 5. Man-woman relationships 6. Middle West 7. Minneapolis, Minnesota 8. 1970s 9. Adaptations, retellings, and spin-offs 10. Contemporary fantasy 11. Fantasy fiction
LC 90049033

This Scottish-based tale for adults offers a pregnant heroine who must rescue the man who seduced her in the woods from his captor, the Fairie Queen.

"This delightful new entry in the Fairy Tale series, featuring children's classics refashioned for adult audiences, adapts the eponymous Scottish ballad to a Midwestern university setting." —*Publishers Weekly*

An original novel based on the classic fairy tale.

Includes text of the Scottish ballad.

Deane, Seamus

Reading in the dark. Seamus Deane. A. A. Knopf, 1997. 245 p.

ISBN 9780394574400

1. Boys 2. Family secrets 3. Betrayal 4. Murder 5. Family relationships 6. Northern Ireland 7. 1940s 8. 1950s 9. Coming-of-age stories 10. Literary fiction
LC 96-49635

ALA Notable Book, 1998; Guardian First Book Award, 1996; Library Journal Best Books, 1997; New York Times Notable Book, 1997; Shortlisted for the Booker-McConnell Prize, 1996

A young boy describes growing up amid the violence and tragedy of Northern Ireland during the 1940s and 1950s, detailing the deadly, unspoken betrayal born out of political enmity that shapes the lives of himself and his family.

"A Catholic boy growing up hard by the border between Donegal and Derry is fascinated by the local ghost stories and neighborhood lore, and this fascination leads him to secrets at the heart of a family feud. His search for the truth runs through a labyrinth of Irish detours and delights: elaborate catechisms, mad poets, mute idiots, drunken hyperbole, deathbed revelations, and a clever reprisal involving an unwitting bishop." —*The New Yorker*

Originally published: London: Jonathan Cape, 1996.

Deaver, Jeffery

★ The **coffin** dancer. Jeffery Deaver. Simon & Schuster, 1998. 358 p. (Lincoln Rhyme mysteries, 2)

ISBN 9780684852850

1. Serial murderers 2. Violence 3. Forensic scientists 4. People with quadriplegia 5. Rhyme, Lincoln (Fictitious character) 6. New York City 7. Mysteries
LC 98-13537

Detective Lincoln Rhyme and his protege have 48 hours to keep three federal witnesses alive, as they frantically search for an elusive murderer.

"Quadriplegic forensic specialist Lincoln Rhyme is called in to track down a contract killer, known as the Coffin Dancer, who has been hired to eliminate three witnesses in the upcoming federal trial of Philip Hansen. The trial is set to begin just 48 hours from the novel's (literally) explosive beginning. Rhyme and his beautiful assistant, detective Amelia Sachs, have just that much time to ID the Dancer and keep him from murdering the remaining witnesses.... The pace, energized by Deaver's precise attention, never flags." —*Publishers Weekly*

Edge: a novel. Jeffery Deaver. Simon & Schuster, 2010. 397 p.

ISBN 9781439156353

1. Detectives 2. Criminals 3. Kidnapping 4. Torture 5. Revenge 6. Washington, D.C. 7. Thrillers and suspense 8. First person narratives

Targeted by a ruthless hired criminal seeking to extract information for a mysterious employer, Washington, D.C. police detective Ryan Kessler places the safety of his family in the hands of a federal protection officer who takes incrementally extreme measures to outmaneuver his adversary.

The **empty** chair. By Jeffrey Deaver. Simon & Schuster, 2000. 411 p. (Lincoln Rhyme mysteries, 3)

ISBN 9780684855639

1. Environmental crimes 2. Innocence (Law) 3. Kidnapping victims 4. Rhyme, Lincoln (Fictitious character) 5. Forensic pathologists 6. North Carolina 7. New York City 8. Mysteries 9. Adult books for young adults
LC 24220

New York Times Notable Mysteries, 2000

Detective Lincoln Rhyme is in North Carolina for an experimental surgery when he is asked by local authorities to search for two young women who have been abducted.

"Deaver is the master of the plot twist, and readers will only drive themselves crazy trying to outguess him. Better just to enjoy the ride. A magnificent thriller." —*Booklist*

Garden of beasts: a novel of Berlin 1936. Jeffery Deaver. Simon & Schuster, 2004. 416 p.
ISBN 9780743222013
1. Assassins 2. Nazis 3. Criminals 4. German Americans 5. Berlin, Germany 6. Germany 7. 1930s 8. Historical mysteries 9. Mysteries 10. Adult books for young adults
LC 2004045206
Ian Fleming Steel Dagger Award, 2004
Reputed for his vow to take only morally righteous assignments in 1936 New York City, a German-American hit man is forced by the government to pose as an Olympic contender and kill a member of Hitler's regime.
"Top Nazis, including Hitler, Himmler and Gring, make colorful cameos, but it's the smart, shaded-gray characterizations of the principals that anchor the exciting plot." —*Publishers Weekly*

★ The **goodbye** man. Jeffery Deaver. G.P. Putnam & Sons, 2020. 416 pages (Colter Shaw novels, 2)
ISBN 9780525535973
1. Trackers 2. Cults 3. Hate crimes 4. Suicide 5. Secrecy 6. Washington (State) 7. Thrillers and suspense
Loan Stars Favourites, 2020
A sequel to The Never Game finds Colter Shaw investigating a mysterious organization in Washington State that is either a therapeutic healing colony or a dangerous cult under the sway of a charismatic leader.
"It's no surprise that the story has a lot of moving parts and just the right amount of twists and turns (Deaver's reputation as a master of the corkscrewing plot is well earned), and fans of the author's Lincoln Rhyme and Kathryn Dance novels will note the same attention to character construction and natural-sounding dialogue here." —*Booklist*

★ The **never** game. Jeffery Deaver. G.P. Putnam's Sons, 2019. 400 p. (Colter Shaw novels, 1)
ISBN 9780525535942
1. Trackers 2. Video games 3. Missing persons investigation 4. Video games industry and trade 5. Business — Corrupt practices 6. Silicon Valley, California 7. Cyber-thrillers 8. Thrillers and suspense
LC 2019003019
Searching for a missing woman in Silicon Valley, an expert tracker is pitted against dark elements in the billion-dollar gaming industry and a serial killer who stages scenes from his favorite game.
"Fans of twisty suspense that pushes the envelope of plausibility without inviting disbelief will be enthralled." —*Publishers Weekly*

The **October** list. Jeffery Deaver. Grand Central Publishing, 2013. 208 p.
ISBN 9781455576647
1. Kidnapping 2. Ransom 3. Secrets 4. Venture capitalists 5. Personal assistants 6. Thrillers and suspense
LC 2013018524
After Gabriela McKenzie's daughter is kidnapped, her abductors demand two things: $400,000 in cash and a document known only as the October List.

The **stone** monkey: a Lincoln Rhyme novel. Jeffery Deaver. Simon & Schuster, 2002. 424 p; (Lincoln Rhyme mysteries, 4)
ISBN 9780743221993
1. Human smuggling 2. Undocumented immigrants 3. Serial murderers 4. Sabotage 5. Attempted murder 6. Chinatown, New York City 7. New York City 8. Mysteries 9. Adult books for young adults
New York Times Notable Mysteries, 2002

Recruited to help the FBI and the INS perform the nearly impossible, Lincoln Rhyme and his partner, Amelia Sachs, manage to track down a cargo ship headed for New York City carrying two dozen illegal Chinese immigrants, as well as the notorious human smuggler and killer known as "the Ghost." But when the Ghost's capture goes disastrously wrong, Lincoln and Amelia find themselves in a horrifying race against time.
"This thriller's protagonist, a quadriplegic forensics genius named Lincoln Rhyme who directs elaborate criminal investigations from his customized bed, is the 'last hope' of government agencies clamoring for his aid in capturing the master criminal who sank a ship of illegal Chinese immigrants off the coast of Long Island. Rhyme's quarry, a sinister shapeshifter known as the Ghost, is 'probably the most dangerous human smuggler in the world,' and two desperate families will die if this fiend is not caught in the next 48 hours." —*New York Times Book Review*

Deb, Siddhartha
The **point** of return: a novel. Siddhartha Deb. Ecco, 2003. 304 p.
ISBN 9780060501518
1. Young men 2. Teenage boys 3. Children of veterinarians 4. Veterinarians 5. Civil service workers 6. India 7. 1970s 8. 1980s 9. Family sagas 10. Adult books for young adults
LC 2002035300
New York Times Notable Book, 2003
A tale told in reverse chronological order is set against the political violence of the 1970s and 1980s in northeast India, during which the willful, curious Babu and his father, a doctor and enigmatic product of British colonial rule and Nehruvian nationalism, find themselves strangers living in the same home.
"To allow Dr. Dam to evolve through most of the book in a self-generated fog of benevolence and to shatter it in the last pages is a brilliant stroke.... Storytelling of the kind Deb lavishes, for most of his book, on Dr. Dam is rare and precious and uplifting." —*New York Times Book Review*

DeCarlo, Melissa
The **art** of crash landing: a novel. Melissa DeCarlo. Harper, 2015. 405 pages
ISBN 9780062390547
1. Mothers and daughters 2. Family secrets 3. Forgiveness 4. Family relationships 5. Pregnant women 6. Oklahoma 7. Domestic fiction
LC 2015010374
LibraryReads Favorites, 2015
Chasing a possible inheritance from her grandmother, Mattie Wallace, homeless and pregnant, travels to her mother's hometown in Oklahoma, where she tries to reconcile the town's memory of her mother with the broken alcoholic she became and stop her own downward spiral.
"DeCarlo bursts on the scene with a fascinating, mysterious novel. The pacing is excellent and the prose fluid as the story unfolds in a combination of flashbacks and present-day scenes. This debut is thick with secrets; it will cause readers to question everyone and everything. The author does an outstanding job combining suspense with heartache, adding a dash of romance and, at the end, hope." —*Library Journal*

Dee, Jonathan
The **locals**: a novel. Jonathan Dee. Random House, 2017. 383 p.
ISBN 9780812993226
1. Small towns 2. Contractors 3. Billionaires 4. Working class families 5. Local government 6. Berkshire Hills, Massachusetts 7. New England 8. Mainstream fiction
LC 2016055310

A rural, working-class town in New England elects as its mayor a New York hedge fund millionaire who slowly transforms the community in his image, triggering unexpected changes in the life of a financially strapped contractor and his extended family.

"An absorbing panorama of small-town life and a study of democracy in miniature, with both the people and their polity facing real and particular contemporary pressures." —*Kirkus*

The **privileges:** a novel. Jonathan Dee. Random House, 2010. 258 p.
ISBN 9781400068678
1. Rich people 2. Families 3. Success (Concept) 4. Husband and wife 5. Ambition in men 6. Manhattan, New York City 7. New York City 8. Mainstream fiction 9. Adult books for young adults
LC 2009012900
New York Times Notable Book, 2010; Pulitzer Prize for Fiction finalist, 2011

Becoming wealthier and more socially connected throughout their marriage, Adam and Cynthia Morey also find themselves increasingly subject to the temptations of excess and risky behavior while their children struggle with their own privilege-based challenges.

"The tale of a family scaling the heights of finance in New York City, a family born, nursed and prep-schooled on the fiscally rich milk of the hedge fund. The novel begins with the wedding of Cynthia and Adamtwo glossy, self-absorbed 22-year-olds.... [They] go on to live the life of insider-trading zillionaires, obtaining the Manhattan penthouse, the villa in Anguilla, the halfhearted charitable trust. But where a lesser novelist might rely on sarcasm and satire, Dee opts for old-fashioned complexity. The wedding scene, a 32-page masterpiece, begins with a panoramic perspective that dips into the brains of all involved, from the wedding planner to her stoned son to Cynthia's jealous mother. His characters are stories in and of themselves, particularly Cynthia, a sexy savant who calls people skanks and pays off her estranged father's girlfriend to leave his deathbed. Yet Dee approaches herand all his characterswith understanding." —*Time Out New York*

A **thousand** pardons: a novel. Jonathan Dee. Random House, 2012. 256 p.
ISBN 9780812993219
1. Public relations 2. Divorced women 3. Business — Corrupt practices 4. Businesspeople 5. Man-woman relationships 6. Satirical fiction 7. Mainstream fiction
LC 2012018513
Forced back into the working world after her corporate lawyer husband's spectacular downfall, Helen discovers a talent for public relations and is tempted away from her dysfunctional family by her childhood crush, now a movie star who needs her professional assistance.

Defoe, Daniel
★ **Moll** Flanders. Daniel Defoe; with an introduction by John Mullan. Knopf, 1991. Xxxiii, 338 p.
ISBN 9780679405481
1. Prostitutes 2. Great Britain 3. Picaresque fiction 4. Books to movies 5. Classics
Moll is born in Newgate prison to a petty thief and is soon left at the mercy of whoever will take her in. From this unfavorable beginning, the lusty, resourceful Moll loves and bargains her way from rags to riches, from prostitution in the streets of London to prosperity on a Virginia plantation. Along the way, she offers a charmingly candid view of her life and times.
Original ed. published in 1722 under title: The fortunes and misfortunes of the famous Moll Flanders.

★ **Robinson** Crusoe. Daniel Defoe. TOR, 1996. 340 p.

ISBN 9780812557367
1. Survival (after airplane accidents, shipwrecks, etc.) 2. Friday (Fictitious character) 3. Crusoe, Robinson (Fictitious character) 4. Shipwrecks 5. Solitude 6. Adventure stories 7. Survival stories 8. Books to movies
In 1659, after becoming the sole survivor of a shipwreck, Englishman Robinson Crusoe lives on a deserted island for more than twenty-eight years.
Robinson Crusoe has been closely adapted into the films Robinson Crusoe (1997), Crusoe (1988), and Adventures of Robinson Crusoe (1954). In 1975 the film Man Friday satirized contemporary race relations using the plot of Robinson Crusoe.
Originally published in 1719.

Deighton, Len
Berlin game. By Len Deighton. Knopf, 1984. 345 p; (Bernard Samson novels, 1)
ISBN 9780394534077
1. Moles (Spies) 2. Intelligence service 3. Secret service 4. International intrigue 5. Cold War 6. Berlin, Germany 7. London, England 8. Spy fiction
LC 83048104
East is East and West is West—and they meet in Berlin. He was the best source the Department ever had, but now he desperately wanted to come over the Wall. 'Brahms Four' was certain a high-ranking mole was set to betray him. There was only one Englishman he trusted any more: someone from the old days. So they decided to put Bernard Samson back into the field after five sedentary years of flying a desk. The field is Berlin. The game is as baffling, treacherous and lethal as ever.
"This novel is a decent entertainment that rattles swiftly along to its payoff. Two things especially recommend ita devious contrivance of plot that has probably never been used before in an espionage novel; and the city of Berlin, mecca to spies and spy novelists. The second is the greater asset. Although the book is elaborately plotted, its best moments derive from the setting and from the force of this particular setting upon behavior and psychology." —*New York Times Book Review*
Sequel: Mexico set.
Originally published: [London] : Hutchinson, 1983.

London match. Len Deighton. A. A. Knopf, 1985. 407 p. (Bernard Samson novels, 3)
ISBN 9780394549378
1. Intelligence service 2. Defectors 3. Suspicion 4. Spies 5. Moles (Spies) 6. England 7. Chaucer, Geoffrey
LC 85040454
British agent Bernard Samson discovers compelling evidence that there is yet another traitor at the highest level of British intelligence and finds himself in direct confrontation with this British KGB agent
"The strength of (this novel) is not in its plot but its characterization.... Mr. Deighton portrays each character of his large cast fully and sympathetically. However, the best character is the city of Berlin. It is a living presence, and in some of the descriptions one can almost hear the stones breathing." —*New York Times Book Review*
Sequel to: Mexico set.

Dekker, Ted
Black: the birth of evil. Ted Dekker. WestBow Press, 2004. 408 p; (Books of history chronicles, 1)
ISBN 9780849917905

1. Generals 2. Insomniacs 3. Men's dreams 4. Authors 5. Parallel universes 6. Denver, Colorado 7. Christian fantasy 8. Christian suspense 9. Gateway fantasy

LC 2003020542

Thomas Hunter narrowly survives a shooting attempt only to awaken in an alternate universe of green forests, a world to which he subsequently travels every time he goes to sleep.

Series inferred from bk. 2 and bk. 3, spine.

A trilogy-book one—Spine.

The **girl** behind the red rope. Ted Dekker and Rachelle Dekker. Revell, 2019. 336 p.

ISBN 9780800736538

1. Cults 2. Questioning 3. Good and evil 4. Belief and doubt 5. Religious communities 6. Tennessee 7. Christian suspense

LC 2018057275

Christy Award for Suspense Category, 2020

Grace lives in the hills of Tennessee in a religious community with strict rules meant to keep everyone safe, but her brother's questions and the appearance of outsiders for the first time in decades force her to re-think her truth.

"In this mind-bending inspirational thriller, father-daughter writing team Ted Dekker and Rachelle Dekker triumph in their faultlessly structured and deconstructed world of religious extremism." —*Booklist*

Red: the heroic rescue. Ted Dekker. WestBow Press, 2004. 381 p; (Books of history chronicles, 2)

ISBN 9780849917912

1. Generals 2. Biological terrorism 3. Virus diseases 4. Authors 5. Insomniacs 6. Christian suspense 7. Christian fantasy 8. Gateway fantasy

LC 2004004529

Thomas Hunter finds himself in a desperate quest to rescue two worlds from collapse. In one world, he's a battle-scarred general commanding an army of primitive warriors. In the other, he's racing to out wit sadistic terrorists intent on creating global chaos through an unstoppable virus.

White: the great pursuit. Ted Dekker. WestBow Press, 2004. Xv, 370 p; (Books of history chronicles, 3)

ISBN 9780849917929

1. Authors 2. Chases 3. Virus diseases 4. Generals 5. Insomniacs 6. Christian fantasy 7. Christian suspense 8. Gateway fantasy

LC 2004010579

Time is running out in two realities. In one world, a lethal virus threatens to destroy all life as scientists and governments scramble to find an antidote. In the other, a forbidden love could forever destroy the ragtag resistance known as The Circle. Thomas can bridge both worlds, but he is quickly realizing that he may not be able to save either.

Dektar, Molly

The **Ash** family. Molly Dektar. Simon & Schuster, 2019. 352 pages

ISBN 9781501144868

1. Environmentalists 2. Communes 3. Counterculture 4. Cult leaders 5. Young women 6. Great Smoky Mountains (N.C. and Tenn.) 7. North Carolina 8. Literary fiction 9. Adult books for young adults

Drawn by a mysterious stranger to a remote farming community that lives off the fertile mountain lands, a North Carolina teen is seduced by their high ideals before new friends begin to disappear.

Del Amo, Jean-Baptiste

Animalia. Jean-Baptiste Del Amo; translated by Frank Wynne. Grove Press, 2019. 410 pages

ISBN 9780802147578

1. Farm life 2. Pigs 3. Rural families 4. Animal welfare 5. Pig farming 6. France 7. 20th century 8. Translations

Enduring a hardscrabble childhood on her family's farm in southwest France, a woman becomes the matriarch of a large industrial pig farm, where the casual brutality inflicted on animals reflects the horrors of the 20th century's wars and diseases.

Translation of: "Regne animal."

Originally published: Paris : Gallimard, 2016.

Translated from the French.

Del Vecchio, John M.

The **13th** valley: a novel. John Del Vecchio. Bantam Books, 1982. 606 p.

ISBN 9780553050226

1. Vietnam War, 1961-1975 2. War stories

LC 81070920

"The novel is almost documentary in style and conveys to an extraordinary degree the very 'feel' of ground combat in I Corps.... Two elements in this well-written novel are especially praiseworthy: the depiction of the explosive relations between white and black GIs, and the moral corruption by war of a decent, sensitive young man.... Despite the presence of too much historical exposition, this is one of the finest novels to come out of the Vietnam War." —*Publishers Weekly*

Includes end-paper maps.

Delaney, J. P.

Believe me: a novel. JP Delaney. Ballantine Books, 2018. 334 p.

ISBN 9781101966310

1. Baudelaire, Charles 2. Actors and actresses 3. British in the United States 4. Undercover operations 5. Women murder victims 6. College teachers 7. New York City 8. Psychological suspense

LC 2018009618

LibraryReads Favorites, 2018

An out-of-work British actress plays both sides of a murder investigation while working as a decoy for unfaithful husbands for a New York City divorce firm.

The **girl** before: a novel. JP Delaney. Ballantine Books, 2017. 336 p.

ISBN 9780425285046

1. Landlord and tenant 2. Control (Psychology) 3. Obsession 4. Architects 5. Widowers 6. London, England 7. England 8. Psychological suspense 9. Parallel narratives 10. Multiple perspectives 11. Adult books for young adults

LibraryReads Favorites, 2017

A psychological thriller that spins one woman's seemingly good fortune, and another woman's mysterious fate, through duplicity, death, and deception. Reeling from a traumatic break-in, Emma moves to One Folgate Street. After a personal tragedy, Jane wants a fresh start at One Folgate Street, and soon she learns about the untimely death of the home's previous tenant, Emma. She begins to investigate the girl before.

"This haunting Big Brotheresque novel will consume psychological thriller enthusiasts and keep them thinking long after the final page." —*Library Journal*

The **perfect** wife: a novel. JP Delaney. Ballantine Books, 2019. 432 p.

ISBN 9781524796747

1. Androids 2. Deception 3. Accident victims 4. Married women 5. Married people and secrets 6. Psychological suspense 7. Science fiction

LC 2019007619

A woman miraculously restored to health by the innovations of her tech icon husband struggles with fragmented memories of a past that differs from her husband's accounts.

Playing nice. J. P. Delaney. Ballantine Books, 2020. 416 p. ISBN 9781984821348

1. Deception 2. Infants switched at birth 3. Hospitals 4. Family secrets 5. Suing (Law) 6. Thrillers and suspense 7. Psychological suspense 8. Multiple perspectives

Informed by a stranger that his son was switched at birth with another baby, Pete struggles to adjust to the needs of two families before an investigation unearths disturbing questions about the hospital and the night the exchange occurred.

"Readers will be surprised at the twists the story takes and by an ending they won't see coming. Recommended for psychological-thriller fans who enjoy family dramas." —*Booklist*

Delany, Samuel R.

Aye, and Gomorrah: stories. Samuel R. Delany. Vintage Books, 2003. 383 p.

ISBN 9780375706714

1. Life on other planets 2. Aliens 3. Far future 4. Short stories 5. Science fiction 6. Fantasy fiction

LC 2002035854

An expanded edition of the classic anthology, this collection of science fiction and fantasy tales includes the Nebula and Hugo Award-winning "Time Considered as a Helix of Semi-Precious Stones.

Rev. ed. of Driftglass, with 4 new stories added.

Dhalgren. Samuel R. Delany. Vintage Books, 2001. Xiii, 801 p. ISBN 9780375706684

1. Post-apocalypse 2. Survival (after disaster) 3. Extinct cities 4. Adventurers 5. Identity (Psychology) 6. United States 7. Literary fiction 8. Apocalyptic fiction 9. African American fiction

LC 67412

Journeying to the central United States city of Bellona, where all have fled save madmen and criminals, a poet and adventurer known only as the Kid wonders at the strange portents that appear in the city's cloud-covered sky.

Originally published in the United States by Bantam Books in 1975—Title page verso.

Stars in my pocket like grains of sand. Samuel R. Delaney. Bantam Books, 1984. 368 p.

ISBN 9780553050530

1. Gender role 2. Science fiction 3. African American fiction 4. Afrofuturism

LC 84041580

Set against exotic landscapes and strange cultures, this saga concerns a great information war involving every world inhabited by humanity and two people whose relationship shakes civilization to its core.

"Reading this novel is like learning another language, only to realize how much it teaches you about your own, and how relative it makes your cultural assumptions." —*Publishers Weekly*

Delany, Vicki

Deadly summer nights. Vicki Delany. Berkley, 2021. 304 p. (Catskill summer resort mysteries, 1)

ISBN 9780593334379

1. Women bookkeepers 2. Widows 3. Mother and adult daughter 4. Resorts 5. Hotel management 6. Catskill Mountains Region, New York 7. New York (State) 8. 1950s 9. Historical mysteries

In the summer of 1953 at Haggerman's Catskills Resort, daring young widow Elizabeth must solve the mystery surrounding the death of a reclusive guest whose body was found in the lake on the grounds in order to save the business from going under.

"An immersive setting with details of running a Catskills resort in the 1950s (think Kellerman's in Dirty Dancing) beautifully frame a story with plot twists and a cast of well-delineated characters." —*Booklist*

A Berkley Prime Crime mystery.

Murder in a teacup. Vicki Delany. Kensington Pub Corp, 2021. 304 p. (Tea by the Sea mysteries, 2)

ISBN 9781496725097

1. Tearooms 2. Women business owners 3. Grandmother and granddaughter 4. Women amateur detectives 5. Poisons 6. Cape Cod, Massachusetts 7. Massachusetts 8. Cozy mysteries 9. Culinary mysteries 10. Gentle reads

When her tearoom becomes the site of a family feud that results in murder, Lily Roberts finds herself in hot water and must, with the help of her friends, solve this case and bag the real killer.

"Delany expertly blends a cunning mystery plot with diverting characters and sparkling dialogue. Laura Childs fans will have fun." —*Publishers Weekly*

Tea & treachery. Vicki Delany. Kensington Pub Corp, 2020. 304 p. (Tea by the Sea mysteries, 1)

ISBN 9781496725066

1. Tearooms 2. Women business owners 3. Grandmother and granddaughter 4. Bed-and-breakfast 5. Pastry chefs 6. Cape Cod, Massachusetts 7. Massachusetts 8. Cozy mysteries 9. Culinary mysteries 10. Gentle reads

Lily Roberts is kept busy as the proprietor and pastry chef of Tea by the Sea, a traditional English tearoom on the bluffs of Cape Cod, while her grandmother, Rose, runs the Victorian B & B adjacent to Lily's tearoom. A pushy estate developer, Jack Ford, wants to rezone the land and build a golf course, which would put Rose and Lily out of business. When Ford is found dead at the foot of Rose's property and the police suspect her, Lily starts her own investigation to find the real killer in order to prove her grandmother innocent.

"Details about tea, baking, and running a tea shop and bed-and-breakfast are woven throughout a satisfying cozy with a beautifully described setting and a cast of charming, small-town characters." —*Booklist*

DeLillo, Don

Falling man: a novel. Don DeLillo. Scribner, 2007. 246 p. ISBN 9781416546023

1. September 11 Terrorist Attacks, 2001 2. Terrorism — Psychological aspects 3. Separated couples 4. Escapes 5. Victims of terrorism 6. Manhattan, New York City 7. New York City 8. Psychological fiction 9. Literary fiction

LC 2006052306

Booklist Editors' Choice, 2007; New York Times Notable Book, 2007

Escaping from the World Trade Center during the September 11 attacks, Keith makes his way to the uptown apartment where his ex-wife and young son are living and considers how the day's events have irrevocably changed his perception of the world.

Libra. Don DeLillo. Viking, 1988. 456 p. ISBN 9780670823178

1. Oswald, Lee Harvey 2. Presidents — Assassination 3. Assassination 4. Assassins 5. Defectors 6. Former CIA agents 7. United States 8. Dallas, Texas 9. 1960s 10. Biographical fiction 11. Literary fiction

LC 87040649

National Book Award for Fiction finalist, 1988; National Book Critics Circle Award for Fiction finalist, 1988

The scheme of two disgruntled CIA agents to stage an unsuccessful attempt on the life of President Kennedy and link it to Cuba backfires when the erratic Lee Harvey Oswald goes too far.

"This novel provokes the reader with its clever use of history, its dramatic pacing and its immaculate and detailed construction." —*Publishers Weekly*

The **names**. Don DeLillo. A. A. Knopf, 1982. 339 p.
ISBN 9780394528144

1. Americans in Greece 2. Cults 3. Murder 4. Language and languages 5. Political risk insurance 6. Literary fiction

LC 82048012

In an expatriate's world of turmoil and danger, American risk analyst James Axton learns of a ritual-murder cult in the Aegean and follows the trail to its secret meanings in the ancient city of Lahore.

"Nearly every page testifies to DeLillo's exceptional gifts as a writer." —*The New Republic*

The **silence**. Don DeLillo. Scibner, 2020. 128 pages
ISBN 9781982164553

1. Disasters 2. Apartment house life 3. Digital communications 4. Conversation 5. Social isolation 6. Manhattan, New York City 7. New York City 8. 2020s 9. Literary fiction

Five people gathered together in a Manhattan apartment in 2022 react to a mysterious, catastrophic event that severs all of modern life's digital connections in this new novel from the National Book Award-winning author of White Noise.

"The writing is spare and almost playlike, especially in the second section, which concludes with a series of monologues. This is a small but vivid book, and in its evocation of people in the throes of social crisis, it feels deeply resonant." —*Kirkus*

Underworld. Don DeLillo. Scribner, 1997. 827 p.
ISBN 9780684842691

1. Baseball — History 2. Cold War 3. African Americans 4. African American teenage boys 5. Professional baseball teams 6. New York City 7. United States 8. 1950s 9. Literary fiction 10. Multiple perspectives

LC 97-13825

Booklist Editors' Choice, 1997; Library Journal Best Books, 1997; National Book Award for Fiction finalist, 1997; National Book Critics Circle Award for Fiction finalist, 1997; Pulitzer Prize for Fiction finalist, 1998; Shortlisted for the International IMPAC Dublin Literary Award, 1999

A work combining fiction and history in a collaboration that encompasses fifty years gives readers a glimpse into the realities upon which America's modern culture is based and explores the complex relationship between "waste analyst" Nick Shay and artist Klara Sax.

"The dialogue is a rockingly comic attack on our mental excreta: the distortions and sound bites of the television age. DeLillo was absent from his fiction before, an unbodied intelligence, but here is an undertow of personal pain he has never touched. This is his most demanding novel and yet his most transparent, giving the reader the privileged intimacy that comes from seeing a writer whole." —*New York Times Book Review*

Prologue also published separately in 2001 under the title Pafko at the wall.

Earlier version of prologue published in Harper's magazine (October 1992).

★ **White** noise. Don DeLillo. Viking, 1985. 326 p.
ISBN 9780670803736

1. Industrial accidents 2. Universities and colleges 3. College teachers 4. Poisonous gases 5. Husband and wife 6. Middle West 7. Literary fiction 8. Black humor 9. Satirical fiction

LC 84040375

National Book Award for Fiction, 1985; National Book Critics Circle Award for Fiction finalist, 1985

A Midwestern family navigates the rocky passages of family life while a lethal cloud resulting from an industrial accident hovers over them.

"This is a stunning performance from one of our finest and most intelligent novelists. DeLillo's reach is broad and deep, combining acute observation of the textures of American life and analytic rigor." —*The New Republic*

Zero K: a novel. Don DeLillo. Scribner, 2016. 288 p.
ISBN 9781501135392

1. Cryonics 2. Scientists 3. Fathers and sons 4. Death 5. Billionaires 6. Kyrgyzstan 7. Social science fiction

LC 2015040210

New York Times Notable Book, 2016

Jeffrey Lockhart's father, Ross, is a George Soros-like billionaire now in his sixties, with a younger wife, Artis, whose health is failing. Ross is the primary investor in a deeply remote and secret compound where death is controlled and bodies are preserved until a future moment when medicine and technology can reawaken them. Jeffrey joins Ross and Artis at the compound to say {34an uncertain farewell{34 to her as she surrenders her body.

"DeLillo's rich language and rhythmic prose draw readers deep into a rumination on both the inescapability and alluring possibilities of the eternal return." —*Library Journal*

Delinsky, Barbara

Lake news: a novel. Barbara Delinsky. Simon & Schuster, 1999. 380 p.
ISBN 9780684864327

1. Women singers 2. Journalists 3. Rumor 4. Malicious accusation 5. Journalism 6. New Hampshire 7. Psychological fiction

After being unjustly accused by a reporter of having had an affair with a newly-appointed Cardinal, famous singer Lily Blake returns to her home town to recover and escape further attention from the press. There she forms an unlikely alliance with a big-city reporter whose career ended disastrously, sending him to the same town to edit the local newspaper.

"The author plots this satisfying, gentle romance with the sure hand of an expert, scattering shady pasts and dark secrets among some of her characters, while giving others destructive family patterns and difficult family dynamics to contend with." —*Publishers Weekly*

Author's An Accidental Woman, 2002 shares the fictional Lake Henry setting.

A **week** at the shore. Barbara Delinsky. St Martins Pr 2020. 400 p.
ISBN 9781250119513

1. Homecomings 2. Single mothers 3. Coastal towns 4. Family secrets 5. Women photographers 6. Rhode Island 7. First person narratives 8. Relationship fiction

LC 2019054413

Returning to her family's Rhode Island beach home after a 20-year estrangement, a real estate photographer navigates painful family secrets that test her bonds with her sisters, while her 13-year-old daughter pursues desperately wanted family ties.

"This well-crafted story, buoyed by descriptions of the weathered beach town and nicely drawn characters, will delight Delinsky's fans." —*Publishers Weekly*

Dell'Antonia, K. J.

The **chicken** sisters. K. J. Dell'Antonia. Putnam Pub Group, 2020. 320 p.

ISBN 9780593085141

1. Family feuds 2. Reality television programs 3. Restaurants 4. Sisters 5. Competition 6. Johnson, Ziggy 7. Relationship fiction

A more than three-decade feud between two Kansas families implodes when a daughter who left one of the families to marry into the other brings the story of their fried-chicken competition to the attention of a popular reality show.

"Dell'Antonia deftly deals with issues of mental illness, marriage troubles, and dreams deferred, all the while telling a funny satire of reality TV. An utter delight from start to finish." —*Booklist*

Dell, Kari Lynn

Fearless in Texas. Kari Lynn Dell. Sourcebooks Inc 2018. 416 p. (Texas rodeo, 4)

ISBN 9781492658115

1. Bar owners 2. Secrets 3. Interpersonal attraction 4. Man-woman relationships 5. Texas 6. Western romances 7. Contemporary romances

Refusing to make the same mistakes twice, Melanie Brookman, while trying to rebuild her life, helps smooth-talking rodeo man Wyatt Darrington save his failing bar, and as they work

"The hidden depths of their personal tragedies add complexity to their characters. Chock full of drama, romantic angst, and magnetic supporting characters, Dell's latest is not to be missed." —*Publishers Weekly*

Mistletoe in Texas. Kari Lynn Dell. Sourcebooks Inc, 2018. 448 p. (Texas rodeo, 5)

ISBN 9781492658146

1. Bullfighters 2. Rodeos 3. Interpersonal attraction 4. Man-woman relationships 5. Wounds and injuries 6. Texas 7. Western romances 8. Contemporary romances

"With only a smattering of Christmas window dressing, this touching tale of redemption and forgiveness immerses readers in a world they won't want to leave." —*Publishers Weekly*

Reckless in Texas. Kari Lynn Dell. Sourcebooks Casablanca, 2016. 411 p. (Texas rodeo, 1)

ISBN 9781492631941

1. Single mothers 2. Bullfighters 3. Rodeos 4. Interpersonal attraction 5. Man-woman relationships 6. Texas 7. Western romances 8. Contemporary romances

When single mom Violet Jacobs hires a hotshot rodeo bullfighter to take her family's rodeo production company into the big time, she discovers a man who is not afraid to let his guard down around her—and a man who is determined to create a life of his own—with her.

DeLuca, Jen

Well matched. Jen DeLuca. Jove, 2021. 336 p. (Well met novels, 3)

ISBN 9780593200445

1. Renaissance fairs 2. Single mothers 3. Divorced women 4. Insecurity in men 5. High school teachers 6. Maryland 7. Romantic comedies

LC 2021007531

An upbeat rom-com filled with Renaissance Faire flower crowns, sword fights, tavern wenches, and an accidentally-in-love romance.

"This sexy, witty, fast-paced romantic comedy has surprising emotional depth. It can be read as a standalone or as part of DeLuca's 'Well Met' series." —*Library Journal*

★ **Well** met. Jen DeLuca. Berkley Jove, 2019. 328 p. (Well met novels, 1)

ISBN 9781984805386

1. Teachers 2. Renaissance fairs 3. Women volunteers 4. Actors and actresses 5. Role playing 6. Maryland 7. Romantic comedies 8. Contemporary romances

LC 2019001004

LibraryReads Favorites, 2019

While in the small town of Willow Creek, Maryland, to help her sister, Emily is roped into volunteering for the local Renaissance Faire with her teenaged niece where she, after meeting an irritating, yet handsome, schoolteacher, finally finds a place to call home.

"DeLuca turns in an intelligent, sexy, and charming debut romance sure to resonate with Renaissance Faire enthusiasts and those looking for an upbeat, lighter read." —*Library Journal*

Deluca, Marjorie

The **Savage** Instinct. Marjorie Deluca. Inkshares, 2021. 300 p.

ISBN 9781947848672

1. Cotton, Mary Ann 2. Serial murders 3. Women serial murderers 4. Women prisoners 5. Psychiatric hospitals 6. Mental illness 7. Great Britain 8. Victorian era (1837-1901) 9. 1870s 10. Historical fiction

In the lineage of Margaret Atwood's Alias Grace and Hannah Kent's Burial Rites, THE SAVAGE INSTINCT is the chilling story of one woman's struggle for her sanity, set against the backdrop of the arrest and trial of Mary Ann Cotton, England's first female serial killer.

"DeLuca gives Mary Ann a gentler treatment than the history books, but delivers a fascinating portrayal of womanhood in Victorian England that is also a nail-biting thriller that will keep readers riveted until the very last page." —*Booklist*

DeMille, Nelson

★ The **Cuban** affair: a novel. Nelson DeMille. Simon & Schuster, 2017. 416 p.

ISBN 9781501101724

1. Treasure hunting 2. Veterans 3. Fishing boat captains 4. Ocean travel 5. Fishing 6. Cuba 7. Mainstream fiction

LC 2017017727

When his shaky finances compel him to accept a lucrative job for a 10-day fishing tournament to Cuba, Army combat veteran-turned-charter boat captain Mac learns that one of his clients is seeking to claim millions hidden by her grandfather, who was forced to flee Castro's revolution years earlier.

★ The **deserter:** a novel. Nelson DeMille and Alex DeMille. Simon & Schuster, 2019. 448 p.

ISBN 9781501101755

1. Assassins 2. Missing persons 3. Military police 4. Veterans 5. Special forces 6. Thrillers and suspense

LC 2019013504

A year after a trained assassin with classified Army intelligence disappears under suspicious circumstances, an Army investigator's efforts to capture the man alive are complicated by his partner's inexperience and suspected role as a CIA spy.

Wild fire. Nelson DeMille. Warner Books, 2006. 519 p. (John Corey novels, 4)

ISBN 9780446579674

1. Nuclear terrorism 2. Government investigators 3. Husband-and-wife detectives 4. Corey, John (Fictitious character) 5. Detectives 6. Adirondack Mountains, New York 7. 2000s (Decade) 8. Thrillers and suspense

LC 2006020982

LIST OF FICTIONAL WORKS

While investigating the death of a member of the Federal Anti-Terrorist Task Force, Detective John Corey and his wife, FBI Agent Kate Mayfield, stumble into the middle of a terrifying nuclear conspiracy that leads them to the inner circle of the Custer Hill Club, a luxurious Adirondack hunting lodge whose members include America's most powerful leaders.

"As usual, DeMille appears to have done a ton of research; what sets his thrillers apart from those of some of his competitors is the way he seamlessly incorporates real technology and real government organizations into his stories." —*Booklist*

Demirtas, Selahattin

Dawn: stories. Selahattin Demirtas; translated by Amy Spangler and Kate Ferguson. SJP for Hogarth, 2019. 176 pages
ISBN 9780525576938
1. War and society 2. Distress (Psychology) 3. Women and war 4. Persistence 5. Turkey 6. Middle East 7. Political fiction 8. Short stories 9. Translations
LC 2018038558
An extraordinary short-story collection from the imprisoned pro-Kurdish human-rights lawyer, activist and politician offers a powerful portrait of Turkey and the Middle East that shares insights into the violence, cultural beliefs and humanity shaping the region today.
Originally published in Turkish under title: Seher.
Includes bibliographical references.
Originally published: Kizilay, Ankara : Dipnot Yayinlari, 2017.
Translated from the Turkish.

Dennis-Benn, Nicole

Here comes the sun. Nicole Y. Dennis-Benn. Liveright, 2016. 349 p.
ISBN 9781631491764
1. Island life 2. Prostitutes 3. Lesbians 4. Sisters 5. Self-fulfillment in women 6. Jamaica 7. 1990s 8. Political fiction 9. LGBTQIA fiction 10. Coming-of-age stories
Lambda Literary Award for Lesbian Fiction, 2017; New York Times Notable Book, 2016
Working as a prostitute near the pristine beaches and turquoise seas of Jamaica to pay for a younger sister's education, Margot hopes that a new hotel that is reshaping her home will grant her financial independence and allow her to pursue a forbidden affair with another woman.
"Haunting and superbly crafted, this is a magical book from a writer of immense talent and intelligence." —*Kirkus*

★ **Patsy:** a novel. Nicole Dennis-Benn. Liveright Publishing Corporation, a division of W.W. Norton & Company, 2019. 400 p.
ISBN 9781631495632
1. Undocumented immigrants 2. Jamaican Americans 3. Unrequited love 4. Lesbians 5. Consequences 6. New York City 7. Jamaica 8. Literary fiction 9. Psychological fiction 10. Multiple perspectives
LC 2018055787
Lambda Literary Award for Lesbian Fiction, 2020; Loan Stars Favourites, 2019
Receiving her long-coveted visa to America, Patsy leaves behind her family in Jamaica, only to discover that life as an undocumented immigrant is not what her best friend had described.

Deon, Natashia

Grace. Natashia Deón. Counterpoint, 2016. 404 p.
ISBN 9781619027206
1. Slavery 2. Mothers and daughters 3. Violence against women 4. African American women — Psychology 5. Women murder victims 6. Southern States 7. 19th century 8. Family sagas 9. Literary fiction 10. Historical fiction
Library Journal Best Books, 2016; BCALA Literary Award for First Novelist, 2017
The dual stories of a mother, a runaway plantation slave and the child she never knew are woven through the historic events of the mid-19th century, including the Civil War and the Emancipation Proclamation.
"Deón stays in control of her complex material, from its clever parallel structure to the womens psychological reactions to relentless tension." —*Booklist*

The **perishing:** a novel. Natashia Deón. Counterpoint, 2021. 304 p.
ISBN 9781640093027
1. African American women 2. Journalists 3. Time travel 4. Immortality 5. Fate and fatalism 6. Los Angeles, California 7. 1930s 8. Science fiction 9. Science fiction mysteries 10. Parallel narratives
LC 2021012290
Lou, a young Black woman, wakes up in an alley in 1930s Los Angeles, nearly naked and with no memory of how she got there or where she's from, only a fleeting sense that this isn't the first time she's found herself in similar circumstances. When she befriends a firefighter at a downtown boxing gym, Lou is shocked to realize that though she has no memory of ever meeting him she's been drawing his face for years. Increasingly certain that their paths have previously crossed—perhaps even in a past life—and coupled with unexplainable flashes from different times that have been haunting her dreams, Lou begins to believe she may be an immortal sent to this place and time for a very important reason.
"Deón follows the critically acclaimed Grace with a provocative if unruly adventure through time featuring an immortal Black woman struggling to discover her destiny." —*Publishers Weekly*

Depestre, Rene

Hadriana in all my dreams. Rene Depestre; introduction by Edwidge Danticat. Akashic Books, 2017. 160 p.
ISBN 9781617755330
1. Voodoo 2. Zombies 3. Race relations 4. Weddings 5. Creole women 6. Haiti 7. 1930s 8. Magical realism 9. Literary fiction 10. Translations
"Legendary Haitian author Depestre combines magic, fantasy, eroticism, and delirious humor to explore universal questions of race and sexuality." —Provided by the publisher.
"Depestre presents a rich and nuanced exploration of large and significant themes expertly couched in one fantastical, expertly translated tale." —*Booklist*
Originally published in 1988 as Hadriana dans tous mes reves by Gallimard.
Translated from the French by Kaiama L. Glover.

DePoy, Phillip

Sidewalk saint. Phillip Depoy. Severn House, 2019. 192 p; (Foggy Moskowitz novels, 4)
ISBN 9780727889577
1. Amateur detectives 2. Missing children 3. Social workers 4. Jewish men 5. Children of criminals 6. Florida 7. 1970s 8. Mysteries
Foggy Moscowitz knows he's having a bad night when he wakes to find a gun pressed to his face. Nelson Roan has busted out of his prison cell and broken into Foggy's house, demanding Foggy finds his eleven-year-old daughter, Etta. But as Foggy searches for Etta, it seems her father is not the only person who wants her found...

Dermansky, Marcy

Very nice. Marcy Dermansky. Alfred A Knopf, 2019. 304 pages
ISBN 9780525655633

1. Creative writing 2. Rich people 3. Mothers and daughters 4. Love triangles 5. College teachers 6. Black humor 7. Multiple perspectives

A darkly humorous tale of privilege, race and bad behavior find a wealthy Connecticut divorcée and her college-age daughter becoming unlikely rivals in a romantic triangle involving the latter's creative writing professor.

DeRoux, Margaux

The **lost** diary of Venice. Margaux DeRoux. Ballantine, 2020. 320 pages
ISBN 9781984819482

1. Lomazzo, Giovanni Paolo 2. Bookbinding 3. Diary writing 4. Art criticism 5. Rare books 6. Books — Conservation and restoration 7. Venice, Italy 8. 16th century 9. Historical fiction 10. Love stories 11. Parallel narratives

Navigating her attraction to a married customer who has brought her a 16th century treatise, a book restorer uncovers the story of a forbidden romance between a courtesan and a Renaissance artist who is losing his sight.

"DeRoux brilliantly evokes the 16th-century Venetian art world and pays tribute to Gio's early effort at art criticism, illustrating how 'writing about art can be an art form.' This will satisfy bibliophiles and Renaissance art lovers alike." —*Publishers Weekly*

Desai, Anita

Clear light of day. Anita Desai. Harper and Row, 1980. 183 p.
ISBN 9780060109844

1. Women 2. Middle class 3. Sisters 4. Delhi 5. India 6. Literary fiction
LC 80007603

Shortlisted for the Booker-McConnell Prize, 1980

Explores the traumatic history of India after the departure of the British in a story of an estranged Hindu family in Old Delhi and their complex relationships.

"This work does what only the best novels can do: it totally submerges us. It takes us so deeply into another world that we almost fear we won't be able to climb out again." —*New York Times Book Review*

Fire on the mountain. Anita Desai. Harper & Row, 1977. 145 p.
ISBN 9780060110666

1. Great-grandmothers 2. Women 3. Mothers and daughters 4. India 5. Literary fiction
LC 77003788

Nanda Kaul, a woman remote in her self-imposed solitude among the Simla hills of India, her strange and silent great-granddaughter, and the broken old woman who is her only friend are touched in varying ways by the violence of living

"This is a delicate wisp of a story that nevertheless possesses great tensile strength." —*Booklist*

Desai, Kiran

The **inheritance** of loss. Kiran Desai. Atlantic Monthly Press, 2006. 336 p.
ISBN 9780871139290

1. Grandfather and granddaughter 2. Insurgency 3. Interethnic relations 4. Nationalism 5. Modernization (Social sciences) 6. India 7. New York City 8. 1980s 9. Political fiction 10. Literary fiction 11. Multiple perspectives
LC 2005052416

ALA Notable Book, 2007; Booker Prize, 2006; National Book Critics Circle Award for Fiction, 2006; New York Times Notable Book, 2006; Shortlisted for The Orange Prize for Fiction, 2007

In a crumbling house in the remote northeastern Himalayas, an embittered, elderly judge finds his peaceful retirement turned upside down by the arrival of his orphaned granddaughter, Sai.

"This novel is set in the nineteen-eighties in the northeast corner of India, where the borders of several Himalayan states—Bhutan and Sikkim, Nepal and Tibet—meet. At the head of the novels teeming cast is Jemubhai Patel, a Cambridge-educated judge who has retired from serving a country he finds too messy for justice. He lives in an isolated house with his cook, his orphaned seventeen-year-old granddaughter, and a red setter, whose company Jemubhai prefers to that of human beings. The tranquillity of his existence is contrasted with the life of the cook's son, working in grimy Manhattan restaurants, and with his granddaughter's affair with a Nepali tutor involved in an insurgency that irrevocably alters Jemubhai's life. Briskly paced and sumptuously written, the novel ponders questions of nationhood, modernity, and class, in ways both moving and revelatory." —*The New Yorker*

DeSilva, Bruce

Providence rag. Bruce DeSilva. Forge Books, 2014. 351 pages : (Liam Mulligan mysteries, 3)
ISBN 9780765374295

1. Teenage serial murderers 2. Investigative journalists 3. Parole 4. Investigative journalism — Moral and ethical aspects 5. Murder investigation 6. Providence, Rhode Island 7. Rhode Island 8. Mysteries
LC 2013025786

A tale inspired by a true story finds Mulligan, his friend Mason, and the newspaper they work for confronting an ethical dilemma involving a juvenile serial murderer's parole and corrupt police activities.

"[T]here is real suspense here. And Mulligan's character, played off the vicissitudes of his job, is skillfully layered and engaging." —*Booklist*

Rogue Island. Bruce DeSilva. Forge, 2010. 302 p. : Illustration (Liam Mulligan mysteries, 1)
ISBN 9780765327260

1. Investigative journalists 2. Arson 3. Grimke, Sarah Moore 4. Murder 5. Police 6. Providence, Rhode Island 7. Rhode Island 8. Mysteries
Edgar Allan Poe Award for Best First Novel by an American Author, 2011; Macavity Award for Best First Mystery Novel, 2011

When journalist Liam Mulligan realizes that someone is systematically burning down his childhood neighborhood in Providence, Rhode Island, he ignores his bosses and his budding relationship to figure out the firebug's identity.

A **scourge** of vipers. Bruce DeSilva. Forge, 2015. 368 pages (Liam Mulligan mysteries, 4)
ISBN 9780765374318

1. Gambling 2. Investigative journalists 3. Sports betting — Corrupt practices 4. Murder 5. Corruption 6. Providence, Rhode Island 7. Rhode Island 8. Mysteries

Investigating an upsurge in organized crime when Rhode Island's colorful governor proposes the legalization of sports gambling, rogue journalist Liam Mulligan is targeted by shadowy forces when he unearths suspicious clues in the death of a powerful senator.

"DeSilva is spot-on, as only a journalist with a 40-year newspaper career behind him can be, when it comes to corruption. His dialogue, however, has everyone, including the former nun, sounding as if theyve just completed a 'Talk like a Martin Scorsese thug' course." —*Booklist*

Deutermann, Peter T.

The **Iceman**. P.T. Deutermann. St. Martin's Press, 2018. 304 p. (World War II novels (P. T. Deutermann), 5)
ISBN 9781250181374
1. World War II — Naval operations 2. Risk 3. Submarines 4. Armed Forces — Officers 5. Sailors 6. Pacific Area 7. Second World War era (1939-1945) 8. Historical thrillers

LC 2018003988

A decorated submarine commander haunted by a violent youth unsettles his crew with the incrementally risky measures he takes to sink Japanese ships in the western Pacific during World War II.

"Deutermann packs authentic information on submarine tactics and naval warfare in between the taut underwater action. Fans of old-school submarine novels like Run Silent, Run Deep will be rewarded." —*Publishers Weekly*

The **nugget**: a novel. P. T. Deutermann. St Martins Press, 2019. 320 p. World War II novels (P. T. Deutermann), 6)
ISBN 9781250205889
1. World War II 2. Fighter pilots 3. Prisoners of war 4. Search and rescue operations 5. Friends' death 6. Second World War era (1939-1945) 7. Historical thrillers

LC 2019021340

Compelled by the Pearl Harbor attack to serve in some of World War II's most dangerous air battles, a young naval aviator leads a mission to rescue prisoners from a secluded POW camp.

"Deutermann knows how to reveal navy life to even the casual reader.... [R]eaders who enjoy WWII stories, especially those involving the air war, will be entranced by Steele's story, which is told in a gripping first-person narrative that extends from the Battle of Midway to a mission in which Steele is charged with rescuing POWs from a Japanese internment camp and, finally, to his appearance in an American military court." —*Booklist*

Pacific glory: a novel. Peter T. Deutermann. St. Martin's Press, 2011. 336 p. (World War II novels (P. T. Deutermann), 1)
ISBN 9780312599447
1. Love triangles 2. Pilots 3. Nurses 4. Widows 5. Soldiers 6. Second World War era (1939-1945) 7. Historical fiction 8. War stories
Library Journal Best Books, 2011; W. Y. Boyd Literary Award, 2012

Their military careers forever transformed by the attack on Pearl Harbor, Navy nurse Glory grieves for the loss of her husband while ship officer Marsh battles his way toward Leyte Gulf and fighter pilot Mick struggles with the drinking problem for which he was grounded.

Dev, Sonali

★ A **Bollywood** affair. Sonali Dev. Kensington Books, 2014. Viii, 288 pages
ISBN 9781617730139
1. Arranged marriage 2. East Indians in the United States 3. Film producers and directors 4. Film industry and trade 5. Villages 6. Michigan 7. India 8. Multicultural romances 9. Contemporary romances

LC 2015296688

RUSA Reading List, 2015

Coming to America on a scholarship, Mili Rathod, who has been bound by marriage since she was four years old to a man she has never met, is drawn into the world of her husband's playboy filmmaker brother who has been sent across the world to keep an eye on her.

"Dev's heartfelt debut novel is rich in scenes and images illuminating Indian culture, leaving readers with a greater understanding and appreciation of Indian traditions while beautifully capturing the struggle between familial duty and self-discovery." —*Booklist*

The **Bollywood** bride. Sonali Dev. Kensington, 2015. 352 p.
ISBN 9781617730153
1. Actors and actresses 2. First loves 3. East Indian Americans 4. Second chances 5. Lovers' reunions 6. Chicago, Illinois 7. India 8. Multicultural romances 9. Contemporary romances

Traveling home to Chicago to attend a family wedding and ride out a scandal, Bollywood star Ria Parkar reunites with Vikram Jathar, whose heart she broke to pursue her career.

A **distant** heart. Sonali Dev. Kensington Books, 2017. 302 p.
ISBN 9781496705761
1. Interclass romance 2. Sick persons 3. Social isolation 4. Romantic love 5. Social classes 6. Mumbai, India 7. India 8. Contemporary romances 9. Multicultural romances

Stricken with a rare illness, Indian woman of privilege Kimaya grows up isolated in an ivory tower, until she builds a relationship with window washer Rahul Savant, whom she inspires to join the police force; but when Rahul uncovers a gang-run organ ring at the same time Kimaya gets a chance at a life-changing heart transplant, their world gets turned upside down.

"Thrilling action sequences and a complex, weighty romance propel this smart, sensitive story. A natural wordsmith, Dev dives into the psyches of disparate characters with voice-driven prose that includes both chilling insights and quirky humor. She also paints a vivid picture of modern Mumbai, from Kimi's pristine mansion to Rahul's overcrowded chawl (tenement), and the many personalities who inhabit it. Subplots and characters overlap in Dev's novels, so even though this is a stand-alone, encourage patrons to read her earlier novels for an even-more-enriching experience. This poignant, sensual, and exciting tale captures a range of emotions and conflicts." —*Booklist*

★ **Incense** and sensibility. Sonali Dev. William Morrow & Co, 2021. 400 pages (The Rajes, 3)
ISBN 9780063051805
1. East Indian Americans 2. Politicians 3. Stress management 4. Yoga 5. Cossio y Cisneros, Evangelina 6. California 7. Multicultural romances 8. Contemporary romances 9. Romantic comedies

The author of Recipe for Persuasion adds an Indian American twist to Jane Austen's classic Sense and Sensibility in this delightful retelling that is a feast for the senses.

"Dev's latest is a deeply emotional story of responsibility and impossible love that will appeal to fans of Austen's classic. It also provides an incisive look at a current political landscape of division and violence, while adding an ultimately hopeful spin." —*Library Journal*

★ **Pride,** prejudice, and other flavors: a novel. Sonali Dev. William Morrow Paperbacks, 2019. 368 pages (The Rajes, 1)
ISBN 9780062839053
1. East Indian Americans 2. Immigrant families 3. Interracial dating 4. Classism 5. Racism 6. San Francisco, California 7. Contemporary romances 8. Multicultural romances 9. Adaptations, retellings, and spin-offs

LC 2019009606

LibraryReads Favorites, 2019

A neurosurgeon from a politically ambitious immigrant family clashes with a talented dessert chef who would prove he is more than his pedigree.

"A workaholic, socially inept Indian-American brain surgeon is caught off guard by her attraction to a Rwandan/Anglo-Indian chef in this rewrite of Pride and Prejudice." —*Kirkus*

★ **Recipe** for persuasion. Sonali Dev. William Morrow & Co, 2020. 368 p. (The Rajes, 2)
ISBN 9780062839077
1. Women cooks 2. Restaurateurs 3. Professional soccer players 4. Celebrities 5. Reality television programs 6. California 7. Palo Alto, California 8. Contemporary romances 9. Romantic comedies 10. Multicultural romances
LibraryReads Favorites, 2020
The author of Pride, Prejudice and Other Flavors adapts Jane Austen's Persuasion in the story of a chef who partners with her celebrity first love during a reality-show competition she hopes will save her restaurant.
"Clever allusions to Persuasion aside (even Jane Austen fans will be challenged to spot them all), this is a sumptuously multilayered story about the ways love gets tangled in family life and romantic relationships." —*Library Journal*

Deveraux, Jude

Someone to love. Jude Deveraux. Atria Books, 2007. 320 p; (Montgomery and Taggert clans series)
ISBN 9780743437165
1. Grief in men 2. Fiances — Death 3. Man-woman relationships 4. Haunted houses 5. Women war correspondents 6. England 7. Margate, England 8. Contemporary romances
LC 2006101700
Still grieving three years after his fiancee's mysterious suicide, Jace Montgomery discovers a clue about her death that leads him to purchase an English fortress, where he encounters a headstrong ghost who died under similar circumstances.
"Deveraux never raises the pitch very high, and harmonizes the whole satisfactorily." —*Publishers Weekly*

A **willing** murder. Jude Deveraux. Mira Books, 2018. 384 p. (Medlar mysteries, 1)
ISBN 9780778369295
1. Senior women 2. Aunt and niece 3. Amateur detectives 4. Boarders 5. Renovation (Architecture) 6. Florida 7. Mysteries
The discovery of two bodies in a quiet Florida community exposes old secrets and deadly grudges, prompting a group of improbable friends to try to uncover the truth.

Dewes, J. S.

The **last** watch. J. S. Dewes. Tor Books, 2021. 464 p. (Divide (Dewes), 1)
ISBN 9781250236340
1. Soldiers 2. Space exploration 3. End of the universe 4. Exiles 5. Aliens 6. Science fiction 7. Space opera
The Divide. It's the edge of the universe. Now it's collapsing—and taking everyone and everything with it. The only ones who can stop it are the Sentinels—the recruits, exiles, and court-martialed dregs of the military. At the Divide, Adequin Rake commands the Argus. She has no resources, no comms—nothing, except for the soldiers that no one wanted. Her ace in the hole could be Cavalon Mercer—genius, asshole, and exiled prince who nuked his grandfather's genetic facility for {34reasons.{34 She knows they're humanity's last chance.
"Dewes's debut is an exciting, fast-paced ride around the edges of the universe, where those rejected by much of humanity are the only ones who can save it. Fans of K. B. Wagers's 'Farian Wars' series and John Scalzi's Old Man's War will welcome this military science fiction thriller." —*Library Journal*

deWitt, Patrick

The **Sisters** brothers: a novel. Patrick Dewitt. Ecco Press, 2011. 328 p.
ISBN 9780062041265
1. Gold rush 2. Revenge 3. Gunfighters 4. Assassination 5. Greed in men 6. The West (United States) 7. Westerns 8. Literary fiction 9. Canadian fiction 10. Adult books for young adults
ALA Notable Book, 2012; Canadian Authors Association Literary Awards, MOSAID Technologies Inc. Award for Fiction, 2012; CBA Libris Award for Fiction Book of the Year, 2012; Governor General's Literary Award for English-Language Fiction, 2011; Oregon Book Awards, Ken Kesey Award for Fiction, 2012; Rogers Writers' Trust Fiction Prize, 2011; Stephen Leacock Memorial Medal for Humour, 2012; Shortlisted for the Man Booker Prize, 2011; Shortlisted for the Walter Scott Prize for Historical Fiction, 2012; Shortlisted for the Giller Prize, 2011
When a frontier baron known as the Commodore orders Charlie and Eli Sisters, his hired gunslingers, to track down and kill a prospector named Herman Kermit Warm, the brothers journey from Oregon to San Francisco, and eventually to Warm's claim in the Sierra foothills, running into a witch, a bear, a dead Indian, a parlor of drunken floozies, and a gang of murderous fur trappers.
"A novel about the life and times of two gunslingers, Eli and Charlie Sisters. Contracted by their boss, the mysterious Commodore, the brothers are ordered to hightail it out of 1851 Oregon City and head to California's gold-rush camps. There, they'll meet a dandy named Henry Morris (a man who is not above biting) who will lead them to their intended target: prospector Hermann Kermit Warm. The brothers don't really know why the Commodore wants Warm dead, or even whether he's innocent (it wouldn't surprise them if he was), but taking lives is their job, and they set out on the trail with two ramshackle horses. It seems like a plot straight out of a spaghetti western, but from the start, deWitt has more than a few tricks in his saddlebag. Narrated in delicious deadpan by Eli, the kinder of the two brothers, (Our blood is the same, we just use it differently, Eli explains) the two men embark on a series of picaresque misadventures.... When the brothers finally get to California and find their victim, all expectations are gleefully reversed. The brothers discover that nothing is really what it seems to be, that a career change could be in the works, and the plot peels away like onion skin, revealing startling secrets that lead to a transformative ending as unexpectedly moving as it is satisfying." —*Boston Globe*

Undermajordomo Minor. Patrick Dewitt. Ecco Press, 2015. 320 p.
ISBN 9780062281203
1. Household employees 2. Dishonesty 3. Imaginary places 4. Castles 5. Barons and baronesses 6. Coming-of-age stories 7. Canadian fiction 8. Adult books for young adults
A dark fable by the award-winning author of The Sisters Brothers follows the adventures of an eccentric liar who upon taking a job at the village manor confronts colorful residents, bitter secrets and murderous agendas.
"DeWitt has delivered another intriguing, compelling, and thought-provoking winner that will appeal to anyone who wants to be captivated by a smart, entertaining read." —*Booklist*

DeWoskin, Rachel

Big girl small: a novel. Rachel DeWoskin. Farrar, Straus and Giroux, 2011. 294 p.
ISBN 9780374112578
1. Teenage girls — Sexuality 2. Date rape 3. Humiliation 4. Little people 5. High school students 6. Coming-of-age stories 7. Adult books for young adults
LC 2010033106

Alex Award, 2012; Booklist Editors' Choice: Adult Books for Young Adults, 2011

Sixteen-year-old Judy Lohden finds her three feet nine inches tall, incredibly talented self in the middle of a scandal, with the national media on her trail and the students at Darcy Academy, a local performing arts high school, involved in the mayhem.

"Bright and sardonic Judy Lohden, a 16-year-old dwarf freshly enrolled in Ann Arbor's Darcy Arts Academy, falls victim to the worst Steven King Carrie prank in the history of dating at the hands of popular boy Jeff Legassic, who becomes an object of desire as soon as he and Judy meet cute the first week of school. The book opens with Judy hiding out in a seedy motel; throughout the novel, she slowly unveils her secret and reveals her two visions of herself—that of a pretty teenage girl with an hourglass figure who happens to be three feet nine inches tall, and that of a sideshow attraction. It's a rare author who is willing to subject her protagonist to the extreme ranges of degradation and redemption to which DeWoskin subjects Judy; thankfully, she manages it beautifully." —*Publishers Weekly*

Dexter, Colin

The **daughters** of Cain. Colin Dexter. Crown Publishers, 1995. 295 p. (Inspector Morse mysteries, 11)

ISBN 9780517700679

1. College teachers 2. Household employees 3. Murder investigation 4. Prostitutes 5. Morse, Inspector (Fictitious character) 6. Oxford, England 7. England 8. Mysteries 9. Police procedurals

Chief Inspector Morse and Detective Sergeant Lewis probe the baffling murder of Dr. Felix McClure, late of Wolsey College, Oxford, and follow a trail that leads to Edward Brooks, who himself disappears following a museum theft.

"Mr. Dexter is a superb technician who torments the reader with logistical details that contradict every previously established point in his puzzle. Red herrings are a specialty. But the canny author also strews the path with literary quotations to think on, polysyllabic words to look up and characters whose lives are so complicated they turn into richly distracting mini-dramas." —*New York Times Book Review*

The **remorseful** day. Colin Dexter. Crown Publishers, 1999. 363 p. (Inspector Morse mysteries, 13)

ISBN 9780609606223

1. Cold cases (Criminal investigation) 2. Women murder victims 3. Murder investigation 4. Murder 5. Morse, Inspector (Fictitious character) 6. Lower Swinstead, England 7. Oxford, England 8. Mysteries 9. Police procedurals

New York Times Notable Mysteries, 2000

An unsolved murder case yields new clues that could implicate Inspector Morse even as he seeks to solve the case

"This finale to a grand series presents a moving elegy to one of mystery fiction's most celebrated and popular characters.... Dexter has fashioned another brilliantly intricate puzzle, one of his finest, with the valedictory tone of the narrative lending a particularly rich texture to the tale. Morse leaves us on the highest possible note, perfectly pitched." —*Publishers Weekly*

The final Inspector Morse novel.

The **way** through the woods. Colin Dexter. Crown, 1993. 296 p. (Inspector Morse mysteries, 10)

ISBN 9780517594445

1. Missing persons 2. Vacations 3. Newspapers 4. Missing persons investigation 5. Morse, Inspector (Fictitious character) 6. Oxford, England 7. England 8. Mysteries 9. Police procedurals

LC 92040762

Gold Dagger Award for Best Crime Novel of the Year, 1992

When a young woman mysteriously vanishes in North Oxford, Chief Inspector Morse unsuccessfully sets out to prove that it is a case of murder, until the arrival of an anonymous letter containing a cryptic poem provides a bizarre clue.

"To say that the investigation is tricky is only to hint at the technical density of the plot, which, once all the tantalizing enigmas have been packed up, hinges on the most basic human frailties. Dazzling." —*New York Times Book Review*

Originally published: London : Macmillan, 1992.

Dexter, Pete

★ **Deadwood**. Pete Dexter. Random House, 1986. 365 p.

ISBN 9780394536699

1. Hickok, Wild Bill 2. Cowboys 3. Gunfighters 4. Roosevelt, Eleanor 5. Fate and fatalism 6. The West (United States) 7. Deadwood, South Dakota 8. 19th century 9. Westerns 10. Books to movies

LC 85019635

When Wild Bill Hickok takes a wagon train of prostitutes through Deadwood, a pimp hires someone to kill him.

"This novel is unpredictable, hyperbolic and, page after page, uproarious; a joshing book written in high spirits and a raw appreciation for the past." —*New York Times Book Review*

This book was released as a movie entitled Wild Bill.

Paris Trout. Pete Dexter. Random House, 1988. 306 p.

ISBN 9780394563701

1. Murder 2. Racism 3. Married people 4. Race relations 5. Psychopaths 6. Georgia 7. 1940s 8. Historical fiction 9. Literary fiction

LC 87043314

National Book Award for Fiction, 1988; National Book Critics Circle Award for Fiction finalist, 1988

In Cotton Point, Georgia, the murder of a Black girl by a white man, Paris Trout, becomes the catalyst in a tale of obsession, racism, and murder that centers on Trout, an intimidating, unremorseful bully who warps the attitudes of everyone he touches.

"Mr. Dexter has created a character whose racism is a blunt, unregenerate fact, as primitive and willful as an earthquake or a rainstorm—and just as sealed off from argument, examination or questions of mercy. What the town's polite society takes care to disguise in Sunday-go-to-meeting euphemisms, Paris sets in defiant, ugly relief; he makes it easy for them to believe they are innocent of racism." —*New York Times Book Review*

Spooner. Pete Dexter. Grand Central Pub, 2009. 480 p.

ISBN 9780446540728

1. Fathers and sons 2. Stepfathers 3. Bad luck 4. Twins 5. Grief 6. Philadelphia, Pennsylvania 7. Washington (State) 8. Psychological fiction 9. Adult books for young adults

LC 2009006087

ALA Notable Book, 2010; Library Journal Best Books, 2009

Losing his father shortly after birth, Warren Spooner endures a troubled childhood and even more troubled young adulthood that is marked by his dishonorably discharged stepfather, whose inexhaustible patience is tested by the difficult Warren.

Diachenko, Serhii

Vita nostra. Sergiy Dyachenko and Maryna Shyrshova-Dyachenko; translated from the Russian by Julia Meitov Hersey. HarperCollins 2018. 416 pages

ISBN 9780062694591

1. Magic 2. Schools 3. Teenage girls 4. Coercion 5. Obedience 6. Coming-of-age stories 7. Fantasy fiction 8. Translations 9. Adult books for young adults

A young girl falls under the spell of a strange, sinister man who asks her to perform odd tasks before convincing her to enroll in a strange and magical school called The Institute of Special Technologies.

Originally published in Ukraine, 2007.

Translated from the Russian.

Diamant, Anita

The **Boston** girl: a novel. Anita Diamant. Scribner, 2015. 256 p.
ISBN 9781439199350
1. Jewish women 2. Reminiscing in old age 3. Children of immigrants 4. Gender role 5. Female friendship 6. Boston, Massachusetts 7. 20th century 8. Historical fiction 9. Adult books for young adults
LC 2014019284

Amelia Bloomer List, 2016

Recounting the story of her life to her granddaughter, octogenarian Addie describes how she was raised in early-twentieth-century America by Jewish immigrant parents in a teeming multicultural neighborhood.

★ The **red** tent. Anita Diamant. St.Martin's Press, 1997. 321 p.
ISBN 9780312169787
1. Dinah 2. Women in the Bible 3. Matriarchy 4. Gender role 5. Mothers and daughters 6. Betrayal 7. Bible novels 8. Historical fiction 9. Books to TV
LC 9716825

Book Sense Book of the Year Adult Fiction, 2001

The story of Dinah, a tragic character from the Bible whose great love, a prince, is killed by her brother, leaving her alone and pregnant. The novel traces her life from childhood to death, in the process examining sexual and religious practices of the day, and what it meant to be a woman.

"Diamant's fiction debut links the passions of the early Israelites to the ongoing traditions of modern Jews, while the red tent of her title (where women retreat for menstruation, childbirth and illness) becomes a resonant symbol of womanly strength, love and wisdom. Despite a few unprofitable digressions, Diamant succeeds admirably in depicting the lives of women in the age that engendered our civilization and our most enduring values." —*Publishers Weekly*

Adapted into a TV series by Lifetime in 2014.

Diamond, Elizabeth

An **accidental** light. Elizabeth Diamond. Other Press, 2009. 288 p.
ISBN 9781590513019
1. Life change events 2. Police 3. Daughters — Death 4. Tragedy 5. Grief in families 6. London (England) 7. Mainstream fiction
LC 2008019397

This heartbreaking and redemptive novel explores the ripple effects of a single moment of tragedy—the journey from guilt to peace, from vengeance to forgiveness, from sorrow to hope—and even, ultimately, to joy.

Diaz, Hernan

★ **In** the distance. Hernan Diaz. Coffee House Press, 2017. 256 pages
ISBN 9781566894883
1. Immigrants 2. Frontier and pioneer life 3. Outlaws 4. Swedes in the United States 5. Desert survival 6. The West (United States) 7. 19th century 8. American Westward Expansion (1803-1899) 9. Adventure stories 10. Westerns
LC 2017000413

William Saroyan International Prize for Writing, Fiction category, 2018; Pen/Faulkner Award Finalist, 2018; Pulitzer Prize for Fiction finalist, 2018

After a young Swedish boy finds himself alone in California, he travels east to find his brother, having a series of adventures and encountering naturalists, criminals, religious fanatics, Indians, and lawmen along the way.

"Stitched through with humor, this often-unpredictable novel will keep readers running along with every step of Hakans odd escapades." —*Booklist*

Diaz, Junot

★ The **brief** wondrous life of Oscar Wao. Junot Diaz. Riverhead Books, 2007. 336 p.
ISBN 9781594489587
1. Misfits (Persons) 2. Family curses 3. Eccentrics and eccentricities 4. Loss (Psychology) 5. Persistence 6. New Jersey 7. Literary fiction 8. Adult books for young adults
LC 2007017251

Booklist Editors' Choice, 2007; Hurston/Wright Legacy Award: Fiction, 2008; Library Journal Best Books, 2007; Massachusetts Book Awards, Fiction Award, 2008; National Book Critics Circle Award for Fiction, 2007; New York Times Notable Book, 2007; Pulitzer Prize for Fiction, 2008; Shortlisted for the International IMPAC Dublin Literary Award, 2009

Living with an old-world mother and rebellious sister, an urban New Jersey misfit dreams of becoming the next J. R. R. Tolkien and believes that a long-standing family curse is thwarting his efforts to find love and happiness.

"In this novel Diaz presents a slice of the vast history of Santo Domingo and the intricate past and present of a doomed family.... Diaz weaves the stories of Lola, his troubled but supportive sister, and Belicia, his hardened mother, along with various other family members, to portray a colorful and complex portrait of mad love, old-world superstition, and the continual strivings of a diaspora." —*Christian Science Monitor*

★ **This** is how you lose her. Junot Diaz. Riverhead Books, 2012. 240 p.
ISBN 9781594487361
1. Social behavior 2. Loss (Psychology) 3. Intimacy (Psychology) 4. Love 5. Companionship 6. United States 7. Literary fiction 8. Short stories 9. Adult books for young adults

ALA Notable Book, 2013; Booklist Editors' Choice, 2012; New York Times Notable Book, 2012; Andrew Carnegie Medal for Excellence in Fiction finalist, 2013; National Book Award for Fiction finalist, 2012

A collection of stories that explores the heartbreak and radiance of love as it is shaped by passion, betrayal and the echoes of intimacy.

Dibdin, Michael

Ratking. Michael Dibdin. Bantam Books, 1989. 266 p. (Aurelio Zen mysteries, 1)
ISBN 9780553053371
1. Kidnapping 2. Political corruption 3. Families 4. Detectives 5. Police 6. Italy 7. Perugia, Italy 8. Police procedurals 9. Mysteries 10. Books to TV
LC 88047832

Gold Dagger Award for Best Crime Novel of the Year, 1988

Police Commissioner Aurelio Zen of Rome becomes involved in a kidnapping case that quickly plummets into a case of murder and leads Zen into dangerous and shocking territory in the ancient city.

The TV miniseries Zen is based on the books Vendetta, Cabal, and Ratking.

LC 2018059657
Librarians' Choice (Australia), 2017

A cold case investigator looks into a possible murder that the coroner pegged as a suicide and a doctor who killed three women and left no evidence.

"Disher, the prolific Australian great, best known for the Inspector Challis series (Signal Loss, 2017), offers a stand-alone about a veteran detective faced with thorny moral choices.... As always, Disher writes with clear eyes and a sure hand." —*Booklist*

Originally published: Melbourne, Vic. : The Text Publishing Company, 2017.

Divakaruni, Chitra Banerjee

Oleander girl: a novel. Chitra Banerjee Divakaruni. Free Press, 2013. 304 p.

ISBN 9781451695656

1. Engaged persons 2. Family secrets 3. Fathers and daughters 4. East Indians in the United States 5. Young women 6. India 7. Kolkata, India 8. Coming-of-age stories 9. Mainstream fiction

LC 2012025671

Enjoying a sheltered childhood with adoring grandparents but troubled by the silence surrounding her parents' deaths, 17-year-old Korobi is prompted by a love note among her mother's possessions and a fiance's shattering revelation to travel from India to post-September 11 America in search of her true identity.

"Divakaruni... introduces a cast of characters who defy their stereotypes... [and] has crafted a beautiful, complex story in which caste, class, religion, and race are significant factors informing people's world views." —*Library Journal*

Divya, S. B.

Machinehood. S.B. Divya. Saga Press, 2021. 416 p.

ISBN 9781982148065

1. Women bodyguards 2. Near future 3. Rich people 4. Designer drugs 5. Addiction 6. Science fiction

LC 2020028891

Welga Ramirez, executive bodyguard and ex-special forces, is about to retire early when her client is killed in front of her. It's 2095 and people don't usually die from violence. Humanity is entirely dependent on pills that not only help them stay alive, but allow them to compete with artificial intelligence in an increasingly competitive gig economy. Daily doses protect against designer diseases, flow enhances focus, zips and buffs enhance physical strength and speed, and juvers speed the healing process. All that changes when Welga's client is killed by The Machinehood, a new and mysterious terrorist group that has simultaneously attacked several major pill funders. The Machinehood operatives seem to be part human, part machine, something the world has never seen. They issue an ultimatum: stop all pill production in one week.

"This stunning near-future thriller from Divya (Runtime) tackles issues of economic inequality, workers' rights, privacy, and the nature of intelligence.... Divya keeps the pace rapid, and her crack worldbuilding and vivid characters make for a memorable, page-turning adventure, while the thematic inquiries into human and AI labor rights offer plenty to chew on for fans of big idea sci-fi." —*Publishers Weekly*

Dixon, Stephen

Interstate: a novel. Stephen Dixon. H. Holt, 1995. 374 p.

ISBN 9780805026542

1. Drive-by shootings 2. Child murder victims 3. Daughters — Death 4. Fathers and daughters 5. Roads 6. Mainstream fiction

LC 94040174
Booklist Editors' Choice, 1995; Library Journal Best Books, 1995; National Book Award for Fiction finalist, 1995

A father mentally replays, in eight variations, the shooting of his daughters on an interstate highway.

"Italo Calvino and Alain Robbe-Grillet have also written novels that begin again and again, revising themselves, but the subjects of these novels are only themselves. Neither of them has brought off anything like the broken eloquence of Nathan's voice, which is as distinct and original and American as Mark Twain's, if otherwise very different.... Neither Italo Calvino nor Alain Robbe-Grillet ever brought off anything so cruelly audacious (although they tried) or so upsetting as 'Interstate' or even attempted the muted beauty of the novel's last few pages, as Nathan performs the ordinary rituals of fatherhood, haunted by everything that has gone before." —*New York Times Book Review*

Djavadi, Negar

Disoriental. Négar Djavadi; translated from the French by Tina Kover. Europa Editions, 2018. 338 pages :

ISBN 9781609454517

1. Memories 2. Women immigrants 3. Intergenerational relations 4. Immigrants — Identity 5. Families — History 6. Iran 7. Paris, France 8. Family sagas 9. Literary fiction 10. Translations

Lambda Literary Award for Bisexual Fiction, 2019; National Book Award for Translated Literature finalist, 2018; Shortlisted for the International Dublin Literary Award, 2020

25-year-old Iranian expat Kimia Sadr, facing the future she has built for herself after leaving her family behind, is inundated by her own memories and the stories of her ancestors in the waiting room of a Parisian fertility clinic.

"The novel convincingly and powerfully explores the enormous weight of ones family and culture on individual identity, especially the exile's." —*Publishers Weekly*

Originally published by Liana Levi in 2016.

Translated from the French.

Doan, Amy Mason

The **summer** list. Amy Mason Doan. Graydon House, 2018. 384 p.

ISBN 9781525804250

1. Teenage girls 2. Female friendship 3. Betrayal 4. Best friends 5. Memories 6. Relationship fiction

Returning home after being away for 17 years, Laura is reunited with her former best friend, Casey, and as they embark on one last scavenger hunt, a devastating secret threatens to tear them apart once again.

Dobmeier, Tracy

★ **Girls** with bright futures: a novel. Tracy Dobmeier and Wendy Katzman. Sourcebooks Landmark, 2021. 400 p.

ISBN 9781728216461

1. Mothers 2. Competition 3. Universities and colleges — Admission 4. Ambition 5. Daughters 6. Thrillers and suspense

LC 2020001705

Alicia is a tech giant, wealthy beyond compare. Kelly is a stay-at-home mother and Stanford legacy. Maren makes three: single, broke, and out of place among the rich and elite. All their daughters are natural choices for Stanford: except the school can only recommend one student. As the competition heats up, an attempt is made on one of the girl's lives and the community spirals into panic. Now the mothers have to decide if one of them is capable of murder, or even worse, one of their own children.

"Fans of domestic suspense about rich people behaving badly—and readers who couldn't look away from the Varsity Blues college-admissions scandal—will devour this one." —*Booklist*

Dobyns, Stephen

Saratoga payback. Stephen Dobyns. Blue Rider Press, 2017. 352 p. (Charlie Bradshaw mysteries, 11)

ISBN 9780399576577

1. Former private investigators 2. Former police 3. Retirement 4. Horse thefts 5. Murder investigation 6. Saratoga Springs, New York 7. New York (State) 8. Mysteries

LC 2016041987

Torn between helping and breaking the law when a local troublemaker is found dead on the sidewalk near his home, erstwhile detective Charlie Bradshaw becomes entangled in a mission to rescue an old acquaintance's stolen horse.

Doctorow, Cory

Radicalized. Cory Doctorow. Tor, 2019. 304 pages

ISBN 9781250228581

1. Corporate power 2. Corporate greed 3. Social classes 4. Hacking 5. Hackers 6. Science fiction 7. Dystopian fiction 8. Social science fiction

Four cyberpunk novellas that look at our predicaments and at the humanity that may redeem us.

Rapture of the nerds. Cory Doctorow and Charles Stross. Tor, 2012. 349 p.

ISBN 9780765329103

1. Potters 2. Jury 3. Conspiracies 4. Near future 5. Interplanetary relations 6. 21st century 7. Cyberpunk 8. Canadian fiction 9. Science fiction

LC 2012019450

At the end of the 21st century, humans who have abandoned Earth to join densethinker clades are carelessly circulating technologies which can change entire cultures and spiritual systems. Huw Jones, a technophobe, is chosen to serve on the tech jury that evaluates new inventions before they are released.

A Tom Doherty Associates book.

Walkaway. Cory Doctorow. Tor Books, 2017. 379 p.

ISBN 9780765392763

1. Social classes 2. Inequality 3. Hierarchy (Social sciences) 4. Social structure 5. Identity (Psychology) 6. Canada 7. Science fiction 8. Techno-thrillers 9. Canadian fiction

Abandoning formal society to pursue a minimalist counterculture life in a near-future world wrecked by climate change, a disenchanted senior and his heiress paramour inspire a host of followers who become obsessed with cheating death in ways that turn the world upside down.

"Doctorow sticks the landing with a multigenerational saga that extends this tale of the 'first days of a better nation' to a thrilling and unexpected finale. A truly visionary techno-thriller that not only depicts how we might live tomorrow, but asks why we don't already." —*Kirkus*

Doctorow, E. L.

All the time in the world: new and selected stories. E. L. Doctorow. Random House, 2011. X, 277 p.

ISBN 9781400069637

1. Literary fiction 2. Short stories

A collection of short works includes the stories of a couple who become estranged after a mysterious man claims he grew up in their house, and a Russian bus boy who is entangled with an organized crime ring.

"In the preface to his new book, [Doctorow] reiterates a position he has advocated many times: You write to find out what you're writing.... . The surprises in this book come at you as slaps on the back of the head. Even while the plots make the surprises seem inevitable the moment you see them, you have to imagine Doctorow's own shock and relief that the story has come so far from its premise. You can only imagine it, though, because the writer and his agenda are nowhere to be found. At the emotional heights of this book, you communicate less with Doctorow than with the presiding god of the world of the story. Doctorow is only the medium. The effect is egoless, frank, spontaneous and altogether wonderful." —*San Francisco Chronicle*

Andrew's brain. E. L. Doctorow. Random House, 2014. 200 pages

ISBN 9781400068814

1. Memory 2. Identity (Psychology) 3. Scientists 4. Cognitive science 5. Brain 6. Psychological fiction 7. Literary fiction

A psychological tale recounts the experiences of Andrew, who confesses to an unknown recipient the memory- and truth-challenging events, loves, and tragedies that have led him to a mysterious act.

★ **Billy** Bathgate: a novel. E.L. Doctorow. Random House, 1989. 323 p.

ISBN 9780394525297

1. Schultz, Dutch 2. Gangsters 3. Organized crime 4. Crime 5. Fifteen-year-old boys 6. Revenge 7. New York City 8. 1930s 9. Historical fiction 10. Coming-of-age stories 11. Literary fiction

LC 88042820

National Book Critics Circle Award for Fiction, 1989; PEN/Faulkner Award, 1990; National Book Award for Fiction finalist, 1989; Pulitzer Prize for Fiction finalist, 1990

Young Billy Bathgate witnesses atrocities of the crime world in his introduction to a brutal and unsparing life that takes him through the heart of the city and the rural underworld in Depression-era America.

"Doctorow brings a nice sense of moral ambiguity and creates characters who develop or deteriorate at an appropriate pace. His fecund run-on sentences are a pleasure to read. It all adds up to that rarity: a formal literary work that's also hugely entertaining." —*Newsweek*

★ The **book** of Daniel: a novel. E. L. Doctorow. Plume, 1996. 303 p.

ISBN 9780452275669

1. Rosenberg, Ethel 2. Spies 3. Parent and child 4. Trials (Espionage) 5. Hypocrisy 6. Jewish Americans 7. United States 8. 1950s 9. Psychological fiction 10. Literary fiction 11. Books to movies

In 1967, Daniel, the son of two convicted spies executed by their own country, ponders his life, his sister's radicalism, his appreciation for his wife and son, and the hypocrisy of the moralistic ideals upon which this country was based.

Book made into a movie called Daniel.

Doctorow: collected stories. E.L. Doctorow. Random House, 2016. 321 pages

ISBN 9780399588358

1. Literary fiction 2. Short stories

LC 2016006619

Fifteen stories, written from the 1960s to the early twenty-first century.

Homer and Langley: a novel. E.L. Doctorow. Random House, 2009. 208 p.

ISBN 9781400064946

1. Collyer, Homer Lusk 2. Brothers 3. Recluses 4. Compulsive behavior in men 5. Eccentrics and eccentricities 6. Men who are blind 7. New

York City 8. Biographical fiction 9. Literary fiction 10. First person narratives

LC 2009006959

Booklist Editors' Choice, 2009

A tale inspired by a true story finds the blind Homer Collyer closeted within a once-grand Fifth Avenue mansion with his damaged brother and remembering a life marked by colorful characters, political events, and technological achievements.

"Toward the end of E.L. Doctorow's novel Homer & Langley, narrator Homer Collyer, the real-life Manhattanite notorious for his and his brother Langley's reclusive lifestyle and hoarding of sundry objects, frets about their legacy: For what could be more terrible than being turned into a mythic joke? How could we cope, once dead and gone, with no one available to reclaim our history? In attempting to recover the Collyer brothers' history from those who would reduce their existence to eccentricities, Doctorow probes the inner workings of the brothers' minds and extends their lives well beyond 1947, when the real Collyers died." —*San Antonio Express-News*

Cunningly panoramic.... Doctorow has packed this tale with episodes of existential wonder that capture the brothers in all their fascinating wackiness." —*Elle*

The march: a novel. E.L. Doctorow. Random House, 2005. 363 p.
ISBN 9780375506710
1. Sherman, William Tecumseh 2. Sherman's March to the Sea 3. Confederate soldiers 4. Pillage 5. Freed people 6. Slaveholders 7. Georgia 8. South Carolina 9. American Civil War era (1861-1865) 10. 1860s 11. Historical fiction 12. War stories 13. Literary fiction 14. Adult books for young adults

LC 2005046452

Booklist Editors' Choice, 2005; Michael Shaara Prize for Excellence in Civil War Fiction, 2006; National Book Critics Circle Award for Fiction, 2005; New York Times Notable Book, 2005; PEN-Faulkner Award, 2006; Pulitzer Prize for Fiction finalist, 2006; National Book Award for Fiction finalist, 2005

Chronicles Union General William Tecumseh Sherman's devastating march through Georgia and the Carolinas during the final years of the Civil War and the profound impact it had on the marchers, those in their path, and the outcome of the war.

"The march in question is that of General William Tecumseh Sherman and his Union soldiers as they slash and burn their way through Georgia and the Carolinas, and the march to freedom as liberated slaves fall in step with the liberating army. But it is also, given the poetic depth of Doctorow's vision, the great march of time and of humanity in all its cruelty and glory. As Doctorow dramatizes the fury, conviction, and chaos of the Civil War, he portrays historical figures, as he is wont to do, most electrifyingly Sherman himself. But he focuses most on brilliantly imagined characters who embody the epic conflicts of that cataclysmic era, including Pearl, the smart and courageous daughter of a slave and slave owner; an excessively clinical military surgeon; the valiant daughter of a Southern judge; a freed slave who becomes a war photographer; and Arly, a scheming Rebel soldier who provides shrewdly comic relief. Doctorow writes with blazing clarity about the brutal romance of war and its gruesome realities, with lyrical splendor about nature, and with wry wisdom and nimble satire about human folly." —*Booklist*

★ **Ragtime**. By E.L. Doctorow. Random House, 1975. 270 p.
ISBN 9780394469010
1. Racism — History 2. Violence 3. Families 4. Family relationships 5. Jewish American families 6. New Rochelle, New York 7. United States 8. 1900s (Decade) 9. Historical fiction 10. Literary fiction 11. First person narratives

LC 75009613

National Book Critics Circle Award for Fiction, 1975

In America at the beginning of this century three families become entwined with Henry Ford, Emma Goldman, Harry Houdini, Theodore Dreiser, Sigmund Freud, and Emiliano Zapata.

World's Fair. E.L. Doctorow. Random House, 1985. 288 p.
ISBN 9780394525280
1. Depressions 2. Caravaggio, Michelangelo Merisi da 3. Family relationships 4. Nine-year-old boys 5. Growing up 6. Bronx, New York City 7. New York City 8. 1930s 9. Literary fiction 10. Historical fiction 11. First person narratives

LC 85010728

National Book Award for Fiction, 1986

A nostalgic novel evokes a world where fiction and reality meet within the 1930s Bronx childhood of Edgar, growing up through the intensity of the Depression and the dazzling hope of the 1939 New York World's Fair.

Dodd, Christina

Because I'm watching. Christina Dodd. St. Martin's Press, 2016. 336 p. (Virtue Falls, 3)
ISBN 9781250130648
1. Veterans 2. Women authors 3. Conspiracies 4. Manipulation (Social sciences) 5. Suicide 6. Romantic suspense

Struggling to build the courage to commit suicide to escape the horrors of his past, veteran Jacob finds his life turned upside-down by a local eccentric who drives her car through the front of his house and who hides her own traumas.

"The tautly written novels plot proves that Dodd knows exactly how to keep readers nerves jangling; at the same time, her irresistibly dry wit helps lighten some of the darker twists and turns. Scary, sexy, and smartly written, Dodd is at the top of her game." —*Booklist*

Dead girl running. Christina Dodd. Harlequin Books 2018. 384 p. (Cape Charade, 1)
ISBN 9781335017437
1. Abused women 2. Murder investigation 3. Runaway wives, husbands, etc. 4. Resorts 5. Amnesia 6. Washington (State) 7. Pacific Northwest 8. Thrillers and suspense

Surviving a gunshot wound to the head and struggling to remember an entire year of her life, Kellan Adams finds herself on the run from a husband she hopes is dead and takes a job at a Pacific Coast resort, where she is embroiled in a murder investigation that makes her question both her past and her sanity.

Obsession Falls. Christina Dodd. St Martin's Press, 2015. 384 p. (Virtue Falls, 2)
ISBN 9781250028471
1. Women witnesses 2. Fugitives 3. Secret identity 4. Frameups 5. Hiding 6. Idaho 7. Washington (State) 8. Romantic suspense
Library Journal Best Books, 2015

Sacrificing herself to protect a young boy from a death threat, Taylor subsequently endures a ruined life in the wilderness before seeking the help of an unlikely ally to defeat a man who would prevent her from reclaiming her life.

Strangers she knows. Christina Dodd. HQN Books, 2019. 335 p. (Cape Charade, 3)
ISBN 9781335016614
1. Islands 2. Serial murderers 3. Protectiveness in women 4. Obsession 5. Families 6. California 7. Thrillers and suspense

Living on an obscure technology-free island off California to escape a murderer who hunts her and her new family, Kellen Adams must face off against him one last time when he somehow finds them.

"With a fascinating island setting that includes a spooky old mansion, a secondary storyline involving World War II, and an antagonist who could give Villanelle from Killing Eve a pointer or two, this is Dodd at her brilliant best." —*Booklist*

Virtue Falls. Christina Dodd. St. Martin's Press, 2014. 448 pages (Virtue Falls, 1)
ISBN 9781250028419
1. Reunions 2. Murder witnesses 3. False imprisonment 4. Secrets 5. FBI agents 6. Washington (State) 7. Thrillers and suspense 8. Multiple perspectives
LC 2014016827
Romantic Times Reviewer's Choice Award, 2014
Growing up believing that her father was responsible for murdering her mother twenty years earlier, Elizabeth returns to her hometown in search of answers and discovers evidence of her father's innocence and the ongoing agenda of the real killer.

What doesn't kill her. Christina Dodd. HQN, 2019. 384 p. (Cape Charade, 2)
ISBN 9781335005786
1. Women with amnesia 2. Chases 3. Wilderness survival 4. Mothers and daughters 5. Memories 6. Washington (State) 7. Pacific Northwest 8. Thrillers and suspense
Kellen Adams suffers from a yearlong gap in her memory. A bullet to the brain will cause that. But she's discovering the truth, and what she learns changes her life, her confidence and her very self. She finds herself in the wilderness, on the run, unprepared, her enemies unknown—and she is carrying a priceless burden she must protect at all costs. The consequences of failure would break her.

The **woman** who couldn't scream. Christina Dodd. St Martins Pr, 2017. 352 p. (Virtue Falls, 4)
ISBN 9781250028488
1. Trophy wives 2. Former lovers 3. Revenge in women 4. Violence against women 5. Sheriffs 6. Romantic suspense
Loan Stars Favourites, 2017
Following her wealthy husband's death, Merida reinvents herself and vows revenge on those responsible for a traumatic accident years earlier that cost her the ability to speak and left her bound to her elderly partner's obsessions.
"Dodd's (Because I'm Watching, 2017, etc.) new title delivers complex storytelling, a rollicking pace, and surprising twists and turns, plus sly humor, a touch of the supernatural, and a full cast of interesting and diverse characters." —*Kirkus*

Doerr, Anthony
★ **All** the light we cannot see: a novel. Anthony Doerr. Scribner, 2014. 448 pages
ISBN 9781476746586
1. People who are blind 2. War and society 3. World War II 4. Personal conduct 5. Coastal towns 6. France 7. Germany 8. Second World War era (1939-1945) 9. Historical fiction 10. Literary fiction 11. Multiple perspectives 12. Adult books for young adults
LC 2013034107
ALA Notable Book, 2015; Alex Award, 2015; Andrew Carnegie Medal for Excellence in Fiction, 2015; Australian Book Industry Awards, International Book of the Year, 2015; Booklist Editors' Choice, 2014; Goodreads Choice Award, 2014; Indies' Choice Book Awards, Adult Fiction, 2015; Library Journal Best Books, 2014; LibraryReads Favorites, 2014; New York Times Notable Book, 2014; Pulitzer Prize for Fiction, 2015; School Library Journal Best Books:

Best Adult Books 4 Teens, 2014; National Book Award for Fiction finalist, 2014
A blind French girl on the run from the German occupation and a German orphan-turned-Resistance tracker struggle with their respective beliefs after meeting on the Brittany coast.
"Doerr captures the sights and sounds of wartime and focuses, refreshingly, on the innate goodness of his major characters." —*Kirkus*
Includes bibliographical references and index.

★ **Cloud** cuckoo land: a novel. Anthony Doerr. Scribner, 2021. 656 p.
ISBN 9781982168438
1. Books and reading 2. Space and time 3. Lost books 4. Growing up 5. Imagination 6. Istanbul, Turkey 7. Idaho 8. Byzantine Empire (330-1453) 9. 15th century 10. Literary fiction
LC 2021002936
LibraryReads Favorites, 2021; Loan Stars Favourites, 2021; National Book Award for Fiction finalist, 2021
Follows four young dreamers and outcasts through time and space, from 1453 Constantinople to the future, as they discover resourcefulness and hope amidst peril in the new novel by the Pulitzer Prize—winning author All the Light We Cannot See.
"The descriptions of Constantinople, Idaho, and the Argos are each distinct and fully realized, and the protagonists of each are united by a determination to survive and a hunger for stories, which in Doerr's universe provide the greatest nourishment. This is a marvel." —*Publishers Weekly*

Doerr, Harriet
★ **Stones** for Ibarra. Harriet Doerr. Viking Press, 1984. 214 p.
ISBN 9780670192038
1. Americans in Mexico 2. Husband and wife 3. Married people 4. Copper mines and mining 5. Villages 6. Mexico 7. Domestic fiction
LC 83047861
National Book Critics Circle Award for Fiction finalist, 1984
Richard and Sara Everton move to Ibarra, Mexico to reopen Richard's grandfather's copper mine and learn that Richard is dying of leukemia.

Doetsch, Richard
Half-past dawn. Richard Doetsch. Atria Books, 2011. 356 p.
ISBN 9781439183977
1. Men with amnesia 2. Missing persons 3. District attorneys 4. Conspiracies 5. Thrillers and suspense
Library Journal Best Books, 2011
Waking up with suspicious injuries and no memory of the previous night, attorney Harper Keller is horrified to discover that he has been reported murdered and that his wife is missing.

Doiron, Paul
Almost midnight. Paul Doiron. Minotaur Books, 2019. 320 p. (Mike Bowditch novels, 10)
ISBN 9781250102416
1. Game wardens 2. Prisoners 3. Conspiracies 4. Prisons 5. Wolves 6. Maine 7. Mysteries
LC 2019005587
When his best friend is released from prison under suspicious circumstances, warden investigator Mike Bowditch races to protect his friend's family only to uncover a violent criminal conspiracy.

Bad Little Falls: a novel. Paul Doiron. Minotaur Books, 2012. 320 p. (Mike Bowditch novels, 3)
ISBN 9780312558482

1. Game wardens 2. Murder investigation 3. Wilderness areas 4. Drug dealers 5. Blizzards 6. Maine 7. Thrillers and suspense

LC 2012007787

Summoned to a rustic cabin during a blizzard, Maine game warden Mike Bowdich embarks on a dangerous investigation involving a notorious drug dealer, a beautiful woman with a dark past and her troubled young son.

★ **Dead** by dawn. Paul Doiron. Minotaur Books, 2021. 320 p. (Mike Bowditch novels, 12)

ISBN 9781250235107

1. Game wardens 2. Law enforcement 3. College teachers 4. Death 5. Drowning victims 6. Maine 7. Carrington, Leonora

LC 2020057549

Mike Bowditch is ambushed and forced off the road into a frozen river on his way back from investigating the suspicious drowning of a wealthy professor in the twelfth novel of the series following One Last Lie.

"Once again, Doiron provides brilliant characterizations and a compelling narrative as Maine game warden Mike Bowditch struggles to stay alive and solve a mystery in his twelfth outing.... This series just keeps getting better." —*Booklist*

One last lie. Paul Doiron. Minotaur Books, 2020. 320 p. (Mike Bowditch novels, 11)

ISBN 9781250235077

1. Game wardens 2. Law enforcement 3. Missing men 4. Missing persons investigation 5. Cold cases (Criminal investigation) 6. Maine 7. Mysteries

When his beloved mentor disappears amid the discovery of an antique badge, Mike Bowditch investigates the presumed death of an undercover warden before the cold case is upended by dangerous secrets and a daughter's return.

"Doiron's masterful plotting pulls it all together, and the reader gets to meet an odd assortment of extraordinarily well-defined characters—good guys and bad—while learning more about both the natural and the political history of the Pine Tree State." —*Booklist*

The **poacher's** son. Paul Doiron. Minotaur Books, 2010. 336 p. (Mike Bowditch novels, 1)

ISBN 9780312558468

1. Game wardens 2. Poachers 3. Fathers and sons 4. Fugitives 5. Murder suspects 6. Maine 7. Thrillers and suspense

LC 2009041136

Desperate and alone, game warden Mike Bowditch strikes up an uneasy alliance with a retired warden pilot, and together the two men journey deep into the Maine wilderness in search of a runaway fugitive—Mike's father. But the only way for Mike to save his father is to find the real killer—which could mean putting everyone he loves in the line of fire.

"Along with nostalgic laments about the old-growth woods and modest settlements that have already fallen to civilization, Doiron provides wonderful scenes of present-day bear-tracking and man-hunting through the kind of terrain that attracts hikers, hunters and the odd paranoid militia freak like the one causing so much trouble in this story." —*New York Times Book Review*

The **precipice**. Paul Doiron. Minotaur Books, 2015. 320 p. (Mike Bowditch novels, 6)

ISBN 9781250063694

1. Game wardens 2. Wilderness areas 3. Hikers 4. Murder investigation 5. Murder 6. Maine 7. Thrillers and suspense

LibraryReads Favorites, 2015

When a pair of lovers are declared the victims of a coyote attack on a remote stretch of the Appalachian Trail, Mike Bowditch clashes with his biologist girlfriend, who believes that the victims were murdered.

"Bowditch is an uncomplicated good guy who might even be considered boring except for the lively conversations on topics as diverse as atheism, sexuality, and animal rights. This unexpected thoughtfulness makes his character appealing enough for readers to cheer him on." —*Library Journal*

Stay hidden. Paul Doiron. Minotaur Books, 2018. 320 p. (Mike Bowditch novels, 9)

ISBN 9781250102386

1. Game wardens 2. Women murder victims 3. Islands 4. Communities 5. Sisters 6. Maine 7. Mysteries

LC 2018004439

When a woman is killed in an apparent hunting accident on an island off the coast of Maine, newly promoted Warden Investigator Mike Bowditch discovers that the victim, a controversial author writing about a local recluse, died of other causes.

"The plot is complex, and the action intense, made all the more so by forbidding terrain. The characters are well developed and clearly defined despite the dense fog that surrounds them, literally and figuratively." —*Booklist*

Dolan-Leach, Caite

We went to the woods: a novel. Caite Dolan-Leach. Random House, 2019. 352 pages

ISBN 9780399588884

1. Communes 2. Farm life 3. Idealism 4. Social isolation 5. Twenties (Age) 6. New York (State) 7. First person narratives 8. Literary fiction 9. Adult books for young adults

Convinced that society is on the brink of collapse, five disillusioned twenty-somethings create a self-sustaining socialist commune, before their utopian vision is marred by desire, suspicion and betrayal.

"Equal parts slow-burning thriller and intelligent analysis of the pros and cons of intentional communities, the novel will appeal to those who would rather read about such endeavors from a safe distance than be immersed in their messy reality." —*Kirkus*

Doller, Trish

Float plan. Trish Doller. St. Martin's Griffin, 2021. 272 p.

ISBN 9781250799760

1. Sailing 2. Sailors 3. Grief in women 4. Survivors of suicide victims 5. Life change events 6. Caribbean Area 7. Contemporary romances

LC 2020042059

LibraryReads Favorites, 2021

Hiring a sailor to navigate the boat trip she planned before her fiancé's death, Anna begins healing from a broken heart in the wake of an unexpected romance.

"Doller's expert balance of the sweet and the serious make this touching romance a sure success." —*Publishers Weekly*

Donati, Sara

Where the light enters. Sara Donati. Berkley, 2019. Xi, 652 pages : Illustration; Map (Gilded hour novels, 2)

ISBN 9780425271827

1. Women physicians 2. Violence against women 3. Multiracial women 4. Abortion 5. Serial murderers 6. New York (State) 7. Gilded Age (1865-1898) 8. Historical fiction

LC 2019008855

A black obstetrician returns to Manhattan in 1884 to move in with her best friend and fellow physician after the tragic loss of her family.

"As she brings the sights, sounds, smells, and social mores of 1884 New York into sharp focus, Donati creates a timely tale of the past that illuminates the ongoing struggle for women's reproductive rights and sheds light on the passionate, centuries-long fight over abortion." —*Booklist*

Dongala, Emmanuel Boundzeki

The **Bridgetower** Sonata: Sonata Mulattica. Emmanuel Dongala; translated by Marjolijn de Jager. Schaffner Press, 2021. 352 p.

ISBN 9781943156887

1. Bridgetower, George Augustus Polgreen 2. Boy prodigies 3. Violinists 4. Composers 5. Multiracial men 6. Africans in Europe 7. Paris, France 8. London, England 9. Revolutionary France (1789-1799) 10. Georgian era (1714-1837) 11. Biographical fiction 12. Historical fiction 13. Translations

In this vividly imagined historical novel, acclaimed Congolese author Emmanuel Dongala has focused his laser-sharp wit on the life and times of George Bridgetower, a young violin prodigy, who, at the age of nine, took the courtly world of 18th century Europe by storm—and surprise, given the youth's unusual origins: for George was of mixed-race parentage, known in the parlance of the day as a mulatto. Though his opportunistic father and de facto manager was Barbadan and dark-skinned, while his mother was a Polish handmaiden in the Viennese court, this young virtuoso, proclaimed as the "Black Mozart," was welcomed into the high society of Tout-Paris on the eve of the French Revolution.

"Charming in its details and sharply perceptive in its intent, this fluidly translated work is not just for music lovers but for everyone interested in the culture and history of its setting, and in the risks of friendship." —*Library Journal*

Originally published: Arles : Actes Sud, 2016.

Translated from the French.

Donoghue, Emma

Akin. Emma Donoghue. Little Brown & Co, 2019. 304 pages

ISBN 9780316491990

1. Retirees 2. Widowers 3. French Americans 4. Guardian and ward 5. Coastal towns 6. Nice, France 7. France 8. 21st century 9. Literary fiction 10. Canadian fiction

Noah, a retired chemistry professor from New York City, finds his life thrown into chaos when he takes his great nephew, whom he has never met, to Nice, in hopes of uncovering his own mother's wartime secrets.

★ **Frog** music. Emma Donoghue. Little, Brown & Co, 2014. 405 p.

ISBN 9780316324687

1. Murder investigation 2. Mothers 3. Amateur detectives 4. Friendship 5. Identity (Psychology) 6. San Francisco, California 7. The West (United States) 8. Gilded Age (1865-1898) 9. 1870s 10. Historical mysteries 11. Literary fiction 12. Canadian fiction

Booklist Editors' Choice, 2014; LibraryReads Favorites, 2014

Burlesque dancer Blanche Beunon tries to discover who murdered her friend Jenny, who was shot through a window in a railroad saloon in 1876 San Francisco, amidst a record-breaking heat wave and smallpox epidemic.

"[A]n engrossing and suspenseful tale about moral growth, unlikely friendship, and breaking free from the past." —*Booklist*

★ **Room**: a novel. By Emma Donoghue. Little, Brown and Co, 2010. Ix, 321 p.

ISBN 9780316098335

1. Antisocial personality disorders 2. Captives 3. Boys 4. Mother and child 5. Captivity 6. Psychological fiction 7. Literary fiction 8. Canadian fiction 9. Adult books for young adults

LC 2010006983

ALA Notable Book, 2011; Alex Award, 2011; CBA Libris Award for Fiction Book of the Year, 2011; Commonwealth Writers' Prize, Caribbean and Canada: Best Book, 2011; Evergreen Award (Ontario), 2011; Goodreads Choice Award, 2010; Indies' Choice Book Awards, Adult Fiction, 2011; Kentucky Bluegrass Award for Grades 9-12, 2012; Library Journal Best Books, 2010; New York Times Notable Book, 2010; Rogers Writers' Trust Fiction Prize, 2010; Shortlisted for the Man Booker Prize, 2010; Shortlisted for The Orange Prize for Fiction, 2011; Governor General's Literary Awards, English-language Fiction finalist

A 5-year-old narrates a riveting story about his life growing up in a single room where his mother aims to protect him from the man who has held her prisoner for seven years since she was a teenager.

"Though the story's chilling circumstances reflect the horrors endured by tabloid-famous abductees, Donoghue avoids all sensationalism. Instead, she gracefully distills what it means to be a mother and what it's like for a child whose entire world measures just 11 x 11." —*Entertainment Weekly*

This book was made into film under the same name in 2015, directed by Lenny Abrahamson, and starring Brie Larson, Joan Allen, William H. Macy and Jacob Tremblay.

Slammerkin. Emma Donoghue. Harcourt, 2001. 336 p.

ISBN 9780151006724

1. Saunders, Mary 2. Teenage prostitutes 3. Women murderers 4. Young women 5. Clothing 6. Great Britain 7. London, England 8. Georgian era (1714-1837) 9. 18th century 10. Biographical fiction 11. Historical fiction 12. Literary fiction

LC 49867

New York Times Notable Book, 2001

Born to poverty in eighteenth-century London, Mary Saunders' love of fine clothes and a dream of a better life take her from the world of prostitution to life as a household seamstress in Monmouth to a search for true freedom.

"In her storytelling, the author shrewdly alternates the point of view, a technique that, rather than feeling gratuitous and shticky as it so often does these days, works to put Mary in a delicious pickle, since the satisfaction of her deepest desires, and the revelation of her secret career, could crush those for whom she—and we—come to feel real affection." —*New York Times Book Review*

Originally published: London : Virago, 2000.

★ The **wonder**. Emma Donoghue. Little, Brown and Company, 2016. 291 pages

ISBN 9780316393874

1. Belief and doubt 2. Faith (Christianity) 3. Villages 4. Fasting 5. Miracles 6. Ireland 7. 1850s 8. Historical fiction 9. Literary fiction 10. Canadian fiction

Shortlisted for the Giller Prize, 2016

Hired to care for a small Irish village girl said to have miraculously survived on nothing but "manna from heaven" for months, a journalist and nurse veteran of Florence Nightingale's Crimean campaign quickly finds herself fighting to save the child's life.

"Donoghue's most recent offering is as startlingly rewarding as her celebrated novel Room. Heart-hammering suspense builds as Lib monitors Anna's quickening pulse, making this book's bracing conclusion one of the most satisfying in recent fiction." —*Library Journal*

Donohue, Keith

The **stolen** child. Keith Donohue. Nan A. Talese, Doubleday, 2006. 336 p.

ISBN 9780385516167

1. Boy kidnapping victims 2. Goblins 3. Identity (Psychology) 4. Changelings 5. Doppelgangers 6. New England 7. Contemporary fantasy 8. Multiple perspectives 9. Adult books for young adults
LC 2005053828

Library Journal Best Books, 2006

Stolen from his family by changelings, Henry Day is given the name "Aniday" by the ageless and magical beings, who replace him with another child who takes his place with his parents, a young boy who possesses an extraordinary gift of music.

"On the surface, Donohue may seem to have written a clever debut novel about fairies. But the real triumph of the book is that, while our backs were turned, he has performed a switch and delivered a luminous and thrilling novel about our humanity." —*Washington Post Book World.*

Dorey-Stein, Beck

Rock the boat: a novel. Beck Dorey-Stein. The Dial Press, 2021. 288 p.
ISBN 9780525509158

1. Homecomings 2. Coastal towns 3. Friendship 4. Deception 5. Family businesses 6. Coming-of-age stories
LC 2020051561

When a developer tries to cash in on Sea Point, three friends Kate, Miles and Ziggy must wade through—and overcome—the white lies and long-buried secrets that threaten to erode the bonds between them as well as the landscape of the beachside community they call home.

"First-time novelist Dorey-Stein has written the perfect beach read, filled with delicious heart and meaty observations about knotty relationship issues and offering surprises and delights with every chapter." —*Library Journal*

Dorn, L. R.

The **anatomy** of desire. L.R. Dorn. HarperCollins 2021. 320 p.
ISBN 9780063041929

1. Women entrepreneurs 2. Personal trainers 3. Success (Concept) 4. Influencers 5. Self-fulfillment in women 6. Los Angeles, California 7. Thrillers and suspense 8. Adaptations, retellings, and spin-offs
LC 2020040857

Claire Griffith has it all, a thriving career, a gorgeous boyfriend, glamorous friends. She always knew she was destined for more than the life her conservative parents preached to her. Arriving in Los Angeles flat broke, she has risen to become a popular fitness coach and social media influencer. Having rebranded herself as Cleo Ray, she stands at the threshold of realizing her biggest dreams. One summer day, Cleo and a woman named Beck Alden set off in a canoe on a serene mountain lake. An hour later, Beck is found dead in the water and Cleo is missing. Told in the form of an immersive investigative docuseries, L. R. Dorn's brilliant reimagining of Theodore Dreiser's classic crime drama An American Tragedy captures the urgency and poignance of the original and rekindles it as a very contemporary and utterly mesmerizing page-turner.

"For fans of true crime and podcasts such as Serial, this riveting mock podcast docudrama ratchets up the suspense as readers glimpse every angle of the story from a 360-degree view." —*Library Journal*

From Theodore Dreiser's An American Tragedy

Dos Passos, John

1919. John Dos Passos. Houghton Mifflin, 2000. Xv, 380 p; (U.S.A. series, 2)
ISBN 9780618056828

1. Edison, Thomas A. 2. Sailors 3. Manners and customs 4. Jewish Americans 5. Poets, American 6. Social problems 7. United States 8. First World War era (1914-1918) 9. Literary fiction 10. Modern classics
LC 27609

"'1919' is literally what so many books are erroneously called, 'a slice of life.' With infinite skill that slicing is done by the author, and the raw surface which meets the reader's eye is the actual living, breathing record of a period in its most intense manifestation." —*Chicago Daily Tribune*

Originally published: New York : Harcourt, Brace and Company, 1932.
A Mariner book.

The **42nd** parallel. John Dos Passos; illustrated by Reginald Marsh; with an introduction by Alfred Kazin. Signet Classics 1969. 414 p. (U.S.A. series, 1)
ISBN 9780451524577

1. United States 2. Literary fiction 3. Modern classics

Slowly, in stories artfully spliced together, the lives and fortunes of five characters unfold. Mac, Janey, Eleanor, Ward, and Charley are caught on the storm track of this parallel and blown New Yorkward. As their lives cross and double back again, the likes of Eugene Debs, Thomas Edison, and Andrew Carnegie make cameo appearances.

Manhattan transfer. John Dos Passos. Houghton Mifflin Co, 2000. 342 p. : Portrait
ISBN 9780618381869

1. City life 2. Alienation (Social psychology) 3. Social change 4. Fate and fatalism 5. Modernization (Social sciences) 6. New York City 7. 1920s 8. XXXXXXXX 9. Experimental fiction 10. Literary fiction
LC 2003272269

Vignettes in the lives of numerous characters create a picture of life in New York City during the early twenties.

Originally published: New York : Harper & Brothers, 1925.

Doshi, Avni

Burnt sugar: a novel. Avni Doshi. The Overlook Press, 2021. 240 p.
ISBN 9781419752926

1. Mothers and daughters 2. Betrayal 3. Caregivers 4. Dementia 5. Family relationships 6. Pune, India 7. India 8. Literary fiction
LC 2020944988

Shortlisted for the Booker Prize, 2020

"Burnt Sugar is an unsettling, sinewy debut, startling in its venom and disarming in its humour from the very first sentence." —*The Guardian*

Originally published in India in 2019 with title: Girl in white cotton.

Dostoyevsky, Fyodor

The **best** short stories of Dostoevsky. Fyodor Dostoyevsky; translated with an introduction by David Magarshack. Modern Library, 1992. 348 p.
ISBN 9780679600206

1. Russia 2. Classics 3. Psychological fiction 4. Short stories
LC 55010655

Offers a collection of the Russian author's shorter fiction that features both his best known works and less familiar writing, including early sketches that reveal the development of his style and his understanding of psychology.

7 short stories.

★ The **brothers** Karamazov. Fyodor Dostoevsky; translated from the Russian by Richard Pevear and Larissa Volokhonsky; introduced by Malcolm V. Jones. Knopf, 1992. Xxxiii, 796 p.
ISBN 9780679410034

1. Brothers 2. Parricide 3. Peasantry 4. Fathers and sons 5. Sibling rivalry 6. Russia 7. Romanov Dynasty (1613-1917) 8. Classics 9. Psychological fiction 10. Translations

Driven by intense, uncontrollable emotions of rage and revenge, the four Karamazov brothers all become involved in the brutal murder of their despicable father.

Includes bibliographical references (p. [779]-796).

★ **Crime** and punishment. Fyodor Dostoyevsky; translated by Constance Garnett. Dover Publications, 2001. Xii, 430 p.
ISBN 9780486415871
1. Murderers — Psychology 2. Conscience 3. Guilt in men 4. Criminals 5. Murder 6. Russia 7. St. Petersburg, Russia 8. 19th century 9. Roth, Philip 10. Translations 11. Classics

Believing he can commit the perfect crime, Roderick Raskolnikov robs and murders an elderly pawnbroker. He eventually finds himself engaged in a battle of wits with inspector Porfiry, a policeman who is determined to wring a confession from the once confident Raskolnikov, a killer whose conscience is slowly beginning to destroy him.

Originally published: London : Heinemann, 1914.

Notes from underground. Fyodor Dostoevsky; translated from the Russian by Richard Pevear and Larissa Volkhonsky [sic]; with an introduction by Richard Pevear. Alfred A. Knopf, 2004. Xxxi, 126 p.
ISBN 9781400041916
1. Suffering in men 2. Social isolation 3. Humiliation 4. Middle-aged men 5. Individuality 6. Russia 7. Romanov Dynasty (1613-1917) 8. Psychological fiction 9. Black humor 10. First person narratives
LC 2003059216

Written in 1864, this classic novel recounts the apology and confession of a minor nineteenth-century official, an account of the man's separation from society, and his descent "underground.

First published in 1864.

Includes bibliographical references (p. xxiii-xxiv).

Dovlatov, Sergei

Pushkin Hills. Sergei Dovlatov. Counterpoint Press, 2014. 160 p.
ISBN 9781619022454
1. Authors, Russian 2. Alcoholic men 3. Divorced men 4. Tour guides (Persons) 5. Literary fiction 6. Satirical fiction 7. First person narratives
LC 2013028859

An unsuccessful writer and an inveterate alcoholic, Boris Alikhanov has recently divorced his wife Tatyana, and he is running out of money. The prospect of a summer job as a tour guide at the Pushkin Hills Preserve offers him hope of regaining some balance in life as his wife makes plans to emigrate to the West with their daughter Masha, but during Alikhanov's stay in the rural estate of Mikhaylovskoye, his life continues to unravel.

Translated from Russian to English.

Dow, David R.

Confessions of an innocent man. David R. Dow. Dutton, 2019. 304 pages
ISBN 9781524743888
1. Death row prisoners 2. Judicial error 3. Criminal justice system 4. Innocence (Law) 5. Women murder victims 6. Houston, Texas 7. Texas 8. Legal thrillers 9. Thrillers and suspense

When an Austin billionaire is murdered, her husband, Rafael Zhettah, the son of poor Mexican immigrants, is sent to death row, only to have DNA evidence vindicate him six years later, spurring him to take revenge on the people that ruined his life.

Dowlatabadi, Mahmoud

The **colonel**. Mahmoud Dowlatabadi; translated from the Persian by Tom Patterdale. Melville House, 2012. V, 247 p.
ISBN 9781612191324
1. Father and child 2. Political corruption 3. Soldiers 4. Ayatollahs 5. Islam and state 6. Iran 7. Political fiction 8. Psychological fiction 9. Translations

In a small Iranian town on a dark rain-soaked night, the Colonel paces back and forth waiting for the inevitable knock on the door. The secret police take him to the tortured body of his youngest daughter, for the Islamic revolution is devouring its own children. This shocking diatribe leaves no taboo unbroken.

Translated from the Persian; first published in Germany under the title: Kolonel.

Translated from Persian.

Downes, Anna

The **safe** place: a novel. Anna Downes. Minotaur Books, 2020. 384 pages
ISBN 9781250264800
1. Actors and actresses 2. Dysfunctional families 3. Family secrets 4. Vacation homes 5. Housekeepers 6. France 7. Gothic fiction 8. Psychological suspense
Loan Stars Favourites, 2020

Losing her job and agent on the same miserable day, Emily accepts a nanny position on a remote French estate before discovering that her employer, a successful CEO, and his wife are hiding dangerous secrets.

"British actress Downes' debut novel is a slow burn of a story with Emily picking up on snippets of conversations as a breadcrumb trail leads her to an astounding conclusion. A great read for those looking for a side of mystery with their women's fiction." —*Booklist*

Also published in Australia: Affirm Press, 2020.

Downing, David

Diary of a dead man on leave. David Downing. Soho Press, 2019. 312 pages
ISBN 9781616958435
1. World War II 2. Spies 3. Soldiers 4. Espionage 5. Undercover operations 6. Germany 7. Second World War era (1939-1945) 8. Spy fiction 9. Historical thrillers 10. Diary novels
LC 2018046837

Stumbling across the hidden diary of a boarder who had been a father figure to him half a century earlier, Walter discovers the man's life-risking undercover work as an anti-Nazi Moscow spy.

"This is a quiet, largely introspective spy novel, very different in mood from Downing's adventure-fueled Jack McColl novels, but it packs an equal if not greater emotional wallop." —*Booklist*

Downing, Samantha

He started it. Samantha Downing. Berkley, 2020. 384 p.
ISBN 9780451491756
1. Inheritance and succession 2. Siblings 3. Family secrets 4. Automobile travel 5. Funerals 6. Thrillers and suspense
LC 2019050012
LibraryReads Favourites, 2020

In the latest thrillingly savage stand-alone from the twisted mind behind mega hit My Lovely Wife comes the story of a family—not unlike your own—just with a few more violent tendencies thrown in....

"With our need to know ramped up through a series of teasers offering more to come, this tale is virtually impossible to put down." —*Booklist*

My lovely wife. Samantha Downing. Berkley, 2019. 384 pages
ISBN 9780451491725
1. Husband and wife 2. Murderers 3. Marriage burn out 4. Married people — Psychology 5. Married people and secrets 6. Psychological suspense 7. First person narratives
LibraryReads Favorites, 2019; Loan Stars Favourites, 2019
A seemingly typical suburban husband discloses the secret ways that his wife of 15 years and he keep their marriage alive and chase away domestic boredom by orchestrating creative ways to get away with murder.

Doyle, Arthur Conan

★ The **complete** Sherlock Holmes. Sir Arthur Conan Doyle; with a preface by Christopher Morley. Doubleday, 1930. 1323 p. (Sherlock Holmes mysteries)
ISBN 9780385006897
1. Criminal investigation 2. Amateur detectives 3. Private investigators 4. Watson, John H. (Fictitious character) 5. Holmes, Sherlock (Fictitious character) 6. London, England 7. 19th century 8. Short stories 9. Mysteries 10. Classics
LC 30023546
Here, collected in one volume, are all four full-length novels and 56 short stories chronicling the colorful adventures of Sherlock Holmes—every word Sir Arthur Conan Doyle ever wrote about Baker Street's most famous resident.

★ The **hound** of the Baskervilles. Sir Arthur Conan Doyle; illustrated by Pam Smy. Candlewick Press, 2006. 271 pages : Illustration; Color (Sherlock Holmes mysteries, 5)
ISBN 9780763630645
1. Curses 2. Amateur detectives 3. Dogs 4. Private investigators 5. Moors and heaths 6. Devon, England 7. Dartmoor, England 8. 19th century 9. Mysteries 10. Books to movies 11. Classics
Sherlock Holmes and Dr. Watson journey to unpopulated regions of bracken and fog to solve a mystery at an isolated manor house.
This text is taken from the original version first published in The Strand magazine (London), vols. XXII, XXIII (August, 1901 - April, 1902)—Copyright p.
Originally published: 1902.

Doyle, Brian

The **plover**: a novel. Brian Doyle. Thomas Dunne Books, 2014. 311 p.
ISBN 9781250034779
1. Ship captains 2. Self-discovery 3. Voyages and travels 4. Ocean travel 5. Interpersonal relations 6. Oregon 7. Sea stories
LC 2013032101
Voyaging into the Pacific to escape his troubled life in Oregon, Declan O'Donnell bonds with his crewmates and learns of their own respective quests for self, exchanges that lead to a shared celebration of life's unexpected paths.
"Doyle...has written a novel in the adventurous style of Jack London and Robert Louis Stevenson but with a gentle mocking of their valorization of the individual as absolute. Readers will enjoy this bracing and euphoric ode to the vastness of the ocean and the unexpectedness of life." —*Library Journal*

Doyle, Rob

Threshold. Rob Doyle. Bloomsbury, 2020. 316 pages
ISBN 9781635574142

1. Voyages and travels 2. Travelers 3. Authors 4. Writing 5. Creativity in men 6. Literary fiction 7. Epistolary novels
An uninhibited portrait of the artist as a perpetual drifter and truth-seeker—a funny, profound, compulsive read that's like traveling with your wildest and most philosophical friend.
"Doyle's musings are always intriguing and often enlightening, offering a glimpse of the anxious yet pleasing rationale of a mind struggling to live in a rational world." —*Publishers Weekly*

Doyle, Roddy

The **guts**. Roddy Doyle. Viking Press, 2013. 327 p. (Barrytown novels, 4)
ISBN 9780670016433
1. Musicians 2. Middle-aged men 3. Fathers and sons 4. Middle age 5. People with cancer 6. Dublin, Ireland 7. Ireland 8. Humorous stories
A follow-up to The Commitments finds a middle-aged Jimmy battling cancer and reconnecting with his musical past by tracking down the resurrected albums of old bands, practicing the trumpet, reuniting with his long-lost brother and rediscovering the joys of fatherhood.
Sequel to: The van.
Originally published: London: Jonathan Cape, 2013.

Love. Roddy Doyle. Viking Press, 2020. 304 pages
ISBN 9781984880451
1. Childhood friends 2. Male friendship 3. Middle-aged men 4. Lomazzo, Giovanni Paolo 5. Drinking 6. Dublin, Ireland 7. Ireland 8. Literary fiction
Attending his father's deathbed in hospice, a man reconnects with a drinking buddy from his Dublin youth while reflecting on a long-ago love, his wife's role in upending his life and the truth about his departure from Ireland.
"Doyle's latest novel (after Smile) brilliantly highlights his ear for speech, especially the recursive fluency of inebriation." —*Library Journal*

Paddy Clarke, ha-ha-ha. Roddy Doyle. Viking, 1993. 282 p.
ISBN 9780670853458
1. Working class families 2. Childhood 3. Catholic boys 4. Growing up 5. Family relationships 6. Dublin, Ireland 7. 1960s 8. Literary fiction 9. Coming-of-age stories 10. Adult books for young adults
LC 93216955
Booker Prize, 1993
Paddy Clarke, a ten-year-old boy who longs to be a missionary, experiences life's joys and setbacks—specifically his parent's fights—as he grows up in the north of Liffey, Ireland, in the late 1960s.
"Doyle's triumph in this novel is to replenish our sense of how children think and speak and explain the adult world to themselves." —*London Review of Books*

Smile. Roddy Doyle. Viking, 2017. 214 pages
ISBN 9780735224445
1. Memory 2. Psychic trauma 3. Men — Psychology 4. Marital conflict 5. Former friends 6. Ireland 7. Psychological fiction
Approached by a man he does not remember who claims they attended secondary school together, a man on his own for the first time in years reluctantly reflects on unhappy memories from the past, including those of a brutal teacher who left him traumatized and struggling to hold fast to his sanity.
"Doyle's ability to convey so much meaning through rapid-fire dialog in the Irish vernacular is unsurpassed. His commentary about the Catholic Church, sexuality, and repression is searing." —*Library Journal*

A **star** called Henry. Roddy Doyle. Viking, 1999. 343 p. (The last roundup (Roddy Doyle), 1)

ISBN 9780670887576

1. Easter Rising, 1916 2. Rebels — History 3. Irish resistance and revolts 4. Smart, Henry (Fictitious character) 5. Dublin, Ireland 6. Ireland 7. Picaresque fiction 8. Historical fiction

LC 99-25310

ALA Notable Book, 2000

Offers a portrait of an adventuresome Irishman named Henry Smart, an IRA assassin and 1916 Easter Rebellion fighter, from his Dublin birth to his adulthood, when he becomes the father of a young rebel.

"In Doyle's hands, the grand patriotic narrative is tempered with a sharp sense of humanity and human frailty." —*Times Literary Supplement*

★ The **woman** who walked into doors. Roddy Doyle. Viking, 1996. 226 p. (Paula Spencer novels, 1)

ISBN 9780670867752

1. Working class women 2. Middle-aged women 3. Alcoholic women 4. Abused women 5. Ireland 6. Psychological fiction

LC 95-418650

ALA Notable Book, 1997; Library Journal Best Books, 1996

Relates the story of Paula Spencer, a woman approaching forty and struggling with alcoholism and a violent marriage.

"Doyle is a very, very good writer. 'The Woman Who Walked Into Doors' honors not the female experience in the abstract, but the experience of this one woman, Paula Spencer; it examines it with tenderness, but with fearless clearsightedness. And it's funny in places too. Paula Spencer is neither a victim nor a flawless Madonna; she inhabits the complexity of her mind and history; she acts to buy a better future for her children." —*New York Times Book Review*

Sequel: Paula Spencer.

Drabble, Margaret

★ The **dark** flood rises. Margaret Drabble. Farrar, Straus and Giroux, 2017. 336 p.

ISBN 9780374134952

1. Aging 2. Caregivers 3. Senior women 4. May-December romances 5. Man-woman relationships 6. England 7. Canary Islands 8. Literary fiction 9. Psychological fiction

LC 2016025620

New York Times Notable Book, 2017

Driven to live life to its fullest while she still can, a housing expert for the elderly balances her challenging career with the cares of her loved ones, in a tale that juxtaposes her interconnected social circle in England against her contacts in an idyllic expat community in the Canary Islands.

"For women of a certain age, it is a pure pleasure to grow older alongside Drabble... For all others, there's plenty of joy to be had in this thoughtful meditation on aging and mortality." —*Library Journal*

Originally published in 2016 by Canongate Books.

A **day** in the life of a smiling woman: complete short stories. Margaret Drabble; edited by Jose Francisco Fernandez. Houghton Mifflin Harcourt, 2011. 208 p.

ISBN 9780547550404

1. Female friendship 2. Interpersonal relations 3. Short stories

LC 2010049798

A single-volume compilation of the 2008 Dame of the British Empire's previously uncollected short works offers insight into her use of irony, female friendships and personal passions and is complemented by an introduction that places her works in a context of her life and novels.

"The discursive spaciousness of Margaret Drabble's voice and vision lends itself to the long form, as her 17 splendid novels demonstrate. This may help to explain why her complete short stories make up so slender a volume. Drabble, it seems, just didn't have enough time to write short stories (with apologies to Mark Twain). Of those collected here, 14 in all, the earliest dates from the 1950s, the most recent from the 1990s. Some are reed slim, but many glimmer with the irony, lyricism, moral vision and (despite their page counts) amplitude we associate with Drabble's novels. They reflect back to us the last half of the 20th century, albeit in Drabble's often 19th-century voice." —*New York Times Book Review*

The **pure** gold baby. Margaret Drabble. Houghton Mifflin Harcourt, 2013. 291 p.

ISBN 9780544158900

1. Mothers of children with disabilities 2. Women anthropologists 3. Children with disabilities 4. Female friendship 5. Motherhood 6. London, England 7. Literary fiction 8. Psychological fiction 9. First person narratives

LC 2013021736

Her promising career in 1960s London interrupted by an affair with a married professor that renders her a single mother, anthropology student Jessica Speight faces wrenching questions about responsibility, potential and compassion when her sunny child reveals unique needs.

The **sea** lady. Margaret Drabble. Harcourt, Inc, 2007. 352 p.

ISBN 9780151012633

1. Reunions 2. Social acceptance 3. Memories 4. Marine biologists 5. Women scholars and academics 6. England 7. Psychological fiction 8. Literary fiction

LC 2006023778

Traveling separately to Ornemouth, England, a town by the North Sea where they had spent a summer together as children, Humphrey Clark and Ailsa Kelman reassess the course of their individual lives and decisions over the past thirty years of separation.

"The author has a keen sense of the past and the ways in which intellectual fashions evolve. She is pitiless—and very funny—about the flimsiness of Ailsa's various posturings. Where Humphrey craves knowledge, Ailsa craves exposure. Their love affair mirrors the age they are living through.... Drabble writes beautifully about the passing of time and the sad, incomplete experience of human love." —*New Statesman*

The **witch** of Exmoor. Margaret Drabble. Harcourt Brace, 1996. 281 p.

ISBN 9780151003631

1. Families 2. Eccentric women 3. Women authors 4. Grandmothers 5. Misfits (Persons) 6. England 7. Satirical fiction 8. Psychological fiction

LC 97-10952

Frieda, the peculiar matriarch of the Palmer family, makes her family wonder what escapade she will think of next and whether her foreign grandson will inherit all her money or if the sinister atmosphere of Exmoor has caused her to lose her mind

"Can politics ever amount to more than the conspiracies we hatch against our parents and the spells we cast on our children? The humbling surprise of Drabble's novel is not that it refuses to resolve this question but that we gradually lose our lofty perspective and begin to have an emotional stake in the answer." —*The New Yorker*

Drake, Laura

The **sweet** spot. Laura Drake. Forever, 2013. 384 p. (Sweet on a cowboy novels, 1)

ISBN 9781455521951

1. Divorced couples 2. Lovers' reunions 3. Cowboys 4. Second chances 5. Children — Death 6. Texas 7. Contemporary romances 8. Western romances

RITA Award for Best First Book, 2014

Everything changed the day their son died. Driven apart by guilt and grief, Charla Rae and JB go their separate ways... but a cowboy's love doesn't die easily. A chance encounter a year later, JB wants nothing more than to be the man that Charla needs but can she see beyond her broken heart? Can this cowboy get her to love again?

Drake, Olivia

When a duke loves a governess. Olivia Drake. St Martins Press, 2021. 336 p. (Unlikely duchesses, 3)
ISBN 9781250174499
1. Dukes and duchesses 2. Governesses 3. Single women 4. Interclass romance 5. Ambition in women 6. Regency period (1811-1820) 7. Regency romances 8. Historical romances

Working as a governess for the new Duke of Corlin, Tessa Grey is unexpectedly led down a path to love with this passionate man until a private scandal goes public and all evidence points to Tessa.

"With suspects and motives aplenty and the heat steadily rising between the alluring pair, this proves impossible to put down." —*Publishers Weekly*

Draper, Sharon M.

★ **Forged** by fire. Sharon M. Draper. Atheneum Books for Young Readers, 1997. 151 p. (Hazelwood High trilogy, 2)
ISBN 9780689806995
1. Mother-separated boys 2. Stepsiblings 3. Incest victims 4. African American teenage boys 5. Sexually abused children 6. Cincinnati, Ohio 7. Realistic fiction 8. African American fiction 9. Books for reluctant readers
LC 962763
Coretta Scott King Award, Author Category, 1998; Young Hoosier Book Award, Middle Books, 2001; YALSA Quick Picks for Reluctant Young Adult Readers, 1998; YALSA Best Books for Young Adults, 1998

After surviving a fire, Gerald experiences separation from his mother, the loss of his great aunt, and life with his stepsister's abusive father.

Companion volume to: Tears of a tiger.

Draven, Grace

Phoenix unbound. Grace Draven. Ace, 2018. 384 p. (Fallen empire, 1)
ISBN 9780451489753
1. Imaginary empires 2. Heaney, Seamus 3. Magic 4. Executions and executioners 5. Interpersonal attraction 6. Fantasy romances
LC 2018018971
A woman with power over fire and illusion and an enslaved son of a chieftain battle a corrupt empire.

Drayson, Nicholas

A **guide** to the birds of East Africa. Nicholas Drayson. Houghton Mifflin Co, 2008. 201 p. : Illustration
ISBN 9780547152585
1. Ornithologists 2. Bird watching 3. Love triangles 4. Wildlife watching 5. Wildlife refuges 6. Kenya 7. Mainstream fiction 8. Australian fiction
LC 2008017183
ACT Book of the Year, 2009
Working up the nerve to invite Rose Mbikwa to the Nairobi Hunt Club Ball, Mr. Malik, a reserved, honorable widower, is suddenly confronted by the return of his school nemesis, the flashy Harry Kahn, who also sets his sights on Rose.

"With captivating character sketches and glimpses into Kenyan life and politics, Drayson meets the inevitable comparisons to Alexander McCall Smith without breaking a sweat." —*Publishers Weekly*

Dreiser, Theodore

★ An **American** tragedy. Theodore Dreiser; with a new introduction by Richard Lingeman. Signet Classic, 2000. Xv, 859 p.
ISBN 9780451527707
1. Ambition in men 2. Success (Concept) 3. Poor children 4. Murder 5. Man-woman relationships 6. Literary fiction 7. Books to movies 8. Classics

The author's classic vision of the dark side of American life looks at the failings of the American dream, in the story of the rise and fall of Clyde Griffiths, who sacrifices everything in his desperate quest for success.

The movie called A place in the sun was inspired by the book.
Originally published: New York : Boni & Liveright, 1925.

★ **Sister** Carrie. Theodore Dreiser. Penguin, 1994. 499 p.
ISBN 9780140188288
1. Mistresses 2. Success (Concept) 3. Actors and actresses 4. Moving to a new city 5. Extramarital affairs 6. 19th century 7. Coming-of-age stories 8. Books to movies 9. Classics
LC 78183140
Young Caroline Meeber leaves home for the first time and experiences work, love, and the pleasures and responsibilities of independence in late-nineteenth-century Chicago and New York.

Title of later film version: Carrie (1952).
Originally published: New York : Doubleday, Page & Co, 1900.

Drndic, Dasa

Trieste. Dasa Drndic; translated from the Croatian by Ellen Elias-Bursac. Houghton Mifflin Harcourt, 2014. 359 pages
ISBN 9780547725147
1. Women Holocaust survivors 2. Mother and adult son 3. World War II 4. Jewish women 5. Senior women 6. Italy 7. Trieste, Italy 8. Literary fiction 9. Translations

An old Italian woman seeks a reunion with her son, fathered by an SS officer and taken away by German authorities 62 years ago while she remembers and discusses the atrocities committed in Northern Italy during World War II.

"Trieste's originality lies not just in its structure and forceful, unflinching imagery...but also in how it brings the lingering effects of the Nazis' merciless racial policies forward into the present." —*Booklist*

Originally published: Zagreb : Fraktura, 2007.
Translated from the Croatian.

Druon, Maurice

The **iron** king. By Maurice Druon; translated from the French by Humphrey Hare. Scribner's, 1956. 269 p. (Accursed kings, 1)
ISBN 9780712608763
1. Philip 2. Curses 3. Feudalism 4. Rulers 5. France 6. Medieval period (476-1492) 7. 14th century 8. Historical fiction 9. Biographical fiction
LC 56010197
Originally published in France in 1955, this sweeping 1st volume in a seven-book saga about the Hundred Years' War finally makes its English-language debut. Set in the year 1314, the story takes place during the reign of despotic French King Philip the Fair and focuses on disenfranchised Lord Robert of Artois, whose attempts to reclaim his birthright ignite a conflict that will engulf all of France and destroy a dynasty. Steeped in sex, violence, and political intrigue, this book will captivate readers of sprawling, dramatic, and intricately plotted historical fiction.

First published in Great Britain by Rupert Hart-Davis 1956.

Dubus, Andre

Dirty love. Andre Dubus III.. W. W. Norton & Company, 2013. 320 p.
ISBN 9780393064650
1. Desire 2. Extramarital affairs 3. Small towns 4. Life change events 5. Sexuality 6. Massachusetts 7. Psychological fiction 8. Short stories
LC 2013017214
New York Times Notable Book, 2013
A collection of short stories examines the lives of suburbanites seeking solace and gratification in food, sex, work, and love.

Due, Tananarive

Ghost summer: stories. Tananarive Due; introduction by Nalo Hopkinson. Prime Books, 2015. 256 p.
ISBN 9781607014539
1. Fantasy fiction 2. Science fiction 3. Short stories
In this collection of 15 short stories and a novella, award-winning author Tananarive Due portrays human depravity in the guise of monstrous creatures. With a liberal dollop of ghosts (including the story titled "Summer"), occasional zombies ("Patient Zero" and "Danger World"), werewolves ("Afternoon"), and glimpses into the future, Due expertly reveals what lies under the surface. With an introduction by Nalo Hopkinson and an afterword by Steven Barnes, Ghost Summer offers a terrifying sampler of gourmet treats.

Duenas, Maria

The **time** in between: a novel. Maria Duenas; translated by Daniel Hahn. Atria, 2011. 624 p.
ISBN 9781451616880
1. Seamstresses 2. Spaniards in Morocco 3. World War II 4. Espionage 5. Courage in women 6. Spain 7. Morocco 8. 1930s 9. Historical fiction 10. First person narratives
Booklist Editors' Choice, 2011
The Time In Between follows the story of a seamstress who becomes the most sought-after couturiere during the Spanish Civil War and World War II.
Translated from the Spanish.

Duffy, Brendan

House of echoes: a novel. Brendan Duffy. Ballantine Books, 2015. 384 p.
ISBN 9780804178112
1. Houses 2. Markham, Beryl 3. Moving, Household 4. Life change events 5. Small town life 6. New York State 7. Gothic fiction
LC 2014024343
LibraryReads Favorites, 2015
Frustrating career setbacks and a heartbreaking diagnosis challenge the lives of Ben and Caroline, who after starting over in a nostalgic new hometown encounter disconcerting secrets that threaten their survival.
"Debut author Duffy has delivered a fluid, suspenseful yet subtle thriller, with touches of humor, evocative writing, and characters that are both familiar and uniquely fascinating. A wonderfully tense and heart-wrenching debut." —*Kirkus*

Dugoni, Robert

The **conviction**. Robert Dugoni. Touchstone, 2012. 384 p. (David Sloane thrillers, 5)
ISBN 9781451606720
1. Widowers 2. Fathers and sons 3. Juvenile corrections 4. Judicial corruption 5. Lawyers 6. Seattle, Washington 7. Washington (State) 8. Thrillers and suspense 9. Legal thrillers
Bringing his teenage son on a camping trip with an old friend and his friend's son, lawyer David Sloane embarks on a legal rescue mission when the boys are caught vandalizing a general store and sentenced to six months in a detention camp with ties to a corrupt judge.

The **eighth** sister: a thriller. Robert Dugoni. Thomas & Mercer, 2019. 478 pages (Charles Jenkins novels, 1)
ISBN 9781503903036
1. Espionage 2. CIA agents 3. International intrigue 4. Intelligence service 5. Assassins 6. United States 7. Russia 8. Spy fiction 9. Thrillers and suspense
A pulse-pounding thriller of espionage, spy games, and treachery by the New York Times bestselling author of the Tracy Crosswhite Series.

★ The **extraordinary** life of Sam Hell. Robert Dugoni. Lake Union Press, 2018. 448 pages
ISBN 9781503949003
1. Growing up 2. Misfits (Persons) 3. Small town life 4. Small towns 5. Albinos and albinism 6. Coming-of-age stories
Born with ocular albinism, small-town eye doctor Sam Hill, who was called 'Devil Boy' in his youth, must finally face a past tragedy that caused him to turn his back on his friends, his hometown and the life he'd always known—a journey that makes him realize what truly matters.

In her tracks. Robert Dugoni. Thomas and Mercer, 2021. 383 p. (Tracy Crosswhite novels, 8)
ISBN 9781542008372
1. Women detectives 2. Cold cases (Criminal investigation) 3. Child kidnapping victims 4. Missing persons 5. Investigations 6. Washington (State) 7. Police procedurals 8. Mysteries
Reopening the cold case of an abducted child whose parents were once prime suspects, detective Tracy Crosswhite is simultaneously partnered with Kinsington Rowe to investigate a jogger's disappearance from a North Seattle trail.
"Returning to active duty, Seattle Detective Tracy Crosswhite gets shunted off to cold cases just in time for a fresh series of disappearances to spark her interest in a five-year-old kidnapping.... A warmhearted procedural about some ice-cold crimes." —*Kirkus*

Murder one. Robert Dugoni. Simon & Schuster 2011. 384 p. (David Sloane thrillers, 4)
ISBN 9781451606690
1. Murder investigation 2. Drug traffic 3. Widowers 4. Wrongful death 5. Drugs — Overdose 6. Seattle, Washington 7. Washington (State) 8. Thrillers and suspense 9. Legal thrillers
Library Journal Best Books, 2011
A year after the murder of his wife, attorney David Sloane reconnects with former adversary Barclay Reid, who upon losing her daughter to a drug overdose has launched a campaign against Russian drug trafficking, only to be accused of murdering a dealer.
"While many will anticipate the ending twist, Dugoni conveys the legalese in digestible form." —*Publishers Weekly*

My sister's grave. Robert Dugoni. Thomas & Mercer, 2014. 416 p. (Tracy Crosswhite novels, 1)
ISBN 9781477825570
1. Women detectives 2. Missing women 3. Cold cases (Criminal investigation) 4. Murderers 5. Sisters 6. Seattle, Washington 7. Washington (State) 8. Mysteries 9. Police procedurals
Library Journal Best Books, 2014
Twenty years after Seattle homicide detective Tracy Crosswhite's sister, Sarah, was murdered, Tracy sees a chance to find the real killer when

Sarah's remains are discovered near their hometown in the northern Cascade mountains of Washington State.

Dumas, Alexandre

★ **Camille**. The Modern Library, 1925. 270 p.
ISBN 9780451529206
1. Prostitutes 2. Ford, Robert 3. Counts and countesses 4. Courtesans 5. Nobility 6. Paris, France 7. 19th century 8. Classics 9. Love stories 10. Translations
LC 26008619
Camille, a fashionable Paris courtesan, escapes to the country with her poor lover Armand Duval, from a Count who wants her as his mistress, but she later leaves Duval to placate his family.
Translation of: La dame aux camelias, originally published in 1848.

★ **The count** of Monte Cristo. Alexandre Dumas. Modern Library, 1996. Xiv, 1462 p.
ISBN 9780679601999
1. Escapes 2. Prisoners 3. Revenge 4. Sailors 5. Treason 6. France 7. 19th century 8. Adventure stories 9. Translations 10. Books to TV
LC 96-3397
The Count of Monte Cristo is the story of Edmond Dantes, who is imprisoned in the island fortress of the Chateau d'If on a false political charge; after escaping, he finds the fabulous treasure of Monte Cristo and sets upon the course of revenge against his old enemies.
First published in 1845.
Movie entitled Forever mine is inspired by this book.
Television series entitled Revenge is inspired by this book.

★ **The man** in the iron mask. Alexandre Dumas; translated by Joachim Neugroschel; introduction by Francine du Plessix Gray. Penguin Books, 2003. Xxv, 470 p; (Three musketeers series, 6)
ISBN 9780140439243
1. Man in the Iron mask 2. Rulers 3. Prisoners 4. Musketeers 5. Twin brothers 6. Political corruption 7. France 8. 17th century 9. Historical fiction 10. Swashbuckling tales 11. Adventure stories
Deep inside the dreaded Bastille, a twenty-three-year-old prisoner called merely "Philippe" has languished for eight long, dark years. He does not know his real name or what crime he is supposed to have committed. But Aramis, one of the original Three Musketeers, has bribed his way into the cell to reveal the shocking secret that has kept Philippe locked away from the world. That carefully concealed truth could topple Louis XIV, king of France, which is exactly what Aramis is plotting to do! A daring jailbreak, a brilliant masquerade, and a terrifying fight for the throne may make Aramis betray his sacred vow, "All for one, and one for all!
First published in 1848.
Translated from the French.

★ **The three** musketeers. Alexandre Dumas; translated from the French with an introduction by Richard Pevear. Viking, 2006. Xxiii, 704 p.
ISBN 9780670037797
1. Louis 2. Musketeers 3. Soldiers 4. Male friendship 5. Revenge 6. Swordplay 7. France 8. Swashbuckling tales 9. Adventure stories 10. Historical fiction
A major new translation depicts the epic adventures of musketeer-hopeful d'Artagnan and his swordsmen companions in a faithful rendition that endeavors to preserve the original author's wit, romance, and rollicking pace.
"Richard Pevear's brisk, agile new translation succeeds, I think, because it does justice to the pure nuttiness of Dumas's writing: the nonindustrial, nonformulaic, downright peculiar qualities that make a work of popular fiction memorable." —*New York Times Book Review*
Translated from the French.

Twenty years after. Alexandre Dumas. Oxford University Press, 2009. Xxv, 845 p. (Three musketeers series, 3)
ISBN 9780199537266
1. Musketeers 2. Swordplay 3. Political corruption 4. Soldiers 5. France 6. Paris, France 7. 17th century 8. Swashbuckling tales 9. Adventure stories 10. Historical fiction
Two decades have passed since the musketeers triumphed over Cardinal Richelieu and Milady. Time has weakened their resolve, and dispersed their loyalties. But treasons and strategems still cry out for justice: civil war endangers the throne of France, while in England Cromwell threatens to send Charles I to the scaffold. But their greatest test is a titanic struggle with the son of Milady, who wears the face of Evil.
Sequel to: The three musketeers.

Dumas, Henry

Echo tree: the collected short fiction of Henry Dumas. Edited and with a foreword by Eugene B. Redmond; critical introduction by John S. Wright. Coffee House Press, 2003. 381 pages
ISBN 9781566891493
1. African Americans 2. United States 3. Southern States 4. Short stories 5. African American fiction
LC 2003055120
Gothic romance, ghost story, parable, psychological thriller, inner-space fiction—Dumas's stories form a vivid, expansive portrait of African-American life.
"The work of a late, lamented, and influential icon of the 1960s Black Arts Movement is brought back into print to connect with a post-millennial Black Lives Matter generations of readers and writers." —*Kirkus*
Reprinted by Coffee House Press, 2021.
The collected short fiction of Henry Dumas.

Du Maurier, Daphne

Frenchman's creek. Daphne Du Maurier. Sourcebooks Landmark, 2009. 283 p.
ISBN 9781402217104
1. Pirates 2. Nobility — History 3. Man-woman relationships 4. Cornwall, England 5. Great Britain 6. Restoration England (1660-1688) 7. Stuart period (1603-1714) 8. Historical fiction 9. Books to movies
During the reign of Charles II, a rebellious noblewoman abandons her Cornwall estate to sail with her pirate lover.
"The lovely Lady St. Columb fled by coach from the boredom of London society, and an unloved husband to their wild and unused Cornish coast estate. There she discovered an aristocratic French pirate who secreted his ship and crew in the hidden creek and as a game preyed gaily upon the dull Cornish gentry. [The book describes] the love between the two and the thrilling adventure they shared." —*Booklist*
Originally published: London: Gollancz, 1941.
Originally published: London : V. Gollancz, 1941.

Jamaica Inn. Daphne Du Maurier. Avon Books, 1971. 302 p.
ISBN 9780380000722
1. Smuggling 2. Murder 3. Secrets 4. Wreckers (Plunderers of ships) 5. Shipwrecks 6. Cornwall, England 7. Historical romances 8. Romantic suspense

After her mother dies, Mary Yellan goes to live with her aunt and uncle at the mysterious Jamaica Inn where she is terrified by the ruthless lawbreakers that frequent the roadhouse.

Originally published: London: Gollancz, 1936.

Originally published in the U.S.: Garden City, N.Y. : Doubleday, Doran & Co, 1936.

★ **Rebecca**. Daphne Du Maurier. Avon Books, 1997. 410 p.
ISBN 9780380730407

1. Remarriage 2. Family estates 3. Rich people 4. Widowers 5. Household employees 6. Cornwall, England 7. Gothic fiction 8. Psychological suspense 9. Books to movies

A classic novel of romantic suspense finds the second Mrs. Maxim de Winter entering the home of her mysterious and enigmatic new husband and learning the story of the house's first mistress, to whom the sinister housekeeper is unnaturally devoted.

Sequel: Mrs. de Winter, by Susan Hill.

Originally published: London : V. Gollancz, 1938.

Dunant, Sarah

The **birth** of Venus: a novel. Sarah Dunant. Random House, 2004. 400 p.
ISBN 9781400060733

1. Savonarola, Girolamo 2. Women painters 3. Married women 4. Man-woman relationships 5. Teenage girls 6. Painters 7. Florence, Italy 8. 15th century 9. Historical fiction 10. Adult books for young adults
LC 2003046932

Turning fifteen in Renaissance Florence, Alessandra Cecchi becomes intoxicated with the works of a young painter whom her father has brought to the city to decorate the family's Florentine palazzo.

"Part feverish thriller, part historical romance, the story of the outspoken heroine's sentimental education—a comprehensive curriculum including every conceivable transgression—sometimes comes off as a heady blend of Browning's My Last Duchess and Anaïs Nin. But Dunant's skill lies in combining these elements with a finely textured and pertinent depiction of a cultured citizenry in the grip of rampant fundamentalism." —*The New Yorker*

Blood and beauty: a novel. Sarah Dunant. Random House, 2013. 506 p.
ISBN 9781400069293

1. Borgia, Lucrezia 2. Political corruption 3. Nobility 4. Church and state 5. Siblings 6. Ambition 7. Italy 8. Renaissance (1300-1600) 9. 16th century 10. Biographical fiction 11. Historical fiction
LC 2012042215

A tale inspired by the lives of Borgia siblings Lucretia and Cesare traces the family's rise in the aftermath of Rodrigo Borgia's rise to the papacy, during which war, a terrifying sexual plague, and the family's notorious reputation forge an intimate bond between brother and sister.

"An impressively confident, capable sweep through the corrupt politics and serpentine relationships of a legendary family." —*Kirkus*

In the company of the courtesan: a novel. Sarah Dunant. Random House, 2006. 400 p.
ISBN 9781400063819

1. Courtesans 2. Little people 3. Courts and courtiers 4. Women who are blind 5. Lovers 6. Venice, Italy 7. Renaissance (1300-1600) 8. 16th century 9. Historical fiction 10. First person narratives
LC 2005051649

In 1527, when the city of Rome is sacked and burned by an invading army, the famed courtesan Fiammetta Bianchini and her dwarf companion, Bucino Teodoldi, escape to the wealthy and powerful city of Venice in order to rebuild their business.

"This historical novel follows the fortunes of a beautiful, flame-haired courtesan, Fiammetta Bianchini, who, after escaping from the 1527 pillage of Rome, sets up shop in Venice. The novel, narrated by Fiammetta's servant, a dwarf, chronicles the pair's horrific scrapes and their dizzying triumphs, which include Fiammetta's becoming Titian's model for his Venus of Urbino. Along the way, Dunant presents a lively and detailed acccount of the glimmering palaces and murky alleys of Renaissance Venice, and examines the way the city's clerics and prostitutes alike are bound by its peculiar dynamic of opulence and restraint." —*The New Yorker*

Sacred hearts: a novel. Sarah Dunant. Random House, 2009. 432 p.
ISBN 9781400063826

1. Nuns 2. Imprisonment 3. Convents 4. Interpersonal conflict 5. Women — Social conditions 6. Italy 7. Ferrara, Italy 8. 16th century 9. Historical fiction
LC 2009002246

Shortlisted for the Walter Scott Prize for Historical Fiction, 2010

1570 in the Italian city of Ferrara. Sixteen-year-old Serafina is ripped by her family from an illicit love affair and forced into the convent of Santa Caterina, renowned for its superb music. Serafina's one weapon is her glorious voice, but she refuses to sing. Madonna Chiara, an abbess as fluent in politics as she is in prayer, finds her new charge has unleased a power play rebellion, ecstasies and hysterias within the convent. However, watching over Serafina is Zuana, the sister in charge of the infirmary, who understands and might even challenge her incarceration.

Originally published: 2009.

Duncan, Glen

By blood we live. Glen Duncan. Alfred A. Knopf, 2014. 357 p. (The last werewolf trilogy, 3)
ISBN 9780307595102

1. Werewolves 2. Vampires 3. Animal behavior 4. Supernatural 5. London, England 6. Literary fiction 7. Horror 8. First person narratives

A conclusion to the best-selling saga finds Talulla settling down with her werewolf family only to be tormented by a fanatical cult and nagging thoughts about ancient vampire Remshi, who believes he knows Talulla from another time.

"[T]here are plenty of battles, blood, and sexy escapades; but the real treats continues to be Duncan's beautifully twisted way with language and the profound thesis he poses about humanity." —*Booklist*

The **last** werewolf. Glen Duncan. Alfred A. Knopf, 2011. 293 p. (The last werewolf trilogy, 1)
ISBN 9780307595089

1. Werewolves 2. Self-destructive behavior in men 3. Animal behavior 4. Human behavior 5. Love 6. London, England 7. Horror 8. Literary fiction 9. First person narratives

New York Times Notable Book, 2011

Rendered the last of his kind after a colleague's death, two-hundred-year-old werewolf Jake struggles with depression and contemplates suicide until powerful forces that have personal agendas and the power to keep him alive take over his life.

"A yarn about a Kant-quoting lycanthrope on the run from monster hunters bent on rendering his species extinct. Take that, True Blood fans! Duncan creates a world that is completely imagined, if occasionally implausible." —*Entertainment Weekly*

Sequel: Talulla Rising.

Talulla rising. Glen Duncan. Alfred A. Knopf, 2012. 368 p. (The last werewolf trilogy, 2)
ISBN 9780307595096

1. Werewolves 2. Single mothers 3. Mother and child 4. Protectiveness in women 5. Animal behavior 6. London, England 7. Literary fiction 8. Horror 9. First person narratives

After losing her werewolf lover Jake and giving birth to a son, Talullah confronts a psychotic new WOCOP leader, an unlikely human lover, blood-drinking religious fanatics, a pack of London werewolves, and the world's oldest living vampire.

Sequel to: The Last Werewolf.

Dundas, Chad
The **blaze**. Chad Dundas. G. P. Putnam's Sons, 2020. 374 p.
ISBN 9780399176098
1. Veterans 2. Amnesia 3. Psychic trauma 4. Women journalists 5. Murder investigation 6. Montana 7. Thrillers and suspense

One man knows the connection between two extraordinary acts of arson, 15 years apart, in his Montana hometown—if only he could remember it.

"Dundas's insightful look at a former soldier's attempts to reenter civilian life elevates this poignant, action-packed story. The plot soars with each believable twist and realistic characters worth rooting for." —*Publishers Weekly*

Dunmore, Evie
★ **Bringing** down the duke. Evie Dunmore. Berkley Jove, 2019. 368 p. (League of extraordinary women novels, 1)
ISBN 9781984805683
1. Suffragist movement 2. McKinley, William 3. Universities and colleges 4. Gender role 5. Rich men 6. Oxford, England 7. England 8. Victorian era (1837-1901) 9. Victorian romances 10. Historical romances
LC 2018060569
Library Journal Best Books, 2019; LibraryReads Favorites, 2019

Recruiting men of influence to champion the rising women's suffrage movement of 1879 England, a daring Oxford rebel targets a cold and calculating duke before their unexpected romance threatens to upend the British social order.

Dunmore, Helen
Exposure. Helen Dunmore. Atlantic Monthly Press, 2016. 391 p.
ISBN 9780802124937
1. Cold War 2. Espionage 3. Secrets 4. Spies 5. England 6. 1960s 7. Spy fiction 8. Historical thrillers

A missing top-secret file poses a terrible dilemma for colleagues Giles Holloway and Simon Callington at the height of the Cold War in London, where Simon's wife, Lily, resolves to protect their family, only to be devastatingly exposed.

"Dunmore deftly creates a noir atmosphere, revealing layers of complexity in personal relationships darkened by non-battlefield conflict and blending psychological observations reminiscent of Henry James with le Carre-esque betrayals." —*Publishers Weekly*

The **lie**. Helen Dunmore. Atlantic Monthly Press, 2014. 294 pages
ISBN 9780802122544
1. Veterans 2. Memories 3. World War I 4. Villages 5. Loss (Psychology) 6. England 7. France 8. Between the Wars (1918-1939) 9. 1920s 10. Historical fiction
Shortlisted for the Walter Scott Prize for Historical Fiction, 2015

Returning to the small Cornish town where he was born after surviving World War I, Daniel is haunted by memories of his closest friend and his first love before suffering the unforeseen consequences of a lie.

"From the first page, Dunmore shares Daniel's inner life, building an increasing sense of dread while exposing the tragedy of great promise thwarted by forces beyond Daniel's control. Dunmore's crystalline prose is almost too good; the pain she describes is often unbearable to read, yet the emotional power resonates, and Daniel is impossible to forget." —*Kirkus*
First published: London: Hutchinson, 2014.

Dunn, Kate
The **Dragonfly**. Kate Dunn. Aurora Metro, 2017. 320 p.
ISBN 9781911501039
1. Fathers and sons 2. Grandfather and granddaughter 3. Dysfunctional families 4. Widowers 5. Nine-year-old girls 6. Mainstream fiction

When Colin discovers his son is being held on a murder charge in France, he trails his boat, The Dragonfly, across the channel to help. There he meets his granddaughter for the first time, and they embark on a journey through the French canals, where they land big fish and uncover burning secrets. But can Colin get his son off the hook?

Dunn, Katherine
Geek love. Katherine Dunn. A. A. Knopf, 1989. 347 p.
ISBN 9780394569024
1. Little people 2. Birth defects 3. People with disabilities 4. Carnivals 5. Sideshows 6. Black humor 7. Transgressive fiction 8. Picaresque fiction
LC 88045776
National Book Award for Fiction finalist, 1989

Aloysious and Lillian Binewski, proprietors of a traveling carnival, attempt to reduce overhead by breeding their own freak show, with tragic results.

"This raw, shocking view of the human condition, a glimpse of the tormented people who live on the fringe, makes readers confront the dark, mad elements in every society.... A brilliant, suspenseful, heartbreaking tour de force." —*Publishers Weekly*

Dunn, Mark
Ella Minnow Pea: a progressively lipogrammatic epistolary fable. Mark Dunn. MacAdam/Cage Pub, 2001. 205 p.
ISBN 9780967370163
1. Communes 2. Islands 3. Lipograms 4. South Carolina 5. Epistolary novels 6. Adult books for young adults
LC 2001042585

Recounts what happens when the citizens of an island must rely on all their ingenuity to communicate in an increasingly limited language when the goverment progressively bans letters from the alphabet.

Dunne, Dominick
People like us: a novel. Dominick Dunne. Crown Publishers, 1988. 403 p.
ISBN 9780345430540
1. Rich people 2. Upper class 3. Divorced men 4. Journalists 5. Scandals 6. Manhattan, New York City 7. 1980s 8. Satirical fiction
LC 88000353

Gus Bailey, the confidant of New York society, observes the social repercussions of socialite Justine Altemus's engagement to TV anchorman Bernie Slatkin and inadvertently precipitates a social explosion.

"Engaging us in his characters' concerns and then pulling multiple story strands into a tight knot, Dominick Dunne demonstrates with wit and accuracy the delicate, merciless distinction between 'people like that' and 'people like us'." —*New York Times Book Review*

Sequel: Too much money.

Too much money. Dominick Dunne. Crown Publishers, 2009. 275 p. ISBN 9780609603871

1. Rich people 2. Upper class 3. Journalists 4. Authors 5. Senior men 6. Manhattan, New York City 7. New York City 8. Satirical fiction

Writer Gus Bailey witnesses the disappearance of the old-money society that once occupied him and investigates the murder of one of the world's wealthiest men, an effort that is sabotaged by the man's calculating wife and schemers within Gus's own set.

"The novel opens with an Easter luncheon in a vast Park Avenue apartment that ironically marks the decline of its owner, a well-bred old guard woman named Lil Altemus. Gus Bailey, Dunne's alter ego, is in attendance. He's a journalist who works for a high-society magazine and is about to write a novel about widowed Perla Zacharias, one of the wealthiest women in the world, who, because of dubious origins, has been held down from New York society's highest ranks. Zacharias is not happy with the news about the novel and takes appropriate measures to block it.... Dunne shows a little more affection for his subjects than Capote, but not that much. Too little sympathy and you have acid satire. Too much and you have a sentimental portrait. Dunne does it just about right. After you finish his portrayal of the very rich, you may somehow be satisfied with the knowledge of just how poorly they live." —*San Francisco Chronicle*

Sequel to: People like us.

Dunnett, Dorothy

Niccolo rising. Dorothy Dunnett. Random House, 1999. Viii, 470 p. : Map (House of Niccolo, 1)
ISBN 9780375704772

1. Widows 2. Heirs and heiresses 3. Apprentices 4. Mercenaries 5. Upper class 6. Europe 7. Renaissance (1300-1600) 8. 15th century 9. Family sagas 10. Historical fiction 11. Adventure stories

LC 86045306

Sent to Italy by his guardian Marian, the widowed owner of a Bruges trading house, Claes, a reckless boy and seeming simpleton, develops into a sophisticated adventurer known as Niccolo, in a colorful novel of late fifteenth-century Europe.

Includes endpaper maps.

Originally published: London : Michael Joseph, 1986.

Dupont, Eric

The **American** fiancee: a novel. Eric Dupont; translated from the French by Peter McCambridge. HarperCollins, 2020. 608 p.
ISBN 9780062947451

1. Families 2. War 3. Love 4. Womanizers 5. Generations 6. Quebec (Province) 7. 20th century 8. Literary fiction 9. Family sagas 10. Translations

LC 2019030730

Follows three generations of the Lamontagnes family as they travel the world experiencing passion, jealousy, revenge and death, from the family patriarch, Louis, who served in World War II to his ladies' man grandson, Gabriel.

"While the intensity of Dupont's prose can be maddening, the sweet, sour, and salty world he creates is thoroughly addictive." —*Kirkus*

Translation of: La fiancee americaine.

Originally published: Montreal : Marchand de feuilles, 2012.

Translated from the French.

Durham, David Anthony

★ **Gabriel's** story. David Anthony Durham. Doubleday, 2001. 291 p. ISBN 9780385498142

1. African American families 2. African American cowboys 3. Pioneer men 4. Young men 5. Homesteaders 6. Kansas 7. Westerns 8. Coming-of-age stories 9. African American fiction 10. Adult books for young adults

LC 25291

Alex Award, 2002; BCALA Literary Award for First Novelist, 2002; Booklist Editors' Choice, 2001; Hurston/Wright Legacy Award: Debut Fiction, 2002; New York Times Notable Book, 2001

Reluctantly moving with his mother and younger brother from the urban East to join his stepfather, a Kansas homesteader, Gabriel hates their primitive, harsh new life and runs away to seek adventure as a cowboy, in a coming-of-age story of a young black man in the American West of the 1870s.

"The moral gravity of Durham's narrative is offset by his attentiveness to the primacy of nature in the Western landscape." —*The New Yorker*

Durrell, Lawrence

★ **Justine**. Lawrence Durrell. Penguin Books, 1991. 253 p. (Alexandria quartet, 1)
ISBN 9780140153194

1. Extramarital affairs 2. Authors 3. Jewish women 4. Married women 5. Copts 6. Alexandria, Egypt 7. Egypt 8. Between the Wars (1918-1939) 9. Literary fiction 10. Modern classics

Justine is the first volume of the author's Alexandria quartet, four interlinked novels set in Alexandria, Egypt just before the Second World War.

"Set in Alexandria the story concerns the amorous adventures of a penniless young man, a prostitute who lives with him, the rich and beautiful Justine with whom he has an affair, and Justine's husband." —*Publishers Weekly*

Originally published: London : Faber & Faber, 1957.

Durrow, Heidi W.

The **girl** who fell from the sky: a novel. Heidi W. Durrow. Algonquin Books of Chapel Hill, 2010. 264 p.
ISBN 9781565126800

1. Multiracial children 2. Identity (Psychology) 3. Intergenerational relations 4. Children of suicide victims 5. Abandoned girls 6. Psychological fiction 7. Coming-of-age stories 8. Literary fiction 9. Adult books for young adults

LC 2009027572

Bellwether Prize for Fiction, 2008

After a family tragedy orphans her, Rachel, the daughter of a Danish mother and a black G.I, moves into her grandmother's mostly black community in the 1980s, where she must swallow her grief and confront her identity as a biracial woman in a world that wants to see her as either black or white.

"Set in the 1980s and focusing luminously on one unusually sympathetic girl overcoming apocalyptic tragedy and navigating her way through nascent sexuality and racial tensions, Durrow's novel transcends topicality." —*Christian Science Monitor*

Durst, Sarah Beth

The **queen** of blood. Sarah Beth Durst. Harper Voyager, 2016. 353 p. (Queens of Renthia, 1)
ISBN 9780062413345

1. Women students 2. Warriors 3. Quests 4. Women rulers 5. Spirits 6. Epic fantasy 7. Adult books for young adults

LC 2015044319

Alex Award, 2017

Daleina, a young student, joins forces with a disgraced warrior, Ven, to embark on an epic and treacherous quest to save their realm from the spirits that want to rid it of all human life.

"In addition to a solid cast of characters and great political intrigue, Durst delivers some fascinating worldbuilding, and the spirits are malevolent, cunning, wild, and mysterious antagonists." —*Publishers Weekly*

Race the sands. Sarah Beth Durst. Harper Voyager, 2020. 368 p.
ISBN 9780062888617
1. Imaginary places 2. Abused women 3. Monsters 4. Training 5. Reincarnation 6. Epic fantasy

Life, death, and rebirth: in Becar, who you are in this life will determine your next life. Yet there is hope—you can change your destiny with the choices you make. But for the darkest individuals, there is no redemption: you come back as a kehok, a monster, and are doomed to be a kehok for the rest of time. Unless you can win the Races.

"Durst consistently defies expectations in both plot and characterization while exploring sophisticated themes of found family, integrity, and morality. This excellent epic fantasy will appeal to adult fans of YA authors Tamora Pierce and Megan Whalen Turner." —*Publishers Weekly*

Dybek, Nick

The **Verdun** affair: a novel. By Nick Dybek. Scribner, 2018. 320 p.
ISBN 9781501191763
1. Postwar life 2. War casualties 3. People with amnesia 4. Widows 5. Missing in action 6. France 7. Verdun, France 8. Between the Wars (1918-1939) 9. 1950s 10. Historical fiction 11. Parallel narratives

LC 2017061760

A sweeping novel, set in Europe in the aftermath of World War I and Los Angeles in the 1950s follows a lonely young man, a beautiful widow and the amnesiac soldier whose puzzling case binds them together even as it tears them apart.

Dybek, Stuart

I sailed with Magellan. Stuart Dybek. Farrar, Straus and Giroux, 2003. 307 p.
ISBN 9780374174071
1. Polish American boys 2. Polish American men 3. Polish Americans 4. Polish American families 5. Neighborhoods 6. South Side, Chicago, Illinois 7. Chicago, Illinois 8. 1950s 9. 1960s 10. Short stories 11. Adult books for young adults

LC 2003049052

ALA Notable Book, 2005; Booklist Editors' Choice, 2003; New York Times Notable Book, 2003

A collection of eleven short works is set in the urban areas of Chicago's South Side, where imaginative protagonist Perry Katzek encounters such events as a boy's musical performances on behalf of a drinking uncle, and a thug's distraction by multiple ex-girlfriends.

"The episodes that intersect and surround young Perry Katzek's upbringing in the Polish-Mexican ghetto of Chicago's South Side are simultaneously daring and compassionate, intimate in detail and mythic in scale. Dybek has the rare ability to dart back and forth in time and slide around recklessly in space while carrying the reader effortlessly with him." —*Washington Post Book World.*

11 interlocking short stories.

Dyer, Geoff

Jeff in Venice, death in Varanasi. Geoff Dyer. Pantheon Books, 2009. 296 p.
ISBN 9780307377371
1. Journalists 2. British in India 3. Desire in men 4. Forties (Age) 5. Man-woman relationships 6. Venice, Italy 7. India 8. Literary fiction

LC 2008023759

New York Times Notable Book, 2009

Jeff Atman is a British journalist on assignment in Venice who feels disillusioned with his hedonistic way of living, while a narrator in the Indian holy city of Varanasi practices detachment and meditates on art and spiritual matters.

"This novel is zany and deceptively light, even as Atman explores the meaning of life and enlightenment. Does it matter whether the unnamed hero of the second part is Jeff or Geoff? Or whether the stories in Venice and Varanasi are the same story? You can read this novel as if you're munching a burger or savoring a ribeye." —*St. Louis Post-Dispatch*

Dykes, Amanda

Whose waves these are. Amanda Dykes. Bethany House, 2019. 361 pages
ISBN 9780764234132
1. War memorials 2. Loss (Psychology) 3. Women anthropologists 4. Great-uncles 5. Letter carriers 6. Maine 7. Christian historical fiction 8. Parallel narratives 9. Family sagas

LC 2018048925

Christy Award for Book of the Year, 2020; Christy Award for Contemporary (Stand Alone) Category, 2020

In the wake of WWII, a grieving fisherman submits a poem to a local newspaper asking readers to send rocks in honor of loved ones to create something life-giving—but the building halts when tragedy strikes. Decades later, Annie returns to the coastal Maine town, where stone ruins spark her curiosity and her search for answers faces a battle against time.

E

Earley, Tony

Jim the boy: a novel. Tony Earley. Little, Brown, 2000. 227 p.
ISBN 9780316199643
1. Ten-year-old boys 2. Boys 3. Small town life 4. Families 5. Father-separated boys 6. North Carolina 7. Depression era (1929-1941) 8. Historical fiction 9. Coming-of-age stories 10. Southern fiction

LC 9942901

Booklist Editors' Choice: Adult Fiction for Young Adults, 2000; New York Times Notable Book, 2000

Describes the life of a young boy in a small southern town in the early twentieth century as he begins to explore the confusing adult world that surrounds him and begins to take his own first steps toward maturity.

"The genius of a novel like this is Earley's trust in the purity of his style and the plainness of his story. Perhaps all things done very well look simple." —*Christian Science Monitor*

Sequel: The blue star.

Mr. Tall: a novella and stories. Tony Earley. Little, Brown & Co, 2014. 242 p.
ISBN 9780316246125

1. Small towns 2. Couples 3. Interpersonal relations 4. Southern states 5. Short stories 6. Literary fiction

A collection of short stories and one novella features tales about a widow being visited by Bigfoot and an elderly woman plagued by Jesse James' ghost.

Eason, K.

How Rory Thorne destroyed the multiverse. K. Eason. DAW Books, 2019. 408 p. (Thorne chronicles, 1)

ISBN 9780756415297

1. Princesses 2. Royal pretenders 3. Magic 4. Inheritance and succession 5. Space stations 6. Space opera 7. Science fiction

Rory Thorne is a princess with thirteen fairy blessings, the most important of which is to see through flattery and platitudes. As the eldest daughter, she always imagined she'd inherit her father's throne and govern the interplanetary Thorne Consortium. Then her father is assassinated, her mother gives birth to a son, and Rory is betrothed to the prince of a distant world. When Rory arrives in her new home, she uncovers a treacherous plot to unseat her newly betrothed and usurp his throne. An unscrupulous minister has conspired to name himself Regent to the minor (and somewhat foolish) prince. With only her wits and a small team of allies, Rory must outmaneuver the Regent and rescue the prince.

Ebershoff, David

The **19th** wife: a novel. David Ebershoff. Random House, 2008. 514 p. ISBN 9781400063970

1. Young, Ann Eliza 2. Mormons 3. Polygamy 4. Fundamentalists 5. Gay men 6. Families 7. Utah 8. 19th century 9. 21st century 10. Parallel narratives 11. Historical fiction 12. Multiple perspectives

LC 2008000074

The complex history of polygamy in the Mormon Church intertwines the story of Ann Eliza Young, the nineteenth and final wife of Brigham Young, who in 1875 leaves her husband and embarks on crusade to end polygamy, and a modern-day murder mystery in which a polygamous man has been found dead and one of his wives is accused of the crime.

"This novel tells two parallel stories of polygamy. The first recounts Brigham Young's expulsion of one of his wives, Ann Eliza, from the Mormon Church; the second is a modern-day murder mystery set in a polygamous compound in Utah. Unfolding through an impressive variety of narrative forms—Wikipedia entries, academic research papers, newspaper opinion pieces—the stories include fascinating historical details.... Ebershoff demonstrates abundant virtuosity, as he convincingly inhabits the voices of both a nineteenth-century Mormon wife and a contemporary gay youth excommunicated from the church, while also managing to say something about the mysterious power of faith." —*The New Yorker*

The **Danish** girl: a novel. By David Ebershoff. Viking, 2000. 270 p. ISBN 9780670888085

1. Elbe, Lili 2. Painters 3. Trans women 4. Transitioning (Gender identity) 5. Love 6. Married men — Sexuality 7. Biographical fiction 8. Psychological fiction 9. Historical fiction

LC 99034890

Lambda Literary Award for Transgender/Bisexual, 2000; New York Times Notable Book, 2000

Set in decadent 1920s Copenhagen, this tender tale of love and marriage in the midst of fundamental crisis introduces a man who discovers he's a woman and the woman who will do anything for him.

"Ebershoff's poignant and visionary conclusion is a fitting one for what is, above all, and despite its sensationalist trimmings, a profound and beautifully realized love story." —*Publishers Weekly*

The Danish Girl was adapted into a movie of the same name in 2015.

Eco, Umberto

Baudolino. Umberto Eco; translated from the Italian by William Weaver. Harcourt, Inc, 2002. 528 p.

ISBN 9780151006908

1. Storytelling 2. Dishonesty 3. Courts and courtiers 4. Adopted children 5. Crusades 6. Europe 7. Medieval period (476-1492) 8. 12th century 9. Historical fiction 10. Literary fiction 11. Translations

LC 2002002345

Booklist Editors' Choice, 2002; New York Times Notable Book, 2002

Born a simple peasant in northern Italy, Baudolino narrates the story of his life, from his adoption by Emperor Frederick Barbarossa and his education in Paris to his arrival in Constantinople during the turmoil of the Fourth Crusade.

"In this whimsical yet deadly earnest tale, Eco puts forth the question that perpetually beguiles him and with which he beguiles the rest of us: If a teller of tales tells us he's telling the truth, how can we know for sure what really happened?" —*The New Yorker*

★ **Foucault's** pendulum. Umberto Eco; translated from the Italian by William Weaver. Harcourt Brace Jovanovich, 1989. 641 p.

ISBN 9780151327652

1. Conspiracy theories 2. Elbe, Lili 3. Missing persons 4. Literary fiction 5. Translations

LC 89032212

A wily group of editors devises a mock formula for tapping the mystical powers of the universe, only to set off a series of mysterious disappearances.

"This book is not meant to be easy.... [But] great are the rewards for those who actually manage to read it. For while it is not a novel in the strict sense of the word, it is a truly formidable gathering of information delivered playfully by a master manipulating his own invention in effect, a long, erudite joke." —*New York Times Book Review*

The **island** of the day before. Umberto Eco; translated from the Italian by William Weaver. Harcourt Brace & Co, 1995. 515 p.

ISBN 9780151001514

1. Shipwrecks 2. Flashbacks 3. Paradoxes 4. Missing persons 5. Europe 6. 17th century 7. Literary fiction 8. Translations

LC 95007594

A panoramic historical novel set in the seventeenth century follows a young aristocrat who goes to sea to find love and an old Jesuit with a boundless scientific knowledge

"Umberto Eco's narrative surface is sensually alluring, cool and glittery, but for all its lucidity and charm, there is always something else going on.... This novel is really a book about telling, reminding us that the only clarity we are capable of reaching is the story we tell to compel time and the universe to take on meaning." —*New York Times Book Review*

Translation of L'isola del giorno prima.

The **mysterious** flame of Queen Loana: an illustrated novel. Umberto Eco; translated from the Italian by Geoffrey Brock. Harcourt, 2005. 480 p.

ISBN 9780151011407

1. People with amnesia 2. Memory 3. Memories 4. Antiquarian booksellers 5. Amnesia 6. Italy 7. Milan, Italy 8. Psychological fiction 9. Literary fiction 10. Translations

LC 2004029105

Booklist Editors' Choice, 2005

Having suffered a complete loss of memory regarding every aspect of his identity, Yambo withdraws to a family home outside of Milan, where he sorts through boxes of old records and experiences memories in the form of a graphic novel.

"Those who don't enjoy the occasional ramble through Bartlett's Quotations may quickly lose patience with Queen Loana, but bookworms

will get an added kick out of puzzling out the dozens of literary allusions." —*Christian Science Monitor*
Includes bibliographical references.

★ The **name** of the rose. Umberto Eco; translated from the Italian by William Weaver. Harcourt Brace, 1994. 536 p. Illustration
ISBN 9780156001311
1. Librarians 2. Monastic libraries 3. Murder 4. Monks 5. European Renaissance 6. Italy 7. Medieval period (476-1492) 8. 14th century 9. Medieval mysteries 10. Historical mysteries 11. Literary fiction
LC 94013818
In 1327, finding his sensitive mission at an Italian abbey further complicated by seven bizarre deaths, Brother William of Baskerville turns detective.
"This novel is an antidetective-story detective story; as a semiotic murder mystery it is superbly entertaining; it is also an extraordinary work of novelistic art." —*Harper's*
A Helen and Kurt Wolff book.
This translation originally published: London;: Secker & Warburg, 1983. Originally published in Italy in 1980 under the title Il nome della rose.

Numero zero. Umberto Eco; translated from the Italian by Richard Dixon. Houghton Mifflin Harcourt, 2015. 191 p.
ISBN 9780544635081
1. Journalism 2. Corruption 3. Newspapers 4. Journalists 5. Ghostwriters 6. Italy 7. 1990s 8. Political fiction 9. Satirical fiction 10. Literary fiction
Follows the employees of a mudslinging newspaper in 1992 as they try to identify a dead body that appears in a back alley in Milan.
"Eco combines his delight in suspense with astute political satire in this brainy, funny, neatly lacerating thriller." —*Booklist*
Originally published in Italian: Milan : Bompiani, 2015.

Edgerton, Clyde
★ **Walking** across Egypt: a novel. Clyde Edgerton. Algonquin Books of Chapel Hill, 1987. 216 p.
ISBN 9780912697512
1. Juvenile delinquents (Boys) 2. Intergenerational relations 3. Widows 4. Senior women 5. Septuagenarians 6. North Carolina 7. Southern States 8. Books to movies 9. Southern fiction 10. Gentle reads
LC 86020645
Mattie Rigsbee, seventy-eight and set in her ways, decides to help out Wesley Benfield, a troubled adolescent just out of reform school for car theft.
"This novel is warm, innocent, and has a charming central character." —*Booklist*
Sequel : Killer diller.

Edghill, India
Queenmaker: a novel of King David's Queen. India Edghill. St. Martin's Press, 2002. 376 p.
ISBN 9780312289188
1. Michal 2. Women in the Bible 3. Women rulers 4. Political intrigue 5. Rulers 6. Bible novels 7. Adult books for young adults
LC 2001048603
Romantic Times Reviewers' Choice Award, 2002
A retelling of the biblical story of King David and Queen Michal follows Michal, who lived and reigned in David's court for more than forty years, as she speaks about her hopes and fears while war, betrayal, death, and prophecy rage through the Promised Land.

"With its excellent writing, dynamic characters, and galloping pace, Edghill's work is highly recommended for all historical fiction collections." —*Library Journal*
Sequel: Wisdom's daughter.

Edugyan, Esi
Half-blood blues. Esi Edugyan. Picador, 2012. 321 pages
ISBN 9781250012708
1. Multiracial men 2. Jazz musicians 3. Race (Social sciences) 4. Secrets 5. Betrayal 6. Berlin, Germany 7. Paris, France 8. 1940s 9. 1990s 10. Literary fiction 11. Historical fiction 12. Canadian fiction
ALA Notable Book, 2013; BC Book Prizes, Ethel Wilson Fiction Prize, 2012; Hurston/Wright Legacy Award: Fiction, 2013; Library Journal Best Books, 2012; Scotiabank Giller Prize, 2011; Governor General's Literary Awards, English-language Fiction finalist; Rogers Writers' Trust Fiction Prize finalist, 2011; Shortlisted for the Man Booker Prize, 2011; Shortlisted for The Orange Prize for Fiction, 2012; Shortlisted for the Walter Scott Prize for Historical Fiction, 2012
Sid, the only one to witness his bandmate's disappearance at the hands of the Gestapo, breaks his silence on the incident over fifty years later when the men are reunited at a documentary premiere.
Originally published: London: Serpent's Tail : 2011.

★ **Washington** Black: a novel. Esi Edugyan. Alfred A. Knopf, 2018. 333 p.
ISBN 9780525521426
1. Enslaved people 2. Betrayal 3. Fugitives 4. Science 5. Airships 6. Barbados 7. 1830s 8. 19th century 9. Historical fiction 10. Canadian fiction 11. Black Canadian fiction 12. Adult books for young adults
LC 2017058436
ALA Notable Book, 2019; Booklist Editors' Choice, 2018; Booklist Editors' Choice: Adult Books for Young Adults, 2018; New York Times Notable Book, 2018; Scotiabank Giller Prize, 2018; Andrew Carnegie Medal for Excellence in Fiction finalist, 2019; Shortlisted for the Man Booker Prize, 2018; Shortlisted for the International Dublin Literary Award, 2020
Unexpectedly chosen to be a family manservant, an 11-year-old Barbados sugar-plantation slave is initiated into a world of technology and dignity before a devastating betrayal propels him throughout the world in search of his true self.

Edwards, Kim
The **memory** keeper's daughter. Kim Edwards. Viking, 2005. 401 p.
ISBN 9780670034161
1. Children with Down syndrome 2. Fraternal twins 3. Family secrets 4. Abandoned children 5. Married people 6. Lexington, Kentucky 7. Pittsburgh, Pennsylvania 8. Psychological fiction 9. Books to movies 10. Mainstream fiction
LC 2005042257
British Book Award for Popular Fiction, 2008
In a tale spanning twenty-five years, a doctor delivers his newborn twins during a snowstorm and, rashly deciding to protect his wife from their baby daughter's affliction with Down Syndrome, turns her over to a nurse, who secretly raises the child.

Edwards, Louis
Ramadan Ramsey: a novel. By Louis Edwards. Amistad Press, 2021. 384 p.
ISBN 9780063012035

1. Children of immigrants 2. Refugees 3. Fathers 4. Voyages and travels 5. Betrayal 6. New Orleans, Louisiana 7. Syria 8. Historical fiction 9. Southern fiction 10. Literary fiction

LC 2020054365

When Ramadan Ramsey, the son of a ninth generation New Orleans African American and a Syrian refugee, turns 17, he sets off to find the father he has never known—an adventure-filled journey filled that takes him from NOLA to Egypt, Istanbul and finally Syria.

"A young Southern boy travels to the Middle East to find his father in this delightful and intimate modern epic." —*Kirkus*

Edwards, Rachel

Darling. Rachel Edwards. Fourth Estate, 2018. 352 p.

ISBN 9780008281113

1. Teenage girls 2. Resentfulness 3. Stepmothers 4. Stepdaughters 5. Racism in teenagers 6. England 7. Psychological suspense 8. Adult books for young adults

Lola doesn't particularly want a new stepmother. Especially not one who has come out of nowhere and only been with her dad for three months. And she's not racist or anything but since when did her dad fancy black women anyway? Darling didn't particularly want a new stepdaughter. Especially not one as spiteful and spoilt as Lola. She does want Lola's dad though. And he wants her, so that's that: Darling and Lola will just have to get used to each other. Unless Lola can find a way to get rid of Darling.

Edwards, Yvvette

The mother. Yvvette Edwards. Amistad Press, 2016. 192 p.

ISBN 9780062440778

1. Mothers 2. Grief in women 3. Trials (Murder) 4. Mothers of murder victims 5. Criminal evidence 6. Psychological fiction

A mother copes with the death of her murdered teen after learning disturbing truths about the killer's dysfunctional family.

Egan, Greg

Perihelion summer. Greg Egan. St Martins Pr 2019. 208 p.

ISBN 9781250313782

1. Disasters 2. Black holes (Astronomy) 3. Global environmental change 4. Science — Public opinion 5. Climate change 6. Australia 7. Earth 8. Hard science fiction 9. Apocalyptic fiction 10. Science fiction

Taraxippus is coming: a black hole one tenth the mass of the sun is about to enter the solar system. By the time it leaves, the conditions of life across the globe will be changed forever.

Phoresis. Greg Egan. Subterranean Press, 2018. 168 p.

ISBN 9781596068667

1. Planets 2. Women 3. Aliens (Humanoid) 4. Space colonies 5. Intergenerational relations 6. Hard science fiction

Welcome to Tvibura and Tviburi, the richly imagined twin planets that stand at the center of Greg Egan's extraordinary new novella.

Schild's ladder. By Greg Egan. EOS, 2002. 342 p. : Illustration

ISBN 9780061050930

1. Far future 2. Scientists 3. Space flight 4. Vacuum 5. Research 6. Space 7. Hard science fiction 8. Science fiction 9. Watson, Edgar J.

LC 2001055583

Twenty-thousand years in the future, a dangerous experiment in quantum physics creates an expanding vacuum in space that threatens to wipe out all humanity.

"Egan writes rather forbidding novels, always grounded in real science and imbued with serious scientific speculations. This is his most uncompromising book to date." —*Booklist*

Egan, Jennifer

The **keep**. By Jennifer Egan. Alfred A. Knopf, 2006. 239 p.

ISBN 9781400043927

1. Castles 2. Revenge 3. Prisoners 4. Cousins 5. Thirties (Age) 6. Eastern Europe 7. Thrillers and suspense 8. Gothic fiction 9. Novels-within-novels 10. Adult books for young adults

LC 2006011573

New York Times Notable Book, 2006

Two decades after taking part in a childhood prank whose devastating repercussions changed their lives forever, two cousins are reunited to work on the renovation of a medieval castle in Eastern Europe, a remote, eerie site profoundly influenced by its bloody past, where the two are cut off from the outside world and doomed to reenact the horrific event from their past.

"This novel makes us think hard about one of the murkiest mysteries of all: the mystery of perception, that uncertain border where reality and imagination meet.... In a novel full of unexpected shifts and interruptions, it's amazing how deftly Egan builds a logic for her characters." —*Los Angeles Times*

★ **Manhattan** Beach: a novel. Jennifer Egan. Scribner, 2017. 352 p.

ISBN 9781476716732

1. World War II 2. Young women 3. Corruption 4. Deals 5. Divers 6. New York City 7. Second World War era (1939-1945) 8. Historical fiction 9. Literary fiction

LC 2017029043

Andrew Carnegie Medal for Excellence in Fiction, 2018; Booklist Editors' Choice, 2017; LibraryReads Favorites, 2017; Loan Stars Favourites, 2017; New York Times Notable Book, 2017; Longlisted for the National Book Award for Fiction, 2017; Longlisted for The Women's Prize for Fiction, 2018; Shortlisted for the Walter Scott Prize for Historical Fiction, 2018

Years after she is placed in the hands of a stranger vital to her family's survival, Anna takes a job at the Brooklyn Naval Yard during the war while meeting with the man who helped them and learning important truths about her father's disappearance.

"Realistically detailed, poetically charged, and utterly satisfying: apparently there's nothing Egan can't do." —*Kirkus*

Map on endpapers.

★ A **visit** from the Goon Squad. Jennifer Egan. Alfred A. Knopf, 2010. 273 p.

ISBN 9780307592835

1. Punk rock musicians 2. Music industry and trade 3. Change 4. Sound recording executives and producers 5. Senior men 6. Psychological fiction 7. Literary fiction

LC 2009046496

ALA Notable Book, 2011; Booklist Editors' Choice, 2010; Library Journal Best Books, 2010; Los Angeles Times Book Prize for Fiction, 2010; National Book Critics Circle Award for Fiction, 2010; New York Times Notable Book, 2010; Pulitzer Prize for Fiction, 2011; Shortlisted for the International IMPAC Dublin Literary Award, 2012

Working side-by-side for a record label, former punk rocker Bennie Salazar and the passionate Sasha hide illicit secrets from one another while interacting with a motley assortment of equally troubled people from 1970s San Francisco to the post-war future.

"This novel is centered, nominally, on the aging owner of an independent record label and his comely, kleptomania-prone assistant. But it is in fact a frequently dazzling piece of layer-cake meta-fiction, told via a sprawling constellation of characters and linked vignettes that spill from the late'70s Bay Area punk scene to the African plains, the dissolute slums of Naples, and the flush New York suburbs of the '90s boom. Egan's expert flaying of human foibles has the compulsive allure of poking at a sore tooth: excruciating but exhilarating, too." —*Entertainment Weekly*

Eggers, Dave

The **circle**. Dave Eggers. Knopf, 2013. 504 p.
ISBN 9780385351393
1. Near future 2. Technology 3. Surveillance 4. Internet industry and trade 5. Social media 6. Satirical fiction 7. Books to movies
LC 2013032894
Booklist Editors' Choice, 2013; New York Times Notable Book, 2013
Hired to work for the Circle, the world's most powerful Internet company, Mae Holland begins to questions her luck as life beyond her job grows distant, a strange encounter with a colleague leaves her shaken, and her role at the Circle becomes increasingly public.
Adapted into a film by the same title in 2016.

A **hologram** for the king: a novel. Dave Eggers. McSweeney's Books, 2012. 312 p.
ISBN 9781936365746
1. Americans in Saudi Arabia 2. Businesspeople 3. Recession (Economics) 4. Household finances 5. Interracial friendship 6. Saudi Arabia 7. Social science fiction 8. Science fiction 9. Books to movies
New York Times Notable Book, 2012; ALA Notable Book, 2013; National Book Award for Fiction finalist, 2012
In a Saudi Arabian city, far from weary, recession-scarred America, a struggling businessman attempts to avoid foreclosure, pay his daughter's college tuition, and finally do something great.
Adapted into a film in 2016 under the same title.

How we are hungry: stories. By Dave Eggers. Vintage, 2005. 240 p.
ISBN 9781400095568
1. Friendship 2. Family relationships 3. Interpersonal relations 4. Man-woman relationships 5. Social acceptance 6. Psychological fiction 7. Short stories
LC 2005042321
New York Times Notable Book, 2005
A debut collection of short stories presents a compelling cast of characters who struggle with inconvenient revelations, from the deserts of Egypt to the side of Interstate 5.

What is the what: the autobiography of Valentino Achak Deng. By Dave Eggers. McSweeney's, 2006. 386 p.
ISBN 9781932416640
1. Deng, Valentino Achak 2. Father-separated boys 3. Civil war 4. Survival 5. Refugees, Sudanese 6. Poverty 7. Sudan 8. Biographical fiction 9. First person narratives 10. Adult books for young adults
Booklist Editors' Choice, 2006; New York Times Notable Book, 2007; National Book Critics Circle Award for Fiction finalist, 2006
A biographical novel traces the story of Valentino Achak Deng, who as a boy was separated from his family when his village in southern Sudan was attacked, and became one of the estimated 17,000 "lost boys of Sudan" before relocating from a Kenyan refugeecamp to Atlanta in 2001.
"Eggers has made the outlines of the tragedy in East Africa—so vague to so many Americans—not only sharp and clear but indelible. An eloquent testimony to the power of storytelling, What Is the What is an extraordinary work of witness, and of art." —*New York Times Book Review*

Ehirim, Nnamdi

Prince of monkeys. Nnamdi Ehirim. Counterpoint, 2019. 304 p.
ISBN 9781640091672
1. Young men 2. Friendship 3. Social mobility 4. Political persecution 5. Corruption 6. Lagos, Nigeria 7. Nigeria 8. Coming-of-age stories 9. Literary fiction 10. Adult books for young adults
LC 2018044345
Growing up in middle-class Lagos, Nigeria during the late 1980s and early 1990s, Ihechi forms a band of close friends discovering Lagos together as teenagers with differing opinions of everything from film to football, Fela Kuti to spirituality, sex to politics. They remain close-knit until tragedy unfolds during an anti-government riot. Nnamdi Ehirim's debut novel, Prince of Monkeys, is a lyrical, meditative observation of Nigerian life, religion, and politics at the end of the twentieth century.

Eisenberg, Deborah

The **twilight** of the superheroes. Deborah Eisenberg. Farrar, Straus and Giroux, 2006. 225 p.
ISBN 9780374299415
1. Families 2. Friendship 3. Man-woman relationships 4. New York City 5. Short stories 6. Literary fiction
LC 2005042659
New York Times Notable Book, 2006
A collection of short works includes the tales of a group of friends whose efforts to acquire a luxurious Manhattan sublet are halted by the September 11 attacks, a teacher's Roman holiday in the wake of her husband's life-threatening illness, and a brother's painful love for his schizophrenic sister.
"Using her playwright's ear for dialogue and a journalistic eye for the askew detail, Ms. Eisenberg gives us—in just a handful of pages—a visceral sense of these characters' daily routines, the worlds they inhabit and the families they rebel against or allow to define them.... Instead of forcing her characters' stories into neat, arbitrary, preordained shapes, she allows them to grow asymmetrical narratives—narratives that possess all the surprising twists and dismaying turns of real life." —*New York Times*
Six short stories.

Eisler, Barry

All the devils. Barry Eisler. Thomas & Mercer, 2019. 364 pages (Livia Lone novels, 4)
ISBN 9781542094238
1. Women detectives 2. Serial rapists 3. Missing girls 4. Government investigators 5. Thai Americans 6. Thrillers and suspense
Ordered against investigating a series of disappearances linked to his daughter's unsolved kidnapping a decade earlier, a Homeland Security agent pleads for help from Seattle detective Livia Lone, who follows leads to a twisted pair of Special Forces veterans.

The **god's** eye view. Barry Eisler. Thomas & Mercer, 2016. 374 p.
ISBN 9781503951518
1. National security 2. Intelligence service 3. Secrecy in government 4. Spies 5. Intrigue 6. Spy fiction 7. Political thrillers 8. Thrillers and suspense
Working as a camera surveillance tech for a zealous security director, Evelyn stumbles on a mysterious program code connected to a string of journalist and whistle-blower deaths before finding herself and her deaf son in the crosshairs of a sadistic bomber and her boss's enforcer.
"The agent sent to monitor her is not quite what the boss thinks, and the personal and cyberfink stories are blended beautifully." —*Booklist*

The **killer** collective. Barry Eisler. Thomas & Mercer, 2019. 401 p. (John Rain novels, 10; Livia Lone novels, 3; Ben Treven thrillers, 4)

ISBN 9781503904262

1. Tussaud, Marie 2. Elite operatives 3. Women detectives 4. Sex crimes 5. Conspiracies 6. Spy fiction 7. Thrillers and suspense

When a joint FBI-Seattle Police investigation into an international child pornography ring gets too close to powerful enemies, sex-crimes detective Livia Lone becomes the target of a hit that is offered to a retired John Rain.

Livia Lone. Barry Eisler. Thomas & Mercer, 2016. 368 p. (Livia Lone novels, 1)

ISBN 9781503939660

1. Sisters 2. Detectives 3. Human trafficking 4. Police 5. Revenge 6. Seattle, Washington 7. Thrillers and suspense

RUSA Reading List Short List, 2017

Seattle PD sex-crimes detective, and former human-trafficking victim, Livia Lone must relive the horrors of the past when she gets a fresh lead as to the whereabouts of her little sister, Nason.

The **night** trade. Barry Eisler. Thomas & Mercer, 2018. 320 p. (Livia Lone novels, 2)

ISBN 9781477820049

1. Women detectives 2. Former Marines 3. Conspiracies 4. Intelligence service 5. Human trafficking 6. Thailand 7. Thrillers and suspense

When an effort to arrest a trafficking kingpin goes violently wrong, sex-crimes detective Livia Lone forges a partnership with a former Marine sniper who is tracking the same criminal, only to uncover a conspiracy with ties to the highest levels of American intelligence.

Ekwuyasi, Francesca

Butter honey pig bread: a novel. Francesca Ekwuyasi. Arsenal Pulp Press, 2020. 368 pages

ISBN 9781551528236

1. Mothers and daughters 2. Options, alternatives, choices 3. Home (Concept) 4. Spirits 5. Twin sisters 6. Lagos, Nigeria 7. Montreal, Quebec 8. Family sagas 9. Canadian fiction 10. Relationship fiction

Governor General's Literary Awards, English-language Fiction finalist, 2020

Told through the interwoven stories of twin sisters, Kehinde and Taiye, and their mother, Kambirinachi, this is a story of choices and their consequences, of motherhood, of the malleable line between the spirit and the mind, of finding new homes and mending old ones, of voracious appetites, of queer love, of friendship, faith, and above all, family.

"Ekwuyasi's magical debut delves into the reverberating effects of a Nigerian mother's choices on her twin daughters' lives." —*Publishers Weekly*

El Akkad, Omar

American war. Omar El Akkad. Alfred A. Knopf, 2017. 333 p.

ISBN 9780451493583

1. Civil war 2. Near future 3. Child soldiers 4. Refugee camps 5. Child refugees 6. United States 7. Lincoln, Abraham 8. 21st century 9. Political fiction 10. War stories 11. Dystopian fiction 12. Adult books for young adults

LC 2016963038

ALA Notable Book, 2018; LibraryReads Favorites, 2017; New York Times Notable Book, 2017; Oregon Book Awards, Ken Kesey Award for Fiction, 2018; Longlisted for the Andrew Carnegie Medal for Excellence in Fiction, 2018; Rogers Writers' Trust Fiction Prize finalist, 2017; Shortlisted for the James Tait Black Memorial Prize for Fiction, 2017

A second American Civil War and devastating plague in the late 21st century forces a family into a camp for displaced people, where a young woman is befriended by a mysterious functionary who would transform her into a living weapon.

"El Akkad has created a brilliantly well-crafted, profoundly shattering saga of one family's suffering in a world of brutal power struggles, terrorism, ignorance, and vengeance." —*Booklist*

What strange paradise. Omar El Akkad. Alfred A Knopf, 2021. 256 p.

ISBN 9780525657903

1. Refugees 2. Shipwreck survivors 3. Rescues 4. Islands 5. Shipwrecks 6. Mediterranean Region 7. Political fiction 8. Coming-of-age stories 9. Canadian fiction

Loan Stars Favourites, 2021; Scotiabank Giller Prize, 2021

Looking at the global refugee crisis through the eyes of a child, this dramatic story follows Vanna who comes to the rescue of a 9-year-old Syrian boy who has washed up on the shores of her small island and is determined to do whatever it takes to save him..

"Akkad (American War) delivers a stirring if straightforward account of a young boy's flight from Syria during the country's civil war." —*Publishers Weekly*

El-Mohtar, Amal

★ **This** is how you lose the time war. Amal El-Mohtar and Max Gladstone. Saga Press, 2019. 198 pages

ISBN 9781534431003

1. Space and time 2. Imaginary wars and battles 3. Romantic love 4. Enemies 5. Letter writing 6. Science fiction 7. Epistolary novels 8. Love stories

Booklist Editors' Choice, 2019; Ignyte Awards: Best Novella, 2020

Two time-traveling agents from warring futures, working their way through the past, begin to exchange letters—and soon fall in love.

"The authors pack their narrative full of fanciful ideas and poignant moments, weaving a tapestry stretching across the millennia and through multiple realities thats anchored with raw emotion and a genuine sense of wonder. This short novel warrants multiple readings to fully unlock its complexities." —*Publishers Weekly*

Elias, Gerald

Danse macabre. Gerald Elias. Minotaur Books, 2010. 304 p. (Daniel Jacobus mysteries, 2)

ISBN 9780312541897

1. Violin teachers 2. Murder investigation 3. Murder suspects 4. Violin 5. Violinists 6. New York City 7. Mysteries

LC 2010021994

Library Journal Best Books, 2010

When a beloved violinist is brutally murdered and a rival performer sentenced to death for the crime, blind concert master and amateur sleuth Daniel Jacobus reluctantly reopens the investigation at his own peril.

★ **Death** and transfiguration: a Daniel Jacobus novel. Gerald Elias. Minotaur Books, 2012. 320 p. (Daniel Jacobus mysteries, 4)

ISBN 9780312678357

1. Conductors (Music) 2. Suicide investigation 3. Violin teachers 4. Jacobus, Daniel (Fictitious character) 5. Violinists 6. New York City 7. Mysteries

LC 2012005488

When an aspiring concertmaster commits suicide after being dismissed by the tyrannical conductor of a world-famous touring orchestra, blind violin teacher Daniel investigates allegations about the conductor's harassment.

Eliasberg, Jan

★ **Hannah's** war. Jan Eliasberg. Little Brown & Co, 2020. 320 p. ISBN 9780316537469

1. Women physicists 2. Jewish women 3. Armed forces — Officers 4. Options, alternatives, choices 5. Nazis 6. Germany 7. Berlin, Germany 8. Second World War era (1939-1945) 9. Historical fiction 10. Spy fiction

As a female scientist works to develop the first atomic bomb during World War II, a young military investigator is determined to uncover her secret past.

"Eliasberg moves effortlessly between Hannah's past and present to deliver a historical love story full of intrigue and suspense. Hannah's War shines a much-needed light on one of the most influential women in history." —*Booklist*

Eliot, George

★ **Adam** Bede. George Eliot; introduction by Joanna Trollope; notes by Hugh Osborne. Modern Library, 2002. Xvii, 592 p.

ISBN 9780375759017

1. Carpenters 2. Love triangles 3. Rural life 4. Clergywomen 5. Rich men 6. England 7. Literary fiction 8. Classics

LC 2001044873

Arthur's seduction of an innocent, young country girl results in remorse, suffering, and regret.

Originally published: 1859.

★ **Middlemarch:** a study of provincial life. George Eliot; with a new introduction by Michael Faber. Signet Classic, 2003. Xx, 892 p.

ISBN 9780451529176

1. Women's role 2. Young women — Relations with older men 3. Inheritance and succession 4. Physicians 5. Scholars and academics 6. England 7. 1830s 8. Psychological fiction 9. Classics 10. Domestic fiction

LC 200354205

A sensitive young woman marries a bitter, despotic scholar 30 years her senior, who lives just long enough to blight her spirit. She inherits his fortune, only to learn she will forfeit it if she marries her husband's young cousin, whom she loves. When Dorothea tries to find happiness without Ladislaw, the intricate plots, subplots and character portraits lead to a satisfying conclusion in this masterpiece of 19th-century morals and social issues.

Originally published: 1872.

★ **The mill** on the Floss. George Eliot; edited with an introduction and notes by A.S. Byatt. Penguin, 2003. 579 p.

ISBN 9780141439624

1. Women's role 2. Siblings 3. Family relationships 4. Self-fulfillment in women 5. Growing up 6. 19th century 7. Psychological fiction 8. Books to TV 9. Alexander, the Great, 356 B.C.-323 B.C

Evokes nineteenth-century rural England through the story of Maggie Tulliver, who attempts to adapt to her life until her brother forbids her to see the one person who understands her after she is found in a compromising situation.

First published in 1860.

★ **Silas** Marner: the weaver of Raveloe. George Eliot. Knopf, 1993. Xxx, 206 p.

ISBN 9780679420309

1. Recluses 2. Malicious accusation 3. Abandoned children 4. Rural life 5. Stealing 6. 19th century 7. Psychological fiction 8. Domestic fiction 9. Books to movies

Here is a tale straight from the fireside. We are compelled to follow the humble and mysterious figure of the linen weaver Silas Marner, on his journey from solitude and exile to the warmth and joy of family life. His path is a strange one; when he loses his hoard of hard-earned coins all seems to be lost, but in place of the golden guineas come the golden curls of a child and from desolate misery comes triumphant joy.

The 1994 film A simple twist of fate is loosely based on Silas Marner. Originally published: Edinburgh : William Blackwood & Sons, 1861.

Elison, Meg

The **book** of Etta. Meg Elison. 47North, 2017. 314 p. (Road to Nowhere, 2)

ISBN 9781503941823

1. Post-apocalypse 2. Midwives 3. Far future 4. Survival (after epidemics) 5. Dictators 6. Apocalyptic fiction 7. Social science fiction 8. Science fiction

Etta comes from Nowhere, a village of survivors of the great plague that wiped away the world that was. In the world that is, women are scarce and childbearing is dangerous—yet desperately necessary for humankind's future. Mothers and midwives are sacred, but Etta has a different calling. As a scavenger. Loyal to the village but living on her own terms, Etta roams the desolate territory beyond: salvaging useful relics of the ruined past and braving the threat of brutal slave traders, who are seeking women and girls to sell and subjugate.

"Elison continues to startle her readers with unexpected gender permutations and fascinating relationships worked out in front of a convincingly detailed landscape." —*Publishers Weekly*

The **book** of Flora. Meg Elison. 47North, 2019. 332 pages (Road to Nowhere, 3)

ISBN 9781542042093

1. Post-apocalypse 2. Far future 3. Gender identity 4. Belief and doubt 5. Survival (after epidemics) 6. Apocalyptic fiction 7. Social science fiction 8. Science fiction

Navigating a blighted landscape, Flora—an outsider everywhere she goes—her friends, and a sullen young slave she adopts as her own child leave their oppressive pasts behind to find their place in a post-apocalyptic world. When the promise of a miraculous hope for humanity's future tears Flora's makeshift family asunder, she must choose: protect the safe haven she's built or risk everything to defy oppression, whatever its provenance.

The **book** of the unnamed midwife. Meg Elison. Sybaratic Press, 2014. 185 p. (Road to Nowhere, 1)

ISBN 9781495116360

1. Post-apocalypse 2. Midwives 3. Sex discrimination 4. Survival (after epidemics) 5. Male impersonators 6. Apocalyptic fiction 7. Social science fiction 8. Science fiction

Philip K. Dick Award for Science Fiction, 2015

"Elison takes readers on an exciting and often excruciating journey, navigating issues of gender and sex in a scorched, disease-ridden world." —*Booklist*

Elliott, Kate

Servant mage. Kate Elliott. Tordotcom, 2022. 176 p.

ISBN 9781250769053

1. Women wizards 2. Conspiracies 3. Magic 4. Imaginary empires 5. Rebels 6. Fantasy fiction

LC 2021033447

A lowly fire mage finds herself entangled in an empire-spanning conspiracy on her way to discovering her true power. They choose their laws to secure their power. Fellion is a Lamplighter, able to provide illumination through magic. A group of rebel Monarchists free her from indentured servitude and take her on a journey to rescue trapped compatriots from an underground complex of mines. Along the way they get caught up in a conspiracy to kill the latest royal child and wipe out the Monarchist movement for good. But Fellion has more than just her Lamplighting skills up her sleeve.

"In limited space, Elliott builds a refreshingly complex world with a magic system not linked to familial lineage and with realistically thorny politics, as neither the Liberationists nor the Monarchists are depicted as infallibly good for the people." —*Publishers Weekly*

A Tom Doherty Associates book.

Unconquerable sun. Kate Elliott. Tor Books, 2020. 528 p. (Sun chronicles, 1)
ISBN 9781250197245
1. Princesses 2. Space flight 3. Nobility 4. Political intrigue 5. Women engineers 6. Science fiction 7. Space opera 8. Multiple perspectives

A high-adventure space opera inspired by Alexander the Great follows the coming of age of Princess Sun, a legendary queen-marshal's daughter who navigates a plot by conniving nobles to prevent her ascent to the throne.

The upshot is a maelstrom of palace intrigue, interstellar back-stabbing, devious plots, treachery, blistering action, ferocious confrontations—and a heroine for the ages, tough, resourceful, loyal, intelligent, honorable, courageous, and utterly indomitable. Enthralling, edge-of-your-seat stuff hurtling along at warp speed. Grab! Kirkus

Elliott, Lexie

The **missing** years. Lexie Elliott. Berkley, 2019. 320 pages
ISBN 9780399586958
1. Women television producers and directors 2. Half-sisters 3. Manors 4. Missing persons investigation 5. Missing men 6. Highlands, Scotland 7. Scotland 8. Gothic fiction
LC 2018043170

When Ailsa Calder inherits her childhood home in the craggy peaks of the Scottish Highlands, she must contend with memories of her 27-years-gone father, a half-sister she's hardly known, the fact that neighborhood animals avoid the garden—and the nighttime intruder.

Ellis, Bella

The **vanished** bride. Bella Ellis. Berkley, 2019. 304 pages (Bronte sisters mystery, 1)
ISBN 9780593099056
1. Bronte, Charlotte 2. Women amateur detectives 3. Women authors, English 4. Gender role 5. Missing women 6. Sisters 7. Yorkshire, England 8. England 9. Victorian era (1837-1901) 10. 1840s 11. Historical mysteries
LC 2019015852

In 1845 Yorkshire, a young wife and mother has gone missing from her home, leaving behind two small children and a large pool of blood, and it is up to the Bronte sisters to investigate.

Ellis, Bret Easton

Imperial bedrooms. By Bret Easton Ellis. Alfred A. Knopf, 2010. 288 p.
ISBN 9780307266101
1. Middle-aged men 2. Generation X 3. City life 4. Conspiracies 5. Friendship 6. Los Angeles, California 7. Psychological fiction
LC 2009041690

With his screenwriting career at its peak, Clay returns to Los Angeles to hire the cast for an upcoming blockbuster. There he comes across his former girlfriend Blair and her philandering husband Trent, whose night-life and sexual tastes have made him the talk of the town. He also comes into contact with Julian, an old friend turned junkie, and his sinister drug dealer. However, when his life starts spiraling out of control, Clay is forced to face his own past.

"As with Chandler's work, the details of the twists and turns are beside the point particularly since Ellis puckishly reveals at the start which character is going to wind up as a corpse in a Tom Ford suit. But the author uses the thriller framework to infuse nerve-rending unease into this look at Tinseltown mores, a dissection that also comes nicely weighted with both bleak hilarity and firsthand authorial experience." —*Entertainment Weekly*

Sequel to: Less than zero.

Lunar Park. Bret Easton Ellis. Knopf, 2005. 307 p.
ISBN 9780375412912
1. Ellis, Bret Easton 2. Suburban life 3. Drug abuse 4. Missing boys 5. Fathers and sons 6. Murder 7. Autobiographical fiction 8. Psychological fiction 9. Domestic fiction
LC 2005040923

International Horror Guild Award for Best Novel, 2005; New York Times Notable Book, 2005

Becoming a best-selling novelist and wealthy celebrity while still in college, only to have his fame disintegrate in a sea of booze, drugs, and vilification, the narrator gets a new chance at life married to the mother of a previously unacknowledged son and living in suburbia, but now his new life unravels in the wake of a series of grotesque murders and the disappearance of young boys.

"The whole book swirls, surreally, pushing the limits of tolerable confusion while sending up laughably familiar horror story shticks. For a while, it looks as if nothing will be resolved. It works precisely because it is a ghost story, replete with eviscerated livestock, freshly dug graves, and messages written in ashand because everything, ultimately, is resolved." —*New Criterion*

Ellis, David

In the company of liars. David Ellis. G.P. Putnam's Sons, 2005. 378 p.
ISBN 9780399152474
1. Women authors 2. Women authors 3. Women murder suspects 4. Divorced persons 5. Former husbands 6. Thrillers and suspense
LC 2004057342

Library Journal Best Books, 2005

A thriller told in reverse centers on a woman who is undergoing a murder trial that is being overseen by a prosecutor who is strongly pursuing a death penalty and an FBI agent who would force the defendant to betray her family.

Ellis, Helen

American housewife: stories. Helen Ellis. Doubleday, 2016. Xi, 188 pages
ISBN 9780385541039
1. Women 2. Married women 3. Femininity 4. Anger in women 5. Revenge 6. Satirical fiction 7. Short stories
LC 2015021779

LibraryReads Favorites, 2016; Library Journal Best Books, 2016

A collection of stories featuring conventional, if ruthless, housewives features a rigged reality television show, a unique book club initiation ritual, and the fitting room of a legendary lingerie shop.

"With monstrous children and cats, hopeless husbands, and covertly dangerous women, Ellis takes down the entire housewife concept with a sniper's precision. These are delectably revved up, marauding, sometimes macabre tales of ruined marriages, illness, infertility, crass commercialism (literary product placement), desperation, ghosts, even murder, featuring women of shrewd calculation, secret sorrows, and deep sympathy." —*Booklist*

Ellison, J. T.

Good girls lie. J. T. Ellison. MIRA, 2019. 464 pages
ISBN 9780778309185
1. Girls' boarding schools 2. Teenage girls 3. Murder 4. Transfer students 5. Prep schools 6. United States 7. Virginia 8. Psychological suspense 9. Multiple perspectives
LibraryReads Favorites, 2019
In a follow-up to Lie to Me and Tear Me Apart, a popular transfer student at an elite prep school races to protect a dangerous secret when a killer sets her up for a string of murders.

Tear me apart. J. T. Ellison. MIRA Books, 2018. 368 p.
ISBN 9780778308263
1. Teenage girls 2. Daughters 3. Infants switched at birth 4. Skiers 5. Accident victims 6. Colorado 7. Psychological suspense
When a life-threatening illness reveals that she is not related to her parents, a competitive skier uncovers the sinister impact of lies and desperation on two families.

Ellison, Ralph

★ **Invisible** man. Ralph Ellison. Vintage International, 1995. Xxiii, 581 p.
ISBN 9780679732761
1. Race relations 2. African Americans 3. Identity (Psychology) 4. African American men 5. New York City 6. Harlem, New York City 7. African American fiction 8. Literary fiction 9. Modern classics
National Book Award for Fiction, 1953
An African-American man's search for success and the American dream leads him out of college to Harlem and a growing sense of personal rejection and social invisibility.
Originally published: New York : Random House, 1952.

★ **Juneteenth**. Ralph Ellison; edited by John F. Callahan. Random House, 1999. 368 p.
ISBN 9780593242100
1. Race relations 2. Assassins 3. Identity (Psychology) 4. Secrets 5. African American clergy 6. Southern States 7. Literary fiction 8. African American fiction 9. Modern classics
Booklist Editors' Choice, 1999; New York Times Notable Book, 1999
In Washington D.C., in the 1950s, Senator Sunraider is mortally wounded by an assassin's bullet. From his deathbed, he calls out for Hickman, an old black minister. As the two men relive their memories of a shared history, they gradually reveal the secrets of their past.
"Ellison's fans will nevertheless find much to savor and can only wonder about the unseen chapters. For all fiction collections." —*Library Journal*
First published in the USA by Random House Inc, 1999.

Three days before the shooting... Ralph Ellison; edited by John Callahan. Modern Library, 2010. 896 p.
ISBN 9780375759536
1. Attempted assassination 2. Race relations 3. Politicians 4. Caretakers 5. African Americans — Identity 6. Literary fiction 7. African American fiction
Booklist Editors' Choice, 2010
"Culled from Ellison's drafts, his notes, and those of his wife, Fanny, this book brings together four decades of work, a portion of which was published posthumously as Juneteenth in 1999. The allegorical, lyrical novel is presented in three books in various stages of completion. It cen-

ters on the complex relationship between A. Z. Hickman, a blues musician turned preacher, and Bliss, an orphan of undetermined race, whom Hickman raises as a boy preacher.... He is masterful at evoking the language of common black folks, preachers, press and politicians, and charlatans and flimflammers." —*Booklist*

Ellmann, Lucy

Ducks, Newburyport. Lucy Ellmann. Biblioasis, 2019. 728 p.
ISBN 9781771963077
1. Mothers 2. Obsession 3. Popular culture 4. Family relationships 5. Anxiety 6. Ohio 7. 21st century 8. Literary fiction 9. Experimental fiction 10. First person narratives
James Tait Black Memorial Prize for Fiction, 2019; New York Times Notable Book, 2019; Shortlisted for the Booker Prize, 2019
Peeling apple after apple for the tartes tatin she bakes for local restaurants, an Ohio mother wonders how to exist in a world of distraction and fake facts, besieged by a tweet-happy president and trigger-happy neighbors, and all of them oblivious to what Dupont has dumped into the rivers and what's happening at the factory farm down the interstate—not to mention what was done to the land's first inhabitants.

Ellroy, James

American tabloid: a novel. James Ellroy. A.A. Knopf, 1995. 571 p. (Underworld U.S.A. trilogy, 1)
ISBN 9780679403913
1. Kennedy, John F. 2. Political corruption 3. Criminals 4. Labor unions 5. Savonarola, Girolamo 6. United States 7. 1960s 8. Noir fiction 9. Political fiction

LC 94042898
Offers a story of the dark secrets behind Kennedy's election and assassination, the Bay of Pigs, and the roles of the underworld, the CIA, Howard Hughes, Hoover, and three renegade law-enforcement officers.
"It's as if Ellroy injects us with a mainline pop of the undiluted power that surges through the veins of his obsessed characters. Though he is thought of as a crime novelist, Ellroy is really a political novelist, and like the best of the breed, his work has no politics. Is his version of who killed JFK believable? Probably, but the real message behind this profoundly disturbing, utterly intoxicating book is how trivial a question that really is." —*Booklist*
Reprinted in 2019 with "The Cold Six Thousand."

Blood's a rover. James Ellroy. Knopf, 2019. 583 p. (Underworld U.S.A. trilogy, 3)
ISBN 9781101908143
1. Organized crime 2. Political corruption 3. Conspiracies 4. Assassination 5. Racism 6. United States 7. 1960s 8. Noir fiction 9. Political fiction
Blood's A Rover takes us into the seventies. MLK and RFK are dead. The Democratic National Convention in Chicago has spawned chaos. There's a punk-kid private eye in L.A. He's clashing with a mob goon and an enforcer for J. Edgar Hoover. There's an armored-car heist and a cache of missing emeralds. There's bad voodoo in the Dominican Republic and Haiti. Amidst it all is a revolutionary, Joan Rosen Klein. The kid P.I, the mob goon, and Hoover's enforcer love her unto death. Blood's A Rover gives us the private nightmare of public policy on an epic scale.
"Ellroy employs a huge cast and hyper-pulp prose to create a convincingly horrific universe run by the F.B.I, the Mob, and a host of other sinister organizations." —*The New Yorker*
Originally published in 2009.

The **cold** six thousand: a novel. By James Ellroy. Knopf, 2001. 669 p; (Underworld U.S.A. trilogy, 2)

ISBN 9780679403920

1. King, Martin Luther 2. Political corruption 3. Conspiracies 4. Assassins 5. Drug smugglers 6. Police 7. United States 8. 1960s 9. Noir fiction 10. Political fiction 11. Multiple perspectives
New York Times Notable Book, 2001

Politics and conspiracies are interwoven in this story of a young policeman from Las Vegas who becomes intangled with the events and people who shaped the Sixties.

"A look at the dark side of American life during the 1960s, focusing on a Las Vegas police officr, Wayne Tedrow Jr, and his inadvertent role in the cover-up of John F. Kennedy's assassination. The narrative spans a five-year period and traces Tedrow's dealings with the Mafia, the Ku Klux Klan, and various political and cultural icons of that time period." —Library Journal

Reprinted in 2019 with "American Tabloid."

★ **L.A.** confidential. James Ellroy. Warner Books, 1997. 496 p. (L. A. quartet, 3)

ISBN 9780446674249

1. Police 2. Detectives 3. Police corruption 4. Mass murder 5. Los Angeles, California 6. 1950s 7. Crime fiction 8. Books to movies

Three troubled cops— Ed Exley, desperately seeking glory; vengeful Bud White, a witness to his mother's murder by his father; and Jack Vincennes, a shakedown artist with a dark secret— tread a fine line between right and wrong in 1950s Los Angeles.

"The author merges raw-edged period detail with sleazy celluloid lore, producing a dark and dazzling descent into the criminal underworld of the 1950s." —Booklist

Originally published: New York : Mysterious Press, 1990.

Perfidia. James Ellroy. Random House Inc, 2014. 608 p. (Second L. A. quartet, 1)

ISBN 9780307956996

1. Japanese Americans — Forced removal and incarceration, 1942-1945 2. World War II 3. Violence against marginalized people 4. Forced relocations 5. Man-woman relationships 6. Los Angeles, California 7. Second World War era (1939-1945) 8. 1940s 9. Police procedurals 10. Historical mysteries

A debut entry in a second L.A. Quartet follows a post-Pearl Harbor murder of a Japanese family that entangles a brilliant Japanese-American forensic chemist, an adventurous woman, a future police chief and an arch villain.

"Regardless of what Ellroy intends or means, what hes achieved is a disturbing, unforgettable, and inflammatory vision of how the men in charge respond to the threat of war." —Booklist

This storm: a novel. James Ellroy. Alfred A. Knopf, 2019. 589 p. (Second L. A. quartet, 2)

ISBN 9780307957009

1. Police 2. Military intelligence 3. Murder investigation 4. Murder 5. Profiteering 6. Los Angeles, California 7. 1940s 8. Second World War era (1939-1945) 9. Police procedurals 10. Historical mysteries
LC 2018048538

A corrupt vice cop, a crime-lab whiz facing Japanese internment, a fascist police consultant to Army Intelligence and a rogue profiteer investigate a historically relevant murder in 1942 Los Angeles.

"Just when it seems that things couldn't get darker, Ellroy peels back a deeper level of corruption. This obsessive, wholly satisfying probing of 20th-century American history deserves a wide readership." —Publishers Weekly

★ **Widespread** panic: a novel. James Ellroy. Alfred A. Knopf, 2021. 336 p.

ISBN 9780593319345

1. Otash, Fred 2. Conspiracies 3. Private investigators 4. Secrets 5. Celebrities 6. Investigations 7. Los Angeles, California 8. 1950s 9. Hardboiled fiction 10. Historical mysteries 11. Biographical fiction
LC 2020050847

In the 1950s, Freddy Otash, the Tattle Tyrant for Confidential magazine who held Hollywood hostage, decides to tell all, in this tale of pervasive paranoia teeming with communist conspiracies, FBI finks, celebrity smut films, and strange bedfellows.

"Ellroy's total command of the jazzy, alliterative argot of the era never fails to astonish. This is a must for L.A. noir fans." —Publishers Weekly

Emezi, Akwaeke

★ The **death** of Vivek Oji. Akwaeke Emezi. Riverhead Books, 2020. 256 p.

ISBN 9780525541608

1. Gender fluid 2. Dead 3. Familial love 4. Identity (Psychology) 5. Misfits (Persons) 6. Nigeria 7. Literary fiction 8. Multiple perspectives 9. First person narratives
New York Times Notable Book, 2020

In the wake of a southeastern Nigerian mother's discovery of her son's body on her doorstep, a family struggles to understand the enigmatic nature of a youth shaped by disorienting blackouts, diverse friendships and a cousin's worldly influence.

"Following Pet, a finalist for the National Book Award for Young People's Literature, this achingly beautiful probe into the challenges of living fully as a nonbinary human being, is an illuminating read." —Library Journal

Freshwater. Akwaeke Emezi. Grove Press, 2018. 229 p.

ISBN 9780802127358

1. Emezi, Akwaeke 2. Women with mental illnesses 3. Identity (Psychology) 4. Self 5. Nigerians in the United States 6. Igbo (African people) 7. Nigeria 8. Virginia 9. Autobiographical fiction 10. Literary fiction 11. Adult books for young adults
LC 2017028925

Otherwise Award, 2019; New York Times Notable Book, 2018; Longlisted for The Women's Prize for Fiction, 2019

Traces the experiences of a deeply troubled young woman who alarms her devout Nigerian family as she succumbs to multiple personality disorder and begins to display increasingly dark and dangerous traits in accordance with her fractured personalities.

"Emezi's brilliance lies not just in her expert handling of the conflicting voices in Ada's head but in delivering an entirely different perspective on just what it means to go slowly mad. Complex and dark, this novel will simultaneously challenge and reward lovers of literary fiction. A must-read." —Booklist

Enard, Mathias

Compass. Mathias Enard; translated by Charlotte Mandell. New Directions, 2017. 464 p.

ISBN 9780811226622

1. Obsession 2. Voyages and travels 3. Interpersonal relations 4. Musicologists 5. Learning and scholarship 6. Literary fiction 7. Translations
LC 2016039665

Shortlisted for the International Dublin Literary Award, 2019

Franz Ritter, an insomniac musicologist, spends a restless night drifting between dreams and memories, revisiting the important chapters of his life, including his elusive, unrequited love, Sarah, a brilliant French scholar caught in the complex tension between Europe and the Middle East.

Endicott, Marina

The **voyage** of the morning light. Marina Endicott. W W Norton & Co, 2020. 383 p.

ISBN 9781324007067

1. Sisters 2. Merchant ships 3. Ocean travel 4. Adoption racket 5. Miscarriage 6. Micronesia 7. Nova Scotia 8. 1910s 9. Historical fiction 10. Canadian fiction 11. Sea stories

Two sisters, Thea and Kay, live aboard one of the last merchant ships to sail the South Pacific in the early 1900s. After the death of their father, Thea is free to marry her love, a ship captain. Kay comes aboard too, and together they embark on a life-changing voyage through the South Pacific and around the Cape of Good Hope. After Thea experiences a devastating miscarriage, she "purchases" a young boy from an island in Micronesia for four tins of tobacco, adopting him as her own. The repercussions of this act reverberate through the story.

"Endicott artfully combines a bracing world voyage and the equally transformative journey of a young woman discovering and honoring her genuine nature. With her passion for all the creatures and cultures she encounters, Kay shines as a timely embodiment of the solace of human connection across time and space." —*Booklist*

Originally published with the title The difference : Toronto : Alfred A. Knopf Canada, 2019.

Endo, Shusaku

Deep river. Shusaku Endo; translated by Van C. Gessel. New Directons, 1994. 216 p.

ISBN 9780811212892

1. Japanese in India 2. Pilgrims and pilgrimages 3. Ganges River 4. Leonardo da Vinci 5. Translations

LC 94038913

Library Journal Best Books, 1995

Offers a religious vision combining Christian faith with Buddhist acceptance in the story of a group of Japanese tourists who converge at the Ganges River in India

"This is a beautifully wrought, lyrically suggestive story.... If Christianity holds up to us the lonely individual challenged by a God who entered history, Buddhism gives us people who are ready to surrender, finally, a measure of their human and spiritual particularity and who, with acceptance, join their fellow creatures as part of the great tide of humanity. Mr. Endo manages to merge both of these streams of faith, bringing them together in a flow that is, indeed, deep. His work is a soulful gift to a world he keeps rendering as unrelievedly parched." —*New York Times Book Review*

Originally published: Tokyo : Kodansha, 1993.

Silence. Shusaku Endo; translated by William Johnston. Sophia University; in cooperation with the C.E. Tuttle Co, Rutland, Vt, 1969. 306 p.

ISBN 9780800871864

1. Christian missionaries 2. Priests 3. Nabokov, Vladimir Vladimirovich 4. Religious persecution 5. Portuguese in Japan 6. Japan 7. 17th century 8. Translations 9. Christian historical fiction 10. Christian fiction

LC 68058912

Sustained by dreams of glorious martyrdom, a seventeenth-century Purtuguese missionary in Japan administers to the outlawed Christians until Japanese authorities capture him and force him to watch the torture of his followers, promising to stop if he will renounce Christ.

Adapted into a 2016 film directed by Martin Scorsese.

Japanese original title on cover romanized: Chinmoku.

This translation first published 1969 by Sophia University Press, Tokyo.

Engel, Patricia

★ **Infinite** country. Patricia Engel. Avid Reader Press, 2021. 192 p.

ISBN 9781982159467

1. Families 2. Deportation 3. Undocumented immigrants 4. Separated friends, relatives, etc. 5. Juvenile jails 6. Bogota, Colombia 7. Literary fiction 8. Bronte, Patrick Branwell

Moving their family to what they believe will be a safer but temporary home in Houston, two young parents are forced to choose between an undocumented status in America and returning to the violence of war-torn Bogata.

"Engel's sharp, unflinching narrative teems with insight and dazzles with a confident, slyly sophisticated structure. This is an impressive achievement." —*Publishers Weekly*

Enger, Leif

Virgil Wander. Leif Enger. Grove Press, 2018. 300 p.

ISBN 9780802128782

1. Film theater managers 2. Survival (after automobile, truck, train accidents, etc.) 3. Amnesia 4. Memory 5. Interpersonal communication 6. Minnesota 7. Mainstream fiction 8. Psychological fiction 9. First person narratives

LC 2018026619

LibraryReads Favorites, 2018; Library Journal Best Books, 2018

Emerging from an accident with damaged memories and compromised language skills, a movie-house owner from a small Midwestern town pieces together his story against a backdrop of community history, which is shaped by a prodigal son's return.

Enger, Lin

The **high** divide: a novel. By Lin Enger. Algonquin Books of Chapel Hill, 2014. 304 pages

ISBN 9781616203757

1. Father-deserted families 2. Frontier and pioneer life 3. Voyages and travels 4. Families 5. Wilderness areas 6. The West (United States) 7. 1880s 8. Westerns 9. Literary fiction

LC 2014014702

Abandoned by her husband and her two sons who went out to search for him, Gretta Pope must follow her family across the rugged badlands of 1880s Montana.

Undiscovered country: a novel. Lin Enger. Little, Brown and Co, 2008. 320 p.

ISBN 9780316006941

1. Fathers and sons 2. Suicide 3. Revenge 4. Family secrets 5. Married people 6. Minnesota 7. Domestic fiction 8. Adult books for young adults

LC 2007030138

While hunting in the cold Minnesota woods, 17-year-old Jesse Matson's life is forever changed when he discovers his father, dead by a self-inflicted gunshot wound. But would easygoing Harold Matson really kill himself? If so, why? And just where was Jesse's uncle Clay—always jealous of Harold, and a bit too friendly with Jesse's mother—that cold afternoon?

"A modern-day Hamlet story set in rural northern Minnesota. Teenage Jesse's father, the mayor of Battlepoint, apparently committed suicide with his own hunting rifle. But Jesse suspects his Uncle Clay, who had more than one motive for murder. Is Jesse's suspicion simply his inability to accept his father's senseless act? Or is Clay really guiltyand how complicit is Jesse's mother? If Clay is guilty, what should he do about it? The obvious parallels with Shakespeare's play are even acknowledged by some of the characters, but Enger doesn't let this conceit overwhelm the story. He skillfully draws a portrait of small-town life and all its barely concealed secrets and effectively narrates Jesse's torment." —*Library Journal*

Englander, Nathan

The **ministry** of Special Cases. Nathan Englander. Alfred A. Knopf, 2007. 352 p.

ISBN 9780375404931

1. Missing persons 2. Missing children 3. Human rights 4. Jews 5. Loss (Psychology) 6. Argentina 7. Political fiction 8. Literary fiction
LC 2006048731

Booklist Editors' Choice, 2007; New York Times Notable Book, 2007; Sophie Brody Medal, 2008

In the heart of Argentina's Dirty War, Kaddish Poznan struggles with a son who won't accept him; strives for a wife who forever saves him; and spends his nights protecting the good name of a community that denies his existence—and denies a checkered history that only Kaddish holds dear.

"The author bravely wrangles the themes of political liberty and personal loss with the swift style and knowing humor of folklore. In the spirit of the simple ambiguity of its title, The Ministry of Special Cases is carefully contradictory, wise and off-kilter, funny and sad." —*New York Observer*

What we talk about when we talk about Anne Frank: stories. Nathan Englander. Knopf, 2012. 288 p.

ISBN 9780307958709

1. Jews 2. Mother and child 3. Holocaust (1933-1945) 4. Holocaust survivors 5. Jewish way of life 6. Literary fiction 7. Short stories
LC 2011033756

New York Times Notable Book, 2012; Pulitzer Prize for Fiction finalist, 2013

A collection of short stories includes the title story about two marriages in which the Holocaust is played out as a devastating parlor game, and a dark story of vigilante justice undertaken by a troop of geriatric campers.

Enjeti, Anjali

★ The **parted** Earth. Anjali Enjeti. Hub City Press, 2021. 272 p.

ISBN 9781938235771

1. East Indian Americans 2. East Indians 3. Families 4. Religious persecution 5. Violence 6. Atlanta, Georgia 7. India 8. British Raj (1858-1947) 9. Family sagas 10. Historical fiction 11. Parallel narratives
LC 2020046269

When a pregnancy loss uproots her life, Shan begins the search for her estranged grandmother and, piecing together her family history shattered by the Partition of India, discovers how little she actually knows about the women in her family and what they endured.

"Though an author's note says that only the historical aspects of this story are nonfictional, the fact that a character shares a name with one of Enjeti's grandmothers (as seen in the dedication) underlines the pulse of truth that makes this book feel so urgent and important. Illuminating, absorbing, and resonant." —*Kirkus*

Enright, Anne

Actress: a novel. Anne Enright. W. W. Norton & Co, 2020. 264 p.

ISBN 9781324005629

1. Mothers and daughters 2. Theater actors and actresses 3. Celebrities 4. Children of actors and actresses 5. Fame 6. Ireland 7. Family sagas 8. Literary fiction
LC 2019046238

When her Irish-theater-legend mother succumbs to alcohol and instability, Norah draws on her experiences of surviving a crime and growing up in the wings of her mother's career to rediscover herself as a wife, mother and writer.

"Another triumph for Enright: a confluence of lyrical prose, immediacy, warmth, and emotional insight." —*Kirkus*

The **forgotten** waltz. Anne Enright. W. W. Norton & Co, 2011. 263 p.

ISBN 9780393072556

1. Memories 2. Extramarital affairs 3. Desire 4. Boredom in women 5. Fathers and daughters 6. Ireland 7. Psychological fiction 8. Literary fiction

Andrew Carnegie Medal for Excellence in Fiction, 2012; Booklist Editors' Choice, 2011; Shortlisted for The Orange Prize for Fiction, 2012

During a peaceful snowfall in a suburb in Dublin, a woman remembers her younger days spent with her lover in various hotel rooms as she awaits the arrival of his 12-year-old daughter.

"The Forgotten Waltz meditates on the way personal responsibility can twist the most well-meaning, loving relationship into a holding tank for accusations and tears.... Enright allows her main character the thrill of remembered joys, without letting her slip away from blame." —*A.V. Club*

★ The **gathering**. Anne Enright. Black Cat, 2007. 260 p.

ISBN 9780802170392

1. Middle-aged women 2. Brothers — Death 3. Catholics 4. Resentfulness 5. Unhappiness in women 6. Dublin, Ireland 7. Ireland 8. Psychological fiction 9. Literary fiction

Booklist Editors' Choice, 2007; Man Booker Prize, 2007; New York Times Notable Book, 2007

Veronica—once an attention-deprived middle child among 12 siblings, and now an unfulfilled wife and mother—has come to London to claim the body of her beloved yet estranged brother Liam who drowned himself at sea. As the nine surviving members of the Hegarty clan converge in Dublin for Liam's wake, Veronica wants to protect the past—and the secret of what transpired in her grandmother's house during the winter of 1968.

"You will love this book or loathe it. It doesn't take prisoners, it doesn't simper or seek to be liked. Abrasively honest and toweringly moving, it grabs and shakes you, rabbiting on in a manic monologue, comical, tragic, lost and profound." —*The Scotsman*

First published in Great Britain in 2007 by Jonathan Cape.

The **Green** Road: a novel. Anne Enright. W. W. Norton & Co, 2015. 304 p.

ISBN 9780393248210

1. Mothers 2. Home (Concept) 3. Voyages and travels 4. Mother and adult child 5. Growing up 6. Ireland 7. Family sagas 8. Literary fiction 9. Multiple perspectives

Shortlisted for the Baileys Women's Prize for Fiction, 2016; Shortlisted for the International Dublin Literary Award, 2017

When Christmas day reunites the Madigan children, who all left their mother Rosaleen behind to follow their dreams, under one roof in County Clare, Ireland, they each must confront the terrible weight of family ties and the journey that brought them home.

"Long introductions to the principal characters precede the theatrical format of the reunion, allowing Enright plenty of space to convey her brilliant ear for dialogue, her soft wit, and piercing, poetic sense of life's larger abstractions." —*Kirkus*

Yesterday's weather: stories. By Anne Enright. Grove Press, 2008. 308 p.
ISBN 9780802118745
1. Change — Psychological aspects 2. Ireland 3. Short stories
LC Bl2008017676
New York Times Notable Book, 2008
A collection of short fiction chronicles the lives of ordinary men and women struggling to cope with the bonds of love, family, and community, in an increasingly disconnected, transient, and changing Ireland.
"Enright's subjects are family, children, love, domestic horror. The stories are strong and hard bitten. Something in them is always snagging and catching on grief, large or small. She is a confident writer, letting stories unfold at their own speed. Her best pieces have a fluid shape that feels close to the way we actually think, choose, muse." —*Washington Post Book World*.

Epstein, Jennifer Cody
★ **Wunderland:** a novel. Jennifer Cody Epstein. Crown Publishing, 2019. 371 pages
ISBN 9780525576907
1. Mothers and daughters 2. World War II 3. Women and war 4. Persecution by Nazis 5. Kristallnacht, 1938 6. Berlin, Germany 7. Germany 8. 20th century 9. Historical fiction 10. Parallel narratives
A German-American woman in 1989 New York City evaluates her relationship with her late mother, whose childhood best friendship was shattered in the wake of a betrayal involving the Hitler Youth movement and a family secret.
"A vividly written and stark chronicle of Nazism and its legacies." —*Kirkus*

Epstein, Joseph
The **love** song of A. Jerome Minkoff, and other stories. Joseph Epstein. Houghton Mifflin Harcourt, 2010. 260 p.
ISBN 9780618721955
1. Jewish Americans 2. Jewish American men 3. Family relationships 4. Man-woman relationships 5. Chicago, Illinois 6. Short stories
LC 2009034898
A collection of short stories features everyday Jewish men in Chicago who confront life-defining moments during complex love affairs, unspoken rivalries, and family triumphs.
"It's a rare and welcome thing to find a collection of short stories that define a place.... Epstein delivers one about a neighborhood on the far north of Chicago called West Rogers Park. It is a polyglot area, but Epstein has chosen to write about the Jews who dominate it.... If his voice is wry, it is also sympathetic. Life is hard, and he knows it. He invests his collection with a peerless take on a particular slice of Jewish life today. Each story stands strong as a discrete work, but together they become profound." —*Boston Globe*

Erdrich, Louise
The **beet** queen: a novel. Holt, 1986. 338 p.
ISBN 9780805000580
1. Native American women 2. Loneliness 3. Abandonment (Psychology) 4. Jealousy 5. Mothers and daughters 6. North Dakota 7. Literary fiction 8. Coming-of-age stories 9. Multiple perspectives
LC 86004788
National Book Critics Circle Award for Fiction finalist, 1986

Orphaned fourteen-year-old Carl and his eleven-year-old sister, Mary, travel to Argus, North Dakota, to live with their mother's sister, in this tale of abandonment, sexual obsession, jealousy, and unstinting love.
Sequel to: Love Medicine.
Sequel: Tracks.

Four souls: a novel. Louise Erdrich. Harper Collins Publishers, 2004. 210 p.
ISBN 9780066209753
1. Land tenure 2. Revenge in women 3. Native American women 4. Ojibwa Indians 5. Indian reservations 6. Minneapolis, Minnesota 7. North Dakota 8. Psychological fiction 9. Literary fiction
LC 2003065243
Booklist Editors' Choice, 2004; New York Times Notable Book, 2004
After taking her mother's name, Four Souls, for strength, the strange and compelling Fleur Pillager walks from her Ojibwe reservation to the cities of Minneapolis and Saint Paul. She is seeking restitution from and revenge on the lumber baron who has stripped her tribe's land. But revenge is never simple, and her intentions are complicated by her dangerous compassion for the man who wronged her.
"The shifting of voices and stories, ranging back and forth in time and place, may sound dauntingly complicated; luckily, it doesn't read that way. In fact, the progression of events feels natural and unforced, full of satisfying yet unexpected twists. The book begins with clean, spare prose, but finishes in gorgeous incantation and poetry." —*New York Times Book Review*
Sequel to: Tracks.

Future home of the living god. Louise Erdrich. Harper 2017. 368 p.
ISBN 9780062694058
1. Ojibwa Indians 2. Pregnant women 3. Human evolution 4. Adoption 5. Fugitives 6. Minnesota 7. Dystopian fiction 8. Literary fiction 9. Apocalyptic fiction
Booklist Editors' Choice, 2017; LibraryReads Favorites, 2017; New York Times Notable Book, 2017; Longlisted for the Andrew Carnegie Medal for Excellence in Fiction, 2018
A tale set in a world of reversing evolution and a growing police state follows pregnant twenty-six-year-old Cedar Hawk Songmaker, who investigates her biological family while awaiting the birth of a child who may emerge as a member of a primitive human species.
"A tornadic, suspenseful, profoundly provoking novel of lifes vulnerability and insistence." —*Booklist*

★ **LaRose**. Louise Erdrich. HarperCollins, 2016. 256 p.
ISBN 9780062277022
1. Sons 2. Atonement 3. Hunting accidents 4. Grief 5. Families 6. North Dakota 7. Literary fiction 8. Magical realism 9. Domestic fiction
Booklist Editors' Choice, 2016; National Book Critics Circle Award for Fiction, 2016; New York Times Notable Book, 2016; Pen/Faulkner Award Finalist, 2017
Horrified when he accidentally kills his best friend's 5-year-old son while hunting, Landreaux Iron gives away his own young son to his friend's family according to ancient tradition, a decision that helps both families reach a tenuous peace that is threatened by a vengeful adversary.
"Electric, nimble, and perceptive, this novel is about 'the phosphorous of grief' but also, more essentially, about the emotions men need, but rarely get, from one another." —*Kirkus*

The **last** report on the miracles at Little No Horse. Louise Erdrich. Harper Collins, 2001. 361 p.
ISBN 9780060187279
1. Ojibwa Indians 2. Impostors 3. Indian reservations 4. Priests 5. Male impersonators 6. North Dakota 7. Literary fiction 8. Multiple perspectives
LC 47198

Booklist Editors' Choice, 2001; Library Journal Best Books, 2001; Minnesota Book Award for Novel & Short Story, 2002; New York Times Notable Book, 2001; National Book Award for Fiction finalist, 2001

As a priest nears the end of his life, he is asked to prove or disprove the sainthood of a woman he knows well and struggles to guard his own secret identity in the process.

"Even the small incidents in this novel are moments of tremendous power, stripped of sentimentality or pretension. Erdrich has developed a style that can sound as serious as death or ring with the haunting simplicity of ancient legend." —*Christian Science Monitor*

Illustrations on lining papers.

Love medicine: a novel. Louise Erdrich. Harper Perennial, 1993. 272 p.

ISBN 9780805027983

1. Extended families 2. Indian reservations 3. Family secrets 4. Grandparents 5. Love potions 6. North Dakota 7. Literary fiction

LC 84003774

Los Angeles Times Book Prize for Fiction, 1985; National Book Critics Circle Award for Fiction, 1984

Expanded to include previously unpublished chapters, this collection of interrelated stories of love, betrayal, mystery, and madness concerns men and women bound by blood, legend, tradition, and need.

"This reissue of Erdrich's exquisite first novel includes five new sections that color and complement the original multigenerational saga of two extended families who live on and around a Chippewa reservation in North Dakota....By placing us right inside the heads of her remarkable characters, Erdrich allows us to feel the despair that insensitive government policies, poverty, and alcoholism have brought them. For those who have yet to discover this magical novel and for those who will have the pleasure of reexperiencing its heartbreak and its hope, this new version is highly recommended." —*Library Journal*

Sequel: The Beet Queen.

The **Master** Butchers Singing Club: a novel. Louise Erdrich. HarperCollins, 2002. 389 p.

ISBN 9780066209777

1. Married people 2. Widows 3. Immigrants 4. Love triangles 5. Caesar, Julius 6. North Dakota 7. The West (United States) 8. Literary fiction 9. Historical fiction 10. Love stories

LC 2002068501

Booklist Editors' Choice, 2003; New York Times Notable Book, 2003

Returning to his quiet German village home after World War I, trained killer Fidelis Waldvogel, accompanied by his new wife, starts a new life in America and finds his life irrevocably changed by a new relationship.

★ The **night** watchman: a novel. Louise Erdrich. Harper, 2020. 451 pages

ISBN 9780062671189

1. Guards 2. Factories 3. Ojibwa Indians 4. Uncles 5. Native American men 6. North Dakota 7. 1950s 8. Literary fiction 9. Historical fiction

Pulitzer Prize for Fiction, 2021

A historical novel based on the life of the author's grandfather traces the experiences of a Chippewa Council night watchman in mid-19th-century rural North Dakota who fights Congress to enforce Native American treaty rights.

"National Book Award winner Erdrich once again calls upon her considerable storytelling skills to elucidate the struggles of generations of Native people to retain their cultural identity and their connection to the land." —*Library Journal*

The **painted** drum: a novel. Louise Erdrich. HarperCollins, 2005. 277 p.

ISBN 9780060515102

1. Multiracial women 2. Ojibwa Indians — Antiquities 3. Grief 4. Divorced women 5. Women travelers 6. New England 7. North Dakota 8. Psychological fiction 9. Domestic fiction 10. Literary fiction

LC 2005040227

Booklist Editors' Choice, 2005; Minnesota Book Award for Novel & Short Story, 2006; New York Times Notable Book, 2005

Discovering a cache of valuable Native American artifacts while appraising a family estate in New Hampshire, Faye Travers investigates the history of a ceremonial drum, which possesses spiritual powers and changes the lives of people who encounter it.

"There is searing pain and loss aplenty in this book, but one of Erdrich's strengths as a writer is the way in which she controls emotion.... Readers familiar with her works will recognize characters from the North Dakota native families who populate other of her works. But again, it doesn't really matter. Her themes transcend that terrain." —*Christian Science Monitor*

The **plague** of doves. Louise Erdrich. HarperCollins, 2008. 313 p.

ISBN 9780060515126

1. Small town life 2. Lynching 3. Multiracial women 4. Grandfather and granddaughter 5. Indian reservations 6. North Dakota 7. Domestic fiction 8. Literary fiction 9. Multiple perspectives

LC 2007033626

ALA Notable Book, 2009; Booklist Editors' Choice, 2008; Minnesota Book Award for Novel & Short Story, 2009; Pulitzer Prize for Fiction finalist, 2009

Unaware of a violent event that marked the beginning of her mixed ancestry, ambitious young Evelina Harp, a part-Ojibwe, part-white girl prone to falling hopelessly in love, learns disturbing truths from her gifted storyteller grandfather, while a sentimental judge weighs the legacy of a century-old crime as reflected by his own love life.

"This novel is about the unsolved murder of a farm family, but it is also an allegory about blood (and bloody) connections that develop as the descendants of killers and victims continue to live alongside one another near the Ojibwe reservation in North Dakota. As always with Erdrich, the bloodlines are both white and Native American, churned by the passions of characters with wonderful names like Mooshum Milk and Holy Track, whose lives and stories make the question of whodunit seem like an afterthought. Mooshum, one of three Indians falsely accused of the 1911 crime and the only one who survives the lynch mob tells of finding the murdered farm family and the infant who lived. Evelina, his granddaughter, becomes the central narrator of Mooshum's story amidst the intertwining tales of deathless romantic encounters that follow. Evelina and others detail the dramas of her family, including her own budding romantic encounters with the descendant of the murdered family and a nun whose lineage goes back to the lynch mob." —*New York Daily News*

The **red** convertible: selected and new stories, 1978-2008. Louise Erdrich. HarperCollins, 2009. X, 496 p.

ISBN 9780061536076

1. Literary fiction 2. Short stories

LC Bl2008029054

A collection of three dozen short works includes six previously unpublished pieces and offers insight into the author's use of plot twists and contrasting psychological landscapes.

"Louise Erdrich is an immensely satisfying storyteller who molds her novels from the clay of her short fiction.... This anthology returns 30 of those stories, which eventually became parts of 11 novels, to their original, unentangled forms. The book also includes six other stories, some of which are being published for the first time. Like Faulkner, Erdrich has created a fictional community an Ojibwe reservation in North Dakota from which her work can unfold. Her stories stretch back 100 years or more and venture as far away as New Hampshire, looping elliptically, intersecting through a priest, a place, a hidden parentage. But where her novels develop these relationships, The Red Convertible, in dislodging the stories, creates a new arc between them." —*Los Angeles Times Book Review*

★ The **round** house: a novel. Louise Erdrich. Harper, 2012. 336 p.
ISBN 9780062065247
1. Ojibwa Indians 2. Life change events 3. Indian reservations 4. Revenge 5. Teenage boys 6. North Dakota 7. Literary fiction 8. Coming-of-age stories 9. Adult books for young adults
LC 2012005381
ALA Notable Book, 2013; Alex Award, 2013; Booklist Editors' Choice, 2012; Indies' Choice Book Awards, Adult Fiction, 2013; Minnesota Book Award for Novel & Short Story, 2013; National Book Award for Fiction, 2012; New York Times Notable Book, 2012; Andrew Carnegie Medal for Excellence in Fiction finalist, 2013

When his mother, a tribal enrollment specialist living on a reservation in North Dakota, slips into an abyss of depression after being brutally attacked, fourteen-year-old Joe Coutz sets out with his three friends to find the person that destroyed his family.

★ The **sentence**. Louise Erdrich. HarperCollins, 2021. 416 p.
ISBN 9780062671127
1. Ojibwa Indians 2. Haunted places 3. Former convicts 4. Women booksellers 5. Bookstores 6. Minneapolis, Minnesota 7. Minnesota 8. 2010s 9. 2020s 10. Literary fiction 11. Ghost stories
LibraryReads Favorites, 2021

The Pulitzer Prize and National Book Award-winning author presents this unusual novel in which a small independent bookstore in Minneapolis is haunted from November 2019 to November 2020 by the store's most annoying customer.

"The many-hued, finely patterned weave of Erdrich's funny, evocative, painful, and redemptive ghost story includes strands of autobiography and even cameo appearances." —*Booklist*

★ **Shadow** tag: a novel. Louise Erdrich. Harper, 2010. 255 p.
ISBN 9780061536090
1. Husband and wife 2. Family relationships 3. Identity (Psychology) 4. Marriage 5. Artists 6. Psychological fiction 7. Literary fiction 8. Diary novels
LC 2009033699
New York Times Notable Book, 2010

After she discovers that her husband has been reading her diary, Irene America turns it into a manipulative farce, while secretly keeping a second diary that includes her true thoughts, through which the reader learns of Irene's shaky marriage, its affect on her children and her struggles with alcohol.

"Erdrich is a muscular and fearless writer, and she explores her characters with both compassion and criticism and through lyrical and visceral prose." —*BookPage*

Tracks: a novel. Louise Erdrich. Harper Perennial, 2004. 226 p.
ISBN 9780060972455
1. Indians of North America — Relations with European-Americans 2. Widowers 3. Pride and vanity 4. Man-woman relationships 5. Multiracial women 6. North Dakota 7. Literary fiction
LC 88009321

Set in North Dakota at a time in the past century when Indian tribes were struggling to keep what little remained of their lands, Tracks is a tale of passion and deep unrest. Over the course of ten crucial years, as tribal land and trust between people erode ceaselessly, men and women are pushed to the brink of their endurance—yet their pride and humor prohibit surrender.

"Ms. Erdrich is, as always, the generous kind of storyteller, passing along not only everything her characters know, but the story of the stories as well. Giving life and shape and sense to what's happened, she lets the designs spring clear." —*New York Times Book Review*
Sequel to: The Beet Queen.
Sequel: The Bingo Palace.

Eriksson, Kjell

The **deathwatch** beetle: a mystery. Kjell Eriksson; translated from the Swedish by Paul Norlen. Minotaur Books, 2021. 288 p. (Ann Lindell novels, 9)
ISBN 9781250766168
1. Former detectives 2. Retirees 3. Island life 4. Rural life 5. Missing women 6. Sweden 7. Scandinavian crime fiction 8. Mysteries 9. Translations
LC 2021021936

Even though she is no longer with the police, when Ann Lindell receives a tip that Cecilia Karlsson, who disappeared four years ago from the island of Graso in Roslagen, has been seen alive, cannot help getting involved.

"Eriksson's excellent ninth series mystery.... The plot slowly and steadily builds to a genuinely shocking denouement. Fans of literary fiction will be equally rewarded." —*Publishers Weekly*
Originally published in Sweden by Ordfront forlag under the title Dodsuret

Erpenbeck, Jenny

The **book** of words. . New Directions, 2007. 93 p. (New Directions paperbook, 1092)
ISBN 9780811217064
1. State-sponsored terrorism 2. Political violence 3. Teenage girls 4. Immigrant families 5. Totalitarianism 6. Tropics 7. Political fiction 8. Literary fiction 9. First person narratives

"Erpenbeck...eschews specific geographical detail, letting the eeriness rise to the universal. Susan Bernofsky's remarkably fluid translation does a seamless job of capturing Erpenbeck's swirl of language as the voice of her narrator trips along like uninterrupted thought..... This is writing so intense you don't even notice the brevity." —*Guardian (UK)*

Go, went, gone: a novel. Jenny Erpenbeck; translated from the German by Susan Bernofsky. New Directions Books, 2017. 286 p.
ISBN 9780811225946
1. Refugees 2. Retirees 3. Psychic trauma 4. Immigration and emigration 5. Former college teachers 6. Berlin, Germany 7. Literary fiction 8. Translations
LC 2017013730
New York Times Notable Book, 2018

Richard is a widower and a retired classics professor who lives in Berlin, and whose life is routine until the day he spies some African refugees staging a hunger strike. As he visits their shelter, interviews them, and becomes embroiled in their harrowing fates, he finds he has more in common with them than he realizes.
First published in German as Gehen, ging, gegangen. Munich : Albrecht Knaus Verlag, 2015.
Translated from the German.

Escandon, Maria Amparo

★ **L.A.** weather. Maria Amparo Escandon. Flatiron Books, 2021. 352 p.
ISBN 9781250802569

1. Mexican American families 2. Parent and adult child 3. Interfaith families 4. Marital conflict 5. Divorce 6. Los Angeles, California 7. Southern California 8. Domestic fiction

LC 2021024208

Follows the Los Angeles-based Alvardo family as they take critical looks at their internal and external relationships while struggling with a fierce local drought, impending evacuations, secrets, deception, betrayal and making some tough decisions.

"Escandon (Gonzalez & Daughter Trucking Co.) returns with a rollicking and hilarious family drama of telenovela-esque proportions that doubles as a fiery love letter to Los Angeles." —*Publishers Weekly*

Escobar, Mario

The **librarian** of Saint-Malo: a novel. Mario Escobar; translated from the Spanish by Gretchen Abernathy. Thomas Nelson, 2021. 384 p.

ISBN 9780785239918

1. World War II 2. Military occupation 3. Letter writing 4. Librarians 5. Nazis 6. France 7. Second World War era (1939-1945) 8. Historical fiction 9. Translations

LC 2020056697

Through letters with a famous author, one French librarian tells her love story and describes the brutal Nazi occupation of her small coastal village.

"This is a powerful portrait of a woman fighting to preserve knowledge in a crumbling world." —*Publishers Weekly*

Translation of: La bibliotecaria de Saint-Malo.

Originally published : HarperCollins Espanol, 2020.

Translated from the French.

Eskens, Allen

Nothing more dangerous: a novel. Allen Eskens. Mulholland Books, 2019. Vii, 293 pages

ISBN 9780316509725

1. Race relations 2. Male friendship 3. Small town life 4. Racism 5. Missing women 6. Ozark Mountain region 7. 1970s 8. Coming-of-age stories 9. Mysteries 10. Adult books for young adults

A high school boy growing up in the Ozark hills rethinks his understanding of the world, race and class when he befriends a black family that moves in across the street.

Esquivel, Laura

★ **Like** water for chocolate: a novel in monthly installments, with recipes, romances, and home remedies. Laura Esquivel; translated by Carol Christensen and Thomas Christensen. Doubleday, 1992. 245 p.

ISBN 9780385420167

1. Cooking, Mexican 2. Responsibility 3. Love triangles 4. Families 5. Women cooks 6. Mexico 7. Magical realism 8. Love stories 9. Translations

LC 91047188

Book Sense Book of the Year Adult Trade, 1994

Despite the fact that she has fallen in love with a young man, Tita, the youngest of three daughters born to a tyrannical rancher, must obey tradition and remain single and at home to care for her mother

"A poignant, funny story of love, life, and food which proves that all three are entwined and interdependent." —*Library Journal*

Translation of: Como agua para chocolate (1989).

Includes recipes.

Previously published as Like water for hot chocolate.

Essbaum, Jill Alexander

Hausfrau: a novel. Jill Alexander Essbaum. Random House, 2015. 324 p.

ISBN 9780812997538

1. Married women 2. Extramarital affairs 3. Self-fulfillment in women 4. Americans in Switzerland 5. Marital conflict 6. Switzerland 7. Psychological fiction

LC 2014026118

Enduring private misery in spite of a well-appointed life in suburban Zurich with her distant Swiss banker husband and young children, Anna Benz experiments with unfulfilling hobbies before engaging in a series of surprising sexual affairs.

"Isolated and tormented, Anna shares more than her name with that classic adulteress, Anna Karenina, but Essbaum has given a deft, modern facelift to the timeless story of a troubled marriage and tragic love." —*Booklist*

Estleman, Loren D.

The **adventures** of Johnny Vermillion: a novel. Loren D. Estleman. Forge, 2006. 272 p.

ISBN 9780765309143

1. Swindlers and swindling 2. Outlaws 3. Tricksters 4. Criminals 5. Bank robbers 6. 1870s 7. Westerns

LC 2006042532

Heading a theater troupe that journeys throughout the wild western frontier, Johnny Vermillion uses their performances as a clever cover-up for a bank robbery operation that is investigated by a suspicious Pinkerton agent.

"Johnny Vermillion, operator and featured performer of the Prairie Rose Repertory Company, travels the Wild West putting on plays in towns like Lockjaw, Diablo, and Purgatory. But that's just his cover: in fact, he and his small troop are bank robbers. And when a determined Pinkerton agent tips to what Johnny has been up to, an all-out pursuit results, culminating in a wickedly clever trap. Once again, Estleman proves why he is among the best of our contemporary western novelists .... Johnny and his merry band of thieves are thoroughly delightful characters, a bunch of good-natured rogues, colorful without being cartoony." —*Booklist*

A Tom Doherty Associates book.

Republished in 2016 with The Long High Noon.

★ **Amos** Walker: the complete story collection. Loren D. Estleman. Tyrus Books, 2010. 637 p; (Amos Walker novels)

ISBN 9781935562245

1. Private investigators 2. Crime 3. Criminals 4. Detroit, Michigan 5. Michigan 6. Hardboiled fiction 7. Mysteries

Collects every short story featuring Detroit detective Amos Walker, including a brand-new story never before published.

"All the elements that have made Estleman one of the best hard-boiled writers of all time—just a notch below Chandler and Hammett—are present in these 32 short stories. Remarkably, he has kept his Detroit-based Amos Walker series (Motor City Blue) fresh after three decades and 20 novels, and any fan of the genre who has yet to encounter the ex-cop turned PI will get a great introduction through this collection. What's most impressive is Estleman's ability to blend sharp-edged language, cynical characters, betrayals, twists, and a memorable narrative voice within the short story format. He also manages to inject dark humor into his work that keeps the violence, corruption, and double-crosses from becoming too grim.... Longtime fans will welcome the author's informative introduction." —*Publishers Weekly*

Frames. Loren D. Estleman. Forge, 2008. 272 p. (Valentino mysteries, 1)

ISBN 9780765315755

1. Archivists 2. Murder investigation 3. Film — Preservation 4. Film industry and trade — History 5. Women law students 6. Hollywood, California 7. California 8. Gentle reads 9. Cozy mysteries

LC 2008004505

Discovering a skeleton in a decrepit movie palace he hopes to restore, UCLA firm archivist Valentino also finds a priceless original director's cut of a long-lost classic film and must solve the mystery of the skeleton before the police claim the film as evidence and doom it to destruction.

"Estleman first introduced Valentino in a series of short stories for Ellery Queen Mystery Magazine and promises that Frames is the first in a series of novels featuring the film detective. As with every Estleman novel, Frames is written in crisp, vivid prose, the characters well-drawn. And the author's meticulous research of movie history adds another layer of richness." —San Francisco Chronicle

A Tom Doherty Associates book.

★ **Gas** City. Loren D. Estleman. Forge, 2008. 304 p.
ISBN 9780765319562
1. Mafia 2. Serial murders 3. Police 4. Police chiefs 5. Husband and wife 6. Noir fiction 7. Crime fiction

LC 2007034927

The black heart of a seemingly stable well-run city is pitched into violence and chaos when a serial killer's rampage pits the police chief, a mafia boss and the press against each other.

"The shades of Frank Norris and Upton Sinclair must have been looking over Loren D. Estleman's shoulder when he wrote Gas City. Set in a Midwestern metropolis that grew up around a refinery, his muscular novel initially takes a long view of the cynical bargain struck between civic leaders and organized crime—and only moves in for the kill when a key figure in this devil's dance decides to reform. Like earlier muckraking writers, Estleman is always looking for the tipping point where our frontier values of independent entrepreneurship and community justice tumble into criminality. And his characters never stop asking whether it's possible to go back and get it right." —New York Times Book Review

A Tom Doherty Associates book.

★ **Indigo:** a Valentino mystery. Loren D. Estleman. Forge Books, 2020. 224 p. (Valentino mysteries, 6)
ISBN 9781250258359
1. Amateur detectives 2. Film collectors and collecting 3. Organized crime 4. Missing persons 5. Actors and actresses 6. California 7. Hollywood, California 8. Mysteries

Collecting a valuable, never-before-released noir film that was shelved for its possible mob ties, film detective Valentino searches for clues about the film's believed-dead star as part of a mainstream marketing campaign.

"The solution to the cold case is both clever and surprising. Film noir buffs will be in heaven." —Publishers Weekly

Infernal angels. Loren D. Estleman. Forge, 2011. 304 p. (Amos Walker novels, 21)
ISBN 9780765319555
1. Private investigators 2. Murder investigation 3. Drug smuggling 4. Criminals 5. Walker, Amos (Fictitious character) 6. Detroit, Michigan 7. Hardboiled fiction 8. Mysteries 9. First person narratives 10. Adult books for young adults

Detroit private investigator Amos Walker is hired to recover HDTV converter boxes stolen from a retailer whose shop also does vintage resale business. Before long, the case turns old school: both a suspect and the man who lost the boxes are murdered, and Walker ends up working with both the local police and the feds.

"A novel featuring Detroit PI Amos Walker.... Reuben Crossgrain, proprietor of Past Presence (Everything you require for the Modern Regressive Lifestyle), hires Walker to recover 25 TV converter boxes that allow the owner to watch HDTV on an analog set, although the total value of the loss isn't much more than Walker's standard retainer. The detective hits the pavement to identify the likely recipients of the hot items, and his digging soon attracts the attention of ex-Detroit police detective Mary Ann Thaler, who now works in D.C. on homeland security. As the bodies start to drop, Estleman presents a powerful view of the battered inner city, where federally funded housing ends up derelict. Three decades on, Estleman and Walker show no signs of slowing down." —Publishers Weekly

★ The **master** executioner. Loren D. Estleman. Forge, 2001. 270 p.
ISBN 9780312869700
1. Capital punishment 2. Executions and executioners 3. Civil War veterans 4. Frontier and pioneer life 5. The West (United States) 6. 19th century 7. Westerns 8. Psychological fiction

LC 2001023181

Western Heritage Award for Outstanding Western Novel, 2002

Hangman Oscar Stone is a master executioner, who prides himself on his careful and exacting work, until a sudden moment of realization and devastating truth forces him to come to terms with himself and his profession.

"Estleman has created an unforgettable character in Stone.... A dark, compelling journey into a previously unexplored facet of the old West." —Booklist

A **smile** on the face of the tiger. Loren D. Estleman. Mysterious Press, 2000. 295 p. (Amos Walker novels, 14)
ISBN 9780892967063
1. Private investigators 2. Mystery story writing 3. Missing persons 4. Murder investigation 5. Walker, Amos (Fictitious character) 6. Detroit, Michigan 7. Hardboiled fiction 8. Mysteries 9. First person narratives

LC 22284

Detroit private detective Amos Walker is hired by scheming book editor Louise Starr to find the missing Eugene Booth, an aging pulp fiction writer from the 1950s, to uncover why he has turned down his first book contract in forty years.

"Detroit gumshoe Amos Walker, a serious drinker-thinker who lives by a tough-guy code that went out of fashion with the Edsel, is sick of hearing that he looks as if he just slouched out of a 1950's paperback novel. But when a publisher hires him to find Eugene Booth, a has-been pulp legend who skipped out on a lucrative contract to reissue his best book, Walker finds himself staring at a streaky mirror image of himself—if he lives so long.... Estleman pays handsome homage to Goodis and Woolrich and all the other 'paper tigers' to whom he dedicates this wonderful book." —New York Times Book Review

★ **Something** borrowed, something black. Loren D. Estleman. Forge, 2002. 236 pages; (Peter Macklin novels, 4)
ISBN 9780312878634
1. Assassins 2. Honeymoons 3. Macklin, Peter (Fictitious character) 4. Los Angeles, California 5. San Antonio, Texas 6. Thrillers and suspense

LC 2001054752

Retired hit man Peter Macklin is enjoying his honeymoon with his beautiful new wife Laurie when his past catches up to him, and he is forced to leave to take care of old business that will not wait.

"The story vibrates with letter-perfect details, and the plot, with changing locations and changing points of view, is deftly handled." —Publishers Weekly

A Tom Doherty Associates book.

Eugenides, Jeffrey

Fresh complaint: stories. Jeffrey Eugenides. Farrar, Straus and Giroux, 2017. 285 p.

ISBN 9780374203061

1. Misfits (Persons) 2. Life change events 3. Human nature 4. Embezzlers 5. Travelers 6. Short stories 7. Literary fiction

LC 2017007576

Booklist Editors' Choice, 2017; New York Times Notable Book, 2017; Longlisted for the Andrew Carnegie Medal for Excellence in Fiction, 2018

A first collection of short stories by the Pulitzer Prize winner includes the tales of a failed poet-turned-embezzler, a young traveler seeking enlightenment, and a high schooler whose drastic decision upends a British physicist's life.

"Pulitzer Prizewinning Eugenides first story collection...is gifted with the strong voices and luminous prose his novels are known for." —*Booklist*

★ The **marriage** plot. Jeffrey Eugenides. Farrar Straus & Giroux, 2011. 406 p.

ISBN 9780374203054

1. Compulsive behavior in men 2. Love triangles 3. Man-woman relationships 4. Semiotics 5. Loners 6. 1980s 7. Literary fiction 8. Psychological fiction

Booklist Editors' Choice, 2011; Indies' Choice Book Awards, Adult Fiction, 2012; Library Journal Best Books, 2011; New York Times Notable Book, 2011; National Book Critics Circle Award for Fiction finalist, 2011

Madeleine Hanna breaks out of her straight-and-narrow mold when she enrolls in a semiotics course and falls in love with charismatic loner Leonard Morten, a time which is complicated by the resurfacing of a man who is obsessed with the idea that Madeleine is his destiny.

"In capturing the heady spirit of youthful intellect on the verge, Eugenides revives the coming-of-age novel for a new generation. The book's fidelity to its young heroes and to a superb supporting cast of enigmatic professors, feminist theorists, neo-Victorians, and concerned mothers, and all of their evolving investment in ideas and ideals is such that the central argument of the book is also its solution: the old stories may be best after all, but there are always new ways to complicate them." —*Publishers Weekly*

★ **Middlesex.** Jeffrey Eugenides. Farrar, Straus, and Giroux, 2002. 544 p.

ISBN 9780374199692

1. People who are intersex 2. Greek Americans 3. Identity (Psychology) 4. City life 5. Suburban life 6. Detroit, Michigan 7. Coming-of-age stories 8. Literary fiction 9. LGBTQIA fiction

LC 2002019921

Great Lakes Book Awards, Fiction category, 2003; Library Journal Best Books, 2002; Pulitzer Prize for Fiction, 2003; National Book Critics Circle Award for Fiction finalist, 2002; Shortlisted for the International IMPAC Dublin Literary Award, 2004; Shortlisted for the James Tait Black Memorial Prize for Fiction, 2003

Calliope's friendship with a classmate and her sense of identity are compromised by the adolescent discovery that she is a hermaphrodite, a situation with roots in her grandparent's desperate struggle for survival in the 1920s.

"Eugenides pitches a big tent, but one of the delights of 'Middlesex' is how soundly it's constructed, with motifs and characters weaving through the novel's various episodes, pulling it tight." —*New York Times Book Review*

★ The **virgin** suicides. Jeffrey Eugenides. Farrar Straus Giroux, 1993. 249 p.

ISBN 9780374284381

1. Suicide 2. Suburban families 3. Teenage boys 4. Teenage girls 5. Sisters 6. Detroit, Michigan 7. 1970s 8. Coming-of-age stories 9. Psychological fiction 10. Literary fiction

LC 92033466

ALA Notable Book, 1994

The narrator and his friends piece together the events that led up to suicides of the Lisbon girls, brainy Therese, fastidious Mary, ascetic Bonnie, libertine Lux, and saintly Cecilia.

"The author's engrossing writing style keeps one reading despite a creepy feeling that one shouldn't be enjoying it so much. A black, glittering novel that won't be to everyone's taste but must be tried by readers looking for something different." —*Library Journal*

Evanovich, Janet

★ **Game** on: tempting twenty-eight. Janet Evanovich. Atria Books, 2021. 320 p. (Stephanie Plum mysteries, 28)

ISBN 9781982154875

1. Bounty hunters 2. Computer crimes 3. Hackers 4. Computer crime investigation 5. Crime 6. Trenton, New Jersey 7. Mysteries 8. Chick lit 9. First person narratives

Unsure if he is her partner or her competition, Stephanie Plum and Oswald Wednesday try to hunt down a master cyber criminal in Trenton.

"A hilariously madcap, action-packed caper filled with crazy twists and some nail-biting suspense.... All in all, this finds the irrepressible Stephanie and cohorts in absolutely top form." —*Booklist*

Look alive twenty-five. Janet Evanovich. G.P. Putnam's Sons, 2018. 311 p. (Stephanie Plum mysteries, 25)

ISBN 9780399179228

1. UFO abductions 2. Missing persons investigation 3. Women bounty hunters 4. Women bail bond agents 5. Bounty hunters 6. New Jersey 7. Trenton, New Jersey 8. Mysteries 9. Chick lit 10. First person narratives

LC 2018038157

When three consecutive managers from a famous deli go missing, leaving no clues behind but a single shoe each, latest manager Stephanie Plum navigates Lula's theories about alien abductions to avoid becoming the next victim.

One for the money. Janet Evanovich. C. Scribner's Sons, 1994. 290 p. (Stephanie Plum mysteries, 1)

ISBN 9780684196398

1. Women bounty hunters 2. Fugitives 3. Family businesses 4. Police 5. Cousins 6. Trenton, New Jersey 7. Mysteries 8. Chick lit 9. First person narratives

LC 9350733

John Creasey Memorial Award (Best First Crime Novel), 1995; Dilys Award, 1995

When Stephanie Plum needs money (she's been laid off, her Miata has been repossessed, her rent is due, etc.), she turns to bounty hunting for quick cash...even though she has no idea what to do and doesn't own a gun. Luckily, her first quarry, an ex-cop accused of murder, turns out to be her first lover, with whom she still shares a powerful chemistry; unluckily, he's better at getting away than she is at catching him. With the help of a mysterious (and hot!) new friend, Ranger, who shows her some tricks of the trade, Stephanie just might turn this new job into a career.

"A wonderful sense of humor, an eye for detail, and a self-deprecating narrative endow Stephanie Plum with the easy-to-swallow believability that accounts for her appeal as heroine.... A witty, well-written, and gutsy debut." —*Library Journal*

Turbo twenty-three. Janet Evanovich. Bantam Books, 2016. 288 p. (Stephanie Plum mysteries, 23)

ISBN 9780345543004

1. Women bounty hunters 2. Women bail bond agents 3. Man-woman relationships 4. Bounty hunters 5. Plum, Stephanie (Fictitious character) 6. New Jersey 7. Trenton, New Jersey 8. Mysteries 9. Chick lit 10. First person narratives

Bounty hunter Stephanie Plum receives support from prostitute-turned-bounty hunter Lula, gun-toting Grandma Mazur, on-again-off-again paramour Joe Morelli, and mentor Ranger.

Evanovich, Stephanie

Under the table. Stephanie Evanovich. William Marrow, 2019. 336 pages

ISBN 9780062415929

1. Women caterers 2. Computer programmers 3. Millionaires 4. Separation (Marital relations) 5. Self-discovery 6. New York City 7. Chick lit

The best-selling author of Big Girl Panties presents a modern adaptation of My Fair Lady in the story of a canny young divorcee who makes over her socially awkward millionaire client, with unexpected results.

Evans, Danielle

★ The **office** of historical corrections: a novella and stories. Danielle Evans. Riverhead Books, 2020. 240 p.

ISBN 9781594487330

1. Race relations 2. Interpersonal relations 3. Racism 4. Loss (Psychology) 5. United States 6. African American fiction 7. Literary fiction 8. Short stories

LC 2019058284

ALA Notable Book, 2021; LibraryReads Favorites, 2020

The award-winning author examines race, grief and apology in a history-inspired anthology that complements the title novella.

"Each detail meticulously builds on the last, leading to satisfying, unforeseeable plot twists. The language is colorful and drenched with emotion. Readers won't be able to look away from the page as Evans captivates them in a world all her own." —Booklist

Evans, Diana

Ordinary people: a novel. Diana Evans. Liveright Publishing, 2018. 326 p.

ISBN 9781631494819

1. Husband and wife 2. New mothers 3. Marital conflict 4. Identity (Psychology) 5. Extramarital affairs 6. London (England) 7. Mainstream fiction

Shortlisted for The Women's Prize for Fiction, 2019

In South London and the surrounding suburbs, two couples—longtime friends whose bonds are no longer clearly defined—struggle through a year of marital crisis.

Evans, Nicholas

★ The **horse** whisperer: a novel. Nicholas Evans. Delacorte Press, 1995. 404 p.

ISBN 9780385315234

1. Accidents 2. Horse whisperers 3. Human/animal communication 4. Ranchers 5. Humans and horses 6. Montana 7. Mainstream fiction 8. Love stories 9. Books to movies

LC 95-37603

After her daughter and the girl's horse are injured in a tragic accident, Annie Graves journeys across the continent in search of Tom Booker, the Horse Whisperer, hoping he can use his ancient gift to help both the horse and the maimed girl.

"Evans can give equally clipped but clear descriptions of a prosthetic device or a Montana vista, and the lead characters emerge through carefully constructed, seemingly effortless scenes and dialog, not in histrionics." —Library Journal

Evaristo, Bernardine

★ **Girl,** woman, other. Bernardine Evaristo. Grove Press, 2019. 452 pages

ISBN 9780802157706

1. Identity (Psychology) 2. Women — Social life and customs 3. Black British 4. England 5. Great Britain 6. Literary fiction 7. Multiple perspectives

ALA Notable Book, 2020; Booklist Editors' Choice, 2019; Man Booker Prize, 2019; Shortlisted for the International Dublin Literary Award, 2021; Shortlisted for The Women's Prize for Fiction, 2020

From one of Britain's most celebrated writers of color, a magnificent portrayal of the intersections of identity among an interconnected group of Black British women.

"Anglo-Nigerian writer Evaristo's (Mr. Loverman, 2014) courageous and intersectional novel explores Black British identity and unfolds in a single night, or over the course of 100 years, depending on how readers look at it." —Booklist

12 interconnected short stories.

Originally published in London by Hamish Hamilton, 2019.

Everett, Elizabeth

★ A **lady's** formula for love. Elizabeth Everett. Berkley Pub Group, 2021. 336 p. (Secret scientists of London, 1)

ISBN 9780593200629

1. Women scientists 2. Bodyguards 3. Associations, institutions, etc. 4. Secrets 5. Gender role 6. Historical romances 7. Victorian romances

LC 2020030432

.Lady Violet Hughes is keeping secrets. First, she founded London's first social club for ladies to provide sanctuary for England's most brilliant female scientists. Second, she is using her genius on a clandestine mission for the Crown. But the biggest secret of all? Her feelings for protection officer Arthur Kneland. The most guarded of men, Kneland learned the hard way to put duty first. But the more time spent in the company of Violet and the eccentric club members, the more his best intentions go up in flames. Literally. When a shadowy threat infiltrates Violet's laboratories, endangering her life and her work, scientist and bodyguard will find all their theories put to the test—and learn that the most important discoveries are those of the heart.

"With its beguiling blend of danger, desire, and deliciously dry wit, the brilliantly conceived and smartly executed A Lady's Formula for Love is an exciting debut and a first-rate launch for Everett's The Secret Scientists of London series. Fans of Evie Dunmore's A League of Extraordinary Women books or Olivia Waite's historical romances will savor this fiercely feminist, achingly romantic, and intensely sensual love story." —Booklist

Everett, Percival L.

Erasure: a novel. Percival Everett. University Press of New England, 2001. 265 p.

ISBN 9781584650904

1. Identity (Psychology) 2. Fiction writing 3. African American authors 4. African American men 5. Mothers and sons 6. Washington, D.C. 7. Satirical fiction 8. Literary fiction 9. Novels-within-novels

LC 2001002535

ALA Notable Book, 2002; Hurston/Wright Legacy Award: Fiction, 2002

Thelonious "Monk" Ellison's writing career has bottomed out: his latest manuscript has been rejected by seventeen publishers, which stings all the more because his previous novels have been "critically acclaimed." He seethes on the sidelines of the literary establishment as he watches the meteoric success of We's Lives in Da Ghetto, a first novel by a woman who once visited "some relatives in Harlem for a couple of days." In his rage and despair, Monk dashes off a novel meant to be an indictment of Juanita Mae Jenkins's bestseller. He doesn't intend for My Pafology to be published, let alone taken seriously, but it is—under the pseudonym Stagg R. Leigh—and soon it becomes the Next Big Thing.

God's country. Percival Everett. Faber and Faber, 1994. 219 p.

ISBN 9780571198320

1. African American men 2. Women kidnapping victims 3. Kidnapping 4. Frontier and pioneer life 5. Race relations 6. The West (United States) 7. 1870s 8. Westerns 9. Satirical fiction 10. Literary fiction

The unlikely narrator through this tale of misadventures is one Curt Marder: gambler, drinker, cheat, and would-be womanizer. It's 1871, and he's lost his farm, his wife, and his dog to a band of marauding hooligans. With nothing to live on but a desire to recover what is rightfully his, Marder is forced to enlist the help of the best tracker in the West: a black man named Bubba.

I am Not Sidney Poitier. Percival L. Everett. Graywolf Press, 2009. 234 p.

ISBN 9781555975272

1. Race relations 2. African American men — Identity 3. Identity (Psychology) 4. Class conflict 5. Orphans 6. Georgia 7. Alabama 8. Satirical fiction 9. Literary fiction 10. African American fiction

Hurston/Wright Legacy Award: Fiction, 2010

Rendered an orphan at a young age, Not Sidney Poitier bears an uncanny resemblance to the actor who inspired his name, grows up in the home of a less-than-watchful foster father, and struggles to balance his considerable fortune with the inherent disadvantages of his skin color.

"Not only is the novel smart and without a trace of pretentiousness, it shows Everett as a novelist at the height of his narrative and satirical powers." —Publishers Weekly

Evison, Jonathan

All about Lulu: a novel. Jonathan Evison. Soft Skull Press, 2008. 340 p.

ISBN 9781593761967

1. Blended families 2. Stepsisters 3. Unrequited love 4. Grief 5. Teenage boys 6. Los Angeles, California 7. United States 8. Coming-of-age stories 9. Mainstream fiction

LC 2007046761

Loner William Miller tries to cope after his mother dies of cancer, his bodybuilding father remarries a grief counselor, and he falls in love with his stepsister Lulu.

"Evison provides readers a viciously funny and deeply felt portrayal of a blended family and one man's thwarted longing." —Publishers Weekly

★ **Lawn** boy: a novel. Jonathan Evison. Algonquin Books of Chapel Hill, 2018. 312 p.

ISBN 9781616202620

1. Mexican Americans 2. Working class 3. American Dream 4. Libraries 5. Librarians 6. Washington (State) 7. Coming-of-age stories 8. Adult books for young adults

LC 2017032613

Alex Award, 2019; Booklist Editors' Choice, 2018

Faced by a life of menial prospects in the years after high school, Mike Munoz, a young Mexican-American, attempts over and over to change his life for the better and achieve the American dream, only to be stymied by social-class distinctions and cultural discrimination.

Legends of the North Cascades: a novel. Jonathan Evison. Algonquin Books of Chapel Hill, 2021. 336 p.

ISBN 9781643750101

1. Fathers and daughters 2. Caves 3. Wilderness survival 4. Secrets 5. Veterans 6. Historical fiction 7. Literary fiction 8. Parallel narratives

LC 2020040903

After his wife's death, a man brings his young daughter to live in a cave he has found in the Cascade mountains. Once there, his daughter begins to sense the presence of other people in the cave, a mother and son who retreated there during the last ice age in an effort to survive.

"Evison masterfully delivers subtle yet pointed commentary on how society marginalizes veterans and how we profess to admire yet distrust the individualist ethos while also offering a profound meditation on the human spirit." —Booklist

The **revised** fundamentals of caregiving: a novel. By Jonathan Evison. Algonquin Books of Chapel Hill, 2012. 288 p.

ISBN 9781616200398

1. Caregivers 2. Teenagers with muscular dystrophy 3. Automobile travel 4. Loss (Psychology) 5. People with muscular dystrophy 6. Washington (State) 7. Mainstream fiction

LC 2012002956

After losing virtually everything meaningful in his life, Benjamin trains to be a caregiver, but his first client, a fiercely independent teen with muscular dystrophy, gives him more than he bargained for and soon the two embark on a road trip to visit the boy's ailing father.

★ **Small** world. Jonathan Evison. E.P. Dutton, 2022. 480 p.

ISBN 9780593184127

1. American dream 2. Ancestors 3. Railroads 4. Travelers 5. Family history 6. Antebellum America (1820-1861) 7. 1850s 8. Historical fiction 9. Parallel narratives

In this epic historical novel set in multiple time periods, present-day travelers on a train and their ancestors more than a century before are brought together by the history they share against such iconic backdrops as the California gold rush and the development of the Continental Railroad.

"The sweeping panorama is the perfect canvas on which Evison explores the diversity of the nation's character while limning contours and adding textures to bring to vivid life his memorable characters." —Booklist

West of here: a novel. By Jonathan Evison. Algonquin Books of Chapel Hill, 2011. 496 p.

ISBN 9781565129528

1. Men and nature 2. Small town life 3. Eccentrics and eccentricities 4. Dams 5. Consequences 6. Washington (State) 7. 1880s 8. 2000s (Decade) 9. Literary fiction 10. Parallel narratives

Booklist Editors' Choice, 2011

The stories of the people who first inhabited the mythical town of Port Bonita in Washington State from 1887-1891, and then who live there in 2005-2006 and must deal with the damage done by their predecessors.

Extence, Gavin

The **universe** versus Alex Woods. Gavin Extence. Orbit, 2013. 320 p.
ISBN 9780316246576
1. Misfits (Persons) 2. Teenage boys 3. Intergenerational friendship 4. Books and reading 5. Widowers 6. Coming-of-age stories 7. Mainstream fiction 8. Adult books for young adults
Alex Award, 2014; School Library Journal Best Books: Best Adult Books 4 Teens, 2013

Alex Woods was struck by a meteorite when he was ten years old, leaving scars that marked him for an extraordinary life. The son of a fortune teller, bookish, and an easy target for bullies, he hasn't had the most conventional childhood. When he meets curmudgeonly widower Mr. Peterson, he finds an unlikely friend. Someone who teaches him that that you only get one shot at life. That you have to make it count. So when, aged seventeen, Alex is stopped at Dover customs with 113 grams of marijuana, an urn full of ashes on the passenger seat, and an entire nation in uproar, he's fairly sure he's done the right thing.

"Most teens think the universe is against them at some point. Seventeen-year-old Alex Woods has plenty of evidence for his case: a tarot-reading witch for a mother, his father a one-night Solstice stand long since forgotten, a chunk of meteorite crashing through the roof and smashing into him, the onset of epileptic seizures, and school bullies eager to target him...A bittersweet, cross-audience charmer, this debut novel will appeal to guys, YA readers, and Vonnegut and coming-of-age fiction fans." —*Library Journal*

A tale of unlikely friendship—Cover.

F

Faber, Michel

The **book** of strange new things. Michel Faber. Hogarth Press, 2014. 500 p.
ISBN 9780553418842
1. Clergy 2. Life on other planets 3. Husband and wife 4. Married men 5. Environmental disasters 6. Literary fiction 7. Science fiction
New York Times Notable Book, 2014

Called to perform missionary work in a world light years away where the natives are fascinated by the concepts he introduces, man of faith Peter Leigh finds his beliefs tested when he learns of natural disasters that are tearing Earth apart.

The **crimson** petal and the white. Michel Faber. Harcourt, 2002. 838 p.
ISBN 9780151006922
1. Rich men 2. Prostitutes 3. Social status 4. Young women — History 5. Married men — Relations with single women 6. London, England 7. Great Britain 8. Victorian era (1837-1901) 9. 19th century 10. Historical fiction
LC 2002024138
Booklist Editors' Choice, 2002; New York Times Notable Book, 2002; Shortlisted for the James Tait Black Memorial Prize for Fiction, 2003

Yearning to escape her life of prostitution in 1870s London, Sugar finds her fate entangled in the complicated family life of patron William, an egotistical perfume magnate.

"The large themes that interwine the characters with one another—religion, health, sexuality, death, and, reluctantly, love—are juxtaposed against the most minute and intimate details of Victorian life...This massive work is startling and absorbing." —*Booklist*

Originally published: Edinburgh : Canongate, 2002.

Fabry, Chris

Looking into you. Chris Fabry. Thorndike Press, 2017. 400 pages
ISBN 9781432839604
1. Birthmothers — Identification 2. Mothers and daughters 3. Adopted girls 4. Regret in women 5. College teachers 6. Christian fiction
Christy Award for Contemporary (Series, Sequels, and Novellas) Category, 2017

Every day, Paige Redwine is haunted by a choice she made when she was only seventeen. Now, just past forty, still single, she lives a tidy, controlled life as a well-respected English professor at a college in Nashville. Nothing could prepare her for the day Treha Langsam—the daughter she secretly placed for adoption—walks into her classroom as a student, unknowingly confronting Paige with both her greatest longing and her greatest fear.

The **promise** of Jesse Woods. Chris Fabry. Tyndale House Publishers, Inc, 2016. 400 p.
ISBN 9781414387772
1. Life change events 2. Family secrets 3. Friendship 4. Reunions 5. Children of clergy 6. West Virginia 7. Christian fiction 8. Coming-of-age stories 9. First person narratives
LC 2016005373
Christy Award for Contemporary (Stand Alone) Category, 2017

Matt Plumley moves to West Virginia and falls in love with an Appalachian girl, Jesse Woods, but she ends their relationship after he joins her in a rescue that causes a death, and years later, Matt returns to find out the truth about that night.

War room: prayer is a powerful weapon. By Chris Fabry. Tyndale House Pub 2015. 424 pages
ISBN 9781496407290
1. Marital conflict 2. Suburban life 3. Prayer 4. Faith (Christianity) 5. Working mothers 6. Domestic fiction 7. Christian fiction 8. Media tie-ins
LC 2015011970
When real-estate agent Elizabeth Jordan meets elderly widow Clara Williams, a visit to the elder woman's prayer room helps Elizabeth realize that her mounting problems at home are surmountable with the help of God.

Based on the screenplay by Alex Kendrick and Stephen Kendrick.

Fairstein, Linda A.

Blood oath. Linda A. Fairstein. Dutton, an imprint of Penguin Random House LLC, 2018. 400 p. (Alexandra Cooper novels, 20)
ISBN 9781524743109
1. Women assistant district attorneys 2. Sex crimes 3. Sexually abused women 4. Detectives 5. Biomedical engineering 6. New York City 7. Thrillers and suspense 8. Legal thrillers

A key witness' revelation about a sexual assault at the hands of a prominent official is complicated by rumors about a colleague's abusive conduct and another associate's violent, mysterious collapse.

Entombed. Linda Fairstein. Scribner, 2005. 416 p. (Alexandra Cooper novels, 7)
ISBN 9780743254885
1. Poe, Edgar Allan 2. Women lawyers 3. Serial rape 4. Murder 5. Women public prosecutors 6. Literary societies 7. New York City 8. Upper East Side, New York City 9. Thrillers and suspense 10. Legal thrillers
LC 2004052189
Romantic Times Reviewers Choice Award, 2005

When a former residence of Edgar Allan Poe is demolished, a human skeleton is found behind the walls. Soon, Cooper is digging into Poe's tormented life, hoping to discover a clue that will break open the case.

"It's a tribute to Fairstein's integrity and her clear, measured prose that the novel never tips into prurience. Her methodical presentation of authentic detail engages reader interest more than narrative flourish or cheap thrills." —*Publishers Weekly*

Fajardo-Anstine, Kali

★ **Sabrina** & Corina: stories. Kali Fajardo-Anstine. One World, 2019. 212 p.

ISBN 9780525511298

1. Hispanic American women 2. Mothers and daughters 3. Social marginality 4. Poverty 5. Racism 6. Denver, Colorado 7. The West (United States) 8. Literary fiction 9. Short stories

LC 2018023965

ALA Notable Book, 2020; Library Journal Best Books, 2019; National Book Award for Fiction finalist, 2019

A debut story collection about female relationships and the deep-rooted truths of our homelands features Latina protagonists of indigenous descent who cautiously navigate the violence and changes in a Denver, Colorado community.

"These stories are stirring meditations on the lives of Latinas of indigenous ancestry; Fajardo-Anstine's collection is vividly alive with the love and pain of its characters, while echoing with the spiritual power of their pasts." —*Publishers Weekly*

Fallada, Hans

Every man dies alone. . Melville House Pub, 2009. 544 p.
ISBN 9781933633633

1. Hampel, Otto Hermann 2. World War II 3. Nazism 4. Civil disobedience 5. Resistance to government 6. Grief 7. Germany 8. Biographical fiction 9. Historical fiction 10. Books to movies

LC 2008027489

New York Times Notable Book, 2009

Tells the story of a working-class German couple who lose their son to war and begin to a small resistance against Nazi power.

"This is a readable, suspense-driven novel from an author who a) knew what he was doing when it came to writing commercial fiction, and b) had lived through, and so knew intimately, the period he was writing about. This is an extraordinary combination. I hesitate to use a word like serendipity, but cruelly enough, that's exactly what it was. Thus, the characters and what characters they are, the good, the bad and the ugly of the Berlin working class during the war are drawn from life. They are alive." —*Globe and Mail*

First published in German as Jeder stirbt fur sich allein. Berlin : Aufbau, 1947.

Also known as Alone in Berlin: London : Penguin Classics, 2009.

Fallon, Siobhan

You know when the men are gone. Siobhan Fallon. G.P. Putnam's Sons, 2011. 240 p.

ISBN 9780399157202

1. Military spouses 2. Families of military personnel 3. Iraq War, 2003-2011 4. Military life 5. Coping in women 6. Texas 7. Short stories

LC 2010029597

A collection of interconnected stories relate the experiences of Fort Hood military wives who share a poignant vigil during which they raise children while waiting for their husbands to return.

"In this book of eight stories, connected by young families stationed at Fort Hood, Texas, Siobhan Fallon sees military life as an alternate universe. It can be many times better and so much worse than its civilian counterparts.... Fallon is a superb writer with a delicate perception of this raw material. Her characters may be invented or based on people she herself knew as an army wife. In either case, the stories are powerful." —*Providence Journal*

Amy Einhorn books.

Farah, Nuruddin

Crossbones. Nuruddin Farah. Riverhead Books, 2011. 400 p. (Link trilogy, 3)

ISBN 9781594488160

1. Americans in Somalia 2. Journalists 3. College teachers 4. Political refugees 5. Somali Americans 6. Somalia 7. Mogadishu, Somalia 8. Political fiction 9. Literary fiction

Jeebleh returns to Mogadiscio to discover that it is being rigidly controlled by white-robed oppressors; while Ahl searches for his missing stepson, who he fears has been recruited for a religious insurgency.

"Gripping but utterly humane thriller set in one of the least-understood regions on earth." —*Kirkus*

Knots. Nuruddin Farah. Riverhead Books, 2007. 432 p. (Links trilogy 2)

ISBN 9781594489242

1. Americans in Somalia 2. Warlords 3. Feminism 4. Muslim women 5. Peace activists 6. Mogadishu, Somalia 7. Political fiction 8. Literary fiction

LC 2006023107

New York Times Notable Book, 2007

Returning to her native home in Somalia after being raised in North America and suffering a failed marriage, self-reliant Cambara struggles to reclaim her family's home from a warlord and finds support from a group of women activists.

"Despite its weaknesses, there is beauty in this story of reclamation and resurrection. When Farah's heroine sheds her veil of conformity, it is as if Somalia itself is emerging from a cocoon of despair." —*Time Out New York*

Farrell, Henry

★ **What** ever happened to Baby Jane? Henry Farrell. Carroll & Graf 1991. 245 p.

ISBN 9780881847253

1. Sisters 2. Former film actors and actresses 3. Sibling rivalry 4. Psychological fiction 5. Books to movies

Baby Jane, a former child star of early vaudeville who resented having to grow up in the shadow of her prettier sister, Blanche, is now casting her own sinister shadow over Blanche, an invalid who must rely on Jane for her care.

Originally published: New York : Rinehart, 1960.

Farrow, John

The storm murders: a thriller. John Farrow. St Martins Pr 2015. 384 p (Emile Cinq-Mars mysteries, 4; Storm murders trilogy, 1)

ISBN 9781250057686

1. Blizzards 2. Weather 3. Farms 4. Murder 5. Murder investigation 6. Quebec (Province) 7. Mysteries 8. Canadian fiction

City of Ice, John Farrow's first book in his acclaimed Emile Cinq-Mars series, which has been hailed by Booklist as "the best series in crime fiction today," has been published in over 17 countries. Now with

The Storm Murders, the series continues. On the day after a massive blizzard, two policemen are called to an isolated farm house sitting all by itself in the middle of a pristine snow-blanketed field. Inside the lonely abode are two dead people. But there are no tracks in the snow leading either to the house or away. What happened here? Is this a murder/suicide case? Or will it turn into something much more sinister? John Farrow is the pen name of Trevor Ferguson, a Canadian writer who has been named Canada's best novelist in both Books in Canada and the Toronto Star. This is the first of a trilogy he is writing for us called The Storm Murders trilogy. Each book features Emile Cinq-Mars, the Hercule Poirot of Canada, and extreme weather conditions.

"Farrow (a pseudonym for Canadian author Trevor Ferguson) brings a literary fiction writer's sensitivity to nuance and feel for landscape to this fine, character-rich thriller with a bang-up finish." —*Booklist*

Faulkner, William

★ **Absalom,** Absalom!. William Faulkner. Vintage Books, 1990. 313 p.
ISBN 9780679732181
1. Poor people 2. Vermeer, Johannes 3. Yoknapatawpha County (Miss. : Imaginary place) 4. Sutpen family (Fictitious characters) 5. Mississippi 6. Literary fiction 7. Family sagas 8. Historical fiction
The story of Thomas Sutpen, an enigmatic stranger who came to Jefferson in the early 1830s to wrest his mansion out of the muddy bottoms of the north Mississippi wilderness. He was a man, Faulkner said, "who wanted sons and the sons destroyed him.

★ **As** I lay dying: the corrected text. William Faulkner. Modern Library, 1992. Vii, 261 p.
ISBN 9780375504525
1. Death 2. Farm life 3. Dysfunctional families 4. Yoknapatawpha County (Miss. : Imaginary place) 5. Southern Gothic 6. Southern fiction 7. Literary fiction
LC 56254
The members of a Southern family contribute their individual tribulations to this encompassing impression of rural poverty.
Originally published: 1930.

★ **Go** down, Moses. William Faulkner. Vintage Books, 1990. 365 p.
ISBN 9780679732174
1. Race relations 2. Plantation life 3. Slavery 4. Nature 5. Yoknapatawpha County (Miss. : Imaginary place) 6. Mississippi 7. Literary fiction 8. Short stories 9. Modern classics
LC 90050209
Set in mythical Yoknapatawpha County, seven interrelated stories deal with the complex, changing relationships between Blacks and whites and between man and nature.
Originally published by Random House, Inc, in 1942—Title page verso.

The **hamlet**. William Faulkner. Random House, 1940. 366 p. (Snopes Family, 1)
ISBN 9780394427591
1. Small town life 2. Obsession 3. Family relationships 4. Sharecroppers 5. Snopes family (Fictitious characters) 6. Mississippi 7. Family sagas 8. Literary fiction 9. Books to movies
LC 64007972
Traces the growing power of Flem Snopes, a white-trash farmer, in the Mississippi town of Frenchman's Bend.
Later film version: Long hot summer

Intruder in the dust. William Faulkner. Vintage International, 1991. 241 p.
ISBN 9780679736516

1. Trials (Murder) 2. African American defendants 3. Racism 4. Race relations 5. Lynching 6. Mississippi 7. Literary fiction 8. Books to movies 9. Modern classics
LC 91050014
Dramatizes the events that surround the murder of a white man in a volatile Southern community.
Originally published in 1948.

★ **Light** in August. William Faulkner. Modern Library, 2002. Vii, 512 p.
ISBN 9780679642480
1. Racism 2. Pregnant women 3. Multiracial men 4. Drifters 5. Misfits (Persons) 6. Mississippi 7. Literary fiction 8. Modern classics 9. Southern Gothic
LC 67012716
In a novel about hopeless perseverance in the face of mortality, guileless Lena Grove searches for the father of her unborn child, Reverend Hightower is plagued by visions of Confederate horsemen, and drifter Joe Christmas is consumed by his mixed ancestry.
Originally published: Harrison Smith and Robert Haas, 1932.

The **reivers:** a reminiscence. William Faulkner. Random House, 1962. 305 p.
ISBN 9780394442297
1. Automobile travel 2. Eleven-year-old boys 3. Boys and men 4. African American men 5. Automobile thefts 6. 1900s (Decade) 7. Coming-of-age stories 8. Literary fiction 9. Books to movies
LC 62010335
Pulitzer Prize for Fiction, 1963
Boon Hogganbeck persuades Lucius Priest, 11, to borrow his grandfather's car in 1905, and after they arrive at a bordello, the black Ned McCaslin trades the car for a horse.

Requiem for a nun. William Faulkner. Random House 1951. 286p.
ISBN 9780394442747
1. Child murders 2. Household employees 3. African American women 4. Rape victims 5. Nurses 6. Literary fiction 7. Modern classics 8. Southern fiction
LC 51012731
In order to save a nurse convicted of murder, Temple Stevens decides to confess that she killed her own daughter.
Sequel to: Sanctuary

★ **Sanctuary**. William Faulkner. Vintage, 1993. 309 p.
ISBN 9780679748144
1. Crimes against women 2. Rape 3. Kidnapping 4. Murder 5. College students 6. Mississippi 7. Literary fiction 8. Modern classics 9. Southern fiction
An assortment of perverse characters act out this dramatic story of the kidnapping of a Mississippi debutante
Sanctuary was the basis for the films The story of Temple Drake (1933) and Sanctuary (1960).
Sequel: Requiem for a nun.
First published: [London] : Chatto & Windus, 1931.

★ The **sound** and the fury. William Faulkner. Random House, 1929. 401 p.
ISBN 9780394532417
1. Men with developmental disabilities 2. Dysfunctional families 3. Incest 4. Suicide 5. African Americans 6. 1920s 7. Literary fiction 8. Psychological fiction 9. Multiple perspectives
Retells the tragic times of the Compson family, including beautiful, rebellious Caddy; manchild Benjy; haunted, neurotic Quentin; Jason, the brutal cynic; and Dilsey, their Black servant.

Uncollected stories of William Faulkner. William Faulkner; edited by Joseph Blotner. Random House, 1979. 716 p.

ISBN 9780394400440

1. Family relationships 2. Small towns 3. Rural life 4. Yoknapatawpha County (Miss. : Imaginary place) 5. Mississippi 6. Short stories 7. Literary fiction 8. Modern classics

LC 78021803

Forty-six stories never before published in any collection include twenty that were incorporated into longer works after magazine publication, eleven that appeared in periodicals, and fifteen never published at all
BT

Faulks, Sebastian

★ **Birdsong**. Sebastian Faulks. Random House, 1993. 402 p. (French trilogy, 2)

ISBN 9780091773731

1. World War I 2. Soldiers — History 3. Extramarital affairs 4. Trench warfare 5. British in France 6. France 7. First World War era (1914-1918) 8. War stories 9. Historical fiction 10. Literary fiction

LC 9523721

In 1910, Stephen Wraysford, a young Englishman, journeys to France and becomes embroiled in a series of traumatic events, including a clandestine love affair, and is later trapped amid the horrors of the First World War.

"[The author] proves himself a grand storyteller here." —*Publishers Weekly*

Charlotte Gray: a novel. Sebastian Faulks. Random House, 1998. 399 p. (French trilogy, 3)

ISBN 9780375501692

1. British in France 2. World War II 3. Resistance to military occupation 4. Holocaust (1933-1945) 5. Nazi collaborators 6. France 7. England 8. Second World War era (1939-1945) 9. 1940s 10. Historical fiction 11. War stories 12. Literary fiction

LC 9833658

A young Scottish woman who falls in love with a World War II RAF pilot shortly before his plane is lost over France joins the Resistance movement to find him, only to discover a larger meaning in her new role.

"Faulks has written one of those rare books that is adventurous enough to attract a popular audience while thoughtful enough to sustain the more serious reader." —*Library Journal*

Jeeves and the wedding bells. Sebastian Faulks. St. Martin's Press, 2013. 336 p.

ISBN 9781250047595

1. Butlers 2. Misadventures 3. Rich people 4. Man-woman relationships 5. Weddings 6. Roosevelt, Eleanor 7. Humorous stories 8. Gentle reads

When young man about town Bertie Wooster, nursing a broken heart, agrees to help his old friend Peregrine Woody Beeching, whose own romance is failing, hilarity and chaos ensue as Jeeves, the very epitome of the modern manservant, steps in to save Bertie from himself.

"The heartwarming denouement, which reveals how the godlike Jeeves has manipulated the action from behind the scenes, humanizes Bertie and Jeeves as Wodehouse never did. In my humble opinion, Faulks has outdone Wodehouse." —*Publishers Weekly*

Originally published: London: Hutchinson, 2013.

On Green Dolphin Street: a novel. Sebastian Faulks. Random House, 2001. 351 p.

ISBN 9780375502255

1. British in the United States 2. Extramarital affairs 3. Diplomats' spouses 4. Married women 5. Young, Ann Eliza 6. Washington, D.C. 7. New York City 8. 1960s 9. Love stories 10. Literary fiction

LC 2001041753

In 1960, Mary van der Linden, a loyal wife and mother approaching forty, moves with her family from London to Washington, D.C, where she escapes her narrow world for the larger issues of politics and the Cold War with the help of Frank, a New York journalist.

"The outline of this archetypal love story may sound familiar, but everything about Faulks' telling of it is fresh.... It is a love story above all, but it is also a New York story, the sights, sounds, and smells of the city perfectly evoked to capture one of those moments when the forces of change collide with the proprieties of the past." —*Booklist*

Paris echo: a novel. Sebastian Faulks. Henry Holt and Company, 2018. 272 p.

ISBN 9781250305657

1. Women historians 2. Americans in Paris, France 3. Immigrants 4. History 5. Identity (Psychology) 6. Paris, France 7. France 8. Literary fiction 9. Psychological fiction

LC 2018013873

An American historical researcher in World War II Paris and a Moroccan teen who risked his life to enter France find the realities of the Nazi occupation transforming their ideas about sacrifice and happiness.

A week in December. Sebastian Faulks. Doubleday, 2010. 392 p.

ISBN 9780385532914

1. Rich people 2. Dinners and dining 3. Banks and banking 4. Reality 5. Greed 6. London, England 7. Literary fiction 8. Psychological fiction 9. Multiple perspectives

LC 2009030109

A novel set in 2007 London follows seven diverse characters, exploring the complex patterns and crossings of modern urban life and culminating in a climax where each character is forced to confront the true nature of the world they inhabit.

Originally published: London: Hutchinson, 2009.

Faust, Christa

Choke hold. Christa Faust. Hard Case Crime, 2011. 256 p.

ISBN 9780857682857

1. Former erotic film actors and actresses 2. Murder 3. Sex industry and trade 4. Federal Witness Protection Program 5. Violence 6. Crime fiction 7. Pulp fiction

After a shoot-out at the restaurant where she works leaves a former costar dead, Angel Dare begins to protect his son Cody, a mixed martial artist, and they wind up on the run from drug dealers who think that Cody stole drugs from them.

Sequel to: Money Shot.

Money shot. Christa Faust. Hard Case Crime, 2008. 250 p.

ISBN 9780843959581

1. Former erotic film actors and actresses 2. Revenge 3. Sex industry and trade 4. Pornographic film actors and actresses 5. Murder 6. Crime fiction 7. Pulp fiction

Angel Dare, a retired porn star and owner of an adult modeling agency, seeks revenge on the people who framed her for murder after locking her in the trunk of a car, battered, raped, and shot.

"Former porn star Angel Dare (nee Gina Moretti), who stopped acting to establish Daring Angels, a firm that manages women in the business, is lured to perform once more by a hot young male star. Instead, she's beaten, raped, shot, and left for dead in the trunk of a car, and that's just the start—all because of money from the international sex trade. With the help of her company's ex-cop security escort, Lalo Malloy, Angel untangles the plot and players, depending finally on nothing but her own resources for the vengeance she craves. A rip-roaring story with nonstop action and an inside look at X-rated movie making, this is clearly not for all readers or collections; but the title (which originated in the porn industry) and cover art are indicators of its contents." —*Library Journal*

Sequel: Choke Hold.

Fay, Juliette

The **shortest** way home. Juliette Fay. Penguin Books, 2013. 368 p.
ISBN 9780143121916
1. Siblings 2. Small town life 3. Family relationships 4. Huntington's disease 5. Interpersonal relations 6. Massachusetts 7. Pelham, Massachusetts 8. Mainstream fiction

LC 2012025149

Library Journal Best Books, 2012

Sean, burnt out after spending twenty years in the Third World, returns home to Massachusetts and reconnects with his family and a woman from his past, who may just rewrite his future.

Faye, Gael

★ **Small** country: a novel. Gael Faye. Hogarth Press, 2018. 183 p.
ISBN 9781524759872
1. Boys 2. Civil war 3. Childhood innocence (Concept) 4. Genocide 5. Survival 6. Burundi 7. Rwanda 8. 1990s 9. Coming-of-age stories 10. Literary fiction 11. Translations
Library Journal Best Books, 2018

In Burundi in 1992, ten-year-old Gabriel enjoys carefree days with his friends, but his idyllic existence and his innocence come to a brutal end when Burundi and neighboring Rwanda are hit by civil war and genocide.

Faye, Lyndsay

The **gods** of Gotham. Lyndsay Faye. G. P. Putnam's Sons, 2012. 432 p. (Gods of Gotham, 1)
ISBN 9780399158377
1. Police 2. Serial murderers 3. Irish Americans — Discrimination 4. Immigrants, Irish 5. Crimes against children 6. New York City 7. 1840s 8. Historical mysteries 9. Mysteries 10. Adult books for young adults
RUSA Reading List, 2013

Joining the newly formed NYPD in 1845, Timothy reluctantly assumes his duties near the notorious Five Points slum, where in the middle of the night he hears a little girl's claim that dozens of bodies have been buried in a local forest.

Jane Steele. Lyndsay Faye. G. P. Putnam's Sons, 2016. 400 p.
ISBN 9780399169496
1. Murderers 2. Inheritance and succession 3. Governesses 4. Women murderers 5. Orphans 6. London, England 7. England 8. 19th century 9. Adaptations, retellings, and spin-offs 10. Gothic fiction 11. Adult books for young adults
LibraryReads Favorites, 2016

A reimagining of Jane Eyre as a gutsy, heroic serial killer, from the author whose work The New York Times described as "riveting" and The Wall Street Journal called "thrilling."

"Fayes skill at historical mystery was evident in her nineteenth-century New York trilogy, but this slyly satiric stand-alone takes her prowess to new levels. A must for Bronte devotees; wickedly entertaining for all." —*Booklist*

★ The **king** of infinite space. Lyndsay Faye. G. P. Putnam's Sons, 2021. 384 p.
ISBN 9780525535898

1. Fathers — Death 2. Suspicion 3. Ambition 4. Revenge 5. Male friendship 6. New York City 7. Contemporary fantasy 8. Adaptations, retellings, and spin-offs 9. Multiple perspectives

LC 2021021036

After his Broadway theater baron father dies mysteriously, Ben Dane, his best friend Horatio and his artist ex-fiance Lia, on one explosive night, are drawn into otherworldly events where the only outcome is death.

"Ophelia finally gets some agency in this contemporary reboot of Hamlet—with a few characters from other Shakespearean works thrown in for good measure.... Smart and suspenseful; top-notch popular fiction." —*Kirkus*

★ The **Paragon** Hotel. Lyndsay Faye. G.P. Putnam's Sons, 2018. 432 p.
ISBN 9780735210752
1. Women fugitives 2. Racism 3. Hotels 4. Gunshot victims 5. Mafia 6. New York City 7. Portland, Oregon 8. 1920s 9. Historical mysteries 10. First person narratives

LC 2018012903

Loan Stars Favourites, 2019

Fleeing to 1921 Oregon, Alice takes refuge in the city's only black hotel and helps new friends search for a missing child, hide from KKK violence and navigate painful secrets.

"A riveting multilevel thriller of race, sex, and mob violence that throbs with menace as it hums with wit." —*Kirkus*

Seven for a secret. Lyndsay Faye. G. P. Putnams Sons, 2013. 464 p. (Gods of Gotham, 2)
ISBN 9780399158384
1. Free African Americans 2. Slave trade 3. Missing persons investigation 4. Kidnapping 5. Underground Railroad 6. New York City 7. Antebellum America (1820-1861) 8. 1840s 9. Historical mysteries 10. Mysteries 11. Adult books for young adults

LC 2013008127

A police officer investigates a ring of "blackbirders" who kidnap free people of color in the North and sell them to Southern plantations.

The **whole** art of detection: lost mysteries of Sherlock Holmes. Lyndsay Faye. Mysterious Press, 2017. 388 p.
ISBN 9780802125927
1. Criminal investigation 2. Private investigators 3. Crime 4. Holmes, Sherlock (Fictitious character) 5. Watson, John H. (Fictitious character) 6. London, England 7. England 8. Victorian era (1837-1901) 9. 1880s 10. Adaptations, retellings, and spin-offs 11. Short stories 12. Victorian mysteries

LC 2016037116

In this superb short story collection, Edgar Award-nominated Lyndsay Faye presents a collection of 15 Sherlock Holmes tales, including two new works (such as the clever "The Adventure of the Thames Tunnel" as well as stories that were previously published. Though Sherlock Holmes pastiches abound, not very many place him in his prime on Baker Street as Lyndsay Faye often does here. Read and enjoy, Sherlockians.

"Fans and neophytes alike should cheer Faye's reinvigoration of Conan Doyle's hero and his panoramic world." —*Kirkus*

Feehan, Christine

Dark illusion. Christine Feehan. Berkley, 2019. 432 pages (Dark series, 33)
ISBN 9781984803467
1. Women wizards 2. Vampires 3. Interspecies romance 4. Mate selection 5. Good and evil 6. Carpathian Mountains 7. Paranormal romances

LC 2019003736

Fleeing her controlling family to warn the Carpathians of an imminent threat, mage Julija Brennan resists her explosive connection to centuries-old warrior Isai Florea, who recognizes her as his lifemate.

Shadow rider. Christine Feehan. Jove Books, 2016. 432 p. (Shadow riders novels, 1)

ISBN 9780515156133

1. Organized crime 2. Psychic ability 3. Secrets 4. Determination in men 5. Rich families 6. Chicago, Illinois 7. Paranormal romances

Library Journal Best Books, 2016

Gifted with the ability to manipulate light and dark, shadow rider Stefano Ferraro, the head of a Chicago crime family, meets his match in Francesca Cappello, a mysterious—and dangerously beautiful—woman whose powers rival his own.

Feeney, Alice

★ **I** know who you are: a novel. Alice Feeney. Flatiron Books, 2019. 304 p.

ISBN 9781250147349

1. Actors and actresses 2. Married women 3. Stalkers 4. Missing men 5. Secrets 6. Psychological suspense

LC 2018037893

Loan Stars Favourites, 2019

An actress on the brink of fame finds her sense of reality thrown into question by her husband's baffling disappearance at the same time a young runaway lands in mortal danger.

★ **Sometimes** I lie. Alice Feeney. Flatiron Books, 2018. 272 p.

ISBN 9781250144843

1. Coma — Patients 2. Married women 3. Betrayal 4. Sisters 5. Secrets 6. London, England 7. Psychological suspense

LC 2017045151

LibraryReads Favorites, 2018

Depicts the harrowing experiences of a coma patient with shut-in syndrome who while unable to move or speak must listen to those around her to figure out what happened and who is responsible for her injuries.

Feldman, Ellen

Paris never leaves you. Ellen Feldman. St. Martin's Griffin, 2020. 368 p.

ISBN 9781250759894

1. Jewish women 2. Nazis 3. Identity (Psychology) 4. Military occupation 5. Single mothers 6. Paris, France 7. New York City 8. Second World War era (1939-1945) 9. 1950s 10. Historical fiction

LC 2019054415

Hiding her fateful past with a German officer during World War II, a Parisian bookstore clerk builds a new life for herself in the clubby, eccentric world of Manhattan publishing, before her daughter begins asking dangerous questions.

"Fans of Anthony Doerr's All the Light We Cannot See (2014) and Kristin Hannah's The Nightingale (2015) may want to pick this up, and book groups are sure to find much to dissect and discuss." —*Booklist*

Feng, Linda Rui

Swimming back to Trout River. Linda Rui Feng. Simon & Schuster, 2021. 272 p.

ISBN 9781982129392

1. Social change 2. Families 3. Separated friends, relatives, etc. 4. Family secrets 5. Immigrants, Chinese 6. China 7. United States 8. Chinese Cultural Revolution (1966-1976) 9. 20th century 10. Literary fiction 11. Canadian fiction

Set against the backdrop of China's Cultural Revolution, this lyrical novel follows a father's determination to reunite his family before his daughter Junie's 12th birthday, even if it means bringing painful family secrets to light.

"With the lightest of touches, Feng vividly portrays the experience of living in China during Mao's rule as well as the pressures of being a new immigrant." —*Booklist*

Longlisted for the Scotiabank Giller Prize, 2021.

Ferber, Edna

So big. Edna Ferber; introduction by Maria K. Mootry. University of Illinois Press, 1995. Xvi, 212 p.

ISBN 9780252063763

1. Gamblers 2. Children of gamblers 3. Fathers and daughters 4. Mothers and sons 5. Families 6. Chicago, Illinois 7. Coming-of-age stories 8. Modern classics 9. Domestic fiction

LC 94024615

Pulitzer Prize for Fiction, 1925

Follows a Chicago gambler's daughter as she tries to hold on to her dignity in the face of terrible challenges.

Originally published: Garden City, N. Y. : Doubleday, Page & Company, 1924.

Ferencik, Erica

Into the jungle. Erica Ferencik. Scout Press, 2019. 320 p.

ISBN 9781501168925

1. Jungles 2. Foster teenagers 3. Runaway teenagers 4. Indians of South America 5. Determination (Personal quality) 6. Bolivia 7. Survival stories 8. Thrillers and suspense 9. Adult books for young adults

LC 2018047677

Taking a job in Bolivia to escape foster care and group homes, Lily apprehensively follows the man she loves into a ruthless, life-threatening jungle region of lawless poachers, bullheaded missionaries and desperate indigenous tribes.

Fernandez, Nona

The **twilight** zone. Nona Fernandez; translated from the Spanish by Natasha Wimmer. Graywolf Press, 2021. 192 p.

ISBN 9781644450475

1. State-sponsored terrorism 2. Torturers 3. Violence — Psychological aspects 4. Memory 5. Disappeared persons 6. Chile 7. 20th century 8. 21st century 9. Translations 10. Literary fiction 11. First person narratives

National Book Award for Translated Literature finalist, 2021

An engrossing, incantatory novel about the legacy of historical crimes by the author of Space Invaders.

"Fernandez is emerging as a major voice in South American letters, and this slender but rich story shows why." —*Kirkus*

Translated from the Spanish.

Ferrante, Elena

The **lost** daughter. By Elena Ferrante; translated from the Italian by Ann Goldstein. Europa, 2008. 125 p.

ISBN 9781933372426

1. Mothers and daughters 2. Divorced women 3. Motherhood 4. Parent and child 5. Vacations 6. Italy 7. Domestic fiction 8. Mahmood, Zaved 9. Books to movies

When Leda's daughters leave home to be with their father, she decides to take a trip to a small coastal town in Italy, but soon after she arrives memories from her unsettled past come back to haunt her.

"In this brutally frank novel of maternal ambivalence, the narrator, a forty-seven-year-old divorcee summering alone on the Ionian coast, becomes obsessed with a beautiful young mother who seems ill at ease with her husband's rowdy, slightly menacing Neapolitan clan. When this woman's daughter loses her doll, the older woman commits a small crime that she can't explain even to herself. Although much of the drama takes place in her head, Ferrante's gift for psychological horror renders it immediate and visceral." —*The New Yorker*

Original title: La figlia oscura.
The author revisits the story of this book in her children's book, The Beach at Night.
Made into a movie of the same name, 2021.

The **lying** life of adults. Elena Ferrante; translated by Ann Goldstein. Europa Editions, 2020. 336 pages
ISBN 9781609455910
1. Middle-class families 2. Growing up 3. Teenage rebels 4. Teenage girls 5. Social classes 6. Naples, Italy 7. Italy 8. 1990s 9. Coming-of-age stories 10. Literary fiction 11. Translations
Kirkus Prize for Fiction finalist, 2020
Presents the story of an Italian teen who searches for a sense of identity and clear perspectives when she finds herself torn between the refinements and excesses of a divided Naples.

"Fans of Ferrante's first two Neopolitan novels, My Brilliant Friend (2012) and The Story of a New Name (2013), will especially revel in Giovanna's confessional, perceptive, gut-wrenching, and often funny narration of what she calls her arduous approach to the adult world." —*Booklist*

Translation of: La vita bugiarda degli adulti.
Originally published in Italy, 2019.
Translated from the Italian.

My brilliant friend. Elena Ferrante; translated from the Italian by Ann Goldstein. Europa Editions, 2012. 336 p. (Neapolitan novels, 1)
ISBN 9781609450786
1. Growing up 2. Teenage girls — Friendship 3. Poverty 4. Violence 5. Inner city 6. Italy 7. Naples, Italy 8. 1950s 9. Mainstream fiction 10. Translations 11. Adult books for young adults
Beginning in the 1950s Elena and Lila grow up in Naples, Italy, mirroring two different aspects of their nation.
Translation of: L'amica geniale.
Originally published: Rome : Edizioni, 2011.

The **story** of a new name. Elena Ferrante; translated from the Italian by Ann Goldstein. Europa Editions, 2013. 480 p. (Neapolitan novels, 2)
ISBN 9781609451349
1. Marriage 2. Unhappiness in women 3. Self-discovery in women 4. Female friendship 5. Childhood friends 6. Italy 7. Naples, Italy 8. Mainstream fiction 9. Translations
In this follow-up to My Brilliant Friend, Lila is imprisoned by marriage, while Elena continues her journey of self-discovery, until their friendship, which is at the center of their emotional lives, forces them both to mature into women.
"Ferrante's writing is captivating and insightful. She delves deeply into the character of the girls' friendship, ushering them into womanhood with an honesty that is acutely personal." —*Booklist*
Translation from the Italian of: Storia del nuovo cognome.
Originally published: Rome : Edizione, 2012.

The **story** of the lost child. Elena Ferrante; translated from the Italian by Ann Goldstein. Europa Editions, 2015. 464 p. (Neapolitan novels, 4)
ISBN 9781609452865

1. Female friendship 2. Middle-aged women 3. Women authors 4. Independence in women 5. Childhood friends 6. Italy 7. Naples, Italy 8. 1970s 9. 1980s 10. Mainstream fiction 11. Translations
New York Times Notable Book, 2015; Booklist Editors' Choice, 2015
Follows the continuing story of the friendship between fiery Lina and bookish Elena, now grown with children and successful in their chosen careers, and both again living in Naples, the city of their birth.
"Although the eponymous child is of profound importance here, it's the disappearance revealed at the series' onset and to which Ferrante returns, after navigating the 40-plus-year span covered in the story, that will compel readers forward, puzzling over it and anticipating resolution. As Elena ages, struggling to understand her relationship to her books success, she writes—and we read, a level removed—a story about story and its authorship. A friendship so reflective and yet so repellent, so truthfully plumbed, is a rare thing written." —*Booklist*
Translation from the Italian of: Storia della bambina perduta
Originally published: Rome : E/O, 2014.

Those who leave and those who stay. Elena Ferrante; translated from the Italian by Ann Goldstein. Europa Editions, 2014. 400 p. (Neapolitan novels, 3)
ISBN 9781609452339
1. Self-fulfillment in women 2. Female friendship 3. Creativity in women 4. Women authors 5. Women employees 6. Italy 7. Naples, Italy 8. Mainstream fiction 9. Translations
Booklist Editors' Choice, 2014; New York Times Notable Book, 2014
Continues the story of Lina and Elena as they push against boundaries in 1970s Italy, where Lina has left her husband and is working in a factory while taking care of her son and Elena has graduated college and published a novel.
"Ferrante continues to imbue this growing saga with great magic, treating the girls' years of marriage and motherhood with breathtaking honesty while envisaging the turbulence of political and social unrest in 1970s Italy." —*Booklist*
Translation from the Italian of: Storia di chi fugge e di chi resta.
Originally published: Rome : E/O, 2013.

Ferraris, Zoe
Finding Nouf. Zoe Ferraris. Houghton Mifflin, 2008. 320 p. (Katya Hijazi novels, 1)
ISBN 9780618873883
1. Sixteen-year-old girls 2. Gender role 3. Murder investigation 4. Teenage girl murder victims 5. Siblings 6. Saudi Arabia 7. Middle East 8. Mysteries 9. Adult books for young adults
LC 2007038411
Alex Award, 2009; Los Angeles Times Art Seidenbaum Award for First Fiction, 2008
When sixteen-year-old Nouf goes missing and is found drowned in the desert outside Jeddah, Nayir—a desert guide hired by her prominent family to search for her—feels compelled to find out what really happened.
"Sixteen-year-old Nouf ash-Shrawi, daughter of a wealthy Saudi Arabian family, mysteriously disappears and is eventually found drowned in the desert.... Nouf's brother, Othman, asks his friend Nayir Sharqi, a local desert guide, to find out what happened to his sister. Nayir's investigation leads him into unknown territorynotably, the secret realm of women in a segregated Middle Eastern society. In an unusual partnership that challenges his traditional ideas, Nayir works on the case with Othman's fiancée, a laboratory technician in the medical examiner's office. Ferraris's debut novel gives a fascinating peek into the lives and minds of

devout Muslim men and women while serving up an engrossing mystery."
—*Library Journal*
Sequel : City of veils.

Kingdom of strangers: a novel. Zoe Ferraris. Little, Brown and Company, 2012. 304 p. (Katya Hijazi novels, 3)
ISBN 9780316074247
1. Crimes against women 2. Serial murders 3. Murder investigation 4. Missing persons 5. Extramarital affairs 6. Saudi Arabia 7. Middle East 8. Mysteries 9. Adult books for young adults
LC 2011046158
Saudi lead inspector Ibrahim Zahrani discovers that a serial killer has been burying women's bodies in Jeddah for more than 10 years at the same time his mistress disappears and seeks assistance from Katya, one of the few women on the force.
Sequel to: City of veils.

Ferrell, Carolyn

Dear Miss Metropolitan. Carolyn Ferrell. Henry Holt & Co, 2021. 400 p.
ISBN 9781250793614
1. Captives 2. Psychic trauma 3. Torture 4. Violence against women 5. Violence in men 6. Queens, New York City 7. New York City 8. 1990s 9. 21st century 10. African American fiction 11. Multiple perspectives 12. Literary fiction
After being abducted by Boss Man and held captive in a dilapidated house in Queens, three rescued girls rage against a local newspaper columnist who missed their tale of horror as it unfolded right across the street.
"Ferrell's debut novel is a brave examination into the accumulation of unresolved generational trauma and its detrimental outcomes." —*Booklist*

Ferris, Joshua

A **calling** for Charlie Barnes. Joshua Ferris. Little Brown & Co 2021. 320 p.
ISBN 9780316333535
1. Storytelling 2. Fathers and sons 3. Failure (Psychology) 4. Authors 5. Dysfunctional families 6. Literary fiction 7. Metafiction
With help from his storyteller son, Charlie Barnes, a lifelong schemer and eternal romantic who would like out of his present circumstances, is granted a second act and, at last, through an act of selflessness and love, becomes the man his son always knew he could be.
"Good old-fashioned faux metafiction about death and family, full of panic and glee." —*Kirkus*

To rise again at a decent hour: a novel. Joshua Ferris. Little, Brown and Company, 2014. 337 pages
ISBN 9780316033978
1. Dentists 2. Compulsive behavior in men 3. Identity (Psychology) 4. False personation 5. Online identity theft 6. Psychological fiction 7. Literary fiction 8. Satirical fiction
Shortlisted for the Man Booker Prize, 2014
After noticing his identity has been stolen and used to create various social media accounts, a man with a troubled past, Paul O'Rourke, begins to wonder if his virtual alter ego is actually a better version of himself.
"The protagonist's sharp inner dialogues are laugh-out-loud hilarious, combining New York nihilism with an Ivy League vocabulary." —*Booklist*

The **unnamed**. Joshua Ferris. Little, Brown and Co, 2010. 320 p.
ISBN 9780316034012
1. Compulsive behavior 2. Husband and wife 3. Identity (Psychology) 4. Lawyers 5. Diseases 6. Domestic fiction 7. Mainstream fiction

LC 2009010264
Booklist Editors' Choice, 2010
Their wealthy lifestyle marred only by a two-time occurrence of a short-lived illness, Tim and Jane Farnsworth are devastated when the illness returns in ways that frighteningly alter Tim's behavior and test Jane's endurance.
"Audacious, risky and powerfully bleak, with the author's unflinching artistry its saving grace." —*Kirkus*

Fesperman, Dan

Safe houses: a novel. Dan Fesperman. Alfred A. Knopf, 2018. 336 p.
ISBN 9780525520191
1. Intelligence service 2. Conspiracies 3. Cold War 4. Children of murder victims 5. Mothers and daughters 6. Berlin, Germany 7. West Germany 8. 1970s 9. Spy fiction 10. Thrillers and suspense
LC 2017058898
RUSA Reading List, 2019
A CIA safe house inspector uncovers a nefarious secret at the heart of Agency operations in postwar Berlin, triggering a life on the run, her brutal murder and her daughter's search for answers.

ffitch, Madeline

Stay and fight. Madeline ffitch. Farrar, Straus and Giroux, 2019. 320 p.
ISBN 9780374268121
1. Homesteading 2. Sustainable living 3. Counterculture 4. Wilderness areas 5. Alternative lifestyles 6. Ohio 7. Appalachian Region 8. Political fiction 9. Multiple perspectives
LC 2018046442
This hilarious, truth-telling debut upends notions of family, protest, and Appalachia, and forces us to reimagine an America we think we know.

Fforde, Jasper

★ **Early** riser: a novel. Jasper Fforde. Viking Press, 2019. 402 pages : Illustration
ISBN 9780670025039
1. Winter 2. Civil service workers 3. Sleep 4. Misfits (Persons) 5. Hibernation 6. Wales 7. Dystopian fiction 8. First person narratives
The best-selling author of the Nursery Crimes series imagines the reader as a first-winter employee with the misfit Winter Consuls, who protect the world's hibernating masses until an outbreak of viral nightmares starts triggering mysterious deaths.
"Readers familiar with Fforde's (The Woman Who Died a Lot, 2012) gleefully pun-heavy world building will relish this stand-alone novel, confident that everything will work out in the end for the underdog." —*Booklist*

The **Eyre** affair: a novel. Jasper Fforde. Viking, 2002. 374 p. (Thursday Next novels, 1)
ISBN 9780670030644
1. Fathers and daughters 2. Censorship 3. Time travel 4. Women detectives 5. Crimean War, 1853-1856 6. England 7. Wales 8. 1980s 9. Fantasy mysteries 10. First person narratives 11. Metafiction 12. Adult books for young adults
LC 2001043775
Alex Award, 2003; School Library Journal Best Books: Best Adult Books 4 Teens, 2002
In a world where one can literally get lost in literature, Thursday Next, a Special Operative in literary detection, tries to stop the world's Third Most Wanted criminal from kidnapping characters, including Jane Eyre, from works of literature.

"This rambunctious caper could be taken as a warning about what might happen if society considered literature really important—like, say, energy futures or accounting." —*The New Yorker*

Lost in a good book: a Thursday Next novel. Jasper Fforde. Viking, 2002. 416 p. (Thursday Next novels, 2)
ISBN 9780670031900
1. Women detectives 2. Multinational corporations 3. Time travel 4. Characters and characteristics in literature 5. Literary historians 6. England 7. Great Britain 8. 1980s 9. Fantasy mysteries 10. First person narratives 11. Metafiction 12. Adult books for young adults
LC 2002071304
Dilys Award, 2004; New York Times Notable Book, 2003
In order to rescue the love of her life from the corrupt multinational Goliath, Thursday seeks out a believed-vanquished enemy from the pages of The Raven and finds unexpected assistance from Great Expectation's Miss Havisham.
"Time flies—and leaps and zigzags—while reading this wickedly funny and clever fantasy. Would-be wordsmiths and mystery fans will find the surreal genre-buster irresistible." —*Publishers Weekly*

Shades of grey: a novel. Jasper Fforde. Viking, 2009. 400 p. (Chromatacia novels, 1)
ISBN 9780670019632
1. Color blindness 2. Dystopias 3. Social classes 4. Technology — Social aspects 5. Post-apocalypse 6. England 7. Fantasy fiction 8. Literary fiction 9. Adult books for young adults
LC 2009030813
Booklist Editors' Choice: Adult Books for Young Adults, 2010
Color Control Agency employee and House of Red member Eddie Russet experiences discontent with his limited vision when he meets Gray Nightseer Jane, who suggests that their color-blind world was brought about by a disaster that nobody is allowed to acknowledge.
"The world is wildly but closely imagined, so the result is as internally coherent as it is unlikely. Distinctive wordplay abounds. All the fooling around is built on a good mystery, and Fforde telegraphs no punches. In short, Shades of Grey is everything that Fforde fans love, and distinctly different from what has come before." —*Denver Post*

Fielding, Helen
★ **Bridget** Jones's diary: a novel. Helen Fielding. Viking, 1998. 271 p. (Bridget Jones, 1)
ISBN 9780670880720
1. Single women 2. Dieting for women 3. Dating (Social customs) 4. Female friendship 5. Single people 6. London, England 7. Chick lit 8. Diary novels 9. Books to movies
LC 9818687
British Book Award for Book of the Year, 1998; New York Times Notable Book, 1998
The daily chronicle of a 30-something single English woman who is convinced her life would be perfect if she could lose weight, stop smoking and develop "Inner Poise."
"Brimming with a deliciously irreverent sense of humor and a keen sense of women's deepest insecurities, Bridget Jones's Diary is a must-read." —*Booklist*
Sequel: Bridget Jones : the edge of reason.

Fielding, Henry
★ The **history** of Tom Jones, a foundling. Henry Fielding; edited with explanatory notes by Thomas Keymer and Alice Wakely with an introduction by Thomas Keymer. Penguin Books, 2005. Xlvii, 975 p. : Map
ISBN 9780140436228

1. Elopement 2. Interclass romance 3. Abandoned children 4. Illegitimacy 5. Social classes 6. England 7. Picaresque fiction 8. Satirical fiction 9. Classics
A foundling of mysterious parentage, Tom Jones is brought up by the benevolent and wealthy Squire Allworthy as his own son. Tom falls in love with the beautiful and unattainable Sophia Western, a neighbor's daughter, whose marriage has already been arranged. When Tom's sexual misadventures around the countryside get him banished, he sets out to make his fortune and find his true identity. Against the vivid background of eighteenth-century London, Tom encounters passion, corruption, danger, and intrigue before finally claiming his fortune, legitimacy, and true love.
Title of later film version: Tom Jones.
Originally published: London : A. Millar, 1749.

Fielding, Joy
All the wrong places: a novel. Joy Fielding. Ballantine Books, 2019. 240 p.
ISBN 9780399181559
1. Murderers 2. Online dating 3. Crimes against women 4. Women — Interpersonal relations 5. Dating (Social customs) 6. Thrillers and suspense
LC 2018051132
Loan Stars Favourites, 2019
Driven to desperation by divorce, boredom, infidelity and loss, four women turn to online dating for companionship, only to find themselves in the crosshairs of a tech-savvy killer.

The **bad** daughter: a novel. Joy Fielding. Ballantine Books, 2018. 368 p.
ISBN 9780399181528
1. Family secrets 2. Home invasions 3. Homecomings 4. Women psychotherapists 5. Blended families 6. California 7. Thrillers and suspense 8. Canadian fiction
LC 2017051448
Loan Stars Favourites, 2018
Estranged from her family because of her difficulties getting along with her stepmother, Robin returns home in the aftermath of a brutal home invasion, hoping to mend fences, only to uncover horrible family secrets that may have led to the attack.

Fields, Hilary
Last Chance Llama Ranch. Hilary Fields. Orbit, 2015. 350 p.
ISBN 9780316277426
1. Women journalists 2. Ranches 3. Cowboys 4. Former athletes 5. Llamas 6. Romantic comedies
From Olympic skier to llama farmer? Now that is a serious jump. When a close encounter with an eighty-foot spruce steals Merry's dreams of Olympic gold, the former ski champ finds herself falling into a career she never expected—the life of a travel writer. Picturing glamorous trips to exotic places, Merry is speechless when her boss assigns her to the blog, "Don't Do What I Did," and sends her to, place of all places, a llama ranch. Soon she's eyeball-deep in alpacas, llamas, goats and more. But when Last Chance Llama Ranch starts to grow on her, Merry finds that ranch life, while still just as gross, might be just what she's been missing. You know what they say... When life gives you llamas...

Finch, Charles
A **beautiful** blue death. Charles Finch. St. Martin's Minotaur, 2007. 320 p. (Charles Lenox chronicles, 1)

ISBN 9780312359775

1. Amateur detectives 2. Murder investigation 3. Murder 4. Deception 5. Butlers 6. London, England 7. England 8. Victorian era (1837-1901) 9. 19th century 10. Historical mysteries 11. Victorian mysteries 12. Mysteries

LC 2007011273

Library Journal Best Books, 2007

When Victorian gentleman Charles Lenox begins to investigate the apparent suicide of a friend's former servant, he suspects murder—but to find the killer, he must untangle a complex web of loyalties and animosities before it's too late.

The **last** passenger. Charles Finch. Minotaur Books, 2020. 304 p. (Charles Lenox chronicles, 13)

ISBN 9781250312204

1. Private investigators 2. Trains 3. Impostors 4. Murder investigation 5. Locomotive engineers 6. England 7. London, England 8. 1850s 9. 19th century 10. Historical mysteries

LC 2019049215

Finds Victorian detective Charles Lenox defying Scotland Yard and navigating the dual challenges of royal obstinance and class prejudice to investigate the murder of a first-class passenger at Paddington Station.

"Set 10 years before series debut A Beautiful Blue Death (2007), this tightly plotted mystery, winding through the back alleys of Whitechapel to the halls of Parliament itself, is rich in historical detail and quite enjoyable on its own merits but will be of particular interest to fans of the series, as it provides useful backstory to favorite characters." —*Booklist*

The **September** Society. Charles Finch. St. Martin's Minotaur, 2008. 310 p. (Charles Lenox chronicles, 2)

ISBN 9780312359782

1. Amateur detectives 2. Missing persons investigation 3. College students 4. Murder 5. Secret societies 6. London, England 7. England 8. Victorian era (1837-1901) 9. 1860s 10. Historical mysteries 11. Victorian mysteries 12. Mysteries 13. Adult books for young adults

LC 2008003452

Amateur detective and Victorian gentleman Charles Lenox heads for his alma mater at Oxford to investigate the disappearance of a student and encounters a series of bizarre clues, including a card bearing the name The September Society.

"Finch, a superb hand at plotting, gives nothing away, and even the most astute reader will be guessing to the end." —*Library Journal*

The **vanishing** man. Charles Finch. Minotaur Books, 2019. 320 p. (Charles Lenox chronicles, 12)

ISBN 9781250311368

1. Davidman, Joy 2. Aristocracy 3. Art thefts 4. Scandals 5. Rich families 6. London, England 7. England 8. 1850s 9. 19th century 10. Victorian mysteries 11. Historical mysteries

A second entry in a prequel trilogy to the best-selling series finds the theft of an antique painting sending a young Charles Lenox on a hunt for a criminal mastermind.

Finder, Joseph

Buried secrets. Joseph Finder. St. Martin's Press, 2011. 400 p. (Nick Heller novels, 2)

ISBN 9780312379148

1. Kidnapping 2. Missing persons 3. Secrets 4. Criminal investigation 5. Greed 6. Boston, Massachusetts 7. Financial thrillers

LC 2011004443

Hoping to set up his own spy operation in his Boston home town, Nick Heller is contacted by a desperate family friend to rescue his kidnapped daughter, whose terrifying incarceration in an underground crypt is being broadcast on the Internet.

"Finder's compulsively readable sequel to Vanished opens fast and never slows down. When 17-year-old Alexa Marcus, the spoiled daughter of Marshall Marcus, a wildly successful money manager, is kidnapped from a Boston club and buried alive in a coffin equipped with an air hose and a video camera (for Internet streaming, of course!), Marshall asks his old intelligence expert friend, Nick Heller, to find her. The search leads into an expanding world of buried secrets, from Marshall's gold-digging trophy wife, Belinda, and his crumbling investment empire to allegations of government funding for covert operations and the Russian mafia.... Self-effacing, wry, and ridiculously competent, Heller makes a reasonably engaging protagonist, but this thriller's real star is the suspenseful, expertly paced plot." —*Publishers Weekly*

The **fixer**. Joseph Finder. Dutton/Penguin Random House, 2015. 416 p.

ISBN 9780525954613

1. Family secrets 2. Fathers and sons 3. Life change events 4. People who have had strokes — Family relationships 5. Hiding-places (Secret chambers, etc.) 6. Massachusetts 7. Financial thrillers 8. Adult books for young adults

LC 2015006982

Forced to move to the ramshackle home of his youth after a career setback, Rick Hoffman begins a laborious renovation only to make a discovery that threatens his life and challenges everything he thought he knew about his late father.

Guilty minds. Joseph Finder. Penguin, 2016. 400 p. (Nick Heller novels, 3)

ISBN 9780525954620

1. Security consultants 2. Intrigue 3. Conspiracies 4. Criminal investigation 5. Corruption 6. Political thrillers 7. Thrillers and suspense 8. Adult books for young adults

Summoned to investigate potentially explosive charges of corruption levied by a gossip website against the chief justice of the Supreme Court, private intelligence operative Nick Heller is given 48 hours to prove that the story is baseless.

★ **House** on fire: a novel. Joseph Finder. Dutton, 2020. 384 p.

ISBN 9781101985847

1. Veterans 2. Drug industry and trade — Corrupt practices 3. Opioid epidemic 4. Rich families 5. Whistle blowers 6. Thrillers and suspense

LC 2019039182

Eagerly accepting a job investigating whistleblower claims about the manufacturer of an opioid that contributed to an army buddy's death, Nick Heller uncovers dangerous secrets implicating a powerful family.

"This thriller is not only topical but beautifully driven by the intricacies of personal agendas, both obvious and hidden. Easily read as a stand-alone as well as part of the series, this is sure to captivate a new audience and bring them to the Joseph Finder backlist." —*Library Journal*

Originally published in Great Britain by Head of Zeus, 2019.

★ **Judgment**. Joseph Finder. Dutton, 2019. 384 p.

ISBN 9781101985816

1. Women judges 2. Strangers 3. One-night stands (Interpersonal relations) 4. Married women 5. Extramarital affairs 6. Boston, Massachusetts 7. Chicago, Illinois 8. Legal thrillers 9. Thrillers and suspense

LC 2018026165

Sharing a one-night stand with a gentle stranger during a moment of weakness, a state superior court judge reencounters the man during a high-profile case and discovers that a conspiracy is threatening her family and federal court prospects.

Suspicion. Joseph Finder. Dutton Adult, 2014. 384 pages
ISBN 9780525954606
1. Drug traffic 2. Single fathers 3. Options, alternatives, choices 4. Drug enforcement agents 5. Undercover operations 6. Boston, Massachusetts 7. Financial thrillers
LC 2013049012
Unable to afford the private school his daughter adores, single father Danny Goodman reluctantly accepts a loan from a wealthy man only to be forced to choose between false drug charges and an undercover DEA assignment targeting his best friend.

The **switch**: a novel. Joseph Finder. Dutton, 2017. 384 p.
ISBN 9781101985786
1. Intelligence service 2. Government cover-ups 3. National security 4. Politicians 5. Security classification (Government documents) 6. Boston, Massachusetts 7. Political thrillers 8. Thrillers and suspense 9. Adult books for young adults
LC 2017006234
Picking up a politician's laptop by mistake, Michael Tanner discovers stolen files before finding himself targeted by an unscrupulous fixer at the same time the owners of the files hatch a deadly plot.

Vanished. Joseph Finder. St. Martin's Press, 2009. 400 p. (Nick Heller novels, 1)
ISBN 9780312379087
1. Security consultants 2. Missing persons 3. Brothers 4. Corporate culture 5. Former Special Forces members 6. Washington, D.C. 7. Financial thrillers
LC 2009013029
After an assault leaves his estranged brother nowhere to be found and his sister-in-law in a coma, security investigator and ex-intelligence agent Nick Heller is forced to seek help even from his despised convict father as Nick contends with one of the most powerful and secretive corporations in the world, an endeavor which may get him and everyone he's trying to protect killed.
"The first title in a new series featuring Nick Heller, a high-powered international investigator and corporate security consultant. Through a brilliant piece of detection, Heller has just tracked down 12 cargo containers packed with $1 billion in cash when he gets a call from his nephew Gabe in Washington, DC." — *Library Journal*

Fine, Julia
The **upstairs** house. Julia Fine. HarperCollins, 2021. 240 p.
ISBN 9780062975829
1. Brown, Margaret Wise 2. New mothers 3. Infants 4. Postpartum 5. Women graduate students 6. Ghosts 7. United States 8. Gothic fiction
Recovering from a difficult childbirth, a woman caring for her newborn alone while her husband travels for work suffers a psychological unraveling that causes her to see the ghost of famed children's book author, Margaret Wise Brown.
"This white-knuckle depiction of the essential scariness of new motherhood will captivate readers." —*Publishers Weekly*

What should be wild. Julia Fine. Harper, 2018. 350 p.
ISBN 9780062684134
1. Family curses 2. Family estates 3. Social isolation 4. Superhuman abilities 5. Forests 6. Coming-of-age stories 7. Gothic fiction 8. Multiple perspectives 9. Adult books for young adults
Born with the power to kill or restore life at a touch, a young woman endures a childhood of objectification and a complete inability to experience physical contact before she ventures into the woods at the edge of her village to remove a curse that has plagued the women in her family for centuries.

Finlay, Mick
The **murder** pit. Mick Finlay. Harlequin MIRA, 2019. 336 p. (Arrowood novels (Mick Finlay), 2)
ISBN 9780778369301
1. Private investigators 2. Missing women 3. Missing persons investigation 4. Working class 5. Poverty 6. London, England 7. Victorian era (1837-1901) 8. 1890s 9. Victorian mysteries 10. Hardboiled fiction 11. Historical mysteries
Receiving less recognition and income than his contemporary, Sherlock Holmes, private detective William Arrowood investigates a simple missing person's case that turns into a complicated murder investigation.
"This is a welcome grittier take on a familiar genre trope." —*Publishers Weekly*

Finn, A. J.
★ The **woman** in the window. A. J. Finn. William Morrow & Co, 2018. 368 p.
ISBN 9780062678416
1. Women recluses 2. Neighbors 3. Surveillance 4. Obsession 5. Agoraphobia 6. New York City 7. Psychological suspense 8. Books to movies
Librarians' Choice (Australia), 2017; LibraryReads Favorites, 2018
An agoraphobic recluse languishes in her New York City home, drinking wine and spying on her neighbors, before witnessing a terrible crime through her window that exposes her secrets and raises questions about her perceptions of reality.
"An astounding debut from a truly talented writer, perfect for fans in search of more like Gone Girl and The Girl on the Train." —*Booklist*
Made into a movie of the same name in 2021.

Fisher, Helen
Space hopper. Helen Fisher. Simon & Schuster (UK), 2021. 304 p.
ISBN 9781982142674
1. Married women 2. Mothers 3. Orphans 4. Time travel (Past) 5. Boxes 6. London, England 7. Relationship fiction
A debut novel examines loss, faith, and love as it follows a grown woman who travels back in time to be reunited with the mother she lost when she was a child.
"Fisher's achingly authentic characters leap off the page and capture readers' hearts. This addictive, emotionally heavy page-turner marks a delightful spin on the time travel genre." —*Publishers Weekly*
Originally published as Faye, Faraway in 2021 by Gallery Books in New York.

Fisher, Tarryn
The **wives**. Tarryn Fisher. Graydon House, 2019. 320 p.
ISBN 9781525805127
1. Polygamy 2. Married men 3. Partner abuse 4. Married women 5. Nurses 6. Clemenc, Ana K. 7. Seattle, Washington 8. Psychological suspense
LibraryReads Favorites, 2019
A married woman shares her husband with two other wives, yet she has never met them. When she accidentally comes across information about one of the others her curiosity is aroused and she seeks her out.
"Fisher smoothly inserts moments of self-doubt, longing, paranoia, and triumph into her unsettling narrative as she draws the reader into Thursday s conflicted and increasingly complicated life." —*Publishers Weekly*

Fitch, Janet

Paint it black: a novel. Janet Fitch. Little, Brown, 2006. 400 p.
ISBN 9780316182744
1. Young women 2. Art students 3. First loves 4. Punk rock music
5. Suicide 6. Los Angeles, California 7. 1980s 8. Psychological fiction
9. Adult books for young adults

LC 2006010211

Following the suicide of her lover, art student Michael Faraday, Josie Tyrell, an art model and teenage runaway, struggles to come to terms with his death and to deal with his mother, Meredith, who holds her responsible for the tragedy.

"Fitch has given us a courageous and interesting young woman who handles the bad cards she has been dealt with grace and resolve. No one, not even Cinderella, knows better than Josie Tyrell that life isn't fairand no one, despite some very long odds, seems more likely to transcend the role of victim and succeed with or without her fairy-tale prince." —*Washington Post Book World.*

White oleander: a novel. Janet Fitch. Little, Brown, 1999. 390 p.
ISBN 9780316569323
1. Women poets 2. Children of prisoners 3. Identity (Psychology)
4. Women murderers 5. Single mothers 6. California 7. Los Angeles, California 8. Psychological fiction 9. Literary fiction 10. Books to movies

LC 9850371

At the age of 12, Astrid has her world blown away when her mother is sentenced to life in prison for murdering her lover. Sharpened by harsh foster home environments, Astrid remakes herself as a survivor, and ultimately, an artist.

"This sensitive exploration of the mother daughter terrain...offers a convincing look at what Adrienne Rich has called 'this womanly splitting of self,' in a poignant, virtuosic, utterly captivating narrative." —*Publishers Weekly*

Fitzgerald, F. Scott

★ The **beautiful** and damned. By F. Scott Fitzgerald. Scribner, 1922. 449 p.
ISBN 9781471239847
1. Inheritance and succession 2. Married people 3. Rich people
4. Socialites 5. Alcoholics 6. New York City 7. Psychological fiction
8. Satirical fiction 9. Modern classics

LC 22004437

Set in the heady Jazz Age of New York, "The beautiful and damned" chronicles the relationship between Anthony Patch, a Harvard-educated aspiring aesthete, and his beautiful trophy wife, Gloria, as they wait to inherit his grandfather's fortune. Anticipating easy millions, they embrace the glittering, hedonistic lifestyle of the pretentious nouveaux riches, but find that they are living a dream that is all too fleeting.

★ The **last** tycoon: an unfinished novel. F. Scott Fitzgerald. Scribner, 1958. 163 p.
ISBN 9780007574902
1. Film industry and trade executives 2. Man-woman relationships 3. American dream 4. Workaholism 5. Failure (Psychology) 6. Hollywood, California 7. 1930s 8. Love stories 9. Books to movies 10. Modern classics

LC 58014792

In this tragic tale, unfinished at the time of his death, F. Scott Fitzgerald exposes the corruption, sex and towering ambition at the dark heart of 1930s Hollywood.
The Last Tycoon inspired the film The Last Tycoon in 1976.
Features Life & Times - a fascinating insight into the author, their

work and the time of publication - and glossary of classic literature.
Original ed. published in 1941 by Scribner, New York.

Novels and stories, 1920-1922. F. Scott Fitzgerald. Library of America, 2000. 1082 p.
ISBN 9781883011840
1. College students 2. Rich people 3. Manners and customs 4. New Jersey 5. United States 6. 1920s 7. Short stories 8. Books to movies
9. Modern classics

LC 24287

A compilation of the novelist's work, including This Side of Paradise, The Beautiful and Damned and his short stories reflects American society during the 1920s and portrays the aristocratic class of the era.
Includes bibliographical references.

★ The **short** stories of F. Scott Fitzgerald: a new collection. Edited and with a preface by Matthew J. Bruccoli. Scribner, 1989. Xix, 775 p.
ISBN 9780684191607
1. Manners and customs 2. United States 3. Short stories 4. Books to movies 5. Modern classics

LC 89006351

Gathers more than forty Fitzgerald stories and provides brief background information on each piece.
43 short stories.

Six tales of the jazz age and other stories. F. Scott Fitzgerald. Scribner, 1960. 192 p.
ISBN 9780684717623
1. Manners and customs 2. United States 3. 1920s 4. Short stories
5. Books to movies 6. Modern classics

LC 60006410

Tales of the Jazz Age, F. Scott Fitzgerald's second book of 11 short stories, including "The Curious Case of Benjamin Button," a humorous satire of the wealthy, is a perfect length for a long commute—and for a return to a golden, bygone era.

★ **This** side of paradise. F. Scott Fitzgerald. Scribner, 1970. 282 p.
ISBN 9780684101644
1. Debutantes 2. Interclass romance 3. Social status 4. Young men
5. Classism 6. Coming-of-age stories 7. Literary fiction 8. Modern classics

A young man searches for himself in the American upper-class society of the pre- and post-World War I era.

Fitzgerald, Penelope

The **means** of escape: stories. Penelope Fitzgerald. Houghton Mifflin, 2000. 117 p.
ISBN 9780618079940
1. Social classes 2. Interpersonal relations 3. Short stories 4. Literary fiction

LC 38914

New York Times Notable Book, 2000
A collection of stories skips across the globe from England to New Zealand between the seventeenth century and the modern day, exploring the shifting fortunes of class and wealth.

"Strange, whimsical, sometimes gothic or bizarre, these tales demonstrate Fitzgerald's cool and civilized wit and the merciless eye she casts on worldly pretensions." —*Publishers Weekly*

Fitzpatrick, Lydia

Lights all night long: a novel. Lydia Fitzpatrick. Penguin Press, 2019. 352 p.

ISBN 9780525558736
1. Exchange students 2. Brothers 3. Culture shock 4. Russians in the United States 5. Murder suspects 6. Louisiana 7. Russia 8. Coming-of-age stories 9. Adult books for young adults
LC 2018034986

With the help of his American host family's daughter, Sadie, who has secrets of her own, Russian exchange student Ilya embarks on a mission to prove his brother Vladimir's innocence in the murders of three girls back in Russia.

Flagg, Fannie

★ **Fried** green tomatoes at the Whistle Stop Cafe. Fannie Flagg. Random House, 1987. 403 p.
ISBN 9780394561523
1. Reminiscing in old age 2. Female friendship 3. Self-discovery in women 4. Women 5. Lesbians 6. Alabama 7. 1930s 8. 1980s 9. Humorous stories 10. Relationship fiction 11. Parallel narratives
LC 87012813

Mrs. Threadgoode's tale of two high-spirited women of the 1930s, Idgie and Ruth, helps Evelyn, a 1980s woman in a sad slump of middle age, to begin to rejuvenate her own life.

"This novel is set in a rural hamlet outside of Birmingham, Alabama. Bulletins from a gossipy town newsletter produced in the 1940s by Dot Weems are interspersed with the recollections of Mrs. Cleo (Vinnie) Throughgoode uttered (40 years later) in a nursing home to a depressed, menopausal visitor, Evelyn Couch (whose life is rejuvenated by these Sunday afternoon chats). Flagg also supplies basic narrative passages illuminating the news shared by Dot and Vinnie. The pace of the novel is as swift as the life of the small town is slow—at least it seems slow until Vinnie drops hints of a murder and of riotous pranks played upon the local minister. The story is carefully plotted, with the moods and people of pre- and post-World War II Alabama splendidly evoked." —*Booklist*

Includes recipes.

Book made into movie called Fried green tomatoes.

Standing in the rainbow: a novel. Fannie Flagg. Random House, 2002. 464 p.
ISBN 9780679426158
1. Women radio broadcasters 2. Pharmacists 3. Gospel singers 4. Mothers and sons 5. People who are blind 6. Missouri 7. 1940s 8. Humorous stories 9. Southern fiction 10. Gentle reads 11. Adult books for young adults
LC 2002021977

As the story begins, it is 1945, the war is over, the American economy is booming, and there is no better place in the world than Elmwood Springs, Missouri. Ten-year-old Bobby Smith's father is the town pharmacist and his mother is a local radio personality. Over the next several decades, the plot expands to include numerous beguiling characters who interact with the Smith family—among them, the Oatman Family Southern Gospel Singers.

"Beneath the sentimentality, there's a real celebration of life here, an affirmation that success and happiness are the results of simple kindness gratituder and courage." —*Christian Science Monitor*

Sequel to: Welcome to the world, Baby Girl!.

★ The **wonder** boy of Whistle Stop: a novel. Fannie Flagg. Random House, 2020. 272 p.
ISBN 9780593133842
1. Senior men 2. Reminiscing in old age 3. Memories 4. Self-discovery in men 5. Mothers and sons 6. Alabama 7. 1930s 8. 1990s 9. Humorous stories 10. Southern fiction 11. Parallel narratives
LC 2020002438

LibraryReads Favorites, 2020

Taking a final visit to the ghost town where his mother Ruth's Whistle Stop Cafe made its famous fried green tomatoes, Bud Threadgoode discovers new friends and surprises about the community's women while triggering unexpected changes in his daughters' lives.

"All the down-home characters, rural wisdom, and effervescent charm of Flagg's endearing 1987 novel, Fried Green Tomatoes at the Whistle Stop Cafe come back to life in this return to one of the most beloved locales in Southern fiction." —*Booklist*

Flanagan, Richard

Gould's book of fish: a novel in twelve fish. By Richard Flanagan. Grove Press, 2001. 404 p. : Color illustration
ISBN 9780802117113
1. Gould, William Buelow, 1803-1853 2. Marine animals in art 3. Prisoners 4. Penal colonies 5. Fishes in art 6. Prisoners — History 7. Australia 8. Colonial Australia (1788-1901) 9. Historical fiction 10. Literary fiction 11. Australian fiction
LC 2001055747

Australian Literature Society Gold Medal, 2002; Commonwealth Writers' Prize for Best Book, 2002; Commonwealth Writers' Prize, South East Asia and South Pacific: Best Book, 2002; New York Times Notable Book, 2002; Victorian Premier's Literary Awards, Vance Palmer Prize for Fiction, 2002; Shortlisted for the Miles Franklin Literary Award, 2002

In the early nineteenth century, forger and thief William Buelow Gould lands in prison in Australia, where the prison doctor utilizes his painting talents to create an illustrated taxonomy of the country's exotic sea creatures.

"This remarkable novel is a meditation on colonialism—indeed, on history itself—couched in the story of an English guttersnipe." —*The New Yorker*

Originally published: Sydney, N.S.W.: Picador, 2001.

The **living** sea of waking dreams. Richard Flanagan. Random House Inc 2021. 288 p.
ISBN 9780593319604
1. Families 2. Wildfires 3. Climate change 4. Environmental degradation 5. Senior women 6. Tasmania 7. Australia 8. Magical realism 9. Australian fiction
LC 2020045408

In a novel of family, climate change and the resilience of the human spirit, Anna, whose aged mother is dying in a world of perennial fire and growing extinctions, escapes into visions of horror and delight through the ever-widening hospital window.

"This is a timely, unforgettable work of climate fiction, unrelenting in its focus on the horrors of climate change, but one that also offers some hope." —*Booklist*

★ The **narrow** road to the deep north. Richard Flanagan. Knopf, 2014. 467 pages
ISBN 9780385352857
1. Lovers 2. Forced labor 3. World War II — Prisoners and prisons, Japanese 4. Violence 5. Guilt in men 6. Thailand 7. Australia 8. 1940s 9. Literary fiction 10. Love stories 11. Historical fiction
ALA Notable Book, 2015; Man Booker Prize, 2014; New York Times Notable Book, 2014; Tasmania Book Prizes, Margaret Scott Prize, 2015; Prime Minister's Literary Awards: Fiction, 2014; Queensland Literary Awards, Fiction Book Award, 2014; Western Australian Premier's Book Awards, Fiction category, 2014; Western Australian Premier's Book Awards, Premier's Prize, 2014; Shortlisted for the Miles Franklin Literary Award, 2014; Shortlisted for the International Dublin Literary Award, 2015

Haunted by the death of his wife while attending brutally sick and injured soldiers at a World War II Japanese POW camp, surgeon Dorrigo Evans receives a letter that irrevocably shapes the subsequent decades of his life in Australia.

"A supple meditation on memory, trauma, and empathy that is also a sublime war novel." —*Publishers Weekly*

Originally published: North Sydney, N.S.W.: Knopf, 2013.

The **unknown** terrorist. Richard Flanagan. Grove, 2007. 336 p.
ISBN 9780802118516
1. Terrorism 2. Hysteria (Social psychology) 3. Stripteasers 4. Mass media — Social aspects 5. Malicious accusation 6. Sydney, New South Wales 7. Australia 8. Political fiction 9. Australian fiction

What would you do if you turned on the television and saw you were the most wanted terrorist in the country? After spending a night with an attractive stranger, Gina Davies becomes a prime suspect in an attempted terrorist attack. When police find three unexploded bombs at a stadium, Gina goes on the run and witnesses every truth of her life turned into a betrayal. A devastating picture of a world where the ceaseless drumbeat of terror alerts, news breaks, and fear of the unknown push one woman ever closer to breaking point.

"A page-turning thriller worthy of John le Carre, with a plot so credible a reader might feel it's nonfiction, except for a few too many coincidences. But even those can't dampen the chilling effect of the story, written in a fresh, exhilarating prose style in which the author makes each sentence a small work of art." —*Seattle Times*

Originally published: Sydney : Picador, 2006.

Flanery, Patrick

Absolution: a novel. Patrick Flanery. Riverhead Books, 2012. 388 p.
ISBN 9781594488177
1. Women authors 2. Apartheid 3. Forgiveness 4. Biographers 5. Truth 6. South Africa 7. Cape Town, South Africa 8. Literary fiction

Shortlisted for the International IMPAC Dublin Literary Award, 2014

In modern-day South Africa, Clare Walde tells the story of her sister's death and disappearance of her daughter during apartheid 20 years earlier.

Flaubert, Gustave

★ **Madame** Bovary: provincial ways. Gustave Flaubert; a new translation by Lydia Davis. Viking Press, 2010. 342 p.
ISBN 9780670022076
1. Married women — History 2. Physicians' spouses 3. Boredom in women 4. Extramarital affairs 5. Married people 6. France 7. Domestic fiction 8. Translations 9.

A new translation of Flaubert's classic tale, in which the title character turns to spending and a series of affairs to combat the boredom of married life and, heartbroken and crippled by debts, takes drastic action that results in tragedy.

"The power of Madame Bovary stems from Flaubert's determination to render each object of his scrutiny exactly as it looks, or sounds or smells or feels or tastes.... Given the pressure Flaubert applied to each sentence, there is no greater test of a translator's art than Madame Bovary. Faithful to the style of the original, but not to the point of slavishness, Davis's effort is transparent the reader never senses her presence. For Madame Bovary, hers is the level of mastery required." —*New York Times Book Review*

Sentimental education. Gustave Flaubert; translated with an introduction by Robert Baldick. Penguin Books, 1964. 429 p.
ISBN 9780140441413

1. Flaubert, Gustave 2. Disillusionment in men 3. Alienation in men 4. Idealism 5. Young men 6. Married women 7. France 8. Paris, France 9. 19th century 10. Translations 11. Classics

Based on Flaubert's own youthful passion for an older woman, Sentimental Education was described by its author as 'the moral history of the men of my generation.' It follows the amorous adventures of Frederic Moreau, a law student who, returning home to Normandy from Paris, notices Mme Arnoux, a slender, dark woman several years older than himself.

Originally published in French as L'education sentimentale: 1869.

Fleischmann, Raymond

How quickly she disappears. Raymond Fleischmann. Berkley, 2020. 320 p.
ISBN 9781984805171
1. Twin sisters 2. Missing women 3. Violent crimes 4. Crimes against women 5. Strangers 6. Alaska 7. 1940s 8. Second World War era (1939-1945) 9. Historical thrillers
LC 2019019798
LibraryReads Favorites, 2020

A woman whose twin disappeared 30 years earlier is approached in her small Alaskan town by a dangerous man claiming to know what happened to her sister, but requesting from her three specific gifts in exchange for the information.

"As the narrative toggles between the present of 1941-42 and the past, shortly before Jacqueline disappeared, Elizabeth is forced to make dreadful choices, leading to a pulse-pounding climax. Fleischmann proves to be an author to watch on the literary-thriller scene." —*Booklist*

Fleming, Ian

★ **Casino** royale: a James Bond novel. By Ian Fleming. Penguin Books, 2002. 181 p; (James Bond series, 1)
ISBN 9780142002025
1. Secret service 2. Spies 3. Gambling 4. International intrigue 5. France 6. Spy fiction 7. Adventure stories 8. Books to movies
LC 2002024602

In his first mission, James Bond (Agent 007) must neutralize a Russian agent known as "Le Chiffre" by ruining him at the baccarat table, thus forcing his "retirement." However, a beautiful female agent leads him to disaster—and an unexpected savior.

Doctor No. Ian Fleming. Macmillan, 1973. 256 p. (James Bond series, 6)
ISBN 9789997512338
1. Spies 2. Churchill, Winston, 1874-1965 3. Sadists 4. Murder 5. Intelligence service 6. Jamaica 7. Spy fiction 8. Adventure stories 9. Books to movies

Hidden on a tropical island paradise is the evil empire of Dr. No. Dr. No's obsession is power. His only gifts are strictly pain-shaped. He will be a worthy adversary for James Bond.

From Russia with love. Ian Fleming. J. Cape, 1972. 253 p. (James Bond series, 5)
ISBN 9789997407191
1. Spies 2. Betrayal 3. Encoding machines 4. Intelligence officers 5. Bond, James (Fictional character) 6. Europe 7. Istanbul, Turkey 8. Spy fiction 9. Adventure stories 10. Books to movies

The light nudge at his ankle wakes Bond. He doesn't move. His senses come to life like an animal's. What has woken him? The spectral eye of the nightlight casts its deep velvet sheen over the little room. No sound comes from the upper bunk. By the window, Captain Nash sits in his place, his book open on his lap, a flicker of moonlight from the edge of the blind showing white on the double page.

First published: [London]: Jonathan Cape, 1957.

★ **Goldfinger**. Ian Fleming. Charter Books 1987. 262 p. (James Bond series, 7)

ISBN 9780441298068

1. Gold thefts 2. Robbery 3. Spies 4. Women murder victims 5. Bond, James (Fictional character) 6. Kentucky 7. Spy fiction 8. Adventure stories 9. Books to movies

A friendly game of two-handed canasta that turns out thoroughly crooked. And a beautiful golden girl who ends up thoroughly dead...In Bond's first encounter with the world's cleverest, cruellest criminal, useful lessons are learned. Soon the game will change and the stakes will rise...to fifteen billion dollars' worth of US government bullion. But 007 knows that Auric Goldfinger's rules remain brutally simple—Heads I win, tails you die.

Originally published: London : Cape, 1959.

The **man** with the golden gun. Ian Fleming. New American Library, 1965. 235 p. (James Bond series, 13)

ISBN 9780859974400

1. Spies 2. Assassins 3. Undercover operations 4. Secret service 5. Jamaica 6. Spy fiction 7. Adventure stories 8. Books to movies

Pitted against the sophisticated and deadly villain Scaramanga and his arch rival Hi Fat, Bond is assigned to recover a small piece of equipment which can be utilized to harness the sun's energy.

On Her Majesty's secret service. Ian Fleming. New American Library, 1963. 190 p. (James Bond series, 11)

ISBN 9780451154323

1. Spies 2. Mafia 3. Undercover operations 4. Conspiracies 5. Chases 6. Spy fiction 7. Adventure stories 8. Books to movies

In this tale, Secret Agent James Bond finds himself once again against the SPECTRE archfiend, Blofeld, and his plot to destroy the world. Bond also finds himself falling for Tracy, the daughter of Marc-Ange Draco, head of the Corsican mafia.

You only live twice. Ian Fleming. J. Cape, 1964. 255 p. (James Bond series, 12)

ISBN 9780685116319

1. Codes (Communication) 2. Assassination 3. Recluses 4. Spies 5. Intelligence service 6. Japan 7. Spy fiction 8. Adventure stories 9. Books to movies

After the death of his wife, Bond leaves for Japan to accomplish an impossible mission far removed from his usual duties.

"Bond, near-prostrate from his bride's death, is given a Japanese assignment to snap him out of his torpor.... [The story] involves Bond's making up as a Japanese and venturing into the den of a foreign 'death collector,' a madman who has set up a poisonous garden complete with noxious plants, volcanic geysers, snakes, and, in a lake, piranha fish. Very grisly and chilling. The ending is an epitome of horror." —*Publishers Weekly*

Flint, Emma

★ **Little** deaths: a novel. Emma Flint. Hachette Books, 2017. 304 p.

ISBN 9780316272476

1. Single mothers 2. Child murder victims 3. Public opinion 4. Malicious accusation 5. Journalists 6. New York City 7. Queens, New York City 8. 1960s 9. Literary fiction 10. Isherwood, Christopher

LC 2016037331

Librarians' Choice (Australia), 2017; Longlisted for The Baileys Women's Prize for Fiction, 2017

A tale set in 1960s New York and inspired by true events follows the investigation of a cocktail waitress whose two young children have been brutally murdered and a rookie tabloid reporter who would uncover the truth.

"This accomplished debut novel will intrigue fans of both true crime and noir fiction. Flint, a technical writer in London, is a welcome addition to the world of literary crime fiction." —*Library Journal*

Flores, Fernando A.

Tears of the trufflepig. Fernando A. Flores. Farrar, Straus and Giroux, MCD x FSG Originals, 2019. 336 p.

ISBN 9780374538330

1. Mexican Americans 2. Widowers 3. Criminals 4. Cartels 5. Conspiracies 6. Mexican-American Border Region 7. Texas 8. Magical realism

LC 2018044001

A surreal debut novel set on the Texas-Mexico border, blending magical realism, sci-fi, and political parable to tell the story of an everyday man's tumble into a bizarre and sinister criminal underworld.

Florio, Gwen

Best laid plans. Gwen Florio. Severn House Publishers, 2021. 256 pages (Nora Best novels, 1)

ISBN 9781780297156

1. Women authors 2. Separated women (Marital relations) 3. Cheating (Interpersonal relations) 4. Recreational vehicles 5. Voyages and travels 6. Wyoming 7. Mysteries

When Nora Best's plans on exploring the US in an Airstream trailer with her husband go up in smoke upon finding him in a compromising position with her friend, she sets off on her own. Nora ends up drowning her sorrows in a campsite in the Wyoming mountains, but soon finds herself in trouble when blood is found around the campsite and she is accused of murder.

"Baffling circumstances combine with life-changing adventures in this breathtaking page-turner." —*Kirkus*

Silent hearts. Gwen Florio. Atria Books, 2018. 336 p.

ISBN 9781501181924

1. Women interpreters 2. Americans in Afghanistan 3. Female friendship 4. Humanitarian assistance 5. Cultural differences 6. Kabul, Afghanistan 7. Afghanistan 8. 2000s (Decade) 9. Literary fiction 10. Political fiction

LC 2017057630

An American aid worker and her local interpreter forge an unexpected friendship in spite of disparate life experiences and the increasing violence that surrounds them in 2001 Kabul. By the author of the Lola Wicks series.

Flournoy, Angela

The **Turner** house. Angela Flournoy. Houghton Mifflin Harcourt, 2015. 320 p.

ISBN 9780544303164

1. African American families 2. Intergenerational relations 3. Houses 4. Families 5. Change 6. Detroit, Michigan 7. Domestic fiction 8. African American fiction

LC 2014034423

BCALA Literary Award for First Novelist, 2016; New York Times Notable Book, 2015; Finalist for the Hurston/Wright Legacy Awards for Fiction, 2016; National Book Award for Fiction finalist, 2015

Learning after a half-century of family life that their house on Detroit's East Side is worth only a fraction of its mortgage, the members of the Turner family gather to reckon with their pasts and decide the house's fate.

"Flounoy's debut is a lively, thoroughly engaging family saga with a cast of fully realized characters.... [She] evokes the intricacies of domestic situations and sibling relationships, depicting how each of the Turners lives has been shaped by the social history of their generation." —*Publishers Weekly*

Fluke, Joanne

★ **Christmas** cupcake murder. Joanne Fluke. Kensington Pub Corp, 2020. 288 p. (Hannah Swensen mysteries, 26)
ISBN 9781496729125
1. Christmas 2. Women bakers 3. Cupcakes 4. Baking 5. Men with amnesia 6. Minnesota 7. Holiday mysteries 8. Culinary mysteries 9. Cozy mysteries

Firing up the Cookie Jar's ovens to attend a lengthy holiday checklist, Hannah Swensen helps loved ones manage seasonal doldrums before she is challenged to identify a skilled antique restorer found near death outside her bakery.

"Fans of Fluke's wildly popular cozy series featuring cookie baker Hannah Swensen and her family in Lake Eden, Minnesota, will be thrilled with this twenty-sixth entry, which offers a kind of origin story, as the action takes place before Hannah solves her first missing-person case." —*Booklist*

Flynn, Gillian

Dark places. Gillian Flynn. Shaye Areheart Books, 2009. 368 p.
ISBN 9780307341563
1. Children of murder victims 2. Teenage murderers 3. Siblings 4. Crimes against family 5. Secret societies 6. Missouri 7. Kansas City, Missouri 8. Psychological suspense 9. Books to movies
LC 2008040244

After witnessing the murder of her mother and sisters, 7-year-old Libby Day testifies against her brother Ben, but twenty-five years later she tries to profit from her tragic history and admit that her story might not have been accurate.

★ **Gone** girl: a novel. Gillian Flynn. Crown, 2012. 416 p.
ISBN 9780307588364
1. Murder suspects 2. Missing women 3. Marital conflict 4. Husband and wife 5. Married people 6. Psychological suspense 7. First person narratives 8. Multiple perspectives 9. Adult books for young adults
LC 2011041525
Goodreads Choice Award, 2012; Library Journal Best Books, 2012; Romantic Times Reviewer's Choice Award, 2012; RUSA Reading List, 2013

When beautiful Amy Dunne disappears from her Missouri home, it looks as if her husband Nick is to blame. But though he protests his innocence, it's clear that he's not being entirely truthful. Gone Girl is not only the story of a disappearance, but a truly frightening glimpse of a souring marriage.

★ **Sharp** objects: a novel. Gillian Flynn. Shaye Areheart Books, 2006. 272 p.
ISBN 9780307341549
1. Self-harm 2. Women journalists 3. Girl murder victims 4. Murder investigation 5. Missouri 6. Psychological suspense 7. First person narratives 8. Books to TV
LC 2005035046

Ian Fleming Steel Dagger Award, 2007; New Blood Dagger Award, 2007

Returning to her hometown after a long absence to investigate the murders of two girls, reporter Camille Preaker is reunited with her neurotic mother and enigmatic half-sister as she works to uncover the truth about the killings.

"The author offers up a literary thriller that's a doozy...and she does it with wit and grit, a sort of Hitchcock visits Stephen King, with plenty of the former's offstage and often only implied violence, and the latter's sense of pacing and facility with dialogue.... This is not a comfortable novel of touchy-feely family fun. Rather, it is a tough tale told with remarkable clarity and dexterity." —*Denver Post*

Flynn, Michael

Eifelheim. Michael Flynn. Tor Books, 2006. 320 p.
ISBN 9780765300966
1. Historians 2. Women physicists 3. Research 4. Villages 5. Space vehicles 6. Germany 7. Earth 8. 14th century 9. Alternate histories 10. Hard science fiction 11. Science fiction
LC 2006005468

Tom, a contemporary historian and his physicist girlfriend Sharon become interested in a one small town in Germany that disappeared in 1349 and was never resettled. Father Deitrich the priest of the village is the first contact between humanity and an alien race from a distant star when their interstellar ship crashes in the nearby forest in 1348, the year the Black Death spread across Europe.

"Tom, a young historian, obsesses about Eifelheim, a German village that mysteriously disappeared from all maps in 1349. His lover Sharon, a theoretical physicist, occupies herself with testing the limits of conventional theories of time and space. Their interests merge when they discover the remarkable story of Father Dietrich, Eifelheim's parish priest during the Black Death and a believer in travelers from the stars. With a sure grasp of both speculative science and medieval history, Flynn...compellingly weaves past and present together in a dialog of faith and science." —*Library Journal*

A Tom Doherty Associates book.

The **January** dancer. Michael Flynn. Tor, 2008. 352 p. (January dancer, 1)
ISBN 9780765318176
1. Antiquities, Prehistoric 2. Space flight 3. Collectors and collecting 4. Life on other planets 5. Life after death 6. Science fiction 7. Space opera
LC 2008029772

Follows the adventures of Captain Amos January and a host of rivals struggling to obtain an ancient pre-human artifact of great power that incites murderous actions in those who seek it.

"The characters zip through so many worlds that it's hard to keep track of them, but Flynn includes enough clever references to the long-abandoned Earth to keep the journey amusing.... The balladic framework can be heavy-handed at times, but it adds a mythical quality to what could have been run-of-the-mill space fantasy." —*Washington Post Book World.*

A Tom Doherty Associates book.

Flyte, Magnus

City of dark magic: a novel. Magnus Flyte. Penguin Books, 2012. 368 p. (City of dark magic, 1)
ISBN 9780143122685

1. Music students 2. Magic 3. Mentors 4. Murder 5. Murder investigation 6. Prague, Czech Republic 7. Thrillers and suspense 8. Urban fantasy

LC 2012028676

A music student working in Prague cataloging Beethoven's manuscripts discovers clues that her deceased mentor may not have committed suicide and becomes involved with a time-travel drug, a 400-year-old dwarf, a handsome Prince and a powerful U.S. senator.

City of lost dreams: a novel. Magnus Flyte. Penguin Books, 2013. 368 p. (City of dark magic, 2)

ISBN 9780143123279

1. Music students 2. Magic 3. Mentors 4. Enemies 5. Paranormal phenomena 6. Prague, Czech Republic 7. Thrillers and suspense 8. Urban fantasy

LC 2013031311

A sequel to City of Dark Magic finds Sara and Nicolas's search for an alchemical cure for a gravely ill friend threatened by an old enemy and a bloodthirsty horseman, while Prince Max tries to explain the strange reappearance of a saint while outmaneuvering a scheming historian.

"Sensual, witty and sometimes laugh-out-loud funny, set forth in sparkling prose and inhabited by characters well-worth getting to know." —*Kirkus*

Maps on inside cover.

Foer, Jonathan Safran

Everything is illuminated: a novel. Jonathan Safran Foer. Houghton Mifflin Co, 2002. 276 p.

ISBN 9780618173877

1. Grandfather and child 2. Holocaust (1933-1945) 3. Translators 4. World War II. 5. Guilt in men 6. Ukraine 7. Novels-within-novels 8. Epistolary novels 9. Magical realism

LC 2001051610

Guardian First Book Award, 2002; National Jewish Book Award for Fiction, 2001; New York Times Notable Book, 2002; William Saroyan International Prize for Writing, Fiction category, 2003

Hilarious, energetic, and profoundly touching, a debut novel follows a young writer as he travels to the farmlands of eastern Europe, where he embarks on a quest to find Augustine, the woman who saved his grandfather from the Nazis, and, guided by his young Ukrainian translator, he discovers an unexpected past that will resonate far into the future.

"Foer deftly handles the intricate story-within-a-story plot, and the layers of suspense build as the shtetl hurtles toward the devastation of the 20th century while Alex and Jonathan and Grandfather close in on the object of their search. An impressive, original debut." —*Publishers Weekly*

Extremely loud and incredibly close. Jonathan Safran Foer. Houghton Mifflin, 2005. 368 p.

ISBN 9780618329700

1. Fathers — Death 2. Loss (Psychology) 3. Quests 4. Locks and keys 5. Boys 6. New York City 7. Dresden, Germany 8. 21st century 9. Multiple perspectives 10. First person narratives 11. Books to movies 12. Adult books for young adults

LC 2004065131

ALA Notable Book, 2006; School Library Journal Best Books: Best Adult Books 4 Teens, 2005; Shortlisted for the International IMPAC Dublin Literary Award, 2007

Oskar Schell, the nine-year-old son of a man killed in the World Trade Center attacks, searches the five boroughs of New York City for a lock that fits a black key his father left behind.

"The author's depiction of Oskar's reaction to phone messages left by his father as he awaited rescue in the burning World Trade Center, his description of Oskar's grandfather's love affair...and his experiences during

the bombing of Dresden—these passages underscore Mr. Foer's ability to evoke, with enormous compassion and psychological acuity, his characters' emotional experiences, and to show how these private moments intersect with the great public events of history." —*New York Times*

Here I am: a novel. Jonathan Safran Foer. Farrar, Straus and Giroux, 2016. 512 p.

ISBN 9780374280024

1. Dysfunctional families 2. Jewish families 3. Family relationships 4. Jewish Americans 5. Self-discovery in men 6. Washington, D.C. 7. Israel 8. Domestic fiction

LC 2016007096

New York Times Notable Book, 2016

A tale told over four tumultuous weeks in present-day Washington, D.C traces the fracturing of a family in crisis when the three sons of Jacob and Julia confront the paradoxes between the lives they think they want and the lives they are actually living.

"That he can provide such a redemptive denouement, at once poignant, inspirational, and compassionate, is the mark of a thrillingly gifted writer." —*Publishers Weekly*

Foley, Bridget

Just get home. Bridget Foley. Mira Books, 2021. 336 p.

ISBN 9780778331599

1. Teenage girls 2. Foster children 3. Single mothers 4. Earthquakes 5. Mother-separated girls 6. Los Angeles, California

Racing through an earthquake-devastated Los Angeles to find her 3-year-old daughter, a single mom finds her fate bound to that of a smart-talking 15-year-old assault survivor who becomes her partner in a quest for survival.

"This story is told with artful suspense-building, with main characters who are heavily defined by the traumatic events of each of their pasts. The duo's journey across the sprawling metropolis will compel the reader, and the development of Beegie and Dessa's relationship brings redemption to a story set in a very harsh and unforgiving world." —*Booklist*

Foley, Lucy

The **guest** list. Lucy Foley. William Morrow & Co, 2020. 320 p.

ISBN 9780062868930

1. Weddings 2. Islands 3. Storms 4. Celebrities 5. Murder 6. Ireland 7. Thrillers and suspense

LibraryReads Favorites, 2020

An expertly planned celebrity wedding between a rising television star and an ambitious magazine publisher is thrown into turmoil by petty jealousies, a college drinking game, the bride's ruined dress and an untimely murder.

"Only a handful of thriller writers can accomplish what Foley does here: weave a complex plot from the perspectives of eight characters plus an omniscient narrator without causing confusion or reader exhaustion when the plot bounces from one person to the next." —*Library Journal*

The **hunting** party. Lucy Foley. William Morrow Co, 2019. 327 pages

ISBN 9780062868909

1. Country homes 2. Blizzards 3. Flashbacks 4. Thirties (Age) 5. Winter 6. Highlands, Scotland 7. Scotland 8. Psychological suspense 9. Multiple perspectives

A group of thirty-something Oxford friends celebrate New Year's Eve in the Scottish Highlands as a historic blizzard hits, trapping and isolating them, only to discover one of them is a murderer.

Follett, Ken

A **column** of fire. Ken Follett. Viking, 2017. 1024 p. (Pillars of the Earth, 3)

ISBN 9780525954972

1. Church and state 2. Man-woman relationships 3. Interpersonal attraction 4. Ambition 5. Humanism (14th-16th centuries) 6. Great Britain 7. Elizabethan era (1558-1603) 8. Tudor period (1485-1603) 9. Historical fiction

LC 2017025384

The relationship between a man in service to Elizabeth I and a woman on the opposing side of England's religious divide is challenged by violent ideological power shifts, torn loyalties, and the queen's circle of spies.

"Follett's sprawling novel is a fine mix of heart-pounding drama and erudite historicism." —*Publishers Weekly*

Edge of eternity. Ken Follett. Dutton, 2014. 1120 p. (Century trilogy, 3)

ISBN 9780525953098

1. World politics 2. Social change 3. Civil Rights Movement 4. Vietnam War, 1961-1975 5. Assassination 6. 20th century 7. Historical fiction 8. Family sagas 9. Epic fiction

Continues the experiences of five intertwined international families as they confront the social, political, and economic turmoil of the second half of the twentieth century.

"This mesmerizing final installment is an exhaustive but rewarding reading experience dense in thematic heft, yet flowing with spicy, expertly paced melodrama, character-rich exploits, familial histrionics, and international intrigue." —*Publishers Weekly*

★ The **evening** and the morning. Ken Follett. Viking, 2020. 928 p. (Pillars of the Earth, 4)

ISBN 9780525954989

1. Civilization, Medieval 2. Married women 3. Romantic love 4. Vikings 5. Nobility 6. England 7. Great Britain 8. Anglo-Saxon period (449-1066) 9. 10th century 10. Historical fiction

LC 2019051791

A prequel to the best-selling The Pillars of the Earth follows the experiences of a young boatbuilder, a scholarly monk and a Norman noblewoman against a backdrop of the Viking attacks at the end of the 10th century in England.

"Follett has done it again. Readers will gobble up this exciting prequel to his 1989 classic, The Pillars of the Earth." —*Library Journal*

Eye of the needle. Ken Follett. Dark Alley, 2005. 339, 14 p.

ISBN 9780060748159

1. Spies 2. Intelligence service 3. World War II. 4. Germans in Great Britain 5. Married women 6. Scotland 7. Second World War era (1939-1945) 8. 1940s 9. Spy fiction 10. Historical thrillers 11. Books to movies

LC 2004061876

Edgar Allan Poe Award for Best Mystery Novel, 1979

One enemy spy knows the secret of the Allies' greatest deception, a brilliant aristocrat and ruthless assassin—code name: "The Needle"—who holds the key to the ultimate Nazi victory. Only one person stands in his way: a lonely Englishwoman on an isolated island, who is coming to love the killer who has mysteriously entered her life. Ken Follett's unsurpassed and unforgettable masterwork of suspense, intrigue, and dangerous machinations of the human heart.

"An absolutely terrific thriller, so pulse-pounding, so ingenious in its plotting, and so frighteningly realistic that you simply cannot stop reading, this World War II espionage tale is right up there with the best of them." —*Publishers Weekly*

Includes bibliographical references (p. 13 (2nd)).

Published in England as: Storm Island.

Originally published: London : Futura, 1978.

Fall of giants. Ken Follett. Dutton, 2010. Xiv, 985 p. : Color; Map (Century trilogy, 1)

ISBN 9780525951650

1. World War I 2. World politics 3. Suffrage 4. War — History 5. Families 6. First World War era (1914-1918) 7. 20th century 8. Historical fiction 9. Family sagas 10. Epic fiction

LC 2010009279

Goodreads Choice Award, 2010

Follows the fates of five interrelated families—American, German, Russian, English, and Welsh—as they move through the dramas of the First World War, the Russian Revolution, and the struggle for women's suffrage.

"Follett entwines fiction and factual events well. Creating characters of numerous, actual historical figures is a big risk. How do you write about Trotsky without being facile? Follett successfully assails the dilemma from a couple of angles, most importantly by knowing a lot about the period but not making the reader aware of how arduously he is working." —*Chicago Sun-Times*

Sequel: Winter of the World.

Col. map on endpapers.

Hornet flight. Ken Follett. Dutton, 2002. 420 p.

ISBN 9780525946892

1. Spies 2. Military intelligence — History 3. World War II — Radar 4. Radar — History 5. Nazis 6. Denmark 7. Great Britain 8. Second World War era (1939-1945) 9. 1940s 10. War stories 11. Spy fiction 12. Thrillers and suspense 13. Adult books for young adults

In June 1944, with the war not going well for the British, the lives of three people on both sides of the English Channel intertwine as one of them makes a discovery that could change the course of the war.

"Tale of amateur spies pursued by Nazi collaborators in occupied Denmark in 1941. Harald Olufsen is an 18-year-old physics student who stumbles into espionage when he accidentally discovers a secret German radar installation on the island where he lives.... Follett starts out fast and keeps up the pace, revealing how ordinary people who want to do the right thing are undone by their own enthusiasm and inexperience. He also paints a vivid and convincing picture of life in occupied Denmark, of easy collaboration with the Nazis and of the insidious, creeping persecution of the Jews." —*Publishers Weekly*

Jackdaws. Ken Follett. Dutton, 2001. 384 p.

ISBN 9780525946281

1. Women spies 2. Military intelligence 3. World War II. 4. Secret service 5. Telephones 6. France 7. Second World War era (1939-1945) 8. 1940s 9. War stories 10. Spy fiction 11. Historical thrillers

LC 2001037087

On the eve of World War II, Special Operations agent, Felicity 'Flick' Clairet sent undercover to destroy the German lines of communication. An all woman team dubbed the Jackdaws is hastily trained to aid her in this very difficult mission.

"This thriller is about a mission to take out a German telephone exchange near Reims in the last few hours before D-Day.... All of this may sound like cliched melodrama, but when Follett starts the clock and slips the narrative gearshift into synchromesh, one's literary misgivings are abandoned in the wake of the plot's forward thrust." —*Booklist*

★ The **pillars** of the earth. Ken Follett. W. Morrow, 1989. 973 p. : Illustration (Pillars of the Earth, 1)

ISBN 9780688046590

1. Church and state 2. Revenge 3. Betrayal 4. Cathedrals 5. Stone building 6. Great Britain 7. Medieval period (476-1492) 8. Norman period (1066-1154) 9. Historical fiction 10. Books to TV

LC 89009405

Set in twelfth-century England, this epic of kings and peasants juxtaposes the building of a magnificent church with the violence and treachery that often characterized the Middle Ages.

"Follett has skillfully crafted an extraordinary epic buttressed by a succession of suspenseful subplots. A towering triumph of romance, rivalry, and spectacle from a major talent." —*Booklist*

Sequel: World without end (2007).

★ **Whiteout**. Ken Follett. Dutton, 2004. 374 p.
ISBN 9780525948438
1. Biological terrorism 2. Competition 3. Betrayal 4. Drug industry and trade 5. Animal rights advocates 6. Scotland 7. Thrillers and suspense

LC 2004010373

A missing canister containing a deadly virus forms the center of a deadly storm that traps Stanley Oxenford, director of a medical research firm; his greedy grown children; Toni Gallo, the firm's security director; an ambitious local TV reporter; and a violent trio of thugs in a remote house during a Christmas Eve blizzard.

Winter of the world. Ken Follett. Dutton, 2012. 1008 p. (Century trilogy, 2)
ISBN 9780525952923
1. Atomic bomb 2. World War II 3. War 4. Families 5. Nazism 6. Spain 7. 20th century 8. Historical fiction 9. Family sagas 10. Epic fiction

LC 2012004653

A follow-up to Fall of Giants continues the stories of five interrelated families from different world regions who struggle with social, political and economic turmoil in the years leading up to World War II, during which Carla considers a dangerous act against the Nazis, brothers Woody and Chuck pursue separate paths to key world events and Lloyd takes a stand against Communism.

Sequel to: Fall of Giants.
Maps on lining papers.
Originally published: London : Macmillan, 2012.

World without end. Ken Follett. Dutton, 2007. 992 p. (Pillars of the Earth, 2)
ISBN 9780525950073
1. Church and state 2. Greed 3. Ambition 4. Humanism (14th-16th centuries) 5. European Renaissance 6. Great Britain 7. Plantagenet period (1154-1485) 8. 14th century 9. Historical fiction

A war that lasts a hundred years. A plague that ravages a continent. A rivalry that could destroy everything. On the day after Halloween, in the year 1327, four children slip away from the cathedral city of Kingsbridge. In the forest they see two men killed. As adults, their lives become braided together by desire, determination, avarice and retribution. They will see prosperity and famine, plague and war. Yet they will always live under the shadow of the unexplained killing on that fateful childhood day."—back cover.

"Populated with an immense cast of truly remarkable characters-the rich and powerful, the weak and downtrodden, clergy, guildsmen and nobility-this novel explores the lives and fortunes of the ancestors of the original inhabitants of Kingsbridge." —*Library Journal*

Sequel to: The pillars of the Earth (1989)
Sequel to: The pillars of the earth.
First published: London : Macmillan, 2007.

Forbes, Curdella
A **tall** history of sugar. Curdella Forbes. Akashic Books, 2019. 372 p.

ISBN 9781617757518
1. Artists 2. Adopted children 3. Misfits (Persons) 4. Childhood friends 5. Political activists 6. Jamaica 7. England 8. 20th century 9. Magical realism 10. Love stories 11. Literary fiction
Hurston/Wright Legacy Award: Fiction, 2020

Tells the story of Moshe Fisher, a man who was "born without skin," so that no one is able to tell what race he belongs to; and Arrienne Christie, his quixotic soul mate who makes it her duty in life to protect Moshe from the social and emotional consequences of his strange appearance.

Force, Marie
Deceived by desire. Marie Force. Zebra Books, 2019. 320 pages (Gilded novels, 2)
ISBN 9781420147872
1. Industrialists 2. Housekeepers 3. Rich men 4. Dukes and duchesses 5. Vacations 6. Newport, Rhode Island 7. Regency period (1811-1820) 8. Regency romances 9. Historical romances

From New York Times bestselling author Marie Force comes a glittering tale of star-crossed romance set amid the lavish mansions and decadent lifestyles of early 20th century Newport, Rhode Island. But even in an age of great fortune, the heart has its own idea of true riches . . .

Five years gone. Marie Force. Zebra Books, 2018. 325 p.
ISBN 9781420149036
1. Love triangles 2. Soldiers 3. Lovers 4. Options, alternatives, choices 5. Loss (Psychology) 6. New York City 7. Contemporary romances 8. First person narratives 9. Multiple perspectives

The most brazen terrorist attack in history. A country bent on revenge. A love affair cut short. A heart that never truly heals.

Ford, Ford Madox
★ The **good** soldier: a tale of passion. Ford Madox Ford. Knopf 1991. 220 p.
ISBN 9780679406655
1. Americans in Germany 2. Extramarital affairs 3. Friendship 4. British in Germany 5. Leisure class 6. Bad Nauheim, Germany 7. Germany 8. Literary fiction 9. Psychological fiction 10. Classics

LC 91052977

Four wealthy and socially prominent individuals are forced to see each other realistically

Ford, Kelli Jo
★ **Crooked** hallelujah. Kelli Jo Ford. Grove Press, 2020. 304 p.
ISBN 9780802149121
1. Native American women 2. Family relationships 3. Mothers and daughters 4. Cherokee women 5. Cherokee Indians 6. United States 7. Literary fiction 8. Short stories 9. Family sagas

LC 2020026007

LibraryReads Favorites, 2020

A first collection by an award-winning Cherokee writer traces four generations of Native American women as they navigate cultural dynamics, religious beliefs, the 1980s oil bust, devastating storms and unreliable men to connect with their ideas about home.

"The theme of the weather as villain illustrates the unopposable forces Cherokee women must contend with, including the tyranny of society and of men. A riveting and important read." —*Booklist*

Ford, Richard
Canada. Richard Ford. Ecco Press, 2012. 432 p.

ISBN 9780061692048

1. Fifteen-year old boys 2. Children of prisoners 3. Coping in teenage boys 4. Violence in men 5. Self-fulfillment in teenage boys 6. Saskatchewan 7. Psychological fiction 8. Literary fiction

ALA Notable Book, 2013; Andrew Carnegie Medal for Excellence in Fiction, 2013; New York Times Notable Book, 2012

After his parents are arrested and imprisoned for robbing a bank, 15-year-old Dell Parsons is taken in by Arthur Remlinger who, unbeknownst to Dell, is hiding a dark and violent nature that interferes with Dell's quest to find grace and peace on the prairie of Saskatchewan.

★ **Independence** Day. Richard Ford. A.A. Knopf, 1995. 451 p. (Frank Bascombe novels, 2)

ISBN 9780679492658

1. Fathers and sons 2. Divorced men 3. Real estate agents 4. Teenage boys 5. Families 6. New Jersey 7. 1980s 8. Psychological fiction 9. Literary fiction 10. First person narratives

LC 95003126

PEN-Faulkner Award, 1996; Pulitzer Prize for Fiction, 1996; National Book Critics Circle Award for Fiction finalist, 1995

Real estate agent Frank Bascombe moves into his newly married ex-wife's old home, and is looking forward to the upcoming Fourth of July weekend, but somehow nothing turns out the way he expects.

"One is constantly struck by the rich, dense mixture of Ford's narrative. No one writes better—and with more inventive brio—about the bland wasteland of US suburbia; that shopping-malled, subdivisioned terrain that has rapidly become the true defining landscape of late 20th-century America." —*New Statesman*

Sequel to: The sportswriter.

Sequel: The lay of the land.

The **lay** of the land. By Richard Ford. Alfred A. Knopf, 2006. 496 p. (Frank Bascombe novels, 3)

ISBN 9780679454687

1. Remarriage 2. Mortality 3. Aging 4. Man-woman relationships 5. Fathers and sons 6. New Jersey 7. 2000s (Decade) 8. Psychological fiction 9. Literary fiction 10. First person narratives

LC 2006025570

Booklist Editors' Choice, 2006; Library Journal Best Books, 2006; New York Times Notable Book, 2006; National Book Critics Circle Award for Fiction finalist, 2006

In the fall of 2000, with the results of the presidential election still hanging in the balance, Frank Bascombe confronts the perils of Thanksgiving as he contends with health, marital, and family issues and works as a realtor at the Jersey shore.

"This is as vibrant a book as any that Richard Ford has written. It bristles with energy, with a natural assurance on the part of its writer.... And what a slice of life at the turn of the century and millennium this novel is. There is so much trenchant criticism of what is wrong with American society: the economic royalism, the greed, the lack of common decency and civility in so many walks of life, and above all perspective.... As people today read Theodore Dreiser for his acute portraits of industrialized America in its gilded age and Sinclair Lewis for his insights into his nation's struggles to come to terms with 20th-century changes in its social structures, one day readers will turn to Richard Ford to discover just what the United States was like on the homefront during his particular fin de siecle." —*Christian Science Monitor*

Sequel to: Independence Day.

Let me be Frank with you. Richard Ford. Ecco Press, 2014. 240 pages; (Frank Bascombe novels, 4)

ISBN 9780061692062

1. Hurricanes 2. Sixties (Age) 3. Mortality 4. Aging 5. Voyages and travels 6. New Jersey 7. Psychological fiction 8. Literary fiction 9. First person narratives

New York Times Notable Book, 2014; Pulitzer Prize for Fiction finalist, 2015

In the aftermath of Hurricane Sandy, Frank Bascombe travels to the site of his former home on the shore, visits his ex-wife, who is suffering with Parkinson's, and meets a dying former friend.

"In each neatly linked tale, Frank ruminates misanthropically, wittily, and wisely about love, family, friendship, race, politics, and the mystery of the self." —*Booklist*

A **multitude** of sins: stories. Richard Ford. Alfred A. Knopf : 2001. 286 p.

ISBN 9780375412127

1. Man-woman relationships 2. Intimacy (Psychology) 3. Interpersonal relations 4. Failure (Psychology) 5. Love 6. Blake, William 7. Grand Canyon 8. Psychological fiction 9. Short stories

LC 2001038402

New York Times Notable Book, 2002

A collection of short stories that explores the theme of love and intimacy looks inside the relationships between men and women—both in and out of marriage—and the sense of right and wrong.

"Tracing the blueprint of human interaction in this latest collection...Ford signals the master text of lust standing behind the multitude of small sins he so tersely and poignantly chronicles. To err is human, and, in Ford's worldview, little is so human as the act of cheating on a wife or husband." —*Publishers Weekly*

Originally published in Great Britain by The Harvill Press, London—Title page verso.

Sorry for your trouble: stories. Richard Ford. Ecco Press, 2020. 320 pages

ISBN 9780062969804

1. Loss (Psychology) 2. Identity (Psychology) 3. Interpersonal relations 4. Short stories 5. Literary fiction

A new short-story collection by the award-winning author of Independence Day includes the novella, "The Run of Yourself," in which a New Orleans lawyer tackles the challenges of living beyond his Irish wife's death.

"Powerfully unsettling stories in which men nearing the end of their lives wonder, befuddled, if that's all there is." —*Kirkus*

Forester, C. S.

Admiral Hornblower in the West Indies. C.S. Forester. Little, Brown, 1989. 329 p. (Horatio Hornblower saga, 10)

ISBN 9781405936958

1. Sailing ships 2. Ship captains 3. British in the West Indies 4. Hornblower, Horatio (Fictitious character) 5. Great Britain 6. Adventure stories 7. Sea stories 8. Historical fiction

LC 58007862

Horatio Hornblower faces a new Bonapartist uprising in the West Indies while trying to stamp out slave trade and piracy.

The **African** Queen. C.S. Forester. Little, Brown, 1984. 307 p.

ISBN 9780316289108

1. World War I 2. Women Christian missionaries 3. River boat pilots 4. British in Africa 5. Man-woman relationships 6. Africa 7. First World War era (1914-1918) 8. Adventure stories 9. Historical fiction 10. Books to movies

The African Queen tells the story of Rose Sayer, a respectable missionary who is in Africa with her brother the Reverend Samuel Sayer, and Charles Alnutt the hard-bitten and disreputable skipper of the African

Queen. Upon the death of her brother the pair become the unlikeliest of allies as marooned in German Central Africa during the First World War, they fight their ramshacle old launch, laden with explosives, downriver to strike a blow for England.

Originally published: 1935.

Beat to quarters. C.S. Forester. Little, Brown, 1985. 324 p. (Horatio Hornblower saga, 5)

ISBN 9780316289320

1. Sailing ships 2. Naval battles 3. Napoleonic Wars, 1800-1815 — Naval operations, British 4. Hornblower, Horatio (Fictitious character) 5. Great Britain 6. 19th century 7. Adventure stories 8. Sea stories 9. Historical fiction

LC 85-11609

Hornblower sails the South American waters and comes face to face with a mad revolutionary in a novel that ripples with risk and gripping adventure. Through his escapades Forester's hero remains resourceful and courageous.

"There is plenty of action. But there is also an unusual character study." —*New York Times Book Review*

Plot elements of Horatio Hornblower saga titles Beat to quarters, Ship of the line, and Flying colours were used in the 1951 movie "Captain Horatio Hornblower."

Originally published as The happy return: London : Michael Joseph, 1937.

Commodore Hornblower. C.S. Forester. Little, Brown, 1989. 320 pages (Horatio Hornblower saga, 8)

ISBN 9780316289382

1. Napoleonic Wars, 1800-1815 2. Military campaigns 3. Sailing ships 4. Ship captains 5. Naval battles 6. Spain 7. Great Britain 8. 19th century 9. Historical fiction 10. Adventure stories 11. Sea stories

Commodore Hornblower's new mission is a delicate one because he must maintain good diplomatic relations with Russia and Sweden at all costs and, at the same time, keep Napoleon's forces out of the Baltic.

"It is a spirited piece of work, and full of interesting detail where matters naval, military, and diplomatic in that year of decision are concerned."
—*Times Literary Supplement*

Originally published as The Commodore: London : Michael Joseph, 1945.

Flying colours. C.S. Forester. Little, Brown, 1986. 294 pages; (Horatio Hornblower saga, 7)

ISBN 9780316289399

1. Napoleonic Wars, 1800-1815 — Naval operations, British 2. Sailing ships 3. Naval battles 4. Prisoners of war, British 5. Hornblower, Horatio (Fictitious character) 6. Great Britain 7. 19th century 8. Adventure stories 9. Historical fiction 10. Sea stories

James Tait Black Memorial Prize for Fiction, 1938

Hornblower becomes a national hero when he escapes a French firing squad. But the Terror of the Mediterranean becomes Europe's most wanted man, forced to fight alone for England—and liberty.

Plot elements of Horatio Hornblower saga titles Beat to quarters, Ship of the line, and Flying colours were used in the 1951 movie "Captain Horatio Hornblower."

Originally published: London : Michael Joseph, 1938.

Hornblower and the Atropos. C.S. Forester. Little, Brown, 1985. 325 p. (Horatio Hornblower saga, 4)

ISBN 9780316289290

1. Salvage 2. Naval battles 3. Napoleonic Wars, 1800-1815 — Naval operations, British 4. Sailing ships 5. Ship captains 6. Great Britain 7. 19th century 8. Adventure stories 9. Sea stories 10. Historical fiction

Captain Horatio Hornblower takes his 22-gun sloop into the Mediterranean, where he and his crew search for sunken treasure, harass Napoleon's fleet, and face off against a Spanish frigate.

Originally published: London : Michael Joseph, 1953.

Hornblower and the Hotspur. C.S. Forester. Little, Brown, 1998. 344 p. (Horatio Hornblower saga, 3)

ISBN 9780316290463

1. Naval battles 2. Napoleonic Wars, 1800-1815 — Naval operations, British 3. Sailing ships 4. Ship captains 5. Hornblower, Horatio (Fictitious character) 6. Great Britain 7. 19th century 8. Adventure stories 9. Sea stories 10. Historical fiction

LC 62013907

In the midst of his wedding reception, Hornblower receives orders to report the next day to his command in the Channel Fleet and help protect England against Napoleon's threatened invasion.

Originally published: London : Michael Joseph, 1962.

Lieutenant Hornblower. C.S. Forester. Little, Brown, 1998. 306 p. (Horatio Hornblower saga, 2)

ISBN 9780316290630

1. Sailing ships 2. Napoleonic Wars, 1800-1815 — Naval operations, British 3. Naval battles 4. Resourcefulness in young men 5. Courage in young men 6. Great Britain 7. 19th century 8. Adventure stories 9. Sea stories 10. Historical fiction

LC 52005530

His cool judgement under fire shows that young Hornblower is maturing as he repeatedly defeats the Spanish warships.

"The author interprets the navy, certainly in its Napoleonic period, with the help of a character that represents the navy at its best and action that is grandly exciting without being melodramatic; helped, too, by a sense of order and a mastery of technique that puts his work on a high plane of artistry." —*Christian Science Monitor*

Originally published: London : Michael Joseph, 1952.

Lord Hornblower. C.S. Forester. Little, Brown, 1989. 322 p. (Horatio Hornblower saga, 9)

ISBN 9780316289436

1. Sailing ships 2. Napoleonic Wars, 1800-1815 — Naval operations, British 3. Naval battles 4. Ship captains 5. Hornblower, Horatio (Fictitious character) 6. Great Britain 7. Bordeaux (Nouvelle-Aquitaine, France) 8. 19th century 9. Adventure stories 10. Sea stories 11. Historical fiction

The Admiral's face was grim as he gave Commodore Hornblower his orders. The situation was critical: mutiny was an infection that could spread through the fleet like the plague and, furthermore, the crew were threatening to go over to the French.

Originally published: London : Michael Joseph, 1946.

Mr. Midshipman Hornblower. C.S. Forester. Little, Brown, 1984. 310 p. (Horatio Hornblower saga, 1)

ISBN 9780316289122

1. Sailing ships 2. Napoleonic Wars, 1800-1815 — Naval operations, British 3. Naval battles 4. Ship captains 5. Hornblower, Horatio (Fictitious character) 6. Great Britain 7. Adventure stories 8. Sea stories 9. Historical fiction

Horatio Hornblower rises to lieutenant after serving as a midshipman

Originally published: London : Michael Joseph, 1950.

Ship of the line. C.S. Forester. Little, Brown, 1985. 323 p. (Horatio Hornblower saga, 6)

ISBN 9780316289368

1. Napoleonic Wars, 1800-1815 — Naval operations, British 2. Sailing ships 3. Naval battles 4. Hornblower, Horatio (Fictitious character)

5. Great Britain 6. 19th century 7. Adventure stories 8. Sea stories 9. Historical fiction

LC 85-12856

James Tait Black Memorial Prize for Fiction, 1938

Her Majesty's ship *Sutherland* is a humdrum ship of the line. But in command none other than the heroic Captain Hornblower and, with his crew from the *Lydia*, looks set to take on commando raids, hurricanes at sea and Napoleons's gun batteries.

Plot elements of Horatio Hornblower saga titles Beat to quarters, Ship of the line, and Flying colours were used in the 1951 movie "Captain Horatio Hornblower."

Originally published: London : Michael Joseph, 1938.

Forman, Gayle

Leave me: a novel. Gayle Forman. Algonquin Books of Chapel Hill, 2016. 352 p.

ISBN 9781616206178

1. Working mothers 2. Self-fulfillment in women 3. Workaholics 4. Married women 5. People who have had heart attacks 6. Relationship fiction

LC 2016006430

LibraryReads Favorites, 2016

A harried working mom, who is so busy that she fails to recognize the signs of a heart attack, leaves the family that resents helping her recover and gradually confronts the painful secrets she has been ignoring.

"With humor and pathos, Forman depicts Maribeths complicated situation and her thoroughly satisfying arc, leaving readers feeling as though theyve really accompanied Maribeth on her journey." —*Publishers Weekly*

Forster, E. M.

★ **Howards** End. E.M. Forster; introduction and notes by David Lodge. Penguin Books, 2000. Xxx, 302 p.

ISBN 9780141182131

1. Rich people — Relations with poor people 2. Social classes 3. Family estates 4. Classism 5. Women 6. England 7. Literary fiction 8. Domestic fiction 9. Modern classics

Howards End, an English country house, passes to the moneyed, the cultured, and then to the lower class.

Originally published: London : Edward Arnold, 1910.

★ A **passage** to India. E.M. Forster. Harcourt Brace Jovanovich, 1984. 322 p.

ISBN 9780156711425

1. British in India 2. Imperialism, British 3. Trials (Rape) 4. Physicians 5. British Raj (1858-1947) 6. Psychological fiction 7. Literary fiction 8. Books to movies

LC 8422375

James Tait Black Memorial Prize for Fiction, 1924

Two women come to Chandrapore, India, and their lack of understanding of the culture causes one of them to make an unjust accusation.

Originally published: London : E. Arnold & Co, 1924.

★ A **room** with a view. E.M. Forster. Knopf, 1968. 318 p.

ISBN 9781444736281

1. British in Italy 2. Young women 3. Middle class 4. Upper class 5. Classism 6. England 7. Literary fiction 8. Modern classics 9. Love stories

Lucy Honeychurch falls in love while on a visit to Florence and must choose between fulfilling her social role or following her heart.

Originally published: 1908.

Forsyth, Frederick

The **fox**. Frederick Forsyth. G. P. Putnam's Sons, 2018. Xiii, 286 pages

ISBN 9780525538424

1. Hackers 2. International intrigue 3. Espionage 4. Political intrigue 5. Spies 6. Cyber-thrillers 7. Thrillers and suspense

When America's intelligence agencies are breached by a teen hacker, a British MI6 leader endeavors to use the boy's talents to safeguard both nations from unseen enemies.

The **kill** list. Frederick Forsyth. G. P. Putnam's Sons, 2013. 352 p.

ISBN 9780399165276

1. Undercover operations 2. Fathers — Death 3. Assassins 4. Government missions 5. Fundamentalism 6. Thrillers and suspense 7. Spy fiction

LC 2013015342

A counter-terrorist unit hunts down the Preacher, a terrorist who radicalizes young muslims into carrying out assassinations.

Fossey, Brooke

The **big** finish. Brooke Fossey. Berkley Pub Group, 2020. 336 p.

ISBN 9781984804938

1. Senior men 2. Grouches 3. Granddaughters 4. Partner abuse 5. Assisted living for seniors 6. Humorous stories 7. Relationship fiction

LC 2019031857

A curmudgeonly senior who would avoid a nursing home forges an unexpected bond with his estranged granddaughter, an abused child who is rapidly succumbing to the alcoholism that once painfully overshadowed his own life.

"Fossey manages to depict the struggles of the elderly, whose concerns aren't often examined in fiction, in a way that's both respectful and entertaining." —*Kirkus*

Foster, Alan Dean

Relic. Alan Dean Foster. Del Rey, 2018. 304 p.

ISBN 9781101967638

1. Humans 2. Quests 3. Aliens 4. Loneliness in men 5. Epidemics 6. Space 7. Science fiction

LC 2018009535

A lone surviving human of a destructive engineered virus is rendered a research subject by his alien rescuers, who outmaneuver his reluctance by offering to help him find the mythical planet Earth.

Foster, Brooke Lea

Summer darlings. Brooke Lea Foster. Gallery Books, 2020. 368 pages

ISBN 9781982115029

1. Nannies 2. Rich families 3. Women college students 4. Summer 5. Options, alternatives, choices 6. Martha's Vineyard, Massachusetts 7. Massachusetts 8. 1960s 9. Historical fiction

Set during the splendid summer days of 1960s Martha's Vineyard, a historical novel pulls back the curtain on a mysterious and wealthy family, as seen through the eyes of their nanny—a college student who, while falling in love on the elegant island, is also forced to reckon with the dark underbelly of privilege.

"Foster's musings on money and class, along with her believable depictions of over-the-top behavior, elevate this tale above typical summer fare." —*Publishers Weekly*

Foster, Fiona King

The **captive**: a novel. Fiona King Foster. Ecco Press, 2021. 256 p.
ISBN 9780062990976
1. Women bounty hunters 2. Escaped convicts 3. Hiding 4. Winter
5. Escapes 6. Noir fiction
LC 2020041843

A woman with elite skills from her violent past travels with her family and an escaped criminal through a harsh winter landscape to claim a bounty and safeguard her loved ones from murderous rivals.

"Exuding that irresistible blend of courage and vulnerability that defined Daniel Woodrell's Ree Dolly in Winter's Bone (2006), Brooke drives this propulsive wilderness adventure, made all the more chilling by its shockingly realistic vision of a country ravaged by culture wars." —*Booklist*

Foster, Lori

Sisters of summer's end. Lori Foster. Harlequin Books 2019. 304 p. (Love at the resort, 2)
ISBN 9781335007681
1. Single mothers 2. Businesspeople 3. Female friendship
4. Man-woman relationships 5. Family relationships 6. Contemporary romances

Abandoning her stressful life to take a job at a lakeside resort, a single mom reconsiders romance at the urging of a new friend, a dedicated businesswoman who also starts wondering what she might be missing.

Founds, Kathleen

When mystical creatures attack!. Kathleen Founds. University of Iowa Press, 2014. 206 p.
ISBN 9781609382834
1. High school teachers 2. Teacher-student relationships 3. Nervous breakdown 4. Women with mental illnesses 5. Texas 6. Short stories
7. Surrealist fiction
New York Times Notable Book, 2014

Set against a South Texas landscape where cicadas hum and the air smells of taco stands and jasmine flowers, these stories range from laugh-out-loud funny to achingly poignant. This surreal, exuberant collection mines the dark recesses of the soul while illuminating the human heart.

"Each story adds a layer of feeling, understanding and history to the characters as they slide back and forth through time and relationships. They handle, gracefully, the whiplash switch between depression and hilarity, between the ghost of a suicidal mother and a love-struck boy promising to invent a time machine. A surreal, dark and very funny collection that has the emotional punch of a novel." —*Kirkus*

Fountain, Ben

★ **Billy** Lynn's long halftime walk. Ben Fountain. Ecco Press, 2012. 307 p.
ISBN 9780060885595
1. Soldiers 2. Young men — Personal conduct 3. Iraq War, 2003-2011
4. Self-discovery in men 5. Patriotism 6. Dallas, Texas 7. Texas
8. Satirical fiction 9. Literary fiction 10. Books to movies 11. Adult books for young adults
ALA Notable Book, 2013; Booklist Editors' Choice, 2012; Library Journal Best Books, 2012; Los Angeles Times Book Prize for Fiction, 2012; National Book Critics Circle Award for Fiction, 2012; New York Times Notable Book, 2012; School Library Journal Best Books: Best Adult Books 4 Teens, 2012; National Book Award for Fiction finalist, 2012

Asked to be part of the Dallas Cowboys' halftime show on Thanksgiving, Specialist Billy Lynn, one of the eight surviving men of Bravo Squad, finds his life forever changed by this event that will help him understand difficult truths about himself.

Billy Lynn's Long Halftime Walk inspired the 2016 movie of the same name, directed by Ang Lee and starring Kristen Stewart, Garrett Hedlund, and Vin Diesel.

Fowler, Christopher

Bryant & May: hall of mirrors : a Peculiar Crimes Unit mystery. Christopher Fowler. Bantam, 2018. 432 p. (Bryant and May mysteries, 15)
ISBN 9781101887097
1. Eccentrics and eccentricities 2. Whistle blowers 3. Bodyguards
4. Detectives 5. Country homes 6. England 7. 1960s 8. Mysteries
LC 2018023627

An early Peculiar Crimes Unit case from 1969 London finds a younger Bryant and May struggling to protect a playboy star witness and solve a murder mystery at an old-fashioned manor house estate.

"The inspired idea of revisiting the youth of his aged sleuths in swinging England is matched by Fowler's customary gusto in sweating the details. More fully fleshed-out suspects, clues, red herrings, twists, and honest mystery and detection than in the last three whodunits you read." —*Kirkus*

Bryant & May: oranges and lemons. Christopher Fowler. Bantam, 2021. 464 p. (Bryant and May mysteries, 17)
ISBN 9780525485926
1. Criminal investigation 2. Occultism 3. Detectives 4. Politicians
5. Octogenarians 6. England 7. London, England 8. Mysteries
LC 2020012950

Investigating the bizarre death of a high-profile politician, senior detectives Arthur Bryant and John May overcome insurmountable odds to reunite the Peculiar Crimes Unit and stop a dangerous plot against London's churches.

"Fowler again tests his leads with a bizarre series of crimes while devising a satisfying resolution. This long-running series remains as vital as ever." —*Publishers Weekly*

Bryant & May: strange tide. Christopher Fowler. Random House, 2016. 448 p. (Bryant and May mysteries, 13)
ISBN 9781101887035
1. Detectives 2. Drowning victims 3. Police 4. Refugees 5. Occultism
6. London, England 7. Mysteries

When a woman is found drowned in the Thames after being roped to a pillar at low tide, the Peculiar Crimes Unit is baffled to discover only the victim's footprints leading to the spot where she was killed.

"Fowler once again perfectly balances farce and deduction." —*Publishers Weekly*

Bryant & May: the lonely hour. Christopher Fowler. Bantam, 2019. 448 pages (Bryant and May mysteries, 16)
ISBN 9780525485827
1. Detectives 2. Octogenarians 3. Serial murders 4. Serial murder investigation 5. Night 6. England 7. London, England 8. Mysteries
LC 2019034750

Tangled in a cat-and-mouse hunt with a killer who has been performing ritual murders at 4 A.M, Bryant and May explore technological and academic leads that are bizarrely connected by arson, kidnapping and blackmail.

"Perfect for fans of police procedurals with nontraditional, especially older, detectives." —*Library Journal*

Fowler, Karen Joy

The **Jane** Austen book club. Karen Joy Fowler. G. P. Putnam's Sons, 2004. 256 p.

ISBN 9780399151613

1. Austen, Jane 2. Book clubs 3. Friendship 4. Books and reading 5. Fiction — Appreciation 6. California 7. 21st century 8. Humorous stories 9. Relationship fiction 10. Multiple perspectives

LC 2003047244

New York Times Notable Book, 2004

Six Californians join to discuss Jane Austen's novels. Over the six months they meet, marriages are tested, affairs begin, unsuitable arrangements become suitable, and love happens.

"This novel is essentially a character study of six people who meet regularly over several months to discuss six of Austen's works. Jocelyn, in her 50s and never married, is the originator of the club, a control freak who handpicked all the members; Sylvia, her good friend, is in a funk because her husband of 32 years has just left her for another woman; Sylvia's daughter, Allegra, is an attractive 30-year-old lesbian who recently broke up with her lover; Prudie is a twentysomething high school French teacher; the much-married Bernadette, 67, is now single; and Grigg, in his 40s, would love to get married." —*Library Journal*

A Marian Wood book.

Originally published: 2004.

★ **We** are all completely beside ourselves. Karen Joy Fowler. Marian Wood, 2013. 320 p.

ISBN 9780399162091

1. Sisters 2. Bonding (Human/animal) 3. Humans and chimpanzees 4. Familial love 5. Animal rights 6. Literary fiction 7. First person narratives 8. Adult books for young adults

Library Journal Best Books, 2013; New York Times Notable Book, 2013; PEN-Faulkner Award, 2014; School Library Journal Best Books: Best Adult Books 4 Teens, 2013; Shortlisted for the Man Booker Prize, 2014

Coming of age in middle America, 18-year-old Rosemary evaluates how her entire youth was defined by the presence and forced removal of an endearing chimpanzee who was secretly regarded as a family member and who Rosemary loved as a sister.

"A fantastic novel: technically and intellectually complex, while emotionally gripping." —*Kirkus*

Fowler, Therese

★ A **good** neighborhood. Therese Anne Fowler. St. Martin's Press, 2020. 288 p.

ISBN 9781250237279

1. Racism 2. Suburbs 3. Teenage romance 4. Ecology 5. Multiracial boys 6. North Carolina 7. Relationship fiction 8. Neruda, Pablo 9. Multiple perspectives 10. Adult books for young adults

LC 2019035018

LibraryReads Favorites, 2020; Loan Stars Favourites, 2020

The single mother of a mixed-race college student and a thriving business owner with a troubled daughter clash over a historic oak tree on their property line and the blossoming romance between their children.

"This page-turner delivers a thoughtful exploration of prejudice, preconceived notions, and what it means to be innocent in the age of an opportunistic media." —*Publishers Weekly*

A **well-behaved** woman: a novel of the Vanderbilts. Therese Anne Fowler. St. Martin's Press, 2018. 352 p.

ISBN 9781250095473

1. Belmont, Alva 2. Rich women 3. Ambition in women 4. Women's role 5. Suffragist movement 6. Socialites 7. New York City 8. New York (State) 9. Gilded Age (1865-1898) 10. Historical fiction 11. Biographical fiction

LC 2018019687

RUSA Reading List Short List, 2019

Marrying into the newly rich but socially scorned Vanderbilt clan, a formerly impoverished Alva navigates society snubs and dark undercurrents in the lives of her in-laws and friends while testing the limits of her ambitious rule-breaking.

"Though the novels lavish sweep and gorgeous details evoke a vanished world, Fowler's exploration of the way powerful women are simultaneously devalued and rewarded resonates powerfully." —*Publishers Weekly*

★ **Z**: a novel of Zelda Fitzgerald. Therese Anne Fowler. St. Martin's Press, 2013. 352 p.

ISBN 9781250028655

1. Fitzgerald, Zelda 2. Alcoholism 3. Authors' spouses 4. Marital conflict 5. Socialites 6. Women with mental illnesses 7. United States 8. 1920s 9. Biographical fiction 10. Historical fiction

A tale inspired by the marriage of F. Scott and Zelda Fitzgerald follows their union in defiance of her father's opposition and her scandalous transformation into a Jazz Age celebrity in the literary party scenes of New York, Paris, and the French Riviera.

Fowles, John

★ The **French** lieutenant's woman. John Fowles. Back Bay Books, 1998. 467 p.

ISBN 9780316291163

1. Love triangles 2. Scientists 3. Women 4. Man-woman relationships 5. Interpersonal attraction 6. England 7. Great Britain 8. Victorian era (1837-1901) 9. 1860s 10. Historical fiction 11. Literary fiction 12. Love stories

Charles Smithson, a conventional young scientist, breaks his proper Victorian engagement upon becoming involved with the devastating Sarah Woodruff, whom the townspeople have linked with scandal and forbidden pleasures.

Originally published: Boston : Little, Brown, 1969.

The **magus**. John Fowles. Little Brown 1966. 582 p.

ISBN 9780316290975

1. Manipulation (Social sciences) 2. Hallucinations and illusions 3. Sexuality 4. Islands 5. Freedom 6. Greece 7. Islands of the Aegean 8. Psychological fiction 9. Literary fiction 10. Modern classics

LC 65021357

Nicholas Urfe, a young Englishman, accepts a teaching position on a remote Greek island, where an eccentric millionaire manipulates him with hallucinations, riddles, and psychological tests.

"With the narrative skill and literary sleight of hand...Fowles again provides hours of engrossing entertainment for an audience susceptible to a massive blend of sensuous realism, suspenseful romanticism, hypertheatrical mystification, psychic intervention, and a gallery of unusual or exotic characters in the vivid setting of the golden, craggy, threatening beauty of an isolated Greek island." —*Booklist*

Fox, Candice

Crimson Lake. Candice Fox. Forge, 2018. 304 p. (Crimson Lake, 1)

ISBN 9780765398482

1. Former police 2. Private investigators 3. Missing persons investigation 4. Missing persons 5. Innocence (Law) 6. Australia 7. Thrillers and suspense 8. Australian fiction

RUSA Reading List Short List, 2019

A Sullivan's Island beekeeper navigates her demanding hypochondriac mother and flamboyant rival sister while immersing herself in the lives of two young neighbor boys and their widowed father.

Frankel, Laurie

Goodbye for now: a novel. Laurie Frankel. Doubleday, 2012. 288 p.
ISBN 9780385536189
1. Computer programmers 2. Loss (Psychology) 3. Online dating 4. Social networks 5. Soul mates 6. Satirical fiction 7. Mainstream fiction
LC 2011051266
Creating an algorithm to improve his Internet dating employer's match success rate only to be fired for being too effective, Sam Elliot, who used his innovation to meet the love of his life, develops a computer program that creates compelling human simulations that allow people to say final goodbyes to lost loved ones.
First published in Great Britain in 2012.

One two three: a novel. Laurie Frankel. Henry Holt and Company, 2021. 400 p.
ISBN 9781250236777
1. Triplets 2. Teenagers with disabilities 3. High schools 4. Enemies 5. Chemical spills 6. Coming-of-age stories 7. Multiple perspectives
LC 2020013981
The Mitchell sisters—teenage triplets—find everything changing in their town when a handsome new student enrolls at Bourne Memorial High who happens to be their family's sworn enemy..
"Frankel has given us another socially conscious 21st-century fable in a voice that is part pastor, part political speechwriter, and part Fannie Flagg." —*Kirkus*

This is how it always is. Laurie Frankel. Flatiron Books, 2017. 327 p.
ISBN 9781250088550
1. Transgender children 2. Family secrets 3. Identity (Psychology) 4. Social acceptance 5. Families 6. Domestic fiction 7. Adult books for young adults
LC 2016037633
A family reshapes their ideas about family, love and loyalty when youngest son Claude reveals increasingly determined preferences for girls' clothing and accessories and refuses to stay silent.
"This is a wonderfully contradictory storyheartwarming and generous, yet written with a wry sensibility." —*Publishers Weekly*

Franklin, Ariana

★ **Death** and the maiden. . William Morrow & Co, 2020. 416 pages (Adelia Aguilar series, 5)
ISBN 9780062562388
1. Henry 2. Women healers 3. Daughters 4. Courtship 5. Voyages and travels 6. Missing girls 7. England 8. Medieval period (476-1492) 9. Plantagenet period (1154-1485) 10. Historical mysteries 11. Medieval mysteries
A long-anticipated series conclusion finds a young healer dispatched to the Cambridgeshire village of Ely, where her courtship with a young aristocrat is complicated by her investigation into the disappearances of several local girls.
"This is a fascinating, page-turning historical mystery, with dashes of twelfth-century politics and religion, intriguing period ambience, charismatic characters, and a completely unexpected ending." —*Booklist*

Mistress of the art of death. Ariana Franklin. G. P. Putnam's Sons, 2007. 384 p. : Map (Adelia Aguilar series, 1)
ISBN 9780399154140
1. Henry 2. Women physicians 3. Child murder victims 4. Blame 5. Serial murder investigation 6. Rulers 7. Cambridge, England 8. England 9. Medieval period (476-1492) 10. Plantagenet period (1154-1485) 11. Historical mysteries 12. Mysteries
LC 2006024710
Ellis Peters Historical Dagger Award, 2007; RUSA Reading List, 2008; Sue Feder Historical Mystery Award, 2008
Sent to medieval Cambridge in order to exonerate Jewish prisoners with financial ties to King Henry II, University of Salerno medical examiner Adelia struggles to avoid being accused of witchcraft and discovers that the killer may be a former crusader.
"This novel will surely please mystery fans as well as lovers of historical fiction." —*Library Journal*

The **serpent's** tale. Ariana Franklin. G. P. Putnam's Sons, 2008. 371 p; (Adelia Aguilar series, 2)
ISBN 9780399154645
1. Henry 2. Women physicians 3. Murder 4. Mistresses 5. Man-woman relationships 6. Interpersonal relations 7. Great Britain 8. Medieval period (476-1492) 9. Plantagenet period (1154-1485) 10. Historical mysteries 11. Mysteries 12. Adult books for young adults
LC 2007038585
Ordered by Henry II to establish the possible role of Eleanor of Aquitaine in the poisoning death of Henry's mistress, a reluctant Adelia Aguilar joins forces with her infant daughter's father, the Bishop of St. Albans, during the investigation.
"This excellent adventure delivers high drama and lively scholarship from its heroine's feminist perspective." —*New York Times Book Review*
Also published as: "The Death Maze."

The **siege** winter. . William Morrow & Co, 2015. 352 p.
ISBN 9780062282569
1. Matilda 2. Apprentices 3. War and society 4. Political intrigue 5. Rulers 6. Kidnapping victims 7. Great Britain 8. Medieval period (476-1492) 9. Norman period (1066-1154) 10. Historical fiction 11. Adult books for young adults
LibraryReads Favorites, 2015
A traumatized apprentice archer, disguised as a boy, and the young chatelaine of a strategically important fortress risk their lives to support the Empress Matilda's campaign for the throne of mid-12th-century England.
"The cheeky wit and precise descriptions that were Franklins hallmarks are as sharp as ever, and the major characters are delightfully human. The book also has a genuine feel for medieval life and times. This unique collaboration is a worthy conclusion to one remarkable career and a promising beginning to another." —*Booklist*

Franklin, Miles

My brilliant career. Miles Franklin. St. Martin's Press, 1980. 232 p.
ISBN 9780312555993
1. Franklin, Miles 2. Teenage nonconformists 3. Independence in teenage girls 4. Women marriage resisters 5. Teenagers — Career aspirations 6. Teenage girls 7. Australia 8. 19th century 9. Autobiographical fiction 10. Australian fiction 11. Books to movies
LC 80052658
This captivating Australian novel transcends time and genre in the classic tale of an extraordinarily ambitious young woman who passionately evades marriage to pursue her envisioned brilliant career
Sequel: My career goes bung.
Originally published: Edinburgh : William Blackwood & Sons, 1901.

Franklin, Tom

Crooked letter, crooked letter: a novel. Tom Franklin. William Morrow, 2010. 288 p.

ISBN 9780060594664

1. Male friendship 2. Small town life 3. Missing girls 4. Reconciliation in men 5. Childhood friends 6. Mississippi 7. Psychological suspense 8. Southern Gothic 9. Southern fiction

LC 2010005423

ALA Notable Book, 2011; Gold Dagger Award for Best Crime Novel of the Year, 2011; Los Angeles Times Book Prize for Mystery or Thriller, 2010; Romantic Times Reviewers' Choice Award, 2010

African-American Constable Silas Jones must confront his white former friend Larry Ott, who has lived under suspicion for twenty years since a girl disappeared while on a date with him, after another girl disappears and Larry is blamed once again.

"Franklin writes with quiet economy. There are no great flights of dialogue or rambling description; everything is sharply focused to achieve its purpose. The resulting novel winds through its path as crookedly as the letters of its title, and arrives at a nicely achieved ending. It's an ending that isn't without complication but, given what precedes it, a conclusion that is fitting and right." —*Denver Post*

Frantz, Laura

The **lacemaker**. Laura Frantz. Revell, 2018. 416 p.

ISBN 9780800726638

1. Revolutionaries 2. Jilted women 3. Protectiveness in men 4. Malicious accusation 5. Loyalty 6. Williamsburg, Virginia 7. United States 8. Revolutionary America (1775-1783) 9. Christian historical romances 10. Historical romances

LC 2017031367

Christy Award for Historical Romance Category, 2018

On the eve of her wedding, Lady Elisabeth Lawson's world is shattered, as surely as the fine glass windows of her colonial Williamsburg home. In a town seething with Patriots ready for rebellion, her protection comes from an unlikely source—now if she could only protect her heart.

Franzen, Jonathan

★ The **corrections**. Jonathan Franzen. Farrar, Straus and Giroux, 2001. 576 p.

ISBN 9780374129989

1. People with Parkinson's disease 2. Parent and adult child 3. Dysfunctional families 4. Family relationships 5. Married women 6. Middle West 7. Philadelphia, Pennsylvania 8. Literary fiction 9. Psychological fiction

LC 2001033478

ALA Notable Book, 2002; Booklist Editors' Choice, 2001; James Tait Black Memorial Prize for Fiction, 2002; Library Journal Best Books, 2001; National Book Award for Fiction, 2001; National Book Critics Circle Award for Fiction finalist, 2001; Pulitzer Prize for Fiction finalist, 2002; Shortlisted for the International IMPAC Dublin Literary Award, 2003

Enid Lambert begins to worry about her husband when he begins to withdraw and lose himself in negativity and depression as he faces Parkinson's disease.

"The novel has the absorbing treacheries of married life, the comic squalors of cruise-shop travel and the shenanigans of global capitalism. It also has language that builds in powerful, rolling strides. And it has characters, the separately unraveling Lamberts, who get very deeply under your skin." —*Time*

★ **Crossroads**. Jonathan Franzen. Farrar, Straus and Giroux, 2021. 592 p. (Key to all mythologies, 1)

ISBN 9780374181178

1. Families 2. Clergy 3. Secrets 4. Marital conflict 5. Drug traffic 6. Chicago, Illinois 7. 1970s 8. Literary fiction 9. Bruno, Giordano 10. Historical fiction

LC 2021019919

Crossroads is the first novel in Jonathan Franzen's A Key to All Mythologies. The trilogy tells the story of a Midwestern family across three generations, mirroring the preoccupations and dilemmas of the United States from the Vietnam War to the 2020s.

"Franzen (Purity) returns with a sweeping and masterly examination of the shifting culture of early 1970s America, the first in a trilogy." —*Publishers Weekly*

★ **Freedom**. Jonathan Franzen. Farrar, Straus and Giroux, 2010. 576 p.

ISBN 9780374158460

1. Husband and wife 2. Love triangles 3. Dysfunctional families 4. Family relationships 5. Neighbors 6. St. Paul, Minnesota 7. Literary fiction

LC 2010010273

ALA Notable Book, 2011; Booklist Editors' Choice, 2010; Library Journal Best Books, 2010; New York Times Notable Book, 2010; National Book Critics Circle Award for Fiction finalist, 2010

The idyllic lives of civic-minded environmentalists Patty and Walter Berglund come into question when their son moves in with aggressive Republican neighbors, green lawyer Walter takes a job in the coal industry, and go-getter Patty becomes increasingly unstable and enraged.

"Franzen performs a kind of literary MRI on the marriage, micro-slicing its many nuances. He innately grasps how desires can shift in an instant, and how getting what we want can lead to disappointment or self-doubt. And he remains a keen observer of modern culture.... Freedom isn't flawless: Patty's journal reads more like Franzen than his character, and he gets sidetracked by quirky tangents. But this is a deep dive into a fascinating family that feels very real, and fully grounded in our time." —*Entertainment Weekly*

Purity. Jonathan Franzen. Farrar, Straus and Giroux, 2015. 563 pages

ISBN 9780374239213

1. Identity (Psychology) 2. Internet 3. Whistle blowing 4. Young women 5. Interpersonal relations 6. Literary fiction 7. Psychological fiction 8. Adult books for young adults

Booklist Editors' Choice, 2015; New York Times Notable Book, 2015; School Library Journal Best Books: Best Adult Books 4 Teens, 2015

Struggling with identity issues and student loans as the daughter of a mother who hides a mysterious past, Pip takes an internship with an illicit activist group and falls for its charismatic fugitive leader.

"...Franzen is burrowing deep into each person's questionable sense of his or her own goodness and suggests that the moral rot can metastasize to the levels of corporations and government. And yet the novel's prose never bogs down into lectures, and its various back stories are as forceful as the main tale of Purity's fate. Franzen is much-mocked for his primacy in the literary landscape (something he himself mocks when Charles grouses about a plague of literary Jonathans). But here, he's admirably determined to think big and write well about our darkest emotional corners. An expansive, brainy, yet inviting novel that leaves few foibles unexplored." —*Kirkus*

Frayn, Michael

Spies: a novel. Michael Frayn. Metropolitan Books, 2002. 261 p.

ISBN 9780805070583

1. Boys — Friendship 2. Friendship 3. World War II — Children 4. Secrets 5. Women spies 6. London, England 7. Thrillers and suspense 8. Adult books for young adults

LC 2001039840

Commonwealth Writers' Prize, South Asia and Europe: Best Book, 2003; New York Times Notable Book, 2002; Whitbread Book Award for Novel, 2002

When a long-forgotten scent forces Stephen Wheatley to confront his past, he starts to remember a troubling childhood summer in wartime London where an imaginative child's game of playing spies wreaked havoc upon innocent lives.

"A compelling story about secrecy and betrayal.... What is truly remarkable about this novel, though, is the way Frayn perfectly captures the dynamics of childhood friendships." —*Booklist*

Frazier, Charles

★ **Cold** Mountain. Charles Frazier. Atlantic Monthly Press, 1997. 356 p.

ISBN 9780871136794

1. Confederate soldiers 2. Deserters 3. Farm life 4. Lovers' reunions 5. Soldiers 6. North Carolina 7. American Civil War era (1861-1865) 8. 1860s 9. Historical fiction 10. Literary fiction 11. Multiple perspectives 12. Adult books for young adults

LC 97275

ALA Notable Book, 1998; Booklist Editors' Choice, 1997; Book Sense Book of the Year Adult Trade, 1998; National Book Award for Fiction, 1997; New York Times Notable Book, 1997; Sir Walter Raleigh Award for Fiction, 1997; School Library Journal Best Books: Best Adult Books 4 Teens, 1997; National Book Critics Circle Award for Fiction finalist, 1997

After Inman escapes from a war hospital in 1864 and starts walking to Cold Mountain, Ada struggles to save her mountain farm with the help of Ruby, an illiterate but efficient farmer.

"This novel's landscape is finely drawn, full of dark beauty and presentiment, and so are its characters. They give voice to a classical, peculiarly American feeling of nostalgia—the pain of returning home." —*The New Yorker*

Illustrated with endpaper map.

Nightwoods: a novel. Charles Frazier. Random House, 2011. 272 p.
ISBN 9781400067091

1. Children who are mute 2. Aunts 3. Orphans 4. Rural women 5. Solitude 6. North Carolina 7. Appalachian Region 8. 1960s 9. Rural noir 10. Literary fiction 11. Southern fiction

LC 2011014629

Sir Walter Raleigh Award for Fiction, 2012

Named the guardian of her murdered sister's troubled twins, Luce struggles to build a family with the children before being targeted by the twins' father—her sister's killer—who believes that the children are in possession of a stolen cache of money.

"Not surprisingly, things get messy, but Nightwoods is no typical thriller. It hits hard because you come to care so much about the characters, all of them drawn with that precise enchanted prose. By the book's climactic scenes in the shadowy mountain forest that gives Nightwoods its title, the unhurried, poetic suspense is both difficult to bear and impossible to shake." —*Entertainment Weekly*

Thirteen moons: a novel. Charles Frazier. Random House, 2006. 422 p.
ISBN 9780375509322

1. Interracial romance 2. Indians of North America 3. Cherokee Indians 4. Courage in men 5. Loss (Psychology) 6. 19th century 7. Coming-of-age stories 8. Historical fiction 9. Southern fiction

From the age of twelve, when he is sent alone into the wilderness to run an Indian trading post, Will's life becomes intertwined with the destiny of the Cherokee Indians, as he falls in love with a girl named Claire, and builds a friendship with a chief named Bear.

"The author uses his sense of time and place and his lyrical, pointillist prose to give the reader an aching appreciation of the Indians' plight.... [He] recounts Will's melancholy adventures with plenty of narrative brio, giving the reader a succession of suspensefuland in some cases touchingset pieces." —*New York Times*

Varina. Charles Frazier. Ecco, 2018. 288 p.
ISBN 9780062405982

1. Davis, Varina 2. Civil War 3. Married women 4. Politicians' spouses 5. War 6. Social conflict 7. United States 8. Confederate States of America 9. American Civil War era (1861-1865) 10. Biographical fiction 11. Historical fiction

LC Bl2018002826

Forced by limited prospects to marry much-older widower Jefferson Davis, teenaged Varina Howell finds her expectations as the wife of a Mississippi landowner upended by his appointment as the leader of the Confederacy, a situation that renders her and her children fugitives in a divided and increasingly hostile nation.

Frazier, Jean Kyoung

Pizza girl. Jean Kyoung Frazier. Doubleday, 2020. 198 p.
ISBN 9780385545723

1. Pregnant teenagers 2. Delivery drivers 3. Dysfunctional families 4. Fathers — Death 5. Boyfriends 6. Los Angeles, California 7. Literary fiction 8. First person narratives

Eighteen years old, pregnant, and working as a pizza delivery girl in suburban Los Angeles, our charmingly dysfunctional heroine is deeply lost and in complete denial about it all. She's grieving the death of her father (whom she has more in common with than she'd like to admit), avoiding her supportive mom and loving boyfriend, and flagrantly ignoring her future. Her world is further upended when she becomes obsessed with Jenny, a stay-at-home mother new to the neighborhood, who comes to depend on weekly deliveries of pizzas for her son's happiness. As one woman looks toward motherhood and the other toward middle age, the relationship between the two begins to blur in strange, complicated, and ultimately heartbreaking ways.

"This infectious evocation of a young woman's slackerdom will appeal to fans of Halle Butler and Ottessa Moshfegh, and will make it difficult not to root for the troubled and spirited pizza girl." —*Publishers Weekly*

Frear, Caz

Stone cold heart. Caz Frear. HarperCollins, 2019. 368 pages (Cat Kinsella, 2)
ISBN 9780062849885

1. Women detectives 2. Women murder victims 3. Murder investigation 4. Marital conflict 5. Dishonesty 6. London, England 7. England 8. Police procedurals 9. Thrillers and suspense

When a coffee-shop owner is implicated in the death of a young Australian woman, DC Cat Kinsella of the London Metropolitan Police investigates the chief suspect's hostile wife to discern which of them is telling the truth.

Sweet little lies. Caz Frear. Harper, 2018. 480 pages (Cat Kinsella, 1)
ISBN 9780062823199

1. Fathers and daughters 2. Women detectives 3. Missing persons 4. Murder investigation 5. Trust 6. London, England 7. England 8. 1990s 9. Police procedurals 10. Thrillers and suspense

A London policewoman from a troubled family is forced to investigate dark secrets in her estranged father's past to solve the murder of a young housewife and the disappearance of a teen girl years earlier.
Originally published: London : Zaffre, 2017.

Fredericks, Mariah

Death of a new American: a mystery. Mariah Fredericks. Minotaur Books, 2019. 304 p. (Jane Prescott novels, 2)
ISBN 9781250152992
1. Upper class 2. Household employees 3. Women amateur detectives 4. Weddings 5. Mafia 6. Long Island, New York 7. 1910s 8. Historical mysteries
LC 2018049423
A follow-up to A Death of No Importance finds ladies' maid Jane Prescott accompanying her employers to a family wedding in Long Island that is threatened by a nanny's murder, mafia threats against their host and dark secrets.
"Fredericks has a sharp eye for the complexities of human nature and how even good people are capable of committing terrible deeds to protect the ones they love. This is a touching portrait of early-20th-century New York in all its glory and ugliness." —*Publishers Weekly*

Death of a showman. Mariah Fredericks. Minotaur Books, 2021. 288 p. (Jane Prescott novels, 4)
ISBN 9781250210906
1. Former lovers 2. Household employees 3. Investigative journalists 4. Theatrical producers and directors 5. Murder investigation 6. New York City 7. Historical mysteries
LC 2020047623
Forced to spend time with an ex whose new Broadway production is being financed by her employer, lady's maid Jane Prescott teams up with tabloid reporter Michael Behan to uncover the truth about a producer's suspicious demise.
"With a spirited, intelligent heroine; pitch-perfect descriptions of pre-World War I New York; and believable characters, Fredericks's latest historical mystery is a delight." —*Library Journal*

Freedman, Benedict

Mrs. Mike: the story of Katherine Mary Flannigan. Benedict and Nancy Freedman. Berkley Books, 2002. 313 p. (Mrs. Mike series, 1)
ISBN 9780425183236
1. Flannigan, Katherine Mary 2. Frontier and pioneer life 3. Irish American women 4. Police 5. Man-woman relationships 6. Canada 7. Historical fiction 8. Biographical fiction
Mrs. Mike is the love story of Katherine Mary O'Fallon, a young Irish girl from Boston, and Sergeant Mike Flannigan of the Canadian Mounted Police, who is a priest, doctor and magistrate to all in the great Canadian wilderness area under his supervision.
Sequel: The search for joyful.
Originally published: New York : Coward-McCann, 1947.

Freeman, Anna

The **fair** fight: a novel. Anna Freeman. Riverhead Books, 2015. 480 p.
ISBN 9781594633294
1. Boxing 2. Social classes 3. Poor women 4. Women boxers 5. Gambling 6. England 7. Bristol, England 8. Georgian era (1714-1837) 9. Historical fiction 10. Multiple perspectives 11. First person narratives
LC 2014019046
Library Journal Best Books, 2015

Born in a Bristol whorehouse, scrappy Ruth stumbles into a career as a pugilist after a brawl with her half-sister attracts a betting audience. As Ruth enters the gritty, brutal world of professional prize-fighters, she encounters aspiring boxer Charlotte Sinclair, for whom the ring serves as an escape from her abusive marriage and a place where her smallpox scars do not attract notice; and gambler George Bowden, who hopes that backing the right fighter will make him a wealthy man. Bouncing between brothel and boxing ring, this debut skillfully depicts the seamy underbelly of Georgian England.
"Freeman doesnt shy away from the grim realities of sexism, homophobia, and illness that afflict the lives of her characters, and readers will appreciate her blunt look at the English caste system. Freeman is at her best in moments when the characters transcend their societal roles and break free of expectations." —*Booklist*
Originally published: London: Weidenfeld & Nicolson, 2014.

Freeman, Brian

Goodbye to the dead. Brian Freeman. Quercus, 2016. 448 pages (Jonathan Stride novels, 7)
ISBN 9781623659110
1. Widowers 2. Murder witnesses 3. Innocence (Law) 4. Women murder suspects 5. Human trafficking 6. Minnesota 7. Duluth, Minnesota 8. Thrillers and suspense
When fellow detective Serena witnesses a brutal murder with ties to a case from the last year of his wife's life, detective Stride investigates human-trafficking activity in the Duluth port and struggles with the possibility that he may have sent an innocent woman to prison.
"Freeman skillfully weaves together diverse story lines, from the old murder to a sex-slavery operation, with twists that build suspense, in this fine, character-driven addition to a strong series." —*Booklist*
First published in Great Britain in 2015 by Quercus.

Marathon. Brian Freeman. Quercus, 2017. 408 p. (Jonathan Stride novels, 8)
ISBN 9781681442419
1. Bombings 2. Terrorism 3. Criminal investigation 4. Marathons 5. Fugitives 6. Minnesota 7. Duluth, Minnesota 8. Thrillers and suspense
When a bombing at the Duluth Marathon kills and injures numerous victims, detective Jonathan Stride teams up with Serena Dial, Maggie Bei and their FBI contacts to track down a suspicious man with a backpack in the wake of media misinformation. By the award-winning author of Immoral.

The **night** bird. Brian Freeman. Thomas & Mercer, 2017. 350 pages (Frost Easton novels, 1)
ISBN 9781503943568
1. Memory 2. Psychoses 3. Serial murders 4. Serial murder investigation 5. Mental illness — Treatment 6. San Francisco, California 7. Thrillers and suspense 8. Adult books for young adults
Homicide detective Frost Easton doesn't like coincidences, so when a series of bizarre deaths rock San Francisco—during which seemingly random women suffer violent psychotic breaks—Frost looks for a connection that leads him to controversial psychiatrist Francesca Stein.
"In his latest stand-alone thriller, Freeman (Goodbye to the Dead, 2016) once again shows a slick knack for creating enough tension without relying too heavily on gore—just the right amount of nastiness that will not scare away more-genteel thriller readers." —*Booklist*

Thief River Falls. Brian Freeman. Thomas and Mercer, 2020. 314 p.
ISBN 9781542093361
1. Women authors 2. Child witnesses 3. Runaways 4. Protectiveness in women 5. Runaway boys 6. Minnesota 7. Psychological suspense

A best-selling writer living in seclusion after losing her family to a series of tragedies risks her life to protect a child who is being targeted by both killers and police who would cover up the murder he witnessed.

"Readers will admire the skillful way Freeman plays tricks with thriller conventions." —*Publishers Weekly*

Freeman, Castle

All that I have: a novel. Castle Freeman Jr. Steerforth Press, 2009. 176 p.
ISBN 9781586421519
1. Small-town life 2. Sheriffs 3. Middle-aged men 4. Criminals 5. Personal conduct 6. Vermont 7. Psychological fiction

LC 2008043223

Sheriff Lucian Wing deals with unexpected crises in his quiet Vermont jurisdiction, including the theft of a safe from Russian mobsters by a local bad boy, a deputy who wants Lucian's job, and marital problems.

"Sheriff Lucian Wing, the narrator of Freeman's wonderfully wry fourth novel, is a laconic, old-fashioned lawman who discovers an outpost of nefarious Russians in his sleepy Vermont county. Wing's Fargo-esque delivery is hysterical, but what makes this spare tale a standout is Freeman's keen ear for dialogue and his affection for the quietly complex characters of small-town life." —*People*

Freeman, Dianne

A **fiancee's** guide to first wives and murder. Dianne Freeman. Kensington Pub Corp, 2021. 304 p. (Countess of Harleigh mysteries, 4)
ISBN 9781496731609
1. Counts and countesses 2. Women amateur detectives 3. Americans in Great Britain 4. Engaged persons 5. Scandals 6. London, England 7. Great Britain 8. Victorian era (1837-1901) 9. 1890s 10. Victorian mysteries 11. Historical mysteries

In a mystery series set in Victorian England, the American-born Countess of Harleigh uncovers more deadly intrigue among the uppercrust.

"Freeman delivers it all: clever plotting, charming characters, plausible suspects, and red herrings galore. This historical is pure unadulterated fun." —*Publishers Weekly*

A **lady's** guide to etiquette and murder. Dianne Freeman. Kensington Pub Corp 2018. 304 p. (Countess of Harleigh mysteries, 1)
ISBN 9781496716873
1. Counts and countesses 2. Independence in women 3. Women amateur detectives 4. Americans in Great Britain 5. Murder investigation 6. London, England 7. Victorian era (1837-1901) 8. Victorian mysteries 9. Historical mysteries
Agatha Award for Best First Novel, 2018

A wealthy young widow encounters the pleasures—and scandalous pitfalls—of a London social season.

Freitas, Donna

The **nine** lives of Rose Napolitano. Donna Freitas. Pamela Dorman Books, 2021. 384 p.
ISBN 9781984880598
1. Motherhood 2. Marital conflict 3. Decision-making 4. Consequences 5. Identity (Psychology) 6. Kepler, Johannes 7. Relationship fiction

A woman who never wanted to be a mother reconnects with her estranged husband in the wake of unexpected news and is challenged to reevaluate herself in an unanticipated role.

"Freitas's prose is engaging and precise, and her what-if format proves ideal for elegantly unpacking the tensions of the plot. She balances tightly written scenes of confrontation with Rose's poignant reflections on how much she can compromise without losing herself completely. This isn't one to miss." —*Publishers Weekly*

French, Albert

Billy. Albert French. Viking, 1993. 214 p.
ISBN 9780670850136
1. Racism 2. African American boys 3. Ten-year-old boys 4. Murder 5. Mothers and sons 6. Mississippi 7. 1930s 8. Historical fiction 9. African American fiction

LC 93014676

An anonymous observer narrates the tale of spirited ten-year-old Billy Lee, a Black boy who is convicted and executed for the murder of a white girl in Banes, Mississippi, in the 1930s.

French, Jonathan

The **free** bastards. Jonathan French. Del Rey, 2021. 464 p. (Lot lands, 3)
ISBN 9780593156681
1. Alliances 2. Enemies 3. Imaginary wars and battles 4. Half-human hybrids 5. Orcs 6. Sword and sorcery 7. Epic fantasy

LC 2021013692

As war comes to the Lot Lands, Oats, once the strongest Bastard, finds his faith wavering after a grievous loss, which leads him on a perilous journey to Hispartha where he must bet the Lots' fate—and his own—on the promises of the Bastards' wiliest adversary.

"One of the most original fantasy sagas to come along in years; like Tolkien on a bender." —*Kirkus*

★ The **Grey** Bastards. Jonathan French. Crown Publishing, 2018. 424 p. (Lot Lands, 1)
ISBN 9780525572442
1. Half-human hybrids 2. Quests 3. Orcs 4. Goblins 5. Secrets 6. Sword and sorcery 7. Apocalyptic fiction 8. Horror
Library Journal Best Books, 2018

Jackal, a proud member of a group of half-orcs tasked with protecting human civilization from their full-blooded brethren, discovers a dark secret that threatens to dissolve the tenuous peace between species.

The **true** Bastards. Jonathan French. Crown Publishers, 2019. 583 pages; (Lot lands, 2)
ISBN 9780525572473
1. Half-human hybrids 2. Women warriors 3. Alliances 4. Orcs 5. Wanderers and wandering 6. Sword and sorcery 7. Apocalyptic fiction

Fetching—the female leader of her own hoof, a loyal group of orcs sworn to her—fights off famine, desertions, other orcs and humans who are plotting against her.

"The many cultures are richly detailed, adding depth. This installment will more than satisfy fantasy readers who like deadly battles balanced with intricate worldbuilding and skilled characterization." —*Publishers Weekly*
Sequel to: The Grey Bastards.

French, Marilyn

★ The **women's** room. Marilyn French. Summit Books, 1977. 471 p.
ISBN 9780671400101
1. Women graduate students 2. Sexism 3. Self-awareness in women 4. Middle-aged women 5. Feminists 6. 1970s 7. Literary fiction

LC 77024918

A portrait of Mira Ward, erstwhile suburban doctor's wife and mother of two and latter-day Harvard graduate student, depicts a 1950s world of men and women in bondage to one another and the 1970s world of liberation and radical reassessment.

"[The author's] dialogue, her characterizations, her knowledge of the changing relationships, sexual and otherwise, between men and women in a complex world of shifting values, are all extraordinary." —*Publishers Weekly*

French, Nicci

★ **Blue** Monday. Nicci French. Pamela Dorman Books/Viking 2012. 400 pages (Frieda Klein novels, 1)
ISBN 9780670023363
1. Missing children 2. Psychotherapists 3. Psychotherapist and patient 4. Captives 5. Missing persons investigation 6. London, England 7. Psychological suspense

Frieda Klein is a brilliant psychotherapist who finds herself hunting down a kidnapper. When five-year-old Matthew Farraday goes missing, all of London is in an uproar—including Frieda, who recalls a patient haunted by dreams of snatching a child matching Matthew's description. To find the child before it's too late, Frieda must journey to a very dangerous place—the mind of a psychopath.

"With its smart plot, crisp prose, and a stunning final twist, this is psychological suspense at its best. Absolutely riveting." —*Booklist*

Originally published in UK in 2011 (London: Michael Joseph)

Dark Saturday. Nicci French. William Morrow & Co, 2017. 390 pages (Frieda Klein novels, 6)
ISBN 9780062676665
1. Murder suspects 2. Women psychotherapists 3. Cold cases (Criminal investigation) 4. Murder investigation 5. Murderers 6. Great Britain 7. Psychological suspense

Reluctantly agreeing to assess a woman who was incarcerated in a secure psychiatric hospital a decade earlier for murder, psychotherapist Frieda Klein begins to suspect that the girl is innocent, only to find herself targeted by someone who would keep the truth hidden.

★ The **day** of the dead: a novel. Nicci French. William Morrow, 2018. 304 p. (Frieda Klein novels, 8)
ISBN 9780062846082
1. Murder suspects 2. Women psychotherapists 3. Satie, Erik 4. Stalking 5. Murder investigation 6. Great Britain 7. Psychological suspense
LC 2017061678

Finds psychologist Frieda Klein driven into hiding by obsessed psychopath Dean Reeve, while criminology student Lola Hayes places herself at risk to follow in Frieda's footsteps.

Series complete in 8 volumes.

Friday on my mind: a Frieda Klein mystery. Nicci French. Penguin Books, 2016. 352 pages (Frieda Klein novels, 5)
ISBN 9780143127222
1. Women psychotherapists 2. Murder suspects 3. Fugitives 4. Suspicion 5. Former boyfriends 6. Suffolk, England 7. Psychological suspense
LC 2016013489

When the body of her ex-boyfriend turns up in the Thames, London psychotherapist Frieda Klein becomes the prime suspect in the murder investigation and goes on the run to save herself and find the real killer, who she believes is a man who has never stopped haunting her, but who the police think has been dead for years.

"This series' mix of psychological suspense and social commentary makes it a great shelfmate for Scandinavian thrillers, like those of Camilla Lackberg and Karin Fossum." —*Booklist*

Maps on end papers.

★ **House** of correction. Nicci French. William Morrow & Co, 2020. 432 p.
ISBN 9780063021341
1. Women murder suspects 2. Women with depression 3. Memories 4. Homecomings 5. Villages 6. England 7. Great Britain 8. Psychological suspense 9. Legal thrillers

Attempting to solve her own case from the confines of prison, a reclusive murder suspect from an English village uncovers evidence that calls her own sanity into question.

"French, the British husband-and-wife writing team of Nicci Gerrard and Sean French, seamlessly shifts from prison drama to procedural to legal thriller—and finally to an ingenious twist on the locked-room mystery. French continues to impress." —*Publishers Weekly*

"The writing team of Nicci Gerrard and Sean French delivers another winner (following The Living Room, 2019), combining an impeccably constructed, secrecy-prone English village with masterful plotting and an indefatigable protagonist who carries on, no matter the cost." —*Booklist*

★ The **lying** room. Nicci French. William Morrow & Co, 2019. 304 p.
ISBN 9780062676726
1. Married women 2. Extramarital affairs 3. Deception 4. Murder victims 5. Murderers 6. England 7. Psychological suspense

In this thrilling standalone from the internationally bestselling author of the Frieda Klein series, a married woman's affair with her boss spirals into a dangerous game of chess with the police when she discovers he's been murdered and she clears the crime scene of all evidence.

Sunday silence. Nicci French. William Morrow & Co, 2018. 403 p. (Frieda Klein novels, 7)
ISBN 9780062819840
1. Murder suspects 2. Women psychotherapists 3. Stalking 4. Psychopaths 5. Murder investigation 6. Great Britain 7. Psychological suspense

Declared a person of interest when a body is discovered beneath the floorboards of her own home, London psychologist Frieda Klein realizes that a copycat killer of the chief suspect is responsible before she finds herself in a deadly game of tug-of-war between two obsessive murderers.

Maps on endpapers.

Originally published: London : Penguin, 2017 as Sunday morning coming down.

Thursday's children. Nicci French. Michael Joseph, 2014. 420 p. (Frieda Klein novels, 4)
ISBN 9780718156992
1. Women psychotherapists 2. Rape investigation 3. Hometowns 4. Murder 5. Police 6. Suffolk, England 7. Psychological suspense

When psychotherapist Frieda Klein left the sleepy Suffolk coastal town in which she grew up she never intended to return. Left behind were friends, family, lives and loves but alongside them, painful memories; a past she wouldn't allow to destroy her.

"A skillfully woven plot and deftly drawn characters complement the central mystery, which engages and satisfies while developing the series arc." —*Publishers Weekly*

Tuesday's gone. Nicci French. Pamela Dorman Books/Viking, 2013. 384 pages (Frieda Klein novels, 2)
ISBN 9780670025671
1. Swindlers and swindling 2. Women psychotherapists 3. Fraud 4. Detectives 5. False personation 6. London, England 7. Psychological suspense 8. Thrillers and suspense
LC 2012040052

Psychotherapist Frieda Klein is called upon by DCI Karlsson to help solve a grisly murder in which the prime suspect is afflicted with a strange mental disorder. As the pair dig into the dead man's past, they find plenty of motive for murder, but questions remain about whether the real killer is still on the loose.

First published: Michael Joseph, 2012.

Waiting for Wednesday: a Frieda Klein mystery. Nicci French. Pamela Dorman Books/Viking, 2014. 384 pages (Frieda Klein novels, 3)

ISBN 9780670015771

1. Murder investigation 2. Innocence (Law) 3. Women psychotherapists 4. Sabotage 5. Secrets 6. London, England 7. Psychological suspense

While consulting on the murder of housewife, who was hiding a shocking secret, brilliant psychotherapist Frieda Klein is brought closer to a serial killer who has long escaped detection and wonders if she is solving both cases or if she just the victim of her own paranoid, fragile mind.

"French's darkly ambitious tale piles on the complications until you beg for mercy. Hard-core fans of detective work as a vehicle for revealing the depths of the human soul will find it irresistible." —*Kirkus*

Originally published: London : Michael Joseph, 2013.

French, Tana

★ **Broken** harbor. Tana French. Viking, 2012. 464 p. (Dublin Murder Squad novels, 4)

ISBN 9780670023653

1. Police 2. Murder investigation 3. Memories 4. Families of murder victims 5. Dublin, Ireland 6. Psychological suspense 7. Police procedurals

LC 2011042397

Library Journal Best Books, 2012; Los Angeles Times Book Prize for Mystery or Thriller, 2012

In the aftermath of a brutal attack that left a woman in intensive care and her husband and young children dead, brash cop Scorcher Kennedy and his rookie partner, Richie, struggle with perplexing clues and Scorcher's haunting memories of a shattering incident from his childhood.

Faithful place: a novel. Tana French. Viking, 2010. 464 pages (Dublin Murder Squad novels, 3)

ISBN 9780670021871

1. Police 2. Missing persons 3. First loves 4. Family relationships 5. Dysfunctional families 6. Dublin, Ireland 7. Psychological suspense 8. Police procedurals

LC 2010003212

Detective Frank Mackey finds himself straight back in the dark tangle of relationships he left behind twenty-two years ago when the suitcase belonging to his first love, Rosie Daly, shows up behind a fireplace in a derelict house on Faithful Place.

"The first thing that Ms. French does so well in Faithful Place is to inhabit fully a scrappy, shrewd, privately heartbroken middle-aged man. The second is to capture the Mackey family's long-brewing resentments in a way that's utterly realistic on many levels. Sibling rivalries, class conflicts, old grudges, adolescent flirtations and memories of childhood violence are all deftly embedded in this novel, as is the richly idiomatic Dublinese." —*New York Times*

Frank Mackey appeared in The Likeness.

Sequel to: The Likeness.

In the woods. Tana French. Viking, 2007. 464 p. (Dublin Murder Squad novels, 1)

ISBN 9780670038602

1. Coworkers 2. Girl murder victims 3. Detectives 4. Cold cases (Criminal investigation) 5. Murder investigation 6. Dublin, Ireland 7. Police procedurals 8. Psychological suspense 9. First person narratives

LC 2006033498

Anthony Award for Best First Novel, 2008; Edgar Allan Poe Award for Best First Novel by an American Author, 2008; Macavity Award for Best First Mystery Novel, 2008

Twenty years after witnessing the violent disappearances of two companions from their small Dublin suburb, detective Rob Ryan investigates a chillingly similar murder that takes place in the same wooded area, a case that forces him to piece together his traumatic memories.

"French sets a vivid scene for her complex characters, who seem entirely capable of doing the unexpected. Drawn by the grim nature of her plot and the lyrical ferocity of her writing, even smart people who should know better will be able to lose themselves in these dark woods." —*New York Times Book Review*

Adapted into the television series Dublin Murders, Fall 2019.

The **likeness**. Tana French. Viking, 2008. 448 p. (Dublin Murder Squad novels, 2)

ISBN 9780670018864

1. Graduate students 2. Undercover operations 3. Women murder victims 4. Women detectives 5. Murder investigation 6. Police procedurals 7. Psychological suspense 8. First person narratives

LC 2008003940

This novel finds Detective Cassie Maddox still scarred by her last case. When her boyfriend calls her to a chilling murder scene, Cassie is forced to face her inner demons. A young woman has been found stabbed to death outside Dublin, and the victim looks just like Cassie.

"Cassie Maddox, the partner of the self-destructing detective who narrated In the Woods, is drawn into a menage a cinq of college students living a seeming charmed existence in an Irish country house. One of the five, a girl who is Cassie's doppelganger and has been living under an alias Cassie once used as an undercover narcotics agent, turns up murdered in a ruined cottage. Cassie is given the unlikely task of pretending to be a woman who was pretending to be a woman whom Cassie once pretended to be. As you might expect, The Likeness wrestles with matters of identity and intimacy as its heroine comes to prefer this triply false life to her real one. The hypnotic prose and eerie atmosphere conspire to make this ostensible mystery novel much, much more than it appears to be." —*Salon.com*

Cassie Maddox appeared in In the Woods.

Sequel to: In the woods.

Sequel: Faithful Place.

Adapted into the television series Dublin Murders, Fall 2019.

★ The **searcher**. Tana French. Viking, 2020. 464 p.

ISBN 9780735224650

1. Americans in Ireland 2. Former police 3. Missing teenagers 4. Villages 5. Divorced men 6. Ireland 7. Mysteries

LC 2020032206

Loan Stars Favourites, 2020

Looking to start a new life in a small Irish village, former Chicago police officer Cal Hooper comes out of retirement to help find a missing kid and uncovers layers of darkness beneath his picturesque retreat.

"Insightful characterizations, even of minor figures, and a devastating reveal help make this a standout." —*Publishers Weekly*

★ The **secret** place. Tana French. Viking, 2014. 464 pages (Dublin Murder Squad novels, 5)

ISBN 9780670026326

1. Girl boarding school students 2. Boarding schools 3. Cliques 4. Teenage girls 5. Police 6. Dublin, Ireland 7. Psychological suspense 8. Police procedurals 9. Adult books for young adults

LC 2014004500

LibraryReads Favorites, 2014

Investigating a photograph of a boy whose murder was never solved, aspiring Murder Squad member Stephen Moran partners with detective

Antoinette Conway to search for answers in the cliques and rivalries at a Dublin boarding school.

"Beyond the murder mystery, which leaves the reader in suspense throughout, the novel explores the mysteries of friendship, loyalty and betrayal, not only among adolescents, but within the police force as well. Everyone is this meticulously crafted novel might be playing—or being played by—everyone else." —*Kirkus*

★ The **witch** elm: a novel. Tana French. Viking, 2018. 509 p.
ISBN 9780735224629
1. Family secrets 2. Life change events 3. Assault and battery 4. Uncles 5. Secrets 6. Ireland 7. Thrillers and suspense
LC 2018022167
LibraryReads Favorites, 2018; Library Journal Best Books, 2018; Loan Stars Favourites, 2018; New York Times Notable Book, 2018
Left for dead by burglars while partying with friends, a happy-go-lucky charmer takes refuge at his dilapidated ancestral home before a grisly discovery reveals an unsuspected family history.
Published in the UK as The Wych Elm, 2018.

Freudenberger, Nell

The **dissident**. Nell Freudenberger. ECCO, 2006. 448 p.
ISBN 9780060758714
1. Performance artists 2. Psychiatrists 3. Teenagers 4. Host families of foreign students 5. Dysfunctional families 6. Los Angeles, California 7. China 8. Mainstream fiction
LC 2006042617
New York Times Notable Book, 2006
Accepting an artist residency from a wealthy Beverly Hills family, a famous performance artist and political activist becomes increasingly entangled in the lives of his hosts and reveals the artistic subculture that shaped his Beijing past.
"Freudenberger demonstrates great talent for capturing the subtleties of cross-cultural and intergenerational relationships, as the dissident's struggles with his past and with his art intersect with Cece's unravelling." —*The New Yorker*

★ **Lost** and wanted: a novel. Nell Freudenberger. Alfred A Knopf, 2019. 336 pages
ISBN 9780385352680
1. Ghosts 2. Female friendship 3. Grief 4. Women scientists 5. College teachers 6. Literary fiction 7. Psychological fiction
Loan Stars Favourites, 2019
Receiving an unsettling phone call from her late college roommate, a rationally minded MIT professor reflects on their once-close friendship, her friend's tragic death and her own rediscovered feelings for a fellow scientist.
"Narrator Helen, a theoretical physicist who graduated from Harvard and is now an MIT professor of repute, must ponder her place among those in her orbit when she begins, inexplicably, receiving text and email messages from her recently deceased best friend's telephone." —*Library Journal*

The **newlyweds**. Nell Freudenberger. Knopf, 2012. 304 p.
ISBN 9780307268846
1. Muslim women 2. Interethnic marriage 3. Arranged marriage 4. Newlyweds 5. Interethnic romance 6. Rochester, New York 7. New York (State) 8. Literary fiction
LC 2011044116
Leaving her Bangladesh home to marry a New Yorker who wooed her online, Amina finds the marriage challenged by secrets and her struggles to find a place for herself in America.

Fridlund, Emily

★ **History** of wolves: a novel. Emily Fridlund. Atlantic Monthly Press, 2017. 288 pages
ISBN 9780802125873
1. Teenage girls 2. Belonging 3. Options, alternatives, choices 4. Fourteen-year-old girls 5. Social acceptance 6. Minnesota 7. Psychological fiction 8. Literary fiction 9. Coming-of-age stories 10. Adult books for young adults
LC 2016027800
New York Times Notable Book, 2017; Booklist Editors' Choice: Adult Books for Young Adults, 2017; Longlisted for the Andrew Carnegie Medal for Excellence in Fiction, 2018; Shortlisted for the International Dublin Literary Award, 2019; Shortlisted for the Man Booker Prize, 2017
Living with her parents in a nearly abandoned counterculture commune, 14-year-old Linda finds her perspectives and desires changed by the scandal-marked arrest of a teacher and the secrets of a new neighbor family as she wrestles with the consequences of actions and failures in the name of love.
"The novel has a tinge of fairy tale, wavering on the blur between good and evil, thought and action. But the sharp consequences for its characters make it singe and singa literary tour de force." —*Kirkus*
Includes bibliographical references and index.

Friedland, Elyssa

The **floating** Feldmans. Elyssa Friedland. Berkley Pub Group, 2019. 368 p.
ISBN 9780399586897
1. Family vacations 2. Pleasure cruises 3. Dysfunctional families 4. Senior women 5. Grandmothers 6. Domestic fiction 7. Humorous stories 8. Multiple perspectives
Organizing a family reunion cruise for her 70th birthday in the hopes of resolving long estrangements, Annette reveals difficult secrets that challenge long-held perceptions about the more troublesome members of her clan.

The **intermission**. Elyssa Friedland. Penguin Group USA 2018. 368 p.
ISBN 9780399586866
1. Separation (Marital relations) 2. Married people and secrets 3. Married people 4. Marital conflict 5. Husband and wife 6. New York City 7. Los Angeles, California 8. Domestic fiction 9. Multiple perspectives
A novel told from the alternating perspectives of a husband and wife who both have something to hide pulls back the curtain on a seemingly-happy marriage, posing the question: how much do we really know—and how much should we want to know—about the people we love the most?

Last summer at the Golden Hotel. Elyssa Friedland. Berkley, 2021. 368 p.
ISBN 9780593199725
1. Dysfunctional families 2. Hotels 3. Business partners 4. Vacations 5. Jewish families 6. Catskill Mountains Region, New York 7. New York (State) 8. Mainstream fiction 9. Multiple perspectives
LC 2020046445
A family reunion in the Catskills brings hilarity and nostalgia when two clans convene for the summer at their beloved getaway. In its heyday, the Golden Hotel was the crown jewel of the hotter-than-hot Catskills vacation scene. For more than sixty years, the Goldman and Weingold families—best friends and business partners—have presided over this glamorous resort, which served as a second home for well-heeled guests and celebrities. But the Catskills are not what they used to be—and neither is the relationship between the Goldmans and the Weingolds. As the facil-

ities and management begin to fall apart, a tempting offer to sell forces the two families together again to make a heart-wrenching decision. Long-buried secrets emerge, new dramas and financial scandal erupt, and everyone from the traditional grandparents to the millennial grandchildren wants a say in the hotel's future.

"Written with Friedland's signature wit and sharp dialogue, Last Summer at the Golden Hotel is an incisive novel that touches on family legacies, nostalgia, and multigenerational dynamics." —*Booklist*

Friedman, Daniel

★ **Don't** ever get old. Daniel Friedman. Minotaur Books, 2012. 304 p. (Buck Schatz mysteries, 1)
ISBN 9780312606930
1. Senior men 2. Nazi plunder 3. Former police 4. Former prisoners of war 5. Private investigators 6. Memphis, Tennessee 7. Mysteries
LC 2012005485
Macavity Award for Best First Mystery Novel, 2013
Learning that an old adversary may have escaped Germany with a fortune in stolen gold, retired Memphis cop Buck Schatz teams up with his plugged-in, smart-alecky grandson in a vigilante investigation involving a Mississippi loan shark, a 7-foot-tall Hasidic Jewish man and a bloodthirsty maniac.

Riot most uncouth: a Lord Byron mystery. Daniel Friedman. Minotaur Books, 2015. 304 pages (Lord Byron mysteries, 1)
ISBN 9781250027597
1. Byron, George Gordon Byron 2. Poets, English 3. Amateur detectives 4. College students 5. Murder 6. Murder investigation 7. England 8. Cambridge, England 9. Georgian era (1714-1837) 10. Historical mysteries
LC 2015033767
When a young woman is found murdered in a local boarding house, Trinity College student Lord Byron resolves to prove his genius by solving the case while finding time for his regular pursuits of excessive drinking, seducing women and causing mischief.

"Friedman manages to make one of the most obnoxious leads in recent memory oddly endearing and even sympathetic." —*Publishers Weekly*
A Thomas Dunne book.

Running out of road. Daniel Friedman. Minotaur Books, 2020. 288 p. (Buck Schatz mysteries, 3)
ISBN 9781250058485
1. Death row prisoners 2. Senior men 3. Retirees 4. Jewish men 5. Former police 6. Memphis, Tennessee 7. Mysteries 8. First person narratives
LC 2019041960
Retired Memphis detective Buck Schatz must confront a new challenge in NPR producer Carlos Watkins, who claims that Buck coerced a confession out of a man slated for execution.

"Should you, will you, and how can you fight the reaper are questions Friedman handles with amazing grace. Screamingly funny and achingly sad." —*Kirkus*

Fu, Kim

For today I am a boy. Kim Fu. Houghton Mifflin Harcourt, 2014. 256 p.
ISBN 9780544034723
1. Transgender persons 2. Chinese Canadians 3. Siblings 4. Fathers and sons 5. Chinese in Canada 6. 1970s 7. Coming-of-age stories 8. LGBTQIA fiction 9. Canadian fiction 10. Adult books for young adults

LC 2013027720
Peter, the only boy among four siblings born to Chinese immigrants, is convinced he is a girl and must fight the confines of a small town as well as the expectations of his parents to forge his own path into adulthood.

Fuentes, Carlos

The **crystal** frontier: a novel in nine stories. By Carlos Fuentes; translated from the Spanish by Alfred Mac Adam. Farrar, Straus and Giroux, 1997. 266 p.
ISBN 9780374132774
1. Families 2. Mexicans in the United States 3. Entrepreneurs 4. Maquiladoras 5. Cooks 6. Mexico 7. Rio Grande 8. Short stories 9. Translations
LC 9711230
New York Times Notable Book, 1997
Presents a fictional portrait of the relationship between the United States and Mexico, as played out in a Mexican dynasty led by a powerful oligarch with complex ties north of the border.

"Leonardo Barroso is an unscrupulous Mexican oligarch whose fortress of a villa is only a short drive from the 'crystal frontier' of the title, and each one of the nine stories comprising this work explores the life of someone touched by him." —*Library Journal*
Translation of La frontera de cristal: una novela en neuve cuentos (1995).

The **death** of Artemio Cruz. Carlos Fuentes; translated from the Spanish by Alfred MacAdam. Farrar, Straus and Giroux, 2009. 307 p.
ISBN 9780374531805
1. Death 2. Businesspeople 3. Memories 4. Rich men 5. Man-woman relationships 6. Mexico 7. Historical fiction 8. Translations
As the novel opens, Artemio Cruz, the all-powerful newspaper magnate and land baron, lies confined to his bed and, in dreamlike flashes, recalls the pivotal episodes of his life.
Translation of: Muerte de Artemio Cruz
Originally published: Mexico : Fondo de cultura economica, 1952
Translated from the Spanish.

Destiny and desire: a novel. Carlos Fuentes; translated by Edith Grossman. Random House, 2011. 416 p.
ISBN 9781400068807
1. Beheading 2. Friendship 3. Revenge 4. Orphans 5. Mexico 6. Magical realism 7. Literary fiction 8. Translations
LC 2010015078
The severed head of Josue Nadal, floating in the Pacific Ocean off the shore of Mexico, remembers his life, friends, enemies, and lovers, and his involvement in the drug trade and the corruption frequently encountered in his country.

"A towering work. No character enters its pages lightly, and escape for each carries a price. Fuentes's language is rich, evoking character, place and, perhaps most memorably, the human decisions that propel society. It is a novel of wheels turning within wheels and of convoluted but ultimately meaningful connections." —*Denver Post*
Originally published in Spanish as La voluntad y la fortuna by Alfaguara, Mexico City, in 2008.

The **eagle's** throne: a novel. Carlos Fuentes; translated by Kristina Cordero. Random House, 2006. 384 p.
ISBN 9781400062478
1. Presidents 2. Oil industry and trade 3. Armed Forces 4. Revenge 5. Communication technology 6. Mexico 7. United States 8. Letters 9. Political fiction 10. Satirical fiction
LC 2006040806
Booklist Editors' Choice, 2006

"While Fuentes is concerned, as always, about the destiny of his native country, his story focuses more on down-and-dirty political means than serious political ends, leaving us to draw our own conclusions about what sort of good can possibly come of his characters' byzantine strategies and counterstrategiestheir opportunistic alliances, their calculated secret-keeping and secret-leaking, their posturing, their watchful waiting, their sly brutalities. What results is the most wickedly entertaining novel of Fuentes's career." —*New York Times Book Review*

Translation of: Silla del aguila.

Originally published: Mexico, D.F. : Alfaguara, 2003.

★ The **old** gringo. Carlos Fuentes; translated by Margaret Sayers Peden. Farrar Straus Giroux, 1985. 199 p.

ISBN 9780374225780

1. Bierce, Ambrose 2. Americans in Mexico 3. Soldiers 4. Revolutionaries 5. Authors 6. Revolutions 7. Mexico 8. United States 9. Mexican Revolution (1910-1920) 10. Biographical fiction 11. Translations 12. Books to movies

LC 85016266

"We have in this novel a fastidious American governess stranded in Pancho Villa's revolution, where she attracts the erotic interest of an intellectual fellow countryman and a nature-boy Mexican general. On this inanely trite foundation Mr. Fuentes has erected a narrative of brilliant complexity and sophistication, describing brisk military action and philosophically contrasting national character, or social tradition, or styles of revolt, or regional strengths, weaknesses, and prejudices." —*The Atlantic*

Originally published in Spanish as El Gringo viejo: Mexico : Fondo de cultura economica, 1985.

The **years** with Laura Diaz. Carlos Fuentes; translated from the Spanish by Alfred Mac Adam. Farrar, Straus and Giroux, 2000. 518 p.

ISBN 9780374293413

1. Kahlo, Frida 2. Women artists 3. Mexican Americans 4. Political science 5. Women 6. Mexico 7. Mexican Revolution (1910-1920) 8. Political fiction 9. Literary fiction 10. Translations

LC 37648

Shortlisted for the International IMPAC Dublin Literary Award, 2002

The life and fate of Laura Díaz becomes entwined in the history, culture, and politics of Mexico, in a novel that chronicles her life from 1905 to 1978 as she becomes a politically active artist, wife, mother, and lover.

"Fuentes's emotional commitment to his subject shows in the lucidity of the book's underlying intellectual dialogues—the opposition of communism and fascism, the corrosion of individual identities by historical processes—which Fuentes is able to animate with a learned lyricism that should make this volume one of his most admired and memorable." —*Publishers Weekly*

Originally published in Spanish as Anos con Laura Diaz: Madrid : Santillana, 1999.

Fuller, Claire

★ **Bitter** orange. Claire Fuller. Tin House Books, 2019. 320 p.

ISBN 9781947793156

1. Manors 2. Neighbors 3. Voyeurism 4. Friendship 5. Deception 6. England 7. 1960s 8. 1980s 9. Domestic fiction 10. Gothic fiction 11. Gellhorn, Martha

LC 2018024161

An architect spending the summer of 1969 in a dilapidated English country mansion discovers a peephole that allows her to observe the increasingly sinister private lives of her hedonist neighbors.

"Desmond Elliott Prize-winning Fuller's stunning third novel (after Swimming Lessons) is a masterpiece that takes us to the dark places of human emotions." —*Library Journal*

Our endless numbered days: a novel. Claire Fuller. Tin House Books, 2015. 386 pages

ISBN 9781941040171

1. Fathers and daughters 2. Wilderness survival 3. Survivalists 4. Parental kidnapping 5. Family secrets 6. England 7. Germany 8. Coming-of-age stories 9. Literary fiction 10. First person narratives 11. Adult books for young adults

LC 2014037937

Peggy is eight when her survivalist father tells her that the world has been destroyed and takes her to live in a remote cabin, but years later, her search for the owner of a pair of found boots unwittingly leads her back to civilization.

Unsettled ground. Claire Fuller. Tin House, 2021. 330 pages

ISBN 9781951142483

1. Mothers — Death 2. Fifties (Age) 3. Twins 4. Rural life 5. Social isolation 6. England 7. Domestic fiction

LC 2020056873

Costa Book of the Year Award, 2021; Shortlisted for The Women's Prize for Fiction, 2021

When their mother dies suddenly, 51-year-old twins Jeanie and Julius, who have limited exposure to the outside world, strive to find a way forward until secrets from their mother's past come to light, forcing them to question who they are.

"A gripping, unsettling narrative that ultimately offers a journey of resilience and hope, with unforgettable results." —*Library Journal*

Fuqua, Jonathon Scott

Gone and back again. By Jonathon Scott Fuqua. Soft Skull Press, 2007. 176 p.

ISBN 9781933368771

1. Children with depression 2. Divorce 3. Sixth-graders 4. Eleven-year-old boys 5. Coping in children 6. Virginia 7. Florida 8. 1970s 9. Coming-of-age stories 10. Psychological fiction 11. Adult books for young adults

LC 2007028305

Caley tries to survive as he deals with his parents' divorce, moving from place to place, insomnia, and an eventual descent into depression.

Furst, Alan

Blood of victory: a novel. Alan Furst. Random House, 2002. 288 p. (Night soldiers, 7)

ISBN 9780375505744

1. Journalists 2. Oil industry and trade 3. Spies 4. Resistance to government 5. Government investigators 6. Romania 7. Second World War era (1939-1945) 8. 1940s 9. Historical thrillers 10. War stories 11. Spy fiction

LC 2002021312

In 1940, Russian emigre journalist I.A. Serebin is recruited by the British secret service to take part in a desperate operation to prevent Hitler's conquest of Europe by stopping the export of Romanian oil to Germany.

"As usual, Furst adheres strictly to the rules of the genre: the protagonist, a Russian expatriate writer, is seduced into service both by the prospect of heroism and by a mysterious Frenchwoman, and embarks on a globetrotting, spy-versus-spy adventure. But his debts to convention work in his favor. Densely atmospheric and genuinely romatic, the novel is most reminiscent of the Hollywood films of the forties, when moral choices were rendered not in black-and-white but in smoky shades of gray." —*The New Yorker*

Dark voyage: a novel. Alan Furst. Random House, 2004. 272 p. (Night soldiers, 8)
ISBN 9781400060184
1. Ship captains 2. Merchant sailors 3. Refugees 4. Dutch in Sweden 5. Shipping 6. Sweden 7. 1940s 8. War stories 9. Spy fiction 10. Sea stories
LC 2004046674
"The author lulls us into the atmosphere, allows us to imbibe his descriptions and then, in the last 50 pages, turns the screws. The denouement of Dark Voyage is both breathless and utterly relaxed, not so pellmell that Furst can't stop to be amused at the ironies of shifting alliances. If he ever breaks a sweat, it doesn't show." —*New York Times Book Review*

The **foreign** correspondent: a novel. Alan Furst. Random House, 2006. 288 p. (Night soldiers, 9)
ISBN 9781400060191
1. Nazis 2. Secrets 3. Attempted murder 4. Expatriates 5. Murder 6. Europe 7. 1930s 8. Historical thrillers 9. Spy fiction
LC 2006040417
In 1939 Paris, the murder of an Italian political émigré by OVRA, Mussolini's secret police, brings new danger to his successor, Carlo Weisz, who finds himself the target of OVRA, MI6, Stalin's NKVD, and Hitler's Gestapo.
"In an interview in 2002, Furst said that he had difficulty understanding why none of his bestselling novels had yet been filmed. With no apparent preciousness about what might be lost in a transfer to the screen, he added, These really are movies. In a sense, this is true. He has the ability to invent plots that work all on their own, which is, as Somerset Maugham once pointed out, a very rare gift indeed." —*The Atlantic*

★ A **hero** of France. Alan Furst. Random House, 2016. 256 p. (Night soldiers, 13)
ISBN 9780812996494
1. French Resistance (World War II) 2. Nazis 3. Resistance to government 4. National liberation movements 5. Fascism — History 6. France 7. 1940s 8. Second World War era (1939-1945) 9. Spy fiction 10. War stories 11. Historical thrillers
A tale set in World War II occupied Paris follows the experiences of French Resistance network members from diverse walks of life who engage in clandestine actions to regain the country's freedom.

★ **Mission** to Paris. Alan Furst. Random House, 2012. 272 p. (Night soldiers, 12)
ISBN 9781400069484
1. Film actors and actresses 2. Films — Production and direction 3. Woolf, Virginia 4. Fascism — History 5. Spies 6. France 7. 1930s 8. Spy fiction 9. War stories 10. Historical thrillers
Arriving in Paris on the eve of the Munich Appeasement in 1938, Hollywood star Frederic Stahl is unwittingly entangled in the region's shifting political currents when he discovers that his latest film is linked to the destinies of fascists, German Nazis and Hollywood publicists.

Spies of the Balkans: a novel. Alan Furst. Random House, 2010. 256 p. (Night soldiers, 11)
ISBN 9781400066032
1. Police 2. World War II 3. Resistance to military occupation 4. Nazis 5. Spies 6. Greece 7. Balkan Peninsula 8. 1940s 9. Historical thrillers 10. Spy fiction
LC 2010007755
As war approaches northern Greece, the spies begin to circle—from the Turkish legation to the German secret service. In the ancient port of Salonika, Costa Zannis, a senior police official, head of an office that handles special "political" cases, risks everything to secure an escape route for those hunted by the Gestapo.

"Furst is not in the least imitative—he has own style, and intricate sense of detail—but in his hands the mastery of the traditional spy novel has firmly passed to the other side of the Atlantic, and all I can say is that Eric Ambler and Graham Greene would have read his books with pleasure, and that somebody like Orson Welles (think of him playing Harry Lime in The Third Man) or Otto Preminger could have made a marvelous movie out of Spies of the Balkans. A pity that it probably won't happen—somehow, Furst seems to write in black and white, not Technicolor, just as Greene did—but in the meantime, this is a book, written for adults, to sit down and read in one gulp if you can." —*Daily Beast*

The **spies** of Warsaw. Alan Furst. Random House, 2008. 256 p. (Night soldiers, 10)
ISBN 9781400066025
1. Double agents 2. Soldiers 3. Spies 4. Engineers 5. Warsaw, Poland 6. Poland 7. 1930s 8. Historical thrillers 9. Spy fiction 10. Books to TV.
In 1937 Warsaw, on the eve of World War II, intelligence operatives on both sides of the forthcoming struggle wage their own espionage battle in a world of betrayal, intrigue, and abduction.
"Rather than Eric Ambler thrillers or Graham Greene entertainments, the comparisons Mr. Furst's novels most often draw, they might more accurately be seen as extended series of Talk of the Town pieces. There's the same soupçon of irony, the expert deployment of detail and, above all, a thick helping of knowingness—only with military secrets, machine pistols and Gestapo agents instead of celebrity quirks or outer-borough oddities." —*New York Observer*

★ **Under** occupation: a novel. Alan Furst. Random House, 2019. 224 p.
ISBN 9780399592300
1. Authors 2. French Resistance (World War II) 3. Spies 4. World War II 5. World War II — Prisoners and prisons, German 6. France 7. Paris, France 8. Second World War era (1939-1945) 9. Spy fiction 10. War stories 11. Historical thrillers
LC 2019010340
A historical novel based on the true stories of Polish prisoners in Nazi Germany finds a young member of the French resistance in occupied Paris navigating increasingly dangerous assignments and the machinations of an enigmatic spy.

G

Gabaldon, Diana
★ A **breath** of snow and ashes. Diana Gabaldon. Delacorte Press, 2005. 992 p. (Outlander novels, 6)
ISBN 9780385324168
1. Fate and fatalism 2. Dilemmas 3. Loyalty 4. Options, alternatives, choices 5. Scots in America 6. North Carolina 7. United States 8. Revolutionary America (1775-1783) 9. 1770s 10. First person narratives 11. Time travel romances 12. Historical fiction
LC 2005051948
In 1772, on the eve of the American Revolution, Jamie Fraser is asked by the governor to help protect the colonies for King and Crown, but, thanks to his time-traveling twentieth-century wife, Claire, Jamie is aware of the ultimate result of the rebellion.
"This vivid and haunting novel, therefore, brings an aching sadness, but it is balanced with sheer joy, revelation, and solace. The large scope of

the novel allows Gabaldon to do what she does best, paint in exquisite detail the lives of her characters." —*Booklist*

Made into a TV series on Starz beginning in 2014.

★ **Dragonfly** in amber. Diana Gabaldon. Delacorte Press, 1992. 743 p. (Outlander novels, 2)

ISBN 9780385302319

1. Charles Edward 2. Mothers and daughters 3. Time travel (Past) 4. Jacobites 5. Dueling 6. Prisoners 7. Scotland 8. France 9. Jacobite Rebellions (1689-1746) 10. 18th century 11. First person narratives 12. Multiple perspectives 13. Time travel romances

LC 92004904

Twenty years after her voyage to Scotland, Claire Randall, now a doctor, returns to Scotland with her daughter to locate the stone that sent her on her magical journey years before.

Made into a TV series on Starz beginning in 2014.

★ **Drums** of autumn. Diana Gabaldon. Delacorte Press, 1997. 880 p. (Outlander novels, 4)

ISBN 9780385311403

1. Quests 2. Time travel (Past) 3. Mothers and daughters 4. Scots in America 5. Husband and wife 6. Charleston, South Carolina 7. Colonial America (1600-1775) 8. 18th century 9. First person narratives 10. Time travel romances 11. Historical fiction

LC 9614035

Twice, Claire has used an ancient stone circle to travel back to the 18th century. The first time she found love with a Scottish warrior but had to return to the 1940s to save their unborn child. The second time, twenty years later, she reunited with her lost love but had to leave behind the daughter that he would never see. Now Brianna, from her 1960s vantage point, has found a disturbing obituary and will risk everything in an attempt to change history.

Made into a TV series on Starz beginning in 2014.

An **echo** in the bone. Diana Gabaldon. Delacorte Press, 2009. 992 p. (Outlander novels, 7)

ISBN 9780385342452

1. Protectiveness in women 2. Ocean travel 3. Scots in America 4. Dilemmas 5. Love 6. North Carolina 7. United States 8. Revolutionary America (1775-1783) 9. 1770s 10. First person narratives 11. Time travel romances 12. Degas, Edgar

Goodreads Choice Award, 2009

While Jacobite Jamie Fraser reluctantly participates in the American rebellion with a foreknowledge of the fledgling country's victory, his time-traveling wife, Claire, worries about the ultimate price of the war while struggling to safeguard her family.

★ The **fiery** cross. Diana Gabaldon. Delacorte Press, 2001. Ix, 979 p; (Outlander novels, 5)

ISBN 9780385315272

1. Militias and irregular armies 2. Insurgency 3. Mothers and daughters 4. Scots in America 5. Love 6. North Carolina 7. Colonial America (1600-1775) 8. 1770s 9. First person narratives 10. Time travel romances 11. Historical fiction

LC 2001047063

Romantic Times Reviewers Choice Award, 2001

In 1771, Scotsman James Fraser and his wife Claire Randall, a time-traveler from the twentieth century, have emigrated to the Royal County of North Carolina. Dissidents are stirring throughout the colonies. Claire forewarns James of the impendng war and the dangers it may bring them. Will her knowledge of America's tumultuous revolution be enough to guide them through a dangerously uncertain future?

Made into a TV series on Starz beginning in 2014.

★ **Outlander**. Diana Gabaldon. Delacorte Press, 1991. 627 p. (Outlander novels, 1)

ISBN 9780385302302

1. Time travel (Past) 2. Nurses 3. Jacobites 4. Love 5. Clans 6. Scotland 7. Jacobite Rebellions (1689-1746) 8. 18th century 9. First person narratives 10. Time travel romances 11. Historical fiction

LC 90019122

RITA Award for Best Romance of 1991

Hurtled back through time more than two hundred years to Scotland in 1743, Claire Randall finds herself caught in the midst of an unfamiliar world torn apart by violence, pestilence, and revolution and haunted by her growing feelings for James Fraser, a young soldier.

First published in Great Britain by Century in 1991 as Cross stitch.

Made into a TV series on Starz beginning in 2014.

★ **Voyager**. Diana Gabaldon. Delacorte Press, 1994. Viii, 870 p. (Outlander novels, 3)

ISBN 9780385302326

1. Voyages and travels 2. Shipwrecks 3. Women physicians 4. Culloden, Battle of, 1746 5. Randall, Claire (Fictitious character) 6. Scotland 7. West Indies 8. 18th century 9. First person narratives 10. Historical fiction 11. Time travel romances

LC 93021907

Time-travelling Claire Randall returns to her own time, pregnant and weary, and resumes her life, but her memories of her eighteenth-century Scottish lover Jamie Fraser will not die, leading her to a desperate decision to return to him.

Made into a TV series on Starz beginning in 2014.

Written in my own heart's blood. Diana Gabaldon. Delacorte Press, 2014. 832 p. (Outlander novels, 8)

ISBN 9780385344432

1. Protectiveness in women 2. Family secrets 3. Scots in America 4. Dilemmas 5. Love 6. United States 7. Revolutionary America (1775-1783) 8. 1770s 9. First person narratives 10. Historical fiction

Goodreads Choice Award, 2014; Romantic Times Reviewer's Choice Award, 2014

After being presumed dead, Jamie Fraser returns to find that his best friend has married his wife, his illegitimate son has discovered who his father is, and his nephew has decided to marry a Quaker.

Gabel, Aja

The **ensemble**: a novel. Aja Gabel. Riverhead Books, 2018. 352 p.

ISBN 9780735214767

1. Musicians 2. Stringed instruments 3. Ambition 4. String quartets (Groups) 5. Friendship 6. San Francisco, California 7. 1990s 8. Coming-of-age stories 9. Adult books for young adults

LC 2017004103

LibraryReads Favorites, 2018; Library Journal Best Books, 2018

Forging a familial bond over their shared artistic talents and secrets, four young people navigate a cutthroat world and their complex relationships with each other, as ambition, passion and love reinforce and divide them throughout the course of their lives.

Gaddis, William

Agape agape. William Gaddis; foreword by Matthew Gaddis; afterword by Joseph Tabbi. Viking, 2002. 128 p.

ISBN 9780670031313

1. Men with terminal illnesses 2. Fathers and daughters 3. Technology — Social aspects 4. Inheritance and succession 5. Player-piano 6. Psychological fiction 7. Literary fiction

LC 2002020676

New York Times Notable Book, 2002

A dying man lies in bed thinking about how he will write a book and grumbling about the pending fall of civilization.

"Gaddis has compressed 50 years of research on the social history of the player piano into a novel narrated by a dying elderly man who is as concerned with his own physical collapse as he is with his piano-based literary project.... As usual, Gaddis's avant-garde style requires patience and staying power from readers, who must parse long, elliptical sentences that wander from idea to idea while barely advancing the narrative. But his thoughts and ruminations remain fascinating and challenging." —*Publishers Weekly*

A **frolic** of his own: a novel. William Gaddis. Poseidon Press, 1994. 586 p.

ISBN 9780671669843

1. College teachers 2. Copyright 3. Dramatists, American 4. Lawyers 5. Greed 6. Satirical fiction 7. Literary fiction

LC 9326098

National Book Award for Fiction, 1994; National Book Critics Circle Award for Fiction finalist, 1994

A satirically jaundiced view of modern law and justice chronicles the fortunes of Oscar Crease, a middle-aged college instructor and playwright, as he sues a Hollywood producer for pirating a play.

"The medium is exceptionally dense. The mere effort of sorting out the voices, of tracking them, can be exhausting.... In any case, I hope the reader will persevere. 'A Frolic of His Own' is an exceptionally rich, even important novel." —*New York Times Book Review*

★ **J R**: a novel. William Gaddis. Penguin Books, 1993. Xxi, [5], 725 p.

ISBN 9780140187076

1. Free enterprise 2. Capitalists and financiers 3. Eleven-year-old boys 4. Wealth 5. Satirical fiction 6. Literary fiction

National Book Award for Fiction, 1976

A humorous take on the American dream as JR, an eleven-year-old boy, uses his newfound knowledge of business and the stock market to build a huge and exploitive business empire.

Originally published: New York : A.A. Knopf, 1975.

★ The **recognitions**. William Gaddis; with an introduction by William H. Gass. Penguin Books, 1993. 956 p.

ISBN 9780140187083

1. Art forgeries 2. Painters 3. Painting, Flemish — Forgeries 4. Paranoia 5. Literary fiction 6. Modern classics

LC 85556

Presents four novels which tell the terrifying story of a good man tortured, pursued, driven into revolt, and ruined as far as the world is concerned by the clever devices of a jealous and lying wife. Christopher Tietjens is the last of a breed, the Tory gentleman, which the Great War, and the qualities inherent in his nature define and unravel.

Originally published by Harcourt Brace in 1955.

Gaige, Amity

Schroder. Amity Gaige. Twelve, 2013. 288 p.

ISBN 9781455512133

1. Fathers and daughters 2. Child custody 3. Identity (Psychology) 4. Immigrants 5. Family relationships 6. Psychological fiction 7. First person narratives

LC 2012013882

New York Times Notable Book, 2013

Ensconced in a correctional facility at the height of a custody battle with his estranged wife, Eric, a first-generation East German immigrant who changed his name as a youth, surveys his life to consider the disparity between his original and assumed identities.

Sea wife. Amity Gaige. Alfred A Knopf, 2020. 288 pages

ISBN 9780525656494

1. Seafaring life 2. Sailboats 3. Marital conflict 4. Life change events 5. Husband and wife 6. First person narratives 7. Multiple perspectives 8. Psychological fiction

New York Times Notable Book, 2020

A young family escapes suburbia for a year-long sailing trip that upends all of their lives

"From the challenges of two people finding themselves on opposite ends of the political spectrum to Juliet's depression, which leads her to give up on her dissertation, and the challenges of life at sea, this surprising novel is stunning and deep." —*Booklist*

Gailey, Sarah

The **echo** wife. Sarah Gailey. Tor, 2021. 256 p.

ISBN 9781250174666

1. Clones and cloning — Moral and ethical aspects 2. Extramarital affairs 3. Murder 4. Abusive men 5. Women scientists 6. Science fiction thrillers 7. Psychological suspense

LC 2020042347

LibraryReads Favorites, 2021

A precarious arrangement between a man, his wife and his wife's clone explodes in a violent confrontation that forces the two women to figure out a creative way to stay out of prison.

"The Echo Wife is a slow burn, but the emotional intensity simmering under Evelyn's skin and the revelations that spin out of the plot are well worth the investment. Gailey's expertise with suspense and their success in presenting the reader with impossible choices about the ethics of cloning, biological programming and editing, and of Evelyn's specific, difficult situation, will leave the reader thinking about the novel long after the final page." —*Booklist*

A Tom Doherty Associates book.

Magic for liars. Sarah Gailey. Tor Books, 2019. 320 pages

ISBN 9781250174611

1. Women private investigators 2. Women wizards 3. Twin sisters 4. Schools 5. Teachers 6. California 7. Urban fantasy 8. Supernatural mysteries 9. First person narratives 10. Adult books for young adults

LibraryReads Favorites, 2019

A private investigator and talented liar embarks on a search for a killer at a California private academy for mages where her estranged, magically gifted twin hides in plain sight.

"There's something for almost all readers here: family drama, romance, high-school gossip, fantasy-world building. Above all, Gailey shows us that humans are humans, even when they are magic, and they are still flawed, damaged, and oh so interesting." —*Booklist*

Gaiman, Neil

★ **American** gods: a novel. Neil Gaiman. W. Morrow, 2001. 465 p.

ISBN 9781117970486

1. Gods and goddesses 2. National characteristics, American 3. Spiritual warfare 4. Former convicts 5. Bodyguards 6. Contemporary fantasy 7. Mythological fiction 8. Books to TV

LC 2001030407

Bram Stoker Award for Best Novel, 2001; Hugo Award for Best Novel, 2002; Locus Award for Fantasy Novel, 2002; Nebula Award for Best Novel, 2002

Days before his release from prison, Shadow learns that his wife has been killed in an accident. On the plane ride back home for the funeral, he meets Mr. Wednesday, who offers Shadow a job. Shadow accepts but soon discovers that Mr. Wednesday is far more dangerous than he could ever have imagined.

"A noirish sci-fi road trip novel in which the melting pot of the United States extends not merely to mortals but to a motley assortment of disgruntled gods and deities." —*New York Times Book Review*

Adapted into a television series on the Starz network in 2017.

Annotated edition released: New York : William Morrow, 2020.

★ **Anansi** boys: a novel. Neil Gaiman. William Morrow, 2005. 368 p.
ISBN 9780060515188
1. Tricksters 2. Gods and goddesses, African 3. Magic 4. Anansi (Legendary character) 5. Fathers and sons 6. England 7. Florida 8. Mythological fiction 9. Fantasy fiction 10. Adult books for young adults

LC 2005047176

Alex Award, 2006; Locus Award for Fantasy Novel, 2006; Mythopoeic Award for Adult Literature, 2006; YALSA Best Books for Young Adults, 2006

His past marked by his father's embarrassing taunts and untimely death, Fat Charlie meets the brother he never knew and is introduced to new and exciting ways to spend his time.

"A fun book with a little of everything—horror, mystery, magic, comedy, song, romance, ghosts, scary birds, ancient grudges, and trademark British wit." —*Library Journal*

★ **Fragile** things: short fictions and wonders. Neil Gaiman. William Morrow, 2006. 400 p.
ISBN 9780060515225
1. Horror 2. Fantasy fiction 3. Short stories 4. Adult books for young adults 5. Poetry

LC 2006048135

Booklist Editors' Choice: Adult Books for Young Adults, 2006; Locus Award for Best Collection, 2007

A collection of more than twenty-five short fictional works follows a theme of the intersections between life and death, perception and reality, and darkness and light

"Gaiman follows no overarching theme, but that is what makes these stories charming, at times creepy, and good fun. They read like dreams and meditations, with a stream-of-consciousness quality to their presentation. Gaiman also explains some of the inspiration behind the stories to help put them in perspective." —*Library Journal*

Collects approximately twenty previously published pieces of short fiction - stories, verse, and an American Gods novella - plus one new piece written especially for this volume — Author's website.

★ **Good** omens: the nice and accurate prophecies of Agnes Nutter, witch. Neil Gaiman and Terry Pratchett. William Morrow, 2006. 384 p.
ISBN 9780060853969
1. End of the world 2. Demons 3. Angels 4. Fantasy fiction 5. Humorous stories 6. Books to TV 7. Adult books for young adults

LC 2006-41944

The world is going to end next Saturday, but there are a few problems—the Antichrist has been misplaced, the Four Horseman of the Apocalypse ride motorcycles, and the representatives from heaven and hell decide that they like the human race.

"The end of the world is nigh! At least according to the prophecies of Agnes Nutter, a witch whose predictions are usually accurate but seldom heeded. Eleven years before the deadly Last Saturday Night, the ancient rivals of good and evil personified by the angelic Aziraphale (otherwise living as a London book dealer) and the demonic devil and former serpent Crowley clash in substituting the Antichrist during the birth of a baby. But the babies are switched as an unexpected third child enters the picture. The confusion picks up pace as witch hunters Sgt. Shadwell and Newton Pulsifer pursue modern Nutter follower Anathema Device. Along the way, countless puns, humorous footnotes, and satirical illusions enliven the story." —*School Library Journal*

Originally published: New York : Workman Pub, 1990.

★ **Norse** mythology. Neil Gaiman. W.W. Norton & Co, 2017. 256 p.
ISBN 9780393609097
1. Gods and goddesses, Norse 2. Heroes and heroines, Norse 3. Mythology, Norse 4. End of the world 5. Mythical creatures 6. Mythological fiction 7. Mythology, folklore, and legends 8. Adult books for young adults

Booklist Editors' Choice: Adult Books for Young Adults, 2017; LibraryReads Favorites, 2017

Presents a rendering of the major Norse pantheon that traces the genesis of the legendary nine worlds and the exploits of its characters, illuminating the characters and natures of iconic figures Odin, Thor, and Loki.

"Just the thing for the literate fantasy lover and the student of comparative religion and mythology alike." —*Kirkus*

★ The **ocean** at the end of the lane. Neil Gaiman. HarperCollins, 2013. 192 p.
ISBN 9780062255655
1. Good and evil 2. Memories 3. Farms 4. Funerals 5. Senior women 6. England 7. Sussex, England 8. Fantasy fiction 9. Contemporary fantasy 10. First person narratives 11. Adult books for young adults

Booklist Editors' Choice: Adult Books for Young Adults, 2013; British Book Award for Book of the Year, 2013; Goodreads Choice Award, 2013; Locus Award for Fantasy Novel, 2014; School Library Journal Best Books: Best Adult Books 4 Teens, 2013

Returning to his childhood home in the English countryside for a funeral, the unnamed middle-aged narrator of this haunting, lyrical fable finds himself drawn to an ordinary-looking farmhouse that's anything but. As long-buried memories surface, he recalls events that occurred at Hempstock Farm when he was seven. When the malevolent Ursula Monkton insinuates herself into the fabric of his close-knit family, the farm's inhabitants, especially 11-year-old Lettie, offer their friendship and later their protection to the lonely, abused boy. However, their aid comes at a price, requiring a sacrifice he's unprepared to make.

★ **Stardust**. Neil Gaiman; illustrated by Charles Vess. Spike/Avon Books, 1999. 238 p.
ISBN 9780380977284
1. Quests 2. Fairies 3. Magic 4. Walls 5. Gems 6. Victorian era (1837-1901) 7. Historical fantasy 8. Gateway fantasy 9. Boleyn, Jane 10. Adult books for young adults

LC 988773

Alex Award, 2000; Booklist Editors' Choice: Adult Books for Young Adults, 1999; Mythopoeic Award for Adult Literature, 1999; YALSA Best Books for Young Adults, 2000

Living in a Victorian countryside town overshadowed by an imposing stone barrier, Tristran is compelled to retrieve a fallen star for the woman he loves and crosses to the wondrous other side of the barrier, where he encounters dangerous rivals for the star.

Includes reading group questions.

Trigger warning: short fictions and disturbances. Neil Gaiman. HarperCollins 2015. 400 p.
ISBN 9780062330260
1. Ghosts 2. Death 3. Months 4. Magic 5. Characters and characteristics in literature 6. Fantasy fiction 7. Horror 8. Short stories

Locus Award for Best Collection, 2016

A latest collection of short fiction by the #1 best-selling author of Fragile Things includes previously published stories, verses and a 50th anniversary Doctor Who tale, as well as an original short story. Reading-group guide available.

"Full of all manner of witches and monsters and things that creep in the night, this collection will thoroughly satisfy faithful fans and win new onesif there's anyone out there left unconverted." —*Kirkus*

Gaines, Ernest J.

★ The **autobiography** of Miss Jane Pittman. Ernest J. Gaines. Bantam Books, 1996. X, 245 p. : Illustration
ISBN 9780553263572
1. African American women 2. Race relations 3. Leadership in women 4. Enslaved women 5. African Americans — Civil rights 6. Louisiana 7. 19th century 8. 20th century 9. Historical fiction 10. Family sagas 11. African American fiction
LC 96208552
Presents the story of the long life of Miss Jane Pittman, who began her life as a slave in the South and who marched for her civil rights in the 20th century at the age of 110.
Originally published: New York : Dial Press, 1971.

★ A **gathering** of old men. Ernest J. Gaines. Knopf, 1983. 213 p.
ISBN 9780394514680
1. Race relations 2. Revenge 3. Rural African Americans 4. African American men 5. Senior men 6. Louisiana 7. 1970s 8. Literary fiction 9. African American fiction 10. Multiple perspectives
LC 83049000
When Sheriff Mapes is summoned to a sugarcane plantation to find a dead Cajun farmer, he knows who committed the crime. Mapes finds himself powerless, however, when nearly 20 elderly black men confess to the murder. Can justice be served, or will the dead man's brutish father pass judgment his way?

Gainza, Maria

The **optic** nerve. Maria Gainza; translated from the Spanish by Thomas Bunstead. Catapult, 2019. 208 p.
ISBN 9781948226165
1. Women 2. Art 3. Observing things 4. Art museums 5. Obsession 6. Buenos Aires, Argentina 7. Buenos Aires (Argentina) 8. Psychological fiction 9. Literary fiction 10. Translations
New York Times Notable Book, 2019
"With playfulness and startling psychological acuity, Gainza explores the spaces between others, art, and the self, and how what one sees and knows form the ineffable hodgepodge of the human soul." —*Publishers Weekly*
Originally published: Buenos Aires : Mansalva, 2014.
Translated from the Spanish.

Gaitskill, Mary

Don't cry: stories. Mary Gaitskill. Pantheon Books, 2009. 240 p.
ISBN 9780375424199
1. Life change events 2. Personal conduct 3. Sex crimes 4. One-night stands (Interpersonal relations) 5. Interpersonal relations 6. United States 7. Literary fiction 8. Psychological fiction 9. Short stories
LC 2008025231
New York Times Notable Book, 2009
A collection of stories unfolding against the backdrop of American life over the last thirty years includes "College Town 1980," "The Little Boy," and "Mirrorball," in which a young man steals a girl's soul during a one-night stand.
"There is always a moment in a Mary Gaitskill story when you wince. And then you shrug. The wince means, Wow, that's a pretty creepy aspect of human nature to point out, while the shrug is a way of acknowledging,

But it's true. Life's really like that, isn't it? The Gaitskill two-step that wince-and-shrug maneuver her work inspires is what elevates her above other fiction writers who, though talented, are content to give us surfaces. Gaitskill never stops at surfaces. She's too adventurous for that, too reckless." —*Newsday*

The **mare**: a novel. Mary Gaitskill. Pantheon Books, 2015. 400 p.
ISBN 9780307379740
1. Girls and horses 2. Interethnic relations 3. Life change events 4. Hispanic American girls 5. Horses 6. Brooklyn, New York City 7. New York (State) 8. Coming-of-age stories 9. Multiple perspectives 10. Adult books for young adults
LC 2015007973
New York Times Notable Book, 2015; Longlisted for The Baileys Women's Prize for Fiction, 2017
Taken in by a near-alcoholic artist and a jaded academic, a young Dominican girl in Brooklyn's Fresh Air Fund program explores the contrasts between her inner-city life and her hosts' privileged world and finds her realities powerfully shaped by her relationship with a horse.
"Gaitskill explores the complexities of love (mares, meres) to bring us a novel that gallops along like a bracing bareback ride on a powerful thoroughbred." —*Kirkus*

Veronica. Mary Gaitskill. Pantheon Books, 2005. 240 p.
ISBN 9780375421457
1. Female friendship 2. Memories 3. Young women 4. Fashion models 5. Middle-aged women 6. Manhattan, New York City 7. New York City 8. 1980s 9. Literary fiction 10. Psychological fiction 11. Short stories
LC 2005043143
ALA Notable Book, 2006; New York Times Notable Book, 2005; National Book Critics Circle Award for Fiction finalist, 2005; National Book Award for Fiction finalist, 2005
As a teenager on the streets of San Francisco, Alison is discovered by a photographer and swept into the world of fashion modelling in Paris and Rome. When her career crashes and a love affair ends disastrously, she moves to New York City to build a new life. There she meets Veronica—an older wisecracking eccentric with her own ideas about style, a proofreader who comes to work with a personal "office kit" and a plaque that reads "Still Anal After All These Years." Improbably, the two women become friends. Their friendship will survive not only Alison's reentry into the seductive nocturnal realm of fashion, but also Veronica's terrible descent into the then-uncharted realm of AIDS. The memory of their friendship will continue to haunt Alison years later, when she, too, is aging and ill and is questioning the meaning of what she experienced and who she became during that time.
"The author's fierce, night-blooming new novel is about a close friendship between two women. But it should not be confused with anything cozy. Imagine a buddy story from the mind of William S. Burroughs, illustrated with images by Robert Mapplethorpe or David Cronenberg, and you get some idea of the tenderness to be found here.... Ms.Gaitskill writes so radiantly about violent self-loathing that the very incongruousness of her language has shocking power." —*New York Times*
With a new introduction by the author—Cover.
Originally published: USA : Pantheon Books, 2005.

Gala, Marcial

★ The **Black** Cathedral. Marcial Gala; translated from the Spanish by Anna Kushner. Farrar, Straus and Giroux, 2020. 192 pages
ISBN 9780374118013
1. Cathedrals 2. Religious fanatics 3. Neighborhoods 4. Race relations 5. Neighbors 6. Cuba 7. Literary fiction 8. Multiple perspectives 9. Translations
LC 2019037907

After the Stuart family moves to Cienfuegos, Cuba, Arturo Stuart—a charismatic, visionary preacher—discovers soon after arriving that God has given him a mission: to build a temple that surpasses any before seen in Cuba, and to make of Cienfuegos a new Jerusalem.

"Gala's raw, compelling, and highly readable novel lays bare a Cuba that, just like everywhere else, has not found an answer to human desperation, envy, or evil." —*Booklist*

Originally published in Spanish in 2012 by Letras Cubanas, Cuba, as La catedral de los negros.

Translated from the Spanish.

Galbraith, Robert

Career of evil. Robert Galbraith. Mulholland Books, 2015. 464 p. (Cormoran Strike novels, 3)

ISBN 9780316349932

1. Private investigators 2. Enemies 3. Secrets 4. Murder 5. Murder investigation 6. Mysteries 7. Books to TV

When a mysterious package is delivered to Robin Ellacott, she is horrified to discover that it contains a woman's severed leg, and Cormoran Strike must look to his past to determine who is behind the horrid parcel.

"The real appeal here...is Robin and Strikes relationship. A contemporary thriller with characters whose emotional journey is just as page-turningly gratifying as the most high-stakes manhunt." —*Booklist*

Adapted into the TV series C. B. Strike in 2018.

J. K. Rowling writing under the name Robert Galbraith

The **cuckoo's** calling. Robert Galbraith. Mulholland Books, 2013. 464 p. (Cormoran Strike novels, 1)

ISBN 9780316206846

1. Private investigators 2. Fashion models 3. Suicide investigation 4. Celebrities 5. Rich people 6. Mysteries 7. Books to TV

Los Angeles Times Book Prize for Mystery or Thriller, 2013

Private investigator Cormoran Strike has a day he'll not soon forget. The 35-year-old, who lost a leg in Afghanistan, spends the night in his bare-bones London office after a relationship-ending fight with his girlfriend. That morning, he sports a cut on his face (she threw an ashtray) as he rushes out the door, barreling into a new temp secretary he can't afford, almost sending her down a staircase. The forgiving temp, Robin, quickly proves useful when they get a case: a famous young model supposedly jumped from the top of her penthouse apartment, but her brother believes she was murdered. Entering the realm of the mega-rich, Strike and Robin question celebrities and fashionistas, trying to uncover the truth in a beautifully written book that was pseudonymously written by none other than J.K. Rowling.

Adapted into the TV series C. B. Strike in 2017.

J. K. Rowling writing under the name Robert Galbraith

Lethal white. Robert Galbraith. Mulholland Books, 2018. 656 p. (Cormoran Strike novels, 4)

ISBN 9780316422734

1. Private investigators 2. Cold cases (Criminal investigation) 3. Secrets 4. Murder 5. Murder investigation 6. Mysteries 7. Books to TV

LC Bl2018157218

When a troubled young man asks him to investigate a crime he thinks he saw as a child, Cormoran Strike sets off on a twisting trail that leads from London's backstreets, into a secretive inner sanctum within Parliament, and to a country manor house.

Adapted into the TV series C. B. Strike in 2020.

Originally published: London: Sphere, 2018.

The **silkworm**. Robert Galbraith. Mulholland Books, 2014. 464 pages (Cormoran Strike novels, 2)

ISBN 9780316206877

1. Private investigators 2. Authors — Death 3. Secrets 4. Murder 5. Murder investigation 6. Mysteries 7. Books to TV

Cormoran Strike investigates the disappearance of a novelist who, in his most recent book, unflatteringly portrayed people from his life.

"In her Galbraith persona, author J.K. Rowling has created memorable characters who develop and grow throughout the course of the novel. The mystery itself is clever, and the frequent darts aimed at the publishing world are entertaining." —*Library Journal*

Adapted into the TV series C. B. Strike in 2017.

J. K. Rowling writing under the name Robert Galbraith

Galchen, Rivka

American innovations: stories. Rivka Galchen. Farrar, Straus and Giroux, 2014. 176 p.

ISBN 9780374280475

1. Short stories 2. Literary fiction 3. Canadian fiction

LC 2013039912

New York Times Notable Book, 2014

Reimagines the themes of canonical short stories from the perspectives of female characters and includes the tales of a young woman whose furniture walks out on her and a property transaction that illuminates painful family dynamics.

"Galchen's stories feel remarkably believable, despite their suggestion of alternate worlds and lives." —*Kirkus*

Everyone knows your mother is a witch. Rivka Galchen. Farrar, Straus and Giroux, 2021. 272 p.

ISBN 9780374280468

1. Kepler, Johannes 2. Trials (Witchcraft) 3. Hysteria (Social psychology) 4. Misogyny 5. Communities 6. Malicious accusation 7. Germany 8. Holy Roman Empire 9. 17th century 10. Historical fiction 11. Canadian fiction

LC 2020058349

Atwood Gibson Writers' Trust Fiction Prize finalist, 2021

Drawing on real historical documents but infused with the intensity of imagination, sly humor, and intellectual fire for which award-winning author Rivka Galchen's writing is known, Everyone Knows Your Mother Is a Witch is a tale for our time-the story of how a community becomes implicated in collective aggression and hysterical fear.

"Dazzling in its humor, intelligence, and the richness of its created world." —*Kirkus*

Galen, Shana

Third son's a charm. Shana Galen. Sourcebooks Inc 2017. 384 p. (Survivors (Shana Galen), 1)

ISBN 9781492657033

1. Veterans 2. Kidnapping 3. Dukes and duchesses 4. Napoleonic Wars veterans 5. Napoleonic Wars, 1800-1815 6. England 7. Regency period (1811-1820) 8. Regency romances 9. Historical romances

Taking a job watching the Duke of Ridington's stubbornly independent daughter, former soldier Ewan Mostyn, who is trying desperately trying to settle back into peaceful Society, is drawn into a world of subterfuge and betrayal as he tries to save Lady Lorraine from kidnappers—and from herself.

Gallagher, Stephen

The **bedlam** detective: a novel. Stephen Gallagher. Crown Publishers, 2012. 256 p. (Sebastian Becker mysteries, 2)

ISBN 9780307406644

1. Detectives 2. Murder investigation 3. Monsters 4. Rich people 5. Eccentrics and eccentricities 6. England 7. Edwardian era (1901-1914) 8. 1910s 9. Supernatural mysteries

LC 2011018605

Investigating a wealthy landowner whose sanity has come into question, Sebastian Becker stumbles on a murder case involving two young girls, a traumatized suffragette and monsters who hide in plain sight.

The **kingdom** of bones: a novel. Stephen Gallagher. Shaye Areheart Books, 2007. 368 p. (Sebastian Becker mysteries, 1)

ISBN 9780307382801

1. Detectives 2. Serial murderers 3. Vampires 4. Sadism 5. Theater — History 6. Victorian era (1837-1901) 7. 19th century 8. Supernatural mysteries

LC 2007013288

Escaping from custody after being arrested for the serial killings of pauper children, former boxing champion Tom Sayers, desperate to prove himself innocent and to reveal the true murderer, searches for the dark truth and ancient evil behind the murders.

"Vividly set in England and America during the booming industrial era of the late 19th and early 20th centuries, this stylish thriller conjures a perfect demon to symbolize the age and its appetites, an entity that inhabits characters eager to barter their souls for fame and fortune." —*New York Times Book Review*

Gallen, Michelle

Big girl, small town: a novel. Michelle Gallen. Algonquin Books of Chapel Hill, 2020. 320 p.

ISBN 9781643750897

1. Twenties (Age) 2. Everyday life 3. Small town life 4. Postwar life 5. Women with autism 6. Northern Ireland 7. Coming-of-age stories 8. Literary fiction

LC 2020019698

Follows the experiences of a plucky chip-shop worker whose coming-of-age in the post-Troubles years is upended by abandonment and growing tensions between local Catholics and Protestants.

"Infused with local diction, inflection, and slang, her voice envelops readers in the sounds of small-town Ireland." —*Booklist*

Galligan, John

Bad moon rising. John Galligan. Atria Books, 2021. 336 p. (Bad Axe County novels, 3)

ISBN 9781982166533

1. Women sheriffs 2. Murder victims 3. Homeless men 4. Premature burial 5. Heat waves (Meteorology) 6. Wisconsin 7. Thrillers and suspense 8. Police procedurals

A record heat wave suffocates remote rural Wisconsin as the local sheriff tracks down a killer hidden in the depths of the community in this atmospheric, race-to-the-finish mystery.

"The plot is gritty and propulsive, the prose well crafted, the finale satisfyingly bizarre. Intriguing characters take a wild ride through backwoods Wisconsin in this irresistible mystery." —*Kirkus*

Galloway, Gregory

As simple as snow. Gregory Galloway. G. P. Putnam's Sons, 2005. 308 p.

ISBN 9780399152313

1. High school students 2. Teenage boys 3. Teenage girls 4. Teenagers 5. Teenage boy/girl relations 6. Psychological fiction 7. Coming-of-age stories 8. First person narratives 9. Adult books for young adults

LC 2004044500

Alex Award, 2006; Booklist Editors' Choice: Adult Books for Young Adults, 2005; YALSA Best Books for Young Adults, 2006

In awe of high school girl Anna Cayne and her penchant for affectionate magic tricks and riddles, a man is baffled by her mysterious disappearance just before Valentine's Day and retraces the time they spent together for clues to her fate.

Galsworthy, John

★ The **Forsyte** saga. John Galsworthy. Scribner, 2002. 878 p. (Forsyte saga)

ISBN 9780743245029

1. Middle class families 2. Lawyers 3. Husband and wife 4. Women — Social conditions 5. Personal property 6. London, England 7. Great Britain 8. Victorian era (1837-1901) 9. Family sagas 10. Modern classics

The saga begins with Soames Forsyte, a successful solicitor who buys land at Robin Hill on which to build a house for his wife Irene and future family. Eventually, the Forsyte family begins to disintegrate when Timothy Forsyte, the last of the old generation, dies at the age of 100.

Collects the original trilogy: The man of property, In chancery and To let, as well as the related short stories "The Indian Summer of a Forsyte" and "Awakening."

First published together: London : Penguin Books, 1978.

Originally collected: New York : C. Scribner's, 1922.

Gamboa, Santiago

Necropolis. Santiago Gamboa; translated from the Spanish by Howard Curtis. Europa Editions, 2012. 500 p.

ISBN 9781609450731

1. Professional conferences 2. Drinking 3. Sexuality 4. Lust 5. Former convicts 6. Israel 7. Literary fiction 8. Surrealist fiction 9. Translations

An author attends a conference featuring a series of extraordinary life stories, where the story of formerly troubled evangelical pastor José Maturana captures his imagination and causes him to seek answers when Maturana is later found dead.

Ganshert, Katie

Life after. Katie Ganshert. WaterBrook Press, 2017. 352 pages

ISBN 9781601429025

1. Accident victims 2. Widowers 3. Life change events 4. Survival — Psychological aspects 5. Guilt 6. Chicago, Illinois 7. Christian fiction 8. Relationship fiction

LC 2016053315

Christy Award for Contemporary (Stand Alone) Category, 2018; Romantic Times Reviewer's Choice Award, 2017

A bomb goes off on a Chicago train, killing 22 people. Autumn Manning survives, but a year later still can't remember what happened, and can't seem to move on either. Wondering why God let her live when so many lost their lives, she's drawn to the victims' families and records them sharing memories of their loved ones. Autumn connects with one family in particular, a husband and kids who lost their wife and mother—but secrets from the past complicate matters for everyone. Addressing grief and guilt, this poignant, thought-provoking book is unputdownable.

★ **No** one ever asked: a novel. Katie Ganshert. WaterBrook, 2018. 368 p.

ISBN 9781601429049

1. Schools 2. Prejudice 3. Class conflict 4. Income inequality 5. Christian women 6. Missouri 7. Christian fiction

LC 2017048918

Christy Award for Contemporary (Stand Alone) Category, 2019

The absorbtion of an impoverished school district by the affluent community of Crystal Ridge brings three women together as tensions rise, leading to an unforeseen event that impacts them all.

"Ganshert's (Life After) emotionally charged and powerful novel will have readers examining their own personal biases. Recommended for book groups looking for a story with loads of discussion potential." —*Library Journal*

Includes bibliographical references and index.

Gao, Xingjian

Soul mountain. Gao Xingjian; translated from the Chinese by Mabel Lee. Harper Collins, 2000. Xi, 510 p. : Illustration

ISBN 9780066210827

1. Semantics (Philosophy) 2. Revolutions 3. Villages 4. Wanderers and wandering 5. Spiritual journeys 6. China 7. Literary fiction 8. Allegories 9. Translations

Threatened with time on a prison farm for defying his country's laws of cultural conformity, artist/writer Gao Xingjian embarked on an epic search for his inner self and for his freedom. The author's journey through southern China's ancient mountains and forests inspired this story.

"It is not easy to say what the novel is aboutand it is lacking in plot, descriptions and character developmentand yet the marvel is that somehow it is still both engaging and elegant." —*New York Times Book Review*

Translation of: Ling shan.

Gappah, Petina

★ **Out** of darkness, shining light. Petina Gappah. Scribner, 2019. 320 p.

ISBN 9781982110338

1. Livingstone, David 2. Colonialism 3. Voyages and travels 4. Slavery 5. Colonized peoples 6. Exploration 7. Africa 8. 19th century 9. Historical fiction

A sharp-tongued cook and a rigidly pious freed slave confront complicated race dynamics to join the followers of the late Dr. Livingstone on a 19th century voyage from Africa to the doctor's home in England.

Garcia Marquez, Gabriel

★ The **autumn** of the patriarch. Gabriel Garcia Marquez; translated from the Spanish by Gregory Rabassa. Harper & Row, 1976. 269 p.

ISBN 9780060114190

1. Dictators 2. Senior men 3. Death 4. Patriarchs 5. Despotism 6. South America 7. Magical realism 8. Translations 9. Literary fiction

LC 75030349

The discovery of a South American dictator's rotting corpse in the deserted tangle of his crumbling palace prompts a search through his past and a colorful chronicle of his progression from popular, beloved, unafraid ruler to isolated, frightened despot.

Translation of: El otono del patriarca.

Chronicle of a death foretold. Gabriel Garcia Marquez; translated from the Spanish by Gregory Rabassa. Knopf, 1983. 120 p.

ISBN 9780394530741

1. Murder 2. Siblings 3. Villages 4. Passivity (Psychology) 5. Apathy 6. Colombia 7. Translations 8. Literary fiction 9. Modern classics

LC 82048884

The Nobel laureate weaves a story of a fantastic wedding, the return of the bride to her parents, her brothers' resolve to murder her corruptor, and the townspeoples' refusal to depart from routine.

"This investigation of an ancient murder takes on the quality of a hallucinatory exploration, a deep groping search into the gathering darkness of human intentions for a truth that continually slithers away." —*The New York Review of Books*

Collected novellas. Gabriel Garcia Marquez. Harpercollins, 1999. 281 p.

ISBN 9780060932664

1. Magical realism 2. Translations 3. Literary fiction

Three novellas deal with such themes as life in Colombia and the effects of violence

The **general** in his labyrinth. Gabriel Garcia Marquez; translated from the Spanish by Edith Grossman. A. A. Knopf, 1990. 285 p.

ISBN 9780394582580

1. Bolivar, Simon 2. Politicians 3. Death — Psychological aspects 4. Men with terminal illnesses 5. Assassination 6. Unhappiness in men 7. South America 8. 19th century 9. Literary fiction 10. Modern classics 11. Biographical fiction

LC 90052957

In his last days, Simon Bolivar, the Liberator of South America, is prematurely aged, but though he has announced his exile, he hopes to be restored to power.

"Seldom has there been a more fitting match between author and subject. Mr. Garcia Marquez wades into his flamboyant, often improbable and ultimately tragic material with enormous gusto, heaping detail upon sensuous detail, alternating grace with horror." —*New York Times Book Review*

Translation of: El general en su laberinto (1989).

In evil hour. Gabriel Garcia Marquez; translated from the Spanish by Gregory Rabassa. Harper & Row, 1978. 183 p.

ISBN 9780060114145

1. Mayors 2. Gossiping and gossips 3. Villages 4. Good and evil 5. Paranoia 6. Translations 7. Literary fiction 8. Modern classics

The acclaimed Colombian writer's earlier novel about the slanders, defamations, infidelities, and torrential rains that afflict a small town and the sacrifice of a boy that brings torment and chaos to an end.

"The reader is carried along effortlessly in the current of this gifted storyteller's prose. Both heroes and villains elicit sympathy because their basic human foibles, while true to local circumstances, can be recognized by people of any culture." —*Library Journal*

Leaf storm, and other stories. Gabriel Garcia Marquez; translated from the Spanish by Gregory Rabassa. Harper & Row, 1972. 146 p.

ISBN 9780060127794

1. Magical realism 2. Short stories 3. Translations

LC 76' 6784

In a new edition of the Nobel laureate's first book, seven sh゙ stories, including the title story, "The Handsomest Drowned Man in ᵗe World," "A Very Old Man with Enormous Wings," "The Last Voya゙ of the Ghost Ship," and "Nabo," reflect the author's concern with th complexities of human nature.

★ **Love** in the time of cholera. Gabriel Ꮐarcia Marquez; translated from the Spanish by Edith Grossman. A. A. ' nopf, 1988. 348 p.

ISBN 9780394561615

1. Romantic love 2. Unrequited lo゙ 3. Love triangles 4. Courtship 5. Man-woman relationships 6 Latin America 7. Love stories 8. Translations 9. Literary fictio..

LC 87040484

Los Angeles Times Book Prize for Fiction, 1988

Florentino Ariza has never forgotten his first love. He has waited nearly a lifetime in silence since his beloved Fermina married another man. But now her husband is dead. Finally Florentino has another chance to declare his eternal passion and win her back. Will love that has survived half a century remain unrequited?

Translation of: El amor en los tiempos del colera.

This English translation first published in the United States by Alfred A. Knopf, 1988.

Memories of my melancholy whores. Gabriel Garcia Marquez; translated by Edith Grossman. Knopf, 2005. 128 p.
ISBN 9781400044603
1. Senior men — Sexuality 2. Teenage prostitutes 3. Reminiscing in old age 4. Aging 5. Nonagenarians 6. Colombia 7. 1950s 8. Translations 9. First person narratives 10. Literary fiction
LC 2005043591
Booklist Editors' Choice, 2005; Los Angeles Times Book Prize for Fiction, 2005; New York Times Notable Book, 2005

Having decided to celebrate his ninetieth birthday by spending the night with a young virgin, an old man falls deeply in love for the first time in his life when he spots the girl at a local brothel.

★ **One** hundred years of solitude. Gabriel Garcia Marquez; translated from the Spanish by Gregory Rabassa. Harper & Row, 1970. 422 p.
ISBN 9780072434231
1. Families 2. Villages 3. Ghosts 4. Murder 5. Good and evil 6. Latin America 7. Magical realism 8. Literary fiction 9. Family sagas
LC 74083632
The evolution and eventual decadence of a small South American town is mirrored in the family history of the Buendias.

★ **Strange** pilgrims: twelve stories. By Gabriel Garcia Marquez; translated from the Spanish by Edith Grossman. A. A. Knopf, 1993. 188 p.
ISBN 9780679425663
1. Latin Americans in Europe 2. Expatriates 3. Loss (Psychology) 4. Disorientation 5. Fear 6. Magical realism 7. Short stories 8. Literary fiction
LC 93012257
Twelve stories recount the peculiar experiences of Latin Americans visiting or residing in Europe

"Exile and loss are the principal subjects of these 12 stories...which capture with lyrical precision the emotions of disorientation and fear, coupled with a sense of new possibility, experienced by Latin Americans in Europe." —*Publishers Weekly*

12 stories written over the last 18 years.

Garcia Saenz, Eva

The **silence** of the white city. Eva Garcia Saenz; translated from the Spanish by Nick Caistor. Vintage Crime/Black Lizard, 2020. 528 p. (White city trilogy, 1)
ISBN 9781984898593
1. Widowers 2. Archaeologists 3. Serial murders 4. Serial murderers 5. Murder investigation 6. Basque Provinces 7. Spain 8. Mysteries 9. Parallel narratives 10. Translations
LC 2019058952
RUSA Reading List Short List, 2021

A young Inspector investigating a series of ritualistic murders that are strikingly similar to ones that previously terrified Vitoria must determine if the convicted man had an accomplice or he has been wrongly incarcerated for twenty years.

"Fascinating local color, a handsomely crafted plot, and exquisite characterization make this a standout. Readers will eagerly await the next volume in the series." —*Publishers Weekly*

Originally published in Spain as El silencio de la ciudad blanca by Editorial Planeta S.A, Barcelona, in 2016—Title page verso.

Translated from the Spanish

Garcia, Cristina

The **Aguero** sisters. Cristina Garcia. A. A. Knopf, 1997. 299 p.
ISBN 9780679450900
1. Businesspeople 2. Cuban American women 3. Families 4. Family secrets 5. Rembrandt Harmenszoon van Rijn 6. Cuba 7. Florida 8. Family sagas
LC 9652204
ALA Notable Book, 1998; New York Times Notable Book, 1997

Explores the complexities of Cuban-American family life in the story of two middle-aged Cuban sisters—one living in Havana, one in New York City—who have been estranged for more than thirty years.

"Unmoored by the reverberating effects of the revolution, Garcia's characters search for stability and meaning in a world where fatalism is their only belief. They all endure 'the fidelity of certain, unshakable pain,' but sudden insights illuminate their different routes to salvation." —*Publishers Weekly*

Dreaming in Cuban. By Cristina Garcia. A. A. Knopf, 1992. 245 pages
ISBN 9780345381439
1. Cuban American women 2. Cubans 3. Home (Concept) 4. Voodoo 5. Black magic 6. Cuba 7. Brooklyn, New York City 8. Relationship fiction
LC 91020755
National Book Award for Fiction finalist, 1992

A vivid and funny first novel about three generations of a Cuban family divided by conflicting loyalties over the Cuban revolution, set in the world of Havana in the 1970s and '80s and in an emigre neighborhood of Brooklyn. It is a story of immense charmabout women and politics, women and witchcraft, women and their men.

"While taking very seriously those ideas that have truly riven so many families in recent years, leaving many obsessed with the politics of Cuba, Ms. Garcia also portrays the costliness of such an obsession and the fading of the light between mothers and daughters, between lovers, as communication fails." —*New York Times Book Review*

Spanish translation published 1993 under title: Sonar en Cubano.

King of Cuba: a novel. Cristina Garcia. Scribner, 2013. 256 p.
ISBN 9781476710242
1. Dictators 2. Cubans in the United States 3. Senior men 4. Revolutions 5. Revenge 6. Havana, Cuba 7. Miami, Florida 8. Political fiction 9. Multiple perspectives
LC 2012037553
A tale told from the alternating viewpoints of an aging Castro-like dictator and a Miami exile obsessed with avenging himself against the dictator for personal betrayals traces the impact of a six-decade revolution on their lives and a homeland that has paid the price of constant violence.

The **Lady** Matador's hotel: a novel. Cristina Garcia. Scribner 2010. 224 p.
ISBN 9781439181744
1. Hotels 2. Unhappiness 3. Political science 4. Revenge 5. Desire 6. Latin America 7. Political fiction
A novel about the intertwining lives of the denizens of a hotel in an unnamed Latin American country in the midst of political turmoil.

"Garcia has created a half-magical world in which blood runs close to the surface and flesh is transitory, opening the door to the big questions of existence: Who am I, and what is my purpose in life? The answers she offers—such as they are—come with a sly wit and strong visual style that explodes with color and life." —*Miami Herald*

Garcia, Gabriela

Of women and salt. Gabriela Garcia. Flatiron Books, 2021. 176 pages
ISBN 9781250776686
1. Cuban American women 2. Mothers and daughters 3. Immigrants 4. Family relationships 5. Family secrets 6. Miami, Florida 7. Cuba 8. 2010s 9. 1860s 10. Family sagas 11. Multiple perspectives
LC 2020047459
A sweeping, masterful debut about a daughter's fateful choice, a mother motivated by her own past, and a family legacy that begins in Cuba before either of them were born.
"Garcia's dexterous debut chronicles the travails of a Cuban immigrant family.... This riveting account will please readers of sweeping multigenerational stories." —*Publishers Weekly*

Garcia-Roza, L. A.

Alone in the crowd: an Inspector Espinosa mystery. Luiz Alfredo Garcia-Roza; translated from the Portuguese by Benjamin Moser. Henry Holt and Co, 2009. 240 p. (Inspector Espinosa mysteries, 7)
ISBN 9780805079593
1. Fatal traffic accidents 2. Criminal psychology 3. Loners 4. Detectives 5. Espinosa, Inspector (Fictitious character) 6. Rio de Janeiro, Brazil 7. Mysteries 8. Hardboiled fiction 9. Translations
LC 2008050135
After leaving the precinct in Copacabana without speaking to the chief, Dona Laureta is killed when she is hit by a bus two hours later, leading veteran police chief inspector Espinosa to investigate the strange accident and the woman's personal connection to a new suspect involved in an old murder.
Originally published as Na Multidao: Sao Paulo : Companhia das Letras, 2007.
Translated from the Portuguese.

December heat. Luiz Alfredo Garcia-Rosa; translated from the Portuguese by Benjamin Moser. H. Holt, 2003. 288p. (Inspector Espinosa mysteries, 2)
ISBN 9780805068900
1. Espinosa, Inspector (Fictitious character) 2. Police 3. Detectives 4. Former police 5. Prostitutes 6. Rio de Janeiro, Brazil 7. Mysteries 8. Hardboiled fiction 9. Translations
LC 2002038825
Library Journal Best Books, 2003
Inspector Espinosa agrees to take on the case of an old friend and retired police officer, who awoke one morning to find his prostitute girlfriend murdered, his wallet and keys missing, and no memory of the previous night's occurrences.
"An exciting procedural, infused with exotic ambience, sympathetic detectives, and a little romance." —*Library Journal*

Gardam, Jane

The **flight** of the maidens. Jane Gardam. Carroll & Graf, 2001. 278 p.
ISBN 9780786708796
1. Young women 2. Life change events 3. Yorkshire, England 4. England 5. 1940s 6. Coming-of-age stories 7. Adult books for young adults

New York Times Notable Book, 2001
Follows three unforgettable Yorkshire women—independent Hetty Fallowes, rebellious Una Vane, and Jewish refugee Liselotte Klein—as they prepare for their departure for university in Cambridge and London in 1946.
"Gardam has thrown out the usual too-sensitive-for-you boilerplate of the coming-of-age novel, for which we can be thankful. Luckily, the generational conflict that remains is usually all the better for her wry indirection." —*New York Times Book Review*
Originally published: London : Chatto & Windus, 2000.

God on the rocks. Jane Gardam. Europa Editions, 2010. 195 p.
ISBN 9781933372761
1. Children of rich people 2. Conflict in families 3. Child neglect 4. Gifted girls 5. Family relationships 6. England 7. 1930s 8. Coming-of-age stories
Shortlisted for the Booker-McConnell Prize, 1978
To escape her religious father and bitter mother, Margaret Marsh roams the meadows and beaches of coastal England, where she meets childhood friends of her mother that expose her to a side of her mother Margaret has never known.
"This novel dexterously exposes the misapprehensions wrought by class, sex, love, and religion among the members of two families in a seaside town in the north of England during the interwar years. Gardam has been compared to Anita Brookner, but her view, though equally dark, is far less dreary. Few can present tragedy with such humor." —*The Atlantic*
Originally published: London : H. Hamilton, 1978.

Last friends. Jane Gardam. Europa Editions, 2013. 304 p. (Old Filth trilogy, 3)
ISBN 9781609450939
1. Reminiscing in old age 2. Lawyers 3. Social classes 4. Trials 5. Competition 6. England 7. Psychological fiction 8. Literary fiction
The marriage of Edward Feathers and Betty as seen through the eyes of Edwards friend and Betty's lover Terry Veneering.
Originally published: London: Little, Brown, 2013.

Old Filth. Jane Gardam. Europa, 2006. 289 p. (Old Filth trilogy, 1)
ISBN 9781933372136
1. Lawyers 2. Reminiscing in old age 3. Personal conduct 4. Boy orphans 5. Seniors 6. London, England 7. Great Britain 8. Psychological fiction 9. Literary fiction
New York Times Notable Book, 2006; Shortlisted for The Orange Prize for Fiction, 2005
FILTH is a lawyer with a practice in the Far East. A few remember that his nickname stands for Failed In London Try Hong Kong. But Old Filth is not as pompous as people imagine, and his past contains many secrets and dark hiding places. —Publisher.
"Gardam's prose is so economical that no moment she describes is either gratuitous or wasted." —*The New Yorker*

The **people** on Privilege Hill and other stories. Jane Gardam. Europa Editions, 2008. 196 p.
ISBN 9781933372525
1. Manners and customs 2. England 3. Short stories
"The 14 stories in Gardam's marvelously titled new collection, The People on Privilege Hill, focus to a large extent on members of her generation (she was born July 11, 1928, soon to turn 80) or that of her parents. These generally feisty individuals recall sometimes troubling events from their prime while they cope with the affronts of aging in a changing world. Not all the stories are winners, but even the slightest offer the pleasures of Gardam's brisk, sharp sensibility. The title story brings back the splendid character Filth from her last novel. He's approaching 90, a widower who's

retired to Dorset and misses the warm tropical rains of the Orient, where he practiced law for many years." —*Christian Science Monitor*

Originally published: London : Chatto & Windus, 2007.

Gardiner, Meg

The **dark** corners of the night. Meg Gardiner. Blackstone Pub, 2020. 352 p. (Unsub novels, 3)

ISBN 9781982627515

1. Women FBI agents 2. Criminal profilers 3. Psychic trauma 4. Family-killing 5. FBI agents 6. Los Angeles, California 7. Thrillers and suspense

Hunting a serial killer who has been murdering parents in front of their children, FBI behavioral analyst Caitlin Hendrix discovers that the killer holds a devastating secret from Caitlin's own past.

"Gardiner has mastered the art of the serial-killer saga without an ounce of fat." —*Kirkus*

The **Dirty** Secrets Club. By Meg Gardiner. Dutton, 2008. 304 p. (Jo Beckett series, 1)

ISBN 9780525950660

1. Women forensic psychiatrists 2. Suicide 3. Secrets 4. Beckett, Jo (Fictitious character) 5. Forensic sciences 6. San Francisco, California 7. California 8. Mysteries

LC 2007046757

Romantic Times Reviewers' Choice Award, 2008

In the wake of an ongoing string of high-profile murder-suicides in San Francisco, forensic psychiatrist Jo Beckett is hired by the SFPD to perform investigative autopsies and discovers a harrowing commonality among the suicide victims.

"As Beckett gets in touch with her inner Rambo, Ericksen's acid-tinged delivery suddenly works just fine." —*Publishers Weekly*

Into the black nowhere. Meg Gardiner. Dutton, 2018. 384 p. (Unsub novels, 2)

ISBN 9781101985557

1. Women FBI agents 2. Criminal profilers 3. Women murder victims 4. Serial murderers 5. Serial murder investigation 6. Texas 7. Thrillers and suspense

LC 2017045253

An FBI profiler is forced to navigate the twisted mind of a charismatic, ruthless serial killer responsible for the murders of a series of women in southern Texas, in a thriller inspired by the case of Ted Bundy.

Phantom instinct. Meg Gardiner. Dutton, 2014. 368 pages

ISBN 9780525954316

1. Lovers — Death 2. Former police 3. Investigations 4. Murderers 5. People with brain injuries 6. Los Angeles, California 7. California 8. Thrillers and suspense

LC 2013048812

Struggling to rebuild after a club shooting, bartender Harper Flynn searches for the escaped gunman with the help of L.A. Deputy Sheriff Aiden Garrison, whose injuries in the same incident left him with a rare type of perception blindness.

Unsub: a novel. Meg Gardiner. Dutton, 2017. 384 p. (Unsub novels, 1)

ISBN 9781101985526

1. Serial murderers 2. Women detectives 3. Serial murder investigation 4. Obsession 5. Revenge in women 6. San Francisco Bay Area 7. Northern California 8. Thrillers and suspense

LC 2016041608

A psychological thriller inspired by the unsolved case of the Zodiac Killer follows the efforts of a young detective who resolves to apprehend the serial murderer who destroyed her family and terrorized a city 20 years earlier.

Gardner, Lisa

Alone. Lisa Gardner. Bantam Books, 2005. 336 pages (Detective D. D. Warren novels, 1)

ISBN 9780553802535

1. Snipers 2. Police 3. Girl kidnapping victims 4. State police 5. Former convicts 6. Boston, Massachusetts 7. Thrillers and suspense 8. Psychological suspense

LC 2004057577

When Bobby Dodge, a sniper with the Massachusetts State Police SWAT team, saves a woman and her young son from her armed husband, he finds himself investigating the shooting of a man who had accused his wife of poisoning their son.

"The protagonist of this thriller is Massachusetts police sniper Bobby Dodge. He meets his match in Catherine Gagnon, who as a girl was snatched, raped and nearly murdered. Now she's the wife of erratic, rich Jimmy Gagnon and mother of perpetually ill four-year-old Nathan. When Bobby kills Jimmy during a hostage situation at the Gagnons, he does it to save Catherine and Nathan. But was it a righteous shoot, or did Catherine engineer the killing? Judge James Gagnon and his wife, Maryanne, think Bobby murdered their son out of lust for Catherine. As other people start dying, very messily, and the DA and cops come down hard on Bobby, Gardner keeps the tension high and the pace fast." —*Publishers Weekly*

★ **Before** she disappeared: a novel. Lisa Gardner. Dutton 2021. 400 p. (Frankie Elkin novels, 1)

ISBN 9781524745042

1. Cold cases (Criminal investigation) 2. Missing teenagers 3. Haskell, Katharine Wright 4. Policewomen 5. Middle-aged women 6. Boston, Massachusetts 7. Massachusetts 8. Police procedurals

LC 2020042627

Investigating the cold-case disappearance of a Haitian teen in a gritty Boston neighborhood, Frankie Elkin navigates resident and police resistance as well as the challenges of her own sobriety before risking her life to uncover the truth.

"Tense and immersive, Gardner's latest (hopefully a series starter) is a sure bet both for readers drawn to gritty gumshoe fiction and for the growing legion of true-crime podcast fans." —*Booklist*

Fear nothing: a Detective D. D. Warren Novel. Lisa Gardner. Penguin, 2014. 400 pages (Detective D. D. Warren novels, 7)

ISBN 9780525953081

1. Murder investigation 2. Women detectives 3. Vigilantes 4. Memory 5. Deception 6. Boston, Massachusetts 7. Thrillers and suspense

Seriously injured after stumbling into a crime scene she cannot remember, Boston Detective D. D. Warren learns about a second murder with the same characteristics only to discover that she is being personally targeted by the killer.

Find her. Lisa Gardner. Dutton, 2016. 402 pages (Detective D. D. Warren novels, 8)

ISBN 9780525954576

1. Missing persons investigation 2. Vigilantes 3. Murder investigation 4. Women detectives 5. Rape victims 6. Boston, Massachusetts 7. Thrillers and suspense

LC 2015038503

LibraryReads Favorites, 2016

Requesting the assistance of a survivor of an extended abduction experience who has become obsessed with the cases of girls who never made it home, Boston detective D. D. Warren becomes suspicious of the woman's agenda upon discovering her relationships with other victims.

"A gritty, complicated heroine like Flora Dane deserves a better plot than this needlessly complicated story." —*Kirkus*

★ **Look** for me: a novel. Lisa Gardner. Dutton, 2018. 400 p. (Detective D. D. Warren novels, 9)

ISBN 9781524742058

1. Family-killing 2. Missing teenage girls 3. Women vigilantes 4. Women detectives 5. Foster care 6. Boston, Massachusetts 7. Thrillers and suspense

LC 2017042389

Librarians' Choice (Australia), 2018

Detective D. D. Warren teams up with Flora Dane from Find Her in an investigation involving the sinister disappearance of a 16-year-old girl whose family has been brutally murdered.

Love you more: a Detective D.D. Warren novel. Lisa Gardner. Bantam Books, 2011. 368 pages (Detective D. D. Warren novels, 5; Tessa Leoni novels, 1)

ISBN 9780553807257

1. Murder investigation 2. Women detectives 3. Abused women 4. Family secrets 5. Missing girls 6. Boston, Massachusetts 7. Thrillers and suspense

Library Journal Best Books, 2011; Romantic Times Reviewers' Choice Award, 2011

Brian Darby lies dead on the kitchen floor. His wife, state police trooper Tessa Leoni, claims to have shot him in self-defense, and bears the bruises to back up her tale. For veteran detective D. D. Warren, it should be an open-and-shut case. But where is their six-year-old daughter? As the homicide investigation ratchets into a frantic statewide search for a missing child, D. D. Warren must partner with former lover Bobby Dodge to break the case.

"Gardner sprinkles plenty of clues and inventive twists to keep readers off-kilter as the suspense builds to a realistic, jaw-dropping finale." —*Publishers Weekly*

The **neighbor**. Lisa Gardner. Bantam Books, 2009. 373 pages; (Detective D. D. Warren novels, 3)

ISBN 9780553807233

1. Missing persons 2. Murder investigation 3. Mother-separated families 4. Husband and wife 5. Young women 6. Boston, Massachusetts 7. Thrillers and suspense 8. First person narratives 9. Multiple perspectives

Library Journal Best Books, 2009; Thriller Award for Best Novel, 2010

A young mother, blond and pretty, disappears without a trace from her South Boston home, leaving behind her four-year-old daughter as the only witness and her handsome, secretive husband as the prime suspect.

★ **Never** tell: a novel. Lisa Gardner. Dutton, 2019. 416 p. (Detective D. D. Warren novels, 10)

ISBN 9781524742089

1. Women vigilantes 2. Women detectives 3. Women murder suspects 4. Secrets 5. Murder 6. Boston, Massachusetts 7. Thrillers and suspense

LC 2018042977

While D. D. Warren investigates a pregnant woman's suspicious role in the murders of her father and husband, Flora draws on her own haunted past to identify an unsettling link to one of the victims.

★ **When** you see me: a novel. Lisa Gardner. Dutton, 2020. 400 pages

ISBN 9781524745004

1. Women FBI agents 2. Women detectives 3. Serial murderers 4. Cold cases (Criminal investigation) 5. Secrets 6. Georgia 7. Thrillers and suspense

LC 2019041316

FBI Special Agent Kimberly Quincy and Sergeant Detective DD Warren join forces with Flora Dane and true-crime savant Keith Edgar to investigate the secrets of a deceased serial killer.

"A frightening climax provides an appropriate wrap-up to the Ness saga and the story of evil flourishing in a small mountain town. This is top-notch suspense by a best-selling master of the genre." —*Booklist*

Garey, Juliann

Too bright to hear too loud to see. Juliann Garey. Soho Press, 2012. 224 p.

ISBN 9781616951290

1. Film industry and trade executives 2. Bipolar disorder 3. Self-discovery in men 4. Fathers and daughters 5. Marriage 6. 1980s 7. First person narratives 8. Mainstream fiction 9. Psychological fiction

LC 2012026028

ALA Notable Book, 2014

In a look at mental illness that weaves together three timelines, Greyson Todd leaves his successful Hollywood career and wife and young daughter to travel the world, giving free reign to the bipolar disorder he has been forced to keep hidden for almost twenty years.

Garner, Helen

The **spare** room. Helen Garner. Text Publishing Co, 2008. 195 p.

ISBN 9781921351396

1. Women with cancer 2. Death — Psychological aspects 3. Female friendship 4. Women with terminal illnesses 5. Women caregivers 6. Melbourne, Victoria 7. Literary fiction 8. First person narratives 9. Australian fiction

Queensland Premier's Literary Awards, Fiction Book Award, 2008; Victorian Premier's Literary Awards, Vance Palmer Prize for Fiction, 2008; Barbara Jefferis Award, 2009

Offering a room to an old friend who is undergoing treatment for cancer, Helen finds her advice disregarded in the face of her friend's faith in alternative medicine, a situation that turns both of their lives upside-down.

"Humour is not just an occasional relief in The Spare Room, it's actually the lifeblood of the book. The old cliche that you've got to laugh in the face of tragedy is given new meaning by Garner. For all the sickness and suffering and thankless service involved in the story, it's only an acute sense of the absurdity of the situation that keeps the heroine...sane. Garner's dealings with terminal illness are truly refreshing. Instead of focusing on the sufferer, Nicola, she delves inwards, exploring the impact on the carer. And she dares to express the unspeakable thoughts we often think when confronted by another's illness." —*PopMatters*

Garrett, Kellye

★ **Hollywood** homicide. Kellye Garrett. Midnight Ink, 2017. 312 p. (Detective by day novels, 1)

ISBN 9780738752617

1. Women amateur detectives 2. Women witnesses 3. Poor women 4. Actors and actresses 5. Murder investigation 6. Hollywood, California 7. California 8. Mysteries 9. First person narratives 10. African American fiction 11. Adult books for young adults

LC 2017007797

Agatha Award for Best First Novel, 2017; Anthony Award for Best First Novel, 2018

After witnessing a deadly hit-and-run, broke actress Dayna investigates and pursues the reward money in an effort to help her parents keep their house, but she soon finds herself wanting justice for the victim even more.

"TV writer Garrett (Cold Case) makes a smart, sassy debut, introducing an appealing protagonist with amusing friends who deliver one-liners and toss back drinks while solving the case." —*Library Journal*

Garriott, Leah

Promised. Leah Garriott. Shadow Mountain, 2020. 368 pages
ISBN 9781629726144
1. Young women 2. Nobility 3. Arranged marriage 4. Breaking up (Interpersonal relations) 5. Mate selection 6. England 7. Regency period (1811-1820) 8. Regency romances 9. Historical romances 10. Adult books for young adults
LC 2019019684

After the heartbreak and humiliation of a broken engagement, Margaret Brinton is determined to never allow her heart to be hurt again. But will her resolve hold when her father arranges for her to marry Lord Williams, a man who had once publically snubbed her, but who might be more than he appears?

"Garriott's impressive debut distinguishes itself with its expertly evoked Regency setting, a cast of realistically flawed yet eminently relatable characters, and a sweetly satisfying love story." —*Booklist*

Garvin, Eileen

The music of bees. Eileen Garvin. Dutton, 2021. 336 p.
ISBN 9780593183922
1. Strangers 2. Grief 3. Bereavement in women 4. Beekeeping 5. Farms 6. Oregon 7. Relationship fiction
LC 2020043236
LibraryReads Favorites, 2021

Three strangers navigating grief and devastating setbacks cross paths in a rural Oregon town, where they find unexpected friendship, healing and new chances on local honeybee farm.

"Both buoyant and bittersweet, Garvin's impressive first novel, a luscious paean to the bonds of friendship and limitations of family, is the kind of comforting yet thought-provoking tale that will appeal to fans of Anne Tyler and Sue Miller." —*Booklist*

Garwood, Julie

The bride. Julie Garwood. Pocket Books, 1989. 358 p; (MacAlister family, 1)
ISBN 9780671737795
1. Widowers 2. Arranged marriage 3. Man-woman relationships 4. Nobility 5. Sexuality 6. England 7. Medieval period (476-1492) 8. Medieval romances 9. Highland romances 10. Historical romances
Scottish laird Alec Kincaid—in his quest for an English bride—weds Jamie Jamison, and thus begins their long and heated battle of wills and the passion to which they eventually succumb.

Wired. Julie Garwood. Berkley, 2017. 336 p. (Buchanan novels (Julie Garwood), 13)
ISBN 9780525954460
1. Technology 2. Protectiveness in men 3. Computer programmers 4. Siblings 5. Man-woman relationships 6. Boston, Massachusetts 7. Romantic suspense
LibraryReads Favorites, 2017

A beautiful computer hacker and a bad-boy FBI agent must collaborate—in more ways than one—in the sizzling new novel from #1 New York Timesbestselling author Julie Garwood. Allison Trent doesn't look like a hacker. In fact, when she's not in college working on her degree, she models on the side. But behind her gorgeous face is a brilliant mind for computers and her real love is writing—and hacking—code. Her dream is to write a new security program that could revolutionize the tech industry. Hotshot FBI agent Liam Scott has a problem: a leak deep within his own department. He needs the skills of a top-notch hacker to work on a highly sensitive project: to secretly break into the FBI servers and find out who the traitor is. But he can't use one of his own. He finds the perfect candidate in Allison. Only, there's one problem—she wants nothing to do with his job and turns him down flat. What Liam doesn't know is that Allison is hiding secrets that she doesn't want the FBI to uncover. But Liam will do nearly anything to persuade her to join his team, even break a few rules if that's what it takes. A temptation that could put his job—and both of their futures—on the line.

"Engaging and easily relatable characters and a compelling plot that seems to have been ripped from todays headlines." —*Booklist*

Gaskell, Elizabeth Cleghorn

★ **Cranford**. Elizabeth Gaskell; edited with an introduction by Elizabeth Porges Watson. Oxford University Press, 1972. Xix, 200 p.
ISBN 9780192553515
1. Rural life 2. Women — History 3. Sisters 4. England 5. Literary fiction 6. Classics 7. Books to TV

A comic portrait of early Victorian life in a country town which describes with poignant wit the uneventful lives of its lady-like inhabitants, offering an ironic commentary on the separate spheres and diverse experiences of men and women.
Originally serialized in Household Words, 1851-1853.
Adapted into three separate British television series.

★ **North** and South. Elizabeth Gaskell; edited by Angus Easson; with an introduction by Sally Shuttleworth. Oxford University Press, 1998. Xlii, 452 p.
ISBN 9780192831941
1. Factories 2. Young women 3. Class conflict 4. Manners and customs 5. Factory owners 6. England 7. Literary fiction 8. Love stories 9. Books to TV

Moving from the industrial riots of discontented millworkers through to the unsought passions of a middle-class woman, and from religious crises of conscience to the ethics of naval mutiny, the novel poses fundamental questions about the nature of social authority and obedience. Through the story of Margaret Hale, the middle-class southerner who moves to the northern industrial town of Milton, Gaskell skilfully explores issues of class and gender in the conflict between Margaret's ready sympathy with the workers and her growing attraction to the charismatic mill owner, John Thornton.
Originally serialized in Household Words, 1854-1855.

Gaspar de Alba, Alicia

Desert blood: the Juarez murders. By Alicia Gaspar de Alba. Arte Publico Press, 2005. 352 p.
ISBN 9781558854468
1. Women amateur detectives 2. Women college teachers 3. Lesbians 4. Americans in Mexico 5. Serial murders 6. Mexican-American Border Region 7. El Paso, Texas 8. Mysteries 9. LGBTQIA fiction
LC 2004055417
Lambda Literary Award for Lesbian Mystery, 2005; Library Journal Best Books, 2005

Ivon Villa, a women's studies professor who travels to Mexico to arrange for an adoption of a baby for herself and her female lover, discovers the pregnant mother has been murdered, an apparent victim of a serial killer, and vows to find the person responsible for the killings.

Gass, William H.

Middle C. William H. Gass. Alfred A. Knopf, 2013. 352 p.
ISBN 9780307701633
1. Deception 2. Human nature 3. College teachers 4. False personation 5. Mediocrity 6. Middle West 7. Historical fiction 8. Black humor

Investigates the multifaceted nature of human identity and follows the experiences of Joseph, who flees Austria in 1938 and pretends to be Jewish before disappearing from London under mysterious circumstances.

A Borzoi book.

Gates, Eva

Deadly ever after. Eva Gates. Crooked Lane Books, 2021. 304 p. (Lighthouse library mysteries, 8)

ISBN 9781643855882

1. Small towns 2. Coastal towns 3. Murder investigation 4. Cat/dog relations 5. Librarians 6. North Carolina 7. Outer Banks, North Carolina 8. Cozy mysteries 9. Gentle reads 10. First person narratives

When her engagement celebration is marred by murder, librarian Lucy Richardson must once against don her detective's hat to save both her family and her impending nuptials, while chaos ensues at Lighthouse Library between Charles the library cat and a dog named Fluffy.

"Plenty of unexpected plot twists and characters the reader can really care about help make this cozy a winner. Gates (a pen name of Vicki Delany) consistently entertains." —*Publishers Weekly*

A **death** long overdue. Eva Gates. Crooked Lane Books, 2020. 372 p. (Lighthouse library mysteries, 7)

ISBN 9781643854588

1. Librarians 2. College friends 3. Reunions 4. Exhibitions 5. Women murder victims 6. North Carolina 7. Outer Banks, North Carolina 8. Cozy mysteries 9. Gentle reads 10. First person narratives

Bertie James's college class is having their 40th anniversary reunion on the Outer Banks of North Carolina. The opening reception is held at the Lighthouse Library. Some of the women walk down to the pier afterwards, using flashlights to illuminate the dark path, when they find the former library director floating lifeless in the water. Helena Sanchez, the former director, wasn't much loved. Lucy finds herself in deep water as she questions several suspects. But she'll have to batten down the hatches and fast before she's left high and dry... and right in the killer's crosshairs.

"Lucy and her clever cat, Charles, form an amusing sleuthing team, and the lively and endearing supporting characters add to the fun. Cozy queen Gates (a pen name of Vicki Delany) is at the top of her game." —*Publishers Weekly*

Read and buried. Eva Gates. Crooked Lane Books, 2019. N/A (Lighthouse library mysteries, 6)

ISBN 9781643852331

1. Women amateur detectives 2. Librarians 3. Maps 4. Treasure hunting 5. Murder 6. Outer Banks, North Carolina 7. North Carolina 8. Cozy mysteries 9. Gentle reads 10. First person narratives

Librarian Lucy Richardson unearths a mysterious map dating back to the Civil War. But if she can't crack its code, she may end up read and buried.

Gay, Roxane

★ **Ayiti**. Roxane Gay. Grove Press, 2018. 320 p.

ISBN 9780802128263

1. African diaspora 2. Immigrants 3. Interpersonal relations 4. Ethnic identity 5. Culture conflict 6. Haber, Fritz 7. United States 8. Literary fiction 9. African American fiction 10. Short stories

Released for the first time to mainstream readers, a debut story collection by the award-winning author of An Untamed State is a poignant exploration of the Haitian diaspora experience and is complemented by several new stories.

Originally published: New York : Artistically declined press, 2011.

★ **Difficult** women. Roxane Gay. Grove Press, 2017. 272 p.

ISBN 9780802125392

1. Independence in women 2. Women — Psychology 3. Women — Interpersonal relations 4. Short stories 5. Literary fiction

BCALA Literary Award for Fiction, 2018

Telling the stories of strong, imperfect, fully realized women, award-winning author Roxane Gay offers diverse protagonists and settings and unusual, often troubling situations in which women are haunted by pain and loss. In "The Mark of Cain," a woman pretends not to know that her abusive husband and his gentler identical twin have switched places; women participate in fight clubs in another story, while a priest refuses to feel bad about an affair in a third. With complex characters and straightforward writing, this collection stands out.

"Whether focusing on assault survivors, single mothers, or women who drown their guilt in wine and bad boyfriends, Gay's fantastic collection is challenging, quirky, and memorable." —*Publishers Weekly*

★ An **untamed** state. Roxane Gay. Black Cat, 2014. 368 p.

ISBN 9780802122513

1. Kidnapping 2. Ransom 3. Women kidnapping victims 4. Rape 5. Mental illness 6. Haiti 7. Literary fiction

Library Journal Best Books 2014

A novel about a woman kidnapped for ransom, her captivity as her father refuses to pay and her husband fights for her release over thirteen days, and her struggle to come to terms with the ordeal in its aftermath.

"Among the strongest achievements of this novel is that Mireille's story feels complete and whole while emphasizing its essential brokenness. A cutting and resonant debut." —*Kirkus*

Gaylin, Alison

Never look back. Alison Gaylin. William Morrow & Co, 2019. 384 pages

ISBN 9780062884350

1. Teenage murderers 2. Podcasts 3. Amateur detectives 4. Families of murder victims 5. Murder investigation 6. Psychological suspense 7. Multiple perspectives

More than four decades after a 1976 killing spree by two teens, a young podcaster blames his troubled upbringing on the murders before receiving a terrifying message that one of the killers may still be alive.

"A mind-bending mystery, an insightful exploration of parent-child relationships, and a cautionary tale about bitterness and blame." —*Kirkus*

Gaynor, Hazel

The **lighthouse** keeper's daughter. Hazel Gaynor. HarperCollins 2018. 384 p.

ISBN 9780062869302

1. Hurricanes 2. Lighthouses 3. Teenage girls 4. Search and rescue operations 5. Lighthouse keepers 6. Northumberland, England 7. Newport, Rhode Island 8. 1930s 9. 1830s 10. Historical fiction 11. Parallel narratives 12. Adult books for young adults

Pregnant and disgraced, a 1938 Irish teen is sent to stay with a lighthouse keeper relative, where she discovers an unfinished portrait and delves into the story of a woman who lived there a hundred years prior.

Meet me in Monaco: a novel. Hazel Gaynor and Heather Webb. William Morrow, 2019. 384 pages

ISBN 9780062913548

1. Grace 2. Film actors and actresses 3. Friendship 4. Second chances 5. Paparazzi 6. Perfumes industry and trade 7. Monaco 8. France 9. 1950s 10. Historical fiction 11. Love stories

LC 2018059053

A struggling perfumer who has forged an unlikely friendship with Grace Kelly against a backdrop of the latter's high-profile wedding considers what she is prepared to sacrifice when she falls in love with a British press photographer.

Three words for goodbye. . William Morrow & Co, 2021. 384 p.
ISBN 9780063082335
1. Sisters 2. Voyages and travels 3. Sibling rivalry 4. Family secrets 5. Letters 6. Europe 7. Paris, France 8. Between the Wars (1918-1939) 9. 1930s 10. Historical fiction

Estranged sisters Clara and Madeleine Sommers reunite to honor their grandmother's dying wish—to travel across Europe together and deliver three farewell letters, a journey during which they are constantly at odds with each other until a shocking family secret brings them closer than ever before.

"As the sisters learn to embrace the unexpected, from a hot-air-balloon ride to the men they meet on their travels, they grapple with their own futures as they learn more about their grandmother's past. Charming historical fiction." —*Booklist*

Gelernter, J. H.

Hold fast. J. H. Gelernter. W.W. Norton & Company, 2021. 242 p.
ISBN 9780393867046
1. Intelligence service 2. Napoleonic Wars, 1800-1815 3. Former spies 4. Widowers 5. Transatlantic voyages 6. Great Britain 7. Malta 8. Georgian era (1714-1837) 9. 1800s (Decade) 10. Spy fiction 11. Sea stories 12. Historical fiction
LC 2020052181

The year is 1803, and the British Secret Service is contending with a belligerent France under Napoleon. The service suffers a blow in the loss of a prime agent, Thomas Grey, who—despondent at his wife's untimely death—resigns from British Intelligence and departs England for Boston, where he intends to become a lumber merchant. His plan to start a new life is thrown abruptly off course when a French intelligence network attempts to recruit him as an informer, and, in the process, exposes a grave new threat to Britain that Grey can't ignore. Confronting it seems likely to grant the grief-stricken widower a chance of extracting a personal revenge.

"Gelernter's first novel is a pleasing romp through James Bond territory, set back a century and several decades and moved to Napoleonic France." —*Library Journal*

Gelman, Laurie

Class mom: a novel. Laurie Gelman. Henry Holt & Company, 2017. 290 pages; (Class Mom, 1)
ISBN 9781250124692
1. Middle-aged women 2. Kindergarten 3. Parenting 4. Mothers 5. Competition 6. Kansas City, Missouri 7. Missouri 8. Domestic fiction 9. Relationship fiction
LC 2016052495

Loan Stars Favourites, 2017

Frowned upon by conservative fellow PTA members for her past as a single parent, Jen reluctantly agrees to become class mom during her youngest child's kindergarten year, a role that is challenged by parent drama, hypersensitive allergies and a former flame.

"Gelman pens an uproariously funny first novel with a relatable protagonist. Moms will clamor for this story, trying to hold back tears of laughter as Jen establishes her voice and place as the class mom." —*Library Journal*

Yoga pant nation: a novel. Laurie Gelman. Henry Holt and Company, 2021. 288 p. (Class Mom, 3)

ISBN 9781250777577
1. Middle-aged women 2. Parenting 3. Mothers and sons 4. Elementary schools 5. Mother and adult daughter 6. Missouri 7. Relationship fiction
LC 2020052631

The hilarious, irreverent Jen Dixon is class mom-again-for her son's fifth grade year, and a class bully, spin-teacher training, and her irresistible granddaughter keep her on her toes and perpetually in yoga pants.

"Jen's struggles will be amusingly familiar to many women living in the sandwich generation, and fans of previous books in the series will be delighted to follow along with this latest outing of the mom who says the things they wish they could." —*Booklist*

You've been volunteered: a class mom novel. By Laurie Gelman. Henry Holt & Co, 2019. 304 pages (Class Mom, 2)
ISBN 9781250301857
1. Middle-aged women 2. Third graders 3. Parenting 4. Mothers and sons 5. Mother and adult daughter 6. Missouri 7. Kansas City, Missouri 8. Relationship fiction
LC 2018050182

A follow-up to Class Mom finds Jen Dixon agreeing to school-parent her son's third-grade class only to find herself overwhelmed by her husband's late hours, her daughters' early adulthood and the needs of her aging parents.

"The tone and pacing are excellent, and new characters, who come with their own issues and snark, are delightful." —*Library Journal*

Gendry-Kim, Keum Suk

★ The **waiting**. Keum Suk Gendry-Kim; Janet Hong. Drawn & Quarterly, 2021. 480 p.
ISBN 9781770464575
1. Riccio, David 2. Separated friends, relatives, etc. 3. War and society 4. Women authors 5. Senior women 6. Korea 7. 1940s 8. Historical comics 9. Comics and Graphic novels 10. Translations

The Waiting is the fictional story of Gwija, told by her novelist daughter Jina. When Gwija was 17 years old, after hearing that the Japanese were seizing unmarried girls, her family married her in a hurry to a man she didn't know. Japan fell, Korea gained its independence, and the couple started a family. But peace didn't come. The young family of four fled south. On the road, while breastfeeding and changing her daughter, Gwija was separated from her husband and son. Then seventy years passed. Seventy years of waiting. Gwija is now an elderly woman and Jina can't stop thinking about the promise she made to help find her brother.

"Gendry-Kim's masterful black-and-white drawings and innovative layouts convey an uncanny sense of longing in this unforgettable account of the Korean War's lasting impact." —*Library Journal*

Translation of: Kidarim.
Translated from the Korean.

Geni, Abby

The **lightkeepers**: a novel. Abby Geni. Counterpoint, 2016. 375 p.
ISBN 9781619026001
1. Women photographers 2. Social isolation 3. Wildlife refuges 4. Interpersonal relations 5. Islands 6. Mysteries
LC 2015037125

Traveling to a dangerous archipelago off the coast of California for a one-year residency, photographer Miranda is assaulted by a local who is later found dead, an event that leaves Miranda speculating about the region's wild beauty and the natures of her companions.

"As the plot turns violent and suspenseful, and the mesmerizingly vivid descriptions reach shivery crescendos of shocking revelations, Geni dramatically meshe's the grand, menacing power of the ruthless wild with the mysteries and aberrations of the equally untamed human psyche." —*Booklist*

The wildlands: a novel. Abby Geni. Counterpoint, 2018. 288 p.
ISBN 9781619022348
1. Orphans 2. Domestic terrorism 3. Animal rights advocates 4. Siblings 5. Animal rights 6. Oklahoma 7. Literary fiction 8. Multiple perspectives

LC 2018008262

Losing her home and parents to a tornado, a young girl becomes her radical older brother's unwitting accomplice as he declares war on humanity and engages in acts of increasing violence.

Genova, Lisa

Every note played. Lisa Genova. Gallery Books, 2018. 307 p.
ISBN 9781476717807
1. Pianists 2. Reconciliation 3. Amyotrophic lateral sclerosis — Patients 4. Nervous system — Degeneration 5. Degeneration (Pathology) 6. Mainstream fiction

LibraryReads Favorites, 2018; Librarians' Choice (Australia), 2018

A once-celebrated concert pianist who is gradually succumbing to ALS is forced to accept help from the estranged wife he pushed away, a situation that forces the couple to reconcile their past before time runs out.

Inside the O'Briens: a novel. Lisa Genova. Gallery Books, 2015. 320 p.
ISBN 9781476717777
1. People with terminal illnesses — Family relationships 2. Life change events 3. Parent and adult child 4. People with Huntington's disease 5. Children of people with terminal illnesses 6. Massachusetts 7. Domestic fiction 8. Multiple perspectives

LC 2014034832

LibraryReads Favorites, 2015; Library Journal Best Books, 2015

When a beloved Irish Catholic police officer is diagnosed with Huntington's Disease, his grown children witness their father's demise and consider whether they want to be tested to see if they have inherited the condition.

Left neglected: a novel. Lisa Genova. Gallery Books, 2011. 320 p.
ISBN 9781439164631
1. Life change events 2. Self-fulfillment in women 3. Women with brain injuries 4. Caretakers 5. Convalescence 6. Massachusetts 7. Mainstream fiction 8. First person narratives

LC 2010025568

Presents the story of a woman in her thirties who suffers a traumatic brain injury in a car accident that leaves her unable to perceive left-side information, a disability that prompts her struggle to recover and heal an estrangement.

"Some readers will likely find a few of the plot elements a bit too neat.... Despite these contrivances, Left Neglected is a novel worth reading for the way it informs a little-known medical condition, as well as the engaging story of a character who transcends what could have been a tragedy to find a fresh appreciation for life." —*Boston Globe*

Gentill, Sulari

Crossing the lines. Sulari Gentill. Poisoned Pen Press, 2017. 268 p.
ISBN 9781464209147
1. Women authors 2. Characters and characteristics in literature 3. Creation (Literary, artistic, etc.) 4. Married people 5. Authors 6. Experimental fiction 7. Psychological fiction

Ned Kelly Award for Best Novel, 2018; Librarians' Choice (Australia), 2017

A successful writer, Madeleine, creates a character, Edward, and begins to imagine his life. As Madeline engages more with Edward, he begins to engage back. A crisis comes when Madeleine chooses the killer in Edward's story and her husband begins to question her immersion in her novel.

"This mystery won the 2018 Ned Kelly Award under the title Crossing the Lines. Now available in the United States, it's a twisted masterpiece about writing and the loss of identity while writing." —*Library Journal*

Reprinted as "After She Wrote Him" in 2020 by Poisoned Pen Press.

Gentry, Amy

Last woman standing. Amy Gentry. 2019. 288 p.
ISBN 9780544962538
1. Betrayal 2. Revenge in women 3. Sexual harassment 4. Computer programmers 5. Sexism in employment 6. Thrillers and suspense

LC 2018017517

Prompted by sexual harassment and assaults to exact revenge, an aspiring comedienne and her tough computer-programmer friend engage in an escalating series of betrayals that trigger unexpected consequences.

George, Alex

The Paris hours: a novel. Alex George. St Martins Pr 2020. 272 p.
ISBN 9781250307187
1. Loss (Psychology) 2. Loneliness 3. Secrets 4. Household employees 5. Refugees 6. Paris, France 7. France 8. Between the Wars (1918-1939) 9. Historical fiction

LC 2019054653

Four individuals share an extraordinary day in Paris between the wars, including a maid in possession of a lone surviving Marcel Proust manuscript and a lovesick artist who would repay an impossible debt through a partnership with Gertrude Stein.

"George has captured the ethos of 1920s Paris with a feel similar to Anthony Doerr's All the Light We Cannot See. This title is not to be missed." —*Library Journal*

George, Elizabeth

A banquet of consequences. Elizabeth George. Viking, 2015. 736 p. (Thomas Lynley mysteries, 19)
ISBN 9780525954330
1. Criminal investigation 2. Detectives 3. Police 4. Lynley, Thomas (Fictitious character) 5. Havers, Barbara (Fictitious character) 6. London, England 7. England 8. Mysteries 9. Police procedurals

LibraryReads Favorites, 2015

As Inspector Thomas Lynley investigates the London angle of an ever more darkly disturbing case, his partner, Barbara Havers, is looking behind the peaceful façade of country life to discover a twisted world of desire, deceit, and murder. The suicide of William Goldacre is devastating to those left behind. But what was the cause of his tragedy and how far might the consequences reach? Is there a link between the young man's leap from a Dorset cliff and a horrific poisoning in Cambridge? After various career-threatening issues with her department, Barbara Havers is desperate to redeem herself. So when a past encounter with a bestselling feminist writer and her pushy personal assistant gives her a connection to the Cambridge murder, Barbara begs Thomas Lynley to let her pursue the crime.

"This nineteenth Lynley novel is a sterling addition to George's acclaimed character-centered series: even the most minor characters are full-bodied...." —*Booklist*

Believing the lie. Elizabeth George. Dutton, 2012. 624 p. (Thomas Lynley mysteries, 17)

ISBN 9780525952589

1. Undercover operations 2. Murder investigation 3. Family secrets 4. Drowning 5. Recovering drug abusers 6. London, England 7. England 8. Mysteries 9. Police procedurals

In this novel Inspector Thomas Lynley is mystified when he's sent undercover to investigate the death of Ian Cresswell at the request of the man's uncle, the wealthy and influential Bernard Fairclough. The death has been ruled an accidental drowning, and nothing on the surface indicates otherwise. But when Lynley enlists the help of his friends Simon and Deborah St. James, the trio's digging soon reveals that the Fairclough clan is awash in secrets, lies, and motives. Deborah's investigation of the prime suspect, Bernard's prodigal son Nicholas, a recovering drug addict, leads her to Nicholas' wife, a woman with whom she feels a kinship, a woman as fiercely protective as she is beautiful. Lynley and Simon delve for information from the rest of the family, including the victim's bitter ex-wife and the man he left her for, and Bernard himself. As the investigation escalates, the Fairclough family's veneer cracks, with deception and self-delusion threatening to destroy everyone from the Fairclough patriarch to Tim, the troubled son Ian left behind.

"Although an American, George stands shoulder to shoulder with P. D. James and Ruth Rendell as a grande dame of the British mystery. The ongoing success of the Lynley mysteries on PBS continues to bring in new fans." —*Booklist*

Careless in red. Elizabeth George. Harper Collins Publishers, 2008. 640 p. (Thomas Lynley mysteries, 15)

ISBN 9780061160875

1. Murder investigation 2. Murder suspects 3. Police 4. Women detectives 5. Loss (Psychology) 6. Cornwall, England 7. England 8. Mysteries 9. Police procedurals

LC 2007044629

Scotland Yard's Thomas Lynley discovers the body of a young man who appears to have fallen to his death. The closest town, better known for its tourists and its surfing than its intrigue, seems an unlikely place for murder. However, it soon becomes apparent that a clever killer is indeed at work, and this time Lynley is not a detective but a witness and possibly a suspect.

"As with George's other books, the reader is soon plunged into a vast back story of relationships and psychologically complex characters. It's a level of literary sophistication readers have come to expect from George." —*Seattle Times*

Just one evil act. Elizabeth George. Dutton, 2013. 736 p. (Thomas Lynley mysteries, 18)

ISBN 9780525952961

1. Child kidnapping victims 2. Kidnapping investigation 3. British in Italy 4. Policewomen 5. Parents' rights 6. London, England 7. England 8. Mysteries 9. Police procedurals

Supporting a friend who has lost custody of his young daughter, Barbara and her partner, Inspector Thomas Lynley, are further shocked when the girl's mother reports that the child has been kidnapped from an Italian marketplace as part of a complex plot that risks Barbara's career.

The **punishment** she deserves. Elizabeth George. Viking, 2018. 692 p. (Thomas Lynley mysteries, 20)

ISBN 9780525954347

1. Police 2. Women detectives 3. Suicide investigation 4. Politicians 5. Murder investigation 6. London, England 7. England 8. Mysteries 9. Police procedurals

Loan Stars Favourites, 2018

Inspector Thomas Lynley of Scotland Yard and the pugnacious but loyal detective sergeant Barbara Havers tackle one of the most sinister murder cases they have ever encountered.

This body of death: an Inspector Lynley novel. Elizabeth George. HarperCollins, 2010. 692 p. (Thomas Lynley mysteries, 16)

ISBN 9780061160882

1. Murder investigation 2. Crimes against women 3. Police 4. Women detectives 5. Murder suspects 6. London, England 7. England 8. Mysteries 9. Police procedurals

LC 2009035547

After a woman is found dead in an isolated cemetery, Inspector Thomas Lynley and his former partner, Barbara Havers, find that the roots of the crime trace to a long-ago act of violence that has poisoned subsequent generations.

"As always, [George's] story is credible and commanding, and her characters—particularly Lynley and Havers—continue to evolve while remaining the reader's old and dear friends. George's perceptive characterizations find a worthy complement in her descriptive powers, which evoke a strong sense of place.... A book for neither the faint of heart nor the short of patience, This Body of Death is a rich, unsettling work, one whose darkness is lightened by Lynley's steady emergence from grief." —*Richmond Times-Dispatch*

What came before he shot her. Elizabeth George. Harper Collins, 2006. 560 p. (Thomas Lynley mysteries, 14)

ISBN 9780060545628

1. Boy murderers 2. Drug traffic 3. Revenge 4. Dysfunctional families 5. Protectiveness in children 6. London, England 7. England 8. Mysteries 9. Police procedurals 10. Adult books for young adults

LC 2006043520

In North Kensington three orphaned mixed-race children are bounced from one home to another. The middle child Joel takes care of the youngest, Toby, who isn't quite right. When a local gang threatens Toby, Joel makes a pact with the devil that ends in the murder of Thomas Lynley's wife.

"This is crime writing at its finest, with an almost painfully sharp view of the world and evil." —*Rocky Mountain News*

Novel tells of the events prior to the murder of Thomas Lynley's wife. Thomas Lynley and Barbara Havers do not appear in this book.

George, Margaret

The **confessions** of young Nero. Margaret George. Berkley Books, 2017. 528 p. (Nero novels, 1)

ISBN 9780451473387

1. Nero 2. Rulers 3. Inheritance and succession 4. Political intrigue 5. Mothers and sons 6. Ambition in women 7. Rome 8. Roman Empire (27 BCE-476 CE) 9. Historical fiction 10. Biographical fiction

LC 2016024945

Loan Stars Favourites, 2017; RUSA Reading List Short List, 2018

Lucius Domitius Ahenobarbus was born to rule. At least, that's what his mother Agrippina (a woman with a penchant for poisoning her husbands) believes. An intelligent, sensitive boy who loves music and chariot races, Lucius can only be an improvement over his uncle, Caligula. Even as he benefits from Agrippina's scheming, Lucius strives to break free of his family's influence; by age 16, he's Emperor Nero. However, he quickly discovers that staying in power requires a certain amount of ruthlessness. This unusual coming-of-age story imagines the life of a notorious ruler.

"Highly acclaimed for the detail and personality she gives to epic subjects, George's heavily researched novel flows dynamically among multiple points of view." —*Library Journal*

Elizabeth I: a novel. Margaret George. Viking, 2011. 688 p.
ISBN 9780670022533
1. Elizabeth I, Queen of England, 1533-1603 2. Women rulers 3. Courts and courtiers 4. Cousins 5. Man-woman relationships 6. Great Britain 7. Elizabethan era (1558-1603) 8. 16th century 9. Historical fiction 10. Biographical fiction 11. First person narratives

LC 2010035382

Growing up at the side of her cousin, Elizabeth I, Lettice Knollys struggles to regain power and position for her family while competing against the queen for the love of Robert Dudley, a rivalry that is set against a backdrop of the flourishing Elizabethan age.

"Set in the final 20 years of Elizabeth's reign, George's novel is the portrait of an aging powerful woman, one who struggles at times with her waning sexual allure even as she refuses to let its loss diminish her power.... This historical novel has considerable strengths, from impressive detail and a wonderfully evocative setting to dialogue that feels appropriately old without ever veering into hokeyness. George brings the queen's two major foreign-policy challenges—conflict with Spain and with Ireland—to life in a way that feels both immediate and relevant. But these achievements are at times outweighed both by the inclusion of (seemingly) everything that happened in England during the time period covered, and by the jarring choice to divide the story between two first-person narrators: Elizabeth herself, and her cousin, Lettice Knollys, who was wife to one of Elizabeth's favorite courtiers and mother to another. The two narrators slow the pace down—a problem in such a lengthy tome—and the stories don't intersect enough for a reader to gain traction.... Nevertheless, the contrast between the two narrative voices successfully illustrates two very different modes of female power: the Virgin Queen vs. the seductive noblewoman." —*Boston Globe*

Includes bibliographical references.

Helen of Troy. Margaret George. Viking, 2006. 624 p.
ISBN 9780670037780
1. Helen of Troy (Greek mythology) 2. Trojan War 3. Self-sacrifice 4. Love triangles 5. War 6. Mycenae (Extinct city) 7. Troy (Extinct city) 8. Biographical fiction 9. Historical fiction

LC 2005058473

Married at a tender age to the Spartan king Menelaus, the beautiful Helen bears him a daughter and anticipates a passionless marriage before falling in love with the Trojan prince Paris, with whom she flees to Troy with devastating consequences.

"George's characters are precisely crafted, and the lovely Helen, clear-eyed and intelligent, is a sympathetic narrator. Despite the novel's length, the pages practically turn themselves. An absorbing retelling of the classic Trojan War myth, and a sobering look at the utter futility of trying to change one's fate." —*Booklist*

The **splendor** before the dark: a novel of the Emperor Nero. Margaret George. Berkley, 2018. 528 p. (Nero novels, 2)
ISBN 9780399584619
1. Nero 2. Roman emperors 3. Political intrigue 4. Power (Social sciences) 5. Fire 6. Betrayal 7. Rome 8. Roman Empire (27 BCE-476 CE) 9. Historical fiction 10. Biographical fiction

LC 2017060014

When a fire engulfs ancient Rome, Nero Augustus is targeted with suspicion about his complicity, forcing him to navigate a web of false friends and spies to save the empire, in a follow-up to The Confessions of a Young Nero.

George, Nina

The **book** of dreams. Nina George. Crown Publishing, 2019. 352 pages
ISBN 9780525572534

1. Fathers and sons 2. People in comas 3. Former lovers 4. Hospitals 5. Romantic love 6. London, England 7. Mainstream fiction 8. Multiple perspectives 9. Translations

Rendered comatose after an act of heroism, a man revisits memories of his British youth, while his ex forges an unexpected, profound friendship with the teenage son he has never known.

Translated from the German.

The **little** Paris bookshop. Nina George; translated by Simon Pare. Crown, 2015. 320 p.
ISBN 9780553418774
1. Booksellers 2. Books 3. Lost love 4. Voyages and travels 5. Rivers 6. Paris, France 7. France 8. Relationship fiction 9. Translations
LibraryReads Favorites, 2015

A book is both doctor and medicine. It makes diagnoses and provides therapy. Bringing the right novels together with the appropriate people is the way I sell books.

"Through its well-drawn characters, this novel carefully explores these relationships between lovers, friends, and family, and the painful sacrifices made selflessly for them." —*Booklist*

Originally published in Germany as Das Lavendelzimmer by Knaur Verlag in 2013.

Gerritsen, Tess

The **apprentice**: a novel. Tess Gerritsen. Ballantine Books, 2002. 344 p; (Jane Rizzoli and Maura Isles series, 2)
ISBN 9780345447852
1. Serial murders 2. Imitation 3. Escaped convicts 4. Rizzoli, Jane, Detective (Fictitious character) 5. Police 6. Boston, Massachusetts 7. Medical thrillers

It's a boiling summer in Boston. Adding to the city's woes is a series of shocking crimes that end in abduction and death. The pattern suggest "the Surgeon," serial killer Warren Hoyt. But Hoyt is behind bars, so this time it's a copycat killer. Detective Jane Rizzoli is on the case, determined to finally end Hoyt's influence.

"Boston detective Jane Rizzoli is called to a crime scene out of her jurisdiction. The victim is a wealthy doctor, found with his throat slashed, sitting on the floor of his living room in his pajamas, with a teacup in his lap. His wife is missing, but her nightgown is found folded neatly on a chair in the bedroom. There are unmistakable similarities to the work of serial killer Warren Hoyt, nicknamed 'the Surgeon,' but he is in prison, which leads Rizzoli to suspect a copcat killer." —*Library Journal*

Sequel to: The surgeon.
Sequel: The sinner.

The **bone** garden. Tess Gerritsen. Ballantine Books, 2007. 368 p.
ISBN 9780345497604
1. Serial murders 2. Forensic sciences 3. Women detectives 4. Divorced women 5. Murder 6. Boston, Massachusetts 7. 19th century 8. 1830s 9. Thrillers and suspense

The discovery of the skeleton of a woman murdered nearly two centuries earlier sends Boston medical examiner Maura Isles on the trail of a long-dead serial killer who terrorized Boston with crimes in which Norris Marshall, a Harvard Medical School student and reluctant resurrectionist, had become the prime suspect and enlisted the help of classmate Oliver Wendell Holmes to find and stop the murderer.

Choose me. . Thomas & Mercer, 2021. 334 p.
ISBN 9781542026154
1. Women college students 2. Suicide investigation 3. Falls (Accidents) 4. Women detectives 5. Breaking up (Interpersonal relations) 6. Boston, Massachusetts 7. Police procedurals 8. Multiple perspectives

Detective Frankie Loomis investigates a pregnant college student's fatal fall off her apartment balcony and believing there is more to the story than suicide, uncovers a number of sordid secrets that implicate one of her professors.

"With deceitful characters and plenty of twists, this novel is highly recommended for fans of Gerritsen or Braver, and readers who love suspense stories." —*Library Journal*

I know a secret. Tess Gerritsen. Ballantine, 2017. 336 p. (Jane Rizzoli and Maura Isles series, 12)
ISBN 9780345543882
1. Serial murder investigation 2. Women detectives 3. Horror films 4. Filmmakers 5. Fans 6. Medical thrillers
Jane Rizzoli and Maura Isles—the crime-solving duo who inspired the smash hit TNT series—return to investigate the gruesome staged murder of a horror film producer in this edge-of-your-seat thriller.

"One character's statement that "sometimes up really is down" applies to this complex and enjoyable story. It's a worthy addition to the series." —*Kirkus*

Playing with fire. Tess Gerritsen. Ballantine Books, 2015. 288 p.
ISBN 9781101884348
1. Change (Psychology) 2. Violence 3. Music 4. Women violinists 5. Mothers and daughters 6. Thrillers and suspense
Discovering an old and strikingly unusual musical composition that causes her to black out and has a violently transformative effect on her daughter, Julia Ansdell travels to Venice to find the man behind the music and uncovers a dark secret dating back to the Holocaust.

"Gerritsen's narrative weaves back and forth between Julia's time and that of musical prodigy Lorenzo Todesco, who faces the growing anti-Semitism in WWII Italy. These story lines arch, intertwine, and combust in a riveting finale." —*Booklist*

★ The **shape** of night: a novel. Tess Gerritsen. Ballantine Books, 2019. 268 p.
ISBN 9781984820952
1. Haunted houses 2. Ghosts 3. Single women 4. Guilt 5. Seduction 6. Maine 7. Gothic fiction
LC 2019013895
Moving to a coastal community in Maine, a woman trying to outrun her past is confronted by a string of murders and the ghost of a sea captain who is haunting her isolated home.

The **surgeon**. Tess Gerritsen. Ballantine Books, 2001. 359 p; (Jane Rizzoli and Maura Isles series, 1)
ISBN 9780345447838
1. Serial murders 2. Mutilation 3. Rape victims 4. Women heart surgeons 5. Stalkers 6. Boston, Massachusetts 7. Medical thrillers
LC 2001035901
Romantic Times Reviewers Choice Award, 2001; RITA Award for Best Romantic-Suspense Gothic, 2002
A female heart surgeon, terrorized by a serial killer in Boston using the same MO as a killer who attacked her during her internship years in Savannah, works with a detective to solve the crime while trying to stay alive.

"A fascinating story with a gripping plot and believably human characters." —*Booklist*
Sequel: The apprentice.

Gessen, Keith

A **terrible** country. Keith Gessen. Penguin Group USA, 2018. 352 p.
ISBN 9780735221314

1. Grandmother and grandson 2. Seniors — Care 3. Capitalism 4. Communism 5. Senior women 6. Moscow, Russia 7. Russia 8. 2000s (Decade) 9. Satirical fiction 10. Literary fiction
After Andrei Kaplan returns to Moscow to care for his ailing grandmother, he becomes entangled with a group of leftists and he is forced to come to terms with the Russian society he was born into and the American one he has enjoyed since he was a kid.

"With a realistic approach that nods to William Dean Howells and Tolstoy in equal measure, and like the fiction of his n+1 cohorts Chad Harbach and Benjamin Kunkel, Gessen presents a measured, socially engaged novel that is moving, often funny, and deeply thought-provoking." —*Booklist*

Ghaffari, Rabeah

★ **To** keep the sun alive. Rabeah Ghaffari. Catapult, 2019. 176 p.
ISBN 9781948226097
1. Extended families 2. Social change 3. Revolutions 4. Orchards 5. Family estates 6. Iran 7. 1970s 8. Political fiction 9. Family sagas
A cinematic novel about an Iranian family and their fruit orchard, caught up in the Revolution of 1979.

Ghosh, Amitav

Flood of fire. Amitav Ghosh. Farrar, Straus & Giroux, 2015. 528 p. (Ibis trilogy, 3)
ISBN 9780374174248
1. Voyages and travels 2. Opium industry and trade 3. Sailors 4. Schooners 5. Seafaring life 6. China 7. India 8. 19th century 9. 1830s 10. Historical fiction 11. Literary fiction
It is 1839 and tension has been rapidly mounting between China and British India following the crackdown on opium smuggling by Beijing. With no resolution in sight, the colonial government declares war. One of the vessels requisitioned for the attack, the Hind, travels eastwards from Bengal to China, sailing into the midst of the First Opium War. The turbulent voyage brings together a diverse group of travellers, each with their own agenda to pursue.

"Forbidden and betrayed love are the primary forces here, enacted with bawdy comedy and outright melodrama amid family concerns, secret deals, brutality, military battles, and the horrors of the drug trade. This feverishly detailed, vividly panoramic, tumultuous, funny, and heartbreaking tale offers a vigorous conclusion to Ghosh's astutely complex and profoundly resonant geopolitical saga." —*Booklist*
First published in Great Britain in 2015 by John Murray (Publishers).

The **glass** palace. Amitav Ghosh. Random House, 2001. 512 p.
ISBN 9780375501487
1. Courts and courtiers 2. Exiles 3. Colonialism 4. Political intrigue 5. Friendship 6. Burma 7. India 8. 1880s 9. 20th century 10. Historical fiction 11. Literary fiction 12. Family sagas
LC 41477
New York Times Notable Book, 2001
Unable to forget the girl he befriended during the British invasion of 1885 when soldiers forced the royal family of Burma into exile, Rajkumar is lifted on the tides of political and social chaos to create an empire in the Burmese teak forests.

"Ghosh renders the polite imprisonment of the Burmese royal family in India and the lush, dangerous atmosphere of teak camps in the Burmese forest with fine detail—a perfect balance for the broad stroke of romance and serendipity that drive the story forward." —*The New Yorker*

★ **Gun** Island. Amitav Ghosh. Farrar Straus & Giroux, 2019. 288 p.
ISBN 9780374167394

1. Storytelling 2. Climate change 3. East Indian Americans 4. Voyages and travels 5. Antiquarian booksellers 6. Literary fiction

A rare books dealer unexpectedly embarks on a journey of discovery through nations and cultures where the people he meets impart insights into the Bengali legends of his childhood.

The **hungry** tide. Amitav Ghosh. Houghton Mifflin, 2005. 352 p. ISBN 9780618329977

1. Dolphins 2. Women marine biologists 3. Wildlife conservation 4. Americans in Sundarbans (Bangladesh and India) 5. Fishers 6. Sundarbans (Bangladesh and India) 7. India 8. Psychological fiction 9. Literary fiction

LC 2004060942

ALA Notable Book, 2006

Off the eastern coast of Inda lies an extraordinary cluster of islands known as the Sundarbans. It is a raw but a beautiful sea—a place of man-eating tigers, river dolphins, huge crocodiles and devistating tides that sweep across the terrain without remorse. In this exotic land, marine biologist Piya, fisherman Fokir and translator Kanai meet. As they travel deep into the remote archipelago, they experience a territory at risk not only from natural disaster, but also from human foolishness and volatile politics.

River of smoke. Amitav Ghosh. Farrar, Straus & Giroux, 2011. 528 p. (Ibis trilogy, 2)
ISBN 9780374174231

1. Voyages and travels 2. Opium industry and trade 3. Sailors 4. Schooners 5. Cyclones 6. China 7. Mauritius 8. 19th century 9. 1830s 10. Historical fiction 11. Literary fiction

Amid a cyclone in the Bay of Bengal, three vessels, and the diverse occupants within, converge on Canton's Fanqui-Town, or Foreign Enclave, which is a powder keg awaiting a spark to ignite the Opium Wars.

"Ghosh's fascination with the multicultural ferment of Canton inspires thrilling descriptions of everything from local cuisine to the geopolitics of the opium wars. And his delight in language, especially the inventiveness of pidgin, further vitalizes his canny and dazzling tale, which, for all its historical exactitude, subtly reflects the hypocrisy and horrors of today's drug trafficking." —*Booklist*

Sea of poppies. Amitav Ghosh. Farrar, Straus and Giroux, 2008. 528 p. (Ibis trilogy, 1)
ISBN 9780374174224

1. Schooners 2. Opium industry and trade 3. Sailors 4. Voyages and travels 5. Travelers 6. India 7. 1830s 8. Historical fiction 9. Literary fiction

LC 2008030854

Shortlisted for the Man Booker Prize, 2008

Preparing to fight China's nineteenth-century Opium Wars, a motley assortment of sailors and passengers establish family-like ties that eventually span continents, races, and generations.

"An adventure story set in nineteenth-century Calcutta against the backdrop of the Opium Wars. On the Ibis, a ship engaged in transporting opium across the Bay of Bengal, varied life stories converge. A fallen raja, a half-Chinese convict, a plucky American sailor, a widowed opium farmer, a transgendered religious visionary are all united by the smoky paradise of the opium seed. Ghosh writes with impeccable control, and with a vivid and sometimes surprising imagination." —*The New Yorker*

First published, 2008.

Gibb, Camilla

Sweetness in the belly. Camilla Gibb. Penguin Press, 2006. 432 p. ISBN 9781594200847

1. Muslim women 2. Muslims 3. Immigrants 4. British in Ethiopia 5. Harer, Ethiopia 6. London, England 7. Psychological fiction 8. Political fiction 9. Canadian fiction

LC 2005053451

Trillium Book Award, 2005; Shortlisted for the Giller Prize, 2005

"Utterly convincing and authentic...a novel that will take you to a place so far from yourself that you may wonder, from time to time, whether you are ever coming back." —*San Francisco Chronicle*

Gibbon, Maureen

The **lost** notebook of Edouard Manet: a novel. Maureen Gibbon. W. W. Norton & Company, 2021. 240 p.
ISBN 9780393867152

1. Manet, Edouard 2. Painters 3. Artists 4. Art 5. Syphilis 6. Men with terminal illnesses 7. Paris, France 8. 19th century 9. 1880s 10. Historical fiction 11. Biographical fiction 12. Diary novels

LC 2021022100

Set in the richly drawn art world of nineteenth-century Paris, this stunning historical novel imagines Édouard Manet's last days in an indelible snapshot of genius, illness, and the dying embers of passion.

"This compelling and revealing book furthers a cultural understanding of Manet's place in time and art, a difficult task for a difficult character." —*Library Journal*

Gibbons, Kaye

Charms for the easy life. Kaye Gibbons. HarperCollins, 2005. 254 p. ISBN 9780060760250

1. Grandmother and granddaughter 2. Independence in women 3. Mother and adult daughter 4. Midwives 5. Boleyn, Mary 6. North Carolina 7. Family sagas 8. First person narratives 9. Southern fiction

LC 92040690

A tale of three generations of North Carolina women that has charmed readers from coast to coast. Their men may come and go— but for Margaret, Sophia and Charlie Kate, the hopes, hurts, large losses and small victories are the stuff that bind family together.

"A touching picture of female bonding and solidarity. Related with the simple, tart economy of a folktale, the narrative brims with wisdom and superstition, with Southern manners and insights into human nature." —*Publishers Weekly*

★ **Ellen** Foster: a novel. Kaye Gibbons. Algonquin Books of Chapel Hill, 1987. 146 p. (Ellen Foster duology, 1)
ISBN 9781565122055

1. Foster children 2. Child abuse victims 3. Identity (Psychology) 4. Runaways 5. Eleven-year-old girls 6. Southern States 7. North Carolina 8. Coming-of-age stories 9. Domestic fiction 10. Southern fiction

LC 86022136

Having suffered abuse and misfortune for much of her life, a young child searches for a better life and finally gets a break in the home of a loving woman with several foster children.

"What might have been grim, melodramatic material in the hands of a less talented author is instead filled with lively humor,...compassion and intimacy. This short novel focuses on Ellen's strengths rather than her victimization, presenting a memorable heroine who rescues herself." —*New York Times Book Review*

Sequel: The life all around me by Ellen Foster.

The **life** all around me by Ellen Foster. Kaye Gibbons. Harcourt, 2006. 224 p; (Ellen Foster duology, 2)
ISBN 9780151012046

1. Gifted teenagers 2. Independence (Personal quality) 3. Self-fulfillment in teenage girls 4. Teenage girls 5. Fifteen-year-old girls 6. North Carolina 7. Domestic fiction 8. Coming-of-age stories 9. Southern fiction 10. Adult books for young adults

LC 2005014552

Now fifteen, Ellen Foster is settled into a permanent home with a new mother. Strengthened by adversity and blessed with enough intelligence to design a salvation for herself, she still feels ill at ease in the world. While she holds fast to the shreds of her childhood, humoring her best friend Stuart who is determined to marry her. She protects her old neighbor, slow-witted Starletta and sells her poetry for money to pay her way to a camp for gifted students.

"This book lacks the strong story arc of its predecessor, which may make some readers impatient. But Ellen is still a remarkable creation, and her narrative voice, while it has matured and grown more sophisticated, remains compelling and unique." —*Booklist*

Sequel to: Ellen Foster.

Gibson, Claire

Beyond the point: a novel. Claire Gibson. HarperCollins Publishers, 2019. 528 p.
ISBN 9780062853745

1. Women soldiers 2. Female friendship 3. September 11 Terrorist Attacks, 2001 4. Women's role 5. Sexism 6. United States 7. Relationship fiction

In this powerful debut novel set at the U.S. Military Academy at West Point, three women-a nationally-ranked point guard, the granddaughter of an Army general, and a rebellious Homecoming Queen-are brought together in an enthralling story of friendship, heartbreak, and resilience.

Gibson, William

★ **Agency**. William Gibson. Berkley, 2020. 496 p. (Peripheral, 2)
ISBN 9781101986936

1. Artificial intelligence 2. Space and time 3. End of the world 4. High technology 5. Consequences 6. 21st century 7. 22nd century 8. Parallel narratives 9. Cyberpunk 10. Multiple perspectives

LC 2019023019

Verity Jane is hired to test a digital assistant that is accessed through a pair of ordinary glasses for a San Francisco start-up. One hundred years in the future and a different timeline, Wilf Netherton works amid survivors of the slow and steady apocalypse known as the jackpot. His employer can look into alternate pasts and nudge their ultimate directions. Verity has become his boss's current project, which will lead to their own version of the jackpot.

"Gibson blurs the line between real and speculative technology in a fast-paced thriller that will affirm to readers that it was well worth the wait." —*Booklist*

Sequel to: The Peripheral.

Originally published in Great Britain, 2019.

★ **Neuromancer**. William Gibson; with an afterword by Jack Womack. Ace Books, 2000. 276 p; (Sprawl trilogy, 1)
ISBN 9780441007462

1. Hackers 2. Cyberspace 3. Betrayal 4. Computers 5. Near future 6. Cyberpunk 7. Canadian fiction 8. Science fiction classics
Nebula Award for Best Novel, 1984; Phillip K. Dick Award for Science Fiction, 1984; Hugo Award for Best Novel, 1985

The Matrix unfolds like neon origami beneath clusters and constellations of data. Constructs, AIs, live here. Somewhere, concealed by ice, Neuromancer is evolving. As entropy goes into reverse, Molly's surgical implants broadcast trouble from the ferro-concrete geodesic of the Sprawl. Maelcum, Rastafarian in space, is her best hope of rescue. But she and Case, computer cowboy, are busy stealing data from the almighty Megacorps. If the Megacorps do not get them both, perhaps Case will fall prey to the cheap treachery of Linda Lee, someone as lost as himself.

"An adventure story much enlivened by elaborate technical jargon and sleazy, streetwise characters: the pioneering cyberpunk novel and arguably the most influential SF novel of the 1980s." —*Anatomy of Wonder, 5th edition*

Sequel: Count Zero.

Originally published: 1984.

Contains an exerpt from "Count zero."

Originally published: New York : Ace Books, 1984.

Pattern recognition. By William Gibson. G.P. Putnam's Sons, 2003. 368 p. (Blue Ant trilogy, 1)
ISBN 9780399149863

1. Marketing research 2. Pattern perception 3. Hackers 4. Fathers and daughters 5. Grief 6. London, England 7. Tokyo, Japan 8. 21st century 9. Cyberpunk 10. Science fiction mysteries 11. Science fiction 12. Adult books for young adults

LC 2002067955

New York Times Notable Book, 2003

Hired to investigate a mysterious video collection that has been appearing on the Internet, market research consultant Cayce Pollard realizes that there is more to the assignment when her computer is hacked.

"Cayce Pollard is a brand consultant whose father disappeared on September 11th. She becomes fascinated by mysterious scraps of film footageseemingly random scenes, luminously shotthat are disseminated on the Web and have spawned cults of viewers. Gibson wisely avoids addressing the import of 9/11 head on, but he somehow establishes a powerful correlative for it in Cayce's strange questthrough the Tokyo red-light district and the Moscow underworldto find the anonymous filmmaker. In Gibson's eerie vision of our time, the future has come crashing upon us, fragmentary and undecipherable." —*The New Yorker*

The **peripheral**. William Gibson. Putnam's Sons, 2014. 400 p. (Peripheral, 1)
ISBN 9780399158445

1. Dystopias 2. Siblings 3. Computer software — Testing 4. Murder 5. Intrigue 6. Shakespeare, William 7. Science fiction 8. Parallel narratives

LC 2014028558

Library Journal Best Books 2014

Whenever she can, gamer Flynne Fisher tries to help her brother Burton, a disabled veteran. So when Burton asks her to beta-test a virtual reality game as part of his lucrative but illegal part-time job, Flynne agrees to sub in. During her shift, Flynne witnesses a murder and soon realizes that she's not playing a game, she's seeing the future. But how? Cutting-edge technology and crossed time lines create an intricately plotted and thought-provoking science fiction story that slowly builds suspense through parallel, yet intersecting, narratives.

"All of Gibson's characters are intensely real, and Flynne is a clever, compelling, stereotype-defying, unhesitating protagonist who makes this novel a standout. —*Publishers Weekly*

Gide, Andre

★ The **immoralist**. Andre Gide; translated from the French by Richard Howard. Knopf, 1970. 171 p.
ISBN 9780394605005

1. Gay men — Relations with women 2. Gay men — Sexuality 3. Married men 4. Gay men's wives 5. Unhappiness in men 6. Translations 7. Modern classics 8. Literary fiction

LC 70098648

Michel, a young Frenchman living in an Algerian village, nearly succumbs to a fatal illness and, after recovering, rebels against his former standards of morality.

Gideon, Melanie

Wife 22. Melanie Gideon. Ballantine, 2012. 480 p.
ISBN 9780345527950
1. Marital conflict 2. Husband and wife 3. Boredom in women 4. Self-discovery in women 5. Family relationships 6. Relationship fiction 7. First person narratives
Library Journal Best Books, 2012
Baring her soul in an anonymous survey for a marital happiness study, Alice catalogues her stale marriage, unsatisfying job and unfavorable prospects and begins to question virtually every aspect of her life.

Gilb, Dagoberto

The **Flowers**: a novel. Dagoberto Gilb. Grove, 2008. 250 p.
ISBN 9780802118592
1. Apartment house life 2. Mexican American teenage boys 3. Mothers and sons 4. Prejudice 5. Blended families 6. Coming-of-age stories 7. Domestic fiction 8. Adult books for young adults
Booklist Editors' Choice: Adult Books for Young Adults, 2008
Sonny Bravo is a tender, unusually smart fifteen-year-old who is living with his vivacious mother in a large city where intense prejudice is not just white against black, but also brown. When his mother, Silvia, suddenly marries an Okie building contractor named Cloyd Longpre, they are uprooted to a small apartment building, Los Flores. As Sonny sweeps its sidewalks, he meets his neighbors and becomes ensnared in their lives.
"A tightly woven narrative about a boy coming of age in a community bubbling with racial tension. It's beautifully rendered in part because Mr. Gilb nails the voice of 15-year-old narrator Sonny Bravo with pinpoint accuracy." —*Dallas Morning News*

Gilbers, Harald

Germania: a novel of Nazi Berlin. Harald Gilbers; translated from the German by Alexandra Roesch. Thomas Dunne Books, 2020. 432 p. (Richard Oppenheimer novels, 1)
ISBN 9781250246936
1. World War II 2. Jewish men 3. Detectives 4. Serial murder investigation 5. Nazis 6. Second World War era (1939-1945) 7. Historical mysteries 8. Translations
LC 2020028401
Reactivated against his will by the Gestapo in the bombed-out capital of the Reich in 1944, Jewish detective Richard Oppenheimer investigates a serial killer who has been leaving Nazi-connected victims at war memorials.
"As is the case with much WWII noir, atmosphere is the real draw here, and the novel splendidly evokes Berlin in ruins and the fall of the Nazis." —*Booklist*
Translation of : Germania.
Originally published : Germany : Droemer Knaur, 2013.
Translated from the German.

Gilbert, David

& sons: a novel. David Gilbert. Random House, 2013. 496 p.
ISBN 9780812993967
1. Dysfunctional families 2. Authors, American 3. Fathers and sons 4. Family relationships 5. Rich people 6. New York City 7. Upper East Side, New York City 8. Literary fiction

LC 2012031308
A novel about a famous reclusive writer and his three sons finds their bond tested by the weight of long-held secrets and a cumbersome legacy shaped by boarding school, Hollywood and the elite circles of the publishing world.

Gilbert, Elizabeth

★ **City** of girls. Elizabeth Gilbert. Riverhead Books, 2019. 432 p.
ISBN 9781594634734
1. Theater companies 2. Memories 3. Female friendship 4. Reminiscing in old age 5. Scandals 6. New York City 7. 1940s 8. Historical fiction
LibraryReads Favorites, 2019; Loan Stars Favourites, 2019
Eighty-nine-year-old Vivian recounts her life after being kicked out of Vassar College, living in Manhattan with her Aunt Peg and the personal mistake that resulted in a professional scandal.
"Tart-voiced Vivian and her adventures in 20th-century Manhattan will please readers who enjoyed Kathleen Rooney's Lillian Boxfish Takes a Walk." —*Library Journal*

★ The **signature** of all things: a novel. Elizabeth Gilbert. Viking, 2013. 512 p.
ISBN 9780670024858
1. Painters 2. Women botanists 3. Man-woman relationships 4. Women — Spiritual life 5. Interpersonal attraction 6. Philadelphia, Pennsylvania 7. 18th century 8. Family sagas 9. Epic fiction 10. Historical fiction
LC 2013017045
New York Times Notable Book, 2013; Booklist Editors' Choice, 2013
A multi-generational saga of the Whittaker family, whose progenitor makes a fortune in the quinine trade before his daughter, a gifted botanist, researches the mysteries of evolution while falling in love with an utopian artist against a backdrop of the Age of Enlightenment and the Industrial Revolution.

Gilchrist, Ellen

★ **Collected** stories. Ellen Gilchrist. Little,Brown, 2000. 563 p.
ISBN 9780316299480
1. Manning, Rhoda Katherine (Fictitious character) 2. Women 3. Human nature 4. Southern States 5. Short stories
New York Times Notable Book, 2001
Presents a collection of stories selected by the author from her fifteen previous collections of short fiction.
"Gilchrist is an important voice in contemporary Southern fiction, and this book belongs in every library." —*Library Journal*
34 short stories.

Gillham, David R.

City of women. David R. Gillham. Amy Einhorn Books, 2012. 400 p.
ISBN 9780399157769
1. Military spouses 2. Married women 3. Nazis 4. World War II 5. Secrets 6. Berlin, Germany 7. Germany 8. Second World War era (1939-1945) 9. 1940s 10. Historical fiction
LC 2012011002
Hiding her clandestine activities behind the persona of a model Nazi soldier's wife at the height of World War II, Sigrid Schroeder dreams of her former Jewish lover and risks everything to hide a mother and two young children who she believes might be her lover's family.

Gilligan, Ruth

The **butchers'** blessing. Ruth Gilligan. Tin House, 2020. 312 pages
ISBN 9781947793781
1. Butchers 2. Rites and ceremonies 3. Family traditions 4. Cattle 5. Social change 6. Ireland 7. 2010s 8. 1990s 9. Literary fiction 10. Coming-of-age stories
LC 2020013302
RSL Ondaatje Prize, 2021

A modern tale inspired by Irish folklore traces the experiences of a butcher's family that is shaped by loneliness, faith, young love, a difficult promise, fading cultural practices and a photographer's image of an unspeakably violent murder.

"With beautifully crafted prose, suspenseful plotting, and imaginative scope, Gilligan's off to a blazing start." —*Publishers Weekly*

Gilman, Carolyn Ives

Dark orbit. Carolyn Ives Gilman. St. Martin's Press, 2015. 304 p.
ISBN 9780765336293
1. Women scientists 2. Aliens (Non-humanoid) 3. Aliens 4. Exiles 5. Prophets 6. Space 7. Science fiction

Recruited to monitor an unstable scientist who is investigating a habitable new planet, exoethnologist Sara Callicot navigates the culture of the planet's extrasensory indigenous race while her charge battles delusions to warn their crewmates of an impending danger.

"Blending mystery, philosophy, and science gracefully in a twisty plot, Gilman (Ison of the Isles) has written a challenging but ultimately satisfying space adventure that explores how the most basic preconceptions can distort our outlook. It's a winner for any sf fan, of special appeal to those with interests in epistemology, ethics, or physics." —*Library Journal*

Gilman, Charlotte Perkins

Herland. Charlotte Perkins Gilman; with an introduction by Ann J. Lane. Pantheon Books, 1979. Xxiv, 147 p.
ISBN 9780394736655
1. Utopias 2. Sexism 3. Prejudice 4. Explorers 5. Culture conflict 6. 1910s 7. Science fiction classics 8. Social science fiction 9. Science fiction
LC 78020418

On the eve of World War I, an all-female society is discovered somewhere in the distant reaches of the earth by three male explorers who are now forced to re-examine their assumptions about women's roles in society. —Publisher's description.

Jacket subtitle: A lost feminist utopian novel.
Originally published: 1915.

★ The **yellow** wallpaper and selected writings. By Charlotte Perkins Gilman with an introduction by Kate Bolick. Penguin Classics, 2020. 367 p.
ISBN 9780143134794
1. Gilman, Charlotte Perkins 2. Married women — Psychology 3. Women with mental illnesses 4. Gender role 5. Control (Psychology) 6. Short stories 7. Classics 8. Psychological fiction 9. Poetry

A collection of the groundbreaking feminist writer's most famous works, with a thought-provoking introduction by bestselling author Kate Bolick.

Gilman, Felix

The **half-made** world. Felix Gilman. Tor, 2010. 480 p. (Half-made world novels, 1)
ISBN 9780765325525
1. Magic 2. Dystopias 3. Industries 4. Machinery 5. Terrorism 6. Weird Westerns 7. Steampunk 8. Historical fantasy
LC 2010032564

A steampunk reimagining of the American West follows the efforts of a spiritually protected doctor to analyze two rival factions that are oppressing the world's people, a study that leads to her discovery of a broken general from a mythological resistance force.

"Sick of predictable books that fill your subgenre bingo card with the same subgenre elements over and over? .... Felix Gilman has blended elements from alternate history, Steampunk, Westerns, and epic fantasy to create something truly original." —*io9*

A Tom Doherty Associates book.

Gilman, Laura Anne

The **cold** eye. Laura Anne Gilman. Saga Press, 2017. 400 p. (Devil's West, 2)
ISBN 9781481429719
1. Frontier and pioneer life 2. Devil 3. Voyages and travels 4. Young women 5. Power (Social sciences) 6. The West (United States) 7. American Westward Expansion (1803-1899) 8. Weird Westerns 9. Historical fantasy
LC 2016029456

While serving as the Left Hand of the Devil, Isobel has her power tested as she tries to figure out the cause of a growing and mysterious danger throughout the Territory, in a sequel to Silver on the Road.

Flesh and fire. Laura Anne Gilman. Pocket Books, 2009. 384 p. (Vineart war trilogy, 1)
ISBN 9781439101414
1. Wizards 2. Wine and wine making 3. Magic potions 4. Power (Social sciences) 5. Vineyards 6. Fantasy fiction 7. Coming-of-age stories
LC 2009012786
Library Journal Best Books, 2009

Jerzy—a young slave who has just begun an apprenticeship to become a Vineart, a mage who can create spell-making wines—must work with his master to stop a plot to complete the work of the dreaded Sin-Washer and rid the world of the last few Vinearts.

Hard magic. Laura Anne Gilman. Luna, 2010. 352 p. (Paranormal scene investigations, 1)
ISBN 9780373803132
1. Murder investigation 2. Magic 3. Spells (Magic) 4. Detectives 5. Bisexual women 6. Urban fantasy 7. Mysteries 8. First person narratives

Bonnie Torres and four other paranormal investigators are hired to prove that the deaths of two Talents were murder, not suicide, while dealing with a vast array of high-profile people who want to shut them down.

"Spinning off a minor character from the Retrievers books (Staying Dead, etc.), Gilman launches an entertaining new series set in her Cosa Nostradamus world of magic-using Talented humans. Following up on a mysterious job lead, college grad Bonita Torres joins the Private Unaffiliated Paranormal Investigations (PUPI), a freelance CSI-style unit for Talent-related crimes. The puppies refine and practice spells until they get their first big case: an apparent double suicide. As they follow the evidence, trail and interrogate suspects, and defend themselves against attacks, the investigators develop comfortable and engaging team dynamics and create the field of forensic magic. Gilman's deft plotting and first-class characters complement her agile blend of science and spell craft." —*Publishers Weekly*

Silver on the road. Laura Anne Gilman. Saga Press, 2015. 400 p. (Devil's West, 1)
ISBN 9781481429689

1. Young women 2. Devil 3. Manipulation (Social sciences) 4. Deals 5. Faustian bargains 6. The West (United States) 7. American Westward Expansion (1803-1899) 8. Weird Westerns 9. Historical fantasy 10. Adult books for young adults

Taking a job in the untamed American West serving a being of immense power who makes deals with people and gives them exactly what they deserve, Izzy receives training in the manipulations of human desire and travels throughout the territory to spread magical chaos.

"Refreshingly, her vision of the American West includes respectful portrayals of Native Americans. Isobel's coming-of-age story is very accessible to teens, and there's plenty for adventure-minded adults to enjoy as well." —*Publishers Weekly*

Gilman, Susan Jane

Donna has left the building. Susan Jane Gilman. Grand Central Publishing, 2019. 384 p.

ISBN 9781538762417

1. Automobile travel 2. Decision-making 3. Recovering alcoholics 4. Transformations, Personal 5. Married women 6. Relationship fiction
LC 2018048056

Leaving behind her family and her suburban home when her world implodes, forty-five-year-old Donna Koczynski sets off on a road trip to rebuild her life.

The **ice** cream queen of Orchard Street: a novel. Susan Jane Gilman. Grand Central Publishing, 2014. 512 pages

ISBN 9780446578936

1. Immigrants 2. Entrepreneurs 3. People with disabilities 4. Abandoned girls 5. Street vendors 6. United States 7. 20th century 8. Mainstream fiction
LC 2013030543

LibraryReads Favorites, 2014

Russian immigrant Malka arrives in 1913 Manhattan, where she struggles to survive and learns trade secrets from an Italian ices peddler before setting off across America in an ice cream truck with a handsome, illiterate radical to seek their fortunes.

"With its vivid depictions of old New York City tenement life and its tale of the American ice cream business set against the backdrop of the major events of the 20th century, this rags-to-riches saga will appeal greatly to readers of American historical novels." —*Library Journal*

Ginzburg, Natalia

A **family** lexicon. By Natalia Ginzburg; translated by Jenny McPhee; afterword by Peg Boyers. New York Review of Books, 2017. 224 pages (New York Review Books classics)

ISBN 9781590178386

1. Ginzburg, Natalia 2. Authors 3. Families 4. Intimacy (Psychology) 5. Family relationships 6. Friendship 7. Italy 8. Autobiographical fiction 9. Domestic fiction 10. Family sagas
LC 2016026803

Re-creates with extraordinary objectivity the small world of a family enduring some of the most difficult years of the twentieth century, the period from the rise of Mussolini through World War II and its immediate aftermath.

Originally published: Turin : Einaudi, 1963.
Translated from the Italian.

Voices in the evening. Natalia Ginzburg; translated from the Italian by D. M. Low; with an introduction by Colm Toibin. New Directions Publishing, 2021. Xvii, 125 p.

ISBN 9780811231008

1. Single women 2. Villages 3. Mother and adult daughter 4. Young men 5. Rich families 6. Italy 7. Literary fiction 8. Love stories 9. Translations
LC 2021001798

In a quiet Italian town after World War Two, Elsa lives with her parents in the house where she was born. Twenty-seven and unmarried, she is a constant concern to her obsessive, hypochondriac mother. But her mother does not know that Elsa has fallen in love with Tommasino, the elusive youngest son of the De Francisci family, who own the textile factory that dominates the town. Over the course of their secret meetings, Elsa begins to imagine a future with Tommasino, free from the constraints of expectations and burdensome history. But this is all threatened by exposure. An elegant and beautifully restrained novel that scratches at the fragility of postwar consciousness, Voices in the Evening is an unforgettable story about first love and lost chances.

"Ginzburg's efficient, lyrical prose and ear for dialogue make for an expansive and beautifully rendered study of individuals and community in wartime. With this latest resurrected masterpiece, the late author's work continues to prove irresistible and relevant." —*Publishers Weekly*

Originally published: Turin : Einaudi Editore, 1961.
Translated from the Italian.

Giordano, Mario

★ **Auntie** Poldi and the lost Madonna. Mario Giordano; translated by John Brownjohn. Houghton Mifflin Harcourt 2021. 352 p. (Auntie Poldi novels, 4)

ISBN 9780358251392

1. Women amateur detectives 2. Expatriate women 3. Senior women 4. Widows 5. Alcoholic women 6. Sicily, Italy 7. Italy 8. Mysteries 9. First person narratives 10. Translations
LC 2020034218

Strange dealings are afoot in the Apostolic Palace—a nun leapt to her death shortly after participating in a seemingly routine exorcism. But when a priest clad in Gammarelli and a Vatican commissario with an almost unholy level of sex appeal turn up at her door, Poldi is shocked to hear that she's a suspect in their case. Poldi will need all the help she can get to clear her name, but her nephew has been distracted by a love affair gone sour, someone in the town has been spraying graffiti death threats on her front door, and her local friends seem to be avoiding her. And even Vito Montana balks when Poldi discovers that the case hinges on a lost Madonna statue, stolen years ago from the pope himself.

"Poldi's devil-may-care attitude and Nephew's witty, self-deprecating narration are as entertaining as ever, but this series' fourth entry is anchored by Poldi's evolution as she faces both her future and her conflicted past." —*Booklist*

Originally published: Cologne : Bastei Lubbe AG, 2019.
Translated from the German.

Auntie Poldi and the Vineyards of Etna. Mario Giordano; translated by John Brownjohn. Houghton Mifflin Harcourt, 2019. 352 pages (Auntie Poldi novels, 2)

ISBN 9781328919021

1. Women amateur detectives 2. Senior women 3. Vineyards 4. Nephews 5. Murder investigation 6. Sicily, Italy 7. Italy 8. Mysteries 9. First person narratives 10. Translations

A follow-up to Auntie Poldi and the Sicilian Lions finds Prosecco-loving Auntie Poldi defending her community when a dog is poisoned and a respected handyman goes missing amid a rise in local Mafia activities.

"Readers will look forward to the further adventures of the irrepressible Auntie Poldi." —*Publishers Weekly*

Published in the UK by Bitter Lemon Press as Auntie Poldi and the fruits of the Lord, 2018.

Originally published by Bastei, 2016.

Translated from the German Tante Poldi und die Früchte des Herrn by John Brownjohn.

Giordano, Paolo

Heaven and earth. Paolo Giordano; translated by Anne Milano Appel. Pamela Dorman Books/Viking, 2020. 404 pages
ISBN 9781984877314

1. Summer 2. Family estates 3. Male friendship 4. First loves 5. Sects 6. Italy 7. 20th century 8. 21st century 9. Translations 10. Literary fiction 11. Coming-of-age stories

Forging close ties with three brothers from a neighboring farm in Italy, Teresa discovers a dark secret when the brother she secretly loves commits a brutal act of revenge.

"Lush regional details, indelible characters, and a riveting story line make this an overwhelmingly emotional read. Giordano's captivating tale is a magnificent testament to the lingering impact of a charged romance." —*Publishers Weekly*

Translation of: Divorare il cielo.

Originally published in Italy, 2018.

Translated from the Italian.

The **human** body. Paolo Giordano; translation from the Italian by Anne Milano Appel. Pamela Dorman Books/Viking, 2014. 336 p.
ISBN 9780670015641

1. Afghan War, 2001-2021 2. Soldiers 3. War — Psychological aspects 4. Young men 5. Military missions 6. War stories 7. Literary fiction 8. Psychological fiction

LC 2014006927

A platoon in one of the world's most dangerous war zones—the Forward Operating Base in the Gulistan district of Afghanistan—endure deadly engagements and psychological trauma before a mission gone wrong changes everything.

"[A] memorable entry in the literature of the Afghan war, the characters crisply drawn and the writing full of telling details." —*Booklist*

Like family. Paolo Giordano; translated from the Italian by Anne Milano Appel. Pamela Dorman Books/Viking, 2015. 160 p.
ISBN 9780525428763

1. Housekeepers 2. People with terminal illnesses 3. Families 4. Widows 5. Scientists 6. Literary fiction 7. Translations 8. First person narratives

The delicate fabric of a young family unravels when a beloved maid who has become the glue in their household falls ill and reveals poignant incidents from her past, including a tragically short marriage. By the best-selling author of The Solitude of Prime Numbers.

"And at his best, Giordano muses gorgeously on our inability to blend our life essences; even love leaves us lonely. A lovely remembrance played in a minor key." —*Kirkus*

Translation from the Italian of: Nero e l'argento.

Originally published: Torino : Einaudi, 2014.

★ The **solitude** of prime numbers: a novel. Paolo Giordano; translated from the Italian by Shaun Whiteside. Pamela Dorman Books/Viking, 2010. 288 p.
ISBN 9780670021482

1. Life change events — Psychological aspects 2. Solitude 3. Loss (Psychology) 4. Anorexia nervosa 5. Anger in women 6. Italy 7. Psychological fiction 8. Love stories 9. Literary fiction

LC 2009041165

Misfits Alice and Mattia bond as teens over shared experiences of suffering before mathematically gifted Mattia accepts a research position that takes him far away, a situation that restores their isolation before they meet by chance years later.

"This is a book about communication: in lacking a facility for self-expression, our stunted protagonists exist almost solely, and safely, in their own minds. Despite its heavy subject matter, it reads easily, due in part to the almost seamless translation. A quietly explosive ending completes the novel in just the fashion it was started, as an intimate psychological portrait of two prime numbers—together alone and alone together." —*Booklist*

Originally published: Milano : Mondadori, 2008.

Translation of La solitudine dei numeri primi from the Italian.

Gladstone, Max

★ **Empress** of forever. Max Gladstone. Tor, 2019. 480 p.
ISBN 9780765395818

1. Women computer scientists 2. Time travel (Future) 3. Dystopias 4. Women rulers 5. Artificial intelligence 6. Space opera 7. Science fiction

LC 2018054087

After being thrown into a dark future ruled by the powerful Empress, radical billionaire tech genius Vivian Liao assembles a group of unlikely allies to aid in her attempt to break free of the Empress's stranglehold and save the galaxy.

A Tom Doherty Associates Book.

Glass, Jenna

The **women's** war. Jenna Glass. Del Rey, 2019. 560 pages (Women's war, 1)
ISBN 9781984817204

1. Spells (Magic) 2. Reproductive rights 3. Women rulers 4. Women exiles 5. Magic 6. Epic fantasy

LC 2018015835

When a world-altering spell gives women the ability to control their own fertility, a disinherited princess and a powerless queen trigger changes in their patriarchal kingdoms before a caravan of exiles stumbles on a new source of women's magic.

"Glass's substantial debut stands out as both social commentary on contemporary issues of bodily autonomy, gender, and social power and as feminist retribution fantasy, made manifest through an appealing epic fantasy setting and grounded in a carefully designed magic system." —*Publishers Weekly*

Glass, Julia

★ **Three** Junes. Julia Glass. Pantheon Books, 2002. 368 p.
ISBN 9780375421440

1. Family relationships 2. Loss (Psychology) 3. Fathers and sons 4. Familial love 5. Scots in the United States 6. Long Island, New York 7. Scotland 8. Multiple perspectives 9. Psychological fiction 10. First person narratives

LC 2001055448

National Book Award for Fiction, 2002; New York Times Notable Book, 2002

Reveals the interconnected lives, loves, and relationships of different generations of the McLeod family over the course of three crucial summers.

"Free of gimmickry, Three Junes brilliantly rescues, then refurbishes, the traditional plot-driven novel." —*New York Times Book Review*

The **whole** world over. Julia Glass. Pantheon Books, 2006. 528 p.
ISBN 9780375422744

1. Women cooks 2. Marital conflict 3. Women bakers 4. Husband and wife 5. Psychiatrists 6. Manhattan, New York City 7. New Mexico 8. Psychological fiction 9. Domestic fiction 10. Literary fiction

LC 2005054043

Hired as the personal chef to the governor of New Mexico, Greenie Duquette leaves behind her Greenwich Village pastry business and her husband to head west with her four-year-old son, prompting a period of upheaval and reflection for herself.

"Glass is too capable to need recipes and four-legged friends to make her fiction a pleasure. It's a tribute to this unassuming but conspicuously talented novelist that even with far too many of them, The Whole World Over so often manages to sing." —*New York Times Book Review*

Fenno McLeod found in this book was first mentioned in the author's debut novel, Three Junes.

The **widower's** tale. Julia Glass. Pantheon Books, 2010. 448 p.

ISBN 9780307377920

1. Senior men 2. Family relationships 3. Father and adult child 4. Widowers 5. Former librarians 6. Literary fiction

Enjoying an active but lonely rural life, 70-year-old Percy haplessly allows a progressive preschool to move into his barn and transform his quiet home into a lively, youthful community that compels him to reexamine the choices he made in the decades after his wife's death.

"Percy Darling, 70, is the titular widower, a rigid man still sorely missing his long-deceased wife. He holds the center of Glass' [novel],...set in a bucolic town outside of Boston. Orbiting around Percy are two grown daughters: one a divorced flibbertigibbet and the other a renowned oncologist who is as stern with her family as she is open and available to her patients. Add to the mix a wayward Harvard grandson, a Guatemalan gardener, a gay preschool teacher, and a salt-of-the-earth artist who reminds Percy that he is still very much alive. It's a large, endearing cast, bursting with emotional and social issues, and Glass slips effortlessly between their individual and enmeshed dramas." —*Entertainment Weekly*

Glass, Seraphina Nova

Someone's listening. Seraphina Nova Glass. MIRA Books, 2020. 336 p.

ISBN 9781525836749

1. Psychologists 2. Women authors 3. Missing men 4. Threat (Psychology) 5. Anonymous letters 6. Mysteries

A talented psychologist and best-selling author is shattered when her food critic husband goes missing and she begins receiving threatening notes that are ripped from the pages of her own book that helps victims leave their abusers.

"Exceptionally well-drawn characters set this above the psychological thriller pack. Readers will eagerly await Glass's next." —*Publishers Weekly*

Glass, Seressia

★ The **love** con. Seressia Glass. Jove, 2021. 336 p.

ISBN 9780593199053

1. African American women 2. Cosplay 3. Costume 4. Ambition in women 5. Interracial romance 6. Romantic comedies 7. Multicultural romances 8. Contemporary romances

LC 2021022683

LibraryReads Favorites, 2021

He's cosplaying as her boyfriend but their feelings for each other are real in this romantic comedy from Seressia Glass.

"This sassy, sexy romantic comedy explores geek culture and issues in that community regarding diversity. Kenya and Cam are fully realized three-dimensional characters who are clearly meant to be together. The plot yields well-written surprises and emotional depth, and readers will find it hard to put this book down." —*Library Journal*

Gleason, Colleen

Murder at the capitol. C. M. Gleason. Kensington Pub Corp, 2020. 304 pages (Lincoln's White House mysteries, 3)

ISBN 9781496723987

1. Lincoln, Abraham 2. Presidents 3. Espionage 4. Private investigators 5. Murder 6. Murder investigation 7. Washington, D.C. 8. United States 9. American Civil War era (1861-1865) 10. 1860s 11. Historical mysteries

In July 1861, just months after the Battle of Fort Sumter plunges the young nation into civil war, President Lincoln's top priority is to unite the country, while Adam Quinn finds himself on the trail of a murderer . . .

"Gleason follows Murder in the Oval Library with a riveting historical mystery set on the eve of the first major battle of the Civil War. Fans of descriptive historical mysteries will appreciate the mix of real people and intriguing fictional characters." —*Library Journal*

Glover, Nicole

★ The **conductors**. Nicole Glover. John Joseph Adams/Mariner Books, 2020. 432 p. (Murder and Magic, 1)

ISBN 9780358197058

1. Magic 2. Husband and wife 3. Detectives 4. African Americans 5. Murder investigation 6. Philadelphia, Pennsylvania 7. Pennsylvania 8. Historical fantasy 9. Fantasy fiction

LC 2020009019

LibraryReads Favorites, 2021

As a conductor on the Underground Railroad, Hetty Rhodes helped usher dozens of people north with her wits and magic. Now that the Civil War is over, Hetty and her husband, Benjy, have settled in Philadelphia, solving murders and mysteries that the white authorities won't touch. When they find one of their friends slain in an alley, Hetty and Benjy bury the body and set off to find answers. But the secrets and intricate lies of the elites of Black Philadelphia only serve to dredge up more questions. To solve this mystery, they will have to face ugly truths all around them, including the ones about each other.

"The Conductors juggles a lot of elements, including segregated magic systems, romance, a large cast of characters, and several deep, dark secrets. Hetty and Benjy's relationship as they work together to find out more about the crimes is a highlight of the novel, as is the constellation-based magic system that Hetty and her friends use. The magical Reconstruction setting should appeal to fantasy and history buffs alike, especially for fans of Ring Shout, by P. Djèlí Clark (2020) and An Extraordinary Union, by Alyssa Cole (2017)." —*Booklist*

The **undertakers**. Nicole Glover. Mariner Books/Houghton Mifflin Harcourt, 2021. 384 p. (Murder and Magic, 2)

ISBN 9780358197102

1. Magic 2. Husband and wife 3. Detectives 4. African Americans 5. Murder investigation 6. Philadelphia, Pennsylvania 7. Pennsylvania 8. Historical fantasy 9. Fantasy mysteries 10. Fantasy fiction

LC 2021014685

Nothing bothers Hetty and Benjy Rhodes more than a case where the answers, motives, and the murder itself feel a bit too neat. Raimond Duval, a victim of one of the many fires that have erupted recently in Philadelphia, is officially declared dead after the accident, but Hetty and Benjy's investigation points to a powerful Fire Company known to let homes in the Black community burn to the ground. Before long, another death breathes new life into the Duval investigation: Raimond's son, Valentine, is also found dead.

"Glover has written another fast-paced story of luck, fate, and betrayal. Readers will be engrossed by its celestial magic, hidden tunnels leading to unexpected places, and cliffhanger ending." —*Library Journal*

A John Joseph Adams book.

Glynn, Alan

Receptor. Alan Glynn. St Martins Pr 2019. 288 p. (Limitless novels, 2)
ISBN 9781250061805
1. Mind control 2. Power (Social sciences) 3. Experimental drugs 4. Addiction 5. Elitism 6. 1950s 7. 2010s 8. Techno-thrillers
LC 2018036692

From the author of Limitless comes Receptor, an irresistible thriller that reveals the origins of MDT-48 and the consequences of unlocking the human mind.

Originally published as "Under the Night" by Faber & Faber, 2018.

Gnuse, A. J.

Girl in the walls: a novel. A.J. Gnuse. Ecco Press, 2021. 256 p.
ISBN 9780063031807
1. Orphans 2. Houses 3. Hiding 4. Families 5. Secrets 6. Thrillers and suspense 7. Coming-of-age stories
LC 2021002237

After her parents die, Elise lives within in the walls of their house, secretly hiding, until a new family moves in, placing her existence in danger and bringing a far more real threat to their doorstep.

"Gnuse has done a brilliant job of making the implausible plausible and of creating characters, especially Eddie, who are simply unforgettable. The Louisiana setting is evocative and a marvel of verisimilitude." —*Booklist*

Originally published in Great Britain in 2021 by 4th Estate, an imprint of HarperCollins Publishers.

Goddard, Robert

Beyond recall: a novel. Robert Goddard. Henry Holt, 1998. 310 p.
ISBN 9780805051100
1. Cold cases (Criminal investigation) 2. Innocence (Law) 3. Secrets 4. Men 5. Greed in men 6. Cornwall, England 7. England 8. Thrillers and suspense 9. First person narratives
LC 97-28895

New York Times Notable Mysteries, 1998

The suicide of the black sheep of the family at a wedding party in Cornwall, England, drives Chris Napier into his clan's dark past, where he discloses more than one skeleton, including child abuse and old-fashioned revenge.

"There's an elegant arc to Goddard's fluid style, which gracefully orchestrates the story over its broad time span and through the ambiguous testimony of its complex characters." —*New York Times Book Review*

Originally published: London: Bantam, 1997.

★ **Into** the blue. Robert Goddard. Poseidon Press, 1990. 415 p; (Harry Barnett series, 1)
ISBN 9780671704827
1. Frameups 2. British in Greece 3. Missing persons investigation 4. Betrayal 5. Extortion 6. Greece 7. England 8. Psychological suspense 9. Thrillers and suspense
LC 90042481

A disgraced caretaker on the island of Rhodes is suspected in the murder of a woman, and his quest to clear his name leads him to his native England, where he investigates the victim's past and regains his self-esteem.

"During this quest, Harry's courage is tested as well as his judgment of peopleall of whom turn out to be totally and depressingly human. An everyman's hero, against all mental and emotional odds, Harry finds Heather and renewed self-respect. A very satisfying novel in every way." —*Booklist*

★ **Long** time coming: a novel. Robert Goddard. Bantam Books Trade Paperbacks, 2010. 432 p.
ISBN 9780385343619
1. Former convicts 2. Art forgeries 3. World War II 4. Diamond industry and trade 5. War crimes — History 6. England 7. Mysteries
LC 2009044547

Edgar Allan Poe Award for Best Paperback Original, 2011

Astonished to learn that the uncle he believed was killed in the Blitz has been in prison for nearly four decades, Stephen Swan finds himself in the middle of a conspiracy involving forged Picassos and the disinherited family an Antwerp diamond dealer.

Never go back. Robert Goddard. Bantam Dell, 2007. 336 p; (Harry Barnett series, 3)
ISBN 9780385340632
1. Suspicion 2. Senior men 3. Human experimentation in medicine 4. Heydrich, Reinhard 5. Secrets 6. Scotland 7. Psychological suspense 8. Thrillers and suspense
LC 2007006336

"Goddard's latest offering marks the return of unlikely hero Harry Barnett, star of Into the Blue (1990) and Out of the Sun (1997). It's a crackling good read, with clipped prose, complex characters, and a smart, sinuous plot." —*Booklist*

Godden, Rumer

The **greengage** summer: a novel. Viking, 1958. 218p.
ISBN 9781447211013
1. British in France 2. France 3. Literary fiction 4. Classics
LC 58007066

When five English children are forced to fend for themselves in a small French village it requires all their combined courage and strength to manage.

Originally published: London: Macmillan, 1958.

Godwin, Gail

Flora: a novel. Gail Godwin. Bloomsbury, 2013. 288 p.
ISBN 9781620401200
1. Loss (Psychology) 2. Family secrets 3. Girls 4. Guardian and ward 5. World War II 6. North Carolina 7. 1940s 8. Historical fiction 9. Coming-of-age stories 10. Literary fiction
LC 2012036741

Isolated in a decaying family home while her father performs secret work at the end of World War II, 10-year-old Helen, grieving the losses of her mother and grandmother, bonds with her sensitive young aunt while desperately clinging to the ghosts and stories of her childhood.

Grief cottage: a novel. Gail Godwin. Bloomsbury USA, 2017. 324 p.
ISBN 9781632867056
1. Cottages 2. Recluses 3. Eleven-year-old boys 4. Ghosts 5. Island life 6. South Carolina 7. Southern Gothic 8. Literary fiction 9. Coming-of-age stories 10. Adult books for young adults
LC 2016036527

Moving in with his reclusive artist aunt after his mother's death, 11-year-old Marcus learns the story of a local cottage from which a family disappeared during a hurricane half a century earlier, a tragedy that compels him to explore the cottage, where he meets a ghost with a mysterious agenda.

"The book moves between the fantastical and the everyday with ease; Marcus is just as likely to shop for his elderly neighbors as to whisper encouragement to loggerhead hatchlings or offer friendship to the restless spirits of the island. But nothing and no one on the island can break free of the forces that build and destroy, that give life and bring death. As time pushes him forward, Marcus must decide how to grieve: to raze his identity completely or memorialize his tragedies. His choice and its consequences will echo with readers, and Godwins forceful prose captivates with the quiet, renewing power of a persistent tide." —*Publishers Weekly*

Old Lovegood girls. Gail Godwin. St Martins Pr 2020. 288 p.
ISBN 9781632868220
1. Female friendship 2. Women college friends 3. Loss (Psychology) 4. Women authors 5. Families 6. Literary fiction
LC 2019042321
Separated by a devastating loss, two estranged college roommates reach out to each other years later in the face of unpredictable hardships before discovering the power of their unbreakable bond to transform their lives.

"Godwin's mastery and following grow with each book, and literary fiction lovers will seek out this intricately structured and emotionally rich tale." —*Booklist*

Unfinished desires. Gail Godwin. Random House, 2009. 416 p.
ISBN 9780345483201
1. Competition in girls 2. Nuns 3. Scandals 4. Girls' schools 5. Friendship 6. North Carolina 7. Literary fiction 8. First person narratives 9. Multiple perspectives 10. Adult books for young adults
Sparking enthusiasm for a play about the founding of their North Carolina mountains Catholic girls' school, a charismatic ninth grader and her recently orphaned best friend set in motion a series of events that have decades-long ramifications.

"Told from multiple points of view, Unfinished Desires puts the author's twin talents—storytelling and characterization—on dazzling display. Godwin brings each of the girls and women fully alive and tells her well-conceived and well-executed story in a leisurely but suspenseful fashion." —*Richmond Times-Dispatch*
Working title was originally: The Red Nun: A Tale of Unfinished Desires.

Goenawan, Clarissa

The **perfect** world of Miwako Sumida. Clarissa Goenawan. Soho Press, 2020. 278 pages
ISBN 9781641291194
1. College students 2. Suicide victims 3. Friends' death 4. Villages 5. Friendship 6. Japan 7. Psychological fiction
LC 2019036361
A Japanese university student investigates the mysterious suicide of a classmate in a remote mountainside village, discovering secrets that may lead to his own unraveling.

"Goenawan's luminous prose captures the deep emotions of her characters as they grapple with questions about family history, gender, and sexuality. The tug of Miwako's strange, troubled spirit will wrench readers from the beginning." —*Publishers Weekly*

Rainbirds. Clarissa Goenawan. Soho Press, 2018. 336 p.
ISBN 9781616958558
1. Siblings 2. Sisters — Death 3. Murder 4. Murder investigation 5. Teachers 6. Japan 7. Literary fiction 8. Psychological fiction
LC 2017055165

After his sister, Keiko, is mysteriously murdered in a desolate, small town far from Tokyo, Ren finds himself stepping into her shoes, accepting her teaching position and a job reading to the catatonic wife of a wealthy politician while investigating what really happened.

Gogol, Nikolai Vasilievich

The **collected** tales of Nikolai Gogol. Nikolai Vasilevich Gogol; translated and annotated by Richard Pevear and Larissa Volokhonsky. Pantheon Books, 1998. Xxii, 435 p.
ISBN 9780679430230
1. Russia 2. St. Petersburg, Russia 3. Short stories 4. Anthologies 5. Translations
LC 97037228
A new translation offers thirteen satirical and fantastic stories of downtrodden characters who are set upon by the powers that be.

"Pevear's informative Preface persuasively emphasizes the personal, nonpolitical, and, to some degree, haphazard nature of the distinctive alchemy by which a deeply flawed and troubled soul managed to create some of the most colorful and haunting fiction of his century." —*Kirkus*

★ **Dead** souls. . Modern Library, 1997. 674 p.
ISBN 9780679602651
1. Swindlers and swindling 2. Social classes 3. Serfdom 4. Gossiping and gossips 5. Political corruption 6. Russia 7. Romanov Dynasty (1613-1917) 8. Translations 9. Classics
LC 9629784
Chichikov, an amusing, and often confused schemer, buys deceased serfs' names from landholders' poll tax lists hoping to mortgage them for profit.
Originally published: 1842.
Translated from the Russian.

Gohlke, Cathy

Promise me this. Cathy Gohlke. Tyndale House Publishers, 2012. 416 p.
ISBN 9781414353074
1. Promises 2. Long-distance romance 3. Interpersonal attraction 4. Last words 5. Siblings 6. First World War era (1914-1918) 7. Christian historical romances
LC 2011034977
Library Journal Best Books, 2012
Michael, a *Titanic* survivor living in New Jersey, develops a friendly correspondence with Annie, an Englishwoman whose brother died in the disaster, that evolves into love, but their budding relationship is threatened by the onset of World War I.

Goldberg, Lee

Bone canyon. Lee Goldberg. Thomas and Mercer, 2021. 288 p. (Eve Ronin novels, 2)
ISBN 9781542042710
1. Cold cases (Criminal investigation) 2. Women detectives 3. Crime scenes 4. Wildfires 5. Sexism 6. Los Angeles, California 7. Police procedurals
A catastrophic wildfire scorches the Santa Monica Mountains, exposing the charred remains of a woman who disappeared years ago. The investigation is assigned to Eve Ronin, the youngest homicide detective in the Los Angeles County Sheriff's Department, a position that forces her to prove herself again and again. Eve tirelessly digs into the past, unearthing dark secrets that reveal nothing about the case is as it seems. With almost

no one she can trust, her relentless pursuit of justice for the forgotten dead could put Eve's own life in peril.

"The tension ratchets up in this fast-paced police procedural, which addresses sexism, cronyism, and corrupt officers, while also dealing with the investigative process." —*Library Journal*

Fake truth. Lee Goldberg. Thomas & Mercer, 2020. 298 pages (Ian Ludlow novels, 3)

ISBN 9781542014694

1. Authors 2. Dissenters 3. Actors and actresses 4. Women CIA agents 5. Fake news 6. United States 7. Spy fiction 8. Thrillers and suspense

When author Ian Ludlow helps a Chinese movie star defect to the United States, he accidentally winds up becoming the hero in a real-life espionage thriller in the latest addition to the series following Killer Thriller.

"Who says preventing global destruction can t be funny? Goldberg continues to inject a welcome dose of levity into the thriller genre." —*Publishers Weekly*

Goldberg, Myla

Feast your eyes. Myla Goldberg. Scribner, 2019. 326 pages

ISBN 9781501197840

1. Women photographers 2. Mothers and daughters 3. Creativity in women 4. Obscenity (Law) 5. Photographs 6. 20th century 7. Literary fiction

Booklist Editors' Choice, 2019; Andrew Carnegie Medal for Excellence in Fiction finalist, 2020; National Book Critics Circle Award for Fiction finalist, 2019

The life of a controversial mid-20th-century photographer is chronicled through her daughter's memories, interviews with her intimates and excerpts from journals and letters documenting her quest for artistic legitimacy in the face of public notoriety.

"This is a novel of infinite depth, of caring authenticity both intimate and societal, of mothers and daughters, art and pain, and transcendent love." —*Booklist*

Goldberg, Tod

Gangsterland: a novel. Tod Goldberg. Counterpoint, 2014. 464 p.

ISBN 9781619023444

1. Gangsters 2. Assassins 3. Deception 4. Crime 5. Rabbis 6. Chicago, Illinois 7. Las Vegas, Nevada 8. Crime fiction

LC 2014014920

After his botched assassination attempt leaves three FBI agents dead, hit man Sal Cupertine agrees to the Chicago Mafia's insane plan to save his skin—several reconstructive surgeries and a new identity as "Rabbi David Cohen" of Las Vegas—but just as he is settling into his new life, he learns of the mafia's intentions to use the synagogue cemetery in a crime scheme.

"Clever plotting, a colorful cast of characters and priceless situations make this comedic crime novel an instant classic." —*Kirkus*

Goldbloom, Goldie

On division. Goldie Goldbloom. Farrar, Straus and Giroux, 2019. 240 p.

ISBN 9780374175313

1. Jewish families 2. Pregnant women 3. Middle-aged women — Sexuality 4. Extended families 5. Hasidism 6. Brooklyn, New York City 7. New York City 8. Literary fiction 9. Religious fiction

LC 2018060811

Anticipating the birth of her first great-grandchild, a 57-year-old Chasidic woman in Williamsburg, Brooklyn feels exposed and ashamed by a late-in-life pregnancy that slowly separates her from her community.

Golden, Arthur

★ **Memoirs** of a geisha: a novel. Arthur Golden. A. A. Knopf, 1997. 434 p.

ISBN 9780375400117

1. Geishas 2. Artisans 3. Competition in women 4. Women entertainers 5. Sisters 6. Kyoto, Japan 7. 1930s 8. 1940s 9. Historical fiction 10. Books to movies

LC 9774747

Booklist Editors' Choice, 1997; New York Times Notable Book, 1997

The "memoirs" of one of Japan's most celebrated geishas describes how, in 1929, as a little girl, she is sold into slavery; her efforts to learn the arts of the geisha; the impact of World War II; and her struggle to reinvent herself to win the man she loves.

"Rarely has a world so closed and foreign been evoked with such natural assurance, from the aesthetics of the Kyoto geisha's art—to the fetishized sexuality of Gion in the thirties and forties, at once delicate and crude, repressed and flagrant." —*The New Yorker*

Originally published: London : Chatto & Windus, 1997.

Also published: Toronto : Vintage Canada, 1999.

Golden, Christopher

Ararat. Christopher Golden. St. Martin's Press, 2017. 305 p. (Ben Walker novels, 1)

ISBN 9781250117052

1. Survival (after disaster) 2. Archaeological expeditions 3. Archaeologists 4. Mountains 5. Caves 6. Mount Ararat 7. Turkey 8. Horror

Bram Stoker Award for Best Novel, 2017; RUSA Reading List Short List, 2018

fter an avalanche uncovers an ancient boat (maybe Noah's Ark) on Turkey's Mt. Ararat, an archaeological team finds human-like remains inside a coffin—and the skeleton has horns! Then the explorers are trapped by a blizzard, and terrifying things happen. Is the evil coming from a supernatural power

The **pandora** room: a novel. Christopher Golden. St. Martin's Press, 2019. 320 pages (Ben Walker novels, 2)

ISBN 9781250192103

1. International intrigue 2. Extinct cities 3. Archaeologists 4. Plague 5. Militants 6. Horror

LC 2018041160

When what appears to be the original Pandora's box of mythological fame is discovered in an ancient city, neighboring countries fight for ownership before chaos-minded jihadi forces unleash a terrible plague.

"Golden provides a detailed setting and excellent character development. Where this novel shines is in the horror. The tension and fear are eerily realistic, while the supernatural monsters are unique and utterly terrifying." —*Booklist*

Red hands. Christopher Golden. St. Martin's Press, 2020. 320 p. (Ben Walker novels, 3)

ISBN 9781250246301

1. Elite operatives 2. Communicable diseases 3. Death 4. Biological weapons 5. Secrecy in government 6. New Hampshire 7. Horror 8. Thrillers and suspense

LC 2020028407

Loan Stars Favourites, 2020

Ben Walker, an expert in weird phenomena is asked by the Global Science Research Coalition to locate a woman who has been the victim of a devastating bioweapon that causes every person she touches to drop dead.

"The neck-whipping action and shifting points of view give the reader a wide-angle perspective on the complicated, terrifying situation, invoking maximum terror on every page." —*Booklist*

Goldin, Megan

The **escape** room. Megan Goldin. St. Martin's Press, 2019. 368 pages
ISBN 9781250219657
1. Resentfulness 2. Murderers 3. Secrets 4. Feuds 5. Office politics 6. Wall Street, New York City 7. Thrillers and suspense 8. Australian fiction
LibraryReads Favorites, 2019
Ordered to participate in a corporate team-building exercise that requires them to escape from a locked elevator, four ruthless Wall Street high-flyers struggle to put aside rivalries shaped by workplace intimidation, deception, and sexual harassment.
Originally published: North Sydney, Australia : Penguin Random House Australia, 2018.

The **night** swim. Megan Goldin. St. Martin's Press, 2020. 368 p.
ISBN 9781250219688
1. Podcasters 2. Trials (Rape) 3. Letters 4. Cold Cases (Criminal investigation) 5. Secrets 6. North Carolina 7. Psychological suspense 8. Australian fiction
LC 2020010738
LibraryReads Favorites, 2020
A popular true-crime podcaster finds an unsettling note on her windshield begging for help before she uncovers dark community secrets from the past and present, including one involving the disappearance of her own sister.
"This novel is haunting, yet somehow, after tearing at the reader's heart, it offers a good laugh at the end. Rachel delivers justice for all. Well done." —*Booklist*

Golding, Melanie

The **hidden:** a novel. Melanie Golding. Crooked Lane Books, 2021. 304 p.
ISBN 9781643852973
1. Women detectives 2. Mothers and daughters 3. Motherhood 4. Criminal investigation 5. Mythology, Celtic 6. England 7. Adaptations, retellings, and spin-offs 8. Psychological suspense
While investigating the brutal murder of Gregor, a seemingly single man, DS Joanna Harper discovers that her estranged daughter Ruby is somehow involved in this case that is steeped in Celtic mythology.
"Long before the end, readers will be questioning all their assumptions about who are the victims, who are the criminals, and exactly which facts really are the facts. As dexterously shape-shifting as the legends it draws from." —*Kirkus*

Little darlings. Melanie Golding. Crooked Lane Books, 2019. 304 p.
ISBN 9781683319979
1. New mothers 2. Changelings 3. Motherhood 4. Bergman, Ingmar 5. Twins 6. England 7. Psychological suspense
LibraryReads Favorites, 2019
Discounted by everyone when after the traumatizing birth of her twins she is threatened by a mysterious being, an exhausted mother risks the unthinkable when she becomes convinced that her infants have been replaced by changelings.

Golding, William

Close quarters. William Golding. Farrar, Straus, Giroux, 1987. 281 p; (Sea trilogy, 2)
ISBN 9780374125103
1. Ocean travel — History 2. Shipwrecks 3. Young men 4. Nobility 5. Classism 6. Atlantic Ocean 7. Indian Ocean 8. 1810s 9. Historical fiction 10. Sea stories 11. Literary fiction
LC 87005351
In the sequel to Rites of Passage, an old ship transporting cargo and passengers from England to Australia in the 19th century disintegrates after a sailor's error.
"This second volume of the trilogy begun with Rites of passage is a tale of the tragic misadventures befalling an 18th century fighting ship now converted to transporting cargo and passengers on the treacherous voyage from England to Australia. The novel is cast as a journal written by Edmund FitzHenry Talbot, a well-meaning, somewhat uncertain, slightly pompous officer and gentleman enroute to Sydney and a career in His Majesty's service. As a result of a green sailor's blunder, the ship's masts shatter, and it founders. Golding's principal achievement is the vivid, detailed depiction of a disintegrating vessel in the tropical seas, its progressive decay, and the wretchedness and despair of its passengers." —*Publishers Weekly*

★ **Darkness** visible. William Golding. Farrar Straus Giroux, 2007. 259 p.
ISBN 9780374530518
1. People with disfigurements 2. Mental illness 3. Religious fanaticism 4. Loneliness 5. Burn victims 6. Great Britain 7. Literary fiction 8. Psychological fiction
James Tait Black Memorial Prize for Fiction, 1979
Wartime firestorms in London mutilate a child, Matty, whose physical appearance keeps others from forming relationships with him.
"A child hideously maimed in the bombing of London during World War II grows up to inspire the messianic fantasies of the people with whom he comes in contact. In Golding's dark world the horrors of the physically deformed are mirrored in—but are no match for—the spiritual monsters who inhabit the novel's strange vision of contemporary life. A powerful contemplation of the evil at the root of human behavior." —*Booklist*
Originally published: London : Faber and Faber, 1979.

Fire down below. William Golding. Farrar, Straus, Giroux, 1989. [5], 313 p; (Sea trilogy, 3)
ISBN 9780374253813
1. Ocean travel — History 2. Sailors 3. Young men 4. Nobility 5. Classism 6. Australia 7. Indian Ocean 8. 1810s 9. Historical fiction 10. Sea stories
LC 88018079
Edmund Talbot learns about survival in a terrible storm off the Cape of Good Hope, in the sequel to Close Quarters.
"Golding is translucent and economical. In his writing, allegorical motifs are revealed fleetingly in the everyday and in the ordinary. He is at once a complex and highly readable novelist." —*The Economist*

The **inheritors**. William Golding. Harcourt, Brace & World, 1962. 233 p.
ISBN 9780156443791
1. Prehistoric humans 2. Cave dwellers 3. Stone age 4. Prehistoric women 5. Survival 6. Historical fiction 7. Literary fiction
LC 62016724

A happy group of mild-mannered Neanderthals cannot survive when the more technologically advanced beings, homo sapiens, arrive at their campsite.

Reprint. Originally published in London : Faber and Faber, 1955.

★ **Lord** of the flies: a novel. William Golding. Coward-McCann, 1955. 243 p.

ISBN 9780884116950

1. Survival (after airplane accidents, shipwrecks, etc.) 2. Human nature 3. Child castaways 4. Teenage boys 5. Boys 6. Psychological fiction 7. Literary fiction 8. Books to movies 9. Adult books for young adults

LC 55010081

The classic study of human nature which depicts the degeneration of a group of schoolboys marooned on a desert island.

First published: 1954.

William Golding centenary—Cover.

Originally published: 1954.

Reprint. Originally published in London : Faber and Faber, 1954.

Rites of passage. William Golding. Farrar, Straus, Giroux, 1980. 278 p; (Sea trilogy, 1)

ISBN 9780374250867

1. Ocean travel — History 2. Clergy 3. Immigrants 4. Nobility 5. Young men 6. Atlantic Ocean 7. England 8. 1810s 9. Historical fiction 10. Sea stories 11. First person narratives

LC 80016809

Booker Prize, 1980

Edmund Talbot recounts his voyage from England to the Antipodes, and the humiliating confrontation between the stern Captain Anderson and the nervous parson, James Colley, which leads to the latter's death.

"In a sense the novel seems highly artificial, not only in its careful, detailed recreation of the period, but also in the elaborate system of correspondences and parallels—some clear, some obscure—which underpins the narration. Yet at the same time it is an extremely lively, enjoyable piece of work. Readers who know only the early Golding will be surprised by its humor." —*Times Literary Supplement*

Goldman, Matt

Dead West. Matt Goldman. Forge, 2020. 304 p. (Nils Shapiro novels, 4)

ISBN 9781250191342

1. Private investigators 2. Divorced men 3. Grief 4. Suspicion 5. Murder investigation 6. Hollywood, California 7. Hardboiled fiction 8. Mysteries

Visiting Hollywood to investigate Beverly Mayer's heartbroken grandson's reckless spending activities, Minneapolis private detective Nils Shapiro infiltrates the grieving man's disorienting inner circle to uncover the truth about a fiancée's tragic death.

"Goldman continues to please with interesting twists, great peripheral characters, insights into specific communities, and enough peril to keep readers turning pages past bedtime." —*Booklist*

The **shallows**. Matt Goldman. Forge, 2019. 320 pages (Nils Shapiro novels, 3)

ISBN 9781250191311

1. Private investigators 2. Divorced men 3. Murder suspects 4. Law firms 5. Suspicion 6. Minnesota 7. Hardboiled fiction 8. Mysteries

Investigating the brutal murder of a Minnesota lawyer, private investigator Nils Shapiro and his partners are unexpectedly overwhelmed by an influx of complicated cases, additional murders and an unknown adversary that would keep the truth hidden.

"Fans of classic hard-boiled crime novels of the 1930s and 1940s will appreciate Nils's intelligence and likable coworkers, who star in a novel

that is timely, not old-fashioned, and featuring a riveting story." —*Library Journal*

Sequel to: Broken ice.

Goldman, William

★ The **princess** bride: S. Morgenstern's classic tale of true love and high adventure : the. Abridged by [i.e. written by] William Goldman. Harcourt Brace Jovanovich, 1973. 308 p.

ISBN 9780151730858

1. Princesses 2. Swordfighters 3. Kidnapping 4. Imaginary kingdoms 5. Agricultural laborers 6. Fantasy fiction 7. Humorous stories 8. Metafiction

LC 73006812

A classic swashbuckling romance retells the tale of a drunken swordsman and a gentle giant who come to the aid of Westley, a handsome farm boy, and Buttercup, a princess in dire need of rescue from the evil schemers surrounding her.

"This comes on like the hip fairy tales on TV—the best ones—with that constant finger-popping humorousness. But it is a real fairy tale and that is how it affects you—the men in the black capes especially, although there is also intrigue, love and danger. And if that isn't enough, it's 'being retold' in one of those elaborate narrative setups that gets things going on more cogitative levels." —*Kirkus*

Originally published: New York : Harcourt Brace Jovanovich, c1973.

Goldstein, Rebecca

36 arguments for the existence of God: a work of fiction. Rebecca Newberger Goldstein. Pantheon Books, 2010. 416 p.

ISBN 9780307378187

1. Faith and reason 2. Psychology teachers 3. Men — Religious life 4. Man-woman relationships 5. Love triangles 6. Humorous stories 7. Literary fiction

LC 2009017022

Elevated to celebrity by his best-selling book, psychology professor Cass Seltzer finds his relationship with a fellow theorist challenged by a former girlfriend's invitation to join her biochemistry experiment in immortality, an effort that is further complicated by his ongoing quest to understand religion.

"This is without a doubt the funniest work of existential philosophy you'll read.... Thoughtful, witty, and—really entertaining, 36 Arguments is part campus comedy, part romantic farce, part philosophical treatise." —*Christian Science Monitor*

Goldstone, Lawrence

Assassin of shadows. Lawrence Goldstone. Pegasus Books, 2019. 352 pages

ISBN 9781643131306

1. McKinley, William 2. Assassins 3. Presidents — Assassination 4. Anarchists 5. Assassination 6. Conspiracy theories 7. 1900s (Decade) 8. Historical thrillers

The latest historical thriller by New York Times Notable mystery author Lawrence Goldstone plunges readers into the dramatic events surrounding the assassination of President William McKinley.

Gonzalez, Christopher

I'm not hungry but I could eat. Christopher Gonzalez. Santa Fe Writer's Project, 2021. 115 p.

ISBN 9781951631215

1. Gay men 2. Bisexual men 3. Men 4. Food 5. Hunger 6. Short stories

Long nights, empty stomachs, and impulsive cravings haunt the stories of I'm Not Hungry But I Could Eat. Exploring the lives of bisexual and gay Puerto Rican men, these fifteen stories show a vulnerable, intimate world of yearning and desire. The stars of these narratives linger between living their truest selves and remaining in the wings, embarking on a journey of self-discovery to satisfy their hunger for companionship and belonging.

"Gonzalez's debut collection crackles with humor and tension in brilliantly crafted stories about food and relationships." —*Publishers Weekly*

Goodis, David

Nightfall. David Goodis. Vintage Books, 1991. 139 p.
ISBN 9780679734741
1. Fugitives 2. Gangsters 3. Police 4. Chases 5. Lost articles 6. Crime fiction

LC 90050592

"Nightfall's real story is about Vanning's despair about how to behave rationally when he knows he's being watched and the detective's self-questioning about whether a man can ever act with integrity without falling under suspicion. It's a relatively big theme for a noir, but Goodis keeps the story earthbound, rooting it in cynical observations designed to keep the mood of paranoia going." —*Washington City Paper*

Goodman, Allegra

The **cookbook** collector: a novel. Allegra Goodman. Dial Press, 2010. 352 p.
ISBN 9780385340854
1. Self-fulfillment in women 2. Rare books 3. Trust 4. Greed 5. Man-woman relationships 6. California 7. Cambridge, Massachusetts 8. Mainstream fiction

LC 2009047594

While executive Emily questions her choices about her career and a long-distance relationship with a successful man, her environmental activist sister, Jessamine, struggles with her own doubts about her beliefs and love affair.

"As the story opens in 1999, twentysomething sisters Emily and Jessamine Bach are a study in contrasts: One's a driven tech executive in Silicon Valley; the other, an impoverished Berkeley grad student/bookstore employee with a penchant for sprout sandwiches and seductive tree huggers. A revolving constellation of characters— Emily's golden-boy fiance and instant-millionaire colleagues, Jess' brusque, ponytailed boss, George— are made fully flesh and blood by Goodman; sometimes more so, even, than her protagonists. She especially excels at capturing the precipitous rush of the then-nascent tech boom, with its breakneck innovations and backroom intrigues, while simultaneously recounting Jess' increasing absorption into the ornate and distinctly analog world of high-end bibliophilia. Even as Cookbook strikes a rare bum note with a late, left-field revelation, Goodman delivers a novel of impressive elan and real emotional resonance." —*Entertainment Weekly*

Goodman, Carol

The **sea** of lost girls. Carol Goodman. William Morrow, 2020. 336 pages
ISBN 9780062979636
1. Women teachers 2. Married people 3. Sons 4. Boarding schools 5. Murder 6. United States 7. Maine 8. Psychological suspense

A teacher with a secret past endures attacks on her family when her son is implicated in the death of his girlfriend just before she discovers her husband's involvement.

"Readers will have a hard time putting this one down thanks to Goodman?'s storytelling powers." —*Publishers Weekly*

Goodman, Jo

In want of a wife. Jo Goodman. Berkley, 2014. 384 p.
ISBN 9780425264171
1. Frontier and pioneer life 2. Mail-order brides 3. Ranches 4. Determination in women 5. Interpersonal attraction 6. Wyoming 7. 1890s 8. Western romances 9. Historical romances

Responding to an ad for a mail-order bride needed in Bitter Springs, Wyoming, Jane Middlebourne arrives on the Morning Star ranch where she must prove to her new husband that she is the perfect woman to stand by his side.

A **touch** of forever. Jo Goodman. Jove, 2019. 402 pages (Cowboys of Colorado, 3)
ISBN 9780440000648
1. Independence in women 2. Young widows 3. Tubman, Harriet 4. Frontier and pioneer life 5. Railroad engineers 6. Colorado 7. The West (United States) 8. 1900s (Decade) 9. Western romances 10. Historical romances

Lily Salt has sworn off men. After finally gaining her independence, the last thing she needs is another man telling her what to do. But the handsome railroad engineer from New York isn't at all what she expected. He's kind, gentle...and tempting enough to make her wonder what a second chance at love might be worth.

"Crisp descriptions, insightful character development, and four savvy kids bring depth to this romantic historical charmer that is pure gold." —*Library Journal*

Goodwin, Bobi Gentry

Revelation. Bobi Gentry Goodwin. She Writes Press, 2019. 256 pages
ISBN 9781631526060
1. Family secrets 2. Addiction 3. Social workers 4. Family problems 5. Faith (Christianity) 6. San Francisco, California 7. African American fiction 8. Mainstream fiction 9. Multiple perspectives

When Angela walked into her social work office for the first time, she vowed her work with traumatized families would be meaningful. But when one family intrudes into her personal life, all bets are off. Discovering her father's picture alongside an overdosed client is just the beginning as her life and family unravels as she searches to uncover the truth.

"Wonderfully realistic dialogue and relatably fallible characters mark Goodwin's debut for readers who appreciate Vanessa Davis Griggs and Kimberla Lawson Roby." —*Booklist*

Goodwin, Daisy

The **American** heiress. Daisy Goodwin. St. Martin's Press, 2011. 480 p.
ISBN 9780312658656
1. Heirs and heiresses 2. Aristocracy — History 3. Americans in England 4. Dukes and duchesses 5. Cultural differences 6. Great Britain 7. England 8. Gilded Age (1865-1898) 9. 1890s 10. Historical fiction
Library Journal Best Books, 2011

Presents the story of vivacious Cora Cash, whose early twentieth-century marriage to England's most eligible duke is overshadowed by his secretive nature and the traps and betrayals of London's social scene.

"A shrewd, spirited historical romance with flavors of Edith Wharton, Daphne du Maurier, Jane Austen, Upstairs, Downstairs and a dash of

People magazine that charts a bumpy marriage of New World money and Old World tradition." —*Kirkus*

Originally published as My Last Duchess, London : Headline Review, 2010.

Goodwin, S. M.

Absence of mercy. S. M. Goodwin. Crooked Lane Books, 2020. 320 pages (Lightner and Law novels, 1)

ISBN 9781643855219

1. Crimean War veterans 2. Detectives 3. British in the United States 4. Police 5. Serial murders 6. New York City 7. 1850s 8. Historical mysteries

Forced by his father's political connections to relocate to pre-Civil War New York, a former Crimean War hero teams up with a misfit detective to investigate a philanthropist's murder and wrongful charges targeting an innocent woman. A first novel.

"An ingeniously clued and perfectly executed plot, a full cast of memorable characters, including the intriguingly flawed Lightner, and an expertly evoked setting, New York City circa 1857 in all its gritty and seedy splendor, add up to a must-read noir historical mystery." —*Booklist*

Goonan, Kathleen Ann

In war times. Kathleen Ann Goonan. Tor, 2007. 400 p.

ISBN 9780765313553

1. World War II 2. Saxophonists 3. Time travel (Future) 4. Technology 5. Jazz music 6. 1940s 7. Alternate histories 8. Science fiction 9. Adult books for young adults

LC 2007005165

John W. Campbell Memorial Award for Best Science Fiction Novel, 2008; RUSA Reading List, 2008

In an alternate-universe depiction of World War II, Sam enlists in the military after his brother is killed at Pearl Harbor and receives plans for a mysterious device from one of his instructors that he spends the war constructing, with unexpected and bizarre results.

"Goonan weaves a remarkable tale of quantum physics, human nature and jazz." —*SF Signal*

Sequel: This Shared Dream.

A Tom Doherty Associates Book.

Gordimer, Nadine

The **conservationist**. Nadine Gordimer. Penguin, 1978. 267 p.

ISBN 9780140047165

1. Industrialists 2. Farms 3. Injustice 4. Conservation of natural resources 5. Superiority and inferiority (Psychology) 6. South Africa 7. 1970s 8. Literary fiction 9. Multiple perspectives 10. First person narratives

Booker Prize, 1974

Mehring, a wealthy, dominating South African industrialist moves to preserve his way of life, his power, and his possessions in the face of massive injustice and suffering, changing times, and death.

"The author probes the way of life that exists in South Africa today, and some aspects of the tensions that exist among English and Afrikaaners, Blacks, coloreds, Indian shopkeepers.... Mehring is rich, white, bored. His farm is a weekend pleasure place to which he once brought the mistress whose flirtations with left wing causes have now exiled her forever. His teenage son won't even come home for the holidays and wants out of all that South Africa stands for. Mehring is kind enough to his blacks, keeps them in their place, avoids his Boer neighbors with whom he has nothing in common. A loner, living for himself, deliberately isolated from any unpleasantness that might intrude, only gradually does he begin to perceive that there are forces at work in nature, in the closeness between the blacks and the land by which some day his way of life will be forever changed." —*Publishers Weekly*

Originally published: London : Cape, 1974.

Get a life. By Nadine Gordimer. Farrar, Straus and Giroux, 2005. 208 p.

ISBN 9780374161705

1. Ecologists 2. People with cancer — Family relationships 3. Mortality 4. Quarantine 5. Parent and adult child 6. South Africa 7. Mexico 8. Literary fiction 9. Psychological fiction 10. Domestic fiction

LC 2005007199

Paul Bannerman, an ecologist living in South Africa, begins to re-examine his life after he is diagnosed with thyroid cancer and begins radiation treatments—an isolating experience that forces him to confront his relationships with family and friends.

"Gordimer confronts the reader with questions of conservation, social welfare, and emotional ecosystems. The austere Gordimer's mastery of her craft means she never needs to point at herself, thus highlighting the difference between art and performance." —*Harper's*

★ **July's** people. Nadine Gordimer. Viking, 1981. 160 p.

ISBN 9780140061406

1. Household employees 2. Insurgency 3. Families 4. Race relations 5. Villages 6. South Africa 7. Literary fiction

LC 80024877

When South Africa is riven by war and the Smales, a white couple, take refuge in the village of their former servant July, their relationships are completely transformed

Life times: stories, 1952-2007. Nadine Gordimer. Farrar, Straus and Giroux, 2010. 560 p.

ISBN 9780374270537

1. Politics and culture 2. Sexuality 3. Race (Social sciences) 4. South Africa 5. Short stories

LC 2010023403

A collection of short fictional works offers insight into the author's use of rich language to convey themes ranging from politics and sexuality to race and family life, in a volume that includes such pieces as "Friday's Footprint" and "Something Out There." BT

"Gordimer has been writing for more than 60 years now, but her concerns have been constant: race, justice, the South African land.... Four of the stories are new, an added pleasure for admirers of Gordimer's work. A welcome collection by a master of English prose—lucid and precisely written, if often bringing news only of disappointment, fear and loss." —*Kirkus*

★ **My** son's story. Nadine Gordimer. Farrar Straus Giroux, 1991. 277 p.

ISBN 9780374217518

1. Human rights activists 2. Fathers and sons 3. Interracial romance 4. Interracial families 5. Extramarital affairs 6. South Africa 7. Literary fiction

LC 9083232

Will, an adolescent black South African, finds his already unsettled relationship with his father further confused by his father's political activism and his affair with a young white woman.

"This is a thoughtful, poised, quietly poignant novel that not only recognizes the value and cost of political commitment, but also takes account of recent developments in South Africa and Eastern Europe in a way that Gordimer's previous work did not." —*Christian Science Monitor*

No time like the present: a novel. Nadine Gordimer. Farrar, Straus and Giroux, 2012. 421 p.

ISBN 9780374222642

1. Interracial marriage 2. Race relations 3. London, Jack 4. Post-apartheid era 5. Collective memory 6. South Africa 7. Multiple perspectives 8. Literary fiction 9. Psychological fiction

LC Bl2012005508

Gordimer trains her keen eye on Steve and Jabulile, an interracial couple living in a newly, tentatively, free South Africa. They have a daughter, Sindiswa; they move to the suburbs; Steve becomes a lecturer at a university; Jabulile trains to become a lawyer; there is another child, a boy this time. There is nothing so extraordinary about their lives, and yet, in telling their story and the stories of their friends and families, Gordimer manages to capture the tortured, fragmented essence of a nation struggling to define itself post-apartheid. —Publisher's website.

None to accompany me. Nadine Gordimer. Farrar, Straus and Giroux, 1994. 324 p.

ISBN 9780374222970

1. Women lawyers 2. Man-woman relationships 3. Marriage 4. Political violence 5. Family problems 6. South Africa 7. Literary fiction

LC 94-7553

Booklist Editors' Choice, 1994

Set in South Africa during the last days of the white regime, the heroine Vera Stark, a white lawyer, works to restore land taken from blacks by the government.

"A novel that raises more questions than it answers, 'None to Accompany Me' is an unflinching and perceptive exploration of people living on the brink of changes—political and personal—with little but their own sense of self-reliance to guide them." —Christian Science Monitor

The **pickup**. Nadine Gordimer. Farrar, Straus and Giroux, 2001. 270 p.

ISBN 9780374232108

1. Undocumented immigrants 2. Interethnic relations 3. Women 4. Man-woman relationships 5. Immigrants, Arab 6. Arab countries 7. Literary fiction

LC 2001023041

ALA Notable Book, 2002; Booklist Editors' Choice, 2001; Commonwealth Writers' Prize, Africa: Best Book, 2002; New York Times Notable Book, 2002

Julie is from an affluent white family and is always searching for new ideas and adventures. When her car breaks down in a South African city she is immediately drawn to Abdu the mechanic who comes to her aid. He has left his home and family in the north to find work in the new South Africa. As their relationship develops into passionate love, they must both confront the prejudices of their past and the uncertainties of the future.

"Gordimer writes so tenderly and so searchingly about Julie's gradual transcendence of her western self that she manages to hold sceptism at bay." —Women's Review of Books

Gordon, Jaimy

★ **Lord** of misrule: a novel. By Jaimy Gordon. McPherson & Co, 2010. 296 p.

ISBN 9780929701837

1. Horse trainers 2. Race horses 3. Deception 4. Horse racing 5. Race tracks 6. West Virginia 7. 1970s 8. Literary fiction

Booklist Editors' Choice, 2010; National Book Award for Fiction, 2010

Set in 1970s West Virginia, this National Book Award winner examines the bottom rung of the sport of kings. In the ruthless and often violent world of cheap horse racing, trainers and jockeys, grooms and hotwalkers, loan sharks and touts all struggle to take an edge, or prove their luck, or just survive.

"Gordon clearly loves the subculture of grifters and ne'er-do-wells whose lives center on a venue that obviously has never and will never bring them success. Her lowlifes have names like Two-Tie, Medicine Ed, Kidstuff and Deucey, and they're capable of speaking a kind of racetrack patois occasionally reminiscent of Damon Runyon characters.... Exceptional writing and idiosyncratic characters make this an engaging read." —Kirkus

Gorman, Edward

Riders on the storm : a Sam McCain mystery. Ed Gorman. Pegasus Books, 2014. 252 p. (Sam McCain mysteries, 10)

ISBN 9781605986258

1. Vietnam veterans 2. Violence against radicals 3. Murder investigation 4. Male friendship 5. Peace activists 6. Iowa 7. 1970s 8. Mysteries

Returning to his hometown after recovering from his Vietnam War injuries, lawyer Sam McCain investigates a charge against a veteran friend who has been accused of murdering a peace protestor.

"This is an extended, nuanced fictional biography with an occasional mystery thrown in. Great reading." —Booklist

Gornichec, Genevieve

★ The **witch's** heart. Genevieve Gornichec. Ace, 2021. 368 p.

ISBN 9780593099940

1. Mythology, Norse 2. Loki (Norse deity) 3. Witches 4. Monsters 5. Mothers 6. Mythological fiction 7.

LC 2020022385

LibraryReads Favorites, 2021

A subversive reimagining of Norse mythology traces the experiences of a banished witch whose unexpected passionate relationship with the trickster Loki produces three remarkable offspring before her family is targeted by wrathful gods.

"Gornichec's spellbinding story breathes life into a minor character from Norse myth, delving into the complexities of Angrboda's familial relationships and the lengths to which she'll go for both love and vengeance." —Publishers Weekly

Gortner, C. W.

The **first** actress: a novel of Sarah Bernhardt. C. W. Gortner. Ballantine Books, 2020. 384 pages

ISBN 9781524799076

1. Bernhardt, Sarah 2. Actors and actresses 3. Independence in women 4. Ambition in women 5. Determination in women 6. Single mothers 7. France 8. 19th century 9. Biographical fiction 10. Historical fiction 11. First person narratives

A historical tale inspired by the life of French actress Sarah Bernhardt traces the rise of a courtesan's daughter whose rebellious style and refusal to give up her child lead her to become the most acclaimed performer of her time.

"Skillful first-person narration evokes Bernhardt's fierce energy and tempestuous liaisons, the vulnerability borne of her wounding childhood, and her struggles against misogyny and anti-Semitism. Gortner does justice to this trailblazing celebrity and her fascinating era." —Publishers Weekly

Gosling, Victoria

Before the ruins: a novel. Victoria Gosling. Henry Holt and Company, 2020. 288 p.

ISBN 9781250759153

1. Manors 2. Friendship 3. Strangers 4. Games 5. Missing men 6. England 7. 1990s 8. 2010s 9. Literary fiction 10. Psychological suspense

LC 2020002138

A multilayered debut by the founder of The Reader Berlin finds a woman forced to confront a haunting summer from the past shaped by a stolen diamond necklace, a man on the run and a devastating betrayal.

"Read it for the characters, the prose, the story of complicated relationships, and the regrets of long-held secrets." —*Library Journal*

Goss, Theodora

The **sinister** mystery of the mesmerizing girl. Theodora Goss. Saga Press, 2019. 416 p. (Extraordinary adventures of the Athena Club, 3)
ISBN 9781534427877
1. Characters and characteristics in literature 2. Secret societies 3. Conspiracies 4. Kidnapping victims 5. Enemies 6. London, England 7. Great Britain 8. Victorian era (1837-1901) 9. Historical fantasy 10. Adaptations, retellings, and spin-offs 11. Adult books for young adults

Mary Jekyll and the Athena Club race to save Alice—and foil a plot to unseat the Queen—in the conclusion to the trilogy that began with the Nebula Award finalist and Locus Award winner The Strange Case of the Alchemist's Daughter.

The **strange** case of the alchemist's daughter. Theodora Goss. Saga Press, 2017. 352 p. (Extraordinary adventures of the Athena Club, 1)
ISBN 9781481466509
1. Characters and characteristics in literature 2. Secret societies 3. Alchemists 4. Fugitives 5. Monsters 6. London, England 7. Great Britain 8. Victorian era (1837-1901) 9. Historical fantasy 10. Adaptations, retellings, and spin-offs 11. Adult books for young adults
Locus Award for First Novel, 2018

Alone and penniless, Mary Jekyll hunts for her father's killer, a former friend named Edward Hyde, along with help from Sherlock Holmes and Dr. Watson resulting in the discovery of a secret society of immoral and power-crazed scientists.

Gottlieb, Eli

Best boy: a novel. Eli Gottlieb. Liveright Publishing Corporation, 2015. 248 p.
ISBN 9781631490477
1. People with autism 2. Roommates 3. Escapes 4. People with disabilities 5. Housing 6. Psychological fiction 7. First person narratives

LC 2014048573

LibraryReads Favorites, 2015; Library Journal Best Books, 2015; Booklist Editors' Choice, 2015

A middle-aged autistic resident of a therapeutic community where he was sent as a young child rebels against changes in his environment by attempting to return to a family home and younger sibling he only partially remembers.

"Gottlieb merits praise for both the endearing eloquence of Todd's voice and a deeply sympathetic parable that speaks to a time when rising autism rates and long-lived elders force many to weigh tough options." —*Kirkus*

Gowar, Imogen Hermes

The **mermaid** and Mrs. Hancock. Imogen Hermes Gowar. HarperCollins, 2018. 488 pages
ISBN 9780062859952
1. Courtesans 2. Mermaids 3. Captives 4. Unhappiness in women 5. Merchants 6. England 7. London, England 8. Georgian era (1714-1837) 9. Historical fantasy 10. Literary fiction

Shortlisted for The Women's Prize for Fiction, 2018

When one of his trading vessels returns to 18th-century London with the remarkable body of a mermaid, Jonah gains entry into high society and falls in love with a highly accomplished courtesan, with unexpected consequences.

Gowdy, Barbara

Helpless: a novel. Barbara Gowdy. Metropolitan Books, 2006. 320 p.
ISBN 9780805082883
1. Kidnapping victims 2. Obsession in men 3. Stalkers 4. Nine-year-old girls 5. Single mothers 6. Thrillers and suspense 7. Canadian fiction

LC 2006047348

Trillium Book Award, 2007; Governor General's Literary Awards, English-language Fiction finalist

"There is a clean urgency to Gowdy's tale. We are helpless before her sure and beguiling hand because ultimatelyand breathlesslywe are drawn in." —*Vancouver Sun*

Gracie, Anne

Marry in scandal. Anne Gracie. Berkley, 2018. 320 p. (Marriage of convenience romances, 2)
ISBN 9780425283820
1. Rogues 2. Nobility 3. Heirs and heiresses 4. Inheritance and succession 5. Shyness in women 6. England 7. Great Britain 8. Regency period (1811-1820) 9. Regency romances 10. Historical romances 11. Australian fiction
Australian Romance Readers Awards, Favourite Historical Romance, 2018

Shy young heiress, Lady Lily Rutherford, is in no hurry to marry. She dreams of true love and a real courtship. But when disaster strikes, she finds herself facing a scandal-forced marriage to her rescuer, Edward Galbraith, a well known rake. As heir to a title, Galbraith knows he must wed, so a convenient marriage suits him perfectly. But there is a darkness in his past, and secrets he refuses to share with his tender-hearted young bride.?

Graedon, Alena

The **word** exchange: a novel. Alena Graedon. Doubleday, 2014. 304 pages
ISBN 9780385537650
1. Dystopias 2. Language and technology 3. Missing persons 4. English language 5. Technology — Social aspects 6. North America 7. Literary fiction 8. Dystopian fiction 9. Science fiction

LC 2013033165

In a world where the "death of print" has become a near reality, Anana Johnson, an employee at the North American Dictionary of the English Language (NADEL), searches for her missing father and stumbles upon the spiritual home of the written world and a pandemic "word flu." BT.

"A wildly ambitious, darkly intellectual and inventive thriller about the intersection of language, technology and meaning." —*Kirkus*

Graff, Andrew J.

Raft of stars. Andrew J. Graff. Ecco Press, 2021. 304 pages
ISBN 9780063031906
1. Child abuse victims 2. Runaway boys 3. Wilderness survival 4. Rafts 5. Shooting 6. Wisconsin 7. 1990s 8. Coming-of-age stories

Fleeing into the woods believing that they have accidentally murdered an abusive parent, two young boys, unaware that they have become the focus of a desperate search, navigate dangerous natural threats in their effort to survive.

"Graff's narrative voice is lyrical, with a Southern Gothic edge that fits surprisingly well with the Wisconsin Northwoods setting. Exploring the necessity of the stories we tell ourselves to survive, Raft of Stars is a clever, compelling coming-of-age tale." —*Booklist*

Grafton, Sue

A is for alibi. Sue Grafton. Holt, Rinehart, and Winston, 1982. 274 p. (Kinsey Millhone mysteries, 1)

ISBN 9780805013344

1. Women private investigators 2. Frameups 3. Murder investigation 4. Widows 5. Murder 6. Santa Teresa (Calif. : Imaginary place) 7. California 8. Mysteries 9. Adult books for young adults

LC 81007128

After serving time for the murder of her husband, Nikki Fife is out on parole and wants private investigator Kinsey Millhone to find the real killer.

"Kinsey Millhone is a cut above the usual woman private eye who flounces through fiction. Millhone is neither a sex bomb nor a detached cerebrum, but a believable, straightforward character." —*Booklist*

X. Sue Grafton. G. P. Putnam's Sons, 2015. 400 p. (Kinsey Millhone mysteries, 24)

ISBN 9780399163845

1. Serial murderers 2. Psychopaths 3. Women private investigators 4. Murder investigation 5. Millhone, Kinsey (Fictitious character) 6. California 7. 1980s 8. Mysteries 9. Adult books for young adults

A serial killer who leaves no trace of his crimes challenges Kinsey Milhone's skills to solve the case before she becomes his next victim.

"Grafton's endless resourcefulness in varying her pitches in this landmark series (W Is for Wasted, 2013, etc.), graced by her trademark self-deprecating humor, is one of the seven wonders of the genre." —*Kirkus*

Y is for yesterday. Sue Grafton. Marian Wood, 2017. 483 p. (Kinsey Millhone mysteries, 25)

ISBN 9780399163852

1. Rapists 2. Extortion 3. Criminals 4. Psychopaths 5. Women private investigators 6. California 7. 1980s 8. Mysteries 9. Adult books for young adults

Kinsey Millhone monitors the release from prison of a sociopath who is determined to exact revenge on a fellow perpetrator who went missing after they sexually assaulted a fourteen-year-old classmate.

"The series may be coming to a close, but Grafton (W Is for Wasted) constructs an intricate plot following two time lines with at least a dozen characters in play while rarely slowing the pace. Kinseys fans may have to take notes to keep up with her as she untangles a web of lies and cover stories to solve the current blackmail case as well as the older murder." —*Library Journal*

Series complete in 25 volumes.

Graley, Lisa

The current that carries: stories. By Lisa Graley. The University of Georgia Press, 2016. 176 p.

ISBN 9780820349879

1. Rural life 2. Loss (Psychology) 3. Interpersonal relations 4. Appalachian region 5. Short stories 6. Literary fiction 7. Southern fiction

LC 2015047529

This collection bristles and hums with the rugged resilience one encounters in southern and Appalachian fiction, where ghosts of loved ones and livestock alike haunt an underworld of lonely trails.

"Eight stories that give voice to incommunicable aspects of love and loss." —*Kirkus*

Grames, Juliet

The seven or eight deaths of Stella Fortuna. Juliet Grames. Ecco Press, 2019. 445 p.

ISBN 9780062862822

1. Teenage girls 2. Sisters 3. Protectiveness in teenagers 4. Immigration and emigration 5. Italian-American women 6. Italy 7. Connecticut 8. 20th century 9. 21st century 10. Historical fiction 11. Domestic fiction 12. Coming-of-age stories

LibraryReads Favorites, 2019

Believed cursed in her rugged Italian village, a tough, intelligent teen protects her younger sister during World War II, enduring challenges that transform her views about survival and independence.

"With her story of an ordinary woman who is anything but, Grames explores not just the immigrant experience but the stages of a womans life. This is a sharp and richly satisfying novel." —*Publishers Weekly*

Gran, Sara

Claire DeWitt and the city of the dead. Sara Gran. Houghton Mifflin Harcourt, 2011. 288 p. (Claire DeWitt mysteries, 1)

ISBN 9780547428499

1. Women private investigators 2. Missing persons investigation 3. Drug use 4. Murder investigation 5. Public prosecutors 6. Brooklyn, New York City 7. New Orleans, Louisiana 8. Hardboiled fiction 9. Mysteries

LC 2010021449

Library Journal Best Books, 2011; Macavity Award for Best Mystery Novel, 2012

Augmenting her brilliant deductive skills with dream analysis, marijuana, and the written work of a mysterious French detective, private investigator Claire DeWitt reluctantly returns to post-Katrina New Orleans to solve the disappearance of an unpopular prosecutor.

"The novel is is difficult to categorize, offering a strangely appealing mix of the mystical and the hardboiled. The book is beautifully written in a tight, quirky style that distinguishes Gran as one of the more original writers working today." —*Miami Herald*

The infinite blacktop: a novel. Sara Gran. Atria Books, 2018. 304 p. (Claire DeWitt mysteries, 3)

ISBN 9781501165719

1. Women private investigators 2. Hit-and-run accidents 3. King, Martin Luther, 1929-1968 4. Missing persons investigation 5. Murder investigation 6. Hardboiled fiction 7. Mysteries

LC 2018026234

Acclaimed detective Claire DeWitt navigates three cases from different turning points in her life, including the disappearance of a childhood friend, the cold-case double murder that shaped her PI license, and a near-fatal attack by a homicidal driver.

Includes bibliographical references and index.

Grant, Helen

The glass demon. Helen Grant. Bantam Dell, 2011. 320 p.

ISBN 9780385344203

1. Fathers and daughters 2. Relics 3. Demons 4. Supernatural 5. Teenage girls 6. Germany 7. Horror 8. Adult books for young adults

Booklist Editors' Choice, 2011; School Library Journal Best Books: Best Adult Books 4 Teens, 2011

When seventeen-year-old Lin and her family move to an ancient German castle for a year while her medievalist father searches for the famed Allerheiligen glass—lost stained glass windows that are said to be haunted by a terrifying demon—she becomes involved in a horrific murder mystery.

"With its fascinating information on medieval folklore, unique setting, and increasingly claustrophobic sense of terror, this is an exhilarating page-turner that offers a cerebral blend of horror and mystery." —*Booklist*

The **vanishing** of Katharina Linden. Helen Grant. Delacorte, 2010. 304 p.
ISBN 9780385344173
1. Villages 2. Missing persons 3. Secrets 4. Ten-year-old girls 5. Bullying and bullies 6. Germany 7. Mysteries 8. Coming-of-age stories 9. Adult books for young adults
Alex Award, 2011; Booklist Editors' Choice: Adult Books for Young Adults, 2010

Reviled in her German village home where her only friends are a fellow outcast and an elderly storyteller, eleven-year-old Pia investigates the disappearances of three local girls whom she believes are tied to unsolved missing persons cases from decades earlier.

"Set in the small German town of Bad Mnstereifel during a cold, dreary winter when little girls seem to be disappearing left and right, this dark story gains immeasurably from Grant's choice of narrator: Pia Kolvenbach, who is socially ostracized (shunned as the Potentially Explosive Schoolgirl) after her grandmother dies in a bizarre accident. Feeling even more isolated when her English mother and German father begin quarreling, Pia finds companionship with StinkStefan, the most unpopular boy in the class, and Herr Schiller, a kindly old gent who spins terrifying but oddly comforting horror stories. Although thin on plot, the novel has nice atmosphere and takes a tender view of lonely children trying to make sense of a grown-up world." —*New York Times Book Review*

Grant, Mira

Blackout. Mira Grant. Orbit, 2012. 560 p. (Newsflesh, 3)
ISBN 9780316081078
1. Conspiracies 2. Viruses 3. Zombies 4. Near future 5. Dystopias 6. Apocalyptic fiction 7. Horror
In 2041, Georgia Mason, held hostage by a team of CDC researchers, must find her way back to Shaun Mason, who is dealing with his own problems, such as zombie bears, mad scientists and rogue government agencies, before things get worse in her post-zombie, post-resurrection America.

Deadline. Mira Grant. Orbit, 2011. 560 p. (Newsflesh, 2)
ISBN 9780316081061
1. Conspiracies 2. Viruses 3. Zombies 4. Near future 5. Dystopias 6. Apocalyptic fiction 7. Horror
When a CDC researcher, after faking her own death, arrives on his doorstep with a ravenous pack of zombies in tow, Shaun Mason, the head of a news organization, is plunged into the biggest story of his life.

Feed. Mira Grant. Grand Central Pub, 2010. 560 p. (Newsflesh, 1)
ISBN 9780316081054
1. Conspiracies 2. Viruses 3. Zombies 4. Near future 5. Mind control 6. Apocalyptic fiction 7. Horror
Goodreads Choice Award, 2010
In the year 2014, a new virus emerges, taking over bodies and minds with one, unstoppable command, FEED, and, now, 20 years later, two re-

porters will stop at nothing to expose the dark conspiracy behind the infected.

"Shunning misogynistic horror tropes in favor of genuine drama and pure creepiness, McGuire has crafted a masterpiece of suspense with engaging, appealing characters who conduct a soul-shredding examination of what's true and what's reported." —*Publishers Weekly*

Feedback. Mira Grant. Orbit, 2016. 512 p. (Newsflesh, 4)
ISBN 9780316379342
1. Viruses 2. Zombies 3. Journalists 4. Dystopias 5. Near future 6. Apocalyptic fiction 7. Horror
LC 2016013017
Loan Stars Favourites, 2016

Twenty years after the Rising—the start of an infection that caused people to have a single uncontrollable impulse to feed—a team of scrappy underdog reporters relentlessly pursue dangerous truths on the presidential campaign trail.

"This mashup of medical and media ethics, politics and the living undead, is a whip-smart thriller overflowing with sharp ideas and social commentary." —*Kirkus*
Story overlaps the timeline of Feed (2010).

Into the drowning deep. Mira Grant. Orbit, 2017. 512 p. (Into the drowning deep, 1)
ISBN 9780316379403
1. Shipwrecks 2. Vanished ships 3. Sea monsters 4. Ocean travel 5. Scientists 6. Mariana Trench 7. Contemporary fantasy 8. Horror
LC 2017020686

Victoria Stewart and her crew sail to the Mariana Trench in the hopes of discovering the fate of the Atargatis, which, along with its crew, including Victoria's sister, was lost at sea during the crew's attempt to film a mockumentary on ancient sea creatures of legend.
This novel is a sequel to the author's 2015 novella Rolling in the deep.

Parasite. Mira Grant. Little, Brown, 2013. 608 p. (Parasitology, 1)
ISBN 9780316218955
1. Parasites 2. Near future 3. Genetic engineering 4. Amnesia 5. Immunity 6. Bio-thrillers 7. Science fiction 8. Science fiction thrillers
LibraryReads Favorites, 2013

In the future, a genetically engineered tapeworm protects most of the human populace from illness, boosts everyone's immune system and even secretes designer drugs, but now the organisms have begun to change and want out of human bodies they occupy—at all costs.

Grass, Gunter

The **box**: tales from the darkroom. Gunter Grass; translated from the German by Krishna Winston. Houghton Mifflin Harcourt, 2010. 208 p.
ISBN 9780547245034
1. Photography 2. Childhood 3. Growing up 4. Father and child 5. Memories 6. Literary fiction
LC 2010008479

Grass writes in the voices of his eight children as they record memories of their childhoods and of their father.

Crabwalk. Gunter Grass; translated from the German by Krishna Winston. Harcourt, 2002. 240 p.
ISBN 9780151007646
1. Shipwrecks 2. Journalists 3. Fathers and sons 4. Guilt 5. Memories 6. Literary fiction 7. First person narratives 8. Translations
LC 2002013205
New York Times Notable Book, 2003

Presents a fictional exploration of the worst maritime disaster in history, the 1945 sinking of a German cruise ship packed with refugees by a Soviet sub—a disaster that killed nine thousand people.

"A writer who refuses to avert his eyes from unpleasant truths, Grassremains an eloquent explorer of his country's troubled 20th-century history." —*Publishers Weekly*

Too far afield. Gunter Grass; translated from the German by Krishna Winston. Harcourt, 2000. 658 p.
ISBN 9780151002306
1. Senior men 2. German reunification 3. Berlin, Germany 4. East Germany 5. Political fiction 6. Translations
LC 29586
Library Journal Best Books, 2000; New York Times Notable Book, 2000

Follows two old German men—one a former Eastern diplomat, the other a Prussian spy who has served many masters—as they make their way in modern Germany.

"The narrative's focus is German reunification, in particular, the fate of the German Democratic Republic after the Wall came down in 1989. At the center of the novel are two characters, locked in a sort of political marriage: Theo Wuttke, a former East German cultural figure and long-winded raconteur, and Ludwig Hoffstaller, a professional spy who served for years as Wuttke's shadow. They are both about to turn 70 in this new Germany and are now both employees of the agency responsible for privatizing state-held companies." —*Booklist*

Gratton, Tessa

The **queens** of Innis Lear. Tessa Gratton. Tom Doherty Associates Book, 2018. 544 p. (Queens of Innis Lear, 1)
ISBN 9780765392466
1. Princesses 2. Rulers — Succession 3. Inheritance and succession 4. Magic 5. Prophecy 6. Epic fantasy 7. Adaptations, retellings, and spin-offs 8. Adult books for young adults
LC 2017039670
Booklist Editors' Choice: Adult Books for Young Adults, 2018; Loan Stars Favourites, 2018

A fantasy inspired by Shakespeare's "King Lear" depicts a once-bountiful isle decimated by a prophecy-obsessed king's erratic decisions, where three rival princesses prepare for a war that will determine their realm's leadership and survival.

Grau, Shirley Ann

The **keepers** of the house. Shirley Ann Grau. Knopf, 1969. 309 p.
ISBN 9780394431826
1. Interracial marriage 2. Interracial families 3. Small town life 4. Politicians 5. Race relations 6. Southern States 7. Literary fiction 8. Southern fiction
LC 64012306
Pulitzer Prize for Fiction, 1965

Abigail is the last keeper of the house, the last to know the Howland family's secrets. Now in the name of all her brothers and sisters, she must take her bitter revenge on the small-minded Southern town that shames them.

Graves, Robert

Claudius the god and his wife Messalina: the troublesome reign of Tiberius Claudius Caesar, Emperor of the Romans(born B.C. 10, died A.D. 54), as described by himself : also his murder at the hands of thenotorious Agrippina (mother of the Emperor Nero) and his subsequent deification as described by others. By Robert Graves. Vintage, 1989. Viii, 533 p. : Table
ISBN 9780679725732
1. Claudius 2. Roman emperors 3. Rome 4. Roman Empire (27 BCE-476 CE) 5. Historical fiction
James Tait Black Memorial Prize for Fiction, 1934

Depicts the turbulent life of a Roman emperor, reconstructing the decadence of the Roman world

A vivid picture of profligate Rome during the years in which Claudius conquered Britain and instituted many reforms at home. A story complete in itself, though a continuation of 'I, Claudius.' Booklist.
Sequel to: I, Claudius.
Originally published: London : Arthur Barker, 1934.

★ **I,** Claudius: from the autobiography of Tiberius Claudius, born 10 B.C, murdered and deified A.D. 54. Robert Graves. Vintage Books, 1989. X, 468 p.
ISBN 9780679724773
1. Claudius 2. Roman emperors 3. Rome 4. Roman Empire (27 BCE-476 CE) 5. Biographical fiction 6. Historical fiction 7. Modern classics
James Tait Black Memorial Prize for Fiction, 1934

Claudius, born weak and with a stutter, was shamed and dismissed by his family as an idiot. This allowed him to live under the public radar and avoid his family's scandals and murders to become the emperor of Rome in 41 A.D.
Sequel: Claudius the god and his wife Messalina.
Originally published: London : Arthur Barker, 1934.

Graves, Stephanie

Olive Bright, Pigeoneer. Stephanie Graves. Kensington Pub Corp, 2020. 304 pages
ISBN 9781496731517
1. World War II home front 2. Young women 3. Pigeons 4. Women amateur detectives 5. Villages 6. England 7. Second World War era (1939-1945) 8. Historical mysteries

Tending her veterinarian father's Hertfordshire racing pigeons while waiting for her best friend to return from World War II, Olive is recruited into the Baker Street covert branch of British Intelligence before investigating the murder of a local busybody.

"A delightful classic village mystery studded with little-known World War II facts: a promising series debut." —*Kirkus*

Gray, Anissa

The **care** and feeding of ravenously hungry girls. Anissa Gray. Berkley Books, 2019. 294 p.
ISBN 9781984802439
1. Aunt and niece 2. Mothers and daughters 3. African American families 4. Sisters 5. Women prisoners 6. Michigan 7. 2010s 8. Literary fiction 9. Domestic fiction 10. Multiple perspectives
LC 2018018552
LibraryReads Favorites, 2019

When their formidably strong-willed eldest sister is arrested, abruptly transitioning their family from respectability to disgrace, two younger sisters confront complicated dynamics in their family and identities to uncover what really happened.

Gray, Erick S.

Love & a gangsta: a novel. By Erick S. Gray. Augustus Pub, 2009. 261 p. : Illustration (Crave all, lose all novels, 2)

ISBN 9780979281648
1. Drug traffic 2. Ambition in men 3. Criminals 4. Gangsters 5. Man-woman relationships 6. New York City 7. Queens, New York City 8. Urban fiction 9. African American fiction

LC Bl2010011393

Soul completes a four-year stint in prison but rejects America's request for him to live honestly, returning to the Queens drug scene and severely testing the strength of their relationship.

Sequel to: Crave all, lose all. New York : Augustus, c2008.

Greaves, Chuck

Hush money: a mystery. Chuck Greaves. Minotaur Books, 2012. 304 p. (Jack MacTaggart mysteries, 1)

ISBN 9781250005236
1. Insurance fraud 2. Show jumping 3. Horses 4. Lawyers 5. Fraud investigation 6. Mysteries

LC 2012004489

Investigating a socialite's insurance claim for a champion show horse's sudden death, elite Pasadena law firm newcomer Jack MacTaggart uncovers links to an old blackmail scheme before he is falsely accused of murder.

Grebe, Camilla

After she's gone: a novel. Camilla Grebe; translated from the Swedish by Elizabeth Clark Wessel. Ballantine Books, 2019. 304 p. (Psychological profiler novels (Camilla Grebe), 2)

ISBN 9780425284407
1. Criminal profilers 2. Cross-dressers 3. Women with amnesia 4. Secrets 5. Cold cases (Criminal investigation) 6. Sweden 7. Scandinavian crime fiction 8. Translations

LC 2018050773

Finds an amnesia-stricken psychological profiler struggling to figure out what happened, while a teen with a difficult secret considers exposing himself to save the profiler's life.

"Grebe delivers an unflinching, heart-wrenching message about the plight of refugees in this scorching thriller." —*Publishers Weekly*

Sequel to: The Ice Beneath Her

Originally published in Swedish in Sweden by Wahlstrom & Widstrand, a division of the Bonnier Group, Stockholm, Sweden, in 2017.

Translated from the Swedish.

The **ice** beneath her: a novel. Camilla Grebe; translated from the Swedish by Elizabeth Clark Wessel. Ballantine Books, 2016. 368 p. (Psychological profiler novels (Camilla Grebe), 1)

ISBN 9780425284322
1. Missing persons 2. Murder investigation 3. Criminal profilers 4. Dementia 5. Murder suspects 6. Thrillers and suspense 7. Scandinavian crime fiction 8. Translations

LC 2016013298

Loan Stars Favourites, 2016

Investigating a grisly murder in a business tycoon's Stockholm residence, detective Peter Lindgren and psychological profiler Hanne Lagerlind-Schon navigate complications in their own relationship while tracking down the businessman, who may have been having an affair with the victim.

"A tour de force that lifts its author to the front rank among the increasingly crowded field of Nordic noir." —*Kirkus*

Translation of: Alskaren fran huvudkontoret.

Originally published: Stockholm : Wahlstrom & Widstrand, 2015.

Translated from the Swedish.

Grecian, Alex

The **saint** of wolves and butchers. Alex Grecian. G.P. Putnam's Sons, 2018. 388 p.

ISBN 9780399176111
1. Nazis 2. Nazi hunters 3. War criminals 4. Nazism 5. Deception 6. Kansas 7. Thrillers and suspense

LC 2017012118

An enigmatic hunter and his highly skilled dog track a Nazi concentration-camp administrator who has been hiding in the United States, a case that is complicated by the man's secret ongoing work and his band of fanatical followers.

Also published in Great Britain under the title The Wolf.

Greeley, Molly

The **clergyman's** wife. Molly Greeley. William Morrow & Co, 2019. 304 p.

ISBN 9780062942913
1. Married women 2. Romantic love 3. Spouses of clergy 4. Options, alternatives, choices 5. Interclass friendship 6. England 7. Great Britain 8. Regency period (1811-1820) 9. Historical fiction 10. Adaptations, retellings, and spin-offs

When she makes the acquaintance of Mr. Travis, the tenant of her vicar husband's condescending patroness, Charlotte, for the first time in her life, feels appreciated, heard and seen and must question the role of love and passion in her life.

"With tight prose and expert characterization (and, sadly, a finale true to those times), Greeley easily draws readers into the world she's created while largely staying true to Pride and Prejudice's original plot." —*Publishers Weekly*

A Pride & Prejudice novel—Cover.

Green, Amy Lynn

Things we didn't say. Amy Lynn Green. Bethany House, 2020. 416 p.

ISBN 9780764237874
1. Women translators 2. World War II home front 3. Prisoners of war 4. Helpfulness in women 5. Concentration camps 6. Minnesota 7. Second World War era (1939-1945) 8. Epistolary novels 9. Christian historical fiction

LC 2020023530

Carol Award for Best Historical, 2021; Carol Award for Best Debut, 2021

In this epistolary novel from the WWII home front, Johanna Berglund is forced to return to her small Midwestern town to become a translator at a German prisoner of war camp. There, amid old secrets and prejudice, she finds that the POWs have hidden depths. When the lines between compassion and treason are blurred, she must decide where her heart truly lies.

"Green's debut is a memorable and moving exploration of prejudice and friendship across ethnic and gender lines. For readers who enjoy tales of ordinary people thrust into extraordinary historical situations a la Susan Meissner and Lisa Wingate." —*Library Journal*

Green, Hank

An **absolutely** remarkable thing: a novel. Hank Green. Penguin Group USA 2018. 320 p. (Absolutely remarkable thing novels, 1)

ISBN 9781524743444
1. Fame 2. Social media 3. Young women 4. Self-discovery 5. Robots 6. New York City 7. Science fiction 8. Coming-of-age stories 9. Adult books for young adults

LC 2018010156

YALSA Quick Picks for Reluctant Young Adult Readers, 2020

The first to document the appearance of the Carls, giant robot-like statues popping up around the world, April May finds herself at the center of an intense international media spotlight that puts her relationships, identity and safety at risk.

"At once funny, exciting, and a tad terrifying, this exploration of aliens and social-media culture is bound to have wide appeal to readers interested in either theme." —*Booklist*

Sequel: A beautifully foolish endeavor

Green, Jocelyn

The **mark** of the king. Jocelyn Green. Bethany House, 2017. 400 p.
ISBN 9780764219061
1. Midwives 2. Exiles 3. Voyages and travels 4. Colonists 5. New France 6. 1720s 7. Colonial America (1600-1775) 8. Christian historical fiction

LC 2016034521

Christy Award for Historical Category, 2017

After being unjustly imprisoned for the death of her client, midwife Julianne Chevalier trades her life sentence for exile to the French colony of Louisiana in 1720. She marries a fellow convict in order to sail, but when tragedy strikes—and a mystery unfolds—Julianne must find her own way in this dangerous new land while bearing the brand of a criminal.

Veiled in smoke. Jocelyn Green. Bethany House, 2020. 384 pages (Windy City saga, 1)
ISBN 9780764233302
1. Sisters 2. Homeless persons 3. Civil War veterans 4. Post-traumatic stress disorder 5. Murder victims 6. 1870s 7. Christian historical fiction 8. Christian mysteries

LC Bl2019036930

As Chicago's Great Fire destroys their bookshop, Meg and Sylvie Townsend make a harrowing escape from the flames with the help of reporter Nate Pierce. But the trouble doesn't end there—their father is committed to an asylum after being accused of murder, and they must prove his innocence before the asylum truly drives him mad.

"History, mystery, romance, and faith combine in the first book in the Christy Award-winning Green's Windy City Saga. Recommend to readers who enjoy Lisa Wingate and Elizabeth Camden." —*Booklist*

Greenberg, Joanne

I never promised you a rose garden: a novel. By Hannah Green. Holt, Rinehart and Winston, 1964. 300 p.
ISBN 9780030437250
1. Greenberg, Joanne 2. Teenage girls with mental illnesses 3. Psychotherapist and patient 4. Teenage girls — Psychology 5. Teenagers with schizophrenia 6. Psychiatric hospital patients 7. Autobiographical fiction 8. Psychological fiction 9. Books to movies

LC 64011018

Chronicles the three-year battle of a mentally ill, but perceptive, teenage girl against a world of her own creation, emphasizing her relationship with the doctor who gave her the ammunition of self-understanding with which to destroy that world of fantasy.

"The hospital world and Deborah's fantasy world are strikingly portrayed, as is the girl's violent struggle between sickness and health, a struggle given added poignancy by youth, wit, and courage." —*Library Journal*

Greene, Amy

Long Man. Amy Greene. Alfred A Knopf, 2014. 272 p.

ISBN 9780307593436
1. Rivers 2. Missing children 3. Farms 4. Small town life 5. Dams 6. Tennessee 7. Joyce, James 8. Historical fiction 9. Literary fiction 10. Southern fiction

Booklist Editors' Choice, 2014

Refusing to evacuate the East Tennessee hometown that is being flooded by a newly constructed dam, Annie Clyde Dodson battles with a husband who would start over elsewhere only to begin a frantic search when their toddler goes missing.

"A smart and moody historical novel that evokes the best widescreen Southern literature." —*Kirkus*

Greene, Graham

★ **Brighton** Rock. Graham Greene; introduction by J.M. Coetzee. Penguin Books : 2004. Xvi, 270 p.
ISBN 9780142437971
1. Psychopaths 2. Murder 3. Gangsters 4. Journalists 5. Teenage murderers 6. England 7. Brighton, England 8. Psychological suspense 9. Literary fiction 10. Crime fiction

LC 2004275123

Set in Brighton among the criminal rabble, the story depicts the tragic career of a 17 year-old boy named Pinkie whose primary ambition is to lead a gang to rival that of the wealthy and established Calleoni.

Graham Greene Centennial, 1904-2004—Cover.
Originally published: New York : The Viking press, 1938.
Originally published in Great Britain: William Heinemann, 1938.
Originally published: 1938.
Includes bibliographical references (p. xv-xvi).

The **captain** and the enemy. Graham Greene. Penguin, 2005. 154 p.
ISBN 9780143039297
1. Foster fathers 2. Gun smugglers 3. Abandoned boys 4. Father-separated boys 5. Impostors 6. England 7. Psychological fiction 8. Literary fiction

This evocative novel centers on the life of Victor Baxter, a young boy growing up amid odd and touching circumstances, and on his relationships with various unusual and enigmatic people.

"The author wastes not a word in distilling the fictional preoccupations of a lifetime, omitting descriptive padding and elaborate transitions. But stripped down, the narrative runs fast and true across that bleak and poignant emotional landscape that is uniquely, immortally his." —*Time*

Vintage Greene—Cover.
Originally published: London: Reinhardt, 1988.
Originally published: New York: Viking, 1988.

Collected stories: including May we borrow your husband? A sense of reality, Twenty-one stories. Graham Greene. Viking Press, 1973. Xii, 561 p.
ISBN 9780670229116
1. Violence 2. Vandalism 3. Gay men 4. Honeymoons 5. Man-woman relationships 6. Great Britain 7. Short stories 8. Literary fiction

LC 73002334

Forty stories by the popular British novelist show his mastery of narrative, suspense, and atmosphere.

★ The **end** of the affair. Graham Greene. Penguin, 2004. 192 p.
ISBN 9780142437988
1. Love triangles 2. Extramarital affairs 3. Loss (Psychology) 4. Former lovers 5. Authors, English 6. London, England 7. Psychological fiction 8. Love stories 9. Literary fiction

LC 51013559

The love affair between Maurice Bendix and Sarah, flourishing in the turbulent times of the London Blitz, ends when she suddenly and without explanation breaks it off. After a chance meeting rekindles his love and jealousy two years later, Bendix hires a private detective to follow Sarah, and slowly his love for her turns into an obsession.

"A close, intense experience which flails the fallibility and vulnerability of human love, cauterizes despair with faith, provides a drama which—if it is more superficial in substance—continues the implications of The Heart of the Matter." —*Kirkus*

Originally published : London : Heinemann, 1951.

Originally published: London : Heinemann, 1951

★ The **heart** of the matter. Graham Greene. Penguin Books, 1999. 242 p.

ISBN 9780140283327

1. British in West Africa 2. Extramarital affairs 3. Personal conduct 4. Catholic men 5. Police 6. West Africa 7. Love stories 8. Psychological fiction 9. Literary fiction

LC 48007530

James Tait Black Memorial Prize for Fiction, 1948

Scobie, a police officer serving in a war-time West African state, is distrusted, being scrupulously honest and immune to bribery. But then he falls in love, and in doing so he is forced to betray everything he believes in, with drastic and tragic consequences.

Originally published: London : Heinemann, 1948.

The **honorary** consul. Graham Greene. Simon and Schuster 1973. 315 p.

ISBN 9780671215699

1. Hostage taking 2. Diplomats 3. International intrigue 4. Physicians 5. Political science 6. Argentina 7. Paraguay 8. Thrillers and suspense 9. Literary fiction 10. Books to movies

LC 73005254

Although Paraguayan revolutionaries make the mistake of kidnapping the British Consul instead of the American Ambassador, they continue to threaten violence.

Book made into a movie called Beyond the limit.

The **human** factor. Graham Greene. Knopf, 1992. 338 p.

ISBN 9780679409922

1. Spies 2. Double agents 3. Interracial marriage 4. Defectors 5. Intelligence service 6. Spy fiction 7. Literary fiction 8. Books to movies

The senior officers of Britain's secret service move to plug a leak by eliminating a junior colleague, unmindful of a veteran intelligence processor whose decency, courage, and capacity for love threaten all security.

Originally published: London : The Bodley Head, 1978.

The **last** word and other stories. Graham Greene. Penguin Books, 1999. Vii, 149 p.

ISBN 9780141181578

1. Spies 2. Human nature 3. Senior men 4. People with amnesia 5. Christianity 6. Great Britain 7. Short stories 8. Literary fiction

LC 99200035

"This modest volume gathers uncollected stories from the entire range of Greene's career. The earliest dates from 1923 (!) and the latest from 1989." —*Library Journal*

Collection of stories dating from 1923-89, of which only four have appeared before in book form and none of which are included in Collected short stories, published in 1972—Pref.

Our man in Havana. Graham Greene; introduction by Christopher Hitchens. Penguin, 2007. 247 p.

ISBN 9780142438008

1. Single fathers 2. Intelligence service 3. Spies 4. Fathers and daughters 5. British in Cuba 6. Havana, Cuba 7. Satirical fiction 8. Spy fiction 9. Books to movies

Follows the plight of Wormold, a former vacuum cleaner salesman, who becomes a slave to the expensive whims of his thirteen-year-old daughter, Milly, and takes on a job for MI6 as Secret Agent 5920015 to pay for them.

This edition first published by Collector's Library 2015—Title page verso.

Originally published: New York : Viking Press, 1958.

The **power** and the glory. By Graham Greene. Viking Press, 1990. Xviii, 295 p.

ISBN 9780670835362

1. Religious persecution 2. Priests 3. Faith (Christianity) 4. Faith in men 5. Alcoholic priests 6. Mexico 7. 1930s 8. Literary fiction 9. Books to movies 10. Modern classics

The time is 1938 and the place is one of Mexico's southern states. They are undergoing a religious purge, arresting every Catholic priest they can find, charging them with treason and then killing them in a firing squad. Those that aren't caught get married or go into hiding. One such priest has tried to escape through the jungles, villages, and plantations. A policeman is after him and shooting a hostage in each village until someone turns in the priest.

Movies inspired by this book are: The fugitive and The power and the glory.

Originally published: London : W. Heinemann, 1940.

★ The **quiet** American. Graham Greene; text and criticism edited by John Clark Pratt. Penguin Books, 1996. 515 p.

ISBN 9780140243505

1. Love triangles 2. Americans in Vietnam 3. War correspondents 4. British in Vietnam 5. Husband and wife 6. Vietnam 7. Indochina 8. 1950s 9. Political fiction 10. War stories 11. Psychological fiction

LC 95023183

This novel is a study of New World hope and innocence set in an Old World of violence. The scene is Saigon in the violent years when the French were desperately trying to hold their footing in the Far East. The principal characters are a skeptical British journalist, his attractive Vietnamese mistress, and an eager young American sent out by Washington on a mysterious mission.

"Mr. Greene has always been a master of suspense, and the particular excellence of 'The Quiet American' lies in the way in which he builds up the situation finally to explode the moral problem which for him lies at the heart of the matter. In so doing he uses with complete mastery something of the method of the detective-story writer, only at the end he exposes, as well as a murderer, a problem of far-reaching significance. The effect is powerful and long-lasting, and it is by this effect that the whole book must be judged." —*Times Literary Supplement*

Originally published in 1955.

Includes bibliographical references (p. [509]-515).

The **tenth** man. Graham Greene. Simon and Schuster, 1985. 157 p.

ISBN 9780671507947

1. Rich men 2. World War II — Prisoners and prisons, German 3. Cowardice in men 4. Shame in men 5. Good and evil 6. France 7. 1940s 8. Psychological fiction 9. Literary fiction

LC 84029830

This recently recovered novel, written in 1944, focuses on Jean-Louis Charlot, who returns to his home after a four-year absence knowing that strangers live there and that one moment of panic has cost him the right to call it his own.

"A fatal series of events follows, entwining narrative excitement with broader questions of identity, fate, and morality. As always with Greene, the basic plot is heightened by the novelist's compelling view of the human condition." —*Library Journal*

Greengrass, Jessie

Sight: a novel. Jessie Greengrass. Hogarth, 2018. 198 pages
ISBN 9780525574606
1. Motherhood 2. Mother and child 3. Identity (Psychology) 4. Loss (Psychology) 5. Grief 6. Literary fiction 7. First person narratives

LC 2017060526

Shortlisted for the James Tait Black Memorial Prize for Fiction, 2018; Shortlisted for The Women's Prize for Fiction, 2018

A first novel by an award-winning writer draws on the history of psychoanalysis and the origins of modern surgery to explore the complexities and poignant birth-and-death cycles of being a child, choosing to become a parent and letting go.

Greenidge, Kaitlyn

★ **Libertie:** a novel. Kaitlyn Greenidge. Algonquin Books of Chapel Hill, 2021. 304 p.
ISBN 9781616207014
1. Gender role 2. Color of African Americans 3. Mother and adult daughter 4. Reconstruction (United States history) 5. Independence in women 6. United States 7. Brooklyn, New York City 8. 1860s 9. 1870s 10. Coming-of-age stories 11. Literary fiction 12. Historical fiction 13. Adult books for young adults

LC 2020040086

LibraryReads Favorites, 2021

Coming of age as a free-born Black girl in Reconstruction-era Brooklyn, Libertie Sampson is all too aware that her mother, a physician, has a vision for their future together: Libertie will go to medical school and practice alongside her. But Libertie feels stifled by her mother's choices and is constantly reminded that, unlike her mother, Libertie has skin that is too dark. When a young man from Haiti proposes to Libertie and promises she will be his equal on the island, she accepts, only to discover that she is still subordinate to him and all men. As she tries to parse what freedom actually means for a Black woman, Libertie struggles with where she might find it-for herself and for generations to come.

Greenidge creates a richly layered tapestry of Black communal life, notably Black female life, and the inevitable contradictions and compromises of 'freedom.' Booklist

This book is inspired by Susan Smith McKinney Steward (1847-1918), the first female African American doctor in New York State.

We love you, Charlie Freeman: a novel. Kaitlyn Greenidge. Algonquin Books of Chapel Hill, 2016. 368 p.
ISBN 9781616204679
1. Families 2. Sign language 3. Human-animal relationships 4. Chimpanzees 5. African American families 6. Massachusetts 7. Coming-of-age stories 8. Literary fiction 9. African American fiction 10. Adult books for young adults

LC 2015031336

School Library Journal Best Books: Best Adult Books 4 Teens, 2016

An African-American, sign-language-fluent family is hired by a private research institute-with a shocking, secret past-to teach sign language to a chimpanzee who will live as part of their household.

"A vivid and poignant coming-of-age story that is also an important exploration of family, race, and history." —*Kirkus*

Greenwell, Garth

Cleanness. Garth Greenwell. Farrar, Straus and Giroux, 2020. 208 p. (What belongs to you, 2)
ISBN 9780374124588

1. Gay men — Sexuality 2. Teachers 3. Americans in Eastern Europe 4. Intimacy (Psychology) 5. Sexual attraction 6. Bulgaria 7. LGBTQIA fiction 8. Psychological fiction 9. Literary fiction

LC 2019028457

New York Times Notable Book, 2020

In a follow-up to What Belongs to You, set in Sofia, Bulgaria—a landlocked city in Southern Europe—an American teacher grapples with the intimate encounters that have marked his years abroad as he prepares to leave the place he's come to call home.

"Greenwell's writing on language, desire, and sex in all their complex choreography vibrates with intensity, reading like brainwaves and heartbeats as much as words." —*Booklist*

Sequel to: What belongs to you.

What belongs to you: a novel. Garth Greenwell. Farrar, Straus and Giroux, 2016. 208 p. (What belongs to you, 1)
ISBN 9780374288228
1. Men/men relations 2. Obsession 3. Gay men 4. Self-destructive behavior 5. Americans in Bulgaria 6. Bulgaria 7. LGBTQIA fiction 8. Psychological fiction 9. Literary fiction

LC 2015003932

Shortlisted for the James Tait Black Memorial Prize for Fiction, 2016; Pen/Faulkner Award Finalist, 2017

Drawn by hunger, loneliness, and risk, an American teacher embarks on a sexual relationship with a young hustler and discovers that desire has far-reaching consequences when he is forced to grapple with his own fraught history and that of the lover with whom he is obsessed.

"The book breaks up the adult protagonist's story with a long middle section devoted to exploring the professor's difficult childhood, as well as his first love, and it is here that the man's struggles—sexual and emotional—come alive." —*Publishers Weekly*

Part one of What Belongs to You was originally published in a very different form as a novella, 'Mitko', in June 2011 by the Miami University Press—Title page verso.

Sequel: Cleanness.

Greenwood, Kerry

Death in Daylesford. Kerry Greenwood. Poisoned Pen Press, 2021. 336 pages (Phryne Fisher mysteries, 21)
ISBN 9781728234564
1. Health resorts 2. Missing persons 3. Crimes against women 4. Murder investigation 5. Fisher, Phryne (Fictitious character) 6. Australia 7. Historical mysteries 8. Australian fiction 9. Mysteries 10. Adult books for young adults

When a mysterious invitation arrives for the redoubtable Miss Phryne Fisher from an unknown retired Captain Herbert Spencer, Phryne's curiosity is piqued. Spencer runs a retreat in Victoria's rural spa country for shell-shocked veterans of World War I. It's a cause after Phryne's own heart, but what can Spencer want from her? Phryne and her faithful servant Dot set out for Daylesford, viewing their rural sojourn as a short holiday. But the pair barely have time to unpack before they are thrown into treacherous Highland gatherings, a mysterious case of disappearing women, and a string of murders committed under their very noses. With her usual pluck, deft thinking and several satisfying costume changes, Phryne methodically investigates the strange goings-on in this anything-but-tranquil spa town.

"This is the most complicated tapestry Greenwood has woven for Phryne yet, but all parties are up for the challenge. The real star is the fabulous Phryne, with her Jazz Age fashions, devil-may-care attitude, and dry narrative wit." —*Booklist*

Originally published: Crows Nest, NSW : Allen & Unwin, 2020.

Out of the Black Land. Kerry Greenwood. Poisoned Pen Press, 2013. 250 p.
ISBN 9781464200380
1. Nefertiti 2. Political intrigue 3. Women priests 4. Rulers 5. Scribes 6. Ancient Egypt 7. Ancient Egypt (3100 BCE-640 CE) 8. Historical mysteries 9. Australian fiction

Appointed by a dream-plagued young pharaoh to the unwanted position of Great Royal Scribe, peasant boy Ptah-hotep finds himself surrounded by envious rivals; while the beautiful Nefertiti participates in a shocking scheme to bear children to an impotent king; and zealous monotheist Akhnaten plots to suppress the worship of all other gods in the Black Land.

Unnatural habits. Kerry Greenwood. Poisoned Pen Press, 2013. 250 p. (Phryne Fisher mysteries, 19)
ISBN 9781464201233
1. Missing persons 2. Teenage pregnancy 3. Women journalists 4. Women amateur detectives 5. Human trafficking 6. Australia 7. 1920s 8. Historical mysteries 9. Australian fiction 10. Mysteries 11. Adult books for young adults

In 1929 Melbourne, Australia, three unmarried pregnant girls working at a convent laundry go missing weeks before they are due to give birth—and then an ambitious reporter, Polly Kettle, who was investigating the girls' whereabouts, disappears, too. It's a good thing for them all that brave, intelligent Honourable Miss Phryne Fisher, who'd just met Polly, decides to sort it all out. Phryne, who's wealthy, glamorous, and a good shot, uses her skills and connections to solve a case that is dark at its core. Unnatural Habits is part of a fun, vibrant flapper-era series, which inspired the Australian TV program Miss Fisher's Murder Mysteries.
Sequel to: Dead man's chest.
Sequel: Murder and Mendelssohn.
Originally published: 2012.

Greenwood, T.

Rust & stardust. T. Greenwood. St. Martin's Press, 2018. 336 p.
ISBN 9781250164193
1. Horner, Sally 2. Girl kidnapping victims 3. Former convicts 4. Child abusers 5. Eleven-year-old girls 6. Deception 7. 1940s 8. Historical fiction
LC 2018001891
LibraryReads Favorites, 2018; Library Journal Best Books, 2018; Loan Stars Favourites, 2018

Traces the story of the 11-year-old kidnapping victim whose 1948 abduction inspired Nabokov's Lolita, recreating in chilling detail Sally Horner's exploitation and assault by predatory former inmate Frank LaSalle.

Greer, Andrew Sean

The **impossible** lives of Greta Wells. Andrew Sean Greer. Ecco, 2013. 304 p.
ISBN 9780062213785
1. Electric shock therapy 2. Time travel (Past) 3. Loss (Psychology) 4. Parallel universes 5. Identity (Psychology) 6. San Francisco, California 7. Psychological suspense 8. Literary fiction
New York Times Notable Book, 2013

After the death of her beloved twin brother, Felix, and the breakup with her longtime lover, Nathan, Greta Wells embarks on a radical psychiatric treatment to alleviate her suffocating depression. But the treatment has unexpected effects, and Greta finds herself transported to the lives she might have had if she'd been born in different eras. —from publisher's description.

"Philosophically intriguing as well as gorgeously imagined and executed, this novel will catch fire with the same audience that propelled Audrey Niffenegger's The Time Traveler's Wife (2003) to the top of the best-seller list." —Booklist

★ **Less**. Andrew Sean Greer. Lee Boudreaux Books/Little, Brown and Company, 2017. 263 p.
ISBN 9780316316125
1. Americans in foreign countries 2. Middle-aged men 3. Gay men 4. Birthdays 5. Authors 6. LGBTQIA fiction 7. Romantic comedies 8. Literary fiction
ALA Notable Book, 2018; Australian Book Industry Awards, International Book of the Year, 2019; Librarians' Choice (Australia), 2018; New York Times Notable Book, 2017; Pulitzer Prize for Fiction, 2018; Longlisted for the Andrew Carnegie Medal for Excellence in Fiction, 2018

Receiving an invitation to his ex-boyfriend's wedding, Arthur, a failed novelist on the eve of his 50th birthday, embarks on an international journey that finds him falling in love, risking his life, reinventing himself and making connections with the past.

Greer, Robert O.

First of state. Robert Greer. North Atlantic Books, 2010. 400 p. (C. J. Floyd mysteries, Prequel)
ISBN 9781556439155
1. African American men 2. Murder investigation 3. Stealing 4. Automobile license plates 5. Vietnam veterans 6. Denver, Colorado 7. 1970s 8. Mysteries 9. African American fiction
LC 2010020235

It is 1972 and CJ returns from Vietnam with PTSD, but quickly befriends a fellow vet and collector of western memorabilia; however, the friend and a mysterious Chinese man are soon found murdered, prompting CJ to take on the first case of his life.

"This prequel to Greer's always thoughtful and multilayered Floyd series reveals the pain behind the protagonist's curmudgeonly, emotionally guarded personality and his reluctance to employ violence. CJ Floyd is one of crime fiction's hidden gems, and this is a satisfying entry in a rewarding, underappreciated series." —Booklist

Gregory, Daryl

Afterparty. Daryl Gregory. Tor Books, 2014. 320 pages
ISBN 9780765336927
1. Mental illness 2. Drug control 3. Near future 4. Lesbians 5. Prisons 6. Medical thrillers 7. Science fiction
LC 2013025194

When a girl who was addicted to a drug she helped develop dies in a detention facility, Lyda Rose, a scientist and patient at the same facility, receives help from an imaginary, drug-induced doctor to make things right while finding the other survivors of her development team.

"This taut, brisk, gripping narrative, dazzlingly intercut with flashbacks and sidebars, oozes warmth and wit. A hugely entertaining, surprising and perhaps prophetic package." —Kirkus

The **devil's** alphabet. Daryl Gregory. Ballantine Books, 2009. 384 p.
ISBN 9780345501172
1. Small town life 2. Mutants 3. Secrets 4. Syndromes 5. Human evolution 6. Tennessee 7. Mysteries 8. Horror

Returning to his small hometown in the aftermath of a neighbor's suicide, Paxton Martin remembers how the community was radically transformed by a mysterious retrovirus that mutated many of its survivors, a seemingly short-lived incident that he discovers has caused additional changes.

"Small-town peace and quiet are turned upside-down when Transcription Divergence Syndrome (TDS) kills a third of the inhabitants of Switchcreek, Tennessee, and transforms most of the rest into mutants: argos (gray-skinned giants), betas (seal-like people whose women get pregnant spontaneously), and charlies (the morbidly obese whose males leak a narcotic called the vintage). One of the few unaffected is 14-year-old Paxton Martin. After losing his mother and watching his father (a charlie) hideously changed by the disease, Paxton leaves for Chicago. Fifteen years later, following news of a friend's death, he returns, forced to revisit the horror of his previous lifeand to solve a murder. Bookmarks,The larger question, of what eventually might become of these evolutionary exiles as they move into second and third generations, seems to move us back into Theodore Sturgeon territory, and it's fortunately a territory that Gregory has mastered well. The novel's quiet ending, in a snowbound South Dakota winter, is haunting." —*Locus Magazine*

We are all completely fine. Daryl Gregory. Tachyon Publications, 2014. 192 p.
ISBN 9781616961718
1. Supernatural 2. Good and evil 3. Victims 4. Survival 5. Psychotherapists 6. Horror
A group of outcasts with questionable states of mental health—including Stan, who was partially eaten by cannibals, and Greta, who may be a mass-murdering arsonist—are sought by a psychotherapist to uncover internal and external monsters.
"Blending the stark realism of pain and isolation with the liberating force of the fantastic, Gregory (Afterparty) makes it easy to believe that the world is an illusion, behind which lurks an alternative truthdark, degenerate, and sublime." —*Publishers Weekly*

Gregory, Philippa

The **Boleyn** inheritance. Philippa Gregory. Touchstone, 2006. 416 p. (Tudor novels (Philippa Gregory), 3)
ISBN 9780743272506
1. Boleyn, Jane 2. Marriages of royalty and nobility 3. Courts and courtiers 4. Ladies-in-waiting 5. Nobility 6. Ambition 7. Great Britain 8. Tudor period (1485-1603) 9. 16th century 10. Biographical fiction 11. Historical fiction 12. Multiple perspectives
Romantic Times Reviewers Choice Award, 2006
An only survivor of the ambitious Boleyn family, lady-in-waiting Jane Boleyn testifies against Henry VIII's latest queen, Anne of Cleves, and conspires to place her young cousin, Katherine Howard, on the throne.
"Rich in intrigue and irony, this is a tale where readers will already know who was divorced, beheaded or survived, but will savor Gregory's sharp staging of how and why." —*Publishers Weekly*

The **constant** princess. Philippa Gregory. Simon & Schuster, 2005. 400 p. (Tudor novels (Philippa Gregory), 1)
ISBN 9780743272483
1. Catharine 2. Marriages of royalty and nobility 3. Catholic women 4. Determination in women 5. Widows 6. Brothers 7. Great Britain 8. Tudor period (1485-1603) 9. 16th century 10. Biographical fiction 11. Historical fiction 12. Multiple perspectives
LC 2005052303
I am Catalina, Princess of Spain, daughter of the two greatest monarchs the world has ever known...and I will be Queen of England." Thus, bestselling author Philippa Gregory introduces one of her most unforgettable heroines: Katherine of Aragon. Daughter of Queen Isabella and King Ferdinand of Spain, Katherine has been fated her whole life to marry Prince Arthur of England. When they meet and are married, the match becomes as passionate as it is politically expedient.
A Touchstone book.

The **kingmaker's** daughter. Philippa Gregory. Simon & Schuster, 2012. 432 p. (Cousins' war, 4)
ISBN 9781451626070
1. Edward 2. Conspiracies 3. Ambition in men 4. Fathers and daughters 5. Power (Social sciences) 6. Royal houses 7. Great Britain 8. Medieval period (476-1492) 9. Plantagenet period (1154-1485) 10. Historical fiction 11. Biographical fiction
Presents a tale inspired by the daughters of "Kingmaker" Richard, 15th-century Earl of Warwick, who uses his daughters as political pawns before their strategic marriages place them on opposing sides in a royal war that will cost them everyone they love.

The **lady** of the rivers. Philippa Gregory. Simon & Schuster, 2011. 448 p. (Cousins' war, 3)
ISBN 9781416563709
1. Henry 2. Ambition 3. Greed 4. Women psychics 5. Wars of the Roses, 1455-1485 6. Loyalty 7. Great Britain 8. Historical fiction 9. Biographical fiction
The duchess—kin to half the crowned heads of Europe and mother of England's White Queen—walks a perilous path through the battle lines of the tumultuous War of the Roses.

The **last** Tudor. Philippa Gregory. Simon & Schuster 2017. 432 p. (Cousins' war, 7)
ISBN 9781476758763
1. Grey, Jane 2. Inheritance and succession 3. Religious persecution 4. Women rulers 5. Executions and executioners 6. Courts and courtiers 7. Great Britain 8. England 9. Tudor period (1485-1603) 10. 16th century 11. Historical fiction 12. Biographical fiction
Reimagines the lives of Lady Jane Grey and her two sisters, who respectively endure imprisonment, a secret marriage and marginalization under the suspicious eyes of Tudor queens Mary and Elizabeth.

The **other** Boleyn girl: a novel. Philippa Gregory. Scribner Paperback Fiction, 2002. 664 p; (Tudor novels (Philippa Gregory), 2)
ISBN 9780743227445
1. Boleyn, Mary 2. Mistresses 3. Nobility 4. Sibling rivalry 5. Ambition 6. Siblings 7. Great Britain 8. Tudor period (1485-1603) 9. Biographical fiction 10. Historical fiction 11. Books to movies
LC 2001057646
Romantic Times Reviewers' Choice Award, 2002
The daughters of a ruthlessly ambitious family, Mary and Anne Boleyn are sent to the court of Henry VIII to attract the attention of the king, who first takes Mary as his mistress, in which role she bears him an illegitimate son, and then Anne as his wife.
"This is as much a tale of love and lust as it is a saga about an ambitious family who used their kin as negotiable assets.... Absorbing tale of a Renaissance family determined to climb as high as they can, whatever the cost." —*Kirkus*

The **red** queen: a novel. Philippa Gregory. Simon & Schuster, 2010. 382 p. : Map; Table (Cousins' war, 2)
ISBN 9781416563723
1. Beaufort, Margaret 2. Ambition 3. Power (Social sciences) 4. Conspiracies 5. Widows 6. Deception 7. Great Britain 8. Medieval period (476-1492) 9. Plantagenet period (1154-1485) 10. Historical fiction 11. Biographical fiction
Determined to see her son Henry on the throne of England, pious Margaret Beaufort arranges politically advantageous marriages, sends her

son out of the country for his safety and lays secret plans for a battle between the houses of York and Lancaster.

The **taming** of the queen. Philippa Gregory. Touchstone, 2015. 432 p.
ISBN 9781476758794
1. Catharine Parr 2. Women rulers 3. Forced marriage 4. Royal houses 5. Widows 6. Independence in women 7. Great Britain 8. Tudor period (1485-1603) 9. 16th century 10. Biographical fiction 11. Historical fiction
LC 2015018375
Reimagines the story of Henry VIII's sixth wife, Kateryn Parr, who after being forced to marry the king struggles against dangerous adversaries to observe her own faith and promote religious reforms.
"Tracing Kateryn's path to intellectual independence requires more religious discussion than some readers will prefer, but Gregory's portrait of the complex, aging king and his sensual, scholarly bride will satisfy Tudor enthusiasts." —*Publishers Weekly*

Tidelands. Philippa Gregory. Atria Books, 2019. 480 p. (Fairmile novels, 1)
ISBN 9781501187155
1. English Civil War, 1642-1649 2. Women healers 3. Independence in women 4. Midwives 5. Priests 6. Great Britain 7. England 8. Stuart period (1603-1714) 9. Historical fiction 10. Family sagas
LC 2019005706
During England's 17th century civil war, Alinor, a woman without a husband and skilled with herbs, helps a young man on the run and unwittingly brings disaster into the heart of her life.
Includes bibliographical references and index.

The **white** princess. Philippa Gregory. Simon & Schuster, 2013. 400 p. (Cousins' war, 5)
ISBN 9781451626094
1. Elizabeth 2. Arranged marriage 3. Lovers 4. Rulers 5. Ambition 6. Loyalty 7. Great Britain 8. Medieval period (476-1492) 9. Plantagenet period (1154-1485) 10. Historical fiction 11. Biographical fiction
Passionately in love with Richard III in spite of her arranged marriage to pretender to the throne Henry Tudor, Princess Elizabeth of York is forced to marry the man who murdered her lover and create a royal family.

Grenville, Kate

Sarah Thornhill. Kate Grenville. Grove Press, 2011. 307 p.
ISBN 9780802120243
1. Young women 2. Family secrets 3. Families — History 4. Winthrop, Elizabeth 5. Postcolonialism 6. Australia 7. New Zealand 8. Colonial Australia (1788-1901) 9. Historical fiction 10. Love stories 11. Australian fiction
Australian Book Industry Awards, General Fiction Book of the Year, 2012
Sarah is the youngest child of William Thornhill, an uneducated ex-convict from London who has built his fortune on the blood of Aboriginal people. With a fine stone house and plenty of money, Thornhill has re-invented himself. As he tells his daughter, he "never looks back," and Sarah grows up learning not to ask about the past. Instead her eyes are on handsome Jack Langland, whom she's loved since she was a child. Their romance seems destined, but the ugly secret in Sarah's family is poised to ambush them both.
Sequel to: The secret river
Originally published: Melbourne, Vic. : Text Publishing, 2011.

The **secret** river. Kate Grenville. Canongate U.S., 2006. 352 p.
ISBN 9781841957975

1. Exiles 2. Criminals 3. Prisoners 4. Penal colonies 5. Serfdom 6. New South Wales 7. Australia 8. Colonial Australia (1788-1901) 9. Historical fiction 10. Literary fiction 11. Australian fiction 12. Adult books for young adults
ALA Notable Book, 2007; Australian Book Industry Awards, Book of the Year, 2006; Australian Book Industry Awards, Literary Fiction Book of the Year, 2006; Commonwealth Writers' Prize for Best Book, 2006; Commonwealth Writers' Prize, South East Asia and South Pacific: Best Book, 2006; Nielsen BookData Australian Booksellers' Choice Award, 2006; NSW Premier's Literary Awards, Christina Stead Prize for Fiction, 2006; School Library Journal Best Books: Best Adult Books 4 Teens, 2006; Shortlisted for the Man Booker Prize, 2006; Shortlisted for the Miles Franklin Literary Award, 2006
Moving between the slums of nineteenth-century London and the convict colonies of Australia, a compelling historical novel chronicles the lives and fortunes of the early pioneers of New South Wales, in a volume based on the author's own family history.
"[A]n unflinching exploration of modern Australia's origins. Like the settlers, we instinctively turn away from the ugly truths behind every cleared riverbank and every posted fence. But Grenville's psychological acuity, and the sheer gorgeousness of her descriptions of the territory being fought over, pulls us ever deeper into a time when one community's opportunity spelled another's doom." —*The New Yorker*

Grey, Zane

★ **Riders** of the purple sage. Zane Grey. Penguin Books 1990. 280 p.
ISBN 9780140184402
1. Outlaws 2. Women ranchers 3. Gunfighters 4. Mormon women 5. Polygamy 6. Utah 7. Westerns
LC 89-29702
Refusing to marry the grim, brutal Elder Tull, Jane Withersteen is dismayed when her Utah ranch and hired hands are targeted in retaliation, and the mysterious gunfighter Lassiter offers Jane protection and a chance at love.
"Well handled melodramatic story of hairbreadth escapes from Mormon vengeance in southwestern Utah in 1871." —*Booklist*
Collected with The Rainbow Trail and Desert Gold in an omnibus entitled Western Colors by Forge, 2014.
Released in one volume with The Rainbow Trail in 2015 by Tor Books. ISBN 9780765382399.
First published 1912 by Harper & Brothers.

Woman of the frontier: a western story. Zane Grey. Five Star, 1998. 320 p.
ISBN 9780786211562
1. Frontier and pioneer life 2. Abandoned girls 3. Apache Indians 4. Families 5. Homesteaders 6. Arizona (Territory) 7. Westerns
LC 9822717
Details the harsh realities of frontier life in the story of a former Army scout and his wife, settling in central Arizona, where they deal with oppressive loneliness, the wife's rape, and their twenty-year struggle to achieve prosperity BT
"This tale, written in 1934, was rejected by magazines because of its vivid portrayal of the hardships of pioneer life, including the rape of Grey's heroine by a renegade Apache. A heavily edited version called 30,000 on the Hoof was finally published in 1940, a year after the author's death. This version, completely restored by Grey's son, Loren, recounts the trials and tribulations of Arizona rancher Logan Huett, his heroic wife, Lucinda, their three sons, and a girl named Barbara, who is abandoned by wagon-train travelers and raised by the Huetts." —*Booklist*

Griffin, Anne

When all is said: a novel. Anne Griffin. Thomas Dunne Books, 2019. 352 p.

ISBN 9781250200587

1. Senior men 2. Life change events 3. Reminiscing in old age 4. Options, alternatives, choices 5. Loss (Psychology) 6. Ireland 7. Psychological fiction

LC 2018041302

An 84-year-old loner, sitting at a grand hotel bar in Ireland, toasts the five people who have meant the most to him while recalling unspoken losses and joys, a tragic secret and a fierce love.

"Newcomer Griffin's storytelling, while economical, is rich and evocative, and her deft pacing maintains suspense across several narrative arcs spanning multiple time lines...Highly recommended; this unforgettable first novel introduces Griffin as a writer to watch." —*Library Journal*

Griffith, Nicola

Hild: a novel. Nicola Griffith. Farrar, Straus and Giroux, 2013. 560 p.

ISBN 9780374280871

1. Hilda 2. Women saints 3. Civilization, Medieval 4. Bisexual women 5. Christian saints 6. Christian women 7. England 8. Great Britain 9. Anglo-Saxon period (449-1066) 10. 7th century 11. Historical fiction 12. Biographical fiction

LC 2013022510

Daughter of a poisoned prince and a crafty noblewoman, quiet, bright-minded Hild arrives at the court of King Edwin of Northumbria, where the six-year-old takes on the role of seer/consiglieri for a monarch troubled by shifting allegiances and Roman emissaries attempting to spread their new religion.

Griffiths, Elly

The crossing places. Elly Griffiths. Houghton Mifflin Harcourt, 2009. 304 p. (Ruth Galloway mysteries, 1)

ISBN 9780547229898

1. Missing girls 2. Bogs 3. Women archaeologists 4. Detectives 5. Criminal investigation 6. Norfolk, England 7. Mysteries

LC 2009007006

Edgar Allan Poe Awards: Mary Higgins Clark Award, 2011

When a child's bones are found near an ancient henge in the wild saltmarshes of Norfolk's north coast, Ruth Galloway, a university lecturer in forensic archaeology, is asked to date them by DCI Harry Nelson who thinks they may be the bones of a child called Lucy who has been missing for ten years.

First published in Great Britain in 2009 by Quercus.

The dark angel. Elly Griffiths. Houghton Mifflin Harcourt, 2018. 336 p. (Ruth Galloway mysteries, 10)

ISBN 9780544750326

1. Women archaeologists 2. Murder 3. Forensic sciences 4. Murder investigation 5. Archaeology 6. Italy 7. Mysteries

LC 2017057874

Asked by archaeologist Angelo Morelli for help in identifying bones found in the tiny hilltop town of Fontana Liri in Italy, Ruth Galloway soon realizes that there is darkness lurking in this seemingly picturesque town when she discovers a link between the bones and a modern-day murder.

"A sure bet for fans of strong-minded women and wry humor in the tradition of Rhys Bowen and M. C. Beaton." —*Booklist*

A dying fall: a Ruth Galloway mystery. Elly Griffiths. Houghton Mifflin Harcourt 2013. 240 p. (Ruth Galloway mysteries, 5)

ISBN 9780547798165

1. Arthur 2. Women archaeologists 3. Forensic sciences 4. Murder investigation 5. Universities and colleges 6. Skeleton 7. Lancashire, England 8. England 9. Mysteries

An old friend's death sends Ruth to Lancaster to investigate an important archaeological discovery, but what she finds is a mystery that may have gotten her friend murdered.

Originally published: London : Quercus, 2012.

The house at sea's end: a Ruth Galloway mystery. Elly Griffiths. McClelland & Stewart, 2011. 356 p. : Illustration (Ruth Galloway mysteries, 3)

ISBN 9780771036002

1. Forensic sciences 2. New mothers 3. Skeleton 4. Galloway, Ruth (Fictitious character) 5. Women archaeologists 6. Norfolk, England 7. Mysteries

"Solid characterization, believable forensic science, great atmosphere, and a mystery that stretches back decades all make this another winner from the talented Griffiths." —*Booklist*

The Janus stone. Elly Griffiths. Houghton Mifflin Harcourt, 2011. 336 p. (Ruth Galloway mysteries, 2)

ISBN 9780547237442

1. Child murder victims 2. Criminal investigation 3. Galloway, Ruth (Fictitious character) 4. Pregnant women 5. Women archaeologists 6. Norfolk, England 7. Mysteries

LC 2010005740

Library Journal Best Books, 2011

Ruth Galloway is called in to investigate when builders, demolishing a large old house in Norwich to make way for a housing development, uncover the bones of a child beneath a doorway—minus the skull. Is it some ritual sacrifice or just plain straightforward murder? DCI Harry Nelson would like to find out—and fast. It turns out the house was once a children's home. Nelson traces the Catholic priest who used to run the home. Father Hennessey tells him that two children did go missing from the home forty years before—a boy and a girl. They were never found. When carbon dating proves that the child's bones predate the home and relate to a time when the house was privately owned, Ruth is drawn ever more deeply into the case. But as spring turns into summer it becomes clear that someone is trying very hard to put her off the scent by frightening her half to death.

"Griffiths nimbly weaves the mythological aspects of her story—particularly the Roman god Janus, who represents doorways as well as beginnings and endings—with the complicated life of her feisty heroine." —*Publishers Weekly*

The lantern men: a Dr. Ruth Galloway mystery. Elly Griffiths. Houghton Mifflin Harcourt, 2020. 356 p. (Ruth Galloway mysteries, 12)

ISBN 9780358237044

1. Women archaeologists 2. Forensic sciences 3. Cold cases (Criminal investigation) 4. Fens 5. Paranormal phenomena 6. England 7. Great Britain 8. Police procedurals

LC 2020003633

When a convicted murderer offers to lead her to the bodies of four additional cold-case victims, Ruth Galloway embarks on a search in a fens-bordering village reputed to be haunted by mysterious lantern-carrying beings.

"Once again expertly incorporating myth and folklore into the story—this time, it's the menacing Lantern Men, said to haunt the local fens and who may be responsible for the killings—Griffiths has delivered a perfect Halloween read." —*Booklist*

The night hawks. Elly Griffiths. Houghton Mifflin Harcourt, 2021. 352 p. (Ruth Galloway mysteries, 13)

ISBN 9780358237051

1. Women archaeologists 2. Forensic sciences 3. Detectives 4. Metal detectors 5. Scavenging 6. Norfolk, England 7. Great Britain 8. Mysteries

LC 2020057664

When a group of amateur archaeologists called the Night Hawks uncover Bronze Age artifacts and a dead body along the shore, Ruth Galloway and DCI Nelson, after another murder is discovered, probe into both cases that eventually intertwine and point to Ruth's new lecturer, David Brown.

"Griffiths once again presents a well-plotted mystery, nicely blending historical elements with a contemporary take on the classic whodunit.... A strong addition to the series; recommended for readers who enjoy a mystery investigated by relatable characters." —*Library Journal*

The **postscript** murders. Elly Griffiths. Houghton Mifflin Harcourt, 2021. 352 p. (Harbinder Kaur novels :, 2)
ISBN 9780358418610
1. Women detectives 2. Books and reading 3. Mystery story writers 4. Amateur detectives 5. Murder victims 6. England 7. Scotland 8. Mysteries 9. Multiple perspectives 10. Adult books for young adults

LC 2020033853

"Bibliophile genre fans will enjoy the insider's look at publishing and relish the intoxicating, often intoxicated, milieu of the festival. All readers will devour the cleverly constructed story, replete with Griffiths' trademark engaging prose, well-placed humor, and always-endearing characters." —*Booklist*
Originally published: 2020.

The **stone** circle. Elly Griffiths. Houghton Mifflin Harcourt, 2019. 368 p. (Ruth Galloway mysteries, 11)
ISBN 9781328974648
1. Women archaeologists 2. Forensic sciences 3. Murder investigation 4. Archaeological sites 5. Cold cases (Criminal investigation) 6. England 7. Great Britain 8. Police procedurals

LC 2019001733

The past returns in ominous ways when both Ruth Galloway and DCI Nelson begin receiving threatening letters from the man responsible for their partnership, Ruth's believed-dead former mentor.

"This superb series (The Dark Angel, 2018, etc.) never disappoints. Its' patented combination of mysterious circumstances, police procedure, and agonizing relationship problems will keep you reading, and feeling, all night." —*Kirkus*

The **stranger** diaries. Elly Griffiths. Houghton Mifflin Harcourt, 2019. 352 p. (Harbinder Kaur novels :, 1)
ISBN 9781328577856
1. Literature teachers 2. Murder investigation 3. Women amateur detectives 4. Women 5. Authors, English 6. England 7. West Sussex, England 8. Gothic fiction 9. Mysteries 10. Multiple perspectives 11. Adult books for young adults

LC 2018035768

Loan Stars Favourites, 2019; Edgar Allan Poe Award for Best Novel, 2020

A high-school English teacher chronicles her suspicions about the murder of a colleague before discovering a sinister message in her own diary.

"Alternating among the voices of Clare, Georgia, and Det. Sgt. Harbinder Kaur, who investigates the killings, Griffiths weaves a tale replete with ghosts, the occult, forbidden desire, and murder." —*Publishers Weekly*
Originally published: London : Quercus, 2018.

Grippando, James

The **girl** in the glass box. James Grippando. Harper, 2019. 352 p. (Jack Swyteck novels, 15)
ISBN 9780062657831
1. Undocumented immigrants 2. Lawyers 3. Deportation 4. Legal assistance to poor people 5. Women immigrants 6. Miami, Florida 7. Florida 8. Legal thrillers 9. Thrillers and suspense

LC 2018022312

Miami attorney Jack Swyteck lands in the heart of the contentious immigration debate when he takes on the heart-wrenching case of an undocumented immigrant who fled to America to protect her daughter and save herself, in this timely and pulse-pounding thriller that explores the stories behind the headlines.

Grisham, John

The **client**. John Grisham. Doubleday, 1993. 421 p.
ISBN 9780385424714
1. Trials (Murder) 2. Mafia 3. Witnesses 4. Secrets 5. Eleven-year-old boys 6. New Orleans, Louisiana 7. Thrillers and suspense 8. Legal thrillers 9. Books to movies 10. Adult books for young adults

LC 92039079

Colorado Blue Spruce YA Book Award, 1995

Present at the suicide of a New Orleans defense attorney, a young boy hires a lawyer to protect himself, sharing with her the dead attorney's shocking last words and hiding from her some dangerous information.

"This thriller is unique in its theme and in its suspense mixed with humor. A sure all-night read." —*School Library Journal*

★ The **firm**. John Grisham. Doubleday, 1991. 421 p.
ISBN 9780385416344
1. Mafia 2. FBI informants 3. Law firms 4. Lawyers 5. Corruption investigation 6. Tennessee 7. Memphis, Tennessee 8. Thrillers and suspense 9. Legal thrillers 10. Books to movies

LC 90003945

Mitch McDeere, a Harvard Law graduate, becomes suspicious of his Memphis tax firm when mysterious deaths, obsessive office security, and the Chicago mob figure into its operations.

"The aphorism between a rock and a hard place aptly describes the dilemma of a young attorney pressed by the FBI to reveal crime-related secrets of his firm, while also hounded by his employers to simply take his huge salary and zip his lip. No aphorism, though, can convey the suspense, wit, and polished writing of this laser-sharp candidate for the best recent updating of the David and Goliath story." —*Library Journal*

★ The **guardians**. John Grisham. Doubleday, 2019. 368 pages
ISBN 9780385544184
1. Lawyers 2. African American prisoners 3. Innocence (Law) 4. Frameups 5. Murder 6. Legal thrillers

Guardian handles only a few innocence cases at a time, and Cullen Post is its only investigator. He travels the South fighting wrongful convictions and taking cases no one else will touch. With Quincy Miller, though, he gets far more than he bargained for. Powerful, ruthless people murdered Keith Russo, and they do not want Quincy exonerated. They killed one lawyer twenty-two years ago, and they will kill another one without a second thought.

"Grisham's readers are legion, and they will be prepped for his latest, which finds the perennial chart-topper in great form." —*Booklist*

The **last** juror. John Grisham. Doubleday : 2004. 355 p.
ISBN 9780385510431
1. Former convicts 2. Murderers 3. Jurors 4. Newspaper publishers and publishing 5. Rape 6. Mississippi 7. 1970s 8. Thrillers and suspense

LC 2004043818

The future of a bankrupt paper looked grim until a young mother was brutally raped and murdered by a member of the notorious Padgitt family. Willie Traynor reported all the gruesome details, and his newspaper began to prosper. Nine years after Danny Padgitt was convicted, he managed to get himself paroled. He returned to Ford County and the retribution began.

★ The **pelican** brief. John Grisham. Doubleday, 1992. 371 p.
ISBN 9780385421980
1. Assassination 2. Government cover-ups 3. Witnesses 4. Crimes against judges 5. Women law students 6. Washington, D.C. 7. Louisiana 8. Legal thrillers 9. Thrillers and suspense 10. Books to movies
LC 91033235
Two members of the Supreme Court are assassinated by a professional killer on the same night. A law student thinks that she has figured it out, and must protect herself and her theory.

"Mr. Grisham has written a genuine page-turner. He has an ear for dialogue and is a skillful craftsman. Like a composer, he brings all his themes together at the crucial moment for a gripping, and logical, finale." —*New York Times Book Review*

A **time** to kill. John Grisham. Doubleday, 1993. 415 p. (Jack Brigance novels, 1)
ISBN 9780385470810
1. Revenge 2. Trials (Murder) 3. Race relations 4. African American defendants 5. Defense attorneys 6. Mississippi 7. Legal thrillers 8. Books to movies
LC 89005760
Criminal lawyer Jake Brigance faces the fight of his life when he is asked to defend Carl Hailey, who, in a rage of anger, shot and killed the men on trial for the rape of his daughter.

Sequel to: Sycamore row (2013).

Grodstein, Lauren

Our short history. Lauren Grodstein. Algonquin Books of Chapel Hill, 2017. 352 pages
ISBN 9781616206222
1. Mothers and sons 2. Mortality 3. Parenthood 4. Six-year-old boys 5. Mothers with terminal illnesses 6. New York City 7. Washington (State) 8. Domestic fiction 9. Literary fiction

Karen Neulander has always been fiercely protective of her son, Jacob, now six. She's had to be: when Jacob's father, Dave, found out Karen was pregnant and made it clear that fatherhood wasn't in his plans, Karen walked out of the relationship. But now Jake is asking to meet his dad, and with good reason: Karen is dying. Lauren Grodstein has created an unforgettable story about parenthood, sacrifice, and life itself.

"Grodstein's...heartbreaking, character-driven story is told in the remarkable, believable voice of a courageous, sympathetic character." —*Library Journal*

Groen, Hendrik

On the bright side: the new secret diary of Hendrik Groen, 85 years old. Hendrik Groen; translated from the Dutch by Hester Velmans. Grand Central Pub 2019. 384 p. (Secret diary of Hendrik Groen, 2)
ISBN 9781538746639
1. Seniors 2. Senior men 3. Retirement communities 4. Clubs 5. Aging 6. Amsterdam, Netherlands 7. Netherlands 8. Humorous stories 9. Diary novels 10. Translations

Finds octogenarian curmudgeon Hendrik emerging from a year of mourning to help the Old-But-Not-Dead Club save their homes from demolition plans.

Translated from the Dutch Zolang er leven is: het tweede geheime dagboek van Hendrik Groen, 85 jaar.

Groff, Lauren

★ **Arcadia:** a novel. Lauren Groff. Hyperion, 2012. 291 p.
ISBN 9781401340872
1. Communes 2. Hippies 3. Introspection 4. Growing up 5. Epidemics 6. New York (State) 7. 1960s 8. Literary fiction 9. Coming-of-age stories
LC 2011009956
Booklist Editors' Choice, 2012; New York Times Notable Book, 2012
In a haunting story of the American dream, Bit, born in a back-to-nature commune in 1970s New York State, must come to grips with the outside world when the commune eventually fails.

Delicate edible birds and other stories. Lauren Groff. Hyperion, 2009. 320 p.
ISBN 9781401340865
1. Scandals 2. Epidemics 3. Interpersonal relations 4. Short stories 5. Literary fiction
LC 2008044002
Presents a volume of nine stories that reflects the use of different styles and structures, including a recreation of the tale of Abelard and Heloise during the 1918 New York flu epidemic, and the experiences of a group of war correspondents in France.

"An innovative and beautifully written collection that covers a wide swath of humanity, from east coast resort towns, to the early 20th century flu epidemic, to WWII Europe.... Even in the less successful stories, Groff's prose is lovely, and when she nails a storylike the title story about journalists fleeing Nazi-occupied Paristhe results are sublime." —*Publishers Weekly*

Short stories.

★ **Fates** and furies. Lauren Groff. Riverhead Books, 2015. 390 p.
ISBN 9781594634475
1. Marriage 2. Husband and wife 3. Married people and secrets 4. Love 5. Families 6. Maine 7. Literary fiction 8. Domestic fiction 9. Multiple perspectives
LC 2015013565
Booklist Editors' Choice, 2015; Indies' Choice Book Awards, Adult Fiction, 2016; LibraryReads Favorites, 2015; Library Journal Best Books, 2015; New York Times Notable Book, 2015; National Book Award for Fiction finalist, 2015; National Book Critics Circle Award for Fiction finalist, 2015; Kirkus Prize for Fiction finalist, 2015
Marrying in a glamorous whirlwind amid predictions of future greatness, Lotto and Mathilde are shaped throughout a subsequent shared decade by complications, secrets and powerful creative drives.

"The first half of the novel, entitled "Fates," gives lanky lothario Lotto's perspective on the marriage. He sees nothing but Mathilde's goodness ('the best person I know') and her unerring belief in his talent, and, after some years of struggling as an actor, Lotto finds great success as a playwright, which brings the couple both fame and wealth. The second half of the novel, "Furies," turns the lens on Mathilde and will upend readers' expectations, for she is possessed of a cold calculation that will surprise and even dismay." —*Booklist*

★ **Florida**. Lauren Groff. Riverhead Books, 2018. 272 p.
ISBN 9781594634512
1. Florida 2. Short stories 3. Literary fiction
LC 2017042916
National Book Award for Fiction finalist, 2018; Kirkus Prize for Fiction finalist, 2018
A collection of stories spanning centuries of time in mercurial Florida examines the decisions and connections behind life-changing events in characters ranging from two abandoned sisters to a conflicted family woman.

"The flora and fauna of the Sunshine State vine and prowl through Groffs second short story collection and first book since the smash-hit novel Fates and Furies (2015). With sympathy for her characters and a keen sensitivity to the natural world, Groff gets readers wondering who or what will triumph or succumb." —*Booklist*

★ **Matrix**. Lauren Groff. Penguin, 2021. 272 pages
ISBN 9781594634499
1. Marie 2. Women poets 3. Abbesses 4. Social change 5. Visions 6. Power (Social sciences) 7. England 8. Medieval period (476-1492) 9. 12th century 10. Literary fiction 11. Historical fiction
Loan Stars Favourites, 2021; Andrew Carnegie Medal for Excellence in Fiction finalist, 2022; National Book Award for Fiction finalist, 2021
Cast out of the royal court, 17-year-old Marie de France, born the last in a long line of women warriors, is sent to England to be the new prioress of an impoverished abbey where she vows to chart a bold new course for the women she now leads and protects.
"Transcendent prose and vividly described settings bring to life historic events, from the Crusades to the papal interdict of 1208. Groff has outdone herself with an accomplishment as radiant as Marie's visions." —*Publishers Weekly*

Groom, Winston

El Paso: a novel. Winston Groom. Liveright Publishing, 2016. 477 p.
ISBN 9781631492242
1. Villa, Pancho 2. Kidnapping 3. Outlaws 4. Capitalists and financiers 5. Frontier and pioneer life 6. Railroads 7. Texas 8. Mexico 9. Mexican Revolution (1910-1920) 10. 1910s 11. Westerns
LC 2016021007
After feared outlaw and revolutionary Pancho Villa kidnaps his grandchildren, railroad tycoon John Shaughnessy, known as the Colonel, ventures to El Paso with his adopted son and a band of hired cowboys on a rescue mission.
"An engaging epic that could be headed for the best-seller lists and then the big screen." —*Booklist*

Groot, Tracy

Flame of resistance. Tracy Groot. Tyndale House, 2012. 416 p.
ISBN 9781414359472
1. Spies 2. Undercover operations 3. Prostitutes 4. Fighter pilots 5. French Resistance (World War II) 6. Normandy 7. 1940s 8. War stories 9. Christian historical fiction
LC 2011052924
Christy Award for Historical Category, 2013
Years of Nazi occupation have stolen much from Brigitte Durand, but that changes the day American fighter pilot Tom Jaeger is shot down over occupied France and is picked up by the Resistance, giving her hope for a new future.
"This is a superior, page-turning entry." —*Publishers Weekly*

Gross, Andrew

Button man. Andrew Gross. Minotaur Books, 2018. 371 p.
ISBN 9781250179982
1. Jewish families 2. Organized crime 3. Immigrant families 4. Betrayal 5. Brothers 6. New York City 7. 1930s 8. Between the Wars (1918-1939) 9. Historical fiction
LC 2018013607

A disadvantaged but once happy immigrant family is brought together and torn apart by the birth of organized crime in 1930s New York City.

The **one** man. Andrew Gross. Minotaur Books, 2016. 384 p.
ISBN 9781250079503
1. Physicists 2. Intelligence service 3. Holocaust (1933-1945) 4. Concentration camp inmates 5. Undercover operations 6. Poland 7. United States 8. Second World War era (1939-1945) 9. Historical thrillers
LC 2016007570
Library Journal Best Books, 2016; RUSA Reading List Short List, 2017
When a World War II physics professor with information vital to Allied forces is sent to a Nazi concentration camp, intelligence officer Nathan Blum is sent undercover to infiltrate Auschwitz and bring the professor to safety.
"Alternating between scenes of American hope-against-hope optimism and Nazi brutality, Blum's deadly odyssey into and out of this 20th-century hell drives toward a compelling celebration of the human will to survive, remember, and overcome." —*Publishers Weekly*

Gross, Max

The **lost** shtetl. Max Gross. HarperVia, 2019. 304 p.
ISBN 9780062991126
1. Shtetl 2. Social isolation 3. Small towns 4. Marriage 5. Interpersonal conflict 6. Poland 7. Literary fiction 8. Historical fiction
LC 2019060200
A tiny Jewish shtetl that has peacefully escaped the devastations of the Holocaust and Cold War is wrenchingly forced into the 21st century by a marriage dispute that spins out of control. A first novel.
"The narrator, a present-day villager, is well versed in Jewish traditions and human foibles, alternately reminiscent of early Isaac Bashevis Singer and a Catskills comedian. Gross's entertaining, sometimes disquieting tale delivers laugh-out-loud moments and deep insight on human foolishness, resilience, and faith." —*Publishers Weekly*

Grossman, David

Be my knife. David Grossman. Farrar, Straus and Giroux, 2002. 320 p.
ISBN 9780374299774
1. Middle-aged men 2. Middle-aged women 3. Antiquarian booksellers 4. Rare books — Collectors and collecting 5. Extramarital affairs 6. Literary fiction 7. Translations
LC 2001033645
New York Times Notable Book, 2002
When Yair, an awkward, neurotic seller of rare books, encounters a gorgeous stranger named Miriam at a class reunion, he begins writing her letters, which ignites a powerful love affair of words between these two people who are dissatisfied with their lives.
"When a thirty-three-year-old man named Yair catches a glimpse of Miriam at a class reunion, he senses a bond with her that goes beyond sexual attraction; because he is a practiced philanderer who is in search of something extraordinary, he implores her to enter a ruthlessly honest correspondence with him, on the understanding that they will never meet.... Most of the book is devoted to Yair's letters, and so we don't get to hear Miriam's responses until near the end. But it is Grossman's achievement that we understand from the start that Yair's vision of Miriam (and thus ours) is almost painfully incomplete." —*The New Yorker*

Falling out of time. By David Grossman; translated by Jessica Cohen. Alfred A. Knopf, 2014. 208 p.
ISBN 9780385350136

1. Bereavement 2. Death 3. Parent and child 4. Grief 5. Tragedy 6. Joan of Arc 7. Translations

LC 2013017532

Booklist Editors' Choice, 2014

Announcing that he must embark on a journey in search of his dead son, a man walks in ever-widening circles around his town and beyond, picking up similarly bereaved companions with whom he explores questions about the potential for overcoming death and reconnecting with lost loved ones.

"Grossman's lyrical approach to the silent suffering of mourning is both a literary study in processing grief and a reminder that healing often comes through the action of putting into words the pain we thought was unspeakable." —*Library Journal*

Originally published in Hebrew as Nofel mi-huts la-zeman.

★ A **horse** walks into a bar. By David Grossman; translated from the Hebrew by Jessica Cohen. Alfred A. Knopf, 2016. 208 p.

ISBN 9780451493972

1. Comedians 2. Autobiography 3. Stand-up comedy 4. Jokes 5. Judges 6. Israel 7. Psychological fiction 8. Literary fiction 9. Translations

LC 2016014688

New York Times Notable Book, 2017; Man Booker International Prize, 2017; National Jewish Book Award, 2017

An Israeli comedian a bit past his prime conveys with semi-questionable humor anecdotes from his violence-stricken youth during a night of standup, while a judge in the audience wrestles with his own part in the comedian's losses.

"In this latest from award-winning Israeli author Grossman, a stand-up comedy routine quickly turns into a harrowing and soul-searching experience for both audience and performer.... Dov's emotions are thoroughly spent as this oral memoir reaches its climax, a defining moment in his life told with such power and resonance that the audience is shocked and becomes totally submissive to this significant performance." —*Library Journal*

Previously published as Sus ehad nikhnas le-bar in 2011.

Translated from the Hebrew.

★ **More** than I love my life: a novel. David Grossman; translated by Jessica Cohen. 2021. 288 p.

ISBN 9780593318911

1. Concentration camp inmates 2. Mothers and daughters 3. Grandmothers 4. Psychic trauma 5. Coping 6. Yugoslavia 7. Croatia 8. Literary fiction 9. Translations

Thirty-year-old Gili seeks to make a film that might help explain her life and embarks on an unlikely journey with her grandmother Vera to a barren island off the coast of Croatia where Vera was imprisoned and tortured for not denouncing her husband as an enemy of the state.

"Grossman performs a deft exploration of how trauma impacts succeeding generations." —*Booklist*

Originally published in Israel as Iti ha'chayim mesachek harbeh by Ha'kibbutz Ha'meuchad, Tel Aviv, in 2019.

Translated from the Hebrew.

★ **To** the end of the land. By David Grossman; translated from the Hebrew by Jessica Cohen. Alfred A. Knopf, 2010. 592 p.

ISBN 9780307592972

1. Coping in women 2. Family relationships 3. War and society 4. Man-woman relationships 5. Hiking 6. Israel 7. Translations 8. Literary fiction 9. Psychological fiction

LC 2010003915

Booklist Editors' Choice, 2010; Library Journal Best Books, 2010; National Jewish Book Award for Fiction, 2010; New York Times Notable Book, 2010; National Book Critics Circle Award for Fiction finalist, 2010

Fleeing to Galilee in despair when her son voluntarily rejoins the Israeli army, Ora drags along estranged family friend Avram, a tortured former POW to whom she relates her experiences of motherhood against a backdrop of constant war and fear.

"Grossman weaves the essences of private life into the tapestry of history with deliberate and delicate skill; he has created a panorama of breathtaking emotional force, a masterpiece of pacing, of dedicated storytelling, with characters whose lives are etched with extraordinary, vivid detail. While his novel has the vast sweep of pure tragedy, it is also at times playful, and utterly engrossing." —*New York Times Book Review*

This is a Borzoi book.

Translation from the Hebrew of: Ishah borahat mi-besorah.

Grossman, Lev

The **magician** king: a novel. Lev Grossman. Viking, 2011. 400 p; (Magician novels (Lev Grossman), 2)

ISBN 9780670022311

1. Magic 2. Wizards 3. Rulers 4. Voyages and travels 5. Young men 6. Massachusetts 7. Contemporary fantasy 8. Gateway fantasy 9. Adult books for young adults

LC 2011019733

School Library Journal Best Books: Best Adult Books 4 Teens, 2011

After Quentin and his old friend Julia leave Fillory on a magical sailing ship, they end up back in Quentin's home in Chesterton, Massachusetts, and only Julia's dark magic can get them back to the realm they have grown to love.

"Quentin Coldwater, the wizard who traveled to a mythical land to be its king in the first book, has gotten past most of his misery and settled into bored complacency, wondering whether hanging out in a castle and getting drunk is really all there is to rulership. Isn't he meant for great things? Shouldn't he be carrying out some giant quest? In the book's opening chapter, the quest he's already on unravels disappointingly, so he decides to embark to the farthest edge of the land he rules, a speck of an island in the middle of the sea, and he winds up on an even stranger journey. The Magicians was terrific, but loose, with a plot that moved from incident to incident with only the barest connecting material. The Magician King, which is better in almost every way, feels as if it might be even looser in the early going, with plenty of opportunities to worry whether Grossman can pull his narrative together. But once he reaches his devastating climax, neatly knitting together story threads readers won't have even realized were major plot points, the novel reaches a level of poignancy the first could only hope to attain." —*A. V. Club*

Sequel to: The magicians.

The **magician's** land: a novel. Lev Grossman. Viking, 2014. 416 p. (Magician novels (Lev Grossman), 3)

ISBN 9780670015672

1. Magic 2. Wizards 3. Rulers 4. Voyages and travels 5. Young men 6. Massachusetts 7. Contemporary fantasy 8. Adult books for young adults

Booklist Editors' Choice: Adult Books for Young Adults, 2014; LibraryReads Favorites, 2014; New York Times Notable Book, 2014; School Library Journal Best Books: Best Adult Books 4 Teens, 2014

Quentin Coldwater has been cast out of Fillory, the secret magical land of his childhood dreams. With nothing left to lose he returns to where his story began, the Brakebills Preparatory College of Magic. But he can't hide from his past, and it's not long before it comes looking for him. Along with Plum, a brilliant young undergraduate with a dark secret of her own, Quentin sets out on a crooked path through a magical demimonde of gray magic and desperate characters. But all roads lead back to Fillory, and his new life takes him to old haunts, like Antarctica, and to buried secrets and old friends he thought were lost forever. He uncovers the key to a sorcery masterwork, a spell that could create magical utopia, a new Fillory—but casting it will set in motion a chain of events that will bring Earth and Fillory crashing together. To save them he will have to risk sacrificing everything.

"This novel serves as an elegantly written third act to Quentin's bildungsroman, in which he at last learns responsibility and to not simply put childish things aside but understand them—and himself—anew." —*Publishers Weekly*

★ The **magicians**: a novel. Lev Grossman. Viking, 2009. 402 p. (Magician novels (Lev Grossman), 1)
ISBN 9780670020553
1. Teenage wizards 2. Magic — Study and teaching 3. Young men 4. Good and evil 5. Schools 6. New York (State) 7. Contemporary fantasy 8. Books to TV 9. Adult books for young adults
LC Bl2009000464
Alex Award, 2010; Booklist Editors' Choice: Adult Books for Young Adults, 2009
Harboring secret preoccupations with a magical land he read about in a childhood fantasy series, Quentin Coldwater is unexpectedly admitted into an exclusive college of magic and rigorously educated in modern sorcery.

"Quentin Coldwater is a geeky high-school senior in Brooklyn who is convinced that happiness and the life he should be living are elsewhere—for example, in the series of nineteen-thirties British adventure novels that he was obsessed with as a child. When Quentin stumbles on a portal that takes him to a college for magicians in upstate New York, he learns that the world depicted in these novels, known as Fillory, is real, and he is forced to square his youthful ideas with the realities that exist there, too—boredom, regret, shame, and despair. Quentin's journey becomes an unexpectedly moving coming-of-age story in which he learns that magical worlds are much like the real one." —*The New Yorker*
Sequel: The magician king.

Grossman, Paul

Children of wrath. Paul Grossman. St. Martin's Press, 2012. 320 pages (Willi Kraus novels, Prequel)
ISBN 9780312601911
1. Crimes against children 2. Serial murderers 3. Serial murder investigation 4. Jews, German 5. Detectives 6. Germany 7. Berlin, Germany 8. 1920s 9. Historical mysteries 10. Mysteries
Detective Willi Kraus investigates the 1929 discovery of a burlap sack filled with children's bones and enclosed with a biblical phrase, a grisly finding with links to the dark side of Germany's capital.

Gruber, Michael

The **book** of air and shadows. Michael Gruber. William Morrow, 2007. 480 p.
ISBN 9780060874469
1. Shakespeare, William 2. Lost books 3. Antiquities 4. Booksellers 5. Books 6. Rare books 7. England 8. New York City 9. Thrillers and suspense
LC 2006046767
Desperately typing out the details of a case that puts him at the center of a deadly conspiracy, intellectual property lawyer Jake Mishkin recounts how a bookstore fire led to the discovery of the whereabouts of one of the most valuable historical items in the world.

"Few thrillers will surpass [this book] when it comes to energetic writing, compellingly flawed characters, literary scholarship and mathematical conundrums." —*USA Today*

The **forgery** of Venus: a novel. Michael Gruber. William Morrow, 2008. 336 p.

ISBN 9780060874483
1. Art forgeries 2. Delusions 3. Extortion 4. Painters 5. Art dealers 6. Thrillers and suspense
LC 2008002363
Although Chaz Wilmot's father is a famed illustrator, and Chaz has far surpassed his father in talent. Desperately in need of money, Chaz accepts a job restoring an antique fresco in a European castle. But when he gets there, he finds that there is so little to restore, it will really be more of a forgery—one that Chaz can pull off perfectly.

"Gruber writes passionately and knowledgeably about art and its historyand he writes brilliantly about the shadowy lines that blur reality and unreality. Fans of intelligent, literate thrillers will be well rewarded." —*Publishers Weekly*

Night of the jaguar: a novel. Michael Gruber. Morrow, 2006. 384 p. (Jimmy Paz series, 3)
ISBN 9780060577681
1. Police 2. Paz, Jimmy (Fictitious character) 3. Supernatural 4. Shamanism 5. Shamans 6. Miami, Florida 7. Thrillers and suspense
LC 2005040011
Miami detective Jimmy Paz risks everything to save his daughter and stop a series of murders involving the gruesome killings of affluent Cuban-American businessmen, crimes that could be tied to the murder in Colombia of an American priest.

"Hotly spiced with hit men and guns, demon gods and piranhas, this one offers more social satire than its predecessors, mostly at the expense of do-gooder environmentalists." —*Publishers Weekly*

The **return**: a novel. Michael Gruber. Henry Holt and Co, 2013. 320 p.
ISBN 9780805091298
1. Revenge 2. Violence in men 3. Ethics 4. Editors 5. Justice 6. Mexico 7. New York, City 8. Thrillers and suspense
LC 2012045307
When a shattering piece of news awakens his buried desire for vengeance, Richard Marder, with nothing left to lose, sets out to punish the people whose actions, years earlier, changed his life and, with an old army buddy by his side, encounters a colorful cast of dangerous characters along the way.

Valley of bones: a novel. Michael Gruber. William Morrow, 2005. 448 p. (Jimmy Paz series, 2)
ISBN 9780060577667
1. Police 2. Supernatural 3. Women psychiatric hospital patients 4. Paz, Jimmy (Fictitious character) 5. Cuban American men 6. Miami, Florida 7. Africa 8. Thrillers and suspense
LC 2004045756
Investigating the murder of an oil tycoon, detective Jimmy Paz interviews an unlikely suspect in pious young Emmylou Dideroff, whose claim about her ability to commune with saints places her sanity in question.

"The author is at least as eager to fathom the violent and the unknown as he is to exploit these things. Some books simply relish the darker sides of human nature. Mr. Gruber summons them with troubled inquisitiveness, with both brio and regret." —*New York Times*
Sequel to: Tropic of night.

Gruen, Sara

The **ape** house. Sara Gruen. Spiegel & Grau, 2010. 320 p.
ISBN 9780385523219
1. Bonobos 2. Apes 3. Human-animal relationships 4. Human/animal communication 5. American Sign Language 6. Literary fiction 7. Canadian fiction 8. Adult books for young adults
LC 2010008928

A group of apes are kidnapped from a language laboratory and subsequently cast on a reality television show that calls into question scientific assumptions about common DNA that is shared by apes and people.

"This novel portrays a group of six bonobo apes housed in the fictional Great Ape Language Lab in Kansas City and the humans who either come to love them or seek to profit from their surprisingly advanced communication skills. Led by Bonzi, the matriarch and undisputed leader, the bonobo group includes Sam, the charismatic oldest male, Jelani, an adolescent showoff, and Makena, Jelani's biggest fan, who is pregnant and due any day. Isabel Duncan is a research scientist overseeing the bonobos and their unique ability to communicate via lexigrams on their computers, supplemented by American Sign Language.... Gruen enlivens this charming story of their emotional bonding with multiple villains—including Isabel's fiance, the head of the Great Ape Language Lab, who she discovers has a history of animal cruelty and a desire to profit from the bonobos under his control. There's also a purveyor of porn who sees the bonobos as the perfect stars for his new reality TV show, enticing viewers with their healthy sex lives 24 hours a day. Ape House turns into a romp, but Gruen never loses the thread of the enviable bond Isabel has nurtured with her ape friends." —*BookPage*

Also published: Toronto : Bond Street Books, 2010.

★ **Water** for elephants: a novel. By Sara Gruen. Algonquin Books, 2006. 352 p.
ISBN 9781565124998
1. Circus performers 2. Reminiscing in old age 3. Depressions 4. Human-animal relationships 5. Parents — Death 6. Literary fiction 7. Canadian fiction 8. First person narratives 9. Adult books for young adults

LC 2005052700

Alex Award, 2007; Book Sense Book of the Year Adult Fiction, 2007; Great Lakes Book Awards, Fiction category, 2007

Ninety-something-year-old Jacob Jankowski remembers his time in the circus as a young man during the Great Depression, and his friendship with Marlena, the star of the equestrian act, and Rosie, the elephant, who gave them hope.

"Life is good for Jacob Jankowski. He's about to graduate from veterinary school and about to bed the girl of his dreams. Then his parents are killed in a car crash, leaving him in the middle of the Great Depression with no home, no family, and no career. Almost by accident, Jacob joins the circus. There he falls in love with the beautiful performer Marlena, who is married to the circus' psychotic animal trainer. He also meets the other love of his life, Rosie the elephant. This lushly romantic novel travels back and forth in time between Jacob's present day in a nursing home and his adventures in the surprisingly harsh world of 1930s circuses. The ending of both stories is a little too cheerful to be believed, but just like a circus, the magic of the story and the writing convince you to suspend your disbelief. The book is partially based on real circus stories and illustrated with historical circus photographs." —*Booklist*

Grushin, Olga
The **line**. Olga Grushin. G.P. Putnam's Sons, 2010. 336 p.
ISBN 9780399156168
1. Hope 2. Rumor 3. Friendship 4. Interpersonal relations 5. Music 6. Moscow, Russia 7. Literary fiction

LC 2009042733

When rumors about an exiled composer's return to Moscow for a farewell symphony spark power abuses among officials and bureaucrats, a disparate gaggle of strangers evolves into a community of friends bonded by long-buried memories and unexpected acts of kindness.

"In the world of The Line, no desire, no matter how trifling, is met without a herculean struggle, and Anna's stymied attempts to present her family with something as simple as a date cake sometimes devolve into farce. But for the most part, Grushin expertly maintains a dreamlike tone to sell the novel's more preposterous (albeit historically grounded) elements, and characters who initially appear one-dimensional become intensely empathetic by the novel's end, as they bristle or cave under a society that grinds down the exceptional to make way for the pedestrian." —*A. V. Club*

Guhrke, Laura Lee
Governess gone rogue. Laura Lee Guhrke. Avon Books, 2019. 352 p. (Dear Lady Truelove, 3)
ISBN 9780062890689
1. Tutors 2. Deception 3. Male impersonators 4. Seduction 5. Aristocracy 6. England 7. Great Britain 8. Victorian era (1837-1901) 9. Victorian romances 10. Historical romances

Disguising herself as a man to score her dream job—being the tutor for the Earl of Kenyon's wild young sons—Miss Amanda Leighton, when her deception is exposed, vows to teach the Earl some lessons in love, seduction and second chances.

"Witty, sensual, and just plain fun, Guhrke's latest foray into the late Victorian world of "Lady Truelove" cleverly refreshes the classic cross-dressing heroine trope; highlights the cruel disparity between opportunities for men and women; and gives a deserving pair their happy ending." —*Library Journal*

How to lose a duke in ten days. Laura Lee Guhrke. Avon Books, 2014. 384 p. (An American heiress in London, 2)
ISBN 9780062118196
1. Heirs and heiresses 2. Dukes and duchesses 3. Husband and wife 4. Separated couples 5. Homecomings 6. England 7. London, England 8. Historical romances

"A spirited yet emotionally fragile heroine and a resourceful hero find love in this flawlessly written, lushly sensual tale that balances sexual abuse issues with flashes of humor and treats readers to a beautifully depicted and tender courtship." —*Library Journal*

The **trouble** with true love. Laura Lee Guhrke. Avon Books, 2018. 384 p. (Dear Lady Truelove, 2)
ISBN 9780062469878
1. Advice columnists 2. Womanizers 3. Mate selection 4. Aristocracy 5. Interpersonal attraction 6. England 7. Great Britain 8. Victorian era (1837-1901) 9. Victorian romances 10. Historical romances

When he is forced into an alliance with Clara Deverill, a stand-in for the real Lady Truelove, Rex Galbraith finds his life turned upside down by this advice columnist who makes him question everything he thought he knew about women and himself.

"Engaging prose, witty barbs, and sigh-worthy sensuality make this humorous Victorian charmer an excellent addition to Guhrke's series and a most diverting read." —*Library Journal*

The **truth** about love and dukes. Laura Lee Guhrke. Avon Books, 2017. 369 p. (Dear Lady Truelove, 1)
ISBN 9780062469854
1. Dukes and duchesses 2. Advice columnists 3. Newspaper publishers and publishing 4. Women columnists 5. Scandals 6. England 7. Great Britain 8. Victorian era (1837-1901) 9. Victorian romances 10. Historical romances

When his mother elopes after receiving advice from columnist Lady Truelove, causing a huge scandal, Henry, Duke of Torquil, is determined to expose the author's true identity before she can ruin any more lives, but his plan backfires when he, instead, embarks on an affair with the beauty.

When the marquess met his match. Laura Lee Guhrke. Avon, 2013. 384 p. (An American heiress in London, 1)
ISBN 9780062118172

1. Matchmakers 2. Womanizers 3. Heirs and heiresses 4. Marquis and marchionesses 5. Nobility 6. England 7. London, England 8. Historical romances

Nicholas, Marquess of Trubridge, wants to marry a rich American heiress—until he meets the beautiful matchmaker, Lady Belinda Featherstone.

"Graced with an abundance of memorable characters and rich in lush sensuality." —*Booklist*

Guillory, Jasmine

Party of two. Jasmine Guillory. Berkley, 2020. 320 p. (Wedding dates, 5)

ISBN 9780593100813

1. Women lawyers 2. Politicians 3. Interracial romance 4. Dating (Social customs) 5. Mass media 6. Los Angeles, California 7. California 8. Contemporary romances 9. Multicultural romances

LC 2020009944

Going against her better judgement, LA lawyer Olivia Monroe secretly starts dating a hotshot junior senator until their romance is made public and her life falls under intense media scrutiny, jeopardizing everything.

"Best-selling Guillory specializes in tales of modern love featuring high-powered professionals' relationships.... Perfect for readers who enjoy uplifting, steamy, and diverse romances similar to those of Jamie Pope and Talia Hibbert." —*Booklist*

A Jove book—Title page verso.

The **proposal**. Jasmine Guillory. Jove/Berkley, 2018. 336 p. (Wedding dates, 2)

ISBN 9780399587689

1. Interracial romance 2. Dating (Social customs) 3. Social media 4. Physicians 5. Women authors 6. Los Angeles, California 7. California 8. Multicultural romances 9. Contemporary romances 10. African American fiction

LC 2018022593

LibraryReads Favorites, 2018; Loan Stars Favourites, 2018; Library Journal Best Books, 2018

After a handsome doctor helps Nikole escape a ridiculous, public proposal, she starts having a series of hookups with him, but when things begin to get out of hand, one of them has to put the brakes on things.

Royal holiday. Jasmine Guillory. Berkley, 2019. 304 pages (Wedding dates, 4)

ISBN 9781984802217

1. Christmas 2. Middle-aged couples 3. Dating (Social customs) 4. Personal assistants 5. Women fashion designers 6. England 7. Holiday romances 8. Multicultural romances 9. Contemporary romances

LC 2019024644

A spontaneous holiday vacation turns into an unforgettable romance.

★ The **wedding** date. Jasmine Guillory. Berkley, 2018. 304 p. (Wedding dates, 1)

ISBN 9780399587665

1. Women politicians 2. Physicians 3. Interracial romance 4. Long-distance romance 5. African American women 6. California 7. Multicultural romances 8. Contemporary romances 9. African American fiction

LC 2017034041

LibraryReads Favorites, 2018; RUSA Reading List Short List, 2019

Stranded together in an elevator during a power outage, Drew and Alexa agree to pose as a couple at an ex's wedding and discover afterwards that they are unable to forget each other.

"This incredibly delicious meet-cute brings two people together who would not have met otherwise, and though it could have become predictable, Guillory keeps this contemporary romance fresh with well-drawn multicultural characters navigating the perils of long-distance relationships." —*Booklist*

The **wedding** party. Jasmine Guillory. Jove, 2019. 320 pages (Wedding dates, 3)

ISBN 9781984802194

1. Wedding planning 2. Interpersonal conflict 3. One-night stands (Interpersonal relations) 4. Aversion 5. Friendship 6. California 7. Multicultural romances 8. Contemporary romances 9. African American fiction

LC 2018057817

Maddie and Theo have two things in common: Alexa is their best friend, and they hate each other. After an "oops, we made a mistake" night together, neither one can stop thinking about the other. With Alexa's wedding rapidly approaching, Maddie and Theo both share bridal party responsibilities that require more interaction than they're comfortable with.

★ **While** we were dating. Jasmine Guillory. Berkley, 2021. 336 p. (Wedding dates, 6)

ISBN 9780593100844

1. Advertising executives 2. Actors and actresses 3. Publicity 4. Fame 5. Flirtation 6. Hollywood, California 7. California 8. Multicultural romances 9. Contemporary romances 10. African American fiction

LC 2021003777

Loan Stars Favourites, 2021

Featuring Ben Stephens, Theo's brother from The Wedding Party, this charming and hilarious new Romance finds Ben and a famous actress struggling to keep their working relationship strictly professional.

"Guillory's latest 'Wedding Date' series installment (after Party of Two) weaves serious issues, including mental health and parental abandonment, through a believable romance that features relatable, good-hearted protagonists." —*Library Journal*

Guinn, Matthew

The **scribe**: a novel. Matthew Guinn. W. W. Norton & Company, 2015. 304 p.

ISBN 9780393239294

1. Serial murder investigation 2. Crimes against African Americans 3. Police 4. Racism 5. Mutilation 6. Atlanta, Georgia 7. Gilded Age (1865-1898) 8. 1880s 9. Historical mysteries

LC 2015013780

LibraryReads Favorites, 2015

Investigating a series of murders targeting post-Civil War Atlanta's wealthiest black entrepreneurs, a disgraced former detective partners with the city's first African-American officer in a case marked by fierce racial, political, and personal tensions.

"This is an absorbing historical mystery filled with evocative period detail, a brooding atmosphere of corruption and pervasive evil, and compelling characters who could be developed further." —*Booklist*

Gunaratne, Guy

In our mad and furious city. Guy Gunaratne. MCD x FSG Originals, 2018. 288 p.

ISBN 9780374175771

1. City life 2. Immigrants 3. Public housing 4. Riots 5. Inner city 6. London, England 7. Literary fiction 8. Political fiction 9. Multiple perspectives

LC 2018039534

Longlisted for the Man Booker Prize, 2018

While Selvon, Ardan, and Yusuf organize their lives around soccer, girls, and grime, Caroline and Nelson struggle to overcome pasts that haunt them. Each voice is uniquely insightful, impassioned, and unforgettable, and when stitched together, they trace a brutal and vibrant tapestry of today's London. In a forty-eight-hour surge of extremism and violence, their lives are inexorably drawn together in the lead-up to an explosive, tragic climax.

Gundar-Goshen, Ayelet

Waking lions. Ayelet Gundar-Goshen; translated from the Hebrew by Sondra Silverston. Little, Brown and Company, 2017. 352 p.

ISBN 9780316395434

1. Hit-and-run accidents 2. Hit-and-run drivers 3. Extortion 4. Refugees 5. Surgeons 6. Israel 7. Psychological suspense 8. Multiple perspectives
New York Times Notable Book, 2017

After neurosurgeon Eitan Green hits and kills an African migrant while driving on a deserted road late at night, the victim's wife tracks him down and confronts him the next day, and her price for silence shatters his safe existence.

"As characters reveal previously hidden facets, Gundar-Goshens mesmerizing novel, her first to be published in English, moves continually into unexpected territory." —*Booklist*

Originally published in Hebrew as "Leha'ir arajot" in 2014.

Published by arrangement with The Institute for the Translation of Hebrew Literature—Title page verso.

Gunday, Hakan

The **few**. Arcade Publishing, 2018. 335 p.

ISBN 9781628727098

1. Human trafficking 2. Eleven-year-olds 3. Immigrants, Turkish 4. Adult child abuse victims 5. Authors 6. London, England 7. Turkey 8. Literary fiction 9. Coming-of-age stories 10. Translations

Sold by her mother as a wife to a conservative tribesman, Derda, after five years of abuse in London, escapes only to find herself preyed upon by Turkish immigrants in London's underworld; while, in Turkey, an unstable writer targets two authors whom he believes stole his fame.

Translation of: Az

Originally published:Istanbul : Dogan Kitap, 2015

Translated from the Turkish

Gunesekera, Romesh

★ **Suncatcher:** a novel. Romesh Gunesekera. The New Press, 2020. 312 pages

ISBN 9781620975596

1. Teenage boys 2. Friendship 3. Families 4. Entitlement attitudes 5. Class consciousness 6. Sri Lanka 7. 1960s 8. Historical fiction 9. Literary fiction 10. Coming-of-age stories 11. Adult books for young adults

LC 2019051382

Set in post-independence Sri Lanka, a coming-of-age novel follows young Kairo as he discovers a world of privilege through his new friend, Jay, a budding naturalist and a born rebel, and embarks on a journey of devastating consequences.

"A lyrical and evocative portrait of a Sri Lankan boyhood friendship and the life lessons that came." —*Kirkus*

Originally published: London : Bloomsbury Publishing, 2019.

Gunn, James E.

Transcendental. James Gunn. Tor Books, 2013. 320 p. (Transcendental novels, 1)

ISBN 9780765335012

1. Far future 2. Pilgrims and pilgrimages 3. Faith 4. Space flight 5. Veterans 6. Space opera 7. Hard science fiction 8. Science fiction

LC 2013023856

As it travels to its destination at the end of the galaxy, where a Prophet offers guidance in achieving Transcendence, dilapidated spaceship Geoffrey plays host to a motley crew of pilgrims who pass the time by telling their stories. In addition to Aldebaran "flower child" 4107 (a sentient plant), heavy-world tripod Tordor, "weasel-faced" alien Xi, and captive-born human Asha, there's also mercenary Riley, a war veteran hired by anonymous but powerful employers to identify the Prophet and kill him. Fans of Dan Simmons' Hyperion, which also draws inspiration from The Canterbury Tales to present multiple narratives from diverse perspectives, should enjoy this richly detailed, thought-provoking novel.

A Tom Doherty Associates Book.

Gunning, Sally

Painting the light. Sally Cabot Gunning. William Morrow & Co, 2021. 368 pages

ISBN 9780062916242

1. Women artists 2. Absence and presumption of death 3. Widows 4. Curie, Marie 5. Farm life 6. Martha's Vineyard, Massachusetts 7. Massachusetts 8. Gilded Age (1865-1898) 9. 1890s 10. Historical fiction

In 1898, after her inattentive and unreliable husband's tragic death, artist Ida Pease must sift through the remnants of his life and work, separating the truth from lies and what matters from what doesn't.

"This is one that lingers well after the final page is turned." —*Publishers Weekly*

Gurganus, Allan

★ **Local** souls: novellas. Allan Gurganus. Liveright Publishing Corporation, 2013. 352 p.

ISBN 9780871403797

1. Interpersonal relations 2. Small town life 3. North Carolina 4. Southern States 5. Short stories

LC 2013016662

New York Times Notable Book, 2013

Returning to his mythological Falls, North Carolina home of Widow, the author presents three novellas set in today's South, a place revolutionized around freer sexuality, looser family ties and superior telecommunications.

Oldest living Confederate widow tells all. A. A. Knopf, 1989. 718 p.

ISBN 9780394545370

1. Antietam, Battle of, Md, 1862 2. Husband and wife 3. Widows 4. Nonagenarians 5. Senior women 6. Southern States 7. Historical fiction 8. Southern fiction

LC 88045870

Sir Walter Raleigh Award for Fiction, 1990

"In a way, 'Oldest Living Confederate Widow Tells All' is as much about language and myth-making as it is about love and war. Whether one feels that it succeeds depends on how much leeway one is willing to give to this indomitable 'veteran of the veteran,' as Lucy describes herself." —*New York Times Book Review*

The **practical** heart: four novellas. Allan Gurganus. Knopf, 2001. 322 p.

ISBN 9780679437635
1. Women immigrants 2. Houses — Remodeling 3. Fathers 4. Villages 5. United States 6. Short stories

LC 2001032665

Lambda Literary Award for Gay Men's Fiction, 2001; New York Times Notable Book, 2001; Sir Walter Raleigh Award for Fiction, 2002

A collection of four novellas includes "He's One, Too," about a pillar of the community whose attraction to boys turns him into a pariah, and "Saint Monster," a love story that celebrates one boy's feelings for his father.

White people: stories and novellas. Allan Gurganus. Vintage Books, 2000. 252 p.

ISBN 9780375704277
1. European Americans 2. Short stories

Los Angeles Times Book Prize for Fiction, 1991

A collection of eleven comic short stories by the author of The Oldest Living Confederate Widow Tells All features tales of love and money among American WASPs.

Originally published: New York : Knopf, 1990.

Guskin, Sharon

The **forgetting** time. Sharon Guskin. Flatiron Books, 2016. 304 p.

ISBN 9781250076427
1. Single mothers 2. Mothers and sons 3. Memory 4. Men with terminal illnesses 5. Missing persons 6. Literary fiction

While a mother's life abruptly stops after receiving an emergency phone call from her son's preschool, a driven former Ivy League professor confronts the realities of his terminal diagnosis and helps a woman whose child has been missing for years.

Gustine, Amy

You should pity us instead: stories. Amy Gustine. Sarabande Books, 2016. 256 p.

ISBN 9781941411193
1. Interpersonal relations 2. Family relationships 3. Literary fiction 4. Short stories

LC 2015017017

Debut story collection explores love in its many guises—family, romance, friendship—through the lens of religion, international conflict, and complicated relationships.

"Gustine's language is uniformly remarkable for its clarity and forthrightness." —Publishers Weekly

Guterson, David

The **other**. David Guterson. Alfred A. Knopf, 2008. 272 p.

ISBN 9780307263155
1. Male friendship 2. Recluses 3. Men and nature 4. Class conflict 5. Secrets 6. Washington (State) 7. Psychological fiction 8. Literary fiction 9. Multiple perspectives

LC 2007041098

New York Times Notable Book, 2008

A deeply engrossing story about friendship, youth, and idealism from the bestselling author of Snow falling on cedars. When John William Barry and Neil Countryman met in 1972, the 16-year-old boys find they share a youthful idealism and a love of the outdoors. But after high school, their paths diverge. John William eventually drops out of society, and only Neil knows his whereabouts. He remains loyal to his oath of secrecy, until years later, when a shocking truth is revealed.

Our Lady of the Forest. David Guterson. Alfred A. Knopf, 2003. 336 p.

ISBN 9780375412110
1. Mary 2. Manipulation (Social sciences) 3. Homeless teenagers 4. Visions 5. Teenage abuse victims 6. Runaway teenagers 7. Washington (State) 8. Psychological fiction 9. Literary fiction 10. Adult books for young adults

LC 2002043322

New York Times Notable Book, 2003

Sixteen-year-old runaway and unlikely spiritual candidate Ann Holmes, surviving by living in a tent and working as a mushroom picker, experiences a vision of the Virgin Mary in the foggy woods of a Washington November afternoon.

"When Ann Holmes starts having visions of the Virgin Mary, the bedraggled teen runaway becomes the last hope for the inhabitants of a dank, economically depressed logging town and the hordes of miracle-seekers who descend on it. In this panoramic, psychologically dense novel, she also becomes a symbol of the intimate intertwining of the sacred and the profane in American life." —Publishers Weekly

★ **Snow** falling on cedars. David Guterson. Harcourt Brace, 1994. X, 345 p.

ISBN 9780151001002
1. Japanese Americans 2. Trials (Murder) 3. Racism 4. Journalists 5. People who have had amputations 6. Washington (State) 7. 1950s 8. Literary fiction 9. Psychological suspense 10. Books to movies

LC 94007535

Book Sense Book of the Year Adult Trade, 1994; PEN-Faulkner Award, 1995

Presents a tense courtroom drama, a poignant love story, and a haunting reflection on the delicate balance between the mind and heart.

Originally published: 1995.

Guthrie, A. B.

★ The **big** sky. . Houghton Mifflin, 2002. 386 p. : Map (Western saga (A.B. Guthrie, Jr.), 1)

ISBN 9780618154630
1. Frontier and pioneer life 2. Adventurers 3. Indians of North America — Relations with missionaries, traders, etc. 4. Mountain men 5. Piegan Indians 6. The West (United States) 7. Oregon Trail 8. American Westward Expansion (1803-1899) 9. 19th century 10. Westerns

Relates the adventures of Boone Caudill, a mountain man in the American West of the mid-nineteenth century.

Sequel: The way west.

Includes map.

Gyasi, Yaa

★ **Homegoing**: a novel. Yaa Gyasi. Alfred A. Knopf, 2016. 304 p.

ISBN 9781101947135
1. Half-sisters 2. Race relations 3. Separated friends, relatives, etc. 4. Slavery 5. Ancestors 6. Africa 7. Ghana 8. 18th century 9. 19th century 10. Historical fiction 11. Family sagas 12. African American fiction 13. Adult books for young adults

LC 2015039411

ALA Notable Book, 2017; Hemingway Foundation/PEN Award, 2017; Indies' Choice Book Awards, Adult Debut, 2017; Library Journal Best Books, 2016; LibraryReads Favorites, 2016; Loan Stars Favourites, 2016; New York Times Notable Book, 2016; School Library Journal Best Books: Best Adult Books 4 Teens, 2016; RUSA Reading List Short List, 2017

Two half-sisters, unknown to each other, are born into different villages in 18th-century Ghana and experience profoundly different lives and legacies throughout subsequent generations marked by wealth, slavery, war, coal mining, the Great Migration and the realities of 20th-century Harlem.

"Gyasi's characters are vividly drawn, sympathetic yet not simplistically heroic. It's wrenching to leave them behind, but readers will be quickly enthralled by the next generation's story." —*Library Journal*

★ **Transcendent** kingdom. Yaa Gyasi. Alfred A. Knopf, 2020. 288 p.
ISBN 9780525658184
1. Immigrants 2. Women graduate students 3. Women scientists 4. Suffering 5. Ambition in women 6. Ghana 7. Alabama 8. Psychological fiction 9. Literary fiction 10. African American fiction
LC 2019039844
LibraryReads Favorites, 2020; Shortlisted for The Women's Prize for Fiction, 2021

A novel about faith, science, religion, and family that tells the deeply moving portrait of a family of Ghanaian immigrants ravaged by depression and addiction and grief, narrated by a fifth year candidate in neuroscience at Stanford school of medicine studying the neural circuits of reward seeking behavior in mice.

"Though it's a departure from her gorgeous historical debut, Homegoing, winner of the NBCC's John Leonard Prize, Gyasi's contemporary novel of a woman's struggle for connection in a place where science and faith are at odds is a piercingly beautiful tale of love and forgiveness." —*Library Journal*

This is a Borzoi book.

H

Hackwith, A. J.

The **library** of the unwritten. A.J. Hackwith. Ace Books, 2019. 336 p. (Hell's library novels, 1)
ISBN 9781984806376
1. Librarians 2. Magical books 3. Angels 4. Hell 5. Demons 6. Adventure stories 7. Fantasy fiction
LC 2019012345
Library Journal Best Books, 2019; LibraryReads Favorites, 2019

Assigned to watch the restless characters of books left unfinished by their authors, a head librarian of Hell's neutral Unwritten Wing tracks an escaped Hero before an angel attack reveals the existence of a powerful literary weapon.

Haddam, Jane

Cheating at solitaire: a Gregor Demarkian novel. Jane Haddam. St. Martin's Minotaur, 2008. 391 p. (Gregor Demarkian mysteries, 23)
ISBN 9780312343088
1. Celebrities 2. Paparazzi 3. Actors and actresses 4. Demarkian, Gregor (Fictitious character) 5. Armenian American men 6. Massachusetts 7. Philadelphia, Pennsylvania 8. Mysteries
LC 2007049770
Former FBI agent Gregor Demarkian, fleeing from his own wedding preparations, is hired to review a case—one that he finds has little evidence and twisted by an out-of-control media—in what may be the most compelling case of his entire career.

"Moving slowly through the landscape of her story, Haddam turns the island and its ambiance into a vividly visual experience for readers. Brilliantly introspective, intellectual ruminations and multiple narrators—who fully convey the craziness of the paparazzi and the cutthroat attitudes of those with power—intersperse with Haddam's own unique and frequently unexpected conclusions." —*Library Journal*

Hardscrabble road. By Jane Haddam. St. Martin's Minotaur, 2006. 320 p. (Gregor Demarkian mysteries, 21)
ISBN 9780312353735
1. Radio talk show hosts and guests 2. Right-wing extremists 3. Prescription drug abuse 4. Homeless men 5. Nuns 6. Philadelphia, Pennsylvania 7. Mysteries
LC 2005054793
Retired FBI agent Gregor Demarkian probes the circumstances surrounding the death of a former client, following a maze of clues that could be tied to the arrest of a local Philadelphia right-wing radio talk-show host for illegal drugs.

"Those new to Haddam will snap up her earlier work based on this captivating literate mystery, which shows how well a classic fair play whodunit can work in a contemporary setting." —*Publishers Weekly*

Haddon, Mark

★ The **curious** incident of the dog in the night-time: a novel. Mark Haddon. Doubleday, 2003. 256 p.
ISBN 9780385512107
1. Fifteen-year-old boys 2. Autism 3. Savant syndrome 4. Dogs — Death 5. Neighbors 6. England 7. Mysteries 8. Psychological fiction 9. First person narratives 10. Adult books for young adults
LC 2002031355
ALA Notable Book, 2004; Alex Award, 2004; British Book Award for Children's Book of the Year, 2004; British Book Award for Literary Fiction, 2004; Booklist Editors' Choice: Adult Books for Young Adults, 2003; Commonwealth Writers' Prize for Best First Book, 2004; Commonwealth Writers' Prize, South Asia and Europe: Best First Book, 2004; Garden State Teen Book Award (New Jersey), Fiction (Grades 9-12), 2006; Library Journal Best Books, 2003; Los Angeles Times Art Seidenbaum Award for First Fiction, 2003; New York Times Notable Book, 2003; School Library Journal Best Books: Best Adult Books 4 Teens, 2003; Whitbread Book Award for Novel, 2003; Whitbread Book of the Year Award, 2003; YALSA Best Books for Young Adults, 2004; Shortlisted for the James Tait Black Memorial Prize for Fiction, 2003

Despite his overwhelming fear of interacting with people, Christopher, a mathematically-gifted, autistic fifteen-year-old boy, decides to investigate the murder of a neighbor's dog and uncovers secret information about his mother.

"Unable to feel emotions himself, his story evokes emotions in readers: heartache and frustration for his well-meaning but clueless parents and deep empathy for the wonderfully honest, funny, and lovable protagonist. Readers will never view the behavior of an autistic person again without more compassion and understanding." —*School Library Journal*

Hadley, Tessa

Bad dreams and other stories. Tessa Hadley. HarperCollins, 2017. 288 p.
ISBN 9780062476661
1. Human nature 2. Family relationships 3. Interpersonal relations 4. Families 5. Life 6. Short stories 7. Literary fiction
New York Times Notable Book, 2017

A collection of stories by the award-winning author of The Past explores a theme of the exceptional nature of seemingly mundane things, depicting such characters as sisters who quarrel over an inheritance and new baby, a child who explores her home in the middle of the night and a housekeeper who uncovers an elderly charge's secrets.

"Achingly lovely, though never sentimental, Hadley's collection renders common lives with exquisite grace." —*Kirkus*

Clever girl. Tessa Hadley. HarperCollins, 2014. 272 p.
ISBN 9780062270399
1. Middle-aged women 2. Memory 3. Arthur, King 4. Teenage mothers 5. Growing up 6. England 7. Literary fiction

Captures the beauty, innocence, and irony of ordinary life in a story that follows a woman named Stella from her childhood growing up with a single mother in a Bristol bedsit in the 1960s to middle age.
Originally published: London: Jonathan Cape, 2013.

The **past**. Tessa Hadley. HarperCollins, 2015. 320 p.
ISBN 9780062270412
1. Adult children of dysfunctional families 2. Siblings 3. Family secrets 4. Intergenerational relations 5. Family relationships 6. Domestic fiction
Hawthornden Prize, 2016

Over five novels and two collections of stories Tessa Hadley has earned a reputation as a fiction writer of remarkable gifts, and been compared with Elizabeth Bowen and Alice Munro. In her new novel three sisters and a brother meet up in their grandparents' old house for three long, hot summer weeks. The house is full of memories of their childhood and their past—their mother took them there when she left their father—but now they may have to sell it. And under the idyllic surface, there are tensions. Roland has come with his new wife and his sisters don't like her. Kasim, the twenty-year-old son of Alice's ex-boyfriend, makes plans to seduce Molly, Roland's teenage daughter. Fran's children uncover an ugly secret in a ruined cottage in the woods. Passion erupts where it's least expected, blasting the quiet self-possession of Harriet, the oldest sister. A way of life—bourgeois, literate, ritualised—winds down to its inevitable end. With uncanny precision and extraordinary sympathy, Tessa Hadley charts the squalls of lust and envy disrupting this ill-assorted house party, as well as the consolations of memory and affection, the beauty of the natural world, the shifting of history under the social surface. From the first page the reader is absorbedand enthralled, watching a superb craftsman at work.

Hadley is the patron saint of ordinary lives; her trademark empathy and sharp insight are out in force here. Kirkus.

Hagberg, David

Gambit. David Hagberg. Forge, 2021. 288 p. (Kirk McGarvey adventures, 26)
ISBN 9780765394231
1. Former CIA agents 2. Assassins 3. Intrigue 4. Billionaires 5. Revenge 6. Thrillers and suspense 7. Spy fiction

Targeted by an American billionaire and a Russian oligarch who want him dead, Kirk McGarvey is confronted by an escalating series of hired killers before resolving to turn the tables on his assassination conspirators.

"The open ending promises that McGarvey and the other members of his team will be back. His faithful readers will be waiting." —*Publishers Weekly*

Hage, Rawi

Beirut Hellfire Society: a novel. Rawi Hage. W. W. Norton & Company, 2019. 288 pages
ISBN 9781324002918
1. Undertakers 2. Existentialism 3. Death 4. Misfits (Persons) 5. Burial 6. Beirut, Lebanon 7. Lebanon 8. 1970s 9. Literary fiction 10. Canadian fiction

It's 1978 in Beirut, Lebanon. When his father dies, Pavlov is approached by a member of the mysterious Beirut Hellfire Society, and agrees to take up his father's work for the Society, arranging burial or cremation for those have been denied last rites.
Previously published in Toronto : Alfred A. Knopf Canada, 2018.

De Niro's game. Rawi Hage. Steerforth Press, 2007. 277 p.
ISBN 9781581952230
1. Civil war 2. Militias and irregular armies 3. War and society 4. Young men 5. Best friends 6. Beirut, Lebanon 7. Lebanon 8. 1980s 9. Political fiction 10. War stories 11. Literary fiction
International IMPAC Dublin Literary Award, 2008; Quebec Writers' Federation Literary Awards, Hugh MacLennan Prize for Fiction, 2006; Quebec Writers' Federation Literary Awards, McAuslan First Book Prize, 2006; Governor General's Literary Awards, English-language Fiction finalist; Shortlisted for the Giller Prize, 2006

Follows the lives and choices of two best friends, Bassam and George, caught in Lebanon's civil war. Both men are desparate to escape Beirut but choose different paths to accomplish their goals.

"This is a grim, flat book. Hage's flatness gives it the right tone of bruised emotion, disconnectedness, and violence; it's what makes this such an effective debut." —*Quill & Quire*
Originally published: Canada: House of Anansi, 2006.

Hahn, Sumi

The **mermaid** from Jeju: a novel. Sumi Hahn. Alcove Press, 2020. 300 pages
ISBN 9781643854403
1. Divers 2. Deep diving 3. Korean War, 1950-1953 4. Growing up 5. Military occupation 6. Korea 7. 20th century 8. Coming-of-age stories 9. Historical fiction

A talented young deep-sea diver from occupied 1948 Korea's neighboring Jeju Island visits Mt. Halla for her family's annual trading trip before her romance with a mountain youth is upended by family tragedy and political turbulence.

"With constant tension, the novel masterfully captures the devastating effects of loss and grief, and what people must do to survive war." —*Publishers Weekly*

Haig, Francesca

The **fire** sermon: a novel. Francesca Haig. Gallery Books, 2015. 320 p. (Fire sermon, 1)
ISBN 9781476767185
1. Dystopias 2. Post-apocalypse 3. Twins 4. Perfection 5. Power (Social sciences) 6. Dystopian fiction 7. Science fiction 8. Adult books for young adults
LC 2014031292

In a world turned primitive following a nuclear fire, every person is born with a twin and of each pair, one is an Alpha, perfect in every way, and the other is an Omega, burdened with a deformity that makes them ostracized; and psychic Cass, a rare Omega, dares to envision a world of equality.

"Haig's experience as a poet shows in her writing, which is clear, forceful and laced with bright threads of beauty. [A] well-built world [with] vivid characters and [a] suspenseful plot." —*Kirkus*

Haig, Matt

The **humans**: a novel. Matt Haig. Simon & Schuster, 2013. 256 p.
ISBN 9781476727912

1. Aliens 2. Mathematicians 3. Immortality 4. Disguises 5. Human/alien encounters 6. Social science fiction 7. Science fiction 8. Adult books for young adults

LC 2013003203

Regarding humans unfavorably upon arriving on Earth, a reluctant extraterrestrial assumes the identity of a Cambridge mathematician before realizing that there is more to the human race than he suspected and embarking on a darkly comic effort to save humanity from itself.

Includes bibliographical references and index.

The **midnight** library. Matt Haig. Viking Press, 2020. 336 p.
ISBN 9780525559474
1. Libraries 2. Parallel universes 3. Young women 4. Options, alternatives, choices 5. Depression 6. Science fiction
LibraryReads Favorites, 2020

Somewhere out beyond the edge of the universe there is a library that contains an infinite number of books, each one the story of another reality. One tells the story of your life as it is, along with another book for the other life you could have lived if you had made a different choice at any point in your life. Nora Seed finds herself faced with the possibility of changing her life for a new one, following a different career, undoing old breakups, realizing her dreams of becoming a glaciologist; she must search within herself as she travels through the Midnight Library to decide what is truly fulfilling in life, and what makes it worth living in the first place.

"Haig treats the subject of suicide with a light touch, and the book's playful tone will be welcome to readers who like their fantasies sweet if a little too forgettable. A whimsical fantasy about learning what's important in life." —*Kirkus*

Haigh, Jennifer

Baker Towers: a novel. Jennifer Haigh. William Morrow, 2005. 352 p.
ISBN 9780060509415
1. Coal mining towns 2. Working class families 3. Small town life 4. Ambition 5. Single mothers 6. Pennsylvania 7. Historical fiction 8. Family sagas 9. Adult books for young adults

LC 2004049073

L. L. Winship/PEN New England Award for Fiction, 2006

The decade following World War II becomes one of tragedy, excitement, and unexpected change for the five Novak children and the residents of their western Pennsylvania community of company houses, church festivals, union squabbles, and firemen's parades.

"This novel is set in Bakerton, a mining town in post-World World II Pennsylvania. Haigh's focus is the Novak family, particularly the five children being raised by their Italian mother after their Polish father drops dead. All five make attempts to escape Bakerton at one point or another; some are successful, others are not. George, a veteran of WW II, neglects his Bakerton fiancee and marries a cold socialite. Dorothy goes to the nation's capital to work, but a nervous breakdown brings her home. Brilliant, cold Joyce thinks her future lies with the military, but she is sorely disappointed. Sandy is the golden son who escapes to dubious success. And Lucy is the youngest, who finds herself in college despite the nagging feeling that she never wanted to leave home in the first place. Haigh creates a real sense of a community and brings her mining town to life through a large cast of minor characters who pass in and out of the Novaks' lives." —*Booklist*

Mrs. Kimble: a novel. Jennifer Haigh. Morrow, 2003. 400 p.
ISBN 9780060509392
1. Man-woman relationships 2. Strength and weakness 3. Quarreling 4. Married men 5. Married women 6. Literary fiction

LC 2002070304

Hemingway Foundation/PEN Award, 2004

Follows twenty-five years in the life of a charismatic opportunist as seen through the eyes of his three wives.

"Original and compelling." —*Library Journal*

Hairston, Andrea

Master of poisons. Andrea Hairston. Tor Books, 2020. 512 p.
ISBN 9781250260543
1. Exiles 2. Deserts 3. Women magicians 4. Spells (Magic) 5. Droughts 6. Epic fantasy 7. African American fiction 8. Afrofantasy

The world is changing. Poison desert eats good farmland. Once-sweet water turns foul. The wind blows sand and sadness across the Empire. To get caught in a storm is death. To live and do nothing is death. There is magic in the world, but good conjure is hard to find. Djola, righthand man and spymaster of the lord of the Arkhysian Empire, is desperately trying to save his adopted homeland, even in exile. Awa, a young woman training to be a powerful griot, tests the limits of her knowledge and comes into her own in a world of sorcery, floating cities, kindly beasts, and uncertain men.

"In stirring prose ('As long as sweet water fell from the sky every afternoon and mist rolled in on a night wind, everybody promised to change—tomorrow or next week. Then crops failed and rivers turned to dust.'), Hairston weaves a rich tapestry of folklore and adventure, inviting readers into a well-developed, non-Western fantasy world, while navigating pressing issues of climate change and personal responsibility." —*Publishers Weekly*

Hajdu, David

Adrianne Geffel: a fiction. David Hajdu. W. W. Norton & Company, 2020. 207 pages
ISBN 9780393634228
1. Women musicians 2. Missing women 3. Experimental music 4. Oral histories 5. Creativity 6. New York City 7. 1980s 8. Satirical fiction 9. Literary fiction

LC 2020008287

Decades after a music artist with a rare neurological condition transforms American pop culture with her pure sensory masterworks, her surviving loved ones piece together what they have come to understand about her life, work and exploitation by others.

"The story unfolds as oral history, delivered mostly by those who celebrate their stake in her—her clueless parents, a controlling self-styled boyfriend—resulting in a portrait that's as much about the exploitation of the gifted as it is about the gift of music, of the artist's exterior situation as it is about the artist's interior world. Hajdu is excellent at articulating the vitality of Geffel's music while leaving what it actually sounds like to our imagination." —*Library Journal*

Haldane, Sean

The **devil's** making. Sean Haldane. Minotaur Books, 2015. 367 pages; (From sea to sea, 1)
ISBN 9781250069405
1. Police 2. Frontier and pioneer life 3. Race relations 4. Colonists 5. British in Canada 6. Victoria, British Columbia 7. 1860s 8. Historical mysteries 9. Canadian fiction
Arthur Ellis Award for Best Novel, 2014

In 1869 Victoria, British Columbia, policeman Chad Hobbes, recently arrived from England, must solve the murder of an American alienist, whose methods included phrenology, Mesmerism and sexual-mystical magnetation, and discovers that everyone who knew him seems to have something to hide.

"A good match for readers who relish suspense drawn out at a leisurely pace, lavish details of Pacific Northwest Coast Indian life, and the particular edginess of unreliable narrators." —*Booklist*

Haldeman, Joe W.

★ The **forever** war. Joe Haldeman. EOS, 2003. 277 p. (Forever series (Joe W. Haldeman), 1)

ISBN 9780345324894

1. Space warfare 2. Space flight 3. Aging 4. Aliens 5. War — Moral and ethical aspects 6. Military science fiction 7. Hard science fiction 8. Science fiction classics

Hugo Award for Best Novel, 1976; Locus Award for Best Science Fiction Novel, 1976; Nebula Award for Best Novel, 1975

Drafted into the ranks of Earth's interstellar warriors, private William Mandella finds his fight against the Taurans secondary to the side-effects of faster-than-light space travel, which affects the rate at which he ages.

Originally published: New York : St Martin's Press, 1974.

Hale, Shannon

Austenland: a novel. Shannon Hale. Bloomsbury, 2007. 197 p. (Austenland novels, 1)

ISBN 9781596912854

1. Single women 2. Idealism in women 3. Gardeners 4. Thirties (Age) 5. Romantic love 6. England 7. New York City 8. Chick lit 9. Books to movies 10. Adult books for young adults

LC 2006034165

Because her obsession with Jane Austen's Mr. Darcy, as played by Colin Firth in the BBC adaptation of "Pride and Prejudice," is ruining her love life, Jane Hayes is delighted when she gets the chance to take a trip to an English resort catering to Austen-crazed women.

"The author's charming first book for adults is chick lit with soul. Though there's a laugh on nearly every page. Hale, like Austen, is adept at subtly skewering the ridiculousthere's also the more serious story of a woman learning the difference between fantasy and reality, and discovering that real life can be better than your dreams." —*BookPage*

Title adapted into a film by the same name (2013).

Halfon, Eduardo

Mourning. Eduardo Halfon; translated by Lisa Dillman & Daniel Hahn. Bellevue Literary Press, 2018. 192 p. (Polish boxer novels, 3)

ISBN 9781942658443

1. Family history 2. Family secrets 3. Identity (Philosophical concept) 4. Jews 5. Immigrant families 6. Literary fiction 7. Translations

LC 2017059202

Edward Lewis Wallant Award, 2018; Kirkus Prize for Fiction finalist, 2018

A mysterious family tragedy inspires a journey across the globe, into the past, and through the tangled memories of childhood.

Originally published in Spanish in 2017 as Duelo by Libros del Asteroide.

Translation of: "Duelo"

Translated from the Spanish.

Hall, Adam

The **quiller** memorandum. Adam Hall. Forge, 2004. 220 p; (Quiller adventures, 1)

ISBN 9780765309679

1. Quiller (Fictitious character) 2. Spies 3. Nazis 4. Intelligence officers 5. British in Germany 6. Berlin, Germany 7. Great Britain 8. Spy fiction 9. Adventure stories

LC 2003069455

Edgar Allan Poe Award for Best Mystery Novel, 1966

Set in West Berlin fifteen years after the end of World War II, a British agent takes on a neo-Nazi underground organization and its war-criminal leader.

A Tom Doherty Associates book.

Also known as: The Berlin memorandum.

Hall, Alexis

★ **Boyfriend** material. Alexis Hall. Sourcebooks Casablanca, 2020. 368 p.

ISBN 9781728206141

1. Gay men 2. Fame 3. Self-esteem 4. Adult children of celebrities 5. Lawyers 6. London, England 7. LGBTQIA romances 8. Romantic comedies 9. First person narratives

LC 2020014702

LibraryReads Favorites, 2020

Fabricating a respectable relationship with a man with whom he shares nothing in common when his rock-star father's comeback leads to unwanted attention, Luc stages publicity-friendly dates that become complicated by all-too-real feelings.

"The writing is witty, and Luc and Oliver's chemistry is irresistible, but it's Hall's insights about trust and self-worth that set the story apart. This is a triumph." —*Publishers Weekly*

For real. Alexis Hall. Riptide Publishing, 2015. 470 p. (Spires novels, 3)

ISBN 9781626492806

1. Gay men 2. Men-men relations. 3.Sexual dominance and submission 4. Middle-aged men — Relations with younger men 5. Leather lifestyle (Sexuality) 6. LGBTQIA romances 7. Contemporary romances 8. LGBTQIA fiction

RITA Award for Best Erotic Romance, 2016

"A complex, poignant look at modern love, loneliness and sexual identity." —*Washington Post*

Rosaline Palmer takes the cake. Alexis Hall. Forever, 2021. 368 p. (Winner bakes all, 1)

ISBN 9781538703328

1. Women bakers 2. Single mothers 3. Bisexual women 4. Reality television programs 5. Self-fulfillment in women 6. Great Britain 7. Romantic comedies 8. LGBTQIA romances

LC 2020054048

Fans of Casey McQuiston, Christina Lauren, and Abby Jimenez will love this scrumptious and sweet romantic comedy.

"Hall balances the adorable love story and witty narration with incisive critiques of classism and the fetishization of bisexual women. As Rosaline learns to trust her instincts and stand up for herself, the tension of the competition keeps the plot flying, and the vibrant cast—including vivacious baker Anvita and Rosaline's ex-girlfriend, Lauren—couches her journey toward self-actualization in encouraging community." —*Publishers Weekly*

Hall, Araminta

Imperfect women: a novel. Araminta Hall. MCD/Farrar, Straus and Giroux, 2020. 304 p.

ISBN 9780374272586

1. Murder 2. Female friendship 3. Secrets 4. Grief 5. Socialites 6. Psychological suspense 7. Multiple perspectives

LC 2020003430

When their best friend, the gorgeous and wealthy Nancy Hennessy, is murdered, Eleanor and Mary wrestle with their grief while dealing with how little they knew their friend, each other and maybe even themselves as the investigation lays bare all of Nancy's secrets.

"Hall's astute novel unravels a gripping mystery and explores the complicated shifts of personal and familial relationships and the conflicts between societal expectations and inner desires." —*Booklist*

Hall, Louisa

Speak. Louisa Hall. HarperCollins, 2015. 352 p.
ISBN 9780062391193
1. Artificial intelligence 2. Robots 3. Technology and civilization 4. Communication 5. Science fiction 6. Social science fiction 7. Multiple perspectives

Exploring the creation of artificial intelligence and illuminating the very human need for communication, connection and understanding, a thought-provoking novel is told from the perspectives of five very different people from different times and places.

"Hall subtly weaves a thread through a temporally diverse cast of narrators. Like all good robot novels, Speak raises questions about what it means to be human as well as the meaning of giving voice to memory." —*Booklist*

Hall, Parnell

Lights! Camera! Puzzles!. Parnell Hall;; with puzzles from ... Will Shortz. Pegasus Crime, 2019. 263 p. : Illustration (Puzzle lady mysteries, 20)
ISBN 9781643130590
1. Crossword puzzles 2. Crossword puzzle makers 3. Women amateur detectives 4. Filmmaking 5. Biographical films 6. Williams, Tennessee 7. Hobby mysteries 8. Cozy mysteries

When her ex's sensational tell-all about their lives is optioned for a movie, Puzzle Lady Cora Felton reluctantly accepts a producer role's in the much-despised production before a body is found on set, staged with a crossword puzzle clue.

Sequel to: The purloined puzzle.

Hall, Rachel Howzell

And now she's gone. Rachel Howzell Hall. Forge, 2020. 384 pages
ISBN 9781250753175
1. Women private investigators 2. African American women 3. Missing women 4. Abused women 5. Family violence 6. Los Angeles, California 7. Thrillers and suspense

When a desperate family implores her to track down a woman who may not want to be found, Grayson Sykes unravels violent secrets that embroil her in an increasingly dangerous game of cat and mouse.

"Full of wry, dark humor, this nuanced tale of two extraordinary women is un-put-downable." —*Publishers Weekly*

These toxic things. Rachel Howzell Hall. Thomas & Mercer, 2021. 430 p.
ISBN 9781542027472
1. Women Professional employees 2. Women archivists 3. Souvenirs (Keepsakes) 4. Memories 5. Patron and client 6. Thrillers and suspense 7. First person narratives 8. African American fiction

Mickie Lambert creates "digital scrapbooks" for clients, ensuring that precious souvenirs aren't forgotten or lost. When her latest client, Nadia Denham, a curio shop owner, dies from an apparent suicide, Mickie honors the old woman's last wish and begins curating her peculiar objets d'art. A music box, a hair clip, a key chain—twelve mementos in all that must have meant so much to Nadia, who collected them on her flea market scavenges across the country. But these tokens mean a lot to someone else, too. Mickie has been receiving threatening messages to leave Nadia's past alone. It's becoming a mystery Mickie is driven to solve. Discovering the truth means crossing paths with a long-dormant serial killer and navigating the secrets of a sinister past. One that might, Mickie fears, be inescapably entwined with her own.

"This cleverly plotted, surprise-filled novel offers well-drawn and original characters, lively dialogue, and a refreshing take on the serial killer theme. Hall continues to impress." —*Publishers Weekly*

Hall, Steven

Maxwell's demon. Steven Hall. Grove Press, 2021. 352 p.
ISBN 9780802149206
1. Authors 2. Books and reading 3. Fathers — Death 4. Jealousy 5. Father and adult son 6. Literary fiction 7. Experimental fiction 8. Metafiction

Failed novelist Thomas Quinn's life isn't going well when he gets a voicemail from his father, who has been dead for seven years.

"Part fantasy, part mystery, it is altogether delightful and filled with surprises—in a word, exceptional." —*Booklist*

Hall, Tarquin

The **case** of the deadly butter chicken: a Vish Puri mystery. Tarquin Hall. McClelland & Stewart 2012. 288 p. (Vish Puri mysteries, 3)
ISBN 9780771038297
1. Detectives 2. Murder investigation 3. Secrets 4. Poisoning 5. Cricket (Sports) 6. Pakistan 7. India 8. Mysteries 9. Adult books for young adults

Mustachioed sleuth Vish Puri tackles his greatest fears in a case involving the poisoning death of the elderly father of a leading Pakistani cricketer, whose demise is linked to the Indian and Pakistani mafias and the violent 1947 partition of India.

Previously published Great Britain : Hutchinson, 2012.

The **case** of the love commandos: from the files of Vish Puri, India's most private investigator. Tarquin Hall. Simon & Schuster, 2013. 310 p. (Vish Puri mysteries, 4)
ISBN 9781451613261
1. Private investigators 2. Social classes 3. Missing persons 4. Romantic love 5. Families 6. Pakistan 7. India 8. Mysteries

LC 2013009100

Coming to the rescue of Ram and Tulsi, only to have Ram disappear, India's Love Commandos, a real-life group of volunteers dedicated to helping mixed-caste couples, asks Vish Puri, India's Most Private Investigator, to help them reunite the star-crossed lovers.

Includes recipes and glossary p.297-310.

Hallberg, Garth Risk

★ **City** on fire. Garth Risk Hallberg. Alfred A. Knopf, 2015. 944 pages
ISBN 9780385353779
1. Interpersonal relations 2. Punk culture 3. Detectives 4. Betrayal 5. Power failures 6. New York City 7. 1970s 8. Multiple perspectives 9. Literary fiction

LC 2014041963

Booklist Editors' Choice, 2015; LibraryReads Favorites, 2015; Library Journal Best Books, 2015; New York Times Notable Book, 2015

A tale set against a backdrop of the infamous 1977 blackout follows the experiences of two New York heirs, their paramours, two punk-loving teens, an obsessive reporter and a detective who would learn what any of them have to do with a Central Park shooting.

"Graceful in execution, hugely entertaining, and most concerned with the longing for connection, a theme that reaches full realization during the blackout of 1977, this epic tale is both a compelling mystery and a literary tour de force." —*Booklist*

Halliday, Lisa

★ **Asymmetry**. Lisa Halliday. Simon & Schuster, 2018. 275 p. ISBN 9781501166761
1. Art 2. Writing 3. Inequality 4. Interpersonal relations 5. Man-woman relationships 6. Literary fiction 7. Multiple perspectives
New York Times Notable Book, 2018

Explores the imbalances that drive dramatic human relations, tracing the overlapping stories of a young American editor's relationship with a famous older writer during the early years of the Iraq War, and an Iraqi-American man who is detained by immigration officers in Heathrow.

Hallinan, Timothy

Fields where they lay. Timothy Hallinan. Soho Crime, 2016. 384 pages (Junior Bender mysteries, 6)
ISBN 9781616957469
1. Thieves 2. Christmas 3. Shopping malls 4. Gangsters 5. Shoplifting 6. Hollywood, California 7. Mysteries

It's the week before Christmas in Tinsel Town, and the Edgerton Mall isn't exactly full of holiday cheer, despite its two Santas. The mall is a fossil of an industry in decline; many of its stores are closed, and to make matters worse, there is a rampant shoplifting problem. Enter burglar Junior Bender, the unwilling fixer for LA's various underworld bosses. The murderous Russian gangster who owns the mall hires Junior to look into the shoplifting problem for him. But Junior's surveillance operation doesn't go well: within two days, two people are dead. It's obvious that shoplifting is the least of the mall's problems. Meanwhile, Junior must confront his own deep-seated melancholy at the very notion of Christmas—both present and past.

"A plum pudding stuffed with cynical disillusionment, organized and disorganized crime, two Santas, a seasonal miracle, and an ending that earns every bit of its uplift." —*Kirkus*

Fools' river. Timothy Hallinan. Soho Crime, 2017. 360 pages (Poke Rafferty Bangkok thrillers, 8)
ISBN 9781616957506
1. Travel writers 2. Amateur detectives 3. Kidnapping victims 4. Missing persons investigation 5. Thieves 6. Bangkok, Thailand 7. Thailand 8. Thrillers and suspense
LC 2017011761

When his daughter's friend begs for help tracking down his father, Bangkok writer Poke Rafferty discovers that the missing man has been abducted by a pair of killers who kidnap people and drain their accounts before murdering them, a finding that triggers a desperate race against time.

Halls, Stacey

The **lost** orphan. Stacey Halls. Mira Books, 2020. 352 p.
ISBN 9780778309321
1. Adoption 2. Mother separated children 3. Illegitimacy 4. Deception 5. Widows 6. London, England 7. Georgian era (1714-1837) 8. Historical fiction 9. Literary fiction 10. Multiple perspectives

In 1754 London, six years after leaving her illegitimate newborn at the Foundling Hospital, Bess Bright returns to reclaim her daughter, only to find that she has already been picked up by someone else.

"The characters are quirky, and their personalities will keep readers invested. The Georgian setting also plays a huge role, as does the formidable hospital. This is a page-turner with a satisfying and harmonious ending." —*Library Journal*

Hambly, Barbara

House of the patriarch. Barbara Hambly. Severn House, 2021. 256 pages (Benjamin January mysteries, 18)
ISBN 9780727889904
1. Freed people 2. Amateur detectives 3. Missing teenage girls 4. Voyages and travels 5. Religion 6. New York (State) 7. New Orleans, Louisiana 8. Antebellum America (1820-1861) 9. 1840s 10. Historical mysteries

When Eve Russell vanishes into thin air, her frantic parents call on free man of color Benjamin January for help. Did the teenager run away—or was she kidnapped? The answer lies in distant New York, a hotbed of new religions, of human circuses . and of dangerous slave traders. If January uncovers the truth, will he ever get home to tell it?

"Hambly's masterful historical detail, scrupulous character portrayal, and psychological analysis of human frailties contribute handsomely to her storytelling. This long-running series shows no signs of losing steam." —*Publishers Weekly*

Lady of perdition. Barbara Hambly. Severn House, 2020. 246 p. (Benjamin January mysteries, 17)
ISBN 9780727889096
1. Freed people 2. Amateur detectives 3. African American men 4. Musicians 5. Violence against women 6. Texas 7. Antebellum America (1820-1861) 8. Historical mysteries

Risking his freedom in New Orleans to help a loved one in the Republic of Texas in 1840, Benjamin January navigates land disputes and racism to locate a kidnapped girl while proving the innocence of a murdered landowner's widow.

"It's a stark and occasionally brutal story, and Hambly tells it superbly, in prose that is vivid and empathetic." —*Booklist*
First published in 2019.

Scandal in Babylon. Barbara Hambly. Severn House, 2021. 240 p. (Silver screen historical novels, 1)
ISBN 9780727890382
1. Young widows 2. Sisters-in-law 3. Women amateur detectives 4. Actors and actresses 5. Film industry and trade 6. Hollywood, California 7. California 8. Between the Wars (1918-1939) 9. 1920s 10. Historical mysteries

In 1924 Hollywood, young British widow Emma Blackstone must help her actress sister-in-law Kitty Flint prove her innocence in the murder of her first husband and discovers that Kitty is hiding something that could blow this case wide open.

"An educated British woman's work at a Tinseltown studio is exhilarating, exasperating, and dangerous.... A sparkling series launch featuring Hollywood hijinks and a clever sleuth." —*Kirkus*

Hamer, Kate

The **girl** in the red coat. Kate Hamer. Melville House, 2016. 378 pages
ISBN 9781612195001
1. Missing girls 2. Single mothers 3. Eight-year-old girls 4. Captives 5. Captivity 6. England 7. Great Britain 8. Cotton, Mary Ann 9. Multiple perspectives 10. Adult books for young adults
LibraryReads Favorites, 2016

When her daughter Carmel disappears during an outdoor festival, Beth, despite being told by authorities she may be gone for good, embarks on a mission to find her.

"Telling the story in two remarkable voices, with Beth's chapters unfurling in past tense and Carmel's in present tense, the author weaves a page-turning narrative. The trajectories of the novel's two leads—through despair, hope, and redemption—are believable and nuanced, resulting in a morally complex, haunting read." —*Publishers Weekly*

Originally published: London : Faber and Faber, 2015.

Hamid, Mohsin

★ **Exit** west: a novel. Mohsin Hamid. Riverhead Books, 2017. 240 p.
ISBN 9780735212176
1. Couples 2. Refugees 3. Political violence 4. Civil war 5. Culture conflict 6. Literary fiction 7. Love stories 8. War stories 9. Adult books for young adults

LC 2016036296

ALA Notable Book, 2018; Booklist Editors' Choice, 2017; Los Angeles Times Book Prize for Fiction, 2017; New York Times Notable Book, 2017; Kirkus Prize for Fiction finalist, 2017; Shortlisted for the Man Booker Prize, 2017; Longlisted for the Andrew Carnegie Medal for Excellence in Fiction, 2018; National Book Critics Circle Award for Fiction finalist, 2017; Shortlisted for the International Dublin Literary Award, 2019

Presents the story of two young lovers whose furtive affair is shaped by local unrest on the eve of a civil war that erupts in a cataclysmic bombing attack, forcing them to abandon their previous home and lives.

"Hamid's storytelling is stripped down, and the books sweeping allegory is timely and resonant." —*Publishers Weekly*

Hamill, Pete

Forever. Pete Hamill. Little, Brown and Co, 2003. 624 p.
ISBN 9780316341110
1. Revenge 2. Orphans 3. Immortality 4. Peasant men 5. Earls and countesses 6. Ireland 7. Manhattan, New York City 8. Urban fantasy 9. Adult books for young adults

LC 2002114241

Moving from Ireland to New York City in 1741, Cormac O'Connor witnesses the city's transformation into a thriving metropolis while he explores the mysteries of time, loss, and love.

"In 1740, an Irish Jew named Cormac O'Connor heads to New York in pursuit of the man who killed his father and gets tangled up in a rebellion against the English. Through a series of events involving an African slave with shamanistic powers, he is granted eternal life, provided that he never leaves Manhattan. There follows a tour of the city's history through Cormac's eyes: the political corruption and the poverty, but also the majestic growth of the metropolis through its culture, its buildings, and its people." —*The New Yorker*

Hamill, Shaun

A **cosmology** of monsters. Shaun Hamill. Pantheon Books, 2019. 336 p.
ISBN 9781524747671
1. Monsters 2. Family problems 3. Obsession 4. Supernatural 5. Sexuality 6. Texas 7. Horror 8. Coming-of-age stories

Shielded by his mother and sisters from his father's obsessive construction of a haunted house attraction, young Noah considers an ultimate sacrifice when he chooses to acknowledge a monster that his family members have tried to ignore.

Hamilton, Jane

A **map** of the world. Jane Hamilton. Doubleday, 1994. 389 p.
ISBN 9780385473101
1. Dante Alighieri 2. Drowning 3. Women prisoners 4. Scapegoats (Persons) 5. Mothers 6. Wisconsin 7. Middle West 8. Mainstream fiction 9. Books to movies

LC 94-42531

Booklist Editors' Choice, 1994

On a dairy farm in the midwest, Alice is watching her neighbor's daughter when she drowns in the pond. This marks the beginning of a series of events that turns Alice into a scapegoat and brings about her family's downfall.

"This is not an easy or light read; indeed, it takes on some of the toughest issues of modern life. But the writer's skill in describing a community and a way of life, as well as her insight into the hearts of her characters, render this story difficult to forget." —*Christian Science Monitor*

Hamilton, Karen

The **last** wife. Karen Hamilton. Graydon House, 2020. 384 p.
ISBN 9781525804632
1. Female friendship 2. Betrayal 3. Promises 4. Jealousy 5. Last words 6. Psychological suspense

Promising to look after her late friend's family, Marie is drawn into the routines of their countryside home before the reappearance of a college friend reveals sinister truths about a suspicious accident from the past.

"Everybody has a nasty side, but that's just one of the pleasures of this cunning whodunit. A devious plot is another. Hamilton knows how to keep the pages turning." —*Publishers Weekly*

Hamilton, Peter F.

The **dreaming** void. Peter F. Hamilton. Del Rey/Ballantine Books, 2008. 640 p. (Void trilogy, 1)
ISBN 9780345496539
1. Telepathy 2. Religious fanatics 3. Life on other planets 4. Visions 5. Space vehicles 6. 34th century 7. Space opera 8. Science fiction

LC 2007029244

At the center of the galaxy is the Dreaming Void, an artificial black hole that may hold paradise within its walls. When a human named Inigo begins dreaming of what lies within the Void, the word spreads, triggering a religious pilgrimage into the Void and possibly a catastrophic expansion that threatens the peace of the Commonwealth Universe.

"There is a generous cast of characters and a handful of storylines involved here and it takes the overall story a while to get going. But once it does, it feels like putting on a comfortable jacket; space opera is what Hamilton does and he does it well." —*SF Signal*

Originally published: London : Macmillan, 2007.

Great North Road. Peter F. Hamilton. Del Rey/Ballantine Books, 2012. 976 p.
ISBN 9780345526663
1. Serial murder investigation 2. Clones and cloning 3. Rich families 4. Human/alien encounters 5. Life on other planets 6. 22nd century 7. Science fiction mysteries 8. Science fiction

LC 2012033593

In 2143 Newcastle, a naked corpse is dredged from the River Tyne. Although there's no physical evidence, police detective Sidney Hurst must discover the identity of both the murderer and the victim, who seems to be one of the hundreds of clones comprising the North family. Their wealthy and powerful dynasty began with three brothers who pioneered technology allowing humans access to other star systems—and the off-world production of Earth's primary fuel source, bioil. In this deadly web of money, politics, and family secrets, Hurst has just one lead: a decades-old crime with striking similarities to his present-day case.

Pandora's star. Peter F. Hamilton. Del Rey, 2004. 768 p. (Commonwealth saga, 1)
ISBN 9780345461629
1. Wormholes (Astrophysics) 2. Aliens (Non-humanoid) 3. Space exploration 4. Humans 5. Space flight 6. 24th century 7. Science fiction 8. Space opera 9. Adult books for young adults
LC 2003068753

The year is 2380. The Intersolar Commonwealth, a sphere of stars some four hundred light-years in diameter, contains more than six hundred worlds, interconnected by a web of transport "tunnels" known as wormholes. At the farthest edge of the Commonwealth, astronomer Dudley Bose observes the impossible: Over one thousand light-years away, a star...vanishes. It does not go supernova. It does not collapse into a black hole. It simply disappears. Since the location is too distant to reach by wormhole, a faster-than-light starship, the Second Chance, is dispatched to learn what has occurred and whether it represents a threat.

"By the 24th century, the vast human Commonwealth has spread from Earth via artificial wormholes. Various benign or seemingly indifferent alien races have been encountered during exploration of new planets, but an astronomer sparks curiosity by announcing that a pair of stars is enclosed by a mysterious energy barrier. Unfortunately, a space expedition discovers that the shield was created to imprison an insatiably greedy mass mind that sees any other race as a mortal threat. When the barrier somehow is lowered, the alien immediately attacks the largely unprepared Commonwealth, while humans begin wondering if yet another inhuman power has manipulated events that unleashed this threat. The author deftly juggles many characters in multiple plot lines." —*Publishers Weekly*

Sequel: Judas unchained.

Originally published: London: Macmillan, 2004.

Hamilton, Steve

★ The **lock** artist. Steve Hamilton. Minotaur Books, 2010. 304 p.
ISBN 9780312380427
1. Safecrackers 2. Men who are mute 3. Psychic trauma in men 4. Former convicts 5. Criminals 6. Crime fiction 7. Adult books for young adults
LC 2009034523

Alex Award, 2011; Edgar Allan Poe Award for Best Novel, 2011; Ian Fleming Steel Dagger Award, 2011

Traumatized at the age of eight and pushed into a life of crime by reason of his unforgiveable talent—lock picking—Michael sees his chance to escape, and with one desperate gamble risks everything to come back home to the only person he ever loved, and to unlock the secret that has kept him silent for so long.

The **second** life of Nick Mason: a novel. Steve Hamilton. Putnam Pub. Group, 2015. 304 p. (Nick Mason novels, 1)
ISBN 9780399574320
1. Organized crime 2. Former convicts 3. Thieves 4. Manipulation (Social sciences) 5. Control (Psychology) 6. Chicago, Illinois 7. Crime fiction
LC 2015022076

Library Journal Best Books, 2016

Reprieved from a long prison term in exchange for committing increasingly dangerous crimes on behalf of a criminal kingpin, Nick Mason is relentlessly haunted by the detective who initially placed him behind bars.

Hammad, Isabella

★ The **Parisian**, or, Al-Barisi: a novel. Isabella Hammad. Grove Press, 2019. Ix, 566 pages : Map
ISBN 9780802129437
1. Palestinians — Identity 2. Immigrants, Arab 3. Social conflict 4. Lost love 5. Colonialism 6. Paris, France 7. Palestine 8. 1910s 9. First World War era (1914-1918) 10. Literary fiction 11. Historical fiction
LC 2018058113

New York Times Notable Book, 2019; Shortlisted for the Walter Scott Prize for Historical Fiction, 2020

Studying medicine and falling in love in 1914 France, the son of a wealthy Palestinian textile merchant finds his loyalties tested by conflicts between the British government and the independence-minded nationalists of his community.

"Richly textured prose drives the novels spellbinding themes of the ebb and flow of cultural connections and people who struggle with love, familial responsibilities, and personal identity." —*Publishers Weekly*

Hammett, Dashiell

The **glass** key. Dashiell Hammett. Vintage Books 1989. 214 p.
ISBN 9780679722625
1. Frameups 2. Politicians 3. Heirs and heiresses 4. Male friendship 5. Gamblers 6. Hardboiled fiction 7. Mysteries 8. Mystery classics
LC 88040517

This classic work of detective fiction combines an airtight plot, authentically venal characters, and writing of telegraphic crispness. —Amazon

Originally published by A. A. Knopf in 1931.

★ The **Maltese** falcon. Dashiell Hammett. Vintage Books, 1992. 217 p.
ISBN 9780679722649
1. Femmes fatales 2. Private investigators 3. Spade, Sam (Fictitious character) 4. Business partners 5. Widows 6. San Francisco, California 7. 1920s 8. Hardboiled fiction 9. Mysteries 10. Books to movies
LC 85672450

Sam Spade's partner is murdered while working on a case, and it is Spade's responsibility to find the killer. In his search, Spade runs mortal risks as he comes closer to the answer.

★ The **thin** man. Dashiell Hammett. Vintage Books, 1992. 201 p.
ISBN 9780679722632
1. Husband-and-wife detectives 2. Married people 3. Missing persons 4. Private investigators 5. Charles, Nick (Fictitious character) 6. New York City 7. Noir fiction 8. Books to movies
LC 9150920

Nick Charles searches for a wealthy inventor who is the prime suspect in a New York City murder case BT

Originally published: New York : Knopf; London : Barker, 1934.

Hampton, Brenda

Stalker. Brenda Hampton. Urban Books, 2017. 288 p.
ISBN 9781622867974
1. Divorced women 2. Stalkers 3. Threat (Psychology) 4. Man-woman relationships 5. Interpersonal attraction 6. Drama lit 7. Thrillers and suspense 8. African American fiction

After a brutal divorce, Abigal Wilson vowed to never love again, but when Brent Carson crosses her path, she simply can't resist his good-guy persona that exemplifies perfection, but then he gives her the bad news.

Hamya, Jo

Three rooms. Jo Hamya. Houghton Mifflin Harcourt, 2021. 224 p.
ISBN 9780358572091

1. Young women 2. Millennials 3. Brexit, 2016-2020 4. Identity (Psychology) 5. Home ownership 6. England 7. Great Britain 8. 21st century 9. Literary fiction 10. Pasternak, Boris Leonidovich

LC 2021007529

Forced to return home jobless and alone, a young woman, searching an apartment of her own, struggles to live a meaningful life on her terms, unsure if she'll ever be able to afford to do so.

"Hamya's debut, a tight story of privilege and neoliberalism, rakes the muck of a wealth-hoarding society." —*Booklist*

Han, Kang

★ **Human** acts: a novel. Han Kang; translated from the Korean and introduced by Deborah Smith. Hogarth, 2017. 218 pages
ISBN 9781101906729

1. Protests, demonstrations, vigils, etc. 2. Political violence 3. Consequences 4. Life change events 5. Dissenters 6. South Korea 7. 20th century 8. 21st century 9. Political fiction 10. Literary fiction 11. Translations

ALA Notable Book, 2018; Booklist Editors' Choice, 2017; Longlisted for the Andrew Carnegie Medal for Excellence in Fiction, 2018; Shortlisted for the International Dublin Literary Award, 2018

Follows the aftermath of a young boy's shocking death during a violent student uprising as told from the perspectives of the event's victims and their loved ones.

"A fiercely written, deeply upsetting, and beautifully human novel." —*Kirkus*

Originally published as: Sonyon i onda = The boy is coming : Changbi Publishers, 2014.
Translated from the Korean.

The **white** book. Han Kang; translated from the Korean by Deborah Smith. Hogarth, 2019. 157 pages : Illustration
ISBN 9780525573067

1. Han, Kang 2. White (Color) 3. Infant death 4. Grief 5. Loss (Psychology) 6. Death 7. Autobiographical fiction 8. Literary fiction 9. First person narratives

Shortlisted for the Man Booker International Prize, 2018

An exploration of personal grief, conveyed through the prism of the color white, finds a nameless writer grappling with a haunting family tragedy involving the infancy death of her older sister.

"Though thin on conventional narrative, the novel resonates as a prayer for the departed, and only gains power upon rereading." —*Publishers Weekly*

Originally published in Korean: Seoul: Munhak Dongne, 2016.
This translation originally published in Great Britain by Portobello Books, London in 2017. This edition published by arrangement with Portobello Books—Title page verso.
Translated from the Korean.

Hand, Elizabeth

Available dark: a thriller. Elizabeth Hand. Minotaur Books, 2012. 256 p. (Cass Neary novels, 2)
ISBN 9780312585945

1. Women photographers 2. Violence 3. Serial murders 4. Photographs 5. Death 6. Finland 7. Iceland 8. Thrillers and suspense 9. Scandinavian crime fiction

LC 2011032833

Romantic Times Reviewer's Choice Award, 2012

Fleeing for her life after she is shown photographs of ritual killings during a mysterious job in Helsinki, Cass Neary encounters a former lover and exiled musician in Iceland only to be inundated by a series of unsolved murders.

Sequel to: Generation loss

The **book** of lamps and banners: a novel. Elizabeth Hand. Mulholland Books, 2020. 344 p; (Cass Neary novels, 4)
ISBN 9780316485937

1. Women photographers 2. Rare books 3. Antiquarian booksellers 4. Manuscripts 5. Murder victims 6. London, England 7. Sweden 8. Thrillers and suspense

LC 2020934680

Photographer Cass Neary is desperate to get home, and she's already lost her camera—like losing a limb. Now her only chance is to cash in on a deal that a friend is about to cut for a legendary illuminated manuscript: The Book of Lamps and Banners. Rumored to have been rescued from the Library at Alexandria, the Book is said to contain ancient esoteric knowledge, even an otherworldly power. So when an intruder brazenly steals the manuscript, Cass and her ex-con lover Quinn must get it back-plunging headlong into a shady underworld where antiquarian booksellers, unhinged tech entrepreneurs, and brutal nationalists all converge.

"It's a wild ride that defies comparison: pill-popping idealist Cass Neary's obsessive hunt piles on teeth-grinding, story-propelling tension, and Hand's gifted portrayal of subcultures seamlessly links Cass' past in New York's '80s punk scene, London's rare-book dealers, and Odinist neo-Nazis." —*Booklist*

Curious toys. Elizabeth Hand. Mulholland Books, 2019. 336 p.
ISBN 9780316485883

1. Darger, Henry 2. Male impersonators 3. Violence in men 4. City life 5. Misfits (Persons) 6. Amusement parks 7. Chicago, Illinois 8. 1910s 9. Historical mysteries 10. Multiple perspectives 11. Adult books for young adults

Joining a gang near the famous Riverview amusement park in 1915 Chicago, the daughter of a fortune teller teams up with a reclusive artist to track down a serial killer responsible for a child's disappearance.

★ **Generation** loss: a novel. Elizabeth Hand. Small Beer Press : 2007. 320 p. (Cass Neary novels, 1)
ISBN 9781931520218

1. Women photographers 2. Secrets 3. Redemption 4. Self-destructive behavior in women 5. Islands 6. New York City 7. Maine 8. Thrillers and suspense

LC 2006102024

Shirley Jackson Awards, Novel, 2007

Cass, a photographer who made a name for herself in the seventies, now finds herself adrift when someone sends her on a mercy gig where she stumbles across an old mystery that is still claiming victims.

"This is a crossover novel, difficult to classify, uncomfortable, spiky. Hand is one of those writers who has challenged the restrictions of genre writing. Here, she both fights with and against the conventions of the thriller genre to get at an evil deeper than its mere perpetrator.... So although Generation Loss moves like a thriller, it detonates with greater resound. It's a dark and beautiful novel that should not be read by anyone under the age of 30." —*Washington Post Book World*.

Sequel: Available dark

Hard light. Elizabeth Hand. Minotaur Books, 2016. 336 p. (Cass Neary novels, 3)
ISBN 9781250030382

1. Women photographers 2. Violence 3. Smuggling 4. Photographs 5. Death 6. London, England 7. Thrillers and suspense

As the story opens Cass arrives in London where she's arranged to meet her long-lost lover, Quinn O'Boyle. When Quinn fails to show at eir rendezvous point, Cass meets the eccentric couple Mallo and Mor-en Dunfries. When Mallo catches Cass rifling his medicine cabinet in earch of drugs, he threatens to turn her in to the authorities, then puts her o work as a runner for his illegal goods.

Handke, Peter

Don Juan: his own version. Peter Handke; translated from the German y Krishna Winston. Farrar, Straus and Giroux, 2010. 112 p.
ISBN 9780374142315
1. Cooks 2. Don Juan (Legendary character) 3. Seduction 4. Innkeepers 5. France 6. Literary fiction
LC 2009029526
"In this quick and airy fantasia, the quintessential womanizer be-omes instead a sad and mostly passive man, possessing a certain magne-sm but emphatically not a seducer, who feels pursued by time itself. Handke's multilayered structure has a sympathetic narrator relaying Don uan's account of travel through contemporary Europe, the Middle East, nd North Africa.... The novel's action is obscured behind screens of hilosophically tinted analysis touching on the nature of relationships, torytelling, and time. And yet the story itself is suffused with the fresh-ess of the French countryside in which it largely takes place." —*The New Yorker*

Hankin, Laura

Happy & you know it. Laura Hankin. Berkley, 2020. 384 p.
ISBN 9781984806239
1. Women musicians 2. Rich people 3. Mothers 4. Play groups 5. Social media 6. New York City 7. Satirical fiction
LC 2019039595
LibraryReads Favorites, 2020
Accepting a job as a playgroup musician for Park Avenue infants af-er her band rises to stardom without her, Claire is drawn into the glamor-us world of wealthy clients who hide secrets and betrayals beneath competitive social-media stardom.
"A slow build to hidden motives and a clever sense of humor make his a fast read, but it's Claire's thoughtful look at our expectations of women and mothers that give the novel its depth." —*Booklist*

Hannah, Kristin

The great alone. Kristin Hannah. St. Martin's Press, 2018. 464 p.
ISBN 9780312577230
1. Vietnam veterans 2. Wilderness survival 3. Moving, Household 4. Post-traumatic stress disorder 5. Communities 6. Alaska 7. 1970s 8. Domestic fiction 9. Adult books for young adults
LC 2017036271
Goodreads Choice Award, 2018; LibraryReads Favorites, 2018; Loan Stars Favourites, 2018
When her volatile, former POW father impulsively moves the family o mid-1970s Alaska to live off the land, young Leni and her mother are orced to confront the dangers of their lack of preparedness in the wake of a dangerous winter season.
"[The novel is] a heart-tugger written in borderline young adult style, combining terrible troubles with notes of overripe romance...[The book] s packed with rapturous descriptions of Alaskan scenery, which are the most reliably alluring part of it.... Characters are good or bad in The Great Alone, happy or miserable." —*New York Times*

Home front. Kristin Hannah. St. Martin's Press, 2012. 400 p.
ISBN 9780312577209

1. Married people 2. Husband and wife 3. Marital conflict 4. Defense attorneys 5. Helicopter pilots 6. United States 7. Washington (State) 8. Domestic fiction 9. Relationship fiction
LC 2011033805
Struggling with a marital estrangement that is further complicated when one of them is deployed, military couple Michael and Joleen Zarkades are forced to confront their problems while protecting the security of their family.

The nightingale. Kristin Hannah. St. Martin's Press, 2015. 384 p.
ISBN 9780312577223
1. Sisters 2. War and society 3. World War II 4. Rescues 5. Resistance to military occupation 6. France 7. Second World War era (1939-1945) 8. Historical fiction 9. Adult books for young adults
LC 2014033303
Library Journal Best Books, 2015; School Library Journal Best Books: Best Adult Books 4 Teens, 2015; RUSA Reading List Short List, 2016
Reunited when the elder's husband is sent to fight in World War II, French sisters Vianne and Isabelle find their bond as well as their respective beliefs tested by a world that changes in horrific ways.

Hannah, Sophie

Keep her safe. Sophie Hannah. HarperCollins, 2017. 384 p.
ISBN 9780062388322
1. Frameups 2. Witnesses 3. Teenage girl murder victims 4. Staged deaths 5. Deception 6. Thrillers and suspense
A British woman's relaxing holiday at a sunny Arizona resort transforms into a dark, obsessive quest for the truth when she becomes convinced that another guest is the woman who disappeared in a sensational headline case years earlier.

The killings at Kingfisher Hill. Sophie Hannah. William Morrow, 2020. 320 p. (New Hercule Poirot mysteries, 4)
ISBN 9780062792372
1. Private investigators 2. Women murder suspects 3. Upper class 4. Family estates 5. Engaged persons 6. England 7. Between the Wars (1918-1939) 8. 1930s 9. Historical mysteries 10. Adult books for young adults
Hired to discretely investigate murder allegations against a wealthy client's wife, Hercule Poirot swaps seats with a nervous train passenger before a second killing is complicated by a series of impossible confessions.
"Bestseller Hannah displays her superior ability to devise mind-blowing setups in her fourth authorized continuation of Agatha Christie's Hercule Poirot series.... Fans of classic fair-play puzzle mysteries will clamor for more." —*Publishers Weekly*
At head of title: Agatha Christie.
Agatha Christie—Cover.

The mystery of three quarters: the new Hercule Poirot mystery. Sophie Hannah. William Morrow, 2018. 320 p. (New Hercule Poirot mysteries, 3)
ISBN 9780062792341
1. Private investigators 2. Murder suspects 3. Malicious accusation 4. Murder victims 5. Murder investigation 6. Between the Wars (1918-1939) 7. 1920s 8. Historical mysteries 9. Adult books for young adults
LC 2018019740
Accused by strangers of trying to set them up for murder, Hercule Poirot teams up with Scotland Yard policeman Edward Catchpool to investigate the drowning death of an elderly man.
"In her third Poirot mystery, Hannah, authorized to continue the series by Agatha Christie's estate, once again nails the style and substance of

her beloved predecessor, producing another treat for Christie fans." —*Booklist*

At head of title: Agatha Christie.

Agatha Christie—Cover.

Perfect little children. Sophie Hannah. William Morrow, 2020. 416 pages

ISBN 9780062978202

1. Former friends 2. Mothers 3. Children 4. Aging 5. Snooping 6. England 7. Cambridge, England 8. Psychological suspense

Spying on a former best friend she has not seen in years, Beth is alarmed when she discovers that the woman's children do not appear to have aged.

"A tightly wound tale of love gone awry." —*Booklist*

Hannaham, James

★ **Delicious** foods. James Hannaham. Little Brown & Co, 2015. 371 p.

ISBN 9780316284943

1. Widows 2. Drug addiction 3. Captivity 4. Mother separated boys 5. Farms 6. Psychological fiction 7. Literary fiction 8. African American fiction

ALA Notable Book, 2016; Hurston/Wright Legacy Award: Fiction, 2016; LibraryReads Favorites, 2015; New York Times Notable Book, 2015; PEN-Faulkner Award, 2016

A young widow with an addiction is lured away to a remote farm by a shady company called Delicious Foods, where she is held captive and forced into hard labor while she struggles to become reunited with her young son.

"If the plot sounds like tough going, Hannahams masterpiece is anything but. The writing makes it 'great,' and the themes of pain, forgiveness, exploitation, and self-creation make it American." —*Booklist*

Hansen, Ron

★ The **assassination** of Jesse James by the coward Robert Ford. Ron Hansen. A. A. Knopf, 1983. 304 p.

ISBN 9780394516479

1. Ford, Robert 2. Outlaws 3. Enemies 4. Obsession in men 5. Biographical fiction 6. Westerns 7. Books to movies

LC 83047851

Jesse James was a fabled outlaw, a charismatic, spiritual, larger-than-life bad man whose bloody exploits captured the imagination and admiration of a nation hungry for antiheroes. Robert Ford was a young upstart torn between dedicated worship and murderous jealousy, the "dirty little coward" who coveted Jesse's legend. The story of their interweaving paths— and twin destinies that would collide in a rain of blood and betrayal.

"Hansen's Jesse is in no way romanticized; his interest derives from the complexity of his psychopathology. The Jesse that emerges here is prematurely decrepit; he'll murder when he doesn't need to, but he reads his Bible and talks about God's peace. Canny, intuitive, he seems to welcome the disciple who will betray him, even gives him the pistol for the job.... The novel works not despite our knowledge of what will happen, but because of it a sense of fatality hangs over every scene." —*Newsweek*

Mariette in ecstasy. Ron Hansen. HarperPerennial, 1991. 179 p.

ISBN 9780060182144

1. Teenage nuns 2. Stigmatization 3. Christian church controversies 4. Nuns 5. Teenage girls 6. New York (State) 7. Historical fiction 8. Psychological fiction 9. Books to movies

When miraculous wounds appear on a seventeen-year-old postulant in an upstate New York convent who claims to have been seduced by God, a religious controversy ensues.

"The novel pulls its taut plot-thread smartly along from start to finish, weaving flash-forward patches of dialogue from the investigation of Mariette's case into the unfolding action of her entry into the life of the convent. The finale is a stunner." —*New York Times Book Review*

Hanson, Hart

The **driver**. Hart Hanson. E.P. Dutton, 2017. 327 p.

ISBN 9781101986363

1. Veterans 2. Murder suspects 3. Intuition 4. Chauffeurs 5. Special forces 6. Los Angeles, California 7. Mysteries 8. Hardboiled fiction

A debut thriller by the award-winning creator of Bones traces the experiences of an Army special forces sergeant turned limo driver who, after hearing a ghost's warning of imminent danger, finds himself implicated in a murder, a situation that is further complicated by his crush on the case's lead detective.

Hao, Jingfang

Vagabonds: a novel. Hao Jingfang; translated by Kenneth Liu. Saga Press, 2020. 640 pages

ISBN 9781534422087

1. Imaginary wars and battles 2. Ambassadors 3. Teenagers 4. Student exchange programs 5. XXXXXXXX 6. Earth 7. Mars (Planet) 8. Science fiction 9. Social science fiction

LC 2019047897

Sent to Earth a century after the Martian war of independence, a group of young delegates becomes caught between two worlds, unable to reconcile the beauty and culture of Mars with the realities of a violent Earth.

"Hugo Award?winner Jingfang's cerebral, futuristic debut explores the interplay between societal values and individual dreams in crisp, gorgeous prose." —*Publishers Weekly*

Haratischvili, Nino

The **eighth** life: (for Brilka). Nino Harastischvil; translated by Charlotte Collins and Ruth Martin. Scribe Publications, 2020. 944 pages

ISBN 9781950354153

1. Families 2. Interpersonal relations 3. Recipes 4. Chocolate 5. Ecstasy 6. Soviet Union 7. Russia 8. 20th century 9. Historical fiction 10. Family sagas 11. Translations

At the start of the twentieth century, on the edge of the Russian empire, a family prospers. It owes its success to a delicious chocolate recipe, passed down the generations with great solemnity and caution. A caution which is justified: this is a recipe for ecstasy that carries a very bitter aftertaste.

"Haratischvili seamlessly weaves the political upheaval around the characters into the love and loss in their lives. Haratischivili's epic portrait of a close-knit family doubles as a stunning tribute to the power of resilience." —*Publishers Weekly*

Translation of: Das achte Leben (fur Brilka) : Roman.

Originally published: Frankfurt : Frankfurter Verlagsanstalt, 2014

Translated from the German.

Harbison, Beth

The **Cookbook** Club. Beth Harbison. William Morrow & Co, 2020. 384 p.

ISBN 9780062958624

1. Recipes 2. Clubs 3. Cookbooks 4. Cooking 5. Female friendship 6. Washington, D.C. 7. Relationship fiction

New York Times bestselling author Beth Harbison whips together a witty and charming—and delicious—story about the secrets we keep, the friends we make, and the food we cook.

"Through recipes and easy reading, Harbison's pleasant tale shines a light on her characters' successes and failures." —*Publishers Weekly*

Tasty recipes inside!—Cover.

Hardiman, Rebecca

Good eggs. Rebecca Hardiman. Atria Books, 2021. 304 pages
ISBN 9781982164294
1. Women thieves 2. Women caregivers 3. Families 4. Generation gap 5. Octogenarians 6. Ireland 7. Domestic fiction 8. Humorous stories

Three generations of a boisterous Irish family are upended by a matriarch's shoplifting activities and an upbeat American home aide whose initial support catapults the family into the worst crisis they have ever faced.

"Full of surprises, Hardiman's endearing novel stands out for its brilliant insight into the mixed blessings of family bonds." —*Publishers Weekly*

Harding Thornton, Christina

Pickard County atlas. Chris Harding Thornton. MCD/Farrar, Straus and Giroux, 2021. 288 p.
ISBN 9780374231255
1. Sheriffs 2. Boy murder victims 3. Secrets 4. Families 5. Dysfunctional families 6. Nebraska 7. 1970s 8. Rural noir
LC 2020034898

While following the local town miscreant, a dusty Nebraska town's sheriff's deputy, Harley Jensen, runs into Pam Reddick, a young woman looking for an escape from the chains of motherhood, marriage and her husband's dark family history.

"Thornton's superior gift for evocative prose augurs well for her next work. Fans of Lou Berney will be pleased." —*Publishers Weekly*

Harding, Lisa

Bright burning things. Lisa Harding. HarperVia, 2021. 336 pages
ISBN 9780063097148
1. Single mothers 2. Unemployed women 3. Alcoholism 4. Motherhood 5. Addiction 6. Mainstream fiction
LibraryReads Favorites, 2021; Loan Stars Favourites, 2021

Haunted by her failed career and lingering childhood trauma, a former stage performer turns to alcohol but is saved from the brink of the abyss by her son whose love redirects her towards rehabilitation and redemption.

"Through Harding's realistic writing, one feels the profound desperation and pain of addiction. Readers won't soon forget this viscerally raw immersion into addiction." —*Library Journal*

Originally published: London : Bloomsbury Publishing, 2017.

Harding, Paul

Tinkers. Paul Harding. Bellevue Literary Press, 2009. 192 p.
ISBN 9781934137123
1. Fathers and sons 2. Reminiscing in old age 3. People with dementia 4. Grandfathers 5. Seniors — Identity 6. New England 7. Psychological fiction 8. Literary fiction
LC 2008039887

ALA Notable Book, 2010; Library Journal Best Books, 2009; Pulitzer Prize for Fiction, 2010

On his deathbed, surrounded by his family, George Washington Crosby's thoughts drift back to his childhood and the father who abandoned him when he was twelve.

"In Harding's skillful evocation, Crosby's life, seen from its final moments, becomes a mosaic of memories." —*The New Yorker*

Hardy, Thomas

★ **Far** from the madding crowd. Thomas Hardy. Vintage Books, 2015. 434 p.
ISBN 9780345804006
1. Rural life 2. Courtship 3. Classism 4. Man-woman relationships 5. Shepherds 6. England 7. Victorian era (1837-1901) 8. Classics 9. Psychological fiction 10. Love stories

After an unfortunate marriage to Sergeant Troy and an affair with Farmer Boldwood, Bathsheba Everdene finally becomes the wife of the man who has always loved her.

Originally published serially in 1874 in "Cornhill Magazine.

★ **Jude** the obscure. Thomas Hardy. Bantam Books, 1996. 444 p.
ISBN 9780553211917
1. Cousins 2. Extramarital affairs 3. Stonemasons 4. Great-aunts 5. Husband and wife 6. England 7. Love stories 8. Books to movies 9. Classics

The story of the tragic relationship between Jude Fawley, a village stonemason who is thwarted in his aspirations to the ministry, and Sue Bridehead, a free-thinking cousin who is shunned by society for her social and sexual rebellion.

This book was released as a movie entitled Jude.

First published in the United Kingdom in 1895 by Osgood, McIlvaine, & Co.

★ The **return** of the native. Thomas Hardy. Bantam, 1991. 512 p.
ISBN 9780553212693
1. Moors and heaths 2. Lovers 3. Rural life 4. Women 5. England 6. Love stories 7. Psychological fiction 8. Classics

A young beauty who feels trapped living in the country with her grandfather plots her escape with a dashing suitor. But her plans are shaken when a handsome local man returns from Paris, hoping to make her his bride. Torn by her passion for two men, and a dream she will never abandon, Eustacia Vye learns that fate holds all the answers.

First published in 1878.

★ **Tess** of the d'Urbervilles: a pure woman faithfully presented. Thomas Hardy. Oxford University Press, 2005. L, 443 p. : Map
ISBN 9780192840691
1. Young women — Relations with older men 2. Rape victims 3. Unplanned pregnancy 4. Guilt in women 5. England 6. Wessex, England 7. Psychological fiction 8. Books to TV 9. Books to movies

Tess Durbeyfield is driven by family poverty to claim kinship with the wealthy D'Urbevilles, and meeting her "cousin" Alec proves to be her downfall. When Angel Clare offers her his love and salvation, she must choose whether to reveal her past or remain silent in the hope of a peaceful future.

The movie "Trishna" is loosely based on this book.

Originally serialized in The Graphic, 1891.

Originally published in 1891. This revised edition first published in 1912.

Hargrave, Kiran Millwood

The **mercies**: a novel. Kiran Millwood Hargrave. Little Brown & Co, 2020. 336 pages
ISBN 9780316529259

1. Storms 2. Men — Death 3. Independence in women 4. Survival 5. Fishing villages 6. Norway 7. 17th century 8. Historical fiction
New York Times Notable Book, 2020

In Finnmark, Norway, 1617, after 40 fishermen are drowned in the sea, the women of the tiny Arctic town of Vardo must fend for themselves especially when a sinister figure arrives, bringing with him a mighty evil that threatens their very existence.

"Hargrave presents a moving tale of women given no choice but independence who are then persecuted for the 'choice' they have made." —*Booklist*

Harkaway, Nick

Angelmaker. Nick Harkaway. Alfred A. Knopf, 2012. 477 p.
ISBN 9780307595959
1. Women spies 2. International intrigue 3. End of the world 4. Clocks and watches — Repairing and adjusting 5. Children of gangsters 6. London, England 7. Spy fiction 8. Science fiction mysteries 9. Science fiction

LC 2011028261

Booklist Editors' Choice, 2012

Avoiding the lifestyle of his late gangster father by working as a clock repairman, Joe Spork fixes an unusual device that turns out to be a former secret agent's doomsday machine and incurs the wrath of the government and a diabolical South Asian dictator.

Gnomon: a novel. Nick Harkaway. Alfred A. Knopf, 2018. 560 p.
ISBN 9781524732080
1. Dystopias 2. Dissenters 3. Government investigators 4. Subversive activities 5. Murder investigation 6. Dystopian fiction 7. Literary fiction 8. Science fiction

LC 2017039289

Booklist Editors' Choice, 2018

A tale set in a near-future, high-tech surveillance state follows the suspicious death of a dissident in custody and finds state inspector Mielikki Neith immersing herself in the victim's world, where she encounters a panorama of characters and innovations that transform her perspectives.

The **gone-away** world. By Nick Harkaway. Alfred A. Knopf, 2008. 512 p.
ISBN 9780307268860
1. End of the world 2. Power (Social sciences) 3. Friendship 4. Conspiracies 5. Greed 6. Apocalyptic fiction 7. Science fiction 8. Humorous stories

LC 2008008701

With a fire burning along the Jorgmund Pipe, a vital protection from the bandits and monsters left in the wake of the Go-Away War, Gonzo Lubitsch and his colleagues at the Haulage and HazMat Emergency Civil Freebooting Company are hired to put it out.

"This novel is set in a dystopian future where humanity huddles in the shadow of the Jorgmund Pipe. The ragtag bunch of heroes are sent to put out a fire on the Pipe, a mission both dangerous and imperative, since the Pipe, like a vast futuristic Glade room-freshener, releases the only substance that keeps the psychic stinks and foul odours of this post-apocalyptic world at bay. On the way there, the unnamed narrator reminisces about his upbringing, college days, military service, the Go Away Bombs that created their surreal present, and above all his friend Gonzo, to whom he's always felt closer than a brother. Somehow their story brings in ninjas, first loves, pirate-kings, mime-artists, human monsters and, well, monster monsters.... The revelation of Gonzo's relationship to his nameless best friend (and the ways in which Harkaway keeps on teasing around us not knowing his name) is one of the novel's joys) is both unexpected and obvious. The Gone-Away World is brakes-off fiction." —*The Scotsman*

Tigerman. Nick Harkaway. Alfred A. Knopf, 2014. 384 p.
ISBN 9780385352413
1. Veterans 2. Vigilantes 3. Comic book fans 4. Islands 5. Pollution 6. Asia 7. Superhero stories 8. Apocalyptic fiction
ALA Notable Book, 2015

Assigned to a ceremonial post in Mancreu, British consul and Afghanistan war veteran Lester Ferris is compelled to disregard widespread underworld activities while bonding with a comic-addicted youth who during a violent uprising desperately relies on him for help.

"Harkaway has created an immensely likable hero who rises to the occasion in amusing and spectacularly improbable fashion." —*Publishers Weekly*

Harkness, Deborah E.

The **book** of life. Deborah Harkness. Viking, 2014. 560 p. (All souls trilogy, 3)
ISBN 9780670025596
1. Women scholars and academics 2. Witches 3. Vampires 4. Alchemy 5. Manuscripts 6. Contemporary fantasy 7. Books to TV
Goodreads Choice Award, 2014

Historian and witch Diana Bishop and her vampire scientist husband Matthew Clairmont return from a trip to the past still searching for the elusive alchemy tome Ashmole 782 in the final installment of the best-selling trilogy following Shadow of Night.

"There is no shortage of action in this sprawling sequel, and nearly every chapter brings a wrinkle to the tale. The storytelling is lively and energetic, and Diana remains an appealing heroine even as her life becomes ever more extraordinary." —*Publishers Weekly*
Made into the TV series Discovery of Witches beginning in 2018.

A **discovery** of witches: a novel. Deborah Harkness. Viking, 2011. 579 p; (All souls trilogy, 1)
ISBN 9780670022410
1. Women scholars and academics 2. Witches 3. Manuscripts 4. Vampires 5. Alchemy 6. Contemporary fantasy 7. Books to TV

LC 2010030425

Discovering a magical manuscript in Oxford's library, scholar Diana Bishop, a descendant of witches who has rejected her heritage, inadvertently unleashes a fantastical underworld of daemons, witches and vampires whose activities center around an enchanted treasure.

"A riveting tale full of romance and danger that will have you on the edge of your seat, yet its chief strength lies in the wonderfully rich and ingenious mythology underlying the story. Entwining strands of science and history, Harkness creates a fresh explanation for how such creatures could arise that is so credible, you'll have to keep reminding yourself this is fiction." —*BookPage*

Shadow of night. Deborah Harkness. Viking, 2012. 592 p. (All souls trilogy, 2)
ISBN 9780670023486
1. Women scholars and academics 2. Witches 3. Vampires 4. Alchemy 5. Time travel (Past) 6. 16th century 7. Historical fantasy 8. Books to TV

LC 2012005843

Goodreads Choice Award, 2012

A follow-up to A Discovery of Witches finds Oxford scholar and reluctant witch Diana and vampire geneticist Matthew Clairmont in Elizabethan London, where Diana seeks a magical tutor and Matthew confronts elements from his past at the same time the mystery of Ashmole 782 deepens.

Made into the TV series Discovery of Witches beginning in 2018.

Time's convert. Deborah Harkness. Viking, 2018. 436 pages; (All souls universe, 1)
ISBN 9780399564512
1. Surgeons 2. Vampires 3. American Revolution, 1775-1783 4. Men — Personal conduct 5. Transformations (Magic) 6. Paris, France 7. London, England 8. Revolutionary America (1775-1783) 9. Historical fantasy 10. Adult books for young adults

A Revolutionary War-era doctor seizes a chance to become a vampire, only to find the ancient traditions governing his new life clashing with the deeply held beliefs of his former one.

The **world** of all souls: the complete guide to a Discovery of Witches, Shadow of Night, and the Book of Life. . Vikings Press, 2018. Ix, 484 pages : Illustration
ISBN 9780735220744
1. Witches 2. Vampires 3. Magic 4. Alchemy 5. Contemporary fantasy 6. Arts and Entertainment — Writing and Publishing

In The World of All Souls, Harkness shares the rich sources of inspiration behind her bewitching novels. She draws together synopses, character bios, maps, recipes, and even the science behind creatures, magic, and alchemy—all with her signature historian's touch. Bursting with fascinating facts and dazzling artwork, this essential handbook is a must-have for longtime fans and eager newcomers alike.

Harman, Patricia

The **midwife** of Hope River: a novel. By Patricia Harman. HarperCollins, 2012. 320 p. (Hope River novels, 1)
ISBN 9780062198891
1. Midwives 2. Poverty 3. Home birth 4. Depressions 5. Secrets 6. West Virginia 7. Appalachian Region 8. Depression era (1929-1941) 9. 1930s 10. Historical fiction
LC 2012010944

Midwife Patience Murphy has a gift: a talent for escorting mothers through the challenges of bringing children into the world. Working in the hardscrabblle conditions of Appalachia during the Depression, Patience takes the jobs that no one else wants, helping those most in need.

Harmel, Kristin

The **room** on Rue Amelie. Kristin Harmel. Gallery Books, 2018. 368 p.
ISBN 9781501171406
1. World War II 2. Military occupation 3. Survival 4. War 5. Soldiers 6. Paris, France 7. Second World War era (1939-1945) 8. War stories 9. Historical fiction 10. Multiple perspectives
LC 2017047966

An American newlywed whose romantic dreams are shattered by the realities of war, an 11-year-old Jewish girl witnessing the horrors of mass deportations and a British Royal Air Force soldier who wonders if he is making a difference are brought together by fate and loss in Nazi-occupied Paris, where together they find the courage to survive.

Harmon, Amy

Where the lost wander. Amy Harmon. Lake Union Press, 2020. 340 pages
ISBN 9781542017961

1. Voyages and travels 2. Man-woman relationships 3. Widows 4. Grief 5. Prejudice 6. The West (United States) 7. Overland Trails 8. American Westward Expansion (1803-1899) 9. Historical fiction 10. Westerns

Set on Overland Trail in 1853, a young widow sets off with her family for a life out West—a journey fraught with hardship, fear, death and terrible sacrifice that leads her into the arms of a half-Pawnee man straddling two worlds.

"The love story of John and Naomi is filled with tension and honest reflection, as well as missteps and disappointments, all of which add a rich realism to this sumptuous historical novel." —*Booklist*

Harper, Jane

The **dry**. Jane Harper. Flatiron Books, 2017. 320 p. (Aaron Falk novels, 1)
ISBN 9781250105608
1. Alibi 2. Deception 3. Revenge 4. Government investigators 5. Droughts 6. Australia 7. Mysteries 8. Australian fiction 9. Books to movies
Australian Book Industry Awards, Book of the Year, 2017; Australian Book Industry Awards, General Fiction Book of the Year, 2017; Davitt Awards, Best Adult Novel, 2017; Davitt Awards, Readers' Choice, 2017; Gold Dagger Award for Best Crime Novel of the Year, 2017; LibraryReads Favorites, 2017; Ned Kelly Award for Best First Novel, 2017; RUSA Reading List Short List, 2018

Receiving a sinister anonymous note after his best friend's suspicious death, federal agent Aaron Falk is forced to confront the fallout of a twenty-year-old false alibi against a backdrop of the worst drought Melbourne has seen in a century.

"From the ominous opening paragraphs, all the more chilling for their matter-of-factness, Harper, a journalist who writes for Melbourne's Herald Sun, spins a suspenseful tale of sound and fury as riveting as it is horrific." —*Publishers Weekly*
Originally published: Australia : Macmillan, 2016.

The **lost** man. Jane Harper. Flatiron Books, 2019. 340 pages
ISBN 9781250105684
1. Cattle ranches 2. Rural life 3. Family problems 4. Brothers 5. Ranches 6. Queensland 7. Australia 8. Mysteries 9. Australian fiction
Davitt Awards, Readers' Choice, 2019; Library Journal Best Books, 2019; Ned Kelly Award for Best Novel, 2019; Thriller Award for Best Paperback Original, 2019

Meeting at the remote fence line separating their cattle ranches on an isolated belt of the Australian outback, two brothers navigate the haunting realities of the isolation that ended their third brother's life.

"The mystery of Cam's death is at the dark heart of an unfolding family drama that will leave readers reeling, and the final reveal is a heartbreaker. A twisty slow burner by an author at the top of her game." —*Kirkus*
Originally published: Pan Macmillan Australia, 2018.

The **survivors**. Jane Harper. Flatiron Books, 2021. 320 pages
ISBN 9781250232427
1. Brothers — Death 2. Murder suspects 3. Missing teenage girls 4. Guilt 5. Homecomings 6. Tasmania 7. Mysteries 8. Australian fiction
LC 2020037495
Loan Stars Favourites, 2021

Haunted by guilt for a reckless and consequential mistake in his youth, Kieran returns to his coastal hometown and his struggling fishing-industry parents, before the discovery of a body on the beach reveals long-held secrets.

"While this novel isn't quite as suspenseful as Harper's previous books, she's a master at creating atmospheric settings, and it's easy to fall under her spell. A layered and nuanced mystery." —*Kirkus*

Originally published: Sydney : Pan Macmillan, 2020.

Harper, Karen

The **queen's** secret: a novel of England's World War II queen. Karen Harper. William Morrow & Co, 2020. 384 p.

ISBN 9780062979650

1. Elizabeth 2. Royal houses 3. Determination in women 4. Husband and wife 5. Political intrigue 6. War and society 7. Great Britain 8. Second World War era (1939-1945) 9. Historical fiction

Endearing herself to the British people with her kindness and strength, Elizabeth the Queen Mother, the wife of George VI and mother of a future Elizabeth II, orchestrates Edward VIII's exile while hiding damaging secrets.

"Harper's novel draws attention to the heroism and strength of the royal family during a trying time in history. A strong selection for those interested in a more personal imagining of royal life at that time." —*Library Journal*

Harrigan, Stephen

The **leopard** is loose: a novel. Stephen Harrigan. Alfred A. Knopf, 2022. 304 p.

ISBN 9780525655770

1. Leopard 2. Postwar life 3. Boys 4. Growing up 5. Fear 6. Oklahoma City, Oklahoma 7. 1950s 8. Historical fiction 9. Literary fiction

LC 2021028338

The fragile, 1952 postwar tranquility of a five-year-old boy's world explodes one summer day when a leopard escapes from the zoo, throwing all of Oklahoma City into dangerous excitement, in this evocative story of a child's confrontation with his deepest fears.

"That the novel is told retrospectively by Grady, now in his seventies, adds an element of nostalgia to this slightly old-fashioned family story, which, in its quiet way, is quite captivating." —*Booklist*

Harrington, Anna

An **extraordinary** lord. Anna Harrington. Sourcebooks Casablanca, 2021. 384 p. (Lords of the Armory, 3)

ISBN 9781728200149

1. Veterans 2. Lawyers 3. Women thieves 4. Rich families 5. Secret identity 6. London, England 7. Great Britain 8. Regency period (1811-1820) 9. Regency romances 10. Historical romances

Soldier turned solicitor Lord Merritt Rivers has dedicated his life to upholding the law. He patrols the streets faithfully, hoping to stop crimes before they can happen. While hunting an escaped convict, he encounters a woman also hunting thieves. She's a delicious distraction, until he discovers that she is the criminal he's after. Veronica Chase has hidden her past as a nobleman's daughter. She confesses to a crime to keep her adopted brother out of prison. Forming an uneasy alliance, Veronica and Merritt work together to protect innocent Londoners during the city's riots. Moving between her world and his, they grow closer to each other and to the mob's dangerous leaders. But their newfound trust won't be enough, until each face their demons and ask what's worth saving—the lives they've chosen to lead or the love that leaves them yearning for more.

"Harrington's vivid vision of London reaches from its darkest corners to the glittering halls of the aristocracy, making for an immersive outing.

The three-dimensional characters and rich romance will keep Regency fans riveted from the first page." —*Publishers Weekly*

An **inconvenient** duke. Anna Harrington. Sourcebooks Casablanca, 2020. 352 pages (Lords of the Armory, 1)

ISBN 9781728200088

1. Dukes and duchesses 2. Veterans 3. Young women 4. Sisters — Death 5. Best friends 6. England 7. Great Britain 8. Regency period (1811-1820) 9. Historical romances 10. Regency romances

Marcus Braddock, former general and newly appointed Duke of Hampton, is back from war. Now, not only is he surrounded by the utterly unbearable ton, he's mourning the death of his beloved sister, Elise. Marcus believes his sister's death wasn't an accident, and he's determined to learn the truth—starting with Danielle Williams, his sister's beautiful best friend.

"Action, suspense, seduction, and two determined lovers fighting for what is right provide a host of reasons to read well into the night. Danielle is an extremely compelling heroine who is willing to forgo her own prospects to correct wrongdoing. When combined with Marcus's conviction and refusal to abandon those he cares about, they make a perfect pair to kick off Harrington's (How I Married a Marquess) latest Regency series." —*Library Journal*

Harris, C. S.

Good time coming. C. S. Harris. Severn House Pub, 2016. 309 p.

ISBN 9780727886491

1. Families 2. Civil War 3. Women and war 4. Confederate soldiers 5. Oppression (Psychology) 6. Louisiana 7. Mississippi 8. American Civil War era (1861-1865) 9. Historical fiction 10. War stories 11. Adult books for young adults

As the Civil War comes ever closer to her vulnerable village of St. Francisville in Louisiana, young Amrie St. Pierre is forced to grow up quickly when she encounters a Union captain named Gabriel who threatens to destroy all she holds dear.

"Harris offers an evocative, intimate, disturbing, mesmerizing tale of the American Civil War, seen through the eyes of a 12-year-old girl, Amrie St. Pierre.... When two Federals attack Amrie's home, she defends it with all her might, but the results are as terrifying as they are shocking. This story of love, loss, and growing up under some of the most difficult circumstances imaginable is beautifully written, superbly researched, emotionally engaging, and gripping from first page to last. A must for old-school fans of historical fiction." —*Booklist*

A novel of the American Civil War—Cover.

What the devil knows: a Sebastian St. Cyr mystery. C.S. Harris. Berkley, 2021. 336 p. (Sebastian St. Cyr mysteries, 16)

ISBN 9780593102664

1. Murder investigation 2. Judicial error 3. Serial murderers 4. Serial murders 5. Amateur detectives 6. London, England 7. England 8. Regency period (1811-1820) 9. Historical mysteries

LC 2020030401

Investigating the suspicious murder of a lead investigator, Sebastian St. Cyr uncovers clues that suggest that the wrong man was arrested for a serial murder case three years earlier.

"An intricate puzzle, based on a series of real-life murders, that indicts social injustices that continue to this day." —*Kirkus*

Harris, E. Lynn

Basketball Jones: a novel. E. Lynn Harris. Doubleday, 2009. 256 p.

ISBN 9780767926270

1. African American gay men 2. Professional basketball players 3. Extortion 4. Homosexuality 5. Identity (Psychology) 6. United States 7. LGBTQIA fiction 8. African American fiction 9. Drama lit

Aldridge James "AJ" Richardson's comfortable life with his longtime lover, famed NBA star Dray Jones, is threatened by the need to hide their relationship to maintain Dray's public image and by Dray's marriage to Judi, a beautiful and ambitious woman.

I say a little prayer: a novel. By E. Lynn Harris. Doubleday, 2006. 256 p.
ISBN 9780385512725
1. Bisexual African American men 2. African American singers 3. African American churches 4. African Americans 5. African American gay men 6. Georgia 7. Atlanta, Georgia 8. LGBTQIA fiction 9. African American fiction 10. Mainstream fiction
LC 2005055452

Chauncey Greer, the bisexual owner of a thriving card company in Atlanta, is inspired to pursue his old dream of a musical career, a career that had ended in scandal thanks to a teenage love affair with his fellow bandmate in a popular boy band.

Invisible life: a novel. E. Lynn Harris. Anchor Books, 1994. 268 p. (Invisible life trilogy, 1)
ISBN 9780385469685
1. African American men — Sexuality 2. Bisexual African American men 3. Sexuality 4. Identity (Psychology) 5. Love triangles 6. African American fiction 7. LGBTQIA fiction 8. Mainstream fiction
LC 93008731

A young man graduating from college discovers his bisexuality and spends the next eight years alternately trying to face and deny the truth of his passions.

Not a day goes by: a novel. E. Lynn Harris. Doubleday, 2000. 271 p.
ISBN 9780385498241
1. Separation (Psychology) 2. Bisexual African American men 3. African American men/women relations 4. African American actors and actresses 5. African-American sports agents 6. Romantic comedies 7. Drama lit 8. African American fiction
LC 38368

John "Basil" Henderson and Yancey Harrington Braxton believe that they have found the perfect mate in each other. A lavish wedding is planned but just before the nuptials, fate and a little comeuppance from the past threaten the happy couple's future.

"When John 'Basil' Henderson, ex-football player and sports agent on the rise, falls in love with haughty, ambitious Broadway star Yancey Harrington Braxton, it seems like a perfect match. But on the couple's wedding day, which opens the book, the extravagant nuptials are suddenly canceled. The narrative retraces the couple's rocky courtship.... Determined to mary, have children, and keep his homosexual proclivities a secret, Basil doesn't realize that Yancey has a few secrets of her own." —*Publishers Weekly*

Harris, Joanne
★ **Chocolat:** a novel. Joanne Harris. Viking, 1999. 242 p. (Chocolat novels (Joanne Harris), 1)
ISBN 9780670881796
1. Single mothers 2. Mothers and daughters 3. Chocolate 4. Small town life 5. Villages 6. France 7. Literary fiction 8. Books to movies
LC 9821771
New York Times Notable Book, 1999

When an exotic stranger, Vianne Rocher, arrives in the French village of Lansquenet and opens a chocolate boutique directly opposite the church, Father Reynaud identifies her as a serious danger to his flock—especially as it is the beginning of Lent, the traditional season of self-denial. War is declared as the priest denounces the newcomer's wares as the ultimate sin.

"Harris' writing conveys a multitude of images and captures the self-absorption of small town life in France." —*Booklist*
Sequel: The girl with no shadow (which has also been published as: The Lollipop Shoes).
Originally published: London: Doubleday, 1999.

Harris, Nathan
The **sweetness** of water. Nathan Harris. Little, Brown & Co, 2021. 368 pages
ISBN 9780316461276
1. Freed people 2. African Americans 3. Brothers 4. Farmers 5. Veterans 6. Georgia 7. 1860s 8. 19th century 9. Historical fiction 10. African American fiction
Loan Stars Favourites, 2021

"Harris' first novel is an aching chronicle of loss, cruelty, and love in the wake of community devastation." —*Booklist*

Harris, Oliver
A **shadow** intelligence. Oliver Harris. Houghton Mifflin Harcourt, 2020. 359 p. (Elliot Kane novels, 1)
ISBN 9780358206651
1. Spies 2. Missing women 3. Intelligence service 4. Psychological warfare 5. Data encryption (Computer science) 6. Kazakhstan 7. Spy fiction 8. Thrillers and suspense
LC 2019041570

A modern but classically styled spy novel in the spirit of John Le Carré and Chris Pavone, A Shadow Intelligence follows a mercurial MI6 agent, Elliot Kane, as he goes off script to find his lover, who went missing while embroiled in a dangerous scheme in Kazakhstan.

"An absorbing, superbly written novel likely to stand as one of the best spy novels of the year." —*Kirkus*

Harris, Robert
Archangel: a novel. Robert Harris. Random House, 1999. 373 p.
ISBN 9780679428886
1. Stalin, Joseph 2. Spies 3. Americans in Moscow, Russia 4. Sovietologists 5. Stalinism 6. Soviet Union 7. Russia 8. Thrillers and suspense 9. Books to TV
LC 9833655

While in Moscow, historian Fluke Kelso is approached by someone claiming to have been present when Stalin died, but a simple check into the old man's story turns into a murderous chase into the dark forests of northern Russia near the White Sea port of Archangel.

"The sinewy plot never slackens, but what makes the book memorable are the vividly observed backgrounds.... No less authentic are the fragmented but undead relics of the old Soviet system." —*The National Review*
Originally published: London : Hutchinson, 1998.

Enigma. Robert Harris. Random House, 1995. 320 p.
ISBN 9780679428879
1. Enigma machine 2. World War II 3. Cryptographers 4. Secret service 5. Cryptography 6. England 7. War stories 8. Spy fiction 9. Historical thrillers 10. Adult books for young adults
LC 95-47628
School Library Journal Best Books: Best Adult Books 4 Teens, 1996

A fictional account of the desperate efforts to break the Nazi's Enigma code takes place in a British railway town, a struggle that becomes complicated by the pivotal disappearance of a beautiful cryptographer

"As one expects from a thriller-writer, Harris ensures the tension builds inexorably as the plot unfolds. Unlike some, however, he creates characters that linger in the mind, and he never bores his readers with gratuitous technical detail." —*The New Scientist*

★ **Fatherland**. Robert Harris. Random House, 1992. 338 p.
ISBN 9780679412731
1. Hitler, Adolf 2. Nazism 3. Nazis 4. Conspiracies 5. Police 6. Holocaust (1933-1945) 7. Germany 8. Mysteries 9. Alternate histories 10. Books to movies
LC 91051026
"Fatherland is a bleak book. But what concerns the author is the indestructibility of the human spirit, as exemplified by Xavier March. If Hitler's Germany is hell, at least a few angels are floating around." —*New York Times Book Review*
Illustrated with maps and endpaper drawings.

The **ghost**: a novel. Robert Harris. Simon & Schuster, 2007. 352 p.
ISBN 9781416551812
1. Ghostwriters 2. Political corruption 3. Deception 4. Spies 5. Former prime ministers 6. London, England 7. England 8. Thrillers and suspense 9. Books to movies
LC 2007029670
Thriller Award for Best Novel, 2008
Having served as Great Britain's longest-enduring prime minister, Adam Lang accepts a large cash advance to write a tell-all memoir of his life and controversial political career, an effort for which he hires a ghostwriter who uncovers dangerous secrets about the former leader's term.
"From the first paragraph, Harris' novel tugs the reader on through a thriller blessedly short on shoot'emup and long on character nuance, dead-on media satire and the damned-either-way consequences of wielding power in the murky wake of 9/11." —*Pittsburgh Post-Gazette*
Book adapted into a film entitled The ghost writer.

An **officer** and a spy. Robert Harris. Random House, 2014. 304 p.
ISBN 9780385349581
1. Dreyfus, Alfred 2. Dreyfus Affair, 1894-1906 3. Antisemitism 4. Spies 5. Exiles 6. Espionage 7. France 8. Belle Epoque (1871-1914) 9. 19th century 10. Historical thrillers
British Book Award for Popular Fiction, 2013; Ian Fleming Steel Dagger Award, 2014; Walter Scott Prize for Historical Fiction, 2014
Paris, 1895: Captain Alfred Dreyfus, a Jewish army officer, is convicted of treason, stripped of his rank, and sentenced to a lifetime of hard labor on Devil's Island, French Guiana. Ordered to investigate the case on behalf of the military's new counter-espionage force, Colonel Georges Picquart uncovers evidence of anti-Semitism as well as a conspiracy that reaches the highest levels of the government. Inspired by the events of the Dreyfus Affair, a real-life political scandal that engulfed Europe in the late 19th century, this gripping tale brings history to life.
"Harris combats the predictability that can haunt fictional accounts of well-known events by teasing out the tale through Picquart's training in espionage and investigation, his unsanctioned detecting, and the complex intrigues he navigates to secure a reexamination of Dreyfus' case." —*Booklist*
First published: London: Hutchinson, 2013.

Pompeii: a novel. Robert Harris. Random House, 2003. 288 p.
ISBN 9780679428893

1. Pliny, the Elder 2. Civilization, Ancient 3. Aqueducts 4. Coastal towns 5. Engineers 6. Civil engineers 7. Italy 8. Pompeii (Extinct city) 9. 1st century 10. Historical fiction 11. Adult books for young adults
LC 2003058446
When the aqueduct that brings fresh water to thousands of people around the bay of Naples fails, Roman engineer Marius Primus heads to the slopes of Mount Vesuvius to investigate, only to come face to face with an impending catastrophe.
"Lively writing, convincing but economical period details and plenty of intrigue keep the pace quick." —*Publishers Weekly*

The **second** sleep: a novel. Robert Harris. Knopf, 2019. 464 pages
ISBN 9780525656692
1. Civilization, Medieval 2. Priests 3. Heretics 4. Young men 5. Funerals 6. England 7. Apocalyptic fiction 8. Mysteries
LC 2019012429
Arriving in a remote mid-15th-century Exmoor village, a young priest discovers his late predecessor's possibly fatal obsession with the ancient coins, glass and human bones strewn throughout the region.

Harris, Sarah J.

The **color** of Bee Larkham's murder: a novel. Sarah J. Harris. Touchstone, 2018. 448 p.
ISBN 9781501187896
1. Synesthesia 2. Perception 3. Missing persons 4. Senses and sensation 5. Clues 6. London, England 7. Literary fiction 8. Mysteries 9. First person narratives
Librarians' Choice (Australia), 2018
A boy with synesthesia—a condition that causes him to see colors when he hears sounds—tries to uncover what happened to his beautiful neighbor, and if he was ultimately responsible.
Originally published: London : Harper Collins, 2018.

Harris, Thomas

Hannibal. Thomas Harris. Delacorte, 1999. 486 p. (Hannibal Lecter novels, 4)
ISBN 9780385299299
1. Violence against women 2. Women murder victims 3. Psychiatrists with mental illnesses 4. Serial murderers 5. Men with mental illnesses 6. Italy 7. Psychological suspense 8. Multiple perspectives 9. Horror
New York Times Notable Book, 1999
A showdown between two psychopathic killers with a beautiful FBI agent caught in the middle. From his respirator, Mason Verger orders the capture of Hannibal Lecter, the man who put him there, and the bait is Clarice Starling with whom Lecter crossed swords in The Silence of the Lambs.
"Where Silence haunted and tantalized, Hannibal grosses out and gratifies. Yet there's still a basso ostinato of serious questions, and the answers are darker than in Silence." —*The Nation*

Hannibal rising. Thomas Harris. Delacorte, 2006. 336 p. (Hannibal Lecter novels, 1)
ISBN 9780385339414
1. Child abuse victims 2. Uncle and nephew 3. Revenge 4. Childhood 5. Sisters — Death 6. France 7. Coming-of-age stories 8. Psychological suspense 9. Horror
The villainous Hannibal Lecter—from Red Dragon and Silence of the Lambs—returns in a chilling new novel that describes the cannibalistic serial killer's early life in Eastern Europe, from the ages of six to twenty, following the loss of his entire family during World War II.

"There are images of morbid beauty here.... Harris' handling of the wartime violence is also impressive, as swift and vicious as the blitzkrieg itself." —*Los Angeles Times*

This novel is a prequel to: Red Dragon.

Red dragon. Thomas Harris. G. P. Putnam's Sons, 1981. 348 p. Hannibal Lecter novels, 2)

ISBN 9780399124426

1. Serial murderers 2. Adult child abuse victims 3. Psychopaths 4. People with disabilities 5. Cleft palate 6. Psychological suspense 7. Multiple perspectives 8. Books to movies

LC 81008674

Will Graham's unusual, fearful ability to project himself into the minds of psychopaths puts him on the trail of Francis Dolorhyde, whose bizarre and bloody murders of two suburban families have been triggered by his viewing of a William Blake watercolor.

Red Dragon inspired the film Manhunter in 1986, which was remade into the more faithfully-adapted film Red Dragon in 2002.

★ The **silence** of the lambs. Thomas Harris. St. Martin's Press, 1988. 338 p. (Hannibal Lecter novels, 3)

ISBN 9780312022822

1. Women FBI agents 2. Violence against women 3. Psychopaths 4. Women murder victims 5. Psychiatrists 6. Psychological suspense 7. Multiple perspectives 8. Books to movies

LC 88018203

Bram Stoker Award for Best Novel, 1988; Anthony Award for Best Novel, 1989

FBI trainee Clarise Starling is assigned to interview a brilliant, imprisoned psychopathic killer, Dr. Hannibal Lecter. She needs him to bring in a psychotic serial killer.

"Harris places his clues with precision, and his characterizations...are superbly developed and richly complex." —*Booklist*

Harris, Zakiya Dalila

The **other** Black girl: a novel. Zakiya Dalila Harris. Atria Books, 2021. 288 p.

ISBN 9781982160135

1. African American women 2. Editors 3. Racism in employment 4. Microaggressions 5. Office politics 6. Thrillers and suspense 7. African American fiction

LC 2020048720

LibraryReads Favorites, 2021

Tired of being the only Black employee at Wagner Books, 26-year-old editorial assistant Nella Rogers is thrilled when Harlem-born and bred Hazel is hired until she after a string uncomfortable events, is elevated to Office Darling, leaving Nella in the dust.

"While the novel overflows with witty dialogue and skillfully drawn characters, its biggest strength lies in its penetrating critique of gatekeeping in the publishing industry and the deleterious effects it can have on Black editors. This insightful, spellbinding book packs a heavy punch." —*Publishers Weekly*

Harrison, Cora

Beyond absolution: a mystery set in 1920s Ireland. Cora Harrison. Severn House, 2017. 249 pages; (Reverend Mother mysteries, 3)

ISBN 9780727887139

1. Nuns 2. Women amateur detectives 3. Clergy 4. Murder investigation 5. Antiques 6. Cork, Ireland 7. Ireland 8. 1920s 9. Historical mysteries

LC Bl2017031596

Reverend Mother Aquinas aids in the investigation of the murder of a beloved priest, which may be linked to a string of antique thefts.

Harrison, Jamie

The **center** of everything: a novel. Jamie Harrison. Counterpoint, 2020. 320 p.

ISBN 9781640092341

1. Head injury survivors 2. Healing 3. Family reunions 4. Accidents 5. Missing persons 6. Montana 7. New York (State) 8. 1960s 9. 2000s (Decade) 10. Historical fiction 11. Parallel narratives

LC 2019040742

While recovering from a traumatic head injury, Polly Schuster struggles to find her way through one chaotic week in July when her entire extended family descends upon the bucolic town of Livingston, Montana for their annual gathering. As she contents with a series of unexpected events and the haunting echoes of her past inconveniently resurfacing as a result of her injury, Polly soon learns that her perception of her family and their life together is far from objective. Eventually Polly comes to understand the truths of her tragic, talented clan and the strange events of one year of her childhood in New York that continue to echo through to her current life.

"Against the backdrop of Polly's family history and the author's exploration of the vagaries of the human mind, Harrison plumbs complex family relationships and sheds insight on the power of memories and how they shape her characters." —*Publishers Weekly*

Harrison, Jim

The **great** leader. Jim Harrison. Grove Press, 2011. 288 p. (Detective Sunderson novels, 1)

ISBN 9780802119704

1. Religious fanatics 2. Cults 3. Sex offenders 4. Pedophiles 5. Former sheriffs 6. Michigan 7. Arizona 8. Black humor 9. Noir fiction 10. Literary fiction

Retired Detective Sunderson must get past his troubles with alcohol if he and an unlikely 16-year-old sidekick are ever going to expose an elusive cult leader called The Great Leader.

"Some of the funniest and profoundest bits in The Great Leader are the detective's alcohol-soaked musings just before he passes out. The novel serves up Sunderson's old-school field notes, which range from serious case observations to stream-of-consciousness ramblings. This is all the better, for it is fun to hear police quote Marx to each other in the field, where the outlaw and his pursuer find they have things in common, and where religion and sex intersect under the canopy of trees in the Upper Peninsula." —*Cleveland Plain Dealer*

Harrison, M. John

Light. M. John Harrison. Gollancz, 2002. 336 p.

ISBN 9780553382952

1. Physicists 2. Quantum computers 3. Serial murderers 4. Options, alternatives, choices 5. Aliens 6. 1990s 7. 25th century 8. Space opera 9. Science fiction

James Tiptree, Jr. Award, 2002

The stories of three people—modern-day Michael Kearney who plays a part in a discovery that will make interstellar travel possible; Seria Mau Genlicher, a spaceship pilot modified to interact directly with her ship; and Ed Chainese, a down-and-out drifter and adventurer, living in New Venusport—are linked by the mysteries of the Kefahuchi Tract.

Companion to: Nova Swing.

Nova swing. M. John Harrison. Victor Gollancz, 2006. 304 pages

ISBN 9780575070271

1. Young women 2. Police 3. Detectives 4. Aliens 5. Tourism 6. Cyberpunk 7. Science fiction

Arthur C. Clarke Award, 2007; Philip K. Dick Award for Science Fiction, 2007

Years after Ed Chianese's trip into the Kefahuchi Tract, the Tract begins to expand and change, with pieces falling to Earth and transforming the landscape with strange artifacts and organisms that threaten surrounding areas.

Companion to: Light.

Harrison, Mette Ivie

The **bishop's** wife. Mette Ivie Harrison. Soho Crime, 2014. 352 pages (Linda Wallheim mysteries, 1)

ISBN 9781616954765

1. Mormons 2. Married women 3. Missing persons 4. Families 5. Faith 6. Utah 7. Mysteries 8. Mormon fiction

LibraryReads Favorites, 2015

In the predominantly Mormon city of Draper, Utah, some seemingly perfect families have deadly secrets. Inspired by an actual crime and written by a practicing Mormon, The Bishop's Wife is both a fascinating look at the lives of modern Mormons as well as a grim and cunningly twisted mystery. Linda Wallheim is the mother of five grown boys and the wife of a Mormon bishop. As bishop, Kurt Wallheim is the ward's designated spiritual father, and that makes Linda the ward's unofficial mother, and her days are filled with comfort visits, community service, and informal counseling. But Linda is increasingly troubled by the church's patriarchal structure and secrecy, especially as a disturbing situation takes shape in the ward. One cold winter morning, a neighbor, Jared Helm, appears on the Wallheims' doorstep with his five-year-old daughter, claiming that his wife, Carrie, disappeared in the middle of the night, leaving behind everything she owns. The circumstances surrounding Carrie's disappearance become more suspicious the more Linda learns about them, and she becomes convinced that Jared has murdered his wife and painted himself as an abandoned husband. Kurt asks Linda not to get involved in the unfolding family saga, but she has become obsessed with Carrie's fate, and with the well-being of her vulnerable young daughter. She cannot let the matter rest until she finds out the truth. Is she wrong to go against her husband, the bishop, when her inner convictions are so strong?

"This decidedly adult tale adds twists aplenty to an insider's look at a religion replete with its own mysteries." —*Kirkus*

The **prodigal** daughter. Mette Ivie Harrison. Random House Inc 2021. 264 p. (Linda Wallheim mysteries, 5)

ISBN 9781641292450

1. Mormons 2. Bishops' spouses 3. Clergy 4. Married women 5. Marital conflict 6. Salt Lake City, Utah 7. Utah 8. Mysteries 9. Mormon fiction

LC 2020052768

Linda Wallheim, who is increasingly jaded with the Mormon church, has begun marriage counseling with her bishop husband, Kurt, hoping to reconcile their household and philosophical disagreements. On other days, Linda occupies herself with happier things, like visits to see her five grown sons and their families. When Linda's eldest son, Joseph, tells her his infant daughter's babysitter, a local teenager named Sage Jensen, has vanished, Linda can't help but ask questions. Her casual inquiries form the portrait of a girl under extreme pressure from her parents to be the perfect Mormon daughter, and it eventually emerges that Sage is the victim of a terrible crime at the hands of her own classmates—including the high school's academic and athletic superstars.

"Harrison follows Not of This Fold with a believable story about teen runaways, violence, sexual assault, and her ongoing examination of the Church of Jesus Christ of Latter-day Saints. While the ending might not satisfy some readers, it is realistic." —*Library Journal*

Harrison, Nicola

Montauk. Nicola Harrison. St. Martin's Press, 2019. 400 p.

ISBN 9781250200112

1. Self-fulfillment in women 2. Married women 3. Social classes 4. Islands 5. Resorts 6. Montauk, New York 7. Long Island, New York 8. 1930s 9. Historical fiction

LC 2018055447

Distancing herself from her unfaithful spouse and her fellow society wives at seaside Montauk Manor, Bea Bordeaux is drawn by the village's natural beauty and community spirit before falling for a man who is nothing like her husband.

Harrison, Rachel

The **return**. Rachel Harrison. Berkley, 2020. Viii, 296 pages

ISBN 9780593098660

1. Missing women 2. Female friendship 3. Women with amnesia 4. Change (Psychology) 5. Reunions 6. Catskill Mountains Region, New York 7. Gothic fiction 8. First person narratives 9. Horror 10. Adult books for young adults

LC 2019027223

LibraryReads Favorites, 2020; RUSA Reading List Short List, 2021

When their friend returns ill and haggard from a two-year absence with no memory of what happened, a circle of women, trapped inside a hotel by bad weather, become targeted by malevolent otherworldly phenomena.

"This girls' trip has teeth. A stylish and well-crafted horror debut." —*Kirkus*

Harrison, Thea

Dragon bound. Thea Harrison. Berkley Sensation, 2011. 336 p. (Elder races, 1)

ISBN 9780425241509

1. Stealing 2. Dragons 3. Sexual attraction 4. Thieves 5. Extortion 6. Paranormal romances

RITA Award for Best Paranormal Romance, 2012; Romantic Times Reviewers' Choice Award, 2011

When she is blackmailed into stealing a coin from the hoard of a dragon, Pia Giovanni, half human and half wyr, goes up against Dragos Cuelebre, who, after catching her in the act, spares her life, but claims her as his own.

Harrod-Eagles, Cynthia

Cruel as the grave. Cynthia Harrod-Eagles. Severn House, 2021. 252 pages (Inspector Bill Slider mysteries, 22)

ISBN 9780727890856

1. Detectives 2. Husband and wife 3. Pregnant women 4. Murder victims 5. Murder suspects 6. London, England 7. England 8. Police procedurals 9. Mysteries

Bill Slider investigates the murder of a fitness trainer whose head was smashed in with a dumbbell and looks for additional suspects despite the girlfriend's clothes being covered in blood.

"Sparkling dialogue complements a plot that provides satisfyingly shifting motives and persons of interest. However, it's Harrod-Eagles's ability to create authentic relationships between Slider and his colleagues and family that lifts this series into a league of its own." —*Publishers Weekly*

Headlong. Cynthia Harrod-Eagles. Severn House, 2018. 256 pages (Inspector Bill Slider mysteries, 21)

ISBN 9780727888365

1. Murder 2. Literary agents 3. Murder investigation 4. Detectives 5. Secrets 6. London, England 7. Mysteries 8. Police procedurals

Bill Slider and his team investigate the death of a prominent literary agent.

Old bones. Cynthia Harrod-Eagles. Severn House, 2017. 256 p. (Inspector Bill Slider mysteries, 19)

ISBN 9780727886651

1. Bones 2. Cold cases (Criminal investigation) 3. Missing teenage girls 4. Detectives 5. Murder investigation 6. London, England 7. England 8. Police procedurals

A couple discover human remains buried in the garden of their new house: could this be the resting place of 14-year-old Amanda Knight, who disappeared from the same garden two decades before? With a murder twenty years in the past, this is the coldest of cold cases. Most of the suspects are now dead too, and all passion is long spent. Or is it? SALS

"Another sterling entry in a truly outstanding series." —*Booklist*

Hart, Carolyn G.

Ghost blows a kiss. Carolyn Hart. Severn House, 2022. 192 p. (Bailey Ruth mysteries, 10)

ISBN 9781780297897

1. Ghosts 2. Women amateur detectives 3. Women murder suspects 4. Spirits 5. Mediums 6. Oklahoma 7. Supernatural mysteries 8. Cozy mysteries

Sent down to Earth by Heaven's Department of Good Intentions, ghost Bailey Ruth breaks the rules of Earthly Visitation by intervening in a drowning in the tenth novel of the series following Ghost Ups Her Game.

"Fans of paranormal mysteries will appreciate this 10th 'Bailey Ruth Ghost' case (after Ghost Ups Her Game), a template for a traditional mystery in the style of Agatha Christie." —*Library Journal*

Originally published: 2021.

Letter from home. Carolyn Hart. Berkley Prime Crime, 2003. 272 p.

ISBN 9780425191798

1. Small town life 2. Crimes against women 3. Women journalists 4. Teenage girls 5. Teenage girl journalists 6. Oklahoma 7. 1940s 8. Letters 9. Historical mysteries 10. Mysteries

LC 2003051953

Agatha Award for Best Novel, 2004

Working at the local newspaper during the summer of 1944, Gretchen Gilman investigates the mysterious death of Faye Tatum, found dead in her own living room, supposedly murdered by her husband, a World War II veteran.

"Set in a small-town America that lives only in memory, this artfully narrated whodunit observes the residents of an unnamed Oklahoma hamlet over the hot and dusty summer of 1944 as they ration their food, count their war dead and turn on their neighbors." —*New York Times Book Review*

Hart, Elsa

The **cabinets** of Barnaby Mayne. Elsa Hart. Minotaur Books, 2020. 352 p.

ISBN 9781250142818

1. Herbalists 2. Women scientists 3. Collectors and collecting 4. Murder investigation 5. Women amateur detectives 6. Stuart period (1603-1714) 7. Historical mysteries

LC 2019059161

Edgar Allan Poe Awards: Mary Higgins Clark Award, 2021

Visiting a formidable science-book collector's home in the hopes of identifying plant specimens, 18th-century herbalist Cecily Kay finds her-self investigating her host's untimely murder when she observes unsettling inconsistencies.

"Hart's juicy character portraits and graceful prose make for a delightful period whodunit." —*Kirkus*

City of ink: a mystery. Elsa Hart. Minotaur Books, 2018. 352 p. (Li Du novels, 3)

ISBN 9781250142795

1. Former librarians 2. Mentors 3. Intrigue 4. Homecomings 5. Memories 6. China 7. 1700s (Decade) 8. Historical mysteries

LC 2018004086

Forced to return home to unravel the mystery surrounding his mentor's execution, Li Du confronts painful memories while investigating a double murder, the secrets of several Beijing residents and threats against his safety.

Hart, Erin

The **book** of Killowen. Erin Hart. Scribner, 2013. 302 p. (Nora Gavin and Cormac Maguire series, 4)

ISBN 9781451634846

1. Cold cases (Criminal investigation) 2. Women pathologists 3. Murder investigation 4. Television personalities 5. Archaeologists 6. Ireland 7. Mysteries

LC 2012028465

Returning to the bogs after a year away from the field, archaeologist Cormac Maguire and pathologist Nora Gavin investigate a ninth-century corpse found in the trunk of a car along with the body of a provocative television philosopher, a case that is tied to an ancient volume of philosophical heresy.

Haunted ground: a crime novel. Erin Hart. Scribner, 2003. 328 p. (Nora Gavin and Cormac Maguire series, 1)

ISBN 9780743235051

1. Bogs 2. Family estates 3. Women pathologists 4. Landowners 5. Archaeologists 6. Ireland 7. Mysteries

LC 2002030679

Romantic Times Reviewers' Choice Award, 2003

The Irish landscape holds secrets past and present as archaeologist Cormac Maguire and pathologist Nora Gavin encounter a mystery when a decapitated woman is found in the bogs who may be related to a recent mother/child disappearance.

Hart, John

Down river. John Hart. Thomas Dunne Books/St. Martin's Minotaur, 2007. 352 p.

ISBN 9780312359317

1. Small town life 2. Murder suspects 3. Family secrets 4. Forgiveness 5. Families 6. North Carolina 7. Mysteries 8. Southern fiction

LC 2007021540

Edgar Allan Poe Award for Best Novel, 2008

Five years after fleeing to New York in the wake of a murder acquittal, Adam Harston returns to North Carolina, only to find himself trapped in the middle of a new case of murder as the people around him begin to die and he becomes the prime suspect in the crimes.

"This work is reminiscent of Raymond Chandler's novels, hardboiled and rich with evocative metaphors." —*Library Journal*

Iron house. John Hart. Thomas Dunne Books/St. Martin's Press, 2011. 352 p.

ISBN 9780312380342

1. Organized crime 2. Second chances 3. Revenge 4. Secrets 5. Brothers 6. North Carolina 7. New York City 8. Thrillers and suspense 9. Crime fiction

LC 2011006909

At the Iron Mountain Home for Boys, there was nothing but time. Time to burn and time to kill, time for two young orphans to learn that life isn't won without a fight. Julian survives only because his older brother, Michael, is fearless and fiercely protective. When tensions boil over and a boy is brutally killed, there is only one sacrifice left for Michael to make: He flees the orphanage and takes the blame with him. For two decades, Michael has been an enforcer in New York's world of organized crime, a prince of the streets so widely feared he rarely has to kill anymore. But the life he's fought to build unravels when he meets Elena, a beautiful innocent who teaches him the meaning and power of love. He wants a fresh start with her, the chance to start a family like the one he and Julian never had. But someone else is holding the strings. And escape is not that easy... The mob boss who gave Michael his blessing to begin anew is dying, and his son is intent on making Michael pay for his betrayal. Determined to protect the ones he loves, Michael spirits Elena—who knows nothing of his past crimes, or the peril he's laid at her door—back to North Carolina, to the place he was born and the brother he lost so long ago. There, he will encounter a whole new level of danger, a thicket of deceit and violence that leads inexorably to the one place he's been running from his whole life: Iron House. —From book jacket.

"Hart deftly interweaves a complex family history story with Stevan's intense, bloody quest for vengeance." —*Publishers Weekly*

The **king** of lies. John Hart. St. Martin's Press, 2006. 320 p.
ISBN 9780312341619
1. Murder suspects 2. Fathers and sons 3. Lawyers 4. Defense attorneys 5. Families of murder victims 6. North Carolina 7. Legal thrillers 8. Psychological suspense 9. First person narratives 10. Adult books for young adults

LC 2005049774

When Work Pickens finds his father murdered, the investigation pushes a repressed family history to the surface and he sees his own carefully constructed façade begin to crack. Work's troubled sister, her combative girlfriend, his gold digging socialite wife, and an unrequited lifelong love join a cast of small town characters that create no shortage of drama in this extraordinary, fast-paced suspense novel.

"More than anything elsemore than a terrific whodunit, an unsentimental, clear-eyed story of love and forgiveness, and a gripping family saga: The King of Lies is a masterful piece of writing." —*Raleigh News & Observer*

The **last** child. John Hart. Minotaur Books, 2009. 373 p.
ISBN 9780312359324
1. Missing children 2. Twins 3. Small town life 4. Detectives 5. Dysfunctional families 6. North Carolina 7. Psychological suspense 8. Adult books for young adults

LC 2008045678

Ian Fleming Steel Dagger Award, 2009; Edgar Allan Poe Award for Best Novel, 2010

After his twin sister Alyssa disappears, thirteen year-old Johnny Merrimon is determined to find her. When a second girl disappears from his rural North Carolina town, Johnny makes a discovery that sends shock waves through the community in this multi-layered tale of broken families and deadly secrets.

"The author has produced a novel that is elegant, haunting, and memorable. His characters are given an emotional depth that genre characters seldom have, and the graceful, evocative prose lifts his stories right out of

their genre and into the realm of capital-L literature. A must-read for every variety of fiction reader." —*Booklist*

A Thomas Dunne book for Minotaur Books—Title page verso.

Redemption road. John Hart. Thomas Dunne Books, 2016. 432 p.
ISBN 9780312380366
1. Murder 2. Revenge 3. Women detectives 4. Former convicts 5. Boys 6. Thrillers and suspense
LibraryReads Favorites, 2016

Over 2 million copies of his books in print. The first and only author to win back-to-back Edgars for Best Novel. Every book a New York Times bestseller. Now after five years, John Hart is back with a stunning literary thriller. Imagine: A boy with a gun waits for the man who killed his mother. A troubled detective confronts her past in the aftermath of a brutal shooting. After thirteen years in prison, a good cop walks free. But for how long? And deep in the forest, on the altar of an abandoned church,the unthinkable has just happened... This is a town on the brink. This is a road with no mercy. Since his debut bestseller, The King of Lies, reviewers across the country have heaped praise on John Hart, comparing his writing to that of Pat Conroy, Cormac McCarthy and Scott Turow. With each novel Hart has climbed higher on the New York Times bestseller list, with his last two books—The Last Child and Iron House—landing squarely in the top ten. His masterful writing and assured evocation of place havewon readers around the world and earned history's only consecutive Edgar Awards for Best Novel. After five years, John Hart returns with Redemption Road, his most powerful story yet.

"Hart plays brilliantly on the tradition of the southern gothic, but his grasp of character gives this novel—and all his works—the extra dimension that extends his audience well beyond adrenaline junkies." —*Booklist*

The **unwilling**. John Hart. St. Martin's Press, 2020. 400 p.
ISBN 9781250167729
1. Brothers 2. Veterans 3. Kidnapping 4. Murder investigation 5. Vietnam War, 1961-1975 6. Thrillers and suspense 7. Historical fiction

LC 2019058395

The younger brother of a wrongly implicated Vietnam veteran and ex-con races to uncover the truth about a young woman's murder and the brutal realities of war that shaped his brother's darker nature.

"Award-winning Hart (The Hush) offers another propulsive crime novel that features fully realized, multifaceted characters and a strong sense of place." —*Library Journal*

Hart, Josephine

Damage: a novel. Josephine Hart. Virago, 2011. 195 p.
ISBN 9781844087181
1. Fathers and sons 2. Love triangles 3. Extramarital affairs 4. Obsession in men 5. Politicians 6. England 7. Psychological suspense 8. Books to movies 9. First person narratives

LC 90053393

The narrator's erotic obsession with a woman who wields a dominant sexual and psychological power over him draws him into a headlong plunge toward tragedy for his family and his own self-destruction.

This book was released as a movie entitled Fatale.

Originally published: London: Chatto & Windus, 1991.

Hart, Rob

The **warehouse**: a novel. Rob Hart. Crown Publishing, 2019. 358 pages
ISBN 9781984823793

1. Near future 2. Corporations 3. Undercover operations 4. Dystopias 5. Online shopping 6. Dystopian fiction 7. Multiple perspectives 8. Thrillers and suspense
LibraryReads Favorites, 2019

Set in a near-future America wracked by violence, unemployment and climate change, two employees of a world-saving global giant discover their employers' true agenda.

"Part video game, part Sinclair Lewis, part Michael Crichton; it adds up to a terrific puzzle." —*Kirkus*

Harte, Bret

★ The **best** short stories of Bret Harte. . Modern Library, 1947. X, 517 p.
ISBN 9780394602509
1. Frontier and pioneer life 2. Gold rush 3. California 4. The West (United States) 5. 1860s 6. Westerns 7. Short stories
LC 47030278

Twenty-five stories of the Western frontier

Haruf, Kent

Benediction. Kent Haruf. Alfred A. Knopf, 2013. 272 p.
ISBN 9780307959881
1. Family relationships 2. Men with terminal illnesses — Family relationships 3. People with cancer 4. Bereavement in families 5. Death 6. Colorado 7. Psychological fiction
LC 2012028744
Shortlisted for the James Tait Black Memorial Prize for Fiction, 2013

A terminally ill cancer patient is attended throughout his final days by his wife and daughter while the trio contemplates their relationships with an estranged son, a situation that stirs up painful memories for a new next-door neighbor who has recently lost her mother.

This is a Borzoi book.

Eventide. Kent Haruf. Alfred A. Knopf, 2004. 320 p.
ISBN 9780375411588
1. Ranchers 2. Single men 3. Brothers 4. Boys 5. Single mothers 6. Colorado 7. Psychological fiction 8. Domestic fiction 9. Adult books for young adults
LC 2003060480
A novel of small-town life in the high plains region around Holt, Colorado, follows the challenges, emotional upheaval, tragedies, and intertwined destinies of the local inhabitants as they cope with the changes they encounter.

"This novel takes up where the author's Plainsong left off, in the windy high-plains country in and around the tiny town of Holt, Colorado.... It's rare that such slow, deliberate prose is this highly charged, but Haruf's writing draws power from his sense of characterits limitations and its possibilitiesand how it propels action." —*The New Yorker*
Sequel to: Plainsong.

★ **Our** souls at night. Kent Haruf. Alfred A. Knopf, 2015. 176 p.
ISBN 9781101875896
1. Widowers 2. Small town life 3. Loneliness 4. Friendship 5. Memories 6. Colorado 7. Literary fiction 8. Love stories
LibraryReads Favorites, 2015
Addie Moore and Louis Waters, a widow and widower each living alone, forge a loving bond over their shared loneliness, provoking local gossip and the disapproval of their grown children in ways that are further complicated by an extended visit by a sad young grandchild.

"Haruf, who died in 2014, returns to the landscape and daily life of Holt County, Colo. where his previous novels (Plainsong, Eventide, The Tie That Binds) have also been set, this time with a stunning sense of all

thats passed and the precious importance of the days that remain." —*Publishers Weekly*

★ **Plainsong**. Kent Haruf. A. A. Knopf, 1999. 301 p.
ISBN 9780375406188
1. Small town life 2. High school teachers 3. Ranchers 4. Single men 5. Pregnant teenagers 6. Colorado 7. Domestic fiction 8. Psychological fiction 9. Literary fiction 10. Adult books for young adults
LC 9915606
Alex Award, 2000; Booklist Editors' Choice: Adult Books for Young Adults, 1999; New York Times Notable Book, 1999; YALSA Best Books for Young Adults, 2001; National Book Award for Fiction finalist, 1999

An unlikely extended family is formed when a high school teacher helps a pregnant student make a home with two elderly bachelor ranchers.

"From simple strands of language and cuttings of talk, from the look of the high Colorado plains east of Denver almost to the place where Nebraska and Kansas meet, Haruf has made a novel so foursquare, so delicate and lovely, that it has the power to exalt the reader." —*New York Times Book Review*
Sequel: Eventide.

Harvey, John

Cold in hand. John Harvey. William Heinemann, 2008. 405 p; (Charlie Resnick mysteries, 11)
ISBN 9780434016945
1. Police 2. Human trafficking 3. Teenage murder victims 4. Murder investigation 5. Private investigators 6. Nottingham, England 7. England 8. Police procedurals
LC 2008396522
"Resnick is now living with a much younger DI, Lynn Kellog, and their relationship is one of the best aspects of this fine crime novel, subtly described and convincing.... Cold in Hand reveals modern England in all its most depressing messiness while engaging the reader with characters whose warmth and humanity give real pleasure. There is no melodrama here; all the actions and motives that are eventually revealed are rooted in reality; and yet at the heart of the novel is an event so shocking in the context that it could rival anything in the most lurid thriller." —*Times Literary Supplement*

A **darker** shade of blue: stories. John Harvey. Pegasus Books, 2012. 368 p.
ISBN 9781605982847
1. Detectives 2. Criminal investigation 3. Former police 4. Private investigators 5. Resnick, Charlie (Fictitious character) 6. England 7. Short stories 8. Mysteries
This collection of short stories from a master of British crime fiction feature tales of ex-cops, private eyes and investigators who wade through broken families, revenge, prostitution, drugs and corruption in their search for justice.

Darkness, darkness. John Harvey. Pegasus Books, 2014. 352 p. (Charlie Resnick mysteries, 12)
ISBN 9781605986166
1. Dead 2. Strikes 3. Miners 4. Police 5. Missing women 6. Nottingham, England 7. England 8. 1980s 9. 21st century 10. Police procedurals 11. Parallel narratives
LC Bl2014031493
In 1984, young police inspector Charlie Resnick ran an intelligence gathering team during the British Miners' Strike, a terrible time of civil unrest that pitted close friends and family members against each other; back then, a vocal young supporter of the strike, Jenny Hardwick, went missing. Now her body's been discovered, and though he's retired, Char-

lie teams up with DS Catherine Njoroge, who has problems of her own, to dig into the past and solve the case.

"Harvey's first Resnick novel, 1989's Lonely Hearts, is one of the London Times List of 100 Best Crime Novels of the last century and there has been no diminishment in quality in the 11 books since. This is Resnick's final case, and every reader of contemporary mystery fiction should be acquainted with this outstanding series and its jazz-loving protagonist whose stories limn the changing world around him. Increasingly, Charlie is an observer more than an actor, but he remains an unforgettable creation." —*Library Journal*

Resnick's last case—Cover.

Harvey, Michael T.

Brighton. Michael Harvey. Ecco, 2016. 304 p.
ISBN 9780062442970
1. Male friendship 2. Investigative journalists 3. Murder suspects 4. Organized crime 5. Murder 6. Boston, Massachusetts 7. Thrillers and suspense 8. Crime fiction

Before he became a Pulitzer Prize-winning journalist, Kevin Pearce grew up in gritty Brighton, MA, where he committed a horrible act of violence—one that he got away with. Nearly three decades on, having avoided Brighton ever since, he's returned to a neighborhood embroiled in a series of murders that could bring to light his own bloody past. Told from multiple points of view, this is an intense and descriptive novel.

"Sharp as the blades used to gut the guilty and innocent alike, Harvey's fierce stand-alone is a blood-soaked tribute to finding your past and living with the consequences." —*Kirkus*

The **Chicago** way. By Michael Harvey. Knopf, 2007. 320 p. (Michael Kelly mysteries, 1)
ISBN 9780307266866
1. Private investigators 2. Cold cases (Criminal investigation) 3. Police cover-ups 4. Police 5. Deception 6. Chicago, Illinois 7. Hardboiled fiction 8. Mysteries
LC 2007007796

A former Chicago cop and tough, street-smart private detective, Michael Kelly is hired by his former partner, John Gibbons, to solve an eight-year-old rape and battery case, a crime that is complicated by Gibbons's own murder.

"Harvey's tightly plotted evocation of the Chicago underworld is set in the present but brings to mind the voices of Chandler and Hammett." —*New York Magazine*

Sequel: The Fifth Floor
This is a Borzoi book.

The **fifth** floor. Michael Harvey. Alfred A. Knopf, 2008. 288 p. (Michael Kelly mysteries, 2)
ISBN 9780307266873
1. Political corruption 2. Cold cases (Criminal investigation) 3. Private investigators 4. Frameups 5. Kelly, Michael (Fictitious character) 6. Chicago, Illinois 7. Hardboiled fiction 8. Mysteries
LC 2008001484

Hired by a former lover to follow her abusive husband, private detective Michael Kelly follows the subject to an old house on Chicago's North Side, where he stumbles upon a body and a possible answer to the mystery about who actually started the Great Chicago Fire of 1871, in the atmospheric sequel to The Chicago Way.

"This Michael Kelly thriller has the ex-Chicago cop taking on what he thinks is a simple domestic violence case. But when he tails Johnny Woods, a fixer for the city's powerful mayor, to what turns out to be a grisly murder scene, Kelly realizes he's stumbled onto a scandal that began with the great Chicago Fire of 1871. Digging deeper, Kelly unearths what was once considered an urban legend: two of Chicago's most emi-

nent families conspiring to eradicate Irish immigrants by burning down the city's slums. As more bodies pile up and he becomes romantically involved with a judge with secrets of her own, Kelly vows to expose the conspiracy, even if that means putting himself on the wrong side of the city's most powerful men. Harvey's plot twists in all the right places, and his noir-inspired dialogue crackles without sounding showy. Marlowe and Spade would readily welcome Michael Kelly into their fold." —*Publishers Weekly*

Sequel to: The Chicago way

The **governor's** wife. By Michael Harvey. Alfred A. Knopf, 2015. 256 p. (Michael Kelly mysteries, 5)
ISBN 9780307958648
1. Private investigators 2. Political corruption 3. Ambition 4. Missing persons investigation 5. Secrets 6. Chicago, Illinois 7. Hardboiled fiction 8. Mysteries
LC 2014014535

Receiving a lucrative anonymous offer to track down an escaped criminal, private investigator Michael Kelly unwinds the past of the fugitive's wife, who harbors deeply complicated and dangerous reasons for standing by her husband.

"Harvey makes political corruption personal: this isn't a story of anonymous millions being shuffled between various offshore accounts. The consequence of every decision in Kelly's gritty world bleeds." —*Kirkus*

Pulse. Michael Harvey. HarperCollins 2018. 304 p.
ISBN 9780062443038
1. Psychic ability 2. Murder investigation 3. College football players 4. Police 5. Visions 6. Boston, Massachusetts 7. 1970s 8. Mysteries 9. Police procedurals 10. Supernatural mysteries

Investigating the murder of a Harvard football star, a pair of veteran detectives are stunned when the victim's teen-runaway brother arrives at the scene, claiming to have metaphysical knowledge of the crime before it occurred.

We all fall down. Michael Harvey. Alfred A. Knopf, 2011. 320 p. (Michael Kelly mysteries, 4)
ISBN 9780307272515
1. Private investigators 2. Biological terrorism 3. Terrorism — Prevention 4. Gangs 5. Former police 6. Chicago, Illinois 7. Hardboiled fiction 8. Mysteries
LC 2011004681

When Chicago is targeted by a brutal biological attack that threatens millions of lives, Michael Kelly begins a desperate search through the tangled underworld of the city's West Side gangs, where he confronts the covert practices of dark science in one of the nation's premiere laboratories.

"A gripping crime novel with a frightening message about very plausible biological warfare." —*Booklist*

Hashemzadeh Bonde, Golnaz

What we owe. Golnaz Hashemzadeh Bonde; translated from the Swedish by Elizabeth Clark Wessel. Mariner Books/Houghton Mifflin Harcourt, 2018. 200 p.
ISBN 9781328995087
1. Women 2. Mothers and daughters 3. Women with cancer 4. Pregnant women 5. Immigrants 6. Iran 7. Sweden 8. Domestic fiction 9. Literary fiction 10. Translations
LC 2017058741

Standing on the precipice of her own death, 50-year-old Nahid, who has never had the ability or opportunity to live life to the fullest, is filled with both new fury and long dormant rage when she learns that her daughter Aram is pregnant with her first child.

"Hashemzadeh Bonde, unafraid of ugliness and seemingly unconcerned with likability, has produced a startling meditation on death, national identity, and motherhood. Always arresting, never sentimental; gut-wrenching, though not without hope." —*Kirkus*
Originally published: Stockholm : Wahlstrom & Widstrand, 2017.
Translated from the Swedish.

Haslett, Adam

★ **Imagine** me gone: a novel. Adam Haslett. Little, Brown and Company, 2016. 368 p.
ISBN 9780316261357
1. Depression 2. Married people 3. Family and mental illness 4. Coping 5. Fathers 6. Psychological fiction 7. Literary fiction 8. First person narratives
LC 2015028890
Los Angeles Times Book Prize for Fiction, 2016; Kirkus Prize for Fiction finalist, 2016; National Book Critics Circle Award for Fiction finalist, 2016; Pulitzer Prize for Fiction finalist, 2017
Electing to marry the fiancé who is hospitalized for depression, a woman commits to decades of love and faith involving their brilliant musical eldest son, their responsible daughter and a tightly controlled younger son who helps her care for her increasingly troubled husband.
"This touching chronicle of love and pain traces half a century in a family of five from the parents' engagement in 1963 through a father's and son's psychological torments and a final crisis." —*Kirkus*

Union Atlantic. Adam Haslett. Nan A. Talese/Doubleday, 2010. 304 p.
ISBN 9780385524476
1. Social classes 2. Banks and banking 3. Personal conduct 4. Interpersonal relations 5. Arthur, King 6. Massachusetts 7. Literary fiction
Lambda Literary Award for Gay Men's Fiction, 2010
Banker Doug Fanning begins building a massive mansion on land formerly owned by retired teacher Charlotte Graves' grandfather. The land was once donated to the local town, and now Charlotte is trying to stop Doug's construction efforts by any means necessary.
"A novel about Doug Fanning, a handsome, renegade Boston securities trader whose imprudent bets on the Japanese markets threaten to cause systemic bank failure.... Unfolding in the fictional town of Finden, Massachusetts, the novel's central narrative pits Doug in an oblique battle of wills with his neighbor Charlotte Graves, a former history teacher and dismayed old-school liberal who resents the size and style of his massive new house. While the two ostensibly wrangle over property rights, the real stakes of their disagreement is not taste but ideologyor perhaps better, pathology.... Set during the run-up to the invasion of Iraq, Union Atlantic is like a pressure-compacted version of a Tom Wolfe zeitgeist doorstop, complete with a diffuse cast of characters (bankers, pot-smoking teenagers, a conflicted corporate whistle-blower, the president of the Federal Reserve Bank of New York) and myriad cultural obsessions: about the corporatization of war, the joyless hedonism of American society and the soullessness of suburban life." —*Time Out New York*

Hassib, Rajia

A **pure** heart: a novel. Rajia Hassib. Viking, 2019. 320 pages
ISBN 9780525560050
1. Sisters 2. Muslim women 3. Egyptian-Americans 4. Women 5. Women archaeologists 6. Cairo, Egypt 7. New York City 8. Literary fiction
LC 2018060355
Follows the divergent fates of two Egyptian sisters—Rose, married to an American journalist and living in New York City, and Gameela, a devout Muslim who remained in Cairo—when Rose returns to Egypt after Gameela is killed in a suicide bombing.
"...A multifaceted look at the complicated legacies of identity, religion, and politics in Egypt after the Arab Spring emerges. Even the story of the suicide bomber is given careful consideration in this enlightening, heartrending novel." —*Booklist*

Hatcher, Robin Lee

Cross my heart. Robin Lee Hatcher. Thomas Nelson, 2019. 320 pages (Legacy of faith novels, 2)
ISBN 9780785219309
1. Horse farms 2. Recovering alcoholics 3. Trust 4. Faith (Christianity) 5. Man-woman relationships 6. Idaho 7. Christian romances
LC 2018059440
Ashley and Ben have a lot in common and a possible love connection, but Ben is a recovering alcoholic and after dealing with her drug addicted brother, Ashley refuses to enter a relationship where addiction is present.

Who I am with you. Robin Lee Hatcher. Thomas Nelson, 2018. 320 p. (Legacy of faith novels, 1)
ISBN 9780785219262
1. Pregnant women 2. Widows 3. Politicians 4. Scandals 5. Loss (Psychology) 6. Idaho 7. Christian romances
LC 2018031310
A pregnant woman embittered by the deaths of her husband and daughter finds healing and renewal in her great-grandfather's Bible before opening her heart to a disgraced businessman who would withdraw from the world.

Hauck, Rachel

How to catch a prince. Rachel Hauck. Zondervan, 2015. 320 p. (Royal wedding novels, 3)
ISBN 9780310315544
1. Friends' death 2. Former lovers 3. Married people 4. Man-woman relationships 5. Heirs and heiresses 6. Florida 7. Christian romances
LC 2014033423
Corina Del Rey's life as a journalist in Melbourne, Florida, is complicated when professional rugby player and prince Stephen of Brighton Kingdom re-enters her life.
"Hauck has written a sensitive, emotion-filled story about the effects of war on a relationship. Her characters are flawed and realistic. This engaging, faith-based book is part of the Royal Wedding Series." —*Booklist*

Once upon a prince. Rachel Hauck. Zondervan, 2013. 320 p. (Royal wedding novels, 1)
ISBN 9780310315476
1. God (Christianity) — Will 2. Faith (Christianity) 3. Royal weddings 4. Princes 5. Life change events 6. St. Simon's Island, Georgia 7. Christian romances 8. Adult books for young adults
LC 2013001023
When a jilted girlfriend meets a reluctant crown prince, they discover the power of God's love to heal hearts and change a nation.

The **wedding** chapel. Rachel Hauck. Zondervan, 2015. 352 p.
ISBN 9780310341529
1. Retirees 2. Women photographers 3. Husband and wife 4. Advertising executives 5. Marital conflict 6. New York City 7. Tennessee 8. Christian romances
LC 2015023680
Christy Award for Contemporary Romance Category, 2016
When photographer Taylor Branson elopes with top ad man Jack Forester and then returns to her home town in Tennessee, her doubts about her

relationship are put into perspective by a retired football coach who has been holding onto a dream since 1949.

Hausmann, Romy

★ **Dear** child. Romy Hausmann; translated from the German by Jamie Bulloch. Flatiron Books, 2020. 336 p.
ISBN 9781250768537
1. Young women 2. Child kidnapping victims 3. Captivity 4. Kidnappers 5. Mother and child 6. Germany 7. Psychological suspense 8. Multiple perspectives 9. Translations

LC 2020031677

A windowless shack in the woods. A dash to safety. But when a woman finally escapes her captor, the end of the story is only the beginning of her nightmare. She says her name is Lena. Lena, who disappeared without a trace 14 years prior. She fits the profile. She has the distinctive scar. But her family swears that she isn't their Lena. The little girl who escaped the woods with her knows things she isn't sharing, and Lena's devastated father is trying to piece together details that don't quite fit. Lena is desperate to begin again, but something tells her that her tormentor still wants to get back what belongs to him—and that she may not be able to truly escape until the whole truth about what happened in the woods finally emerges.

"Tiny clues are steadily inserted into this fast-paced, shivery tale with an unforeseen denouement. Inevitably likened to Emma Donoghue's Room, also suggest Sarah Pinborough's Behind Her Eyes." —*Library Journal*

Originally published: Munich : Deutscher Taschenbuch-Verlag, 2019. Translated from the German.

Hawke, Ethan

A **bright** ray of darkness. Ethan Hawke. Alfred a Knopf, 2021. 256 p.
ISBN 9780385352383
1. Actors and actresses 2. Extramarital affairs 3. Theater 4. Fatherhood 5. Masculinity 6. Literary fiction

Hawke's narrator is a young man in torment, disgusted with himself after the collapse of his marriage, still half-hoping for a reconciliation that would allow him to forgive himself and move on as he clumsily, and sometimes hilariously, tries to manage the wreckage of his personal life with whiskey and sex. What saves him is theater: in particular, the challenge of performing the role of Hotspur in a production of *Henry IV* under the leadership of a brilliant director, helmed by one of the most electrifying—and narcissistic—Falstaff's of all time. Searing, raw, and utterly transfixing, A Bright Ray of Darkness is a novel about shame and beauty and faith, and the moral power of art.

"A brilliant insider's account of the joys and terrors of acting, the trials of celebrity, and the secrets of *Henry IV*." —*Kirkus*

Hawkins, Paula

★ The **girl** on the train: a novel. Paula Hawkins. Riverhead Books, 2015. 336 p.
ISBN 9781594633669
1. Divorced women 2. Secrets 3. Murder witnesses 4. Crime 5. Murder victims 6. London, England 7. Multiple perspectives 8. Psychological suspense 9. Books to movies 10. Adult books for young adults

LC 2014027001

LibraryReads Favorites, 2015

Obsessively watching a breakfasting couple every day to escape the pain of her losses, Rachel witnesses a shocking event that inextricably entangles her in the lives of strangers.

"The novel is alternately narrated by three equally unlikable women, and Hawkins very deliberately doles out tantalizing information, but what really gives this novel its compulsive readability is the way she so expertly mines female archetypes: the jealous ex-wife, the smug mistress, the emotionally damaged femme fatale." —*Booklist*

Adapted into a film in 2016 under the same title.

Hawkins, Scott

★ The **library** at Mount Char. Scott Hawkins. Crown Publishers, 2015. 400 p.
ISBN 9780553418606
1. Orphans 2. Libraries 3. Imprisonment 4. Gods and goddesses 5. Secrets 6. Fantasy fiction 7. Adult books for young adults

Carolyn and a dozen other children being raised by "Father," a cruel man with mysterious powers, begin to think he might be God, so when he dies, they square off against each other to determine who will inherit his library, which they believe holds the power to all Creation.

"Hawkins's cunning plotting is backed up by crisp dialogue, a sensation of constant dread, and a solid, subtly weird setting." —*Publishers Weekly*

Hawks, Arlem

Georgana's secret. Arlem Hawks. Shadow Mountain, 2021. 320 p.
ISBN 9781629727929
1. Sailors 2. Warships 3. Women impostors 4. Disguises 5. Secret identity 6. Regency period (1811-1820) 7. Historical romances 8. Sea stories

LC 2020030172

As a young girl, Georgana Woodall dreamed of beautiful dresses, fancy balls, and falling in love, but when her mother dies, she cannot face a future under the guardianship of her abusive grandmother and instead chooses to join her father on his ship disguised as his cabin boy, "George," where see meets Lieutenant Dominic Peyton and quickly losing her heart to Dominic's compassion and care.

"Fans of sweet love stories as well as readers who fondly remember those marvelous old traditional Signet Regencies will quickly succumb to the siren song of Hawk's expertly crafted novel, which delivers the perfect blend of Jane Austen-smart romance and Patrick O'Brian-flavored seafaring adventure." —*Booklist*

Hawley, Noah

Before the fall. Noah Hawley. Grand Central Pub, 2016. 384 p.
ISBN 9781455561780
1. Airplane accidents 2. Accident victims 3. Rich people 4. Four-year-old boys 5. Business — Corrupt practices 6. Massachusetts 7. Thrillers and suspense
Edgar Allan Poe Award for Best Novel, 2017; New York Times Notable Book, 2016; Thriller Award for Best Novel, 2017

The stories of ten wealthy victims of a plane crash intertwine with those of a down-on-his-luck painter and a four-year-old boy, the tragedy's only survivors, as odd coincidences surrounding the crash point to a possible conspiracy.

"This is a gritty tale of a man overwhelmed by unwelcome notoriety, with a stunning, thoroughly satisfying conclusion." —*Publishers Weekly*

The **good** father. By Noah Hawley. Doubleday, 2012. 320 p.
ISBN 9780385535533
1. Parents of children with mental illnesses 2. Children of divorced parents 3. Father and adult son 4. Physicians 5. Assassination 6. Psychological suspense

LC 2011017657
Establishing a specialty in diagnosing otherwise abandoned patients with conflicting symptoms, Chief of Rheumatology Paul Allen is placed in the impossible position of having to unlock the mind of his 20-year-old son, who has attempted to assassinate a presidential candidate.

Hawthorne, Nathaniel

★ The **house** of the seven gables. Nathaniel Hawthorne. Modern Library, 2001. Xix, 312 p.
ISBN 9780375756870
1. Curses 2. Families 3. Haunted houses 4. Revenge 5. Greed in men 6. Salem, Massachusetts 7. New England 8. Family sagas 9. Gothic fiction 10. Books to movies
The sins of the Pyncheon father are visited upon his children over a period of several generations, until such time as one of his descendants unites with a member of the family he has wronged. Love conquers hate, and new blood washes away the original crime. This intriguing and insightful novel truly deserves its significant place in the canon of American literature.
First published 1851.
Book inspired a 1940 film of the same name but differs dramatically from the plot of the novel.

★ The **scarlet** letter: a romance. Nathaniel Hawthorne; with an introduction by Alfred Kazin. Knopf, 1992. Xxvii, 273 p.
ISBN 9780679417316
1. Married women 2. Puritans 3. Revenge 4. Husband and wife 5. Pariahs 6. Massachusetts 7. Colonial America (1600-1775) 8. Historical fiction 9. Books to movies 10. Classics 11. Adult books for young adults
LC 92052902
In early colonial Massachusetts, a young woman endures the consequences of her sin of adultery and spends the rest of her life in atonement.
First published in 1850.
Includes bibliographical references (p. xvii).
Originally published: Boston: J.R. Osgood and company, 1878.

Hay, Elizabeth

Late nights on air. Elizabeth Hay. McClelland & Stewart, 2007. 376 p.
ISBN 9780771038112
1. Radio newscasters and commentators 2. Fuel industry and trade 3. Land claims 4. Women radio newscasters and commentators 5. Radio stations 6. Yellowknife, Northwest Territories 7. Northwest Territories 8. 1970s 9. Literary fiction 10. Canadian fiction
CBA Libris Award for Fiction Book of the Year, 2008; Ottawa Book Award for English Fiction, 2008; Scotiabank Giller Prize, 2007
Accepting a position at a northern Canadian radio station in 1975, Dido Paris disarms a hard-bitten broadcaster with her beauty and vocal talents before controversy surrounding a proposed gas pipeline triggers call-in-listener debates on the air.
"The plot of this novel is a faint signal, a series of short moments, sometimes funny, sometimes poignant, often flecked with intimations of tragedy. Hay's writing is so alluring and her lost souls so endearing that you'll lean in to catch the story's delicate developments as these characters shuffle along through quiet desperation and yearning." —*Washington Post Book World.*

Hayder, Mo

Gone. Mo Hayder. Atlantic Monthly Press, 2011. 416 p. (Detective Inspector Jack Caffery mysteries, 5)

ISBN 9780802119643
1. Carjacking 2. Kidnapping 3. Missing girls 4. Eleven-year-old girls 5. Detectives 6. England 7. Bristol, England 8. Police procedurals 9. Mysteries
Edgar Allan Poe Award for Best Novel, 2012
Investigating a serial carjacker whose actual targets are young children in back seats, Jack Caffery teams up once again with police diver Sergeant Flea Marley, whose life is endangered by a discovery in an abandoned, half-submerged tunnel.
"A crime novel featuring Detective Inspector Jack Caffery of Bristol's Major Crime Investigation Unit and Sgt. Flea Marley, who heads up the Underwater Search Unit. This artfully constructed procedural opens with a car-jacking that becomes a kidnapping after the thief drives off with a little girl in the back seat. The narrative takes its first chilling turn when Caffery's team detects a pattern of other accidental kidnappings, indicating that the carjacker was stalking little girls all along. More shocks are in store, but for once the visceral thrills don't come at the expense of character. By giving her villain the intelligence to inflict as much emotional as physical pain, Hayder makes him less of a monster and more of a terror." —*New York Times Book Review*
Originally published: London : Bantam, 2010.

Hanging hill. Mo Hayder. Grove/Atlantic, 2012. 432 p.
ISBN 9780802120069
1. Murder investigation 2. Pornography 3. Teenage girls 4. Policewomen 5. Sisters 6. Bath, England 7. England 8. Thrillers and suspense
After a popular Bath teen's murder, police detective Zoe Benedict looks beyond the usual motives to solve the crime; while her divorced sister, Sally, takes a housekeeping job for a wealthy entrepreneur who behaves in increasingly suspicious ways.

Poppet. Mo Hayder. Grove/Atlantic, 2013. 400 p. (Detective Inspector Jack Caffery mysteries, 6)
ISBN 9780802121073
1. Detectives 2. Escapes 3. Psychiatric hospitals 4. Self-harm 5. Psychiatric hospital patients 6. England 7. Bristol, England 8. Mysteries 9. Police procedurals
When a dangerous mental patient named Isaac, who is linked to a series of unexplained episodes of self-harm among the ward's patients, is released in error, Detective Jack Caffery must track him down before he kills again.
The new Jack Caffery thriller—Cover.

Haydon, Elizabeth

The **Merchant** Emperor. Elizabeth Haydon. Tor Books, 2014. 384 p. (Symphony of Ages, 7)
ISBN 9780765305664
1. Women rulers 2. Motherhood 3. Demons 4. Intrigue 5. Imaginary wars and battles 6. Epic fantasy 7. Adult books for young adults
While Ashe, Gwydion Navarne, and Lord Marshal Anborn prepare to combat the forces of throne-seeking Talquist, the Merchant Emperor of Sorbold forges an alliance with two demons and Rhapsody goes into hiding to protect her infant son.
"For those familiar with the history of Rhapsody and Ashe, two of the main characters from previous books, this volume will provide additional depth to their personalities as they are forced to make difficult decisions to save not only themselves and those they love but also perhaps the world they live in... followers of the series will be delighted with it." —*Booklist*

Hayes, Terry

I am Pilgrim. Terry Hayes. Atria Books, 2014. 608 p.

ISBN 9781439177723
1. Genius 2. Terrorists 3. Antiterrorists 4. Former spies 5. Crime prevention 6. Middle East 7. Turkey 8. Spy fiction 9. Thrillers and suspense
British Book Award for Crime Thriller of the Year, 2014
Suspense Fiction. This explosive thriller starts with the perfect murder—the victim has had her teeth removed, her identifiable features have been destroyed by acid, and the scene has been liberally sprayed with DNA-destroying disinfectant. But more alarmingly, a jihadist is building a biological weapon he's planning on letting loose in the U.S. The connection between the two is Pilgrim, a retired CIA operative, who's called in to stop the terrorist—and whose textbook on criminal investigations may have been the blueprint for the murder.
"[T]he race against time to save the world has been done before but seldom this well.... [A] taut and muscular thriller." —*Library Journal*
First published: London: Bantam Press, 2013.

Haynes, Natalie
A **thousand** ships. Natalie Haynes. HarperCollins, 2021. 368 pages
ISBN 9780063065390
1. Trojan War 2. Women and war 3. Mythology, Greek 4. Gods and goddesses, Greek 5. Heroes and heroines, Greek 6. Troy (Extinct city) 7. Ancient Greece 8. Ancient Aegean civilizations (3000?1000 BCE) 9. Historical fiction
Shortlisted for The Women's Prize for Fiction, 2020
A feminist retelling of the Trojan War—giving voices to the women the myths forgot.
"Haynes shines by twisting common perceptions of the Trojan War and its aftermath in order to capture the women's experiences. Readers who enjoyed Madeline Miller's Circe will want to take a look." —*Publishers Weekly*
Originally published: London, Mantle, c2019.

Haywood, Gar Anthony
Cemetery Road. Gar Anthony Haywood. Severn House, 2010. 224 p.
ISBN 9780727868510
1. Murder investigation 2. Drug dealers 3. Revenge 4. Repairers 5. Friendship 6. Los Angeles, California 7. Mysteries 8. African American fiction
When Errol "Handy" White returns to his native Los Angeles to attend the funeral of his old friend R. J. Burrow, who has been brutally murdered, a terrible secret threatens to reveal itself.

Haywood, Sarah
The **cactus**. Sarah Haywood. Park Row, 2018. 368 p.
ISBN 9780778318996
1. Mothers — Death 2. Loss (Psychology) 3. Pregnant women 4. Self-discovery in women 5. Coping 6. Relationship fiction
Susan has a hard time adjusting when her mother dies and she discovers she's about to become a mother herself.

Hazelwood, Ali
The **love** hypothesis. Ali Hazelwood. Berkley Publishing Group, 2021. 336 p.
ISBN 9780593336823
1. Doctoral students 2. College teachers 3. Dating (Social customs) 4. Universities and colleges 5. Harassment 6. Contemporary romances 7. Romantic comedies
LibraryReads Favorites, 2021

"This smart, sexy contemporary should delight a wide swath of romance lovers." —*Publishers Weekly*

Hazzard, Shirley
★ The **great** fire. Shirley Hazzard. Farrar, Straus and Giroux, 2003. 352 p.
ISBN 9780374166441
1. Soldiers 2. World War II veterans 3. Girls 4. Children with terminal illnesses 5. Siblings 6. England 7. Japan 8. 1940s 9. Literary fiction 10. Australian fiction
LC 2003049189
Booklist Editors' Choice, 2003; Library Journal Best Books, 2003; Miles Franklin Award, 2004; National Book Award for Fiction, 2003; New York Times Notable Book, 2003; Shortlisted for the International IMPAC Dublin Literary Award, 2005; Shortlisted for The Orange Prize for Fiction, 2004
In war-torn Asia and stricken Europe, men and women, still young but veterans of harsh experience, must reinvent their lives and expectations, and learn, from their past, to dream again. Some will fulfill their destinies, others will falter. At the center of the story, a brave and brilliant soldier find that survival and worldly achievement are not enough. His counterpart, a young girl living in occupied Japan and tending her dying brother, falls in love, and in the process discovers herself.
"The time is 1947-48, and the place is, primarily, East Asia.... Our hero, and indeed he fills the requirements to be called one, is Aldred Leith, who is English and part of the occupation forces in Japan; his particular military task is damage survey. He has an interesting past, including, most recently, a two-year walk across civil-war-torn China to write a book. In the present. . .he meets the teenage daughter and younger son of a local Australian commander. And, as Helen is growing headlong into womanhood, this novel of war's aftermath becomes a story of love—or more to the point, of the restoration of the capacity for love once global and personal trauma have been shed." —*Booklist*

★ The **transit** of Venus. Shirley Hazzard. Viking Press, 1980. 337 p.
ISBN 9780670724260
1. Sisters 2. Man-woman relationships 3. Romantic love 4. Australians in foreign countries 5. Literary fiction 6. Australian fiction
LC 79021754
National Book Critics Circle Award for Fiction, 1980; National Book Award for Fiction finalist, 1981
"This is an exceedingly ambitious novel; a stunning and at times bewildering galaxy of ideas. From a literary and intellectual standpoint it is a challenge.... Miss Hazzard's greatest achievement in this novel is the suspense she creates from unfinished relationships. Instead of spinning off in different directions through space, these characters collide once again, drawn together by an ineluctable magnetism." —*Christian Science Monitor*
First published in the United States by Viking 1980 and in Great Britain by Macmillan & Co 1980.

Heaberlin, Julia
We are all the same in the dark: a novel. Julia Heaberlin. Ballantine Books, 2020. 288 p.
ISBN 9780525621676
1. Policewomen 2. Teenage girls who are mute 3. Missing persons 4. Suspects (Criminal investigation) 5. Abandoned teenagers 6. West Texas 7. Texas 8. Mysteries
LC 2020000513

The discovery of an unknown girl found by the side of the road a decade after an unsolved disappearance compels a young police officer's investigation into dangerous local and personal secrets.

"Heaberlin sensitively addresses issues of survival and vulnerability in this heart-wrenching gothic tale." —*Publishers Weekly*

Heacox, Kim

Jimmy Bluefeather: a novel. Kim Heacox. Alaska Northwest Books, 2015. 256 p.

ISBN 9781941821688

1. Grandfather and grandson 2. Spiritual journeys 3. Indians of North America 4. Canoes 5. Villages 6. Alaska 7. Literary fiction 8. Adventure stories 9. First person narratives

LC 2015007906

National Outdoor Book Award for Outdoor Literature, 2015

Canoe carver Keb Wisting and his grandson James, who is despondent after a logging injury derails the future he envisioned, embark on a great canoe journey into the wild Alaska.

"Heacox does a superb job of transcending his characters unique geography to create a heartwarming, all-American story. Jinkaat, Alaska, can stand beside Twain's Missouri and Anderson's Winesburg, Ohio." —*Booklist*

Headley, Maria Dahvana

The **mere** wife. Maria Dahvana Headley. Farrar, Straus and Giroux, 2018. 308 p.

ISBN 9780374208431

1. Mothers and sons 2. Gated communities 3. Misfits (Persons) 4. Women veterans 5. Stay-at-home mothers 6. Literary fiction 7. Adaptations, retellings, and spin-offs

LC 2017058628

A modern retelling of Beowulf recasts classic themes from the perspectives of the attackers and finds a suburban housewife and a battle-hardened veteran navigating dark realities to protect the sons they love.

Healey, Emma

★ **Elizabeth** is missing. Emma Healey. HarperCollins, 2014. 303 p.

ISBN 9780062309662

1. Female friendship 2. Memory disorders 3. People with dementia 4. Missing persons 5. Memory 6. England 7. Psychological suspense 8. First person narratives

Costa First Novel Award, 2014; LibraryReads Favorites, 2014

When Maud, an aging grandmother who is slowly losing her memory, is convinced that her best friend Elizabeth is missing and in terrible danger, she becomes obsessed with saving her beloved friend despite the fact that no one believes her.

"Part mystery, part meditation on memory, part Dickensian revelation of how apparent charity may hurt its recipients, this is altogether brilliant." —*Booklist*

Healey, Jane

The **animals** at Lockwood Manor. Jane Healey. Houghton Mifflin Harcourt, 2020. 304 p.

ISBN 9780358106401

1. World War II home front 2. Natural history museums 3. Manors 4. Rural life 5. Secrets 6. England 7. Second World War era (1939-1945) 8. Gothic fiction 9. Historical fiction 10. Multiple perspectives

LC 2019033904

When a young woman is tasked with safeguarding a natural history collection as it is spirited out of London during World War II, she discovers her new manor home is a place of secrets and terror instead of protection.

"Healey excels at creating disquiet through descriptions of crushed feathers, disintegrating fur, teeth shining in the half-light, and the living creatures that prey upon the taxidermied animals: mice gnawing, insects scrabbling in sawdust innards. Billed for fans of Kate Morton, Healey's novel will offer a satisfying scratch for those with an itch for a gothic read." —*Booklist*

Heath, Lorraine

Falling into bed with a duke. Lorraine Heath. Avon Books, 2015. 384 p. (Hellions of Havisham, 1)

ISBN 9780062391018

1. Dukes and duchesses 2. Heirs and heiresses 3. Lovers 4. Secret identity 5. Mate selection 6. England 7. Great Britain 8. Victorian era (1837-1901) 9. Victorian romances 10. Historical romances

Choosing spinsterhood over fortune-hungry suitors, Miss Minerva Dodger decides to enjoy one night of pleasure at the Nightingale Club where she is drawn into an intimate affair with the Duke of Ashebury, who, once he discovers her true identity, sets out to win her heart.

"With her usual flair for richly nuanced characters and elegant writing, RITA Award-winning Heath launches her new Hellions of Havisham historical series with a tale that simply sizzles with sensuality." —*Booklist*

Heger, Amanda

Crazy cupid love. Amanda Heger. Sourcebooks Casablanca, 2019. 352 p. (Let's get mythical, 1)

ISBN 9781492672753

1. Enchantment 2. Family businesses 3. Matchmaking 4. Mentors 5. Characters and characteristics in mythology 6. California 7. Romantic comedies 8. Paranormal romances

In a magical rom-com, the descendants of Greek mythology must learn to live and love in a mundane world where Aphrodite's blessing can sure feel like a real pain in the quiver.

Heggen, Thomas

Mister Roberts. Thomas Heggen; illustrated by Samuel Hanks Bryant. Houghton Mifflin, 1946. 221 pages.

ISBN 9781557507235

1. World War II — Naval operations 2. World War II — Naval operations, American 3. Seafaring life 4. Pacific Ocean 5. 1940s 6. War stories 7. Sea stories 8. Historical fiction

LC 46025229

The popular First Lieutenant of a cargo ship leads the otherwise idle crew in a fight against boredom and the captain.

"The leisurely narrative is told in a very few incidents, all centering about an admirable young lieutenant miserably defeated in his desire to get into fighting. A quiet, credible story of the corroding effects of apathy and boredom on men who, in battle, might have been heroes." —*The New Yorker*

Hegi, Ursula

Children and fire: a novel. Ursula Hegi. Simon & Schuster 2011. 272 p.

ISBN 9781451608298

1. Family secrets 2. Nazism 3. Women teachers 4. Fear in women 5. School children 6. Germany 7. 1930s 8. Historical fiction

Protecting her beloved students from the devastating world outside of their 1934 Berlin classroom, Thekla Jansen sacrifices some of her personal freedoms to retain her teaching position until activities within Hitler's early regime test her moral courage.

"A thoughtful, sidelong approach to the worst moment in Germany's history that invites us to understand how decent people come to collaborate with evil." —*Kirkus*

Stones from the river. Ursula Hegi. Poseidon Press, 1994. 507 p. ISBN 9780671780753

1. Small town life 2. Librarians 3. Secrets 4. Women librarians 5. World War II 6. West Germany 7. 20th century 8. Literary fiction

LC 93033533

A dwarf becomes the librarian of a small German town. The work makes her privy to many of the town's secrets and she uses them to set people against each other. It's her way of paying them back for the taunts and humiliations.

"The author imbues her novel with a strong spirit of place. When Trudi wrestles with despair, she goes to the nearby Rhine for help. It never fails her.... Americans still tend to view Germany with horror or (sometimes gleeful) condescension. This moving, elegiac novel commands our compassion and respect for the wisdom and courage to be found in unlikely places, in unlikely times." —*New York Times Book Review*

The **vision** of Emma Blau. Ursual Hegi. Simon & Schuster, 2000. 432 p.

ISBN 9780684829975

1. Family relationships 2. Young women 3. Deception 4. Runaways 5. Ambition in men 6. New Hampshire 7. Family sagas 8. Literary fiction

LC 99056392

A novel of immigration and love follows a German man who flees to the U.S. at the start of the century and makes a life for himself, spawning four generations of descendants

"Hegi has created a milieu full of sexual energy—the book is often erotic—and has captured both the tension and love endemic to all tight-knit families. Compelling and absorbing, this old-fashioned saga is rife with passion, tragedy, and redemption." —*Library Journal*

Heinlein, Robert A.

The **moon** is a harsh mistress. Robert A. Heinlein. T. Doherty, 1997. 382 p.

ISBN 9780312863555

1. Artificial intelligence 2. Space warfare 3. Revolutions 4. Computers 5. Supercomputers 6. Moon 7. Hard science fiction 8. Dystopian fiction 9. Science fiction classics

LC 9553750

Hugo Award for Best Novel, 1967

The moon, 2075. Working to produce wheat for earth, lunar residents live like sharecroppers, kept prisoners of the mother planet by a tight web of control. A small group of dissidents are planning a revolution that will change this relationship forever.

★ **Starship** troopers. Robert A. Heinlein. G. P. Putnam's Sons, 1959. 309 p.

ISBN 9781473616110

1. Aliens (Non-humanoid) 2. Space warfare 3. Human/alien encounters 4. Life on other planets 5. Violence 6. First person narratives 7. Books to movies 8. Science fiction

LC 59012950

Hugo Award for Best Novel, 1960

With Earth embroiled in a vast interplanetary war with the "Bugs," a young recruit in the Federal Reserves relates his experiences training in boot camp and as a junior officer in the Terran Mobile Infantry.

A much abridged version...was published in Fantasy and science fiction magazine under the title "Starship soldier."

Originally published: New York: Putnam, 1959; Great Britain: New English Library, 1960.

★ **Stranger** in a strange land. Robert A. Heinlein. G. P. Putnam's Sons, 1961. 408 p.

ISBN 9780399107726

1. Messiahs 2. Sexual freedom 3. Religion 4. Rich men 5. Men psychics 6. Mars (Planet) 7. Science fiction classics 8. Social science fiction 9. Science fiction

LC 61011702

Hugo Award for Best Novel, 1962

A nonhuman visitor brings into doubt the values and self-evident truths of Western society.

Heiny, Katherine

★ **Early** morning riser. Katherine Heiny. Alfred A. Knopf, 2021. 336 p.

ISBN 9780525659341

1. Couples 2. Divorced couples 3. Womanizers 4. Small town life 5. Teachers 6. Michigan 7. 21st century 8. Relationship fiction

LC 2020014650

A new novel explores love, disaster and unconventional family.

"With sharply drawn portraits and acerbic wit, Heiny captures emotions, bonds, revelations, and heartbreak in this tale of unconventional interactions." —*Booklist*

Heley, Veronica

Murder in law. Veronica Heley. Severn House Pub Ltd, 2021. 224 p. (Ellie Quicke mysteries, 21)

ISBN 9780727890979

1. Victorian houses 2. Women amateur detectives 3. Married people 4. Children 5. Home invasions 6. England 7. Cozy mysteries

While Ellie's away, murder will play...Is the death of Ellie's son-in-law really the result of a burglary gone wrong?

"Susan lacks confidence in her abilities and feels like an underappreciated, frumpy housewife—until she beats the cops at their own game. An entertaining plot, lively characterizations, and a quick-fire ending make this a good choice for most mystery collections." —*Booklist*

Heller, Joseph

★ **Catch-22**. By Joseph Heller. Simon & Schuster Paperbacks, 2004. 463 p.

ISBN 9780684833392

1. Soldiers 2. World War II 3. Survival 4. Military missions 5. Mental illness 6. Italy 7. 1940s 8. Satirical fiction 9. Black humor 10. War stories

LC 2004558446

Presents the contemporary classic depicting the struggles of a United States airman attempting to survive the lunacy and depravity of a World War II airbase

Sequel: Closing time.

Originally published: New York: Simon & Schuster, 1961.

Good as Gold. Joseph Heller. Simon and Schuster, 1979. 447 p.
ISBN 9780671229238

1. Jewish men 2. Middle-aged men 3. Midlife crisis in men 4. Jewish American families 5. Fathers and sons 6. United States 7. 1970s 8. Domestic fiction 9. Satirical fiction 10. Political fiction

LC 78023894

Dr. Bruce Gold, a forty-eight-year-old Jewish professor of English, faces the possibilities of being appointed to a high State Department position and being disowned by his family.

Heller, L. Alison

The **neighbor's** secret. L. Alison Heller. Flatiron Books, 2021. 336 p.
ISBN 9781250205810

1. Planned communities 2. Rich families 3. Book clubs 4. Women — Books and reading 5. Married women 6. Colorado 7. Psychological suspense

LC 2021025632

With its sprawling yards and excellent schools, Cottonwood Estates is the perfect place to raise children. The Cottonwood Book Club serves as the subdivision's eyes and ears, meeting once a month for discussion, gossip, and cocktails. If their selections trend toward twisty thrillers and salacious murder mysteries, it's only because the members feel secure that such evil has no place in their own cul-de-sacs. Or does it? When late-night acts of vandalism target the women of the book club in increasingly violent and personal ways, they will be forced to decide how far to go to keep their secrets. At least they all agree on what's most important: protecting their children at any cost—even if it means someone has to die.

"With its imaginative plot, charismatic characters, and wealth of dramatic revelations, this addictive tale is one of those novels that demands to be gobbled up in a single sitting. Great for book clubs (whose members may or may not have their own secrets) and for domestic-thriller lovers in general." —*Publishers Weekly*

Heller, Peter

Celine: a novel. Peter Heller. Alfred A. Knopf, 2017. 352 pages
ISBN 9780451493897

1. Missing persons investigation 2. Women private investigators 3. Senior women 4. Cold cases (Criminal investigation) 5. Families of missing persons 6. Yellowstone National Park 7. Wyoming 8. Mysteries

LC 2016026943

Establishing an excellent record as a missing-persons tracker who specializes in reuniting families to make amends for a loss in her own past, Celine searches for a presumed-dead photographer in Yellowstone, only to be targeted by a shadowy figure who would keep the case unsolved.

"Heller (The Painter) blends suspense with beautiful descriptive writing of both nature and civilization to create a winner." —*Library Journal*

★ The **dog** stars: a novel. Peter Heller. Alfred A. Knopf, 2012. 272 p.
ISBN 9780307959942

1. Pilots 2. End of the world 3. Survival 4. Risk 5. Epidemics 6. Apocalyptic fiction

LC 2011050429

ALA Notable Book, 2013

Surviving a pandemic disease that has killed everyone he knows, a pilot establishes a shelter in an abandoned airport hangar before hearing a random radio transmission that compels him to risk his life to seek out other survivors.

This is a Borzoi book.

The **Guide.** Peter Heller. Alfred A. Knopf, 2021. 272 p.
ISBN 9780525657767

1. Hotels 2. Grief 3. Fishing guides 4. Young men 5. Singers 6. Thrillers and suspense

Loan Stars Favourites, 2021

Trying to return to normalcy after a young life filled with loss, Jack takes a job as a guide for the elite Kingfisher Lodge where he, while guiding a well-known singer, discovers that this idyllic fishing lodge may be a cover for a far more sinister operation.

"Masterful evocations of nature are not surprising, given Heller's award-winning nonfiction about his own outdoor experiences, while his ability to inject shocking menace into a novel that might otherwise serve as a lyrical paean to nature is remarkable." —*Publishers Weekly*

The **painter:** a novel. Peter Heller. Alfred A. Knopf, 2014. 363 p.
ISBN 9780385352093

1. Twain, Mark 2. Violence in men 3. Former convicts 4. Abstract expressionism 5. Life change events 6. Psychological fiction 7. First person narratives

LC 2013045522

Struggling with dark impulses after serving time for attempted murder, a successful artist gives in to his obsessions to kill an abusive troublemaker before fleeing authorities and the man's vengeful clan.

"[E]mbraces themes of personal loss and growth, drama and suspense, while also including plenty for those who enjoy art or nature fiction." —*Library Journal*

The **river:** a novel. Peter Heller. Alfred A. Knopf, 2019. 253 pages
ISBN 9780525521877

1. Canoeing 2. Male friendship 3. Wilderness survival 4. Survival 5. Friendship 6. Canada 7. Survival stories 8. Psychological fiction
LibraryReads Favorites, 2019

Two college students on a wilderness canoe trip find their survival skills and longtime best friendship tested by a wildfire, white-water hazards and two mysterious strangers.

"An exhilarating tale delivered with the pace of a thriller and the wisdom of a grizzled nature guide." —*Kirkus*

Heller, Zoe

What was she thinking?: notes on a scandal. Zoe Heller. Henry Holt, 2003. 256 p.
ISBN 9780805073331

1. Women teachers 2. Senior women 3. Middle-aged women 4. Female friendship 5. Teacher-student relationships 6. London, England 7. 1990s 8. Psychological fiction 9. Satirical fiction 10. Books to movies

LC 2002038809

New York Times Notable Book, 2003; Shortlisted for the Man Booker Prize, 2003

Schoolteacher Barbara Covett has known none but the most solitary of lifestyles until new teacher Sheba Hart joins St. George's. Starting by sharing lunches, then family events, the new art teacher draws Barbara into a touching confidence. Sheba has begun a passionate affair with an underage male student. When the details come to light and Sheba falls prey to the inevitable media circus, Barbara decides to write an account in her friend's defense, revealing not only Sheba's secrets but her own.

"Barbara Covett, a sixtyish history teacher, is the kind of unmarried-woman-with-cat whose female friends sooner or later decide she is 'too intense.' Thus when a beautiful new pottery teacher, Sheba Hart. . .chooses Barbara as a confidante, she is deeply, even rather sinisterly, gratified. Sheba's secret is explosive: married with two kids, she is having an affair with a fifteen-year-old student.... Equally adroit at satire and at psychological suspense, Heller charts the course of a predatory friendship and demonstrates the lengths to which some people go for human company." —*The New Yorker*

Book made into a movie called Notes on a scandal.

Helprin, Mark

In sunlight and in shadow. Mark Helprin. Houghton Mifflin Harcourt, 2012. 752 p.

ISBN 9780547819235

1. Veterans 2. Love triangles 3. Heirs and heiresses 4. Courtship 5. Engagement 6. New York City 7. 1940s 8. Love stories 9. Historical fiction 10. Literary fiction

LC 2012016242

Returning home after serving in World War II to run his family business in New York, paratrooper Harry Copeland falls in love with young singer and heiress Catherine Thomas Hale, who risks everything to break off her engagement to another man.

Paris in the present tense. Mark Helprin. Overlook Press, 2017. 394 p.

ISBN 9781468314762

1. Holocaust survivors 2. Personal conduct 3. Widowers 4. Cellists 5. Seniors 6. Paris, France 7. France 8. Literary fiction

When faced with a series of challenges to his principles, livelihood and home, Jules—a 74-year-old maitre at Paris-Sorbonne, cellist, widow, veteran of the war in Algeria and child of the Holocaust—must confront his complex past and find a way forward.

★ **Winter's** tale. Mark Helprin. Harcourt, 2005. 748 p. : Illustration

ISBN 9780156031196

1. Love 2. Death 3. Mortality 4. Irish Americans 5. Thieves 6. Upper West Side, New York City 7. New York City 8. Gilded Age (1865-1898) 9. Magical realism 10. Literary fiction 11. Books to movies

LC 2006272912

When master mechanic Peter Lake attempts to rob a mansion on the Upper West Side, he is caught by young Beverly Penn, the terminally ill daughter of the house, and their subsequent love sends Peter on a desperate personal journey

Originally published: San Diego : Harcourt Brace Jovanovich, 1983.

This book was adapted into film in 2014, directed by Akiva Goldsman and stars Colin Farrell, Russell Crowe, Jessica Brown Findlay, Jennifer Connelly and Will Smith.

Hemingway, Ernest

★ A **farewell** to arms. Ernest Hemingway. Scribner, 1995. 332 p.

ISBN 9780684801469

1. Americans in Italy 2. World War I 3. Ambulance drivers — History 4. British women in Italy 5. Nurses — History 6. Italy 7. War stories 8. Love stories 9. Historical fiction

An American's love for an English nurse during the First World War ends in tragedy.

First published: [New York] : Charles Scribner's Sons, 1929.

For whom the bell tolls. Ernest Hemingway. Scribner, 1995. 471 p.

ISBN 9780684803357

1. Americans in Spain 2. Disillusionment in men 3. Soldiers 4. Guerrillas 5. Anti-fascism 6. Spain 7. War stories 8. Historical fiction 9. Books to movies

LC 95-15746

The story of an American fighting in the Spanish Civil War, his loyalty and courage and his eventual disillusionment with love and defeat.

The **Nick** Adams stories. Ernest Hemingway; preface by Philip Young. Scribner, 1972. 268 p.

ISBN 9780684124858

1. Young men 2. Adams, Nick (Fictitious character) 3. Coming-of-age stories 4. Short stories 5. Modern classics

LC 77159759

Events in the life of Hemingway's memorable character are presented chronologically in this arrangement of the stories.

"The volume presents Nick as a child in the northern woods, as adolescent, as soldier, veteran, writer, husband and parent. The last Nick Adams story appeared in 1933, and what surprises here, in these...[stories] of varying length, quality and intent, is their freshness and immediacy." —*Publishers Weekly*

Eight of these stories never before published.

★ The **old** man and the sea. Ernest Hemingway; illustrations by C.F. Tunnicliffe and Raymond Sheppard. Scribner, 1996. 93 p. : Illustration

ISBN 9780684830490

1. Fishers 2. Marlin fishing 3. Courage in men 4. Senior men 5. Male friendship 6. Cuba 7. Coming-of-age stories 8. Allegories 9. Books to movies

LC 96011419

Pulitzer Prize for Fiction, 1953

Santiago is a Cuban fisherman who encounters a giant marlin in the Gulf Stream and the battle for his catch becomes one of survival against a band of marauding sharks.

The Old Man and the Sea was closely adapted into the film The Old Man and the Sea in 1958.

First published: London : Jonathan Cape, 1952.

Vintage Hemingway.

Originally published: New York : Scribner, 1952.

The **short** stories. Ernest Hemingway. Scribner Classics, 1997. 457 p.

ISBN 9780684837864

1. Manners and customs 2. Short stories

Forty-nine stories reflect much of the intensity of Hemingway's own life and environment.

The **snows** of Kilimanjaro and other stories. Ernest Hemingway. Scribner, 1995. 143 p.

ISBN 9780684862217

1. Safaris 2. Death — Psychological aspects 3. Kilimanjaro 4. Short stories 5. Adventure stories 6. Modern classics

Contains ten of Hemingway's classic stories including "The snows of Kilimanjaro," "A day's wait," "Fathers and sons," "The killers," and "The short happy life of Francis Macomber" BT

★ The **sun** also rises. Ernest Hemingway. Scribner, 1995. 251 p.

ISBN 9780684800714

1. Expatriates 2. Americans in Europe 3. Disillusionment 4. Bullfights 5. Alienation (Social psychology) 6. Europe 7. 1920s 8. Books to movies 9. Modern classics 10. Literary fiction

LC 95-130282

The story of a group of Americans and English on a sojourn from Paris to Paloma, evokes in poignant detail, life among the expatriates on Paris's Left Bank, during the 1920s and conveys in brutally realistic descriptions the power and danger of bullfighting in Spain.

To have and have not. Ernest Hemingway. Scribner, 1999. 174 p.

ISBN 9780684859231

1. Smuggling 2. Fishing boat captains 3. Married people 4. Americans in Cuba 5. Havana, Cuba 6. Key West, Florida 7. 1930s 8. Books to movies 9. Modern classics 10. Literary fiction

In an attempt to keep his family above water, Harry Morgan runs contraband rum shipments between Cuba and Key West during the 1930s, in a humorous tale that also follows an unlikely love affair.

Titles of later film versions: To have and have not (1944), The breaking point (1950), and The gun runners (1958).

Hemmings, Kaui Hart

The **possibilities**: a novel. Kaui Hart Hemmings. Simon & Schuster, 2014. 288 p.
ISBN 9781476725796
1. Sons — Death 2. Bereavement 3. Families 4. Life change events 5. Grief 6. Breckenridge, Colorado 7. Colorado 8. Mainstream fiction 9. First person narratives
LC 2013027385
A grieving mother struggles to overcome her son's death, when a strange girl enters her life with a secret that changes them both forever.
"Hemmings writes a piercing, empathetic story about parenthood and unfathomable heartbreak and manages to bring humor and hope to her characters. Emotionally complex and relatable to all." —*Kirkus*

Hempel, Amy

Sing to it: new stories. Amy Hempel. Scribner, 2019. 149 p.
ISBN 9781982109110
1. Interpersonal relations 2. Family relationships 3. Options, alternatives, choices 4. Short stories 5. Literary fiction
LC 2018045523
Finely tuned and brilliantly written, a heartbreaking new collection of 15 stories introduces characters, lonely and adrift, searching for connection.
Includes bibliographical references.

Henderson, Smith

Fourth of July Creek. Smith Henderson. Ecco Press, 2014. 512 p.
ISBN 9780062286444
1. Social workers 2. Survivalists 3. Wilderness areas 4. Missing persons 5. Eleven-year-old boys 6. Montana 7. 1980s 8. Literary fiction
Montana Book Award, 2014; New Blood Dagger Award, 2015; New York Times Notable Book, 2014; Shortlisted for the James Tait Black Memorial Prize for Fiction, 2014
Set in the mountains, valleys and close-knit communities of rural Montana in the early 1980s, this novel is about a young social worker called Pete, who struggles to hold together the lives of the most dysfunctional inhabitants of the town of Tenmile, as his own life begins to fall apart.

Henderson, Susan

The **flicker** of old dreams. Susan Henderson. Perennial, 2018. 320 p.
ISBN 9780062834072
1. Funeral homes 2. Misfits (Persons) 3. Change (Psychology) 4. Undertakers 5. Small town life 6. Montana 7. Modern Westerns
Spur Awards, Best Western Contemporary Novel, 2019; WILLA Literary Awards: Contemporary Fiction, 2019
Finding fulfillment in her job as an embalmer in her father's small town mortuary, outsider Mary bonds with a villainized local who was blamed for a fatal accident twenty years earlier, a friendship that compels her to consider what might happen if she were to leave their fading community.

Hendricks, Greer

An **anonymous** girl. Greer Hendricks and Sarah Pekkanen. St. Martin's Press, 2019. 352 p.
ISBN 9781250133731
1. Makeup artists 2. Psychology teachers 3. Psychology — Experiments 4. Ethics 5. Obsession 6. New York City 7. Manhattan, New York City 8. Psychological suspense 9. Multiple perspectives 10. Second person narratives
LC 2018029126
LibraryReads Favorites, 2019; Loan Stars Favourites, 2019
Participating in a psychological study under the mysterious Dr. Shields, Jessica endures intense, invasive sessions and oppressive behavioral restrictions before she begins to lose her grasp on reality.
"The movement here from small tests to bigger ones masterfully escalates the suspense. The juxtaposed points of view, with reactions of each protagonist to the other, keep the reader guessing until the end." —*Booklist*
Originally published: PanMacmillan, 2018.

★ **You** are not alone. Greer Hendricks and Sarah Pekkanen. St. Martin's Press, 2020. 352 p.
ISBN 9781250202031
1. Loneliness in women 2. Popularity 3. Sisters 4. Deception 5. Female friendship 6. Psychological suspense
LC 2019049429
Loan Stars Favourites, 2020
A lonely misfit with a dead-end job quietly envies a circle of popular sisters who hide dangerous vengeful truths beneath a veneer of friendship, glamour and accomplishments.
"Lots of frenzied flipping back and forth for readers who like to figure out the puzzle." —*Kirkus*

Hendrix, Grady

The **final** girl support group. Grady Hendrix. Berkley, 2021. 400 p.
ISBN 9780593201237
1. Support groups 2. Psychic trauma 3. Violence against women 4. Paranoia 5. Massacres 6. Los Angeles, California 7. Southern California 8. Horror
LC 2021002704
LibraryReads Favorites Top Ten, 2021
A real-life "final girl"—the one girl always left standing at the end of a horror movie, Lynette Tarkington, who survived a massacre 22 years ago, along with five other final girls, works to overcome her past until someone becomes determined to take their lives apart again, piece by piece.
"A bloody and grotesque but ultimately entertaining and inspiring take on horror movies, trauma, and self-determination." —*Kirkus*

My best friend's exorcism. Grady Hendrix. Quirk Books, 2016. 336 pages
ISBN 9781594748622
1. Female friendship 2. Demonic possession 3. Exorcism 4. Exorcists 5. Best friends 6. Charleston, South Carolina 7. 1980s 8. Horror 9. Adult books for young adults
Booklist Editors' Choice: Adult Books for Young Adults, 2016; RUSA Reading List Short List, 2017
The year: 1988. The place: Charleston, South Carolina. Abby and Gretchen have been BFFs since fifth grade, but now that they're in high school, Gretchen seems different. After a series of bizarre events, Abby realizes that Gretchen has a demon living inside her—and it's up to Abby to rescue her friend. Author Grady Hendrix hits a home run with his spectacular, gripping exorcism scene. Don't miss this terrifying tale, filled with spot-on 1980s popular culture references and framed at the beginning and end with yearbook-style layouts.

The **southern** book club's guide to slaying vampires. Grady Hendrix. Quirk Books, 2020. 336 pages
ISBN 9781683691433

1. Book clubs 2. Homemakers 3. Strangers 4. Vampires 5. Protectiveness in women 6. South Carolina 7. 1990s 8. Horror 9. Southern fiction

LC 2019037437

LibraryReads Favorites, 2020; RUSA Reading List Short List, 2021

A supernatural thriller set in South Carolina in the '90s about a women's book club that must protect its suburban community from a mysterious stranger who turns out to be a real monster.

"This powerful, eclectic novel both pays homage to the literary vampire canon and stands singularly within it." —*Publishers Weekly*

Henkin, Joshua

Morningside Heights. Joshua Henkin. Pantheon Books, 2020. 304 p.

ISBN 9781524748357

1. Married people 2. Alzheimer's disease 3. Families 4. Jewish women 5. Orthodox Jews 6. Literary fiction 7. Jewish fiction

Marrying a prestigious Shakespeare professor after moving to 1976 New York, a Yale graduate navigates feelings for another man, the reappearance of her ailing husband's estranged son and her own feelings of unfulfillment in the ensuing decades.

Caring for a spouse with Alzheimers is an ever more common heartbreak, illuminated by this tender portrait of a marriage. Kirkus Reviews.

Henry, Emily

Beach read. Emily Henry. Jove, 2020. 384 pages

ISBN 9781984806734

1. Women authors 2. Authors 3. Neighbors 4. Writer's block 5. Writing 6. Contemporary romances

LC 2019044690

LibraryReads Favorites, 2020; Loan Stars Favourites, 2020

An acclaimed but blocked literary master and a best-selling novelist who has stopped believing in true love agree to a summer-long writing project that challenges them write well in each others' styles.

"There are more than enough steamy scenes to sustain the slow-burn romance, and smart commentary on the placement and purpose of 'women's fiction' joins with crucial conversations about mental health to add multiple intriguing layers to the plot. A heartfelt look at taking second chances, in life and in love." —*Kirkus*

People we meet on vacation. Emily Henry. Jove, 2021. 384 p.

ISBN 9781984806758

1. Best friends 2. Summer 3. Vacations 4. Interpersonal conflict 5. Romantic love 6. Romantic comedies

LC 2020036305

LibraryReads Favorites, 2021; LibraryReads Favorites Top Ten, 2021; Loan Stars Favourites, 2021

With one week to win back the best friend she might just be in love with, a travel writer plans the trip of a lifetime.

"Flashbacks to each past summer trip make for fun travelogues that highlight both characters' understandable but frustrating refusal to discuss their feelings. Watching them dance around the inevitable grows tiresome as things drag on, but Henry's skills with sensory detail and lovable characters shine through." —*Publishers Weekly*

Henry, O.

★ The **complete** works of O. Henry. O. Henry; foreword by Harry Hansen. Doubleday 1960. 1692p.

ISBN 9780385009614

1. Short stories 2. Christmas stories 3. Anthologies

LC 60051825

Entertaining collection of two hundred eighty-six stories and poems generally about simple people in various situations with surprise endings.

286 stories and poems.

Includes "The gift of the Magi."

O. Henry: 101 stories. O. Henry; edited by Ben Yagoda. Library of America, 2021. 750 p.

ISBN 9781598536904

1. Short stories 2. Anthologies

Collects 101 of the master storyteller's very best short stories that represent all of his collections, and captures the genius and range of a gifted humorist who deserves to be ranked among the best in our literature.

"Most of the stories, 'Red Chief' foremost among them, read as if freshly written, although there are a few dated ethnic categorizations and outright slurs. Overall, though, the volume provides ample evidence for why one of American literature's most eminent literary awards should be named for the author." —*Kirkus*

Henry, Patti Callahan

★ **Becoming** Mrs. Lewis: the improbable love story of Joy Davidman and C. S. Lewis. Patti Callahan. Thomas Nelson, 2018. 432 p.

ISBN 9780785224501

1. Davidman, Joy 2. Authors 3. Faith (Christianity) 4. Literature 5. Divorced women 6. College teachers 7. Historical fiction 8. Love stories 9. Biographical fiction

Christy Award for Book of the Year, 2019; Christy Award for Historical Romance Category, 2019

Fictionalizes the romance between beloved author C.S. Lewis and his wife Joy Davidman, as she begins writing letters to Lewis searching for spiritual answers and eventually finds love.

Hensher, Philip

Scenes from early life: a novel. Philip Hensher. Faber and Faber, 2013. 312 p.

ISBN 9780865477612

1. Mahmood, Zaved 2. Families — History 3. Culture conflict 4. Social conflict 5. Bangladeshi families 6. Genocide 7. Bangladesh 8. Biographical fiction 9. Literary fiction 10. First person narratives

RSL Ondaatje Prize, 2013

Traces the experiences of young Zaved's upper-middle-class Bengali family, whose strong bond is made more resilient in the face of brutal violence as Bangladesh fights for independence.

Originally published: London: Fourth Estate, 2012.

Henson, Pene

Into the blue. Pene Henson. Interlude Press, 2016. 236 p.

ISBN 9781941530849

1. Surfers 2. Professional athletes 3. Roommates 4. Best friends 5. Misunderstanding 6. Hawaii 7. LGBTQIA romances 8. Contemporary romances 9. New adult fiction

Lambda Literary Award for Gay Romance, 2017

"Readers eager for more diversity in romance will appreciate the nuanced portrayals of the leads (one gay, one demisexual) and the women they live with (one bisexual, one asexual) but may wish that Tai's Samoan heritage and its meaning for him had been explored, rather than just repeatedly referred to in passing." —*Publishers Weekly*

Hepworth, Sally

The **secrets** of midwives. Sally Hepworth. St. Martin's Press, 2015. 352 p.

ISBN 9781250051899

1. Midwives 2. Pregnant women 3. Family secrets 4. Mothers and daughters 5. Granddaughters 6. New England 7. Relationship fiction 8. Multiple perspectives 9. Australian fiction

LC 2014033628

Determined to hide the identity of her baby's father from others, a third-generation midwife is separated from and bound to her mother and grandmother by a similar secret from the past.

"Hepworth makes some interesting, though not always successful, choices in her narratives (chapters alternate among Neva, Grace and Floss), painting an irksome portrait of Grace and a rather opaque picture of Neva, whose secret is kept from the reader until the finale. Fans of Call the Midwife will enjoy the vignettes of childbirth and the multigenerational female saga." —*Kirkus*

Herbert, Frank

★ **Dune**. Frank Herbert. G. P. Putnam's Sons, 1984. 517 p. (Dune novels, 1)

ISBN 9780399128967

1. Revolutions 2. Psychic ability 3. Rulers 4. Dukes and duchesses 5. Sabotage 6. Science fiction classics 7. Space opera 8. Coming-of-age stories 9. Adult books for young adults

LC 83016030

Hugo Award for Best Novel, 1966; Nebula Award for Best Novel, 1965

Set on the desert planet Arrakis, this is the story of the boy Paul Atreides, who would become the mysterious man known as Muad'Dib, avenge the traitorous plot against his noble family, and bring to fruition humankind's most ancient and unattainable dream.

A deluxe hardcover edition was published in 2019 by Ace Books.
A movie tie-in paperback was published in 2021 by Ace Books.
Includes map.
Adapted into movies in 1984 and 2021.
Originally published: Philadelphia : Chilton Books, 1965.

Herbert, Julian

Bring me the head of Quentin Tarantino: stories. . Graywolf Press, 2020. 192 p.

ISBN 9781644450413

1. Everyday life 2. Eccentrics and eccentricities 3. Doppelgangers 4. Secrets 5. Murder 6. Literary fiction 7. Short stories

Julian Herbert brings to vivid life people who struggle to retain a measure of sanity in an insane world. Here we become acquainted with a vengeful "personal memories coach" who tries to get even with his delinquent clients; a former journalist with a cocaine habit who travels through northern Mexico impersonating a famous author of Westerns; the ghost of Juan Rulfo; a man who discovers music in his teeth; and, in the deliriously pulpy title story, a drug lord who looks just like Quentin Tarantino, who kidnaps a mopey film critic to discuss Tarantino's films while he sends his goons to find and kill the doppelganger that has colonized his consciousness. Herbert's astute observations about human nature in extremis feel like the reader's own revelations.

"While not for the faint of heart or weak of stomach, Herbert's stories use a light touch to explore the dilemma of the intellectual enmeshed in a crudely vicious world. This provocatively cerebral volume should amuse those with a taste for literary horror." —*Publishers Weekly*

Translation of : Traiganme la cabeza de Quentin Tarantino.
Originally published: Barcelona : Literatura Random House, 2017.
Translated from the Spanish.

Heron, Farah

Accidentally engaged. Farah Heron. Forever, 2021. 384 p.

ISBN 9781538734988

1. Muslim women 2. Women bakers 3. Arranged marriage 4. Contests 5. Neighbors 6. Toronto, Ontario 7. Romantic comedies

LC 2020042919

A delightful romantic comedy featuring a Muslim woman who fakes an engagement to the boy next door in the hopes of winning a couples cooking contest.

"Heron enhances the love story with mouthwatering descriptions of Indian cuisine and a rich glimpse into Toronto's Indian Muslim community and Reena's family culture. Equally sweet and spicy, this is sure to leave readers smiling." —*Publishers Weekly*

Herrera, Adriana

★ **American** dreamer. Adriana Herrera. Carina Press, 2019. 288 p; (Dreamers (Adriana Herrera), 1)

ISBN 9781335006875

1. Moving, Household 2. Food trucks 3. Caribbean Americans 4. Gay men 5. Librarians 6. Ithaca, New York 7. New York City 8. Multicultural romances 9. LGBTQIA romances 10. Contemporary romances

No one ever said big dreams come easy.

American fairytale. Adriana Herrera. Carina Press, 2019. 361 pages; (Dreamers (Adriana Herrera), 2)

ISBN 9781335215963

1. Gay men 2. Social workers 3. Businesspeople 4. Interclass romance 5. Money 6. New York City 7. Multicultural romances 8. LGBTQIA romances 9. Contemporary romances

LC 2018660216

Fairytale endings don't just happen; they have to be fought for.

American love story. Adriana Herrera. Carina Press, 2019. 288 p; (Dreamers (Adriana Herrera), 3)

ISBN 9781335215970

1. College teachers 2. Political activists 3. Lawyers 4. Gay men 5. Racism 6. Ithaca, New York 7. New York (State) 8. Multicultural romances 9. LGBTQIA romances 10. Contemporary romances

No one should have to choose between love and justice.

Herron, Mick

Dolphin junction: collected stories. Mick Herron. Soho Crime, 2021. 312 p.

ISBN 9781641293020

1. Crime 2. Criminal investigation 3. Short stories 4. Thrillers and suspense 5. Mysteries

LC 2021018971

Five standalone crime fiction tales and four mystery stories featuring Oxford wife-and-husband detective team of Zoe Boehm and Joe Silvermann will delight fans of thrillers, in this collection of short stories from the award-winning author of the Slough House novels.

"Herron, best known for his Jackson Lamb espionage series, is also a gifted short-story writer. His latest collection contains 11 outstanding tales that range from taut and terrifying to cleverly ironic and subtly humorous." —*Booklist*

Hersey, John

★ A **bell** for Adano. John Hersey. Vintage Books, 1988. 269 p.
ISBN 9780394756950
1. Soldiers 2. World War II 3. Americans in Italy 4. Small towns 5. Italian Americans 6. Sicily, Italy 7. War stories 8. Historical fiction 9. Literary fiction

LC 8745943

Pulitzer Prize for Fiction, 1945
An American major attempts to rebuild ravaged Italian town during the World War II occupation.
Originally published: New York : A.A. Knopf, 1944.

Hertmans, Stefan

★ The **convert**: a novel. Stefan Hertmans; translated from the Dutch by David McKay. Pantheon Books, 2019. 304 pages
ISBN 9781524747084
1. Hertmans, Stefan 2. Young women 3. Jewish men 4. Jews — Persecutions 5. Conversion to Judaism 6. Voyages and travels 7. France 8. Egypt 9. 11th century 10. Historical fiction 11. Translations

LC 2019025351

Abandoning her privileged life after falling in love with a Jewish man, a Medieval Christian noblewoman embarks on a dangerous journey to southern France, where their brief happiness is upended by the vicious anti-Semitism of the First Crusade.
"The horrors of anti-Semitism and the unintended consequences of the First Crusade are pitilessly portrayed, resulting in a story that is tragic and harrowing, yet beautifully told, with an ambience that is fully realized for both the eleventh century and our own." —*Booklist*
Originally published: Amsterdam : De Bezige Bij, 2016.
English translations originally published London : Harvill Secker, 2019.
Translated from the Dutch.

Hesse, Hermann

The **fairy** tales of Hermann Hesse. Hermann Hesse; translated and with an introduction by Jack Zipes; woodcut illustrations by David Frampton. Bantam Books, 1995. Xxxi, 266 p. : Illustration
ISBN 9780553377767
1. Belonging 2. Normality (Psychology) 3. Individuality 4. Social acceptance 5. Allegories 6. Anthologies 7. Translations

LC 94049166

A collection of twenty-two fairy tales by the Nobel Prize winning novelist, most translated into English for the first time, show the influence of German Romanticism, psychoanalysis, and Eastern religion on his development as an author
"Quirky and evocative, Hesse's fairy tales stand alone, but also amplify the ideas and utopian longings of such counterculture avatars as Siddhartha and Steppenwolf." —*Publishers Weekly*
Translation from the German of: Marchen.

Narcissus and Goldmund. Hermann Hesse; translated from the German by Ursule Molinaro. Random House, 1992. 320 p.
ISBN 9780553275865
1. Monasticism and religious orders for men 2. Civilization, Medieval 3. Meaning (Psychology) 4. Young men 5. Artists 6. Germany 7. Medieval period (476-1492) 8. Coming-of-age stories 9. Historical fiction 10. Literary fiction

Narcissus, an ascetic instructor at a cloister school, has devoted himself solely to scholarly and spiritual pursuits. One of his students is the sensual, restless Goldmund, who is immediately drawn to his teacher's fierce intellect and sense of discipline. When Narcissus persuades the young student that he is not meant for a life of self-denial, Goldmund sets off in pursuit of aesthetic and physical pleasures, a path that leads him to a final, unexpected reunion with Narcissus.
Translation of Narziss und Goldmund.
Translated from the German.

★ **Siddhartha:** a new translation. Hermann Hesse; translated from the German by Sherab Chodzin Kohn; with an introduction by Paul W. Morris. Shambhala, 2002. Xxiii, 159 p. : Illustration
ISBN 9781570629709
1. Gautama Buddha 2. Spiritual life — Buddhism 3. Self-fulfillment 4. Enlightenment (Buddhism) 5. Buddhism 6. Courtesans 7. India 8. Psychological fiction 9. Translations 10. Modern classics

LC 2002073423

Blends elements of psychoanalysis and Asian religions to probe an Indian aristocrat's efforts to renounce sensual and material pleasures and discover spiritual truths.
Translated from the German.
Originally published: Berlin : S. Fischer, 1922.

★ **Steppenwolf**. By Hermann Hesse; introduction by Joseph Mileck. H. Holt, 1990. Vi, 218 p.
ISBN 9780805012477
1. Alienation in men 2. Men with mental illnesses 3. Self-discovery in men 4. Middle-aged men 5. Intellectuals 6. Germany 7. 1920s 8. Psychological fiction 9. Literary fiction 10. Translations
Harry Haller is a sad and lonely figure, a reclusive intellectual for whom life holds no joy. He struggles to reconcile the wild primeval wolf and the rational man within himself without surrendering to the bourgeois values he despises. His life changes dramatically when he meets a woman who is his opposite, the carefree and elusive Hermine. With its blend of Eastern mysticism and Western culture, Hesse's best-known and most autobiographical work, originally published in English in 1929, Steppenwolf continues to speak to our souls and marks it as a classic of modern literature.

Hession, Ronan

Leonard and Hungry Paul. Ronan Hession. Melville House, 2020. 254 p.
ISBN 9781612198484
1. Single men 2. Kindness 3. Thirties (Age) 4. Personal conduct 5. Purpose in life 6. Literary fiction
Two friends—who still live with their parents, are resolutely kind, and like to read and play board games—discover that they are not considered {34normal{34 and struggle to protect their concept of what's meaningful in life.
"Dublin-based songwriter Hession has written a tender and hilarious debut. The title characters are unforgettable, and their shared amazement of the world is a gift to readers. Essential reading, especially in these times." —*Library Journal*

Hewson, David

The **garden** of angels. David Hewson. Severn House, 2021. 320 pages
ISBN 9781780297569
1. Grandfather and grandson 2. Family secrets 3. World War II — Underground movements 4. Protectiveness 5. Interfaith friendship 6. Venice, Italy 7. Italy 8. 1940s 9. Second World War era (1939-1945) 10. Historical thrillers 11. Coming-of-age stories

At his beloved Nonno Paolo's deathbed, fifteen-year-old Nico receives a gift that will change his life forever: a yellowing manuscript which tells the haunting, twisty tale of what really happened to his grandfather in Nazi-occupied Venice in 1943.

"A good read for those who love their World War II thrillers with a bit of history included. Followers of Donna Leon's 'Commissario Brunetti' mysteries may appreciate the atmosphere and the intrigue." —*Booklist*

The **garden** of evil. David Hewson. Delacorte Press, 2008. 416 p. (Nic Costa mysteries, 6)
ISBN 9780385339575
1. Art 2. Murder investigation 3. Violence against prostitutes 4. Murder 5. Costa, Nic (Fictitious character) 6. Rome, Italy 7. Italy 8. Mysteries
LC 2007045762
RUSA Reading List, 2009
The discovery of two corpses next to an unknown Caravaggio masterpiece in an art studio in Rome sends Detective Nic Costa on a quest to uncover the truth about a modern-day crime and a centuries-old secret concealed in the painting.

"A thought-provoking blend of art history and mystery, The Garden of Evil is...a treat for readers who like their entertainment literate." —*Richmond Times-Dispatch*

A **season** for the dead. David Hewson. Delacorte Press, 2004. 386 p. (Nic Costa mysteries, 1)
ISBN 9780385337229
1. Women college teachers 2. Former lovers 3. Religious corruption 4. Religious fanatics 5. Serial murders 6. Vatican 7. Rome, Italy 8. Mysteries
LC 2003062522
The first installment in a new crime series features detective Nic Costa on the trail of a serial killer who stalks and kills victims according to a heavenly play book—Catholic martyrs—leaving behind a trail of clues that read like bloody chapters from Lives of the Saints.

"Outsized, eccentric characters, a complex story and an abundance of historical detail make this engrossing book more than just another cookie-cutter, religious-nut serial killer thriller." —*Publishers Weekly*

Heyer, Georgette

Black sheep. Georgette Heyer. Sourcebooks, 2008. 279 p.
ISBN 9781402210785
1. Aunts 2. Single women 3. Mate selection 4. Black sheep 5. Fortune hunters 6. Bath, England 7. Regency period (1811-1820) 8. Regency romances 9. Historical romances
LC 2007050205
"A lovely young spinster is both charmed and infuriated by the wealthy, unconventional black sheep uncle of the fortune hunter on whom her young niece has her heart set. This character-driven novel...is considered one of Heyer's best." —*Library Journal*
Originally published: London : Bodley Head, 1966.

The **grand** Sophy. Georgette Heyer. Sourcebooks Casablanca, 2009. 372 p.
ISBN 9781402218941
1. Independence in women 2. Cousins 3. Engagement 4. Helpfulness in women 5. Man-woman relationships 6. London, England 7. England 8. Regency period (1811-1820) 9. Regency romances 10. Historical romances 11. Gentle reads
When Lady Ombersley agrees to take in her young niece, no one expects Sophy, who sweeps in and immediately takes the ton by storm. Sophy discovers that her aunt's family is in desperate need of her talent for setting everything right: Cecila is in love with a poet, Charles has tyrannical tendencies that are being aggravated by his grim fiancee, her uncle is

of no use at all, and the younger children are in desperate need of some fun and freedom. By the time she's done, Sophy has commandeered Charles's horses, his household, and finally, his heart.

These old shades. Georgette Heyer. Sourcebooks Casablanca, 2009. 378 p.
ISBN 9781402219474
1. Dukes and duchesses 2. Mistaken identity 3. Man-woman relationships 4. Guardian and ward 5. Nobility 6. Paris, France 7. Georgian era (1714-1837) 8. 1770s 9. Georgian romances 10. Historical romances
Set in the Georgian period, about 20 years before the Regency, "These Old Shades" features two of Heyer's most memorable characters: Justin Alastair, the Duke of Avon, and Leonie, whom he rescues from a life of ignominy and comes to love and marry.
Sequel: The Devil's Cub.
First published 1926.

Hiaasen, Carl

Bad monkey. Carl Hiaasen. Alfred A. Knopf, 2013. 368 p. (Andrew Yancy novels, 1)
ISBN 9780307272591
1. Real estate development 2. Police 3. Murder investigation 4. Widows 5. Florida 6. Crime fiction 7. Humorous stories
LC 2013005863
Anticipating his retirement from the Key West Police, Andrew Yancy tackles a murder case involving a human arm in his freezer, an investigation that pits him against a twitchy widow, a clueless real estate developer and a voodoo witch with a string of hapless lovers.

Basket case. Carl Hiaasen. Alfred A. Knopf, 2002. 317 p.
ISBN 9780375411076
1. Obituary writers 2. Investigative journalists 3. Newspaper publishers and publishing 4. Rock musicians — Death 5. Women newspaper editors 6. Florida 7. Mysteries 8. First person narratives 9. Humorous stories
LC 2001038317
Once a hotshot investigative reporter, middle-aged Jack Tagger now bangs out obituaries for a South Florida daily. When Jimmy Stoma, the infamous front man of Jimmy and the Slut Puppies, dies in a diving "accident," Jack uses clues from the singer's own music to unravel the mystery and resurrect his career in the process.

"Hiaasen skewers both corporate media operations and the world of pop stardom." —*New York Times Book Review*

Lucky you: a novel. Carl Hiaasen. A. A. Knopf, 1997. 353 p.
ISBN 9780679454441
1. Women lottery winners 2. Stolen property recovery 3. Newspapers 4. Journalists 5. Militia movement 6. Florida 7. Humorous stories
LC 9736885
New York Times Notable Book, 1997
A romantic comedy featuring two people recovering a stolen $14-million lottery ticket. It belongs to JoLayne Lucks, a black veterinary assistant in Florida and was stolen by white supremacists. With the help of reporter Tom Krome, JoLayne goes after the thieves and love blooms.

"Hiaasen writes witty dialogue that crackles, and his characters are eccentrically colorful." —*New York Times Book Review*

Nature girl. Carl Hiaasen. Alfred A. Knopf, 2006. 320 p.
ISBN 9780307262998
1. Mistresses 2. Real estate agents 3. Tour guides (Persons) 4. Mothers and sons 5. Twelve-year-old boys 6. Florida 7. Everglades, Florida 8. Humorous stories 9. Mysteries
LC 2006049360

Honey Santana, the bipolar, self-proclaimed "queen of lost causes," has plans to give Boyd Shreave and his mistress a lesson in civility, unaware that she is being followed by her obsessed ex-employer and her one-time drug runner ex-husband.

"As usual, Hiaasen throws his colorful characters into an increasingly frenetic mix, and the fun lies in watching how, or if, they'll manage to extricate themselves. One reason Nature Girl works so well is the fact that much of the action is confined to a single island, allowing the characters to intermingle and weave in and out of view." —*San Francisco Chronicle*

Skin tight. Carl Hiaasen. Ballantine, 1990. 373 p.
ISBN 9780449219416
1. Retirees 2. Attempted murder 3. Plastic surgery 4. Criminals 5. Political corruption 6. Florida 7. Black humor 8. Thrillers and suspense

A man with a gun foolishly enters retired PI Mike Stranahan's house with bad intentions and ends up fatally gored by a taxidermied blue marlin. Now, the laid-back Stranahan needs to figure out who wants him dead and why. As he tries to sort out the mystery, more wild and crazy things happen.

Skinny dip: a novel. By Carl Hiaasen. Alfred A. Knopf, 2004. 368 p. (Skink novels (Carl Hiaasen), 5)
ISBN 9780375411083
1. Former police 2. Married women 3. Marine scientists 4. Marine biologists 5. Married people 6. Everglades, Florida 7. Florida 8. Thrillers and suspense 9. Satirical fiction
LC 2004044106

Doctoring water samples to help his corrupt agribusiness employer continue illegal dumping in the Everglades, biologist Chaz Perrone attempts to murder his wife, who has figured out his scam and who survives to plot her husband's downfall.

"The squirm-inducing mayhem that follows in this sometimes side-splitting novel almost makes you feel sorry for Chaz. It has rarely been this much fun to read about the act of revenge. All of the trademark characters and Florida locales are used to maximum effect." —*Library Journal*

Story includes the character Mick Stranahan, who first appeared in Skin tight.

★ **Squeeze** me: a novel. Carl Hiaasen. Alfred A. Knopf, 2020. 352 p.
ISBN 9781524733452
1. Women murder victims 2. Presidents 3. Political intrigue 4. Pythons 5. Blame 6. Palm Beach, Florida 7. Florida 8. Political fiction 9. Satirical fiction 10. Crime fiction
LC 2020018516

LibraryReads Favorites, 2020

When a high-society dowager murdered at the height of Palm Beach's charity gala season is declared a political martyr by the colorful president she supported, a talented wildlife wrangler uncovers the truth amid the discovery of a controversial affair.

"This exuberant elegy for Florida's paved-over paradise performs the near miracle of making us laugh even as we despair." —*Kirkus*

Star Island. Carl Hiaasen. Alfred A. Knopf, 2010. 337 p; (Skink novels (Carl Hiaasen), 6)
ISBN 9780307272584
1. Celebrities 2. Mistaken identity 3. Kidnapping 4. Pop musicians 5. Second chances 6. Florida 7. Mysteries 8. Humorous stories 9. Adult books for young adults
Booklist Editors' Choice: Adult Books for Young Adults, 2010

Ann DeLuisa, body double for drug-addled pop star Cherry Pye, is kidnapped by an obsessed paparazzo, and Cherry's entourage must rescue her while keeping her existence a secret from Cherry's public—and from Cherry herself.

"Trying to follow the plot, which involves a supporting cast of crooked politicians and predatory developers, is a little like walking a puppy. But the outlandish events soar on the exuberance of Hiaasen's manic style, a canny blend of lunatic farce and savage satire." —*New York Times Book Review*

Strip tease: a novel. Carl Hiaasen. A. A. Knopf, 1993. 353 p.
ISBN 9780679419815
1. Politicians 2. Stripteasers 3. Extortion 4. Sugar industry and trade 5. Sugar industry and trade — Corrupt practices 6. Florida 7. Humorous stories 8. Books to movies
LC 93012358

A Florida congressman falls for a gorgeous stripper who's also a damsel in distress. In pursuit of this woman, the congressman ripples through the strip club, sugar cane fields in South Florida, and some powerful political careers.

"In among Hiaasen's freaks and obsessives, his corrupters and corrupted, his brain-dead and his frenetically active, the author has dropped a real honest-to-God human being, an appealing young woman named Erin Grant. Her presence, her history and goals, make the cartoon nastiness around her less cartoony and more nasty than in previous Hiaasen novels." —*New York Times Book Review*

Book adapted into a 1996 film called Striptease.

Hibbert, Talia

★ **Act** your age, Eve Brown. Talia Hibbert. Avon Books, 2021. 320 p. (The Brown sisters, 3)
ISBN 9780062941275
1. Bed and breakfast 2. Innkeepers 3. Women cooks 4. Unemployed women 5. Accidents 6. England 7. Contemporary romances 8. Multicultural romances 9. Romantic comedies

When his life is taken over by a purple-haired tornado of a woman named Eve Brown, B&B owner Jacob Wayne tries to fight his attraction to this sunny, chaotic woman who is his natural-born enemy.

"This satisfying conclusion to Hibbert's 'Brown Sisters' trilogy provides a happily ever after for the third Brown sister. Through Jacob and Eve, both characters on the autism spectrum, Hibbert explores themes of self-discovery and belonging with her trademark humor and sensitivity, providing plenty of heat as her characters begin to understand each other." —*Library Journal*

★ **Get** a life, Chloe Brown. Talia Hibbert. Avon Books, 2019. 384 pages (The Brown sisters, 1)
ISBN 9780062941206
1. People with chronic illnesses 2. Repairers 3. Lists 4. Geeks (Computer enthusiasts) 5. Artists 6. England 7. Contemporary romances 8. Multicultural romances 9. Romantic comedies
LibraryReads Favorites, 2019

Emerging from a life-threatening illness, a fiercely organized but unfulfilled computer geek recruits a mysterious artist to help her establish meaning in her life, before finding herself engaged in reckless but thrilling activities.

A **girl** like her. Talia Hibbert. Nixon House, 2018. 296 p; (Ravenswood, 1)
ISBN 9781916404304
1. Single women 2. Veterans 3. Neighbors 4. Villages 5. Ostracism 6. England 7. Contemporary romances 8. Multicultural romances

After years of military service, Evan Miller wants a quiet life. The small town of Ravenswood seems perfect—until he stumbles upon a vicious web of lies with his new neighbour at its centre. Ruth Kabbah is rude, awkward, and—according to everyone in town—bad news.... The more Evan's isolated, eccentric neighbour pushes him away, the more he wants her. Her—and all her secrets.

★ **Take** a hint, Dani Brown. Talia Hibbert. Avon Books, 2020. 320 pages (The Brown sisters, 2)
ISBN 9780062941237
1. Women graduate students 2. Private security services 3. Rugby football 4. Black British 5. Muslim men 6. England 7. Contemporary romances 8. Multicultural romances 9. Romantic comedies
LibraryReads Favorites, 2020; RUSA Reading List Short List, 2021
A young woman who agrees to fake-date her friend after a video of him "rescuing" her from their office building goes viral.
"Hibbert's follow up to Get a Life, Chloe Brown, featuring Dani's sister, is another superb and emotionally rich romance. Grief and turmoil are expertly balanced with hilarious wit, making the story both complex and immensely readable. The characters are vibrant, and their chemistry is scorching. Remarkable." —*Library Journal*

Hicks, Robert
The **widow** of the South. Robert Hicks. Warner Books, 2005. 409 p.
ISBN 9780446500128
1. McGavock, Caroline E. Winder 2. Franklin, Battle of, 1864 3. Plantation owners' spouses 4. Women caregivers 5. Cemetery managers 6. Plantation owners 7. Williamson County (Tenn.) 8. American Civil War era (1861-1865) 9. 1860s 10. Biographical fiction 11. War stories 12. Historical fiction
LC 2005010568
A story based on the true experiences of a Civil War heroine finds Carrie McGavock witnessing the bloodshed of the Battle of Franklin, falling in love with a wounded man, and dedicating her home as a burial site for fallen soldiers.

Higashino, Keigo
★ The **devotion** of suspect X. Keigo Higashino; translated from the Japanese by Alexander O. Smith. St. Martin's Minotaur, 2011. 304 p. (Detective Galileo mysteries, 1)
ISBN 9780312375065
1. Mathematics teachers 2. Abused women 3. Murder 4. Former husbands 5. Murder suspects 6. Japan 7. Mysteries 8. Psychological suspense
LC 2010039022
RUSA Reading List, 2012
Ishigami is a lonely Japanese math teacher infatuated with his next-door neighbor Yasuko, a lovely woman who has killed her deadbeat ex-husband to protect her daughter. Not only does Ishigami help her dispose of the body, he also devises a clever cover story for her when the police begin to investigate. But problems build as the involvement of an old colleague threatens to destabilize both Ishigami's ability to counter every police move and his plans for himself and Yasuko, who begins to break down—and pull away.

Malice. Keigo Higashino; translated by Alexander O. Smith. Minotaur Books, 2014. 276 p. (Kyoichiro Kaga mysteries)
ISBN 9781250035608
1. Detectives 2. Authors, Japanese 3. Police 4. Enemies 5. Strangling 6. Japan 7. 1990s 8. Mysteries 9. Translations
LC 2014019885
LibraryReads Favorites, 2014
When a best-selling Japanese novelist is found murdered the night before he was scheduled to move to another country, police detective Kyochiro Kaga uncovers a deadly game involving the victim's best friend and rival.

"Each time you're convinced Higashino's wrung every possible twist out of his golden-age setup, he comes up with a new one. If you still miss the days of The Murder of Roger Ackroyd, you can't do better than this fleet, inventive retro puzzler." —*Kirkus*
Malice was originally published fourth in the Kyoichiro Kaga mystery series, but is the first to have been translated into English. This translation originally published: London: Little, Brown, 2014. Originally published in Japanese as Akui by Kodansha. Originally published: Tokyo : Kodansha, 2001. Translation from the Japanese.

The **miracles** of the Namiya General Store. Keigo Higashino; translated from the Japanese by Sam Bett. Yen ON, 2019. 314 p.
ISBN 9781975382575
1. Shopkeepers 2. Retail stores 3. Thieves 4. Juvenile delinquents 5. Letter writing 6. Japan 7. Magical realism 8. Translations 9. Adult books for young adults
LC 2019023608
When three delinquents hole up in an abandoned general store after their most recent robbery, to their great surprise, a letter drops through the mail slot in the store's shutter. This seemingly simple request for advice sets the trio on a journey of discovery as, over the course of a single night, they step into the role of the kindhearted former shopkeeper who devoted his waning years to offering thoughtful counsel to his correspondents.
"More than a time travel mystery, the story is a rather earnest tale of human decision-making, and the author is adept at drawing an emotional response from readers. Inventive and always surprising, this book is easy to get drawn into and difficult to put down. An endearing tale about a magical correspondence." —*Kirkus*
Translated from the Japanese.

Newcomer. Keigo Higashino. Minotaur Books, 2018. 320 p. (Kyoichiro Kaga mysteries)
ISBN 9781250067869
1. Murder suspects 2. Detectives 3. Police 4. Secrets 5. Strangling 6. Japan 7. Tokyo, Japan 8. 1990s 9. Mysteries 10. Translations
LibraryReads Favorites, 2018
Newly transferred to a precinct in the Nihonbashi area of Tokyo, Detective Kyochiro Kaga, while investigating the puzzling murder of a woman, soon discovers that nearly all the people living and working in the business district of Nihonbashi are suspects.
Newcomer is the second Kyoichiro Kaga mystery published in English by Minotaur Books. It was originally published in Japanese as Shinzanmono in 2009, the seventh book in the Police Detective Kaga series.
Translated from the Japanese by Giles Murray.

Higgins, C. A.
Lightless. C.A. Higgins. Del Rey, 2015. 304 p. (Lightless, 1)
ISBN 9780553394429
1. Women engineers 2. Terrorists 3. Space travelers 4. Space vehicles 5. Space opera 6. Hard science fiction 7. Science fiction
LC 2014037514
A female engineer, Althea, fights for her life when her small space-craft is invaded by two mysterious terrorists on a dark mission, one of whom is a revolutionary harboring deep secrets.
"A suspenseful, emotional story that asks plenty of big questions about identity and freedom." —*Kirkus*

Higgins, George V.
The **friends** of Eddie Coyle. George Higgins. Knopf, 1972. 183 p.
ISBN 9780394473277

1. Criminals 2. Swindlers and swindling 3. Informers 4. Assassins 5. Illegal arms transfers 6. Massachusetts 7. Boston, Massachusetts 8. Thrillers and suspense

LC 71163134

A crime classic about gunrunner Eddie Coyle and his dangerous relations with bank robber Jimmy Scalisi, a cop named Foley, and Dillon, a bartending hitman.

Higgins, Jack

Confessional. Jack Higgins. Stein and Day, 1985. 278p. (Liam Devlin thrillers, 3)

ISBN 9780812830255

1. John Paul 2. Undercover operations 3. Assassins 4. Spies 5. Impostors 6. Intelligence service 7. Ukraine 8. Thrillers and suspense 9. War stories 10. Spy fiction

LC 84040777

"This novel is tense. It is riveting. It is what a thriller should be. If Mr. Higgins's prose is dull and his understanding of humanity shallow, it may only be because good prose and a deeper understanding would inhibit the race to the plot's final twist." —*New York Times Book Review*

Harry Patterson writing as Jack Higgins.

The **eagle** has flown. Jack Higgins. Simon and Schuster 1991. 335 p. (Liam Devlin thrillers, 4)

ISBN 9780330321990

1. Churchill, Winston 2. Search and rescue operations 3. Betrayal 4. World War II 5. Secret service 6. Hostage taking 7. Norfolk, England 8. 1940s 9. War stories 10. Historical thrillers

LC 91004368

IRA assassin Liam Devlin returns to Britain in an attempt to effect the escape of German soldier Kurt Steiner from the Tower of London and return with him to Berlin.

"Mr. Higgins is an expert storyteller, and he goes about The Eagle Has Flown with typical gusto. Everything is carefully arranged, little pieces fitting into other little pieces to form an action-packed mosaic." —*New York Times Book Review*

Harry Patterson writing as Jack Higgins.

The **eagle** has landed. Jack Higgins. Holt, Rinehart and Winston, 1975. 352 p. (Liam Devlin thrillers, 1)

ISBN 9780030137464

1. Churchill, Winston 2. Undercover operations 3. Hostage taking 4. World War II 5. Secret service 6. Devlin, Liam (Fictitious character) 7. Norfolk, England 8. 1940s 9. War stories 10. Historical thrillers 11. Books to movies

LC 74015475

Combines fact and speculation in a fictionalized reconstruction of the events leading up to and including the November 1943 mission of a small force of German paratroopers landed in Britain to capture Prime Minister Winston Churchill

"There are elements of heroism, duplicity, and heavy irony, plus considerable bloodshed, in this action-oriented yarn." —*Christian Science Monitor*

This novel was made into the 1976 film The Eagle Has Landed directed by John Struges and starring Michael Caine, Donald Sutherland, and Robert Duvall.

Harry Patterson writing as Jack Higgins.

Eye of the storm. Jack Higgins. G. P. Putnam's Sons 1992. 320 p. (Sean Dillon thrillers, 1)

ISBN 9780399137587

1. Major, John 2. Attempted assassination 3. International intrigue 4. Undercover operations 5. Secret service 6. Spies 7. London, England 8. Thrillers and suspense 9. Spy fiction 10. Political thrillers

LC 91046736

Elusive master terrorist Sean Dillon reemerges during the Gulf War when Saddam Hussein hires him to assassinate Margaret Thatcher, and only Martin Brosnan can stop him.

"Early in 1991, while the Gulf war is in full bloom, operatives of Saddam Hussein hire legendary terrorist Sean Dillon to take the war to the enemy. A master of disguise and subterfuge, Dillon began his career with the IRA, earning the enmity of Liam Devlin—the unforgettable antihero of The Eagle Has Landed, who makes a featured appearance here—and of Martin Brosnan, an American Special Forces hero and IRA member turned college professor. After Dillon's attempt to assassinate former Prime Minster Margaret Thatcher during a visit to France fails, he decides to go after her successor John Major.... Although readers can be sure that Dillon's scheme will be foiled, fun remains in the how and why." —*Publishers Weekly*

Harry Patterson writing as Jack Higgins.

Also published under the title: Midnight man.

Touch the devil. Jack Higgins. Stein and Day 1982. 251 p. (Liam Devlin thrillers, 2)

ISBN 9780007283316

1. Kidnapping 2. International intrigue 3. Spies 4. Terrorism 5. Secret service 6. Ireland 7. War stories 8. Spy fiction 9. Thrillers and suspense

LC 82040080

Retired agent Liam Devlin is forced to undertake a deadly mission that involves British and Soviet intelligence, hired killer Martin Brosnan, and combat photographer Anne-Marie Audin.

Harry Patterson writing as Jack Higgins.

Higgins, Kristan

Always the last to know. Kristan Higgins. Berkley, 2020. 400 pages

ISBN 9780593199855

1. Husband and wife 2. Mothers and daughters 3. People who have had strokes 4. Sisters 5. Secrets 6. Connecticut 7. Multiple perspectives 8. Relationship fiction

LC 2019050000

After their father suffers a stroke, two sisters must return home and deal with the paths both their lives have taken as well as their parents' relationship.

"The plot, told in shifting perspectives from the three women, expertly intertwines each of their dilemmas and moves along briskly thanks to the charming, snappy prose. Most importantly, Higgins excels at creating multidimensional, sympathetic characters, an ability that is on full display throughout." —*Publishers Weekly*

★ The **best** man. Kristan Higgins. HQN, 2013. 432 p. (Blue Heron romances, 1)

ISBN 9780373777921

1. Homecomings 2. Jilted women 3. Police chiefs 4. Interpersonal attraction 5. Wineries 6. New York (State) 7. Contemporary romances

Library Journal Best Books, 2013

Finally ready to return to the Blue Heron Winery, her family's vineyard, and face her past, Faith Holland is drawn to Levi Cooper, the local police chief and best friend of her former fiancé, but has a hard time forgetting his role in ruining her wedding years ago.

★ **Life** and other inconveniences. Kristan Higgins. Berkley, 2019. 448 p.

ISBN 9780451489425

1. Grandmother and adult child 2. Single mothers 3. Reconciliation 4. Terminal illness 5. Family relationships 6. Relationship fiction 7. Multiple perspectives
LibraryReads Favorites, 2019

A blue-blood grandmother and her black-sheep granddaughter discover they are truly two sides of the same coin.

Now that you mention it. Kristan Higgins. HQN Books, 2017. 406 p.
ISBN 9781335915276
1. Homecomings 2. Family problems 3. Near-death experience 4. Hometowns 5. Reconciliation 6. Maine 7. Boston, Massachusetts 8. Relationship fiction
RITA Award, 2018

Returning to her hometown in the hopes of reconciling with her estranged family, a woman who recently survived a brush with death makes discoveries with the potential to heal the rift or permanently separate her from her surviving relatives.

★ **Pack** up the moon. Kristan Higgins. Berkley, 2021. 480 p.
ISBN 9780593335369
1. Husband and wife 2. Women with terminal illnesses 3. People with autism 4. Letter writing 5. Grief 6. Relationship fiction
LC 2020042953

When his wife leaves him letters, one for every month in the year after her death, Joshua is led on a journey of pain, anger and denial that eventually makes room for laughter and new relationships.

"Perfect pacing and plotting lift Higgins's masterly latest. This is going to break (and restore) plenty of hearts." —*Publishers Weekly*

Highsmith, Patricia

The **Highsmith** reader: selected novels and short stories. Patricia Highsmith; edited with an introduction by Joan Schenkar. W. W. Norton & Co, 2010. Xvi, 644 p.
ISBN 9780393080131
1. Short stories 2. Psychological suspense
LC 2010034589

Features key works in the psychological thriller genre from the author of The Talented Mr. Ripley, including Strangers on a Train which was made into a legendary Alfred Hitchcock film and The Price of Salt.

★ The **talented** Mr. Ripley. Patricia Highsmith. Vintage Books 1992. 295 p. (Ripley novels, 1)
ISBN 9780679742296
1. Americans in Italy 2. Psychopaths 3. Impostors 4. Murderers 5. Ripley, Tom (Fictitious character) 6. Italy 7. Psychological suspense 8. Thrillers and suspense 9. Modern classics
LC 92053511

In order to convince his son to come home, Herbert Greenleaf, a rich shipbuilder, sends Tom Ripley to Italy, but is unaware of his son's friend's criminal activities.

"The virtuosity here—more than anything else—will pin you to the page." —*Kirkus*
Originally published: New York : Coward-McCann, 1955.

Hijuelos, Oscar

Beautiful Maria of my soul. Oscar Hijuelos. HarperCollins, 2010. 352 p.
ISBN 9781401323349
1. First loves 2. Cuban American women 3. Cubans in the United States 4. Reminiscing in old age 5. Man-woman relationships 6. New York City 7. 1950s 8. Literary fiction
Booklist Editors' Choice, 2010

In a part sequel and part retelling of "The Mambo Kings Play Songs of Love," the inspiration for the Mambo King's biggest hit, Maria, now 60 years old, reminisces about her days and nights in Havana, offering a completely different perspective on the Mambo Kings' story.

"The rare sequel that can be enjoyed independently of the original work or as a complement to it.... There's a simmering backdrop of revolution in the middle of the book that provides the story with historical heft. And, in the novel's bold ending, Hijuelos seamlessly welds fact and fiction, with the author himself making an appearance to discuss his books with the characters that inhabit them." —*Cleveland Plain Dealer*
Companion to The Mambo Kings Play Songs of Love

★ The **mambo** kings play songs of love: a novel. Oscar Hijuelos. Farrar, Straus, Giroux, 1989. 407 p.
ISBN 9780374201258
1. Cubans in the United States 2. Reminiscing in old age 3. Man-woman relationships 4. First loves 5. Commitment (Psychology) 6. New York City 7. 1950s 8. Literary fiction 9. Books to movies
LC 89001248
Pulitzer Prize for Fiction, 1990; National Book Critics Circle Award for Fiction finalist, 1989; National Book Award for Fiction finalist, 1989

"The novel alternates crisp narrative with opulent musings—the language of everyday and the language of longing. When Mr. Hijuelos falters, as from time to time he does, it's through an excess of self-consciousness: he strives too hard for all-encompassing description or grows distant and dutiful in an effort to get period details just right." —*New York Times Book Review*
The Mambo Kings Play Songs of Love inspired the movie The Mambo Kings in 1992.

Twain & Stanley enter paradise. Oscar Hijuelos. Grand Central Pub, 2015. 592 p.
ISBN 9781455561490
1. Twain, Mark 2. Male friendship 3. Voyages and travels 4. Journalists 5. Intellectual life 6. Women artists 7. United States 8. Cuba 9. 19th century 10. Historical fiction 11. Biographical fiction 12. Diary novels
Booklist Editors' Choice, 2015

Chronicles the sojourn of journalist-explorer Henry Stanley; his wife, the painter Dorothy Tennant; and Mark Twain, Stanley's longtime friend, as they head for Cuba in search of Stanley's father.

Hilderbrand, Elin

★ **28** summers. Elin Hilderbrand. Little Brown & Co, 2020. 432 pages
ISBN 9780316420044
1. Summer 2. Weekends 3. Extramarital affairs 4. Sick mothers 5. Family secrets 6. Nantucket, Massachusetts 7. 20th century 8. 21st century 9. Love stories 10. Relationship fiction

Presents a tale inspired by the film, Same Time Next Year, that follows a man's discovery of his mother's long-term relationship with the husband of a Presidential frontrunner.

"In her 25th novel, Hilderbrand gets everything right and leaves her ardent fans hungry for No. 26. Oh for the days when life was a picnic on the beach: Hilderbrand sets the gold standard in escapist fiction."—*Kirkus*

The **perfect** couple. Elin Hilderbrand. Little Brown & Co, 2018. 471 p.
ISBN 9780316375269
1. Weddings 2. Rich families 3. Couples 4. Vacation homes 5. Summer 6. Massachusetts 7. Nantucket, Massachusetts 8. Mysteries 9. Relationship fiction

When a bride-to-be is found dead in the harbor, Chief of Police Ed Kapenash searches for the killer within her own wedding party.

★ **Summer** of '69. Elin Hilderbrand. Little Brown & Co, 2019. 432 p.
ISBN 9780316420013
1. Family secrets 2. Siblings 3. Vietnam War, 1961-1975 4. Families 5. Social change 6. Nantucket, Massachusetts 7. 1960s 8. Historical fiction 9. Relationship fiction

As a man flies to the moon and Ted Kennedy sinks a car in Chappaquiddick, four siblings experience the drama, intrigue and upheaval along with the rest of the country during the summer of 1969.

★ **Troubles** in paradise. Elin Hilderbrand. Little, Brown and Company, 2020. 272 p. (Paradise (Elin Hilderbrand), 3)
ISBN 9780316435581
1. Widows 2. Island life 3. Adult children 4. Coping in women 5. Mothers and sons 6. West Indies 7. Virgin Islands of the United States 8. Relationship fiction

As drama unfolds around her and her family after the death of her husband, who was leading a double life, Irene Steele gets some help from a mysterious source and a new beginning in the paradise of St. John after the truth is finally revealed.

"Nobody sets a scene like Hilderbrand, and readers will relish the satisfying conclusion to this vividly escapist trilogy that is as aspirational as it is emotional." —*Booklist*

★ **What** happens in paradise: a novel. Elin Hilderbrand. Little Brown & Co, 2019. Vii, 323 pages; (Paradise (Elin Hilderbrand), 2)
ISBN 9780316435574
1. Widows 2. Adult children 3. Secrets 4. Truth 5. Coping in women 6. West Indies 7. Virgin Islands of the United States 8. Relationship fiction

LC 2019943388
A follow-up to Winter in Paradise finds Irene and her sons returning to St. John to investigate her late husband's secret double life before uncovering surprising truths about their own realities and futures.

★ **Winter** in paradise: a novel. Elin Hilderbrand. Little Brown & Co, 2018. Viii, 310 pages; (Paradise (Elin Hilderbrand), 1)
ISBN 9780316435512
1. Married people and secrets 2. Extramarital affairs 3. Coping in women 4. Secrets 5. Betrayal 6. West Indies 7. Virgin Islands of the United States 8. Relationship fiction

A suburban wife confronts the loss of everything at the same time her husband is found dead on the beaches of St. John, where he harbored a secret second family.

"As usual, Hilderbrand's characters are as familiar as old friends, and her smooth prose is as tender and welcoming...Readers will be happy to lose themselves in paradise while getting to know these irresistible new characters." —*Publishers Weekly Annex*

Hill Gumbao, Toni

The **good** suicides: a thriller. Antonio Hill; translation by Laura McGloughlin. Crown Publishers, 2014. 338 pages (Inspector Hector Salgado mysteries, 2)
ISBN 9780770435905
1. Suicide victims 2. Suicide investigation 3. Business — Corrupt practices 4. Cold cases (Criminal investigation) 5. Detectives 6. Barcelona, Spain 7. Mysteries 8. Translations

LC 2013019691
A follow-up to The Summer of Dead Toys finds Inspector Salgado infiltrating the icy personal lives of a group of young executives who committed suicide after returning from a team-building retreat and receiving grisly e-mail photos.

"The characters are intriguingly complex and the author skillfully pulls the rug out with a flourish at the end." —*Library Journal*

Originally published in Spanish as Los Buenos Suicidas in June 2012 by Random House Mondadori.

This translation originally published, in slightly different form, in Great Britain by Doubleday, an imprint of Transworld Publishers, a division of Random House, Inc, London, in 2013.

The **summer** of dead toys. Antonio Hill. Doubleday, 2012. 320 p. (Inspector Hector Salgado mysteries, 1)
ISBN 9780857520821
1. Falls (Accidents) 2. Human trafficking 3. Elite (Social sciences) 4. Corruption 5. Witnesses 6. Spain 7. Barcelona, Spain 8. Mysteries 9. Translations

Inspector Hector Salgado is sent to investigate the death of a high society Barcelona teenager and manages to uncover some dangerous secrets from among the city's most powerful families.

Translated from the Spanish by Laura McGlouglin.

Translation of El verano de los juguetes muertos, originally published Barcelona : Debolsillo, 2011.

Hill, Donna

★ **Confessions** in B-flat. Donna Hill. Entangled Sideways, 2020. 400 p.
ISBN 9781640638297
1. Civil rights workers 2. Women poets 3. African Americans — Civil rights 4. Civil Rights Movement 5. Ideology 6. Harlem, New York City 7. New York City 8. 1960s 9. Historical romances 10. Multicultural romances 11. African American fiction

Follows the 1964 Civil Rights-era relationship between a passive-resistance protege of Martin Luther King, Jr. and a Harlem black culture supporter of Malcolm X.

"Meticulous research, achingly real characters, and convincing romance power this enthralling tale, which ultimately lands on a message of love and compromise." —*Publishers Weekly*

Hill, Edwin J.

Little comfort. Edwin Hill. Kensington Books, 2018. 343 p. (Hester Thursby novels, 1)
ISBN 9781496715906
1. Librarians 2. Women private investigators 3. Swindlers and swindling 4. Missing men 5. Rich people 6. Boston, Massachusetts 7. Mysteries

Harvard librarian Hester Thursby must track down charismatic—and deadly—con man Sam Blaine before he bilks another widow out of her life savings.

Hill, Joe

The **Fireman:** a novel. Joe Hill. William Morrow, 2016. 608 p.
ISBN 9780062200631
1. Spontaneous combustion 2. End of the world 3. Plague 4. Fires 5. Spores 6. New Hampshire 7. Apocalyptic fiction 8. Horror 9. Adult books for young adults

LC 2015042212
Goodreads Choice Award, 2016; LibraryReads Favorites, 2016; Locus Award for Dark Fantasy-Horror Novel, 2017; RUSA Reading List Short List, 2017

When a bizarre virulent plague breaks out in the world's major cities, causing victims to spontaneously combust, a dedicated nurse resolves to urvive until her baby is born and receives protection from a mysterious nfected man who uses his fire symptoms to help others.

"This is a long book, but with a curiously ominous tone set from the very first line, a brisk pace throughout, and dozens of detailed action scenes, readers will be hard-pressed to stop turning the pages." —*Booklist*

★ **Full** throttle: stories. Joe Hill. William Morrow, 2019. 480 p.
ISBN 9780062200679
1. Horror 2. Short stories

LC 2019014759

New York Times Notable Book, 2019

Dissects timeless human struggles in thirteen relentless tales of supernatural suspense.

Heart-shaped box. Joe Hill. William Morrow, 2007. 384 p.
ISBN 9780061147937
1. Ghosts 2. Rock musicians 3. Supernatural 4. Secrets 5. Man-woman relationships 6. Ghost stories 7. Horror 8. Adult books for young adults

LC 2006046548

Bram Stoker Award for Best First Novel, 2007; Locus Award for First Novel, 2008; Thriller Award for Best First Novel, 2008; RUSA Reading List, 2008

A collector of obscure and macabre artifacts, unscrupulous metal band musician Judas Coyne is unable to resist purchasing a ghost over the Internet, which turns out to be the vengeful spirit of his late girlfriend's stepfather.

"The author has created a wild, mesmerizing, perversely witty tale of horror. In a book much too smart to sound like the work of a neophyte, he builds character invitingly and plants an otherworldly surprise around every corner." —*New York Times*

With a new introduction by the author—Back cover.

Horns. Joe Hill. William Morrow & Co, 2010. 384 p.
ISBN 9780061147951
1. Lovers — Death 2. Transformations (Magic) 3. Revenge 4. Grief in men 5. Devil 6. New Hampshire 7. Horror 8. Books to movies

After his childhood sweetheart is brutally killed and suspicion falls on him, Ig Parrish goes on a drinking binge and wakes up with horns on his head, hate in his heart, and an incredible new power which he uses in the name of vengeance.

"The strange thing about Horns is that its opening scenes aren't all that strange. Its author, Joe Hill, is able to make Ig's problem seem like the most natural thing in the world. Mr. Hill writes with such palpable enthusiasm that he has no trouble hooking readers.... [He] is able to combine intrigue, editorializing, impassioned romance and even fiery theological debate in one well-told story." —*New York Times*

Title adapted into a film by the same name (2013).

★ **NOS4A2**. Joe Hill. William Morrow & Co, 2013. 384 p.
ISBN 9780062200570
1. Secret places 2. Boy kidnapping victims 3. Transformations, Magic 4. Monsters 5. Christmas 6. Horror 7. Books to TV 8. Adult books for young adults
Library Journal Best Books, 2013; School Library Journal Best Books: Best Adult Books 4 Teens, 2013

When Charles Talent Manx, an unstoppable monster who transforms children into his own terrifying likeness, kidnaps her son, Victoria McQueen, the only person to ever escape his unmitigated evil, must engage in a life-and-death battle of wills to get her son back.

Strange weather: four short novels. Joe Hill. William Morrow & Co, 2017. 432 pages : Illustration
ISBN 9780062663115
1. Supernatural 2. Paranormal phenomena 3. Horror 4. Short stories

Bram Stoker Award for Best Fiction Collection, 2017; Booklist Editors' Choice, 2017; Librarians' Choice (Australia), 2017; LibraryReads Favorites, 2017

"Hill is back with a collection of four short novels that each showcases his talent for mining modern lives for fear." —*Booklist*

Hill, Lawrence

Someone knows my name: a novel. Lawrence Hill. W.W. Norton & Co, 2007. 384 p.
ISBN 9780393065787
1. Child kidnapping victims 2. Slavery 3. African American loyalists (United States history) 4. Black Canadian women 5. Enslaved girls 6. Nova Scotia 7. United States 8. Revolutionary America (1775-1783) 9. 18th century 10. Historical fiction 11. Literary fiction 12. Black Canadian fiction 13. Adult books for young adults
Commonwealth Writers' Prize for Best Book, 2008; Commonwealth Writers' Prize, Caribbean and Canada: Best Book, 2008; Evergreen Award (Ontario), 2008; Rogers Writers' Trust Fiction Prize, 2007; School Library Journal Best Books: Best Adult Books 4 Teens, 2008

Kidnapped at the age of 11 by British slavers, Aminata survives the Middle Passage and is reunited in South Carolina with Chekura, a boy from a village near hers. Her story gets entwined with his, and with those of her owners: nasty indigo producer Robinson Appleby and, later, Jewish duty inspector Solomon Lindo. During her long life of struggle, she does what she can to free herself and others from slavery, including learning to read and teaching others to, and befriending anyone who can help her, black or white.

"What makes this novel extraordinary is Hill's ability to transcend the facts—to make something magical out of them. Despite the unpalatable subject matter, he compels our attention and manages to delight. His Aminata is a heroic figure, a little larger than life, residing within and outside of history. You can never forget this character. She embeds herself in your heart." —*Toronto Star*

Originally published as The Book of Negroes in Canada (Toronto : HarperCollins, 2007).

Hill, Nathan

The **nix:** a novel. Nathan Hill. Knopf, 2016. 512 p.
ISBN 9781101946619
1. Family secrets 2. Mothers and sons 3. Self-fulfillment 4. Women criminals 5. Loss (Psychology) 6. 1960s 7. 2010s 8. Literary fiction 9. Multiple perspectives

LC 2015046704

ALA Notable Book, 2017; Booklist Editors' Choice, 2016; Library Journal Best Books, 2016; Los Angeles Times Art Seidenbaum Award for First Fiction, 2016; New York Times Notable Book, 2016

Astonished to see the mother who abandoned him in childhood throwing rocks at a presidential candidate, a bored college professor struggles to reconcile the radical media depictions of his mother with his small-town memories and decides to draw her out by penning a tell-all biography.

"As more subplots build, including the mesmerizing tale of young Samuels relationships with twins fearless Bishop and violin prodigy Bethany, Hill takes aim at hypocrisy, greed, misogyny, addiction, and vengeance with edgy humor and deep empathy." —*Booklist*

Hill, Reginald

The **woodcutter:** a novel. Reginald Hill. Harper, 2011. 528 p.
ISBN 9780062060747

1. Innocence (Law) 2. Betrayal 3. Family secrets 4. Revenge 5. Former convicts 6. Cumbria, England 7. England 8. Psychological suspense 9. Thrillers and suspense

LC 2010053608

"Near the end, a character refers to the fate of the dreadful, drab English. There's nothing drab about this dark and compelling novel, although some of its characters are dreadful human beings." —*Kirkus*

Originally published: London: HarperCollins, 2010.

Hill, Ruth Beebe

Hanta Yo. Ruth Beebe Hill. Doubleday, 1979. 834 p.

ISBN 9780385135542

1. Dakota Indians 2. Dakota men 3. Male friendship 4. Indians of North America 5. 18th century 6. 19th century 7. Family sagas 8. Historical fiction

LC 77016922

Western Heritage Award for Outstanding Western Novel, 1980

"The practice of using the multi-generational family story to reflect changing times and/or historical events is almost a genre unto itself. This is such a novel.... The historical accuracy, linguistic acrobatics, and ethnological acuity do not limit the book's appeal. A superb style transcends the few minor flaws, and despite the scholarly impression given by the introduction, chronology notes, and glossaries, this book is first and foremost a well-written story." —*Library Journal*

Hill, Susan

The **pure** in heart: a Simon Serrailler crime novel. Susan Hill. Overlook Press, 2007. 370 p; (Simon Serrailler crime novels, 2)

ISBN 9781585679287

1. Kidnapping investigation 2. Stalking 3. Police 4. Detectives 5. Nine-year-old boys 6. England 7. Mysteries 8. Police procedurals

Detective Chief Inspector Simon Serrailler investigates the kidnapping of a young boy, a case that is influenced by a critically ill disabled woman and an ex-con who is struggling to stay honest.

"A nine-year-old boy is kidnapped in broad daylight while waiting for his school ride outside his home in the British cathedral town of Lafferton, and the case falls squarely in the lap of Detective Chief Inspector Serrailler. It's a copper's worst nightmarebroken and grieving parents, intense media interest, and extreme pressure from the top police brass to solve the case yesterday. But there are few leads and no apparent motive, and as the days go by and the child isn't found, hope drains away. Although the case hits Simon and his team exceptionally hard, he has other problems to deal with.... This is realistic, gritty, and gut-wrenching crime fiction, but it's also a poignant and thoughtful character study." —*Booklist*

Originally published: London : Chatto & Windus, 2005.

The **shadows** in the street: a Simon Serrailler mystery. Susan Hill. Overlook, 2010. 372 p. (Simon Serrailler crime novels, 5)

ISBN 9781590204085

1. Missing women 2. Murder investigation 3. Women murder victims 4. Missing persons investigation 5. Crimes against prostitutes 6. England 7. Scotland 8. Mysteries 9. Psychological suspense 10. Police procedurals

Simon Serrailler has just wrapped up a particularly exhausting and difficult case and is on sabbatical on a far-flung Scottish island when he is called back to Lafferton by the Chief Constable. Two local prostitutes have been found strangled. When the wife of the St. Michael's Cathedral Dean goes missing and then another respectable woman is taken on her way to work, the townspeople grow angry and afraid. Serrailler is in the greatest danger of his life.

Simultaneously published in the UK: London : Chatto & Windus, 2010.

Hillerman, Tony

The **shape** shifter. Tony Hillerman. Harper Collins, 2006. 288 p. (Joe Leaphorn and Jim Chee mysteries, 18)

ISBN 9780060563455

1. Native American men 2. Former police 3. Criminal investigation 4. Murder investigation 5. Navajo Indians 6. New Mexico 7. Mysteries 8. Police procedurals

LC 2005052602

Spur Award for Best Western Novel (Short Novel), 2007

Retired Police Lieutenant Joe Leaphorn returns to put together the clues from his last unsolved case—a mystery involving the disappearance of a priceless Navajo rug—without the help of Jim Chee and Bernie Manuelito, who are on their honeymoon.

"Only Hillerman could so masterfully connect such disparate elements as an ancient cursed weaving, two stolen buckets of pion sap and the Vietnam War. The conclusion is sure to startle longtime fans of this acclaimed mystery series." —*Publishers Weekly*

The **sinister** pig. Tony Hillerman. HarperCollins, 2003. 304 p. (Joe Leaphorn and Jim Chee mysteries, 16)

ISBN 9780060194437

1. Smuggling 2. Native American men 3. Former police 4. Detectives 5. Tribal police 6. New Mexico 7. Dickens, Charles 8. Police procedurals 9. Adult books for young adults

LC 2003042316

Discovering a link between the woman he loves and a political murder and a twisted conspiracy, Navajo tribal police Sergeant Chee joins a map-wielding Joe Leaphorn on the heels of a fleeing Washington power broker.

"With his usual up-front approach to issues concerning Native Americans such as endlessly overlapping jurisdictions, Hillerman delivers a masterful tale that both entertains and educates." —*Publishers Weekly*

The **wailing** wind. Tony Hillerman. HarperCollins, 2002. 224 p. (Joe Leaphorn and Jim Chee mysteries, 15)

ISBN 9780060194444

1. Navajo shamans 2. Murder suspects 3. Police 4. Manuelito, Bernadette (Fictitious character) 5. Tribal police 6. New Mexico 7. Mysteries 8. Police procedurals 9. Adult books for young adults

LC 2001051734

The mishandling of a murder scene places Navajo Tribal Police sergeant Jim Chee on the bad side of the FBI and brings ex-lieutenant Joe Leaphorn out of retirement into an old crime he hoped to forget involving an obsessive love and memories of a missing woman.

"Hillerman is never better than when he is circling a puzzle from various angles, playing with the perceptions of his detectives as well as the reader's." —*New York Times Book Review*

Hilton, James

★ **Good-bye,** Mr. Chips. James Hilton. Little, Brown, and Co, 2004. 132 p.

ISBN 9780316010139

1. Boarding schools 2. Boys' schools 3. Teachers 4. England 5. Classics 6. Books to TV 7. Books to movies

Depicts the life of Mr. Chipping, a gentle English schoolmaster known familiarly to the schoolboys at Brookfield as Mr. Chips.

★ **Lost** horizon: a novel. James Hilton. Perennial, 2004. 241 p.
ISBN 9780060594527
1. Utopias 2. Survival (after airplane accidents, shipwrecks, etc.)
3. Shangri-La (Imaginary place) 4. Himalaya Mountains region
5. Adventure stories 6. Classics 7. Books to movies
Following a plane crash in the Himalayan mountains, a lost group of Englishmen and Americans stumble upon the dream-like, utopian world of Shangri-La, where life is eternal and civilization refined.
Originally published: New York : W. Morrow & Co, 1933.

Random harvest. James Hilton. Carroll and Graf, 1985. 326 p.
ISBN 9780818841255
1. Men with amnesia 2. Politicians 3. World War I veterans 4. England
5. Love stories 6. Books to movies
Charles Rainier, a prosperous Briton, loses his memory as a result of shellshock in the First World War.

Hilton, L. S.
Maestra. L.S. Hilton. Penguin Group USA, 2016. 320 p. (Maestra novels, 1)
ISBN 9780399184260
1. Femmes fatales 2. Women swindlers 3. Art industry and trade
4. Murder 5. Sexuality 6. London, England 7. Crime fiction 8. Erotic fiction
Maestra is the beginning of a razor-sharp trilogy that introduces the darkly irresistible Judith Rashleigh, a femme fatale for the ages whose vulnerability and ruthlessness will keep you guessing until the last page.
"With the book already optioned for a movie, interest will be high for this scandalous, thrilling tour through Europe and the art world." —*Library Journal*

Hirahara, Naomi
★ **Clark** and Division. Naomi Hirahara. Soho Crime, 2021. 312 p.
ISBN 9781641292498
1. Japanese American families 2. Japanese Americans — Forced removal and incarceration, 1942-1945 3. Moving to a new city 4. Young women 5. Sisters — Death 6. Chicago, Illinois 7. Second World War era (1939-1945) 8. Historical mysteries
LC 2021000576
Released from a Japanese internment camp in 1944, Aki Ito moves to Chicago to be with her sister, Rose, only to lose her in subway train accident on the even of their reunion and vows to learn what really happened.
"Hirahara does a masterly job of incorporating extensive historical research into an emotionally compelling story. Highly recommended for readers who enjoy high-quality historical fiction with well-drawn characters and an engrossing plot." —*Library Journal*

Ho, Lauren
Last Tang standing. Lauren Ho. Putnam Pub Group, 2020. 368 pages
ISBN 9780593187814
1. Women lawyers 2. Single women 3. Expectation (Psychology) 4. Thirties (Age) 5. Coworkers 6. Singapore 7. Relationship fiction 8. Chick lit
Crazy Rich Asians meets Bridget Jones's Diary in this funny and irresistible debut novel about the pursuit of happiness, surviving one's thirties intact, and opening oneself up to love.
"A lush portrayal of Singapore life filled with vibrant characters and a lovable leading lady readers will root for." —*Kirkus*

Hoang, Helen
★ The **bride** test. Helen Hoang. Jove, 2019. 300 p. (Kiss quotient novels, 2)
ISBN 9780451490827
1. Romantic love 2. People with autism 3. Arranged marriage
4. Multiracial women 5. Vietnamese Americans 6. California
7. Multicultural romances 8. Treat, Mary
LC 2018053953
Library Journal Best Books, 2019; LibraryReads Favorites, 2019; Loan Stars Favourites, 2019
Believing he cannot experience big emotions—like love, or grief, Khai Diep avoids relationships, until his mother travels to Vietnam and returns with Esme Tran.

★ The **heart** principle. Helen Hoang. Berkley, 2021. 320 p. (Kiss quotient novels, 3)
ISBN 9780593197837
1. Burn out (Psychology) 2. Women violinists 3. Romantic love
4. Expectation (Psychology) 5. Couples 6. Multicultural romances
7. Contemporary romances
LC 2021016848
When she suddenly loses her ability to play the violin, Anna Sun must learn to listen to her heart and falls in love with a man her parents disapprove of, forcing her to choose between meeting expectations and finding happiness in who she really is.
"Readers shouldn't expect a typical rom-com, but many will still swoon for this sensitive love story." —*Publishers Weekly*

★ The **kiss** quotient. Helen Hoang. Berkley/Jove, 2018. 336 p. (Kiss quotient novels, 1)
ISBN 9780451490803
1. People with Asperger's syndrome 2. Dating (Social customs)
3. Women mathematicians 4. Escort services (Prostitution) 5. Autism
6. Contemporary romances 7. Erotic romances
LC 2017061141
Goodreads Choice Award, 2018; Librarians' Choice (Australia), 2018; LibraryReads Favorites, 2018; RUSA Reading List Short List, 2019
A 30-year-old math whiz with Asperger's tries to make her love life as rich as her career by hiring an escort to help her with her lack of knowledge and experience in the dating department.
"A compulsively readable erotic romance that is equal parts sugar and spice. Highly recommended." —*Library Journal*

Hobson, Brandon
★ The **removed**: a novel. Brandon Hobson. Ecco, 2021. 288 pages
ISBN 9780062997548
1. Cherokee Indians 2. Native American families 3. Grief 4. Holidays
5. Foster children 6. Oklahoma 7. Literary fiction 8. Multiple perspectives
LC 2020040868
A Cherokee family takes in a remarkable foster child on the eve of the Cherokee National Holiday and anniversary of a loved one's death.
"Hobson is a master storyteller and illustrates in gently poetic prose how for many Native Americans the line between this world and the next isn't so sharp." —*Publishers Weekly*

Hockman, Angie
Shipped. Angie Hockman. Gallery Books, 2021. 336 p.
ISBN 9781982151591

1. Women professional employees 2. Workaholics 3. Cruise ships 4. Marketing 5. Enemies 6. Galapagos Islands 7. Seattle, Washington 8. Contemporary romances 9. Romantic comedies

LibraryReads Favorites, 2021

Between taking night classes for her MBA and her demanding day job at a cruise line, marketing manager Henley Evans barely has time for herself, let alone family, friends, or dating. But when she's shortlisted for the promotion of her dreams, all her sacrifices finally seem worth it. The only problem? Graeme Crawford-Collins, the remote social media manager and the bane of her existence, is also up for the position. Although they've never met in person, their epic email battles are the stuff of office legend. Their boss tasks each of them with drafting a proposal on how to boost bookings in the Galapagos—best proposal wins the promotion. There's just one catch: they have to go on a company cruise to the Galapagos Islands... together.

"Does this book do anything to separate itself from many others of the same ilk? Not really, but it's a solid entry in the workplace enemies-to-lovers canon. Henley and Graeme's rivalry is overstated, though Henley's doggedness will feel familiar to any woman who's dealt with subtle (or even outright) sexism when vying for career advancement. Like a tropical cocktail: a little overcomplicated but goes down easy." —*Kirkus*

Hodges, Cheris F.

Rumor has it. Cheris Hodges. Dafina 2015. 368 p. (Rumor novels (Cheris F. Hodges), 1)

ISBN 9781617733796

1. Revenge 2. Cheating (Interpersonal relations) 3. Engaged persons 4. Best friends 5. Women lawyers 6. North Carolina 7. Contemporary romances 8. Multicultural romances 9. African American fiction

RUSA Reading List Short List, 2016

Public relations professional Liza Palmer is proud to work for North Carolina senatorial candidate Robert Montgomery, who also happens to be her best friend Chante's fiancé—until she catches him in flagrante delicto with a woman who's not his bride-to-be. Armed with enough information to destroy his political career, Liza approaches Robert's opponent, Jackson Franklin. But Jackson refuses to play dirty, at least when it comes to elections. The bedroom, however, is a whole other story. As their relationship heats up, Liza and Jackson must learn to balance their personal lives and professional ambitions, and without compromising their integrity.

Hodgson, Antonia

The **last** confession of Thomas Hawkins. Antonia Hodgson. Houghton Mifflin Harcourt, 2016. 388 p; (Tom Hawkins novels, 2)

ISBN 9780544639683

1. Innocence (Law) 2. Murder suspects 3. Murder 4. Mistresses 5. Rulers 6. London, England 7. 1720s 8. Historical mysteries

LC 2015028196

An early 18th-century gentleman with a penchant for trouble, facing hanging for a crime he did not commit, endeavors to secure his freedom while reflecting on the careless choices that led to his condemnation, including placing trust in a calculating royal.

"Hodgson maintains pitch-perfect suspense, craftily constructs a fairly clued whodunit, and convincingly evokes the period." —*Publishers Weekly*

Sequel to: The Devil in the Marshalsea.

First published in Great Britain in 2015 by Hodder & Stoughton—Title page verso.

Hoeg, Peter

★ **Smilla's** sense of snow. Peter Hoeg; translated from the Danish by Tiina Nunnally. Farrar Straus and Giroux, 1993. 453 p.

ISBN 9780374266448

1. Conspiracies 2. Women detectives 3. Murder investigation 4. Inuit women 5. Inuit children 6. Copenhagen, Denmark 7. Greenland 8. Crime fiction 9. Translations 10. Books to movies

LC 93017742

Dilys Award, 1994; Silver Dagger Award for Fiction, 1994

When her six-year-old neighbor falls to his death, and no one is willing to suspect foul play, Smilla Qaavigaaq Jasperson finds her own investigation taking her into the files of a Danish company

"Selfishness, menace and systematic corruption form the fabric of this mysterious novel. Relationships are all based on suspicion, and love has to be 'like a military operation.'... Peter Hoeg has a remarkable feeling for sinister surprises." —*Times Literary Supplement*

Winner of the Glass Key Award in 1993.

Originally published: Copenhagen : Rosinante, 1992.

Hoffman, Alice

The **book** of magic. Alice Hoffman. Simon & Schuster 2021. 384 p. (Practical magic novels, 2)

ISBN 9781982151485

1. Witches 2. Witchcraft 3. Spells (Magic) 4. Sisters 5. Protectiveness 6. Magical realism 7. Literary fiction

The Owens family has been cursed in matters of love for over three-hundred years but all of that is about to change. The novel begins in a library, the best place for a story to be conjured, when beloved aunt Jet Owens hears the deathwatch beetle and knows she has only seven days to live. Jet is not the only one in danger—the curse is already at work.

"Hoffman concludes her Practical Magic series about the Owens family women, cursed by 17th-century ancestor Maria, with an illuminating story of their inherited witchcraft." —*Publishers Weekly*

The **ice** queen: a novel. Alice Hoffman. Little, Brown and Co, 2005. 224 p.

ISBN 9780316058599

1. Loss (Psychology) 2. Wishing and wishes 3. Self-acceptance in women 4. Secrets 5. Women librarians 6. Psychological fiction 7. Literary fiction 8. First person narratives

LC 2004026610

After a small town librarian survives a lightning strike, she seeks out a fellow survivor in a quest for meaning, only to begin an obsessive love affair between two opposites joined by a single common thread.

"As Hoffman's spellbinding and wonderfully insightful tale unfurls, she pays charming tribute to librarians, revels in metaphors of hot and cold, and poetically explores the meaning of trust, the chemistry of healing, and the reach of love." —*Booklist*

The **marriage** of opposites: a novel based on the life of Rachel Pizzarro. Alice Hoffman. Simon & Schuster, 2015. 369 p.

ISBN 9781451693591

1. Pissarro, Camille 2. Gender role 3. Scandals 4. Ambition in girls 5. Refugees, Jewish 6. Widows 7. West Indies 8. France 9. 19th century 10. Magical realism 11. Historical fiction 12. Love stories

LC 2014047743

LibraryReads Favorites, 2015

Dreaming of an exotic life in Paris while coming of age in a St. Thomas refugee community, young Rachel is forced to marry a widower before falling scandalously in love and becoming the mother of Impressionist master Camille Pissarro.

"As witty as she is lyrical, she writes ricocheting dialogue. This rhapsodic blend of keenly observed historical elements and vibrantly fabulistic invention generates an entrancing saga of sacrifice, forbidden loves, betrayals, and family tragedies endured in a world fractured by religion, class, and race and redeemed by art and by love. Hoffman is at her resplendent best in this trenchant and revelatory tale of a heroic woman and her world-altering artist son.... Given the resounding success of her previous two novels, Hoffman's latest, with zealous publisher support, will lure her fans and readers curious about the lives of artists." —*Booklist*

The **Museum** of Extraordinary Things: a novel. Alice Hoffman. Scribner, 2014. 384 pages
ISBN 9781451693560
1. Freak shows 2. Fires 3. Young women 4. Photographers 5. Missing women 6. Coney Island, New York City 7. New York City 8. 1900s (Decade) 9. Historical fiction 10. Parallel narratives 11. Adult books for young adults
LC 2013036572
The daughter of a Coney Island boardwalk curiosities museum's front man pursues an impassioned love affair with a Russian immigrant photographer who after fleeing his Lower East Side Orthodox community has captured poignant images of the infamous Triangle Shirtwaist Factory fire.

The **river** king. Alice Hoffman. G. P. Putnam's Sons, 2000. 324 p.
ISBN 9780399145995
1. Superstition 2. Private schools 3. Small town life 4. Murder 5. Prep school students 6. Massachusetts 7. Magical realism 8. Literary fiction 9. Books to movies 10. Adult books for young adults
LC 23870
New York Times Notable Book, 2000
A town divided by class lines is thrown into turmoil by a mysterious death, which begins to unravel the lives of a fifteen-year-old girl, a young boy, and a woman running from her own destiny.
"It can be hard to find an example of good old-fashioned storytelling these days, but storytelling, refreshingly, is Alice Hoffman's strength." —*New York Times Book Review*

The **rules** of magic: a novel. Alice Hoffman. Simon & Schuster, 2017. 367 pages; (Practical magic novels, Prequel)
ISBN 9781501137471
1. Sisters 2. Witches 3. Spells (Magic) 4. Witchcraft 5. Siblings 6. New England 7. New York City 8. 1950s 9. Magical realism 10. Books to movies 11. Literary fiction 12. Adult books for young adults
LC 2016054138
Loan Stars Favourites, 2017; LibraryReads Favorites, 2017; Librarians' Choice (Australia), 2017
A prequel to Practical Magic traces the story of the children of Susanna Owens, who, in spite of their mother's fierce edicts against witchcraft, develop powerful abilities while struggling to escape the family curse that leads to tragedy if they fall in love.
"The spellbinding story, focusing on the strength of family bonds through joy and sorrow, will appeal to a broad range of readers." —*Publishers Weekly*

★ The **world** that we knew. Alice Hoffman. Simon & Schuster, 2019. 384 pages
ISBN 9781501137570
1. Golem 2. Protectiveness 3. Holocaust (1933-1945) 4. Jewish girls 5. Persecution by Nazis 6. Berlin, Germany 7. France 8. Second World War era (1939-1945) 9. Magical realism 10. Literary fiction 11. Historical fiction
Sent away to 1941 Paris when Berlin becomes too dangerous for Jewish families, a young girl bonds with her protective mystical golem; while her friend, a rabbi's daughter, rises to become a defender of their people.

Hoffmann, R. J.

Other people's children: a novel. R. J. Hoffmann. Simon & Schuster, 2021. 352 p.
ISBN 9781982159092
1. Mothers and daughters 2. Adoption 3. Teenage pregnancy 4. Miscarriage 5. Birthmothers 6. Chicago, Illinois 7. Psychological suspense
LC 2020031134
A pregnant teen who would go to college, a determined grandmother and a desperate would-be adoptive parent are pitted against one another in their respective efforts to protect their families.
"Hoffmann's believable characters don't disappoint, and his engrossing look at fraught issues piques. This sharp tale of heartache, loss, and redemption resonates." —*Publishers Weekly*

Hogan, Ruth

Queenie Malone's paradise hotel. Ruth Hogan. William Morrow & Co, 2020. 304 pages
ISBN 9780062979643
1. Eccentrics and eccentricities 2. Mothers and daughters 3. Homecomings 4. Boarding schools 5. Women and dogs 6. England 7. Mainstream fiction
When her mother dies, Tilda goes back to Brighton and with the help of her beloved Queenie sets about unravelling the mystery of her exile from The Paradise Hoteland discovers that her mother was not the woman she thought she knew at all.
"In her third novel, Hogan (The Wisdom of Sally Red Shoes, 2019) once again creates a captivating story full of endearing characters." —*Booklist*
Originally published: London : Hodder & Stoughton, 2019.

Holahan, Cate

Her three lives. Cate Holahan. Grand Central Pub 2021. 336 p.
ISBN 9781538736340
1. Engaged persons 2. Architects 3. Influencers 4. Caribbean Americans 5. Interracial couples 6. Psychological suspense 7. Tiffany, Louis Comfort
LC 2020053584
Greg Hamlin's kids think he's having a mid-life crisis. With his youngest off to college, the wealthy architect has divorced his wife and begun designing a new life with Anya, a struggling lifestyle blogger whose Bronx-upbringing and Caribbean roots seem an odd match for a suburban-Connecticut dad. But before Greg's second act can truly start, a savage home invasion leaves him housebound with a traumatic brain injury and glued to the live feeds from his omnipresent security cameras. The more Greg watches, the less safe he feels. Soon, he and his kids suspect his fiance of hiding something. Greg begins monitoring Anya's every move, watching her on the cameras, tracking her phone, and digging into her past. Anya is keeping secrets. But do they relate to her involvement in the break-in? Or, is Greg's battered brain playing tricks, pushing him to terrorize the only person who truly loves him?
"Fans of soapy domestic suspense will be well satisfied." —*Publishers Weekly*

Holbert, Bruce

Whiskey. Bruce Holbert. MCD/Farrar, Straus and Giroux, 2018. 255 p.
ISBN 9780374289188

1. Family relationships 2. Brothers 3. Dysfunctional families
4. Religious fanaticism 5. Runaways 6. Washington (State) 7. The West
(United States) 8. 1990s 9. Literary fiction

LC 2017040456

Two self-destructive, but fiercely loyal adult brothers find themselves
entwined in domestic troubles, alcoholic benders, their parents' ongoing
tangles with the law and religious fanaticism and must work together after
one of their daughters runs off with a zealot.

Holdstock, Pauline

Here I am!. Pauline Holdstock. Biblioasis, 2019. 292 p.

ISBN 9781771963091

1. Boys 2. Mothers — Death 3. Stowaways 4. Ocean travel
5. Intergenerational relations 6. England 7. France 8. Literary fiction
9. Canadian fiction 10. Multiple perspectives

After Frankie's mother dies, he can't seem to get anyone to listen to
him. So the six-year-old comes up with a plan: go to France, find a police
station, and ask the officers to ring his father.

"A wide range of readers from late adolescence on will find this compelling story of one youngster's adventure full of psychological depth and
rich characterization." —*Library Journal*

A John Metcalf book.

Holland, Cecelia

Jerusalem. Cecelia Holland. Forge, 1996. 318 p.

ISBN 9780312859565

1. Crusades 2. Power (Social sciences) 3. Knights and knighthood
4. People with leprosy 5. Crusaders (Middle Ages) 6. Jerusalem, Israel
7. 12th century 8. Historical fiction 9. Franchise books 10. Media tie-ins

LC 9538814

A recreation of the Crusader Kingdom of Jerusalem captures the religious passions and political intrigues of the Holy Land in A.D. 1187, as
seen through the eyes of Rannulf Fitzwilliam, a Knight Templar who
loves the princess Sibylla BT

"The narrative structure may be simple, but Holland's masterful lay-
ering of subplots, historical detail and multiple perspectives makes for a
great read." —*Publishers Weekly*

Hollis, Lee

Poppy Harmon investigates. Lee Hollis. Kensington Books, 2018. 282
p. (Desert Flowers mysteries, 1)

ISBN 9781496713889

1. Women amateur detectives 2. Retirement communities 3. Women
retirees 4. Widows 5. Jewelry theft 6. California 7. Palm Springs,
California 8. Cozy mysteries 9. Gentle reads

Poppy Harmon and her friends find that life after retirement can be
much busier—and deadlier—than any of them ever anticipated.

Holmes, J. M.

How are you going to save yourself. J. M. Holmes. Little Brown & Co,
2018. 248 p.

ISBN 9780316514880

1. African American men 2. Working class 3. Male friendship
4. Multiracial men 5. Social classes 6. Rhode Island 7. Literary fiction
8. Coming-of-age stories 9. Multiple perspectives

Four friends come of age in a Rhode Island postindustrial enclave and
struggle to liberate themselves from the limitations imposed on African
Americans while navigating the dynamics of sex, drugs, class and family.

Holmes, Linda

★ **Evvie** Drake starts over: a novel. Linda Holmes. Ballantine Books,
2019. 304 p.

ISBN 9780525619246

1. Widows 2. Young women 3. Baseball players 4. Coastal towns
5. Pitchers (Baseball) 6. Maine 7. Relationship fiction

LC 2018051134

Booklist Editors' Choice, 2019; LibraryReads Favorites, 2019

Young widow Evvie Drake and major league pitcher Dean Tenney,
who has lost his game and needs a chance to reset his life, form an unlikely
relationship when Dean moves into an apartment at the back of Evvie's
house.

"The charm of Holmes novel comes not only from a genuine friendship turned sweet romance between Evvie and Dean but also from watching amiable Evvie stumble through the process of finding herself. A warm
and funny book that will captivate fans of Abbi Waxman and Taylor
Jenkins Reid." —*Booklist*

Holmes, Shannon

★ **B-more** careful: a novel. By Shannon Holmes. Meow Meow
Productions, 2001. 281 p.

ISBN 9780967224916

1. African American young women 2. African American families 3.
African Americans 4. Inner city 5. Street life 6. Baltimore, Maryland
7. Maryland 8. Urban fiction 9. African American fiction

LC 2002113967

Street Lit Book Award Medal: Adult Fiction, 2002

Fatherless and with an addict mother, Netta, the leader of the Pussy
Pound, relies on her body and her wiles to survive the harsh streets of Baltimore, but finds there is more to life after her heartbroken lover Black
swears revenge on her.

Holroyde, Claire

The effort. Claire Holroyde. Grand Central Publishing, 2021. 368 p.

ISBN 9781538717615

1. Astronomers 2. Comets 3. Comet collisions 4. Near future 5.
Scientists 6. Apocalyptic fiction 7. Social science fiction

LC 2020030171

A novel of love and sacrifice follows people around the world as they
unite to prevent a global catastrophe.

"With fascinating scientific concepts and nuanced situations on both
global and individual levels, Holroyde's tale, arriving during a pandemic,
will attract fans of end-of-world disaster novels, going back to Lucifer's
Hammer and on to Station Eleven (2014)." —*Booklist*

Holsinger, Bruce W.

The gifted school: a novel. Bruce Holsinger. Riverhead Books, 2019.
304 p.

ISBN 9780525534969

1. Schools 2. Social conflict 3. Parents — Psychology 4. Competition
5. Class conflict 6. Colorado 7. Mainstream fiction 8. Domestic fiction
9. Multiple perspectives

LC 2018057642

The students and parents of a tight-knit community find their bonds
nearly destroyed by competitiveness when an exclusive school for gifted
children opens nearby, in a story told from both adult and child perspectives.

Holt, Victoria

The **black** opal. Victoria Holt. Fawcett Crest, 1994. 373 p.
ISBN 9780449222713
1. Abandoned children 2. Family secrets 3. Murder 4. Scandals 5. Illegitimacy 6. England 7. Romantic suspense 8. First person narratives

Returning to England many years after a murder had taken away her adoptive family, Carmel March searches her memory for the truth behind her past and wonders about the role played by her childhood friend, Lucian.

Jean Plaidy writing as Victoria Holt.
Originally published: New York : Doubleday, 1993.

Holton, India

The **Wisteria** Society of lady scoundrels. India Holton. Jove, 2021. 352 p. (Dangerous damsels, 1)
ISBN 9780593200162
1. Women's organizations 2. Women thieves 3. Assassins 4. Great-aunts 5. Misogyny 6. Great Britain 7. Victorian era (1837-1901) 8. Victorian romances 9. Swashbuckling tales 10. Historical fantasy
LC 2020043100

A prim and proper lady thief must save her aunt from a crazed pirate and his dangerously charming henchman in this fantastical historical romance.

"Holton debuts with a delightful alternate-Victorian-era romp replete with swashbuckling, skulduggery, and sly romance." —*Publishers Weekly*

Hooper, Elise

Fast girls: a novel of the 1936 women's Olympic team. Elise Hooper. William Morrow & Company, 2020. 432 p.
ISBN 9780062937995
1. Robinson, Betty 2. Women Olympic athletes 3. Track and field athletes 4. Discrimination 5. Women track and field athletes 6. Sexism 7. United States 8. Berlin, Germany 9. 1930s 10. Biographical fiction 11. Historical fiction

Traces the lesser-known stories of such athletes as Betty Robinson, Louise Stokes and Helen Stephens to detail the barriers they overcame to become the first integrated women's Olympic team at the 1936 games in Berlin.

"For fans of Daniel James Brown's The Boys in the Boat (2015), historical fiction about real people, and stories about little-known female heroes breaking through barriers." —*Booklist*

Hooper, Emma

Etta and Otto and Russell and James: a novel. Emma Hooper. Simon & Schuster, 2014. 320 p.
ISBN 9781476755670
1. Walking 2. Memories 3. Octogenarians 4. Voyages and travels 5. Senior couples 6. Canada 7. Literary fiction 8. Canadian fiction

Embarking on a more than 3,000-kilometer walking journey from rural Canada to the East coast so that she can see the ocean for the first time in her life, an octogenarian woman has experiences that blur her perspectives between illusion, memory and reality.

"Hooper has written an irresistibly enchanting debut novel that explores mysteries of love old and new, the loyalty of animals and dependency of humans, the horrors of war and perils of loneliness, and the tenacity of time and fragility of memory." —*Booklist*

Hoover, Colleen

All your perfects. Colleen Hoover. Atria Books, 2018. 308 pages
ISBN 9781501193323
1. Husband and wife 2. Marital conflict 3. Infertility 4. Communication 5. Promises 6. New adult fiction 7. Contemporary romances

A damaged couple in a troubled marriage grapple with the memories and mistakes they've made and secrets they've kept as they try to repair their love.

It ends with us. Colleen Hoover. Atria Books, 2016. 320 p.
ISBN 9781501110368
1. Adult children of dysfunctional families 2. Women florists 3. Surgeons 4. Family violence 5. Former boyfriends 6. Boston, Massachusetts 7. New adult fiction 8. Contemporary romances 9. First person narratives
Goodreads Choice Award, 2016

With this bold and deeply personal novel, Colleen Hoover delivers a heart-wrenching story that breaks exciting new ground for her as a writer. Combining a captivating romance with a cast of all-too-human characters, It Ends With Us is an unforgettable tale of love that comes at the ultimate price.

Horan, Nancy

Loving Frank: a novel. Nancy Horan. Ballantine Books, 2007. 384 p.
ISBN 9780345494993
1. Borthwick, Mamah Bouton 2. Architects 3. Women intellectuals 4. Extramarital affairs 5. Scandals 6. Married women 7. Illinois 8. Wisconsin 9. Biographical fiction 10. Historical fiction 11. Love stories
James Fenimore Cooper Prize, 2009; Romantic Times Reviewers' Choice Award, 2007

Fact and fiction blend in a historical novel that chronicles the relationship between seminal architect Frank Lloyd Wright and Mamah Cheney, from their meeting, when they were each married to another, to the clandestine affair that shocked Chicago society.

"In 1904, Frank Lloyd Wright started work on a house for an Oak Park couple, Edwin and Mamah Cheney, and, before long, he and Mamah had begun a scandalous affair. In her first novel, Horan, viewing the relationship from Mamah's perspective, does well to avoid serving up a bodice-ripper for the smart set. If anything, she cleaves too faithfully to the sources, occasionally giving her story the feel of a dissertation masquerading as a novel. But she succeeds in conveying the emotional center of her protagonist, whom she paints as a proto-feminist, an educated woman fettered by the role of bourgeois matriarch. Horan best evokes Mamah's troubled personality by means of delicately rendered reflections on the power of the natural world, from which her lover drew inspiration." —*The New Yorker*

Horn, Dara

Eternal life: a novel. Dara Horn. W. W. Norton & Co, 2018. 236 p.
ISBN 9780393608533
1. Faustian bargains 2. Jewish women 3. Immortality 4. Death 5. Families 6. New York City 7. Jerusalem, Israel 8. Literary fiction
LC 2017044684
Booklist Editors' Choice, 2018; LibraryReads Favorites, 2018; New York Times Notable Book, 2018

Ever since she made a deal to save her son's life in Roman-occupied Jerusalem, Rachel has been doomed to live eternallyhaving hundreds of children and being stalked by an obsessed manbut as her descendants develop new technologies for immortality, she realizes that, for them to live fully, she must die.

"Horn constructs a deeply satisfying novel, rich not only in history and the great philosophical conundrums of living and dying but also in humor and passion." —*Booklist*

Hornby, Gill

Miss Austen. Gill Hornby. St Martins Pr 2020. 304 p.
ISBN 9781250252203
1. Austen, Cassandra 2. Sisters 3. Letters 4. Secrets 5. Memories 6. Women authors 7. England 8. 19th century 9. Biographical fiction 10. Historical fiction

LC 2019052573

Cassandra Austen hunts down a trove of letters written by her deceased sister, Jane, and confronts the buried secrets they hold, secrets not only about Jane but also about Cassandra herself.

"Cassandra herself is similarly fascinating, a woman who never ceases her efforts to carve out a life of her own in a world that is not kind to unmarried women. The pacing is leisurely, but the thoughtful characterization makes this a worthy addition to most collections." —*Booklist*

Hornby, Nick

High fidelity. Nick Hornby. Riverhead Books, 1995. 323 p.
ISBN 9781573220163
1. Popular music 2. Self-fulfillment in men 3. Music 4. Man-woman relationships 5. Vintage record store owners 6. London, England 7. Humorous stories 8. Books to movies 9. Relationship fiction

LC 95008469

Booklist Editors' Choice, 1995

A pop music junkie ponders life, love, and hangs out with the two offbeat clerks who work at his semi-failing record store.

"Happily, Hornby does not rely on pop-cultural allusion to limn his characters' inner lives, but uses it instead to create a rich, wry backdrop for them." —*Time*

This book was adapted into a TV show on Hulu, in February 2020.

Just like you. Nick Hornby. Riverhead Books, 2020. 464 pages
ISBN 9780593191385
1. May-December romances 2. Middle-aged women — Relations with younger men 3. Interpersonal attraction 4. Separated women (Marital relations) 5. Black British men 6. Relationship fiction

The person you are with is just like you- same background, same age, same interests. The perfect match. And it is an unmitigated disaster. Then, when, and where, you least expect it, you meet someone new. You seem to have nothing in common and yet, somehow, it feels totally right. Nick Hornby's brilliantly observed, tender but also brutally funny new novel gets to the heart of what it means to fall surprisingly and headlong in love with the best possible person—someone who is not just like you at all.

"Filled with laugh-out-loud charm, Hornby's movie-ready follow-up to State of the Union is a hopeful balm for our unsettled postpandemic times." —*Library Journal*

Horowitz, Anthony

The **House** of Silk: a Sherlock Holmes novel. Anthony Horowitz. Mulholland Books, 2011. 320 p. (Sherlock Holmes novels (Anthony Horowitz), 1)
ISBN 9780316196994
1. Detectives 2. Organized crime 3. Train robberies 4. Conspiracies 5. Murder 6. London, England 7. Boston, Massachusetts 8. 1890s 9. Adaptations, retellings, and spin-offs 10. Historical mysteries 11. First person narratives

LC 2011030839

It is 1890. A year after Holmes's death, Watson—now in a retirement home—narrates a tale of Sherlockian detection that could tear apart the very fabric of society. The story opens with a train robbery in Boston, and moves to the innocuous setting of Wimbledon.

★ **Magpie** murders. Anthony Horowitz. Harper, 2017. 368 p. (Magpie murders, 1)
ISBN 9780062645227
1. Detectives 2. Editors 3. Holocaust survivors 4. Accidental death 5. Murder investigation 6. England 7. 1950s 8. Mysteries 9. Metafiction

LC 2016045021

LibraryReads Favorites, 2017; Macavity Award for Best Mystery Novel, 2018; RUSA Reading List Short List, 2018

From New York Times bestselling author Anthony Horowitz comes Magpie Murders, a brilliant and strikingly original reimagining of the classic whodunit (a la Agatha Christie) with a contemporary mystery wrapped around it.

"Fans who still mourn the passing of Agatha Christie, the model who's evoked here in dozens of telltale details, will welcome this wildly inventive homage /update/commentary as the most fiendishly clever puzzle—make that two puzzles—of the year." —*Kirkus*

Originally published: London : Orion, 2016.

★ **Moonflower** murders. Anthony Horowitz. HarperCollins Publishers, 2020. 400 p. (Magpie murders, 2)
ISBN 9780062955456
1. Women editors 2. Retirees 3. Books and reading 4. Innocence (Law) 5. Murder suspects 6. Crete 7. England 8. Mysteries 9. Novels-within-novels

LC 2020022623

Helping run her boyfriend's small Greek island hotel, a homesick London editor is irresistibly drawn to the story of a murder on the Suffolk coast and the wrongful incarceration of an innocent immigrant.

"Horowitz, who matches a baffling puzzle with a sympathetic, flawed lead, has never been better at surprising the reader and playing fair. This is a flawless update of classic golden age whodunits." —*Publishers Weekly*

★ The **sentence** is death. Anthony Horowitz. HarperCollins, 2019. 464 pages (Daniel Hawthorne novels, 2)
ISBN 9780062676832
1. Detectives 2. Authors 3. Mystery story writers 4. Secrets 5. Deception 6. England 7. Mysteries 8. Metafiction 9. First person narratives

Detective Daniel Hawthorne and his literary sidekick risk their lives to expose dangerous secrets while investigating the murder of a celebrity divorce lawyer and teetotaler who was bludgeoned to death with an expensive bottle of wine.

"Horowitz plays fair with the reader all the way to the surprise reveal of the killers identity. Fans of traditional puzzle mysteries will be enthralled." —*Publishers Weekly*

Also published as Another word for death: HarperCollins Canada, 2019.

★ The **word** is murder. Anthony Horowitz. Harper, 2018. 400 p. (Daniel Hawthorne novels, 1)
ISBN 9780062676788
1. Grey, Jane 2. Authors 3. Mystery story writers 4. Secrets 5. Deception 6. England 7. Mysteries 8. Metafiction 9. First person narratives

LibraryReads Favorites, 2018

When a wealthy woman is found murdered after planning her own funeral service, disgraced police detective Daniel Hawthorne and his sidekick, author Anthony Horowitz, investigate.

"Deduction and wit are well-balanced, and fans of Peter Lovesey and other modern channelers of the spirit of the golden age of detection will clamor for more." —*Publishers Weekly*

Originally published: London : Cornerstone, 2017.

Horrocks, Caitlin

Life among the terranauts. Caitlin Horrocks. Little Brown & Co, 2021. 320 p.

ISBN 9780316316972

1. Everyday life 2. Small towns 3. Experiments 4. Interpersonal relations 5. Death 6. Short stories 7. Surrealist fiction

A new story collection that move boldly between the real and the surreal.

"Horrocks's linguistic finesse and narrative range is impressive, and she brings incisive humor, pathos, and wit to her characters and their predicaments." —*Publishers Weekly*

The **vexations**. Caitlin Horrocks. Little Brown & Co, 2019. 451 pages
ISBN 9780316316910

1. Satie, Erik 2. Obsession 3. Composers 4. Siblings 5. Genius 6. Loyalty 7. Paris, France 8. Belle Epoque (1871-1914) 9. Biographical fiction 10. Historical fiction 11. Multiple perspectives

Devoted to her talented composer brother after becoming orphaned in childhood, Louise is forced to confront the realities of her brother's obsessions in the wake of a devastating loss.

"Finely written and deeply empathetic, a powerful portrait of artistic commitment and emotional frustration." —*Kirkus*

Hosking, Jay

Three years with the rat: a novel. Jay Hosking. Thomas Dunne Books, 2017. 271 p.

ISBN 9781250116307

1. Siblings 2. Graduate students 3. Missing persons 4. Missing persons investigation 5. Rats 6. Toronto, Ontario 7. Science fiction 8. Canadian fiction 9. First person narratives

Alarmed by his sister's raging meltdowns that point to a serious mental illness, a young man embarks on a quest for answers when his sister goes missing, an effort that is complicated by her seemingly devoted boyfriend's suspicious knowledge.

"A potent, sophisticated combination of science-fiction novel and psychological thriller." —*Kirkus*

Originally published: Toronto, Ontario : Hamish Hamilton, 2016.

Hossain, Saad Z.

Cyber mage: a novel. Saad Z. Hossain. Unnamed Press, 2021. 288 p.
ISBN 9781951213282

1. Near future 2. Dystopias 3. Mercenaries 4. Hackers 5. Nanotechnology 6. Bangladesh 7. Science fantasy 8. Dystopian fiction

LC 2021039688

A mercenary, Djibrel, searches for answers about what happened to a magical super-race of genies who seem to have disappeared in 2089 Dhaka, Bangladesh, a city that has survived a global climate apocalypse using biological nanotech.

Hosseini, Khaled

★ The **kite** runner. Khaled Hosseini. Riverhead Books, 2003. 368 p.
ISBN 9781573222457

1. Boys — Friendship 2. Afghan War, 2001-2021 3. Social classes 4. Rich boys 5. Household employees 6. Afghanistan 7. Kabul, Afghanistan 8. Vidocq, Francois Eugene 9. Coming-of-age stories 10. First person narratives 11. Adult books for young adults

LC 2003043106

Alex Award, 2004; ALA Notable Book, 2004; School Library Journal Best Books: Best Adult Books 4 Teens, 2003

Afghanistan, 1975: Twelve-year-old Amir is desperate to win the local kite-fighting tournament and his loyal friend Hassan promises to help him. But neither of the boys can foresee what will happen to Hassan that afternoon, an event that is to shatter their lives. After the Russians invade and the family is forced to flee to America, Amir realises that one day he must return to Afghanistan under Taliban rule to find the one thing that his new world cannot grant him: redemption.

"Khaled Hosseini gives us a vivid and engaging story that reminds us how long his people have been struggling to triumph over the forces of violence." —*New York Times Book Review*

★ **Sea** prayer. Khaled Hosseini. Riverhead Books, 2018. 48 p.
ISBN 9780525539094

1. Refugees, Syrian 2. Fathers and sons 3. Child refugees 4. Children and war 5. Family and war 6. Syria 7. War stories 8. Illustrated books 9. Epistolary novels 10. Adult books for young adults

LC 2018022980

Booklist Editors' Choice: Adult Books for Young Adults, 2018

Presents an evocatively illustrated tribute to the tragic human realities of today's refugee crisis in the form of a father's letter to his young son on the eve of a dangerous journey.

Hostin, Sunny

★ **Summer** on the bluffs. Sunny Hostin. William Morrow & Co, 2021. 432 p. (Oak Bluffs, 1)

ISBN 9780062994172

1. Summer 2. Rich people 3. Ambition in women 4. Godmothers 5. African American women 6. Martha's Vineyard, Massachusetts 7. Relationship fiction 8. African American fiction

Emmy Award winner, renowned lawyer and journalist, and The View cohost Sunny Hostin makes her literary debut with this dazzling novel about a life-changing summer along the beaches of Martha's Vineyard.

"Come for the debut novel from an Emmy-winning cohost of The View, stay for the diverse cast of characters in an aspirational, beachy escape." —*Booklist*

Houellebecq, Michel

Submission. Michel Houellebecq; Translated from the French by Lorin Stein. Farrar Straus & Giroux, 2015. 256 pages
ISBN 9780374271572

1. Near future 2. Elections 3. College teachers 4. Muslims 5. Social change 6. France 7. Literary fiction 8. Satirical fiction 9. Translations

New York Times Notable Book, 2015

In a near-future France, François, a middle-aged academic, is watching his life slowly dwindle to nothing. His sex drive is diminished, his parents are dead, and his lifelong obsession—the ideas and works of the novelist Joris-Karl Huysmans—has led him nowhere. In a late-capitalist society where consumerism has become the new religion, François is spiritually barren, but seeking to fill the vacuum of his existence. And he is not alone. As the 2022 Presidential election approaches, two candidates emerge as favorites: Marine Le Pen of the Front National, and Muhammed Ben Abbes of the nascent Muslim Fraternity. Forming a controversial alliance with the mainstream parties, Ben Abbes sweeps to power, and overnight the country is transformed. Islamic law comes into force: women are veiled, polygamy is encouraged and, for François, life is set on a new course.

"Submission is well crafted, but the pornographic sex scenes are as tired as their rationale. Houellebecqs faltering is Franois failure writ large: the inability to believe there might be any meaning in or meaningful differences between diverse points of view or ways of life." —*Booklist*

Translation of: Soumission.

Originally published: Paris : Flammarion, 2015.

Translated from the French.

Howard, Ravi

Driving the king: a novel. Ravi Howard. Harper, 2015. 336 p.

ISBN 9780060529611

1. Cole, Nat 2. Racism 3. Chauffeurs 4. African Americans — Social conditions 5. Racism in the judicial system 6. Violence against marginalized people 7. United States 8. Montgomery, Alabama 9. 1950s 10. Biographical fiction 11. Historical fiction 12. African American fiction

LC 2014015054

Explores race and class in 1950s America, witnessed through the experiences of Nat King Cole and his driver, Nat Weary.

"Alternating between the cities and Wearys past and present, Howard explores race relations in the pre-civil rights era and the strong ties forged between two extraordinary men." —*Booklist*

Howarth, Paul

Dust off the bones. Paul Howarth. Harper, 2021. 336 p.

ISBN 9780063076006

1. Frontier and pioneer life 2. Lange, Dorothea 3. Ranches 4. Cattle industry and trade 5. Separated brothers 6. Queensland 7. Australia 8. 1890s 9. Historical fiction

The author of Only Killers and Thieves returns to turn-of-the-century Australia in this powerful sequel that follows the story of brothers Tommy and Billy McBride, the widow of their family's killer, Katherine Sullivan, and the sadistic Native Police officer Edmund Noone.

"A classic cowboy saga is transformed into a complex, sophisticated morality play." —*Kirkus*

Sequel to: Only killers and thieves.

Only killers and thieves: a novel. Paul Howarth. Harper, 2018. 319 p.

ISBN 9780062690968

1. Frontier and pioneer life 2. Wilderness areas 3. Atrocities 4. Aboriginal Australians 5. Racism 6. Australia 7. 1880s 8. Historical fiction 9. Coming-of-age stories 10. Adult books for young adults

It is 1885, and a crippling drought threatens to ruin the McBride family. Their land is parched, their cattle starving. When the rain finally comes, it is a miracle that renews their hope for survival. But returning home from an afternoon swimming at a remote waterhole filled by the downpour, fourteen-year-old Tommy and sixteen-year-old Billy meet with a shocking tragedy.

Sequel: Dust off the bones.

Howland, Bette

Calm sea and prosperous voyage. Bette Howland. A Public Space, 2019. 230 p.

ISBN 9780998267500

1. Women 2. Family relationships 3. Interpersonal relations 4. Autobiographical fiction 5. Short stories

Calm sea and prosperous voyage restores to the literary canon an extraordinarily gifted writer, who was recognized as a major talent, with

Guggenheim and MacArthur "genius" fellowships, before all but disappearing from public view for decades. With direct and powerful use of language in the tradition of Lucia Berlin, Kathleen Collins, and Grace Paley, Bette Howland chronicles the tensions of her generation.

Howrey, Meg

The wanderers. Meg Howrey. G. P. Putnam's Sons, 2017. 400 p.

ISBN 9780399574634

1. Astronauts 2. Family relationships 3. Introspection 4. Space flight to Mars 5. Ambition 6. Utah 7. Literary fiction 8. Psychological fiction 9. Multiple perspectives

LibraryReads Favorites, 2017

Station Eleven meets The Martian in this brilliantly inventive novel about three astronauts training for the first-ever mission to Mars, an experience that will push the boundary between real and unreal, test their relationships, and leave each of them—and their families—changed forever In an age of space exploration, we search to find ourselves. In four years Prime Space will put the first humans on Mars. Helen Kane, Yoshi Tanaka, and Sergei Kuznetsov must prove they're the crew for the job by spending seventeen months in the most realistic simulation ever created. Retired from NASA, Helen had not trained for irrelevance. It is nobody's fault that the best of her exists in space, but her daughter can't help placing blame. The MarsNOW mission is Helen's last chance to return to the only place she's ever truly felt at home. For Yoshi, it's an opportunity to prove himself worthy of the wife he has loved absolutely, if not quite rightly. Sergei is willing to spend seventeen months in a tin can if it means travelling to Mars. He will at least be tested past the point of exhaustion, and this is the example he will set for his sons. As the days turn into months the line between what is real and unreal becomes blurred, and the astronauts learn that the complications of inner space are no less fraught than those of outer space. The Wanderers gets at the desire behind all exploration: the longing for discovery and the great search to understand the human heart.

"Although the contours of a space drama may seem familiar to a 21st-century readership, Howrey, through the poetry of her writing and the richness of her characters, makes it all seem new. A lyrical and subtle space opera." —*Kirkus*

Hoyt, Elizabeth

Not the duke's darling. Elizabeth Hoyt. Forever, 2018. 368 p. (Greycourt novels, 1)

ISBN 9781538763520

1. Parties 2. Dukes and duchesses 3. Independence in women 4. Secret societies 5. Revenge 6. Great Britain 7. Georgian era (1714-1837) 8. Georgian romances 9. Historical romances

A member of the secret order of Wise Women, Freya de Moray, the daughter of disgraced nobility, finds her plans of revenge against the man who destroyed her family thwarted by an attraction she cannot deny.

Includes a bonus story by Grace Burrowes!—Cover.

When a rogue meets his match. Elizabeth Hoyt. Forever, 2020. 368 p. (Greycourt novels, 2)

ISBN 9781538763568

1. Dukes and duchesses 2. Arranged marriage 3. Henchmen 4. Uncle and niece 5. Class conflict 6. Great Britain 7. Georgian era (1714-1837) 8. Georgian romances 9. Historical romances

When he offers the Duke of Windemere's niece, Messalina Greycourt, a devil's bargain to avoid an arranged marriage, Gideon Hawthorne, who has performed the Duke's dirty work for years, finally has the chance to win her affections.

"Historical romance fans will be gratified by the way Hoyt highlights social issues, focusing on Gideon and Messalina's struggle against pov-

erty and 18th-century gender roles. Credible characters, steamy romance, and heart-pounding action set this romance apart." —*Publishers Weekly*
Includes a bonus story by Kelly Bowen—Cover.

Hozar, Nazanine

Aria. Nazanine Hozar. Pantheon Books, 2020. 434 p.
ISBN 9781524749033
1. Abandoned children 2. Adoptive parents 3. Child-separated mothers 4. Intergenerational relations 5. Revolutions 6. Iran 7. Tehran, Iran 8. 1950s 9. 20th century 10. Historical fiction 11. Canadian fiction
Abandoned as an infant in a corrupt and divided Iran, Aria is raised by three mother figures of disparate class levels and temperaments before becoming a mother herself against a backdrop of the 1979 revolution.
"Making an impressive fiction debut, Hozar creates a vibrant, unsettling portrait of her native Iran from the 1950s to 1981, a period beset by poverty and oppression, chaos and revolution." —*Kirkus*
Originally published: Toronto : Alfred A. Knopf Canada, 2019.

Huang, S. L.

Burning roses. S.L. Huang. Tor, 2020. 160 p.
ISBN 9781250763990
1. Archers 2. Magic 3. Monster hunters 4. Middle-aged women 5. Monsters 6. Fantasy fiction 7. Adaptations, retellings, and spin-offs
LC Bl2020018900
A wolf-weary Red Riding Hood and a middle-aged Hou Yi the Archer join forces when deadly sunbirds begin to ravage the countryside, threatening everything the pair have grown to love.
A Tom Doherty Associates book.

Zero sum game. S. L. Huang. Tor, 2018. 336 p. (Cas Russell novels, 1)
ISBN 9781250180254
1. Mathematics 2. Telepathy 3. Mercenaries 4. Corporations 5. Conspiracies 6. Science fiction
LC 2018023931
Cas Russell wields her math skills like a superpower, using vector calculus to dodge bullets and beat up armed men, but is very surprised to find someone with a power more dangerous than her own, the ability to control minds.
A Tom Doherty Associates Book.

Huber, Anna Lee

Penny for your secrets. Anna Lee Huber. Kensington Books, 2019. 304 p. (Verity Kent novels, 3)
ISBN 9781496713193
1. Postwar life 2. Women spies 3. Female friendship 4. Newlyweds 5. Aristocracy 6. England 7. Great Britain 8. Between the Wars (1918-1939) 9. 1910s 10. Historical mysteries
A former Secret Service agent investigates two murders in post-World War I England: the first of a friend's husband and the other the sister of a colleague
"In the follow-up to Treacherous Is the Night, Huber focuses on characters who are struggling with postwar memories, depicting the upper-class life more typical of Downton Abbey than books by Charles Todd or Jacqueline Winspear. Readers looking for atmospheric mystery set in the period following the Great War will savor the intricate plotting and captivating details of the era." —*Library Journal*

Huchu, Tendai

The **library** of the dead. T. L. Huchu. Tor, 2021. 288 p. (Edinburgh nights, 1)
ISBN 9781250767769
1. Ghosts 2. Occultism 3. Libraries 4. Secret societies 5. Women mediums 6. Edinburgh, Scotland 7. Urban fantasy 8. Supernatural mysteries 9.
LC 2020055857
Ropa dropped out of school to become a ghost talker, and she now speaks to Edinburgh's dead—carrying messages to the living—but when she learns someone is bewitching children she investigates and discovers an occult library, a taste for hidden magic,and a wealth of Edinburgh's dark secrets.
"Expertly blending elements of Zimbabwean and Scottish culture, Huchu's occult thriller is as entertaining as it is thought-provoking." —*Publishers Weekly*

Hughes, Caoilinn

Orchid and the wasp. Caoilinn Hughes. Hogarth, 2018. 368 p.
ISBN 9781524761103
1. Independence in women 2. Ambition in women 3. Swindlers and swindling 4. Creativity 5. Art 6. 2000s (Decade) 7. Coming-of-age stories 8. Literary fiction
An iron-willed young woman comes of age while traveling through London, Dublin and New York to secure her dysfunctional family's future after the departure of her career-oriented father.
"Debut novelist Hughes, an award-winning poet, employs wry, crackling prose to proffer existential questions about what constitutes a meaningful life." —*Library Journal*

Hughes, Langston

Not without laughter. Langston Hughes; with a new introduction by Maya Angelou; foreword by Arna Bontemps. Scribner Paperback Fiction, 1995. 299 p.
ISBN 9780020209850
1. Growing up 2. African American boys 3. Small town life 4. Kansas 5. African American fiction 6. Coming-of-age stories 7. Modern classics
Depicts a Black family's attempts to deal with life in a small Kansas town BT
"A sympathetic portrayal, unmarred by bitterness or sentimentality, of a people to whom life, no matter how hard, was not without laughter." —*Booklist*
Originally published: New York : Knopf, 1930.

★ **Short** stories. Langston Hughes; edited by Akiba Sullivan Harper; with an introduction by Arnold Rampersad. Hill and Wang, 1996. 299 p.
ISBN 9780809016037
1. African Americans — Social life and customs 2. Race relations 3. Social classes 4. Man-woman relationships 5. Survival 6. New York City 7. Harlem, New York City 8. Short stories 9. Autobiographical fiction 10. African American fiction
LC 95-19554
Offers a collection of stories written between 1919 and 1963 that follow Hughes' literary development and the growth of his personal and political concerns.
"[T]hese pieces vary in theme... If you crave good reading don't pass up this gem." —*Library Journal*
47 short stories.

Hugo, Victor

★ The **hunchback** of Notre Dame. Victor Hugo; revised translation and notes by Catherine Liu; introduction by Elizabeth McCracken. Modern Library, 2002. Xxviii, 483 p.

ISBN 9780679642572

1. People with disfigurements 2. Romani women 3. Love 4. Frameups 5. Jealousy in men 6. Paris, France 7. France 8. Historical fiction 9. Translations 10. Books to TV

The archdeacon of Notre Dame, Claude Frollo, falls in lust with Esmerelda, a gypsy dancer who is much admired in Paris and convinces Quasimodo, the hunchbacked bell-ringer of Notre Dame, to kidnap her. Esmerelda is rescued by the Captain of the Royal Archers and falls mistakenly in love with his bravery when he is in reality, something of a rogue and a braggart.

The Hunchback of Notre-Dame was loosely adapted into a silent film titled "The Darling of Paris" in 1917, but the film is presumed lost. The 1922 silent film "Esmeralda" and the 1997 film "The Hunchback" are also based on The Hunchback of Notre-Dame. Further loosely-adapted films of the same title as the book were released in 1939 and 1996.

Television mini-series of the same title as the book were based on The Hunchback of Notre-Dame in 1966 and 1977, and a television movie in 1982.

First published in French as Notre Dame de Paris in 1831.

Originally published: Paris : Gosselin, 1831.

★ **Les** miserables. Victor Hugo; translated from the French by Charles E. Wilbour; with an introduction by Peter Washington. Knopf, 1997. Xxxvii, 1432 p.

ISBN 9780375403170

1. French Revolution, 1789-1799 2. Fate and fatalism 3. Revolutions 4. State-sponsored terrorism 5. Revolutionaries 6. France 7. Literary fiction 8. Classics 9. Translations

Story of Valjean, the ex-convict who rises against all odds from galley slave to mayor, and the fanatical police inspector who dedicates his life to recapturing Valjean.

Book adapted into a 4 part television mini-series in 2000.

Originally published: Paris : J. Hetzel, 1862.

Huisman, Violaine

The **book** of mother. Violaine Huisman; translated from the French by Leslie Camhi. Scribner, 2021. 240 p.

ISBN 9781982108786

1. Mothers and daughters 2. Growing up 3. Children of people with mental illnesses 4. Women with bipolar disorder 5. Psychiatric hospital patients 6. Autobiographical fiction 7. Literary fiction 8. Translations

When their Maman returns from being hospitalized for a breakdown, Violaine and her sister find their home turning into an emotional landmine due to Maman's violent mood swings and flagrant disregard for personal boundaries.

"Huisman's storytelling ability is immense: Violaine unfurls the wide-ranging narrative like a raconteur at a party, and develops a kaleidoscopic portrait of Catherine." —*Publishers Weekly*

Originally published in France in 2018 by Editions Gallimard as Fugitive parce que reine.

Hulme, Keri

★ The **bone** people: a novel. By Keri Hulme. Louisiana State University Press, 1985. 450 p.

ISBN 9780807112847

1. Maori (New Zealand people) 2. Love triangles 3. Multiracial women 4. Interpersonal relations 5. Foster child abuse 6. New Zealand 7. Literary fiction 8. Magical realism 9. Multiple perspectives

LC 85012937

New Zealand Book Award for Fiction, 1984; Booker Prize, 1985

A novel of the charged relationships between European and Polynesian descendents in New Zealand explores the fluctuating bonds connecting three South Sea natives as they struggle to endure.

"This novel is unforgettably rich and pungent.... Set on the harsh South Island beaches of New Zealand, bound in Maori myth and entwined with Christian symbols, Miss Hulme's provocative novel summons power with words, as in a conjurer's spell." —*New York Times Book Review*

Originally published: Wellington : Spiral, 1983.

Hulse, S. M.

★ **Black** River. S. M. Hulse. Houghton Mifflin Harcourt, 2015. 256 p.

ISBN 9780544309876

1. Widowers 2. Correctional personnel 3. Confrontation (Interpersonal relations) 4. Prison riots 5. Redemption 6. Montana 7. Psychological fiction 8. Literary fiction

LC 2014027025

ALA Notable Book, 2016

Meditative and Montana-set, this debut is a modern American Western that tells the story of former prison guard Wes Carver, tortured 20 years ago by an inmate who's now up for parole, claiming to have found religion. Though Wes moved away, he's back in Black River (with his wife's ashes) to speak against the parole hearing. He's also got some work to do in repairing his damaged relationship with his stepson. Awash in bluegrass music, this is a wrenching story of a broken man trying to find his way back.

"Hulse clearly loves Montana, and her own experience playing the fiddle and knowledge of horses shine through the novel. She maintains suspense and manages to avoid the cliches of redemption stories." —*Booklist*

Eden mine. S.M. Hulse. Farrar, Straus and Giroux, 2020. 256 pages

ISBN 9780374146474

1. People with disabilities 2. Siblings 3. Bombing 4. Domestic terrorism 5. Sheriffs 6. Montana 7. Literary fiction 8. Westerns 9. Multiple perspectives

LC 2019036405

After the state seizes through eminent domain the home near Den Mine that she and her brother, Samuel, inherited, she is packing up her things when a tragedy rocks the town—and the lives of those she loves.

"Especially fine is her rendering of a person of faith struggling with doubt and the nature of evil. Fans of Annie Proulx may appreciate the novel's pensive mood and the exploration of a place where people have few options and little hope." —*Booklist*

Hummel, Maria

Lesson in red. Maria Hummel. Counterpoint, 2021. 320 p.

ISBN 9781640094314

1. Art students 2. Artists 3. Museums 4. Secret societies 5. Suicide 6. Los Angeles, California 7. Southern California 8. Mysteries

Brenae Brasil is a rising star at Los Angeles Art College, the most prestigious art school in the country, and her path to art world celebrity is all but assured. Until she is found dead on campus, just after completing a provocative documentary about female bodies, coercion, and self-defense. Maggie Richter's return to L.A. and her job at the Rocque Museum was supposed to be about restarting her career and reconnecting with old friends. With mounting pressure to keep the museum open, the last thing she needs is to find herself at the center of another art world mystery. But when she uncovers a number of cryptic clues in Brasil's video art, Maggie is suddenly caught up in the shadowy art world of Los Angeles, playing a very dangerous game with some very influential people.

"The cutthroat arts milieu, precisely and knowingly rendered, is magnetizing, while the intricately knotted plot and the characters' nuanced psychology are stoked by Hummel's evisceration of privilege, greed, exploitation, and criminality. Scathing, sexy, suspenseful, and righteous." —*Booklist*

Humphreys, Sara Taney

Trouble walks in. Sara Humphreys. Sourcebooks Casablanca, 2016. 309 p. (McGuire brothers, 2)
  ISBN 9781402293702
1. Police 2. Women real estate agents 3. Threat (Psychology) 4. Protectiveness in men 5. Police dogs 6. New York City 7. Contemporary romances

When an old friend moves into his jurisdiction, K-9 cop Ronan McGuire will do anything to get Maddy Morgan's attention, and when his work places her life in danger, his resolve is tested beyond anything he's experienced before.

Hunt, April

Deadly obsession. April Hunt. Forever, 2019. 336 p. (Steele ops, 1)
  ISBN 9781538763339
1. Former Army Rangers 2. Women detectives 3. Private security services 4. Crime scenes 5. Protectiveness in men 6. Romantic suspense
The latest installment in the heart-stopping romantic suspense series Steele Ops.

"Despite a predictable damsel-in-distress ending, the depiction of a strong woman with health vulnerabilities trying to achieve independence definitely makes this a cut above the rest." —*Booklist*

Hunt, Laird

The **evening** road. Laird Hunt. Little, Brown and Company, 2017. 278 pages
  ISBN 9780316391283
1. Race relations 2. Small towns 3. African American women 4. Lynching 5. Married women 6. Indiana 7. 1920s 8. Historical fiction

In the summer of 1920 in small-town Indiana, two extraordinary women—beautiful Ottie Lee Henshaw and Calla Destry, a young black woman—cross paths and they soon move through an America plagued by fear and hatred, determined to flee the secrets they have left behind.

"Though the novels meandering odysseys sometimes feel frustrating, Hunts striking prose and visionary imagery capture Americas community bonds, violent prejudices, falling darkness, and searing light." —*Publishers Weekly*

Zorrie. Laird Hunt. Bloomsbury Pub, 2021. 176 pages
  ISBN 9781635575361
1. Orphans 2. Women farmers 3. Rural life 4. Farmers 5. Communities 6. Indiana 7. Middle West 8. 20th century 9. Literary fiction 10. Historical fiction
National Book Award for Fiction finalist, 2021

Spanning an entire lifetime, a life convulsed and transformed by the events of the 20th century, Laird Hunt's extraordinary novel offers a profound and intimate portrait of the dreams that propel one tenacious woman onward and the losses that she cannot outrun.

"A beautifully written ode to the rural Midwest." —*Booklist*

Hunt, Samantha

The **dark** dark: stories. Samantha Hunt. Farrar, Straus & Giroux, 2017. 256 pages
  ISBN 9780374282134
1. Paranormal phenomena 2. Magic 3. Loneliness 4. Lust 5. Anxiety 6. Literary fiction 7. Magical realism
                LC 2016050909
Pen/Faulkner Award Finalist, 2018

A first collection of stories by the award-winning author of The Invention of Everything Else imagines lives that are disrupted by otherworldly manifestations, from a woman who inadvertently cheats on her husband when she turns into a deer by night, to an FBI agent who falls in love with a robot built for a suicide mission.

"This excellent, inventive collection...is rife with observant asides, sly humor, and surprises." —*Publishers Weekly*

Hunter, Megan

The **harpy**. Megan Hunter. Grove Press, 2020. 194 pages
  ISBN 9780802148162
1. Married people 2. Cheating (Interpersonal relations) 3. Betrayal 4. Revenge 5. Punishment 6. Psychological suspense

Lucy has set her career aside in order to devote her life to her children and her home. But then a man calls one afternoon with a shattering message: his wife has been having an affair with Lucy's husband, Jake. The revelation marks a turning point: Lucy and Jake decide to stay together, but make a special arrangement designed to even the score and save their marriage—she will hurt him three times. As the couple submit to a delicate game of crime and punishment, Lucy herself begins to change, surrendering to a transformation of both mind and body from which there is no return.

"The tension ratchets up as Lucy spirals downward. Short, spare chapters, interspersed with harpy folklore and memories of an abusive childhood, heighten the sense of dread that pervades Hunter's intriguing take on revenge, which follows her debut, The End We Start From." —*Library Journal*

Hunter, Stephen

The **47th** samurai. Stephen Hunter. Simon & Schuster, 2007. 480 p. (Bob Lee Swagger novels, 4)
  ISBN 9780743238090
1. Greed 2. Murder investigation 3. Revenge 4. Vietnam veterans 5. Voyages and travels 6. Tokyo, Japan 7. Japan 8. Thrillers and suspense
                LC 2007006627

With a high opinion of loyalty as well as a need to bring about justice—by any means necessary—Bob Lee Swagger is a former Marine whose skills are frequently required as he rights wrongs and clears conspiracies. The 47th Samurai takes him to Japan to return a samurai sword to the son of the rightful owner. After he does so, someone slaughters the entire family in order to get the historic sword. Vowing to avenge their murders and retrieve the sword, Bob Lee is drawn into the world of the samurai.

"Although heavy on both the explanations of Japanese customs and the sordid world of incredibly savage Japanese criminals, this work is compelling, exciting, and satisfying, a dark adventure that will appeal to thriller fans." —*Library Journal*

Game of snipers: a Bob Lee Swagger novel. By Stephen Hunter. G. P. Putnam's'S Son, 2019. 400 p. (Bob Lee Swagger novels, 11)
  ISBN 9780399574573

1. Snipers 2. Extremists 3. Tracking and trailing 4. Guns 5. Assassins 6. Middle East 7. Idaho 8. Thrillers and suspense

LC 2018044740

Obsessively tracking a sniper with skills that match his own, Bob Lee Swagger teams up with the Mossad, the FBI and local law enforcement to identify the killer's next target.

Soft target: a thriller. Stephen Hunter. Simon & Schuster, 2011. 384 p. (Ray Cruz novels, 2)

ISBN 9781439138700

1. Snipers 2. Terrorism — Prevention 3. Hostages 4. Former Marines 5. Minneapolis, Minnesota 6. Thrillers and suspense

Black Friday. America's largest shopping mall, suburban Minneapolis. 3:00 pm. Twelve gunmen open fire in the mall corridors, and take more than a thousand hostage. Cruz, a retired Marine sniper, is taken captive along with his fiancée and her family. Hehas a plan— now all he needs is a gun...

Ray Cruz first appeared in Stephen Hunter's Dead zero.

Hunting, Helena

Handle with care. Helena Hunting. St Martins Pr, 2019. 320 pages
ISBN 9781250183996

1. Chief executive officers 2. Women public relations consultants 3. Families 4. Family businesses 5. Fathers — Death 6. Contemporary romances

He wants to lose control... She's trying to hold it together.

Hurley, Andrew Michael

Devil's Day. Andrew Michael Hurley. Houghton Mifflin Harcourt, 2018. 295 p.
ISBN 9781328489883

1. Newlyweds 2. Superstition 3. Grandfathers — Death 4. Devil 5. Sheep 6. England 7. Lancashire, England 8. Horror 9. Gothic fiction

LC 2018000259

John Pentecost returns to his family farm each autumn to gather the sheep down from the moors, but this year his grandfather has died, and with him the village's protection from the Devil.

"[T]his beautifully told gothic story of love, obligation, and legacy blends genres superbly. Hurley is considered one of the leading figures in what is called the British folk-horror revival." —*Booklist*

Originally published: London : John Murray, 2017.

Hurley, Kameron

★ The **light** brigade. Kameron Hurley. SAGA Press, 2019. 356 pages
ISBN 9781481447966

1. Women soldiers 2. Teleportation 3. Imaginary wars and battles 4. War 5. Time travel 6. Mars (Planet) 7. Military science fiction 8. Science fiction

To fight a war on Mars, soldiers are broken down into particles of light, but those who survive are experiencing an alarming type of combat madness.

"...this book is both a gripping story of future warfare and an incisive antiwar fable. Readers will savor this striking novels ambitious structure and critique of rapacious, militarized capitalism." —*Publishers Weekly*

The **stars** are legion. Kameron Hurley. Simon & Schuster, 2017. 400 p.
ISBN 9781481447935

1. Imaginary wars and battles 2. Royal houses 3. Armistices 4. Sisters 5. Intrigue 6. Space 7. Space opera 8. Science fiction

Amnesiac Zan is a prisoner, although her family insists that it's for her own good. They also claim that she represents their best hope for saving the Legion, their dying civilization of "world-ships." Yet Zan can't shake the feeling she's been here before, and that her family isn't really her family. Flawed characters and inventive world-building make this novel a good bet for fans of Iain M. Banks' Culture novels.

Hurston, Zora Neale

Hitting a straight lick with a crooked stick: stories from the Harlem Renaissance. Zora Neale Hurston. Amistad Press, 2020. 192 pages
ISBN 9780062915795

1. African Americans 2. Race relations 3. Social classes 4. Prejudice 5. Racism 6. Short stories 7. Literary fiction 8. African American fiction

Featuring eight lesser-known stories, a collection of Harlem Renaissance tales by the revered folklorist and author of Their Eyes Were Watching God explores subjects ranging from class and migration to racism and sexism.

"With biting wit, Hurston gets to the heart of the human condition, including racism, sexism, and classism, through the circuitous path of her characters, that is, the straight lick with a crooked stick." —*Booklist*

★ **Their** eyes were watching God. Zora Neale Hurston; with a foreword by Edwidge Danticat. Harper Collins, 2000. Xxii, 231 p.
ISBN 9780060199494

1. Independence in African American women 2. Scandals 3. Self-fulfillment in African American women 4. African American women 5. Women murder suspects 6. Florida 7. 1930s 8. Modern classics 9. Literary fiction 10. Psychological fiction

LC 58186

When Janie Starks returns home, she seeks identity and independence as the small southern black community buzzes with gossip about the outcome of her affair with a younger man.

Originally published: Philadelphia : J.B. Lippincott Co, 1937.

Hurwitz, Gregg Andrew

★ **Into** the fire. Gregg Hurwitz. Minotaur Books, 2020. 400 p. (Evan Smoak thrillers, 5)
ISBN 9781250120458

1. Former assassins 2. Money laundering 3. Protectiveness in men 4. Murder victims 5. Murder 6. Thrillers and suspense

LC 2019035900

Helping a murder victim's cousin who is being violently pursued for a mysterious key, Nowhere Man Evan Smoak eliminates a series of dangerous threats before discovering that he is being personally targeted.

"Another exceptional installment in the Orphan X series, full of action, excitement, and adventure. A must-read for thriller fans." —*Library Journal*

★ **Out** of the dark: the return of Orphan X. Gregg Hurwitz. Minotaur Books, 2019. 400 p. (Evan Smoak thrillers, 4)
ISBN 9781250120427

1. Assassins 2. Former assassins 3. Presidents — Assassination plots 4. Secrecy in government 5. Assassination 6. Thrillers and suspense

LC 2018029794

Evan Smoak, a.k.a, the Nowhere Man, is pitted against one of his own for the future of the country when a murderous President Bennett activates the Orphan program's first recruit.

Huxley, Aldous

★ **Brave** new world. Aldous Huxley. Perennial Classics, 1998. Xvii, 270 p.
ISBN 9780060929879

1. Dystopias 2. Far future 3. Totalitarianism 4. Passivity (Psychology) 5. Genetic engineering 6. 26th century 7. Dystopian fiction 8. Science fiction 9. Science fiction classics

LC 98008385

Cloning, feel-good drugs, anti-aging programs, and total social control through politics, programming and media—has Aldous Huxley accurately predicted our future? With a storyteller's genius, he weaves these ethical controversies in a compelling narrative that dawns in the year 632 A.F. (After Ford, the deity). When Lenina and Bernard visit a savage reservation, we experience how Utopia can destroy humanity.

Originally published: Garden City, N.Y. : Doubleday, Doran & company, inc, 1932.

Hyde, Catherine Ryan

My name is Anton. Catherine Ryan Hyde. Lake Union Press, 2020. 364 p.

ISBN 9781542023481

1. Protectiveness 2. Neighbors 3. Abused women 4. Family violence 5. Married women 6. Coming-of-age stories 7. Relationship fiction

Realizing that a neighbor is trapped in an abusive marriage, a smitten 18-year-old youth, haunted by his brother's accidental death, offers the woman shelter and a means to escape.

"A great choice for fans of Hyde and a fine introduction to Hyde's brand of uplifting story of people thrown together by chance and united by love." —*Library Journal*

I

Ide, Joe

★ **Hi** five: an IQ novel. Joe Ide. Mulholland Books, 2020. 341 pages; (IQ novels, 4)

ISBN 9780316509534

1. African Americans 2. Private investigators 3. Dissociative identity disorder 4. Women witnesses 5. Women murder suspects 6. Los Angeles, California 7. Mysteries

Finds genius private investigator Isaiah Quintabe's efforts to build a quiet life with Grace challenged by unexpected new threats.

"Ide goes dark with the skill of a noir master, leaving Isaiah in a very bad place and the reader gasping for breath. A stunning change of pace from one of crime fiction's new stars." —*Booklist*

Iggulden, Conn

The **abbot's** tale. Conn Iggulden. Pegasus Books, 2018. 480 p.

ISBN 9781681777306

1. Alfred 2. Rulers 3. Clergy 4. Ambition in men 5. Political intrigue 6. Battles 7. Great Britain 8. Medieval period (476-1492) 9. Anglo-Saxon period (449-1066) 10. Historical fiction

At the side of Alfred the Great in 973, priest Dunstan of Glastonbury helps guide England into a unified country.

Igharo, Jane

The **sweetest** remedy. Jane Igharo. Jove, 2021. 296 p.
ISBN 9780593101964

1. Multiracial women 2. African American women 3. Fathers — Death 4. Funerals 5. Abandonment (Psychology) 6. Lagos, Nigeria 7. Nigeria 8. Relationship fiction 9. Canadian fiction 10. Multiple perspectives

LC 2021025767

Hannah Bailey has never had a relationship with her father, the Nigerian businessman who had a fling with her white mother, so she's always felt clueless about part of her identity. When her father dies, she's invited to Nigeria for the funeral. Though she wants to hate the man who abandoned her, deep down she can't help feeling curious about where he was from and what he was like. Searching for answers, Hannah boards a plane to Lagos, Nigeria. In Banana Island, one of Nigeria's most affluent areas, Hannah meets the Jolades, her late father's prestigious and famed family—some who accept her and some who think she doesn't belong. But in the chaotic days leading up to the funeral, Hannah is shaped by a family she never thoughtshe would have, a culture she never thought she would understand or appreciate, and a love interest who makes her see herself in a new light.

"Captivating love story meets generational saga in this novel about forging an identity and forgiving the sins of the past." —*Kirkus*

Ignatius, David

The **increment**: a novel. David Ignatius. W. W. Norton & Co, 2009. 400 p.

ISBN 9780393065046

1. Nuclear weapons 2. Nuclear physicists 3. Intelligence officers 4. Spies 5. Codes (Communication) 6. Tehran, Iran 7. Spy fiction

LC 2008053857

When a Tehrani scientist sends encrypted messages to the CIA about Iran's secret nuclear program, Harry Pappas commences communication with him, positive that his information is legitimate. As the agency looks into pretexts for attacking Iran, the scientist grows certain that his life is in danger. Therefore, Pappas enlists the help of British operatives, the Increment, who possess licenses to kill. As the ordeal grows in complexity, Pappas may have to betray his country to find a resolution.

"The author immerses readers in a totally believable universe. Jargon, geography and detail all ring true as his meticulously crafted, tightly woven tale moves from Washington to London and Iran. The plot grabs everything in its path like a snowball rolling down a hill." —*Kirkus*

Iles, Greg

The **bone** tree: a novel. Greg Iles. William Morrow, an imprint of HarperCollinsPublishers, 2015. 816 p. (Penn Cage novels, 5)

ISBN 9780062311115

1. Malicious accusation 2. Police corruption 3. Father and adult son 4. Race relations 5. Justice 6. Flaubert, Gustave 7. Natchez, Mississippi 8. Thrillers and suspense 9. Legal thrillers

LC 2014042113

LibraryReads Favorites, 2015

A follow-up to Natchez Burning finds Southern lawyer Penn Cage desperately struggling to protect his father from false charges and corrupt officers by confronting the puppet master behind the Double Eagles terrorist group.

"In a scenario swarming with FBI agents...villains, reporters, and a red herring or two, Iles allows Cage and Masters plenty of room to operate—and so they do, with all the missteps of ordinary people, unlike the supercops and superagents of so many other procedurals." —*Kirkus*

Cemetery road: a novel. Greg Iles. William Morrow, 2019. 752 p.
ISBN 9780062824615

1. Investigative journalists 2. Secret societies 3. Small town life 4. Amateur detectives 5. Rich people 6. Mississippi 7. Mysteries

His father's terminal illness, his family's struggling newspaper, and a politically charged murder trial force a Washington journalist to return to his small Mississippi hometown.

"Iles once again delivers a sweeping tale of family dysfunction, sexually charged secrets, and the power of wealth, with an overlay of violence and Southern sensibility. Despite the novels length, it all goes by in a flash." —*Publishers Weekly*

Mississippi blood: a novel. Greg Iles. William Morrow, 2017. 694 p. (Penn Cage novels, 6)
ISBN 9780062311153
1. Hate groups 2. Murder suspects 3. Father and adult son 4. African American authors 5. Murder investigation 6. Mississippi 7. Natchez, Mississippi 8. Thrillers and suspense 9. Legal thrillers
LC 2016043631

Grief-stricken and with his world collapsing around him, Penn Cage is shut out of trial preparations by his once-revered Southern doctor father, who is about to be tried for murder in the wake of revelations about a mixed-race child and KKK associations.

"Iles wraps up his massively ambitious Natchez Burning trilogy with a book that is (in keeping with its predecessors) compelling, dark, surprising, and morally ambiguous." —*Booklist*

Natchez burning: a novel. Greg Iles. William Morrow, 2014. 656 pages (Penn Cage novels, 4)
ISBN 9780062311078
1. Father and adult son 2. Malicious accusation 3. Cold cases (Criminal investigation) 4. Race relations 5. Justice 6. Mississippi 7. Natchez, Mississippi 8. Thrillers and suspense 9. Legal thrillers
LC 2013031971

Penn Cage must investigate when his father, a beloved family doctor and pillar of the community, is accused of murdering Viola Turner, the beautiful nurse with whom he worked in the dark days of the early 1960s.

"Much more than a thriller.... This superlative novel's main strength comes from the lead's struggle to balance family and honor." —*Publishers Weekly*

Imamura, Natsuko

The **woman** in the purple skirt: a novel. Natsuko Imamura; translated from the Japanese by Lucy North. Penguin Books, 2021. 224 p.
ISBN 9780143136026
1. Single women 2. Loneliness 3. Hotel workers 4. Manipulation (Social sciences) 5. Obsession 6. Psychological suspense
LC 2020055640

Explores envy, loneliness, power dynamics, and the vulnerability of unmarried women in a taut, suspenseful narrative about the sometimes desperate desire to be seen.

"A subtly ominous story about voyeurism and the danger of losing yourself in someone else." —*Kirkus*

Originally published in Japanese as Murasaki no sukato no onna by Asahi Shimbun Publications, Inc in 2019.
Translated from the Japanese.

Indriðason, Arnaldur

The **darkness** knows. Arnaldur Indridason; [translated by Victoria Cribb].. Minotaur Books, 2021. 352 p. (Detective Konrad novels, 1)
ISBN 9781250765468
1. Former detectives 2. Retirees 3. Cold cases (Criminal investigation) 4. Glaciers 5. Dead 6. Iceland 7. Scandinavian crime fiction 8. Translations
LC 2021015678

When the frozen body of a businessman who disappeared 30 years earlier is found in the icy depths of the Langjokull glacier, former detective Konrad is called out of retirement to reopen this case that has weighed on his mind for decades.

"Indridason methodically builds a portrait of Iceland with a large cast of nuanced characters unsettled by past events. In dredging up the past, Konrad must also confront his complex relationship with his own abusive father, whose murder was unsolved as well." —*Kirkus*
Originally published: Reykjavik : Vaka-Helgafell, 2017.
Translated from the Icelandic.

Outrage. Arnaldur Indridason; translated from the Icelandic by Anna Yates. St Martin's Minotaur, 2012. 288 p. (Erlendur Sveinsson mysteries, 7)
ISBN 9780312659110
1. Secrets 2. Cold cases (Criminal investigation) 3. Drug traffic 4. Policewomen 5. Murder investigation 6. Reykjavik, Iceland 7. Iceland 8. Mysteries 9. Translations 10. Scandinavian crime fiction

When Detective Erlender places her in charge during his leave of absence, Elinborg tackles a disturbing serial rapist case that has the local police racing against time to prevent another attack.
Translation of: Myrka.
Originally published in Icelandic as: Myrka: Reykjavik : Vaka-Helgafell, 2008.

Reykjavik nights: an Inspector Erlendur novel. Arnaldur Indridason; translated from the Icelandic by Victoria Cribb. Minotaur Books, 2015. 288 p. (Erlendur Sveinsson mysteries, 10)
ISBN 9781250048424
1. Police 2. Young men 3. Drowning victims 4. Crime 5. Murder 6. Reykjavik, Iceland 7. Iceland 8. Mysteries 9. Translations 10. Scandinavian crime fiction
LC 2014044425

Erlendur is a young, budding detective who is introduced to Reykjavik's dark underworld while investigating the death of a homeless man.
This title is a prequel to the Erlendur Sveinsson mysteries, but the recommended reading order is tenth in the series.
Originally published in Icelandic as Reykjavikurnaetur: Reykjavik : Vaka-Helgafell, 2012.
Translated from the Icelandic.

The **shadow** district: a thriller. Arnaldur Indridason; translated from the Icelandic by Victoria Cribb. Minotaur Books, 2017. 304 p. (Reykjavik wartime mysteries, 1)
ISBN 9781250124029
1. World War II 2. Murder investigation 3. Cold cases (Criminal investigation) 4. Murder 5. Former detectives 6. Iceland 7. Reykjavik, Iceland 8. Second World War era (1939-1945) 9. 1940s 10. Historical mysteries 11. Parallel narratives 12. Scandinavian crime fiction
LC 2017025692
LibraryReads Favorites, 2017

Investigating the murder of a 90-year-old man, a retired detective discovers unsettling links between the victim, the World War II case of a strangled woman and a pair of attacks that suggest the wrong man may have been arrested decades earlier.

"With minimalist prose, Indridason skillfully weaves the present-day murder with the past in this classic whodunit that ends with a satisfying and logical resolution." —*Kirkus*
A Thomas Dunne Book.
First published with the title Skuggasund in Iceland by Vaka-Helgafell in 2013.
Translated from the Icelandic.

Strange shores: an Inspector Erlendur novel. Arnaldur Indridason; translated from the Icelandic by Victoria Cribb. Minotaur Books, 2014. 304 pages (Erlendur Sveinsson mysteries, 9)

ISBN 9781250000408

1. Missing persons 2. Cold cases (Criminal investigation) 3. Loss (Psychology) 4. Detectives 5. Blizzards 6. Reykjavik, Iceland 7. Iceland 8. Mysteries 9. Translations 10. Scandinavian crime fiction

LC 2014007876

Decades after a woman disappears from the Icelandic fjords amid a tempest of lies, betrayal and revenge, Detective Erlendur searches the same region for his long-lost brother, only to uncover disturbing secrets.

First published with the title Furdustrandir in Iceland by Vaka-Helgafell in 2010.

Translated from the Icelandic.

Irvin, Kelly

Tell her no lies. Kelly Irvin. Thomas Nelson, 2018. 352 p.

ISBN 9780785223115

1. Women journalists 2. Uncles — Death 3. Malicious accusation 4. Family relationships 5. Lawyers 6. San Antonio, Texas 7. Texas 8. Christian romantic suspense

LC 2018028548

Nina Fischer carries a camera wherever she goes—so she can view life through a filter. Safely. After her mother abandoned her to the streets, Nina has kept people at a distance, including her uncle, who adopted Nina and her sister. Wealthy and proud, he is a good man, a fair judge, and someone many in San Antonio admire. But when he is murdered, and the detective assigned to the case accuses Nina of the crime, she knows she must act. She's determinedto use her journalism background to find the real killer. The two men in her life want to help, but can she trust them? She's known Rick since they were children, but now he's an attorney whose political aspirations seem more important than Nina's tragic loss. And then there's Aaron, a news videographer; using their friendship could break the biggest story of his career. Following the evidence leads Nina on a journey of discovery into her father's shocking masquerade as a law-abiding, family-loving Christian. Unlocking these secrets could prove fatal, but it's the only way Nina will ever be able to trust love again..

Irving, John

Avenue of mysteries: a novel. John Irving. Simon & Schuster, 2015. 460 p.

ISBN 9781451664164

1. Fate and fatalism 2. Memory 3. Dreams 4. Aging 5. Voyages and travels 6. Philippines 7. Mexico 8. Literary fiction 9. Psychological fiction

LC 2015005193

Embarking on a trip to the Philippines, senior-aged Juan Diego reflects on dreams and memories of his childhood in Mexico before his past and present intersect in unexpected ways.

"Irving works his familiar themes—Catholicism, sex, death—with a light and assured touch, and though the dream-narrative construct is a little shelf-worn, it serves the story well. Though not as irresistible as early works such as The World According to Garp and The Hotel New Hampshire, a welcome return to form." —*Kirkus*

★ The **Cider** House rules: a novel. John Irving. W. Morrow, 1985. 560 p.

ISBN 9780688030360

1. Orphans 2. Orphanages 3. Physician drug abusers 4. Obstetricians 5. Rural life 6. Maine 7. Literary fiction 8. Books to movies 9. Modern classics

LC 84027195

Set in rural Maine in the first half of the 20th century, it tells the story of Dr. Wilbur Larch—saint and obstetrician, founder and director of the orphanage in the town of St. Cloud's, ether addict and abortionist. It is also the story of Dr. Larch's favorite orphan, Homer Wells, who is never adopted.

"The Cider House Rules is filled with people to love and to feel for.... The characters in John Irving's novel break all the rules, and yet they remain noble and free-spirited. Victims of tragedy, violence, and injustice, their lives seem more interesting and full of thought-provoking dilemmas than the lives of many real people." —*Houston Post*

★ A **prayer** for Owen Meany: a novel. John Irving. W. Morrow, 1989. 543 p.

ISBN 9780688077082

1. Misfits (Persons) 2. Messiahs 3. Christians 4. Tallness and shortness 5. Male friendship 6. New Hampshire 7. 1950s 8. Psychological fiction 9. Books to movies 10. Modern classics

LC 88013839

ALA Notable Book, 1990

Owen Meany hits a foul ball while playing baseball in the summer of 1953 that kills his best friend's mother, an accident that Owen is sure is the result of divine intervention.

"Despite its theological proppings, A Prayer for Owen Meany is a fable of political predestination. As usual, Irving delivers a boisterous cast, a spirited story line and a quality of prose that is frequently underestimated even by his admirers. On the other hand, the novel invites trespass by symbol hunters.... To get lost in critical rummage would be to miss the point. Irving's litany of error and folly may strike some as too righteous; but it is effective." —*Time*

A prayer for Owen Meany was the inspiration for the movie Simon Birch.

★ The **world** according to Garp: a novel. By John Irving. Modern Library, 1998. Xvi, 688 p.

ISBN 9780679603061

1. Authors, American 2. Feminism 3. Eccentrics and eccentricities 4. Mothers and sons 5. Children of single parents 6. Coming-of-age stories 7. Modern classics 8. Books to movies

National Book Critics Circle Award for Fiction finalist, 1978

T. S. Garp, a man with high ambitions for an artistic career and with obsessive devotion to his wife and children, and Jenny Fields, his famous feminist mother, find their lives surrounded by an assortment of people including teachers, whores, and radicals.

"This is a long family novel, spanning four generations and two continents, crammed with incidents, characters, feelings and craft. The components of black comedy and melodrama, pathos and tragedy, mesh effortlessly in a tale that can also be read as a commentary on art and the imagination." —*Time*

40th anniversary edition published by EP Dutton, 2018.

Irwin, Stephen M.

The broken ones: a novel. Stephen M. Irwin. Doubleday, 2012. 368 p.

ISBN 9780385534659

1. Detectives 2. Life after death 3. Serial murder investigation 4. Police corruption 5. Ghosts 6. Supernatural mysteries 7. Australian fiction

When everyone in the world finds themselves suddenly accompanied by a personal ghost that only the haunted can see, the situation throws society into chaos and creates complications for homicide detective Oscar Mariani.

Isaac, Kara

Then there was you. Kara Isaac. Bellbird Press, 2017. 344 p.

ISBN 9780473396534

1. Musicians 2. Americans in foreign countries 3. Big churches 4. Contemporary Christian music 5. Church management 6. Sydney, New South Wales 7. Christian romances 8. Romantic comedies 9. New Zealand fiction

RITA Award, 2018

When Josh and Paige are thrown together to organize his band's next tour, the sparks fly. But can they find a way to bridge the differences that pull them apart? Or will they choose the safety and security of what they know over taking a chance on something that will require them to risk everything?

Isherwood, Christopher

★ The **Berlin** stories: The last of Mr. Norris, Goodbye to Berlin. Christopher Isherwood. James Laughlin, 1946. 191, 207 p.

ISBN 9780811218047

1. Isherwood, Christopher 2. City life 3. British in Germany 4. Gay men 5. Berlin, Germany 6. 1930s 7. Literary fiction 8. Historical fiction 9. Autobiographical fiction

LC 46002158

A two-in-one volume containing the works The Last of Mr. Norris and Goodbye to Berlin finds the characters of Sally Bowles, Fräulein Schroeder, and the doomed Landauers caught up by the nightlife, danger, and mystique of 1931 Berlin.

Two previously published novels reissued here together under a new collective title.

"A New directions book."

Ishiguro, Kazuo

An **artist** of the floating world. Kazuo Ishiguro. Faber and Faber, 1986. 206 p.

ISBN 9780571136087

1. World War II — Art and the war 2. Fathers and daughters 3. Artists 4. Senior men 5. Responsibility 6. Japan 7. Historical fiction 8. Literary fiction 9. Brown, John, 1800-1859

LC 86214424

Whitbread Book Award for Novel, 1986; Whitbread Book of the Year, 1986; Shortlisted for the Booker-McConnell Prize, 1986

This is the story of an artist as an aging man, struggling through the wreckage of Japan's World War II experience. Ishiguro's first novel.

"The tensions stay tight. And this is what makes Mr. Ishiguro not only a good writer but also a wonderful novelist." —*New York Times Book Review*

The **buried** giant: a novel. Kazuo Ishiguro. Alfred A. Knopf, 2015. 304 p.

ISBN 9780307271037

1. Quests 2. Memory 3. Husband and wife 4. Loss (Psychology) 5. Characters and characteristics in literature 6. Great Britain 7. Anglo-Saxon period (449-1066) 8. Arthurian fantasy 9. Historical fantasy 10. Literary fiction

LC 2014028378

As the wars that have ravaged Britain fade into the past, Axl and Beatrice, a couple of elderly Britons, set out on a journey to find the son they have not seen in years, and are joined in their travels by a Saxon warrior, his orphaned charge, and a knight.

"Ishiguros story is a deceptively simple one, for enfolded within its elemental structure are many profound truths, including its beautiful and memorable portrait of a long-term marriage and its subtle commentary on

the eternity of war, all conveyed in the authors mesmerizing prose." —*Booklist*

This is a Borzoi book.

★ **Klara** and the sun. Kazuo Ishiguro. Alfred A. Knopf, Inc, 2021. 304 p.

ISBN 9780593318171

1. Artificial intelligence 2. Companionship 3. Love 4. Robots 5. Solar energy 6. Literary fiction 7. Science fiction

Waiting to be chosen by a customer, an Artificial Friend programmed with high perception observes the activities of shoppers while exploring fundamental questions about what it means to love.

"A haunting fable of a lonely, moribund world that is entirely too plausible." —*Kirkus*

★ **Never** let me go. Kazuo Ishiguro. Alfred A. Knopf, 2005. 304 p.

ISBN 9781400043392

1. Clones and cloning 2. Organ donors 3. Ethics 4. Women 5. Young women 6. England 7. 1970s 8. 1990s 9. Literary fiction 10. Science fiction 11. Books to movies 12. Adult books for young adults

LC 2004048966

ALA Notable Book, 2006; Alex Award, 2006; Library Journal Best Books, 2005; New York Times Notable Book, 2005; School Library Journal Best Books: Best Adult Books 4 Teens, 2005; Shortlisted for the Man Booker Prize, 2005; Shortlisted for the James Tait Black Memorial Prize for Fiction, 2005; National Book Critics Circle Award for Fiction finalist, 2005

A reunion with two childhood friends—Ruth and Tommy—draws Kath and her companions on a nostalgic odyssey into the supposedly idyllic years of their lives at Hailsham, an isolated private school in the serene English countryside, and a dramatic confrontation with the truth about their childhoods and about their lives in the present.

"Ishiguro serves up the saddest, most persuasive science fiction you'll read. Set in England, late 1990s, the novel posits a technological breakthrough whose effect is to condemn the children of Hailsham to a fate that was, until this novel, unthinkable. Ishiguro's imagining of the children's misshapen little world is profoundly thoughtful, and their hesitant progression into knowledge of their plight is an extreme and heartbreaking version of the exodus of all children from the innocence in which the benevolent but fraudulent adult world conspires to place them." —*The Atlantic*

★ The **remains** of the day. Kazuo Ishiguro. A. A. Knopf, 1989. 245 p.

ISBN 9780394573434

1. Butlers 2. Social classes 3. Men — Psychology 4. Loyalty 5. Country homes 6. England 7. Psychological fiction 8. Literary fiction 9. Books to movies

LC 89080445

Booker Prize, 1989; ALA Notable Book, 1990

Stevens, an aging butler dedicated to the dignity of his profession, takes to the road to convince Ms. Bent—a now-married former housekeeper—to resume her duties at Darlington Hall. As Stevens journeys, he reflects on their prior acquaintance; his memories reveal Stevens' deeply personal desires, and how he has rewritten events to maintain his ideal image of service and discretion.

Originally published: 1989.

Originally published in Great Britain by Faber and Faber Limited, London—Title page verso.

The **unconsoled**. Kazuo Ishiguro. A. A. Knopf, 1995. 535 p.

ISBN 9780679404255

1. Pianists 2. Celebrities 3. Memory 4. Interpersonal relations 5. Expectation (Psychology) 6. Europe 7. Surrealist fiction 8. Literary fiction

LC 9515829

ALA Notable Book, 1996

Arriving in an European city with significant gaps in his memory, Ryder, a renowned pianist, is overwhelmed by an onslaught of strangers who seem to know him and of whom he has vague, dreamlike recollections.

"In this novel, prominent concert pianist Ryder is at odds with his surroundings. Ryder arrives in an unidentified European city at a bit of a loss. Everyone he meets seems to assume that he knows more than he knows, that he is well acquainted with the city and its obscure cultural crisis. A young woman he kindly consents to advise seems to have been an old lover and her son quite possibly his own; he vaguely recalls past conversations. The world he has entered is a surreal, Alice-in-Wonderland place where a door in a cafe can lead back to a hotel miles away. The result is at once dreamy, disorienting, and absolutely compelling; Ishiguro's paragraphs, though Proust-like, are completely lucid and quite addictive to read." —*Library Journal*

When we were orphans. Kazuo Ishiguro. A. A. Knopf, 2000. 335 p.
ISBN 9780375410543
1. Detectives 2. British in China 3. Orphans 4. Parent-separated boys 5. Cold cases (Criminal investigation) 6. Shanghai, China 7. 1930s 8. Mysteries 9. Literary fiction 10. Psychological fiction
LC 26120

New York Times Notable Book, 2000; Shortlisted for the Booker-McConnell Prize, 2000

Christopher Banks, an English boy born in early-20th-century Shanghai, is orphaned at age nine when both his mother and father disappear under suspicious circumstances. He grows up to become a renowned detective, and more than 20 years later, returns to Shanghai to solve the mystery of the disappearances.

"For all its ellipses and evasions, When We Were Orphans, will linger in the mind as an often fascinating, imaginative work of surpassing intelligence and taste." —*Times Literary Supplement*

Itami, Emily

Fault lines: a novel. Emily Itami. Custom House, 2021. 224 p.
ISBN 9780063099807
1. Married women 2. Homemakers 3. Restaurateurs 4. Extramarital affairs 5. Options, alternatives, choices 6. Mainstream fiction
LC 2021024232

A bored, frustrated Japanese housewife begins living two lives when she meets a successful restaurateur and rediscovers the freedom and the electric pulse of her beloved Tokyo and realizes that she has to make a choice.

"While a somewhat pat ending feels unworthy of the novel's provocative premise, Itami makes palpable Mizuki's loneliness and her need to feel seen. Itami's brave, frank portrayal of Japan's societal expectations of women is worth a look." —*Publishers Weekly*

Iweala, Uzodinma

★ **Speak** no evil. Uzodinma Iweala. Harper, 2018. 214 p.
ISBN 9780061284922
1. Gay teenagers 2. Homophobia 3. Nigerian Americans 4. Immigrants 5. Interethnic friendship 6. Washington, D.C. 7. Nigeria 8. Literary fiction 9. LGBTQIA fiction 10. Multiple perspectives 11. Adult books for young adults
Booklist Editors' Choice: Adult Books for Young Adults, 2018; Library Journal Best Books, 2018

An Ivy League-bound star athlete from a prestigious private school in Washington, D.C, and his best friend, the daughter of prominent government insiders, struggle with brutal responses to the young man's sexual

orientation before finding themselves speeding toward a violent and senseless future.

J

Jackson, Brenda

Forged in desire. Brenda Jackson. HQN, 2017. 384 p. (The Protectors (Brenda Jackson), 1)
ISBN 9780373790005
1. Bodyguards 2. Heirs and heiresses 3. Women jurors 4. Threat (Psychology) 5. Protectiveness in men 6. Romantic suspense 7. Multicultural romances 8. African American fiction

Jury duty isn't usually this exciting: soon after Margo Connelly and her fellow jurors deliver a guilty verdict, people involved in the trial start dying. Once the judge, the court clerk, and the bailiff are gunned down in cold blood outside the courthouse, it becomes clear that Margo needs protection, too. Tasked with protecting Margo from a crime boss' hired killer, bodyguard Lamar "Striker" Jennings must stay by her side, day and night. Naturally, Margo and Lamar get to know each other very, very well. But Lamar has reservations about a relationship: not only is Margo his mentor's niece, but Lamar fears that his law-breaking past may change her mind about him.

"Jackson's deft plotting and effective red herrings keep the suspense high as her multidimensional characters command the readers attention." —*Publishers Weekly*

Jackson, Charles

The **lost** weekend. By Charles Jackson. R. Bentley, 1979. 244 p.
ISBN 9780837604305
1. Middle-aged men 2. Alcoholics 3. Alcoholism 4. Depression 5. Family relationships 6. Psychological fiction 7. Books to movies
LC 78026163

The famous novel of five harrowing days in the life of an alcoholic. Originally published: New York : Farrar & Rinehart, 1944.

Jackson, Joshilyn

Never have I ever. Joshilyn Jackson. William Morrow, 2019. 352 pages
ISBN 9780062855312
1. Secrets 2. Paul, the Apostle, Saint 3. Book clubs 4. Diving 5. Families 6. Southern States 7. Thrillers and suspense 8. Southern fiction 9. Relationship fiction
Booklist Editors' Choice, 2019

When her loved ones are put in danger by a blackmailer who threatens to expose dangerous secrets, a devoted family woman struggles to keep the upper hand in an escalating war of betrayal.

Jackson, K. M.

How to marry Keanu Reeves in 90 days. K.M. Jackson. Forever, 2021. 336 p.
ISBN 9781538703502
1. Reeves, Keanu 2. African Americans 3. Women artists 4. Swift, Kay 5. Single men 6. Job offers 7. Romantic comedies 8. Multicultural romances 9. Contemporary romances
LC 2021023035

Bethany Lu Carlisle is devastated when the tabloids report actor Keanu Reeves is about to tie the knot. What?! How could the world's perfect boyfriend and forever bachelor, Keanu not realize that making a move like this could potentially be devastating to the equilibrium of... well... everything! Not to mention he's never come face to face with the person who could potentially be his true soulmate—her. Desperate to convince Keanu to call off the wedding, Lu and her ride-or-die BFF Truman Erikson take a wild road trip to search for the elusive Keanu so that Lu can fulfill her dream of meeting her forever crush and confess her undying love.

"It would be enough if Jackson's latest (after Real Men Knit) were simply a charming rom-com replete with laugh-out-loud one liners and pop-culture references, but it's also a moving, heartfelt story about coping with grief, stress, and major life changes." —*Publishers Weekly*

Jackson, Shirley

★ The **haunting** of Hill House. Shirley Jackson. Penguin, 1984. 246 p.
ISBN 9780140071085
1. Haunted houses 2. Loners 3. Paranormal phenomenon investigation 4. Poltergeists 5. Ghosts 6. Horror 7. Gothic fiction 8. Books to movies

An 80-year-old mansion harboring dark secrets comes to menacing life in this classic spine-tingling tale from Shirley Jackson. Anthropologist and ghost hunter Dr. John Montague invites three strangers to stay in haunted Hill House for the summer. One of the guests is 32-year-old Eleanor, for whom three months in a haunted house is preferable to caring for her invalid mother. Soon, Eleanor begins to see and hear things that the other guests cannot. Is it all in her imagination, or is she the only one who can perceive the evil that lurks in Hill House.

Later editions published as: The Haunting.

Book made into a movie called The haunting.

Originally published: New York : Viking, 1959.

★ The **lottery:** and other stories. Shirley Jackson. Farrar, Straus, Giroux, 2005. 306 p.
ISBN 9780141191430
1. Manners and customs 2. Villages 3. Stoning 4. Small town life 5. Lotteries 6. Horror 7. Classics 8. Short stories

A collection of stories including "The Lottery."

"The particular talents of Shirley Jackson are shown off to even greater advantage in this collection of short stories (some from *The New Yorker*) than in her last year's The Road Through The Wall." —*Kirkus*

Original title: The lottery, or, The adventures of James Harris.

We have always lived in the castle. Shirley Jackson. Penguin Books, 1984. 214 p.
ISBN 9780140071078
1. Family estates 2. Eccentric families 3. Poisoning 4. Social isolation 5. Superstition 6. Horror 7. Gothic fiction

A deliciously unsettling novel about a perverse, isolated, and possibly murderous family and the dramatic struggle that ensues when an unexpected visitor interrupts their unusual way of life.

Jackson-Brown, Angela

★ **When** stars rain down: a novel. Angela Jackson-Brown. Thomas Nelson, 2021. 368 p.
ISBN 9780785240440
1. African American women 2. Racism 3. Families 4. Birthdays 5. Hate crimes 6. Georgia 7. 1930s 8. African American fiction 9. Historical fiction 10. Coming-of-age stories
LC 2020045148

A young woman's coming of age against a backdrop of an unseasonably hot summer in 1936 Georgia is upended by KKK activities that raise questions about her community's unacknowledged racism and the kind of person she wants to be.

Jakes, John

Love and war. John Jakes. Harcourt Brace Jovanovich, 1984. 1019 p. (North and South trilogy, 2)
ISBN 9780151544967
1. Family relationships 2. Abolitionists — History 3. War 4. Slavery 5. Revenge 6. Confederate States of America 7. United States 8. American Civil War era (1861-1865) 9. 1860s 10. War stories 11. Family sagas 12. Historical fiction
LC 84012895

"This sequel to North and South carries forward the entwined sagas of the Hazards of Pennsylvania, industrialists, and the Mains of South Carolina, plantation owners.... The story moves from action on the battlefield to the corridors of Washington to the shipyards of Liverpool. It encompasses deeds heroic and dastardly; passions licit and illicit; spying, assassination plotting and cynical profiteering; and the trying out of new military interventions." —*Publishers Weekly*

★ **North** and South. John Jakes. Harcourt Brace Jovanovich, 1982. 740 p. (North and South trilogy, 1)
ISBN 9780151669981
1. Family relationships 2. Abolitionists — History 3. Slavery 4. Revenge 5. Confederate States of America 6. West Point, New York 7. 1940s 8. War stories 9. Family sagas 10. Historical fiction
LC 81047898

Chronicles two great American dynasties over three generations. Though brought together in a friendship that neither jealousy nor violence could shatter, the Hazards and the Mains are torn apart by the storm of event that has divided the nation.

Jalaluddin, Uzma

★ **Ayesha** at last. Uzma Jalaluddin. Berkley, 2019. 368 p.
ISBN 9781984802798
1. Muslim families 2. Expectation (Psychology) 3. Women poets 4. Women teachers 5. Independence in women 6. Toronto, Ontario 7. Canada 8. Chick lit 9. Romantic comedies 10. Canadian fiction 11. Adult books for young adults
LC 2018058488

Booklist Editors' Choice, 2019; Library Journal Best Books, 2019; LibraryReads Favorites, 2019

A modern Muslim adaptation of Pride and Prejudice finds a reluctant teacher who would avoid an arranged marriage setting aside her literary ambitions before falling in love with her perpetually single cousin's infuriatingly conservative fiance.

Hana Khan carries on. Uzma Jalaluddin. Jove, 2021. 336 p.
ISBN 9780593336366
1. Restaurants 2. Waitresses 3. Podcasters 4. Hate crimes 5. Competition 6. Toronto, Ontario 7. Contemporary romances 8. Canadian fiction
LC 2020050115

When the halal restaurant where she waitresses is threatened by new competition, a rising podcaster uncovers a long-buried family secret and falls for a rival before their community is upended by a hate attack.

"The social dynamics at the radio station and in Toronto's Indian communities are the real highlights, bound by just enough plot to move the story forward smoothly." —*Publishers Weekly*

James, Eloisa

★ **Seven** minutes in heaven. Eloisa James. Avon Books, 2017. 384 p. (Desperate duchesses by the numbers, 3)
ISBN 9780062660121
1. Widows 2. Inventors 3. Abduction 4. Guardian and ward 5. Governesses 6. England 7. Great Britain 8. Georgian era (1714-1837) 9. 1800s (Decade) 10. Historical romances 11. Georgian romances

Eugenia Snowe's professional reputation depends on supplying the upper classes with England's finest governesses. So when one of her placements proves unsuitable, she takes a personal interest in rectifying the situation. Edward "Ward" Reeve is desperate to find someone who can handle his rambunctious younger half-siblings, whose behavior threatens his status as their guardian. A witty and heartfelt tale of opposites attracting.

"Another bright, delightful read from a queen of historical romance." —*Kirkus*

Story takes place in 1801.

Three weeks with Lady X. Eloisa James. Avon Books, 2014. 384 p. (Desperate duchesses by the numbers, 1)
ISBN 9780062223890
1. Rich men 2. Women mentors 3. Nobility 4. Aristocracy 5. Social status 6. London, England 7. Great Britain 8. Georgian era (1714-1837) 9. Georgian romances 10. Historical romances
Romantic Times Reviewer's Choice Award, 2014

Having sworn off marriage to start her own business, Lady Xenobia India St. Clair has made quite the name for herself as society's most in-demand interior designer. Hired by Tobias "Thorn" Dautry, illegitimate son of the Duke of Villiers, to refurbish his newly acquired country house, India finds herself drawn to Thorn, who's equally enchanted by "Lady X." However, since Thorn has employed India for the express purpose of designing a comfortable home for his future bride, their steadily escalating flirtation proves problematic. Readers who enjoy this installment of the Desperate Duchesses series will want to read more about Thorn's childhood in A Duke of Her Own.

"Emotionally rewarding and elegantly written, with textured characters and a captivating plot." —*Kirkus*

The **ugly** duchess. Eloisa James. Avon Books, 2012. 384 p. (Happily ever afters (Eloisa James), 4)
ISBN 9780062021731
1. Dukes and duchesses 2. Separated couples 3. Married people and secrets 4. Romantic love 5. Feminine beauty (Aesthetics) 6. London, England 7. England 8. Regency period (1811-1820) 9. Regency romances 10. Historical romances

When she discovers that her husband James married her only for her dowry, Theodora Saxby, known by the town as The Ugly Duchess, is devastated until James launches a campaign to prove that he really loves her.

Wilde in love. Eloisa James. Avon Books, 2017. 384 p. (Wildes of Lindow Castle, 1)
ISBN 9780062697288
1. Adventurers 2. Celebrities 3. Aristocracy 4. Mate selection 5. Independence in women 6. England 7. Great Britain 8. Georgian era (1714-1837) 9. Georgian romances 10. Historical romances

After returning home from dangerous adventures, the notoriously rakish Lord Alaric Wilde, son of the Duke of Lindow, finds himself drawn to the very private, but very witty, Miss Willa Ffynche.

Includes a note about bogs, Egyptian ducks, and melodramatic plays.

James, Henry

Complete stories, 1864-1874. Henry James. Library of America, 1999. 972 p.

ISBN 9781883011703
1. Bolano, Roberto 2. Manners and customs 3. United States 4. Europe 5. Short stories 6. Anthologies
LC 98053919

The complete stories of Henry James spans the creative life of the writer and includes his first twenty-four published stories, including thirteen never collected by him.

Complete stories, 1874-1884. Henry James. Library of America, 1999. 941 p.
ISBN 9781883011635
1. Americans in Europe 2. Europe 3. 19th century 4. Short stories 5. Psychological fiction 6. Classics
LC 9819252

A collection of nineteen stories from the middle period of Henry James's writing career features some of his most famous works examining the relationship between the United States and Europe, including the classic "Daisy Miller" and the satiric "Lady Barbarina.

Second volume in The Library of America's complete, five-volume edition.

Complete stories, 1884-1891. Library of America, 1999. 904 p.
ISBN 9781883011642
1. Americans in Europe 2. Europe 3. 19th century 4. Short stories 5. Psychological fiction 6. Classics
LC 9819250

A gathering of seventeen of the classic short stories of Henry James, covering the middle period of his career, contains some of his greatest writing, including the novella "The Aspern Papers" and the unforgettable supernatural story "Sir Edmund Orne."

Third volume in the Library of America's complete, five-volume edition.

Complete stories, 1892-1898. Henry James. Library of America, 1996. 948 p.
ISBN 9781883011093
1. Americans in Europe 2. Europe 3. 19th century 4. Short stories 5. Psychological fiction 6. Classics

Twenty-one stories include "The Turn of the Screw," and "The Figure in the Carpet."

Complete stories, 1898-1910. Henry James. Library of America, 1996. 946 p.
ISBN 9781883011109
1. Americans in Europe 2. Europe 3. Short stories 4. Psychological fiction 5. Classics
LC 95-23462

Gathers thirty-one stories, including "The Great Good Place," "The Jolly Corner," and "The Beast in the Jungle."

Daisy Miller. Henry James. Dover Publications, 1995. 59 p.
ISBN 9780486287737
1. Americans in Europe 2. Scandals 3. Voyages and travels 4. Young women 5. Rich women 6. Europe 7. Psychological fiction 8. Books to movies 9. Classics
LC 95021203

Daisy Miller, a young American girl, flirts and partakes of young life to its fullest while visiting Europe. Daisy meets the more subtle and self-aware Winterbourne and their romance ends in misfortune.

An unabridged republication of the work originally published in The Cornhill magazine, 1878—Title page verso.

The **golden** bowl. Henry James. A.A. Knopf, 1992. 596 p.
ISBN 9780679417330

1. Father and adult daughter 2. Extramarital affairs 3. Marriage 4. Deception 5. Psychological fiction 6. Books to movies 7. Classics

LC 92052927

The close relationship between American millionaire Adam Venuer and his daughter Maggie threatens their respective marriages.

Originally published 1904.

The **portrait** of a lady. Henry James. Alfred A. Knopf, 1991. 626 p.
ISBN 9780679405627
1. Heirs and heiresses 2. Americans in England 3. Marriage 4. Manors 5. Young women 6. Italy 7. Psychological fiction 8. Coming-of-age stories 9. Books to movies

LC 91052999

When Isabel Archer, a beautiful, spirited American, is brought to Europe by her wealthy Aunt Touchett, it is expected that she will soon marry. But Isabel, resolved to determine her own fate, does not hesitate to turn down two eligible suitors. She then finds herself irresistibly drawn to Gilbert Osmond, who, beneath his veneer of charm and cultivation, is cruelty itself.

First published: 1881.

★ The **turn** of the screw. Henry James. Dover Publications, 1991. 87 p.
ISBN 9780486266848
1. Ghosts 2. Governesses 3. Orphans 4. Man-woman relationships 5. Supernatural 6. England 7. Ghost stories 8. Gothic fiction 9. Psychological fiction

LC 90-20572

The story unfolds with the arrival of a new governess at a remote country estate, who has been hired by the uncle of two young orphans to take complete charge of the children's lives and upbringing. Her first peaceful weeks are disturbed by the apparition of the ghosts of two evil servants who once served in the house.

The turn of the screw has been adapted several times into movies of the same name and inspired the following films: The innocents (1961), The haunting of Helen Walker (1995), Presence of mind (1999), The others (2001), In a dark place (2006), and The turning (2020)

New introduction and notes (c)2000.

The **wings** of the dove. Henry James. Modern Library, 1993. 711 p.
ISBN 9780679600671
1. Americans in Europe 2. Heirs and heiresses 3. Manipulation (Social sciences) 4. Terminal illness 5. Upper class 6. London (England) 7. Venice (Italy) 8. Psychological fiction 9. Books to movies 10. Classics

LC 93015338

Beautiful Kate Croy may have been left penniless by her relatives, but her bold, ambitious nature ensures she will not succumb meekly to a life of poverty. If the financial circumstances of Merton Densher, the man she is passionately in love with, are not sufficient to secure her future, perhaps her cunning will. Her scheming is flawed, though, for it fails to take into account the inconstancies of the human heart.

The wings of the dove was closely adapted to a film of the same name in 1997. It was loosely interpreted in the later film Under heaven (1998).

James, Lorelei

I want you back. Lorelei James. Berkley, 2019. 320 p. (Want you series, 1)
ISBN 9780451492746

1. Former girlfriends 2. Former hockey players 3. Single mothers 4. Coparenting 5. Life change events 6. Minneapolis, Minnesota 7. Sports romances 8. Contemporary romances

When former NHL star Jaxson Lund returns home, he is determined to prove to Lucy, his ex-girlfriend and mother of his daughter, that he is ready to be a father and the man she has always wanted.

James, Marlon

★ **Black** leopard, red wolf. Marlon James. Riverhead Books, 2019. 720 pages (Dark star trilogy (Marlon James), 1)
ISBN 9780735220171
1. Missing boys 2. Quests 3. Shapeshifters 4. Private investigators 5. Imaginary creatures 6. Epic fantasy 7. Literary fiction 8. Afrofantasy

LC 2018035102

Los Angeles Times Book Prize, Ray Bradbury Prize for Science Fiction, Fantasy & Speculative Fiction, 2019; Loan Stars Favourites, 2019; Locus Award for Dark Fantasy-Horror Novel, 2020; Minnesota Book Award for Genre Fiction, 2020; National Book Award for Fiction finalist, 2019

Hired to find a mysterious boy who disappeared three years before, Tracker joins a search party that is quickly targeted by deadly creatures.

"James's first foray into fantasy demonstrates epic sweep, an intensely layered structure, and raw if luscious language that pins readers to the page with enough concrete detail to discourage a breezy skim-through. Placed firmly in the genre by its dark magic, unstoppable twists and turns, dangerous kingly aspirations, and imperfect but essential fellow-creature bonding, the narrative is refreshingly distinctive in its grounding in African history and folklore." —*Library Journal*

★ **A brief** history of seven killings: a novel. Marlon James. Riverhead Books, 2014. 704 p.
ISBN 9781594486005
1. Marley, Bob 2. Reggae musicians 3. Drug traffic 4. Assassins 5. Attempted murder 6. Political corruption 7. Jamaica 8. New York City 9. 20th century 10. Historical fiction 11. Literary fiction 12. Multiple perspectives

LC 2014018475

Booklist Editors' Choice, 2014; Library Journal Best Books 2014; Man Booker Prize, 2015; Minnesota Book Award for Novel & Short Story, 2015; New York Times Notable Book, 2014; Shortlisted for the International Dublin Literary Award, 2016; National Book Critics Circle Award for Fiction finalist, 2014

A tale inspired by the 1976 attempted assassination of Bob Marley spans decades and continents to explore the experiences of journalists, drug dealers, killers and ghosts against a backdrop of period social and political turmoil.

"This is a breakthrough novel not only for the author but also for Caribbean and world literature. The Kingston milieu (and its extensions, including New York) is made horrifyingly believable; the patois is rhythmic, slangy, and often quite funny." —*Booklist*

Includes bibliographical references and index.

James, Miranda

What the cat dragged in. Miranda James. Berkley Prime Crime, 2021. 304 p. (Cat in the stacks mysteries, 14)
ISBN 9780593199466
1. Librarians 2. Cats 3. Amateur detectives 4. Grandfathers 5. Inheritance and succession 6. Mississippi 7. Gentle reads 8. Cozy mysteries

LC 2021016850

Librarian Charlie Harris and his faithful feline companion, Diesel, have inherited Charlie's grandfather's house, along with a deadly legacy: a decades-old crime scene. As he and Diesel check out the house he remembers fondly from his childhood, he is pleasantly surprised that it is in better condition than expected. That is, until they find a literal skeleton in a closet. While the sheriff's department investigates the mysterious remains, Charlie digs deeper into the past for clues to the identity of the bones and why they are there. But the cold case heats up quickly when a family friend is found dead on the farm. As Charlie delves into his own family history, he encounters many people who might have been motivated to take a life. But Charlie and Diesel know that things are not always what they seem, and that secrets seemingly lost to time have a way of finding their way back to haunt the present.

"The solution's both fair and satisfying, and Charlie is a plausible investigator and the supporting cast realistic. This entry reinforces James's place in the top rank of cozy authors." —*Publishers Weekly*

James, P. D.

Death of an expert witness. P. D. James. Scribner, 1977. 322 p. (Adam Dalgliesh mysteries, 6)

ISBN 9780684152677

1. Police 2. Forensic scientists 3. Murder investigation 4. Dalgliesh, Adam (Fictitious character) 5. Crime laboratories 6. Mysteries 7. Police procedurals

LC 77021530

A community of forensic scientists are taken by surprise when a member of their own team is found in a bloody pool on the laboratory floor. Dalgliesh faces too many suspects as he tries to discover who might have wanted to kill the universally hated Edward Lorrimer.

"Basically James is a novelist who happens to put her character into mystery stories. She is just as much interested in people and their relationships as she is in the conventions of the genre. And being the perceptive and sensitive writer she is, she constructs books that can be read on several levels." —*New York Times Book Review*

The **lighthouse**. P.D. James. Knopf, 2005. 320 p. (Adam Dalgliesh mysteries, 13)

ISBN 9780307262912

1. Seaside resorts 2. Police 3. Murder investigation 4. Policewomen 5. Resorts 6. Mysteries 7. Police procedurals

LC 2005051039

Commander Adam Dalgliesh and his team are called in to solve a sensitive high profile case on Combe island off the Cornish coast of England at a time when Dalgliesh is dealing with his uncertain future with Emma Lavenham, Kate Miskin struggles with her own personal turmoil, and Sergeant Francis Benton-Smith must cope with resentment over a female superior.

"This novel is too rooted in genre conventions to count originality as its strong suit. But it has deviousness to burn, and it also offers other enticements. It's the kind of book that boasts a wryly humorous Scrabble scene, not to mention a Scrabble-lover's vocabulary." —*New York Times Book Review*

Original sin. P.D. James. A. A. Knopf, 1995. 416 p. (Adam Dalgliesh mysteries, 9)

ISBN 9780679438892

1. Police 2. Murder investigation 3. Dalgliesh, Adam (Fictitious character) 4. Publishers and publishing 5. Revenge 6. Thames River 7. London, England 8. Mysteries 9. Police procedurals

LC 9426094

As Commander Adam Dalgliesh and his team probe the bizarre death of publishing magnate Gerard Etienne, a ruthless man with many enemies,

they uncover a complex web of dark secrets and revenge and a desperate killer prepared to strike again

"A mystery featuring Commander Adam Dalgliesh of Scotland Yard. Innocent House, a nineteenth-century pile on the Thames that accommodates the Peverell Press, presides over this novel of revenge. After Gerard Etienne, the new chairman of the press, announces his plan to sell the house, he ends up dead, with the head of a toy snake stuffed in his mouth. In this elaborate novel, the author...does what she does best: shows that guilt and blame have no single address." —*The New Yorker*

The **private** patient. P.D. James. Alfred A. Knopf, 2008. 368 p. (Adam Dalgliesh mysteries, 14)

ISBN 9780307270771

1. Women journalists 2. Murder investigation 3. Plastic surgery 4. Police 5. Policewomen 6. Dorset, England 7. Mysteries 8. Police procedurals

LC 2008027137

When investigative journalist Rhoda Gradwyn turns up dead after seeing renowned plastic surgeon George Chandler-Powell for a routine surgical procedure, Commander Adam Dalgliesh is called in to investigate.

"The book begins by introducing investigative journalist Rhoda Gradwyn, whose face is marked by a disfiguring scar. She chooses prominent plastic surgeon George Chandler-Powell to remove it at his private clinic in Cheverell Manor.... It's a place where the comfortably situated can have their cosmetic work done in privacy and not everyone welcomes the arrival of a professional snoop. The evening after her surgery, Gradwyn is murdered. Dalgliesh and his team are called in to solve the mystery, then have to deal with a second murder.... The investigation disrupts lives and disturbs secrets far beyond the little group at the manor. James is in excellent form in Patient. She engages the brain as she entertains with apt descriptions and wry asides, and sets the reader to thinking beyond the obvious." —*St. Louis Post-Dispatch*

This is a Borzoi book—Title page verso.

The **skull** beneath the skin. P.D. James. Scribner, 1982. 416 p. (Cordelia Gray mysteries, 2)

ISBN 9780684177731

1. Women private investigators 2. Murder investigation 3. Anonymous letters 4. Actors and actresses 5. Islands 6. England 7. Mysteries

LC 82005981

Hired as a bodyguard to faded actress Clarissa Lisle, the recent recipient of numerous death threats, Cordelia Gray accompanies the actress to an island castle, whose owner collects funeral paraphernalia.

"Fading actress Clarissa Lisle has been receiving frightening notes and is terrified of failing in her comeback performance, a revival of 'The Duchess of Malfi', held on a small private island off Dorset. Her husband hires detective Cordelia Gray to stop the notes. Once on the island, Cordelia discovers that nearly everyone there has a good reason to hate Clarissa, who is soon found gruesomely battered to death. The isolated group of suspects, hidden clues, and macabre atmosphere of an island castle complete with skulls and underground passageways make a pleasant traditional mystery. But James is never superficial, and her in-depth characterizations and excellent writing reveal complex relationships, motives, and human frailties." —*Library Journal*

A **taste** for death. P.D. James. Knopf, 1986. 459 p. (Adam Dalgliesh mysteries, 7)

ISBN 9780394555836

1. Police 2. Murder investigation 3. Social classes 4. Hoboes 5. Aristocracy 6. London, England 7. Mysteries 8. Police procedurals

LC 86045273

Macavity Award for Best Mystery Novel, 1987; Silver Dagger Award for Fiction, 1986

Commander Adam Dalgleish investigates the throat-slash murders, in a London Church, of Sir Paul Berowne, former Minister of State, and a tramp named Harry Mack, murders that lead Dalgleish onto surprising English pathways

"This book is about murder and the way murder changes everything.... It is also about the human condition in London today, enlarged by a sense of the British past that stretches back like a rich and barely dwindling perspective." —*New York Times Book Review*

An **unsuitable** job for a woman. P.D. James. Scribner, 2001. 250 p. (Cordelia Gray mysteries, 1)
ISBN 9780743219556
1. Women private investigators 2. College students 3. Murder investigation 4. Suicide 5. Dalgliesh, Adam (Fictitious character) 6. Cambridge, England 7. Mysteries

LC 200118202
Left alone by her partner's suicide, Cordelia Gray struggles to manage the private detective agency they once shared.

James, Rebecca
The **woman** in the mirror. Rebecca James. Minotaur Books, 2020. 351 pages
ISBN 9781250230058
1. Family secrets 2. Adoption 3. Mansions 4. Young women 5. Secrets 6. Cornwall, England 7. England 8. Psychological suspense 9. Gothic fiction 10. Parallel narratives

LC 2019046418
Investigating her birth family upon inheriting a centuries-old English manor, an adopted art gallery curator uncovers the story of a mid-20th-century governess who was cruelly treated by the curator's unknown ancestors.

"This thrilling gothic endeavor keeps the pages turning with tense scenes and lush depictions." —*Booklist*
Originally published in Great Britain by HQ, an imprint of HarperCollinsPublishers, Ltd. in 2018.

James, Wendy
A **little** bird. Wendy James. Lake Union Press, 2021. 319 pages
ISBN 9781542026482
1. Homecomings 2. Family secrets 3. Mother deserted families 4. Father and adult daughter 5. Hometowns 6. Australia 7. Mysteries 8. Australian fiction 9. Multiple perspectives

A homecoming snares a young woman in a dangerous tangle of lies, secrets, and bad blood in this gripping novel by the bestselling author of An Accusation.

"A Little Bird is a solid mystery with interesting characters, and although it may be considered a slow-burn of a story, it lands the ending with a few twists that are sure to surprise as well as tie up all loose ends." —*Booklist*

Janowitz, Brenda
The **Grace** Kelly dress. Brenda Janowitz. Graydon House, 2020. 384 pages
ISBN 9781525804663
1. Wedding dress 2. Mothers and daughters 3. Options, alternatives, choices 4. Dressmakers 5. Imitation 6. 1950s 7. 2010s 8. Relationship fiction 9. Family sagas

The iconic wedding dress of Grace Kelly inspires three generations of women to forge their own paths, including a Parisian atelier who is hired to sew a look-alike gown before confronting an impossible choice.

"Alternating between the timelines of the three women, Janowitz gives each of them a unique voice and weaves a delightful tale of mothers and daughters and the delicate balance of keeping tradition while still forging your own path." —*Booklist*

Jaswal, Balli Kaur
Erotic stories for Punjabi widows. Balli Kaur Jaswal. William Morrow & Co, 2017. 304 p.
ISBN 9780062645128
1. Multiculturalism 2. Creativity 3. Books and reading 4. Communities 5. Female friendship 6. London, England 7. Literary fiction

A lively, sexy, and thought-provoking East-meets-West story about community, friendship, and women's lives at all ages—a spicy and alluring mix of Together Tea and Calendar Girls.

"Jaswal's charming debut features an engaging protagonist who longs to break free from her more traditional mothers expectations and who is still smarting from her fathers death, but its the portrayal of the women in Nikkis' class that is the highlight: these women are considered invisible, but through their writing they can be seen and their desires and dreams can be acknowledged." —*Publishers Weekly*

Jayatissa, Amanda
★ **My** sweet girl. Amanda Jayatissa. Berkley, 2021. 400 p.
ISBN 9780593335086
1. Secrets 2. Memories 3. Hallucinations and illusions 4. Orphanages 5. Adoption 6. Sri Lanka 7. San Francisco, California 8. 21st century 9. Psychological suspense

LC 2021019902
Paloma thought her perfect life would begin once she was adopted and made it to America, but she's about to find out that no matter how far you run, your past always catches up to you.

"In her debut novel, Sri Lanka-based Jayatissa is a master of first-person narration as she delves into questions of identity—how individuals perceive themselves, and the tendency not to see others for who they really are." —*Library Journal*

Jedrowski, Tomasz
Swimming in the dark. Tomasz Jedrowski. William Morrow & Co, 2020. 208 pages
ISBN 9780062890009
1. Communism 2. Social change 3. Gay men 4. Politicians 5. Political activists 6. Poland 7. 1980s 8. LGBTQIA fiction 9. Second person narratives 10. Coming-of-age stories

In early 1980s Poland during the violent decline of communism, two young men fall in love but eventually find themselves on opposite sides of the political divide.

"Jedrowski's portrayal of Poland's tumultuous political transformation over several decades makes this a provocative, eye-opening exploration of the costs of defying as well as complying with social and political conventions." —*Publishers Weekly*

Jeffers, Honoree Fanonne
★ The **love** songs of W. E. B. Du Bois. Honoree Fanonne Jeffers. HarperCollins, 2021. 797 p.
ISBN 9780062942937
1. Du Bois, W. E. B. 2. African American families 3. Psychic trauma 4. Ancestors 5. Family history 6. African American women — Identity 7. United States 8. Family sagas 9. Coming-of-age stories 10. African American fiction

Kirkus Prize for Fiction finalist, 2021

To come to terms with who she is and what she wants, Ailey, the daughter of an accomplished doctor and a strict schoolteacher, embarks on a journey through her family's past, helping her embrace her full heritage, which is the story of the Black experience in itself.

"Poet Jeffers reinvigorates the multigenerational saga in her first novel, an audacious, mellifluous love song to an African American family." —*Booklist*

Jeffries, Sabrina

Project Duchess. Sabrina Jeffries. Zebra Books, 2019. 352 p. (Duke Dynasty, 1)

ISBN 9781420148558

1. Dukes and duchesses 2. Nobility 3. Debutantes 4. Funerals 5. Arrogance in men 6. England 7. Great Britain 8. Darwin, Charles 9. Historical romances

Being prepared for her debut by the Duke of Greycourt at the behest of his mother, Beatrice Wolf, as she gets to know the man beneath the arrogant facade, must decide where her loyalties lie—with her family or with him—when her family's secrets come to light.

Jemc, Jac

★ The **grip** of it. Jac Jemc. Farrar, Strauss and Giroux, 2017. 272 p.

ISBN 9780374536916

1. Suspicion 2. Paranoia 3. Psychoses 4. Married people 5. Homeowners 6. Psychological suspense 7. Horror 8. Multiple perspectives

LC 2016041347

Julie and James settle into a house in a small town outside the city where they met. As they settle into their home and their marriage, the house and its surrounding terrain become the locus of increasingly strange happenings. Together the couple embark on a panicked search for the source of their mutual torment, a journey that mires them in the history of their peculiar neighbors and the mysterious residents who lived in the house before them.

"Shivery and smart. A book that brings the legacy of Henry James into the modern world with great effect." —*Kirkus*

Jemisin, N. K.

★ The **city** we became. N.K. Jemisin. Orbit, 2020. 448 p. (Great cities trilogy, 1)

ISBN 9780316509848

1. Cities and towns 2. Good and evil 3. Gentrification of cities 4. Imaginary creatures 5. Race relations 6. New York City 7. Manhattan, New York City 8. Urban fantasy 9. African American fiction

LC 2019043382

Locus Award for Fantasy Novel, 2021; BSFA Award for Best Novel, 2020; Loan Stars Favourites, 2020; RUSA Reading List Short List, 2021

Takes readers into the dark underbelly of New York City where a roiling, ancient evil stirs in the halls of power, threatening to destroy the city and her six newborn avatars.

"Jemisin (The Broken Earth) writes a harsh love story to one of America's most famous places. As raw and vibrant as the city itself, the prose pushes the boundaries of fantasy and brings home what residents already know—their city is alive." —*Library Journal*

The **fifth** season. N. K. Jemisin. Orbit, 2015. 498 pages; (Broken Earth novels, 1)

ISBN 9780316229296

1. End of the world 2. Mothers 3. Superhuman abilities 4. Imaginary empires 5. Murder 6. Social science fiction 7. Apocalyptic fiction 8. African American fiction

Hugo Award for Best Novel, 2016; Library Journal Best Books, 2015; New York Times Notable Book, 2015; RUSA Reading List Short List, 2016

When her husband murders their son and abducts their daughter, grief-stricken and vengeful Essun pursues him across The Stillness, a vast and dynamic super-continent on the brink of catastrophe that will usher in a "fifth season," a time of uncertainty and hardship. But Essun is as formidable as the land she traverses—she's an orogene, which means that she can shape the contours of the land. Although she's spent much of her life hiding from those who would kill her on account of her race, Essun is about to prove how dangerous a woman on a mission can be. Set in a richly detailed, fully realized world inhabited by numerous well-drawn and complex cultures, The Fifth Season launches the Broken Earth series.

"Jemisin's graceful prose and gritty setting provide the perfect backdrop for this fascinating tale of determined characters fighting to save a doomed world." —*Publishers Weekly*

How long 'til black future month? N. K. Jemisin. Orbit, 2018. 400 pages

ISBN 9780316491341

1. Magic 2. African Americans 3. Short stories 4. Science fiction 5. Fantasy fiction 6. Adult books for young adults

LC 2018034027

Alex Award, 2019; LibraryReads Favorites, 2018; Locus Award for Best Collection, 2019

Offers a collection of the author's short fiction, including "The City Born Great," where a young street kid fights to give birth to an old metropolis's soul.

"In this career-spanning collection, Jemisin (The Broken Earth" trilogy) delivers 22 thrilling stories of black strength in the face of worldly and otherworldly adversity.... This robust collection is a worthy introduction to three-time Hugo Award winner Jemisin's powerful work for curious newcomers and is sure to delight the author's many fans." —*Library Journal*

The **obelisk** gate. N. K. Jemisin. Orbit, 2016. 433 pages : Map (Broken Earth novels, 2)

ISBN 9780316229265

1. End of the world 2. Mothers 3. Superhuman abilities 4. Imaginary empires 5. Murder 6. Social science fiction 7. Apocalyptic fiction 8. African American fiction

Romantic Times Reviewer's Choice Award, 2016; Hugo Award for Best Novel, 2017

In this sequel to the Hugo Award-winning novel The Fifth Season, the world known as Stillness is on the verge of collapse. Essun, who can harness geological forces to physically reshape her surroundings, may be able to prevent the apocalype. However, Essun's priority is searching for her lost daughter, Nassun, who travels with her father—Essun's ex-husband who murdered their son and attempted to kill Essun for possessing an orogene's abilities. Complex characters, detailed world-building, and thought-provoking meditations on identity and human nature make this book a must-read.

"The Stillness and those who dwell there are vividly drawn, and the threats they face are both timely and tangible. Once again Jemisin immerses readers in a complex and intricate world of warring powers, tangled morals, and twisting motivations." —*Publishers Weekly*

The **stone** sky. N. K. Jemisin. Orbit, 2017. 445 pages : Map (Broken Earth novels, 3)

ISBN 9780316229241

1. End of the world 2. Mothers 3. Superhuman abilities 4. Imaginary empires 5. Murder 6. Social science fiction 7. Apocalyptic fiction 8. African American fiction

Hugo Award for Best Novel, 2018; Locus Award for Fantasy Novel, 2018; Nebula Award for Best Novel, 2017; New York Times Notable Book, 2017; Romantic Times Reviewer's Choice Award, 2017

In this concluding volume of N.K. Jemisin's acclaimed Broken Earth trilogy, orogene Essun and her daughter Nassun find themselves on opposite sides of an ideological battle for the future of the Stillness. Like its predecessors, this novel boasts a vivid apocalyptic setting and thoughtful explorations of the nature of personhood and the ways in which systems of oppression operate. Due to the complexity of the story, newcomers will want to start with the first of the series, The Fifth Season.

"Vivid characters, a tautly constructed plot, and outstanding worldbuilding meld into an impressive and timely story of abused, grieving survivors fighting to fix themselves and save the remnants of their shattered home." —Publishers Weekly

Jen, Gish

★ The **resisters**. Gish Jen. Knopf, 2020. 320 pages
ISBN 9780525657217
1. Near future 2. Families 3. Social classes 4. Totalitarianism 5. Artificial intelligence 6. United States 7. Dystopian fiction 8. Science fiction 9. Mainstream fiction

Enduring life on the margins in a near-future world ruthlessly divided between the employed and unemployed, a once-professional couple give birth to an athletically gifted child, whose attention by the government compels her mother to challenge society's foundations.

"While some of Jen's fans might miss the overt humor of her previous work, her intelligence and control shine through in a chilling portrait of the casual acceptance of totalitarianism." —Publishers Weekly

★ **Thank** you, Mr. Nixon: stories. Gish Jen. Alfred A. Knopf, 2022. 256 p.
ISBN 9780593319895
1. Chinese Americans 2. Chinese American families 3. Culture conflict 4. Family relationships 5. Immigration and emigration 6. United States 7. China 8. Literary fiction 9. Short stories
LC 2021027612

In her first collection of stories since the acclaimed Who's Irish?, the author of The Resisters refracts the fifty years since the opening of China through the lives of ordinary people. Beginning with a cheery, kindly letter penned by a Chinese girl in heaven to "poor Mr. Nixon" in hell, Gish Jen embarks on an eleven-story journey through U.S.-Chinese relations, capturing not only the excitement of a world on the brink of tectonic change, but the all-too-human encounters that ensue as East meets West. With their profound compassion, equally profound humor, and unexpected connections, these masterful stories reflect history's shifting shadow over our boldest decisions and most intimate moments.

"Jen (The Resisters, 2020) distills five decades of cultural collision, confusion, and collaboration between the U.S. and China into 11 gorgeously comedic and heartbreaking stories cleverly linked through family and friends." —Booklist

Jenkins, Beverly

Forbidden. Beverly Jenkins. Avon Books, 2016. 384 p. (Old West series, 1)
ISBN 9780062389008
1. Women cooks 2. Multiracial men 3. Passing (Identity) 4. Secret identity 5. Civil War veterans 6. Nevada 7. The West (United States)

8. 1870s 9. Western romances 10. Historical romances 11. Multicultural romances
RUSA Reading List, 2017; Romantic Times Reviewer's Choice Award, 2016

The son of a slave and a plantation owner, Union Army veteran Rhine Fontaine moves to Virginia City, Nevada, where his light skin and green eyes enable him to pass for white. Convinced that passing is his best bet for helping the local black community, Rhine questions his choice after meeting cook and aspiring restaurant owner Eddy Carmichael. Eddy insists that she's bound for California as soon as she can save enough money; Rhine wants her stay, but convincing her would mean sacrificing the life he's built for himself. Fans of Beverly Jenkins' African-American historical romances will recognize Rhine from his supporting role in Through the Storm.

"The characters are strong and appealing in this excellent western historical romance, with its fascinating background and modern implications." —Booklist

Rebel. Beverly Jenkins. Avon Books, 2019. 373 p. (Women who dare, 1)
ISBN 9780062861689
1. Postwar life 2. Determination in women 3. Architects 4. Protectiveness in men 5. Ambition in women 6. New Orleans, Louisiana 7. 1860s 8. Multicultural romances 9. Historical romances 10. African American fiction

After the Civil War, Captain Drake LeVeq, an architect from an old New Orleans family, is drawn into an irresistible intrigue when he encounters a rebellious young woman who is on a mission to help the newly emancipated community survive and flourish.

"So often, stories drawn from the African-American past deal largely with struggle, and Jenkins does not shy away from depictions of injustice and violence. But she also gives us characters who are able to thrive and love and find their ways to happy endings. A satisfying start to a new historical series from one of romance's finest writers." —Kirkus

Tempest. Beverly Jenkins. Avon Books, 2018. 373 p. (Old West series, 3)
ISBN 9780062389046
1. Mail order brides 2. Widowers 3. African Americans 4. Single fathers 5. Fathers and daughters 6. Wyoming 7. The West (United States) 8. American Westward Expansion (1803-1899) 9. Historical romances 10. Western romances 11. Multicultural romances
RUSA Reading List Short List, 2019

When Regan Carmichael, his mail-order bride, arrives, widower Dr. Colton Lee, who is in need of someone to care for his daughter, gets the unexpected in the form of this independent beauty who makes him believe in second chances.

Wild rain. Beverly Jenkins. Avon Books, 2021. 384 p. (Women who dare, 2)
ISBN 9780062861719
1. Women ranchers 2. Postwar life 3. Independence in women 4. Determination in women 5. Journalists 6. Wyoming 7. 1860s 8. American Westward Expansion (1803-1899) 9. Multicultural romances 10. Historical romances 11. African American fiction

In the wake of the Civil War, Spring Lee, running her own ranch in Paradise, Wyoming, second guesses her resolve to avoid men when a reporter arrives to interview her brother and becomes enamored with her instead.

"This second in the 'Women Who Dare' series presents a solid entry point for readers new to the legendary Jenkins's oeuvre. Longtime fans will appreciate the appearance of a couple from an earlier book, Tempest. Jenkins's excellent storytelling skills, paired with fascinating American history, makes the narrative shine." —Library Journal

Jenner, Natalie

The **Jane** Austen society. Natalie Jenner. St. Martin's Press, 2020. 320 p.

ISBN 9781250248732

1. Austen, Jane 2. Postwar life 3. War — Psychological aspects 4. Loss (Psychology) 5. Villages 6. Fans (Persons) 7. England 8. 1940s 9. Historical fiction 10. Canadian fiction

LC 2019051879

LibraryReads Favorites, 2020

A group of disparate bibliophiles bands together in the small English village of Chawton in the hopes of restoring the final home of Jane Austen, revealing their respective losses along the way.

"Readers won't need previous knowledge of Austen and her novels to enjoy this tale's slow revealing of secrets that build to a satisfying and dramatic ending, while devoted Austen fans will pore over these pages, savoring the deeper connections between the lives of Jenner's postwar characters and of Austen's creations. The pleasures are many in this clever tribute to the beloved and endlessly influential Austen and the English village tale." —*Booklist*

Jenoff, Pam

The **lost** girls of Paris. Pam Jenoff. Park Row, 2019. 377 p.

ISBN 9780778308614

1. Postwar life 2. Women spies 3. Women and war 4. World War II 5. Photographs 6. 1940s 7. Historical fiction

After discovering an abandoned, photograph-filled suitcase in Grand Central Station in 1946 a young widow sets out to discover who the people in the pictures are.

Jensen, Nancy

In our midst. Nancy Jensen. Dzanc Books, 2020. 352 pages

ISBN 9781950539161

1. World War II home front 2. Immigrants, German 3. Suspicion 4. Concentration camps 5. War — Psychological aspects 6. United States 7. Second World War era (1939-1945) 8. Historical fiction

A family of German immigrants who own a popular restaurant must make awful choices to stay together after their mother is seized by FBI agents and interned in the wake of the attack on Pearl Harbor.

"Jensen's satisfying fictional account of a lesser-known chapter of U.S. history resonates chillingly with today's headlines." —*Publishers Weekly*

Jewell, Lisa

The **family** upstairs. Lisa Jewell. Atria Books, 2019. 320 p.

ISBN 9781501190100

1. Orphans 2. Birthparents 3. Inheritance and succession 4. Young women 5. Mansions 6. London, England 7. Great Britain 8. Thrillers and suspense 9. Multiple perspectives

Loan Stars Favourites, 2019

Inheriting an abandoned mansion on the banks of the Thames in London's fashionable Chelsea neighborhood, 25-year-old Libby Jones is soon on a collision course with her birth family's past that is linked to long-ago murders.

Then she was gone: a novel. Lisa Jewell. Atria Books, 2018. 359 p.

ISBN 9781501154645

1. Single fathers 2. Divorced women 3. Parents of missing children 4. Cold cases (Criminal investigation) 5. Man-woman relationships 6. London, England 7. Psychological suspense 8. Multiple perspectives

LC 2017032784

LibraryReads Favorites, 2018; Loan Stars Favourites, 2018

Struggling to put her life back together a decade after her beloved teen daughter's disappearance, a divorced woman bonds with a charming single father whose young child eerily resembles the woman's own lost daughter and who compels a wrenching search for answers.

Watching you. Lisa Jewell. Pocket Books, 2018. 324 p.

ISBN 9781501190070

1. Headmasters 2. Obsession 3. Neighborhoods 4. Secrets 5. Murder 6. England 7. Thrillers and suspense

LibraryReads Favorites, 2019

When a murder occurs in Melville Heights, one of the nicest neighborhoods in Bristol, England, dangerous obsessions come to light involving the headmaster at a local school, in this place where everyone has a secret.

"Expert misdirection keeps the reader guessing, and the rug-pulled-out-from-beneath-your-feet conclusioncoupled with one final, bone-chilling revelationis stunning." —*Booklist*

Jhabvala, Ruth Prawer

At the end of the century: the stories of Ruth Prawer Jhabvala. Ruth Prawer Jhabvala; introduction by Anita Desai. Counterpoint, 2019. 448 p.

ISBN 9781640091375

1. Human nature 2. Europeans in India 3. Man-woman relationships 4. Social classes 5. India 6. Short stories 7. Literary fiction

LC 2018041024

In this vivid collection of stories, pathos, despair, sensuality and liberation are explored with sensitivity, wit and affection.

Includes bibliographical references and index.

★ **Heat** and dust. Ruth Prawer Jhabvala. Harper & Row, 1976. 181 p.

ISBN 9780060121976

1. Extramarital affairs 2. Women nonconformists 3. Sex scandals 4. Race relations 5. Interracial sex 6. India 7. Literary fiction 8. Parallel narratives 9. Books to movies

LC 72025088

Booker Prize, 1975

In a narrative intermingling past and present, a young English woman journeys to India to reconstruct the behavior of her grandfather's first wife, Olivia, who left husband and friends in 1923 out of love for an Indian prince.

Originally published: London : J. Murray, 1975.

Jiles, Paulette

News of the world: a novel. Paulette Jiles. William Morrow, 2016. 213 p.

ISBN 9780062409201

1. Voyages and travels 2. Widowers 3. Families 4. Friendship 5. Orphans 6. Texas 7. San Antonio, Texas 8. American Westward Expansion (1803-1899) 9. 1870s 10. Historical fiction 11. Books to movies 12. Adult books for young adults

LC 2015041173

Booklist Editors' Choice, 2016; LibraryReads Favorites, 2016; RUSA Reading List Short List, 2017

A live news reader traveling the Antebellum South is offered $50 to bring an orphan girl, who was kidnapped and raised by Kiowa raiders, back to her family in San Antonio.

Sequel to: The Color of Lightning.

Jimenez, Abby

The **friend** zone. Abby Jimenez. Forever, 2019. 367 pages

ISBN 9781538715604

1. Women business owners 2. Fire fighters 3. Friendship 4. Weddings 5. Secrets 6. Contemporary romances 7. Fry, Varian

Kristen Peterson doesn't do drama, will fight to the death for her friends, and has no room in her life for guys who just don't get her. She's also keeping a big secret: facing a medically necessary procedure that will make it impossible for her to have children.

"Biting wit and laugh-out-loud moments take priority, but the novel remains subtle in its sentimentality and sneaks up on the reader with unanticipated depth." —*Publishers Weekly*

★ The **happy** ever after playlist. Abby Jimenez. Forever, 2020. 388 pages

ISBN 9781538715642

1. Hitler, Adolf 2. Rock musicians 3. Pet adoption 4. Rescue dogs 5. Fiances — Death 6. United States 7. Australia 8. Contemporary romances 9. Romantic comedies

LC 2019026595

LibraryReads Favorites, 2020

Adopting a rescue puppy to help her get her life back on track two years after losing her fiance, Sloan clashes with the mischievous pup's original owner, Jason, a rising musician who challenges Sloan to make difficult choices.

"Following her exceptional debut (The Friend Zone, 2019), author Jimenez has written Sloan's story with elegant, compassionate success, showcasing a romance that navigates deep grief and healing while exploring the unexpected stressors placed on a celebrity relationship." —*Kirkus*

Life's too short. Abby Jimenez. Forever, 2021. 384 p.

ISBN 9781538754580

1. Voyages and travels 2. Nieces 3. Child custody 4. Women travelers 5. Infants 6. Contemporary romances 7. Romantic comedies

LibraryReads Favorites, 2021

Gaining an unexpected online following after quitting her job to travel the world, a woman anticipating a short life becomes the guardian of her infant niece before her resolve to avoid relationships is tested by a baby-savvy lawyer.

"Jimenez masterfully blends heavy issues and humor, lacing the tear-jerking heartache with sass and sarcasm." —*Publishers Weekly*

Jimenez, Simon

★ The **vanished** birds. Simon Jimenez. Del Rey, 2020. 400 p.

ISBN 9780593128985

1. Space flight 2. Space and time 3. Decision-making 4. Boys who are mute 5. Music 6. Space 7. Space opera 8. Science fiction

LC 2019034925

A lone space traveler who has outlived everyone she has ever known takes in a mysterious, traumatized boy who falls from the sky and communicates through the haunting music he plays on an old wooden flute.

"This powerful, suspenseful story asks us to consider what we'd sacrifice for progress—or for the ones we love. The best of what science fiction can be: a thought-provoking, heart-rending story about the choices that define our lives." —*Kirkus*

Jin, Ha

The **boat** rocker: a novel. Ha Jin. Pantheon Books, 2016. 256 p.

ISBN 9780307911629

1. Journalists 2. Chinese in the United States 3. Personal conduct 4. Asian Americans 5. Communism 6. New York City 7. 2000s (Decade) 8. Political fiction 9. Black humor 10. Literary fiction

LC 2016007449

Rendered famous for his explosive anti-Communist expose, a fiercely principled Chinese expatriate reporter endures an excruciating assignment investigating his own ex-wife, an unscrupulous novelist who has become a pawn of the Chinese government.

"Ha Jin's prose is always pleasurable to read." —*Publishers Weekly*

A **map** of betrayal: a novel. Ha Jin. Pantheon, 2014. 320 pages

ISBN 9780307911605

1. Former CIA agents 2. Diary writing 3. Chinese American women 4. Loyalty 5. Parents — Death 6. China 7. United States 8. Literary fiction 9. Spy fiction 10. Parallel narratives

LC 2014008892

From the award-winning author of Waiting: a spare, haunting tale of espionage and conflicted loyalties that spans half a century in the entwined histories of two countries—China and the United States—and two families as it explores the complicated terrain of love and honor. When Lilian Shang, born and raised in America, discovers her father's diary after the death of her parents, she is shocked by the secrets it contains. She knew that her father, Gary, convicted decades ago of being a mole in the CIA, was the most important Chinese spy ever caught. But his diary—an astonishing chronicle of his journey from 1949 Shanghai to Okinawa to Langley, Virginia—reveals the pain and longing that his double life entailed. The trail leads Lilian to China, to her father's long-abandoned other family, whose existence she and her Irish American mother never suspected. As Lilian begins to fathom her father's dilemma—torn between loyalty to his motherland and the love he came to feel for his adopted country—she sees how his sense of duty distorted his life. But as she starts to understand that Gary, too, had been betrayed, she finds that it is up to her to prevent his tragedy from damaging yet another generation of her family.

"A sharply ironic, stealthily devastating tale of the tragic cost of 'blind' patriotism, told by a master of clarifying fiction, that unites the personal and the geopolitical." —*Booklist*

★ **Waiting**. Ha Jin. Pantheon Books, 1999. 308 p.

ISBN 9780375406539

1. Love triangles 2. Man-woman relationships 3. Waiting 4. Physicians 5. Arranged marriage 6. China 7. Literary fiction

LC 9921334

ALA Notable Book, 2000; National Book Award for Fiction, 1999; PEN/Faulkner Award, 2000; New York Times Notable Book, 1999; Pulitzer Prize for Fiction finalist, 2000

An ambitious and dedicated Chinese doctor, Lin Kong finds himself torn between two very different women—the educated and dynamic nurse with whom he has fallen in love and the traditional, meek, and humble woman to whom his family married him when they were both very young.

"This novel provides a dual education: a crash course in Chinese society during and since the Cultural Revolution, and more leisurely but nonetheless compelling exploration of the less exotic terrain that is the human heart." —*New York Times Book Review*

Jin, Meng

Little gods. Meng Jin. Custom House, 2020. 279 pages

ISBN 9780062935953

1. Chinese American women 2. Mothers and daughters 3. Ambition in women 4. Love triangles 5. Mothers — Death 6. China 7. Literary fiction 8. Multiple perspectives

Explores the complex web of grief, memory, time, physics, history and selfhood in the immigrant experience, and the complicated bond between daughters and mothers.

"Artfully composed and emotionally searing, Jin's debut about lost girls, bottomless ambition, and the myriad ways family members can hurt and betray one another is gripping from beginning to end." —*Publishers Weekly*

Jin, Yong

A **hero** born: a novel. Jin Yong; translated from the Chinese by Anna Holmwood. St. Martin's Press, 2019. 394 p. (Legends of the condor heroes, 1)
ISBN 9781250220608
1. Genghis Khan 2. Heroes and heroines 3. Kung fu 4. Warriors 5. Martial arts 6. Political intrigue 7. China 8. Translations 9. Historical fantasy 10. Epic Fantasy
LC 2019016755
A U.S. release of an epic Chinese classic is set in the years between the Song Empire and the rise of Genghis Khan and traces the story of a murdered patriot's son who fulfills his destiny in a divided China.
"Filled to the brim with characters and action, this translation will allow English-speaking readers to finally enjoy a classic of the wuxia fantasy genre, and hopefully whet their appetites for more." —*Booklist*
Translated from the Chinese.

Johnson, Alaya Dawn

Trouble the saints. Alaya Dawn Johnson. Tor Books, 2020. 320 p.
ISBN 9781250175342
1. Women assassins 2. Campbell, Enid 3. Death threats 4. Love 5. City life 6. Harlem, New York City 7. Second World War era (1939-1945) 8. Literary fiction 9. Historical fantasy 10. African American fiction
World Fantasy Award, 2021
Forced to give up her identity and the man she loves after a decade in the glittering underworld of Manhattan, a Harlem assassin fights the ghosts of her past at the dawn of World War II.
"With a sweeping but overstuffed plot, dynamic characters, and style to spare, this alternate history demands the reader's full attention. Fans of challenging, diverse fantasy will enjoy this literary firecracker." —*Publishers Weekly*

Johnson, Caleb

Treeborne. Caleb Johnson. Picador, 2018. 308 p.
ISBN 9781250169082
1. Women 2. Small towns 3. Change 4. Orchards 5. Home (Concept) 6. Alabama 7. Southern states 8. Southern fiction 9. Family sagas
LC 2017060104
Anticipating the end of her small Alabama community, an orchard keeper seeks to preserve its story by imparting the experiences of the ancestors who endured hardships and loss against a backdrop of regional history.

Johnson, Charles Richard

★ **Middle** Passage. Charles Johnson. Atheneum, 1990. 209 p.
ISBN 9780689119682
1. Monroe, Marilyn 2. Mutiny 3. Freed people 4. Middle passage (Atlantic slave trade) 5. Slave trade 6. New Orleans, Louisiana 7. Atlantic Ocean 8. 19th century 9. Sea stories 10. Adventure stories 11. Diary novels
LC 90032713
National Book Award for Fiction, 1990; National Book Critics Circle Award for Fiction finalist, 1990
In 1830, seeking to escape an unwanted marriage, Rutherford Calhoun, a newly freed slave, becomes a stowaway aboard "The Republic," unaware that the ship is a slave clipper bound for West Africa BT

"Johnson's exciting sea narrative provides an unusual historical look at the horrifying Middle Passage experience.... Like *Moby-Dick*'s Ahab, the captain of the *Republic* is on his own special quest (in this case, the capture of the African trickster god).... Above all, the book is valuable in offering a rare perspective of the shocking experience of the slave trade and the consequences of that event for American blacks." —*Choice*

Johnson, Craig

Daughter of the morning star. Craig Johnson. Viking, 2021. 336 p. (Walt Longmire mysteries, 17)
ISBN 9780593297254
1. Death threats 2. Sheriffs 3. Law enforcement 4. Teenage girls 5. Teenage girl basketball players 6. Montana 7. Modern Westerns 8. Mysteries 9. Media tie-ins
LC 2021016947
When Lolo Long's niece Jaya begins receiving death threats, Tribal Police Chief Long calls on Absaroka County Sheriff Walt Longmire along with Henry Standing Bear as lethal backup. Jaya "Longshot" Long is the phenom of the Lame Deer Lady Stars High School basketball team and is following in the steps of her older sister, who disappeared a year previously, a victim of the scourge of missing Native Woman in Indian Country. Lolo hopes that having Longmire involved might draw some public attention to the girl's plight, but with this maneuver she also inadvertently places the good sheriff in a one-on-one with the deadliest adversary he has ever faced in both this world and the next.
After a Native high school basketball star whose sister disappeared begins receiving death threats, Tribal Police Chief Long, Absaroka County Sheriff Walt Longmire and Henry Standing Bear investigate in the latest novel of the series following Next to Last Stand.
"The sheriff of Absaroka County, Wyoming, has solved many an odd case, but none so odd as his search for a missing girl.... A mysterious adventure that spotlights the horrific experiences of Native women whose abuse is often unseen and unreported." —*Kirkus*

Land of wolves. Craig Johnson. Viking Press, 2019. 336 pages (Walt Longmire mysteries, 15)
ISBN 9780525522508
1. Sheriffs 2. Suicide investigation 3. Wolves 4. Shepherds 5. Vietnam veterans 6. Wyoming 7. Modern Westerns 8. Mysteries 9. Media tie-ins
LC 2019014874
Investigating the suspicious suicide of a Wyoming shepherd, sheriff Walt Longmire uncovers disturbing connections to a violent family before the case is further complicated by the appearance of a giant wolf.

Next to last stand. Craig Johnson. Viking, 2020. 336 p. (Walt Longmire mysteries, 16)
ISBN 9780525522539
1. Sheriffs 2. Law enforcement 3. Art thefts 4. Murder 5. Murder investigation 6. Wyoming 7. Modern Westerns 8. Mysteries 9. Media tie-ins
LC 2020013739
Walt Longmire visits the 7th Calvalry Headquarters of 1946 Fort Bliss, Texas to investigate links between a fatal heart attack, a fire that has destroyed a high-profile work of American art and a shoebox containing a million dollars.
"The author's poetic turns of phrase, witty dialog, and one of the funniest, most memorable chase scenes in a novel combine to make this a winner." —*Library Journal*

Spirit of steamboat: a Walt Longmire story. Craig Johnson. Viking, 2013. 112 p. (Walt Longmire mysteries)
ISBN 9780670015788

1. Sheriffs 2. Reunions 3. Christmas 4. World War II veterans 5. Accident victims 6. Mysteries 7. Modern Westerns

LC 2013017053

A holiday entry in the best-selling series finds Sheriff Walt Longmire making the acquaintance of a scarred young woman who raises questions about his predecessor while imparting the story of a tragic car accident during a blizzard that marked Walt's first year as sheriff.

Johnson, D. E.

Detroit shuffle. D.E. Johnson. Minotaur Books, 2013. 336 p. (Will Anderson novels, 4)

ISBN 9781250006769

1. Attempted murder 2. Detectives 3. Suffragists 4. Protectiveness in men 5. Conspiracies 6. Detroit, Michigan 7. Historical mysteries 8. Mysteries

LC 2013013935

Thwarting an attempt on Elizabeth Hume's life only to be accused of having a hallucination, Will Anderson resolves to prove his sanity against a backdrop of key suffrage legislation that is further complicated by a suspicious death and Detective Riordan's secretive behavior.

Johnson, Daisy

Everything under. Daisy Johnson. Graywolf Press, 2018. 264 p.

ISBN 9781555978266

1. Mother-separated girls 2. Mothers and daughters 3. Lexicographers 4. Canals 5. Houseboats 6. Oxfordshire, England 7. Great Britain 8. Literary fiction 9. Horror

New York Times Notable Book, 2018; Shortlisted for the Man Booker Prize, 2018

An eerie, watery reimagining of the Oedipus myth set on the canals of Oxford, from the author of Fen. In this electrifying reinterpretation of a classical myth, Daisy Johnson explores questions of fate and free will, gender fluidity, and fractured family relationships.

"Johnsons harrowing, singular first novel (following the story collection Fen) retells the myth of Oedipus Rex, putting a modern spin on a familiar tale." —*Publishers Weekly*

Sisters. Daisy Johnson. Riverhead Books, 2020. 224 p.

ISBN 9780593188958

1. Sisters 2. Moving, Household 3. Social isolation 4. Psychic trauma 5. Family estates 6. Northern England 7. England 8. Gothic fiction 9. Literary fiction 10. Multiple perspectives

New York Times Notable Book, 2020

Moving in the aftermath of a school bullying incident to an abandoned family home near the shore, two fiercely loyal siblings find the nature of their bond changing in the wake of a series of revelatory encounters.

"The story is beautifully written, the characters expertly drawn, as is the setting, the house becoming a character in itself. A memorable and haunting novel." —*Booklist*

Johnson, Denis

The **largesse** of the sea maiden: stories. Denis Johnson. Random House, 2018. 208 p.

ISBN 9780812988635

1. Purpose in life 2. Mortality 3. Aging 4. Short stories 5. Literary fiction

LC 2017027298

New York Times Notable Book, 2018; National Book Critics Circle Award for Fiction finalist, 2018

A posthumous story collection by the National Book Award-winning author contemplates subjects ranging from old age and mortality to the unexpected ways the mysteries of the universe manifest, depicting haunted characters who would atone for the past, remember departed loved ones or come to terms with lifelong obsessions.

"The second story collection from the late Johnson (Jesus' Son) is a masterpiece of deep humanity and astonishing prose." —*Publishers Weekly*

Johnson, Jocelyn Nicole

★ **My** Monticello: fiction. Jocelyn Nicole Johnson. Henry Holt and Company, 2021. 256 p.

ISBN 9781250807151

1. African American families 2. Racism 3. Life change events 4. Violence against marginalized people 5. Identity (Psychology) 6. Short stories 7. African American fiction

LC 2021002249

Kirkus Prize for Fiction finalist, 2021

A young woman descended from Thomas Jefferson and Sally Hemings driven from her neighborhood by a white militia. A university professor studying racism by conducting a secret social experiment on his own son. A single mother desperate to buy her first home even as the world hurtles toward catastrophe. Each fighting to survive in America. An irresistibly accessible yet startlingly bold book of short stories and a novella, inspired by Black lives in America and featuring the gripping eponymous work "My Monticello.

"The author's riveting storytelling and skill at rendering complex characters yield rich social commentary on Monticello and Jefferson's complex ideologies of freedom, justice, and liberty. This incandescent work speaks not just to the moment, but to history." —*Publishers Weekly*

Johnson, Julia Claiborne

Better luck next time: a novel. Julia Claiborne Johnson. Custom House, 2021. 304 p.

ISBN 9780062916365

1. Divorce 2. Ranchers 3. Marriage 4. Ranches 5. Women pilots 6. Reno, Nevada 7. Between the Wars (1918-1939) 8. Historical fiction

LC 2020019558

Follows the experiences of a former Yale student whose life at a 1930s Reno divorce ranch is upended by a shy woman and a thrice-divorced pilot.

"This brims with the clever banter and farcical situations of a classic Capra film, and is deepened by dramatic scenes and portrayals of the hardworking ranchers. Johnson's novel soars." —*Publishers Weekly*

Johnson, Keith Lee

★ **Little** black girl lost. Keith Lee Johnson. Urban Books, 2005. 324 p. (Little black girl lost, 1)

ISBN 9780974702551

1. Prostitution 2. Race relations 3. African American women 4. Enslaved girls 5. Mothers and daughters 6. New Orleans, Louisiana 7. 1950s 8. Urban fiction 9. Thrillers and suspense

In 1950s New Orleans, beautiful fifteen-year-old Johnnie Wise is sold to a corrupt white insurance man named Earl Shamus, while being pursued by a crime boss who will stop at nothing to possess her, against a backdrop of murder, greed, jealousy, and lust.

Johnson, Kij

★ The **dream-quest** of Vellitt Boe. Kij Johnson. Tor.com, 2016. 169 p.

ISBN 9780765391414
1. Women college teachers 2. Quests 3. Dreams 4. Gods and goddesses 5. Women students 6. Fantasy fiction

Professor Vellitt Boe teaches at the prestigious Ulthar Women's College. When one of her most gifted students elopes with a dreamer from the waking world, Vellitt must retrieve her. But the journey sends her on a quest across the Dreamlands and into her own mysterious past, where some secrets were never meant to surface.

"Superb worldbuilding and gorgeous prose will hold readers rapt." —*Publishers Weekly*

Johnson, Micaiah

The **space** between worlds. Micaiah Johnson. Del Rey, 2020. 288 p.
ISBN 9780593135051
1. Survival 2. Parallel universes 3. Doppelgangers 4. Murder 5. Dystopias 6. Science fiction thrillers

LC 2019059324
RUSA Reading List, 2021

A cross-dimensional examination of identity, privilege and belonging follows the adventures of a rare survivor whose counterparts in other realities have died and who stumbles on a dangerous secret threatening her new home and fragile place in it.

"This exciting debut is intelligently built, with clever characters, surprise twists, plenty of action, subtly detailed worlds, and a plot that highlights social and racial inequities in astute prose." —*Library Journal*

Johnson, Nancy

The **kindest** lie. Nancy E. Johnson. William Morrow and Co, 2021. 320 p.
ISBN 9780063005631
1. African American engineers 2. African American women 3. Adoption 4. Family secrets 5. Racism 6. 2000s (Decade) 7. Relationship fiction 8. African American fiction
LibraryReads Favorites, 2021

Needing to reconnect with the baby she gave up for adoption years earlier, an Ivy League-educated Black engineer uncovers devastating family secrets before her bond with a young white misfit scandalizes her racially torn community.

"Through well-developed characters, Johnson provides a realistic portrayal of middle America in the tumultuous era of economic collapse." —*Booklist*

Johnson, Sadeqa

★ **Yellow** wife. Sadeqa Johnson. Simon & Schuster 2021. 288 p.
ISBN 9781982149109
1. Plantation life 2. Slavery 3. Enslaved women 4. Multiracial women 5. Women healers 6. Virginia 7. Antebellum America (1820-1861) 8. African American fiction 9. Historical fiction

Born on a plantation but set apart from the others by her mother's position as a medicine woman, a young slave is forced to leave home at 18 and unexpectedly finds herself in an infamously cruel jail.

"A horrifying but ultimately moving story anchored by a complex narrator." —*Kirkus*

Johnson, Tara

Engraved on the heart. Tara Johnson. Tyndale House Pub 2018. 400 p.
ISBN 9781496428318

1. Debutantes 2. Physicians 3. Underground Railroad 4. Abolitionists 5. Women with epilepsy 6. Savannah, Georgia 7. Pennsylvania 8. American Civil War era (1861-1865) 9. Christian historical fiction
LC 2017043706

Reluctant debutante Keziah Montgomery lives beneath the weighty expectations of her staunch Confederate family, forced to keep her epilepsy secret for fear of a scandal. As the tensions of the Civil War arrive on their doorstep in Savannah, Keziah sees little cause for balls and courting. Despite her discomfort, she cannot imagine an escape from her familial confines—until her old schoolmate Micah shows her a life-changing truth that sets her feet on a new path...as a conductor in the Underground Railroad.

Johnston, Tim

The **current:** a novel. Tim Johnston. Algonquin Books of Chapel Hill, 2019. 352 p.
ISBN 9781616206772
1. College students 2. Traffic accidents 3. Cold cases (Criminal investigation) 4. Accident investigation 5. Murder investigation 6. Minnesota 7. Thrillers and suspense
LC 2018020534
LibraryReads Favorites, 2019

Surviving the accident that killed her friend, a young woman delves into the case of another victim from a decade earlier to identify a killer among her neighbors.

"An apt title that functions as a beautiful metaphor for all the secrets and emotions roiling beneath the surface of every human life." —*Kirkus*

Johnstone, Carole

Mirrorland. Carole Johnstone. Scribner, 2021. 320 p.
ISBN 9781982136352
1. Sisters 2. Adult child abuse victims 3. Missing women 4. Houses 5. Imaginary places 6. Los Angeles, California 7. Edinburgh, Scotland 8. Gothic fiction 9. Psychological suspense
Loan Stars Favourites, 2021

Cat lives in Los Angeles, far away from 36 Westeryk Road, the imposing gothic house in Edinburgh where she and her estranged twin sister, El, grew up. As girls, they invented Mirrorland, a dark, imaginary place under the pantry stairs full of pirates, witches, and clowns. These days Cat rarely thinks about their childhood home, or the fact that El now lives there with her husband Ross. But when El mysteriously disappears after going out on her sailboat, Cat is forced to return to 36 Westeryk Road, which has scarcely changed in twenty years. And someone (El?) has left Cat clues in almost every room: a treasure hunt that leads right back to Mirrorland, where she knows the truth lies crouched and waiting...

"This bar-raising debut exposes the gray areas in an often-misunderstood disorder and defies readers to root against its psychopathic antiheroes. Kurian's highly anticipated thriller will undoubtedly lead fans of Gone Girl, Jeff Lindsay's Dexter series, and Patricia Highsmith's Tom Ripley novels to hope for Chloe's return." —*Booklist*

Jónasson, Ragnar

★ The **girl** who died. Ragnar Jónasson; translated from the Icelandic by Victoria Cribb. Minotaur Books, 2021. 336 p.
ISBN 9781250793737
1. Teachers 2. Villages 3. Thomas, Dorothy Kirwan 4. Ghosts 5. Secrets 6. Iceland 7. 1980s 8. Translations 9. Psychological suspense 10. Ghost stories

LC 2021004753

From Ragnar Jónasson, the award-winning author of the international bestselling Ari Thor series, The Girl Who Died is a standalone thriller about a young woman seeking a new start in a secluded village where a small community is desperate to protect its secrets.

"The isolated village and the pre-smartphone 1980s setting create a sense of claustrophobia that combines with the villagers' secrecy and the hint of supernatural elements to infuse strong foreboding throughout what is ultimately revealed to be a story about trust. A draw for Jónasson's growing fan base, along with fans of Jennifer McMahon, Yrsa Sigurdardottir, and Camilla Lackberg." —*Booklist*

Translation of: Þorpið.

Translated from the Icelandic.

The **island**. Ragnar Jónasson. Minotaur Books, 2019. 352 p. (Inspector Hulda Hermannsdottir, 2)
ISBN 9781250193377
1. Hunting lodges 2. Islands 3. Women detectives 4. Wilderness areas 5. Reunions 6. Iceland 7. Scandinavian crime fiction 8. Translations

Autumn of 1987 takes a young couple on a romantic trip in the Westfjords holiday—a trip that gets an unexpected ending and has catastrophic consequences. Ten years later a small group of friends go for a weekend to an old hunting lodge in Ellidaey. A place completely cut off from the outside world, to reconnect. But one of them isn't going to make it out alive. And Detective Inspector Hulda Hermannsdottir is determined to find the truth in the darkness.

Prequel to: The darkness.

Originally published: Reykjavik : Verold, 2016.

Translated from the Icelandic.

The **mist**. Ragnar Jónasson; translated from the Icelandic by Victoria Cribb. Minotaur Books, 2020. 336 pages (Inspector Hulda Hermannsdottir, 3)
ISBN 9781250768117
1. Women detectives 2. Psychic trauma 3. Farmhouses 4. Blizzards 5. Murder victims 6. Iceland 7. 1980s 8. Scandinavian crime fiction 9. Translations

In this gripping conclusion of the Hidden Iceland series, Detective Hulda is haunted forever by the events that occurred in an isolated farm house in the east of Iceland that opened its doors to a killer.

"No one is who they seem to be in this fast-paced, character-rich thriller about murder and isolation during the brutal Icelandic winter." —*Library Journal*

Originally published in Iceland under the title Mistur by Verold Publishing—Title page verso.

Translated from the Icelandic.

Jones, Cherie

How the one-armed sister sweeps her house. Cherie Jones. Little Brown & Co, 2021. 240 p.
ISBN 9780316536981
1. Married people 2. Criminals 3. Grief 4. Greed 5. Expatriates 6. Barbados 7. Literary fiction 8. Multiple perspectives
Shortlisted for The Women's Prize for Fiction, 2021

Lala must deal with a chain of events that have terrible consequences when her petty criminal husband is interrupted in his attempt to rob one of the mansions in their "paradise" home of Baxter Beach, Barbados.

"Rich characters and pulsing backstories add a great deal of flavor to the drama." —*Publishers Weekly*

Jones, Cynan

Stillicide. Cynan Jones. Catapult, 2020. 176 p.

ISBN 9781646220137
1. Climate change 2. Protests, demonstrations, vigils, etc. 3. Water 4. Interpersonal relations 5. Scientists 6. Literary fiction 7. Apocalyptic fiction

Water is commodified. The Water Train that serves the city increasingly at risk of sabotage. As news breaks that construction of a gigantic Ice Dock will displace more people than first thought, protestors take to the streets and the lives of several individuals begin to interlock.

Jones, Darynda

A **bad** day for Sunshine. Darynda Jones. St. Martin's Press, 2020. 352 p. (Sunshine Vicram, 1)
ISBN 9781250149442
1. Women sheriffs 2. FBI agents 3. Missing girls 4. Kidnapping 5. Small towns 6. New Mexico 7. Police procedurals
LC 2019048698
LibraryReads Favorites, 2020; Loan Stars Favourites, 2020

Challenged to prove herself when her New Mexico community becomes the center of a nationwide manhunt, police chief Sunshine Vicram is seduced by an alluring FBI agent and a sultry U.S. Marshal who test her feelings for a childhood crush.

"Compelling characters and a sexy, angst-filled bunch of mysteries add up to a winning series debut." —*Kirkus*

A **good** day for chardonnay. Darynda Jones. St. Martin's Press, 2021. 400 p. (Sunshine Vicram, 2)
ISBN 9781250233110
1. Women sheriffs 2. Small towns 3. Mothers and daughters 4. Crushes (Interpersonal relations) 5. Serial murder investigation 6. New Mexico 7. Police procedurals
LC 2021006926

The sheriff of a small-town police force in the New Mexico mountains tackles a crazy bar fight and her teenager hunting a serial killer in the second novel of the series following A Bad Day for Sunshine.

"Snappy dialogue and appealing characters enhance the crazy, stop-and-go plot, and a bit of a cliffhanger points to more fun ahead. Fans of zanier mysteries will welcome Sunshine's further adventures." —*Publishers Weekly*

Jones, Douglas C.

The **court-martial** of George Armstrong Custer. Douglas C. Jones. Scribner, 1976. 291 p.
ISBN 9780684147383
1. Custer, George A. 2. Courts-martial and courts of inquiry 3. Little Big Horn, Battle of the, 1876 4. Indians of North America 5. 19th century 6. Westerns
LC 76012606
Spur Award for Best Western Novel (Short Novel), 1977

An alternative historical novel considers the life of George Armstrong Custer if he had lived beyond his 7th Cavalry battles and places him on trial, where he is called upon to explain what really happened at Little Bighorn.

"Slowly building the cases for the prosecution and defense, Jones does well by mixing the drama of courtroom proceedings with the color of a controversial incident." —*Booklist*

Jones, Gayl

★ **Palmares**. Gayl Jones. Beacon Press, 2021. 492 p.
ISBN 9780807033494

1. Magic 2. Freedom seekers 3. Escapes 4. Enslaved people 5. Slavery — History 6. Brazil 7. 17th century 8. Coming of age stories 9. Historical fiction 10. Magical realism

LC 2021012710

The epic rendering of a Black woman's journey through slavery and liberation, set in 17th-century colonial Brazil.

"Jones seems to have come through a life as tumultuous as her heroine's with her storytelling gifts not only intact, but enhanced and enriching. It is marvelous, in every sense, to have a new Gayl Jones novel to talk about." —*Kirkus*

Jones, James

★ **From** here to eternity. James Jones. Delta, 1998. 850 p.
ISBN 9780385333641
1. World War II 2. War 3. Soldiers 4. War stories 5. Literary fiction 6. Modern classics
National Book Award for Fiction, 1952

Two young soldiers and the women they love are caught up in the events preceding the bombing of Pearl Harbor BT

"Mr. Jones has grappled with a variety of materials and handles some of them less successfully than others. There is a good deal of weak stuff in the two love affairs and the characterizations of the women, and the sorties into the field of general ideas are unimpressive. The book as a whole, however, is a spectacular achievement; it has tremendous vitality and driving power and graphic authenticity." —*The Atlantic*

Originally published: New York : Scribner, 1951.

★ **The thin** red line. James Jones. The Dial Press, 1998. 510 p.
ISBN 9780385324083
1. Soldiers 2. Guadalcanal, Battle of, 1942-1943 3. Military campaigns 4. World War II 5. 1940s 6. War stories 7. Historical fiction 8. Books to movies

LC 62012099

C-for-Charlie, an Army rifle company, struggles against death, depression, and cowardice during the invasion of Guadalcanal.

Originally published: New York: Scribner, 1962.

Jones, Robert

★ **The prophets:** a novel. . G. P. Putnam's Sons, 2021. 400 p.
ISBN 9780593085684
1. Enslaved people 2. Gay men 3. Plantation life 4. Clergy 5. Betrayal 6. Mississippi 7. Southern States 8. Antebellum America (1820-1861) 9. Historical fiction 10. Literary fiction 11. LGBTQIA fiction

LC 2020042100

National Book Award for Fiction finalist, 2021

Two enslaved young men on a Deep South plantation find refuge in each other while transforming a quiet shed into a haven for their fellow slaves, before an enslaved preacher declares their bond sinful.

"A masterfully told story that will haunt readers from beginning to end." —*Booklist*

Jones, Sandie

The **other** woman. Sandie Jones. Minotaur Books, 2018. 294 p.
ISBN 9781250191984
1. Mother and adult son 2. Possessiveness 3. Manipulation by women 4. Couples 5. Widows 6. London, England 7. Psychological suspense

LC 2018011480

LibraryReads Favorites, 2018

A blissful romance between Adam and Emily is challenged by Adam's manipulative mother, who resorts to dire measures to keep all other women out of her son's life.

Jones, Sherry

Four sisters, all queens. Sherry Jones. Gallery Books, 2012. 434 p. : Illustration; Map
ISBN 9781451633245
1. Marguerite, Queen, consort of Louis IX, King of France, 1221-1295 2. Eleanor, of Provence, Queen, consort of Henry III, King of England, 1223 or 1224-1291 3. Beatrice, of Provence, Queen of Sicily, consort of Charles I, King of Naples, 1234-1267 4. Sancha, of Provence, Queen, consort of Richard, King of the Romans, 1225-1261 5. Sisters 6. Courts and courtiers 7. Women rulers 8. Europe 9. 13th century 10. Biographical fiction 11. Historical fiction

LC 2011044484

Advised by their mother to place their family first in all things, medieval royal sisters Marguerite, Eleanor, Sanchia and Beatrice become influential queens who further their kingdoms' respective agendas and advance family power until the death of their father tears them apart.

Jones, Stephen Graham

My heart is a chainsaw. Stephen Graham Jones. Saga Press, 2021. 320 p.
ISBN 9781982137632
1. Multiracial teenage girls 2. Native American teenage girls 3. Horror films 4. Psychic trauma 5. Social classes 6. Idaho 7. Horror

LC 2021014273

LibraryReads Favorites, 2021

Protected by horror movies—especially the ones where the masked killer seeks revenge on a world that wronged them, Jade Daniels, an angry, half-Indian outcast, pulls us into her dark mind when blood actually starts to spill into the waters of Indian lake.

★ **The only** good Indians: a novel. Stephen Graham Jones. Saga Press, 2020. 320 p.
ISBN 9781982136451
1. Native American men 2. Siksika Indians 3. Indian Reservations 4. Hunting 5. Elk 6. Montana 7. Blackfeet Indian Reservation, Montana 8. Horror 9. Multiple perspectives 10. Adult books for young adults

LC 2019032510

Alex Award, 2021; Bram Stoker Award for Best Novel, 2020; LibraryReads Favorites, 2020; Los Angeles Times Book Prize, Ray Bradbury Prize for Science Fiction, Fantasy & Speculative Fiction, 2020; RUSA Reading List, 2021; Shirley Jackson Awards, Novel, 2020

Seamlessly blending classic horror and a dramatic narrative with sharp social commentary, The Only Good Indians follows four American Indian men after a disturbing event from their youth puts them in a desperate struggle for their lives. Tracked by an entity bent on revenge, these childhood friends are helpless as the culture and traditions they left behind catch up to them in a violent, vengeful way.

"A violent tale of vengeance, justice, and generational trauma from a prolific horror tinkerer." —*Kirkus*

Jones, Stephen Mack

Dead of winter. Stephen Mack Jones. Soho Crime 2021. 312 p. (August Snow novels, 3)
ISBN 9781641291026

1. Former police 2. Death threats 3. Billionaires 4. Extortion 5. Multiracial men 6. Hardboiled fiction 7. African American fiction

LC 2020052288

Detroit ex-cop August Snow must fight for both his life and the soul of Mexicantown itself when a local business owner is targeted by an anonymous entity that is linked to a dangerous net of ruthless billionaire developers.

"Like Walter Mosley and Joe Ide, Jones builds a raucous and endearing cast of characters from his inner-city setting, fusing neighborhood camaraderie with streetwise know-how and head-banging action." —*Booklist*

Jones, Tanen

The **better** liar: a novel. Tanen Jones. Ballantine Books, 2020. 306 pages

ISBN 9781984821225

1. Sisters 2. Impersonation 3. Wills 4. Swindlers and swindling 5. Fathers — Death 6. Psychological suspense 7. Multiple perspectives

LC 2019034777

Desperate to safeguard a much-needed inheritance that is dependent on the legacy of a long-estranged runaway sibling, Leslie orchestrates a reckless bargain with an imposter who hides her own dangerous secrets.

"A stunning twist ending will leave readers waiting to see what Jones will give them next." —*Booklist*

Jones, Tayari

★ An **American** marriage: a novel. Tayari Jones. Algonquin Books of Chapel Hill, 2018. 308 p.

ISBN 9781616201340

1. Marriage 2. African American families 3. False imprisonment 4. Husband and wife 5. Life change events 6. Atlanta, Georgia 7. Louisiana 8. Literary fiction 9. Southern fiction 10. Domestic fiction

LC 2017030582

ALA Notable Book, 2019; BCALA Literary Award for Fiction, 2019; Library Journal Best Books, 2018; LibraryReads Favorites, 2018; New York Times Notable Book, 2018; Women's Prize for Fiction, 2019; Shortlisted for the International Dublin Literary Award, 2020

When her new husband is arrested and imprisoned for a crime she knows he did not commit, a rising artist takes comfort in a longtime friendship, only to encounter unexpected challenges in resuming her life when her husband's sentence is suddenly overturned.

"Jones crafts an affecting tale that explores marriage, family, regret, and other feelings made all the more resonant by her well-drawn characters and their intricate conflicts of heart and mind." —*Booklist*

Silver sparrow: a novel. By Tayari Jones. Algonquin Books of Chapel Hill, 2011. 352 p.

ISBN 9781565129900

1. African American families 2. Polygamy 3. Family secrets 4. African American teenage girls 5. Betrayal 6. Atlanta, Georgia 7. 1980s 8. Literary fiction 9. Coming-of-age stories 10. Adult books for young adults

LC 2010048098

BCALA Literary Award for Fiction, 2012; Library Journal Best Books, 2011

In 1980s Atlanta, James Witherspoon is living a double life. He has two families, a public one and a secret one. When the daughters from each family become friends, James' secrets are revealed and lives are changed forever.

"A tense, layered and evocative tale.... Jones explores the rivalry and connection of siblings, the meaning of beauty, the perils of young womanhood, the complexities of romantic relationships and the contemporary African-American experience." —*Minneapolis Star Tribune*

Jong, Erica

★ **Fear** of flying: a novel. Erica Jong. Holt, Rinehart and Winston, 1973. 340 p.

ISBN 9780030107313

1. Women poets 2. Marital conflict 3. Self-fulfillment in women 4. Extramarital affairs 5. Man-woman relationships 6. Erotic fiction 7. Psychological fiction

LC 73003697

Records the erotic fantasies and outrageous adventures of Isadora Wing who travels constantly in spite of her phobia of flight.

"At times, Jong gets caught in cliches about women, men, sex, and Jewish mothers, all [of] which she could do without. However, when she takes herself more seriously, the language is penetrating, paying tribute to her worth as a poet." —*Library Journal*

Sequel: How to save your own life.

Jordan, Hillary

Mudbound: a novel. Hillary Jordan. Algonquin Books Of Chapel Hill, 2008. 328 p.

ISBN 9781565125698

1. Racism 2. Farm life 3. African American veterans 4. World War II veterans 5. Prejudice 6. Mississippi 7. 1940s 8. Historical fiction 9. Multiple perspectives 10. First person narratives 11. Adult books for young adults

LC 2007044471

Alex Award, 2009; Bellwether Prize for Fiction, 2006

In 1946, Laura McAllan tries to adjust after moving with her husband and two children to an isolated cotton farm in the Mississippi Delta.

"With authentic, earthy prose...Jordan picks at the scabs of racial inequality that will perhaps never fully heal and brings just enough heartbreak to this intimate, universal tale, just enough suspense, to leave us contemplating how the lives and motives of these vivid characters might have been different." —*San Antonio Express-News*

Jordan, Sophie

The **duke** goes down. Sophie Jordan. HarperCollins, 2021. 384 p. (Duke hunt novels, 1)

ISBN 9780063035638

1. Illegitimacy 2. Heirs and heiresses 3. Homecomings 4. Children of clergy 5. Revenge 6. England 7. Great Britain 8. Victorian era (1837-1901) 9. Victorian romances 10. Historical romances

The virtuous daughter of a senile vicar, Imogen Bates, a pillar of the community, is determined to sabotage Peregrine Butler's attempts to land an heiress by any means necessary until she realizes that she wants him all to herself.

"Jordan (Rogue Effect) launches the Duke Hunt Victorian romance series with an enticing premise and a dashing hero who suffers from an ill-matched eventual partner." —*Publishers Weekly*

This Scot of mine. Sophie Jordan. Avon, 2019. 384 p. (Rogue files, 4)

ISBN 9780062463661

1. Family curses 2. Pregnancy 3. Reputation 4. Deception 5. Clans 6. Scotland 7. Highland romances 8. Historical romances

Fleeing to Scotland, disgraced Lady Clara is resigned to her fate as a spinster until she meets the powerful and devilishly handsome Laird Hunt MacLarin who believes that she is the answer to the curse that has plagued his family for years.

Joseph, Fabiola

Niya: rainbow dreams. Fabiola Joseph. Urban Books, 2016. 288 p.
ISBN 9781622867851
1. Lesbian teenagers 2. Friendship 3. Love triangles 4. Self-discovery
5. Coping 6. Urban fiction 7. LGBTQIA fiction 8. African American
fiction

Do you know who you are? Are you comfortable in your skin? Outed by her best friend in front of the whole neighborhood, Niya is trying to come to terms with being a lesbian. When she falls for her straight neighbor, Jamilla, there is no more denying who she really is. Niya will do whatever it takes to prove her love, even if it means taking a life. What will happen when family issues, fame, the struggle for love, and reality set in? How will Niya deal with a Hip-Hop career as she tries to repair her broken heart and family issues?

Joshi, Alka

The **henna** artist. Alka Joshi. Mira Books, 2020. 368 pages (Henna artist, 1)
ISBN 9780778309451
1. Women artists 2. Runaway wives, husbands, etc. 3. Abusive men
4. Young women 5. Arranged marriage 6. India 7. 1950s 8. Historical fiction

A talented henna artist for wealthy confidantes finds her efforts to control her own destiny in 1950s Jaipur threatened by the abusive husband she fled as a teenage girl.

"Joshi has constructed a bewitching glimpse into the not-so-distant past with a tough heroine well worth cheering on." —*Booklist*

Joukhadar, Zeyn

★ The **thirty** names of night: a novel. Zeyn Joukhadar. Atria Books, 2020. 320 p.
ISBN 9781982121495
1. Syrian Americans 2. Rare and endangered birds 3. Trans men 4.
Mothers — Death 5. Extended families 6. New York City 7. Syria 8.
21st century 9. 20th century 10. Literary fiction 11. Coming-of-age stories
LC 2020020267
Lambda Literary Award for Transgender Fiction, 2021; Stonewall Book Award for the Barbara Gittings Literature Award, 2021

Follows three generations of Syrian Americans who are linked by a mysterious species of bird and the truths they carry close to their hearts.

"Joukhadar conveys the protagonist's gender confusion with such a sense of turmoil and angst that the reader can also become a bit confused, but overall this is a brilliant novel from the author of the celebrated The Map of Salt and Stars." —*Library Journal*

Joyce, James

★ **Dubliners**. James Joyce. A. A. Knopf, 1991. 287 p.
ISBN 9780679405740
1. Dublin, Ireland 2. Ireland 3. Short stories 4. Books to movies
5. Modern classics
LC 91053001
In this collection of masterful stories, steeped in realism, James Joyce creates an exacting portrait of his native city, showing how it reflects the general decline of Irish culture and civilization.
Dubliners first published 1914.
Originally published: London : Grant Richards, 1914.

★ **Finnegans** wake. James Joyce. Penguin Books, 1999. 628 p.
ISBN 9780141181264

1. Senior men 2. Dreams 3. Men's dreams 4. Men — Psychology
5. Dublin, Ireland 6. Ireland 7. Psychological fiction 8. Experimental fiction 9. Modern classics

'Riverrun past Eve and Adam's, from swerve of shore to bend of bay, brings us by a commodius vicus of recirculation back to Howth Castle and Environs ..." So starts Finnegans wake, the greatest challenge in twentieth-century literature. Who is Humphrey Chimpden Earwicker? And what did he get up to in Phoenix Park? And what did Anna Livia Plurabelle have to say about it? In the rich night time language of dreams here is history, anecdote, myth, folk tale—and above all, a wondrous sense of humour coloured by a clear sense of humanity.

★ A **portrait** of the artist as a young man. James Joyce. Knopf, 1991.
Xli, 318 p.
ISBN 9780679405757
1. Joyce, James 2. Young men 3. Artists 4. Families 5. Catholics
6. Self-fulfillment in men 7. Ireland 8. Dublin, Ireland
9. Coming-of-age stories 10. Autobiographical fiction 11. Books to movies

Stephen Dedalus, a sensitive and creative youth, rebels against his family, his education, and his country by committing himself to the artist's life.
Originally serialized in The Egoist, 1914-1915 and collected in book form in 1916.
This edition first published: United States : Vintage International, 1993.

★ **Ulysses**. James Joyce. Modern Library, 1992. 783 pages
ISBN 9780679600114
1. Men — Personal conduct 2. Married people 3. City life 4. Alienation (Social psychology) 5. Bloom, Leopold (Fictitious character) 6. Dublin, Ireland 7. Ireland 8. Psychological fiction 9. Multiple perspectives 10. Books to movies

A day in the life of Leopold Bloom, whose odyssey through the streets of turn-of-the-century Dublin leads him through trials that parallel those of Ulysses on his epic journey home.
Originally published: Paris : Shakespeare & Company, 1922.

Joyce, Rachel

Miss Benson's beetle. Rachel Joyce. The Dial Press, 2020. 352 p.
ISBN 9780812996708
1. Postwar life 2. Single women 3. Middle-aged women 4. Beetles
5. Quests 6. 1950s 7. Historical fiction 8. Relationship fiction
LC 2020006856
LibraryReads Favorites, 2020
Leaving London behind, Margery Benson, a schoolmarm and spinster in 1950, embarks on a quest to the other side of the world in search of her childhood obsession—the golden beetle of New Caledonia—with the help of a fun-loving assistant who changes her life forever.

"A hilarious jaunt into the wilderness of women's friendship and the triumph of outrageous dreams." —*Kirkus*

K

K'wan

Animal. K'wan. Cash Money Content, 2012. 407 p; (Animal novels (K'wan), 1)
ISBN 9781936399253

1. Street life 2. Revenge 3. Fugitives 4. Attempted murder 5. Secrets 6. New York City 7. Harlem, New York City 8. Urban fiction 9. African American fiction

LC Bl2012025014

Library Journal Best Books, 2012; Street Lit Book Award Medal: Adult Fiction, 2013; Street Lit Book Award Medal: Emerging Classic, 2013

When Animal returns to Harlem and learns of the attempt on his soul mate's life, he wages a personal war against those responsible, only to discover the frightening truth in the process.

Animal II: the omen. K'Wan. Cashmoney, 2013. 336 p. (Animal novels (K'wan), 2)

ISBN 9781936399291

1. Street life 2. Revenge 3. Father and adult son 4. Cooperation 5. Enemies 6. New York City 7. Harlem, New York City 8. Urban fiction 9. African American fiction

When Animal returns to Harlem, he is captured by Shai Clark and sentenced to death by the crime boss, only to discover that the executioner is actually his missing father, and the two band together to defeat a common enemy.

The **Diamond** empire. K'wan. St Martin's Griffin, 2017. 260 p. (Diamonds and Pearl, 2)

ISBN 9781250102638

1. Drug lords 2. Business competition 3. African Americans 4. Street life 5. Drug traffic 6. New York City 7. New Orleans, Louisiana 8. Urban fiction 9. African American fiction

When his crew is usurped by an ambitious rival, an exiled Diamond carefully plans his comeback only to be outmaneuvered by an unexpected enemy from the past; while a grieving Pearl finds herself pushed into the very life her father worked to prevent.

★ **Diamonds** and Pearl. K'wan. St Martin's Griffin, 2016. 320 p. (Diamonds and Pearl, 1)

ISBN 9781250102614

1. Street life 2. Criminals 3. African Americans 4. Murder 5. Survival 6. New York City 7. New Orleans, Louisiana 8. Urban fiction

LC 2016021589

Library Journal Best Books, 2016

"They say that good girls like bad boys, and this was especially true for Pearl Stone. A child born of privilege to a drug baron and reputed killer known in the streets as Big Stone. Although the flashy, fast-paced nature of the streets calls to Pearl, she's been brought up to look but not touch. But when a young hustler named Diamonds crawls up from the swamps of Louisiana and sets up shop in New York City, everything Pearl was taught flies out the window." —Provided by publisher.

The **fix**. K'wan. Urban Books, 2014. 288 pages (Fix novels, 1)

ISBN 9781601625854

1. Street life 2. Drug use 3. Life change events 4. Addiction 5. African Americans 6. Harlem, New York City 7. New York City 8. Urban fiction

LC Bl2014000550

Persia reunites with her old Harlem friends, a situation that becomes dangerous when she starts dating a drug dealer who brings her into his world of sex, money, and drugs.

Gangsta. K'wan. Urban Books, 2013. 263 p; (Gangsta novels, 1)

ISBN 9781601625762

1. Gang members 2. African American men 3. Friendship 4. African American authors 5. African Americans 6. California 7. New York City 8. Urban fiction 9. African American fiction

Crip assassin Lou-Loc, who wants to be a writer, and his sociopath counterpart Gutter, who has dreams of being a kingpin, leave Los Angeles for New York, each with his dream in tow.

Sequel: Gutter.

Originally published: Columbus, Ohio : Triple Crown, 2003.

Gutter. K'wan. St. Martin's Griffin, 2008. 416 p. (Gangsta novels, 2)

ISBN 9780312360092

1. Gang members 2. African American men 3. Violence in men 4. Street life 5. Best friends 6. Harlem, New York City 7. Urban fiction 8. James, Henry

LC 2008021526

After Lou-loc's brutal murder, his best friend, Gutter, vows to seek revenge on the entire Blood faction in New York City in retaliation, despite the pleas of his pregnant girlfriend, Sharell, unaware that a vicious adversary named Major Blood has plans to shut down the Harlem Crips and eliminate Gutter and all those who matter to him.

Sequel to: Gangsta

Hoodlum. K'wan. St. Martin's Griffin, 2005. 336 p.

ISBN 9780312333089

1. African American young men 2. Street life 3. Organized crime 4. Young men 5. African American brothers 6. Harlem, New York City 7. Urban fiction 8. African American fiction

Street Lit Book Award Medal: Adult Fiction, 2006

After waging a war on the streets that lasts nearly three years, Shai feels that he can finally try to legitimize his family's business, but when enemies old and new come out of the woodwork, it becomes clear that the previous battle was just a warm-up.

Later published as The good son. Write 2 Eat Concepts, 2017.

Lawless. K'wan. Urban Books, 2019. 266 p.

ISBN 9781601621245

1. Murder investigation 2. African American women 3. Married people and secrets 4. Marketing consultants 5. African Americans 6. Atlanta, Georgia 7. New Orleans, Louisiana 8. Urban fiction 9. African American fiction

Atlanta marketing mogul Bernadette "Bernie" Hunt falls for and marries high-powered lawyer Keith Davis, but when she and Keith must go to his native New Orleans to solve a murder mystery, she begins to learn about his dark past.

Revelations. K'wan. Cashmoney, 2014. 336 p. (Animal novels (K'wan), 3)

ISBN 9781936399932

1. Street life 2. Protectiveness in men 3. Single mothers 4. Former lovers 5. Enemies 6. New York City 7. Harlem, New York City 8. Urban fiction 9. African American fiction

Forced to return to street life by the shocking revelation that he has fathered a child, Animal embarks on a deadly mission to stop a powerful drug dealer, who would kill Animal's daughter and the girl's mother.

Street dreams. K'wan. St. Martin's Griffin, 2004. 310 p.

ISBN 9780312333065

1. African American young men 2. Ghettoes, African American 3. Ambition in men 4. African American men 5. Young men 6. Harlem, New York City 7. Coming-of-age stories 8. Urban fiction 9. African American fiction

LC 2004046805

Two young people—Darius, a.k.a. Rio, the hustler son of an alcoholic singer who did prison time for a friend, and his soulmate, Trinity, the daughter of an abusive father—find solace in their love from the troubled realities of their lives, all the while dreaming of an escape from the mean streets of ghetto Harlem.

Kadare, Ismail

★ The **three-arched** bridge. Ismail Kadare; translated from the Albanian by John Hodgson. Arcade Publishing, 1997. 184 p.

ISBN 9781559703680

1. Bridges — Design and construction 2. Monks 3. Villages 4. Prophecies (Occultism) 5. Men with mental illnesses 6. Balkan Peninsula 7. 14th century 8. Allegories 9. Literary fiction 10. First person narratives

New York Times Notable Book, 1997

When engineers build a bridge in Albania, a monk records its construction and the people's belief that a body buried in it gave the bridge a soul.

"In this matter-of-fact parable, a fourteenth-century Albanian monk attempts to 'record the lie we saw and the truth we did not see' about the building of a stone bridge that is a threatening wonder to the local people. The lie is the myths and legends exploited by the foreign builders to destroy their competitors; the truth is the mercenary nature of their crime. Kadare manages to appeal to a sense of outrage and hunger for evidence even as he suggests the outlines of today's Balkans." —*The New Yorker*

Kadrey, Richard

The **grand** dark. Richard Kadrey. HarperCollins 2019. 400 p.

ISBN 9780062672490

1. Ambition 2. Postwar life 3. Class conflict 4. Power (Social sciences) 5. Bicycle messengers 6. Science fantasy 7. Science fiction 8. Steampunk

The Great War is over. The city of Lower Proszawa celebrates the peace with a decadence and carefree spirit as intense as the war's horrifying despair. Unlike others who live strictly for fun, Largo is an addict with ambitions. Dreams can be a dangerous thing in a city whose mood is turning dark and inward. Others have a vision of life very different from Largo's, and they will use any methods to secure control. The threat of new war always looms.

Kafka, Franz

★ **Collected** stories. Franz Kafka; edited and introduced by Gabriel Josipovici. Knopf, 1993. Lv, 503 pages

ISBN 9780679423034

1. Identity (Psychology) 2. Purpose in life 3. Belonging 4. Short stories 5. Parables 6. Anthologies

LC 93001858

Collects Kafka's short stories and parables, each reflecting his concern for modern man's search for identity, place, and purpose.

Includes bibliographical references (page xli).

★ The **metamorphosis**. By Franz Kafka; translated and edited by Stanley Corngold. Bantam Books, 1986. Xxii, 201 p.

ISBN 9780553213690

1. Loneliness in men 2. Transformations (Magic) 3. Insects 4. Coping 5. Rejection (Psychology) 6. Allegories 7. Modern classics 8. Literary fiction

A seemingly typical man wakes up one morning to discover that he has been transformed into a gigantic insect, and must deal with the depression over his new physical alteration, as well as the rejection of his family.

Originally published: Leipzig : Kurt Wolff Verlag, 1915.

★ The **trial**. Knopf, 1992. Xxxiii, 299 p.

ISBN 9780679409946

1. Trials 2. Bureaucracy 3. Totalitarianism 4. Alienation (Social psychology) 5. Guilt 6. Allegories 7. Literary fiction 8. Surrealist fiction

LC BL 99729791

Narrates the experiences and reactions of a respectable bank functionary after his abrupt arrest on an undisclosed charge

Translation of: Der Prozess.

Includes bibliographical references (p. xx-xxi).

Translated from the German.

Kagen, Lesley

Every now and then. Lesley Kagen. Alcove Press, 2020. 296 p.

ISBN 9781643853543

1. Women authors 2. Psychiatric hospitals 3. Memories 4. Secrets 5. Small towns 6. Relationship fiction 7. Coming-of-age stories

A best-selling novelist reflects on a traumatizing experience she shared with two friends during the summer of 1960 in Wisconsin, where their innocence was upended by long-kept secrets and the escape of three patients from a mental institution.

"Kagan thoughtfully captures the spirit of early '60s small-town America, showing both the idyllic, rosy past that inspires nostalgia and its troubling underbelly, which includes small-mindedness, racism, homophobia, and mistreatment of the mentally ill." —*Booklist*

Kamal, Sheena

It all falls down. Sheena Kamal. William Morrow & Co, 2018. 384 p. (Nora Watts novels, 2)

ISBN 9780062565778

1. Fathers and daughters 2. Family and suicide 3. Drug traffic 4. First Nations (Canada) 5. Private investigators 6. British Columbia 7. Detroit, Michigan 8. Thrillers and suspense 9. Canadian fiction

To find the truth about her father's life and violent death, Nora Watts, focused on the mysterious events of her father's past and the clues they provide to her own fractured identity, is led to a private investigator whose latest is case is somehow connected to her.

Kamal, Soniah

Unmarriageable: a novel. Soniah Kamal. Ballantine Books, 2019. 342 p.

ISBN 9781524799717

1. Marriage 2. Teachers 3. Families 4. Man-woman relationships 5. Mate selection 6. Pakistan 7. Chick lit 8. Romantic comedies 9. Adaptations, retellings, and spin-offs

LC 2018036398

LibraryReads Favorites, 2019

A retelling of Pride and Prejudice, set in modern-day Pakistan, finds a practical-minded teacher from a family of sisters evaluating her resolve never to marry after encountering a brusque but compelling man during a series of lavish wedding parties.

"This love letter to Austen reexamines sisterhood, society, and marriage in Pakistani culture and includes a fleshed-out epilogue that will satisfy today's readers." —*Booklist*

Kamali, Marjan

★ The **stationery** shop. Marjan Kamali. Gallery Books, 2019. 312 pages

ISBN 9781982107482

1. Teenage romance 2. Political violence 3. Fate and fatalism 4. Engagement 5. Jilted women 6. Tehran, Iran 7. Iran 8. 1950s 9. 2010s 10. Historical fiction

LC 2018052061

A young couple who meet and fall in love at a neighborhood stationery shop in 1953 Tehran are separated by a violent coup d'etat on the eve of their marriage and reunite by chance after more than half a century.

"The unfurling stories in Kamali's sophomore novel (after Together Tea) will stun readers as the aromas of Persian cooking wafting throughout convince us that love can last a lifetime. For those who enjoy getting caught up in romance while discovering unfamiliar history of another country." —*Library Journal*

Kaminsky, Stuart M.

Dancing in the dark. Stuart M. Kaminsky. Mysterious Press, 1996. 228 p. (Toby Peters mysteries, 19)

ISBN 9780892965281

1. Astaire, Fred 2. Murder investigation 3. Gangsters 4. Women murder victims 5. Dancing 6. Film actors and actresses 7. Hollywood, California 8. 1940s 9. Historical mysteries 10. Hardboiled fiction 11. First person narratives

LC 95013095

In 1940s Hollywood, PI Toby Peters is hired by Fred Astaire to serve as a dancing partner for a gangster's moll learning to dance. A strenuous assignment as Peters is no dancer, but before you know it the moll is killed and Peters is once again in his element.

"The author effortlessly choreographs Hollywood history, colorful cast and dirty doings." —*Publishers Weekly*

Includes appearance by Fred Astaire.

Murder on the Trans-Siberian Express. Stuart M. Kaminsky. Mysterious Press, 2001. 277 p; (Inspector Porfiry Rostnikov mysteries, 14)

ISBN 9780892967476

1. Police 2. Murder investigation 3. Kidnapping 4. Railroad travel 5. Murder 6. Siberia 7. Moscow, Russia 8. Mysteries 9. Hardboiled fiction

LC 2001026218

Chief Inspector Rostnikov heads for Vladivostok aboard the Trans-Siberian Express to find an extortionist who may possess information that could bring down the Russian government.

"The action reaches back to Siberia in 1894, when one man in a band of starving, disease-ridden convicts, sentenced to work on constructing the great rail line from Moscow to Vladivostok, buries his treasurea leather pouch containing a tiny gold box with a letter inside. More than a century later, Inspector Porfiry of the Moscow Police is sent on the 6,000-mile rail line to find this box. Porfiry leaves behind two other investigations: the kidnapping of a skinhead rock star and a series of murders in the Moscow Metro. How Kaminsky weaves these tangled plot lines into a taut suspense fabric, while providing fascinating, sad-funny commentary on his characters and the tensions inherent in the new Russian social order, is a matter of wonder." —*Booklist*

To catch a spy: a Toby Peters mystery. Stuart M. Kaminsky. Carroll & Graf Publishers, 2002. 230 p; (Toby Peters mysteries, 22)

ISBN 9780786710232

1. Grant, Cary 2. Murder investigation 3. Nazis 4. Spies 5. Film actors and actresses 6. Private investigators 7. Hollywood, California 8. 1940s 9. Historical mysteries 10. Hardboiled fiction 11. First person narratives

LC 2002067254

While trying to deliver a package for film superstar Cary Grant, private detective Toby Peters stumbles upon a corpse and joins forces with the movie star to follow a trail of clues that leads them to a gang of Nazi sympathizers.

An Otto Penzler book.

Kandasamy, Meena

When I hit you, or, A portrait of the writer as a young wife. Meena Kandasamy. Europa Editions, 2020. 210 p.

ISBN 9781609455996

1. Abused women 2. Married women 3. Women authors 4. Partner abuse 5. Courage in women 6. India 7. Literary fiction 8. Autobiographical fiction

Shortlisted for The Women's Prize for Fiction, 2018

Set in modern India, the unnamed narrator falls in love with a university professor and agrees to be his wife. Based on the author's own experience of marriage, soon the newly-wed experiences extreme violence at her husband's hands and finds herself socially isolated.... Yet hope keeps her alive. Writing becomes her salvation, a supreme act of defiance.

"Kandasamy (The Gypsy Goddess, 2014, etc.) divides her time between Chennai and London, and the novel was shortlisted for the Women's Prize for Fiction and the Jhalak Prize and longlisted for the Dylan Thomas Prize." —*Kirkus*

Originally published: London : Atlantic Books, 2017.

Kane, Ben

Spartacus: the gladiator. Ben Kane. St. Martin's Press, 2012. 466 p. ; Map

ISBN 9781250001160

1. Spartacus 2. Gladiators 3. Soldiers 4. Jealousy in men 5. Women priests 6. Escapes 7. Rome 8. Roman Empire (27 BCE-476 CE) 9. Historical fiction 10. War stories

Returning to his village after escaping the Roman army, Spartacus is betrayed by his jealous king and forced into life as a gladiator before executing a daring overthrow and assuming leadership over an army of escaped slaves.

Sequel: Spartacus: the rebellion.

Kane, Darby

Pretty little wife. Darby Kane. William Morrow & Co, 2020. 384 pages

ISBN 9780063016408

1. Married women 2. Women murderers 3. Pedophiles 4. Criminal evidence 5. Missing men 6. New York (State) 7. Psychological suspense

LibraryReads Favorites, 2020

Debut author Darby Kane thrills with this twisty domestic suspense novel that asks one central question: shouldn't a dead husband stay dead?

"Debut mystery author Kane blends tense domestic suspense with procedural details and legal thriller?like verbal sparring. A page-turner built on skilfully layered plotting and an intriguing protagonist." —*Booklist*

Kane, Jessica Francis

Rules for visiting. Jessica Francis Kane. Penguin Press, 2019. 304 p.

ISBN 9780525559221

1. Women gardeners 2. Middle age 3. Loners 4. Female friendship 5. Vacations 6. Relationship fiction

A talented but reclusive gardener is inspired by her love of classic literature to embark on a female odyssey to reconnect with her four once-close friends through simple activities and digital encounters that unexpectedly catapult her into viral fame.

Kantaria, Annabel

I know you: a novel of suspense. Annabel Kantaria. Crooked Lane Books, 2019. 384 pages
ISBN 9781643851105
1. Stalkers 2. Friendship 3. Social media 4. Moving, Household 5. Moving to a new country 6. England 7. Psychological suspense
A twisted domestic thriller in the vein of B. A. Paris and Shari Lapena that asks: How well do you know your friends?
Originally published: London : HQ, 2018.

Kantor, MacKinlay

★ **Andersonville**. MacKinlay Kantor. Plume, 1993. 766 p. : Map
ISBN 9780452269569
1. Prisoners of war, Confederate 2. Prisons 3. Civil war 4. United States Civil War, 1861-1865 5. United States 6. American Civil War era (1861-1865) 7. Historical fiction 8. War stories 9. Literary fiction
LC 9235802
Pulitzer Prize for Fiction, 1956
In 1864, thirty-three thousand Yankee prisoners of war suffer the horrors of imprisonment at the Confederate prison of Andersonville.
Originally published: New York : New American Library, 1955.

Kantra, Virginia

Beth & Amy. Virginia Kantra. Berkley, 2021. 352 p.
ISBN 9780593100363
1. March family (Fictitious characters) 2. Families 3. Sisters 4. Weddings 5. Interpersonal relations 6. Domestic fiction 7. Contemporary romances 8. Relationship fiction
LC 2020050421
Four sisters face new beginnings in this heartfelt modern take on Little Women. With the March women reunited, this time with growing careers and families, they must once again learn to lean on one another as they juggle the changes coming their way.
"Kantra (Meg and Jo) continues her delightful 21st-century retelling of Little Women, set in Bunyan, N.C, with characters that hew closely to the versions that inspired them." —*Publishers Weekly*

★ **Meg** and Jo. Virginia Kantra. Berkley, 2019. 400 pages
ISBN 9780593100349
1. Sisters 2. Mothers and daughters 3. Family relationships 4. Young women 5. Ambition in women 6. North Carolina 7. Mainstream fiction 8. Domestic fiction 9. Adaptations, retellings, and spin-offs
LC 2019022562
LibraryReads Favorites, 2019; Loan Stars Favourites, 2019
When their mother falls ill, the March sisters—reliable Meg, independent Jo, stylish Amy and shy Beth, return home to North Carolina for the holidays where they'll rediscover what really matters.
"Kantra blends just enough of Alcott's story of four close-knit sisters and their myriad tribulations with clever and timely new elements (unexpected pregnancies, the girls father as a military chaplain, parents separating), a mix that will satisfy Alcott fans as well as entice Kantra s existing fans." —*Publishers Weekly*

Kaplan, Mitchell James

Rhapsody. Mitchell James Kaplan. Gallery Books, 2021. 352 p.
ISBN 9781982104009
1. Swift, Kay 2. Married women 3. Women pianists 4. Composers 5. Extramarital affairs 6. Jazz music 7. New York City 8. 1920s 9. 1930s 10. Biographical fiction 11. Historical fiction

One evening in 1924, Katharine "Kay" Swift—the restless but loyal society wife of wealthy banker James Warburg and a serious pianist who longs for recognition—attends a concert. The piece: Rhapsody in Blue. The composer: a brilliant, elusive young musical genius named George Gershwin. Kay is transfixed, helpless to resist the magnetic pull of George's talent, charm, and swagger. Their ten-year love affair, complicated by her conflicted loyalty to her husband and the twists and turns of her own musical career, ends only with George's death from a brain tumor at the age of thirty-eight.
"This spellbinding and luminous tale will linger in readers' minds long after the final page is turned." —*Publishers Weekly*

Kasulke, Calvin

Several people are typing. Calvin Kasulke. Doubleday, 2021. 224 p.
ISBN 9780385547222
1. Labor productivity 2. Corporate culture 3. Consciousness 4. Public relations personnel 5. Coworkers 6. Satirical fiction 7. Epistolary novels
When his consciousness is uploaded into his company's internal Slack channels, boosting his productivity, Gerald, who works for a PR firm, as his reality becomes more absurd, enlists the help of a co-worker to help him escape—and to find out what happened to his body.
"Kasulke turns what sounds like a gimmicky premise, and a limiting one at that, into a poignant depiction of the always-on nature of the contemporary workplace. Kasulke's ear for dialogue is remarkable as he truly captures the in-jokes, asides, and odd language of Slack communication. Funny, relatable, and incredibly timely, this is a hugely entertaining read." —*Booklist*

Kate, Jessica

A girl's guide to the Outback: a novel. Jessica Kate. Thomas Nelson, 2020. 358 p.
ISBN 9780785229612
1. Clergy 2. Church work 3. Women entrepreneurs 4. Dairy farms 5. Farm life 6. Australia 7. United States 8. Christian romances 9. Contemporary romances 10. Australian fiction
LC 2019032265
How far will a girl go to win back a guy she can't stand?
"Kate (Love and Other Mistakes) brings the outback to life in this stand-alone Christian romance that features two people struggling to figure out what they want." —*Library Journal*

Katsu, Alma

The **deep**. Alma Katsu. G.P. Putnam's Sons,, 2020. 420 pages
ISBN 9780525537908
1. Ocean travel 2. Ocean liners 3. Paranormal phenomena 4. Nurses 5. Shipwreck survivors 6. 1910s 7. Historical horror 8. Multiple perspectives 9. Adult books for young adults
Surviving the sinking of the *Titanic*, Annie takes a job as a nurse on the *Britannic* before encountering a fellow survivor who forces her to reckon with past demons.
"A riveting, seductively menacing tale of love, loss, and betrayal set amid the glamour of the *Titanic*, filled with seances, sea witches, and second chances." —*Library Journal*

The **hunger**: a novel. Alma Katsu. G. P. Putnam's Sons, 2018. 400 p.
ISBN 9780735212510
1. Donner Party 2. Wagon trains 3. Good and evil 4. Cannibalism 5. Supernatural 6. The West (United States) 7. American Westward

Expansion (1803-1899) 8. 1840s 9. Horror 10. Historical horror 11. Weird Westerns 12. Adult books for young adults

LC 2017019689

Western Heritage Award for Outstanding Western Novel, 2019

A supernatural reimagining of the Donner Party story follows a group of wagon-train pioneers who navigate sanity-testing misfortunes, including the mysterious death of a little boy and a series of disappearances that cause a beautiful member of the group to be accused of witchcraft.

Katz, Erica

The **boys'** club. Erica Katz. Harper, 2020. 416 p.
ISBN 9780062961488
1. Women lawyers 2. Overachievers 3. Sexism in employment 4. Law firms 5. Competition 6. Manhattan, New York City 7. New York City 8. Legal thrillers

An Ivy League overachiever accepts a job at a prestigious Manhattan law firm where the dynamics of workplace sexism force her to choose between her career and doing what is right.

"A knowing, nuanced #MeToo story from the world of corporate law, with juicy The Wolf of Wall Street-type action." —*Kirkus*

Katzenbach, John

What comes next. John Katzenbach. Mysterious Press, 2012. 320 p.
ISBN 9780802126115
1. Women kidnapping victims 2. Internet 3. Torture 4. Missing persons investigation 5. Sadism 6. Psychological suspense

After the police falter in their investigation, a retired college professor vows to track down a young woman he witnessed being snatched off the street, kidnapped by a sadistic couple who put their victim's slow torture up for public display on the Internet.

Kaufman, Bel

Up the down staircase. Bel Kaufman. Prentice Hall 1965. 340p.
ISBN 9781912854615
1. Teaching — Philosophy 2. High school teachers 3. High schools 4. New York City 5. Mainstream fiction

LC 64024258

Chronicles the goings-on in a large metropolitan high school, detailing the experiences of an idealistic first-year teacher who is plagued by difficulties arising from an overwhelming bureaucracy, inadequate facilities, and some unforgettable students.

Kaufman, Charlie

Antkind: a novel. Charlie Kaufman. Random House, 2020. 705 pages
ISBN 9780399589683
1. Film critics 2. Films 3. Memory 4. Creativity 5. Loss (Psychology) 6. Florida 7. New York City 8. Satirical fiction 9. Picaresque fiction

LC 2020001684

A neurotic and underappreciated film critic becomes sole witness to a film he's convinced will change his career trajectory and rock the world of cinema to its core.

"With this surprisingly breezy read, given its length, Kaufman proves to be a masterful novelist, delivering a tragic, farcical, and fascinating exploration of how memory defines our lives." —*Booklist*

Kaufman, Sue

Diary of a mad housewife. By Sue Kaufman. Thunder's Mouth Press : 2005. 311 p.

ISBN 9781560256878
1. Homemakers 2. Identity (Psychology) 3. Gender role 4. Women — Identity 5. Husband and wife 6. New York City 7. Manhattan, New York City 8. 1960s 9. Diary novels 10. Books to movies

First published in 1967, this novel of life in New York is written in the form of a diary of a disenchanted housewife who offers a frank, unsparing portrait of her terrors and passions.

Originally published: New York : Random House, c1967.

Kawabata, Yasunari

The **sound** of the mountain. Yasunari Kawabata; translated from the Japanese by Edward M. Seidensticker. Vintage, 1996. 276 p.
ISBN 9780679762645
1. Senior men 2. Emotions 3. Anxiety 4. Memory 5. Mountains 6. Japan 7. Historical fiction 8. Literary fiction 9. Translations

LC 77098666

Focuses on the anxieties, desires, and emotions of a sensitive old Japanese man

"The language is delicate, allusive, intensely Japanese; and, since plot and character development count for little, the style is all-important. We are fortunate that it should have been a writer with Mr. Seidensticker's gifts who ventured to convey [Kawabata's] rarefied novels into English." —*New York Times Book Review*

Kawaguchi, Toshikazu

Before the coffee gets cold. Toshikazu Kawaguchi; translated from the Japanese by Geoffrey Trousselot. Hanover Square Press, 2020. 240 p. (Before the coffee gets cold, 1)
ISBN 9781335430991
1. Coffee shops 2. Time travel 3. Families 4. Interpersonal relations 5. Options, alternatives, choices 6. Magical realism 7. Literary fiction 8. Translations

LibraryReads Favorites, 2020

At a century-old Tokyo coffee shop rumored to offer patrons the chance to travel back in time, four customers reevaluate their formative life choices.

"Kawaguchi's tender look at the beauty of passing things, adapted from one of his plays, makes for an affecting, deeply immersive journey into the desire to hold onto the past." —*Publishers Weekly*

Originally published: Tokyo : Sunmark Publishing, 2015.

Translated from the Japanese.

Kawakami, Mieko

Ms. Ice Sandwich. Mieko Kawakami; translated by Louise Heal Kawai. Pushkin Press, 2018. 160 pages
ISBN 9781782273301
1. Women merchants 2. Strangers 3. Crushes in boys 4. Friendship 5. Portraits 6. Literary fiction 7. Coming-of-age stories 8. Translations

Obsessed with a woman who sells sandwiches, a young boy, who endlessly draws her portrait, finds his hopes dashed when a friend hears about his hesitant adoration, which changes everything.

Translated from the Japanese

Kay, Guy Gavriel

★ A **brightness** long ago. Guy Gavriel Kay. Berkley, 2019. 422 p.
ISBN 9780451472984
1. Courts and courtiers 2. Women assassins 3. Social classes 4. Counts and countesses 5. Rebels 6. Epic fantasy 7. Canadian fiction

LC 2018039450

A brilliant servant under a despotic count and a would-be assassin who has forfeited a life of comfort join an extraordinary group of companions when a rivalry between two mercenary commanders threatens the world balance.

"Fans of Kay's previous work will find his usual elements in play: strong historical research and worldbuilding, a vast cast of characters, world-changing events, and prose that sometimes gets carried away with itself. An epic tale filled with characters compelling enough to bear the weight of the high stakes." —*Kirkus*

★ **Children** of earth and sky. Guy Gavriel Kay. New American Library, 2016. 560 p.
ISBN 9780451472960
1. Voyages and travels 2. Interpersonal relations 3. Imaginary wars and battles 4. Revenge 5. Intrigue 6. Fantasy fiction 7. Historical fantasy 8. Canadian fiction
LC 2015047832
RUSA Reading List Short List, 2017
A khalif from the Ottoman Empire sends an enormous army to attack the fortress that separates the Western World from the Turkish lands.
"This intricately plotted literary novel will appeal to Kays many fans as well as readers who enjoy character-driven historical fiction with just a touch of fantasy." —*Booklist*

The **summer** tree. Guy Gavriel Kay. Roc, 2001. 383 p. : Map (Fionavar Tapestry, 1)
ISBN 9780451458223
1. Parallel universes 2. Imaginary wars and battles 3. Magic 4. College students 5. Good and evil 6. Epic fantasy 7. Gateway fantasy 8. Canadian fiction
LC 45803
Five young professionals and students are dramatically precipitated out of their lives in this world into the realm of Fionavar, the true world, of which our own is only shadow. Led by Silvercloak, the wizard, the five are caught up in the opening forays of a devastating war as the renegade god, Rakoth Maugrim, breaks free from his thousand-year imprisonment. In a world gripped by the timeless war between the forces of Light and Dark, a rich tapestry is woven as the five are confronted by wood and water spirits, dwarves, supernatural animals and the titanic magics of the gods, against which the strengths of humans seem weak and small.
Originally published: New York : Arbor House, 1984.

Tigana. Guy Gavrial Kay. Penguin Books, 1990. 673 p.
ISBN 9780451450289
1. Magic 2. Wizards 3. Psychological warfare 4. Singers 5. Guilt 6. Epic fantasy 7. Canadian fiction
LC 90034423
Prix Aurora: Best Novel, 1991
Allesan, son of the king of Tigana, and other survivors of the forgotten world band together to plot the demise of Brandin of Ygrath.
"Memorable characters and cultures add depth to a gracefully plotted story." —*Library Journal*
Includes end-paper maps.

Kayode, Femi
★ **Lightseekers.** Femi Kayode. Mulholland Books, 2021. 480 p.
ISBN 9780316536615
1. Psychologists 2. College students 3. Murder victims 4. Torture victims 5. Fathers and sons 6. Nigeria 7. Mysteries
When Dr. Philip Taiwo is called on by a powerful Nigerian politician to investigate the public torture and murder of three university students in Port Harcourt, he has no idea that he's about to be enveloped by a perilous case that is far from cold. Philip is not a detective. He's an investigative

psychologist, an academic more interested in figuring out the why of a crime than actually solving it. But when he steps off the plane and into the dizzying frenzy of the provincial airport, he soon realizes that the mob-driven murder of the Okriki Three isn't as straight forward as he thought. With the help of his loyal and streetwise personal driver, Chika, Philip must work against those actively conspiring against him to parse together the truth of what happened to these students.
"With alluring characters, including a chillingly psychotic villain; an original, many-faceted plot; and blazing psychological and social insights, Kayode's commanding and thought-provoking first crime novel launches a profoundly promising series." —*Booklist*

Kazantzakis, Nikos
The **last** temptation of Christ. Nikos Kazantzakis; translated from the Greek by P.A. Bien. Simon and Schuster, 1960. 506 p.
ISBN 9780671407100
1. Jesus Christ 2. Historical fiction 3. Translations 4. Books to movies
LC 60010985
Novel which portrays Christ as a sensitive human being who is torn between his own passionates desires and his triumphant destiny on the cross.

Keesey, Anna
Little century: a novel. Anna Keesey. Farrar, Straus and Giroux, 2012. 304 p.
ISBN 9780374192044
1. Eighteen-year-old women 2. Range wars 3. Loyalty 4. Homesteading 5. Orphans 6. Oregon 7. Westerns 8. Adult books for young adults
LC 2011046308
School Library Journal Best Books: Best Adult Books 4 Teens, 2012
After she moves near the lawless frontier town of Century, Oregon, to become a homesteader, eighteen-year-old Esther Chambers finds herself in a full-out range war that tests her loyalty to her cousin, rancher Ferris Pickett.

Keller, Julia
★ **Bone** on bone. Julia Keller. Minotaur Books, 2018. 304 p. (Bell Elkins mysteries, 7)
ISBN 9781250190925
1. Former lawyers 2. Former convicts 3. Drug addiction 4. People with paraplegia 5. Former sheriffs 6. West Virginia 7. Mysteries 8. Southern fiction
LC 2018023688
An investigation involving the suspicious deaths of a drug addict's parents is complicated by former deputy Jake Oakes' struggles to adjust to his physical challenges and Bell's grief over the loss of her sister.
"This haunting, thought-provoking story proves Keller is one of a kind. Readers of Julia Spencer-Fleming's mysteries of communities torn apart by crime may also want to try." —*Library Journal*

A **killing** in the hills. Julia Keller. Minotaur Books, 2012. 416 p. (Bell Elkins mysteries, 1)
ISBN 9781250003485
1. Teenage girls 2. Murder witnesses 3. Small town life 4. Mothers and daughters 5. Crimes against seniors 6. West Virginia 7. Mysteries 8. Southern fiction
LC 2012016583
Prosecuting attorney Bell Elkins and her estranged teenage daughter, Carla, try to protect their town and each other in the aftermath of a shock-

ing triple murder committed by an unknown shooter whose identity is gradually realized by Carla.

First published in the United Kingdom in 2012 by Headline Publishing Group.

Kellerman, Jonathan

Bones: an Alex Delaware novel. Jonathan Kellerman. Ballantine Books, 2008. 368 p. (Alex Delaware novels, 23)

ISBN 9780345495136

1. Crimes against women 2. Marshes 3. Psychologists 4. Delaware, Alex (Fictitious character) 5. Sturgis, Milo (Fictitious character) 6. California 7. Mysteries 8. Psychological suspense 9. Adult books for young adults

LC Bl2008020492

When an anonymous tip leads to the skeletal remains of victims whose right hands have been removed and a box containing six human hands, LAPD detective Milo Sturgis calls in Alex Delaware, whose investigation takes them to a reclusive tycoon's mansion.

"Kellerman's strength is that he can set up an intriguing situation and keep things moving at a breakneck pace. He can also, when he wants to, write well. He's good at short, vivid descriptions.... I don't think the plot of Bones will withstand scrutiny, but most readers probably won't care. The story sweeps them along, offering plenty of snappy dialogue and cheap thrills, plus a fair amount of suspense that is relieved by the final unveiling of the killer." —*Washington Post Book World.*

Gone. Jonathan Kellerman. Ballantine Books, 2006. 384 p. (Alex Delaware novels, 20)

ISBN 9780345452610

1. Art students 2. Hoaxes 3. Psychologists 4. Police 5. California 6. Mysteries 7. Psychological suspense 8. Adult books for young adults

Psychologist Alex Delaware and L.A.P.D. detective Milo Sturgis investigate the bizarre case of two students whose claims of abduction are revealed to be a hoax, a case that takes an odd turn when one student is found murdered and the other vanishes.

"While the murderer's identity may not be that surprising, the author's ability to convey the unrelenting sadness of his characters' lives and his deep psychological insights will satisfy those looking for more than mere thrills." —*Publishers Weekly*

★ **Half** Moon Bay: a novel. Jonathan Kellerman and Jesse Kellerman. Ballantine Books, 2020. 354 pages (Clay Edison novels, 3)

ISBN 9780525620082

1. Coroners 2. Crime scenes 3. Cold cases (Criminal investigation) 4. Missing persons 5. Murder 6. Berkeley, California 7. Mysteries

LC 2019048621

When the decades-old skeleton of a child is discovered at the site of a park demolition, Deputy Coroner Clay Edison unearths devastating community secrets surrounding the long-ago disappearance of his sister.

"Clay's thoughtful narration is procedural gold in this latest from the father-son Kellerman writing team." —*Booklist*

Kells, Claire

Vanishing edge. Claire Kells. Crooked Lane Books, 2021. 288 p.

ISBN 9781643858678

1. Sequoia National Park 2. National parks and reserves 3. Park rangers 4. Former Navy SEALs 5. Government investigators 6. California 7. Mysteries

Brought in as chief investigator when a party of campers go missing, 32-year-old Felicity Harland must place her trust in a Navy SEAL turned park ranger when the investigation takes them from the wilderness to the streets of Los Angeles, where the grisly truth comes to light.

"Sharply drawn characters and striking descriptions of park scenery more than compensate for less than assured plotting. Fans of Scott Graham's National Parks mysteries will want to check this one out." —*Publishers Weekly*

Kelly, Cathy

Secrets of a happy marriage. Cathy Kelly. Grand Central Publishing, 2018. 464 p.

ISBN 9781538728796

1. Newlyweds 2. Husband and wife 3. Stepdaughters 4. Dysfunctional families 5. Resentfulness 6. Ireland 7. Relationship fiction

While planning her new husband's big birthday celebration, Bess, finds her May-December romance going into a tailspin as she quickly realizes that joining his family isn't going to be as easy as she thought.

Originally published as an ebook in the U.K. by Orion, 2017.

Kelly, Erin

Broadchurch: a novel. . Minotaur Books, 2014. 433 p.

ISBN 9781250055507

1. Women detectives 2. Child murder victims 3. Small town life 4. Murder 5. Secrets 6. England 7. Dorset, England 8. Police procedurals 9. Mysteries 10. Media tie-ins

A novelization of the hit television show follows detectives Alec Hardy and Ellie Miller as they search for a young boy's killer among numerous suspects and a brewing media storm.

"Kelly's novelization of the eponymous British TV series...works as both a classic puzzle and an unnerving portrait of a little English town wracked by a young boy's murder." —*Kirkus*

The **burning** air: a novel. Erin Kelly. Pamela Dorman Books, 2013. 336 p.

ISBN 9780670026722

1. Family secrets 2. Revenge 3. Rich families 4. Country homes 5. Bereavement in families 6. England 7. Psychological suspense 8. Multiple perspectives

LC 2012029302

Old wounds and long-buried family secrets come crashing down on the seemingly untouchable MacBride clan not long after matriarch Lydia MacBride dies. Connecting everything is a mysterious confession in Lydia's extensive diaries and an outsider bent on exacting terrible revenge on the MacBrides.

Watch her fall. Erin Kelly. Mobius, 2021. 400 p.

ISBN 9781473680838

1. Ballet dancers 2. Ballet 3. Ambition in women 4. Stalkers 5. Wounds and injuries 6. London, England 7. England 8. Psychological suspense 9. Multiple perspectives

Ballerina Ava Kirilova has reached the very top of her profession, but now there's someone who wants to see her fall.

"This fresh approach to the story of a dancer facing the inevitable decline of her body will resonate with many." —*Publishers Weekly*

Kelly, Greta

The **frozen** crown. Greta Kelly. Harper Voyager, 2021. 384 p. (Warrior witch duology, 1)

ISBN 9780062956958

1. Imaginary kingdoms 2. Heirs and heiresses 3. Women magicians 4. Magic 5. Armies 6. High fantasy 7. Fantasy fiction

Fleeing to her allies in the south when her realm is overrun by the forces of a mad emperor, a young heiress is embroiled in labyrinthine political games that threaten to expose her secret magical nature.

"Filled with magic, war, and intrigue, this thrilling high fantasy questions how much a ruler should be willing to sacrifice for the sake of duty. Vivid worldbuilding, high stakes, and just a hint of romance propel the twisty plot to a cliffhanger finale." —*Publishers Weekly*

Kelly, Julia

The **last** dance of the debutante. Julia Kelly. Gallery Books, 2021. 320 p.

ISBN 9781982171636

1. Debutantes 2. Mothers and daughters 3. Socialites 4. Female friendship 5. Family secrets 6. 1950s 7. Historical fiction

LC 2021030501

In 1958, the last year debutantes are to be presented in court, Lily Nichols, while attending a glittering and grueling string of countless parties and balls, discovers a devastating secret about her entire family, forcing her to choose between her legacy or her own happiness.

"The story is full of allure, society scandals, and the determination for these young women to eschew the dying traditions of the time." —*Booklist*

The **light** over London. Julia Kelly. Gallery Books, 2019. 288 p.
ISBN 9781501196416

1. Antique dealers 2. Baudelaire, Charles 3. World War II 4. Man-woman relationships 5. Antiaircraft guns 6. Cornwall, England 7. London, England 8. Second World War era (1939-1945) 9. Parallel narratives 10. Historical fiction

LC 2018010178

Unable to confront the challenges in her own life, Cara Hargraves immerses herself in work for her antiques-dealer boss, uncovering relics from the life of World War II British "Gunner Girl" Louise Keene and her complicated relationship with a man named Paul.

Kelly, Martha Hall

Lilac girls. Martha Hall Kelly. Ballantine Books, 2016. 496 p. (Caroline Ferriday, 1)

ISBN 9781101883075

1. World War II 2. Women 3. Secrets 4. Nazis 5. Teenage girls 6. Paris, France 7. Germany 8. Second World War era (1939-1945) 9. Historical fiction

LibraryReads Favorites, 2016; Library Journal Best Books, 2016

On a September day in Manhattan in 1939, twenty-something Caroline Ferriday is consumed by her efforts to secure the perfect boutonniere for an important French diplomat and resisting the romantic advances of a married actor. Meanwhile across the Atlantic, Kasia Kuzmerick, a Polish Catholic teenager, is nervously anticipating the changes that are sure to come since Germany has declared war on Poland. As tensions rise abroad—and in her personal life—Caroline's interest in aiding the war effort in France grows and she eventually comes to hear about the dire situation at the Ravensbruck all-female concentration camp. At the same time, Kasia's carefree youth is quickly slipping away, only to be replaced by a fervor for the Polish resistance movement. Through Ravensbruck—and the horrific atrocities taking place there told in part by an infamous German surgeon, Herta Oberheuser—the two women's lives will converge in unprecedented ways and a novel of redemption and hope emerges that is breathtaking in scope and depth.

Lost roses: a novel. Martha Hall Kelly. Ballantine Books, 2019. 448 p; (Caroline Ferriday, 2)

ISBN 9781524796372

1. Female friendship 2. Voyages and travels 3. Revolutions 4. Friendship 5. Life change events 6. Russia 7. United States 8. First

World War era (1914-1918) 9. Russian Revolution and Civil War (1917-1921) 10. Historical fiction

LibraryReads Favorites, 2019

Based on true events, a tale set a generation before Lilac Girls traces the stories of three women, including Caroline Ferriday's mother, a Romanov cousin and a fortune-teller's daughter, against a backdrop of the Russian revolution and World War I.

Originally published: North Sydney, NSW : Michael Joseph, 2019.

Kelly, Stephen

The **wages** of desire: a World War II mystery. Stephen Kelly. Pegasus Books, 2016. 314 p. (Inspector Lamb novels, 2)

ISBN 9781681771496

1. Detectives 2. Villages 3. World War II 4. Cold cases (Criminal investigation) 5. Conscientious objectors 6. England 7. 1940s 8. Second World War era (1939-1945) 9. Historical mysteries

Detective Chief Inspector Thomas Lamb risks his life to uncover links between a series of killings from the past and present in a Hampshire village brimming with dark secrets.

Kelman, James

How late it was, how late. James Kelman. W. W. Norton, 1995. 373 p.
ISBN 9780393038170

1. Working class men 2. Men who are blind 3. Former convicts 4. Missing persons 5. Glasgow, Scotland 6. Literary fiction

Booker Prize, 1994

Sammy, an ex-convict living in Glasgow, gets into a fight with some soldiers, only to regain consciousness in a jail cell and be questioned by the police about his girlfriend's disappearance.

"The novel is a tour de force, both in its convincingly claustrophobic rendering of what it's like to be newly sightless and in its rhythmic prose." —*Newsweek*

Kelton, Elmer

Hard ride. Elmer Kelton. Forge, 2018. 411 p.
ISBN 9781250161284

1. Ranchers 2. Outlaws 3. Rodeos 4. Justice 5. Gunfights 6. The West (United States) 7. Short stories 8. Westerns

LC 2018044737

Imbued with an adventurous spirit, Hard Ride is filled with many heartfelt glimpses into the authentic experience of the American West. These stories encompass an enormous array of scenes from the early days of the Wild West into the twentieth century.

Collects stories originally published in the 1950s.

A Tom Doherty Associates Book.

★ The **way** of the coyote. Elmer Kelton. Forge, 2001. 283 p; (Texas Rangers (Elmer Kelton), 3)

ISBN 9780312873189

1. Kidnapping 2. Loyalty 3. Political corruption 4. Dickinson, Emily 5. Boy orphans 6. Texas 7. 1860s 8. Westerns

LC 2001040482

Spur Award for Best Western Novel (Short Novel), 2002

Former Comanche captive Rusty Shannon tries to resume a normal life after the end of the Civil War, but instead finds himself confronted by racial tension, murderous outlaws, brutal Comanche bands, and his nemesis—the deadly Oldham brothers.

"Kelton covers a wide swath of history with aplomb, illuminating a little-known period in Western history. California is still Mexican, Indians are a real threat and outlaws rule the land in this rough-riding adventure tale." —*Publishers Weekly*

Kemelman, Harry

Monday the rabbi took off. G. P. Putnam's Sons, 1972. 316 p. (Rabbi David Small mysteries, 4)
ISBN 9780449210017
1. Americans in Israel 2. Criminal investigation 3. Murder 4. Murder investigation 5. Rabbis 6. Israel 7. Barnard's Crossing, Massachusetts 8. Mysteries

LC 75175264

Equipped with the ability to see the third side of every question, Rabbi David Small, determined to have a peaceful day at the park, unexpectedly finds himself in the middle of an international incident.

One fine day the rabbi bought a cross. Harry Kemelman. W. Morrow, 1987. 234 p. (Rabbi David Small mysteries, 9)
ISBN 9780688056315
1. Illegal arms transfers 2. Criminal investigation 3. Murder 4. Murder investigation 5. Vacations 6. Jerusalem, Israel 7. Barnard's Crossing, Massachusetts 8. Mysteries

LC 86023571

As a favor, the rabbi looks in on Jordan Goodman, son of the local grocer. Jordan has adopted the beliefs of a fundamentalist Jewish group, and before long, he is the only suspect in a local murder.

Keneally, Thomas

★ The **daughters** of Mars. Tom Keneally. Atria Books, 2013. 544 p.
ISBN 9781476734613
1. Military nurses 2. Sisters 3. World War I 4. Military campaigns 5. Battle casualties 6. Gallipoli, Turkey 7. France 8. First World War era (1914-1918) 9. Historical fiction 10. War stories 11. Literary fiction
Colin Roderick Award (Australia), 2012; Library Journal Best Books, 2013; Shortlisted for the Walter Scott Prize for Historical Fiction, 2013

Joining the war effort as nurses in 1915, two spirited Australian sisters, carrying a guilty secret, become the friends they never were at home and find themselves courageous in the face of extreme danger as they serve alongside remarkable women during the first World War.

"Keneally must have done copious research, but historical details and information about wartime medical treatment are presented organically, without the weight of historical retrospection... Highly recommended." —*Library Journal*

Includes author's note.

Originally published: North Sydney, N.S.W. : Vintage Books, 2012.

★ **Schindler's** list. Thomas Keneally. Simon and Schuster, 1994. 398 p.
ISBN 9780671516888
1. Schindler, Oskar 2. Holocaust (1933-1945) 3. Righteous Gentiles in the Holocaust 4. Ghettoes, Jewish 5. Holocaust survivors 6. World War II — Jews 7. Poland 8. Germany 9. Historical fiction 10. Mason, Charles 11. Literary fiction
Booker Prize, 1982; Los Angeles Times Book Prize for Fiction, 1983

A wealthy German-Catholic industrialist and Nazi Party member named Oskar Schindler builds a factory near a concentration camp to save the lives of over 1,300 Jews.

Simultaneously published in 1982: New York : Simon and Schuster, as Schindler's list; and, London : Hodder and Stoughton, as Schindler's ark.

Shame and the captives: a novel. Thomas Keneally. Atria Books, 2015. 400 p.
ISBN 9781476734644
1. Escapes 2. Prisoners of war, Japanese 3. Prisoners of war, Australian 4. World War II 5. Prisoners' spouses 6. Australia 7. New South Wales 8. Literary fiction 9. Historical fiction 10. Roth, Philip

LC 2014034535

A tale inspired by true events follows the experiences of a World War II prisoner's wife who befriends an Italian anarchist in the hopes of alleviating her husband's suffering, only to be swept up in a violent prison break.

"Keneally explores multiple and multifaceted themes of courage, loyalty, empathy, and cultural dissonance." —*Booklist*

Originally published: North Sydney, NSW : Random House Australia, 2013.

Woman of the inner sea. Thomas Keneally. Nan A. Talese/Doubleday, 1993. 277 p.
ISBN 9780385467957
1. Runaway wives, husbands, etc. 2. Small town life 3. Wilderness areas 4. Women 5. Grief in women 6. Australia 7. Psychological fiction 8. Australian fiction

LC 92028554

Distraught after a family crisis, Kate Gaffney-Kozinski disappears into the Australian outback, where she assumes a new identity and works as a barmaid, while her wealthy husband's enforcer tries to track her down.

"This novel succeeds on many fronts. It is a picaresque and often hilarious adventure story, recounting one woman's unforgettable if improbable travels. It is a series of love stories, as Kate meets the man who is appropriate for her at each stage of her life, and it is a mystery story as well. But the novel is also very much an exploration of ethics." —*New York Times Book Review*

Originally published: Sydney : Hodder & Stoughton, 1992.

Kennedy, James

Dare to know. James Kennedy. Quirk Books, 2021. 336 p.
ISBN 9781683692607
1. Sales personnel 2. Death 3. Near future 4. Corporations 5. Accidents 6. Thrillers and suspense

LC 2021004469

The most gifted salesperson at a strange company that developed the technology to predict the exact moment of anyone's death violates company policy and forecasts his own only to discover he actually died 23 minutes ago.

"Kennedy ties the very personal quirks of his main character to the eccentricities of the universe, incorporating the lost city of Cahokia and the Crab Nebula supernova of 1054 into the mystery of the algorithm's error. Readers with a taste for the synchronicity of the cosmic with the commonplace are sure to be entertained." —*Publishers Weekly*

Kennedy, Randy

Presidio. Randy Kennedy. Simon & Schuster, 2018. 304 p.
ISBN 9781501153860
1. Drifters 2. Automobile thefts 3. Girl kidnapping victims 4. Stolen money 5. Thieves 6. Texas 7. Texas Panhandle 8. 1970s 9. Crime fiction 10. Modern Westerns 11. Multiple perspectives

Two brothers in the 1970s Texas panhandle steal a car to search for one's wife who ran off with their tiny amount of money and accidentally kidnap a Mennonite girl who was asleep in the backseat.

Kennedy, William

★ **Ironweed:** a novel. By William Kennedy. Viking Press, 1983. 227 p; (Albany cycle, 3)

ISBN 9780670401765

1. Alcoholic men 2. Darrow, Clarence 3. Phelan family (Fictitious characters) 4. Former baseball players 5. Murderers 6. Albany, New York 7. 1930s 8. Noir fiction 9. Historical fiction 10. Literary fiction

LC 82040370

National Book Critics Circle Award for Fiction, 1983; Pulitzer Prize for Fiction, 1984

"With this tale of skid-row life in the Depression, Kennedy adds another chapter to his Albany cycle." —*Booklist*

Kenney, John

Talk to me. John Kenney. Penguin Group, 2019. 320 p.

ISBN 9780735214378

1. Reputation 2. Life change events 3. Television newscasters and commentators 4. Families 5. Discontent 6. New York City 7. Mainstream fiction 8. Domestic fiction

Losing his job and reputation in the wake of an ill-timed live tirade, a disgraced television anchor finds himself reconnecting with his family and the man he used to be.

Kent, Kathleen

The **burn.** Kathleen Kent. Mulholland Books, 2020. 352 p. (Detective Betty novels, 2)

ISBN 9780316450584

1. Drug cartels 2. Women detectives 3. Narcotics investigation 4. Women/women relations 5. Organized crime 6. Dallas, Texas 7. Police procedurals 8. Thrillers and suspense 9. LGBTQIA fiction

A Dallas detective struggles to adjust at work and home after a run-in with an apocalyptic cult while trying to track down crooked cops and the cult leader who had taken her hostage.

"Betty's struggles with PTSD and challenges to her identity as a cop spark compelling character evolution as she lowers walls to bond with a pair of old souls she meets on the streets. A gripping, powerfully human procedural." —*Booklist*

The **pledge.** Kathleen Kent. Mulholland Books, 2021. 400 pages (Detective Betty novels, 3)

ISBN 9780316280457

1. Women detectives 2. Organized crime 3. Cults 4. Revenge 5. Missing persons 6. Dallas, Texas 7. Thrillers and suspense 8. Police procedurals 9. LGBTQIA fiction

Things are looking up for Detective Betty Rhyzik. She's settled into a happy marriage and been promoted to Sergeant in the Dallas Police Department. But when a hostage stand-off puts her on the phone with legendary cartel leader The Knife, things take a turn. The Knife has heard a rival is making a play for the streets of Dallas—none other than Evangeline Roy. The matriarch of a ruthless cult, Evangeline also happens to hold a personal vendetta against Betty. So who better to draw Evangeline out of hiding? Betty's got two weeks to catch her. Or else.

Strong women, sharp dialogue, and a vulnerable, kick-ass heroine combine for another satisfying adventure. Follows the formula, but the formula's still fun! Kirkus

Kepler, Lars

The **sandman.** Lars Kepler; translated from the Swedish by Neil Smith. Alfred A. Knopf, 2018. 443 p. (Detective Inspector Joona Linna mysteries, 4)

ISBN 9781524732240

1. Cold cases (Criminal investigation) 2. Serial murders 3. Detectives 4. Police 5. Psychiatric hospital patients 6. Sweden 7. Stockholm, Sweden 8. Translations 9. Mysteries 10. Scandinavian crime fiction

During a cold winter night in Stockholm a man is found walking alongside a railway bridge, suffering from hypothermia and legionella. After he's rushed to the hospital, it's discovered that, according to a death certificate, the man has been dead for over seven years. He is believed to be a victim of notorious serial killer Jurek Walter, who was arrested years ago by Detective Inspector Joona Linna and sentenced to a life of total isolation in forensic psychiatric care. As Joona Linna investigates where the "dead man" has been all these years, some unexpected evidence leads to the reopening of a cold case.

Originally published in 2012 by Albert Bonniers Forlag, Sweden, as Sandmannen.

Kerangal, Maylis de

The **heart:** a novel. Maylis de Kerangal; translated by Sam Taylor; British edition translated by Jessica Moore. Farrar, Straus and Giroux, 2016. 256 pages

ISBN 9780374240905

1. Transplantation of organs, tissues, etc. 2. Organ donors 3. Traffic accidents 4. Grief 5. Loss (Psychology) 6. France 7. Literary fiction 8. Psychological fiction 9. Translations

LC 2015023340

"The Heart" takes place over the twenty-four hours surrounding a fatal accident and a resulting heart transplant as life is taken from a young man and given to a woman close to death. In gorgeous, ruminative prose it examines the deepest feelings of everyone involved—grieving parents, hardworking doctors and nurses—as they navigate decisions of life and death.

"It's clear de Kerangal has done extensive research, and the novel contains a wealth of medical knowledge. But her prose is more than just technical; the writing is uncommonly beautiful and never lacking humanity." —*Publishers Weekly*

Originally published in French in 2014 by Verticales, an imprint of Editions Gallimard, France, as Reparer les vivants—Title page verso. Also translated by Jessica Moore under the title Mend the living, 2016

Translated from the French.

Kerley, Jack

★ The **death** collectors. Jack Kerley. Dutton, 2005. 336 p. (Carson Ryder and Harry Nautilus mysteries, 2)

ISBN 9780525948773

1. Psychopaths 2. Serial murder investigation 3. Collectors and collecting 4. Police 5. Brothers 6. Alabama 7. Mobile, Alabama 8. Mysteries

LC 2004028816

Thirty years after a renowned artist and serial killer is shot dead in the courtroom on the day of his sentencing, homicide detectives Carson Ryder and Harry Nautilus investigate a murder scene that resembles the work of the long-dead killer.

Kerouac, Jack

The **dharma** bums. Jack Kerouac. Penguin Books, 1990. Xxviii, 187 p.

ISBN 9780140042528

1. Kerouac, Jack 2. Young men 3. Zen Buddhism 4. Counterculture 5. Hedonism 6. Dharma (Buddhism) 7. Sierra Nevada Mountains 8. San

Francisco, California 9. Literary fiction 10. Autobiographical fiction 11. Modern classics

During the 1950s the search for Buddhist truths takes two young Bohemians through a series of bizarre experiences in California BT

"This novel deals with Zen Buddhism. It's about two young men who are seeking to find themselves through meditation, voluntary poverty, separation from society, and intimate contact with nature, especially the Western mountains.... Sometimes Kerouac seems a little foolish, often he is extreme, but he is genuine, he is alive, and he is native." —*Library Journal*

Sequel: Desolation Angels.
Originally published: New York : Viking Press, 1958.

★ **On** the road. Jack Kerouac. Penguin Books, 1975. 310 p.
ISBN 9780140042597
1. Kerouac, Jack 2. Travelers 3. Counterculture 4. Friendship 5. Hitchhiking 6. Companionship 7. 1950s 8. Autobiographical fiction 9. Books to movies 10. Modern classics

On the Road is a thinly fictionalized autobiography, filled with a cast made of Kerouac's real life friends, lover, and fellow travelers. Narrated by Sal Paradise, one of Kerouac's alter-egos, On the Road is a cross-country bohemian odyssey that not only influenced writing in the years since its 1957 publication but penetrated into the deepest level of American thought and culture.

"The biggest immediate difference between the first draft and the finished product...is that while we know On the Road as a novel—the great novel of the Beat Generation—the scroll is essentially nonfiction, a memoir that uses real names and is far less self-consciously literary. It is a dazzling piece of writing for all of its rough edges, and, stripped of affectations that in the novel can sometimes verge on bathos, as well as of gratuitous punctuation supplied by editors more devoted to rules than to music, it seems much more immediate and even contemporary. The scroll clarifies the book's connection to the past—to Mark Twain and tramp narratives and Woody Guthrie and cowboy sagas—and underlines the features it shares with its nearest contemporaneous cultural relative, Robert Frank's great photographic road book The Americans." —*New York Times Book Review*

Originally published: New York : Viking Press, 1957.

★ **Road** novels 1957-1960. Jack Kerouac; edited by Douglas Brinkley. Library of America, 2007. 864 p.
ISBN 9781598530124
1. Counterculture 2. Beat culture 3. Beat generation 4. Wanderers and wandering 5. 1950s 6. Literary fiction 7. Autobiographical fiction 8. Modern classics
LC 2007924522
A collector's edition of five works by the late Beat Generation classic writer.

"Kerouac's work marked the articulation of a new voice far more interesting for what the author had to say and the way in which he said it than for the technical breakthroughs that it was heralded—and scorned—for at the time." —*San Francisco Chronicle*

Kerr, Laurel
Wild on my mind. Laurel Kerr. Sourcebooks Casablanca, 2018. 384 p. (Where the wild hearts are, 1)
ISBN 9781492670858
1. Zoos 2. Single fathers 3. Helpfulness in women 4. Animals 5. Animal rescue 6. Contemporary romances

Love runs wild at the Sagebrush Flats Zoo, where a motley crew of big-hearted animals helps the most unlikely couples find love.

Kerr, Philip
★ **Greeks** bearing gifts: a Bernie Gunther novel. Philip Kerr. G.P. Putnam's Sons, 2018. 511 p. (Bernhard Gunther mysteries, 13)
ISBN 9780399177064
1. Nazi plunder 2. Former detectives 3. Insurance companies 4. Murderers 5. Postwar life 6. Germany 7. 1950s 8. Second World War era (1939-1945) 9. Historical mysteries 10. Hardboiled fiction
LC 2017037137
Working undercover in 1956 Munich, Bernie Gunther investigates a murder with ties to Nazi plunder that prompts his collaboration with a lieutenant who has been looking for an opportunity to bring a killer to justice.
A Marian Wood book.

★ **Metropolis:** a Bernie Gunther novel. Philip Kerr. G.P. Putnam's Sons, 2019. 400 pages (Bernhard Gunther mysteries, 14)
ISBN 9780735218895
1. Police 2. Young men 3. Serial murder investigation 4. Murder investigation 5. World War I veterans 6. Germany 7. Berlin, Germany 8. 1920s 9. Between the Wars (1918-1939) 10. Historical mysteries 11. Hardboiled fiction
LC 2018046712
A Bernie Gunther origin story is set during his first weeks on Berlin's Murder Squad and finds a twentysomething Bernie investigating a particularly violent wave of murders targeting the city's vulnerable prostitutes and homeless veterans.

"The banter is priceless. Going against the grainas usual—by writing an origin novel as his swan song, Kerr leaves his fans happy." —*Kirkus*

★ **Prussian** blue. Philip Kerr. Marian Wood Books/Putnam, 2017. 544 pages (Bernhard Gunther mysteries, 12)
ISBN 9780399177057
1. Former detectives 2. Coercion 3. Hamilton, Alexander 4. Nazi fugitives 5. Murder investigation 6. French Riviera 7. France 8. 1950s 9. Second World War era (1939-1945) 10. Hardboiled fiction 11. Historical mysteries
LC 2016046341
Longlisted for the Walter Scott Prize for Historical Fiction, 2018
When his cover is blown, Bernie Gunther plays a game of cat-and-mouse with an old enemy before escaping to Berlin seeking help from a group of former allies.

"As always, Kerr lets Bernie have fun with genre conventions without losing sight of the horror behind the tough talk. At the top of everyones WWII mystery list." —*Booklist*
A Marian Wood book.

Kesey, Ken
★ **One** flew over the cuckoo's nest. Ken Kesey. Viking, 2002. Xxiv, 281 p. : Illustration
ISBN 9780670030583
1. Psychiatric hospitals 2. Psychiatric hospital care 3. People with mental illnesses — Care and treatment 4. Mental illness — Treatment 5. Psychiatric hospital patients 6. Oregon 7. Satirical fiction 8. Modern classics 9. Literary fiction
LC 200146923
McMurphy, a criminal who feigns insanity, is admitted to a mental hospital where he challenges the autocratic authority of the head nurse.
Originally published: Viking, 1962.

Sometimes a great notion: a novel. Ken Kesey. Penguin Books, 1988. 628 p.
ISBN 9780140045291

1. Strikebreakers 2. Lumber workers 3. Strikes 4. Small town life 5. Lumber industry and trade 6. Oregon 7. Multiple perspectives 8. Modern classics 9. Literary fiction

LC 87029184

A family determines to fight the unionization of their northwestern lumber empire.

Originally published: New York : Viking Press, 1964.

Khadivi, Laleh

★ A **good** country: a novel. Laleh Khadivi. Bloomsbury, 2017. 239 pages; (Khourdi trilogy, 3)

ISBN 9781632865847

1. Iranian Americans 2. Friendship 3. Radicalism 4. Jihad 5. Growing up 6. Coming-of-age stories 7. Literary fiction 8. First person narratives 9. Adult books for young adults

LC 2016050042

Booklist Editors' Choice: Adult Books for Young Adults, 2017

Alireeza Courdee, son of Iranian immigrants, changes from a typical American teenager to a political radical, making his way to Syria with two of his friends, and is soon faced with the harsh reality of his choice.

"The story unfolds deftly, beautifully capturing the psychology of an American teen who goes down the path of radicalization; readers will understand what would motivate a sheltered, shortsighted young person to run away to join extremists." —*School Library Journal*

Khadra, Yasmina

★ **Khalil:** a novel. Yasmina Khadra; translated from the French by John Cullen. Nan A. Talese; 2021. 288 p.

ISBN 9780385545914

1. Terrorism 2. Suicide bombers 3. Purpose in life 4. Muslim men 5. Identity (Psychology) 6. Belgium 7. Europe 8. 21st century 9. Translations 10. First person narratives 11. Literary fiction

LC 2020008874

Reevaluating his choices when the ISIS suicide bomb he attempted to detonate malfunctions, a young Moroccan in Belgium learns that the assignment had been part of a training test and that his terrorist cell has another mission for him.

"With Khalil's fate-and those of countless potential victims-perpetually hanging in the balance, the book becomes a gripping existential inquiry that earns the author comparisons with Camus. An exciting work of fiction rooted in docu-like reality." —*Kirkus*

Translated from the French.

The **swallows** of Kabul: a novel. Yasmina Khadra; translated from the French by John Cullen. Nan A. Talese/Doubleday, 2004. 208 pages.

ISBN 9780385510011

1. Prison guards 2. Women prisoners 3. State-sponsored terrorism 4. Married people 5. Life change events 6. Afghanistan 7. Kabul, Afghanistan 8. Literary fiction 9. Translations

LC 2003050769

ALA Notable Book, 2005; Booklist Editors' Choice, 2004; Shortlisted for the International IMPAC Dublin Literary Award, 2006

Their lives as a diplomat and lawyer frozen by the ascendancy of the Taliban, Moshen and Zunaira find their situation becoming a nightmare when Zunaira is arrested and condemned to death.

"The author is intimately familiar with the consequences that war and religious extremism have on people's daily lives, and in this book he gives the reader a tactile sense of what life under the Taliban might have been like." —*New York Times*

Khalfah, Khlid

Death is hard work: a novel. Khaled Khalifa; translated from the Arabic by Leri Price. Farrar, Straus and Giroux, 2019. 192 p.

ISBN 9780374135737

1. Civil war 2. Siblings 3. Fathers — Death 4. Father and child 5. Cemeteries 6. Syria 7. Literary fiction 8. War stories 9. Translations

LC 2018033289

National Book Award for Translated Literature finalist, 2019

Draws on first-person experiences in the story of three siblings who set aside their differences and risk their lives during the Syrian civil war to honor their late father's final wishes.

"Flawlessly translated and exquisitely written, this novel from the winner of the Naguib Mahfouz Prize is a genuine tour de force as well as a thoughtful and provocative examination of what it means to be alive." —*Library Journal*

Translation of: Mawt 'amal shaq.

Translated from the Arabic.

Khan, Ausma Zehanat

Among the ruins. Ausma Zehanat Khan. Minotaur Books, 2017. 336 p. (Rachel Getty and Esa Khattak novels, 3)

ISBN 9781250096739

1. Political prisoners 2. Muslim men 3. Detectives 4. Missing persons investigation 5. Women murder victims 6. Iran 7. Toronto, Ontario 8. Police procedurals 9. Canadian fiction

Investigating the murder of a filmmaker in Iran at a notorious prison, detectives Esa Khattak and Rachel Getty become embroiled in the country's tumultuous politics and a conspiracy linked to the Shah and the decades-old murders of famous dissidents.

"Khan uses an involving mystery in a vividly portrayed setting to illustrate unspeakable violations undertaken by governments in religious and political chaos. In Khans hands, mysteries carry powerful messages." —*Booklist*

The **unquiet** dead. Ausma Zehanat Khan. Minotaur Books, 2015. 336 p. (Rachel Getty and Esa Khattak novels, 1)

ISBN 9781250055118

1. War criminals 2. Deception 3. Muslim men 4. Detectives 5. Murder investigation 6. Toronto, Ontario 7. Canada 8. Police procedurals 9. Canadian fiction

LC 2014032396

Arthur Ellis Award for Best First Novel, 2016; Romantic Times Reviewer's Choice Award, 2015

Detective Esa Khattack and his partner, Detective Rachel Getty, investigate the death of a local man who may have been a Bosnian war criminal with ties to the Srebrenica massacre of 1995.

"Khan's stunning debut is a poignant, elegantly written mystery laced with complex characters who force readers to join them in dealing with ugly truths." —*Kirkus*

Khan, Vaseem

The **perplexing** theft of the jewel in the crown. Vaseem Khan. Redhook Books, 2016. 362 p. (Baby Ganesh Agency investigations, 2)

ISBN 9780316386845

1. Former police 2. Jewelry theft 3. Elephants 4. Diamonds 5. Crown jewels 6. India 7. Mumbai, India 8. Mysteries

Shamus Award for Best P.I. Paperback Original, 2017

When the priceless Koh-i-noor diamond is stolen from an exhibition of the British Crown Jewels in Mumbai, Inspector Chopra and his elephant are left with the task of discovering the perpetrators of the seemingly impossible heist.

"The second in the Baby Ganesh Agency series, following last years The Unexpected Inheritance of Inspector Chopra, is every bit as captivating as its predecessor. The reason has much to do with Khans ability to craft such quirky, three-dimensional characters and the fact that he places them in such believable difficulties amid the rich stew of Mumbai." —*Booklist*

Khaw, Cassandra

Nothing but blackened teeth. Cassandra Khaw. Nightfire, Tom Doherty Associates Book, 2021. 128 p.

ISBN 9781250759412

1. Mansions 2. Ghosts 3. Human sacrifice 4. Brides 5. Weddings 6. Japan 7. Horror

LC 2021033056

LibraryReads Favorites, 2021

A Heian-era mansion stands abandoned, its foundations resting on the bones of a bride and its walls packed with the remains of the girls sacrificed to keep her company. It's the perfect venue for a group of thrill-seeking friends, brought back together to celebrate a wedding. A night of food, drinks, and games quickly spirals into a nightmare as secrets get dragged out and relationships are tested. But the house has secrets too. Lurking in the shadows is the ghost bride with a black smile and a hungry heart. And she gets lonely down there in the dirt.

"Japanese mythological creatures come to life in this dynamic, unique tale that will satisfy horror readers eager for fresh blood." —*Booklist*

Khoury, Raymond

Empire of lies. Raymond Khoury. Forge, 2019. 448 p.

ISBN 9781250210968

1. Time travel 2. History 3. Civilization 4. Caliphate 5. Culture 6. Paris, France 7. Europe 8. Science fiction 9. Alternate histories

Paris, 2017: Ottoman flags have been flying over the great city for three hundred years, ever since its fall—along with all of Europe—to the empire's all-conquering army. Notre Dame has been renamed the Fatih Mosque. Public spaces are segregated by gender. And Kamal Arslan Agha, a feted officer in the sultan's secret police, is starting to question his orders.

Published in the U.K. under the title The Ottoman secret, Michael Joseph, 2019.

Kibler, Julie

Home for erring and outcast girls. Julie Kibler. Random House Inc 2019. 336 p.

ISBN 9780451499332

1. Female friendship 2. Women's shelters 3. Women — Social conditions 4. Librarians 5. Friendship 6. Texas 7. 1900s (Decade) 8. Historical fiction 9. Parallel narratives

Inspired by historical events, a follow-up to the best-selling Calling Me Home follows the deep friendship between two women at an early 20th-century rehabilitation home for cast-out single mothers, and the reclusive librarian who discovers their story a century later.

Kidd, Jess

★ **Things** in jars. Jess Kidd. Simon & Schuster, 2020. 384 p.

ISBN 9781982121280

1. Aristocracy 2. Supernatural 3. Eccentrics and eccentricities 4. Anatomy 5. Detectives 6. London, England 7. Victorian era (1837-1901) 8. Historical fantasy 9. Adult books for young adults

Woman detective Bridie Devine investigates the kidnapping of a nobleman's illegitimate daughter, whose reputed supernatural powers have captured the attention of sinister collectors in the underworld's curiosities trade.

"With so much detail and so many clever, Dickensian characters, readers might petition Kidd to give Bridie her own series. Creepy, violent, and propulsive; a standout gothic mystery." —*Kirkus*

Previously published in Great Britain, 2019.

Kidd, Sue Monk

★ The **book** of longings. Sue Monk Kidd. Viking, 2020. 384 p.

ISBN 9780525429760

1. Jesus Christ 2. Ethics 3. Marriage 4. Ambition in women 5. Women authors 6. Writing 7. Roman Empire (27 BCE-476 CE) 8. Historical fiction 9. First person narratives

LC 2019049624

LibraryReads Favorites, 2020; Loan Stars Favourites, 2020

A first-century intellectual fights the limitations imposed on women before an encounter with an 18-year-old Jesus leads to their marriage, his dangerous public ministry and her flight to safety in Alexandria.

"Kidd is a library favorite, and the bold subject of this novel will increase buzz tenfold." —*Booklist*

★ The **invention** of wings: a novel. Sue Monk Kidd. Viking, 2014. 384 p.

ISBN 9780670024780

1. Grimke, Sarah Moore 2. Anti-slavery movements 3. Feminists 4. Women's rights 5. Women abolitionists 6. Slavery 7. South Carolina 8. Charleston, South Carolina 9. Antebellum America (1820-1861) 10. 19th century 11. Historical fiction 12. Biographical fiction 13. Multiple perspectives

LC 2013028185

Library Journal Best Books, 2014

Traces more than three decades in the lives of a wealthy Charleston debutante who longs to break free from the strictures of her household and pursue a meaningful life; and the urban slave, Handful, who is placed in her charge as a child before finding courage and a sense of self.

★ The **secret** life of bees. Sue Monk Kidd. Viking, 2002. Xii, 301 p.

ISBN 9780670894604

1. African American women 2. Interracial friendship 3. Teenage girls 4. Sisters 5. Beekeepers 6. South Carolina 7. 1960s 8. Coming-of-age stories 9. Books to movies 10. Mainstream fiction 11. Adult books for young adults

LC 2001026310

Book Sense Book of the Year Paperback, 2004; YALSA Best Books for Young Adults, 2003; School Library Journal Best Books: Best Adult Books 4 Teens, 2002

After her stand-in mother, a bold black woman named Rosaleen, insults the three biggest racists in town, Lily Owens joins Rosaleen on a journey to Tiburon, South Carolina, where they are taken in by three black, bee-keeping sisters.

"While racial tensions simmer around them, the women help Lily accept her loss and learn the power of forgiveness. There is a wonderful sense of the strength of female friendship and love throughout the story." —*School Library Journal*

Kiernan, Caitlin R.

The **very** best of Caitlin R. Kiernan. Caitlin R. Kiernan; introduction by Richard Kadrey. Tachyon Publications, 2019. Xi, 424 pages

ISBN 9781616963026

1. Horror 2. Fantasy fiction 3. Anthologies

Caitlin R. Kiernan is one of dark fantasy and horror's most acclaimed and influential short fiction writers. Her powerful, unexpected stories shatter morality, gender, and sexuality.

"This versatile retrospective offers something for nearly every fan of the strange and macabre, and cements Kiernan's legacy as the reigning queen of dark fantasy." —*Kirkus*

Kiernan, Stephen P.
Universe of two. Stephen P. Kiernan. William Morrow & Company, 2020. 448 p.

ISBN 9780062878441

1. Fisk, Charles B. 2. Atomic bomb 3. Mathematicians 4. Husband and wife 5. World War II 6. Nuclear weapons 7. Los Alamos, New Mexico 8. United States 9. Second World War era (1939-1945) 10. Historical fiction 11. Biographical fiction

A novel of conscience, love, and redemption—a fascinating fictionalized account of the life of Charlie Fisk, a gifted mathematician who was drafted into the Manhattan Project and ordered against his morals to build the detonator for the atomic bomb.

"Kiernan recreates the zeitgeist of America leading up to the atomic bomb on a national and personal level: the eager anticipation of wartime's end, the grimly fascinating science, and the growing sense of guilt and dread. Simultaneously tender and hard-hitting, this riveting story offers much to reflect upon." —*Booklist*

Kilalea, Katharine
Ok, Mr. Field: a novel. Katharine Kilalea. Tim Duggan Books, 2018. 218 p.

ISBN 9780525573630

1. Pianists 2. Wounds and injuries 3. Architecture 4. Houses 5. Men with mental illnesses 6. Cape Town, South Africa 7. Literary fiction 8. First person narratives

LC 2018003397

Retiring to a Cape Town beachhouse inspired by Le Corbusier's Villa Savoye, an injured concert pianist begins to experience the psychological consequences of the house's unusual design.

Kim, Angie
Miracle Creek. Angie Kim. Sarah Crichton Books/Farrar, Straus and Giroux, 2019. 352 p.

ISBN 9780374156022

1. Secrets 2. Trials (Murder) 3. Human experimentation in medicine 4. Rural life 5. Small towns 6. Virginia 7. Legal stories

LC 2018037096

Edgar Allan Poe Award for Best First Novel by an American Author, 2020; Library Journal Best Books, 2019; LibraryReads Favorites, 2019; Loan Stars Favourites, 2019; Thriller Award for Best First Novel, 2020

A dramatic murder trial in the aftermath of an experimental medical treatment and a fatal explosion upends a rural Virginia community where personal secrets and private ambitions complicate efforts to uncover what happened.

"Intricate plotting and courtroom theatrics, combined with moving insight into parenting special needs children and the psychology of immigrants, make this book both a learning experience and a page-turner." —*Kirkus*

Kim, Bo Young
★ **I'm** waiting for you: and other stories. Bo-young Kim. Harper Voyager, 2021. 336 p.

ISBN 9780062951465

1. Interpersonal relations 2. Time travel 3. Gods and goddesses 4. Humans 5. Short stories 6. Science fiction

Four tales of speculative fiction includes the story of an engaged couple trying to fight time and space to get married and a story featuring god-like beings who created Earth and humanity and pass judgement on them.

"In four paired short stories, Korean science-fiction doyenne Kim imagines the vanishingly distant future.... Playing with notions of immortality and toying with improbable transgressions of the laws of physics, Kim delivers a suite of stories that is at once lyrical and full of foreboding, keeping dramatic tension tight among poetic evocations of a home planet that is 'our hall of learning, our cradle of experiences, our short-term interactive training ground,' if one we have also destroyed." —*Kirkus*

Kim, Crystal Hana
If you leave me. Crystal Hana Kim. William Morrow & Co, 2018. 417 p.

ISBN 9780062645173

1. Love triangles 2. War and society 3. Korean War, 1950-1953 4. Refugees 5. Life change events 6. Korea 7. 1950s 8. 1960s 9. Family sagas 10. Multiple perspectives 11. Historical fiction

Booklist Editors' Choice, 2018

Forced into the life of a refugee when the North Korean army invades her home, 16-year-old Haemi is forced to choose between love and security in ways that resonate throughout generations of her family.

Kim, Eugenia
The **kinship** of secrets. Eugenia Kim. Houghton Mifflin Harcourt, 2018. 292 p.

ISBN 9781328987822

1. Separated sisters 2. Immigrant families 3. Koreans in the United States 4. Sisters 5. Life change events 6. United States 7. South Korea 8. 20th century 9. Family sagas 10. Historical fiction 11. Adult books for young adults

LC 2017061490

LibraryReads Favorites, 2018

The story of two sisters separated by the Korean War follows Miran, who grows up living with her parents in a prosperous American suburb, and her sister Inja who struggles with life in war-torn Korea and ties to a family she doesn't remember.

"How she copes with the cultural change, and how the sisters gradually forge the bond they had only dreamed about, make up the remainder of Kim's heartfelt story, one which will greatly appeal to readers who enjoy the multicultural novels of Lisa See and Amy Tan, stories that enlighten as well as entertain." —*Booklist*

Kim, Nancy Jooyoun
The **last** story of Mina Lee. Nancy Jooyoun Kim. Park Row Books, 2020. 381 p.

ISBN 9780778310174

1. Korean American women 2. Mothers and daughters 3. Mothers — Death 4. Family secrets 5. Korean-Americans 6. Koreatown (Los Angeles, Calif.) 7. Los Angeles, California 8. Domestic fiction

"As a personal immigration narrative Kim's novel largely succeeds, but as a mystery novel or a mother-daughter drama it fails to connect." —*Publishers Weekly*

Kim, Young-ha

Diary of a murderer: and other stories. Young-ha Kim; translated by Krys Lee. Mariner Books, 2019. 224 p.

ISBN 9781328545428

1. Murder 2. Sexuality 3. Writing 4. Short stories 5. Literary fiction 6. Translations

LC 2018042555

"An electric collection that captivates and provokes in equal measure, exploring what it means to be on the edge—between life and death, good and evil." —Provided by publisher.

Translated from the Korean by Krys Lee.

Kimani, Peter

Dance of the Jakaranda. Peter Kimani. Akashic Books, 2017. 342 pages

ISBN 9781617754968

1. Railroads 2. Social change 3. Intergenerational communication 4. Interethnic relations 5. Racism 6. Kenya 7. 1900s (Decade) 8. 1960s 9. Historical fiction 10. Literary fiction 11. Multiple perspectives

New York Times Notable Book, 2017

Set in the shadow of Kenya's independence from Great Britain, Kimani reimagines the rise and fall of colonialism in Africa, and the special circumstances that brought black, brown, and white men together to lay the railroad that heralded the birth of the nation.

"Kimani's complex novel will leave readers questioning the meanings of citizenship and belonging during an era of significant social upheaval in Kenya's history." —*Booklist*

Kimmel, Fran

No good asking: a novel. Fran Kimmel. ECW Press, 2018. 300 p.

ISBN 9781770414389

1. Former police 2. Family relationships 3. Family problems 4. Women with depression 5. Moving to a new state 6. Canada 7. Domestic fiction 8. Multiple perspectives 9. Canadian fiction

"Kimmel's novel has only a few characters, but they all possess presence and depth and experience honest changes. The strong sense of place serves as an additional relationship for the characters to negotiate." —*Library Journal*

Kincaid, Jamaica

★ **Annie** John. Jamaica Kincaid. Farrar, Straus, Giroux, 1985. 148 p.

ISBN 9780374105211

1. Teenage girls 2. Family relationships 3. Self-discovery in teenage girls 4. West Indians 5. Girl rebels 6. Antigua and Barbuda 7. Coming-of-age stories 8. Domestic fiction 9. Literary fiction

LC 84028630

"Episodes from the young life of Annie John, aged 10 to 17, as she grows up on the Caribbean island of Antigua. This is a magical coming-of-age tale, ripe with the special ambience of its tropical setting and sustained by Annie's far from naive awareness of the world around her. Death, illness, and poverty intrude on the narrator's perceptive sensibility from time to time, but even these experiences instruct her and expand her understanding of life and its shifting reality.... A poetic and intensely moving work." —*Booklist*

The **autobiography** of my mother. Jamaica Kincaid. Farrar Straus Giroux, 1996. 228 p.

ISBN 9780374107314

1. Island life 2. Multiracial persons 3. Power (Social sciences) 4. Women 5. West-Indian women 6. Dominica 7. Literary fiction

LC 9424580

Shortlisted for the International IMPAC Dublin Literary Award, 1998; National Book Critics Circle Award for Fiction finalist, 1996

"In Kincaid's poised and crystalline prose, precise and serene as a knife drawn through water, she now gives us this starkly memorable 'self-portrait' of a calm, thoughtful, utterly alienated woman who has learned to lead a life devoid of love, but not devoid of dignity." —*Christian Science Monitor*

★ **Lucy**. Jamaica Kincaid. Farrar, Straus, Giroux, 2002. 176 p.

ISBN 9780374527358

1. Young women 2. Au pairs 3. Culture shock 4. West Indian women 5. Women immigrants 6. Literary fiction 7. Coming-of-age stories

Lucy, a nineteen-year-old girl from the West Indies, comes to North America to work as an au pair and observes the unhealthy realities of the seemingly happy family that employs her.

"The great motifs of Western literature, like goodness and evil, innocence and experience, resonate in Kincaid's novel in a completely updated and unselfconscious way. In other hands, this story of a West Indian au pair would just be sociology. In Kincaid's recasting, it is both art and argument." —*Christian Science Monitor*

See now then. Jamaica Kincaid. Farrar, Straus and Giroux, 2013. 176 p.

ISBN 9780374180560

1. Marriage 2. Family relationships 3. Anger in women 4. Archetype (Psychology) 5. Romantic love 6. Literary fiction

LC 2012029932

A mother and father and their two children, living in a small village in New England, move, in their own minds, between the present, the past and the future.

King, Laurie R.

Castle shade. Laurie R. King. Bantam Books, 2021. 384 p. (Mary Russell and Sherlock Holmes mysteries, 17)

ISBN 9780525620860

1. Marie 2. Women rulers 3. Women private investigators 4. Husband-and-wife detectives 5. Castles 6. Rumor 7. Romania 8. 1920s 9. Between the Wars (1918-1939) 10. Historical mysteries 11. Adaptations, retellings, and spin-offs

LC 2021001133

Queen Marie of Romania, granddaughter to both Queen Victoria and Tsar Alexander II calls on Mary Russell and Sherlock Holmes to investigate a series of strange accidents in Castle Bran.

"King smoothly slips in fascinating historical details about the life of Marie of Roumania, all the while keeping the plot galloping along at high speed. This is a treat for old fans and newcomers alike." —*Publishers Weekly*

King, Lily

Writers & lovers: a novel. Lily King. Grove Press, 2020. 320 p.

ISBN 9780802148537

1. Grief 2. Women authors 3. Love triangles 4. Moving to a new city 5. Waitresses 6. Massachusetts 7. 1990s 8. Literary fiction 9. Coming-of-age stories 10. Love stories

LC 2019045257

New York Times Notable Book, 2020

Blindsided by her mother's sudden death, and wrecked by a recent love affair, Casey Peabody has arrived in Massachusetts in the summer of 1997 without a plan. When she falls for two very different men at the same time, her world fractures even more. Casey's fight to fulfill her creative ambitions and balance the conflicting demands of art and life is challenged in ways that push her to the brink.

Read this for insights about writing, about losing one's mother, about dealing with a cranky sous-chef and a difficult four-top. Kirkus. Reviews

King, Stephen

11/22/63. Stephen King. Scribner, 2011. 960 p.
ISBN 9781451627282
1. Kennedy, John F. 2. Time travel (Past) 3. High school teachers 4. Man-woman relationships 5. Rescues 6. Life change events 7. Dallas, Texas 8. Maine 9. 1950s 10. Alternate histories 11. Thrillers and suspense
Goodreads Choice Award, 2011; Los Angeles Times Book Prize for Mystery or Thriller, 2011; New York Times Notable Book, 2011; Thriller Award for Best Novel, 2012
Receiving a horrific essay from a GED student with a traumatic past, high-school English teacher Jake Epping is enlisted by a friend to travel back in time to prevent the assassination of John F. Kennedy, a mission for which he must befriend troubled loner Lee Harvey Oswald.
"Though his scenarios aren't always plausible in strictest terms, King's imagination, as always, yields a most satisfying yarn." —*Kirkus*

★ **Billy** Summers. Stephen King. Scribner, 2021. 528 p.
ISBN 9781982173616
1. Assassins 2. Iraq War veterans 3. Snipers 4. Murder 5. Ethics 6. Noir fiction
Billy Summers is a man in a room with a gun. He's a killer for hire and the best in the business. But he'll do the job only if the target is a truly bad guy. And now Billy wants out. But first there is one last hit. Billy is among the best snipers in the world, a decorated Iraq war vet, a Houdini when it comes to vanishing after the job is done. So what could possibly go wrong? How about everything.
"King has multiple novels in play here—a thriller, at least two coming-of-age stories, and a knockout road novel—and he knits them together beautifully, never missing a stitch.... King has never been better than he is here at wrapping readers into a propulsive, many-tentacled narrative—complete with a perfectly orchestrated, moving ending." —*Booklist*

★ **Carrie**. Stephen King. Doubleday, 1974. 199 p.
ISBN 9780812419726
1. Psychokinesis 2. Bullying and bullies 3. Teenage psychics 4. High school students 5. Teenage girls 6. Maine 7. Horror 8. Books to movies
LC 73009037
A repressed teenager uses her telekinetic powers to avenge the cruel jokes of her classmates.
"A terrifying treat for both horror and parapsychology fans." —*School Library Journal*

Cujo. Stephen King. Viking Press, 1981. 319 p.
ISBN 9780670451937
1. Dogs 2. Rabies in animals 3. Animal attacks 4. Alcoholic men 5. Families 6. Maine 7. Horror 8. Books to movies
LC 81050265
A family's two-hundred-pound Saint Bernard is transformed by rabies and the insidious guidance of demonic forces into a terrifying monster.

Doctor Sleep: a novel. Stephen King. Scribner, 2013. 544 p.
ISBN 9781476727653
1. Good and evil 2. Psychics 3. Supernatural 4. Psychic ability 5. Telepathy 6. New Hampshire 7. Horror 8. Books to movies 9. Adult books for young adults
LC 2013000431
Bram Stoker Award for Best Novel, 2013; Goodreads Choice Award, 2013; New York Times Notable Book, 2013

After decades as an itinerant alcoholic, middle-aged Dan Torrance uses his remnant powers to assist the dying before coming to the aid of a twelve-year-old girl being tortured by a tribe of murderous paranormals.
Sequel to: The shining (1977).
Adapted into a film entitled "Doctor Sleep" in 2019.

Dolores Claiborne. Stephen King. Viking, 1993. 305 p.
ISBN 9780670844524
1. Husband-killing 2. Incest 3. Household employees 4. Family violence 5. Women murderers 6. Maine 7. Psychological suspense 8. Books to movies
LC 92015467
Forced by overwhelming evidence to confess her life of crime, Dolores Claiborne, a foul-tempered New Englander, describes how her disintegrating marriage years before caused her heart to turn murderous.
"What drives Dolores Claiborne is a powerful characterization of the title figure, a cranky old Maine islander who takes no guff from life or death.... King's mimicry is startlingly good." —*Time*

Elevation. Stephen King. Scribner, 2018. 144 p.
ISBN 9781982102319
1. Prejudice 2. Body weight 3. Weightlessness 4. Divorced men 5. Diseases 6. Maine 7. Contemporary fantasy
Goodreads Choice Award, 2018
The latest from legendary master storyteller Stephen King, a riveting, extraordinarily eerie, and moving story about a man whose mysterious affliction brings a small town together—a timely, upbeat tale about finding common ground despite deep-rooted differences.

End of watch: a novel. By Stephen King. Scribner, 2016. 496 p. (Bill Hodges novels, 3)
ISBN 9781501129742
1. Psychic ability 2. People with brain injuries 3. Private investigators 4. Psychopaths 5. Suicide 6. Middle West 7. Thrillers and suspense 8. Adult books for young adults
LC 2015039639
Goodreads Choice Award, 2016; New York Times Notable Book, 2016
A conclusion to the trilogy finds mental patient Brady Hartsfield manifesting powers to commit deadly acts without leaving his hospital room, while retired detective Bill Hodges and his partner investigate a suicide with ties to the Mercedes Massacre.
"King's mystery experiment has been page-flipping fun from the start, and no ones going to want to miss seeing how it all pans out." —*Booklist*

Finders keepers. Stephen King. Simon & Schuster, 2015. 448 p. (Bill Hodges novels, 2)
ISBN 9781501100079
1. Books and reading 2. Obsession 3. Authors 4. Recluses 5. Fans (Persons) 6. Middle West 7. Thrillers and suspense
After Morris Bellamy discovers that notebooks and money belonging to his favorite author were taken by Pete Saubers, only Bill Hodges, Holly Gibney, and Jerome Robinson can rescue the Saubers family from the deranged and vengeful criminal.
"This being a King novel, the narrative hums and roars along like a high-performance vehicle, even though there are times when its readers may find themselves several tics ahead of the book's plot developments. But such qualms are overcome by the plainspoken, deceptively simple King style, which has once again fashioned a rip-snorting entertainment; one that also works as a sneaky-smart satire of literary criticism and how even the most attentive readers can often miss the whole point behind making up characters and situations. Reading a King novel as engrossing as this is a little like backing in a car with parking assist: after a while, you

just take your hands off the wheel and the pages practically turn themselves." —*Kirkus*

Firestarter. Stephen King. Viking Press, 1980. 428 p.
ISBN 9780670315413
1. Psychic ability 2. Psychokinesis 3. Fires 4. Supernatural 5. Seven-year-old girls 6. Horror 7. Books to movies
LC 80014793
Andy and Vicky McGee's eight-year-old daughter, Charlie, has the ability to set things on fire and a secret government agency is determined to make use of Charlie's horrifyingly destructive gift.

"This is your advanced post-Watergate cynical American thriller with some eerie parapsychological twists, and it's been done so distinctively well that we'd better talk about genius rather than genre." —*Quill & Quire*

The **girl** who loved Tom Gordon. Stephen King. Scribner, 1999. 224 p.
ISBN 9780684867625
1. Lost girls 2. Professional baseball players 3. Wilderness survival 4. Children of divorced parents 5. Girl hikers 6. Appalachian Trail 7. Maine 8. Thrillers and suspense 9. Adult books for young adults
LC 9913109
Booklist Editors' Choice: Adult Books for Young Adults, 1999; YALSA Best Books for Young Adults, 2000.
When a 9-year-old girl becomes lost on a hike on the Appalachian Trail, she relies on her courage and faith, as she imagines her hero, baseball pitcher Tom Gordon, is with her.

"Nine-year-old Trisha McFarland is hopelessly lost in the woods. Out for a morning hike with her bickering mother and brother, she runs off to relieve herself and discovers she can't find her way back to the path.... Trisha wanders for a week in the mosquito-infested forest with nothing but her wits, her Walkman and the pitching prowess of her hero, the dreamy Red Sox reliever Tom Gordon, to guide her. As Trisha fights to stay alive, King demonstrates his empathy for the inner lives of children and an outdoorsman's knowledge of the edible wild flora of Maine." —*New York Times Book Review*

If it bleeds. Stephen King. Scribner, 2020. 436 pages
ISBN 9781982137977
1. Horror
LC 2020123456
A collection of four new novellas.
"Longtime readers and new King fans alike will love the fresh tales in this wonderful collection." —*Library Journal*

The **Institute**. Stephen King. Scribner, 2019. 576 p.
ISBN 9781982110567
1. Children 2. Superhuman abilities 3. Captivity 4. Torture 5. Manipulation (Social sciences) 6. Thrillers and suspense 7. Horror
Goodreads Choice Award, 2019; New York Times Notable Book, 2019
Abducted youth Luke Ellis is imprisoned in an inescapable institute, where children with the abilities of telekinesis and telepathy are subjected to torturous manipulation.

It. Stephen King. Viking, 1986. 1138 p.
ISBN 9780670813025
1. Children 2. Murder 3. Clowns 4. Fear in children 5. Crimes against children 6. Maine 7. Horror 8. Books to TV 9. Books to movies 10. Adult books for young adults
LC 85041062
Colorado Blue Spruce YA Book Award, 1994
They were seven teenagers when they first stumbled upon the horror. Now they were grown-up men and women who had gone out into the big world to gain success and happiness. But none of them could withstand the force that drew them back to Derry, Maine to face the nightmare without an end, and the evil without a name.

"Six adults, living separately in a blessed fog of forgetfulness, are summoned back to their hometown to complete the destruction of a horrific, shape-changing entity who breakfasts on the city's children. This same group first encountered the menace more than a quarter century before, as schoolchildren in the 1950s. Their quest breeds some riveting chase scenes as adults and children alike flee from an assortment of menacing humans and slavering monsters—most of which are manifestations of an evil so vile its true nature can never be known. King's considerable talent for grounding this supernatural stuff in the minutiae of everyday life is evident." —*Booklist*
Book adapted into a 1990 TV miniseries called Stephen King's It. Book was later adapted into a two-part film called It Chapter One (2017) and It Chapter Two (2019).

★ **Misery**. Stephen King. Viking, 1987. 310 p.
ISBN 9780670813643
1. Obsession in women 2. Captives 3. Fans (Persons) 4. Horror story authors 5. Captivity 6. Psychological suspense 7. Horror 8. Books to movies
LC 86040504
Bram Stoker Award for Best Novel, 1987
Rescued from a car crash by a psychotic woman claiming to be a fan, novelist Paul Sheldon becomes a captive invalid in her secluded Colorado farmhouse.

"Even if 'Misery' is less terrifying than his usual work—no demons, no witchcraft, no nether-world horrors—it creates strengths out of its realities. Its excitements are more subtle. And, as such, it is an intriguing work." —*New York Times Book Review*

Mr. Mercedes: a novel. Stephen King. Scribner, 2014. 496 pages (Bill Hodges novels, 1)
ISBN 9781476754451
1. Mass murder 2. Former police 3. Psychopaths 4. Retirees 5. Mass murderers 6. Middle West 7. Thrillers and suspense 8. Adult books for young adults
LC 2013046172
Edgar Allan Poe Award for Best Novel, 2015; Goodreads Choice Award, 2014
In a mega-stakes, high-suspense race against time, three of the most unlikely and winning heroes Stephen King has ever created try to stop a lone killer from blowing up thousands. In the frigid pre-dawn hours, in a distressed Midwestern city, hundreds of desperate unemployed folks are lined up for a spot at a job fair. Without warning, a lone driver plows through the crowd in a stolen Mercedes, running over the innocent, backing up, and charging again. Eight people are killed; fifteen are wounded. The killer escapes. In another part of town, months later, a retired cop named Bill Hodges is still haunted by the unsolved crime. When he gets a crazed letter from someone who self-identifies as the "perk" and threatens an even more diabolical attack, Hodges wakes up from his depressed and vacant retirement, hell-bent on preventing another tragedy. Brady Hartfield lives with his alcoholic mother in the house where he was born. He loved the feel of death under the wheels of the Mercedes, and he wants that rush again. Only Bill Hodges, with a couple of highly unlikely allies, can apprehend the killer before he strikes again. And they have no time to lose, because Brady's next mission, if it succeeds, will kill or maim thousands. Mr. Mercedes is a war between good and evil, from the master of suspense whose insight into the mind of this obsessed, insane killer is chilling and unforgettable.

"This exists outside of the usual Kingverse (Pennywise the Clown is referred to as fictive); add that to the atypical present-tense prose, and this feels pretty darn fresh. Big, smashing climax, too." —*Booklist*

Night shift. Stephen King. Doubleday, 1978. Xxii, 336 p.
ISBN 9780385129916
1. Supernatural 2. Paranormal phenomena 3. Horror 4. Books to movies
LC 77075146

More than twenty-five stories of horror and nightmarish fantasy transform everyday situations into experiences of compelling terror in the worlds of the living, the dying, and the nonliving.
"Boogeyman," "Children of the corn," "The lawnmower man," "Mangler," and "Graveyard shift" were each released as a movie under the same title as the short story. The 1985 film Cat's eye was inspired by "The ledge," and "Quitters, Inc."

Pet sematary. Stephen King. Doubleday, 1983. 373 p.
ISBN 9780385182447
1. Undead 2. Sons — Death 3. Loss (Psychology) 4. Cemeteries 5. Supernatural 6. Maine 7. Horror 8. Books to movies 9. Adult books for young adults
LC 82045360
Colorado Blue Spruce YA Book Award, 1991

hen the Creed family's beloved cat, Winston Churchill, dies, Dr. Louis Creed—on the instructions of his elderly neighbor—buries the animal not in the "Pet Sematary" where local children inter their deceased pets, but rather in the haunted Indian burial ground behind it. The next day, a changed Churchill comes back, a little smellier and more vicious than before. What will happen when a person dies and is buried in the same are
Republished in 2019 by Gallery Books.

Salem's lot. Stephen King. Doubleday, 1975. 439 p.
ISBN 9780385007511
1. Vampires 2. Small towns 3. Authors 4. Good and evil 5. Supernatural 6. Maine 7. Rivers, William 8. Horror 9. Books to movies

When a writer returns to his small Maine hometown, he discovers that the peaceful hamlet is being overrun by vampires and sets out to curb this ancient evil before it can spread.

★ The **shining**. Stephen King. Doubleday, 1977. 447 p.
ISBN 9780385121675
1. Haunted hotels 2. Caretakers 3. Supernatural 4. Boy psychics 5. Telepathy 6. Colorado 7. Horror 8. Books to movies
LC 76024212

Jack Torrance sees his stint as winter caretaker of a Colorado hotel as a way back from failure, his wife sees it as a chance to preserve their family, and their five-year-old son sees the evil waiting just for them.
"In a fast-paced and gory denouement, the terror comes to a violent end. King is a masterful technician of suspense whose readers as well as characters are the victims of his relentless heightening of horror." —*Library Journal*
Sequel: Doctor Sleep (2013).

Sleeping beauties: a novel. Stephen King and Owen King. Scribner, 2017. 720 p.
ISBN 9781501163401
1. Epidemics 2. Near future 3. Small towns 4. Poverty 5. Violence 6. Appalachian region 7. Horror 8. Apocalyptic fiction 9. Social science fiction
LC 2017002473
Goodreads Choice Award, 2017

In a near-future where women succumb to a sleeping disease and men revert to their primal natures, one mysteriously immune woman struggles to survive in an Appalachian town where she is treated as both a demon and a lab specimen.

★ The **stand**. Stephen King. Doubleday, 1990. Xix, 1153 p. : Illustration

ISBN 9780385199575
1. Plague 2. Epidemics 3. Survival (after epidemics) 4. Influenza 5. Good and evil 6. Horror 7. Books to movies 8. Apocalyptic fiction
LC 89027548

A monumentally devastating plague leaves only a few survivors who, while experiencing dreams of a battle between good and evil, move toward an actual confrontation as they migrate to Boulder, Colorado.
"That said, the extra 400 or so pages of subplots, character development, conversation, interior dialogue, spiritual soul-searching, blood, bone and gristle make King 's best novel better still. A new beginning adds verisimilitude to an already frighteningly believable story, while a new ending opens up possibilities for a sequel. Sheer size makes an Everest of the whole deal." —*Publishers Weekly*

Kingsolver, Barbara

★ The **bean** trees: a novel. By Barbara Kingsolver. Harper & Row, 1988. 232 p.
ISBN 9780060158637
1. Abandoned children 2. Single mothers 3. Friendship 4. Female friendship 5. Cherokee girls 6. Tucson, Arizona 7. Relationship fiction
LC 87045633

Taylor Greer hits the road wanting only to get as far away from Kentucky as possible, ending up in Arizona with a 3-year-old Cherokee girl she has inherited from a woman in a bar.
"This book gives readers something that's increasingly hard to find today—a character to believe in and laugh with and admire." —*Christian Science Monitor*
Sequel: Pigs in heaven.

★ **Flight** behavior. Barbara Kingsolver. HarperCollins, 2012. 400 p.
ISBN 9780062124265
1. Global warming 2. Small towns 3. Women farmers 4. Mothers 5. Poverty 6. Tennessee 7. Appalachian Region, Southern 8. Literary fiction
Booklist Editors' Choice, 2012; New York Times Notable Book, 2012; Shortlisted for The Women's Prize for Fiction, 2013

Tired of living on a failing farm and suffering oppressive poverty, bored housewife Dellarobia Turnbow, on the way to meet a potential lover, is detoured by a miraculous event on the Appalachian mountainside that ignites a media and religious firestorm that changes her life forever.

Pigs in heaven. By Barbara Kingsolver. Harper Collins, 1993. 343 p.
ISBN 9780060168018
1. Single mothers 2. Runaways 3. Self-acceptance in women 4. Cherokee girls 5. Cherokee Indians 6. Relationship fiction
LC 92054739
Los Angeles Times Book Prize for Fiction, 1993; Western Heritage Award for Outstanding Western Novel, 1994

When a six-year-old child named Turtle is the sole witness to a freak accident at the Hoover Dam, she and her adoptive mother Taylor have a moment of celebrity that will change their lives forever. Turtle is claimed by Annawake Fourkiller, a Cherokee activist, to have been wrongly taken from the Cherokee nation. Fear of losing Turtle sends Taylor fleeing across the country with her mother Alice, pursued by Annawake. In the course of their journey, the three find love and wisdom in surprising places.
"Possessed of an extravagantly gifted narrative voice, [Kingsolver] blends a fierce and abiding moral vision with benevolent, concise humor." —*New York Times Book Review*
Sequel to: The bean trees.

★ The **Poisonwood** Bible: a novel. Barbara Kingsolver. HarperFlamingo, 1998. 546 p.

ISBN 9780060175405
1. Christian missionaries 2. Americans in Africa 3. Culture conflict 4. Christian families 5. Americans in Congo (Democratic Republic) 6. Congo (Democratic Republic) 7. Historical fiction 8. Literary fiction 9. Multiple perspectives

LC 9819901

Booklist Editors' Choice, 1998; Booklist Editors' Choice: Adult Books for Young Adults, 1998; Book Sense Book of the Year Adult Fiction, 2000; Pulitzer Prize for Fiction finalist, 1999; Shortlisted for The Orange Prize for Fiction, 1999

The family of a fierce evangelical Baptist missionary—Nathan Price, his wife, and his four daughters—begins to unravel after they embark on a 1959 mission to the Belgian Congo, where they find their lives forever transformed over the course of three decades by the political and social upheaval of Africa.

"Buttressing her suspenseful chronicle with authentic background detail, Kingsolver's narrative is at once a compelling family saga and an astute look at Western imperialism in Africa." —*Publishers Weekly*
Includes bibliographical references (p. 545-546).

★ **Unsheltered**. Barbara Kingsolver. Harper, 2018. 464 p.
ISBN 9780062684561
1. Treat, Mary 2. Home (Concept) 3. Utopias 4. Social change 5. Houses — History 6. Ethics 7. New Jersey 8. 21st century 9. 19th century 10. Literary fiction 11. Political fiction 12. Parallel narratives
LibraryReads Favorites, 2018; Booklist Editors' Choice, 2018

Traces the experiences of a woman whose efforts to protect her family from sudden unemployment are shaped by the story of an ostracized 19th-century science teacher.

Kirkpatrick, Jane

One more river to cross. Jane Kirkpatrick. Revell, 2019. 368 p.
ISBN 9780800727024
1. Overland journeys to the Pacific 2. Wagon trains 3. Winter storms 4. Disaster victims 5. Survival 6. Sierra Nevada Mountains 7. The West (United States) 8. American Westward Expansion (1803-1899) 9. 1840s 10. Christian historical fiction

LC 2019006997

Based on true events, this compelling survival story by award-winning novelist Jane Kirkpatrick is full of grit and endurance. Beset by storms, bad timing, and desperate decisions, 8 women, 17 children, and one man must outlast winter in the middle of the Sierra Nevada Mountains in 1844.

"Sibling disagreements, marital stress, faith-based doubts, and fear all bear witness to the gumption, solidarity, and effort vital to the pioneering experience. Kirkpatrick is a commanding innovator of the historical genre with her depth of research and lifelike characters." —*Booklist*

Kirshenbaum, Binnie

Rabbits for food. Binnie Kirshenbaum. Soho Press, 2019. 371 pages
ISBN 9781641290531
1. Women authors 2. Women with depression 3. Nervous breakdown 4. Women with mental illnesses 5. Psychiatric hospitals 6. New York City 7. Literary fiction 8. First person narratives
LC 2018059655

New York Times Notable Book, 2019

A clinically depressed writer who has a breakdown on New Year's Eve chronicles the lives of her fellow "lunatics" in the psych ward of a prestigious New York hospital.

Kitamura, Katie M.

Intimacies. Katie Kitamura. Riverhead Books, 2021. 240 p.
ISBN 9780399576164
1. Women interpreters 2. Lovers 3. Married men 4. War criminals 5. War crime trials 6. The Hague, Netherlands 7. Netherlands 8. Psychological fiction 9. Literary fiction
LC 2021006487

Seeking a fresh start an interpreter takes a position at the International Court at The Hague and is drawn into numerous personal dramas, including her lover's ongoing entanglement in his marriage and her friend witnessing a random act of violence.

"The novel takes place so deeply within her that it's truly personlike, at once forthright and mysterious, a piercing and propulsive meditation on closeness of many sorts." —*Booklist*

Klay, Phil

★ **Missionaries**. Phil Klay. Penguin Press, 2020. 416 p.
ISBN 9781984880659
1. Violence — Psychological aspects 2. War — Psychological aspects 3. Power (Social sciences) 4. Americans in South America 5. International relations 6. Colombia 7. Political fiction 8. Multiple perspectives 9. Literary fiction
LC 2020016830

New York Times Notable Book, 2020

Examines the globalization of violence through the interconnected stories of a U.S. Army Special Forces medic, a foreign correspondent, a Colombian officer and a militia lieutenant who navigate the realities of modern warfare.

"As the characters' lives begin to intersect in a rewarding, yet tension-filled denouement, the author's prodigious skill and deep understanding of the region provide the scaffolding to explore essential questions of human dignity and sacrifice." —*Booklist*

Kleeman, Alexandra

Something new under the sun. Alexandra Kleeman. Hogarth, 2021. 351 p.
ISBN 9781984826305
1. Authors 2. Married men 3. Screenplay writing 4. Films — Production and direction 5. Actors and Actresses 6. Hollywood, California 7. Los Angeles, California 8. Literary fiction 9. Dystopian fiction

While in Hollywood overseeing the production of a film adaptation of one of his books, novelist Patrick Hamlin discovers that a company behind a mysterious new brand of synthetic water is responsible for the recent droughts and wildfires and teams up with a starlet to investigate the city's darker side.

"While a few plot twists are telegraphed, the action is propulsive and entertaining even as the horrors of climate change smolder around every corner. Readers will be captivated by this intelligent, rip-roaring story." —*Publishers Weekly*

Kleypas, Lisa

Cold-hearted rake. Lisa Kleypas. Avon Books, 2015. 384 p. (The Ravenels, 1)
ISBN 9780062371812
1. Earls and countesses 2. Widows 3. Inheritance and succession 4. Family estates 5. Womanizers 6. England 7. Great Britain 8. Victorian era (1837-1901) 9. Victorian romances 10. Historical romances
Romantic Times Reviewer's Choice Award, 2015

When the death of his cousin, an earl, lands him with responsibility for an estate riddled with debt and the late earl's three sisters, Devon

Ravenel finds himself drawn to his cousin's widow and committed to restoring the estate.

"Kleypas begins a new historical romance series with two damaged characters who might find happiness if they can ever learn to trust themselves and one another. Intricately and elegantly crafted, intensely romantic, and with secondary characters and an epilogue that will leave readers anxiously awaiting more." —*Kirkus*

★ **Devil** in disguise. Lisa Kleypas. Avon Books, 2021. 384 p. (The Ravenels, 7)
ISBN 9780063082168
1. Aristocracy 2. Young widows 3. Independence in women 4. Distilling industry and trade 5. Shipping industry and trade 6. England 7. Great Britain 8. Victorian era (1837-1901) 9. Victorian romances 10. Historical romances
LibraryReads Favorites, 2021

A young widow, Lady Merritt Sterling, tries to avoid London society scandals while running her late husband's shipping business, but her sensible plans disappear when she meets a rugged Scotch whisky distiller who is running from danger.

"While Kleypas takes no risks to push her oeuvre in new directions, the novel abounds in the vintage pleasures of her writing: finely drawn characters; a tactile, sensuous style in both the sex scenes and the landscape descriptions; banter that illustrates the emotional compatibility of romantic partners; dual points of view that show both the hero's and the heroine's interior lives; moving moments of familial ties; and glimpses of couples from other novels to assure us that love lasts forever." —*Kirkus*

Klune, TJ
The **house** in the cerulean sea. TJ Klune. Tor, 2020. 320 p.
ISBN 9781250217288
1. Social workers 2. Orphanages 3. Prejudice 4. Suspicion 5. Magic 6. Contemporary fantasy 7. Adult books for young adults
LC 2019050452
Mythopoeic Award for Adult Literature, 2021; Alex Award, 2021; RUSA Reading List, 2021

A magical island. A dangerous task. A burning secret. Linus Baker leads a quiet, solitary life. At forty, he lives in a tiny house with a devious cat and his old records. As a Case Worker at the Department in Charge Of Magical Youth, he spends his days overseeing the well-being of children in government-sanctioned orphanages. When Linus is unexpectedly summoned by Extremely Upper Management he's given a curious and highly classified assignment: travel to Marsyas Island Orphanage, where six dangerous children reside: a gnome, a sprite, a wyvern, an unidentifiable green blob, a were-Pomeranian, and the Antichrist. Linus must set aside his fears and determine whether or not they're likely to bring about the end of days. But the children aren't the only secret the island keeps...

"A delightful tale about chosen families, and how to celebrate differences. Klune's (The Extraordinaries) quirky tone and appealing cast will remind readers of both the Miss Peregrine and Mysterious Benedict Society series." —*Library Journal*
A Tom Doherty Associates book.

★ **Under** the whispering door. TJ Klune. TOR, 2021. 400 p.
ISBN 9781250217349
1. Death 2. Magic 3. Lawyers 4. Soul 5. Grim Reaper (Symbolic character) 6. Contemporary fantasy 7. LGBTQIA romances
LC 2021028510
LibraryReads Favorites, 2021; LibraryReads Favorites Top Ten, 2021

After he dies, a curious and powerful being gives Wallace one week to cross over to the land of the dead, and Wallace, who finally starts to learn about all the things he missed in life, sets about living a lifetime in seven days.

"Tenderness, wit, and skillful worldbuilding elevate this delightful tale. Fans of queer fantasy won't want to miss this." —*Publishers Weekly*
A Tom Doherty Associates book.

Knausgaard, Karl Ove
The **morning** star. Karl Ove Knausgaard; translated from the Norwegian by Martin Aitken. Penguin Press, 2021. 688 p.
ISBN 9780399563423
1. Summer 2. Stars 3. Curiosities and wonders 4. Everyday life 5. Interpersonal relations 6. Norway 7. Translations 8. Literary fiction
LC 2021033640

It's a typical summer night in August. Literature professor Arne and artist Tove are with their children at a summer house in southern Norway. Their friend Egil is staying nearby. Kathrine, a priest, is on her way home from a seminar, journalist Jostein is out on the town, and his wife, Turid, an assistant nurse, is on the night shift. Above them all, a huge star suddenly appears blazing in the sky. No one knows what this phenomenon might be. Is it a star burning itself out? But why, then, has no one seen it before? Is it a brand new star? Life goes on, but not quite as before, as strange things start to happen on the fringes of human existence.

"Readers hungry for more of this author's immersive storytelling will burn through this tome, while those new to Knausgaard may find it a compelling point of entry to his other works." —*Booklist*
Originally published in Norwegian under the title Morgenstjernen by Forlaget Oktober, Oslo in 2020.
Originally published Oslo : Forlaget, 2020.
Translated from the Norwegian.

Knight, Renee
The **secretary**: a novel. Renee Knight. Harper, 2019. 292 p.
ISBN 9780062362353
1. Personal assistants 2. Loyalty 3. Rich women 4. Secrets 5. Celebrities 6. London, England 7. England 8. Psychological suspense 9. First person narratives

Serving 20 years as the Personal Assistant to the celebrated Mina Appleton, and amassing many, many secrets, Christine Butcher, discovering that years of loyalty and discretion come with a high price, shows everyone why they should never underestimate a steadfast woman.

"Knight (Disclaimer) builds tension in this page-turning story about misplaced loyalty, secrets, manipulation, and class with an alternating time line, slowly revealing what happens when one woman's desire to be helpful and needed ruins her life." —*Library Journal*

Knopf, Chris
You're dead. Chris Knopf. Permanent Press, 2018. 288 pages
ISBN 9781579625665
1. Frameups 2. Psychologists 3. Aerospace industry and trade 4. Murder 5. Murder suspects 6. Connecticut 7. New Haven, Connecticut 8. Mysteries
LC 2018039060

"Knopf plays fair as he matches well-developed characters with a crafty whodunit plot, one whose resolution few readers will anticipate." —*Publishers Weekly*

Knott, Robert
Robert B. Parker's Buckskin. Robert Knott. G.P. Putnam's Sons, 2019. 304 p. (Virgil Cole and Everett Hitch, 10)
ISBN 9780735218277

1. Serial murderers 2. United States marshals 3. Mines and mineral resources 4. Blizzards 5. Gunfighters 6. The West (United States) 7. Westerns 8. First person narratives

LC 2019001337

A campaign for sheriff in Appaloosa is thrown into turmoil by a nearby gold strike and a dangerous snowstorm, pitting marshals Virgil Cole and Everett Hitch against rival mining factions and a vicious serial killer.

Knowles, John

★ A **separate** peace. By John Knowles. Scribner Classics, 1996. 204 p.

ISBN 9780684833668

1. Teenage boys 2. Betrayal 3. Friendship 4. Prep school students 5. Prep schools 6. New Hampshire 7. Second World War era (1939-1945) 8. 1940s 9. Coming-of-age stories 10. Modern classics 11. Literary fiction

LC 96025844

A conflict of loyalties between Gene and his fearless friend, Phineas, leads to tragedy.

Originally published: London : Secker & Warburg, 1959.

Ko, Lisa

The **leavers**. Lisa Ko. Algonquin Books of Chapel Hill, 2017. 352 pages

ISBN 9781616206888

1. Undocumented immigrants 2. Mothers and sons 3. Abandonment (Psychology) 4. Parent-separated boys 5. Assimilation (Sociology) 6. New York City 7. China 8. Coming-of-age stories 9. Literary fiction 10. Adult books for young adults

Asian Pacific American Award for Literature: Adult Fiction, 2018; Bellwether Prize for Fiction, 2016; LibraryReads Favorites, 2017; National Book Award for Fiction finalist, 2017

One morning, Deming Guo's mother, an undocumented Chinese immigrant named Polly, goes to her job at the nail salon and never comes home. With his mother gone, eleven-year-old Deming is left with no one to care for him. He is eventually adopted by two white college professors who move him from the Bronx to a small town upstate. Set in New York and China, The leavers is the story of how one boy comes into his own when everything he's loved has been taken away—and how a mother learns to live with the mistakes of her past.

"Ko's stunning tale of love and loyalty—to family, to country—is a fresh and moving look at the immigrant experience in America, and is as timely as ever." —*Publishers Weekly*

Ko-eun, Yun

The **disaster** tourist. Yun Ko-eun; translated from the Korean by Lizzie Buehler. Counterpoint Press, 2020. 208 p.

ISBN 9781640094161

1. Women travel agents 2. Travel agencies 3. Voyages and travels 4. Islands 5. Resorts 6. Satirical fiction 7. Translations

CWA Crime Fiction in Translation, 2021

"Yun cleverly combines absurdity with legitimate horror and mounting dread. With its arresting, nightmarish island scenario, this work speaks volumes about the human cost of tourism in developing countries." —*Publishers Weekly*

Koepp, David

Cold storage: a novel. David Koepp. Ecco, 2019. 256 p.

ISBN 9780062916433

1. Epidemics 2. Biological terrorism 3. Government investigators 4. Mutation (Biology) 5. Predation (Biology) 6. Bio-thrillers 7. Thrillers and suspense

LC 2018057661

When Pentagon bioterror operative Roberto Diaz was sent to investigate a suspected biochemical attack, he found something far worse: a highly mutative organism capable of extinction-level destruction. He contained it and buried it in cold storage deep beneath a little-used military repository.

Koestler, Arthur

Darkness at noon. Arthur Koestler; translated by Daphne Hardy. Macmillan, 1987. 267 p.

ISBN 9780025652101

1. Political prisoners 2. Revolutionaries 3. Moscow, Russia, Trials, 1936-1937 4. Stalinism 5. Trials 6. Soviet Union 7. 1930s 8. Historical fiction 9. Political fiction 10. Translations

An aging revolutionary is imprisoned by his own political party and forced to confess to crimes he never committed. Where once he saw promise for humanity, he now sees only darkness.

Originally published: London : J. Cape, 1940.

Kohnstamm, Thomas B.

Lake City. Thomas Kohnstamm. Counterpoint, 2019. 256 p.

ISBN 9781640091429

1. Gentrification of cities 2. Ambition in men 3. Class conflict 4. Underclass 5. Birthmothers 6. Seattle, Washington 7. 2000s (Decade) 8. Humorous stories

The setting is Seattle's Lake City neighborhood during the 2001 holiday season. In the wake of the 9/11 tragedy and at the peak of Seattle's first wave of tech-boom gentrification—a wave that never quite made it to his neighborhood—Lane Bueche schemes how to win back his wife (and her trust fund). In his childhood bedroom in his mother's decrepit old house, the idealistic but self-serving striver Lane licks his wounds and hatches a plot.

Konar, Affinity

Mischling: a novel. Affinity Konar. Little, Brown and Company, 2016. 344 pages

ISBN 9780316308106

1. Mengele, Josef 2. Twin sisters 3. Human experimentation in medicine 4. Holocaust, 1933-1945 5. Concentration camp survivors 6. Persecution by Nazis 7. Poland 8. Second World War era (1939-1945) 9. Historical fiction 10. Literary fiction 11. Adult books for young adults

New York Times Notable Book, 2016

Arriving at Auschwitz in 1944, twin sisters Pearl and Stasha Zagorski take refuge in each other when they become part of the experimental population of twins known as Mengele's Zoo, where they experience horrors unknown to other inmates.

"Konar makes every sentence count; its to her credit that the girls never come across as simply victims: they're flawed, memorable characters trying to stay alive. This is a brutally beautiful novel." —*Publishers Weekly*

Koontz, Dean R.

The **darkest** evening of the year. Dean Koontz. Bantam, 2007. 416 p.

ISBN 9780739327425

1. Trust 2. Secrets 3. Female friendship 4. Crimes against girls 5. Hotels 6. Romantic suspense

LC 2015016234

Library Journal Best Books, 2015

Reuniting at the hotel where one of them was brutally attacked as a child decades earlier, Madeline and Daphne are forced to confront painful memories and truths in order to solve the mysterious death of Madeline's father.

"Krentz scores another winner with complex characters and seamless plotting." —*Publishers Weekly*

When all the girls have gone. Jayne Ann Krentz. Berkley Books, 2016. 304 p. (Cutler, Sutter & Salinas, 1)
ISBN 9780399174490

1. Stepsisters 2. Missing women 3. Investment clubs 4. Private investigators 5. Conspiracies 6. Seattle, Washington 7. Romantic suspense

LibraryReads Favorites, 2016

When Charlotte Sawyer is unable to contact her step-sister, Jocelyn, to tell her that one her closest friends was found dead, she discovers that Jocelyn has vanished. Beautiful, brilliant—and reckless—Jocelyn has gone off the grid before, but never like this. In a desperate effort to find her, Charlotte joins forces with Max Cutler, a struggling PI who recently moved to Seattle after his previous career as a criminal profiler went down in flames—literally. Burned out, divorced and almost broke, Max needs the job. After surviving a near-fatal attack, Charlotte and Max turn to Jocelyn's closest friends, women in a Seattle-based online investment club, for answers. But what they find is chilling...When her uneasy alliance with Max turns into a full-blown affair, Charlotte has no choice but to trust him with her life. For the shadows of Jocelyn's past are threatening to consume her—and anyone else who gets in their way....

"Krentz returns with an intricately plotted romantic suspense novel that satisfies on every level, includes some clever twists with the senior community, and may open the door for a sequel. A terrific read by a stellar author." —*Kirkus*

Kress, Nancy

Beggars in Spain. Nancy Kress. William Morrow, 1993. 438 p. (Beggars trilogy, 1)
ISBN 9780380718771

1. Perfectionism in children 2. Genetic engineering 3. Prejudice 4. Millionaires 5. Envy 6. 21st century 7. Hard science fiction 8. Science fiction classics 9. Science fiction

LC 92025070

The product of an experiment in genetic manipulation, superintelligent Leisha Camden is forced to live a life apart from most "ordinary" people and seeks the companionship of other superhumans.

"This book is an intellectual roller-coaster ride, supplying no simple conclusions about right and wrong, and racing along with its brisk prose, stimulating ideas, and a variety of challenging characters." —*School Library Journal*

If tomorrow comes. Nancy Kress. Tor, 2018. 288 p. (Yesterday's kin, 2)
ISBN 9780765390325

1. Aliens 2. Scientists 3. Epidemics 4. Human/alien encounters 5. Disasters — Prevention 6. Hard science fiction 7. Science fiction

Ten years after the Aliens left Earth, humanity succeeds in building a ship, Friendship, to follow them home to Kindred. Aboard are a crew of scientists, diplomats, and a squad of Rangers to protect them. But when the Friendship arrives, they find nothing they expected. No interplanetary culture, no industrial base—and no cure for the spore disease.

Tomorrow's kin. Nancy Kress. Tor, 2017. 349 p. (Yesterday's kin, 1)
ISBN 9780765390295

1. Aliens 2. Scientists 3. Xenophobia 4. Human/alien encounters 5. Disasters — Prevention 6. New York City 7. Hard science fiction 8. Science fiction

Follows the arrival of alien embassies who meet with the United Nations amid human fear and speculation before obscure scientist Dr. Marianne Jenner is secretly invited to visit the aliens and prevent an imminent disaster.

Tomorrow's Kin is an expansion of the author's 2014 novella Yesterday's Kin.

Krivak, Andrew

The **bear**. Andrew Krivak. Bellevue Literary Press, 2020. 221 pages
ISBN 9781942658702

1. Post-apocalypse 2. Wilderness survival 3. Fathers and daughters 4. Human-animal relationships 5. Voyages and travels 6. Apocalyptic fiction 7. Coming-of-age stories

LC 2018061687

LibraryReads Favorites, 2020; Massachusetts Book Awards, Fiction Award, 2020

Living close to the land in an Eden-like post-civilization world, a girl learns the secrets of hunting and star navigation before finding herself in an unknown landscape, where a bear imparts powerful natural-world lessons.

"Poignant but not tragic, this end-of-civilization story shows that there's no loneliness in this world when we are one with nature." —*Library Journal*

The **signal** flame: a novel. Andrew Krivak. Scribner, 2017. 288 p. (Sojourn novels (Andrew Krivak), 2)
ISBN 9781501126376

1. Small towns 2. Grief 3. Families 4. Soldiers 5. Veterans 6. Pennsylvania 7. 20th century 8. Family sagas 9. Historical fiction

In a small town in Pennsylvania's Endless Mountains Hannah and her son Bo mourn the loss of the family patriarch, Jozef Vinich. They were three generations under one roof. Three generations, but only one branch of a scraggy tree; they are a war-haunted family in a war-torn century. Having survived the trenches of World War I as an Austro-Hungarian conscript, Vinich journeyed to America and built a life for his family. His daughter married the Hungarian-born Bexhet Konar, who enlisted to fight with the Americans in the Second World War but brought disgrace on the family when he was imprisoned for desertion. He returned home to Pennsylvania a hollow man, only to be killed in a hunting accident on the family's land. Finally, in 1971, Hannah's prodigal younger son, Sam, was reported MIA in Vietnam. And so there is only Bo, a quiet man full of conviction, a proud work ethic, and a firstborn's sense of duty. He is left to grieve but also to hope for reunion, to create a new life, to embrace the land and work its soil through the seasons.

"This family saga is quiet at its core, but it's Krivak's gorgeous prose and deep grasp of the relationship between longing and loss that make the book such a stunner." —*Publishers Weekly*

Kroese, Robert

The **last** iota. Robert Kroese. Thomas Dunne Books, 2017. 302 p. (Erasmus Keane novels, 2)
ISBN 9781250088468

1. Private investigators 2. Lost articles 3. Near future 4. Eccentrics and eccentricities 5. Film industry and trade executives 6. Los Angeles, California 7. 21st century 8. Science fiction mysteries

LC 2017001074

Hired by a movie mogul to find rare coins lost somewhere in the Disincorporated Zone of LA, eccentric private investigator Erasmus Keane struggles to unravel the mystery while his partner, Blake, is framed for murder, which plunges them both into a conspiracy that reaches the highest levels of government.

Krueger, Paul

Steel crow saga. Paul Krueger. Del Rey, 2019. 516 p.

ISBN 9780593128220

1. Princes 2. Imaginary empires 3. Magic 4. Women soldiers 5. Thieves 6. Fantasy fiction 7. Asian-influenced fantasy

LC 2019014522

A band of rogues and royals that should be enemies join forces for a common purpose—to defeat an unstoppable killer who defies the laws of magic in a battle that forges bonds of friendship and love that will change their lives and the world.

"With a well-realized world and strong characters, many of whom are queer, Krueger's novel will feel as fast-paced and exciting as its animated influences and leave the reader longing for more." —*Booklist*

Krueger, William Kent

★ **Lightning** strike. William Kent Krueger. Atria Books, 2021. 336 p. (Cork O'Connor mysteries, 18)

ISBN 9781982128685

1. Ojibwa Indians 2. Multiracial boys 3. Twelve-year-old boys 4. Fathers and sons 5. Race relations 6. Minnesota 7. 1960s 8. Mysteries

In this prequel to the acclaimed Cork O'Connor series, 12-year-old Cork stumbles upon the body of a man hanging in a tree—the first in a series of events that cause him to question everything he took for granted about his hometown, his family and himself.

"Krueger makes the youthful version of his lead plausible, as well as his detective abilities. Longtime fans will relish Cork's rich backstory." —*Publishers Weekly*

This tender land: a novel. William Kent Krueger. Atria Books, 2019. 464 pages

ISBN 9781476749297

1. Orphans 2. Voyages and travels 3. Native American children 4. Separated friends, relatives, etc. 5. Schools 6. Minnesota 7. Depression era (1929-1941) 8. 1930s 9. Historical fiction 10. Adventure stories 11. Coming-of-age stories

LC 2019015067

LibraryReads Favorites, 2019

Fleeing the Depression-era school for Native American children who have been taken from their parents, four orphans share a summer marked by struggling farmers, faith healers and lost souls.

Kuang, R. F.

★ The **dragon** republic. R. F. Kuang. Harper Voyager, 2019. 560 pages (Poppy war, 2)

ISBN 9780062662637

1. Shamans 2. Opium addiction 3. Gods and goddesses 4. Rulers 5. Betrayal 6. 20th century 7. Asian-influenced fantasy 8. Historical fantasy 9. Military fantasy

A sequel to The Poppy War finds shaman-warrior Rin haunted by personal demons including the choice she made to save her people, an atrocity that compels a precarious alliance to defeat the Empress.

The **poppy** war. R.F. Kuang. Harper Voyager, 2018. 530 pages (Poppy war, 1)

ISBN 9780062662569

1. Orphans 2. Apprentices 3. Shamans 4. Gods and goddesses 5. Martial arts 6. 20th century 7. Asian-influenced fantasy 8. Historical fantasy 9. Military fantasy 10. Adult books for young adults

Library Journal Best Books, 2018; RUSA Reading List Short List, 2019

An epic historical military fantasy, inspired by the violent history of China's 20th century, follows the efforts of an unexpected, dark-skinned war orphan to obtain an education at Nikan's most elite military school in spite of prejudice and the challenges of her lethal shaman skills, which raise her awareness about the existence of gods and the imminence of war.

Kubica, Mary

★ The **other** Mrs. Mary Kubica. Park Row, 2020. 384 p.

ISBN 9780778369110

1. Inheritance and succession 2. Coastal towns 3. Neighbors 4. Secrets 5. Moving to a new city 6. Maine 7. Psychological suspense

LibraryReads Favorites, 2020

Unnerved by her husband's inheritance of a decrepit coastal property and the presence of a disturbed relative, community newcomer Sadie uncovers harrowing facts about her family's possible role in a neighbor's murder.

"What is satisfying and most effective is the oppressive sense of unease that permeates this intense psychological suspense drama. For fans of A.J. Finn and Gillian Flynn." —*Library Journal*

Kuhn, M. J.

Among thieves. M. J. Kuhn. Saga Press, 2021. 352 p.

ISBN 9781982142148

1. Assassins 2. Mercenaries 3. Imaginary kingdoms 4. Secrets 5. Alliances 6. Epic fantasy

In just over a year's time, Ryia Cautella has already earned herself a reputation as the quickest, deadliest blade in the dockside city of Carrowwick—not to mention the sharpest tongue. But Ryia Cautella is not her real name. Ryia's path now leads directly into the heart of the Guildmaster's stronghold, and against every instinct she has, it's not a path she can walk alone. Forced to team up with a crew of assorted miscreants, smugglers, and thieves, Ryia must plan her next moves very carefully. If she succeeds, her freedom is won once and for all... but unfortunately for Ryia, her new allies are nearly as selfish as she is, and they all have plans of their own.

"This fantasy heist's fast pace, multiple points of view, and intriguing twists will leave readers clamoring for the next book. Rich worldbuilding adds to the standard Western epic fantasy conventions." —*Library Journal*

Kundera, Milan

★ **Immortality**. Milan Kundera; translated from the Czech by Peter Kussi. Grove Weidenfeld 1991. 345p.

ISBN 9780802111111

1. Love 2. Sexuality 3. Immortality 4. Identity (Psychology) 5. Man-woman relationships 6. Literary fiction 7. Translations 8. First person narratives

LC 90028628

Through the actions of three characters—Agnes, her husband, and her sister—and others in contemporary France and Weimar Germany, the author reflects on the image of the individual, the Western cult of sentiment, and the meaning of love.

"Immortality swings easily, almost imperceptibly, from narrative to rumination and back again, collapsing the distinction between action and concepts.... Out of a story about contemporary neuroses, Kundera has fabricated a context in which everything, literally, can be claimed to matter. What is more, the author indulges this obsessiveness without ever droning or turning out a dull page. In its inventiveness and its dazzling display of what written words can convey, Immortality gives fiction back its good name." —*Time*

Translation of Nesmrtelnost.

★ The **unbearable** lightness of being. Milan Kundera; translated from the Czech by Michael Henry Heim. Harper & Row, 1984. 314 p.

ISBN 9780060152581

1. Man-woman relationships 2. Totalitarianism 3. Sexuality 4. Jealousy 5. Czechoslovakia 6. 1960s 7. Literary fiction 8. Translations 9. Books to movies

LC 83048363

Los Angeles Times Book Prize for Fiction, 1984

After the 1968 Soviet invasion of Czechoslovakia, a married surgeon, Tomas, becomes a window washer while trying to reconcile himself to decisions that he and his wife must make about their relationship.

Kunsken, Derek

The **House** of Styx. Derek Kunsken. Solaris, 2021. 500 p. (Venus ascendant, 1)

ISBN 9781781088050

1. Humans 2. Christie, Agatha 3. Space colonies 4. Survival 5. Secrets 6. Venus (Planet)

Life can exist anywhere. And anywhere there is life, there is home. In the swirling clouds of Venus, the families of la colonie live on floating plant-like trawlers, salvaging what they can in the fierce acid rain and crackling storms. Outside is dangerous, but humankind's hold on the planet is fragile and they spend most of their days simply surviving. But Venus carries its own secrets, too. In the depths, there is a wind that shouldn't exist. And the House of Styx wants to harness it.

"This electrifying planetary adventure features a hardscrabble family that earnestly addresses issues of addiction, gender, sexuality, and disability while surviving storms of all sorts in the hostile clouds of Venus." —*Library Journal*

Kunzru, Hari

Red pill: a novel. Hari Kunzru. Alfred A. Knopf, 2020. 283 p.

ISBN 9780451493712

1. Authors 2. Midlife crisis 3. Television programs 4. Local history 5. Americans in Germany 6. Germany 7. 2010s 8. Literary fiction 9. Political fiction

LC 2019053311

New York Times Notable Book, 2020

Navigating an existential crisis in a haunted Berlin suburb after accepting a prestigious writing fellowship, an aspiring author becomes locked in a cosmic, Darwinian rivalry against the creator of a popular television series.

"As Kunzru's protagonist slowly loses his hold on reality, he questions if what he's seeing is just another whitewashed version of the truth. Kunzru has created a complex, challenging, and bold story about a world gone amok and a middle-aged man coming to terms with his one truth: his mediocrity." —*Booklist*

White tears. Hari Kunzru. Alfred A. Knopf, 2017. 288 p.

ISBN 9780451493699

1. Hoaxes 2. Blues music 3. Cultural appropriation 4. Racism 5. Rich families 6. Mississippi 7. New York City 8. Literary fiction 9. Coming-of-age stories

LC 2016011904

New York Times Notable Book, 2017; Kirkus Prize for Fiction finalist, 2017; Longlisted for the Andrew Carnegie Medal for Excellence in Fiction, 2018; Shortlisted for the James Tait Black Memorial Prize for Fiction, 2017

Two ambitious young musicians, one shy, the other a glamorous heir, are drawn into the dark underworld of blues-record collecting while navigating the ghosts of a repressive past and the fallout of a scam involving one's claim that a viral video of an unknown singer is long-lost recording of a famous blues musician.

"Record collecting turns dangerous in a smart, time-bending tale about cultural appropriation." —*Kirkus*

This is a Borzoi book.

Kupersmith, Violet

★ **Build** your house around my body. Violet Kupersmith. Random House, 2021. 378 p.

ISBN 9780812993325

1. Vietnamese American women 2. Expatriates 3. Americans in Vietnam 4. English language teachers 5. Missing women 6. Vietnam 7. Literary fiction 8. Franklin, Jane

The fate of an unhappy woman who disappears in 2011 while living in Saigon is entwined with a teenager who gets lost in an abandoned rubber plantation in 1986 and a woman who captures a two-headed cobra in 2009.

"Magic can be both benevolent and monstrous in Kupersmith's work, and here she indelibly illustrates the ways in which Vietnam's legacies of colonialism, war, and violence against women continue to haunt." —*Publishers Weekly*

Kurian, Vera

Never saw me coming. Vera Kurian. Park Row, 2021. 352 p.

ISBN 9780778311553

1. Psychopaths 2. Women college students 3. Murder victims 4. Clinical trials 5. Universities and colleges 6. Washington, D.C. 7. Psychological suspense 8. First person narratives

LibraryReads Favorites, 2021

College student and psychopath Chloe Sevre is one of seven students at her DC-based college who are part of a clinical study for psychopaths that tracks their moods and movements. When one of the students in the study is found dead in the psychology building, Chloe goes from hunter to prey. As she tries to identify the murderer and put her own plan for revenge against her childhood friend who wronged her into action, she'll be forced to decide if she can trust any of the other psychopaths.

"Seriously brilliant, seriously flawed, ambitious, and delicious." —*Kirkus*

Kushner, Rachel

The **Mars** room. Rachel Kushner. Scribner, 2018. 338 p.

ISBN 9781476756554

1. Single mothers 2. Women prisoners 3. Prisons 4. Women murderers 5. Prison sentences 6. San Francisco, California 7. California 8. 2000s (Decade) 9. First person narratives 10. Literary fiction

LC 2017061764

ALA Notable Book, 2019; Booklist Editors' Choice, 2018; New York Times Notable Book, 2018; National Book Critics Circle Award for Fiction finalist, 2018; Shortlisted for the Man Booker Prize, 2018

A woman begins serving two life sentences at Stanville Women's Correctional Facility deep in 2003 California's Central Valley, reflecting on the San Francisco of her youth and her relationship with her young son while navigating the harsh realities of a bare-essentials life of casual violence at the hands of the guards and her fellow inmates.

"This is a gorgeously eviscerating novel of incarceration writ large, of people trapped in the wrong body, the wrong family, poverty, addiction, and prejudice. The very land is chained and exploited. Rooted in deeply inquisitive thinking and executed with artistry and edgy wit, Kushner's dramatic and disquieting novel investigates with verve and compassion societal strictures and how very difficult it is to understand each other and to be truly free." —*Booklist*

Kutsukake, Lynne

The **translation** of love: a novel. Lynne Kutsukake. Doubleday, 2016. 318 p.

ISBN 9780385540674

1. Deportation 2. Japanese Canadians 3. Letter writing 4. Culture conflict 5. Female friendship 6. Tokyo, Japan 7. Japan 8. 1940s 9. Historical fiction 10. Canadian fiction 11. Multiple perspectives 12. Adult books for young adults

Booklist Editors' Choice, 2016; Canada-Japan Literary Awards, 2016

Deported back to post-war Japan with her father after their release from a Canadian internment camp, thirteen-year-old Aya Shimamura struggles at school, where she is bullied for being foreign, before one of her tormentors asks for Aya's help in finding her missing sister.

"A vivid delight chronicling a fascinating—and little-discussed—chapter in world history." —*Kirkus*

Kuznetsov, Anatolii Petrovich

Babi Yar: a document in the form of a novel. By A. Anatoli (Kuznetsov). Translated by David Floyd. Farrar, Straus and Giroux, 1970. 477 p.

ISBN 9780374107611

1. Babi Yar Massacre, 1941 2. Atrocities 3. Soviet Union 4. 1940s 5. Historical fiction 6. Translations

LC 70125154

The author documents the German massacre from 1941 to 1943 of two million people, including 50,000 Jews, outside Kiev.

Kwan, Kevin

China rich girlfriend. Kevin Kwan. Knopf Doubleday, 2015. 400 p. (Rich novels (Kevin Kwan), 2)

ISBN 9780385539081

1. Heirs and heiresses 2. Weddings 3. Birthfathers 4. Father-separated families 5. Rich people 6. China 7. Relationship fiction

Feeling incomplete because her unknown birth father cannot walk her down the aisle, Rachel Chu, on the brink of marrying one of Asia's richest bachelors, is brought into the elite circles of Shanghai by a shocking revelation.

"Lovers of clothes, cuisine, and cars will find themselves at home in Kwans second smart and snarky send-up of the Chinese jet set." —*Booklist*

Sequel to: Crazy rich Asians.

Crazy rich Asians. Kevin Kwan. Doubleday, 2013. 416 p. (Rich novels (Kevin Kwan), 1)

ISBN 9780385536974

1. Engaged persons 2. Americans in Singapore 3. Rich families 4. Social conflict 5. Chinese American women 6. Singapore 7. Relationship fiction 8. Books to movies

LC 2012032395

Envisioning a summer vacation in the humble Singapore home of a boy she hopes to marry, Chinese American Rachel Chu is unexpectedly introduced to a rich and scheming clan that strongly opposes their son's relationship with an American girl.

Title adapted into a film in 2018.

Rich people problems. Kevin Kwan. Doubleday, 2017. 384 p. (Rich novels (Kevin Kwan), 3)

ISBN 9780385542234

1. Rich people 2. Inheritance and succession 3. Families 4. Divorced persons 5. Family relationships 6. Singapore 7. Manila, Philippines 8. Relationship fiction

Rushing to the deathbed of his grandmother, Nicholas Young encounters a massive clan eager to claim a share of the family fortune, win the hearts of loved ones, destroy each other's reputations and outmaneuver professional rivals.

"The fairy tale/soap opera/lux-a-thon that began with Crazy Rich Asians (2013) and China Rich Girlfriend (2015) comes to a fittingly majestic and hilarious end in Kwan's third novel." —*Kirkus*

Sex and vanity: a novel. Kevin Kwan. Doubleday, 2020. 315 p.

ISBN 9780385546270

1. Love triangles 2. Rich people 3. Engaged persons 4. Chinese American women 5. Deception 6. East Hampton, New York 7. New York City 8. Relationship fiction 9. Adaptations, retellings, and spin-offs

LC 2020011658

When George, the man with whom she had brief fling several years earlier, unexpectedly appears in East Hampton, newly engaged Lucie Churchill is drawn to him again and spins a web of deceit in an attempt to block him from her life—and her heart.

"The resolution adds another satisfying layer to this frothy, escapist delight." —*Booklist*

Kwok, Jean

Searching for Sylvie Lee. Jean Kwok. William Morrow & Co, 2019. 304 pages

ISBN 9780062834300

1. Missing persons 2. Sisters 3. Children of immigrants 4. Family secrets 5. Immigrants, Chinese 6. New York City 7. Netherlands 8. Literary fiction 9. Multiple perspectives

A poignant and suspenseful drama that untangles the complicated ties binding three women—two sisters and their mother—in one Chinese immigrant family and explores what happens when the eldest daughter disappears, and a series of family secrets emerge, from the New York Times bestselling author of Girl in Translation.

Kwon, Yo-son

Lemon. Kwon Yeo-sun; translated from the Korean by Janet Hong. Other Press, 2021. 160 p.

ISBN 9781635420883

1. Teenage girl murder victims 2. Sisters 3. Murder suspects 4. Cold cases (Criminal investigation) 5. Suspicion 6. South Korea 7. Psychological fiction 8. Multiple perspectives 9. Translations

LC 2021006077

In this piercing psychological portrait that takes the shape of a crime novel, a woman haunted by her sister's unsolved murder transforms herself in order to cope with the pain of absence and unknowing. In the summer of 2002, when Korea is abuzz over hosting the FIFA World Cup, nineteen-year-old Kim Hae-on is killed in what becomes known as the High School Beauty Murder. Although two suspects quickly emerge, the case goes cold. Seventeen years pass without any resolution for those who knew and loved Hae-on, and the grief and uncertainty take a cruel toll on her younger sister, Da-on, in particular. Unable to move on with her life, Da-on tries in her own twisted way to recover some of what she's lost, ultimately setting out to find the truth of what happened.

"Those ready to sink into a creepy and intense yet understated emotional experience will find that this story hits and sticks." —*Publishers Weekly*

Originally published: Paju : Changbi, 2019.

Translated from the Korean.

L

L'Amour, Louis

★ **Bendigo** Shafter. Louis L'Amour. Bantam, 1983. 323 p.
ISBN 9780553264463

1. Frontier and pioneer life 2. Brothers 3. Eighteen-year-old men 4. Widows 5. The West (United States) 6. Wyoming 7. Westerns

Bendigo Shafter and his followers build a town in the heart of Wyoming Indian country, where the crack-shot leader falls in love with two women: the dignified Widow Macken and the beautiful Ninon.

The **Californios**. Louis L'Amour. Bantam Books, 1996. 188 p.
ISBN 9780553253221

1. Widows 2. Ranches 3. Gold prospecting 4. Native American mystics 5. Brothers 6. California 7. The West (United States) 8. Westerns

The Mulkerin Brothers, in a desperate attempt to settle the debt on their ranch, follow an Indian mystic to California in search of gold, with a gang of greedy gunfighters riding hard on their heels.

"An expert blend of the fascinating settling of California in the 1840's; strong, self-reliant characters...and a plot of evil doings but triumphant good. The theme of mysticism and the legends of The Old Ones is what lifts this book above the typical western. Intriguing even for those who aren't westerns fans." —*Library Journal*

End of the drive. Louis L'Amour. Bantam Books, 1997. 257 p. (The Sacketts, 7)
ISBN 9780553578980

1. Frontier and pioneer life 2. The West (United States) 3. Westerns

Eight exciting tales, by one of American's most beloved Western writers, chronicles the adventures of the men and women who faced the dangers, challenges, and trials of Westward settlement with courage, strength, and humor.

"An unexpected and entertaining treat for L'Amour fans." —*Booklist*
Comprised of seven unforgettable, never-before-published tales, together with one complete novella.

"The courting of Griselda" is part of L'Amour's Sacketts series. This story takes place between The Daybreakers and Lando.

The **last** of the breed. Louis L'Amour. Bantam Books, 1986. 358 p.
ISBN 9780553051629

1. Test pilots 2. Native American men 3. Airplane accidents 4. Military secrets 5. Wilderness survival 6. Siberia 7. Adventure stories
LC 86003622

When his experimental aircraft is forced down over the Bering Sea by Russians, U.S. Air Force Major Joseph "Joe Mack" Makatozi must seek his safety in the uncharted wilds of Siberia, pursued by Colonel Zamatev of the GRU and by a Yakut tracker BT

"Joe Mack is a classic American hero, thrown back into the wilderness and forced to rely on his wits and his ancestral skills to survive the deadly cold and elude his Soviet pursuers, including his nemesis, a Siberian tracker. L'Amour brings the same colorful realism to this sweeping adventure that has made his Westerns so beloved." —*Publishers Weekly*
Includes end-paper maps.

To the far blue mountains. Louis L'Amour. Bantam Books, 1977. 287 p. (The Sacketts, 2)
ISBN 9780553027570

1. Frontier and pioneer life 2. British in the United States 3. Fugitives 4. Sackett family (Fictitious characters) 5. Virginia 6. Blue Ridge Mountains 7. Colonial America (1600-1775) 8. 17th century 9. Westerns 10. Family sagas
LC 75029190

Wanted by the law, Barnabas Sackett leaves England to seek his fortune in the New World and heads west with his wife Abigail and a few friends to begin a new life in the wilderness.

"This tale is much more leisurely and nonviolent than the usual L'Amour story, but it has its share of suspense and gives us a different kind of look at colonial America." —*Publishers Weekly*

Labatut, Benjamin

When we cease to understand the world. Benjamin Labatut; translated by Adrian Nathan West. New York Review Books, 2021. 192 p.
ISBN 9781681375663

1. Haber, Fritz 2. Heisenberg uncertainty principle 3. Quantum theory 4. Science — Moral and ethical aspects 5. Scientific discoveries 6. Scientists 7. 20th century 8. 19th century 9. Biographical fiction 10. Translations 11. Literary fiction
LC 2021005101

National Book Award for Translated Literature finalist, 2021

A fictional examination of the lives of real-life scientists and thinkers whose discoveries resulted in moral consequences beyond their imagining. When We Cease to Understand the World is a book about the complicated links between scientific and mathematical discovery, madness, and destruction. Fritz Haber, Alexander Grothendieck, Werner Heisenberg, Erwin Schrodinger: these are some of luminaries into whose troubled lives Labatut's book thrusts the reader, showing us how they grappled with the most profound questions of existence.

"Reading like an episodic digest, Chilean writer Labatut's stylish English-language debut offers an embellished, heretical, and thoroughly engrossing account of the personalities and creative madness that gave rise to some of the 20th century's greatest scientific discoveries." —*Publishers Weekly*

Translation of: Un verdor terrible.

Originally published Barcelona : Anagrama, 2020.

Translated from the Spanish.

Lacey, Catherine

★ **Pew**: a novel. Catherine Lacey. Farrar, Straus and Giroux, 2020. 192 p.
ISBN 9780374230920

1. Identity (Psychology) 2. Strangers 3. Christians 4. Churches 5. People who are mute 6. Southern States 7. Literary fiction
LC 2019056415

Racially ambiguous, genderless, mute, and of unknown age, Pew is named by where they were found—sleeping in a church. Pew's muteness allows the townspeople to project whatever they wish; Pew's own thoughts are communicated to readers alone. But fear of the unknown is strong, and soon the town's generosity turns to suspicion and mistrust.

"She shines a light on how complicated people are and the dangers of judging others based on appearance, as Pew's ambiguity reveals the true nature of the novel's characters." —*Booklist*

Lackberg, Camilla

The **golden** cage. Camilla Lackberg; translated from the Swedish by Neil Smith. Knopf, 2020. 400 p.

ISBN 9780525657972

1. Rich families 2. Betrayal 3. Revenge 4. Witchcraft 5. Curses 6. Psychological suspense 7. Translations

Discovering that the privileged husband for whom she sacrificed everything has been having an affair, an emotionally and financially devastated woman orchestrates a daring plot for revenge.

"A darkly glamorous and utterly absorbing departure from Läckberg's atmospheric Fjallbacka series." —*Booklist*

Sequel: Silver tears.

Also published as The gilded cage: London : HarperCollins, 2020.

Translated from the Swedish.

Silver tears. Camilla Lackberg; translated by Ian Giles. Alfred A. Knopf, 2021. 288 p.

ISBN 9780525657996

1. Rich families 2. Divorced women 3. Women chief executive officers 4. Former husbands 5. Former convicts 6. Psychological suspense 7. Translations

LC 2021006392

In this riveting novel of seduction, deceit and female power, three generations of women, who have survived in hiding from the men who sought to destroy them, find that secrets always end in tears.

"Lackberg's second novel about the brilliant economist who overcame a stifling marriage certainly draws on the strengths of the first: The plot careens at breakneck speed through steamy sex scenes, startling revelations, and flashbacks to Faye's very dark childhood riddled with rape and murder.... A scandal-filled page-turner sure to delight the beach-read crowd." —*Kirkus*

Sequel to: The golden cage.

Originally published: Stockholm : Bokforlaget Forum, 2020.

Translated from the Swedish.

Lafferty, Mur

Six wakes. Mur Lafferty. Little Brown & Co 2017. 352 p.

ISBN 9780316389686

1. Clones and cloning 2. Space vehicles 3. Murder victims 4. Murder investigation 5. Military missions 6. 25th century 7. Science fiction thrillers 8. Science fiction

Awakening in a cloning vat, streaked with blood and possessing no memory of how she died, new clone Maria Arena discovers the clones of six former starship crew members and must identify their murderers before the killer strikes again.

Lafferty delivers a tense nail-biter of a story fueled by memorable characters and thoughtful worldbuilding. This space-based locked-room murder mystery explores complex technological and moral issues...Publishers Weekly.

Lagercrantz, David

The **girl** who lived twice: a Lisbeth Salander novel. David Lagercrantz. Knopf, 2019. 416 pages (Millennium novels (Stieg Larsson), 6)

ISBN 9780451494344

1. Political intrigue 2. Hackers 3. Investigative journalists 4. Organized crime 5. Violence against women 6. Sweden 7. Scandinavian crime fiction 8. Mysteries 9. Translations

The best-selling author of The Girl in the Spider's Web presents a latest entry in the internationally acclaimed series starring punk hacker heroine, Lisbeth Salander.

Continuing Stieg Larsson's Millenium series—Cover.

Translated from the Swedish.

The **girl** who takes an eye for an eye. David Lagercrantz. Knopf, 2017. 416 p. (Millennium novels (Stieg Larsson), 5)

ISBN 9780451494320

1. Political intrigue 2. Hackers 3. Investigative journalists 4. Organized crime 5. Violence against women 6. Sweden 7. Scandinavian crime fiction 8. Mysteries 9. Translations

Accepting help from Mikael Blomkvist to uncover the truth about her traumatic childhood, Lisbeth Salander navigates obstacles in the form of an anti-Muslim gang, her mafia-connected twin, and the conductors of a pseudoscientific experiment.

Continuing Stieg Larsson's Millenium series—Cover.

Originally published in Sweden as Mannen som sökte sin skugga by Norstedts, Stockholm, in 2017—Title page verso.

Lahiri, Jhumpa

The **lowland**: a novel. Jhumpa Lahiri. Alfred A. Knopf, 2013. 339 pages

ISBN 9780307265746

1. Brothers 2. Love triangles 3. Loss (Psychology) 4. Insurgency 5. Widows 6. India 7. Psychological fiction 8. Literary fiction 9. Family sagas

LC 2012043878

Booklist Editors' Choice, 2013; LibraryReads Favorites, 2013; New York Times Notable Book, 2013; National Book Award for Fiction finalist, 2013; Shortlisted for The Baileys Women's Prize for Fiction, 2014; Shortlisted for the Man Booker Prize, 2013

Brothers Subhash and Udayan Mitra pursue vastly different lives—Udayan in rebellion-torn Calcutta, Subhash in a quiet corner of America—until a shattering tragedy compels Subhash to return to India, where he endeavors to heal family wounds.

★ The **namesake**. Jhumpa Lahiri. Houghton Mifflin, 2003. 304 p.

ISBN 9780395927212

1. East Indian Americans — Social life and customs 2. Culture conflict 3. Immigrant families 4. College students 5. Young men 6. Massachusetts 7. Cambridge, Massachusetts 8. 20th century 9. Literary fiction 10. Books to movies 11. Adult books for young adults

LC 2003041718

New York Times Notable Book, 2003; School Library Journal Best Books: Best Adult Books 4 Teens, 2003

A portrait of the immigrant experience follows the Ganguli family from their traditional life in India through their arrival in Massachusetts in the late 1960s and their difficult melding into an American way of life.

"Its incorrigible mildness and its ungilded lilies aside, Lahiri's novel is unfailingly lovely in its treatment of Gogol's relationship with his father. This is the classic American parent-child bond." —*New York Times Book Review*

First published in Great Britain by Flamingo, 2003.

★ **Whereabouts**. Jhumpa Lahiri. Alfred A. Knopf, 2021. 176 p.

ISBN 9780593318317

1. Middle-aged women 2. College teachers 3. City life 4. Single women 5. City dwellers 6. Italy 7. Translations 8. Literary fiction 9. Psychological fiction

Follows the routines of a misfit city dweller who experiences a year of remarkable transformation in the aftermath of a parent's death.

"With a painterly interplay of light and shadows, Lahiri creates an in-isive and captivating evocation of the nature and nexus of place and elf." —*Booklist*

Translated from the Italian.

ai, Larissa

The **tiger** flu. Larissa Lai. Arsenal Pulp Press. 2018. 296 p.
ISBN 9781551527314
1. Survival 2. Epidemics 3. Women exiles 4. Quests 5. Villages 6. 22nd century 7. Apocalyptic fiction 8. Science fiction 9. Canadian fiction
Lambda Literary Award for Lesbian Fiction, 2019

After her lover dies of the tiger flu brought into their village, Kirilow, doctor, travels to the city to find a new "starfish," a person capable of egrowing organs.

alami, Laila

★ The **Moor's** account: a novel. Laila Lalami. Pantheon Books, 2014. 23 pages
ISBN 9780307911667
1. Narvaez, Panfilo de 2. Voyages and travels 3. Survival 4. Enslaved people 5. Slavery 6. Explorers 7. North America 8. Morocco 9. Historical fiction 10. Political fiction
LC 2013045255
Hurston/Wright Legacy Award: Fiction, 2015; New York Times Notable Book, 2014; Pulitzer Prize for Fiction finalist, 2015

A tale inspired by the experiences of the New World's first explorer of African descent describes how Moroccan slave Estebanico barely survives his early 16th-century expedition's encounters with storms, disease and hostile natives while traveling to the Gulf Coast and beyond.

"Estebanicos' account alternates between this disastrous mission and his past as a merchant, with the two threads combining to create a deeply layered, complex portrait of all-too-familiar characters in an unfamiliar world. The result is a totally engrossing and captivating novel that reconsiders the overlooked roles of Africans in New World exploration." —*Booklist*

Includes bibliographical references.

The **other** Americans: a novel. Laila Lalami. Pantheon Books, 2019. 20 pages
ISBN 9781524747145
1. Immigrant families 2. Family relationships 3. Hit-and-run accidents 4. Accident investigation 5. Immigration and emigration 6. Mojave Desert 7. California 8. Mysteries 9. Literary Fiction 10. Multiple perspectives
Kirkus Prize for Fiction finalist, 2019; National Book Award for Fiction finalist, 2019

The suspicious death of a Moroccan immigrant impacts the lives of a diverse cast of characters, including his jazz-composer daughter, an undocumented witness and an Iraqi War veteran. By the award-winning author of The Moor's Account.

"Though structured like a murder mystery, the novel delves into much deeper themes." —*Library Journal*

Lalli, Sonya

A **holly** jolly Diwali. Sonya Lalli. Berkley, 2021. 352 p.
ISBN 9780593100950
1. East Indian American women 2. Employees — Dismissal 3. Vacations 4. Divali 5. Cultural differences 6. Mumbai, India 7. Seattle, Washington 8. Holiday romances 9. Romantic comedies 10. Multicultural romances

LC 2021022207
A very practical, straightlaced twenty-eight-year-old, Niki Randhawa, attends a friend's wedding in India where she arrives in time to celebrate Diwali and meets a free-spirited London musician who helps her get in touch with her passionate and creative side.

"Funny and heartwarming, with lush descriptions of Indian beach resorts and chaotic city streets, Lalli's (Serena Singh Flips the Script, 2021) latest multicultural romance is extremely satisfying; her characters are refreshingly relatable." —*Booklist*

The **matchmaker's** list. Sonya Lalli. Berkley Books, 2019. 329 p.
ISBN 9780451490940
1. Immigrant families 2. Matchmaking 3. Grandmother and granddaughter 4. Harnack-Fish, Mildred 5. Culture conflict 6. Toronto, Ontario 7. Canada 8. Canadian fiction 9. Romantic comedies 10. Multicultural romances

Navigating a series of disastrous dates, Raina Anand attempts to balance her Indian-immigrant community's expectations with her personal idea of modern romance.

"Lalli's sharp-eyed tale of cross-cultural dating, family heartbreak, the strictures of culture, and the exuberance of love is both universal and timeless." —*Publishers Weekly*

Serena Singh flips the script. Sonya Lalli. Berkley, 2021. 352 p.
ISBN 9780593100936
1. Single women 2. Independence in women 3. Expectation (Psychology) 4. Success (Concept) 5. Thirties (Age) 6. Washington, D.C. 7. Relationship fiction 8. Canadian fiction
LC 2020045201
Serena Singh is tired of everyone telling her what she should want—and she is ready to prove to her mother, her sister, and the aunties in her community that a woman does not need domestic bliss to have a happy life.

"Heartfelt and forthright, Lalli's culturally rich work of women's fiction is exceptional." —*Booklist*

Landau, Alexis

Those who are saved. Alexis Landau. G. P. Putnam's Sons, 2021. 448 p.
ISBN 9780593190531
1. Jews, Russian 2. Separated friends, relatives, etc. 3. Family and war 4. Mothers and daughters 5. Rich people 6. France 7. United States 8. Second World War era (1939-1945) 9. 1940s 10. Historical fiction
LC 2020050296
Given hours to report to an internment camp when Nazis occupy France, a Jewish-Russian emigre places her young daughter in the care of a trusted governess before an unexpected opportunity to escape to America leads to a heartbreaking separation.

"Landau brilliantly explores the blurred lines between good and evil as the characters wrestle with their own dire decisions and the choices of those they love. Once this magnetic book takes hold, it doesn't let go." —*Publishers Weekly*

Landon, Sydney

Wishing for us. Sydney Landon. Berkley Sensation, 2016. 260 p. (Danvers novels, 9)
ISBN 9780399583209
1. Single fathers 2. Executives 3. Single women 4. Fiances — Death 5. Interpersonal attraction 6. Contemporary romances

When, after a wild Vegas bachelorette party, Lydia Cross wakes up next to corporate hotshot Jacob Hay—as his wife—she is shocked, especially when Jacob doesn't seem inclined to end their hasty merger, but instead wants to give her everything she's been missing in her life.

Landragin, Alex

★ **Crossings:**consisting of three manuscripts : The education ofa monster : City of ghosts : Tales of thealbatross. Alex Landragin. St. Martin's Press, 2020. Xviii, 359 pages
ISBN 9781250259042
1. Books and reading 2. Booksellers 3. Manuscripts 4. Rich women 5. World War II 6. Paris, France 7. France 8. Historical fiction 9. Australian fiction

LC 2019059177

A Parisian bookbinder stumbles across a manuscript containing three stories, each as unlikely as the other. The first, 'The Education of a Monster', is a letter penned by the poet Charles Baudelaire to an illiterate girl. The second, 'City of Ghosts', is a noir romance set in Paris in 1940 as the Germans are invading. The third, 'Tales of the Albatross', is the strangest of the three: the autobiography of a deathless enchantress. Together, they tell the tale of two lost souls peregrinating through time. An unforgettable tour de force, Crossings is a novel in three parts, designed to be read in two different directions, spanning a hundred and fifty years and seven lifetimes.

"This highly imaginative novel allows the reader to decide the order of the narrative. Read sequentially, the book is a related set of intersecting tales. Read as defined by a note to the reader, the book assumes an interleaved wholeness, with the end of the story occurring in the middle." —*Library Journal*

Originally published by Pan Macmillan Australia, 2019.

Landvik, Lorna

Chronicles of a radical hag: with recipes. Lorna Landvik. University of Minnesota Press, 2019. 320 p.
ISBN 9781517905996
1. Columnists 2. Newspapers 3. Small town life 4. Secrets 5. Journalists 6. Minnesota 7. Humorous stories 8. Relationship fiction 9. Gentle reads 10. Adult books for young adults

When beloved columnist Haze Evans falls into a coma, Susan McGrath, filling the void with Haze's past columns, stumbles upon secrets that have been locked in the files for decades.

Lane, Byron

★ **A star** is bored. Byron Lane. Henry Holt & Co 2020. 352 pages
ISBN 9781250266491
1. Actors and actresses 2. Personal assistants 3. Austen, Cassandra 4. Fame 5. Addiction 6. Hollywood, California 7. California 8. Relationship fiction

LC 2019057802

A debut novel by Carrie Fisher's former personal assistant follows the experiences of an assistant to an award-winning celebrity who becomes a close friend and possibly more as she conducts him through the wonders of Hollywood life.

"A funny, tender-hearted, and humane Hollywood story." —*Booklist*

Langan, Sarah

Good neighbors. Sarah Langan. Atria Books, 2021. 288 p.
ISBN 9781982144364
1. Neighborhoods 2. Female friendship 3. Suburban life 4. Musicians 5. Secrets 6. Literary fiction

A too-fast friendship between a repressed queen bee and the ostracized wife of a once-famous rock musician explodes into a community uprising involving a dangerous sinkhole, a trapped child and shocking accusations.

"This sharp, propulsive novel pulls off a maximalist variation on suburban gossip gone wrong." —*Publishers Weekly*

Lange, Tracey

★ **We** are the Brennans. Tracey Lange. Celadon Books, 2021. 274 p.
ISBN 9781250796226
1. Catholic families 2. Irish Americans 3. Single women 4. Separated friends, relatives, etc. 5. Drunk drivers 6. Westchester County, New York 7. Los Angeles, California 8. Literary fiction 9. Domestic fiction
LC 2021005982

Returning to the east coast to recover from a drunk driving accident she caused, 29-year-old Sunday Brennan must protect her family from a man from her past who brings her family's pub business to the brink of financial ruin.

"Lange's narrative perspectives are keenly realized, and she keeps all of the Brennans sizzling with humanity while they grapple with familial loyalty. Fans of intense family dramas are in for a treat." —*Publishers Weekly*

Lansdale, Joe R.

The **bottoms**. Joe R. Lansdale. Mysterious Press, 2000. 328 p.
ISBN 9780892967049
1. Serial murders 2. Depressions 3. Serial murderers 4. Eleven-year-old boys 5. Nine-year-old girls 6. East Texas 7. Texas 8. 1930s 9. Mysteries 10. Coming-of-age stories 11. Southern fiction 12. Adult books for young adults

LC 32886

Edgar Allan Poe Award for Best Mystery Novel, 2001; New York Times Notable Mysteries, 2000

When young Harry Crane stumbles upon a mutilated body in the local river bottoms, the region becomes trapped in a nightmare of fear and racial tension, as a vicious serial killer stalks the town.

"An emotionally charged tale very reminiscent of To Kill a Mockingbird. Effectively combining mystery and family history, it offers a vivid, multifaceted glimpse back to a simpler, but not necessarily better, time." —*Booklist*

Devil red. Joe R. Lansdale. Knopf, 2011. 288 p. (Hap Collins and Leonard Pine novels, 8)
ISBN 9780307270986
1. Cults 2. Cold cases (Criminal investigation) 3. Serial murders 4. Inheritance and succession 5. Vampires 6. Texas 7. Mysteries
LC 2010047476

Investigating a cold-case double murder to earn extra cash, amateur detectives Hap and Leonard discover that one of the victims was a member of a vampire cult and that many similar killings have taken place.

"Nobody's better at smacking us with the look, feel, and smell of derring-do. Along the way, there is the usual camaraderie, banter, and sex." —*Library Journal*

Edge of dark water. Joe R. Lansdale. Mulholland Books/Little, Brown and Co, 2012. 288 p.
ISBN 9780316188432
1. Female friendship 2. Friends' death 3. Small towns 4. Murder victims 5. Murder investigation 6. Depression era (1929-1941) 7. 1930s 8. Historical fiction 9. Adult books for young adults
LC 2011030557

Booklist Editors' Choice: Adult Books for Young Adults, 2012

Trying to escape her worthless life leads to unexpected and disastrous consequences when Sue Ellen steals money and a raft and embarks on a journey to dig up her best friend's body, burn it, and sprinkle the ashes in Hollywood.

Honky tonk samurai. Joe R. Lansdale. Mulholland Books, 2016. 352 p. (Hap Collins and Leonard Pine novels, 11)
ISBN 9780316329408
1. Cold cases (Criminal investigation) 2. Missing persons investigation 3. Prostitutes 4. Extortion 5. Interracial friendship 6. Texas 7. Mysteries
Blackmailed into accepting a missing-persons cold case, rebel Hap and gay veteran Leonard search for their client's long-missing grand-daughter, who they discover was involved in a prostitution ring.
"This shambolic, action-packed novel will ensnare new readers and satisfy devoted fans alike." —*Publishers Weekly*

More better deals. Joe R. Lansdale. Mulholland Books, 2020. 288 p.
ISBN 9780316479912
1. Multiracial men 2. Passing (Identity) 3. Used car selling 4. Femmes fatales 5. Extramarital affairs 6. East Texas 7. Texas 8. 1960s 9. Noir fiction 10. Adaptations, retellings, and spin-offs
Dispatched to repossess a Cadillac from a deadbeat pet-cemetery owner and his beautiful wife, an unscrupulous used-car salesman embarks on an affair that tests the limits of his character. By the Edgar Award-winning author of The Bottoms.
"Populated with an admirable array of laughable miscreants, this droll, savage novel is vintage Lansdale. The author's storytelling powers remain as strong as ever." —*Publishers Weekly*

★ **Paradise** sky. Joe R. Lansdale. Mullholland Books, 2015. 416 p.
ISBN 9780316329378
1. Love, Nat 2. African American cowboys 3. Frontier and pioneer life 4. African Americans — Social conditions 5. Misunderstanding 6. Race relations 7. Texas 8. South Dakota 9. Westerns 10. Biographical fiction
Library Journal Best Books, 2015; Spur Awards, Best Western Historical Novel, 2016; RUSA Reading List Short List, 2016
On the run after an infamous landowner murders his father, Willie becomes an expert marksman before turning Buffalo Soldier, befriending Wild Bill Hickok and earning the nickname "Deadwood Dick."
"Loosely based on the true story of African American cowboy Nat Love (1854-1921), this fast-paced Western with its multicultural cast of characters is a winner." —*Library Journal*

Sunset and sawdust. Joe R. Lansdale. Alfred A. Knopf, 2004. 320 p.
ISBN 9780375414534
1. Women sheriffs 2. Pregnant women 3. Depressions 4. Murder investigation 5. Policewomen 6. East Texas 7. Depression era (1929-1941) 8. Historical mysteries 9. Mysteries
LC 2003060478
Sunset Jones has just killed her husband. Never mind that he was raping her. Pete Jones was constable of a small sawmill settlement called Camp Rapture, where no woman refuses her husband. So everyone is angrily surprised when, thanks to the amazing understanding of her mother-in-law—who owns three-quarters of the mill—Sunset becomes the new constable and begins to investigate the murders of a woman and unborn baby in which her late husband might be implicated. Yet, no one is more surprised than Sunset when the murders lead her—through a labyrinth of greed, corruption, and unspeakable malice—not only to the conclusion of the case, but to a well of inner strength she never knew she had.
The mystery is only mildly engrossing here; the great pleasure of Lansdale's work lies in his pitch-perfect vernacular prose.... The book opens with a cyclone, ends with a plague of grasshoppers and in between there's insanity, extreme violence, sex, grotesques aplenty and an excellent dog. What's not to like? Publishers Weekly.

The **thicket**. Joe R. Lansdale. Mulholland Books, 2013. 288 p.
ISBN 9780316188456
1. Orphans 2. Kidnapping 3. Outlaws 4. Siblings 5. Bounty hunters 6. East Texas 7. 1930s 8. Adventure stories 9. Historical mysteries 10. Adult books for young adults
LC 2013016949
Library Journal Best Books, 2013
Recently orphaned, Jack Parker witnesses his grandfather's murder and his sister's kidnapping by bank robbers while traveling to his uncle's farm in East Texas and vows revenge.

Larison, John
Whiskey when we're dry. John Larison. Viking Press, 2018. 400 p.
ISBN 9780735220447
1. Women sharpshooters 2. Male impersonators 3. Outlaws 4. Orphans 5. Teenage girls 6. The West (United States) 7. American Westward Expansion (1803-1899) 8. Westerns 9. Coming-of-age stories 10. Literary fiction 11. Adult books for young adults
Facing starvation and worse when she is orphaned on her family's 1885 homestead, a 17-year-old sharpshooter cuts off her hair and disguises herself as a boy to journey across the mountains in search of her outlaw brother.

Larkin, Allie
The **people** we keep. Allison Larkin. Gallery Books, 2021. 352 p.
ISBN 9781982171292
1. Teenage girl musicians 2. Voyages and travels 3. Home (Concept) 4. Belonging 5. Growing up 6. New York (State) 7. 1990s 8. Coming-of-age stories
Chronicling her life in the songs she writes, April Sawicki, after leaving home for good, finds her way to Ithaca, New York where she finally finds a sense of belonging but cannot shake the feeling that she'll hurt her new friends that way she's been hurt.
"The depiction of the mid-1990s is pitch-perfect and will invoke feelings of nostalgia, especially in Gen Xers who came of age during this era." —*Booklist*

Larkwood, A. K.
The **unspoken** name. A. K. Larkwood. Tor, 2020. 448 p. (Serpent Gates, 1)
ISBN 9781250238900
1. Wizards 2. Women bodyguards 3. Interdimensional travel 4. Women warriors 5. Gods and goddesses 6. Fantasy fiction 7. Adult books for young adults
LC 2019042768
Destined to become a sacrifice on behalf of her superstitious people, Csorwe accepts a powerful mage's alternate offer to become his bodyguard and spy to help him reclaim his power in the land from where he was exiled.
"Larkwood's intricately woven plot is jam-packed with intrigue and excitement. Lyrical, immersive prose masterfully conveys complex worldbuilding. Epic fantasy fans are sure to be impressed by this expertly crafted adventure." —*Publishers Weekly*

Larsen, Nella
Passing. By Nella Larsen. Modern Library, 2002. 215 p.
ISBN 9780375758133
1. African American women — Identity 2. Identity (Psychology) 3. Race relations 4. Middle class women 5. Married women 6. Harlem,

New York City 7. New York City 8. 1920s 9. Books to movies 10. Psychological fiction 11. Literary fiction

LC 29009990

Irene Redfield is living an affluent life with her husband and children in the thriving African American enclave of Harlem in the 1920s—until she runs into her childhood friend, Clare Kendry. Clare has been passing for a white woman, married to a racist man who does not know about his wife's real identity. Irene is both fascinated and repulsed by Clare's secret, and in turn, Clare yearns for Irene's sense of ease and security with her Black identity. Clare begins to insert herself and her deception into every part of Irene's stable existence, and their complex reunion sets off a chain of events that dynamically alters both women forever.

"This is a shrewdly conceived and finely executed novella that raises questions not only of racial identity in a realistically rendered middle and upper-middle-class Negro society (in Harlem and Chicago, 1927) but of the murderous rage one woman might feel for another who has passed beyond her." —*The New York Review of Books*

Originally published: New York : A.A. Knopf, 1929.

This book was made into the 2021 film of the same name.

Larsen, Reif

I am Radar: a novel. Reif Larsen. Penguin Press, 2015. 656 p.

ISBN 9781594206160

1. Protest art 2. Secret societies 3. Human skin color 4. Puppetry 5. Young men 6. New Jersey 7. Norway 8. Literary fiction

Born inexplicably to white parents, black youth Radar falls in with a secretive group of scientific puppeteers who stage experimental art in the world's war zones, where he is forced to confront the true nature of his identity.

"If Larsen's story makes demands of its readers, it also offers plenty of rewards. Imaginative, original, nicely surreal—and hyperpigmentarily so." —*Kirkus*

Larsson, Stieg

★ The **girl** who kicked the hornet's nest. By Stieg Larsson; translated from the Swedish by Reg Keeland. Alfred A. Knopf, 2010. 512 pages (Millennium novels (Stieg Larsson), 3)

ISBN 9780307269997

1. Political corruption 2. Revenge 3. Gunshot wounds 4. Murder investigation 5. Conspiracies 6. Sweden 7. Mysteries 8. Translations 9. Books to movies

LC 2010006361

Goodreads Choice Award, 2010; New York Times Notable Book, 2010

Lisbeth Salander is in the intensive care unit of a provincial Swedish city hospital, fighting for her life in more ways than one: when she's well enough, she'll stand trial for a triple murder. While journalist Mikael Blomkvist helps to prove her innocence, Lisbeth plots her revenge against the man who tried to kill her, and the government institutions that very nearly destroyed her life.

Sequel to: The girl who played with fire.

Translation of Luftslottet som sprangdes. Originally published: Stockholm : Norstedts, 2007.

The **girl** who played with fire. By Stieg Larsson; translated from the Swedish by Reg Keeland. Alfred A. Knopf, 2009. 512 pages (Millennium novels (Stieg Larsson), 2)

ISBN 9780307269980

1. Sexual slavery 2. Murder 3. Police misconduct 4. Murder investigation 5. Sex industry and trade 6. Sweden 7. Mysteries 8. Translations 9. Books to movies

Goodreads Choice Award, 2009

On the eve of the publication of a sex-trafficking exposé, two reporters responsible for the magazine story are murdered, and the fingerprints on the murder weapon belong to Lisbeth Salander, a genius hacker, prompting the magazine's publisher, Mikael Blomkvist, to launch his own investigation to vindicate Lisbeth, just as she becomes the prey of a murderous hunt.

"For all the complications of the melodramatic story, which advances at a brisk, violently cinematic clip in Reg Keeland's translation, it's clear where Larsson's strongest interests lie in his heroine and the ill-concealed attitudes she brings out in men." —*New York Times Book Review*

Translation from the Swedish of: Flickan som lekte med elden.

Originally published: Stockholm : Norstedts, 2006.

The **girl** with the dragon tattoo. By Stieg Larsson; translated from the Swedish by Reg Keeland. Alfred A. Knopf, 2008. 480 pages (Millennium novels (Stieg Larsson), 1)

ISBN 9780307269751

1. Murder investigation 2. Missing persons 3. Violence against women 4. Cold cases (Criminal investigation) 5. Investigative journalists 6. Sweden 7. Scandinavian crime fiction 8. Mysteries 9. Translations

LC 2008017771

Anthony Award for Best First Novel, 2009; British Book Award for Crime Thriller of the Year, 2009; Library Journal Best Books, 2008; Macavity Award for Best First Mystery Novel, 2009

Journalist Mikael Blomkvist and hacker Lisbeth Salander investigate the disappearance of Harriet Vanger, which took place forty years ago.

"First title in the author's Millennium trilogy. Convicted of libeling a prominent businessman and awaiting imprisonment, financial journalist Mikael Blomkvist agrees to industrialist Henrik Vanger's request to investigate the 40-year-old disappearance of Vanger's 16-year-old niece, Harriet. In return, Vanger will help Blomkvist dig up dirt on the corrupt businessman. Assisting in Blomkvist's investigation is 24-year-old Lisbeth Salander, a brilliant but enigmatic computer hacker." —*Library Journal*

Originally published as: Man som hatar kvinnor. Stockholm : Norstedt, 2005.

Lasdun, James

Afternoon of a faun: a novel. James Lasdun. W. W. Norton & Co, 2019. 160 p.

ISBN 9781324001942

1. Rape 2. Truth 3. Journalists 4. Loyalty 5. Secrets 6. New York City 7. 2010s 8. Literary fiction 9. Psychological fiction 10. First person narratives

LC 2018057124

When his expat journalist friend is accused of sexual assault in a former girlfriend's memoir, a man finds himself caught between loyalty and an urgent desire to uncover the truth.

Laskowski, Tara

The **mother** next door. Tara Laskowski. Graydon House, 2021. 320 p.

ISBN 9781525804700

1. Mothers 2. Women journalists 3. Suburban life 4. Cliques 5. Suburbs 6. Washington, D.C. 7. Psychological suspense 8. Multiple perspectives

"Smartly paced, menacing, full of bizarre twists, and offering a collection of thoroughly fascinating (if sometimes a mite loathsome) characters, this is a fine domestic thriller." —*Booklist*

Lattari, Katie

Dark things I adore. Katie Lattari. Sourcebooks, 2021. 400 p.
ISBN 9781728229843
1. Graduate students 2. Women painters 3. Secrets 4. Ambition 5. College teachers 6. Maine 7. 1990s 8. 2010s 9. Psychological suspense 10. First person narratives
LC 2020056407

Loan Stars Favourites, 2021

A group of outcasts gather at an arts camp in the Maine woods, but secrets and dark ambitions rise like smoke from a campfire, and the truths they tell will come back to haunt them in ways more deadly than they dreamed.

"Lattari's unreliable narrator pivots between present and past. This vengeful tale that pits artistic genius against mental health and happiness will captivate fans of dark suspense." —*Library Journal*

Lau, Jackie

Donut fall in love. Jackie Lau. Jove, 2021. 304 p.
ISBN 9780593334300
1. Actors and actresses 2. Women bakers 3. Loss (Psychology) 4. Interpersonal attraction 5. Baking 6. Toronto, Ontario 7. Romantic comedies 8. Contemporary romances
LC 2021012850

Actor Ryan Kwok is back in Toronto after the promotional tour for his latest film, a rom-com that is getting less-than-stellar reviews. After the sudden death of his mother and years of constant work, Ryan is taking some much-needed time off. But as he tries to be supportive to his family, he struggles with his loss and doesn't know how to talk to his dad—who now trolls him on Twitter instead of meeting him for dim sum. Innovative baker Lindsay McLeod meets Ryan when he knocks over two dozen specialty donuts at her bakery. Their relationship is off to a messy start, but there's no denying their immediate attraction. When Ryan signs up for a celebrity episode of Baking Fail, he asks Lindsay to teach him how to bake and she agrees. As Lindsay and Ryan spend time together, bonding over grief and bubble tea, it starts to feel like they're cooking up something sweeter than cupcakes in the kitchen.

"While the connection between Ryan and Lindsay takes center stage, author Lau tackles big issues—Asian representation in media, male body image, grief, postpartum depression, complicated family dynamics—with skill and heart. A warm treat with just enough spice and complexity to temper the sweetness." —*Kirkus*

Laukkanen, Owen

Deception Cove. Owen Laukkanen. Mulholland Books 2019. 372 p. (Neah Bay novels, 1)
ISBN 9780316448703
1. Widows 2. Police corruption 3. Afghan War veterans 4. Sheriffs 5. Rescues 6. Thrillers and suspense

A recently widowed marine suffering PTSD from her time in Afghanistan has her service dog kidnapped by a corrupt deputy sheriff who wants to blackmail her into delivering goods allegedly stolen by her husband before his death.

Gale force. Owen Laukkanen. G. P. Putnam's Sons, 2018. 384 p.
ISBN 9780735212633
1. Women ship captains 2. Organized crime 3. Ocean travel 4. Deep-sea sounding 5. Salvage 6. Alaska 7. Thrillers and suspense
LC 2017020483

Playing it safe in spite of significantly reduced profits after witnessing her father's death in a freak maritime accident and assuming his rank as captain of an Alaskan salvage boat, McKenna and her crew take a last-chance job helping an imperiled freighter only to discover that it contains valuable cargo that is being targeted by powerful enemies.

Lone Jack Trail. Owen Laukkanen. Mulholland Books, 2020. 352 p. (Neah Bay novels, 2)
ISBN 9780316448758
1. Women veterans 2. Women detectives 3. Couples 4. Former convicts 5. Women and dogs 6. Washington (State) 7. Thrillers and suspense 8. Canadian fiction

A veteran Marine and an ex-convict find themselves on opposite sides of the law.

"Laukkanen brilliantly integrates psychological depth into a suspenseful whodunit plot in his superior sequel to 2019's Deception Cove." —*Publishers Weekly*

Laureano, C. E.

★ The **Saturday** Night Supper Club. Carla Laureano. Tyndale House Pub 2018. 416 p. (Saturday Night Supper Club novels, 1)
ISBN 9781496428271
1. Women cooks 2. Ambition in women 3. Journalists 4. Reputation 5. Dinners and dining 6. Denver, Colorado 7. Christian romances
LC 2017049829

RITA Award, 2019

After an essay he writes results in chef Rachel Bishop's firing, a repentent Alex Kanin partners with Rachel to host an exclusive pop-up dinner party that they hope will restore her career.

Lauren, Christina

Dating you / Hating you. Christina Lauren. Gallery Books, 2017. 320 p.
ISBN 9781501165818
1. Talent agents 2. Coworkers 3. Workaholics 4. Competition 5. Love-hate relationships 6. Hollywood, California 7. Contemporary romances 8. Romantic comedies

Sparks fly when Hollywood agents Carter and Evie meet at a party (dressed as Harry Potter and Hermione Granger, respectively). Then their agencies merge, turning them into bitter rivals as they compete for the same job.

First published in the US in 2017 by Gallery Books, an imprint of Simon & Schuster, Inc.

In a holidaze. Christina Lauren. Gallery Books, 2020. 320 pages
ISBN 9781982163631
1. Single women 2. Brothers 3. Wishing and wishes 4. Life change events 5. Crushes (Interpersonal relations) 6. Utah 7. Romantic comedies 8. Holiday romances

One Christmas wish, two brothers, and a lifetime of hope are on the line for hapless Maelyn Jones.

"Down-on-her-luck Maelyn is a likable protagonist, and it's easy to relate to her desire to fix her life (even if most readers don't have the benefit of time travel). Her conversations with Andrew are adorably banter-filled, and her relationship with her parents' friend Benny, an aging, wacky stoner, is sweetly charming." —*Kirkus*

Roomies. Christina Lauren. Gallery Books, 2017. 358 p.
ISBN 9781501165832
1. Irish in the United States 2. Musicians 3. Women authors 4. Visas 5. Immigrants 6. New York City 7. Contemporary romances
LC 2017036788

When a struggling musician on the brink of stardom reveals he is in the country illegally, besotted Holland Bakker enters a marriage of convenience that becomes more real than either anticipated.

The **soulmate** equation. Christina Lauren. Gallery Books, 2021. 368 p. ISBN 9781982123963
1. Women statisticians 2. Single mothers 3. Matchmaking 4. Application software 5. Geneticists 6. San Diego, California 7. California 8. Romantic comedies 9. Contemporary romances
Perfect for fans of The Rosie Project and One Plus One, this entertaining novel follows single mom and data and statistics wizard Jess Davis as she, using a revolutionary new scientific dating app, is matched with the app's arrogant creator who is not what he seems.
"With the laugh-out-loud voice that Lauren's die-hard fans adore, this sweet, charming, and humorous book is a perfect match for readers looking for a low-stakes, high swoon-factor romance, but some readers may have concerns about the ethical implications of DNA-based matchmaking." —*Library Journal*

Laurens, Stephanie

The **pursuits** of Lord Kit Cavanaugh. Stephanie Laurens. Harlequin Books 2019. 330 p. (Cavanaughs (Stephanie Laurens), 2)
ISBN 9780778369899
1. Schools 2. Nobility 3. Sabotage 4. Yachts 5. Business competition 6. England 7. Victorian era (1837-1901) 8. 19th century 9. Victorian romances 10. Historical romances 11. Australian fiction
Kit Cavanugh and Sylvia Buckleberry fight to secure her school and to expose the blackguard trying to sabotage his yacht business; yet an even more dastardly villain lurks, one who threatens the future both discover they now hold dear.
"Laurens' subtle nods to forgiveness, community-building, and second chances lend extra character and warmth to a winning love story." —*Kirkus*

Lawler, Liz

Don't wake up. Liz Lawler. Harper Paperbacks, 2019. 368 p. ISBN 9780062886224
1. Rape victims 2. Violence against women 3. Skepticism 4. Women physicians 5. Memory 6. England 7. Psychological suspense
Dr. Alex Taylor awakens after an assault with no physical proof of the attack and must try to convince everyone of what really happened.
Originally published: London : Twenty7 Books, 2017.

Lawrence, D. H.

★ **Lady** Chatterley's lover. D.H. Lawrence; with an afterword by Harry T. Moore. Penguin, 1962. 299 p.
ISBN 9780451524980
1. Extramarital affairs 2. Interclass romance 3. Married women 4. Sexual ethics 5. Sexuality 6. England 7. Literary fiction 8. Erotic fiction 9. Modern classics
Bold, passionate, and erotic, this classic tale of love and discovery pits the paralyzed and callous Clifford Chatterley against his indecisive wife and her persuasive lover.

Sons and lovers. D.H. Lawrence. Penguin Classics, 2010. 420 p.
ISBN 9780141195445
1. Mothers and sons 2. Young men 3. Family relationships 4. Marriage 5. Sexuality 6. England 7. Nottingham, England 8. Literary fiction 9. Coming-of-age stories 10. Books to movies
LC 13021105

Under the shadow of his parents' unsatisfactory marriage and the profound influence of his mother, Paul Morel faces a painful struggle to emancipate himself. His spiritual friendship with Miriam Lievers and a passionate sexual awakening with Clara Dawes together with the anguish caused by his mother's death, brings Paul Morel to manhood.

Women in love. Cambridge University Press, 1988. 448 p.
ISBN 9780521235655
1. Women — Sexuality 2. Man-woman relationships 3. Ideas (Philosophy) 4. Sisters 5. Sexuality 6. Saunders, Mary 7. 1900s (Decade) 8. Love stories 9. Literary fiction 10. Books to movies
LC 85031367
Women in Love follows the passionate relationships of two sisters Gudrun and Ursula Brangwen, with their respective lovers, the ominous Gerald Crich and the charismatic but fragile Rupert Birkin. Beginning in a narrow-minded English colliery town and culminating amidst the ice and snow of the Alps, the abortive alliance between the two men and the couples' affairs are played out against the derangements of industrialism and the need to find new ways of living and better ways of dying.
The 2nd volume of the author's trilogy, the 1st of which in The rainbow, and the 3rd, Aaron's rod.
Originally published: London : Thomas Seltzer, 1920.

Lawrence, David

The **dead** sit round in a ring. David Lawrence. Thomas Dunne Books, 2004. 448 p. (Stella Mooney mysteries, 1)
ISBN 9780312327101
1. Policewomen 2. Police 3. Mafia 4. Prostitutes 5. Serbs in England 6. London, England 7. Mysteries
LC 2004041878
"This mystery offers a perspective on London that is darker and grittier than in conventional treatments. But the writing is the thing. Whether he's describing a bizarre death scene...or observing a group of streetwalkers plying their night trade...Lawrence, a published poet, writes with a delicacy and restraint rare in the genre." —*New York Times Book Review*
Published in 2005 in paperback as: Circle of the dead.

Lawson, Mary

Crow Lake. Mary Lawson. Dial Press, 2002. 288 p.
ISBN 9780385336116
1. Women zoologists 2. Siblings 3. Rural families 4. Farm life 5. Orphans 6. Ontario 7. Psychological fiction 8. Canadian fiction 9. Adult books for young adults
LC 2001053779
Alex Award, 2003; Books in Canada First Novel Award, 2002; Evergreen Award (Ontario), 2005; New York Times Notable Book, 2002
"Lawson achieves a breathless anticipatory quality in her surprisingly adept first novel, in which a child tells the story, but tells it very well indeed." —*Booklist*

Lawton, John

Hammer to fall. John Lawton. Atlantic Monthly Press, 2020. 352 p. (Joe Wilderness novels, 3)
ISBN 9780802148124
1. Espionage 2. Intelligence service 3. International intrigue 4. Smuggling 5. KGB agents 6. London, England 7. Finland 8. 1960s 9. Thrillers and suspense 10. Spy fiction
LC 2019045235

Posted in disgrace to remote northern Finland under the guise of a cultural exchange representative, 1960s MI6 spy Joe Wilderness earns money on the side as a vodka smuggler before uncovering a mining operation with possible atomic ties.

"Lawton does a brilliant job of incorporating backstory here, deepening our understanding of and feelings for rule-breaking Joe, who cares more for people than governments, while delivering a jaw-dropping finale that will leave readers palpitating for more." —*Booklist*

Then we take Berlin. John Lawton. Grove/Atlantic, 2013. 400 p. (Joe Wilderness novels, 1)
ISBN 9780802121967
1. Private investigators 2. Swindlers and swindling 3. Former spies 4. Smuggling 5. Royal Air Force veterans 6. Berlin, Germany 7. 1960s 8. Historical fiction 9. Crime fiction
In 1963, freelance P.I. Joe Wilderness, a former MI6 agent and black market con-artist, agrees to one last Berlin scam, which involves smuggling people and brings the old gang back together once again.

Layden, Emily
All girls. Emily Layden. St. Martin's Press, 2021. 320 p.
ISBN 9781250270894
1. Teenage girls 2. Rape 3. Girl boarding school students 4. Rape suspects 5. Scandals 6. Connecticut 7. Coming-of-age stories 8. Multiple perspectives
LC 2020037485
Nine young women embark on personal and scholarly journeys of self-discovery at a prestigious New England prep school, where their evolving voices are shaped by a scandal that the administration would cover up.
"An important take on sexuality and #MeToo from the perspective of the young, including many references to pop culture and social media." —*Library Journal*

Laymon, Kiese
Long division. Kiese Laymon. Bolden, 2013. 270 pages
ISBN 9781932841725
1. Contests 2. Missing persons 3. Books 4. Small towns 5. Internet broadcasting 6. Mississippi 7. 1960s 8. 1980s 9. Coming-of-age stories 10. African American fiction 11. Southern fiction 12. Adult books for young adults
School Library Journal Best Books: Best Adult Books 4 Teens, 2013; William Saroyan International Prize for Writing, Fiction category, 2014
A teenager in post-Katrina Mississippi discovers the whereabouts of a missing young girl after finding a strange, authorless book that describes how a young couple time travel from 1964 to 1985 to help a friend.
"A revised version of Laymon's elliptical, time-folding work of metafiction about Southern racism. The first novel by Laymon, initially published in 2013, is effectively two novels, both potent yet often funny character studies." —*Kirkus*

Layne, Lauren
Passion on Park Avenue. Lauren Layne. Gallery Books, 2019. 288 p. (Central Park pact, 1)
ISBN 9781501191572
1. Women executives 2. Rich men 3. Interpersonal attraction 4. Elite (Social sciences) 5. Misfits (Persons) 6. Upper East Side, New York City 7. New York City 8. Contemporary romances
LC 2018045881

Naomi Powell, the strong-willed CEO of one of the biggest jewelry empires in the country, fights to find her place in Manhattan's upper class while engaging in a battle of wits with her new neighbor—and former childhood tormentor—Oliver Cunningham.

Le Carre, John
Agent running in the field. John Le Carre. Viking Press, 2019. 281 pages
ISBN 9781984878878
1. Political intrigue 2. Spies 3. Intelligence service 4. Middle-aged persons 5. Young men 6. London, England 7. 2010s 8. Spy fiction
LC 2019037844
Desperate to resist the political turbulence of his 2018 London home, a young man establishes connections that lead him down a dark and dangerous path.

The **constant** gardener: a novel. John Le Carre. Scribner, 2010. 492 p.
ISBN 9780743215053
1. International businesses — Corrupt practices 2. Diplomats 3. Pharmaceutical research — Corrupt practices 4. Conspiracies 5. Business — Corrupt practices 6. Kenya 7. Political thrillers 8. Thrillers and suspense 9. Books to movies
LC 53340
When the young and beautiful wife of a much older embassy worker and amateur gardener is found murdered near northern Kenya's Lake Turkana, his personal pursuit of the killers not only sets him up as their next target, but as a suspect among his embassy colleagues.
"Globalization in its uglier aspects...has replaced the Cold War as the moral backdrop in Le Carre's work. His Cold War novels did not spare the conscience even of citizens on the 'right' side, confronting them with crimes committed in their names, and the globalization novels do not spare the stockholder." —*The Atlantic*
Also published: Toronto : Penguin Group Canada, 2010, c2001.

★ A **delicate** truth. John Le Carre. Viking, 2013. 432 p.
ISBN 9780670014897
1. Terrorism — Prevention 2. Government cover-ups 3. Arms dealers 4. Political corruption 5. Conspiracies 6. Spy fiction
Three years after the launch of a delicate counter-terrorist operation organized to capture a high-value jihadist arms buyer, a disgraced Special Forces solider delivers a message that raises questions about the operation's success and a possible cover-up, a situation that forces the soldier to choose between his conscience and his duty.

★ The **honourable** schoolboy. John le Carre. Knopf, 1977. 533 p; (George Smiley novels, 6)
ISBN 9780394416458
1. Spies 2. Intelligence service 3. Cold War 4. Smiley, George (Fictitious character) 5. 1970s 6. Spy fiction
LC 77075001
Gold Dagger Award for Best Crime Novel of the Year, 1977; James Tait Black Memorial Prize for Fiction, 1977
George Smiley, of England's Secret Service, goes onto the attack, manipulating old Asian hand Jerry Westerby through the Far East and a tangle of money, defection, passion, loyalty, and love that tests severely Westerby's hitherto unfaltering allegiances.
"This is superbly well-organized, combining a grandiose sweep with an intricate pattern. It has hard-edged reality instead of fuzzy near-fantasy, a host of sharply etched characters instead of a few eccentric caricatures, and a style which, subtle and flexible...never obtrudes, yet never goes unnoticed." —*Times Literary Supplement*

A **most** wanted man: a novel. John Le Carre. Scribner, 2008. 323 p.
ISBN 9781416594888

1. Intelligence officers 2. War on Terrorism, 2001-2009 3. Spies 4. Terrorism 5. Muslims 6. Germany 7. Thrillers and suspense 8. Spy fiction 9. Books to movies

LC 2008030704

New York Times Notable Book, 2008

Smuggled into Hamburg, Issa, a young Russian man carrying a large amount of cash and claiming to be a devout Muslim, forms an unlikely alliance with Annabel, an idealistic young German civil rights lawyer, and Tommy Brue, a sixty-year-old scion of a failing British bank, as they become victims of rival intelligence operations in the War on Terror.

"Le Carre's dialogue has snap, rhythm and wit, particularly in those passages where intelligence chiefs maneuver to gain an edge on each other. Too, his immaculate timing helps him fold in different plot lines without smudging narrative pace and tone. Ever the spymaster, he also differentiates the challenges faced by spies today from those of their Cold War counterparts." —*St. Louis Post-Dispatch*

Title adapted into a film by the same name (2013).

★ **Our** kind of traitor: a novel. John Le Carre. Viking, 2010. 305 p.
ISBN 9780670022243
1. Mafia 2. Spies 3. Money laundering 4. Defectors 5. Vacations 6. Antigua and Barbuda 7. Spy fiction 8. Thrillers and suspense

LC 2010019513

Vacationing at a posh tennis resort in Antigua, Perry and Gail are recruited by big-time Russian money launderer Dima to help him defect, an arrangement for which Dima promises to expose financial corruption but renders the hapless couple pawns in a deadly international scheme.

"Le Carre seems positively re-invigorated in a retro sort of way. The story carries on with an extra spring in the step that harkens back, both in the manner of plotting and the style, to Le Carre's earliest and still greatest novels. That's due in large part to how he engages with current events: the teetering economy, Britain (and Europe's) austerity-oriented response, and the rise of state surveillance even as the events of September 11 grow more distant." —*Daily Beast*

Smiley's people. John le Carre. Knopf, 1980. 374 p; (George Smiley novels, 7)
ISBN 9780394508436
1. Spies 2. Intelligence service 3. International intrigue 4. Smiley, George (Fictitious character) 5. Spy fiction 6. Books to TV

LC 79002299

"This novel is a complete winner, exciting, well-paced, and convincing.... There is a lot of the Le Carre gloom, but now it seems almost elegiac and touching. Absolutely not to be missed." —*Library Journal*

The **spy** who came in from the cold. John Le Carre. Coward, McCann & Geoghegan, 1978. 256 p. (George Smiley novels, 3)
ISBN 9780698109162
1. Spies 2. Intelligence service 3. Double agents 4. Cold War 5. Smiley, George (Fictitious character) 6. Berlin, Germany 7. Spy fiction 8. Books to movies

LC 78001799

Edgar Allan Poe Award for Best Mystery Novel, 1965; Gold Dagger Award for Best Crime Novel of the Year, 1963; Somerset Maugham Award, 1964

Secret agent Leamas is on a mission in East Berlin, but he has doubts about the organization he serves.

"The story of Alec Leamas, 50-year-old professional secret agent who has grown stale in espionage, who longs to come in from the cold and how he undertakes one last assignment before that hoped-for retirement. Over the years Leamas has grown unsure where his workday carapace ends and his real self begins.... Recalled from Berlin after the death of his last East German contact at the Wall, Leamas lets himself be seduced into a pretended defection—thereby providing the East Germans with data

from which they can deduce that the head of their own spy apparatus is a double agent." —*New York Times Book Review*

Originally published: London : Victor Gollancz, 1963.
First published: London : Victor Gollancz, 1963.

The **tailor** of Panama. John le Carre. Alfred A. Knopf, 1996. 331 p. : Map
ISBN 9780679454465
1. Conspiracies 2. Spies 3. Secret identity 4. British in Panama 5. Tailors 6. Panama 7. 1980s 8. Spy fiction 9. Books to movies

LC 96034802

Seldom has the hidden eye of British Intelligence selected such an unlikely champion as Harry Pendel, a British tailor living in Panama City.

"Le Carre reveals in the contortions of British diplomats, aghast at the arriviste spy masters whom they pretend to accept, all the while struggling to extricate themselves from absurd but inevitable catastrophe. Readers who wonder whether Graham Greene was not here 40 years ago are right, and Mr le Carre acknowledges his debt to Our Man in Havana. This tale, told with wit and ingenuity, is a splendid homage from one master of political thrillers to another." —*The Economist*

First published by Hodder & Stoughton 996.

★ **Tinker,** tailor, soldier, spy. John Le Carre. Knopf, 1974. 355 p; (George Smiley novels, 5)
ISBN 9780241323410
1. Spies 2. Intelligence service 3. Husband and wife 4. Extramarital affairs 5. Spy fiction 6. Books to movies

LC 74005084

George Smiley, who is a troubled man of infinite compassion, is also a single-mindedly ruthless adversary as a spy. The scene which he enters is a Cold War landscape of moles and lamplighters, scalp-hunters and pavement artists, where men are turned, burned or bought for stock. Smiley's mission is to catch a Moscow Centre mole burrowed thirty years deep into the Circus itself.

"Smiley instinctively realises from the outset who the traitor is but refuses to confront the embarrassing truth. A perceptive reader will sense the secret too, but one goes on reading entranced not so much by the ramifications of the plot, beautifully engineered though it is, as by concern for the characters, a rare thing in thrillers." —*New Statesman*

Originally published: London: Hodder & Stoughton, 1974.

Le Guin, Ursula K.

The **beginning** place. Ursula K. LeGuin. Tor, 2005. 230 p.
ISBN 9780765346254
1. Quests 2. Imaginary places 3. Magic 4. Growing up 5. Happiness 6. Coming-of-age stories 7. Fantasy fiction

Two young people who cross over from everyday reality and meet in the magical village of Tembreadbrezi volunteer to take on and destroy the unknown malevolent force that is threatening the village with destruction.

The **birthday** of the world: and other stories. Ursula K. Le Guin. Harper Collins, 2002. 362 p.
ISBN 9780066212531
1. Life on other planets 2. Aliens (Humanoid) 3. Human/alien encounters 4. Gender role 5. Women's role 6. Short stories 7. Social science fiction 8. Science fiction 9. Adult books for young adults

LC 2001039508

A collection of stories that are filled with love, lust, sex, marriage, gender, and other annoying problems that people must deal with no matter where they reside in the universe.

"Le Guin appears to have the most fun with her investigations of sex and gender...but the costs of revolution, religious bliss, and technology are also provicatively explored, and one returns to the current headlines with a fresh awareness of the exotic providional nature of human arrangements." —*The New Yorker*

★ The **dispossessed:** an ambiguous utopia. Ursula K. Le Guin. Harper & Row, 1974. 341 p. (Hainish series, 1)
ISBN 9780060125639
1. Dystopias 2. Utopias 3. Far future 4. Life on other planets 5. Anarchists 6. Dystopian fiction 7. Science fiction classics 8. Social science fiction
LC 73018667
Hugo Award for Best Novel, 1975; Locus Award for Best Science Fiction Novel, 1975; Nebula Award for Best Novel, 1974
A physicist from isolated Anarres travels to the mother planet, Urras, in hopes of dissolving the hatred that exists between them.

Four ways to forgiveness. Ursula Le Guin. HarperPrism, 1995. 228 p. (Hainish series, 7)
ISBN 9780061052347
1. Enslaved people's resistance and revolts 2. Sexism 3. Far future 4. Life on other planets 5. Enslaved people 6. Social science fiction 7. Science fiction
LC 95011459
Locus Award for Best Collection, 1996
Four interconnected novellas are set on the twin planets Werel and Yeowe and follow the stories of such characters as the disgraced revolutionary Abberkam, the callow "space brat" Solly, and the androgynous artist Batikam
"Four interrelated novellas deal with the Hainish culture on the twin planets of Werel and Yeowe and examine the relationship between love, freedom and forgiveness." —*Publishers Weekly*
4 novellas.

The **lathe** of heaven. By Ursula K. Le Guin. Scribner, 1971. 184 p.
ISBN 9780684125299
1. Near future 2. Dreams 3. Psychiatrist and patient 4. Psychic ability 5. Portland, Oregon 6. Oregon 7. Books to movies 8. Science fiction classics 9. Science fiction
LC 77162760
Locus Award for Best Science Fiction Novel, 1972
George Orr discovers that his dreams possess the remarkable ability to change the world, and when he falls into the hands of a power-mad psychiatrist, he counters by dreaming up a perfect world that can overcome his nightmares.
First published in Amazing stories magazine.

★ The **left** hand of darkness. Ursula Le Guin. Ace Books, 1969. 286 p. (Hainish series, 6)
ISBN 9780441007318
1. Far future 2. Androgyny (Psychology) 3. Life on other planets 4. Culture conflict 5. Ethnologists 6. Science fiction classics 7. Social science fiction 8. Science fiction
Hugo Award for Best Novel, 1970; James Tiptree, Jr. Award, 1995; Nebula Award for Best Novel, 1969
While on a mission to the planet Gethen, earthling Genly Ai is sent by leaders of the nation of Orgoreyn to a concentration camp from which the exiled prime minister of the nation of Karhide tries to rescue him.

Orsinian tales. By Ursula K. LeGuin. Harpercollins, 2004. 179 p.
ISBN 9780060763435
1. Freedom 2. State-sponsored terrorism 3. Political persecution 4. Eastern Europe 5. Short stories 6. Historical fiction
LC 76005545
The universal need for human freedom and love and the horrors of government oppression are recurring themes in this collection of eleven haunting pieces of short fiction, all set in the imaginary Eastern European country of Orsinia.
"This is a cycle of interrelated short stories. Set in a vaguely Middle-European country, Le Guin's tales deal with love, freedom, and tyranny in a society which over a series of historical periods appears to be perpetually in the last stages preceding cataclysm." —*Booklist*
Originally published: New York : Harper, 1976.

The **other** wind. By Ursula K. Le Guin. Harcourt, 2001. 256 p. (Earthsea series, 6)
ISBN 9780151006847
1. Dragons 2. Wizards 3. Magic 4. Rulers 5. Ged (Fictitious character) 6. High fantasy 7. Fantasy fiction
LC 2001024632
New York Times Notable Science Fiction, 2001; World Fantasy Award, 2002
Haunted by dreams of the dead who seek to invade Earthsea through him, the sorcerer Alder enlists the aid of Ged, a former Archmage, who advises him to find the holiest place in the world, which holds the key to preserving Earthsea.

The **telling.** Ursula Le Guin. Harcourt, 2000. 272 p. (Hainish series, 8)
ISBN 9780151005673
1. Life on other planets 2. Aliens (Humanoid) 3. Far future 4. Social science fiction 5. Science fiction 6. Adult books for young adults
LC 29574
Library Journal Best Books, 2000; Locus Award for Best Science Fiction Novel, 2001
On a world in which ancient beliefs and customs are banned, Sutty journeys deep into the countryside and discovers the Telling, the old faith of the Akans, a banned religion that teaches her about the meaning of her own existence
"This parable of the modern world's headlong rush toward monocultural sterility exemplifies the author's elegant simplicity and keen insight." —*Library Journal*

Leavitt, David

★ **Shelter** in place. David Leavitt. Bloomsbury, 2020. 224 pages
ISBN 9781620404874
1. Presidential election, 2016 2. Rich people 3. Elite (Social sciences) 4. Houses 5. Liberals 6. United States 7. New York City 8. 2010s 9. Literary fiction 10. Political fiction
Unsuccessfully challenging her influential friends in New York to perform an online search for tips on how to assassinate Donald Trump, a salon hostess impulsively purchases a grand if dilapidated apartment in Venice, triggering an unexpected affair.
"None of the main characters gets a pass in this dark comedy, and it's a lot of fun: Democrats, Republicans, writers, and even one magazine editor who binges on sugar-dusted sticks of butter—Leavitt skewers them all in this delectable novel. A humane, knowing comedy perfect for a moment when no one in America seems to like one another." —*Kirkus*

The **two** Hotel Francforts: a novel. David Leavitt. Bloomsbury, 2013. 257 p.
ISBN 9781596910423
1. Life change events 2. Expatriates 3. Marital conflict 4. Extramarital affairs 5. Gay men 6. Lisbon, Portugal 7. Portugal 8. 1940s 9. Historical fiction 10. LGBTQIA fiction
LC 2013015952
New York Times Notable Book, 2013
As Europe prepares for war during the summer of 1940, two couples—expatriate Americans fleeing Paris and wealthy bohemians beset by the social and sexual anxieties of their class—arrive in Portugal where

their lives become inexplicably entwined in unimaginable—and dangerous—ways.

"Leavitt's clever, engaging tale of marriage's hidden shadows, lies, and half-truths demonstrates that husbands and wives are only as happy as they've already decided to allow themselves to be." —*Publishers Weekly*

Lebbon, Tim

Eden. Tim Lebbon. Titan Books, 2020. 384 pages
ISBN 9781789092936
1. Climate change 2. Nature — Effect of humans on 3. Wilderness areas 4. Adventurers 5. Wildlife 6. Horror

Earth's rising oceans contain enormous islands of refuse, the Amazon rainforest is all-but destroyed, and countless species edge towards extinction. Humanity's last hope to save the planet lies with The Virgin Zones, thirteen vast areas of land off-limits to people and given back to nature. Extreme sports enthusiasts target these dangerous zones for illicit races. When one such team enters the oldest Zone, Eden, they find nature has returned to Eden in a primeval way. And here, nature is no longer humanity's friend. A horror eco thriller from the bestselling author of The Silence.

"Jurassic Park meets catastrophic climate change in this creepy, cinema-ready story." —*Kirkus*

Lebrecht, Norman

The **song** of names. Norman Lebrecht. Anchor Books, a division of Penguin Random House LLC, 2019. 311 pages
ISBN 9780593082485
1. Refugees 2. Jews 3. Boys — Friendship 4. Self-discovery 5. Violinists 6. London, England 7. 20th century 8. Literary fiction 9. Historical fiction 10. Books to movies
Whitbread Book Award for First Novel, 2002

Martin is growing up as an only child in wartime London until Dovidl, a refugee violinist from Warsaw, comes to stay. His arrival brings merriment and love, mischief and menace. Blood-brothers, they roam the ruined city, finding tragedy and triumph, sex and crime, until Dovidl disappears.

"Lebrecht's story delves into the horrors of the Holocaust and the Blitz, as well as the quiet communities of Hasidic Judaism that developed in Britain after the flight of so many refugees. What emerges is a vivid and outstanding story that sings about artistry, genius, music, love, envy, friendship, and revenge." —*Booklist*

Originally published: London : Headline Review, c2002.

Leckie, Ann

Ancillary justice. Ann Leckie. Orbit, 2013. 432 p. (Imperial Radch, 1)
ISBN 9780316246620
1. Aliens 2. Space flight 3. Revenge 4. Immortalism 5. Rulers 6. Space opera 7. Science fiction
LC 2012051135
Arthur C. Clarke Award, 2014; BSFA Award for Best Novel, 2013; Hugo Award for Best Novel, 2014; Locus Award for First Novel, 2014; Nebula Award for Best Novel, 2013

One Esk—an electronic artificial intelligence—once commanded an entire starship, the formidable Justice of Tore. Now confined to a mortal body cobbled together from interchangeable human parts as the entity called "Breq," the AI must survive as a multisegmented, ancillary humanoid being in a galactic empire ruled by an oppressive government—without disobeying the law that forbids AIs from harming their creators.

"Using the format of sf military adventure blended with hints of space opera, Leckie explores the expanded meaning of human nature and the un-

easy balance between individuality and membership in a group identity.' —*Library Journal*

Ancillary mercy. Ann Leckie. Orbit, 2015. 432 p. (Imperial Radch, 3)
ISBN 9780316246682
1. Aliens 2. Space flight 3. Revenge 4. Immortalism 5. Rulers 6. Space opera 7. Science fiction
LC 2015020915
Locus Award for Best Science Fiction Novel, 2016

Housed in a composite human body not her own, Fleet Captain Breq is the last remaining "ancillary" fragment of a fallen starship's AI, as well as the commander of her own vessel. With civil war raging throughout the rapidly fracturing Radchaai Empire, Breq and her crew devise a plan to defend Atheok Station from ancient nemesis Anaander Mianaai, Lord of the Radch. Action-packed heroics unfold side-by-side with reflections on identity and personhood in this dramatic conclusion of the Imperial Radch trilogy, which begins with Ancillary Justice and Ancillary Sword.

"Leckie creates a grand backdrop to tell an intimate, cerebral story about identity and empowerment. She devotes as much attention to the characters' personal relationships and their mental and emotional difficulties as she does to the wider conflict." —*Kirkus*

Ancillary sword. Ann Leckie. Orbit, 2014. 432 p. (Imperial Radch, 2)
ISBN 9780316246651
1. Aliens 2. Space flight 3. Revenge 4. Immortalism 5. Rulers 6. Space opera 7. Ballard, J. G.
LC 2014018730
BSFA Award for Best Novel, 2014; Library Journal Best Books, 2014; Locus Award for Best Science Fiction Novel, 2015

Fleet Captain Breq Mianaai has acquired both a human body and command of a starship. Not the worst fate in the universe for a several-thousand-year-old AI component (or "ancillary) separated from her former vessel's hive mind. Sent to the planet Athoek as an envoy of the many-bodied Lord of the Radch, Breq must prevent a civil war that threatens the stability of the Radchaai Empire while engaging in a more personal quest for answers about the past.

"Breq's struggle for meaningful justice in a society designed to favor the strong is as engaging as ever." —*Publishers Weekly*

Provenance. Ann Leckie. Orbit, 2017. 432 p.
ISBN 9780316388672
1. Ambition in women 2. Political intrigue 3. Material culture 4. Thieves 5. Prisoners 6. Space opera 7. Science fiction
LC 2017018846
Ingray Aughskold has never been her mother's favorite child; that distinction belongs to her brother, who will almost certainly be named heir. But will a scheme to shame one of her family's political rivals win Ingray enough plaudits to change her fate? Although set in the universe of the author's Imperial Radch trilogy, Provenance stands on its own.

"Leckie again uses large-scale worldbuilding to tell a deeply personal story—in this case, to explore what binds children to their families. As always, she impels the reader to consider the power language, and specifically names, has to shape perception and reality." —*Kirkus*

★ The **Raven** tower. Ann Leckie. Orbit, 2019. 432 p.
ISBN 9780316388696
1. Imaginary kingdoms 2. Gods and goddesses 3. Rulers 4. Warriors 5. Secrets 6. Epic fantasy 7. Second person narratives 8. First person narratives
LC 2018040311
The kingdom of Iraden, under the protection of a god known as the Raven, faces unrest and challenges from invaders when a usurper takes over the throne and discovers that the Raven's power is weakening.

"Sharp, many layered, and, as always for Leckie, deeply intelligent." —*Kirkus*

Lee, Andrea

Red Island House. Andrea Lee. Scribner, 2021. 320 p.
ISBN 9781982137809
1. African American women 2. Husband and wife 3. Interracial families 4. Vacation homes 5. Island life 6. Madagascar 7. Italy 8. Literary fiction 9. African American fiction

Shay is surprised when her husband Senna declares his intention to build her a spectacular dream house on an idyllic beach in the tropical island nation of Madagascar. But the Red Island House casts a spell from the moment she sees it, and before she knows it Shay has become the somewhat reluctant mistress of a sprawling household, caught between her privileged American upbringing and education, and her connection to the continent of her ancestors. A sweeping novel about marriage and loyalty, identity and heritage, fate and freedom, Red Island House reintroduces readers to a powerhouse literary voice and an extravagantly lush, enchanted world.

"An utterly captivating, richly detailed, and highly critical vision of how the one percent lives in neocolonial paradise." —*Kirkus*

Lee, Chang-Rae

★ **My** year abroad. Chang-Rae Lee. Riverhead Books, 2021. 496 p.
ISBN 9781594634574
1. College students 2. Chinese American men 3. Boredom 4. Businesspeople 5. Studying abroad 6. Satirical fiction 7. Picaresque fiction 8. Literary fiction

An everyday American college student finds his life transformed by a Chinese-American businessman who unexpectedly takes him under his wing on a series of whimsical, heartbreaking and darkly shocking adventures throughout Asia.

"Lee is supreme, and this high-velocity, shocking, and wise novel, avidly promoted, is emitting an irresistible magnetic force." —*Booklist*

Lee, Chang-rae

★ **On** such a full sea. Chang-rae Lee. Riverhead Books, 2014. 336 pages
ISBN 9781594486104
1. Social classes 2. Dystopias 3. Quests 4. Post-apocalypse 5. Missing persons 6. United States 7. Dystopian fiction 8. Literary fiction
LC 2013036600
ALA Notable Book, 2015; Booklist Editors' Choice, 2014; Andrew Carnegie Medal for Excellence in Fiction finalist, 2015; National Book Critics Circle Award for Fiction finalist, 2014

In a class-divided future America where urban neighborhoods function as labor colonies for elite charter villages, Fan, a female fish-tank diver, embarks on what becomes a legendary quest to find the man she loves in a region overcome by anarchic forces.

"A harrowing and fully imagined vision of dystopian America.... Welcome and surprising proof that there's plenty of life in end-of-the-world storytelling." —*Kirkus*

★ **The surrendered**. Chang-rae Lee. Riverhead Books, 2010. 480 p.
ISBN 9781594489761
1. Orphans 2. Soldiers 3. Women missionaries 4. Secrets 5. Korean War, 1950-1953 6. Korea 7. Epic fiction 8. Literary fiction
LC 2009030887
ALA Notable Book, 2011; New York Times Notable Book, 2010; Pulitzer Prize for Fiction finalist, 2011

At the end of the Korean War, the lives of orphan June Han and American soldier Hector Brennan collide. Thirty years later, they meet again and are forced to come to terms with the secrets of their devastating past.

"In its ineffably quiet way, there really is something Tolstoyan in this searching fiction's determination to understand the characters specifically as members of families and products of other people's influences. The characterizations of Hector and Sylvie are astonishingly rich and complex, and the risktaken in depicting the adult June as the woman readers will hope she would not become is triumphantly vindicated." —*Kirkus*

Lee, Fonda

★ **Jade** City. Fonda Lee. Orbit, 2017. 498 p. (Green Bone saga, 1)
ISBN 9780316440868
1. Jade 2. Organized crime 3. Power (social sciences) 4. Imaginary wars and battles 5. Cities and towns 6. Epic fantasy 7. Asian-influenced fantasy 8. Canadian fiction 9. Adult books for young adults
Prix Aurora: Best Novel, 2018; World Fantasy Award, 2018

In this action-packed series opener, Green Bone warriors use the magic-enhancing powers of jade to protect their island nation of Kekon and its capital, Janloon. But times are changing, as rival syndicates headed by the feuding Ayt and Kaul families go to extreme lengths to consolidate their power and gain control of the city. Detailed world-building and exciting martial-arts battles enhance this gritty crime drama, which takes place in an East Asia-inspired fantasy world.

Jade war. Fonda Lee. Orbit, 2019. 512 p. (Green Bone saga, 2)
ISBN 9780316440929
1. Jade 2. Power (Social sciences) 3. Imaginary wars and battles 4. International relations 5. Siblings 6. Epic fantasy 7. Asian-influenced fantasy 8. Canadian fiction 9. Adult books for young adults
LC 2019000760

In a sequel to Jade City, the Kaul siblings forge new and dangerous alliances to fight political rivals and mercenary kingpins for control over the capital city and its supply of magical jade.

Lee, Harper

★ **Go** set a watchman. Harper Lee. HarperCollins, 2015. 288 p. (To kill a mockingbird, 2)
ISBN 9780062409850
1. Homecomings 2. Independence in women 3. Fathers and daughters 4. Race relations 5. Racism 6. Alabama 7. Southern States 8. 1950s 9. Literary fiction 10. Southern fiction

Twenty years after the trial of Tom Robinson, Scout returns home to Maycomb to visit her father and struggles with personal and political issues as her small Alabama town adjusts to the turbulent events beginning to transform the United States in the mid-1950s.

★ **To** kill a mockingbird. Harper Lee. Lippincott, 1960. 296 p; (To kill a mockingbird, 1)
ISBN 9780397001514
1. Racism 2. Single-parent families 3. Fathers and daughters 4. Race relations 5. Trials (Rape) 6. Southern States 7. Alabama 8. Coming-of-age stories 9. Modern classics 10. Literary fiction
LC 60007847
Pulitzer Prize for Fiction, 1961

Scout Finch, daughter of the town lawyer, likes to spend her summers building treehouses, swimming, and catching lightning bugs with her big brother Jem. But one summer, when a black man is accused of raping a white woman, Scout's carefree days come to an end. In the county courtroom, she will join her father in a desperate battle against ignorance and prejudice.

Lee, Ji-min

The **starlet** and the spy. Ji-min Lee; translated from the Korean by Chi-Young Kim. HarperCollins 2019. 256 p.

ISBN 9780062930262

1. Monroe, Marilyn 2. Postwar life 3. Interpreters 4. Actors and actresses 5. Friendship 6. Women and war 7. South Korea 8. Seoul, Korea 9. 1950s 10. Historical fiction 11. Translations

A Korean war survivor is assigned as translator for Marilyn Monroe during a 1954 USO tour to a Korea still struggling to return to normalcy and develops a deep kinship with the star.

Published in the UK as Marilyn and Me, 2019.

Translated from the Korean.

Lee, Jonathan

The **great** mistake. Jonathan Lee. Alfred A. Knopf, 2021. 272 p.

ISBN 9780525658498

1. Green, Andrew Haswell 2. Murder victims 3. City life 4. Secrets 5. Urban planning 6. Urban planners 7. New York City 8. 19th century 9. 1900s (Decade) 10. Historical fiction 11. Biographical fiction

LC 2020044828

From the acclaimed author of High Dive comes a novel of New York City at the turn of the 20th century, a story of one man's rise to fame and fortune, and his mysterious murder.

"Give this entrancing story of an exceptional man to novel-reading fans of Erik Larson and those who enjoy a little mystery with their historical fiction." —*Library Journal*

Lee, Min Jin

★ **Pachinko**. Min Jin Lee. Grand Central Publishing, 2017. 496 p.

ISBN 9781455563937

1. Families 2. Unplanned pregnancy 3. Intergenerational relations 4. Identity (Psychology) 5. Immigrant families 6. Korea 7. Japan 8. 20th century 9. 1910s 10. Family sagas 11. Historical fiction

LC 2016023353

ALA Notable Book, 2018; Loan Stars Favourites, 2017; New York Times Notable Book, 2017; National Book Award for Fiction finalist, 2017; RUSA Reading List Short List, 2018

In early 1900s Korea, prized daughter Sunja finds herself pregnant and alone, bringing shame on her family until a young tubercular minister offers to marry her and move with her to Japan, in the saga of one family bound together as their faith and identity are called into question.

"Those who enjoy historical fiction with strong characterizations will not be disappointed as they ride along on the emotional journeys offered in the author's latest page-turner." —*Library Journal*

Lee, Patrick

Runner. Patrick Lee. Minotaur Books, 2014. Vii, 328 pages (Sam Dryden novels, 1)

ISBN 9781250030733

1. Retired military personnel 2. Escapes 3. Amnesia 4. Special forces 5. Girls 6. California 7. Southern California 8. Thrillers and suspense 9. Techno-thrillers

LC 2013032586

In this series debut starring retired special forces soldier Sam Dryden, our hero is out for a run (at 3am) when he encounters a young girl being chased by a group of men who are armed to the teeth. Of course he helps her, putting himself in immediate danger. The girl—who can remember only her first name and the last two months of her life—appears to have been imprisoned for most of her 11 years, and has a skill that makes her extremely dangerous to a lot of powerful people.

"Tension mounts right from the start in this nonstop action-packed narrative and seldom flags, as Lee...continually blurs the lines between the good guys and the bad guys." —*Library Journal*

Lee, Yoon Ha

Ninefox gambit. Yoon Ha Lee. Solaris, 2016. 384 p. (Machineries of empire, 1)

ISBN 9781781084496

1. Imaginary empires 2. Women soldiers 3. Space warfare 4. Trust 5. Traitors 6. Space 7. Military science fiction 8. Space opera 9. Science fiction

Locus Award for First Novel, 2017

Given the opportunity to redeem herself for past crimes, Captain Kel Cheris is tasked with retaking the Fortress of Scattered Needles, a star fortress under the control of heretics, a mission that requires her to partner with an untrustworthy ally.

Raven stratagem. Yoon Ha Lee. Solaris, 2017. 400 p. (Machineries of empire, 2)

ISBN 9781781085370

1. Imaginary empires 2. Power (Social sciences) 3. Space warfare 4. Political intrigue 5. Military strategy 6. Space 7. Military science fiction 8. Space opera 9. Science fiction

When Kel Cheris, a young captain, summons the ghost of a long-dead General Shuos Jedao to stop a rebellion, the general possesses her and takes over General Khiruev's fleet.

"This follow up to the Nebula- and Hugo-nominated Ninefox Gambit combines exciting space opera action with dazzling, imaginative worldbuilding." —*Library Journal*

Revenant gun. Yoon Ha Lee. Solaris, 2018. 400 p. (Machineries of empire, 3)

ISBN 9781781086070

1. Imaginary empires 2. Imaginary wars and battles 3. Power (Social sciences) 4. Space warfare 5. Political intrigue 6. Space 7. Military science fiction 8. Space opera 9. Science fiction

Shuos Jedao wakes up thinking he is a seventeen-year-old cadet, but his body is that of an older man. The soldiers he commands hate him thanks to a massacre he can't remember committing. Even worse, he is being hunted by an enemy who knows more about Jedao and his crimes than he does himself...

Lefteri, Christy

The **beekeeper** of Aleppo: a novel. Christy Lefteri. Ballantine Books, 2019. 317 pages

ISBN 9781984821218

1. Beekeepers 2. Refugees 3. Voyages and travels 4. Blindness 5. Women who are blind 6. Syria 7. Great Britain 8. Mainstream fiction

A beekeeper and his artist wife have their lives upended and must flee after war destroys their home in Aleppo, Syria, and they set off on a dangerous journey through Turkey and Greece, towards an uncertain future in England.

"Lefteri perceptively and powerfully documents the horrors of the Syrian civil war and the suffering of innocent civilians. Readers will find this deeply affecting for both its psychological intensity and emotional acuity." —*Publishers Weekly*

Lehane, Dennis

★ The **given** day. Dennis Lehane. William Morrow, 2008. 704 p. (Coughlin novels, 1)

ISBN 9780688163181

1. Strikes 2. Race relations 3. Civil rights 4. Police 5. Social classes 6. Boston, Massachusetts 7. 1910s 8. Historical fiction

Booklist Editors' Choice, 2008; Library Journal Best Books, 2008

An epic tale set at the end of World War I follows the experiences of a family whose lives mirror the political unrest of an America caught between its well-patterned past and an unpredictable future.

"Lehane laces his narrative with melodrama—two brothers in love with the same woman, who harbors a secret past; a viciously racist cop out to destroy Luther and frame the burgeoning N.A.A.C.P.and a subplot, involving Babe Ruth, feels stale and unnecessary. But he brings vividly to life the struggles that the working classes faced in pursuit of decent working conditions and a fair wage." —*The New Yorker*

Sequel: Live by Night.

Live by night. Dennis Lehane. William Morrow & Co, 2012. 401 p; (Coughlin novels, 2)

ISBN 9780060004873

1. Prohibition 2. Gangsters 3. Betrayal 4. Violence 5. Bootleggers 6. United States 7. 1920s 8. Historical fiction 9. Crime fiction 10. Books to movies

Edgar Allan Poe Award for Best Novel, 2013

In 1926, during the Prohibition, Joe Coughlin defies his strict law-and-order upbringing by climbing a ladder of organized crime that takes him from Boston to Cuba where he encounters a dangerous cast of characters who are all fighting for their piece of the American dream.

Sequel to: The Given Day.

Title adapted into a film by the same name in 2017.

★ **Mystic** river. Dennis Lehane. William Morrow, 2001. 401 p.

ISBN 9780688163167

1. Adult child sexual abuse victims 2. Men — Psychology 3. Blue collar families 4. Working class neighborhoods 5. Murder 6. Boston, Massachusetts 7. Back Bay, Boston, Massachusetts 8. Noir fiction 9. Thrillers and suspense 10. Psychological fiction

Anthony Award for Best Novel, 2002; Dilys Award, 2002; Massachusetts Book Awards, Fiction Award, 2002; New York Times Notable Mysteries, 2001

Sean Devine must confront the world of violence and pain he tried to forget when his childhood friend's daughter is murdered, and the investigation brings him face-to-face with a vigilante killer and a man with a dangerous secret.

"Lehane spares nothing in his wrenching descriptions of how a crime in the neighborhood kills the neighborhood, taking it down house by house, family by family." —*New York Times Book Review*

Shutter Island. Dennis Lehane. Morrow, 2003. Ix, 325 p.

ISBN 9780688163174

1. Psychiatric hospitals 2. United States marshals 3. Escaped convicts 4. Criminals with mental illnesses 5. Islands 6. Massachusetts 7. 1950s 8. Psychological suspense 9. Books to movies

U.S. Marshal Teddy Daniels and his partner, Chuck Aule, come to Shutter Island's Ashcliffe Hospital in search of an escaped mental patient, but uncover true wickedness as Ashcliffe's mysterious patient treatments propel them to the brink of insanity.

"The atmosphere is properly dark and moody, and so long as Teddy and Chuck stick to the manhunt and their investigation of Ashecliffe's creepy medical staff, they play their roles with muscle and grace." —*New York Times Book Review*

Since we fell. Dennis Lehane. Ecco Press, 2017. 400 p.

ISBN 9780062129383

1. Married women 2. Agoraphobia in women 3. Psychic trauma 4. Deception 5. Betrayal 6. Boston, Massachusetts 7. Thrillers and suspense 8. Literary fiction

LibraryReads Favorites, 2017

Retreating from the world in the aftermath of a traumatizing reporting assignment, Rachel finds happiness with a raffish businessman before witnessing activities surrounding a conspiracy that tests the limits of her fragile psyche.

"He produces one of crime fiction's most exciting and well-orchestrated finales—rife with dramatic tension and buttressed by rich psychological interplay between the characters." —*Booklist*

World gone by: a novel. Dennis Lehane. William Morrow, 2015. 416 p. (Coughlin novels :, 3)

ISBN 9780060004903

1. Organized crime 2. Spies 3. Criminals 4. Single fathers 5. Fathers and sons 6. Tampa, Florida 7. Cuba 8. Second World War era (1939-1945) 9. Historical thrillers 10. Crime fiction

LC 2014027026

Working as a consigliere to the Bartolo crime family, traveling between Tampa and Cuba, former crime kingpin Joe Coughlin, who has everything—money, power, anonymity and a beautiful mistress, is forced to pay for his lifetime of sin when the dark truth of his past emerges.

"A multilayered, morally ambiguous novel of family, blood and betrayal." —*Kirkus*

Leigh, Eva

Forever your earl. Eva Leigh. Avon Books, 2015. 384 p. (Wicked quills of London, 1)

ISBN 9780062358622

1. Gossip columnists 2. Earls and countesses 3. Gossiping and gossips 4. Womanizers 5. Deception 6. London, England 7. England 8. Regency period (1811-1820) 9. Regency romances 10. Historical romances

Gossip writer Eleanor Hawke is invited to indulge in the illicit pursuits of Daniel Balfour, the notorious Earl of Ashford, but when Daniel falls for Eleanor, she discovers that the earl's true scandal may involve herself.

"Leigh (the pseudonym of best-selling romance author Zoe Archer) launches the Wicked Quills of London series on a high note with this fabulously fun Regency-set historical that superbly showcases the authors flair for mixing sharp wit and sexy romance." —*Booklist*

Scandal takes the stage. Eva Leigh. Avon Books, 2015. 370 p. (Wicked quills of London, 2)

ISBN 9780062358646

1. Women dramatists 2. Viscounts and viscountesses 3. Writer's block 4. Country homes 5. Nobility 6. London, England 7. England 8. Regency period (1811-1820) 9. Regency romances 10. Historical romances

When writer's block threatens the delivery of her new play, playwright Maggie Delamere accepts the offer of the theater-loving Viscount Marwood to write at his country estate, where passion sparks between them.

"This lighthearted romp is full of rambunctious characters, witty repartee, and believable emotional development." —*Publishers Weekly*

Temptations of a wallflower. Eva Leigh. Avon Books, 2016. 384 p. (Wicked quills of London, 3)

ISBN 9780062358660

1. Clergymen 2. Women erotica writers 3. Husband and wife 4. Newlyweds 5. Secret identity 6. London, England 7. England 8. Regency period (1811-1820) 9. Regency romances 10. Historical romances

Lady Sarah Frampton has a scandalous secret: she is A Lady of Dubious Quality, the pseudonymous author of bestselling erotica. Country vicar Jeremy Cleland has no idea that the demure wallflower he's falling in love with is the woman whose identity he's been ordered to publicly expose by his father, the Earl of Hutton, as part of the elder man's crusade against immorality.

"Leigh's latest is a thoughtful and sensuous romance." —*Publishers Weekly*

Leilani, Raven

★ **Luster**. Raven Leilani. Farrar, Straus and Giroux, 2020. 208 p.
ISBN 9780374194321
1. African American women 2. Open marriage 3. Women artists 4. Race relations 5. Adopted children 6. New York City 7. New Jersey 8. Literary fiction 9. African American fiction 10. First person narratives

LC 2020012289

Kirkus Prize for Fiction, 2020; New York Times Notable Book, 2020

A young black artist falls into an affair with a man in an open marriage before gradually befriending his wife and adopted daughter against a backdrop of dynamic racial politics.

"Edie's ability to navigate the complicated relationships with the Walkers exhibits Leilani's mastery of nuance, and the narration is perceptive, funny, and emotionally charged. Edie's frank, self-possessed voice will keep a firm grip on readers all the way to the bitter end." —*Publishers Weekly*

Leitch, Will

★ **How** lucky. Will Leitch. HarperCollins, 2021. 304 p.
ISBN 9780063073098
1. Wheelchair users 2. Kidnapping 3. Witnesses 4. Spinal muscular atrophy 5. Men with disabilities 6. Southern fiction 7. Mysteries 8.

Unable to speak or move without a wheelchair, Daniel, spending hours observing his neighborhood from his front porch, believes he has witnessed the kidnapping of a young college student and vows to solve this mystery.

"It's rare that a crime novel could be described as lovely but this is a lovely book.... It is also beautifully written and suspenseful, at the same time being all about goodness and caring without once being sappy or, well, sentimental." —*Booklist*

Leithauser, Brad

The **promise** of elsewhere. Brad Leithauser. Alfred a Knopf, 2019. 336 p.
ISBN 9780525655039
1. Travelers 2. Midlife crisis 3. Voyages and travels 4. Americans in foreign countries 5. Men with bipolar disorder 6. Rome, Italy 7. London, England 8. Humorous stories

In the face of devastating existential crisis stemming from a collapsing marriage and a health scare, a Midwestern professor decides to tour the world's most beautiful architectural sites and becomes sidetracked with a jilted bride in Rome.

Lelchuk, Saul

Save me from dangerous men: a novel. Saul Lelchuk. Flatiron Books, 2019. 320 p. (Nikki Griffin novels, 1)
ISBN 9781250170248
1. Women private investigators 2. Women vigilantes 3. Bookstores 4. Books and reading 5. Violence against women 6. San Francisco Bay Area 7. California 8. Thrillers and suspense

LC 2018046994

Operating a private investigator business from an office above her bookstore, bibliophile and part-time vigilante Nikki Griffin becomes the target of dangerous adversaries when she breaks cover to save a woman's life.

"A credible plot and solid prose are pluses, but the books real appeal stems from its powerful, distinctive protagonist." —*Publishers Weekly*

Lem, Stanislaw

His master's voice. Stanislaw Lem; translated from the Polish by Michael Kandel. Harcourt Brace Jovanovich, 1983. 199 p.
ISBN 9780156403009
1. Scientists 2. Interstellar communication 3. Cosmic background radiation 4. Aliens 5. Cold war 6. Diary novels 7. Translations 8. Hard science fiction

LC 82015765

A secret team of scientists study a pulsating stream of radiation from outer space and attempt to determine if it is a message from another world.

"This thorough, intellectual take on a classic hard sci-fi trope is Lem at his best." —*Publishers Weekly*

Translation of: Gos pana.
Translated from the Polish.

★ **Solaris**. Stanislaw Lem; afterword by Darko Suvin; translated from the French by Joanna Kilmartin and Steve Cox. Walker, 1970. 204 p.
ISBN 9780802755261
1. Scientists 2. Consciousness 3. Aliens (Non-humanoid) 4. Oceans 5. Memories 6. Hard science fiction 7. Books to movies 8. Literary fiction

LC 75123267

Upon landing at an interplanetary station, Kris Kelvin discovers that an advanced power has taken over.
Translated from the French.

Leon, Donna

Beastly things: a Commissario Guido Brunetti mystery. Donna Leon. Atlantic Monthly Press, 2012. 288 p. (Guido Brunetti mysteries, 21)
ISBN 9780802120236
1. Police 2. Murder investigation 3. Men with disfigurements 4. Animal rights 5. Brunetti, Guido (Fictitious character) 6. Venice, Italy 7. Italy 8. Mysteries 9. Police procedurals

Commissario Brunetti investigates the death of an animal lover whose decomposed body was found in a Venice canal.

Drawing conclusions: a Commissario Guido Brunetti mystery. Donna Leon. Grove/Atlantic, 2011. 256 p. (Guido Brunetti mysteries, 20)
ISBN 9780802119797
1. Widows 2. Heart attack 3. Old age homes 4. Murder investigation 5. Police 6. Venice, Italy 7. Italy 8. Mysteries 9. Police procedurals
Library Journal Best Books, 2011

When Anna Maria Giusti returns from holiday to find her elderly neighbour Constanza Altavilla dead, with blood on the floor near her head, she immediately alerts the police. Commissario Brunetti is called to the scene and it seems the woman has suffered a fatal heart attack. Patta, the Vice-Questore, is eager to dismiss the case as a death from natural causes.

"This installment epitomizes what we treasure most about this series: a feeling for the life of a sublimely beautiful city and a sensitivity to the forces that are reshaping it. Not to mention the pleasure of being in Brunetti's company when this shrewd but scrupulously honest man is having a crisis of ethics at the flower market or trying to pry information from a hostile nun." —*New York Times Book Review*

Falling in love: a Commissario Guido Brunetti mystery. Donna Leon. Atlantic Monthly Press, 2015. 264 p. (Guido Brunetti mysteries, 24)

ISBN 9780802123534
1. Police 2. Stalking 3. Opera singers 4. Obsession 5. Fans 6. Venice, Italy 7. Italy 8. Mysteries 9. Police procedurals

Attending a performance by a opera star he saved in Death at La Fenice, Brunetti learns that the singer is being stalked by an obsessed fan who subsequently attacks a fellow performer.

The **golden** egg. Donna Leon. Atlantic Monthly Press, 2013. 256 p. (Guido Brunetti mysteries, 22)
ISBN 9780802121011
1. Police 2. Murder investigation 3. Extortion 4. Scandals 5. Men with developmental disabilities 6. Venice, Italy 7. Italy 8. Mysteries 9. Police procedurals

Commissario Guido Brunetti investigates the death of a man who never existed on paper.
Maps on cover linings and endpapers.

A **question** of belief: a Commissario Guido Brunetti mystery. Donna Leon. Atlantic Monthly, 2010. 288 p. (Guido Brunetti mysteries, 19)
ISBN 9780802119421
1. Political corruption 2. Police 3. Murder investigation 4. Justice 5. Violence 6. Venice, Italy 7. Italy 8. Mysteries 9. Police procedurals

Under the stifling summer sun, Venice is flooded with tourism. Commissario Guido Brunetti is planning the perfect mountain vacation where he can catch up on his reading. However, before he can go, an old friend has him look into a court corruption case. As he probes deeper, Commissario Brunetti quickly becomes embroiled in a shocking murder case that is linked to his own investigation.

Trace elements. Donna Leon. Atlantic Monthly Press, 2020. 320 pages (Guido Brunetti mysteries, 29)
ISBN 9780802148674
1. Detectives 2. Last words 3. Public health 4. Murder investigation 5. Criminal investigation 6. Italy 7. Venice, Italy 8. Police procedurals

A woman's cryptic dying words in a Venetian hospice lead Guido Brunetti to uncover a threat to the entire region in Donna Leon's haunting twenty-ninth Brunetti novel.

"As usual, Leon adroitly portrays the complex questions of what constitutes justice and the sad consequences that can result from its pursuit." —*Publishers Weekly*

★ **Transient** desires. Donna Leon. Atlantic Monthly Press, 2021. 288 p. (Guido Brunetti mysteries, 30)
ISBN 9780802158178
1. Detectives 2. Boating accidents 3. Women 4. Criminal investigation 5. Crime 6. Italy 7. Venice, Italy 8. Police procedurals

investigating a mysterious boating accident outside his jurisdiction, commissario Guido Brunetti and his colleague, Claudia Griffoni, discover that one of the suspects is associated with Laguna's sinister underworld.

"All the introspective human drama we expect from Leon, with an adrenaline booster as well!...This landmark thirtieth Guido Brunetti novel demonstrates that Leon's beloved series shows no signs of aging." —*Booklist*

Uniform justice. Donna Leon. Atlantic Monthly Press, 2003. 280 p. (Guido Brunetti mysteries, 12)
ISBN 9780871139030
1. Police 2. Military cadets 3. Political corruption 4. Brunetti, Guido (Fictitious character) 5. Detectives 6. Venice, Italy 7. Italy 8. Mysteries 9. Police procedurals
LC 2003044326

Commissario Guido Brunetti is called in to investigate when a young cadet at an elite military academy is found hanged, a presumed suicide.

"As a thinking man, Brunetti reads Cicero for moral direction, looks to his wife for doses of cynical realism and humbly consults his secretary, the terrifyingly efficient Signorina Elettra, on practical matters. But it is as a man of sensibility that this endearing detective most engages us." —*New York Times Book Review*

Unto us a son is given. Donna Leon. Atlantic Monthly Press, 2019. 320 p. (Guido Brunetti mysteries, 28)
ISBN 9780802129116
1. Murder investigation 2. Family relationships 3. Detectives 4. Inheritance and succession 5. Criminal investigation 6. Italy 7. Venice, Italy 8. Police procedurals
LC 2018058492

When an elderly family friend is urged to bequeath his fortune to a specific heir before suddenly dropping dead, Commissario Guido Brunetti untangles a disturbing mystery from the victim's past.

"Far more than whodunit, the real subject of this novel (and Leons work in general) is what we all do to one another." —*Booklist*

Leonard, Elmore

★ **Be** cool: everyone is looking for the next big hit. Elmore Leonard. Delacorte Press, 1999. 292 p.
ISBN 9780385333917
1. Film producers and directors 2. Record industry and trade 3. Film industry and trade 4. Cool (Personal quality) 5. Entertainment industry and trade 6. Hollywood, California 7. Caper novels 8. Books to movies 9. Crime fiction
LC 989836601

New York Times Notable Book, 1999

Chili Palmer is ready to move into the recording industry, but his next big singing star may have ties to the mob.

"Aside from the wit, the fun and the colorful figures that populate Elmore Leonard's novels, the real magic of his work is in the language.... This is Elmore Leonard at his best, the sweeping synaptic prose effortlessly echoing the argot of the gutter." —*New York Times Book Review*

Sequel to: Get Shorty.

Charlie Martz and other stories: the unpublished stories. Elmore Leonard. William Morrow, 2015. 300 p.
ISBN 9780062364920
1. Crime 2. Outlaws 3. Law enforcement 4. Gangsters 5. United States marshals 6. New Mexico 7. Detroit, Michigan 8. Westerns 9. Thrillers and suspense 10. Short stories
LC 2015008625

An anthology of 15 stories by the award-winning author include 11 previously unpublished tales and selections from the early years of his career.

"[T]his posthumous collection showcases the early writing of the author of westerns and crime stories, revealing his particular genius in embryonic, pulpish form." —*Publishers Weekly*

★ The **complete** Western stories of Elmore Leonard. William Morrow, 2004. 544 p.
ISBN 9780060724252
1. Indians of North America 2. Frontier and pioneer life 3. Apache Indians 4. Arizona 5. Southwest (United States) 6. 19th century 7. Westerns 8. Short stories 9. Books to movies
LC 2004055969

A collection of short fiction features pieces written over the course of five decades and includes the author's first short story, "The Trail of the Apache."

Seven of the titles were later published as: Trail of the Apache and other stories.

★ **Get** Shorty. Elmore Leonard. HarperTorch, 2002. 359 p.
ISBN 9780385301411

1. Money lenders 2. Horror film producers and directors 3. Film industry and trade — Corrupt practices 4. Gamblers 5. Hollywood, California 6. Caper novels 7. Books to movies 8. Crime fiction

Chili Palmer, a Miami loanshark, and Harry Zimm, a film producer in debt, become reluctant partners as they become embroiled in the seductive but deadly Hollywood scene.

"Leonard's strongest books make you stand up and sit down a lot during their tight moments, but Get Shorty, despite its occasional white-knuckle passages, belongs to that vast vinegary canon known as the Hollywood novel.... Best of all is the portrait Leonard gives us of a seven-million-dollar-a-picture star named Michael Weir." —*The New Yorker*

Sequel: Be cool.

Originally published: New York : Delacorte Press, 1990.

Glitz. Elmore Leonard. Arbor House, 1985. 251 p.
ISBN 9780877956327
1. Former convicts 2. Revenge 3. Police 4. Atlantic City, New Jersey 5. Miami, Florida 6. Mysteries 7. Books to movies
LC 84016794

When Miami Beach detective Vincent Mora's quirky girl friend turns up dead, only seven days after taking a hostess job in Atlantic City, Mora investigates the circumstances and comes up against La Cosa Nostra BT

"There is a steady flow of intrigue and action set just outside the law in a world both dirty and glamorous. Several characters develop into complex personalities, but Mora is never quite clear." —*Library Journal*

The **Hot** Kid. Elmore Leonard. William Morrow, 2005. 304 p.
ISBN 9780060724221
1. United States deputy marshals 2. Fame 3. Criminals 4. Gangsters 5. Former convicts 6. Oklahoma 7. Depression era (1929-1941) 8. 1930s 9. Westerns
LC 2004063578

New York Times Notable Book, 2005

Having made his name by killing notorious bank robber Emmet Long, Deputy U.S. Marshal Carl Webster embarks on a dangerous search for Jack Belmont, the son of an oil millionaire who dreams of becoming Public Enemy Number One.

"Where so much of Leonard's recent fiction has a sharp, almost hyperrealistic quality, The Hot Kid is noirish and even a little pulpy at times, in the fashion of 30's movies and detective magazines.... Tony Antonelli isn't a portrait of the artist as young man, exactly, but rather a fond wink at the tradition of potboilers and genre writing that gave rise to Leonard himself and from which, for all his success, he has never cut himself off." —*New York Times Book Review*

★ **Killshot**. Elmore Leonard. Warner Books, 1990. 321 p.
ISBN 9781557100412
1. Witnesses 2. Federal Witness Protection Program 3. Vermeer, Johannes 4. Terrorism 5. Assassins 6. Crime fiction 7. Books to movies

Armand Degas and Richie Nix combine their criminal credentials, their ease with killing, and their lust for adventure and take off on a spree that has innocent victims running for cover.

Originally published: New York : Arbor House, 1989.

LaBrava. Elmore Leonard. Arbor House 1983. 283 p.
ISBN 9780877955276
1. Photographers 2. Film actors and actresses 3. Man-woman relationships 4. South Miami Beach, Florida 5. Thrillers and suspense
LC 83072676

Edgar Allan Poe Award for Best Mystery Novel, 1984

Joe LaBrava, a photographer and former Secret Service agent, observes a murder and becomes involved in an unusual confidence scheme in South Miami Beach BT

"What makes the author's work memorable is his uncompromisingly direct prose, his affectionately crafted yet very real characters, and, of course, the fact that Leonard knows that providing entertainment is the novelist's first commandment. Nobody brings the illogic of crime and criminals to life better." —*Christian Science Monitor*

Pagan babies. Elmore Leonard. Delacorte Press, 2000. 263 p.
ISBN 9780385333924
1. Americans in Rwanda 2. Swindlers and swindling 3. Criminals 4. Priests 5. Women stand-up comedians 6. Detroit, Michigan 7. Rwanda 8. Crime fiction
LC 29506

Father Terry Dunn returns to Detroit from a stint in Rwanda, and begins a search for the perfect money-raising scam.

"This is one of Mr. Leonard's funniest books, with a typically colourful cast of oddballs. The dialogue, too, is snappy.... Mr. Leonard steers the reader effortlessly through a maze of plots and counterplots, then brings the whole thing in with a bravura flourish and stops on a dime." —*The Economist*

★ **Raylan**. Elmore Leonard. William Morrow, 2012. 263 pages (Raylan Givens thrillers, 3)
ISBN 9780062119469
1. United States marshals 2. Drug dealers 3. Human body parts industry and trade 4. Criminal investigation 5. Brothers 6. Kentucky 7. Harlan County, Kentucky 8. Crime fiction
LC 2011024392

After discovering his quarry naked in the bathtub, doped up and missing his kidneys, Federal Marshall Raylan Givens becomes involved, both literally and figuratively, in a case involving the harvesting of organs for sale on the black market where this time the bad guys are girls.

Rum punch. Elmore Leonard. Delacorte 1992. 297 p.
ISBN 9780385301435
1. Gun smugglers 2. Bail bond agents 3. Betrayal 4. Flight attendants 5. Thrillers and suspense 6. Books to movies
LC 91038738

When the feds arrest her for running machine guns for gun dealer Ordell Robbie, former flight attendant Jackie Burke must decide whether to keep quiet about her boss or spill the beans and face his wrath BT

"Mr. Leonard never tells you; he shows you. The story is all action, a scam within a scam.... His style is the absence of style, stripped of fancy baggage...the absence, as far as it's possible, of an authorial ego." —*New York Times Book Review*

Book adapted into the 1997 film: Jackie Brown.

Tishomingo blues: a novel. Elmore Leonard. Morrow, 2002. 308 p.
ISBN 9780060008727
1. Murder witnesses 2. Divers 3. Daredevils (Stunt performers) 4. Crime 5. Casinos 6. Southern States 7. United States 8. Crime fiction
LC 2001044405

New York Times Notable Book, 2002

Warned by the local Dixie underworld to keep silent after witnessing a murder, daredevil diver Dennis Lenahan is recruited by Detroit gangster Robert Taylor for a showdown that takes place during a Civil War reenactment.

When the women come out to dance: stories. Elmore Leonard. William Morrow, 2002. 228 p.
ISBN 9780060083977
1. Law enforcement 2. Criminals 3. Man-woman relationships 4. Short stories 5. Crime fiction 6. Westerns
LC 2002026426

New York Times Notable Book, 2003

A collection of stories includes two novella-length works featuring surprising plot twists.

"Reading the clipped, unfailingly accurate dialogue that comes out of the mouths of Leonard's characters can make you feel as if you're in the presence of a writer who is both ventriloquist and psychic. It's not just that Leonard captures the cadences and elisions of each character's speech, it's that he has an uncanny sense of knowing what each will say next." —*New York Times Book Review*

Lepionka, Kristen

The **last** place you look. Kristen Lepionka. Minotaur Books, 2017. 320 p. (Roxane Weary novels, 1)
ISBN 9781250120519
1. Judicial error 2. Death row prisoners 3. Missing teenage girls 4. Missing persons investigation 5. Women private investigators 6. Ohio 7. Mysteries
Shamus Award for Best First P.I. Novel, 2018

Nine months after her cop father died on duty, PI Roxane Weary is still a mess. Even so, she agrees to help the desperate sister of a man on death row. The woman thinks she's seen her black brother's white girlfriend, who could clear his name... but if it's really her, where's she been for the last 15 years, gone since the day her parents were murdered? Roxane finds solace in whiskey and sex, but also finds purpose in her search, even as she gets harassed by cops and links the missing girl to one of her late father's cases. This accomplished debut set in Columbus, Ohio has a hardboiled feel, great dialogue, complex characters, and a tough female detective.

"Introducing a fascinating protagonist who combats her emotional demons with the aid of sugar, booze, and sex, this suspenseful, original, and confident debut will please fans of the hard-boiled PI genre." —*Library Journal*

Once you go this far: a mystery. Kristen Lepionka. Minotaur Books, 2020. 312 pages (Roxane Weary novels, 4)
ISBN 9781250309372
1. Women private investigators 2. Women murder victims 3. Secrets 4. Threat (Psychology) 5. Conspiracies 6. Columbus, Ohio 7. Ohio 8. Mysteries
LC 2019055285

Believing that her father, a well-connected ex-cop, killed her mother, Maggie turns to PI Roxane Weary for help, drawing Roxane into a situation that doesn't add up, and Roxane must find a way to connect the pieces before a dangerous secret gets someone else killed.

"Along the way to the surprise ending, Roxane learns a shocking truth about her own father's past. Roxane, with her vibrant narrative voice, stands as a worthy successor to Sue Grafton's Kinsey Millhone." —*Publishers Weekly*

Lerner, Ben

★ The **Topeka** school. Ben Lerner. Farrar Straus & Giroux, 2019. 272 pages
ISBN 9780374277789
1. Middle-class families 2. Violence — Psychological aspects 3. High school students 4. Debates and debating 5. Identity (Psychology) 6. Kansas 7. Middle West 8. 1990s 9. Literary fiction 10. Multiple perspectives
ALA Notable Book, 2020; Los Angeles Times Book Prize for Fiction, 2019; New York Times Notable Book, 2019; National Book Critics Circle Award for Fiction finalist, 2019; Pulitzer Prize for Fiction finalist, 2020

A family drama set in the American Midwest at the turn of the century: a tale of adolescence, transgression, and the conditions that have given rise to the trolls and tyrants of the new right.

Lescroart, John T.

Guilt. John Lescroart. Delacorte Press, 1997. 462 p.
ISBN 9780385316552
1. Guilt 2. Trials (Murder) 3. Ethics 4. Married men 5. Extramarital affairs 6. San Francisco, California 7. Legal thrillers 8. Thrillers and suspense
LC 96-43756

When Mark Dooher becomes a suspect in his wife's murder, all the San Francisco attorney—who gets what he wants, including a beautiful mistress and the power of the Church behind him—has to fear is the truth BT

A standalone novel starring attorneys Wes Farrell and Mark Dooher and homicide detective Abe Glitsky set in the same San Francisco milieu as the Dismas Hardy novels.

Lessing, Doris May

★ The **fifth** child. Doris Lessing. A. A. Knopf 1988. 133 p.
ISBN 9780394571058
1. Violence in boys 2. Family problems 3. Misfits (Persons) 4. Mothers and sons 5. Large families 6. London, England 7. Psychological fiction 8. Literary fiction
LC 88002680

A self-satisfied couple intent on raising a happy family is shocked by the birth of an abnormal and brutal fifth child.

Sequel: Ben, in the world.

★ The **golden** notebook. Doris Lessing; with an introduction by the author. Harper Perennial, 1994. Xxix, 623 p.
ISBN 9780060975906
1. Women authors 2. Communism 3. Feminists 4. Identity (Psychology) 5. London, England 6. Psychological fiction 7. Literary fiction 8. Diary novels
LC 93044125

The experiences of two women provide the framework for an intense literary study of liberated womanhood.

A **proper** marriage. Doris Lessing. Plume, 1991. 345 p; (Children of violence series, 2)
ISBN 9780452265776
1. Extramarital affairs 2. Arthur, King 3. British in South Africa 4. Quest, Martha (Fictitious character) 5. Marital conflict 6. Africa 7. 1930s 8. Psychological fiction 9. Literary fiction 10. Domestic fiction
LC 90022046

Feeling trapped and alienated by her husband, Martha Quest must choose between the security of marriage and the sacrifices of independence.

The **sweetest** dream. Doris Lessing. Harper Collins Publishers, 2002. 478 p.
ISBN 9780066213347
1. Extended families 2. Self-sacrifice in women 3. Widows 4. Runaway wives, husbands, etc. 5. Daughters-in-law 6. London, England 7. Africa 8. 1960s 9. Family sagas 10. Psychological fiction 11. Literary fiction 12. Adult books for young adults
New York Times Notable Book, 2002

As Frances Lennox and her two sons try to make the best of their situation living with her conservative mother-in-law, her ex-husband dumps his second wife's problem child at her feet, in a novel that recreates the tumultuous political landscape of the 1960s.

Lethem, Jonathan

Chronic city. Jonathan Lethem. Doubleday, 2009. 480 p.
ISBN 9780385518635
1. Women astronauts 2. Socialites 3. Social criticism 4. Celebrities 5. Critics 6. Manhattan, New York City 7. Literary fiction
New York Times Notable Book, 2009

Exchanging love letters with a fiancee who is trapped on the Space Station, Chase Insteadman apathetically attends social engagements before pop critic Perkus Tooth introduces him to a side of Manhattan that causes Chase to question everything he believes

Dissident gardens. Jonathan Lethem. Doubleday, 2013. 468 p.
ISBN 9780385534932
1. Dysfunctional families 2. Jewish women 3. Communism 4. Mothers and daughters 5. Interracial romance 6. New York City 7. Family sagas 8. Literary fiction 9. Political fiction
New York Times Notable Book, 2013

A multigenerational saga focuses on two extraordinary women, including Rose, a tyrannical Communist who terrorizes her neighborhood with her absolute beliefs, and her daughter Miriam, who embraces the counterculture of Greenwich Village.

"The cast makes for a heady, swirly mix of fascinating, lonely people. Lethem's writing, as always, packs a witty punch." —*Publishers Weekly*

★ **Motherless** Brooklyn. Jonathan Lethem. Doubleday, 1999. 311 p.
ISBN 9780788751837
1. Tourette syndrome 2. Private investigators 3. Murder investigation 4. Orphans 5. Brooklyn, New York City 6. Hardboiled fiction 7. Literary fiction 8. Books to movies
ALA Notable Book, 2000; Booklist Editors' Choice, 1999; Gold Dagger Award for Best Crime Novel of the Year, 2000; National Book Critics Circle Award for Fiction, 1999; New York Times Notable Book, 1999

A walk on the wild side of Brooklyn's criminal underclass with a hero known as "The Human Freakshow," a would-be detective also answering to the name of Lionel Essrog. Essrog is a victim of Tourette's Syndrome; hapless and veering out of control, he fights himself and his disease.

"The short and shady life of Frank Minna ends in murder, shocking the four young men employed by his dysfunctional Brooklyn detective agency/limo service. The 'Minna Men' have centered their lives around Frank.... Tourette's-afflicted Lionel had found security as a Minna Man and is shattered by Frank's death. Lionel determines to become a genuine sleuth and find the killer. The ensuing plot twists are marked by clever wordplay, fast-paced dialog, and nonstop irony." —*Library Journal*

Adapted into a film entitled "Motherless Brooklyn" in 2019.

Levin, Adam

Bubblegum. Adam Levin. Bubblegum, 2020. 784 pages
ISBN 9780385544962
1. Robots 2. Alienation (Social psychology) 3. Fathers and sons 4. Living and non-living things 5. 1980s 6. 2010s 7. Alternate histories 8. Experimental fiction

In an alternate present-day word in which the Internet doesn't exist, one of the first owners of a popular interactive "flesh and bone" robot called Curio grapples with the outside world as he attempts to write his memoir.

"While breathtakingly bizarre, this relentlessly inventive novel teems with humanity, humor, and pathos like few other recent works and is a book many will obsess over and delight in." —*Booklist*

Levin, Ira

The **boys** from Brazil: a novel. Ira Levin. Random House, 1976. 312 p.
ISBN 9780394402673
1. Hitler, Adolf 2. Racism 3. Conspiracies 4. Clones and cloning 5. Nazis 6. Antisemitism 7. Thrillers and suspense 8. Books to movies

Six former SS men, dispatched from Brazil by the notorious former commandant of Auschwitz to kill ninety-four men, become the targets of aging, increasingly shortsighted Nazi-hunter Yakov Liebermann.

A **kiss** before dying. Ira Levin. Simon and Schuster, 1953. 244 p.
ISBN 9780786711642
1. Psychopaths 2. Antisocial personality disorders 3. Deception 4. Twin sisters 5. Ambition in men 6. Noir fiction 7. Thrillers and suspense 8. Books to movies
LC 53002041
Edgar Allan Poe Award for Best First Mystery Novel, 1954

A charming young man who will stop at nothing, including murder, to get to where he wants to go, must deal with Dorothy, his pregnant girlfriend, and the solution involves some desperate measures.

★ **Rosemary's** baby: a novel. Ira Levin. Penguin, 1997. 319 p.
ISBN 9780451194008
1. Husband and wife 2. Rape 3. Antichrist 4. Apartment houses 5. Unplanned pregnancy 6. Manhattan, New York City 7. Horror 8. Books to movies 9. Books to TV

Witchcraft and terror await Rosemary and Guy Woodhouse when they move into the ominous Bramford apartment building.

Sequel: Son of Rosemary.
Originally published: New York : Random House, 1967.

★ The **Stepford** wives: a novel. Ira Levin. Random House, 1972. 145 p.
ISBN 9780394481999
1. Suburban life 2. Gender role 3. Men's organizations 4. Homemakers 5. Robots 6. Horror 7. Books to movies
LC 72002481

For Joanna, her husband, Walter, and their children, the move to beautiful Stepford seems almost too good to be true. It is. For behind the town's idyllic facade lies a terrible secret—a secret so shattering that no one who encounters it will ever be the same.

"There is a broad current of humor beneath the horrific surface of this little ambush of Women's Lib, life and the pursuit of happiness." —*New York Times Book Review*

Levine, David D.

Arabella of Mars. David D. Levine. Tor, 2016. 320 p. (Adventures of Arabella Ashby, 1)
ISBN 9780765382818
1. Space flight 2. Young women 3. Male impersonators 4. Space vehicles 5. Frontier and pioneer life 6. Mars (Planet) 7. 18th century 8. Science fiction 9. Alternate histories 10. Steampunk 11. Adult books for young adults
Nebula Awards: Andre Norton Award for YA Science Fiction and Fantasy, 2016

Arabella Ashby loves her life on the British colony of Mars. Her parents, however, despair of Arabella's refusal to act like a proper English lady and sends her to Oxfordshire, where she must endure an endless succession of social events for the purpose of finding a husband. But when Arabella receives word that her brother, still on Mars, is in danger, she disguises herself as a boy and joins the crew of the Diana, a Mars Trading Company vessel. But will she arrive in time to save him? With its Steampunk-infused Regency-era setting and swashbuckling adventure among the stars, Arabella of Mars should appeal to fans of Jules Verne and Edgar Rice Burroughs.

"The alternate-world science is novel, the plot thrilling, and the romance appropriately chaste, but with her wits, resourcefulness, and courage, Arabella cuts a dashing figure as the heroine of this story." —*Booklist*

Levy, Andrea

The **long** song. Andrea Levy. Farrar, Straus and Giroux, 2010. 320 p.
ISBN 9780374192174
1. Slavery 2. Master and servant 3. Enslaved women 4. Race relations 5. Plantation life 6. Jamaica 7. Historical fiction
LC 2009043181
Walter Scott Prize for Historical Fiction, 2011; New York Times Notable Book, 2010; Shortlisted for the Man Booker Prize, 2010

You do not know me yet but I am the narrator of this work. My son Thomas, who is publishing this book, tells me it is customary at this place in a novel to give the reader a little taste of the story that is held within these pages. As your storyteller, I am to convey that this tale is set in Jamaica during the last turbulent years of slavery and the early years of freedom that followed.

"For all its power to disturb, this is a beautifully written and cleverly constructed novel that projects convincing personal relationships on to the feral backdrop of the Jamaican plantations." —*Times (London)*
A Frances Coady book.
Contains reading group questions.

Small island. Andrea Levy. Review, 2004. 448 p.
ISBN 9780755307494
1. Racism 2. Prejudice 3. Race relations 4. Interracial friendship 5. Husband and wife 6. England 7. 1940s 8. Historical fiction 9. Literary fiction 10. Multiple perspectives 11. Adult books for young adults
Commonwealth Writers' Prize for Best Book, 2005; Commonwealth Writers' Prize, South Asia and Europe: Best Book, 2005; Orange Prize for Fiction, 2004; Whitbread Book Award for Novel, 2004; Whitbread Book of the Year Award, 2004; National Book Critics Circle Award for Fiction finalist, 2005

Returning to England after the war Gilbert Joseph is treated very differently now that he is no longer in an RAF uniform. Joined by his wife Hortense, he rekindles a friendship with Queenie who takes in Jamaican lodgers. Can their dreams of a better life in England overcome the prejudice they face?

"The narrative voice jumps between the characters, a technique that embeds familiar cultural observations in closely observed and surprising lives. If the plot sometimes verges on the operatic, Levy's writing deftly illuminates the complex and contradictory motives behind each character's behavior." —*The New Yorker*

Levy, Deborah

Hot milk: a novel. Deborah Levy. Bloomsbury USA, 2016. 217 p.
ISBN 9781620406694
1. Parent and adult child 2. Mothers and daughters 3. Self-fulfillment in women 4. Uncertainty 5. Purpose in life 6. Spain 7. Literary fiction
LC 2016001369
New York Times Notable Book, 2016; Shortlisted for the Man Booker Prize, 2016

Driven to cure her mother's inexplicable illness, a young anthropologist seeks the advice of a famous but controversial consultant on the arid coast of southern Spain, where the transient desert environment shapes her own desires.

"Levy has crafted a great character in Sofia, and witnessing a pivotal point in her life is a pleasure." —*Publishers Weekly*

Swimming home: a novel. Deborah Levy; with an introduction by Tom McCarthy. Bloomsbury USA, 2012. 157 p.
ISBN 9781620401699
1. Middle class families 2. Family vacations 3. Strangers 4. Interpersonal relations 5. Poets 6. Nice, France 7. French Riviera 8. 1990s 9. Psychological fiction 10. Literary fiction
LC 2011535684
New York Times Notable Book, 2012; Shortlisted for the Man Booker Prize, 2012

A mysterious woman who suffers from mental illness suddenly appears at a vacation villa where two families are staying and her interactions with them reveal secret details about their past and tensions within their relationships with each other.
Originally published: High Wycombe, England : And Other Stories, c2011.

Lewis, Beverly

The **brethren**. Beverly Lewis. Bethany House, 2006. 352 p. (Annie's people, 3)
ISBN 9780764202315
1. Children of clergy 2. Family secrets 3. Amish families 4. Women artists 5. Amish — Social life and customs 6. Pennsylvania 7. Christian fiction 8. Domestic fiction
LC 2006019314
Christy Award for Contemporary (Series, Sequels, and Novellas) Category, 2007; Library Journal Best Books, 2006

Annie Zook, the Amish preacher's daughter, is caught between two worlds. Living with shunned friend Esther, Annie longs to return to her forbidden art and the idyllic days spent with Englisher Ben Martin, before her father ordered her never to see him again. Stunned when family secrets come to light, Ben determines to solve the mystery of his past. Will his future include Annie—or will the Brethren always stand between them?
Sequel to: The Englisher.

The **ebb** tide. Beverly Lewis. Baker Pub Group 2017. 352 p.
ISBN 9780764219092
1. Amish 2. Amish women 3. Nannies 4. College students 5. Man-woman relationships 6. Cape May, New Jersey 7. Christian romances
LC 2016041992
Spending the summer working as a nanny in Cape May, young Amish woman Sallie meets a marine biology student and makes discoveries about herself and the world outside her community that compel her to question her commitments to the home she has always loved.

The **missing**. Beverly Lewis. Bethany House, 2009. 332 p. (Seasons of grace (Beverly Lewis), 2)
ISBN 9780764207242
1. Amish 2. People with terminal illnesses 3. Mothers and daughters 4. Female friendship 5. Missing women 6. Pennsylvania 7. Christian fiction
Library Journal Best Books, 2009

Longing to find her missing mother and uncover the secrets that led to her leaving three weeks earlier, 21-year-old Grace Byler strikes up a fast friendship with Heather Lang, an "Englisher" contemplating her own grave medical prognosis, and the two young women travel together in hopes of finding Grace's mother and bringing her home.

The **preacher's** daughter. Beverly Lewis. Bethany House, 2005. 349 p; (Annie's people, 1)
ISBN 9780764201059

1. Amish women 2. Children of clergy 3. Women artists 4. Pen pals 5. Women art teachers 6. Pennsylvania 7. 1890s 8. Christian historical fiction 9. Domestic fiction 10. Coming-of-age stories

LC 2005018581

Library Journal Best Books, 2005

Annie Zook's greatest passion is drawing, but it's forbidden by her father, an Old Order Amish preacher in Paradise, Pennsylvania. She must even sacrifice marriage and happiness with the love of her life, Rudy Esh, in order to secretly practice her art. But when longtime pen pal, fellow artist and "Englisher" Louisa Stratford visits seeking solace after a broken engagement, Annie must come to terms with her unhappiness and decide whether to stay with her Plain community or pursue her dream.

Collected in 2014 with The Englisher and The Brethren under the title Annie's People.

Lewis, C. S.

Till we have faces: a myth retold. C.S. Lewis; drawings by Fritz Eichenberg. Harcourt Brace & Co, 1984. 313 p. : Illustration

ISBN 9780156904360

1. Love 2. Identity (Psychology) 3. Princesses 4. Psyche (Greek deity) 5. Cupid (Roman deity) 6. Mythological fiction 7. Fantasy fiction

This reinterpretation of the tale of Cupid and Psyche, combines elements of barbarism and fantasy with an understanding of human nature and psychology.

Originally published in 1956.

Lewis, Linden A.

The first sister: a novel. Linden A. Lewis. Skybound Books, 2020. 352 p. (First Sister novels, 1)

ISBN 9781982126995

1. Space vehicles 2. Women priests 3. Comfort women 4. Soldiers 5. Space flight 6. Multiple perspectives 7. Science fiction 8. Military science fiction

LC 2019026611

A Sisterhood priestess whose soldiers own the rights to her body confronts a difficult choice between duty and her heart, while an elite Venus soldier questions his allegiances when he is ordered to kill his former partner.

"Despite a bit of clunky exposition early on, Lewis skillfully handles the tale's many moving pieces, maintaining pace, nuance, and clarity throughout. Lewis's lush prose creates an immersive, richly textured world with complex social dynamics and solid LGBTQ and multicultural representation." —Publishers Weekly

Lewis, Sinclair

Babbitt. Sinclair Lewis. Harcourt 1950. 401 p.

ISBN 9780140189025

1. Hypocrisy 2. Real estate agents 3. Conformity 4. Middle class men 5. 1920s 6. Satirical fiction 7. Books to movies 8. Modern classics

On the surface, everything is all right with Babbitt's world of the solid, successful businessman. But in reality, George F. Babbit is a lonely, middle-aged man. He doesn't understand his family, has an unsuccessful attempt at an affair, and is almost financially ruined when he dares to voice sympathy for some striking workers. Babbitt finds his only safety lies deep in the fold of those who play it safe. He is a man who has added a new word to our language: a "Babbitt," meaning someone who conforms unthinkingly, a sheep.

Originally published in 1922.

Dodsworth. Sinclair Lewis. Harcourt, 1929. 377 p.

ISBN 9789997412379

1. Middle-aged men 2. Executives 3. Climacteric, Male 4. Automobile industry and trade 5. Rich men 6. United States 7. Domestic fiction 8. Satirical fiction 9. Books to movies

Touring Europe with his beautiful but spoiled wife Fran, millionaire Sam Dodsworth, known as the American Captain of Industry, witnesses the clash of American and English cultures at the same time his marriage falls apart.

★ **Elmer** Gantry. Sinclair Lewis. New American Library, 1980. 430 p.

ISBN 9780451522511

1. Ambition 2. Hypocrisy 3. Revivals 4. Itinerant preachers 5. Evangelists 6. Modern classics 7. Satirical fiction 8. Books to movies

A vulgar and licentious college football captain becomes a messenger of God as a suave evangelist preacher, in this classic story that is universally recognized as a landmark in American literature.

Originally published: New York : Harcourt, Brace and Co, 1927.

★ **It** can't happen here. New American Library, 1963. 331 p.

ISBN 9780451216588

1. State-sponsored terrorism 2. Newspaper editors 3. Extremism 4. Totalitarianism 5. Dictators 6. United States 7. Fascism 8. 1930s 9. Political fiction

It is 1936. America has just elected Berzelius Windrip to the presidency-and his fascist policies turn the U.S. into a totalitarian state.

"In an enigmatic election year, Sinclair Lewis's 1935 political satire It Can't Happen Here holds unexpectedly fresh warnings." —Chronicle of Higher Education

★ **Main** street: the story of Carol Kennicott. Sinclair Lewis; with an introduction and notes by Martin Bucco. Penguin Books, 1995. 415 p.

ISBN 9780140189018

1. Physicians' spouses 2. Small town life 3. Hypocrisy 4. Gossiping and gossips 5. Greed 6. Minnesota 7. 1920s 8. Satirical fiction 9. Modern classics

LC 95016373 //r96

Raised in free-thinking St. Paul, Carol Milford is slightly disheartened when she marries Dr. Will Kennicott, moves to a rural town, and reverts to a life of domesticity. Although her husband is not to blame for her unhappiness, Carol quickly becomes disillusioned and begins to contemplate leaving the good doctor.

Originally published: New York : Harcourt, Brace, 1920.

Li, Yiyun

The vagrants: a novel. Yiyun Li. Random House, 2009. 337 p.

ISBN 9781400063130

1. Communism 2. Executions and executioners 3. Human body parts industry and trade 4. Violence 5. Friendship 6. China 7. Chinese Cultural Revolution (1966-1976) 8. 1970s 9. Historical fiction

LC 2008023467

ALA Notable Book, 2010; Shortlisted for the International IMPAC Dublin Literary Award, 2011

In 1979 Muddy River, a provincial Chinese city, the Gu family struggles to deal with the imminent loss of their daughter, Gu Shan, about to be executed as a counterrevolutionary, while their neighbors deal with the realities of life in China.

"Li offers both a bleak view of a historical moment when people were the most dangerous animals in the world and a meditation on the act of martyrdom, which is presented both as a duty and as a luxury that few could afford." —The New Yorker

Liardet, Frances

We must be brave. Frances Liardet. G.P. Putnam's Sons, 2019. 464 p.
ISBN 9780735218864
1. Childlessness 2. Married women 3. Lost children 4. Loss (Psychology) 5. Villages 6. England 7. 20th century 8. Historical fiction
LC 2018041587

Caring for a lost child during the chaotic 1940 evacuation of her once-quiet Southampton village, a woman who never believed she wanted children finds herself unexpectedly at a loss when the child is taken away.

Lightman, Alan P.

The **diagnosis**. By Alan Lightman. Pantheon Books, 2000. 369 p.
ISBN 9780679436157
1. Identity (Psychology) 2. Amnesia 3. Technology — Social aspects 4. Executives 5. Men with amnesia 6. Boston, Massachusetts 7. Psychological fiction
LC 24543

Booklist Editors' Choice, 2000; New York Times Notable Book, 2000; National Book Award for Fiction finalist, 2000

Businessman Bill Chalmers descends into a nightmare as he pursues a diagnosis for his strange illness, which involves a bizarre memory loss and a strange numbness that gradually affects his entire body.

"A work of vivid sensuousness, sparkling intelligence, and poignant beauty, Lightman's gripping tale contrasts the needs of the body and spirit with the acquisitiveness of the mind and ponders the potential lethality of ideologies, be they cultural or technological." —*Booklist*

★ **Einstein's** dreams. By Alan Lightman. Pantheon Books, 1993. 179 p.
ISBN 9780679416463
1. Einstein, Albert 2. Dreams 3. Time 4. General relativity (Physics) 5. Physicists 6. Physics 7. Literary fiction
LC 92050465

A fictional recreation of Einstein's discovery of the nature of time follows the young Albert through 1905 Bern, Switzerland, as he sorts through the dreams that have persisted in his mind for several months BT

"Lightman starts out with commonplaces, neurological conditions or abstractions of our personal experience of time. Then, with one or two exceptions, he embodies the concept in brilliant, folkloric tales with extraordinary assurance." —*New Statesman*

Lim, Roselle

Natalie Tan's book of luck and fortune. Roselle Lim. Berkley, 2019. 304 p.
ISBN 9781984803252
1. Women cooks 2. Chinese Americans 3. Families 4. Cooking, Chinese 5. Women — Family relationships 6. Chinatown, San Francisco, California 7. San Francisco, California 8. Relationship fiction
LC 2018041137

LibraryReads Favorites, 2019

Inheriting her grandmother's restaurant in a crumbling San Francisco Chinatown neighborhood, Natalie Tan is advised by the local seer to prepare three recipes from her grandmother's cookbook to help their struggling community.

"Readers will fall in love with Natalie, her multifaceted supporting cast, and the sights, sounds, and smells of San Francisco. This bighearted and deeply-felt story stirs together mourning, nostalgia, and the freedom of new possibilities." —*Booklist*

Vanessa Yu's magical Paris tea shop. Roselle Lim. Berkley, 2020. 304 p.
ISBN 9781984803276
1. Chinese American families 2. Women psychics 3. Clairvoyance 4. Single women 5. Tearooms 6. Paris, France 7. France 8. Romantic comedies 9. Canadian fiction
LC 2019059053

LibraryReads Favorites, 2020

From the critically acclaimed author of Natalie Tan's Book of Luck and Fortune comes a new delightful novel about exploring all the magical possibilities of life in the most extraordinary city of all: Paris.

"Still, the characters sparkle, the magic successfully enchants, and Lim skewers the anti-Asian racism the Yus face in France with pointed and timely commentary. This feast for the senses will especially appeal to hopeless romantics." —*Publishers Weekly*

Limon, Martin

The **line**. Martin Limon. Soho Press, 2018. 336 p. (George Sueno and Ernie Bascom mysteries, 13)
ISBN 9781616959661
1. Murder investigation 2. Racism 3. Racism in the military 4. Innocence (Law) 5. Scapegoats (Persons) 6. Korean Demilitarized Zone 7. Korea 8. 1970s 9. First person narratives 10. Mysteries 11. Political fiction
LC 2018016742

After discovering a body on the Korean Demilitarized Zone in the 1970s, Sueño and Bascom try to find the perpetrator despite little cooperation between the two countries' governments.

"Limn has never been better at incorporating a logical mystery plot into the politics of his chosen time and place." —*Publishers Weekly*

War women. Martin Limon. Soho Crime, 2021. 288 p. (George Sueno and Ernie Bascom mysteries, 15)
ISBN 9781641292795
1. Military police 2. Americans in Korea 3. Missing men 4. Security classification (Government documents) 5. Defectors 6. Korean Demilitarized Zone 7. Korea 8. 1970s 9. First person narratives 10. Mysteries
LC 2021027163

South Korea, 1970s: Sergeant First Class Cecil B. Harvey, a senior NCO in charge of 8th Army's classified documents, has long been a friend (willing or unwilling) to Sergeants George Sueno and Ernie Bascom. So when he goes missing with a top-secret document that even a glance at could get an officer court-martialed, Sueno and Bascom take it upon themselves to find him. Meanwhile, *Overseas Observer* reporter Katie Byrd Worthington is back to make life difficult for top Army brass. When she lands in a Korean jail cell, Sueno and Bascom are sent to get her out—and negotiate against the publication of an incriminating story that could land important military officials in hot water.

"Through 15 episodes, Limon continues to balance old-school, Chandlerian action with crisp historical detail and penetrating insight into military malfeasance." —*Booklist*

Lin, Jeannie

The **lotus** palace. Jeannie Lin. HQN, 2013. 384 p. (Lotus Palace, 1)
ISBN 9780373777730
1. Nobility 2. Murder investigation 3. Civilization, Medieval 4. Interclass romance 5. Deception 6. China 7. Tang dynasty (618-907) 8. Medieval period (476-1492) 9. Historical romances

Even without her disfiguring birthmark, maidservant Yue-ying knows she could never attract the attention of Lord Bai Huang—not when he could have her mistress, Mingyu, the Lotus Palace's most desirable courtesan and one of the Four Beauties of the Pingkang li, the famed entertainment district of capital city Chang'an. However, as Yue-ying discovers when they're thrown together during a murder investigation, Bai is more than the charming wastrel he seems at first. Can their mutual attraction overcome their different stations in life? Set in during China's 9th-century Tang Dynasty, The Lotus Palace delivers romance loaded with lavish, atmospheric historical details.

"Lin once again effortlessly evokes the colorful, intriguing world of Tang dynasty China in her latest dazzlingly different romance, and the books mystery-rich plot and exotic historical setting also make The Lotus Palace an excellent read-alike suggestion for fans of Laura Joh Rowlands mysteries." —*Booklist*

Linden, Rachel

Ascension of larks. Rachel Linden. Thomas Nelson, 2017. 336 p.
ISBN 9780718095734
1. Family secrets 2. Self-discovery in women 3. Women photographers 4. Loss (Psychology) 5. Widows 6. Relationship fiction

LC 2017004213

Risking her career to care for the widow and young children of the only man she's ever loved, globetrotting photographer Magdalena Henry finds joy after tragedy and embraces the beauty of an unexpected life.

The **enlightenment** of bees. Rachel Linden. Thomas Nelson, 2019. 336 p.
ISBN 9780785221401
1. Humanitarian assistance 2. Self-fulfillment in women 3. Breaking up (Interpersonal relations) 4. Volunteers 5. Food relief 6. Hungary 7. Mumbai, India 8. Christian fiction

LC 2019002201

Rachel Linden's newest story speaks to the universal struggle of what it means to live a meaningful life where the passions we have meet the needs of the world.

Lindsay, Jeffry P.

Just watch me. Jeffry P. Lindsay. E.P. Dutton, 2019. 320 pages (Riley Wolfe novels, 1)
ISBN 9781524743949
1. Thieves 2. Jewelry theft 3. Ambition 4. Parkour 5. Diamonds 6. Caper novels
Loan Stars Favourites, 2019

Targeting a crown jewel collection that is protected by airtight security, a Robin Hood-type master thief finds his efforts complicated by an equally skilled nemesis cop and an expert forger with dubious loyalties.

Lindsey, Odie

Some go home: a novel. Odie Lindsey. W W Norton & Co Inc 2020. 295 pages
ISBN 9780393249521
1. Women veterans 2. Pregnancy 3. Racism 4. Trials (Murder) 5. Prisoners 6. Mississippi 7. Southern fiction

LC 2019052107

A pregnant Iraq War veteran, the son of a man undergoing retrial and a correction officer's family navigate media hype, community secrets and racial tensions at the antebellum estate where a civil rights murder occurred half a century earlier.

"In dazzling prose, the author lassos complex subjects with acuity, from the legacy of racism in Mississippi to internecine class wars, the horror of combat, and the joy and terror of becoming a mother. This is a con-summate portrait of human fragility and grim determination.' —*Publishers Weekly*

Includes bibliographical references (page 295).

Lipman, Elinor

The **dearly** departed. Elinor Lipman. Random House, 2001. 256 p.
ISBN 9780679463122
1. Self-discovery 2. Siblings 3. Funerals 4. Mothers — Death 5. Family secrets 6. New Hampshire 7. Relationship fiction

LC 67368

The untimely death of her single mother, Margaret Batten, brings Sunny back to small-town King George, New Hampshire, the scene of her unhappy adolescence, where she discovers old family secrets and a possible half-brother she never knew she had.

Good riddance. Elinor Lipman. Houghton Mifflin Harcourt, 2019. 290 p.
ISBN 9780544808256
1. School yearbooks 2. Neighbors 3. Family secrets 4. Mothers — Death 5. Class reunions 6. New York City 7. New Hampshire 8. Romantic comedies 9. Relationship fiction

LC 2018006362

LibraryReads Favorites, 2019

Discarding her late mother's cherished and heavily annotated high school yearbook, Daphne is entangled in a series of absurdities when the yearbook is discovered by a busybody documentary filmmaker.

The **pursuit** of Alice Thrift: a novel. Elinor Lipman. Random House, 2003. 269 p.
ISBN 9780679463139
1. Courtship 2. Swindlers and swindling 3. Self-discovery 4. Self-fulfillment 5. Women physicians 6. Boston, Massachusetts 7. Relationship fiction

LC 2002031864

Workaholic wallflower Alice Thrift, a socially inept surgical intern at a Boston hospital, is pursued romantically by Ray Russo, a social-climbing, somewhat shady purveyor of carnival fudge, until her roommate, nurse Leo Frawley, and neighbor, Dr. Sylvie Schwartz, decide to take on the task of guiding Alice through the social complexities of life.

"The eponymous Alice is a sleep-deprived surgical intern at a Boston hospital. A graduate of MIT and Harvard and a congenital workaholic, she's also devoid of social skills, a sense of humor or elementary tact. Though miserably unequipped with self-esteem, Alice is an intelligent, well-brought-up offspring of upper-middle-class parents. Why, then, does she fall prey to the romantic blandishments of Ray Russo, a vulgar loudmouth and con artist whoit turns outlies every time he opens his mouth? That Lipman can make this story plausible, and tell it with humor, pschological insight and rising suspense, is a triumph." —*Publishers Weekly*

Lippman, Laura

★ **After** I'm gone. Laura Lippman. William Morrow, 2014. 334 p.
ISBN 9780062083395
1. Missing men 2. Coping 3. Family relationships 4. Cold cases (Criminal investigation) 5. Women murder victims 6. Baltimore, Maryland 7. Psychological suspense

LC 2013018550

Anthony Award for Best Novel, 2015; LibraryReads Favorites, 2014; Romantic Times Reviewer's Choice Award, 2014

Working a twenty-six-year-old cold case involving the murder of a convicted felon's mistress, retired Baltimore detective Roberto Sanchez discovers a web of bitterness, jealousy, and greed involving five women which spans five decades.

"Lippman incisively explores marriage, Jewish family life, class distinctions, and the power and liability of physical beauty, thus creating an involving and elegant novel of the psychological ravages of crime." —*Booklist*

★ **And** when she was good. Laura Lippman. William Morrow, 2012. 384 p.

ISBN 9780061706875

1. Madams (Prostitution) 2. Crimes against prostitutes 3. Death threats 4. Murderers 5. Former lovers 6. Thrillers and suspense

Suburban madam Heloise, with no one left to trust, decides to get out of the game when another suburban madam is brutally murdered, forcing her to stay one step ahead of a killer—and the father of her child—who is just as lethal behind bars as he was on the outside.

★ **Dream** girl. Laura Lippman. William Morrow & Company, 2021. 384 p.

ISBN 9780062390073

1. Authors 2. Accident victims 3. Convalescence 4. Telephone calls 5. Women in literature 6. Baltimore, Maryland 7. Psychological suspense

Injured in a freak fall, novelist Gerry Andersen is confined to a hospital bed in his glamorous high-rise apartment, dependent on two women he barely knows: his incurious young assistant, and a dull, slow-witted night nurse. Then late one night, the phone rings. The caller claims to be the "real" Aubrey, the alluring title character from his most successful novel, Dream Girl. Isolated from the world, drowsy from medication, Gerry slips between reality and a dreamlike state in which he is haunted by his own past: his faithless father, his devoted mother; the women who loved him, the women he loved. And now here is Aubrey, threatening to visit him, suggesting that she is owed something. Is the threat real or is it a sign of dementia? Which scenario would he prefer?

"Lippman never stops twisting the plot into a deliciously intricate pretzel, right up to the jaw-dropping finale. This is both a beguiling look at the mysteries of authorship and a powerful #MeToo novel, but that's only the tip of a devilishly jagged iceberg that asks us to look very deeply into the hearts of its multidimensional characters." —*Booklist*

★ **Hush** hush. Laura Lippman. HarperCollins, 2015. 384 p. (Tess Monaghan mysteries, 12)

ISBN 9780062083425

1. Infanticide 2. Child-separated mothers 3. Parent and child 4. Mental illness 5. Child custody 6. Baltimore, Maryland 7. Mysteries

Hush blends mystery with an unflinching look at new parenthood. HBeautiful, upper-crust Melisandre Dawes purposefully left her baby in a hot car ten years ago; scandalously found not guilty of murder by reason of insanity, she fled the country. Now D back in Baltimore, Dawes has hired a down-and-out documentary filmmaker to tell her story and hopes to mend matters with her 15- and 17-year-old daughters. PI Tess Monaghan, worn out from caring for her strong-willed three-year-old daughter, must discover who's sending Dawes threatening notes and track down a killer in this excellent series installment.

"With an intriguing cast of characters, stinging dialogue, hilarious moments, and a superbly convoluted and suspenseful plot, Lippman has created an incisive and provocative tale about parents good and evil." —*Booklist*

★ **Lady** in the lake: a novel. Laura Lippman. William Morrow, 2019. 384 p.

ISBN 9780062390011

1. Journalists 2. Race relations 3. Murder investigation 4. Ghosts 5. Racism 6. Baltimore, Maryland 7. 1960s 8. Historical thrillers 9. Multiple perspectives

LC 2018058807

Booklist Editors' Choice, 2019

A divorced reporter in racially torn 1966 Baltimore triggers unanticipated consequences for vulnerable community members while investigating the murder of an African-American party girl.

No good deeds. Laura Lippman. William Morrow, 2006. 352 p. (Tess Monaghan mysteries, 9)

ISBN 9780060570729

1. Homeless teenagers 2. Murder investigation 3. Witnesses 4. Detectives 5. Women private investigators 6. Baltimore, Maryland 7. Mysteries

LC 2005058358

Anthony Award for Best Novel, 2007

For Tess Monaghan, the unsolved murder of a young federal prosecutor is nothing more than a theoretical problem, one of several cases to be deconstructed in her new gig as a consultant to the local newspaper. But then her boyfriend brings home a street kid who doesn't even realize he holds an important key to the man's death. Tess agrees to protect the boy's identity no matter what, especially when one of his friends is killed in an apparent case of mistaken identity. But with federal agents determined to learn the boy's name at any cost, Tess finds out just how far even official authorities will go to get what they want. Soon she's facing felony charges—and her boyfriend has gone into hiding with his protégé, so Tess can't deliver the kid to investigators even if she wants to. —From publisher description.

"Lippman has pulled off the near-impossible: writing a conventional procedural that still feels fresh. It's impossible not to like the complex, all-too-real Monaghan, a strong, wry detective prone to derailing my own gravy train." —*Washington Post Book World.*

★ **Sunburn**. Laura Lippman. William Morrow & Co, 2018. 292 p.

ISBN 9780062389923

1. Strangers 2. Lovers 3. Femmes fatales 4. Wanderers and wandering 5. Married women 6. Delaware 7. 1990s 8. Noir fiction 9. Adaptations, retellings, and spin-offs

Librarians' Choice (Australia), 2018; LibraryReads Favorites, 2018; Library Journal Best Books, 2018

A pair of travelers, one of whom may be playing a dangerous psychological game with the other, embark on a steamy summertime affair that is thrown into chaos by dark secrets and a suspicious death, in a story inspired by the classics of James M. Cain.

What the dead know. Laura Lippman. William Morrow, 2007. 376 p.

ISBN 9780061128851

1. Police 2. Cold cases (Criminal investigation) 3. Kidnapping 4. Detectives 5. Girl kidnapping victims 6. Baltimore, Maryland 7. Maryland 8. Mysteries 9. Adult books for young adults

LC 2006052495

Anthony Award for Best Novel, 2008; Macavity Award for Best Mystery Novel, 2008

Interviewing a distressed and disoriented woman who has fled the scene of an accident, Baltimore County police department detective Kevin Infante is amazed when she claims to be the younger of a pair of sisters who were abducted thirty years earlier, a statement that she seems completely unable to prove.

"As artful as she is at interweaving disarming scenes of two spirited girls on the day they vanished with painful moments in the lives of their parentsmaintaining all the while a thread of continuity in the current-day police investigationLippman pulls off something more ambitious than a high-wire act of technical virtuosity. With great thought and compassion, she uses her fractured narrative style to delve into the ways in which every serious crime tears to shreds the lives of its victims." —*New York Times Book Review*

Wilde Lake. Laura Lippman. William Morrow & Co, 2016. 352 p.
ISBN 9780062083456

1. Trials (Murder) 2. District attorneys 3. Cold cases (Criminal investigation) 4. Women district attorneys 5. Siblings 6. Maryland 7. Psychological suspense 8. Adult books for young adults
LibraryReads Favorites, 2016

Luisa "Lu" Brant is the newly elected— and first female— state's attorney of Howard County, Maryland, a job in which her widower father famously served. Fiercely intelligent and ambitious, she sees an opportunity to make her name by trying a mentally disturbed drifter accused of beating a woman to death in her home. It's not the kind of case that makes headlines, but peaceful Howard County doesn't see many homicides. As Lu prepares for the trial, the case dredges up painful memories, reminding her small, but tight-knit, family of the night when her brother, AJ, saved his best friend at the cost of another man's life. Only eighteen, AJ was cleared by a grand jury. Now, Lu wonders if the events of 1980 happened as she remembers them. What details might have been withheld from her when she was a child?

"As shocking secrets are revealed, the reader realizes that nothing and no one can be taken at face value in Lippman's brainy, witty, socially conscious, and all-consuming inquiry into human nature and our slowly evolving sense of justice and equality." —*Booklist*

Lipsyte, Sam

The **ask**. Sam Lipsyte. Farrar, Straus and Giroux, 2010. 304 p.
ISBN 9780374298913

1. Marriage 2. Failure (Psychology) 3. Family relationships 4. Artists 5. Classism 6. Satirical fiction
LC 2009029508

Booklist Editors' Choice, 2010; New York Times Notable Book, 2010

After he loses his job as a development officer at a university, family man Milo Burke is given a chance to regain his position, but only if he can reel in a potential donor, one who has requested his involvement and turns out to be his sinister college classmate.

"The Ask's narrative heft comes from the reappearance of a wealthy friend from Milo's college days and the tragicomic scenarios that follow the plight of socialist daycare workers and legless Iraq-war vets among them. But the gift is Sam Lipsyte's writing: a chewy, corrosive, and syntactically dazzling prose style that doesn't so much run across the page as pick it up and throttle it. You may want to throttle Milo yourself frequently, but you won't stop reading." —*Entertainment Weekly*

Littell, Robert

The **company:** a novel of the CIA. Robert Littell. Overlook Press, 2002. 894 p.
ISBN 9781585671977

1. International relations 2. Intelligence officers 3. Cold War 4. International intrigue 5. CIA agents 6. Spy fiction 7. Books to TV
LC 2001051383

A novel of Cold War espionage traces the struggles of two generations of CIA operatives fighting Communism and battling one another in the complex world of international intrigue.

"There is plenty here to amuse anyone with even a network news interest in current events—and a gold mine for true conspiracy theorists." —*New York Times Book Review*

The **Mayakovsky** tapes: a novel. Robert Littell. Thomas Dunne Books, 2016. 243 p.
ISBN 9781250100566

1. Mayakovsky, Vladimir 2. Creativity in men 3. Poets 4. Memories 5. Former lovers 6. Suicide victims 7. Soviet Union 8. Historical fiction 9. Biographical fiction
LC 2016010551

Loan Stars Favourites, 2016

A tale inspired by the life of 20th-century Russian poet Vladimir Mayakovsky is told from the perspectives of four women who loved him and share with each other memories of pivotal moments in his life, from his early years as a Futurist leader, to his work as a Revolution propagandist, to the censorship battles that turned him against the State.

"...Littell uses four sophisticated women who had relationships with the poet to illuminate his life and character.... Separately and together they paint a vivid picture of a gifted poet, a tireless womanizer, and a man beset by wild mood swings. The ladies narration is both raunchy and often hilarious. It also illuminates a tumultuous period of Russian history." —*Booklist*

Littlejohn, Emily

Inherit the bones. Emily Littlejohn. Minotaur, 2016. 336 p. (Detective Gemma Monroe novels, 1)
ISBN 9781250089397

1. Small towns 2. Women detectives 3. Pregnant women 4. Secret identity 5. Circus 6. Colorado 7. Mysteries
Loan Stars Favourites, 2016

While investigating a traveling circus, detective Gemma Monroe discovers that a murdered clown is actually the mayor's missing son and must trace back a chain of events that began nearly 40 years ago.

Lost Lake: a detective Gemma Monroe mystery. Emily Littlejohn. Minotaur Books, 2018. 304 p. (Detective Gemma Monroe novels, 3)
ISBN 9781250178305

1. Women detectives 2. Missing women 3. Lakes 4. Friendship 5. Museum curators 6. Colorado 7. Mysteries
LC 2018025709

Detective Gemma Monroe must figure out who is lying to her after three friends make a missing person's report about the fourth member of their camping party.

"The mysteries involved, one of which hints at the supernatural, are satisfying and wrapped up in a way that readers won't see coming." —*Booklist*

Liu, Cixin

Ball lightning. Cixin Liu; translated by Joel Martinsen. Tor, 2018. 352 p.
ISBN 9780765394071

1. Scientific discoveries 2. Parents — Death 3. Weapons 4. Physicists 5. Soldiers 6. China 7. Science fiction 8. Translations 9. First person narratives

After witnessing his parents' bizarre death by ball lightning, Chin uncovers a new frontier in particle physics that pits him against a weapons-obsessed army major and an unscrupulous physicist.

★ The **dark** forest. Cixin Liu; translated from the Chinese by Joel Martinsen. Tor Books, 2015. 480 p. (Remembrance of Earth's past, 2)
ISBN 9780765377081

1. Aliens 2. Human nature 3. Research 4. Physicists 5. Life on other planets 6. China 7. Hard science fiction 8. Science fiction 9. Translations

A continuation of a near-future trilogy follows humanity's desperate plan to outmaneuver alien invaders by placing all defensive strategies in the hands of four men, including an anonymous astrologer who is baffled by his new status.

"The book's large cast of characters form a latticework of precisely placed focal points around which the story weaves and connects to wonderful moments of revelation." —*Booklist*
Translated from the Chinese.

★ **Death's** end. Cixin Liu; translated from the Chinese by Ken Liu. Tor, 2016. 604 p. (Remembrance of Earth's past, 3)
ISBN 9780765377104
1. Aliens 2. Scientists 3. Human nature 4. Life on other planets 5. Space flight 6. China 7. Hard science fiction 8. Science fiction 9. Translations
Locus Award for Best Science Fiction Novel, 2017
Half a century after the Doomsday Battle, twenty-first-century aerospace engineer Cheng Xin awakens from hibernation, bringing with her knowledge of a long-forgotten program that threatens the peaceful co-existence of humans and Trisolarans.
"The time scale is an obstacle to emotional engagement, but there are emotionally moving moments that ground the intriguing speculations about science and human nature." —*Publishers Weekly*
First published in Chinese in 2010 by Chongqing Publishing Group.
Translated from the Chinese.

★ The **three-body** problem. Cixin Liu; translated by Ken Liu. Tor Books, 2014. 336 p. (Remembrance of Earth's past, 1)
ISBN 9780765377067
1. Aliens 2. Revolutions 3. Physics 4. Loss (Psychology) 5. Human nature 6. China 7. Chinese Cultural Revolution (1966-1976) 8. Hard science fiction 9. Science fiction 10. Translations
Hugo Award for Best Novel, 2015
Set against the backdrop of China's Cultural Revolution, a secret military project's signal is received by an alien civilization on the brink of destruction, which plans to invade Earth; meanwhile, on Earth, different camps start forming, planning to either welcome the superior beings and help them take over a world seen as corrupt, or to fight against the invasion.
"The narrative will grab readers attention with its passionate and fascinating critique of early Communist China, augmented by translator Lius can but informative footnotes for the likely uninformed English readers. But the high-minded premise is really just a vessel for a collection of surreal and hauntingly beautiful scenes that will hook you deep and drag you relentlessly across every page." —*Booklist*
Originally published: 2007.
Translated from the Chinese.

Liu, Ken
★ The **grace** of kings. Ken Liu. Saga Press, 2015. 800 p; Map (Dandelion dynasty, 1)
ISBN 9781481424271
1. Rebels 2. Insurgency 3. Friendship 4. Imaginary wars and battles 5. Gods and goddesses 6. Epic fantasy 7. Asian-influenced fantasy
LC 2014019957
Locus Award for First Novel, 2016
Warrior Mata Zyndu, scion of his once-powerful Clan, believes that it is his destiny to rule. His best friend, wily bandit Kuni Garu, just wants to get rich and have a grand time doing so. Although they bond during the rebellion against the empire, their different goals and philosophies will ultimately make them bitter adversaries. Author Ken Liu has won Hugo, Nebula, Locus, and World Fantasy awards for his short fiction and his translations (most notably of Cixin Liu's The Three-Body Problem). This first book in the Dandelion Dynasty series, which vividly evokes the politics and culture of China's Han dynasty, marks his novel-writing debut.

Invisible planets: contemporary Chinese science fiction in translation. Ken Liu. Tor, 2016. 383 pages

ISBN 9780765384195
1. Social problems 2. Dystopias 3. Technology — Social aspects 4. Totalitarianism 5. Science fiction 6. Science fiction 7. Social science fiction 8. Translations
"A phenomenal anthology of short speculative fiction." —*Kirkus*

★ The **veiled** throne. Ken Liu. Saga Press, 2021. 1008 pages (Dandelion dynasty, 3)
ISBN 9781481424332
1. Political leadership 2. Identity (Psychology) 3. Assimilation (Sociology) 4. International relations 5. Quests 6. Epic fantasy 7. Asian-influenced fantasy
With the invasion of Dara complete, and the Wall of Storms breached, the world has opened to new possibilities for the gods and peoples of both empires as the sweeping saga of the award-winning Dandelion Dynasty continues.
"Hugo and Nebula Award winner Liu's masterful third Dandelion Dynasty fantasy (after The Wall of Storms) returns to a world steeped in myth, philosophy, and East Asian culture with a densely woven story of cultural conflict, political intrigue, and family rivalry." —*Publishers Weekly*

The **wall** of storms. Ken Liu. Simon & Schuster, 2016. 600 p. (Dandelion dynasty, 2)
ISBN 9781481424301
1. Rulers 2. Imaginary empires 3. Imaginary wars and battles 4. Aggression (International relations) 5. Adult children of politicians 6. Epic fantasy 7. Asian-influenced fantasy
A sequel to Grace of Kings finds newly declared Emperor Kuni Garu struggling to meet the demands of his people and vision before an unexpected invading force compels him to dispatch his grown children to defend the shores of Dara.
"This tale of divided loyalties, deadly ambition, and 'silkpunk' technology delivers enough excitement and sense of wonder to enchant any fan of epic fantasy." —*Publishers Weekly*

Lively, Penelope
★ **Moon** tiger. By Penelope Lively. Grove Press, 1987. 208 p.
ISBN 9780802110275
1. Women historians 2. Senior women authors 3. Women with terminal illnesses 4. Psychological fiction 5. Literary fiction
LC 87023798
Booker Prize, 1987
Claudia Hampton, writer of best-selling popular history books, lies in a London hospital bed and looks back on her own life, including an unforgettable love affair.
Originally published: London : Deutsch, 1987.

Livesay, Tracey
Like lovers do. Tracey Livesay. Avon Books, 2020. 384 p. (Girls trip, 2)
ISBN 9780062979568
1. Women surgeons 2. Workaholics 3. Businesspeople 4. Interracial romance 5. African American women 6. Martha's Vineyard, Massachusetts 7. Massachusetts 8. Contemporary romances 9. Multicultural romances 10. African American fiction
Tracey Livesay continues her fun-filled Girls Trip series with this romance that will tug at your heartstrings.
"The steady pace, smooth progression from friends to lovers, and natural, witty dialogue make this a winner. Readers will be wowed." —*Publishers Weekly*

Livesey, Margot

★ The **boy** in the field. Margot Livesey. HarperCollins, 2020. 272 p.
ISBN 9780062946393
1. Violence against teenagers 2. Siblings 3. Violence — Psychological aspects 4. Self-discovery 5. Consequences 6. England 7. Canadian fiction 8. Coming-of-age stories 9. Literary fiction
New York Times Notable Book, 2020
Saving the life of a young boy, three siblings find their bond challenged by their parents' troubled marriage and their respective efforts to identify the boy's attacker, manage a new relationship and search for a birth parent.
"Every character rings true; every observation and reaction feels real. Braiding three separate views of the same incident, Livesey (Mercury, 2016) weaves a masterful tapestry of emotion and action focused on the indelible impact of random events." —*Booklist*

Criminals: a novel. Margot Livesey. Knopf, 1996. 271 p.
ISBN 9780679444879
1. Abandoned children 2. Women with mental illnesses 3. Bankers 4. Voyages and travels 5. Siblings 6. London, England 7. Scotland 8. Novels-within-novels 9. Psychological suspense
LC 9531512
Booklist Editors' Choice: Adult Books for Young Adults, 1996
The discovery of a baby girl abandoned in a bus station restroom becomes the catalyst for linking five distinct lives in a web of responsibility, affection, and filial, maternal, and romantic love BT
"The reader becomes enmeshed in the complex windings of Ms. Livesey's plot, a web of criminal circumstance and moral consequence that conveys the awful randomness of life even as it offers the abiding pleasures of artfully constructed fiction." —*New York Times Book Review*

Llewellyn, Richard

★ **How** green was my valley. Richard Llewellyn. Scribner 1997. 495 p.
ISBN 9780684825557
1. Coal miners' families 2. Families 3. Boys 4. Young men 5. Coal miners 6. Wales 7. Great Britain 8. 1880s 9. 1890s 10. Coming-of-age stories 11. Family sagas 12. Historical fiction
The youngest son of a Welsh coal-mining family recalls the tender and tragic experiences of his youth at the turn of the century with his courageous and loving parents and brothers and sisters.
"A remarkably beautiful novel of Wales. And although it follows stirringly in the romantic traditions, there is the resonance of a profound and noble realism in its evocation, its intensity and reach of truth." —*New York Times Book Review*
Sequel: Up into the singing mountain.
Originally published: London : M. Joseph, 1939.

Lloyd, Catherine

Death comes to the nursery. Catherine Lloyd. Kensington Pub Corp, 2020. 304 p. (Kurland St. Mary mysteries, 7)
ISBN 9781496723222
1. Pregnant women 2. Husband and wife 3. Amateur detectives 4. Ovid 5. Deception 6. Great Britain 7. Regency period (1811-1820) 8. Historical mysteries
When their new nursery maid from London is found dead, Lady Lucy, who is expecting another child, and Major Sir Robert Kurland suspect foul play and set out to find the truth, which leads them to the London theater world—and into great danger.

"A charming Regency mystery/romance with plenty of local color and unexpected twists and turns." —*Kirkus*

Death comes to the rectory. Catherine Lloyd. Kensington Pub Corp, 2021. 304 p. (Kurland St. Mary mysteries, 8)
ISBN 9781496723253
1. Clergy 2. Murder investigation 3. Baptism 4. Debt 5. Amateur detectives 6. Regency period (1811-1820) 7. Historical mysteries
When her father, the rector, is implicated in the death of his wife's son-in-law, a very disagreeable man, Lady Lucy Kurland, with her daughter's christening marred by murder, must clear his name and expose the real culprit.
"Complex characters and a shoal of red herrings add up to a delightful period read." —*Kirkus*

Locke, Attica

★ **Bluebird,** bluebird. Attica Locke. Mulholland Books, 2017. 336 p. (Highway 59, 1)
ISBN 9780316363297
1. African American men 2. Detectives 3. Race relations 4. Murder investigation 5. Small towns 6. Texas 7. Mysteries 8. African American fiction 9. Adult books for young adults
Anthony Award for Best Novel, 2018; Edgar Allan Poe Award for Best Novel, 2018; Ian Fleming Steel Dagger Award, 2018
In a rural East Texas town of fewer than 200 people, the body of an African American lawyer from Chicago is found in a bayou, followed several days later by that of a local white woman. What's going on? African American Texas Ranger Darren Mathews hopes to find out, which means talking to relatives of the deceased, including the woman's white supremacist husband—and Mathews soon discovers things are more complex than they seem. With fully realized characters and a timely look at race relations in the U.S, this book by award-winning novelist Attica Locke (who's also written and produced for TV's Empire) is the 1st in her Highway 59 series.
"Locke...deserves a career breakthrough for this deftly plotted whodunit whose writing pulses throughout with a raw, blues-inflected lyricism." —*Kirkus*

The **cutting** season. Attica Locke. Harper, 2012. 384 p.
ISBN 9780061802058
1. Migrant workers 2. Families — History 3. Plantations 4. Farms 5. Murder 6. Louisiana 7. Southern States 8. Mysteries
Library Journal Best Books, 2012
When the dead body of a young woman is found on the grounds of Belle Vie, the estate's manager, Caren Gray, launches her own investigation into Belle Vie's history, which leads her to a centuries old mystery involving the plantation's slave quarters—and her own past.

★ **Heaven,** my home. Attica Locke. Mulholland Books, 2019. 304 p. (Highway 59, 2)
ISBN 9780316363402
1. African American men 2. Detectives 3. Missing boys 4. Missing persons investigation 5. Race relations 6. Texas 7. Southern States 8. Mysteries 9. African American fiction
In this follow-up to Bluebird, Bluebird, Texas Ranger Darren Mathews must battle centuries-old suspicions and prejudices, as well as threats that have been reignited in the current political climate, to find a missing boy and save himself.

Locke, Thomas

Emissary. Thomas Locke. Revell, 2015. 304 p. (Legends of the realm 1)

ISBN 9780800723859

1. Young men 2. Fate and fatalism 3. Quests 4. Magic 5. Outlaws 6. Christian fantasy

LC 2014029802

With magic largely outlawed, and its legitimate practitioners tightly controlled, a young man begins to find that the astonishing powers he has discovered in himself may be the key to facing a growing menace from beyond the badlands.

"Locke (a pseudonym for Christy-winning inspirational thriller author Davis Bunn) launches the Legends of the Realm fantasy series with this competent story that owes more to the Lord of the Rings trilogy than the Bible...Even if fans of Bunn's international thrillers dont follow him over to the fantasy realm, readers of inspirational fantasy will enjoy his foray into a new genre." —*Publishers Weekly*

Lockridge, Ross Franklin

Raintree County. Ross Lockridge Jr. Chicago Review Press, 2007. 1066 p.

ISBN 9781556527104

1. Rural life 2. Civil war 3. United States Civil War, 1861-1865 4. United States 5. Indiana 6. Books to movies 7. Modern classics

LC 48000245

Throughout a single day in 1892, John Shawnessy recalls the great moments of his life—from the love affairs of his youth in Indiana, to the battles of the Civil War, to the politics of the Gilded Age, to his homecoming as schoolteacher, husband, and father. Shawnessy is the epitome of the place and period in which he lives, a rural land of springlike women, shady gamblers, wandering vagabonds, and soapbox orators. Yet here on the banks of the Shawmucky River, which weaves its primitive course through Raintree County, Indiana, he also feels and obeys ancient rhythms.

Originally published: Boston, Mass. : Houghton Mifflin, 1948.

Lodato, Victor

Edgar and Lucy: a novel. Victor Lodato. St. Martin's Press, 2017. 533 pages

ISBN 9781250096982

1. Mothers and sons 2. Boy kidnapping victims 3. Survivors of suicide victims 4. Kidnappers 5. Grief in boys 6. New Jersey 7. Literary fiction 8. Domestic fiction

A grieving little boy who had been cared for by his late grandmother during his mother's dysfunctional episodes becomes an at-risk youth in the New Jersey Pine Barrens home of an unsettlingly attentive adult who harbors dubious intentions.

"Lodatos remarkable novel traces a broken familys spiritual journey toward healing in moving, magical prose." —*Booklist*

Mathilda Savitch. Victor Lodato. Farrar, Straus and Giroux, 2009. 304 p.

ISBN 9780374204006

1. Grief in families 2. Worry in girls 3. Alcoholic mothers 4. Loss (Psychology) 5. Compassion in teenagers 6. Psychological fiction 7. Literary fiction 8. First person narratives 9. Adult books for young adults

LC 2009004719

Booklist Editors' Choice, 2009; Booklist Editors' Choice: Adult Books for Young Adults, 2009

Mathilda investigates her older sister's shattering death and learns perplexing truths when she accesses her sister's computer journals and reads about a secret underworld life.

"A novel about a preteen whose older sister has died, pushed off a train platform. Logging in to her sister's e-mail, Mathilda eventually adopts her sister's life, contacting her old boyfriends and trying to retrace the footsteps of her last days.... Trying to provoke her parents, Mathilda dresses up in her dead sister's birthday dress. Numb, in search of deeper numbness, her mother downs the vodka, and crawls on the kitchen floor, howling, in search of another bottle. Mathilda's original observations carry these incidentsblending imagination, intelligence and kookily beautiful imagery.... For the most part, this is a delight and a devil of a book, a tale that fills you with despair and pleasureoften at the same time." —*Time Out New York*

Loedel, Daniel

Hades, Argentina. Daniel Loedel. Riverhead Books, 2021. 304 p.

ISBN 9780593188644

1. Medical students 2. Women revolutionaries 3. Guerrillas 4. Childhood friends 5. Crushes (Interpersonal relations) 6. Buenos Aires, Argentina 7. Argentina 8. 1970s 9. 1980s 10. Literary fiction

A medical student in 1970s Buenos Aires must decide how far he's willing to go for his childhood crush and the group of insurgents she's joined as more and more people like her are disappeared by an oppressive military junta.

"Loedel's unflinching look at human frailty adds a revelatory new chapter to South American Cold War literature." —*Publishers Weekly*

Logan, Kylie

The **secrets** of bones: a mystery. Kylie Logan. St Martins Pr 2020. 320 p. (Jazz Ramsey novels, 2)

ISBN 9781250180599

1. Working dogs 2. Dog trainers 3. Women amateur detectives 4. Dead 5. Women murder suspects 6. Cleveland, Ohio 7. Mysteries

LC 2019055293

A follow-up to The Scent of Murder finds Jazz Ramsey giving a cadaver dog demonstration at a school career day before her canine companion uncovers the body of a former teacher who went missing under suspicious circumstances.

"Red herrings, a developing romance, and just the right amount of information about cadaver dogs help make this a winner." —*Publishers Weekly*

Logan, T. M.

The **vacation**. T.M. Logan. St. Martin's Press, 2020. 374 p.

ISBN 9781250270771

1. Vacations 2. Friendship 3. Married people 4. Extramarital affairs 5. Social classes 6. France 7. Psychological suspense 8. Multiple perspectives

Spending a week with loved ones in an opulent villa in southern France, Kate finds her life upended by an incriminating text that reveals her husband is having an affair with one of her three best friends.

"The tantalizing twists, enjoyably written from various characters' viewpoints, culminate in an unexpected ending that will leave readers thinking about their own relationships and what they would do to save those they love." —*Booklist*

Loigman, Lynda Cohen

The **wartime** sisters: a novel. Lynda Cohen Loigman. St. Martin's Press, 2019. 304 p.

ISBN 9781250140708

1. Sisters 2. Family and war 3. World War II — Women 4. Family relationships 5. Women and success 6. Brooklyn, New York City 7. Massachusetts 8. Second World War era (1939-1945) 9. Historical fiction

LC 2018029127

Reunited after an estrangement at the beginning of World War II, two Brooklyn sisters, one an officer's wife, the other a widow and factory laborer, are shattered by the revelations of a mysterious figure from the past.

Lombardo, Claire

The **most** fun we ever had: a novel. Claire Lombardo. Doubleday, 2019. 544 pages

ISBN 9780385544252

1. Married people 2. Sisters 3. Family relationships 4. Daughters 5. Sibling rivalry 6. Chicago, Illinois 7. Illinois 8. Family sagas 9. Literary fiction

LC 2018036701

The four adult daughters of two Chicago parents who have been madly in love for decades recklessly ignite old rivalries, until a long-buried secret threatens to shatter the lives they built.

"The result is an affectionate, sharp, and eminently readable exploration of the challenges of love in its many forms." —*Booklist*

London, Jack

★ The **call** of the wild. Jack London; illustrations by Philippe Munch. Viking, 1996. 126 p. : Illustration; Color

ISBN 9780670869183

1. Sled dogs 2. Wolves 3. Prospectors 4. Men and dogs 5. Dogs 6. Klondike gold fields 7. Alaska 8. Adventure stories 9. Books to movies 10. Classics

LC 95-61728

The adventures of an unusual dog, part St. Bernard, part Scotch Shepherd, that was kidnapped and shipped off to Alaska to work on the Klondike Gold Rush. Buck the dog quickly learns how to survive in the wild and also learns the call of the wolf.

The Call of the Wild has inspired three films, released in 1923, 1935, and 1972.

An unabridged republication of the story originally published in book form by the Macmillan Co, New York, in 1903—Title page verso.

Martin Eden. Jack London. Penguin Books, 1993. 482 p.

ISBN 9780140187724

1. London, Jack 2. Sailors 3. Working class men 4. Social status 5. Interclass romance 6. Individualism in men 7. Autobiographical fiction 8. Classics

Recounts the story of Martin Eden, a young seaman struggling to obtain social and intellectual recognition as a writer BT

Originally serialized in Pacific Monthly, September 1908-September 1909. Published in book format: New York, Macmillan, 1909.

★ **White** Fang. Jack London. Scholastic, 2001. 252 p.

ISBN 9780439236195

1. Wild animals as pets 2. Men and dogs 3. Gold rush 4. Human-animal relationships 5. Mixed-breed dogs 6. Yukon Territory 7. Klondike River Valley, Yukon Territory 8. Adventure stories 9. Books to TV 10. Books to movies

The adventures in the northern wilderness of a dog who is part wolf and how he comes to make his peace with man.

White Fang is about a dog, a cross-breed, sold to Beauty Smith. This owner tortures the dog to increase his ferocity and value as a fighter. A new owner Weedon Scott, brings the dog to California, and, by kind treatment, domesticates him. White Fang later sacrifices his life to save Scot Thesaurus of Book Digests

Originally serialized in The Outing Magazine, May-October 1906. White Fang has been closely adapted into a movie of the same name (1991) and loosely adapted into a television series of the same name (1993).

London, Joan

The **golden** age. Joan London. Europa Editions, 2016. 221 p.

ISBN 9781609453329

1. People with poliomyelitis 2. Hospital patients 3. Refugees Hungarian 4. Boy/girl relations 5. Poetry writing 6. Perth, Western Australia 7. Australia 8. 1950s 9. Historical fiction 10. Australia fiction 11. Love stories

Nita B. Kibble Literary Award, 2015; NSW Premier's Literary Awards, People's Choice Award for Fiction, 2015; Queensland Literary Awards, Fiction Book Award, 2015; Prime Minister's Literary Awards: Fiction, 2015; Western Australian Premier's Book Awards, Fiction category, 2016; Shortlisted for the Stella Prize, 2015; Shortlisted for the Miles Franklin Literary Award, 2015

Escaping the perils of World War II to the safety of Australia 13-year-old Jewish Hungarian Frank is diagnosed with polio and sent to a sprawling children's hospital, where he falls in love with incandescent fellow patient Elsa while their families back home struggle to adjust to life in a new culture.

"Like Sister Penny, London sees past people's exteriors to their complex and desirous interiors, and she generously offers those people to us in all their fullness. The novel was a recipient of multiple awards in London's native Australia, and deservedly so: it is pretty much perfect." —*Publishers Weekly*

Originally published: North Sydney, N.S.W. : Vintage Australia, 2014.

London, Julia

The **charmer** in chaps. Julia London. Berkley Pub Group, 2019. 336 pages (Princes of Texas, 1)

ISBN 9780451492357

1. Rich men 2. Self-discovery 3. Homecomings 4. Womanizers 5. Men with dyslexia 6. Texas 7. Western romances 8. Contemporary romances

A Texas prince meets his match...

Wild wicked Scot. Julia London. HQN Books, 2016. 352 p. (Highland grooms, 1)

ISBN 9780373789665

1. Political intrigue 2. Seduction 3. Espionage 4. Aristocracy 5. English in Scotland 6. Highlands, Scotland 7. Scotland 8. Jacobite Rebellions (1689-1746) 9. Stuart period (1603-1714) 10. Highland romance 11. Historical romances

Forced to return to her husband, whom she fled three years earlier English beauty Margot Armstrong must outmaneuver Arran McKenzie in games of espionage and seduction as their respective countriesÆ fragile unity threatens to unravel.

"This absorbing and passionate romance bodes well for future Highland Grooms titles." —*Booklist*

London, Stefanie

The **Aussie** next door. Stefanie London. Entangled Amara, 2019. 350 pages (Patterson's Bluff, 1)

ISBN 9781640636682

1. Americans in Australia 2. Neighbors 3. Single women 4. Former foster children 5. Options, alternatives, choices 6. Australia 7. Contemporary romances 8. Australian fiction

To stay in the tiny seaside town of Margaret River, Australia, Angie Donovan, who has finally found a place to call home—and whose 6-month visa is about to run out, asks her neighbor for help in finding a man whom she can marry.

Each book in the Patterson's Bluff series can be read standalone.

Long, Julie Anne

Angel in a devil's arms. Julie Anne Long. Avon Books, 2019. 352 pages (Palace of rogues, 2)

ISBN 9780062867490

1. Nobility 2. Inheritance and succession 3. Revenge 4. Rumor 5. Courtship 6. London, England 7. England 8. Regency period (1811-1820) 9. Regency romances 10. Historical romances

Sweeping into London with vengeance on his mind, Lucien Durand, seeking to reclaim his true birthright, finds himself brought to his knees by the beautiful Angelique Breedlove and the dangerous passion they share.

"With a sizzling romance, an intriguing revenge plot, and a cast of quirky Palace guests, this next installment of Long's luscious new series is smart and deliciously sensual." —*Library Journal*

★ **Lady** Derring takes a lover. Julie Anne Long. Avon Books, 2019. 384 p. (Palace of rogues, 1)

ISBN 9780062867469

1. Widows 2. Boarding houses 3. Ship captains 4. Counts and countesses 5. Debt 6. London, England 7. England 8. Regency period (1811-1820) 9. Regency romances 10. Historical romances

Booklist Editors' Choice, 2019; Library Journal Best Books, 2019

On the hunt for a notorious smuggler, Captain Tristan Hardy is led to the Rogue's Palace, a London boarding house, and sets out to seduce its beautiful blue-blooded proprietress, the Countess of Derring, to get the answers he seeks.

Longworth, M. L.

Murder on the Ile Sordou: a Verlaque and Bonnet Provencal mystery. M.L. Longworth. Penguin Books, 2014. 303 p. (Verlaque and Bonnet mysteries, 4)

ISBN 9780143125549

1. Husband and wife 2. Vacations 3. Hotels 4. Storms 5. Wine and wine making 6. France 7. Mysteries

LC 2014010451

While vacationing at the opulent Locanda Sordou hotel, Judge Antoine Verlaque and his girlfriend, law professor Marine Bonnet, investigate a murder and find things going from bad to worse when a violent storm cuts off all communication with the mainland, trapping them with a killer.

"Longworth once again immerses readers in French culture with this whodunit, which will delight Francophiles and fans of Donna Leon and Andrea Camilleri. The setting will also appeal to readers who enjoy trapped-on-the-island mysteries in the tradition of Agatha Christie's And Then There Were None." —*Library Journal*

A Penguin mystery.

Lopez Barrio, Cristina

The house of the impossible loves. Cristina Lopez Barrio; translated from the Spanish by Lisa Carter. Houghton Mifflin Harcourt, 2013. 319 pages

ISBN 9780547661193

1. Curses 2. Mothers and daughters 3. Father-deserted children 4. Hope 5. Jilted women 6. Spain 7. France 8. Magical realism 9. Literary fiction 10. Family sagas

Cursed to suffer tragic love affairs and give birth to equally cursed daughters, a family of women in 20th-century Spain and France and their colorful inner circle watch over a youngest daughter's passionate affair with a landowner who leaves her pregnant and determined to make redemptive changes.

Translated from the Spanish.

Loren, Roni

★ The **one** for you. Roni Loren. Sourcebooks Casablanca, 2019. 352 pages (Ones who got away, 4)

ISBN 9781492693192

1. Single women 2. Best friends 3. School shootings 4. Life change events 5. Psychic trauma 6. Contemporary romances

Still haunted by a school shooting on prom night years earlier, Kincaid Breslin runs into an old classmate with whom she embarks on a romantic relationship until she discovers the truth about that night—and his involvement in it.

"Loren nimbly addresses heavy topics, emphasizing emotional resilience and recovery." —*Publishers Weekly*

The **one** you can't forget. Roni Loren. Sourcebooks, 2018. 352 p. (Ones who got away, 2)

ISBN 9781492651437

1. Douglass, Frederick 2. Divorced men 3. Secrets 4. Mugging 5. Man-woman relationships 6. Contemporary romances

"Loren's second title in a series that revolves around survivors of a high school shooting (The Ones Who Got Away, 2018) maintains the complexity and emotional intensity that earned the first book huge acclaim but never loses its way as a sexy, captivating romance." —*Kirkus*

The **one** you fight for. Roni Loren. Sourcebooks Casablanca, 2019. 352 p. (Ones who got away, 3)

ISBN 9781492651468

1. Women college teachers 2. Athletic trainers 3. New identities 4. Interracial romance 5. Siblings 6. Austin, Texas 7. Multicultural romances 8. Contemporary romances

When Taryn, whose younger sister was killed in a school shooting, and Shaw, whose brother was one of the shooters, meet years later, they find themselves falling in love despite their positions on opposite sides of the tragedy.

"Loren delivers another stunning and moving addition to her series about survivors of a school shooting. She realistically and vividly depicts guilt and loneliness while also showcasing the power and importance of love and friendship." —*Booklist*

Louis, Edouard

The **end** of Eddy: a novel. Edouard Louis; translated from the French by Michael Lucey. Farrar, Straus and Giroux, 2017. 192 p.

ISBN 9780374266653

1. Young men 2. Working class families 3. Self-acceptance in gay men 4. Working poor people 5. Gay teenagers 6. France 7. LGBTQIA fiction 8. Autobiographical fiction 9. Coming-of-age stories 10. Adult books for young adults

LC 2016041340

Traces how a young gay man in a violent French factory village navigates his orientation and intellectually precocious nature while enduring pressure to become a strong man in accordance with local beliefs.

"In this excellent autobiographical novel, a middle school boy struggles to forge an identity in a French industrial town hostile in every way to his homosexuality." —*Publishers Weekly*

First published in French as *En finir avec Eddy Bellegueule* (Paris : Editions du Seuil, 2014).

Translated from the French.

Lourey, Jess

★ **January** thaw: a murder-by-month mystery. Jess Lourey. Midnight Ink, 2014. 288 pages (Murder by month mysteries, 9)

ISBN 9780738738758

1. Women amateur detectives 2. Murder investigation 3. Small town life 4. Women librarians 5. Women journalists 6. Minnesota 7. Mysteries

LC 2013027483

In her new home in small town Minnesota, private-detective-in-training Mira James must investigate a 150-year cold case, as well as a present-day spate of drug-trafficking.

Lovecraft, H. P.

★ **Tales**. H.P. Lovecraft. Library of America : 2005. 850 p.

ISBN 9781931082723

1. Cthulhu (Fictitious character) 2. Short stories 3. Horror 4. Horror classics

LC 2004048979

"If you spend enough time in Lovecraft's lonely landscapes, fear really does develop: not the fear that you will come across unearthly creatures, but the fear that you will come across little else. And what first seems horridly overdone accumulates a creepy minimalism. Taken as a whole, Lovecraft's work exhibits a hopeless isolation not unlike that of Samuel Beckett: lonely man after lonely man, wandering aimlessly through a shadowy city or holing up in rural emptiness, pursuing unspeakable secrets or being pursued by secret unspeakables, all to little avail and to no comfort. There is something funny about this—in small doses. But by the end of this collection, one does not hear giggling so much as the echoes of those giggles as they vanish into the ether lonely, desperate and, yes, very, very scary." —*New York Times Book Review*

Lovely, Lutishia

Blind ambition. Lutishia Lovely. Dafina Books, 2021. 279 p.

ISBN 9781496724458

1. African American families 2. African American sisters 3. Separated sisters 4. African American women singers 5. African American celebrities 6. Los Angeles, California 7. Missouri 8. Drama lit 9. Relationship fiction

Since childhood, Chantel has idolized her older sister, Jett, a superstar performer. But she's seldom seen her Hollywood-based sibling. More on the shy side, Chantel is perfectly happy with her own modest singing career and quiet Missouri hometown life. But when their mother dies and Chantel's world is upended, she hopes that moving to Los Angeles will give her a fresh start—and a chance to know Jett better. But the truth is, she doesn't know Jett at all. When Jett rebuffs her efforts to bond, Chantel learns a devastating secret she never could have imagined. Reeling and angry, Chantel soon comes up with the perfect vengeful weapon: a bestselling tell-all book that will reveal Jett's stormy past—and wreak havoc on the stardom she prizes more than anything or anyone.

"Money, sex, and a behind-the-scenes look at celebrity life in L.A. keep the pages turning." —*Booklist*

Lovesey, Peter

Beau death. Peter Lovesey. Soho Crime, 2017. 416 pages (Peter Diamond mysteries, 17)

ISBN 9781616959050

1. Nash, Richard 2. Dead 3. Detectives 4. Building sites 5. Cold case (Criminal investigation) 6. Murder investigation 7. England 8. Bath England 9. Police procedurals 10. Mysteries

When human remains in 18th-century clothing are discovered on a demolition site, Chief Inspector Peter Diamond eagerly embarks on a mission to prove that a scandal-marked fashion icon from Bath may have had quite a different end than the one popularly believed.

Diamond solitaire. Peter Lovesey. Mysterious Press 1993. 345 p (Peter Diamond mysteries, 2)

ISBN 9780892965359

1. Abandoned children 2. Children with autism 3. Guards 4. Diamond Peter (Fictitious character) 5. Former police 6. England 7. London England 8. Mysteries 9. Police procedurals

LC 92050660

When an autistic Japanese child is mysteriously abducted in London ex-police detective Peter Diamond begins a desperate search that sends him from the sumo wrestling world of Japan to New York's high finance district

"Peter Diamond is plagued by bad karma. Formerly detective superintendent of police in Bath, he's sunk to being a security guard at Harrod's until a small Asian child is found in the area of the store Peter patrols. Out of a job once again (security breaches are no laughing matter at terrorist-obsessed Harrod's), Diamond becomes intrigued by the Asian child, who is autistic and who remains unclaimed despite massive publicity. What starts out as a kindly effort to restore the child to her parents turns into an international adventure as Diamond travels from London to New York to Japan and confronts millionaire sumo wrestlers, unethical drug researchers, and corrupt businessmen." —*Booklist*

★ The **last** detective. Peter Lovesey. Doubleday, 1991. 331 p. (Peter Diamond mysteries, 1)

ISBN 9780385421140

1. Murder investigation 2. Murder suspects 3. Police 4. Diamond, Peter (Fictitious character) 5. Forensic sciences 6. Bath, England 7. England 8. Mysteries 9. Police procedurals

LC 91011859

Anthony Award for Best Novel, 1992

Challenged by departmental red tape and a dearth of clues, British detective Peter Diamond must solve the murder of a down-on-her-luck soap opera actress, who was found floating face down in a reservoir

"An intricate, many-tiered examination of police work, especially modern forensic technology, complete with computers and genetic finger printing. Everything meshe's perfectly in this airtight tale." —*Booklist*

A Perfect crime book.

The **tooth** tattoo. Peter Lovesey. Soho Press, 2013. 348 pages (Peter Diamond mysteries, 13)

ISBN 9781616952303

1. Crimes against women 2. Violinists 3. Classical music industry and trade 4. Detectives 5. Murder investigation 6. Bath, England 7. London England 8. Mysteries 9. Police procedurals

LC 2012043412

Investigating the murder of a young woman whose only identifying mark is a tattoo on one of her teeth, British criminal investigator Peter Diamond teams up with violinist Mel Farran, who is being scouted by a mysterious and elite classical quartet that reveals frightening truths about fandom and the cutthroat world of professional music.

Lovett, Charles C.

The **lost** book of the Grail: or a visitor's guide to Barchester Cathedral. Charlie Lovett. Viking, 2017. 320 pages

ISBN 9780399562518

1. Grail 2. Obsession 3. College teachers 4. Libraries 5. Searching 6. England 7. Mysteries

An obsessive bibliophile and Holy Grail fanatic combs through centuries of history to uncover a long-lost secret about the medieval Barchester Cathedral library at the side of a young American charged with digitizing the library's manuscripts.

"A solidly built, innocently bookish diversion with a distinct Masterpiece Theater flavor." —*Kirkus*

Lowe, Kathryn A.

The **furies**. Katie Lowe. St. Martin's Press, 2019. 352 pages

ISBN 9781250297891

1. Witchcraft 2. Revenge 3. Boarding schools 4. Murder 5. Friendship 6. England 7. 1990s 8. Thrillers and suspense 9. Coming-of-age stories 10. Adult books for young adults

LC 2019016759

In 1990s England, at an elite boarding school connected to seventeenth-century witch trials, troubled sixteen-year-old Violet is drawn into a circle of friends dabbling in witchcraft to avenge wrongs done to them.

Lu, S. Qiouyi

In the watchful city. S. Qiouyi Lu. Tor, 2021. 192 p.

ISBN 9781250792983

1. Superhuman abilities 2. Cities and towns 3. Protectiveness 4. Networks 5. Strangers 6. Cyberpunk 7. Science fiction 8. Asian-influenced fantasy

Anima is an extrasensory human tasked with surveilling and protecting Ora's citizens via a complex living network called the Gleaming. Although ær world is restricted to what æ can see and experience through the Gleaming, Anima takes pride and comfort in keeping Ora safe from harm. When a mysterious outsider enters the city carrying a cabinet of curiosities from around with the world with a story attached to each item, Anima's world expands beyond the borders of Ora to places—and possibilities—æ never before imagined to exist. But such knowledge leaves Anima with a question that throws into doubt ær entire purpose: What good is a city if it can't protect its people?

"Lu's full-length debut (after the collection Inhalations) combines beautiful prose, a complex structure, and well-wrought Asian-influenced worldbuilding into a powerful, futurist work." —*Publishers Weekly*

Lucashenko, Melissa

Too much lip. Melissa Lucashenko. HarperVia, 2020. 320 p.

ISBN 9780063032538

1. Aboriginal Australians 2. Families 3. Home (Concept) 4. Rural life 5. Loss (Psychology) 6. Black humor 7. Australian fiction

LC 2020021739

Queensland Literary Awards, Queensland Premier's Award for a work of State Significance, 2019; Miles Franklin Award, 2019; Shortlisted for the Stella Prize, 2019

Sneaking back to Bundjalung country to attend her father's deathbed, an outspoken, queer First Nations Australian woman confronts the ghosts of her ancestors to prevent her family's spiritual home from being turned into a prison.

"An award-winning Australian author explores family dysfunction and the legacy of colonial oppression in her American debut." —*Kirkus*

Originally published: University of Queensland Press, 2018.

Luchette, Claire

Agatha of Little Neon. Claire Luchette. Farrar, Straus and Giroux, 2021. 208 p.

ISBN 9780374265267

1. Nuns 2. Group homes 3. Female friendship 4. Moving to a new city 5. Mill towns 6. Relationship fiction 7. Literary fiction

LC 2021008693

Agatha has lived every day of the last nine years with her sisters: they work together, laugh together, pray together. Their world is contained within the little house they share. The four of them are devoted to Mother Roberta and to their quiet, purposeful life. But when the parish goes broke, the sisters are forced to move. They land in Woonsocket, a former mill town now dotted with wind turbines. They take over the care of a halfway house, where they live alongside their charges, such as the jawless Tim Gary and the headstrong Lawnmower Jill. Agatha is forced to venture out into the world alone to teach math at a local all-girls high school, where for the first time in years she has to reckon all on her own with what she sees and feels. Who will she be if she isn't with her sisters? These women, the church, have been her home. Or has she just been hiding?

"Employing short, clipped chapters and shimmering prose, Luchette garnishes each scene with tender and nuanced descriptions of longing and chastity, creating a lovely story of how cross-cultural exchange can foster hope and fruitful advancements." —*Publishers Weekly*

Ludlum, Robert

★ The **Bourne** identity. Robert Ludlum. R. Marek Publishers, 1980. 535 p. (Jason Bourne series, 1)

ISBN 9780399900709

1. Amnesia 2. Assassins 3. International intrigue 4. Spies 5. Bourne, Jason (Fictitious character) 6. Thrillers and suspense 7. Books to movies

LC 79023638

A shooting victim, suffering from amnesia, finds himself with a Swiss bank account in the name of Jason Bourne, a professional assassin being manipulated by a top-secret American government organization to kill his arch rival, the dreaded Carlos.

The **Bourne** supremacy. Robert Ludlum. Random House, 1986. 597 p. (Jason Bourne series, 2)

ISBN 9780394543963

1. Impostors 2. International intrigue 3. Assassins 4. Bourne, Jason (Fictitious character) 5. China 6. Thrillers and suspense 7. Books to movies

LC 85018318

Super-diplomat Raymond Havilland sets up the kidnapping of Jason Bourne's wife, in order to draw Bourne out of retirement and into a Taiwanese plot to seize Hong Kong and incite China against the West.

The **Bourne** ultimatum. Robert Ludlum. Random House, 1990. 611 p. (Jason Bourne series, 3)

ISBN 9780394584089

1. Carlos 2. International intrigue 3. Assassins 4. Spies 5. Bourne, Jason (Fictitious character) 6. Thrillers and suspense 7. Books to movies

LC 89043201

Professor David Webb must once again become his alter ego, assassin Jason Bourne, as he approaches a final confrontation with his archnemesis, terrorist Carlos the Jackal.

Ludwig, Benjamin

Ginny Moon. Benjamin Ludwig. Park Row, 2017. 368 p.

ISBN 9780778330165

1. Girls with autism 2. Foster children 3. Birthmothers 4. Autism 5. Adoption 6. Mainstream fiction 7. Adult books for young adults

Librarians' Choice (Australia), 2017; LibraryReads Favorites, 2017; Library Journal Best Books, 2017; School Library Journal Best Books: Best Adult Books 4 Teens, 2017

Despite being placed in the ideal foster home, autistic 14-year-old girl Ginny Moon is intent on running back to her abusive, drug-addict birth mother, Gloria.

"Ludwigs excellent debut is both a unique coming-of-age tale and a powerful affirmation of the fragility and strength of families." —*Publishers Weekly*

Luesse, Valerie Fraser

Missing Isaac. Valerie Fraser Luesse. Baker Pub Group 2018. 341 pages

ISBN 9780800728786

1. Missing persons investigation 2. Race relations 3. African Americans 4. Small towns 5. Searching 6. Alabama 7. 1960s 8. Christian historical fiction

LC 2017032966

Christy Award for First Novel Category, 2018

When Pete McLean's close friend Isaac, who is African American, goes missing in 1960s Alabama, Pete's efforts to find him lead him into parts of their small town he has never seen before, and to a girl who will change his life.

Under the bayou moon: a novel. Valerie Fraser Luesse. Revell, a division of Baker Publishing Group, 2021. 352 p.

ISBN 9780800737511

1. Women teachers 2. Rural life 3. Courtship 4. Cajun men 5. Uncle and nephew 6. Louisiana 7. Atchafalaya River 8. 1940s 9. Christian historical fiction 10. Southern fiction

LC 2021002491

A young, restless Alabama teacher searching for a sense of purpose accepts a position at a tiny Louisiana bayou school, where a lonely Cajun fisherman, a tight-knit community, and a legendary white alligator will change her life forever.

"Luesse's multifaceted, lyrical tale dazzles with larger-than-life villains searching for a big payday, a mythical albino alligator, a mysterious 'esprit Blanc' that allegedly roams the swamps, and a lovable cast. Faith themes are organic and subtle, and the sweet romance between Raphe and Ellie unfolds nicely against the backdrop of Ellie's introduction to the community." —*Publishers Weekly*

Includes bibliographical references.

Luiselli, Valeria

★ **Lost** children archive: a novel. Valeria Luiselli. Alfred A. Knopf, 2019. 416 p.

ISBN 9780525520610

1. Cross-country automobile trips 2. Child immigrants 3. Apache Indians 4. Undocumented immigrants 5. Marital conflict 6. United States 7. Literary fiction

LC 2018018390

ALA Notable Book, 2020; Andrew Carnegie Medal for Excellence in Fiction, 2020; Booklist Editors' Choice, 2019; International IMPAC Dublin Literary Award, 2021; New York Times Notable Book, 2019; National Book Critics Circle Award for Fiction finalist, 2019; Kirkus Prize for Fiction finalist, 2019; Longlisted for the Booker Prize, 2019; Longlisted for The Women's Prize for Fiction, 2019

A novel about a family of four, on the cusp of fracture, who take a trip across America—a story told through varying points of view, and including archival documents and photographs.

"Intense and keenly timely, Luiselli's latest work is perhaps her most politically relevant, and themes of translation and migration resonate, making it one of few novels that fully and powerfully convey the urgency of this unsettling situation." —*Booklist*

Lukas, Michael David

The **last** watchman of Old Cairo: a novel. Michael David Lukas. Spiegel & Grau, 2018. 288 p.

ISBN 9780399181160

1. Synagogues 2. Ancestors 3. Family secrets 4. Torah scrolls 5. College students 6. Cairo, Egypt 7. California 8. Literary fiction 9. Family sagas

LC 2017007153

National Jewish Book Award, 2018; Sophie Brody Medal, 2019; Middle East Book Award, Honorable Mention, 2019

A Berkeley literature student from a mixed-faith family receives a mysterious package that draws him into a quest to uncover his ancestors' tangled history as watchmen for Old Cairo's storied Ibn Ezra Synagogue.

"Lukas enlivens a fascinating epoch when Jews and Muslims bridged cultural divides for a common cause. Part mystery, part character study, yet historically accurate, this book should appeal to a broad swath of readers." —*Library Journal*

Luna, Louisa

The **Janes**. Louisa Luna. Doubleday, 2020. 368 pages (Alice Vega novels, 2)

ISBN 9780385545518

1. Women private investigators 2. Human trafficking 3. Sex crimes 4. Teenage girl murder victims 5. Private investigators 6. San Diego, California 7. Thrillers and suspense

Private investigator Alice Vega and her partner, Cap, search for clues in the murders of two unidentified young women who might be victims of a San Diego sex-trafficking ring.

"In contrast with her debut, Luna this time develops the burgeoning attraction between empathetic Cap and Jack Reacher-esque Vega, resulting in a series duo with legs. Luna's latest entertains while subverting gender stereotypes and confronting the politics of immigration." —*Kirkus*

Lunde, Maja

The **end** of the ocean: a novel. Maja Lunde; translated from the Norwegian by Diane Oatley. HarperCollins, 2020. 304 p. (Climate novels, 2)

ISBN 9780062951366

1. Climate change 2. Refugees 3. Droughts 4. Sailboats 5. Ocean travel 6. Europe 7. 21st century 8. Translations 9. Literary fiction 10. Apocalyptic fiction

LC 2019030722

Explores the threat of a devastating worldwide drought, witnessed through the lives of a father, a daughter and a woman who will risk her life to save the future.

"Two stories on the impact of climate change intersect in this thoughtful and suspenseful novel." —*Kirkus*

Translation of: Bla.

Translated from the Norwegian.

undrigan, Nicole

Glass boys: a novel. Nicole Lundrigan. Douglas & McIntyre, 2011.)0 p.

ISBN 9781553657972

1. Abandonment (Psychology) 2. Stepfathers 3. Murder 4. Forgiveness 5. Family problems 6. Newfoundland and Labrador 7. Mysteries 8. Canadian fiction

When Roy Trench is killed in a drunken prank gone wrong, his rother Lewis blames alcoholic Eli Fagan. Though the courts rule the eath an accident, the event causes ongoing hate between the two families f Knife's Point, Newfoundland.

urie, Alison

Foreign affairs. Alison Lurie. Random House, 1984. 291 p.

ISBN 9780394540764

1. College teachers 2. Americans in London, England 3. Extramarital affairs 4. Middle-aged women — Relations with younger men 5. Single men 6. London, England 7. England 8. Psychological fiction 9. Literary fiction

LC 84042657

Pulitzer Prize for Fiction, 1985; National Book Award for Fiction finalist, 1984; National Book Critics Circle Award for Fiction finalist, 1984

Vinnie Miller, a professor of children's literature, and Fred Turner, an ssistant professor at the same American university, pursue their separate ffairs in London during the same six-month period BT

utz, Lisa

The **Spellman** files: a novel. Lisa Lutz. Simon & Schuster, 2007. 368 (Spellman files, 1)

ISBN 9781416532392

1. Missing persons 2. Women private investigators 3. Cold cases (Criminal investigation) 4. Sisters 5. Familial love 6. San Francisco, California 7. Humorous stories 8. Mysteries 9. Adult books for young adults

LC 2006049161

Alex Award, 2008

Isabel "Izzy" Spellman, a San Francisco private eye with a checkered ast, has been working for her family's firm, Spellman Investigations, nce age 12. Now 28, Izzy thinks she wants out of the family business, but lects to take on a cold case while dealing with her 14-year-old sister Rae, nightmarish Nancy Drew, and parents who have no qualms about bug-ing their children's bedrooms. When Rae suddenly disappears, Izzy and er family must learn some serious lessons in order to find her.

Sequel: Curse of the Spellmans (2008).

The **swallows**: a novel. Lisa Lutz. Ballantine Books, 2019. 416 pages

ISBN 9781984818232

1. Private schools 2. Misogyny 3. Entitlement attitudes 4. Creative writing teachers 5. Boarding school students 6. New England 7. 2000s (Decade) 8. Black humor 9. Thrillers and suspense 10. Multiple perspectives 11. Adult books for young adults

LC 2019011519

LibraryReads Favorites, 2019; Alex Award, 2020

When a creative writing assignment leads to unsettling allegations bout her school's indifference to sexual assault, a new teacher organizes group of marginalized girls in an escalating gender war.

Lyons, Annie

The **brilliant** life of Eudora Honeysett. Annie Lyons. William Morrow & Co,, 2020. 372 pages

ISBN 9780063026063

1. Senior women 2. Girls 3. Intergenerational friendship 4. Assisted suicide 5. Octogenarians 6. England 7. Relationship fiction

Wanting to organize an assisted death on her own terms, a world-weary octogenarian forges an unexpected bond with an exuberant 10-year-old who drags her to tea parties, shopping sprees and other social excursions.

"As Eudora's hardened exterior softens with this newfound kinship, she is still adamant about getting on with her plans ('If I can have the choice of how I live my own life, why can't I choose how to die my own death?'). Lyons strikes a winning balance, reaching deep feelings while avoiding the traps of sentimentality." —*Publishers Weekly*

Lyons, Jenn

The **name** of all things. Jenn Lyons. Tor Books, 2019. 587 pages : Illustration; Map (Chorus of dragons, 2)

ISBN 9781250175533

1. Nobility 2. Dragons 3. Prophecies 4. Fugitives 5. Wizards 6. Epic fantasy

A sequel to The Ruin of Kings finds a fugitive Kihrin navigating a se-cret rebellion and a formidable dragon to help a mysterious Joratese woman prevent the wizard Relos Var from obtaining an artifact of extraor-dinary power.

The **ruin** of kings. Jenn Lyons. Tor, 2019. 560 p. (Chorus of dragons, 1)

ISBN 9781250175489

1. Prisoners 2. Political intrigue 3. Power (Social sciences) 4. Nobility 5. Family secrets 6. Epic fantasy

LC 2018045774

Raised on storybook tales of royal adventure, Kihrin discovers his identity as the illegitimate son of a treasonous prince and is rendered a pawn in the royal family's power schemes before embracing his anti-hero destiny.

"Although a cast of well-developed characters and an impressively intricate storyline power this novel, it's Lyons' audacious worldbuilding that makes for such an unforgettable read." —*Kirkus*

A Tom Doherty Associates book.

M

Ma Jian

Beijing coma. Ma Jian; translated from the Chinese by Flora Drew. Farrar, Straus and Giroux, 2008. 592 p.

ISBN 9780374110178

1. Political activists 2. Social change 3. Change (Psychology) 4. People in comas 5. Freedom 6. China 7. 1980s 8. Historical fiction 9. Translations

LC 2008925628

New York Times Notable Book, 2008

Dai Wei lies in his bedroom, a prisoner in his body, after he was shot in the head at the Tiananmen Square protest ten years earlier and left in a coma. As his mother tends to him, and his friends bring news of their lives in an almost unrecognisable China, Dai Wei escapes into his memories.

"A valuable work. Ma's writing can be lively, and his use of dialogue that embraces everyday chitchat gives the book a sense of reality. The idealism of youth is ably captured. Indeed, the students' frequently lofty and at times naive emotions are touching." —*The New Leader*

First published in Great Britain by Chatto & Windus, 2008.

China dream. Ma Jian; translated from the Chinese by Flora Drew. Counterpoint, 2019. 176 pages

ISBN 9781640092402

1. Politicians 2. Totalitarianism 3. Dreams 4. Social change 5. Mistresses 6. China 7. Political fiction 8. Satirical fiction

LC 2018057990

One of the year's most anticipated novels in translation, written by an acclaimed Chinese author whose entire body of work has been banned by his home country, and published in the thirtieth-anniversary year of the Tiananmen Square Massacre.

First published in the United Kingdom by Chatto & Windus in 2018.

Ma, Ling

Severance. Ling Ma. Farrar, Straus and Giroux, 2018. 291 p.

ISBN 9780374261597

1. Children of immigrants 2. Survival (after epidemics) 3. End of the world 4. Chinese Americans 5. Capitalism 6. New York City 7. 2010s 8. Apocalyptic fiction 9. Satirical fiction

LC 2017038340

Kirkus Prize for Fiction, 2018; New York Times Notable Book, 2018

A survivor of an apocalyptic plague maintains a blog about a decimated Manhattan before joining a motley group of survivors to search for a place to rebuild, a goal that is complicated by an unscrupulous group leader.

Maaren, Kari

★ **Weave** a circle round. Kari Maaren. Tor, 2017. 336 p.

ISBN 9780765386281

1. Misfits (Persons) 2. Time travel (Past) 3. High school students 4. Chaos 5. Neighbors 6. Gateway fantasy 7. Fantasy fiction 8. Canadian fiction 9. Adult books for young adults

Loan Stars Favourites, 2017

When she runs afoul of her eccentric new neighbors, teen Freddy is sent traveling through time where she encounters numerous versions of her neighbors, Josiah and Cuerva, and she realizes that she might be the third in their group of immortals.

"This is an ambitious, intricate, joyful coming-of-age tale, with memorable characters and a powerful sense of wonder." —*Publishers Weekly*

Mabanckou, Alain

★ **Black** Moses. Alain Mabanckou; translated from the French by Helen Stevenson. The New Press, 2017. 199 p.

ISBN 9781620972939

1. Boy orphans 2. Self-discovery 3. Survival 4. Escapes 5. Gangs 6. Congo (Brazzaville) 7. Literary fiction 8. Political fiction 9. Satirical fiction 10. Adult books for young adults

Hurston/Wright Legacy Award: Fiction, 2018

Three orphans in 1970s Africa escape their orphanage to the busy port town of Pointe-Noire where they form a gang of petty thieves and become part of the underworld.

"A small book with a big narrative voice, this wacky new novel by Mabanckou follows the existential misfortunes of an orphan whose kilometrically extended name means Thanks be to God, the black Moses is born on the earth of our ancestors.... This mythic, beguiling novel is a journey to discover what is hard-wired in us and what we make up about ourselves." —*Publishers Weekly*

Originally published: Paris : Editions Seuil, 2015.

Translated from the French.

Macallister, Greer

★ The **Arctic** fury. Greer Macallister. Sourcebooks Landmark, 2020. 300 p.

ISBN 9781728229058

1. Franklin, Jane 2. Women adventurers 3. Courage in women 4. Wilderness areas 5. Quests 6. Northwest Passage 7. Arctic Regions 8. Victorian era (1837-1901) 9. Historical fiction

LC 2020015957

Secretly hired by an eccentric Lady Franklin to lead a team of women explorers into the Arctic to recover Captain Sir John Franklin's lost expedition, Virginia Reeve survives a harrowing quest only to find herself on trial for murder.

"Moving from the present to the past and from one woman's voice to another, Macallister captures the suspenseful journey from all angles as readers uncover the truth about what really happened out on the ice." —*Booklist*

MacBride, Stuart

Cold granite. Stuart MacBride. St. Martin's Minotaur, 2005. 464 p. (Logan McRae mysteries, 1)

ISBN 9780312339951

1. Police 2. Child murders 3. Serial murders 4. Detectives 5. Crimes against children 6. Aberdeen, Scotland 7. Scotland 8. Mysteries 9. Police procedurals

LC 2005042786

Returning to duty after recovering from being stabbed by a murder suspect, Detective Sergeant Logan McRae becomes involved in the ritualistic murder of a three-year-old boy, whose body is found months after being reported missing.

MacDonald, Andrew

When we were Vikings. Andrew David MacDonald. Gallery Books, 2020. 336 pages

ISBN 9781982126766

1. Vikings 2. Siblings 3. Fetal alcohol syndrome 4. Obsession 5. Twenties (Age) 6. Coming-of-age stories 7. Canadian fiction

LibraryReads Favorites, 2020; Loan Stars Favourites, 2020

When 21-year-old Viking enthusiast Zelda finds out that her older brother, Gert, has resorted to some questionable—and dangerous—methods to make enough money to keep them afloat, Zelda decides to launch her own quest.

"MacDonald avoids oversentimentality and a too-neat resolution, instead depicting Zelda's desire to shape her own life and be the hero of her own legend with frankness and humor." —*Publishers Weekly*

MacDonald, John D.

Cinnamon skin: the twentieth adventure of Travis McGee. John D. MacDonald. Harper & Row, 1982. 275 p; (Travis McGee novels, 20)

ISBN 9780060149901

1. Terrorists 2. Bombings 3. Private investigators 4. Murder 5. Chases 6. Fort Lauderdale, Florida 7. Rio Grande Valley 8. Mysteries 9. First person narratives

LC 8104815

Travis McGee investigates the explosion of a cruise boat in the Florida Keys, supposedly the work of a Chilean underground organization.

"Travis McGee and his friend Meyer search for Meyer's niece's new husband, who has killed his wife and faked his own death in an explosion. The search is plodding and long, but MacDonald makes it interesting through the diverse and lively characters involved. The showdown, on Mexico's Yucatn Peninsula, is a bit slow but colorful and original." —*Library Journal*

The **green** ripper. John D. MacDonald. Lippincott, 1979. 221 p; (Travis McGee novels, 18)
ISBN 9780891907794
1. Cults 2. Terrorists 3. Private investigators 4. Murder 5. Chases 6. Fort Lauderdale, Florida 7. California 8. Mysteries 9. First person narratives
LC 79012063
Beautiful girls always grace the Florida beaches, strolling, sailing, relaxing at the many parties on Travis McGee's houseboat, The Busted Flush. McGee was too smart—and had been around too long—for many of them to touch his heart. Now, however, there was Gretel. She had discovered the key to McGee—to all of him—and now he had something to hope for. Then, terribly, unexpectedly, she was dead. From a mysterious illness, or so they said. But McGee knew the truth, that Gretel had been murdered. And now he was out for blood...

"MacDonald is unsurpassed at showing the American brand of loneliness. He catches foibles in a phrase and gives us many-sided, wounded but courageous, characters." —*Booklist*

★ The **lonely** silver rain. John D. MacDonald. A.A. Knopf, 1985. 231 p; (Travis McGee novels, 21)
ISBN 9780394538990
1. Middle-aged men 2. Cocaine smuggling 3. Private investigators 4. Yachts 5. Murder 6. Fort Lauderdale, Florida 7. Miami, Florida 8. 1970s 9. Mysteries 10. First person narratives
LC 84023373
Someone is trying to kill Travis McGee, someone linked to southern Florida's drug traffickers—either Miami's old-time underworld or the new generation of Latino drug barons—and in order to save his own life, McGee must detonate a drug war.

The **long** lavender look. John D. MacDonald. Lippincott, 1972. 264 p; (Travis McGee novels, 12)
ISBN 9780397007394
1. Police misconduct 2. Private investigators 3. Malicious accusation 4. Murder 5. Secrets 6. Fort Lauderdale, Florida 7. Everglades, Florida 8. Mysteries 9. First person narratives
LC 78037010
Featuring an introduction by best-selling author, Carl Hiaasen, another colorful adventure sends freewheeling detective Travis McGee on the trail of millions and murder in a deadly Florida town.

A **purple** place for dying. John D. MacDonald. Lippincott, 1976. 204 p; (Travis McGee novels, 3)
ISBN 9780449224380
1. Snipers 2. Deserts 3. Private investigators 4. Murder 5. Married women 6. Fort Lauderdale, Florida 7. Nevada 8. 1960s 9. Mysteries 10. First person narratives
LC 76004096
While on vacation in the Southwest, Travis McGee reluctantly agrees to help Mona Yeoman retrieve her estate from a wayward husband, only to become an eyewitness to her sudden death.

"Travis McGee is pondering whether to take on the beautiful Mona Yeoman as a client when someone decides for him by shooting her in the back and hiding the body. Mona's husband soon dies of poison, and the killers might have been in the clear if they had not tried to add McGee (and one of those lovely women he always attracts) to their list. The usual literate and fast-paced stuff expected from MacDonald." —*Booklist*

The **scarlet** ruse. John D. MacDonald. Lippincott & Crowell, 1980. 262 p; (Travis McGee novels, 14)
ISBN 9780690018875
1. Stamp thefts 2. Private investigators 3. Counterfeits and counterfeiting 4. Murderers 5. Senior men 6. Fort Lauderdale, Florida 7. 1970s 8. Mysteries 9. First person narratives
LC 79024843
Travis McGee agrees to investigate a case involving a rare-stamps swindle and finds himself confronting death, deception, a tantalizing affair, and an ambush aboard a houseboat aground at No Name Island.

The **turquoise** lament. By John D. MacDonald. Lippincott, 1973. 287 p; (Travis McGee novels, 15)
ISBN 9780397009879
1. Private investigators 2. Attempted murder 3. Wife-killing 4. Suspicion 5. Fear in women 6. Fort Lauderdale, Florida 7. Hawaii 8. Mysteries 9. First person narratives
LC 73014806
Believing either that her husband is out to kill her or that she is insane, Pidge Brindle contacts a friend of her late father for help.
"One of the best McGee adventures." —*Publishers Weekly*

MacDonald, Philip
The **list** of Adrian Messenger. Philip MacDonald. Vintage Books, 1983. 224 p; (Anthony Gethryn mysteries, 12)
ISBN 9780394717128
1. Murder investigation 2. Detectives 3. Lists 4. Airplane accidents 5. Murder suspects 6. England 7. Mysteries
LC 83005806
"If some readers find Mr. MacDonald's style a bit stiff and old-fashioned, they will also find that he provides such other old-fashioned elements as honest clues, characters who stick in the mind from page to page, an original idea, and, in Anthony Gethryn, a detective who inspires utter confidence." —*The New Yorker*
An Anthony Gethryn mystery—Cover.
Reprint. Originally published: 1st ed. Garden City, N.Y. : Published for the Crime Club by Doubleday, 1959.

Macdonald, Ross
The **drowning** pool. Ross Macdonald. Vintage Crime/Black Lizard, 1996. 244 p; (Lew Archer novels, 2)
ISBN 9780679768067
1. Archer, Lew (Fictitious character) 2. Private investigators 3. Mysteries 4. Mystery classics
When a millionaire matriarch is found floating face down in the family pool, the prime suspects are her good-for-nothing son and his seductive teenage daughter. In The Drowning Pool, Lew Archer takes this case in the Los Angeles suburbs and encounters a moral wasteland of corporate greed and family hatred—and sufficient motive for a dozen murders.
Originally published: New York : Knopf, 1950.

The **far** side of the dollar. Ross Macdonald. Knopf, 1965. 247 p. (Lew Archer novels, 12)
ISBN 9780679768654
1. Archer, Lew (Fictitious character) 2. Private investigators 3. Mysteries
LC 65010103
Gold Dagger Award for Best Crime Novel of the Year, 1965

To reach the Barcelona Hotel you took Sunset and the coast highway. Once starlets and Navy boys had rubbed shoulders with tycoons and hustlers there, but for Lew Archer the old, closed-up palace held the key to a missing teenager and a hot murder. Archer knew that twenty years ago a handful of dreamers and losers had come together in the barcelona. The only question now was what kind of deal had gone down there, and why a mixed-up rich kid and a beautiful blonde were the first to pay the price ...

The **Galton** case. Ross Macdonald. Warner Books 1990. 198 p. (Lew Archer novels, 8)
ISBN 9780679768647
1. Archer, Lew (Fictitious character) 2. Private investigators 3. California 4. Mysteries 5. Mystery classics

Almost twenty years have passed since Anthony Galton disappeared, along with a suspiciously streetwise bride and several thousand dollars of his family's fortune. Now Anthony's aging and very rich mother wants him back and has hired Lew Archer to find him. What turns up is a headless skeleton, a boy who claims to be Galton's son, and a con game whose stakes are so high that someone is still willing to kill for them.

The **goodbye** look. Ross Macdonald. Vintage Books, 2000. 243 p; (Lew Archer novels, 15)
ISBN 9780375708657
1. Archer, Lew (Fictitious character) 2. Private investigators 3. Rich people 4. California 5. Mysteries
LC 78308610

In searching for a gun used to commit two murders fifteen years apart, Lew Archer is introduced to California hobos and the nouveau riche in his attempt to solve the murder of another private eye.
Ross Macdonald is the pseudonym of Kenneth Millar.
Originally published: New York : Alfred A. Knopf, 1969.

Sleeping beauty. Ross Macdonald. Vintage Books, 2000. 271 p; (Lew Archer novels, 17)
ISBN 9780375708664
1. Private investigators 2. Rich people 3. Missing persons 4. Extortion 5. Murder 6. California 7. Mysteries
LC 72011037

Private detective Lew Archer challenges the power and ruthlessness of a wealthy oil dynasty responsible for a spill on the Southern California coast and linked to a missing girl, a six-figure ransom, and murder.
Originally published: New York : Alfred A. Knopf, 1973.

The **underground** man. Ross Macdonald. Vintage Crime/Black Lizard, 1996. 273 p. (Lew Archer novels, 16)
ISBN 9780679768081
1. Fires 2. Missing persons investigation 3. Missing children 4. Private investigators 5. Secrets 6. Southern California 7. California 8. Mysteries 9. Mystery classics

As a mysterious fire rages through the hills above a privileged town in Southern California, Lew Archer tracks a missing child who may be the pawn in a marital struggle or the victim of a bizarre kidnapping. What he uncovers amid the ashes is murder—and a trail of motives as combustible as gasoline.

Machado, Carmen Maria

Her body and other parties: stories. Carmen Maria Machado. Graywolf Press, 2017. 245 p.
ISBN 9781555977887
1. Women 2. Sexuality 3. Short stories 4. Literary fiction 5. Horror
Indies' Choice Book Awards, Adult Debut, 2018; Lambda Literary Award for Lesbian Fiction, 2018; Shirley Jackson Awards, Single-Author Collection, 2017; Kirkus Prize for Fiction finalist, 2017; National Book Award for Fiction finalist, 2017

Contains short stories about the realities of women's lives and the violence visited upon their bodies.

"Machado creates eerie, inventive worlds shimmering with supernatural swerves in this engrossing debut collection. Her stories make strikingly feminist moves by combining elements of horror and speculative fiction with womens everyday crises." —*Publishers Weekly*

★ The **low,** low woods. . DC Comics, 2020. 160 p.
ISBN 9781779504524
1. Best friends 2. Amnesia 3. Secrets 4. Memories 5. Teenage girl 6. Pennsylvania 7. Horror comics 8. Comics and Graphic novels
LC 20200226?

YALSA Great Graphic Novels for Teens, 2021
When your memories are stolen, what would you give to remember Follow El and Vee as they search for answers to the questions everyone else forgot. Shudder-to-Think, Pennsylvania, is plagued by a mysterious illness that eats away at the memories of those affected by it. El and Octavia are two best friends who find themselves the newest victims of this disease after waking up in a movie theater with no memory of the past few hours. As El and Vee dive deeper into the mystery behind their lost memories, they realize the stories of their town hold more dark truth than they could've imagined. It's up to El and Vee to keep their town from falling apart...to keep the world safe from Shudder-to-Think's monsters.

"This will surely call out to fans of Machado's searing prose, and will also hit the spot for comics fans who like their horror heartfelt" —*Publishers Weekly*
Originally published in single magazine form in "The Low, Low Woods" 1-6.
The Low, Low Woods created by Carmen Maria Machado; curated for Hill House Comics by Joe Hill

Mackintosh, Anneliese

Bright and dangerous objects. Anneliese Mackintosh. Tin House 2020. 240 p.
ISBN 9781951142100
1. Divers 2. Planets — Colonization 3. Married people 4. Options, alternatives, choices 5. Ambition in women 6. Science fiction
LC 202001315

Commercial deep-sea diver Solvig has a secret. She wants to be one of the first human beings to colonize Mars, and she's one of a hundred people shortlisted by the Mars Project to do just that. But to fulfil her ambition, she'll have to leave behind everything she's ever known-for the rest of her life. As the prospect of heading to space becomes more real, thirty-seven-year-old Solvig is forced to define who she really is.

"A perceptive and nuanced study of a woman's search for self-fulfillment, reaching from the ocean floor to outer space." —*Kirkus*

Mackintosh, Clare

After the end. Clare Mackintosh. G.P. Putnam's Sons, 2019. 400 p.
ISBN 9780451490568
1. Husband and wife 2. Sick children 3. Decision-making 4. Parenthood 5. Options, alternatives, choices 6. England 7. Mainstream fiction 8. Multiple perspectives
LC 201900345?

Disagreeing for the first time when their son falls ill and they receive conflicting doctor recommendations, a devoted couple finds a unique way for both of their preferences to become possible.

MacLaughlin, Nina

Wake, siren: Ovid resung. Nina MacLaughlin. FSG/Farrar, Straus and Giroux, 2019. X, 342 pages

ISBN 9780374538583

1. Ovid 2. Metamorphosis — Mythology 3. Mythology, Classical 4. Heroes and heroines 5. Women — Mythology 6. Short stories 7. Adaptations, retellings, and spin-offs

LC 2019020215

The women of Ovid's Metamorphoses claim their stories and challenge the power of myth.

MacLaverty, Bernard

★ **Blank** pages: and other stories. Bernard MacLaverty. W. W. Norton & Company, 2022. 272 p.

ISBN 9780393881592

1. Love 2. Death 3. Loss (Psychology) 4. Grief 5. Families 6. Short stories

LC 2021037010

A collection of twelve powerful and moving new stories from one of Ireland's most celebrated writers. Tinged with melancholy but rooted in resiliency, the exquisite stories of Bernard MacLaverty's Blank Pages display the perseverance of the human spirit. Blank Pages elegantly probes MacLaverty's signature themes-domestic love, Catholicism, the Troubles, aging-with compassion and insight..

"A fine collection by a true craftsman, thematically rich and deeply humane." —*Kirkus*

MacLean, Sarah

★ **Bombshell**. Sarah MacLean. Avon Books, 2021. 288 p. (Hell's belles, 1)

ISBN 9780063118973

1. Scandals 2. Aristocracy 3. Women vigilantes 4. Secret societies 5. Reputation 6. London, England 7. Great Britain 8. Victorian era (1837-1901) 9. Victorian romances 10. Historical romances

No stranger to scandal, Lady Sesily Talbot embraces her bad reputation and continues luring men from Mayfair ballrooms for late night escapades but finds herself pining for what she can't seem to have—her brother's best friend.

"This book is a complete pleasure as it seamlessly shifts from nail-biting action to aching romance. It's a celebration of finding joy through living and loving with truth and authenticity. The characters are rich and complex, and the pining between Sesily and Caleb is top-notch." —*Kirkus*

★ **Brazen** and the Beast. Sarah MacLean. Avon Books, 2019. 400 pages (Bareknuckle bastards, 2)

ISBN 9780062912978

1. Single women 2. Independence in women 3. Swindlers and swindling 4. Brothers 5. Secrets 6. England 7. Georgian era (1714-1837) 8. Georgian romances 9. Historical romances

Henrietta Sedley, who wants to take over her father's shipping company but is passed over in favor of her roguish brother, indulges in a night of passion with a king of smugglers known as Beast, only to find their fates linked.

"When it comes to crafting unforgettable romances that are both emotionally and thematically complex, nobody does it quite like RITA Award-winning MacLean (Wicked and the Wallflower, 2018), and the latest brilliantly written and boldly sensual addition to her Bareknuckle Bastards series is another exquisitely constructed and exceptionally entertaining celebration of the power of love to transform lives." —*Booklist*

No good duke goes unpunished. Sarah MacLean. Avon Books, 2013. 384 p. (Rules of scoundrels, 3)

ISBN 9780062068545

1. Dukes and duchesses 2. Murder suspects 3. Scandals 4. Casinos 5. Missing women 6. England 7. London, England 8. Regency period (1811-1820) 9. Regency romances 10. Historical romances

LibraryReads Favorites, 2013; RITA Award for Best Historical Romance, 2014; Romantic Times Reviewer's Choice Award, 2013

When her brother gets deep in debt to Temple, a disgraced duke who now owns an exclusive casino, Mara Lowe agrees to come forward and clear Temple, who has been accused of her murder, if he will forgive what her brother owes him.

"MacLean once again creates compelling and complex characters and sets them on a path toward love and reconciliation that begins with seemingly impossible odds and ends with exquisite fulfillment." —*Kirkus*

The **rogue** not taken. Sarah MacLean. Avon Books, 2015. 432 p. (Scandal & scoundrel, 1)

ISBN 9780062379412

1. Marquis and marchionesses 2. Pariahs 3. Womanizers 4. Scandals 5. Reputation 6. England 7. Great Britain 8. Regency period (1811-1820) 9. Regency romances 10. Historical romances

After stowing away in the Marquess of Eversley's carriage to escape London and scandal, Lady Sophie Talbot must convince the Marquess that she is not trying to trick him into marriage as they try to resist their mutual attraction.

"Readers will be intoxicated by the emotional connection between the lovers, which makes their banter that much more amusing and their eventual physical passion that much more satisfying. Sophie's delightful family will leave readers eager for future installments in the series." —*Publishers Weekly*

★ **Wicked** and the wallflower. Sarah MacLean. Avon Books, 2018. 360 pages; (Bareknuckle bastards, 1)

ISBN 9780062842640

1. Single women 2. Swindlers and swindling 3. Dishonesty 4. Dukes and duchesses 5. Mate selection 6. England 7. Historical romances

Finding the perfect way to exact a revenge years in the making, Devil, bastard son of a duke and king of London's dark streets, offers to help Lady Felicity Faircloth land a suitable husband by transforming her into an irresistible temptress who will destroy his enemy.

MacLeod, Alison

Tenderness. Alison MacLeod. Bloomsbury, 2021. 288 p.

ISBN 9781635576108

1. Lawrence, D. H. 2. Books and reading 3. Sexuality 4. Extramarital affairs 5. Censorship 6. Authors, British 7. Great Britain 8. United States 9. 20th century 10. Literary fiction 11. Historical fiction 12. Canadian fiction

A Booker Prize-longlisted author brilliantly recreates the origins of D.H. Lawrence's Lady Chatterley's Lover and boldly reimagines its journey to freedom through the story of Jackie Kennedy, who was known to be an admirer.

"Sinuous storytelling, escalating stakes, and an avalanche of bad decisions propel the tale to a gratifying if far-fetched conclusion." —*Publishers Weekly*

Macmillan, Gilly

The **nanny**. Gilly Macmillan. William Morrow & Co, 2019. 384 pages

ISBN 9780062875556

1. Nannies 2. Aristocracy 3. Dead — Identification 4. Rich families 5. Mother and adult daughter 6. England 7. California 8. Psychological suspense 9. Multiple perspectives

Leaving her home after the mysterious disappearance of her beloved nanny, an embittered woman is forced to return decades later when the discovery of human remains forces her to question everything she thought she knew.

The **perfect** girl. Gilly Macmillan. William Morrow & Co, 2016. 448 p.

ISBN 9780062567482

1. Gifted teenagers 2. Teenage musicians 3. Mothers — Death 4. Teenage girls 5. Former convicts 6. Psychological suspense

Fighting to start over after serving time for her role in a fatal accident, teen musical prodigy Zoe is horrified when her mother is found dead after a career-launching recital, in a high-suspense tale told over the course of 24 hours.

Macneal, Elizabeth

The **doll** factory. Elizabeth Macneal. Emily Bestler Books/Atria, 2019. 362 p.

ISBN 9781982106768

1. Artists' models 2. Painters 3. Women's role 4. City life 5. Poor people 6. Victorian era (1837-1901) 7. Historical fiction

In 1850s London beautiful young aspiring artist Iris is asked to model for Pre-Raphaelite artist Louis Frost, whose dark obsession may destroy her world forever.

MacNeal, Susan Elia

The **king's** justice. Susan Elia MacNeal. Bantam Books, 2020. 352 p. (Maggie Hope mysteries, 9)

ISBN 9780399593840

1. World War II home front 2. Intelligence service 3. Conscientious objectors 4. Serial murders 5. Serial murder investigation 6. England 7. Second World War era (1939-1945) 8. Historical mysteries 9. Adult books for young adults

LC 2019038115

Secret agent and spy Maggie Hope, traumatized by her past and living dangerously, gets entangled in another crime when a stolen violin is linked to a serial killer terrorizing London during World War II.

"Irresistibly readable and brilliantly crafted, this is a story both historical mystery and fiction fans will adore." —*Library Journal*

Includes bibliographical references.

Macomber, Debbie

If not for you: a novel. Debbie Macomber. Ballantine Books, 2017. 400 p.

ISBN 9780553391961

1. Life change events 2. Music teachers 3. Mechanics 4. Self-fulfillment 5. Moving to a new city 6. Portland, Oregon 7. Chicago, Illinois 8. Contemporary romances

LC 2016042032

LibraryReads Favorites, 2017

Moving away from her oppressive parents in hopes of taking charge of her own life, Beth takes a job as a school music teacher and initially resists her attraction to a tattooed mechanic who is the epitome of everything her conservative parents fear.

"A likable supporting cast keep the action moving and the plot intriguing in a well-crafted story that includes several romantic relationships and is rich with unresolved interpersonal issues. Wholesome and thoughtful." —*Library Journal*

Maguire, Gregory

The **brides** of Maracoor. Gregory Maguire. William Morrow & Company, 2021. 320 p. (Another day, 1)

ISBN 9780063093966

1. Girls with amnesia 2. Castaways 3. Witches 4. Islands 5. Imaginary kingdoms 6. Fantasy fiction

LC 2021002176

Volume one of Maguire's new series finds Elphaba's granddaughter, Rain, washing ashore on a foreign island. Comatose from crashing into the sea, Rain is taken in by a community of single women committed to obscure devotional practices. As the mainland of Maracoor sustains an assault by a foreign navy, the island's civil-servant overseer struggles to understand how an alien arriving on the shores of Maracoor could threaten the stability and wellbeing of an entire nation. Is it myth or magic at work, for good or for ill? The trilogy Another Day will follow this green-skinned girl from the island outpost into the unmapped badlands of Maracoor before she learns how, and becomes ready, to turn her broom homeward, back to her family and her lover, back to Oz, which—in its beauty, suffering, mystery, injustice, and possibility—reminds us all too clearly of the troubled yet sacred terrain of our own lives.

"The larger world of Maracoor Abiding, with its priestesslike brides, mysterious artifacts, and its own systems of magic, myth, and politics, has echoes of Greek mythology and looks to be fertile ground as a setting for more books. An expertly crafted introduction to a new series of magic and adventure." —*Kirkus*

Son of a witch: a novel. Gregory Maguire. Harper Collins 2005. 352 p. (Wicked years, 2)

ISBN 9780060548933

1. Witches 2. Good and evil 3. Wickedness 4. Young men 5. Teenage boys 6. Adaptations, retellings, and spin-offs 7. Fantasy fiction 8. Adult books for young adults

LC 2005046232

The sequel to Wicked returns to the land of Oz to tell the story of Liir, an adolescent boy last seen hiding in the shadows of the castle after Dorothy did in Elphaba, the Wicked Witch of the West. Bruised, comatose, and left for dead in a gully, Liir is shattered in spirit as well as in form. But he is tended at the Cloister of Saint Glinda by the silent novice called Candle, who wills him back to life with her musical gifts. What dark force left Liir in this condition? Is he really Elphaba's son? He has her broom and her cape, but what of her powers? Can he find his supposed half-sister, Nor, last seen in the forbidding prison, Southstairs? Can he fulfill the last wishes of a dying princess? In an Oz that, since the Wizard's departure, is under new and dangerous management, can Liir keep his head down long enough to grow up?

"This sequel to the adult fairy tale Wicked (1995)...begins ten years after the destruction of Elphaba, a.k.a. the Wicked Witch of the West. In Maguire's dark version of the Land of Oz, there's not much to ring the bells for in the Emerald City, despite the tyrannical Wizard's departure. Corruption is rife, political factions compete for power, and radicals proclaim Elphaba lives! Elsewhere, a horribly injured young man called Liir wakes in the religious House of Saint Glinda to many puzzles.... Above all, was Elphaba his mother? These and other questions drive a tale that adroitly mixes drama, humor, and political satire into a well-knit examination of good and evil-and leaves several doors open for future journeys over the rainbow into this cleverly constructed dystopia." —*Library Journal*

Sequel to: Wicked.

★ **Wicked:** the life and times of the wicked witch of the West : a novel. Gregory Maguire; illustrations by Douglas Smith. ReganBooks, 1995. 406 p. : Illustration (Wicked years, 1)

ISBN 9780060391447

1. Witches 2. Wickedness 3. Social acceptance 4. Wicked Witch of the West (Fictitious character) 5. Oz (Imaginary place) 6. Adaptations, retellings, and spin-offs 7. Fantasy fiction

LC 95000669

Set in an Oz where a morose Wizard battles suicidal thoughts, the story of the green-skinned Elphaba, otherwise known as the Wicked Witch of the West, profiles her as an animal rights activist striving to avenge her dear sister's death.

"Born with green skin and huge teeth, like a dragon, the free-spirited Elphaba grows up to be an anti-totalitarian agitator, an animal-rights activist, a nun, then a nurse who tends the dyingand, ultimately, the headstrong Wicked Witch of the West in the land of Oz. Maguire's strange and imaginative postmodernist fable uses L. Frank Baum's Wonderful Wizard of Oz as a springboard to create a tense realm inhabited by humans, talking animals (a rhino librarian, a goat physician), Munchkinlanders, dwarves and various tribes." —*Publishers Weekly*

Sequel: Son of a witch.

Includes endpaper maps.

Mahfuz, Najib

★ **Palace** walk. Naguib Mahfouz; translated from the Arabic by William M. Hutchins with Olive E. Kenny. Doubleday, 1990. 498 p. (Cairo trilogy, 1)

ISBN 9780385264662

1. Muslim families 2. Cairo, Egypt 3. Translations 4. Political fiction 5. Family sagas

LC 89023348

ALA Notable Book, 1991

"This is the first volume in the author's trilogy dealing with three generations of a Cairo family in the first half of the twentieth century. The emotional and physical struggles of these middle-class people are depicted with a great deal of sympathy and honesty, from the torments of adolescent love through the banked passions of an established marriage. The novel begins with a series of domestic scenes featuring the five children of a merchant and his wife; later, the setting shifts to Cairo nightclubs, coffee shops, and stores as Mahfouz re-creates the everyday existence of his characters in almost Dickensian detail." —*Booklist*

Originally published in Arabic in 1956.

Mahmoud, Lena

Amreekiya: a novel. Lena Mahmoud. The University Press of Kentucky, 2018. 178 p.

ISBN 9780813176376

1. Palestinian American women 2. Newlyweds 3. Marriage 4. Miscarriage 5. Women's role 6. California 7. Domestic fiction 8. Literary fiction

LC 2018027377

After her mother is killed and her father disappears, Isra Shadi, whose parents were Palestinian and white, lives with her aunt and uncle, but when she is encouraged to leave and marry, she chooses a love from her past, as she is caught between two cultures and struggles for identity.

Mailer, Norman

★ The **executioner's** song. Norman Mailer. Little, Brown, 1979. 1056 p.

ISBN 9780316544177

1. Gilmore, Gary Mark 2. Murderers 3. Capital punishment 4. Violence in men 5. Man-woman relationships 6. Utah 7. Biographical fiction 8. Psychological fiction 9. Books to movies

LC 79017193

Pulitzer Prize for Fiction, 1980; National Book Award for Fiction finalist, 1980; National Book Critics Circle Award for Fiction finalist, 1979

Reconstructs the crime and fate of Gary Gilmore, the convicted murderer who sought his own execution in Utah, based on taped interviews with relatives, friends, lawyers, and law-enforcement officials.

★ The **naked** and the dead. Norman Mailer. H. Holt, 1998. Xiii, 721 p. : Map

ISBN 9780805060188

1. World War II 2. Soldiers 3. Self-awareness 4. Self-perception 5. War 6. Islands of the Pacific 7. Second World War era (1939-1945) 8. War stories 9. Modern classics 10. Literary fiction

Portrays the contrasting personalities and nostalgic reminiscences of a group of World War II American soldiers engaged in a combat operation against the Japanese BT

The Naked and the Dead inspired the film The Naked and the Dead in 1958.

Maizes, R. L.

Other people's pets. R.L. Maizes. St Martins Pr 2020. 292 pages

ISBN 9781250304131

1. Thieves 2. Pets 3. Human-animal relationships 4. Human-animal communication 5. Fathers and daughters 6. Mainstream fiction

LC 2020002701

Abandoned by her mother and thief father, a woman who empathically relates more to animals than people drops out of veterinary school and turns burglar, targeting houses where ailing pets can benefit from her care.

Majors, Inman

Penelope Lemon: game on!. Inman Majors. Louisiana State University Press, 2018. 264 p.

ISBN 9780807169513

1. Divorced women 2. Online dating 3. Misfits (Persons) 4. Single mothers 5. Waitresses 6. Virginia 7. Relationship fiction 8. Humorous stories

Audacious and laugh-out-loud funny, Inman Majors's new novel holds up a fun-house mirror to the relatable challenges of being a single parent in the digital age. All those who live by the beat of their own drum gain a coconspirator, an accomplice, and a champion in the unstoppable Penelope Lemon.

Majumdar, Megha

A **burning**. Megha Majumdar. Alfred A. Knopf, 2020. 240 p.

ISBN 9780525658696

1. Muslim girls 2. Terrorism 3. Inequality 4. Suspects (Criminal investigation) 5. Social media 6. India 7. Literary fiction 8. Multiple perspectives 9. Thrillers and suspense

LC 2019039498

New York Times Notable Book, 2020; Andrew Carnegie Medal for Excellence in Fiction finalist, 2021

An opportunistic gym teacher and a starry-eyed misfit find the realization of their ambitions tied to the downfall of an innocent Muslim girl who has been wrongly implicated in a terrorist attack.

"A polyphonic novel that sharply observes class and religious divisions in India." —*Kirkus*

Makkai, Rebecca

The **borrower**: a novel. Rebecca Makkai. Viking, 2011. 336 p.
ISBN 9780670022816
1. Librarians 2. Boys 3. Books and reading 4. Automobile travel 5. Intergenerational friendship 6. Mainstream fiction 7. Adult books for young adults

LC 2010052432

Lucy Hull is an accidental children's librarian who routinely gives her favorite patron, 10-year-old Ian, books that do not conform to the rigid rules his overbearing, fundamentalist mother has set for him. When Ian's parents force him to attend behavior-modification classes that will "cure" his burgeoning homosexuality, Ian determines to run away—and Lucy decides to go with him. Though this set-up may leave you feeling incredulous, it's actually the start of a warm, moving, and frequently funny book full of literary references and paeans to the power of reading.

"A crime farce about a hapless librariancumaccidental kidnapper. Lucy Hull is a 26-year-old whose rebellion against her wealthy Russian mafia parents has taken the form of her accepting a children's librarian job in smalltown Missouri. After an unnecessarily long-winded first act, the novel picks up when Lucy discovers her favorite library regular, 10-year-old Ian Drake, hiding out in the stacks one morning after having run away from his evangelical Christian parents, who censor his book choices and are pre-emptively sending him to SSAD (Same-Sex Attraction Disorder) rehab, and Lucy soon aids and abets his escape. The tale of their subsequent jaunt across several state lines dodging cops, a persistent suitor of Lucy's, and a suspicious black-haired pursuer is fast-paced, suspenseful, and thoroughly enjoyable." —*Publishers Weekly*

★ The **great** believers. Rebecca Makkai. Viking, 2018. 421 p.
ISBN 9780735223523
1. AIDS (Disease) 2. Homophobia 3. Epidemics 4. Mothers and daughters 5. Siblings 6. Chicago, Illinois 7. Paris, France 8. 1980s 9. 2010s 10. LGBTQIA fiction 11. Literary fiction 12. Parallel narratives
ALA Notable Book, 2019; Andrew Carnegie Medal for Excellence in Fiction, 2019; Booklist Editors' Choice, 2018; New York Times Notable Book, 2018; Library Journal Best Books, 2018; Los Angeles Times Book Prize for Fiction, 2018; Stonewall Book Award for the Barbara Gittings Literature Award, 2019; Pulitzer Prize for Fiction finalist, 2019

A novel set in 1980s Chicago and contemporary Paris follows the director of a Chicago art gallery and a woman looking for her estranged daughter in Paris who both struggle to come to terms with the ways AIDS has affected their lives.

"As her intimately portrayed characters wrestle with painful pasts and fight to love one another and find joy in the present in spite of what is to come, Makkai carefully reconstructs 1980s Chicago, WWI-era and present-day Paris, and scenes of the early days of the AIDS epidemic. A tribute to the enduring forces of love and art, over everything." —*Booklist*

Makumbi, Jennifer Nansubuga

★ A **girl** is a body of water. Jennifer Nansubuga Makumbi. Tin House, 2020. 545 pages
ISBN 9781951142049
1. Witches 2. Villages 3. Abandonment (Psychology) 4. Mothers and daughters 5. Teenage girls 6. Uganda 7. Literary fiction 8. Magical realism 9. Coming-of-age stories

LC 2020013151

Coming of age with the support of the women in her Ugandan village, a girl struggling with abandonment seeks answers at the side of a local witch who shares stories about their culture's heritage of female strength.

Kintu. Jennifer Nansubuga Makumbi; introduction by Aaron Bady. Transit Books, 2017. 400 p.
ISBN 9781945492013
1. Family curses 2. Clans 3. Heredity 4. Families 5. National characteristics 6. Uganda 7. Family sagas 8. Literary fiction 9. Afrofantasy

Though Kintu opens with the death of a man in 2004, this sweeping, literary family saga immediately jumps to 1750, when ambitious Kintu Kidda inadvertently kills his adopted son; the boy's father curses Kintu Kidda, a legacy that generations of his family cannot escape. First published in Kenya in 2014, this debut weaves the history of Uganda into the lives of the members of the Kintu clan.

"Makumbis debut novel is a sprawling family chronicle that explores Ugandas national identity through a brilliant interlacing of history, politics, and myth." —*Publishers Weekly*

Originally published: Nairobi : Kwani Trust, 2014.

Malamud, Bernard

The **assistant**. Bernard Malamud. Farrar, Straus and Giroux, 2003. Xi, 246 p.
ISBN 9780374504847
1. Italian American men 2. Interfaith romance 3. Immigrants 4. Family businesses 5. Families 6. Brooklyn, New York City 7. Modern classics 8. Literary fiction

LC 57007397

National Jewish Book Award for Fiction, 1958

A struggling neighborhood Jewish grocer takes on a helper who falls in love with his daughter and steals from his store.

Originally published: New York: Farrar, Straus and Giroux, 1957.

★ The **complete** stories. Bernard Malamud; edited and introduced by Robert Giroux. Farrar, Straus and Giroux, 1997. Xv, 634 p.
ISBN 9780374126391
1. Jews 2. Short stories

LC 9712394

New York Times Notable Book, 1997

Brings together all of the late author's short fiction from the past four decades—fifty-three stories in all—ranging from his early work, taken from the National Book Award-winning "The Magic Barrel," to his latest BT

"Whether, stark, comic or fanciful, Malamud's stories give us immigrant Jews and their descendants pondering moral questions and experiencing moments of magical intervention while enduring life's ridiculous situations. Yet the stories transcend their ethnic settings and achieve a universal resonance." —*Publishers Weekly*

55 short stories.

Includes bibliographical references (p. 633-634).

★ The **fixer**. Bernard Malamud. Farrar, Straus and Giroux, 2004. Xi, 335 p.
ISBN 9780374529383
1. Antisemitism 2. Self-discovery 3. Malicious accusation 4. Loneliness in men 5. Jews, Eastern European 6. Russia 7. Literary fiction 8. Books to movies
National Book Award for Fiction, 1967; Pulitzer Prize for Fiction, 1967

A Jew in Tsarist Russia is accused of murdering a Catholic boy and suffers from mistreatment in prison.

Originally published: New York : Farrar, Straus & Giroux, 1966.

The **natural**. Bernard Malamud. Farrar, Straus and Giroux, 2003. 231

.
ISBN 9780374502003
1. Pitchers (Baseball) 2. Baseball 3. Professional baseball players
4. Purpose in life 5. Magic 6. Books to movies
LC 2003104942
This sports novel follows the career of baseball player Roy Hobbs, a
atural with a bat whose dreams of playing in the big leagues are deferred
y a youthful indiscretion, but who finally becomes a hero.
Originally published: New York: Harcourt, Brace, 1952.

Malerman, Josh
Bird box: a novel. Josh Malerman. Ecco Pr, 2014. 272 p. (Bird Box
ovels, 1)
ISBN 9780062259653
1. Survival 2. Monsters 3. Sensory deprivation 4. Hysteria (Social
psychology) 5. Mother and child 6. Horror 7. Apocalyptic fiction
8. Books to movies
LibraryReads Favorites, 2014
In Bird Box, brilliantly imaginative debut author Josh Malerman cap-
ures an apocalyptic near-future world, where a mother and her two small
hildren must make their way down a river, blindfolded. One wrong
hoice and they will die. And something is following them—but is it man,
nimal, or monster? Within these tracks, Malerman, a professional musi-
ian, discusses his love of horror and invokes an ethereal and atmospheric
xperience in an homage to Orson Welles à la War of the Worlds.
"The author uses understatement and allusion to create a lean, spell-
inding thriller." —*Publishers Weekly*

Goblin: a novel in six novellas. Josh Malerman. Del Rey, 2021. 368 p.
ISBN 9780593237809
1. Monsters 2. Paranormal phenomena 3. Small towns 4. Secrets
5. Horror 6. Short stories
LC 2020036061
The town of Goblin seems like any other ordinary small town. But
ith the master storyteller Josh Malerman as your tour guide, you'll dis-
over the secrets that hide behind the town's closed doors. These six no-
ellas tell the story of a place where the rain is always falling, nighttime is
lways near, and your darkest fears and desires await. Welcome to
oblin...
"This is must-read horror." —*Publishers Weekly*
Originally published in paperback in the United States by Earthling
Publications, 2017.

Malorie: a Bird Box novel. Josh Malerman. Del Rey, 2020. 299 pages;
Bird Box novels, 2)
ISBN 9780593156858
1. Survival 2. Mother and teenager 3. Dystopias 4. Monsters 5. Sensory
deprivation 6. Michigan 7. United States 8. Horror 9. Apocalyptic
fiction
LC 2019059282
A highly anticipated sequel to the best-selling Bird Box focuses on
e story of main character, Malorie, as she confronts the dangers of her
ear-future apocalypse world head-on.
"Malerman will no doubt add to his legions of fans with this title ripe
r readers of any genre seeking an intensely thrilling ride." —*Library
ournal*
Originally published: 2019.

Unbury Carol. Josh Malerman. Del Rey, 2018. 362 p.
ISBN 9780399180163

1. Coma 2. Rich women 3. Premature burial 4. Murder 5. Outlaws
6. The West (United States) 7. American Westward Expansion
(1803-1899) 8. 19th century 9. Horror 10. Weird Westerns
LibraryReads Favorites, 2018
A woman prone to secret temporary comas that make her appear to be
dead receives protection from a redemption-seeking former lover who
would save her from being buried alive by her fortune-hunting husband.

Mallery, Susan
Best of my love. Susan Mallery. HQN, 2016. 384 p. (Fools Gold series
(Susan Mallery), 22)
ISBN 9780373789191
1. Women bakers 2. Single men 3. Small towns 4. Friendship 5. Trust in
women 6. California 7. Contemporary romances
LibraryReads Favorites, 2016
A heartbroken baker and a charming but womanizing tour guide embark on an experiment to prove their respective gender's quality and trust-
worthiness while regaining self-respect, only to become the subject of
gossip in their small hometown.

California girls. Susan Mallery. MIRA, 2019. 461 pages
ISBN 9780778368960
1. Sisters 2. Mother and adult daughter 3. Breaking-up (Interpersonal
relations) 4. Jilted women 5. Marital conflict 6. California
7. Relationship fiction
Three sisters wrestling with difficulties in their personal and professional lives tackle secrets and old wounds while helping their mother relocate from the family home to a condo.
"Mallery fans and newcomers alike will adore this tale about the
bonds of sisterhood and friendship tested by lifes ups and downs." —*Publishers Weekly*

The **summer** of Sunshine and Margot. Susan Mallery. HQN Books,
2019. 356 pages
ISBN 9781335659972
1. Twin sisters 2. Self-fulfillment in women 3. Determination in women
4. Summer 5. Family relationships 6. Relationship fiction
Descended from a long line of women with disastrous luck in love,
twin sisters Margot and Sunshine transform their controversial relationships with a client's son and an employer into unexpected sources of
happiness.
"Mallery's approach to the alternating stories of the sisters and their
attraction to their powerful employers makes for an enjoyable diversion,
perfect for a summer read." —*Booklist*

★ **When** we found home. Susan Mallery. Harlequin Books, 2018. 416
p.
ISBN 9780373802500
1. Family secrets 2. Siblings 3. Blended families 4. Family relationships
5. Wealth 6. Washington (State) 7. Contemporary romances
Three very different people navigate the complicated discovery that
they share the same late father and a wealthy grandfather who would surround himself with his blended family.

Malliet, G. M.
A **demon** summer: a Max Tudor mystery. G.M. Malliet. Minotaur
Books, 2014. 304 p. (Max Tudor mysteries, 4)
ISBN 9781250021410
1. Clergy 2. Amateur detectives 3. Dinners and dining 4. Vicars
5. Poisons 6. England 7. Cozy mysteries 8. Gentle reads
LC 2014019884

Investigating what appears to be an attempt on the life of the reviled earl of Lislelivet, former MI5 agent turned vicar Max Tudor interrupts wedding plans and concludes that the event was accidental before a body is discovered in the cloister well.

"The fourth fun entry (after Pagan Spring) in this charming English cozy series is delightful in tone. Think Agatha Christie meets Ian Fleming." —*Library Journal*

Pagan spring: a mystery. G.M. Malliet. Minotaur Books, 2013. 304 p. (Max Tudor mysteries, 3)
ISBN 9781250021403
1. Clergy 2. Amateur detectives 3. Dinners and dining 4. Vicars 5. Murder 6. England 7. Cozy mysteries 8. Gentle reads
LC 2013016676
To restore peace in the quaint village of Nether Monkslip, Vicar Max Tudor must unravel the clues, which are linked to long-ago crimes, after one of the village's residents is murdered.
A Thomas Dunne book for Minotaur Books.

Mallon, Thomas

Finale: a novel. Thomas Mallon. Pantheon Books, 2015. 464 p.
ISBN 9780307907929
1. Reagan, Ronald 2. Presidents 3. Cold War 4. Politicians 5. Political science 6. United States 7. Iceland 8. 1980s 9. Political fiction
LC 2014044333
New York Times Notable Book, 2015
An analysis of the Reagan Administration shares insights into the 40th President's character and decisions while evaluating key historical events and the influences of such figures as Margaret Thatcher, Jimmy Carter and Richard Nixon.
"Despite all the scene-jumping, the transitions are seamless; There's a whirlwind of activity and abundant snappy dialogue." —*Booklist*

Landfall: a novel. Thomas Mallon. Pantheon Books, 2019. 480 p.
ISBN 9781101871058
1. Bush, George W. 2. Presidents 3. Iraq War, 2003-2011 4. Hurricane Katrina, 2005 5. Politicians 6. Women politicians 7. United States 8. 2000s (Decade) 9. Political fiction
The award-winning author of Watergate reimagines the turbulent second term and political relationships of a mercurial President George W. Bush from the perspectives of two West Texans with disparate ideological views.

Malone, Minx

Bad blood. M. Malone. CrushStar Romance, 2018. 224 p. (Left at the altar, 5)
ISBN 9781938789670
1. McCarthy, Joseph 2. Sexual attraction 3. Man-woman relationships 4. Contemporary romances
RITA Award, 2019
She's his best friend and business partner's sister. Plus she's engaged to another man. But when she's left at the altar, he steps in to help her out. But will he be able to stop there?

Malouf, David

Ransom. David Malouf. Pantheon Books, 2010. 224 p.
ISBN 9780307378774
1. Achilles (Greek mythology) 2. Priam (Greek mythology) 3. Grief in men 4. Loss (Psychology) 5. War — Psychological aspects 6. Troy (Extinct city) 7. Ancient Greece 8. Ancient Greece (800 BCE-640 CE) 9. Historical fiction 10. Epic fiction 11. Literary fiction

Adelaide Festival Award for Fiction (South Australia), 2010; Australian Literature Society Gold Medal, 2010; Shortlisted for the International IMPAC Dublin Literary Award, 2011
A tale of suffering, sorrow, and redemption, "Ransom" is a retelling of one of the most famous stories in all of literature—Achilles's slaughter and desecration of Hector, and Priam's attempt to ransom his son's body in Homer's "The Iliad.
"A retelling of Achilles' desecration of Hector's corpse and his capitulation to Priam's appeal for proper rites and burial for the Trojan hero. Malouf's prose is triumphantly sure, and his characterizations of the subtle and complex bonds between Priam and Achilles, gods and mortals, wives and husbands, parents and children, nobles and commoners, and beasts and men resonate with authority." —*Library Journal*
Originally published: North Sydney, N.S.W. : Knopf, 2009.

Remembering Babylon. David Malouf. Vintage Books, 1994. 200 p.
ISBN 9780679749516
1. Frontier and pioneer life 2. Difference (Psychology) 3. Strangers 4. Racism 5. Aboriginal Australians 6. Queensland 7. Australia 8. Colonial Australia (1788-1901) 9. Historical fiction 10. Australian fiction 11. Literary fiction
LC 93007888
ALA Notable Book, 1994; Commonwealth Writers' Prize, South East Asia and South Pacific: Best Book, 1994; International IMPAC Dublin Literary Award, 1996; Los Angeles Times Book Prize for Fiction, 1994; NSW Premier's Literary Awards, Christina Stead Prize for Fiction, 1993; Shortlisted for the Booker-McConnell Prize, 1993; Shortlisted for the Miles Franklin Literary Award, 1994
Thirteen-year-old Gemmy Fairley is cast ashore in northern Australia and adopted by Australian aborigines during the mid-1840s
"The book is more reflective than polemic. Without excusing the actions of the townsfolk,...Malouf shows how difficult original thought is for members of a community that perceives itself as surrounded by danger. The book is a joy to read: richly layered, complex, and dense." —*Christian Science Monitor*
Originally published: London : Chatto & Windus, 1993.

Malpas, Jodi Ellen

Leave me breathless. Jodi Ellen Malpas. Forever, 2019. 390 p.
ISBN 9781538745212
1. Secret identity 2. Bodyguards 3. Women artists 4. Cabins 5. Handicraft shops 6. England 7. Romantic suspense
LC 2019017664
Taking a respite in his secluded cabin after an exhausting job, bodyguard Ryan unexpectedly falls for the owner of a local arts and crafts store before uncovering dangerous secrets that risk both their lives.
"Readers will enjoy the multilayered main and supporting characters...sizzling erotic scenes, and a taut plot loaded with plenty of twists and turns. Malpas will charm her current fans and win new ones with this strong romantic thriller, perfect for those who love a good alpha male and a damsel in distress who doesn't wait for someone else to rescue her." —*Publishers Weekly*

Mamet, David

Chicago: a novel. David Mamet. Custom House, 2018. 332 p.
ISBN 9780062797193
1. Mafia 2. Women murder victims 3. Revenge 4. World War I veterans 5. Journalists 6. Chicago, Illinois 7. 1920s 8. Between the Wars (1918-1939) 9. Crime fiction 10. Historical fiction
LC 201704400

A novel set against the backdrop of the 1920s Chicago mob scene follows the experiences of a World War I veteran who seeks vigilante justice against the man responsible for killing the woman he loved.

Manansala, Mia P.

★ **Arsenic** and adobo. Mia P. Manansala. Berkley Publishing, 2021. 304 p. (Tita Rosie's kitchen, 1)

ISBN 9780593201671

1. Women amateur detectives 2. Filipino American women 3. Family businesses 4. Restaurants 5. Food columnists 6. Illinois 7. Culinary mysteries 8. Cozy mysteries 9. Gentle reads

LC 2020050117

LibraryReads Favorites, 2021

The first book in a new culinary cozy series full of sharp humor and delectable dishes—one that might just be killer....

"This debut introduces readers to Filipino American food and culture, with its emphasis on family. There are cozy tropes (the close-knit community, the food business), but the emphasis on the Tagalog language, the culture, and drug dealing in a small town add gravity and individuality to this outstanding series kick-off." —*Library Journal*

Mandanipour, Shahriar

Moon brow. Shahriar Mandanipour; translated from the Farsi by Khalili Sara. Restless Books, 2018. 452 p.

ISBN 9781632061287

1. War 2. Angels 3. Soldiers 4. People with post-traumatic stress disorder 5. People who have had amputations 6. Iran 7. Tehran, Iran 8. War stories 9. Literary fiction 10. Magical realism

Library Journal Best Books, 2018

A novel steeped in Persian folklore and contemporary Middle Eastern history tells the story of playboy Amir whose whole life changes when his left arm is severed during the Iran-Iraq War and he begins to be haunted by the vision of a mysterious woman.

"The novel's halting narrative flow, alternating as it does between two scribes on Amir's left and right shoulders, respectively, is disorienting at first, but the patient reader will be rewarded with a dazzling mosaic of a troubled young man and a troubled yet gloriously rich nation." —*Booklist*

Translated from the Farsi.

Mandel, Emily St. John

★ The **glass** hotel: a novel. Emily St. John Mandel. Alfred A. Knopf, 2020. 320 p.

ISBN 9780525521143

1. Bartenders 2. Missing women 3. Ponzi schemes 4. Hotel owners 5. Greed 6. New York City 7. Vancouver, British Columbia 8. Literary fiction 9. Magical realism 10. Multiple perspectives

LC 2019023840

LibraryReads Favorites, 2020; Shortlisted for the Scotiabank Giller Prize, 2020

From the author of 'Station Eleven' comes a captivating novel of money, beauty, white-collar crime, ghosts and moral compromise in which a woman disappears from a container ship off the coast of Mauritania and a massive Ponzi scheme implodes in New York, dragging countless fortunes with it.

"With superb writing and an intricately connected plot that ticks along like clockwork, Mandel offers an unnerving critique of the twinned modern plagues of income inequality and cynical opportunism." —*Library Journal*

The **singer's** gun: a novel. Emily St. John Mandel. Unbridled Books, 2010. 287 p.

ISBN 9781936071647

1. Forgery 2. Former criminals 3. Criminal investigation 4. Conflict in families 5. Extramarital affairs 6. Noir fiction 7. Canadian fiction

Anton's newly constructed life as a newlywed and manager is in jeopardy after his cousin Aria threatens to expose his criminal past if he does not do one more heist for her.

"This is a gripping story, full of moral ambiguities, where deception and betrayal become the norm, and where the expression, a riddle wrapped in a mystery, inside an enigma, is lifted to new heights." —*St. Louis Post-Dispatch*

★ **Station** Eleven. Emily St. John Mandel. Alfred A. Knopf, 2014. 272 p.

ISBN 9780385353304

1. Epidemics 2. End of the world 3. Post-apocalypse 4. Actors and actresses 5. Fame 6. Toronto, Ontario 7. Canada 8. Apocalyptic fiction 9. Literary fiction 10. Science fiction 11. Adult books for young adults

ALA Notable Book, 2015; Arthur C. Clarke Award, 2015; Booklist Editors' Choice, 2014; LibraryReads Favorites, 2014; Toronto Book Awards, 2015; National Book Award for Fiction finalist, 2014

One snowy night a famous actor slumps over and dies onstage during a production of *King Lear.* Hours later, the world as we know it begins to dissolve. Moving back and forth in time—from the actor's early days as a film star to twenty years in the future, when a theater troupe known as the Traveling Symphony roams the wasteland of what remains—this elegiac novel charts the strange twists of fate that connect five people: the actor, the man who tried to save him, the actor's first wife, his oldest friend, and a young actress with the Traveling Symphony, caught in the crosshairs of a dangerous self-proclaimed prophet.

"In this unforgettable, haunting, and almost hallucinatory portrait of life at the edge, those who remain struggle to retain their basic humanity and make connections with the vanished world through art, memory, and remnants of popular culture." —*Library Journal*

Mangan, Christine

Palace of the drowned. Christine Mangan. Flatiron Books, 2021. 272 p.

ISBN 9781250788429

1. Women authors 2. Nervous breakdown 3. Scandals 4. British in Italy 5. Middle-aged women 6. Venice, Italy 7. Italy 8. 1960s 9. Psychological suspense

LC 2020056386

After a public breakdown over a scathing review, a failing writer retreats to a friend's vacant palazzo in 1966 Venice to rest, where she discovers she has a stalker on the eve of a catastrophic flood.

"Against the grim backdrop of off-season Venice, literary rivalry can be menacing." —*Kirkus*

Mankell, Henning

Before the frost: a Linda Wallander mystery. Henning Mankell; translated by Ebba Segerberg. New Press; Distributed by W.W. Norton, 2005. 383 p. (Linda Wallander mysteries, 1)

ISBN 9781565848351

1. Police 2. Father and adult daughter 3. Murder investigation 4. Missing persons investigation 5. Wallander, Kurt (Fictitious character) 6. Sweden 7. Translations 8. Mysteries 9. Scandinavian crime fiction

LC 2004055197

Just graduated from the police academy, Linda Wallander returns to Skane to join the police force, and she already shows all the hallmarks of her father—the maverick approach, the flaring temper. Before she even starts work she becomes embroiled in the case of her childhood friend, Anna, who has inexplicably disappeared. As the case that her father is working on dovetails with her own, something far more dangerous than either could have imagined begins to emerge. They soon find themselves forced to confront a group of extremists bent on punishing the world's sinners. —Publisher's website.

First in series featuring Kurt Wallander's daughter, Linda, although Kurt appears throughout the book.

The **dogs** of Riga. Henning Mankell; translated by Laurie Thompson. Vintage Books, 2004. 336 p. (Kurt Wallander mysteries, 2)
ISBN 9781400031528
1. Police 2. Murder investigation 3. Shakespeare, William 4. Wallander, Kurt (Fictitious character) 5. Detectives 6. Soviet Union 7. Latvia 8. 1990s 9. Mysteries 10. Translations 11. Scandinavian crime fiction
LC 2003068869

On the Swedish coastline, two bodies, victims of grisly torture and cold execution, are discovered in a life raft; after the victims are traced to Latvia, Major Liepa of the Riga police takes over the investigation. Thinking his work done, Detective Kurt Wallander slips into the routine once more, until he is called suddenly to Riga and plunged into an alien world in which shadows are everywhere, everything is watched, and old regimes will do anything to stay alive.

"Set against the chaotic backdrop of eastern Europe after the fall of the Berlin Wall, Mankell's intense, accomplished mystery, the last in his Kurt Wallander series...explores one man's struggle to find truth and justice in a society increasingly bereft of either. Here the provincial Swedish detective takes on a probably fruitless task: investigating the murders of two unidentified men washed up on the Swedish coast in an inflatable dinghy." —Publishers Weekly

A Kurt Wallander mystery.

This title was adapted into an episode of the BBC televion version of the series.

Originally published: Stockholm; Ordfront, 1992.

Firewall. Henning Mankell; translated from the Swedish by Ebba Segerberg. New Press, 2002. 405 p; (Kurt Wallander mysteries, 8)
ISBN 9781565847675
1. Police 2. Murder investigation 3. Cyberterrorism 4. Hackers 5. Wallander, Kurt (Fictitious character) 6. Sweden 7. Mysteries 8. Translations 9. Scandinavian crime fiction
LC 2002025543

Inspector Kurt Wallander begins to suspect that there is a connection between a series of crimes tormenting Sweden—the brutal murder of a taxi driver by two teenage girls, the escape of one of the culprits from police custody, the sudden death of man who drops dead at an ATM, a bizarre power blackout, and a grisly discovery at the malfunctioning power station.

"Although things get pretty tense at the end in Ebba Segerberg's well-paced translation, this a thinking man's thriller bearing the messsage that no infernal machine is a match for a decent man with a sense of good and evil." —New York Times Book Review

English translation of: Brandvagg.

This title was adapted into an episode of the BBC televion version of the series.

Originally published: Stockholm; Ordfront, 1998.

The **man** from Beijing. Henning Mankell; translated from the Swedish Laurie Thompson. Alfred A. Knopf, 2010. 365 p.
ISBN 9780307271860

1. Women judges 2. Grandparents — Death 3. Murder 4. Diaries 5. Murder investigation 6. Sweden 7. Mysteries 8. Translations 9. Scandinavian crime fiction

In the aftermath of the 2006 massacre of 19 people in a Swedish village, Judge Birgitta Roslin, a granddaughter of two of the victims, discovers the 19th-century diary of a gang leader that reveals the case's eerie connections to the abuse of Chinese slave workers.

"A sweepingly ambitious tale of corruption, injustice and revenge that ranges over three continents and 140 years.... Breathtakingly bold in its scope. If Mankell never links his far-flung, multigenerational horrors closely together, that's an important part of his point." —Kirkus

Originally published under title Kinesen : Stockholm : Leopard, 2008. English translation originally published: London: Harvill Secker, 2010.

The **man** who smiled: a Kurt Wallander mystery. Henning Mankell; translated from the Swedish by Laurie Thompson. New Press; distributed by W. W. Norton & Co, 2006. 336 p. (Kurt Wallander mysteries, 4)
ISBN 9781565849938
1. Police 2. Murder investigation 3. Accidental death 4. Wallander, Kurt (Fictitious character) 5. Detectives 6. Sweden 7. Mysteries 8. Translations 9. Scandinavian crime fiction
LC 2006021925

A disillusioned Inspector Kurt Wallander is thrown back into the fray when he becomes both hunter and hunted. Crestfallen, dejected, and spiraling into an alcohol-fuelled depression after killing a man in the line of duty, Inspector Wallander has made up his mind to quit the police force for good. When an old acquaintance, a solicitor, seeks Wallander's help and later turns up dead, Wallander realizes that he was wrong not to listen.

"When the bleak landscapes of Henning Mankell's Swedish police procedurals start to look like home, it's time to head for the hills. Either that, or confront the grim truths about modern society that give weight to this author's absorbing but disquieting existential mysteries." —New York Times Book Review

Originally published in Sweden in 1994 as Mannen son log.

This title was adapted into an episode of the BBC televion version of the series.

★ **One** step behind. Henning Mankell; translated from the Swedish by Ebba Segerberg. New Press, 2002. 408 p. (Kurt Wallander mysteries, 7)
ISBN 9781565846524
1. Police 2. Murder investigation 3. College students 4. Serial murder 5. Wallander, Kurt (Fictitious character) 6. Sweden 7. Mysterie 8. Translations 9. Scandinavian crime fiction
LC 200103425

Chief Inspector Kur Wallander investigates the deaths of three young celebrants after the Midsummer's Eve ritual.

"The sweep and complexity of Mankell's plot are reason enough fo tackling this dense book, thoughtfully translated by Ebba Segerberg. Bu his meditations on surprising subjects like time travel and 'man's relation ship to monsters' make him something special." —New York Times Boo Review

This title was adapted into an episode of the BBC televion version of the series.

Originally published: Stockholm : Ordfront, 1997.

★ The **return** of the dancing master. Henning Mankell; translated b Laurie Thompson. New Press, 2004. 391 p. : Map
ISBN 9781565848603
1. Police 2. Neo-Nazism 3. Murder investigation 4. People with cance 5. Villages 6. Sweden 7. 1990s 8. 1940s 9. Translations 10. Mysterie 11. Scandinavian crime fiction

Fifty-four years after war criminals are hanged in ruined Nazi Ge many, a retired police officer is found slaughtered on his farm in Swede leading a former colleague to investigate and uncovering the links between the death and global Neo-Nazi activity.

"With its expansive time frame and meticulous procedural details, the story (as translated by Laurie Thompson) has a density that demands—and rewards—intellectual involvement." —*New York Times Book Review*

English translation of: Danslararens aterkomst.

The **troubled** man. By Henning Mankell; translated by Laurie Thompson. Knopf, 2011. 384 p. (Kurt Wallander mysteries, 10)
ISBN 9780307593498
1. Police 2. International intrigue 3. Missing persons 4. Spies 5. Cold War 6. Sweden 7. Translations 8. Thrillers and suspense 9. Scandinavian crime fiction
LC 2010049169

When his father-in-law, a retired naval officer, disappears under suspicious circumstances, Kurt Wallander uncovers disturbing evidence of Cold War espionage, a case that forces him to confront dark truths about his own nature.

"Not only does this novel widen the scope of the detective's investigations into the world of international geopolitics and the relationship of Sweden to the United States and Russia, it is a work of genuine heft and substance, a melancholy, elegiac book that is thoughtful and perceptive about memory, regret and the unfathomability of human nature." —*PopMatters*

Originally published as: Den orolige mannen, by Leopard Förlag, Stockholm, 2009.

Mann, Thomas

Buddenbrooks. Thomas Mann; translated from the German by John E. Woods. Vintage International, 1994. 731 p.
ISBN 9780679752608
1. Middle class 2. Family relationships 3. Small town life 4. Germany 5. 19th century 6. Family sagas 7. Psychological fiction 8. Literary fiction

A new translation of Mann's classic story of four generations of a wealthy bourgeois family in northern Germany captures the triumphs and tragedies, successes and failures, relationships, loves, and ordinary events of middle-class life.

Death in Venice and seven other stories. Thomas Mann; translated from the German by H.T. Lowe-Porter. Modern Library, 1992. 461 p.
ISBN 9780679600404
1. Homosexuality 2. Obsession in men 3. Authors 4. Senior men 5. Venice, Italy 6. Psychological fiction 7. Literary fiction 8. Short stories
LC 92-253225

Eight complex stories illustrative of the author's belief that "a story must tell itself," highlighted by the high art style of the famous title novella.

Includes biographical note.
This translation originally published: United States : Bantam, 1988.

Doctor Faustus. Thomas Mann; translated from the German by John E. Woods. A. A. Knopf, 1997. 534 p.
ISBN 9780375400544
1. Devil 2. Musicians 3. Faustian bargains 4. Soul 5. Composers 6. Literary fiction 7. Modern classics 8. Translations

A new translation of one of Thomas Mann's novel, written in 1948, offers a modern rendering of the Faust legend in which Leverkuhn, a musical genius, promises his body and soul to the devil in exchange for twenty-four years of musical triumph.

The **Magic** Mountain. Thomas Mann; translated from the German by John E. Woods. Vintage International, 1996. 706 p.
ISBN 9780679772873
1. Sanatoriums 2. Civilization, Western 3. World War I 4. Soldiers 5. Science 6. Coming-of-age stories 7. Psychological fiction 8. Allegories

A sanatorium in the Swiss Alps reflects the societal ills of pre-twentieth-century Europe, and a young marine engineer rises from his life of anonymity to become a pivotal character in a story about how a human's environment affects self identity.

Translation of Der Zauberberg.

Manning, Corinne

We had no rules: stories. Corinne Manning. Arsenal Pulp Press, 2020. 167 p.
ISBN 9781551527994
1. LGBTQIA persons 2. Transgender persons 3. Gender identity 4. Gay men 5. Lesbians 6. LGBTQIA fiction 7. Literary fiction 8. Short stories

In Corinne Manning's stunning debut story collection, a cast of queer characters explore the choice of assimilation over rebellion. Spanning the years 1992 to 2019, and moving from New York to North Carolina to Seattle, the eleven first-person stories in We Had No Rules feature characters who feel the promise of a radically reimagined world but face complicity instead.

"This enriching view of queer worlds unpacks narratives that have always been there, even if they're not often seen." —*Publishers Weekly*

Manning, Max

The **victim:** a novel. Max Manning. Sourcebooks Landmark, 2019. 336 pages
ISBN 9781492667018
1. Public relations consultants 2. Carjacking 3. Criminals 4. Options, alternatives, choices 5. Life change events 6. London, England 7. Psychological suspense
LC 2018052448

When public relations executive Gem Golding becomes the victim of a carjacking at the hands of a dangerous criminal bent on her destruction, she must make a choice: Does she surrender to her attacker, or does she stand her ground and fight for her life?What follows are the two strands Gem's life can take, and the chain of causes and effects that leads to Gem's survival...or her eventual demise. — Provided by publisher.

Mantel, Hilary

★ **Bring** up the bodies: a novel. Hilary Mantel. Henry Holt and Co, 2012. 432 p. (Wolf Hall trilogy, 2)
ISBN 9780805090031
1. Cromwell, Thomas 2. Conspiracies 3. Courts and courtiers — History 4. Extramarital affairs 5. Treason 6. Ambition in men 7. Great Britain 8. Tudor period (1485-1603) 9. Renaissance (1300-1600) 10. Historical fiction 11. Literary fiction 12. Books to TV
LC 2012006335

Booklist Editors' Choice, 2012; Costa Book of the Year Award, 2012; Costa Novel Award, 2012; Man Booker Prize, 2012; New York Times Notable Book, 2012; RUSA Reading List, 2013; Shortlisted for the Walter Scott Prize for Historical Fiction, 2013; Shortlisted for The Women's Prize for Fiction, 2013

Depicts the downfall of Anne Boleyn at the hands of Henry VIII and Thomas Cromwell as Anne and her powerful family fight back while she is on trial for adultery and treason.

Sequel to: Wolf Hall.

Adapted along with the author's Wolf Hall into a BBC TV series called Wolf Hall in 2015.

★ **Wolf** Hall. Hilary Mantel. Henry Holt & Co, 2009. 672 p. (Wolf Hall trilogy, 1)

ISBN 9780805080681

1. Cromwell, Thomas 2. Courts and courtiers — History 3. Ambition in men 4. Political corruption 5. Politicians 6. Great Britain 7. Tudor period (1485-1603) 8. 16th century 9. Historical fiction 10. Literary fiction 11. Books to TV

Library Journal Best Books, 2009; Man Booker Prize, 2009; National Book Critics Circle Award for Fiction, 2009; New York Times Notable Book, 2009; Walter Scott Prize for Historical Fiction, 2010; Shortlisted for The Orange Prize for Fiction, 2010; Shortlisted for the James Tait Black Memorial Prize for Fiction, 2009

Assuming the power recently lost by the disgraced Cardinal Wolsey, Thomas Cromwell counsels a mercurial Henry VIII on the latter's efforts to marry Anne Boleyn against the wishes of Rome and many of his people, a successful endeavor that comes with a dangerous price.

"Set in 16th-century Tudor England, Wolf Hall thrusts the reader into Henry VIII's seething court, where the players include Anne Boleyn, her sister Mary, Cardinal Wolsey, Thomas More and Jane Seymour. At the book's center: Thomas Cromwell, the ruthless blacksmith's son who rose to power under Henry VIII because of his intelligence, cunning and work ethic.... Mantel's novel is less about Henry's sex life and more about power: how to get it, wield it, keep it, particularly if you like the lowborn Cromwell lived in a merciless world ruled by the rich and titled. Cromwell usually is presented as a bully utterly lacking scruples, but Mantel's Cromwell is a sympathetic character modern readers will understand." —USA Today

Sequel: Bring Up the Bodies.

Adapted into a BBC TV series in 2015.

Also published: Toronto : HarperCollins, 2011, c2009.

Mapson, Jo-Ann

Bad Girl Creek: a novel. Jo-Ann Mapson. Simon & Schuster, 2001. 381 p; (Bad Girl Creek trilogy, 1)

ISBN 9780743202565

1. Women with disabilities 2. Boarding houses 3. Flower gardening 4. Single women 5. Women gardeners 6. California 7. Relationship fiction 8. Multiple perspectives

LC 2001027006

Four wounded women heal their hearts by opening a flower farm together, where they rediscover the importance of friendship.

"Mapson combines poignancy with the good-natured banter of girlfriends in her tale of women in transition, waiting to be reborn." —Publishers Weekly

Marcelo, Tif

In a book club far away. Tif Marcelo. Gallery Books, 2021. 400 p.

ISBN 9781982148096

1. Army spouses 2. Betrayal 3. Former friends 4. Book clubs 5. Parenthood 6. Relationship fiction

Regina Castro, Adelaide Wilson-Chang, and Sophie Walden used to be best friends. As Army wives at Fort East, they bonded during their book club and soon became inseparable. But when an unimaginable betrayal happened amongst the group, the friendship abruptly ended, and

they haven't spoken since. That's why, eight years later, Regina and Sophie are shocked when they get a call for help from Adelaide. Adelaide's husband is stationed abroad, and without any friends or family near her new home of Alexandria, Virginia, she has no one to help take care of her young daughter when she has to undergo emergency surgery. For the sake of an innocent child, Regina and Sophie reluctantly put their differences aside to help an old friend.

"Themes of friendship, forgiveness, and women's independence make this propulsive, feel-good story a gem." —Publishers Weekly

March, Emily

Jackson. Emily March. St Martins Press, 2019. 336 pages (Eternity Springs: McBrides of Texas, 1)

ISBN 9781250314918

1. Young widows 2. Women booksellers 3. Divorced men 4. Songwriters 5. Ranches 6. Texas 7. Contemporary romances

Sometimes it takes a new beginning...to reach a happily-ever-after.

March, Nev

Murder in old Bombay. Nev March. Minotaur Books, 2020. 386 p.

ISBN 9781250269546

1. Multiracial men 2. Women murder victims 3. Veterans 4. War wounds 5. Suspicion 6. Mumbai, India 7. India 8. British Raj (1858-1947) 9. Historical mysteries 10. First person narratives

LC 2020026248

LibraryReads Favorites, 2020

Investigating the double murder of two women in 1892 Bombay, Captain Jim Agnihotri is confronted by suspicion on both sides of a divided land before his investigation triggers unexpected consequences.

"Based on true events, March's crisply written debut combines fascinating historic details with a clever puzzle." —Kirkus

March, William

The **bad** seed: a novel. By William March; with a new introduction by Elaine Showalter. Harper Perennial, 2005. 256 p.

ISBN 9780060795481

1. Mothers and daughters 2. Moving to a new city 3. Drowning victims 4. Eight-year-old girls 5. Schools 6. Thrillers and suspense

A seemingly normal and attractive young girl, Rhoda Penmark uses her strange powers and talent for evil to force others to give her what she wants.

"Rhoda Penmark at 8 years of age had a mind of her own and a will to match. Aged people doted on her splendid manners, but rogues knew her as one of themselves while older children were afraid of her. Christine, her mother suddenly discovers her daughter's horrible tendencies and also finds out that she is the murderess of two people who stood in her way. Christine resolves to check back and finds that she had been adopted and that the mother she had never known had also been a successful killer. Christine tries to stop the pattern in her daughter, but in the process dies herself." —Library Journal

Originally published: New York : Rinehart, 1954.

Marcom, Micheline Aharonian

The **new** American. Micheline Aharonian Marcom. Simon & Schuster, 2020. 288 p.

ISBN 9781982120726

1. Undocumented immigrants 2. Deportation 3. Voyages and travel 4. College students 5. Guatemalans in the United States 6. United States 7. California 8. Coming-of-age stories 9. Multiple perspectives

LC 2019049302

A young Guatemalan-American college student gets deported and decides to make his way back home to California.

"Marcom masterfully navigates the graphic ugliness of deportation and anguished immigration with entreaties to a remote and capricious God, creating a tough but necessary and beautiful novel." —*Booklist*

Marias, Javier

The **infatuations**. Javier Marias; translated from the Spanish by Margaret Jull Costa. Alfred A. Knopf, 2013. 352 p.

ISBN 9780307960726

1. Young women 2. Murder 3. Obsession 4. Widows 5. Murderers 6. Spain 7. Madrid, Spain 8. Psychological suspense 9. Literary fiction 10. First person narratives

LC 2013016429

New York Times Notable Book, 2013; National Book Critics Circle Award for Fiction finalist, 2013

At the Madrid cafe where she stops for breakfast each day before work, Maria Dolz finds herself drawn to a couple who is also there every morning. Though she can hardly explain it, observing what she imagines to be their "unblemished" life lifts her out of the doldrums of her own existence. But what begins as mere observation turns into an increasingly complicated entanglement when the man is fatally stabbed in the street.

Originally published as Los enamoramientos: Alfaguara, Santillana Ediciones Generales-S. L. : Madrid, 2011.

Translated from the Spanish.

Thus bad begins: a novel. By Javier Marias; translated by Margaret Jull Costa. Alfred A. Knopf, 2016. 464 pages

ISBN 9781101946084

1. Married people 2. Personal assistants 3. Family secrets 4. Rumor 5. Civil war 6. Madrid, Spain 7. 1980s 8. Literary fiction 9. Psychological suspense 10. Translations

LC 2015049902

Taking a job under an eccentric film director while completing his university degree in 1980 Madrid, Juan de Vere is asked to investigate unsavory rumors surrounding a family friend and uncovers complications in his employer's marriage and wartime activities.

"Another challenging, boundary-stretching work from Maras, complete with a jaw-dropping last-chapter revelation." —*Kirkus*

This translation first published by Hamish Hamilton, 2016.

Originally published as Asi empieza lo malo: Madrid : Alfaguara, 2014.

Translation from the Spanish.

Marillier, Juliet

Daughter of the forest. Juliet Marillier. TOR, 2000. 400 p; (Sevenwaters fantasies, 1)

ISBN 9780312848798

1. Young women 2. Witches 3. Fathers and daughters 4. Siblings 5. Families 6. Ireland 7. Fantasy fiction 8. Mythological fiction 9. Celtic fantasy 10. Adult books for young adults

LC 25216

Alex Award, 2001; Booklist Editors' Choice: Adult Fiction for Young Adults, 2000; Romantic Times Reviewer's Choice Award, 2000; YALSA Best Books for Young Adults, 2001

To reclaim the lives of her brothers, Sorcha leaves the only safe place she has known and starts on a journey of pain, loss, and terror.

"The author's keen understanding of Celtic paganism and early Irish Christianity adds texture to a rich and vibrant novel that belongs in most fantasy collections." —*Library Journal*

Mark, David John

Cruel mercy. David J. Mark. Penguin Group USA, 2017. 352 p. (Aector McAvoy novels, 6)

ISBN 9780399185113

1. Police 2. Detectives 3. Scots in the United States 4. Murder investigation 5. People in comas 6. New York City 7. Mysteries 8. Police procedurals

A first U.S. case for Detective Sergeant McAvoy finds the British investigator assisting the NYPD in the aftermath of a shooting attack that has killed a promising young boxer and left his legendary coach in a coma.

"Beautifully crafted, filled with flashbacks, horror, angst, and chilling detail, this one is his most complex and best yet." —*Kirkus*

Markley, Stephen

Ohio. Stephen Markley. Simon & Schuster, 2018. 496 p.

ISBN 9781501174476

1. Homecomings 2. Drug addiction 3. Recession (Economics) 4. Memories 5. Secrets 6. Ohio 7. Middle West 8. 2010s 9. Literary fiction

LC 2017040397

Four former classmates converge on their recession- and opioid-ravaged hometown on a fateful summer night that finds them pursuing respective goals based on haunting memories from their shared past.

Marlantes, Karl

Deep river. Karl Marlantes. Atlantic Monthly Pr, 2019. 820 p.

ISBN 9780802125385

1. Logging 2. Immigrants, Finnish 3. Siblings 4. Labor unions 5. Imperialism, Russian 6. Washington (State) 7. Finland 8. 1900s (Decade) 9. Literary fiction 10. Historical fiction

In the early 1900s, as the oppression of Russia's imperial rule takes its toll on Finland, the Koski siblings—Ilmari, Matti and the politicized young Aino—flee to the U.S, settling in a logging community in southern Washington.

★ **Matterhorn:** a novel of the Vietnam War. Karl A. Marlantes. Grove/Atlantic, 2010. 592 p.

ISBN 9780802119285

1. Vietnam War, 1961-1975 2. Soldiers 3. Marines 4. War 5. Jungles 6. Vietnam 7. 1960s 8. War stories 9. Historical fiction 10. Literary fiction

Indies' Choice Book Awards, Adult Debut, 2011; James Fenimore Cooper Prize, 2011; W. Y. Boyd Literary Award, 2011; ALA Notable Book, 2011; New York Times Notable Book, 2010; Shortlisted for the International IMPAC Dublin Literary Award, 2012

Lieutenant Waino Mellas and his fellow Marines venture into the mountain jungle of Vietnam as boys and fight their way into manhood, confronting external obstacles as well as racial tension, competing ambitions, and underhanded officers.

"Matterhorn is one of those countless hills in Vietnam that makes young men's lives so cheap. In this case, it's the Marines of Bravo Company and the hardened NVA (North Vietnamese Army) soldiers. The story revolves around a young Marine lieutenant, Waino Mellas, who must quickly learn the difference between officer candidate school and the reality of life in the bush. Lt. Mellas tries to straddle the line between being one of the guys and a platoon commander. This division between the troops and a low-ranking officer like Mellas (who is only a few years older than his men) can become too vague if he is overly friendly. In combat, that can be disastrous. The delicate balance between life and death resonates throughout Matterhorn, as it does in real combat. What is so fresh and fascinating about this novel is Marlantes' depiction of the specific ac-

tivities and conflicting motivations that take place in a war zone."
—*BookPage*

Maron, Margaret

Bootlegger's daughter. Margaret Maron. Mysterious Press, 1992. 261 p; (Deborah Knott mysteries, 1)
ISBN 9780892964451
1. Elections 2. Small town life 3. Fathers and daughters 4. Women lawyers 5. Women judges 6. North Carolina 7. Mysteries 8. Southern fiction
LC 91058021
Agatha Award for Best Novel, 1993; Anthony Award for Best Novel, 1993; Edgar Allan Poe Award for Best Mystery Novel, 1993; Macavity Award for Best Mystery Novel, 1993
Deborah Knott, an attorney attempting to infiltrate the old boy network of tobacco country by running for district judge, is distracted from the race, and almost eliminated, when she finds new evidence to an old small-town murder BT

Up jumps the Devil. Margaret Maron. Mysterious Press, 1996. 278 p; (Deborah Knott mysteries, 4)
ISBN 9780892965687
1. Former husbands 2. Murder investigation 3. Real estate development 4. Knott, Deborah (Fictitious character) 5. Women judges 6. North Carolina 7. Mysteries 8. Southern fiction
LC 96007715
Agatha Award for Best Novel, 1997; Booklist Editors' Choice: Adult Books for Young Adults, 1996
Colleton County, North Carolina judge Deborah Knott embarks on a Thanksgiving Day investigation into the murder of a man from her father's moonshine-making past.
"The droll characters and their lilting regional humor seem ever more endearing because we sense their days are numbered." —*New York Times Book Review*

Marra, Anthony

★ A **constellation** of vital phenomena: a novel. Anthony Marra. Hogarth, 2013. 400 p.
ISBN 9780770436407
1. Women physicians 2. Civil war 3. Eight-year-old girls 4. Hospitals 5. Father-separated children 6. Russia 7. Chechnya, Russia 8. 2000s (Decade) 9. War stories 10. Literary fiction
LC 2012017444
ALA Notable Book, 2014; Booklist Editors' Choice, 2013; Indies' Choice Book Awards, Adult Debut, 2014; Library Journal Best Books, 2013; New York Times Notable Book, 2013
This debut novel by Pushcart Prize-winning author Anthony Marra is set in rural Chechnya during the region's war with Russia. Though events shift in time, the main focus is a five-day period in 2004, when an eight-year-old girl witnesses her father's abduction by Russian soldiers. Swearing to protect the girl, local doctor Akhmed (whose true passion is portraiture), brings her to a crumbling hospital, run by a hardened but dedicated surgeon, for safety.

The **tsar** of love and techno: stories. Anthony Marra. Hogarth, 2015. 256 p.
ISBN 9780770436438
1. Families 2. War and society 3. Art 4. Self-sacrifice 5. Interpersonal relations 6. Russia 7. Literary fiction 8. Short stories
ALA Notable Book, 2016; Booklist Editors' Choice, 2015; New York Times Notable Book, 2015; National Book Critics Circle Award for Fiction finalist, 2015

A collection of interwoven tales explores themes of family, sacrifice, war, and the redemptive power of art.
"As in his previous novel, Marra is deft at managing different characters at different points in time, but the book's brilliance and humor are laced with the somber feeling that the country is allergic to evolution: KGB thugs then, drug dealers and Internet scammers now, with a few stray moments of compassion in between. A powerful and melancholy vision of a nation with long memories and relentless turmoil." —*Kirkus*

Marsh, Ngaio

A **man** lay dead. Ngaio Marsh. St. Martin's Paperbacks, 1997. 214 p; (Roderick Alleyn mysteries, 1)
ISBN 9780312963583
1. Murder parties 2. Family estates 3. Nobility 4. Murder 5. Roosevelt, Eleanor 6. England 7. New Zealand fiction 8. Mysteries 9. Mystery classics
Scotland Yard's Inspector Roderick Alleyn arrives at Sir Hubert Handesley's country house party only to discover a real corpse has appeared during the guests' parlor game of "Murder.
Originally published: London : G. Bles, 1934.

Marsh, Nicola

The **boy** toy. Nicola Marsh. Jove, 2020. 352 p.
ISBN 9780593198629
1. Interracial romance 2. Divorced women 3. Homecomings 4. Casual sex 5. Stunt performers 6. Melbourne, Victoria 7. Australia 8. Australian fiction 9. Multicultural romances 10. Romantic comedies
LC 2020025761
LibraryReads Favorites, 2020
A woman ready to give up on love meets her match in a man she never expected to fall for.
"Marsh eschews intense drama in favor of slow-burning anticipation, drawing readers in with vivid descriptions, witty dialogue, and a fleshed out depiction of Indian family culture." —*Publishers Weekly*

Marshall, Catherine

Christy. Catherine Marshall. Avon Books, 1968. 501 p.
ISBN 9780380001415
1. Mountain life 2. Women teachers 3. Christian women 4. Christian teachers 5. Love triangles 6. Appalachian Region 7. Great Smoky Mountains (N.C. and Tenn.) 8. 1910s 9. Christian historical romances
LC 67024957
A nineteen-year-old woman leaves her home to teach school in Cutter Gap, Tennessee, in 1912.
Previously published by McGraw.

Marske, Freya

A **marvellous** light. Freya Marske. Tom Doherty Associates, 2021. 384 p. (Last binding, 1)
ISBN 9781250788870
1. Civil service workers 2. Magic 3. Missing persons 4. Gay men 5. Curses 6. Great Britain 7. Edwardian era (1901-1914) 8. Historical fantasy
LC 2021033050
LibraryReads Favorites, 2021
Robin Blyth is accidentally named the civil service liaison to a hidden magical society and is forced to contend with the beauty and danger operating beneath normal reality while uncovering what happened to his predecessor.

LIST OF FICTIONAL WORKS

"Sensual erotic scenes, an intriguing magic system, and a puzzling mystery combine to make this novel a wonder. Fans of C.L. Polk's Witchmark, period queer novels, and creative fantasy will all clamor for more." —*Publishers Weekly*

Marston, Edward

The **roaring** boy: a novel. Edward Marston. St. Martin's Press, 1995. 260 p. (Nicholas Bracewell mysteries, 7)
ISBN 9780312131555
1. Mathematicians 2. Murder investigation 3. Riots 4. Lord Westfield's Men (Fictitious characters) 5. Actors and actresses 6. Great Britain 7. Elizabethan era (1558-1603) 8. 16th century 9. Historical mysteries 10. Mysteries
LC 95008568
An Elizabethan theater mystery finds theater manager Nicholas Bracewell trying to save his company by solving the murder their play—a domestic drama about a sensational murder case—is based on
"Marston's colorful (and convincing) characterizations shine as Nicholas chases the secrets of the murder in order to save the company. The plot, except for one transparently finagled episode, is expertly wrought, with the suspense building steadily to breathtaking climax and some surprises saved for the very end." —*Publishers Weekly*

The **wanton** angel: a novel. Edward Marston. St. Martin's Press, 1999. 279 p. (Nicholas Bracewell mysteries, 10)
ISBN 9780312203917
1. Revenge 2. Landlords 3. Young women — Relations with older men 4. Lord Westfield's Men (Fictitious characters) 5. Actors and actresses 6. Great Britain 7. Elizabethan era (1558-1603) 8. 16th century 9. Historical mysteries 10. Mysteries
LC 99-22062
Nicholas Bracewell attempts to save Lord Westfield's Men, a theatrical group threatened by the murder of a star actor and by the elusive identity of a mysterious patron

Martel, Yann

★ **Life** of Pi: a novel. Yann Martel. Harcourt, 2001. 319 p.
ISBN 9780151008117
1. Survival (after airplane accidents, shipwrecks, etc.) 2. Human-animal relationships 3. Tigers 4. Storytelling 5. Teenage boys 6. Pacific Ocean 7. Psychological fiction 8. Literary fiction 9. Survival stories
LC 2001039737
Asian Pacific American Award for Literature: Adult Fiction, 2004; Booker Prize, 2002; Library Journal Best Books, 2002; New York Times Notable Book, 2002; Quebec Writers' Federation Literary Awards, Hugh MacLennan Prize for Fiction, 2001; Governor General's Literary Awards, English-language Fiction finalist
Possessing encyclopedia-like intelligence, unusual zookeeper's son Pi Patel sets sail for America, but when the ship sinks, he escapes on a life boat and is lost at sea with a dwindling number of animals until only he and a hungry Bengal tiger remain.
An impassioned defense of zoos, a death-defying trans-Pacific sea adventure la 'Kon-Tiki,' and a hilarious shaggy-dog story starring a four-hundred-and-fifty-pound Bengal tiger named Richard Parker: this audacious novel manages to be all of these.... This breezily aphoristic, unapologetically twee saga of man and cat is a convincing hands-on, how-to guide for dealing with what Pi calls, with typically understated brio, 'major lifeboat pests.' The New Yorker.
Originally published: Toronto : Alfred A. Knopf Canada, 2001.

Martell, Nick

The **kingdom** of liars. Nick Martell. Saga Press, 2020. 608 p. (Legacy of the mercenary king novels, 1)
ISBN 9781534437784
1. Regicide 2. Secrets 3. Betrayal 4. Political intrigue 5. Memory 6. Fantasy fiction
LC 2019047936
Michael is branded a traitor as a child because of the murder of the king's nine-year-old son, by his father David Kingman. Ten years later on Michael lives a hardscrabble life, with his sister Gwen, performing crimes with his friends against minor royals in a weak attempt at striking back at the world that rejects him and his family. What the truth holds is a set of shocking revelations that will completely change the Hollows, if Michael and his friends and family can survive long enough to see it.
"Though the abundance of characters becomes overwhelming at times, their political maneuvers and varied motivations form a satisfying web. This smart, briskly told high fantasy entertains all the way until the unexpected end." —*Publishers Weekly*

Martin, Alexa

Fumbled. Alexa Martin. Berkley, 2019. 320 pages (Playbook (Alexa Martin), 2)
ISBN 9780451491978
1. Professional football players 2. Multiracial women 3. Single mothers 4. Professional football 5. Man-woman relationships 6. Denver, Colorado 7. Sports romances 8. Multicultural romances 9. Contemporary romances
LC 2018045172
Successful single mom, Poppy Patterson, crosses paths with her high school sweetheart, now the hard-partying starting wide receiver for the Denver Mustangs and is shocked to find her feelings rushing back to her in the follow-up to Intercepted.
A Jove Book.

★ **Intercepted**. Alexa Martin. Penguin Group USA 2018. 320 p. (Playbook (Alexa Martin), 1)
ISBN 9780451491954
1. Professional football players 2. African American women 3. Businesspeople 4. Gossiping and gossips 5. Reputation 6. Sports romances 7. Multicultural romances 8. Contemporary romances
LC 2017060279
RUSA Reading List, 2019
Marlee thought she scored the man of her dreams only to be scorched by a bad breakup. But there's a new player on the horizon, and he's in a league of his own...

Martin, Charles

The **water** keeper. Charles Martin. Thomas Nelson, 2020. 352 pages (Murphy Shepherd novels, 1)
ISBN 9780785230915
1. Former clergy 2. Helpfulness in men 3. Human trafficking 4. Kidnapping victims 5. Loss (Psychology) 6. Florida 7. Christian suspense
Tending the grounds of an island church with no parishioners, retired priest Murphy Shepherd voyages down the Intracoastal waterway to scatter a friend's ashes before agreeing to help a woman whose daughter has been abducted into the world of trafficking.

Martin, George R. R.

★ A **clash** of kings. George R.R. Martin. Bantam Books, 1999. 761 p. (Song of ice and fire, 2)

ISBN 9780553108033

1. Ambition 2. Political corruption 3. Magic 4. Nobility 5. Dragons 6. Epic fantasy 7. Multiple perspectives 8. Books to TV

LC 9837954

Locus Award for Fantasy Novel, 1999

Five separate factions vie for control of the Seven Kingdoms, while an ancient form of magic, an everlasting winter, and an unearthly army threaten to return.

"The novel is notable particularly for the lived-in quality of its world, created through abundant detail that dramatically increases narrative length even as it aids suspension of disbelief; for the comparatively modest role of magic...and for its magnificent action-filled climax." —*Publishers Weekly*

The TV series Game of thrones: season 2 is based on the book A clash of kings.

Sequel to: A Game of Thrones.

Special 20th anniversary illustrated edition was published by Bantam books in 2019 with illustrations by Lauren K. Cannon

★ A **dance** with dragons. George R. R. Martin. Spectra, 2011. 1008 p. (Song of ice and fire, 5)

ISBN 9780553801477

1. Ambition 2. Political corruption 3. Nobility 4. Power (Social sciences) 5. Dragons 6. Epic fantasy 7. Multiple perspectives 8. Adult books for young adults

Goodreads Choice Award, 2011; Library Journal Best Books, 2011; Locus Award for Fantasy Novel, 2012

New threats emerge to endanger the future of the Seven Kingdoms, as Daenerys Targaryen fights off a multitude of enemies, while Jon Snow faces his foes both in the Watch and beyond the great Wall of ice and stone.

"The heart-hammering conclusion hints that the next installment will see a return to the fiery battles and icy terror that earned the series its fanatic following. Even ostensibly disillusioned fans will be caught up in the interweaving stories, especially when Martin drops little hints around long-debated questions such as Jon's parentage." —*Publishers Weekly*

★ A **feast** for crows. George R.R. Martin. Spectra, 2004. 1024 p. (Song of ice and fire, 4)

ISBN 9780553801507

1. Ambition 2. Political corruption 3. Magic 4. Nobility 5. Nefertiti 6. Epic fantasy 7. Multiple perspectives

The uneasy peace is threatened by new plots, intrigues, and alliances that once again will plunge the Seven Kingdoms into all-out war for control of the Iron Throne.

"The author introduces plot twists and characters that continue to flesh out one of the genre's most detailed and intriguing worlds. A must-purchase for libraries owning the series, this panoramic fantasy adventure is highly recommended." —*Library Journal*

Fire & blood: 300 years before a Game of Thrones (a Targaryen history). George R. R. Martin; illustrated by Doug Wheatley. Bantam Dell Pub Group, 2018. 640 p. (Song of ice and fire)

ISBN 9781524796280

1. Royal houses 2. Dragons 3. Rulers 4. Imaginary wars and battles 5. Imaginary kingdoms 6. Epic fantasy

The thrilling history of the Targaryens comes to life in this masterly work by the author of A Song of Ice and Fire, the inspiration for HBO's Game of Thrones.

George R. R. Martin writing as Archmaester Gyldayn.

Also published Nov. 2018 in the UK by HarperCollins as Fire and Blood: a history of the Targaryen kings from Aegon the conqueror to Aegon III as scribed by Archmaester Gyldayn.

★ A **game** of thrones. George R. R. Martin. Bantam Books, 1996. 694 p. (Song of ice and fire, 1)

ISBN 9780553103540

1. Ambition 2. Political corruption 3. Magic 4. Nobility 5. Knights and knighthood 6. Epic fantasy 7. Multiple perspectives 8. Books to TV.

LC 95-43936

Locus Award for Fantasy Novel, 1997

The aristocratic Stark family faces its ultimate challenge in the onset of a generation-long winter, the poisonous plots of the rival Lannisters, the emergence of the Neverborn demons, and the arrival of barbarian hordes.

"The first volume in A Song of Ice and Fire saga, combines intrigue, action, romance, and mystery in a family saga. The family is the Starks of Winterfell, a society in crisis due to climatic change that has created decades-long seasons, and a society almost without magic but with human perversity abundant and active. Martin reaches a new plateau in terms of narrative technique, action scenes, and integrating...his political views into the story." —*Booklist*

20th anniversary illustrated edition published: New York : Random House, 2016.

★ A **storm** of swords. George R.R. Martin. Bantam Books, 2000. 800 p. (Song of ice and fire, 3)

ISBN 9780553106633

1. Ambition 2. Political corruption 3. Magic 4. Nobility 5. Knights and knighthood 6. Epic fantasy 7. Multiple perspectives 8. Books to TV

LC 60827

Locus Award for Fantasy Novel, 2001

The Seven Kingdoms are torn by strife as the three surviving contenders for the throne continue their struggle for power, Robb Stark defends his fledgling kingdom from the ravaging Greyjoys, Winterfell lies in ruins and Jon Snow confronts an escalating threat from behind the Wall, and Danerys Stormborn and her dragon allies continue to grow in power.

"The author's ability to interweave dozens of plot lines and to create memorable characters makes this a rousing saga that should appeal to most fans of grand-scale fantasy. Recommended for most libraries, along with its predecessors, A Game of Thrones and A Clash of Kings." —*Library Journal*

The TV series Game of thrones: season 3 and season 4 are based on the book A storm of swords.

Special 20th anniversary illustrated edition released by Bantam Books in 2020, with illustrations by Gary Gianni.

Martin, Steve

Shopgirl. Hyperion, 2000. 130 p.

ISBN 9780786866588

1. Department store employees 2. Clerks (Retail industry and trade) 3. Department stores 4. Prescription drug abuse 5. Young women 6. Beverly Hills, California 7. Books to movies 8. Mainstream fiction 9. Psychological fiction

LC 38874

Mirabelle is the shopgirl who sells gloves at Neiman Marcus. She meets Ray Porter, a wealthy businessman twice her age. Together they embark on a relationship and try to decipher the language of love.

"There is an impressive gravity about Shopgirl. Its glints of comedy are sharp and dry.... The novella has an edge to it, and a deep, unassuageable loneliness." —*New York Times Book Review*

LIST OF FICTIONAL WORKS

Martine, Arkady

★ A **desolation** called peace. Arkady Martine. Tor Books, 2021. 416 p. (Teixcalaan novels, 2)

ISBN 9781250186461

1. Interstellar relations 2. Cultural differences 3. Women diplomats 4. Imaginary empires 5. Political intrigue 6. Space opera 7. Science fiction mysteries 8. Multiple perspectives 9. Adult books for young adults

An alien armada lurks on the edges of Teixcalaanli space. No one can communicate with it, no one can destroy it, and Fleet Captain Nine Hibiscus is running out of options. In a desperate attempt at diplomacy with the mysterious invaders, the fleet captain has sent for a diplomatic envoy. Now Mahit Dzmare and Three Seagrass—still reeling from the recent upheaval in the Empire—face the impossible task of trying to communicate with a hostile entity.

"Multiple points of view add depth to the narrative as each character is rendered in exquisite detail, and that in turn propels the varied plot lines of diplomatic strategy, space conflicts, interpersonal relationships, and self-discovery. Elaborate and complex, with a diverse cast of characters, this saga will appeal to those who enjoy the detailed history-based world building of Guy Gavriel Kay combined with the intimate camaraderie and grand adventure of James S. A. Corey's Expanse series." —*Booklist*

★ A **memory** called empire. Arkady Martine. Tor, 2019. 464 p. (Teixcalaan novels, 1)

ISBN 9781250186430

1. Ambassadors 2. Poetry writing 3. Imperialism 4. Cultural differences 5. Imaginary empires 6. Space opera 7. Science fiction mysteries 8. Adult books for young adults

LC 2018046933

Hugo Award for Best Novel, 2020; Library Journal Best Books, 2019

After discovering that the previous ambassador in her post may have been murdered, Mahit Dzmare arrives in the capital of the Teixcalaanli Empire determined to find the killer, as she hides a secret which may save her station from the Teixcalaan's desirefor expansion.

"Politics and personalities blend with an immersive setting and beautiful prose in a debut that weaves threads of identity, assimilation, technology, and culture to offer an exceedingly well-done sf political thriller." —*Library Journal*

A Tom Doherty Associates Book.

Martineau, Maxym M.

Kingdom of exiles. Maxym M. Martineau. Sourcebooks Casablanca, 2019. 448 pages (Beast Charmer, 1)

ISBN 9781492689386

1. Mythical creatures 2. Human/animal communication 3. Women exiles 4. Assassins 5. Human/animal telepathy 6. Fantasy romances

LibraryReads Favorites, 2019

Forced to sell her beloved magical beasts on the black market—an offense punishable by death, exiled beast charmer Leena Edenfrell, with a price on her head, makes a devil's bargain with the realm's most talented assassin in exchange for her life.

Martinson, T. J.

The **reign** of the Kingfisher: a novel. T. J. Martinson. Flatiron Books, 2019. 320 p.

ISBN 9781250170217

1. Superheroes 2. Hostages 3. Staged deaths 4. Vigilantes 5. Villains 6. Chicago, Illinois 7. Superhero stories 8. Crime fiction

LC 2018030160

30 years ago a superhero tried to save Chicago. Now the city is again under siege.

Mas, Victoria

The **Mad** Women's Ball. Victoria Mas; translated by Frank Wynne. Harry N Abrams, 2021. 224 p.

ISBN 9781419757594

1. Women psychiatric hospital patients 2. Psychiatric hospitals 3. Women spiritualists 4. Balls (Parties) 5. Gender role 6. Paris, France 7. France 8. 1880s 9. 19th century 10. Translations 11. Historical fiction 12. Gothic fiction

Under the cover of the Madwomen's Ball—when the great and good come to gawk at the patients of the Salpetriere Asylum in Paris—19-year-old Eugenie, who can see spirits, is determined to escape and seek those who will believe in her.

"Mas elegantly blends feminist history and spiritualism, and poignantly demonstrates how the hospital is both prison and refuge for its residents, as Genevieve simultaneously grows disillusioned and empowered. Mas's dark tale will have readers transfixed." —*Publishers Weekly*

Translation of: Le Bal des folles.

Made into a movie of the same name, 2021.

Originally published: France : Albin Michel, 2019.

Translated from the French.

Masad, Ilana

All my mother's lovers: a novel. Ilana Masad. E.P. Dutton, 2020. 336 p.

ISBN 9781524745974

1. Lesbians 2. Mothers — Death 3. Family secrets 4. Lincoln, Abraham 5. Extramarital affairs 6. United States 7. LGBTQIA fiction 8. Multiple perspectives 9. Literary fiction

LC 2019031340

Shattered by revelations about the recently deceased mother who never entirely accepted her sexuality, a gay woman tracks down the men in her mother's hidden second life while coming to terms with new understandings about monogamy.

"A sort of mother-daughter road-trip novel, this explores the idea that we're all incomplete and forever subject to change, especially to those we love." —*Booklist*

Mason, Bobbie Ann

Dear Ann: a novel. Bobbie Ann Mason. Harper, 2020. 304 p.

ISBN 9780062986658

1. Options, alternatives, choices 2. Reminiscing in old age 3. Memories 4. Obsession 5. Misfits (Persons) 6. 1960s 7. 2010s 8. Literary fiction

LC 2019058961

A woman facing a life crisis reflects on her past as a naïve graduate student who set aside her educational ambitions at the height of the Summer of Love to pursue an obsessive relationship.

"Mason's time-shifting narrative can be difficult to follow, but she vividly recreates those heady counterculture days as a poignant backdrop for the regrets one often faces when one follows one's head instead of one's heart." —*Booklist*

Patchwork. Bobbie Ann Mason; introduction by George Saunders. University Press of Kentucky, 2018. 478 p.

ISBN 9780813175454

1. Human nature 2. Interpersonal relations 3. Family relationships 4. Kentucky 5. Tennessee 6. Short stories 7. Literary fiction 8. Domestic fiction

LC 2018011975

Patchwork contains short stories first published in the New Yorker and other leading periodicals; chapters from Mason's novels, including In Country, An Atomic Romance, and The Girl in the Blue Beret; and excerpts from Mason's eclectic nonfiction. Some examples of Mason's recent explorations in flash fiction appear here in print for the first time.

"Admirable in its broad sweep of Mason's estimable career as a writer and likely as good a gathering as there could be—if, for a fan, too short." —*Kirkus*

Shiloh and other stories. Bobbie Ann Mason. Modern Library, 2001. 240 p.
ISBN 9780375758430
1. Rural life 2. Kentucky 3. Short stories

LC 82047541

Hemingway Foundation/PEN Award, 1983; National Book Critics Circle Award for Fiction finalist, 1982; National Book Award for Fiction finalist, 1983

A collection of stories, mostly about people raised in western Kentucky, that portrays, in carefully observed detail, their struggle to reconcile family traditions and religion with new societal pressures and lifestyles and charts their search for understanding.

"Capturing in vivid detail the emotional frustrations of her characters and the unsettling ambience of her small-town Kentucky settings, Mason portrays the uneasy feelings of people who don't know what they want out of life but who do know that what they have isn't it." —*Booklist*

Originally published: New York : Harper & Row, 1982.

Mason, Daniel

The **piano** tuner. Daniel Mason. Knopf, 2002. 336 p.
ISBN 9780375414657
1. Piano tuners 2. Colonialism 3. British in Burma 4. Quests 5. Diplomats 6. Burma 7. Historical fiction
New York Times Notable Book, 2002

In 1886, piano tuner Edgar Drake leaves London for the jungles of Burma, where he has been asked to repair a grand piano belonging to a British army officer who uses the piano and music to help keep the peace among warring local Burmese princes.

"Mason proves himself equally adept at scenes of wry humor and moments of rapture; most remarkable, he has written a profound adventure story with an unexpected climax, as the mild piano tuner finally becomes the hero of his own life." —*The New Yorker*

Originally published: New York : Alfred A. Knopf, 2002.

A **registry** of my passage upon the Earth: stories. Daniel Mason. Little Brown & Co, 2020. 336 pages
ISBN 9780316477635
1. Short stories 2. Historical fiction 3. Literary fiction
Pulitzer Prize for Fiction finalist, 2021

At times funny and irreverent, always moving and deeply urgent, these stories—among them a National Magazine Award and a Pushcart Prize winner—cap a fifteen-year project.

"Each story is informed and deepened by scientific inquisitiveness, and rewards readers with understated philosophical insight. This showcases Mason's wide range and mastery of lyrical precision." —*Publishers Weekly*

Mason, Jamie

The **hidden** things. Jamie Mason. Gallery Books, 2019. 352 pages
ISBN 9781501177316
1. Art thefts 2. Social media 3. Fourteen-year-old girls 4. Victims of violent crimes 5. Self-defense 6. Thrillers and suspense 7. Multiple perspectives

A hair-raising, atmospheric thriller from the acclaimed author of Three Graves Full is inspired by the real-life unsolved theft of a 17th-century painting.

Mason, Meg

Sorrow and bliss. Meg Mason. HarperCollins, 2021. 240 p.
ISBN 9780063049581
1. Homecomings 2. Eccentrics and eccentricities 3. Women with depression 4. Forties (Age) 5. Self-discovery 6. London, England 7. England 8. Relationship fiction 9. First person narratives 10. Brown, Margaret Wise

Pushing away her devoted husband, a once-successful writer moves back into her bohemian childhood home, where she struggles to come to terms with the mental illness that has overshadowed her life.

"English writer Mason excels in her heartbreaking U.S. debut, an account of a woman's self-discovery amid her struggle with mental illness." —*Publishers Weekly*

Mason, Timothy

The **Darwin** affair. By Tim Mason. Algonquin Books of Chapel Hill, 2019. 336 p.
ISBN 9781616206345
1. Darwin, Charles 2. Attempted assassination 3. Psychopaths 4. Conspiracies 5. Detectives 6. Investigations 7. London, England 8. Great Britain 9. Victorian era (1837-1901) 10. 1860s 11. Victorian mysteries 12. Historical mysteries

LC 2018037996

Unsettling connections between an assassination attempt on Queen Victoria and the gruesome murder of a petty thief lead Chief Detective Inspector Charles Field to a shocking conspiracy related to the publication of Darwin's On the Origin of Species.

Masood, Syed M.

The **bad** Muslim discount. Syed M. Masood. Doubleday, 2020. 336 p.
ISBN 9780385545259
1. Immigrant families 2. Muslim families 3. Belief and doubt 4. Identity (Psychology) 5. Neighbors 6. San Francisco, California 7. California 8. 1990s 9. 2000s (Decade) 10. Relationship fiction

A homesick Pakistani immigrant chafing against the strictures of his family's new devout Muslim life in California and a young woman who barely escaped war-torn Baghdad upend their community in the aftermath of a fateful chance encounter. A first novel.

"A moving, comic take on the immigrant experience." —*Booklist*

Massey, Sujata

★ The **Bombay** prince. Sujata Massey. Soho Crime, 2021. 360 p. (Perveen Mistry novels, 3)
ISBN 9781641291057
1. Women lawyers 2. Murder investigation 3. Political intrigue 4. Families 5. Colonialism 6. India 7. Mumbai, India 8. 1920s 9. British Raj (1858-1947) 10. Historical mysteries

LC 2020052762

India's only female lawyer in 1920s Bombay, India, Perveen Mistry, as the streets erupt in riots to protest British colonial rule, investigates the murder of Parsi student at the behest of their suffering family while trying to save her own.

"Massey has never been better at pairing her redoubtable and impressive lead with a challenging murder to unravel." —*Publishers Weekly*

The **Satapur** moonstone. Sujata Massey. Soho Crime 2019. 384 pages (Perveen Mistry novels, 2)
ISBN 9781616959098
1. Women lawyers 2. Rulers — Succession 3. Courts and courtiers 4. Princes 5. Political intrigue 6. India 7. Mumbai, India 8. 1920s

9. British Raj (1858-1947) 10. Historical mysteries 11. Adult books for young adults

LC 2018046843

India's only female lawyer in 1922 helps the royal ladies of Satapur by getting involved in the power plays and ancient vendettas of the palace.

"Edgar finalist Masseys second whodunit featuring Bombay attorney Perveen Mistry is even better than the series impressive debut...The winning, self-sufficient Perveen should be able to sustain a long series." —*Publishers Weekly*

★ The **widows** of Malabar Hill: a mystery of 1920s Bombay. Sujata Massey. Soho Crime, 2018. 400 p. (Perveen Mistry novels, 1)
ISBN 9781616957780
1. Wills 2. Women lawyers 3. Murder investigation 4. Purdah 5. Muslim women 6. Mumbai, India 7. India 8. 1920s 9. Historical mysteries 10. Adult books for young adults

LC 2017021391

Agatha Award for Best Historical Novel, 2018; Edgar Allan Poe Awards: Mary Higgins Clark Award, 2019; Sue Feder Historical Mystery Award, 2019; RUSA Reading List, 2019

Introduces Bombay's first female lawyer, Oxford graduate Perveen Mistry, as she investigates a suspicious will on behalf of three Muslim widows living in strict purdah seclusion who become subject to a murderous guardian's schemes for their inheritances.

Matar, Hisham

In the country of men. Hisham Matar. Dial Press, 2007. 256 p.
ISBN 9780385340427
1. Nine-year-old boys 2. Deception in men 3. Political prisoners 4. Exiles 5. Childhood 6. Libya 7. 1970s 8. Coming-of-age stories 9. Political fiction 10. Adult books for young adults

LC 2006050649

Commonwealth Writers' Prize, South Asia and Europe: Best First Book, 2007; Library Journal Best Books, 2007; New York Times Notable Book, 2007; RSL Ondaatje Prize, 2007; Shortlisted for the Man Booker Prize, 2006; National Book Critics Circle Award for Fiction finalist, 2007

On a hot day in Tripoli in the summer of 1979, nine-year-old Suleiman spots his father, supposedly away on business, across from the market square and wearing dark glasses, the first portent of grave danger in a previously unsuspected world.

"A remarkably perceptive and affecting portrait of a young boy's premature political awakening.... [Matar] expertly builds an atmosphere of palpable tension, and though this novel never delves directly into politics, the menacing pall cast by political tyranny looms over the proceedings." —*Miami Herald*

Matheson, Richard

★ **I** am legend. Richard Matheson. TOR, 1997. 317 p.
ISBN 9780312865047
1. Survival (after epidemics) 2. Vampires 3. Vampire slayers 4. Loners 5. Survival 6. 1970s 7. Horror 8. Books to movies 9. Apocalyptic fiction

A lone human survivor in a world that is overrun by vampires, Robert Neville leads a desperate life in which he must barricade himself in his home every night and hunt down the starving undead by day.

Adapted to films entitled: The last man on Earth (1964), The omega man (1971), and I am legend (2007). It was also an inspiration for Night of the living dead (1968).

Originally published: Garden City, N.Y, : Nelson Doubleday, 1954.

Mathis, Ayana

The **twelve** tribes of Hattie. Ayana Mathis. Alfred A. Knopf, 2013. 256 p.
ISBN 9780307959423
1. African Americans — Migrations 2. African American families 3. Family relationships 4. African American women 5. African American gay men 6. Philadelphia, Pennsylvania 7. Historical fiction 8. Family sagas

LC 2012010779

New York Times Notable Book, 2013; BCALA Literary Award for First Novelist, 2013

Ayana Mathis tells the story of the children of the Great Migration through the trials of one unforgettable family.

Matthews, Jason

★ The **Kremlin's** candidate. Jason Matthews. Scribner, 2018. 434 p. (Dominika Egorova and Nathaniel Nash novels, 3)
ISBN 9781501140082
1. Putin, Vladimir Vladimirovich 2. Women spies 3. Double agents 4. Spies 5. Espionage 6. CIA agents 7. Russia 8. United States 9. Spy fiction 10. Thrillers and suspense

Overhearing a Kremlin plot to install a spy in a high intelligence position so that the Russians can identify CIA assets in Moscow, Dominika launches a desperate mole hunt, only to be exposed and arrested before recklessly immersing herself in Kremlin palace intrigues in the hopes of stealing as much information as possible before her time runs out.

Red sparrow: a novel. Jason Matthews. Scribner, 2013. 448 p. (Dominika Egorova and Nathaniel Nash novels, 1)
ISBN 9781476706122
1. Seduction 2. Women spies 3. Spies 4. CIA agents 5. Kerouac, Jack 6. Russia 7. United States 8. Spy fiction 9. Thrillers and suspense 10. Books to movies

LC 2012031933

Edgar Allan Poe Award for Best First Novel by an American Author, 2014; RUSA Reading List, 2014; Thriller Award for Best First Novel, 2014

Former ballerina Dominika Egorova serves Vladimir Putin's regime by seducing, then spying on, enemies of the state. CIA officer Nate Nash has been reassigned to Helsinki after nearly blowing the cover of a highly valuable Russian mole, and this is where Dominika latches on, determined to learn the mole's identity. But Dominika is more than a pretty lady—she's smart, and her synesthesia allows her to tell when someone is lying. As they try to outwit and out-spy each other, readers are treated to vivid, authentic details of spycraft. Author Jason Matthews knows his stuff—he worked for the CIA for more than 30 years—and there are shades of John le Carré in his writing.

Sequel: Palace of treason

Title adapted into a film by the same name in 2017.

Matthews, Mimi

★ The **siren** of Sussex. Mimi Matthews. Jove, 2022. 336 p. (Belles of London, 1)
ISBN 9780593337134
1. Women equestrians 2. Tailors 3. Multiracial men 4. Fashion design 5. Racism 6. London, England 7. Great Britain 8. Victorian era (1837-1901) 9. Victorian romances 10. Historical romances 11. Multicultural romances

LC 2021019358

London's daring new equestrienne finds love and an unexpected ally in her fight for independence in the strong arms of Victorian society's most sought after and devastatingly handsome half-Indian tailor.

"The societal obstacles to their relationship and thoughtful exploration of multiracial identity ground the romance, striking a delicate balance between grim period-typical attitudes and fluffy joy. Ahmad and Evelyn both marry impressive fierceness with understandable insecurities, making them a couple to root for." —*Publishers Weekly*

Matthiessen, Peter

Shadow country: a new rendering of the Watson legend. Peter Matthiessen. Modern Library, 2008. Xvi, 892 p. : Map

ISBN 9780679640196

1. Watson, Edgar J. 2. Frontier and pioneer life 3. Murderers 4. Violence in men 5. Neighbors 6. Murder victims 7. Florida 8. Everglades, Florida 9. Casement, Roger 10. Historical fiction 11. Family sagas 12. Literary fiction

LC 2007025117

National Book Award for Fiction, 2008

Inspired by a near-mythic event of the wild Florida frontier at the turn of the twentieth century, Shadow Country reimagines the legend of the inspired Everglades sugar planter and notorious outlaw E. J. Watson, who drives himself relentlessly toward his own violent end at the hands of neighbors who mostly admired him, in a killing that obsessed his favorite son. —From publisher description.

"Matthiessen is meticulous in creating characters, lyrical in describing landscapes, and resolute in dissecting the values and costs that accompanied the development of this nation." —*Seattle Times*

Maturin, Charles Robert

Melmoth the wanderer: a tale. Charles Maturin; edited with an introduction and notes by Victor Sage. Penguin Books, 2001. 704 p.

ISBN 9780140447613

1. Immortality 2. Jews, Spanish 3. Wanderers and wandering 4. Uncles 5. Betrayal 6. Ireland 7. Gothic fiction 8. Classics

After striking a deal with the Devil, Sebastian Melmoth spends his extended lifetime searching the world for someone to take his place in the Faustian bargain. Written in 1820 by an Anglican priest, this Gothic novel consists of several tales-within-a-tale. Enthusiasts of the brooding melodrama include Balzac, Poe, Dostoyevsky, and Baudelaire.

First published 1820.

Maugham, W. Somerset

The moon and sixpence. W. Somerset Maugham; introduction by Robert Calder. Penguin Books, 2005. 216 p.

ISBN 9780143039341

1. Gauguin, Paul 2. Painters 3. Ambition 4. Middle-aged men 5. Artists 6. British in Tahiti 7. London, England 8. Paris, France 9. Psychological fiction 10. First person narratives 11. Modern classics

A British stockbroker abandons his wife and career to pursue a simple life as an artist in Tahiti.

★ **Of** human bondage. W. Somerset Maugham; introduction by Gore Vidal. Modern Library, 1999. Xxxix, 611 p.

ISBN 9780375753152

1. Artists 2. People with disabilities 3. Unrequited love 4. Orphans 5. Clubfoot men 6. London, England 7. England 8. Coming-of-age stories 9. Psychological fiction 10. Literary fiction

LC 98046169

Considered by many to be W. Somerset Maugham's masterpiece, Of Human Bondage traces the travels of Philip Carey to Germany, Paris, and London while exploring his intellectual, emotional, and psychological development and, later, his destructive relationship with a tawdry waitress.

Originally published: London : W. Heinemann, 1915.

Maxwell, Everina

Winter's orbit. Everina Maxwell. Tor, 2021. 384 p.

ISBN 9781250758835

1. Political intrigue 2. Conspiracies 3. Imaginary empires 4. Princes 5. Counts and countesses 6. Social science fiction 7. LGBTQIA fiction 8. Multiple perspectives 9.

LC 2020042322

Prince Kiem—the Emperor's least favorite grandchild—is commanded to renew the empire's bonds with its newest vassal planet. The prince must marry Count Jainan, the recent widower of another royal prince of the empire. But Jainan suspects his late husband's death was no accident. And Prince Kiem discovers that Jainan is a suspect himself. But broken bonds between the empire and its vassal planets leaves the entire empire vulnerable, so together they must prove that their union is strong while uncovering a possible conspiracy. In the shadows of a secret past and an insecure future, Kiem and Jainan must come together to protect both of their worlds.

"The intricate royal protocol of The Crown intertwines with the adventure of Louis McMasters Bujold's Vorkosigan Saga series in Maxwell's gorgeously plotted LGBTQ space opera debut." —*Publishers Weekly*

May, Peter

The blackhouse. Peter May. SilverOak, 2012. 432 p. (Lewis trilogy, 1)

ISBN 9781454901273

1. Murder investigation 2. Detectives 3. Murder 4. Sons — Death 5. Grief in men 6. Scotland 7. Hebrides 8. Mysteries

LC 2012016939

Library Journal Best Books, 2012

When a grisly murder occurs on a Scottish island, Edinburgh detective Fin Macleod must confront his past if he is ever going to discover if the killing has a connection to another one that took place on the mainland.

Mayer, Mark

Aerialists: stories. Mark Mayer. Bloomsbury Publishing, 2019. 290 p. : Illustration

ISBN 9781635572179

1. Circus 2. Short stories 3. Literary fiction

LC 2018006312

Through nine surreal stories, a carnival caravan of ordinary misfits grapple with finding happiness, including a sad boy who finds a mentor in a tough female bodybuilder and a navy recruit who builds his childhood neighborhood in code.

"Mayer's high-wire debut exposes the weirdness of everyday life.... Mayer wittily subverts reader expectations with stories told in a realistic manner about characters or situations that all share a slightly surreal bent, resulting in a clever collection." —*Publishers Weekly*

Maynard, Joyce

Count the ways. Joyce Maynard. William Morrow & Company, 2021. 464 p.

ISBN 9780062398277

1. Married women 2. Husband and wife 3. Families 4. Siblings 5. Accidents 6. New Hampshire 7. New England 8. Domestic fiction 9. Mainstream fiction

LC 2020033202

The story of Eleanor and Cam, whose marriage and family is shattered by tragedy and infidelity and how, during the decades that follow, they make surprising discoveries and decisions that bring them together, and tear them apart.

Maynard creates a world rich and real enough to hold the pain she fills it with. Kirkus

Mayor, Archer

★ **Marked** man. Archer Mayor. Minotaur Books, 2021. 304 p. (Joe Gunther mysteries, 32)

ISBN 9781250224163

1. Government investigators 2. Cold cases (Criminal investigation) 3. Mafia 4. Greed 5. Private investigators 6. Vermont 7. Rhode Island 8. Police procedurals 9. Mysteries

LC 2021015938

While Joe Gunther looks into the mafia-related murders linked to the death of a local philanthropist and millionaire, PI Sally Kravitz teams up with a reporter to expose the truth behind this tangled and expanding web duplicity, greed and obsession.

"Bestseller Mayor expertly juggles four plotlines, which may or may not be related, in his superb 32nd mystery featuring Vermont Bureau of Investigation agent Joe Gunther.... This is a perfect jumping-on point for newcomers." —*Publishers Weekly*

Red herring: a Joe Gunther novel. Archer Mayor. Minotaur Books, 2010. 320 p. (Joe Gunther mysteries, 21)

ISBN 9780312381936

1. Anne Boleyn 2. Betrayal 3. Murder investigation 4. Deception 5. Serial murders 6. Brattleboro, Vermont 7. Vermont 8. Mysteries 9. Police procedurals

VBI (Vermont Bureau of Investigation) head Joe Gunther and his team are called in to investigate a series of violent deaths that appear unrelated until telltale clues reveal a link among them.

"With cool forensic details for CSI fans, Mayor's heart-racing tale ends in a dramatic finish that will leave readers gasping." —*Library Journal*

Tag man: a Joe Gunther novel. Archer Mayor. Minotaur Books, 2011. 320 p. (Joe Gunther mysteries, 22)

ISBN 9780312681944

1. Assassins 2. Murder investigation 3. Frameups 4. Police 5. Thieves 6. Brattleboro, Vermont 7. Mysteries 8. Police procedurals

LC 2011018779

When a nuisance burglar who breaks into the heavily secured homes of wealthy Vermont citizens but steals nothing discovers evidence of a string of murders in one of the homes, Joe Gunther and his team struggle to untangle conflicting pieces of evidence while the burglar flees for his life.

"Vermont's history and geography again serve Mayor well in this deadly and highly entertaining entry." —*Publishers Weekly*

Mbue, Imbolo

How beautiful we were. Imbolo Mbue. Random House, 2020. 368 p.

ISBN 9780593132425

1. Villages 2. Environmental degradation 3. Resistance to government 4. Women revolutionaries 5. Oil industry and trade 6. Literary fiction 7. Multiple perspectives

A young revolutionary risks everything to secure her people's freedom when her small African village is decimated by an American oil company that reneges on promises of reparation.

"Among the many virtues of Mbue's novel is the way it uses an ecological nightmare to frame a vivid and stirring picture of human beings' asserting their value to the world, whether the world cares about them or not." —*Kirkus*

McAllister, Tom

How to be safe: a novel. Tom McAllister. Liveright Publishing Corporation, 2018. 232 p.

ISBN 9781631494130

1. High school teachers 2. School shootings 3. Blame 4. Malicious accusation 5. Employees — Dismissal 6. Pennsylvania 7. Literary fiction 8. Satirical fiction

LC 2017054671

LibraryReads Favorites, 2018

When high school teacher Anna Crawford is suspended just before a shooting at her school, she is horrified to see that she is considered a suspect, and even though she is exonerated, her moment in the public eye draws judgment and scrutiny, as the community lapses into familiar reactions.

McBain, Ed

Alice in jeopardy. Ed McBain. Simon & Schuster, 2005. 304 p.

ISBN 9780743262507

1. Kidnapping 2. Ransom 3. Life insurance 4. Widows 5. Household employees 6. Florida 7. Thrillers and suspense

LC 2004052478

When her children are stolen by a kidnapper who demands her late husband's life insurance premiums in exchange for their return, widowed real estate agent Alice Glendenning turns for help to new friend Charlie Hobbs.

"This is a skilled performance from a master of the genre, the pacing and tone just right to keep you tense, curious and amused at each step." —*Washington Post Book World.*

McBride, James

★ **Deacon** King Kong: a novel. James McBride. Riverhead Books, 2020. 384 p.

ISBN 9780735216723

1. Drug traffic 2. Communities 3. Murder 4. Gangsters 5. Mafia 6. Brooklyn, New York City 7. 1960s 8. African American fiction 9. Historical fiction 10. Farcical fiction

LC 2019045146

ALA Notable Book, 2021; Andrew Carnegie Medal for Excellence in Fiction, 2021; New York Times Notable Book, 2020; Loan Stars Favourites, 2020; Kirkus Prize for Fiction finalist, 2020

In the aftermath of a 1969 Brooklyn church deacon's public shooting of a local drug dealer, the community's African-American and Latinx witnesses find unexpected support from each other when they are targeted by violent mobsters.

"McBride has a flair for fashioning comedy whose buoyant outrageousness barely conceals both a steely command of big and small narrative elements and a river-deep supply of humane intelligence." —*Kirkus*

Five-carat soul. James McBride. Riverhead Books, 2017. 288 p.

ISBN 9780735216693

1. Interpersonal relations 2. Interpersonal conflict 3. Race relations 4. Material culture 5. Literary fiction 6. Short stories 7. African American fiction

LC 2017007480

New York Times Notable Book, 2017; Longlisted for the Andrew Carnegie Medal for Excellence in Fiction, 2018

Presents a collection of insightful and unpredictable stories that explore the ways people learn from the world and the people around them.

"A versatile, illustrious author brings out his first short-fiction buffet for sampling, and the results are provocatively varied in taste and texture; sometimes piquant, other times zesty." —*Kirkus*

★ The **good** lord bird. James McBride. Riverhead Books, 2013. 432 p.
ISBN 9781594486340
1. Brown, John 2. Abolitionists 3. Female impersonators 4. Freedom seekers 5. Self-perception in men 6. Children and adults 7. Harper's Ferry, West Virginia 8. Antebellum America (1820-1861) 9. Historical fiction 10. Literary fiction 11. African American fiction 12. Adult books for young adults

LC 2013004014

BCALA Literary Award for Fiction, 2014; Booklist Editors' Choice, 2013; Library Journal Best Books, 2013; National Book Award for Fiction, 2013; New York Times Notable Book, 2013

Mistaken for a girl on account of his curly hair, delicate features, and sackcloth smock, 12-year-old slave Henry Shackleford realizes that his accidental disguise affords him greater safety and decides to remain female. Dubbed "Little Onion" by his liberator, abolitionist John Brown, Henry accompanies the increasingly fanatical Brown on his crusade to end slavery—a picaresque journey that takes them from Bloody Kansas to Rochester, New York, where they attempt to enlist the support of such notables as Frederick Douglass and Harriet Tubman before embarking on the infamous, ill-fated 1859 raid on Harpers Ferry.

Adapted into a TV series of the same name in 2020.

McCaffrey, Anne

★ **Acorna:** the unicorn girl. Anne McCaffrey and Margaret Ball. HarperPrism, 1997. 291 p. (Acorna series, 1)
ISBN 9780061052965
1. Magic 2. Difference (Psychology) 3. Abandoned children 4. Child abuse 5. Alien children (Humanoid) 6. Science fiction 7. Science fantasy

LC 9711099

"Found in a survival pod in space by prospectors, the infant Acorna soon exhibits the ability to analyze deficiencies in plants by taste, purify water and air, and heal. Taken to the planet Kezdet to avoid scientists who want to study her, Acorna discovers barbaric child-labor practices and vows to rescue the children. McCaffrey and Ball have created a magical alien in this fantasy/science fiction story." —*Library Journal*

Dragonflight. Anne McCaffrey. Ballantine Books, 1968. 303 p. (Dragonriders of Pern, 1)
ISBN 9780345276940
1. Women rulers 2. Household employees 3. Dragons 4. Biological invasions 5. Survival 6. Churchill, Winston, 1874-1965 7. Science fantasy 8. Adult books for young adults

At a time when the number of Dragonriders has fallen too low for safety and only one Weyr trains the creatures and their riders, the Red Star approaches Pern, threatening it with disaster.

The short stories Weyr Search and Dragonrider are incorporated in this book.

McCall Smith, Alexander

Blue shoes and happiness. Alexander McCall Smith. Pantheon Books, 2006. 240 p. (No. 1 Ladies' Detective Agency, 7)
ISBN 9780375422720
1. Women thieves 2. Witchcraft 3. Shoes 4. Women private investigators 5. Women administrative assistants 6. Botswana 7. Cozy mysteries 8. Gentle reads

LC 2005052122

Precious Ramotswe and her able assistant, Grace Makutsi, launch an investigation into local advice columnist Aunty Emang, who somehow may be linked to trouble at a local medical clinic and the cobra that somehow ended up in Precious's office, while Grace confronts her own troubles with her greedy uncles and her wealthy fiancé, Phuti Radiphuti.

"McCall Smith renders brisk, seamless tales that are both wry and profound. Amidst the mayhem (like the cobra that slithers its way into the detective agency's headquarters) are eloquent descriptions of the serene African country that holds a special place in his heart." —*Booklist*

The **comforts** of a muddy Saturday: an Isabel Dalhousie novel. Alexander McCall Smith. Pantheon Books, 2008. 256 p. (Isabel Dalhousie mysteries, 5)
ISBN 9780375425134
1. Middle-aged women 2. Physicians 3. Medical malpractice 4. Women editors 5. Americans in Scotland 6. Scotland 7. Hildegard von Bingen 8. Gentle reads

LC 2008018573

Isabel Dalhousie comes to the aid of a renowned, much respected doctor whose reputation is at stake following the death of a patient because of allegations of scientific fraud in respect to a newly marketed drug.

"While the truth isn't straightforward, the motives of the guilty party prove to be both plausible and rational. The strengths of the book...lie in its protagonist's determination to treat others without judgment and in the author's revealing glimpses into the human soul." —*Publishers Weekly*

★ The **Department** of Sensitive Crimes: a Detective Varg novel. Alexander McCall Smith. Pantheon Books, 2019. 208 p. (Detective Varg novels, 1)
ISBN 9781524748210
1. Police 2. Detectives 3. Criminal investigation 4. Eccentrics and eccentricities 5. Sweden 6. Malmo, Sweden 7. Mysteries 8. Humorous stories 9. Gentle reads

LC 2018040221

Tasked with their Swedish Police Department's most unusual cases, lead detective Ulf Varg and his colorful associates investigate a bizarre stabbing, a lost imaginary boyfriend and a haunted spa.

The **Double** Comfort Safari Club. Alexander McCall Smith. Pantheon Books, 2010. 224 p. (No. 1 Ladies' Detective Agency, 11)
ISBN 9780375424502
1. Women private investigators 2. Marriage 3. Murder investigation 4. Overweight women 5. Husband and wife 6. Botswana 7. Africa 8. Cozy mysteries 9. Gentle reads

LC 2009049060

Traveling to northern Botswana where they are impressed by the natural beauty of the Okavango Delta, Mma Ramotswe and Mma Makutsi visit a safari lodge where they encounter discontented locals and struggle with untimely wedding issues.

"It's not in the stories themselves, but in the telling of them, that the secret of McCall Smith's appeal lies. His Botswana may indeed be a kindly place, but he has an ability— a very rare one— to write with kindness too. This world, he says, is only ours for a short time, and we realise that more and more with age. And when we cry, he'll point out, how odd it is that we rock forward and back, as our mothers comforted us, as if we were trying to comfort ourselves. Such apecus are, of themselves, not original. What is, is the way McCall Smith effortlessly weaves them into stories of fun and laughter and heartfelt love of place and character." —*The Scotsman*

The **forgotten** affairs of youth. Alexander McCall Smith. Pantheon Books, 2011. 272 p. (Isabel Dalhousie mysteries, 8)
ISBN 9780307379184
1. Birthparents — Identification 2. Aunt and niece 3. Engagement 4. Household employees 5. Man-woman relationships 6. Scotland 7. Edinburgh, Scotland 8. Mysteries 9. Gentle reads
When a visiting Australian philosopher on sabbatical in Edinburgh asks for Isabel's help to discover the identity of her father, of course Isabel obliges.
Originally published: London: Little, Brown, 2011.

The **full** cupboard of life. Alexander McCall Smith. Pantheon Books, 2004. 208 p. (No. 1 Ladies' Detective Agency, 5)
ISBN 9780375422188
1. Mate selection 2. Courtship 3. Women private investigators 4. Women administrative assistants 5. Secretaries 6. Botswana 7. Africa 8. Cozy mysteries 9. Gentle reads 10. Adult books for young adults
LC 2003062379
Worrying about her upcoming marriage, Precious Ramotswe is confronted by the challenges of running her No. 1 Ladies' Detective Agency and an investigation into the would-be suitors of a wealthy woman to determine if any are fortune hunters.
Originally published: Edinburgh : Polygon, 2003.

★ The **geometry** of holding hands. Alexander McCall Smith. Random House Inc 2020. 223 pages : Color; Illustration (Isabel Dalhousie mysteries, 13)
ISBN 9781524748944
1. Women philosophers 2. Elizabeth, Queen, consort of Henry VII, King of England, 1465-1503 3. Women amateur detectives 4. Married women 5. Investigations 6. Edinburgh, Scotland 7. Mysteries 8. Gentle reads
LC 2020010147
One of the author's most beloved characters is back—and once again she will have to call upon her powers of deduction and her unflappable moral code to unravel a new philosophical mystery.
"The elegant resolution of both problems makes this the ethicist's best in more than a decade." —*Kirkus*

The **good** husband of Zebra Drive. Alexander McCall Smith. Pantheon Books, 2007. 240 p. (No. 1 Ladies' Detective Agency, 8)
ISBN 9780375422737
1. Resourcefulness in women 2. Women private investigators 3. Husband and wife 4. Women administrative assistants 5. No. 1 Ladies' Detective Agency (Imaginary organization) 6. Botswana 7. Cozy mysteries 8. Gentle reads 9. Adult books for young adults
LC 2006039047
Mma Ramotswes devoted husband, J. L. B. Matekoni tries his hand at the detective business, catering to a rude client who suspects her husband of infidelity.
"The author's subtlety of touch and humane portrayal of figures at all levels of society will continue to win him new readers even as his deepening of the ties binding the main figures will satisfy those who have followed the lady detectives from their first recorded case." —*Publishers Weekly*
Originally published: Edinburgh: Polygon, 2007.

In the company of cheerful ladies. Alexander McCall Smith. Pantheon Books 2005. 240 p. (No. 1 Ladies' Detective Agency, 6)
ISBN 9780375422713

1. Dancing — Study and teaching 2. Burglary 3. Extramarital affairs 4. Women private investigators 5. Women administrative assistants 6. Botswana 7. Africa 8. Cozy mysteries 9. Gentle reads
LC 2004056827
Overwhelmed by work at the No. 1 Ladies' Detective Agency, Precious Ramotswe is further challenged by a strange intruder at her home, the appearance in her yard of a mysterious pumpkin, troubles at her husband's motorworks, and a visitor who forces her to confront a painful secret from her past.
Originally published: Edinburgh : Polygon, 2004.

The **Joy** and Light Bus Company. Alexander McCall Smith. Pantheon Books, 2021. 240 p. (No. 1 Ladies' Detective Agency, 22)
ISBN 9780593315736
1. Women private investigators 2. Communities 3. Women business owners 4. Female friendship 5. Women owned businesses 6. Botswana 7. Africa 8. Cozy mysteries 9. Gentle reads
LC 2021027552
While enjoying all that life has to offer with her loving family, good friends and a thriving business doing what she enjoys most—helping people, Mma Ramotswe finds herself up to her neck in mysterious trouble.
"As ever, Smith's mix of solving minor crimes and kindhearted philosophical ruminations enchants." —*Publishers Weekly*
No. 1 Ladies' Detective Agency (22)—Title page.
Originally published in hardcover in Great Britain by Little, Brown, an imprint of Little, Brown Book Group, a Hachette UK company, London, in 2021.

The **Kalahari** typing school for men. Alexander McCall Smith. Pantheon Books, 2003. 186 p. (No. 1 Ladies' Detective Agency, 4)
ISBN 9780375422171
1. Secretaries 2. Sexism 3. Ethics 4. Women private investigators 5. No. 1 Ladies' Detective Agency (Imaginary organization) 6. Botswana 7. Africa 8. Cozy mysteries 9. Gentle reads
LC 2002030709
Now that the No. 1 Ladies' Detective Agency is firmly established, founder Precious Ramotswe faces new challenges at home and at work—from problems with her adopted son, to an assistant who dreams of opening a Kalahari Typing School for Men, to a sexist rival who is opening a Satisfaction Guaranteed Detective Agency across town.
Originally published: Edinburgh : Polygon, 2002.

The **Limpopo** Academy of Private Detection. Alexander McCall Smith. Pantheon Books, 2012. 224 p. (No. 1 Ladies' Detective Agency, 13)
ISBN 9780307378408
1. Newlyweds 2. Schools 3. Authors 4. Women private investigators 5. No. 1 Ladies' Detective Agency (Imaginary organization) 6. Botswana 7. Africa 8. Cozy mysteries 9. Gentle reads
The formidable talents of Precious Ramotswe are put to the test in the face of a mysterious disciplinary problem at her adopted daughter's school, assistant Grace Makutsi's early marital adjustments and the appearance of the No. 1 Ladies' hero detective.
Originally published: London: Little, Brown, 2012.

The **lost** art of gratitude. Alexander McCall Smith. Pantheon Books, 2009. 272 p. (Isabel Dalhousie mysteries, 6)
ISBN 9780375425141
1. Investment bankers 2. Fraud 3. Plagiarism 4. Birthday parties 5. Women editors 6. Scotland 7. Edinburgh, Scotland 8. Mysteries 9. Gentle reads
LC 2009022618
Encountering high-flying financier Minty Auchterlonie while attending a birthday party, Isabel learns of Minty's complicated monetary troubles and wonders if the ambitious woman is perpetuating a fraud, a

situation that is further complicated by a plagiarism battle with Professor Dove and Cat's problematic new man.

"Smith's trademark humor and telling observations about people heighten the appeal." —*Publishers Weekly*

★ The **man** with the silver Saab: a Detective Varg novel. Alexander McCall Smith. Pantheon Books, 2021. 240 p. (Detective Varg novels, 3)
ISBN 9780593316108
1. Eccentrics and eccentricities 2. Criminal investigation 3. Detectives 4. Crime 5. Men and dogs 6. Sweden 7. Malmo, Sweden 8. Mysteries 9. Humorous stories 10. Gentle reads
LC 2021007281

Perplexing, unfathomable, and perhaps unimportant, the cases that Malmo's Department of Sensitive Crimes take on will test them to their limits. Life—and crime—is not always as it seems for Ulf Varg and the other fearless detectives in Malmo's Department of Sensitive Crimes. There are always surprising new cases to take on, and the latest batch is no exception. And that's not to mention Ulf's struggle to contain his feelings for his colleague Anna Bengsdotter. All in all, things are distinctly difficult in Malmo, and it seems up to Ulf and the Department to set them right.

"What appears, at first, to be a 'nothing' series of crimes expands into an incisive character analysis with a wow of a resolution, all while sustaining its comic bent. The Varg series is a nice antidote to Nordic noir." —*Booklist*

★ The **No.** 1 Ladies' Detective Agency. Alexander McCall Smith. Anchor Books, 2002. 226 p; (No. 1 Ladies' Detective Agency, 1)
ISBN 9781400031344
1. Women private investigators 2. Missing children 3. Shamans 4. Kidnapping 5. Physicians 6. Botswana 7. Africa 8. Cozy mysteries 9. Gentle reads

Working in Gaborone, Botswana, Precious Ramotswe investigates several local mysteries, including a search for a missing boy and the case of the clinic doctor with different personalities for different days of the week.

Originally published: Edinburgh : Polygon, 1998.

The **Saturday** big tent wedding party. Alexander McCall Smith. Pantheon Books, 2011. 256 p. (No. 1 Ladies' Detective Agency, 12)
ISBN 9780307378392
1. Missing men 2. Weddings 3. Poisoning 4. Cattle 5. Women private investigators 6. Botswana 7. Africa 8. Cozy mysteries 9. Gentle reads

Hoping to reclaim a van that was featured in a possible prophetic dream, Precious and Grace find themselves helping an apprentice of Phuti Radiphuti, investigating a cattle poisoning and considering Grace's possible marriage to Phuti.

Originally published: London: Little, Brown, 2011.

Tiny tales: stories of romance, ambition, kindness, and happiness. Alexander McCall Smith; illustrated by Iain McIntosh. Pantheon Books, 2021. 240 pages
ISBN 9780593316009
1. Gods and goddesses, Greek 2. Gods and goddesses, Norse 3. Cats 4. Politicians 5. Short stories 6. Humorous stories
LC 2020045181

A delightful compendium of short fiction celebrating the joy and absurdity of the human experience. From conflict between the Greek Gods of Olympus and the Norse Gods, to a handy unintended benefit of cosmetic surgery; from a rather droll cat named Stanley, to Good President Wenceslas, benevolent leader of a snowy land: these stories are by turns funny, poignant, and deliciously wicked, each one a gift begging to be unwrapped and enjoyed again and again.

"McCall Smith's gift for quick characterization and his ability to conjure a range of moods, from philosophical to madcap, are on full display here." —*Booklist*

McCammon, Robert R.

Boy's life. Robert R. McCammon. Pocket Books, 1991. 440 p.
ISBN 9780671742263
1. Twelve-year-old boys 2. Murder witnesses 3. Family violence 4. Boys 5. Fathers and sons 6. Alabama 7. 1960s 8. Coming-of-age stories 9. Mysteries
Bram Stoker Award for Best Novel, 1991; World Fantasy Award, 1992

The witnesses to a horrific murder, Cory Mackenson and his father investigate and come face to face with the vicious Blaylock clan, a secret society united by racial hatred, and a reptilian creature inhabiting the river BT

"McCammon is both a precise and lush writer, and thus the trail Cory takes to deciphering the puzzle the dead man represents quickly firms up into a compelling, even haunting yarn of adult demons being faced and fathomed by the young. This look at life's blacker sides is neither cloying nor jejune." —*Booklist*

McCann, Colum

★ **Apeirogon:** a novel. Colum McCann. Random House, 2020. 464 p.
ISBN 9781400069606
1. Arab-Israeli relations 2. Fathers and daughters 3. Grief 4. Violence 5. Suicide bombings 6. Political fiction 7. Literary fiction 8. Biographical fiction
LC 2019022848

National Jewish Book Award, 2020; Shortlisted for the International Dublin Literary Award, 2021

Two fathers, a Palestinian and an Israeli, navigate the physical and emotional checkpoints of their conflicted world before devastating losses compel them to work together to use their grief as a weapon for peace.

"National Book Award winner McCann (Let the Great World Spin) bases this masterful novel on the lives of two real men working together toward Middle Eastern peace." —*Publishers Weekly*

★ **Transatlantic:** a novel. Colum McCann. Random House, 2013. 304 p.
ISBN 9781400069590
1. Douglass, Frederick 2. Transatlantic voyages 3. Politicians 4. Freed people 5. Ireland 6. United States 7. 1840s 8. 1910s 9. Literary fiction 10. Family sagas 11. Historical fiction
LC 2012043294

Shortlisted for the International Dublin Literary Award, 2015

Spanning 150 years and two continents, this literary family saga from National Book Award-winning author Colum McCann ties Frederick Douglass' 1845 journey to Ireland with the first trans-Atlantic flight made in 1919 by two British aviators and the work of U.S. Senator George Mitchell on the 1998 Good Friday Agreement. These great men and the events they're connected to are also linked to a servant girl named Lily, who in 1846 leaves Dublin for New York, and her descendants. Transatlantic is a complex meditation on time, memory, freedom, and war.

McCarthy, Cormac

★ **All** the pretty horses. Cormac McCarthy. A. A. Knopf, 1992. 301 p. (Border trilogy (Cormac McCarthy), 1)
ISBN 9780394574745
1. Horse training 2. Americans in Mexico 3. Sixteen-year-old boys 4. Boys and horses 5. Horses 6. Northern Mexico 7. West Texas 8. 1940s 9. Coming-of-age stories 10. Literary fiction 11. Books to movies 12. Adult books for young adults
LC 91058560

ALA Notable Book, 1993; National Book Award for Fiction, 1992; National Book Critics Circle Award for Fiction, 1992; Western Heritage Award for Outstanding Western Novel, 1993

Cut off from the life of ranching he has come to love by his grandfather's death, John Grady Cole flees to Mexico, where he and his two companions embark on a rugged and cruelly idyllic adventure.

"Though some readers may grow impatient with the wild prairie rhythms of McCarthy's language, others will find his voice completely transporting." —*Publishers Weekly*

★ **Blood** meridian, or, The evening redness in the West. Cormac McCarthy. Vintage Books, 1992. 337 p.
ISBN 9780679728757
1. Outlaws 2. Massacres 3. Apache Indians 4. Teenage boys 5. Mexico 6. Texas 7. 1850s 8. 19th century 9. Westerns 10. Literary fiction 11. Southern Gothic

LC 91050742

Based on incidents that took place in the southwestern United States and Mexico around 1850, this novel chronicles the crimes of a band of desperados, with a particular focus on one, "the kid," a boy of fourteen.

The **crossing**. Cormac McCarthy. A.A. Knopf, 1994. 425 p. (Border trilogy (Cormac McCarthy), 2)
ISBN 9780394574752
1. Wolves 2. Americans in Mexico 3. Sixteen-year-old boys 4. Boys and wolves 5. Brothers 6. New Mexico 7. 1930s 8. Coming-of-age stories 9. Literary fiction 10. Adult books for young adults

LC 94004281

Booklist Editors' Choice, 1994

In the 1930s, Billy and his family come to Hidalgo County, New Mexico, where he becomes obsessed with a wild wolf that lives a precarious existence threatened by the region's ranchers BT

★ **No** country for old men. Cormac McCarthy. Knopf, 2005. 320 p.
ISBN 9780375406775
1. Heroin traffic 2. Violence 3. Vietnam veterans 4. Sheriffs 5. World War II veterans 6. Texas 7. Mexico 8. 1980s 9. Literary fiction 10. Crime fiction 11. First person narratives

LC 2004064903

ALA Notable Book, 2006; New York Times Notable Book, 2005; Shortlisted for the International IMPAC Dublin Literary Award, 2007

Stumbling upon a bloody massacre, a cache of heroin, and more than $2 million in cash during a hunting trip, Llewelyn Moss removes the money, a decision that draws him and his young wife into the middle of a violent confrontation.

"As devised and refined by James M. Cain, Jim Thompson and their gloomy paperback peers, the crime novel aimed its cheap handgun at the heart of America's most prized beliefs about its destiny: that the loot we've scooped up will belong to us forever and that history allows clean getaways. Cormac McCarthy's No Country for Old Men is as bracing a variation on these noir orthodoxies as any fan of the genre could expect." —*New York Times Book Review*

★ The **road**. Cormac McCarthy. Knopf, 2006. 256 p.
ISBN 9780307265432
1. Fathers and sons 2. Survival (after nuclear warfare) 3. Familial love 4. Hunger 5. Cannibalism 6. United States 7. Apocalyptic fiction 8. Literary fiction 9. Books to movies

LC 2006045158

ALA Notable Book, 2007; Booklist Editors' Choice, 2006; James Tait Black Memorial Prize for Fiction, 2006; Library Journal Best Books, 2006; New York Times Notable Book, 2006; Pulitzer Prize for Fiction, 2007; National Book Critics Circle Award for Fiction finalist, 2006

Apocalypse grips the earth; wildlife has disappeared; and starvation prevails. Amidst this bleak backdrop, a man and his young son slowly make their way toward the coast. Avoiding roves of marauding cannibals and fighting off starvation, they gain hope and stamina in knowing they are some of the remaining few virtuous people.

McCarthy, Jesse

The **fugitivities**. Jesse Mccarthy. Random House, 2021. 256 pages
ISBN 9781612198064
1. African American men 2. High school teachers 3. Teacher-student relationships 4. Basketball coaches 5. Voyages and travels 6. New York City 7. African American fiction 8. Literary fiction

An Ivy Leaguer disillusioned with his apathetic students while teaching at a Manhattan public school jumps at the chance to escape to South America with a friend and winds up on a journey of self-discovery and growth.

"In his insightful debut, writer, editor, and Harvard professor McCarthy explores the tension between community and individual perceptions of Black identity in different cultures." —*Booklist*

McClure, James

The **steam** pig. James McClure. Soho Crime, 2010. 272 p. (Kramer and Zondi mysteries, 1)
ISBN 9781569476529
1. Apartheid 2. Murder investigation 3. Detectives 4. Music teachers 5. Murder 6. South Africa 7. 1970s 8. Police procedurals 9. Mysteries

LC 72000410

Gold Dagger Award for Best Crime Novel of the Year, 1971

When a young music teacher is murdered, Lieutenant Kramer and Sergeant Zondi attempt to solve the case.

"Mr. McClure is a new writer with a raffish vigor, humor and originality all within the very easy reach of his talent while so-called "serious" novels could hardly give you a sharper lesson in apartheid." —*Kirkus*

Originally published: London : Gollancz, 1971.

McConaghy, Charlotte

Migrations. Charlotte McConaghy. Flatiron Books, 2020. 240 p.
ISBN 9781250204028
1. Birds — Migration 2. Women environmentalists 3. Climate change 4. Ocean travel 5. Fishing boats 6. Literary fiction 7. Australian fiction

LC 2020001233

A woman who has dedicated her life to protecting the environment convinces a fishing captain and his salty crew to follow the world's last flock of Arctic terns on a migration of dark revelations.

"Some may find this darkly enrapturing work of ecofiction too heavily plotted, but all the violence, shock, and loss Franny navigates do aptly, and unnervingly, foreshadow a possible environmental apocalypse." —*Booklist*

Once there were wolves: a novel. Charlotte McConaghy. Flatiron Books, 2021. 272 p.
ISBN 9781250244147
1. Wildlife reintroduction 2. Wolves 3. Environmentalism 4. Rare and endangered animals 5. Women biologists 6. Scotland 7. Literary fiction 8. Australian fiction

LC 2021005981

When a farmer is mauled to death after she reintroduces 14 gray wolves into the remote Scottish Highlands, Inti Flynn knows where the town will lay blame and makes a reckless decision to protect them no matter what the cost.

"The bleak landscape is gorgeously rendered and made tense by its human and animal inhabitants, each capable of killing. Throughout, McConaghy avoids melodrama by maintaining a cool matter-of-factness. This is a stunner." —*Publishers Weekly*

McCorkle, Jill

★ **Hieroglyphics:** a novel. Jill McCorkle. Algonquin Books of Chapel Hill, 2020. 288 p.

ISBN 9781616209728

1. Husband and wife 2. Retirees 3. Parenthood 4. Family secrets 5. Memories 6. North Carolina 7. Mainstream fiction

LC 2019059067

Bonding over the mutual losses of their parents in childhood, a couple determined to leave a history for their own children respectively sift through family records and obsess over a possible childhood home before uncovering troubling memories.

"McCorkle testifies to the ageless nobility of human beings who want the next generation to do better. A deeply moving and insightful triumph." —*Booklist*

McCormack, Mike

★ **Solar** bones. Mike McCormack. Soho Press, 2017. 224 p.

ISBN 9781616958534

1. Memories 2. Introspection 3. Meaning (Psychology) 4. Ghosts 5. Civilization 6. Ireland 7. Literary fiction 8. Psychological fiction

LC 2017007611

ALA Notable Book, 2018; International IMPAC Dublin Literary Award, 2018; Longlisted for the Man Booker Prize, 2017

A man's spirit ruminates on his life and all the entwined events and circumstances in the vast systems of time and history that lead him to that exact moment.

"Deserving a readership far larger than Irish-literature devotees, this is a work of bold risks and luminous creativity." —*Booklist*

Originally published: Dublin : Tramp Press, 2016.

McCracken, Elizabeth

★ **Bowlaway:** a novel. Elizabeth McCracken. Ecco, 2019. 384 p.

ISBN 9780062862853

1. Eccentrics and eccentricities 2. Bowling alleys 3. Family lore 4. Family secrets 5. Love 6. Massachusetts 7. 20th century 8. Family sagas 9. Historical fiction

LC 2018025083

An unconventional New England family faces scandal, inheritance battles and questions of paternities as viewed through their three generations of owning and operating a candlepin bowling alley in the town of Salford, Massachusetts.

The **souvenir** museum: stories. Elizabeth McCracken. Ecco, 2021. 256 p.

ISBN 9780062971289

1. Families 2. Family relationships 3. Interpersonal relations 4. Atonement 5. Intergenerational relations 6. Short stories 7. Literary fiction

LC 2020040870

The award-winning author of presents a story collection that includes entries about a fear-testing Texas water park venture, a widower's puffin search and a villain actress's New Year celebration.

"Each story opens to reveal a whole life spent within the web of a family, chosen or not. Full of gems, this collection is a winner." —*Publishers Weekly*

McCreight, Kimberly

Friends like these. Kimberly McCreight. HarperCollins 2021. 400 p.

ISBN 9780063061569

1. College friends 2. Secrets 3. Reunions 4. Murder 5. Friendship 6. Catskill Mountains Region, New York 7. New York state 8. Psychological suspense

Five college friends meet up in the Catskills ten years after graduation bringing their shared past, betrayals and secrets with them.

"Whether describing the majestic beauty of the natural world or the heartbreaking nuances of neurological deficit, McGregor's luminous prose brings the world brilliantly to life." —*Booklist*

McCrumb, Sharyn

★ The **ballad** of Frankie Silver. Sharyn McCrumb. Dutton, 1998. 386 p. (Ballad novels, 5)

ISBN 9780525939696

1. Sheriffs 2. Death row prisoners 3. Pioneer women 4. Abused women 5. Women murderers 6. North Carolina 7. Tennessee 8. Historical mysteries 9. Parallel narratives 10. Southern fiction

LC 9724867

New York Times Notable Mysteries, 1998

As a convicted killer awaits execution in Tennessee, Sheriff Spencer Arrowood wonders if he arrested the right man years ago. Searching for answers, he discovers shocking parallels with a case more than a century old—the controversial hanging of a 19-year-old North Carolina woman. Suddenly he finds himself in a frantic struggle to stop history from repeating itself.

"By working in two time frames and alternating the narrative voice, McCrumb threads both stories into a single pattern, a dense and lovely but very dark design that illustrates the social hypocrisy of the legal system as much as the harshness of mountain justice—then and now." —*New York Times Book Review*

★ **If** ever I return, pretty Peggy-O. Sharyn McCrumb. Ballantine Books, 1991. 263 p. (Ballad novels, 1)

ISBN 9780345369062

1. Class reunions 2. Small town life 3. Women folk singers 4. Murder investigation 5. Sheriffs 6. Appalachian Region 7. Tennessee 8. Mysteries 9. Southern fiction 10. Adult books for young adults

Macavity Award for Best Mystery Novel, 1991

Sheriff Spencer Arrowood investigates the threatening messages being sent to Peggy Muryan, a famous folksinger of the 1960s, who has returned to her hometown of Hamelin, Tennessee, in search of peace and quiet.

"The author's strongly individualized characters give serious and intelligent thought to the ghosts raised by the reunionincluding the tangible spector of a murderer." —*New York Times Book Review*

Originally published: New York : Scribner, 1990.

McCullers, Carson

★ The **heart** is a lonely hunter. Carson McCullers. Houghton Mifflin, 2000. 359 p.

ISBN 9780618526413

1. Misfits (Persons) 2. Social isolation 3. Racism 4. Men who are deaf and mute 5. Interpersonal relations 6. Southern States 7. 1940s 8. Literary fiction 9. Books to movies 10. Modern classics

LC 40010298

A quiet, sensitive girl searches for beauty in a small, but damned Southern town.

Originally published: Boston: Houghton Mifflin, 1940.

The **member** of the wedding. Carson McCullers. Houghton Mifflin, 2004. 163 p.

ISBN 9780618492398

1. Social isolation 2. Twelve-year-old girls 3. Loneliness 4. Belonging 5. Siblings 6. Southern States 7. Georgia 8. Coming-of-age stories 9. Literary fiction 10. Southern Gothic

LC 46002022

Presents a drama about Frankie, a motherless twelve-year old girl who sees a solution to her unhappiness in the approaching wedding of her elder brother.

Reflections in a golden eye. Carson McCullers. Houghton Mifflin, 2000. 136 p.

ISBN 9780618084753

1. Husband and wife 2. Compulsive behavior 3. Love triangles 4. Military life 5. Men — Sexuality 6. Southern States 7. 1930s 8. Literary fiction 9. Southern Gothic 10. Southern fiction

LC 41002706

Transfered to an army base in the American South of the 1930's, Alison Langdon watches her husband, his commanding officer, and the officer's wife get caught up in a web of passion and jealousy.

McCullough, Colleen

The **first** man in Rome. Colleen McCullough. W. Morrow, 1990. 896 p. (Masters of Rome, 1)

ISBN 9780688093686

1. Marius, Gaius 2. Politics and culture 3. Political corruption 4. Ambition in men 5. Social classes 6. Families 7. Rome 8. Roman Republic (509-27 BCE) 9. Historical fiction 10. Australian fiction

LC 90037080

McCullough's epic tale of ancient Rome explores the power struggle between an ambitious military man and a man who lost his fortune to pleasure.

Sequel: The grass crown.

Includes end-paper maps.

An **indecent** obsession. Colleen McCullough. Harper and Row, 1981. 317 p.

ISBN 9780060149208

1. War — Psychological aspects 2. Duty 3. Jealousy 4. Nurses 5. People with mental illnesses 6. Pacific Area 7. Historical fiction 8. Psychological fiction 9. Australian fiction

LC 81047547

At the end of World War II, decorated sergeant Michael Wilson enters the mental war of a Pacific military hospital, which contains five remaining patients united by their devotion to their nurse, Honour Langtry

McDermid, Val

The **distant** echo. Val McDermid. St. Martin's Minotaur, 2003. 404 p; (Karen Pirie novels, 1)

ISBN 9780312301996

1. Cold cases (Criminal investigation) 2. College students 3. Murder suspects 4. Friendship 5. Police 6. Scotland 7. St. Andrews, Scotland 8. Mysteries 9. Adult books for young adults

LC 2003052902

The first novel in the bestselling Karen Pirie seriesThe award-winning Number One bestseller and Queen of crime fiction Val McDermid carves out a stunning psychological thriller.

"Individually, the characters are sensitively drawn. Collectively, they present the inscrutable face of closed-off communities so terrified of change they would kill for peace." —*New York Times Book Review*

How the dead speak: a Tony Hill and Carol Jordan novel. Val McDermid. Atlantic Monthly Press, 2019. 410 pages (Tony Hill and Carol Jordan mysteries, 11)

ISBN 9780802147615

1. Former policewomen 2. Prisoners 3. Corruption 4. Lawyers 5. Churchill, Clementine 6. England 7. Mysteries

LC 2019040561

Loan Stars Favourites, 2019

When skeletal remains are found on the site of an orphanage renovation, imprisoned psychological profiler Tony Hill painfully reunites with ex-DCI Carol Jordan to investigate the discovery of a victim who is believed to be behind bars.

"Series fans will be pleased to see Tony and Carol reunite after a long separation... McDermid is writing at the top of her game." —*Publishers Weekly*

A **place** of execution. Val McDermid. St. Martin's Minotaur, 2000. 403 p.

ISBN 9780312266325

1. Police 2. Missing children 3. Small town life 4. Women journalists 5. Murder 6. England 7. Mysteries 8. Books to movies

LC 59145

Anthony Award for Best Novel, 2001; Dilys Award, 2001; Los Angeles Times Book Prize for Mystery or Thriller, 2000; Macavity Award for Best Mystery Novel, 2001; New York Times Notable Mysteries, 2000

Police Inspector George Bennet, who investigated the never-solved disappearance of thirteen-year-old Alison Carter from her cloistered village decades ago, finds shattering new evidence, leading writer Catherine Heathcote to investigate further.

"When a 13-year-old English schoolgirl goes missing from her Derbyshire village in the winter of 1963, George Bennett, the police inspector in charge of the case, quickly realizes that the secrets of the child's life and possible death are locked in the collective mind of Scardale, an isolated hamlet of inbred families united by their common surnames and their hostility to strangers. Through Bennett's exhaustive efforts, the likely villain is caught and hangedor so it seems, until the story reaches 35 years into the future for its chilling resolution." —*New York Times Book Review*

★ **Still** life. Val McDermid. Atlantic Monthly Press, 2020. 436 pages; (Karen Pirie novels, 6)

ISBN 9780802157447

1. Women detectives 2. Cold cases (Criminal investigation) 3. Dead 4. Art forgeries 5. Murder investigation 6. Scotland 7. Mysteries 8. Police procedurals

LC 2020033628

DCI Karen Pirie is drawn into a murder investigation involving a historic disappearance, art forgery and secret identities, while dealing with the release of the man responsible for the death of the love of her life from prison.

"In the sixth in her 'Karen Pirie' series (after Broken Ground), McDermid rewards readers with a timely and cracking good mystery that keeps the pages flying. New readers are brought up to speed and will join longtime fans cheering on the well-drawn characters." —*Library Journal*

McDermott, Alice

After this. Alice McDermott. Farrar, Straus and Giroux, 2006. 288 p.

ISBN 9780374168094

1. Family relationships 2. Middle class families 3. Vietnam War, 1961-1975 4. Parent and child 5. Siblings 6. United States 7. 1960s 8. 1970s 9. Domestic fiction 10. Literary fiction 11. Adult books for young adults

LC 2006005598

Booklist Editors' Choice, 2006; New York Times Notable Book, 2006; Pulitzer Prize for Fiction finalist, 2007

A portrait of an American family during the middle decades of the twentieth century evokes the social, spiritual, and political turmoil of the era as seen through the experiences of a middle-class couple and their children.

"McDermott's easy authority with this material, combined with her clear-eyed sympathy for her characters, results in a moving, old-fashioned story about longing and loss and sorrow." —*New York Times*

At weddings and wakes. Alice McDermott. Farrar Straus Giroux, 1992. 213 p.

ISBN 9780374106744

1. Siblings 2. Irish American families 3. Catholic families 4. Family relationships 5. Long Island, New York 6. 1960s 7. Domestic fiction 8. Literary fiction

LC 91042070

Pulitzer Prize for Fiction finalist, 1993

The bittersweet, lovable, human story of an Irish-Catholic family on Long Island as seen through the eyes of two sisters and a brother.

"Set in Brooklyn during the sixties, this novel tells the story of an extended Irish-American family observed primarily through the eyes of the children, son and two daughters. Time. circles backwards and forwards around a variety of family rituals: holiday meals, vacations at the shore, the wedding of a favorite aunt. The poignant middle-aged romance that develops between the aunt, a former nun, and her suitor, a shy mailman, exacerbates already pronounced family tensions. As they listen to oft-repeated stories about poverty, disease, and early deaths, the children are solemn witnesses to the Irish immigrant experience in America." —*Library Journal*

★ **Charming** Billy. Alice McDermott. Farrar, Straus and Giroux, 1998. 280 p.

ISBN 9780374120801

1. Alcoholic men 2. Irish Americans 3. Unrequited love 4. Alcoholics 5. Death 6. New York City 7. Literary fiction

LC 9777089

ALA Notable Book, 1999; Booklist Editors' Choice, 1998; Library Journal Best Books, 1998; National Book Award for Fiction, 1998; New York Times Notable Book, 1998; Shortlisted for the International IMPAC Dublin Literary Award, 2000

When the late Billy Lynch's relatives and friends gather together to keep his memory alive, stories are woven and memories relived detailing his life in the close Irish-American community and the intricate feelings that resurface BT

"This novel opens at the wake of the debonair Billy Lynch—gifted talker, abandoned suitor, faithful husband, devout Catholic, raging alcoholic. It then ranges back and forth through dozens of family theories and anecdotes to answer the question of what did or didn't make him who he was. At once a love story, a portrait of Irish Catholic Queens, and an ode to an edenic postwar East Hampton, this novel honors the consequences of everyday decisions, both sacred and profane, burnishing them in the retelling to a high shine." —*The New Yorker*

Child of my heart. Alice McDermott. Farrar Straus Giroux, 2002. 242 p.

ISBN 9780374121235

1. Working class families 2. Babysitters 3. Beauty 4. Teenage girls 5. Senior men 6. New York (State) 7. Long Island, New York 8. 1960s 9. Coming-of-age stories 10. Literary fiction 11. Adult books for young adults

LC 2002069764

Booklist Editors' Choice, 2002; New York Times Notable Book, 2002

A teenage girl, raised on the east end of Long Island among the country estates of the rich, reflects on her understanding of the complexities and contradictions of human nature during a seemingly idyllic summer spent with her eight-year-old cousin Daisy.

"Child of My Heart is a golden and luminous memory retrieved by a narrator who has achieved a cool and slightly ironic distance from one of those summers in the late fifties or early sixties." —*Commonweal*

★ The **ninth** hour. Alice McDermott. Farrar, Straus and Giroux, 2017. 240 p.

ISBN 9780374280147

1. Irish Americans 2. Nuns 3. Family and suicide 4. Immigrants 5. Children of suicide victims 6. Brooklyn, New York City 7. New York City 8. 20th century 9. Literary fiction 10. Family sagas 11. Historical fiction

LC 2017011508

New York Times Notable Book, 2017; Library Journal Best Books, 2017; Booklist Editors' Choice, 2017; Kirkus Prize for Fiction finalist, 2017; Longlisted for the Andrew Carnegie Medal for Excellence in Fiction, 2018; National Book Critics Circle Award for Fiction finalist, 2017

A portrait of the Irish-American experience is presented through the story of an Irish immigrant's suicide and how it reverberates through innumerable lives in early twentieth-century Catholic Brooklyn.

"National Book Award winner McDermott (Someone) delivers an immense, brilliant novel about the limits of faith, the power of sacrifice, and the cost of forgiveness." —*Publishers Weekly*

Someone. Alice McDermott. Farrar, Straus and Giroux, 2013. 232 p.

ISBN 9780374281090

1. Irish Americans 2. Siblings 3. Self-discovery in women 4. Catholic women 5. Growing up 6. Brooklyn, New York City 7. Literary fiction 8. Psychological fiction

LC 2013014938

New York Times Notable Book, 2013; Shortlisted for the International Dublin Literary Award, 2015; National Book Critics Circle Award for Fiction finalist, 2013

Chronicles the ordinary life of a woman named Marie, from her childhood to old age, as she experiences the changing world of her Irish-American enclave in Brooklyn, in this novel that speaks of life as it is daily lived.

★ **That** night. Alice McDermott. Farrar, Straus, and Giroux, 1987. 183 p.

ISBN 9780385333306

1. Man-woman relationships 2. Suburban life 3. Violence 4. Teenagers 5. Long Island, New York 6. 1960s 7. Literary fiction 8. Books to movies

LC 84045765

National Book Award for Fiction finalist, 1987; Pulitzer Prize for Fiction finalist, 1988

"In spite of its brevity, That Night is a wonderfully unfettered, ample novel, one that celebrates voice, personality and feeling when so much fiction avoids those rewarding characteristics. Ms. McDermott has invested her novel with a strong sense of historical authority, rendering with sure clarity a time and place marked by both a cultural innocence and the premonition of its inevitable loss." —*New York Times Book Review*

McDevitt, Jack

The **engines** of God. Jack McDevitt. Ace Books, 1994. 419 p. (Priscilla Hutchins series, 1)

ISBN 9780441000777

1. Terraforming 2. Monuments 3. Women spaceship captains 4. Space flight 5. Aliens (Non-humanoid) 6. Hard science fiction 7. Science fiction thrillers 8. Adult books for young adults

LC 94007131

An unknown race called the Monument-Makers creates a stunning array of gorgeous statues, scattering them throughout the galaxy and encoding them with strange inscriptions that hold the key to the survival of humankind.

McDonald, Christina

Behind every lie. Christina McDonald. Gallery Books, 2020. 320 pages

ISBN 9781501184031

1. Mothers and daughters 2. Mothers — Death 3. Murder suspects 4. Lightning strike victims 5. Amnesia 6. United States 7. Seattle, Washington 8. Multiple perspectives 9. Thrillers and suspense

Awakening in the hospital with no memory at the same time her mother is found murdered, Eva visits her childhood home for answers, only to find herself targeted by a killer who guards dangerous secrets.

"Readers who enjoy character-driven thrillers will be pleased." —*Publishers Weekly*

McDonald, Ian

New moon. Ian McDonald. Tor, 2016. 428 p. (Luna novels (Ian McDonald), 1)

ISBN 9780765375513

1. Siblings 2. Mines and mineral resources 3. Greed 4. Heirs and heiresses 5. Competition 6. Moon 7. Science fiction 8. Cyberpunk 9. Financial thrillers

When her corporation, Corta Helio, which controls the Moon's Helium-3 industry, is confronted by the many enemies she made during her meteoric rise, Adriana Corta and her five children must navigate a world of corporate warfare to save the family empire from those who want to destroy it.

McDowell, Christina

The **cave** dwellers: a novel. Christina McDowell. 2021. 320 p.

ISBN 9781982132781

1. Upper class 2. Socialites 3. Murder 4. Families 5. Privilege (Social psychology) 6. Washington, D.C. 7. Psychological fiction 8. Satirical fiction

LC 2020027812

Only socializing within their inner circle, and living free of consequences, Washington, D.C.'s elite find everything about their legacy called into question when one of their own is held hostage and brutally murdered.

"Through blunt caricatures and sharp characterizations, McDowell archly demonstrates her disdain for the superficiality of such an existence and combines social satire with moral outrage to offer a masterfully crafted, absorbing read that can simply entertain on one level and provoke reasoned discourse on another." —*Booklist*

Includes bibliographical references.

McElroy, Alex

The **Atmospherians**. Alex McElroy. Atria Books, 2021. 304 p.

ISBN 9781982158309

1. Women entrepreneurs 2. Influencers 3. Humiliation 4. Reputation 5. Childhood friends 6. Satirical fiction

When her oldest childhood friend hatches a plan for her to restore her reputation, hilarity ensues as former social media sensation Sasha Marcus becomes the resident female leader of a group of washed up, desperate men who need to be rid of their toxic masculinity.

"Exploring the complexities of friendship, a culture of toxic masculinity, and the perils of constantly being online, this is an ambitious, timely, and dazzling debut." —*Booklist*

McEwan, Ian

★ **Amsterdam**. Ian McEwan. Nan A. Talese/Doubleday, 1999. 193 p. ISBN 9780385494236

1. Former lovers — Death 2. Sex scandals 3. Ambition in men 4. Newspaper editors 5. Composers 6. Amsterdam, Netherlands 7. London, England 8. Satirical fiction 9. Psychological fiction 10. Literary fiction

LC 9841401

Booker Prize, 1998; New York Times Notable Book, 1999

Two old friends, Clive Linley and Vernon Halliday, both former lovers of of the late Molly Lane, meet to pay their last respects and make a pact that will have unforeseen consequences

★ **Atonement**: a novel. Ian McEwan. Nan A. Talese, Doubleday, 2002. 351 p.

ISBN 9780385503952

1. Sisters 2. Guilt in women 3. Rich families 4. Shame 5. Thirteen-year-old girls 6. England 7. 1930s 8. Psychological fiction 9. Historical fiction 10. Literary fiction 11. Adult books for young adults

LC 2001044291

Commonwealth Writers' Prize, South Asia and Europe: Best Book, 2002; Los Angeles Times Book Prize for Fiction, 2002; National Book Critics Circle Award for Fiction, 2002; ALA Notable Book, 2003; Shortlisted for the Booker-McConnell Prize, 2001

In 1935 England, thirteen-year-old Briony Tallis witnesses an event involving her sister Cecilia and her childhood friend Robbie Turner, and she becomes the victim of her own imagination, which leads her on a lifelong search for truth and absolution.

"This is a work of astonishing depth and humanity.... The upper-class milieu, the sense of place and time, are rendered with an exactitude worthy of Elizabeth Bowen.... Mr McEwan has achieved the difficult task of combining literary sophistication with moral gravity." —*The Economist*

Originally published: London: Jonathan Cape, 2001.

Black dogs. Ian McEwan. Nan A. Talese, Doubleday, 1992. 149 p. ISBN 9780385425414

1. Husband and wife 2. Parents-in-law 3. Berlin Wall — Dismantling, 1989 4. Orphans 5. Communism 6. England 7. Psychological fiction 8. Literary fiction

LC 92007418

Shortlisted for the Booker-McConnell Prize, 1992

Writing a memoir of his parents-in-law, Jeremy describes how June and Bernhard Iremaine met, fell in love, and committed themselves to the Communist party, in a narrative that spans from post-World War II to the present.

"This novel is compassionate without resorting to sentimentality, clever without ever losing its honesty, an undisguised novel of ideas which is also Ian McEwan's most human work." —*Times Literary Supplement*

The **child** in time. Ian McEwan. Anchor Books, 1999. 263 p. ISBN 9780385497527

1. Kidnapping 2. Missing children 3. Grief in men 4. Loss (Psychology) 5. Guilt 6. England 7. Psychological fiction 8. Literary fiction

LC 87008603

Whitbread Book Award for Novel, 1987

The abduction of his only child destroys Stephen Lewis' marriage and painfully forces him to look back on his own childhood.

"Many of the plot turns in the novel may seem improbable and even fanciful, but the feelings expressed by the characters and their sense of time (running up, running down and running out) are, without exception, genuine.... [This is an] astonishing book." —*Time*

Originally published: London : Cape, 1987.

★ **On** Chesil Beach. Ian McEwan. Nan A. Talese, Doubleday, 2007. 176 p.
ISBN 9780385522403
1. Newlyweds 2. Intimacy (Psychology) 3. Musicians 4. Women musicians 5. Man-woman relationships 6. England 7. London, England 8. 1960s 9. 20th century 10. Love stories 11. Literary fiction 12. Books to movies

LC 2006100720

ALA Notable Book, 2008; Booklist Editors' Choice, 2007; British Book Award for Book of the Year, 2008; New York Times Notable Book, 2007; Shortlisted for the Man Booker Prize, 2007

On their wedding day, a young couple—Florence, daughter of an Oxford academic and a successful businessman, and Edward, an earnest history student with little experience of women—looks forward to the future while worrying about their upcoming wedding night

Title adapted into a film in 2017.

First published: London : Jonathan Cape, 2007.

Solar: a novel. Ian McEwan. Nan A. Talese/Doubleday, 2010. 287 p.
ISBN 9780385533416
1. Physicists 2. Nobel Prize winners 3. Egotism in men 4. Selfishness in men 5. Intellectual property 6. Arctic regions 7. New Mexico 8. Satirical fiction 9. Literary fiction

LC 2009046508

New York Times Notable Book, 2010

Nobel Prize-winning scientist Michael Beard is coasting through his professional life, making no real contribution since he won his award, while his fifth marriage is in danger due to his, and his wife's, infidelities; but he gets a chance at redemption when he is called on to save humanity from environmental disaster.

McFadden, Bernice L.

The **Book** of Harlan. Bernice L. McFadden. Akashic, 2016. 400 p.
ISBN 9781617754456
1. African Americans 2. Prisoners of war 3. Nazis 4. Musicians 5. Concentration camps 6. Europe 7. Second World War era (1939-1945) 8. Historical fiction 9. Adult books for young adults
Booklist Editors' Choice: Adult Books for Young Adults, 2016

In WWII, two African American musicians are captured by the Nazis in Paris and imprisoned at the Buchenwald concentration camp.

"Playing with themes of divine justice and the suffering of the righteous, McFadden presents a remarkably crisp portrait of one average mans extraordinary bravery in the face of pure evil." —*Booklist*

McFarland, Jeni

The **house** of deep water. Jeni McFarland. Penguin Group USA 2020. 352 p.
ISBN 9780525542353
1. Divorced women 2. Homecomings 3. Small towns 4. Multiracial women 5. Middle class 6. Michigan 7. Domestic fiction 8. Literary fiction 9. African American fiction

LC 2019049488

River Bend, Michigan, is the kind of small town most can't imagine leaving, but three women couldn't wait to escape. When each must return—Linda Williams, never sure what she wants; her mother, Paula, always too sure; and Beth DeWitt, one of River Bend's only black daughters, now a mother of two who'd planned to raise her own children anywhere else—their paths collide under Beth's father's roof. As one town struggles to contain all of their love affairs and secrets, a local scandal forces Beth to confront her own devastating past. Filled with the voices of mothers and daughters, husbands, lovers, and fathers, The House of Deep Water explores motherhood, trauma, love, loss, and new beginnings found in a most unlikely place: home.

"She deftly weaves in issues of race and consent. Perfect for those who like books about family dysfunction, this would also make a great book discussion selection." —*Booklist*

McFarlane, Mhairi

Don't you forget about me. Mhairi McFarlane. William Morrow, 2019. 432 p.
ISBN 9780062958464
1. First loves 2. Reunions 3. Women — Interpersonal relations 4. Lost love 5. Coping in women 6. Romantic comedies 7. Relationship fiction
LibraryReads Favorites, 2019

Fired and dumped on the same night, Georgina takes a new job before realizing that her boss is her first love, and does not recognize her.

If I never met you: a novel. Mhairi McFarlane. William Morrow & Co, 2020. 412 p.
ISBN 9780062958501
1. Lawyers 2. Women lawyers 3. Revenge 4. Breaking up (Interpersonal relations) 5. Interracial romance 6. Manchester, England 7. Contemporary romances 8. Romantic comedies
LibraryReads Favorites, 2020

Humiliated when her long-time boyfriend breaks up with her amid rumors of an illicit pregnancy, Laurie agrees to pretend she is seriously dating the office playboy, who needs a steady girlfriend to protect his professional integrity.

"McFarlane's gift is writing romantic comedy that depicts a recognizable world—in this case, the culturally diverse world of young professionals in Manchester, England—without dimming the luster of shining moments of humor, love, and connection. McFarlane has created a very funny, very romantic story with deep emotional impact." —*Kirkus*

Originally published in Great Britain, 2019.

McGhee, Alison

The **opposite** of fate. Alison McGhee. Houghton Mifflin Harcourt, 2020. 256 p.
ISBN 9781328518439
1. Rape victims 2. Pregnancy 3. Missing children 4. Options, alternatives, choices 5. Autonomy 6. New York (State) 7. Relationship fiction 8. Adult books for young adults

Rendered comatose and pregnant by a violent attack, a young woman emerges from her long state of unresponsiveness, only to find herself reckoning with the consequences of decisions that were made about her body without her consent.

"Like its comparable titles, The Opposite of Fate is a prime book-group choice." —*Booklist*

McGregor, Jon

Lean fall stand. Jon McGregor. Random House, 2021. 288 p.
ISBN 9781646220991

1. Scientific expeditions 2. Polar expeditions 3. Geological research 4. Traumatic brain-injury 5. Blame 6. Antarctica 7. Chile

After a catastrophic Antarctic expedition, Robert Wright is so distressed he becomes unable to communicate the truth and must learn a whole new way to be in the world, in a new novel from the award-winning author of Reservoir 13.

"Lyrical and terse, funny and tragic-a marvelous addition to the McGregor canon." —*Kirkus*

The **reservoir** tapes. Jon McGregor. Catapult, 2018. 176 p. (Reservoir novels, 2)
ISBN 9781936787913
1. Villages 2. Interviewing 3. Missing teenage girls 4. Memories 5. Small town life 6. England 7. Literary fiction 8. Adult books for young adults
Booklist Editors' Choice, 2018

Returns readers to the territory of the award-winning author's Reservoir 13, tracing the efforts of an interviewer who collects stories throughout a secretive English village to piece together the fate of a missing girl.

"McGregor demonstrates an extraordinary ability to create complex, multidimensional characters in only a few spare sentences. He is also a master of mood, investing his stories with an air of the ominous while proving also to be a superb stylist." —*Booklist*

McGuane, Thomas

★ **Cloudbursts:** collected and new stories. Thomas McGuane. Knopf, 2018. 512 p.
ISBN 9780385350211
1. Wilderness areas 2. Literary fiction 3. Short stories
LC 2017039288
Booklist Editors' Choice, 2018

An abundant collection of 45 short stories by the acclaimed author of Crow Fair depicts protagonists on the fringes of society whose twisted pasts complicate their future prospects, in a volume set in the seedy corners of Key West, the remote shores of the Bahamas and McGuane's hallmark Big Sky country.

"McGuane is a master, choosing his words with a lapidary's precision and setting them in sentences that burn brightly, finishing his stories with epiphanies to treasure." —*Booklist*

Crow fair: stories. Thomas McGuane. Alfred A. Knopf, 2015. 272 p.
ISBN 9780385350198
1. Family relationships 2. Friendship 3. Interpersonal relations 4. Montana 5. Mainstream fiction 6. Short stories
LC 2014018360

A collection of stories set in Big Sky country explores the ties of family and friendship and the many challenges and complications of these relationships.

"The conflicts throughout this book are age-old—indeed, the title story evokes 'Oedipus'—but McGuane's clean writing and psychological acuity enliven them all. A slyly cutting batch of tales." —*Kirkus*

McGuire, Ian

The **abstainer:** a novel. Ian McGuire. Random House, 2020. 272 p.
ISBN 9780593133873
1. Irish American men 2. Secret societies 3. Civil War veterans 4. Revenge 5. Secrets 6. Manchester, England 7. England 8. 1860s 9. Victorian era (1837-1901) 10. Historical thrillers
LC 2019040115

An Irish-American veteran of the Civil War, Stephan Doyle, return to England where he joins a secret society intent on ending British rule in Ireland by any means necessary and must choose sides out of when his nephew arrives on his doorstep from America, imperiling his new life.

"This tightly wound historical tale is full of the grit and grime of industrial England that is bleeding Ireland dry and setting the stage for the rebellion of the next century. More a noir thriller than historical fiction, it is driven by a thirst for retribution and freedom." —*Library Journal*

McGuire, Seanan

★ **Beneath** the sugar sky. Seanan McGuire. Tor, 2018. 160 p. (Wayward children, 3)
ISBN 9780765393586
1. Interdimensional travel 2. Boarding schools 3. Prophecies 4. Magic 5. Boarding school students 6. Fantasy fiction 7. Gateway fantasy 8. Adult books for young adults
LibraryReads Favorites, 2018

Beneath the Sugar Sky returns to Eleanor West's Home for Wayward Children. At this magical boarding school, children who have experienced fantasy adventures are reintroduced to the "real" world. Sumi died years before her prophesied daughter Rini could be born. Rini was born anyway, and now she's trying to bring her mother back from a world without magic.

Chimes at midnight: an October Daye novel. Seanan McGuire. DAW Books, 2013. 357 p. (October Daye novels, 7)
ISBN 9780756408145
1. Murder investigation 2. Poisoning 3. Fairies 4. Supernatural 5. Magic 6. San Francisco, California 7. Urban fantasy

When she is exiled by the Queen of the Mists, the only way that Toby Daye can escape the sentence is to locate the legendary Library of the Stars, find the rightful heir to the Kingdom of Mists, and overthrow the Queen.

★ **Down** among the sticks and bones. Seanan McGuire. Tor, 2017. 187 pages; (Wayward children, 2)
ISBN 9780765392039
1. Interdimensional travel 2. Boarding schools 3. Twin sisters 4. Magic 5. Teenage girls 6. Fantasy fiction 7. Gateway fantasy 8. Adult books for young adults
Alex Award, 2018; Amelia Bloomer List, 2018; LibraryReads Favorites, 2017; Library Journal Best Books, 2017; Rainbow List, 2018; RUSA Reading List, 2018; School Library Journal Best Books: Best Adult Books 4 Teens, 2017

Shares the story of Jack and Jill before they tumbled into Eleanor West's Home for Wayward Children, relating their experiences in a childhood world of monsters, mad scientists and fateful choices.

"Beautifully crafted and smartly written, this fairy-tale novella is everything that speculative fiction readers look for: fantastical worlds, diverse characters, and prose that hits home with its emotional truths." —*Library Journal*
Sequel to: Every heart a doorway.

★ **Every** heart a doorway. Seanan McGuire. Tor, 2016. 160 p. (Wayward children, 1)
ISBN 9780765385505
1. Interdimensional travel 2. Boarding schools 3. Imaginary places 4. Magic 5. Murder 6. Fantasy fiction 7. Gateway fantasy 8. Adult books for young adults
Alex Award, 2017; LibraryReads Favorites, 2016; Library Journal Best Books, 2016; Rainbow List, 2017

Children have always disappeared from Eleanor West's Home for Wayward Children under the right conditions; slipping through the shadows under a bed or at the back of a wardrobe, tumbling down rabbit holes and into old wells, and emerging somewhere...else. But magical lands have little need for used-up miracle children. Nancy tumbled once, but now she's back. The things she's experienced...they change a person. The children under Miss West's care understand all too well. And each of them is seeking a way back to their own fantasy world. But Nancy's arrival marks a change at the Home. There's a darkness just around each corner, and when tragedy strikes, it's up to Nancy and her new-found schoolmates to get to the heart of the matter. No matter the cost.

★ **In** an absent dream. Seanan McGuire. Tor, 2019. 176 p. (Wayward children, 4)
ISBN 9780765399298
1. Nonconformists 2. Parallel universes 3. Deals 4. Consequences 5. Imaginary places 6. Gateway fantasy 7. Fantasy fiction 8. Adult books for young adults
LC 2018044548
Traces the origin story of studious Lundy, who discovers a world founded on logic, reason and riddles before making a fateful bargain.
A Tom Doherty Associates Book.

★ **Middlegame**. Seanan McGuire. Tor, 2019. 528 p.
ISBN 9781250195524
1. Twins 2. Alchemy 3. Magic 4. Time travel 5. Mathematics 6. Fantasy fiction 7. Adult books for young adults
Alex Award, 2020; Locus Award for Fantasy Novel, 2020
In an alternate-reality world under the shadow of a magical government bent on transmuting the fabric of reality, two alchemical twins, one skilled with language and the other with math, become catalysts in their creator's grab for power.
"Shifts and alterations in timelines demand close attention from readers, but McGuire's rigorous plotting pulls everything together by the end. This is a fascinating novel by an author of consummate skill." —*Publishers Weekly*

McHugh, Laura

What's done in darkness: a novel. Laura McHugh. Random House, 2021. 256 p.
ISBN 9780399590313
1. Former captives 2. Teenage kidnapping victims 3. Courage in women 4. Determination in women 5. Homecomings 6. Ozark Mountains 7. First person narratives 8. Thrillers and suspense 9. Southern Gothic
LC 2020036215
Struggling to keep her past buried, 22-year-old Sarabeth, who was abducted as a teenager, is dragged back by to the last place she wants to go where she must face her estranged family and her darkest fears to help a detective solve a similar case.
"As incredible as the plot's harrowing twists may seem, any number of true crime accounts testify otherwise. Fortunately, there's a light amid all this darkness—courageous, determined Sarah. Readers will hope to encounter her again." —*Publishers Weekly*

The **wolf** wants in: a novel. Laura McHugh. Spiegel & Grau, 2019. 260 pages
ISBN 9780399590283
1. Small towns 2. Brothers — Death 3. Murder investigation 4. Sisters 5. Teenage girls 6. Kansas 7. Thrillers and suspense
A woman confronts a dark secret about her brother's death while a teen becomes increasingly desperate to escape their opioid-ravaged community.

McIlvanney, William

The **dark** remains: Laidlaw's first case. . World Noir, 2021. 208 p. (Jack Laidlaw, Prequel)

ISBN 9781609457198
1. Laidlaw, Jack (Fictitious character) 2. Police 3. Detectives 4. Murder 5. Gangs 6. Glasgow (Scotland) 7. Mysteries
LC Bl2021015682
In this searing crime prequel, two crime-writing legends team up for the first ever case of D.I. Laidlaw, Glasgow's original gritty detective who is standing in the midst of gangs, organized crime bosses, crooked politicians, corrupt police and innocent battlers caught in the crossfire.
"Rankin has finished a fourth Laidlaw novel, working from a handwritten manuscript found by McIlvanney's widow, after the writer's death.... McIlvanney's gift for evoking the bruised humanity in Glasgow's underclass will remind readers not only of Rankin and his Scottish contemporaries, but also of Englishman John Harvey and, across the pond, Michael Connelly." —*Booklist*

McKenzie, Alecia

A **million** aunties. Alecia McKenzie. Akashic Books, 2020. 160 p.
ISBN 9781617758928
1. Artists 2. Painters 3. Widowers 4. Jamaican Americans 5. Life change events 6. Jamaica 7. New York City 8. Literary fiction 9. Multiple perspectives
After a personal tragedy upends his world, American-born artist Chris travels to his mother's homeland in the Caribbean hoping to find some peace and tranquility. He plans to spend his time painting in solitude and coming to terms with his recent loss and his fractured relationship with his father. Instead, he discovers a new extended and complicated 'family,' with their own startling stories, including a love triangle. The people he meets help him to heal, even as he supports them in unexpected ways, through his art.
"Racial identity, nonfamilial relationships, and the restorative nature of art are all explored as McKenzie considers the possibility of regeneration of the human spirit even as we grapple with the tragedies of lost loves and changing worlds. McKenzie successfully integrates various speech patterns in Caribbean patois and a mixture of English and French as she takes readers on a hopeful journey across continents." —*Booklist*

McKenzie, Elizabeth

The **portable** Veblen. Elizabeth McKenzie. Penguin Press, 2015. 304 p.
ISBN 9781594206856
1. Engaged persons 2. Family relationships 3. Dysfunctional families 4. Values 5. Ambition 6. Palo Alto, California 7. Literary fiction 8. Satirical fiction 9. Adult books for young adults
Shortlisted for the Baileys Women's Prize for Fiction, 2016
An aimless amateur translator struggling under the thumb of an oppressive parent and an ambitious medical researcher from a hippie family endure tests to their bond and question their priorities as their wedding approaches.
"McKenzie's idiosyncratic love story scampers along on a wonderfully zig-zaggy path, dashing and darting in delightfully unexpected directions as it progresses toward its satisfying end and scattering tasty literary passages like nuts along the way." —*Kirkus*

McKevett, G. A.

A **few** drops of bitters. G. A. McKevett. Kensington Pub Corp, 2021. 304 p. (Savannah Reid mysteries, 26)
ISBN 9781496720160
1. Women private investigators 2. Foster children 3. Celebrities 4. Overweight women 5. Birthday parties 6. California 7. Cozy mysteries 8. Gentle reads

After the jet-setting, brain surgeon husband of her veterinarian friend dies after making a champagne toast at a star-studded party, plus-sized private eye Savannah Reid investigates in the latest novel of the series following And the Killer Is?

"Red herrings abound, and McKevett smoothly blends the sleuthing with serious social issues. Series fans and newcomers alike will enjoy spending time with Savannah and friends." —*Publishers Weekly*

Murder at Mabel's motel. G. A. McKevett. Kensington Pub Corp, 2021. 288 p. (Granny Reid mysteries, 3)
ISBN 9781496729064
1. Women amateur detectives 2. Gangs 3. Murder 4. Senior women 5. Murder investigation 6. Georgia 7. 1980s 8. Cozy mysteries 9. Gentle reads

When a notorious gang leader is found poisoned in small-town McGill, Georgia, Stella "Granny" Reid investigates a flood of suspects who reveal dark secrets about the victim and several respected locals.

"McKevett poignantly evokes how difficult and all-consuming raising seven children can be, but in Stella she has created a woman strong and loving enough to do it." —*Publishers Weekly*

Murder in the corn maze. G. A. McKevett. Kensington Pub Corp 2019. 304 p. (Granny Reid mysteries, 2)
ISBN 9781496716293
1. Women amateur detectives 2. Grandchildren 3. Halloween 4. Murder investigation 5. Senior women 6. Georgia 7. Cozy mysteries 8. Gentle reads

During Halloween festivities, Granny Reid and her granddaughter make it to the center of a corn maze on Judge Patterson's antebellum mansion where they discover a human skull.

Chronicles McKevett's character Savannah Reid as a 12-year-old child being raised by her amateur sleuth grandmother, Stella Reid.

McKinlay, Jenn

The **good** ones. Jenn McKinlay. Berkley Pub Group, 2019. 304 p. (Happily ever after (Jenn McKinlay), 1)
ISBN 9780451492432
1. Architects 2. Women college teachers 3. Single fathers 4. Renovation (Architecture) 5. Bookstores 6. North Carolina 7. Contemporary romances 8. Adult books for young adults

Hired by Maisy Kelly to convert her late aunt's Victorian house into a romance bookstore, architect and single father Ryder Copeland finds his plans of leaving this small town behind thwarted by his attraction to this shy, curly haired professor.

Killer research. Jenn McKinlay. Berkley Prime Crime, 2021. 304 p. (Library lover's mysteries, 12)
ISBN 9780593101773
1. Women librarians 2. Libraries 3. Women amateur detectives 4. Murder 5. Murder investigation 6. Connecticut 7. Cozy mysteries 8. Gentle reads

LC 2021023867

When she finds the body of a man in her trunk whom she dated 40 years ago, librarian and mayoral candidate Ms. Cole refuses to go down without a fight and asks Lindsay, Sully, and the rest of the crafternoon pals to figure out who is trying to frame her.

"Plenty of well-defined characters add charm and bite to a thorny mystery." —*Kirkus*

McKinney, Chris

Midnight, Water City. Chris McKinney. Soho Crime, 2021. 312 pages (Water City novels, 1)

ISBN 9781641292405
1. Near future 2. Underwater cities 3. High technology 4. Conspiracies 5. Intrigue 6. 22nd century 7. Science fiction mysteries 8. Science fiction 9. First person narratives

LC 2020055355

Through a future of underwater cities, floating suburbs, skin-dyed teenagers, and a wealth gap that has outlived a near-apocalypse, McKinney's cinematic novel is the perfect blend of dark cyberpunk and thrilling detective procedural, all while posing the ultimate question of what we are willing to sacrifice to engineer the world we want.

"Set In the 22nd century, this exceptional mystery-SF hybrid from McKinney (The Tattoo), a trilogy kickoff, boasts impressive worldbuilding and a classic morally compromised lead thrust into a high-stakes homicide investigation." —*Publishers Weekly*

McKinney-Whetstone, Diane

Leaving Cecil Street: a novel. Diane McKinney-Whetstone. William Morrow, 2004. 304 p.
ISBN 9780688163853
1. African American community life 2. Teenage pregnancy 3. Abortion 4. African American teenage girls 5. African American musicians 6. Pennsylvania 7. Philadelphia, Pennsylvania 8. 1960s 9. Historical fiction 10. Domestic fiction 11. African American fiction 12. Adult books for young adults

LC 2003055845

BCALA Literary Award for Fiction, 2005

Surrounded by block parties that liven up the summer nights of their 1969 Philadelphia home, Joe and Louise find their marriage falling apart, a situation that is complicated by the tragic illegal abortion of their daughter's best friend.

"Cecil Street is a quiet, tree-lined haven in West Philadelphia, a place where everyone knows everyone else, a place removed from the turmoil and violence of the late 1960s. Yet the residents of Cecil Street have their problems. Joe and Louise's marriage is strained; Johnetta's sexy niece has arrived, ripe for trouble; and teenaged Shay tries to help best friend Neet deal with an unwanted pregnancy. When Neet's abortion goes tragically wrong, everyone on the street must rally around her, while Joe, Louise, and Neet's mother, Alberta, discover how their pasts have now drawn them together. McKinney-Whetstone's portrayal of African American family life is sensitive and compassionate, with characters who love, work, live, and die without veering into soap opera." —*Library Journal*

McKinty, Adrian

★ The **chain**. Adrian McKinty. Mulholland Books, 2019. 357 p.
ISBN 9780316531269
1. Kidnapping 2. Parent and child 3. Mothers of kidnapping victims 4. Death threats 5. Consequences 6. Massachusetts 7. Thrillers and suspense
Booklist Editors' Choice, 2019; Macavity Award for Best Mystery Novel, 2020; Theakston Old Peculier Crime Novel of the Year Award, 2020; Thriller Award for Best Novel, 2020

A parent receives a panicked phone call from a stranger who reveals that both of their children have been kidnapped by someone who demands that they abduct another child to prevent the murders of their own.

In the morning I'll be gone: a Detective Sean Duffy novel. By Adrian McKinty. Seventh Street Books, 2014. 315 p. (Sean Duffy novels, 3)
ISBN 9781616148775
1. Detectives 2. Revenge 3. Police 4. Veterans 5. Catholic men 6. Belfast, Northern Ireland 7. Northern Ireland 8. 1980s 9. Police procedurals

LC 2013037740

Ned Kelly Award for Best Novel, 2014

Recruited by MI5 to hunt down Dermot McCann, an IRA master bomber who has escaped from Maze Prison, Sean Duffy, a conflicted Catholic cop, must solve another mystery first in order to discover Dermot's whereabouts before Mrs. Thatcher's keynote speech.

"The Troubles' first two novels were exceptionally smart police procedurals, and McKinty applies the same expertise here, contrasting a classic locked-room puzzle with the gritty, violent Belfast backdrop." —*Booklist*

McLain, Paula

Circling the sun. Paula McLain. Random House, 2015. 368 p.
ISBN 9780345534187
1. Markham, Beryl 2. Women pilots 3. Independence in women 4. British in Africa 5. Love triangles 6. Horse breeders 7. Kenya 8. East Africa 9. 1920s 10. Historical fiction 11. Biographical fiction
LibraryReads Favorites, 2015

Raised by her father and the Kipsigis tribe in 1920s Kenya, Beryl endures painful losses before entering a passionate love triangle and discovering her unconventional true calling.

"McLain's...latest showcases her immersive command of setting and character, fictionalizing the exploits of real-life aviator and author Beryl Markham in British Kenya in the early 20th century.... Markham's true life was incredibly adventurous, and it's easy for readers to identify with this woman who refused to be pigeonholed by her gender." —*Publishers Weekly*

Map on endpapers.

Love and ruin. Paula McLain. Ballantine Books, 2018. 352 p.
ISBN 9781101967386
1. Gellhorn, Martha 2. Women journalists 3. War correspondents 4. Independence in women 5. Authors 6. Husband and wife 7. Spain 8. Madrid, Spain 9. 1930s 10. 1940s 11. Biographical fiction 12. Historical fiction

LC Bl2018020577

LibraryReads Favorites, 2018

The author of The Paris Wife returns to her fan-favorite subject, Ernest Hemingway, in a tale set on the eve of World War II that is inspired by his passionate, stormy marriage to a fiercely independent, ambitious young Martha Gellhorn, who would become one of the 20th century's leading war correspondents.

The **Paris** wife: a novel. Paula McLain. Ballantine Books, 2011. Xii, 320 p.
ISBN 9780345521309
1. Hemingway, Ernest 2. Authors' spouses 3. Authors, American 4. Husband and wife 5. Americans in France 6. Expatriate authors 7. Paris, France 8. 1920s 9. Biographical fiction 10. Historical fiction
LC 2010037878

Goodreads Choice Award, 2011

Meeting through mutual friends in Chicago, Hadley is intrigued by brash "beautiful boy" Ernest Hemingway, and after a brief courtship and small wedding, they take off for Paris, where Hadley makes a convincing transformation from an overprotected child to a game and brave young woman who puts up with impoverished living conditions and shattering loneliness to prop up her husband's career.

McLain's vivid, clear-voiced novel is a conjecture, an act of imaginary autobiography on the part of the author. Yet her biographical and geographical research is so deep, and her empathy for the real Hadley Richardson so forthright (without being intrusively femme partisan), that the account reads as very real indeed. Big things happen: Hadley is there as Hemingway meets Gertrude Stein and Scott Fitzgerald, as he writes

The Sun Also Rises, as he falls in love with bullfighting. But a thousand less glamorous, more quotidian things happen too, as Hadley tries to find a way to live her own life (she's a fine pianist) and support her moody husband, and keep up with hard-drinking company, and run a household in a country not her own. By making the ordinary come to life, McLain has written a beautiful portrait of being in Paris in the glittering 1920s as a wife and one's own woman. Entertainment Weekly.

Originally published: 2011.

★ **When** the stars go dark: a novel. Paula McLain. Ballantine Books, 2021. 336 p.
ISBN 9780593237892
1. Women detectives 2. Missing teenage girls 3. Kidnapping victims 4. Loss (Psychology) 5. Psychic trauma 6. Northern California 7. California 8. Mysteries 9. Literary fiction
LC 2020034008

Loan Stars Favourites, 2021

Retreating to her childhood foster home in the wake of a tragedy, a veteran missing-persons detective becomes entwined in the search for a local teen whose disappearance eerily resembles an unsolved case from the detective's past.

"Most memorable of all are the girls, past and present, who emerge here not as convenient victims but as vulnerable, believable characters. A muted yet thrilling multilayered mystery enriched by keen psychological and emotional insight." —*Kirkus*

Mclaughlin, Danielle

The **art** of falling. Danielle Mclaughlin. Random House, 2021. 384 p.
ISBN 9780812998443
1. Sculptors 2. Betrayal 3. Extramarital affairs 4. Art — Exhibitions 5. Women art curators 6. Literary fiction

A woman finds her precarious marriage and career thrown into turmoil by a reckoning with an old friend and an enigmatic woman's claim that she is the true creator of a famous work of art.

"The art-world mystery is nicely balanced with family and interpersonal drama, and the climactic ending is authentic and believable." —*Booklist*

McLaughlin, Emma

The **nanny** diaries: a novel. Emma McLaughlin and Nicola Kraus. St. Martin's Press, 2002. 305 p.
ISBN 9780312278588
1. Rich people 2. Nannies 3. Upper class 4. Four-year-old boys 5. Women college students 6. Manhattan, New York City 7. Park Avenue, New York City 8. Satirical fiction 9. Chick lit 10. Books to movies 11. Adult books for young adults
LC 2001048652

Romantic Times Reviewers' Choice Award, 2002

A satirical glimpse into Manhattan's upper class follows Nanny, a struggling NYU student who takes a position caring for the son of the rich and glamorous X family, as she learns how to juggle a vast array of tasks so that a Park Avenue wife never has to lift a well-manicured finger.

"This is a diabolically funny New York story.... [Nanny] is a vastly entertaining narrator and impromptu social critic.... Not surprisingly, The Nanny Diaries fades slightly when the X's are out of sight, despite the boyfriend and family matters that are meant to fill out Nanny's story. The heart of the matter remains perfectly pitched social satire.... This book is saved from self-righteousness not only by the authors' cleverness but also by their compassion. For oblivious parents, lonely offspring and overworked, underpaid employees alike, they're out to fix something that's broken." —*New York Times*

Sequel: Nanny returns

McLaughlin, James A.

Bearskin. James A. McLaughlin. Ecco Press, 2018. 352 p.
ISBN 9780062742797
1. Poachers 2. Drug cartels 3. Forest conservation 4. Wilderness areas 5. Bears 6. Appalachian Region 7. Virginia 8. Thrillers and suspense

Edgar Allan Poe Award for Best First Novel by an American Author, 2019; RUSA Reading List Short List, 2019

Hiding out from the Mexican drug cartels he betrayed in Arizona, Rice More, while protecting a remote forest preserve in Virginian Appalachia, exposes a bear-poaching scheme that reveals his location to the criminals he was running from in the first place.

McLean, Felicity

The **Van** Apfel girls are gone. Felicity McLean. Algonquin Books of Chapel Hill, 2019. 297 pages
ISBN 9781616209643
1. Suburban life 2. Teenage girls 3. Missing persons 4. Suburbs 5. Crimes against girls 6. Australia 7. 1990s 8. Psychological fiction 9. Literary fiction 10. Australian fiction 11. Adult books for young adults

Librarians' Choice (Australia), 2019

Follows the efforts of two sisters who return to their suburban hometown to make sense of the unsolved disappearances of three girls from a strict evangelical family.

"This debut, part coming-of-age story and part crime thriller, is both forceful and unnerving." —*Publishers Weekly*

McMahon, Jennifer

The **invited**: a novel. Jennifer McMahon. Doubleday, 2019. 336 p.
ISBN 9780385541381
1. Ghosts 2. Local history 3. Historic buildings 4. History 5. Couples 6. Vermont 7. Ghost stories 8. Horror 9. Thrillers and suspense
LC 2018037320

Library Journal Best Books, 2019; LibraryReads Favorites, 2019

When an inspired effort to build her dream home is overshadowed by discoveries about her rural property's violent past, a former history teacher becomes obsessed with the stories of three generations of local women who died under suspicious circumstances.

"A city couple trades their fast-paced lifestyle for rural Vermont, running headlong into a few ghosts along the way." —*Kirkus*

McMillan, Terry

★ **How** Stella got her groove back. Terry McMillan. Viking, 1996. 368 p.
ISBN 9780670869909
1. Interethnic romance 2. Young men — Relations with older women 3. Divorced mothers 4. African American women — Friendship 5. African American women investment advisers 6. Jamaica 7. African American fiction 8. Books to movies 9. Relationship fiction

Presents a humorous novel about a woman who unexpectedly finds love but who just might be losing her mind BT

"Readers who have been yearning for a Judith Krantz of the black bourgeoisie—albeit one with a dirty mouth and a more ebullient spirit—will be pleased with this fantasy of sexual fulfillment." —*Publishers Weekly*

★ **It's** not all downhill from here: a novel. Terry McMillan. Ballantine Books, 2020. 368 p.
ISBN 9781984823748
1. Senior women 2. Aging 3. Female friendship 4. Loss (Psychology) 5. Women with diabetes 6. Southern California 7. California 8. African American fiction 9. Relationship fiction
LC 2019038586

Confident that her best days are still ahead, a successful businesswoman relies on close friends and her resourcefulness when an unexpected loss turns her world upside down.

"McMillan's writing is smart and witty, throwing readers right into the action, and her dialogue is coated with humor that breathes life into her characters." —*Booklist*

★ **Waiting** to exhale. Terry McMillan. Viking 1992. 409 p.
ISBN 9780670839803
1. Dating (Social customs) 2. African American women — Friendship 3. Friendship 4. Self-discovery in women 5. African American men/women relations 6. Phoenix, Arizona 7. African American fiction 8. Books to movies 9. Relationship fiction
LC 91046564

Four African-American women console and support one another in a complex friendship that helps each of them face the middle of their lives as single women BT

"Terry McMillan's heroines are so well drawn that by the end of the novel, the reader is completely at home with the four of them. They observe men—and contemporary America—with bawdy humor, occasional melancholy and great affection. But the novel is about more than four lives; the bonds among the women are so alive and so appealing they almost seem a character in their own right." —*New York Times Book Review*

Sequel: Getting to happy.

McMurtry, Larry

Boone's Lick: a novel. Larry McMurtry. Simon & Schuster, 2000. 287 p.
ISBN 9780684868868
1. Hickok, Wild Bill 2. Family relationships 3. Voyages and travels 4. Runaway wives, husbands, etc. 5. Shoshoni Indians 6. Fifteen-year-old boys 7. The West (United States) 8. Westerns 9. First person narratives 10. Adult books for young adults
LC 56342

Fifteen-year-old Shay describes his family's arduous journey from Boone's Lick, Missouri, to Fort Kearny in Wyoming, in search of Shay's father.

Comanche moon: a novel. Larry McMurtry. Simon & Schuster, 1997. 752 p; (Lonesome Dove saga, Second Prequel)
ISBN 9780684807546
1. Comanche Indians — Relations with European-Americans 2. Horse stealing 3. Frontier and pioneer life 4. Male friendship 5. Trackers 6. Texas 7. The West (United States) 8. Westerns 9. Literary fiction 10. Epic fiction
LC 9729609

Spur Award for Best Novel of the West (Long Novel), 1998

As Buffalo Hump becomes older, his Comanche children rise to power, but his son Blue Duck breaks away to form a renegade group favoring guns over bows and arrows, in a prequel to Lonesome Dove.

The final volume of the Lonesome Dove saga.

First published 1997 by Simon & Schuster, Inc, New York.

The **evening** star: a novel. Larry McMurtry. Simon & Schuster, 1999. 637 p; (Houston series, 4)

ISBN 9780684857510

1. Seniors — Sexuality 2. Grandmother and adult child 3. Aging — Psychological aspects 4. Senior women 5. Female friendship 6. Texas 7. Black humor 8. Literary fiction 9. Books to movies

LC 2003265645

This is the sequel to Terms of endearment, and follows the ongoing trials and tribulations of a woman raising her grandchildren after the death of her daughter.

"The success of a book like this one depends on the tone the author manages to muster up. Mr. McMurtry's is sentimentality laced with comic irony, and it works very well.... And if, in the end, Aurora Greenway and her extended and highly dysfunctional family turn out to be more entertaining than genuinely moving, it's reassuring to know that they—and the reader—are in the hands of a real pro." —*New York Times Book Review*

Sequel to: Terms of endearment.

Originally published: New York : Simon & Schuster, 1992.

★ **Lonesome** Dove: a novel. By Larry McMurtry. Simon and Schuster, 1985. 843 p. (Lonesome Dove saga, 1)

ISBN 9780671504205

1. Cowboys 2. Cattle drives 3. Frontier and pioneer life 4. Male friendship 5. Comanche Indians — Relations with European-Americans 6. Texas 7. The West (United States) 8. 19th century 9. Westerns 10. Literary fiction 11. Epic fiction

LC 85002192

Pulitzer Prize for Fiction, 1986; Spur Award for Best Western Novel (Short Novel), 1986; National Book Critics Circle Award for Fiction finalist, 1985

Set in the late-nineteenth century, this novel chronicles a cattle drive from Texas to Montana, and follows the lives of Gus and Call, the cowboys heading the drive, Gus's woman, Lorena, and Blue Duck, a sinister Indian renegade BT

Sequel: Streets of Laredo.

★ **Streets** of Laredo: a novel. By Larry McMurtry. Simon & Schuster, 1993. 589 p; (Lonesome Dove saga, 2)

ISBN 9780671792817

1. Bounty hunters 2. Frontier and pioneer life 3. Thieves 4. Outlaws 5. Comanche Indians — Relations with European-Americans 6. Texas 7. The West (United States) 8. Westerns 9. Literary fiction 10. Epic fiction

LC 93019279

Captain Call, a bounty hunter hired to catch bandit Joey Garza, assembles a group of unlikely assistants and travels to Crowtown, Texas BT

"This sequel to Lonesome Dove takes place 20 years after the death of Gus McCrae. In this novel, Captain Woodrow Call, McCrae's old partner, tracks a young Mexican train robber, Joe Garza, with the help of a railroad accountant named Brookshire, a Texas deputy named Ted Plunkett and Pea Eye Parker, who is trying to build a family life with his wife Lorena and their children. Across the Texas Panhandle and into northern Mexico, Call pursues his prey. America,As in some great 19th-century saga, the story has more than its share of improbable coincidencesbut these seem only mild contrivances to shape a story packed with action, terror, humor and pathos. Laredo is a fitting conclusion to a remarkable feat of reconstruction and sheer storytelling genius." —*Publishers Weekly*

Sequel to: Lonesome dove.

★ **Terms** of endearment: a novel : with a new preface. By Larry McMurtry. Scribner Paperback Fiction, 1999. 410 p; (Houston series, 3)

ISBN 9780684853901

1. Women with cancer 2. Mothers and daughters 3. Husband and wife 4. Widows 5. Marriage 6. Texas 7. Houston, Texas 8. Literary fiction 9. Books to movies

LC 265299

Aurora Greenway is the kind of woman who makes the whole world orbit around her, including a string of devoted suitors. Widowed and over-protective of her daughter, Aurora adapts at her own pace until life sends two enormous challenges her way. Her daughter Emma marries hastily and subsequently battles with cancer. Terms of Endearment is the story of an unforgettable mother and her feisty daughter and their struggle to find the courage and humour to live through life's hazards—and to love each other as never before.

"Suddenly, just when we are enjoying ourselves the most, McMurtry changes his style, and we are plunged into a moving but agonizing realistic account of daughter Emma's death from cancer at 37 and the way in which her family and old friends react.... The shift of pace may throw some readers off stride badly. McMurtry certainly remains, however, one of our most exciting novelists." —*Publishers Weekly*

Sequel to: All my friends are going to be strangers.

Sequel: Evening star.

Originally published: New York : Simon & Schuster, Inc, 1975.

The acclaimed novel that inspired the Academy Award-winning film—Cover.

McPherson, Catriona

Quiet neighbors: a novel. Catriona McPherson. Midnight Ink, 2016. 336 p.

ISBN 9780738747620

1. Secrets 2. Bookstores 3. Runaways 4. Small town life 5. Separated couples 6. Scotland 7. Mysteries

LC 2015044401

It's the oldest bookshop in a town full of bookshops; rambling and disordered, full of treasures if you look hard. Jude found one of the treasures when she visited last summer, the high point of a miserable vacation. Now, in the depths of winter, when she has to run away, Lowell's chaotic bookshop in that backwater of a town is the safe place she runs to.

"McPhersons literary observations are delightful, her quirky collection of characters intriguing, and the unfolding mystery highly satisfying." —*Publishers Weekly*

Scot & soda. Catriona McPherson. Midnight Ink, 2019. 288 p. (Last Ditch mysteries, 2)

ISBN 9780738754123

1. Scots in the United States 2. Women amateur detectives 3. Cold cases (Criminal investigation) 4. Murder investigation 5. Marriage counseling 6. California 7. Southern California 8. Mysteries

"Peppered with clever red herrings, the mystery gleefully revels in the absurd, but it's Lexy's friendships with the Last Ditch's unusual residents that give this series its big heart." —*Publishers Weekly*

★ A **step** so grave. Catriona McPherson. Quercus, 2019. 336 pages (Dandy Gilver murder mysteries, 13)

ISBN 9781473682351

1. Women private investigators 2. Superstition 3. Family estates 4. Engaged persons 5. Women murder victims 6. Scotland 7. Between the Wars (1918-1939) 8. 1930s 9. Historical mysteries 10. First person narratives

Dandy Gilver investigates after discovering Lady Lavinia, the mother of his son's betrothed, murdered in the middle of her famous knot garden.

Originally published by Hodder & Stoughton, 2018.

Strangers at the gate. Catriona McPherson. Minotaur Books, 2019. 304 pages

ISBN 9781250070012
1. Husband and wife 2. Clergywomen 3. Crime scenes 4. Secrets 5. Options, alternatives, choices 6. Scotland 7. Psychological suspense

Moving into her boss's gatehouse in the wake of a law partnership, a deacon's wife is alarmed by otherworldly noises on the property before her boss is brutally murdered. By the Anthony Award-winning author of Quiet Neighbors.

McQuiston, Casey

★ **One** last stop. Casey McQuiston. St. Martin's Griffin, 2021. 432 p.
ISBN 9781250244499
1. Moving to a new city 2. Cynicism 3. Bisexual women 4. Crushes (Interpersonal relations) 5. Subway passengers 6. New York City 7. LGBTQIA romances 8. Romantic comedies 9. Contemporary romances
LC 2020056428
LibraryReads Favorites, 2021

Cynical August starts to believe in the impossible when meets Jane on the subway, a mysterious punk rocker she forms a crush on, who is literally displaced in time from the 1970s and is trying to find her way back.

"McQuiston's joyful sophomore romp mixes all the elements that made Red, White & Royal Blue so outstanding—quirky characters, coming-of-age confusion, laugh-out-loud narration, and hilarious pop-cultural references ('Bella Swan, eat your horny little Mormon heart out')—into something totally its own." —*Publishers Weekly*

★ **Red,** white & royal blue: a novel. Casey McQuiston. Wednesday Books, 2019. 352 p.
ISBN 9781250316776
1. Children of presidents 2. Princes 3. Ambition in men 4. International relations 5. Women presidents 6. Washington, D.C. 7. Great Britain 8. Romantic comedies 9. LGBTQIA romances 10. Adult books for young adults
LC 2018055526
Booklist Editors' Choice, 2019; Library Journal Best Books, 2019; LibraryReads Favorites, 2019; Goodreads Choice Award, 2019; Alex Award, 2020

The First Son falls in love with the Prince of Wales after an incident of international proportions forces them to pretend to be best friends.

"The drama, which involves political rivals, possible betrayals, and even a meeting with the queen, is both irresistible and delicious." —*Publishers Weekly*

Meacham, Leila

Dragonfly: a novel. Leila Meacham. Grand Central Publishing, 2019. 576 pages
ISBN 9781538732229
1. Espionage 2. Americans in Europe 3. French Resistance (World War II) 4. Spies 5. Women spies 6. Paris, France 7. Second World War era (1939-1945) 8. Historical fiction
LC 2019001971

Teamed together to infiltrate Nazi ranks in occupied Paris, five idealistic American spies from diverse backgrounds begin questioning who they can trust when one of their number is killed.

"Complex, epic, and rich in historical detailan uplifting story of finding friendship behind enemy lines." —*Kirkus*

Meader, Kate

Playing with fire. Kate Meader. Pocket Books, 2015. 384 p. (Hot in Chicago novels, 2)

ISBN 9781476785929
1. Women fire fighters 2. Mayors 3. Rescues 4. Political campaigns 5. Former foster children 6. Chicago, Illinois 7. Contemporary romances
Romantic Times Reviewer's Choice Award, 2015

"Meader packs the flawless second Hot in Chicago romance (after Flirting with Fire) with superb relationship development and profane but note-perfect dialogue." —*Publishers Weekly*

Meadows, Rae

I will send rain: a novel. Rae Meadows. Henry Holt and Co, 2016. 256 p.
ISBN 9781627794268
1. Rural families 2. Farm life 3. Droughts 4. Dust Bowl Era, 1931-1939 5. Marital conflict 6. Oklahoma 7. Mann, Thomas 8. 1930s 9. Historical fiction 10. Domestic fiction
LC 2015046689

In 1934, as the earliest storms of the Dust Bowl descend on the Bell farm in Mulehead, Oklahoma, Annie Bell and her husband and children struggle against hardship as the wheat harvest dries out and people around them pack up to leave.

"When tragedy strikes or hope emerges, it makes sense and comes to fruition organically. This makes for a vibrant, absorbing novel that stays with the reader." —*Publishers Weekly*

Means, David

★ **Hystopia:** a novel. David Means. Farrar, Straus & Giroux, 2016. 336 p.
ISBN 9780865479135
1. Post-traumatic stress disorder 2. Vietnam veterans 3. Memories 4. Vietnam War, 1961-1975 — Psychological aspects 5. Authors 6. United States 7. 1960s 8. Alternate histories 9. Novels-within-novels
LC 2015035421
Longlisted for the Man Booker Prize, 2016

Describes an alternate history where JFK survived and created an enormous federal agency, the Psych Corps, charged with keeping American citizens happy, even if it means erasing their memories, a practice that is particularly handy for returning Vietnam veterans.

"Means' first novel is a compelling portrait of an imagined counterhistory that feels entirely real." —*Kirkus*

★ **Instructions** for a funeral: stories. David Means. Farrar Straus & Giroux, 2019. 176 p.
ISBN 9780374279813
1. Regret 2. Human nature 3. Interpersonal relations 4. Desire 5. Literary fiction 6. Short stories
LC 2018019100

A collection of harrowing and personal stories by the O. Henry Prize-winning author David Means.

Medie, Peace A.

His only wife: a novel. By Peace Adzo Medie. Algonquin Books of Chapel Hill, 2020. 278 pages
ISBN 9781616209155
1. Arranged marriage 2. Mistresses 3. Seamstresses 4. Women — Identity 5. Rich people 6. Ghana 7. Relationship fiction 8. First person narratives
LC 2020009732
New York Times Notable Book, 2020; RUSA Reading List Short List, 2021

Enduring a life of minimal prospects among her uncles many wives, a young seamstress relocates to Accra when she is married in absentia to a wealthy man whose family would separate him from the woman he loves.

"Medie's busy debut turns on a family drama caused by polygamy in Ghana.... This stirring tale sings when Afi learns to flex her limited power." —*Publishers Weekly*

Mehta, Rahul

No other world: a novel. Rahul Mehta. Harper, 2017. 286 p.
ISBN 9780062020468
1. Identity (Psychology) 2. Gay teenagers 3. Immigrant families 4. Immigrants — Identity 5. East Indian Americans 6. New York State 7. India 8. 1980s 9. 1990s 10. LGBTQIA fiction 11. Coming-of-age stories 12. Literary fiction 13. Adult books for young adults
LC 2016032306

A 1980s Indian-American immigrant family struggles with cultural differences, past secrets, arranged marriage and a gay son's coming-of-age in a homophobic community.

"Buried secrets, suppressed desires, and the hardships of western New York threaten to tear apart an Indian-American immigrant family in Mehtas (Quarantine, 2011) ruminative first novel of identity and loss.... Mehta uses vivid, memorable imagery to present likable, complex characters whose conflicts are mostly internal, the invisible things we hold in our hearts, as Pooja puts it. The result is a plot that feels muted and ultimately secondary to shimmering descriptions of emotionally resonant moments." —*Booklist*

Meier, Leslie

Silver anniversary murder. Leslie Meier. Kensington Books, 2018. 304 p. (Lucy Stone mysteries, 25)
ISBN 9781496710338
1. Weddings 2. Small towns 3. Women amateur detectives 4. Divorced women 5. Murder investigation 6. Maine 7. Cozy mysteries 8. Gentle reads

Devastated to learn that her strong-willed maid of honor has died under suspicious circumstances while finalizing a fourth divorce, Lucy Stone embarks on a determined investigation through New York in pursuit of a desperate killer.

Meltzer, Brad

The escape artist. Brad Meltzer. Grand Central Publishing, 2018. 384 p. (Zig and Nola novels, 1)
ISBN 9781455559527
1. Conspiracies 2. Government cover-ups 3. Secrecy in government 4. Women artists 5. Women soldiers 6. Thrillers and suspense
LC 2017041729

Discovering that a military artist-in-residence who has been officially declared dead by the government is actually alive and on the run, Zig, a worker at Dover Air Force Base, uncovers disturbing facts about the young woman's past before learning that she witnessed something she was not supposed to see.

The **inner** circle. Brad Meltzer. Grand Central Pub, 2011. Ix, 449 p; (Culper Ring novels (Brad Meltzer), 1)
ISBN 9780446577892
1. Archivists 2. Conspiracies 3. Deception 4. Man-woman relationships 5. Secrets 6. Washington (D.C.) 7. Thrillers and suspense 8. Political thrillers 9. Adult books for young adults

After an archivist goes against security protocol to show an ex-crush the president's private room at the National Archives, the two stumble upon a dictionary once owned by George Washington, and are soon entangled in a web of conspiracy and murder.

"Meltzer expertly develops the story, throwing in twists and turns at appropriate intervals, and he does an excellent job of putting us in Beecher's corner and making us care about what happens to him." —*Booklist*
Sequel: The fifth assassin

The **tenth** justice. Brad Meltzer. R. Weisbach Books, 1997. 389 p.
ISBN 9780688150891
1. Extortion 2. Betrayal 3. Confidential communications 4. Trust 5. Law clerks 6. Washington, D.C. 7. Thrillers and suspense 8. Political thrillers 9. Legal thrillers
LC 9644815

When Ben Addison, a new clerk for a Supreme Court justice, makes an error in judgement that leaves him open to blackmail, he turns for help to Lisa, a fellow clerk, and his housemates, who work in the State Department, a senator's office, and a Washington newspaper BT

"Meltzer moves the story along at a crisp pace, spicing the action and legalese with lively banter and intriguing D.C. arcana." —*Publishers Weekly*

The **zero** game. Brad Meltzer. Warner Books, 2004. 496 p.
ISBN 9780446530989
1. Political corruption 2. Congressional aides 3. Gambling 4. Capitol pages 5. Teenagers 6. Washington, D.C. 7. Capitol Hill (Washington, D.C.) 8. Thrillers and suspense 9. Political thrillers 10. Legal thrillers
LC 2003015157

Bored with their jobs as senior staffers to a respected congressman, Matthew Mercer and Harris Sandler become involved in the clandestine Zero Game, but when someone close to them turns up dead, they discover the sinister intent of the "game."

"This thriller is packed with plenty of backroom D.C. ambience and lots of action." —*Booklist*

Meltzer, Jean

★ The **Matzah** Ball. Jean Meltzer. Mira Books, 2021. 336 p.
ISBN 9780778312130
1. Women authors 2. Jewish families 3. Hanukkah 4. Chronic fatigue syndrome 5. Secrets 6. Holiday romances 7. Romantic comedies 8. Contemporary romances

Hiding her career as the bestselling author of Christmas romance novels from her family, chronically ill Rachel Rubenstein-Goldblatt, a "nice Jewish girl," needing inspiration for her Hanukkah romance, must attend a high-end Jewish music celebration but her summer camp arch enemy stands in her way.

"A sparkling holiday romance told with both honesty and heart." —*Kirkus*

Melville, Herman

The **complete** shorter fiction. Herman Melville; with an introduction by John Updike. Alfred A. Knopf, 1997. Xli, 478 p.
ISBN 9780375400681
1. Short stories 2. Classics
LC 98102392

Gathers all of Melville's short stories and novellas, including "Billy Budd, Sailor," "Bartleby, the Scrivener," and "Benito Cereno.

The **confidence-man:** his masquerade. Herman Melville; edited with an introduction and notes by Stephen Matterson. Penguin Books, 1990. 351 p.
ISBN 9780140445473

1. Swindlers and swindling 2. Impostors 3. River boats 4. River travel 5. Mississippi River 6. Satirical fiction 7. Classics

LC 91205777

On April Fool's Day in 1856, a shape-shifting grifter boards a Mississippi riverboat to expose the pretenses, hypocrisies, and self-delusions of his fellow passengers. Melville's comic allegory addresses themes of sincerity, identity, and morality in its challenge to the optimism and materialism of mid-nineteenth-century America. Misunderstood by the author's contemporaries, the novel is praised today for its stunningly modern techniques.

First published 1857.

★ **Moby-Dick;** or, The whale. Herman Melville. Modern Library, 1992. Xxxv, 822 p.
ISBN 9780679600107
1. Whaling 2. Humans and whales 3. Ahab, Captain (Fictitious character) 4. Moby Dick (Whale) 5. Obsession in men 6. Sea stories 7. Allegories 8. Books to movies
The classic American novel about the doomed voyage of the *Pequod* in pursuit of the enigmatic white whale.

First published 1851.

Mendez, Paul

Rainbow milk. Paul Mendez. Doubleday, 2021. 368 p.
ISBN 9780385547062
1. Moving to a new city 2. Sex workers 3. Religious communities 4. Boxers (Sports) 5. Racism 6. 1950s 7. LGBTQIA fiction 8. Coming-of-age stories 9. Literary fiction

Seeking a fresh start in London after escaping a repressive religious community, Jesse finds himself at a lost for a new center of gravity and turns to sex work, music and art to create his own notions of love, masculinity and spirituality.

"Mendez dazzles with his debut, an explosive bildungsroman drawing on the legacy of Britain's Windrush generation of 1950s migrants from the West Indies." —*Publishers Weekly*

Mengestu, Dinaw

★ **All** our names. Dinaw Mengestu. Alfred A. Knopf, 2014. 255 p.
ISBN 9780385349987
1. Revolutionaries 2. Identity (Psychology) 3. Alienation (Social psychology) 4. Women social workers 5. Flaubert, Gustave 6. Africa 7. United States 8. Political fiction 9. Psychological fiction

LC 2013031632

New York Times Notable Book, 2014; Kirkus Prize for Fiction finalist, 2014

Coming of age during an African revolution, a brilliant university student-turned-fighter eventually flees the escalating violence of his country to resettle in America, where he is haunted by his past and the memory of a charismatic leader's devastating sacrifice.

"Mengestu...portrays the intersection of cultures experienced by the immigrant with unsettling perception." —*Publishers Weekly*

Mengiste, Maaza

★ The **shadow** king: a novel. Maaza Mengiste. W. W. Norton & Company, 2019. 448 p.
ISBN 9780393083569
1. Women and war 2. World War II — Women 3. Resistance to military occupation 4. False personation 5. Military occupation 6. Ethiopia 7. 1930s 8. Second World War era (1939-1945) 9. Historical fiction 10. Literary fiction

LC 2019020502

Library Journal Best Books, 2019; New York Times Notable Book, 2019; Shortlisted for the Booker Prize, 2020

Tending the wounded when her nation is invaded by Mussolini, an orphaned servant in 1935 Ethiopia helps disguise a gentle peasant as their exiled emperor to rally her fellow women in the fight against fascism.

Menon, Lily

Make up break up: a novel. Lily Menon. Griffin, 2021. 336 p.
ISBN 9781250799951
1. Women computer programmers 2. Computer programs 3. Competition 4. Love-hate relationships 5. Application software 6. Romantic comedies 7. Contemporary Romances

LC 2020037476

Rendered instantly famous when his break-up app becomes meteorically successful, Hudson Craft moves into a new office adjoining the workspace of a commitment-minded woman with whom he once shared a Las Vegas summer fling.

"Though the abrupt ending offers a frustratingly meager glimpse of the lovers portion of their enemies-to-lovers arc, the witty banter and electric sexual tension throughout will keep readers hooked." —*Publishers Weekly*

Merbeth, K. S.

★ **Fortuna**. Kristyn Merbeth. Orbit, 2019. 448 p. (Nova vita protocol, 1)
ISBN 9780316453998
1. Smugglers 2. Family businesses 3. Space vehicles 4. Massacres 5. Conspiracies 6. Space 7. Space opera 8. Science fiction

LC 2019015305

Scorpia Kaiser has always stood in Corvus's shadow until the day her older brother abandons their family to participate in a profitless war. When a deal turns deadly and Corvus returns from the war, Scorpia's plans to take over the family business are interrupted, and the Kaiser siblings are forced to make a choice: take responsibility for their family's involvement in a devastating massacre or lay low and hope it blows over. Too bad Scorpia was never any good at staying out of a fight...

"Merbeth 's world building is fascinating—five human-settled planets, each distinct and littered with alien technology—but her multifaceted characters and their troubled relationships give this action-packed family drama its heart." —*Booklist*

Merullo, Roland

The **talk-funny** girl: a novel. Roland Merullo. Crown, 2011. 320 p.
ISBN 9780307452924
1. Teenage girl abuse victims 2. Isolationism 3. Self-fulfillment in young women 4. Courage in young women 5. Cult leaders 6. New Hampshire 7. Psychological suspense 8. Adult books for young adults

LC 2011003328

Alex Award, 2012

Raised by parents so intentionally isolated that they speak their own hybrid dialect, abused youth Marjorie witnesses a nearby town's economic ruin and her parents' submission to a sadistic cult leader before she is rescued by another abuse survivor who teaches her stoneworking skills.

Messud, Claire

★ The **woman** upstairs: a novel. Claire Messud. Alfred A. Knopf, 2013. 272 p.
ISBN 9780307596901

1. Obsession in women 2. Women artists 3. Teacher-student relationships 4. Elementary school teachers 5. Ambition in women 6. Massachusetts 7. Cambridge, Massachusetts 8. Psychological fiction 9. Literary fiction 10. Canadian fiction

LC 2012017806

New York Times Notable Book, 2013; ALA Notable Book, 2014

Relegated to the status of schoolteacher and friendly neighbor after abandoning her dreams of becoming an artist, Nora advocates on behalf of a charismatic Lebanese student and is drawn into the child's family until his artist mother's careless ambition leads to a shattering betrayal.

This Is A Borzoi book.

Meuleman, Sarah

Find me gone. Sarah Meuleman. HarperCollins, 2018. 304 p.

ISBN 9780062870704

1. Missing persons 2. Women journalists 3. Memories 4. Secrets 5. Friendship 6. Belgium 7. New York City 8. 1960s 9. 2010s 10. Thrillers and suspense

A successful fashion magazine columnist investigates the mysterious disappearances of Agatha Christie, Barbara Follett and Virginia Woolf before endeavoring to figure out what happened to a friend who went missing during their teen years.

Meyer, Deon

Icarus. Deon Meyer. Atlantic Monthly Pr, 2015. 352 p. (Benny Griessel novels, 5)

ISBN 9780802124005

1. Detectives 2. Internet — Social aspects 3. Murder investigation 4. Extramarital affairs 5. Businesspeople 6. South Africa 7. Thrillers and suspense 8. Translations

Captain Benny Griessel takes on a high profile murder case after a young tech wiz and the founder of an internet service for cheating spouses is discovered dead in Cape Town.

Meyer, Nicholas

The **adventure** of the peculiar protocols: adapted from the journals of John H. Watson, M.D.. Nicholas Meyer. Minotaur Books, 2019. 238 p. (Memoirs of John Watson)

ISBN 9781250228956

1. Spies 2. Murder 3. Secret societies 4. Conspiracies 5. Antisemitism 6. France 7. Russia 8. 1900s (Decade) 9. Diary novels 10. Historical mysteries 11. Mysteries

LC 2019029073

Investigating the murder of a Secret Service agent, Sherlock and Watson, accompanied by an enigmatic woman, uncover a plot by a covert group intent on taking over the world.

"Director and author Meyer puts his own stamp on the Holmes and Watson tradition, basing his story on historic events with contemporary relevance, as lies become accepted as truth by means of willful ignorance. Holmes enthusiasts will relish this well-crafted novel." —*Library Journal*

Meyer, Philipp

★ The **son:** a novel. Philipp Meyer. Ecco Press, 2013. Viii, 561 pages

ISBN 9780062120397

1. Frontier and pioneer life 2. Indian captivities 3. Ambition in men 4. Families 5. Ranchers 6. Texas 7. The West (United States) 8. Family sagas 9. Westerns 10. Epic fiction

Library Journal Best Books, 2013; New York Times Notable Book, 2013; Western Heritage Award for Outstanding Western Novel, 2014; Pulitzer Prize for Fiction finalist, 2014

An epic of the American West and a multigenerational saga of power, blood, land, and oil that follows the rise of one Texas family, from the Comanche raids of the 1800s to the to the oil booms of the 20th century.

Meyerson, Amy

The **imperfects**. Amy Meyerson. Park Row, 2020. 368 pages

ISBN 9780778305071

1. Siblings 2. Diamonds 3. Grandmothers — Death 4. Jewelry 5. Family secrets 6. Multiple perspectives 7. Family sagas

A family's discovery of a priceless inheritance leads them on a pursuit for the truth that transforms their lives in unexpected ways.

"A solidly entertaining multigenerational saga about sacrifice, self-reliance, and what it means to be family." —*Kirkus*

Michener, James A.

★ The **bridges** at Toko-Ri. James A. Michener. Random House, 1953. 146 p.

ISBN 9780394417806

1. Korean War, 1950-1953 — Aerial operations, American 2. Fighter pilots 3. Bridges 4. Sabotage 5. Bombing 6. Korea 7. 1950s 8. War stories 9. Historical fiction 10. Books to movies

LC 52007129

A naval task force tries to destroy the bridges at Toko-ri with jet bombers so that supplies will not reach communist front lines during the Korean War.

Caribbean. James A. Michener. Random House, 1989. 672 p. : Illustration; Color; Map

ISBN 9780394565613

1. Island life 2. Rastafarians 3. Culture conflict 4. Cuban resistance and revolts 5. Pirates 6. Caribbean Area 7. Historical fiction

LC 89042785

An epic tale of Caribbean history from the 15th century to the present, following the Rastafarians, Cuban revolution, and nationalism.

"A novel about the Caribbean islands from the days when the peace-loving Arawak Indians were overpowered by cannibalistic Caribs, to a ship's tour of today's still lush, but troubled, paradise. Sir Francis Drake, pirate Henry Morgan, Horatio Nelson, Haitian General Toussaint L'Ouverture, Fidel Castro march across the pages, and while the pace is sometimes achingly slow, the dialogue stilted and the characterization skimpy, Michener laces the whole with fiery Caribbean drama." —*Publishers Weekly*

The maps are on lining papers.

Includes bibliographical references (p. [669]-672).

★ **Centennial**. James A. Michener. Random House, 1974. 909 p. : Illustration

ISBN 9780394479705

1. Indians of North America — Relations with missionaries, traders, etc. 2. Frontier and pioneer life 3. Homesteaders 4. Arapaho Indians 5. Paleontology 6. Colorado 7. The West (United States) 8. American Westward Expansion (1803-1899) 9. Westerns 10. Books to TV

LC 74005164

Western Heritage Award for Outstanding Western Novel, 1975

The story of Centennial, Colorado, begins when the earth formed the area and ends in the 1970s with human disregard for its benefits and beauties, and also tells the history of relations between the white settlers and Native Americans.

Includes maps on end papers.

Chesapeake. James A. Michener. Random House, 1978. 865 p. ISBN 9780394500799

1. Human settlements 2. Indians of North America 3. Racism 4. Immigration and emigration 5. Rich families 6. Chesapeake Bay Region 7. Chesapeake Bay 8. Family sagas 9. Historical fiction
LC 78002892

The Eastern shore of Maryland and Virginia evolves from prehistory into the 20th century and influences the lives of Native Americans, African Americans, and Irish immigrants who live there.

"Through the interwoven stories of three families and the Indians, Blacks, and Irish immigrants with whom they interact, Michener chronicles four centuries of life on Maryland's Eastern Shore.... Michener elaborates...variations on his themes of personal accountability for social change, man's self-expulsion from paradise, and the interrelated ecological network of all things." —*Library Journal*

Includes end-paper maps.

Space. James A. Michener; [cartography by Jean Paul Tremblay].. Random House, 1982. 622 p. : Map
ISBN 9780394505558

1. Space programs 2. Astronautics 3. Space exploration 4. Rocketry — History 5. Swindlers and swindling 6. United States 7. Moon 8. Historical fiction 9. Books to TV
LC 82040127

During World War II, scientists and politicians become involved in the program that eventually takes humans into space.

Maps on lining papers.

★ **Tales** of the South Pacific. By James A. Michener. Macmillan, 1986. 326 p.
ISBN 9780025845404

1. World War II. 2. Interethnic romance 3. Military bases, American 4. Man-woman relationships 5. Interethnic relations 6. South Pacific Ocean 7. Oceania 8. Second World War era (1939-1945) 9. War stories 10. Historical fiction 11. Books to movies
LC 86028450

Pulitzer Prize for Fiction, 1948

The people and beauty of the South Pacific's coral islands are viewed through the eyes of a young naval lieutenant.

Tales of the South Pacific was the inspiration for the movie "South Pacific."

Mieville, China

★ The **city** & the city. China Mieville. Del Rey/Ballantine Books, 2009. 416 p.
ISBN 9780345497512

1. Murder investigation 2. Parallel universes 3. City life 4. Missing persons 5. Hallucinations and illusions 6. Eastern Europe 7. Hardboiled fiction 8. Fantasy mysteries 9. Adult books for young adults
LC 2009013775

Arthur C. Clarke Award, 2010; BSFA Award for Best Novel, 2009; Hugo Award for Best Novel, 2010; Locus Award for Fantasy Novel, 2010; World Fantasy Award, 2010

Inspector Tyador Borlu must travel to Ul Qoma to search for answers in the murder of a woman found in the city of Beszel.

"A murder mystery set in two cities, Ul Qoma and Beszel, one rich and one poor, where residents have been trained to unsee each other in order to coexist.... The story takes the form of a police procedural as the protagonist, Inspector Tyador Borl of the Extreme Crime Squad, tries to crack the murder case. There are no elves or UFOs. Instead, the story focuses on the lengths to which people will go to enforce borders and maintain separate cultural identities. Evoking such writers as Franz Kafka and Mikhail Bulgakov, Mr. Mieville asks readers to make conceptual leaps and not to simply take flights of fancy." —*The Wall Street Journal*

Embassytown. China Mieville. Ballantine Books, 2011. 368 p. ISBN 9780345524492

1. Human/alien encounters 2. Life on other planets 3. Space warfare 4. Far future 5. Genetic engineering 6. Social science fiction 7. Science fiction

Locus Award for Best Science Fiction Novel, 2012; Romantic Times Reviewers' Choice Award, 2011

Embassytown: a city of contradictions on the outskirts of the universe. Avice is an immerser, a traveller on the immer, the sea of space and time below the everyday, now returned to her birth planet. Here on Arieka, humans are not the only intelligent life, and Avice has a rare bond with the natives, the enigmatic Hosts—who cannot lie. Only a tiny cadre of unique human Ambassadors can speak Language, and connect the two communities. But an unimaginable new arrival has come to Embassytown. And when this Ambassador speaks, everything changes. Catastrophe looms. Avice knows the only hope is for her to speak directly to the alien Hosts. And that is impossible.

"It's a joy to find this young author coming into his own, and bringing the craft of science fiction out of the backwaters where it's been caught lately between the regressive drag of publishers marketing to a safe readership and the bewildering promises of change and growth offered by postmodernism in all its forms and formlessness. Embassytown is a fully achieved work of art. Only the trash forms of science fiction are undemanding and predictable; the good stuff, like all good fiction, is not for lazy minds. Where the complexity of realistic novels is moral and psychological, in science fiction it's moral and intellectual; individual character is seldom the key. But Mieville's characters are deftly sketched, and his narrator-protagonist, Avice, is a subtler portrait than she seems at first." —*The Guardian (UK)*

Originally published: London: Macmillan, 2011.

★ **Perdido** Street Station. China Mieville. Del Rey, 2001. 710 p; (New Crobuzon series, 1)
ISBN 9780345443021

1. Dystopias 2. Scientists 3. Flight 4. Garuda (Mythical bird) 5. Caterpillars 6. Science fantasy 7. Steampunk 8. Science fiction 9. Adult books for young adults
LC 67474

Arthur C. Clarke Award, 2001

In the squalid, gothic city of New Crobuzon, a mysterious half-human, half-bird stranger comes to Isaac, a gifted but eccentric scientist, with a request to help him fly, but Isaac's obsessive experiments and attempts to grant the request unleash a terrifying dark force on the entire city.

"Scientist Isaac Dan der Grimnebulin and his lover, an insectlike creature named Lin, discover the risks of meddling in the affairs of mobsters, renegades, and revolutionaries when they fall afoul of the powers that rule the sprawling city of New Crobuzon. The author...delivers a powerful tale about the power of love and the will to survive in a dystopian universe that combines Victorian elements with a fantasy version of cyberpunk." —*Library Journal*

Illustrated with a map.

Mihalic, Susan

Dark horses. Susan Mihalic. Simon & Schuster, 2021. 352 pages ISBN 9781982133849

1. Teenage equestrians 2. Abusive men 3. Ambition in teenage girls 4. Sexually abused teenagers 5. Family violence 6. Psychological fiction 7. First person narratives

A teenage girl struggles to reclaim her life from her abusive father.

"Deftly sketching the relationships here (including the relationship between horse and rider), Mihalic gives a powerful and insightful account of Roan's abuse and her path to freedom." —*Library Journal*

Milan, Courtney

The **duchess** war. Courtney Milan. CreateSpace, 2012. 268 p. (The Brothers Sinister, 1)

ISBN 9781481207478

1. Jack, the Ripper 2. Single women 3. Secrets 4. Nobility 5. Poor women 6. England 7. Great Britain 8. Victorian era (1837-1901) 9. 1860s 10. Victorian romances 11. Historical romances

Miss Minerva Lane is a quiet, bespectacled wallflower, and she wants to keep it that way. After all, the last time she was the center of attention, it ended badly—so badly that she changed her name to escape her scandalous past. Wallflowers may not be the prettiest of blooms, but at least they don't get trampled. So when a handsome duke comes to town, the last thing she wants is his attention. But that is precisely what she gets. Because Robert Blaisdell, the Duke of Clermont, is not fooled. When Minnie figures out what he's up to, he realizes there is more to her than her spectacles and her quiet ways. And he's determined to lay her every secret bare before she can discover his. But this time, one shy miss may prove to be more than his match.

Miles, Jonathan

Anatomy of a miracle. Jonathan Miles. Hogarth Press, 2018. 355 p.

ISBN 9780553447583

1. Veterans 2. People with paraplegia 3. Miracles 4. Belief and doubt 5. Religion and science 6. Mississippi 7. Biloxi, Mississippi 8. 21st century 9. Satirical fiction

Confined to a wheelchair after a paralyzing injury, an Afghanistan War veteran endures a hardscrabble existence in his sister's ramshackle Mississippi home before spontaneously regaining his ability to walk, an apparent miracle that subjects him to scientific and religious debates and exposes his most private secrets.

Miles, Terry

Rabbits. Terry Miles. Del Rey, 2021. 448 p.

ISBN 9781984819659

1. Alternate reality games 2. Conspiracies 3. Competition 4. Missing men 5. Obsession 6. Science fiction 7. Techno-thrillers 8. Media tie-ins

Set in the same world as the popular Rabbits podcast, this fast-paced technothriller takes readers into an underground alternate reality game where the future of the world depends on a player named K.

Miller, Andrew

Oxygen. Andrew Miller. Harcourt, 2001. 323 p.

ISBN 9780151007219

1. Parents with terminal illnesses 2. Mothers and sons 3. Translators 4. Dramatists 5. Actors and actresses 6. Paris, France 7. England 8. Psychological fiction 9. Parallel narratives

LC 2001051459

New York Times Notable Book, 2002; Shortlisted for the Booker-McConnell Prize, 2001

As Alec Valentine and his brother Larry return to England to care for their ailing mother, Laszlo Lazar, whose play Alec is translating, finds that he cannot stop thinking about past mistakes.

"Written in elegant, resonant prose, this book breathes with compassion and honesty, and with the rare quality called hope." —*Publishers Weekly*

Miller, Derek B.

★ **American** by day. Derek B. Miller. Houghton Mifflin Harcourt, 2018. 338 p. (Sheldon Horowitz novels, 2)

ISBN 9781328876652

1. Women detectives 2. Siblings 3. Missing persons investigation 4. Police 5. Culture shock 6. Adirondack Mountains, New York 7. New York (State) 8. Mysteries

LC 2017045332

Police Chief Inspector Sigrid Odegard from Norwegian by Night departs Oslo for the United States to search for her missing brother, a quest that plunges her into the political minefields and backwoods undercurrents of the Adirondacks.

★ The **girl** in green. Derek B. Miller. Houghton Mifflin Harcourt, 2017. 336 p.

ISBN 9780544706255

1. Life change events 2. War — Psychological aspects 3. Captives 4. Muslim girls 5. Journalists 6. Syria 7. Iraq 8. War stories

LC 2016005409

Middle East Book Award, Honorable Mention, 2017

A tale set in the aftermath of Desert Storm finds a British journalist who avoids his family and a reckless American private seeking redemption after failing to save the life of a young girl.

"A penetrating, poetic, and unexpectedly disarming book about the ageless conflict in the Middle East by a writer who has made that topic his specialty." —*Kirkus*

First published: 2016.

How to find your way in the dark. Derek B Miller. Houghton Mifflin Harcourt, 2021. 320 p. (Sheldon Horowitz novels, prequel)

ISBN 9780358269601

1. Orphans 2. Antisemitism 3. Children of murder victims 4. Jewish families 5. Loss (Psychology) 6. New England 7. 20th century 8. Coming-of-age stories 9. Historical fiction

LC 2020057651

Twelve-year old Sheldon Horowitz is still recovering from the tragic loss of his mother only a year ago when a suspicious traffic accident steals the life of his father near their home in rural Massachusetts.

"Diverting subplots track America's entry into WWII and the birth of modern stand-up comedy, as shown by Lenny's hilarious forays into showbiz." —*Publishers Weekly*

Miller, Henry

★ **Tropic** of Cancer. Henry Miller. Grove Press, 1980. 318 p.

ISBN 9780802131782

1. Miller, Henry 2. Americans in France 3. Writing 4. Authors 5. Expatriates 6. Americans in Paris, France 7. Paris, France 8. France 9. 1930s 10. Transgressive fiction 11. Modern classics 12. Erotic fiction

Chronicles the bawdy adventures of a young expatriate writer, his friends, and the characters they meet in Paris in the 1930s.

Sequel: Tropic of Capricorn.

Originally published: Paris : Obelisk Press, 1934.

★ **Tropic** of Capricorn. Henry Miller. Grove Press, 1961. 348 p.

ISBN 9780802151827

1. Miller, Henry 2. Writing 3. Masculinity 4. Bohemianism 5. Sex customs 6. Sexuality 7. Brooklyn, New York City 8. New York City 9. 1920s 10. Transgressive fiction 11. Modern classics 12. Erotic fiction

Presents Miller's controversial work candidly depicting the life of an American expatriate in Paris, following the narrator from the ethnic neighborhoods of New York City through a series of sexual adventures to Europe in the 1920s.

Sequel to: Tropic of Cancer.

Originally published: Paris : Obelisk Press, 1938.

Miller, Holly

★ The **sight** of you. Holly Miller. G. P. Putnam's Sons, 2020. 320 p.
ISBN 9780593085585
1. Psychic ability 2. Precognition 3. Options, alternatives, choices 4. Romantic love 5. Grief 6. Love stories 7. Multiple perspectives 8. Mainstream fiction

LC 2020003145

Unable to help falling in love with a woman who offers him a second chance, a man who secretly experiences dreams about the future makes a difficult choice in the face of a daunting premonition about their future together.

"Miller paints big emotions with nuance and subtlety, exploring complex family dynamics, grief, and anxiety with expert skill that lends realism to her tale, despite its supernatural conceit." —*Publishers Weekly*

Miller, Karen E. Quinones

An **angry-ass** black woman. Karen E. Quinones Miller. Gallery Books, 2012. 288 p.
ISBN 9781451607826
1. Miller, Karen E. Quinones 2. People in comas 3. African American authors 4. Growing up 5. Poverty 6. Forties (Age) 7. Harlem, New York City 8. New York City 9. Autobiographical fiction 10. African American fiction

LC 2011047077

Library Journal Best Books, 2012

Traces the impoverished early years of Ke-Ke, who awakens from a coma in her midlife to confront events that shaped her resolve to leave Harlem, earn an education, and pursue a writing career.

Miller, Kei

★ **Augustown**. Kei Miller. Pantheon Books, 2017. 256 p.
ISBN 9781101871614
1. Women 2. Women who are blind 3. Rastafari Movement 4. Poverty 5. Religion 6. Jamaica 7. 20th century 8. Literary fiction 9. Historical fiction 10. Parallel narratives
Longlisted for the Andrew Carnegie Medal for Excellence in Fiction, 2018

Possessing strong intuitive powers in spite of being unable to see, Ma Taffy comforts her stricken great-nephew while recalling a fantastical story with ties to Jamaican history, the birth of the Rastafari and the human drive for a better life.

"Fusing facts with what-could-have-well-been, Augustown is a gorgeously plotted, sharply convincing, achingly urgent novel deserving widespread attention." —*Booklist*

Miller, Madeline

★ **Circe**. Madeline Miller. Little Brown & Co, 2018. 393 p.
ISBN 9780316556347

1. Exiles 2. Witches 3. Gods and goddesses, Greek 4. Supernatural 5. Titans (Mythology) 6. Ancient Greece 7. Ancient Aegean civilizations (3000?1000 BCE) 8. Mythological fiction 9. Historical fantasy 10. Literary fiction 11. Adult books for young adults
Alex Award, 2019; Goodreads Choice Award, 2018; Indies' Choice Book Awards, Adult Fiction, 2019; Librarians' Choice (Australia), 2018; LibraryReads Favorites, 2018; Loan Stars Favourites, 2018; RUSA Reading List Short List, 2019; Shortlisted for The Women's Prize for Fiction, 2019

Follows the banished witch daughter of Titans as she hones her powers and interacts with famous mythological beings before a conflict with one of the most vengeful Olympians forces her to choose between the worlds of the gods and mortals.

The **song** of Achilles. Madeline Miller. Ecco Press, 2012. 352 p.
ISBN 9780062060617
1. Princes 2. Exiles 3. Young men — Interpersonal relations 4. Warriors 5. Trojan War 6. Troy (Extinct city) 7. Ancient Greece 8. Ancient Aegean civilizations (3000?1000 BCE) 9. Historical fiction 10. War stories 11. Literary fiction 12. Adult books for young adults
Library Journal Best Books, 2012; Orange Prize for Fiction, 2012; Rainbow List, 2013; School Library Journal Best Books: Best Adult Books 4 Teens, 2012

Patroclus, an awkward young prince, follows Achilles into war, little knowing that the years that follow will test everything they have learned, everything they hold dear. And that, before he is ready, he will be forced to surrender his friend to the hands of Fate. Set during the Trojan War.

"With language both evocative of her predecessors and fresh, and through familiar scenes that explore new territory, this first-time novelist masterfully brings to life an imaginative yet informed vision of ancient Greece featuring divinely human gods and larger-than-life mortals." —*Publishers Weekly*

Originally published: London : Bloomsbury, c2011.

Miller, Mary

Biloxi: a novel. Mary Miller. Liveright Publishing Corp, 2019. 224 pages
ISBN 9781631492167
1. Divorced men 2. Men and dogs 3. Options, alternatives, choices 4. Sixties (Age) 5. Human-animal relationships 6. Biloxi, Mississippi 7. Mississippi 8. Literary fiction 9. Southern fiction

LC 2018056974

Mary Miller seizes the mantle of Southern literature with this wry tale of middle age and the unexpected turns a life can take.

Miller, Rebecca

★ **Jacob's** folly: a novel. Rebecca Miller. Farrar, Straus and Giroux, 2013. 352 p.
ISBN 9780374178543
1. Reincarnation 2. Judaism 3. Fathers and sons 4. Hospital patients 5. Transformations, Personal 6. Long Island, New York 7. 18th century 8. 21st century 9. Literary fiction 10. Historical fiction

LC 2012022882

Jacob is a Jewish peddler living in eighteenth-century France; Leslie and Deirdre Senzatimore are a settled American couple; and Masha is an alluring young ultra-Orthodox Jew who is gravely ill. In Jacob's Folly, these four individuals will find their fates intertwined and the courses of their lives irrevocably altered when Jacob is reincarnated as a house fly in contemporary Long Island.

First published in the USA in 2013 by Farrar, Straus and Giroux, New York.

Includes reading group questions.

Miller, Sue

The **good** mother. Sue Miller. Harper and Row, 1986. 310p.
ISBN 9780060155513
1. Child custody 2. Psychiatrists 3. Parenting 4. Trials (Child custody) 5. Mothers and daughters 6. Psychological fiction 7. Relationship fiction 8. First person narratives

LC 85045475

"The fulcrum on which the novel's plot pivots is the allegation by Anna's ex-husband that Anna's lover has molested Molly, and the ensuing custody trial. Miller's treatment of this high point of tension in the novel is dramatic, discreet, compassionate. Each development in the legal process increases the tension. The drama heightens, the suspense builds, character is further developed, and the latitude for choice logically narrowed. Like a final judgment, the custody decision breaks over reader and character alike." —*Christian Science Monitor*

★ **Monogamy**. Sue Miller. HarperCollins, 2020. 368 pages
ISBN 9780062969651
1. Widows 2. Remarriage 3. Extramarital affairs 4. Secrets 5. Women photographers 6. Massachusetts 7. Literary fiction
LibraryReads Favorites, 2020; New York Times Notable Book, 2020

Derailed by the sudden passing of her husband of 30 years, an artist on the brink of a gallery opening struggles to pick up the pieces of her life before discovering harrowing evidence of her husband's affair.

The **senator's** wife. By Sue Miller. Alfred A. Knopf, 2008. 320 p.
ISBN 9780307264206
1. Dilemmas 2. Adult children of dysfunctional families 3. Politicians' spouses 4. Married people 5. Marriage 6. New England 7. Relationship fiction

LC 2007014659

Two unconventional women, neighbors in adjacent New England townhouses—Meri Fowler, pregnant, newly married, and discovering the gap between reality and expectation, and Delia Naughton, wife of a notoriously unfaithful liberal senator—confront the costs and challenges of love.

This is a Borzoi book—Title page verso.

Miller, Walter M.

★ A **canticle** for Leibowitz. . Bantam Books, 2007. 338 p.
ISBN 9780553273816
1. Survival (after nuclear warfare) 2. End of the world 3. Monks 4. Monasticism and religious orders for men 5. Mutants 6. Utah 7. Apocalyptic fiction 8. Science fiction classics 9. Social science fiction

LC 85045444

Hugo Award for Best Novel, 1961

A monk struggles to preserve spiritual life and wisdom in the years following a nuclear holocaust BT

Sequel: Saint Leibowitz and the wild horse woman (1997).

Miller, Xander

Zo: a novel. Xander Miller. Alfred A. Knopf, 2020. 327 p.
ISBN 9781101874127

1. Poor men 2. Nursing students 3. Man-woman relationships 4. Haiti Earthquake, Haiti, 2010 5. Fathers and daughters 6. Haiti 7. Love stories 8. Literary fiction 9. Magical realism

LC 2015045682

An impoverished orphan coming of age in a 1990s Haitian fishing village runs away with a beautiful nursing student whose father does not approve of their relationship, before the couple is separated by the 2010 earthquake.

"Miller's debut is a provocative modern rendition of the Romeo and Juliet story. Set against the backdrop of a country ravaged by nature, and written in raw and affecting prose, Zo's story takes the reader to the very limits of what a person will do for love." —*Booklist*

Millhauser, Steven

Martin Dressler: the tale of an American dreamer. Steve Millhauser. Crown Publishers, 1996. 294 p.
ISBN 9780517703199
1. Obsession in men 2. Entrepreneurs 3. Hotel management 4. Siblings 5. Visions 6. New York City 7. Gilded Age (1865-1898) 8. Historical fiction 9. Literary fiction

LC 96683

Pulitzer Prize for Fiction, 1997; National Book Award for Fiction finalist, 1996

Portrays a businessman at the turn of the century, starting out as a clerk in his father's cigar store, and eventually becoming the proprietor of several hotels, looking at the lessons he learns on his rise to fortune, and after his collapse.

"This wonderful, wonder-full book is a fable and phantasmagoria of the sources of our century: 'There once lived a man named Martin Dressler, a shopkeeper's son, who rose from modest beginnings to a height of dreamlike good fortune. . . . But this is a perilous privilege, which the gods watch jealously.' 'Perilous privilege' is the core of Mr. Millhauser's analysis of that subgenre of fairy tale, the American Dream." —*New York Times Book Review*

Mina, Denise

Conviction. Denise Mina. Mulholland Books, 2019. 376 pages
ISBN 9780316528504
1. Podcasts 2. Stay-at-home mothers 3. Intrigue 4. Family-killing 5. Crime 6. Scotland 7. Europe 8. Thrillers and suspense

LC 2019930999

An upper-class Edinburgh housewife who enjoys listening to the sordid details of true-crime podcasts has her world turned upside down when a new podcast turns out to have connections to her own dark past.

Originally published in Great Britain by Harvill Secker, an imprint of Penguin Random House UK: May 2019.

The **less** dead. Denise Mina. Mulholland Books, 2020. 240 pages
ISBN 9780316528511
1. Pregnant women 2. Women physicians 3. Birthmothers 4. Mothers and daughters 5. Single women 6. Glasgow, Scotland 7. Scotland 8. Thrillers and suspense

Navigating burnout, an unfaithful ex and a relative's recent death, Margo reaches out to her birth family before discovering that her biological mother was murdered years earlier by a killer who begins sending her threatening letters.

"Mina is a master of the genre, with wide appeal, especially for those who appreciate character-driven stories with literary weight, like those of Tana French, Karin Slaughter, and Laura Lippman." —*Booklist*

★ **Rizzio**. Denise Mina. Pegasus Crime, 2021. 144 p.
ISBN 9781643138459

1. Riccio, David 2. Women rulers 3. Courts and courtiers 4. Political intrigue 5. Assassins 6. Conspiracies 7. Scotland 8. Scottish Stewart period (1371-1603) 9. 16th century 10. Historical thrillers 11. Political thrillers

In this radical new take on one of the darkest episodes in Scottish history, the New York Times bestselling author revisits the brutal murder of David Rizzio, the private secretary of Mary, Queen of Scots, telling the infamous story as it was never told before.

"This superior historical thriller reads like a real-life episode of Game of Thrones." —*Publishers Weekly*

Minato, Kanae
Confessions. Kanae Minato; translated from the Japanese by Stephen Snyder. Mulholland Books, 2014. 288 p.
ISBN 9780316200929
1. Accidental death 2. Middle school students 3. Bullying and bullies 4. Revenge 5. Middle schools 6. Japan 7. Psychological suspense 8. Multiple perspectives 9. First person narratives 10. Adult books for young adults
Alex Award, 2015

After calling off her engagement in wake of a tragic revelation, Yko Moriguchi had nothing to live for except her only child, four-year-old Manami. Now, following an accident on the grounds of the middle school where she teaches, Yko has given up and tendered her resignation. But first she has one last lecture to deliver. She tells a story that upends everything her students ever thought they knew about two of their peers, and sets in motion a maniacal plot for revenge. Narrated in alternating voices, with twists you'll never see coming, Confessions explores the limits of punishment, despair, and tragic love, culminating in a harrowing confrontation between teacher and student that will place the occupants of an entire school in danger.

"This award-winning debut novel is a creepy and mesmerizing psychological thriller that challenges the conventions of right vs. wrong, good vs. evil, and law vs. justice. There are no happy endings here, but Minato has pieced together an intriguing puzzle that will keep readers glued to their seats." —*Library Journal*
Translated from the Japanese.

Minh, Drew
Neon empire. Drew Minh. Rare Bird Books, 2019. 220 pages
ISBN 9781947856769
1. Dystopias 2. Social media 3. Near future 4. Filmmakers 5. Missing women 6. Cyberpunk 7. Science fiction

"Minh creates a nonstop social media frenzy amid a rich cyberpunk landscape in this vivid debut...With shifting points of view and sharply detailed descriptions, Minh sets up a gripping, if uneven, dynamic between the characters, spicing the intrigue with action. Fans of SF thrillers will enjoy this colorful high-tech mystery and its echoes of the present-day hunger for likes, favorites, and going viral." —*Publishers Weekly*

Mishima, Yukio
The **sound** of waves. Yukio Mishima; translated by Meredith Weatherby; drawings by Yoshinori Kinoshita. Vintage Books, 1994. 182 p. : Illustration
ISBN 9780679752684
1. Fishers 2. Teenage boys 3. Fathers and daughters 4. Teenage romance 5. Teenage boy/girl relations 6. Japan 7. Love stories 8. Translations
LC 94019314

A poor fisherman longs to meet the young and beautiful pearl diver who has enthralled his Japanese village.
Translation of: Shiosai.

Spring snow. Yukio Mishima; translated from the Japanese by Michael Gallagher. A. A. Knopf, 1972. 389 p. (Sea of fertility, 1)
ISBN 9780394442396
1. Aristocracy 2. Upper class 3. Japan 4. Psychological fiction 5. Translations
LC 74154940

In Tokyo at the beginning of the 20th century, Satoko is betrothed to an imperial prince but immediately starts an affair with the son of a newly elite family.
Originally published in Japan as Haru no yuki (1968).

The **temple** of dawn. Translated from the Japanese by E. Dale Saunders and Cecilia Segawa Seigle. A. A. Knopf, 1973. 334 p. (Sea of fertility, 3)
ISBN 9780394466149
1. Senior men 2. Reincarnation 3. Voyeurism 4. Psychological fiction 5. Translations
LC 73007277

In the sequel to Runaway Horses, Honda goes to Bangkok and India in the 1940s to better understand reincarnation.
Originally published in Japan as Akatsuki no tera (1970).

Mitchell, David
Black Swan Green: a novel. David Mitchell. Random House, 2006. 294 p.
ISBN 9781400063796
1. Thirteen-year-old boys 2. Stutterers 3. Teenage boys — Psychology 4. Small town life 5. Family problems 6. England 7. Worcestershire, England 8. 1980s 9. Literary fiction 10. Coming-of-age stories 11. First person narratives 12. Adult books for young adults
LC 2005052914
Alex Award, 2007; ALA Notable Book, 2007; Booklist Editors' Choice: Adult Books for Young Adults, 2006; New York Times Notable Book, 2006; School Library Journal Best Books: Best Adult Books 4 Teens, 2006; YALSA Best Books for Young Adults, 2007

Follows a single year in the life of thirteen-year-old Jason Taylor as he grows up in what is for him the sleepiest village in Worcestershire, England, in 1982.

"The author does not pull any punches when it comes to the casual cruelty that adolescent boys can inflict on one another, but it is this very brutality that underscores the sweetness of which they are also capable. With its British slang and complex twists and turns, this title is not a selection for reluctant readers, but teens who enjoy multifaceted coming-of-age stories will be richly rewarded." —*School Library Journal*

The **bone** clocks: a novel. David Mitchell. Random House, 2014. 624 p.
ISBN 9781400065677
1. Paranormal phenomena 2. Mystics 3. Time 4. Voyages and travels 5. Imaginary wars and battles 6. 20th century 7. 21st century 8. Literary fiction 9. Contemporary fantasy 10. Multiple perspectives
LC 2014008517
ALA Notable Book, 2015; Booklist Editors' Choice, 2014; Library Journal Best Books 2014; New York Times Notable Book, 2014; World Fantasy Award, 2015

Beginning in 1984 and moving in linear fashion through the years before ending in the 2040s, this complex, layered novel interweaves several different narratives to tell the story of a secret war between those who would steal souls and those who try to stop them. But it's also the story of

Holly Sykes, who belongs to neither of these groups but whose life is nevertheless bound up in them. An expansive, globe-trotting book that takes on themes of aging, youth, and death, The Bone Clocks also features characters who have appeared in author David Mitchell's other books and incorporates genres from absolute realism to heady fantasy.

"From gritty realism to far-out fantasy, each section has its own charm and surprises." —*Publishers Weekly*

★ **Cloud** atlas: a novel. David Mitchell. Random House, 2004. 509 p.
ISBN 9780375507250
1. Fate and fatalism 2. Reincarnation 3. Musicians 4. People who are blind 5. Colonialism 6. California 7. Great Britain 8. Experimental fiction 9. Literary fiction 10. Multiple perspectives
LC 2003069314
ALA Notable Book, 2005; British Book Award for Literary Fiction, 2005; British Book Award for the Richard & Judy Best Read of the Year, 2005; Library Journal Best Books, 2004; New York Times Notable Book, 2004; Shortlisted for the Man Booker Prize, 2004; National Book Critics Circle Award for Fiction finalist, 2004

Many characters live out their lives from 1850 to a postapocalyptic Iron Age Hawaii and eventually their disparate lives intertwine.

"The author presents six narratives that evoke an array of genres, from Melvillean high-seas drama to California noir and dystopian fantasy. There is a naive clerk on a nineteenth-century Polynesian voyage; an aspiring composer who insinuates himself into the home of a syphilitic genius; a journalist investigating a nuclear plant; a publisher with a dangerous bestseller on his hands; and a cloned human being created for slave labor. These five stories are bisected and arranged around a sixth, the oral history of a post-apocalyptic island, which forms the heart of the novel. Only after this do the second halves of the stories fall into place, pulling the novels themes into focus: the ease with which one group enslaves another, and the constant rewriting of the past by those who control the present. Against such forces, Mitchell's characters reveal a quiet tenacity." —*The New Yorker*

The **thousand** autumns of Jacob De Zoet: a novel. David Mitchell. Random House, 2010. 496 p.
ISBN 9781400065455
1. East and West 2. Trading posts 3. Islands 4. Man-woman relationships 5. Cultural differences 6. Japan 7. Deshima (Nagasaki-shi, Japan) 8. 19th century 9. Historical fiction 10. Literary fiction
LC 2009047296
ALA Notable Book, 2011; Booklist Editors' Choice, 2010; Commonwealth Writers' Prize, South Asia and Europe: Best Book, 2011; New York Times Notable Book, 2010; Shortlisted for the Walter Scott Prize for Historical Fiction, 2011

Dispatched to the influential Japanese port of Dejima in 1799, ambitious clerk Jacob de Zoet resolves to earn enough money to deserve his wealthy fiancee, an effort that is challenged by his relationship with the midwife daughter of a Samurai.

"Mitchell's meticulously reconstructed the lost world of Edo-era Japan, and in doing so he's created his most conventional but most emotionally engaging novel yet: it's as if an acrobatic but show-offy performance artist, adept at mimicry, ventriloquism and cerebral literary gymnastics, had decided to do an old-fashioned play and, in the process, proved his chops as an actor." —*New York Times*

★ **Utopia** Avenue: a novel. David Mitchell. Random House, 2020. 608 p.
ISBN 9780812997439
1. Bands (Music) 2. Fame 3. Musicians 4. Music 5. Drug use 6. Great Britain 7. 1960s 8. Literary fiction 9. Historical fiction
LC 2020002646

The members of a music band in 1967 London navigate the era's parties, drugs and politics as well as their own egos and tragedies while exploring transformative perspectives about youth, art and fame.

"Utopia Avenue, while leaving behind neither the complexity nor the genre-bending pyrotechnics of The Bone Clocks (2014), is by far the most accessible of Mitchell's broad-canvas novels." —*Booklist*

Mitchell, Margaret
★ **Gone** with the wind. By Margaret Mitchell. Warner Books, 1993. 1024 p.
ISBN 9780446365383
1. Reconstruction (United States history) 2. Love triangles 3. Survival 4. War 5. O'Hara, Scarlett (Fictitious character) 6. Georgia 7. United States 8. American Civil War era (1861-1865) 9. War stories 10. Epic fiction 11. Historical fiction
Pulitzer Prize for Fiction, 1937

A spoiled young Southern belle vows to rebuild her family plantation home after the Civil War and is swept off her feet by a man who infuriates her.

Famously adapted to the big-screen as Gone with the Wind (1939), starring Clark Gable and Vivien Leigh; Academy Award for Best Picture, 1940.
Sequel: Scarlett, by Alexandra Ripley (1991).
Originally published: New York : Scribner, 1936.

Mitford, Nancy
Love in a cold climate. Nancy Mitford. Vintage Books, 2010. 304 p.
ISBN 9780307740823
1. Aristocracy 2. Young women 3. Mate selection for women 4. Marriage 5. Rich families 6. England 7. Satirical fiction 8. Modern classics
LC 2010021927
'How lovely green velvet and silver. I call that a dream, so soft and delicious, too.' She rubbed a fold of the skirt against her cheek. 'Mine's silver lame, it smells like a bird cage when it gets hot but I do love it. Aren't you thankful evening skirts are long again?' Ah, the dresses! But oh, the monotony of the Season, with its endless run of glittering balls. Even fabulously fashionable Polly Hampton with her startling good looks and excellent social connections is beginning to wilt under the glare. Groomed for the perfect marriage by her mother, fearsome Lady Montdore, Polly instead scandalises society by declaring her love for her uncle 'Boy' Dougdale, the Lecherous Lecturer, and promptly eloping to France. But the consequences of this union no one could quite expect. Love in a Cold Climate is the wickedly funny follow-up to The Pursuit of Love.
Sequel to: The pursuit of love.
Sequel: The blessing.
First published by Hamish Hamilton in 1949. Reissued in this edition 2015.
Originally published: London : H. Hamilton, 1949.

★ The **pursuit** of love: a novel. Nancy Mitford. Vintage Books, 2010. 214 p.
ISBN 9780307740816
1. Rural life 2. Mate selection for women 3. Young women 4. Rich families 5. Aristocracy 6. England 7. Satirical fiction 8. Modern classics 9. Books to TV
Nancy Mitford's The Pursuit of Love is one of the funniest, sharpest novels about love and growing up ever written. Oh, the tedium of waiting to grow up! Longing for love, obsessed with weddings and sex, Linda and her sisters and cousin Fanny are on the lookout for the perfect lover. But

finding Mr Right is much harder than any of the sisters had thought. Linda must suffer marriage first to a stuffy Tory MP and then to a handsome and humourless communist, before finding real love in war-torn Paris.

Sequel: Love in a cold climate.

First published: 1945.

Originally published: London : H. Hamilton, 1945.

Mizushima, Margaret

Killing trail. Margaret Mizushima. Crooked Lane Books, 2015. 352 p. (Timber Creek K-9 novels, 1)

ISBN 9781629533810

1. Small town life 2. Girl murder victims 3. Murder investigation 4. Policewomen 5. Police dogs 6. Colorado 7. Mysteries 8. Police procedurals

When she is assigned to investigate the murder of a young girl, Timber Creek Officer Mattie Cobb and her partner, K-9 police dog Robo, discovers that her hometown holds many secrets and that the daughter of a local veterinarian and single father holds the key to solving this mystery that could get them all killed.

Mohamed, Nadifa

The **orchard** of lost souls: a novel. Nadifa Mohamed. Farrar, Straus & Giroux, 2014. 336 p.

ISBN 9780374209148

1. Civil war 2. War and society 3. Women 4. Nine-year-old girls 5. Women soldiers 6. Somalia 7. 1980s 8. Political fiction 9. Literary fiction 10. Adult books for young adults

LC 2013034411

Booklist Editors' Choice, 2014; Somerset Maugham Award, 2014

The fall of Somalia in the late 1980s is witnessed firsthand by three women in the province of Hargeisa, including Deqo, who left a refugee existence for city security; widow Kawsar, who has been brutalized by the police; and Filsan, a young soldier who helps suppress the growing rebellion.

"Mohamed evokes the burgeoning unrest of a city on the brink of chaos with vibrant, evocative language and imagery, crafting a story that will stay with readers long after the final page is turned." —*Booklist*

Originally published: London : Simon & Schuster, 2013.

Molloy, Aimee

The **perfect** mother: a novel. Aimee Molloy. Harper, 2018. 317 p.

ISBN 9780062696793

1. New mothers 2. Infant kidnapping victims 3. Motherhood 4. Female friendship 5. Secrets 6. Brooklyn, New York City 7. New York City 8. Psychological suspense 9. Multiple perspectives

LibraryReads Favorites, 2018; Librarians' Choice (Australia), 2018

A group of new moms who all gave birth in the month of May gather twice weekly at the park to offer support and companionship before one of the babies is shatteringly abducted, subjecting his traumatized mother to invasive questions and prompting the others to go to increasingly risky lengths to help.

Momaday, N. Scott

The **ancient** child: a novel. N. Scott Momaday. Doubleday, 1989. 313 p.

ISBN 9780385279727

1. Billy 2. Kiowa women shamans 3. Native American mysticism 4. Middle-aged men — Relations with younger women 5. Sexuality —

Spiritual aspects 6. Native American painters 7. Oklahoma 8. Love stories 9. Literary fiction 10. Mythological fiction

LC 89031304

Based on an Indian myth about a boy who turns into a bear, this mystic novel concerns a young artist who confronts his unusual destiny with the aid of the beautiful medicine woman who loves him.

"Momaday's prose is not just memorable, it's haunting, and it haunts on many levels. There is a multilayered story line and vivid, believable characters, but Momaday's poetic vision is flush on every page, making almost every sentence something to savor." —*Booklist*

House made of dawn. By N. Scott Momaday. Perennial Classics, 1999. 198 p.

ISBN 9780060931940

1. Indian reservations 2. Culture conflict 3. Native American veterans 4. Native American men 5. Indians of North America 6. 1940s 7. 1950s 8. Literary fiction 9. Books to movies

Pulitzer Prize for Fiction, 1969

A young American Indian returning from World War II searches for his place on his old reservation and in urban society.

Originally published: New York : Harper & Row, 1968.

Moniz, Dantiel W.

Milk blood heat. Dantiel W. Moniz. Grove Press, 2021. 208 p.

ISBN 9780802158154

1. Race (Social sciences) 2. Femininity 3. Faith 4. Forgiveness 5. Families 6. Florida 7. Short stories 8. Literary fiction

Depicts the sultry lives of Floridians in intergenerational tales that contemplate human connection, race, womanhood, inheritance, and the elemental darkness in us all. Set among the cities and suburbs of Florida, each story delves into the ordinary worlds of young girls, women, and men who find themselves confronted by extraordinary moments of violent personal reckoning. These intimate portraits of people and relationships scour and soothe and blast a light on the nature of family, faith, forgiveness, consumption, and what we may, or may not, owe one another.

"Focusing on marginalized communities and limning relationships, longing, and our uneasy passage through a world that often confounds us, she nails aching moments of naked human emotion in direct if luscious language." —*Library Journal*

Moniz, Tomas

Big familia. Tomas Moniz. Acre Books, 2019. 192 p.

ISBN 9781946724229

1. Divorced men 2. Bisexual men 3. Commitment (Psychology) 4. Teenage pregnancy 5. Children of divorced parents 6. Psychological fiction 7. First person narratives

Follows Juan Gutierrez, a self-employed single father, as he navigates a tumultuous year of inescapable change.

Monroe, Mary

★ **God** don't like ugly. Mary Monroe. Dafina Books, 2000. 340 p. (God don't novels, 1)

ISBN 9781575666075

1. Overweight girls 2. African American girls 3. Child abuse victims 4. Girls — Friendship 5. Best friends 6. Ohio 7. Coming-of-age stories 8. Drama lit 9. African American fiction

LC 2001274884

Frightened and ashamed, budding teenager Annette Goode, a shy, awkward, overweight girl hides the devastating secret that her mother's boarder has been sexually abusing her, until her life is changed forever by the beautiful and worldly Rhoda Nelson.

"In using a young girl's innocent voice to narrate, Monroe recounts a tale of extreme hardship with a hopeful, uplifting tone." —*Publishers Weekly*

Sequel: God still don't like ugly.

God still don't like ugly. Mary Monroe. Dafina Books, 2003. 320 p. (God don't novels, 2)

ISBN 9781575669120

1. Fathers and daughters 2. African American men/women relations 3. Self-discovery 4. Overweight African American women 5. African American young women 6. Ohio 7. Miami, Florida 8. Drama lit 9. African American fiction 10. Gable, Clark

LC 2003103715

Annette, who has recently reconciled with the father she never knew, finds solace with her childhood sweetheart after a dark secret from her past destroys her engagement and a troubled friend unexpectedly comes back into her life.

Sequel to: God don't like ugly.

Sequel: God don't play.

★ **Mrs.** Wiggins. Mary Monroe. Dafina Books, 2021. 320 p. (Wiggins novels, 1)

ISBN 9781496732583

1. African American families 2. Identity (Psychology) 3. Racism 4. Children of prostitutes 5. Children of clergy 6. Alabama 7. 20th century 8. Historical fiction 9. African American fiction 10. Southern fiction

The daughter of a prostitute mother and an alcoholic father, Maggie Franklin knew her only way out was to marry someone upstanding and church-going. Someone like Hubert Wiggins, the most eligible man in Lexington, Alabama—and the son of its most revered preacher. Proper and prosperous, Hubert is glad to finally have a wife, even one with Maggie's background. For Hubert has a secret he desperately needs to stay hidden. And Maggie's unexpected charm, elegance, and religious devotion makes her the perfect partner in lies...

"Although scenes of rape and sexual abuse shape Monroe's unflinching dramatization of difficult but important themes of sexuality, sexual trauma, and survival, they do not weigh down the story, but rather enrich its resonance." —*Booklist*

Monroe, Mary Alice

Beach house reunion. Mary Alice Monroe. Simon & Schuster 2018. 416 p. (Isle of Palms novels, 5)

ISBN 9781501193293

1. Aunt and niece 2. Vacation homes 3. Self-fulfillment in women 4. Surfing 5. Reunions 6. South Carolina 7. Isle of Palms, South Carolina 8. Relationship fiction 9. Southern fiction

Cara Rutledge returns to her Southern home on the idyllic Isle of Palms. Everything is comfortingly the same, yet each detail is rife with painful memories. Only through reconnecting with family, friends, and the rhythms of the lowcountry can Cara release the hold of the past and open herself to the possibility of a new love, career, and hope for the future.

★ The **summer** of lost and found. Mary Alice Monroe. Simon & Schuster 2021. 368 p. (Isle of Palms novels, 7)

ISBN 9781982148348

1. COVID-19 Pandemic, 2019- 2. Lovers 3. Uncertainty 4. Life change events 5. Coastal towns 6. South Carolina 7. Isle of Palms, South Carolina 8. 2020s 9. Relationship fiction 10. Southern fiction

LC 2021001556

With her family, finances, emotions, relationships and health teetering on the brink, Linnea Rutledge finds her life further complicated by her feelings for John, an old flame who turns up from California and is quarantining next door.

"The intimate island atmosphere keeps the focus on family and romantic relationships, as the characters deal with a global pandemic. Monroe's book acknowledges some of the hardships that real people endured over the past year, addresses loss and change, and finds hope where it's possible, which gives depth to this timely story." —*Library Journal*

Monsarrat, Nicholas

The **cruel** sea. Nicholas Monsarrat. Burford Books, 2000. 509 p.

ISBN 9781580800464

1. Military campaigns 2. World War II 3. Naval battles 4. North Atlantic Ocean 5. Second World War era (1939-1945) 6. Sea stories 7. Adventure stories 8. War stories

Based on the author's own vivid experiences, The Cruel Sea is the nail-biting story of the crew of *HMS Compass Rose,* a corvette assigned to protect convoys during World War II. Darting back and forth across the icy North Atlantic, *Compass Rose* played a deadly cat-and-mouse game with packs of German U-boats lying in wait beneath the ocean waves. Packed with tension and vivid descriptions of agonizing U-boat hunts, this tale of the most bitter and chilling campaign of the war tells of ordinary men who had to master their own fears before they could face a brutal menace-one which would strike without warning from the deep.

Originally published: New York : Knopf, 1951.

Montag, Kassandra

After the flood: a novel. Kassandra Montag. William Morrow, 2019. 400 p.

ISBN 9780062889362

1. Post-apocalypse 2. Floods 3. Survival (after environmental catastrophe) 4. Mothers and daughters 5. Mothers of kidnapping victims 6. Apocalyptic fiction 7. Science fiction

LC 2018044621

Booklist Editors' Choice, 2019

A tale set in an anarchic near-future America of mountaintop colonies surrounded by rising oceans finds an independent woman trading for supplies and information about the daughter who was stolen from her eight years earlier.

Montclair, Allison

The **right** sort of man. Allison Montclair. Minotaur Books, 2019. 336 p. (Sparks & Bainbridge mysteries, 1)

ISBN 9781250178367

1. Postwar life 2. Matchmakers 3. Women amateur detectives 4. Former spies 5. Murder suspects 6. London, England 7. 1940s 8. Historical mysteries

LC 2019004332

Organizing a matchmaking business together in spite of their differences, two women from 1946 London find their promising company endangered when one of their clients is arrested for the murder of another.

"Fans of M. C. Beaton will relish the wit, and followers of Susan Elia MacNeal and Jacqueline Winspear will enjoy the depth and the period detail." —*Booklist*

A **rogue's** company. Allison Montclair. Minotaur Books, 2021. 288 p. (Sparks & Bainbridge mysteries, 3)

ISBN 9781250750327

1. Murder 2. Kidnapping 3. Matchmaking 4. Women-owned businesses 5. Child custody 6. London, England 7. 1940s 8. Historical mysteries

LC 2020056397

Business becomes personal for the Right Sort Marriage Bureau when a new client, a brutal murder, two kidnappings, and the recently returned from Africa Lord Bainbridge threatens everything that one of the principals holds dear...

"An artfully constructed puzzle and dry humor lift Montclair's excellent third mystery featuring professional matchmakers and amateur sleuths Iris Sparks and Gwen Bainbridge in post-WWII London (after 2020's A Royal Affair)." —*Publishers Weekly*

A **royal** affair. Allison Montclair. Minotaur Books, 2020. 320 p. (Sparks & Bainbridge mysteries, 2)

ISBN 9781250178398

1. Postwar life 2. Women amateur detectives 3. Matchmaking 4. Royal houses 5. Women-owned businesses 6. London, England 7. England 8. 1940s 9. Historical mysteries

LC 2020001337

A sequel to The Right Sort of Man finds Iris and Gwendolyn of The Right Sort of Marriage Bureau investigating the past of a dashing Greek prince who has captured the heart of the Princess Elizabeth.

"An irresistible mix of period thrills, international intrigue, unquenchable friendship, and a royal betrothal." —*Kirkus*

Montgomery, Jess

The **stills**. Jess Montgomery. Minotaur Books, 2021. 352 p. (Kinship novels, 3)

ISBN 9781250623409

1. Widows 2. Women sheriffs 3. Bootleggers 4. Moonshining (Illegal distilling) 5. Criminals 6. Ohio 7. Appalachian Region 8. 1920s 9. Historical fiction

LC 2020042045

Ohio, 1927: Moonshining is a way of life in rural Bronwyn County, and even the otherwise upstanding Sheriff Lily Ross has been known to turn a blind eye when it comes to stills in the area. But when thirteen-year-old Jebediah Ranklin almost dies after drinking tainted moonshine, Lily knows that someone has gone too far, and—with the help of organizer and moonshiner Marvena Whitcomb—is determined to find out who.

"Like Sharyn McCrumb's and Julia Keller's thrillers, this third Lily Ross tale (following The Hollows, 2020) is a fine example of Appalachian storytelling, thoughtfully portraying characters at the intersections of kinship, poverty, power, and survival." —*Booklist*

The **widows**. Jess Montgomery. Minotaur Books, 2019. 320 p. (Kinship novels, 1)

ISBN 9781250184528

1. Jones 2. Widows 3. Women sheriffs 4. Coal miners 5. Prohibition 6. Communities 7. Ohio 8. Appalachian Region 9. 1920s 10. Historical fiction

LC 2018029795

Vowing revenge against her sheriff husband's killers in 1924 Ohio, Lily offers help to a fellow widow and uncovers dangerous evidence revealing her husband's corrupt secret life and the complexities that triggered his death.

"Inspired by the true story of Maude Collins, Ohio's first female sheriff, and prominent labor and community organizer Mary Harris Mother Jones, Montgomery's debut novel features two tough-as-nails, strong-willed women whose empathy leaves a lasting impression. A simultaneous examination of women's rights, coal mining, prohibition, and Appalachian life, make this is a fantastic choice for historical fiction fans." —*Library Journal*

Montimore, Margarita

Oona out of order. Margarita Montimore. Flatiron Books, 2020. 338 pages

ISBN 9781250236609

1. Time travel 2. New Year's Eve 3. Women 4. Memories 5. Reality 6. Science fiction 7. Relationship fiction

LC 2019036420

LibraryReads Favorites, 2020; RUSA Reading List, 2021

As the countdown to the New Year begins, soon-to-be-19 Oona Lockhart faints and awakens 32 years in the future in her 51-year-old body; and, greeted by a friendly stranger in a beautiful house she's told is her own, Oona learns that with each passing year she will leap to another age at random.

"Read this to get a bit lost, to root for a character with a strong love for herself, and to connect on a deeply human level with the fear of leading an incomplete life." —*Kirkus*

Published in the UK as "The rearranged life of Oona Lockhart" by Orion, 2020.

Mooney, Chris

Blood world. Chris Mooney. Berkley, 2020. 436 p.

ISBN 9780593197639

1. Drugs 2. Policewomen 3. Child kidnapping victims 4. Undercover operations 5. Blood 6. Los Angeles, California 7. California 8. Thrillers and suspense 9. Bio-thrillers

LC 2019057674

In a world where people with a rare gene are kidnapped for their blood's wonder-cure abilities, an LAPD officer fighting the activities of illegal blood farms is pitted against a madman who has modified healing blood to unstoppable levels.

"Several tense scenes will keep readers on edge as they race with Batista toward a satisfying cliff-hanger ending. Given our current circumstances, biotech story lines are bound to intrigue patrons for the next while." —*Booklist*

Moor, Jessica

The **keeper**. Jessica Moor. Viking,, 2020. 336 pages

ISBN 9780143134527

1. Partner abuse 2. Family violence 3. Women murder victims 4. Women's shelters 5. Police 6. England 7. Mysteries 8. Police procedurals

LC 2019055793

A detective looking into the apparent suicide of a woman who lived at a domestic violence shelter discovers evidence that she was not who she appeared to be and sets out to prove it was actually murder.

"Set in rural England, Moor's clever debut presents a movingly sympathetic portrait of the victims of domestic violence." —*Publishers Weekly*

Moore, Alan

Jerusalem: a novel. Alan Moore. Liveright Publishing Corporation, 2016. 1184 p. : Illustration

ISBN 9781631491344

1. Space and time 2. Slums 3. Mortality 4. Public housing 5. Eternity 6. England 7. Northamptonshire, England 8. Literary fiction 9. Fantasy fiction

LC 2016014957

A novel employing a kaleidoscope of literary forms and styles provides a rich cast of characters includes the living, the dead, the celestial, and the infernal in an intricately woven tapestry that presents a vision of an absolute and timeless human reality in all of its exquisite, comical and heartbreaking splendor.

"Moore bundles all his ruminations about space, time, life, and death into an immense interconnected narrative that spans all human existence within the streets of his native Northampton, U.K. Reading this sprawling collection of words and ideas isnt an activity; its an experience." —*Publishers Weekly*

Moore, Alison

The **lighthouse**. Alison Moore. Salt Publishing, 2012. 183 p.
ISBN 9781907773174
1. Middle-aged men 2. Memories — Psychological aspects 3. Abandonment (Psychology) 4. Compulsive behavior in men 5. Neuroses in men 6. Germany 7. Psychological fiction 8. Literary fiction
Shortlisted for the Man Booker Prize, 2012
On the outer deck of a North Sea ferry stands Futh, a middle-aged and newly separated man, on his way to Germany for a restorative walking holiday. As he contemplates an earlier trip to Germany and the things he has done in his life, he does not foresee the potentially devastating consequences of things not done.

Moore, Graham

The **holdout**: a novel. Graham Moore. Random House, 2020. 336 p.
ISBN 9780399591778
1. Race relations 2. African American men 3. Trials (Murder) 4. Jurors 5. Frameups 6. Legal thrillers 7. Multiple perspectives
LC 2019029712
RUSA Reading List, 2021
A woman is wrongly implicated in a murder one decade after convincing the members of a deadlocked jury to return a not-guilty verdict.

"The twists are sharp and the flashbacks that uncover what each juror knows are placed for maximum impact in this rollicking legal thriller." —*Library Journal*

Moore, Liz

Long bright river. Liz Moore. Riverhead Books, 2020. 496 p.
ISBN 9780525540670
1. Policewomen 2. Women drug abusers 3. Sisters 4. Opioid epidemic 5. Addiction 6. Philadelphia, Pennsylvania 7. Police procedurals
LC 2018051652
LibraryReads Favorites, 2020
A suspense novel that also looks at the anatomy of a Philadelphia family rocked by the opioid crisis and the relationship between two sisters—one, suffering from addiction, who has suddenly gone missing amid a series of mysterious murders; the other a police officer who patrols the neighborhood from which she disappeared: a story about the formidable ties between place, family, and fate.

"In her fourth novel (following The Unseen World), Rome Prize-winning author Moore blends the reality of today's deadly opioid crisis with a complicated family dynamic to create an intense mystery with stunning twists and turns. Impossible to put down, impossible to forget." —*Library Journal*

The **unseen** world. Liz Moore. W. W. Norton & Co, 2016. 416 p.
ISBN 9780393241686
1. Fathers and daughters 2. Identity (Psychology) 3. Computer scientists 4. Alzheimer's disease 5. Girl prodigies 6. Boston, Massachusetts 7. 1980s 8. Literary fiction 9. Coming-of-age stories 10. Adult books for young adults
LC 2016011031
ALA Notable Book, 2017; LibraryReads Favorites, 2016; Loan Stars Favourites, 2016
Accompanying her eccentric, socially inept father to his 1980s Boston computer science lab every day, Ada, a shy, homeschooled prodigy, is sheltered by a colleague when her father's mental health and reputation deteriorate in ways that compel her to investigate his hidden past.

Moore, Lorrie

A **gate** at the stairs: a novel. By Lorrie Moore. Alfred A. Knopf, 2009. 336 p.
ISBN 9780375409288
1. Racism 2. Adoption 3. Nannies 4. College students 5. Rich families 6. Literary fiction 7. First person narratives 8. Coming-of-age stories 9. Adult books for young adults
LC 2009003091
Booklist Editors' Choice, 2009; New York Times Notable Book, 2009; Shortlisted for The Orange Prize for Fiction, 2010
In the Midwest just after the September 11 attacks, twenty-year-old Tassie Keltjin comes of age amid such challenges as racism, the War on Terror, and cruelty in the name of love, as she leaves her family's farm to attend college and takes a part-time job as a nanny.

"The novel concludes in a tone of wan hope, with Tassie wiser and stronger, though forever sadder.... This book is—not above all, but in the service of all—funny. Moore is not shy about the bad joke, and never pushes a great one too far. Her humor, always pointed at insight and elaboration, strikes the perfect balance between taste and feeling." —*PopMatters*

Moore, Meg Mitchell

The **islanders**. Meg Mitchell Moore. William Morrow, 2019. 416 p.
ISBN 9780062840066
1. Islands 2. Secrets 3. Friendship 4. Writing 5. Divorce 6. Rhode Island 7. Block Island, Rhode Island 8. Mainstream fiction
A writer struggling with a second book, the divorced owner of a café and an unfulfilled stay-at-home mom share a season of unexpected romance and secrets on scenic Block Island.

Morante, Elsa

Arturo's island: a novel. Elsa Morante; translated by Ann Goldstein. Liveright Publishing Corporation, 2019. 384 p.
ISBN 9781631493294
1. Solitude 2. Stepmothers 3. Fathers and sons 4. Growing up 5. Teenage boys 6. Italy 7. Between the Wars (1918-1939) 8. Modern classics 9. Coming-of-age stories 10. First person narratives
LC 2018046181
Imbued with a spectral grace, as if told through an enchanted looking glass, the novel follows the adolescent Arturo through his days on the isolated Neapolitan island of Procida, where—his mother long deceased, his father often absent, and a dog as his sole companion—he roams the countryside and the beaches or reads in his family's lonely, dilapidated mansion. This quiet, meandering existence is upended when his father brings home a beautiful sixteen-year-old bride, Nunziatella.
Translation of: Isola di Arturo.
Originally published: 1957.
Translated from the Italian.

Morelli, Laura

The **stolen** lady. Laura Morelli. William Morrow & Co, 2021. 384 p.

ISBN 9780062993595

1. Leonardo 2. Household employees 3. Secrets 4. World War II 5. Women archivists 6. Nazis 7. Second World War era (1939-1945) 8. Renaissance (1300-1600) 9. Historical fiction 10. Parallel narratives

Separated by 500 years, two women—Anne Guichard, a young archivist at the Louvre, who at the dawn of WWII must keep treasures safe from the Nazis; and house servant, Bellina Sardi, who is tasked with keeping an impossible secret—each hide Leonardo da Vinci's Mona Lisa with unintended consequences.

"Morelli makes both story lines richly drawn, revealing the remarkable fortitude of two women who saved a masterpiece, each during a moment of upheaval. This will pull in readers from the very first page." —*Publishers Weekly*

Moreno, Gus

This thing between us: a novel. Gus Moreno. MCD x FSG Originals / Farrar, Straus and Giroux, 2021. 256 p.

ISBN 9780374539238

1. Widowers 2. Grief in men 3. High technology 4. Good and evil 5. Hispanic Americans 6. Chicago, Illinois 7. Illinois 8. Horror 9. First person narratives

LC 2021019887

A widower battles his grief, rage, and the mysterious evil inhabiting his home smart speaker, in this mesmerizing horror thriller from newcomer Gus Moreno.

"Harrowing existential horror that lingers like a nightmare." —*Kirkus*

Moreno-Garcia, Silvia

★ **Gods** of jade and shadow: a novel. Silvia Moreno-Garcia. Del Rey, 2019. 352 p.

ISBN 9780525620754

1. Gods and goddesses, Mayan 2. Young women 3. Quests 4. Families 5. Cousins 6. Mexico 7. Mexican-American Border Region 8. 1920s 9. Historical fantasy 10. Mythological fiction 11. Canadian fiction

LC 2019007450

Ignyte Awards: Best Adult Novel, 2020; LibraryReads Favorites, 2019; Sunburst Award for Excellence in Canadian Literature of the Fantastic, 2020

A dark fairy tale inspired by folklore is set against the Jazz age in Mexico's underworld, where a young dreamer is sent by the Mayan God of Death on a life-changing journey.

Mexican Gothic. Silvia Moreno-Garcia. Del Rey, 2020. 352 pages
ISBN 9780525620785

1. Socialites 2. Family estates 3. Family secrets 4. Newlyweds 5. Cousins 6. Mexico 7. 1950s 8. Gothic fiction 9. Historical fantasy 10. Canadian fiction

LC 2019048648

LibraryReads Favorites, 2020; Loan Stars Favourites, 2020; Locus Award for Dark Fantasy-Horror Novel, 2021; Prix Aurora: Best Novel, 2021; RUSA Reading List Short List, 2021

A reimagining of the classic gothic suspense novel follows the experiences of a courageous socialite in 1950s Mexico who is drawn into the treacherous secrets of an isolated mansion.

"Moreno-Garcia offers a terrifying twist on classic gothic horror, set in 1950s Mexico." —*Kirkus*

★ **Velvet** was the night. Silvia Moreno-Garcia. Del Rey, 2021. 288 p.
ISBN 9780593356821

1. Secretaries 2. Missing women 3. Intrigue 4. State sponsored terrorism 5. Missing persons investigation 6. Mexico City 7. Mexico 8. 1970s 9. Noir fiction 10. Historical fiction 11. Canadian fiction

LC 2021005283

Loan Stars Favourites, 2021

In 1970s Mexico City, Maite, a secretary with a penchant for romance novels, searches for her missing neighbor, Leonora, a beautiful art student, which leads her to an eccentric gangster who longs to escape his own life, and together, they set out to discover the dangerous truth.

"Moreno-Garcia keeps the suspense high and the action intense, all while sharing a bit of 1970s Mexican history in this perfectly pitched novel." —*Library Journal*

Morgan Jones, Chris

The **silent** oligarch. Christopher Morgan Jones. Penguin Press, 2012. 336 p. (Ben Webster novels, 1)

ISBN 9781594203190

1. Business intelligence 2. Money laundering 3. Political corruption 4. Upper class 5. Lawyers 6. Moscow, Russia 7. Thrillers and suspense

Hired to expose the criminal networks of a Russian bureaucrat who has amassed an illicit fortune, London investigator Benjamin Webster uncovers evidence that his target may also be responsible for the murder of a colleague.

Sequel: The jackal's share

Morgan, C. E.

★ The **sport** of kings. C. E. Morgan. Farrar, Straus & Giroux, 2016. 480 p.

ISBN 9780374281083

1. Horse breeding 2. Horse racing 3. Fathers and daughters 4. Thoroughbred horses 5. African American men 6. Kentucky 7. Literary fiction

LC 2015038512

ALA Notable Book, 2017; Booklist Editors' Choice, 2016; Kirkus Prize for Fiction, 2016; New York Times Notable Book, 2016; Pulitzer Prize for Fiction finalist, 2017; Shortlisted for The Baileys Women's Prize for Fiction, 2017; Shortlisted for the James Tait Black Memorial Prize for Fiction, 2016

The trailblazing patriarch of a proud Kentucky clan, his daughter, and a black ex-prisoner embark on an effort to reclaim the family's near-mythic legacy by breeding champion horses, an endeavor that is challenged by divided ambitions, the farm's ugly past, and a willful thoroughbred filly.

"A dense meditation on the ugliness that undergirds much of the sublime we as humans strive for and admire in life." —*Library Journal*

Morgenstern, Erin

★ The **night** circus: a novel. By Erin Morgenstern. Doubleday, 2011. 387 p.

ISBN 9780385534635

1. Magicians 2. Magicians' apprentices 3. Competition 4. Circus 5. Games 6. 19th century 7. Historical fantasy 8. Adult books for young adults

LC 2010050546

Alex Award, 2012; Booklist Editors' Choice: Adult Books for Young Adults, 2011; Library Journal Best Books, 2011; Locus Award for First Novel, 2012; RUSA Reading List, 2012; School Library Journal Best Books: Best Adult Books 4 Teens, 2011

Waging a fierce competition for which they have trained since childhood, circus magicians Celia and Marco unexpectedly fall in love with each other and share a fantastical romance that manifests in fateful ways.

★ The **starless** sea. Erin Morgenstern. Doubleday, 2019. 498 pages

ISBN 9780385541213

1. Libraries 2. Secret societies 3. Imaginary places 4. Graduate students 5. Magic 6. Fantasy fiction 7. Multiple perspectives

LC 2018053215

LibraryReads Favorites, 2019; Loan Stars Favourites, 2019

Discovering a mysterious book of prisoner tales, a Vermont graduate student recognizes a story from his own life before following clues to a magical underground library that is being targeted for destruction.

Moriarty, Jaclyn

Gravity is the thing. Jaclyn Moriarty. HarperCollins, 2019. 402 p.

ISBN 9780062883735

1. Self-help psychology 2. Loss (Psychology) 3. Missing persons 4. Grief 5. Coping 6. Australia 7. Relationship fiction 8. Australian fiction

Librarians' Choice (Australia), 2019

Follows a single mother's heartfelt search for more meaningful truths about the universe, her family and herself.

"With an eye as keen for human idiosyncrasies as Miranda July's, and a sense of humor as bright and surprising as Maria Semple's, this is a novel of pure velocity; it sucks the reader into Abi's problems and her joys in equal, brilliant measure. A complex dissection of the self-help industry, as well as a complete and moving portrait of a difficult, delightful woman, Moriarty proves her adult novels can live up to her YA work's reputation." —*Publishers Weekly*

Previoulsy published by Macmillan Australia, 2019.

Moriarty, Liane

Big little lies. Liane Moriarty. Amy Einhorn Books, 2014. 416 p.

ISBN 9780399167065

1. Suburban life 2. Murder 3. Parents 4. Schools 5. Family relationships 6. Mainstream fiction 7. Australian fiction 8. Books to TV

Davitt Awards, Best Adult Novel, 2015; Library Journal Best Books 2014; LibraryReads Favorites, 2014

An annual school Trivia Night ends in a disastrous riot leaving one parent dead in what appears to be a tragic accident, but evidence shows it might have been premeditated.

"Moriarty demonstrates an excellent talent for exposing the dark, seedy side of the otherwise 'perfect' family unit while keeping the characters believable enough to be someone you might know." —*Library Journal*

The **husband's** secret. Liane Moriarty. Amy Einhorn Books, 2013. 416 p.

ISBN 9780399159343

1. Husband and wife 2. Life change events 3. Secrets 4. Mothers 5. Schools 6. Australia 7. Sydney, New South Wales 8. Mainstream fiction 9. Multiple perspectives 10. Australian fiction

LC 2013009340

Discovering a tattered letter that says she is to open it only in the event of her husband's death, Cecelia, a successful family woman, is unable to resist reading the letter and discovers a secret that shatters her life and the lives of two other women.

"There is real darkness here, but it is offset by the author's natural wit...and irrepressible goodwill toward her characters." —*Kirkus*

We all have secrets. But not like this——Cover.

Nine perfect strangers. Liane Moriarty. Flatiron Books, 2018. 432 p.

ISBN 9781250069825

1. Health resorts 2. Strangers 3. Wellness lifestyle 4. Women authors 5. Secrets 6. Australia 7. Mainstream fiction 8. Australian fiction 9. Books to TV

Librarians' Choice (Australia), 2018; Loan Stars Favourites, 2018

Gathering at a remote health resort for a 10-day fitness program, nine strangers and their enigmatic host become subjects of interest to a brokenhearted novelist who develops uncomfortable doubts about the resort's real agenda.

Truly madly guilty. Liane Moriarty. Flatiron Books, 2016. 416 p.

ISBN 9781250069795

1. Married people 2. Life change events 3. Consequences 4. Barbecues 5. Friendship 6. Sydney, New South Wales 7. Australia 8. Mainstream fiction 9. Australian fiction

Goodreads Choice Award, 2016; LibraryReads Favorites, 2016

A busy couple formerly on the brink of realizing their dreams reflects on a fortuitous gathering with their best friends and another couple, in a tale that explores the role of guilt in relationships and the power of everyday moments in family life.

"This novel sheds light on the truths that we all fear as parents, spouses, and friends. It's perfect for those long summer days, but readers will have to pace themselves to not devour it in one sitting." —*Library Journal*

Morrell, David

Ruler of the night. David Morrell. Mulholland Books, 2016. 342 p. (Thomas De Quincey mysteries, 3)

ISBN 9780316307901

1. De Quincey, Thomas 2. Trains 3. Fathers and daughters 4. Intrigue 5. Power (Social sciences) 6. Nobility 7. London, England 8. Victorian era (1837-1901) 9. Victorian mysteries 10. Historical mysteries

Opium addict Thomas De Quincey and his irrepressible daughter Emily investigate the strangling of a lawyer in what is the first murder on an English train, and they uncover a dangerous secret that reaches the highest levels of British society.

Sequel to: Inspector of the dead.

Morris, Heather

Cilka's journey. Heather Morris. St Martin's Press, 2019. 343 pages

ISBN 9781250265708

1. Survival (in concentration camps, prisons, etc.) 2. Consequences 3. Resilience (Personal quality) 4. Beauty 5. Holocaust survivors 6. Poland 7. Siberia 8. 20th century 9. Historical fiction 10. Australian fiction

LibraryReads Favorites, 2019

Follows a Russian woman who is forced by a concentration-camp commandant to become his lover and is subsquently sent to Siberia after being found guilty of collaborating with the enemy.

"Morris weaves a fast-paced story that captures the immediacy of Cilka's duties caring for prisoners while appeasing guards at every step." —*Publishers Weekly*

Morrison, Toni

★ **Beloved**: a novel. Toni Morrison. Knopf, 1987. 275 p.

ISBN 9780394535975

1. Freed people 2. Children — Death 3. Coping in women 4. African American women 5. Mothers and daughters 6. Ohio 7. 19th century 8. Historical fiction 9. Magical realism 10. Literary fiction

LC 86026157

Pulitzer Prize for Fiction, 1988; Robert F. Kennedy Book Award, 1988; National Book Critics Circle Award for Fiction finalist, 1987; National Book Award for Fiction finalist, 1987

Sethe, an escaped slave living in post-Civil War Ohio with her daughter and mother-in-law, is persistently haunted by the ghost of her dead baby girl.

"Ms. Morrison's versatility and technical and emotional range appear to know no bounds. If there were any doubts about her stature as a pre-eminent American novelist, of her own or any other generation, Beloved will put them to rest. In three words or less, it's a hair-raiser." —*New York Times Book Review*

★ The **bluest** eye: a novel. Toni Morrison. Holt, Rinehart and Winston, 1970. 164 p.
ISBN 9780030850745
1. Social acceptance 2. Self-acceptance in girls 3. Self-esteem in girls 4. African Americans 5. Family problems 6. Ohio 7. Coming-of-age stories 8. African American fiction 9. Literary fiction
LC 79117270
Eleven-year-old Pecola Breedlove, an African-American girl in an America whose love for blonde, blue-eyed children can devastate all others, prays for her eyes to turn blue, so that she will be beautiful, people will notice her, and her world will be different.

★ **God** help the child. Toni Morrison. Knopf, 2015. 192 p.
ISBN 9780307594174
1. Mothers and daughters 2. Child abuse 3. Psychic trauma 4. Color of African Americans 5. Human skin color 6. Psychological fiction 7. Literary fiction 8. African American fiction
BCALA Literary Award for Fiction, 2016; New York Times Notable Book, 2015
Traces the impact of childhood trauma on the lives of a beautiful multiracial woman, the man she loves, and an abused white girl who looks to her for help.

"There are some moves here that may seem obvious, but the pieces all fit together seamlessly in a story about beating back the past, confronting the present, and understanding one's worth." —*Library Journal*

Home. Toni Morrison. Knopf, 2012. 144 p.
ISBN 9780307594167
1. African American veterans 2. Siblings 3. Korean War veterans 4. Psychic trauma in men 5. Racism 6. Georgia 7. Psychological fiction 8. Literary fiction 9. African American fiction
LC 2011043441
New York Times Notable Book, 2012; Booklist Editors' Choice, 2012
A Korean War veteran living a shattered life embarks on a quest to save his younger sister.

Jazz. Toni Morrison. A. A. Knopf, 1992. 229 p.
ISBN 9780679411673
1. Murder 2. Violence in men 3. Extramarital affairs 4. African American men/women relations 5. African American teenage girls 6. Harlem, New York City 7. New York City 8. 1920s 9. Love stories 10. Literary fiction 11. First person narratives
LC 91058555
ALA Notable Book, 1993
In Harlem, 1926, Joe Trace, a door-to-door salesman in his fifties, kills his teenage lover. A profound love story which depicts the sights and sounds of Black urban life during the Jazz Age.

"This novel tells the story of Violet and Joe Trace, married for over 20 years, residents of Harlem in 1926.... Violet works as an unlicensed hairdresser, doing ladies hair in their own homes, and Joe sells Cleopatra cosmetics door to door.... When the novel opens, Joe has shot his 18-year-old lover, Dorcas, and Violet has disfigured the dead girl's body at her funeral in a fit of rage. Joe, who was not caught, is in mourning, crying all day in his darkened apartment, and Violet has taken on the task of finding out whatever she can about Dorcas." *Voice Lit Suppl*

"As the story unfolds, we come to understand, if not excuse, what happened. The characters themselves cannot excuse their own behavior, which baffles them. Violet is obsessed by the memory of the dead girl whose face she slashed: What was it about her that Joe found so special? She is driven to visit the girl's aunt Alice, who is understandably frightened.... Some of the most interesting scenes in the book are the subsequent meetings of these two very different women who come to respect each other, even before they learn to understand each other." —*Christian Science Monitor*

Love. Toni Morrison. Knopf, 2003. 208 p.
ISBN 9780375409448
1. Community life 2. African American women 3. African American men 4. Hotel owners 5. African American men/women relations 6. Florida 7. Psychological fiction 8. Literary fiction 9. African American fiction
LC 2003052737
ALA Notable Book, 2004; Booklist Editors' Choice, 2003; New York Times Notable Book, 2003
The epitome of a group of women's ideals about love, fatherhood, and friendship, wealthy hotel owner Bill Cosey finds his life compromised by his troubled past and his feelings about a spellbinding woman named Celestial.

A **mercy**: a novel. By Toni Morrison. Knopf, 2008. 176 p.
ISBN 9780307264237
1. Slavery 2. Prejudice 3. African American girls 4. Interracial adoption 5. Racism 6. 17th century 7. Historical fiction 8. Literary fiction 9. African American fiction
LC 2008021067
ALA Notable Book, 2010; Booklist Editors' Choice, 2008; Library Journal Best Books, 2008; New York Times Notable Book, 2008; Shortlisted for the James Tait Black Memorial Prize for Fiction, 2008
In exchange for a bad debt, an Anglo-Dutch trader takes on Florens, a young slave girl, who feels abandoned by her slave mother and who searches for love—first from an older servant woman at her master's new home, and then from a handsome free blacksmith, in a novel set in late seventeenth-century America.

"The fate of a slave child abandoned by her mother animates this allusive novel part Faulknerian puzzle, part dream-song about orphaned women who form an eccentric household in late-17th-century America. Morrison's farmers and rum traders, masters and slaves, indentured whites and captive Native Americans live side by side, often in violent conflict, in a lawless, ripe American Eden that is both a haven and a prison an emerging nation whose identity is rooted equally in Old World superstitions and New World appetites and fears." —*New York Times Book Review*

Paradise. Toni Morrison. A. A. Knopf, 1998. 318 p.
ISBN 9780679433743
1. African American communities 2. Community life 3. African American men/women relations 4. African Americans 5. Women's shelters 6. Oklahoma 7. 1890s 8. 1970s 9. Poe, Edgar Allan 10. Literary fiction 11. Modern classics
New York Times Notable Book, 1998; Shortlisted for the International IMPAC Dublin Literary Award, 2000; Shortlisted for The Orange Prize for Fiction, 1999
Tells the story of Ruby, Oklahoma, an all Black town settled by a dozen families in the 1890s when they were turned away from other communities. But now it's the 1970s and the men of the town blame the women and the women's shelter for the change in their community's character.

★ **Song** of Solomon. Toni Morrison. A. A. Knopf, 1977. 337 p.
ISBN 9780394497846

1. African Americans — Identity 2. Self-discovery in men 3. Self-acceptance in men 4. African American fathers and sons 5. Rich African American families 6. Detroit, Michigan 7. Family sagas 8. Literary fiction 9. African American fiction

LC 77000874

National Book Critics Circle Award for Fiction, 1977

Milkman Dead was born shortly after a neighborhood eccentric hurled himself off a rooftop in a vain attempt at flight. For the rest of his life he, too, will be trying to fly.

"Toni Morrison's Song of Solomon belongs in [the]... small company of special books that are a privilege to review... It builds, out of history and language and myth, to music. It takes off. If Ralph Ellison's Invisible Man went underground, Toni Morrison's Milkman flies."—*New York Times Book Review*

Sula. Toni Morrison; with a new foreword by the author. Vintage International, 2004. Xvii, 174 p.

ISBN 9781400033430

1. African American women 2. Small town life 3. Friendship 4. African American women — Friendship 5. Female friendship 6. Ohio 7. Literary fiction 8. African American fiction 9. Modern classics

LC 2004555327

At the heart of Sula is a bond between two women, a friendship whose intensity first sustains, then injures. Sula and Nel are both black, both smart, and both poor. Through their girlhood years, they share everything. All this changes when Sula gets out of the Bottom, the hilltop neighborhood where there hides a fierce resentment at the invisible line that cannot be overstepped.

Tar baby. Toni Morrison. A. A. Knopf, 1981. 305 p.

ISBN 9780394423296

1. Community life 2. Caribbean Area 3. African American fiction 4. Literary fiction 5. Modern classics

LC 80022821

On a tropical island paradise, six people interact with each other in all the tender or hateful ways that human beings are capable of. Rich and poor, black and white, young and old, male and female, each has something to teach the others—and each has something to learn.

"Each of the characters in Toni Morrison's Tar Baby comes with a history, quite a complete history that is given to us in a series of stunning performances." —*The New Republic*

Morton, Brian

Florence Gordon. Brian Morton. Houghton Mifflin Harcourt, 2014. 256 p.

ISBN 9780544309869

1. Senior women 2. Women radicals 3. Independence in women 4. Intellectual life 5. Authors 6. New York City 7. Upper West Side, New York City 8. 2000s (Decade) 9. Literary fiction

LC 2014011676

Booklist Editors' Choice, 2014; Kirkus Prize for Fiction finalist, 2014

A wise and entertaining novel about a woman who has lived life on her own terms for seventy-five defiant and determined years, only to find herself suddenly thrust to the center of her family's various catastrophes..

"Morton's characters are sharply drawn, vivid in temperament and behavior, and his prose smartly reveals Florence's strength and dignity." —*Publishers Weekly*

Morton, Kate

The distant hours: a novel. Kate Morton. Atria Books, 2010. 480 p.

ISBN 9781439152782

1. Mothers and daughters 2. Family secrets 3. World War II 4. Evacuation of civilians 5. Castles 6. England 7. Kent, England 8. Gothic fiction 9. Psychological suspense 10. Parallel narratives

LC 2010033472

Australian Book Industry Awards, General Fiction Book of the Year, 2011

Edie Burchill and her mother have never been close, but when a long-lost letter arrives one Sunday afternoon with the return address of Milderhurst Castle, Kent, printed on its envelope, Edie begins to suspect that her mother's emotional distance masks an old secret. Evacuated from London as a thirteen-year-old girl, Edie's mother is chosen by the mysterious Juniper Blythe, and taken to live at the grand and glorious Milderhurst Castle, where she discovers the joys of books and fantasy and writing, but also, ultimately, the dangers. Fifty years later, as Edie chases the answers to her mother's riddle, she, too, is drawn to Milderhurst Castle and the eccentric Sisters Blythe. Inside the decaying castle, Edie begins to unravel her mother's past. But there are other secrets hidden in the stones of Milderhurst Castle, and Edie is about to learn more than she expected. The truth of what happened in the distant hours has been waiting a long time for someone to find it.

The house at Riverton: a novel. Kate Morton. Atria Books, 2008. Vi, 473 p.

ISBN 9781416550518

1. Family estates 2. Sisters 3. Household employees 4. Reminiscing in old age 5. Secrets 6. Essex, England 7. Great Britain 8. 1920s 9. Historical fiction 10. Australian fiction

Australian Book Industry Awards, General Fiction Book of the Year, 2007

Living out her final days in a nursing home, ninety-eight-year-old Grace remembers the secrets surrounding the 1924 suicide of a young poet during a glittering society party hosted by Grace's English aristocrat employers, a family that is shattered by war.

"A suspenseful and beautifully atmospheric novel capturing the transitional time from the end of the Edwardian era through World War I into the Roaring Twenties." —*Library Journal*

Originally published in Australia in 2006 as The Shifting Fog by Allen & Unwin—Title page verso.

Moshfegh, Ottessa

★ **Death** in her hands: a novel. Ottessa Moshfegh. Penguin Press, 2020. 272 p.

ISBN 9781984879356

1. Widows 2. Senior women 3. Forests 4. Obsession 5. Women amateur detectives 6. Literary fiction 7. Mysteries

LC 2019045121

Discovering a note and grave while walking her dog in the woods, an elderly widow becomes obsessed with learning the victim's story before her grip on reality is shaken by what she uncovers.

"Cleverly unraveling, linguistically brilliant, and limning the limits of reality, this will speak to fans of literary psychological suspense." —*Booklist*

Eileen. Ottessa Moshfegh. Penguin Press, 2015. 260 pages

ISBN 9781594206627

1. Loneliness in women 2. Crime 3. Female friendship 4. Self-hate in women 5. Obsession 6. Massachusetts 7. 1960s 8. Psychological fiction 9. Literary fiction 10. First person narratives

Hemingway Foundation/PEN Award, 2016; National Book Critics Circle Award for Fiction finalist, 2015; Shortlisted for the Man Booker Prize, 2016

Dreaming of life in the city while caring for her alcoholic father and working in a 1960s boys' prison, a disturbed young woman is manipulated into committing a psychologically charged crime during the holiday season.

"Moshfegh keeps all options on the table while keeping her heroine coherent. A shadowy and superbly told story of how inner turmoil morphs into outer chaos." —*Kirkus*

My year of rest and relaxation. Ottessa Moshfegh. Penguin Press, 2018. 288 p.
ISBN 9780525522119
1. Young women 2. Social isolation 3. Alienation (Social psychology) 4. Drugs 5. Orphans 6. New York City 7. Upper East Side, New York City 8. 2000s (Decade) 9. Literary fiction 10. Psychological fiction 11. First person narratives
New York Times Notable Book, 2018
After losing her parents, a young college graduate in New York City spends a year alienating the world under the influence of a crazy combination of drugs.

Mosley, Walter

All I did was shoot my man: a Leonid McGill mystery. Walter Mosley. Riverhead, 2012. 336 p. (Leonid McGill mysteries, 4)
ISBN 9781594488245
1. Redemption 2. Frameups 3. Robbery investigation 4. Conflict in families 5. Father and adult child 6. New York City 7. Mysteries 8. African American fiction
When Zella Grisham is accused of both shooting her boyfriend and stealing more than six million dollars from the Rutgers Assurance Corp, Leonid McGill investigates, while his own family life begins to unravel around him.

And sometimes I wonder about you: a Leonid McGill mystery. Walter Mosley. Doubleday, 2015. 304 p. (Leonid McGill mysteries, 5)
ISBN 9780385539180
1. Missing persons investigation 2. Inheritance and succession 3. Husband and wife 4. Extramarital affairs 5. Family relationships 6. New York City 7. Mysteries 8. African American fiction
Investigating the murder of a client he initially refused to help, Leonid navigates difficult personal elements in his own life while uncovering dark secrets about the victim's old-money family and its missing heiress.

"While Mosley is best known for his Easy Rawlins novels, set in the post-WWII and later twentieth-century era, this gritty, present-day series deserves serious attention from all fans of mainstream hard-boiled detective fiction." —*Booklist*

★ The **awkward** black man: stories. Walter Mosley. Grove Press, 2020. 336 p.
ISBN 9780802149565
1. African American men 2. United States 3. Short stories 4. First person narratives 5. Literary fiction
LC 2020026945
A masterful collection of stories that showcases one of the country's most beloved and acclaimed writers—award-winning author, Walter Mosley.

"In this collection of simple and complex portraits of a wide range of Black men, Mosley, whose many honors include a PEN America Lifetime Achievement Award, defies the stereotypical images that abound in American culture." —*Booklist*

Black Betty: an Easy Rawlins mystery. By Walter Mosley. W.W. Norton, 1994. 255 p. (Easy Rawlins mysteries, 4)
ISBN 9780393036442
1. African American men 2. Missing women 3. Race relations 4. Rawlins, Easy (Fictitious character) 5. Private investigators 6. Los Angeles, California 7. 1960s 8. Historical mysteries 9. African American fiction 10. Mysteries
LC 94-6839
On the shady side of LA in 1961, African-American private eye Easy Rawlins can go places a white detective cannot. So when Saul Lynx needs a missing woman found, he hires Easy to do his dirty work.

"Mosley gives us a recognizable moment in American history viewed through the eyes of a single black man. This perspective, rare in crime fiction, vivifies not only the black experience but the larger event as well. Here we feel the hot winds that would eventually ignite the Watts riots not as abstract issues in race relations, but as emotions in the hearts of individuals we have come to know and care about." —*Booklist*

★ **Blood** grove. Walter Mosley. Mulholland Books, 2021. 320 p. (Easy Rawlins mysteries, 15)
ISBN 9780316491181
1. Vietnam veterans 2. Detectives 3. Missing persons investigation 4. Stolen money 5. Race relations 6. Los Angeles, California 7. California 8. 1960s 9. Historical mysteries 10. African American fiction 11. Mysteries
LC Bl2020073213
Unlicensed private investigator-turned-hardboiled detective Easy Rawlins navigates sex clubs, the mafia and dangerous friends when he reluctantly accepts the racially charged case of a traumatized Vietnam War veteran in late-1960s Los Angeles.

"As always, Easy's finely calibrated understanding of and commentary on the social and racial climate around him gives the novel its defining texture and power." —*Booklist*

Charcoal Joe: an Easy Rawlins mystery. Walter Mosley. Doubleday, 2016. 304 p. (Easy Rawlins mysteries, 14)
ISBN 9780385539203
1. African American men 2. Hostages 3. Kidnappers 4. Ransom 5. Boxers (Sports) 6. Los Angeles, California 7. 1960s 8. Historical mysteries 9. African American fiction 10. Mysteries
LC 2015044304
Easy Rawlins' plans to marry his girlfriend and start a new detective agency are interrupted by the case of a promising Stanford student who has been charged with the race-related murder of a white man.

Devil in a blue dress. Walter Mosley. W. W. Norton, 1990. 219 p. (Easy Rawlins mysteries, 1)
ISBN 9780393028546
1. African American men 2. Organized crime 3. Rawlins, Easy (Fictitious character) 4. Working class African Americans 5. African American World War II veterans 6. Los Angeles, California 7. Watts, Los Angeles, California 8. 1940s 9. Historical mysteries 10. African American fiction 11. Books to movies
LC 89025503
John Creasey Memorial Award (Best First Crime Novel), 1991; Shamus Award for Best First P.I. Novel, 1991
1948, Los Angeles: The mortgage payment's coming due, so Easy Rawlins accepts the assignment of finding Daphne Monet, a blonde torch singer with a penchant for jazz and criminal black consorts. In his search through a sleazy, fearful city, he is lucky to be under the protection of the murderous Mouse who wants a piece of the action.

"Mosley's prose is a little stiff and his plot is far too complicated. But he has a keen eye for period details.... And his lowdown humor never deserts him." —*Newsweek*
First published: New York : Norton; London : Serpent's Tail, 1990.

Down the river unto the sea. Walter Mosley. Little Brown & Co 2018. 336 p.
ISBN 9780316509640

1. Frameups 2. Police corruption 3. Private investigators 4. Injustice 5. Police brutality 6. New York City 7. Mysteries 8. African American fiction

Edgar Allan Poe Award for Best Novel, 2019

Framed by corrupt enemies within the NYPD and forced to serve a decade in prison, private detective Joe King Oliver receives a confession from a woman who helped set him up, a situation that compels him to investigate his own case at the same time he assists a black radical journalist who has been wrongly accused of murdering two corrupt cops.

Fortunate son: a novel. Walter Mosley. Little, Brown and Co, 2006. 320 p.

ISBN 9780316114714

1. Race relations 2. Stepsiblings 3. Trust 4. Rich boys 5. Boys with disabilities 6. Boston, Massachusetts 7. Psychological suspense 8. African American fiction 9. Adult books for young adults

LC 2005024477

Booklist Editors' Choice: Adult Books for Young Adults, 2006

Sharing a close bond in spite of very different backgrounds, Eric, a handsome white man of privilege, and Tommy, an impoverished black youth with poor health, are separated by tragedy and reunited by a common enemy years later.

"The writing is crisp and the plotting impeccable." —*Library Journal*

★ **John** Woman. Walter Mosley. Atlantic Monthly Press, 2018. 377 p.

ISBN 9780802128416

1. Multiracial men 2. College teachers 3. Identity (Psychology) 4. Anonyms and pseudonyms 5. Intellectuals 6. Literary fiction 7. Psychological fiction 8. African American fiction

LC 2018012867

A young man reinvents himself as a professor to share his late father's wisdom at an unorthodox university, only to encounter fellow intellectuals who have insights into his father's hidden past.

Includes bibliographical references and index.

Little Scarlet: an Easy Rawlins mystery. Walter Mosley. Little, Brown and Co, 2004. 320 p. (Easy Rawlins mysteries, 9)

ISBN 9780316073035

1. Coetzee, J. M. 2. Murder investigation 3. Rawlins, Easy (Fictitious character) 4. Detectives 5. Watts Riot, Los Angeles, California, 1965 6. Los Angeles, California 7. Watts, Los Angeles, California 8. 1960s 9. Historical mysteries 10. African American fiction 11. Mysteries

LC 2003023002

When a man who fled the 1965 Watts riots is suspected of killing a woman in a nearby apartment building, Easy Rawlins begins a murder investigation and learns that the case has sobering racial origins.

"This is Mosley's best novel to date: the plot is streamlined and the language simple yet strong, allowing the serpentine story line to support Easy's amazingly complex character and hypnotic narration as Mosley plunges us into his world and, by extension, the world of all blacks in white-run America. Fierce, provocative, expertly entertaining, this is genre writing at its finest." —*Publishers Weekly*

The **right** mistake: the further philosophical investigations of Socrates Fortlow. Walter Mosley. Basic Books, 2008. 288 p. (Socrates Fortlow novels, 3)

ISBN 9780465005253

1. Former convicts 2. Gangs 3. Violence 4. African American men 5. Meetings 6. Los Angeles, California 7. Psychological fiction 8. Political fiction 9. African American fiction

LC Bl2008020384

After serving nearly three decades in prison for his deadly crimes, Socrates returns to the streets of South Central L.A. to connect with old

friends and encourage new ones to join him in his campaign to get to the heart of gang violence.

Trouble is what I do: a Leonid McGill mystery. Walter Mosley. Mulholland Books, 2020. 176 pages (Leonid McGill mysteries, 6)

ISBN 9780316491136

1. Private investigators 2. Blues musicians 3. Assassins 4. Family secrets 5. Criminals 6. New York City 7. Hardboiled fiction 8. Mysteries 9. African American fiction

Detective Leonid McGill is forced to confront the ghost of his felonious past when a nonagenarian Mississippi bluesman is targeted by an infamous assassin.

"Spieled in a powerful, streamlined voice, this wrenching American noir will stick with readers long after the final page." —*Booklist*

Moss, Sarah

Ghost wall: a novel. Sarah Moss. Farrar, Straus and Giroux, 2019. 144 p.

ISBN 9780374161927

1. Historical reenactments 2. Archaeology 3. Working-class families 4. Iron age 5. Abusive men 6. Northern England 7. England 8. Literary fiction 9. Coming-of-age stories 10. Adult books for young adults

LC 2018026605

Rise: A Feminist Book Project List, 2020; Longlisted for The Women's Prize for Fiction, 2019; Shortlisted for the RSL Ondaatje Prize, 2019

Spending her father's vacations at an Iron Age reenactment anthropology field site that requires participants to use period tools and knowledge to survive, Silvie begins to envision her own future before a spiritual ritual involving human sacrifice raises disturbing questions.

"Moss' slender novel follows a working-class family of three from Northern England as they take a proverbial trip back in time, joining an archaeology professor and three of his students on a journey to the wilds of the country to live in the fashion of Iron Age Britons." —*Booklist*

Originally published by Granta Books, 2018.

Summerwater. Sarah Moss. Farrar Straus & Giroux, 2021. 176 pages

ISBN 9780374105938

1. Summer 2. Rain and rainfall 3. Vacations 4. Strangers 5. Cabins 6. Highlands, Scotland 7. Scotland 8. Literary fiction 9. Multiple perspectives

LC 2020039382

A series of vignettes offer the idle thoughts of a group of strangers vacationing in a Scottish holiday park during a very rainy day, lost in their own little worlds, until a shocking event unites them.

"The novel that began at dawn ends at nightfall with a satisfying though awful denouement that steers clear of melodrama. A psychologically acute depiction of modern Britain through the lens of one rainy summer day." —*Kirkus*

Moss, Tara

The **war** widow. Tara Moss. E.P. Dutton, 2020. 368 p. (Billie Walker mysteries, 1)

ISBN 9780593182659

1. Women private investigators 2. Widows 3. Missing persons investigation 4. Postwar life 5. Gangsters 6. Australia 7. Sydney, New South Wales 8. 1940s 9. Historical mysteries 10. Australian fiction 11. Canadian fiction

LC 2019045177

When her career is sidelined by returning male soldiers, World War II correspondent Billie Walker reopens her late father's private investigation agency, only to be swept up in a dangerous missing-persons case.

"Thoroughly researched and anchored by the spunky, sympathetic heroine at its heart, this is a perfect read for fans of Kerry Greenwood's Phryne Fisher series, and readers will finish the book clamoring for Billie's next case." —*Booklist*

Originally published: Sydney : HarperCollins Publishers Australia, 2019.

Mosse, Kate

The **city** of tears. Kate Mosse. Minotaur Books, 2020. 480 pages (Burning chambers, 2)

ISBN 9781250202185

1. Marriages of royalty and nobility 2. Husband and wife 3. Enemies 4. Saint Bartholomew's Day, Massacre of, France, 1572 5. Relics 6. France 7. Paris, France 8. Renaissance (1300-1600) 9. 16th century 10. Historical fiction

A continuation of the story that began with The Burning Chambers is set in Paris, London and Amsterdam and follows the failed efforts of a royal marriage to end a decade-long religious conflict.

"Mosse presents another absorbing historical yarn that mixes intrigue, action, and family drama with aplomb." —*Booklist*

Mott, Jason

Hell of a book. Jason Mott. E.P. Dutton, 2021. 336 pages

ISBN 9780593330968

1. African Americans 2. Authors 3. Publishers and publishing 4. Voyages and travels 5. Psychic trauma 6. United States 7. Metafiction 8. Literary fiction 9. African American fiction

National Book Award for Fiction, 2021

A work of fiction goes to the heart of racism, police violence, and the hidden costs exacted upon Black Americans, and America as a whole.

"Mott's poetic, cinematic novel tackles what it means to live in a country where Black people perpetually 'live lives under the hanging sword of fear.' Absurdist metafiction doesn't get much better." —*Publishers Weekly*

Moyes, Jojo

The **girl** you left behind. Jojo Moyes. Pamela Dorman Books/Viking, 2013. 384 p.

ISBN 9780670026616

1. Loss (Psychology) 2. Family and war 3. Portraits 4. Soldiers 5. Widows 6. France 7. First World War era (1914-1918) 8. 1910s 9. Historical fiction 10. Parallel narratives 11. Relationship fiction

Unwillingly rendered an object of obsession by the Kommandant occupying her small French town in World War I, Sophie risks everything to reunite with her husband a century before a widowed Liv tests her resolve to claim ownership of Sophie's portrait.

First published: 2012.

Originally published: London : Michael Joseph, 2012.

★ The **giver** of stars: a novel. Jojo Moyes. Pamela Dorman Books/Viking, 2019. 400 pages

ISBN 9780399562488

1. Volunteers 2. Libraries 3. Traveling libraries 4. Women librarians 5. Independence in women 6. Kentucky 7. Depression era (1929-1941) 8. 1930s 9. Historical fiction 10. Relationship fiction

LC 2019030049

English bride Alice Wright volunteers for Eleanor Roosevelt's new traveling library in small-town Kentucky, joining a group of independent women whose commitment to their job transforms the community and their relationships.

Me before you: a novel. Jojo Moyes. Pamela Dorman Books, 2012. 384 p. (Me before you, 1)

ISBN 9780670026609

1. Resentfulness in men 2. Wheelchair users 3. Caregivers 4. Young women 5. Moods and moodiness 6. England 7. Multiple perspectives 8. First person narratives 9. Books to movies 10. Adult books for young adults

LC 2012029301

RUSA Reading List, 2014

Taking a job as an assistant to extreme sports enthusiast Will, who is wheelchair bound after a motorcycle accident, Louisa struggles with her employer's acerbic moods and learns of his shocking plans before demonstrating to him that life is still worth living.

Sequel: After You.

The **peacock** emporium. Jojo Moyes. Penguin Books, 2019. 432 p.

ISBN 9780735222335

1. Mothers and daughters 2. Socialites 3. Women business owners 4. Coffee shops 5. Married women 6. England 7. Great Britain 8. Multiple perspectives 9. Relationship fiction

LC 2018058360

Struggling to find refuge from her late mother's shameful legacy, Suzanna Peacock finds friendship and escape at her coffee bar and shop, the Peacock Emporium.

Originally published: London : Hodder & Stoughton, 2004.

Mozley, Fiona

★ **Elmet**. Fiona Mozley. Algonquin Books, 2017. 320 p.

ISBN 9781616208424

1. Poor people 2. Father and child 3. Social conflict 4. Violence in men 5. Belonging 6. Yorkshire, England 7. England 8. Literary fiction 9. First person narratives 10. Psychological fiction 11. Adult books for young adults

Somerset Maugham Award, 2018; Shortlisted for the Man Booker Prize, 2017; Longlisted for The Women's Prize for Fiction, 2018

Cathy and Daniel live with their father, John, in the remote woods of Yorkshire, in a house the three of them built themselves. John is a gentle brute of a man, a former enforcer who fights for money when he has to, but who otherwise just wants to be left alone to raise his children. When a local landowner shows up on their doorstep, their precarious existence is threatened, and a series of actions is set in motion that can only end in violence.

Originally published: London : JM Originals, 2017.

Mueenuddin, Daniyal

In other rooms, other wonders: connected stories. Daniyal Mueenuddin. W.W. Norton, 2009. 224 p.

ISBN 9780393068009

1. Social classes 2. Pakistan 3. Short stories 4. Political fiction

LC 2008040632

Commonwealth Writers' Prize, South Asia and Europe: Best First Book, 2010; New York Times Notable Book, 2009; National Book Award for Fiction finalist, 2009; Pulitzer Prize for Fiction finalist, 2010

A volume of linked stories describes the intertwined lives of landowners and their retainers on the Gurmani family farm in Pakistan, in a collection that explores such themes as culture, class power, and desire.

"In eight beautifully crafted, interconnected stories, Mueenuddin explores the cutthroat feudal society in which a rich Lahore landowner is entrenched.... An elegant stylist with a light touch, Mueenuddin invites the reader to a richly human, wondrous experience." —*Publishers Weekly*

Muir, Tamsyn

Harrow the Ninth. Tamsyn Muir. Tor.com, 2020. 512 p. (Ninth House, 2)

ISBN 9781250313225

1. Imaginary empires 2. Women wizards 3. Undead 4. Training 5. Sick women 6. Space opera 7. Science fantasy 8. New Zealand fiction
LibraryReads Favorites, 2020

A sequel to Gideon the Ninth continues the story of Harrowhark Nonagesimus, whose failing health and uncooperative magic are complicated by the schemes of a would-be assassin in the twisted halls of the Emperor.

"An incredible journey into the chaos of the mind, Muir's latest (after Gideon the Ninth) doubles down on all the wonderfully queer and pulpy moments, body horror, and macabre humor of her debut—and exceeds it." —*Library Journal*

Mukherjee, Abir

Death in the East. Abir Mukherjee. Pegasus Crime, 2020. 352 pages (Sam Wyndham novels, 4)

ISBN 9781643134680

1. Roebling, Emily Warren 2. World War I veterans 3. Opium addiction 4. Enemies 5. Prejudice 6. India 7. British Raj (1858-1947) 8. 1920s 9. Historical mysteries
CWA Historical Dagger Award, 2020

Calcutta police detective Captain Sam Wyndham and his quick-witted Indian Sergeant,Surrender-Not Banerjee, are back for another exotic adventure set in 1920s India.

"This clever tale of interwoven locked-room mysteries may be the best yet in a series that boasts gifted storytelling and full-sensory, Raj-era details." —*Booklist*
Originally published in Great Britain, 2019.

The **shadows** of men. Abir Mukherjee. Pegasus Crime, 2021. 352 p. (Sam Wyndham novels, 5)

ISBN 9781643137445

1. Detectives 2. World War I veterans 3. Secrecy in government 4. Theologians 5. Murder victims 6. India 7. British Raj (1858-1947) 8. 1920s 9. Historical mysteries

When a Hindu theologian is found murdered in his home, the city is on the brink of all-out religious war. Can the officers of the Imperial Police Force—Captain Sam Wyndham and Sergeant "Surrender-Not" Banerjee—track down those responsible in time to stop a bloodbath? Set at a time of heightened political tension, beginning in atmospheric Calcutta and taking the detectives all the way to bustling Bombay, the latest instalment in this remarkable series presents Wyndham and Banerjee with an unprecedented challenge.

"Increasing tensions in 1923 colonial India provide the backdrop for Edgar finalist Mukherjee's superb fifth mystery featuring Capt. Sam Wyndham and Det. Sgt. Surendranath Bannerjee of the Calcutta CID.... This is a sterling example of a riveting whodunit plot coupled with a vivid portrayal of a seminal historical moment." —*Publishers Weekly*

Smoke and ashes: a novel. Abir Mukherjee. Pegasus Books, 2019. 332 p; (Sam Wyndham novels, 3)

ISBN 9781643130149

1. Detectives 2. World War I veterans 3. Serial murder investigation 4. Police 5. Colonialism 6. Calcutta, India 7. India 8. British Raj (1858-1947) 9. 1920s 10. Historical mysteries

Haunted by his memories of the Great War, Captain Sam Wyndham is battling a serious addiction to opium that he must keep secret from his superiors in the Calcutta police force.

"This series' third installment...is pivotal for Sam and Surrender-Not's characters and for colonial India; Mukherjee skillfully manipu-

lates that tension as he darkens the atmosphere in this thoughtful narrative. Definitely the series' best entry so far." —*Booklist*
Sequel to: A necessary evil.
Originally published: London : Random House, c2018.

Mukherjee, Neel

The **lives** of others. Neel Mukherjee. W. W. Norton & Co, 2014. 516 pages : Map; Table

ISBN 9780393247909

1. Social classes 2. Social conflict 3. Rich families 4. Family relationships 5. Generation gap 6. Calcutta, India 7. India 8. 1960s 9. Literary fiction
Shortlisted for the Man Booker Prize, 2014

Chronicles the vicissitudes of the extended Ghosh family as internal rivalries accompany the implosion of the family business and external social unrest.

"This is an immensely accomplished, steady-handed achievement, Victorian in its solidity, quietly enthralling in its insightful observation of the ties that bind." —*Kirkus*

★ A **state** of freedom. Neel Mukherjee. W. W. Norton & Co, 2018. 278 p.

ISBN 9780393292909

1. Interpersonal relations 2. Caste 3. Poverty 4. Poor people 5. Cooks 6. India 7. Literary fiction
New York Times Notable Book, 2018

Five characters in very different circumstances—from a domestic cook in Mumbai to a vagrant and his dancing bear—find the meanings of dislocation and the desire to get more out of life.

"Mukherjees diverse perspectives and narrative treatments offer an honest, uncompromising look at the realities of his characters circumstances and, most pointedly, their lack of control over them, as well as a compelling exploration of disparity and identity." —*Booklist*

Mullen, Thomas

Darktown: a novel. Thomas Mullen. 37 Ink/Atria, 2016. 384 p. (Darktown novels, 1)

ISBN 9781501133862

1. Police misconduct 2. Racism 3. Murder 4. Race relations 5. African Americans 6. Atlanta, Georgia 7. 1940s 8. Historical mysteries 9. Police procedurals

LC 2015041687

LibraryReads Favorites, 2016; Library Journal Best Books, 2016;
Loan Stars Favourites, 2016; RUSA Reading List, 2017

Hired resentfully into the Atlanta Police Department of 1948, war veterans Lucious Boggs and Tommy Smith confront deep hostility from their white peers and are significantly limited in their ability to do their jobs before confronting a corrupt officer who complicates their investigation into the murder of a black woman.

"Mullens writing is extremely evocative in bringing the precivil rights South to life." —*Booklist*

Lightning men: a novel. Thomas Mullen. 37 INK/Atria Books, 2017. 384 p. (Darktown novels, 2)

ISBN 9781501138799

1. Segregation 2. Racism 3. Hate crimes 4. Hate groups 5. Race relations 6. Atlanta, Georgia 7. 1950s 8. Historical mysteries 9. Police procedurals

LC 2017004468

In this highly anticipated follow-up to last year's Darktown, African American police officers Tommy Smith and Lucius Boggs find themselves once again navigating volatile racial tensions in Atlanta. This time, it's 1950, and their attempt to stop the influx of illegal alcohol and drugs is complicated by the involvement of whites, whom they're not allowed to arrest. Meanwhile, neo-Nazis are in town stirring up trouble as black families move into formerly whites-only neighborhoods. Examining the cops' professional and personal lives, Lightning Men provides a well-rounded look at fascinating characters in an explosive setting.

"Mullen effectively uses the police-procedural format to shine a light on the daily indignities and violence blacks suffered in the precivil rights South, while delivering a plot that never lets up on suspense." —*Booklist*

Muller, Marcia

Dead midnight. Marcia Muller. Mysterious Press, 2002. 289 p; (Sharon McCone mysteries, 21)
ISBN 9780892967650
1. Women private investigators 2. Business sabotage 3. Suicide 4. E-zines 5. Hazing 6. San Francisco, California 7. Mysteries 8. First person narratives 9. Hardboiled fiction
LC 2002020097
Sharon McCone takes on a wrongful-death case in which a grieving family is suing a company for the suicide of a young employee, but as her investigation progresses, she discovers that there may have been more to the death than meets the eye.

"This mystery has Sharon McCone gathering evidence for a wrongful-death suit brought by the family of a sensitive young man driven to kill himself by the deplorable working conditions at a trendy online magazine. But events never advance in a straight line in Muller's complicated narratives, and the job that McCone took on because she thought it would help her come to grips with her own brother's suicide turns into a lethal game of industrial sabotage." —*New York Times Book Review*

Ice and stone. Marcia Muller. Grand Central Publishing, 2021. 272 p. (Sharon Mccone mysteries, 34)
ISBN 9781538733165
1. Violence against marginalized women 2. Indigenous women 3. Murder investigation 4. Undercover operations 5. Racism 6. Hardboiled fiction 7. Mysteries
LC 2021010626
Hired by Crimes Against Indigenous Sisters, private investigator Sharon McCone goes undercover in Eiwok county on the Oregon border to determine who killed two women.

"Muller's McCone set the standard for fictional women detectives; after 35 installments, the detective's character has not diminished but continues to evolve and grow and meet all challenges head on." —*Library Journal*

Munro, Alice

Dear life: stories. By Alice Munro. Alfred A. Knopf, 2012. 336 p.
ISBN 9780307596888
1. Interpersonal relations 2. Fate and fatalism 3. Small town life 4. Lake Huron region 5. Canada 6. Short stories 7. Canadian fiction 8. Literary fiction
LC 2012020455
New York Times Notable Book, 2012; Booklist Editors' Choice, 2012; Trillium Book Award, 2012
A collection of stories illuminates moments that shape a life, from a dream or a sexual act to simple twists of fate, and is set in the countryside and towns of Lake Huron.
This is a Borzoi book.

Family furnishings: selected stories, 1995-2014. Alice Munro. Alfred A. Knopf, 2014. 620 p.
ISBN 9781101874103

1. Small town life 2. Interpersonal relations 3. Canada 4. Ontario 5. Literary fiction 6. Short stories 7. Canadian fiction
LC 2014023046
These stories illuminate the extraordinary in the lives of men and women, parents and children, friends and lovers as they discover sex, fall in love, part, quarrel, suffer defeat, set off into the unknown, or find a way to be in the world.

"Certainly few, if any, narrators are less trustworthy than Munro's; among many other things, she is the ascended master of quiet betrayals, withheld information and unforeseeable reversals of fortune... As is true of so many of Munro's tales, taken straight from the pages of quotidian life, its end is heartbreaking, tragic, not a little mysterious—and entirely unexpected. In fact, all that can be expected from these economical, expertly told stories is that they're near peerless, modern literary fiction at its very best." —*Kirkus*
This is a Borzoi book—Title page verso.

Hateship, friendship, courtship, loveship, marriage: stories. Alice Munro. Alfred A. Knopf, 2001. Vii, 323 p.
ISBN 9780375413001
1. Borthwick, Mamah Bouton 2. Women 3. Friendship 4. Canada 5. Literary fiction 6. Canadian fiction 7. Short stories
LC 2001029870
Commonwealth Writers' Prize, Caribbean and Canada: Best Book, 2002; Library Journal Best Books, 2001; National Book Critics Circle Award for Fiction finalist, 2001
A collection of short fiction explores the complexities of human relationships and emotions in stories about a housekeeper entering old-maidhood whose life is transformed by a practical joke and a lifelong philanderer who finds the tables turned.

"Opulent in their beauty and gem-bright psychology, the extraordinary stories in [this] collection span the spectrum from romance to tales of manners to deep meditations on love and mortality, and all evince Munro's profound understanding of the power of memories and the stories we tell ourselves." —*Booklist*
The short story "The bear came over the mountain" was later made into the motion picture "Away from her."
Published by Penguin Canada in 2007 under the title: Away from her.

Lives of girls and women. Alice Munro. Vintage Contemporaries, 2001. 277 p.
ISBN 9780375707490
1. Small town life 2. Young women 3. Self-discovery in women 4. Women — Identity 5. Eccentric men 6. Canada 7. 1940s 8. Coming-of-age stories 9. Literary fiction 10. Canadian fiction
LC 63412
The story of a young woman who journeys from the carelessness of childhood through an uneasy adolescence in search of love and sexual experience.
Originally published: Toronto : McGraw-Hill Ryerson, 1971.

Open secrets: stories. Alice Munro. A.A. Knopf, 1994. 293 p.
ISBN 9780679435754
1. Women 2. Small town life 3. Canada 4. Literary fiction 5. Short stories 6. Canadian fiction
LC 942099
ALA Notable Book, 1995; Governor General's Literary Awards, English-language Fiction finalist
8 short stories that evoke the devastating power of old love suddenly recollected.

"The author peoples these exquisite tales with sad, lonely eccentrics leading lives of quiet self-deception. Her heroines are often troubled souls with the unforgiving task of fitting into the rigorously confining community that spawned them.... Munro expertly captures the vagaries of history and geography in this satisfying and immensely pleasurable collection." —*Booklist*

Eight short stories.

Runaway: stories. Alice Munro. Knopf, 2004. 352 p.
ISBN 9781400042814

1. Senior women 2. Women 3. Young women 4. Married women 5. Family relationships 6. British Columbia 7. Canada 8. Literary fiction 9. Canadian fiction 10. Short stories

LC 2004046539

ALA Notable Book, 2005; Booklist Editors' Choice, 2005; Commonwealth Writers' Prize, Caribbean and Canada: Best Book, 2005; Giller Prize, 2004; New York Times Notable Book, 2004; Rogers Writers' Trust Fiction Prize, 2004; Governor General's Literary Awards, English-language Fiction finalist, 2004

A collection of short fiction captures the lives of women of all ages and circumstances, as they deal with the limits and lies of passion, unfulfilled dreams, motherhood, betrayal, and the bonds of love.

"Munro's spare style belies the psychological depth of the stories, which feature characters running away from someone or something (often representative of the past) or telling a lie by commission or omission (another form of running away)." —*Library Journal*

Three of these short stories ("Chance," "Soon," and "Silence") later published in an omnibus entitled: Julieta (2016) and made into a Spanish film by the same name.

Selected stories. Alice Munro. A. A. Knopf, 1996. 545 p.
ISBN 9780679446279

1. Women 2. Small town life 3. Man-woman relationships 4. Parent and child 5. Canada 6. Literary fiction 7. Short stories 8. Canadian fiction

LC 96004145

Library Journal Best Books, 1996

A selection of short fiction drawn from the author's seven collections spans almost thirty years of work and includes twenty-eight tales dealing with such themes as love, parents and children, seduction, marriage, sex, murder, dreams, and death BT

"Little gems from one of Canada's best writers, drawn from seven collections." —*Library Journal*

First published in Great Britain: Chatto & Windus, 1996.
Winner of the Man Booker International prize—Cover.
Winner of the Nobel Prize in Literature 2013—Cover.

Too much happiness: stories. By Alice Munro. Alfred A. Knopf, 2009. 320 p.
ISBN 9780307269768

1. Women mathematicians 2. Interpersonal relations 3. Women 4. Small town life 5. Canada 6. Literary fiction 7. Short stories 8. Canadian fiction

LC 2009020010

Booklist Editors' Choice, 2009; New York Times Notable Book, 2009; Governor General's Literary Awards, English-language Fiction finalist, 2009

Nine new short works by the National Book Critics Circle-winning author of Love of a Good Woman include the stories of a grieving mother who is aided by a surprising source, a woman's response to a humiliating seduction, and a nineteenth-century Russian emigre's winter journey to the Riviera.

"The collection's 10 stories take on some sensational subjects. In fact, a quick tally yields all the elements of pulp fiction: violence, adultery, extreme cruelty, duplicity, theft, suicide, murder. But while in pulp fiction the emotional climax coincides with the height of external drama, a Munro story works according to a different scheme. Here the nominally momentous event is little more than an anteroom to an echo chamber filled with subtle and far-reaching thematic reverberations." —*New York Times Book Review*

Also published: Toronto : Douglas Gibson Books, 2009.

The **view** from Castle Rock: stories. By Alice Munro. Knopf, 2006. 368 p.
ISBN 9781400042821

1. Families 2. Immigrants 3. Frontier and pioneer life 4. Women 5. Small town life 6. Canada 7. Literary fiction 8. Shakespeare, William 9. Short stories

LC 2006045261

New York Times Notable Book, 2007; Shortlisted for the James Tait Black Memorial Prize for Fiction, 2006

A collection of short stories in which Munro traces the generations of her Laidlaw ancestors.

"This collection differs from Munro's usual examinations of women in rural Canada leaving home to remake their possibilities. She draws instead on family documents, historical records, and what feels like memoir to piece together, in 12 parts, a fictionalized chronicle of how her tough-minded clan got from the Ettrick Valley near Edinburgh, Scotland, to America. The book shows how much can be done in a simple short story but breaks every rule ever taught in a writing seminar, setting up a writing master class along the way." —*Time*

Murakami, Haruki

★ **1Q84**. Haruki Murakami; translated from the Japanese by Jay Rubin and Philip Gabriel. Alfred A. Knopf, 2011. 928 p.
ISBN 9780307593313

1. Authors, Japanese 2. Parallel universes 3. Cults 4. Self-discovery 5. Secret societies 6. Tokyo, Japan 7. 1980s 8. Literary fiction 9. Surrealist fiction 10. Translations

LC 2011014274

Booklist Editors' Choice, 2011; Goodreads Choice Award, 2011; Library Journal Best Books, 2011; New York Times Notable Book, 2011; Shortlisted for the International IMPAC Dublin Literary Award, 2013

An ode to George Orwell's "1984" told in alternating male and female voices relates the stories of Aomame, an assassin for a secret organization who discovers that she has been transported to an alternate reality, and Tengo, a mathematics lecturer and novice writer.

"In typical Murakami fashion, the result is deeply weirdand surprisingly convincing." —*Entertainment Weekly*

Originally published in three volumes with the title 1Q84 in 2009 and 2010 by Shinchosa Publishing Co Ltd, Tokyo.

After dark. By Haruki Murakami; translated from the Japanese by Jay Rubin. Alfred A. Knopf, 2007. 208 p.
ISBN 9780307265838

1. Sisters 2. Prostitutes 3. Night 4. Alienation (Social psychology) 5. Supernatural 6. Tokyo, Japan 7. Japan 8. Translations 9. Literary fiction

LC 2007004828

New York Times Notable Book, 2007

Two sisters—Eri, a fashion model sleeping her way to oblivion, and Mari, a young student—form the center of a novel that documents a series of encounters in Tokyo during the witching hours between midnight and dawn.

"The narrative flows like a jazz ballad, excruciatingly slow yet hypnotically entrancing .... Each character is unique in his or her form of loneliness, yet each possesses a capacity for momentary empathy that is both sweet and heartbreaking. Murakami's genius, on both large and small canvases, is to create worlds both utterly alien and disconcertingly familiar." —*Booklist*

Originally published in Japan as Afutadaku by Kodansha, Tokyo, in 2004—Title page verso.

A Borzoi book.

This translation first published in Great Britain by Harvill Secker, 2007.

First published with the title Afutadaku by Kodansha, Tokyo 2004.

After the quake: stories. Haruki Murakami; translated from the Japanese by Jay Rubin. Alfred A. Knopf, 2002. 181 p.

ISBN 9780375413902

1. Earthquakes 2. Terrorism 3. Poisonous gases 4. Man-woman relationships 5. Japan 6. 1990s 7. Surrealist fiction 8. Short stories 9. Translations

LC 2001038829

New York Times Notable Book, 2002

A collection of stories inspired by the January 1995 Kobe earthquake and the poison gas subway attacks two months later takes place between the two disasters and follows the experiences of people who found their normal lives undone by surreal events.

"These six stories, all loosely connected to the disastrous 1995 earthquake in Kobe, are Murakami...at his best. The writer, who returned to live in Japan after the Kobe earthquake, measures his country's suffering and finds reassurance in the inevitability that love will surmount tragedy, mustering his casually elegant prose and keen sense of the absurd in the service of healing." —*Publishers Weekly*

Translation of: Kami no kodomotachi wa mina odoru.

Blind willow, sleeping woman: 24 stories. By Haruki Murakami. Knopf, 2006. 352 p.

ISBN 9781400044610

1. Human behavior 2. Paranormal phenomena 3. Identity (Psychology) 4. Supernatural 5. Loneliness 6. Short stories 7. Surrealist fiction 8. Translations

LC 2005044544

Kiriyama Prize for Fiction, 2007; ALA Notable Book, 2007

From the surreal to the mundane, an anthology of short fiction captures a full range of human experience, emotion, and relationship in works that chronicle a chance reunion in Italy, a holiday in Hawaii, and a romantic exile in Greece.

"Murakami's first collection of short stories in more than a decade again demonstrates his fabulous talent for transporting readers and making the world fade away with a few short strokes of his pen.... Murakami's characters are as alienated as any in Albert Camus, and as lost as any in J.D. Salinger.... What shines in all of [the stories] is Murakami's love for the open-ended mystery at the core of existence and his willingness to give himself up to the flow in order to capture some of the magic in the mundane." —*Christian Science Monitor*

This translation originally published: London: Harvill Secker, 2006.

Colorless Tsukuru Tazaki and his years of pilgrimage. Haruki Murakami; translated by Philip Gabriel. Alfred A. Knopf, 2014. 208 p.

ISBN 9780385352109

1. Friendship 2. Self-discovery in men 3. Voyages and travels 4. Identity (Psychology) 5. Sexuality 6. Japan 7. Europe 8. Literary fiction 9. Surrealist fiction 10. Translations

Booklist Editors' Choice, 2014; New York Times Notable Book, 2014

Thirty-six-year-old Tsukuru Tazaki meets a woman named Sara who raises questions about a painful incident from his youth in which his closest friends all cut off relations with him without explanation, and inspires him to find out why.

"A a trademark [Murakami] story that blends the commonplace with the nightmarish in a Japan full of hollow men." —*Kirkus*

Translation from the Japanese of: Shikisai o motanai Tazaki Tsukuru to kare no junrei no toshi.

Originally published in Japan: 2013.

★ **First** person singular: stories. Haruki Murakami; translated by Philip Gabriel. Alfred A. Knopf, 2021. 256 p.

ISBN 9780593318072

1. Baseball 2. Nostalgia 3. Identity (Psychology) 4. Magical realism 5. Literary fiction 6. Translations

The eight masterly stories in this new collection are all told in the first person by a classic Murakami narrator. From nostalgic memories of youth, meditations on music, and an ardent love of baseball to dreamlike scenarios and invented jazz albums, together these stories challenge the boundaries between our minds and the exterior world. Occasionally, a narrator who may or may not be Murakami himself is present. Is it memoir or fiction? The reader decides.

"A new collection of stories from the master of the strange, enigmatic twist of plot.... An essential addition to any Murakami fan's library." —*Kirkus*

Translated from the Japanese.

★ **Kafka** on the shore. Haruki Murakami; translated from the Japanese by Philip Gabriel. Knopf, 2005. 448 p.

ISBN 9781400043668

1. Runaway teenage boys 2. Eccentrics and eccentricities 3. Cats 4. Senior men 5. Fate and fatalism 6. Japan 7. Surrealist fiction 8. Translations 9. Parallel narratives

LC 2004048907

ALA Notable Book, 2006; New York Times Notable Book, 2005; World Fantasy Award, 2006

An unlikely alliance forms between Kafka Tamura, a fifteen-year-old runaway, and the aging Nakata, a man who has never recovered from a wartime affliction, as they embark on a surreal odyssey through a strange, fantastical world.

"Like his characters' quests, Murakami's expeditions off the worn path of literature can be both rewarding and terrifying. Finishing Kafka on the Shore is like waking from a great dream. Nothing has changed, but everything about the world looks different." —*Newsweek*

Killing commendatore: a novel. Haruki Murakami; translated from the Japanese by Philip Gabriel and Ted Goossen. Alfred A. Knopf, 2018. 681 p.

ISBN 9780525520047

1. Artists 2. Painting 3. Lovers 4. Secrets 5. Girls 6. Japan 7. Literary fiction 8. Surrealist fiction 9. Translations

Library Journal Best Books, 2018; Booklist Editors' Choice, 2018

A portrait painter deals with the upcoming divorce from his wife by moving into an old house in rural Japan that used to belong to a famous artist.

Translation of: Kishi dancho-goroshi.

Translated from the Japanese.

Men without women: stories. Haruki Murakami; translated from the Japanese by Philip Gabriel and Ted Goossen. Alfred A. Knopf, 2017. 240 p.

ISBN 9780451494627

1. Human behavior 2. Loneliness 3. Men — Psychology 4. Short stories 5. Surrealist fiction 6. Literary fiction

LC 2016037304

A major new collection of stories by the internationally acclaimed author of Colorless Tsukuru Tazaki and His Years of Pilgrimage features male protagonists who find themselves alone in a smoky bar, in a baseball game, in the face of Beatles music, in the presence of women and in the wake of a vanishing cat.

Originally published in Japanese as: Onna no inai otokotachi. Tokyo : Bungei Shunju Ltd, 2014.

Translated from the Japanese.

South of the border, west of the sun. Haruki Murakami; translated from the Japanese by Philip Gabriel. A. A. Knopf, 1999. 213 p.
ISBN 9780375402517
1. Extramarital affairs 2. First loves 3. Missing persons 4. Bar owners 5. Interpersonal relations 6. Japan 7. Psychological fiction 8. Translations 9. Literary fiction
LC 9749459
New York Times Notable Book, 1999

Years after their separation, two Japanese childhood sweethearts are reunited, and happily married Hajime finds himself prepared to risk everything for the chance to be with his now mysterious first love, Shimamoto.

"The narrative unfolds as an introspective ghost story in which Hajime must exorcise his past in the person of the enigmatic Shimamoto before he can affirm the new direction of his life. The ending, at once tender and hopeful, shows Murakami in a more mellow aspect than his work has exhibited before." —*Publishers Weekly*

The **wind-up** bird chronicle. Haruki Murakami; translated from the Japanese by Jay Rubin. A. A. Knopf, 1997. 611 p.
ISBN 9780679446699
1. Runaway wives, husbands, etc. 2. Husband and wife 3. Missing women 4. Alienation (Social psychology) 5. Mystics 6. Japan 7. Surrealist fiction 8. Translations 9. Literary fiction
LC 972813
ALA Notable Book, 1998; Booklist Editors' Choice, 1997; New York Times Notable Book, 1997; Shortlisted for the International IMPAC Dublin Literary Award, 1999

The saga of a mysteriously disintegrating marriage, suppressed memories of the tragedies of war, and a young man's search for his personal and national identity is set against the turbulent backdrop of twentieth-century Japan.

"Murakami's protagonist is a harmless fellow who merely wants to recover his cat and his wife. The troubles, real and delusional, that he encounters can be seen as extravagant metaphors for every ill from personal isolation to mass murder. The novel is a deliberately confusing, illogical image of a confusing, illogical world. It is not easy reading, but it is never less than absorbing." —*The Atlantic*

Murakami, Ryu

In the miso soup. Ryu Murakami; translated by Ralph McCarthy. Kodansha International, 2003. 180 p.
ISBN 9784770029577
1. Men 2. Americans in Japan 3. Americans in Tokyo, Japan 4. Teenage girls 5. Psychopaths 6. Tokyo, Japan 7. Japan 8. Transgressive fiction 9. Thrillers and suspense 10. Translations

"Through simple yet chilling language, Murakami doesn't condemn his characters. Instead he takes aim at rampant consumerism and the dumbing-down of Japanese and American culture. No one, Murakami seems to say, is completely guilty because we are shaped by the world around us." —*USA Today*

English translation of: In za miso supu.

Murata, Sayaka

Earthlings: a novel. Sayaka Murata; translated from the Japanese by Ginny Tapley Takemori. Grove Press, 2020. 240 p.
ISBN 9780802157003

1. Misfits (Persons) 2. Nonconformists 3. Expectation (Psychology) 4. Cousins 5. Alienation (Social psychology) 6. Japan 7. Coming-of-age stories 8. Literary fiction 9. Translations
LC 2020033625
New York Times Notable Book, 2020

As a child, Natsuki doesn't fit in with her family. Her parents favor her sister, and her best friend is a plush toy hedgehog named Piyyut, who talks to her. He tells her that he has come from the planet Popinpobopia on a special quest to help her save the Earth. One summer, on vacation with her family and her cousin Yuu in her grandparents' ramshackle wooden house in the mountains of Nagano, Natsuki decides that she must be an alien, which would explain why she can't seem to fit in like everyone else. Later, as a grown woman, living a quiet life with her asexual husband, Natsuki is still pursued by dark shadows from her childhood, and decides to flee the 'baby factory' of society for good, searching for answers about the vast and frightening mysteries of the universe—answers only Natsuki has the power to uncover.

"Murata again confronts and devastates so-called 'normal,' 'proper' behavior to create an unflinching expose of society." —*Booklist*

Originally published as Chikyu seijin. Japanese edition published by Shinchosha Publishing Co, Ltd, Tokyo
Originally published: 2018.
Translated from the Japanese.

Murdoch, Iris

An **accidental** man. Iris Murdoch. Viking 1972. 442 p.
ISBN 9780670102082
1. Vietnam War, 1961-1975 2. Americans in England 3. Draft resisters 4. Rich people 5. England 6. Psychological fiction 7. Literary fiction
LC 79171893

Austin Gibson Grey, an American living in London, blames fate when he is drafted during the Vietnam War.

The central figure of this novel is one of those accident-prone figures whose...misfortune becomes a substitute source of strength.... Ever since his brother injured his hand in a childhood incident, the world owes Austin a blank cheque to cover subsequent reverses—which do not fail to arrive. But someone is always sorry for him, always getting him out of trouble even at the price of their own. His self-pity destroys others in accordance with what Miss Murdoch...calls 'whatever deep mythological forces control the destinies of men.' New Statesman.

The **book** and the brotherhood. Iris Murdoch. Penguin, 1988. 607 p.
ISBN 9780140104707
1. Friendship 2. Murder 3. Guilt 4. Universities and colleges 5. Interpersonal relations 6. England 7. Literary fiction
LC 87040294
Shortlisted for the Booker-McConnell Prize, 1987

In a study of obsession, love, betrayal, and friendship, a group of friends gathers at a midsummer ball at Oxford and the actions of one of them—a radical genius named David Crimond—sets off a crisis.

"Despite its excessive length and passages that can seem almost as self-indulgent as the characters they represent, The Book and The Brotherhood demonstrates again and again that Iris Murdoch is among the most gifted descriptive and narrative writers in English—and certainly one of the most consistently entertaining." —*New York Rev Books*

The **green** knight. Iris Murdoch. Viking Press, 1994. 472 p.
ISBN 9780670852291
1. Self-defense (Law) 2. Brothers 3. Murder 4. Strangers 5. Guilt in men 6. London, England 7. Literary fiction 8. Modern classics
LC 93030618

When an attempt by the sharp, feral, uncommonly intelligent Lucas to murder his brother, Clement, backfires and Lucas kills a stranger, the stranger reappears with specific demands for reparation.

"That a cold, dark, evil act should open up a gap through which warmth and light can flood into the world is a paradox characteristic of Iris Murdoch's deeply meditated insight into the nature of the good." —London Review of Books

The **nice** and the good. Iris Murdoch. Penguin, 1978. 378 p.
ISBN 9780140030341
1. Married people 2. Murder 3. Spies 4. Extortion 5. Man-woman relationships 6. Psychological fiction 7. Literary fiction
Shortlisted for the Booker-McConnell Prize, 1969

A novel originally published in 1968, revolving around a happily married couple and telling of a violent death, blackmail, suspected espionage, Black Arts, stress and terror, over which love conquers all.

"The action begins with a violent death in the chambers of Whitehall faintly suggestive of a Le Carr thriller.... At times hilariously funny, slightly shivery (intimations of blackmail, suicide, dabblings in black magic) The Nice and the Good is first and foremost a delightful love story. The friends, relatives, hanger-ons, whose lives revolve around the happily married Octavian and Kate Gray are all seeking after love in their own ways. They find it, too, and sometimes in the most amazing places. The characterizations are superb, the mood that of a happy fairy tale crossed with highly sophisticated sexual comedy." —Publishers Weekly

The **philosopher's** pupil. Iris Murdoch. Viking Press, 1982. 505 p.
ISBN 9780670551866
1. Teacher-student relationships 2. Philosophers 3. Small towns 4. Health resorts 5. Ethics 6. England 7. Literary fiction
LC 82045901

"This collaboration between Murdoch and her imagination is both challenging and irresistible: a combination of gossip and profundity, modern times and ancient edicts." —Time
Originally published: London : Chatto & Windus, 1980.

The **sea,** the sea. Iris Murdoch. Penguin Books, 2001. Xxvii, 495 p.
ISBN 9780141186160
1. Senior men 2. Obsession in men 3. Recluses 4. Reminiscing in old age 5. Single men 6. England 7. Literary fiction 8. Ghost stories 9. Psychological fiction
Booker Prize, 1978

After a brilliant and fulfilling career, Charles Arrowby revels in his perfect refuge, an isolated home by the sea, but soon his complex past makes unbidden visits.

"The narrator of this novel is Charles Arrowby, a former actor and director who has retired from the theater to take up solitary residence in a remote house on a northern coast. His tale begins as a mixture of diary and memoir: alternately he records his first impressions of his new home and reviews his past life as though the better to understand the man he has become.... His recollections largely concern a succession of love-affairs with actresses; but before all these, and dwarfing them in its importance to his development, was an unconsummated but passionate childhood relationship with a girl named Hartley, who disappeared abruptly and woundingly from his life before he was twenty and married another man." —Times Literary Supplement
Originally published: London: Chatto & Windus, 1978.

Murphy, Devin
Tiny Americans. Devin Murphy. Harper Perennial, 2019. 336 p.
ISBN 9780062886248

1. Father-deserted children 2. Father and adult child 3. Reconciliation 4. Adult children of alcoholics 5. Siblings 6. New York (State) 7. 1970s 8. 2010s 9. Literary fiction 10. Domestic fiction

Abandoned by the alcoholic father who idealized the natural world without imparting any survival skills to his children, three siblings in 1970s New York embark on difficult adult lives before their father attempts a reconciliation.

Murphy, Julie
If the shoe fits. Julie Murphy. Hyperion Avenue, 2021. 304 p. (Meant to be, 1)
ISBN 9781368050388
1. Fashion 2. Body image 3. Overweight women 4. Stepmothers 5. Shoes 6. Fairy tale and folklore-inspired fiction 7. Contemporary romances 8. Romantic comedies
LC 2020043723
LibraryReads Favorites, 2021

A fashion-obsessed plus-size woman fills in for a no-show contestant on her executive producer stepmother's popular dating reality show and becomes a body-positivity viral sensation overnight and could actually picture herself falling for the eligible suitor.

"In Murphy's breezy and fun rom-com, there's enough of Cinderella in the story to be charming, yet overall it sparkles like an exciting new tale. One particularly refreshing update is that the stepfamily is caring and supportive, not evil. Cindy is immensely lovable, and readers will root for all her dreams to come true." —Booklist

Murphy, Sara Flannery
The **possessions**. Sara Flannery Murphy. HarperCollins, 2017. 320 p.
ISBN 9780062458322
1. Mediums 2. Spiritualism 3. Spirits 4. Grief 5. Loss (Psychology) 6. Psychological suspense 7. Contemporary fantasy
Booklist Editors' Choice, 2017

In an unnamed city, Edie works for the Elysian Society, a private service that allows grieving clients to reconnect with lost loved ones. She and her fellow workers, known as "bodies," wear the discarded belongings of the dead and swallow pills called lotuses to summon their spirits—numbing their own minds and losing themselves in the process. Edie has been with the company for five years, an unusual record. Her success is the result of careful detachment: she seeks refuge in the lotuses' anesthetic effects and avoids personal contact with her clients. But when Edie channels Sylvia, the deceased wife of Patrick Braddock, she becomes obsessed with the glamorous couple.

"This poignant tale is a study of grief and obsession told by a person who will do anything to forget while surrounded by those who refuse to move on." —Library Journal

Murr, Naeem
The **perfect** man: a novel. Naeem Murr. Random House, 2007. 429 p.
ISBN 9780812977011
1. Abandoned boys 2. Multiracial boys 3. Children — Friendship 4. East Indians in the United States 5. Secrets 6. Missouri 7. 1950s 8. Coming-of-age stories 9. Adult books for young adults
LC 2006043088
Commonwealth Writers' Prize, South Asia and Europe: Best Book, 2007; School Library Journal Best Books: Best Adult Books 4 Teens, 2007

Follows the life of Rajiv Travers, the child of an East Indian mother and an English father but who is raised by an American romance novel author in Pisgah, Missouri, in the 1950s, and whose presence unsettles the small community.

"This novel succeeds in recreating an entire world with a full spectrum of human emotions in a small Missouri town, as Faulkner did in the imaginary Yoknapatawpha County in Mississippi." —*Times Literary Supplement*

Murray, Paul

Skippy dies. Paul Murray. Faber & Faber, 2010. 672 p.
ISBN 9780865479432
1. Teacher-student relationships 2. Boarding schools 3. Teenage boys — Death 4. Prescription drug abuse 5. Roommates 6. Dublin, Ireland 7. Ireland 8. Coming-of-age stories 9. Literary fiction 10. Adult books for young adults
ALA Notable Book, 2011; Booklist Editors' Choice, 2010; Booklist Editors' Choice: Adult Books for Young Adults, 2010; National Book Critics Circle Award for Fiction finalist, 2010

After fourteen-year-old Skippy ends up dead on the floor of a local donut shop, a number of suspects emerge at Skippy's school in Dublin, in a hilarious portrait of the pain, joy, and occasional beauty of adolescence.

"First off, the title of Skippy Dies should come with a spoiler alert, because Skippy does in fact die. And oh, the humanity! He dies like a fish on the floor of Ed's Doughnut House, where he's been locked in a doughnut-eating contest with his tubby, brilliant, but unhinged prep-school buddy Ruprecht.... Essentially, though, the novel's about a fusty old Catholic school trying to cope and connive after the Skippy Doughnut Tragedy, while dealing with the more commonplace tragedy that being an adolescent sucks, as do being middle-aged and being old. Murray's humor and inventiveness never flag. And despite a serious theme what happens to boys and men when they realize the world isn't the sparkly planetarium they had hoped for Skippy Dies leaves you feeling hopeful and hungry for life. Just not for doughnuts." —*Entertainment Weekly*

Musil, Robert

The **man** without qualities. [by] Robert Musil; translated from the German by Eithne Wilkins and Ernst Kaiser. Vintage Books, 1996. 1774 p.
ISBN 9780394510521
1. Men 2. Character 3. Character in men 4. Meaning (Psychology) 5. Fascism 6. Vienna, Austria 7. Austria 8. Translations 9. Psychological fiction 10. Modern classics
LC 80471287
Library Journal Best Books, 1995

A novel in three volumes on the dying culture of pre-World War I Vienna. The man without qualities of the title is Ulrich, a skeptical type who views with an amused eye all attempts by the rulers of the Austro-Hungarian Empire to instill in their subjects the nationalistic fervor of neighboring Germany.

Translation of Der Mann ohne Eigenschaften.
Originally publised: Berlin: Rohwolt, 1930.

N

Nabokov, Vladimir Vladimirovich

King, queen, knave: a novel. Vladimir Nabokov; translated from the Russian by Dmitri Nabokov in collaboration with the author. McGraw-Hill, 1968. 272 p.

ISBN 9780070457164
1. Love triangles 2. Extramarital affairs 3. Husband and wife 4. Lovers 5. Uncle and nephew 6. Major, John 7. 1920s 8. Literary fiction 9. Satirical fiction 10. Modern classics

Berlin in the late twenties provides the setting for this novel about a woman's scheme to murder her husband to live on his money with his nephew.

Originally published as Korol', dama, valet: Berlin : Slovo, 1928.

★ **Lolita**. Vladimir Nabokov; with an introduction by Martin Amis. Knopf, 1992. Xxxi, 335 p.
ISBN 9780679410430
1. Pedophilia 2. Obsession in men 3. Pedophiles 4. Men — Sexuality 5. Sexuality 6. Literary fiction 7. First person narratives 8. Books to movies
LC 92052931

A novel that studies the moral disintegration of a man whose obsessive desire to possess his step-daughter destroys the lives of those around him.

Includes bibliographical references (p. xxvii).
Originally published: Paris : Olympia Press, 1955.

Look at the harlequins!. Vladimir Nabokov. Vintage Books, 1990. 253 p.
ISBN 9780679727286
1. Authors 2. Exiles 3. Reminiscing in old age 4. Men with terminal illnesses 5. Literary fiction 6. Modern classics
LC 74010677

This is a fictional autobiography narrated by Vadim Vadimovich N. (VV), a Russian-American writer with uncanny biographical likenesses to the novel's author, Vladimir (Vladimirovich) Nabokov. 'Look at the harlequins... Play! Invent the world! Invent reality'. This is the childhood advice given by an aunt to Russian born writer Vadim Vadimovich, who emigrates to England, then Paris, then Germany and then the US, and, now dying, reconstructs his past. He remembers Iris his first wife, Annette his long-necked typist and Bel his daughter, as well as his own bizarre numerical nimbus syndrome.

"This is a book to enchant Nabokov fans and irritate everybody else.... [It] is part roman a clef, part fantasy, a tale of 'wives and books interlaced monogrammatically.' It is full of erudite allusions, Russian words in various stages of translation and absurd mistranslation, puns, anagrams, acronyms. Also opinions.... Comic, polished, international, [Nabokov] offers sophisticated entertainment, a concoction of romantic and literary matters." —*Christian Science Monitor*

Originally published: New York : McGraw-Hill, 1974.

Novels and memoirs, 1941-51. Vladimir Nabokov. Library of America, 1996. 710 p.
ISBN 9781883011185
1. Nabokov, Vladimir Vladimirovich 2. Authors, Russian 3. Russian Americans 4. Refugees, Russian 5. Authors, American 6. Half-brothers 7. Autobiographies and memoirs 8. Anthologies 9. Modern classics 10. Arts and entertainment — Writing and publishing 11. Life stories — Arts and culture — Writing — Authors
LC 96-15237

Includes: The real life of Sebastian Knight; Bend sinister; Speak, memory.
Illustrated with black-and-white photos.
Includes chronology.

Pale fire. Vladimir Nabokov. A. A. Knopf 1992. 315 p.
ISBN 9780679410775
1. Poetry — History and criticism 2. College teachers 3. Obsession in men 4. Immigrants 5. Criticism 6. Satirical fiction 7. Literary fiction 8. Modern classics

LC 91053217 //r92
Nabokov's parody, half poem and half commentary on the poem, deals with the escapades of the deposed king of Zemala in a New England college town.

Originally published: New York : G.P. Putnam's Sons, 1962.

Pnin. Vladimir Nabokov. R. Bentley, 1982. 191 p.
ISBN 9780837604657
1. Exiles 2. Russian Americans 3. College teachers 4. Immigrants 5. New York (State) 6. Satirical fiction 7. Literary fiction 8. Modern classics
LC 82001208
Professor Timofey Pnin, previously of Tsarist Russia, ia now precariously perched at the heart of an American campus. Battling with American life and language, Pnin must face great hazards in this new world: the ruination of his beautiful lumber-room-as-office; the removal of his teeth and the fitting of new ones; the search for a suitable boarding house; and the trials of taking the wrong train to deliver a lecture in a language he has yet to master. Wry, intelligent and moving, Pnin reveals the absurd and affecting side of one man in exile.

"Not a novel, not really a collection of short stories, but rather a series of sketches, all of them dealing with Timofey Pnin, professor of Russian in a small American university. Each one finds Pnin valiantly trying to cope with the daily crises of American societyPnin on the wrong train, Pnin learning to drive, Pnin giving a party, Pnin and the washing machine. They are all gently amusing, affectionate portraits of a Russian expatriate of the old school caught up in the inexplicable complexities of daily life." —*Library Journal*

Originally published: Garden City, N.Y.: Doubleday; London: Heinemann, 1957.

The **stories** of Vladimir Nabokov. . Alfred A. Knopf, 1995. 659 p.
ISBN 9780679729976
1. Literary fiction 2. Short stories 3. Translations
LC 95023466
Booklist Editors' Choice, 1995; Library Journal Best Books, 1995
A collection of 65 stories about human relations, human nature, and political satire includes 13 first-time English translations.
65 stories, including eleven never before translated into English.

Nagamatsu, Sequoia

How high we go in the dark. Sequoia Nagamatsu. William Morrow & Company, 2022. 256 p.
ISBN 9780063072640
1. Global warming 2. Plague 3. Near future 4. Epidemics 5. People with terminal illnesses 6. Apocalyptic fiction 7. Social science fiction
LC 2021018637
Beginning in 2030, a grieving archeologist arrives in the Arctic Circle to continue the work of his recently deceased daughter at the Batagaika crater, where researchers are studying long-buried secrets now revealed in melting permafrost, including the perfectly preserved remains of a girl who appears to have died of an ancient virus. Once unleashed, the Arctic Plague will reshape life on earth for generations to come, quickly traversing the globe, forcing humanity to devise a myriad of moving and inventive ways to embrace possibility in the face of tragedy. Sequoia Nagamatsu takes readers on a wildly original and compassionate journey, spanning continents, centuries, and even celestial bodies to tell a story about the resiliency of the human spirit, our infinite capacity to dream, and the connective threads that tie us all together in the universe.

"As with his story collection Where We Go When All We Were Is Gone (a BuzzFeed Notable Book and Entropy Best Book), Nagamatsu blends literary and visionary verve in a narrative winning comparison to Cloud Atlas and Station Eleven." —*Library Journal*

Naipaul, V. S.

A **bend** in the river. V.S. Naipaul. Vintage International, 1989. 278 p.
ISBN 9780679722021
1. East Indians in Africa 2. Disillusionment in men 3. Villages 4. Colonialism 5. Extramarital affairs 6. Africa 7. Sub-Saharan Africa 8. Political fiction 9. Literary fiction 10. Modern classics
Shortlisted for the Booker-McConnell Prize, 1979
In an African country that has suffered revolution and civil war and that is headed by a man of almost insane energy and crudity, one restless, reflective, and isolated villager and his friends uneasily submit to the tide of events.
First published in Great Britain by Andre Deutsch, 1979.

Guerrillas. V. S. Naipaul. Vintage Books, 1990. 248 p.
ISBN 9780679731740
1. Guerrillas 2. Love triangles 3. Class conflict 4. European Africans 5. British in the West Indies 6. West Indies 7. Political fiction 8. Literary fiction
LC 90-50147
A former hero of the South African resistance and his English mistress arrrive on a troubled Caribbean island, where their involvement with a young mulatto revolutionary leader leads to violence
"This is a novel without a villain, and there is not a character for whom the reader does not at some point feel deep sympathy and keen understanding, no matter how villainous or futile he may seem." —*New York Times Book Review*

A **house** for Mr. Biswas. V.S. Naipaul. Knopf, 1995. Xxxi, 564 p.
ISBN 9780679444589
1. East Indians 2. Married men 3. Middle-aged men 4. Identity (Psychology) 5. Home (Concept) 6. Trinidad and Tobago 7. Literary fiction 8. Psychological fiction 9. Modern classics
This is the story of Mohun Biswas, an Indo-Trinidadian who continually strives for success and mostly fails, who marries into the Tulsi family only to find himself dominated by it, and who finally sets the goal of owning his own house. Drawing some elements from the life of the author's father, the work is primarily a sharply drawn look at life that uses postcolonial perspectives to view a vanished colonial world.
First published in a different edition: London: Andre Deutsch, 1961.

Magic seeds. V.S. Naipaul. Alfred A. Knopf, 2004. 280 p.
ISBN 9780375407369
1. Revolutionaries 2. Underground movements 3. Middle-aged men 4. East Indians in England 5. Siblings 6. England 7. India 8. 1950s 9. Psychological fiction 10. Political fiction 11. Literary fiction
LC 2004048964
Booklist Editors' Choice, 2004; New York Times Notable Book, 2004
Willie Chandran feels as though the life he lives is not his own. But his listlessness washes away in a flood of encouragement from his radically political sister. Inspired, he joins an underground liberation movement in India. But after years of revolution and incarceration, he grows disillusioned and returns to England, still hoping to find his true self.
"The author has written a calculated polemic.... Naipaul is suggesting that our racial and ethnic fate is sealed; we can never escape who we are, and must learn to live with our unchosen identities whether we like them or not. It's not a consoling vision; neither is it despairing. It simply is." —*New York Times Book Review*
Sequel to: Half a life.

Napolitano, Ann

Dear Edward. Ann Napolitano. The Dial Press, 2020. 340 p.
ISBN 9781984854780

1. Airplane accidents 2. Survival (after airplane accidents, shipwrecks, etc.) 3. Boys 4. Life change events 5. Loss (Psychology) 6. Mainstream fiction 7. Adult books for young adults

LC 2019000400

LibraryReads Favorites, 2020

A 12-year-old lone survivor of a plane crash investigates the stories of his less-fortunate fellow passengers before making a profound discovery about his life purpose in the face of transcendent losses.

"It is a skillful and satisfying examination of not only what it means to survive, but of what it means to truly live." —*Booklist*

Narayan, R. K.

Malgudi days. R.K. Narayan. Penguin Books, 2006. Xx, 264 p. : Map
ISBN 9780143039655
1. Malgudi (India : Imaginary place) 2. India 3. Short stories

LC 81052204

"This selection distills, magically, Malgudi's vibrancy, its mythological-animistic throb, the large and small corruptions of its citizensfrom bureaucrats to back-street peopleand the reassuring backdrop of its cyclical rhythms. Distinguished writing; rewarding reading." —*Booklist*
Originally published: New York : Viking Press, 1982.

Natsukawa, Sosuke

The **cat** who saved books. Sosuke Natsukawa; translated from the Japanese by Louise Heal Kawai. HarperVia, 2021. 208 p.
ISBN 9780063095724
1. Talking cats 2. Booksellers 3. High school students 4. Books 5. Quests 6. Contemporary fantasy 7. Translations

LC 2021022643

LibraryReads Favorites, 2021

When a talking cat named Tiger demands that he help save books with him, high school student Rintaro Natsuki and Tiger embark on an amazing journey, liberating books from their neglectful owners and meeting a colorful cast of characters along the way.

"Lovers of traditional literature and books themselves will find validation in the lessons Rintaro learns (and teaches), while the story's structure and fanciful nature may hold appeal for a young adult audience more familiar with the conventions of gaming." —*Kirkus*
Originally published in 2017 as Hon o mamoro to suru neko no hanashi.

Nava, Michael

★ **Carved** in bone. Michael Nava. Persigo Press, 2019. 374 p. (Henry Rios mysteries, 8)
ISBN 9781733609111
1. Lawyers 2. Public defenders 3. Gay men 4. Mexican American men 5. Criminal investigation 6. Los Angeles, California 7. 1980s 8. Mysteries 9. LGBTQIA fiction 10. Legal stories
Lambda Literary Award for Gay Mystery, 2020

Set in San Francisco in 1984, Henry Rios is hired by an insurance company to investigate the apparently accidental death by carbon monoxide poisoning of Bill Ryan in his Castro Street apartment, but Rios becomes convinced Ryan's death was no accident, and that his young lover is implicated.

Naylor, Gloria

Mama Day. Gloria Naylor. Ticknor & Fields, 1988. 312 p.
ISBN 9780899197166

1. Independence in women 2. Islands 3. Married people 4. African American senior women 5. African Americans 6. South Carolina 7. New York City 8. Literary fiction 9. African American fiction

LC 87018157

Miranda Day, matriarch of an island off the coast of the U.S, fights a mortal combat with dark forces that threaten her great-niece, Cocoa, who has married and gone to the mainland BT

"When she is not didactically fostering our spiritual instruction, Gloria Naylor serves another worthy purpose beautifully: she invites us to imagine the lives of complex characters at work and play, and gives us a faithfully rendered community in all its seasons." —*Ms*

Nelson, Christina Suzann

If we make it home: a novel of faith and survival in the Oregon wilderness. Christina Suzann Nelson. Kregel Publications, 2017. 272 pages
ISBN 9780825444951
1. Women college friends 2. Wilderness survival 3. Hiking 4. Blizzards 5. Mountain survival 6. Christian suspense
Library Journal Best Books, 2017

After learning that Hope, their friend from college has died, Jenna, Ireland, and Vicky embark on a wilderness adventure in her honor.

Nesbo, Jo

The **leopard**. Jo Nesbo; translated from the Norwegian by Don Bartlett. Alfred A. Knopf, 2011. 528 p. (Detective Harry Hole, 8)
ISBN 9780307595874
1. Police 2. Crimes against women 3. Serial murder investigation 4. Opium addiction 5. Hole, Harry (Fictitious character) 6. Oslo, Norway 7. Mysteries 8. Translations 9. Scandinavian crime fiction

In the depths of winter, a killer stalks the city streets. His victims are two young women, both found with twenty-four inexplicable puncture wounds, both drowned in their own blood. The crime scenes offer no clues, the media is reaching fever pitch, and the police are running out of options. There is only one man who can help them, and he doesn't want to be found. Deeply traumatised by an investigation that threatened the lives of those he holds most dear, Inspector Harry Hole has lost himself in the squalor of Hong Kong's opium dens. But with his father seriously ill in hospital, Harry reluctantly agrees to return to Oslo. He has no intention of working on the case, but his instinct takes over when an MP is found brutally murdered in a city park.

First published in Great Britain : Harvill Secker, 2011.
First published with the title Panserhjerte in Oslo : H. Aschehong, 2009.
Translated from the Norwegian.

Phantom. Jo Nesbø; translated from the Norwegian by Don Bartlett. Alfred A. Knopf, 2012. 400 p. (Detective Harry Hole, 9)
ISBN 9780307960474
1. Former detectives 2. Former police 3. Murder suspects 4. Murder investigation 5. Drug traffic 6. Oslo, Norway 7. Norway 8. Mysteries 9. Translations 10. Scandinavian crime fiction

LC 2012019892

Former cop Harry Hole returns to Oslo to prove the innocence of a young man. He embarks on a dangerous investigation linked to Oslo's most virulent street drug.

This is a Borzoi book.
Title page verso.
Originally published as: Gjenferd, by Aschehoug : Oslo, 2011.
Translated from the Norwegian.

The **redeemer**. Jo Nesbø; translated from the Norwegian by Don Bartlett. Alfred A. Knopf, 2013. 464 p. (Detective Harry Hole, 6)

ISBN 9780307595850

1. Serial murderers 2. Police 3. Murder investigation 4. Detectives 5. Hole, Harry (Fictitious character) 6. Oslo, Norway 7. Norway 8. Mysteries 9. Translations 10. Scandinavian crime fiction

One freezing night in Oslo Christmas shoppers gather to listen to a Salvation Army street concert. An explosion cuts through the music, and a man in uniform falls to the ground, shot in the head at point-blank range. Harry Hole and his team have little to work with: no immediate suspect, no weapon and no motive.

Translation of Frelseren. Originally published: Oslo : Aschehoug, 2005.

Neubauer, Erica Ruth

Murder at the Mena House. Erica Ruth Neubauer. Kensington Pub Corp, 2020. 304 pages (Jane Wunderly novels, 1)

ISBN 9781496725851

1. Young widows 2. Independence in women 3. Americans in Egypt 4. Women murder victims 5. Women murder suspects 6. Egypt 7. Cairo, Egypt 8. Between the Wars (1918-1939) 9. Historical mysteries

Agatha Award for Best First Novel, 2020

Well-heeled travelers from around the world flock to the Mena House Hotel—an exotic gem in the heart of Cairo where cocktails flow, adventure dispels the aftershocks of World War I and deadly dangers wait in the shadows.

"Stunning revelations, romance, adventure, and intrigue abound in this multilayered, delightfully entertaining whodunit. Neubauer's debut dazzles, with a smart plot, remarkable scenery, and skilled execution." —Library Journal

Newitz, Annalee

Autonomous. Annalee Newitz. Tor, 2017. 304 p.

ISBN 9780765392077

1. Far future 2. Smugglers 3. Medicine 4. Scientists 5. Women scientists 6. Hard science fiction 7. Science fiction

Lambda Literary Award for Lesbian/Gay Science Fiction-Fantasy-Horror, 2018; Library Journal Best Books, 2017

Big Pharma is watching you. In a near-future society dominated by multinational corporations, drug pirate Jack Chen reverse-engineers expensive medications and distributes free copies to those who can't afford the real thing. As a result, her activities have attracted the attention of the International Property Coalition, which sends military robot Paladin and Paladin's human partner, Eliasz, to apprehend Jack. With its noir-tinged dystopian setting, suspenseful plot, and themes of bioethics and artificial intelligence, this debut may remind readers of William Gibson's Neuromancer.

"In a phenomenal debut thats sure to garner significant awards attention, Newitz, cofounder of io9, sends three fascinating characters on an action-packed race against time through a strange yet familiar futuristic landscape." —Publishers Weekly

Newland, Courttia

A **river** called time. Courttia Newland. Akashic Books, 2021. 448 p.

ISBN 9781617759260

1. Survival 2. End of the world 3. Astral projection 4. Soul 5. Supernatural 6. London, England 7. Dystopian fiction 8. Alternate histories 9. Science fiction

The Ark was built to save the lives of the many, but rapidly became a refuge for the elite, the entrance closed without warning. Years after the Ark was cut off from the world, a chance of survival within its confines is granted to a select few who can prove their worth. Among their number is

Markriss Denny, whose path to future excellence is marred only by a closely guarded secret: without warning, his spirit leaves his body, allowing him to see and experience a world far beyond his physical limitations.

"This is an ambitiously imagined book that, by removing the European lens on African cultures, creates a new reality that allows us to question how we view our own. Complex and multilayered, this novel opens the door to the possibilities of noncolonial worlds." —Kirkus

Newman, Sandra

The **heavens**. Sandra Newman. Grove Press, 2019. 272 p.

ISBN 9780802129024

1. Dreams 2. Consequences 3. Time travel (Past) 4. Fate and fatalism 5. Purpose in life 6. New York City 7. England 8. 2000s (Decade) 9. 16th century 10. Literary fiction

LC 2018028231

New York Times Notable Book, 2019

A New Yorker named Kate often dreams she is transported to the past—where she lives a second life as Emilia, the mistress of a nobleman in Elizabethan England—but soon, the dream becomes increasingly real and compelling until it threatens to overwhelm her life.

"A complex, unmissable work from a writer who deserves wide acclaim." —Kirkus

Ng, Celeste

★ **Everything** I never told you: a novel. Celeste Ng. Penguin Press, 2014. 304 pages

ISBN 9781594205712

1. Daughters — Death 2. Loss (Psychology) 3. Interracial families 4. Chinese Americans 5. Drowning 6. Ohio 7. 1970s 8. Psychological fiction 9. Adult books for young adults

LC 2013039961

Alex Award, 2015; Asian Pacific American Award for Literature: Adult Fiction, 2015; Booklist Editors' Choice, 2014; Massachusetts Book Awards, Fiction Award, 2015; New York Times Notable Book, 2014; School Library Journal Best Books: Best Adult Books 4 Teens, 2014

Explores the fallout of a favorite daughter's shattering death on a Chinese-American family in 1970s Ohio.

"Ng constructs a mesmerizing narrative that shrinks enormous issues of race, prejudice, identity, and gender into the miniaturist dynamics of a single family." —Library Journal

★ **Little** fires everywhere: a novel. Celeste Ng. Penguin Press, 2017. 384 p.

ISBN 9780735224292

1. Landlord and tenant 2. Adoption 3. Interpersonal conflict 4. Consequences 5. Secrets 6. Cleveland, Ohio 7. Ohio 8. Literary fiction 9. Multiple perspectives 10. Books to TV 11. Adult books for young adults

LC 2016056762

Goodreads Choice Award, 2017; Loan Stars Favourites, 2017; LibraryReads Favorites, 2017; School Library Journal Best Books: Best Adult Books 4 Teens, 2017

Fighting an ugly custody battle with an artistic tenant who has little regard for the strict rules of their progressive Cleveland suburb, a straitlaced family woman who is seeking to adopt a baby becomes obsessed with exposing the tenant's past, only to trigger devastating consequences for both of their families.

"The characters she creates here are wonderfully appealing, and watching their paths connect...is mesmerizing, casting into new light ideas about creativity and consumerism, parenthood and privilege." —*Kirkus*
Adapted into a TV series of the same name in 2020.

Nguyen, Kevin

★ **New** waves. Kevin Nguyen. One World, 2020. 288 p.
ISBN 9781984855237
1. New businesses 2. Racism 3. Asian American men 4. African American women 5. Twenties (Age) 6. Satirical fiction 7. Adult books for young adults

LC 2019034574

Fed up with discriminating bosses, an Asian-American customer service representative and a talented African-American programmer conspire to steal their employer's user database before an unexpected setback exposes a secret double life.

"Nguyen's stellar debut is a piercing assessment of young adulthood, the tech industry, and racism." —*Publishers Weekly*

Nguyen, Lena

We have always been here. Lena Nguyen. Daw Books, 2021. 368 pages
ISBN 9780756417291
1. Women psychologists 2. Androids 3. Paranoia 4. Space vehicles 5. Space exploration 6. Science fiction thrillers 7. Science fiction

The behavioral psychologist onboard a survey ship headed to a planet ripe for colonization, Dr. Grace Park must determine the origin of a strange phenomenon that is causing the crew to suffer mental breaks without losing her own mind in the process.

"Nguyen immerses readers in a chilling landscape while effortlessly softening the more sinister moments with wistful, dreamlike flashbacks." —*Publishers Weekly*

Nguyen, Phan Que Mai

★ The **mountains** sing: a novel. Nguyn Phan Que Mai. Algonquin Books of Chapel Hill, 2020. 352 p.
ISBN 9781616208189
1. War — Psychological aspects 2. Violence — Psychological aspects 3. Loss (Psychology) 4. Vietnam War, 1961-1975 5. Families 6. Vietnam 7. 20th century 8. Translations 9. Family sagas 10. Literary fiction

LC 2019030591

Years after a family is forced by Vietnam's Communist Land Reforms to abandon their farm, a granddaughter comes of age as her loved ones depart for the Ho Chi Minh Trail.

"This brilliant, unsparing love letter to Vietnam will move readers." —*Publishers Weekly*
Translated from the Vietnamese.

Nguyen, Viet Thanh

★ The **committed**. Viet Thanh Nguyen. Grove Press, 2021. 400 p.
ISBN 9780802157065
1. Refugees 2. Drug traffic 3. Spies 4. Psychic trauma 5. Vietnamese in France 6. Paris, France 7. 1980s 8. Literary fiction

The Committed follows the unnamed Sympathizer as he arrives in Paris in the early 1980s with his blood brother Bon. The pair try to overcome their pasts and ensure their futures by engaging in capitalism in one of its purest forms: drug dealing.

★ The **refugees**. Viet Thanh Nguyen. Grove Press, 2017. 192 p.
ISBN 9780802126399
1. Vietnamese Americans 2. Home (Concept) 3. Self-fulfillment 4. Families 5. Human nature 6. California 7. Literary fiction 8. Short stories

New York Times Notable Book, 2017; Booklist Editors' Choice, 2017

Author Viet Thanh Nguyen's debut novel The Sympathizer won both the Pulitzer Prize and the Carnegie Medal, among other accolades; readers hungry for more will appreciate the eight stories collected here, written before The Sympathizer was published. While the stories, mostly set in the Vietnamese community in California, represent Vietnamese refugee experiences in the US, the topics they explore—relationships, grief, the desire for fulfillment—speak to the human experience. Check them out if you're interested in sympathetic characters, cultural dislocation, or the experiences of refugees.

"Nguyen is the foremost literary interpreter of the Vietnamese experience in America, to be sure. But his stories, excellent from start to finish, transcend ethnic boundaries to speak to human universals." —*Kirkus*

★ The **sympathizer**. Viet Thanh Nguyen. Grove/Atlantic, 2015. 371 p.
ISBN 9780802123459
1. Spies 2. Identity (Psychology) 3. Vietnam War, 1961-1975 4. Vietnamese in the United States 5. Double agents 6. Vietnam 7. 1970s 8. 20th century 9. Historical fiction 10. Literary fiction 11. Psychological fiction

ALA Notable Book, 2016; Andrew Carnegie Medal for Excellence in Fiction, 2016; Asian Pacific American Award for Literature: Adult Fiction, 2016; Booklist Editors' Choice, 2015; Edgar Allan Poe Award for Best First Novel by an American Author, 2016; Library Journal Best Books, 2015; New York Times Notable Book, 2015; Pulitzer Prize for Fiction, 2016; Shortlisted for the International Dublin Literary Award, 2017

Follows a Viet Cong agent as he spies on a South Vietnamese army general and his compatriots as they start a new life on 1975 Los Angeles.

"Nguyen's probing literary art illuminates how Americans failed in their political and military attempt to remake Vietnam—but then succeeded spectacularly in shrouding their failure in Hollywood distortions. Compelling—and profoundly unsettling." —*Booklist*

Nicholls, David

Us: a novel. David Nicholls. Harper, 2014. 400 p.
ISBN 9780062365583
1. Middle-aged men 2. Husband and wife 3. Families 4. Man-woman relationships 5. Family vacations 6. England 7. Europe 8. Psychological fiction 9. Domestic fiction 10. First person narratives

LC 2014015360

Booklist Editors' Choice, 2014; Library Journal Best Books 2014; LibraryReads Favorites, 2014

The highly anticipated new novel from David Nicholls, author of the mega-bestselling fiction sensation One Day, which follows one man's efforts to salvage his marriage—and repair his troubled relationship with his teenaged son—during the course of a trip around Europe.

"This is Nicholls's most ambitious work to date, and his realistically flawed characters are somehow endearing despite the many bruises they inflict upon each other." —*Publishers Weekly*

Nicholls, Owen

Love, unscripted: a novel. Owen Nicholls. Ballantine Books, 2020. 384 pages
ISBN 9781984826879

1. Film projectionists 2. Dating (Social customs) 3. Breaking up (Interpersonal relations) 4. Depression 5. Memories 6. England 7. London, England 8. Love stories 9. Mainstream fiction

LC 2019038100

A romantic movie buff and film projectionist is devastated when his four-year relationship with the leading lady of his dreams ends, compelling him to rewrite history to come to terms with what went wrong.

"Their relationship has cinematic highs and believable lows, with fully rounded characters and smart, snappy, romantic comedy-worthy dialogue. Nick's and Ellie's real lives aren't a movie, but as Nicholls tells it, they might have a happily-ever-after anyway. A delightfully sweet, funny, and heartbreaking ode to love stories, both onscreen and off." —*Kirkus*

Originally published in Great Britain in 2019 by Headline Review, an imprint of the Headline Publishing Group.

Nichols, Peter

The **rocks**. Peter Nichols. Riverhead Books, 2015. 432 p.
ISBN 9781594633317
1. Family secrets 2. Coastal towns 3. Former lovers 4. Man-woman relationships 5. Islands 6. Spain 7. Majorca, Spain 8. Love stories

LC 2014022801

Two honeymooners, Gerald and Lulu, abruptly split in 1948, and despite residing on the same island for more than sixty years, they live separately, never interacting until children from their rivaling families fall in love.

Nicieza, Fabian

Suburban dicks. Fabian Nicieza. Putnam Pub Group, 2021. 400 pages
ISBN 9780593191262
1. Pregnant women 2. Stay-at-home mothers 3. Suburban life 4. Murder victims 5. Journalists 6. New Jersey 7. Mysteries 8. Satirical fiction

A mystery featuring two amateur sleuths examines the racial tensions exposed in a New Jersey suburb after the murder of a gas station attendant.

"Nicieza, a comics writer best known as co-creator of the wisecracking antihero Deadpool for Marvel, pivots to his first mystery here but keeps the comic-book energy and zaniness.... Scathing and timely social commentary in a comic mystery." —*Booklist*

Nickson, Chris

Come the fear. Chris Nickson. Creme de la Crime, 2012. 214 p. : Map (Richard Nottingham mysteries, 4)
ISBN 9781780290300
1. Murder investigation 2. Police 3. Arson 4. Women murder victims 5. Rich men 6. England 7. Leeds, England 8. 1730s 9. Historical mysteries 10. Mysteries

LC Bl2012039732

Investigating the deaths of a young woman and a baby whose bodies were found in a deliberately set fire, Richard Nottingham conducts a search through the streets of Leeds before discovering a link to a wealthy wool merchant.

Niffenegger, Audrey

The **time** traveler's wife: a novel. By Audrey Niffenegger. MacAdam/Cage Pub, 2002. 518 p.
ISBN 9781931561464
1. Time travel 2. Husband and wife 3. Fate and fatalism 4. Marriage 5. Fathers and daughters 6. Chicago, Illinois 7. Michigan 8. Literary fiction 9. Multiple perspectives 10. First person narratives 11. Adult books for young adults

LC 2003010159

Alex Award, 2004; British Book Award for Popular Fiction, 2006

Passionately in love, Clare and Henry vow to hold onto each other and their marriage as they struggle with the effects of Chrono-Displacement Disorder, a condition that casts Henry involuntarily into the world of time travel.

"Niffenegger writes with the unflinching yet detached clarity of a war correspondent standing at the sidelines of an unfolding battle. She possesses a historian's eye for contextual detail. This is no romantic idyll." —*USA Today*

Nin, Anais

Cities of the interior. Anais Nin; introduction by Sharon Spencer. Swallow Press/Ohio University Press, 1991. Xx, 588 p. : Illustration
ISBN 9780804006668
1. Women 2. Self-discovery in women 3. Literary fiction 4. Psychological fiction 5. Anthologies

LC 91014523

Five interconnected Symbolist and modernist novels in which the inner worlds and lives of three women, Lillian, Djuna, and Sabina, and the relationships they influence are meticulously explored and celebrated.

North, Alex

The **shadows**. Alex North. Celadon Books, 2020. 336 p.
ISBN 9781250318039
1. Homecomings 2. Teenage murderers 3. Copycat murders 4. Dreams 5. Lucid dreams 6. England 7. Thrillers and suspense 8. Police procedurals

LC 2020002697

Forced by his mother's failing health to return to the hometown where a misfit friend committed a shocking murder 25 years earlier, Paul learns about an investigation into a local copycat before realizing he is being followed.

"This second stunning thriller firmly establishes North as a rapturous teller of tales." —*Booklist*

The **Whisper** Man. Alex North. Celadon Books, 2019. 368 pages
ISBN 9781250317995
1. Fathers and sons 2. Moving household 3. Serial murderers 4. Detectives 5. Widowers 6. England 7. Thrillers and suspense 8. Police procedurals
LibraryReads Favorites, 2019

Mourning the death of his wife, a father and his young son move to Featherbank for a fresh start but find their new town has a dark past involving a serial killer named "The Whisper Man."

North, Anna

The **life** and death of Sophie Stark. Anna North. Blue Rider Press, 2015. 270 pages
ISBN 9780399173394
1. Fame 2. Filmmakers 3. Humiliation 4. Documentary films — Production and direction 5. College basketball players 6. Multiple perspectives 7. Literary fiction
Lambda Literary Award for Bisexual Literature

An unapologetic filmmaker uses the stories of those around her to create movies that bring her both critical acclaim and ire from the people whose secrets she has exposed.

"As taut and artistically ambitious as its title character, North's novel upends the trope of the lone, tortured genius, considering instead the deeply human consequences of one person's uncompromising vision." —*Booklist*

North, Claire

Notes from the burning age. Claire North. Orbit, 2021. 464 p.
ISBN 9780316498838
1. Dystopias 2. Political intrigue 3. Imaginary wars and battles 4. End of the world 5. Post-apocalypse 6. Dystopian fiction 7. Science fiction

Once, we lived through the Burning Age—the time when we cared so little for the world that it went up in flames. It was a punishment. But it was also a gift, and centuries of peace followed. Once, Ven was a holy man, studying texts from the ashes of the past, sorting secrets from heresies. But when he gets caught up in the political scheming of the Brotherhood, he finds himself in the middle of a war, fueled by old knowledge and forbidden ambition. There was a time when the world burned. Now, some want to set the fire again . . .

"World Fantasy Award winner North (The Sudden Appearance of Hope) spins a riveting tale of subterfuge and deadly self-indulgence in this postapocalyptic thrill ride." —*Publishers Weekly*

The **pursuit** of William Abbey. Claire North. Orbit, 2019. 432 pages
ISBN 9780316316842
1. Physicians 2. Curses 3. Imperialism 4. Shadows 5. Guilt 6. 19th century 7. 20th century 8. Historical fantasy

A hauntingly powerful novel about how the choices we make can stay with us forever, by the award-winning author of The First Fifteen Lives of Harry August and 84K.

Novic, Sara

Girl at war. Sara Novic. Random House, 2015. 320 p.
ISBN 9780812996340
1. War — Psychological aspects 2. Loss (Psychology) 3. Memory 4. Yugoslav War, 1991-1995 5. Secrets 6. Croatia 7. New York City 8. 1990s 9. Coming-of-age stories 10. Adult books for young adults
Alex Award, 2016; Longlisted for the Baileys Women's Prize for Fiction, 2016

When her happy life in 1991 Croatia is shattered by civil war, 10-year-old Ana Juric is embroiled in a world of guerilla warfare and child soldiers before making a daring escape to America, where years later she struggles to hide her past.

"Elegiac, and understandably if unrelievedly so, with a matter-of-factness about death and uprootedness. A promising start." —*Kirkus*

Novik, Naomi

A **deadly** education: a novel. Naomi Novik. Del Rey, 2020. 272 p. (Scholomance, 1)
ISBN 9780593128480
1. Witches 2. Magic 3. Monsters 4. Good and evil 5. Misfits (Persons) 6. Great Britain 7. Fantasy fiction 8. First person narratives
LC 2020008102
RUSA Reading List Short List, 2021

An unwilling dark sorceress destined to rewrite the rules of magic clashes with a popular combat sorcerer while resolving to spare the lives of innocents.

"Novik (Spinning Silver) puts a refreshingly dark, adult spin on the magical boarding school setting of the spellbinding first fantasy in her Scholomance trilogy.... Readers will delight in the push-and-pull of El and Orion's relationship, the fantastically detailed world, the clever magic system, and the matter-of-fact diversity of the student body." —*Publishers Weekly*

His majesty's dragon. By Naomi Novik. Del Rey Books, 2006. 384 p. (Temeraire, 1)
ISBN 9780345481283
1. Ship captains 2. Dragons 3. Napoleonic Wars, 1800-1815 4. Military life 5. Military tactics 6. England 7. 19th century 8. Historical fantasy 9. Military fantasy 10. Fantasy fiction 11. Adult books for young adults
LC 2005046342

When the HMS Reliant captures a French ship and its priceless cargo, an unhatched dragon egg, Captain Will Laurence is swept into an unexpected kinship with an extraordinary creature and joins the elite Aerial Corps as a master of the dragon Temeraire, in which role he must match wits with the powerful dragon-borne forces of Napoleon Bonaparte.

"A completely authentic tale, brimming with all the detail and richness one looks for in military yarns as well as the impossible wonder of gilded fantasy." —*Entertainment Weekly*

The **last** graduate: a novel. Naomi Novik. Del Rey, 2021. 336 p. (Scholomance, 2)
ISBN 9780593128862
1. Graduation (School) 2. Witches 3. Magic 4. Monsters 5. Good and evil 6. Great Britain 7. Fantasy fiction 8. First person narratives
LC 2020055382
Loan Stars Favourites, 2021

A budding dark sorceress determined not to use her formidable powers uncovers yet more secrets about the workings of her world in the sequel to A Deadly Education.

"Sardonic students, gruesome monsters, growing friendships, and a touch of romance create a highly readable story. Some questions remain to be answered in the trilogy's last volume. The end of this installment ensures that book three can't come fast enough." —*Library Journal*

★ **Spinning** silver. Naomi Novik. Del Rey, 2018. 466 p.
ISBN 9780399180989
1. Debt 2. Money lenders 3. Pride and vanity 4. Elves 5. Magic 6. Adaptations, retellings, and spin-offs 7. Fantasy fiction 8. Multiple perspectives 9. Adult books for young adults
LC 2018005791
Alex Award, 2019; Amelia Bloomer List, 2019; Librarians' Choice (Australia), 2018; LibraryReads Favorites, 2018; Library Journal Best Books, 2018; Locus Award for Fantasy Novel, 2019; Mythopoeic Award for Adult Literature, 2019; New York Times Notable Book, 2018

Deciding to collect on the outstanding debts owed her family of moneylenders, a young woman is overheard boasting about being able to turn silver into gold by the creatures who haunt the wood, in a reimagining of the Rumpelstiltskin story.

★ **Uprooted**. Naomi Novik. Del Rey, 2015. 438 pages
ISBN 9780804179034
1. Curses 2. Witches 3. Wizards 4. Magic 5. Quests 6. Fantasy fiction 7. Coming-of-age stories 8. Adaptations, retellings, and spin-offs 9. Adult books for young adults
Nebula Award for Best Novel, 2015; LibraryReads Favorites, 2015; Library Journal Best Books, 2015; Locus Award for Fantasy Novel, 2016; Mythopoeic Award for Adult Literature, 2016; RUSA Reading List, 2016

A tale inspired by the "Beauty and the Beast" story follows the experiences of Agnieszka, who becomes the latest girl chosen to serve an immortal wizard who protects their village from the malevolent forces of a nearby forest.

"Novik's use of language is supremely skillful as she weaves a tale that is both elegantly grand and earthily humble, familiar as a Grimm fairy tale yet fresh, original, and totally irresistible." —*Publishers Weekly*

Nugent, Benjamin

Fraternity: stories. Benjamin Nugent. Farrar Straus & Giroux, 2020. 160 p.
ISBN 9780374158606
1. Fraternities 2. Campus life 3. College students 4. Universities and colleges 5. Young men 6. Massachusetts 7. Short stories 8. Satirical fiction

Navigating their respective transitions from adolescence to adulthood, the members of a dilapidated fraternity house in a Massachusetts college town hide their fears of exclusion behind drunken antics, hazing dares, solemn confessions and sexual encounters.

"This is a book about the awkward, awful passage between adolescence and adulthood and about the way these unwary, ill-prepared boys negotiate it, or try not to. Nugent manages—the mark of the master satirist—to be simultaneously compassionate and ruthless. Splendid." —*Kirkus*

Nunez, Sigrid

★ The **friend**. Sigrid Nunez. Riverhead Books, 2018. 212 p.
ISBN 9780735219441
1. Friends' death 2. Grief in animals 3. Human-animal relationships 4. Survivors of suicide victims 5. Loss (Psychology) 6. Psychological fiction 7. Literary fiction
LC 2017011191
National Book Award for Fiction, 2018; New York Times Notable Book, 2018; Shortlisted for the International Dublin Literary Award, 2020

Becoming the guardian of her late best friend's enormous Great Dane, a grieving woman is evicted from her no-pets apartment and forges a deep bond with the equally distraught animal in ways that initially disturb her friends.

"This elegant novel explores both rich memories and day-to-day mundanity, reflecting the way that, especially in grief, the past is often more vibrant than the present." —*Publishers Weekly*

The **last** of her kind: a novel. Sigrid Nunez. Farrar, Straus and Giroux, 2006. 384 p.
ISBN 9780374183813
1. Interclass friendship 2. Idealism in women 3. Women radicals 4. Women college students 5. Women roommates 6. New York City 7. Psychological fiction 8. Coming-of-age stories 9. Adult books for young adults
LC 2005040098
Chronicles the lives of two women who meet as freshmen in 1968 at Columbia University—Georgette George and her idealistic, radical roommate Ann Drayton—from their first encounter, through the fight that ends their friendship, to Ann's arrest for murder in 1976 and Georgette's search for answers to the riddle of Ann's life.

"In previous works, Nunez has proved herself a master of psychological acuity. Here her ambitions are grander, and the result is a remarkable and disconcerting vision of a troubled time in American history, and of its repercussions for national and individual identity." —*The New Yorker*

Salvation city. Sigrid Nunez. Riverhead Books, 2010. 288 p.
ISBN 9781594487668
1. Epidemics 2. Teenage boys 3. Orphans 4. Forgiveness 5. Salvation 6. Indiana 7. Psychological suspense 8. Coming-of-age stories 9. Adult books for young adults
LC 2010001989
Seeking refuge in the home of an evangelical pastor after a flu pandemic decimates the planet's populations, thirteen-year-old orphan Cole witnesses the community's preparations for a prophesied religious cataclysm and struggles with memories of a very different world.

"The great success of Nunez's book is that the end of the world is filtered through Cole's imperfect perspective, so that the collapse of society is no more devastating than first love, and deeply felt conflict rages as a young man tries to find something worth preserving in a place determined to obliterate the past." —*Publishers Weekly*

What are you going through. Sigrid Nunez. Riverhead Books, 2020. 208 pages
ISBN 9780593191415
1. Interpersonal communication 2. Listening 3. Women with cancer 4. Assisted suicide 5. Female friendship 6. Literary fiction 7. First person narratives
LC 2020022836
A woman who is content to listen to the people she encounters talk about themselves is asked by one to do something extraordinary, in a novel by the New York Times-best-selling, National Book Award-winning author of The Friend.

"Deeply empathetic without being sentimental, this novel explores women's lives, their choices, and how they support one another, particularly when they don't have spouses or children or those relationships have become strained. Highly recommended for readers who favor emotional resonance over escapism during difficult times." —*Library Journal*

Nussbaum, Susan

Good kings, bad kings: a novel. Susan Nussbaum. Algonquin Books of Chapel Hill, 2013. 336 p.
ISBN 9781616202637
1. Institutional care — Employees 2. Teenagers with disabilities 3. Children with developmental disabilities 4. Children with disabilities 5. Wheelchair users 6. Chicago, Illinois 7. Multiple perspectives 8. Mainstream fiction 9. First person narratives 10. Adult books for young adults
LC 2013001350
Bellwether Prize for Fiction, 2012
The residents at a facility for disabled young people in Chicago build trust and make friends in an effort to fight against their living conditions and mistreatment in this debut novel from the playwright behind "Mishuganismo."

"Nussbaum charms, outrages, and enlightens readers as she cycles among these and other characters, boldly contrasting the transcendence of love with the harsh realities of a negligent for-profit nursing home." —*Booklist*

O

O'Brian, Patrick

Master and commander. Patrick O'Brian. W. W. Norton, 1990. 411 p. : Illustration (Jack Aubrey and Stephen Maturin novels, 1)
ISBN 9780393307054
1. Napoleonic Wars, 1800-1815 — Naval operations 2. Naval tactics 3. Sailing ships 4. Ship captains 5. Seafaring life 6. Great Britain 7. Sea stories 8. Historical fiction 9. Adventure stories
LC 77085111

First in the series of Jack Aubrey novels. Establishes the friendship between Captain Aubrey, R.N, and Stephen Maturin, ship's surgeon and intelligence agent, against the backdrop of the Napoleonic wars.

Originally published : London: Collins, 1970.

O'Brien, Edna

★ **Girl**. Edna O'Brien. Farrar, Straus and Giroux, 2019. 208 p.
ISBN 9780374162559
1. Women kidnapping victims 2. Rape victims 3. Escapes 4. Violence against women 5. Girl kidnapping victims 6. Nigeria 7. Literary fiction
LC 2019020325
New York Times Notable Book, 2019

Abducted by Boko Haram, a young woman makes a hair-raising escape from her northeast Nigerian prison before confronting the hostility and bureaucracy of being the mother of a child fathered by enemies.

O'Brien, Perry Edmond

Fire in the blood. Perry O'Brien. Random House. 2020. 288 p.
ISBN 9780812988581
1. Soldiers 2. Widowers 3. Hit-and-run accidents 4. Absent without leave 5. Murder investigation 6. New York City 7. Bronx, New York City 8. Thrillers and suspense

A traumatized Army soldier in Afghanistan goes AWOL and finds the limits of his military training tested when he tries to uncover the truth behind his wife's fatal hit-and-run accident.

"In addition to his background as a soldier in Afghanistan, debut author O'Brien's ability to express the human experience of inner turmoil and atonement, revenge and justice, displays his powerful and engaging talent as a writer.... Fans of Michael Connelly's 'Harry Bosch' series will appreciate Coop's brusque, principled personality." —*Library Journal*

O'Brien, Tim

Going after Cacciato: a novel. By Tim O'Brien. Delacorte Press/S. Lawrence, 1978. 338 p.
ISBN 9780440029489
1. Vietnam War, 1961-1975 2. Deserters 3. Soldiers 4. War and society 5. Courage 6. Vietnam 7. War stories 8. Literary fiction 9. Metafiction
LC 77011723
National Book Award for Fiction, 1979

Cacciato leaves his unit in Vietnam, announcing that he is going to Paris, but the men chasing him see India and Iran as well.

★ The **things** they carried: a work of fiction. Tim O'Brien. Houghton Mifflin, 1990. 273 p.
ISBN 9780395515983
1. Vietnam veterans 2. XXXXXXXX 3. Soldiers — Psychology 4. Vietnam War, 1961-1975 — Casualties 5. Writing 6. Psychological fiction 7. War stories 8. Short stories
LC 89039871
ALA Notable Book, 1991; National Book Critics Circle Award for Fiction finalist, 1990; Pulitzer Prize for Fiction finalist, 1991

A collection of award-winning and utterly moving stories about the madness of the Vietnam war.

"This book may be self-conscious...but through its determination to treat these men with dignity and decency it proves immensely affecting." —*Newsweek*

O'Connor, Carlene

Murder in an Irish bookshop. Carlene O'Connor. Kensington Publishing, 2021. 304 p. (Irish village mysteries, 7)
ISBN 9781496730794
1. Bookstores 2. Authors 3. Murder 4. Women amateur detectives 5. Murder investigation 6. Ireland 7. Cork County, Ireland 8. Cozy mysteries 9. Gentle reads
Loan Stars Favourites, 2021

The grand opening of a new bookstore in Kilbane becomes the closing chapter of an author's life—and a whodunit that tests even Garda Siobhan O'Sullivan's deductive reasoning.

"Aided by a garda trainee, Siobhan pursues a puzzling investigation full of misdirection and enlivened by the input of her five rambunctious siblings. O'Connor reinforces her place as the queen of the cozy police procedural." —*Publishers Weekly*

O'Connor, Flannery

★ **Collected** works. Flannery C'Connor; edited by Sally Fitzgerald. Library of America; distributed by Viking Press 1988. 1281 p.
ISBN 9780940450370
1. Letters 2. Essays 3. Short stories
LC 87037829

This collection includes all the short stories, both novels, the essays, and selected letters of one of the most unique and important writers in the southern tradition.

The **complete** stories. Flannery O'Connor. Farrar, Straus and Giroux, 1971. Xvii, 555 p.
ISBN 9780374127527
1. Southern States 2. Short stories 3. Literary fiction 4. Southern Gothic
LC 72171492
National Book Award for Fiction, 1972

Thirty-one tales depicting the humorous, if near tragic conditions of life in the Deep South during the fifties.

"This collection is arranged in chronological order from the story she wrote for her master's thesis at the University of Iowa to 'Judgement Day' .... The stories here include the original openings and other chapters of her two novels Wise Blood and The Violent Bear It Away." —*New York Times Book Review*

★ The **violent** bear it away. Flannery O'Connor. Farrar, Straus & Cudahy, 1960. 243 p.
ISBN 9780374505240
1. Redemption 2. Prophets 3. Religious fanaticism 4. Families 5. Children with Down syndrome 6. Southern States 7. Literary fiction 8. Modern classics 9. Southern Gothic

A back country orphan struggles to defy his uncle's prophesy that he will become a Baptist prophet.

★ **Wise** blood. Flannery O'Connor. Farrar, Straus and Giroux, 1996. 232 p.
ISBN 9780374505844
1. Veterans 2. Prophets 3. Grace (Theology) 4. Christianity 5. Eccentrics and eccentricities 6. Southern States 7. Literary fiction 8. Books to movies 9. Modern classics

The passengers on the train to Taulkinham show mixed reactions when Haze questions their belief in Jesus.

O'Connor, Frank

Collected stories. Introduction by Richard Ellmann. A. A. Knopf, 1981. 701p.
ISBN 9780394516028

1. Short stories

LC 81001253

"The author grew up with 'the troubles,' but the Ireland he evokes in these 72 stories...is the provincial life of his Cork boyhood." —*Library Journal*

O'Connor, Joseph

Star of the Sea. Joseph O'Connor. Harcourt, 2003. Xxiii, 386 p. ISBN 9780151009084

1. Murderers 2. Ships 3. Ocean travel 4. Immigrants 5. Household employees 6. Ireland 7. England 8. Irish Potato Famine (1845-1852) 9. 19th century 10. Historical mysteries

LC 2003001984

ALA Notable Book, 2004; New York Times Notable Book, 2003

In the middle of the Atlantic Ocean during the summer of 1847, a boatload of Irish refugees heading for the promise of America is stalked by a killer in their ranks who seems bent on some kind of revenge.

"The author brillantly weaves together an intriguing plot, a cast of memorable characters, and some stunningly realistic dialog. Universal themes of love, loyalty, vengeance, and violence are explored in the context of a troubled class-ridden society convulsed by the catastropic potato blight." —*Library Journal*

O'Dell, Claire

A **study** in honor: a novel. Claire O'Dell. Harper Voyager, 2018. 293 pages; (Janet Watson chronicles, 1)

ISBN 9780062699305

1. Civil War 2. Veterans 3. Near future 4. Artificial limbs 5. Military surgeons 6. Washington, D.C. 7. Social science fiction 8. Science fiction mysteries 9. Adaptations, retellings, and spin-offs

Lambda Literary Award for Lesbian Mystery, 2019

Homeless and jobless after being dishonorably discharged during the New Civil War, Dr. Janet Watson returns to Washington, D.C, where she is offered a place to stay by mysterious covert agent Sara Holmes.

O'Donnell, Lisa

The **death** of bees: a novel. Lisa O'Donnell. Harper, 2013. 320 p. ISBN 9780062209849

1. Sisters 2. Neighbors 3. Family secrets 4. Orphans 5. Teenage girls 6. Glasgow, Scotland 7. Coming-of-age stories 8. Literary fiction 9. Black humor 10. Adult books for young adults

LC 2012031882

Commonwealth Book Prize, 2013; Commonwealth Book Prize: Canada and Europe, 2013; Alex Award, 2014

Hazlehurst housing estate, Glasgow, Christmas Eve 2006. 15-year-old Marnie and her little sister Nelly have just finished burying their parents in the back garden. Only Marnie and Nelly know how they got there.

This book was originally published in Great Britain in 2012 by William Heinemann, an imprint of the the Random House Group—Title page verso.

O'Donnell, Paraic

The **house** on Vesper Sands: a novel. Paraic O'Donnell. Tin House, 2021. 368 pages

ISBN 9781951142247

1. College students 2. Women columnists 3. Women — Death 4. Poor women 5. Snow 6. London, England 7. Victorian era (1837-1901)

8. 1890s 9. Historical mysteries 10. Victorian mysteries 11. Gothic fiction

LC 2020034643

LibraryReads Favorites, 2021

A Victorian-inspired supernatural mystery follows the experiences of a Cambridge dropout and his savvy detective partner, who connect a paramour's disappearance to a bizarre suicide.

"An intriguing, unexpected gothic mashup with elements of Dorothy Sayers, Wilkie Collins, and Josephine Tey." —*Kirkus*

Originally published: London: Weidenfeld & Nicolson, 2018.

O'Donohue, Clare

The **lover's** knot: a Someday Quilts mystery. Clare O'Donohue. Plume, 2008. 304 p. (Someday Quilts mysteries, 1)

ISBN 9780452289796

1. Quilting 2. Murder 3. Friendship 4. Small town life 5. Women amateur detectives 6. New York (State) 7. Cozy mysteries 8. Gentle reads 9. Hobby mysteries

LC 2008016909

Overjoyed to receive a handmade quilt from her grandmother as an engagement gift until her fiance calls off the wedding, Nell seeks refuge at her grandmother's home in picturesque Archers Rest, until the body of a local handyman turns up in the quilt shop and Nell is drawn into the investigation—and to the handsome police chief.

O'Farrell, Maggie

Hamnet. Maggie O'Farrell. Alfred A Knopf, 2020. 304 p. ISBN 9780525657606

1. Shakespeare, William 2. Dramatists 3. Herbalists 4. Plague 5. Children — Death 6. Grief 7. Stratford-Upon-Avon, England 8. England 9. Elizabethan era (1558-1603) 10. 16th century 11. Historical fiction 12. Literary fiction

LC 2019030390

ALA Notable Book, 2021; Loan Stars Favourites, 2020; National Book Critics Circle Award for Fiction, 2020; New York Times Notable Book, 2020; Women's Prize for Fiction, 2020; Shortlisted for the Walter Scott Prize for Historical Fiction, 2021

A moving story about the death of William Shakespeare's 11-year-old son Hamnet, and the years leading up to the production of his great play, Hamlet.

"While O'Farrell encapsulates atmosphere through small sensory details—golden honey dripping from a comb, the smell of lavender sprinkled into a vat of soap—she is laser-focused on human connections, their ebb and flow, and how they can drown a person. This striking, painfully lovely novel captures the very nature of grief." —*Booklist*

The **hand** that first held mine: a novel. Maggie O'Farrell. Houghton Mifflin Harcourt, 2010. 341 p.

ISBN 9780547330792

1. Women painters 2. Motherhood 3. Family secrets 4. Man-woman relationships 5. Parenthood 6. London, England 7. Psychological fiction 8. Love stories

LC 2009042058

Costa Novel Award, 2010

Fifty years after an unconventional reporter of genteel origins becomes a single mother, present-day London painter Elina navigates the first weeks of motherhood upon surviving a dangerous labor and learns that her life is disconcertingly linked to the woman from the past.

"O'Farrell constantly fiddles with perspective. Her knowing narrator is so intimate with Lexie, Elina, Ted, and Innes that the story seems to spill directly from their conscious and unconscious voices. She flashes back and forward, revealing secrets about pasts and futures unknown to characters." —*Boston Globe*

This must be the place. Maggie O'Farrell. Alfred A. Knopf, 2016. X, 382 pages : Illustration
ISBN 9780385349420
1. College teachers 2. Americans in Ireland 3. Divorced men 4. Former actors and actresses 5. Voyages and travels 6. Ireland 7. Literary fiction 8. Multiple perspectives

LC 2015044361

Recovering from an ugly divorce and custody battle by marrying a sexual icon who would escape her life of fame, Daniel is threatened by a secret from his past in a story told through his voice and the perspectives of those who have influenced his life.

"There is enough possibility and randomness for three books, yet the story never feels overstuffed, and when it ends, the reader is stunned and grateful, relieved that in the face of all that can go (and have gone) wrong, some things have come right." —*Publishers Weekly*

The **vanishing** act of Esme Lennox. Maggie O'Farrell. Harcourt, 2007. 245 p.
ISBN 9780151014118
1. Family secrets 2. Institutionalized persons 3. Life change events 4. Senior women 5. Reunions 6. Scotland 7. 2000s (Decade) 8. 1930s 9. Historical fiction 10. Psychological suspense 11. Multiple perspectives

LC 2007006079

Iris Lockhart is stunned when she receives news that her great-aunt Esme, a previously unknown woman edited out of her family's history, is being released from Cauldstone Hospital, where she has been confined for more than sixty years, and soon discovers that Esme holds the key to long-hidden family secrets that could change her life forever.

"At the heart of this fantastic new novel is a mystery you want to solve until you start to suspect the truth, and then you read on in a panic, horrified that you may be right." —*Washington Post Book World*.

O'Hara, John

Appointment in Samarra. John O'Hara. Penguin Classics, 2013. 269 p.
ISBN 9780143107071
1. Self-destructive behavior 2. Couples 3. Small towns 4. Pennsylvania 5. 1930s 6. Modern classics 7. Literary fiction

Julian and Caroline English are at the center of the social elite until Julian makes a fateful decision to break with polite society and embarks on a rapid spiral toward self-destruction.

Originally published 1934.

O'Keefe, Megan E.

Velocity weapon. Megan E. O'Keefe. Orbit, 2019. 533 pages; (The Protectorate, 1)
ISBN 9780316419598
1. Siblings 2. Space warfare 3. Artificial intelligence 4. Space flight 5. Women soldiers 6. Space opera 7. Science fiction 8. Multiple perspectives

LC 2019000293

Sanda and Biran Greeve were siblings destined for greatness. A high-flying sergeant, Sanda has the skills to take down any enemy combatant. Biran is a savvy politician who aims to use his new political position to prevent conflict from escalating to total destruction. However, on a routine maneuver, Sanda loses consciousness when her gunship is blown out of the sky. Instead of finding herself in friendly hands, she awakens 230 years later on a deserted enemy warship controlled by an AI who calls himself Bero. The war is lost. The star system is dead. Ada Prime and its rival Icarion have wiped each other from the universe. Now, separated by time and space, Sanda and Biran must fight to put things right.

"The short chapters and alternating points of view create strong pacing, the character interaction seamlessly moves from fluid battle scenes and sinister scheming to sarcastic and deeply funny dialogue. The inevitable convergence of disparate story lines will leave readers both satisfied by the ending and eagerly awaiting the next installment." —*Booklist*

O'Leary, Beth

The **flatshare**: a novel. Beth O'Leary. Flatiron Books, 2019. 336 pages
ISBN 9781250295637
1. Roommates 2. Shared housing 3. Apartment house life 4. Man-woman relationships 5. Sexual attraction 6. London, England 7. England 8. Romantic comedies

LC 2019004158

LibraryReads Favorites, 2019

Entering a flatshare arrangement with a man on an opposite work shift, a heartbroken woman begins exchanging notes with the roommate she has never met and becomes his best friend, and possibly soulmate, through their correspondence.

The **switch**. Beth O'Leary. Flatiron Books, 2020. 320 pages
ISBN 9781250769862
1. Grandmother and granddaughter 2. Single women 3. Grief 4. Loss (Psychology) 5. Sisters — Death 6. Yorkshire, England 7. London, England 8. Relationship fiction 9. Romantic comedies
LibraryReads Favorites, 2020

Ready for an adventure in the months after her husband of 60 years departs, a woman from a picture-postcard Yorkshire village offers to swap places with her burned-out adult granddaughter to pursue romance in bustling London.

"The Switch brilliantly encompasses all the humor and whimsy of The Flatshare while delving into emotional topics like grief and the importance of watching out for neighbors. Charismatic Eileen stands out as the star of this witty, joyful show, illustrating that mature women need love, too." —*Booklist*

O'Mara, Tim

Crooked numbers. Tim O'Mara. Minotaur Books, 2013. Ix, 306 pages; (Raymond Donne novels, 2)
ISBN 9781250009005
1. Murder investigation 2. Former police 3. Teachers 4. Gangs 5. Violence in gangs 6. New York City 7. Mysteries

When one of Raymond Donne's former students is found stabbed to death under the Williamsburg Bridge, Ray draws on his past as a cop to find the truth in Tim O'Mara's second New York mystery. Raymond Donne's former student Douglas Lee had everything going for him thanks to a scholarship to an exclusive private school in Manhattan, but all of that falls apart when his body is found below the Williamsburg Bridge with a dozen knife wounds in it. That kind of violence would normally get some serious attention from the police and media except when it's accompanied by signs that it could be gang related. When that's the case, the story dies and the police are happy to settle for the straightforward explanation. Dougie's mom isn't having any of that and asks Ray, who had been a cop before an accident cut his career short, to look into it, unofficially. He does what he can, asking questions, doling out information to the press, and filling in some holes in the investigation, but he doesn't get far before one of Dougie's private school friends is killed and another is put in the hospital. What kind of trouble could a couple of sheltered kids get into that would end like that? And what does is have to do with Dougie's death?

None of it adds up, but there's no way Ray can just wait around for something to happen. Following on the heels of his acclaimed debut, Tim O'Mara's Crooked Numbers is another outstanding mystery that brings the streets of Brooklyn and Manhattan to life and further solidifies O'Mara's place among the most talented new crime fiction writers working today.

O'Nan, Stewart

Henry, himself. Stewart O'Nan. Penguin Group USA 2019. 352 p. ISBN 9780735223042

1. Senior men 2. Septuagenarians 3. Reminiscing in old age 4. Aging 5. Memory 6. Pittsburgh, Pennsylvania 7. 1990s 8. Psychological fiction

A 75-year-old retired engineer looks out on 1998 and sees a world he suspects has passed him by, and weighs his life's dreams against his regrets.

Prequel to: Wish You Were Here and Emily, Alone.

O'Neill, Heather

★ The **Lonely** Hearts Hotel: a novel. Heather O'Neill. Riverhead Books, 2017. 416 p.

ISBN 9780735213739

1. First loves 2. Soul mates 3. Child prodigies 4. Separated couples 5. Organized crime 6. Montreal, Quebec 7. Depression era (1929-1941) 8. Love stories 9. Historical fiction 10. Canadian fiction

LC 2016036295

Quebec Writers' Federation Literary Awards, Hugh MacLennan Prize for Fiction, 2017; Longlisted for The Baileys Women's Prize for Fiction, 2017

Two orphaned soul mates in Montreal—one a piano prodigy, the other a dancing savant—dream up a plan for the most extraordinary circus show the world has ever seen against a backdrop of the Great Depression.

"O'Neill's prose is crisp and strange, arresting in its frankness; much like the novel itself, her writing is both gleefully playful and devastatingly sad. Big and lush and extremely satisfying; a rare treat." —*Kirkus*

O'Rawe, Richard

Northern heist. Richard O'Rawe. Melville House, 2021. 272 pages ISBN 9781612199030

1. Bank robbers 2. Bank robberies 3. Kidnappers 4. Violent crimes 5. Deception 6. Belfast, Northern Ireland 7. Northern Ireland 8. 1990s 9. Crime fiction

A former IRA bank robber bases his fast-paced thriller on one of the biggest (and still unsolved) bank-robberies in history.

"O'Rawe channels both Elmore Leonard and Guy Ritchie in this heist thriller full of sharp twists and gritty dialogue, emerging with a style all his own. His reimagining of the real-life bank heist feels so authentic readers will hope he has a strong alibi." —*Publishers Weekly*

Oakley, Colleen

The **invisible** husband of Frick Island. Colleen Oakley. Berkley, 2021. 352 p.

ISBN 9781984806482

1. Absence and presumption of death 2. Widows 3. Pretending 4. Island life 5. Journalists 6. Chesapeake Bay Region 7. Maryland 8. Relationship fiction

LC 2020040641

LibraryReads Favorites, 2021

USA Today bestselling author Colleen Oakley delivers an unforgettable love story about an eccentric community, a grieving widow, and an outsider who slowly learns that sometimes faith is more important than the facts.

"Fans of the delightfully bizarre and quaintly humorous will love Oakley's (You Were There Too) hopeful tale about the powerful bond of community and how far people will go to protect someone they love." —*Library Journal*

You were there too. Colleen Oakley. Berkley, 2020. 352 p. ISBN 9781984806468

1. Married women 2. Strangers 3. Love triangles 4. Dreams 5. Women artists 6. Pennsylvania 7. Love stories 8. Relationship fiction

LC 2019017291

LibraryReads Favorites, 2020

When she and her husband move to a small town in Pennsylvania, Mia Graydon encounters the stranger she has been dreaming about for years —who, it turns out, has been dreaming of her, too—and together, determined to understand, they search for answers.

"Fans of relationship fiction that explores women's inner lives and choices by Jennifer Weiner or Amy Hatvany will be unable to put this book down." —*Booklist*

Oates, Joyce Carol

The **(other)** you: stories. Joyce Carol Oates. Ecco Press, 2021. 304 p. ISBN 9780063035201

1. Options, alternatives, choices 2. Fate and fatalism 3. Life change events 4. Remorse 5. Literary fiction 6. Short stories

In this stirring, reflective collection of short stories, Joyce Carol Oates ponders alternate destinies: the other lives we might have led if we'd made different choices. An accomplished writer returns to her childhood home of Yewville, but the homecoming stirs troubled thoughts about the person she might have been if she'd never left. A man in prison contemplates the gravity of his irreversible act. A student's affair with a professor results in a pregnancy that alters the course of her life forever. Even the experience of reading is investigated as one that can create a profound transformation.

"Oates's mastery of the form remains fierce and formidable in this unsettling collection of lamentations and missed opportunities." —*Publishers Weekly*

Because it is bitter, and because it is my heart. Joyce Carol Oates. Dutton, 1990. 405 p.

ISBN 9780525248606

1. Interracial romance 2. Murder 3. Racism 4. Families 5. African Americans 6. New York (State) 7. 1950s 8. Psychological fiction 9. Literary fiction

LC 89025965

National Book Award for Fiction finalist, 1990

Iris Courtney, a young white woman living in upstate New York in the decade prior to the Civil rights movement, begins a clandestine relationship with Jinx Fairchild, a black man who had defended her in a fatal street fight with a white man

"At its best, the novel awakens the reader to something like the unexpected new comprehensions of the universe that Iris experiences." —*The New York Review of Books*

Blonde: a novel. Joyce Carol Oates. Ecco Press, 2000. 738 p. ISBN 9780060196073

1. Monroe, Marilyn 2. Film actors and actresses 3. Adult child abuse victims 4. Man-woman relationships 5. Sexuality 6. Mothers and daughters 7. Hollywood, California 8. Biographical fiction 9. Literary fiction

New York Times Notable Book, 2000; National Book Award for Fiction finalist, 2000; Pulitzer Prize for Fiction finalist, 2001

A fictional recreation of the life of Marilyn Monroe recounts the tale of her rise to stardom, as seen from Marilyn's perspective.

"Joyce Carol Oates takes the boldest path to comprehending 'the riddle, the curse of Monroe' by proceeding directly and frankly to fiction. Her novel 'Blonde' is fat, messy and fierce. It's part Gothic, part kaleidoscopic novel of ideas, part lurid celebrity potboiler, and it is seldom less than engrossing." —*New York Times Book Review*

Breathe. Joyce Carol Oates. Ecco Press, 2021. 364 pages
ISBN 9780063085473
1. Married people 2. Widows 3. Loss (Psychology) 4. Identity (Psychology) 5. Grief in women 6. New Mexico 7. Psychological fiction 8. Literary fiction

After her husband comes down with a mysterious illness, Michaela contemplates widowhood at age 37 and refuses to surrender her love.

"Fecund with fear and anguish, and driven by raw, breathless narration, this hallucinatory tale will not disappoint. Oates is on a roll." —*Publishers Weekly*

The **falls:** a novel. Joyce Carol Oates. Ecco, 2004. Xiv, 481 p.
ISBN 9780060722289
1. Widows 2. Survivors of suicide victims 3. Community life 4. Lawyers 5. Husband and wife 6. New York (State) 7. Niagara Falls 8. 20th century 9. Psychological fiction 10. Domestic fiction 11. Literary fiction

LC 2004043310
New York Times Notable Book, 2004

Follows the interconnected and secretive lives of parents and their children when they are challenged by circumstances outside their family, in a tale set against a backdrop of Niagara Falls in the mid-twentieth century.

"The broad canvas, frank carnality and family melodrama of 'The Falls' may not signal literary sublimity, but they do propel Ms. Oates into the mainstream. This novel could easily be mistaken for the work of a more visceral, less august storyteller. And if she strains to incorporate chemical waste into an otherwise intimate and high-strung narrative, the mixture is as effective as it is forced." —*New York Times*

A **garden** of earthly delights. Joyce Carol Oates. Modern Libary, 2003. Ix, 404 p.
ISBN 9780812968347
1. Children of migrant workers 2. Fathers and daughters 3. Poor women 4. Independence in women 5. Women's role 6. 1930s 7. Psychological fiction 8. Domestic fiction 9. Literary fiction

LC 2002038012
The daughter of a migrant worker finds her life in the deprived and ugly transient world shaped by her father, lover, husband, and son.

"The book has much to say of society's indifference to the plight of the disadvantaged, and of the shallowness of a way of life based entirely on getting and spending." —*Library Journal*

This complete revision of Oates' book by the same title (originally published in 1967) includes a new afterword.

The **gravedigger's** daughter: a novel. Joyce Carol Oates. Ecco, 2007. 592 p.
ISBN 9780061236822
1. Gravediggers 2. Children of immigrants 3. Mothers and sons 4. Jewish American families 5. Husband and wife 6. New York (State) 7. 1960s 8. First person narratives 9. Psychological fiction 10. Literary fiction 11. Adult books for young adults

LC 2006048546
National Book Critics Circle Award for Fiction finalist, 2007

The daughter of a German high school teacher who was forced to work as a gravedigger after immigrating to upstate New York, Rebecca begins a life-changing pilgrimage throughout America in the wake of a prejudice-motivated tragedy.

"This is neither a depressing story nor an uplifting one. Oates succeeds here, as she often does, in making such judgments feel simpleminded. What it all seems is true and therefore moving and somewhat terrible, but in an exhilarating way. Every aspect of the ungainly plot feels right, including its ungainliness." —*Washington Post Book World*.

★ **My** life as a rat. Joyce Carol Oates. HarperCollins, 2019. 304 p.
ISBN 9780062899835
1. Dysfunctional families 2. Murder witnesses 3. Racism 4. Family secrets 5. Regret 6. Psychological fiction 7. Literary fiction 8. Multiple perspectives 9. Adult books for young adults

Exiled from her family and church since the age of 12 for testifying honestly about a racist murder, a young woman reflects on the wrenching choice she was forced to make between her family and the truth.

Night. sleep. death. the stars. Joyce Carol Oates. Ecco Press, 2020. 752 pages
ISBN 9780062797582
1. Patriarchs 2. Grief in families 3. Dysfunctional families 4. People who have had strokes 5. Psychic trauma 6. New York (State) 7. Literary fiction 8. Domestic fiction

An intimate exploration of race, class warfare and healing follows the unexpected reactions of a wife and her adult children to a powerful patriarch's death.

"While Oates purposefully plumbs the depths of each family member's agonizing loss, her perceptive study of Jessalyn's widowhood stands out as an impressive and impassioned portrait of this distressing life journey." —*Booklist*

Pursuit. Joyce Carol Oates. Mysterious Press, 2019. 144 p.
ISBN 9780802147912
1. Newlyweds 2. Nightmares 3. Husband and wife 4. Accidents 5. Secrets 6. Psychological suspense

As a child, Abby had the same recurring nightmare night after night, in which she wandered through a field ridden with human skulls and bones. Now an adult, Abby thinks she's outgrown her demons, until, the evening before her wedding, the terrible dream returns and forces her to confront the dark secrets from her past she has kept from her new husband, Willem. The following day—less than 24 hours after exchanging vows—Abby steps out into traffic. As his wife lies in her hospital bed, sleeping in fits and starts, Willem tries to determine whether this was an absentminded accident or a premeditated plunge, and he quickly discovers a mysterious set of clues about what his wife might be hiding.

★ **Them**. Joyce Carol Oates. Modern Library, 2006. Xxxiv, 546 p.
ISBN 9780345484406
1. Dysfunctional families 2. Young women 3. Race relations 4. Working class families 5. Poor women 6. Detroit, Michigan 7. Michigan 8. 1960s 9. Psychological fiction 10. Caesar, Julius
National Book Award for Fiction, 1970

From the 1930s through the race riots of 1967, the members of the Wendall family, living in inner-city Detroit, struggle to understand the obscure forces constantly tearing at their lives and happiness. Winner of the National Book Award.

Originally published: New York : Vanguard Press, 1969.

★ **We** were the Mulvaneys. Joyce Carol Oates. Dutton 1996. Viii, 454 p.
ISBN 9780525942238

1. Rural life 2. Date rape 3. Family problems 4. Family relationships 5. New York (State) 6. 20th century 7. Psychological fiction 8. Literary fiction 9. Books to movies

LC 9617267

Judd Mulvaney, now age 30, and the youngest of the four Mulvaney children, looks back through his memories to tell the secrets that eventually ripped apart the fabric of his storybook family.

"Oates has written an uncharacteristically cathartic book with a provocatively happy ending.... Oates eloquently employs daily details, cataloguing Corinne's antiques, mapping Patrick's Ithaca jogging route, calculating the number of paint gallons required to spruce up High Point Farm. She is a vivid storyteller, and the occupations, names and places are rich in allusive imagery.... Oates is fascinated by the markings of kinship. Particularly impressive is her shaping of siblings' passions, allegiances and resentments." —*The Nation*

Obioma, Chigozie

★ The **fishermen**: a novel. Chigozie Obioma. Little, Brown & Co, 2015. 297 pages : Illustration

ISBN 9780316338370

1. Brothers 2. Life change events 3. Tragedy 4. Prophecies 5. Family relationships 6. Nigeria 7. 1990s 8. Literary fiction 9. Political fiction 10. First person narratives

Library Journal Best Books, 2015; Los Angeles Times Art Seidenbaum Award for First Fiction, 2015; New York Times Notable Book, 2015; Shortlisted for the Man Booker Prize, 2015

In a Nigerian town in the mid 1990s, four brothers encounter a madman whose mystic prophecy of violence threatens the core of their close-knit family.

"Obioma excels at juxtaposing sharp observation, rich images of the natural world, and motifs from biblical and tribal lore; his novel succeeds as a convincing modern narrative and as a majestic reimagining of timeless folklore." —*Publishers Weekly*

★ An **orchestra** of minorities. Chigozie Obioma. Little Brown & Co, 2019. 400 p.

ISBN 9780316412391

1. Farmers 2. Determination in men 3. Fate and fatalism 4. Free will and determinism 5. Interclass romance 6. Nigeria 7. Cyprus 8. Literary fiction 9. Adaptations, retellings, and spin-offs

Shortlisted for the Booker Prize, 2019

In a contemporary twist of Homer's The Odyssey, a guardian spirit recounts the tragic story of a Nigerian poultry farmer who sacrifices everything for the wealthy woman he loves.

"Influences like Homer's Odyssey, Shakespeare's Othello, and The Divine Comedy inform Obioma's examination of the Igbo tribe's cosmology of destiny vs. the Christian tenet of free will." —*Library Journal*

Obregon, Nicolas

Blue light Yokohama. Nicolas Obregon. Minotaur Books, 2017. 352 p. (Inspector Iwata novels, 1)

ISBN 9781250110480

1. Family-killing 2. Signs and symbols 3. Workaholics 4. Detectives 5. Nightmares 6. Tokyo, Japan 7. Japan 8. Police procedurals

Newly reinstated Tokyo Homicide Division Police Inspector Iwata works with reluctant colleagues to investigate the brutal murder of an entire family and other deaths that are identified as the work of the same killer.

"Obregon's full-bodied prose is by turns gritty and poetic, and it's consistently energetic. Given the terrific chemistry between the two lead detectives, here's hoping this debut novel kicks off a new series." —*Kirkus*

Obreht, Tea

Inland: a novel. Tea Obreht. Random House, 2019. 384 pages

ISBN 9780812992861

1. Pioneer women 2. Outlaws 3. Droughts 4. Loss (Psychology) 5. Sons 6. Arizona (Territory) 7. Southwest (United States) 8. American Westward Expansion (1803-1899) 9. Literary fiction 10. Historical fiction 11. Multiple perspectives

LC 2018050729

Library Journal Best Books, 2019; LibraryReads Favorites, 2019

An unexpected relationship between a frontierswoman riding out the Arizona Territory drought of 1893 and a former outlaw, who has the ability to see ghosts, inspires an epic journey across the West.

The **tiger's** wife: a novel. Tea Obreht. Dial Press, 2011. 352 p.

ISBN 9780385343831

1. Women physicians 2. Orphanages 3. Grandparent and child 4. Family secrets 5. Balkan Peninsula 6. Literary fiction 7. Parallel narratives 8. Adult books for young adults

ALA Notable Book, 2012; Indies' Choice Book Awards, Adult Debut, 2012; Library Journal Best Books, 2011; New York Times Notable Book, 2011; Orange Prize for Fiction, 2011; School Library Journal Best Books: Best Adult Books 4 Teens, 2011; National Book Award for Fiction finalist, 2011

Struggling to understand why her beloved grandfather left his family to die alone in a field hospital far from home, a young doctor in a war-torn Balkan country takes over her grandfather's search for a mythical ageless vagabond while referring to a worn copy of Rudyard Kipling's "The Jungle Book.

"Every word, every scene, every thought is blazingly alive in this many-faceted, spellbinding, and rending novel of death, succor, and remembrance." —*Booklist*

Oe, Kenzaburo

The **changeling**. Kenzaburo Oe; translated from the Japanese by Deborah Boliver Boehm. Grove, 2010. 336 p.

ISBN 9780802119360

1. Brothers-in-law 2. Suicide 3. Loss (Psychology) 4. Male friendship 5. Grief in men 6. Literary fiction 7. Translations

After he rekindles a decades-lost friendship with his brother-in-law, Goro Hanawa, and receives a series of tapes on which Goro has recorded his reflections on their friendship, writer Kogito Choko hears his friend commit suicide on one of the recordings, prompting him to travel to Berlin to confront ghosts from his own past, and that of his friend.

★ **Death** by water. Kenzaburo Oe; translated from the Japanese by Deborah Boliver Boehm. Grove Press, 2015. 424 pages

ISBN 9780802124012

1. Senior men 2. Authors 3. Loss (Psychology) 4. Writer's block 5. Fathers — Death 6. Japan 7. Literary fiction 8. Translations

The recurring and literary alter ego of the Nobel Prize-winning author, Kogito Choko, searches for a red suitcase that may hold documents related to the details of his father's death during World War II.

"This novel, teeming with crises and disclosures, proceeds almost exclusively via conversation made up of intricate, literarily and dramaturgically knowledgeable, politically progressive, long speeches. And it is enchanting." —*Booklist*

Translation from the Japanese of: Suishi.

Originally published: Tokyo : Kodansha, 2009.

Nip the buds, shoot the kids. Kenzaburo Oe; translated and introduced by Paul St. John Mackintosh and Maki Sugiyama. Marion Boyars, 1995. 189 p.

ISBN 9780714529974

1. Juvenile delinquents 2. Mountain life 3. Plague 4. Teenage boys 5. Japan 6. Translations 7. First person narratives

LC 94040897

A group of deliquent boys are abandoned in a remote village during the Korean war and manage to survive by stealing food and hunting, only to face the possibility of death when the villagers return

Translation of Memushiri kouchi.

★ A **quiet** life. Kenzaburo Oe; translated from the Japanese by Kunioki Yanagishita and William Wetherall. Grove Press, 1996. 240 p.

ISBN 9780802115973

1. Families 2. Young women 3. Savant syndrome 4. Men with developmental disabilities 5. Young men 6. Japan 7. Literary fiction 8. Translations

LC 9625795

At the age of twenty, Ma-chen, a young woman, is forced to redefine her family and her life when she finds herself the head of the household due to her father's acceptance of a visiting professorship at an American university

"A famous Japanese writer whose first name begins with K takes off with his wife for a year to become writer in residence at 'one of the several campuses of the University of Carolina,' leaving their almost equally famous son, an idiot savant who is a remarkable composer, in the care of their daughter, Ma-chan. It is Ma-chan, a conscientious young woman acutely aware of the responsibility that devolves on her during her parents' absence, who tells the story related in Kenzaburo Oe's novel A Quiet Life, and the translators, Kunioki Yanagishita and William Wetherall, admirably succeed in conveying a certian archness of style that infuses the work with Ma-chan's personality." —*New York Times Book Review*

Originally published in Japan Shizuka-na seikatsu by Kodansha.

Somersault: a novel. Kenzaburo Oe; translated from the Japanese by Philip Gabriel. Grove Press, 2003. 570 p.

ISBN 9780802117380

1. New religious movements 2. Religion 3. Spirituality 4. Faith 5. Charisma 6. Literary fiction 7. Translations

LC 2002029746

Ten years after recanting their teachings and abandoning their zealous and violent congregation, two men known only as the Patron and Guide of Humankind seek to overcome a radical faction while leading peaceful followers toward a new future.

"Through the believers' motivations for joining the cult, Oe explores the struggle of contemporary Japanese to situate themselves between a traditional culture and the bullet-train pace of the boom years." —*The New Yorker*

Offill, Jenny

Dept. of speculation. Jenny Offill. Knopf, 2014. 176 p.

ISBN 9780385350815

1. Marriage 2. Families 3. Marital conflict 4. Interpersonal relations 5. College teachers 6. Literary fiction

LC 2013019367

New York Times Notable Book, 2014; Shortlisted for the International Dublin Literary Award, 2016

The unnamed narrator of this novel writes in short vignettes, starting with odd facts, memories of boys she loved, and recollections from her travels. But as a whole the book itself is a moving portrait of a marriage and a relationship, from early days filled with possibilities to recent difficulties and fears. Wide-ranging and speculative, this novel focuses on the role of a wife and mother.

"The 46 short chapters are told mostly in brief fragments and fly through the life of the nameless heroine. Her mind wanders from everyday tasks and struggles, the beginnings of her marriage, the highs and lows with her husband, the joys of having a daughter." —*Publishers Weekly*

★ **Weather**. Jenny Offill. Alfred A. Knopf, 2020. 224 p.

ISBN 9780385351102

1. Social obligations 2. Anxiety in women 3. Families 4. Librarians 5. Marital conflict 6. New York City 7. Literary fiction

LC 2019032408

Shortlisted for The Women's Prize for Fiction, 2020

Hired by her famous podcaster mentor to answer letters from increasingly polarized fans, a librarian who has acquired her education from a lifetime spent reading struggles between the limits of her knowledge and growing crises in the outside world.

"The tension between mundane daily concerns and looming apocalypse, the weather of our days both real and metaphorical, is perfectly captured in Offill's brief, elegant paragraphs, filled with insight and humor." —*Kirkus*

Offutt, Chris

Country dark. Chris Offutt. Grove Press, 2018. 231 p.

ISBN 9780802127792

1. Life change events 2. Bootleggers 3. Veterans 4. Parents of children with disabilities 5. Social workers 6. Kentucky 7. 20th century 8. Southern Gothic 9. Historical fiction 10. Literary fiction

LC 2017051048

In rural Kentucky in the years after the Korean War, Tucker, a young veteran and bootlegger, is pushed into a life-altering act of violence by threats against his family.

★ The **killing** hills. Chris Offutt. Grove Press, 2021. 224 p.

ISBN 9780802158413

1. Women sheriffs 2. Siblings 3. Veterans 4. Betrayal 5. Murder investigation 6. Kentucky 7. Thrillers and suspense

Agreeing to secretly help his sister, the new sheriff, investigate her first murder case, Mick Hardin, a combat veteran now working as an Army CID agent, tries to stay under the radar as he attempts to head off further murders while preparing for the birth of his first child.

"In place of plot convolutions, Offutt offers those of Appalachian folkways. The result is a fast-paced, satisfying read. Rural crime fiction that kicks like a mule." —*Kirkus*

Ogawa, Yoko

The **housekeeper** and the professor. Yoko Ogawa; translated from the Japanese by Stephen Snyder. Picador, 2009. 192 p.

ISBN 9780312427801

1. Men with brain injuries 2. Short-term memory 3. Household employees 4. College teachers 5. Mothers and sons 6. Psychological fiction 7. Translations

LC 2006041568

A strange relationship blossoms between a brilliant math professor suffering from short-term memory problems following a traumatic head injury and the young housekeeper, the mother of a ten-year-old son, hired to care for him, in an enchanting novel that explores what it means to live in the present and to be part of a family, albeit an unusual one.

"This is the intimate story of a young housekeeper and her ten-year-old son who come to care for an aging math professor with a peculiar problem: he lives with only eighty minutes of short-term memory. Asian Pages,A mysterious, suspenseful, and radiant fable.... The smart and resourceful housekeeper, the single mother of a baseball-crazy 10-year-old boy the Professor adores, falls under the spell of the beautiful mathematical phenomena the Professor elucidates, as will the reader, and the three create an indivisible formula for love." —*Booklist*

★ The **memory** police: a novel. Yoko Ogawa; translated from the Japanese by Stephen Snyder. Pantheon Books, 2019. 288 pages
ISBN 9781101870600
1. Memory 2. Authors 3. Lost articles 4. Missing persons 5. Loss (Psychology) 6. Dystopian fiction 7. Translations
LC 2018057224
Library Journal Best Books, 2019; New York Times Notable Book, 2019; National Book Award for Translated Literature finalist, 2019
An Orwellian novel about the terrors of state surveillance finds a young novelist hiding her editor from mysterious authorities who would erase all memories of people who once existed.
Translation of: Hisoyaka na kessho.
Originally published: Toyko : Kodansha, 1994.
Translated from the Japanese.

Ogden, Aimee

Sun-daughters, Sea-daughters. Aimee Ogden. Tor, 2021. 128 p.
ISBN 9781250782120
1. Landforms 2. Oceans 3. Love 4. Quests 5. Space flight 6. Science fiction 7. Adaptations, retellings, and spin-offs
Gene-edited human clans have scattered throughout the galaxy, adapting themselves to environments as severe as the desert and the sea. Atuale, the daughter of a Sea-Clan lord, sparked a war by choosing her land-dwelling love and rejecting her place among her people. Now her husband and his clan are dying of a virulent plague, and Atuale's sole hope for finding a cure is to travel off-planet. The one person she can turn to for help is the black-market mercenary known as the World Witch—and Atuale's former lover. Time, politics, bureaucracy, and her own conflicted desires stand between Atuale and the hope for her adopted clan.
"Sun-Daughters, Sea-Daughters is a short page-turner that feels epic in its world-building craft and the depth of its protagonists. At once a fairy-tale retelling and a lyrical space opera, it straddles many genres to tell one nostalgic yet utterly new story." —*Booklist*

Ohlsson, Kristina

Unwanted: a novel. Kristina Ohlsson; translated from the Swedish by Sarah Death. Emily Bestler Books/Atria, 2012. 357 p; (Fredrika Bergman mysteries, 1)
ISBN 9781439198896
1. Missing children 2. Murder investigation 3. Kidnapping 4. First impressions 5. Serial murderers 6. Sweden 7. Translations 8. Mysteries 9. Multiple perspectives
LC 2011031787
Inspector Fredericka Bergman investigates the kidnapping and murder of a child who had been separated from her mother on a crowded train on a rainy Swedish summer day, a case that points to the work of a brilliant and ruthless killer.
Originally published as Askungar: Stockholm : Pocketforlaget, 2009.
Translated from the Swedish.

Okorafor, Nnedi

★ **Binti**. Nnedi Okorafor. Tom Doherty Associates, 2015. 106 p. (Binti, 1)
ISBN 9780765385253

1. Young women 2. Space warfare 3. Conflict resolution 4. Aliens 5. Space flight 6. Space opera 7. Science fiction 8. African American fiction
Her name is Binti, and she is the first of the Himba people ever to be offered a place at Oomza University, the finest institution of higher learning in the galaxy. But to accept the offer will mean giving up her place in her family to travel between the stars among strangers who do not share her ways or respect her customs. The world she seeks to enter has long warred with the Meduse, an alien race that has become the stuff of nightmares.
Trilogy published together in one volume, 2019.

Binti: home. Nnedi Okorafor. Tom Doherty Asociates, 2015. 106 p. (Binti, 2)
ISBN 9780765393111
1. Young women 2. Diplomacy 3. Aliens 4. Xenophobia 5. Space warfare 6. Space opera 7. Science fiction 8. African American fiction
It's been a year since Binti and Okwu enrolled at Oomza University. A year since Binti was declared a hero for uniting two warring planets. A year since she found friendship in the unlikeliest of places. And now she must return home to her people, with her friend Okwu by her side, to face her family and face her elders. But Okwu will be the first of his race to set foot on Earth in over a hundred years, and the first ever to come in peace. After generations of conflict can human and Meduse ever learn to truly live in harmony?
Trilogy published together in one volume, 2019.

Binti: the night masquerade. Nnedi Okorafor. Tor Books, 2018. 208 p. (Binti, 3)
ISBN 9780765393135
1. Young women 2. Diplomacy 3. Aliens 4. Xenophobia 5. Homecomings 6. Space opera 7. Science fiction 8. African American fiction
Library Journal Best Books, 2018
Binti has returned to her home planet, believing that the violence of the Meduse has been left behind. Unfortunately, although her people are peaceful on the whole, the same cannot be said for the Khoush, who fan the flames of their ancient rivalry with the Meduse. Far from her village when the conflicts start, Binti hurries home, but anger and resentment has already claimed the lives of many close to her. Once again it is up to Binti, and her intriguing new friend Mwinyi, to intervene—though the elders of her people do not entirely trust her motives—and try to prevent a war that could wipe out her people, once and for all.
Series complete in 3 volumes.
Trilogy published together in one volume, 2019.

★ **Noor**. Nnedi Okorafor. Daw Books, 2021. 224 p.
ISBN 9780756416096
1. Biotechnology 2. Near future 3. Cyborgs 4. Determination in women 5. Intrigue 6. Nigeria 7. Science fiction 8. Afrofuturism
LibraryReads Favorites, 2021; Loan Stars Favourites, 2021
When everything goes wrong on a trip to the local market, AO, a woman with a ton of major and necessary body augmentations, must race against time across the deserts of Northern Nigeria with a Fulani herdsman named DNA in a world where everything is streamed.
"The newest novel from acclaimed African futurist Okorafor is a rich story of climate, capitalism, and biotech." —*Booklist*

★ **Remote** control. Nnedi Okorafor. Tor, 2021. 160 p.
ISBN 9781250772800
1. Death 2. Memory 3. Human/animal communication 4. Touch 5. Magic 6. Ghana 7. Science fiction 8. African American fiction 9. Afrofuturism
LC 2020038238
LibraryReads Favorites, 2021

The day Fatima forgot her name, Death paid a visit. From here on in she would be known as Sankofa—a name that meant nothing to anyone but her, the only tie to her family and her past. Her touch is death, and with a glance a town can fall. And she walks-alone, except for her fox companion-searching for the object that came from the sky and gave itself to her when the meteors fell and when she was yet unchanged; searching for answers. But is there a greater purpose for Sankofa, now that Death is her constant companion?

"Okorafor (Binti) builds a stunning landscape of futuristic technology and African culture, with prose that will grab readers from the first sentence. Sankofa is at once innocent and experienced, facing a world forever changed for and by her." —*Library Journal*

★ **Who** fears death. Nnedi Okorafor. Daw Books, 2010. 304 p.
ISBN 9780756406172
1. Genocide 2. Far future 3. Women shamans 4. Survival (after nuclear warfare) 5. Interethnic conflict 6. Africa 7. Science fantasy 8. Coming-of-age stories 9. Apocalyptic fiction
Amelia Bloomer List, 2011; Romantic Times Reviewers' Choice Award, 2010; World Fantasy Award, 2011
Born into post-apocalyptic Africa by a mother who was raped after the slaughter of her entire tribe, Onyesonwu is tutored by a shaman and discovers that her magical destiny is to end the genocide of her people.
Title adapted into a TV series in 2018.
Prequel: The Book of Phoenix.

Okparanta, Chinelo
★ **Under** the udala trees. Chinelo Okparanta. Houghton Mifflin Harcourt, 2015. 328 pages
ISBN 9780544003446
1. Civil war 2. Lesbians 3. Interethnic romance 4. Prejudice 5. Household employees 6. Nigeria 7. Political fiction 8. Coming-of-age stories 9. LGBTQIA fiction 10. Adult books for young adults
LC 2014044506
Amelia Bloomer List, 2017; Lambda Literary Award for Lesbian Fiction, 2016; Shortlisted for the International Dublin Literary Award, 2017
A young Nigerian girl, displaced during their civil war, begins a powerful love affair with another refugee girl from a different ethnic community until the pair are discovered and must learn the cost of living a lie amidst taboos and prejudices.
"The fact that Nigeria criminalized same-sex marriages in 2014 makes Okparanta's tale that much more sobering and urgent. It is especially gratifying that one of the defining tag lines of the feminist movement, 'a woman without a man,' just might be co-opted here in another time and place." —*Booklist*

Okri, Ben
Prayer for the living. Ben Okri. Akashic Books, 2021. 216 p.
ISBN 9781617758638
1. Supernatural 2. Characters and characteristics in mythology 3. Characters and characteristics in fairy tales 4. Reality 5. Short stories 6. Literary fiction
Playful, frightening, shocking—these stories from a writer at the height of his power will make you think, or make you laugh. Sometimes they'll make you want to look away, but they will always hold your gaze. Topical and timely, Booker Prize-winning author Ben Okri's new collection of short stories blurs parallel realities and walks the line between darkness and magic.

"Okri often plays with form, as in two stories written in a flash-fiction style he calls 'stoku,' a portmanteau of story and haiku. But throughout, Okri skillfully embeds abstract ideas in concrete, engaging storytelling. A diverse yet consistent collection, mind-bending and provocative in a host of styles and milieus." —*Kirkus*
Originally published: 2019.

Okuizumi, Hikaru
The **stones** cry out. Hikaru Okuizumi; translated from the Japanese by James Westerhoven. Harcourt Brace, 1998. 138 p.
ISBN 9780151003655
1. World War II veterans 2. Geologists 3. Guilt in men 4. Memory 5. Japan 6. Psychological fiction 7. Translations
LC 98-14434
Japanese World War II veteran Tsuyoshi Manase, troubled by memories of the war's end, returns to civilian life, marries, and has children, but when his eldest son is gouged to death in a cave, suspicion falls on Manase, and his life begins to unravel
"A monstrous tale, The Stones Cry Out is written with a lyrical beauty that only underscores the horror Manase's life becomes. As Okuizumi elegantly plays Manase's nightmare out, Manase is compelled to reenact the real atrocities he has tried so desperately to forget." —*Booklist*

Ólafsdóttir, Auður A.
Butterflies in November. Auour Ava Olafsdottir; translated from the Icelandic by Brian FitzGibbon. Black Cat, 2014. 304 p.
ISBN 9780802123183
1. Thirties (Age) 2. Automobile travel 3. Life change events 4. Self-fulfillment in women 5. Children who are deaf and mute 6. Iceland 7. Mainstream fiction 8. First person narratives 9. Translations
After being dumped and then winning the lottery, a woman in her thirties, along with her best friend's four-year-old deaf-mute son, takes a transformative road trip through Iceland, encountering eccentrics and finding herself.
Originally published: Reykjavik : Salka, 2004.
Translated from the Icelandic.

Ólafsson, Ólafur Jóhann
The **sacrament**: a novel. Olaf Olafsson. Ecco Press, 2019. 292 p.
ISBN 9780062899873
1. Nuns 2. Memory 3. Catholic schools 4. Clergymen child sexual abusers 5. Child sexual abuse 6. Iceland 7. France 8. Psychological fiction 9. Literary fiction 10. Translations
LC Bl2019028916
Tells the haunting, vivid story of a nun whose past returns to her in unexpected ways, all while investigating a mysterious death and a series of harrowing abuse claims.
"Emotionally gratifying and spiritually challenging—a compelling novel that grabs the reader's psyche and won't let go." —*Kirkus*
Translated from the Icelandic.

Oliveras, Priscilla
Anchored hearts. Priscilla Oliveras. Zebra Books, 2021. 352 p. (Keys to love, 2)
ISBN 9781420150193
1. Hispanic American families 2. Former lovers 3. Photographers 4. Women fire fighters 5. Women paramedics 6. Key West, Florida 7. Florida 8. Contemporary romances 9. Multicultural romances

Sparks fly for a second time when award-winning photographer and prodigal son Alejandro ends up back home, forced to face the familia—and the girl he left behind—for the first time in years. Can these two Key West natives learn to put away old hurts and embrace a new future under the tropical sun?

"Oliveras has perfected the second-chance romance trope with Alejandro and Anamaria. Their anguish is so real that the book should come with tissues. The Key West setting is vibrant, adding a blessed touch of armchair travel to the current global circumstances. Wonderfully soapy, this is a romance to read in one sitting." —*Kirkus*

Olmstead, Robert
★ **Coal** black horse. Robert Olmstead. Algonquin Books of Chapel Hill, 2007. 224 p.
ISBN 9781565125216
1. Civil war 2. Teenage boys and horses 3. Quests 4. Teenagers and war 5. Rescues 6. United States 7. American Civil War era (1861-1865) 8. Historical fiction 9. Adult books for young adults
LC 2006042914
YALSA Best Books for Young Adults, 2008
When Robey Childs's mother experiences a premonition about her husband, a Civil War soldier, she sends her only son to retrieve his father from the battlefield, accompanied by a horse that becomes his only companion as he makes his way through the destruction of war.

This novel is mostly memorable as an exquisite corpse, a fictive vision of war so vivid and gruesome that it remains in the memory—grotesque, stiff and gape-mouthed—after every other detail of Olmstead's tale fades away. —*Paste*

Olson, Neil
Before the devil fell. Neil Olson. Hanover Square Press, 2019. 320 p.
ISBN 9781335217554
1. College teachers 2. Children of aging parents 3. Witchcraft 4. Spirits 5. Secrets 6. New England 7. Boston, Massachusetts 8. Supernatural mysteries
Returning to his Boston village hometown to care for an aging parent, Will is embroiled in the case of a mysterious death and the New England witchcraft traditions upheld by his mother's spirit circle.

Ondaatje, Michael
★ **Warlight**. Michael Ondaatje. Alfred A Knopf, 2018. 288 p.
ISBN 9780525521198
1. Postwar life 2. Siblings 3. Guardian and ward 4. Eccentrics and eccentricities 5. Mentors 6. London, England 7. 20th century 8. Coming-of-age stories 9. Literary fiction 10. Canadian fiction 11. Adult books for young adults
ALA Notable Book, 2019; Booklist Editors' Choice, 2018; Loan Stars Favourites, 2018; New York Times Notable Book, 2018; Longlisted for the Man Booker Prize, 2018; Shortlisted for the Walter Scott Prize for Historical Fiction, 2019
Years after growing up in the care of a group of mysterious protectors who served in unspecified ways during World War II, a young man endeavors to piece together the truth about his parents and the unconventional education he received.

"The multi-award-winning author of The English Patient turns in a new novel both mysterious and dramatic, featuring 14-year-old Nathaniel and older sister Rachel, whose parents leave them in the care of a shadowy and possibly criminal individual called the Moth when they move to Singapore in 1945. The Moth's friends, connected by wartime service, have

lots to teach the siblings, who face more confusion when the siblings' mother returns, mum about their father." —*Library Journal*

Ono, Masatsugu
Echo on the bay. Masatsugu Ono; translated by Angus Turvill. Two Lines Press, 2020. 160 pages
ISBN 9781949641035
1. Fishing villages 2. Small town life 3. Police 4. Coastal towns 5. Elections 6. Japan 7. Literary fiction 8. Translations
LC 2019044396
Tells the story of a small fishing village in Japan-with the untreated wounds of the town's history in the foreground.

"The stories quickly turn dark, echoing far beyond in time and location, reverberating with evidence of horrific inhumanity. Understated, yet unforgettably stunning." —*Booklist*
Translation of: Nigiyakana wan ni seowareta fune.
Original Japanese edition published by Asahi Shimbun Publications Inc, 2015.
Translated from the Japanese.

Onuzo, Chibundu
Sankofa: a novel. Chibundu Onuzo. Catapult Publishing, . 296 p.
ISBN 9781646220830
1. Belonging 2. Birthfathers 3. Multiracial women 4. Black British women 5. Self-discovery 6. West Africa 7. 1960s 8. Literary fiction
When Anna, wondering who she really is, discovers that the African father she never knew is still alive, she embarks on a journey to a small nation in West Africa where she searches for her family's hidden roots.

"Though the quest for identity has become a conventional staple of contemporary fiction, it feels fresh and new in Onuzo's capable hands." —*Library Journal*

Onyebuchi, Tochi
★ **Riot** baby. Tochi Onyebuchi. Tor, 2020. 176 pages
ISBN 9781250214751
1. Violence against African Americans 2. Psychic ability 3. Siblings 4. African American families 5. Racism 6. United States 7. 20th century 8. 21st century 9. Political fiction 10. Dystopian fiction 11. Literary fiction 12. Adult books for young adults
LC 2019041049
Alex Award, 2021; Ignyte Awards: Best Novella, 2021
Ella and Kev are brother and sister, both gifted with extraordinary power. Their childhoods are defined and destroyed by structural racism and brutality. Their futures might alter the world. When Kev is incarcerated for the crime of being a young black man in America, Ella-through visits both mundane and supernatural-tries to show him the way to a revolution that could burn it all down.

Orange, Tommy
★ **There** there. Tommy Orange. Alfred A. Knopf, 2018. 294 pages
ISBN 9780525520375
1. Native American families 2. Culture conflict 3. Multiracial persons 4. Indians of North America 5. Powwows 6. Oakland, California 7. California 8. Literary fiction 9. Multiple perspectives 10. Adult books for young adults
LC 2017038125
ALA Notable Book, 2019; Booklist Editors' Choice, 2018; Hemingway Foundation/PEN Award, 2019; Indies' Choice Book Awards, Adult Debut, 2019; Library Journal Best Books, 2018;

LibraryReads Favorites, 2018; Loan Stars Favourites, 2018; New York Times Notable Book, 2018; Society of American Historians Prize for Historical Fiction (formerly the James Fenimore Cooper Prize), 2019; Andrew Carnegie Medal for Excellence in Fiction finalist, 2019; Pulitzer Prize for Fiction finalist, 2019; Shortlisted for the International Dublin Literary Award, 2020

A novel which grapples with the complex history of Native Americans; with an inheritance of profound spirituality; and with a plague of addiction, abuse and suicide, follows 12 characters, each of whom has private reasons for traveling to the Big Oakland Powwow.

Orczy, Emmuska Orczy

The **old** man in the corner. Baroness Orczy. Pushkin Vertigo, 2018. 284 p. : Illustration

ISBN 9781782275237

1. Amateur detectives 2. Tearooms 3. London, England 4. Great Britain 5. Edwardian era (1901-1914) 6. Mysteries 7. Short stories 8. Anthologies

"This welcome reissue of a 1908 collection by Orczy (The Scarlet Pimpernel) opens with a story in which the eponymous lead, whose real name is never revealed, sits down uninvited at the table of reporter Polly Burton in a London tea shop. As arrogantly as Sherlock Holmes, the interloper proclaims that 'there is no such thing as a mystery in connection with any crime, provided intelligence is brought to bear upon its investigation.'"—*Publishers Weekly*

★ The **Scarlet** Pimpernel. Baroness Orczy. Modern Library, 2002. Xviii, 271 p; (Scarlet Pimpernel series, 3)

ISBN 9780812966114

1. Rescues 2. Secret identity 3. Heroes and heroines, English 4. Dandies 5. Disguises 6. France 7. England 8. Revolutionary France (1789-1799) 9. 1790s 10. Adventure stories 11. Books to TV 12. Books to movies

LC 8015153

In 1792, during the French Revolution's Reign of Terror, an English aristocrat known to be an ineffectual fop is actually a master of disguises who, with a small band of dedicated friends, undertakes dangerous missions to save members of the French nobility from the guillotine.

Originally published: Hutchinson, 1905.

Orenstein, Hannah

Love at first like. Hannah Orenstein. Atria Books, 2019. 320 p.

ISBN 9781982117795

1. Women business owners 2. Social media 3. Engagement rings 4. Deception 5. Sisters 6. Brooklyn, New York City 7. New York City 8. Romantic comedies

LC 2019005677

When her Instagram following skyrockets over a mistaken rumor about her mystery engagement, a young jewelry shop owner hires an actor to keep up the ruse, which is complicated by her growing feelings for someone else.

"Orenstein's (Playing With Matches, 2018) writing is quick, witty, and compulsively readable, even when Eliza's desperate actions evoke cringes. Although the story is over the top, the feelings are real, and readers will be able to relate to Eliza's struggle to find her soul mate in the age of apps and social media. A classic wacky rom-com and an ideal summer read." —*Kirkus*

Includes bibliographical references and index.

Orringer, Julie

★ The **flight** portfolio: a novel. Julie Orringer. Alfred A. Knopf, 2019. 448 pages

ISBN 9780307959409

1. Fry, Varian 2. Righteous Gentiles in the Holocaust 3. World War II — Jews 4. World War II — Refugees 5. Journalists 6. Jews, French 7. France 8. Vichy (France) 9. Second World War era (1939-1945) 10. Biographical fiction 11. Historical fiction

LC 2018044985

Presents a long-anticipated novel based on the story of Varian Fry's extraordinary effort to save the lives and work of Jewish artists fleeing the Holocaust.

"Brilliantly conceived, impeccably crafted, and showcasing Orringer's extraordinary gifts, this is destined to become a classic." —*Publishers Weekly*

This is a Borzoi book.

★ The **invisible** bridge: a novel. Julie Orringer. Alfred A. Knopf, 2010. X, 602 p.

ISBN 9781400041169

1. World War II 2. Students 3. Jews 4. Brothers 5. Jews — Persecutions 6. Europe 7. Budapest, Hungary 8. Second World War era (1939-1945) 9. 1930s 10. Historical fiction 11. Love stories 12. Literary fiction

LC 2009046498

Booklist Editors' Choice, 2010; Edward Lewis Wallant Award, 2010; New York Times Notable Book, 2010; RUSA Reading List, 2011

A story of three brothers, of history and love, of marriage tested by disaster, of a Jewish family's struggle against annihilation, and of the dangerous power of art in a time of war.

"Andras is a Hungarian Jew studying in Paris as Hitler's influence begins to spread across a continent already riddled with anti-Semitism and bloodlust. He falls for fellow emigre Klara, and their world is soon rocked by war. Other characters weave in and out of the story line, but it's the love tethering Andras and Klara that powers the narrative's massive machinery. The Invisible Bridge is without a doubt an ambitious slice of literature, but Orringer fulfills her ambitions with crisp writing that never wanders far from the story's path. World War II is hardly undiscovered literary territory. Still, this stunning work manages to feel both original and part and parcel of the well-blazed tradition of historical novels that came before it." —*Entertainment Weekly*

Orwell, George

★ **1984:** a novel. George Orwell. Harcourt Brace Jovanovich, 1984. 314 p.

ISBN 9780151660384

1. Dystopias 2. Totalitarianism 3. Near future 4. Resistance (Psychology) 5. Identity (Psychology) 6. Dystopian fiction 7. Science fiction 8. Science fiction classics

LC 8318442

Portrays life in a future time when a totalitarian government watches over all citizens and directs all activities.

Originally published: London: Secker & Warburg, 1949.

★ **Animal** farm. George Orwell. Signet Classics, 1996. 140 p.

ISBN 9780451526342

1. Totalitarianism 2. Dystopias 3. Farm animals 4. Talking animals 5. Domestic animals 6. Political fiction 7. Allegories 8. Satirical fiction

A satire on totalitarianism in which farm animals overthrow their human owner and set up their own government.

Animal Farm has been loosely adapted to film in 1954 and 1999.

Originally published: [London] : Martin Secker & Warburg, 1945.

LIST OF FICTIONAL WORKS

Osborne, Lawrence

The **glass** kingdom: a novel. Lawrence Osborne. Hogarth, 2020. 272 p.
ISBN 9781984824301
1. Apartment house life 2. Rich people 3. Expatriates 4. Americans in Thailand 5. Political violence 6. Bangkok, Thailand 7. Thailand 8. Thrillers and suspense
LC 2020002452
New York Times Notable Book, 2020

Fleeing to Bangkok with a suitcase of money to hide in plain sight in a luxury high-rise, Sarah bonds with a circle of ex-pat women before political chaos and military coup attempts turn the apartment's residents against each other.

"It's a masterfully drawn, mesmerizing novel in which the ghosts of the past—like the bats, lizards, and geckos who gain free access to the Kingdom—refuse to vacate the premises. A seductive, darkly atmospheric thriller with a spine-tingling climax." —*Kirkus*

Only to sleep: a Philip Marlowe novel. Lawrence Osborne. Hogarth, 2018. 256 p. (Philip Marlowe mysteries, 9)
ISBN 9781524759612
1. Retirees 2. Senior men 3. Private investigators 4. Widows 5. Rich people 6. California 7. United States 8. 1980s 9. Mysteries 10. Hardboiled fiction 11. First person narratives
LC 2018017511
New York Times Notable Book, 2018

In 1988, 72-year-old Philip Marlowe must come out of retirement to investigate the death of Donald Zinn—supposedly drowned off his yacht, and leaving behind a much younger and now very rich wife.

Osman, Richard

The **man** who died twice: a Thursday Murder Club mystery. Richard Osman. Pamela Dorman Books, Viking, 2021. 368 pages (Thursday Murder Club novels, 2)
ISBN 9781984880994
1. Seniors 2. Amateur detectives 3. Retirement communities 4. Former spies 5. Diamonds 6. England 7. Mysteries 8. Multiple perspectives
LC 2021021660
LibraryReads Favorites, 2021; Loan Stars Favourites, 2021

Richard Osman is back with everyone's favorite mystery-solving quartet, and the second installment of The Thursday Murder Club series is just as clever and warm as the first-an unputdownable, laugh-out-loud pleasure of a read.

When an old friend, who has been accused of stealing millions of dollars' worth of diamonds, desperately needs her help leaving a dead body in his wake, Elizabeth and her friends go up against a ruthless murderer who wouldn't bat an eyelid at knocking off four septuagenarians.

"Osman follows The Thursday Murder Club (2020), his supremely entertaining debut, with an even better second installment.... A clever, funny mystery peopled with captivating characters that enhance the story at every quirky turn." —*Kirkus*

★ The **Thursday** Murder Club. Richard Osman. Pamela Dorman Books/Viking, 2020. 355 p. (Thursday Murder Club novels, 1)
ISBN 9781984880963
1. Retirees 2. Seniors 3. Amateur detectives 4. Clubs 5. Retirement communities 6. England 7. Mysteries 8. Multiple perspectives
LC 2020008501

Meeting weekly in their retirement village's Jigsaw Room to exchange theories about unsolved crimes, four savvy septuagenarians propose a daring but unorthodox plan to help a woman rookie cop solve her first big murder case.

"British TV celebrity Osman mixes mirth and murder in his exceptional debut, a series launch featuring the four members of the Thursday Murder Club, residents of the Coopers Chase Retirement Village in Kent." —*Publishers Weekly*

First published in hardcover in Great Britain by Viking, an imprint of Penguin Books, a division of Penguin Random House Ltd, London.

Osondu, E. C.

This house is not for sale: a novel. E.C. Osondu. Harper, 2015. 182 pages
ISBN 9780061990885
1. Large families 2. Houses 3. Family problems 4. Family relationships 5. Extramarital affairs 6. Africa 7. Domestic fiction 8. Literary fiction
LC 2014013856

A young member of an extraordinary African-American family observes the larger-than-life people who shape his house's vibrant history, from his contradictory grandfather to the longtime rival owners of competing convenience stores.

Voice of America: stories. E.C. Osondu. Harper, 2010. 215 p.
ISBN 9780061990861
1. Nigeria 2. United States 3. Short stories
LC 2010005729

An acclaimed African writer offers a debut collection of stories set both in Nigeria and the United States, which moves from the fears and dreams of boys and girls in African villages and refugee camps, to the disillusionment and confusion of young married couples living in America.

"These richly shaded tales explore old ways and new, wealth and poverty, myth and misapprehension. Though there is sadness here, the tone is deadpan, and the reader can imagine the storyteller's eyes crinkled in a smile." —*Booklist*

Collects 18 short stories.

Otsuka, Julie

The **Buddha** in the attic. Julie Otsuka. Alfred A. Knopf, 2011. 144 p.
ISBN 9780307700001
1. Mail order brides 2. Japanese in the United States 3. Assimilation (Sociology) 4. Identity (Psychology) 5. World War II 6. San Francisco, California 7. Second World War era (1939-1945) 8. Historical fiction 9. Literary fiction 10. First person narratives
David J. Langum, Sr. Prize in American Historical Fiction, 2011; Library Journal Best Books, 2011; New York Times Notable Book, 2011; PEN-Faulkner Award, 2012; Shortlisted for the International IMPAC Dublin Literary Award, 2013; National Book Award for Fiction finalist, 2011

Presents the stories of six Japanese mail-order brides whose new lives in early twentieth-century San Francisco are marked by backbreaking migrant work, cultural struggles, children who reject their heritage, and the prospect of wartime internment.

When the emperor was divine: a novel. By Julie Otsuka. Knopf, 2002. 141 p.
ISBN 9780375414299
1. Japanese Americans — Forced removal and incarceration, 1942-1945 2. World War II 3. Concentration camps 4. Japanese American families 5. Family relationships 6. California 7. Second World War era (1939-1945) 8. 1940s 9. Historical fiction 10. War stories 11. Multiple perspectives 12. Adult books for young adults
LC 2002020814
Alex Award, 2003; Booklist Editors' Choice, 2002; Booklist Editors' Choice: Adult Books for Young Adults, 2002; New York Times Notable Book, 2002

A story told from five different points of view, chronicles the experiences of Japanese Americans caught up in the nightmare of the World War II internment camps.

"Otsuka demonstrates a breathtaking restraint and delicacy throughout this supple and devastating first novel." —*Booklist*

Overton, Hollie

The **runaway**. Hollie Overton. Redhook Books/Orbit, 2019. 439 p.
ISBN 9780316482257

1. Missing teenage girls 2. Foster mothers 3. Manipulation by women 4. Teenage girls 5. Runaways 6. Los Angeles, California 7. Thrillers and suspense

LC 2019002121

The search for a teenage runaway sends her foster mother, a psychologist working for the LAPD, on a dangerous journey through Los Angeles' criminal underworld.

"Readers will root for the deeply empathetic Becca, who's devoted to helping society's most vulnerable, and Overton shines a light on the plight of the mentally ill, foster children, and the homeless while building plenty of tension. Fans of bighearted thrillers will find a lot to like." —*Publishers Weekly*

Originally published in England, 2018.

Owens, Delia

Where the crawdads sing. Delia Owens. G.P. Putnam's Sons, 2018. 320 p.
ISBN 9780735219090

1. Hermits 2. Marshes 3. Suspicion 4. Loners 5. Coasts 6. North Carolina 7. 1960s 8. Literary fiction 9. Coming-of-age stories 10. Adult books for young adults

LC 2018010775

Viewed with suspicion in the aftermath of a tragedy, a beautiful hermit who has survived for years in a marsh becomes targeted by unthinkable forces.

"Owens memorably depicts the small-town drama and courtroom theatrics, but perhaps best of all is her vivid portrayal of the singular North Carolina setting." —*Publishers Weekly*

Oyeyemi, Helen

Boy, Snow, Bird: a novel. Helen Oyeyemi. Riverhead Hardcover, 2014. 320 pages
ISBN 9781594631399

1. Mothers and daughters 2. Identity (Psychology) 3. Beauty 4. Mirrors 5. Passing (Identity) 6. 1950s 7. 1960s 8. Adaptations, retellings, and spin-offs 9. Magical realism 10. Literary fiction

LC 2013025053

New York Times Notable Book, 2014

A reimagining of the Snow White story recast as a story of family secrets, race, beauty, and vanity set in the United States during the 1950s and 1960s.

"Dense with fully realized characters, startling images, original observations and revelatory truths, this masterpiece engages the reader's heart and mind as it captures both the complexities of racial and gender identity in the 20th century and the more intimate complexities of love in all its guises." —*Kirkus*

Gingerbread: a novel. Helen Oyeyemi. Riverhead Books, 2019. 258 p.
ISBN 9781594634659

1. Mothers and daughters 2. Family recipes 3. Characters and characteristics in fairy tales 4. Gingerbread 5. Family history 6. London, England 7. Literary fiction 8. Magical realism 9. Adaptations, retellings, and spin-offs 10. Adult books for young adults

LC 2018019890

Finalist for the Hurston/Wright Legacy Awards for Fiction, 2020

Draws on the classic fairy-tale element of gingerbread in the story of a British family whose surprising legacy and secret past are tied to a favorite recipe.

"Readers familiar with Oyeyemi's work will not be surprised to learn that her latest plot sets off in one direction and immediately takes a hairpin curve in another (and another, and still another). The effect is heady, surreal, and disarming—you have to be willing to surrender to Oyeyemi's vision and the delicious twists and turns of her prose." —*Kirkus*

Mr. Fox. Helen Oyeyemi. Riverhead Books, 2011. 324 p.
ISBN 9781594488078

1. Authors 2. Writing 3. Muses (Persons) 4. Heroes and heroines 5. Death 6. Metafiction 7. Love stories

LC 2011013747

New York Times Notable Book, 2011; Hurston/Wright Legacy Award: Fiction, 2012

Unable to stop killing off the heroines of his novels, celebrated writer Mr. Fox is confronted by a living embodiment of his muse, Mary, who challenges him to join her in fairy-tale stories where they must stay together in spite of disparate character traits.

"Each character is so superbly formed, and they are believable people whose habits of thought and language are so perfectly pitched and entertaining that they become instantly lovable, that is until we learn more about them. The combination of intensity and changeability in all three characters reflect many of the archetypal baddies from myth and batty old fairy-fables, the most prominent of which is Bluebeard, with his many bloodbaths, and the Furies, with their readiness to punish crime." —*Chicago Sun-Times*

The **opposite** house. Helen Oyeyemi. Nan A. Talese, Doubleday, 2007. 257 p.
ISBN 9780385513845

1. Young women 2. Cubans in Great Britain 3. Identity (Psychology) 4. Faith 5. Magic 6. London, England 7. Psychological fiction 8. Mythological fiction

LC 2006036812

An exploration of the thin wall that exists between myth and reality chronicles the alternating stories of two young women—Maja Carmen Carrerra, the daughter of a black Cuban couple living in England who longs for a connection to her African roots, and Yemaya Saramgua, a Yoruba goddess in the Somewherehouse—in search of the meaning of faith and identity.

"The novel is insightful, urgently and sometimes painfully so. What Oyeyemi shows us about cultural alienation, about what makes and marks a migrant, needs to be seen.... At times, it's true, Maja's skin feels thin, stretched, raw. We can feel Oyeyemi writing through her character. But those times are rare; on most of the pages in this novel Maja lives, and it matters that she lives. This is her life." —*Strange Horizons*

Peaces. Helen Oyeyemi. Riverhead Books, 2021. 272 p.
ISBN 9780593192337

1. Gay couples 2. Honeymoons 3. Railroad travel 4. Mongooses 5. Trains 6. Literary fiction 7. Magical realism

Honeymooning aboard a historic former tea-smuggling train, newlyweds Otto and Xavier enjoy the locomotive's fantastical accommodations before encountering a secretive fellow passenger, who imparts a surprising message.

"Oyeyemi (Gingerbread, 2019) has once again crafted a layered modern-day fairy tale replete with interlinked stories and unexpected connections among its vibrant characters." —*Booklist*

What is not yours is not yours: stories. Helen Oyeyemi. Riverhead Books, 2016. 325 pages
ISBN 9781594634635
1. Locks and keys 2. Literary fiction 3. Magical realism 4. Short stories 5. Adult books for young adults
A collection of stories by the award-winning author of Boy, Snow, Bird features entries about literal and metaphorical keys that open or shut the fates of lovers, the heart of a puppeteering student and the doors of a house of locks that holds unobservable developments.

Oz, Amos
Fima. Amos Oz; translated from the Hebrew by Nicholas de Lange. Harcourt, Brace, 1993. 322 p.
ISBN 9780151898510
1. Poets, Israeli 2. Middle-aged men 3. Jerusalem, Israel 4. Psychological fiction 5. Translations
LC 92044200
"Not only does Mr. Oz strive toward a Chekhovian compassion for his characters, but his novel depends...on making us believe in the possibility of last-minute grace. When tragedy strikes, we watch Fima rise to the occasion and begin to tap his own resources of generosity, humility, common sense, and his sense of purpose." —*New York Times Book Review*

Ozeki, Ruth L.
The **book** of form and emptiness: a novel. Ruth Ozeki. Penguin Books, 2021. 512 p.
ISBN 9780399563645
1. Auditory hallucinations 2. Fathers — Death 3. Loss (Psychology) 4. Books and reading 5. Zen Buddhism 6. Coming-of-age stories 7. Literary fiction 8. Magical realism
LC 2021008787
Thirteen-year-old Benny Oh starts to hear voices after the death of his musician father. The voices belong to the things in his house such as a sneaker, a broken Christmas ornament, a piece of wilted lettuce. At first, Benny tries to ignore them, but soon the voices drive him to seek sanctuary in the silence of a large public library, where objects are quieter. There, Benny encounters a homeless philosopher-poet, who encourages him to ask important questions and find his own voice amongst the many. And he finds his very own Book, who narrates Benny's life and teaches him to listen to the things that are important.
"This enthralling, poignant, funny, and mysterious saga, thrumming with grief and tenderness, beauty and compassion, offers much wisdom." —*Booklist*

★ A **tale** for the time being. Ruth Ozeki. Viking, 2013. 432 p.
ISBN 9780670026630
1. Women authors 2. Diary writing 3. Compassion 4. Loneliness 5. Tsunamis 6. Tokyo, Japan 7. Vancouver Island 8. Literary fiction 9. Metafiction
LC 2012039878
ALA Notable Book, 2014; Asian Pacific American Award for Literature: Adult Fiction, 2014; Booklist Editors' Choice, 2013; Canada-Japan Literary Awards, 2014; Los Angeles Times Book Prize for Fiction, 2013; Sunburst Award for Excellence in Canadian Literature of the Fantastic, 2014; Shortlisted for the Man Booker Prize, 2013; National Book Critics Circle Award for Fiction finalist, 2013

A novelist on a remote island in the Pacific is linked to a bullied and depressed Tokyo teenager after discovering a Hello Kitty lunchbox that washed ashore.
Includes bibliographical references.

Ozick, Cynthia
Foreign bodies. Cynthia Ozick. Houghton Mifflin Harcourt, 2010. 272 p.
ISBN 9780547435572
1. Divorced women 2. Americans in France 3. Nephews 4. Siblings 5. Fifties (Age) 6. Paris, France 7. 1950s 8. Literary fiction 9. Psychological fiction
LC 2010005757
New York Times Notable Book, 2010; Shortlisted for The Orange Prize for Fiction, 2012
Presents a retelling of Henry James's "The Ambassadors" that follows the efforts of divorced schoolteacher Bea Nightingale to navigate a turbulent year spent with her estranged brother's family.
"Ozick is a craggy writer, with strenuous climbs, momentary slides and startling views. Some of Bea's confrontations, feeling out her new independence back in the United States, seem contrived, even stagy. But her vision of Europe and its tragic history is profound; and Lili is a creation of stunning depth. It is not Jamesian, it is Ozickian." —*Boston Globe*

Heir to the glimmering world. Cynthia Ozick. Houghton Mifflin, 2004. 320 p.
ISBN 9780618470495
1. Children of authors 2. Refugees, Jewish 3. Young women 4. Jewish families 5. Benefactors 6. New York City 7. Bronx, New York City 8. Depression era (1929-1941) 9. 1930s 10. Historical fiction 11. Domestic fiction 12. Adult books for young adults
LC 2004042723
Booklist Editors' Choice, 2004; New York Times Notable Book, 2004
James A'bair, whose father is the author of the popular series "The Bear Boy," has taken in the eccentric Mitwisser family and the orphaned Rose Meadows, who must resist the pull of the actual Bear Boy, in a novel of Depression-era New York.
"In 1933, the Mitwissers, a family of German Jews, arrive in America after a narrow and eccentric escape from Berlin.... After landing somewhat haphazardly in New York, they place an ad for help in a local paper. The only applicant for the job is an eighteen-year-old orphan, Rose Meadows, who narrates the story, and who observes the Mitwissers with the dry neutrality of an invisible servant. Her duties are vaguely defined—part nanny, part secretary—and her salary comes intermittently, the family's sole source of income being the whimsy of a troubled benefactor. Ozick portrays this ramshackle household to dazzling effect, as it adjusts to its many states of exile—from a sense of security, from cherished ideas, and from the consolations of each other." —*The New Yorker*

The **Puttermesser** papers. Cynthia Ozick. Alfred A. Knopf, 1997. 235 p.
ISBN 9780679454762
1. Jewish women 2. Women mayors 3. Life change events 4. Golem 5. Interpersonal relations 6. New York City 7. Picaresque fiction 8. Literary fiction
Booklist Editors' Choice, 1997; Shortlisted for the International IMPAC Dublin Literary Award, 1999; National Book Award for Fiction finalist, 1997
A female Don Quixote transplanted to modern-day Manhattan, Ruth Puttermesser yearns for a life of the mind, only to find herself hopelessly mired in the eternal circle of city bureaucracy when she is unexpectedly elected mayor of the Big Apple BT

"This entertaining fable is a social commentary as well as a comic tour de force, and it bristles with Ozick's formidable intelligence and wit." —*Publishers Weekly*

P

Packer, Ann

The **children's** crusade. Ann Packer. Scribner, 2015. 464 p.
ISBN 9781476710457
1. Siblings 2. Women artists 3. Adult children of dysfunctional families 4. Mother-deserted children 5. Married people 6. San Francisco Bay Area 7. California 8. Family sagas 9. Literary fiction 10. Multiple perspectives

When their younger sibling returns, the three oldest Blair children find their lives disrupted in ways they could have never imagined as they each tell their story that is interwoven with portraits of their family at crucial points in their history.

"Packer fully captures the intimacy of this familys life and, by extension, the way the childrens interactions impact their adult lives. A masterful portrait of indelible family bonds." —*Booklist*

The **dive** from Clausen's pier. Ann Packer. Alfred A. Knopf, 2002. 369 p.
ISBN 9780375412820
1. Self-discovery 2. Engaged persons 3. Small town life 4. Self-fulfillment 5. Young women 6. Wisconsin 7. New York City 8. Coming-of-age stories 9. Books to movies 10. Adult books for young adults
LC 2001042522
Alex Award, 2003; Great Lakes Book Awards, Fiction category, 2002; New York Times Notable Book, 2002

When her fiance Mike is left paralyzed following a tragic accident, Carrie Bell begins to question her familiar world, from her everyday life in Wisconsin to her relationships, as she sets out to rediscover her own identity.

Songs without words. By Ann Packer. Knopf, 2007. 352 p.
ISBN 9780375412813
1. Friendship 2. Self-perception 3. Loss (Psychology) 4. Grief 5. Interpersonal relations 6. California 7. Domestic fiction 8. Adult books for young adults
LC 2006100512
This chronicles the long-time friendship between Liz and Sarabeth, a relationship that is forged in childhood and sustained through the decades that follow, until both women are forced to reexamine their lives in the wake of a devastating crisis.

"[Packer] shows a deft touch in framing emotional dilemmas, such as whether it is the duty of those who have been raised with affection to compensate those who have gone without." —*The New Yorker*

Palahniuk, Chuck

Choke: a novel. Chuck Palahniuk. Doubleday, 2001. 293 p.
ISBN 9780385501569
1. Get-rich-quick ventures 2. Women with Alzheimer's disease 3. Sex addiction in men 4. Mother and adult son 5. Swindlers and swindling 6. Psychological fiction 7. Books to movies
LC 63905

Medical school dropout Victor Mancini comes up with a complicated but ingenious scam to pay for his mother's elder care, cruises sex addiction groups for action, and visits his zany mother, whose Alzheimer's disease hides the bizarre truth about his parentage.

Fight Club. By Chuck Palahniuk. W. W. Norton & Company, 1996. 208 p.
ISBN 9780393039764
1. Secret societies 2. Violence 3. Man-woman relationships 4. Poe, Edgar Allan 5. Young men 6. Transgressive fiction 7. Books to movies
LC 95047591
Oregon Book Awards, Fiction Award, 1997

In a confusing world poised on the brink of mayhem, Tyler Durden, a projectionist, waiter, and anarchic genius, comes up with an idea to create clubs in which young men can escape their humdrum existence and prove themselves in barehanded fights.

Has a graphic novel sequel released in 2016, Fight Club 2.

The **invention** of sound. Chuck Palahniuk. Grand Central Publishing, 2020. 256 p.
ISBN 9781538718001
1. Fathers 2. Missing girls 3. Frightful sounds 4. Horror films 5. Suffering 6. Hollywood, California 7. California 8. Transgressive fiction
LC 2020008872
A father on the brink of uncovering his missing daughter's fate and a talented Foley sound artist find themselves on a collision course with Hollywood's violent underworld.

"Palahniuk's heralded return to fiction will galvanize his many avid readers." —*Booklist*

Lullaby: a novel. Chuck Palahniuk. Doubleday, 2002. 260 p.
ISBN 9780385504478
1. Incantations 2. Journalists 3. Sudden Infant Death Syndrome 4. Widowers 5. Paranormal phenomena 6. Horror 7. Transgressive fiction
LC 2001052979
Assigned to a story on sudden infant death syndrome, journalist Carl Streator finds a poetry anthology that contains an African chant that becomes lethal when spoken or thought in someone's direction.

"This is vintage Palahniuk: weird, creepy, twisted, upsetting, and ultimately a great read for anyone who wants to be scared for pleasure." —*Library Journal*

Pygmy. Chuck Palahniuk. Doubleday, 2009. 240 p.
ISBN 9780385526340
1. Foreign students 2. Terrorists 3. Terrorism 4. Young adults 5. International relations 6. Middle West 7. Satirical fiction 8. Thrillers and suspense 9. Adult books for young adults
Booklist Editors' Choice, 2009

Pygmy—a young adult from a totalitarian state, disguised as an exchange student—plans a terrorist attack and depicts U.S. Midwestern life through the eyes of a hateful, indoctrinated little killer, in a satire of American xenophobia.

"The story unfolds in a series of dispatches from an unnamed 13-year-old agent, dubbed Pygmy by the locals.... The frisson around his internal, target-acquiring narrative, the locals' unwitting perception of him, and his outsider's view of the routine humiliations inflicted upon high-school youth is so spot-on it produces a sense of deja vu: surely someone would have thought of this before." —*Booklist*

Paley, Grace

★ The **collected** stories. Grace Paley. Farrar Straus Giroux, 1994. 386 p.

ISBN 9780374126360
1. Short stories 2. Literary fiction

LC 93042230

ALA Notable Book, 1995; National Book Award for Fiction finalist, 1994; Pulitzer Prize for Fiction finalist, 1995

An introduction by Paley accompanies a comprehensive collection of short fiction by the author of "Later the same day," "Enormous changes at the last minute," and "The little disturbances of man."

45 short stories

From The little disturbances of man, Enormous changes at the last minute, and Later the same day.

Palliser, Charles

The **quincunx**. Charles Palliser. Ballantine Books 1990. 788 p.
ISBN 9780345364630
1. Inheritance and succession 2. Identity (Psychology) 3. Revenge 4. Men — Identity 5. England 6. 19th century 7. Historical mysteries 8. Literary fiction 9. Mysteries

LC 89091787

This meditation on the Victorian novel and sprawling epic tale of a man's quest for his identity follows John as he journeys to the heart of the Quincunx to reveal his elusive past

"This is not an ironic parody a la Barth, not an echo of Eco, but a genuine reproduction of a full-bodied 19th-century page-turner of a novel, set in late Regency England, thick with characters of all classes, with plots, counterplots, fore-bodings, reversals and interpolated tales.... Mr. Palliser's re-creation of this period is absolutely convincing, his dialogue never jars, his command of details never falters." —*New York Times Book Review*

Palmer, Ada

Too like the lightning. Ada Palmer. Tor, 2016. 400 p. (Terra Ignota, 1)
ISBN 9780765378002
1. Far future 2. Criminals 3. Spirituality 4. Political science 5. Utopias 6. 25th century 7. Science fiction

In the 25th century, human civilization is divided into philosophical sects based on technologically generated abundance and inspired by the 18th-century European Enlightenment. In this utopia, convicted felon Mycroft Canner serves his sentence by carrying out the orders of everyone he meets, while sensayer Carlyle Foster acts as a spiritual counselor in a world where organized religion has been outlawed. Their paths converge when they encounter Bridger, a young boy whose unusual abilities could destroy their hard-won world of peace and prosperity.

"Although the primary plot centers around a stolen list ranking the most powerful people on the planet and its political ramifications, the overarching theme of the book is philosophy, from the debate about gendered pronouns to thoughts about the afterlife." —*Booklist*

Palmer, Daniel

The **new** husband. D. J. Palmer. St. Martin's Press, 2020. 384 p.
ISBN 9781250107497
1. Single mothers 2. Control (Psychology) 3. Widowers 4. Deception 5. Teenage girls 6. New Hampshire 7. Psychological suspense

LC 2019048512

After meeting Simon Fitch, a teacher from her daughter Maggie's middle school, widow Nina Garrity has hopes of putting her shattered life back together, but her friends aren't so sure that Simon has the best of intentions.

"A well-crafted, increasingly tense page-turner." —*Kirkus*

Palmer, Dexter Clarence

★ **Mary** Toft; or, the rabbit queen: a novel. Dexter Palmer. Pantheon Books, 2020. 320 p.
ISBN 9781101871935
1. Curiosities and wonders 2. Childbirth 3. Hoaxes 4. Rabbits 5. Apprentices 6. London, England 7. 18th century 8. Historical fiction 9. Psychological fiction

LC 2019013815

The award-winning author of Version Control presents a novel based on true events depicting a young woman who baffles the medical community of early 18th-century England when she begins giving birth to dead rabbits.

Includes bibliographical references.

Version control. Dexter Palmer. Pantheon Books, 2016. Viii, 495 pages
ISBN 9780307907592
1. Near future 2. Married people 3. Physics — Experiments 4. Time machines 5. Consequences 6. New York City 7. Hard science fiction 8. Science fiction 9. Adult books for young adults

Convinced that "nothing is as it should be; everything is upside down," Rebecca Wright struggles to explain her conviction to her husband, physicist Philip Steiner, who's skeptical to say the least. Could the "wrongness" that Rebecca perceives have something to do with Philip's work? Philip has spent the better part of ten years developing a causality violation device. The CVD is NOT a time machine, although the way it works (if it, in fact, works) seems remarkably similar to how a time machine might behave, disrupting the space-time continuum in subtle, yet powerful ways.

"A Mobius strip of a novel in which time is more a loop than a path and various possibilities seem to exist simultaneously." —*Kirkus*

Palmer, Lindsey J.

Otherwise engaged. Lindsey J. Palmer. Skyhorse Publishing, 2019. 304 p.
ISBN 9781510732391
1. Couples 2. Engagement 3. Authors 4. Engaged persons 5. Wedding planning 6. New York City 7. Chick lit

After her fiance authors a sensational and best-selling novel loosely based on his torrid love affair with his ex-girlfriend, Molly's paranoia that she will come back and try to rekindle their romance sends her into a downward spiral.

Pamuk, Orhan

The **museum** of innocence. Orhan Pamuk; translated from the Turkish by Maureen Freely. Alfred A. Knopf, 2009. 535 p.
ISBN 9780307266767
1. Lindbergh, Anne Morrow 2. Love triangles 3. Rich families 4. Men 5. Man-woman relationships 6. Istanbul, Turkey 7. 1970s 8. Translations 9. Literary fiction

LC 2009019475

Booklist Editors' Choice, 2009; New York Times Notable Book, 2009

Ending his engagement to pursue a married cousin, Kemal unsuccessfully woos the woman over the course of nine years, during which he amasses personal effects that reflect his obsession and render him a laughingstock among his peers.

"Pamuk is brilliant at the human parade, and especially at humiliation in its masculine forms, frequently played out in Istanbul along East-West tensions." —*Cleveland Plain Dealer*

Translated from the Turkish Masumiyet muzesi.

Translated from the Turkish.

The **red-haired** woman. Orhan Pamuk; translated from the Turkish by Ekin Oklap. Alfred A. Knopf, 2017. 253 p.

ISBN 9780451494429

1. Blue collar workers 2. Young men 3. Jack, the Ripper 4. Apprentices 5. Intergenerational friendship 6. Istanbul, Turkey 7. Literary fiction 8. Translations

LC 2016057733

Hired to find water on a barren plain during the hot summer, a master well digger and his young apprentice develop a filial bond neither has known until the boy becomes fatefully attracted to a red-haired actress from a traveling theatre company.

"As usual, Pamuk handles weighty material deftly, and the result is both puzzling and beautiful." —*Booklist*

Originally published in Turkey as Kirmizi Sacli Kadin by Yapi Kredi Yayinlari, Istanbul, in 2016.

Translated from the Turkish.

Silent house. Orhan Pamuk; translated from the Turkish by Robert Finn. Alfred A. Knopf, 2012. 334 p.

ISBN 9780307700285

1. Widows 2. Families 3. Memories 4. Coups d'etat 5. Household employees 6. Turkey 7. 1980s 8. Translations 9. Literary fiction

LC 2012005468

New York Times Notable Book, 2012

Awaiting the arrival of her grandchildren in her home outside Istanbul, bed-ridden widow Fatma shares memories and grievances with her late husband's illegitimate son until his cousin, a right-wing nationalist, involves the family in the Turkish military coup of 1980.

This is a Borzoi book.

★ **Snow**. Orhan Pamuk; translated from the Turkish by Maureen Freely. Knopf, 2004. 448 p.

ISBN 9780375406973

1. Islam and women 2. Suicide 3. Poets, Turkish 4. Married women 5. Actors and actresses 6. Turkey 7. Translations 8. Political fiction 9. Literary fiction

LC 2003065935

New York Times Notable Book, 2004

After years of lonely political exile, Turkish poet Ka returns to Istanbul to attend his mother's funeral and learns about a series of suicides among pious girls forbidden to wear headscarves.

"Pamuk's sometimes exhaustive conversations and descriptions create a stark picture of a too-little-known part of the world, where politics, religion and even happiness can seem alternately all-consuming and irrelevant. A detached tone and some dogmatic abstractions make for tough reading, but Ka's rediscovery of God and poetry in a desolate place makes the novel's sadness profound and moving." —*Publishers Weekly*

★ A **strangeness** in my mind: a novel. Orhan Pamuk; translated by Ekin Oklap. Alfred A. Knopf, 2015. 599 p.

ISBN 9780307700292

1. Self-fulfillment in men 2. City life 3. Growing up 4. Men — Psychology 5. Street vendors 6. Turkey 7. Istanbul, Turkey 8. 20th century 9. 21st century 10. Coming-of-age stories 11. Literary fiction 12. Political fiction

LC 2015006769

Shortlisted for the International Dublin Literary Award, 2017

Selling Turkish spirits on the street and dreaming of becoming rich in a rapidly developing Istanbul, street youth Melvut Karatas elopes with the wrong woman and builds a family over decades marked by a series of dead-end jobs and an enduring sense of his unique destiny.

"If anything, Pamuk recalls the great Victorian novelists as he ranges confidently from near-documentary passages on real estate machinations and the privatization of electrical service to pensive meditations on the gap between people's public posturing and private beliefs. The oppression of women is quietly but angrily depicted as endemic... As Pamuk follows his believably flawed protagonist and a teeming cast of supporting players across five decades, Turkey's turbulent politics provide a thrumming undercurrent of unease. Rich, complex, and pulsing with urban life: one of this gifted writer's best." —*Kirkus*

Includes index.

Originally published in Turkish as Kafamda bir tuhaflik by Yapi Kredi Publications. First published in the UK in 2015.

Pandya, Sameer

Members only. Sameer Pandya. Houghton Mifflin Harcourt, 2020. 288 p.

ISBN 9780358098546

1. East Indian Americans 2. Racism 3. College teachers 4. Athletic clubs 5. Identity (Psychology) 6. California 7. Literary fiction

LC 2019033955

First the white members of Raj Bhatt's posh tennis club call him racist. Then his life falls apart. Along the way, he wonders: where does he, a brown man, belong in America?

"This realistic, character-driven novel with multiple, exceptionally well developed, threads of suspense engages contemporary identity politics and what it means to belong—to a club, to a racial group, to a country, and to various cultures and subcultures." —*Booklist*

Panowich, Brian

Bull Mountain. Brian Panowich. Putnam Adult, 2015. 304 p. (Bull Mountain, 1)

ISBN 9780399173967

1. Sheriffs 2. Drug traffic 3. Mountain life 4. Outlaws 5. Brothers 6. Georgia 7. Appalachian region 8. Rural noir 9. Multiple perspectives 10. Literary fiction

LC 2015002115

Thriller Award for Best First Novel, 2016

Taking a job as sheriff to distance himself from his drug-running family and keep the peace in their Georgia mountain territory, Clayton Burroughs is approached by a federal agent who claims he wants to help shut down the family's operations.

Sequel: Like lions.

Hard cash valley. Brian Panowich. St Martins Pr 2020. 320 p.

ISBN 9781250206923

1. People with autism 2. Former detectives 3. Women FBI agents 4. Murder 5. Criminals 6. Florida 7. Georgia 8. Crime fiction

LC 2019059173

Investigating a murder in a Jacksonville motel room, Dane Kirby and his FBI counterpart, Special Agent Roselita Velasquez, find themselves in a race against time to save a boy on the autism spectrum whose savant talents are being violently exploited.

"Make room for this splendid genre-bender, a crime novel with emotional resonance and a steady flow of fine writing. Plus staggering plot twists, jaw-dropping revelations, and enough suspense to fill two books." —*Booklist*

Like lions. Brian Panowich. St Martins Pr 2019. 320 p. (Bull Mountain, 2)

ISBN 9781250206947

1. Sheriffs 2. Organized crime 3. Family relationships 4. Crime 5. Criminals 6. Catharine Parr 7. Appalachian region 8. Rural noir 9. Literary fiction 10. Southern fiction

A follow-up to the award-winning Bull Mountain finds sheriff and father Clayton Burroughs struggling to recover from the shooting that ended his brothers' lives before violent rivals compel his return to the criminal past he would leave behind.

Sequel to: Bull Mountain.

Paolini, Christopher

★ **To** sleep in a sea of stars. Christopher Paolini. Tor Books, 2020. 688 pages

ISBN 9781250762849

1. Women scientists 2. Space exploration 3. Alien artifacts 4. Engaged persons 5. Aliens 6. Space opera 7. Science fiction

A space voyager living her dream of exploring new worlds lands on a distant planet ripe for colonization before her discovery of a mysterious relic transforms her life and threatens the entire human race.

"This one clocks in at close to 900 pages, but the rollicking pace, rapidly developing stakes, and Paolini's confident worldbuilding make them fly by. Perhaps not the most impressive prose, but a worthwhile adventure story." —*Kirkus*

Paretsky, Sara

★ **Dead** land. Sara Paretsky. William Morrow & Co, 2020. 304 p. (V. I. Warshawski mysteries, 20)

ISBN 9780062435927

1. Women private investigators 2. Grandmother and granddaughter 3. Corruption 4. Windsor, Edward 5. Real estate development 6. Chicago, Illinois 7. Kansas 8. Mysteries 9. Adult books for young adults

Dragged by her impetuous goddaughter into a legal battle over a clandestine deal that is threatening community land, V. I. Warshawski uncovers a developer scheme that ends the life of the young man her goddaughter is dating.

"A high point in Paretsky's long-running and much-loved series." —*Booklist*

Indemnity only: a novel. Sara Paretsky. Dell, 1982. 244 p. (V. I. Warshawski mysteries, 1)

ISBN 9780385272131

1. Labor unions — Corrupt practices 2. Missing persons 3. Women private investigators 4. Criminal investigation 5. Murder 6. Chicago, Illinois 7. Mysteries

"Chicago private eye V. I. Warshawski is hired to locate a young woman and instead comes across the body of her boyfriend, a crooked union, and an insurance scam. Thugs beat V. I. up, and another man is murdered. This is all standard hard-boiled detective stuff, except that V. I. is a woman—tough, independent, good looking, and believable. Paretsky has done an excellent job of presenting a real female private eye, without falling into parody." —*Library Journal*

Love & other crimes: stories. Sara Paretsky. William Morrow & Co, 2020. 288 pages

ISBN 9780062915542

1. Crime 2. Social justice 3. Mysteries 4. Short stories

A New York Times best-selling author offers a collection of thrilling crime and detective short stories, many featuring legendary detective V.I. Warshawski, V. I. (Fictitious character)—including a brand-new V.I. story.

"The well-wrought plots and densely imagined worlds make this the most distinguished mystery collection so far this year." —*Kirkus*

Shell game. Sara Paretsky. William Morrow, 2018. 304 p. (V. I. Warshawski mysteries, 19)

ISBN 9780062435866

1. Women private investigators 2. White collar crime 3. International intrigue 4. Law firms 5. Greed 6. Chicago, Illinois 7. Mysteries 8. Adult books for young adults

LC 2018018513

Returning to Chicago to prevent an erroneous murder charge, V. I. Warshawski traces a stolen artifact with links to an network of international mobsters, terrorist financiers, scammers and art thieves.

Parini, Jay

The **Damascus** road: a novel of Saint Paul. Jay Parini. Doubleday, 2019. 368 p.

ISBN 9780385522786

1. Paul 2. Apostles 3. Christianity 4. Conversion to Christianity 5. Church history 6. Voyages and travels 7. 1st century 8. Bible novels 9. Christian historical fiction

The best-selling author of The Last Station presents a historical novel inspired by the Apostle Paul, who at the side of gospel writer Luke becomes Christianity's most influential messenger in an ancient world on the brink of epochal change.

The **passages** of H.M.: a novel of Herman Melville. Jay Parini. Doubleday, 2010. 464 p.

ISBN 9780385522779

1. Melville, Herman 2. Authors, American 3. Alcoholism 4. Marital conflict 5. Husband and wife 6. Male friendship — History 7. United States 8. Biographical fiction 9. Historical fiction

LC 2010006291

A tale inspired by the life of Herman Melville finds the aging author's wife witnessing his descent into alcoholism and obscurity in the decades after the failure of *Moby Dick*, a work of creative genius shaped by memories of youthful seafaring adventures.

Paris, B. A.

Behind closed doors. B. A. Paris. St. Martin's Press, 2016. 293 p.

ISBN 9781250121004

1. Husband and wife 2. Suburban life 3. Deception 4. Married people 5. Newlyweds 6. Psychological suspense 7. Adult books for young adults

LibraryReads Favorites, 2016

The friends of a seemingly perfect socialite couple begin to see cracks in the facade when they realize that the husband and wife are never apart and that there are bars on one of their upstairs windows.

The **breakdown**. B. A. Paris. St. Martin's Press, 2017. 328 p.

ISBN 9781250122469

1. Murder witnesses 2. Memory 3. Stalking 4. Murder 5. Guilt 6. Thrillers and suspense

LC 2017002673

Loan Stars Favourites, 2017

Unable to forget a murder she witnessed when she was where she was not supposed to be, Cass struggles with an increasingly compromised memory before she begins receiving silent, sinister phone calls.

Bring me back: a novel. B.A. Paris. St. Martin's Press, 2018. 291 p.

ISBN 9781250151339

1. Missing women 2. Sisters 3. Former lovers 4. Loss (Psychology) 5. Deception 6. Psychological suspense

LC 2017060169

LibraryReads Favorites, 2018; Loan Stars Favourites, 2018

A decade after a man's wife disappears without a trace, his new fianc? makes a discovery that raises questions about what happened and whether his first wife may still be alive.

★ The **dilemma**. B.A. Paris. St. Martin's Press, 2020. 304 p.
ISBN 9781250151360

1. Family secrets 2. Birthday parties 3. Airplane accidents 4. Guilt 5. Deception 6. England 7. Psychological suspense

LC 2019054419

Organizing a lavish birthday party after decades of hardship, a woman hiding a secret about a daughter who cannot attend is forced to confront a devastating truth when her husband arranges a surprise.

"Paris constructs an unusual and compelling premise and masterfully maintains suspense about what happened and when it will be revealed. A breathtaking story, nearly impossible to put down." —*Booklist*

Park, Ishle Yi

Angel & Hannah: a novel in verse. Ishle Park. One World, 2021. 96 p.
ISBN 9780593134320

1. Korean American teenage girls 2. Teenage boys 3. City life 4. Teenage romance 5. First loves 6. 1990s 7. Coming-of-age stories 8. Novels in verse

LC 2020042202

Told in seasons, this hip-hop love story follows Hannah, a Korean American girl from Queens, New York, and Angel, a Puerto Rican boy from Brooklyn, as their forbidden love wildly blooms along the Jackie Robinson Expressway in the spring of 1993.

"With an energy and attitude closer to Lin-Manuel Miranda's In the Heights than West Side Story, the spoken-word style of Park's wildly creative rendition will entrance readers." —*Booklist*

Park, Sang Young

★ **Love** in the big city: a novel. Sang Young Park; translated from the Korean by Anton Hur. Grove Press, 2021. 240 p.
ISBN 9780802158789

1. Gay men 2. City life 3. Friendship 4. Loneliness in men 5. People with HIV 6. Seoul, Korea 7. South Korea 8. LGBTQIA fiction 9. Literary fiction 10. Translations

When his female best friend and roommate, Jaehee, leaves him to settle down, Young, a cynical gay man living in the lonely city of Seoul, tries to make sense of his life and his relationships as he finds himself torn between two very different men.

"The strength of the narrator, notably his flexibility of voice and expansiveness, carries the narrative to great heights, making this a standout among queer literature." —*Publishers Weekly*

Originally published in 2019 as Daedosiui Sarangbeop.

Parker, Lucy

The **Austen** playbook. Lucy Parker. Carina Press, 2019. 400 p.
(London celebrities, 4)
ISBN 9781335006899

1. Actors and actresses 2. Theater critics 3. Interpersonal attraction 4. Man-woman relationships 5. England 6. Romantic comedies 7. Contemporary romances 8. New Zealand fiction

"In the delightful fourth in Parker's contemporary London Celebrities series (after Making Up), readers will easily immerse themselves into the passionate world of actor Frederica 'Freddy' Carlton and critic James 'Griff' Ford-Griffin.... There's more drama offstage than on, the writing is outstanding, and the bit of mystery blends well into the romance." —*Publishers Weekly*

Battle royal. Lucy Parker. Avon Books, 2021. 384 p. (Palace insiders, 1)
ISBN 9780063040069

1. Baking 2. Bakers 3. Nobility 4. Reality television programs 5. Fame 6. London, England 7. Great Britain 8. Romantic comedies 9. Contemporary romances 10. New Zealand fiction

LibraryReads Favorites, 2021

After being kicked off by judge Dominic De Vere on a baking-competition show, an otherwise successful London baker, Sylvie Fairchild, returns to Operation Cake as a judge, setting off an intense rivalry and maybe a bit of romance.

"The slow burn of the romance is tantalizing and well paced, though there is plenty of setting and detail to take in while readers await the inevitable happily-ever-after." —*Kirkus*

Parker, Robert B.

Appaloosa. Robert B. Parker. G.P. Putnam's Sons, 2005. 288 p. (Virgil Cole and Everett Hitch, 1)
ISBN 9780399152771

1. United States deputy marshals 2. Wanderers and wandering 3. Honor in men 4. Ranchers 5. Male friendship 6. The West (United States) 7. Westerns 8. First person narratives 9. Books to movies

LC 2004058745

Arriving in a small nineteenth-century western town only to discover that its sheriff has been killed and its residents placed at the mercy of renegade rancher Randall Bregg, itinerant lawmen Virgil Cole and Everett Hitch find themselves facing an unusually challenging adversary who works by playing psychological games.

"The story gallops along to a surprise ending, but beneath the trappings of this gunfighter novel, Parker really has something to say about the nature of men and women in the Old West." —*Library Journal*

Blue-eyed devil. Robert B. Parker. G.P. Putnam's Sons, 2010. 288 p. (Virgil Cole and Everett Hitch, 4)
ISBN 9780399156489

1. Police chiefs 2. Police corruption 3. Protection racket 4. Honor in men 5. Gunfighters 6. The West (United States) 7. Westerns 8. First person narratives

Refusing recruitment by ambitious new chief Amos Callico, itinerant lawmen Virgil Cole and Everett Hitch protect local merchants who the chief is harassing for protection money, a situation that escalates to the shooting of a politically connected landowner's son.

"More shifting allegiances, moral dilemmas and characters capable of change than Virgil and Everett's fans may be used to. It's a shame that this youngest of the late Parker's franchises has to end so soon." —*Kirkus*

Death in paradise. Robert B. Parker. G.P. Putnam's Sons, 2001. 294 p. (Jesse Stone mysteries, 3)
ISBN 9780399147791

1. Police chiefs 2. Small town life 3. Teenage girl murder victims 4. Murder investigation 5. Former baseball players 6. Massachusetts 7. Mysteries 8. Hardboiled fiction

LC 2001031874

Jesse Stone, Chief of Police in the quiet New England town of Paradise, is enjoying a beer when he receives a call for help. The body of a teenage girl has been found in a nearby lake. Stone must figure out who would want to kill her, all the while fighting to keep his personal life in order as he struggles with alcoholism and strong feelings for his ex-wife.

Night passage. Robert B. Parker. G. P. Putnam's Sons, 1997. 322 p. (Jesse Stone mysteries, 1)

ISBN 9780399143045

1. Organized crime 2. Small town life 3. Police chiefs 4. Divorced men 5. Alcoholic men 6. Massachusetts 7. Mysteries 8. Hardboiled fiction

LC 97-6901

An otherwise washed-up LAPD cop with a drinking problem gets a job offer from a small Massachusetts town that is too good to be true, and Jesse Stone finds himself with no one to trust and a town full of moral and political corruption.

"This mystery features complex, expertly shaded relationships, especially romantic, as Jesse flails and fails at loving both his ex-wife and his new girlfriend. The most powerful romance here, though, is between Parker and the written word." —*Publishers Weekly*

Previous ed.: New York : G.P. Putnam's, 1997; Harpenden, Hertfordshire : No Exit Press, 1999.

Painted ladies. Robert B. Parker. G.P. Putnam's Sons, 2010. 304 p. (Spenser novels, 38)

ISBN 9780399156854

1. Private investigators 2. Art thefts 3. Bombing 4. Ransom 5. Secrets 6. Boston, Massachusetts 7. Massachusetts 8. Mysteries 9. Hardboiled fiction

LC 2010020027

Hired by a museum to provide protection during a ransom exchange for a stolen painting, Spenser is personally outraged when the ransom fails and the painting is not recovered, a case that makes him suspect the innocence of the art scholar who retained him.

"The focus on Susan comes at the expense of the plot, which, as Spenser novels go, is fairly pedestrian.... The story gives us extended looks at two of the most-beloved Spenser side characters, homicide Capt. Martin Quirk and Sgt. Frank Belson, as well as brief nods to many of the others who have stood at Spenser's side in the past Hawk, Vinnie, Chollo, Lee Farrell, Epstein, Tedy Sapp, the Grey Man. Mostly, though, what Painted Ladies gives us is Spenser being Spenser. And he couldn't do that without Susan." —*Chicago Sun-Times*

Sixkill. Robert B. Parker. G. P. Putnam's Sons, 2011. 304 p. (Spenser novels, 39)

ISBN 9780399157264

1. Private investigators 2. Murder investigation 3. Bodyguards 4. Actors and actresses 5. Women murder victims 6. Boston, Massachusetts 7. Massachusetts 8. Mysteries 9. Hardboiled fiction

LC 2010048041

When infamous actor Jumbo Nelson is accused of rape and murder, the Boston PD calls on Spenser to make heads or tails of the case. Although the evidence is mounting against Jumbo, Spenser makes a break when he teams up with Jumbo's bodyguard, Zebulon Sixkill, and uncovers some secrets involving the murder victim.

"The story has the depth of a puddle, but it's a well-designed puddle, so when it ripples, the clean, steady rolling of the waves is like a shimmering poem." —*Chicago Sun-Times*

Trouble in Paradise. Robert B. Parker. G. P. Putnam's Sons, 1998. 324 p. (Jesse Stone mysteries, 2)

ISBN 9780399144332

1. Police chiefs 2. Former convicts 3. Small town life 4. Man-woman relationships 5. Recovering alcoholics 6. Massachusetts 7. Mysteries 8. Hardboiled fiction

LC 987354

Jesse Stone, police chief of the Massachusetts coast town of Paradise, finds two of his lovers and an entire island threatened by a maniacal ex-convict BT

Parker, T. Jefferson

The **blue** hour. T. Jefferson Parker. Hyperion, 1999. 359 pages (Merci Rayborn mysteries, 1)

ISBN 9780786862887

1. Former police 2. People with cancer 3. Serial murderers 4. Policewomen 5. Women detectives 6. California 7. Southern California 8. Mysteries 9. Police procedurals

In a picturesque southern California beach community, a brutal serial killer is on the loose. His only victims are beautiful young women. His only adversaries are two cops haunted by problems of their own: the tough Tim Hess who is batting a life threatening illness, and the brash Merci Rayborn who has a rep for causing trouble. Now this unlikely team must put aside their personal issues to stop a ruthless madman before he strikes again.

"Solid police work, beefed up with some ingenious devices from Parker's bottomless bag of tricks, makes it all come out rightbut not before the wondrously weird characters have taken this lurid plot to its outer limits." —*New York Times Book Review*

Sequel: Red light.

L.A. outlaws: a novel. T. Jefferson Parker. Dutton, 2008. 372 p. (Charlie Hood thrillers, 1)

ISBN 9780525950554

1. Teachers 2. Criminals 3. Secret identity 4. Thieves 5. Police 6. California 7. Los Angeles, California 8. Thrillers and suspense

LC 2007033722

Investigating the latest crime scene of a celebrity thief who has been staging lucrative heists and donating the spoils to charity, rookie deputy Charlie Hood is forced to make an ethics-testing decision when the thief is targeted by a professional killer.

"Parker writes with an understanding of the West's essential character: in Outlaws, he casts Los Angeles as an eternally sprawling, brawling camp town, populated by bandits and bigots, the quick and the dead, where the poor who once rendered tallow now work the deep fryer at KFC.... His concise prose, at once low-key and lyrical, plays almost like cowboy poetry." —*Los Angeles Times*

Parker-Chan, Shelley

★ **She** who became the sun. Shelley Parker-Chan. Tor, 2021. 416 p. (Radiant emperor, 1)

ISBN 9781250621801

1. Fate and fatalism 2. Siblings 3. Determination (Personal quality) 4. Ambition 5. Gender identity 6. China 7. 14th century 8. Historical fantasy 9. Asian-influenced fantasy

LC 2021009142

LibraryReads Favorites, 2021

When the Zhu family's eighth-born son, Zhu Chongban, given the fate of greatness, dies during a brutal attack, his sister, escaping her own fated death, uses her brother's identity to claim another future altogether—her brother's abandoned greatness.

"Parker-Chan's fascinating debut, the first in the Radiant Emperor duology, gives the historical Red Turban Rebellion a grimdark fantasy twist." —*Publishers Weekly*

A Tom Doherty Associates book.

Parks, Brad

Closer than you know. Brad Parks. E.P. Dutton, 2018. 416 p.

ISBN 9781101985625

1. Foster care 2. Malicious accusation 3. Frameups 4. Cocaine 5. Rape victims 6. Virginia 7. Thrillers and suspense

Enduring a brutal foster-care upbringing, Melanie embarks on an adult life that she hopes will allow her to leave the past behind, only to be framed for drug charges that threaten her ability to keep her baby, a situation that is aided by an attorney who wants to solve the cold case of a serial rapist.

The **player:** a mystery. Brad Parks. Minotaur Books, 2014. 336 p. (Carter Ross mysteries, 5)
ISBN 9781250044082
1. Investigative journalism 2. Environmental protection 3. Organized crime 4. Ross, Carter (Fictitious character) 5. Diseases 6. Newark, New Jersey 7. New Jersey 8. Mysteries
LC 2013045900
Investigating an outbreak of a bizarre and occasionally fatal disease in a Newark neighborhood, investigative reporter Carter Ross contracts the illness himself before discovering mob ties to a local construction project.

Say nothing: a novel. Brad Parks. Dutton, 2017. 448 p.
ISBN 9781101985595
1. Extortion 2. Child kidnapping victims 3. Families of kidnapping victims 4. Trials 5. Judges 6. Legal thrillers 7. Thrillers and suspense 8. First person narratives 9. Adult books for young adults
LC 2016018767
Library Journal Best Books, 2017; LibraryReads Favorites, 2017
When their children are abducted by a man who blackmails them to follow instructions at the risk of the children's lives, a judge and his wife endure a terrorizing ordeal of no-holds-barred deceit and bond-breaking suspicions.
"The nerve-shredding never lets up for a minute as Parks picks you up by the scruff of the neck, shakes you vigorously, and repeats over and over again till a climax so harrowing that you'll be shaking with gratitude that it's finally over." —*Kirkus*

Parks, Gordon
★ The **learning** tree. Gordon Parks. Ballantine Books, 1989. 240 p.
ISBN 9780449215043
1. Growth (Psychology) 2. Teenage boys 3. Charles Edward 4. Racism 5. Murder witnesses 6. Kansas 7. African American fiction 8. Coming-of-age stories 9. Books to movies
A black youth in rural Kansas of the 1920's must make a difficult decision after he witnesses a murder.
The Learning Tree was closely adapted into a film of the same name, alternatively titled Learn, Baby, Learn in 1969.

Parmar, Priya
Vanessa and her sister. Priya Parmar. Ballantine Books, 2014. 368 p.
ISBN 9780804176378
1. Bell, Vanessa 2. Intellectual life 3. Sisters 4. Bloomsbury group 5. Artists 6. Authors 7. London, England 8. England 9. Edwardian era (1901-1914) 10. 1900s (Decade) 11. Biographical fiction 12. Historical fiction 13. Diary novels
LibraryReads Favorites, 2015; New York Times Notable Book, 2015
Set in early 1900s London, this historical novel examines the adult lives of sisters Virginia Woolf and Vanessa Bell, focusing on the controversial and popular circle of artists and writers known as the Bloomsbury Group.
"Parmar's novel sparkles, intrigues, and attracts, just as the Stephen sisters must have done in their time. It should inspire readers to revisit the works of the Bloomsbury crowd in a new light, especially Virginia Woolf's." —*Booklist*

Parnell, Sean
Left for dead. Sean Parnell. HarperCollins, 2021. 400 p. (Eric Steele novels, 4)
ISBN 9780062986610
1. Biological weapons 2. Coronaviruses 3. Women scientists 4. Biological terrorism 5. Elite operatives 6. Techno-thrillers 7. Thrillers and suspense
Back in action as a special operative for the Program, Eric Steele investigates the theft of a very dangerous, new Chinese bioweapon.
"Parnell creates real, compassionate characters and puts them into a well-developed story, and the Eric Steele series deserves all the recognition it has received. Readers of military thrillers should be encouraged to check it out." —*Booklist*

Man of war: an Eric Steele novel. Sean Parnell. William Morrow, 2018. 400 p. (Eric Steele novels, 1)
ISBN 9780062668783
1. Special forces 2. Intelligence officers 3. Nuclear weapons thefts 4. Intelligence service 5. Nuclear weapons 6. Techno-thrillers
LC 2017049082
An intelligence operative draws on the elite skills he learned as a Special Forces soldier when an adversary from his past steals a nuclear weapon.

Parris, S. J.
★ The **dead** of winter. S. J. Parris. Pegasus Crime, 2020. 352 p. (Giordano Bruno novels)
ISBN 9781643136547
1. Bruno, Giordano 2. Conspiracies 3. Autopsy 4. Secrecy 5. Churches 6. Pregnant women 7. England 8. 16th century 9. Historical mysteries 10. Mysteries 11. Biographical fiction
Naples, 1566. During a sweltering summer, eighteen-year-old Giordano Bruno takes his final vows at San Domenico Maggiore and is admitted to the Dominican Order—despite doubts over his tendency to ask difficult questions. Assisting in the infirmary, Bruno witnesses an illicit autopsy performed on the body of a young woman. Her corpse reveals a dark secret, and Bruno suspects that hers may not have been an accidental death.
"This is historical mystery at its absolute strongest, and quite possibly the best prequel ever in crime fiction." —*Booklist*

Sacrilege. S. J. Parris. Doubleday, 2012. 432 p. (Giordano Bruno novels, 3)
ISBN 9780385535472
1. Bruno, Giordano 2. Spies — History 3. Murder investigation 4. Cults 5. England 6. 16th century 7. Biographical fiction 8. Historical mysteries 9. Mysteries
Agreeing to help former paramour Sophia Underhill clear her name of a wrongful murder charge, 16th-century radical philosopher and spy Giordano Bruno uncovers secrets with ties to the cult of Thomas Becket and the legend surrounding the disappearance of the saint's body.

Treachery. S.J. Parris. Pegasus Books, 2019. 592 pages (Giordano Bruno novels, 4)
ISBN 9781643132242
1. Bruno, Giordano 2. Rulers 3. Conspiracies 4. Murder investigation 5. Secrecy 6. Spies 7. England 8. 16th century 9. Biographical fiction 10. Historical mysteries 11. Mysteries
When Sir Francis Drake's daring 1585 expedition against the Spanish is sabotaged by an on-board murder, Giordano Bruno uncovers multiple deadly plots in Plymouth's murky underworld.
"Fans of the series will relish the violent and suspenseful adventures; believable relationships, both personal and political; and, especially, the

author s skillful and unobtrusive re-creation of the historical period, filth and all." —*Booklist*

Originally published: Toronto, Ontario : Doubleday Canada, 2014.

Parrish, Christa

Still life. Christa Parrish. Thomas Nelson, 2015. 352 p.
ISBN 9781401689032
1. Newlyweds 2. Married women 3. Airplane accidents 4. Life change events 5. Female friendship 6. Relationship fiction 7. Christian fiction
LC 2014029129

Five months after leaving her family's fringe religious sect to elope with a mysterious stranger, Ada is left widowed in a strange world, while Katherine struggles with a loveless marriage just as an artistic young man brings the two women together.

Parrish, Roan

Better than people. Roan Parrish. Carina Adores, 2020. 256 p. (Garnet Run, 1)
ISBN 9781335542823
1. Gay men 2. Pet owners 3. Children's book illustrators 4. Grouches 5. Graphic designers 6. Wyoming 7. Contemporary romances 8. LGBTQIA romances

Simon Burke has always preferred animals to people. When the countdown to adopting his own dog is unexpectedly put on hold, Simon turns to the PetShare app to find the fluffy TLC he's been missing. Meeting a grumpy children's book illustrator who needs a dog walker isn't easy for the man whose persistent anxiety has colored his whole life, but Jack Matheson's menagerie is just what Simon needs. Four dogs, three cats and counting. Jack's pack of rescue pets is the only company he needs. But when a bad fall leaves him with a broken leg, Jack is forced to admit he needs help. That the help comes in the form of the most beautiful man he's ever seen is a complicated, glorious surprise.

"Parrish nails both the throat-closing hell of Simon's anxiety disorder and his palpable desire to have a healthy relationship, as well as Jack's frustration at not always being able to soothe Simon's fears. Superb supporting characters—especially Simon's firecracker of a grandmother, Jean, and Jack's doting older brother, Charlie—add considerable charm. This sensitive tale will leave readers with big smiles on their faces." —*Publishers Weekly*

Parry, Ambrose

The **way** of all flesh. Ambrose Parry. Canongate, 2018. 407 pages; (Way of all flesh, 1)
ISBN 9781786893789
1. Medical students 2. Housekeepers 3. Social classes 4. Women murder victims 5. Physicians 6. Edinburgh, Scotland 7. Scotland 8. Victorian era (1837-1901) 9. 1840s 10. Victorian mysteries 11. Historical mysteries
LC Bl2018182031

An apprentice to a mid-19th-century anesthesia pioneer unexpectedly partners with a quick-witted housemaid in order to survive an investigation in the Edinburgh underworld to solve a string of grisly deaths.

"Parry provides a fascinating look at how medicine was practiced at a period when anesthetics were still not widely used or understood, as well as certain things that have changed little over time: mansplaining, the subservience expected of women of any social class, and religious leaders demanding their God-given right to control reproductive health." —*Publishers Weekly*

Parry, H. G.

A **declaration** of the rights of magicians. H. G. Parry. Orbit, 2020. 544 p. (Shadow histories, 1)
ISBN 9780316459082
1. Enlightenment (European intellectual movement) 2. Magic 3. Freedom 4. Slavery 5. Insurgency 6. 17th century 7. Historical fantasy 8. Alternate histories 9. New Zealand fiction

It is the Age of Enlightenment—of new and magical political movements. But amidst all of the upheaval of the early modern world, there is an unknown force inciting all of human civilization into violent conflict. And it will require the combined efforts of revolutionaries, magicians, and abolitionists to unmask this hidden enemy before the whole world falls to darkness and chaos.

"Give this alternative history to fans of Naomi Novik's Temeraire series and fans of Susanna Clark's Jonathan Strange & Mr Norrell (2004), as well as to historical fiction fans willing to embrace a little magic. Impeccably researched and epically written, this novel is a stellar start to what promises to be a grand new fantasy series." —*Booklist*

The **unlikely** escape of Uriah Heep. H. G. Parry. Redhook Books/Orbit, 2019. 456 p.
ISBN 9780316452717
1. Characters and characteristics in literature 2. Superhuman abilities 3. Brothers 4. Family secrets 5. Books and reading 6. Contemporary fantasy 7. Fantasy fiction 8. New Zealand fiction
LC 2019000762

A young scholar with a secret uncontrollable magical ability to bring literary characters into the world is overseen by a protective older sibling before an unknown stranger unleashes literary characters throughout their city.

"Fun, witty, and full of insights about the powerful effect of stories on our lives, this book is highly recommended. Give it to readers who devoured Jasper Fforde, Jim C. Hines' Libriomancer (2012), and Genevieve Cogman's The Invisible Library (2016), and to readers looking for adventurous fantasy with a soupcon of family drama." —*Booklist*

Pastan, Rachel

In the field. Rachel Pastan. Delphinium Books, 2021. 240 p.
ISBN 9781953002037
1. Women scientists 2. College students 3. Genetics 4. Corn 5. Lesbians 6. Historical fiction 7. Relationship fiction 8. LGBTQIA fiction

Inspired by the life of the scientist who won the Nobel Price in 1983, follows Kate Croft who attends college in 1920 and, confused by her own sexuality, finds refuge in the rationality of biology and genetics.

"Untold-until-now tales of trailblazing women in the sciences capture the popular imagination, and Pastan's novel about determined geneticist Kate Croft is a worthy addition to this compelling and inspiring trend." —*Booklist*

Pasternak, Boris Leonidovich

★ **Doctor** Zhivago. Boris Pasternak; translation by Max Hayward and Manya Harrari. Pantheon Books, 1991. Xxiii, 558 p.
ISBN 9780679774389
1. Physicians 2. Poets, Russian 3. Churchill, Winston, 1874-1965 4. Civil war 5. Idealism in men 6. Russia 7. Soviet Union 8. Russian Revolution and Civil War (1917-1921) 9. Love stories 10. Translations 11. Books to movies
LC 58008005

Epic novel of post-revolutionary Russia focuses on the torments and dreams of a doctor-poet who attempts to avoid the struggles of his turbulent era.

The poems of Yurii Zhivago" translated by Bernard Guilbert Guerney.
Originally published in English: London : Collins, 1958.
Originally published: Milan : Feltrinelli, 1957.

Patchett, Ann

★ **Bel** canto: a novel. Ann Patchett. HarperCollins, 2001. 304 p.
ISBN 9780060188733
1. Hostages 2. Victims of terrorism 3. Diplomats 4. Women opera singers 5. Singing 6. South America 7. Psychological fiction 8. Literary fiction 9. Books to movies

LC 53671

Book Sense Book of the Year Paperback, 2003; Orange Prize for Fiction, 2002; PEN-Faulkner Award, 2002; Shortlisted for the International IMPAC Dublin Literary Award, 2003; National Book Critics Circle Award for Fiction finalist, 2001

When terrorists seize hostages at an embassy party, an unlikely assortment of people is thrown together, including American opera star Roxanne Coss, and Mr. Hosokawa—a Japanese CEO and her biggest fan.

"An impoverished South American country hosts a birthday extravaganza for a Japanese industrialist in the hope of securing new foreign investment. The lure? An internationally renowned lyric soprano. Indeed, when Roxane Coss sings, even the ragtag terrorists who are about to flood through the air-conditioning vents and take the guests hostage hold their breath, transported by the beauty of her voice. Patchett's tragicomic novela fantasia of guns and Puccini and Red Cross negotiations invokes the glorious, unreliable promises of art, politics, and love." —*The New Yorker*

★ **Commonwealth**. Ann Patchett. HarperCollins, 2016. 322 p.
ISBN 9780062491794
1. Extramarital affairs 2. Stepsiblings 3. Blended families 4. Family secrets 5. Family history 6. Byron, George Gordon Byron 7. Virginia 8. Family sagas 9. Multiple perspectives
Australian Book Industry Awards, International Book of the Year, 2017; LibraryReads Favorites, 2016; New York Times Notable Book, 2016; National Book Critics Circle Award for Fiction finalist, 2016

A five-decade saga tracing the impact of an act of infidelity on the parents and children of two Southern California families traces their shared summers in Virginia and the disillusionment that shapes their lasting bond.

"A satisfying meat-and-potatoes domestic novel from one of our finest writers." —*Kirkus*

★ The **Dutch** house: a novel. Ann Patchett. Harper, 2019. 352 pages
ISBN 9780062963673
1. Houses 2. Siblings 3. Family relationships 4. Mother-deserted children 5. Stepmothers 6. Philadelphia, Pennsylvania 7. Pennsylvania 8. Literary fiction 9. Family sagas 10. Coming-of-age stories

LC 2019024072

LibraryReads Favorites, 2019; New York Times Notable Book, 2019; Pulitzer Prize for Fiction finalist, 2020

A tale set over the course of five decades traces a young man's rise from poverty to wealth and back again as his prospects center around his family's lavish Philadelphia estate.

Run. Ann Patchett. Harper Collins Publishers, 2007. 304 p.
ISBN 9780061340635
1. Families 2. Adopted children 3. Adoptees 4. Protectiveness in men 5. Rich families 6. Boston, Massachusetts 7. Massachusetts 8. Domestic fiction 9. Psychological fiction

LC 2006041297

Bernadette and Bernard Doyle share a great love for family. Already blessed with a son, they adopt two black children, Teddy and Tip. Even after Bernadette dies, she continues to exert a profound influence over the family. And then Tip is pushed out of a car's path in a sudden act of heroism, and lives are bound by this selfless act.

"Ms. Patchett gives her readers much to contemplate when genetics, privilege, opportunity and nurture come into play. And to her credit she is neither vague nor reductive about any of these things; she creates a genuinely rich landscape of human possibility." —*New York Times*

★ **State** of wonder: a novel. Ann Patchett. Harper, 2011. 353 p.
ISBN 9780062049803
1. Change (Psychology) 2. Kinship-based society 3. Transformations, Personal 4. Fertility drugs 5. Pharmaceutical research 6. Amazon Valley 7. Psychological fiction

LC 2010029229

Shortlisted for The Orange Prize for Fiction, 2012

A researcher at a pharmaceutical company, Marina Singh journeys into the heart of the Amazonian delta to check on a field team that has been silent for two years—a dangerous assignment that forces Marina to confront the ghosts of her past.

"The book's dreamlike claustrophobia weaves a spell even when far-fetched plot twists tip toward absurdity. Though it ultimately can't match the subtler pleasures of Patchett's previous voyage to South America, 2001's gorgeous Bel Canto, it's still a trip well worth taking." —*Entertainment Weekly*

Paton, Alan

Ah, but your land is beautiful. Alan Paton. Scribner, 1982. 271 p.
ISBN 9780684173368
1. Astaire, Fred 2. Anti-apartheid movements 3. Race relations 4. Political parties — History 5. South Africa 6. 1950s 7. 1960s 8. Political fiction 9. Historical fiction 10. Multiple perspectives

LC 81013547

Dramatizes the public and private lives of contemporary South Africa, tracing the multifarious reactions of the human spirit to life in a racially divided society and perceptively sketching heroes, victims, and the self-absorbed ordinary citizen

"Alan Paton's considerable practical life in South Africa aside, his place in the literature of social protest has been secured by his steady devotion to the ideal of the empathetic imagination in fiction." —*New York Times Book Review*

★ **Cry,** the beloved country. Alan Paton. Scribner Classics, 2003. 316 p.
ISBN 9780743261951
1. Apartheid 2. Race relations 3. South Africans 4. Fathers and sons 5. Clergymen 6. South Africa 7. 1940s 8. Political fiction 9. Literary fiction 10. Books to movies

LC 86009674

A novel depicting the racial ferment in the beautiful country of South Africa in 1948.
Originally published: New York : C. Scribner's and Sons, 1948.

Too late the phalarope. Alan Paton. Scribner, 1995. 253 p.
ISBN 9780684818955
1. Racism 2. Police 3. Race relations 4. Apartheid 5. South Africa 6. Political fiction

Portrays a police lieutenant's struggle with his conscience when he violates a strict South African law concerning relationships between Blacks and whites

"The book is written with superb simplicity. It is cadenced but unaffected; it will inevitably be called Biblical and yet there is no conscious parodying of scriptural prose. It flows relentlessly to its crisis, and sometimes we cry out at its power. The people are all clear and real, the South African backgrounds are colorfully and deeply etched. The conflicts are diverse but they all contribute to the basic struggle; father and son, races, languages, prejudices." —*Christian Science Monitor*

Originally published: J. Cape, 1953.

Patrick, Phaedra

★ The **secrets** of love story bridge. Phaedra Patrick. Park Row, 2020. 352 pages

ISBN 9780778309789

1. Single fathers 2. Missing women 3. Second chances 4. Locks and keys 5. Bridges 6. England 7. Relationship fiction

A single father's brave act of saving a woman's life sparks an unexpected journey that helps him find a second chance at love.

"Patrick blends romance, mystery, and quirkiness to highly entertaining effect." —*Booklist*

Patterson, James

1st to die: a novel. By James Patterson. Little Brown, 2001. 424 pages (Women's Murder Club, 1)

ISBN 9780316666008

1. Women detectives 2. Women coroners 3. Serial murderers 4. Female friendship 5. Serial murders 6. San Francisco, California 7. Mysteries 8. Books to movies

LC 61123

Four women friends—a homicide detective, a medical examiner, an assistant DA, and a crime desk reporter—form a Women's Murder Club to stop a killer who has been stalking newlyweds in San Francisco.

"The story opens in San Francisco with the gruesome murder of a bride and groom on their wedding night. Detective Lindsay Boxer is called to the scene, just after learning she is suffering from a rare and potentially life-threatening blood disease. For help with the case, she calls on her best friend, Claire, a medical examiner, and, reluctantly at first, Cindy, a newspaper reporter who is covering the story.... Patterson keeps up the suspense until the very last page." —*Booklist*

★ **Along** came a spider: a novel. James Patterson. Little, Brown 1993. 435 p. (Alex Cross novels, 1)

ISBN 9780446364195

1. African American men 2. Kidnapping 3. Murder investigation 4. Men with dissociative identity disorder 5. Murder investigation 6. Washington, D.C. 7. Thrillers and suspense 8. Books to movies

LC 92024581

Washington, D.C, police detective Alex Cross becomes caught up in a kidnapping case that may involve Gary Soneji, a teacher at an elite private school who is also a schizophrenic psychopath and serial murderer.

"Patterson's storytelling talent is in top form in this grisly escapist yarn." —*Library Journal*

Kiss the girls: a novel. James Patterson. Little, Brown, 1995. 451 p. (Alex Cross novels, 2)

ISBN 9780316693707

1. Serial murderers 2. African American men 3. Police psychologists 4. Missing teenage girls 5. African American psychologists 6. North Carolina 7. Washington, D.C. 8. Thrillers and suspense 9. Books to movies

LC 94014177

As two serial killers terrorize different regions of America, the FBI begins to suspect that the two are competing with each other, and Washington, D.C, police detective Alex Cross embarks on a personal quest to find the perpetrators.

★ **Private**. James Patterson and Maxine Paetro. Little, Brown and Co, 2010. 400 p. (Private Detective Agency novels, 1)

ISBN 9780316096157

1. Scandals 2. Cold cases (Criminal investigation) 3. Murder investigation 4. Crimes against girls 5. Revenge 6. California 7. Thrillers and suspense

LC 2009052188

Former CIA agent Jack Morgan inherits his father's elite Los Angeles detective agency and along with it such cases as an NFL gambling scandal, eighteen unsolved schoolgirl slayings, and the murder of his best friend's wife.

Patterson, Molly

Rebellion. Molly Patterson. Harper, 2017. 548 p.

ISBN 9780062574046

1. Missionaries 2. Sisters 3. Married women 4. Widows 5. Extramarital affairs 6. China 7. United States 8. 1890s 9. 1950s 10. Historical fiction 11. Family sagas

A mid-20th-century widow struggles to manage her farm and raise her children while reflecting on the intertwined experiences of her farm wife mother, her missionary aunt and a Chinese student whose lives were shaped by the Boxer Rebellion.

Patterson, Richard North

Balance of power. Richard North Patterson. Ballantine Books, 2003. 624 pages (Kerry Kilcannon trilogy, 3)

ISBN 9780345450173

1. Gun control 2. Presidents 3. Family violence 4. Kilcannon, Kerry (Fictitious character) 5. Presidents' spouses 6. Washington, D.C. 7. United States 8. Political thrillers 9. Thrillers and suspense 10. Legal thrillers 11. Adult books for young adults

LC 2003051848

The marriage of President Kerry Kilcannon and TV journalist Lara Costello is marred by a massacre of innocent civilians by gunfire, setting in motion events that reveal the hidden connections among guns, money, and power in Washington.

"This complex novel has a fascinating debate at its heart. To his credit, Patterson has done his research, and though it's clear which side he's on, he does a good job of presenting all the arguments." —*Booklist*

Dark lady. Richard North Patterson. Alfred A. Knopf 1999. 371 p.

ISBN 9780679450436

1. Political corruption 2. Cities and towns 3. Ruthlessness in women 4. Murder 5. Greed 6. Middle West 7. Thrillers and suspense 8. Legal thrillers

LC 99023565

Two prominent men are found dead in Steelton, a small town struggling with an economic turnaround. Enter Assistant County Prosecutor Stella Marz, referred to as Dark Lady by her fellow lawyers. As she makes her way through the maze of corruption, deceit, and greed to get at the truth behind these murders, Stella comes to believe that the history of the small town is involved and may threaten her own life.

"Patterson is familiar with the civic shenanigans that can destroy a community, and he draws wisely on the history and geography of Cleveland to portray a city struggling to escape its bondage to organized crime, racial conflict and the entrenched corruption of its elected officials." —*New York Times Book Review*

Eclipse. Richard North Patterson. Henry Holt & Co, 2009. 384 p.

ISBN 9780805087727

1. Lawyers 2. Oil 3. Frameups 4. Murder 5. Divorced men 6. West Africa 7. San Francisco, California 8. Thrillers and suspense 9. Legal thrillers

LC 2008017386

An American lawyer takes on a nearly impossible case—the defense of an African freedom fighter against his corrupt government's charge of murdering three PetroGlobal workers.

"Eclipse aspires to be any number of books: a novel of political intrigue, an international conspiracy thriller, a courtroom drama, a romance, even a straightforward murder mystery.... To Patterson's credit, the novel succeeds on all counts." —*Washington Post Book World.*

No safe place. Richard North Patterson. Alfred A. Knopf, 1998. 497 pages (Kerry Kilcannon trilogy, 1)

ISBN 9780679450429

1. Scandals 2. Pro-life Movement 3. Presidential candidates 4. Legislators 5. Kilcannon, Kerry (Fictitious character) 6. California 7. Political thrillers 8. Thrillers and suspense

LC 9814573

As Senator Kerry Kilcannon campaigns in the California presidential primary, he struggles to cope with memories of his older brother's assassination during his own run for the nomination twelve years before and becomes the target of a deranged anti-abortion activist on the ultimate mission BT

"The main character, Kerry Kilcannon, is an Irish Catholic U.S. senator, reminiscent of the Kennedy brothers. Embroiled in a close campaign with the vice president for the Democratic presidential nomination, Kilcannon struggles to maintain his honesty and upright values in a sleazy world where everything depends on image and the proper spin. At the same time, a militant right-to-lifer vows to kill Kilcannon for his pro-choice stance on abortion. Throughout the constant twists and turns of the plot, Patterson builds realistic supporting characters and brings to life the surrealistic world of a presidential campaign." —*Library Journal*

Protect and defend. Richard North Patterson. Knopf 2000. 544 pages (Kerry Kilcannon trilogy, 2)

ISBN 9780679450443

1. Pro-life movement 2. Presidents 3. Abortion 4. Kilcannon, Kerry (Fictitious character) 5. Women lawyers 6. Washington, D.C. 7. United States 8. Thrillers and suspense 9. Political thrillers 10. Adult books for young adults

In San Francisco, a fifteen-year-old girl wants to sue for permission to have a late-term abortion over the opposition of her pro-life parents. In Washington, the President is about to nominate a woman as the next Chief Justice. She's shadowed by a personal secret. But the politics and medical dilemmas of abortion threatens to tear both women and the nation apart.

"Patterson skillfully juggles a large cast of characters and controversies." —*School Library Journal*

Pattison, Eliot

Bones of the earth: an Inspector Shan Tao Yun mystery. Eliot Pattison. Minotaur Books, 2019. 320 p. (Shan Tao Yun mysteries, 10)

ISBN 9781250169686

1. Corruption 2. Secrecy in government 3. Archaeological sites 4. Justice 5. Military occupation 6. Tibet 7. China 8. Mysteries

LC 2018050880

Bones of the Earth is Edgar Award-winning author Eliot Pattison's much anticipated tenth and final installment in the internationally acclaimed Inspector Shan series.

"Pattison's tenth and final Inspector Shan novel is a pitch-perfect series ending, leaving readers with a satisfying last look at the scrupulously ethical investigator as well as further insight into a recent era of Asian history little known in the West." —*Kirkus*

The **skull** mantra. Eliot Pattison. St. Martin's Minotaur, 1999. 403 p. (Shan Tao Yun mysteries, 1)

ISBN 9780312204785

1. Conspiracies 2. Murder investigation 3. Political prisoners 4. Forced labor 5. Former police 6. Himalaya Mountains region 7. Tibet 8. Mysteries

Edgar Allan Poe Award for Best First Mystery Novel, 2000

When a headless corpse turns up on a Tibetan mountainside, inspector Shan Tao Yun is released from prison to investigate the crime, and he quickly uncovers a conspiracy involving American mining interests, corrupt Party officials, and Tibetan sorcerers.

"Set against a background that is alternately bleak and blazingly beautiful, this is at once a topnotch thriller and a substantive look at Tibet under siege." —*Publishers Weekly*

Paul, Gill

★ The **lost** daughter. Gill Paul. William Morrow & Company, 2019. 469 p.

ISBN 9780062843272

1. Maria Nikolaevna 2. Princesses 3. Exile (Punishment) 4. Family relationships 5. Man-woman relationships 6. Family secrets 7. Soviet Union 8. 20th century 9. Historical fiction 10. Biographical fiction 11. Parallel narratives

LC 2018059051

Heartbreaking and gripping novel of a Russian princess and a journey to solve a mystery that might change everything we know about the tragic Romanov family.

Pava, Sergio de la

Lost empress: a novel. Sergio De La Pava. Pantheon, 2018. 623 p.

ISBN 9781524747220

1. Football teams 2. Women business owners 3. Criminal justice system 4. Football team owners 5. Inheritance and succession 6. Satirical fiction 7. Literary fiction

LC 2017049323

Shocked when her brother inherits their father's NFL team in spite of her pivotal role in building the family dynasty, Nina takes over a small indoor football franchise and resolves to take the NFL by storm, an ambition that is challenged by a criminal mastermind who prepares to commit an audacious act.

A **naked** singularity. By Sergio de la Pava. University of Chicago Press, 2012. 696 p.

ISBN 9780226141794

1. Children of immigrants 2. Public defenders 3. Judicial system 4. Existentialism 5. Lawyers 6. New York City 7. Experimental fiction 8. Satirical fiction 9. Books to movies

Casi, the child of Colombian immigrants, lives in Brooklyn but works in Manhattan as a public defender. Casi has never lost a trial, but then his world ruptures when a case goes bad. Increasingly disillusioned, the young lawyer finds himself involved in a scheme that might be the perfect crime—or his undoing.

Made into a movie of the same name, 2021.

Originally self-published in 2008.

Personae: a novel. Sergio De La Pava. University of Chicago Press, 2013. 201 p.

ISBN 9780226078991

1. Detectives 2. Fate and fatalism 3. Ideas (Philosophy) 4. Women detectives 5. College teachers 6. Literary fiction 7. Experimental fiction 8. Mysteries

LC 2013016557

"Game readers should have as much fun with this clever experiment as the author seems to have had inventing it, and be challenged by his more serious and troubling questions." —*Publishers Weekly*

Pavone, Chris

★ The **expats**: a novel. Chris Pavone. Crown, 2012. 336 p. (Kate Moore novels, 1)

ISBN 9780307956354

1. Former CIA agents 2. Secrets 3. Married people 4. Deception 5. FBI agents 6. Luxembourg 7. Spy fiction 8. Thrillers and suspense

LC 2011046207

Anthony Award for Best First Novel, 2013; Edgar Allan Poe Award for Best First Novel by an American Author, 2013

An international spy thriller about a former CIA agent who moves with her family to Luxembourg where everything is suspicious and nothing is as it seems.

The **Paris** diversion: a novel. Chris Pavone. Crown Publishing, 2019. 373 pages : Illustration (Kate Moore novels, 2)

ISBN 9781524761509

1. Former CIA agents 2. Terrorism 3. Suicide bombers 4. Deception 5. Undercover operations 6. Paris, France 7. Spy fiction 8. Thrillers and suspense 9. Multiple perspectives

Loan Stars Favourites, 2019

Kate Moore partners with a French agent to investigate a bombing threat in Paris, a race against time that is complicated by her husband's missing nemesis and a suspicious absence of orders from Langley.

"Pavone gives us a fresh, pulsating, and introspective thriller that delivers on its tourist-heavy Parisian setting and expands and connects territory from his previous novels." —*Library Journal*

Sequel to: The expats.

Pawel, Rebecca

Death of a nationalist. Rebecca Pawel. Soho Press, 2003. 262 p; (Carlos Tejada Alonso y Leon investigations, 1)

ISBN 9781569473047

1. Police 2. Men 3. Postwar life 4. Tejada Alonso y Leon, Carlos (Fictitious character) 5. Nationalists 6. Madrid, Spain 7. Spain 8. 1930s 9. Historical mysteries 10. Police procedurals 11. Mysteries

LC 2002026921

Edgar Allan Poe Award for Best First Mystery Novel, 2004

"Madrid in 1939 is filled with bomb craters, desecrated churches and nearly abandoned streets, while black markets are just about the only markets with anything to sell. The hatreds and atrocities shared by the Nationalists (supported by the Communists) still simmer and erupt in sporadic violence. The Guardia Civil has the responsibility to maintain authority—and their enthusiasm and ruthlessnesss for enforcing order terrorizes the citizens. The intertwined fates of Sergeant Tejada Alonzo Leon of the Guardia Civil and that of Gonzalo Llorente, a wounded Republican in hiding are handled with unusual skill and subtlety." —*Publishers Weekly*

Peace, David

Occupied city. David Peace. Alfred A. Knopf, 2010. 288 p. (Tokyo trilogy, 2)

ISBN 9780307263759

1. Massacres 2. Bank robberies 3. Mass murder investigation 4. Murder suspects 5. Biological warfare 6. Japan 7. Tokyo, Japan 8. 1940s 9. Noir fiction 10. Literary fiction

LC 2009043254

Booklist Editors' Choice, 2010

A tale inspired by a true story follows the murder of a dozen people in 1948 Tokyo by a man who claimed he was providing government-directed medical care, an event recounted from the disparate perspectives of the victims.

"Powerful and ambitious, this British import is deepened by a multiperspective, Rashomon-like approach. But reader be warned: The immensely talented Peace...is not in the business of making his work easy." —*Kirkus*

Originally published: London : Faber and Faber, 2009.

Pearl, Matthew

The **Dante** chamber. Matthew Pearl. Penguin Press, 2018. 368 p. (Dante Club novels (Matthew Pearl), 2)

ISBN 9781594204937

1. Dante Alighieri 2. Authors, English 3. Amateur detectives 4. Poets, English 5. Women poets 6. Serial murder investigation 7. London, England 8. 1870s 9. Historical mysteries

LC 2018006196

Poets Robert Browning and Alfred Tennyson team up to decode literary clues after a murder victim is discovered in a London park with a verse from the Divine Comedy around his neck.

Sequel to: The Dante Club.

The **Dante** Club: a novel. Matthew Pearl. Random House, 2003. 384 p. (Dante Club novels (Matthew Pearl), 1)

ISBN 9780375505294

1. Dante Alighieri 2. Authors 3. Banned books 4. Serial murder investigation 5. Censorship 6. Book clubs 7. Boston, Massachusetts 8. Cambridge, Massachusetts 9. 1860s 10. Historical mysteries 11. Mysteries

LC 2002017886

In 1865, the preparations of the Dante Club—led by Henry Wadsworth Longfellow and Oliver Wendell Holmes—to release the first translation of Dante's "The Divine Comedy" are threatened by a series of murders that re-create episodes from "Inferno.

"A literary thriller about a serial murderer who draws gory inspiration from the torments of Dante's Inferno.... The author sets this novel in Boston in 1865, when Henry Wadsworth Longfellow, James Russell Lowell, and Oliver Wendell Holmes were translating Dante into English. As they work through the cantos, the Dante-inspired corpses arrive on cue, and the versifiers must turn detective." —*The New Yorker*

Sequel: The Dante chamber, Penguin, 2018.

The **last** Dickens: a novel. Matthew Pearl. Random House, 2009. 400 p.

ISBN 9781400066568

1. Osgood, James R. 2. Publishers and publishing 3. Authors — Death 4. London, England 5. 19th century 6. Historical mysteries 7. Mysteries 8. Adult books for young adults

LC 2008046962

The news of the untimely death of Charles Dickens reaches his American publisher. James R Osgood, a junior partner there, suspicious of unscrupulous New York publishers and their ruthless agents intent on stealing Dickens' last novel "The Mystery of Edwin Drood, Osgood sends his trusted young clerk, Daniel Sands, to await its arrival.

"Pearl is too smart to hinge his plot on mere publishing rights. Like Dickens, he finds compelling stories in every social stratum, viewing the downtrodden with sympathy and the upper crust with a gimlet eye." —*New York Daily News*

The **Poe** shadow: a novel. Pearl Matthew. Random House, 2006. 384 p.
ISBN 9781400061037
1. Poe, Edgar Allan 2. Authors, American 3. Fanaticism 4. Lawyers 5. Death 6. Impostors 7. Virginia 8. Baltimore, Maryland 9. 1840s 10. Historical mysteries 11. Mysteries
LC 2005057998
In 1849, the body of Edgar Allan Poe has been buried in an unmarked grave in Baltimore. Concluded by everyone as a second-rate writer who met a disgraceful end, one lone admirer, Quentin Clark, puts his own career and reputation at risk in a crusade to salvage Poe's. Quentin soon finds himself enmeshed in sinister machinations involving international political agents and the lost secrets of Poe's final hours, and must himself turn master investigator to escape Poe's grisly fate.

The **technologists:** a novel. Matthew Pearl. Random House, 2012. 480 p.
ISBN 9781400066575
1. College students 2. Paranormal phenomena 3. Scholars and academics 4. Secret societies 5. Civil war veterans 6. Boston, Massachusetts 7. Cambridge, Massachusetts 8. 1860s 9. 19th century 10. Historical mysteries 11. Mysteries
LC 2011014628
Massachusetts Book Awards, Fiction Award, 2013
The first graduating class at the Massachusetts Institute of Technology is thrown into turmoil by bizarre phenomena that cause instruments to inexplicably spin out of control, challenging enterprising students to protect lives while combating Harvard rivals.

Pearlman, Edith

Binocular vision: new & selected stories. Edith Pearlman. Lookout Books/University of North Carolina Wilmington, 2011. 392 p.
ISBN 9780982338292
1. New England 2. Short stories 3. Literary fiction
LC 2010033376
Edward Lewis Wallant Award, 2011; National Book Critics Circle Award for Fiction, 2011; National Book Award for Fiction finalist, 2011
Presents a collection of short stories that focus on the trials and tribulations of a group of Northeasterners.
"Short stories are like miniatures: A delicate touch makes all the difference. In Edith Pearlman's world, that light hand means choosing the perfect phrase to capture a moment or a mood. Often it leaves the reader breathless. In Binocular Vision, a hefty collection of 34 stories, including 13 new ones,...Pearlman shows her unerring sense for the right words.... Set all over the world, in different times during the last hundred years, and involving characters of all ages, these tales focus on the precise pivotal moments when life changes often for the worse. Death and dying are common themes, while ill-fated liaisons, frequently involving incest, occur with regularity." —*Boston Globe*

Honeydew: stories. Edith Pearlman. Little Brown & Co, 2015. 279 p.
ISBN 9780316297226
1. Misfits (Persons) 2. Interpersonal relations 3. Loss (Psychology) 4. Identity (Psychology) 5. Teenage drug abusers 6. Literary fiction 7. Short stories
New York Times Notable Book, 2015; Booklist Editors' Choice, 2015
This new collection of short stories from the National Book Critics Circle Award-winning author of Binocular Vision, who describes tales full of teenage drug use, anorexia, cruise-ship stowaways and a widowed nail tech who finds herself falling for a client.

"Ovid is a subtle influence throughout, as Pearlman imagines gentle metamorphoses catalyzed by longing, as in the ravishing title story about the headmistress of a private girls' day school and an anorexic, ant-loving student. Pearlman not only writes with bewitching clarity, she also fathoms much about our inner lives and relationships that is unexpectedly wondrous." —*Booklist*

Pears, Iain

Death and restoration. Iain Pears. Scribner, 1996. 223 p. (Jonathan Argyll and Flavia DiStefano mysteries, 6)
ISBN 9780684814612
1. Caravaggio, Michelangelo Merisi da 2. Art historians 3. Art thefts 4. Monasteries 5. Argyll, Jonathan (Fictitious character) 6. Di Stefano, Flavia (Fictitious character) 7. Rome, Italy 8. Mysteries
LC 97-39932
A tale of intrigue and murder set in the heart of Italy's art world pits Jonathan Argyll and art squad investigator Flavia de Stefano against a wily band of thieves that steals a painting reputed to have miraculous powers.
Sequel to: Giotto's hand.
Sequel: The immaculate deception.

The **dream** of Scipio. Iain Pears. G. P. Putnam's Sons, 2002. 608 p.
ISBN 9781573222020
1. World War II 2. Black Death 3. Nazi collaborators 4. Aristocracy 5. Cardinals 6. Provence, France 7. Rome 8. Roman Empire (27 BCE-476 CE) 9. Medieval period (476-1492) 10. Historical fiction 11. Love stories 12. Parallel narratives
Booklist Editors' Choice, 2002
An ancient manuscript called "The Dream of Scipio" links three separate centuries—the fifth, the end of the Roman Empire; the fourteenth, the time of the Black Death; and the twentieth during World War II—and three stories of love, all set in Provence.
"Pears builds a multilayered tale of moral choice, love, danger and loss. Like an archaeologist, he uncovers worlds beneath worlds in a few square miles of Provencal earth." —*New York Times Book Review*

The **immaculate** deception. Iain Pears. Scribner, 2000. 221 p. (Jonathan Argyll and Flavia DiStefano mysteries, 7)
ISBN 9780743212571
1. Art historians 2. Art thefts 3. Murder investigation 4. Argyll, Jonathan (Fictitious character) 5. Di Stefano, Flavia (Fictitious character) 6. Rome, Italy 7. Italy 8. Mysteries
Flavia di Stefano, the acting head of Italy's Art Theft Squad, attempts to track down the thief who stole a politically sensitive painting on loan from a foreign museum, a search that soon becomes a hunt for a killer.
Sequel to: Death and restoration.

An **instance** of the fingerpost. Iain Pears. Riverhead Books, 1998. 691 p.
ISBN 9781573220828
1. Murder 2. Italians in England 3. Physicians 4. Mathematicians 5. Students 6. Oxford, England 7. Great Britain 8. Restoration England (1660-1688) 9. 17th century 10. Historical mysteries 11. Multiple perspectives 12. First person narratives
LC 9723899
Booklist Editors' Choice, 1998; New York Times Notable Book, 1998
In the 1660s, as Charles II and the Church of England try to quell residual opposition, Robert Grove, fellow of New College, is murdered, and four different people give their versions of the incident.
"Robert Boyle, the devout chemist, and John Thurloe, Cromwell's inscrutable spymaster, are among the historical characters who figure in this richly imagined mystery set in Oxford in the sixteen-sixties, after Charles

II has been restored to the throne. A Fellow of New College is found dead, and a woman accused of whoring and witchcraft is sentenced to hang for the murder. Three narrators—all unreliable and all self-interested—tell their versions of the story, which unfolds in a turbulent atmosphere of scientific, political, and religious dissent. Not until a fourth, and final, narrator speaks are the mysteries, including the meaning of the book's title, revealed." —*The New Yorker*

The **last** judgement. Iain Pears. Scribner, 1996. 224 p. (Jonathan Argyll and Flavia DiStefano mysteries, 4)
ISBN 9780684814599
1. Art historians 2. French Resistance (World War II) 3. Murder investigation 4. Argyll, Jonathan (Fictitious character) 5. Di Stefano, Flavia (Fictitious character) 6. Rome, Italy 7. Paris, France 8. Mysteries
LC 9538120
Art dealer Jonathan Argyll has found a buyer for an 18th century painting of the death of Socrates. However when he arrives in Rome to deliver the painting, the purchaser, Mr. Muller seems disinterested in it and asks Jonathan to arrange its resale. But if he is no longer interested in the painting, someone else is—enough to commit murder to possess it.
"A sophisticated, adventurous, and gripping story that is sure to hold wide appeal." —*Booklist*
Sequel to: The Bernini bust.
Sequel: Giotto's hand.
Originally published: London : Gollancz, 1993.

Stone's fall. Iain Pears. Spiegel & Grau, 2009. 608 p.
ISBN 9780385522847
1. Capitalists and financiers 2. Arms transfers 3. International finance 4. Death 5. Europe 6. 19th century 7. Historical mysteries
LC 2009000472
Shortlisted for the Walter Scott Prize for Historical Fiction, 2010
In this dazzling historical mystery, John Stone, financier and arms dealer, dies falling out of a window at his London home. The quest to uncover the truth behind his death plays out against the backdrop of high-stakes international finance, Europe's first great age of espionage, and the start of the twentieth century's arms race.
"Pears manages his complicated structure with a confidence and dexterity possible only to a master of the craft of fiction. It is a novel which frequently and daringly challenges credibility, skating on the thinnest of ice, and yet meets that challenge successfully every time." —*The Scotsman*

Pearson, Allison
★ **How** hard can it be? Allison Pearson. St. Martin's Press, 2018. 352 p. (Kate Reddy novels, 2)
ISBN 9781250086082
1. Middle-aged women 2. Working mothers 3. Menopause 4. Women employees 5. Husband and wife 6. London, England 7. Chick lit 8. Diary novels 9. First person narratives
LC 2017059419
LibraryReads Favorites, 2018
The heroine from I Don't Know How She Does It is forced by her husband's flaky unemployment to reinvent herself as a younger, hip professional to secure a job with the hedge fund she founded.
"Tackling sexism, growing older, and understanding ones needs when catering to those of so many others, Pearson writes realism with all the fun of escapism." —*Booklist*

Pearson, Ridley
The **risk** agent. Ridley Pearson. G.P. Putnam's Sons, 2012. 432 p. (Grace Chu and John Knox novels, 1)

ISBN 9780399158834
1. Hostages 2. Hostage negotiations 3. Security consultants 4. Real estate development 5. International intrigue 6. Shanghai, China 7. China 8. Adventure stories 9. Thrillers and suspense 10. Spy fiction
LC 2012001184
When a Chinese national working for an American-owned construction company is kidnapped along with his one-man security detail, Rutherford Risk, a firm specializing in hostage recovery, recruits two outsiders to aide in the victims return.

Pearson, Robin W.
A **long** time comin'. Robin W. Pearson. Tyndale House, 2020. 425 p.
ISBN 9781496441881
1. Grandmother and granddaughter 2. Family secrets 3. Women with terminal illnesses 4. Pregnant women 5. Faith (Christianity) 6. North Carolina 7. Christian fiction 8. Southern fiction 9. African American fiction
LC 2019025105
Christy Award for First Novel Category, 2020
To hear Beatrice Agnew tell it, she entered the world with her mouth tightly shut. Just because she finds out she's dying doesn't mean she can't keep it that way. If any of her children have questions about their daddy and the choices she made after he abandoned them, they'd best take it up with Jesus. There's no room in Granny B's house for regrets or hand-holding. Or so she thinks.
"Though it is perhaps overlong, the writing is strong, and the story is engaging, and readers will be pleased to discover a new voice in southern inspirational fiction. Libraries with Christian-fiction collections will want to add this novel to their shelves." —*Booklist*

Peebles, Frances de Pontes
The **air** you breathe. Frances De Pontes Peebles. Penguin Group USA 2018. 464 p.
ISBN 9780735210998
1. Female friendship 2. Ambition in women 3. Interclass friendship 4. Friendship 5. Samba music 6. Brazil 7. 1930s 8. Historical fiction 9. Coming-of-age stories
An orphaned kitchen maid and the reckless daughter of a sugar baron embark on a volatile friendship marked by their ambitions to escape, their changing fortunes and unexpected fame.

Peikoff, Kira
Mother knows best. Kira Peikoff. Crooked Lane Books, 2019. 288 p.
ISBN 9781643850405
1. Grief in mothers 2. Sons — Death 3. Medical genetics 4. Physicians 5. Women scientists 6. Medical thrillers 7. Multiple perspectives
Claire Abrams's dreams became a nightmare when she passed on a genetic mutation that killed her little boy. Now she wants a second chance to be a mother, and finds it in Robert Nash, a maverick fertility doctor who works under the radar with Jillian Hendricks, a cunning young scientist bent on making her mark. Claire, Robert, and Jillian work together to create the world's first baby with three genetic parents—an unprecedented feat that could eliminate inherited disease. But when word of their illegal experiment leaks to the wrong person, Robert escapes into hiding with the now-pregnant Claire, leaving Jillian to serve out a prison sentence that destroys her future.

Pelecanos, George P.

The **big** blowdown. George P. St. Martin's Press, 1996. 313 p. (Marcus Clay and Dimitri Karras novels)

ISBN 9780312142841

1. Immigrants 2. Mafia 3. Gangsters 4. Karras, Dimitri (Fictitious character) 5. Clay, Marcus (Fictitious character) 6. Washington, D.C. 7. 1940s 8. 1950s 9. Hardboiled fiction 10. Mysteries

Karras and Recevo face off when organized crime threatens their old friend's establishment in a story that explores the seamier side of life surrounding Nick's Grill BT

"Set in Washington, D.C. from the 1930s to the 1950s, Pelecanos's...novel traces a group of boyhood friends as they make their way in the richly detailed Greek and Italian neighborhoods of the city. Peter Karras, a Greek, and his friend Joe Recevo, an Italian, grow up together, serve separately in World War II, and reunite for a time after the war as Joe becomes involved in organized crime in the city. Peter cannot stomach the practice of shaking down immigrants for loan vigorish and is brutally cast out by the gangsters, as Joe stands by. The two friends will inevitably cross paths again." —*Library Journal*

This novel features Nick Stefanos in a minor role.

The **cut**: a novel. George Pelecanos. Little, Brown and Co, 2011. 304 p. (Spero Lucas mysteries, 1)

ISBN 9780316078429

1. Private investigators 2. Organized crime 3. Violence in men 4. Stolen property recovery 5. Crime bosses 6. Washington, D.C. 7. Hardboiled fiction 8. Mysteries

LC 2010044937

After returning home from serving in Iraq, Spero Lucas makes a living doing special investigations for a defense attorney and catches the attention of a high-profile crime boss who offers Lucas a high paying job he cannot refuse.

"The novel's story is O.K, but nowhere near as heart-racing as the storytelling." —*New York Times Book Review*

Pelevin, Viktor

The **hall** of singing caryatids. Victor Pelevin; translated from the Russian by Andrew Bromfield. New Directions, 2011. 105 p.

ISBN 9780811219426

1. Elite (Social sciences) 2. Nightclubs 3. Sexploitation 4. Upper class 5. Billionaires 6. Russia 7. Satirical fiction 8. Surrealist fiction 9. Allegories

LC 2011023260

Twelve girls are hired to perform in a posh new nightclub for Russia's elite. There they find things are very strange.

"Pelevin's so funny, sharp and engaging that not only do you forgive him his excesses, you look forward to them." —*Salon.com*

Pellegrino, Amanda

Smile and look pretty. Amanda Pellegrino. Park Row, 2021. 352 p.

ISBN 9780778311126

1. Entertainment industry and trade 2. Personal assistants 3. Blogs 4. Empowerment (Social sciences) 5. Sexual harassment 6. New York City 7. Mainstream fiction

What happens when four assistants risk everything to say enough is enough?

"Readers will cheer Pellegrino's shattering of the glass ceiling in this fast-paced, millennial-centric, you-go-girl novel about workplace empowerment." —*Library Journal*

Pembrooke, Kate

Not the kind of earl you marry. Kate Pembrooke. Forever, 2021. 368 p. (Unconventional ladies of Mayfair, 1)

ISBN 9781538703755

1. Earls and countesses 2. Single men 3. Single women 4. Nobility 5. Politicians 6. London, England 7. Regency period (1811-1820) 8. Regency romances

William Atherton, Earl of Norwood, is as shocked as the rest of London to discover his betrothal via an announcement in the morning paper. Furious at what appears to be a shrewd marriage trap, William tracks down his alleged fiancée before her plans can affect his campaign for a coveted political post. But then William realizes an engagement, however fake, may benefit them both... Miss Charlotte Hurst may be a wallflower, but she&;s no shrinking violet. She would never attempt such an underhanded scheme, especially not with a man as haughty or sought-after as Norwood. Yet his suggestion to play along with the betrothal has its merits...

"Complete with genuine, endearing characters, this charming novel positions Pembrooke as an author to watch." —*Publishers Weekly*

Penelope, L.

Cry of metal & bone: Earthsinger Chronicles, Book 3. L. Penelope. St. Martin's Griffin, 2020. 496 p; Map (Earthsinger chronicles, 3)

ISBN 9781250148117

1. Singers 2. Women singers 3. Magic 4. Rebels 5. Betrayal 6. Epic fantasy 7. Fantasy fiction 8. African American fiction

LC 2019058397

Six weeks after the fall of the Mantle, centuries-old enemies Elsira and Lagrimar struggle to unite. The will of the goddess is that the two nations become one, but while the war may be over, peace is still elusive. As desperate Lagrimari flee their barren land for a chance at a better life in Elsira, a dangerous faction opposed to the unification rises.

"Penelope draws on an array of fantasy tropes, ranging from steampunk to medieval, and deftly blends it all together into something entirely original. But Penelope's writing shines the brightest through her characters?and readers will be eager to see how they continue to grow and work together." —*Booklist*

Song of blood and stone. L. Penelope. St. Martin's Press, 2018. 384 p. (Earthsinger chronicles, 1)

ISBN 9781250148070

1. Pariahs 2. Exiles 3. Spies 4. Magic 5. Soldiers 6. Epic fantasy 7. Fantasy fiction 8. African American fiction 9. Adult books for young adults

LC 2017055114

Enduring life as an outcast from a homeland where her Earthsong talents are feared, orphan Jasminda helps care for an injured spy, Jack, who enlists her help in protecting the protective mantle around two nations that are preparing for war.

Whispers of shadow & flame. L. Penelope. St. Martin's Griffin, 2019. 484 pages (Earthsinger chronicles, 2)

ISBN 9781250148094

1. Singers 2. Women singers 3. Magic 4. Assassins 5. Rebels 6. Epic fantasy 7. Fantasy fiction 8. African American fiction

LC 2019025385

Life in the kingdoms of Elsira and Lagrimar is about to change. Born with a deadly magic she cannot control, Kyara is forced to become an assassin, but secretly seeks freedom from both her untamed power and the blood spell that commands her. Darvyn ol-Tahlyro may be the most powerful Earthsinger in generations, but when he discovers Kyara can unlock the secrets of his past, he can't stay away. Kyara and Darvyn grapple with betrayal, old promises, and older prophecies. And when a new threat emerges, they must beat the odds to save both kingdoms.

"Despite an enticing cliff-hanger, this taut, suspenseful fantasy stands alone, and readers new to the series can comfortably start here. This is a wonderful integration of high-stakes epic fantasy intrigue with intimate personal connections." —*Publishers Weekly*

Penman, Sharon Kay

Here be dragons. Sharon Kay Penman. Holt, Rinehart, and Winston, 1985. Xii, 704 p. : Map (Welsh trilogy, 1)
ISBN 9780030627736
1. Llewelyn ap Iorwerth 2. Rulers 3. Royal houses 4. Civilization, Medieval 5. Princesses 6. Marriages of royalty and nobility 7. Wales 8. Great Britain 9. Medieval period (476-1492) 10. Plantagenet period (1154-1485) 11. Historical fiction 12. Biographical fiction
LC 84023480
King John arranges a marriage between his youngest daughter, Joanna, and his rival, Llewelyn, Prince of North Wales, a young leader who intends to unite all of Wales.

Maps on lining papers.

The **Queen's** man: a medieval mystery. Sharon Kay Penman. H. Holt, 1996. 291 pages. (Justin de Quincy mysteries, 1)
ISBN 9780805038859
1. Eleanor 2. Murder investigation 3. Royal pretenders 4. Goldsmiths 5. Royal houses 6. Secrets 7. England 8. Medieval period (476-1492) 9. Plantagenet period (1154-1485) 10. Historical mysteries 11. Medieval mysteries 12. Mysteries
LC 9615027
YALSA Best Books for Young Adults, 1998
In England in 1193, a dying man gives Justin de Quincy a letter that must be delivered to Eleanor of Aquitaine, a letter that tells the Queen if her son, Richard Lionheart, is living or dead.

"Penman's authentic period details, larger-than-life characters, and fast-paced plot add up to great reading for both mystery fans and history buffs." —*Booklist*

The **sunne** in splendour. Sharon Kay Penman. St. Martin's Griffin, 2008. 936 p.
ISBN 9780312375935
1. Richard 2. Inheritance and succession 3. Rulers 4. Wars of the Roses, 1455-1485 5. Adams, John Quincy 6. Great Britain 7. Medieval period (476-1492) 8. Plantagenet period (1154-1485) 9. Historical fiction
LC 81020149
Departing from the traditional Shakespearian and Tudor historical portraits, this saga depicts the love story of Richard III and Anne Neville against the backdrop of royal family intrigue.

"A historical novel of the first rank." —*Publishers Weekly*
Includes map and family trees.
First published: New York : Holt, Rinehart and Winston, 1982.
Originally published: Ballantine Books, 1982.

When Christ and his saints slept. Sharon Kay Penman. H. Holt, 1995. 746 p. : Illustration; Map (Henry II novels, 1)
ISBN 9780805010152
1. Maude, princess of England 2. Nobility 3. Battles 4. Cousins 5. Civilization, Medieval 6. Royal houses 7. England 8. Medieval period (476-1492) 9. Norman period (1066-1154) 10. Historical fiction 11. Biographical fiction
LC 94022593
A novel depicting a dark period in English history follows the story of Maude, daughter of Henry I and England's uncrowned queen, and her cousin Stephen, as their battles for the crown of England lead to twenty years of anarchy BT

"The author showcases her mastery of the historical novel in this long and thoroughly engrossing study of pragmatic politics, idealism, and the role of women during the 12th century. She brings to life a vast array of unforgettable characters, both historical and invented, all of whose loyalties are being constantly tested by the chaos of the times." —*Library Journal*

Map on lining papers.

Penny, Louise

★ **All** the devils are here. Louise Penny. Minotaur Books, 2020. 448 pages (Inspector Armand Gamache mysteries, 16)
ISBN 9781250145239
1. Godfathers 2. Detectives 3. Crimes against seniors 4. Secrets 5. Rich people 6. Paris, France 7. Police procedurals 8. Mysteries 9. Canadian fiction
LC 2020017253
Agatha Award for Best Novel, 2020
The 16th novel by #1 bestselling author Louise Penny finds Chief Inspector Armand Gamache of the Surete du Quebec investigating a sinister plot in the City of Light.

"Series devotees will revel in both Penny's evocation of Paris—every bit as sumptuous as her rendering of Three Pines—and in the increased role she allots to librarian Reine-Marie, whose research skills are crucial to untying the Gordian knot at the mystery's core." —*Booklist*

★ **A better** man: a Chief Inspector Gamache novel. Louise Penny. Minotaur Books, 2019. 400 p. (Inspector Armand Gamache mysteries, 15)
ISBN 9781250066213
1. Fathers 2. Missing persons 3. Small town life 4. Fathers and daughters 5. Missing persons investigation 6. Quebec (Province) 7. Police procedurals 8. Mysteries 9. Canadian fiction
LC 2019012651
Loan Stars Favourites, 2019
Searching for a missing woman amid a catastrophic flood and blistering social media attacks, a demoted Armand Gamache bonds with the victim's distraught father, who contemplates a murder of his own.

The **cruelest** month: a Three Pines mystery. Louise Penny. St. Martin's Minotaur, 2008. 320 p. (Inspector Armand Gamache mysteries, 3)
ISBN 9780312352578
1. Spiritualism 2. Traitors 3. Small town life 4. Gamache, Armand (Fictitious character) 5. Police 6. Quebec (Province) 7. Canada 8. Police procedurals 9. Mysteries 10. Canadian fiction
LC 2007042422
Agatha Award for Best Novel, 2008
Chief Inspector Armand Gamache of the Surete du Quebec is called to investigate the death of a villager at an Easter seance that was held at the Old Hadley House.

"Penny paints a vivid picture of the French-Canadian village, its inhabitants and a determined detective who will strike many Agatha Christie fans as a 21st-century version of Hercule Poirot." —*Publishers Weekly*

★ The **madness** of crowds. Louise Penny. Minotaur Books, 2021. 448 p. (Inspector Armand Gamache mysteries, 17)
ISBN 9781250145260
1. Women college teachers 2. Statistics 3. Deception 4. Ethics 5. Popularity 6. Quebec (Province) 7. 2020s 8. Police procedurals 9. Mysteries 10. Canadian fiction
LC 2021015666
Loan Stars Favourites, 2021

When a visiting professor spreads lies so that fact and fiction are so confused it's near impossible to tell them apart, leading to murder, Chief Inspector Armand Gamache must investigate this case as well as this extraordinary popular delusion—and the madness of crowds.

"Seamlessly integrating debates about scientific experimentation and morality into a fair-play puzzle, Penny excels at placing her characters in challenging ethical quandaries. This author just goes from strength to strength." —*Publishers Weekly*

Still life. Louise Penny. St. Martin's Minotaur, 2006. 288 p. (Inspector Armand Gamache mysteries, 1)
ISBN 9780312352554
1. Small town life 2. Victims of violent crimes 3. Murder investigation 4. Police 5. Detectives 6. Quebec (Province) 7. Canada 8. Mysteries 9. Canadian fiction 10. Police procedurals
LC 2006041992
Anthony Award for Best First Novel, 2007; Arthur Ellis Award for Best First Novel, 2006; Dilys Award, 2007
Chief Inspector Armand Gamache of Canada's Surete du Quebec is called to Three Pines, a tiny hamlet south of Montreal, just north of the U.S. border, to investigate the suspicious hunting "accident" that claimed the life of Jane Neal, a local fixture in the village.

"The residents of a tiny Canadian village called Three Pines are shocked when the body of Miss Jane Neal is found in the woods. Miss Neal, the village's retired schoolteacher and a talented amateur artist, has been a good friend to most of the townsfolk, so her loss is keenly felt. At first, her death appears to be a tragic accident—it's deer-hunting season, and it looks a stray hunter's arrow killed her. But some folks are suspicious, and Chief Inspector Armand Gamache of the Montreal Surete is called in to investigate." —*Booklist*

Penrose, Andrea

Murder at half moon gate. Andrea Penrose. Kensington, 2018. 304 p. (Wrexford and Sloane historical mysteries, 2)
ISBN 9781496710796
1. Scientists 2. Women artists 3. Murder suspects 4. Political cartoons 5. Inventors 6. London, England 7. England 8. Historical mysteries
A wealthy lord who happens to be a brilliant scientist...an enigmatic young widow who secretly pens satirical cartoons...a violent killing disguised as a robbery...Nothing is as it seems in Regency London, especially when the Earl of Wrexford and Charlotte Sloane join forces to solve a shocking murder.

★ **Murder** at Kensington Palace. Andrea Penrose. Kensington, 2019. 304 pags (Wrexford and Sloane historical mysteries, 3)
ISBN 9781496722812
1. Scientists 2. Women artists 3. Murder investigation 4. Earls and countesses 5. Secret identity 6. London, England 7. England 8. Regency period (1811-1820) 9. Historical mysteries
Wrexford and Sloane must unravel secrets within secrets—including a few that entangle their own hearts—when they reunite to solve a string of shocking murders that have horrified Regency London.

Murder on Black Swan Lane. Andrea Penrose. Kensington, 2017. 304 p. (Wrexford and Sloane historical mysteries, 1)
ISBN 9781496710772
1. Scientists 2. Women artists 3. Murder suspects 4. Political cartoons 5. Clergy 6. London, England 7. England 8. Regency period (1811-1820) 9. Historical mysteries
In Regency London, an unconventional scientist and a fearless female artist form an unlikely alliance to expose unspeakable evil.

Percy, Walker

★ The **moviegoer**. Walker Percy. Vintage International, 1998. 241 p.
ISBN 9780375701962
1. Self-discovery in men 2. Redemption 3. Purpose in life 4. Catholics 5. Young men 6. New Orleans, Louisiana 7. Louisiana 8. Psychological fiction 9. First person narratives 10. Modern classics
National Book Award for Fiction, 1962
"...the tale of Binx Bolling, a small-time stockbroker who lives quietly in suburban New Orleans, pursuing an interest in the movies, affairs with his secretaries, and living out his days. But soon he finds himself on a 'search' for something more important, some spiritual truth to anchor him. Binx's life floats casually along until one fateful Mardi Gras week, when a bizarre series of events leads him to his unlikely salvation. In his half-brother Lonnie, who is confined to a wheelchair and soon to die, and his stepcousin Kate, whose predicament is even more ominous, Binx begins to find the sort of 'certified reality' that had eluded him everywhere but at the movies. —Publisher's web site.

The **second** coming. Walker Percy. Farrar, Straus, Giroux, 1980. 359 p.
ISBN 9780374256746
1. Jesus Christ 2. People with mental illnesses 3. End of the world 4. Second coming of Christ 5. Catholics 6. Widowers 7. Psychological fiction 8. Multiple perspectives 9. Southern fiction
LC 80012899
Los Angeles Times Book Prize for Fiction, 1980; National Book Critics Circle Award for Fiction finalist, 1980; National Book Award for Fiction finalist, 1981
Widower Will Barrett, with very little interest in money and much concern for all the unhappiness in the world, inherits forty million dollars from his late wife. Will, who has some episodes of blacking out, is drawn into a rewakening, "a second coming," with the help of a young escapee from a mental hospital. She becomes for him the light at the end of a long, dark tunnel. Some strong language.

"A beautiful...exploration of Percy's recurrent theme—an individual man's search for the hand of God in the meaningless muddle of contemporary life." —*Booklist*
Sequel to: The last gentleman.

Perez-Reverte, Arturo

The **Club** Dumas. Arturo Perez-Reverte; translated from the Spanish by Sonia Soto. Harcourt Brace, 1997. 362 p.
ISBN 9780151001828
1. Dumas, Alexander 2. Rare books 3. Demons 4. Book collectors 5. Antiquarian booksellers 6. Freytag-Loringhoven, Elsa von 7. Madrid, Spain 8. Paris, France 9. Adventure stories 10. Mysteries 11. Literary fiction
New York Times Notable Book, 1997
"Corso, a tough-guy bibliophile living in Madrid, is hired by a wealthy client to track down a rare seventeenth-century book on how to summon the Devil. He soon finds himself in noir metafiction in which he's been cast as D'Artagnan and is threatened by characters suspiciously like Richelieu's agents—a menacing man with a scar and a blonde with a fleur-de-lis tattoo. Even a reader armed with a Latin dictionary and a copy of 'The Three Musketeers' cannot anticipate the thrilling twists of this stylish, Escher-like mystery." —*The New Yorker*
This book was released as a movie entitled The ninth gate.
Originally published in Spanish under the title El Club Dumas: Madrid : Santillana, 1993.

What we become. Arturo Perez-Reverte; translated by Nick Caistor and Lorenza Garcia. Atria Books, 2016. 512 p.
ISBN 9781476751986

1. Tango (Dance) 2. Extramarital affairs 3. Married women 4. Thieves 5. Upper class 6. Buenos Aires, Argentina 7. Marie, de France, active 12th century 8. 1920s 9. 1930s 10. Love stories 11. Historical fiction 12. Translations

LC 2015037715

A dangerous and passionate love affair between an accomplished tango dancer turned elegant thief and a beautiful, intelligent society woman bursts off the page in this epic historical tale of romance and espionage.

"Prez-Reverte summons the romantic spirit of an old black-and-white movie: impossibly glamorous, undeniably wistful." —*Kirkus*

Originally published in Spain in 2012 by Santillana Ediciones Generales, S. L. as El tango de la Guardia Vieja—Title page verso.

Perkins, S. C.

Murder once removed. S.C. Perkins. Minotaur Books, 2019. 318 p. (Ancestry detective novels, 1)
ISBN 9781250189035
1. Women genealogists 2. Ancestors 3. Women amateur detectives 4. Family secrets 5. Murder 6. Austin, Texas 7. Texas 8. Cozy mysteries 9. Gentle reads

LC 2018046203

When a high-profile billionaire makes a history-changing claim on live television, genealogist Lucy Lancaster of Austin, Texas begins an investigation dating back to the mid-19th century before she is confronted by a modern descendant who would protect family secrets.

"The winner of Minotaur's Malice Domestic Best First Traditional Mystery Novel competition, this debut features an intelligent genealogist detective, a strong supporting cast, some romantic tension, and information about Texas history that should appeal to readers of Rett MacPherson's genealogy mysteries as well as cozy lovers who prefer a dash of history in their mysteries." —*Library Journal*

Perrotta, Tom

The **abstinence** teacher. Tom Perrotta. St. Martin's Press, 2007. 336 p.
ISBN 9780312358334
1. High school teachers 2. Sex education for teenagers 3. Divorced parents 4. Fathers 5. Fathers and daughters 6. Mainstream fiction

LC 2007021961

New York Times Notable Book, 2007

Teaching human sexuality from a perspective that information and pleasure are top priorities, divorced mom Ruth Ramsey butts heads with the local soccer coach, a divorced former addict who became an evangelical Christian after hitting rock bottom.

"Perrotta, an accomplished satirist who has made the suburbs his personal stomping ground, turns Stonewood Heights...into a battleground for the hearts and minds (and, need I add, souls) of his characters. While Perrotta does do more than give lip service to both sides, it's pretty clear where his allegiance lies.... What keeps the book from getting too heavy-handed, besides the sharply written humor, is the fact that Perrotta makes his evangelical Christian protagonist less of a zealot than the atheist." —*Christian Science Monitor*

The **leftovers**. Tom Perrotta. St. Martin's Press, 2011. 336 p.
ISBN 9780312358341
1. Life change events 2. Mayors 3. Conflict in families 4. Disappeared persons 5. Anxiety 6. New Jersey 7. Satirical fiction 8. Books to TV 9. Adult books for young adults

New York Times Notable Book, 2011

When a bizarre phenomenon causes the cataclysmic disappearances of numerous people all over the world, Kevin Garvey, the new mayor of a once-comfortable suburban community, struggles to help his neighbors heal while enduring the fanatical religious conversions of his wife and son.

"Perrotta has a gifted ear for dialogue and a distinct appreciation for the particularities of suburban life." —*Minneapolis Star Tribune*

Title adapted for an HBO television series by the same name (2013).

Little children. Tom Perrotta. St. Martin's Press, 2004. 368 p.
ISBN 9780312315719
1. Suburban life 2. Married people 3. Bradley, Omar N. 4. Former police 5. Mothers 6. Psychological fiction 7. Books to movies 8. Mainstream fiction

LC 2003015947

Library Journal Best Books, 2004; New York Times Notable Book, 2004

A group of young suburban parents, including a handsome stay-at-home dad, a former feminist, an internet surfer, and an over-structured mom, finds its sleepy existence shattered when a convicted child molester moves back into town and two of the parents have an affair.

"The eponymous children in this satirical novel are actually adults who, chafing at the burdens of parenthood, try to recreate their unencumbered youth. Sarah, an overeducated young homemaker, likens her tantrum-prone daughter to a brooding Russian epileptic out of Dostoevsky, and pines for lost college days of feminism and bisexuality. While her husband orders used panties online, she has furtive sex with a stay-at-home dad whose repeated failure to pass the bar has earned him the contempt of his gorgeous wife. The humor is sometimes cruel, but Perrotta never betrays the complexity of his characters." —*The New Yorker*

Perry, Anne

A **dangerous** mourning. Anne Perry. Fawcett Columbine, 1991. 330p. (William Monk and Hester Latterly mysteries, 2)
ISBN 9780747245261
1. Murder investigation 2. Police 3. Nurses 4. Women's role 5. Monk, William (Fictitious character) 6. London, England 7. Victorian era (1837-1901) 8. 19th century 9. Historical mysteries 10. Victorian mysteries 11. Police procedurals

LC 91070655

Inspector Monk returns to the scene of another Victorian era murder mystery when the daughter of an upper-crust family is stabbed in her own home.

Dark tide rising: a William Monk novel. Anne Perry. Ballantine Books, 2018. 289 p. (William Monk and Hester Latterly mysteries, 24)
ISBN 9780399179914
1. Police 2. Suspicion 3. Betrayal 4. Ransom 5. Loyalty 6. London, England 7. Victorian era (1837-1901) 8. 1860s 9. Victorian mysteries 10. Historical mysteries 11. Police procedurals

LC 2018014439

A ransom exchange gone violently wrong forces Commander William Monk to investigate the unthinkable possibility that one of his own men has betrayed him.

"The 24th title in Perry's long-running William Monk series delivers an excellent atmospheric Victorian mystery. While astute readers will identify the villain long before Monk does, longtime fans will delight in the camaraderie among the series regulars and the return to the dark underbelly of polite British society." —*Library Journal*

★ A **darker** reality. Anne Perry. Ballantine Books, 2021. 320 p. (Elena Standish, 3)
ISBN 9780593159361
1. Women spies 2. Women photographers 3. Family secrets 4. Crazy Horse, approximately 1842-1877 5. Scientists 6. Washington D.C.

7. Between the Wars (1918-1939) 8. 1930s 9. Spy fiction 10. Historical thrillers

LC 2021015449

Elena Standish investigates the mysterious death of Lila Worth, who she discovers is a British spy, at an anniversary party for her parents in Washington, D.C.

"It would be easy to believe that Elena Standish really did exist, and that the books are actual biographical stories. Perry proves once again why she is among the top writers of historical mysteries." —*Booklist*

★ **Death** in focus: an Elena Standish novel. Anne Perry. Ballantine Books, 2019. 305 pages (Elena Standish, 1)

ISBN 9780525620983

1. Women photographers 2. International intrigue 3. Families 4. Spies 5. Assassination plots 6. England 7. Italy 8. Between the Wars (1918-1939) 9. 1930s 10. Historical mysteries

LC 2019011797

An intrepid young photographer carries her imperiled lover's final, urgent message into the heart of pre-World War II Berlin as Hitler is ascending to power.

"Obvious comparisons to Charles Todd's Bess Crawford and Jacqueline Winspear's Maisie Dobbs are warranted, but this novel also hearkens back to Helen MacInnes's classic spy thrillers and Mary Stewart's romantic suspense novels. At turns heartbreaking and action-packed, this gripping and superbly written story proves Perry still has what it takes." —*Library Journal*

★ **Death** with a double edge: a Daniel Pitt novel. Anne Perry. Ballantine, 2021. 320 p. (Daniel Pitt novels (Anne Perry), 4)

ISBN 9780593159330

1. City life 2. Lawyers 3. Detectives 4. Father and adult son 5. Suspicion 6. London, England 7. England 8. 1910s 9. Edwardian era (1901-1914) 10. Historical mysteries

LC 2020045206

Joining forces with Toby Kitteridge to investigate the murder of a senior barrister, Daniel Pitt follows leads through London's teeming underworld, before hostile adversaries begin targeting his loved ones.

"Perry has written a cracking story, with characters, even minor ones, deftly drawn to show nuanced personalities, and with dialogue evoking the atmosphere of prewar London." —*Booklist*

The **face** of a stranger. Anne Perry. Fawcett Columbine, 1990. 328 p. (William Monk and Hester Latterly mysteries, 1)

ISBN 9780449905302

1. People with amnesia 2. Police 3. Monk, William (Fictitious character) 4. Murder investigation 5. Social classes 6. London, England 7. Victorian era (1837-1901) 8. 19th century 9. Victorian mysteries 10. Historical mysteries 11. Police procedurals

LC 90034169

William Monk, a member of the London police force in 1856, develops amnesia after an accident, and, while trying to solve the murder of an aristocrat, he looks at his own character.

"The author understands her amnesiac sleuth so intimately that she knows he can rediscover himself only in moments of inspiration along the trail of his quarry. This, and the fact that Monk has more to learn about himself even as the story concludes, are brilliant touches that effectively blend contemporary understanding of character with a Victorian sensibility." —*New York Times Book Review*

One fatal flaw: a Daniel Pitt novel. Anne Perry. Random House Inc 2020. 304 p. (Daniel Pitt novels (Anne Perry), 3)

ISBN 9780593129524

1. Lawyers 2. Women scientists 3. Defense attorneys 4. Murder 5. Murder suspects 6. London, England 7. England 8. 1910s 9. Edwardian era (1901-1914) 10. Historical mysteries

LC 2019050997

Teaming up with brilliant scientist Miriam fford Croft to prove the innocence of a murder suspect, lawyer Daniel Pitt rules the case an accident before his client is found dead in the same manner, bringing Miriam's test methods into question.

Reliable Edwardian legal suspense, liberally flavored with contemporary feminism, from an old pro. —*Kirkus*

Originally published in Great Britain, 2019.

A **question** of betrayal. Anne Perry. Ballantine Books, 2020. 304 p. (Elena Standish, 2)

ISBN 9780593129555

1. Women spies 2. Women photographers 3. International intrigue 4. Former lovers 5. Missing men 6. Italy 7. England 8. Between the Wars (1918-1939) 9. 1930s 10. Spy fiction 11. Historical thrillers

LC 2020011439

A sequel to Death in Focus finds daring young MI6 photographer Elena Standish embarking on a first mission in Mussolini's Italy to rescue and uncover the truth about a former lover who betrayed her six years earlier.

"This manages to be a winning mix of crime story and espionage drama, boat chase and seaplane rescue included." —*Booklist*

Perry, Sarah

The **Essex** serpent. Sarah Perry. Custom House, 2017. 432 p.

ISBN 9780062666376

1. Widows 2. Clergy 3. Belief and doubt 4. Social classes 5. Single mothers 6. England 7. Victorian era (1837-1901) 8. Historical fiction

New York Times Notable Book, 2017; Longlisted for The Baileys Women's Prize for Fiction, 2017; Longlisted for the Walter Scott Prize for Historical Fiction, 2017

Freed from an unhappy marriage by her husband's death, Victorian widow Cora Seaborne settles in Colchester, where she pursues her interest in natural history by searching the Blackwater estuary for evidence of the Essex Serpent, a winged serpent dismissed as superstition by vicar Will Ransome, but greatly feared by the locals. With its heady atmosphere and lush descriptions, the novel vividly explores Victorian English society and culture through the experiences of its ensemble cast.

"Stuffed with smarts and storytelling sorcery, this is a work of astonishing breadth and brilliance." —*Kirkus*

Originally published: London : Serpent's Tail, 2016.

Melmoth: a novel. Sarah Perry. Custom House, 2018. 271 p.

ISBN 9780062856395

1. Characters and characteristics in fairy tales 2. Guilt 3. Superstition 4. Suffering 5. Women translators 6. Prague, Czech Republic 7. Czech Republic 8. Gothic fiction 9. Horror 10. Literary fiction

LC 2018029870

RUSA Reading List Short List, 2019

Helen, an English translator working in Prague, disregards an obscure local monster legend before a friend's disappearance reveals that Helen is being watched.

Perry, Thomas

The **bomb** maker. Thomas Perry. Pgw 2018. 384 p.

ISBN 9780802127488

1. Bomb threats 2. Bombings 3. Police 4. Terrorism 5. Former police 6. Los Angeles, California 7. Thrillers and suspense

LC 2017025438

A lethally clever designer of explosives tests the skills and collective strength of the highly skilled LAPD Bomb Squad.

Death benefits: a novel. Thomas Perry. Random House, 2001. 384 p.
ISBN 9780679453055
1. Insurance investigators 2. Fraud investigation 3. Insurance fraud 4. Missing women 5. Deception in men 6. San Francisco, California 7. New Hampshire 8. Mysteries

LC 41476

When gruff and intimidating security consultant Max Stillman appears without warning in the San Francisco office of McClaren Life and Casualty and begins asking questions and scrutinizing files, the employees can't help wondering just which of them he's been hired to investigate.

"San Francisco insurance data analyst John Walker is sleepwalking through his young life when the boss assigns him to assist a private detective on an inside job involving Walker's ex-girlfriend, a claims adjuster who disappeared after being implicated in a $12 million scheme to defraud the company. Judicious applications of Perry's knowing wit energize the tutor-pupil dynamics between Walker and Max Stillman, the crafty and somewhat sinister P.I. who calls the shots on this case." —*New York Times Book Review*

Fidelity. Thomas Perry. Harcourt, 2008. 368 p.
ISBN 9780151012923
1. Murder investigation 2. Assassins 3. Secrets 4. Detectives 5. Mysteries 6. Multiple perspectives

LC 2007026507

When Emily Kramer's husband Phil is murdered, she finds herself with an empty bank account and many questions. Jerry Hobart did not know why he was hired to kill Phil Kramer, but now being ordered to kill Kramer's widow, he has questions of his own. In searching for Phil's secret, both Hobart and Emily must decide where their loyalties are.

"Perry's characters are uncannily good at sizing one another up and anticipating what the next moves will be. Though he briefly equates Hobart's tactics to the ways a coyote slinks through a neighborhood, Mr. Perry need not even articulate this. It's always built into his storytelling, and it's already on the page." —*New York Times*

An Otto Penzler Book.

★ The **left-handed** twin. Thomas Perry. Mysterious Press, 2021. 321 p. (Jane Whitefield novels;, 9)
ISBN 9781613162590
1. Whitefield, Jane (Fictitious character) 2. Indians of North America 3. Native American women 4. Seneca women 5. Seneca Indians 6. Los Angeles, California 7. Thrillers and suspense

When Jane, who helps disappear people, agrees to help a woman escape a crazed ex-boyfriend who is friends with members of a Russian organized crime brotherhood, thus begins a bloodthirsty chase through the northeast where nothing—and no one—can be trusted.

"Hits the ground running and never lets up. Be sure to take a few deep breaths before plunging in." —*Kirkus*

The **old** man. Thomas Perry. Grove Press, 2017. 352 p.
ISBN 9780802125866
1. Seniors 2. Veterans 3. Fugitives 4. Assassins 5. Intelligence service 6. Vermont 7. United States 8. Thrillers and suspense

Decades after taking millions of dollars during a mission in Libya and starting over in Vermont under a new name, former Army intelligence officer Dan Chase is forced back on the run after eluding two attackers with an interest in obtaining the loot.

Vanishing act. Thomas Perry. Random House, 1995. 289 p. (Jane Whitefield novels, 1)
ISBN 9780679435365
1. Protectiveness 2. New identities 3. Deception 4. Whitefield, Jane (Fictitious character) 5. Witnesses 6. New York (State) 7. Thrillers and suspense

LC 94017413

Jane Whitefield helps people disappear by giving them a new identity—new appearance, new social security card—and her clientele ranges from bankrupt businessmen to fleeing wives. On this occasion, things backfire and she must resort to her Native American talents to track a dangerous customer she helped disappear.

"This is all very satisfying and quite scenic... ." —*New York Times Book Review*

Persaud, Ingrid

Love after love: a novel. Ingrid Persaud. Random House Inc 2020. 304 p.
ISBN 9780593157565
1. Mothers and sons 2. Boarders 3. Leaving home 4. Closeted gay men 5. Undocumented immigrants 6. Trinidad and Tobago 7. New York City 8. Literary fiction 9. Family sagas 10. Multiple perspectives

LC 2019027894

Costa First Novel Award, 2020

An award-winning Trinidadian author offers a novel that looks at a complicated marriage, an unconventional family and the shocking secrets that unite them.

"Writing in vibrant Trinidadian dialect, Persaud renders her characters with great empathy and care." —*Kirkus*

Persson Giolito, Malin

Beyond all reasonable doubt: a novel. Malin Persson Giolito; translated from the Swedish by Rachel Willson-Broyles. Other Press, 2019. 452 p.
ISBN 9781590519196
1. Judicial error 2. Women lawyers 3. Criminal justice system 4. Teenage girl murder victims 5. Scientists 6. Sweden 7. Legal thrillers 8. Scandinavian crime fiction 9. Translations

LC 2018049563

From the award-winning author of Quicksand, a gripping legal thriller that follows one woman's conflicted efforts to overturn what may be a wrongful conviction.

Originally published: 2005.
Translated from the Swedish.

Quicksand. By Malin Persson Giolito; translated from the Swedish by Rachel Willson-Broyles. Other Press, 2017. 512 pages
ISBN 9781590518571
1. High school girls 2. Teenage prisoners 3. School shootings 4. Prep schools 5. Prisons 6. Stockholm, Sweden 7. Coming-of-age stories 8. Psychological fiction 9. Scandinavian crime fiction

LC 2016032468

After spending nine months in jail awaiting trial for her involvement in a mass shooting that took the lives of her boyfriend and best friend in a prep school in Stockholm's richest suburb, Maja finally reveals the circumstances that brought her there.

"Giolitos astonishing English-language debut...is a dark exploration of the crumbling European social order and the psyches of rich Swedish teens." —*Booklist*

Translation of: Storst av allt
Originally published: Sweden : Wahlstrom & Widstrand, 2016
Translated from the Swedish

Persson, Leif G. W.

Another time, another life: the story of a crime. Leif GW Persson; translated from the Swedish by Paul Norlen. Pantheon Books, 2012. 404 p. (Story of a crime trilogy, 2)

ISBN 9780307377463

1. Conspiracies 2. Secrets 3. Murder 4. Politicians 5. Secret service 6. Sweden 7. 1990s 8. Political thrillers 9. Translations 10. Thrillers and suspense

LC 2011017394

An investigation into the murder of a Swedish civil servant is put on indefinite hold by a corrupt senior official before Swedish Security Police newcomer Lars Johansson reopens the case and follows leads to the highest levels of government.

Translation from the Swedish.

Originally published: En annan tid, ett annat liv (2003).

The **dying** detective: a mystery. Leif G.W. Persson; translated from the Swedish by Neil Smith. Pantheon Books, 2017. 426 p.

ISBN 9780307907639

1. Former police 2. People who have had strokes 3. Girl murder victims 4. Cold cases (Criminal investigation) 5. Retirees 6. Sweden 7. Translations 8. Mysteries

LC Oc2016039400

Duncan Lawrie International Dagger, 2017

After suffering a stroke that reveals additional health problems, Swedish homicide detective Lars Martin Johansson launches an investigation into a cold case murder from his hospital bed with the help of a rebellious young woman.

Translation of: Doende detektiven.

Originally published: Stockholm : Bonnier, 2010.

Translated from the Swedish.

Free falling, as if in a dream: the story of a crime. Leif GW Persson; translated from the Swedish by Paul Norlen. Pantheon Books, 2014. 592 p. (Story of a crime trilogy, 3)

ISBN 9780307377470

1. Palme, Olof 2. Prime ministers 3. Assassination investigation 4. Cold cases (Criminal investigation) 5. Murder 6. Murder investigation 7. Sweden 8. Political thrillers 9. Thrillers and suspense 10. Scandinavian crime fiction

LC 2012050987

Lars Martin Johansson investigates the unsolved 1986 murder of Swedish prime minister Olof Palme, only to be seduced by his own ambitions and a shady political spin doctor.

"Strong characterization, a solid grasp of investigatory complexities, and an appreciation of the elusive, chimerical nature of truth make this a fine example of a conspiracy thriller." —*Publishers Weekly*

Translation from the Swedish.

Originally published in Sweden as Faller fritt som i en drom, by Albert Bonniers Forlag, Stockholm, in 2007—Title page verso.

Pesci, David

Amistad: a novel. David Pesci. Marlowe, 1997. 292 p.

ISBN 9781569247488

1. Adams, John Quincy 2. Amistad Case, 1839-1841 3. Enslaved people 4. Slavery 5. Trials (Mutiny) — History 6. Slave trade 7. Connecticut 8. United States 9. 19th century 10. Antebellum America (1820-1861) 11. Historical fiction 12. Adult books for young adults

LC 9654050

Tells the story of an African farmer who is sold into slavery and stages a rebellion aboard the slave ship, the Amistad.

"Pesci deftly blends the facts of this fascinating historical episode with story." —*School Library Journal*

Pessl, Marisha

Night film: a novel. Marisha Pessl. Random House, 2013. 624 p.

ISBN 9781400067886

1. Suicide 2. Fathers and daughters 3. Subcultures 4. Investigative journalism 5. Murder 6. New York City 7. Psychological suspense 8. Literary fiction 9. Illustrated books

LC 2012041163

Booklist Editors' Choice, 2013; LibraryReads Favorites, 2013

When the daughter of a cult horror film director is found dead in an abandoned Manhattan warehouse, investigative journalist Scott McGrath, disbelieving the official suicide ruling, probes into the strange circumstances of the young woman's death.

First published in Great Britain in 2013 by Hutchinson.

Includes bibliographical references and index.

Special topics in calamity physics. Marisha Pessl. Viking, 2006. 528 p.

ISBN 9780670037773

1. Fathers and daughters 2. Murder investigation 3. Teenage girls 4. Teenagers — Death 5. Teachers — Death 6. North Carolina 7. Coming-of-age stories 8. Mysteries 9. Literary fiction 10. Adult books for young adults

LC 2005058474

New York Times Notable Book, 2006

"Even the physics equation on the book's back cover has outsized verve. And what begins as a dubious proposition, in a world wholly without need for additions to its Prep School Confidential bibliography, becomes a whirling, glittering, multifaceted marvel, delivered in an irrepressibly smart and flamboyant new voice." —*New York Times*

Peters, Ellis

Brother Cadfael's penance. Ellis Peters. Mysterious Press, 1994. 292 p. (Brother Cadfael medieval mysteries, 20)

ISBN 9780892965991

1. Monks 2. Prisoners of war 3. Fathers and sons 4. Rescues 5. Amateur detectives 6. Great Britain 7. Medieval period (476-1492) 8. Norman period (1066-1154) 9. Historical mysteries 10. Medieval mysteries 11. Mysteries

LC 94027140

Medieval Benedictine monk Brother Cadfael journeys to save his thirty-year-old-son, who has been taken prisoner in the Civil War between Empress Maud and King Stephen

Edith Pargeter writing as Ellis Peters.

The **holy** thief. Ellis Peters. Mysterious Press, 1994. 237 p. (Brother Cadfael medieval mysteries, 19)

ISBN 9780446403634

1. Monks 2. Amateur detectives 3. Christian relic thefts 4. Stolen property recovery 5. Murder investigation 6. Great Britain 7. Shrewsbury, England 8. Medieval period (476-1492) 9. Norman period (1066-1154) 10. Historical mysteries 11. Medieval mysteries 12. Mysteries

Brother Cadfael must solve a puzzling murder case and locate the sacred bones stolen from the Benedictine Abbey of Saint Peter and Saint Paul in Shrewsbury.

"Twelfth-century Shropshire comes vividly alive when peopled with Peters' aristocratic ladies, sturdy lawmen, eager squires and, above all, devout—and devious—monks." —*Publishers Weekly*

Edith Pargeter writing as Ellis Peters.

Originally published: London : Headline, 1992.

Peters, Torrey

★ **Detransition,** baby. Torrey Peters. One World, 2021. 272 p.

ISBN 9780593133378

1. Trans women 2. Separated couples 3. Transitioning (Gender identity) 4. Men 5. Women 6. New York City 7. LGBTQIA fiction 8. Relationship fiction

A trans woman, her detransitioned ex and his cisgender lover build an unconventional family together in the wake of heartbreak and an unplanned pregnancy.

"Trans women will be matching their experiences against Reese's, but so will cis women-and so will anyone with an interest in the human condition. Smart, funny, and bighearted." —*Kirkus*

Petersen, Todd Robert

Picnic in the ruins. Todd Robert Petersen. Counterpoint, 2021. 352 pages

ISBN 9781640093225

1. Indians of North America — Material culture 2. Land use 3. Historic preservation 4. Women anthropologists 5. Criminals 6. Utah 7. The West (United States) 8. Caper novels 9. Crime fiction

A madcap caper across the RV-strewn vacation lands of southern Utah meets a meditation on mythology, authenticity, the ethics of preservation, and one nagging question: "who owns the past?

"Petersen keeps piling on plot twists, eccentric characters, and well-described settings, and beneath the plot's pandemonium there's an intriguing meditation on 'authenticity,' on 'ownership,' and on the legacy of violence in the remote West. A fast-paced, highly entertaining hybrid of Tony Hillerman and Edward Abbey." —*Kirkus*

Peterson, Tracie

What comes my way. Tracie Peterson. Bethany House Pub, 2019. 384 p. (Brookstone brides, 3)

ISBN 9780764233395

1. Trick riding 2. Wild West shows 3. Cowgirls 4. Independence in women 5. Alcoholism 6. The West (United States) 7. Montana 8. 1900s (Decade) 9. Christian historical romances

Only while trick riding can Ella Fleming forget the truth about who she really is—the daughter of a murderer. Phillip DeShazer buries the guilt he feels for his father's death in work and drink, and his guilt continues to grow the more Ella Fleming comes to his rescue. Will they be able to overcome their pasts and trust God to guide their futures?

Petrie, Nicholas

The breaker. Nick Petrie. Putnam Pub Group, 2021. 400 p. (Peter Ash novels, 6)

ISBN 9780525535478

1. Gunshot victims 2. Iraq War veterans 3. Technology 4. Missing persons 5. Fugitives 6. Milwaukee, Wisconsin 7. Thrillers and suspense

Interrupting a shooting in a crowded marketplace, Peter Ash is approached by an old associate who offers him a clean record in exchange for help tracking down the gunman and the intended victim.

"Fans of Petrie's previous 'Ash' novels and Lee Child's 'Jack Reacher' series will fly through this exciting story and wait eagerly for the next installment." —*Library Journal*

Burning bright. Nicholas Petrie. G.P. Putnam's Sons, 2017. 432 p. (Peter Ash novels, 2)

ISBN 9780399174575

1. Iraq war veterans 2. Journalists 3. Artificial intelligence 4. Veterans 5. Former marines 6. California 7. Thrillers and suspense

LC 2016011425

Afghan war veteran Peter Ash is hiking through northern California's redwoods when he's forced up a tree to escape a grizzly. What he finds in that tree is an elaborate network of ropes, with a pretty blonde on the platform at the top. June Cassidy is no treehugger, however—she's an investigative journalist on the run from fake government agents who believe she's in possession of a powerful algorithm created by her mother, who'd recently been killed. June hires Peter to discover who's behind the threat, and they uncover far more than expected. The 2nd in a series that started with The Drifter (with promises of at least two more to come), Burning Bright is a fast-paced, action-packed read that also addresses the effects of PTSD.

The drifter. Nicholas Petrie. G.P. Putnam's Sons, 2016. 384 p. (Peter Ash, 1)

ISBN 9780399174568

1. Iraq war veterans 2. Post-traumatic stress disorder 3. Conspiracies 4. Claustrophobia 5. Widows 6. Milwaukee, Wisconsin 7. Thrillers and suspense

Thriller Award for Best First Novel, 2017; Wisconsin Library Association Literary Award, 2017

Like Jack Reacher, Marine Corps veteran Peter Ash stays constantly on the move. In Ash's case, however, PTSD prevents him from settling down—or even staying indoors. When a close friend and fellow Marine commits suicide, Ash heads to Milwaukee to look after his family however he can. This includes home repair, which is when he finds a suitcase packed full of money—and explosives. Figuring out his friend's last few days leads Ash straight into a complex situation that allows both a pulse-pounding plot and a sympathetic look at the challenges veterans face at home.

Tear it down. Nick Petrie. G.P. Putnam's Sons, 2019. 373 p. (Peter Ash novels, 4)

ISBN 9780399575662

1. Iraq War veterans 2. Post-traumatic stress disorder 3. Death threats 4. Street musicians 5. Women photojournalists 6. Tennessee 7. Memphis, Tennessee 8. Thrillers and suspense

LC 2018018176

Peter Ash tackles two difficult cases in Memphis involving an attack on a war photographer, a homeless street musician, a stolen cache of watches, vengeful gangsters and a valuable Civil War heirloom.

"...[T]here's no denying that Petrie is hell on wheels at mounting lethal action face-offs. A close cousin to Lee Childs's more analytical Jack Reacher, Peter Ash is one of today's more exciting action heroes." —*Publishers Weekly*

The wild one. Nick Petrie. G. P. Putnam's Sons, 2020. 400 p. (Peter Ash novels, 5)

ISBN 9780525535447

1. Iraq War veterans 2. Post-traumatic stress disorder 3. Kidnapping 4. Fugitives 5. Child kidnapping victims 6. Iceland 7. Tennessee 8. Thrillers and suspense

LC 2019046077

Traumatized war veteran Peter Ash tracks a murderer from a criminal family through the icy landscapes of Reykjavik, where he is confronted by government officials who would block his investigation.

"This kinetic, breathless masterpiece illustrates why Petrie is here to stay." —*Publishers Weekly*

Petry, Ann

★ The **street**. Ann Petry. Houghton Mifflin, 1998. 435 p.

ISBN 9780395901496

1. Ghettoes, African American 2. Single-parent families 3. Poverty 4. African American women 5. Inner city 6. Harlem, New York City 7. New York City 8. 1940s 9. Urban fiction 10. Literary fiction 11. African American fiction

Explores the life and dreams of a young woman who struggles to raise her son in a suffocating ghetto world of racism, human degradation, and uncontrolled violence

Petterson, Per

I curse the river of time. Per Petterson; translated from the Norwegian by Charlotte Barslund. Farrar Straus & Giroux, 2010. 224 p.

ISBN 9781555975562

1. Mothers with terminal illnesses 2. Life change events 3. Divorce 4. Family relationships 5. Guilt in men 6. 1980s 7. Literary fiction 8. Psychological fiction 9. Translations

New York Times Notable Book, 2010

Anticipating a divorce against a backdrop of the fall of communism, Arvid Jansen is further dismayed by his mother's diagnosis with cancer, a situation that prompts his emotionally charged quest for understanding and balance.

"Needless to say, it's a sad book, and at times it'll feel alien to readers who've never been young Communists or hung out in, say, Nittedal or Eidsvoll. (The translation can also be quite a rickety bridge.) But there's no denying the novel's Raymond Carver-like power as Arvid and his mother come to terms with how life hands you hope just before it hands you disappointment and tragedy." —*Entertainment Weekly*

Translation of Jeg forbanner tidens elv.

English translation originally published: London : Harvill Secker, 2010.

Originally published: Oslo : Forlaget Oktober, 2008.

I refuse. Per Petterson; translated from the Norwegian by Don Bartlett. Graywolf Press, 2015. 224 p.

ISBN 9781555976996

1. Male friendship 2. Psychic trauma 3. Family problems 4. Adult children of dysfunctional families 5. Betrayal 6. Psychological fiction 7. Literary fiction 8. Translations

A chance encounter between two childhood friends, including one who escaped an abusive father, reveals how their fortunes have reversed.

"Without pyrotechnics, Petterson brings his characters and working-class Norway vividly, even passionately, to life; days after they finish the novel, readers may still have dreams of ice cracking." —*Kirkus*

Translation of: Jeg nekter.

Originally published: Oslo : Forlaget Oktober, 2012.

Out stealing horses: a novel. Per Petterson; translated from the Norwegian by Anne Born. Graywolf Press, 2007. 288 p.

ISBN 9781555974701

1. Senior men 2. Neighbors 3. Memories 4. Fathers and sons 5. Boys — Friendship 6. Norway 7. 1940s 8. Coming-of-age stories 9. Translations 10. Literary fiction 11. Adult books for young adults

LC 2006938263

ALA Notable Book, 2008; International IMPAC Dublin Literary Award, 2007; Library Journal Best Books, 2007; New York Times Notable Book, 2007

Sixty-seven-year-old Trond Sander lives secluded in a far corner of Norway. Casting his mind back to 1948, he recalls a horse stealing prank with his best friend that turned tragic and changed his life forever.

"Petterson's spare and deliberate prose has astonishing force, and the narrative gains further power from the artful interplay of Trond's childhood and adult perspectives." —*The New Yorker*

Translation of: Ut og stjaele hester.

Originally published: Oslo : Forlaget Oktober, 2003.

Peynado, Brenda

The **rock** eaters: stories. Brenda Peynado. Penguin Books, 2021. 288 p.

ISBN 9780143135623

1. Love 2. Loss (Psychology) 3. Immigration and emigration 4. Social classes 5. Social marginality 6. Magical realism 7. Literary fiction 8. Short stories

LC 2020033789

What does it mean to be other? What does it mean to love in a world determined to keep us apart? These questions murmur in the heart of each of Brenda Peynado's strange and singular stories. Threaded with magic, transcending time and place, these stories explore what it means to cross borders and break down walls, personally and politically. With elements of science fiction and fantasy, fabulism and magical realism, Brenda Peynado uses her stories to reflect our flawed world, and the incredible, terrifying, and marvelous nature of humanity.

"Sixteen genre-bending stories as substantial as they are superbly crafted? A sparkling, strange, and enthralling debut from a vivid new voice in contemporary fiction." —*Kirkus*

Phillips, Arthur

★ The **king** at the edge of the world: novel. Arthur Phillips. Random House, 2020. 264 pages

ISBN 9780812995480

1. Elizabeth I, Queen of England, 1533-1603 2. Physicians 3. Undercover operations 4. Inheritance and succession 5. Spies 6. Religion 7. England 8. Elizabethan era (1558-1603) 9. Tudor period (1485-1603) 10. Historical thrillers 11. Spy fiction

LC 2019019018

New York Times Notable Book, 2020

A secret Muslim warrior from the height of England's religious battles is sent to Scotland to uncover the true nature of James VI's actual religious beliefs while an heirless Elizabeth I lies on her deathbed.

"Readers will flock to the latest from esteemed best-seller Phillips, whose signature literary prowess and nimble imagination remain ascendant." —*Booklist*

The **tragedy** of Arthur: a novel. By Arthur Phillips. Random House, 2011. 432 p.

ISBN 9781400066476

1. Shakespeare, William 2. Dramatists 3. Art forgeries 4. Fathers and sons 5. Family relationships 6. Writing 7. Satirical fiction 8. Metafiction

LC 2010021192

ALA Notable Book, 2012; Library Journal Best Books, 2011; New York Times Notable Book, 2011; Shortlisted for the International IMPAC Dublin Literary Award, 2013

When his long-imprisoned con-artist father reaches the end of his life, Arthur and his twin sister become the owners of an undiscovered play by William Shakespeare that their father wants published, a final request that represents either a great literary gift or their father's last great heist.

Phillips, Caryl

Dancing in the dark. Caryl Phillips. Knopf, 2005. 224 p.

ISBN 9781400043965

1. Williams, Bert 2. African American men — Identity 3. African American entertainers 4. African American comedians 5. Bahamian Americans 6. Blackface entertainers 7. Harlem, New York City 8. Broadway, New York City 9. 1900s (Decade) 10. Biographical fiction 11. Historical fiction

LC 2005044106

A fictional re-creation of the life and times of Bert Williams, the first black entertainer in the United States to achieve success, a man who dons blackface to become a headliner in the Ziegfeld Follies.

"As subjects for historical novels go, Bert Williams is an inspired choice; his strange career exemplified all the ironies and paradoxes that confronted the African-American performers of his time.... Dancing in the Dark is riveting when it recreates mores and social conventions our culture has done its best to forget." —*New York Times Book Review*

A **distant** shore. Caryl Phillips. Knopf, 2003. 256 p.
ISBN 9781400041091
1. Retired teachers 2. Senior women 3. Refugees 4. Undocumented immigrants 5. Undocumented workers 6. Africa 7. England 8. Psychological fiction 9. Literary fiction
Booklist Editors' Choice, 2003; Commonwealth Writers' Prize for Best Book, 2004; Commonwealth Writers' Prize, South Asia and Europe: Best Book, 2004; New York Times Notable Book, 2003; National Book Critics Circle Award for Fiction finalist, 2003
Moving into a new bungalow in an English village, retired teacher Dorothy meets night watchman Solomon, an illegal immigrant, in a tale that recounts their experiences as solitary outsiders in a hostile world.

"This muted, sad novel breaks down the distinction between the placed and the displaced, dissolving our sense of security, if we had one, about safely belonging in the world, dispelling our illusion of being at home. We are all adrift, Phillips says, whether we know it or not: a fact not of race or nationality, but of the human condition." —*New York Times Book Review*

Foreigners. Caryl Phillips. Alfred A. Knopf, 2007. 256 p.
ISBN 9781400043972
1. Barber, Frank 2. Enslaved people 3. Boxers (Sports) 4. Africans in Great Britain 5. Stowaways 6. Racism 7. England 8. Biographical fiction 9. Historical fiction 10. Psychological fiction
LC 2007029219
Booklist Editors' Choice, 2007
The life stories of three black men of different times and backgrounds reveals the place and role of the foreigner in English society.

"With great empathy, and through a collage of voices, Phillips has created three distinct portraits. All are superbly crafted and utterly absorbing .... As Phillips suggests, Englishness, like foreignness, is a complex and changeable thing. An important and sobering book, highly relevant today." —*The Daily Mail*

A **view** of the empire at sunset. Caryl Phillips. Farrar, Straus and Giroux, 2018. 324 p.
ISBN 9780374283612
1. Rhys, Jean 2. Women authors 3. Colonialism 4. Misfits (Persons) 5. Cultural differences 6. Race relations 7. Great Britain 8. West Indies 9. 20th century 10. Historical fiction 11. Biographical fiction
LC 2017047959
New York Times Notable Book, 2018
A reimagining of the life of Jean Rhys, author of Wide Sargasso Sea, traces her tempestuous life in Edwardian England and 1920s Paris before a brief visit transforms her views about colonization in the Caribbean of her childhood.

Phillips, Christi

The **Devlin** diary. Christi Phillips. Pocket Books, 2008. 448 p.
ISBN 9781416527398
1. College teachers 2. Serial murders 3. Women physicians 4. Murder investigation 5. Great Britain 6. Restoration England (1660-1688) 7. Stuart period (1603-1714) 8. Mysteries
LC 2008021769

When a Trinity College history professor is found murdered with a torn page of a seventeenth-century diary in his hand, Claire Donovan and historian Andrew Kent believe his death may be linked to a series of unsolved killings in 1670s London.

The **Rossetti** letter: a novel. Christi Phillips. Pocket Books, 2007. 352 p.
ISBN 9781416527374
1. Habsburg, House of 2. Courtesans 3. Letters 4. Conspiracies 5. Women scholars and academics 6. Dissertation writing 7. Venice, Italy 8. Italy 9. 17th century 10. Historical mysteries 11. Parallel narratives 12. Mysteries
Fearing that her research will be rendered useless if a Cambridge professor proves his theory about seventeenth-century Venetian courtesan Alessandra Rossetti, Ph.D. candidate Claire Donovan agrees to chaperone a troubled teen in order to gain passage to the professor's presentation in Venice.

Phillips, Gin

Fierce kingdom: a novel. Gin Phillips. Viking, 2017. 288 p.
ISBN 9780735224278
1. Mothers and sons 2. Survival 3. Zoos 4. Protectiveness in women 5. Life change events 6. Thrillers and suspense
LC 2016057138
Loan Stars Favourites, 2017; RUSA Reading List, 2018
Trapped in a closed zoo after witnessing a life-shattering event, a woman and her 4-year-old son navigate the zoo's hidden pathways and under-renovation exhibits to stay ahead of a dangerous adversary who tests their survival and the limits of the mother-child bond.

"A searing exploration of motherhood at its most basic, this all-too-plausible horror story may haunt even readers with steely nerves and strong stomachs." —*Publishers Weekly*

Phillips, Helen

The **beautiful** bureaucrat: a novel. Helen Phillips. Henry Holt and Co, 2015. 192 p.
ISBN 9781627793766
1. Married women 2. Conspiracies 3. Husband and wife 4. Bureaucracy 5. Data processing — Data entry 6. Satirical fiction 7. Literary fiction
LC 2014045386
New York Times Notable Book, 2015
Becoming increasingly uneasy about suspicious activities at a new job she felt lucky to land, Josephine makes a terrible realization and is forced to confront dangerous and powerful elements in order to protect her loved ones.

"Phillips takes situations and sentiments that will be all too familiar to many readers—a soul-crushingly dull job that callously steals our youth and beauty, the desperate yearning to be free of it, the restoring power of love and food and intimacy and of shared language and laughter—and uses them to explore bigger universal themes of life and death and the choices and compromises they demand. Intense and enigmatic, tense and tender, this novel offers no easy answers—its deeper meanings may mystify—but it grabs you up, propels you along, and leaves you gasping, grasping, and ready to read it again." —*Kirkus*

The **need**: a novel. By Helen Phillips. Simon & Schuster, 2019. 224 pages
ISBN 9781982113162
1. Working mothers 2. Parenting 3. Home invasions 4. Women scientists 5. Maternal love 6. Literary fiction 7. Psychological suspense
LC 2018044381

New York Times Notable Book, 2019; Longlisted for the National Book Award for Fiction, 2019

A woman grapples with the complex dualities of motherhood—joy and dread, tenderness and anxiety—after confronting a masked intruder in her home.

Phillips, Jayne Anne

Lark and Termite: a novel. Jayne Anne Phillips. Alfred A. Knopf, 2009. 272 p.

ISBN 9780375401954

1. Korean War, 1950-1953 2. Family secrets 3. Siblings 4. Family relationships 5. Aunts 6. West Virginia 7. 1950s 8. Domestic fiction 9. Historical fiction 10. Multiple perspectives

LC 2008033453

Library Journal Best Books, 2009; New York Times Notable Book, 2009; National Book Critics Circle Award for Fiction finalist, 2009; National Book Award for Fiction finalist, 2009

Set against the backdrop of the Korean War in the 1950s, a novel about family, the repercussions of war, and the bonds that sustain personal relationships focuses on a single family—Lark, her brother Termite, their mother Lola, and Termite's soldier father, Robert Leavitt.

"Phillips has done in Lark and Termite what she did in previous novels such as Machine Dreams (1984) and Shelter (1994), which is to take a relatively simple, straightforward tale and twist it into something luminous and haunting and singular. This is Phillips' first novel in almost a decade, but it doesn't feel tardy or excessively fussed over. It feels fresh. It feels as if it has been taken straight from the griddle and is still too hot to touch. And because it deals with issues over which people have been arguing for centuries—family and war—the novel's raw immediacy is really quite spectacular." —*PopMatters*

Quiet dell: a novel. Jayne Anne Phillips. Scribner, 2013. 480 p.

ISBN 9781439172537

1. Women journalists 2. Serial murderers 3. Swindlers and swindling 4. Trials 5. Widows 6. Chicago, Illinois 7. Illinois 8. 1930s 9. Historical fiction

LC 2013016013

In 1931, Emily Thornhill, one of the few women in the Chicago press, covers the murders of Asta Eicher and her three children and, obsessed with finding out what happened to this beautiful family, allies herself with the man funding the investigation who is wracked with guilt for not saving Asta himself.

Phillips, Julia

★ **Disappearing** earth. Julia Phillips. Alfred A Knopf, 2019. 304 pages

ISBN 9780525520412

1. Girl kidnapping victims 2. Loss (Psychology) 3. Communities 4. Missing girls 5. Women 6. Russia 7. Literary fiction 8. Thrillers and suspense

Library Journal Best Books, 2019; New York Times Notable Book, 2019; National Book Award for Fiction finalist, 2019

The shattering disappearance of two young girls from Russia's Kamchatka Peninsula compounds the isolation and fears of a tight-woven community, connecting the lives of neighbors, witnesses, family members and a detective throughout an ensuing year of tension.

Phillips, Susan Elizabeth

Call me irresistible. Susan Elizabeth Phillips. HarperCollins 2011. 400 p. (Wynette, Texas romances)

ISBN 9780061351525

1. Mayors 2. Engaged persons 3. Small town life 4. Friendship 5. Weddings 6. Texas 7. Contemporary romances 8. Western romances

Library Journal Best Books, 2011

Ostracized for her role in halting best friend Lucy's wedding, Meg finds herself stranded without family support in a hostile Texas town where she unexpectedly falls for Ted Beaudine.

★ **Dance** away with me. Susan Elizabeth Phillips. William Morrow & Co, 2020. 384 pages

ISBN 9780062973054

1. Widows 2. Midwives 3. Recluses 4. Artists 5. Moving, Household 6. Tennessee 7. Contemporary romances

Seeking refuge in a Tennessee mountain town to recover from heartbreak, a young widow and midwife bonds with an enigmatic artist, a helpless infant and a passel of curious teens in a small and suspicious community.

"Phillips not only sensitively tackles difficult topics such as grief and guilt, she also explores the creative process, sex education in the community, and the state of medicine in rural America, in lively writing liberally laced with multiple layers of delicious wit and snarky charm." —*Booklist*

First star I see tonight. Susan Elizabeth Phillips. William Morrow, 2016. 384 p. (Chicago Stars, 8)

ISBN 9780062405616

1. Former football players 2. Women private investigators 3. Fame 4. Nightclubs 5. Family businesses 6. Contemporary romances 7. Sports romances

LibraryReads Favorites, 2016; Romantic Times Reviewer's Choice Award, 2016

Discovered by the former quarterback she was hired to tail, detective Piper Dove pretends to be the athlete's stalker and is subsequently hired by him, an arrangement threatened by their growing chemistry.

"This thoroughly enjoyable novel delivers a swift kick to the heartan essential summer read." —*Kirkus*

The **great** escape. Susan Elizabeth Phillips. William Morrow, 2012. 432 p. (Wynette, Texas romances)

ISBN 9780062106063

1. Runaway wives, husbands, etc. 2. Voyages and travels 3. Self-fulfillment in women 4. Children of presidents 5. Brides 6. Great Lakes 7. Texas 8. Contemporary romances

Library Journal Best Books, 2012

Lucy Jorik, the daughter of the former president of the United States, jilts her soon-to-be husband at the altar and embarks on the adventure she has been waiting for.

Heroes are my weakness. Susan Elizabeth Phillips. William Morrow, 2014. 384 pages

ISBN 9780062106070

1. Authors 2. Actors and actresses 3. Men recluses 4. Horror story authors 5. Puppeteers 6. Maine 7. Contemporary romances

LC 2014007547

Library Journal Best Books 2014; LibraryReads Favorites, 2014

A down-on-her-luck actress reduced to staging kids' puppet shows finds herself trapped on a remote island off the coast of Maine with a sexy horror novelist who knows a dozen ways to kill with his bare hands.

"Phillips takes all the iconic elements of those classic gothic novels of the 1960s and '70s and deftly combines them with her own signature literary calling cards of realistically quirky yet all too relatable characters, polished writing, tart humor, and an abundance of potent sexual chemistry." —*Booklist*

★ **Natural** born charmer. Susan Elizabeth Phillips. William Morrow, 2007. 400 p. (Chicago Stars, 7)

ISBN 9780060734572

1. Quarterbacks (Football) 2. Mothers and sons 3. Automobile travel 4. Single men 5. Single women 6. Colorado 7. Tennessee 8. Contemporary romances 9. Sports romances

LC 2006049173

RUSA Reading List, 2008

Taking to the road between seasons, attractive Chicago Stars quarterback Dean Robillard meets the beautiful and infuriating Blue under unusual circumstances and draws on his competitive skills to overcome her wariness of relationships.

"While the verbal sparring in this textbook case of opposites attracting feels stagy at first, the rough edges come together in an alluring way." —*Publishers Weekly*

Sequel to: Match me if you can.

What I did for love. Susan Elizabeth Phillips. William Morrow, 2009. 416 p. (Wynette, Texas romances)

ISBN 9780061351501

1. Actors and actresses 2. Divorce 3. Remarriage 4. Celebrities — Press coverage 5. Paparazzi 6. Hollywood, California 7. Texas 8. Contemporary romances 9. Western romances

LC 2008037321

Library Journal Best Books, 2009

When actress Georgie York's film career hits rock bottom along with her marriage, the paparazzi has a field day with her misfortune, which is only complicated by the reappearance of her sexy, unscrupulous former costar, Bramwell Shepard.

★ **When** stars collide. Susan Elizabeth Phillips. William Morrow and Company, 2021. 384 p. (Chicago Stars, 9)

ISBN 9780062973085

1. Women opera singers 2. Secrets 3. Quarterbacks (Football) 4. Protectiveness in men 5. Fans 6. Contemporary romances 7. Sports romances

Opera diva Olivia Shore and Chicago Stars quarterback Thaddeus Walker Bowman Owens embark on a nationwide tour promoting a luxury watch brand and must find a way to get along when they are plagued by a series of dangerous encounters with an overzealous fan.

From savvy characterization, sassy humor, and sparkling dialogue to a smartly composed plot, in which Phillips deftly weaves a thread of chilling danger, to moments of smoldering sensuality and pure passion, this brilliantly conceived contemporary romance will have readers shouting, Brava! Booklist

Philyaw, Deesha

The **secret** lives of church ladies. Deesha Philyaw. West Virginia University Press, 2020. 168 p.

ISBN 9781949199734

1. African American women 2. Christian life 3. Churches 4. Sexuality 5. Family relationships 6. Literary fiction 7. Short stories 8. African American fiction

LC 2020008805

PEN-Faulkner Award, 2021; Los Angeles Times Art Seidenbaum Award for First Fiction, 2020; National Book Award for Fiction finalist, 2020

The Secret Lives of Church Ladies explores the raw and tender places where black women and girls dare to follow their desires and pursue a momentary reprieve from being good. The nine stories in this collection feature four generations of characters grappling with who they want to be in the world, caught as they are between the church's double standards and their own needs and passions.

"No saints exist in these pages, just full-throated, flesh-and-blood women who embrace and redefine love, and their own selves, in power-fully imperfect renditions. Tender, fierce, proudly Black and beautiful, these stories will sneak inside you and take root." —*Kirkus*

Phoenix, Michele

The **space** between words. Michele Phoenix. Harpercollins Christian Pub 2017. 336 p.

ISBN 9780718086442

1. Historic documents 2. Victims of terrorism 3. Religious persecution 4. Coping 5. Huguenots 6. France 7. Christian historical fiction 8. Parallel narratives

LC 2017013000

Michele Phoenix crafts a poignant story of a young woman recovering from the evils of this world through perseverance, hope, and the light in a centuries-old document.

Piccirilli, Tom

The **last** kind words. Tom Piccirilli. Bantam Books, 2012. 352 p.

ISBN 9780553592481

1. Criminals 2. Brothers 3. Murder investigation 4. Families 5. Murder 6. Long Island, New York 7. Thrillers and suspense 8. Crime fiction

Resolving to pursue an honest life after his brother goes on a murderous rampage and is sentenced to execution, Terrier Rand learns that his brother did not commit one of the killings for which he was sentenced and resolves to learn what really happened that day.

Sequel: The Last Whisper in the Dark

The **last** whisper in the dark: a novel. Tom Piccirilli. Bantam Books, 2013. 336 p.

ISBN 9780345529008

1. Criminals 2. Brothers 3. Swindlers and swindling 4. Robbery 5. Enemies 6. Long Island, New York 7. Thrillers and suspense 8. Crime fiction

LC 2012043223

A follow-up to The Last Kind Words finds youngest son Terry, a surviving member of the Rand family of cat burglars and con artists, endeavoring to go straight before becoming enmeshed in a heist gone wrong that pits him against an old nemesis and threatens to permanently estrange him from the woman he once loved.

Sequel to: The Last Kind Words

Pickard, Nancy

The **scent** of rain and lightning: a novel. Nancy Pickard. Ballantine Books, 2010. 319 p.

ISBN 9780345471017

1. Family secrets 2. Dreams 3. Conspiracies 4. Families of murder victims 5. Greed 6. Mysteries 7. Adult books for young adults

The man convicted of murdering Jody's father, Billy Crosby, is being released from prison and returning to the small town of Rose, Kansas. Crosby has been granted a new trial, thanks in large part to the efforts of his son, Collin, a lawyer who has spent most of his life trying to prove his father's innocence. As Jody revisits old wounds, startling revelations compel her to uncover the dangerous truth about her family's tragic past.

"Well-plotted, clearly written mystery novels are always welcome. A novel that simultaneously qualifies as a gripping read, a master character study and as literary is more than welcome it is exceedingly rare." —*Kansas City Star*

Picoult, Jodi

★ The **book** of two ways. Jodi Picoult. Ballantine Books, 2020. 448 pages : Illustration
ISBN 9781984818355
1. Options, alternatives, choices 2. Married women 3. Survival (after airplane accidents, shipwrecks, etc.) 4. Memories 5. Archaeologists 6. Boston, Massachusetts 7. Egypt 8. Relationship fiction

Experiencing memories of a man other than her husband while surviving a plane crash, an end-of-life doula on the brink of a fateful decision envisions two disparate paths that find her staying with her family or reconnecting with the past.

"Picoult plays with the novel's narrative structure in a way that risks leaving readers feeling perplexed or even tricked. Nonetheless, they will find heady themes to consider." —*Booklist*

Change of heart: a novel. By Jodi Picoult. Atria Books, 2008. 460 p.
ISBN 9780743496742
1. Death row prisoners 2. Transplantation of organs, tissues, etc. 3. Repentance 4. Carpenters 5. Murderers 6. Multiple perspectives 7. Relationship fiction
LC 2007035721

Her life shattered by a devastating act of violence, June Nealon is forced to make a pivotal choice that involves her twelve-year-old daughter and a salvation-seeking criminal.

"Picoult moves the story along with lively debates about prisoner rights and religion." —*Publishers Weekly*

House rules: a novel. By Jodi Picoult. Atria Books, 2010. 544 p.
ISBN 9780743296434
1. Asperger's syndrome 2. Children with autism 3. Forensic sciences 4. Murder investigation 5. Boys with autism 6. Mainstream fiction 7. Psychological fiction 8. Adult books for young adults
LC 2009026381

Unable to express himself socially but possessing a savant-like knack for investigating crimes, a teenage boy with Asperger's Syndrome is wrongly accused of killing his tutor when the police mistake his autistic tics for guilty behavior.

"Emma, a single mother, copes just fine with her teenage sons until the day Jacob is arrested for the murder of his tutor. Jacob has Asperger's, and the cops confuse his symptoms—such as avoiding eye contact—with guilt. Jodi Picoult loses points for ruining what could have been a riveting mystery by establishing Jacob's innocence at the outset. (The real story behind the tutor's death is obvious to the careful reader.) The author has delivered a sweet family drama that doubles as a handbook on Asperger's—not exactly a thrill, but hardly a bad thing." —*Entertainment Weekly*

Keeping faith: a novel. Jodi Picoult. W. Morrow, 1999. 422 p.
ISBN 9780688168254
1. Child custody 2. Mothers and daughters 3. Stigmatization 4. Miracles 5. Faith 6. Mainstream fiction
LC 98-43953

Faith, a seven-year-old girl whose family is torn apart by divorce, begins talking to God and performing miracles, and her family enters a media circus of believers, critics, medical professionals, and lawyers BT

Leaving time: a novel. Jodi Picoult. Ballantine Books, 2014. 405 p.
ISBN 9780345544926
1. Mothers and daughters 2. Missing women 3. Animal welfare 4. Missing persons investigation 5. Teenage girls 6. Mainstream fiction 7. Multiple perspectives 8. Adult books for young adults
LC 2014023994

LibraryReads Favorites, 2014

Abandoned by a grief-stricken father and accomplished-scientist mother who disappeared under mysterious circumstances, 13-year-old Jenna Metcalf approaches a disgraced psychic and a jaded detective in the hopes of finding answers.

"A truly engaging read that crosses through the genres of mystery and the supernatural. The interspersing of elephant behavior information and Alice's journal entries about her subjects provide just the right amount of parallelism." —*Library Journal*

★ **My** sister's keeper. Jodi Picoult. Atria Books, 2004. 432 p.
ISBN 9780743454520
1. People with leukemia 2. Sisters 3. Suing (Law) 4. Donation of organs, tissues, etc. 5. Thirteen-year-old girls 6. Mainstream fiction 7. Domestic fiction 8. Multiple perspectives 9. Adult books for young adults
Abraham Lincoln Illinois High School Book Award, 2006; Alex Award, 2005; Black-Eyed Susan Book Award (Maryland), High School, 2007; Booklist Editors' Choice: Adult Books for Young Adults, 2004; Green Mountain Book Award (Vermont), 2007; Heartland Award, 2006; Pennsylvania Young Reader's Choice Awards, Young Adult, 2007; Virginia Readers' Choice Award for High School, 2007; School Library Journal Best Books: Best Adult Books 4 Teens, 2005

Conceived to provide a bone marrow match for her leukemia-stricken sister, teenage Anna begins to question her moral obligations in light of countless medical procedures and decides to fight for the right to make decisions about her own body.

Originally published: London: Hodder & Stoughton, 2004.
Includes book club discussions questions.
First published: 2004.

Nineteen minutes: a novel. By Jodi Picoult. Atria Books, 2007. 464 p.
ISBN 9780743496728
1. Bullying and bullies 2. School shootings 3. Trials (Murder) 4. Seventeen-year-old boys 5. High school students 6. New Hampshire 7. Multiple perspectives 8. Mainstream fiction 9. Adult books for young adults
LC 2006049276

Booklist Editors' Choice: Adult Books for Young Adults, 2007; Iowa High School Book Award, 2010

In the aftermath of a small-town school shooting, lawyer Jordan McAfee finds himself defending a youth who desperately needs someone on his side, while detective Patrick Ducharme works with a primary witness, the daughter of the judge assigned to the case.

Includes book club discussion questions.

Sing you home: a novel. Jodi Picoult. Pocket Books, 2011. 496 p.
ISBN 9781439102725
1. Embryo transfer — Moral and ethical aspects 2. Lesbian couples 3. Reproductive technology 4. Music therapists 5. Lesbians — Rights 6. Psychological fiction 7. Multiple perspectives 8. Mainstream fiction 9. Adult books for young adults

Ten years of infertility issues culminate in the destruction of music therapist Zoe Baxter's marriage, after which she falls in love with another woman, Vanessa, and wants to start a family; but her ex-husband, Max, in the grips of an anti-gay pastor, stands in the way.

"Picoult may have an agenda, but she has written an immensely entertaining melodrama with crackerjack dialogue." —*USA Today*

A **spark** of light: a novel. Jodi Picoult. Ballantine Books, 2018. 352 p.
ISBN 9780345544988
1. Women's health centers and clinics 2. Pregnant women 3. Hostages 4. Women hostages 5. Hostage negotiations 6. Relationship fiction 7. Multiple perspectives 8. Adult books for young adults
LC 2018018966

Loan Stars Favourites, 2018

When a deranged gunman forces his way into the Center, a women's reproductive health services clinic, and takes hostages, the police hostage negotiator discovers his daughter is inside the clinic.

The **storyteller**. Jodi Picoult. Atria Books, 2013. 460 p.
ISBN 9781439102763
1. Intergenerational friendship 2. Guilt in men 3. Holocaust (1933-1945) 4. Retired teachers 5. Former Nazis 6. Psychological fiction 7. Mainstream fiction 8. Parallel narratives
Library Journal Best Books, 2013
Becoming friends with Josef Weber, an old man who's particularly loved in her community, Sage Singer is shocked when one day he asks her to kill him and reveals why he deserves to die, causing her question her beliefs—and to wonder if his request would be murder or justice.

Vanishing acts: a novel. By Jodi Picoult. Atria Books, 2005. 432 p.
ISBN 9780743454544
1. Girl kidnapping victims 2. Recovered memory 3. Kidnapping 4. Adult children of divorced parents 5. Parental kidnapping 6. New Hampshire 7. Arizona 8. Mainstream fiction 9. Multiple perspectives
LC 2004059454
Working with the Search and Rescue bloodhound team to find missing people, single mother Delia Hopkins anticipates her upcoming nuptials, until a series of unsettling flashbacks threatens to devastate her life and the lives of those she loves.
"Picoult weaves together plot and characterization in a landscape that is fleshed out in rich, journalistic detail, so that readers will come away with intriguing questions rather than pat answers." —*Publishers Weekly*

★ **Wish** you were here: a novel. Jodi Picoult. Ballantine Books, 2021. 336 p.
ISBN 9781984818416
1. COVID-19 (Disease) 2. Quarantine 3. Vacations 4. Self-fulfillment in women 5. Life change events 6. Galapagos Islands 7. New York City 8. 2020s 9. Relationship fiction
LC 2021027370
With everything perfectly on track, Diana O'Toole finds things going off the rails when she is quarantined during her dream vacation in the Galapagos due to a virus, forcing her to reevaluate herself and her life when she makes a connection with a local family.
"Stealthily surprising and very moving, Picoult's latest, written while she was confined at home during the pandemic, taps into the trauma and uncertainty of 2020's global crisis." —*Booklist*

Piercy, Marge
Gone to soldiers: a novel. Marge Piercy. Summit Books/Simon & Schuster, 1987. 703 p.
ISBN 9780671634216
1. Women and war 2. World War II — Women's participation 3. Jews 4. Jewish women 5. Lesbians 6. Second World War era (1939-1945) 7. Historical fiction 8. War stories 9. Literary fiction
LC 86030118
During the Second World War, ten extraordinary people win and lose their fierce, passionate private and public battles, in foxholes, in concentration camps, on the home front, or with partisans.

Sex wars. Marge Piercy. William Morrow, 2005. 416 p.
ISBN 9780060789831
1. Stanton, Elizabeth Cady 2. Suffragists 3. Women's rights 4. Power (Social sciences) 5. Immigrants, Russian 6. Immigrants 7. New York City 8. United States 9. Gilded Age (1865-1898) 10. American Civil War era (1861-1865) 11. Historical fiction 12. Literary fiction
LC 2005041499

Coming of age in a post-Civil War New York City tenement flat, Jewish-Russian Freydeh juggles multiple jobs to earn passage for her family, until she learns that her younger sister is adrift somewhere in the city.
"This is an enjoyable book—usually entertaining and, in its best sections, engrossing. In Woodhull and Freydeh, Piercy has created fascinating portraits of women determined to live on their own terms. As the freewheeling Gilded Age gives way to a growing conservatism that traps both women, observant readers will notice obvious parallels to our own time." —*Christian Science Monitor*

Vida: a novel. Marge Piercy. Fawcett Crest 1989. 477 p.
ISBN 9780671401108
1. Marxism 2. Political activists 3. Women radicals 4. Man-woman relationships 5. Sexuality 6. 1960s 7. 1970s 8. Psychological fiction
LC 79019298
Vida, an antiwar activist during the 1960s, goes underground in 1970 after being associated with a bombing.
"This novel is not 'simply' a novel but a political brief. I have my differences with 'Vida,' but I think they are substantive rather than literary. It is an interesting—and challenging—book.... Marge Piercy has written about movement people before but never, I think, as lovingly as here." —*New York Times Book Review*

Pike, Signe
The **forgotten** kingdom: a novel. Signe Pike. Atria Books, 2020. Xiv, 475 pages : Map (Lost queen (Signe Pike), 2)
ISBN 9781501191459
1. Women rulers 2. Civilization, Celtic 3. Rulers 4. Military occupation 5. Battles 6. Scotland 7. 6th century 8. Medieval period (476-1492) 9. Arthurian fantasy 10. Historical fantasy 11. First person narratives
LC 2020022068
Languoreth endures imprisonment while one of the most violent battles of early medieval Scottish history scatters her loved ones, including her young daughter Angharad, who pursues her destiny in the mystical land of the Picts.
"A rich, immersive narrative founded on impeccable scholarship." —*Kirkus*
Sequel to: The lost queen.

The **lost** queen. Signe Pike. Touchstone, 2018. 576 p. (Lost queen (Signe Pike), 1)
ISBN 9781501191411
1. Women rulers 2. Civilization, Celtic 3. Druids and druidism 4. Twins 5. Merlin (Legendary character) 6. Scotland 7. 6th century 8. Medieval period (476-1492) 9. Arthurian fantasy 10. Historical fantasy 11. First person narratives
LC 2018002985
Reveals the untold story of Languoreth—a forgotten queen of sixth-century Scotland and twin sister of the man who inspired the legend of Merlin—as her family fights for the survival of their kingdom against the encroaching forces of Christianity and the Anglo-Saxons.
"Pike's narrative blends court intrigue, romantic interludes, and gritty violence into a literary brew worth savoring to the dramatic finale. The elements of Celtic mysticism will appeal to fantasy fans looking for a Mists of Avalon-type experience, while the setting remains grounded in sixth-century Scotland's political realities. Enthusiastically recommended for readers of female-centered historical sagas and those enamored of Arthurian tales." —*Booklist*

Pilcher, Rosamunde
Coming home. Rosamunde Pilcher. St. Martin's Press, 1995. 728 p.
ISBN 9780312958121

1. Families 2. Growing up 3. World War II 4. Social classes 5. Great Britain 6. Second World War era (1939-1945) 7. 1930s 8. Coming-of-age stories 9. War stories 10. Historical fiction

LC 95021656

Judith Dunbar comes of age while confronting her feelings about love and sadness and journeying back to her childhood home

"The book's heroine is Judith Dunbar, who is a schoolgirl of 13 when the tale begins in 1935. Sent to boarding school in Cornwall because her parents are posted to Singapore, Judith becomes friends with Loveday Carey-Lewis, who introduces her to a family and an estate, Nancherrow, that is to influence her for the rest of her life. Pilcher does a marvelous job of describing life in England before World War II." —*Booklist*

Later printing issued by St. Martin's Paperbacks.

A **place** like home: short stories. Rosamunde Pilcher. St. Martin's Press, 2021. 288 p.

ISBN 9781250274953

1. Interpersonal relations 2. Options, alternatives, choices 3. Love 4. Joy and sorrow 5. Interpersonal attraction 6. Short stories 7. Love stories

LC 2021006925

A Place Like Home is a collection of Rosamunde Pilcher's most enduring short stories, never before published in book form.Each is the perfect slice of romance written with warmth and passion featuring wonderfully memorable, smart, and feisty female characters that will transport the reader to another time and place.

"In this collection of 15 short stories, published together for the first time, Pilcher (1924-2019) has done something remarkable.... This collection about love offers snippets of joy, small and large, and the tart balances the sweet to just the right degree." —*Kirkus*

★ The **shell** seekers. Rosamunde Pilcher. St. Martin's Press, 1987. 530 p.

ISBN 9780312010584

1. Family relationships 2. Motherhood 3. Greed 4. Artists 5. Painting 6. London, England 7. Cornwall, England 8. Family sagas 9. Gentle reads

LC 87028345

"It is a measure of this story's strength and success that a reader can be carried for more than 500 pages in total involvement with Penelope, her children, her past and the painting that hangs in her country cottage. 'The Shell Seekers' is a deeply satisfying story, written with love and confidence." —*New York Times Book Review*

Pinborough, Sarah

★ **Behind** her eyes: a novel. Sarah Pinborough. Flatiron Books, 2017. 320 p.

ISBN 9781250111173

1. Control (Psychology) 2. Secrets 3. Manipulation (Social sciences) 4. Psychologists 5. Husband and wife 6. London, England 7. Psychological suspense 8. Multiple perspectives

LC 2016037630

LibraryReads Favorites, 2017

The secretary of a successful psychiatrist is drawn into the seemingly picture-perfect life of her boss and his wife before discovering a complex web of controlling behaviors and secrets that gradually reveal profound and dangerous flaws in the couple's relationship.

★ **Cross** her heart: a novel. Sarah Pinborough. William Morrow, 2018. 352 p.

ISBN 9780062856791

1. Promises 2. Betrayal 3. Obsession 4. Teenage girls 5. Single mothers 6. Psychological suspense 7. Multiple perspectives

LC 2018002651

A devoted single parent hides the truth about her daughter's absent father and asks her best friend for help when challenges from her past threaten her teenage daughter.

★ **Dead** to her: a novel. Sarah Pinborough. William Morrow, 2020. 352 p.

ISBN 9780062856821

1. Newlyweds 2. Cheating (Interpersonal relations) 3. Upper class 4. Jealousy 5. Revenge 6. Savannah, Georgia 7. Psychological suspense 8. Thrillers and suspense 9. Multiple perspectives

LC 2019032506

Navigating her new husband's complicated social circle and wandering eye, a mistress-turned-wife becomes ruthless when her husband begins an affair with his boss's own second wife.

"With Dead to Her, Pinborough plants her flag as the master of seductively sinister suspense. This absorbing tale will satisfy and even surprise fans of Jennifer McMahon and Gillian Flynn." —*Booklist*

Pineiro, Caridad

One summer night. Caridad Pineiro. Sourcebooks Casablanca, 2017. 352 p. (At the shore novels, 1)

ISBN 9781492649649

1. Family businesses 2. Real estate developers 3. Family feuds 4. Neighbors 5. Vacation homes 6. New Jersey 7. Contemporary romances

To save her family's business, Jersey girl Maggie Sinclair is forced to ask Jax Pierce for help—despite the fact that the Sinclairs and Pierces have been feuding for nearly 30 years—a decision that causes them to both risk everything.

South Beach love: a feel-good romance from Hallmark Publishing. Caridad Pineiro. Hallmark Publishing, 2021. 310 pages

ISBN 9781947892835

1. Quinceanera 2. Restaurateurs 3. Homecomings 4. Hispanic American families 5. Cooking, Cuban 6. Miami, Florida 7. Florida 8. Multicultural romances 9. Belmont, Alva 10. Contemporary romances

Head to Miami for a Hallmark summer romance celebrating family and tradition, from New York Times bestselling author Caridad Pineiro.

What happens in summer. Caridad Pineiro. Sourcebooks, 2018. 352 p. (At the shore novels, 2)

ISBN 9781492649670

1. Weddings 2. Former lovers 3. Second chances 4. Lovers' reunions 5. Coastal towns 6. New Jersey 7. Contemporary romances

As the only daughter of a single mom, Connie Reyes swore she would never put herself or her child in a similar position. But when she runs into oh so tempting Jonathan Pierce at a wedding, she knows she must stay away. She'll fall for him-hard. And he's not the type to stick around. Ever since he left town after their teenaged fling, Jonathan hasn't been able to forget about Connie. He can't wait for the wedding-to show her the man he's become. And when the night finally comes, their mutual desire will lead to unexpected consequences neither of them were prepared for.

Pinsker, Sarah

A **song** for a new day. Sarah Pinsker. Berkley, 2019. 372 pages

ISBN 9781984802583

1. Post-apocalypse 2. Women musicians 3. Social isolation 4. Terrorism 5. Epidemics 6. Social science fiction

LC 2019011852

Nebula Award for Best Novel, 2019

Public gatherings are illegal making concerts impossible, except for those willing to break the law for the love of music, and for one chance at human connection.

Pinter, Jason

Hide away. Jason Pinter. Thomas & Mercer, 2020. 367 pages (Rachel Marin novels, 1)

ISBN 9781542005906

1. Single mothers 2. Widows 3. Women vigilantes 4. Loss (Psychology) 5. Murder investigation 6. Illinois 7. Thrillers and suspense

From the bestselling author of the Henry Parker series comes a page-turning thriller about a vigilante who's desperate to protect her secrets—and bring a killer to justice.

"Pinter does a masterful job of ramping up suspense about the Marin family's past and the current case, spinning an absolutely riveting plot with a cast of full-bodied, fallible characters, in what seems the start of a promising series." —*Booklist*

A **stranger** at the door. Jason Pinter. Thomas & Mercer, 2021. 362 pages (Rachel Marin novels, 2)

ISBN 9781542005944

1. Single mothers 2. Mother and child 3. Families of murder victims 4. High school students 5. Threat (Psychology) 6. Illinois 7. Thrillers and suspense

From the Amazon bestselling author of Hide Away comes the gripping second installment of the Rachel Marin Thriller series.

"This second in the Rachel Marin series maintains the promise of the first (Hide Away, 2020), with full-bodied characters in a compelling plot and graphic elements leavened by doses of humanity." —*Booklist*

Pintoff, Stefanie

Hostage taker: a novel. Stefanie Pintoff. Bantam Books, 2015. 448 p. (Eve Rossi novels, 1)

ISBN 9780345531407

1. Hostages 2. Women FBI agents 3. Hostage taking 4. Guilt 5. Criminals 6. New York City 7. Thrillers and suspense 8. Adult books for young adults

LC 2015001375

Library Journal Best Books, 2015

FBI hostage negotiator Eve Rossi is burned out and on leave when a shooting in Manhattan turns into a hostage situation at the iconic St. Patrick's Cathedral. Called back to work, Eve is hampered by a hostage taker who won't identify himself—and makes only bizarre demands. Also not helping: intense pressure from the Catholic Church, the media, and the mayor. The behind-the-scenes views of St. Patrick's add an unusual element to a well-paced and increasingly tense story (and likely series debut).

"Strong writing, a well-paced plot, and intriguing characters make this one of the best thrillers of the year." —*Library Journal*

Pipkin, John

Woodsburner: a novel. John Pipkin. Nan A. Talese, 2009. 384 p. cm.

ISBN 9780385528658

1. Thoreau, Henry David 2. Forest fires 3. Philosophers 4. Interpersonal relations 5. Walden Pond region, Massachusetts 6. Massachusetts 7. 1840s 8. Biographical fiction 9. Historical fiction

LC 2008033233

Massachusetts Book Awards, Fiction Award, 2010

Henry Thoreau accidentally sets fire to three hundred acres near nineteenth-century Concord, Massachusetts and affects the lives of three people, a Norwegian farmhand, a bookseller and aspiring playwright, and a preacher, as they respond to the disaster.

"Pipkin doesn't underplay Thoreau's horror at what he's done (or overplay the inherent irony of the author of Walden burning down the woods). Instead, he concentrates on the ability of a natural disaster to act as a catalyst in people's minds and lives. The result is, well, transcendent." —*Christian Science Monitor*

Pirie, David

The **patient's** eyes. David Pirie. St. Martin's Minotaur, 2002. Ix, 244 p. : Illustration (Dark beginnings of Sherlock Holmes, 1)

ISBN 9780312290955

1. Doyle, Arthur Conan 2. Physicians 3. Forensic scientists 4. Amateur detectives 5. Heirs and heiresses 6. Women stalking victims 7. Edinburgh, Scotland 8. Scotland 9. 19th century 10. Historical mysteries 11. Mysteries

Young medical student Arthur Conan Doyle teams up with his mentor, Dr. Joseph Bell, to investigate a Victorian murder mystery involving a phantom cyclist and a rich Spanish businessman.

"A 'fictional' account of Arthur Conan Doyle's early life that relates how his association with Edinburgh physician Joseph Bell was the inspiration for his Holmes character. Pirie vividly evokes the dark ambience of Victorian England, his prose is elegant, and his gift for mimicking the slightly haughty tone of Doyle's writing is uncanny." —*Booklist*

Pitoniak, Anna

Necessary people. Anna Pitoniak. Little Brown & Co, 2019. 352 pages

ISBN 9780316451703

1. Ambition in women 2. Class conflict 3. Television industry and trade 4. Competition in women 5. Rich women 6. New York (State) 7. Psychological suspense 8. Adult books for young adults

In a novel set against the fast-paced backdrop of TV news, the author of The Futures offers a work of psychological suspense about ambition and privilege and the thin line between friendship and rivalry.

★ **Our** American friend. Anna Pitoniak. Simon & Schuster, 2022. 336 p.

ISBN 9781982158804

1. Presidents' spouses 2. Former fashion models 3. Women biographers 4. Women journalists 5. Cold War 6. Spy fiction 7. Political fiction

When mysterious first lady Lara Caine asks her to write her official biography, former White House correspondent Sofie Morse is wary when Lara starts sharing sensitive information, which draws her into a game of cat and mouse with explosive consequences.

"This lively political thriller mulls love, loyalty, and the rewards of playing the long game." —*Kirkus*

Pitts, Leonard

Freeman. Leonard Pitts. Agate, 2012. 432 p.

ISBN 9781932841640

1. Searching 2. Forced relocations 3. African American husband and wife 4. Loyalty 5. Slavery 6. United States 7. Historical fiction 8. Love stories 9. War stories

BCALA Literary Award for Fiction, 2013

"At the end of the Civil War, an escaped slave first returns to his old plantation and then walks across the ravaged South in search of his lost wife." —Provided by the publisher.

Plath, Sylvia

★ The **bell** jar. Sylvia Plath; foreword by Frances McCullough; biographical note by Lois Ames; drawings by Sylvia Plath. HarperCollins, 1996. Xviii, 296 p. : Illustration

ISBN 9780060174903

1. Women with depression 2. Mental illness 3. Women with mental illnesses 4. Women authors, American 5. Nervous breakdown 6. Psychological fiction 7. Autobiographical fiction 8. Books to movies

LC 96211742

Presents the American poet's semi-autobiographical account of Esther Greenwood, a talented writer who struggles for intimacy and meaning in her artist life.

Title adapted into a film of the same name in 1979 and 2018.

Originally published: New York : Harper & Row, 1948.

Pobi, Robert

City of windows. Robert Pobi. Minotaur Books, 2019. 336 p. (Dr Lucas Page novels, 1)

ISBN 9781250293947

1. Astrophysicists 2. Former FBI agents 3. People who have had amputations 4. Crime scenes 5. College teachers 6. New York City 7. Mysteries

LC 2019006904

When his former partner is murdered by an unusually skilled sniper, a disabled former FBI agent with an exceptional ability for reading difficult crime scenes struggles to outmaneuver a killer during a historical blizzard.

"Relentless pacing, tight plotting, and a brainy, idiosyncratic new hero make this one a winner." —*Kirkus*

Under pressure. Robert Pobi. Minotaur Books, 2020. 437 pages (Dr Lucas Page novels, 2)

ISBN 9781250293961

1. Bombs 2. Explosives 3. Murder investigation 4. Museums 5. Astrophysicists 6. New York City 7. Mysteries

LC 2020012793

When an explosion rocks the Guggenheim Museum, killing 702 people but causing little damage to the building, Brett Kehoe, Special Agent in Charge of Manhattan, teams up with Dr. Lucas Page, astrophysicist, university professor, and former FBI agent. Page wants nothing to do with the FBI, but with his city under attack and his family at risk, he steps in to find a killer in a haystack before they strike again.

"Fans of Jeffery Deaver's 'Lincoln Rhyme' series will find much to enjoy in this second thriller from Pobi (after City of Windows) featuring astrophysicist, numbers whiz, and sometime FBI consultant Lucas Page." —*Library Journal*

Pochoda, Ivy

★ **These** women. Ivy Pochoda. Ecco Press, 2020. 256 pages

ISBN 9780062656384

1. Women — Psychology 2. Violence against women 3. Serial murderers 4. Poverty 5. Street life 6. Los Angeles, California 7. Thrillers and suspense 8. Literary fiction

Connected by the deadly obsessions of a single man, five very different women endure lives of danger and anguish, including a mother whose daughter's murder remains unsolved.

"This deep dive into the lives of women too often unseen in the shadows makes them vividly unforgettable." —*Publishers Weekly*

"It is complex, intense, and enthralling. Fans of Rachel Kushner's The Mars Room will experience a similar sense of feeling both captivated and bereft." —*Library Journal*

Visitation Street: a novel. Ivy Pochoda. Ecco, 2013. 306 p.

ISBN 9780062249890

1. Missing persons investigation 2. Secrets 3. Life change events 4. Neighborhoods 5. Missing teenage girls 6. Brooklyn, New York City 7. New York City 8. Mysteries 9. Adult books for young adults

When an adventure on the bay takes a tragic turn, resulting in her best friend's disappearance, Val, who was washed ashore semi-conscious, is left to deal with the aftermath, while their teacher, a Julliard drop-out and barfly, must confront a past riddled with sins of omission.

"The prose is so lyrical and detailed that readers will easily imagine themselves in Red Hook. A great read for those who enjoy urban mysteries and thrillers with a literary flair." —*Library Journal*

Poe, Edgar Allan

★ **Complete** stories and poems of Edgar Allan Poe. Doubleday, 1966. Ix, 821 p.

ISBN 9780385074070

1. Anthologies 2. Short stories 3. Horror 4. Poetry

LC 66024310

A complete collection of the writings of Poe, including his mysteries, fantasies, satires, and poems

The **narrative** of Arthur Gordon Pym of Nantucket. Edgar Allan Poe. Dover Publications, 2005. Ix, 155 p.

ISBN 9780486440934

1. Survival (after airplane accidents, shipwrecks, etc.) 2. Stowaways 3. Sailors 4. Whaling ships 5. Young men 6. Nantucket, Massachusetts 7. Sea stories 8. Classics 9. Gothic fiction

LC 2004061804

A horror tale presented in journal form by Pym, a young man who is smuggled aboard the brig Grampus in 1827. Mutiny, cannibalism, fantastic animals and natives of Antarctica, and supernatural happenings comprise a story of adventure in the South Seas.

This Dover edition, first published in 2005, is an unabridged republication of the first edition of the work originally published in 1838 by Harper & Brothers, New York—Title page verso.

Originally published: New York: Harper & Brothers, 1838.

Poeppel, Amy

Musical chairs: a novel. Amy Poeppel. Emily Bestler Books/Atria, 2020. X, 405 p.

ISBN 9781501176418

1. Vacation homes 2. Musicians 3. Summer 4. Parent and adult child 5. Single mothers 6. Connecticut 7. Relationship fiction

LC 2020012003

Envied for her close relationship with a famous music artist and Julliard classmate, a successful chamber group founder finds her summer plans riotously upended by sudden family upheavals, including her elderly father's marriage.

"There is a large cast of characters, but they are all distinct individuals with their own personalities and voices who work together seamlessly in the novel as both soloists and supporting characters. Author Poeppel has created a story that is well thought out, well plotted, well written, and fully developed. A delightful novel that celebrates the messiness and joy to be found in real life." —*Kirkus*

Pohl, Frederik

Chernobyl: a novel. Frederik Pohl. Bantam Books 1987. 355p.

ISBN 9780553052107

1. Chernobyl Nuclear Accident, 1986

LC 86047896

Dramatizes the human stories of the Chernobyl disaster, and chronicles the accident's day-to-day impact on personal lives, the dreadful future toll on the world, and the effect the catastrophe has on Russian political policies BT

"The author re-creates in fiction the massive 1986 Ukrainian nuclear power plant disaster. The book opens during normal days just before the accident; suspense builds, as the reader expects the worst. Characters that would actually have been on the scene are seen being overwhelmed by berserk technology, their lives shattered. The tale is gripping, and the locale well established." —*Library Journal*

Gateway. Frederik Pohl. Ballantine Books, 1977. 313 p. (Heechee saga, 1)
ISBN 9780345346902
1. Alien artifacts 2. Space flight 3. Far future 4. Corporations 5. Voyages and travels 6. Science fiction classics 7. Space opera 8. Science fiction

LC 76-10561

Hugo Award for Best Novel, 1978; John W. Campbell Memorial Award for Best Science Fiction Novel, 1978; Locus Award for Best Science Fiction Novel, 1978; Nebula Award for Best Novel, 1977

The Heechee gateways, remnants of an ancient civilization, provide instantaneous passage to the far reaches of the universe but do not ensure destination, return, wealth, or survival.

Poissant, David James

Lake life. David James Poissant. Simon & Schuster, 2020. 304 p.
ISBN 9781476729992
1. Weekends 2. Lakes 3. Vacation homes 4. Parent and adult child 5. Family secrets 6. North Carolina 7. Domestic fiction 8. Literary fiction 9. Multiple perspectives

The members of the Starling family return for one last weekend to their beloved, but for-sale, summer home in North Carolina, where they witness a tragedy that acts as a catalyst to a series of dramatic revelations.

"Poissant's compassion for his characters generates empathy for even their most disastrous actions. A totally engrossing story of the long shadows cast by troubled relationships and the glimmer of hope that dawns after painful confrontation." —*Booklist*

Polansky, Daniel

The **seventh** perfection. Daniel Polansky. St. Martins Press, 2020. 173 pages
ISBN 9781250767561
1. Women 2. Perfection 3. Gods and goddesses 4. Truth 5. Photographic memory 6. Fantasy mysteries 7. Second person narratives

When a woman with perfect memory sets out to solve a riddle, the threads she tugs on threatens not only the carefully prepared myths of the God-King's ascent, but her own identity and the nature of truth itself.

"While readers will crave more details about this world, the unique, challenging way the mystery unfolds presents a delightful puzzle." —*Publishers Weekly*

Polk, C. L.

The **midnight** bargain. C. L. Polk. Erewhon Trading Company, 2020. 208 p.
ISBN 9781645660071
1. Witches 2. Magic 3. Ambition in women 4. Gender role 5. Spirits 6. England 7. Regency period (1811-1820) 8. Historical fantasy 9. Canadian fiction

A romantic fantasy set in a magical Regency England. A sorceress with the ambition to become the world's first great sorceress is bound by familial duty to be married off.

"Polk expertly balances propulsive pacing, a rich multicultural world, and a vivid and subversive cast of characters. Readers will be swept away by this powerful and passionate fantasy." —*Publishers Weekly*

Soulstar. C.L. Polk. Tor.com, 2021. 272 p. (Kingston cycle series, 3)
ISBN 9781250203571
1. Political intrigue 2. Magic 3. Witches 4. Secrets 5. Assassination 6. Fantasy fiction 7. Steampunk

LC 2020042316

For years, Robin Thorpe has kept her head down, staying among her people in the Riverside neighborhood and hiding the magic that would have imprisoned her by the state. But when Grace Hensley comes knocking on Clan Thorpe's door, Robin's days of hiding are at an end. As freed witches flood the streets of Kingston, scrambling to reintegrate with a kingdom that destroyed their lives, Robin begins to plot a course that will ensure a freer, juster Aeland. At the same time, she has to face her long-bottled feelings for the childhood love who vanished into an asylum twenty years ago.

Stormsong. C.L. Polk. Tor.Com, 2020. 352 p. (Kingston cycle series, 2)
ISBN 9780765398994
1. Revolutions 2. Political intrigue 3. Magic 4. Witches 5. Women photojournalists 6. Steampunk 7. Historical fantasy

LC 2019042696

Loan Stars Favourites, 2020

Dame Grace Hensley helped her brother Miles undo the atrocity that stained her nation, but now she has to deal with the consequences. With the power out in the dead of winter and an uncontrollable sequence of winter storms on the horizon, Aeland faces disaster. Grace has the vision to guide her parents to safety, but a hostile queen and a ring of rogue mages stand in the way of her plans.

"Polk's sequel to Witchmark continues to unwrap an intriguing world of magic, political intrigue, and alternate-Edwardian times. Familiar and favorite characters support the young woman who takes center stage, while Polk's charming prose frames an original and witty story filled with action and romantic tension." —*Library Journal*

Witchmark. C.L. Polk. Tor Books, 2018. 318 p. (Kingston cycle series, 1)
ISBN 9781250162687
1. Magic 2. Veterans 3. Aristocracy 4. Angels 5. Secrets 6. Historical fantasy 7. Steampunk
World Fantasy Award, 2019

After going to war to escape his destiny, Miles Singer is unable to leave his past behind when he, after faking his own death, reinvents himself as a doctor at a cash-strapped veteran's hospital where he can no longer hide what he truly is.

Pollock, Donald Ray

The **devil** all the time. Donald Ray Pollock. Random House Inc 2011. 304 p.
ISBN 9780385535045
1. Veterans 2. Serial murderers 3. Violence 4. Fugitives 5. Religious fanaticism 6. Ohio 7. West Virginia 8. 20th century 9. Rural noir 10. Crime fiction 11. Literary fiction

Presents a dark tale set in rural southern Ohio and West Virginia between World War II and the 1960s that follows the experiences of tormented and violent individuals whose respective struggles culminate in the adult patterns of an orphaned son.

"The flawless cadence of Pollock's gorgeous shadow-and-light prose plays against the heinous acts of his sorrowful and sometimes just sorry characters." —*Elle*

Knockemstiff. Donald Ray Pollock. Doubleday, 2008. 206 p.
ISBN 9780385523820
1. Small town life 2. Ohio 3. Rural noir 4. Short stories 5. Literary fiction

Spanning the era from the mid-1960s to the late 1990s, a collection of stories journeys inside the world of the diverse inhabitants of Knockemstiff, a tough, Midwestern town, as their lives change and intertwine.

"Pollock's writing has been compared to that of Flannery O'Connor, Raymond Carver and Cormac McCarthy. He draws his readers in slowly, tangling them in the mundane toil of small-town life, before smacking them upside the head with something unexpected and primal. Small moments yield big surprises." —*The Oregonian*

Pomerantz, Sharon

Rich boy. Sharon Pomerantz. Twelve, 2010. 528 p.
ISBN 9780446563185
1. Rich people 2. Self-fulfillment 3. Jewish American men 4. Hypocrisy 5. Ambition 6. Manhattan, New York City 7. Philadelphia, Pennsylvania 8. Psychological fiction

LC 2009032386

After he rises from a working-class New York Jewish neighborhood in the 1970s to the cloistered universities of New England to the highest circles of Manhattan society during the Reagan boom, Robert Vishniak sees his carefully crafted identity start to unravel after he bumps into a beautiful woman from the old neighborhood.

"It would spoil Pomerantz's pleasingly soapy narrative to detail too much of Robert's subsequent journey, first in 1960s Boston and then in the go-go Manhattan of the '70s and '80s. But while his tale often feels allegorical...Rich Boy is told with such page-turning skill that its pleasures, if not deep, feel rich indeed." —*Entertainment Weekly*

Pontoppidan, Henrik

Lucky Per. By Henrik Pontoppidan; translated by Naomi Lebowitz; introduction by Garth Risk Hallberg. Everyman's Library, 2019. 608 pages
ISBN 9781101908099
1. Social change 2. Children of clergy 3. Ambition in men 4. Jewish women 5. Engineers 6. Copenhagen, Denmark 7. Denmark 8. 20th century 9. Coming-of-age stories 10. Classics 11. Translations

LC 2018053817

A hardcover edition of the 1904 novel by Nobel Prize-winning Danish author Henrik Pontoppidan, widely considered "the great Danish novel," but not available in English until recently. In a translation by Naomi Lebowitz, with a new introduction by novelist Garth Risk Hallberg, bibliography, and chronology.

Translation of: Lykke-Per
Includes bibliographical references.
Translated from the Danish

Poole, Sara

The **Borgia** mistress. Sara Poole. St. Martin's Griffin, 2012. 416 p. (Poisoner mysteries, 3)
ISBN 9781250023520

1. Borgia family 2. Women poisoners 3. Conspiracies 4. Secrets 5. Lovers 6. Alliances 7. Italy 8. Rome, Italy 9. Renaissance (1300-1600) 10. 15th century 11. Historical mysteries 12. First person narratives 13. Mysteries

Francesca Giordano joins forces with her lover, Cesare Borgia, in order to decrypt a conspiracy against Pope Alexander VI, after he and the papal court is forced to flee from Rome.

"True to its characters and historical facts, Poole's novel immerses readers in a seductive Renaissance environment, full of danger and passion." —*Publishers Weekly*

Poore, Michael

Reincarnation blues. Michael Poore. Del Rey, 2017. 400 p.
ISBN 9780399178481
1. Men 2. Quests 3. Reincarnation 4. Death (Personification) 5. Metaphysics 6. Contemporary fantasy 7. Fantasy fiction
LibraryReads Favorites, 2017

A man who has been reincarnated nearly ten thousand times, living lives in regions from ancient India and Renaissance Italy to outer space and the modern world, searches for the secret to immortality so that he can be with his beloved, the incarnation of Death.

"Poore (Up Jumps the Devil) addresses humans relationship to the universe through a clever, personal story filled with gentle humor, wry sweetness, and perhaps even some wisdom." —*Publishers Weekly*

Pope, Jamie

One warm winter. Jamie Pope. Dafina, 2019. 320 pages (Sunny and warm)
ISBN 9781496718273
1. Heirs and heiresses 2. Women adoptees 3. Bodyguards 4. Family secrets 5. Scandals 6. Contemporary romances 7. Multicultural romances

Wynter Bates, who was adopted as a child by a tech billionaire, tries to ignore her attraction to her bodyguard, Cullen Whelan, whom she is pretending to date, while investigating her true parentage after a scandal is exposed.

Porter, Chana

The **seep**: a novel. Chana Porter. Soho, 2020. 203 pages
ISBN 9781641290869
1. Aliens 2. Utopias 3. Trans women 4. Loss (Psychology) 5. Fifties (Age) 6. Science fiction

LC 2019023457

Living in a utopian world shaped by alien invaders who make any dream possible, a 50-year-old trans woman is devastated by the end of her marriage before an unexpected quest pits her against the aliens' most avid supporters.

"Porter's gripping, subtly hopeful work of literary speculative fiction is shaped by remarkable world-building elements and acute observation of human frailties and impetus." —*Booklist*

Porter, Henry

The **bell** ringers. Henry Porter. Atlantic Monthly Press, 2010. 288 p.
ISBN 9780802119315
1. Women intelligence officers 2. Conspiracies 3. Genghis Khan 4. Terrorism 5. Inheritance and succession 6. England 7. Political thrillers 8. Thrillers and suspense 9. Spy fiction

After her ex-boyfriend, a former head of intelligence, is killed, Kate Lockhart inherits his dangerous secrets, all having to do with the Orwellian reality this near-future England has become, and she soon finds herself on the run from the security-obsessed state.

"The tale is set in England, where cameras identify license plates and faces, computers catalog phone and financial records, and submitting an incomplete form can be a felony. What's to prevent a prime minister from abusing these powers? Just a few committed (if sometimes cliched) characters, some intricately complex plotting and gobs of local color. The world of The Bell Ringers isn't as dystopian as 1984, but it's not that far off." —*Cleveland Plain Dealer*

Originally published as The dying light: London : Orion, 2009.

Firefly. Henry Porter. The Mysterious Press, 2018. 480 p. (Paul Samson novels, 1)

ISBN 9780802128959

1. Teenage refugees 2. Intelligence service 3. International intrigue 4. Terrorists 5. National security 6. North Macedonia 7. Syria 8. Spy fiction 9. Thrillers and suspense

LC 2018026964

An ex-MI6 agent-turned-detective races to find a 13-year-old refugee in the mountains of Macedonia who holds vital intelligence about a terrorist threat targeting the center of Europe.

Originally published by Quercus, 2018.

The **old** enemy. Henry Porter. Atlantic Monthly Press, 2021. 368 p. (Paul Samson novels, 3)

ISBN 9780802158659

1. Former spies 2. Attempted assassination 3. Intelligence service 4. International intrigue 5. Women environmentalists 6. Europe 7. Estonia 8. Thrillers and suspense 9. Spy fiction

In the electrifying third installment in the internationally best-selling series, former MI6 agent Paul Samson, after several attempts are made on his life, goes on the run to Estonia where he must expose a shadowy and dangerous enemy of Western democracy.

"Porter makes brilliant use of material ripped from today's headlines—Russian cultivation of Western assets, nefarious data mining—to construct a riveting thriller, bolstered by a moving love story and a stunning finale in which a second congressional hearing shows that sometimes the good guys can outwit their cutthroat adversaries." —*Booklist*

White hot silence. Henry Porter. Mysterious Press, 2019. 448 p. (Paul Samson novels, 2)

ISBN 9780802147530

1. Mafia 2. Kidnapping victims 3. International intrigue 4. Former lovers 5. Financial intrigue 6. Italy 7. Thrillers and suspense 8. Spy fiction

After being ambushed outside new African refugee centers built by her billionaire husband, a Greek aid worker is kidnapped by the Mafia and her life is threatened in exchange for some explosive information, in the sequel to Firefly.

Porter, Katherine Anne

★ The **collected** stories of Katherine Anne Porter. Katherine Anne Porter. Harcourt, Brace & World, 1979. Viii, 495 p.

ISBN 9780156188760

1. Short stories

National Book Award for Fiction, 1966; Pulitzer Prize for Fiction, 1966

Twenty-seven short stories by the Pulitzer Prize-winning writer BT

"These are perfect examples of the short story and are representative not only of the best American writing but of the best in the world." —*School Library Journal*

Originally published: New York : Harcourt, Brace & World, 1965.

Pale horse, pale rider: three short novels. Katherine Anne Porter. Harcourt Brace Jovanovich, 1990. 208 p.

ISBN 9780151707553

1. Short stories 2. Modern classics

Three short novels deal with turn of the century family life, a new hired hand, and the World War I homefront and the influenza epidemic.

Ship of fools. Katherine Anne Porter. Back Bay Books; Little Brown, 1962. 497 p.

ISBN 9780316713900

1. Voyages and travels 2. Middle-aged women 3. Ocean travel 4. Ocean liners 5. Atlantic Ocean 6. 1930s 7. Allegories 8. Books to movies

LC 629557

An unforgettable voyage of discovery and self-delusion aboard the vessel sailing from Mexico to pre-Hitler Germany. These interlocking stories unfold and give us a cross-section view of humanity.

Porter, Max

★ **Grief** is the thing with feathers. Max Porter. Graywolf Press, 2016. 114 pages

ISBN 9781555977412

1. Fathers and sons 2. Grief 3. Loss (Psychology) 4. Coping 5. Men-headed families 6. London, England 7. Literary fiction

ALA Notable Book, 2017; New York Times Notable Book, 2016

A recently widowed father of two has difficulty dealing with his grief and the overwhelming sadness of his children, until they are visited by Crow, an actual crow, who serves as an antagonist, protector, therapist and babysitter and helps them heal.

"Porter's daringly strange story skirts disbelief to speak, engagingly and effectively, of the pain this world inflicts, of where the ghosts go, and of how we are left to press on and endure it all." —*Kirkus*

Originally published: London : Faber & Faber, 2015.

★ **Lanny:** a novel. Max Porter. Graywolf Press, 2019. 213 p.

ISBN 9781555978402

1. Mythical creatures 2. Missing boys 3. Villages 4. Missing persons investigation 5. Eccentric boys 6. England 7. 21st century 8. Literary fiction

ALA Notable Book, 2020; Longlisted for the Booker Prize, 2019

Follows the awakening of a mythical being in a London village, where he observes the domestic dramas and creative energies surrounding a mischievous, ethereal young newcomer.

Porter, Regina

The **travelers**. Regina Porter. Random House Inc 2019. 320 p.

ISBN 9780525576198

1. Families — History 2. Interpersonal relations 3. Intergenerational relations 4. African Americans — Social conditions 5. African American families 6. United States 7. 1950s 8. 2000s (Decade) 9. Literary fiction 10. African American fiction

A first novel by an award-winning playwright follows the experiences of two American families, one black and one white, against a backdrop of historical events from the 1950s through the first year of Barack Obama's presidency.

Portis, Charles

★ The **dog** of the South. Knopf 1979. 245 p.

ISBN 9780394506142

1. Runaway wives, husbands, etc. 2. Jilted men 3. Chases 4. Former journalists 5. Former husbands 6. Little Rock, Arkansas 7. Humorous stories 8. Picaresque fiction 9. First person narratives

LC 78067580

Ray Midge is on the trail of his wife Norma, who's headed for Mexico with her ex-husband. On the way Ray meets the eccentric Dr. Reo Symes, a man with more get-rich-quick schemes than common sense. Together, they'll have to overcome tropical storms, grifters, and plenty of car trouble en route to their destination—wherever that may be.

"Simultaneously hilarious and heart breakingly odd...you find yourself laughing so hard in sections that tears run down your face." —*Baltimore Sun*

★ **Gringos:** a novel. Charles Portis. Simon and Schuster 1991. 269 p. ISBN 9780671724573
1. Swindlers and swindling 2. Expatriates 3. Cults 4. Archaeological thefts 5. New Age 6. Yucatan Peninsula 7. First person narratives 8. Humorous stories

LC 90042476

Follows the fortunes of Jimmy Burns, an American expatriate living a simple life in Mexico until his peace is shattered by the arrival of a band of hippies seeking psychic happenings and a woman tracking UFO landing sites.

"Gringos, by far, is Portis's most inward-turning book, a story of a grownup trying to grow up, to keep it together with some dignity. Watching him pull it off is one of the finest pleasures afforded by any novel in a long time." —*Newsweek*

★ **Masters** of Atlantis: a novel. Charles Portis. A. A. Knopf, 1985. 247 p. ISBN 9780394546834
1. Delusions 2. Secret societies 3. Occult centers, groups, etc 4. Americans in France 5. Atlantis (Legendary place) 6. France 7. 1910s 8. Humorous stories

LC 85040212

When Lamar Jimmerson "comes across a little book crammed with Atlantean puzzles, Egyptian riddles, and extended alchemical metaphors," he's convinced that he is called to lead the Gnomon Society in the search for truth concerning the lost city of Atlantis.

"The plot spins dizzily along as sly Sydney Hen and antic Austin Popper are drawn into the society, engineer a farcical schism, and espouse assorted crackpot causes.... Those who enjoy deadpan comedy should get a good laugh here." —*Library Journal*

★ **True** grit: a novel. Charles Portis. Simon and Schuster, 1968. 215 p. ISBN 9780671203016
1. Revenge 2. Fathers — Death 3. Outlaws 4. Ford, Gerald R. 5. Independence in teenage girls 6. The West (United States) 7. 1870s 8. Westerns 9. Books to movies

LC 200234552

With her papa's pistol tied to her saddlehorn and a supersized ration of audacity, fourteen-year-old Mattie Ross sets out to avenge her father's murder.

This novel was adapted into two films: "True Grit" (1969) starring John Wayne and Kim Darby, directed by Henry Hathaway, and "True Grit" (2010) starring Jeff Bridges, Matt Damon and Josh Brolin, directed by Joel and Ethan Coen.

Potenza, Carol

Hearts of the missing. Carol Potenza. Minotaur Books, 2018. 368 p. ISBN 9781250178282
1. Tribal police 2. Indians of North America 3. Missing persons 4. Suicide 5. Women detectives 6. New Mexico 7. Mysteries

LC 2018027002

A prize-winning debut novel follows the experiences of Pueblo Police Sergeant Nicky Matthews, who investigates a personally relevant case involving the serial murders of genetic members of the Fire-Sky tribe by a killer who also deliberately violates spiritual laws.

"Potenza's polished, page-turning debut shares Hillerman's thoughtful exploration of Native identity, story-driving cultural tension, and evocative setting." —*Booklist*

Potok, Chaim

★ The **gift** of Asher Lev. Chaim Potok. Fawcett Columbine, 1997. 369 p. ISBN 9780449001158
1. Jewish Americans 2. Hasidim 3. Artists 4. Cultural differences 5. Middle-aged men 6. New York City 7. Brooklyn, New York City 8. Domestic fiction

LC 89043401

National Jewish Book Award for Fiction, 1991

When the death of a beloved uncle brings him back to his native Brooklyn after two decades, painter Asher Lev is plunged into a conflict between the culture into which he was born and the life that he has forged for himself.
Sequel to: My name is Asher Lev.
Originally published: New York : Knopf, 1990.

★ **My** name is Asher Lev. Chaim Potok. Anchor Books, 2003. 369 p. ISBN 9781400031047
1. Jewish families 2. Culture conflict 3. Identity (Psychology) 4. Self-fulfillment in men 5. Art 6. New York City 7. Crown Heights, New York City 8. Coming-of-age stories

LC 70171131

Records the anguish and triumps of a young painter as he emerges into the great world of art and rejects all else.
Sequel: The gift of Asher Lev.
Originally published: New York : Knopf, 1972.

Potzsch, Oliver

The **beggar** king. Oliver Potzsch; translated from the German by Lee Chadeayne. Houghton Mifflin Harcourt 2013. 544 p. (Hangman's daughter tales, 3)
ISBN 9780547992198
1. Murder investigation 2. Innocence (Law) 3. Sisters — Death 4. Man-woman relationships 5. Executions and executioners 6. Germany 7. 1660s 8. 17th century 9. Historical mysteries 10. Translations 11. Mysteries

After the hangman Jakob Kuisl is framed for his sister's murder, his daughter Magdalena and her paramour, Simon, enlist the help of a network of beggars in order to save him from the noose.
Originally published Henkerstochter und der Konig der Bettler: Berlin : Ullstein, 2010.
Translated from the German.

The **dark** monk: a hangman's daughter tale. Oliver Potzsch; translated from the German by Lee Chadeayne. Mariner Books, 2012. 528 p. (Hangman's daughter tales, 2)
ISBN 9780547807683
1. Murder investigation 2. Monks 3. Poisoning 4. Villages 5. Treasure hunting 6. Germany 7. 1660s 8. 17th century 9. Historical mysteries 10. Translations 11. Mysteries

LC 2012014848

A follow-up to The Hangman's Daughter traces the 1648 investigation by hangman Jakob Kuisl, his headstrong daughter and the town physician into the poisoning murder of a priest whose demise is precariously linked to the Crusades and the Knights Templar treasure.

Originally published Henkerstochter und der schwarze Monch: Berlin : Ullstein, 2009.

Translated from the German.

The **hangman's** daughter: a historical novel. Oliver Potzsch; translated from the German by Lee Chadeayne. AmazonCrossing 2010. 435 p. (Hangman's daughter tales, 1)
ISBN 9781935597056
1. Executions and executioners 2. Witchcraft 3. Pariahs 4. Murder investigation 5. Villages 6. Germany 7. 1660s 8. 17th century 9. Historical mysteries 10. Translations 11. Mysteries

Germany, 1659: When a dying boy is pulled from the river with a mark crudely tattooed on his shoulder, hangman Jakob Kuisl is called upon to investigate whether witchcraft is at play in his small Bavarian town. Whispers and dark memories of witch trials and the women burned at stake just seventy years earlier still haunt the streets of Schongau. When more children disappear and an orphan boy is found dead, marked by the same tattoo, the mounting hysteria threatens to erupt into chaos. Before the unrest forces him to torture and execute the very woman who aided in the birth of his children, Jakob must unravel the truth. With the help of his clever daughter, Magdelena, and Simon, the university-educated son of the town's physician, Jakob discovers that a devil is indeed loose in Schongau. But it may be too late to prevent bloodshed. A brilliantly detailed, fast-paced historical thriller, The Hangman's Daughter is the first novel from German television screenwriter Oliver Pötzsch, a descendent of the Kuisls, a famous Bavarian executioner clan.

First published in Germany in 2008 by Ullstein Buchverlage GmbH as Die henkerstochter—Title page verso.

Translated from the German.

The **play** of death. Oliver Potzsch; translated by Lee Chadeayne. Mariner Books, 2017. 544 pages (Hangman's daughter tales, 6)
ISBN 9781328662088
1. Executions and executioners 2. Murder investigation 3. Villages 4. Crucifixion 5. Passion-plays 6. Germany 7. 17th century 8. Historical mysteries 9. Translations
LC 2016051868

Simon Fronwieser and his hangman father-in-law investigate the murder of the actor due to play Christ in a Passion Play, who was found nailed to the set's cross, in the latest addition to the series.

"A veritable Series of Unfortunate Events for adults and perfect for fans of bleak, folktale-laden landscapes and bogeyman heroes ...." —Booklist

Originally published: Berlin : Ullstein, 2016.

Translated from the German.

The **poisoned** pilgrim: a hangman's daughter tale. Oliver Potzsch; translated by Lee Chadeayne. Mariner Books-Houghton Mifflin Harcourt, 2013. 496 p. (Hangman's daughter tales, 4)
ISBN 9780544114609
1. Missing persons 2. Monks 3. Pilgrims and pilgrimages 4. Murder investigation 5. Families 6. Germany 7. 1660s 8. 17th century 9. Historical mysteries 10. Translations 11. Mysteries

In 1666, Magdalena and her physician husband arrive at Andechs Abbey where they, along with the hangman of Schongau, set out to find the mysterious Brother Virgilius, who disappeared after creating an eerie automaton.

Translation from the German of: Hexer und die Henkerstochter.

Originally published: 2012.

The **werewolf** of Bamberg. Oliver Potzsch; translated by Lee Chadeayne. Houghton Mifflin Harcourt 2015. 720 p. (Hangman's daughter tales, 5)

ISBN 9780544610941
1. Murder investigation 2. Voyages and travels 3. Vacations 4. Amputation 5. Werewolves 6. Germany 7. 1660s 8. 17th century 9. Historical mysteries 10. Translations 11. Mysteries

A 1668 family vacation turns into a nightmare when a series of violent murders are thought to be the work of a werewolf.

Translation from the German of: Die henkerstochter und der teurfel von Bamberg.

Originally published: Germany : Ullstein Buchverlag, 2014.

Powell, Mark
Firebird. Mark Powell. Haywire Books, 2020. 312 pages
ISBN 9781950182022
1. Natural gas 2. Corporations 3. Political intrigue 4. International crime 5. Billionaires 6. Ukraine 7. United States 8. 2010s 9. Political thrillers

An arms deal gone south takes you into the underground world of political operatives, Ivy League criminals, and a hedge fund billionaire with eyes on the presidency.

"Powell has created a cast of indelible characters, and he spins an action-packed story of political intrigue and corruption that could be torn from today's headlines." —Booklist

Powell, Padgett
★ **Edisto:** a novel. Padgett Powell. Farrar, Straus, Giroux, 1984. 183 p.
ISBN 9780374146511
1. Boys 2. Atlantic Coast (South Carolina) 3. Mainstream fiction 4. Coming-of-age stories
LC 83025334

A twelve-year-old boy chronicles his coming of age on a rural strip of coast between Savannah and Charleston BT

"This is distinctly a tour de force.... Powell's ear is acute: one of the pleasures of the book is his ability to catch the nuances of Southern speech." —New York Times Book Review

Sequel: Edisto Revisited.

Power, Susan
The **grass** dancer. Susan Power. Putnam's, 1994. 300 p.
ISBN 9780399139116
1. Dakota Indians 2. Powwows 3. Seventeen-year-old boys 4. Spirits 5. Witches 6. North Dakota 7. Mythological fiction 8. Contemporary fantasy 9. Adult books for young adults
LC 93047199

ALA Notable Book, 1995; Booklist Editors' Choice: Adult Books for Young Adults, 1994; Hemingway Foundation/PEN Award, 1995

From the 1860s, when two lovers are separated by death, the cosmic drama of the two spirits desperately seeking to be reunited molds the lives and fates of their descendants, in a lyrical debut novel shaped by the lore of the Sioux.

"This is a passionate portrayal of universal human emotions and a vivid account of Native American history and culture." —School Library Journal

Powers, Kevin
★ The **yellow** birds: a novel. Kevin Powers. Little, Brown, 2012. 192 p.
ISBN 9780316219365
1. War — Psychological aspects 2. Iraq War, 2003-2011 3. Soldiers 4. Military life 5. Stress in men 6. Iraq 7. United States 8. War stories 9. Literary fiction 10. Books to movies 11. Adult books for young adults

LC 2012019435
Guardian First Book Award, 2012; Hemingway Foundation/PEN Award, 2013; New York Times Notable Book, 2012; School Library Journal Best Books: Best Adult Books 4 Teens, 2012; National Book Award for Fiction finalist, 2012

In the midst of a bloody battle in the Iraq War, two soldiers, bound together since basic training, do everything to protect each other from both outside enemies and the internal struggles that come from constant danger.

Adapted into a film by the same name in 2017.

Powers, Richard

★ **Bewilderment:** a novel. Richard Powers. W. W. Norton & Company, 2021. 304 p.

ISBN 9780393881141

1. Exobiology 2. Widowers 3. Fathers and sons 4. Biodiversity 5. Biofeedback 6. Literary fiction

LC 2021008991

Shortlisted for the Booker Prize, 2021

The astrobiologist Theo Byrne searches for life throughout the cosmos while single-handedly raising his unusual nine-year-old, Robin, following the death of his wife. Robin is a warm, kind boy who spends hours painting elaborate pictures of endangered animals. He's also about to be expelled from third grade for smashing his friend in the face. As his son grows more troubled, Theo hopes to keep him off psychoactive drugs. He learns of an experimental neurofeedback treatment to bolster Robin's emotional control, one that involves training the boy on the recorded patterns of his mother's brain.

"With soaring descriptions and forthright observations about our planet and the life it supports, Bewilderment is centered on a devoted father-and-son relationship, but it also offers rich commentary on the complex, often mystifying intersections between science, popular culture, and politics." —*Booklist*

The **echo** maker. Richard Powers. Farrar, Straus and Giroux, 2006. 464 p.

ISBN 9780374146351

1. Siblings 2. People in comas 3. Cognitive disorders 4. Neurologists 5. Medicine 6. Nebraska 7. Psychological fiction 8. Literary fiction

LC 2006000093

Booklist Editors' Choice, 2006; Library Journal Best Books, 2006; National Book Award for Fiction, 2006; New York Times Notable Book, 2006; Pulitzer Prize for Fiction finalist, 2007

Twenty-seven-year-old Mark Schluter, suffering from a rare brain disorder that causes him to believe his sister to be an impostor, endeavors to discover the cause of the motor vehicle accident that resulted in his head injury.

"This novel—a kind of neuro-cosmological adventure—is an exhilarating narrative feat. The ease with which the author controls his frequently complex material is sometimes as thrilling to watch as the unfolding of the story itself." —*Washington Post Book World.*

Generosity: an enhancement. Richard Powers. Farrar, Straus and Giroux, 2009. 304 p.

ISBN 9780374161149

1. College teachers 2. Genetic research 3. Writing 4. Authors 5. Genetics 6. Literary fiction

LC 2008054249

ALA Notable Book, 2010; Booklist Editors' Choice, 2009; New York Times Notable Book, 2009

Intrigued by an Algerian woman whose blissful demeanor contrasts with the horrific environment of her home country, Chicago teacher Russell Stone brings her to the attention of others who become equally entranced.

"Depending on personal philosophy, readers will disagree as to whether Generosity has a happy ending. But few will fail to be moved by Thassadit's joyful vision of human life." —*Dallas Morning News*

Orfeo: a novel. Richard Powers. W.W. Norton & Company, 2014. 352 p.

ISBN 9780393240825

1. Suspicion 2. Time travel 3. Music 4. Retirees 5. Composers 6. Pennsylvania 7. Thrillers and suspense

LC 2013031952

ALA Notable Book, 2015; Booklist Editors' Choice, 2014; LibraryReads Favorites, 2014

An experimental composer becomes a fugitive after his home microbiology lab, set up to find music in surprising patterns, results in a Homeland Security raid.

★ The **overstory:** a novel. Richard Powers. W. W. Norton & Co, 2018. 502 p.

ISBN 9780393635522

1. Trees 2. Nature 3. Forests 4. Humans — Effect of environment on 5. Women and nature 6. Literary fiction

LC 2017051173

ALA Notable Book, 2019; Booklist Editors' Choice, 2018; Library Journal Best Books, 2018; New York Times Notable Book, 2018; Pulitzer Prize for Fiction, 2019; Pen/Faulkner Award Finalist, 2019; Shortlisted for the Man Booker Prize, 2018

Presents an impassioned novel of activism and natural-world power that is comprised of interlocking fables about nine remarkable strangers who are summoned in different ways by trees for an ultimate, brutal stand to save the continent's few remaining acres of virgin forest.

"A magnificent achievement: a novel that is, by turns, both optimistic and fatalistic, idealistic without being nave." —*Kirkus*

Powning, Beth

The **sea** captain's wife: a novel. Beth Powning. A.A. Knopf Canada, 2010. 372 p. : Map

ISBN 9780307397102

1. Married women 2. Seafaring life 3. Ship captains' spouses 4. Ship captains 5. Children of ship captains 6. 19th century 7. 1860s 8. Literary fiction 9. Historical fiction 10. Canadian fiction

As a new wife living on the Bay of Fundy in the 1860s, Azuba craves a life beyond the tea and sewing circles. When her husband, Nathaniel, allows her to join him abroad, she faces tests that only a woman with a tenacious spirit and boundless fortitude could conquer.

Poyer, David

Overthrow: the war with China and North Korea—fall of an empire. David Poyer. St. Martin's Press, 2019. 320 p. (Tales of the Modern Navy, 19)

ISBN 9781250220561

1. Strategic alliances (Military) 2. Nuclear weapons 3. Naval battles 4. War 5. International relations 6. United States 7. China 8. Sea stories 9. Techno-thrillers

LC 2019024272

Admiral Dan Lenson leads an allied invasion in South China in the hopes of ending World War III, while his wife conducts secret negotiations with Beijing rebels and his daughter fights against a dangerous new epidemic.

"Since this novel supplies little backstory, it will be difficult for newbies to connect the dots at various points in the narrative. Fans, however, will continue to enjoy the ride and will want to get their hands on the next one quickly." —*Booklist*

Violent peace: the war with China - aftermath of Armageddon. David Poyer. St. Martin's Press, 2020. 384 p. (Tales of the Modern Navy, 20)
ISBN 9781250220585
1. Survival (after nuclear warfare) 2. Post-apocalypse 3. Admirals 4. Strategic alliances (Military) 5. Women ship captains 6. United States 7. China 8. Sea stories 9. Techno-thrillers
LC 2020024209
Dan Lenson motorcycles across a war-torn America in search of his missing daughter, while his wife negotiates the tenuous reunification of Taiwan with China and a young case officer confronts a devastating choice.

Pratchett, Terry

★ The **color** of magic. Terry Pratchett. Harper, 2005. 240 p; (Discworld, 1)
ISBN 9780060855925
1. Discworld (Imaginary place) 2. Magic 3. Voyages and travels 4. Monsters 5. Dragons 6. Fantasy fiction 7. Books to TV 8. Fantasy classics 9. Adult books for young adults
LC 83009698
A slightly disorganized and somewhat naive interplanetary tourist named Twoflower joins up with a bumbling wizard and embarks on a chaotic voyage through a world filled with monsters and dragons, heroes and knaves.

Equal rites. Terry Pratchett. Harper Paperbacks, 2000. 213 p; (Discworld, 3)
ISBN 9780061020698
1. Discworld (Imaginary place) 2. Wizards 3. Magic 4. Death (Fictitious character : Pratchett) 5. Fantasy fiction 6. Humorous stories 7. Adult books for young adults
A dying wizard hopes to pass his wisdom on to the eighth son of an eighth son, but when the child comes out female, the future of magic could be in jeopardy

The **fifth** elephant: a novel of Discworld. HarperPrism, 2000. 336 p; (Discworld, 24)
ISBN 9780061051579
1. Police 2. Discworld (Imaginary place) 3. Inheritance and succession 4. Dwarves (Fantasy characters) 5. Werewolves 6. Fantasy fiction 7. Humorous stories 8. Adult books for young adults
LC 99043960
A new visit to the satiric Discworld involves a search for the missing elephant from the five who support Discworld on their backs, as a stolen scone, a dwarf coronation, and ruby tights get into the act
"Pratchett cheerfully takes readers on an exuberant tale of mystery and invention.... Along the way, he skewers everything from monarchy to fascism, as well as communism and capitalism, oil wealth and ethnic identities, Russian plays, immigration, condoms and evangelical Christianity—in short, most everything worth talking about." —*Publishers Weekly*
Originally published: London: Doubleday, 1999.

Going postal: a novel of Discworld. Terry Pratchett. Harper Collins, 2004. 320 p. (Discworld, 30)
ISBN 9780060013134
1. Swindlers and swindling 2. Discworld (Imaginary place) 3. Magic 4. Ankh-Morpork (Imaginary place) 5. Postmasters 6. Fantasy fiction 7. Books to TV 8. Humorous stories 9. Adult books for young adults
LC 2004047391
Arch-swindler Moist Van Lipwig never believed his confidence crimes were hanging offenses—until he found himself with a noose tightly around his neck, dropping through a trapdoor, and falling into...a government job? By all rights, Moist should have met his maker. Instead, it's Lord Vetinari, supreme ruler of Ankh-Morpork, who promptly offers him a job as Postmaster. Since his only other option is a nonliving one, Moist accepts the position-and the hulking golem watchdog who comes along with it, just in case Moist was considering abandoning his responsibilities prematurely. Getting the moribund Postal Service up and running again, however, may be a near-impossible task, what with literally mountains of decades-old undelivered mail clogging every nook and cranny of the broken-down post office building; and with only a few creaky old postmen and one rather unstable, pin-obsessed youth available to deliver it. Worse still, Moist could swear the mail is talking to him.
"The author's inventiveness seems to know no end, his playful and irreverent use of language is a delight, and there is food for thought in his parody of fantasyland." —*School Library Journal*
Book adapted into a two-part television series in 2010.

Guards! Guards!. Terry Pratchett. V. Gollancz, 1989. 288 p; (Discworld, 8)
ISBN 9780575046061
1. Dragons 2. Police 3. Discworld (Imaginary place) 4. Ankh-Morpork (Imaginary place) 5. Dwarves (Fantasy characters) 6. Fantasy fiction 7. Humorous stories 8. Adult books for young adults
LC 91172661
In Anhk-Morpork, the blissful alcoholic oblivion of Vimes is disrupted by the arrival of Carrot, an ambitious dwarf cop who goes on an arresting spree, freeing an enormous dragon in the process.

The **last** hero: a discworld fable. By Terry Pratchett & illustrated by Paul Kidby. HarperCollins, 2001. 160 p. : Color illustration (Discworld, 27)
ISBN 9780061040962
1. Discworld (Imaginary place) 2. Magic 3. Heroes and heroines 4. Good and evil 5. Wizards 6. Fantasy fiction 7. Humorous stories 8. Adult books for young adults
LC 2001039188
Cohen the Barbarian. He's been a legend in his own lifetime. He can remember the good old days of high adventure, when being a Hero meant one didn't have to worry about aching backs and lawyers and civilization. But these days, he can't always remember just where he put his teeth. So now, with his ancient (yet still trusty) sword and new walking stick in hand, Cohen gathers a group of his old—very old—friends to embark on one final quest. He's going to climb the highest mountain of Discworld and meet the gods. It's time the Last Hero in the world returns what the first hero stole. Trouble is, that'll mean the end of the world, if no one stops him in time.

Lords and ladies: a novel of Discworld. Terry Pratchett. HarperPrism, 1996. 281 p; (Discworld, 14)
ISBN 9780061056925
1. Discworld (Imaginary place) 2. Witches 3. Good and evil 4. Weatherwax, Granny (Fictitious character) 5. Dwarves (Fantasy characters) 6. Fantasy fiction 7. Humorous stories 8. Adult books for young adults
Irresistibly cute but vicious elves infest the kingdom of Lancre, upsetting plans for a royal wedding and leaving the ordinary citizens helpless, and it is up to the witches, led by Granny Weatherwax, to handle the deadly brutes
Originally published: 1992.

Men at arms: a novel of Discworld. Terry Pratchett. HarperPrism, 1996. 341 p; (Discworld, 15)
ISBN 9780061092183
1. Police 2. Discworld (Imaginary place) 3. Good and evil 4. Assassins 5. Ankh-Morpork (Imaginary place) 6. Fantasy fiction 7. Humorous stories 8. Adult books for young adults

Placed in charge of the new recruits guarding Discworld's greatest city, Corporal Carrot investigates the discovery of an ancient document that reveals the existence of the city's secret sovereign, who is Carrot himself.

Monstrous regiment. Terry Pratchett. HarperCollins, 2003. 368 p; (Discworld, 29)
ISBN 9780060013158
1. Dukes and duchesses 2. Discworld (Imaginary place) 3. Patriotism 4. Hampel, Otto Hermann 5. Women soldiers 6. Fantasy fiction 7. Humorous stories 8. Adult books for young adults
LC 2003050800
Running the family inn despite dwindling resources while her brother is away at war, Polly cuts off her hair to join the army and notices that her fellow recruits seem to be hiding secrets of their own.
"Pratchett revels in pricking pomp and assurance, but it isn't going too far to say that of late his real subject, like Wilfred Owen's, is the pit of war. Pratchett's approach may be less lyrical, but he can move from farce to sadness in seconds." —*New York Times Book Review*

Pyramids: the book of going forth. Terry Pratchett. V. Gollancz, 1989. 272 p. (Discworld, 7)
ISBN 9780575044630
1. Rulers 2. Discworld (Imaginary place) 3. Inheritance and succession 4. Ankh-Morpork (Imaginary place) 5. Fantasy fiction 6. Humorous stories 7. Adult books for young adults
LC 91155566
BSFA Award for Best Novel, 1989
Magic and humor are combined in the whimsical story of the hard life of Teppic, a teenage pharaoh who does not have a clue about what he is supposed to do as the new ruler of the desert kingdom of Djelibeybi.

Reaper man. Terry Pratchett. Victor Gollancz, 1991. 253 p; (Discworld, 11)
ISBN 9780575049796
1. Discworld (Imaginary place) 2. Death (Fictitious character : Pratchett) 3. Wizards 4. Magic 5. Fantasy fiction 6. Humorous stories 7. Adult books for young adults
LC 92231334
When Death is officially retired, chaos ensues on the planet Earth, and Dead Rights activist Reg Shoe is up to his neck in paperwork and poltergeists in his attempts to put Death back on the job.

Small gods: a novel of Discworld. Terry Pratchett. HarperPrism 1994. 344 p; (Discworld, 13)
ISBN 9780061092176
1. Gods and goddesses 2. Magic 3. Discworld (Imaginary place) 4. Fantasy fiction 5. Humorous stories 6. Adult books for young adults
Brutha, a simple man leading a quiet life tending his garden, finds his life irrevocably changed when his god, speaking to him through a tortoise, sends him on a mission of peace.
Originally published: 1992.

Thief of time. Terry Pratchett. Harper Collins, 2001. 336 p; (Discworld, 26)
ISBN 9780060199562
1. Wizards 2. Discworld (Imaginary place) 3. Time 4. Thieves 5. Sixteen-year-old boys 6. Fantasy fiction 7. Humorous stories 8. Adult books for young adults
LC 65347
Carefully reallocating the Time of Discworld to where it is most needed, Monk of History Lu Tze and his apprentice begin a literal race against time when the world's first truly accurate clock threatens to stop Time forever.

"This is Discworld, an adolescent Oz in which far fewer folks are immortal, but long life doesn't entail decrepitude; magic works; and politics and culture are fluid, far off, and mostly for old guys. Spun out of words and wit, it is as light and curiously tasty as cotton candy." —*Booklist*
Originally published: London: Doubleday, 2001.

Thud!: a novel of Discworld. Terry Pratchett. Harper Collins, 2005. 384 p; (Discworld, 31)
ISBN 9780060815226
1. Police 2. Murder investigation 3. Discworld (Imaginary place) 4. Ankh-Morpork (Imaginary place) 5. Magic 6. Fantasy fiction 7. Humorous stories 8. Adult books for young adults
LC 2005046271
A seemingly routine day in the life of City Watch commander Sam Vimes is abruptly interrupted by an unsolved murder, an impending war, an unwanted new recruit, and a pesky government inspector.
"It's all in a day's work for the City Watch in the latest novel set in the author's hilariously surreal Disc World." —*Library Journal*
Where's My Cow? is a companion volume to Terry Pratchett's Discworld novel Thud.

The **truth:** a novel of Discworld. By Terry Pratchett. HarperCollins, 2000. 336 p; (Discworld, 25)
ISBN 9780380978953
1. Journalists 2. Discworld (Imaginary place) 3. Investigative journalism 4. Newspaper publishers and publishing 5. Fantasy fiction 6. Humorous stories 7. Adult books for young adults
LC 31928
William de Worde plunges into the world of investigative journalism after a high official is impeached following a botched murder attempt.
"Pratchett's...Discworld novel takes on the press and investigative journalism in a hilarious romp that examines the fleeting nature of truth and lies." —*Library Journal*
Originally published: London: Doubleday, 2000.

Witches abroad. Terry Pratchett. V. Gollancz, 1991. 252 p; (Discworld, 12)
ISBN 9780575049802
1. Discworld (Imaginary place) 2. Witches 3. Magic 4. Weatherwax, Granny (Fictitious character) 5. Fantasy fiction 6. Humorous stories 7. Adult books for young adults
LC 93136323
Discworld's own version of the three witches—Magrat Garlick, Granny Weatherwax, and Nanny Ogg—grab their broomsticks and journey to Genua to save Princess Emberella from an overzealous fairy godmother.
First published: 1991.

Wyrd sisters. Terry Pratchett. ROC Books, 1988. 319 p; (Discworld, 6)
ISBN 9780451450128
1. Discworld (Imaginary place) 2. Witches 3. Weatherwax, Granny (Fictitious character) 4. Spells (Magic) 5. Black magic 6. Fantasy fiction 7. Books to TV 8. Humorous stories 9. Adult books for young adults
The arrival of a royal infant on their doorstep sets the three witch sisters of Lancre on an adventure that has them wresting a kingdom away from its ruler.
Starring three witches, also kings, daggers, crowns, storms, dwarfs, cats, ghosts, spectres, apes, bandits, demons, forests, heirs, jesters, tortures, trolls, turntables, general rejoicing, and divers alarums.

Prcic, Ismet

Shards: a novel. Ismet Prcic. Black Cat, 2011. 392 p.

ISBN 9780802170811

1. Young men 2. Bosnians in the United States 3. Writing — Psychological aspects 4. Memories — Psychological aspects 5. Guilt in men 6. Bosnia and Hercegovina 7. California 8. 1990s 9. Psychological fiction 10. Literary fiction

Los Angeles Times Art Seidenbaum Award for First Fiction, 2011; New York Times Notable Book, 2011; Oregon Book Awards, Ken Kesey Award for Fiction, 2013

A young Bosnian, Ismet Prcic, who has fled his war-torn homeland for California, uses writing to come to terms with his past, while another Bosnian, Mustafa, stays in his country to fight.

The author's debut is about a young Bosnian, also named Ismet Prcic, who has fled his wartorn homeland and is now struggling to reconcile his past with his present life in California. He is advised that in order to make peace with the corrosive guilt he harbors over leaving his family behind, he must write everything. The result is a great rattlebag of memories, confessions, and fictions: sweetly humorous recollections of Ismet's childhood in Tuzla appear alongside anguished letters to his mother about the challenges of life in this new world. As Ismet's foothold in the present falls away, his writings are further complicated by stories from the point of view of another young man—real or imagined—named Mustafa, who joined a troop of elite soldiers and stayed in Bosnia to fight. When Mustafa's story begins to overshadow Ismet's new-world identity, the reader is charged with piecing together the fragments of a life that has become eerily unrecognizable, even to the one living it. Bookreporter.com.

Prescott, Lara

The **secrets** we kept. Lara Prescott. Alfred A. Knopf, 2019. 304 pages
ISBN 9780525656159

1. Pasternak, Boris Leonidovich 2. Women CIA agents 3. Banned books 4. Authors, Russian 5. International intrigue 6. Man-woman relationships 7. Soviet Union 8. Washington, D.C. 9. 1950s 10. 1960s 11. Historical fiction

Library Journal Best Books, 2019; LibraryReads Favorites, 2019; Sue Feder Historical Mystery Award, 2020

A tale of spycraft, love and sacrifice inspired by the true story of Doctor Zhivago follows the efforts of two CIA agents to help publish Boris Pasternak's censored masterpiece against a backdrop of Cold War politics in Moscow.

Pressfield, Steven

36 righteous men: a novel. Steven Pressfield. W. W. Norton & Company, Inc, 2020. 320 p.
ISBN 9781324002895

1. Near future 2. End of the world 3. Detectives 4. Serial murder investigation 5. Scars 6. Thrillers and suspense

LC 2019014779

Two New York homicide detectives make an apocalyptic discovery before racing to prevent the murder of a last surviving guardian who would protect the world from destruction.

Preston, Caroline

The **scrapbook** of Frankie Pratt. Caroline Preston. Ecco Press, 2011. 240 p.
ISBN 9780061966903

1. Scrapbooks 2. Women authors 3. Man-woman relationships 4. Growing up 5. Moving to a new city 6. 1920s 7. Historical fiction 8. Diary novels 9. Illustrated books 10. Adult books for young adults

Alex Award, 2012

Using an array of vintage memorabilia, a novel told in the form of a scrapbook follows Frankie Pratt, who goes to Vassar in 1920 with dreams of becoming a writer, which becomes a stepping stone to an international adventure.

Preston, Douglas J.

City of endless night. Douglas Preston & Lincoln Child. Grand Central Publishing, 2018. 416 p. (Pendergast novels, 17)
ISBN 9781455536948

1. Beheading 2. FBI agents 3. Serial murder investigation 4. Clues 5. Police 6. Massachusetts 7. Thrillers and suspense 8. Adult books for young adults

LC 2017031496

Heading an investigation into the murder of a wealthy tech billionaire's daughter, Lieutenant CDS Vincent D'Agosta teams up with FBI Special Agent A.X.L. Pendergast, only to uncover the work of a serial killer whose agenda threatens an entire city.

Crooked river. . Grand Central Publishing, 2020. 400 p. (Pendergast novels, 19)
ISBN 9781538747254

1. FBI agents 2. Violence 3. Criminal investigation 4. Foot 5. Oceans 6. Thrillers and suspense

Racing to uncover the mystery of several light green-shoe-clad severed feet found floating in the Gulf of Mexico, Agent Pendergast is faced with the most inexplicable challenge of his career

"There is plenty of suspense, and the action gets bloody. Great storytelling, a quirky hero, and a quirkier plot make this a winner for adventure fans." —*Kirkus*

The **Obsidian** chamber. Douglas Preston & Lincoln Child. Grand Central Publishing, 2016. 416 p. (Pendergast novels, 16)
ISBN 9781455536917

1. Missing persons 2. Kidnapping 3. Kidnapping victims 4. Missing persons investigation 5. Clues 6. Massachusetts 7. Thrillers and suspense 8. Adult books for young adults

LC 2016022192

With special agent Pendergast missing and presumed dead and his ward Constance taken captive by a shadowy figure from the past, Pendergast's bodyguard, Proctor, begins an international pursuit of Constance's kidnapper.

"This twisty and bizarre 16th series installment will puzzle and delight fans as well as readers who enjoy locked-room mysteries, international intrigue, shadowy characters with ambiguous moral compasses, and tales that confound and entertain." —*Library Journal*

Old bones. Douglas Preston & Lincoln Child. Grand Central Publishing, 2019. 384 pages (Nora Kelly novels (Preston & Child), 1)
ISBN 9781538747223

1. Donner Party 2. Women archaeologists 3. Women FBI agents 4. Expeditions 5. Grave robbing 6. California 7. Thrillers and suspense

LC 2019006977

Young curator Nora Kelly leads a team in search of the "Lost Camp" of the Donner Party, but as they expose the real truth of what happened, those ancient horrors lead to present-day violence in a case assigned to rookie FBI agent Corrie Swanson.

Thunderhead. By Douglas Preston & Lincoln Child. Warner Books, 1999. 483 p.
ISBN 9780446523370

1. Women archaeologists 2. Stalking 3. Quests 4. Archaeologists 5. Anasazi Culture 6. Thrillers and suspense 7. Adventure stories 8. Adult books for young adults

LC 98037557

School Library Journal Best Books: Best Adult Books 4 Teens, 1999

Sixteen years after her father's mysterious disappearance, archaeologist Nora Kelly follows in his footsteps, guided by an enigmatic letter, as she embarks on an expedition into the remote canyon country of southeastern Utah to search for Quivira, the fabled Lost City of Gold.

Verses for the dead. . Grand Central Pub 2018. 368 p. (Pendergast novels, 18)
ISBN 9781538747209
1. FBI agents 2. Serial murders 3. Serial murder investigation 4. Suicide 5. Letter writing 6. Miami Beach, Florida 7. Thrillers and suspense

Notoriously rogue Agent Pendergast must accept two new challenges: a partner, and a serial killer leaving cryptic notes—along with his victims' hearts—at the graves of women who committed suicide. As he digs deeper, he realizes the brutal new crimes may be just the tip of the iceberg: a conspiracy of death that reaches back decades.

Price, Reynolds

The **good** priest's son. Reynolds Price. Scribner, 2005. 288 p.
ISBN 9780743254007
1. September 11 Terrorist Attacks, 2001 2. Parent and adult child 3. Homecomings 4. Middle-aged men 5. Children of clergy 6. North Carolina 7. New York City 8. Domestic fiction 9. Literary fiction 10. Psychological fiction
LC 2004065383

Visiting his aging Episcopal priest father when his own home is decimated by the September 11 attacks, art conservator Mabry Kincaid meets his father's caregiver, an ambitious African-American woman, and struggles with mixed feelings about his adult daughter.

"This novel is thematically rich—indeed, it is rather bowed by its meanings—and features many pleasing Southern voices, along with an impeccable depiction of the region's deep-rooted traditions." —*New York Times Book Review*

Roxanna Slade. Reynolds Price. Scribner, 1998. 301 p.
ISBN 9780684832920
1. Women with depression 2. Small town life 3. Family relationships 4. Women 5. Man-woman relationships 6. Southern States 7. Literary fiction 8. Psychological fiction 9. First person narratives
LC 9739167

Booklist Editors' Choice, 1998; New York Times Notable Book, 1998

Roxanna begins her story on her twentieth birthday—a day that introduces her to the harsh realities of adulthood and changes the course of her life forever. From this day on, Roxanna is quick to share with the reader the intimate details of ninety years of life in North Carolina. While she rarely leaves the small town of her youth, Roxanna's vision of the world is shaped by intense passions and loyalties and the certain tragedies of a life long lived.

Price, Richard

Clockers. Richard Price. Houghton Mifflin, 1992. 599 p.
ISBN 9780395537619
1. Crack traffic 2. Detectives 3. Drug dealers 4. Drug traffic 5. African American teenagers 6. New Jersey 7. Mysteries 8. Books to movies
LC 91043318

National Book Critics Circle Award for Fiction finalist, 1992

Certain that the young Black man who has confessed to a recent murder is covering for his drug-dealing half-brother, Striker, veteran cop Rocco Klein decides to make Striker's life a nightmare BT

"This is an incredible course in urban street life, particularly the crack culture." —*Booklist*

Lush life. Richard Price. Farrar, Straus, and Giroux, 2008. 464 p.
ISBN 9780374299255
1. Police questioning 2. Child abuse and crime 3. Robbery 4. Teenagers 5. Teenage boys 6. Lower East Side, New York City 7. New York City 8. Crime fiction

Booklist Editors' Choice, 2008; New York Times Notable Book, 2008

Still living on the Lower East Side and waiting tables, thirty-five-year-old Eric Cash has every reason to be jealous of Ike Marcus, an ambitious young man on the way to the top, until he is supposedly gunned down by street thugs while walking one night with Eric.

"Price has been around for what seems like forever, but there's a reason we still read him. Because every sentence is a pleasure. Because he never puts a foot wrong, and never lingers. He takes just enough time to make you care." —*Esquire*

Samaritan. Richard Price. Knopf, 2003. 377 p.
ISBN 9781400041824
1. Victims of violent crimes 2. Men and success 3. Criminal investigation 4. Public housing 5. Detectives 6. Psychological suspense
New York Times Notable Book, 2003

Ray Mitchell returns to New Jersey to the housing project where he grew up to re-evaluate his life, but when he is found savagely beaten—and refuses to press charges—childhood friend Detective Nerese Ammons must uncover the truth.

Pride, Christine

★ **We** are not like them. Christine Pride and Jo Piazza. Atria Books, 2021. 336 p.
ISBN 9781982181031
1. Female friendship 2. Interracial friendship 3. Best friends 4. African American women journalists 5. Women television newscasters and commentators 6. Philadelphia, Pennsylvania 7. Literary fiction 8. African American fiction 9. Multiple perspectives
LC 2021015882

Riley and Jen have been best friends since they were children. It never mattered to them that Riley is black and Jen is white, and as adults, they remain as close as sisters. Jen is married and pregnant, while Riley is a television journalist poised to become one of the first Black female anchors in Philadelphia. But when Jen's city police officer husband is involved in the shooting of an unarmed Black teenager, Jen's friendship with Riley is thrown into uncertainty. Covering this career-making story, Riley wrestles with the implications of this tragic incident for her Black community, her ambitions, and her relationship with her lifelong friend.

"With its timely premise, clear-cut messages, and appealing female characters, this novel is bound for book-club glory." —*Kirkus*

Priest, Cherie

Boneshaker. Cherie Priest. Tor, 2009. 416 p. (Clockwork century, 1)
ISBN 9780765318411
1. Mothers and sons 2. Zombies 3. Inventors 4. Rescues 5. Mad scientist (Concept) 6. Seattle, Washington 7. Pacific Northwest 8. American Westward Expansion (1803-1899) 9. 19th century 10. Steampunk 11. Alternate histories 12. Horror
LC 2009018700

Locus Award for Best Science Fiction Novel, 2010

Commissioned to build a machine that will promote gold-rush land-breaking efforts between Civil War-era Seattle and Alaska, inventor Leviticus Blue inadvertently triggers the release of a deadly gas that transforms people into the living dead, a situation that prompts his teenage son to restore the family reputation years later.

"Intelligent, exceptionally well written and showcasing a phenomenal strong female protagonist who embodies the complexities inherent in motherhood, this yarn is a must-read for the discerning steampunk fan." —*Publishers Weekly*

Clementine. Cherie Priest. Subterranean, 2010. 208 p. (Clockwork century, 2)
ISBN 9781596063082
1. Women spies 2. Freedom seekers 3. Intelligence service — History 4. Conspiracies 5. Strategic alliances (Military) 6. 1880s 7. 19th century 8. Steampunk 9. Alternate histories 10. Spy fiction 11. Adult books for young adults
Maria Isabella Boyd's success as a Confederate spy has made her too famous for further espionage work, and now her employment options are slim. Exiled, widowed, and on the brink of poverty...she reluctantly goes to work for the Pinkerton National Detective Agency in Chicago. Adding insult to injury, her first big assignment is commissioned by the Union Army. In short, a federally sponsored transport dirigible is being violently pursued across the Rockies and Uncle Sam isn't pleased. The Clementine is carrying a top secret load of military essentials—essentials which must be delivered to Louisville, Kentucky, without delay. Intelligence suggests that the unrelenting pursuer is a runaway slave who's been wanted by authorities on both sides of the Mason-Dixon for fifteen years. In that time, Captain Croggon Beauregard Hainey has felonied his way back and forth across the continent, leaving a trail of broken banks, stolen war machines, and illegally distributed weaponry from sea to shining sea. And now it's Maria's job to go get him.

Dreadnought. Cherie Priest. Tor, 2010. 480 p. (Clockwork century, 3)
ISBN 9780765325785
1. Nurses 2. Zombies 3. Widows 4. Overland journeys to the Pacific 5. Child-separated fathers 6. United States 7. American Westward Expansion (1803-1899) 8. Steampunk 9. Alternate histories 10. Horror
Mercy Lynch is just a frustrated nurse who wants to see her father before he dies. But she'll have to survive both Union intrigue and Confederate opposition if she wants to make it off the Union-operated, Tacoma-bound "Dreadnought" alive.

Ganymede. Cherie Priest. Tor Books, 2011. 400 p. (Clockwork century, 4)
ISBN 9780765329462
1. Pilots 2. Submarines 3. Brothels 4. Zombies 5. Smuggling 6. New Orleans, Louisiana 7. 1880s 8. Steampunk 9. Alternate histories 10. Horror
LC 2011021569
In a new steampunk adventure, air pilot Andan Cly and his crew must retrieve a dangerous submersible called Ganymede from the bottom of Lake Pontchartrain near New Orleans.

The inexplicables. Cherie Priest. Tor, 2012. 320 p. (Clockwork century, 5)
ISBN 9780765329479
1. Greed 2. Zombies 3. Monsters 4. Orphans 5. Drug dealers 6. Seattle, Washington 7. Steampunk 8. Alternate histories 9. Horror
LC 2012024853
Rector "Wreck 'em" Sherman, a drug dealer haunted by the ghost of a kid he used to know, sneaks over the wall into the wasteland of Seattle where he makes a shocking discovery that changes everything.

Pronzini, Bill

Crazybone. Carroll & Graf, 2000. 197 p. (Nameless Detective mysteries, 26)
ISBN 9780786707300

1. Mothers and daughters 2. Ten-year-old girls 3. Private investigators 4. Nameless Detective (Fictitious character) 5. San Francisco, California 6. California 7. Mysteries 8. Hardboiled fiction
The "nameless detective" journeys behind the lush facade of the affluent California community of Greenwood when he investigates an unusual case of insurance fraud and uncovers a complex web of larceny, adultery, betrayal, and murder.
"Pronzini's nameless detective lumbers down the San Francisco Peninsula to a private enclave of wooded estates and walled country clubs to find out why a grieving widow has refused a $50,000 insurance settlement for the accidental death of her husband. The look of 'raw terror' on the woman's face when he confronts her...suggests that she might have something to hide, and the nameless hero does a good job of ferreting out her secret. But the real fun comes from watching the old war horse plod through a hostile social environment, observing the swells at their selfish pursuits and making them regret every condescending sneer they threw in his face." —*New York Times Book Review*

Fever: a Nameless Detective novel. Bill Pronzini. Forge, 2008. 288 p. (Nameless Detective mysteries, 33)
ISBN 9780765318183
1. Husband and wife 2. Missing persons 3. Abused women 4. Marital conflict 5. Organized crime and gambling 6. San Francisco, California 7. California 8. Mysteries 9. Hardboiled fiction
LC 2008005228
Nameless had told Mitchell Krochek that he'd do whatever he could to find his missing wife, Janice. She'd run away before—propelled by a gambling fever that rose ever higher—and Mitch had always taken her back. This time, when Nameless, his partner Tamara, and the agency's chief operative Jake Runyon finally found her in a sleazy San Francisco hotel, she demanded a divorce. A few days later, a beaten and bloody Janice stumbled into the agency begging to go home. No one is surprised when, soon after her homecoming, she disappears again. With Janice missing again, Mitchell is the prime suspect, and as Nameless searches for the truth behind her disappearance, he uncovers a vicious racket that preys on gambling fever victims.
"This insightful novel will appeal to those who like the mean streets portrayed with understatement and subtlety rather than gory violence." —*Publishers Weekly*
A Tom Doherty Associates book.

Hardcase. Delacorte Press, 1995. 215 p. (Nameless Detective mysteries, 22)
ISBN 9780385305068
1. Private investigators 2. Nameless Detective (Fictitious character) 3. Adoptees — Identity 4. Family secrets 5. San Francisco, California 6. Mysteries 7. Hardboiled fiction
LC 95005723
Hired to locate a woman's biological parents, the Nameless Detective discovers that the woman's mother had been an emotionally unstable girl raped by a teenage delinquent who is determined to repeat his crime BT
"This mystery opens as the California PI, approaching 60, marries his longtime girlfriend, Kerry. After a civil ceremony marked by his nervous clumsiness, Nameless takes on a client who wants him to find her birthparents. Melanie Ann Aldrich has just discovered that she was adopted and is sure there's a reason her adoptive parents, who are deceased, kept this information from her. Nameless fairly quickly identifies the woman's birthparents, but that's just the beginning." —*Publishers Weekly*

Hellbox. Bill Pronzini. Forge, 2012. 320 p. (Nameless Detective mysteries, 37)
ISBN 9780765325655

1. Missing persons investigation 2. Missing women 3. Private investigators 4. Nameless Detective (Fictitious character) 5. San Francisco, California 6. Sierra Nevada Mountains 7. Mysteries 8. Hardboiled fiction

LC 2012011650

When his wife goes missing from their Sierra foothills cabin after spotting a suspicious man, Nameless Detective Bill and his associate, Jake Runyon, launch a search and rescue mission that stretches legal boundaries and pits them against uncaring locals and a brutal adversary.

A Tom Doherty Associates book.

Illusions. Carroll & Graf, 1997. 243 p. (Nameless Detective mysteries, 24)

ISBN 9780786704033

1. Private investigators 2. Nameless Detective (Fictitious character) 3. Suicide 4. Suicide investigation 5. Missing persons investigation 6. San Francisco, California 7. Mysteries 8. Hardboiled fiction

LC 97-4274

The "Nameless Detective" investigates the suicide of his estranged friend and detective partner while searching for his missing ex-wife, who holds the secrets to his death BT

"Shaken by the suicide of his former partner and onetime best friend, a pathetic figure whose life had shrunk to 'drinking, brooding, building his own private gallows day by day,' Nameless throws himself into a job for a Santa Fe businessman who wants to contact his former wife. The woman is easily found; but before the shamus can cash his check, a second suicide delivers another body blow to his code of ethics and deposits another load of guilt on his conscience.... The parallel investigations offer prime examples of Pronzini's ace plotting techniques...and if you can take the mood swings, Nameless is a good man to walk you through the noir landscape." —*New York Times Book Review*

Mourners: a nameless detective novel. Bill Pronzini. Forge, 2006. 288 p. (Nameless Detective mysteries, 31)

ISBN 9780765309327

1. Private investigators 2. Nameless Detective (Fictitious character) 3. Financial planners 4. Husband and wife 5. Sisters of murder victims 6. San Francisco, California 7. California 8. Mysteries 9. Hardboiled fiction

LC 2005043510

When a suspicious wife reports her husband's inexplicable attendance at the funerals of murdered strangers, the nameless detective and his companions, Tamara and Jake, find themselves compromised in the face of a stalled investigation.

"Pronzini's series becomes more layered and complex with each entry. This time the primary characters are all in one stage or another of mourning, but the only one who recognizes it is the initial subject of the investigation. He is also the only one who understands the timeless omnipresence of grief.... A dark, foreboding entry in a classic series." —*Booklist*

A Tom Doherty Associates book.

Nemesis. Bill Pronzini. A Tom Doherty Associates Book, 2013. 352 p. (Nameless Detective mysteries, 38)

ISBN 9780765325662

1. Private investigators 2. Extortion 3. Frameups 4. Nameless Detective (Fictitious character) 5. Malicious accusation 6. California 7. Mysteries 8. Hardboiled fiction

LC 2013003644

Agreeing to investigate threats by a mysterious extortionist against a newly rich young woman, Jake Runyon makes a series of surprise discoveries that cause him to be wrongfully accused of a crime and his employers to be subjected to a vicious legal vendetta.

A Tom Doherty Associates book.

Nightcrawlers. Bill Pronzini. Forge Books, 2005. 304 p. (Nameless Detective mysteries, 30)

ISBN 9780765309310

1. Private investigators 2. Nameless Detective (Fictitious character) 3. Seniors 4. African American women 5. Women kidnapping victims 6. San Francisco, California 7. Mysteries 8. Multiple perspectives 9. First person narratives

LC 2004056323

Unaware of links between a series of gay hate crimes and the kidnapping of a young girl, investigators Bill, Jake, and Tamara tackle difficult cases when Jake pursues leads related to an attack on his son's partner.

"The long-running Nameless series continues to evolve. With the novels no longer exclusively first-person narratives by Nameless, parallel plotlines have been introduced from multiple points of view, giving readers a chance to view Nameless as others see him. And, as always, the novels are never just about crime." —*Booklist*

A Tom Doherty Associates book.

Savages: a nameless detective novel. Bill Pronzini. Forge Books, 2007. 304 p. (Nameless Detective mysteries, 32)

ISBN 9780765309334

1. Private investigators 2. Nameless Detective (Fictitious character) 3. Husband and wife 4. Partners of people with breast cancer 5. Sisters 6. San Francisco, California 7. California 8. Mysteries 9. Hardboiled fiction

Investigating the death of a woman that has been ruled accidental by the police but that her sister insists was a murder by a known perpetrator, a reluctant Nameless begins to suspect that the victim's sister is telling the truth when he learns unsettling facts about her life.

"San Francisco detective Nameless is asked by a former client to look into the death of her sister, who was trapped in an unhappy marriage. Although the death had been ruled an accident, Nameless soon finds himself stymied by ethical questions and lack of evidence. Meanwhile, Jake Runyon, a partner in Nameless's agency, is trying to serve a subpoena and gets caught in a case of serial arson and murder. It is hard to find a better crime writer than Pronzini, and his understanding of feminine angst as well as male motivations has made this one of the best detective series ever." —*Library Journal*

Sequel: Fever.

A Tom Doherty Associates book.

Spook. Bill Pronzini. Carroll & Graf, 2003. 240 p. (Nameless Detective mysteries, 28)

ISBN 9780786710867

1. Identity (Psychology) 2. Homeless men 3. Murder victims 4. Murder investigation 5. Homeless people with mental illnesses 6. San Francisco, California 7. Mysteries 8. Hardboiled fiction

LC BL2002012420

After a near brush with death, the Nameless Detective searches for the identity of a gentle, mentally disturbed homeless man who was brutally slain, a search that leads him to a small California town rife with murder and mayhem.

"The case seems simple enough. Spook, a homeless street person, becomes a fixture at a local business; its employees provide assistance as needed for the obviously mentally disturbed individual. He is murdered in an especially heinous assault. His unofficial 'family' wants San Francisco private investigator 'Nameless' to learn his real identity. Nameless hands the case over to his newly hired field operative, Jake Runyon, a former Seattle cop.... A fascinating entry in a series that continues to redefine noir fiction even as it honors its roots." —*Booklist*

The **stolen** gold affair. Bill Pronzini. Forge, 2020. 224 pages (Carpenter and Quincannon novels, 12)

ISBN 9781250216489

1. Private investigators 2. Undercover operations 3. Miners 4. Mines and mineral resources 5. Criminal investigation 6. San Francisco, California 7. California 8. 1890s 9. Historical mysteries

While Quincannon goes undercover to investigate a string of gold thefts in a lucrative mine, his bride-to-be, Sabina, tackles an audacious real-estate scam and an abusive young man's villainous secret.

"Attractive characters, a finely tuned plot, and fascinating snippets of California history distinguish this outing." —*Publishers Weekly*

The **violated**. Bill Pronzini. Bloomsbury USA, 2016. 256 p. ISBN 9781632866608
1. Rapists 2. Small towns 3. Murder victims 4. Police 5. Murder 6. California 7. Mysteries 8. Multiple perspectives 9. First person narratives

LC 2016025590

When a registered sex offender who has been implicated in a string of attacks is found murdered in a small California town, police chief Griffin Less and detective Robert Ortiz are pressured by a results-oriented mayor as they reconstruct events from the testimonies of the offender's wife and the irate husbands of women victims.

"This is a psychological novel dressed up in a thriller suit, which means the teeth are showing, and Pronzinis skill keeps things moving. Another satisfying tale from a crime master." —*Booklist*

Prose, Francine

Blue angel: a novel. Francine Prose. HarperCollins, 2000. 314 p. ISBN 9780060195410
1. Universities and colleges 2. Teacher-student relationships 3. Scandals 4. Authors 5. College teachers 6. New England 7. Satirical fiction 8. Literary fiction 9. Adult books for young adults

LC 99040564

New York Times Notable Book, 2000; National Book Award for Fiction finalist, 2000

An ironic look at modern academia offers the chronicle of the trials and tribulations of Swenson, a frustrated college professor who finds that Angela Argo, a post-punk, oft-pierced student, has a brilliant writing talent.

"An ironic gloss on Von Sternberg's tragedy of erotic abasement.... Prose's retelling focuses less on the ridiculous and self-destructive behavior of the professor...than on the far more laughable (and hazardous) rigidity of the politically correct behavior codes governing his tiny Vermont campus." —*The New Yorker*

Goldengrove: a novel. Francine Prose. HarperCollins, 2008. 288 p. ISBN 9780066214115
1. Grief 2. Sexuality 3. Teenage girls 4. Growing up 5. Loss (Psychology) 6. New England 7. Psychological fiction 8. Coming-of-age stories 9. Literary fiction 10. Adult books for young adults

LC 2008002112

Grieving after the drowning death of her sister, thirteen-year-old Nico falls into a seductive and dangerous relationship with her sister's enigmatic boyfriend during a summer when she realizes that she has moved beyond the help of her parents.

"Nico's introduction into adult situations is accelerated and scary, and Prose doesn't handle the topic with kid gloves. As Nico's relationship with Aaron progresses, her thoughts about physical intimacy run rampant. Prose expertly conveys the newfound sexual desires teenagers experience as they grow into adults." —*Deseret News*

★ The **vixen**. Francine Prose. HarperCollins, 2021. 304 p. ISBN 9780063012141
1. Jewish men 2. Family secrets 3. Editors 4. Women authors 5. Options, alternatives, choices 6. New York state 7. United States 8. 1950s 9. Literary fiction 10. Historical fiction

In 1953, at a distinguished New York publishing firm, Simon Putnam, a recent Harvard graduate, is tasked with editing a steamy bodice-ripper based on the trial of Ethel and Julius Rosenberg—a project that makes him realize that everyone round him are not what they seem.

Simon, our overheated narrator, pulls us along as he stumbles into Cold War intrigue, and we're never sure which way the plot will turn until literally the last sentence. What a delightful read! Library Journal

Proulx, Annie

Bad dirt: Wyoming stories 2. Annie Proulx. Scribner, 2004. 240 p. (Wyoming stories, 2)
ISBN 9780743257992
1. Cowboys 2. Husband and wife 3. Family relationships 4. Ranch life 5. Small town life 6. Wyoming 7. Short stories 8. Westerns 9. Literary fiction

LC 2004056530

An anthology of short stories, all set in Wyoming, features characters who have a profound effect on the people around them, in such tales as "The Trickle Down Effect," "The Contest," and "What Kind of Furniture Would Jesus Pick?"

"This poignant and often humorous collection is packed with well-drawn characters that linger in the mind and heart. As expected, the Wyoming landscape is the enduring character in each story, silently wielding its magical and brutal power." —*Library Journal*

11 short stories.

★ **Barkskins:** a novel. Annie Proulx. Scribner, 2016. 640 p. ISBN 9780743288781
1. Forests 2. Wilderness areas 3. Immigrants, French 4. Families 5. Colonialism 6. New France (1534-1763) 7. 17th century 8. Family sagas 9. Literary fiction 10. Historical fiction

LC 2015030152

Loan Stars Favourites, 2016; New York Times Notable Book, 2016; Longlisted for The Baileys Women's Prize for Fiction, 2017; Kirkus Prize for Fiction finalist, 2016

Working as woodcutters under a feudal lord in 17th-century New France, two impoverished young Frenchmen follow separate journeys, one of extraordinary hardship, the other of wealth and craftiness, that shape their families throughout three centuries.

"Despite the length, nothing seems extraneous, and not once does the reader sense the story slipping from Proulx's grasp, resulting in the kind of immersive reading experience that only comes along every few years." —*Publishers Weekly*

Fine just the way it is: Wyoming stories 3. Annie Proulx. Scribner, 2008. 240 p. (Wyoming stories, 3)
ISBN 9781416571667
1. Family relationships 2. Ranch life 3. Wyoming 4. Short stories 5. Westerns 6. Literary fiction

LC 2008013682

Booklist Editors' Choice, 2008; New York Times Notable Book, 2008

A collection of nine western-themed tales features an array of pioneer country inhabitants from different backgrounds.

"This collection of Wyoming tales, continues [Proulx's] Dickensian delight in memorable nomenclature.... Proulx's writing can be as fine as anything being produced in America today." —*Times Literary Supplement*

Postcards. E. Annie Proulx. Scribner, 1992. 308 p. ISBN 9780684187181

1. Family relationships 2. Farm life 3. Poor families 4. Wanderers and wandering 5. Eccentric families 6. United States 7. Domestic fiction 8. Literary fiction

LC 91025089

PEN-Faulkner Award, 1993

The story of a well-meaning fugitive-at-large provides a glimpse of America's past as it follows Loyal Blood from his home in Vermont, where he mistakenly commits a heinous crime, to the coast of California
BT

★ The **shipping** news. E. Annie Proulx. Scribner, 1993. 337 p.
ISBN 9780684193373
1. Widowers 2. Families 3. Small town life 4. Redemption 5. Psychic trauma 6. Newfoundland and Labrador 7. Literary fiction 8. Books to movies

LC 92030315

National Book Award for Fiction, 1993; Pulitzer Prize for Fiction, 1994; ALA Notable Book, 1994; National Book Critics Circle Award for Fiction finalist, 1993

Quoyle retreats to Newfoundland with his daughters after the death of his unfaithful wife. There, as his family begins anew, Quoyle deals with his personal fears.

"The author blends Newfoundland argot, savage history, impressively diverse characters, fine descriptions of weather and scenery, and comic horseplay without ever lessening the reader's interest in Quoyle's progress from bumbling outsider to capable journalist." —*The Atlantic*

Proust, Marcel

★ **Remembrance** of things past. Marcel Proust; translated by C.K. Scott Moncrieff and Terence Kilmartin. Random House, 1981. 3 v.
ISBN 9780394506449
1. Memories 2. Introspection 3. France 4. Autobiographical fiction 5. Translations 6. Classics 7. Adult books for young adults

LC 79005542

"This is the first complete English version of Proust's masterpiece, translated from the definitive 1954 Pliade edition, Terence Kilmartin has checked the Scott Moncrieff translation (which comprised the first 11 volumes of the English language version and was made from the uneven first French edition) against the impeccable Clarac-Ferre Pliade edition. The 12th volume, Andreas Mayor's 1970 translation of Time Regained was the only English translation based on the Pliade edition prior to this one and has been incorporated into it with only minor changes." —*Library Journal*

Vol. 3's Time regained, translated by Andreas Mayor.
Translation of A la recherche du temps perdu.
Includes bibliographical references.

Swann's way. Marcel Proust; translated by C. K. Scott Moncrieff and Terence Kilmartin. Modern Library, 1992. 615 p. (In search of lost time, 1)
ISBN 9780679600053
1. Villages 2. Growing up 3. Memories 4. France 5. Coming-of-age stories 6. Autobiographical fiction 7. Translations

LC 92025657

In this opening volume of Proust's great novel, the narrator seems at first to be launching a fairly traditional life-story. But after the prelude the narrator travels backwards rather than forwards in time, in order to tell the story of a love affair that had taken place before his own birth. Swann's jealous love for Odette, together with the comic antics of the Verdurins and the adoring members of their 'little clan', provide a prophetic model of the narrator's own love-relationships and peregrinations in salon soci-

ety. All Proust's great themes—time and memory, love and loss, art and the artistic vocation—are here in kernel form.

Originally published in 1913.

Time regained. . Modern Library, 1993. 749 p. (In search of lost time, 7)
ISBN 9780679424765
1. Memories 2. Introspection 3. Grief 4. Love 5. France 6. Autobiographical fiction 7. Translations 8. Classics

LC 93003628 //r94

The narrator returns to Paris after World War I, and reflects on his past life as the raw material for literature, in the final part of the author's cycle of autobiographical novels entitled: A la recherche du temps perdu (Remembrance of things past).

This translation is a revised edition of the 1981 translation of Time regained by Andreas Mayor and Terence Kilmartin.

Within a budding grove. By Marcel Proust; translated from the French by C.K. Scott Moncrieff. The Modern Library, 1930. 356 p. (In search of lost time, 2)
ISBN 9780679600060
1. Girls 2. Boys 3. Growing up 4. Memories 5. Love 6. France 7. Paris, France 8. Autobiographical fiction 9. Coming-of-age stories 10. Translations

Follows the narrator's transition from childhood to adolescence and first love on the beaches of Normandy.

Later English editions published under the title: In the shadow of young girls in flower.
Translated from the French.

Pryor, Mark

Hollow man. Mark Pryor. Seventh Street Books, 2015. 260 p. (Hollow man, 1)
ISBN 9781633880863
1. Psychopaths 2. Stealing 3. Personal conduct 4. Lawyers 5. Musicians 6. Austin, Texas 7. Texas 8. Noir fiction 9. Crime fiction 10. Adult books for young adults

LC 2015011552

Dominic finds his plans of living a normal life unraveling when he, after being demoted at work, meets a beautiful woman who convinces him to unleash his dark side and embark on a life of crime and murder.

Pufahl, Shannon

On swift horses. Shannon Pufahl. Riverhead Books, 2019. 352 p.
ISBN 9780525538110
1. Postwar life 2. Closeted gay men 3. Independence in women 4. Newlyweds 5. Brothers 6. San Diego, California 7. Las Vegas, Nevada 8. 1950s 9. LGBTQIA fiction 10. Literary fiction
Spur Medicine Pipe Bearers Award for Best First Novel, 2020; Spur Awards, Best Western Contemporary Novel, 2020

A lonely newlywed and her wayward brother-in-law follow divergent and dangerous paths through the postwar American West.

Pulley, Natasha

The **Bedlam** stacks. Natasha Pulley. Bloomsbury, 2017. 336 p.
ISBN 9781620409671
1. Smugglers 2. Expeditions 3. Forests 4. Adventure 5. British in South America 6. Peru 7. England 8. Victorian era (1837-1901) 9. 1850s 10. Historical fantasy 11. Steampunk
Longlisted for the Walter Scott Prize for Historical Fiction, 2018

Still recovering from his latest, near-lethal mission abroad, smuggler Merrick Tremayne is tapped by the East India Company to acquire cinchona tree cuttings from Peru, thus breaking the country's monopoly on quinine. But Merrick's expedition to the Andes soon takes a unexpected turn. Although the plot of The Bedlam Stacks is not directly connected to the events of The Watchmaker of Filigree Street, readers can expect brief cameo appearances from some of the previous novel's characters.

"Pulley's beautifully descriptive language sets the stage for a mysterious and dangerous journey reminiscent of the grand scientific expeditions of the nineteenth century." —*Booklist*

★ The **kingdoms**. Natasha Pulley. Bloomsbury, 2021. 384 p.
ISBN 9781635576085
1. Men with amnesia 2. Identity (Psychology) 3. Indentured servants 4. Postcards 5. Clues 6. London, England 7. Scotland 8. 19th century 9. Alternate histories

Diagnosed with a form of epilepsy that causes amnesia and hallucinations, Joe Tournier, in an England that is a peaceful colony under the Republic of France, leaves London to repair a Scottish lighthouse, which changes the way he sees the world, its history and himself.

"All time-travel plots are fraught with paradox, but not all rise to Pulley's level of tricky cleverness, and few of those trickily clever books rise to her level of emotional intensity. Suspenseful, philosophical, and inventive, this sparkling novel explores the power of memory and love." —*Kirkus*

The **lost** future of Pepperharrow. Natasha Pulley. Bloomsbury, 2020. 336 p. (Watchmaker of Filigree Street series, 2)
ISBN 9781635573305
1. Precognition 2. Ghosts 3. Memory 4. Lovers 5. Clocks and watches 6. England 7. Victorian era (1837-1901) 8. 1880s 9. Historical fantasy 10. Steampunk

Finds Thaniel's unexpected posting to the British legation in politically charged 1888 Tokyo complicated by ghostly sightings, Mori's sudden disappearance and bizarre activities at a frozen labor camp.

"Pulley's intricate plot, vibrant setting, entrancing magic, and dynamic ensemble of characters make for an un-put-downable historical fantasy. New readers will be pulled in and series fans will be delighted by this tour de force." —*Publishers Weekly*

Sequel to: The Watchmaker of Filigree Street

The **watchmaker** of Filigree Street. Natasha Pulley. Bloomsbury, 2015. 318 pages; (Watchmaker of Filigree Street series, 1)
ISBN 9781620408339
1. Clocks and watches 2. Precognition 3. Male friendship 4. Bombs 5. Office workers 6. England 7. Victorian era (1837-1901) 8. 1880s 9. Historical fantasy 10. Steampunk 11. Adult books for young adults

Employed as a telegraph operator for the Home Office, synesthete Thaniel Steepleton sees colors in sound and dreams of becoming a musician. But just as Thaniel resigns himself to a dreary life as an underpaid civil servant, someone breaks into his boarding house and leaves a pocket watch on his pillow. The watch leads him to Filigree Street, where he meets gifted Japanese watchmaker Keita Mora who can "remember" the future. However, their budding friendship is complicated by the detonation of a terrorist's bomb, which contains a mechanism strikingly similar to Mori's clockwork creations.

"The story thwarts expectations; whenever an outcome looks as predetermined as clockwork, it might well go another way. Clever and engaging, this impressive first novel will reward both casual readers looking for a fun period adventure and those fascinated by the tension between free will and fate." —*Kirkus*

Punke, Michael

Ridgeline: a novel. By Michael Punke. Henry Holt and Company, 2021. 352 p.
ISBN 9781250310460
1. Crazy Horse 2. Lakota Indians 3. Battles 4. Frontier and pioneer life 5. Violence 6. Forts 7. The West (United States) 8. American Westward Expansion (1803-1899) 9. Historical fiction 10. Multiple perspectives
LC 2020034258
David J. Langum, Sr. Prize in American Historical Fiction, 2021

In 1866, a new war breaks out on the western frontier between a young ambitious nation and the Native tribes who have lived on the land for centuries, in this fascinating saga, based on real people and events, that grapples with essential questions of conquest and justice that still echo today.

"Ridgeline transcends genre categorization—any sophisticated reader would appreciate this novel." —*Booklist*

Purcell, Laura

The **house** of whispers. Laura Purcell. 2020. 384 pages
ISBN 9780143135531
1. Fathers and daughters 2. Physicians 3. Superstition 4. Country homes 5. Tuberculosis 6. Cornwall, England 7. Gothic fiction 8. Historical fiction

Consumption has ravaged Louise Pinecroft's family, leaving her and her father alone and heartbroken. But Dr Pinecroft has plans for a revolutionary experiment- convinced that sea air will prove to be the cure his wife and children needed, he arranges to house a group of prisoners suffering from the same disease in the cliffs beneath his new Cornish home. Forty years later, Hester Why arrives at Morvoren House to take up a position as nurse to the now partially paralysed and almost entirely mute Miss Pinecroft. Hester has fled to Cornwall to try and escape her past, but surrounded by superstitious staff enacting bizarre rituals, she soon discovers that her new home may be just as dangerous as her last.

"Purcell amps up the tension and smartly leaves it up to readers to decide what is real or imagined. This book will appeal to those who like their historical fiction clever, creepy, and gothic." —*Booklist*

Originally published in the UK as "Bone china" by Raven Books, 2019.

The **silent** companions: a ghost story. Laura Purcell. Penguin Books, 2018. 304 p.
ISBN 9780143131632
1. Mansions 2. Women with mental illnesses 3. Women murderers 4. Haunted houses 5. Pregnant women 6. London, England 7. England 8. 17th century 9. 19th century 10. Gothic fiction 11. Historical fiction 12. Parallel narratives
RUSA Reading List, 2019

While residing in her late husband's crumbling estate to see out her pregnancy, newly widowed Elsie is met with resentment and hostility from both the servants and local villagers and soon discovers that she is not alone when she finds a wooden figure that bears a startling resemblance to her—and whose eyes seem to follow her where she goes.

"[Purcell's] novel is reminiscent of the work of all the greats, particularly Shirley Jackson and Daphne du Maurier, but Purcell has a style all her own. A must for all lovers of Gothic literature." —*Library Journal*

Originally published: London : Raven Books, 2017.

Putnam, Jonathan F.

These honored dead. Jonathan Putnam. Crooked Lane Books, 2016. 297 p. (Lincoln and Speed novels, 1)
ISBN 9781629537771

1. Lincoln, Abraham 2. Lawyers 3. Women murder suspects 4. Women murder victims 5. Small town life 6. Murder investigation 7. Illinois 8. 1830s 9. Historical mysteries

Abraham Lincoln has just moved to Springfield, Illinois in 1837 to practice law, and since beds are sparse, he ends up rooming with storekeeper Joshua Speed. When an orphaned girl from a neighboring town is found murdered and suspicion falls on her aunt (Joshua's former lover), Joshua makes it his mission to clear her name and calls upon Lincoln to help. This well-researched, richly detailed debut novel will especially please readers who like a bit of courtroom drama.

Putney, Mary Jo

Loving a lost lord. Mary Jo Putney. Zebra Books, 2009. 352 p; (Lost lords (Mary Jo Putney), 1)
ISBN 9781420103281
1. Deception 2. Inheritance and succession 3. Nobility 4. People with amnesia 5. Interpersonal attraction 6. Regency period (1811-1820) 7. 19th century 8. Regency romances 9. Historical romances
Romantic Times Reviewers' Choice Award, 2009

Mariah Clarke, desperate to escape the grasp of a bullying suitor, stumbles upon a man washed ashore on a desolate beach who has no memory of his past and convinces him that he is her husband.

The **marriage** spell: a novel. Mary Jo Putney. Ballantine Books, 2006. 336 p.
ISBN 9780345449184
1. Wizards 2. Women wizards 3. Women healers 4. Nobility 5. Family secrets 6. England 7. Beaufort, Margaret 8. Paranormal romances 9. Historical romances 10. Adult books for young adults
LC 2005057087
Library Journal Best Books, 2006

Jack Langdon has always suppressed his talent for sorcery. But his marriage to Abigail, a skilled wizard, ignites his passion and opens doorways he never imagined.

No longer a gentleman. Mary Jo Putney. Zebra Books, 2012. 352 p. (Lost lords (Mary Jo Putney), 4)
ISBN 9781420117233
1. Women spies 2. Prisoners 3. Rescues 4. Former spies 5. Nobility — History 6. London, England 7. England 8. Regency period (1811-1820) 9. Regency romances 10. Historical romances
Romantic Times Reviewer's Choice Award, 2012

Cassie Fox, a spy determined to help destroy Napoleon's empire, is distracted from her mission to rescue Grey Sommers, Lord Wyndham, from a French dungeon by her unexpected attraction to him.

Not quite a wife. Mary Jo Putney. Kensington, 2014. 352 p. (Lost lords (Mary Jo Putney), 6)
ISBN 9781617733093
1. Married people 2. Aristocracy 3. Second chances 4. Pregnant women 5. Kidnappers 6. England 7. Regency period (1811-1820) 8. Regency romances 9. Historical romances
Library Journal Best Books 2014

When Laurel Herbert witnessed her husband, James, Lord Kirkland, commit an act of shocking violence, she abandoned him, but a passionate encounter ten years later causes her to rethink their estrangement.

"RITA Award-winning Putney (Sometimes a Rogue, 2013) continues her Lost Lords series with a superbly written historical Regency that borrows a classic romance story line and imbues it with all the elements her readers love: simmering sensuality, subtle wit, a surfeit of danger, and a sophisticated flair for characterization." —*Booklist*

Nowhere near respectable. Mary Jo Putney. Zebra Books, 2011. 352 p. (Lost lords (Mary Jo Putney), 3)

ISBN 9781420117226
1. Gamblers 2. Man-woman relationships 3. Rescues 4. Assassination plots 5. Secrets 6. London, England 7. Historical romances
Library Journal Best Books, 2011

Rescued from smugglers by notorious scoundrel Damien Mackenzie, Lady Kiri Laford finds herself falling in love with her brother's oldest friend as they work together to stop a deadly threat against England's crown.

Once a scoundrel. Mary Jo Putney. Kensington, 2018. 368 p. (Rogues redeemed, 3)
ISBN 9781496703538
1. Aristocracy 2. Rescues 3. Women kidnapping victims 4. Sailing 5. Sexual attraction 6. Georgian era (1714-1837) 7. Historical romances

The disgraced son of a proud naval dynasty embarks on a dangerous mission in hostile waters to rescue an earl's kidnapped daughter from life as a harem slave.

Once a soldier. Mary Jo Putney. Kensington Books, 2016. 368 p. (Rogues redeemed, 1)
ISBN 9781496703514
1. Soldiers 2. Independence in women 3. Courage 4. Napoleonic Wars, 1800-1815 5. Heirs and heiresses 6. Europe 7. Georgian era (1714-1837) 8. Georgian romances 9. Historical romances

After shirking his title and great wealth, Will Masterson is hoping to wrap up his military years, spent fighting the French, until he meets fiercely loyal Athena Markham in the tiny mountain stronghold of San Gabriel.

Puzo, Mario

The **family:** a novel. Mario Puzo; completed by Carol Gino. Regan Books 2001. 304 p.
ISBN 9780060394455
1. Borgia family 2. Nobility 3. Manipulation (Social sciences) 4. Power (Social sciences) 5. Greed 6. Italy 7. Biographical fiction 8. Historical fiction 9. Family sagas
LC 2001031876

The story opens with Cardinal Rodrigo Borgia manipulating papal elections in 1492 to become the new Pope Alexander. Determined to establish a family dynasty, he appoints his son Cesare cardinal in his stead and, after a strategically engineered episode of incest between siblings Cesare and Lucrezia, begins ruthlessly eliminating rivals and marrying his children into alliances with the offspring of noble families of France and Spain.

"The saga is lush, full of detail, with characters who manage to be larger than life while seeming entirely realistic. The dialogue is slightly ornmented but never clumsy, and the plot is appropriately epic in scope, mixing fact and fiction seamlessly." —*Booklist*

★ The **godfather**. Mario Puzo. G. P. Putnam's Sons, 1969. 446 p. (Godfather series (Mario Puzo), 1)
ISBN 9780399103421
1. Organized crime 2. Men-headed families 3. Fathers and sons 4. Violence 5. Gangsters 6. New York (State) 7. Crime fiction 8. Books to movies 9. Family sagas
LC 69011465

The Godfather is an extraordinary novel which has become a modern day classic. Puzo pulls us inside the violent society of the Mafia and its gang wars. The leader, Vito Corleone, is the Godfather. He is a benevolent despot who stops at nothing to gain and hold power. His command post is a fortress on Long Island from which he presides over a vast underground empire that includes the rackets, gambling, bookmaking, and unions. His influence runs through all levels of American society, from the cop on the beat to the nation's mighty.

"Names, places, crimes have been changed, but the Mafia world remains true to fact. Here is Cosa Nostra: the wars of the competing families; their changing 'business enterprises'; their struggle for power and money; their weapons: graft, guns, spies, violence, murder. A wide variety of characters are colorfully drawn. The Don comes though as a person you will remember." —*Library Journal*

The **last** don. Mario Puzo. Random House, 1996. 482 p.
ISBN 9780679401438
1. Mafia 2. Violence 3. Families 4. Cousins 5. Film industry and trade 6. Hollywood, California 7. Las Vegas, Nevada 8. Crime fiction
LC 963401

Don Domenico has a surprise in store for his family—he wants them to create a life free from criminal activities for his grandchildren. There is nothing unusual about that, except that the Clericuzio are the last great Mafia family and there are seeds of evil in the family history, seeds sown by the Don himself. Killing is what the family does best.

"Mr. Puzo wraps up his intricate plot with the same ingenuity he exhibits throughout this satisfying novel." —*New York Times Book Review*

The **Sicilian:** a novel. Linden Press/Simon and Schuster, 1984. 410 p. (Godfather series (Mario Puzo), 2)
ISBN 9780671435646
1. Organized crime 2. Men-headed families 3. Fathers and sons 4. Violence 5. Gangsters 6. Sicily, Italy 7. Books to movies 8. Family sagas 9. Crime fiction

After his three-year exile in Sicily, Michael Corleone is charged to return to America with Salvatore Giuliano, a young Sicilian bandit whose activities have angered the head of the Sicilian Mafia BT

"Perhaps only an American writer with deep Sicilian roots and passions could have succeeded as Mr. Puzo has in symbolizing a desperate society through the deeds of a desperado, and in revealing how thin is the line that often separates a freedom-fighter from a terrorist." —*New York Times Book Review*

Pym, Barbara

★ **Excellent** women. Barbara Pym. Plume Books 1978. 256p.
ISBN 9780452267305
1. Single women 2. England 3. Satirical fiction 4. Classics 5. Gentle reads
LC 88-70110

"Mildred Lathbury, 30ish, a spinster, a clergyman's daughter, is an excellent woman, one who, with no life of her own to speak of, finds herself somewhat unwillingly a part of the lives of others. Her days are made up of small things: church, flowers, dinner with the bachelor vicar and his sister, brief encounters with neighbors.... Pym's singular world is a lonely, bittersweet familiar place. She travels it with rueful wit, views the human landscape with a wise, sharp, compassionate eye." —*Publishers Weekly*
Originally published 1952 by Dutton.

Pynchon, Thomas

Against the day: a novel. Thomas Pynchon. Penguin Press, 2006. 1085 p.
ISBN 9781594201202
1. Human behavior 2. Labor disputes — History 3. Good and evil 4. Uncertainty 5. Sexuality 6. United States 7. Mexico 8. Mexican Revolution (1910-1920) 9. 1890s 10. Historical fiction 11. Satirical fiction
LC 2006050714

Booklist Editors' Choice, 2006; Library Journal Best Books, 2006; New York Times Notable Book, 2006

An epic tale spanning the years between the Chicago World's Fair of 1893 and the end of World War I features a sizable cast of characters who are caught up by such events as the labor troubles of Colorado, the Mexican revolution, and the heyday of silent-movie Hollywood.

"For all its brilliant passages, this is the book that makes you wonder whether even Pynchon knows what lies behind all those veils he's always urging us to part. But wouldn't you know it? Even when he jumps the shark, he does it with an agility that can take your breath away." —*Time*

★ **Bleeding** edge. Thomas Pynchon. The Penguin Press, 2013. 512 p.
ISBN 9781594204234
1. Cromwell, Thomas 2. High technology 3. Billionaires 4. Rich men 5. Businesspeople 6. New York City 7. 2000s (Decade) 8. Literary fiction 9. Mysteries
LC 2013017173
Library Journal Best Books, 2013; New York Times Notable Book, 2013; National Book Award for Fiction finalist, 2013

An average mother of two working in investigation fraud gets drawn into a shady and eccentric underworld after looking into the finances of a billionaire computer geek.

★ The **crying** of lot 49. Thomas Pynchon. Perenial Library, 1986. 183 p.
ISBN 9780060913076
1. Administration of estates 2. Conspiracies 3. Counterculture 4. Paranoia 5. Entropy 6. Southern California 7. 1960s 8. Satirical fiction 9. Literary fiction 10. Modern classics
LC 85045221

When Oedipa Maas is named as the executor of her late lover's will, she discovers that his estate is mysteriously connected with an underground organization.
Originally published: Philadelphia : Lippincott, 1966.

★ **Gravity's** rainbow. Thomas Pynchon. Viking, 1973. 760 p.
ISBN 9780670348329
1. Soldiers 2. Rockets (Ordnance) 3. Americans in Europe 4. Science — Experiments 5. Conditioned response 6. Germany 7. Second World War era (1939-1945) 8. Literary fiction 9. Modern classics 10. Science fiction classics
LC 72083804
National Book Award for Fiction, 1974

Tyrone Slothrop, a GI in London in 1944, is under suspicion by his superiors and soon on the run from enemies through Germany.

"Fiction allows at last what was forbidden to the original suffering poets and novelists of 1914-18: the utmost in obscene description, the limit of masochistic pornography. If Gravity's Rainbow is often nauseating it is in a good cause. This is the war book to end them all." —Anthony Burgess, *99 Novels*

Inherent vice. Thomas Pynchon. Penguin Press, 2009. 384 p.
ISBN 9781594202247
1. Private investigators 2. Kidnapping 3. Rich men 4. Criminals 5. Former girlfriends 6. Los Angeles, California 7. 1960s 8. Noir fiction 9. Experimental fiction 10. Literary fiction
LC 2009007705

Reluctantly investigating a kidnapping threat against his ex-girlfriend's billionaire beau, Doc Sportello tackles a bizarre tangle of nefarious characters before stumbling on a mysterious entity that may actually be a tax shelter for a dental group.

"An account of the adventures of a hippie private eye pursuing assorted nonlucrative commissions in a Southern California beach town around 1970, Inherent Vice is a sun-struck, pot-addled shaggy dog story that fuses the sulky skepticism of Raymond Chandler with the good-natured scrappiness of The Big Lebowski. It's an inspired formula; the mystery plot supplies the novel with a minimum of structure (as well as confidence that there's some point to the enterprise) and the genre provides ample cover for Pynchon's literary weaknesses." —*Salon.com*

Mason & Dixon. Thomas Pynchon. H. Holt, 1997. 773 p.
ISBN 9780805037586
1. Mason, Charles 2. Mason-Dixon Line 3. Surveying — History 4. Surveyors 5. Frontier and pioneer life 6. United States 7. Colonial America (1600-1775) 8. Biographical fiction 9. Historical fiction
LC 976467
Follows mismatched British surveyors Charles Mason and Jeremiah Dixon as they make their way through frontier hardships, Native Americans, warfare, conspiracies, and other perils of eighteenth-century, pre-Revolutionary America BT
"From historical odds and ends and the Field Journal they left behind, Pynchon re-imagines Mason and Dixon before, during and after the four-plus years, 1763-1767, they took to draw their 244-mile-long line through the American wilderness, dividing the proprietorships of the Penns of Pennsylvania and the Calverts of Maryland, ordaining our North and South. From his omnivorous reading, with his diabolical genius for mimicry, he also re-creates their tumultuous era." —*The Nation*

★ **V:** a novel. Thomas Pynchon. Perennial Library, 1986. 492 p.
ISBN 9780060913083
1. Losers (Persons) 2. Women — Identity 3. Imperialism 4. British in the United States 5. Sewer workers 6. New York City 7. 20th century 8. Literary fiction 9. Modern classics
LC 8545222
The search for the mysterious V ranges from New York to Cairo to Alexandria to Malta. Apart from its strange heroine, the book's characters include sailors, spies, priests, philosophers, bums and bawds.
Originally published: Philadelphia : Lippincott, 1963.

Vineland. Thomas Pynchon. Little, Brown, 1990. 385 p.
ISBN 9780316724449
1. The Sixties generation 2. Hippies — Influence 3. Counterculture 4. Obsession in men 5. Northern California 6. 1960s 7. 1980s 8. Satirical fiction 9. Multiple perspectives
LC 89013025
Ex-hippie and unemployed FBI sting specialist Frenesi Gates must confront her past when former commune-mates start disappearing and an old lover turns up after fifteen years BT
"This is manifestly the work of a man of quick intelligence and quirky invention. Many of its episodes flicker with an appealingly far-flung humor. And Pynchon displays throughout Vineland what might be called an internal loyalty: he keeps the faith with the generally feckless and almost invariably inarticulate misfits he assembles, tracking their looping thoughts and indecisive actions with a patience that seems grounded in affection." —*The New York Review of Books*

Pyper, Andrew

The **damned:** a novel. Andrew Pyper. Simon & Schuster, 2015. 304 p.
ISBN 9781476755113
1. Twins 2. Ghosts 3. Life after death 4. Good and evil 5. Near-death experience 6. Detroit, Michigan 7. Horror 8. Canadian fiction
LC 2014016217
Twenty years after his death and resuscitation following a fire, Danny Orchard is still haunted by his twin, Ashleigh, who didn't survive. A psycopath before her death, Ash's ghost proves even more malicious. When Danny gets engaged, Ash (who has sabotaged all of Danny's relationships) threatens mayhem. Canadian author Andrew Pyper enhances

this chiller—set in modern Detroit—with a vivid sense of place and realistic character development.
"Pyper's pacing, as well as the novel's length, is perfect, and his evocative description of Detroit, a city desolate in its decline, comes off as both sad and poetic at the same time. A treat for fans of intelligent treatments of the supernatural and rock-solid writing." —*Kirkus*

The **homecoming:** a novel. Andrew Pyper. Simon & Schuster, 2019. 353 p.
ISBN 9781982108977
1. Wills 2. Family secrets 3. Social isolation 4. Family relationships 5. Fathers — Death 6. Pacific Northwest 7. Psychological suspense 8. Thrillers and suspense 9. Canadian fiction
After learning from their father's will that to claim their inheritance they must stay at the family estate for thirty days with their troubled mother and sister, two brothers are drawn into a world of dark revelations and long-kept secrets.
"Pyper fairly lays the groundwork for the truth behind their experiences, and readers will be invested in the thoughtfully constructed characters." —*Publishers Weekly*

The **residence:** a novel. Andrew Pyper. Gallery Books, 2020. 352 p.
ISBN 9781982149055
1. Pierce, Franklin 2. Ghosts 3. Seances 4. Haunted houses 5. Presidents 6. Railroad accidents 7. Washington, D.C. 8. Ghost stories 9. Historical fiction
LC 2020008538
After losing her son in a train derailment, First Lady Jane Pierce contacts the most notable spiritualists of the day to connect with him in a séance and instead brings forth a malevolent spirit.
"Pyper does a good job of haunting the White House but is less successful at incorporating the real historical horrors of slavery and the looming Civil War. History buffs might take issue with some of the minutiae, but this eerie ghost story is sure to please horror fans." —*Publishers Weekly*

Q

Qiu, Xiaolong

Death of a red heroine. Qiu Xiaolong. Soho, 2000. 463 p; (Inspector Chen Cao mysteries, 1)
ISBN 9781569471937
1. Police 2. Murder investigation 3. Detectives 4. Poets 5. Murder 6. Shanghai, China 7. China 8. Mysteries 9. Police procedurals
LC 20362
Anthony Award for Best Novel, 2001
Inspector Chen must battle the political climate of Shanghai and seek the help of a former lover in order to solve the murder of a National Model Worker.
"An engrossing first novel set in China during the 1990s that begins as a simple police procedural and then just keeps on getting more complex.... Chen is an irresistible protagonist, likable and determined to make the honorable choices, no matter how dangerous." —*Kirkus*

Don't cry Tai Lake: an Inspector Chen novel. Qiu Xiaolong. Minotaur Books, 2011. 336 p. (Inspector Chen Cao mysteries, 7)
ISBN 9780312550646
1. Police 2. Murder investigation 3. Manufacturing industry and trade 4. Murder 5. Crimes against men 6. Shanghai, China 7. Mysteries 8. Police procedurals

Offered a luxury vacation near Lake Tai, Chief Inspector Chen Cao is drawn into the murder investigation of a manufacturing plant director who had been accused of polluting the once-beautiful lake, a case that implicates the leader of a local ecological group.

Enigma of China. Xiaolong Qiu. St. Martin's Minotaur, 2013. 277 pages; (Inspector Chen Cao mysteries, 8)
ISBN 9781250025807
1. Police 2. Suicide investigation 3. Murder 4. Crimes against men 5. Political intrigue 6. Shanghai, China 7. China 8. Mysteries 9. Police procedurals
In line for the top politic position of the Shanghai Police Department, Chief Inspector Chen Cao is drawn into the investigation of a major party member's son, whose suspicious suicide in the face of corruption charges forces Chen to make a difficult choice.

Hold your breath, China. Qiu Xiaolong. Severn House Publishers, 2020. 208 pages; (Inspector Chen Cao mysteries, 10)
ISBN 9780727890436
1. Investigations 2. Environmentalists 3. Serial murders 4. Political corruption 5. Deception 6. Shanghai, China 7. China 8. Mysteries 9. Police procedurals
Inspector Chen is on the case of a serial murderer when he is called away to report on environmentalists trying to tackle the pollution issues in China. .
"Xiaolong writes with both urgency and grace about modern China in another well-crafted mystery." —*Booklist*

Red mandarin dress: an Inspector Chen novel. Qiu Xiaolong. St. Martin's Minotaur, 2007. 310 p; (Inspector Chen Cao mysteries, 5)
ISBN 9780312371074
1. Police 2. Corruption investigation 3. Murder 4. Serial murderers 5. Young women 6. Shanghai, China 7. China 8. Mysteries 9. Police procedurals
LC 2007044109
Chief Inspector Chen Cao of the Shanghai Police Department finds himself caught up in a dangerous case when the bodies of two young women dressed in identical red mandarin dresses turn up, igniting fears of the city's first sexual serial killer.
"The suspense, and the way Qiu weaves in the human wreckage caused by Mao Zedong's Cultural Revolution, gives one of contemporary fiction's best pictures yet of the wrenching changes facing China as it struggles with its recent, wretched past." —*St. Louis Post-Dispatch*

Shanghai redemption: an Inspector Chen novel. Xiaolong Qiu. Minotaur Books, 2015. 308 pages; (Inspector Chen Cao mysteries, 9)
ISBN 9781250065278
1. Investigations 2. Reputation 3. Political corruption 4. Deception 5. Police 6. Shanghai, China 7. China 8. Mysteries 9. Police procedurals
Library Journal Best Books, 2015
Given a bogus promotion and targeted by an assassin after a controversial case, former Shanghai detective and Communist Party secretary Chen Cao risks his life to investigate an increasingly corrupt Party leader.

When red is black. Qiu Xiaolong. Soho Press, 2004. 309 p; (Inspector Chen Cao mysteries, 3)
ISBN 9781569473696
1. Police 2. Murder investigation 3. Crimes against women 4. Translators 5. Real estate developers 6. Shanghai, China 7. China 8. Mysteries 9. Police procedurals
LC 2003023436
When Inspector Chen is made an offer by a triad-connected businessman, he takes a vacation, leaving his partner to investigate a novelist's death, only to apprehend the culprit after Chen returns, who then discovers how the triad has played him.

"This mystery offers a complex and riveting portrait of Shanghai, a city in transition from a proletarian dictatorship to a capitalist playground." —*Washington Post Book World.*

Quade, Kirstin Valdez
★ The **five** wounds: a novel. Kirstin Valdez Quade. W. W. Norton & Company, 2021. 448 p.
ISBN 9780393242836
1. Alcoholic men 2. Pregnant teenagers 3. Hispanic American families 4. Catholic families 5. Communities 6. New Mexico 7. Domestic fiction 8. Literary fiction
LC 2020030288
Andrew Carnegie Medal for Excellence in Fiction finalist, 2022
Finds a man accepting the role of Jesus in his New Mexico community's Good Friday procession, before his personal goals of redemption are challenged by a daughter's pregnancy.
"The well-developed characters convey palpable emotion as Amadeo's failures as a father, partner, entrepreneur, and even as Jesus translate into fits of rage and frustration. Quade's rendering of a singular community is pitch perfect." —*Publishers Weekly*

Night at the fiestas: stories. Kirstin Valdez Quade. W.W. Norton & Company, 2015. 288 p.
ISBN 9780393242980
1. Parent and child 2. Earp, Wyatt 3. Families 4. Catholics 5. Interpersonal relations 6. New Mexico 7. Literary fiction 8. Short stories 9. Adult books for young adults
LC 2014038352
Library Journal Best Books, 2015; New York Times Notable Book, 2015
Exploring the themes of race, class and coming-of-age, a stunning collection of stories about growing up in a land shaped by love, loss and violence introduces a cast of unforgettable characters who protect, betray, wound, undermine, bolster, define and, ultimately, save each other.
"A piercingly perfect debut collection from a young writer who's already arrived; highly recommended." —*Library Journal*

Quartey, Kwei
Children of the street: a novel. Kwei Quartey. Random House Trade Paperbacks, 2011. X, 335 p; (Inspector Darko Dawson mysteries, 2)
ISBN 9780812981674
1. Teenage murder victims 2. Serial murder investigation 3. Street life 4. Detectives 5. Marijuana 6. Ghana 7. Mysteries 8. Police procedurals
A follow-up to Wife of the Gods finds Inspector Darko Dawson investigating a string of murders targeting the street teens of Ghana in a case that takes him through the city's underground, where he is forced to come to terms with the brutal world of the urban poor. —publisher's description.
"A must-read for anyone who follows African crime fiction." —*Booklist*

Gold of our fathers. Kwei Quartey. Soho Crime, 2016. 368 p. (Inspector Darko Dawson mysteries, 4)
ISBN 9781616956301
1. Gold mines and mining 2. Murder 3. Police 4. Corruption 5. Detectives 6. Ghana 7. Mysteries 8. Police procedurals
LC 2015028758
Children's Africana Book Awards, New Adult, 2020
A body has been unearthed in one of the remote Obuasi gold quarries. The list of potential suspects is a long one, and Dawson must pursue it alone, because he can't trust his sergeant partner. He learns very quickly how dangerous it is to pursue justice in this kingdom of illegal gold mines,

where the worst offenders have so much money they have no fear of the law.

The **missing** American. Kwei Quartey. Soho Crime, 2020. 432 p. (Emma Djan novels, 1)
ISBN 9781641290708
1. Private investigators 2. Savonarola, Girolamo 3. Missing persons investigation 4. Computer crimes 5. Widowers 6. Accra, Ghana 7. Ghana 8. Mysteries
LC 2019019288
Shamus Award for Best First P.I. Novel, 2021
Accra private investigator Emma Djan's first missing persons case will lead her to the darkest depths of the email scams and fetish priests in Ghana, the world's Internet capital.
"This promising series debut from the acclaimed Quartey ('Darko Dawson' mysteries) introduces the formidable Emma, and most important, the culture and politics of Ghana. Recommended for readers of mystery, African American and African fiction, and international crime/mystery." —*Library Journal*

Murder at Cape Three Points. Kwei Quartey. Soho Crime, 2014. 336 p. (Inspector Darko Dawson mysteries, 3)
ISBN 9781616953898
1. Crimes against rich people 2. Murder investigation 3. Oil industry and trade 4. Real estate development 5. Beheading 6. Ghana 7. Mysteries 8. Police procedurals
LC 2013038337
"When a prominent couple is found murdered on the Ghanaian coast, Detective Inspector Darko Dawson of the Accra police force is separated from his family while investigating an increasingly dangerous case involving the efforts of real estate and oil interests to force out local fishing villages."

★ **Sleep** well, my lady. Kwei Quartey. Soho Crime, 2021. 336 pages (Emma Djan novels, 2)
ISBN 9781641292078
1. Women private investigators 2. Women murder victims 3. Secrets 4. Rich people 5. Undercover operations 6. Accra, Ghana 7. Ghana 8. Mysteries 9. African American fiction
LC 2020033010
PI Emma Djan investigates the death of a Ghanaian fashion icon and social media celebrity, Lady Araba.
"Quartey skewers Ghanaian politics, religion, and the law. Smooth prose complements the well-wrought plot. This distinctive detective series deserves a long run." —*Publishers Weekly*

Wife of the gods: a novel. By Kwei J. Quartey. Random House, 2009. 336 p. (Inspector Darko Dawson mysteries, 1)
ISBN 9781400067596
1. Murder 2. Missing persons 3. Detectives 4. Murder suspects 5. Villages 6. Ghana 7. Mysteries 8. Police procedurals
LC 2008032579
Investigating the murder of an AIDS worker in an African community from which his mother went missing years earlier, Detective Inspector Darko Dawson collects details about the killing and realizes that he is close to solving the truth about his mother's disappearance.

Quick, Amanda

'Til death do us part. Amanda Quick. Berkley Books, 2016. 342 pages
ISBN 9780399174469
1. Matchmakers 2. Mystery story writers 3. Men recluses 4. Women stalking victims 5. Stalking 6. London, England 7. England 8. Victorian era (1837-1901) 9. Romantic suspense 10. Historical romances 11. Victorian romances

LC 2015037168
LibraryReads Favorites, 2016
Operating an exclusive matchmaking service for nobles in Victorian London, Calista is stalked by a dangerously obsessed individual and turns to a reclusive author, who is fighting mysterious demons from his past, for help.

Close up. Amanda Quick. Berkley, 2020. 320 pages (Burning Cove, California, 4)
ISBN 9781984806840
1. Women photographers 2. Private investigators 3. Crime scenes 4. Forensic photographers 5. Women murder victims 6. Hollywood California 7. California 8. 1930s 9. Historical romances 10. Romantic suspense
LC 2019048129
Welcome to Burning Cove, California, where 1930s Hollywood glamour conceals a ruthless killer.... Vivian Brazier never thought life as an art photographer would include shooting headshots for aspiring male actors or nightly wake-up calls to snap photos of grisly crime scenes. After shooting crime scene photos of a famous actress-the latest victim of the murderer the press has dubbed the "Dagger Killer-Vivian notices eerie similarities to the crime scenes of previous Dagger Killer victims, details that only another photographer would have noticed.... The kind of details that lead Vivian to become a target herself.

Garden of lies. Amanda Quick. G.P. Putnam Sons, 2015. 359 pages
ISBN 9780399165153
1. Murder investigation 2. Amateur detectives 3. Secretaries 4. Crimes against secretaries 5. Widows 6. London, England 7. Victorian era (1837-1901) 8. 19th century 9. Victorian mysteries 10. Historical mysteries
Refusing to believe that her star employee's death was not accidental, Ursula Kern, the owner of a secretarial agency for wealthy clients, hires skeptical adventurer Slater Roxton to investigate the dark side of cultured society.
"The end result is another top-drawer historical romance that delivers the perfect fusion of witty dialogue, intriguing characters, and seductive passion." —*Booklist*

The **girl** who knew too much. Amanda Quick. Berkley, 2017. 352 p. (Burning Cove, California, 1)
ISBN 9780399174476
1. Women journalists 2. Magicians 3. Hotel owners 4. Gossiping and gossips 5. Film industry and trade 6. Hollywood, California 7. 1930s 8. Romantic suspense 9. Historical romances
LC 2016050066
Discovering the body of a beautiful actress at the bottom of a pool at an exclusive California hotel, rookie reporter Irene Glasson investigates the victim's secret about an up-and-coming man and becomes drawn to a once-famous master magician whose career was mysteriously cut short.
"Quick (Jayne Ann Krentz, who also writes as Jayne Castle) transports readers back to the 1930s, showing the grimy truth behind Hollywoods glamorous facades and proving that she is a titan of historical romantic thrillers." —*Publishers Weekly*

★ The **lady** has a past. Amanda Quick. Berkley, 2021. 352 p. (Burning Cove, California, 5)
ISBN 9781984806888
1. Women private investigators 2. Booksellers 3. Undercover operations 4. Psychic ability 5. Health resorts 6. Hollywood California 7. 1930s 8. Historical romances 9. Romantic suspense
LC 2020042166
When her boss disappears while on a health retreat at an exclusive spa, investigative apprentice Lyra Brazier goes undercover with the help

of a man with a unique gift, and together, they are plunged into a world darker and more dangerous than they ever could have imagined.

"This ingeniously plotted, paranormal-spiced novel brilliantly showcases Quick's mastery of concentrated suspense, clever characterization, and combustible sexual chemistry." —*Booklist*

The **other** lady vanishes. Amanda Quick. Berkley, 2018. 340 p. (Burning Cove, California, 2)
ISBN 9780399585326
1. Coastal towns 2. Escapes 3. Secret identity 4. Undercover operations 5. Swindlers and swindling 6. Hollywood, California 7. 1930s 8. Romantic suspense 9. Historical romances
LibraryReads Favorites, 2018
After escaping from a private sanitarium, Adelaide Blake arrives in Burning Cove, California, desperate to start over. Working at an herbal tea shop puts her on the radar of those who frequent the seaside resort town: Hollywood movers and shakers always in need of hangover cures and tonics. One such customer is Jake Truett, a recently widowed businessman in town for a therapeutic rest. But unbeknownst to Adelaide, his exhaustion is just a cover. In Burning Cove, no one is who they seem. Behind facades of glamour and power hide drug dealers, gangsters, and grifters. Into this make-believe world comes psychic to the stars Madame Zolanda. Adelaide and Jake know better than to fall for her kind of con. But when the medium becomes a victim of her own dire prediction and is killed, they'll be drawn into a murky world of duplicity and misdirection. Neither Adelaide nor Jake can predict that in the shadowy underground they'll find connections to the woman Adelaide used to be—and uncover the specter of a killer who's been real all along.

Otherwise engaged. Amanda Quick. G. P. Putnam's Sons, 2014. 342 pages; (Ladies of Lantern Street, 3)
ISBN 9780399165146
1. Spies 2. Voyages and travels 3. Murderers 4. Obsession 5. Kidnappers 6. Romantic suspense 7. Spy fiction
LC 2013042660
Barely escaping a would-be abductor who has left a trail of victims in his wake, world traveler Miss Amity Doncaster discovers that her attacker has become obsessed with gossip that ties Amity to scientist Benedict Stanbridge, a spy for the throne who resolves to bring the killer to justice.

Quincy, D. M.

Murder at the opera. D. M. Quincy. Crooked Lane Books, 2019. 304 p. (Atlas Catesby mysteries, 3)
ISBN 9781643852355
1. Aristocracy 2. Amateur detectives 3. Competition 4. Theater 5. Sisters — Death 6. Regency period (1811-1820) 7. 1810s 8. Historical mysteries
In 1815 London, amateur sleuth Atlas Catesby investigates the murder of a notorious courtesan and discovers a link between this crime and the death of his own sister years ago, leading him down a dark and dangerous path of violence and revenge.

Murder in Mayfair: an Atlas Catesby mystery. D. M. Quincy. Crooked Lane Books, 2017. 304 p. (Atlas Catesby mysteries, 1)
ISBN 9781683312253
1. Rescues 2. Frameups 3. Abusive men 4. Small town life 5. Murder 6. Regency period (1811-1820) 7. 1810s 8. Historical mysteries
Library Journal Best Books, 2017
After rescuing a woman, Lilliana, who was being auctioned off by her husband in a small country village in 1810 England, Atlas Catesby must work to help her to clear her name after the husband is found murdered.

Quincy, Diana

Her night with the duke. Diana Quincy. Avon Books, 2020. 384 pages (Clandestine affairs, 1)
ISBN 9780062986795
1. Dukes and duchesses 2. Nobility 3. Widows 4. One-night stands (Interpersonal relations) 5. Stepdaughters 6. England 7. Great Britain 8. Regency period (1811-1820) 9. Regency romances 10. Multicultural romances 11. Historical romances
After one night of reckless passion with a complete stranger, Lady Delilah Chambers is shocked to discover that he is none other than the duke who is set on wedding her beloved stepdaughter and must find a way to keep him at arm's length.
"Quincy's own background as a first-generation Arab American also allows her to bring indispensable detail to the story, which is enriched by details of Leela's journey to learn about, and come to appreciate, her 'Levantine' heritage—a welcome addition to the overwhelmingly White ranks of Regency romance. An exciting start to a new Regency romance series which promises to highlight new voices from the era." —*Kirkus*

The **viscount** made me do it. Diana Quincy. Avon Books, 2021. 384 p. (Clandestine affairs, 2)
ISBN 9780062986818
1. Viscounts and viscountesses 2. Working class women 3. Ambition in women 4. Women healers 5. Nobility 6. England 7. Great Britain 8. Regency period (1811-1820) 9. Regency romances 10. Multicultural romances 11. Historical romances
Diana Quincy returns with the second novel in her Clandestine Affairs series featuring a steamy romance between a working class London bonesetter who is dangerously attracted to her mysterious noble client.
"As in book one, mutual pining is the driving force here, keeping the romantic tension high and the passion sizzling until the end." —*Publishers Weekly*

Quindlen, Anna

Miller's Valley. Anna Quindlen. Random House, 2016. 257 pages
ISBN 9780812996081
1. Girls 2. Farm life 3. Family relationships 4. Families 5. Growing up 6. Pennsylvania 7. Domestic fiction 8. Coming-of-age stories
LC 2015025157
Coming of age in a dwindling 1960s farming community in eastern Pennsylvania, Mimi struggles with profound family secrets and the pain of falling in love with the wrong person against a backdrop of dynamic historical periods.

Quinn, Julia

★ An **offer** from a gentleman. Julia Quinn. Avon Books, 2001. 377 p; (Bridgerton series, 3)
ISBN 9780380815586
1. Stepmothers 2. Earls and countesses 3. Fathers — Death 4. Household employees 5. Rescues 6. England 7. Regency period (1811-1820) 8. Regency romances 9. Historical romances
Library Journal Best Books, 2001
While searching for a mysterious beauty he met at a masquerade party, Benedict Bridgerton meets Sophie Beckett, a servant in need of his help, and as passion flares between them, he must choose between Sophie and the woman of his dreams.

Quinn, Kate

★ The **huntress**. Kate Quinn. William Morrow & Co, 2019. 400 p.
ISBN 9780062884343

1. Women pilots 2. Nazi hunters 3. Postwar life 4. War correspondents 5. Justice 6. Historical thrillers
LibraryReads Favorites, 2019

Stranded behind enemy lines, brave bomber pilot Nina Markova becomes the prey of a lethal Nazi murderess known as the Huntress and joins forces with a Nazi hunter and British war correspondent to find her before she finds them.

Quinn, Spencer

Dog on it: a Chet and Bernie mystery. Spencer Quinn. Atria Books, 2008. 320 p. (Chet and Bernie mysteries, 1)

ISBN 9781416585831

1. Dogs 2. Missing persons investigation 3. Private investigators 4. Missing teenagers 5. Dog owners 6. Mysteries 7. Stories told by animals

LC 2008015370

Chet and Bernie investigate the disappearance of Madison, a teenage girl who may or may not have been kidnapped, but who has definitely gotten mixed up with some very unsavory characters.

"Chet the Jet is a dog who failed K-9 school (cats in the open country played a role in his demise), but now he is a dedicated PI and works with Bernie, owner of the Little Detective Agency. The story is told entirely from Chet's point of view, which will delight dog-loving mystery readers, but the book is also an excellent PI tale, dogs aside, as Chet and Bernie investigate the disappearance of a teenage girl whose developer dad may be up to no good.... Excellent and fully fleshed primary and secondary characters, a consistently doggy view of the world, and a sprightly pace make this a not-to-be-missed debut." —*Booklist*

Regular print edition published: Sydney : Arena, 2008.

Copyright page from the original book.

★ **It's** a wonderful woof. Spencer Quinn. Forge, 2021. 304 p. (Chet and Bernie mysteries, 12)

ISBN 9781250770325

1. Private investigators 2. Dogs 3. Missing persons investigation 4. Holidays 5. Missing persons 6. Southwest (United States) 7. Stories told by animals 8. Mysteries

LC 2021028490

As the holidays approach, Chet the dog and his human partner, private investigator Bernie Little, search for a fellow investigator who disappeared along with a client, in the 12th novel of the series following Tender Is the Bite.

"Most will find the humor and charm to be icing on the smart whodunit cake. There are enough references to winter holidays and the reasons behind them to provide both a festive feeling and thoughts to ponder." —*Library Journal*

A Tom Doherty Associates book.

Quinonez, Ernesto

Bodega dreams. Ernesto Quinonez. Vintage Contemporaries, 2000. 213 p.

ISBN 9780375705892

1. Puerto Ricans 2. Drug lords 3. Spanish Harlem, New York City 4. Urban fiction 5. Adult books for young adults

LC 99033380

In a stunning narrative combining the gritty rhythms of Junot Diaz with the noir genius of Walter Mosley, Bodega Dreams pulls us into Spanish Harlem, where the word is out: Willie Bodega is king. Need college tuition for your daughter? Start-up funds for your fruit stand? Bodega can help. He gives everyone a leg up, in exchange only for loyalty-and a steady income from the drugs he pushes. Lyrical, inspired, and darkly funny, this powerful debut novel brilliantly evokes the trial of Chino, a smart, promising young man to whom Bodega turns for a favor.

Quirk, Matthew

Cold barrel zero. Matthew Quirk. Mulholland Books, 2016. 373 pages; (John Hayes novels, 1)

ISBN 9780316259217

1. Former Special Forces members 2. Malicious accusation 3. Terrorism 4. Intrigue 5. Physicians 6. Techno-thrillers

Returning from exile to win back his family and take revenge on his accusers, a disgraced Black Ops soldier plots escalating attacks on U.S. soil and is targeted by doctor and former comrade-in-arms Thomas Byrne, who struggles with his loyalties during an explosive confrontation.

"Characters, most known only by their last names, are well drawn and motivated, and their exploits are hair raising. Another hard-to-put-down adventure from Quirk, this is even more chilling for its air of plausibility. A fine thriller." —*Booklist*

Dead man switch. Matthew Quirk. Mulholland Books, 2017. 368 p. (John Hayes novels, 2)

ISBN 9780316259231

1. Former Special Forces members 2. Malicious accusation 3. Assassins 4. Murder 5. Intrigue 6. Techno-thrillers

The suspicious deaths of two members of an elite undercover military team are investigated by Special Ops legend Captain John Hayes, who is horrified to discover that his protege, a brilliant assassin, is the prime suspect.

Quotah, Eman

★ **Bride** of the sea: a novel. Eman Quotah. Tin House, 2021. 312

ISBN 9781951142452

1. Married people 2. Divorce 3. Parental kidnapping 4. Searching 5. Moving to a new country 6. Literary fiction 7. Coming-of-age stories

LC 2020034682

Newlywed university students Muneer and Saeedah are expecting their first child, and he is harboring a secret: the word divorce is whispering in his ear. Soon, their marriage will end, and Muneer will return to Saudi Arabia, while Saeedah remains in Cleveland with their daughter, Hanadi. Consumed by a growing fear of losing her daughter, Saeedah disappears with the little girl, leaving Muneer to desperately search for his daughter for years. The repercussions of the abduction ripple outward, not only changing the lives of Hanadi and her parents, but also their interwoven family and friends—those who must choose sides and hide their own deeply guarded secrets.

"Geopolitics is integral to the story, serving as a backdrop for all the developments. Quotah's deft characterization and pacing, combined with an inside look at Saudi Arabian life, make this debut a compelling and worthy read." —*Booklist*

R

Rabb, Jonathan

Among the living. Jonathan Rabb. Other Press, 2016. 288 p.

ISBN 9781590518038

1. Holocaust survivors 2. Jewish families 3. Communities 4. Postwar life 5. Refugees 6. Georgia 7. Savannah, Georgia 8. 1940s 9. Historical fiction 10. Adult books for young adults

LC 2016008314
A moving novel about a Holocaust survivor's unconventional journey back to a new normal in 1940s Savannah, Georgia. In late summer 1947, thirty-one-year-old Yitzhak Goldah, a camp survivor, arrives in Savannah to live with his only remaining relatives. They are Abe and Pearl Jesler, older, childless, and an integral part of the thriving Jewish community that has been in Georgia since the founding of the colony. There, Yitzhak discovers a fractured world, where Reform and Conservative Jews live separate lives—distinctions, to him, that are meaningless given what he has been through. He further complicates things when, much to the Jeslers' dismay, he falls in love with Eva, a young widow within the Reform community. When a woman from Yitzhak's past suddenly appears—one who is even more shattered than he is—Yitzhak must choose between a dark and tortured familiarity and the promise of a bright new life. Set amid the backdrop of America's postwar south, Among the Living grapples with questions of identity and belonging, and steps beyond the Jewish experience as it situates Yitzhak's story during the last gasp of the Jim Crow era. Yitzhak begins to find echoes of his own experience in the lives of the black family who work for the Jeslers—an affinity he does not share with the Jeslers themselves. This realization both surprises and convinces Yitzhak that his choices are not as clear-cut as he might have thought.

"This stirring, powerful novel never sugarcoats its themes or characters; what emerges is a hard-won realism and a compelling look at one corner of the postwar world." —*Booklist*

Rabe, Peter

★ **Anatomy** of a killer;: A shroud for Jesso. Peter Rabe. Stark House Press, 2008. 308 p.
ISBN 9781933586229
1. Gangsters 2. Organized crime 3. Criminals 4. Spies 5. Assassins 6. Germany 7. Noir fiction

Anatomy of a Killer (1960) is the story of a hitman who learns, too late, what it is to be human. A Shroud for Jesso (1955) is the story of a crime boss who is hijacked on a steamer to Europe, where he quickly learns what it takes to stay alive. Provided by publisher

Originally published by Abelard-Schuman in 1960 (Anatomy of a killer) and Fawcett in 1955 (A shroud for Jesso).

Racculia, Kate

★ **Bellweather** rhapsody. Kate Racculia. Houghton Mifflin Harcourt, 2014. 304 pages
ISBN 9780544129917
1. Hotels 2. Gogh, Vincent van 3. Missing teenage girls 4. Fear 5. Murder 6. 1990s 7. Mysteries 8. Supernatural mysteries 9. Adult books for young adults
LC 2013026339
Alex Award, 2015; Library Journal Best Books 2014; School Library Journal Best Books: Best Adult Books 4 Teens, 2014

A young music prodigy goes missing from a hotel room that was the site of an infamous murder-suicide 15 years earlier, renewing trauma for a bridesmaid who witnessed the first crime and rallying an eccentric cast of characters during a snowstorm that traps everyone on the grounds.

"[A] novel of dueling wills, marked by textured characterization and an ebullient storytelling style." —*Publishers Weekly*

★ **Tuesday** Mooney talks to ghosts: a novel. Kate Racculia. Houghton Mifflin Harcourt, 2019. 368 pages
ISBN 9780358023937
1. Poe, Edgar Allan 2. Treasure hunts (Games) 3. Clues 4. Misfits (Persons) 5. Billionaires 6. Women volunteers 7. Boston,

Massachusetts 8. Adventure stories 9. Mainstream fiction 10. Adult books for young adults
LC 2018046444
LibraryReads Favorites, 2019

A dying billionaire sends one woman and a cast of dreamers and rivals on a citywide treasure hunt.

Rachman, Tom

The **imperfectionists**: a novel. Tom Rachman. The Dial Press, 2010. 288 p.
ISBN 9780385343664
1. Journalists 2. Newspaper publishers and publishing 3. Newspaper editors 4. Americans in Italy 5. Jealousy 6. Italy 7. Psychological fiction 8. Literary fiction 9. Canadian fiction
LC 2009033148
Canadian Authors Association Literary Awards, MOSAID Technologies Inc. Award for Fiction, 2011; New York Times Notable Book, 2010

Preoccupied by personal challenges while running a struggling newspaper in Rome, an obituary writer confronts mortality, an eccentric publisher obsesses over his dog, and other staff members uncover the paper's founding by an impulsive millionaire.

"Rachman's strength lies in his rendering of the characters: all 11 are believable, flawed and loveable. The narrative works and forms a coherent whole." —*The Scotsman*

The **Italian** teacher. Tom Rachman. Viking, 2018. 341 p.
ISBN 9780735222694
1. Fathers and sons 2. Father-deserted families 3. Genius 4. Ambition 5. Artists 6. Europe 7. 20th century 8. 21st century 9. Literary fiction 10. Historical fiction 11. Canadian fiction
LC 2017032493
An Italian youth raised to revere the genius artist father who abandoned their family strives to become worthy of his father's attentions through a series of failed career pursuits before he hatches a scheme to secure his father's legacy.

"Rachman's...haunting addition to the list of novels about children overshadowed by famous parents is a momentous drama of a volatile relationship and the fundamental will to survive." —*Booklist*

Radcliffe, Ann Ward

★ The **mysteries** of Udolpho. Ann Radcliffe; edited by Bonamy Dobree; with an introduction and notes by Terry Castle. Oxford University Press, 1998. Xxxiii, 693 p.
ISBN 9780192825230
1. Guardian and ward 2. Orphans 3. Women prisoners 4. Castles 5. Gothic fiction 6. Classics

Count Montoni, in his gloomy medieval fortress in the Appenines, terror becomes the order of the day. With its dream-like plot and hallucinatory rendering of its characters' psychological states, The Mysteries of Udolpho is a fascinating challenge to contemporary readers.

First published in 1794.

Rademacher, Cay

Deadly Camargue: a Provence mystery. Cay Rademacher; translated from the French by Peter Millar. Minotaur Books, 2018. 293 p. (Provence mysteries, 2)
ISBN 9781250110725

1. Cold cases (Criminal investigation) 2. Art thefts 3. Rural life 4. Journalists 5. Detectives 6. Provence, France 7. France 8. Translations 9. Mysteries

LC 2018013875

Roger Blanc and Marius Tonon investigate after a Parisian political reporter and TV personality is discovered gored to death by a fighting bull in Camargue.

Translation of: Todliche Camargue.

Translated from the French.

Rader-Day, Lori

The **black** hour. Lori Rader-Day. Seventh Street Books, 2014. 330 pages

ISBN 9781616148850

1. Sociology 2. Gunshot victims 3. Women college teachers 4. Graduate students 5. Former boyfriends 6. Chicago, Illinois 7. Psychological suspense

LC 2014003653

Anthony Award for Best First Novel, 2015; LibraryReads Favorites, 2014

For Chicago sociology professor Amelia Emmet, violence was a research topic—until a student she'd never met shot her.

"Chapters that alternate between Amelia and Nath's viewpoints provide an irresistible combination of menace, betrayal, and self-discovery." *—Publishers Weekly*

The **day** I died. Lori Rader-Day. William Morrow, 2017. 408 p.

ISBN 9780062560292

1. Family violence 2. Criminal profiling 3. Missing boys 4. Graphologists 5. Kidnapping investigation 6. Indiana 7. Psychological suspense

Anthony Award for Best Paperback Original, 2018

Using her skills as a handwriting analyst to assist a local murder case, Anna identifies disturbing parallels between the crime and her own struggles to protect her troubled teen son from an abusive ex.

"Beautiful prose and tack-sharp observations round out this slow-burning but thought-provoking meditation on the ravages of domestic violence." *—Publishers Weekly*

Little pretty things. Lori Rader-day. Random House Inc, 2015. 298 p.

ISBN 9781633880047

1. Best friends 2. Friends' death 3. Women amateur detectives 4. Hotels 5. Secrets 6. Mysteries

Edgar Allan Poe Awards: Mary Higgins Clark Award, 2016

OLD RIVALRIES NEVER DIE. BUT SOME RIVALS DO. Juliet Townsend is used to losing. Back in high school, she lost every track team race to her best friend, Madeleine Bell. Ten years later, she's still running behind, stuck in a dead-end job cleaning rooms at the Mid-Night Inn, a one-star motel that attracts only the cheap or the desperate. But what life won't provide, Juliet takes. Then one night, Maddy checks in. Well-dressed, flashing a huge diamond ring, and as beautiful as ever, Maddy has it all. By the next morning, though, Juliet is no longer jealous of Maddy—she's the chief suspect in her murder. To protect herself, Juliet investigates the circumstances of her friend's death. But what she learns about Maddy's life might cost Juliet everything she didn't realize she had.

★ The **lucky** one. Lori Rader-Day. William Morrow and Co, 2020. 416 p.

ISBN 9780062938060

1. Missing persons 2. Murder victims 3. Secret identity 4. Adult children of police 5. Women 6. Thrillers and suspense 7. Psychological suspense

A volunteer for a website called The Doe Pages to help reunite families with their missing loved ones, Alice, who was kidnapped as a child, stumbles upon a post by her own kidnapper and races against time to find him before he hurts someone else.

"The tightly crafted storytelling brings heat back into the familiar cold case plot, digging deep into those aches that never really fade." *—Publishers Weekly*

Ragan, Theresa

Buried deep. T. R. Ragan. Thomas & Mercer, 2019. 275 page (Jessie Cole novels, 4)

ISBN 9781542091480

1. Women private investigators 2. Men with amnesia 3. Missing women 4. Missing persons investigation 5. Heirs and heiresses 6. Sacramento, California 7. California 8. Thrillers and suspense

Two missing persons. One apparent suicide. Three cases pushing PI Jessie Cole and crime reporter Ben Morrison closer to the edge. As the mysteries, puzzles, and lies of three investigations are unearthed, Jessie and Ben will risk everything to bring all that is hidden into the light.

Deadly recall. T. R. Ragan. Thomas & Mercer, 2018. 286 pages (Jessie Cole novels, 2)

ISBN 9781503949232

1. Women private investigators 2. Journalists 3. Revenge 4. Girl kidnapping victims 5. Kidnapping investigation 6. Sacramento, California 7. California 8. Thrillers and suspense

PI Jessie Cole is about to discover that there's no revenge too wicked as New York Times bestselling author T.R. Ragan's gripping series continues.

Deranged. T. R. Ragan. Thomas & Mercer, 2018. 288 p. (Jessie Cole novels, 3)

ISBN 9781503904293

1. Women private investigators 2. Men with amnesia 3. Fathers and sons 4. Prisoners 5. Surveillance 6. Sacramento, California 7. California 8. Thrillers and suspense

Ever since a car accident left reporter Ben Morrison with amnesia, he's been trying to rebuild a future as he puts together the pieces of his past. With the help of PI Jessie Cole, he's getting closer. But few who remember Ben's troubled childhood want to talk. Then Jessie is sidetracked by a surveillance request from a suspicious husband. An ordinary case, until the cheating wife and lover are found murdered. They bear the trademark wounds of an elusive serial killer who's now leading Jessie down a chilling path—one that's about to put a dangerous twist in the search for Ben's identity.

Her last day. T. R. Ragan. Thomas & Mercer, 2017. 305 pages (Jessie Cole novels, 1)

ISBN 9781542046060

1. Women private investigators 2. Missing women 3. Sisters 4. Journalists 5. Men with amnesia 6. Sacramento, California 7. California 8. Thrillers and suspense

Ten years ago, PI Jessie Cole and reporter Ben Morrison each suffered a tragedy that changed their lives—and now these two strangers are about to share a nightmare.

Raheem, Zara

The **marriage** clock: a novel. Zara Raheem. William Morrow Paperbacks, 2019. 342 p.

ISBN 9780062877925

1. Arranged marriage 2. Dating (Social customs) 3. Muslim American families 4. Young women 5. East Indian Americans 6. Los Angeles, California 7. India 8. Chick lit 9. First person narratives

LC 2018059052

Given three months by her traditional parents to find a husband or agree to an arranged marriage, a Muslim-American woman with dreams of Bollywood romance starts dating in hopes of finding love on her own terms.

"Raheem's debut uses chick-lit tropes to smartly skewer modern ways of dating and to bring humor to more traditional South Asian ones." —*Booklist*

Rai, Alisha

★ **First** comes like. Alisha Rai. Avon Books, 2021. 384 p. (Modern love, 3)

ISBN 9780063059436

1. Single women 2. Beauty care 3. Influencers 4. Single men 5. Television actors and actresses 6. Contemporary romances 7. Multicultural romances

A social media influencer and makeup expert finds herself in a public relations jam after the son of a powerful Bollywood family begins private messaging her.

"Rai offers a refreshingly balanced depiction of minor celebrity; her protagonists clearly have money and fans, but in the end, they're still people. The personalities of the couple's families are distinctive, but never so over the top that the novel falls into farce, and the story lands as upbeat, witty, and sincere." —*Publishers Weekly*

★ **Girl** gone viral. Alisha Rai. Avon Books, 2020. 384 p. (Modern love, 2)

ISBN 9780063003989

1. Former fashion models 2. Bodyguards 3. Social phobia 4. Anxiety in women 5. Capitalists and financiers 6. California 7. Contemporary romances 8. Multicultural romances

LibraryReads Favorites, 2020

One minute, Katrina King's enjoying an innocent conversation with a random guy at a coffee shop; the next, a stranger has live-tweeted the entire encounter with a romantic meet-cute spin and #CafeBae has the world swooning. Going viral isn't easy for anyone, but Katrina has painstakingly built a private world for herself, far from her traumatic past. Besides, everyone has it all wrong...that #CafeBae bro? He isn't the man she's hungry for.

"Rai follows up The Right Swipe with a sweet and spicy romance that delves into some deep issues of mental health for both main characters (severe anxiety and PTSD), as well as the effects of social media on people's lives. Essential for public libraries." —*Library Journal*

★ The **right** swipe. Alisha Rai. Avon Books, 2019. 384 p. (Modern love, 1)

ISBN 9780062878090

1. Professional athletes 2. Former lovers 3. Second chances 4. Women entrepreneurs 5. Online dating 6. Contemporary romances 7. Multicultural romances

Library Journal Best Books, 2019; LibraryReads Favorites, 2019

Cynical dating app creator Rhiannon Hunter must decide whether or not to give former pro-football player Samson Lima, who wooed her during one magical night and then disappeared, a second chance despite the fact that his in league with a business rival.

Raimondo, Lynne

Dante's dilemma: a Mark Angelotti novel. Lynne Raimondo. Seventh Street Books, 2015. 290 p. (Mark Angelotti novels, 3)

ISBN 9781633880429

1. Psychiatrists 2. People who are blind 3. Women murderers 4. Frameups 5. College teachers 6. Chicago, Illinois 7. Mysteries

LC 2015004945

After his testimony against the wife of a murdered professor seems to establish her guilt, blind psychiatrist Mark Angelotti becomes unsure of her role when new evidence points to another killer and he discovers that his own life may be in danger.

Dante's poison: a Mark Angelotti novel. Lynne Raimondo. Seventh Street Books, 2014. 271 p. (Mark Angelotti novels, 2)

ISBN 9781616148799

1. Hadrian 2. People who are blind 3. Pharmaceutical research 4. Pharmacology 5. Murder investigation 6. Chicago, Illinois 7. Mysteries

LC 2013045364

While enrolling in a drug trial that could restore his eyesight, blind psychiatrist Mark Angelotti helps an attorney discredit the testimony of a crucial eyewitness in a case involving Big Pharma and a powerful antipsychotic drug that may have been responsible for the death of an investigative journalist.

Dante's wood: a Mark Angelotti novel. By Lynne Raimondo. Seventh Street Books, 2013. 350 p. (Mark Angelotti novels, 1)

ISBN 9781616147181

1. Women murder victims 2. Child sexual abuse 3. Murder investigation 4. Psychologists 5. Teenagers with developmental disabilities 6. Chicago, Illinois 7. Mysteries

LC 2012031725

After looking into a case of possible sexual abuse of a mentally handicapped teen named Charlie Dickerson, psychiatrist Mark Angelotti soon has to testify on Charlie's behalf when the boy's teacher is found murdered.

Rajaniemi, Hannu

The **fractal** prince. Hannu Rajaniemi. Tor Books, 2012. 320 p. (Quantum thief novels, 2)

ISBN 9780765329509

1. Thieves 2. Criminals 3. Fugitives 4. Escapes 5. Prisoners 6. Mars (Planet) 7. Space 8. Hard science fiction 9. Science fiction mysteries 10. Science fiction 11. Adult books for young adults

A sequel to The Quantum Thief finds a physicist receiving mysterious information about how to enable immortality in a city torn by the agendas of "fast ones," shadow players, jinni and two revolution-minded sisters; while a thief on the edges of reality is aided by a sardonic ship to risk his freedom and find his patron.

The **quantum** thief. Hannu Rajaniemi. Tor, 2011. 330 p. (Quantum thief novels, 1)

ISBN 9780765329493

1. Thieves 2. Criminals 3. Fugitives 4. Escapes 5. Prisoners 6. Mars (Planet) 7. Space 8. Science fiction mysteries 9. Hard science fiction 10. Science fiction 11. Adult books for young adults

Library Journal Best Books, 2011

Broken free from a nightmarish distant-future prison by a mysterious woman who offers him his life back if he will complete the ultimate heist he left unfinished, con man Jean le Flambeur is pursued in worlds where people communicate through shared memories.

Ramadan, Ahmad Danny

The **clothesline** swing. Ahmad Danny Ramadan. Nightwood Editions, 2017. 288 pages

ISBN 9780889713321

1. Storytelling 2. Death 3. Memories 4. Gay couples 5. Men with terminal illnesses 6. Arab countries 7. Syria 8. Canadian fiction 9. Literary fiction

Tells the epic story of two lovers anchored to the memory of a dying Syria. One is a Hakawati, a storyteller, keeping life in forward motion by relaying remembered fables to his dying partner.

Ramos, Joanne

The **farm**: a novel. Joanne Ramos. Random House, 2019. 326 pages
ISBN 9781984853752

1. Women immigrants 2. Surrogate mothers 3. Money-making projects 4. Human reproduction 5. American dream 6. New York (State) 7. Mainstream fiction

Booklist Editors' Choice, 2019; LibraryReads Favorites, 2019

Ensconced within a Hudson Valley retreat where expectant birth mothers are given luxurious accommodations and lucrative rewards to produce perfect babies, a Filipino immigrant is forced to choose between a life-changing payment and the outside world.

Ramqvist, Karolina

The **white** city. Karolina Ramqvist; translated from the Swedish by Saskia Vogel. Black Cat, 2017. 161 p.
ISBN 9780802125958

1. Organized crime 2. New mothers 3. Despair 4. Motherhood 5. Life change events 6. Sweden 7. Scandinavian crime fiction 8. Translations
LC 2016030009

Karen must take drastic measures to claim what is rightfully hers when the shady legacy of her high-flying criminal boyfriend sends the authorities after the only thing she has left, the home she lives in with her young daughter.

"The ghostly Scandinavian setting and Karins closely narrated sense of impending doom, baby cooing patiently at her hip, make Swedish star Ramqvists English-language debut an atmospheric and suspenseful read." —*Booklist*

Translation of: Den vita staden.
Originally published: Stockholm : Norstedts, 2015.
Translated from the Swedish.

Ramsay, Frederick

Countdown. Frederick Ramsay. Poisoned Pen Press, 2018. 196 pages (Jesse Sutherlin mysteries, 1)
ISBN 9781464210594

1. Fathers — Death 2. Amateur detectives 3. Murder investigation 4. Sheriffs 5. Stolen property recovery 6. Virginia 7. 1920s 8. Historical mysteries

Sheriff Privette doesn't take a deep interest in this cold crime, but Jesse is not letting it go. His father's body has been found with a money belt fat with fifty dollars, a small fortune. Twenty of the seventy dollars that Sutherlin Sr. was carrying when he was reported dead of the Spanish flu in 1918 is missing. His heirloom watch given to him for "thirty years' service in the AM and O Railroad which is now the Norfolk and Western is also missing. It was gold and big as an onion." What happened to the money and to "the Onion? Was all this the work of a thief? Who was the man who showed up at the Sutherlins' door? There's not much to work with. But that won't stop Jesse who investigates as the 1928 boom progresses relentlessly toward 1929.

Features characters from the authors's Copper Kettle.

Ramsay, Hope

Summer on Moonlight Bay. Hope Ramsay. Forever, 2019. 368 pages (Moonlight Bay, 2)
ISBN 9781538732496

1. Women veterans 2. Veterinarians 3. Dogs 4. Moving, Household 5. Guilt 6. South Carolina 7. Contemporary romances

From USA Today bestselling author Hope Ramsay comes a small-town romance filled with love, laughter, and friendship!
2-in-1 special! Includes a bonus novel by Miranda Liasson—Cover.

Ramzipoor, E. R.

The **ventriloquists**. E. R. Ramzipoor. Park Row, 2019. 544 pages
ISBN 9780778308157

1. Resistance to military occupation 2. Journalists 3. Dissenters 4. World War II 5. Anti-Nazi movement 6. Brussels, Belgium 7. Belgium 8. Second World War era (1939-1945) 9. Historical fiction

A tale based on true events finds a misfit journalist, a forger and a street urchin joining a band of resistance fighters who risk their lives to publish a satiric newspaper mocking the Nazis.

Rand, Ayn

★ The **fountainhead**. Ayn Rand. Plume, 1994. Xiii, 736 p; 23 cm.
ISBN 9780452273337

1. Architects 2. Individualism 3. Creativity 4. Self-interest 5. Egotism 6. Psychological fiction 7. Books to movies
LC 86008760

The story of an intransigent young architect, Howard Roark, of his violent battle against a mindless status quo, and of his explosive love affair with a beautiful woman who worships him yet struggles to defeat him. In order to build his kind of buildings according to his own standards, Roark must fight against every variant of human corruption.

Originally published: New York: Bobbs-Merrill, 1943.

Randall, Alice

★ **Black** Bottom saints. Alice Randall. HarperCollins 2020. 384 p.
ISBN 9780062968623

1. Johnson, Ziggy 2. Reminiscing in old age 3. Nightclubs 4. Middle class African Americans 5. Celebrities 6. Nightlife 7. Detroit, Michigan 8. Literary fiction 9. Biographical fiction 10. African American fiction

A celebrated columnist, nightclub emcee and fine arts philanthropist draws inspiration from the Catholic Saints Day books while reflecting on his encounters with legendary black artists from the Great Depression through the post-World War II years.

"This is an exuberant celebration of the arts, including the arts of living well and caring for others. Each of Randall's books is a literary event, and readers will embrace this radiant celebration of African American art and culture." —*Booklist*

Randisi, Robert J.

Hey there (you with the gun in your hand): a Rat Pack mystery. Robert J. Randisi. Minotaur Books, 2008. 272 p. (Rat pack mysteries, 3)
ISBN 9780312376420

1. Sinatra, Frank 2. Entertainers 3. Film actors and actresses 4. Extortion 5. Casino employees 6. Murder 7. Las Vegas, Nevada 8. 1960s 9. Mysteries
LC 2008030119

In 1961 Las Vegas, Eddie Gianelli, pit boss at the Sands Casino and a friend of members of the Rat Pack, is called in by Frank Sinatra to stop an extortionist targeting Sammy Davis, Jr, only to find himself and New York torpedo Jerry Epstein caught in a conspiracy involving treachery, murder, and the Secret Service.

Rankin, Ian

★ **Black** and blue: an Inspector Rebus novel. Ian Rankin. St. Martin's Press, 1997. 394 p. (Inspector John Rebus mysteries, 8)

ISBN 9780312167837

1. Detectives 2. Malicious accusation 3. Serial murder investigation 4. Police 5. Edinburgh, Scotland 6. Aberdeen, Scotland 7. Mysteries 8. Police procedurals

LC 9725381

Gold Dagger Award for Best Crime Novel of the Year, 1997

Already tackling a murder in Edinburgh, Inspector John Rebus becomes involved when a copy-cat serial rapist called "Bible Johnny" begins striking in Aberdeen and must keep his wits about him in the center of the media circus surrounding the case.

"Rankin has a point to make about the corrosive effects of human wickedness that, if left unchecked, seeps into the bloodstream and poisons the national body—a point well made in his blunt and bruising style." —*New York Times Book Review*

The **black** book. Ian Rankin. O. Penzler books, 1994. 278 p. (Inspector John Rebus mysteries, 5)

ISBN 9781883402778

1. Detectives 2. Murder investigation 3. Cold cases (Criminal investigation) 4. Police 5. Missing persons 6. Edinburgh, Scotland 7. Mysteries 8. Police procedurals

LC 948929

"Rankin's compelling and original plot is almost as intriguing as the gruff, tough, rebellious Rebus, whose rough exterior hides a charming, funny, tenderhearted human being we'd all like to know." —*Booklist*

Originally published in 1993.

Blood hunt: a novel. Ian Rankin. Little, Brown and Company, 2006. 400 p.

ISBN 9780316009119

1. Revenge 2. Murder investigation 3. Former Special Forces members 4. Survivalists 5. Crimes against journalists 6. Scotland 7. San Diego, California 8. Mysteries

LC 2005050419

Determined to exact revenge in the aftermath of his brother's unlikely suicide, professional assassin Gordon Reeve becomes increasingly enraged by a local cop who thwarts his attempts to talk with a friend who last saw Reeve's brother alive.

"Gordon Reeve is an ex-SAS soldier who now makes his living training weekend warriors in rural Scotland. Told that his brother has committed suicide in California, Reeve goes to the funeral and quickly decides that the investigative reporter was murdered. Trying to get the story and then revenge, he finds himself pitted against both an amoral chemical conglomerate and an unwelcome face from his own past.... Not Rankin's best but still awfully good." —*Booklist*

The main character, Gordon Reeve, first appeared in Rankin's book Knots and crosses.

Originally published by Ian Rankin writing as Jack Harvey: England : Headline, 1995.

The **complaints**. Ian Rankin. Orion, 2009. 381 p; (Malcolm Fox mysteries, 1)

ISBN 9780752889511

1. Police 2. Police internal affairs investigation 3. Police misconduct 4. Detectives 5. Fox, Malcolm (Fictitious character) 6. Edinburgh, Scotland 7. Mysteries 8. Police procedurals

LC 2009510086

Nobody likes The Complaints—they're the cops who investigate other cops. It's a department known within the force as "The Dark Side," and it's where Malcolm Fox works. His new case: investigate a cop named Jamie Breck. As Fox takes on the job, he learns that there's more to Breck than anyone thinks—dangerous knowledge, especially when a vicious murder takes place far too close to home.

"This novel is part mystery, part buddy story, part morality essay. Mr. Rankin never lets the reader down for a single page." —*Pittsburgh Post-Gazette*

Sequel: The impossible dead.

Dead souls: an Inspector Rebus novel. Ian Rankin. St. Martin's Minotaur, 1999. 406 p. (Inspector John Rebus mysteries, 10)

ISBN 9780312202934

1. Detectives 2. Pedophiles 3. Missing persons investigation 4. Police 5. Serial murderers 6. Edinburgh, Scotland 7. Mysteries 8. Police procedurals

LC 99044276

John Rebus has trouble in the form of a paroled murderer, a pedophile, and the missing son of a former sweetheart, all coming together in a mystery that could cost him everything

Exit music. Ian Rankin. Little, Brown and Co, 2008. 432 p. (Inspector John Rebus mysteries, 17)

ISBN 9780316057585

1. Detectives 2. Murder investigation 3. Conspiracy theories 4. Retirement 5. Rebus, Inspector (Fictitious character) 6. Edinburgh, Scotland 7. Scotland 8. Mysteries 9. Police procedurals

LC 2008001888

It's late autumn in Edinburgh and late autumn in the career of Detective Inspector John Rebus. As he tries to tie up some loose ends before retirement, a murder case intrudes. A dissident Russian poet has been found dead in what looks like a mugging gone wrong. By apparent coincidence, a high-level delegation of Russian businessmen is in town—and everyone is determined that the case should be closed quickly and clinically. But the further they dig, the more Rebus and DS Siobhan Clarke become convinced that they are dealing with something more than a random attack—especially after a particularly nasty second killing. Meanwhile, a brutal and premeditated assault on a local gangster sees Rebus in the frame. Has the Inspector taken a step too far in tying up those loose ends? Only a few days shy of the end to his long, inglorious career, will Rebus even make it that far?

"The final novel in Rankin's Inspector Rebus series is set during the Edinburgh detective's final week at work. (He is nearing the mandatory retirement age of sixty.) The novel begins with a dissident Russian poet beaten to death, and expands to take in smalltime drug dealers, cloak-wearing women who act in walking mystery tours of the city, international oligarchs, and Scottish bank executives. A contemporary artist who makes sound installations may be in league with politicians agitating for Scotland's independence. Rebus is as gruffly mischievous as ever, and the novel ends in a cliffhanger scene with his archenemy that will have readers gasping into the blank space that follows. Rankin's work is crime fiction at its most consuming, cerebral best." —*The New Yorker*

First published in Great Britain: Orion, 2007.

The **falls:** an Inspector Rebus novel. Ian Rankin. St. Martin's Minotaur, 2001. 399 p; (Inspector John Rebus mysteries, 12)

ISBN 9780312206109

1. Detectives 2. Missing persons investigation 3. Internet games 4. Missing girls 5. Police 6. Edinburgh, Scotland 7. Mysteries 8. Police procedurals

LC 2001041946

When a young student mysteriously disappears, Inspector John Rebus comes up with two bizarre clues—a carved wooden doll in a coffin and an Internet role-playing game—and must follow a deadly trail from Edinburgh's past to a modern-day killer.

"Rankin combines complicated multiple plot lines with finely drawn characters and fascinating Scottish lore and settings." —*Library Journal*

Originally published, 2000.

The **hanging** garden: an Inspector Rebus novel. Ian Rankin. St. Martin's Press, 1998. 335 p. (Inspector John Rebus mysteries, 9)

ISBN 9780312192785

1. Detectives 2. Gangsters 3. Organized crime 4. People in comas 5. War criminals 6. Edinburgh, Scotland 7. Mysteries 8. Police procedurals

The hanging garden: DI Rebus is buried under a pile of paperwork but an escalating dispute between the upstart Tommy Telford and Big Ger Cafferty's gang gives Rebus an escape clause. Telford is known to have close links with a Chechen gangster bringing refugees into Britain as prostitutes. When Rebus takes under his wing a distraught Bosnian call girl, it gives him a personal reason to make sure Telford goes back to Paisley and pronto. Then Rebus's daughter is the victim of an all too professional hit-and-run and Rebus knows that there is now nothing he won't do to bring down prime suspect Tommy Telford—even if it means cutting a deal with the devil. Dead souls: A call from an old friend brings back memories and more than a little guilt for DI John Rebus. An old schoolfriend's son has gone missing, the ghost of Jack Morton is inhabiting Rebus' dreams, a part-time poisoner is terrorising the local zoo and a freed paedophile rouses the vigilantes.

"John Rebus, an Edinburgh detective-inspector and father of a 24-year-old daughter, feels especially protective of a young Serbian woman coerced into prostitution by a local mobster. The woman's inability to communicate adds to the frustration of an unproductive, ongoing police surveillance and the continuation of crimes associated with the mobster. At the same time, Rebus investigates a local ex-Nazi's alleged role in a French war crime." —*Library Journal*

A Rebus omnibus—Cover.

The **impossible** dead. Ian Rankin. Little Brown & Co, 2011. 384 pages (Malcolm Fox mysteries, 2)

ISBN 9780316039772

1. Police corruption 2. Politicians 3. Suicide 4. Police 5. Police internal affairs investigation 6. Edinburgh, Scotland 7. Mysteries 8. Police procedurals

A major inquiry into a neighboring police force sees Malcolm Fox and his colleagues cast adrift, unsure of territory, protocol, or who they can trust. An entire station-house looks to have been compromised, but as Fox digs deeper he finds the trail leads him back in time to the suicide of a prominent politician and activist. There are secrets buried in the past, and reputations on the line.

"Edinburgh Internal Affairs cop Malcolm Fox and his two colleagues receive a frosty reception in Kirkcaldy, where they must decide whether a disgraced officer's three fellow cops helped cover up his misdeeds. Det. Constable Paul Carter, found guilty of sexual misconduct, intrigues Fox because it was Carter's ex-copper uncle, Alan, who turned him in. Since interviewing the belligerent Carter and his mates leads nowhere, Fox turns to Alan for insight. He discovers the elder Carter was hired by a prestigious lawyer to look into the 1985 suicide—or possible murder—of Francis Vernal, a fellow attorney, well-known orator, and vocal supporter of the fringe Scottish separatist movement. Soon Fox's attention is divided between following up scant leads in the Carter investigation and unearthing decades-old secrets about Vernal's life and associates. Rankin elegantly weaves together the two story lines without forcing a connection." —*Publishers Weekly*

Sequel to: The Complaints.

The **naming** of the dead: an Inspector Rebus novel. Ian Rankin. Little, Brown and Co, 2007. 432 p. (Inspector John Rebus mysteries, 16)

ISBN 9780316057578

1. Detectives 2. Murder investigation 3. Organized crime 4. Rebus, Inspector (Fictitious character) 5. Police 6. Edinburgh, Scotland 7. Scotland 8. Mysteries 9. Police procedurals

LC 2006031495

British Book Award for Crime Thriller of the Year, 2007

Sent to man an abandoned police station during an international conference between the leaders of the free world, officer John Rebus investigates the suspicious falling death of a delegate at an Edinburgh banquet.

"In his backhanded, reluctant way Rebus winds up uniting all the book's loose ends, and seeing how he accomplishes this is a pleasure. Besides, The Naming of the Dead isn't really about its detective plot. It's about Rebus's taking stock, not only of his own past but also of the world around him." —*New York Times*

Originally published: London : Orion, 2006.

A **question** of blood: an inspector Rebus novel. Ian Rankin. Little, Brown and Co, 2004. 416 p. (Inspector John Rebus mysteries, 14)

ISBN 9780316095648

1. Detectives 2. Murder investigation 3. School shootings 4. Police 5. Rebus, Inspector (Fictitious character) 6. Edinburgh, Scotland 7. Mysteries 8. Police procedurals

LC 2003059549

At a private school, two teenagers are killed by an ex-Army loner who then turned the gun on himself. Finding the truth will take Detective Inspector John Rebus into the heart of a shattered community. Ex-Army himself, Rebus becomes fascinated by the killer, and finds he is not alone. It seems the man had friends in high places and enemies to spare. And Rebus has secrets of his own. He's fresh out of hospital, with newly bandaged hands, and won't say what happened. But after the death of a criminal he visited, who had been stalking DS Siobhan Clarke, Rebus is the prime suspect.

First published in Great Britain in 2003 by Orion Books.

Originally published: London : Orion Books, 2003.

★ **Rather** be the devil. Ian Rankin. Little Brown & Co, 2017. 400 p. (Inspector John Rebus mysteries, 21)

ISBN 9780316342575

1. Organized crime 2. Women murder victims 3. Cold cases (Criminal investigation) 4. Violence against men 5. Murder 6. Scotland 7. Edinburgh, Scotland 8. Police procedurals

Maverick investigator John Rebus gains dangerous enemies upon reopening a cold case from the 1970s involving the murder of a wealthy socialite.

Originally published: London : Orion, 2016.

Resurrection men: an Inspector Rebus novel. Ian Rankin. Little, Brown, 2003. 448 p. (Inspector John Rebus mysteries, 13)

ISBN 9780316766845

1. Detectives 2. Police internal affairs investigation 3. Police misconduct 4. Police corruption 5. Rebus, Inspector (Fictitious character) 6. Edinburgh, Scotland 7. Mysteries 8. Police procedurals

LC 2002016271

Edgar Allan Poe Award for Best Mystery Novel, 2004; New York Times Notable Mysteries, 2003

Sent to a rehabilitation school after a serious mistake, Inspector John Rebus discovers that his classmates are plotting a drug heist and joins forces with Detective Sergeant Siobhan Clarke to investigate ties to an art dealer's murder.

"We are well and truly in Rankin country—a shady world where good and evil are relative terms and truth is an arbitrary concept." —*New York Times Book Review*

Originally published in 2002.

Set in darkness: an Inspector Rebus novel. Ian Rankin. Minotaur Books, 2000. 320 p. (Inspector John Rebus mysteries, 11)

ISBN 9780312206093

1. Detectives 2. Conspiracy theories 3. Stalkers 4. Rebus, Inspector (Fictitious character) 5. Murder 6. Edinburgh, Scotland 7. Scotland 8. Mysteries 9. Police procedurals

Library Journal Best Books, 2000

Inspector John Rebus investigates a body found in a Queensbury House fireplace, the suicide of a homeless man in possession of a fortune, and the murder of an ambitious politician—three deaths with ties to one of Scotland's most notorious criminals.

"Rebus has been assigned to a bogus task force called the Policing of Parliament Liaison Committee. Things liven up, though, when a body is found inside a bricked-up fireplace in one of the buildings under construction for the new Scottish Parliament. That's a tantalizing enough mystery, but when a top politico is found dead at the construction site, Rebus has something he can sink his teeth into: a decades-old crime whose tentacles touch the present and lead to a new confrontation with Rebus' longtime nemesis, Edinburgh crime boss Big Ger Cafferty.... Nobody writes darker than Rankin." —*Booklist*

★ A **song** for the dark times. Ian Rankin. Little Brown & Co, 2020. 336 p. (Inspector John Rebus mysteries, 23)

ISBN 9780316479257

1. Former police 2. Father and adult daughter 3. Missing men 4. Women detectives 5. Criminals 6. Scotland 7. Edinburgh, Scotland 8. Police procedurals

A thrilling new Rebus novel, from a master of mystery, is about crime, punishment and redemption.

"As the two plots converge, the various credible, complex backstories coalesce into a highly satisfying and unified whole. This fresh entry boasts the kind of storytelling that made Rankin famous." —*Publishers Weekly*

Rao, Shobha

★ **Girls** burn brighter. Shobha Rao. Flatiron Books, 2018. 307 pages

ISBN 9781250074256

1. Female friendship 2. Poor women 3. Ambition in women 4. Arranged marriage 5. Human trafficking 6. India 7. United States 8. 21st century 9. Literary fiction 10. Adult books for young adults

LC 2017045149

Booklist Editors' Choice: Adult Books for Young Adults, 2018; LibraryReads Favorites, 2018; Loan Stars Favourites, 2018

Forging a deep friendship with impoverished but passionate fellow weaver Savitha, motherless Poornima begins to reconnect with the beauty of the world before a devastating act of cruelty drives her friend away, compelling her to leave behind everything she knows to search for her friend in the darkest corners of India's underworld and beyond.

Rash, Ron

Above the waterfall. Ron Rash. Ecco, 2015. 288 p.

ISBN 9780062349316

1. Sheriffs 2. Small town life 3. Drug traffic 4. Park rangers 5. Methamphetamine 6. North Carolina 7. Appalachian Region 8. Rural noir 9. Multiple perspectives 10. Literary fiction 11. Adult books for young adults

Enduring the mistakes and tragedies that have shaped their lives in contemporary Appalachia, a sheriff on the brink of retirement and a haunted park ranger confront violent forces when an elderly local is accused of poisoning a trout stream.

Burning bright: stories. Ron Rash. Ecco, 2010. 205 p.

ISBN 9780061804113

1. Poverty 2. Small town life 3. Appalachian Region 4. Rural noir 5. Short stories 6. Literary fiction

Captures the eerie beauty, stark violence, and rugged character of Appalachia in a collection of stories that spans the Civil War to the present day.

"The stories in this collection are set in the rural, meth-addled hills of North Carolina. Pervaded with desperation pawn shops, gravediggers, arson and a sense of impending death these are not uplifting stories.... Burning Bright is a collection to be read for the quality of the prose, which reflects Rash's intimate knowledge of this region and its history. His heart is clearly in this place the dialect is pitch-perfect and he is a skillful translator of the inner worlds and difficult lifestyles of the unique, hardened-by-necessity breed of people who have populated the area, past and present." —*The Oregonian*

★ The **cove**. Ron Rash. HarperCollins, 2012. 255 p.

ISBN 9780061804199

1. Loneliness 2. Misfits (Persons) 3. Man-woman relationships 4. Small town life 5. World War I 6. Appalachian Region 7. North Carolina 8. First World War era (1914-1918) 9. 1910s 10. Historical fiction 11. Rural noir 12. Literary fiction 13. Adult books for young adults

Booklist Editors' Choice, 2012; David J. Langum, Sr. Prize in American Historical Fiction, 2012; School Library Journal Best Books: Best Adult Books 4 Teens, 2012

Living deep within a cove in the Appalachians of North Carolina during World War I, Laurel Shelton finally finds the happiness she deserves in Walter, a mysterious stranger who's mute, but their love can't protect them from a devastating secret.

★ **In** the valley: stories and a novella based on Serena. Ron Rash. Doubleday, 2020. 288 p.

ISBN 9780385544290

1. Rural life 2. Mountain life 3. Revenge 4. Interpersonal relations 5. North Carolina 6. Appalachian Region 7. Literary fiction 8. Short stories 9. Southern fiction

LC 2019058231

A collection of 10 modern allegorical tales includes such acclaimed entries as "Baptism" and "Neighbors" as well as a novella starring fan-favorite villainess Serena Pemberton, who returns to North Carolina to finish the murderous job she started.

"In simple but eloquent prose, Rash describes the vulnerabilities, fears, and desires of his characters and shows how often they unite persons from vastly different walks of life and social strata. The skillful craftsmanship of these tales and their subtle but powerful climaxes make for profoundly moving reading." —*Publishers Weekly*

Nothing gold can stay: stories. Ron Rash. Ecco Press, 2013. 239 pages

ISBN 9780062202710

1. Change (Psychology) 2. Violence 3. North Carolina 4. Appalachian Region 5. Rural noir 6. Short stories 7. Literary fiction

This collection of stories navigates the emotionally harsh terrain of Appalachia and includes "The Trusty," in which a convict sent to fetch water for the chain gang tries to convince a farmer's young wife to help him escape, but she is trapped in her own prison.

★ **Serena**: a novel. Ron Rash. Ecco, 2008. 384 p.

ISBN 9780061470851

1. Husband and wife 2. Lumber industry and trade 3. Greed 4. Infertility 5. Environmentalism 6. North Carolina 7. 1930s 8. Historical fiction 9. Books to movies 10. Southern fiction

LC 2008000712

Sir Walter Raleigh Award for Fiction, 2009

Traveling to the mountains of 1929 North Carolina to forge a timber business with her new husband, Serena Pemberton champions her mastery of harsh natural and working conditions but turns murderous when she learns she cannot bear children.

"Rash's evocative rendering of the blighted landscape and the tough characters who inhabit it recalls both John Steinbeck and Cormac McCarthy, while the malignant character of Serena, who projects a stark unflinching certainty about her actions, propels his finely paced story." —*The New Yorker*

Film tie-in.

Originally published: New Yorks : Ecco, 2008.

Something rich and strange: selected stories. Ron Rash. Ecco, 2014. 288 p.

ISBN 9780062349347

1. City life 2. Mountain life 3. Men and nature 4. Man-woman relationships 5. Appalachian region 6. Southern states 7. Rural noir 8. Short stories 9. Literary fiction

ALA Notable Book, 2015

A collection of stories set in Appalachia illuminates the tensions between the traditional and the modern, the old and new south, tenderness and violence and man and nature.

"These superbly suspenseful stories evoke a world of hurt, but what makes them so deeply satisfying is that they enlarge our capacity for empathy." —*Booklist*

Collects 30 stories from his previously published collections: Nothing Gold Can Stay, Burning Bright, Chemistry, and The Night New Jesus Fell to Earth.

Ratner, Vaddey

Music of the ghosts. Vaddey Ratner. Touchstone, 2017. 324 p.

ISBN 9781476795782

1. Refugees 2. Genocide 3. Homecomings 4. Musicians 5. Memories 6. Cambodia 7. Literary fiction

LC 2016026793

Returning to the Cambodian homeland she fled as a child refugee decades earlier, Teera finds herself in a country of survivors and perpetrators of the Khmer Rouge holocaust before bonding with a mysterious musician who claims to have known her late father.

"Ratner's descriptions of Teera's confrontation with her past, even as she experiences, once again, the beauty of her homeland, alternate with the old mans memories of his life in captivity with his old friend, Teera's father. The juxtaposition is unnerving and powerful as the reader is transported from scenes of unbearable torture to glimpses of monks arriving at a temple, their saffron robes like a row of candle flames moving across the land. Ratner, herself a Cambodian refugee, has penned another haunting, unforgettable novel." —*Booklist*

Rawles, Nancy

My Jim: a novel. Nancy Rawles. Crown Publishers, 2004. 176 p.

ISBN 9781400054008

1. Reminiscing in old age 2. Freedom seekers 3. Characters and characteristics in literature 4. Separated friends, relatives, etc. 5. Enslaved people 6. Southern States 7. United States 8. Antebellum America (1820-1861) 9. 19th century 10. Adaptations, retellings, and

spin-offs 11. Historical fiction 12. First person narratives 13. Adult books for young adults

LC 2004011606

Alex Award, 2006; Booklist Editors' Choice: Adult Books for Young Adults, 2005; Hurston/Wright Legacy Award: Fiction, 2006; School Library Journal Best Books: Best Adult Books 4 Teens, 2005

Pens a moving story about Huck Finn's slave friend Jim, told through the eyes of the wife Jim was forced to leave behind. Sadie shares her story of loss with her granddaughter as they weave Sadie's most treasured items—her mother's knife, a piece of a bowl from Africa, a piece of Jim's hat found when he was thought to be dead—into a quilt.

Rawlings, David

The **baggage** handler: a novel. David Rawlings. Thomas Nelson, 2019. 240 p.

ISBN 9780785224938

1. Attitude (Psychology) 2. Change (Psychology) 3. Personal conduct 4. Belief and doubt 5. Faith (Christianity) 6. Christian fiction 7. Allegories 8. Australian fiction

LC 2018033737

Christy Award for First Novel Category, 2019

When David, Gillian, and Michael all take the wrong suitcase in baggage claim, they are directed to a mysterious facility where the Baggage Handler shows them that their baggage represents larger problems in their lives.

Ray, Eleanor

The **missing** treasures of Amy Ashton. Eleanor Ray. Simon & Schuster 2021. 320 pages

ISBN 9781982163525

1. Women recluses 2. Collectors and collecting 3. Social isolation 4. New neighbors 5. Children 6. Relationship fiction

A reclusive artist's collection has gotten out of control, but her unexpected friendship with a pair of new neighbors might be just what she needs to start over.

"Though the ending is a tad Hollywood, Ray has a light touch with her prose. Readers who can appreciate a comforting story about nice people will find much to like." —*Publishers Weekly*

Originally published in Great Britain with the title "Everything is beautiful" by Piatkus, 2021.

Raybourn, Deanna

A **curious** beginning: a Veronica Speedwell mystery. Deanna Raybourn. Obsidian, 2015. 352 p. (Veronica Speedwell novels, 1)

ISBN 9780451476012

1. Independence in women 2. Orphans 3. Young women 4. Nobility 5. Kidnapping 6. England 7. Victorian era (1837-1901) 8. 1880s 9. Historical mysteries 10. First person narratives

LC 2015009286

Receiving a warning from a mysterious baron after suffering a home invasion, Veronica Speedwell accepts the baron's shelter and teams up with an ill-tempered naturalist when her host is subsequently murdered.

A **dangerous** collaboration. Deanna Raybourn. Berkley, 2019. 328 p. (Veronica Speedwell novels, 4)

ISBN 9780451490711

1. Women amateur detectives 2. Upper class 3. Butterflies 4. Pretending 5. Missing women 6. England 7. Victorian era (1837-1901) 8. 1880s 9. Historical mysteries 10. First person narratives

LC 2018043155

LibraryReads Favorites, 2019

Attending a party in remote Cornwall as a favor to a colleague, Victorian adventuress Veronica Speedwell races to uncover her host's true agenda when suspicious accidents plague the guests.

"A brooding castle, rain-lashed windows, hidden passages, and a seance all contribute to a delightfully creepy tale with twists that would make Daphne Du Maurier proud." —*Publishers Weekly*

Sequel to: A treacherous curse.

★ A **murderous** relation. Deanna Raybourn. Berkley, 2020. 336 p. (Veronica Speedwell novels, 5)
ISBN 9780451490742
1. Jack 2. Women amateur detectives 3. Nobility 4. Royal houses 5. Naturalists 6. Undercover operations 7. London, England 8. England 9. Victorian era (1837-1901) 10. 1880s 11. Dee, John 12. First person narratives
LC 2019043282

LibraryReads Favorites, 2020

Tasked to prevent a royal scandal involving the prince and a brothel madam, Veronica and Stoker go undercover, only to become embroiled in the Jack the Ripper killings.

"The charming characters and involving story, together with the smoldering heat between Stoker and Veronica, make this one a highlight in a very popular series." —*Booklist*

A **perilous** undertaking: a Veronica Speedwell mystery. Deanna Raybourn. Berkley Books, 2017. 352 p. (Veronica Speedwell novels, 2)
ISBN 9780451476159
1. Women amateur detectives 2. Upper class 3. Malicious accusation 4. Murder investigation 5. Secrets 6. England 7. Victorian era (1837-1901) 8. 1880s 9. Historical mysteries 10. First person narratives
LC 2016019601

Visiting a ladies-only club for intrepid women, Victorian adventuress Veronica Speedwell is challenged to save a society art patron from execution.

"Another exciting installment in Raybourn's promising historical-mystery series, starring a fun heroine who defies convention and embraces intrigue." —*Booklist*

A **treacherous** curse: a Veronica Speedwell mystery. Deanna Raybourn. Berkley, 2018. 308 p. (Veronica Speedwell novels, 3)
ISBN 9780451476173
1. Women amateur detectives 2. Upper class 3. Antiquities thefts 4. Murder investigation 5. Conspiracies 6. England 7. Victorian era (1837-1901) 8. 1880s 9. Historical mysteries 10. First person narratives
LC 2017013413

When the enigmatic Stoker's former expedition partner goes missing from an archaeological dig with a priceless Egyptian diadem, Victorian adventurer Veronica Speedwell investigates mishaps that have plagued the expedition as well as malevolent enemies that threaten Stoker's career.

"A Victorian Phryne Fisher, Veronica is an irresistible, modern, engaging woman who uses scientific observation and natural charm to guide her investigations. Details about Egyptian relics, myths, and curses add an extra layer of intrigue to an already fun, rollicking puzzle. Though A Treacherous Curse can be read on its own, recommend the whole series to fans of upbeat, savvy, historical mysteries." —*Booklist*

Sequel to: A perilous undertaking.
Sequel: A dangerous collaboration.

Reay, Katherine

The **Bronte** plot. Katherine Reay. Thomas Nelson, 2015. 336 p.
ISBN 9781401689759

1. Bronte, Emily 2. Booksellers 3. Business ethics 4. Consequences 5. Rare books 6. Christian life 7. Great Britain 8. Chicago, Illinois 9. Love stories 10. Christian fiction 11. Adult books for young adults
LC 2015022374

When Lucy Alling's secret is unearthed, her world begins to crumble, but it may be the best thing that has ever happened to her after discovering that she is not the only one with ghosts and that she can prevail even in the midst of change.

"The moral ambiguity makes the story more modern than its premise would suggest—and proves how well its source material holds up over time." —*Kirkus*

Reddi, Rishi

Passage west: a novel. Rishi Reddi. Ecco, 2020. 432 p.
ISBN 9780060898793
1. Immigrants, East Indian 2. Sharecroppers 3. Farm life 4. Agriculture 5. Friendship 6. California 7. 20th century 8. Historical fiction
LC 2019050704

Follows a family of Indian sharecroppers at the onset of World War I, revealing a little-known part of California history.

"Reddi's Steinbeck-ian tale adds a valuable contribution to the stories of immigrants in California." —*Publishers Weekly*

Redfield, James

The **celestine** prophecy: an adventure. James Redfield. Warner Books, 1993. 246 p; (Celestine series (James Redfield), 1)
ISBN 9780446518628
1. Quests 2. Manuscripts, Peruvian 3. Prophecies (Occultism) 4. Spiritual life 5. New Age 6. Peru 7. Adventure stories 8. Spiritual fiction 9. Books to movies
LC 93-61754

The unnamed hero takes on the Peruvian government, priests, guerrillas and drug dealers to find an ancient manuscript whose nine insights prophesy New Age spirituality. An adventure story replete with energy transfers and other psychic phenomena.

"Redfield has a real talent for page-turning action." —*Publishers Weekly*

Redondo, Dolores

The **invisible** guardian. Dolores Redondo; translated from the Spanish by Isabelle Kaufeler. Atria Books, 2016. 384 p. (Baztan trilogy, 1)
ISBN 9781501102134
1. Homecomings 2. Women detectives 3. Serial murder investigation 4. Murder 5. Secrets 6. Basque Provinces 7. Spain 8. Police procedurals 9. Mysteries 10. Translations

Homicide investigator Amaia Salazar returns to her hometown in Basque Country in Spain after a murdered teenage girl is found along the riverbank, and must determine if the crime is a result of a ritual killer or a mythological creature known as the Basajuan.

Originally published by Destino, 2013.

The **north** face of the heart. Dolores Redondo; translated from the Spanish by Michael Meigs. AmazonCrossing, 2021. 473 p.
ISBN 9781542022323
1. Young women 2. Women detectives 3. FBI agents 4. Serial murderers 5. Serial murder investigation 6. Virginia 7. New Orleans, Louisiana 8. Police procedurals 9. Mysteries 10. Translations

Amaia Salazar, a young detective from the north of Spain, has joined a group of trainees at the FBI Academy in Virginia. Haunted by her past and having already tracked down a predator on her own, Amaia is no typical rookie. And this is no ordinary student lecture at Quantico. FBI agent Aloisius Dupree is already well acquainted with Amaia's skills, her intuition, and her ability to understand evil. He now needs her help in hunting an elusive serial killer dubbed "the Composer," and in solving another case that's been following him his whole life.

"The mysteries are dark and twisty, and the moments of danger are plentiful. Amaia's trauma gives her insight into other people's thinking; she uses this knowledge to hunt down new demons. Fans of noir fiction will devour this book." —*Library Journal*

Previously published as La cara norte del corazon by Destino in Spain in 2019.

Translated from the Spanish.

Reed, Ishmael

Flight to Canada. Ishmael Reed. Random House, 1976. 179 p.
ISBN 9780394487540
1. Freedom seekers 2. Civil war 3. Slavery 4. African Americans 5. Escapes 6. United States 7. Southern States 8. 1960s 9. Satirical fiction 10. Literary fiction 11. African American fiction
LC 76015598

Raven Quickskill runs away from his master during the Civil War but cannot reach the Canadian border until the war has ended because his master is determined to capture him.

★ **Mumbo** jumbo. Ishmael Reed. Doubleday, 1972. 223 p. Illustration
ISBN 9780241305812
1. Harlem Renaissance 2. African American men 3. African Americans 4. African Americans — Social life and customs 5. Epidemics 6. New Orleans, Louisiana 7. Harlem, New York City 8. 1920s 9. African American fiction 10. Historical fiction 11. Satirical fiction
LC 73171314

A strange psychic epidemic called "Jes Grew" is spreading through the country, affecting millions. People start doing stupid sensual things with abandon, and civilization itself is threatened. PaPa LaBas, a HooDoo detective, is trying to find out the origins of the Jes Grew—not because he wants to cure it, but because he's ready for a new kind of society.

Bibliography: p. [219]-223.

Rees, Matt

The **fourth** assassin. Matt Beynon Rees. Soho, 2010. 336 p. (Omar Yussef mysteries, 4)
ISBN 9781569476192
1. Fathers and sons 2. Murder suspects 3. Beheading 4. Murder investigation 5. Yussef, Omar (Fictitious character) 6. Brooklyn, New York City 7. Mysteries
LC 2009041044

Arriving to visit his son in a heavily Palestinian area of Bay Ridge, Brooklyn, Omar Yussef discovers the beheaded body of one of the boy's roommates; and when his son is arrested as a suspect, Omar must prove his innocence.

Reich, Christopher

★ The **take**. Christopher Reich. Little Brown & Co 2018. 336 p. (Simon Riske novels, 1)
ISBN 9780316342353
1. Spies 2. Espionage 3. Stolen property recovery 4. International intrigue 5. Gangsters 6. Paris, France 7. London, England 8. Spy fiction 9. Political thrillers

Preferring work that allows him to stay under the radar, freelance industrial spy Simon Riske reluctantly takes a high-profile job from the CIA involving a gangster's theft of millions from a visiting Saudi prince and a stolen letter containing highly sensitive information.

Reichs, Kathy

206 Bones. Kathy Reichs. Simon & Schuster, 2009. 320 p. (Temperance Brennan mysteries, 12)
ISBN 9780743294393
1. Women forensic anthropologists 2. Crimes against women 3. Sabotage 4. Murder 5. Bones 6. Chicago, Illinois 7. Montreal, Quebec 8. Mysteries

Forensic anthropologist Tempe Brennan regains consciousness to discover herself bound and trapped in a small enclosed space before remembering an autopsy case that resulted in a murder and an attempt on her life.

Bare bones. Kathy Reichs. Scribner, 2003. 320 p. (Temperance Brennan mysteries, 6)
ISBN 9780743233460
1. Women forensic anthropologists 2. Murder investigation 3. Drug smuggling 4. Brennan, Temperance (Fictitious character) 5. Forensic sciences 6. Charlotte, North Carolina 7. Mysteries
LC 2003040725

Her plans for a romantic vacation interrupted by the discoveries of two murdered bodies and a small plane crash, Tempe Brennan traces leads to an isolated North Carolina farm.

Sequel to: Grave secrets.

Sequel: Monday mourning.

First published: London: William Heinemann, 2003.

Bones of the lost: a Temperance Brennan novel. Kathy Reichs. Simon & Schuster, 2013. 304 p. (Temperance Brennan mysteries, 16)
ISBN 9781439102459
1. Women forensic anthropologists 2. Murder 3. Bones 4. Forensic sciences 5. Murder investigation 6. Montreal, Quebec 7. Mysteries

While examining a bundle of Peruvian dog mummies confiscated by U.S. Customs, forensic anthropologist Tempe Brennan finds herself in the center of a human trafficking conspiracy when she investigates the murder of a teenage girl.

Bones to ashes. Kathy Reichs. Scribner, 2007. 320 p. (Temperance Brennan mysteries, 10)
ISBN 9780743294379
1. Women forensic anthropologists 2. Missing girls 3. Forensic sciences 4. Brennan, Temperance (Fictitious character) 5. Missing persons 6. Canada 7. Mysteries
LC 2007002405

Discovering the skeleton of a young girl in the neighborhood of a childhood best friend who had gone missing thirty years earlier, Tempe Brennan investigates suspicions that the victim and her friend are one and the same.

Break no bones. Kathy Reichs. Scribner, 2006. 352 p. (Temperance Brennan mysteries, 9)
ISBN 9780743233491
1. Women forensic anthropologists 2. Missing persons 3. Murder investigation 4. Brennan, Temperance (Fictitious character) 5. Cemeteries 6. Charleston, South Carolina 7. Mysteries
LC 2006045038

Struggling with a lackluster teaching position at an archaeology field school in South Carolina, Tempe Brennan discovers a fresh skeleton among ancient bones and traces leads to a free street clinic where patients are going missing.

"Reichs's down-to-earth heroine is an appealing creation, who deftly juggles personal problems with professional challenges." —*Publishers Weekly*

★ A **conspiracy** of bones. Kathy Reichs. Scribner, 2020. 336 pages (Temperance Brennan mysteries, 19)
ISBN 9781982138882
1. Women forensic anthropologists 2. Forensic sciences 3. Brain aneurysms 4. Murder victims 5. Supervisors 6. Charlotte, North Carolina 7. North Carolina 8. Mysteries
Forensic anthropologist Temperance Brennan struggles to identify a faceless murder victim in possession of her cell number, a mystery that is entangled with a decade-old missing-child case.
"The novel shows us a more vulnerable side of Brennan, and Reichs' writing style is subtly different, too, as though she were trying to make us feel ever so slightly off-kilter. A complete success." —*Booklist*

Deadly decisions. Kathy Reichs. Scribner, 2000. 333 p; (Temperance Brennan mysteries, 3)
ISBN 9780684859712
1. Women forensic anthropologists 2. Murder investigation 3. Motorcycle gangs 4. Brennan, Temperance (Fictitious character) 5. Bombing 6. Montreal, Quebec 7. North Carolina 8. Mysteries 9. Adult books for young adults
LC 22220
Forensic anthropologist Temperance Brennan divides her time between North Carolina and Montreal. In Canada, a motorcycle gang war claims the life of a nine-year-old girl. Back in the states, the body of a long-missing teenager is found hundreds of miles from her home. Are the two cases related? If so, how? That's what Tempe wonders even as she faces surprising trouble in her love life and with her nephew.
"The author doesn't dumb down the scientific stuff, delivering the full textbook version of subjects like hydrocephalus, blood-spatter analysis, ground-penetrating radar devices and the history of outlaw motorcycle clubs in North America." —*New York Times Book Review*
Sequel to: Death du jour.
Sequel: Fatal voyage.

Death du jour. Kathy Reichs. Scribner, 1999. 379 p; (Temperance Brennan mysteries, 2)
ISBN 9780684841182
1. Brennan, Temperance (Fictitious character) 2. Women forensic anthropologists 3. Burn victims 4. Cults 5. Women cult leaders 6. Montreal, Quebec 7. Texas 8. Mysteries
LC 98048763
Forensic anthropologist Temperance Brennan investigates an occurance of arson, which leads to the work of a controversial professor, a commune, and a primate colony.
Sequel to: Deja dead.
Sequel: Deadly decisions.

★ **Deja** dead. Kathy Reichs. Scribner, 1997. 411 p. : Map (Temperance Brennan mysteries, 1)
ISBN 9780684841175
1. Women forensic anthropologists 2. Women murder victims 3. Serial murder investigation 4. Brennan, Temperance (Fictitious character) 5. Serial murderers 6. Montreal, Quebec 7. Mysteries
LC 97002990
Arthur Ellis Award for Best First Novel, 1998
Temperance Brennan leaves a shaky marriage behind and heads to Quebec on an assignment as director of forensic anthropology that leads her to track down a killer on the loose.
"Except for imparting an excess of lab information, Reichs, also a forensic anthropologist, drives the pace at a heady clip. A first-class writer,

she dazzles readers with sensory imagery that is apt, fresh, and funny." —*Library Journal*
Sequel: Death du jour.

Grave secrets. Kathy Reichs. Scribner, 2002. 416 p. (Temperance Brennan mysteries, 5)
ISBN 9780684859736
1. Women forensic anthropologists 2. Massacres 3. Murder investigation 4. Brennan, Temperance (Fictitious character) 5. Forensic sciences 6. Guatemala 7. Mysteries
LC 2002022695
Summer, 1982: Soldiers enter a Guatemalan village and massacre its women and children. Today, families refer to their lost members as the disappeared. Enter Temperance Brennan, about to confront the most heartbreaking case of her careeer. Out of shallow graves fading clues emerge. Something savage happened in the highlands two decades ago. Is it happening again? Four girls are missing and a human rights investigator is murdered as Tempe listens to her screams on the phone. Will Tempe be the next victim?
Sequel to: Fatal voyage.
Sequel: Bare bones.
First published: London: William Heinemann, 2002.

Monday mourning. Kathy Reichs. Scribner, 2004. 320 p. (Temperance Brennan mysteries, 7)
ISBN 9780743233477
1. Women forensic anthropologists 2. Murder investigation 3. Teenage girl murder victims 4. Brennan, Temperance (Fictitious character) 5. Forensic sciences 6. Montreal, Quebec 7. Mysteries
LC 2004045263
Journeying to wintry Montreal to testify at a murder trial, forensic anthropologist Tempe Brennan discovers three skeletons in the basement of a pizza parlor and realizes that she has stumbled into a crime from the past.
"This Temperance Brennan mystery finds the forensic anthropologist in Montreal to testify in a murder case. Arriving a day early to prepare, she becomes caught up in a new investigation when three sets of human bones are discovered in the basement of a pizza parlor. Examining the remains, she discovers that the victims were Caucasian and female. Antique buttons found near the bodies lead Homicide Detective Claudel to believe that the remains are over a century old, but Tempe is not so convinced and investigates with the help of her friend Anne, who has come to visit while contemplating her marriage. Readers of the series will be pleased to see the relationship between Tempe and Detective Andrew Ryan develop further." —*Library Journal*
Sequel to: Bare bones.

Reid, Ava

The **wolf** and the woodsman. Ava Reid. Harper Voyager, 2021. 368 p.
ISBN 9780062973122
1. Young women 2. Magic 3. Princes 4. Mythology, Judaic 5. Fanaticism 6. Fantasy fiction
Inspired by Hungarian history and Jewish mythology, the unforgettable debut follows Evike, a young pagan woman, as she, rescued by Gaspar, the one-eyed captain of the Woodsmen—and a disgraced prince, makes a tenuous pact to stop his brother from instigating a violent reign.
"The convincing enemies-to-lovers romance, fascinating religion-based magic system, and thoughtful examination of zealotry make this a notable debut." —*Publishers Weekly*

Reid, Iain

I'm thinking of ending things. Iain Reid. Scout Press, 2016. 224 p.
ISBN 9781501126925

1. Automobile travel 2. Abandonment (Psychology) 3. Couples 4. Solitude 5. Threat (Psychology) 6. Psychological suspense 7. First person narratives 8. Books to movies

LC 2015031094

ALA Notable Book, 2017; Loan Stars Favourites, 2016

A thriller about a young woman who is considering what to do about Jake, the man with whom she is driving for hours to and from his parents house in the country.

"Reid's tightly crafted tale toys with the nature of identity and comes by its terror honestly, building a wall of intricately layered psychological torment." —*Kirkus*

Made into a Netflix movie of the same name in 2020.

Reid, Kiley

★ **Such** a fun age. Kiley Reid. G.P. Putnam's Sons, 2019. 310 pages
ISBN 9780525541905

1. Babysitters 2. African American women — Identity 3. White privilege 4. Children 5. Racism 6. Philadelphia, Pennsylvania 7. Literary fiction 8. African American fiction

Australian Book Industry Awards, International Book of the Year, 2021; LibraryReads Favorites, 2019

A story about race and privilege is centered around a young black babysitter, her well-intentioned employer and a surprising connection that threatens to undo them both.

"In her smart and timely debut, Reid has her finger solidly on the pulse of the pressures and ironies inherent in social media, privilege, modern parenting, racial tension, and political correctness." —*Booklist*

Reid, Taylor Jenkins

★ **Daisy** Jones & the Six: a novel. Taylor Jenkins Reid. Ballantine Books, 2019. 336 p.
ISBN 9781524798628

1. Women singers 2. Rock groups 3. Fame 4. Addiction 5. Drug use 6. 1970s 7. Relationship fiction 8. Books to TV

LC 2018051135

Booklist Editors' Choice, 2019; LibraryReads Favorites, 2019; Goodreads Choice Award, 2019

When singer Daisy Jones meets Billy Dunne of the band The Six, the two rising 70s rock-and-roll artists are catapulted into stardom when a producer puts them together, a decision that is complicated by a pregnancy and the seductions of fame.

"Framed as a tell-all biography compiled through interviews and articles, Reids (The Seven Husbands of Evelyn Hugo, 2017) novel so resembles a memoir of a real band and conjures such true-to-life images of the seventies music scene that readers will think they're listening to Fleetwood Mac or Led Zeppelin." —*Booklist*

Forever, interrupted: a novel. Taylor Jenkins Reid. Washington Square Press, 2013. 320 p.
ISBN 9781476712826

1. Grief 2. Loss (Psychology) 3. Friendship 4. Husband and wife 5. Widowers 6. Love stories 7. Relationship fiction

LC 2012035073

After her newlywed husband, Ben, is killed while riding his bike, Elsie realizes the only family she has left is a mother-in-law she does not meet until after Ben's death, and whom she is instantly at odds with, and must forge a bond with the woman if she is ever going to get over the grief.

★ **Malibu** rising. Taylor Jenkins Reid. Ballantine Books, 2021. 384 pages
ISBN 9781524798659

1. Summer 2. Parties 3. Surfing 4. Fires 5. Dysfunctional families 6. Malibu, California 7. 1980s 8. 1950s 9. Historical fiction 10. Parallel narratives 11. Mao, Zedong

LibraryReads Favorites Top Ten, 2021; Loan Stars Favourites, 2021

Four famous siblings throw an epic end-of-summer party that goes dangerously out of control as secrets and loves that shaped this family's generations come to light, changing their lives forever.

"Reid's fan base has grown with each novel, and with multiple books in development for television, Malibu Rising will be the sought-after book of the summer." —*Booklist*

Also published by Doubleday Canada.S

Reimringer, John

Vestments. John Reimringer. Milkweed Editions, 2010. 304 p.
ISBN 9781571310804

1. Priests 2. Self-fulfillment — Religious aspects 3. Temptation 4. Faith in men 5. Minnesota 6. Literary fiction

LC 2010007143

Minnesota Book Award for Novel & Short Story, 2011

Just a few years after his ordination as a priest in the Catholic Church, James Dressler finds himself attracted again to his first love, Betty Garcia, and is torn by his opposing desires for the Church and for Betty.

"Just a few years after his ordination and his first assignment as a parish priest, James Dressler is placed on leave. His housekeeper found some letters from a woman and turned them into the archdiocese. For little more than a kiss, he is relegated to a parish in a backwater burg. He opts instead to live back home with his mother in St. Paul until he can come up with a better game plan. But his gritty hometown has its own temptations, and, broke and in need of work, James finds himself renovating apartments and butting heads with his tough, bad-tempered father and attracted once again to his old highschool lover, Betty Garcia. Through his thoughtful themes and lyrical prose, Reimringer effortlessly restores a measure of dignity to the priesthood even as he pays tender homage to the working-class roots of St. Paul." —*Booklist*

Remarque, Erich Maria

★ **All** quiet on the western front. Erich Maria Remarque; translated from the German by A. W. Wheen. Fawcett Columbine, 1996. 295 p.
ISBN 9780449911495

1. Trench warfare 2. War and society 3. Soldiers 4. Teenage boys 5. War — Psychological aspects 6. Germany 7. First World War era (1914-1918) 8. War stories 9. Modern classics 10. Literary fiction 11. Adult books for young adults

LC 96096745

The testament of Paul Baumer, who enlists with his classmates in the German army of World War I, illuminates the savagery and futility of war.

Translation of: Im Westen nichts neues.

Sequel: The road back.

This translation originally published: London: Jonathan Cape, 1994.

Translation of Im Westen nichts Neues.

Complete & unabridged

Originally published: London : Bodley Head, 1929.

Originally published: Berlin : Propylaen-Verlag, 1929.

The **road** back. Erich Maria Remarque; translated from the German by A.W. Wheen. Ballantine Books, 1998. 313 pages
ISBN 9780449912461

1. Survival — Psychological aspects 2. Postwar life 3. Veterans 4. Food supply 5. Justice 6. Germany 7. 1910s 8. War stories 9. Translations 10. First person narratives

In a sequel to " All quiet on the Western Front," Ernst and the few survivors of his company return home after the war to find food in short supply and their families changed.

"A profoundly moving, a painfully moving, document. Unlike tragedy, it has no katharsis, but, like a tragedy, it has to be looked at open-eyed, honestly, courageously." —*The Spectator*

Sequel to: All quiet on the Western Front.

Also published under the title "The Way Back" in the UK.

Originally published in 1931 under the title Weg zuruck.

A **time** to love and a time to die. Erich Maria Remarque; translated from the German by Denver Lindley. Fawcett Columbine; 1998. 378 p.

ISBN 9780449912508

1. Soldiers 2. Loss (Psychology) 3. World War II 4. Bombing victims 5. Disillusionment 6. Soviet Union 7. Second World War era (1939-1945) 8. Love stories 9. War stories 10. Historical fiction

LC 98096094

"The whole story is told with great restraint, with little sentimentality for those in misery and with little open rage at those who caused it." —*Chicago Tribune*

This novel was adapted into film under the same name in 1958, starring John Gavin and directed by Douglas Sirk.

Renault, Mary

The **bull** from the sea. By Mary Renault. Vintage Books, 1975. 343 p.

ISBN 9780394715049

1. Theseus (Greek mythology) 2. Interpersonal attraction 3. Man-woman relationships 4. Minotaur (Greek mythology) 5. Heroes and heroines, Greek 6. Historical fiction

LC 62008924

Slaying the Minotaur was only the beginning. Theseus's legendary exploits continue in this magnificent novel of mythological adventure in classical Greece. Esteemed author Mary Renault picks up where her classic The King Must Die left off, relating the tale of Theseus's triumphant return from Crete to become King of Athens. Plunge into the thrilling world of the continuing adventures of this mythic ruler, from his famous capture of the Amazon Hippolyta to the bitter twist of fate that loosened the bull from the sea. Renault's writing is rich with color and drama, vividly capturing the heroism and uniquely Greek sense of destiny that characterize this classic tale of a royal ruler who looms larger than life.

Funeral games. Mary Renault. Pantheon Books 1981. 335p. (Alexander the Great trilogy (Mary Renault), 3)

ISBN 9780394520681

1. Alexander 2. Rulers 3. Conspiracies 4. Heirs and heiresses 5. Betrayal 6. Power (Social sciences) 7. Ancient Greece 8. Ancient Greece (800 BCE-640 CE) 9. Biographical fiction 10. Historical fiction

LC 81047273

After the death of Alexander the Great, an extraordinary power struggle, involving intrigue and a series of murders, takes place among the various successors to his reign

Sequel to: The Persian boy (1972)

The **king** must die. Mary Renault. Vintage Books, 1988. 339 p.

ISBN 9780394751047

1. Minotaur (Greek mythology) 2. Heroes and heroines, Greek 3. Theseus (Greek mythology) 4. Man-woman relationships 5. Crete 6. Historical fiction

An adaptation of the legend of Theseus who masters the art of bull leaping and slays the Minotaur in the process of fulfilling his destiny

"Retold by its hero, the legend of Theseus becomes a logical sequence of adventures that befell a slight, wiry, quick-witted youth impelled to prove his manhood in a semibarbaric society that put a premium

on size and brawn. Although, at seventeen, he was already a king and a seasoned warrior, Theseus obeyed his patron god's prompting and voluntarily joined a company of young people conscripted for the bull-dances in Crete, became a renowned bull-leaper, and took advantage of an earthquake to overthrow the Cretan kingdom." —*Booklist*

The **last** of the wine. Mary Renault. Vintage Books, 1975. 446 p.

ISBN 9780394716534

1. Socrates 2. Gay men 3. Peloponnesian War, 431-404 B.C.E. 4. Ballard, J. G. 5. Interpersonal relations 6. Men/men relations 7. Ancient Greece (800 BCE-640 CE) 8. Historical fiction 9. LGBTQIA fiction

LC 754841

Two young Athenians, Alexias and Lysis compete in the palaestra, take part in the Olympic games, fight in the wars against Sparta, and grow to manhood influenced by the friendship of Alkibiades and the wise guidance of Socrates.

Illustrated with map of Greece and the Aegean.

Includes chronological table and glossary.

Originally published by Pantheon Books, New York. 1956

The **Persian** boy. Mary Renault. Vintage Books, 1988. 419 p. (Alexander the Great trilogy (Mary Renault), 2)

ISBN 9780394751016

1. Alexander 2. Gay men 3. Rulers 4. Eunuchs 5. Lovers 6. Battles 7. Iran 8. Biographical fiction 9. Historical fiction 10. LGBTQIA fiction

LC 72003407

A slave-boy in the household of Alexander the Great tells about the adventures of the Macedonian king during the last seven years of his life

"This sequel to Fire From Heaven continues the story of Alexander the Great, focusing upon his momentous expedition into Asia. This time we observe events through the eyes of Bagoas, a beautiful Persian eunuch who was loved by King Darius and then by Alexander himself. The multiple facets of Renault's art, familiar to a host of admirers, are once again apparent: a particularly sensitive depiction of boyhood and youth; an astounding grasp of the facts and the spirit of the ancient world; an unerring sense of the dramatic which, along with her superb descriptive powers, brings to life a great historical period." —*Library Journal*

Sequel to: Fire from heaven.

Sequel: Funeral games.

Includes map, and sources for the general reader.

Rendell, Ruth

The **babes** in the wood: a Chief Inspector Wexford mystery. Ruth Rendell. Crown, 2003. 368 p. (Chief Inspector Wexford mysteries, 19)

ISBN 9781400049301

1. Dysfunctional families 2. Murder investigation 3. Family secrets 4. Wexford, Chief Inspector (Fictitious character) 5. Police 6. England 7. Mysteries 8. Police procedurals

LC 2003001575

New York Times Notable Mysteries, 2003

The mysterious disappearance of two local teenagers and their baby-sitter draws Inspector Wexford into a baffling case involving dark family secrets, violence, a religious cult, adultery, and murder.

★ The **bridesmaid**. Ruth Rendell. Mysterious Press 1989. 259 p.

ISBN 9780892963881

1. Women with mental illnesses 2. Obsession in men 3. Murder 4. Man-woman relationships 5. Bridesmaids 6. Psychological suspense

LC 88043471

Philip Wardman, a young man with an abnormal fear of violence and death, meets beautiful and mysterious Senta, a bridesmaid in his sister's wedding, who insists that he prove his love to her by committing a murder.

"Ms. Rendell is a diabolically subtle writer. For much of this claustrophobic study of mutual obsession, she has us peering into Senta's mind through Philip's eyes, suspiciously analyzing her bizarre statements and mysterious behavior. But, like a cunning old spider, the author has caught two flies in her web; and in the end, Philip proves the more interesting study, with his phobia about violence and his fanaticism for propriety." —*New York Times Book Review*

Collected stories. Ruth Rendell. Pantheon Books, 1987. 536 p.
ISBN 9780394569420
1. Murder 2. Obsession 3. Mental illness 4. Psychological suspense 5. Short stories 6. Mysteries
LC 87035949
Includes nearly forty stories from the author's first four short story collections, among them five Inspector Wexford tales and two Edgar award winners
Collected stories from the author's early career.

End in tears: a Chief Inspector Wexford mystery. Ruth Rendell. Crown Publishers, 2005. 336 p. (Chief Inspector Wexford mysteries, 20)
ISBN 9780307339768
1. Crimes against teenage girls 2. Stalking 3. Murder investigation 4. Serial murderers 5. Wexford, Chief Inspector (Fictitious character) 6. England 7. Mysteries 8. Police procedurals
LC 2005026619
A lump of concrete dropped deliberately from a little stone bridge over a relatively unfrequented road kills the wrong person. The driver behind is spared. But only for a while...One particular member of the local press is gunning for the Chief Inspector, distinctly unimpressed with what he regards as old-fashioned police methods. But Wexford, with his old friend and partner, Mike Burden, along with two new recruits to the Kingsmarkham team, pursue their inquiries with a diligence and humanity that make Ruth Rendell's detective stories enthralling, exciting and very touching.

Harm done. Ruth Rendell. Crown Publishers, 1999. 346 p. (Chief Inspector Wexford mysteries, 18)
ISBN 9780609605479
1. Child sexual abusers 2. Missing persons 3. Murder investigation 4. Violence against women 5. Wexford, Chief Inspector (Fictitious character) 6. England 7. Mysteries 8. Police procedurals
LC 9920432
Inspector Wexford must solve the mysterious disappearances of young girls, protect a pedophile and catch the killer of a wealthy executive found stabbed to death shortly after his child disappears.

★ A **judgement** in stone. Ruth Rendell. Doubleday, 1978. 188 p.
ISBN 9780385132237
1. Rich families 2. Household employees 3. Mass murder 4. Classism 5. Former prostitutes 6. Psychological suspense 7. Thrillers and suspense 8. Books to movies
LC 77076961
When a housekeeper carries out a modern "Valentine's Day Massacre" on the family that employs her, Detective Chief Superintendent William Vetch investigates to uncover evidence of a personal tragedy that precipitated the crime.

Kissing the gunner's daughter. Ruth Rendell. Mysterious Press, 1992. 378 p. (Chief Inspector Wexford mysteries, 15)
ISBN 9780892963904
1. Father and adult daughter 2. Murder investigation 3. Family relationships 4. Wexford, Chief Inspector (Fictitious character) 5. Police 6. England 7. Mysteries 8. Police procedurals
LC 91050615

Detective Chief Inspector Reginald Wexford remains cool in the face of massive media attention as he sets out to investigate the stabbing death of celebrity writer Davina Flory and her husband and daughter.
"This is an intricate story that hinges on vanity and self-deception, a story in which the most minor and seemingly innocent relationships are charged with meaning and malice." —*New York Times Book Review*

Live flesh. Ruth Rendell. Pantheon Books 1986. 272 p.
ISBN 9780394555447
1. Rapists 2. Obsession in men 3. Love triangles 4. Former convicts 5. Men with disabilities 6. Psychological suspense
LC 86004922
Gold Dagger Award for Best Crime Novel of the Year, 1986
After fourteen years in prison, rapist Victor Jenner attempts to pick up the pieces of his life but finds himself involved in an awkward triangle whose conflicts resurrect the buried demons of his violent past.
"The obvious way to write this novel would have been to tell it through the eyes of the crippled policeman; Rendell takes the bolder path of getting inside the mind of Jenner.... [This] is a frightening, resonant novel—an extraordinary achievement." —*New Statesman*

Not in the flesh: a Wexford novel. Ruth Rendell. Crown Publishers, 2008. 304 p. (Chief Inspector Wexford mysteries, 21)
ISBN 9780307406811
1. Murder investigation 2. Dead 3. Missing persons investigation 4. Wexford, Chief Inspector (Fictitious character) 5. Police 6. England 7. Mysteries 8. Police procedurals
LC 2007040945
Searching for truffles in a wood, a man and his dog unearth something less savoury—a human hand. The body, as Chief Inspector Wexford is informed later, has lain buried for ten years or so, wrapped in a purple cotton sheet. The post mortem cannot reveal the precise cause of death. The only clue is a crack in one of the dead man's ribs.
"Rendell has been documenting change in her imaginary Kingsmarkham for 44 years; Not in the Flesh continues to hold a mirror to British society.... [She] also weaves into the story Wexford's heartbreaking attempts to address the tradition of female genital mutilation within the Somali community of Kingsmarkham." —*Los Angeles Times Book Review*

Road rage. Ruth Rendell. Crown Publishers, 1997. 344 p. (Chief Inspector Wexford mysteries, 17)
ISBN 9780609600566
1. Hostages 2. Green movement 3. Murder investigation 4. Resistance to road construction, powerlines, etc. 5. Wexford, Chief Inspector (Fictitious character) 6. England 7. Mysteries 8. Multiple perspectives 9. Police procedurals
LC 97-1200
Chief Inspector Wexford confronts a group of environmental radicals who attempt to stop a highway project by taking five people hostage, including Wexford's wife
"Taking what he vows will be his last walk in the deep woods that border his Sussex village, Chief Inspector Reginald Wexford contemplates with dread the new superhighway that will soon plow it all under.... But whatever sympathy he feels for the militant conservationists who pitch camp in Framhurst Great Wood to protest the highway is lost when a radical splinter group calling itself Sacred Globe kidnaps five innocent people—including Wexford's wife—and threatens to kill them unless the road is stopped." —*New York Times Book Review*

Simisola. Ruth Rendell. Crown Publishers, 1995. 327 p. (Chief Inspector Wexford mysteries, 16)
ISBN 9780440222026

1. Racism 2. Sexual violence 3. Serial murders 4. Nigerians in England 5. Wexford, Chief Inspector (Fictitious character) 6. England 7. Kingsmarkham, England 8. Mysteries 9. Police procedurals

Chief Inspector Wexford's sixteenth case centers on a teenaged African girl, the child of a prosperous doctor, who is found in a shallow grave in her quiet English suburb.

"Rendell's long acquaintance with her characters has not diminished the freshness of her work, nor her consummate storytelling. Rather, in *Simisola*, she offers a finely tuned moral tale that raises questions as it solves crimes." —*Times Literary Supplement*

A **sleeping** life. Ruth Rendell. Vintage Books, 1978. 180 p. (Chief Inspector Wexford mysteries, 10)
ISBN 9780375704932
1. Murder investigation 2. Secret identity 3. Police 4. Wexford, Chief Inspector (Fictitious character) 5. Kingsmarkham (England : Imaginary place) 6. England 7. Mysteries 8. Police procedurals
LC 99-87718
An expensive leather wallet is Inspector Wexford's only clue to the death of a woman whose body is found on the outskirts of Kingsmarkham and whose past is completely dark.

Speaker of Mandarin. Ruth Rendell. Random House, 1990. 212 p. (Chief Inspector Wexford mysteries, 12)
ISBN 9780345302748
1. Murder investigation 2. Voyages and travels 3. British in China 4. Wexford, Chief Inspector (Fictitious character) 5. Police 6. China 7. Mysteries 8. Police procedurals
LC 83047745
The suspects in the murder of wealthy Adela Knighton are the group of travellers with whom, along with Inspector Wexford, the dead woman had recently toured mainland China.
Previous printing issued by Pantheon Books.

The **tree** of hands. Ruth Rendell. Pantheon Books, 1984. 271 p.
ISBN 9780394530987
1. Murder 2. Mental illness 3. Kidnapping 4. Missing children 5. Mother and child 6. England 7. Psychological suspense
LC 84019002
Silver Dagger Award for Fiction, 1984
Benet Archdale's erratic mother Mapsa casts Benet, her baby son James, Carol Stratford, another young single mother, and her son into a maelstrom of kidnapping, fraud, family violence, and death.
"The story explores spectrum of parental feeling against a background of pervasive anxiety and impending doom. This is not a mystery, really, but rather an engrossing psychological thriller." —*Library Journal*

Restrepo, Laura
★ **Delirium**: a novel. Laura Restrepo; translated from the Spanish by Natasha Wimmer. Nan A. Talese, 2007. 336 p.
ISBN 9780385519908
1. Mental illness 2. Personality change 3. Family secrets 4. Husband and wife 5. Married women 6. Colombia 7. Bogota, Colombia 8. 1980s 9. Political fiction 10. Psychological fiction 11. Literary fiction
Aguilar returns from a brief business trip to find that his wife, Agustina, has had a complete mental breakdown, and as he struggles to help her regain her sanity, he begins to realize how little he knows about his wife's troubled past.
"Restrepo manages her tricky, time-hopping, polyphonic structure with uncommon grace. Everything in 'Delirium' flows, like tributaries into a river. And where that mighty stream is meant to take us, I think, is back to that large body of passionate, history-obsessed literature that is, (or was) Latin American fiction. Restrepo's techniques in this novel recall

the favored narrative methods of the so-called Boom years, invoking the spirits of Juan Rulfo, Jose Donoso, Manuel Puig and many others." —*New York Times Book Review*
Translation of: Delirio.
Originally published: Madrid: Alfaguara, 2004.

No place for heroes: a novel. Laura Restrepo; translated from the Spanish by Ernesto Mestre-Reed. Nan A. Talese/Doubleday, 2010. 304 p.
ISBN 9780385519915
1. Journalists 2. Revolutionaries 3. Resistance to government 4. Teenage boys 5. Father-separated teenage boys 6. Argentina 7. Buenos Aires, Argentina 8. 1980s 9. 1990s 10. Political fiction 11. Literary fiction 12. Parallel narratives
LC 2009047858
Lorenza and her son, Mateo, return to Buenos Aires as they try to find Ramon, Mateo's father, who was a political radical with Lorenza in Argentina's "Dirty War," as Lorenza deals with her memories of the past and Mateo, who is not interested in politics, only wants to find his father.
"Ultimately, this coming-of-age dance, the winding stories of Lorenza's past and the search for Ramon all converge in a climax as unexpected as it is moving." —*San Francisco Chronicle*
Originally published in Spain as Demasiados heroes in 2009.

Reyes, Dolores
Eartheater. Dolores Reyes; translated by Julia Sanches. Harpervia, 2020. 208 p.
ISBN 9780062987730
1. Slums 2. Young women 3. Compulsive behavior in women 4. Visions 5. Psychic ability 6. Argentina 7. Literary fiction 8. Coming-of-age stories 9. Magical realism
A woman from an underprivileged region of contemporary Argentina teams up with a withdrawn police officer when she develops uncontrollable pica that triggers visions of murdered and missing people, including her own mother. A first novel.
"Reyes' debut is a strong addition to the growing body of Latin American crime fiction in the U.S. market. A stirring genre blend of fantasy and crime fiction that combines graceful prose and magic realism." —*Booklist*
Translation of: Cometierra.
Originally published: 2019.
Translated from the Spanish.

Reynolds, Alastair
Permafrost. Alastair Reynolds. Tor, 2019. 192 pages
ISBN 9781250303561
1. Climate change 2. Consciousness transfer 3. Time travel (Past) 4. Women teachers 5. Global warming 6. Arctic Regions 7. Science fiction
Fix the past. Save the present. Stop the future. Master of science fiction Alastair Reynolds unfolds a time-traveling climate fiction adventure in Permafrost.

Revelation space. Alastair Reynolds. Ace Books, 2001. 476 p; (Revelation space universe, 1)
ISBN 9780441008353
1. Artificial intelligence 2. Life on other planets 3. Far future 4. Space colonies 5. Aliens 6. 26th century 7. Hard science fiction 8. Space opera 9. Science fiction
LC 50260
Resurgam, Delta Pavonis system; 2551. Dr. Daniel Sylveste discovers the puzzling remains of a civilization annihilated nine hundred thou-

sand years ago. Believing that the truth will save humanity, he seeks answers aboard a starship despite its dangerous cyborg crew.

Originally published: 2000.

★ **Revenger**. Alastair Reynolds. Orbit, 2017. 560 p. (Revenger novels, 1)

ISBN 9780316555562

1. Far future 2. Treasure hunters 3. Spaceship captains 4. Life on other planets 5. Revenge in women 6. Solar system 7. Space 8. Science fiction 9. Space opera 10. Adult books for young adults

LC 2016037813

Locus Young Adult Book Award, 2017

Adrana and Fura Ness are new on Captain Rackamore's ship, and they are using their Bone Reader abilities to their advantage while trying to avoid the feared Bosa Sennen.

"The award-winning Reynolds' newest action-packed science fiction novel is a tale of sisterly devotion, heartbreaking loss, and brutal vengeance." —*Booklist*

Reynolds, Allie

★ **Shiver**. Allie Reynolds. G. P. Putnam's Sons, 2021. 400 p.

ISBN 9780593187838

1. Reunions 2. Ski resorts 3. Competitive snowboarding 4. Revenge 5. Friendship 6. Alps 7. France 8. Psychological suspense 9. Multiple perspectives 10. Australian fiction

LC 2020022012

A reunion weekend in the French Alps turns deadly when five friends discover that someone has deliberately stranded them at a remote mountaintop resort during a snowstorm, where ominous things begin to happen.

"The story alternates between the present and 10 years prior, ratcheting up the suspense and spooling out a cast of intriguing characters drawn together atop a picturesque yet deadly mountain. Reynolds, a former international snowboarder, delivers the thrills in her must-read debut." —*Library Journal*

Rhodes, Jewell Parker

Voodoo dreams: a novel of Marie Laveau. Jewell Parker Rhodes. St. Martin's Press, 1993. 436 p.

ISBN 9780312098698

1. Laveau, Marie 2. Voodoo 3. African American women 4. Family secrets 5. Mambos (Voodooism) 6. Slavery 7. New Orleans, Louisiana 8. Doyle, Arthur Conan 9. Biographical fiction 10. African American fiction

LC 93024283

In mid 19th-century New Orleans, Marie Laveau was the notorious queen of voodoo—worshiped and feared by blacks and whites alike. Voodoo Dreams reimagines the woman behind this legend, a mesmerizing combination of history and storytelling.

Followed by the author's contemporary Voodoo trilogy.

Yellow moon: a novel. By Jewell Parker Rhodes. Atria Books, 2008. 288 p. (Voodoo trilogy, 2)

ISBN 9781416537106

1. Voodoo 2. Vampires 3. Magic (Occultism) 4. Ghosts 5. Good and evil 6. New Orleans, Louisiana 7. Louisiana 8. Supernatural mysteries 9. African American fiction 10. Adult books for young adults

LC 2008015221

Marie Levant, a doctor who is a descendant of a legendary voodoo queen, struggles with an increasing number of violence victims in her New Orleans hospital, a situation that is complicated by her nightmares about an African vampire.

Rhys, Jean

★ **Wide** Sargasso Sea. Jean Rhys. W.W. Norton, 1999. Xiii, 270 p. : Illustration; Map

ISBN 9780393960129

1. Women with mental illnesses 2. Race relations 3. Forced marriage 4. Married people 5. Women 6. West Indies 7. 1830s 8. 19th century 9. Historical fiction 10. Literary fiction 11. Adaptations, retellings, and spin-offs

Beautiful and wealthy Antoinette Cosway's passionate love for an English aristocrat threatens to destroy her idyllic West Indian island existence and her very life; accompanied by notes and criticism

Rhys, Rachel

Fatal inheritance. Rachel Rhys. Washington Square Press, 2019. 400 pages

ISBN 9781982111571

1. Married women 2. Inheritance and succession 3. Mansions 4. Wills 5. Family secrets 6. French Riviera 7. France 8. 1940s 9. Historical mysteries

She didn't have an enemy in the world...until she inherited a fortune.

Ricciardi, David

Warning light. David Ricciardi. Berkley, 2018. 323 p. (Jake Keller novels, 1)

ISBN 9780399585739

1. CIA agents 2. Intrigue 3. Undercover operations 4. Nuclear weapons 5. Torture 6. Middle East 7. Thrillers and suspense 8. Adult books for young adults

LC 2017006920

A routine surveillance job becomes a do-or-die mission in the Middle East for CIA analyst Zac Miller, who, in the wake of an agent's blown cover and an emergency landing, makes his way over the mountains of Iran and through the Persian Gulf while outmaneuvering Islamic Revolutionary Guards and former teammates who believe he has gone rogue.

"Ricciardi's debut thriller is a slow and steady adrenaline flow. Zac's ability to think or fight his way out of seemingly hopeless situations hints at Lee Child's Jack Reacher and Dan Brown's Robert Langdon, while his solo status adds Robert Ludlum's Jason Bourne and John le Carre's George Smiley to the mix. The author does a nice job of highlighting local culture and settings.... Readers of le Carre, Ludlum, Len Deighton, and other authors of Cold War—era espionage thrillers will enjoy this action-packed adventure." —*Library Journal*

Rice, Anne

Blackwood farm. Anne Rice. A.A. Knopf, 2002. 528 p. (Vampire chronicles, 9; Vampire chronicles and Mayfair witches crossovers, 2)

ISBN 9780375411991

1. Vampires 2. Good and evil 3. Immortality 4. Mortality 5. Lestat (Fictitious character) 6. Southern States 7. New Orleans, Louisiana 8. Ancient Greece (800 BCE-640 CE) 9. Gothic fiction 10. Adult books for young adults

Haunted since birth by a mysterious doppelganger known as Goblin, Quinn Blackwood seeks out the legendary vampire Lestat to free him from the horrifying specter that draws him back to Sugar Devil Swamp and its dark secrets.

"Slowly, the dark, Gothic settings and eccentric characters that make Rice's fiction so fascinating emerge." —*Library Journal*

Blood and gold: or, The story of Marius. Anne Rice. A. A. Knopf, 2001. 471 p; (Vampire chronicles, 8)

ISBN 9780679454496

1. Vampires 2. Good and evil 3. Immortality 4. Mortality 5. Lestat (Fictitious character) 6. Kerouac, Jack

LC 2001029869

Marius, the former mentor to the vampire Lestat, tells his story, which begins in the ancient Roman Empire when he is made a "blood god" by the Druids and follows him through the darkest, bloodiest centuries of European history.

"[A] rollicking vampire adventure through time." —*Booklist*

Blood canticle. Anne Rice. A.A. Knopf, 2003. 320 p. (Vampire chronicles, 10; Vampire chronicles and Mayfair witches crossovers, 3)

ISBN 9780375412004

1. Vampires 2. Good and evil 3. Immortality 4. Mortality 5. Lestat (Fictitious character) 6. New Orleans, Louisiana 7. Gothic fiction

LC 2002192475

Continues the crossover events of Blackwood Farm, pitting the vampire Lestat against the ghost of Julian Mayfair, who is out to avenge the transformation of Mona Mayfair, and chronicling Rowan Mayfair's dangerous attraction to Lestat.

Blood communion: a tale of Prince Lestat. By Anne Rice. Alfred A. Knopf, 2018. 272 p. (Vampire chronicles, 13)

ISBN 9781524732646

1. Vampires 2. Leadership 3. Power (Social sciences) 4. Demons 5. Supernatural 6. Gothic fiction

LC 2017058218

Navigating his new leadership of the vampire world, Lestat uncovers the story of a mysterious outcast demon who he traces to 18th-century Petersburg and the court of Empress Catherine.

The Vampire chronicles concludes.

Final Rice book published in author's lifetime.

Christ the Lord: out of Egypt: a novel. By Anne Rice. Knopf, 2005. 336 p. (Christ the Lord, 1)

ISBN 9780375412011

1. Jesus Christ 2. Jews 3. Healers 4. Jewish families 5. Identity (Psychology) 6. Questions and answers 7. Egypt 8. Israel 9. Bible novels 10. Books to movies 11. Adult books for young adults

LC 2005044077

A novel about the childhood of Christ the Lord based on the Gospels and on the most respected New Testament scholarship.

"Rice is a first-rate writer. There are no purple patches in this narrative, and no attempts to sermonize. There is a story to tell, and since we know the story on which it is based, Rice adroitly forces us to think about how she is going to weave in the gospel stories without sounding contrived or forced." —*Commonweal*

Sequel: Christ the Lord: the road to Cana.

Adapted into film in 2016 under the title: The Young Messiah.

Republished in 2016 as The young messiah.

Christ the Lord: the road to Cana: a novel. Anne Rice. Knopf, 2008. 256 p. (Christ the Lord, 2)

ISBN 9781400043521

1. Jesus Christ 2. Jews 3. Healers 4. Jewish families 5. Identity (Psychology) 6. Truth 7. Israel 8. Christian fiction 9. Bible novels

Library Journal Best Books, 2008

A second volume in the author's chronicle of the life of Christ begins prior to his baptism in the Jordan River and concludes with the miracle at Cana, as he leaves Nazareth to confront his destiny and the call to be Israel's liberator from Roman occupation.

"One of the great achievements of Rice's undertaking, thus far, is to reveal Christ's Jewish roots in all their strength and complexity.... Rice has achieved a prose style that is much simpler, much more straightforward,

than that of her earlier works. Yet, in moments of revelation, her old breathless rapture serves her well." —*New Orleans Times-Picayune*

Sequel to: Christ the Lord: out of Egypt.

★ **Interview** with the vampire. Anne Rice. A.A. Knopf, 1976. 371 p. (Vampire chronicles, 1)

ISBN 9780394498218

1. Vampires 2. Good and evil 3. Immortality 4. Redemption 5. Mortality 6. Gothic fiction 7. Books to movies

LC 75036792

Confessions from a vampire of his first two hundred years as one of the living dead.

"A magnificent combination of compulsively readable thriller and philosophical inquiry... A masterful suspense story... From the beginning we are seduced, hypnotized by the voice of the vampire who pours out his life story... The reader feels he has glimpsed experiences no mortal ever had." —*Chicago Tribune*

Sequel: The vampire Lestat.

Motion picture adaptation, 1994.

Memnoch the devil. Anne Rice. A.A. Knopf, 1995. 353 p. (Vampire chronicles, 5)

ISBN 9780679441014

1. Devil 2. Purgatory 3. Vampires 4. Good and evil 5. Pliny, the Elder 6. Gothic fiction

LC 95-77866

Visited by two beings who claim to be God and the Devil, the vampire Lestat is offered an ultimate chance at redemption when he is invited to be a witness at the Creation in a purgatorial land beyond death.

"The author boldly probes the significance of death, belief in the afterlife and other spiritual matters." —*Publishers Weekly*

Merrick: a novel. Anne Rice. A.A. Knopf, 2000. 307 p. (Vampire chronicles, 7; Vampire chronicles and Mayfair witches crossovers, 1)

ISBN 9780679454489

1. Vampires 2. Good and evil 3. Immortality 4. Mortality 5. Witches 6. Gothic fiction

LC 9988556

David Talbot, an adventurer and near-mortal vampire, narrates the saga of Merrick, a descendant of the Mayfair witches, from whom she inherits her magical gifts, and of a mixed African and French background that is steeped in traditions and lore of voodoo.

"This volume merges several long-running plots.... Merrick must revisit the Guatemalan rainforest, where she traveled as a young girl, to locate a secret treasure trove of ominous ancient runes. Displaying her imaginative talents for atmosphere and suspense, Rice creates a riveting scene that shows Merrick's awesome magic at work." —*Publishers Weekly*

Prince Lestat: the vampire chronicles. Anne Rice. Knopf, 2014. 464 p. (Vampire chronicles, 11)

ISBN 9780307962522

1. Vampires 2. Good and evil 3. Immortality 4. Mortality 5. Lestat (Fictitious character) 6. New Orleans, Louisiana 7. Gothic fiction 8. Adult books for young adults

LC 2014009319

Goodreads Choice Award, 2014

A tale spanning periods from the ancient to the modern world reunites fans with beloved characters, from Louis de Pointe Lac and the eternally young Armand to David Talbot and Marius, who hear a mysterious voice urging ancients to destroy increasing populations of maverick vampires.

"Featuring beloved characters from previous installments and spanning continents and centuries, Rice's exciting return to the Vampire Chronicles is bound to please her legions of fans." —*Booklist*

★ The **queen** of the damned. Anne Rice. A. A. Knopf, 1988. 448 p. (Vampire chronicles, 3)
ISBN 9780394558233
1. Vampires 2. Good and evil 3. Immortality 4. Mortality 5. Lestat (Fictitious character) 6. Gothic fiction 7. Books to movies
LC 88045310

The third novel in the Chronicle of the Vampires intertwines the stories of rockstar Lestat, beautiful twins haunted by a gruesome tragedy, and Akasha, mother of all vampires, who dreams of godhood.

"Don't let the title or the subject matter fool you; this is quality fiction written with care and intelligence. There are no false steps or wasted words in the multilayered plot, and the many characters each have a distinct voice. It's not absolutely necessary to have read the other 'Chronicles' to understand this one, but it would add greatly to the richness of the whole." —*Library Journal*

Sequel to: The vampire Lestat.

The **tale** of the body thief. Anne Rice. A. A. Knopf, 1992. 430 p. (Vampire chronicles, 4)
ISBN 9780345419637
1. Vampires 2. Good and evil 3. Immortality 4. Mortality 5. Lestat (Fictitious character) 6. Gothic fiction
LC 92053085

"Desiring to see the sun, to love without taking blood, to seek God as mortals do, Lestat enters blindly into an unholy bargain. In order to experience mortality for one day and two nights, he agrees to switch bodies with the scoundrel Raglan James, a former member of the secret order of scholarly occultists called the Talamasca... But Lestat has given little thought to how James intends to use his body and its vampiric powers. Trapped in the mortal state, Lestat must overcome the human frailties of despair and physical pain to thwart James's evil intentions and...regain his immortal self." —*Publishers Weekly*

"Readers who crave a happy ending, a justice and a moral coherence that transcend the muddle they really live in, may feel [the author] has broken faith with them. After all, isn't that what escapist fiction is supposed to provide? Grown-ups, on the other hand, will be intelligently entertained, and no more disquieted than usual." —*Newsweek*

The **vampire** Armand. By Anne Rice. A. A. Knopf, 1998. 387 p; (Vampire chronicles, 6)
ISBN 9780679454472
1. Vampires 2. Good and evil 3. Immortality 4. European Renaissance 5. Sexuality 6. Kievan Rus 7. Paris, France 8. Gothic fiction
LC 9814579

Follows the story of Armand across the centuries, from his boyhood in ancient Kiev to his relationship with the great vampire Marius, as he struggles to choose between immortality and his eternal soul.

"The sixth volume of the Vampire chronicles follows the vampire Armand from his boyhood in Kiev Rus, a conquered city under the rule of the Mongols, to ancient Constantinople, where he is sold into slavery by vicious Tartars, to the palazzo in Renaissance Venice, where he meets the great vampire Marius, who gives him the gift of the vampire blood and shows him how to be an 'ethical' vampire.... As always, Rice paints a fascinating and dazzling historical tapestry, providing a beautifully written and incredibly absorbing tale." —*Booklist*

★ The **vampire** Lestat. Anne Rice. A. A. Knopf, 1985. 481 p. (Vampire chronicles, 2)
ISBN 9780394534435
1. Vampires 2. Good and evil 3. Immortality 4. Mortality 5. Lestat (Fictitious character) 6. Gothic fiction
LC 85040123

Lestat is a vampire, but not one of the conventional undead. He is vivid, ecstatic, stagestruck, and in this extravagant story he plunges from the Rome of Augustus to the demonic Egypt of prehistory, and from fin-de-siecle New Orleans to the frenetic world of 20th-century rock stardom.

"This novel is ornate and pungently witty. In the classic tradition of Gothic fiction, it teases and tantalizes us into accepting its kaleidoscopic world. Even when they annoy us or tell us more than we want to know, its undead characters are utterly alive. Their adventures and frustrations are funny, frightening and surprising at once." —*New York Times Book Review*

Sequel to: Interview with the vampire.

Rice, Christopher

Blood victory. Christopher Rice. Thomas & Mercer, 2020. 318 p. (Burning girl novels, 3)
ISBN 9781542014724
1. Superhuman abilities 2. Violence in women 3. Truck drivers 4. Serial murderers 5. Conspiracies 6. Texas 7. Thrillers and suspense

A secret weapon of a mysterious consortium, Charlotte Rowe, who baits evil predators and stops them in their tracks, goes after a long-haul truck driver whose cargo bay is a gallery of horrors on wheels.

"[Rice's] story unravels to dramatic effect. Fans of paranormal suspense will be well satisfied." —*Publishers Weekly*

Rice, Craig

Home sweet homicide. Craig Rice; introduction by Otto Penzler. American Mystery Classics, an imprint of Penzler Publishers, 2018. 295 p.
ISBN 9781613161036
1. Amateur detectives 2. Children of authors 3. Crime scenes 4. Women mystery story writers 5. Neighbors 6. Mysteries 7. Mystery classics

The children of a mystery writer play amateur sleuths and matchmakers.

Originally published: New York : Simon & Schuster, 1944.

Rice, Luanne

★ **Last** day. Luanne Rice. Thomas & Mercer, 2020. 412 pages
ISBN 9781542018203
1. Art thefts 2. Women murder victims 3. Sisters 4. Loss (Psychology) 5. Detectives 6. Connecticut 7. Thrillers and suspense

When her sister is murdered amid the theft of a valuable painting, an eerie echo of their mother's murder 20 years earlier, pilot Kate teams up with the case's original detective and childhood friends to identify a killer.

"Strong love overcomes pain in this latest from Rice (Pretend She's Here), which combines suspense with stories of survivors, sisterhood, best friends, and small communities shaken by violence or death." —*Library Journal*

The **lemon** orchard. Luanne Rice. Pamela Dorman Books, 2013. 352 p.
ISBN 9780670025275
1. Grief in women 2. Loss (Psychology) 3. Interracial romance 4. Healing 5. Man-woman relationships 6. California 7. Southern California 8. Mainstream fiction
LC 2013009690

House-sitting a family home in Malibu where she hopes for peace and healing in the aftermath of her daughter's death, Julia is unexpectedly drawn to a handsome man who oversees a lemon orchard, sends his earnings to an extended family in Mexico and hides the pain of his own daughter's loss.

Little night. Luanne Rice. Pamela Dorman Books/Viking, 2012. 336 p.
ISBN 9780670023561

1. Sisters 2. Family relationships 3. Aunt and niece 4. Nieces 5. Forgiveness 6. New York City 7. Relationship fiction 8. Adult books for young adults

LC 2011049237

Estranged from the sister who refused to testify against an abusive husband, Clare pursues a quiet life as a nature blogger in Manhattan only to be approached by her niece, Grit, with whom she confronts a painful shared history.

Rice, Waubgeshig

Moon of the crusted snow: a novel. Waubgeshig Rice. ECW Press, 2018. 224 p.

ISBN 9781770414006

1. First Nations (Canada) 2. Threat (Psychology) 3. Survival 4. Winter 5. Indians of North America 6. Ontario 7. Canada 8. Apocalyptic fiction 9. Canadian fiction

Evergreen Award (Ontario), 2019; Loan Stars Favourites, 2018

Moon of the Crusted Snow imagines a small community on the precipice of winter without power or communication where leaders must grapple with control, restore order, and save their people from a grave fate.

Rice-Gonzalez, Charles

Chulito. Charles Rice-Gonzalez. Magnus Books, 2011. 317 p.

ISBN 9781936833030

1. Hispanic Americans 2. Coming out (Sexual or gender identity) 3. Young gay men 4. Homophobia 5. Bronx, New York City 6. Coming-of-age stories 7. LGBTQIA fiction

Rainbow List, 2013

Chulito rejects his childhood friend Carlos after Carlos comes out and goes away to college, but when Carlos returns for a visit, Chulito cannot continue to bury his romantic feelings for his old friend.

Richardson, C. S.

The **end** of the alphabet. C.S. Richardson. Doubleday, 2007. 139 p.

ISBN 9780385522557

1. Men 2. Women 3. Man-woman relationships 4. Husband and wife 5. Romantic love 6. Literary fiction 7. Canadian fiction

LC 2006036823

Commonwealth Writers' Prize, Caribbean and Canada: Best First Book, 2008

Reeling from the news that his doctor is giving him only one month to live, fifty-year-old Ambrose Zephyr and his loving wife, Zipper, embark on a whirlwind tour from A to Z of all the places he has ever loved or has ever wanted to visit.

"The surprise of this little book is not that it is poignant but that it is delightful: graceful, stylish, humorous, intelligent and lacking even the faintest whiff of sanctimony." —*Washington Post Book World.*

Richardson, Samuel

★ **Clarissa,** or, The history of a young lady. Samuel Richardson; edited with an introduction and notes by Angus Ross. Penguin Books, 1985. 1533 p.

ISBN 9780140432152

1. Young women 2. Captives 3. Nobility 4. Marriage 5. Deception 6. England 7. 18th century 8. Epistolary novels 9. Classics 10. Literary fiction

A rakish city gentleman determines to seduce the youngest daughter of the Harlowe household.

★ **Pamela:** or, Virtue rewarded. Samuel Richardson; edited with explanatory notes by Thomas Keymer and Alice Wakely; with an introduction by Thomas Keymer. Oxford University Press, 2001. Xxlv, 546 p.

ISBN 9780192829603

1. Household employees 2. Seduction 3. Families 4. Marriage 5. Gender role 6. England 7. 18th century 8. Epistolary novels 9. Classics

LC 2001021704

A country gentleman attempts to seduce his maidservant and ends up falling in love with her in this literary landmark, first published in 1740 and regarded as the English language's first novel.

First published 1740-1741.

Includes bibliographical references (p. [xxxviii]-xlii)

Richler, Mordecai

Barney's version: a novel. Mordecai Richler. A. A. Knopf, 1997. 355 p.

ISBN 9780679404187

1. Immigrants, Jewish 2. Septuagenarians 3. Bohemianism 4. Extremism 5. Sherman, William Tecumseh 6. Montreal, Quebec 7. Literary fiction 8. Canadian fiction 9. Satirical fiction

LC 9737033

Commonwealth Writers' Prize, Caribbean and Canada: Best Book, 1998; Giller Prize, 1997; New York Times Notable Book, 1998; Quebec Writers' Federation Literary Awards, Hugh MacLennan Prize for Fiction, 1998; Stephen Leacock Medal for Humour, 1998

The urban sensibility of immigrant Jewish Montreal is chronicled in this darkly satirical portrait of 67-year-old Barney Panofsky, who decides to set the record straight about his Bohemian days in Paris and London in the 1950s, his circle of famous and infamous friends, his career as a television producer, and his wildly unsuccessful relationships with women.

"What entertains and affects us in Barney's Version is the headlong, spendthrift passage of a life, redeemed from oblivion in the unbridled telling. The edge of the grave makes a lively point vantage." —*The New Yorker*

Solomon Gursky was here. Mordecai Richler. Knopf, 1990. 413 p.

ISBN 9780394539959

1. Alcoholic men 2. Authors 3. Wanderers and wandering 4. Airplane accidents 5. Suing (Law) 6. Montreal, Quebec 7. Canadian fiction 8. Literary fiction 9. Family sagas

LC 88094762

Commonwealth Writers' Prize for Best Book, 1990; Commonwealth Writers' Prize, Caribbean and Canada: Best Book, 1990; Quebec Writers' Federation Literary Awards, Hugh MacLennan Prize for Fiction, 1990; Shortlisted for the Booker-McConnell Prize, 1990

While researching a biography of Solomon Gursky, the blacksheep scion of an influential Jewish family in Montreal, Moses Berger becomes obsessed with uncovering the secret and momentous life of his subject BT

"Richler is a ringmaster, making his performers do dazzling backflips without missing a beat. At the same time he is a moralist, recoiling from those who would sentimentalize the Holocaust or make power a sacrament." —*Time*

Originally published: Markham, Ont. : Penguin Books Canada, 1989.

Richler, Nancy

Your mouth is lovely: a novel. Nancy Richler. Ecco, 2002. 357 p.

ISBN 9780060096779

1. Political prisoners 2. Political prisons 3. Single mothers 4. Women prisoners 5. Women murderers 6. Kiev, Ukraine 7. Russia 8. Romanov

Dynasty (1613-1917) 9. Historical fiction 10. Diary novels 11. Canadian fiction 12. Adult books for young adults

LC 2002023521

Canadian Jewish Book Award

A story told through a series of letters to the main character's daughter follows her upbringing in a Russian shtetl by her stepmother after her mother's mysterious suicide, her isolation as an outcast, and her exile to Siberia.

"This novel summons up the lost world of the Russian shtetls around the Pripet marshe's in Ukraine, and shows how those communities were first changed and then annihilated by the events that led, ultimately, to the Russian Revolution. At the center of Richler's tale is Miriam Lev, whose mother drowned herself when she was a day old, and who at age six is taken in hand by her father's new wife, Tsila, a harsh, beautiful seamstress who teaches Miriam the alphabet and dreams of another life. After an ill-starred and and painful series of events, Miriam ends up, at nineteen, in Siberia, having shot an officer of the Tsar at point-blank range. Miriam's hegira is told here as a letter to her own daughter, whom she hasn't seen since she gave birth to her, in prison. Richler's work recalls the stories of Isaac Babel, in which the knowable is charged with mystery." —*The New Yorker*

Richman, Alyson

The **secret** of clouds. Alyson Richman. Berkley, 2019. 371 p.
ISBN 9781984802620

1. Children of immigrants 2. Women teachers 3. Sick children 4. Teacher-student relationships 5. Tutoring 6. Long Island, New York 7. Mainstream fiction

LC 2018016371

An English teacher with haunting childhood memories gains perspective and inspiration while tutoring a young Ukrainian immigrant whose serious health issues prevent him from taking any day for granted.

Richmond, Michelle

No one you know. Michelle Richmond. Delacorte Press, 2008. 320 p.
ISBN 9780385340137

1. Sisters — Death 2. Secrets 3. Family relationships 4. Mathematics 5. Murder 6. San Francisco, California 7. Mysteries 8. Domestic fiction 9. Adult books for young adults

LC 2008013508

Twenty years after the unsolved murder of her sister Lila, Ellie's chance meeting with the man accused of the crime leads to the discovery of Lila's secret notebook, filled with mathematical equations that lead to other enigmas in her sister's life.

"As complex and beautiful as a mathematical proof, this gripping, thought-provoking novel will keep you thinking long after the last page has been turned." —*Family Circle*

Ridley, Erica

The **duke** heist. Erica Ridley. Forever, 2021. 368 pages (Wild Wynchesters, 1)
ISBN 9781538719527

1. Women thieves 2. Dukes and duchesses 3. Stolen property recovery 4. Interpersonal attraction 5. Art thefts 6. Great Britain 7. England 8. Regency period (1811-1820) 9. 19th century 10. Regency romances 11. Historical romances

Chloe Wynchester is completely forgettable—a curse that gives her the ability to blend into any crowd. When the only father she's ever known makes a dying wish for his adopted family of orphans to recover a missing painting, she's the first one her siblings turn to for stealing it back. No one expects that in doing so, she'll also abduct a handsome duke...

"Schemes, heists, and forgeries abound in this charming series starter by Ridley (Forever Your Duke). This unconventional and quirky Regency will have readers falling for the plucky family and rooting for Chloe and Lawrence to buck tradition." —*Library Journal*

★ The **perks** of loving a wallflower. Erica Ridley. Forever, 2021. 368 p. (Wild Wynchesters, 2)
ISBN 9781538719541

1. Nobility 2. Nonconformists 3. Social classes 4. Crushes (Interpersonal relations) 5. Disguises 6. Great Britain 7. England 8. Regency period (1811-1820) 9. 19th century 10. LGBTQIA romances 11. Regency romances 12. Historical romances

A master of disguise, Thomasina Wynchester finds more than her mission at stake when her new client turns out to be the highborn lady she's secretly smitten with.

"Bestseller Ridley's second Wild Wynchesters romance (after The Duke Heist) arguably touches the holy grail for Regency fans: like Georgette Heyer, but with sex. Lesbian sex, in fact, which pairs deliciously with classic Heyer elements like Shakespearian gender bending and exquisitely delineated fashion." —*Publishers Weekly*

Ridpath, Michael

Far north. Michael Ridpath. Minotaur Books, 2012. 376 p. : Map (Fire and ice, 2)
ISBN 9780312675042

1. Murder 2. Conspiracies 3. Crimes against politicians 4. Murder investigation 5. Detectives 6. Iceland 7. Scandinavian crime fiction 8. Police procedurals 9. Mysteries

Generations after two boys from isolated farmsteads witness a haunting act in the Icelandic lava fields, a grassroots revolution sparked by the economic crisis of 2009 challenges Magnus Jonson to unravel a web of conspirators who are killing off blamed bankers and politicians.

Originally published under the title, 66 degrees north (London: Corvus, 2011).

Riley, Lucinda

The **girl** on the cliff: a novel. Lucinda Riley. Atria Books, 2012. 407 p.
ISBN 9781451655827

1. Arthur, King 2. Family secrets 3. Feuds 4. Breaking up (Interpersonal relations) 5. Miscarriage 6. Ireland 7. First World War era (1914-1918) 8. Family sagas

Grania Ryan returns home to Ireland and forms a close friendship with a young girl whose family history is intertwined with Grania's own.

Originally published: Great Britain: Penguin Books, 2011.

Riley, Vanessa

★ A **duke,** the lady, and a baby. Vanessa Riley. Zebra Books, 2020. 320 p. (Rogues and remarkable women, 1)
ISBN 9781420152234

1. Dukes and duchesses 2. Multiracial women 3. Disguises 4. Secret identity 5. Inheritance and succession 6. Great Britain 7. Regency period (1811-1820) 8. Regency romances 9. Historical romances

Created by a shrewd countess, The Widow's Grace is a secret society with a mission: to help ill-treated widows regain their status, their families, and even find true love again—or perhaps for the very first time.

"Riley loads her expertly crafted romance with intrigue, droll banter, and steadily building passion. Readers will be hard-pressed to find a flaw in this big-hearted Regency romance." —*Publishers Weekly*

★ An **earl,** the girl, and a toddler. Vanessa Riley. Zebra Books, 2021. 320 p. (Rogues and remarkable women, 2)
ISBN 9781420152258
1. Shipwreck survivors 2. Women with amnesia 3. Lawyers 4. Black British 5. Daughters 6. England 7. Great Britain 8. Regency period (1811-1820) 9. Regency romances 10. Historical romances
A shipwrecked woman searches for her memories and becomes entangled with a conflicted nobleman who holds more answers than he realizes...
"Fans of the first book will be delighted by this story, which brings the same elaborate storytelling and portrayal of a more diverse Regency world than is traditionally found. Riley's commitment to writing the complex emotions of motherhood remains a crucial part of the series—also a welcome addition to the genre. Well-researched, with a fascinating author's note at the end, this story proves the first was no fluke." —*Kirkus*

★ **Island** Queen. Vanessa Riley. 2021. 416 p.
ISBN 9780063002845
1. Thomas, Dorothy Kirwan 2. Freed people 3. Women entrepreneurs 4. Multiracial women 5. Success (Concept) 6. Slavery — History 7. Caribbean Area 8. West Indies 9. 18th century 10. Historical fiction 11. Biographical fiction 12. African American fiction
"The experiences and achievements of powerful women, especially those whose lives began among the enslaved, are too often overlooked, and Riley's richly engaging novel is a ringing reminder of how much we miss when these stories remain untold." —*Booklist*

Rimmer, Kelly

Before I let you go. Kelly Rimmer. Graydon House, 2018. 379 p.
ISBN 9781525820847
1. Sisters 2. Drug addicts 3. Pregnant women 4. Child welfare 5. Infants 6. Australia 7. Relationship fiction 8. Australian fiction
Librarians' Choice (Australia), 2018
When Lexie Vidler hears from her drug addict sister, Annie, for the first time in years, she finds out that Annie is strung-out, pregnant, and in premature labor, leaving Lexie to help her troubled sister once again, as they face ghosts from the past that neither wants to face.
"Rimmer's timely novel captures the unbreakable bond of two sisters and humanizes the difficult intersection of the opioid epidemic and the justice system." —*Publishers Weekly*

Truths I never told you. Kelly Rimmer. Graydon House, 2020. 352 p.
ISBN 9781525804656
1. Postpartum depression 2. Family secrets 3. New mothers 4. Diary writing 5. Family relationships 6. Seattle, Washington 7. 1950s 8. 1990s 9. Relationship fiction 10. Epistolary novels 11. Australian fiction
Uncovering disturbing evidence that her mother did not die in a car accident when her sisters and she were toddlers, a woman on maternity leave pieces together journal entries to uncover harrowing truths about her father.
"With a mix of engrossing mystery and deep feeling, Rimmer offers a harrowing account of a doomed mother's experience in the 1950s and a family grappling with the truth." —*Publishers Weekly*

★ The **Warsaw** orphan: a WWII novel. Kelly Rimmer. Graydon House, 2021. 352 p.
ISBN 9781525811531
1. Young women 2. Deception 3. Nazis 4. Jewish resistance and revolts 5. Identity (Psychology) 6. Poland 7. Second World War era (1939-1945) 8. Historical fiction
Set during WW II in Poland, this novel, based on real-life heroes, follows Emilia over the course of the war, her involvement with the Resis-

tance, and her love for a young man imprisoned in the Jewish ghetto who's passion leads him to fight in the Warsaw Uprising.

Rindell, Suzanne

The **other** typist. Suzanne Rindell. G. P. Putnam's Sons, 2013. 368 p.
ISBN 9780399161469
1. Prohibition 2. Obsession in women 3. Typists 4. Police 5. Crime 6. 1920s 7. Historical thrillers
Working as a typist for the NYC Police Department in 1923, Rose Baker documents confessions of harrowing crimes and struggles with changing gender roles while clinging to her Victorian ideals and searching for nurturing companionship before becoming obsessed with a glamorous newcomer and her world of bobbed hair, smoking and speakeasies.

★ The **two** Mrs. Carlyles. Suzanne Rindell. 2020. 417 pages
ISBN 9780525539209
1. San Francisco Earthquake and Fire, Calif, 1906 2. Rich people 3. Remarriage 4. Deception 5. Consequences 6. San Francisco, California 7. California 8. 1900s (Decade) 9. Gothic fiction 10. Historical fiction 11. First person narratives
LC 2020014154
Rendered unexpectedly wealthy by the 1906 San Francisco earthquake, Violet reinvents herself as the second wife of the city's most eligible widower only to find her happiness overshadowed by the specter of her predecessor and her own violent past.
"Fans of gothic historical fiction and historical romantic suspense will find much to enjoy here." —*Booklist*

Rinehart, Mary Roberts

The **circular** staircase. Mary Roberts Rinehart. Dover Publications, 1997. Ix, 178 p.
ISBN 9780486297132
1. Securities 2. Default (Finance) 3. Middle-aged women 4. Crime 5. Murder 6. Mysteries
LC 971445
The Circular Staircase is perhaps Mary Roberts Rinehart's most famous story. Wealthy spinster Rachel Innes is persuaded by her niece and nephew Gertrude and Halsey to take a house in the country for the summer. Rachel is unaware that the house holds a secret, and soon unexplained happenings and murder follow.
Play; later adapted as novel, The Bat.
Originally published: New York : Carroll & Graf Publishers, 1908.

Miss Pinkerton. Mary Roberts Rinehart. Kensington Books, 1998. 272 p.
ISBN 9781575662558
1. Informers 2. Nurses 3. Gunshot victims 4. Aunts 5. Detectives 6. Mystery classics
When Herbert Wynne supposedly commits suicide, Miss Pinkerton poses as a private nurse to his aunt Juliet and discovers that his "bedridden" aunt takes midnight jaunts, a stranger skulks about the stairs, and the other nurse on duty is scared of her own shadow, and Miss Pinkerton must unmask a killer before he strikes again.
Republished by American Mystery Classics in 2019.
Originally published: New York : International Readers League, 1932.

Riordan, Kate

The **heatwave.** Kate Riordan. Grand Central Pub, 2020. 272 pages
ISBN 9781538718018

1. Family secrets 2. Lincoln, Mary Todd 3. Forest fires 4. Daughters — Death 5. Small town life 6. Southern France 7. France 8. 1990s 9. Psychological suspense

Returning to the Southern France childhood home she would rather forget, Sylvie endeavors to protect her youngest daughter from a growing threat and toxic family dynamics linked to the death of her enigmatic firstborn.

"Riordan skillfully manipulates the reader through what initially feels like a ghost story and then, after a revelation that totally recasts the situation, the nail-biting if not entirely plausible page-turner that ensues. S.J. Watson fans will want to check this one out." —*Publishers Weekly*

Ripley, Mike

Mr Campion's coven. Mike Ripley. Severn House, 2021. 256 p. (Albert Campion mysteries, 33)

ISBN 9780727890832

1. Amateur detectives 2. Murder investigation 3. College students 4. Dogs 5. Ship captains 6. England 7. 1970s 8. Mysteries 9. Historical mysteries

East coast of England, 1971. Albert Campion is invited to assist Harvard student Mason Clay on a research trip to Wicken-juxta-Mare. But Wicken is already firmly on Campion's radar thanks to Dame Jocasta Upcott's beached luxury yacht, its captain very stuck—and very dead—in the mudbank. Was it a bizarre accident or something more sinister?

"Filled with dry wit, laugh-out-loud banter, well-paced action, and quirky characters, this latest opportunity to follow in the footsteps of the ever-charming Campion will delight series fans old and new." —*Booklist*

Mr Campion's fault. Mike Ripley. Severn House, 2016. 243 p. (Albert Campion mysteries, 28)

ISBN 9780727886255

1. Amateur detectives 2. Boys' schools 3. Class conflict 4. Small town life 5. Social classes 6. England 7. Yorkshire, England 8. 1960s 9. Mysteries

Following the death of the senior English master in a tragic road accident, Mr Campion's son Rupert and daughter-in-law Perdita are helping out at Ash Grange School for Boys in Yorkshire. When Rupert is arrested, Albert Campion heads to Denby Ash to find out what's going on. Was the English master's death really an accident?

"A charming, courtly, slightly eccentric hero; an intricate and unusual plot; and plenty of gentle humor make this an enticing read for old-school cozy fans." —*Booklist*

Featuring Margery Allingham's character Albert Campion.

Mr. Campion's war. Mike Ripley. Severn House, 2018. 243 p; (Albert Campion mysteries, 30)

ISBN 9780727888099

1. Senior men 2. Former intelligence officers 3. Amateur detectives 4. Campion, Albert (Fictitious character) 5. British in France 6. England 7. France 8. 1970s 9. Second World War era (1939-1945) 10. Mysteries

It's Albert Campion's seventieth birthday, and he has decided to enthral his guests at the Dorchester Hotel with his account of his wartime experiences in Vichy France more than twenty-five years before. But in doing so he unveils a series of extraordinary events, the repercussions of which put one of his guests in deadly danger...

Featuring Margery Allingham's character Albert Campion.

Ripper, Kris

The **hate** project. Kris Ripper. Carina Adores, 2021. 336 p. (Love study :, 2)

ISBN 9781335509178

1. Gay men 2. House cleaning 3. Anxiety 4. Casual sex 5. LGBTQIA persons 6. Romantic comedies 7. LGBTQIA romances

Unemployed, and completely over love, romance and relationships, Oscar Nelson, an anxious overthinker, falls victim to the matchmaking grandmother of Jack, the grumpy friend-of-friend he has been casually hooking up with.

"Ripper's sensitive portrayal of Oscar's anxiety blends nicely with the erotic charge to create a tender but still thrilling romance." —*Publishers Weekly*

The **life** revamp. Kris Ripper. Carina Adores, 2021. 288 p. (Love study :, 3)

ISBN 9781335424556

1. Polyamory 2. Married men 3. Single men 4. Fashion designers 5. LGBTQIA persons 6. LGBTQIA romances 7. Romantic comedies

All Mason wants to do is fall in love, get married and live happily ever after. The hunt is beginning to wear him down, until he meets (slightly) famous fashion designer Diego. Everything sparks between them—the banter, the sex, the fiery eye contact across a crowded room. There's just one thing: Diego is already married and living his happily-ever-after, which luckily (or not) for Mason includes outside courtships. Mason thought he knew what would make him happy, but it turns out the traditional life he'd expected has some surprises in store.

"Ripper's smart, sexy, and banter-filled final Love Study romance (after The Hate Project) gets the loving polyamorous 'V' dynamic just right." —*Publishers Weekly*

The **love** study. Kris Ripper. Carina Adores, 2020. 336 pages (Love study :, 1)

ISBN 9781335943194

1. Commitment (Psychology) 2. YouTubers 3. Dating (Social customs) 4. LGBTQIA persons 5. Gender fluid 6. Romantic comedies 7. LGBTQIA romances

Declan has commitment issues. And then he meets a nonbinary YouTuber named Sidney who asks Declan to be involved in a study where he goes on dates and reports back as to how the dates went. The dates aren't great, and Declan finds that the person he feels chemistry with is Sidney.

"Though some readers will long for higher stakes, the casual queerness of the cast and no-fuss treatment of Sidney's nonbinary pronouns is so refreshing that many won't mind the lack of conflict." —*Publishers Weekly*

Ritter, Josh

The **great** glorious goddamn of it all. Josh Ritter. Hanover Square Press, 2021. 304 p.

ISBN 9781335522535

1. Reminiscing in old age 2. Nonagenarians 3. Lumber workers 4. Lumber industry and trade 5. Small towns 6. Idaho 7. 20th century 8. Historical fiction

Filled with heart, humor and magic, this lyrical, sweeping novel about the last days of the lumberjacks is told by of one of the greatest lumberjacks of all who recounts tales rife with murder, mayhem, avalanches and bootlegging in the tiny timber town of Cordelia, Idaho.

"Ritter lyrically evokes a town fused to the logging industry by necessity and devotion through Weldon's anecdotal narration, which resonates with a shimmery, deep-seated humanity." —*Publishers Weekly*

Ritter, Todd

Devil's night. Todd Ritter. Minotaur Books, 2013. 368 p. (Kat Campbell mysteries, 3)

ISBN 9781250028532

1. Arson 2. Women detectives 3. Small town life 4. Museums 5. Policewomen 6. Pennsylvania 7. Mysteries

LC 2013009831

Summoned in the middle of the night to the site of an arson fire at the Perry Hollow museum, Police Chief Kat Campbell examines the murdered body of the curator before glimpsing nemesis Henry Goll in the crowd, a discovery that prompts a harrowing race against time.

Rivero, Melissa

The **affairs** of the Falcons. Melissa Rivero. Ecco, 2019. 277 p.
ISBN 9780062872357
1. Undocumented immigrants 2. Immigrant families 3. Husband and wife 4. Marital conflict 5. Taxicab drivers 6. New York City 7. Peru 8. 1990s 9. Literary fiction

Fleeing the economic and political strife of 1990s Peru, undocumented factory worker Ana struggles to support her family while fending off the challenges of discrimination, sexual harassment and a loan shark's criminal enforcers.

Rivers, Francine

Bridge to haven. Francine Rivers. Tyndale House Publishers, 2014. 500 pages
ISBN 9781414368184
1. Actors and actresses 2. Redemption (Christianity) 3. Christian life 4. Belonging 5. Abandoned infants 6. Northern California 7. California 8. Christian historical fiction

LC 2013040115

Having been abandoned as a newborn and found and raised by Pastor Ezekiel Freeman in the small California town of Haven, Abra Matthews feels like she doesn't belong and at the age of seventeen runs off to Hollywood, becoming starlet Lena Scott.

"Rivers nicely evokes 1950s Hollywood, with its gossip columnists, high-wattage movie stars, and ladder-climbing aspirants; Elvis Presley and Lana Turner put in cameos. This story arc will be particularly resonant for Christian readers, but Rivers has the writing ability to reel in others who enjoy a well-told tale of redemption." —*Publishers Weekly*

The **masterpiece**. Francine Rivers. Tyndale House Publishers, Inc, 2018. 500 p.
ISBN 9781496407900
1. Artists 2. Personal assistants 3. Single mothers 4. Christian women 5. Atheists 6. Los Angeles, California 7. Christian romances

LC 2017033594

Struggling to make a home for herself and her five-month old son Samuel, Grace Moore accepts a position as a personal assistant to Roman Velasco, a temperamental successful artist.

★ **Redeeming** love. Francine Rivers. Multnomah, 1997. 464 p.
ISBN 9781576738160
1. Desire 2. Belief and doubt 3. Forgiveness 4. Redemption 5. Pioneer women 6. San Francisco, California 7. 1850s 8. American Westward Expansion (1803-1899) 9. Christian historical romances 10. Books to movies

LC 97014694

After being beaten, Angel, a young prostitute, decides to accept devout Christian Michael Hosea's offer of marriage and falls in love not only with him, but also with God.

Multnomah women's fiction.

Movie tie-in edition issued in 2022.

This is the "redeemed" version of Redeeming Love, published by Bantam Books in 1991. The original edition is no longer available.

Originally published: Colorado Springs, Colorado : Multnomah, 1997.

Rizzuto, Rahna R.

Shadow child. Rahna Reiko Rizzuto. Grand Central Publishing, 2018. 341 p.
ISBN 9781538711453
1. Twin sisters 2. Families — History 3. World War II 4. Japanese Americans — Forced removal and incarceration, 1942-1945 5. Separated twin sisters 6. Hawaii 7. Japan 8. 1970s 9. Second World War era (1939-1945) 10. Historical fiction

LC 2017053601

Raised in a postwar Hawaiian town and estranged in the wake of a violent betrayal, mixed-race twins Hana and Kei are reunited years later by a life-changing secret.

"National Book Critics Circle finalist Rizzuto (Why She Left Us; Hiroshima in the Morning) blends historical fiction and mystery into a haunting examination of identity and family in this perfect book club choice." —*Library Journal*

Roanhorse, Rebecca

★ **Black** sun. Rebecca Roanhorse. Saga Press, 2020. 464 pages (Between earth and sky, 1)
ISBN 9781534437678
1. Winter solstice 2. Fate and fatalism 3. Political intrigue 4. Clans 5. LGBTQIA persons 6. Epic fantasy 7. Adult books for young adults

LC 2020012273

Alex Award, 2021; Ignyte Awards: Best Adult Novel, 2021; LibraryReads Favorites, 2020; RUSA Reading List Short List, 2021

Xiala, a disgraced Teek who can calm waters or cause madness with her song, arrives and disrupts the holy city of Tova during the winter solstice.

"Roanhorse (the Sixth World series) strikes a perfect balance between powerful worldbuilding and rich thematic exploration as the protagonists struggle against their fates." —*Publishers Weekly*

Storm of locusts. Rebecca Roanhorse. Saga Press, 2019. 384 pages (Sixth world, 2)
ISBN 9781534413535
1. Native American women 2. Monsters 3. Navajo Indians 4. Kidnapping 5. Cults 6. Navajo Indian Reservation 7. Apocalyptic fiction 8. Fantasy fiction 9. Adult books for young adults

Kai and Caleb Goodacre have been kidnapped just as rumors of a cult sweeping across the reservation leads Maggie and Hastiin to investigate an outpost, and what they find there will challenge everything they've come to know in this action-packed sequel to Trail of Lightning.

"She's a groundbreaking writer, weaving Diné language and culture throughout her work in innovative and deeply important ways while at the same time providing a purely joyous reading experience." —*Kirkus*

★ **Trail** of lightning. Rebecca Roanhorse. Saga Press, 2018. 352 pages (Sixth world, 1)
ISBN 9781534413498
1. Native American women 2. Monsters 3. Navajo Indians 4. Shamans 5. Magic (Occultism) 6. Navajo Indian Reservation 7. Apocalyptic fiction 8. Fantasy fiction 9. Adult books for young adults

LC 2017034119

Loan Stars Favourites, 2018; Library Journal Best Books, 2018; Locus Award for First Novel, 2019; RUSA Reading List Short List, 2019

When a small town needs her help in finding a missing girl, Maggie Hoskie, a Dinetah monster hunter, reluctantly enlists the help of an unconventional medicine man to uncover the terrifying truth behind the disappearance and her own past.

"This exciting postapocalyptic debut, with its heady combination of smartly drawn characters, Wild West feel, and twisty plot, is a must-read for fantasy enthusiasts." —*Library Journal*

Robards, Karen

The **ultimatum**. Karen Robards. Mira Books, 2017. 330 p. (Guardian (Karen Robards), 1)

ISBN 9780778330707

1. Women swindlers 2. Women thieves 3. Swindlers and swindling 4. Fathers and daughters 5. Man-woman relationships 6. Romantic suspense

A talented master of disguise who devotes herself to conning thieves and returning stolen money to its rightful owners hides her Robin Hood activities behind a day job as a personal assistant to her thief father's alluring former partner.

Robb, Candace M.

★ A **choir** of crows. Candace M. Robb. Severn House Publishers, 2020. 288 p. (Owen Archer mysteries, 12)

ISBN 9781780291260

1. Conspiracies 2. Murder 3. Secrets 4. Political intrigue 5. Archbishops 6. Medieval period (476-1492) 7. Plantagenet period (1154-1485) 8. Medieval mysteries 9. Historical mysteries

December, 1374. With the great and the good about to descend on York for the enthronement of Alexander Neville as the new archbishop, the city is in a state of high alert. When two bodies are discovered in the grounds of York Minster, Owen Archer is summoned to investigate. But before he can make headway, a third body is fished out of the river ...

"Robb once again effectively blends crime with the politics of 14th-century England." —*Publishers Weekly*

The **cross-legged** knight: an Owen Archer mystery. Candace Robb. Mysterious Press, 2003. 321 p. : Map (Owen Archer mysteries, 8)

ISBN 9780892967728

1. William 2. Political intrigue 3. Government investigators 4. Bishops 5. Husband and wife 6. Civilization, Medieval 7. Great Britain 8. York, England 9. Medieval period (476-1492) 10. Plantagenet period (1154-1485) 11. Historical mysteries 12. Medieval mysteries

LC 2002027248

Owen Archer investigates a suspicious accident that threatened the life of William of Wykeham, the recently deposed Lord Chancellor of England, who has been scheming to get back in the king's good graces despite a feud with the Duke of Lancaster.

"Once again, Robb provides the reader with an evocative and suspenseful whodunit thoroughly bolstered by a wealth of authentic historical detail." —*Booklist*

Includes bibliographical references (p. 318-321).

A **gift** of Sanctuary: an Owen Archer mystery. Candace Robb. St. Martin's Press, 1998. 303 p. (Owen Archer mysteries, 6)

ISBN 9780312192662

1. Chaucer, Geoffrey 2. Archer, Owen (Fictitious character) 3. Civilization, Medieval 4. Murder investigation 5. Great Britain 6. Wales 7. Medieval period (476-1492) 8. Plantagenet period (1154-1485) 9. Historical mysteries 10. Medieval mysteries 11. Mysteries

LC 9841394

"Robb deftly interweaves a complex story of love, passion and murder into the troubled and tangled fabric of Welsh history, fashioning a rich and satisfying novel." —*Publishers Weekly*

A **murdered** peace. Candace M. Robb. Pegasus Books, 2018. 400 p. (Kate Clifford novels, 3)

ISBN 9781681778624

1. Women amateur detectives 2. Independence in women 3. Political intrigue 4. Resistance to government 5. Friendship 6. Great Britain 7. York, England 8. Medieval period (476-1492) 9. Plantagenet period (1154-1485) 10. Medieval mysteries 11. Historical mysteries

Loan Stars Favourites, 2018

Kate defends a friend who may be involved in an uprising against the king and who is also implicated in the murder of a spice seller in 1400 York.

The **riddle** of St. Leonard's: an Owen Archer mystery. St. Martin's Press, 1997. 303 p. (Owen Archer mysteries, 5)

ISBN 9780312169831

1. Hospitals 2. Archer, Owen (Fictitious character) 3. Civilization, Medieval 4. Great Britain 5. Medieval period (476-1492) 6. Plantagenet period (1154-1485) 7. Historical mysteries 8. Medieval mysteries 9. Mysteries

LC 9716231

When there is a spate of deaths and thefts at St. Leonard's Hospital in York that are not related to the plague, the Master of the hospital calls upon one-eyed master spy Owen Archer to solve the mystery BT

"An evocative historical mystery steeped in authentically gritty period detail." —*Booklist*

A **twisted** vengeance. Candace Robb. Pegasus Books, 2017. 297 pages (Kate Clifford novels, 2)

ISBN 9781681774527

1. Widows 2. Independence in women 3. Political intrigue 4. Women amateur detectives 5. Knights and knighthood 6. York, England 7. Great Britain 8. Plantagenet period (1154-1485) 9. Medieval mysteries 10. Historical mysteries

As the fourteenth century comes to a close, York seethes on the brink of civil war—and young widow Kate Clifford, struggling to keep her businesses afloat, realizes that her mother is harboring a dangerous secret...

Robb, J. D.

Connections in death: an Eve Dallas novel. J. D. Robb. St Martins Pr 2019. 384 p. (In Death series, 48)

ISBN 9781250201577

1. Policewomen 2. Near future 3. Addiction 4. Murder 5. Murder investigation 6. New York City 7. 21st century 8. Romantic suspense 9. Williams, Cathay

LC 2018029160

Helping to build a new school and youth shelter, homicide cop Eve Dallas and her husband enlist the aid of a child psychologist whose rehabilitated brother is found dead under suspicious circumstances.

Fantasy in death. J.D. Robb. G.P. Putnam's Sons, 2010. 368 p. (In Death series, 30)

ISBN 9780399156243

1. Women detectives 2. Murder investigation 3. Virtual reality 4. Rich men 5. Policewomen 6. New York City 7. 21st century 8. Romantic suspense 9. Police procedurals

LC 2009041114

Investigating the bizarre murder of a millionaire video game maven within a locked room, NYPSD Lieutenant Eve Dallas is baffled by a lack of suspects and the victim's demise in spite of his considerable resources.

Nora Roberts writing as J.D. Robb—Cover.

Innocent in death. J.D. Robb. G.P. Putnam's Sons, 2007. 400 p. (In Death series, 24)

ISBN 9780399154010

1. Women detectives 2. Murder investigation 3. Poisoning 4. Dallas, Eve (Fictitious character) 5. Policewomen 6. New York City 7. 21st century 8. Romantic suspense 9. Police procedurals

LC 2006025431

Investigating the baffling murder case of an ordinary and much-loved private school teacher, New York City lieutenant Eve Dallas struggles to identify who may have wanted the death of an innocent man.

Sequel to: Born in death.

Nora Roberts writing as J. D. Robb.

Leverage in death: an Eve Dallas novel. J. D. Robb. St Martins Pr 2018. 384 p. (In Death series, 47)

ISBN 9781250161567

1. Policewomen 2. Suicide bombers 3. Corporate mergers 4. Hostages 5. Businesspeople 6. New York City 7. 21st century 8. Romantic suspense 9. Police procedurals

LC 2018012056

Loan Stars Favourites, 2018

When an airline executive is blackmailed into a suicide bombing in his Wall Street office, lieutenant Eve Dallas investigates strange inconsistencies in the case while trying to uncover the blackmailers' true agenda.

Naked in death. J.D. Robb. Berkley Books, 1995. 313 p. (In Death series, 1)

ISBN 9780425148297

1. Women detectives 2. Murder suspects 3. Murder investigation 4. Dallas, Eve (Fictitious character) 5. Policewomen 6. New York City 7. 21st century 8. Romantic suspense 9. Police procedurals

New York City police lieutenant Eve Dallas pursues a romantic relationship with a mysterious and wealthy Irishman while investigating a murder case.

"Naked in Death features Lt. Eve Dallas of the NYPD as she searches for a serial killer of prostitutes. It hints at the isolation, neglect, and sexual abuse that Eve suffered as a child, memories that she tries to suppress. The adult Eve is slow to trust and awkward when faced with affection and kindness. Yet over the course of this series, she acquires a husband, Roark; a partner, Peabody; and a varied host of friends—hardboiled reporter Nadine, humanitarian doctor Louise, and worldly wise, bursting with life, rock star Mavis." —*Library Journal*

Nora Roberts writing as J. D. Robb.

Robbins, David L.

Last citadel: a novel of the Battle of Kursk. David L. Robbins. Bantam Books, 2003. 421 p. : Illustration; Map (World War II (David L. Robbins), 3)

ISBN 9780553801774

1. Soldiers 2. Intelligence Service 3. Battles 4. Bomber pilots 5. Stoker, Bram 6. Kursk, Russia 7. Soviet Union 8. Second World War era (1939-1945) 9. War stories 10. Historical fiction

LC 2003044304

During the greatest tank battle in armored warfare, the Battle of Kursk, Dimitri Berko and Luis de Vega find themselves in the tensions of deadly battle.

"The battle for the Soviet city of Kursk in July 1943 during World War II involved two million soldiers. Code-named Citadel, it was Hitler's frenzied—and final—attempt to defeat Russia on the eastern front and was the largest buildup of German armed power of the war. Robbins re-creates the battle in this rousing novel: its characters being Hitler; his generals and advisers; Russian, German, and Spanish foot soldiers and tank drivers; fighter pilots (both men and women); partisans; and even elderly men and women digging trenches." —*Booklist*

Includes bibliographical references (p. [420]-421).

War of the rats: a novel. David L. Robbins. Bantam Books, 1999. 392 p. (World War II (David L. Robbins), 1)

ISBN 9780553108170

1. Snipers 2. Women assassins 3. World War II. 4. Undercover operations 5. Americans in Russia 6. Soviet Union 7. Second World War era (1939-1945) 8. War stories 9. Historical fiction

LC 98043918

During the siege of Stalingrad at the height of World War II, two master snipers—Chief Master Sergeant Vasily Zaitsev and German marksman Heinz Thorvald—embark on a deadly and calculating competition to destroy each other.

"The final confrontation takes a while to play out, but once Robbins...gets to the heart of the matter, he presents a riveting account of a battle within a battle, and the sniper motif proves an ideal vehicle to analyze the strengths and weaknesses of both sides." —*Publishers Weekly*

Robbins, Tom

Fierce invalids home from hot climates. Tom Robbins. Bantam Books, 2000. 415 p.

ISBN 9780553107753

1. Former CIA agents 2. International intrigue 3. Eccentrics and eccentricities 4. Inca shamans 5. Pedophiles 6. Peru 7. Middle East 8. Humorous stories

LC 99051683

Follows the adventures, across four continents, of a man who is a contradiction for all seasons, as he falls in and out of love and danger.

"In true Robbins style, the writing throughout is lush and sexy, containing a great deal of witty social and political commentary." —*Publishers Weekly*

★ **Jitterbug** perfume. Tom Robbins. Bantam Books 1984. 342 p.

ISBN 9780553348989

1. Perfumes 2. Immortalism 3. Eccentrics and eccentricities 4. Man-woman relationships 5. Gods and goddesses 6. Seattle, Washington 7. Washington (State) 8. Humorous stories

LC 84045233

This philosophical epic, with a large cast of characters, addresses the fervent desire of the human race to overcome the tyranny of aging and physical death

"Robbins is still in top form, still mixing the lunatic and the thoughtful—or rather, doing a literary watusi up every page and jitterbugging back down." —*Publishers Weekly*

Roberts, Bethan

★ **My** policeman. Bethan Roberts. Penguin Books, 2021. 304 p.

ISBN 9780143136989

1. Married men 2. Lovers 3. Closeted gay men 4. Love triangles 5. Gay men — Social conditions 6. Brighton, England 7. England 8. 20th century 9. Historical fiction

Soon to be a motion picture starring Harry Styles and Emma Corrin, an exquisitely told, tragic tale of thwarted love.

"Roberts beautifully captures the devastation of being unable or unwilling to live in one's truth, and the quiet ending offers a poignant moment of respite for everyone." —*Kirkus*

First published in Great Britain by Chatto & Windus, an imprint of Penguin Random House UK, 2012—Title page verso.

Roberts, Nora

★ The **awakening**. Nora Roberts. St. Martin's Press, 2020. 464 p. (Dragon heart legacy, 1)

ISBN 9781250272614

1. Young women 2. Fairies 3. Imaginary places 4. Parallel universes 5. Fate and fatalism 6. Philadelphia, Pennsylvania 7. Pennsylvania 8. Paranormal romances

LC 2020021886

An anxious young woman mired in student debt and working a hated job uses hidden funds to visit Ireland, where she uncovers truths about vivid dreams compelling her to embrace her destiny in a fantastical alternate world.

"Best-selling Roberts (Hideaway, 2020) sets the bar high with the launch of her Dragon Heart Legacy trilogy, a captivating tale that not only vividly showcases her superior storytelling and characterization skills but also brightly illuminates her affinity for all things Irish." —*Booklist*

★ The **becoming**. Nora Roberts. St. Martin's Press, 2021. 400 p. (Dragon heart legacy, 2)

ISBN 9781250272706

1. Young women 2. Teachers 3. African American gay men 4. Friendship 5. Doorways 6. Philadelphia, Pennsylvania 7. Ireland 8. Paranormal romances

LC 2021027402

Able to walk between the world of man and the world of magick called Talamh, Breen Siobhan Kelly must take the next step on the journey to becoming all that she was born to be when one member of her bloodline, the outcast god Odran, plots to destroy Talamh.

"Perennially best-selling Roberts launched her Dragon Heart Legacy trilogy in 2020 with The Awakening and now, in the second installment, conjures up an action-packed, magic-infused tale of dragons, danger, and desire that will have readers who got hooked on the first volume fully engaged until the last page, at which point they'll begin anxiously awaiting the upcoming conclusion to Breen and Keegan's story." —*Booklist*

Chesapeake blue. Nora Roberts. G.P. Putnam's Sons, 2002. 384 p. (Chesapeake Bay saga, 4)

ISBN 9780399149399

1. Extortion 2. Man-woman relationships 3. Adult child abuse victims 4. Poor families 5. Young men 6. Chesapeake Bay Region 7. Eastern Shore, Maryland 8. Contemporary romances

LC 2002024827

Returning as a successful artist to the home of the family that adopted him, Seth Quinn is intrigued by independent newcomer Dru Whitcomb Banks, who is hesitant to trust Seth, while dark secrets from the past threaten the entire Quinn family.

Sequel to: Inner harbor.

Come sundown. Nora Roberts. St. Martin's Press, 2017. 432 p.

ISBN 9781250123077

1. Ranches 2. Family businesses 3. Murder 4. Ranchers 5. Family relationships 6. Montana 7. Romantic suspense

LC 2017002672

When danger lurks in the mountains around Bo's idyllic ranch and resort in western Montana, she turns to new hire Callen Skinner after they discover her estranged aunt badly injured and another woman murdered.

The **obsession**. Nora Roberts. Berkley, 2016. 464 p.

ISBN 9780399175169

1. Women photographers 2. Adult children of murderers 3. Threat (Psychology) 4. Automobile mechanics 5. Family secrets 6. Washington (State) 7. Romantic suspense

LibraryReads Favorites, 2016

Years after discovering her father's predatory double life, successful photographer Naomi Bowes struggles to hide her painful past from her fellow residents in a community thousands of miles away, a situation that introduces her to a new relationship and forces her to confront her demons.

"Roberts retains her impeccably high standards in this excellently executed tale, once again dazzling readers with a sophisticated blend of edge-of-your-seat suspense and sexy romance." —*Booklist*

Sea swept. Nora Roberts. Jove Books, 1998. 342 p. (Chesapeake Bay saga, 1)

ISBN 9780515121841

1. Brothers 2. Social workers 3. Interpersonal attraction 4. Man-woman relationships 5. Boys 6. Chesapeake Bay Region 7. Maryland 8. Contemporary romances

Cameron, a champion boat racer, returns home to the Maryland shore at the behest of his dying father to care for Seth, a troubled young boy.

Sequel: Rising tides.

Shelter in place. Nora Roberts. St. Martin's Press, 2018. 432 p.

ISBN 9781250161598

1. Post-traumatic stress disorder 2. Gunshot victims 3. Mass shootings 4. Serial murders 5. Threat (Psychology) 6. Maine 7. Thrillers and suspense

A group of survivors navigate trauma and recovery challenges in the aftermath of a mass shooting at a movie theater, an event that inspires a career in law enforcement, triggers devastating PTSD and gives way to an escaped killer's plot to orchestrate an event with an even higher death toll.

★ **Under** currents. Nora Roberts. St Martins Pr 2019. 400 p.

ISBN 9781250207098

1. Adult child abuse victims 2. Landscape gardening 3. Lawyers 4. Family problems 5. Abused women 6. North Carolina 7. Blue Ridge Mountains 8. Romantic suspense

LC 2018055444

Discovering unexpected allies when his successful father's rages spiral out of control, Zane draws strength and insights from the darkness of the past to create a healthier family in adulthood.

Robertson, Imogen

Anatomy of murder. Imogen Robertson. Pamela Dorman Books, 2012. 384 p. (Crowther and Westerman mysteries, 2)

ISBN 9780670023172

1. Women amateur detectives 2. Murder investigation 3. Anatomists — History 4. Drowning victims 5. Murder — History 6. London, England 7. England 8. Georgian era (1714-1837) 9. 1780s 10. Historical mysteries 11. Mysteries

LC 2011036291

The streets of London seethe with rumour and conspiracy as the King's navy battles the French at sea. And while the banks of the Thames swarm with life, a body is dragged from its murky waters. In another part of town, where the air seems sweeter, the privileged enjoy a brighter world of complacent wealth and intoxicating celebrity. But as society revels in its pleasures, a darker plot is played out. Yet some are willing to look below the surface to the unsavoury depths. Mrs Harriet Westerman believes passionately in justice. Reclusive anatomist Gabriel Crowther is fascinated by the bones beneath the skin. Invited to seek the true nature of the dead man, they risk censure for an unnatural interest in murder. But when the safety of a nation is at stake, personal reputation must give way to the pursuit of reason and truth.

Originally published: [London] : Headline Review, 2010.

Circle of shadows. Imogen Robertson. Viking, 2013. 384 p. (Crowther and Westerman mysteries, 4)
ISBN 9780670026289
1. Secret societies 2. Murder investigation 3. Poisoning 4. Widows 5. Anatomists 6. London, England 7. England 8. Georgian era (1714-1837) 9. Historical mysteries
LC 2013009688
Library Journal Best Books, 2013

When a beautiful aristocrat is murdered during a Shrove Tuesday masked ball in 1784, the forthright Mrs. Harriet Westerman and her reclusive companion, anatomist Gabriel Crowther, struggle with reluctant witnesses to clear the name of a falsely accused suspect who is facing execution.

Pamela Dorman Books.

Instruments of darkness: a novel. Imogen Robertson. Pamela Dorman Books, 2011. 384 p. (Crowther and Westerman mysteries, 1)
ISBN 9780670022427
1. Women amateur detectives 2. Murder investigation 3. Anatomists 4. Family secrets 5. Murder 6. Sussex, England 7. England 8. Georgian era (1714-1837) 9. 1780s 10. Historical mysteries 11. Mysteries

Discovering a dead neighbor from a menacing local estate, the unconventional Mrs. Westerman of 1780 Sussex enlists a reclusive local anatomist to uncover the family's secrets, which include ties to the American Revolution and links to the murder of a music shop owner.

Island of bones. Imogen Robertson. Pamela Dorman Books, 2012. 384 p. (Crowther and Westerman mysteries, 3)
ISBN 9780670026272
1. Anatomists 2. Men recluses 3. Tombs 4. Dead 5. Investigations 6. Lake District (England) 7. England 8. Georgian era (1714-1837) 9. 18th century 10. Historical mysteries 11. Mysteries
LC 2012003378

Cumbria, 1783. A broken heritage; a secret history. The tomb of the first Earl of Greta should have lain undisturbed on its island of bones for three hundred years. When idle curiosity opens the stone lid, however, inside is one body too many. Gabriel Crowther's family bought the Greta's land long ago, and has suffered its own bloody history. His brother was hanged for murdering their father, the Baron of Keswick, and Crowther has chosen comfortable seclusion and anonymity over estate and title for thirty years. But the call of the mystery brings him home at last. Travelling with forthright Mrs Harriet Westerman, who is escaping her own tragedy, Crowther finds a little town caught between new horrors and old, where ancient ways challenge modern justice. And against the wild and beautiful backdrop of fells and water, Crowther discovers that his past will not stay buried.

Originally published: 2011.

The Paris winter. Imogen Robertson. St. Martin's Press, 2014. 360 p.
ISBN 9781250051837
1. Women painters 2. Revenge 3. Opium addiction 4. Poverty 5. Siblings 6. Paris, France 7. Belle Epoque (1871-1914) 8. 1910s 9. Historical fiction

British painter Maud Heighton, seduced by the elegance and luxury of Paris, is unknowingly caught in a web of deception and revenge at the height of La Belle Epoque.

"For readers of historical fiction looking for a complex story, this is a sure bet." —*Library Journal*

Robertson, Michael

The **Baker** Street letters. Michael Robertson. Minotaur Books, 2009. 320 p. (Baker Street brothers, 1)
ISBN 9780312538125
1. Brothers 2. Letter writing 3. Missing persons investigation 4. Murder investigation 5. Cold cases (Criminal investigation) 6. London, England 7. Los Angeles, California 8. 1990s 9. Mysteries 10. Adult books for young adults
LC 2008045668

Reggie is thrilled when he learns that his new office is in the same space where famous sleuth Sherlock Holmes used to ply his trade. However, when he starts to receive mysterious mail, written for Holmes, his excitement soon turns into intrigue. As Reggie's brother, Nigel, begins to investigate one of these letters, he inexplicably disappears. Now, Reggie must find his brother while simultaneously solving a murder case.

The **Baker** Street translation: a mystery. Michael Robertson. Minotaur Books, 2013. 288 p. (Baker Street brothers, 3)
ISBN 9781250016454
1. Wills 2. Heirs and heiresses 3. Inheritance and succession 4. Kidnappers 5. Murder investigation 6. London, England 7. England 8. 1990s 9. Mysteries 10. Adult books for young adults

When new letters misaddressed to famous former tenant Sherlock Holmes embroil them in a tangle of new cases, brothers Reggie and Nigel Heath are compelled to sort out an American heiress's unconventional will, translate a nursery rhyme and find a missing rival while preventing an attack on an upcoming royal event.

The **brothers** of Baker Street. Michael Robertson. Minotaur Books, 2011. 288 p. (Baker Street brothers, 2)
ISBN 9780312538132
1. Murder investigation 2. Lawyers 3. Murder suspects 4. Crimes against tourists 5. Lawyers 6. London, England 7. England 8. 1990s 9. Mysteries 10. Adult books for young adults
LC 2010042020

When Reggie and Nigel Heath set up their law office at the famed 221B Baker Street, they are forced to respond to letters mailed to Sherlock Holmes, the most famous previous tenet at that address. As the brothers investigate their current case where a cabbie is accused of murdering two American tourists, the letters begin to pile up.

"According to the terms of their lease,...Reggie and Nigel Heath were able to set up their modern-day law practice in the desirable 200 block of Baker Street by agreeing to answer all correspondence addressed to Sherlock Holmes at 221B. Reggie, the less whimsical of the pair, has been neglecting that responsibility, so...that task falls to Nigel, freeing up Reggie to concentrate on defending a young cab driver accused of robbing and killing two American tourists. An anonymous letter to Holmes gives Reggie a valuable tip, but the communications from a certain Professor Moriarty add a more sinister twist to this breezy and entertaining legal mystery." —*New York Times Book Review*

Moriarty returns a letter: a Baker Street mystery. Michael Robertson. Minotaur Books, 2014. 288 p. (Baker Street brothers, 4)
ISBN 9781250016461
1. Brothers 2. Enemies 3. Voyages and travels 4. Lawyers 5. Letter writing 6. London, England 7. Los Angeles, California 8. 1990s 9. Mysteries
LC 2013033400

After an exhibition of vintage Sherlock Holmes letters opens at the Marylebone Hotel, lawyers Reggie and Nigel Heath, who are charged with answering letters to Holmes that arrive at their office, are faced with a whole new set of problems as an enemy from their past returns.

A Thomas Dunne book for Minotaur Books—Title page verso.

Robertson, Robin

The **long** take: a noir narrative. Robin Robertson. Alfred A. Knopf, 2018. 236 pages : Illustration

ISBN 9780525655213

1. Postwar life 2. Social change 3. World War II veterans 4. Journalists 5. Homelessness 6. Los Angeles, California 7. 1940s 8. 1950s 9. Novels in verse 10. Literary fiction

Walter Scott Prize for Historical Fiction, 2019; Longlisted for the Man Booker Prize, 2018

A D-Day veteran with post-traumatic stress disorder makes his way from New York to Los Angeles and San Francisco and as a journalist explores the social and racial divisions, spiraling corruption, and collapse of inner cities in America.

"Robertson transforms the long take into an epic taking of life, liberty, reason, and hope in this saga of a good man broken by war and a city savaged by greed, an arresting and gorgeously lyrical and disquieting tale of brutal authenticity, hard-won compassion, and stygian splendor." —*Booklist*

Also published as The Long Take : Or A Way To Lose More Slowly.

Robinson, Kim Stanley

Antarctica. Kim Stanley Robinson. Bantam Books, 1998. 511 p. : Map

ISBN 9780553100631

1. Conservation of natural resources 2. Greed 3. Sabotage 4. Environmentalists 5. Environmental crimes 6. Antarctica 7. 21st century 8. Science fiction 9. Adult books for young adults

LC 97041701

Alex Award, 1999; New York Times Notable Science Fiction, 1998

When the treaty protecting Antarctica from profiteers is about to dissolve—sending politicians and corporations scrambling to plunder its resources—a radical environmental group embarks on a campaign of sabotage to protect the land's pristine beauty BT

"This is an exhilarating addition to a body of work distinguished by two elements all too rare in modern science fiction: a sense of character and a sense of place. Robinson brings the two together by writing about people who are in love with where they are." —*New York Times Book Review*

Aurora. Kim Stanley Robinson. Orbit, 2015. 466 pages

ISBN 9780316098106

1. Far future 2. Space vehicles 3. Communities 4. Space travelers 5. High technology 6. Space 7. Hard science fiction 8. Science fiction 9. Adult books for young adults

The starship is headed for Tau Ceti, approximately 12 light years away. Launched from Earth in the 26th century, the vessel is nearing its destination after nearly 160 years. Charged with creating a comprehensive narrative of the voyage by chief engineer Devi, the ship's AI narrates this moving, thought-provoking novel, seamlessly blending the technical aspects of the spacecraft with the more personal stories of its passengers—particularly Devi's daughter, Freya, who's expected to succeed her mother as chief engineer just as they reach their new home.

"Robinson's latest well-researched novel exposes the fundamental flaws in one of science fiction's most beloved tropes: the multigenerational space ark traveling at sub-light speed to colonize a planet around a distant star." —*Kirkus*

★ **Blue** Mars. Kim Stanley Robinson. Bantam Books, 1996. 609 p. (Mars trilogy, 3)

ISBN 9780553573350

1. Overpopulation 2. Whitman, Walt 3. Planets — Colonization 4. Human settlements 5. Terraforming 6. Mars (Planet) 7. Science

fiction classics 8. Hard science fiction 9. Science fiction 10. Adult books for young adults

LC 9546700

Hugo Award for Best Novel, 1997; Library Journal Best Books, 1996; Locus Award for Best Science Fiction Novel, 1997

After declaring independence from Earth, Mars still faces problems: an impending ice age, a search for religious meaning, and immigration. New medical discoveries enable people to live 200 years, causing overpopulation on Earth and the Martians object to being swamped by Earthmen. A replay of New World problems in space.

★ **Green** Mars. Kim Stanley Robinson. Bantam Books, 1994. 535 p. (Mars trilogy, 2)

ISBN 9780553096408

1. Revolutionaries 2. Life on other planets 3. Human settlements 4. Planets — Colonization 5. Conservation of natural resources 6. Mars (Planet) 7. 22nd century 8. Science fiction classics 9. Hard science fiction 10. Science fiction 11. Adult books for young adults

LC 93039516

Hugo Award for Best Novel, 1994; Locus Award for Best Science Fiction Novel, 1994

One generation after the first pioneers begin to transform Mars into an Earthlike planet, the first grown children born on Mars, led by Peter Clayborne, rebel against colonization in an effort to preserve Mars' natural state.

The **Martians**. Kim Stanley Robinson. Bantam Books, 1999. 336 p. : Map (Mars trilogy, 4)

ISBN 9780553801170

1. Life on other planets 2. Space colonies 3. Revolutions 4. Martians 5. Space flight 6. Antarctica 7. Mars (Planet) 8. Short stories 9. Science fiction 10. Hard science fiction 11. Adult books for young adults

LC 99013115

Locus Award for Best Collection, 2000; New York Times Notable Science Fiction, 1999

A collection of stories set in the universe of Red Mars, Green Mars, and Blue Mars, tells the story of the colonists of the red planet and their experiences during its terraformation.

"Also included is Green Mars, a previously published novella about climbing Olympus Mons, the highest mountain in the solar system.... Some of the pieces here will be of interest only to those who have already read the trilogy, but the finest of the short fiction stands firmly on its own. As is the norm with Robinson's work, the stories are beautifully written, the characters are well developed and the author's passion for ecology manifests on every page." —*Publishers Weekly*

Companion to: Mars trilogy.

★ The **ministry** for the future. Kim Stanley Robinson. Orbit, 2020. 480 p.

ISBN 9780316300131

1. Technology 2. Climate change 3. Near future 4. Environmental degradation 5. Hard science fiction

LC 2020014375

The Ministry for the Future is a masterpiece of the imagination using fictional eyewitness accounts to tell the story of how climate change will affect us all over the decades to come. Its setting is not a desolate, postapocalyptic world, but a future that is almost upon us—and in which we might just overcome the extraordinary challenges we face.

"A breathtaking look at the challenges that face our planet in all their sprawling magnitude and also in their intimate, individual moments of humanity." —*Booklist*

New York 2140. Kim Stanley Robinson. Orbit, 2017. 480 p.
ISBN 9780316262347

1. Near future 2. Social change 3. Climate change 4. City life 5. Sea level 6. New York City 7. 22nd century 8. Hard science fiction 9. Apocalyptic fiction 10. Science fiction

LC 2016039922

Librarians' Choice (Australia), 2017

When a New York City of the near future is submerged by rising waters, the residents rapidly adapt the thriving metropolis until it becomes a vibrant, though permanently changed, canal region of island skyscrapers and remarkable inhabitants.

"A post-disaster fairy tale that's light on plot...but a thoroughly enjoyable exercise in worldbuilding, written with a cleareyed love for the city's past, present, and future." —*Kirkus*

★ **Red** Mars. Kim Stanley Robinson. Bantam Books, 1993. 572 p. : Map (Mars trilogy, 1)
ISBN 9780553560732
1. Planets — Colonization 2. Cooperation 3. Human settlements 4. Colonies 5. Revolutionaries 6. Mars (Planet) 7. 21st century 8. Multiple perspectives 9. Science fiction classics 10. Hard science fiction 11. Adult books for young adults

LC 92021607

BSFA Award for Best Novel, 1992; Nebula Award for Best Novel, 1993

For centuries, the red planet has enticed the people of Earth. Now an international group of scientists has colonized Mars. Leaving Earth forever, there 100 people have traveled nine months to reach their new home. This is the remarkable story of the world they create.

"A novel fully inhabited both by detailed technical processes and by people whose careers those processes are; it is also a novel with a complex sense of political reality.... This is one of the finest works of American SF because it is one of the few that aspire to the dignity of the genuinely tragic." —*Times Literary Supplement*

The **years** of rice and salt. Kim Stanley Robinson. Bantam Books, 2002. 658 p. : Map
ISBN 9780553109207
1. Black Death 2. War 3. Islam 4. Buddhists 5. Eastern religions 6. China 7. Asia 8. 14th century 9. Alternate histories 10. Adult books for young adults

LC 2001043492

Library Journal Best Books, 2002; Locus Award for Best Science Fiction Novel, 2003; New York Times Notable Science Fiction, 2002

In an alternate history world in which the population of Europe is almost completely wiped out by the Black Death during the fourteenth century, three superpowers—China, India, and the nations of Islam—battle for supremacy in a World War destined to create a new world order.

"Because this alternate history is set in the same lawful universe as ours, its science must be the same. Because its people have the same basic human needs, their societies resemble ours. However, as events march toward the alternative year of 2002, some of his characters come to believe, despite much evidence to the contrary, that they can change the way they live. The reader is left to ponder whether this is an illusion." —*New York Times Book Review*

Robinson, Marilynne

★ **Gilead**. Marilynne Robinson. Farrar, Straus and Giroux, 2004. 256 p. (Gilead novels, 1)
ISBN 9780374153892
1. Fathers and sons 2. Reminiscing in old age 3. May-December romances 4. Slavery — History 5. Faith (Christianity) 6. Iowa 7. Kansas 8. 1950s 9. Literary fiction 10. Historical fiction 11. Epistolary novels

LC 2004047063

ALA Notable Book, 2006; Booklist Editors' Choice, 2004; National Book Critics Circle Award for Fiction, 2004; New York Times Notable Book, 2004; Pulitzer Prize for Fiction, 2005

As the Reverend John Ames approaches the hour of his own death, he writes a letter to his son chronicling three previous generations of his family, a story that stretches back to the Civil War and reveals uncomfortable family secrets.

"Gilead possesses the quiet ineluctable perfection of Flaubert's A Simple Heart as well as the moral and emotional complexity of Robert Frost's deepest poetry. There's nothing flashy in these pages, and yet one regularly pauses to reread sentences, sometimes for their beauty, sometimes for their truth." —*Washington Post Book World.*

Originally published: New York, N.Y. : Farrar, Straus and Giroux, 2004.

Winner of the 2005 Pulitzer prize for fiction—Cover.

Home. Marilynne Robinson. Farrar, Straus and Giroux, 2008. 336 p. (Gilead novels, 2)
ISBN 9780374299101
1. Clergy 2. Homecomings 3. Families 4. Generation gap 5. Reminiscing in old age 6. Iowa 7. 1950s 8. Literary fiction 9. Domestic fiction 10. Gentle reads

LC 2008018301

Library Journal Best Books, 2008; Los Angeles Times Book Prize for Fiction, 2008; New York Times Notable Book, 2008; Orange Prize for Fiction, 2009; National Book Award for Fiction finalist, 2008; National Book Critics Circle Award for Fiction finalist, 2008; Shortlisted for the International IMPAC Dublin Literary Award, 2010

Returning to Gilead to care for her dying father, Glory Boughton is joined by her long-absent brother, with whom she bonds throughout his struggles with alcoholism, unemployment, and their father's traditionalist values.

"There is almost no first-rate American fiction about what happens in a household where religion is the family business, but if you ever wondered what it's like to be a preacher's kid, you can't do better than Home. Robinson's greatest achievement is that she manages to introduce the notions of belief and religious mystery without ever seeming vague. She never shies from uncomfortable truths." —*Newsweek*

★ **Jack**. Marilynne Robinson. Farrar, Straus and Giroux, 2020. 256 p. (Gilead novels, 4)
ISBN 9780374279301
1. Children of clergy 2. Self-hate in men 3. Alcoholics 4. Interracial romance 5. Romantic love 6. St. Louis, Missouri 7. Missouri 8. 20th century 9. Literary fiction 10. Gentle reads

LC 2020012453

New York Times Notable Book, 2020

A new Gilead novel that tells the story of John Ames Boughton, the beloved, erratic, and grieved-over prodigal son of a Presbyterian minister from Gilead, Iowa.

"The newest, avidly awaited novel in National Humanities Medal winner Robinson's acclaimed Gilead saga grapples with urgent questions of race, faith, and equality." —*Booklist*

★ **Lila**. Marilynne Robinson. Farrar Straus & Giroux, 2014. 261 pages; (Gilead novels, 3)
ISBN 9780374187613
1. Drifters 2. Adult child abuse victims 3. Clergy 4. Calvinism 5. Life change events 6. Iowa 7. Literary fiction 8. Gentle reads
Booklist Editors' Choice, 2014; National Book Critics Circle Award for Fiction, 2014; New York Times Notable Book, 2014; National Book Award for Fiction finalist, 2014; Shortlisted for the International Dublin Literary Award, 2016

Triggering a romance and debate by seeking shelter in a church and becoming a minister's wife, homeless Lila reflects on her hardscrabble life on the run with a canny young drifter and her efforts to reconcile her painful past with her husband's gentle Christian worldview.

"A passionate and learned moral and spiritual inquiry, a paean to the earth, and a witty and transcendent love story." —*Booklist*

Robinson, Peter

All the colors of darkness. Peter Robinson. William Morrow, 2009. 351 p. (Inspector Alan Banks mysteries, 18)

ISBN 9780061362934

1. Police 2. Spies 3. Murder investigation 4. Detectives 5. Murder 6. Yorkshire, England 7. London, England 8. Mysteries 9. Canadian fiction 10. Police procedurals

LC 2008019015

When the body of a man is discovered hanging from a tree in the woods near Eastvale, all signs point toward suicide. Inspector Banks finds himself plunged into a case where nothing is as it seems.

Originally published: Toronto : McClelland & Stewart, c2008.

★ **Careless** love. Peter Robinson. William Morrow, 2019. 432 p. (Inspector Alan Banks mysteries, 25)

ISBN 9780062847522

1. Suicide investigation 2. Murder suspects 3. Police 4. Crime scenes 5. Criminal evidence 6. Police procedurals 7. Mysteries 8. Canadian fiction

Detective Superintendent Alan Banks and his crack investigation team investigate two suspicious deaths that are complicated by a shocking revelation and the return of an old enemy.

Originally published: London : Hodder & Stoughton, 2018.

Children of the revolution. Peter Robinson. McClelland & Stewart, 2013. 387 p. (Inspector Alan Banks mysteries, 21)

ISBN 9780771076305

1. Murder suspects 2. College teachers 3. Scandals 4. Banks, Alan (Fictitious character) 5. Police 6. England 7. Katharine, duchess of Lancaster 8. Mysteries 9. Canadian fiction 10. Police procedurals

Inspector Banks investigates the death of a disgraced college professor.

A DCI Banks novel—Cover.

Regular print edition first published: London: Hodder, 2013.

Close to home. Peter Robinson. William Morrow, 2016. 396 pages; (Inspector Alan Banks mysteries, 13)

ISBN 9780062431271

1. Missing persons 2. Missing persons investigation 3. Murder 4. Murder investigation 5. Missing teenage boys 6. England 7. Yorkshire, England 8. Mysteries 9. Canadian fiction 10. Police procedurals

LC 2002071901

When the remains of a childhood friend of Alan Banks are discovered, who disappeared more then 35 years ago, Banks is drawn into an investigation.

"A moody chap on the sunniest of days, Peter Robinson's Yorkshire copper, Inspector Alan Banks, slips into a melancholy funk...when he returns to his boyhood home—indeed, to his own narrow bed in his old room in his parents' house—to help with an investigation into the death of a former schoolmate. Graham Marshall was 14 when he disappeared in 1965, and the belated discovery of his skeletal remains brings a rush of painful memories to the middle-aged detective who had been his best friend and the keeper of their secrets." —*New York Times Book Review*

Also published under the title The summer that never was.

Cold is the grave. Peter Robinson. W. Morrow, 2000. 369 p. (Inspector Alan Banks mysteries, 11)

ISBN 9780380978083

1. Villages 2. Runaway teenage girls 3. Murder investigation 4. Murder 5. Banks, Alan (Fictitious character) 6. England 7. Yorkshire, England 8. Mysteries 9. Canadian fiction 10. Police procedurals

LC 37231

Arthur Ellis Award for Best Novel, 2001

Maverick police inspector Alan Banks finds himself drawn into London's underworld when he aids his archrival Chief Constable Riddle, after the chief's missing daughter turns up on a pornographic website.

"A cunningly constructed plot, enhanced by Robinson's engaging descriptions and insights." —*Booklist*

Sequel to: In a dry season.

The first cut. Peter Robinson. Perennial Dark Alley, 2004. 310 p. : Map

ISBN 9780060735357

1. Victims of violent crimes 2. Women with amnesia 3. Serial murders 4. Women college graduates 5. Women impostors 6. England 7. Whitby, England 8. Psychological suspense 9. Canadian fiction

LC 2003067660

"Recent university graduate Kirsten survives a brutal Jack the Ripper-style attack of which she has no memory. As Kirsten recovers, she becomes fixated on finding the man who nearly killed her. Miles away, Martha has come to the coastal town of Whitby, where she is doing research for a book. Or is she? Carefully surveying her surroundings, Martha grows more obsessed with the object of her trip. The women's stories are told in alternate chapters until the unsettling end. This atmospheric tale of suspense will keep readers wondering what's really going on." —*Library Journal*

Previously published as: Caedmon's song (1990).

Originally published: Canada: Penguin, 1990; London: Pan, 2004.

Friend of the devil. Peter Robinson. William Morrow, 2008. 400 p. (Inspector Alan Banks mysteries, 17)

ISBN 9780060544379

1. Women murder victims 2. Secret identity 3. Identity (Psychology) 4. Teenage murder victims 5. Police 6. England 7. Yorkshire, England 8. Mysteries 9. Canadian fiction 10. Police procedurals

LC 2007021678

Inspector Banks and DI Annie Cabbot investigate the murders of two women and begin to see the connections between them.

In the dark places. Peter Robinson. William Morrow, 2014. 336 p. (Inspector Alan Banks mysteries, 22)

ISBN 9780062240545

1. Murder suspects 2. Crime scenes 3. Missing persons 4. Banks, Alan (Fictitious character) 5. Police 6. Mysteries 7. Canadian fiction 8. Police procedurals

When two boys vanish under mysterious circumstances, the local community is filled with unease. Assigned to the case, DCI Banks and his team soon find themselves in a race against time where it's their turn to become the prey.

Originally published as Abattoir blues, Toronto: McClelland & Stewart, 2014.

Innocent graves: an Inspector Banks mystery. Peter Robinson. Berkley Prime Crime, 1996. 346 p. (Inspector Alan Banks mysteries, 8)

ISBN 9780425153154

1. Murder investigation 2. Crimes against teenage girls 3. Murder suspects 4. Banks, Alan (Fictitious character) 5. Police 6. England 7. Yorkshire, England 8. Mysteries 9. Canadian fiction 10. Police procedurals

LC 95-38218

Arthur Ellis Award for Best Novel, 1997

When the brutal murder of a teenage girl shatters the peace of the small village of Eastvale, Inspector Banks and his colleague, Susan Gay, dig beneath the surface of small-town secrets to uncover the guilty party

"Although the story follows the classical form of a whodunit, the characters have complexity and the issues range broad and deep, raising interesting moral questions about bigotry, class privilege and the terrible crime of being different." —*New York Times Book Review*

Piece of my heart. Peter Robinson. William Morrow, 2006. 378 p. (Inspector Alan Banks mysteries, 16)
ISBN 9780060544355
1. Murder investigation 2. Rock concerts 3. Power failures 4. Fathers and daughters 5. Fathers and sons 6. England 7. Yorkshire, England 8. Mysteries 9. Canadian fiction 10. Police procedurals
LC 2005058363
As he probes the killing of a freelance music journalist, Detective Inspector Alan Banks finds his investigation journeying back in time more than thirty years and into the heart of the mystery surrounding a decades-old crime.

"The author invokes the most disturbing aspects of the 60's—to the point at which even the Manson murders have repercussions in Yorkshire—to sustain the book's ominous mood. There is pathos too, as Banks winds up revisiting characters who were young and energetic in 1969 but are now tea-sipping retirees." —*New York Times*
First published: London: Hodder & Stoughton, 2006.
DCI Banks—Cover.
TV tie-in.

Playing with fire. Peter Robinson. W. Morrow, 2004. 384 p. (Inspector Alan Banks mysteries, 14)
ISBN 9780060198770
1. Art forgeries 2. Arson 3. Former lovers 4. Former wives 5. Women heroin addicts 6. England 7. Yorkshire, England 8. Mysteries 9. Canadian fiction 10. Police procedurals 11. Adult books for young adults
LC 2003056569
Investigating a dual arson case that has claimed three lives on an English canal, Detective Inspector Banks teams up with fellow investigator Annie Cabot and discovers that the victims are linked to an art forgery operation.

"Characterization is Robinson's real strength. Virtually every character is etched with care, precision and emotional insight." —*Publishers Weekly*

Strange affair. Peter Robinson. William Morrow, 2005. 352 p. (Inspector Alan Banks mysteries, 15)
ISBN 9780060544331
1. Families of missing persons 2. Missing persons 3. Lovers 4. Murder 5. Murder investigation 6. England 7. Yorkshire, England 8. Mysteries 9. Canadian fiction 10. Police procedurals
LC 2004053633
Inspector Alan Banks heads to London after receiving a disturbing call from his estranged brother, while back in Eastvale, detective Annie Cabbot's investigation of a young woman's death uncovers a connection to someone close to Annie.

Robotham, Michael
★ **Close** your eyes. Michael Robotham. Little Brown & Co, 2016. Vii, 392 pages; (Joseph O'Loughlin and Vincent Ruiz novels, 8)
ISBN 9780316267946
1. Clinical psychologists 2. Death — Psychological aspects 3. Murder investigation 4. Serial murders 5. O'Loughlin, Joseph (Fictitious

character) 6. London, England 7. Psychological suspense 8. Thrillers and suspense 9. Australian fiction
When a former student bungles the investigation of a mother-daughter double murder, clinical psychologist Joseph O'Loughlin discovers a link between the case and a series of escalating attacks.
Originally published: London : Sphere, 2015.

★ **Good** girl, bad girl: a novel. Michael Robotham. Scribner, 2019. 352 p. (Cyrus Haven novels, 1)
ISBN 9781982103606
1. Secret identity 2. Deception 3. Crime 4. Emancipation of minors 5. Forensic psychologists 6. Thrillers and suspense 7. Australian fiction 8. Adult books for young adults
LC 2019012944
Gold Dagger Award for Best Crime Novel of the Year, 2020
A dangerous young woman with a unique ability to detect lies sues for her emancipation from a secure children's home, while the psychologist on her case finds herself in a battle of wits for survival.

Life or death. Michael Robotham. Mulholland Books, 2015. 432 p.
ISBN 9780316252058
1. Fugitives 2. Escaped convicts 3. Greed 4. Money 5. Flashbacks 6. Texas 7. Crime fiction 8. Australian fiction
LC 2014024896
Gold Dagger Award for Best Crime Novel of the Year, 2015
Brutalized in prison for a decade for his alleged knowledge about where a fortune in stolen money is hidden, Audie mysteriously escapes the day before his scheduled release in a determined effort to save someone else's life.
Due to be released tomorrow. Why escape today?—Cover.

The **night** ferry: a novel. Michael Robotham. Doubleday, 2007. 384 p.
ISBN 9780385517904
1. Sikh women 2. Detectives 3. Murder investigation 4. Police 5. Immigrants 6. London, England 7. England 8. Mysteries
LC 2006019771
When a murder suspect broke her back across a brick wall, Allisha's dreams of being a detective were shattered. Now on her feet again, but her career in limbo, she receives a message from a schoolfriend, Cate, who is pregnant and in trouble. She travels to the the murky underworld of sex trafficking, slavery and exploitation.
The main character in The night ferry, Ali Barba, made her first appearance as Inspector Ruiz's colleague in Michael Robotham's novel Lost.
First published: 2007.

★ The **other** wife. Michael Robotham. Sphere, 2018. 400 p; (Joseph O'Loughlin and Vincent Ruiz novels, 9)
ISBN 9780751562828
1. Clinical psychologists 2. Family secrets 3. Deception 4. Husband and wife 5. O'Loughlin, Joseph (Fictitious character) 6. London, England 7. Psychological suspense 8. Thrillers and suspense 9. Australian fiction
Librarians' Choice (Australia), 2018
When his father, a celebrated surgeon, is brutally attacked and a strange woman shows up at his bedside covered in blood, Joe O'Loughlin is forced to question everything he has always believed about his father and soon discovers that the truth comes with a high price.
Originally published: Sydney, NSW : Hachette Australia, 2018.

★ **Say** you're sorry. Michael Robotham. Mulholland Books, 2012. 448 p. (Joseph O'Loughlin and Vincent Ruiz novels, 6)
ISBN 9780316221245
1. Clinical psychologists 2. Murder investigation 3. Crimes against married people 4. Murder suspects 5. Missing girls 6. London, England

7. Psychological suspense 8. Thrillers and suspense 9. Australian fiction

LC 2012020772

Two young girls. Both taken. Dead? Or alive? When best friends Piper and Tash disappear one Sunday morning, the investigation captivates a nation but the teenage girls are never found. Three years later, during the worst blizzard in a century, a husband and wife are brutally killed in the farmhouse where Tash McBain once lived. A suspect is in custody, a troubled young man who can hear voices and claims that he saw a girl that night being chased by a snowman. Convinced that Piper or Tash might still be alive, clinical psychologist Joe O'Loughlin persuades police to reopen the investigation, but the closer he gets to the truth, the more dangerous it becomes.

★ **Suspect**. Michael Robotham. Doubleday : 2005. 368 p. (Joseph O'Loughlin and Vincent Ruiz novels, 1)
ISBN 9780385508612
1. Psychiatrists 2. People with Parkinson's disease 3. Middle-aged men 4. Murder suspects 5. Married people 6. London, England 7. Psychological suspense 8. Thrillers and suspense

LC 2004050156

Joe O'Loughlin, a successful psychologist faced with a recent diagnosis of Parkinson's disease, confronts a dangerous conspiracy against him after he becomes the prime suspect in the brutal murder of a woman who turns out to be a woman with whom he once had a relationship and must deal with the betrayal and abandonment of those he trusts the most.

Originally published: London : Time Warner, 2004.

★ **When** she was good. Michael Robotham. Scribner, 2020. 352 p. (Cyrus Haven novels, 2)
ISBN 9781982103637
1. Criminal psychology 2. Psychologists 3. Secrets 4. Psychic trauma 5. Murder investigation 6. England 7. Thrillers and suspense 8. Australian fiction 9. Multiple perspectives
Ian Fleming Steel Dagger Award, 2021

A sequel to Good Girl, Bad Girl finds criminal psychologist Cyrus Haven uncovering answers about Evie Cormac's dark past that force the latter to flee and question whether or not her secrets should remain hidden.

"This one's a jewel, and readers who don't know Robotham should immediately catch up." —*Booklist*

★ The **wreckage**. Michael Robotham. Mulholland Books, 2011. 320 p. (Joseph O'Loughlin and Vincent Ruiz novels, 5)
ISBN 9780316126403
1. Former police 2. Banks and banking 3. Bombings 4. Missing persons 5. Swindlers and swindling 6. Thrillers and suspense 7. Australian fiction

After being robbed of his briefcase, ex-cop Vincent Ruiz tracks down the thieves, who had mistaken him for someone else, and becomes unwittingly involved unraveling plots involving bank bombings in Baghdad and a missing VP at an international finance powerhouse.

"This fast-paced, gritty, and violent tale of international crime and investigation, with a sharp political edge, will appeal to readers seeking summer fiction with depth." —*Library Journal*

Rochon, Farrah

The **boyfriend** project. Farrah Rochon. Forever, 2020. 368 p. (Boyfriend project, 1)
ISBN 9781538716625
1. Women computer programmers 2. Female friendship 3. Dating (Social customs) 4. Intrigue 5. Deception 6. Austin, Texas 7. Texas 8. Contemporary romances 9. Multicultural romances 10. African American fiction

LC 2019049288

LibraryReads Favorites, 2020

When a live tweet of a horrific date reveals the unscrupulous dealings of an internet catfisher, three duped women make a pact to invest in themselves for six months, prompting one to pursue a dream career.

"Rochon is a romance master who adeptly writes interesting and dynamic characters.... The conflict is thorny and real without being melodramatic. Notably, the book unflinchingly portrays the obstacles Samiah faces as a black woman in a STEM field and her determination to pull other black women and girls up the ladder. A richly layered conflict adds depth and complexity to this charming workplace romance." —*Kirkus*

The **dating** playbook. Farrah Rochon. Forever, 2021. 368 p. (Boyfriend project, 2)
ISBN 9781538716670
1. Personal trainers 2. Football players 3. African Americans 4. Man-woman relationships 5. Football injuries 6. Romantic comedies 7. African American fiction 8. Contemporary romances

LC 2021010574

When it comes to personal training, Taylor Powell kicks serious butt. Unfortunately, her bills are piling up, rent is due, and the money situation is dire. Taylor needs more than the support of her new best friends, Samiah and London. She needs a miracle. And Jamar Dixon might just be it. The oh-so-fine former pro athlete wants back into the game, and he wants Taylor to train him. There's just one catch—no one can know what they're doing. But when they're accidentally outed as a couple, Taylor's plan's turned completely upside down. Is Jamar just playing to win...or is he playing for keeps?

"This football romance is a total knockout: funny, sexy, and full of heart." —*Kirkus*

Rockaway, Kristin

How to hack a heartbreak. Kristin Rockaway. Graydon House, 2019. 384 p.
ISBN 9781525834257
1. Women computer programmers 2. Sexism in employment 3. Dating (Social customs) 4. Self-fulfillment in women 5. Man-woman relationships 6. Chick lit
LibraryReads Favorites, 2019

A help-desk tech who supports inept "genius" male co-workers tires of sexual harassment and uses her elite coding skills to create a viral app before she is forced to choose between her relationships and career.

Rodrigues Fowler, Yara

Stubborn archivist. Yara Rodrigues Fowler. Mariner Books, 2019. 320 p.
ISBN 9780358006084
1. Brazilians 2. Children of immigrants 3. British in Brazil 4. Difference (Psychology) 5. Identity (Psychology) 6. London, England 7. Brazil 8. Literary fiction 9. Psychological fiction 10. Autobiographical fiction 11. Adult books for young adults

LC 2018042566

A young Brazilian woman from South London, growing up between two cultures, takes us through first love and loss, losing and finding home, trauma and healing and various awakenings of sexuality and identity.

Rodriguez, Linda

Every broken trust: a mystery. Linda Rodriguez. Minotaur Books, 2013. Viii, 294 pages; (Marquitta Skeet Bannion mysteries, 2)
ISBN 9781250030351

1. Women detectives 2. Politicians 3. Murder 4. Detectives 5. Universities and colleges 6. Mysteries

When a party celebrating the arrival of a Kansas City politician is thrown into turmoil by an attack on a friend that left another person dead, half-Cherokee chief of campus police Skeet Bannion investigates allegations that the survivor's husband's accidental death years earlier was actually a murder.

Every hidden fear: a Skeet Bannion mystery. Linda Rodriguez. St. Martin's Press, 2014. Viii, 292 pages; (Marquitta Skeet Bannion mysteries, 3)
ISBN 9781250049155
1. Women detectives 2. Murder 3. Universities and colleges 4. Detectives 5. Indians of North America 6. Mysteries

Adjusting to a household that includes her Cherokee grandmother and teenage ward, Skeet struggles to keep the peace when a wealthy developer makes a shocking paternity claim and announces plans to build a community-devastating mall.

"This is a strong series featuring a multidimensional heroine." —*Booklist*

Every last secret: a mystery. Linda Rodriguez. Minotaur Books, 2012. 304 p. (Marquitta Skeet Bannion mysteries, 1)
ISBN 9781250005458
1. Native American women 2. Universities and colleges 3. Policewomen 4. Murder investigation 5. Multiracial persons 6. Mysteries
LC 2012005484

Leaving her position as the highest-ranking woman officer in the Kansas City Police Department for what she hopes will be a less-stressful job as the chief of a small-town campus police force, half-Cherokee Skeet Bannion investigates the murder of a student editor and untangles ugly involvements at the highest levels of the college.

Rodriques, Elias

All the water I've seen is running: a novel. Elias Rodriques. W. W. Norton & Company, 2021. 288 p.
ISBN 9780393540796
1. Friends' death 2. Grief 3. Homecomings 4. Death 5. High school students 6. Florida 7. Coming-of-age stories
LC 2020053069

After learning that his close friend from high school has died, Daniel returns to North Florida from New York to meet up with his old classmates and try to find meaning in their friend's passing.

"This melancholy story is a startling and necessary addition to the canon of works that parse what it means to grow up in the American South." —*Publishers Weekly*

Rogers, Morgan Callan

★ **Honey** girl. Morgan Rogers. Park Row Books, 2021. 352 p.
ISBN 9780778311027
1. African American women 2. Lesbians 3. Mental illness 4. Marriage 5. Expectation (Psychology) 6. New York City 7. Portland, Oregon 8. Romantic comedies 9. Multicultural romances 10. Contemporary romances
LibraryReads Favorites, 2021

With her newly completed PhD in astronomy in hand, twenty-eight-year-old Grace Porter goes on a girls' trip to Vegas to celebrate. She's a straight A, work-through-the-summer certified high achiever. She is not the kind of person who goes to Vegas and gets drunkenly married to a woman whose name she doesn't know, until she does exactly that. This one moment of departure from her stern ex-military father's plans for her life has Grace wondering why she doesn't feel more fulfilled from completing her degree. Staggering under the weight of her parent's expectations, a struggling job market and feelings of burnout, Grace flees her home in Portland for a summer in New York with the wife she barely knows.

"With a cast of diverse and underrepresented characters, Rogers's debut is a beautiful story of learning to love in so many ways: untraditionally, through deep hurt, through mental illness, and through struggles with which readers can relate." —*Library Journal*

Roisin, Fariha

Like a bird. Fariha Roisin. The Unnamed Press, 2020. 303 p.
ISBN 9781951213091
1. Interracial families 2. East Indian Americans 3. Teenage girls 4. Sisters — Death 5. Survivors of suicide victims 6. New York City 7. Literary fiction

"In her extraordinary first novel, Roisin exposes the damaging effects of colorism through the Chatterjee family, who unconsciously pit their golden child, light-skinned, confident Alyssa, against Taylia, dark and brooding like her immigrant father and an unwelcome reminder of his roots in Calcutta." —*Library Journal*

Rojas Contreras, Ingrid

★ **Fruit** of the drunken tree: a novel. Ingrid Rojas Contreras. Doubleday, 2018. 304 p.
ISBN 9780385542722
1. Families 2. Sisters 3. Household employees 4. Gated communities 5. Teenage girls 6. Bogota, Colombia 7. Colombia 8. 1990s 9. Domestic fiction 10. Coming-of-age stories 11. Adult books for young adults
LC 2017039664
LibraryReads Favorites, 2018

Follows a sheltered girl and a teen maid, who forge an unlikely friendship that threatens to undo them both amid the violence of 1990s Colombia.

Rojstaczer, Stuart

The **mathematician's** shiva: a novel. Stuart Rojstaczer. Penguin Books, 2014. 384 p.
ISBN 9780143126317
1. Mathematicians 2. Mathematics 3. Jewish mourning customs 4. Mathematics teachers 5. Mourning customs 6. Wisconsin 7. Literary fiction 8. Humorous stories
LC 2014012521

A comic, bittersweet tale of family evocative of The Yiddish Policemen's Union and Everything Is Illuminated Alexander "Sasha" Karnokovitch and his family would like to mourn the passing of his mother, Rachela, with modesty and dignity. But Rachela, a famous Polish emigre, mathematician, and professor at the University of Wisconsin, is rumored to have solved the million-dollar, Navier-Stokes Millennium Prize Problem. Rumor also has it that she spitefully took the solution to her grave. To Sasha's chagrin, a ragtag group of socially challenged mathematicians arrives in Madison and crashes the shiva, vowing to do whatever it takes to find the solution—even if it means prying up the floorboards for Rachela's notes. Written by a trained geophysicist, this hilarious and multi-layered debut novel brims with colorful characters and brilliantly captures humanity's drive not just to survive, but to solve the impossible.

"Though Rojstaczer doesn't have the spikey wit of Gary Shteyngart or the inventiveness of Michael Chabon, his steadiness and empathy are appealing in their own ways. A geophysicist, he brings an added dimension to the book's discussions of scientific matters. He's very good at exploring the apparent divide between genius and happiness as well as the intersection of cultures. An enjoyable debut, the book is distinguished by a fluid, lyrical style that is equally at home with serious and comic matters." —*Kirkus*

Rollins, James

Crucible. James Rollins. William Morrow & Co, 2019. Xiv, 461 p. (Sigma Force novels, 14)

ISBN 9780062381781

1. Elite operatives 2. Inquisition 3. Rare books 4. Violence against women 5. Women kidnapping victims 6. Adventure stories

After his home is attacked and his pregnant girlfriend is kidnapped, Commander Gray Pierce and the Sigma Force confront deep spiritual mysteries tracing back to the Spanish Inquisition.

The **demon** crown: a Sigma Force novel. James Rollins. Morrow, 2017. 448 p. (Sigma Force novels, 13)

ISBN 9780062381736

1. Plague 2. Antiquities 3. Secrets 4. Secret societies 5. Enemies 6. Brazil 7. Adventure stories

The members of Sigma Force reluctantly join forces with their most hated enemy to stop a primordial threat with ties to the American Civil War and the secret work of Alexander Graham Bell.

"Rollins' latest Sigma Force novel is one of the best in the series....The mix of science, history, and high-concept adventure is always first-rate in a Rollins novel, and thats true here as well, even with killer wasps in the mix.." —*Booklist*

The **devil** colony. James Rollins. William Morrow, 2011. Xvi, 480 p. : Illustration; Map (Sigma Force novels, 7)

ISBN 9780061784781

1. Alliances 2. Conspiracies 3. Secrets 4. Criminal investigation 5. Deception 6. United States 7. Adventure stories 8. Adult books for young adults

Library Journal Best Books, 2011

After a mountainside massacre yields a grim message, Painter Crowe, director of Sigma Force, must join with Commander Grayson Pierce and an unlikely ally if he is going to get to the root of a conspiracy that stretches back to a lost prehistoric colony in America.

The **eye** of God. James Rollins. William Morrow, 2013. Xviii, 410 pages : Illustration; Map (Sigma Force novels, 9)

ISBN 9780061784804

1. Murder 2. Codes (Communication) 3. National security 4. Prophecies 5. Antiquities 6. Adventure stories 7. Adult books for young adults

Commander Gray Pierce and Sigma Force set out to uncover the truth tied to the fall of the Roman Empire, to a mystery going back to the birth of Christianity, and to a weapon hidden for centuries that holds the fate of humanity.

★ The **last** odyssey. James Rollins. William Morrow & Co, 2020. 448 pages (Sigma Force novels, 15)

ISBN 9780062892898

1. Homer 2. Elite operatives 3. Antiquities 4. Weapons 5. International intrigue 6. Violence in men 7. Mediterranean Region 8. Adventure stories 9. Thrillers and suspense

When a medieval ship containing a clockwork gold atlas by famous Muslim inventor Ismail al-Jazari is discovering beneath Greenland's frozen tundra, Sigma Force is challenged to prevent a regional uprising inspired by the tales of Homer.

"This is a thoughtful, nonstop thrill ride that's an exemplar of an escapist page-turner." —*Publishers Weekly*

The **sixth** extinction: a Sigma Force novel. James Rollins. William Morrow, 2014. 448 p. (Sigma Force novels, 10)

ISBN 9780061784811

1. Murder 2. Codes (Communication) 3. National security 4. Prophecies 5. Antiquities 6. Adventure stories

When a remote military research station is decimated, Commander Gray Pierce and the Sigma Force must solve a mystery from Antarctica's distant past using an ancient map that leads them to a new form of death, which could result in mankind's extinction.

Romain, Theresa

Fortune favors the wicked. Theresa Romain. Zebra Books, 2016. 368 p. (Royal rewards, 1)

ISBN 9781420138658

1. Courtesans 2. Sailors 3. Treasure hunting 4. Men who are blind 5. Treasure troves 6. Derbyshire, England 7. England 8. Regency period (1811-1820) 9. Regency romances 10. Historical romances

The London papers call it the theft of the century. Someone has robbed the Royal Mint of 50,000 pounds and the Crown is offering a substantial reward for its return. Courtesan Charlotte Perry wants the money to start a new life. A chance encounter in a tavern leads to an alliance with blind Royal Navy lieutenant Benedict Frost, who wishes to use the funds to augment his sister's meager dowry. As they join forces to track down the stolen sovereigns, Charlotte and Benedict discover a love more precious than gold.

Romano-Lax, Andromeda

The **Spanish** bow. Andromeda Romano-Lax. Harcourt, 2007. 560 p.

ISBN 9780151015429

1. Cellists 2. Child prodigies 3. Competition in men 4. Musicians 5. Happiness 6. Madrid, Spain 7. Spain 8. 19th century 9. Historical fiction

LC 2006100937

Library Journal Best Books, 2007

Chronicles the lifelong friendship and rivalry between Feliu Delargo, a Catalan cellist, and eccentric piano prodigy Justo Al-Cerraz, a relationship that is dramatically transformed by the arrival in their lives of Aviva, an Italian violinist with a haunted past.

"Expertly woven throughout the book are cameo appearances by Pablo Picasso, Adolf Hitler, Francisco Franco, Bertolt Brecht, and others, but it is the fictional Feliu, Justo, and Aviva who will keep you mesmerized to the last page." —*Christian Science Monitor*

Romero, George A.

The **living** dead. . Tor Books, 2020. 656 p.

ISBN 9781250305121

1. Zombies 2. End of the world 3. Epidemics 4. Horror 5. Apocalyptic fiction 6. Multiple perspectives

A contemporary thriller traces the outbreak of a zombie plague through the fall of humankind and beyond.

"A blockbuster portrayal of the zombie apocalypse and a fitting tribute to the genre's imaginative progenitor." —*Kirkus*

Rooney, Kathleen

★ **Cher** Ami and Major Whittlesey. Kathleen Rooney. Penguin Group USA, 2020. 336 p.

ISBN 9780525507826

1. Homing pigeons 2. Soldiers 3. War — Psychological aspects 4. Men and birds 5. Gay men 6. Europe 7. United States 8. First World War era

(1914-1918) 9. Historical fiction 10. Stories told by animals 11. Multiple perspectives

A tale based on true events follows the experiences of an army officer who answers the call to service during World War I before his life is astonishingly reshaped by his battlefield encounters with a messenger pigeon.

"An unforgettable maelstrom of emotion and bloodshed, this is a plangent antiwar novel, call for sexual equality, celebration of animal intelligence, and tribute to altruism and courage." —*Booklist*

★ **Lillian** Boxfish takes a walk. Kathleen Rooney. St. Martin's Press, 2017. 304 p.

ISBN 9781250113320

1. City life 2. Social change 3. Octogenarians 4. Aging 5. Marriage 6. New York City 7. Manhattan, New York City 8. 20th century 9. 1980s 10. Historical fiction 11. Psychological fiction

Loan Stars Favourites, 2017; RUSA Reading List Short List, 2018

Embarking on a walk across Manhattan on New Year's Eve in 1984, eighty-five-year-old Lillian Boxfish recalls her long and eventful life, which included a brief reign as the highest-paid advertising woman in America, whose career was cut short by marriage and loss.

"Elegantly written, Rooney creates a glorious paean to a distant literary life and timeand an unabashed celebration of human connections that bridge the past and future." —*Publishers Weekly*

Rooney, Sally

★ **Beautiful** world, where are you. Sally Rooney. Farrar, Straus and Giroux, 2021. 240 p.

ISBN 9780374602604

1. Interpersonal relations 2. Sexual attraction 3. Breaking up (Interpersonal relations) 4. Friendship 5. Mental health 6. Literary fiction

LC 2021014281

Alice, a novelist, encounters Felix, who works in a warehouse, and asks him if he'd like to travel to Rome with her. In Dublin, her best friend Eileen is recovering from a break-up and starts flirting with Simon, a man she has known since childhood.

"Writing with her trademark truthfulness and wit, Rooney compels with both these meta-conversations and the actions of her characters' lives: their enthralling, intimate, and consequential grappling with themselves, with one another, with desire, and with the world." —*Booklist*

★ **Conversations** with friends. Sally Rooney. Hogarth Press, 2017. 309 p.

ISBN 9780451499059

1. Best friends 2. Women college students 3. Female friendship 4. Women journalists 5. Poets 6. Dublin, Ireland 7. Ireland 8. Psychological fiction 9. Mainstream fiction 10. First person narratives 11. Adult books for young adults

Shortlisted for the International Dublin Literary Award, 2019

Devoting herself to an intellectual life and the self-possessed lover with whom she performs spoken-word poetry readings, a college student is drawn into the lives of a sophisticated journalist and her husband before the increasingly intimate relationship tests the boundaries of her resolve.

Normal people: a novel. Sally Rooney. Hogarth Press, 2019. 272 pages

ISBN 9781984822178

1. Social classes 2. College students 3. First loves 4. Emotional abuse 5. Universities and colleges 6. Dublin, Ireland 7. Ireland 8. Literary fiction 9. Books to TV. 10. Multiple perspectives 11. Adult books for young adults

ALA Notable Book, 2020; Booklist Editors' Choice, 2019; Costa Novel Award, 2018; LibraryReads Favorites, 2019; New York Times

Notable Book, 2019; Longlisted for the Man Booker Prize, 2018; Longlisted for The Women's Prize for Fiction, 2019

The unconventional secret childhood bond between a popular boy and a lonely, intensely private girl is tested by character reversals in their first year at a Dublin college that render one introspective and the other social, but self-destructive.

Adapted into the Hulu series of the same name.

Originally published in hardcover in the United Kingdom by Faber & Faber, London, in 2018—Title page verso.

Roorbach, Bill

Life among giants: a novel. Bill Roorbach. Algonquin Books of Chapel Hill, 2012. 352 p.

ISBN 9781616200763

1. Children of murder victims 2. Murder investigation 3. Llewelyn ap Iorwerth 4. Women ballet dancers 5. Mansions 6. Connecticut 7. Mysteries 8. Adult books for young adults

LC 2012016965

A star quarterback and his sister spend decades trying to figure out who murdered their parents, uncovering the involvement and possible motives of a ballerina and her rock star husband who lived in a mansion across the street.

Roosevelt, Elliott

★ **Murder** and the First Lady. Elliott Roosevelt. St. Martin's Press, 1984. 227 p. (Eleanor Roosevelt mysteries, 1)

ISBN 9780312552800

1. Roosevelt, Eleanor 2. Women detectives 3. Presidents' spouses 4. Poisoning 5. Murder investigation 6. Washington, D.C. 7. 1930s 8. Historical mysteries 9. Cozy mysteries 10. Gentle reads

LC 83024659

First Lady Eleanor Roosevelt embarks on an undercover investigation into the White House murder of a crooked New Jersey congressman's son after her young British secretary becomes the prime suspect.

"This historical mystery is set just before World War II, when international tensions are at a peak. Philip Garber, a lowly bookkeeper and assistant to the chief usher at the White House, is found murdered. Eleanor Roosevelt turns sleuth when it's discovered that Garber was found dead in the room of her British secretary, Pamela Rush-Hodgeborne." —*Booklist*

Murder at midnight. Elliott Roosevelt. St. Martin's Press, 1997. 216 p. (Eleanor Roosevelt mysteries, 16)

ISBN 9780312965549

1. Roosevelt, Eleanor 2. Women detectives 3. Presidents' spouses 4. Murder investigation 5. Sadists 6. Sadism 7. Washington, D.C. 8. Historical mysteries 9. Cozy mysteries 10. Gentle reads

LC 96-53530

"Judge Horace Blackwell, friend and adviser to the president, is stabbed to death in his White House suite, and Sara Carter, a black maid, is arrested after finding the body. After promising the girl a fair hearing and gaining the confidence of lead investigator Lawrence Pickering, Eleanor takes an active role. Her doubts about Sara's guilt lead to some disturbing discoveries, not least of which is that the judge appears to have been a sadistic womanizer.... Peopled with famous lights of 1933, including Babe Ruth, William Faulkner and Gertrude Stein, Washington, D.C. is bought to life in the mirror of the White House." —*Publishers Weekly*

Murder in the map room: an Eleanor Roosevelt mystery. Elliott Roosevelt. St. Martin's Press, 1998. 251 p. (Eleanor Roosevelt mysteries, 17)

ISBN 9780312181680

1. Roosevelt, Eleanor 2. Presidents' spouses 3. Women detectives 4. Murder investigation 5. Shoe sellers 6. Chinese in Washington, D.C. 7. Washington, D.C. 8. Second World War era (1939-1945) 9. Historical mysteries 10. Cozy mysteries 11. Gentle reads

LC 97-37243

In 1943, First Lady Eleanor Roosevelt finds herself becoming immersed in the dark world of opium trading when, during a visit from Madame Chiang Kai-Shek, a Chinese shoe salesman is found murdered in the White House map room BT

"As usual, Elliot Roosevelt's respectfully playful portrayal of his down-to-earth mother as a clever sleuth is enough to keep the pages turning." —*Booklist*

Murder in the Oval Office. Elliott Roosevelt. St. Martin's Press, 1989. 247 p. (Eleanor Roosevelt mysteries, 6)
ISBN 9780312022594

1. Roosevelt, Eleanor 2. Presidents' spouses 3. Women detectives 4. Murder investigation 5. Politicians 6. 1930s 7. Historical mysteries 8. Cozy mysteries 9. Gentle reads

LC 88018848

An apparent suicide in the Oval Office of the White House leaves a number of unanswered questions and a long list of people who wanted the victim dead, and Eleanor Roosevelt must once again investigate.

Rose, Heather

The **museum** of modern love. Heather Rose. Algonquin Books of Chapel Hill, 2018. 288 p.
ISBN 9781616208523

1. Abramovic, Marina 2. Composers 3. Creativity 4. Self-discovery 5. Roosevelt, Eleanor 6. Sick persons 7. Literary fiction 8. Australian fiction

NSW Premier's Literary Awards, Christina Stead Prize for Fiction, 2017; Stella Prize, 2017; Tasmania Book Prizes, Margaret Scott Prize, 2017

Arky Levin has reached a creative dead end. Guilty and restless after an unexpected separation from his wife, almost by chance he stumbles upon an art exhibit that will change his life. Based on a real piece of performance art, the installation that the fictional Arky Levin discovers is inexplicably powerful. Visitors to the Museum of Modern Art sit across a table from artist Marina Abramovic for as short or long a period of time as they choose. Although some go in skeptical, almost all leave moved. And the participants are not the only ones to find themselves changed by this unusual experience: Arky finds himself returning daily to watch others with Abramovic. As the performance unfolds over the course of 75 days, so too does Arky. As he bonds with other people drawn to the exhibit, he slowly starts to understand what might be missing in his life and what he must do.

"This captivating work explores the meaning of art in our lives and the ways in which it deepens our understanding of ourselves. As Hannah Rothschild did in The Improbability of Love, Australian author Rose also combines intriguing characters with a laser-sharp focus on art to produce a gem of a novel." —*Library Journal*

Originally published: Crows Nest, NSW : Allen & Unwin, 2016.

Rose, M. J.

★ **Cartier's** hope. M. J. Rose. Atria Books, 2020. 334 p.
ISBN 9781501173639

1. Women journalists 2. Women's role 3. Hope Diamond 4. Extortion 5. Intrigue 6. New York City 7. 1910s 8. Historical fiction

Determined to make her mark in Gilded Age New York, a woman journalist investigates rumors and curses swirling around Pierre Cartier's recently acquired Hope Diamond, before attracting the attention of the blackmailer behind her father's death.

"The narrative cleverly explores highlights of early 20-century history and heaps on plenty of intrigue. Rose irresistibly combines elements of mystery, romance, and historical events in this memorable novel." —*Publishers Weekly*

Tiffany blues: a novel. M.J. Rose. Atria Books, 2018. 336 p.
ISBN 9781501173592

1. Tiffany, Louis Comfort 2. Artists 3. Secrets 4. Artists' colonies 5. Women artists 6. Forbidden love 7. Long Island, New York 8. 1920s 9. Historical fiction 10. First person narratives

LC 2017058991

A candidate at Tiffany's Jazz Age artist colony navigates her attraction to her host's grandson and competes for a gallery spot before an unknown rival exposes her traumatic past.

Includes bibliographical references and index.

Rosen, Leonard J.

The **Kortelisy** escape. Leonard Rosen. The Permanent Press, 2018. 302 pages : Illustration
ISBN 9781579625429

1. Parolees 2. Magic tricks 3. Grandfather and granddaughter 4. Criminal evidence 5. Child custody 6. New England 7. Crime fiction 8. Literary fiction

LC 2018027960

After negotiating with prosecutors for an early prison release for testifying against his brother, Nate Larson takes in his orphaned teenage granddaughter, Grace, and starts a traveling magic show in New England.

"Distinctive characters, a tightly woven plot, and polished prose make this a winner." —*Publishers Weekly*

Rosen, Renee

Dollface: a novel of the roaring twenties. Renee Rosen. New American Library, 2013. 416 p.
ISBN 9780451419200

1. Young women 2. Organized crime 3. Murder 4. Flappers 5. Gangsters 6. Chicago, Illinois 7. 1920s 8. Historical fiction 9. Crime fiction

LC 2012051794

Touring the nightclubs of 1920s Chicago in the hopes of enjoying an exciting life, beautiful Vera captures the attentions of two high rollers who admit her into an underworld of jazz, gambling and bootleg bourbon before Vera discovers that they are actually mobsters from rival Beer Wars gangs.

Also released under the title A Living Doll.

The **social** graces. Renee Rosen. Berkley, 2021. 400 p.
ISBN 9781984802811

1. Belmont, Alva 2. Rich families 3. Socialites 4. Upper class 5. Social obligations 6. Elitism 7. New York City 8. Gilded Age (1865-1898) 9. Historical fiction 10. Biographical fiction

LC 2020040654

A tale spanning three decades and based on true events imagines the bitter rivalry between Gilded Age hostess Caroline Astor and family newcomer Alva Vanderbilt against a backdrop of the latter's rejection by the society that both would control.

"Rosen (Park Avenue Summer) paints a vivid and ravishing picture of the Gilded Age, bringing to life some of the people and parties that rocked this particular era, in an altogether believable tale." —*Library Journal*

Rosenfelt, David

Black and blue: a Doug Brock thriller. David Rosenfelt. Minotaur Books, 2019. 290 p. (Doug Brock novels, 3)

ISBN 9781250133144

1. Men with amnesia 2. Cold cases (Criminal investigation) 3. Murder suspects 4. Murder investigation 5. Police 6. New Jersey 7. Thrillers and suspense

LC 2018050881

Struggling with amnesia after surviving a shooting, Doug Brock reinvestigates a cold case involving the DNA of a man he eliminated as a suspect, but can no longer remember.

"Dead ends and red herrings abound as the action builds to a jaw-dropping reveal. Rosenfelt knocks it out of the park with this fiendishly twisty serial killer thriller." —*Publishers Weekly*

Blackout. David Rosenfelt. St. Martin's Press, 2016. 304 p. (Doug Brock novels, 1)

ISBN 9781250055316

1. Police 2. Amnesia 3. Terrorism — Prevention 4. Terrorists 5. Gunshot wounds 6. New Jersey 7. Thrillers and suspense

In the next thrilling standalone from David Rosenfelt, policeman Doug Brock races against the clock to recover his memory after a gunshot to the head before a terror plot can be put into action.

★ **Dog** eat dog. David Rosenfelt. Minotaur Books, 2021. 304 p. (Andy Carpenter novels, 23)

ISBN 9781250257123

1. Lawyers 2. Men and dogs 3. Animal welfare 4. Husband and wife 5. Murder suspects 6. New Jersey 7. Maine 8. Mysteries

LC 2021008171

Lawyer Andy Carpenter and his golden retriever, Tara, work to free a man who risked it all to help a dog in need

"Unpredictable yet credible plot twists, along with Andy's dry sense of humor and wit, keep the pages turning." —*Publishers Weekly*

Rosenfield, Kat

No one will miss her. Kat Rosenfield. William Morrow & Company, 2021. 304 p.

ISBN 9780063057012

1. Small towns 2. State police 3. Married women 4. Pariahs 5. Women murder victims 6. Maine 7. Boston, Massachusetts 8. Psychological suspense

When the town pariah Lizzie Oullette is found dead, with her husband missing, Detective Ian Bird discovers a link to a social media influencer and wife of a disgraced billionaire who had a relationship with Lizzie that cut across class boundaries—and ultimately became deadly.

"The superb character-driven plot delivers an astonishing, believable jolt. Rosenfield shines a searing light on issues of classism, jealousy, and squandered potential." —*Publishers Weekly*

Roslund, Anders

Cell 8. Anders Roslund and Borge Hellstrom; translated from the original Swedish by Kari Dickson. SilverOak, 2012. 370 p; (Ewert Grens thrillers, 3)

ISBN 9781402787157

1. Murderers 2. Criminal evidence 3. Detectives 4. Capital punishment 5. Death row prisoners 6. Sweden 7. Ohio 8. Thrillers and suspense 9. Translations 10. Scandinavian crime fiction

Six years after a seventeen-year-old death-row inmate dies unexpectedly of heart disease, his case is disturbingly linked to that of a man using a false identity who has been arrested for attacking a fellow ferry passenger.

Originally published as Edward Finnigans upprattelse, Stockholm : Piratforlaget, 2006.

Translated from the Swedish.

★ **Knock** knock. Anders Roslund. G.P. Putnam's Sons, 2021. 448 p. (Ewert Grens thrillers, 8)

ISBN 9780593188217

1. Detectives 2. Investigations 3. Witnesses — Protection 4. Cold cases (Criminal investigation) 5. Police 6. Sweden 7. Police procedurals 8. Thrillers and suspense 9. Scandinavian crime fiction

Tells the story of a police inspector and a former criminal informant in a race against time as they attempt to unravel past and present secrets.

"This terrific mash-up of police procedural and crime thriller has strongly imagined characters, explosive action, and a twisty plot with an unexpected conclusion. It's a must for Scandinavian noir fans." —*Publishers Weekly*

Translation of: Jamahonleva.

Originally published: Stockholm : Albert Bonniers Forlag, 2019.

Translated from the Swedish.

Pen 33. Anders Roslund & Borge Hellstrom; translated by Elizabeth Clark Wessel. Quercus, 2017. 311 pages (Ewert Grens thrillers, 1)

ISBN 9781681440132

1. Escaped convicts 2. Vigilantes 3. Child murder investigation 4. Detectives 5. Pedophiles 6. Sweden 7. Mysteries 8. Translations 9. Scandinavian crime fiction

The murderer of two children escapes from prison. Another child is murdered in the nearby town of Strengnas. The father of the murdered child decides he must take revenge. Anger spreads across the whole country and the case is assigned to two detectives. This novel is an exploration of what can happen when we take the law into our own hands.

Originally published in Swedish: Sweden : Piratforlaget, 2004.

First published in English under the title The Beast; Great Britain: Little, Brown, 2005. Translated by Anna Paterson.

This translation first published: 2016.

Rosnay, Tatiana de

★ **Flowers** of darkness. Tatiana de Rosnay. St. Martin's Press, 2021. 240 p.

ISBN 9781250272553

1. Women authors 2. Apartment houses 3. High technology 4. Divorce 5. Betrayal 6. Paris, France 7. Literary fiction 8. Dystopian fiction

LC 2020040117

Moving into an ultra-modern artist residency in scenic Paris, a novelist seeking tranquility in the aftermath of a divorce begins experiencing ominous trepidation about the apartment building and the true agenda of those behind its creation.

"Nearly plotless, this sensitive examination of relationships and the nature of privacy will appeal mainly to readers of literary fiction." —*Publishers Weekly*

★ **Sarah's** key. Tatiana de Rosnay. St. Martin's Press, 2007. 288 p.

ISBN 9780312370831

1. World War II 2. Family secrets 3. Women journalists 4. Americans in France 5. Antisemitism 6. France 7. Paris, France 8. Psychological fiction 9. Historical fiction 10. Parallel narratives

LC 2007010080

On the sixtieth anniversary of the 1942 roundup of Jews by the French police in the Vel d'Hiv section of Paris, American journalist Julia Jarmond is asked to write an article on this dark episode during World War

II and embarks on investigation that leads her to long-hidden family secrets and to the ordeal of Sarah, a young girl caught up in the raid.

First published in the United States of America in 2007.

Rosner, Jennifer

★ The **yellow** bird sings. Jennifer Rosner. Flatiron Books, 2020. 224 p.
ISBN 9781250179760
1. Jews 2. Mothers and daughters 3. Girl prodigies 4. Hiding 5. Persecution by Nazis 6. Poland 7. Second World War era (1939-1945) 8. Historical fiction

LC 2019045279

A mother who goes into hiding when Nazis begin arresting Jewish citizens in Poland considers an impossible choice while struggling to keep her 5-year-old daughter, a musical prodigy, from being overheard.

"This stunning debut novel sings with the power of a mother's love and the heartbreaking risks she'll endure." —*Booklist*

Ross, Adam

Mr. Peanut. By Adam Ross. Alfred A. Knopf, 2010. 304 p.
ISBN 9780307270702
1. Married people 2. Marital conflict 3. Murder investigation 4. Crimes against women 5. Widowers 6. Mysteries

LC 2009041693

New York Times Notable Book, 2010

Having imagined his beloved wife's death in many ways (you name it, he probably thought of it), video game designer David is eventually charged with killing her after she dies from anaphylactic shock. But the New York investigators dealing with David have their own experiences with marital problems and murder.

"Ross is a sorcerer with words, whose David Foster Wallace-like descriptive powers have given him the ability to conjure everything from a pretty Hawaiian beachscape to the slow-motion horror of a car accident with color and lan." —*New York Times*

Ross, Ann B.

Miss Julia delivers the goods: a novel. Ann B. Ross. Viking, 2009. 352 p. (Miss Julia series, 10)
ISBN 9780670020652
1. Conflict resolution 2. Pregnant women 3. Archives 4. Robbery 5. Springer, Julia (Fictitious character) 6. North Carolina 7. Cozy mysteries 8. Gentle reads

LC 2008045609

Miss Julia reckons Mr. J.D. Pickens is the key to solving all of Hazel Marie's problems, especially the female kind. But how can Miss Julia coax the savvy PI back to town—and back into the arms of her 40-something friend Hazel Marie?

★ **Miss** Julia happily ever after. Ann B. Ross. Viking, 2021. 336 p. (Miss Julia series, 23)
ISBN 9780593296462
1. Weddings 2. Female friendship 3. Wedding planning 4. Marriage proposals 5. Life change events 6. North Carolina 7. Cozy mysteries 8. Gentle reads

LC 2020045756

Wedding fever hits Abbotsville and several of Miss Julia's friends have plans to tie the knot. But, as usual, nothing is so simple.

"The final entry in the beloved series has a few unfortunate elements—a side story about an octogenarian proposing marriage to a teenage girl and a bizarre plotline about a streaker terrorizing Miss Julia and her friends late at night—though the elements come together in the end.

But Miss Julia is still Miss Julia, which may be all that longtime fans of the series require."—*Booklist*

Series complete in 23 volumes.

Miss Julia knows a thing or two. Ann B. Ross. Penguin Group USA 2020. 288 p. (Miss Julia series, 22)
ISBN 9780525560555
1. Strangers 2. Grandchildren 3. Sick persons 4. Helpfulness in women 5. Female friendship 6. North Carolina 7. Cozy mysteries 8. Gentle reads

LC 2019046072

Miss Julia's efforts to help a friend escape unemployment are complicated by her husband's mysterious illness and the abrupt appearance of a suspicious grandchild she has never met on her doorstep.

"Written with Ross's signature Southern charm and wit, the newest Miss Julia will delight long-time fans of the series and will entice new readers to get to know her." —*Booklist*

Miss Julia takes the wheel. Ann B. Ross. Viking, 2019. 320 pages (Miss Julia series, 21)
ISBN 9780525560487
1. Physicians 2. Small town life 3. Women amateur detectives 4. Funeral homes 5. Female friendship 6. North Carolina 7. Cozy mysteries 8. Gentle reads

LC 2018051406

Miss Julia's efforts to understand mysteries surrounding an unscrupulous new doctor and his painfully shy wife are complicated by Lloyd's first car and a newly divorced LuAnne's makeover in accordance with a new funeral home job.

Miss Julia throws a wedding. Ann B. Ross. Viking, 2002. 308 p; (Miss Julia series, 3)
ISBN 9780670031054
1. Sheriffs 2. Women lawyers 3. Weddings 4. Widows 5. Small town life 6. North Carolina 7. Cozy mysteries 8. Gentle reads

LC 2001056798

Septuagenarian Julia Springer is back. This time out, Sheriff Coleman Bates and busy attorney Binkie Enloe's casual announcement that they plan to get married spurs Miss Julia, the only person in Abbotsville who knows or cares how things should be done, into action. She's determined to put together a proper and dignified wedding but faces many hurdles, people being what they are. Will Miss Julia be able to pull this wedding off?

"The inimitable Miss Julia pushes an indecisive couple toward matrimong in this Southern comedy-of-manners,...which begins with the protagonist frustrated at the inability of her friend, Miss Hazel, to get her beau to propose. But another opportunity surfaces when Sheriff Coleman Bates proposes to his lawyer girlfriend Binkie Enloe.... Ross gets a bit carried away with wedding details, but her cheeky style works flawlessly once Miss Julia digs into the romantic intrigue and begins to ply her unique combination of common sense and old-fashioned, smalltown wisdom." —*Publishers Weekly*

Rossner, Rena

The **light** of the midnight stars. Rena Rossner. Orbit, 2021. 432 p.
ISBN 9780316483469
1. Rabbis 2. Fathers and daughters 3. Jewish teenage girls 4. Sisters 5. Magic 6. Hungary 7. Historical fantasy 8. Multiple perspectives

Deep in the Hungarian woods, the sacred magic of King Solomon lives on in his descendants. Gathering under the midnight stars, they perform small miracles and none are more gifted than the great Rabbi Isaac and his three daughters. Hannah, bookish and calm, can coax plants to grow even when the weather is bitterly cold. Sarah, defiant and strong, can control the impulsive nature of fire. And Levana, the fey one, can read the path of the stars to decipher their secrets. But darkness is creeping across Europe, threatening the lives of every Jewish person in every village. Each sister will have to make an impossible choice in an effort to survive—and change the fate of their family forever.

"Highly recommended for lovers of Naomi Novik's Spinning Silver and her 'Scholomance' series, as well as readers who enjoy their fantasy steeped in myths from infrequently represented people and places." —*Library Journal*

Roth, Henry

★ **Call** it sleep. Henry Roth; with an introduction by Alfred Kazin and an afterword by Hana Wirth-Nesher. Picador, 2005. 462 p.
ISBN 9780312424121
1. Immigrants, Jewish 2. Jewish way of life 3. Jewish American boys 4. Slums 5. Jewish families 6. Lower East Side, New York City 7. 1910s 8. Coming-of-age stories 9. Modern classics

An imaginative young boy, David Schearl grows up and comes of age in a candid portrayal of Jewish life in the immigrant tenements of New York, in a novel first published in 1934.
Originally published: 1934.

A **diving** rock on the Hudson. Henry Roth. St. Martin's Press, 1995. 418 p. (Mercy of a rude stream, 2)
ISBN 9780312140854
1. Jewish American teenage boys 2. Immigrant families 3. Teenage boys — Psychology 4. Shame 5. Self-hate (Psychology) 6. 1920s 7. Coming-of-age stories

"Simultaneously, we are inside the mind of a troubled adolescent and that of an aged but still mentally vital man, a man engaged with words, with concepts, obsessively reconsidering the role of the artist and in particular his own responsibility in portraying events truthfully." —*Booklist*
Includes glossary of Yiddish and Hebrew words and phrases.

From bondage. Henry Roth. St. Martin's Press, 1996. 397 p. (Mercy of a rude stream, 3)
ISBN 9780312143411
1. Jewish American men 2. Men — Psychology 3. Immigrant families 4. Creativity 5. Shame 6. New York City 7. 1920s 8. Coming-of-age stories
National Book Critics Circle Award for Fiction finalist, 1996

"This third volume of Roth's autobiographical cycle continues the story of Ira Stigman, son of East European Jewish immigrant parents and now college aged, as he struggles to find his way in 1920s New York. But, like the previous volumes, it is also the story of Ira the octogenarian writer who, nearing the end of his life, is trying to come to terms with both the forces and the choices that shaped it. Paralleling Roth's own experience, this volume focuses on the beginnings of what was to become a decade-long affair between Ira and NYU professor Edith Welles." —*Library Journal*
Includes glossary of Yiddish and Hebrew words and phrases.

Requiem for Harlem. Henry Roth. St. Martin's Press, 1998. 291 p. (Mercy of a rude stream, 4)
ISBN 9780312169800
1. Jewish American men 2. College students 3. Immigrant families 4. Young men — Relations with older women 5. Young men — Family relationships 6. Harlem, New York City 7. New York City 8. 1920s 9. Coming-of-age stories
LC 9717824

"Even as we see the older writer commenting ruefully on all that has come to pass, we see the young artist taking in every detail of the world.... And if it is hard to sympathize with either the egocentric youth or the rue-

ful old man, taken together they meld into a living whole. This is Roth's achievement, this double vision of the artist as both young and old man, hungry and regretful, flawed and penitent." —*New York Times Book Review*
Includes a glossary of Yiddish and Hebrew words and phrases.

A **star** shines over Mt. Morris Park. Henry Roth. St. Martin's Press, 1994. 290 p. (Mercy of a rude stream, 1)
ISBN 9780312104993
1. Jewish American boys 2. Immigrant families 3. Identity (Psychology) 4. Jewish Americans 5. Antisemitism 6. Harlem, New York City 7. 1910s 8. Coming-of-age stories
LC 93037270

"Mr. Roth remains an admirable craftsman, and the scenes of immigrant life in the second decade of the century are evoked with persuasive concreteness." —*New York Times Book Review*

Roth, Joseph

The **collected** stories of Joseph Roth. Translated from the German with an introduction by Michael Hofmann. W. W. Norton, 2002. 281 p.
ISBN 9780393043204
1. Short stories 2. Translations
LC 2001044747

"Combining a shrewd reportorial eye with a taste for the fantastic and droll, Roth portrays characters living materially and spiritually impoverished lives in isolated Eastern European villages and those left homeless in their own homes in the tumultuous aftermath of World War I." —*Booklist*
Seventeen short stories.

Roth, Philip

★ **American** pastoral. Philip Roth. Houghton Mifflin, 1997. 423 p. (Zuckerman novels, 6)
ISBN 9780395860212
1. Roth, Philip 2. Women fugitives 3. Fathers and daughters 4. American dream 5. Jewish American families 6. Bombings 7. Newark, New Jersey 8. 1960s 9. Literary fiction 10. Autobiographical fiction 11. First person narratives
LC 9649368
Library Journal Best Books, 1997; Pulitzer Prize for Fiction, 1998; National Book Critics Circle Award for Fiction finalist, 1997

A former athletic star, devoted family man, and owner of a thriving glove factory, Seymour "Swede" Levov finds his life coming apart during the social disorder of the 1960s, when his beloved daughter turns revolutionary terrorist out to destroy her father's world BT

"This cultural horror story is deepened by Roth's genius for blending humor, pathos, sympathy and rage.... You will search the shelf of contemporary fiction long and hard to find a parental nightmare projected with the emotional force and verbal energy that Roth brings to American Pastoral." —*Time*
Film under the same title released in 2016.

★ The **anatomy** lesson. Philip Roth. Vintage International, 1996. 291 p. (Zuckerman novels, 3)
ISBN 9780679749028
1. Roth, Philip 2. Jewish American authors 3. Pain 4. Family relationships 5. Self-discovery in men 6. Middle-aged men 7. 1970s 8. Humorous stories 9. Literary fiction 10. Psychological fiction
National Book Critics Circle Award for Fiction finalist, 1983; National Book Award for Fiction finalist, 1984

In 1973, Nathan Zuckerman, a writer who has lost the ability to create, attempts to console himself with women as he decides to abandon writing and become a doctor BT

"A ferocious, heartfelt book.... One might venture to say that, like a goodly number of Roth's previous works, 'The Anatomy Lesson' revolves around the paradox of incarnation—the astonishing coexistence in one life of infantilism and intelligence, of selfishness and altruism, of sexual appetite and social conscience—and has the form and manner of a monologue conducted under psychoanalysis." —*The New Yorker*

Originally published: New York : Farrar, Straus, and Giroux, 1983.

★ **Everyman**. Philip Roth. Houghton Mifflin, 2006. 162 p.
ISBN 9780618735167
1. Roth, Philip 2. Aging 3. Mortality 4. Senior men 5. Jewish American men 6. Brothers 7. Newark, New Jersey 8. Psychological fiction 9. Literary fiction 10. Autobiographical fiction

LC 2005031538

PEN-Faulkner Award, 2007; New York Times Notable Book, 2006

"From a distance, Everyman looks like a shaggy dog story—a long, quotidian story whose meaning resides in its final pointlessness. Up close, though, it is a parable that captures, as few works of fiction have, the pathos of Being, as it's manifested even in the favored precincts of affluent America." —*Washington Post Book World*.

Exit ghost. Philip Roth. Houghton Mifflin, 2007. 304 p. (Zuckerman novels, 9)
ISBN 9780618915477
1. Roth, Philip 2. Jewish American authors 3. Self-fulfillment in men 4. Aging 5. Jewish American men — Identity 6. Senior men — Sexuality 7. New York City 8. Psychological fiction 9. Literary fiction 10. Autobiographical fiction

LC 2006102467

Booklist Editors' Choice, 2007; New York Times Notable Book, 2007

After eleven years of solitude working on his New England mountain as a writer, Nathan Zuckerman returns to New York to confront a turbulent city in the wake of September 11, as well as the aging Amy Bellette, one-time muse to his first literary hero, E.I. Lonoff.

"Mr. Roth has created a melancholy, if occasionally funny, meditation on aging, mortality, loneliness and the losses that come with the passage of time.... For fans of the Zuckerman books, it provides a poignant coda to Nathan's story, putting a punctuation point to his journey from youthful idealism and passion through midlife confusion and angst toward elderly renunciation." —*New York Times*

The **ghost** writer. Philip Roth. Vintage Books, 1995. 179 p. (Zuckerman novels, 1)
ISBN 9780679748984
1. Roth, Philip 2. Jewish American authors 3. Writing 4. Self-discovery in men 5. Jewish American men — Identity 6. Role models 7. Berkshire Hills, Massachusetts 8. 1950s 9. Humorous stories 10. Literary fiction 11. Autobiographical fiction
National Book Award for Fiction finalist, 1980; National Book Critics Circle Award for Fiction finalist, 1979; Pulitzer Prize for Fiction finalist, 1980

A young writer in search of a spiritual father, Nathan Zuckerman views E. I. Lonoff, who lives with his wife and his student-mistress in rural Massachusetts, as an embodiment of the ideal of artistic integrity and independence.

Originally published: New York : Farrar Straus Giroux, 1979.

★ **Goodbye**, Columbus, and five short stories. Philip Roth. Modern Library, 1995. Xii, 298 p.
ISBN 9780679601593
1. Jewish American men — Identity 2. Assimilation (Sociology) 3. Social classes 4. Identity (Psychology) 5. Self-discovery in men

6. United States 7. 1950s 8. Literary fiction 9. Short stories 10. Books to movies
National Book Award for Fiction, 1960

The contemporary writer provides insight into varied aspects of Jewish-American life.

"The title story in this collection is about a young Radcliffe girl and a Rutgers boy who learn that there is more to love than exuberance and passion. All of the stories dramatize the dilemma of modern American Jews, torn between two worlds." —*Publishers Weekly*

Goodbye, Columbus was adapted to a film of the same name (1969).
Originally published: Boston : Houghton Mifflin, 1959.

The **great** American novel. Philip Roth. Vintage Books, 1995. 400 p.
ISBN 9780679749066
1. Baseball players 2. Baseball teams 3. Scandals 4. Baseball 5. Humorous stories 6. Picaresque fiction 7. Literary fiction

LC 94041584

A third major baseball league tries to survive, but World War II decimates it by 1943.
Originally published: New York : Holt, Rinehart and Winston, 1973.

★ The **human** stain. Philip Roth. Houghton Mifflin, 2000. 361 p. (Zuckerman novels, 8)
ISBN 9780618059454
1. Shakespeare, William 2. African Americans — Identity 3. Passing (Identity) 4. Scandals 5. Prejudice 6. African American men 7. New England 8. United States 9. 1990s 10. Psychological fiction 11. Literary fiction 12. Autobiographical fiction

LC 99089867

National Jewish Book Award for Fiction, 2000; PEN-Faulkner Award, 2001

A college professor with a sexual indiscretion in his past is hounded from his job by academic enemies who label him a racist BT

"Roth is clearly enjoying himself. The Human Stain is as fresh, as angry and as bitterly amused as his early fiction. It vibrates with mockery, disapproval, poetry, and a healthy dose of personal vindictiveness that one would be tempted to dismiss as unworthy if it weren't so funny." —*The New Leader*

I married a Communist. Philip Roth. Houghton Mifflin, 1998. 323 p. (Zuckerman novels, 7)
ISBN 9780395933466
1. Roth, Philip 2. McCarthyism 3. Communists 4. Betrayal 5. Husband and wife 6. Jewish American men — Identity 7. Newark, New Jersey 8. 1940s 9. Domestic fiction 10. Literary fiction 11. Autobiographical fiction

LC 9816797

ALA Notable Book, 1999; Booklist Editors' Choice, 1998; New York Times Notable Book, 1998; Shortlisted for the International IMPAC Dublin Literary Award, 2000

During the McCarthy era, a wife revenges herself on her husband by denouncing him as a Communist. It happens to Iron Rinn, a radio commentator, after he told her he did not want her daughter in the house.

"What Zuckerman/Roth does with this imagined material is constantly mesmerizing. Library shelves groan under the weight of books published about the witch hunts and blacklistings during the Truman and Eisenhower presidencies, but it would be hard to find one among them that presents as nuanced, as humanly complex an account of those years as I Married a Communist." —*Time*

Indignation. Philip Roth. Houghton Mifflin Company, 2008. 256 p.
ISBN 9780547054841
1. Self-fulfillment in men 2. Interclass romance 3. Interpersonal conflict 4. First loves 5. College students 6. Ohio 7. New Jersey 8. 1950s 9. Coming-of-age stories 10. Literary fiction

LC 2008011431

Booklist Editors' Choice, 2008; Library Journal Best Books, 2008; New York Times Notable Book, 2008

In 1951 America, during the second year of the Korean War, Marcus Messner, a studious young man from Newark, New Jersey, escapes his butcher father's fears about the potential dangers facing his beloved son, by attending college at Ohio's pastoral, conservative Winesburg College, where he confronts the confusing customs and constrictions of a different world.

"We are back in nineteen-fifties Newark, and nineteen-year-old Marcus Messner, the son of a kosher butcher, attempts to escape his father's stifling influence by enrolling at a college in Ohio farm country. Messner is a scholarly type, while his new classmates are an unfriendly bunch of churchgoing, beer-swilling louts. Stubbornly disregarding overtures of friendship from members of the school's only Jewish fraternity, Messner devotes his attentions to a troubled Gentile named Olivia Hutton. There's something of Portnoy in the masturbation-filled high jinks that follow, but Messner, fearful that he might wind up a rifleman in Korea, is a far darker creation." —*The New Yorker*

★ **Nemesis**. Philip Roth. Houghton Mifflin Harcourt, 2010. 304 p.
ISBN 9780547318356
1. Young men — Personal conduct 2. Poliomyelitis 3. Epidemics 4. Playgrounds 5. Newark, New Jersey 6. New Jersey 7. 1940s 8. Historical fiction
Booklist Editors' Choice, 2010
In 1944 Newark, devoted playground director Bucky Cantor, sidelined from the war due to his poor eyesight, watches in horror as the city's polio epidemic begins to ravage the children on his playground.

★ The **plot** against America. Philip Roth. Houghton Mifflin Co, 2004. 400 p.
ISBN 9780618509287
1. Lindbergh, Charles A. 2. Presidential election, 1940 3. Antisemitism 4. Isolationism 5. Jewish Americans 6. Jewish American families 7. Newark, New Jersey 8. 1940s 9. Alternate histories 10. Political fiction 11. Literary fiction 12. Adult books for young adults
LC 2004047490
ALA Notable Book, 2005; Booklist Editors' Choice, 2004; James Fenimore Cooper Prize, 2005; New York Times Notable Book, 2004; School Library Journal Best Books: Best Adult Books 4 Teens, 2004; Sidewise Awards for Alternate History, 2004; National Book Critics Circle Award for Fiction finalist, 2004
In a novel of alternative history, aviation hero and isolationist Charles A. Lindbergh defeats Franklin Roosevelt in the 1940 presidential election, negotiating a cordial accord with Adolf Hitler, accepting his conquest of Europe and anti-Semitic policies, and igniting a storm of fear for Jewish families throughout America.
"The novel is sinister, vivid, dreamlike, preposterous and, at the same time, creepily plausible." —*New York Times Book Review*

★ **Portnoy's** complaint. Philip Roth. Vintage International, 1994. 289 p.
ISBN 9780679756453
1. Jewish American men 2. Masturbation 3. Compulsive behavior in men 4. Family relationships 5. Expectation (Psychology) 6. 1940s 7. 1950s 8. Picaresque fiction 9. Literary fiction 10. Books to movies
A New York lawyer, dominated by a demanding Jewish mother, plays out a sexual revenge in fact and fantasy BT
Originally published: New York : Random House, 1969.

Sabbath's theater. Philip Roth. Houghton Mifflin, 1995. 451 p.
ISBN 9780395739822

1. Senior men — Sexuality 2. Compulsive behavior in men 3. Aging 4. Man-woman relationships 5. Reminiscing in old age 6. Humorous stories 7. Literary fiction
LC 95000914
Booklist Editors' Choice, 1995; Library Journal Best Books, 1995; National Book Award for Fiction, 1995; Pulitzer Prize for Fiction finalist, 1996
The death of his mistress sends Mickey Sabbath, an audacious libertine and onetime puppeteer, on a psychic journey into his past.
"There is plenty of the nasty in this virtuoso performance by our best literary stand-up comic.... The verbal play is almost tactile, like slaps, as the narrative moves from third-person comic to first-person perverse confession, but there is a polemical energy that lifts it beyond verbal playfulness; at times the message is painful." —*New York Times Book Review*

Zuckerman bound. Philip Roth. Farrar, Straus and Giroux, 1985. 784 p. (Zuckerman novels)
ISBN 9780374299439
1. Roth, Philip 2. Jewish American authors 3. Writing 4. Self-discovery in men 5. Jewish American men — Identity 6. Artists — Social responsibility 7. Humorous stories 8. Psychological fiction 9. Literary fiction
LC 84023265
A new novella, "The Prague Orgy," takes Nathan Zuckerman to Prague to rescue the stories of an unknown Yiddish writer from oblivion and also forms a startling epilogue to "The Ghost Writer," "Zuckerman Unbound," and "The Anatomy Lesson," all included in this volume BT
Collects the Zuckerman trilogy and its epilogue: The Ghost Writer, Zuckerman Unbound, The Anatomy Lesson, and The Prague Orgy.

Zuckerman unbound. Philip Roth. Vintage International, 1995. 225 p. (Zuckerman novels, 2)
ISBN 9780679748991
1. Roth, Philip 2. Jewish American authors 3. Family relationships 4. Self-discovery in men 5. Writing 6. Fame 7. Marks, Grace 8. Humorous stories 9. Literary fiction 10. Autobiographical fiction
"After three marriages and a respected body of fiction, Nathan Zuckerman has suddenly struck free with the scandalous and subversive success of a book about a Portnoyish complainer called Carnovsky. The promising apprentice of The Ghost Writer who engaged in biographical fantasy, has himself become a creature of public fantasy who cannot cope comfortably even with material success. The consequences range from bizarre comedy (the plague of a ruined quiz show contestant who claims his life has been plagiarized) to the distortion of family relations." —*Library Journal*
Originally published: New York : Farrar, Straus, Giroux, 1981.

Rothfuss, Patrick

★ The **name** of the wind. Patrick Rothfuss. DAW, 2007. 896 p. (Kingkiller chronicles, 1)
ISBN 9780756404079
1. Wizards 2. Magic 3. Demons 4. Quests 5. Loss (Psychology) 6. Epic fantasy 7. Adult books for young adults
Alex Award, 2008; Romantic Times Reviewers' Choice Award, 2007; RUSA Reading List, 2008
A hero named Kvothe, now living under an assumed name as the humble proprietor of an inn, recounts his transformation from a magically gifted young man into the most notorious wizard, musician, thief, and assassin in his world.

★ The **wise** man's fear. Patrick Rothfuss. DAW Books, 2011. 1008 p. (Kingkiller chronicles, 2)
ISBN 9780756404734

1. Heroes and heroines 2. Magicians 3. Fairies 4. Mercenaries 5. Quests 6. Epic fantasy 7. Adult books for young adults

Kvothe takes his first steps on the path of the hero as he attempts to uncover the truth about the mysterious Amyr, the Chandrian, and the death of his parents. Along the way, Kvothe is put on trial by the legendary Adem mercenaries, forced to reclaim the honor of the Edema Ruh, and travels into the Fae realm where he meets Felurian, the faerie woman no man can resist.

"This breathtakingly epic story is heartrending in its intimacy and masterful in its narrative essence, and will leave fans waiting on tenter-hooks for the final installment." —*Publishers Weekly*

Sequel to: The name of the wind.

Rothschild, Hannah

The **improbability** of love: a novel. Hannah Rothschild. Knopf, 2015. 416 p.
ISBN 9781101874141
1. Single women 2. Painting — Collectors and collecting 3. Art dealers 4. Concentration camp survivors 5. Man-woman relationships 6. Literary fiction 7. Satirical fiction

LC 2014047753

LibraryReads Favorites, 2015; Shortlisted for the Baileys Women's Prize for Fiction, 2016; Longlisted for the Baileys Women's Prize for Fiction, 2016

Annie McMorrow, 31 and not recovered from the end of her long-term relationship, is an assistant to film producer Carlo Spinetti and then to his chilling wife Rebecca Winkleman Spinetti whose father started Winkleman Fine Art in Curzon St. Annie has spent her meagre savings on a dusty painting from a junk shop to give to her new, unsuitable, boyfriend who never shows up for his birthday dinner. The painting now hers, talks, but only to us. Shrewd, spoiled, charming, world weary and cynical, he comments perceptively on Annie, and the modern world and tells tales about his previous owners: Louis XV, Voltaire, Catherine the Great among others. The story unfolds through this voice and many others—unexpected, entertaining, and strangely authentic. Annie will have her apartment ransacked and be pursued by dealers, buyers and an auctioneer in an attempt to get back the painting. With The Improbability of Love, Rothschild has spun a dazzling tale—both irreverant and entertainng—of a many-layered, devious world where, in the end, love triumphs.

"For readers anticipating the next irresistible blend of art, mystery, and intrigue along the lines of Donna Tartt's The Goldfinch, the wait is over. This compulsively readable, immensely enjoyable novel will deeply satisfy that craving." —*Library Journal*

Includes bibliographical references and index.

Rouda, Kaira Sturdivant

Best day ever: a novel. Kaira Rouda. Graydon House Books, 2017. 342 p.
ISBN 9781525811401
1. Husband and wife 2. Marital conflict 3. Vacations 4. Secrets 5. Deception in men 6. Ohio 7. Psychological suspense 8. Thrillers and suspense 9. First person narratives

Paul Strom has the perfect life: a glittering career as an advertising executive, a beautiful wife, two healthy boys and a big house in a wealthy suburb. And he's the perfect husband: breadwinner, protector, provider. That's why he's planned a romantic weekend for his wife, Mia, at their lake house, just the two of them. And he's promised today will be the best day ever.

The **favorite** daughter. Kaira Rouda. Graydon House Books, 2019. 384 p.

ISBN 9781525835148
1. Grief in women 2. Mothers and daughters 3. Gated communities 4. Marital conflict 5. Daughters — Death 6. Orange County, California 7. California 8. Psychological suspense

Emerging from a year grieving the tragic death of her older daughter, a woman in a California oceanfront gated community observes the changes in her family while uncovering disturbing truths about her late daughter's final days.

Rous, Emma

The **perfect** guests. Emma Rous. Berkley, 2021. 304 p.
ISBN 9780593201602
1. Secrets 2. Young women 3. Actors and actresses 4. Murder parties 5. Teenage girls 6. Norfolk, England 7. 1980s 8. 2010s 9. Thrillers and suspense 10. Multiple perspectives 11. Gothic fiction

LC 2020018551

LibraryReads Favorites, 2021; Loan Stars Favourites, 2021

A twisty novel features a grand estate with many secrets, an orphan caught in a web of lies, and a young woman playing a sinister game.

"The reader must carefully shuffle the puzzle pieces into a perfect fit until the very end and one more visit to Raven Hall, when the entire board is undone. This is a party suspense fans are advised to crash." —*Booklist*

Row, Jess

Your face in mine: a novel. Jess Row. Penguin Group USA, 2014. 384 p.
ISBN 9781594488344
1. Male friendship 2. Surgery patients 3. Race relations 4. Identity (Psychology) 5. Belonging 6. Baltimore, Maryland 7. Literary fiction

LC 2013038938

A novel about a grieving man who reconnects with a high-school friend who has undergone racial reassignment surgery and finds their chance encounter has potentially devastating consequences for him.

"Row has outdone himself in a first novel that offers great quantities of food for thought and discussion involving, for starters, questions of race and identity. Plunging deeper than common notions of the self and racial distinctions, Row presents wholly credible, if not thoroughly trustworthy, characters and complicated circumstances that will inspire serious reflection." —*Booklist*

Rowell, Rainbow

Landline. Rainbow Rowell. St Martin's Press, 2014. 320 p.
ISBN 9781250049377
1. Magic telephones 2. Marital conflict 3. Women television writers 4. Families 5. Christmas 6. Los Angeles, California 7. Nebraska 8. Relationship fiction

Goodreads Choice Award, 2014; Library Journal Best Books 2014; LibraryReads Favorites, 2014

In New York Times bestselling author Rainbow Rowell's Landline, Georgie McCool knows her marriage is in trouble. That it's been in trouble for a long time. She still loves her husband, Neal, and Neal still loves her, deeply—but that almost seems besides the point now. Maybe that was always besides the point. Two days before they're supposed to visit Neal's family in Omaha for Christmas, Georgie tells Neal that she can't go. She's a TV writer, and something's come up on her show; she has to stay in Los Angeles. She knows that Neal will be upset with her—Neal is always a little upset with Georgie—but she doesn't expect to him to pack up the kids and go home without her. When her husband and the kids leave for the airport, Georgie wonders if she's finally done it. If she's ruined everything. That night, Georgie discovers a way to communicate with Neal in the past.

It's not time travel, not exactly, but she feels like she's been given an opportunity to fix her marriage before it starts. Is that what she's supposed to do? Or would Georgie and Neal be better off if their marriage never happened?

"Rowell knows romance writing and executes many conventions well: Christmastime setting, romantic triangle, and barriers to vital communication. Yet her tinkering with genre to explore love already in progress is the true gem." —*Booklist*

Rowland, Laura Joh

The **hangman's** secret. Laura Joh Rowland. Crooked Lane Books, 2019. 304 p. (Victorian mysteries (Laura Joh Rowland), 3)
ISBN 9781683319023
1. Women photographers 2. Women private investigators 3. Crime scenes 4. Private investigators 5. Murder 6. London, England 7. Victorian era (1837-1901) 8. 19th century 9. Victorian mysteries 10. Historical mysteries 11. First person narratives
From award-winning author Laura Joh Rowland, a story about the darkness that lurks within and the deadly secrets that beg to be revealed.

The **incense** game: a novel of feudal Japan. Laura Joh Rowland. Minotaur Books, 2012. 304 p. (Sano Ichiro mysteries, 16)
ISBN 9780312658533
1. Detectives 2. Murder investigation 3. Women murder victims 4. Shoguns 5. Murder 6. Japan 7. 18th century 8. Historical mysteries 9. Mysteries 10. Adult books for young adults
Romantic Times Reviewer's Choice Award, 2012
When the shogun's carefully regulated court is thrown into chaos by a massive earthquake in 1703 Japan, Sano Ichiro investigates the poisoning murders of a nobleman's daughters to prevent the regime's takeover.

The **iris** fan: a novel of feudal Japan. Laura Joh Rowland. Minotaur Books, 2014. 352 p. (Sano Ichiro mysteries, 18)
ISBN 9781250047069
1. Shoguns 2. Heirs and heiresses 3. Rulers 4. Sano, Ichiro (Fictitious character) 5. Samurai 6. Japan 7. Historical mysteries 8. Mysteries
LC 2014027065
In 1709 Japan, Sano Ichiro, dedicated to the samurai code of honor, is restored to the rank of chief investigator when the shogun is stabbed with a fan made of painted silk with sharp-pointed iron ribs—a case that, if the shogun's heir is displeased with the outcome, will result in his death.

"Rowland's 18th and final mystery set in feudal Japan showcases the series' strengths and weaknesses.... Rowland offers the usual high-stakes suspense, convincing period detail, and nuanced characters you care about. Readers will be sorry to see the last of Sano." —*Publishers Weekly*

The **Ripper's** shadow. Laura Joh Rowland. Crooked Lane Books, 2017. 358 pages (Victorian mysteries (Laura Joh Rowland), 1)
ISBN 9781683310051
1. Jack 2. Women photographers 3. Women murder victims 4. Prostitutes 5. Erotic photographs 6. Sex crimes 7. London, England 8. Victorian era (1837-1901) 9. Victorian mysteries 10. Historical mysteries
Supplementing her meager income by shooting illicit "boudoir photographs" of the local ladies of the night, photographer Miss Sara Bain and her motley crew of friends are embroiled in the crime of the century when two of her clients are murdered by Jack the Ripper.

The **Shogun's** daughter: a novel of Feudal Japan. Laura Joh Rowland. St. Martin's Minotaur, 2013. 336 p. (Sano Ichiro mysteries, 17)
ISBN 9781250028617
1. Detectives 2. Shoguns 3. Heirs and heiresses 4. Death 5. Smallpox 6. Japan 7. 18th century 8. Historical mysteries 9. Mysteries
LC 2013013933

When the shogun is forced to claim an illegitimate son as his heir after the death of his only child, Sano Ichiro, believing the malevolent youth to be part of a plot to seize power, risks the safety and honor of his family to uncover the truth.

The **snow** empress. Laura Joh Rowland. St. Martin's Minotaur, 2007. 293 p. (Sano Ichiro mysteries, 12)
ISBN 9780312365424
1. Boy kidnapping victims 2. Fathers and sons 3. Warlords 4. Bruno, Giordano 5. Samurai 6. Japan 7. 17th century 8. Historical mysteries 9. Mysteries 10. Adult books for young adults
In 1699 Japan, when their son is kidnapped by dangerous rivals jealous over his influence in the shogun's court, Sano Ichiro and his wife, Reiko, search desperately for the boy, only to be trapped by Lord Matsumae, who has been driven mad by the murder of his mistress.

Rowland, Russell

Cold country: a novel. Russell Rowland. Dzanc Books, 2019. 232 pages
ISBN 9781945814921
1. Ranchers 2. Single men 3. Murder 4. Murder suspects 5. Small town life 6. Montana 7. 1960s 8. Mysteries 9. Modern Westerns
LC 2019013630
A small 1968 Montana community is thrown into turmoil over the murder of a notorious bachelor rancher, a crime that implicates an innocent newcomer and reveals a dangerous secret.

Rowley, Steven

★ The **guncle:** a novel. Steven Rowley. G. P. Putnam's Sons, 2021. 336 p.
ISBN 9780525542285
1. Gay men 2. Uncles 3. Parents — Death 4. Former actors and actresses 5. Rules 6. Palm Springs, California 7. Literary fiction 8. LGBTQIA fiction
LC 2020049239
LibraryReads Favorites, 2021
When Patrick, or Gay Uncle Patrick (GUP) for short, takes on the role of primary guardian for his young niece and nephew, he sets {34Guncle Rules,{34 but soon learn that parenting isn't solved with treats or jokes as his eyes are opened to a new sense of responsibility.

"Its somewhat dire premise notwithstanding, Rowley's (The Editor, 2019) sensitive and witty exploration of grief and healing soothes with a delectable lightness and cunning charm." —*Booklist*

Rowling, J. K.

The **casual** vacancy. J.K. Rowling. Little Brown & Co, 2012. 480 p.
ISBN 9780316228534
1. Social classes 2. Interpersonal conflict 3. Deception 4. Elections 5. City council members 6. England 7. Mainstream fiction 8. Books to TV
Goodreads Choice Award, 2012
The early death of a small town councilman reveals deep-rooted conflicts in the seemingly idyllic community of Pagford, which rapidly deteriorates in the face of cultural disputes, generation clashes, and a volatile election.
Adapted into a TV series in 2015 by BBC and HBO.

Roy, Anuradha

All the lives we never lived: a novel. Anuradha Roy. Atria Books, 2018. 272 p.

ISBN 9781982100513

1. Mothers and sons 2. World War II 3. Mother-deserted children 4. Artists 5. Quests 6. India 7. 20th century 8. Literary fiction 9. Historical fiction 10. Parallel narratives 11. Adult books for young adults

LC 2018026734

Loan Stars Favourites, 2018; Shortlisted for the International Dublin Literary Award, 2020

A novel set from World War II India through the present day and following a son's quest to uncover the story of his freedom-craving, rebellious artist mother.

"Roy (Sleeping on Jupiter, 2016) peppers her novel with intricate descriptions of small-town India and weaves an eloquent and tragic story of straitjacketed lives upended when history and personal ambition intersect." —*Booklist*

An **atlas** of impossible longing. Anuradha Roy. Free Press, 2011. 320 p.

ISBN 9781451608625

1. Orphans 2. Families 3. Women with mental illnesses 4. Family relationships 5. Familial love 6. India 7. Family sagas 8. Love stories 9. Adult books for young adults

LC 2010019362

Growing up in the Bengal region of India, motherless daughter Bakul and Mukunda, an orphan, are inseparable, but after they grow older and their relationship turns into something more than friendship, Mukunda is banished to Calcutta, where he prospers during India's Partition, yet yearns to be back with Bakul.

"An incandescently evocative debut novel filled with wrenching tragedy as well as abiding passion, Roy's panoramic, multigenerational tale of desire, revenge, and loss is filled with the rhythms and values of India's rich and varied subcultures." —*Booklist*

First published: 2008.

Roy, Arundhati

★ The **god** of small things. Arundhati Roy. Random House, 1997. 321 p.

ISBN 9780679457312

1. Twins 2. Family visits 3. Social classes 4. Families 5. Cousins 6. India 7. Literary fiction

LC 96-39190

Booker Prize, 1997; Booklist Editors' Choice, 1997; Library Journal Best Books, 1997; New York Times Notable Book, 1997

In 1969, in Kerala, India, Rahel and her twin brother, Estha, struggle to forge a childhood for themselves amid the destruction of their family life, as they discover that the entire world can be transformed in a single moment.

"If the symbolism is a trifle overdone, the lush local color and the incisive characterizations give the narrative power and drama." —*Publishers Weekly*

★ The **ministry** of utmost happiness: a novel. Arundhati Roy. Alfred A. Knopf, 2017. 449 p.

ISBN 9781524733155

1. Villa, Pancho 2. Misfits (Persons) 3. Unrequited love 4. Self-fulfillment 5. People who are intersex 6. Jammu and Kashmir, India 7. Delhi 8. Literary fiction

LC 2017002124

Booklist Editors' Choice, 2017; Librarians' Choice (Australia), 2017; Loan Stars Favourites, 2017; Longlisted for the Man Booker Prize, 2017; Longlisted for the Andrew Carnegie Medal for Excellence in Fiction, 2018; Longlisted for The Women's Prize for Fiction, 2018; National Book Critics Circle Award for Fiction finalist, 2017

A provocative love story meanders through a spectrum of powerful emotions experienced by diverse protagonists, including a grieving father who writes a letter profiling the people who came to his 5-year-old daughter's funeral and two longtime friends at a guest house who sleep wrapped around each other like newlyweds.

"Roy joins Dickens, Naipaul, Garca Mrquez, and Rushdie in her abiding compassion, storytelling magic, and piquant wit as she questions our perceptions of gender, family, home, country, war, freedom, love, and death in this righteous and tender illumination of humankinds paradoxical capacities for cruelty and kindness." —*Booklist*

Roy, Lori

Bent Road. Lori Roy. Dutton, 2011. 368 p.

ISBN 9780525951834

1. Cold cases (Criminal investigation) 2. Rural families 3. Crimes against girls 4. Secrets 5. Rural life 6. Kansas 7. 1960s 8. Psychological suspense

LC 2010037239

Edgar Allan Poe Award for Best First Novel by an American Author, 2012; Library Journal Best Books, 2011

Celia Scott and her family move back to her husband's hometown in Kansas, where his sister died under mysterious circumstances twenty years before and where Celia and two of her children struggle to adjust—especially when a local girl disappears.

"Like Michael Chabon's work, which sometimes crosses genres, Roy's novel could be called literary fiction or mystery. Whatever the label, Bent Road is written with the care and craft of standout storytelling. There's inevitability to the novel's crisis and denouement but plenty of surprise. Psychological acuity, tight plot and in-depth character development keep the reader trying to resist the urge to read ahead." —*Kansas City Star*

★ **Gone** too long: a novel. Lori Roy. Dutton, 2019. 320 p.

ISBN 9781524741969

1. Missing children 2. Family secrets 3. Hate groups 4. Former captives 5. Captives 6. Georgia 7. Thrillers and suspense 8. Multiple perspectives

LC 2018053742

Seven years after a girl with unusual skills goes missing amid a Klan uprising in Georgia, an estranged daughter confronts community secrets when she discovers a child in her father's basement.

Roy, Lucinda

The **freedom** race. Lucinda Roy. TOR, 2021. 416 p. (Dreambird chronicles)

ISBN 9781250258908

1. Dystopias 2. Racism 3. Civil War 4. Enslaved people 5. Slave trade 6. Dystopian fiction 7. African American fiction

LC 2021009144

In the aftermath of a cataclysmic civil war known as the Sequel, ideological divisions among the states have hardened. In the Homestead Territories, an alliance of plantation-inspired holdings, Black labor is imported from the Cradle, and Biracial "Muleseeds" are bred. Raised in captivity on Planting 437, kitchen-seed Jellybean "Ji-ji" Lottermule knows there is only one way to escape. She must enter the annual Freedom Race as a runner. Ji-ji and her friends must exhume a survival story rooted in the collective memory of a kidnapped people and conjure the voices of the dead to light their way hom

"Things get off to a slow start; Roy front-loads the story with extensive background for the 'disunited states' and an elaborate lexicon of new racial classifications, creating a steep learning curve for readers. But once the world is established and Ji-Ji's story takes off, her harrowing but profoundly spiritual quest for sovereignty against all odds impresses." —*Publishers Weekly*

Rozan, S. J.

★ The **art** of violence. S. J. Rozan. Pegasus Crime, 2020. 352 p. (Lydia Chin and Bill Smith mysteries, 13)

ISBN 9781643135311

1. Private investigators 2. Women private investigators 3. Chinese American women 4. Serial murder investigation 5. Artists 6. New York City 7. Mysteries

Approached by a paroled amnesiac to determine his guilt or innocence in two new murders, Bill Smith and Lydia Chin investigate the suspect's private and professional art circles to determine why he may have been framed.

"As always, Rozan's intelligent, witty prose is a treat, and she justifies a choice made in the previous book regarding the relationship between her two leads. Newcomers as well as devotees will be enthralled." —*Publishers Weekly*

★ **Paper** son. S. J. Rozan. Minotaur Books, 2019. 352 pages (Lydia Chin and Bill Smith mysteries, 12)

ISBN 9781643131290

1. Women private investigators 2. Chinese American women 3. Cousins 4. Murder suspects 5. Innocence (Law) 6. Mississippi 7. Delta Region, Mississippi 8. Mysteries

Informed that an unknown cousin is in jail, Chinese-American private detective Lydia Chin and her partner, Bill Smith, travel to the Mississippi Delta, where they confront river-levee disputes, computer scams and questions about her cousin's innocence.

The **Shanghai** Moon: a Lydia Chin/Bill Smith novel. S.J. Rozan. St. Martin's Minotaur, 2009. 384 p. (Lydia Chin and Bill Smith mysteries, 9)

ISBN 9780312245566

1. Private investigators 2. Women private investigators 3. International intrigue 4. Jewelry theft 5. Stolen property recovery 6. Shanghai, China 7. New York City 8. Mysteries

LC 2008033941

Library Journal Best Books, 2009

Chinese-American P. I. Lydia Chin is brought in by former mentor Joel Pilarsky to help with a case that crosses continents, cultures, and decades. In Shanghai, excavation has unearthed a cache of European jewelry dating back to World War II. The jewelry was immediately stolen by a Chinese official who fled to New York City. Hired by a lawyer specializing in the recovery of Holocaust assets, Chin and Pilarsky are to find any and all leads to the missing jewels. Lydia soon learns that there is much more to the story than they've been told.

Winter and night. S.J. Rozan. Minotaur Books, 2002. 338 p; (Lydia Chin and Bill Smith mysteries, 8)

ISBN 9780312245559

1. Secrets 2. Runaway teenagers 3. Private investigators 4. Women private investigators 5. Chinese American women 6. New Jersey 7. Mysteries

LC 2001048659

Edgar Allan Poe Award for Best Mystery Novel, 2003; Macavity Award for Best Mystery Novel, 2003

Private detective Bill Smith is hurtled headlong into the most provocative—and personal—case of his career when he receives a chilling late night phone call from the NYPD, who is holding his fifteen-year-old nephew Gary.

Republished in the U.K. under the title, Blood ties, (Ebury Press, 2011).

Rubart, James L.

★ The **man** he never was. James L. Rubart. Harpercollins Christian Pub 2018. 371 pages

ISBN 9780718099398

1. Anger in men 2. Men — Spiritual life 3. Transformations, Personal 4. Former football players 5. Husband and wife 6. Christian suspense 7. Adaptations, retellings, and spin-offs

LC 2017038970

Christy Award for Allegory/Fantasy/Visionary Category, 2018

When Toren Daniels resurfaces after an eight-month disappearance, his wife and children discover that his violent temper is completely gone, and Toren goes in search of where he has been and how he has transformed so radically.

Includes discussion questions—Page 4 of cover.

Ruff, Matt

★ **88** names. Matt Ruff. HarperCollins, 2020. 320 p.

ISBN 9780062854674

1. Role-playing games 2. Virtual reality 3. Avatars (Virtual reality) 4. Dictators 5. Spies 6. Cyber-thrillers

A romantic cyberthriller set in a world of fluid identities follows the experiences of a paid guide to online role-playing games who comes to believe that an anonymous wealthy new client is actually a violent dictator.

"Set largely in the world of virtual reality gaming, this fun, fast-paced novel from Ruff (Lovecraft Country) is equal parts amateur sleuth mystery and science fiction thriller." —*Publishers Weekly*

Lovecraft Country: a novel. Matt Ruff. Harper, 2016. 372 pages

ISBN 9780062292063

1. Racism 2. Cults 3. African American families 4. Veterans 5. Automobile travel 6. New England 7. Chicago, Illinois 8. 1950s 9. Historical horror 10. Horror 11. Science fiction

Blends multiple genres in a visceral exploration of the Jim Crow era and its legacy, tracing the story of young Army vet Atticus Turner, who in 1954 Chicago travels with his publisher uncle and childhood friend to search for his missing father only to encounter human and supernatural terrors at the estate of a descendant of slave owners.

Ruiz Zafon, Carlos

The **angel's** game. Carlos Ruiz Zafon; translated by Lucia Graves. Doubleday, 2009. 464 p. (Cemetery of forgotten books, 2)

ISBN 9780385528702

1. Obsession in men 2. Journalists 3. Secrets 4. Authors 5. Antiquarian booksellers 6. Barcelona, Spain 7. Spain 8. 1920s 9. Magical realism 10. Historical fiction 11. Literary fiction

Offered a career-making writing deal from an enigmatic publisher in turbulent 1960s Barcelona, David Martin wonders about his capacity for writing a book for which the publisher claims others will live and die.

"This novel operates on so many levels, a brief review can't quite do justice to its many layers." —*Seattle Times*

This book is set in 1920-1930s.

Translated from the Spanish: Juego del angel.

Also published: London : Phoenix, 2010.

The **labyrinth** of the spirits. Carlos Ruiz Zafon. HarperCollins, 2018. 848 p. (Cemetery of forgotten books, 4)

ISBN 9780062668691

1. Women detectives 2. Books and reading 3. Political corruption 4. State-sponsored terrorism 5. Rare books 6. Barcelona, Spain 7. Spain 8. 1950s 9. Historical fiction 10. Magical realism 11. Literary fiction

Library Journal Best Books, 2018

A conclusion to the best-selling series finds enigmatic Alicia Gris, supported by the Sempere family, uncovering one of the most shocking conspiracies in Spanish history.

"Compelling if unevenly paced, this is for readers who savor each word and scene, soaking in the ambience of Barcelona, Zafn's greatest character (after, perhaps, the irrepressible Fermn Romero de Torres)." —*Booklist*

Originally published: Barcelona, Spain : Planeta, 2016.

The **prisoner** of heaven. Carlos Ruiz Zafon. HarperCollins, 2012. 416 p. (Cemetery of forgotten books, 3)

ISBN 9780062206282

1. Booksellers 2. Rare books 3. Inscriptions 4. Enemies 5. Fathers and sons 6. Barcelona, Spain 7. 1950s 8. Historical fiction 9. Magical realism 10. Translations 11. Adult books for young adults

In 1957 Barcelona, Daniel Semper and his close friend Fermin Romero de Torres find their lives violently disrupted by the arrival of a mysterious stranger who threatens to divulge a terrible secret that has been buried for two decades in the city's dark past.

Includes Reading group notes.

First published in Spain as El prisionero del cielo by Editorial Planeta, 2011.

This translation originally published: London: Weidenfeld & Nicolson, 2012.

★ The **shadow** of the wind. Carlos Ruiz Zafon; translated by Lucia Graves. Penguin Press, 2004. 480 p. (Cemetery of forgotten books, 1)

ISBN 9780143126393

1. Rare books 2. Obsession in men 3. Magic 4. Fathers and sons 5. Books and reading 6. Barcelona, Spain 7. 1940s 8. Historical fiction 9. Magical realism 10. Translations 11. Adult books for young adults

LC 2003062376

A literary mystery set in 1945 Barcelona where David Sempere finds a book that will change the course of his life and throw him into a labyrinth of intrigues and buried secrets in the heart of the city.

"[T]he setting—Spain under Franco—injects an air of sobriety into some plot elements that might otherwise seem soap operatic. Part detective story, part boy's adventure, part romance, fantasy, and gothic horror, the intricate plot is urged on by extravagant foreshadowing and nail-nibbling tension." —*Booklist*

This book is set in 1945-1950s.

First published as La sombra del viento: Barcelona : Editorial Planeta, 2001. This edition published 2006.

This edition includes an interview with the author, discussion notes, and an illustrated Shadow of the Wind walk through the streets of Barcelona.

Ruiz, Sarah Grunder

Love, lists, and fancy ships. Sarah Grunder Ruiz. Berkley Publishing Group, 2021. 336 p.

ISBN 9780593335420

1. Single women 2. Cooks 3. Lists 4. Grief 5. Nieces 6. Florida 7. Contemporary romances 8. Romantic comedies

"The sunny setting; chaste, endearing romance; and heartwarming themes of familial devotion will leave readers hungry for more from Ruiz." —*Publishers Weekly*

Runcie, James

Canvey Island. James Runcie. Other Press, 2008. 301 p.

ISBN 9781590512937

1. Communication in families 2. Loss (Psychology) 3. Men 4. Floods 5. Tragedy 6. England 7. Canvey Island, England 8. 1950s 9. Historical fiction 10. Multiple perspectives 11. Literary fiction

LC 2007052431

On 1953 Canvey Island, in the aftermath of a tragic flood that claims his mother's life, Martin abandons his home to study at Cambridge and take up with Claire, a bohemian feminist and radical activist, until her actions drive him back to Canvey Island, into the arms of a teenage love and back into his old life, in a novel set against the backdrop of post-war Britain.

"In highly readable chapters narrated by each family member, the book manages to address class and generational conflict as it travels through the decades." —*Booklist*

The **road** to Grantchester. James Runcie. Bloomsbury, 2019. 320 p. (Grantchester mysteries, prequel)

ISBN 9781635570588

1. Belief and doubt 2. Postwar life 3. World War II veterans 4. World War II 5. Loss (Psychology) 6. England 7. 20th century 8. Historical mysteries 9. Media tie-ins

A prequel to the Grantchester series follows the life, loves and losses of young Sidney Chambers in postwar London, where, as a traumatized veteran, he navigates devastating survivor guilt and a haphazard religious calling.

"A must for fans and a good starting point for others." —*Booklist*

Sidney Chambers and the forgiveness of sins. James Runcie. Bloomsbury, 2015. 405 p. (Grantchester mysteries, 4)

ISBN 9781632861030

1. Amateur detectives 2. Clergymen 3. Forgiveness 4. Betrayal 5. Deception 6. England 7. Grantchester, England 8. 1950s 9. Mysteries

Collects six new stories featuring the priest and part-time detective Sidney Chambers, in which a stranger seeks sanctuary believing he murdered his wife, a group of school boys blow up the science block, and Sidney is accused of stealing a painting while on holiday.

"Chambers is a winning protagonist, fervid in his faith yet prone to human frailty, and his exploits provide multiple pleasures for readers of cozies and beyond. The full Grantchester mystery series, projected to include six novels, will have a new entry in each of the next two years, and readers, as well as fans of the PBS show based on this series, should treasure them." —*Booklist*

Sidney Chambers and the perils of the night. James Runcie. Bloomsbury USA, 2013. 256 p. (Grantchester mysteries, 2)

ISBN 9781608199518

1. Investigations 2. Amateur detectives 3. Clergymen 4. Murder 5. Arson 6. England 7. Grantchester, England 8. 1950s 9. Mysteries 10. Short stories

LC 2012050017

Canon Sidney Chambers investigates the unexpected fall of a Cambridge don from the roof of King's College Chapel; a case of arson at a glamour photographer's studio; and a poisoning in the middle of a crucial game of cricket.

Adapted into the second season of the TV series "Grantchester" in 2016 by ITV. Broadcast in the United States on PBS.

Originally published: 2013.

Sidney Chambers and the persistence of love. James Runcie. Bloomsbury, 2017. 344 pages; (Grantchester mysteries, 6)

ISBN 9781632867940

1. Clergymen 2. Amateur detectives 3. Hippies 4. Rare books 5. Husband and wife 6. England 7. Grantchester, England 8. 1970s 9. Mysteries

Discovering the body of a man in the Cambridgeshire woods, priest and detective Sidney Chambers immerses himself in the 1970s counterculture of psychedelic plants; while his longtime friend, Detective Inspector Geordie Keating, investigates the disappearance of a historic religious text.

Sidney Chambers and the problem of evil. James Runcie. Bloomsbury, 2014. 352 p. (Grantchester mysteries, 3)

ISBN 9781608199525

1. Amateur detectives 2. Clergymen 3. Investigations 4. Murder 5. Detectives 6. England 7. Grantchester, England 8. 1950s 9. Mysteries 10. Short stories

LC 2013043690

Our favorite clerical detective is back with four longer mysteries in which Canon Sidney Chambers attempts to stop a serial killer with a grievance against the clergy; investigates the disappearance of a famous painting after a distracting display of nudity by a French girl in an art gallery; uncovers the fact that an "accidental" drowning on a film shoot may have been something more sinister; and discovers the reasons behind the theft of a baby from a hospital just before Christmas 1963. In the meantime, Sidney wrestles with the problem of evil, attempts to fulfill the demands of his faithful Labrador, Dickens, and contemplates, as always, the nature of love.

Sidney Chambers and the shadow of death. James Runcie. Bloomsbury USA, 2012. 256 p. (Grantchester mysteries, 1)

ISBN 9781608198566

1. Murder investigation 2. Amateur detectives 3. Clergymen 4. Vicars 5. Detectives 6. England 7. Grantchester, England 8. 1950s 9. Mysteries 10. Books to TV

Introduces unconventional clergyman Sidney Chambers, who teams up with roguish Inspector Harry Keating to investigate a suspicious suicide, a jewelry theft, the unexplained demise of a jazz promoter, and a shocking art forgery.

Adapted into the first season of the TV series "Grantchester" in 2014 by ITV. Broadcast in the United States on PBS in 2015.

Rush, Norman

★ **Mating**. Norman Rush. Knopf, 1991. 477 p.

ISBN 9780394544724

1. Americans in Africa 2. Women anthropologists 3. Courtship 4. Women 5. Man-woman relationships 6. Botswana 7. Kalahari Desert 8. Literary fiction

LC 90025752

National Book Award for Fiction, 1991; National Book Critics Circle Award for Fiction finalist, 1991

Two Americans—a thirtyish anthropologist in the pursuit of a man, and a late-forties utopian who has set up a modern-day Eden—search for love in 1980s Botswana, Africa, a land full of political turmoil and local color.

"Mr. Rush has created one of the wiser and wittier fictive meditations on the subject of mating. His novel illuminates why we yield when we don't have to. It seeks to illuminate the nature of true intimacy: how to define it, how to know when one has achieved it. And few books evoke so eloquently that state of love at its apogee." —*New York Times Book Review*

Includes end paper maps.

Rushdie, Salman

The **enchantress** of Florence: a novel. Salman Rushdie. Random House, 2008. 368 p.

ISBN 9780375504334

1. Storytellers 2. Illegitimate children of royalty 3. Women 4. Women rulers 5. Mughal Empire 6. Historical fiction 7. Literary fiction

LC 2008000070

Booklist Editors' Choice, 2008

A traveler from Italy arrives at the court of Emperor Akbar, lord of the Mughal empire, and entertains him with a story about Akbar's great aunt, Qara Kz, the enchantress of Florence: a tale which suggests a larger, secret history interconnecting East and West.

Originally published: London: Jonathan Cape, 2008.

First published in Great Britain in 2008 by Jonathan Cape.

★ The **golden** house. Salman Rushdie. Penguin, 2017. 368 p.

ISBN 9780399592805

1. Rich families 2. Family secrets 3. Ambition 4. Corruption 5. Filmmakers 6. Satirical fiction 7. Political fiction 8. Literary fiction

Booklist Editors' Choice, 2017; Longlisted for the Andrew Carnegie Medal for Excellence in Fiction, 2018

A real estate tycoon and his mysterious, corrupt family become the subjects of an aspiring filmmaker's project before revelations of their criminal past activities give way to the rise of a mad presidential candidate.

"A sort of Great Gatsby for our time: everyone is implicated, no one is innocent, and no one comes out unscathed, no matter how well padded with cash." —*Kirkus*

Haroun and the sea of stories. Salman Rushdie. Granta Books, in association with Viking, 1990. 218 p.

ISBN 9780670838042

1. Fathers and sons 2. Storytellers 3. Storytelling 4. Allegories 5. Literary fiction 6. Adult books for young adults

LC 90045496

Mythopoeic Award for Children's Literature

The author of The Satanic Verses returns with his most humorous and accessible novel yet. This is the story of Haroun, a 12-year-old boy whose father Rashid is the greatest storyteller in a city so sad that it has forgotten its name. When the gift of gab suddenly deserts Rashid, Haroun sets out on an adventure to rescue his print.

★ **Midnight's** children: a novel. Salman Rushdie. A. A. Knopf, 1981. 446 p.

ISBN 9780394514703

1. Children 2. Infants switched at birth 3. Supernatural 4. Islam — Relations 5. Hinduism — Relations 6. India 7. Literary fiction 8. Magical realism 9. Books to movies

LC 80002712

Booker Prize, 1981; James Tait Black Memorial Prize for Fiction, 1981

Born at the stroke of midnight on August 15, 1947, the exact moment of India's independence, Saleem Sinai becomes inextricably linked to that of his nation and is a whirlwind of disasters and triumphs that mirror modern India's course.

First published: London : Jonathan Cape, 1980.

The **moor's** last sigh. Salman Rushdie. Pantheon Books, 1996. 435 p.

ISBN 9780679420491

1. Families 2. Mothers and sons 3. Spice industry and trade 4. India 5. Satirical fiction 6. Family sagas 7. Byron, George Gordon Byron

LC 95024392

Booklist Editors' Choice, 1996; Library Journal Best Books, 1996; Whitbread Book Award for Novel, 1995; Shortlisted for the Booker-McConnell Prize, 1995

A family saga reflecting the troubled state of India. The protagonists are four generations of the da Gama, who became wealthy in the spice trade before declining into gangsterism. Their tale is narrated by the family's last descendant and he attributes their fall to bickering, a reflection of Hindu-Moslem strife plaguing India today.

"This is a marvellously inventive display of verbal dexterity; an exuberant, entertaining, zestful novel which proves, if proof were needed, that Mr Rushdie's spirit remains undiminished." —*The Economist*

★ **Quichotte:** a novel. Salman Rushdie. Random House, 2019. 396 p. ISBN 9780593132982

1. Traveling sales personnel 2. Quests 3. Television programs 4. Automobile travel 5. Fathers and sons 6. United States 7. 21st century 8. Literary fiction 9. Metafiction 10. Adaptations, retellings, and spin-offs

LC 2019016494

Booklist Editors' Choice, 2019; Shortlisted for the Booker Prize, 2019

Presents a modern adaptation of Don Quixote that finds a courtly, addled salesman embarking on a cross-country journey with his imaginary son after falling impossibly in love with a television star.

★ The **satanic** verses. Salman Rushdie. Viking, 1989. 546 p. ISBN 9780670825370

1. East Indians 2. Good and evil 3. Islam 4. Survival (after airplane accidents, shipwrecks, etc.) 5. London, England 6. Magical realism 7. Literary fiction 8. Modern classics

LC 88040266

Whitbread Book Award for Novel, 1988; Shortlisted for the Booker-McConnell Prize, 1988

Just before dawn one winter's morning, a hijacked aeroplane blows apart high above the English Channel and two figures tumble, clutched in an embrace, towards the sea: Gibreel Farishta, India's legendary movie star, and Saladin Chamcha, the man of a thousand voices. Washed up, alive, on an English beach, their survival is a miracle. But there is a price to pay. Gibreel and Saladin have been chosen as opponents in the eternal wrestling match between Good and Evil. But chosen by whom? And which is which? And what will be the outcome of their final confrontation? SALS

First published in Great Britain in 1988.

Shalimar the Clown: a novel. Salman Rushdie. Random House, 2005. 416 p.
ISBN 9780679463351

1. Extremism 2. Revenge 3. Guilt 4. Muslim men 5. Clowns 6. Jammu and Kashmir, India 7. Strasbourg, France 8. Psychological fiction 9. Literary fiction

LC 2005042796

Booklist Editors' Choice, 2005; New York Times Notable Book, 2005; Shortlisted for the International IMPAC Dublin Literary Award, 2007

In 1991, Ambassador Maximilian Ophuls—ex-ambassador to India, and America's counterterrorism chief—is murdered on the Los Angeles doorstep of his illegitimate daughter's home by his Kashmiri Muslim driver, who calls himself Shalimar the Clown.

"Rushdie has written an intensely political novel, infused with recent events, but its emotional scope reaches so far beyond our current crisis and its vision into the vagaries of the heart is so perceptive that one can imagine Shalimar the Clown being read long after this age of sacred terror has faded into history." —*Washington Post Book World.*

Originally published: London : Jonathan Cape, c2005.

Two years eight months and twenty-eight nights: a novel. Salman Rushdie. Random House, 2015. 304 p.

ISBN 9780812998917

1. Genies 2. Imaginary wars and battles 3. Superhuman abilities 4. Half-human hybrids 5. Fundamentalism 6. New York City 7. Literary fiction 8. Fantasy fiction 9. Satirical fiction

LC 2015008158

A modern fairy tale by the award-winning author of Midnight's Children is set in a world of religious dominance where mystical acts and supernatural abilities shape a war over control of Fairyland.

"Rushdie scatters intriguing allusions (Beckett, Magritte, Gogol, Obama) about like fairy dust and coins of the realm while sustaining swiftly flowing, incisive, piercingly funny commentary on everything from religious extremists to reality TV, anti-Semitism and racism, and economic injustice." —*Booklist*

Ruskovich, Emily

Idaho: a novel. Emily Ruskovich. Random House, 2017. 336 p. ISBN 9780812994049

1. Women murderers 2. Husband and wife 3. Memories 4. Dementia 5. Women prisoners 6. Idaho 7. Literary fiction 8. Multiple perspectives

LC 2016006621

International IMPAC Dublin Literary Award, 2019

A tale told from multiple perspectives traces the complicated relationship between Ann and Wade on a rugged landscape and how they came together in the aftermath of his first wife's imprisonment for a violent murder.

"Shocking and heartbreaking, Ruskovich has crafted a remarkable love story and a narrative that will stay with readers." —*Publishers Weekly*

Russell, Karen

Orange world and other stories. Karen Russell. Alfred A. Knopf, 2019. 320 p.

ISBN 9780525656135

1. Short stories 2. Literary fiction

LC 2018054561

A latest collection of short fiction by the award-winning author of Swamplandia! includes the title story, in which a desperate new mother strikes a bargain to breastfeed the devil in exchange for his protection over her baby.

"Heir to Shirley Jackson and a compatriot of T. C. Boyle, virtuoso Russell, gifted with acute insights, compassion, and a daring, free-diving imagination, explores the bewitching and bewildering dynamic between the voracious appetite of nature and its yawning indifference and humankinds relentless profligacy and obliviousness." —*Booklist*

This is a Borzoi book published by Alfred A. Knopf.

★ **Swamplandia!**. Karen Russell. Alfred A. Knopf, 2011. 304 p. ISBN 9780307263995

1. Family relationships 2. Quests 3. Swamps 4. Mother-separated families 5. Amusement parks 6. Everglades, Florida 7. Ten Thousand Islands, Florida 8. Coming-of-age stories 9. Magical realism 10. Literary fiction 11. Adult books for young adults

LC 2010036708

ALA Notable Book, 2012; Booklist Editors' Choice: Adult Books for Young Adults, 2011; New York Times Notable Book, 2011; School Library Journal Best Books: Best Adult Books 4 Teens, 2011; Andrew Carnegie Medal for Excellence in Fiction finalist, 2012; Pulitzer Prize for Fiction finalist, 2012; Shortlisted for the International IMPAC Dublin Literary Award, 2013

The Bigtree children struggle to protect their Florida Everglades alligator-wrestling theme park from a sophisticated competitor after losing their parents.

"When Hilola Bigtree, professional alligator wrestler and star attraction at a Florida venue that calls itself 'the Number One Gator-Themed Park and Swamp Caf in the area,' dies in the vise grip not of some prehistoric behemoth but of unglamorous cancer, the family-owned tourist destination shrivels into insolvency. Likewise, the remaining Bigtree clan unspools in her absence, and Ava, the youngest of three children, can only watch as they drift apart. Her sister, Ossie, obsessed with the afterlife, carries out furtive relationships with the spirits of dead boys she claims possess her. Her brother, Kiwi, runs off to work for the World of Darkness, an amusement park designed to resemble hell. The plot of Swamplandia! tilts toward the odd. Kiwi toils in his ersatz inferno; Ava goes on a quest to save Ossie after she elopes into the otherworldly wetlands with one of her phantom paramours. But Russell isn't a magic realist. In fact, the only truly magical things about this book are its effortless prose and its small, beautifully drawn cast of characters." —*Entertainment Weekly*

Vampires in the lemon grove: stories. By Karen Russell. Alfred A. Knopf, 2013. 256 p.
ISBN 9780307957238
1. Short stories 2. Literary fiction
LC 2012027415
Award-winning author Karen Russell's latest short story collection blends whimsy and horror in equal measure. Her daringly inventive characters range from centuries-old vampires with surprisingly touching human desires, to a former U.S. president now reincarnated as a horse. Russell's dry humor and keen eye for relatable emotional experiences will lure readers deeply into these surreal vignettes.
This is a Borzoi book.

Russell, Kate Elizabeth

★ **My** dark Vanessa. Kate Elizabeth Russell. William Morrow & Co, 2020. 372 p.
ISBN 9780062941503
1. Teenage girls — Relations with older men 2. Teacher-student relationships 3. High school teachers 4. Sex crimes 5. Memories 6. Maine 7. Psychological fiction 8. Parallel narratives 9. Adult books for young adults
LibraryReads Favorites, 2020
Asked to help defend an older high-school English teacher with whom she had an affair at age 15, Vanessa struggles to choose between her romantic teen illusions and harrowing adult perceptions.
"Russell offers readers an introspective narrative that fully captures the complexity and necessity of the #MeToo movement in her powerful debut." —*Publishers Weekly*

Russell, Mary Doria

★ **Children** of God: a novel. Mary Doria Russell. Villard, 1998. 438 pages (Sparrow novels (Mary Doria Russell), 2)
ISBN 9780679456353
1. Religion 2. Life on other planets 3. Revolutions 4. Linguists 5. Space flight 6. 21st century 7. Social science fiction 8. Science fiction 9. Literary fiction
LC 97-42160
Library Journal Best Books, 1998
A priest named Emilio Sandoz embarks on a quest to demystify God's providence that leads him to question the possibility of faith.
"Russell succeeds in painting an alien culture with remarkably detailed verisimilitude." —*New York Times Book Review*
Sequel to: The sparrow.

★ **Doc:** a novel. Mary Doria Russell. Random House, 2011. 400 p. (Doc novels (Mary Doria Russell), 1)

ISBN 9781400068043
1. Holliday, John H. 2. Male friendship 3. Peace officers 4. Dentists 5. Frontier and pioneer life 6. Boy murder victims 7. Dodge City, Kansas 8. American Westward Expansion (1803-1899) 9. Biographical fiction 10. Westerns
LC 2010015062
RUSA Reading List, 2012
After the burned body of mixed-blood boy Johnnie Sanders is discovered in 1878 Dodge City, Kansas, part-time policeman Wyatt Earp enlists the help of his professional-gambler friend Doc Holliday, in a novel that also features Doc's girlfriend, the Hungarian prostitute Kate Katarina Harony.
"An engaging bit of de-mythology, a vivid re-imagining of a more authentic, slightly less wild West than the one we've come to know through dime-store novels." —*Cleveland Plain Dealer*

Dreamers of the day: a novel. Mary Doria Russell. Random House, 2008. 256 p.
ISBN 9781400064717
1. Lawrence, T. E. 2. Spies 3. World War I 4. Independence in women 5. Love 6. Inheritance and succession 7. Middle East 8. Cairo, Egypt 9. Historical fiction 10. Political fiction 11. First person narratives
LC 2007024665
A forty-year-old schoolteacher from Ohio still reeling from the tragedies of the Great War and the influenza epidemic comes into a modest inheritance that allows her to take the trip of a lifetime to Egypt and the Holy Land. Arriving at the Semiramis Hotel, site of the 1921 Cairo Peace Conference, she meets Winston Churchill, T. E. Lawrence, and Lady Gertrude Bell. With her plainspoken American opinions, she becomes a sounding board for these historic luminaries who will, in the space of a few days, invent the nations of Iraq, Syria, Lebanon, Israel, and Jordan. While neither a pawn or a participant at the conference, she is drawn into the geopolitical intrigue surrounding the conference.
"Russell perfectly captures the political and social milieus of the 1920s, driving home how important it is to consider history when dealing with present-day issues.... The fact that Agnes is telling her story after she has—yes—already died does not come across as a literary conceit but as perfectly fitting for this perfectly enchanting tale." —*BookPage*

Epitaph: a novel of the O.K. Corral. Mary Doria Russell. Ecco Press, 2015. 581 pages; (Doc novels (Mary Doria Russell), 2)
ISBN 9780062198761
1. Earp, Wyatt 2. Gunfights 3. Frontier and pioneer life 4. Competition 5. Gunfighters 6. Greed 7. Arizona (Territory) 8. O. K. Corral, Arizona 9. American Westward Expansion (1803-1899) 10. 1880s 11. Biographical fiction 12. Westerns 13. Literary fiction
Library Journal Best Books, 2015
A sequel to Doc is based on the true events of the gunfight at the O.K. Corral and Wyatt Earp's survival against a backdrop of volatile politics in 1881 America.
"The multitude of points of view exemplifies the best of third-person omniscience, revealing innermost secrets, hopes, and fears. Readers of Lyndsay Faye's Gods of Gotham are sure to enjoy this novel, and fans of Westerns ready to branch out beyond Louis L'Amour and Max Brand might see it as a breath of fresh air." —*Library Journal*

★ The **sparrow**. Mary Doria Russell. Villard, 1996. 408 p. (Sparrow novels (Mary Doria Russell), 1)
ISBN 9780679451501
1. Life on other planets 2. Priests 3. Change (Psychology) 4. Near future 5. Linguists 6. 21st century 7. Social science fiction 8. Science fiction 9. Literary fiction
Arthur C. Clarke Award, 1998; Booklist Editors' Choice, 1996; BSFA Award for Best Novel, 1997; James Tiptree, Jr. Award, 1996

The sole survivor of a crew sent to explore a new planet, Jesuit priest Emilio Sandoz discovers an alien civilization that raises questions about the very essence of humanity, an encounter that leads Sandoz to a public inquisition and the destruction of his faith.

Sequel: Children of God (1998).

A **thread** of grace: a novel. Mary Doria Russell. Random House, 2005. 448 p.

ISBN 9780375501845

1. Catholics 2. Resistance to military occupation 3. Nazis 4. World War II — Jews 5. Holocaust (1933-1945) 6. Italy 7. Second World War era (1939-1945) 8. 1940s 9. Historical fiction 10. War stories

LC 2004050942

In September 1943, Claudette Blum and her father flee across the Alps into Italy with other Jews seeking refuge, only to find an open battle ground among the Nazis, Allied forces, resistance fighters, and ordinary Italians struggling to survive.

"This is a morality play that at times uses black humor, and then shifts to solemn reflection or moving portraiture. A Thread of Grace is deft, sensate, ruthless in its moral incisiveness, and affirming in that even in the worst of times, the lamp of humanity cannot be completely extinguished." —*The Hudson Review*

The **women** of the copper country: a novel. Mary Doria Russell. Atria Books, 2019. 339 p.

ISBN 9781982109585

1. Clemenc, Ana K. 2. Copper Miners' Strike, Mich, 1913-1914 3. Women labor leaders 4. Labor movement 5. Young women 6. Coal mines and mining 7. Michigan 8. United States 9. 1910s 10. Historical fiction 11. Biographical fiction

LC 2018051007

Presents a story inspired by the life of Annie Clements, retelling in historically authentic detail how in 1913 she led a courageous strike against the world's largest copper-mining company.

The painstakingly comprehensive narrative and omniscient point of view make for a deliberate pace, but they also ensure readers completely understand what happened. The tale is often bleak, but it serves as a worthwhile counterpoint to historical writing centered on {34great men.{34 Publishers Weekly.

Includes bibliographical references.

Russo, Richard

Bridge of sighs. Richard Russo. Alfred A. Knopf, 2007. 544 p.

ISBN 9780375414954

1. Small towns 2. Small town life 3. Community life 4. Interpersonal relations 5. Senior men 6. New York (State) 7. Literary fiction

LC 2007027970

Booklist Editors' Choice, 2007; New York Times Notable Book, 2007

After sixty years of living in the upstate New York town of Thomaston, Louis Charles and his wife of forty years, Sarah, prepare for a trip to Italy to visit Louis' childhood friend, an artist who had fled his hometown many years earlier.

"Whatever the scale of their lives, Russo's characters—the stars and the walk-ons are gorgeously drawn. The writing is always in service of illuminating them—with one exception. The black characters speak in a corny-sounding dialect, which can make the reader stop to decode sentences. In this case, the reach for authenticity doesn't work. But everything else works brilliantly.... That Russo manages to juggle so many characters, themes, places, and time periods through 528 delicious pages is an astounding achievement. From its lovely beginning to its exquisite, perfect end, Russo has written a masterpiece." —*Boston Globe*

★ **Chances** are...: a novel. Richard Russo. Alfred A. Knopf, 2019. 304 p.

ISBN 9781101947746

1. Sixties (Age) 2. Male friendship 3. Vacations 4. Missing women 5. Secrets 6. Martha's Vineyard, Massachusetts 7. Literary fiction

LC 2019010992

One beautiful September day, three 66-year-old men convene on Martha's Vineyard, friends ever since meeting in college, and must puzzle out a lingering mystery from the summer of 1971.

★ **Empire** Falls. Richard Russo. Knopf, 2001. 483 p.

ISBN 9780679432470

1. Small town life 2. Working class 3. Diners (Restaurants) 4. Divorce 5. Family businesses 6. Maine 7. Literary fiction

LC 1088568

Booklist Editors' Choice, 2001; Library Journal Best Books, 2001; New York Times Notable Book, 2001; Pulitzer Prize for Fiction, 2002

Milo Roby tries to hold his family together while working at the Empire Grill in the once-successful logging town of Empire Falls, Maine, with his partner, Mrs. Whiting, who is the heir to a faded logging and textile legacy.

"Russo is preoccupied with the death of a certain version of the American dream, but his belief in the power of comedy—sometimes low, sometimes high—rescues his work from bathos and elvates it into the realm of literature." —*The New Yorker*

★ **Everybody's** fool. Richard Russo. Alfred A. Knopf, 2016. 480 p. (Nobody's fool, 2)

ISBN 9780307270641

1. Small town life 2. Police chiefs 3. Misadventures 4. Obsession 5. Crime 6. New York (State) 7. 1990s 8. Literary fiction

LC 2015043451

Loan Stars Favourites, 2016; New York Times Notable Book, 2016

Returns to the setting of "Nobody's Fool" to find Sully confronting a daunting health prognosis, which he hides from his loved ones, including his longtime mistress, an increasingly distant best friend, and an obsessive chief of police.

"Russo's reunion with these beloved characters is genius: silly slapstick and sardonic humor play out in a rambling, rambunctious story that poignantly emphasizes that particular brand of loyalty and acceptance that is synonymous with small-town living." —*Booklist*

★ **Nobody's** fool. Richard Russo. Random House, 1993. 549 p. (Nobody's fool, 1)

ISBN 9780394577784

1. Bad luck 2. Unemployed persons 3. Blue collar workers 4. Small town life 5. Literary fiction 6. Books to movies

LC 92056844

ALA Notable Book, 1994

Follows the unexpected operation of grace in a deadbeat, upstate New York town—and in the lives of the unluckiest of its citizens.

"A grand read sparkling with witty dialogue and memorable characters, Russo's novel is a rollicking tale of a born loser on a downward slide. An economically depressed upper New York State community is the setting, and its lower-middle-class and blue-collar inhabitants are portrayed with empathy and a shrewd understanding of human nature." —*Publishers Weekly*

First published in USA in 1993 by Random House.

The **risk** pool. Richard Russo. Random House, 1988. 479p.

ISBN 9780394565279

1. Small town life 2. Fathers and sons 3. Misadventures 4. Drifters 5. New York (State) 6. Domestic fiction 7. Literary fiction

LC 88042666

Ned, the introspective son of the freewheeling World War II veteran Sam Hall struggles for acceptance from his father while trying to avoid adopting the same hedonistic lifestyle BT

"A superbly original, maliciously funny book, peopled by characters that most of us would back away from plenty fast if they ever lurched toward our barstool. It is Mr. Russo's brilliant, deadpan writing that gives their wasted lives and miserable little town such haunting power and insidious charm." —*New York Times Book Review*

Straight man. Richard Russo. Random House, 1997. 391 p. ISBN 9780679432463

1. Middle-aged men 2. Small town life 3. Universities and colleges — Faculty 4. College teachers 5. Communities 6. Pennsylvania 7. Humorous stories 8. Literary fiction

LC 9648578

Booklist Editors' Choice, 1997; Library Journal Best Books, 1997; New York Times Notable Book, 1997

During one tortuous week, Hank Devereaux, head of the English department at the state university in Railton, Pennsylvania, has his nose slashed by a feminist poet, finds his secretary is a better writer than he is, suspects his wife is having an affair, threatens wild fowl, and confronts his father.

Rutherfurd, Edward

London. Edward Rutherfurd. Crown, 1997. 829 p. : Illustration; Map ISBN 9780517591819

1. Shakespeare, William 2. City life 3. Families 4. Normans in England 5. Bombings 6. Black Death 7. London, England 8. Roman Britain (55 BCE-449 CE) 9. Anglo-Saxon period (449-1066) 10. Historical fiction 11. Family sagas 12. Epic fiction

LC 97010176

The triumphs and failures of seven individual family clans span the history of a city from the third-century Roman occupation of Londinium through such eras as the Norman conquest and the Elizabethan period.

"This fictional history of London is told through the experiences of a group of diverse families who, over the generations, meet, mingle, intermarry, and feud. Beginning with prehistory and continuing to the present, Rutherfurd combines geological details, historical events, real people, and his fictional characters to bring London to life." —*Library Journal*

Illustrated with maps

A novel—Cover.

First published in the United Kingdom in 1997 by Century.

Paris. Edward Rutherfurd. Doubleday, 2013. 528 p. ISBN 9780385535304

1. Cities and towns 2. City life 3. Hundred Years' War, 1339-1453 4. Revolutions 5. Eiffel Tower, Paris, France 6. Paris, France 7. France 8. Historical fiction 9. Family sagas 10. Epic fiction

Taking readers on a journey through Parisian history, this sweeping multigenerational saga, filled with romance, danger and rich detail, beautifully illuminates the City of Lights, from its founding under the Romans to the hotbed of cultural activity during the 1920s and 1930s that included Picasso.

The **princes** of Ireland: the Dublin saga. Edward Rutherfurd. Doubleday : 2004. 752 p. (Dublin saga, 1) ISBN 9780385502863

1. Henry 2. Princes 3. Nobility 4. Thoreau, Henry David 5. Monks 6. Soldiers 7. Ireland 8. Dublin, Ireland 9. Historical fiction 10. Family sagas 11. Epic fiction

LC 2003070005

Romantic Times Reviewers' Choice Award, 2004

A fictional account of the history of Ireland recreates such events as the mission of Saint Patrick, the Viking invasion, and the trickery of Henry II that led to England's establishment in Ireland.

"Beginning in the tribal, pre-Christian times of the warrior kings at Tara, this first book in a two-part novelized history of Ireland sweeps readers through the early centuries of Druids, chieftains, monks, Vikings, noblemen, merchants, and mercenaries, ending with the disastrous invasion of England that tragically changed the course of Irish history. Through the eyes of the men and women who built the mighty city that became Dublin, the unfolding of a colorful and turbulent history is told with energy and a meticulous attention to historical detail." —*Library Journal*

Sequel: The Rebels of Ireland: The Dublin Saga.

The **rebels** of Ireland: the Dublin saga. Edward Rutherfurd. Doubleday : 2006. 800 p. (Dublin saga, 2) ISBN 9780385512893

1. Families 2. Famines 3. Immigration and emigration 4. Family relationships 5. British in Ireland 6. Dublin, Ireland 7. Ireland 8. Historical fiction 9. Family sagas 10. Epic fiction

Follows the lives and destinies of several Dublin families, both Catholic and Protestant, from all strata of society, from the sixteenth-century colonization of Ireland by the English to the founding of the Irish Free State in 1922.

Sequel to: The Princes of Ireland: The Dublin Saga.

Published in the UK as Ireland awakening.

Russka: the novel of Russia. Edward Rutherfurd. Crown Publishers, 1991. Viii, 760 p. : Illustration ISBN 9780517580486

1. Ivan 2. Families 3. Farm life 4. Nobility 5. Crimean Tatars 6. Cossacks 7. Soviet Union 8. Russia 9. Historical fiction 10. Family sagas 11. Epic fiction

LC 90034457

The triumphs, tragedies, passions, and struggles of successive generations of four families are shaped by the turbulent events and forces of Russian history, from ancient times to the twentieth century

"The book does provide a sweeping overview of the land whose very vastness and complexity make it overwhelming and fascinating." —*Christian Science Monitor*

Includes map and family tree.

Sarum: the novel of England. Edward Rutherfurd. Gramercy Books, 2004. 897 p. : Map ISBN 9780517223543

1. Families 2. Technology and civilization 3. Human evolution 4. Human settlements 5. Hunters 6. Stonehenge, England 7. England 8. Historical fiction 9. Family sagas 10. Epic fiction

LC 2003067523

"Rutherfurd is strong on the explication of trends and the narration of events. But he relies heavily on the repetition of character types. Nevertheless, Sarum is fascinating and will appeal to Anglophiles, history buffs, and fans of epic-style novels." —*Christian Science Monitor*

Ryan, Anthony

The **waking** fire. Anthony Ryan. Ace Books, 2016. 582 p. (Draconis memoria, 1) ISBN 9781101987858

1. Imaginary empires 2. Dragons 3. Voyages and travels 4. Adventure 5. Blood 6. Fantasy fiction 7. Steampunk

LC 2015039369

With their lines weakening, the drakes, whose prized blood is used to make a powerful elixir, pose a threat to the supremacy of the Ironship Syndicate.

"Ryan handily juggles draconic fantasy, espionage, and steampunk naval fiction with realism and effortless skill." —*Publishers Weekly*

Ryan, Jennifer

The **spies** of Shilling Lane: a novel. Jennifer Ryan. Crown Publishing, 2019. 355 pages

ISBN 9780525576495

1. Family secrets 2. Women and war 3. World War II 4. Women — Family relationships 5. World War II home front 6. London, England 7. England 8. Second World War era (1939-1945) 9. Historical fiction

A follow-up to The Chilbury Ladies' Choir finds scandalous divorcee Mrs. Braithwaite traveling to World War II London in search of her missing daughter, an effort that is complicated by a difficult secret.

"Even with sometimes-vivid descriptions of the horrors of the Blitz, there is a good deal of fun in this cozy caper, and fans of The Chilbury Ladies' Choir will eat it up." —*Booklist*

Ryan, Kennedy

★ **Long** shot. Kennedy Ryan. 2018. 460 p. (Hoops (Kennedy Ryan), 1)

ISBN 9781732144309

1. College athletes 2. Multiracial persons 3. Engaged persons 4. Abused women 5. Love triangles 6. Sports romances 7. Contemporary romances 8. Multicultural romances

RITA Award, 2019

A forbidden love story set in the explosive world of the NBA.

Rølvaag, O. E.

★ **Giants** in the Earth: a saga of the prairie. O.E. Rolvaag; translated from the Norwegian by Lincoln Colcord and the author; with an introduction by Lincoln Colcord. HarperPerennial, 1999. 531 p. (Norwegian pioneers trilogy, 1)

ISBN 9780060931933

1. Norwegians in the United States 2. Immigrants — History 3. Frontier and pioneer life 4. Prairie life 5. South Dakota 6. Historical fiction 7. Translations

After settling in South Dakota, Per Hansa, a Norwegian, tries to change his wife's attitudes about their new life.

S

Sabatini, Rafael

Captain Blood. Rafael Sabatini. Dover Publications, Inc, 2004. Vi, 242 p.

ISBN 9780486436548

1. Physicians 2. Pirates 3. Sailing ships 4. Seafaring life 5. British in the Caribbean Area 6. Caribbean Area 7. 17th century 8. Adventure stories 9. Sea stories 10. Swashbuckling tales

LC 2004055142

Wrongfully arrested following the Monmouth rebellion of 1685, Peter Blood, country physician and former soldier, escapes the hangman's noose only to be exiled to the tropical colonies. Sold into slavery to a cruel plantation owner, his moral fortitude and medical ability soon earn him the favour of the island's governor, and the attentions of Arabella, his master's niece. When the town is attacked by marauding Spanish buccaneers, Blood springs to the rescue, and with a motley yet loyal band of shipmates escapes to begin a life of noble piracy and adventure on the caribbean seas.

"Peter Blood was many things in his time: soldier, country doctor, slave, pirate, and finally Governor of Jamaica. Incidentally, he was an Irishman. Round his humorous-heroic figure Mr. Sabatini has written an exciting romance of the Spanish Main, the facts of which he alleges to have been found in the diary and log books of one Jeremiah Pitt, a follower of Monmouth in 1685 and Blood's faithful companion in adventure." —*Times Literary Supplement*

Originally published as Captain Blood, His Odyssey: New York : Houghton Mifflin, 1922.

Scaramouche: a romance of the French Revolution. Rafael Sabatini. Norton, 2002. X, 406 p.

ISBN 9780393323306

1. Actors and actresses 2. Traveling theater 3. Disguises 4. French Revolution, 1789-1799 5. Swordfighters 6. France 7. Revolutionary France (1789-1799) 8. 1780s 9. Historical fiction 10. Adventure stories 11. Books to movies

When his best friend is struck down by an uncaring aristocrat, French lawyer Andre-Louis Moreau disguises himself as the clown Scaramouche to speak out against an unjust nobility, in a novel of romance and adventure set during the French Revolution.

Originally published: Boston: Houghton Mifflin Co, 1921.

Saberhagen, Fred

Coinspinner's story. Fred Saberhagen. T. Doherty Associates, 1989. 244 p; (Book of Lost Swords, 5)

ISBN 9780312932213

1. Magic swords 2. Quests 3. Princes 4. Swords 5. Magic 6. Fantasy fiction 7. Sword and sorcery

LC 89039878

A host of strange characters—Prince Nurat of Culm, the evil macrowizard Wood, Prince Adrian, and Trilby—become involved in a desperate struggle to possess a sword of chance known as Coinspinner.

Farslayer's story. Fred Saberhagen. T. Doherty Associates, 1989. 252 p; (Book of Lost Swords, 4)

ISBN 9780312931704

1. Magic swords 2. Good and evil 3. Family feuds 4. Quests 5. Swords 6. Fantasy fiction 7. Sword and sorcery

LC 89011638

"Two rival families wage a war of attrition and vengeance for possession of 'Farslayer,' one of the 12 Lost Swords made by the gods and imbued with unearthly powers. A grim sense of fatality underlies the deceptive simplicity of the author's style." —*Library Journal*

Mindsword's story. Fred Saberhagen. Tor Books, 1990. 250 p. (Book of Lost Swords, 6)

ISBN 9780312851286

1. Magic swords 2. Quests 3. Princes 4. Good and evil 5. Magic 6. Fantasy fiction 7. Sword and sorcery

LC 90038899

When the long-lost Mindsword—which gives mindless devotion to the one who wields it—falls into the hands of Prince Murat, Kristen, the beautiful wife of Prince Mark, falls under its spell, and it is up to Mark and his companions to save his wife and his kingdom.

"Saberhagen treads a fine line between fantasy and moral fable in his latest addition to a popular series." —*Library Journal*

Shieldbreaker's story. Fred Saberhagen. TOR, 1994. 255 p; (Book of Lost Swords, 8)

ISBN 9780312850012

1. Magic swords 2. Princes 3. Good and evil 4. Quests 5. Demons 6. Fantasy fiction 7. Sword and sorcery

An unsuspecting fourteen-year-old warrior, Prince Stephen, is forced into manhood, when he uses Sheildbreaker to protect the universe from the greedy hands of Vikata the Dark King.

Sightblinder's story. Fred Saberhagen. T. Doherty Associates 1987. 248 p. (Book of Lost Swords, 2)
ISBN 9780312930325
1. Magic swords 2. Adventure 3. Wizards 4. Swords 5. Magic 6. Fantasy fiction 7. Sword and sorcery
LC 87050477

When Prince Mark and the good wizard Honan-Fu are cast into a hellish enchantment by the Ancient One, Ben and young Zoltan need the help of Sightbinder, the Sword of Power that causes to appear that which a person most desires, or fears.

Stonecutter's story. Fred Saberhagen. Tor, 1988. 247 p; (Book of Lost Swords, 3)
ISBN 9780312930738
1. Magic swords 2. Quests 3. Black magic 4. Adventure 5. Swords 6. Fantasy fiction 7. Sword and sorcery
LC 87051397

Four very different people—Prince al-Farabi, Kasimir, a young physician, the wise magistrate Wen Chang, and Natalia, an inhabitant of a House of Pleasure in the city of Eylan—pursue the stolen Stonecutter, the Sword of Siege.

"The book's virtues include a cast of well-drawn characters and some vividly realized societies, as well as Saberhagen's usual spare prose and sound narrative technique." —*Booklist*

Wayfinder's story. Fred Saberhagen. TOR, 1992. 251 p; (Book of Lost Swords, 7)
ISBN 9780312850005
1. Magic swords 2. Quests 3. Wisdom 4. Wizards 5. Swords 6. Fantasy fiction 7. Sword and sorcery
LC 92000858

When Wayfinder, the Sword of Wisdom, turns up in the hut of Valdemar, a simple grower of grapes, it leads Valdemar on his quest to find a wife

"One of 12 magical swords forged by the Gods, Wayfinder has the power to guide its possessor to whatever the seeker wants. Chance brings Wayfinder to Ben of Purkinje, who uses it to find Woundhealer, the sword with powers to cure the injured wife of Prince Mar of Sarykam. The evil magician Wood also wants the swords; his attack on Ben brings Mark, and even more swords, into the fray.... Saberhagen keeps the plot moving, providing a pleasurable light reading experience." —*Publishers Weekly*

Woundhealer's story. Fred Saberhagen. TOR, 1986. 281 p; (Book of Lost Swords, 1)
ISBN 9780312932435
1. Magic swords 2. Healing 3. Good and evil 4. Quests 5. Princes 6. Fantasy fiction 7. Sword and sorcery
LC 86050319

Prince Mark of Tasavalta sets out to find the Sword Woundhealer—the only cure for his ill son—but the evil wizard Berslam and Baron Amnitor have other ideas BT

"A pleasant adventure that benefits greatly from Saberhagen's narrative gifts as the various strands leapfrog forward, keeping the reader off balance but constantly intrigued." —*Publishers Weekly*

Sackville-West, V.
All passion spent. Vita Sackville-West. Vintage Books, 2017. 169 p.
ISBN 9780525433972

1. Senior women 2. England 3. Modern classics 4. Psychological fiction

After the death of elder statesman Lord Slane—a former prime minister of Great Britain and viceroy of India—everyone assumes that his eighty-eight-year-old widow will slowly fade away in her grief, remaining as proper, decorative, and dutiful as she has been her entire married life. But the deceptively gentle Lady Slane has other ideas. First she defies the patronizing meddling of her children and escapes to a rented house in Hampstead. There, to her offspring's utter amazement, she revels in her new freedom, recalls her youthful ambitions, and gathers some very unsuitable companions—who reveal to her just how much she had sacrificed under the pressure of others' expectations.

"Gentle, charming Lady Slane, her family, and her friends, drawn with wit and skill in this tale of graceful old age, create an impression of subtlety and beauty." —*Booklist*
Originally published: Great Britain: Hogarth Press, 1931.

The **Edwardians**. Vita Sackville-West; new introduction by Victoria Glendinning. Virago, 2003. 349 p.
ISBN 9780860683599
1. Upper class 2. Aristocracy 3. Generation gap 4. Young men — Relations with older women 5. Freedom 6. Great Britain 7. England 8. Edwardian era (1901-1914) 9. Literary fiction

At nineteen, Sebastian is a duke and heir to a vast country estate. A deep sense of tradition binds him to his inheritance, though he loathes the social circus he is a part of. Deception, infidelity and greed hide beneath the glittering surface of good manners. Among the guests at a lavish party are two people who will change Sebastian's life: Lady Roehampton, who will initiate him in the art of love; and Leonard Anquetil, a polar explorer who will lead Sebastian and his free-spirited sister Viola to question their destiny.

Originally published: London : Hogarth Press, 1930.

Sagan, Carl
Contact: a novel. Carl Sagan. Simon and Schuster, 1985. 432 p.
ISBN 9780671434007
1. Life on other planets 2. Women scientists 3. Interstellar communication 4. Mathematics 5. Aliens 6. Books to movies 7. Hard science fiction 8. Science fiction classics
LC 85014645

Locus Award for First Novel, 1986

Astrophysicist Dr. Rebecca Blake deciphers a message from outer space and finds that the message contains directions for the construction of a complicated machine.

"A serious blend of science fact and speculation with a fast-paced and well-crafted story...suggesting that Sagan is more interested in illustrating human relations and human response than depicting alien creatures.... Sagan has provided a novel of ideas, and finds drama in how people interact with them in a situation of challenge and discovery." —*Christian Science Monitor*

Sagan, Francoise
★ **Bonjour** tristesse. Francoise Sagan; translated from the French by Irene Ash; introduction by Diane Johnson. HarperCollins, 2001. X, 130 p.
ISBN 9780066211695
1. Teenage romance 2. Seventeen-year-old girls 3. Fathers and daughters 4. Mistresses 5. Jealousy in teenage girls 6. French Riviera 7. Translations 8. Coming-of-age stories 9. Modern classics

Cecile is the spoiled 17-year-old daughter of Raymond, a wealthy Parisian widower vacationing in a villa on the French Riviera. Their pleasure-seeking existence is threatened when Raymond decides to marry

Cecile's straitlaced godmother, Anne, who disapproves of the teenager's steamy summer affair with Philippe.

Bonjour tristesse first published by Editions Rene Julliard 1954; first published in Great Britain by John Murray 1955.

Sager, Riley

Final girls: a novel. Riley Sager. Dutton, 2017. 352 p.
ISBN 9781101985366
1. Young women 2. Violence against women 3. Victims of violent crimes 4. Murder 5. Coping in women 6. Manhattan, New York City 7. Psychological suspense 8. Multiple perspectives
LC 2016034340
Librarians' Choice (Australia), 2017; LibraryReads Favorites, 2017; Loan Stars Favourites, 2017; Thriller Award for Best Novel, 2018

Emerging a lone survivor of a serial killer's massacre a decade earlier, a former college student struggles to ignore traumatic memories and move on as one of a group of other survivors who look to her for answers when one of them is found dead in a suspicious suicide.

"Sager does an excellent job throughout of keeping the audience guessing until the final twist. A fresh voice in psychological suspense." —*Kirkus*

The last time I lied: a novel. Riley Sager. Dutton, 2018. 370 p.
ISBN 9781524743079
1. Witnesses 2. Young women 3. Summer camps 4. Artists 5. Missing girls 6. Psychological suspense 7. First person narratives 8. Adult books for young adults
LC 2017060923
Loan Stars Favourites, 2018

An artist who witnessed the disappearance of her bunkmates at summer camp as a young girl accepts an opportunity to return to Camp Nightingale as a painting instructor and tries to discover what really happened to her friends.

"Sager's second thriller is as tense and twisty as his best-selling Final Girls (2017), but this one is even more polished, with gut-wrenching plot surprises skillfully camouflaged by Emma's paranoia and confusion, the increasingly creepy setting, and a cast of intriguingly secretive characters." —*Booklist*

Lock every door: a novel. Riley Sager. Dutton, 2019. 368 p.
ISBN 9781524745141
1. Apartment house life 2. Housesitting 3. Secrets 4. Missing women 5. Rules 6. Manhattan, New York City 7. Psychological suspense
LC 2018058455
LibraryReads Favorites, 2019; Loan Stars Favourites, 2019

Follows a young woman whose new job apartment sitting in one of New York's oldest and most glamorous buildings may cost more than it pays.

"Sager (Final Girls) delivers a psychological, creepy, and unputdownable thriller. Likable characters, great writing, just enough twists, and a Rosemary's Baby vibe will make this a summer hit. Purchase for Stephen King and Gillian Flynn fans." —*Library Journal*

Sahota, Sunjeev

The year of the runaways. Sunjeev Sahota. Alfred A. Knopf, 2016. 484 pages
ISBN 9781101946107
1. Undocumented immigrants 2. Life change events 3. Communities 4. East Indians in England 5. Immigration and emigration 6. England 7. Sheffield, England 8. Political fiction 9. Literary fiction
Shortlisted for the Man Booker Prize, 2015

Follows three young men and a woman who journey together from India to England to fulfill respective goals while hiding painful secrets from the past and struggling with financial limitations and the punishing realities of immigrant life.

"Quarrelling, parting, and finding solace in one another in unexpected ways, Sahota's characters are wonderfully drawn, and imbued with depth and feeling." —*Publishers Weekly*

Originally published: London : Picador, 2015.

Saint, Jennifer

Ariadne. Jennifer Saint. Flatiron Books, 2021. 320 p.
ISBN 9781250773586
1. Ariadne (Greek deity) 2. Theseus (Greek mythology) 3. Minotaur (Greek mythology) 4. Phaedra (Greek mythology) 5. Princesses 6. Crete 7. Ancient Greece 8. Literary fiction 9. Mythological fiction 10. Adaptations, retellings, and spin-offs
LC 2020053224
Loan Stars Favourites, 2021

This epic feminist retelling of the Greek Myth of Theseus and the Minotaur follows Ariadne as she, defying the gods, betraying her family and country, and risking everything for love, helps Theseus kill the Minotaur.

"Saint expertly highlights how often the women of this world pay the price for the actions of the men around them. Lovers of mythology should snap this up." —*Publishers Weekly*

Saint-Exupery, Antoine de

★ The **little** prince. Written and drawn by Antoine de Saint-Exupery; translated from the French by Katherine Woods. Harcourt, 1943. 91 p. : Color illustration
ISBN 9780152023980
1. Princes 2. Pride and vanity 3. Pilots 4. Purpose in life 5. Boy adventurers 6. Sahara 7. Allegories 8. Translations 9. Books to movies
LC 82011968

This many-dimensional fable of an airplane pilot who has crashed in the desert is for readers of all ages. The pilot comes upon the little prince soon after the crash. The prince tells of his adventures on different planets and on Earth as he attempts to learn about the universe in order to live peacefully on his own small planet. A spiritual quality enhances the seemingly simple observations of the little prince. Shapiro. Fic for Youth. 3d edition

Translation of Le petit prince.
Book adapted into the 1974 musical film of the same name.
Translated from the French.

Night flight. Antoine de Saint Exupery; translated from the French by Stuart Gilbert. Harcourt Brace Jovanovich, 1974. 87 p.
ISBN 9780156656054
1. Pilots 2. Night flying 3. Air mail service 4. Flight 5. Aviation 6. Argentina 7. 1930s 8. Adventure stories 9. Hickok, Wild Bill

A group of pilots must conquer the savage Andean weather as well as the mechanical shortcomings of early aircraft to establish an air-mail service to South America.

Reprint of the translation of Vol de nuit, originally published by Reynal & Hitchcock, New York, 1932.

Sainz Borgo, Karina

★ **It** would be night in Caracas. Karina Sainz Borgo; translated from the Spanish by Elizabeth Bryer. Harper Via, 2019. 229 pages
ISBN 9780062936868

1. Mothers — Death 2. Revolutionaries 3. Survival 4. Options, alternatives, choices 5. Anarchism 6. Venezuela 7. Caracas (Venezuela) 8. Political fiction 9. Translations

LC 2019013246

A woman tests the limits of what she is willing to do to secure her future in turbulent modern Venezuela overrun by violent revolutionaries.

Translation of: La hija de la espanola.

Originally published: Barcelona : Lumen, 2019.

Translated from the Spanish.

Sakey, Marcus

A **better** world. Marcus Sakey. Thomas & Mercer, 2014. 380 p. (Brilliance saga, 2)

ISBN 9781477823941

1. Terrorism 2. Antiterrorists 3. Superhuman abilities 4. Families 5. Genius 6. 21st century 7. Dystopian fiction 8. Political thrillers 9. Science fiction

In a world where one percent of the population is born with special abilities, a terrorist network led by these "brilliants" devastates three cities, and presidential adviser Nick Cooper must stop the oncoming war between brilliants and humans.

"Sakey's series has been taken as an allegory of America devouring its own. Could be. But recommend it, too, as a first-rate actioner forever pulsing forward, told in vivid, even poetic prose." —*Booklist*

Brilliance. Marcus Sakey. Thomas & Mercer, 2013. 439 p. (Brilliance saga, 1)

ISBN 9781611099690

1. Terrorism 2. Antiterrorists 3. Superhuman abilities 4. Families 5. Genius 6. 21st century 7. Dystopian fiction 8. Political thrillers 9. Science fiction

Starting in 1980, about 1% of all children born in the U.S. were gifted with unusual abilities. Thirty-three years later, these "brilliants" (also called "abnormals" or "abs") are leaders in various fields—including terrorism. Nick Cooper's one of them, though he works for a government agency charged with stopping ab terrorists. To stop them, Nick will have to demolish most of his beliefs about the world he lives in—and maybe most of that world itself. The too-close-for-comfort possibilities of this near-future thriller will linger long after the last page.

Salinger, J. D.

★ The **catcher** in the rye. J. D. Salinger. Little, Brown and Company, 2001. 288 p.

ISBN 9780316769532

1. Alienation in teenagers 2. Runaway teenagers 3. Sensitivity in teenagers 4. Sixteen-year-old boys 5. Caulfield, Holden (Fictitious character) 6. New York City 7. Psychological fiction 8. Modern classics 9. Coming-of-age stories 10. Adult books for young adults

LC 108915

After leaving prep school Holden Caulfield spends three days on his own in New York City.

"This is tender and true, and impossible, in its picture of the old hells of young boys, the lonesomeness and tentative attempts to be mature and secure, the awful block between youth and being grown-up, the fright and sickness that humans and their behavior cause the changeling, the dramatization of the big bang. It is a sorry little worm's view of the off-beat of adult pressure, of contemporary strictures and conformity, of sentiment... A strict report, worthy of sympathy." —*Kirkus*

First published in serial form in the USA, 1945-46; first published in book form in the USA, 1951.

Orginally published: 1951.

★ **Franny** and Zooey. By J. D. Salinger. Little, Brown, 1991. 202 p. ISBN 9780316769495

1. Teenagers — Religious life 2. Siblings 3. Compulsive behavior in women 4. Prayer 5. College seniors 6. Psychological fiction 7. Modern classics

Two children of the Glass family appear in separate stories laid in twentieth-century New York

Two stories, first published in the New Yorker, "about the Glass family of 20th century New York.

★ **Nine** stories. J.D. Salinger. Little, Brown, 1991. 198 p. ISBN 9780316769501

1. Loss (Psychology) 2. Interpersonal relations 3. Short stories

DeDaumier-Smith's Blue Period," "Teddy," and "A Perfect Day for Bananafish" are among the nine works in a collection of Salinger's perceptive and realistic short stories

Originally published: Boston : Little, Brown and Co, 1953.

Raise high the roof beam, carpenters,: and Seymour—an introduction. J. D. Salinger. Little, Brown, 1963. 248 p.

ISBN 9780316769570

1. Jewish Americans 2. Brothers 3. Weddings 4. Glass family (Fictitious characters) 5. Psychological fiction

LC 63008969

Buddy Glass introduces his older brother and describes the events of Seymour's wedding day.

The first of these two stories was originally published in The New Yorker in 1955. The second was originally published in 1959 in the same magazine.

Sallis, James

Drive. James Sallis. Poisoned Pen Press, 2005. 158 p. (Drive novels, 1) ISBN 9781590581810

1. Automobile driving 2. Stunt performers 3. Betrayal 4. Criminals 5. Fugitives 6. Los Angeles, California 7. Arizona 8. Noir fiction 9. Books to movies

LC 2005925325

The story of a man who works as a stunt driver by day and a getaway driver by night. He drives, that's all, until a heist goes sour and a contract is put on his head.

"Sallis gives us his most tightly written mystery to date, worthy of comparison to the compact, exciting oeuvre of French noir giant Jean-Patrick Manchette." —*Publishers Weekly*

This novel was adapted into film in 2011, directed by director Nicolas Winding Refn, starring Ryan Gosling, Carey Mulligan, Bryan Cranston, and Albert Brooks.

Salter, James

Last night. James Salter. Knopf, 2005. 144 p.

ISBN 9781400043125

1. Interpersonal relations 2. Man-woman relationships 3. Short stories

LC 2004057793

Booklist Editors' Choice, 2005

A compilation of short fiction explores the themes of love, honor, friendship, sacrifice, memory, and abandon through the lives of a translator assisting in his wife's suicide, a rare books collector, a profoundly lonely married woman, and other characters.

"All of the stories in Last Night are superb, but the title story is the tautest and most memorable.... This story about the consequences of adultery gives new meaning to the phrase the morning after. Despite its shocking plot twist, the story maintains the exacting, calm narrative voice that has distinguished all of Salter's work. His characters may be haunted by death and disappointment, but Salter never judges them, never even pretends to have them neatly pegged. He lets them stay elliptical, in shadow." —*New York Times Book Review*

Ten short stories.

Sampson, Freya

The **last** chance library. Freya Sampson. Berkley, 2021. 336 p.

ISBN 9780593201374

1. Libraries 2. Librarians 3. Shyness in women 4. Communities 5. Friendship 6. England 7. Relationship fiction

LC 2021001981

LibraryReads Favorites, 2021

June Jones emerges from her shell to fight for her beloved local library, and through the efforts and support of an eclectic group of library patrons, she discovers life-changing friendships along the way.

"A full roster of quirky characters, hijinks (including a cleverly diverted stripper), and a handsome schoolmate come back to town to populate Sampson's debut, a sweet testament to the power of reading, community, and the library." —*Booklist*

Sand, George

Marianne. By George Sand; edited and translated by Sian Miles. Carrol and Graf Publishers, 1988. 171 pages.

ISBN 9780881844153

1. Young women — Relations with older men 2. Matchmakers 3. Independence in women 4. Love triangles 5. Man-woman relationships 6. France 7. 19th century 8. Translations 9. Love stories

LC 88007308

"While very much a period piece, this last scrap of Sand's tremendous oeuvre is a charming bit of entertainment." —*Publishers Weekly*

Sanders, Lawrence

★ The **first** deadly sin. Lawrence Sanders. G.P. Putnam's Sons, 1973. 566 p. (Edward X. Delaney mysteries, 2)

ISBN 9780399112287

1. Police 2. Serial murder investigation 3. Upper class 4. Secrets 5. Delaney, Edward X. (Fictitious character) 6. New York City 7. Mysteries 8. Psychological fiction 9. Books to movies

LC 73082018

Captain Ed Delaney of the New York City police is out to stop a well-dressed man from depopulating Manhattan's priciest neighborhoods with an ice pick, in an early thriller by the author of McNally's Gamble.

★ The **fourth** deadly sin. Lawrence Sanders. G. P. Putnam's Sons, 1985. 313 p. (Edward X. Delaney mysteries, 5)

ISBN 9780399130625

1. Psychiatric hospital patients 2. Murder suspects 3. Extramarital affairs 4. Delaney, Edward X. (Fictitious character) 5. Deception 6. New York City 7. Psychological fiction 8. Mysteries

When saintly New York psychiatrist Simon Ellerbee is murdered, retired Chief of Detectives Edward X. Delaney pursues the murderer on a list of the doctor's six most potentially violent patients, obtained from his beautiful psychologist wife BT

"Delaney displays that combination of computerlike efficiency and human touch that make him such an appealing detective. It's a masterly performance, not only chilling, but thought-provoking and often touching." —*Publishers Weekly*

McNally's dilemma. By Lawrence Sanders and Vincent Lardo. G. P. Putnam's Sons, 1999. 309 p. (Archy McNally mysteries, 8)

ISBN 9780399144905

1. Private investigators 2. Extortion 3. Murder 4. Rich women 5. Husband killing 6. Palm Beach, Florida 7. Mysteries

LC 99-20988

McNally is hired to find out about thefts from the wealth Forsythe estate, and becomes involved in a family power struggle that can lead to death.

★ **McNally's** gamble. Lawrence Sanders. G. P. Putnam's Sons, 1997. 307 p. (Archy McNally mysteries, 7)

ISBN 9780399142482

1. Greed 2. Widows 3. Lust 4. Murder 5. Stanton, Elizabeth Cady 6. Palm Beach, Florida 7. Mysteries

LC 9650369

When well-to-do widow Edythe Westmore is urged to buy a Faberge Imperial egg, her children oppose the investment and hire Archy McNally to stop the deal. Archy is thrust into a whirling vortex of greed, passion, and murder that even he must fight to rise above.

"A comic whodunit featuring Archy McNally, the foppish but likable head of 'discreet inquiries' at his father's law firm in Palm Beach, Fla. This time Archy's task is to investigate the credentials of a suspicious investment adviser, Frederick Clemens, and his secretary, Felix Katz.... Mr. Sanders clearly delights in playing up the bumbling, spoof aspects of this detective yarn, especially during its climactic but unavoidably funny denouement." —*New York Times Book Review*

McNally's luck. Lawrence Sanders. G. P. Putnam's Sons, 1992. 319 p. (Archy McNally mysteries, 2)

ISBN 9780399137624

1. Women psychics 2. Murder 3. Lust 4. Private investigators 5. Murder investigation 6. Palm Beach, Florida 7. Mysteries

LC 921394

It's hazy, hot and humid in the Palm Beach world of the rich and famous, but charming, sophisticated—and street-smart—investigator Archibald McNally keeps his cool, solving discreet cases for a select group of posh clients.

McNally's puzzle. Lawrence Sanders. G. P. Putnam's Sons, 1996. 311 p. (Archy McNally mysteries, 6)

ISBN 9780399141355

1. Private investigators 2. Death threats 3. Heirs and heiresses 4. Father and adult child 5. Murder 6. Palm Beach, Florida 7. Mysteries

LC 96-5398

A pet store owner turns to McNally and Son for answers when he believes his life is in danger, but then he is murdered in his sleep and Archy McNally's manic depressive son is the prime suspect.

McNally's secret. Lawrence Sanders. G. P. Putnam's Sons, 1992. 317 p. (Archy McNally mysteries, 1)

ISBN 9780399136757

1. Robbery 2. Extortion 3. Private investigators 4. Deception 5. Man-woman relationships 6. Palm Beach, Florida 7. Mysteries

LC 91009803

Beneath the glaring sun of Palm Beach—and behind the lowest crimes of high society—McNally is paid to keep family secrets in the closet.

"Four priceless U.S. airmail stamps issued in 1918 and known as 'inverted Jennies' have been stolen from a wealthy matron's mansion in Palm Beach.... McNally's task is to find the thief 'without the barest hint of scandal coming to light.' There are lots of suspects, a couple of deaths, and a fine romance." —*Booklist*

McNally's trial. G.P. Putnam's Sons, 1995. 309 p. (Archy McNally mysteries, 5)

ISBN 9781568952086

1. Private investigators 2. Business — Corrupt practices 3. Funeral homes 4. Deception 5. Rich families 6. Palm Beach, Florida 7. Mysteries

LC 95-5417

At the request of the nubile treasurer of a posh funeral home, Archy McNally and his partner, Binky Watrous, investigate suspicious goings-on and uncover family scandal, criminal conspiracy, business intrigue, and other sinister surprises BT

"The novel boasts a delightful assembly of supporting characters, especially Archy's pal, the totally dissolute, utterly inept would-be detective Binky Watrous. A pleasant diversion." —*Booklist*

The **second** deadly sin. Lawrence Sanders. G. P. Putnam's Sons, 1977. 443 p. (Edward X. Delaney mysteries, 3)

ISBN 9780399120237

1. Former police 2. Greed 3. Murder investigation 4. Murder 5. Delaney, Edward X. (Fictitious character) 6. New York City 7. Mysteries 8. Psychological fiction

LC 77003652

Coming out of retirement to investigate the stabbing murder of acclaimed and hated artist Victor Maitland, ex-Chief of Detectives Edward X. Delaney is faced with a mob of greedy suspects and a tangle of possible motives.

The **sixth** commandment: a novel. G. P. Putnam's Sons, 1978. 312 p.

ISBN 9780399123054

1. Cancer research 2. Scientists 3. Deception 4. Human experimentation in medicine 5. Small towns 6. Mysteries

LC 78013158

"This gloomy escapade about a hard-drinking, chain-smoking, world-pitying investigator...is brimful of juice and excitement, with some insight and much foolishnessa genuinely riveting diversion." —*The New Yorker*

The **tenth** commandment: a novel. G. P. Putnam's Sons, 1980. 385 p.

ISBN 9780425050019

1. Revenge 2. Private investigators 3. Millionaires 4. Law firms 5. Suicide 6. New York City 7. Mysteries

LC 80013002

Joshua Bigg, the very short chief investigator for a very offbeat law firm, finds that the link between one client's apparent suicide and the disappearance of another is a widow-loving lay minister.

★ The **third** deadly sin. Lawrence Sanders. G. P. Putnam's Sons, 1981. 444 p. (Edward X. Delaney mysteries, 4)

ISBN 9780399126147

1. Former police 2. Violence 3. Women murderers 4. Violence against men 5. Psychopaths 6. New York City 7. Psychological fiction 8. Mysteries

LC 80026325

The murders of out-of-town businessmen in large Manhattan hotels, by a bizarre, brilliant psychopath, hurls retired Chief of Detectives Edward X. Delaney into an elusive, horrifying, tragic manhunt.

The **Timothy** files. G. P. Putnam's Sons, 1987. 380 p. (Timothy Cone mysteries, 1)

ISBN 9780399132612

1. Private investigators 2. Violence 3. Stock market 4. Drug addiction 5. Vietnam veterans 6. Wall Street, New York City 7. Mysteries

LC 86025496

Timothy Cone, a detective who works for a firm that investigates companies with whom its clients are contemplating big business deals, becomes involved with three baffling cases.

Timothy's game. Lawrence Sanders. G. P. Putnam's Sons, 1988. 382 p. (Timothy Cone mysteries, 2)

ISBN 9780399133688

1. Private investigators 2. Violence 3. Scandals 4. Stock market 5. Vietnam veterans 6. Wall Street, New York City 7. Mysteries

LC 87029073

Detective Timothy Cone wanders Wall Street seeking mobsters, murderers, and shady Market operators, in a quest to solve a baffling mystery BT

"This novel is set on Wall Street, where clever detective Timothy Cone dresses in Salvation Army chic, chain-smokes Camels, and drinks too much. Cone has a cat named Cleo who eats ham hocks, potato salad, and garlic salami, and a girlfriend named Samantha who sports long, auburn hair. Throw in a foul-mouthed woman who owns a garbage-hauling firm controlled by the mob, an insider-trading leak, murder, and a tong war in Chinatown, and you have the usual brand of Sanders' readable fiction." —*Booklist*

Sandford, John

Bloody genius. John Sandford. G. P. Putnam's Sons, 2019. 372 p. (Virgil Flowers mysteries, 12)

ISBN 9780525536611

1. Campus murders 2. Culture wars 3. Scholars and academics 4. Murder investigation 5. Universities and colleges 6. Minnesota 7. Police procedurals

When a culture war between rival departments at a local state university culminates in the death of a renowned scholar, Virgil Flowers struggles to identify a killer among a group of wildly passionate, diametrically opposed zealots.

Broken prey. John Sandford. G.P. Putnam's Sons, 2005. 400 p. (Prey series, 16)

ISBN 9780399152726

1. Detectives 2. Serial murder investigation 3. Deception 4. Serial murderers 5. Sex offenders 6. Minnesota 7. Minneapolis, Minnesota 8. Thrillers and suspense 9. Police procedurals

LC 2005042981

After a series of killings that disturbingly emulate the works of a trio of inmates currently being held at the Minnesota Security Hospital, Lucas Davenport investigates a missing man who was released from the hospital weeks earlier.

"Lucas Davenport, a Minnesota State Bureau of Criminal Apprehension investigator, had lately been doing political fix-it jobs for the governor, but this time he's got a psychopathic serial killer on his hands.... The first victim, a young woman, was scourged with a wire whip; number two, a young man, had his penis cut off. Evidence first points to recently released sex offender Charlie Pope. Though Charlie is pretty dumb and the killer is extremely smart, it takes Davenport and his series partner, Detective Sloan, a while to realize they're chasing the wrong guy. Sandford introduces some lighter moments, the most entertaining about Davenport's new iPod and his quest to compile a list of the 100 best rock songs ever recorded, which every cop on the force gives him suggestions for. These moments allow readers to catch their breath amid the otherwise nonstop tension." —*Publishers Weekly*

John Camp writing as John Sandford.

Buried prey. John Sandford. G.P. Putnam's Sons, 2011. 390 pages (Prey series, 21)

ISBN 9780399157387

1. Police 2. Detectives 3. Cold cases (Criminal investigation) 4. Serial murders 5. Serial murder investigation 6. Minnesota 7. St. Paul, Minnesota 8. Thrillers and suspense 9. Police procedurals

Investigating the discovery of two bodies in a house demolition, Lucas Davenport identifies the victims as two girls who disappeared in 1985, a cold case that overshadowed the early years of his career.

Certain prey. John Sandford. G. P. Putnam's Sons, 1999. 339 p. (Prey series, 10)

ISBN 9780399144967

1. Police 2. Women assassins 3. Women defense attorneys 4. Women serial murderers 5. Serial murders 6. Minnesota 7. Minneapolis, Minnesota 8. Thrillers and suspense 9. Books to movies 10. Police procedurals

LC 9919048

Clara Rinker is the best hit woman in the business. She's been hired by an attorney in Minnesota who wants a rival eliminated. But the witness survives, the attorney starts acting strangely and a big cop named Lucas Davenport gets on her case. There are loose ends popping up everywhere and Lucas is in for the run of his life.

"Sandford keeps the level of suspense dizzyingly high as he shifts viewpoints between the women and Davenport." —*Booklist*

John Camp writing as John Sandford.

2011 TV movie also known as John Sandford's Certain prey.

Chosen prey. John Sandford. G.P. Putnam's Sons, 2001. 416 p. (Prey series, 12)

ISBN 9780399147289

1. Art history teachers 2. Murder investigation 3. Police 4. Davenport, Lucas (Fictitious character) 5. Serial murderers 6. Minnesota 7. Minneapolis, Minnesota 8. Thrillers and suspense 9. Police procedurals

LC 2001018594

Deputy Chief Lucas Davenport takes on a murder case involving an art history professor who is a suspect in a serial murder case involving the murder of women who have modeled for photographs.

John Camp writing as John Sandford.

★ **Deadline**. John Sandford. G.P Putnam's Sons, 2014. 388 pages; (Virgil Flowers mysteries, 8)

ISBN 9780399162374

1. Government investigators 2. Murder 3. Journalists 4. Detectives 5. Intelligence service 6. Minnesota 7. Police procedurals

In the aftermath of a school board's secret decision to have a local reporter murdered, Virgil Flowers' investigation of a sinister dognapping is interrupted by a suspicious death.

"Sanford balances straight-talking Virgil Flowers often hilariously folksy tone and Trippton's dark core of methamphetamine manufacturers and sociopaths; the result is pure reading pleasure for thriller fans." —*Booklist*

Deep freeze. John Sandford. Penguin Group USA, 2017. 400 p. (Virgil Flowers mysteries, 10)

ISBN 9780399176067

1. Teachers 2. Serial murderers 3. Girl murder victims 4. Murder investigation 5. Detectives 6. Minnesota 7. Police procedurals

When a woman, with connections to a high school class of twenty years ago, is found frozen in a block of ice, Virgil Floweres returns to Trippton, Minnesota to investigate, uncovering years of traumas, feuds, and bad blood.

Easy prey. John Sandford. G. P. Putnam's Sons, 2000. 407 p. (Prey series, 11)

ISBN 9780399146138

1. Police 2. Murder investigation 3. Fashion models 4. Murder 5. Murderers 6. Minnesota 7. Minneapolis, Minnesota 8. Thrillers and suspense 9. Police procedurals

LC 23962

Police Chief Lucas Davenport hunts two separate murderers tied together by one victim, a model who was on the fast-track to superstardom at the time of her murder.

"Although Lucas makes his own strong fashion statement...his smooth professional moves are the best feature of his style. A shrewd gamester who made his personal fortune designing computer games, he follows sound police procedures and devises one intricate ploy after another to draw out the killers." —*New York Times Book Review*

John Camp writing as John Sandford.

Field of prey. John Sandford. G. P. Putnam's Sons, 2014. 416 p. (Prey series, 24)

ISBN 9780399162381

1. Serial murder investigation 2. Serial murders 3. Detectives 4. Murder investigation 5. Davenport, Lucas (Fictitious character) 6. Minnesota 7. St. Paul, Minnesota 8. Thrillers and suspense 9. Police procedurals

LC 2014006595

Lucas Davenport investigates the discovery of several bodies in an abandoned Minnesota farmyard, discovering the work of a local serial killer who has been murdering one victim every summer for years.

★ **Golden** prey. John Sandford. Penguin Group USA 2017. 416 p. (Prey series, 27)

ISBN 9780399184574

1. Gangs 2. Robbery investigation 3. United States marshals 4. Robbery 5. Drug cartels 6. North Dakota 7. Thrillers and suspense 8. Police procedurals

A series of audacious robberies compels newly appointed U.S. marshal Lucas Davenport to investigate the possible return of a gang leader who once killed two FBI agents.

"Sandford's trademark blend of rough humor and deadly action keeps the pages turning until the smile-inducing wrap-up, which reveals the fates of a number of his quirky, memorable characters." —*Publishers Weekly*

Heat lightning. John Sandford. G.P. Putnam's Sons, 2008. 384 p. (Virgil Flowers mysteries, 2)

ISBN 9780399155277

1. Vietnam War, 1961-1975 2. Serial murders 3. Murder investigation 4. Murder 5. Detectives 6. Minnesota 7. Keckley, Elizabeth

LC 2008028339

Summoned by Lucas Davenport to investigate a pair of murders in which the victims are found with lemons in their mouths, Minnesota Bureau of Criminal Apprehension investigator Virgil Flowers struggles to find a connection that could prevent additional killings.

Sequel to: Dark of the moon.

Sequel: Rough country.

Hidden prey. John Sandford. G. P. Putnam's Sons, 2004. 400 p. (Prey series, 15)

ISBN 9780399151804

1. Detectives 2. Russians in the United States 3. Murder investigation 4. Murder 5. Murderers 6. Minnesota 7. Minneapolis, Minnesota 8. Thrillers and suspense 9. Police procedurals

LC 2004044351

"Readers will be pleased with this relaxed version of the moody Minneapolis investigator. In past novels, the womanizing Davenport would have romanced the good-looking Russian lady, but the new Davenport is content to play the part of friend and protector and go back to his cozy family with an unstained and remarkably contented soul." —*Publishers Weekly*

John Camp writing as John Sandford.

Holy ghost. John Sandford. Putnam Pub Group, 2018. 400 p. (Virgil Flowers mysteries, 11)

ISBN 9780735217324
1. Apparitions 2. Mayors 3. Fraud 4. Tourists 5. Murder 6. Minnesota 7. Police procedurals
A mayor's half-baked scheme to revive a floundering Minnesota community by turning it into a religious shrine is thrown into chaos by the discovery of a body.

★ **Invisible** prey. John Sandford. G. P. Putnam's Sons, 2007. 384 p. (Prey series, 17)
ISBN 9780399154218
1. Senior murder victims 2. Sex crimes 3. Murder investigation 4. Crimes against seniors 5. Murder 6. Minnesota 7. Minneapolis, Minnesota 8. Thrillers and suspense 9. Police procedurals
Investigating the seemingly open-and-shut double homicide case involving a pair of wealthy elderly women, Lucas Davenport begins to suspect that the handful of small items that were stolen from the crime scene may have had more significant values.
John Camp writing as John Sandford.

Mad River. John Sandford. G.P. Putnam's Sons, 2012. 400 p. (Virgil Flowers mysteries, 6)
ISBN 9780399157707
1. Government investigators 2. Teenage murderers 3. Mass murder 4. Murder investigation 5. Detectives 6. Cossa, Francesco del 7. Police procedurals
LC 2012025454
When three teenagers with dead-end prospects begin a killing and robbery spree through rural Minnesota, Bureau of Criminal Apprehension investigator Virgil Flowers joins a growing number of cops trying to stop them.

★ **Mind** prey. John Sandford. G.P. Putnam's Sons, 1995. 323 p. (Prey series, 7)
ISBN 9780399140099
1. Women psychiatrists 2. Psychopaths 3. Women kidnapping victims 4. Mothers and daughters 5. Davenport, Lucas (Fictitious character) 6. Minnesota 7. Minneapolis, Minnesota 8. Thrillers and suspense 9. Books to movies 10. Police procedurals
LC 95003790
Lucas Davenport is back on a case involving a therapist who's been kidnapped by a former patient. The kidnapper has also taken the therapist's two young daughters. Deeply ill, he acts out his violent sexual fantasies on the therapist first and is about to go after the daughters so Davenport must figure out the clues to the kidnapper's identity.
"Sandford expertly ratchets up the suspense from beginning to the brutal finish." —*Publishers Weekly*
John Camp writing as John Sandford.
1999 TV movie also known as John Sandford's Mind prey.

Mortal prey. John Sandford. G. P. Putnam's Sons, 2002. 368 p. (Prey series, 13)
ISBN 9780399148637
1. Police 2. Murder investigation 3. Women assassins 4. Revenge 5. Drug lords 6. Minnesota 7. Minneapolis, Minnesota 8. Thrillers and suspense 9. Police procedurals
Minnesota Book Award for Genre Fiction, 2003
Lucas Davenport and Clara Rinker, a hitwoman are tangled together again. It seems the hitwoman is the target of a hit and vows vengeance against a Mexican drug lord who murders her boyfriend and her unborn child. Davenport is supposed to find Rinker before she kills again.
John Camp writing as John Sandford.

★ **Naked** prey. John Sandford. G.P. Putnam's Sons, 2003. 352 p. (Prey series, 14)
ISBN 9780399150432

1. Police 2. Murder investigation 3. Lynching 4. Murder 5. Murderers 6. Minnesota 7. Minneapolis, Minnesota 8. Thrillers and suspense 9. Police procedurals
LC 2003041364
Moving with his boss to state-level cases, Lucas Davenport, having recently become the head of a family, investigates the hanging deaths of an African American man and a white woman, a case that proves more complicated than it appears.
"Lucas Davenport is now Director of Regional Studies in the Minnesota Bureau of Criminal Apprehension, which is a fancy name for the job of investigating difficult crimes as quickly as possible and answering to the governor of the state. Known for his ability to solve the unsolvable, he goes to a remote area of the state to discover why a black man and a white woman were hanged in a groove of trees.... Fast paced and full of surprises, this may be Sandford's best novel yet." —*Library Journal*
John Camp writing as John Sandford.

★ **Night** prey. John Sandford. G.P. Putnam's Sons, 1994. 336 p. (Prey series, 6)
ISBN 9780399139147
1. Women police chiefs 2. Murder investigation 3. Murder 4. Murderers 5. Davenport, Lucas (Fictitious character) 6. Minnesota 7. Carlos Avery State Wildlife Management Area, Minnesota 8. Thrillers and suspense 9. Police procedurals
LC 9407564
Lucas Davenport is asked by a female game warden to investigate a mysterious murder in a Minnesota wildlife refuge, in a case that leads to a confrontation with a skillful and elusive killer BT
"Despite its length, Night Prey is a tight, fast-moving thriller with appealing good guys and a suitably evil villain. Especially fascinating among the characters is Policewoman Connell." —*Library Journal*
John Camp writing as John Sandford.

★ **Phantom** prey. John Sandford. G. P. Putnam's Sons, 2008. 384 p. (Prey series, 18)
ISBN 9780399155000
1. Goth culture 2. Murder investigation 3. Missing persons investigation 4. Detectives 5. Heirs and heiresses 6. Minnesota 7. Minneapolis, Minnesota 8. Thrillers and suspense 9. Police procedurals
Convinced a missing heiress is dead, Lucas Davenport searches for her body. His hunt connects him to the Twin Cities' Goth community, a group of young people fascinated by death and darkness. The deeper he digs, the closer he gets to the killer.
John Camp writing as John Sandford.

★ **Rules** of prey. John Sanford. G. P. Putnam's Sons, 1989. 317 p. (Prey series, 1)
ISBN 9780399134654
1. Serial murder investigation 2. Serial murderers 3. Crimes against women 4. Lawyers 5. Davenport, Lucas (Fictitious character) 6. Minnesota 7. Twin Cities metropolitan area 8. Thrillers and suspense 9. Police procedurals
LC 89004040
Lieutenant Lucas Davenport is determined to track down a diabolically clever serial killer who leads a double life, carefully picks out his female victims, and taunts the police with notes signed "Maddog." BT
"A killer who calls himself the 'maddog' has been murdering Minneapolis women, seemingly without pattern or motive. The crimes are linked only by their brutality and by the slayer's 'signature': at each scene, he leaves a written rule of crime, such as 'Never kill anyone you know,' or, 'Never carry a weapon after it has been used.' Into the case comes Lucas Davenport, a policeman with five kills in the line of duty, a surefire sense

of how to handle the thirsty media and strong instincts about the killer's psyche." —*Publishers Weekly*

John Camp writing as John Sandford.

Shock wave. John Sandford. G.P. Putnam's Sons, 2011. 400 p. (Virgil Flowers mysteries, 5)

ISBN 9780399157691

1. Government investigators 2. Bombing 3. Building 4. Small town life 5. Real estate development 6. Minnesota 7. Police procedurals

LC 2011027848

When protests about a superstore chain's plans to build a location in a Minnesota river town escalate into bombing attacks at the construction site and the company's headquarters, Virgil Flowers races against time to find and stop the bomber.

"Virgil Flowers is a pretty mellow guy. If he isn't casting off in some quiet trout stream, John Sandford's Minnesota crimestopper might be found behind Bob's Bad Boy Barbeque & Bar, watching some well-nourished farm girls playing a cutthroat game of beach volleyball. But when Virgil's troubleshooting skills are called for, as they are...when a bomb-maker initiates a wave of industrial terrorism against the small-town incursions of a big-box chain store, he can move as fast as the next action hero. For someone who casually saunters onto a crime scene in a pink T-shirt, jeans and cowboy boots, Virgil can think on his feet, a valuable asset when the bomber steps up his deadly campaign against Willard Pye's PyeMart empire, which threatens to destroy the small-town character of Butternut Falls." —*New York Times Book Review*

★ **Silent** prey. John Sandford. G. P. Putnam's Sons, 1992. 320 p. (Prey series, 4)

ISBN 9780399137426

1. Serial murderers 2. Serial murder investigation 3. Vigilantes 4. Murder 5. Davenport, Lucas (Fictitious character) 6. New York City 7. Thrillers and suspense 8. Police procedurals

LC 91043696

A brilliant but insane pathologist flees to New York to continue his research on death, and the police call on Lucas Davenport, who merges his investigative talents with an old flame to put an end to the madness.

"Mad pathologist Bekker's face is battered and broken after his encounter with unorthodox Minneapolis cop Lucas Davenport in Eyes of Prey. Now Bekker's on the loose again, having escaped during his trial and landed in New York City. Even more nutso than ever, he's determined to exact revenge on Lucas and to continue his evil experiments, in which he searches the eyes of his victims in the few, pain-creased seconds before death." —*Booklist*

John Camp writing as John Sandford.

★ **Silken** prey. John Sandford. G.P. Putnam's Sons, 2013. 406 pages; (Prey series, 23)

ISBN 9780399159312

1. Political corruption 2. Political campaigns 3. Extortion 4. Heirs and heiresses 5. Police 6. Minnesota 7. St. Paul, Minnesota 8. Thrillers and suspense 9. Police procedurals

Investigating the murder of a political fixer who had blackmailed his ambitious heiress employer during a vicious smear campaign, Lucas Davenport follows disturbing leads to the Minneapolis police department and a ruthless woman who threatens his life.

Storm Front. John Sandford. G. P. Putnam's Sons, 2013. 400 p. (Virgil Flowers mysteries, 7)

ISBN 9780399159305

1. Government investigators 2. Relics 3. Thieves 4. Detectives 5. Intelligence service 6. Minnesota 7. Police procedurals

LC 2013024514

Approached by an Israeli police officer who is tailing a man in possession of a stolen relic, Virgil Flowers learns that the artifact reveals details about the biblical King Solomon and that rivals are killing everyone who would protect it.

Storm prey. John Sandford. G. P. Putnam's Sons, 2010. 408 p. (Prey series, 20)

ISBN 9780399156496

1. Detectives 2. Robbery 3. Women witnesses 4. Robbery investigation 5. Criminals 6. Minnesota 7. St. Paul, Minnesota 8. Thrillers and suspense 9. Police procedurals

Witnessing a robbery gone wrong that has caused the death of a pharmacy employee, Lucas Davenport's surgeon wife, Weather Karkinnen, is targeted by the thieves when they become fearful that she can identify them.

John Camp writing as John Sandford.

Sudden prey. John Sandford. G. P. Putnam's, 1996. 360 p. (Prey series, 8)

ISBN 9780399141386

1. Police 2. Revenge 3. Death 4. Davenport, Lucas (Fictitious character) 5. Minnesota 6. Minneapolis, Minnesota 7. Thrillers and suspense 8. Police procedurals

Lucas Davenport and his men have been tracking a dangerous woman bank robber. When they finally catch her, she does not go quietly and they are forced to kill her. Now her ex-husband swears revenge: he will find out who's responsible for her death and kill those near and dear to them.

"This Lucas Davenport adventure opens with the Candy LaChaise gang's robbery of a Minnesota credit union. When Candy is ambushed and killed by Davenport and his men, Candy's husband, Dick LaChaise, swears vengeance on the spouses and families of all officers involved. A series of attacks ensue in which spouses are killed at work. With the lives of Davenport's own daughter and his fiance threatened, he quickly metamorphoses into a hunting machine himself." —*Library Journal*

John Camp writing as John Sandford.

★ **Winter** prey. John Sandford. G. P. Putnam's Sons, 1993. 338 p. (Prey series, 5)

ISBN 9780399138157

1. Psychopaths 2. Serial murderers 3. Serial murder investigation 4. Former police 5. Winter 6. Wisconsin 7. Thrillers and suspense 8. Police procedurals

LC 92042072

Twin Cities detective Lucas Davenport faces his most determined foe yet, the savage serial killer called Iceman.

"Davenport, a cool, cynical man of action, is entirely in his element in this harsh terrain—so bitter that it turns animals against men, so brutal that it turns men into beasts." —*New York Times Book Review*

John Camp writing as John Sandford.

Sansom, C. J.

★ **Lamentation**. C.J. Sansom. Mullholland, 2015. 592 p. (Matthew Shardlake novels, 6)

ISBN 9780316254960

1. Political corruption 2. Manuscripts 3. Lost articles 4. Criminal investigation 5. Rulers 6. Great Britain 7. Tudor period (1485-1603) 8. 16th century 9. Historical mysteries 10. Mysteries

Library Journal Best Books, 2015

While King Henry VIII lies on his deathbed, Queen Catherine Parr searches for the person who murdered the London printer who had her shocking, confessional memoir.

First published: [London] : Mantle, 2014.

Revelation. C.J. Sansom. Macmillan, 2008. 549 p. : Map (Matthew Shardlake novels, 4)

ISBN 9781405092722

1. Religious fanatics 2. Serial murderers 3. Lawyers 4. Friends' death 5. Men with disfigurements 6. Great Britain 7. Tudor period (1485-1603) 8. 16th century 9. Historical mysteries 10. Mysteries

LC 2008411769

Defending a young religious zealot who is being held in the infamous Bedlam hospital for the insane, Matthew Shardlake investigates a series of murders with disturbing ties to Lady Catherine Parr, a reform sympathizer and future wife of Henry VIII.

★ **Sovereign**. C.J. Sansom. Viking, 2007. 592 p. (Matthew Shardlake novels, 3)
ISBN 9780670038312
1. Henry 2. Conspiracies 3. Nobility 4. Rulers 5. Shardlake, Matthew (Fictitious character) 6. Murder 7. Great Britain 8. Tudor period (1485-1603) 9. 16th century 10. Historical mysteries 11. Mysteries

LC 2006048686

When Henry VIII sets out to quell rebellion in the north and transport a dangerous conspirator back to London for questioning, lawyer Matthew Shardlake finds himself investigating the murder of a local glazier with unsettling ties to the royal family.

"The skill with which C.J. Sansom is able to conjure up the sights, smells, and sounds of Tudor England is unrivalled." —*Birmingham Post*
First published: [London] : Macmillan, 2006.

Tombland. C.J. Sansom. Mulholland Books, 2019. 866 p; (Matthew Shardlake novels, 7)
ISBN 9780316412421
1. Edward 2. Lawyers 3. Political intrigue 4. Murder 5. Leary, Timothy 6. Murder investigation 7. Great Britain 8. Tudor period (1485-1603) 9. 16th century 10. Historical mysteries 11. Mysteries

When a distant relative of Princess Elizabeth is found dead, Matthew Shardlake is sent to investigate the murder, which may have connections reaching to a peasant rebellion sweeping the country.

Originally published: London : Mantle, 2018.

Santiago, Danny

Famous all over town. Danny Santiago. Plume 1983. 284 p.
ISBN 9780671432492
1. Mexican American boys 2. Mexican American families 3. Values 4. Street life 5. Los Angeles, California 6. Urban fiction

LC 83-22020

A fourteen-year-old Mexican American boy struggles to resolve the conflict between the traditional values of his family and life on the streets of Los Angeles.

Originally published: New York : Simon & Schuster, c1983.

Santiago, Esmeralda

Conquistadora: a novel. Esmeralda Santiago. Alfred A. Knopf, 2011. 416 p.
ISBN 9780307268327
1. Plantation life 2. Independence in women 3. Love triangles 4. Twin brothers 5. Slavery 6. Puerto Rico 7. 19th century 8. Historical fiction

LC 2010051324

Booklist Editors' Choice, 2011

Drawn to the exotic island of Puerto Rico by the diaries of an ancestor who traveled there with Ponce de León, Ana Cubillas becomes involved with enamored twin brothers Ramón and Inocente before convincing them to claim a sugar plantation they have inherited.

"The book's greatest strength lies in its dissection of the systematic enslavement and oppression of people without which the large-scale planting, harvesting, processing, and transporting of sugar was impossible. Santiago's language is most animated in her depiction of slavery.... In Ana, Santiago creates a woman consciously at odds with her culture, chafing at her own oppression, and reluctant but willing to oppress others in order to achieve her own freedom. Though the plot of Conquistadora is thin and the characterizations are flat, in Ana's uneasy rationalization of the brutal, unsustainable system on which these dreams depend, Santiago fleetingly achieves the hallmark of great historical fiction she makes her protagonist a woman of her times." —*Boston Globe*

Sapphire

American dreams. Sapphire. Vintage Books, 1996. 177 p.
ISBN 9780679767992
1. City life 2. Violence 3. Street life 4. African American lesbians 5. Dysfunctional families 6. African American fiction 7. African American poetry 8. Poetry

A collection of poetry and prose pieces captures an angry teenager who goes "wilding" in Central Park, a young African American girl gunned down by a Korean storeowner, a sexually abused child, and the power of art to bear witness and heal its creators.

Originally published: New York : High Risk Books/Serpent's Tail, 1994.

★ The **kid:** a novel. Sapphire. Penguin Press, 2011. 384 p.
ISBN 9781594203046
1. African American boys — Identity 2. Orphans 3. Sexually abused boys 4. Dancing 5. Mothers — Death 6. Harlem, New York City 7. New York City 8. African American fiction 9. First person narratives 10. Coming-of-age stories

LC 2011001739

After his mother dies when he is nine years old, Abdul Jones finds his way toward adulthood by overcoming the legacy of physical and sexual abuse he carries with him from his time in a foster home and at a boys' Catholic school.

Sequel to: Push

★ **Push:** a novel. Sapphire. A.A. Knopf, 1996. 141 p.
ISBN 9780679446262
1. Sixteen-year-old girls 2. Incest 3. Teacher-student relationships 4. Teenage mothers 5. African Americans 6. New York City 7. 1980s 8. African American fiction 9. First person narratives 10. Books to movies

LC 9616516

BCALA Literary Award for First Novelist, 1997

A courageous and determined young teacher opens up a new world of hope and redemption for sixteen-year-old Precious Jones, an abused young African American girl living in Harlem who was raped and left pregnant for the second time by her father.

This novel was made into film called Precious: based on the novel Push by Sapphire in 2009, starring Gabourey Sidibe, Mo'Nique, Paula Patton, and Mariah Carey and directed by Lee Daniels.
Includes unpaged section "Life stories."
Sequel: The kid

Saramago, Jose

All the names. Jose Saramago; translated from the Portuguese by Margaret Jull Costa. Harcourt, 1999. 238 p.
ISBN 9780151004218
1. Obsession in men 2. Loneliness 3. Office workers 4. Birth and death records 5. Vital statistics 6. Portugal 7. Lisbon, Portugal 8. Translations 9. Literary fiction

LC

When a clerk in the Central Registry discovers a stray unfiled birth certificate, he decides to investigate the identity of the woman—the first step in an obsession that will lead him to her.

Translation of Todos os nomes.

★ **Blindness**. Jose Saramago; translated from the Portuguese by Giovanni Pontiero. Harcourt Brace, 1997. 294 p.

ISBN 9780151002511

1. People who are blind 2. Epidemics 3. Survival 4. Loss (Psychology) 5. Disorientation 6. Translations 7. Literary fiction 8. Modern classics

Booklist Editors' Choice, 1998; Library Journal Best Books, 1998; New York Times Notable Book, 1998

A city is hit by an epidemic of "white blindness" whose victims are confined to a vacant mental hospital, while a single eyewitness to the nightmare guides seven oddly assorted strangers through the barren urban landscape.

"A man waiting in his car for a red light to turn green is the first of an entire city's population—with one exception—to be blinded by a 'milky sea' of dazzling whiteness. The inexplicably disabled victims grope and stumble their way through nightmarish landscapes: first an asylum where those initially afflicted are quarantined, and then the chaotic, squalid streets to which they return. Saramago's surreal allegory explores the ability of the human spirit to prevail in even the most absurdly unjust of conditions, yet he reinvents this familiar struggle with the stylistic eccentricity of a master." —The New Yorker

Translation of: Ensaio sobre a cegueira (1995).

Cain. Jose Saramago; translated from the Portuguese by Margaret Jull Costa. Houghton Mifflin Harcourt, 2011. 208 p.

ISBN 9780547419893

1. Cain 2. God 3. Fugitives 4. Murderers 5. Voyages and travels 6. Brothers 7. Literary fiction 8. Bible novels 9. Translations

LC 2011028600

In a reimagining of the Old Testament, Cain, condemned to wander forever for murdering his brother, journeys through time and space to witness key biblical events that impress upon him the unjust nature of God's edicts.

"This is the author's final novel, but the story it tells is among the world's first. In this version of several biblical tales, characters lose their initial capitals, and readers follow the adventures and misadventures of adam and eve, cain and abel, lilith and joshua and job—plus those of the lord, also known as god—with new eyes. Typographical diminution is the first of many wonderful acts of estrangement. Like a postmodern Creator of sorts, Saramago crafts a new world by recycling a series of well-known episodes and interpreting them from the viewpoint of a common reader." —San Francisco Chronicle

First published in 2009 by Editorial Caminho, Lisbon. This translation originally published: London: Harvill Secker, 2011.

★ The **cave**. Jose Saramago; translated from the Portuguese by Margaret Jull Costa. Harcourt, 2002. 320 p.

ISBN 9780151004140

1. Senior men 2. Potters 3. Extinction (Biology) 4. Septuagenarians 5. Translations 6. Literary fiction

LC 2002002355

ALA Notable Book, 2004; New York Times Notable Book, 2002

Informed that his clay pots and jugs are no longer needed, elderly potter Cipriano applies his craft to the making of ceramic dolls, but his family's subsequent successes are compromised by a terrible discovery.

"As a further warning against the urge to seek safety on common ground—moving to the center, as it were—the writer highlights the menaces of cliche by parodying the worldly-wise narrative interventions of an earlier era.... Such deft manipulations in Saramago's style are brilliantly

rendered in Margaret Jull Costa's agile English version of his Portuguese." —New York Times Book Review

English translation of: La Caverna.

Death with interruptions. Jose Saramago; translated from the Portuguese by Margaret Jull Costa. Harcourt, 2008. 256 p.

ISBN 9780151012749

1. Death 2. Immortality 3. Romantic love 4. Love 5. Philosophy 6. Psychological fiction 7. Translations 8. Satirical fiction

LC 2008010088

While Death sits in her apartment wondering what would happen if she became human and fell in love, no one dies, raising concerns among politicians, religious leaders, doctors, morticians, and others as they confront the harsh realities of eternal life.

"Starting at the stroke of midnight on New Year's, in an unidentified country in an undetermined year, in Jose Saramago's new novel, death goes on strike. Nobody dies from illness or suicide or, Mr. Saramago writes, from a car accident, so frequent on festive occasions, when blithe irresponsibility and an excess of alcohol jockey for position on the roads to decide who will reach death first. Thus the Saramago sentence: conversational but a conversation with oneself; portentous yet ludicrous, like a solemn address delivered by someone who has forgotten to wear pants. Thus too the Saramago plot: an impossible event like universal blindness, or Portugal's history altered because of a proofreader's error in a history book. Or, as here, death feeling unappreciated and refusing to oblige.... Mr. Saramago, one of the last of the old-line Communists, has written an atheist's religious parable; a story abounding in sentiment and purged of it." —New York Times

★ The **Elephant's** journey. Jose Saramago; translated from the Portuguese by Margaret Jull Costa. Houghton Mifflin Harcourt, 2010. 288 p.

ISBN 9780547352589

1. Elephants 2. Wedding presents 3. Voyages and travels 4. Friendship 5. Adventure 6. 16th century 7. Historical fiction 8. Translations

Booklist Editors' Choice, 2010

A tale inspired by a true story follows the adventures of a neglected elephant who is given by King Joao of Portugal to Archduke Maximilian as a wedding gift and who travels with the archduke through the war-torn storied cities of 16th-century Europe.

"[This] is a tale rich in irony and empathy, regularly interrupted by witty reflections on human nature and arch commentary on the powerful who insult human dignity." —Los Angeles Times

First published with the title A Viagem do Elefante in 2008 by Editorial Caminho, SA, Lisbon—Title page verso.

The **history** of the siege of Lisbon. By Jose Saramago; translated by Giovanni Pontiero. Harcourt Brace, 1996. 314 p.

ISBN 9780151002382

1. Proofreading 2. Single men 3. Man-woman relationships 4. Authors 5. Writing 6. Lisbon, Portugal 7. Translations 8. Literary fiction

LC 96-46826

New York Times Notable Book, 1997

An editor at a Portuguese publishing house, Raimundo Silva, undertakes to rewrite a crucial episode in Portuguese history as a romantic saga, with the amorous encouragement of his supervisor.

"Although the novel's stream-of-consciousness technique, baroque prose and paragraphs that run on for pages may daunt some readers, this hypnotic tale is a great comic romp through history, language and the imagination." —Publishers Weekly

The **manual** of painting and calligraphy. Jose Saramago; translated from the Portuguese by Giovanni Pontiero. Mariner Books, 2012. 224 p.

ISBN 9780547640228

1. Artists 2. Creativity in men 3. Self-discovery in men 4. Political prisoners 5. Totalitarianism — Psychological aspects 6. Portugal 7. Political fiction 8. Literary fiction 9. Translations

In the last years of Salazar's dictatorship, a struggling young artist is commissioned to paint the portrait of a wealthy client and struggles to capture his likeness while acknowleging his artistic limitations.

Translation first published: Manchester : Carcanet Press, 1994.

Saroyan, William

★ The **human** comedy. William Saroyan. Dell, 1971. 192 p.
ISBN 9780440339335
1. Teenage boys 2. Families 3. Small towns 4. World War II 5. Brothers 6. California 7. 1940s 8. Historical fiction 9. Coming-of-age stories

Homer is a night messenger for the Postal Telegraph Office in a small California town during World War II after his father dies and his brother serves in the army.

Originally published: New York : Harcourt, Brace and Co, 1943.

Sarton, May

A **reckoning:** a novel. May Sarton. W. W. Norton, 1978. 254 p.
ISBN 9780393088281
1. Terminal illness 2. Women — Family relationships 3. Lesbians 4. Mothers and daughters 5. Death

LC 78009691

When Laura Spelman learns that she will not get well, she looks on this last illness as a journey during which she must reckon up her life, give up the nonessential, and concentrate on what she calls "the real connections." BT

"Sarton incorporates...the issues of mother/daughter relationships, what it is to be a woman (and a man), and the conflict of art and life." —*Library Journal*

Sartre, Jean Paul

The **age** of reason. Jean Paul Sartre; translated from the French by Eric Sutton. Vintage Books 1973. 397 pages. (Roads to freedom)
ISBN 9780241259696
1. College teachers 2. Philosophy teachers 3. Freedom 4. Existentialism 5. France 6. 1930s 7. Historical fiction 8. Translations

LC 72004476

Following a Parisian philosophy teacher through the cafes and bars of Montparnasse over two days in the sweltering summer of 1938, Sartre's searing novel explores what it truly means to be free.

Sequel: The reprieve.
L'Age de raison first published 1945.
This translation published in Hamish Hamilton 1947.

★ **Nausea.** Jean Paul Sartre; translated from the French by Lloyd Alexander; introduction by Hayden Carruth. Bentley, 1979. 178 pages.
ISBN 9780837604435
1. Existentialism 2. Self-awareness 3. Emotions 4. Authors 5. Diary novels 6. Translations 7. Psychological fiction

LC 79017598

The diary of Antoine Roquentin follows his thoughts as he gradually sinks into a metaphysical crisis of despair, in this the first novel by the leader of French Existentialism.

Translation of La Nausee, first published in 1938.

Troubled sleep. Jean Paul Sartre; translated from the French by Gerard Hopkins. Vintage Books, 1992. 421 pages. (Roads to freedom, 3)
ISBN 9780679740797

1. World War II 2. France 3. Second World War era (1939-1945) 4. Historical fiction 5. War stories 6. Translations

LC 91050896

Sartre portrays the emotional and intellectual impact of the fall of France on one group of citizens

Sequel to: The reprieve.

Sathian, Sanjena

Gold diggers. Sanjena Sathian. Penguin Press, 2021. 352 p.
ISBN 9781984882035
1. East Indian American teenagers 2. Suburbs 3. Magic 4. Ambition 5. Alchemy 6. Georgia 7. 2000s (Decade) 8. Magical realism 9. Coming-of-age stories 10. Literary fiction 11. Adult books for young adults

A satirical coming-of-age story follows the experiences of an Indian-American teen in the Bush-era Atlanta suburbs, who joins his crush's plot to use an ancient alchemical potion to meet high parental expectations, triggering devastating consequences.

"Exploring the many meanings of the clever title, this multilayered work looks at the history of Indians in America since the gold rush, the matrimonial prospects of gold diggers, and the ethical ramifications of stealing gold for use in alchemy, even to help a loved one." —*Library Journal*

Satyal, Rakesh

No one can pronounce my name: a novel. Rakesh Satyal. Picador, 2017. 320 p.
ISBN 9781250112118
1. Suburban life 2. Immigrant families 3. Culture shock 4. East Indian Americans 5. Identity (Psychology) 6. Cleveland, Ohio 7. Ohio 8. Literary fiction

LC 2016058277

Loan Stars Favourites, 2017; Booklist Editors' Choice, 2017

Struggling with cultural divisions in a Cleveland suburb mostly populated by Indian Americans, lonely forty-something Harit dresses up in a sari to comfort his grief-stricken mother before befriending a woman who writes paranormal romances to manage her fears about her husband's affair.

"Satyal captures his characters experiences within a close-knit Indian community, rounded out with excellent supporting characters like Harit's mother and Ranjana's husband, who have their own stories to tell, resulting in a vivid, complex tale." —*Publishers Weekly*

Saul, John

Midnight voices. Ballantine 2002. 320 p.
ISBN 9780345433312
1. Widows 2. Apartment house life 3. Secrets 4. Mother and child 5. Demons 6. Manhattan, New York City 7. Horror 8. Thrillers and suspense 9. Adult books for young adults

Cheryl Evans is a recently widowed mother of two. Things seem to have fallen into place when she meets Anthony Fleming and they are quickly married. She and her two children move into Fleming's luxury apartment on Central Park West despite her son's misgivings about the building and the people who dwell there. The building is home to a monstrously evil secret.

"This is good, drafty atmospheric horror stuff unafraid to indulge in not-at-all subtle gory bits." —*Booklist*

Saums, Mary

Thistle & Twigg. Mary Saums. St. Martin's Minotour, 2007. 288 p. (Thistle & Twigg, 1)

ISBN 9780312360634

1. Widows 2. Female friendship 3. Eccentrics and eccentricities 4. Women amateur detectives 5. Murder suspects 6. Alabama 7. Cozy mysteries 8. Gentle reads

LC 2006048684

Two widows living in sleepy Tullulah, Alabama, newcomer Jane Thistle and lifelong resident Phoebe Twigg, quickly bond after they stumble upon a corpse during a walk in the woods near Jane's new house, discover that someone may be threatening Jane's reclusive neighbor, and a firebomb explodes in Phoebe's kitchen.

Sequel: Mighty old bones.

Saunders, George

In persuasion nation: stories. By George Saunders. Riverhead Books, 2006. 240 p.

ISBN 9781594489228

1. Popular culture 2. Mass media 3. Materialism 4. Consumerism 5. Advertising 6. Literary fiction 7. Satirical fiction 8. Short stories

LC 2005057715

Booklist Editors' Choice, 2006

"The most unnerving fiction boldly envisions the dire consequences of our most hubristic tendencies: our bottomless greed, maniacal competitiveness, hyper-materialism, environmental obliviousness, spiritual callousness, and fear of being different. Following in the footsteps of Orwell, Bradbury, and Atwood, Saunders writes shrewd, off-the-charts speculative fiction.... In his third savagely imaginative collection, his most riveting to date, he considers various forms of diabolical persuasion in a techno-colonized world in which advertising governs every aspect of life." —*Booklist*

★ **Lincoln** in the bardo: a novel. George Saunders. Random House, 2017. 343 p.

ISBN 9780812995343

1. Lincoln, Abraham 2. Loss (Psychology) 3. Presidents 4. Grief 5. Spiritual journeys 6. Family relationships 7. 1860s 8. Biographical fiction 9. Historical fiction 10. Literary fiction

LC 2016004993

ALA Notable Book, 2018; Booklist Editors' Choice, 2017; Library Journal Best Books, 2017; Man Booker Prize, 2017; New York Times Notable Book, 2017; Andrew Carnegie Medal for Excellence in Fiction finalist, 2018; Shortlisted for the International Dublin Literary Award, 2019

Traces a night of solitary mourning and reflection as experienced by the sixteenth president after the death of his eleven-year-old son at the dawn of the Civil War.

"With this book, Saunders asserts a complex and disturbing vision in which society and cosmos blur." —*Kirkus*

★ **Tenth** of December: stories. George Saunders. Random House, 2013. 208 p.

ISBN 9780812993806

1. Soldiers 2. Kidnapping 3. People with cancer 4. Misfits (Persons) 5. Short stories 6. Literary fiction

LC 2012013782

New York Times Notable Book, 2013; National Book Award for Fiction finalist, 2013

A collection of stories includes "Home," a wryly whimsical account of a soldier's return from war; "Victory Lap," a tale about an inventive abduction attempt; and the title story, in which a suicidal cancer patient saves the life of a young misfit.

Saunders, Kate

The **case** of the wandering scholar. Kate Saunders. Bloomsbury, 2019. 352 pages (Laetitia Rodd mysteries, 2)

ISBN 9781632868381

1. Widows 2. Women private investigators 3. Middle-aged women 4. Missing men 5. Friendship 6. England 7. Victorian era (1837-1901) 8. 1850s 9. Victorian mysteries 10. Historical mysteries

Finds Victorian detective Laetitia Rodd assisting a terminally ill gentleman in a search for his long-missing Oxford academic brother, before uncovering a formidable adversary lurking in the English countryside.

"Saunders's exquisite prose and patient storytelling build a convincing Victorian voice, while Mrs. Rodd's shrewd, energetic narration adds further appeal to the rich depiction of 19th-century landscapes and attitudes." —*Publishers Weekly*

The **secrets** of Wishtide. Kate Saunders. Bloomsbury USA, 2016. 334 p. (Laetitia Rodd mysteries, 1)

ISBN 9781632864499

1. Widows 2. Women private investigators 3. Middle-aged women 4. Lawyers 5. Scandals 6. London, England 7. Victorian era (1837-1901) 8. Victorian mysteries 9. Historical mysteries

LibraryReads Favorites, 2016

Archdeacon's widow and private investigator Laetitia Rodd goes undercover as a governess in order to assist her barrister brother during a case involving the illicit affairs of a nobleman's son.

"The book is a sheer delight, with its deliciously intricate puzzle and well-drawn characters whom readers are sure to continue to enjoy in volumes to come." —*Booklist*

Savage, Sam

Firmin: adventures of a metropolitan lowlife. By Sam Savage. Coffee House Press, 2006. 162 p.

ISBN 9781566891813

1. Science fiction authors 2. Books and reading 3. Identity (Psychology) 4. Rats 5. Bookstores 6. Boston, Massachusetts 7. Coming-of-age stories 8. Stories told by animals 9. Fantasy fiction

LC 2005035803

ALA Notable Book, 2007

"Blending philosophy and abundant literary references with originality, Savage crafts a small comic gem about the costs and rewards of literary illusions." —*Booklist*

The **way** of the dog: a novel. By Sam Savage. Coffee House Press, 2013. 152 p.

ISBN 9781566893121

1. Senior men 2. Artists 3. Alienation in men 4. Regret in men 5. Father and adult son 6. Psychological fiction 7. Literary fiction 8. First person narratives

LC 2011046604

Booklist Editors' Choice, 2013

A disillusioned artist looks for meaning in the wreckage of his life, and finds it in unexpected places.

Savas, Aysegul

Walking on the ceiling. Aysegul Savas. Penguin Group USA 2019. 208 p.

ISBN 9780525537410

1. Women — Identity 2. Friendship 3. Memories 4. Belonging 5. Authors, British 6. Paris, France 7. Istanbul, Turkey 8. Literary fiction 9. Coming-of-age stories

A novel set in Paris and a changing Istanbul follows a young Turkish woman grappling with the past—her country's and her own—and her complicated relationship with the famous British writer who longs for her memories.

Sayers, Constance

The **ladies** of the secret circus. Constance Sayers. Orbit, 2021. 448 p.
ISBN 9780316493673
1. Circus 2. Magic 3. Families 4. Young women 5. Family secrets 6. Historical fantasy
LC 2020032854

A magical story spanning from Jazz Age Paris to modern-day America of family secrets, sacrifice and lost love set against the backdrop of a mysterious circus.

"Sayers (A Witch in Time) weaves romance, mystery, and a family curse into a spellbinding historical fantasy that stretches from 1920s Paris to modern-day America." —*Publishers Weekly*

Sayers, Dorothy L.

★ **Busman's** honeymoon. Dorothy L. Sayers. Harper and Row 1995. 403 p. (Lord Peter Wimsey mysteries, 11)
ISBN 9780061043512
1. Murder investigation 2. Newlyweds 3. Honeymoons 4. Wimsey, Peter, Lord (Fictitious character) 5. Vane, Harriet (Fictitious character) 6. England 7. Mysteries

When their plans for a private and romantic honeymoon are disrupted by the untimely murder of their estate's former owner, newlyweds Lord Peter and Harriet Vane are baffled by the strange clues that they discover.

A love story with detective interruptions.

A Lord Peter Wimsey mystery with Harriet Vane.

Originally published in 1937.

★ **Clouds** of witness. Dorothy L. Sayers. HarperCollins, 1995. 279 p. (Lord Peter Wimsey mysteries, 2)
ISBN 9780061043536
1. Murder investigation 2. Siblings 3. Wimsey, Peter, Lord (Fictitious character) 4. Amateur detectives 5. Nobility 6. 1920s 7. Mysteries
LC 86045689

When his future brother-in-law is murdered during a country retreat, Lord Peter Wimsey is shocked when his brother is accused and seeks the truth in a letter from Egypt, a suitcase-bearing fiancee, and a second murder attempt.

Originally published in 1927.

★ The **documents** in the case. Dorothy L. Sayers and Robert Eustace. Avon, 1968. 221 p.
ISBN 9780061043604
1. Poisonous mushrooms 2. Murder investigation 3. Murder 4. Toxins 5. Mycotoxicoses 6. London, England 7. 1920s 8. Mysteries

The clues to the death of a fungi expert who had died after eating enough poisonous mushrooms to kill thirty people, lie in a series of seemingly unimportant documents that nevertheless intrigue the victim's son.

★ The **five** red herrings. Dorothy L. Sayers. Harpercollins, 1995. 306 p. (Lord Peter Wimsey mysteries, 6)
ISBN 9780061043635
1. Murder investigation 2. Artists 3. Murder 4. Painting 5. Amateur detectives 6. Scotland 7. 1930s 8. Mysteries

When an artist is found dead at the bottom of a cliff where he had been painting, a masterpiece in mystery arises, with six artists as suspects,

five of them "red herrings" and one a murderer who baffles even Lord Peter Wimsey.

Originally published under the title Suspicious characters : New York : Harper, 1931.

★ **Gaudy** night. Dorothy L. Sayers. Harpercollins, 1995. 501 p. (Lord Peter Wimsey mysteries, 10)
ISBN 9780061043499
1. Universities and colleges 2. Murder investigation 3. Class reunions 4. Amateur detectives 5. Wimsey, Peter, Lord (Fictitious character) 6. Oxford, England 7. England 8. 1930s 9. Mysteries 10. Mystery classics

Harriet Vane's Oxford reunion is shadowed by a rash of bizarre pranks and malicious mischief that include beautifully worded death threats, burnt effigies, and vicious poison-pen letters, and Harriet finds herself and Lord Peter Wimsey challenged by an elusive set of clues.

Originally published in 1936.

Hangman's holiday. Dorothy L. Sayers. Harpercollins, 1995. 209 p. (Lord Peter Wimsey mysteries)
ISBN 9780061043628
1. Nobility 2. Murder 3. Amateur detectives 4. Murder investigation 5. Wimsey, Peter, Lord (Fictitious character) 6. Short stories 7. Mysteries

Poisoned port ...Pet cats in peril ...Purloined pearls ...Lord Peter Wimsey solves the mysteries of the man who was blown into the fourth dimension and the murder in fancy dress. He pursues miscreants across several countries and into unexpected hiding places. Dorothy L. Sayers' other detective, Montague Egg, encounters a fugitive murderer and uncovers a killer in an Oxford cloister. The travelling salesman extraordinaire solves puzzles with a unique combination of matter-of-fact practicality and brilliant deduction.

A collection of short mysteries.

Originally published: Victor Gollancz, 1933.

First published 1933.

Have his carcase. Dorothy L. Sayers. Harper and Row, 1995. 448p. (Lord Peter Wimsey mysteries, 7)
ISBN 9780061043529
1. Murder investigation 2. Nobility 3. Wimsey, Peter, Lord (Fictitious character) 4. Vane, Harriet (Fictitious character) 5. Soviets in England 6. England 7. 1930s 8. Mysteries 9. Mystery classics

Retreating to a barren beach in order to console her broken heart, mystery writer Harriet Vane is alarmed when she discovers the dead body of a young man and appeals to her friend Lord Peter for assistance in solving the mystery.

Originally published in 1932.

In the teeth of the evidence. Dorothy L. Sayers. Harpercollins, 1995. 265 p. (Lord Peter Wimsey mysteries)
ISBN 9780061043567
1. Nobility 2. Murder 3. Murder investigation 4. Amateur detectives 5. Wimsey, Peter, Lord (Fictitious character) 6. Mysteries 7. Short stories

All that was left of the garage was a heap of charred and smouldering beams. In the driving seat of the burnt-out car were the remains of a body. This is a vintage collection of Sayers' crime and detection stories featuring Lord Peter Wimsey.

Previously published 1940 as: In the teeth of the evidence, and other stories.

First published in Great Britain in 1939 by Victor Gollancz.

★ **Lord** Peter. Dorothy L. Sayers; compiled and with an introduction by James Sandoe; coda by Carolyn Heilbrun; codetta by E.C. Bentley. Harper, 1972. 487 p. (Lord Peter Wimsey mysteries)

ISBN 9780380016945
1. Nobility 2. Murder 3. Murder investigation 4. Amateur detectives 5. Wimsey, Peter, Lord (Fictitious character) 6. Short stories 7. Mysteries

LC 86045694

All the Lord Peter Wimsey short stories are collected in an anthology that features some twenty tales of mystery and detection.

A collection of all the Lord Peter Wimsey stories.

Murder must advertise. Dorothy L. Sayers. Harpercollins, 1995. 344 p. (Lord Peter Wimsey mysteries, 8)

ISBN 9780061043550
1. Murder investigation 2. Advertising agencies 3. Drug traffic 4. Nobility 5. Amateur detectives 6. England 7. 1930s 8. Mysteries 9. Mystery classics

When an ad man dies after an apparent accident, Lord Peter Wimsey goes undercover as an advertising copywriter and discovers a suspicious set of clues that involve cocaine dealing, blackmail, and wanton women.

Originally published in 1933.

The **nine** tailors. Dorothy L. Sayers. Harcourt Brace Jovanovich, 1989. 397 p. (Lord Peter Wimsey mysteries, 9)

ISBN 9780156658997
1. Murder investigation 2. Jewelry theft 3. Churches 4. Amateur detectives 5. Wimsey, Peter, Lord (Fictitious character) 6. England 7. 1930s 8. Mysteries 9. Mystery classics

LC 89038102

Tale of suspense in which the famous Lord Peter Wimsey is called upon to solve the murder of an unknown man in East Anglia.

Thrones, dominations. Dorothy L. Sayers & Jill Paton Walsh. St. Martin's Press, 1998. 312 p. (Lord Peter Wimsey mysteries, 12)

ISBN 9780312181963
1. Murder investigation 2. Newlyweds 3. Amateur detectives 4. Husband and wife 5. Marriage 6. England 7. 1930s 8. Mysteries 9. Adult books for young adults

Newlyweds Lord Peter Wimsey and Harriet Vane explore another mysterious turn of events during the short-lived reign of Edward VIII, in a novel left unfinished and unpublished for almost sixty years.

"Paton Walsh has made a valiant and resourceful stab at mimicry. No devotee of Lord Peter and his novelist wife Harriet Vane will want to miss it." —*New Statesman*

Dorothy Sayers' unfinished Lord Peter Wimsey novel, Thrones, dominations, completed sixty years later by Jill Paton Walsh.

The **unpleasantness** at the Bellona Club. Dorothy L. Sayers. Harper and Row, 1995. 345 p. (Lord Peter Wimsey mysteries, 4)

ISBN 9780060550264
1. Murder investigation 2. Poisoning 3. Inheritance and succession 4. Amateur detectives 5. Wimsey, Peter, Lord (Fictitious character) 6. 1920s 7. Mysteries

A ninety-year-old man's time of death becomes pivotal in deciding upon his half-million-pound estate, and Lord Peter Wimsey must search through such clues as an artificial poppy and an unsolicited telephone repair.

Originally published : New York : Harper and Row, 1928.

★ **Whose** body?: a Lord Peter Wimsey novel. Dorothy L. Sayers. Harper, 1994. 212 p. (Lord Peter Wimsey mysteries, 1)

ISBN 9780061043574
1. Murder investigation 2. Nobility 3. Amateur detectives 4. Wimsey, Peter, Lord (Fictitious character) 5. Veterans 6. England 7. 1920s 8. Mystery classics 9. Mysteries

Sayers's most renowned amateur detective, the engaging and amusing Lord Peter Wimsey, sets out to unravel a puzzling case involving the disappearance of a wealthy financier and the discovery of a nude corpse, wearing a golden pince-nez, in a bathtub.

Originally published: New York : Harper & Row, 1923.

Sayles, John

A **moment** in the sun. John Sayles. McSweeney's, 2011. 600 p.

ISBN 9781936365180
1. Race relations 2. War and society 3. Gold rush 4. Assassination 5. Colonialism 6. United States 7. Philippines 8. 1890s 9. 1900s (Decade) 10. Historical fiction 11. Epic fiction

New York Times Notable Book, 2011

Traces the tales of America and its events in 1897, months before the start of the Spanish American War, and follows the different lives of men at the turn of the century.

"At times, Sayles' research for A Moment in the Sun makes the writing absolutely vivid: His description of a difficult childbirth is so precise that it will have you flinching. But at other times, the historical trivia overcrowds the book: The novel's world can be so cluttered with exterior detail that it feels as though there is insufficient space for its characters' interior lives. This might seem a natural pitfall for a filmmaker writing a novel. Persnickety fans and critics point out any accidental anachronism that slips into a film's frames, and, so, perhaps, he transfers this anxiety to his fiction. But it is wrongheaded to look at Sayles as just a filmmaker writing a book. If anything, his career has been so interesting because it has demonstrated the opposite: how a novelist would think about and make films." —*Daily Beast*

Saylor, Steven

The **house** of the Vestals: the investigations of Gordianus the Finder. By Steven Saylor. St. Martin's Press, 1997. 260 p. (Roma Sub Rosa series, 5)

ISBN 9780312154448
1. Enslaved people 2. Private investigators 3. Criminal investigation 4. Gordianus the Finder (Fictitious character) 5. Rome 6. XXXXXXXX 7. 1st century BCE 8. Historical mysteries 9. Short stories 10. Mysteries

LC 977597

Nine stories featuring the Roman sleuth Gordianus the Finder, set between the end of Sulla's dictatorship and the Spartacus slave revolt, detail the relationship between Gordianus and his adopted son BT

"Saylor serves up a collection of short stories designed to fill in some of the gaps that have piqued the curiosity of devoted fans of his popular Roma Sub Rosa series. Set between the years 80 and 72 B.C, these nine tales document some of the early adventures of Gordianus the Finder.... While each brief mystery presented is a gem in and of itself, readers will delight in the informational overview provided by the collection as a whole. As usual, Saylor does a superb job of seamlessly incorporating the tumultuous history of the Roman Republic into the narrative flow." —*Booklist*

The **judgment** of Caesar: a novel of Ancient Rome. By Steven Saylor. St. Martin's Minotaur, 2004. 288 p. (Roma Sub Rosa series, 14)

ISBN 9780312271190
1. Cleopatra 2. Battles 3. Innocence (Law) 4. Poisoning 5. Private investigators 6. Gordianus the Finder (Fictitious character) 7. Egypt 8. Rome 9. Roman Republic (509-27 BCE) 10. Ancient Egypt (3100 BCE-640 CE) 11. Historical mysteries 12. Mysteries

LC 2003069548

Heading to Egypt in search of a cure for the mysterious illness of his ailing wife, Bethesda, Gordianus the Finder arrives in a country torn by war and power struggles, a situation that worsens when Bethesda vanishes.

"Readers will be equally absorbed by the bloody history unfolding (Saylor's description of the beheading of Pompey is both suspenseful and wrenching); by the historical figures depicted (Ptolemy listening to his flute player with the head of Pompey in a clay jar at his feet is a miniature study in royal pathology); and by the mysteries Gordianus must solve to keep his own head. Wonderful reading." —*Booklist*

A **mist** of prophecies. Steven Saylor. St. Martin's Minotaur, 2002. X, 270 p; (Roma Sub Rosa series, 13)
ISBN 9780312271213
1. Civil war 2. Murder investigation 3. Insurgency 4. Enslaved people 5. Private investigators 6. Rome 7. Roman Republic (509-27 BCE) 8. 1st century BCE 9. Historical mysteries 10. Mysteries
LC 2001058901
When a beautiful seeress is murdered while Julius Caesar and Pompey make war for control of the Roman Empire, Gordianus the Finder investigates the murder amid the larger intrigues of ancient Rome.
"A mystery set in Rome during the Civil War. A beautiful young woman, given the street name Cassandra for her habit of delivering prophesies, is found murdered. Gordianus is disturbed that no one claims her body—even though, he reflects, someone cared enough to murder her. Yet, at Cassandra's funeral pyre, seven of the most powerful women in Rome, including the wives of Caesar, Cicero, and Marc Antony, attend. Gordianus sorts out the tangled motives of the women who watched Cassandra burn, believing one of them to be her murderer. Saylor brings a wealth of historical information lightly to bear on a chilling mystery." —*Booklist*

Raiders of the Nile: a novel of the ancient world. Steven Saylor. Minotaur Books, 2014. 384 pages (Roma Sub Rosa series, 2)
ISBN 9781250015976
1. Romans 2. Kidnapping 3. Young men 4. Enslaved people 5. Tombs 6. Rome 7. Ancient Egypt 8. Roman Republic (509-27 BCE) 9. Ancient Egypt (3100 BCE-640 CE) 10. Historical mysteries 11. Mysteries
LC 2013032463
Finds Gordianus struggling to rescue Bethesda, who has been mistakenly kidnapped as part of a plot to steal the golden sarcophagus of Alexander the Great.
"Gordianus leaps from the pages as a modern trope—a wisecracking, good-hearted charmer—and Saylor frames him against an entrancing interpretation of ancient Egypt." —*Kirkus*

Roma: the novel of ancient Rome. Steven Saylor. St. Martin's Press, 2007. 555 p.
ISBN 9780312328313
1. Caesar, Julius 2. Romans 3. Families 4. Insurgency 5. Generations 6. Romulus (Roman mythology) 7. Rome 8. Roman Empire (27 BCE-476 CE) 9. Roman Republic (509-27 BCE) 10. Epic fiction 11. Historical fiction
LC 2006051179
Spanning a thousand years, and following the shifting fortunes of two families though the ages, this is the epic saga of Rome, the city and its people.
"Livy's Early History of Rome offers fertile material for a crime writer. The body count is high, and Saylor adds plenty more along the way. Even Livy smelt a 'whodunit' in the sudden apotheosis of Romulus in a thunderclap in the middle of a Senatorial meeting. Saylor illuminates the mystery in gory detail as, with unfailing efficiency, he unravels the enigmas. There is plenty of instruction here for students of classical civilization but sometimes the period detail founders in bathos when characters explain to each other facts they must already know, for the reader's benefit. Sometimes, though, with the scalpel-like deftness of a Hollywood di-

rector, Saylor puts his finger on the very essence of Roman history." —*Times Literary Supplement*
Sequel: Empire.

Rubicon. Steven Saylor. St. Martin's Press, 1999. 276 p. (Roma Sub Rosa series, 11)
ISBN 9780312205768
1. Pompey 2. Murder investigation 3. Insurgency 4. Self-sacrifice 5. Murder 6. Civil war 7. Rome 8. Roman Republic (509-27 BCE) 9. 1st century BCE 10. Historical mysteries 11. Mysteries
A story of murder and double-cross during the Roman Civil War puts Gordianus the Finder in a tough spot when Pompey takes his son-in-law hostage, and to save both their lives, Gordianus must prove that his son, who works for Pompey's enemy Caesar, did not kill Pompey's beloved cousin BT
"This novel is an excellent blending of mystery and history." —*Library Journal*

The **seven** wonders: a novel of the ancient world. Steven Saylor. Minotaur Books, 2012. 336 p. (Roma Sub Rosa series, 1)
ISBN 9780312359843
1. Voyages and travels 2. Tutors 3. Eighteen-year-old men 4. Divination 5. Gordianus the Finder (Fictitious character) 6. Rome 7. Europe 8. Roman Republic (509-27 BCE) 9. Historical mysteries 10. Mysteries
LC 2012005475
A prequel to the Roma Sub Rosa series finds 18-year-old Gordianus embarking on a quest in politically restless 92 B.C. to see the world's Seven Wonders and accompanied by a celebrated poet who fakes his own death to travel under an assumed identity.

The **triumph** of Caesar: a novel of ancient Rome. Steven Saylor. St. Martin's Minotaur, 2008. 320 p. (Roma Sub Rosa series, 15)
ISBN 9780312359836
1. Caesar, Julius 2. Assassination 3. Betrayal 4. Attempted murder 5. Private investigators 6. Gordianus the Finder (Fictitious character) 7. Rome 8. Europe 9. Roman Republic (509-27 BCE) 10. 1st century BCE 11. Historical mysteries 12. Mysteries
LC 2008003668
Rome, 46 BC: the Roman civil war has come to its conclusion and Caesar is now dictator for life. Cleopatra is making a state visit to the city in order to convince Caesar to acknowledge their son as his heir. Marc Antony and Caesar are at odds; Cicero is making a fool of himself with a new teenage bride; and Caesar's wife Calpurnia is troubled by prophesies of disaster and fears for her husband's life. To uncover the truth, Calpurnia calls on Gordianus the Finder, recently returned from Egypt with his wife Bethesda. Although essentially retired, and doubting whether Caesar's life is worth saving, he begins the search, hoping to find the murderer of the friend who was first sent out to investigate the plot.
Sequel to: The judgment of Caesar.

Wrath of the furies: a novel of the ancient world. Steven Saylor. Minotaur Books, 2015. 320 p. (Roma Sub Rosa series, 3)
ISBN 9781250015983
1. Romans 2. Rescues 3. International relations 4. Civilization, Ancient 5. Gordianus the Finder (Fictitious character) 6. Rome 7. Ancient Egypt 8. Roman Republic (509-27 BCE) 9. Ancient Egypt (3100 BCE-640 CE) 10. Historical mysteries 11. Mysteries
LC 2015022081
To rescue an old friend, Gordianus must go behind enemy lines, facing unspeakable danger in the greatest war of the ancient world.

Scalzi, John

The **collapsing** empire. John Scalzi. Tor Books, 2017. 336 p. (Interdependency novels, 1)

ISBN 9780765388889

1. Interplanetary relations 2. Imaginary empires 3. Teleportation 4. Life on other planets 5. Spaceship captains 6. Space opera 7. Science fiction

Locus Award for Best Science Fiction Novel, 2018; RUSA Reading List, 2018

When humanity discovers the existence of an extra-dimensional field capable of transporting travelers to different worlds instantly, a significantly depopulated Earth is threatened by a subsequent finding that the field is unstable and may be cutting travelers off on the wrong side of Earth-friendly worlds.

"Fans of Game of Thrones and Dune will enjoy this bawdy, brutal, and brilliant political adventure.." —*Booklist*

Head on. John Scalzi. Tor Books, 2018. 335 pages; (Lock in novels, 3)

ISBN 9780765388919

1. Virus diseases 2. Near future 3. FBI agents 4. Murder investigation 5. Professional athletes 6. Science fiction 7. Adult books for young adults

Finds the near-future world reveling in a violent but seemingly harmless, robot-bodied sport until a star athlete dies unexpectedly on the field, prompting an investigation by two FBI agents into the game's increasingly lucrative competition.

★ **Lock** in. John Scalzi. Tor Books, 2014. 320 p. (Lock in novels, 1)

ISBN 9780765375865

1. Virus diseases 2. Near future 3. FBI agents 4. Murder investigation 5. Epidemics 6. Science fiction 7. Adult books for young adults

LC 2014015247

Alex Award, 2015; LibraryReads Favorites, 2014; School Library Journal Best Books: Best Adult Books 4 Teens, 2014

When a new virus causes one percent of the population to become completely paralyzed in body but not in mind, America pursues a scientific initiative to develop a virtual-reality world for victims, with unexpected consequences.

"[C]ontains plenty of action, great character development, vivid and believable worldbuilding and a thought-provoking examination of disability culture and politics." —*Kirkus*

★ **Old** man's war. John Scalzi. Tor Books, 2005. 320 p. (Old Man's War universe, 1)

ISBN 9780765309402

1. Life on other planets 2. Senior men 3. Space warfare 4. Space colonies 5. Septuagenarians 6. Military science fiction 7. Science fiction

LC 2004057953

Enlisting in the army on his seventy-fifth birthday, John Perry joins an interstellar war between Earth and alien enemies who would stake claims on the few existing inhabitable planets, unaware that the conflict involves much more than he understands.

Sequel: The ghost brigades.

Redshirts: a novel with three codas. John Scalzi. Tor, 2012. 304 p.

ISBN 9780765316998

1. Space warfare 2. Aliens (Humanoid) 3. Interplanetary relations 4. Betrayal 5. Interstellar relations 6. Metafiction 7. Science fiction 8. Humorous stories

LC 2012009383

Romantic Times Reviewer's Choice Award, 2012; Hugo Award for Best Novel, 2013; Locus Award for Best Science Fiction Novel, 2013

Enjoying his assignment with the Xenobiology lab on board the prestigious Intrepid, ensign Andrew Dahl worries about casualties suffered by low-ranking officers during away missions before making a shocking discovery about the starship's actual purpose.

A Tom Doherty Associates book.

Scerbanenco, Giorgio

A **private** Venus. . Hersilia Press, 2012. 285 p. (Milano quartet, 1)

ISBN 9780956379641

1. Murder investigation 2. Women murder victims 3. Drinking 4. Murder 5. Kidnapping 6. Milan, Italy 7. 1960s 8. Mysteries 9. Translations

Duca Lamberti's a doctor who's just been released from prison, where he's spent the last three years for having practiced euthanasia. Unable to work in medicine, he takes a job helping Davide, a young and depressed alcoholic, whose past seems to involve prostitution, pornography, and murder.

Originally published as Venere privata: Milano : Garzanti, 1966.
Translated from the Italian.

Traitors to all. Giorgio Scerbanenco; translated from the Italian by Howard Curtis. Melville House, 2014. 256 p. (Milano quartet, 2)

ISBN 9781612193663

1. Drowning victims 2. Accidental death investigation 3. Former physicians 4. Amateur detectives 5. Antiheroes and antiheroines 6. Milan, Italy 7. 1960s 8. Mysteries 9. Translations

A lawyer who has spent time in prison with Duca is found drowned in one of the Milanese canals. Duca is contacted by a friend of the dead lawyer to perform surgery on a woman who after the operation confesses that although she is due to marry a wealthy butcher, is really in love with another man, the friend of the lawyer. Shortly afterwards, she is killed together with her lover. Duca discovers that the two events are linked and starts to unravel an arms and drugs trafficking business, centered in an understated trattoria, of which the two were part.

Originally published: Milano : Garzanti Editore, 1966.
Translated from the Italian.

Schaefer, Jack

Monte Walsh. Jack Schaefer. University of Nebraska Press, 1981. Vii, 442 p.

ISBN 9780803241244

1. Cowboys 2. Westerns

LC 80025036

Times change. Monte Walsh doesn't. For him, being a cowboy isn't a job, it's a life. And that's something the fenced-in, corporate-bean-counting ways of the onrushing 20th century must never alter.

"His characters seem real, and, according to the author, the characters and the episodes are based upon historical accounts. This is not just another 'Western.' It is worthy of a place alongside the writing of Will James and Eugene Manlove Rhodes." —*Library Journal*

Originally published: Boston : Houghton Mifflin, 1963.

★ **Shane**. Jack Schaefer; illustrated by John McCormack. Houghton, 1982. 214 p. : Illustration

ISBN 9780395070901

1. Gunfighters 2. Fifteen-year-old boys 3. Ranches 4. Ranchers 5. Wyoming 6. 19th century 7. Westerns 8. Books to movies

A mysterious stranger dressed in black rides into the Wyoming valley where Bob Starrett lives with his parents.

Republished in 2020 by Library of America in The Western: Four classic novels of the 1940s & 50s.

Schaffhausen, Joanna

Gone for good. Joanna Schaffhausen. Minotaur Books, 2021. 304 p. (Detective Annalisa Vega novels, 1)

ISBN 9781250264602

1. Women detectives 2. Serial murderers 3. Serial murder investigation 4. Women amateur detectives 5. Love letters 6. Chicago, Illinois 7. Police procedurals

LC 2021005985

Chicago Detective Annalisa Vega investigates when a new tally is added to the body count of the Lovelorn Killer, a notorious, local serial killer who has evaded the police and been dormant for 20 years.

"Schaffhausen, author of the Ellery Hathaway procedurals, seamlessly weaves past and present together and easily manipulates strong romantic and family-loyalty subplots that might otherwise sink a poorly constructed story. In this strong series debut these multiple story lines provide layers to a heroine who sacrifices everything she loves in pursuit of justice." —*Booklist*

Schaitkin, Alexis

Saint X. Alexis Schaitkin. Celadon Books, 2020. Viii, 343 p.
ISBN 9781250219596

1. Sisters — Death 2. Murder suspects 3. Families of murder victims 4. Loss (Psychology) 5. Social classes 6. New York City 7. Caribbean Area 8. Multiple perspectives 9. Psychological suspense

LC 2019036360

LibraryReads Favorites, 2020; New York Times Notable Book, 2020

When a brief but fateful encounter brings her together with one of the men originally suspected of killing her sister, Claire, hoping to gain his trust and learn the truth, forms an unlikely attachment with this man whose life is forever marked by the same tragedy.

"This killer debut is both a thriller with a vivid setting and an insightful study of race, class, and obsession." —*Kirkus*

Schami, Rafik

Sophia: or the beginning of all tales. Rafik Schami; translated by Monique Arav and John Hannon. Interlink Books, 2018. 480 p.
ISBN 9781566560313

1. First loves 2. Social change 3. Exiles 4. Loyalty 5. Mothers and sons 6. Damascus, Syria 7. Rome, Italy 8. Literary fiction 9. Political fiction 10. Translations

LC 2017031326

A murder in Damascus, a love with the power to save a young man's life... In his latest novel, Rafik Schami ventures to the land of his childhood, where he is now unable to safely return: Syria. OCLC

Translation of: Sophia, oder, Der Anfang aller Geschichten.
Originally published: 2017.
Translated from the German.

Schanbacher, Gary Lester

Crossing Purgatory. Gary Schanbacher. Pegasus Books, 2013. 336 p.
ISBN 9781605984438

1. Families — Death 2. Guilt 3. Frontier and pioneer life 4. Loss (Psychology) 5. Widowers 6. The West (United States) 7. American Westward Expansion (1803-1899) 8. 1850s 9. Rosenberg, Ethel

David J. Langum, Sr. Prize in American Historical Fiction, 2013; Spur Awards, Best Western Traditional Novel, 2014

A young farmer in 1858 sets out across the American frontier in an attempt to deal with his guilt at not being home to prevent a devastating family tragedy and finds himself tested in ways he hadn't imagined.

Schanoes, Veronica L.

Burning girls and other stories. Veronica Schanoes. Tordotcom, 2021. 336 p.

ISBN 9781250781505

1. Women 2. Social marginality 3. Women's power 4. Revenge 5. Psychic trauma 6. Fantasy fiction 7. Short stories

LC 2020051955

In Burning Girls and Other Stories, Veronica Schanoes crosses borders and genres with stories of fierce women at the margins of society burning their way toward the center. This debut collection introduces readers to a fantasist in the vein of Karen Russell and Kelly Link, with a voice all her own. Emma Goldman—yes, that Emma Goldman—takes tea with the Baba Yaga and truths unfold inside of exquisitely crafted lies. In "Among the Thorns," a young woman in seventeenth century Germany is intent on avenging the brutal murder of her peddler father, but discovers that vengeance may consume all that it touches. In the showstopping, awards finalist title story, "Burning Girls," Schanoes invests the immigrant narrative with a fearsome fairytale quality that tells a story about America we may not want—but need—to hear. Dreamy, dangerous, and precise, with the weight of the very oldest tales we tell, Burning Girls and Other Stories introduces a writer pushing the boundaries of both fantasy and contemporary fiction.

"The entries in this collection are powered by the quiet rage and strength of women young and old, often Jewish, many queer." —*Booklist*

Scharer, Whitney

The **age** of light. Whitney Scharer. Little Brown & Co, 2019. 384 p.
ISBN 9780316524087

1. Miller, Lee 2. Women photographers 3. Ambition in women 4. Intellectual life 5. Fashion models 6. Artists 7. 20th century 8. Biographical fiction 9. Historical fiction

Loan Stars Favourites, 2019

Inspired by the life of the *Vogue* model-turned-renowned photographer, Lee Miller relocates to 1929 Paris, where she becomes the muse and colleague of the mercurial Surrealist, Man Ray.

Schell, Orville

My old home: a novel of exile. Orville Schell. Pantheon Books, 2021. 624 pages
ISBN 9780593315811

1. Mao, Zedong 2. Fathers and sons 3. Conservatories of music 4. College teachers 5. Communism 6. Penal colonies 7. China 8. 1950s 9. 1960s 10. Historical fiction 11. Political fiction

Presents the story of a rare Chinese student at 1950 San Francisco's Conservatory of Music who upon returning home is confronted by an erratic new government.

"An ambitious journey through history that captivates with its spectacular scenery." —*Kirkus*

Schellman, Katharine

Silence in the library. Katharine Schellman. Crooked Lane Books, 2021. 352 p. (Lily Adler mysteries, 2)
ISBN 9781643857046

1. Widows 2. Upper class 3. Women amateur detectives 4. Murder victims 5. Secrets 6. London,England 7. Great Britain 8. Regency period (1811-1820) 9. Historical mysteries

Regency widow Lily Adler must earn the trust of her father to help her solve the murder of an old family friend who had secrets worth killing for—and who had family with a lot to gain from his death.

"Schellman's gracefully written whodunit is equally a tale of 19th-century female empowerment and societal conventions.... More than a clever murder puzzle, this is an immersion in a bygone era." —*Kirkus*

Schine, Cathleen

The **Grammarians**. Cathleen Schine. Sarah Crichton Books/Farrar, Straus and Giroux, 2019. 256 pages

ISBN 9780374280116

1. Sisters 2. Sibling rivalry 3. Language and languages — Grammars 4. English language 5. Identical twins 6. Relationship fiction

LC 2018060805

New York Times Notable Book, 2019

Follows the experiences of identical twins whose respective literary careers are upended by their battle to claim an heirloom dictionary.

Schlink, Bernhard

Olga. Bernhard Schlink; translated by Charlotte Collins. Harpervia, 2021. 208 p.

ISBN 9780063112926

1. Romantic love 2. Gender role 3. Adventurers 4. Social classes 5. Misfits (Persons) 6. 20th century 7. 21st century 8. Historical fiction 9. Love stories 10. Epistolary novels

A sweeping novel of love and passion from author of the international bestseller The Reader about a woman out of step with her time, whose life is witness to some of the most tumultuous events of modern age.

"Readers who love rich character studies will want to pick this up." —*Publishers Weekly*

Originally published: 2018.

Translated from the German.

The **reader:** a novel. Bernhard Schlink; translated from the German by Carol Brown Janeway. Pantheon Books, 1997. 218 p.

ISBN 9780679442790

1. Former Nazis 2. War crime trials 3. Law students 4. Teenage boys 5. Women prison guards 6. Coming-of-age stories 7. Literary fiction 8. Translations 9. Adult books for young adults

LC 971511

New York Times Notable Book, 1997; Shortlisted for the International IMPAC Dublin Literary Award, 1999

Schoolboy Michael Berg, 15, meets an older woman and they have an affair, which she breaks off and disappears. Seven years later Berg, now a law student attending a trial, sees her in the dock, accused in a crime dating back to World War II and the death camp at Auschwitz.

"This novel raises provocative questions about guilt and responsibility, as well as the power of literature to heal and bind." —*Publishers Weekly*

Translated from the German.

Self's deception. Bernhard Schlink; translated from the German by Peter Constantine. Vintage Crime/Black Lizard, 2007. 334 p. (Gerhard Self mysteries, 2)

ISBN 9780375709081

1. Private investigators 2. Missing persons investigation 3. Secrecy in government 4. Missing women 5. Psychiatric hospitals 6. Germany 7. Mysteries 8. First person narratives 9. Translations

LC 2006042169

Hired to find Leo Salger, private detective Gerhard Self traces the girl to the psych ward of a local hospital where he is told she died following a fatal fall, only to discover that Leo is very much alive.

Sequel to: Self's punishment.

Sequel: Self's murder.

Originally published: Zurich : Diogenes, 1992.

Translation of: Selbs Betrug.

Self's murder. Bernhard Schlink; translated from the German by Peter Constantine. Vintage Crime/Black Lizard, 2009. 262 p. (Gerhard Self mysteries, 3)

ISBN 9780375709098

1. Private investigators 2. Money laundering 3. Business partners 4. Banks and banking 5. Private banks 6. Germany 7. Mysteries 8. Translations 9. First person narratives

When septuagenarian sleuth Gerhard Self is hired by a German bank owner to track down the silent partner in his business, the detective tangles with Nazi youth and uncovers a money laundering ring with connections to the Russian mafia.

Sequel to: Self's deception.

Originally published: Zurich : Diogenes, 2001.

Self's punishment. Bernhard Schlink with Walter Popp. Vintage Books, 2005. 256 p. (Gerhard Self mysteries, 1)

ISBN 9780375709074

1. Private investigators 2. Hackers 3. Guilt in men 4. Murder 5. Justice 6. Germany 7. 1980s 8. Mysteries 9. Translations 10. First person narratives

LC 2004057166

"This mystery features former Nazi prosecutor turned investigator Gerhard Self. It's the early 1980s, and Self has been hired by a boyhood friend to smoke out a hacker who's playing havoc with the computers at Rhineland Chemical Works. But after Self springs a trap that gets the troublemaker murdered, he gradually faces the guilt he still carries for his youthful embrace of National Socialism. His simple refusal to let himself off the hook and step back into his old public prosecutor's role after the war doesn't seem like penance enough anymore.... Self's unwitting participation in the new crime drives him to pursue the path of justice wherever it may lead. A fascinating exploration of how people often manage to carve out normal lives even after being complicit in terrible acts." —*Booklist*

Sequel: Self's deception.

Translated from German.

Schmidt, Sarah

See what I have done. Sarah Schmidt. Atlantic Monthly Press, 2017. 324 pages

ISBN 9780802126597

1. Borden, Lizzie 2. Murder investigation 3. Sisters 4. Single women 5. Murder 6. Family relationships 7. United States 8. Massachusetts 9. 1890s 10. Historical fiction 11. Multiple perspectives 12. Australian fiction

Australian Book Industry Awards, Literary Fiction Book of the Year, 2018; Librarians' Choice (Australia), 2017; Loan Stars Favourites, 2017; Longlisted for The Women's Prize for Fiction, 2018

Lizzie Borden took an axe... and, well, we all know what happened next. Or do we? This unsettling debut by Australian author Sarah Schmidt tells the story from the (conflicting) perspectives of Lizzie, her elder sister, a maid in the Borden household, and a stranger whose surprising connection to the crime is gradually revealed. With its creeping dread and unreliable narrators, See What I Have Done may appeal to fans of Margaret Atwood's Alias Grace.

"Equally compelling as a whodunit, 'whydunit,' and historical novel, the book honors known facts yet fearlessly claims its own striking vision." —*Publishers Weekly*

Originally published: Sydney: Hachette Australia, 2017.

Schulman, Alex

The **survivors:** a novel. Alex Schulman; translated from the Swedish by Rachel Willson-Broyles. Doubleday, 2021. 240 p.

ISBN 9780385547567

1. Brothers 2. Separated friends, relatives, etc. 3. Dysfunctional families 4. Alienation (Social psychology) 5. Mothers — Death 6. Psychological fiction 7. Coming-of-age stories 8. Translations

LC 2020055315

To finally face what really happened that summer day long ago, three estranged brothers return to the lakeside cottage where an unspeakable accident forever altered their family and find a dangerous new current vibrating between them, testing their loyalty.

"The behavior of Mom in particular is portrayed as classic alcoholic personality disorder; but it slowly dawns on the reader that there is far more to it than that. A final truth emerges, forcing the reader to reevaluate all that has gone before. A novel of family dysfunction that veers into startling and original territory." —*Kirkus*

Translation of: Overlevarna.

Originally published : Stockholm : Albert Bonniers Forlag, 2020.

Translated from the Swedish.

Schulman, Helen

Come with me. Helen Schulman. HarperCollins 2018. 320 p.

ISBN 9780062459138

1. Family relationships 2. Computer algorithms 3. Options, alternatives, choices 4. Technology — Social aspects 5. Married people 6. Palo Alto, California 7. California 8. Literary fiction

A part-time employee of a tech company owned by her friend's 19-year-old son acts as his guinea pig to test an algorithm that allows people to access their "multiverses" and see their alternative life choices and paths.

Schultz, Connie

The **daughters** of Erietown. Connie Schultz. Random House, 2020. 466 p.

ISBN 9780525479352

1. Unplanned pregnancy 2. Man-woman relationships 3. Working class families 4. Small towns 5. Family relationships 6. Ohio 7. Literary fiction 8. Historical fiction

1957, Clayton Valley, Ohio. Ellie has the best grades in her class. Her dream is to go to nursing school and marry Brick McGinty. A basketball star, Brick has the chance to escape his abusive father and become the first person in his blue-collar family to attend college. But when Ellie learns that she is pregnant, everything changes. Just as Brick and Ellie revise their plans and build a family, a knock on the front door threatens to destroy their lives. The evolution of women's lives spanning the second half of the twentieth century is at the center of this beautiful novel that richly portrays how much people know—and pretend not to know—about the secrets at the heart of a town, and a family.

"At its best, the novel has an old-fashioned charm and a keen eye for the details of Midwestern life in the fifties, sixties, and seventies." —*Booklist*

Schumacher, Julie

Dear committee members. Julie Schumacher. Doubleday, 2014. 176 pages (Dear committee members, 1)

ISBN 9780385538138

1. Creative writing teachers 2. Employment references 3. Letters 4. Passive-aggressive personality 5. Teacher-student relationships 6. Satirical fiction 7. Epistolary novels

LC 2013043014

Thurber Prize for American Humor, 2015

Enduring budget cuts and the favoritism of other departments at his small liberal arts college, literature professor Jason Fitger despairs of his writing ambitions and imposed role in a star pupil's would-be opus while writing wryly comic, passive-aggressive letters to students and colleagues.

"Schumacher's warm satire of the peculiarities of the Ivory Tower will be recognizable to anyone who has encountered the bureaucracy and internal politics of higher education." —*Booklist*

Sequel: The Shakespeare Requirement.

Schwab, Victoria

A **conjuring** of light. V. E. Schwab. Tor Books, 2017. 624 p. (Darker shade of magic, 3)

ISBN 9780765387462

1. Magic 2. Parallel universes 3. Power (Social sciences) 4. Enemies 5. Magicians 6. London, England 7. Historical fantasy 8. Gateway fantasy 9. Fantasy fiction 10. Adult books for young adults

Loan Stars Favourites, 2017

Londons fall and kingdoms rise while darkness sweeps the Maresh Empire, and the fraught balance of magic blossoms into dangerous territory while heroes struggle.

"Schwab has fully delivered on the promise of this inventive and captivating series." —*Kirkus*

Series complete in 3 volumes.

A **darker** shade of magic. V. E. Schwab. Tom Doherty Associates, 2015. 400 p. (Darker shade of magic, 1)

ISBN 9780765376459

1. Magic 2. Parallel universes 3. Intrigue 4. Thieves 5. Enemies 6. London, England 7. Historical fantasy 8. Gateway fantasy 9. Fantasy fiction 10. Adult books for young adults

LibraryReads Favorites, 2015; Library Journal Best Books, 2015; RUSA Reading List Short List, 2016

Prepare to be dazzled by a world of parallel Londons—where magic thrives, starves, or lies forgotten, and where power can destroy just as quickly as it can create.

"The brisk plot makes this a page-turner that confronts darkness but is never overwhelmed by it. Fantasy fans will love this fast-paced adventure, with its complex magic system, thoughtful hero and bold heroine." —*Kirkus*

Republished by Tor Books in 2017 as a special collector's edition.

A **gathering** of shadows. V.E. Schwab. Tom Doherty Associates, 2016. 512 p. (Darker shade of magic, 2)

ISBN 9780765376473

1. Magic 2. Contests 3. Parallel universes 4. Pirates 5. Enemies 6. London, England 7. Historical fantasy 8. Gateway fantasy 9. Fantasy fiction 10. Adult books for young adults

LC 2015031510

Romantic Times Reviewer's Choice Award, 2016

Experiencing ominous dreams four months after the events of A Darker Shade of Magic, Kell watches Red London excitedly preparing for the Element Games international magic competition only to realize that the threat of Black London is returning.

"New touches such as a bustling magical market enliven already-rich worldbuilding. Tensions rise steadily, culminating with the exciting Element Games, and the finale will leave readers breathless." —*Publishers Weekly*

The **invisible** life of Addie LaRue. V. E. Schwab. Tor Books, 2020. 480 p.

ISBN 9780765387561

1. Faustian bargains 2. Immortality 3. Memory 4. Curses 5. Loneliness in women 6. Baalbergen, Sarah van 7. Historical fantasy 8. Multiple perspectives

LibraryReads Favorites, 2020; Loan Stars Favourites, 2020

Making a Faustian bargain to live forever but never be remembered, a woman from early 18th-century France endures unacknowledged centuries before meeting a man who remembers her name.

"Schwab (A Darker Shade of Magic) returns with another epic story of love and remembrance that probes deep into history while also penetrating profound matters of the heart." —*Library Journal*

Vengeful. V. E. Schwab. Tor, 2018. 400 p. (Villains (V. E. Schwab), 2)
ISBN 9780765387523
1. Superhuman abilities 2. Enemies 3. Revenge 4. Superheroes 5. Former friends 6. Superhero stories
Goodreads Choice Award, 2018

A conclusion to the story that began with Vicious finds Marcella Riggins targeting the city of Merit while manipulating Victor Vale and Eli Ever into a battle against one another.

Vicious. V. E. Schwab. Tor, 2013. 364 p. (Villains (V. E. Schwab), 1)
ISBN 9780765335340
1. Superhuman abilities 2. Former friends 3. Enemies 4. Villains 5. Revenge 6. Superhero stories
LC 2013023963

RUSA Reading List, 2014

Ten years after a thesis experiment designed to tap a human's supernatural abilities goes terribly wrong, Victor breaks out of prison and resolves to track down his former roommate, Eli, who is accompanied by a girl with astonishing abilities and who resolves to eradicate the world's super-powered people.

"In a genre that tends toward the flippant or pretentious, this is a rare superhero novel as epic and gripping as any classic comic. Schwab's tale of betrayal, self-hatred, and survival will resonate with superhero fans as well as readers who have never heard of Charles Xavier or Victor von Doom." —*Publishers Weekly*

A Tom Doherty Associates Book.

Schwartz, John Burnham

The **commoner:** a novel. John Burnham Schwartz. Nan A. Talese, 2008. 304 p.
ISBN 9780385515719
1. Nobility 2. Women 3. Young women 4. Class conflict 5. Social classes 6. Japan 7. Domestic fiction 8. Historical fiction
LC 2007015391

In 1959, Haruko marries the Crown Prince of Japan, becoming the first commoner to enter the mysterious and reclusive world of Japanese royalty, confronting the cruelty and suspicions of the court, until, three decades later, she helps arrange the marriage of her son.

"An American taking on a fictional memoir about a living Japanese empress is a gutsy move, but Schwartz makes it work.... While the external details of life in the palace remain stunning, it's Schwartz's grasp of [Haruko's] internal struggle that resonates after the last page is turned." —*Denver Post*

Schwartz, Lynne Sharon

Truthtelling: stories, fables, glimpses. Lynne Sharon Schwartz. Delphinium Books, 2020. 217 p.
ISBN 9781883285920
1. Married people 2. Fate and fatalism 3. Truth 4. Life change events 5. Vulnerability 6. New York City 7. New York (State) 8. Short stories

A collection of short fiction features New Yorkers whose established routines are disrupted by mishaps or strange twists of fate.

"Though the situations are unbelievable, the emotions are not. Wise, wry, and witty—these stories in all their stylistic variations are perfect." —*Kirkus*

Schwarz, Christina

Drowning Ruth. Christina Schwarz. Doubleday, 2000. 338 p.
ISBN 9780385502535
1. Drowning victims 2. Family secrets 3. Farm life 4. Nurses 5. Mothers and daughters 6. Wisconsin 7. Multiple perspectives 8. Psychological fiction 9. Adult books for young adults
LC 29523

School Library Journal Best Books: Best Adult Books 4 Teens, 2000

Worn out from nursing soldiers at a Milwaukee hospital and struggling to recover from a traumatic love affair, Amanda Starkey returns to her family's rural Wisconsin farm to stay with her beloved sister, Mattie, and young niece, Ruth.

"The vivid realism of the novel's setting adds depth to an already gripping plot.... Schwarz maintains her mystery with an expert hand, arriving at far more than a simple determination of guilt." —*New York Times Book Review*

The **edge** of the Earth. Christina Schwarz. Atria Books, 2013. 288 p.
ISBN 9781451683677
1. Lighthouses 2. Husband and wife 3. Selfishness in men 4. Native American women 5. Ambition in men 6. California 7. 1890s 8. Historical fiction

Feeling restless in spite of her accomplishments and imminent marriage to a respectable young man, Trudy is ostracized by her late 19th-century Milwaukee community when she falls in love with an enigmatic man and relocates to a California lighthouse, where she uncovers a life-changing secret.

Schwarz, Liese O'Halloran

What could be saved. Liese O'Halloran Schwarz. Atria Books, 2021. 448 p.
ISBN 9781982150617
1. Intelligence service 2. Family secrets 3. Missing boys 4. Siblings 5. Americans in Thailand 6. Bangkok, Thailand 7. 2010s 8. 1970s 9. Multiple perspectives 10. Literary fiction

Alternating between past and present as all of the secrets are revealed, this novel is about a family shattered by loss and betrayal, and the beauty that can exist even in the midst of brokenness.

"Bouncing between modern-day D.C. and 1970s Bangkok, the novel is grounded in its deeply realized characters and the relationships among them, but the author layers in a consideration of power dynamics, racism, and privilege in a way that adds an undercurrent of realism and ugliness, particularly regarding the way the Prestons lived in the '70s." —*Kirkus*

Schwarz-Bart, Andre

The **last** of the just: a novel. By Andre Schwarz-Bart; translated from the French by Stephen Becker. Overlook Press, 2000. 374 p.
ISBN 9781585670161
1. Ghettoes, Jewish 2. Jews, Eastern European 3. Jewish families 4. Jews — Persecutions 5. Jews, German 6. France 7. Historical fiction 8. Translations
LC 99059550

On March 11, 1185, in the old Anglican city of York, the Jews of the city were brutally massacred by their townsmen. As legend has it, God blessed the only survivor of this medieval pogrom, Rabbi Yom Tov Levy, as one of the Lamed-Vov, the thirty-six Just Men of Jewish tradition, a blessing which extended to one Levy of each succeeding generation. This terrifying and remarkable legacy is traced over eight centuries, from the Spanish Inquisition, to expulsions from England, France, Portugal, Germany, and Russia, and to the small Polish village of Zemyock, where the Levys settle for two centuries in relative peace. It is in the twentieth century that Ernie Levy emerges, The Last of the Just, in 1920s Germany, as Hitler's sinister star is on the rise and the agonies of Auschwitz loom on the horizon.

Translation of Le dernier des justes.

Originally published: New York : Atheneum Publishers, 1960.

Schweblin, Samanta

Fever dream: a novel. Samanta Schweblin; translated from the Spanish by Megan McDowell. Riverhead Books, 2017. 192 p.

ISBN 9780399184598

1. Women with terminal illnesses 2. Rural life 3. Intergenerational relations 4. Memories 5. Hazardous waste 6. Argentina 7. Literary fiction 8. Psychological suspense 9. Translations

LC 2016026585

Follows the nightmarish experiences of a dying woman and a boy beside her hospital bed, who explore the dynamics of broken souls, toxic relationships and the power and desperation of family.

"A taut, exquisite page-turner vibrating with existential distress and cumulative dread." —*Kirkus*

Translation of: El nucleo del disturbio.

Made into a movie of the same name, 2021.

Originally published: Buenos Aires : Ediciones Destino, c2002.

Translated from the Spanish.

Little eyes. Samanta Schweblin; translated from the Spanish by Megan McDowell. Riverhead Books, 2020. 240 p.

ISBN 9780525541363

1. Stuffed animals (Toys) 2. Webcams 3. Privacy 4. Electronic surveillance 5. Stalking 6. Literary fiction 7. Psychological suspense 8. Translations

LC 2019042368

ALA Notable Book, 2021; New York Times Notable Book, 2020

A metaphorical tale depicts a complex and relatable world where connections with people from all walks of life engage in internet encounters that lead to unexpected love, transformative adventure and unimaginable terror.

"this jittery eye-opener will appeal to a wide range of readers." —*Library Journal*

Originally published in Spanish and in somewhat different form, as "Kentukis" by Literatura Random House in 2018.

Mouthful of birds: stories. Samanta Schweblin; translated from the Spanish by Megan McDowell. Riverhead Books, 2019. 228 pages

ISBN 9780399184628

1. Psychology 2. Human behavior 3. Interpersonal relations 4. Interpersonal conflict 5. Discontent 6. Argentina 7. Short stories 8. Literary fiction 9. Horror

A first English-language collection of stories by the Man Booker International Prize-finalist author incorporates themes of high suspense, psychological tension, unearthly restlessness and distortions in reality.

"These 20 tales have a visceral effect as Schweblin navigates the extremes of her characters actions and thoughts, both healing and destructive." —*Booklist*

Originally published in Spanish in 2010 as Pájaros en la boca by Random House Mondadori.

Scoppettone, Sandra

Everything you have is mine. Sandra Scoppettone. Little, Brown, 1991. 261 p; (Lauren Laurano mysteries, 1)

ISBN 9780316776462

1. Murder investigation 2. Rape investigation 3. Lesbians 4. Feminists 5. Women private investigators 6. New York City 7. Greenwich Village, New York City 8. Mysteries 9. LGBTQIA fiction

LC 90048889

Lauren Laurano, a gay private detective, and her psychotherapist lover, Kip, join forces to solve the brutal murder of a wealthy young woman who had a penchant for computer dating services, in a mystery set in New York's Greenwich Village BT

"Lauren Laurano, a bighearted, wisecracking lesbian who makes her debut here as a Manhattan private eye, brings cunning as well as caring to her investigation of the murder of a young rape victim who might have met her killer by hooking into a dating service on her personal computer." —*New York Times Book Review*

My sweet untraceable you. Sandra Scoppettone. Little, Brown, 1994. 275 p; (Lauren Laurano mysteries, 3)

ISBN 9780316776486

1. Filmmaking 2. Cold cases (Criminal investigation) 3. Murder investigation 4. Lesbians 5. Feminists 6. New York City 7. Greenwich Village, New York City 8. Mysteries 9. LGBTQIA fiction

LC 93047426

In the most puzzling case of her career, lesbian detective Lauren Laurano finds herself sorting through three decades of bad memories and fending off a succession of all-too-present dangers BT

"Scoppettone is a highly entertaining writer with her fingers on current political and commercial pulses. So she ably transmits the modish urban-grit feel of Laurano's encounters with Manhattan's winos, weirdos, and wise guys as she counterpoints the complex case her sleuth is solving with the deterioration from AIDS of the brother of Laurano's lesbian partner of 14 years." —*Booklist*

Scott, A. D.

★ **Beneath** the abbey wall: a novel. By A. D. Scott. Atria Books, 2012. 384 p. (Joanne Ross novels, 3)

ISBN 9781451665772

1. Journalists 2. Murder 3. Innocence (Law) 4. Newspaper employees 5. Single mothers 6. Highlands, Scotland 7. Scotland 8. 1950s 9. Mysteries

LC 2012030071

On a dark, damp Sunday evening, a man taking a shortcut home sees a hand reaching out in supplication from a bundle of sacks. In an instant he knows something terrifying has happened. In the Highlands in the late 1950s, much of the local newspaper's success was due to Mrs. Smart, the no-nonsense office manager who kept everything and everyone in line. Her murder leaves her colleagues in shock and the Highland Gazette office in chaos. Joanne Ross, a budding reporter and shamefully separated mother, assumes Mrs. Smart's duties, but an intriguing stranger provides a distraction not only from the job and the investigation but from everything Joanne believes in.

A double death on the Black Isle: a novel. A. D. Scott. Atria Paperback, 2011. 384 p. (Joanne Ross novels, 2)

ISBN 9781439154946

1. Journalists 2. Murder investigation 3. Betrayal 4. Murder 5. Newspaper employees 6. Highlands, Scotland 7. Scotland 8. 1950s 9. Mysteries

"Set against the bleak beauty of the Highlands,...[this book explores] the slow transformation of Scotland from a highly ordered society while presenting a fine mystery with engaging characters." —*Kirkus*

A **kind** of grief: a novel. A.D. Scott. Atria Paperback, 2015. 336 p. (Joanne Ross novels, 6)
ISBN 9781476756189
1. Journalists 2. Small town life 3. Superstition 4. Witchcraft 5. Trials (Witchcraft) 6. Highlands, Scotland 7. Scotland 8. 1950s 9. Mysteries
LC 2015025918
Joanne Ross investigates the death of an artist and alleged witch, who was found dead in her home on a remote glen in Scotland.

★ The **low** road. By A.D. Scott. Atria, 2014. 336 pages. (Joanne Ross novels, 5)
ISBN 9781476756165
1. Journalists 2. Gangs 3. Missing persons investigation 4. Murder investigation 5. Small town life 6. Highlands, Scotland 7. Scotland 8. 1950s 9. Mysteries
LC 2014005047
Joanne Ross' fiance, John McAllister, is on a fast-paced hunt for his good friend Jimmy McPhee, who is involved in a blood feud with a murderous razor gang in 1950s Glasgow.

Scott, Paul
★ **Staying** on: a novel. Paul Scott. University of Chicago Press, 1998. 215 p.
ISBN 9780226743493
1. British in India 2. Culture conflict 3. Race relations 4. Senior couples 5. Husband and wife 6. India 7. Historical fiction 8. Literary fiction
Booker Prize, 1977
Tusker and Lily Smalley stayed on in India. Given the chance to return 'home' when Tusker, once a Colonel in the British Army, retired, they chose instead to remain in the small hill town of Pangkot, with its eccentric inhabitants and archaic rituals left over from the days of the Empire. Only the tyranny of their landlady, the imposing Mrs Bhoolabhoy, threatens to upset the quiet rhythm of their days.
Originally published: London: Heinemann, 1977.

Scott, Rion Amilcar
★ The **world** doesn't require you: stories. Rion Amilcar Scott. Liveright, 2019. 304 pages
ISBN 9781631495380
1. African American communities 2. African Americans 3. Race relations 4. Local history 5. Communities 6. Maryland 7. Short stories 8. Literary fiction 9. Surrealist fiction
Finalist for the Hurston/Wright Legacy Awards for Fiction, 2020
This collection of short stories, set in fictional Cross River, Maryland, includes the tales of a struggling musician who is God's last son and a Ph.D. candidate whose dissertation about a childhood game sparks a riot in a once-segregated town.
"Mordantly bizarre and trenchantly observant, these stories stake out fresh territory in the nation's literary landscape." —*Kirkus*

Scott, Stephanie
What's left of me is yours: a novel. By Stephanie Scott. Random House Inc 2020. 272 pages
ISBN 9780385544702
1. Mothers — Death 2. Daughters 3. Extramarital affairs 4. Murder 5. Divorce 6. Japan 7. Psychological fiction 8. Multiple perspectives
LC 2019022477

In modern-day Tokyo a young woman searches for the truth about her mother's life—and her murder. A first novel.
"She clearly defines the unfortunate effects of the traditional Japanese legal system on women, and with carefully accumulated details describes a Japan both physically and psychologically teetering on the edge of change." —*Booklist*

Scott, Walter
The **bride** of Lammermoor. Walter Scott; preface by W.M. Parker. Dent; Dutton, 1966. 342 p. (Waverley novels; Tales of my landlord)
ISBN 9780231105729
1. Arranged marriage 2. Heirs and heiresses 3. Murder 4. Stabbing victims 5. Husband and wife 6. Scotland 7. 1700s (Decade) 8. Historical fiction 9. Classics
The most haunting and Shakespearean of Scott's novels, The Bride of Lammermoor is a fast-paced tragedy set on the eve of the 1707 Union.
Originally published, 1819.

★ **Ivanhoe**. Walter Scott; edited with an introduction by Graham Tulloch. Penguin, 2000. Xlv, 496 p; (Waverley novels)
ISBN 9780140436587
1. Richard 2. Chivalry 3. Knights and knighthood 4. Coups d'etat 5. Jews, English 6. Romantic love 7. Great Britain 8. Medieval period (476-1492) 9. Plantagenet period (1154-1485) 10. Epic fiction 11. Historical fiction 12. Adventure stories
Scott's classic historical romance, set in the twelfth-century England of Richard I, depicts the adventures of the heroic Wilfred of Ivanhoe in winning the hand of beautiful Lady Rowena.
Based on the acclaimed Edinburgh edition of the Waverley novels.
Adapted into several theatrical and television films and miniseries.
Originally published: London : A. Constable, 1820.

★ **Rob** Roy. Walter Scott. Tom Doherty Associates, 1998. Lxix, 465 p; (Waverley novels)
ISBN 9780812580433
1. Rob Roy 2. Jacobites 3. Uncle and nephew 4. Rebels 5. Battles 6. Religion 7. Scotland 8. Jacobite Rebellions (1689-1746) 9. 1710s 10. Historical fiction 11. Books to movies 12. Classics
An English gentleman, involved in Jacobite intrigues, journeys to the Trossachs to meet a famous Scottish outlaw
Originally published: Edinburgh : A. Constable, 1817.

Scottoline, Lisa
After Anna. By Lisa Scottoline. St. Martin's Press, 2018. 352 p.
ISBN 9781250099655
1. Widowers 2. Blended families 3. Trials (Murder) 4. Manipulation by teenage girls 5. Mothers and daughters 6. Psychological suspense
LC 2017053395
Marrying a wonderful woman after years of loneliness and single fatherhood, John finds his newfound happiness turned upside-down by the arrival of his beautiful sociopath teen daughter, whose campaign to destroy their family and untimely murder force John to prove his innocence in the face of malevolent discoveries.

★ **Come** home. Lisa Scottoline. St. Martin's Press, 2012. 384 p.
ISBN 9780312380823
1. Divorced women 2. Motherhood 3. Murder investigation 4. Former husbands — Death 5. Stepdaughters 6. Thrillers and suspense
LC 2011046492
Rebalancing her life and career after a painful divorce, pediatrician Jill learns that her ex has died from an alleged overdose that her former

stepdaughter believes was actually murder, a situation that forces Jill to choose between her duty to past circumstances and her future happiness.

Don't go. Lisa Scottoline. St. Martin's Press, 2013. 384 p.
ISBN 9781250010070
1. Military physicians 2. Married women — Death 3. Grief in men 4. Fathers and daughters 5. Family secrets 6. Thrillers and suspense
Fleeing home from his military service in Afghanistan when his wife dies in an apparent freak household accident, Dr. Mike Scanlon struggles with the tragedy, his inability to bond with his new baby daughter and a downsizing in his medical practice only to discover a shocking secret that changes his understanding of everything.

★ **Every** fifteen minutes. Lisa Scottoline. St. Martin's Press, 2015. 352 p.
ISBN 9781250010117
1. Frameups 2. Murder suspects 3. Obsessive-compulsive disorder 4. Single fathers 5. Hospitals 6. Philadelphia, Pennsylvania 7. Thrillers and suspense
LC 2014042835
A single father and head of a successful Philadelphia psychiatric care unit sees his life begin to crumble when a teen patient is implicated in a murder and the doctor himself is wrongly accused of sexual harassment.
"Scottoline casts an unflinching eye on the damaged world of sociopaths in this exciting page-turner.... Many characters who seem to be gunning for Eric are likely candidates for a sociopathic diagnosis. Once the red herrings are dispatched, the identity of the culprit who plots his downfall is a genuine surprise." —*Publishers Weekly*

Feared. Lisa Scottoline. St. Martin's Press, 2018. 386 p. (Rosato and Associates novels, 17)
ISBN 9781250099594
1. Law firms 2. Suing (Law) 3. Women lawyers 4. Enemies 5. Revenge in women 6. Philadelphia, Pennsylvania 7. Pennsylvania 8. Legal thrillers 9. Corey, Dorian
LC 2018022095
When nemesis Nick Machiavelli targets her family with frivolous legal claims and slander that escalate to an unthinkable tragedy, Mary DiNunzio discovers her own unsettling capacity for dark retaliation.

Legal tender. Lisa Scottoline. Harper Collins Publishers, 1996. 452 p; (Rosato and Associates novels, 2)
ISBN 9780060176587
1. Women lawyers 2. Animal rights advocates 3. Murder 4. Police corruption 5. Women murder suspects 6. Philadelphia, Pennsylvania 7. Legal thrillers 8. Thrillers and suspense
LC 967165
When her former lover and partner, Mark Biscardi, turns up murdered and she becomes the prime suspect in the crime, Philadelphia lawyer Benedetta "Bennie" Rosato finds herself framed for murder, on the run from the cops, and searching for the real killer BT

One perfect lie. Lisa Scottoline. St. Martin's Press, 2017. 355 p.
ISBN 9781250099563
1. Single mothers 2. Teenage boys 3. Deception 4. Mothers and sons 5. Teachers 6. Thrillers and suspense 7. Parallel narratives 8. Adult books for young adults
A single mom's efforts to support her shy star athlete son's recruitment into a Division I college are violently complicated by a secretly disturbed young man from an affluent family and a new teacher with a mysterious agenda.
"Scottoline keeps the pace relentless as she drops a looming threat into the heart of an idyllic suburban community, causing readers to hold their breath in anticipation." —*Booklist*

Searles, John
Help for the haunted. John Seales. William Morrow, 2013. 368 p.
ISBN 9780060779634
1. Parents — Death 2. Family secrets 3. Demons 4. Christian men 5. Sisters 6. Psychological suspense 7. First person narratives 8. Adult books for young adults
Alex Award, 2014; Booklist Editors' Choice: Adult Books for Young Adults, 2013; LibraryReads Favorites, 2013; School Library Journal Best Books: Best Adult Books 4 Teens, 2013
Struggling with the loss of her parents, who helped haunted souls find peace, Sylvie Mason pursues the mystery, moving closer to the truth of what happened that night as she comes to terms with her family's past.

Sears, Michael
Black Fridays. Michael Sears. G. P. Putnam's Sons, 2012. 352 p. (Jason Stafford novels, 1)
ISBN 9780399158667
1. Financial services industry and trade — Corrupt practices 2. Former convicts 3. Self-fulfillment 4. Parents of children with autism 5. Corporate crime 6. Wall Street, New York City 7. Financial thrillers
LC 2012011085
Shamus Award for Best First P.I. Novel, 2013
Struggling to rebuild his life after a two-year prison term for unscrupulous choices, former Wall Street hotshot Jason Stafford is tapped by an investment firm to investigate the suspicious death of a junior trader, a dangerous assignment that is complicated by his efforts to reclaim his young autistic son from his unstable ex-wife.

Tower of Babel. Michael Sears. Soho Crime, 2020. 408 pages
ISBN 9781641291958
1. Former lawyers 2. Private investigators 3. Swindlers and swindling 4. City life 5. Criminals 6. Queens, New York City 7. New York City 8. Hardboiled fiction
Scraping by as a foreclosure profiteer after a spectacular fall from grace, a once high-powered Manhattan attorney is implicated in an informant's murder and forced to confront greedy developers, mobsters, activists and rivals to clear his name.
"Razor-edged prose, sharply defined characters, and a fast-paced plot boost this noir-wrought drama. Fans of Raymond Chandler and classic gangster films will be rewarded." —*Publishers Weekly*

Sebald, Winfried Georg
★ **Austerlitz**. W.G. Sebald; translated from the German by Anthea Bell. Random House, 2001. 298 p. : Illustration
ISBN 9780375504839
1. Holocaust (1933-1945) 2. Refugees, Jewish 3. Orphans 4. Exiles 5. World War II 6. Europe 7. Literary fiction 8. First person narratives 9. Translations
LC 2001019785
ALA Notable Book, 2002; National Book Critics Circle Award for Fiction, 2001
In 1939, five-year-old Jacques Austerlitz is sent to England on a Kindertransport and placed with foster parents. This childless couple promptly erase from the boy all knowledge of his identity and he grows up ignorant of his past. Later in life, after a career as an architectural historian, Austerlitz—having avoided all clues that might point to his origin—finds the past returning to haunt him and he is forced to explore what happened fifty years before.
"As so often in Sebald's fiction, direct connections are never highlighted in the vast loops and sudden knottings of his rhetoric, but the reader cannot escape the inference that in the long sweep of history the

Nazis were not alone, but that an inquirer searching for meaning is."
—*New York Times Book Review*

Originally published: Munchen : C. Hanser, 2001.

The **emigrants**. W. G. Sebald; translated by Michael Hulse. New Directions, 1996. 237 p.

ISBN 9780811213387

1. Exiles 2. World War II 3. Holocaust (1933-1945) 4. Germany 5. Literary fiction 6. Psychological fiction 7. Translations

LC 96-22223

Four narratives weave history and fiction together as refugees from the holocaust remember their experiences

"A profound and original work .... W. G. Sebald has created an end-of-century meditation that explores the most delicate, most painful, most nervously repressed and carefully concealed lesions of the last hundred years. Illuminatingly engaged with the history and literature of the modern era, Mr. Sebald's book gains power through its poetic obsessions with the past." —*New York Times Book Review*

Vertigo. W.G. Sebald; translated by Michael Hulse. New Directions Pub, 2000. 263 p. : Illustration

ISBN 9780811214308

1. Travelers 2. Voyages and travels 3. Venice, Italy 4. Bavaria 5. Literary fiction 6. Translations 7. First person narratives

LC 99058955

New York Times Notable Book, 2000

First-person narrative describes a journey from Italy during Napoleon's invasion to a Bavarian village, drawing in the memories of notable thinkers such as Franz Kafka and Casanova.

"W.G. Sebald is unusual for a literary star. He fuses genres (travelogue, biography, the novel, meditation, myth), confounding the categories most readers are used to. The narrator of 'Vertigo' offers a fair account of Mr. Sebald's intricate methods.... This is poetic or philosophical fiction for readers content to follow the path of a remarkable author's thoughts without the guard-rail of an overarching story." —*The Economist*

Sebastian, Cat

It takes two to tumble. Cat Sebastian. Avon Impulse, 2018. 304 p. (Seducing the Sedgwicks, 1)

ISBN 9780062821577

1. Clergy 2. Ship captains 3. Gay men 4. Single fathers 5. Tutors 6. England 7. Regency period (1811-1820) 8. Regency romances 9. LGBTQIA romances 10. Historical romances

"Sebastian's latest elegantly and eloquently written Regency historical, which puts a clever, same-sex spin on the classic employer/governess trope, slowly unfolds into an unforgettable love story that manages to be both sweetly romantic and sizzlingly sensual at the same time." —*Booklist*

The **Lawrence** Browne affair. Cat Sebastian. Avon Impulse, 2017. 336 p. (Turner series (Cat Sebastian), 2)

ISBN 9780062642516

1. Earls and countesses 2. Gay men 3. Men/men relations 4. Manors 5. Scientists 6. Lincoln, Abraham 7. Regency period (1811-1820) 8. Regency romances 9. LGBTQIA romances 10. Historical romances

RUSA Reading List Short List, 2018

Hiding from the world in his family's crumbling estate, Lawrence Browne, brilliant scientist and the Earl of Radnor, finds his life turned upside down when Georgie Turner arrives at Penkellis claiming to be his new secretary.

Unmasked by the marquess. Cat Sebastian. Avon Impulse, 2018. 306 p. (Regency impostors, 1)

ISBN 9780062821607

1. Aristocracy 2. Mate selection 3. Genderqueer 4. Nonbinary people 5. Nonconformists 6. England 7. Regency period (1811-1820) 8. Regency romances 9. LGBTQIA romances 10. Historical romances

Library Journal Best Books, 2018

Robert Selby is determined to see his sister make an advantageous match. But he has two problems: the Selbys have no connections or money and Robert is really a housemaid named Charity Church. Alistair, Marquess of Pembroke, has spent years repairing the estate ruined by his wastrel father, and nothing is more important than protecting his fortune and name. He shouldn't be so beguiled by the charming young man who shows up on his doorstep asking for favors. Can these stubborn souls learn to sacrifice what they've always wanted for a love that is more than they could have imagined?

Sebastian, Tim

Fatal ally. Tim Sebastian. Severn House, 2019. 240 p.

ISBN 9780727889522

1. Women spies 2. Double agents 3. Defectors 4. Betrayal 5. International intrigue 6. Russia 7. Syria 8. Spy fiction 9. Thrillers and suspense

After five years' silence, a British intelligence asset has made contact from Moscow. Claiming to be in possession of an explosive piece of information, he wishes to defect to the West. The carefully-planned operation however goes catastrophically wrong, the would-be defector ruthlessly betrayed by a rogue element at the highest level of US government.

"Posing difficult questions about loyalty and morality, this unputdownable novel boasts a taut and suspenseful plot, vividly drawn characters, and an eye-opening look inside the dirty world of spying." —*Booklist*

Sebold, Alice

The **almost** moon: a novel. By Alice Sebold. Little, Brown and Co, 2007. 304 p.

ISBN 9780316677462

1. Parricide 2. Women with mental illnesses 3. Mother and adult daughter 4. Middle-aged women 5. Divorced women 6. Psychological fiction

LC 2007009917

Having set aside her own life in her support of her parents, husband, and children, Helen Knightly confronts the realities of the choices that were imposed upon her during a harrowing twenty-four-hour period of death and revelation.

"This novel is brilliantly paced, it's brutally honest, and the Gordian knot at its core an abusive mother and her traumatically attached daughter is depicted with such generous intelligence that the fineness of the novel more than surpasses its own horror show of circumstance. Sebold has managed to give us a sympathetic protagonist who smothers her mother in the opening pages, and yet the decades that led up to this black moment are delivered without a shred of sentimentality or melodramatic overkill. It's a tightrope walk of character building." —*Boston Globe*

★ The **lovely** bones. Alice Sebold. Little, Brown, 2002. 288 p.

ISBN 9780316666343

1. Families of murder victims 2. Crimes against teenage girls 3. Murder victims 4. Teenage girl murder victims 5. Rape victims 6. Psychological fiction 7. Literary fiction 8. Books to movies 9. Adult books for young adults

LC 2001050622

Bram Stoker Award for Best First Novel, 2002; Booklist Editors' Choice: Adult Books for Young Adults, 2002; Book Sense Book of the Year Adult Fiction, 2003; British Book Award for the Richard &

Judy Best Read of the Year, 2004; Eliot Rosewater Indiana High School Book Award (Rosie Award), 2005; Gateway Readers Award (Missouri), 2005; Iowa High School Book Award, 2005; Kentucky Bluegrass Award for Grades 9-12, 2004; New York Times Notable Book, 2002; School Library Journal Best Books: Best Adult Books 4 Teens, 2002; South Carolina Book Award, Young Adult Books, 2005; YALSA Best Books for Young Adults, 2003

Looking down from heaven, 14-year-old Susie Salmon recounts her rape and murder and watches her family as they cope with their grief and "the lovely bones" growing around her absence.

"As pleasant as Susie's heaven is, there's no God there, and certainly no Jesus. This is spirituality for an age that's ecumenical to a fault. But emotionally, it's faultless. Sebold never slips as she follows this family. The risks she walks are enough to give you vertigo." —*Christian Science Monitor*

Sedaris, David

Holidays on ice. By David Sedaris. Little, Brown and Co, 2008. 192 p. ISBN 9780316035903

1. Families 2. Holidays 3. Americans in France 4. Family relationships 5. Christmas stories 6. Short stories 7. Essays 8. Life stories — General
LC 2008925927

An anthology of humorous Christmas tales and essays features excerpts from the author's "Barrel Fever" and "Naked," as well as "The Santaland Diaries," "Season's Greetings to Our Friends and Family," and a new tale of holiday mayhem.

"For those dreading the holiday season, bestseller Sedaris (When You Are Engulfed In Flames) makes life a little easier with this re-release of his uproarious essay collection, newly expanded from the original 1997 edition." —*Publishers Weekly*

A classic collection of stories features six additional works on the joys and embarrassments of favorite holidays, including tales of tardy trick-or-treaters, the difficulties of explaining the Easter Bunny to another culture, and a barnyard Secret Santa scheme gone awry.

Sedgwick, Marcus

Mister Memory: a novel. Marcus Sedgwick. Pegasus Crime, 2017. 327 pages
ISBN 9781681773407

1. Murder suspects 2. Psychiatric hospitals 3. Photographic memory 4. Police 5. Dancers 6. Paris, France 7. France 8. Belle Epoque (1871-1914) 9. 1890s 10. Historical mysteries 11. Adult books for young adults

Transferred to a famous asylum after being arrested for his wife's murder at the end of the 19th century, a man with an eidetic memory is investigated by a doctor and a police officer who discover links between the bizarre crime and the highest and lowest establishments in France.

"Marvelously imagined and sure to appeal to readers who enjoy an intelligent thriller." —*Kirkus*

See, Lisa

Dragon bones: a novel. Lisa See. Random House, 2003. Xv, 348 p; (Red princess mysteries, 3)
ISBN 9780679463207

1. Policewomen 2. Archaeological sites 3. Cults 4. Castro, Fidel 5. Antiquities — Collection and preservation 6. China 7. Yangtze River 8. Mysteries 9. Adult books for young adults
LC 2002024871

When the body of an American archaeologist turns up in the Yangtze, Liu Hulan, an agent for the Chinese government, and her American husband, David Stark, investigate and find that the murder may be tied to a missing priceless artifact.

"The novel flows beautifully, engaging readers in the mystery while gently introducing them to China's rich cultural history." —*Library Journal*

Dreams of joy: a novel. Lisa See. Random House, 2011. 336 p. ISBN 9781400067121

1. Family relationships 2. Mothers and daughters 3. Family secrets 4. Birthfathers 5. Communism 6. China 7. 1950s 8. Historical fiction
LC 2011003891

Finds a devastated Joy fleeing to China to search for her real father while her mother, Pearl, desperately pursues her, a dual quest marked by their encounters with the nation's intolerant Communist culture.

"Although the ending betrays Sees roots in genre fiction, this is a riveting, meticulously researched depiction of one of the worlds worst human-engineered catastrophes." —*Kirkus*
Sequel to: Shanghai girls.

The **island** of sea women. By Lisa See. Scribner, 2019. 320 p. ISBN 9781501154850

1. Women divers 2. Fishers 3. Female friendship 4. Family secrets 5. Islands 6. Jeju Island, South Korea 7. South Korea 8. 20th century 9. Historical fiction 10. First person narratives 11. Multiple perspectives

While working as divers with the all-female diving collective on a small Korean island, Mi-ja and Young-sook find their friendship challenged by their differences and forces outside their control.

Peony in love: a novel. Lisa See. Random House, 2007. 304 p. ISBN 9781400064663

1. Women 2. Operas 3. Love 4. Man-woman relationships 5. Interpersonal attraction 6. China 7. 17th century 8. Love stories 9. Historical fiction
LC 2007001623

In seventeenth-century China, three women become emotionally involved with "The Peony Pavilion," a famed opera rumored to cause love-sickness and even death.

"This novel is—for the reader willing to venture a crucial suspension of disbelief—a complex period tapestry inscribed with the age-old tragedy of love and death and bordered round with vignettes from Chinese metaphysics, dynastic history and the intimate chamber tales of women's friendship and rivalry.... See is gifted with a lucid, graceful style and a solid command of her many motifs." —*New York Times Book Review*

Shanghai girls: a novel. Lisa See. Random House, 2009. 336 p. ISBN 9781400067114

1. Chinese American women 2. Immigrants 3. Sisters 4. Immigrants, Chinese 5. Fathers and daughters 6. United States 7. China 8. 1930s 9. Historical fiction 10. Adult books for young adults
LC 2008049245

Forced to leave Shanghai when their father sells them to California suitors, sisters May and Pearl struggle to adapt to life in 1930s Los Angeles while still bound to old customs, as they face discrimination and confront a life-altering secret.

"Pearl and May Chin are Beautiful Girls, models in 1930s Shanghai whose images grace calendars and ads and who party with the young and restless in the Paris of Asia. But the party is soon over.... Their father sells them into arranged marriages with the sons of a Chinese family that emigrated to Los Angeles. The daughters rebel and literally miss the boat until the Japanese attack on Shanghai in 1937 forces them on an Odyssean journey to America. In this moving historical novel, Lisa See explores her Chinese-American roots and those of the Chinese who headed to California in the early 20th century in hopes of a better life, only to find hardship and discrimination." —*USA Today*

Sequel: Dreams of joy.

The **tea** girl of Hummingbird Lane. Lisa See. Scribner, 2017. 352 p.
ISBN 9781501154829
1. Adopted girls 2. International adoption 3. Chinese American girls 4. Tea 5. Families 6. China 7. California 8. Literary fiction
LibraryReads Favorites, 2017

Explores the lives of a Chinese mother and her daughter, who has been adopted by an American couple, tracing the very different cultural factors that compel them to consume a rare native tea that has shaped their family's destiny for generations.

"With vivid and precise details about tea and life in rural China, Li-Yans gripping journey to find her daughter comes alive." —*Publishers Weekly*

Segal, Erich

★ **Love** story. Erich Segal. Bantam Books, 1970. 115 p.
ISBN 9780380017607
1. College students 2. Interclass romance 3. Women with terminal illnesses 4. Boston, Massachusetts 5. Love stories 6. Books to movies
LC 71096003

"A very professionally crafted short first novel. The author makes no great claims of insight for his work. Indeed, the story is all on the surface. But it is funny and sad and generally recommended." —*Library Journal*

Sequel: Oliver's story (1977).

Sekaran, Shanthi

★ **Lucky** boy. Shanthi Sekaran. G.P. Putnam's Sons, 2016. 480 p.
ISBN 9781101982242
1. Undocumented immigrants 2. Determination in women 3. Motherhood 4. Single mothers 5. Foster mothers 6. Berkeley, California 7. Literary fiction 8. Domestic fiction 9. Multiple perspectives
LC 2016008418

Loan Stars Favourites, 2017; Library Journal Best Books, 2017

A wrenching emotional battle ensues between Soli, an undocumented Mexican single mother, and Kavya, an Indian-American chef who cannot have children, when Soli's infant son is placed in Kavya's care during an immigration detention.

"Sekaran is a master of drawing detailed, richly layered characters and relationships; here are the subtly nuanced lines of love and expectation between parents and children; here, too are moments of great depth and insight. A superbly crafted and engrossing novel." —*Kirkus*

Self, Will

The **book** of Dave: a revelation of the recent past and the distant future. Will Self. Bloomsbury Pub. : 2006. 512 p.
ISBN 9781596911239
1. Taxicab drivers 2. Dystopias 3. Rulers 4. Near future 5. Books 6. London, England 7. 21st century 8. Satirical fiction 9. Satirical fiction
LC 2006004750

When cabdriver Dave Rudman's wife of five years deserts him for another man, taking their only child with her, he is thrown into a tailspin of doubt and discontent. Fearing his son will never know his father, Dave pens a gripping text—part memoir, part deranged philosophical treatise, and part handbook of "the Knowledge" learned by all London cab drivers. Meant for the boy when he comes of age, the book captures the frustration and anxiety of modern life. Five hundred years later, the Book of Dave is discovered by the inhabitants on the island of Ham, where it becomes a sacred text of biblical proportion, and its author is revered as a mighty prophet.

"Self achieves an elaborate vision of vicious superstition and hopeless struggle." —*The New Yorker*

Sem-Sandberg, Steve

The **chosen** ones: a novel. Steve Sem-Sandberg; translated from the Swedish by Anna Paterson. Farrar, Straus and Giroux, 2016. 512 p.
ISBN 9780374122805
1. Euthanasia 2. Persecution by Nazis 3. Children with chronic illnesses 4. Nazis 5. Murder 6. Vienna, Austria 7. Austria 8. Second World War era (1939-1945) 9. Historical fiction 10. Literary fiction 11. Translations
LC 2015042554

A tale inspired by a devastating, forgotten incident from annexed Vienna follows the experiences of a young inmate at a reform school for chronically ill children who become subject to the Nazi regime's euthanasia program on the eve of World War II.

"With a gift for finding humanity in even the darkest of stories, Sem-Sanberg has written an indelible, moving novel." —*Publishers Weekly*

Originally published in Swedish in 2014 by Albert Bonniers Forlag, Sweden, as De utvalda. English translation originally published in 2016 by Faber and Faber Ltd, Great Britain—Title page verso.

Semple, Maria

Where'd you go, Bernadette: a novel. Maria Semple. Little, Brown and Co, 2012. 330 pages.
ISBN 9780316204279
1. Women architects 2. Missing persons investigation 3. Phobias 4. Mothers and daughters 5. Agoraphobia in women 6. Antarctica 7. Seattle, Washington 8. Humorous stories 9. Books to movies 10. Relationship fiction 11. Adult books for young adults
LC 2011040639

Alex Award, 2013; Shortlisted for The Women's Prize for Fiction, 2013

When her notorious, hilarious, volatile, talented, troubled and agoraphobic mother goes missing, teenage Bee begins a trip that takes her to the ends of the earth to find her.

Title adapted into a film in 2019.

Senna, Danzy

New people. Danzy Senna. Riverhead Books, 2017. 288 pages
ISBN 9781594487095
1. Multiracial persons 2. Doctoral students 3. Race relations 4. Poets 5. City life 6. Brooklyn, New York City 7. New York City 8. 1990s 9. Literary fiction 10. African American fiction
LC 2016045954

New York Times Notable Book, 2017

Working on her dissertation while planning her wedding to her college sweetheart as the 20th century draws to a close, Maria, a young woman from Brooklyn being featured in a documentary about mixed-heritage couples, risks the life she has worked so hard to achieve by fantasizing about a poet she barely knows.

"Senna combines the clued-in status details you'd find in a New York magazine article with the narrative invention of big-league fiction. Every detail and subplot, including Maria's dissertation on the Jonestown mas-

sacre and her buried secret about a college prank gone awry, is resonant."
—*Kirkus*

Seo, Mi-ae

★ The **only** child. Mi-ae Seo. HarperCollins, 2020. 288 p.
ISBN 9780062905048
1. Psychologists 2. Stepchildren 3. Serial murderers 4. Koreans
5. Children with behavioral disorders 6. Korea 7. Thrillers and suspense
   When serial killer Yi Byeongdo asks to speak to her, and her husband's 11-year-old daughter from a previous marriage shows up at their door, criminal psychologist Seonkyeong starts to unravel the pasts of the two new arrivals in her life and begins to see startling similarities.
   "This strong addition to the growing collection of Asian crime fiction available in English shares unflinching narration and the unsettling atmosphere of a horror film with the work of Kanae Minato, Natsuo Kirino, and Masako Togawa." —*Booklist*

Sepetys, Ruta

★ **Out** of the Easy. Ruta Sepetys. Philomel Books, 2013. 288 p.
ISBN 9780399256929
1. Children of prostitutes 2. Murder investigation 3. Teenage romance
4. Seventeen-year-old girls 5. Teenage girls 6. New Orleans, Louisiana
7. French Quarter (New Orleans, La.) 8. 1950s 9. Historical mysteries
10. Mysteries
                                                    LC 2012016062
YALSA Best Fiction for Young Adults, 2014; YALSA Best Fiction for Young Adults: Top Ten, 2014
   Josie, the seventeen-year-old daughter of a French Quarter prostitute, is striving to escape 1950 New Orleans and enroll at prestigious Smith College when she becomes entangled in a murder investigation.

Serle, Rebecca

In five years: a novel. Rebecca Serle. Atria Books, 2020. 240 p.
ISBN 9781982137441
1. Fate and fatalism 2. Women lawyers 3. Ambition 4. Marriage proposals 5. Type A personality 6. Manhattan, New York City 7. Love stories 8. Relationship fiction
                                                    LC 2019027133
LibraryReads Favorites, 2020
   An ambitious young lawyer on the brink of having it all disregards a vivid dream about how different her life will be in five years, before meeting the man in her vision nearly five years later.
   "While the plot hinges on well-worn tropes, the deadpan prose highlights the author's keen sense of irony. Serle's whimsical tale is book club catnip." —*Publishers Weekly*

Serpell, Namwali

★ The **old** drift. Namwali Serpell. Hogarth Press, 2019. 640 pages
ISBN 9781101907146
1. Race relations 2. Family curses 3. Social change 4. Families
5. Families — History 6. Zambia 7. Africa 8. 20th century 9. 21st century 10. Epic fiction 11. Family sagas 12. Magical realism
Arthur C. Clarke Award, 2020; Los Angeles Times Art Seidenbaum Award for First Fiction, 2019; New York Times Notable Book, 2019
   Three generations of a cursed family traverse from India and Italy to England and ultimately a fantastical Zambia of the near future, where an interstitial Greek chorus of mosquitoes traces their vibrant human experiences as children, parents and grandparents.

Seth, Vikram

★ A **suitable** boy: a novel. Vikram Seth. Harper Collins, 1993. 1349 p.
ISBN 9780060170127
1. Family relationships 2. Extended families 3. Mothers and daughters
4. Rich families 5. Upper class 6. India 7. 1950s 8. Love stories
9. Kingsley, Mary Henrietta
                                                    LC 92054744
Commonwealth Writers' Prize for Best Book, 1994; Commonwealth Writers' Prize, South Asia and Europe: Best Book, 1994
   While a widowed mother agonizes over her daughter's future, the newly independent India of the early 1950s struggles through a time of great crisis when its varied cultures clash
   "This novel is, at its heart an elegy as well as a comedy of manners, about a traditional society in a time of change, and about a leisurely world of graces giving way to a new, more democratic time." —*Times Literary Supplement*

Seton, Anya

Avalon. Anya Seton. Chicago Review Press, 2006. 440 p.
ISBN 9781556526008
1. Princes 2. Shipwreck survivors 3. Voyages and travels
4. Man-woman relationships 5. Avalon (Legendary place) 6. Great Britain 7. Anglo-Saxon period (449-1066) 8. 10th century 9. Historical fiction
   During the period of conflict and exploration in the late-tenth century, a shipwreck brings a French prince into the life of a Cornish peasant.
   "Late tenth- and early eleventh-century life in England and in the lands colonized by the Norsemen [i.e. Iceland] is re-created from early Anglo-Saxon chronicles, French manuscripts, and secondary sources.... The action and milieu are vivid and though the characterization is not strong the psychological and historical motivations are believable. An honest historical novel for enthusiasts of the genre." —*Booklist*
   Originally published: Boston : Houghton Mifflin, 1965.

★ **Dragonwyck**. Anya Seton. Chicago Review Press, 2005. 342 p.
ISBN 9781556525810
1. Governesses 2. Family estates 3. Violence 4. Narcissism 5. Man-woman relationships 6. New York City 7. Hudson River 8. 19th century 9. Gothic fiction
   It was on an afternoon in May 1844 when the letter came from Dragonwyck. Tired of life on her father's farm in Connecticut, Miranda Wells happily accepts the invitation to the luxurious estate of her distant relative, the dashing and mysterious Nicholas Van Ryn. Introduced to a way of life she has only ever dreamed of, the innocent farm girl becomes a great lady. But soon the dark secrets of Dragonwyck begin to unfold.
   Originally published: Boston : Houghton Mifflin, 1944.

Green darkness. Anya Seton. Chicago Review Press, 2005. 591 p.
ISBN 9781556525766
1. Time travel (Past) 2. Reincarnation 3. Visions 4. Fear in women
5. Household employees 6. Great Britain 7. Gothic fiction
   After a young American woman named Celia moves to England with her new husband, she finds herself haunted by a strange dread, a fear she can only escape by traveling four hundred years into the past and reliving her life as a beautiful servant in the sixteenth century.
   "Reincarnation is the theme of [this]...novel. A 16th-century Benedictine monk, Stephen Marsdon, falls prey to a consuming passion for alluring Celia de Bohun and forsakes his vows. The tragic end of the lovers, involving murder and suicide, brings, nearly 400 years later, madness and near death to their reincarnations, newlyweds Celia and Richard Marsdon. Fortunately, a Hindu doctor (himself a reincarnated Italian physician in

Tudor England who longed for warmer climates) hovers nearby to monitor the proceedings and brings the souls to rest." —*Library Journal*

Originally published: Boston : Houghton Mifflin, 1972.

Katherine. Anya Seton. Chicago Review Press, 2004. 500 p.
ISBN 9781556525322
1. Katharine, duchess of Lancaster 2. Knights and knighthood 3. Extramarital affairs 4. Redemption 5. Love triangles 6. Murder 7. Great Britain 8. Plantagenet period (1154-1485) 9. 14th century 10. Biographical fiction 11. Historical fiction 12. Love stories

"It is a story that demands no intellectual or emotional effort from the reader.... But Miss Seton presents her facts accurately. Her research extends as far as visiting what remains of any of John of Gaunt's 30 castles and her zest for her subject communicates itself to the reader." —*San Francisco Chronicle*

Originally published: Boston : Houghton Mifflin, 1954.

★ The **Winthrop** woman. Anya Seton. Chicago Review Press, 2006. 586 p.
ISBN 9781556526442
1. Winthrop, Elizabeth 2. Puritan women 3. Prejudice 4. Independence in women 5. Governors' spouses 6. Theocracy 7. Massachusetts 8. Colonial America (1600-1775) 9. 17th century 10. Biographical fiction 11. Historical fiction

A biographical novel of Elizabeth Winthrop, a courageous woman who defied Puritan conventions and beliefs.

Originally published: Boston : Houghton Mifflin, 1958.

Setterfield, Diane

★ **Once** upon a river. Diane Setterfield. Atria Books, 2018. 480 p.
ISBN 9780743298070
1. Storytelling 2. Identity (Psychology) 3. Drowning victims 4. Interpersonal relations 5. Resurrection 6. Thames River 7. 1870s 8. Victorian era (1837-1901) 9. Historical fiction 10. Magical realism 11. Literary fiction

LibraryReads Favorites, 2019; Loan Stars Favourites, 2018

When the seemingly dead body of a child reanimates hours after arriving at an ancient inn on the Thames, three families try to claim her.

"By combining flavors of some of Britain's very best writers—a hint of Austen's domestic stories, a tinge of Tolkien's more folkloric elements, and a dash of mystery from Christie—Setterfield has created a tale not to be missed." —*Publishers Weekly*

The **thirteenth** tale: a novel. Diane Setterfield. Atria Books, 2006. 406 p.
ISBN 9780743298025
1. Books and reading 2. Twins 3. Women recluses 4. Women authors 5. Booksellers 6. Gothic fiction 7. Adult books for young adults
LC 2006042906

Alex Award, 2007

When her health begins failing, the mysterious author Vida Winter decides to let Margaret Lea, a biographer, write the truth about her life, but Margaret needs to verify the facts since Vida has a history of telling outlandish tales.

Sexton, Margaret Wilkerson

A **kind** of freedom. Margaret Wilkerson Sexton. Counterpoint Press, 2017. 256 pages
ISBN 9781619029224
1. African American families 2. Middle class 3. Racism 4. Matriarchs 5. Single mothers 6. New Orleans, Louisiana 7. Family sagas 8. African American fiction 9. Literary fiction

LC 2017015331

New York Times Notable Book, 2017; BCALA Literary Award for First Novelist, 2018; Longlisted for the National Book Award for Fiction, 2017

Explores the legacy of racial disparity in the South through the story of three generations of an African American family in New Orleans.

"This novel sparked a competition among literary agents, and for good reason. This family is worth every minute of a reader's time." —*Booklist*

The **revisioners:** a novel. Margaret Wilkerson Sexton. Counterpoint, 2019. 288 pages
ISBN 9781640092587
1. Women 2. Race relations 3. African American families 4. Interracial friendship 5. Freed people 6. New Orleans, Louisiana 7. Family sagas 8. Literary fiction 9. African American fiction

LC 2019008282

New York Times Notable Book, 2019

Explores the impact of racism and interracial relationships between women through the story of an early 20th-century farmer and her unemployed single mother descendant.

Shaara, Jeff

Gods and generals: a novel of the Civil War. Jeff Shaara. Ballantine Books, 1996. 498 p. (Civil War trilogy (Jeff Shaara), 1)
ISBN 9780345404923
1. Jackson, Stonewall 2. Generals 3. Battles 4. Command of troops 5. Fredericksburg, Battle of, 1862 6. Chancellorsville, Battle of, 1863 7. United States 8. Confederate States of America 9. American Civil War era (1861-1865) 10. 1860s 11. Historical fiction 12. War stories 13. Biographical fiction

LC 95-53360

W. Y. Boyd Literary Award, 1997

The lives and careers of four great military leaders—Stonewall Jackson, Winfield Scott Hancock, Joshua Chamberlain, and Robert E. Lee—reach a climax as Union and Confederate forces clash on the battlefields of the Civil War

"As should be the case with good historical fiction, Shaara, in taking actual figures from the past, rekindles them; he uses the personal experiences of these four men to meaningfully explore the political and military issues of the day." —*Booklist*

A prequel to Michael Shaara's The killer angels.

Gone for soldiers. Jeff Shaara. Ballantine Books, 2000. Xix, 424 p. : Illustration; Map
ISBN 9780345427502
1. Lee, Robert E. 2. Revolutionaries 3. Revolutions 4. Soldiers 5. Generals 6. Command of troops 7. Mexico 8. United States 9. 19th century 10. Historical fiction 11. War stories

LC 22745

Eight thousand marines land in Vera Cruz bound for a war against the Mexican army, including Winfield Scott, a general who made history in the War of 1812, and Robert E. Lee, a forty-year-old engineer as yet untested in battle BT

"The book is simply wonderful, populated with eminently human heroes who are called upon to perform Herculean tasks in a war muddied beyond redemption by the ambitions of back-home and battlefield politicians." —*Library Journal*

The **last** full measure. Jeff Shaara. Ballantine Books, 1998. 560 p. (Civil War trilogy (Jeff Shaara), 3)
ISBN 9780345404916

1. Chamberlain, Joshua Lawrence 2. Battles 3. Generals 4. Command of troops 5. Civil war 6. United States Civil War, 1861-1865 7. Confederate States of America 8. United States 9. American Civil War era (1861-1865) 10. 1860s 11. Historical fiction 12. War stories 13. Biographical fiction

LC 97-49383

A second companion novel to "The Killer Angels" follows the continuing showdown between Grant and Lee on the battlefields of the Civil War BT

"As characters, Grant and Lee dominate this book.... Civil War buffs will find Shaara nodding on some small details, but they generally will be delighted with this book." —*Library Journal*

Illustrated with maps.

The **rising** tide: a novel of World War II. Jeff Shaara. Ballantine Books, 2006. 576 p. (World War II novels, 1)

ISBN 9780345461414

1. Eisenhower, Dwight D. 2. World War II. 3. Commando operations 4. Military aircraft — History 5. Tanks (Military science) 6. Soldiers 7. Europe 8. Sicily, Italy 9. Second World War era (1939-1945) 10. 1940s 11. Historical fiction 12. War stories 13. Biographical fiction

LC 2006042936

As the forces of Nazi Germany overrun the nations of Europe and America is drawn into the war by the Japanese attack on Pearl Harbor, American troops and their British allies launch a campaign to stop Hitler on battlefields ranging from the deserts of North Africa to the rugged mountains of Sicily.

"Shaara opens this first volume of a projected trilogy in the deserts of North Africa, where Allied troops attempt to match wits and forces with the Desert Fox, wily German commander Field Marshall Erwin Rommel, and his formidable Afrika Korps. After Hitler overruns France, solidifying his position in Western Europe, he turns his attention eastward toward the vast Russian expanse. With the German focus split, the Allies sense the time is right to launch a united second front in North Africa, setting their sights on an eventual invasion of southern Italy. As plans for Operation Torch become a reality, Shaara vividly recreates a cast of military and political heroes and villains, including General Dwight D. Eisenhower, General George Marshall, General George Patton, British general Bernard Montgomery, German field marshal Erwin Rommel, Adolf Hitler, Winston Churchill, and Franklin Roosevelt." —*Booklist*

The **steel** wave: a novel of World War II. Jeff Shaara. Ballantine Books, 2008. 576 p. (World War II novels, 2)

ISBN 9780345461421

1. Bradley, Omar N. 2. World War II 3. Soldiers 4. Nazism 5. Leadership 6. Normandy Invasion, June 6, 1944 7. Europe 8. United States 9. Second World War era (1939-1945) 10. 1940s 11. Historical fiction 12. War stories 13. Biographical fiction

LC 2008004813

RUSA Reading List, 2009

A fictional account of D-Day and the Allied invasion of Europe chronicles the events of the campaign and the personalities who took part, from the ordinary soldiers on the land and in the air, to such leaders as Dwight Eisenhower and George Patton.

"The muscular prose, deft sense of military drama and relentless pacing are well suited for this crackerjack saga." —*Publishers Weekly*

Shaara, Michael

★ The **killer** angels: a novel. Michael Shaara. David McKay Co, Inc, 1974. 374 p. (Civil War trilogy (Jeff Shaara), 2)

ISBN 9780679504665

1. Longstreet, James 2. Gettysburg, Battle of, 1863 3. Confederate soldiers 4. Civil war 5. United States Civil War, 1861-1865 6. United

States 7. American Civil War era (1861-1865) 8. War stories 9. Historical fiction 10. Multiple perspectives

LC 73091120

Pulitzer Prize for Fiction, 1975

"Shaara's version of private reflections and conversations are based on his reading of documents and letters. Although some of his judgments are not necessarily substantiated by historians, he demonstrates a knowledge of both the battle and the area. The writing is vivid and fast moving." —*Library Journal*

This book was the inspiration for Ken Burns' documentary series on the Civil War. This book was also adapted for the screen as the film "Gettysburg" in 1993.

Shafak, Elif

★ **10** minutes 38 seconds in this strange world. Elif Shafak. Bloomsbury Publishing, 2019. 311 pages : Illustration

ISBN 9781635574470

1. Sex workers 2. Memories 3. Sexual violence victims 4. Psychic trauma 5. Women — Social conditions 6. Istanbul, Turkey 7. Turkey 8. Psychological fiction 9. Literary fiction

Shortlisted for the Booker Prize, 2019

In the moments after she has been murdered and left in a dumpster outside Istanbul, Tequila Leila enters a state of heightened awareness. Her heart has stopped beating but her brain is still active—for 10 minutes 38 seconds. While the Turkish sun rises and her friends sleep soundly nearby, she remembers her life—and the lives of others, outcasts like her. In Tequila Leila's death, the secrets and wonders of modern Istanbul come to life, painted vividly by the captivating tales of how Leila came to know and be loved by her friends. As her epic journey to the afterlife comes to an end, it is her chosen family who brings her story to a buoyant and breathtaking conclusion.

The **bastard** of Istanbul. Elif Shafak. Viking, 2007. 368 p.

ISBN 9780670038343

1. Single mothers 2. Tattooing 3. Mothers and daughters 4. Armenians in Turkey 5. Armenian Americans 6. Istanbul, Turkey 7. San Francisco, California 8. Satirical fiction 9. Domestic fiction

LC 2006042116

From one of Turkey's most acclaimed and outspoken writers comes a novel about the tangled histories of two families.

"Shafak's writing is seductive; each chapter of her novel is named for a food, and the warmth of the Turkish kitchen lies at the center of its wide-ranging plot. The Bastard of Istanbul portrays family as more than merely a function of genetics and fate, folding together history and fiction, the personal and the political into a thing of beauty." —*Elle*

Honor: a novel. Elif Shafak. Viking, 2013. 342 p.

ISBN 9780670784837

1. Muslims 2. Culture conflict 3. Mothers — Death 4. Father-deserted families 5. Child immigrants 6. London, England 7. 1970s 8. 1990s 9. Literary fiction

LC 2012039761

Follows the destinies of twin sisters born in a Kurdish village. While Jamila stays to become a midwife, Pembe follows her Turkish husband, Adem, to London, where they hope to make new lives for themselves and their children.

Shaffer, Mary Ann

The **Guernsey** Literary and Potato Peel Pie Society. Mary Ann Shaffer & Annie Barrows. Dial Press, 2008. 288 p.

ISBN 9780385340991

1. Women authors 2. Book clubs 3. Letter writing 4. Interpersonal relations 5. Memories 6. England 7. Guernsey (Channel Islands) 8. Second World War era (1939-1945) 9. Epistolary novels 10. Historical fiction 11. Multiple perspectives

LC 2007047869

Indies' Choice Book Awards, Best Indie Buzz Book, 2009; Library Journal Best Books, 2008

In 1946, writer Juliet Ashton finds inspiration for her next book in her correspondence with a native of Guernsey, who tells her about the Guernsey Literary and Potato Peel Pie Society, a book club born as an alibi during German occupation.

"Juliet's ready wit is enchanting, as are the discussion of authors from Catullus to Shakespeare.... There is the occasional false note.... However, The Guernsey Literary and Potato Peel Pie Society is a labor of love, and it shows on almost every page." —*Christian Science Monitor*

Titled adapted into a British film by the same name in 2018.

Shalev, Meir

Two she-bears: a novel. Meir Shalev; translated from the Hebrew by Stuart Schoffman. Schocken Books, 2016. 304 p.

ISBN 9780805243291

1. Women high school teachers 2. Family history 3. Storytelling 4. Rural life 5. Loss (Psychology) 6. Palestine 7. Israel 8. Literary fiction 9. First person narratives 10. Translations

LC 2016001663

A U.S. release of a best-seller from Israel follows the efforts of teacher Ruta Tavori to promote independent thinking in a small British Palestine farming community by revealing the true story behind the suicides of three 1930s farmers.

"This tale of love and bloodshed resonates with the primal passions of the biblical texts it invokes, while opening provocative new perspectives on modern questions about Israeli politics and gender identity." —*Booklist*

Originally published: 2013.

Translated from the Hebrew.

Shalvis, Jill

Second chance summer. Jill Shalvis. Grand Central, 2015. 354 p. (Cedar Ridge novels, 1)

ISBN 9781455586738

1. Former lovers 2. Second chances 3. Homecomings 4. Wildfire fighters 5. Search and rescue operations 6. Colorado 7. Contemporary romances

LibraryReads Favorites, 2015

Despite hating her home town, Lily Danville must stay where the work is—in this case, a job at the hottest resort in Cedar Ridge, Colorado—and when rescue worker and firefighter Aidan Kincaid regrets letting her walk out of his life, it's all he can do to get her to give Cedar Ridge—and him—a second chance.

Simply irresistible. Jill Shalvis. Forever, 2010. 326 p. (Lucky Harbor novels, 1)

ISBN 9780446571616

1. Inheritance and succession 2. Abused women 3. Man-woman relationships 4. Interpersonal attraction 5. Trust in women 6. Washington (State) 7. Contemporary romances

RITA Award for Best Contemporary Single Title Romance, 2011

After losing both her boyfriend and her job, Maddie Moore, claiming the inheritance left by her free-spirited mother, arrives in the town of Lucky Harbor, Washington where she must convince her two half-sisters

to join her in a business venture as well as convince herself to take a chance on love.

Sweet little lies. Jill Shalvis. Avon Books, 2016. 384 p. (Heartbreaker Bay novels, 1)

ISBN 9780062448026

1. Women ship captains 2. Bar owners 3. Neighbors 4. Secrets 5. Wishing and wishes 6. San Francisco, California 7. California 8. Contemporary romances

When she makes a wish in a wishing well for Finn to fall in love and find the happiness he deserves, Pru finds herself way in over her head—and heart—when he sets his sights on her and she realizes she must tell him the truth, which could ruin everything.

"Shalvis has created a love story romance fans can't help but root for and grounds it in an affable community they'll adore." —*Kirkus*

The **sweetest** thing. Jill Shalvis. Forever, 2011. 370 p; (Lucky Harbor novels, 2)

ISBN 9780446571623

1. Sisters 2. Divorced women 3. Second chances 4. Coastal towns 5. Interpersonal attraction 6. Washington (State) 7. Contemporary romances

LC Bl2011007482

When she returns home to Lucky Harbor, Washington, to help her sisters get their newly renovated inn up and running, Tara unexpectedly finds herself torn between two men—her sexy ex-husband and handsome sailor Ford Walker.

Shames, Terry

★ An **unsettling** crime for Samuel Craddock. Terry Shames. Seventh Street Books, an imprint of Prometheus Books, 2017. 270 p. (Samuel Craddock mysteries, 6)

ISBN 9781633882096

1. Small town life 2. Police chiefs 3. Hate crimes 4. Racism 5. Crimes against African Americans 6. Texas 7. Mysteries 8. Shostakovich, Dmitri Dmitrievich

"In this prequel, a young Samuel Craddock, as the newly elected chief of police in Jarrett Creek, must investigate the murder of five black residents and confront the ingrained prejudices in the small Texas town." —Provided by the publisher.

Shamsie, Kamila

Home fire: a novel. Kamila Shamsie. Riverhead Books, 2017. 240 p.

ISBN 9780735217683

1. Siblings 2. Muslims 3. Politicians 4. Women graduate students 5. Loyalty 6. Great Britain 7. London, England 8. Political fiction 9. Literary fiction

LC 2017003238

Baileys Women's Prize for Fiction, 2018; Library Journal Best Books, 2017; New York Times Notable Book, 2017; Longlisted for the Man Booker Prize, 2017; Shortlisted for the International Dublin Literary Award, 2019

Given a chance to resume a deferred dream years after raising her troubled siblings, Isma worries about the influence of a powerful politician's son who drives the family to choose between love and loyalty, with devastating consequences.

In accessible, unwavering prose and without any heavy-handedness, Shamsie addresses an impressive mix of contemporary issues...Booklist.

Shan, Sa

The **girl** who played Go. Shan Sa; translated by Adriana Hunter. Alfred A. Knopf, 2003. 288 p.

ISBN 9781400040254

1. Teenage girls 2. Obsession 3. Go (Game) 4. Board games 5. Love 6. Manchuria 7. 1930s 8. Translations 9. Historical fiction 10. Adult books for young adults

LC 2003044679

Kiriyama Prize for Fiction, 2004

"The alternating parallel tales add an extra spark of energy to this swift-moving novel, as Sa portrays tenderness and brutality with equal clarity." —*Publishers Weekly*

Translation of: Joueuse de go.

Shanbhag, Vivek

Ghachar ghochar. Vivek Shanbhag; translated from the Kannada by Srinath Perur. Penguin Books, 2017. 128 p.

ISBN 9780143111689

1. Families 2. Spice industry and trade 3. Wealth 4. Success (Concept) 5. Poverty 6. India 7. First person narratives 8. Domestic fiction 9. Translations

LC 2016027137

Follows the changing dynamics of an impoverished Bangalorean family who lived in a bug-infested shack until their family's spice company became an overnight success and ushered them into a new way of life and a brand new set of challenges.

"Absorbing, insightful, and altogether a wonderful read." —*Publishers Weekly*

Translation of: Ghacar ghocar

Originally published: Heggodu : Aksara Prakasana, 2013

Translated from the Kannada

Shannon, Dell

★ **Chaos** of crime. Dell Shannon. Morrow, 1985. 190 p; (Luis Mendoza mysteries, 36)

ISBN 9780688022976

1. Robbery 2. Heat waves (Meteorology) 3. Crimes against prostitutes 4. Police 5. Criminals 6. Los Angeles, California 7. Hardboiled fiction 8. Mysteries

Luis Mendoza and the L.A.P.D. pursue a psychotic sex killer, a gas station heister with an unusual MO, and an escaped convict BT

"A maniac is loose on the streets of Los Angeles, tying prostitutes to their beds, beheading them, disemboweling them, and then surgically dissecting them like laboratory animals. Detective Luis Mendoza and the Los Angeles Police Department are sufficiently stumped in trying to locate this madman who never leaves a clue—until finally the discovery of a rare French wristwatch helps to reveal a seemingly unlikely killer." —*Booklist*

Shannon, Samantha

The **bone** season. Samantha Shannon. Bloomsbury, 2013. 466 p. (Bone season, 1)

ISBN 9781620401392

1. Clairvoyance 2. Women psychics 3. Women prisoners 4. Mentors 5. Enemies 6. London, England 7. Oxford, England 8. 21st century 9. Dystopian fiction 10. Science fantasy 11. First person narratives 12. Adult books for young adults

LC 2012038358

Paige Mahoney is a Dreamwalker, a rare type of clairvoyant employed by the Seven Seals, the powerful criminal syndicate that operates within a dystopian 21st-century London controlled by the Scion government. When she's captured by Scion agents and turned over to the otherworldly Rephaim, Paige—renamed XX-59-40—ends up in Sheol I, a prison camp where she and her fellow "voyants" will be trained to battle the flesh-eating Emim. Placed under the guardianship of Arcturus, Warden of the Mesarthim, Paige must develop her gifts if she wants to survive, let alone escape. This fast-paced, action-packed fantasy boasts extensive world-building, a complex system of magic, and a well-developed cast of characters.

The **mime** order. Samantha Shannon. St. Martin's Press, 2015. 320 p. (Bone season, 2)

ISBN 9781620408933

1. Clairvoyance 2. Women fugitives 3. Women psychics 4. Intrigue 5. Secrets 6. London, England 7. Oxford, England 8. 21st century 9. Dystopian fiction 10. Science fantasy 11. First person narratives 12. Adult books for young adults

Fugitive Paige Mahoney flees Scion while Jaxon Hall and his Seven Seals prepare for a rare assembly of the clairvoyant community that is clouded by dark secrets, the emergence of the Rephaim, and an elusive Warden.

"Shannon creates vividly dilapidated, macabre, and mysterious worlds both urban and within the dreamscapes Paige valiantly enters. The motley, elaborately costumed characters are compelling; the nonstop, often eerie action is riveting." —*Booklist*

The **priory** of the orange tree. Samantha Shannon. Bloomsbury USA, 2019. 830 pages : Illustration; Map

ISBN 9781635570298

1. Royal houses 2. Dragons 3. Women assassins 4. Political intrigue 5. Women rulers 6. Epic fantasy

LibraryReads Favorites, 2019

A queen who would survive assassination attempts to continue her ruling line is protected with forbidden magic by a court outsider, while a secret society works to prevent a dragon war.

"A well-drawn feminist fantasy with broad appeal for fans of the epic and readers of Zen Cho, Naomi Novik, and V. E. Schwab." —*Booklist*

Shapiro, Barbara A.

The **muralist**. B. A. Shapiro. Algonquin Books of Chapel Hill, 2015. 336 p.

ISBN 9781616203573

1. Artists 2. Missing persons 3. Jewish women 4. Aunts 5. Muralists 6. New York City 7. 1940s 8. Historical fiction 9. First person narratives

LibraryReads Favorites, 2015

Auction-house employee Danielle Abrams investigates the unsolved disappearance of her famous-artist great-aunt when she discovers enigmatic paintings hidden behind Abstract Expressionist works created decades earlier.

"Mystery and historical fiction lovers who can accept that many lives and tragic histories can indeed intersect and converge around works of art in New York and France will find this a riveting read." —*Library Journal*

Sharp, Zoe

Fox hunter. Zoe Sharp. Pegasus Books, 2017. 336 p. (Charlie Fox novels, 11)

ISBN 9781681774381

1. Women veterans 2. Private security services 3. Rape victims 4. Missing men 5. Rapists 6. Iraq 7. Thrillers and suspense

In the latest novel in this energetic series, ex-special forces soldier Charlie Fox finds herself on a mission to the Iraqi countryside to track down a missing comrade-in-arms.

Second shot: a Charlie Fox thriller. Zoe Sharp. Thomas Dunne Books/St. Martin's Minotaur, 2007. 320 p. (Charlie Fox novels, 6)

ISBN 9780312358952

1. Women bodyguards 2. Murder 3. Secrets 4. Bodyguards 5. Former Special Forces members 6. New England 7. Mysteries

LC 2007019016

Hired to protect the beautiful Simone and her little girl while searching for Simone's long-lost father, female bodyguard Charlie Fox confronts a ruthless enemy who will do anything to stop her, including leaving her alone and wounded in the middle of a frozen New England woods.

Sharpe, Tess

Barbed wire heart. Tess Sharpe. Grand Central Publishing, 2018. 400 p.

ISBN 9781538744093

1. Organized crime 2. Young women 3. Drug traffic 4. Crime 5. Violence 6. Northern California 7. California 8. Rural noir 9. Crime fiction

LC 2017041580

RUSA Reading List Short List, 2019

In a book set in rural northern California, Harley McKenna has had to work for her North County-criminal father since she was 16, and as she is trying to decide whether to stay in the family business or get out, her family's biggest rivals, the Springfields, come gunning for her.

Sharratt, Mary

Daughters of the Witching Hill. Mary Sharratt. Houghton Mifflin Harcourt, 2010. 352 p.

ISBN 9780547069678

1. Widows 2. Witchcraft 3. Trials (Witchcraft) 4. Witchcraft — History 5. England 6. Lancashire, England 7. Historical fiction

LC 2009042057

A tale inspired by the Pendle witch hunt of 1612 finds the granddaughter of a folk healer targeted by an ambitious local magistrate who plays neighbors and family members against one another until paranoia reaches frenzied levels.

"Based on the infamous 1612 Lancashire witch trials, Sharratt's...novel vividly portrays the religious turmoil and hardscrabble life of 17th-century rural England. It's a familiar premise: an old beggar woman accused of witchcraft is sentenced to hang, along with others of her ilk. What makes this story stand out are the strong voices of the two main characters, stalwart Bess Southerns (aka Demdike) and her feisty granddaughter Alizon Device. Demdike is a cunning woman, able to heal animals and people with herbal folk magic. She strives to do only good, but when she teaches her dear friend the craft, she releases a Pandora's box of resentment, revenge, and evil." —*Library Journal*

Illuminations: a novel of Hildegard von Bingen. Mary Sharratt. Houghton Mifflin Harcourt, 2012. 272 p.

ISBN 9780547567846

1. Hildegard von Bingen 2. Nuns 3. Courage in women 4. Christianity 5. Civilization, Medieval 6. Benedictine nuns 7. Germany 8. Medieval period (476-1492) 9. 12th century 10. Biographical fiction 11. Historical fiction 12. Psychological fiction

LC 2012014252

A tale inspired by the life of the 12th-century abbess, composer and prophet depicts a young girl who upon being given to the Church rejects the order's masochistic piety and finds grace in studying books, growing herbs and rejoicing in divine visions before finding ways to liberate her sisters and herself.

Revelations. Mary Sharratt. Houghton Mifflin Harcourt, 2021. 384 p. ISBN 9781328518774

1. Kempe, Margery 2. Mysticism 3. Childbirth 4. Visions 5. Arranged marriage 6. Pilgrims and pilgrimages 7. Europe 8. Medieval period (476-1492) 9. Biographical fiction 10. Historical fiction

LC 2020033855

A kind of fifteenth-century 'Eat, Pray, Love,' 'Revelations' illuminates the intersecting lives of two female mystics who changed history-Margery Kempe and Julian of Norwich.

"Sharratt's gift for grounding larger issues in everyday lives makes for historical fiction at its best." —*Kirkus*

Includes bibliographical references.

Shaw, Irwin

Beggarman, thief. Delacorte 1977. 436 p.

ISBN 9780440006732

1. Families 2. Family sagas

LC 77024523

"Scenes from the earlier novel are interwoven allowing the unfamiliar reader to complete enjoyment and understanding." —*Booklist*

Sequel to: Rich man, poor man.

★ **Rich** man, poor man. Irwin Shaw. Delacorte, 1970. 723 p.

ISBN 9780385288583

1. Immigrant families 2. Family sagas

LC 74120463

Traces the fortunes of a first generation German-American family who pursue their dreams in a post-World War II United States.

"Each member of the clan is doomed in one way or another. They fight, love, live hard and their fortunes are inevitably intertwined. Mr. Shaw has juxtaposed their rise and fall against a panoramic picture of the times.... This may not be great literature but it certainly has popular appeal." —*Publishers Weekly*

Sequel: Beggarman, thief.

Shaw, M. B.

Murder at the mill: a mystery. M. B. Shaw. Minotaur Books, 2018. 448 p. (Iris Grey novels, 1)

ISBN 9781250189295

1. Women amateur detectives 2. Murder 3. Artists 4. Portrait painting 5. Separated women (Marital relations) 6. Holiday mysteries 7. Cozy mysteries

LC 2018027004

Renting a cottage in picturesque Hampshire village to escape her crumbling marriage, Iris Grey is commissioned to paint the portrait of a celebrated crime writer before a tension-filled Christmas Eve party is thrown into turmoil by an untimely death.

Shaw, Vivian

★ **Dreadful** company. Vivian Shaw. Orbit, 2018. 431 pages; (Greta Helsing novels, 2)

ISBN 9780316434638

1. Physicians 2. Supernatural 3. Imaginary creatures 4. Women physicians 5. Undead 6. Paris, France 7. France 8. Supernatural mysteries 9. Urban fantasy

LC 2018010014

When Greta Helsing, doctor to the undead, is called to Paris to present at a medical conference, she must navigate the darkest corners of the city to escape a coven of bloodthirsty vampires.

★ **Strange** Practice. Vivian Shaw. Orbit, 2017. 320 p. (Greta Helsing novels, 1)

ISBN 9780316434607

1. Physicians 2. Supernatural 3. Imaginary creatures 4. Women physicians 5. Undead 6. London, England 7. England 8. Supernatural mysteries 9. Urban fantasy

Meet Greta Helsing, fast-talking doctor to the undead. Keeping the supernatural community not-alive and well in London has been her family's specialty for generations. Greta Helsing inherited the family's highly specialized, and highly peculiar, medical practice. In her consulting rooms, Dr. Helsing treats the undead for a host of ills—vocal strain in banshees, arthritis in barrow-wights, and entropy in mummies. Although barely making ends meet, this is just the quiet, supernatural-adjacent life Greta's been groomed for since childhood. Until a sect of murderous monks emerges, killing human and undead Londoners alike. As terror takes hold of the city, Greta must use her unusual skills to stop the cult if she hopes to save her practice, and her life.

"In this comic supernatural mystery debut, Wright assembles an appealing, amusing collection of London's modern undead and the humans who care for them." —*Publishers Weekly*

Shaw, William

The **birdwatcher**. William Shaw. Mulholland Books, 2017. 336 pages

ISBN 9780316316248

1. Detectives 2. Bird watchers 3. Secrets 4. Murder investigation 5. Neighbors 6. Kent, England 7. Northern Ireland 8. Police procedurals 9. Mysteries

When a fellow birdwatcher is found murdered in his remote home, Police Sergeant William South, who may have murdered a man when he was a child in Northern Ireland, finds his world turned upside down.

First published in Great Britain in 2016 by riverrun.

Salt lane. William Shaw. Mulholland Books, 2018. 336 p. (Alexandra Cupidi novels, 1)

ISBN 9780316563505

1. Policewomen 2. Marshes 3. Rural life 4. Adoptees 5. Single mothers 6. England 7. Police procedurals

Misfit London metro police officer Alexandra Cupidi investigates the case of a woman who is found dead in a marshland and a homeless woman claiming to be the same person in search of the son she gave up for adoption.

A **song** for the brokenhearted. William Shaw. Mulholland Books, 2016. 403 p. (Breen and Tozer novels, 3)

ISBN 9780316246910

1. Police 2. Detectives 3. Cold cases (Criminal investigation) 4. Murder investigation 5. Sisters — Death 6. London, England 7. Jack, the Ripper 8. Police procedurals 9. Historical mysteries

LC 750274410

The earthshaking year of 1968 comes to sweeping and dangerous close, as Detectives Breen and Tozer battle the most powerful members of London society.

Shaykh, Hanan

★ **One** thousand and one nights: a sparkling retelling of the beloved classic. Hanan al-Shaykh; with an introduction by Mary Gaitskill. Pantheon Books, 2013. 328 p.

ISBN 9780307958860

1. Storytelling 2. Young women 3. Rulers 4. Roth, Philip 5. Power (Social sciences) 6. Adaptations, retellings, and spin-offs

LC 2012039272

A reimagining of 19 tales from the classic story about young queen Shahrazad's efforts to save her life from a brutal husband focuses on female characters at the heart of each tale in a woven sequence that incorporates humor and sensuality.

Shelley, Mary Wollstonecraft

★ **Frankenstein:** or, The modern Prometheus. Mary Shelley. Penguin Classics, 2014. 273 p.

ISBN 9780141393391

1. Monsters 2. Frankenstein's monster (Fictitious character) 3. Scientists 4. Ethics 5. Regeneration (Biology) 6. 19th century 7. Horror 8. Gothic fiction 9. Books to movies

LC 97061744

Obsessed by creating life itself, Victor Frankenstein plunders graveyards for the material to fashion a new being, which he shocks into life by electricity. But his botched creature, rejected by Frankenstein and denied human companionship, sets out to destroy his maker and all that he holds dear.

Shelton, Paige

Thin ice: a mystery. Paige Shelton. Minotaur Books, 2019. 320 p. (Alaska mysteries (Paige Shelton), 1)

ISBN 9781250295217

1. Women kidnapping victims 2. Moving to a new state 3. Women authors 4. Criminals 5. Murder 6. Alaska 7. Mysteries

LC 2019019598

A best-selling writer escapes from an obsessed fan by hiding in Alaska, where she is embroiled in a local murder case.

Shepard, Jim

★ The **book** of Aron. Jim Shepard. Alfred A. Knopf, 2015. 259 p.

ISBN 9781101874318

1. Holocaust (1933-1945) 2. Children 3. Jews 4. Ghettoes, Jewish 5. Physicians 6. Poland 7. Historical fiction 8. First person narratives 9. Adult books for young adults

ALA Notable Book, 2016; Booklist Editors' Choice, 2015; PEN New England Award for Fiction, 2016; Sophie Brody Medal, 2016; Andrew Carnegie Medal for Excellence in Fiction finalist, 2016; Kirkus Prize for Fiction finalist, 2015

Aron and a handful of boys and girls in the Warsaw Ghetto smuggle and trade things through the "quarantine walls" to keep their people alive until he is rescued by a Jewish-Polish doctor and advocate of children's rights who instills within him the importance of letting the world know the atrocities they have all suffered at the hands of the enemy.

"Aron proves to be engaging company as he describes the selfishness that will help him survive as the world becomes increasingly hellish. The horrors are so incremental that Aron—and the reader—might be compared to the lobster dropped into the pot as the temperature keeps rising past the boiling point." —*Kirkus*

Phase six. Jim Shepard. Alfred Knopf, 2021. 240 p.

ISBN 9780525655459

1. Epidemics 2. Survival 3. Guilt 4. Eleven-year-old boys 5. Viruses 6. Medical thrillers

LC 2020038895

One of the few survivors of a mysterious outbreak in Greenland, 11-year-old Aleq must deal with crushing guilt for what he may have unleashed from a mining site, while two Epidemic Intelligence Service agents work together to head off the cataclysm.

"Shepard writes with drilling authority about Greenland, epidemiology, the challenges women doctors and scientists face, and the confounding complexities of the microbial world. With word-by-word artistry, fluid compassion, and deep insights, Shepard emphatically dramatizes epic failures, self-sacrificing dedication, desolation, and love." —*Booklist*

The **world** to come: stories. By Jim Shepard. Alfred A. Knopf, 2017. 256 p.
ISBN 9781524731809
1. Ambition 2. Interpersonal relations 3. Literary fiction 4. Short stories
LC 2016038353

An anthology of 10 stories by the author of The Book of Aron reflects the personal and political challenges of protagonists ranging from English Arctic explorers during one of history's most nightmarish expeditions to 18th-century French balloonists who would invent manned flight.

"With the release of his fifth story collection, Shepard...continues to weave interlacing narrative threads that imaginatively evoke time and place." —*Library Journal*

Shepard, Sam

The **one** inside. Sam Shepard. Alfred A. Knopf, 2017. 172 p.
ISBN 9780451494580
1. Memories 2. Life change events 3. Extortion 4. Visions 5. Actors and actresses 6. Literary fiction

The One Inside is a narrative in which an actor/writer explores and revisits key moments and people from his life—all the while attempting to negotiate with a young woman who threatens to publish recordings of their darkly revealing phone conversations. In his dreams and in visions he sees his late father, sometimes in miniature, sometimes flying planes, sometimes at war. In his childhood memories he sees his father's young girlfriend, with whom the narrator also became involved, setting into motion a tragedy that continues to haunt him.

"Shepard is a master of conflicting emotions and haunting regrets, andgraced with a foreword by Patti Smith (M Train, 2015)this is a ravishing tale of deep-dark cosmic humor, complex tragedy, and self-inflicted exile." —*Booklist*

Shepard, Sara

★ **Reputation**. Sara Shepard. E.P. Dutton, 2019. 368 pages
ISBN 9781524742904
1. Universities and colleges 2. Scandals 3. Hacking 4. College towns 5. Murder victims 6. Pennsylvania 7. Psychological suspense 8. Multiple perspectives
LibraryReads Favorites, 2019

Told in multiple points of view, a story of intrigue, sabotage and secrets follows a tight-knit college community as it is rocked to its core when a hacker dumps 40,000 people's emails onto an easily searchable database, which results in murder.

"From chapter to chapter, Shepard's plotting breathlessly careens between characters, with each cliffhanger swiftly answered by another, ratcheting up the stakes until the killer is finally unmasked." —*Kirkus*

Shepherd, Peng

The **book** of M: a novel. Peng Shepherd. William Morrow, 2018. 485 p.
ISBN 9780062669605
1. Near future 2. Memory 3. Epidemics 4. Identity (Psychology) 5. Husband and wife 6. Apocalyptic fiction 7. Literary fiction
LC 2017050120

In a dangerous near-future world where an unknown phenomenon causes people to gain strange new powers but lose their memories, Ory and his wife Max journey through a perilous, unrecognizable world in a search for answers.

Sherrill, Steven

The **minotaur** takes his own sweet time: a novel. By Steven Sherrill. John F. Blair, 2016. 288 p. (Minotaur novels (Steven Sherrill), 2)
ISBN 9780895876737
1. Minotaur (Greek mythology) 2. Working class 3. Identity (Psychology) 4. Loss (Psychology) 5. Alienation (Social psychology) 6. Pennsylvania 7. Contemporary fantasy 8. Mythological fiction
LC 2016026939

Sixteen years have passed since Steven Sherrill first introduced us to "M," the selfsame Minotaur from Greek mythology, transplanted to the modern American South. M has moved north now, from a life of kitchens and trailer parks, to that of Civil War re-enactor at a run-down living history park in the dying blue-collar rustbelt of central Pennsylvania. Though he dies now, in uniform, on a regular basis, M's world, his daily struggles, remain unchanged.

"This novels juxtaposition of magical realism and the mundane allows for a number of haunting and contemplative moments." —*Kirkus*

Shields, Carol

The **republic** of love. Carol Shields. Viking, 1992. 366 p.
ISBN 9780670838752
1. Women folklorists 2. Radio talk show hosts and guests 3. Self-discovery in men 4. Love 5. Divorced men 6. Canada 7. Love stories 8. Canadian fiction
LC 91016154

A story of the persistence of love in modern times follows Fay, a fickle folklorist falling hard for her neighbor Tom, an all-night disc jockey three times divorced.

"Not only are Fay and Tom exceptionally likable and capable of arresting insights, their worlds are complete and organic. Secondary characters are respectfully but economically drawn via short monologues, and the city of Winnipeg bustles in the background." —*Publishers Weekly*

★ The **stone** diaries. Carol Shields. Viking, 1994. 361 p.
ISBN 9780670853090
1. Women 2. Middle class families 3. Families 4. Quarries and quarrying 5. Growing up 6. Winnipeg, Manitoba 7. Ottawa, Ontario 8. 20th century 9. Literary fiction 10. Multiple perspectives 11. Canadian fiction
LC 9330239

Governor General's Literary Award for English-Language Fiction, 1993; Manitoba Writing and Publishing Awards, McNally Robinson Book of the Year Award, 1993; National Book Critics Circle Award for Fiction, 1994; Pulitzer Prize for Fiction, 1995; Shortlisted for the Booker-McConnell Prize, 1993

From her birth in rural Manitoba, to her journey with her father to southern Indiana, to her years as a wife, mother, and widow, to her old age, Daisy Stone Goodwill struggles to find a place for herself in her own life BT

"This book is a miraculous meeting of intellectual rigour and imaginative flow. On the one hand, it's a sharp-as-tacks investigation into the limits of the autobiographical form; on the other, a novel of effortless pleasure and sensuality. Daisy Goodwill...attempts intermittently to tell the story of a life remarkable only in its large tracts of ordinariness." —*New Statesman*

Unless. Carol Shields. Fourth Estate, 2002. 213 p.

ISBN 9780007141074

1. Teenage girls with mental illnesses 2. Feminism 3. Social advocacy 4. Family problems 5. Women authors 6. Ontario 7. Literary fiction 8. Canadian fiction

BC Book Prizes, Ethel Wilson Fiction Prize, 2003; Booklist Editors' Choice, 2002; New York Times Notable Book, 2002; Governor General's Literary Awards, English-language Fiction finalist, 2002; Shortlisted for the Giller Prize, 2002; Shortlisted for the James Tait Black Memorial Prize for Fiction, 2002; Shortlisted for the Man Booker Prize, 2002; Shortlisted for The Orange Prize for Fiction, 2003

A mother's grief over a daughter's break with the family revises her feminist outlook and pushes her craft as a writer in a new direction.

"Shields's ability to use Reta's darkest fears to reveal the order lurking in chaos, without ever losing her light touch...is nothing short of astonishing." —*The New Yorker*

Shimotakahara, Leslie

After the bloom. Leslie Shimotakahara. Dundurn, 2017. 321 pages
ISBN 9781459737433

1. Japanese Canadians 2. Families 3. World War II. 4. Mothers and daughters 5. Missing persons 6. Toronto, Ontario 7. California 8. Historical fiction 9. Canadian fiction

Booklist Editors' Choice, 2017

Lily Takemitsu goes missing from her home in Toronto in the mid-1980s. Her daughter, Rita sets out to find her. In the course of searching for her mom, Rita is forced to confront a labyrinth of secrets surrounding the family's internment at a camp in the California desert during the Second World War, their postwar immigration to Toronto, and the father she has never known.

Includes bibliographical references.

Shin, Ann

The **last** exiles. Ann Shin. Park Row Books, 2021. 352 p.
ISBN 9780778389415

1. College students 2. Love 3. Class struggle 4. Families 5. Political persecution 6. North Korea 7. Literary fiction 8. Relationship fiction

Falling in love against a backdrop of political turbulence in North Korea, two Pyongyang university students are separated when one makes a desperate choice to save his starving family.

"Shin depicts the incredible resilience of people and the power of love in the grim and oppressive realities of North Korea." —*Booklist*

Shipman, Viola

The **clover** girls. Viola Shipman. Graydon House, 2021. 352 p.
ISBN 9781525811524

1. Female friendship 2. Summer camps 3. Inheritance and succession 4. Friends' death 5. Reunions 6. Michigan 7. Relationship fiction

The new owners of Camp Birchwood—thanks to their late friend, Emily—Elizabeth, Veronica and Rachel must spend a week together remembering the dreams they put aside and find a way to become the women they always swore they'd grow up to be.

"Shipman's (The Heirloom Garden) evocative novel is a love letter to Michigan summers, past and present, and to the value of lifelong friendships." —*Library Journal*

The **heirloom** garden. Viola Shipman. Graydon House, 2020. 384 p.
ISBN 9781525804649

1. Widows 2. Loss (Psychology) 3. Gardens 4. Female friendship 5. Intergenerational friendship 6. Michigan 7. Relationship fiction

Moving to Grand Haven with her traumatized veteran husband, Abby bonds with her reclusive next-door neighbor over a shared love of flowers that they cultivate together, discovering hope and healing along the way.

"Shipman's tale successfully captures these women's resilience and their hopeful desire for new beginnings." —*Publishers Weekly*

Shocklee, Michelle

Under the tulip tree. Michelle Shocklee. Tyndale House Publishers, 2020. 425 p.
ISBN 9781496446077

1. Slavery 2. Teenage girl journalists 3. Senior women 4. Racism 5. Centenarians 6. Depression era (1929-1941) 7. Christian historical fiction

Seven years into the Great Depression, Rena is an unemployed newspaper reporter. Eager for any writing job, Rena accepts a position interviewing former slaves for the Federal Writers' Project. There, she meets Frankie Washington, a 101-year-old woman whose honest yet tragic past captivates Rena. As Frankie recounts her life as a slave, Rena is horrified to learn of all the older woman has endured—especially because Rena's ancestors owned slaves. While Frankie's story challenges Rena's preconceptions about slavery, it also connects the two women whose lives are otherwise separated by age, race, and circumstances.

"Though set years ago, this title resonates today, as many struggle with the same issues and questions of racial reconciliation. With its haunting message of forgiveness, this is a must-buy for any Christian or historical fiction collection." —*Library Journal*

Shoham, Liad

Asylum city: a novel. Liad Shoham ; translated from the Hebrew by Sara Kitai. Harper, 2014. 336 pages
ISBN 9780062237538

1. Policewomen 2. Violence against women 3. Political activists 4. City life 5. Criminals 6. Tel Aviv, Israel 7. Israel 8. Mysteries 9. Translations
LC 2014011217

A Tel Aviv police officer isn't convinced the case is closed when an African man confesses to the murder of a social activist.

Translation from the Hebrew of: Ir Miklat.

Originally published as Ir Miklat in a different form in Israel in 2013 by Kinneret Zmora-Bitan—Title page verso.

Showalter, Gena

Shadow and ice. Gena Showalter. Hqn Books, 2018. 384 p. (Gods of war, 1)
ISBN 9781335080943

1. Gods and goddesses 2. Imaginary wars and battles 3. Warriors 4. Protectiveness in men 5. Mate selection 6. Paranormal romances

The most ruthless Earth-defending warrior in All War history risks his lifetime struggle for freedom from slavery in his unlikely alliance with a street-tough human who is inadvertently drawn into an ancient war.

Shreve, Anita

Eden Close: a novel. Anita Shreve. Harcourt Brace Jovanovich, 1989. 265 p.
ISBN 9780151275823

1. Friendship 2. Rape victims 3. Secrets 4. Coping in women 5. Women who are blind 6. New York (State) 7. Love stories
LC 89034712

"Eden Close' is not a novel of suspense but one of sensibility. Its insights are keen, its language measured and haunting. In it, a sense of loss and then of rupture is everywhere." —*New York Times Book Review*

Fortune's rocks: a novel. Anita Shreve. Little, Brown, 2000. 453 p.
ISBN 9780316781015
1. Young women — Sexuality 2. Extramarital affairs 3. Sex scandals — History 4. Mills and millwork — History 5. Trials (Child custody) — History 6. New England 7. 19th century 8. Coming-of-age stories 9. Historical fiction

Set in the late 1890s in New England, a passionate and idealistic young woman tries to put her life back together after she has been made an outcast because of an affair she has with an older, married man.

"The level of suspense never falters, but becomes breathtaking during a custody court battle.... The astounding denouement of cascading events will leave no reader unmoved." —*Publishers Weekly*

The **last** time they met: a novel. Anita Shreve. Little, Brown, 2001. 313 p.
ISBN 9780316781145
1. Man-woman relationships 2. Romantic love 3. Forgiveness 4. Married people 5. Widows 6. Kenya 7. Massachusetts 8. Love stories 9. Mainstream fiction
LC 53496

At a literary festival, poet Linda Fallon meets, for the first time in years, fellow poet Thomas Janes. Thomas has arranged to be there hoping to reestablish contact with the woman he passionately pursued years earlier, in an affair that ended disastrously. As the story moves backward, it examines their love affair.

"Romantic regret is Anita Shreve's subject in this instantly captivating novel.... Fiction writers could go to school on Shreve's command of scene." —*The Atlantic*

The **pilot's** wife: a novel. Anita Shreve. Little, Brown, 1998. 293 p.
ISBN 9780316789080
1. Married people and secrets 2. Widows 3. Secrets 4. Women high school teachers 5. Fifteen-year-old girls 6. New Hampshire 7. London, England 8. Mainstream fiction 9. Books to movies
LC 9751647

When her husband, a pilot, dies in an airplane crash off the Irish coast, Kathryn Lyons finds herself in the media spotlight as rumors abound of her husband's shocking secret past.

"The climax, less dramatic than meditative, may strike some readers as too muted: understatement is one of this novel's strengths. What haunts us is the way Jack's secret life gradually weakens its hold on Kathryn's imagination and ours." —*Publishers Weekly*

Sea glass: a novel. Anita Shreve. Little, Brown, 2002. 378 p.
ISBN 9780316780810
1. Labor movement — History 2. Purpose in life 3. Massacres — History 4. Depressions 5. Husband and wife 6. New Hampshire 7. Depression era (1929-1941) 8. 1920s 9. Historical fiction

When Honora and Sexton Beecher are rendered penniless by the crash of the stock market, Sexton is forced to work in a nearby mill that is plagued by violence, and as they try to reconstruct their lives, they are confronted by passions of every kind.

"Shreve does not use her characters frivolously. They reveal who they are through their actions, with the author—who writes with admirable economy—rarely having to point a finger or underline the obvious. The true power of her novel comes from the appalling social conditions she describes so vividly, the grim but heroic lives her characters live." —*New York Times Book Review*

Testimony: a novel. Anita Shreve. Little, Brown, 2008. 320 p.
ISBN 9780316059862

1. Boarding schools 2. Scandals 3. Sexuality 4. Students 5. Life change events 6. Vermont 7. New England 8. Multiple perspectives 9. Literary fiction 10. Adult books for young adults
LC 2008005027

A New England boarding school is rocked in the wake of a sex scandal in which participants were caught on videotape, a situation that derails the innocence and best intentions of students, parents, and others in life-shattering ways.

"Shreve arrows in on many targets—underage drinking, instant exposure via the Internet, familial expectations, youthful insecurities, and peer pressure, among them—as she flawlessly weaves a tale that is mesmerizing, hypnotic, and compulsive." —*Library Journal*

The **weight** of water. Anita Shreve. Little, Brown, 1997. 246 p.
ISBN 9780316789974
1. Women photographers 2. Women murder victims 3. Boat living 4. Norwegian Americans 5. Fishers 6. New Hampshire 7. Literary fiction 8. Parallel narratives 9. Books to movies
LC 9621326

L. L. Winship/PEN New England Award, 1997; Shortlisted for The Orange Prize for Fiction, 1998

A photographer who has come to a small island off the coast of New Hampshire to shoot a photo-essay about a double murder that took place there over a century ago, notices parallels between her own life and the lives of the murder victims.

"Deftly moving among almost as many plot lines as there are islands and employing at least two distinct voices, Ms. Shreve unravels themes of adultery, jealousy, crimes of passion, incest, negligence, loss and guilt, and then manages somehow to knit them all together into an engrossing tale." —*New York Times Book Review*

Shriver, Lionel

The **post-birthday** world. Lionel Shriver. Harper Collins Publishers, 2007. 528 p.
ISBN 9780061187841
1. Boredom in women 2. Women's fantasies 3. Extramarital affairs 4. Couples 5. Unmarried couples 6. London, England 7. Parallel narratives 8. Psychological fiction
LC 2006049233

Library Journal Best Books, 2007

A tale told from the parallel perspectives of two possible timelines considers the life of American expatriate Irena McGovern, who in one reality stays faithful to her disciplined American intellectual partner, and in the other runs off with an exuberant British long-time friend.

"Lawrence often verges on being a parody of a judgmental, snobbish prig, while Ramsey often verges on being a parody of a hard-living, irresponsible celebrity.... That we're able to overlook the flaws of Ramsey and Lawrence is, in the end, a testament to Ms. Shriver's ability to make Irina into a thoroughly compelling character, an idiosyncratic yet recognizable heroine about whom it's impossible not to care." —*New York Times*

Should we stay or should we go. Lionel Shriver. HarperCollins, 2021. 288 p.
ISBN 9780063094246
1. Husband and wife 2. Suicide pacts 3. Aging 4. Death control 5. Options, alternatives, choices 6. Great Britain 7. 20th century 8. 21st century 9. Satirical fiction 10. Literary fiction

When her father, who had been ravaged by Alzheimer's for ten years, dies, Kay and her husband Cyril, determined to one day die with dignity, take control of their final years by making a pact to exit the world together at the age of 80.

"An acute and wily satirist, Shriver handles a delicate subject with wry humor, reassuring sensitivity, and bracing realism." —*Booklist*

So much for that. Lionel Shriver. Harper, 2010. 436 p.
ISBN 9780061458583
1. Husband and wife 2. Women with cancer 3. Medical care — Costs 4. Mesothelioma 5. Retirement 6. Mainstream fiction
National Book Award for Fiction finalist, 2010
After his wife is diagnosed with cancer, Shep Knacker sees his dream of retiring to a developing country slip away, along with all the money in his once-plentiful bank account, as he tries to navigate America's labyrinthine health-care system.
"Though there is one farcical plot development that is poorly woven into the emotional fabric of the story, and though some of the asides about health care feel shoehorned into the narrative, the author's understanding of her people is so intimate, so unsentimental that it lofts the novel over such bumpy passages, insinuating these characters permanently into the readers imagination." —*New York Times*

We need to talk about Kevin. Lionel Shriver. Counterpoint, 2003. 400 p.
ISBN 9781582432670
1. School shootings 2. Teenage murderers 3. Mass shootings 4. Violence in schools 5. Parents of criminals 6. New York (State) 7. Psychological fiction 8. Books to movies 9. Adult books for young adults
LC 2002152753
Orange Prize for Fiction, 2005
The mother of a teenage boy who killed seven fellow students and two adults in a high-school shooting writes a series of letters to her estranged husband on their son's upbringing and questions what she fears may be her own part in the tragedy.
"It's a harrowing, psychologically astute, sometimes even darkly humorous novel, with a clear-eyed, hard-won ending and a tough-minded sense of the difficult, often painful human enterprise." —*Publishers Weekly*
First published: New York : Counterpoint, 2003.

Shteyngart, Gary

★ **Lake** Success: a novel. Gary Shteyngart. Random House, 2018. 338 p.
ISBN 9780812997415
1. Midlife crisis 2. Transcontinental journeys 3. Self-discovery in men 4. Marital conflict 5. Rich men 6. Mainstream fiction 7. Satirical fiction 8. Multiple perspectives
LC 2017043962
LibraryReads Favorites, 2018; New York Times Notable Book, 2018; Library Journal Best Books, 2018
A self-made Wall Street millionaire, baffled by the implosion of his seemingly perfect life, takes a cross-country bus trip in search of his college sweetheart and the ideals of his youth.

The **Russian** debutante's handbook. Gary Shteyngart. Riverhead Books, 2002. 452 p.
ISBN 9781573222136
1. Immigrants, Russian 2. Expatriates 3. Russian Americans 4. Young men 5. Immigrants 6. New York City 7. 1990s 8. Coming-of-age stories 9. Satirical fiction
LC 2001047676
National Jewish Book Award for Fiction, 2002-2003; ALA Notable Book, 2003; New York Times Notable Book, 2002
"Shteyngart's playful, carnivalesque sensibility fits within a Russian satirical-fantastic tradition that stretches from Nikolai Gogol in the 19th century to Mikhail Bulgakov in the Stalin period and Vassily Aksyonov in the Soviet twilight. The sturdy conventions of the traditional novel...are blithely disregarded in favor of digressive, madcap inventiveness." —*New York Times Book Review*

★ **Super** sad true love story: a novel. Gary Shteyngart. Random House, 2010. 352 p.
ISBN 9781400066407
1. Equality 2. Pride and vanity 3. Eccentric men 4. Immortality 5. Death 6. Satirical fiction
LC 2009037971
New York Times Notable Book, 2010
In a novel set in the near future, when a beautiful, yet cruel, woman that Lenny Abramov met in Italy says she his coming to stay with him in New York, even the tanks and soldiers stationed in the city and the ongoing war with Venezuela can't get him down.
"Full-tilt and fulminating satirist Shteyngart...is mordant, gleeful, and embracive as he funnels today's follies and atrocities into a devilishly hilarious, soul-shriveling, and all-too plausible vision of a ruthless and crass digital dystopia in which techno-addled humans are still humbled by love and death." —*Booklist*

Shumway, Charity

Ten girls to watch: a novel. Charity Shumway. Washington Square Press, 2012. 320 p.
ISBN 9781451673418
1. Self-discovery in women 2. Single women 3. Women authors 4. Women college graduates 5. Self-acceptance 6. New York City 7. Chick lit
LC 2011048888
When she lands a job tracking down the past winners of Charm magazine's "Ten Girls to Watch" contest, Dawn West is excited to interview hundreds of fascinating women and discovers that success, love and friendship can be found in the most unexpected of places.

Shupe, Joanna

The **courtesan** duchess. Joanna Shupe. Zebra, 2015. 352 p. (Wicked deceptions, 1)
ISBN 9781420135527
1. Dukes and duchesses 2. Separated couples 3. Secret identity 4. Seduction 5. Courtesans 6. Venice, Italy 7. 1810s 8. Historical romances
Disguising herself as a courtesan to get the attention of her husband, who she has not seen in eight years, the Duchess of Colton arrives in Venice where she sets her plan of seduction in motion and is shocked to discover that the man she married just could be the love of her life.

The **heiress** hunt. Joanna Shupe. HarperCollins, 2021. 384 p. (Fifth Avenue rebels, 1)
ISBN 9780063045040
1. Arranged marriage 2. Best friends 3. Dukes and duchesses 4. Secrets 5. Inheritance and succession 6. Historical romances 7. Victorian romances
With their marriages to others looming, Maddie Webster, who is engaged to a duke, and her best friend Harrison Archer, who is engaged to an heiress, wonder if their fate in inescapable or if love will set them free.
"This is friends-to-lovers romance at its finest, with an endearing Gilded Age couple who are clearly made for each other." —*Library Journal*

The **prince** of Broadway. Joanna Shupe. Avon Books, 2019. 384 p. (Uptown girls, 2)

ISBN 9780062906830

1. Casinos 2. Young women 3. Revenge 4. Mentoring 5. Upper class 6. New York City 7. Gilded Age (1865-1898) 8. Historical romances

Using each other for their own means, Clayton Madden, the owner of the city's most exclusive casino, and heiress Florence Greene's finds their mutually beneficial relationship taking a romantic turn, which forces both their hands.

"Shupe...continues her lusciously detailed Gilded Age-set series with a dynamic duo determined to get what they want at any cost. Sensual and passionate and with an unconventional, intriguing story line, this second in the series (after The Rogue of Fifth Avenue) is one readers will clamor for." —*Library Journal*

The **rogue** of Fifth Avenue. Joanna Shupe. Avon Books, 2019. 384 p. (Uptown girls, 1)

ISBN 9780062906816

1. Lawyers 2. Rich families 3. Helpfulness in women 4. City life 5. Independence in women 6. New York City 7. Gilded Age (1865-1898) 8. Historical romances

Determined to help struggling families in the tenements, Mamie Greene, the daughter of a wealthy New York City powerbroker, matches wits with her father's lawyer who threatens her efforts.

Siegel, Jan

Prospero's children. Jan Siegel. Del Rey, 2000. 350 p.

ISBN 9780345439017

1. Atlantis (Legendary place) 2. Fantasy fiction 3. Adult books for young adults

LC 190160

Booklist Editors' Choice: Adult Fiction for Young Adults, 2000; Library Journal Best Books, 2000

Sixteen-year-old Fern Chapel rediscovers the secret and powerful magic of Atlantis BT

Sienkiewicz, Henryk

★ **Quo** vadis: a story of faith in the last days of the Roman Empire. By Henryk Sienkiewicz; introduction and afterword by Joe Wheeler. Tyndale House Publishers, 2000. 606 p.

ISBN 9781561797950

1. Nero 2. Christians 3. Man-woman relationships 4. Church history 5. Rome 6. Roman Empire (27 BCE-476 CE) 7. Historical fiction 8. Translations

LC 36463

Marcus, a Roman officer in Nero's army, risks his career, his family, and even his life when he falls in love with a Christian woman named Callina. In order to win Callina's love, Marcus must come to understand the true meaning of her religion, even as Rome sinks under the excesses of Nero and Christians are thrown to the lions.

Siger, Jeffrey

Mykonos after midnight: a Chief Inspector Kaldis Mystery. Jeffrey Siger. Poisoned Pen, 2013. 250 p. (Greek mysteries (Jeffrey Siger), 5)

ISBN 9781464201813

1. Murder investigation 2. Murder 3. Rich people 4. Nightclubs 5. Kaldis, Andreas (Fictitious character) 6. Mykonos (Island) 7. Greece 8. Mysteries

The murder of a legendary nightclub owner who helped transform Mykonos from an impoverished Greek island into a wealthy, world-renown tourist paradise puts politically explosive secrets into play and Chief Inspector Andreas Kaldis into battle with a powerful, clandestine

international force intent on doing whatever necessary to dominate the island.

Target Tinos: an Inspector Kaldis mystery. Jeffrey Siger. Poisoned Pen Press, 2012. 250 p. (Greek mysteries (Jeffrey Siger), 4)

ISBN 9781590589786

1. Romanies 2. Secret societies 3. Hate crimes 4. Organized crime 5. Murder investigation 6. Tenos, Greece 7. Greece 8. Mysteries

Andreas Kaldis's investigation into the murder of two gypsies on the Aegean island of Tinos leads him to more bodies, a secret society, and questions about the growing number of non-Greeks and gypsies flocking to the island.

Sigurðardóttir, Lilja

Cage. Lilja Sigurdardottir. Orenda Books, 2019. 276 p; (Reykjavik noir novels (Lilja Sigurdardottir), 3)

ISBN 9781912374496

1. Drug smuggling 2. Fraud 3. Revenge 4. Political intrigue 5. Organized crime 6. Iceland 7. Reykjavik, Iceland 8. Scandinavian crime fiction 9. Crime fiction 10. Translations

As Agla finishes her prison sentence and is released, a group of foreign businessmen tries to draw Agla into an ingenious fraud that stretches from Iceland around the world. Agla and her former nemesis, Maria, find the stakes being raised at a terrifying speed. A deadly threat to Sonya and her family brings her from London back to Iceland, where she needs to settle scores with longstanding adversaries if she wants to stay alive. With a shocking crescendo, the lives of these characters collide, as drugs, smuggling, big money and political intrigue rally with love, passion, murder and betrayal until the winner takes all.

"Fans already invested in this Nordic crime series will race through the pages." —*Publishers Weekly*

Silber, Joan

Improvement. Joan Silber. Counterpoint Press, 2017. 227 p.

ISBN 9781619029606

1. Interpersonal relations 2. Consequences 3. Smuggling 4. Prisoners 5. Single mothers 6. New York City 7. Literary fiction

LC 2017025010

National Book Critics Circle Award for Fiction, 2017; PEN-Faulkner Award, 2018; New York Times Notable Book, 2018

A young single mother living with her concerned eccentric aunt in New York makes fateful decisions that have unexpected implications, including her relationship with a Rikers Island inmate who draws her into a cigarette smuggling scheme.

"In Silber's (Fools, 2013) latest, big events in characters lives play out on a small stage in quiet and reflective ways.... Silber's decision to write events of great magnitude from everyday points of view lends realism and universality to her story. Fans of character-driven, literary fiction should be on the lookout for Improvement." —*Booklist*

Secrets of happiness. Joan Silber. Counterpoint, 2021. 288 p.

ISBN 9781640094451

1. Young gay men 2. Lawyers 3. Rich families 4. Family secrets 5. Fathers and sons 6. New York City 7. Bangkok, Thailand 8. Domestic fiction 9. Literary fiction 10. Multiple perspectives

When Ethan, a young lawyer, discovers his father in New York has had another, secret, family—a wife and two kids—the interlocking fates of both families lead to surprise loyalties, love triangles, and a reservoir of inner strength.

"As more layers peel away across continents, the fallout of Gil's affair trickles down through Silber's intricate and emotionally elaborate study of emotional ties." —*Publishers Weekly*

Silko, Leslie Marmon

Almanac of the dead. Leslie Marmon Silko. Simon and Schuster, 1991. 763 p.

ISBN 9780140173192

1. Prophecies 2. Native American resistance and revolts 3. Indians of North America — Relations with missionaries, traders, etc. 4. Political corruption 5. Race relations 6. Tucson, Arizona 7. Southwest (United States) 8. Magical realism 9. Literary fiction

LC 91019978

Seese, a survivor of the dangerous world of drug dealing, takes a job as a secretary to Lecha, an old woman who is suspected of being a witch. Includes endpaper illustrations.

★ **Ceremony**. Leslie Marmon Silko; introduction by Larry McMurtry; with a new preface by the author. Penguin Books, 2006. Xxiii, 243 p.

ISBN 9780143104919

1. Native American men 2. Culture conflict 3. Despair 4. World War II veterans 5. Pueblo Indians 6. Laguna Pueblo Reservation, New Mexico 7. Historical fiction 8. Literary fiction

LC 76046936

On a New Mexico reservation, one Navajo family—including Tayo, a World War II veteran deeply scarred by his experiences as a Japanese POW and by the rejection of his own people—struggles to survive in a world no longer theirs in the years just before and after World War II.

Originally published: New York : The Viking Press, 1977.

Gardens in the dunes: a novel. Leslie Marmon Silko. Simon & Schuster, 1999. 479 p.

ISBN 9780684811543

1. Native American girls 2. Assimilation (Sociology) 3. Identity (Psychology) 4. Indians of North America — Relations with missionaries, traders, etc. 5. Race relations 6. Southwest (United States) 7. 19th century 8. Historical fiction 9. Literary fiction

LC 98-51987

Booklist Editors' Choice, 1999

An Indian girl left orphaned after soldiers raid and destroy her village is adopted by a well-meaning American family, but she cannot forget her past and accept the white traditions and education they expect her to embrace BT

"Set in the 19th century this is the tale of two sisters, the last remaining members of the ancient Sand Lizard tribe. Sister Salt, so called for her light skin, and her younger sister, Indigo, learn all about the hidden, life-sustaining plants of the desert from Grandma Fleet, who teaches them how to live happily with a minimum of material goods and a wealth of knowledge. Such self-sufficiency is essential if they are to stay free from the misery of reservation life, but even so their liberty is put at risk when they travel to the mean little town of Needles, Arizona, where hundreds of Indians gather to dance in anticipation of the arrival of the Messiah. In the chaotic aftermath of the miraculous visitation, the girls lose their mother and grandmother and then are cruelly separated by the authorities." —*Booklist*

Silva, Daniel

★ The **black** widow. Daniel Silva. Harper, 2016. 528 pages : Map (Gabriel Allon novels, 16)

ISBN 9780062320223

1. Intelligence officers 2. International intrigue 3. Spies 4. Bombings 5. Assassination 6. Thrillers and suspense 7. Spy fiction

Art restorer, assassin, and spy Gabriel Allon finds himself poised to become the chief of Israel's secret intelligence service, but not before answering the French government's request to eliminate the person responsible for detonating a massive bomb in Paris.

"Silva proves once again that he can rework familiar genre material and bring it to new life." —*Publishers Weekly*

★ The **kill** artist: a novel. Daniel Silva. Random House, 2000. 428 p; (Gabriel Allon novels, 1)

ISBN 9780375500909

1. Art restorers 2. Fashion models 3. Intelligence officers 4. International intrigue 5. Secret service 6. Israel 7. Middle East 8. Thrillers and suspense 9. Spy fiction

LC 55308

The Israeli intelligence chief recalls two former agents to eliminate a top Palestinian terrorist. The former agents were once lovers and their pasts and their enemies come back to haunt them as the terrorist begins his campaign of murder.

The **new** girl. Daniel Silva. Harper, 2019. 496 pages (Gabriel Allon novels, 19)

ISBN 9780062834836

1. Intelligence officers 2. International intrigue 3. Teenage girl kidnapping victims 4. Enemies 5. Spies 6. Thrillers and suspense 7. Spy fiction

The kidnapping of a mysterious girl from her Swiss boarding school ignites a secret war between Israeli intelligence chief Gabriel Allon and an old enemy who would transform the future of the Middle East.

The **other** woman. Daniel Silva. Harper, 2018. 476 p. (Gabriel Allon novels, 18)

ISBN 9780062834829

1. Intelligence officers 2. International intrigue 3. Spies 4. Revenge 5. Terrorism 6. Thrillers and suspense 7. Spy fiction

After his asset inside Russian intelligence is assassinated, Gabriel's search for the truth leads him to the twentieth century's greatest act of treason.

Silver, Elizabeth L.

The **execution** of Noa P. Singleton: a novel. Elizabeth L. Silver. Crown Publishers, 2013. 304 p.

ISBN 9780385347433

1. Death row prisoners 2. Women prisoners 3. Attorney and client 4. Women lawyers 5. Murder investigation 6. Legal thrillers 7. Psychological suspense

LC 2012040204

Visited by a high-powered attorney who has initiated a clemency petition on her behalf and who is also the mother of her victim, death-row inmate Noa is slowly persuaded to share the events surrounding the murder in spite of her reluctance to reveal the whole story or have her life extended.

Silver, Marisa

Mary Coin: a novel. Marisa Silver. Blue Rider Press, 2013. 336 p.

ISBN 9780399160707

1. Poor people 2. Depressions 3. Photographers 4. Women migrant workers 5. Women photographers 6. Depression era (1929-1941) 7. Historical fiction 8. Parallel narratives 9. Relationship fiction

LC 2012039861

Imagines the lives of the subject of the photograph, photographer, and a college professor who finds a connection to a family legacy in the image of the iconic "Migrant Mother."

Includes bibliographical references and index.

Silvis, Randall

Two days gone: a novel. Randall Silvis. Sourcebooks Landmark, 2017. 400 p. (Ryan DeMarco novels, 1)

ISBN 9781492639732

1. Murder suspects 2. Family killing 3. Friendship 4. Murder investigation 5. Police 6. Pennsylvania 7. Police procedurals 8. Mysteries

LC 2016008657

When a woman and her children are murdered, Sergeant Ryan DeMarco doubts the prime suspect, the woman's fugitive husband, was capable of killing his family and wonders if the half-finished manuscript he left behind contains clues to the killer.

Simenon, Georges

Maigret and the black sheep. Georges Simenon; translated from the French by Helen Thomson. Harcourt Brace Jovanovich, 1976. 158 p. (Jules Maigret mysteries)

ISBN 9780151551460

1. Police 2. Murder 3. Extramarital affairs 4. Letter writing 5. Murder investigation 6. Paris, France 7. France 8. Mysteries 9. Translations 10. Police procedurals

LC 75028384

"The victim is a retired carton manufacturer who has been shot, without apparent motive, while sitting at home in his favorite armchair. To [Chief Inspector Maigret's] chagrin, he can find no crack or crevice in the utter respectability of the dead man's life.... The season is the end of summer. Parisians are drifting back to the city from their vacations, there is a nip in the air.... Maigret sips his beer in several cafs, confers with his faithful colleague Lapointe, and ponders the many facts of this...case." —*The New Yorker*

A Helen and Kurt Wolff book.

Translation of Maigret et les braves gens.

Maigret and the fortuneteller. Georges Simenon; translated by Geoffrey Sainsbury. Harcourt Brace Jovanovich, 1989. 140 p. (Jules Maigret mysteries)

ISBN 9780151555710

1. Police 2. Murder 3. Fortune-tellers 4. Murder investigation 5. Maigret, Jules (Fictitious character) 6. Paris, France 7. France 8. Mysteries 9. Translations 10. Police procedurals

LC 88016301

Inspector Maigret investigates the death of fortuneteller Mademoiselle Jeanne, a case remarkable for its wealth of unconnected suspects and fragmentary clues

"Maigret is forewarned of a murder but fails to prevent it. He tracks down the villain by exercising his famous 'capacity for putting himself in other people's shoes.' In this case, the shoes belong to a woebegone old man, apparently senile, who was found at the scene of the crime. Obviously more terrified of his wife and daughter than he is of the thunderous Maigret, the old man piques the policeman's interest and so leads him to the solution." —*Booklist*

Previously published as: To any lengths.

Translation of Signe Picpus.

★ **Maigret** and the killer. Georges Simenon; translated by Lyn Moir. Harcourt Brace Jovanovich, 1971. 165 p. (Jules Maigret mysteries)

ISBN 9780151551279

1. Murder 2. Murder investigation 3. Detectives 4. Police 5. Criminal investigation 6. Paris, France 7. France 8. Mysteries 9. Translations 10. Police procedurals

LC 91017180

"The witty pace featuring kidnappings and shootings, is effectively sustained throughout." —*Booklist*

Maigret and the madwoman. Georges Simenon; translated from the French by Eileen Ellenbogen. Harcourt, 1972. 176 p. (Jules Maigret mysteries)

ISBN 9780151551385

1. Murder 2. Detectives 3. Police 4. Murder investigation 5. Criminal investigation 6. Paris, France 7. France 8. Mysteries 9. Translations 10. Police procedurals

LC 72075421

A kind but seemingly paranoid old lady turns to Inspector Maigret for help. Against the judgement of his subordinates, he decides to pay a visit to her Parisian apartment to investigate, but is he already too late?

2019 reprint by Penguin Classics, London, was translated by Sian Reynolds.

★ **Maigret** and the Saturday caller. Georges Simenon; translated by Tony White. Harcourt Brace Jovanovich, 1991. 124 p. (Jules Maigret mysteries)

ISBN 9780151555666

1. Police 2. Murder 3. Extramarital affairs 4. Detectives 5. Crimes of passion 6. Paris, France 7. France 8. Mysteries 9. Translations 10. Police procedurals

LC 90046032

Slow-moving psychological detective Jules Maigret is hot on the trail of a crime that has not even happened yet after being visited by Leonard Planchon, a man who confesses that he intends to murder his wife and her lover.

"Maigret is visited by a harelipped man who confesses that he wants to murder his wife and her lover but hasn't yet done so. Needless to say, Maigret cannot dismiss the man's plans as the fantasy of a harmless lunatic and begins to probe around the edges, irritated by the handicaps imposed by the public prosecutor's recent restrictions on police powers." —*Booklist*

★ **Maigret** and the toy village. Georges Simenon; translated by Eileen Ellenbogen. Harcourt, 1979. 139 p. (Jules Maigret mysteries)

ISBN 9780151555543

1. Police 2. Murder 3. Murder investigation 4. Sailors 5. Household employees 6. France 7. Mysteries 8. Translations 9. Police procedurals

LC 79001843

Investigating the murder of Jules Lapie, a sailor nicknamed Peg Leg, Maigret finds Lapie's young housekeeper the most difficult obstacle to solving the case

A Helen and Kurt Wolff book.

Translation of Felicie est la.

Maigret and the wine merchant. Georges Simenon; translated from the French by Eileen Ellenbogen. Harcourt Brace Jovanovich, 1971. 187 p. (Jules Maigret mysteries)

ISBN 9780151551361

1. Murder 2. Detectives 3. Criminal investigation 4. Wine and wine making 5. Murder investigation 6. Paris, France 7. France 8. Mysteries 9. Translations 10. Police procedurals

LC 73142097

When a wealthy wine merchant is shot and killed in Paris, Inspector Maigret must investigate a long list of family, colleagues and lovers to uncover just who could have committed the crime. Delving into the depths of the man's personality, Maigret discovers that the victim may have made one too many enemies on his way to the top.

A Helen and Kurt Wolff book.

Translation of Maigret et le marchand de vin.

★ **Maigret** bides his time. Georges Simenon; translated by Alastair Hamilton. Harcourt Brace Jovanovich 1985. 155 p. (Jules Maigret mysteries)

ISBN 9780151555635

1. Police 2. Jewelry theft 3. Murder 4. Murder investigation 5. Maigret, Jules (Fictitious character) 6. Paris, France 7. France 8. Mysteries 9. Translations 10. Police procedurals

"This novel combines a delight in the sensual world with an exploration of the horrors of human cruelty. Vintage Simenon." —*Booklist*

Translation of Patience de Maigret.

★ **Maigret** goes home. Georges Simenon; translated by Robert Baldick. Harcourt Brace Jovanovich, 1989. 139 p. (Jules Maigret mysteries)

ISBN 9780151551507

1. Police 2. Hometowns 3. Murder 4. Murder investigation 5. Maigret, Jules (Fictitious character) 6. Paris, France 7. France 8. Translations 9. Mysteries 10. Police procedurals

LC 89002011

Chief Inspector Maigret returns to the village of Saint-Fiacre, where he was born, after a note to the police warns that a crime will take place, and soon after he arrives the Countess de Saint-Fiacre dies, leaving Maigret to find the killer.

"The countess of the estate where Maigret grew up drops dead during early mass on All Souls' Day, shocked to death by a fake newspaper report falsely reporting the suicide of her son. Although the estate had been heavily mortgaged to pay for the son's debts and the countess' young lovers, the inheritance is still not inconsiderable, and, of course, there are at least three likely suspects." —*Booklist*

Translation of Affaire Saint-Fiacre.

Also published as: Maigret on Home Ground, The Saint-Fiacre Affair, Death of a countess, and Maigret and the Countess

Maigret in Holland. Georges Simenon; translated by Geoffrey Sainsbury. Harcourt Brace, 1993. 165 p. (Jules Maigret mysteries)

ISBN 9780151551590

1. Police 2. Murder 3. Murder investigation 4. Maigret, Jules (Fictitious character) 5. Detectives 6. Netherlands 7. Mysteries 8. Translations 9. Police procedurals

LC 92030504

When Inspector Maigret arrives in Delfzijl to investigate the murder of Conrad Popinga, he finds a long list of suspects, including a giggling, man-hungry farmer's daughter and a pompous criminologist found holding the murder weapon

"Although Maigret speaks no Dutch, he is called to Holland to assist a compatriot, Jean Duclos. Unfortunately, Duclos was present when Conrad Popinga, a former captain in the merchant marine, was murdered, and the Dutch police think Duclos, along with Popinga's wife and sister-in-law, a young sailor, and a local farm girl, is a prime suspect. Once the capable but long-suffering Maigret arrives, he methodically reviews the evidence and questions suspects.... Readers will marvel at the inspector's brilliant logic." —*Booklist*

Previously published as A Crime in Holland

Maigret's memoirs. Georges Simenon; translated from the French by Jean Stewart. Harcourt Brace Jovanovich, 1985. 134 p. (Jules Maigret mysteries)

ISBN 9780151551484

1. Police 2. Memories 3. Courtship 4. Maigret, Jules (Fictitious character) 5. Detectives 6. Paris, France 7. France 8. Translations 9. Mysteries 10. Police procedurals

LC 85008591

Inspector Maigret shows the ways of police work to a young writer and reveals his rural upbringing, his first assignment as a bicycle messenger, and how he wooed and won Madame Maigret.

"Inspector Maigret, upset by writer Georges Simenon's 'caricature' of him, decides to correct the world's misconception of his personality and his cases by writing his memoirs.... Maigret outlines a few criminal cases, digresses about the Parisian weather, explains his dislike for Simenon, and presents his views on the criminal mind and on life in general in this odd but marvelous 'autobiographical' account." —*Booklist*

Translation of Memoires de Maigret.

My friend Maigret. Georges Simenon; translated by Nigel Ryan. Penguin Books, 2008. 176 p. (Jules Maigret mysteries)

ISBN 9780143112846

1. Detectives 2. Murder 3. Murder investigation 4. Maigret, Jules (Fictitious character) 5. Police 6. France 7. Mysteries 8. Translations 9. Police procedurals

LC 2007025931

A small time crook has been murdered on a Mediterranean island—a thug, drunk, pimp and thief—yet just before he died he was heard boasting about his friend Maigret! Maigret, who is mentoring a Scotland Yard detective, Inspector Pike, travels to sun-drenched Porquerolles Island to investigate.

Translated from the French of: Mon ami Maigret (1949).

First published in French as Mon ami Maigret by Presses de la Cite 1949.

Simmons, Dan

The **abominable**: a novel. Dan Simmons. Little, Brown and Company, 2013. 704 p.

ISBN 9780316198837

1. Missing persons 2. Mountaineering 3. Mountaineers 4. Friendship 5. Secrets 6. Mount Everest 7. 1920s 8. Horror 9. Historical horror

LC 2013017754

Four climbers travel to Mount Everest in 1924 in an attempt to recover the body of a missing adventurer but find themselves being pursued by someone or something.

Drood: a novel. Dan Simmons. Little, Brown and Co, 2009. 784 p.

ISBN 9780316007023

1. Dickens, Charles 2. Authors, English 3. Railroad travel 4. Accidents 5. Railroad accidents — Psychological aspects 6. Secrets 7. London, England 8. 1860s 9. Biographical fiction 10. Historical mysteries 11. First person narratives 12. Adult books for young adults

LC 2008024501

A tale inspired by the mysterious final years of Charles Dickens finds the fifty-three-year-old literary master irrevocably changed when a train journey with his mistress ends in violence.

"The narrative is overlong, with discarded subplots and red herrings, but Simmons, a master of otherworldly suspense, cleverly explores envy's corrosive effects." —*The New Yorker*

Endymion. Dan Simmons. Bantam Books, 1996. 468 p. (Hyperion series, 3)

ISBN 9780553100204

1. Androids 2. Artificial intelligence 3. Messiahs 4. Time travel (Future) 5. Space flight 6. 32nd century 7. Science fiction 8. Space opera

LC 95033191

Trapped in an orbiting prison that will kill him at the slightest sign of tampering, the narrator looks back on events leading up to his impending death.

"The protagonist, a good-hearted soldier named Raul Endymion, sets off on a quest with historic consequences: he must keep from harm a young girl who holds the key to a rebirth of human civilization. Arrayed against him is the power of the Pax, a militarized Catholic Church that offers its adherents a literal resurrection of the body. It is Mr. Simmons's inspiration to embody the Pax in the person of Father Captain Federico de Soya, a starship commander who pursues Endymion and the young girl from one exotic planet to the next." —*New York Times Book Review*

The **fall** of Hyperion. Dan Simmons. Doubleday, 1990. 517 p. (Hyperion series, 2)
ISBN 9780385249508
1. Pilgrims and pilgrimages 2. Space warfare 3. Imaginary empires 4. Priests 5. Detectives 6. 28th century 7. Space opera 8. Multiple perspectives 9. Science fiction classics
LC 89037438
BSFA Award for Best Novel, 1991; Locus Award for Best Science Fiction Novel, 1991
Seven pilgrims continue their fateful mission to Hyperion, a planet that may be humankind's only hope in a galaxy threatened by an all-encompassing war.
"In this sequel to Hyperion, Simmons weaves together many strands of a complex plot with lucidity and poetic imagination." —*Library Journal*
A Foundation book.

The **fifth** heart. Dan Simmons. Little, Brown and Company, 2015. 640 p.
ISBN 9780316198820
1. James, Henry 2. Holmes, Sherlock (Fictitious character) 3. Private investigators 4. Authors, American 5. Characters and characteristics in literature 6. Murder investigation 7. Gilded Age (1865-1898) 8. 1890s 9. Historical mysteries 10. Adaptations, retellings, and spin-offs 11. Multiple perspectives
LC 2014021881
While in America to solve the mystery of the 1885 death of Clover Adams, wife of the esteemed historian Henry Adams, Sherlock Holmes and Henry James find themselves involved in matters of national importance possibly orchestrated by Moriarty. By the author of The Abominable.
Originally published: 2015.

★ **Hyperion**. Dan Simmons. Doubleday, 1989. 481 p. (Hyperion series, 1)
ISBN 9780385249492
1. Pilgrims and pilgrimages 2. Imaginary empires 3. Space warfare 4. Priests 5. Soldiers 6. 28th century 7. Space opera 8. Multiple perspectives 9. Science fiction classics
LC 88033407
Hugo Award for Best Novel, 1990; Locus Award for Best Science Fiction Novel, 1990
A pilgrimage to the realm of the Shrike, a part-god/part-killing machine, provides the travellers the forum to tell their incredible stories.

The **rise** of Endymion. Dan Simmons. Bantam Books, 1997. 579 p. (Hyperion series, 4)
ISBN 9780553106527
1. Messiahs 2. Androids 3. Artificial intelligence 4. Religion 5. Space flight 6. Science fiction 7. Space opera
LC 97-5658
Locus Award for Best Science Fiction Novel, 1998; New York Times Notable Science Fiction, 1997
The conclusion of the author's Hyperion series follows Aenea's emergence as a messiah and her relationship to Raul Endymion and the poet, Martin Silenius.

★ The **Terror:** a novel. Dan Simmons. Little, Brown and Co, 2007. 784 p.
ISBN 9780316017442
1. Survival (after airplane accidents, shipwrecks, etc.) 2. Shipwrecks 3. Sea monsters 4. Ship captains 5. Inuit women 6. Arctic regions 7. Northwest Passage 8. 1840s 9. Sea stories 10. Horror 11. Multiple perspectives 12. Adult books for young adults
LC 2006014608
International Horror Guild Award for Best Novel, 2007
Captain Crozier must find a way for his crew to survive the deadly attacks of a sea monster, in a novel loosely based on the mid-nineteenth-century Arctic expedition originally led by Sir John Franklin.
"A deeply absorbing story that combines awe-inspiring myth, grinding horror and historically accurate adventure." —*Seattle Times*
Adapted into a television series by AMC network in 2017.

Simonson, Helen

Major Pettigrew's last stand: a novel. Helen Simonson. Random House, 2010. 368 p.
ISBN 9781400068937
1. Rural life 2. Retirees 3. Interracial friendship 4. Widowers 5. Widows 6. England 7. Relationship fiction 8. Gentle reads
LC 2009022231
Forced to confront the realities of life in the twenty-first century when he falls in love with Pakistani widow Mrs. Ali, Major Pettigrew finds the relationship challenged by local prejudices that view Mrs. Ali, a Cambridge native, as a perpetual foreigner.
"As with the polished work of Alexander McCall Smith, there is never a dull moment but never a discordant note either. Still, this book feels fresh despite its conventional blueprint. Its main characters are especially well drawn, and Ms. Simonson makes them as admirable as they are entertaining." —*New York Times*

The **summer** before the war: a novel. Helen Simonson. Random House, 2016. 479 p.
ISBN 9780812993103
1. Women teachers 2. Rural life 3. Villages 4. War and society 5. Life change events 6. England 7. Edwardian era (1901-1914) 8. Historical fiction 9. Adult books for young adults
LC 2015016554
LibraryReads Favorites, 2016
Arriving in the village of Rye, England, in 1914, Beatrice Nash, a young woman of good family, becomes the first female teacher of Latin at the local school and falls in love with her sponsor's nephew.
"Aficionados of Downton Abbey and The Guernsey Literary and Potato Peel Pie Society will sigh with pleasure." —*Kirkus*

Simpson, Dorothy

Dead and gone: an Inspector Luke Thanet novel. Scribner, 1999. 247 p. (Inspector Luke Thanet mysteries, 15)
ISBN 9780684863368
1. Detectives 2. Police 3. Murder investigation 4. Thanet, Luke (Fictitious character) 5. Families 6. England 7. Mysteries
LC 99-39091
Inspector Luke Thanet and Detective Sergeant Mike Lineham unravel the intricate events leading up to the drowning of Victoria Mintaur, the wife of a renowned barrister.
"A perfect puzzle, perfectly solved." —*New York Times Book Review*

Dead by morning. Dorothy Simpson. C. Scribner's Sons, 1989. 277 p. (Inspector Luke Thanet mysteries, 9)
ISBN 9780684191232

1. Detectives 2. Murder investigation 3. Suspicion 4. Sisters 5. Thanet, Luke (Fictitious character) 6. Kent, England 7. Mysteries

LC 89006270

Delia and her husband may lose their posh country hotel if her brother, Leo, who has reappeared after a twenty-year absence reclaims his inheritance.

"Inspector Thanet is faced with a murder at a luxurious English country inn and an overzealous superintendent who is busily reorganizing with all the annoying haste of the newly promoted." —*Booklist*

Doomed to die. Dorothy Simpson. C. Scribner's Sons 1991. 245 p. (Inspector Luke Thanet mysteries, 10)
ISBN 9780684193816
1. Detectives 2. Women artists 3. Murder investigation 4. Thanet, Luke (Fictitious character) 5. Police 6. Mysteries

LC 91004185

Inspector Luke Thanet investigates the murder of Perdita Master—a woman who, before her death, had felt a sense of impending doom.

"Confirmed clue-sniffers should be ready for a surprise here: both the solution and the sinner are shockers, though eminently fair ones." —*Booklist*

Last seen alive: a Luke Thanet mystery. Dorothy Simpson. Scribner, 1985. 220 p. (Inspector Luke Thanet mysteries, 5)
ISBN 9780684184357
1. Detectives 2. Resorts 3. Motive (Law) 4. Murder investigation 5. Thanet, Luke (Fictitious character) 6. Kent, England 7. Mysteries

LC 85014530

Silver Dagger Award for Fiction, 1985

Police Inspector Luke Thanet investigates the apparently motiveless murder of Alice Parnall, a guest at the luxurious Black Swan hotel in England's Sturrenden village.

No laughing matter. Scribner, 1993. 262 p. (Inspector Luke Thanet mysteries, 12)
ISBN 9780684196268
1. Detectives 2. Murder investigation 3. Thanet, Luke (Fictitious character) 4. Police 5. Kent, England 6. Mysteries

LC 93019799

Inspector Luke Thanet investigates the grisly death of Zak Randish, winemaker and owner of the Sturrenden Vineyard, whose jugular vein was severed when he was forced through a window pane.

"Simpson turns out her usual high-caliber tale and gives the reader more to ponder than a simple mystery. Her shrewd understanding of what makes humans tick results in a story that is both entertaining and thought-provoking." —*Booklist*

Once too often: an Inspector Luke Thanet novel. Dorothy Simpson. Scribner, 1998. 223 p. (Inspector Luke Thanet mysteries, 14)
ISBN 9780684845784
1. Detectives 2. Thanet, Luke (Fictitious character) 3. Police 4. Fathers and daughters 5. Murder investigation 6. Kent, England 7. Mysteries

LC 9732513

Jessica Manifest's questionable death spirits Inspector Luke Thanet away from his daughter's wedding preparations to investigate the victim's supposedly accidental death, and as he delves into her secretive past, he realizes that there are many people with motives for murdering her.

Simpson, Mona

Anywhere but here. Mona Simpson. A. A. Knopf, 1987. 406 p.
ISBN 9780394552835
1. Mothers and daughters 2. Moving to a new city 3. Eccentric women 4. Ambition 5. Families 6. Los Angeles, California 7. Domestic fiction 8. Books to movies

LC 86045282

This novel about the dreams of three generations of a Midwestern family begins with twelve-year-old Ann August and her ambitious mother, as they travel to California in search of fame and fortune BT

"Any single episode could stand on its own, but Simpson keeps piling them on, building with strength and grace." —*Booklist*

Adapted in 1999 into a film of the same name starring Susan Sarandon and Natalie Portman.

Sequel: The lost father.

Simpson, Rosemary

Let the dead keep their secrets. Rosemary Simpson. Kensington Pub Corp 2018. 304 p. (Gilded Age mysteries (Rosemary Simpson), 3)
ISBN 9781496715739
1. Heirs and heiresses 2. Undercover operations 3. Women amateur detectives 4. Murder investigation 5. Amateur detectives 6. New York City 7. Gilded Age (1865-1898) 8. 1890s 9. Historical mysteries

Heiress Prudence MacKenzie and former Pinkerton agent Geoffrey Hunter attempt to discover the truth behind the death of opera singer Claire Buchanan's twin sister and newborn niece when Claire confides her belief that they were murdered.

★ **What** the dead leave behind. Rosemary Simpson. Kensington Books, 2017. 390 p. (Gilded Age mysteries (Rosemary Simpson), 1)
ISBN 9781496709080
1. Heirs and heiresses 2. Blizzards 3. Engaged persons 4. Murder victims 5. Women amateur detectives 6. New York City 7. Gilded Age (1865-1898) 8. 1890s 9. Historical mysteries 10. Adult books for young adults

When her beloved fiance is found dead after the Great Blizzard of 1888 in New York City, heiress Prudence MacKenzie, suspecting foul play, turns to her fiance's best friend, a former Pinkerton agent, to discover the truth and find protection from sinister forces.

"Launching an atmospheric new series set in Gilded Age New York, Simpson...incorporates historical events and figures to add verisimilitude to this tension-filled story." —*Library Journal*

Simsion, Graeme C.

The **Rosie** effect. Graeme Simsion. Simon & Schuster, 2014. 304 p. (Rosie novels (Graeme Simsion), 2)
ISBN 9781476767314
1. Geneticists 2. Marriage 3. Fatherhood 4. Pregnant women 5. Husband and wife 6. New York City 7. Romantic comedies 8. Australian fiction 9. Adult books for young adults

LibraryReads Favorites, 2015

The highly anticipated sequel to the New York Times bestselling novel The Rosie Project, starring the same extraordinary couple now living in New York and unexpectedly expecting their first child. Get ready to fall in love all over again. Don Tillman and Rosie Jarman are back. The Wife Project is complete, and Don and Rosie are happily married and living in New York. But they're about to face a new challenge because— surprise!—Rosie is pregnant. Don sets about learning the protocols of becoming a father, but his unusual research style gets him into trouble with the law. Fortunately his best friend Gene is on hand to offer advice: he's left Claudia and moved in with Don and Rosie. As Don tries to schedule time for pregnancy research, getting Gene and Claudia to reconcile, servicing the industrial refrigeration unit that occupies half his apartment, helping Dave the Baseball Fan save his business, and staying on the right side of Lydia the social worker, he almost misses the biggest problem of all: he might lose Rosie when she needs him the most. Graeme Simsion first introduced these unforgettable characters in The Rosie Project, which

NPR called "sparkling entertainment along the lines of Where'd You Go Bernadette and When Harry Met Sally." The SanFrancisco Chronicle said, "sometimes you just need a smart love story that will make anyone, man or woman, laugh out loud." If you were swept away by the book that's captivated a million readers worldwide, you will love The Rosie Effect.

★ The **Rosie** project. Graeme Simsion. Simon & Schuster, 2013. 329 p; (Rosie novels (Graeme Simsion), 1)
ISBN 9781476729084
1. Geneticists 2. Dating (Social customs) 3. Birthfathers — Identification 4. Interpersonal attraction 5. Man-woman relationships 6. Australia 7. Romantic comedies 8. Australian fiction 9. Adult books for young adults
Australian Book Industry Awards, Book of the Year, 2014; Australian Book Industry Awards, General Fiction Book of the Year, 2014; LibraryReads Favorites, 2013; School Library Journal Best Books: Best Adult Books 4 Teens, 2013
A socially awkward genetics professor who has never been on a second date sets out to find the perfect wife, but instead finds Rosie Jarman, a fiercely independent barmaid who is on a quest to find her biological father.
"The story lurches from one set piece of deadpan nudge-nudge, wink-wink humor to another: We laugh at, and with, Don as he tries to navigate our hopelessly emotional, nonliteral world, learning as he goes." —*Kirkus*
Originally published: Melbourne : Text Publishing, 2013.

The **Rosie** result. Graeme Simsion. Text Publishing, 2019. 368 p. (Rosie novels (Graeme Simsion), 3)
ISBN 9781925773811
1. Geneticists 2. Marriage 3. Fatherhood 4. Husband and wife 5. Marital conflict 6. New York City 7. Romantic comedies 8. Australian fiction 9. Adult books for young adults
Don and Rosie help their eleven-year-old son who is struggling at school and having trouble fitting in while trying to open a cocktail bar.
"Charming, eloquent, and insightful, The Rosie Result is a triumphant conclusion to Dons story, one that celebrates this remarkable father, husband, and friend in all his complexity and brilliance." —*Booklist*
Series complete in 3 volumes.

Sinclair, Upton
★ The **jungle**. Upton Sinclair. Penguin Books, 1985. Xxxv, 411 p.
ISBN 9780140390315
1. Immigrants 2. Capitalism 3. Meat industry and trade — Corrupt practices 4. Meat workers — Health and safety 5. Corporate accountability 6. Chicago, Illinois 7. United States 8. 1900s (Decade) 9. Political fiction 10. Classics
A documentary novel portraying industry's conditions at the end of the 19th and beginning of the 20th century. Sinclair's novel prompted public outrage which led President Theodore Roosevelt to demand an official investigation. This eventually led to the passage of the Pure Food and Drug laws.
Originally published: New York : Doubleday, Jabber & Co, 1906.

Singer, I. J.
The **brothers** Ashkenazi. By Israel Joshua Singer; a new translation from the Yiddish by Joseph Singer. Atheneum, 1980. 426 pages
ISBN 9780689111020
1. Jews, Polish 2. Brothers 3. Jewish families 4. Social classes 5. Lodz, Poland 6. Poland 7. Translations 8. Family sagas 9. Literary fiction
LC 80066017

With a large cast of characters, this is a social novel, a family saga set against the rise of capitalism and of a Jewish bourgeoisie in Lodz. It tells the story, through an interwoven plot, of the clash between old traditions and growing desires.
"What gives the book its significance is not the picture of nineteenth-century Jewish family life, and not the characterizations of the two brothers, but the clear exposition of the class struggle of which Max and Jacob form unconscious parts." —*The New Yorker*
Translation of: Di brider Ashkenazi.
Originally published in Warsaw, Poland as Di brider Ashkenazi by Farlag H. Bzshoza, in 1936.

Singer, Isaac Bashevis
Collected stories: A friend of Kafka to Passions. Isaac Bashevis Singer. Library of America, 2004. X, 856 p.
ISBN 9781931082624
1. Jews 2. Families 3. Jewish way of life 4. Hope 5. Belonging 6. Short stories 7. Translations
LC 2003066057
Presents a collection of sixty-five short stories.
Ilan Stavans is the editor of this volume—Page [vii].
Includes bibliographical references (p. 842-856).

Collected stories: Gimpel the fool to the Letter writer. Isaac Bashevis Singer. Library of America, 2004. 789 p.
ISBN 9781931082617
1. Jews 2. Families 3. Jewish way of life 4. Hope 5. Belonging 6. Short stories 7. Translations
LC 2003066055
Presents a collection of fifty-four short stories, including "Gimpel the Fool," "Yentl the Yeshiva Boy," and "The Mirror."
Ilan Stavans is the editor of this volume—page after Title page verso.

Enemies, a love story. Isaac Bashevis Singer. Farrar, Straus 1972. 280 p.
ISBN 9780374148300
1. Guilt in men 2. Love triangles 3. Holocaust survivors 4. Concentration camp survivors 5. Jewish Americans 6. New York City 7. 1940s 8. Literary fiction 9. Translations 10. Books to movies
LC 78189337
"The book has the surface gaiety, ribaldry and surprise of a medieval fabliau. Yet the New York subways, telephone calls, Bronx Zoo, bus trip to the Adirondacks are solidly, meticulously real. Herman's three women expand into mythic dimension.... Whether or not you accept its ending, [this] is a brilliant, unsettling novel." —*Newsweek*
First published in The Jewish daily forward in 1966 under the title 'Sonim, di Geshichte fun a Liebe.'

The **family** Moskat. Isaac Bashevis Singer. Knopf, 1950. 611 p. (Family chronicles, 1)
ISBN 9780140186697
1. Family relationships 2. Jews 3. Jewish way of life 4. Antisemitism 5. Family traditions 6. Poland 7. Family sagas 8. Literary fiction 9. Translations
Reb Meshulam Moskat's wealthy family represents the thoughts and concerns of Jews from the end of the 19th century until the beginning of World War II.
Translated from the Yiddish.

★ The **magician** of Lublin. Isaac Bashevis Singer; translated from the Yiddish by Elaine Gottlieb and Joseph Singer. Farrar Straus & Giroux, 2010. 256 p.
ISBN 9780374532543

1. Escape artists 2. Jewish way of life 3. Extramarital affairs 4. Jews 5. Shtetl 6. Poland 7. 1870s 8. Literary fiction 9. Historical fiction 10. Translations

LC 2010926163

Caught between his eagerness to win fame and fortune as a performer and his reluctance to give up his easy life of pleasure, a late-nineteenth-century Polish magician and holy man finds himself on the brink of disaster.

Originally published in Yiddish, 1960.

Singh, Nalini

A **madness** of sunshine. Nalini Singh. Berkley, 2019. 352 pages
ISBN 9780593099131

1. Homecomings 2. Hometowns 3. Women pianists 4. Missing women 5. Maori (New Zealand people) 6. New Zealand 7. Thrillers and suspense 8. New Zealand fiction

LC 2019014381

LibraryReads Favorites, 2019

Returning to her impoverished New Zealand hometown to reconnect with familiar things after a personal tragedy, Anahera Rawiri bonds with detective Will Gallagher to uncover the community secrets behind a missing-persons case.

"Popular romance author Singh shifts to a new genre, New Zealand gothic, in which nearly every character including the dense, ferocious landscape has something to hide, and studying them is nearly as fascinating and compelling as solving the multifaceted mystery." —*Kirkus*

★ **Silver** silence. Nalini Singh. Berkley, 2017. 496 p. (Psy-Changeling trinity, 1)
ISBN 9781101987797

1. Negotiation 2. Shapeshifters 3. Assassination plots 4. Imaginary wars and battles 5. Protectiveness 6. Paranormal romances 7. New Zealand fiction

LC 2016058705

Australian Romance Readers Awards, Favourite Paranormal Romance, 2017; LibraryReads Favorites, 2017; Romantic Times Reviewer's Choice Award, 2017

A first entry in a story arc tied to the Psy-Changeling series finds Silver Mercant, a negotiator for peace for a fledgling Trinity Accord, targeted by an assassination plot and finding protection from Valentin Nikolaev, alpha of the wild StoneWater Bears.

Sinha, Indra

Animal's people. Indra Sinha. Simon & Schuster, 2008. 384 p.
ISBN 9781416578789

1. Bhopal Union Carbide Plant Disaster, Bhopal, India, 1984 2. Chemical spills 3. Accident victims 4. Men with disfigurements 5. Orphans 6. India 7. Humorous stories

LC 2007042118

Commonwealth Writers' Prize, South Asia and Europe: Best Book, 2008; Shortlisted for the Man Booker Prize, 2007; Shortlisted for the International IMPAC Dublin Literary Award, 2009

Ever since That Night, the residents of Khaufpur have lived a perilous existence. Their world is poisoned. Nobody has received compensation or help for the chemical leak, least of all Animal, as he is known, whose spine twisted at a young age, leaving him to walk on all fours. Though he inhabits a dark kind of half-life, he knows what love is. He has long harboured feelings for his friend Nisha but since she is enamoured of his friend Zafar he cannot even allow himself to hope. When Elli Barber arrives, an "Amrikan" keen to set up a free clinic to help the victims of the disaster, deep suspicion arises amongst the community. Animal resolves

to turn the situation to his advantage and starts to investigate Elli's motives.

"Animal is a teenage boy who lives on the streets of the Indian city of Khaufpur. He goes around on all fours since his spine is badly damaged; he cannot walk normally. As an infant, he was one of the thousands of victims of a poison gas leak at an American-owned company, here just called the Kampani. Animal also lost his parents that night (as the local people refer to the horrible event). Animal has a lively mind and a way with words, some of them angry and profane, some of them bitterly funny, as he gets caught up in the struggle of those in Khaufpur who seek long-delayed justice from the Kampani. Sinha...has clearly based his story on the human and environmental disaster at the Union Carbide factory in Bhopal in 1984. The result is a gripping novel that also reminds us of a continuing real-life tragedy." —*Library Journal*

Sister Souljah

★ The **coldest** winter ever: a novel. Sister Souljah. Pocket Books, 1999. 337 p; (Coldest winter ever, 1)
ISBN 9780671025366

1. African American women 2. Street life 3. Drug traffic 4. Inner city 5. City life 6. Brooklyn, New York City 7. African American fiction 8. Urban fiction

LC 99012242

Street Lit Book Award Medal: Adult Fiction, 2000

Winter Santiaga, the daughter of one of Brooklyn's most powerful drug czars, uses her own weapons—including sex and an aggressive attitude—to stay on top, after her father's empire is threatened by a drug war.

Sequel: A deeper love inside

★ A **deeper** love inside: the Porsche Santiaga story. By Sister Souljah. Emily Bestler Books/Atria, 2012. 432 p.
ISBN 9781439165317

1. Street life 2. Problem youth 3. African American teenagers 4. Growing up 5. Inner city 6. New York City 7. Brooklyn, New York City 8. Coming-of-age stories 9. African American fiction 10. Urban fiction

LC 2012029222

Natural-born hustler Porsche Santiaga refuses to accept her new life in juvenile detention after her family is torn apart and fights to regain what she has lost.

Sequel to: The Coldest Winter Ever

Midnight and the meaning of love. Sister Souljah. Atria Books, 2011. 608 p. (Midnight series (Sister Souljah), 2)
ISBN 9781439165355

1. African American men 2. Family relationships 3. Protectiveness in men 4. Martial artists 5. Family fortunes 6. Brooklyn, New York City 7. Love stories 8. Urban fiction 9. African American fiction

Midnight's efforts to rescue his wife trigger unexpected consequences that mark his journey into adulthood.

Sittenfeld, Curtis

Eligible: a novel. Curtis Sittenfeld. Random House, 2016. 384 p.
ISBN 9781400068326

1. Sisters 2. Dysfunctional families 3. Family relationships 4. Mate selection 5. Single women 6. Cincinnati, Ohio 7. New York City 8. Romantic comedies 9. Relationship fiction 10. Adaptations, retellings, and spin-offs 11. Adult books for young adults

LC 2015027778

LibraryReads Favorites, 2016

Returning with her sister, Jane, to their Ohio hometown when their father falls ill, New York magazine editor Lizzy Bennett confronts her younger sisters' football fangirl antics, a creepy cousin's unwanted attentions, and the infuriating standoffish manners of a handsome neurosurgeon.

"Sittenfeld's style is endlessly amusing and, at times, gut-wrenchingly painful. Her take on Austen's iconic characters is skillful, her pacing excellent, and her dialog highly entertaining." —*Library Journal*

A modern retelling of Jane Austen's "Pride and Prejudice."

Prep: a novel. Curtis Sittenfeld. Random House, 2005. 416 p.
ISBN 9781400062317
1. Fourteen-year-old girls 2. Middle class teenage girls 3. Prep school students 4. Boarding school students 5. New students 6. Massachusetts 7. Indiana 8. Coming-of-age stories 9. Chick lit 10. Adult books for young adults
LC 2004046858
Booklist Editors' Choice: Adult Books for Young Adults, 2005; New York Times Notable Book, 2005

"Lee Fiora, a scholarship student at the prestigious Ault School (not Ault Academy, as her parents embarrassingly refer to it), negotiates her days there in a blaze of self-consciousness that is, by turns, hilarious and excruciating... And yet she becomes an expert on the rituals that govern the rarefied microenvironment in which she finds herself: the students fondness for catchphrases like therein lies the paradox and LMC (lower middle class); the taboo against enthusiasm for anything other than sports; the fact that the school always sings God be with you till we meet again at chapel before breaks. In the end, Lees incisive vision of herself and others is her downfall but also—as this richly textured narrative suggests—her greatest gift." —*The New Yorker*

Rodham: a novel. Curtis Sittenfeld. Random House, 2020. 416 p.
ISBN 9780399590917
1. Clinton, Hillary Rodham 2. Independence in women 3. Ambition in women 4. Single women 5. Transformations, Personal 6. Women politicians 7. United States 8. 20th century 9. 21st century 10. Political fiction 11. Alternate histories
LC 2020004610
This powerfully imagined tour de force of fiction of what-might-have-been follows Hillary Rodham as she takes a different path, blazing her own trail—one that unfolds in public as well as in private—and one that crosses paths again and again with Bill Clinton.

"Successfully interspersing fact with fiction, Sittenfeld imagines Rodham's personal and professional life without marriage in aching detail in this captivating novel." —*Library Journal*

Sisterland: a novel. Curtis Sittenfeld. Random House, 2013. 448 p.
ISBN 9781400068319
1. Twin sisters 2. Psychic ability 3. Earthquakes 4. Sisters 5. Identical twins 6. Mainstream fiction
LC 2012043726
When the strongest earthquake in U.S. history occurs just north of their St. Louis home, Kate and Jeremy find the disaster further complicated by Kate's self-proclaimed-medium twin's prediction about a more powerful earthquake, a situation that places Kate under public scrutiny and reveals her own psychic abilities.

"The author turns conventions on their collective head and creates a world that is familiar, maddening, alluring, and, ultimately, guardedly hopeful." —*Library Journal*

★ **You** think it, I'll say it: stories. Curtis Sittenfeld. Random House, 2018. 226 p.
ISBN 9780399592867
1. Short stories 2. Literary fiction 3. Adult books for young adults
LC 2017020945
LibraryReads Favorites, 2018

The best-selling author of Eligible presents a collection of 10 short stories that features both original pieces and two previously published in the New Yorker.

Sjon

The **blue** fox. Sjón; translated from the Icelandic by Victoria Cribb. Farrar, Straus and Giroux, 2013. 128 p.
ISBN 9780374114459
1. Hunting 2. Priests 3. People with Down syndrome 4. Natural history 5. Guardian and ward 6. 19th century 7. Mysteries 8. Translations
LC 2012039701
An elusive fox leads a hunter on a transformative quest, while a naturalist endeavors to build a life for a young woman with Down syndrome whom he rescued from a shipwreck years earlier.
Translation from the Icelandic of: Skugga-Baldur.
Originally published: 2004.

Sjowall, Maj

★ **Cop** killer: the story of a crime. Maj Sjowall and Per Wahloo; translated from the Swedish by Thomas Teal. Pantheon Books, 1975. 296 p; (Martin Beck mysteries, 9)
ISBN 9780394485317
1. Crimes against police 2. Murder investigation 3. Detectives 4. Crimes against women 5. Johnson, Robert 6. Stockholm, Sweden 7. 1960s 8. Mysteries 9. Translations 10. Police procedurals
LC 74026197
In a country town, a woman is brutally murdered and left buried in a swamp. There are two main suspects: her closest neighbor and her ex-husband. Meanwhile, on a quiet suburban street a midnight shootout takes place between three cops and two teenage boys. Dead, one cop and one kid. Wounded, two cops. Escaped, one kid. Martin Beck and his partner Lenart Kollberg are called in to investigate. As Beck digs deeper into the murky waters of the young girl's murder, Kollberg scours the town for the teenager, and together they are forced to examine the changing face of crime.
Translation from the Swedish of: Polismordaren.
Originally published: Stockholm : Norstedt, 1974.

★ The **laughing** policeman. By Maj Sjowall and Per Wahloo; translated from the Swedish by Alan Blair. Vintage Books, 1992. 211 p. (Martin Beck mysteries, 4)
ISBN 9780679742234
1. Mass murder 2. Gunshot victims 3. Detectives 4. Police 5. Beck, Martin (Fictitious character) 6. Stockholm, Sweden 7. 1960s 8. Mysteries 9. Translations 10. Police procedurals
LC 92050005
Edgar Allan Poe Award for Best Mystery Novel, 1971
Superintendent Martin Beck seeks the murderer of nine passengers on a Stockholm bus, one of whom was his best detective
Translation from the Swedish of: Den skrattande polisen.
Originally published: Stockholm : Norstedt, 1968.

★ The **locked** room: the story of a crime. By Maj Sjowall and Per Wahloo. Translated from the Swedish by Paul Britten Austin. Vintage Crime/Black Lizard, 1973. 311 p. (Martin Beck mysteries, 8)
ISBN 9780394485331
1. Bank robberies 2. Murder investigation 3. Detectives 4. Police 5. Beck, Martin (Fictitious character) 6. Stockholm, Sweden 7. 1960s 8. Mysteries 9. Translations 10. Police procedurals
LC 73007027

The eighth classic installment in this genre-changing series of novels starring Detective Inspector Martin Beck.

Translation from the Swedish of: Slutna rummet

Originally published: Stockholm : Norstedt, 1972.

The **man** on the balcony: the story of a crime. Maj Sjowall and Per Wahloo; translated from the Swedish by Alan Blair. Vintage Books, 1993. 180 p; (Martin Beck mysteries, 3)

ISBN 9780679745969

1. Serial murder investigation 2. Murder witnesses 3. Detectives 4. Women murder victims 5. Police 6. Stockholm, Sweden 7. 1960s 8. Mysteries 9. Translations 10. Police procedurals

LC 92050693

Swedish police superintendent Martin Beck conducts a thorough investigation of a series of brutal muggings and child sex murders

"The chief problem is child murder in Stockholm, and it is a macabre race with death when the only clues are disturbing and intangible for Beck and for the 75-man force assigned to help him." —*Library Journal*

Translation from the Swedish of: Mannen pa balkongen.

Originally published: Stockholm : Norstedt, 1967.

★ **Murder** at the Savoy. Maj Sjowall and Per Wahloo; translated from the Swedish by Joan Tate. Harper Perennial, 2007. Xi, 238, 21 pages; (Martin Beck mysteries, 6)

ISBN 9780007242962

1. Industrialists 2. Assassination 3. Detectives 4. Shooting 5. Arms dealers 6. Stockholm, Sweden 7. 1960s 8. Mysteries 9. Translations 10. Police procedurals

"When Viktor Palmgren, a powerful Swedish industrialist is shot during his after-dinner speech in the luxurious Hotel Savoy, it sends a shiver down the spine of the international money markets and terrifies the tiny town of Malmo. No one in the restaurant can identify the gunman, and local police are sheepishly baffled. That's when Beck takes over the scene and quickly picks through Palmgren's background. What he finds is a web of vice so despicable that it's hard for him to imagine who wouldn't want Palmgren dead, but that doesn't stop him and his team of dedicated detectives from tackling one of their most intriguing cases yet." —Provided by publisher

Translation from the Swedish of: Polis, polis, potatismos!

This translation originally published: New York: Pantheon, 1971.

Originally published: Stockholm : Norstedt, 1970.

Skarmeta, Antonio

The **dancer** and the thief: a novel. Antonio Skarmeta; translated from the Spanish by Katherine Silver. W. W. Norton, 2008. 320 p.

ISBN 9780393064940

1. Revenge 2. Thieves 3. Stealing 4. Dancers 5. Entertainers 6. Chile 7. South America 8. Love stories 9. Crime fiction 10. Translations

LC 2007033340

Granted amnesty along with other non-violent Chilean prisoners, Ángel Santiago plots revenge against those who abused him in jail, teaming up with bank robber Nicolás Vergara Grey during a heist that is complicated by the presence of a talented dancer.

"Though Skarmeta scarcely ranks at the very top of Latin America's remarkably distinguished and varied literary elite, he is a serious writer to whom the death and rebirth of democracy in his native Chile is an endlessly compelling subject.... Though the ending that Skarmeta gives his characters falls well short of happy, the Chile that he portrays herein is vibrant and strong." —*Washington Post Book World.*

Skeslien Charles, Janet

The **Paris** library: a novel. Janet Skeslien Charles. Atria Books, 2020. 368 p.

ISBN 9781982134198

1. Librarians 2. French Resistance (World War II) 3. Libraries 4. Books and reading 5. Intergenerational friendship 6. Paris, France 7. Montana 8. Second World War era (1939-1945) 9. 1980s 10. Historical fiction 11. Multiple perspectives

LC 2019043786

LibraryReads Favorites, 2021; Loan Stars Favourites, 2021

Based on a true story, describes how a lonely, 1980s teenager befriends an elderly neighbor and uncovers her past as a librarian at the American Library in Paris who joined the Resistance when the Nazis arrived.

"Historical fiction fans will be drawn to the realistic narrative and the bond of friendship forged between a widow and a lonely young girl." —*Publishers Weekly*

Skyhorse, Brando

Madonnas of Echo Park: a novel. Brando Skyhorse. Free Press, 2010. 224 p.

ISBN 9781439170809

1. Mexican Americans 2. Identity (Psychology) 3. Undocumented immigrants 4. American dream 5. Murder witnesses 6. Los Angeles, California 7. Echo Park, Los Angeles, California 8. Psychological fiction

LC 2009034403

Hemingway Foundation/PEN Award, 2011

Revolving around the random shooting of a young girl, this novel interweaves stories from the barrios of Los Angeles to coalesce into a powerful examination of the Mexican-American experience.

Slaughter, Karin

Cop Town: a novel. Karin Slaughter. Delacorte Press, 2014. 402 p.

ISBN 9780345547491

1. Policewomen 2. Serial murder investigation 3. Police murders 4. Race relations 5. Violence 6. Atlanta, Georgia 7. Georgia 8. 1970s 9. Mysteries

LC 2014005076

Ian Fleming Steel Dagger Award, 2015

Finds reluctant rookie cop Kate Murphy teamed with agenda-seeking Maggie Lawson in a manhunt for a cop killer in 1974 Atlanta.

"Slaughter's first stand-alone thriller is a superb, very gritty look at both a city and era in social and political flux. It's also a searing portrait of family ties and how our pasts can shape our futures, as well as a gripping procedural, with some genuinely terrifying moments.... [T]his title is sure to win over readers new to Slaughter's work while reminding old fans of her enormous talent." —*Library Journal*

Criminal: a novel. Karin Slaughter. Delacorte Press, 2012. 416 p. (Will Trent series, 6)

ISBN 9780345528506

1. Detectives 2. Murder investigation 3. Death threats 4. Secrets 5. Man-woman relationships 6. Georgia 7. Atlanta, Georgia 8. Thrillers and suspense

LC 2012001504

A Georgia Bureau of Investigation search into a shocking crime from 1975 poses unprecedented personal and professional challenges for top agent Will Trent, who encounters threats against his life and everything he thought he understood about his past.

★ **Fallen:** a novel. Karin Slaughter. Delacorte, 2011. 416 p. (Georgia series (Karin Slaughter), 3; Will Trent series, 5)
ISBN 9780345528209
1. Missing persons 2. Mother and adult daughter 3. Women hostages 4. Policewomen 5. Police corruption 6. Georgia 7. Atlanta, Georgia 8. Thrillers and suspense 9. Police procedurals
Library Journal Best Books, 2011
Georgia Bureau of Investigations Detective Faith Mitchell, her partner Will Trent, and trauma doctor Sara Linton join forces to find Faith's mother, missing after a deadly hostage situation that leaves Faith a murder suspect—and the scapegoat for police corruption, bribery, and murder.
"Family-biological, professional, and everything in between-plays a key role in a thriller sure to please Slaughter's many fans." —*Publishers Weekly*
This novel involves characters from her "Will Trent series."

The **good** daughter. Karin Slaughter. William Morrow, 2017. 515 p.
ISBN 9780062430243
1. Cold cases (Criminal investigation) 2. Small town life 3. Women lawyers 4. Secrets 5. Home invasions 6. Georgia 7. Psychological suspense
Librarians' Choice (Australia), 2017
Decades after a shattering confrontation that left her mother dead and her sister traumatized, a New York-based lawyer returns to her Atlanta hometown to help her father save the life of a young woman accused of a school shooting.

The **kept** woman. Karin Slaughter. William Morrow & Co, 2016. 400 p. (Will Trent series, 8)
ISBN 9780062430212
1. Government investigators 2. Professional basketball players 3. Rich people 4. Building sites 5. Former police 6. Atlanta, Georgia 7. Thrillers and suspense
Georgia detective Will Trent faces against the dark forces of a case that threatens to destroy him.

★ The **last** widow. Karin Slaughter. William Morrow & Co, 2019. 400 p. (Will Trent series, 9)
ISBN 9780062858085
1. Epidemics 2. Conspiracies 3. Kidnapping victims 4. Couples 5. Government investigators 6. Atlanta, Georgia 7. Thrillers and suspense
LibraryReads Favorites, 2019
Finds Will and Sara pitted against a mysterious group that would unleash a deadly epidemic.

★ **Pieces** of her. Karin Slaughter. HarperCollins 2018. 400 p.
ISBN 9780062430274
1. Secrets 2. Family secrets 3. Mothers and daughters 4. Domestic terrorism 5. Violence in women 6. Georgia 7. 1980s 8. 2010s 9. Thrillers and suspense 10. Parallel narratives
The daughter of a woman who has wanted nothing more than a quiet life in her small beachside home embarks on a desperate search for answers when she discovers the explosive truth about her mother's true identity.
"Readers will find themselves totally immersed in the suspenseful, alternating story lines and wont want either of them to end." —*Booklist*

★ **Pretty** girls: a novel. Karin Slaughter. William Morrow, 2015. 396 pages
ISBN 9780345547521
1. Corruption 2. Stalkers 3. Murderers 4. Lawyers 5. Sisters 6. Thrillers and suspense
RUSA Reading List, 2016
The story of estranged sisters—Claire and Lydia—reunited by the murder of Claire's husband, whom Lydia had accused of harassment years

ago. Hidden computer files pique Claire's interest and provoke suspicion that he may have known something about the disappearance of their oldest sister, Julia, decades previously. Realistic characters, unexpected humor, poignant chapters from their father's perspective, ample suspense, and the slow healing of damaged relationships make for a tense, unsettling, and utterly compelling read.
"Slaughter (Cop Town, 2014, etc.) is so uncompromising in following her blood trails to the darkest places imaginable that she makes most of her high-wire competition look pallid, formulaic, or just plain fake." —*Kirkus*
The prepublication title of this novel was The truth about pretty girls.

★ The **silent** wife. Karin Slaughter. William Morrow & Co, 2020. 400 p. (Will Trent series, 10)
ISBN 9780062858108
1. Women murder victims 2. Cold cases (Criminal investigation) 3. Government investigators 4. Lovers 5. Judicial error 6. Atlanta, Georgia 7. Thrillers and suspense
LibraryReads Favorites, 2020
Investigating a brutal murder that eerily resembles another from years earlier, Will Trent reopens the case of a possibly wrongly convicted prisoner before teaming up with medical examiner Sara Linton to hunt down the true killer.
"Slaughter adds depth to her best-selling series with the investigations of old and current cases, while also advancing the key personal relationship. Another slam dunk." —*Booklist*

★ **Undone:** a novel. Karin Slaughter. Delacorte Press, 2009. 448 pages (Georgia series (Karin Slaughter), 1; Will Trent series, 3)
ISBN 9780385341967
1. Women physicians 2. Accidents 3. Violence against women 4. Kidnapping 5. Torture 6. Atlanta, Georgia 7. Thrillers and suspense 8. Psychological fiction 9. Police procedurals
LC 2009013477
Fleeing to Atlanta to seek refuge in the aftermath of a violent act, Sara Linton becomes unwittingly enmeshed in a case involving a tortured young ER patient, a situation that is investigated by special agents Will Trent and Faith Mitchell.
This novel involves characters from her "Will Trent series."
Published in the United Kingdom by Century in 2009 under the title: Genesis.

Slimani, Leïla

In the country of others. Leila Slimani; translated from the French by Sam Taylor. Penguin Group USA, 2021. 240 p.
ISBN 9780143135975
1. Marriage 2. Soldiers 3. World War II 4. Colonists 5. National liberation movements 6. Morocco 7. Second World War era (1939-1945) 8. 1950s 9. Relationship fiction 10. Translations
LC 2021006123
After marrying a handsome Moroccan soldier during World War II, a young Frenchwoman is torn as tensions mount between the locals and the French colonists.
"An affecting tale of evolution and revolution." —*Kirkus*
Translation of: Le pays des autres.
Originally published : Paris : Editions Gallimard, 2020.
Translated from the French.

Sloan, Robin

Mr. Penumbra's 24-hour bookstore. Robin Sloan. Farrar, Straus and Giroux, 2012. 288 p.
ISBN 9780374214913

1. Bookstores 2. Codes (Communication) 3. Secret societies 4. Displaced workers 5. Website designers 6. California 7. San Francisco, California 8. Science fiction 9. Literary fiction 10. Adult books for young adults

LC 2012012357

Alex Award, 2013

The Great Recession has shuffled Clay Jannon out of his life as a San Francisco web-design drone and landed him a new gig working the night shift at Mr. Penumbra's 24-Hour Bookstore. But after just a few days on the job, Clay begins to realize that this store is even more curious than the name suggests. There are only a few customers, but they come in repeatedly and never seem to actually buy anything. Soon he embarks on a complex analysis of the customers' behaviour and ropes his friends into helping him figure out just what's going on.

First published: New York : Farrar, Straus and Giroux, 2012.

First published: New York: Farrar, Straus & Giroux, 2012.

Smiley, Jane

Early warning. Jane Smiley. Knopf, 2015. 384 p. (Last hundred years trilogy, 2)

ISBN 9780307700322

1. Family relationships 2. Joy and sorrow 3. Families 4. Farm life 5. Farms 6. United States 7. Iowa 8. 20th century 9. Family sagas

LibraryReads Favorites, 2015

Follows the Langdon family after the sudden death of their patriarch, Walter, as the five Langdon children, now adults, navigate the Cold War years of the 1950s and the social revolution of the '60s and '70s.

"Each of the large cast of characters has sharply individualized traits, and though we're seldom emotionally wrapped up in their experiences...they are unfailingly interesting." —*Kirkus*

Golden age. Jane Smiley. Random House, 2015. 384 p. (Last hundred years trilogy, 3)

ISBN 9780307700346

1. Family relationships 2. Joy and sorrow 3. Family secrets 4. Growing up 5. Farmers 6. United States 7. Iowa 8. 20th century 9. 21st century 10. Family sagas

The third book of a trilogy about a farm family from Iowa, which takes them from the late 1980s through the present and into the future.

"As for Smiley's cantering, far-reaching, yet intimate trilogy, it is both timely in the issues it so astutely raises, especially as Iowa is once again in the presidential election spotlight, and timeless in the rapture of its storytelling and the humanness of its insights into family, self, and our connection to the land. Readers will be reading and rereading Smileys Last Hundred Years far into the next." —*Booklist*

Horse heaven. Jane Smiley. Knopf, 2000. 561 p.

ISBN 9780375406003

1. Horse racing 2. Race horses 3. Humans and horses 4. Equestrians 5. Jack Russell terriers 6. Satirical fiction 7. Mainstream fiction 8. Stories told by animals 9. Adult books for young adults

New York Times Notable Book, 2000; Shortlisted for The Orange Prize for Fiction, 2001

A novel set in the world of thoroughbred racing follows a group of trainers, jockeys, and "track brats" on a two-year journey through the racing cycle BT

"What's remarkable about Smiley's handling of horses as characters is that she manages to bring it off at alland more, she does it brilliantly." —*New York Times Book Review*

★ **Perestroika** in Paris: a novel. Jane Smiley. Alfred A. Knopf, 2020. 288 p.

ISBN 9780525520351

1. Race horses 2. Dogs 3. Human/animal communication 4. Boys 5. Friendship 6. Literary fiction

LC 2019058473

Loan Stars Favourites, 2020

Coexisting in the lush hidden spaces of Paris until cold weather arrives, an escaped racehorse and her companion, a German shorthaired pointer, forge a bond with a boy living in seclusion with his nonagenarian grandmother in an ivy-covered house.

"Readers will flock to the first adult novel from Smiley in five years, especially since this smart and enchanting tale is a guaranteed antidote to stress." —*Booklist*

Republished in 2021 as The Strays of Paris by Pan Macmillan.

Some luck. Jane Smiley. Alfred A. Knopf, 2014. 395 p. (Last hundred years trilogy, 1)

ISBN 9780307700315

1. Farm life 2. Rural families 3. World War I veterans 4. Family relationships 5. Joy and sorrow 6. United States 7. Iowa 8. 20th century 9. 1920s 10. Family sagas

Library Journal Best Books 2014; LibraryReads Favorites, 2014

Follows the triumphs and tragedies of a farm family from post-World War I America through the early 1950s.

"An expansive, episodic tale showing this generally flinty author in a mellow mood: surprising, but engaging." —*Kirkus*

★ **A thousand** acres. Jane Smiley. Knopf, 1991. 371 p.

ISBN 9780394577739

1. Sisters 2. Family problems 3. Farm life 4. Farmers 5. Family farms 6. Iowa 7. Adaptations, retellings, and spin-offs 8. Literary fiction 9. Domestic fiction

LC 91052720

ALA Notable Book, 1993; National Book Critics Circle Award for Fiction, 1991; Pulitzer Prize for Fiction, 1992

Larry Cook, an Iowan farmer who has worked a thousand acre plot owned by his family for generations, abruptly decides to leave his farm to his three daughters and retire. His two eldest daughters are pleased with the decision but his youngest daughter has been cut out by her father and is angry. As the daughters' activity on the land progresses, they notice a change in their father. Events begin to unfold that will threaten and destroy the family and their farm.

"What makes this novel such a triumph is Smiley's brilliant twist on the Lear story: she tells it not from Larry's point of view but from his eldest daughter's.... In the end Smiley does what Shakespeare himself never did: she creates a female heroine who grows through her own anguish until she towers over the hero and conquers him." —*Newsweek*

Smith, Ali

The **accidental**. Ali Smith. Pantheon Books, 2006. 320 p.

ISBN 9780375422256

1. Strangers 2. Twelve-year-old girls 3. Teenage boys 4. Women biographers 5. College teachers 6. Norfolk, England 7. Psychological fiction 8. Domestic fiction 9. Adult books for young adults

LC 2005051031

Whitbread Book Award for Novel, 2005; Shortlisted for the Man Booker Prize, 2005; Shortlisted for The Orange Prize for Fiction, 2006; Shortlisted for the James Tait Black Memorial Prize for Fiction, 2005

Talking her way into the Norfolk cottage that the Smart family is renting for the summer, Amber, an enigmatic, lying con artist insinuates herself into the lives of Eve, her husband Michael, and their children, forcing them to reexamine the events of their lives through her perceptions and forever altering the world around them.

"Smith is a wonderful ventriloquist, adept at throwing her voice into an astonishing array of characters.... [She] can do suicidal teenage angst and middle-aged ennui, a 12-year-old's sardonic innocence and an aging Lothario's randy daydreams with equal aplomb. And in riffing on the stream of consciousness form, pioneered by such highbrow litterateurs as Joyce and Woolf, she manages to make it as accessible and up to the minute (if vastly more entertaining) as talk radio or an Internet chat room." —*New York Times*

★ **Autumn**. Ali Smith. Pantheon Books, 2017. 208 p. (Seasonal (Ali Smith), 1)
ISBN 9781101870730
1. Time 2. Aging 3. Intergenerational friendship 4. Interpersonal relations 5. Social change 6. Great Britain 7. Literary fiction 8. Psychological fiction
New York Times Notable Book, 2017; Shortlisted for the Man Booker Prize, 2017
A debut installment in a series about aging, time, love and the nature of stories examines the dynamics of pop culture, meditation and harvests in a world growing more bordered and exclusive.
"Smith's book is a kaleidoscope whose suggestive fragments and insights don't easily render a pleasing pattern, yet it's compelling in its emotional and historical freight, its humor, and keen sense of creativity and loss." —*Kirkus*
Originally published: London : Hamish Hamilton, 2016.

★ **How** to be both. Ali Smith. Pantheon Books, 2014. 384 p.
ISBN 9780375424106
1. Cossa, Francesco del 2. Art and society 3. Romantic love 4. Injustice 5. Painters 6. Teenage girls 7. Literary fiction 8. Parallel narratives
Baileys Women's Prize for Fiction, 2015; Costa Novel Award, 2014; New York Times Notable Book, 2015; Shortlisted for the Man Booker Prize, 2014
How to be both is a novel all about art's versatility. Borrowing from painting's fresco technique to make an original literary double-take, it's a fast-moving genre-bending conversation between forms, times, truths and fictions. Two tales of love and injustice twist into a singular yarn where time gets timeless, structural gets playful, knowing gets mysterious, fictional gets real—and all life's givens get given a second chance.
"The narratives are captivating, challenging, and often puzzling, as the prose varies among contemporary vernacular English, archaic 15th-century rhetoric interposed with fragments of poetry, and unpunctuated stream-of-consciousness narration.... Smith's two-in-one novel is a provocative reevaluation of the form." —*Publishers Weekly*
Originally published in UK (London: Hamish Hamilton, 2014).

★ **Spring**. Ali Smith. Pantheon Books, 2019. 339 pages; (Seasonal (Ali Smith), 3)
ISBN 9781101870778
1. Spring 2. Social change 3. Social values 4. Political values 5. Pretending 6. Great Britain 7. 2010s 8. Literary fiction 9. Psychological fiction
New York Times Notable Book, 2019
"Smith's work is always challenging and always rewarding." —*Kirkus*

★ **Summer**. Ali Smith. Pantheon Books, 2020. 304 p. (Seasonal (Ali Smith), 4)
ISBN 9781101870792
1. Brexit, 2016-2020 2. Epidemics 3. Social change 4. Immigration and emigration 5. Refugees 6. Great Britain 7. Literary fiction
Orwell Prize, 2021
A highly anticipated concluding entry in the best-selling series features a stand-alone story that is lightly connected to the events in Winter, Spring and the award-winning Autumn.

"A deeply resonant finale to a work that should come to be recognized as a classic." —*Kirkus*

There but for the: a novel. Ali Smith. Pantheon Books, 2011. 256 p.
ISBN 9780375424090
1. Houseguests 2. Social interaction 3. Identity (Psychology) 4. Middle-aged men 5. Personal space 6. England 7. Greenwich, England 8. Literary fiction
LC 2010051377
Hawthornden Prize, 2012; Shortlisted for the James Tait Black Memorial Prize for Fiction, 2011
When Miles Garth locks himself in an upstairs room during a dinner party and communicates only through notes slipped under the door, his involuntary hosts beg help from childhood friend Anna, who is unwittingly thrust into the family's surreal world.
"The novel is ostensibly about a dinner-party guest who locks himself in a spare bedroom and refuses to come out, inadvertently sparking a media frenzy. But the book—packed with jokes and random facts— is really about small stuff like life and death and the meaning of human existence, all told with sharp humor and real insight. The novel itself is a riddle with no solution, which is exactly the point: When you reluctantly come to the end, you can't help going back to the beginning, trying to unravel this beautifully elusive book's mysterious spell." —*Entertainment Weekly*

★ **Winter**. Ali Smith. Pantheon Books, 2018. 208 p. (Seasonal (Ali Smith), 2)
ISBN 9781101870754
1. Social change 2. Winter 3. Christmas 4. Memory 5. Sisters 6. Cornwall, England 7. Great Britain 8. 2010s 9. Literary fiction 10. Psychological fiction
Winter. Bleak. Frosty wind, earth as iron, water as stone, so the old song goes. And now Art's mother is seeing things. Come to think of it, Art's seeing things himself.

Smith, B. J.

All hat: a novel. Brad Smith. Henry Holt and Co, 2003. 308 p.
ISBN 9780805072174
1. Former convicts 2. Farms 3. Cowboys 4. Swindlers and swindling 5. Male friendship 6. Wright, Frank Lloyd 7. Canada 8. Caper novels 9. Crime fiction 10. Canadian fiction
LC 2002027307
Ex-convict Ray Dokes heads to the farm of his friend, Pete Culpepper, a Texas cowboy, and he eventually finds himself up against Sonny Stanton, the rich heir of a thoroughbred dynasty, after a ten-million-dollar thoroughbred goes missing. Stanton is also creating trouble by buying up large amounts of farmland, and threatening family farms.
"Set in rural Ontario and featuring an ensemble cast of delightfully eccentric, even downright loopy, characters, this big-hearted caper novel mixes laugh-out-loud-comedy with streaks of country noir that call to mind Daniel Woodrell." —*Booklist*

Crow's landing: a novel. Brad Smith. Scribner, 2012. 320 p. (Virgil Cain mysteries, 2)
ISBN 9781451678536
1. Police misconduct 2. Drug traffic 3. Evidence (Law) 4. Fishing 5. Ranchers 6. Mysteries 7. Black humor 8. Canadian fiction
LC 2012015809
Drawing the attention of a crooked city cop when he fishes up a mysterious steel cylinder linked to an old crime, Virgil Cain finds his boat and the cylinder confiscated and teams up with an attractive single mom to solve a case involving a cache of pure cocaine, a violent dealer and a wild Russian cowboy.

The **return** of Kid Cooper: a novel. Brad Smith. Arcade Publishing, 2018. 296 pages
ISBN 9781628728712
1. Former convicts 2. Cowboys 3. Personal conduct 4. Values 5. Innocence (Law) 6. Montana 7. 1910s 8. Westerns
LC 2017045572
Spur Awards, Best Western Traditional Novel, 2019
After spending thirty years in prison for a wrongful conviction, Nate Cooper returns to a changed Northern Montana where his search for justice stirs up controversy.

Shoot the dog: a Virgil Cain mystery. Brad Smith. Scribner, 2013. 320 p. (Virgil Cain mysteries, 3)
ISBN 9781439197561
1. Actors and actresses 2. Horses 3. Kidnapping 4. Horse farms 5. Detectives 6. New York (State) 7. Mysteries 8. Black humor 9. Canadian fiction
LC 2013017221
Finds Virgil Cain renting his draft horses to a film crew only to discover the director's irresponsible nature and a casino owner's agenda to replace the film's star, a situation that is further complicated by two murders.

Smith, Betty
★ A **tree** grows in Brooklyn. Betty Smith. Harper Collins Publishers, 2001. Xi, 493 p.
ISBN 9780060001940
1. Poor families 2. Children of immigrants 3. Children of alcoholic fathers 4. City life 5. Girls 6. Brooklyn, New York City 7. 1900s (Decade) 8. Roth, Philip 9. Literary fiction 10. Modern classics
LC 2001039509
A young girl in a shabby neighborhood lives with dreams in an innocent time before the war.
Originally published: New York : Harper, 1943.

Smith, Dodie
★ **I** capture the castle. Dodie Smith. St. Martin's Press, 1998. 343 p.
ISBN 9780312181109
1. Poor families 2. Eccentric families 3. Teenage girls 4. Man-woman relationships 5. Unrequited love 6. England 7. 1930s 8. Diary novels 9. Coming-of-age stories 10. Books to movies 11. Adult books for young adults
LC 9737231
The 1934 journal of seventeen-year-old Cassandra Mortmain reveals her perspective on six stormy months in the eccentric and poverty-stricken life of her family in a ruined Suffolk castle, ending with the revelation that Cassandra is deeply in love.
Originally published: Boston : Little, Brown, 1948.

Smith, Dominic
Bright and distant shores. Dominic Smith. Washington Square Press, 2011. 470 p.
ISBN 9781439198865
1. Collectors and collecting 2. Voyages and travels 3. Orphans 4. Ship captains 5. Ethnological museums 6. Chicago, Illinois 7. Oceania 8. Gilded Age (1865-1898) 9. Historical fiction 10. Literary fiction 11. Australian fiction
When a late-19th-century Chicago insurance magnate sponsors a South Seas expedition to collect various Melanesian artifacts, his schemes

ensnare two orphans including a recently engaged itinerant trader and a mission houseboy who longs to be reunited with his sister.
"Beautifully researched and ripe with symbolisman enthralling narrative peopled by characters both exotic and real." —*Kirkus*
Originally published: Crows Nest, N.S.W. : Allen & Unwin, 2011.

★ The **electric** hotel. Dominic Smith. Sarah Crichton Books, Farrar, Straus and Giroux, 2019. 400 p.
ISBN 9780374146856
1. Cinematographers 2. Films — History 3. Silent films 4. Film industry and trade 5. Reminiscing in old age 6. Hollywood, California 7. 1960s 8. Historical fiction 9. Parallel narratives 10. Australian fiction
LC 2018045335
A French pioneer of silent films who has lived for half a century in a Hollywood hotel is forced to reckon with the reappearance of the lost movie masterpiece that left him bankrupt.

★ The **last** painting of Sara De Vos. Dominic Smith. Sarah Crichton Books, 2016. 288 p.
ISBN 9780374106683
1. Baalbergen, Sarah van 2. Women artists 3. Painting, Dutch 4. Art forgeries 5. Art historians 6. Art forgers 7. Netherlands 8. Brooklyn, New York City 9. 1950s 10. 17th century 11. Biographical fiction 12. Historical fiction 13. Parallel narratives
Australian Book Industry Awards, Literary Fiction Book of the Year, 2017; Longlisted for the Walter Scott Prize for Historical Fiction, 2017
Parallel narratives unfold and eventually converge in this multi-layered novel, which explores the legacy of fictional 17th-century Dutch painter Sara de Vos. The artist's masterpiece, At the Edge of a Wood, is stolen from Manhattan attorney Marty de Groot's Upper East Side residence in 1957 and replaced with a skillfully executed forgery that remains a secret for decades—until museum curator Ellie Shipley, who created the fake, is confronted by the two versions of the painting. Don't miss this richly detailed and complex meditation on art and identity by the author of Bright and Distant Shores.
"Rich in historical detail, the novel explores the immense challenges faced by women in the arts (past and present), provides a glimpse into the seedy underbelly of the art world across the centuries, and illustrates the transformative power and influence of great art." —*Booklist*

Smith, Gregory Blake
★ The **maze** at Windermere: a novel. Gregory Blake Smith. Viking, 2018. 352 p.
ISBN 9780735221925
1. James, Henry 2. Cities and towns 3. Social classes 4. Personal conduct 5. Ambition 6. Self-fulfillment 7. Newport, Rhode Island 8. Rhode Island 9. 17th century 10. 18th century 11. Literary fiction 12. Parallel narratives 13. Historical fiction
LC 2017025390
A reckless, high-stakes wager between a fading tennis pro and a drunken party guest launches a narrative odyssey that brings three centuries of ambition and adversity full circle.
"Taken individually, each story is dramatic and captivating, but as the author makes ever-increasing connections among the stories and shuffles them all into one unbroken narrative, the novel becomes a moving meditation on love, race, class, and self-fulfillment in America across the centuries." —*Publishers Weekly*

Smith, Ian
The **unspoken**. Ian K. Smith. Thomas & Mercer, 2020. 287 p. (Ashe Cayne novels, 1)

ISBN 9781542025270

1. Former detectives 2. Private investigators 3. Missing women 4. Rich families 5. Boyfriends 6. Chicago, Illinois 7. Thrillers and suspense 8. African American fiction

Fired for refusing to cooperate in a police cover-up, Chicago detective-turned-private investigator Ashe Cayne searches for a missing woman who has been hiding dangerous secrets from her wealthy family.

"This fine series launch from bestseller Smith (The Ancient Nine) introduces PI Ashe Cayne, a former Chicago PD detective who has the luxury of being able to pick his cases selectively thanks to a large settlement he won from the city for wrongfully terminating him after he refused to participate in a department cover-up." —*Publishers Weekly*

Wolf Point. Ian K. Smith. Thomas & Mercer, 2021. 348 pages (Ashe Cayne novels, 2)

ISBN 9781542027861

1. Private investigators 2. African Americans 3. Corruption 4. Race relations 5. Suicide investigation 6. Chicago, Illinois 7. Hardboiled fiction 8. Mysteries 9. African American fiction

When Walter Griffin, a prominent Black Chicagoan insider, is found in a watery grave at Wolf Point, his death ruled a suicide, PI Ashe Cayne investigates on behalf of Griffin's children and navigates a city rotting with corruption, racial tensions and sketchy backroom deals where it's every man for himself.

"Smith's love of Chicago is palpable in his rich depictions of its diversity, vitality, and unique pockets.... A brisk and twisty whodunit with a motley cast that includes the city of big shoulders." —*Kirkus*

Smith, Jill Eileen

Star of Persia: Esther's story. Jill Eileen Smith. Revell, 2020. 368 pages

ISBN 9780800734718

1. Esther 2. Women rulers 3. Jewish women 4. Courage in women 5. Faith 6. Women in the Old Testament 7. Persian Empire 8. Christian fiction 9. Bible novels

Esther is poised to save her people from annihilation. Relying on a fragile trust in a silent God, can she pit her wisdom against a vicious enemy and win?

"Smith's latest will be of great interest to fans of historical fiction, especially those interested in biblical times, as well as readers who enjoy new perspectives on women figures of the past." —*Booklist*

Smith, Julie

82 Desire: a Skip Langdon novel. Julie Smith. Fawcett Columbine, 1998. 309 p; (Skip Langdon mysteries, 8)

ISBN 9780449000601

1. Missing persons investigation 2. Murder 3. Revenge 4. Langdon, Skip (Fictitious character) 5. Police 6. New Orleans, Louisiana 7. Mysteries 8. Southern fiction

LC 98022259

Police Detective Skip Langdon investigates the disappearance of a New Orleans councilwoman's husband BT

"Russell Fortier, a prominent businessman, has vanished. His wife asks Langdon, a New Orleans detective, to look into his disappearance. Later, a private detective who was investigating Fortier turns up dead, and one of his employees, a poet and freelance computer expert, wants to know how Fortier's disappearance is connected with the murder.... The novel is intricately constructed, and while Smith keeps nothing important

unfairly hidden from her readers, she manages to spring some nice little surprises." —*Booklist*

Introduces Talba Wallis (aka Baroness Pontalba) who is featured in Smith's Baroness Pontalba novels.

Crescent City kill: a Skip Langdon novel. Julie Smith. Fawcett Columbine, 1997. 326 p. (Skip Langdon mysteries, 7)

ISBN 9780804112734

1. Vigilantes 2. Swindlers and swindling 3. Murder investigation 4. Assassination 5. Langdon, Skip (Fictitious character) 6. New Orleans, Louisiana 7. Mysteries 8. Southern fiction

LC 9722099

"The New Orleans ambiance is less pronounced than in most Skip Langdon mysteries, but Smith's colorful characterizations and the showdown with Jacomine make this an excellent addition to the series." —*Publishers Weekly*

House of blues. Julie Smith. Fawcett Columbine 1995. 343 p. (Skip Langdon mysteries, 5)

ISBN 9780449909362

1. Missing persons 2. Murder investigation 3. Restaurateurs 4. Langdon, Skip (Fictitious character) 5. Policewomen 6. New Orleans, Louisiana 7. Mysteries 8. Southern fiction

LC 9448823

Finding local pressures rising when a crime wave peaks with the murder of a prominent restauranteur, New Orleans homicide detective Skip Langdon begins a detailed search for the killer, as well as for the victim's missing heirs BT

"Arthur Hebert, a prominent restaurateur and domineering patriarch hated by his children, doesn't attend the opening of his restaurant in New Orleans' first casino—because he's been gunned down at home while enjoying his usual Monday evening meal of red beans and rice. Hebert's daughter, his son-in-law and his baby granddaughter have vanished. In the race to find the killer and the missing family, Skip calls on the denizens of the New Orleans underworld.... Smith carries off a tricky balancing act, rendering Skip heroic while imbuing her with a credibly textured emotional life. But the real star of this superb effort is New Orleans, which has never seemed more dangerous or alluring." —*Publishers Weekly*

Jazz funeral. Julie Smith. Fawcett Columbine, 1993. 365p. (Skip Langdon mysteries, 3)

ISBN 9780449907429

1. Runaways 2. Street musicians 3. Murder investigation 4. Langdon, Skip (Fictitious character) 5. Policewomen 6. New Orleans, Louisiana 7. Mysteries 8. Southern fiction

LC 92054997

Policewoman Skip Langdon is drawn to the New Orleans Jazz Festival in her search for the cold-blooded murderer of a music producer.

The **kindness** of strangers: a Skip Langdon novel. Julie Smith. Fawcett Columbine, 1996. 338 p. (Skip Langdon mysteries, 6)

ISBN 9780449909379

1. Mayoral candidates 2. Political corruption 3. Campaigning 4. Langdon, Skip (Fictitious character) 5. Women detectives 6. New Orleans, Louisiana 7. Mysteries 8. Southern fiction

LC 95-52460

Traces Police Detective Skep Langdon's ongoing struggle to expose Errol Jacomine, a candidate for mayor of New Orleans with a reputation for civic spirit, as a psychopath BT

"Langdon takes on the Big Easy's corrupt political machine, as three 'pick the best of the worst' candidates line up for the mayoral race. New Orleans voters, tired of years of corruption and scandal, are leaning toward Errol Jacomine, a Christian right-winger who appears to have the right stuff. But Skip senses evil lurking behind Jacomine's jovial facade, and she figures to discredit him before he gains control of the city.... Smith serves up a gritty, gripping story along with a big helping of action and a pinch of humor." —*Booklist*

Louisiana hotshot. Julie Smith. Forge, 2001. 335 p; (Baroness Pontalba novels, 1)
ISBN 9780765300584
1. Crimes against teenage girls 2. Family relationships 3. Rape 4. Women private investigators 5. African American women 6. New Orleans, Louisiana 7. Mysteries 8. Southern fiction
LC 2001018958
Talba Wallis—African American poet, leader of New Orleans' café society, and fledgling private detective—is hired by veteran sleuth Eddie Valentino to find a dangerous lothario who seduces teenage black girls who then mysteriously vanish.
"A mystery set in New Orleans featuring Talba Wallis (aka Baroness de Pontalba), the black poet/computer expert and would-be investigator.... Answering an unlikely ad with her customary bravado lands her a job as assistant to aging PI Eddie Valentino. The young black female and 65-year-old Italian male have striking similarities that offset their obvious differences. Both are stubborn and strongly attached to, if somewhat alienated from, their families. Throw in a vulnerable young girl, Cassandra, being preyed on by a rap star's hanger-on identified only by the nickname 'Toes,' and you have a story that spans generations, races and lifestyles." —*Publishers Weekly*
Sequel: Louisiana bigshot.
Talba Wallis (aka Baroness Pontalba) is first introduced in Smith's 82 Desire.

★ **Mean** woman blues. Julie Smith. Forge, 2003. 304 p; (Skip Langdon mysteries, 9)
ISBN 9780765305527
1. Evangelists 2. Politicians 3. Attempted murder 4. Television talk show hosts and guests 5. Murder 6. New Orleans, Louisiana 7. Mysteries 8. Southern fiction
LC 2003040018
Having chased corrupt evangelist and dangerous presidential hopeful Errol Jacomine for years, New Orleans detective Skip Langdon finds her loved ones targeted and realizes that Jacomine is so carefully disguised that nobody recognizes him.
"The Formosan termites that infest new Orleans every May haunt police detective Skip Langdon's dreams, an apt image for the gnawing fear that her happiness will collapse. That happiness is based on the fact that her long distance lover, a documentary filmmaker, has moved to New Orleans. Her fear is that her enemy, an evangelical fanatic who aspires to the mind control of Jim Jones, is coming back to kill her, after a disappearance of two years." —*Booklist*
A Tom Doherty Associates book.

New Orleans beat. Julie Smith. Fawcett Columbine 1994. 359 p. (Skip Langdon mysteries, 4)
ISBN 9780449907436
1. Electronic bulletin boards 2. Murder investigation 3. Murder witnesses 4. Langdon, Skip (Fictitious character) 5. Women detectives 6. New Orleans, Louisiana 7. Mysteries 8. Southern fiction
LC 93046506
Detective Skip Langdon believes that TOWN, a computer bulletin board community, holds the key to the "accidental" death of Geoff, a computer genius BT
"Smith is a skilled writer who can evoke the steamy, mysterious ambience of New Orleans while simultaneously proving that computer jargon can be comprehensible even to the 'computer-challenged.' This is a humorous, suspenseful mystery." —*Booklist*

Smith, Lee

★ **Fair** and tender ladies. Lee Smith. G. P. Putnam's Sons, 1988. 316 p.
ISBN 9780399133824
1. Mountain life 2. Family secrets 3. Death 4. Mothers and daughters 5. Sisters 6. Virginia 7. Epistolary novels 8. Southern fiction
LC 88010915
Sir Walter Raleigh Award for Fiction, 1989
A series of letters, written to family and friends, reveals the life and times of Ivy Rowe, as she grows from girlhood to old age, finds love, dreams great visions, and raises a family, in an evocative portrait of Appalachia.
"An exquisite novel.... Through Ivy's curiously spelled and situated letters, we see the growth not only of her own family, but also of wider Appalachia." —*Christian Science Monitor*
Includes bibliographical references.

Family linen. Lee Smith. G. P. Putnam's Sons 1985. 272 p.
ISBN 9780399130809
1. Families 2. Small town life 3. Mother and adult child 4. Siblings 5. Death 6. Virginia 7. Mysteries 8. Southern fiction
LC 85003664
Gathered at Miss Elizabeth's deathbed, the whole Hesse family learns unexpected secrets about Elizabeth and each other BT
"This is a companionable, chatty book populated by people who tell us about themselves in a rambling style and with good humor." —*New York Times Book Review*

On Agate Hill: a novel. Lee Smith. Algonquin Books of Chapel Hill, 2006. 416 p.
ISBN 9781565124523
1. Orphans 2. Plantation life 3. Plantations 4. Uncles 5. Widows 6. North Carolina 7. Southern States 8. 19th century 9. 1860s 10. Coming-of-age stories 11. Historical fiction 12. Southern fiction
LC 2006045859
"Molly is like a grown-up, Southern version of Louisa May Alcott's Jo, only she is thrown into circumstances that test her essentially wholesome nature. For the most part, she battles back not with sass—which modern novels seem to think is universally charming—but pluck. As this is Smith's first historical novel, she deserves credit for understanding this subtle, but essential period point." —*Denver Post*
A Shannon Ravenel book.

Oral history. Lee Smith. G. P. Putnam's Sons, 1983. 286p.
ISBN 9780399127946
1. Oral histories 2. Rural life 3. Mountain life 4. Family relationships 5. Interpersonal relations 6. Virginia 7. Family sagas 8. Southern fiction
LC 82018081
Sir Walter Raleigh Award for Fiction, 1983
"Smith is excellent at making the separate voices distinctive.... Serious fiction readers will be interested in Smith's techniques and will appreciate her decision to utilize this 'oral history' format to best achieve her intentions." —*Booklist*

Smith, Mark Haskell

Baked. Mark Haskell Smith. Grove Press, Black Cat, 2010. 288 p.
ISBN 9780802170767
1. Botanists 2. Marijuana 3. Gunshot victims 4. Inventions 5. Quests 6. Los Angeles, California 7. Crime fiction
Miro Basinas is an experimental botanist who sells his rarefied product to a discerning clientele. Only Miro's not growing heirloom tomatoes or making organic wine—he's growing weed. And when Miro hits the big time by winning Amsterdam's famed Cannabis Cup, cannasseurs and

ganjaficionados aren't the only people who want a piece of him and his mind-blowing pot that tastes like mangoes.

"As cockeyed and riotous as Carl Hiaasen on really good dope." —*Kirkus*

Smith, Martin Cruz

December 6. Martin Cruz Smith. Simon & Schuster, 2002. 352 p. ISBN 9780684872537

1. Pearl Harbor, Attack on, 1941 2. World War II 3. Americans in Japan 4. Swindlers and swindling 5. Pearl Harbor, Hawaii 6. Tokyo, Japan 7. Second World War era (1939-1945) 8. 1940s 9. Historical thrillers 10. Adult books for young adults

New York Times Notable Book, 2002

Harry Niles, a disreputable American businessman with an unknown agenda, seeks to abandon his life in Tokyo while fleeing to the west on the last flight out before the Pearl Harbor attack.

"Smith's plot is more than slightly reminiscent of Casablanca and the spectre of the Second World War seems, at this distance, almost quaint, but the characters are so well drawn and the local color so colorful that these quibbles hardly interfer with the novel's pleasures." —*The New Yorker*

★ **Gorky** Park. Martin Cruz Smith. Random House, 1981. 365 p. (Arkady Renko novels, 1)

ISBN 9780394517483

1. Detectives 2. Murder 3. Government cover-ups 4. FBI agents 5. KGB agents 6. Moscow, Russia 7. Thrillers and suspense 8. Books to movies 9. Police procedurals

LC 80006022

Gold Dagger Award for Best Crime Novel of the Year, 1981

In contemporary Moscow, Chief Homicide Investigator Arkady Renko unravels the mystery of a triple murder complicated by the shadowy and uncooperative presence of the KGB and by his falling in love.

"The author has succeeded in rendering very believable, realistic, and gripping portrayals of certain segments of Soviet society and of one man's search for meaning." —*Christian Science Monitor*

Havana Bay. Martin Cruz Smith. Random House, 1999. 329 p. (Arkady Renko novels, 4)

ISBN 9780679426622

1. International intrigue 2. Detectives 3. Murder investigation 4. Murder 5. Renko, Arkady (Fictitious character) 6. Havana, Cuba 7. Thrillers and suspense 8. Police procedurals

New York Times Notable Book, 1999

When the body of a Russian embassy official turns up floating in Havana Bay, detective Arkady Renko is sent to Cuba to identify it, only to find himself caught up in a dangerous conspiracy that will do anything to seize control of Cuba.

"His earnest unsentimentality and calm tenaciousness on the hunt are what make Renko one of the most interesting detectives in modern fiction. What a clever stroke for Smith to dispatch him to Havana, where sentimentality and passion are in rare abundance." —*New York Times Book Review*

Polar Star. Martin Cruz Smith. Random House, 1989. 386 p. (Arkady Renko novels, 2)

ISBN 9780394578194

1. Detectives 2. International intrigue 3. Murder 4. Murder investigation 5. Food processing plants 6. Soviet Union 7. Thrillers and suspense 8. Police procedurals

LC 88043232

Former Moscow Police Inspector Arkady Renko escapes from a psychiatric "hospital" to Siberia, where he becomes embroiled in an investigation into the death of a female crew member of a fish-processing ship.

"Rich in humor, generous in spirit, endlessly entertaining and deeply serious, 'Polar Star' is not merely the work of our best writer of suspense, but of one of our best writers, period." —*New York Times Book Review*

Rose. Martin Cruz Smith. Random House, 1996. 364 p. ISBN 9780679426615

1. Coal mine accidents 2. Coal miners 3. Man-woman relationships 4. Mining engineers 5. Missing persons 6. England 7. Lancashire, England 8. 1870s 9. 19th century 10. Historical fiction

LC 95037914

In 1872, Jonathan Blair wants only to return to Africa, but his employer demands that he go to Lancashire to find out about a missing minister, which leads to information on a recent mining disaster.

"Rose has everthing a compelling novel needs: Blair is a fascinating protagonist, by turns a hero and a boor; other significant characters are complex and as multifaceted as a chunk of coal; the mystery is gripping. But it is the horrific, mesmerizing portrayal of the dark, hellish Wigan, the mines themselves, and the lives of miners that makes this novel much more than a good read." —*Booklist*

The **Siberian** dilemma. Martin Cruz Smith. Simon & Schuster, 2019. 288 pages (Arkady Renko novels, 9)

ISBN 9781439140253

1. Detectives 2. Women journalists 3. Undercover operations 4. Missing women 5. Missing persons investigation 6. Moscow, Russia 7. Thrillers and suspense 8. Police procedurals

When his lover fails to return from a deep-cover assignment, Moscow investigator Arkady Renko embarks on a dangerous journey involving the rise of a political dissident who threatens Putin's rule.

"This is Smith at his absolute best: black humor, brown bears, and gray souls." —*Booklist*

Stalin's ghost. Martin Cruz Smith. Simon & Schuster, 2007. 352 p. (Arkady Renko novels, 6)

ISBN 9780743276726

1. Detectives 2. Police corruption 3. Murder investigation 4. Renko, Arkady (Fictitious character) 5. Police 6. Moscow, Russia 7. Thrillers and suspense 8. Police procedurals

A high-stakes tale set in Moscow follows the machinations of a group of reactionaries who harbor a nostalgic loyalty to the regime of Joseph Stalin and who plot to create a groundswell for a new dictatorship.

"Every page reeks of Moscow: dirty snow, the stink of cigarette and vodka fumes, the cynicism and tasteless opulence of the mafia, the all-pervasive corruption.... Like the Red Army facing the Nazis, Renko refuses to give up, surrendering neither his investigation nor those he loves. In this subtle, moving book, he is an everyman, whose loyalty and courage speak to all of us." —*The Economist*

Stallion Gate. Martin Cruz Smith. Random House 1986. 321 p. ISBN 9780394530062

1. Oppenheimer, J. Robert 2. Native American soldiers 3. Atomic bomb — Testing 4. Interracial romance 5. Jewish American women 6. Women mathematicians 7. New Mexico 8. Los Alamos, New Mexico 9. Historical mysteries

LC 85024444

Dr. Robert Oppenheimer; General Groves, the director of the Manhattan project; Klaus Fuchs, a German-born British scientist; and Sergeant Joe Pena, a Pueblo Indian, figure in this imagined account of the creation of the first atomic bomb.

"Obviously Stallion Gate is not meant to be taken too literally. There is a touch of the folk hero about Pea as he moves across the New Mexican landscape. A conscious stylist, Smith relies strongly on emotional echoes and calibrated suspense." —*Time*

★ **Tatiana:** an Arkady Renko novel. Martin Cruz Smith. Simon & Schuster, 2013. 304 p. (Arkady Renko novels, 8)
ISBN 9781439140215
1. Government cover-ups 2. Detectives 3. Organized crime 4. Police 5. Women journalists 6. Moscow, Russia 7. Thrillers and suspense 8. Police procedurals
LC 2013026426
When investigative reporter Tatiana Petrovna falls to her death from a sixth-floor window in Moscow the same week that a mob billionaire is shot and buried, investigator Arkady Renko connects the two cases, which leads him to a Cold War secret city and a teenage chess hustler to find the truth.
Includes bibliographical references and index.

Three stations: an Arkady Renko novel. Martin Cruz Smith. Simon & Schuster, 2010. 352 p. (Arkady Renko novels, 7)
ISBN 9780743276740
1. Detectives 2. Police corruption 3. Murder investigation 4. Renko, Arkady (Fictitious character) 5. Police 6. Moscow, Russia 7. Thrillers and suspense 8. Police procedurals
LC Bl2010001966
Struggling with a prosecutor's refusal to send work his way, investigator Arkady Renko of Moscow finds his efforts to watch out for teen chess prodigy Zhenya challenged by a case involving a kidnapped baby, a dead prostitute, and police corruption.
The main investigation underpinning Three Stations doesn't carry the full force of past adventures.... The denouement, in particular, feels rushed and half-hearted. Smith does, however, nail the key to the structure of a detective novel, when Renko thinks there was still time for [him] to walk away from a case he did not fathom and a woman he did not understand. One can trace that very essence back to Hammett and Chandler, who imbued their respective gumshoes with dogged determination no matter what price they paid later. So too must Arkady, who is doomed to repeat this existential cycle in book after book? Los Angeles Times Book Review.

Wolves eat dogs: a novel. Martin Cruz Smith. Simon & Schuster, 2004. 352 p. (Arkady Renko novels, 5)
ISBN 9780684872544
1. Detectives 2. Radiation victims 3. Nuclear accidents 4. Renko, Arkady (Fictitious character) 5. Police 6. Ukraine 7. Moscow, Russia 8. Thrillers and suspense 9. Police procedurals
LC 2004052585
In the wake of a businessman's suicide, Moscow detective Arkady Renko investigates secrets and international plots that may have driven him to his death, in a case that leads Renko to discover crimes in the area surrounding Chernobyl.
"Senior Investigator Arkady Renko must determine whether the defenestration death of a Russian tycoon was suicide or murder. The discovery of radioactive salt in the dead man's apartment leads Renko to the abandoned Ukrainian towns of Chernobyl and Pripyat, still dangerously contaminated 18 years after the world's deadliest nuclear accident. There he finds a ghostly world inhabited by scavengers, elderly villagers, and a small group of Russian militia and scientists. As Renko pursues his investigation, he uncovers a greater crime, the sad legacy of Soviet ineptitude and corruption." —*Library Journal*

Smith, Michael F.
Blackwood. Michael Farris Smith. Little, Brown and Co, 2020. 293 p.
ISBN 9780316529815

1. Homecomings 2. Family history 3. Artists 4. Rural life 5. Small towns 6. Mississippi 7. 1970s 8. Southern gothic 9. Southern fiction
LC 2019946516
In this timeless, mythical tale of unforgiving justice and elusive grace, rural Mississippi townsfolk shoulder the pain of generations as something dangerous lurks in the enigmatic kudzu of the woods.
"Smith's meditation on the darkness of the human heart offers a moving update to the Southern gothic tradition." —*Publishers Weekly*

The **fighter:** a novel. Michael Farris Smith. Little Brown & Co, 2018. 243 p.
ISBN 9780316432344
1. Foster mothers 2. Middle-aged men 3. Bare knuckle boxing 4. Circus performers 5. Boxers (Sports) 6. Mississippi 7. Delta Region, Mississippi 8. Southern gothic 9. Literary fiction 10. Southern fiction
His mind failing from the effects of decades of bare-knuckle fighting, his foster mother's family legacy in the hands of strangers, and overwhelmed with gambling debts, Jack's only chance at redemption is to step into the fighting pit one last time.

Smith, Scott
The **ruins:** a novel. Scott Smith. Alfred A. Knopf, 2006. 336 p.
ISBN 9781400043873
1. Tourists 2. Jungle survival 3. Mayas 4. Jungles 5. Americans in Mexico 6. Cancun, Mexico 7. Horror 8. Holliday, John H. 9. Adult books for young adults
LC 2005057782
Best friends Amy and Stacy (and their boyfriends Jeff and Eric) travel to Cancun, Mexico for a summer they'll never forget. On arrival, the Americans meet German tourist Mathias, whose brother Heinrich is missing. Last seen heading into the jungle with a beautiful woman to join an archaeological expedition to some Mayan ruins, Heinrich hasn't been heard from since...although he did leave behind a crudely drawn map.

A **simple** plan: a novel. Scott Smith. Knopf, 1993. 335 p.
ISBN 9780679419853
1. Airplane accidents 2. Money 3. Greed in men 4. Fathers 5. Brothers 6. Ohio 7. Thrillers and suspense 8. Books to movies 9. First person narratives 10. Adult books for young adults
LC 92042478
When a young man finds a suitcase with a million dollars in cash, his life is changed forever.
"This novel is so cunningly imagined that for the most part Mr. Smith drags us willingly through what in less deft hands could be a morally repugnant story." —*New York Times Book Review*

Smith, Tom Rob
Agent 6. Tom Rob Smith. Grand Central Pub, 2012. 448 p. (Leo Demidov thrillers, 3)
ISBN 9780446550765
1. Former spies 2. Conspiracies 3. Secret service 4. Daughters — Death 5. Communism 6. New York City 7. Soviet Union 8. 1950s 9. Historical thrillers
Former secret police agent Leo Demidov is thrown into a foreign conflict and is forced to question and confront everything he ever thought he knew about his country, his family, and himself.

Child 44. Tom Rob Smith. Grand Central Pub, 2008. 439 p. (Leo Demidov thrillers, 1)
ISBN 9780446402385

1. Secret service 2. Serial murder investigation 3. Political crimes and offenses 4. Police 5. Serial murderers 6. Soviet Union 7. 1950s 8. Historical thrillers 9. Books to movies

LC 2007028272

Ian Fleming Steel Dagger Award, 2008; Thriller Award for Best First Novel, 2009

Rising Soviet state security force officer Leo Demidov encounters the test of his career when a serial killer challenges his beliefs about the paradise of the working world, resulting in his demotion and threats against the lives of his family members.

"Smith captures the rhythm of day-today paranoia in Stalinist Russia and the ways that personal jealousies can balloon into ruthless vendettas. It's hard to fathom which is more grisly, the descriptions of the serial murders or the scenes of torture perpetrated by Leo's colleagues in the MGB. Throughout, Smith's prose is propulsive but plain; his real genius is his careful plotting." —*Entertainment Weekly*

Sequel : The secret speech.

The **secret** speech. Tom Rob Smith. Grand Central Pub, 2009. 416 p. (Leo Demidov thrillers, 2)

ISBN 9780446402408

1. Secret service 2. Political oratory 3. Revenge 4. Murder 5. Political crimes and offenses 6. Soviet Union 7. 1950s 8. Historical thrillers

LC 2008048329

Honored as a hero for his role in stopping a serial killer three years earlier, post-Stalinist Soviet Union MGB officer Leo Demidov is placed at the head of a newly formed Moscow homicide department and is forced to undertake a personal mission in the criminal underworld when dark elements from his past catch up with him.

"Based on real events, The Secret Speech is jam-packed with action—the near-sinking of a prison ship, a violent takeover at a Kolyma gulag, and a rebellion in Hungary—and Smith explores pertinent questions of revenge, morality and responsibility." —*PopMatters*

Sequel to: : Child 44.

Smith, Wilbur A.

Birds of prey. Wilbur A. Smith. St. Martin's Press, 1997. 554 p. (Courtney novels, 9)

ISBN 9780312157913

1. Fathers — Death 2. Betrayal 3. Revenge 4. Deception 5. Fathers and sons 6. Indian Ocean 7. 17th century 8. Adventure stories 9. Historical fiction 10. Sea stories

LC 978192

1667, Sir Francis Courteney and his son Hal are on patrol in their fighting caravel off the Agulhas Cape of South Africa. They are lying in wait there for one of the treasure-laden galleons of the Dutch East India Company returning from the Orient. So begins a quest for adventure and the spoils of war. They are swept from the settlement of Good Hope at the southern tip of Africa to the Great Horn of Ethiopia far to the north at a time when international maritime law permitted acts of piracy, rape, and murder otherwise punishable by death. In this book the author presents a generation of the indomitable Courteney's and thrillingly recreates their part in the struggle for supremacy and riches on the high seas.

"Smith's depiction of the African coast, and of life aboard ship, is vivid and believable. He handles the action sequences well, opting for short, trenchant paragraphs to sustain momentum.... Smith knows what his readers want, and once again he delivers the goods." —*Publishers Weekly*

Monsoon. Wilbur A. Smith. St. Martin's Press, 1999. 613 p. (Courtney novels, 10)

ISBN 9780312203399

1. Sibling rivalry 2. Kidnapping 3. Courtney family (Fictitious characters) 4. Fathers and sons 5. Sailors 6. Africa 7. 18th century 8. Sea stories 9. Adventure stories 10. Historical fiction

LC 9924554

"This sequel to Birds of Prey finds Sir Hal Courtney and his sons up to their bloody sword arms in piracy, intrigue, treachery and civil war in late 17th and early 18th century East Africa and Arabia.... Clever plot twists and lavish historical detail attend the siblings' adventures." —*Publishers Weekly*

Smith, Zadie

The **autograph** man: a novel. Zadie Smith. Random House, 2002.

ISBN 9780375501869

1. Jewish men — Identity 2. Ethnicity 3. Autographs — Collectors and collecting 4. Friendship 5. Misadventures 6. London, England 7. Picaresque fiction

LC 2002069705

New York Times Notable Book, 2002; Shortlisted for The Orange Prize for Fiction, 2003

Alex-Li Tandem is a 27-year-old, half-Jewish, half-Chinese man in search of himself. In his own words, he has "no love, no transportation, no ambitions, no faith," and not much else. An autograph peddler, he hunts down the signatures people want and sells them.

"Smith's pen portraits of the shabby, yobbish autograph trading circle are intermittently funny, but her prose is so busy being clever that the laughter never builds. This is disappointing but, even with its faults, the novel points to a literary talent of a high order." —*Publishers Weekly*

Originally published: London: Hamish Hamilton, 2002.

★ **Grand** union: stories. Zadie Smith. Penguin Press, 2019. 256 pages
ISBN 9780525558996

1. Identity (Psychology) 2. Legacies 3. Interpersonal relations 4. Short stories 5. Literary fiction

Loan Stars Favourites, 2019; New York Times Notable Book, 2019

The award-winning author of White Teeth presents a first collection of 10 original short stories and selections from her most-lauded pieces as first published in The New Yorker and other prestigious literary magazines.

★ **NW**: a novel. Zadie Smith. Penguin Press, 2012. 320 p.
ISBN 9781594203978

1. Young adults 2. Planned communities 3. Social isolation 4. City life 5. Adulthood 6. London, England 7. Literary fiction 8. Coming-of-age stories 9. Psychological fiction

LC 2012015114

New York Times Notable Book, 2012; Library Journal Best Books, 2012; National Book Critics Circle Award for Fiction finalist, 2012; Shortlisted for The Women's Prize for Fiction, 2013

Growing up in the same 1970s urban planning development in Northwest London, four young people pursue independent and reasonably successful lives until one of them is abruptly drawn out of her isolation by a stranger who is seeking her help.

On beauty. Zadie Smith. Penguin Press, 2005. 320 p.
ISBN 9781594200632

1. Rembrandt Harmenszoon van Rijn 2. Extramarital affairs 3. Family relationships 4. Ethnic identity 5. Interracial families 6. College teachers 7. Massachusetts 8. New England 9. Domestic fiction 10. Literary fiction 11. Adult books for young adults

Commonwealth Writers' Prize, South Asia and Europe: Best Book, 2006; Library Journal Best Books, 2005; New York Times Notable Book, 2005; Orange Prize for Fiction, 2006; Somerset Maugham Award, 2006; Shortlisted for the Man Booker Prize, 2005

Howard Belsey, a Rembrandt scholar who doesn't like Rembrandt, is an Englishman abroad and a long-suffering Professor at Wellington College. He has been married for thirty years to Kiki, an American woman who no longer resembles the sexy activist she once was. Their three children passionately pursue their own paths, and faced with the oppressive enthusiasms of his children, Howard feels that the first two acts of his life are over and he has no clear plans for the finale. Then Jerome, Howard's oldest son, falls for Victoria, the stunning daughter of the right-wing icon Monty Kipps. Increasingly, the two families find themselves thrown together in a beautiful corner of America, enacting a cultural and personal war against the background of real wars that they barely register.

"Ms Smith has her shortcomings. The novel's first half is under-edited; surely we do not need to meet every guest at an anniversary party.... Nevertheless, the book gathers momentum, and the second half gallops along." —*The Economist*

Includes author's note.

Originally published: London: Hamish Hamilton, 2005.

★ **Swing** time. Zadie Smith. Penguin Press, 2016. 416 p.
ISBN 9781594203985
1. Female friendship 2. Dancing 3. Multiracial women 4. Competition 5. Race relations 6. London, England 7. West Africa 8. Literary fiction 9. First person narratives
Booklist Editors' Choice, 2016; LibraryReads Favorites, 2016; New York Times Notable Book, 2016; Andrew Carnegie Medal for Excellence in Fiction Finalist, 2017; National Book Critics Circle Award for Fiction finalist, 2016; Longlisted for the Man Booker Prize, 2017

Two dark-skinned dancers with very different talents share a complicated childhood friendship that ends abruptly in early adulthood in a story that transitions from northwest London to West Africa.

"Moving, funny, and grave, this novel parses race and global politics with Fred Astaire's or Michael Jackson's grace." —*Kirkus*

★ **White** teeth: a novel. Zadie Smith. Random House, 2000. 448 p.
ISBN 9780375501852
1. Immigrants 2. Interracial friendship 3. Families 4. Muslim families 5. Gender role 6. London, England 7. Great Britain 8. 1970s 9. Satirical fiction 10. Literary fiction
LC 99043658
ALA Notable Book, 2001; Betty Trask Award, 2001; Commonwealth Writers' Prize for Best First Book, 2001; Commonwealth Writers' Prize, South Asia and Europe: Best First Book, 2001; Guardian First Book Award, 2000; James Tait Black Memorial Prize for Fiction, 2000; Library Journal Best Books, 2000; Whitbread Book Award for First Novel, 2000; Shortlisted for The Orange Prize for Fiction, 2000; National Book Critics Circle Award for Fiction finalist, 2000

White Teeth is a comic epic of multicultural Britain by one of the most exciting young writers of 2000. It tells the story of immigrants in England over a period of 40 years.

"Hopscotching through several continents and 150 years of history, White Teeth encompasses a teeming family saga, a sly inquiry into race and identity and a tender-hearted satire on religious antagonism and cultural bemusement.... Smith holds it all together with a raucous energy and confidence." —*New York Times Book Review*

Snipes, Wesley
Talon of God. Wesley Snipes with Ray Norman. Harper Voyager, 2017. 368 p.
ISBN 9780062668165
1. Demons 2. Good and evil 3. Warriors 4. Physicians 5. Demonic possession 6. Chicago, Illinois 7. Christian fantasy 8. Urban fantasy 9. African American fiction

A fiction debut by the acclaimed actor depicts a holy warrior in a fantastical urban world where he must convince a doctor with no faith to help stop a powerful demon and his minions from establishing a hell on earth.

Snow, C. P.
★ **Strangers** and brothers. C.P. Snow. Scribner, 1960. 309 p. (Strangers and brothers, 1)
ISBN 9780333138533
1. Lewis, Eliot (Fictitious character) 2. Men 3. Lawyers 4. Fraud 5. Families 6. England 7. 1930s 8. Historical fiction
LC 60012605
"Essentially the tragedy of a good man defeated by the mediocrity of his world, the story of George Passant is completed in the novel 'Homecoming.'...Like all the novels in the series, 'Strangers and Brothers' is distinguished by virtue of its analysis of motive and character and its anatomization of a world in which a smooth mediocrity is the greatest virtue." —*Library Journal*

Snow, Jennifer
An **Alaskan** Christmas. Jennifer Snow. HQN Books, 2019. 384 pages (Wild River, 1)
ISBN 9781335041500
1. Women surgeons 2. Search and rescue operations 3. Vacations 4. Best friends 5. Christmas 6. Alaska 7. Contemporary romances 8. Holiday romances 9. Canadian fiction
Arriving in Wild River, Alaska for a much-needed break, workaholic surgeon Erika Sheraton is reunited with her best friend's brother, Reed Reynolds, who makes it his mission to prove to her just how much his search-and-rescue team—and he—needs her.

Snyder, Suleikha
Big bad wolf. Suleikha Snyder. Sourcebooks Casablanca, 2021. 320 p. (Third Shift, 1)
ISBN 9781728214979
1. Gangsters 2. Vigilantes 3. Shapeshifters 4. Sikh women 5. Panjabis (South Asian people) 6. New York City 7. Paranormal romances 8. Romantic suspense
Joe Peluso has blood on his hands. He took out the mobsters responsible for killing his foster brother, and that one act of vigilante justice has earned him countless enemies in New York's supernatural-controlled underworld. He knows that shifters like him deserve the worst. But meeting Neha makes him feel human for the first time in forever. Lawyer and psychologist Neha Ahluwalia knows Joe is guilty, but she's determined to help him craft a solid defense...even if she can't defend her own obsession. Just one look from the wolf shifter makes her skin burn hot and her pulse race. When a payback hit goes wrong, Neha's forced to make a choice: help Joe escape or leave him to his fate. Before long they're on the run—from the monsters who want him dead, from their own traitorous hearts, and from an attraction that threatens to destroy them.

"After a slow beginning, the adventure and romance kick in full blast in Snyder's engrossing and diverse tale of paranormal romantic suspense that launches a promising series." —*Booklist*

So, Anthony Veasna
Afterparties: stories. Anthony Veasna So. Ecco Press, 2021. 256 p.
ISBN 9780063049901
1. Cambodian Americans 2. Immigrants 3. Refugees 4. Psychic trauma 5. Family history 6. California 7. Short stories 8. Literary fiction

Short stories that portray of the lives of Cambodian-Americans still dealing with the inherited weight of the Khmer Rouge genocide including a young, disillusioned teacher obsessed with Moby-Dick and a child whose mother survived a school shooting.

"Nine electrifying stories comprise So's debut, and while many were previously published, when read together their magnificence is enhanced as they create an interconnected Cambodian American community." —*Booklist*

Soderberg, Alexander

The **other** son: a Sophie Brinkmann novel. Alexander Soderberg; translated from the Swedish by Neil Smith. Crown Publishing, 2015. 388 p. (Sophie Brinkman trilogy, 2)

ISBN 9780770436087

1. People in comas 2. Organized crime 3. Single mothers 4. Kidnapping 5. Police corruption 6. Europe 7. Scandinavian crime fiction 8. Crime fiction 9. Translations

A follow-up to The Andalucian Friend finds Sophie Brinkmann using a family murder to plot a daring escape from comatose Hector Guzman's crime family, an effort that compels her to forge dubious alliances and tap darker aspects of her own nature.

Translation from the Swedish of: Den Andre Sonen.

Originally published as: Den Andre Sonen. Stockholm : Norstedts, 2014.

Originally published: Stockholm : Norstedts, 2014.

Sofer, Dalia

Man of my time. Dalia Sofer. Farrar, Straus and Giroux, 2020. 352 p.

ISBN 9780374110062

1. Bronte, Charlotte 2. Exiles 3. Military interrogation 4. Change (Psychology) 5. Violence — Psychological aspects 6. Iran 7. New York City 8. Psychological fiction 9. Literary fiction

LC 2019054566

New York Times Notable Book, 2020

The story of an Iranian man reckoning with his capacity for love and evil.

"A perceptive, humane inquiry into Iran's history and soul." —*Kirkus*

The **Septembers** of Shiraz. Dalia Sofer. Ecco Press, 2007. 336 p.

ISBN 9780061130403

1. Lempicka, Tamara de 2. Jewish families 3. Revolutions 4. Religious persecution 5. Imprisonment 6. Tehran, Iran 7. Iran 8. 1980s 9. Domestic fiction 10. Historical fiction

New York Times Notable Book, 2007

Their serene villa life devastated by a wrongful imprisonment, the wife and children of Tehran gentleman Isaac Amin face potential betrayals within their own household and eventually plan a dangerous escape.

"Sofer paints a complicated picture of postrevolutionary Iran: The Amins (and especially their relatives) aren't entirely innocent, having shut their eyes to brutality and corruption under the shah, but [the author] recoils from the idea of justice by 'collective retribution' voiced by Farnaz's formerly docile housekeeper. While the dialogue can feel overly formal at times, the impression the reader is left with at the end is that of a powerful story honestly told." —*Christian Science Monitor*

Solares, Martin

The **black** minutes. Martin Solares; translated by Aura Estrada and John Pluecker. Grove Press, 2010. 436 p.

ISBN 9780802170682

1. Detectives 2. Murder 3. Crimes against journalists 4. Murder investigation 5. Mexico 6. Mysteries 7. Translations

Follows the investigation of police officer Ramon Cabrera into the murder of a journalist that has unsettling links to a corruption-tainted multiple homicide case from years earlier.

Translation form the Spanish of: Minutos negros.

Don't send flowers. Martin Solares; translated by Heather Cleary. Black Cat 2018. 288 p.

ISBN 9780802128157

1. Former police 2. Police corruption 3. Missing persons investigation 4. Cartels 5. Corruption 6. Mexico 7. Literary fiction 8. Noir fiction 9. Translations

LC 2018015205

A twisty, darkly captivating novel about a police detective hired to investigate the disappearance of a rich businessman's daughter several years after rampant corruption forced him to retire and made him a target of everyone still on the force in cartel-controlled, northern Mexico.

Originally published in 2015 by Literatura Random House.

Translated from the Spanish.

Soli, Tatjana

The **lotus** eaters. Tatjana Soli. St. Martin's Press, 2010. 400 p.

ISBN 9780312611576

1. Women war photographers 2. Vietnam War, 1961-1975 3. Lovers 4. Americans in Vietnam 5. War — Psychological aspects 6. Ho Chi Minh City (Vietnam) 7. Vietnam 8. War stories 9. Historical fiction 10. Love stories 11. Adult books for young adults

LC 2009045697

James Tait Black Memorial Prize for Fiction, 2010; ALA Notable Book, 2011; New York Times Notable Book, 2010

Helen Adams, an American combat photographer during the Vietnam War, captures the wrenching chaos of battle on film and finds herself torn between the love of two men, one an American war correspondent and the other his Vietnamese underling.

"Soli is at her best in conveying the day-to-day mix of adventure, tedium, and violence in wartime. Her descriptions are visceral, almost cinematic.... And she captures the camaraderie and tension among soldiers in a way that seems authentic." —*Boston Globe*

Solomon, Anna

Leaving Lucy Pear. Anna Solomon. Viking Press, 2016. 336 p.

ISBN 9781594632655

1. Life change events 2. Abandoned children 3. Gender role 4. Mothers and daughters 5. Identity (Psychology) 6. New England 7. Between the Wars (1918-1939) 8. 1920s 9. Historical fiction

Inadvertently reunited with the daughter she secretly abandoned and the girl's Irish-Catholic adoptive mother during the height of America's xenophobic Prohibition era, the adult daughter of a Jewish industrialist finds her life turned upside down by her daughter's bold and unconventional personality.

"A beautifully rendered tale of discovering one's true nature." —*Library Journal*

Solomon, Asali

The **days** of Afrekete. Asali Solomon. Farrar, Straus and Giroux, 2021. 176 p.

ISBN 9780374140052

1. Middle-aged women 2. Memories 3. Female friendship 4. Married people 5. African American women 6. African American fiction

LC 2021021361

As Liselle Belmont prepares for a dinner party, she questions her marriage and her choices, while across town, Selena finds her memories of Liselle shifting her path in life, in this deeply human examination of two women coming back to themselves at midlife.

"Solomon charts the social and cultural geography of her native Philadelphia with clear-eyed affection, and gives each woman character a full-throated voice. Unforgettable." —*Booklist*

Disgruntled: a novel. Asali Solomon. Farrar, Straus & Giroux, 2015. 304 p.
ISBN 9780374140342
1. African American girls 2. Ethnic identity 3. Bullying and bullies 4. Racism 5. Vigilantes 6. Philadelphia, Pennsylvania 7. 1980s 8. First person narratives 9. Psychological fiction 10. Coming-of-age stories 11. Adult books for young adults

LC 2014027442
Booklist Editors' Choice: Adult Books for Young Adults, 2015

In a powerful coming-of-age tale that also doubles as a portrait of Philadelphia in the late 80s and early 90s, Kenya Curtis, who knows that she is different, but can't put her finger on why, grows increasingly disgruntled by her inability to find any place, thing or person that feels like home.

"Solomon's cultural references resound, her dialogue stings, and the intricate and surprising relationships she choreographs are saturated with racial, sexual, and political quandaries of intimate and epochal repercussions. A deft, knowing, bold, and witty debut." —*Booklist*

Solomon, Rachel Lynn

★ The **ex** talk. Rachel Lynn Solomon. Jove, 2021. 352 p.
ISBN 9780593200124
1. Radio stations 2. Radio producers and directors 3. Radio programs 4. Radio personalities 5. Coworkers 6. Seattle, Washington 7. Contemporary romances 8. Multicultural romances

LC 2020040938
LibraryReads Favorites, 2021

Shay Goldstein has been a producer at her Seattle public radio station for nearly a decade, and she can't imagine working anywhere else. But lately it's been a constant clash between her and her newest colleague, Dominic Yun, who's fresh off a journalism master's program and convinced he knows everything about public radio. When the struggling station needs a new concept, Shay proposes a show that her boss green-lights with excitement. On The Ex Talk, two exes will deliver relationship advice live, on air. Their boss decides Shay and Dominic are the perfect co-hosts, given how much they already despise each other. Neither loves the idea of lying to listeners, but it's this or unemployment. As the show gets bigger, so does their deception, especially when Shay and Dominic start to fall for each other. In an industry that values truth, getting caught could mean the end of more than just their careers.

"Witty dialogue meets steamy slow-burn tension while fun romance tropes (fake dating! there's only one bed!) take a refreshing turn by making Dominic the less sexually experienced, and more emotionally open, of the two. A vibrant supporting cast of family, friends, and co-workers helps round out the plot. Delightfully romantic and emotionally uplifting." —*Kirkus*

Weather girl. Rachel Lynn Solomon. Jove, 2022. 336 p.
ISBN 9780593200148
1. Meteorologists 2. Sportswriters 3. Gifts 4. Dating (Social customs) 5. Matchmaking 6. Romantic comedies 7. Contemporary romances

LC 2021026243
LibraryReads Favorites, 2022

A TV meteorologist and a sports reporter scheme to reunite their divorced bosses with unforecasted results in this charming romantic comedy from the author of The Ex Talk. Ari Abrams has always been fascinated by the weather, and she loves almost everything about her job as a TV meteorologist. Her boss, legendary Seattle weatherwoman Torrance Hale, is too distracted by her tempestuous relationship with her ex-husband, the station's news director, to give Ari the mentorship she wants. Ari, who runs on sunshine and optimism, is at her wits' end. The only person who seems to understand how she feels is sweet but reserved sports reporter Russell Barringer. In the aftermath of a disastrous holiday party, Ari and Russell decide to team up to solve their bosses' relationship issues. Between secret gifts and double dates, they start nudging their bosses back together. But their well-meaning meddling backfires when the real chemistry builds between Ari and Russell. Working closely with Russell means allowing him to get to know parts of herself that Ari keeps hidden from everyone. Will he be able to embrace her dark clouds as well as her clear skies?

"But with a cast of interesting characters, sensitively explored topics of mental health and family dynamics, and enough steamy scenes to fog up the Seattle skyline, readers will no doubt be satisfied. The forecast predicts a 100% chance of heartfelt rom-com charm." —*Kirkus*

A Jove book—Title page verso.

Solomon, Rivers

The **deep**. Saga Press, 2019. 166 pages
ISBN 9781534439863
1. Underwater cities 2. Memories 3. Mermaids 4. Women 5. Slave trade 6. Fantasy fiction 7. African American fiction 8. Afrofantasy

LC 2020275363
Booklist Editors' Choice, 2019; Lambda Literary Award for LGBTQ Science Fiction/Fantasy/Horror, 2020; LibraryReads Favorites, 2019

The historian of the water-dwelling descendants of pregnant African slaves thrown overboard by slavers keeps all the memories of her people both painful and miraculous, until she discovers that their future lies in returning to the past.

Sorrowland. Rivers Solomon. MCD / Farrar, Straus and Giroux, 2021. 320 p.
ISBN 9780374266776
1. African Americans 2. Albinos and albinism 3. People who are intersex 4. Single mothers 5. Atrocities 6. United States 7. Literary fiction 8. Magical realism 9. Horror

LC 2020053564
Fleeing from the strict religious compound where she was raised, Vern, in the safety of the forest, gives birth to twins, and to keep her small family safe, unleashes incredible brutality far beyond what a person should be capable of.

"As in their debut, An Unkindness of Ghosts, Solomon often packs so much into each image that the result can be overwhelming. They display a maturing control of their craft, employing a breathtaking range of reference that will enable any reader, from horror geek to Derridean academic, to engage with this thrilling tale." —*Publishers Weekly*

An **unkindness** of ghosts. Rivers Solomon. Akashic Books, 2017. 340 p.
ISBN 9781617755880
1. Misfits (Persons) 2. Space vehicles 3. Racism 4. Race relations 5. Social classes 6. Social science fiction 7. Literary fiction
Library Journal Best Books, 2017

Aster lives in the lowdeck slums of the HSS Matilda, a space vessel organized much like the antebellum South. For generations, Matilda has ferried the last of humanity to a mythical Promised Land. On its way, the ship's leaders have imposed harsh moral restrictions and deep indignities on dark-skinned sharecroppers like Aster. Embroiled in a grudge with a brutal overseer, Aster learns there may be a way to improve her lot—if she's willing to sow the seeds of civil war.

"Infused with the spirit of Octavia Butler...An Unkindness of Ghosts will appeal to a wide variety of readers. Solomons impassioned, speculative, literary book is sorely needed on library shelves." —*Booklist*

Solomons, Natasha

House of Gold. Natasha Solomons. G.P. Putnam's Sons, 2018. 432 p.
ISBN 9780735212978
1. Heirs and heiresses 2. War and society 3. Rich families 4. Jewish families 5. Husband and wife 6. England 7. Austria 8. 20th century 9. Historical fiction
LC 2018002308
The outbreak of World War I forces a headstrong Austrian heiress to choose between the family she built and the family she left behind.

Solzhenitsyn, Aleksandr Isaevich

★ **Cancer** ward. Alexander Solzhenitsyn; translated by Nicholas Bethell and David Burg. Modern library, 1995. Vii, 536 p.
ISBN 9780679601630
1. Medical care — Corrupt practices 2. Socialism 3. Collectivism 4. Man-woman relationships 5. Communism 6. Uzbekistan 7. Soviet Union 8. 1950s 9. Translations 10. Political fiction
LC 95003798
Solzhenitsyn's celebrated novel describes the lives of people in the Soviet Union under Stalin who were condemned on health grounds to "internment" or death. It also give a psychological insight into the intensified experience of people under varying degrees of pressure and deprivation.
Translation of: Rakovyi korpus (1968).

In the first circle: a novel : the restored text. Aleksandr I. Solzhenitsyn; translated by Harry T. Willetts. Harper Perennial Modern Classics, 2009. Xxx, 741 p.
ISBN 9780061479014
1. Mathematicians 2. Political prisoners 3. Political persecution 4. Soviet Union 5. 1940s 6. Political fiction 7. Translations
The government orders an imprisoned mathematician and his fellow genius inmates to figure out a turncoat's identity, forcing the prisoners to choose between helping the Stalinist regime that jailed them or being sent to certain death in the Siberian Gulags, in an edition that restores a significant amount of text originally cut by Soviet censors.

"It has taken a half-century for English-language readers to receive the definitive text of In the First Circle... Such is the fate of art created under a totalitarian regime. But now it is finally available in the West as the author envisioned it. The English translator is Harry T. Willetts, renowned for combining fidelity to Aleksandr Solzhenitsyn's rich, complex Russian with supple equivalents in English prose and the only person Solzhenitsyn fully trusted to render his fiction into English." —*The Wall Street Journal*
Previously published (1968) in a shortened and altered ed, with title: The first circle.
The first uncensored edition.—Cover.

One day in the life of Ivan Denisovich. Aleksandr Solzhenitsyn; translated from the Russian by H. T. Willetts; with an introduction by John Bayley. A. A. Knopf, 1995. 159 p.
ISBN 9780679444640
1. Forced labor 2. Concentration camps 3. Political prisoners 4. Communism 5. Soviet Union 6. Translations 7. Literary fiction 8. Modern classics
LC 96121678

Presents a new translation of the fictional account of the daily hardships a prisoner endures in a Stalinist labor camp
Translation of: Odin den' Ivana Denisovicha (1963).

Somer, Mehmet Murat

The **serenity** murders. Mehmet Murat Somer. Penguin Books, 2012. 256 p. (Hop-Ciki-Yaya mysteries, 4)
ISBN 9780143121220
1. Nero, Emperor of Rome, 37-68 2. Murder investigation 3. Television programs 4. Death threats 5. Murder 6. Turkey 7. Istanbul, Turkey 8. Mysteries 9. Translations 10. LGBTQIA fiction
LC 2012030581
During a television show appearance, transvestite Burçak Veral receives a call from an irate man who threatens to kill everyone close to her and then murders the show's host, prompting Burçak to put her sleuthing skills to the test.
Translation from the Turkish of: Huzur cimayetleri.

Sontag, Susan

★ **In** America. Susan Sontag. Farrar, Straus and Giroux, 2000. 387 p.
ISBN 9780374175405
1. Polish Americans 2. Actors and actresses 3. Frontier and pioneer life 4. Theater 5. Utopias 6. 1870s 7. 19th century 8. Historical fiction 9. Biographical fiction 10. Literary fiction
LC 99054641
Booklist Editors' Choice, 2000; National Book Award for Fiction, 2000; New York Times Notable Book, 2000
Poland's greatest living actress leads a utopian community to the wilds of 1876 California, where she will struggle to maintain love, hope, and idealism in the harsh reality of the American West.

"This novel displays Sontag in a relaxed, pleasure-seeking mode, guiding her characters through a long travelogue in time, specifically the beginnings of the gilded age in the brave new world." —*Time*

The **volcano** lover: a romance. Susan Sontag. Farrar Straus Giroux, 1992. 419 p.
ISBN 9780374285166
1. Nelson, Horatio Nelson 2. Love triangles 3. Extramarital affairs 4. Mistresses 5. Man-woman relationships 6. Married people 7. Naples, Italy 8. Vesuvius 9. 18th century 10. Historical fiction 11. Love stories 12. Biographical fiction
LC 92071738
A romance set in eighteenth-century Naples follows the fortunes of a British ambassador, the ravishing woman he marries, and the young British admiral with whom she falls in love BT

"Sontag's narrative deftly blends the magnetism of personality and the suspense of event with shrewd commentary and sly mockery as she contrasts the habits of thought in that age with ours and reflects on the meaning of mercy and vengeance, self-invention and praise, love and obsession. In all, a memorable group portrait and a brilliant, fresh improvisation on classically grand themes." —*Booklist*

Sorenson, Jill

Aftershock. Jill Sorenson. Harlequin Books, 2012. 384 p. (Aftershock (Jill Sorenson), 1)
ISBN 9780373777327
1. Earthquakes 2. Rescues 3. Secrets 4. Paramedics 5. Veterans 6. San Diego, California 7. Romantic suspense 8. Category romances
When she is trapped by an earthquake underneath the freeway with a group of strangers, including Iraq war veteran Garrett Wright, emergency

paramedic Lauren Boyer turns to Garrett for help in saving the others when a gang of escaped convicts goes on the attack.

Sosa, Mia

★ **Acting** on impulse. Mia Sosa. HarperCollins, 2017. 400 p. (Love on cue, 1)

ISBN 9780062690340

1. Vacations 2. Disguises 3. Sexual attraction 4. Personal trainers 5. Actors and actresses 6. Caribbean Area 7. Aruba 8. Contemporary romances

Sparks fly during their vacations when fitness trainer Tori Alvarez and Hollywood heartthrob Carter Stone meet on their way to Aruba for rest & relaxation.

★ The **worst** best man. Mia Sosa. Avon Books, 2020. 359 p.

ISBN 9780062909879

1. Wedding consultants 2. Jilted women 3. Brothers 4. Business competition 5. Interpersonal attraction 6. Romantic comedies 7. Multiple perspectives

LibraryReads Favorites, 2020

A wedding planner left at the altar? Yeah, the irony isn't lost on Carolina Santos, either. But despite that embarrassing blip from her past, Lina's offered an opportunity that could change her life. There's just one hitch: she has to collaborate with the best (make that worst) man from her own failed nuptials.

"Sosa (Acting on Impulse) delivers a steamy and witty enemies-to-lovers romance. Lina and Max's relationship grows against a rich background of Lina's Afro-Latinx culture, and readers will enjoy the complex cast of side characters." —*Library Journal*

Soule, Charles

★ **Anyone**. Charles Soule. Perennial, 2019. 400 p.

ISBN 9780062890634

1. Women scientists 2. Consciousness 3. Mind transfers 4. Human body 5. High technology 6. Techno-thrillers 7. Parallel narratives

When a botched experiment leads to the unexpected development of consciousness-transferring technology, a scientist witnesses the havoc of her innovation throughout two subsequent decades of body-rental violence, entertainment and warfare.

Soule's uncomfortable vision of the future will please readers of cutting-edge speculative fiction. Publishers Weekly.

Soyinka, Wole

Chronicles from the land of the happiest people on earth. Wole Soyinka. Pantheon Books, 2021. 416 p.

ISBN 9780593320167

1. Organ and tissue thefts 2. Abuse of administrative power 3. Entrepreneurs 4. Hospitals 5. Upper class 6. Nigeria 7. Political fiction 8. Literary fiction

LC 2021006092

Duyole Pitan-Payne realizes that someone is trying to stop him from assuming a prestigious job in the United Nations after discovering that a wily entrepreneur is stealing body parts from a Nigerian hospital for use in rituals.

"Both a pointed critique of Nigeria's political elite—and of political abuse worldwide—and a rollercoaster ride of a literary thriller to discover the culprit, this book should make news." —*Library Journal*

Spain, Jo

With our blessing: an Inspector Tom Reynolds mystery. Jo Spain. Crooked Lane Books, 2019. 368 p. (Inspector Tom Reynolds novels, 1)

ISBN 9781683314363

1. Convents 2. Revenge 3. Women murder victims 4. Detectives 5. Murder 6. Ireland 7. Police procedurals 8. Mysteries

After the corpse of a nun is found in a public Dublin park, Detective Inspector Tom Reynolds investigates its connection in this American debut from the best-selling Irish author.

Originally published: London : Quercus, 2015.

Spann, Susan

Blade of the Samurai: a Shinobi mystery. Susan Spann. Minotaur Books, 2014. 293 p. (Shinobi mysteries, 2)

ISBN 9781250027054

1. Political intrigue 2. Ninja 3. Assassination 4. Murder 5. Murder investigation 6. Japan 7. Kyoto, Japan 8. 16th century 9. Historical mysteries 10. Mysteries

LC 2014008766

Learning that the shogun's cousin has been murdered within palace walls, master ninja Hiro Hattori and Father Mateo learn of an assassination plot by a usurping clan and begin to doubt a friend's innocence.

"There are already a couple of good mystery series set in feudal-era Japan, one at the beginning of the historical period and the other at the end; this one's set in between, meaning the been-there-done-that factor is reduced to background noise. A strong second entry in a very promising series." —*Booklist*

★ **Claws** of the cat: a Shinobi mystery. Susan Spann. Minotaur Books, 2013. 288 p. (Shinobi mysteries, 1)

ISBN 9781250027023

1. Ninja 2. Murder 3. Samurai 4. Priests 5. Assassins 6. Japan 7. Kyoto, Japan 8. 16th century 9. Historical mysteries 10. Mysteries

In sixteenth-century Japan, master ninja Hiro and the Jesuit priest he is sworn to protect race against time to prevent a wrongful execution by solving the murder of a samurai whose death is linked to numerous possible suspects.

Trial on Mount Koya: a Hiro Hattori novel. Susan Spann. Seventh Street Books, 2018. 256 p. (Shinobi mysteries, 6)

ISBN 9781633884151

1. Ninja 2. Samurai 3. Buddhism 4. Priests 5. Sacred space 6. Japan 7. Kyoto, Japan 8. 16th century 9. Historical mysteries 10. Mysteries

LC 2018006388

November, 1565: Master ninja Hiro Hattori and Portuguese Jesuit Father Mateo travel to a Buddhist temple at the summit of Mount Koya, carrying a secret message for an Iga spy posing as a priest on the sacred mountain. When a snowstorm strikes the peak, a killer begins murdering the temple's priests and posing them as Buddhist judges of the afterlife—the Kings of Hell. Hiro and Father Mateo must unravel the mystery before the remaining priests—including Father Mateo—become unwilling members of the killer's grisly council of the dead.

Spark, Muriel

Aiding & abetting. Muriel Spark. Doubleday, 2001. Viii, 166 p.

ISBN 9780385501538

1. Lucan, Richard John Bingham 2. Deception 3. Extortion 4. Murderers 5. Fugitives 6. Missing persons 7. England 8. Paris, France 9. Mysteries 10. Literary fiction

LC 55559

New York Times Notable Book, 2001

Psychiatrist Hildegard Wolf is intrigued when two patients begin therapy with her—both claiming to be the notorious Lord Lucan. Lucan disappeared in 1974, shortly after murdering his children's nanny in a botched attempt to kill his wife. It's not just the patients who have secrets, as the doctor has also abandoned a previous life.

"The unsettling wit of 'Aiding and Abetting' hits the funny bone as hard it pricks the conscience.... It's kiln-dried wit that never cracks, with a smile that dares you to laugh. As always [Spark is] breathtakingly deft with the anxieties of well-bred people, people who know how to dress, where to eat, and how to commit the most heinous cruelty. If satire is your cup of tea,...[this is a] perfectly seeped book to be savored." —*Christian Science Monitor*

Originally published: London: Viking, 2000.

The **driver's** seat. Muriel Spark. Knopf, 1970. 117 p.
ISBN 9789997405333
1. Self-destructive behavior 2. Deception 3. Women travelers 4. Women — Psychology 5. Sexuality 6. Italy 7. Psychological fiction 8. Mysteries

LC 79111242

"The author's perspective is cosmically cool and fantastic: she knows no more about her protagonist, Lise, than does the reader.... She follows this woman, another of her slightly bizarre lunatics, through a day's grotesque project, narrating only its circumstances, leaving all motive, all emotion, all inner plan to be inferred. The result is a long, elusive joke that casts as deep an irony on life's arbitrariness as do the more 'compassionate' ironies of, say, E. M. Forster." —*The Nation*

This novel first appeared in the New Yorker.
Originally published: London : Macmillan, 1970.

★ A **far** cry from Kensington. Muriel Spark. New Directions, 2000. 189 p.
ISBN 9780811214575
1. Boarding houses 2. Widows 3. Reminiscing in old age 4. Extortion 5. Eccentrics and eccentricities 6. London, England 7. England 8. 1950s 9. Psychological fiction

LC 88005904

In a post-war London boarding house, kindly Mrs. Hawkins, adept at handling other people's problems, finds herself a player in some very strange events.

"Spark balances devastatingly eccentric characters and funny situations with darker elements, even pathos. Her well-constructed novel has no loose ends and few contrived situations." —*Library Journal*

Originally published: New York : Houghton Mifflin, 1988.

★ The **girls** of slender means. Muriel Spark. New Directions, 1998. 141 p.
ISBN 9780811213790
1. Single women 2. War and society 3. Young women 4. Poor women 5. Boarding houses for women 6. London, England 7. 1940s 8. Satirical fiction 9. Modern classics 10. Literary fiction

LC 89091877

Just after World War II in a London ladies' hostel its lady inhabitants do their best to act as if the world were back to normal, practicing elocution and jostling over suitors and a single Schiaparelli gown.

Originally published: London : Macmillan, 1963.

★ The **Mandelbaum** gate. Muriel Spark. Welcome Rain Pub, 2001. 329 p.
ISBN 9781566492263
1. Young women 2. British in Israel 3. Jewish women 4. Pilgrims and pilgrimages, Christian 5. Interethnic conflict 6. Jerusalem, Israel 7. West Bank (Jordan River) 8. 1960s 9. Literary fiction
James Tait Black Memorial Prize for Fiction, 1965

The Mandelbaum Gate divides the conflict-torn realm of Jerusalem, separating Israel from Jordan. Barbara Vaughan, a stubborn young Englishwoman and half-Jewish Catholic convert, insists upon crossing the divide in order to rendezvous with her fiance, in spite of the very real danger. Not even the threat of bodily harm and fearful admonishments of staid British diplomat Freddy Hamilton can dissuade Barbara from her ill-timed pilgrimage. Her quest sets off a series of bizarre situations and adventures, set against the backdrop of the Eichmann trial of 1961.

Originally published: London: Macmillan, 1965.

★ **Memento** mori. Muriel Spark. New Directions, 2000. 224 p.
ISBN 9780811214384
1. Seniors 2. Mortality 3. Extortion 4. Secrets 5. Extramarital affairs 6. London, England 7. England 8. 1950s 9. Satirical fiction 10. Modern classics 11. Literary fiction

LC 90093171

In late 1950s London, a group of aging eccentrics is brought together by a series of uncanny events. Lettie Colston is the first to receive an anonymous phone call from an insinuating voice reminding her that she must die. Soon, ten of Lettie's friends also receive the call. In the flurry that results from these seemingly supernatural messages, a bizarre investigation is launched that reveals a network of deception binding the group, including such dark secrets as blackmail and adultery.

Originally published: London : Macmillan, 1959.

★ The **prime** of Miss Jean Brodie. Muriel Spark. Harper Perennial, 1999. 150 p.
ISBN 9780060931735
1. Middle-aged women 2. Teacher-student relationships 3. Women teachers 4. Nonconformists 5. Teenage girls 6. Edinburgh, Scotland 7. Scotland 8. 1930s 9. Modern classics 10. Psychological fiction 11. Books to movies
A teacher at a girl's school in Edinburgh during the 1930s comes into conflict with school authorities because of her unorthodox teaching methods

First published in the USA by the New Yorker 1961. First published in Great Britain by Macmillan 1961. Published in Penguin, 1965.

Sparks, Nicholas

Every breath. Nicholas Sparks. Grand Central Publishing, 2018. 496 p.
ISBN 9781538728529
1. Beaches 2. Strangers 3. Birthparents 4. Safari guides 5. Sick fathers 6. North Carolina 7. Love stories 8. Relationship fiction

LC 2018012865

A chance encounter becomes a transcendent turning point for two very different people, including the conflicted surgeon daughter of an ALS patient and a Sunset Beach newcomer from Zimbabwe who aims to meet his birth father.

"Sparks confirms his gifts as he spans the last two decades and transports readers to the bush of Zimbabwe and the Carolina coast in this thoughtfully researched and spellbinding story of love that defies time, a tale both heartbreaking and heartwarming." —*Booklist*

The **guardian**. Nicholas Sparks. Warner Books, 2003. 384 p.
ISBN 9780446527798
1. Love triangles 2. Man-woman relationships 3. Stalking victims 4. Possessiveness 5. Courtship 6. North Carolina 7. Romantic suspense 8. Multiple perspectives 9. Relationship fiction 10. Adult books for young adults

LC 2002192411

Four years after losing her husband, twenty-nine-year-old Julie Barenson considers falling in love again and wonders if she should choose sophisticated Richard, who treats her like a queen, or down-to-earth Mike, who is her best friend.

"On Christmas Eve, Julie Barenson, 25 years old and newly widowed, finds an unexpected presenta Great Dane pup that her late husband, Jim, had arranged for her to receive after her died from a brain tumor.... Julie's new dog, Singer, turns out to be a better judge of character than she, which is unfortunate because the dog nearly gives away the book's ending when he growls warily at Richard Franklin, the new man in Julie's life." —*Publishers Weekly*

★ The **notebook**. Nicholas Sparks. Warner, 1996. 214 p.
ISBN 9780446520805
1. Senior romance 2. Man-woman relationships 3. Single men 4. World War II veterans 5. Former lovers 6. North Carolina 7. Love stories 8. Books to movies 9. Relationship fiction
LC 9633815
An elderly man reads a story from a notebook to a woman who does not know him; the story is of young lovers kept apart by disapproving parents.

"At 80, Noah Calhoun reads daily from a notebook containing the love story of Noah and Allie. We learn of the teenaged lovers, their 14-year separation and reunion in New Bern, North Carolina, just weeks before Allie is to marry another man. Back in the present, we learn that Noah and Allie did marry and were happy for more than 40 years. Now, they are residents of a nursing home, separated both by rooms and, more profoundly, by Allie's Alzheimer's. Noah's daily reading from the notebook is not to himself; he reads aloud to Allie, hoping that the power of their love story will reach her." —*Library Journal*
Sequel: The wedding

A **walk** to remember. Nicholas Sparks. Warner Books, 1999. 240 p.
ISBN 9780446525534
1. First loves 2. Teenage boy/girl relations 3. People with cancer 4. Middle-aged men 5. Teenagers 6. North Carolina 7. 1950s 8. Love stories 9. Books to movies 10. Relationship fiction 11. Adult books for young adults
LC 99012079
Booklist Editors' Choice: Adult Books for Young Adults, 1999; Colorado Blue Spruce YA Book Award, 2003; Iowa High School Book Award, 2004
A nostalgic look back at the 1950s in a story of first love set in a small North Carolina town.

"The author is a master at pulling heartstrings and bringing a tear to his readers' eyes.... Told in Landon's down-home voice, this bittersweet tale will enthrall Sparks' numerous fans." —*Booklist*

Spear, Terry
A **billionaire** wolf for Christmas. Terry Spear. Sourcebooks, 2018. 352 p. (Billionaire wolf (Terry Spear), 2)
ISBN 9781492655848
1. Billionaires 2. Werewolves 3. Physicians 4. Women werewolves 5. Wolf packs 6. Paranormal romances
Wolf shifter Dr. Aidan Denali has been working day and night to find a cure for werewolves' alarmingly sudden decline in lifespan. The key to the problem eludes him. But when Aidan grudgingly leaves his work to do some holiday shopping, he meets a remarkable she-wolf whose mysterious pack could bring him one step closer to the answer.

Speight, Shameek A.
★ A **child** of a crack head. Shameek A. Speight. Amazon Digital Services, 2009. 231 p.
ISBN 9781449966126

1. Crack addicts 2. Mothers and sons 3. Fathers and sons 4. Family violence 5. Urban fiction 6. African American fiction
This story tells the countless beatings, killings, lies, infidelity and betrayals of a crack head and how a mother and child survive the street life.

The **pleasure** of pain. By Shameek A. Speight; editor Kelly Klem. Createspace] : 2011. 228 p; (Pleasure of pain novels (Shameek A. Speight), 1)
ISBN 9781463526245
1. Drug dealers 2. African American women 3. Women criminals 4. Street life 5. Man-woman relationships 6. New York City 7. Urban fiction 8. African American fiction

Speller, Elizabeth
The **return** of Captain John Emmett. Elizabeth Speller. Houghton Mifflin Harcourt, 2011. 384 p. (Laurence Bartram novels, 1)
ISBN 9780547511696
1. World War I veterans 2. Suicide investigation 3. War — Psychological aspects 4. War and society 5. Soldiers 6. London, England 7. England 8. 1920s 9. Historical mysteries 10. Mysteries
LC 2010052590
"An absorbing mystery set in postwar London,...[this book] is brimming with historical details of the period and doesn't shy away from war's atrocities." —*Library Journal*
Sequel: The strange fate of Kitty Easton.
Originally published: 2010.

The **strange** fate of Kitty Easton. Elizabeth Speller. Virago, 2011. 416 p. (Laurence Bartram novels, 2)
ISBN 9781844086313
1. World War I veterans 2. Missing girls 3. Missing persons investigation 4. War and society 5. War — Psychological aspects 6. Wiltshire, England 7. England 8. 1920s 9. Historical mysteries 10. Mysteries
When former infantry officer Laurence Bartram is called to the small village of Easton Deadall, he is struck by the beauty of the place: a crumbling stately home; a centuries-old church; and a recently planted maze, a memorial to the men of the village, almost all of whom died in one heroic battle in 1916. But it soon becomes clear to Laurence that while rest of the country is alight with hope for the first time since the end of the War, as the first Labour government takes power, the Wiltshire village is haunted by its tragic past. In 1911, five-year-old Kitty Easton disappeared from her bed and has not been seen since: only her fragile mother believes still she is alive. When a family trip to the Empire Exhibition in London ends in disaster and things take an increasingly sinister turn, Laurence struggles to find out what has happened as it seems that the fate of the house, the men and of Kitty herself may be part of a much longer, darker story of love, betrayal and violence.
Sequel to: The return of Captain John Emmett.
Originally published: 2011.

Spencer, Elizabeth
The **southern** woman: new and selected fiction. Elizabeth Spencer. Modern Library, 2001. 462 p.
ISBN 9780679642183
1. Women 2. Southern States 3. Italy 4. Short stories
LC 54612
New York Times Notable Book, 2001
The author's most masterful stories and novellas plus more than ten new stories. This collection celebrates a six-decade career devoted to the art of the story and the novella.

"This collection offers selections from the Mississippi native's earlier short fiction together with several new stories. Best known of the earlier fiction is her stunning novella, The Light in the Piazza (1960), the deceptively simple tale of an American mother and daughter in Florence." —*Library Journal*

The **stories** of Elizabeth Spencer. Elizabeth Spencer; with a foreword by Eudora Welty. Doubleday, 1981. 429 p.

ISBN 9780385156974

1. Short stories

LC 79006601

An award-winning Southern writer includes thirty-three short stories spanning four decades of her life, portraying her homeland, Mississippi, and other places she has come to love.

Spencer, Minerva

Barbarous. Minerva Spencer. Zebra Books, 2018. 304 p. (Outcasts (Minerva Spencer), 2)

ISBN 9781420147216

1. Pirates 2. Widows 3. Independence in women 4. Aristocracy 5. Thirties (Age) 6. England 7. Historical romances

When the man whom she thought was dead returns, Lady Daphne Davenport, who secretly cheated him of his title, lands and fortune, must find a way to makes things right despite an unknown enemy standing in her way.

"Deft writing and astute character development sustain a complex plot and a huge cast of characters that could flounder in less accomplished hands, while a touch of humor tempers some darker edges of the nuanced story." —*Kirkus*

Dangerous. Minerva Spencer. Zebra Books, 2018. 304 p. (Outcasts (Minerva Spencer), 1)

ISBN 9781420147193

1. Former captives 2. Misfits (Persons) 3. Widowers 4. Aristocracy 5. Independence in women 6. England 7. Historical romances

What sort of lady doesn't make her debut until the age of thirty-two? A timeless beauty with a mysterious past—and a future she intends to take into her own hands. . .

Scandalous. Minerva Spencer. Zebra Books, 2019. 378 pages; (Outcasts (Minerva Spencer), 3)

ISBN 9781420147209

1. Women missionaries 2. Ship captains 3. Privateers 4. Virgins 5. Rescues 6. Regency period (1811-1820) 7. Historical romances 8. Canadian fiction

When straight-laced missionary Sarah Fisher makes him an outrageous offer, Captain Martin Bouchard is captivated by this brazen beauty and must confront his scandalous past in order to have a future with the first woman to steal his heart.

Spencer, Sally

Backlash. Sally Spencer. Severn House, 2011. 224 p. (Monika Paniatowski mysteries, 4)

ISBN 9780727880550

1. Policewomen 2. Missing persons investigation 3. Missing women 4. Police spouses 5. Women murder victims 6. England 7. 1970s 8. Mysteries

DCI Monika Paniatowski tries to balance searching for both Chief Superintendent Kershaw's wife, Elaine, and young prostitute Grace Meade, who suddenly disappear.

Best served cold. Sally Spencer. Severn House, 2015. 224 p. (Monika Paniatowski mysteries, 9)

ISBN 9780727885074

1. Policewomen 2. Murder investigation 3. Actors and actresses 4. Secrets 5. Revenge 6. England 7. 1970s 8. Mysteries 9. Police procedurals

DCI Monika Paniatowski investigates the death of a member of a theater company and discovers everyone in the company had a reason to want the victim dead.

Dead end. Sally Spencer. Severn House, 2019. 240 p; (Monika Paniatowski mysteries, 13)

ISBN 9780727888747

1. Policewomen 2. Cold cases (Criminal investigation) 3. Murder investigation 4. Paniatowski, Monika (Fictitious character) 5. England 6. Lancashire, England 7. 1970s 8. Mysteries 9. Police procedurals

When a body is discovered on a local allotment after lying buried for years, Monika Paniatowski has no real leads—until she sees possible links with a case she closed four years earlier. Are the two cases connected? All she knows is that she is being watched by an old enemy, and will be killed if she shares her information with her team.

The **dead** hand of history. Sally Spencer. Severn House, 2009. 224 p. (Monika Paniatowski mysteries, 1)

ISBN 9780727868053

1. Extramarital affairs 2. Murder suspects 3. Gender role 4. Single mothers 5. Paniatowski, Monika (Fictitious character) 6. England 7. 1970s 8. Mysteries

On her first day in a new job, DCI Monika Paniatowski finds herself in the middle of a mystery after a severed female hand is found on the riverbank.

Death's dark shadow. Sally Spencer. Severn House, 2013. 208 p. (Monika Paniatowski mysteries, 7)

ISBN 9780727883476

1. Policewomen 2. Murder investigation 3. Crimes against women 4. Police 5. Murder 6. England 7. 1970s 8. Mysteries

Before she can even begin to track down the killer of the old woman dumped on the lonely canalside, Monika Paniatowski needs to find out who she is—but no one seems to know.

★ A **dying** fall. Sally Spencer. Severn House, 2008. 248 p. (Chief Inspector Woodend mysteries, 19)

ISBN 9780727866097

1. Woodend, Charlie (Fictitious character) 2. Detectives 3. Women detectives 4. Women journalists 5. Politicians 6. England 7. 1960s 8. Mysteries

When a charred body is discovered at an abandoned mill, DCI Woodend must attempt to solve a crime with virtually no clues while also fighting against police authority that blocks him at every turn.

Alan Rustage writing as Sally Spencer.

★ **Echoes** of the dead. Sally Spencer. Severn House, 2011. 218 p. (Monika Paniatowski mysteries, 3)

ISBN 9780727869807

1. Police 2. Cold cases (Criminal investigation) 3. False imprisonment 4. Police corruption 5. Policewomen 6. England 7. 1970s 8. Mysteries

LC Oc2010056413

When a recently released prisoner claims in a deathbed confession that he is innocent of the rape and murder of a young girl for which he was convicted twenty-two years earlier, DCI Monika Paniatowski is tasked to lead an unofficial investigation into his claims. At first she is reluctant, but when she learns that her old mentor Charlie Woodend was the lead detective in the case, she knows she must do everything she can to protect his reputation.

★ The **hidden**. Sally Spencer. Severn House, 2017. 186 p. (Monika Paniatowski mysteries, 12)
ISBN 9780727887078
1. Policewomen 2. Murder investigation 3. Murder suspects 4. Secret societies 5. Murder 6. England 7. Mysteries 8. Police procedurals
DCI Paniatowski's team are increasingly convinced that the girl found dead in the woods is the victim of a ritual killing, carried out by a secret society which has been established in the very heart of Whitebridge. Their problem is that without Paniatowski there to back them up, they find it impossible to persuade the ambitious DCI "Rhino" Dixon that treating it as a mere domestic murder will get them nowhere. And so Meadows, Crane and Beresford find themselves out on a limb—cutting corners, ignoring procedure, and running the very real risk that their careers could be brought to an abrupt and dramatic end.

Lambs to the slaughter. Sally Spencer. Severn House, 2012. 208 p. (Monika Paniatowski mysteries, 5)
ISBN 9780727881922
1. Policewomen 2. Murder investigation 3. Small towns 4. Strikes 5. Mines and mineral resources 6. England 7. 1970s 8. Mysteries
Inspector Monika Paniatowski investigates the murder of retired miner Len Hopkins, but progress is hindered by the unwelcoming nature of the mining industry and concerns for the behavior of her partner, Inspector Colin Beresford.

The **ring** of death. Sally Spencer. Severn House, 2010. 240 p. (Monika Paniatowski mysteries, 2)
ISBN 9780727868688
1. Police 2. Serial murder investigation 3. Serial murderers 4. Policewomen 5. Paniatowski, Monika (Fictitious character) 6. England 7. 1970s 8. Miller, Henry
DCI Monika Paniatowski finds herself handicapped by a colleague she doesn't trust and being watched by an old enemy as she tries to unravel a series of clues left by a deranged murderer.
Originally published: 2010.

The **shivering** turn. Sally Spencer. Severn House, 2016. 218 p. (Jennie Redhead novels, 1)
ISBN 9780727886675
1. Women private investigators 2. Missing teenage girls 3. Secret societies 4. Upper class 5. Poetry 6. Oxford, England 7. 1970s 8. Mysteries
Seventeen-year-old Linda Corbet is missing and Jennie is hired to investigate. The only clue Jennie has is a fragment of a 17th century poem she finds in Linda's room. But from that one clue her investigations will lead her to a secret Oxford society—and a hidden world of violence, excess and desire which lies behind the city's dreaming spires.

Thicker than water: a Monika Paniatowski British police procedural. Sally Spencer. Severn House, 2016. 224 p. (Monika Paniatowski mysteries, 10)
ISBN 9780727885616
1. Policewomen 2. Murder investigation 3. Murder suspects 4. New mothers 5. Politicians 6. England 7. Mysteries 8. Police procedurals
Just back from maternity leave, DCI Monika Paniatowski is called in to investigate the murder of a wealthy politician's wife, who is the mother of three small children, a case in which she must make a quick arrest or her career may be on the line.

A **walk** with the dead. Sally Spencer. Severn House, 2013. 208 p. (Monika Paniatowski mysteries, 6)
ISBN 9780727882424

1. Policewomen 2. Murder investigation 3. Crimes against girls 4. Guilt in women 5. Police 6. England 7. 1970s 8. Mysteries
DCI Monica Paniatowski becomes emotionally invested in finding the murderer of a wedding guest who was killed just hours after the investigator saw her alive.

Spencer, Scott

★ **Endless** love. Scott Spencer. Knopf, 1979. 417 p.
ISBN 9780394506050
1. People with mental illnesses 2. Obsession 3. Arson 4. Lovers 5. Man-woman relationships 6. 1960s 7. 1970s 8. Love stories 9. First person narratives 10. Books to movies
LC 79002089
National Book Award for Fiction finalist, 1980
"The author has achieved something quite remarkable in this unabashedly romantic and often harrowing novel. He has created an adolescent love that is believably endless.... Mr. Spencer has an acute grasp of character and situation. He gives us details that make these often tormented people uncommonly convincing." —*New York Times Book Review*
This book was made into film twice — in 1981 directed by Franco Zeffirelli, starring Brooke Shields and Martin Hewitt and in 2014, directed by Shana Feste and staring Alex Pettyfer and Gabriella Wilde.

Man in the woods. Scott Spencer. Ecco Press, 2010. 288 p.
ISBN 9780061466557
1. Murder 2. Guilt in men 3. Animal welfare 4. Carpenters 5. Women authors 6. New York (State) 7. Psychological fiction
Two characters from A Ship Made of Paper, Kate Ellis and her daughter, Ruby, meet a wandering adventurer and offer him stability if he is willing to forgo his deep convictions and make compromises to get along with others.
"A novel about what happens to a couple when the man, Paul Phillips, impulsively decides to stop a stranger from beating his dog.... Paul's partner, Kate Ellis, is successful, sober and blissfully happy in love, a hard-won trifecta. Her collection of essays, Prays Well With Others, chronicling her years as an alcoholic and wayward mother, has become a best seller; Kate's brand of honesty, humor and religion has found a wide audience. She and her young daughter Ruby (both characters from Spencer's novel, A Ship Made of Paper) are living with Paul, a carpenter.... After a stressful meeting with a Manhattan client one day, Paul stops off at a state park to clear his head before driving on to Kate's home in rural New York. He spots the man and the dog. One life-altering moment isn't new in fiction, of course, but Spencer makes it fresh, and compelling." —*Cleveland Plain Dealer*

An **ocean** without a shore. Scott Spencer. HarperCollins, 2020. 341 pages
ISBN 9780062851628
1. Closeted gay men 2. Heterosexual men 3. Male friendship 4. Codependency 5. Obsession 6. Hudson Valley 7. New York (State) 8. 1990s 9. Psychological fiction 10. First person narratives
Kip Woods, infatuated with married father of two Thaddeus Kaufman, must decide how much he is willing to sacrifice for a love that may never be shared.
"Unrequited desire festers for decades, but it's money that ultimately destroys a gay man's relationship with his straight best friend." —*Booklist*
Companion to: River under the road.

Spencer-Fleming, Julia

All mortal flesh. Julia Spencer-Fleming. St. Martin's Minotaur, 2006. 320 p. (Reverend Clare Fergusson mysteries, 5)

ISBN 9780312312640

1. Gossiping and gossips 2. Separation (Marital relations) 3. Innocence (Law) 4. Murder investigation 5. Betrayal 6. Adirondack Mountains, New York 7. Mysteries

Library Journal Best Books, 2006

Police Chief Russ Van Alstyne and Reverend Clare Fergusson have long fought their passion in deference to his marriage, but it's difficult keeping secrets in the small Adirondack town of Millers Kill. When his wife is found brutally murdered in their home, the state police think it's an open-and-shut-case of a disaffected husband, silencing first his wife, then the investigation he controls. But nothing is as it seems in Millers Kill, where betrayal twists old friendships and evil waits inside white-clapboard farmhouses. Russ and Clare struggle against the reach of the law, the authority of the church, and their own guilty hearts.

"In a story as unpredictable as its characters, the resolution takes this series in a direction that should give the good bishop heart palpitations." —*New York Times Book Review*

Hid from our eyes. Julia Spencer-Fleming. Minotaur Books, 2020. 336 p. (Reverend Clare Fergusson mysteries, 9)

ISBN 9780312606855

1. Clergywomen 2. Police chiefs 3. Women murder victims 4. Husband and wife 5. Copycat murderers 6. Adirondack Mountains, New York 7. New York (State) 8. Mysteries

LC 2019049217

Police chief Russ van Alstyne races to solve a baffling murder that eerily resembles two unsolved killings from decades earlier for which he was the prime suspect.

"Spencer-Fleming combines a first-rate mystery with flawed but endearing characters." —*Publishers Weekly*

I shall not want: a Clare Fergusson/Russ Van Alstyne mystery. Julia Spencer-Fleming. Thomas Dunne Books, 2008. 336 p. (Reverend Clare Fergusson mysteries, 6)

ISBN 9780312334871

1. Migrant workers 2. Drug traffic 3. Separated couples 4. Serial murderers 5. Fergusson, Clare (Fictitious character) 6. Adirondack Mountains, New York 7. Mysteries

LC 2008012281

Russ's balance between duty and desire was broken by his wife's tragic death. Now, Russ and Episcopal priest Clare Fergusson are separated by a wall of guilt and grief. When a Mexican farmhand stumbles over a Latino man killed with a single shot to the back of his head, Clare is drawn into the investigation. The discovery of two more bodies ignites fears that a serial killer is loose in the rural town and Russ is plagued by the media hysteria, conflict within the police department, and a series of baffling assaults. Throughout the escalating tensions, he and Clare find themselves seeking each other out even as they intend to keep distant.

In the bleak midwinter. Julia Spencer-Fleming. St. Martin's Minotaur, 2002. 308 p; (Reverend Clare Fergusson mysteries, 1)

ISBN 9780312288471

1. Abandoned infants 2. Police chiefs 3. Moving to a new city 4. Women murder victims 5. Clergywomen 6. Adirondack Mountains, New York 7. Mysteries

LC 2001051303

Agatha Award for Best First Novel, 2003; Anthony Award for Best Novel, 2003; Dilys Award, 2003; Macavity Award for Best First Mystery Novel, 2003

Trying to acclimate herself to her new parish and surroundings, Clare Fergusson, the first female priest of an Episcopal church in Millers Kill, New York, finds herself immersed in murder when a newborn baby is abandoned and a young mother is brutally slain, forcing her to dig deeply into the town's secrets, while fighting her attraction to the married police chief.

"A mystery set in the upstate New York town of Millers Kill. As the new (and first female) priest of St. Alban's Episcopal Church, Clare [Fergusson] faces her first test when an infant is left on the rectory doorstep by an unwed teenage mother who is found frozen to death by the river. More crises follow in this freshly conceived and meticulously plotted whodunit when a police investigation raises suspicions about two parishioners who are frantic to adopt the child, and when Clare's own inquiries within her conservative flock turn up troubling evidence of domestic abuse." —*New York Times Book Review*

Through the evil days: a Clare Fergusson/Russ van Alstyne mystery. Julia Spencer-Fleming. Minotaur Books, 2013. 320 p. (Reverend Clare Fergusson mysteries, 8)

ISBN 9780312606848

1. Fires 2. Clergywomen 3. Police chiefs 4. Murder 5. Kidnapping 6. Adirondack Mountains, New York 7. Mysteries

LC 2013025276

LibraryReads Favorites, 2013

When a raging fire quickly becomes a double homicide and kidnapping, expectant parents Chief of Police Russ Van Alstyne and the Reverend Clare Fergusson must deal with personal and professional issues they never before encountered.

Spiegelman, Peter

Black maps. Peter Spiegelman. Alfred A. Knopf, 2003. 304 p. (John March novels, 1)

ISBN 9781400040759

1. Private investigators 2. Extortion 3. Capitalists and financiers 4. White collar crime 5. Financial intrigue 6. New York (State) 7. Manhattan, New York City 8. Mysteries 9. Hardboiled fiction 10. Financial thrillers

Shamus Award for Best First P.I. Novel, 2004

Manhattan P.I. John March takes on the case of Rick Pierro, a successful banker, who is on the verge of losing everything to a blackmail attempt that threatens to engulf him in a money-laundering scheme under federal investigation.

Spillane, Mickey

The Consummata. Mickey Spillane and Max Allan Collins. Hardcase Crime, 2011. 256 p.

ISBN 9780857682888

1. Double agents 2. Stolen property recovery 3. Rescues 4. Criminals 5. Violence against women 6. Miami, Florida 7. 1960s 8. Mysteries 9. Hardboiled fiction

In a tale completed from an unfinished Spillane outline, Morgan the Raider sets out to clear his name after he is accused of being the mastermind behind a forty million dollar heist and finds himself hiding out in the middle of Miami's Little Havana neighborhood.

"Spillane decided to introduce a new series featuring a master criminal called Morgan the Raider. The first entry, The Delta Factor, came out in '67. So far, so good. Then the business intervened in the form of Hollywood, which decided to make a movie out of the first Morgan book. But the experience left Spillane so upset that he stopped work on the already announced second installment.... Collins finishes this project seamlessly. It is impossible to tell where one great writer left off and another begins." —*BookReporter.com*

The **Goliath** bone. Mickey Spillane; with Max Allan Collins. Harcourt, 2008. 288 p. (Mike Hammer mysteries, 14)
ISBN 9780151014545
1. Goliath 2. Relics 3. Terrorists 4. Right-wing extremists 5. Bones 6. Archaeological thefts 7. New York City 8. Mysteries 9. Hardboiled fiction
LC 2008010091
After preventing the violent robbery of two college sweethearts who stumbled onto a priceless archaeological find, P.I. Mike Hammer takes on Islamic terrorists and Israeli extremists out to seize the relic for their own purposes.
"Much of the jargon is vintage, as is the indomitable Hammer as he strives to protect the kids and prevent the Goliath bone from setting off the next big war. While not on a par with early Spillane classics, this is a fitting capstone to Hammer's career." —*Publishers Weekly*
An Otto Penzler Book.

Kill me, darling. . Titan Books, 2015. 296 p. (Mike Hammer mysteries, 20)
ISBN 9781783291380
1. Private investigators 2. Organized crime 3. Automobile travel 4. Crimes against police 5. Murder 6. Long Island, New York 7. Miami, Florida 8. Hardboiled fiction 9. Mysteries
An inebriated Mike Hammer investigates the murder of an aging police officer who once worked with Mike Hammer's ex-partner Velda, who is reputed to be involved with a powerful Florida gangster.

A **long** time dead: a Mike Hammer casebook. Open Road Media, 2016. 250 p. (Mike Hammer mysteries)
ISBN 9781504036092
1. Private investigators 2. Crime 3. Criminal investigation 4. Hammer, Mike (Fictitious character) 5. New York City 6. Hardboiled fiction 7. Mysteries
The first Mike Hammer short story collection from the twentieth-century bestselling American mystery writer Mickey Spillane.
"Collins has published several Hammer novels, completions of Spillane's original unfinished manuscripts, and, as with those novels, the writing here is so fluid, so very much in Spillane's voice, that its impossible to tell where the original writer's words end and the coauthor's begin. A must for anyone interested in the history of hard-boiled mysteries." —*Booklist*

Spiotta, Dana
Wayward. Dana Spiotta. Alfred A Knopf, 2021. 256 p.
ISBN 9780593318737
1. Middle-aged women 2. Mothers and daughters 3. Presidential election, 2016 4. Separated women (Marital relations) 5. Local history 6. Syracuse, New York 7. New York (State) 8. 2010s 9. Literary fiction
In 2016, 52-year-old Samantha Raymond, as her life begins to unravel, flees her suburban existence—and her family—as she struggles with how to be a wife, a mother and a daughter in a country that is coming apart at the seams.
"An engrossing, interior mother-daughter story that expands into a sharp social commentary." —*Kirkus*

Spufford, Francis
★ **Golden** hill. Francis Spufford. Simon & Schuster, 2017. 336 p.
ISBN 9781501163876
1. Misadventures 2. Escapes 3. Swindlers and swindling 4. Deception 5. New York City 6. Colonial America (1600-1775) 7. 1740s 8. Historical fiction

Costa First Novel Award, 2016; Library Journal Best Books, 2017; RSL Ondaatje Prize, 2017; RUSA Reading List Short List, 2018; Shortlisted for the Walter Scott Prize for Historical Fiction, 2017
When a mysterious man shows up at the countinghouse in 1746 New York with an order for a huge sum of money, the local colonial merchants can't decide if they should trust him, befriend him, arrest him or seduce him.
"Spufford's...spirited 'novel of Old New York,' playfully rendered in simulated eighteenth-century prose, pays homage to the literature of the colonial era." —*Booklist*
Originally published: London : Faber, 2016.

★ **Light** perpetual. Francis Spufford. Scribner, 2021. 352 p.
ISBN 9781982174149
1. Civilians in war 2. Bombings 3. Children — Death 4. Tragedy 5. Paradoxes 6. London, England 7. United States 8. Literary fiction
Lunchtime on a Saturday, 1944: the Woolworths on Bexford High Street in southeast London receives a delivery of aluminum saucepans. A crowd gathers to see the first new metal in ages. An instant later, the crowd is gone; incinerated. Among the shoppers were five young children. Who were they? What futures did they lose? This brilliantly constructed novel lets an alternative reel of time run, imagining the life arcs of these five souls as they live through the extraordinary, unimaginable changes of the bustling immensity of twentieth-century London. Ingenious and profound, full of warmth and beauty, Light Perpetual illuminates the shapes of experience, the extraordinariness of the ordinary, the mysteries of memory and expectation, and the preciousness of life.
"Thanks to Spufford's narrative wizardry, all five protagonists come to vivid life in this spectacularly moving story." —*Publishers Weekly*

St. Aubyn, Edward
At last. Edward St. Aubyn. Farrar, Straus and Giroux, 2012. 264 p. (Patrick Melrose novels, 5)
ISBN 9780374298890
1. Mothers — Death 2. Mother and adult son 3. Funerals 4. Dysfunctional families 5. Melrose, Patrick (Fictitious character) 6. London, England 7. Psychological fiction 8. Books to TV.
LC 2011034964
New York Times Notable Book, 2012
Friends, relatives, and foes trickle in to pay final respects to Patrick's mother, Eleanor. An American heiress, Eleanor married into the British aristocracy, giving up the grandeur of her upbringing for "good works" freely bestowed on everyone but her own son, who finds himself questioning whether his transition to a life without parents will indeed be the liberation he had so long imagined.
First published: 2011.

Double blind. Edward St. Aubyn. Farrar, Straus & Giroux, 2021. 224 p.
ISBN 9780374282196
1. Women scholars and academics 2. College friends 3. Boyfriends 4. Ecologists 5. Venture capitalists 6. Great Britain 7. United States 8. Literary fiction 9. Multiple perspectives
LC 2020057034
When Olivia meets a new lover just as she is welcoming her best friend, Lucy, back from New York, her dedicated academic life expands precipitously. Her connection to Francis, a committed naturalist living off the grid, is immediate and startling. Eager to involve Lucy in her joy, Olivia introduces the two—but Lucy has received shocking news of her own that binds the trio unusually close. Over the months that follow, Lucy's boss, Hunter, Olivia's psychoanalyst parents, and a young man named Sebastian are pulled into the friends' orbit, and not one of them will emerge unchanged.

"St. Aubyn's impressive trove of knowledge of wide-ranging topics like artificial intelligence, epigenetics, climate science, and wilding takes nothing away from an entertaining story about love and friendship." —*Library Journal*

St. George, Harper

The **heiress** gets a duke. Harper St. George. Berkley, 2021. 320 p. (Gilded Age heiresses, 1)
ISBN 9780593197202
1. Single women 2. Heirs and heiresses 3. Rich families 4. Dukes and duchesses 5. Arranged marriage 6. Victorian era (1837-1901) 7. Victorian romances 8. Historical romances

Forced into a marriage of convenience with Evan Sterling, the Duke of Rothschild, to save her sister, American heiress August Crenshaw pulls every stunt in the book to make him call of the wedding.

"St. George (Falling for Her Viking Captive) heartrendingly depicts Victorian women bartered away for wealth and status, but the deep affection and witty dialog August and Evan share outshines a grim if realistic beginning. Fans of Courtney Milan and Scarlett Peckham will enjoy this 'The Gilded Age Heiresses' series opener." —*Library Journal*

St. James, Simone

The **broken** girls. Simone St. James. Berkley, 2018. 336 p.
ISBN 9780451476203
1. Boarding schools 2. Women journalists 3. Murder investigation 4. Sisters 5. Ghosts 6. Vermont 7. Horror 8. Mysteries 9. Ghost stories 10. Adult books for young adults
LC 2017004873
LibraryReads Favorites, 2018; RUSA Reading List Short List, 2019

More than 60 years after one of four friends in a reputedly haunted boarding school goes missing, journalist Fiona Sheridan resolves to learn her sister's fate before a harrowing discovery is made.

The **haunting** of Maddy Clare. Simone St. James. New American Library, 2012. 336 p.
ISBN 9780451235688
1. Ghosts 2. Suicide victims 3. Revenge 4. Paranormal phenomenon investigation 5. Haunted places 6. England 7. 1920s 8. Ghost stories 9. Historical fiction 10. Canadian fiction 11. Adult books for young adults
LC 2011033391
Arthur Ellis Award for Best First Novel, 2013; RITA Award for Best First Book, 2013; RITA Award for Best Novel with Strong Romantic Elements, 2013

In 1920s England, Sarah Piper is sent by her temporary agency to assist a ghost hunter, Alistair Gellis, as he investigates the spirit of Maddy Clare, a young serving maid said to haunt the barn where she committed suicide. The ghost is no hoax, and Sarah is soon caught up in trying to discover who Maddy was, where she came from, and why she is desperate for revenge.

The **Sun** Down motel. Simone St. James. Berkley, 2020. 336 p.
ISBN 9780440000174
1. Young women 2. Motels 3. Missing persons 4. Serial murders 5. Aunts 6. New York (State) 7. United States 8. Horror 9. Parallel narratives
LC 2019026692
A young woman takes a night-clerk job at the same roadside motel from where her aunt went missing decades earlier before uncovering the work of a serial killer.

"Booktalk this one to your mystery-loving readers until you run out of superlatives. What a story!"—*Booklist*

Stabenow, Dana

★ A **deeper** sleep: a Kate Shugak novel. Dana Stabenow. St. Martin's Minotaur, 2007. 240 p. (Kate Shugak mysteries, 15)
ISBN 9780312343224
1. District attorneys 2. Women murder victims 3. Shooting 4. Shugak, Kate (Fictitious character) 5. Former lawyers 6. Alaska 7. Anchorage, Alaska 8. Mysteries 9. Adult books for young adults

Anchorage private detective Kate Shugak and Alaska state trooper Jim Chopin pursue Louis Deem, a man arrested for and acquitted of the murder of his wife, after a witness to the shooting of a woman and her son places Deem at the scene of the crime.

"Private investigator Kate Shugak is determined to find the evidence to convict Louis Deem, who has been arrested and tried for several serious crimes but never convicted. When a double homicide occurs after his latest acquittal, Kate investigates. A witness places Deem at the scene, but Kate wants additional evidence to convince the jury. Deem is a dangerous character who intimidates witnesses, and Kate and her family won't be safe until he is in jail." —*Booklist*
Previously published in Great Britain in 2013.

★ A **fine** and bitter snow: a Kate Shugak novel. Dana Stabenow. St. Martin's Minotaur, 2002. 211 p; (Kate Shugak mysteries, 12)
ISBN 9780312205485
1. Oil well drilling 2. Park rangers 3. State police 4. Women private investigators 5. Shugak, Kate (Fictitious character) 6. Alaska 7. Mysteries 8. Adult books for young adults
LC 2002022863
Aleutian private detective Kate Shugak becomes caught up in a vicious battle between conservationists and developers of Alaska's pristine wilderness when an environmentalist protesting plans for drilling for oil in a nearby wildlife preserve is found poisoned.

"Rich with details about life in this snowbound culture, the story moves at a steady pace to a classic ending." —*Publishers Weekly*

★ A **grave** denied. Dana Stabenow. St. Martin's Minotaur, 2003. 304 p. (Kate Shugak mysteries, 13)
ISBN 9780312306816
1. Guardian and ward 2. Arson 3. Glaciers 4. Shugak, Kate (Fictitious character) 5. Former lawyers 6. Alaska 7. Mysteries 8. Adult books for young adults
LC 2003050605
When the body of a murdered town handyman is discovered, frozen and in the path of a receding glacier, Alaska state trooper Jim Chopin asks Kate Shugak to investigate the victim's background in the hope of finding the killer.

★ **Hunter's** moon. Dana Stabenow. G. P. Putnam's Sons, 1999. 239 p. (Kate Shugak mysteries, 9)
ISBN 9780425172599
1. Big game hunters 2. Hunting 3. Wilderness areas 4. Shugak, Kate (Fictitious character) 5. Park rangers 6. Alaska 7. Mysteries 8. Adult books for young adults
LC 98-33465
Kate Shugak and her boyfriend, Jack, lead a group of German tourists into the wilds of Alaska on a hunting trip, but the expedition begins to go horribly wrong when several of the hunters turn up dead, and Kate discovers that bears are not the only animals being hunted in the bush

Killing grounds: a Kate Shugak mystery. Dana Stabenow. G. Putnam's Sons, 1998. 273 p. (Kate Shugak mysteries, 8)
ISBN 9780399143564
1. Fisheries 2. Fishers 3. Undercover operations 4. Shugak, Kate (Fictitious character) 5. Former lawyers 6. Alaska 7. Mysteries 8. Adult books for young adults

While deckhanding on board a salmon tender, Kate Shugak hauls up the body of a widely disliked fisherman whose apparent murder is greeted with great rejoicing. Drafted by State Trooper Jim Chopin to assist in the investigation, Kate draws up a long list of suspects. Meanwhile, Kate's Aleut aunties are mixed up in some shady dealings of their own, which Kate must prove do not include murder.

★ **Less** than a treason. Dana Stabenow. Head of Zeus, 2017. 336 p. (Kate Shugak mysteries, 21)
  ISBN 9781786695697
  1. Wolfdogs 2. Aleut women 3. Women private investigators 4. Aleuts 5. Survival 6. Alaska 7. Mysteries
  Native Aleut private investigator Kate Shugak finds her and her trusty half-wolf, half-husky dog Mutt in trouble in the Alaskan wilds when they both wind up shot.
  "The book is sprinkled with wit, studded with exquisite descriptions of the rugged landscape, and filled with opinionated and endearing characters, including reality TV show producers, park rangers, geologists, and barkeeps." —*Publishers Weekly*

A **night** too dark: a Kate Shugak novel. Dana Stabenow. Minotaur Books, 2010. 336 p. (Kate Shugak mysteries, 17)
  ISBN 9780312559090
  1. Murder investigation 2. Gold mines and mining 3. State parks 4. Murder 5. Park rangers 6. Alaska 7. Mysteries 8. Adult books for young adults
                                        LC 2009039815
  When a man believed to have committed suicide reappears from the wilderness, Aleut private investigator Kate Shugak and Trooper Jim Chopin struggle to identify the remains of a mysterious victim, a case that is complicated by political factors at the local gold mine.

No fixed line. Dana Stabenow. Head of Zeus, 2020. 336 pages (Kate Shugak mysteries, 22)
  ISBN 9781788549110
  1. Aleut women 2. Women private investigators 3. Wilderness areas 4. Blizzards 5. Airplane accidents 6. Alaska 7. Mysteries
  When a New Year's Eve blizzard blocks access to the site of a plane crash in the Quilak mountains, former trooper Jim Chopin struggles to rescue two child survivors, before Kate Shugak receives an unwelcome accusation from beyond the grave.
  "Stabenow's affection for her characters, in particular Chopin, shines through, as does her fondness for the Alaskan country she knows so well. Fans will hope this series goes on forever." —*Publishers Weekly*

Restless in the grave. Dana Stabenow. Minotaur Books, 2012. 368 p. (Kate Shugak mysteries, 19)
  ISBN 9780312559137
  1. Sabotage 2. Murder investigation 3. Undercover operations 4. State police 5. Conspiracies 6. Alaska 7. Mysteries
                                        LC 2011037662
  Aleut private investigator Kate Shugak and Alaska State Trooper Liam Campbell—the heroes of "New York Times" bestseller Stabenow's most beloved series—team up for the first time ever when Liam needs Kate's help to clear his wife of the murder of a wealthy aviation entrepreneur.

The **singing** of the dead. Dana Stabenow. St. Martin's Minotaur Books, 2000. 272 p. (Kate Shugak mysteries, 11)
  ISBN 9780312209575
  1. Women politicians 2. Senatorial candidates 3. Park rangers 4. Aleut women 5. Former lawyers 6. Alaska 7. Mysteries 8. Adult books for young adults

Kate Shugak joins the staff of a Native woman running for the Alaska State Senate to work security. The candidate has been receiving anonymous threats and Kate's job will be to shadow the candidate. The campaign is rocked when a staff researcher is murdered and it appears linked to a ninety-year-old unsolved murder.
  "With well-drawn characters, splendid scenery and an insider's knowledge of Alaskan history and politics, this fine novel ranks as one of Stabenow's best." —*Publishers Weekly*

So sure of death: a Liam Campbell mystery. Dana Stabenow. Dutton, 1999. 275 p. (Liam Campbell mysteries, 2)
  ISBN 9780525945192
  1. Excavations (Archaeology) 2. Fishing villages 3. State police 4. Campbell, Liam (Fictitious character) 5. Murder investigation 6. Alaska 7. Mysteries 8. Adult books for young adults
                                        LC 99025121
  When the brutally murdered bodies of a local family are found adrift at sea, Alaska State Trooper Liam Campbell suddenly is drawn into a nasty homicide case involving forbidden romance, family scandal, tribal taboos, and adultery.

Spoils of the dead. Dana Stabenow. Head of Zeus, 2021. 400 p. (Liam Campbell mysteries, 5)
  ISBN 9781788549158
  1. State police 2. Bush pilots 3. Married people 4. Archaeology 5. Drug traffic 6. Alaska 7. Mysteries 8. Adult books for young adults
  Restationed in a remote bush town in the aftermath of a fatal judgment call, Trooper Liam Campbell tackles unexpected challenges in the form of a cutthroat local fishing trade, violent drug dealers and a war-gold archaeologist's murder.
  "Stabenow's vivid portraits of the Alaskan landscape, along with the Campbell-Chouinard relationship (these are two people besotted with each other), lighten the tone in this smooth, character-driven mystery featuring Alaskan history and culture and the welcome return of Sergeant Campbell." —*Booklist*

★ **A taint** in the blood. Dana Stabenow. St. Martin's Minotaur, 2004. 305 p; (Kate Shugak mysteries, 14)
  ISBN 9780312306830
  1. Women with cancer 2. Families of murder victims 3. Arson investigation 4. State police 5. Shugak, Kate (Fictitious character) 6. Alaska 7. Anchorage, Alaska 8. Mysteries 9. Adult books for young adults
                                        LC 2004046856
  Hired by Charlotte Mauravieff, who wants to clear her mother's name of the arson fire that killed one of her brothers, private investigator Kate Shugak finds the case complicated by someone who wants the truth to stay hidden.

Though not dead: a Kate Shugak novel. Dana Stabenow. Minotaur Books, 2011. 480 p. (Kate Shugak mysteries, 18)
  ISBN 9780312559113
  1. Wills 2. Family secrets 3. Fathers and sons 4. Material culture 5. Attempted murder 6. Alaska 7. Mysteries 8. Adult books for young adults
                                        LC 2010039080
  Inheriting a homestead from her late uncle, a stunned Kate Shugak receives a cryptic letter from him imploring her to discover his father's fate, a mystery involving a priceless tribal artifact for which Kate is targeted by murderous attacks.
  First published in the UK in 2013 by Head of Zues, Ltd—Title page verso.

Whisper to the blood: a Kate Shugak novel. Dana Stabenow. Minotaur Books, 2009. 368 p. (Kate Shugak mysteries, 16)

ISBN 9780312369743

1. Foster family 2. Mines and mineral resources 3. Robbery 4. Park rangers 5. Aleut women 6. Alaska 7. Mysteries 8. Adult books for young adults

LC 2008033959

The inhabitants of Niniltna are uneasy about the gold-mining company buying up tracts of land nearby, an unease shared by P.I. Kate Shugak as she probes the killings of a mine opponent and a popular ski champion-turned-company spokesperson.

"A dynamite combination of atmosphere, action, and character." —*Booklist*

Stachniak, Eva

The **chosen** maiden: a novel. Eva Stachniak. Doubleday Canada, 2017. 432 p.

ISBN 9780385678568

1. Ballet dancers 2. Sibling rivalry 3. Siblings 4. Determination (Personal quality) 5. Kiev, Ukraine 6. St. Petersburg, Russia 7. Russian Revolution and Civil War (1917-1921) 8. Between the Wars (1918-1939) 9. Historical fiction 10. Canadian fiction

Loan Stars Favourites, 2017

Born on the road to dancer parents, the Nijinsky children seem destined for the stage. Vaslav is an early prodigy, and through single-minded pursuit will grow into arguably the greatest—and most infamous—Russian ballet dancer of the 20th century. His talented younger sister Bronia, however, also longs to dance. Overshadowed by Vaslav, plagued by a body deemed less than ideal and struggling against the constraints of her gender, Bronia will have to work triply hard to prove herself worthy.

"A memorable literary rendering of a remarkable womans life." —*Booklist*

The **Winter** Palace: a novel of Catherine the Great. Eva Stachniak. Bantam Books 2012. 384 p.

ISBN 9780553808124

1. Catherine 2. Women rulers 3. Courts and courtiers 4. Heirs and heiresses 5. Arranged marriage 6. Household employees 7. Russia 8. Romanov Dynasty (1613-1917) 9. 18th century 10. Historical fiction 11. Canadian fiction 12. Biographical fiction

Booklist Editors' Choice, 2011

A reimagining of the early years of Catherine the Great traces the story of two young women: Barbara, a servant who will become one of Russia's most cunning royal spies, and Sophia, a pretty, naive German duchess who will become Catherine the Great.

Stage, Zoje

★ **Baby** teeth: a novel. Zoje Stage. St. Martin's Press, 2018. 304 p.

ISBN 9781250170750

1. People who are mute 2. Mothers and daughters 3. Manipulation (Social sciences) 4. Motherhood — Psychological aspects 5. Seven-year-old girls 6. Psychological suspense 7. Multiple perspectives

LC 2017056740

LibraryReads Favorites, 2018; Library Journal Best Books, 2018

An ailing woman fights to protect her family from her mute daughter's psychologically manipulative schemes, which are complicated by her doting husband's denial about their daughter's true nature.

Getaway. Zoje Stage. Mulholland Books, 2021. 368 p.

ISBN 9780316242509

1. Sisters 2. Hiking 3. Stalking 4. Secrets 5. Jealousy 6. Psychological suspense

Two sisters and a best friend go on a hiking getaway, but tensions from their shared past flare up as someone appears to be stalking them in the new thriller by the best-selling author of Baby Teeth.

"This bildungsroman, mixed with a dark fairy tale and a touch of Kate DiCamillo's The Tale of Despereaux, makes Stage's third triumph, following Wonderland (2020) and Baby Teeth (2018)." —*Booklist*

Wonderland. Zoje Stage. Mulholland Books, 2020. 352 p.

ISBN 9780316458498

1. Rural life 2. Supernatural 3. Moving, Household 4. Trees 5. Good and evil 6. New York (State) 7. Horror

Moving to a rural farmhouse in far upstate New York, Orla, a retired dancer, must protect her family from an unknown entity that is calling to them from the land, in the earth, beneath the trees—and in their minds.

"The horror genre has found an eloquent and unflinching new author." —*Booklist*

Stanley, Michael

A **carrion** death. Michael Stanley. Harper Collins, 2008. 480 p. (Detective Kubu mysteries, 1)

ISBN 9780061252402

1. Detectives 2. Murder investigation 3. Corruption investigation 4. Overweight men 5. Diamond mines and mining 6. Botswana 7. Africa 8. Mysteries

In the aftermath of the murder of an anonymous victim, assistant superintendent David Bengu begins his career in Botswana, where his convivial passions and determined methods earn him a local nickname that likens him to a hippopotamus.

"Readers may be lured to Africa by the landscape, but it takes a great character like Kubu to win our loyalty." —*New York Times Book Review*

Michael Sears and Stanley Trollip writing under the pseudonym, Michael Stanley.

Deadly harvest. Michael Stanley. Bourbon Street Books, 2013. Xiv, 477 p; (Detective Kubu mysteries, 4)

ISBN 9780062221520

1. Detectives 2. Serial murder investigation 3. Missing persons 4. Wiesel, Elie 5. Politicians 6. Botswana 7. Africa 8. Mysteries

Detecive Kubu searches for a possible serial killer targeting girls in Botswana in order to use their bodies in muti, a witch doctor's potion that can be made more potent with the addition of human remains.

"The real-life phenomenon of African witch doctors committing murder to get ingredients for their spells drives the richly atmospheric fourth Detective Kubu mystery (after 2011's Death of the Mantis)...Their investigation takes place during a time of political instability in the country when the prospect that an opposition party could finally be gaining traction spawns violence. The gritty depiction of corruption and obsession serves as a striking counterpoint to Alexander McCall Smith's blood-free No. 1 Ladies' Detective Agency series, also set in Botswana." —*Publishers Weekly*

A **death** in the family. Michael Stanley. Minotaur Books, 2015. 304 p. (Detective Kubu mysteries, 5)

ISBN 9781250070890

1. Mineral industry and trade 2. Public officials 3. Corruption 4. Murder investigation 5. Detectives 6. Botswana 7. Africa 8. Mysteries

Just as Detective Kubu, against orders, begins to inspect the murder of his father in modern-day Africa, a senior official at the Department of Mines is found dead amid a Chinese-owned company's effort to take over part of a village.

Death of the mantis. By Michael Stanley. Harper Paperbacks, 2011. 448 p. (Detective Kubu mysteries, 3)

ISBN 9780062000378

1. Murder investigation 2. Innocence (Law) 3. Detectives 4. Bengu, David (Fictitious character) 5. Police 6. Botswana 7. Africa 8. Mysteries

LC 2011022154

Library Journal Best Books, 2011

In the southern Kalahari area of Botswana, three Bushmen are found standing around a ranger who is dying from a severe head wound in a dry ravine and Dectective David "Kubu" Bengu must figure out, with the help of an old school friend, if the Bushmen were there to help—or were the murderers.

Michael Sears and Stanley Trollip writing under the pseudonym, Michael Stanley.

Dying to live. Michael Stanley. Minotaur Books, 2017. 324 pages (Detective Kubu mysteries, 6)
ISBN 9781250070906
1. Detectives 2. Indigenous peoples 3. Senior murder victims 4. Murder investigation 5. San (African people) 6. Botswana 7. Africa 8. Mysteries

LC 2017024858

A Bushman is discovered dead near the Central Kalahari Game Reserve in Africa. Although the man looks old enough to have died of natural causes, the police suspect foul play. Pathologist Ian MacGregor confirms the cause of death as a broken neck, and calls in Assistant Superintendent David "Kubu" Bengu. When the Bushman's corpse is stolen from the morgue, suddenly the case takes on a new dimension.

Stansel, Ian

The **last** cowboys of San Geronimo. Ian Stansel. Houghton Mifflin Harcourt, 2017. 186 p.
ISBN 9780544963399
1. Fratricide 2. Brothers 3. Widows 4. Horse trainers 5. Sibling rivalry 6. California 7. Modern Westerns 8. Crime fiction

LC 2016047296

A justice-fueled race across the wilds of Northern California reveals the hardscrabble youth and fateful experiences of a preeminent horse trainer who has been murdered by his jealous brother.

Staples, Dennis E.

This town sleeps. Dennis E. Staples. Counterpoint, 2020. 224 pages
ISBN 9781640092846
1. Gay men 2. Ojibwa Indians 3. Prejudice 4. Small town life 5. Urban legends 6. Minnesota 7. Mysteries 8. Literary fiction 9. LGBTQIA fiction

Engaging in a secret affair with a closeted white man, an Ojibwe from a northern Minnesota reservation navigates small-town discrimination before a ghost leads him to the grave of a basketball star whose murder becomes linked to a local legend.

"With its multiple narrators and stories of ghosts, this debut will find its audience in those searching for #ownvoices authors with an authentic view of reservation life and the tragedies that haunt the communities." —*Library Journal*

Stapley, Marissa

The **last** resort. Marissa Stapley. Graydon House, 2019. 384 pages
ISBN 9781525823541
1. Married people 2. Marital conflict 3. Marriage counseling 4. Resorts 5. Hurricanes 6. Mexico 7. Psychological suspense

Description: When two couples head to an intensive marriage therapy program at the Harmony Resort, it soon becomes clear that the getaway is not what it seems, and neither are its celebrity owners.

Stark, Richard

Ask the parrot: a Parker novel. Richard Stark. Mysterious Press, 2006. 279 p. (Parker thrillers, 23)
ISBN 9780892960682
1. Bank robberies 2. Criminals 3. Race tracks 4. Parker (Fictitious character : Stark) 5. Former convicts 6. Crime fiction

LC 2006927625

Racing through the backwoods of Massachusetts and on the verge of being taken down for one of the biggest and most disastrous bank heists the state has ever seen, Parker runs right into the barrel of a gun pointed from the wrong side of the law. A quiet and angry recluse with only a silent parrot for company in his seclusion, Tom Lindahl saves Parker from the police dogs, but enmeshes him in yet another in a long line of dubious, highly dangerous, but seriously profitable jobs. Far more than some aimless indigent, holed up in a shack in the woods, Lindahl is a man built on rage and driven by a thirst for revenge. A whistleblower whom nobody heard, a man tossed aside by a corrupt political establishment, Lindahl plans to rob them of their lucre and needs Parker's help.

Breakout. Richard Stark. Mysterious Press, 2002. 299 p. (Parker thrillers, 21)
ISBN 9780892967797
1. Barber, Frank 2. Escapes 3. Robbery 4. Thieves 5. Parker (Fictitious character : Stark) 6. Crime fiction

LC 2002023492

"Richard Stark (the name that Donald E. Westlake uses when he lets Parker off the leash) writes with ruthless efficiency. His bad guys are polished pros who think hard, move fast and turn on a dime in moments of crisis. And because talk doesn't come cheap, every bit of dialogue counts." —*New York Times Book Review*

Donald E. Westlake writing as Richard Stark.

Comeback. Richard Stark. Mysterious Press, 1997. 292 p. (Parker thrillers, 17)
ISBN 9780892966615
1. Thieves 2. Robbery 3. Betrayal 4. Parker (Fictitious character : Stark) 5. Evangelists 6. Crime fiction

LC 977019

New York Times Notable Mysteries, 1997

The robbery of a Christian crusade comes off without a hitch, but it seems that the evangelist, the cops, the criminals, and the church's security officer are all after the loot, in a dark world where no one can be trusted

Donald E. Westlake writing as Richard Stark.

Dirty money. Richard Stark. Grand Central Pub, 2008. 276 p; (Parker thrillers, 24)
ISBN 9780446178587
1. Bank robberies 2. Criminals 3. Deception 4. Parker (Fictitious character : Stark) 5. Churches 6. Noir fiction 7. Crime fiction

LC 2007931314

Master criminal Parker takes another turn for the worse as he tries to recover loot from a heist gone terribly wrong. Parker and two cohorts stole the assets of a bank in transit, but the police heat was so great they could only escape if they left the money behind. Now Parker and his associates plot to reclaim the loot, which they hid in the choir loft of an unused country church. As they implement the plan, people on both sides of the law use the forces at their command to stop Parker and grab the goods for themselves. Though Parker's new getaway van is an old Ford Econoline with "Holy Redeemer Choir" on its doors, his gang is anything but holy, and Parker will do whatever it takes to redeem his prize, no matter who gets hurt in the process.

The **hunter**: a Parker novel. Richard Stark. University of Chicago Press, 2008. 199 p. (Parker thrillers, 1)

ISBN 9780226770994

1. Thieves 2. Revenge 3. Criminals 4. Parker (Fictitious character : Stark) 5. New York City 6. Books to movies 7. Crime fiction

Parker, a professional thief, comes to New York City seeking revenge on a woman who betrayed him and a man who stole his money.

Donald E. Westlake writing as Richard Stark.

Title of later film version: Point blank.

The **jugger**: a Parker novel. Richard Stark. University of Chicago Press, 2009. X, 211 p. (Parker thrillers, 6)

ISBN 9780226771021

1. Criminals 2. Inheritance and succession 3. Murder 4. Parker (Fictitious character : Stark) 5. Nebraska 6. Crime fiction

Parker is in Sagamore, Nebraska, at the request of Joe Sheer, a retired safe cracker who carries many of Parker's criminal secrets.

Originally published: New York : Pocket Books, 1965.

Starling, Caitlin

The **death** of Jane Lawrence. Caitlin Starling. St. Martin's Press, 2021. 352 p.

ISBN 9781250272584

1. Arranged marriage 2. Manors 3. Physicians 4. Women 5. Paranoia 6. Horror 7. Gothic fiction

LC 2021026475

LibraryReads Favorites, 2021; Loan Stars Favourites, 2021

Set in a dark-mirror version of post-war England, Caitlin Starling crafts a new kind of gothic horror from the bones of the beloved canon. This Crimson Peak-inspired story assembles, then upends, every expectation set in place by Shirley Jackson and Rebecca, and will leave readers shaken, desperate to begin again as soon as they are finished.

"A perfect choice for those who enjoy writers who play with the well-trod gothic trope to create something wholly new, utterly terrifying, and supremely satisfying." —*Booklist*

The **luminous** dead. Caitlin Starling. Harper Voyager, 2019. 352 p.

ISBN 9780062846907

1. Spelunkers 2. Planets 3. Caves 4. Exploration 5. Caving 6. Science fiction

When Gyre Price lied her way into this expedition, she thought she'd be mapping mineral deposits, and that her biggest problems would be cave collapses and gear malfunctions. She also thought that the fat paycheck—enough to get her off-planet and on the trail of her mother—meant she'd get a skilled surface team, monitoring her suit and environment, keeping her safe. Instead, she got Em.

"Starling's riveting near-future debut depicts an intense psychological battle of wills between two damaged, deeply flawed women who forge an unbreakable connection in the dark." —*Publishers Weekly*

Starnone, Domenico

Ties. Europa Editions, 2017. 144 p.

ISBN 9781609453855

1. Abandoned wives 2. Marital conflict 3. Marriage 4. Cheating (Interpersonal relations) 5. Forgiveness 6. Naples, Italy 7. Italy 8. Domestic fiction 9. Multiple perspectives 10. Translations

New York Times Notable Book, 2017

When her husband, who left her for a younger woman, returns home for the sake of the children, a woman, forced to carry on as if nothing ever came between them, wonders if she has the strength to overcome the betrayal or the courage to start over.

"A slim, stunning meditation on marriage, fidelity, honesty, and truth." —*Kirkus*

Translation of: Lacci

Originally published: Torino : Einaudi, 2014

Translated from the Italian

Trick. Europa Editions, 2018. 191 p.

ISBN 9781609454449

1. Grandfather and grandson 2. Four-year-old boys 3. Solitude 4. Babysitting 5. Interpersonal relations 6. Naples, Italy 7. Translations

Library Journal Best Books, 2018; National Book Award for Translated Literature finalist, 2018

A grandfather, used to living in solitude and obsessively focusing on his illustrating career, and his 4-year-old grandson match wits during a 72-hour babysitting stay in Naples.

Translation of: Scherzetto

Originally published: Torino : Giulio Einaudi, 2016

Translated from the Italian

Starr, Melvin R.

Unhallowed ground. Mel Starr. Monarch, 2012. 240 p. (Chronicle of Hugh de Singleton, surgeon, 4)

ISBN 9780857210586

1. Surgeons 2. Murder investigation 3. Suicide investigation 4. Singleton, Hugh de (Fictitious character) 5. Amateur detectives 6. Oxfordshire, England 7. England 8. Medieval period (476-1492) 9. Plantagenet period (1154-1485) 10. Medieval mysteries 11. Historical mysteries 12. Mysteries

While renovating her house, Sarah McKinley finds the remains of dozens of bodies that are linked to current missing-persons cases as well as a long-ago murder, which points toward a killer who has the ability to transcend time.

Statovci, Pajtim

Bolla. Pajtim Statovci; translated from the Finnish by David Hackston. Pantheon Books, 2021. 272 p.

ISBN 9781524749200

1. College students 2. Married men 3. Closeted gay men 4. Secrets 5. War 6. Kosovo (Republic) 7. Kosovo, Serbia 8. Literary fiction 9. LGBTQIA fiction 10. Love stories

LC 2020052280

Kirkus Prize for Fiction finalist, 2021

April 1995. Arsim is a twenty-two-year-old, recently-married student at the University of Pristina, keeping his head down to gain a university degree in a time and place deeply hostile to Albanians. In a cafâe he meets a young man named Milos, a Serb. Before the day is out, everything has changed for both of them, and within a week two milestones erupt in Arsim's married life: his wife announces her first pregnancy, and he begins a life in secret. After these febrile beginnings, Arsim and Milos's unlikely affair is derailed by the outbreak of war, which sends Arsim's fledgling family abroad and the timid Milos spiraling down a dark path. Years later, deported back to Pristina after a spell in prison, Arsim, alone and hopeless, finds himself in a broken reality that completely questions his past.

Originally published: Helsinki : Kustannusosakeyhtio Otava, 2019.

Translated from the Finnish.

Stead, Christina

★ The **man** who loved children. Christina Stead; introduction by Randall Jarrell. Picador USA, 2001. Xli, 527 p.

ISBN 9780312280444

1. Father and child 2. Marriage — Psychological aspects 3. Married women — Psychology 4. Idealism in men 5. Contempt 6. Washington, D.C. 7. Domestic fiction 8. Australian fiction

After ten years of marriage, Sam and Henny Pollit find themselves with too many children, insufficient money, and an abundant loathing for each other.

Originally published: New York : Simon and Schuster, 1940.
Introduction by Michael Schmidt.

Steadman, Catherine

The **disappearing** act. Catherine Steadman. Ballantine Books, 2021. 320 p.

ISBN 9780593158036

1. Actors and actresses 2. British in the United States 3. Auditions 4. Ambition in women 5. Competition 6. Hollywood, California 7. Psychological suspense 8. First person narratives

LC 2020044412

A British actress new to Hollywood, Mia Eliot is forced to play the role of a lifetime when a girl she only met once disappears and an imposter shows up in her place, forcing her to question her sanity as the truth goes beyond anything she could have ever imagined.

"This tale of Hollywood glamour, cruelty, and myth is sure to win Steadman new fans." —*Publishers Weekly*

Mr. Nobody: a novel. Catherine Steadman. Ballantine Books, 2020. 320 p.

ISBN 9781524797683

1. Men with amnesia 2. Women psychiatrists 3. Physician and patient 4. Secrets 5. New identities 6. England 7. Psychological suspense

LC 2019035576

Treating a man found on the beach with no memory of his identity, a neuropsychologist who would hide her own past is confronted by her patient's mysterious knowledge of her secrets.

"Steadman (Something in the Water) strikes an engaging balance between character development and action in this satisfying, intricately plotted thriller that will appeal to fans of Sarah Pinborough and Ruth Ware." —*Library Journal*

Something in the water. Catherine Steadman. Ballantine Books, 2018. 352 p.

ISBN 9781524797188

1. Married people 2. Honeymoons 3. Scuba diving 4. Options, alternatives, choices 5. Greed 6. Bora-Bora (French Polynesia) 7. Psychological suspense 8. Adult books for young adults

LC 2018005086

Erin is a documentary filmmaker on the brink of a professional breakthrough, Mark a handsome investment banker with big plans. Passionately in love, they embark on a dream honeymoon to the tropical island of Bora Bora, where they enjoy the sun, the sand, and each other. Then, while scuba diving in the crystal blue sea, they find something in the water....

Stedman, M. L.

★ The **light** between oceans: a novel. M.L. Stedman. Scribner, 2012. 345 p. : Map

ISBN 9781451681734

1. Social isolation 2. Loss (Psychology) 3. Grief in women 4. Lighthouse keepers 5. Lighthouses 6. Australia 7. Literary fiction 8. Historical fiction 9. Arthur, King

Australian Book Industry Awards, Book of the Year, 2013; Australian Book Industry Awards, Literary Fiction Book of the Year, 2013; Australian Book Industry Awards, Newcomer of the Year, 2013; Goodreads Choice Award, 2012; Nielsen BookData Australian Booksellers' Choice Award, 2013

After moving with his wife to an isolated Australian lighthouse where they suffer miscarriages and a stillbirth, Tom allows his wife to claim an infant that has washed up on the shore, a decision with devastating consequences.

Originally published: North Sydney, N.S.W. : Vintage Australia, 2012.

Steel, Danielle

First sight. Danielle Steel. Delacorte Press, 2013. 384 p.

ISBN 9780385338301

1. Clothing industry and trade 2. Fashion 3. Women executives 4. Physicians 5. Married men 6. Contemporary romances

LC 2006042666

Running a successful fashion empire in Paris and New York that hides the pain of a failed marriage, Timmie O endures a sequence of meaningless relationships before a surprise bout of appendicitis places her under the care of alluring but married French doctor, Jean-Charles Vernier.

Steele, Allen M.

Coyote: a novel of interstellar exploration. Allen M. Steele. Ace Books, 2002. 390 p; (Coyote novels, 1)

ISBN 9780441009749

1. Space colonies 2. Dissenters 3. Time travel 4. Life on other planets 5. Space flight 6. 21st century 7. Space opera 8. Science fiction 9. Political fiction 10. Adult books for young adults

LC 2002074517

Coyote marks a dramatic new turn in the career of Allen Steele, Hugo Award-winning author of Chronospace. Epic in scope, passionate in its conviction, and set against a backdrop of plausible events, it tells the brilliant story of Earth's first interstellar colonists—and the mysterious planet that becomes their home.

"A much-foreshadowed 'surprise' ending is by far the least of the surprises in Steele's bag of tricks. But each page of this novel bears evidence of fresh thought about the opportunities inherent in science fiction to take the familiar and make it new." —*New York Times Book Review*

Sequel: Coyote Rising: A Novel of Interstellar Revolution.

Stegner, Wallace

★ **Angle** of repose. Wallace Stegner. Penguin Books, 1992. 569 p.

ISBN 9780140169300

1. Grandsons 2. Grandmothers 3. Marital conflict 4. Extramarital affairs 5. The West (United States) 6. California 7. Family sagas 8. Literary fiction 9. Modern classics

LC 72144301

Pulitzer Prize for Fiction, 1972

Traces the fortunes of four generations of one family as they attempt to build a life for themselves in the American West BT

"This novel is set mainly in the West in the late 1800's; but the central characters cannot be confined to the West nor to the 19th Century. They have a healing effect on the narrator, their grandson and biographer.... The beautiful, talented, charming Susan and her inarticulate engineer husband Oliver Ward rough it in mining camps and desolate, unfinished irrigation project camps. Their lives are hard and their marriage is strained past redemption. Yet their suffering and their strength do redeem." —*Library Journal*

Originally published: Garden City, N.Y. : Doubleday, 1971.

★ The **Big** Rock Candy Mountain. Wallace Stegner. Penguin Books 1995. 563 p.

ISBN 9780140139396

1. Violence in men 2. Poor families 3. Liquor smuggling 4. Family relationships 5. Ruthlessness in men 6. The West (United States) 7. Northwestern States 8. Autobiographical fiction 9. Domestic fiction 10. Multiple perspectives

"A well-written study of the footloose family.... The life of the household is a misery of continual cruelty and often crushing poverty, alternating with occasional scenes of simple family happiness which stand out beautifully and unforgettably." —*The New Yorker*

Sequel: Recapitulation

First published in 1943.

Crossing to safety. Wallace Stegner; introduction by Terry Tempest Williams; afterword by T.H. Watkins. Modern Library, 2002. Xviii, 335 p.

ISBN 9780375759314

1. Universities and colleges 2. Married people 3. Friendship 4. Women with poliomyelitis 5. Couples 6. Vermont 7. Domestic fiction 8. Literary fiction

LC 2001057942

National Book Critics Circle Award for Fiction finalist, 1987

Two young couples, Sid and Charity and Larry and Sally, from different backgrounds—East and West, rich and poor—befriend each other in 1937 Madison, Wisconsin.

Originally published: New York : Random House, 1987.

Stein, Garth

The **art** of racing in the rain: a novel. Garth Stein. Harper Collins, 2008. 336 pages.

ISBN 9780061537936

1. Dogs 2. Humans and dogs 3. Automobile racing drivers 4. Automobile racing 5. Wishing and wishes 6. Washington (State) 7. Literary fiction 8. Stories told by animals 9. Books to movies 10. Adult books for young adults

LC 2007033890

Booklist Editors' Choice: Adult Books for Young Adults, 2008

Enzo knows he is different from other dogs: a philosopher with a nearly human soul (and an obsession with opposable thumbs), he has educated himself by watching television and by listening closely to the words of his master, Denny Swift, an up-and-coming race car driver. On the night before his death, Enzo takes stock of his life, recalling all that he and his family have been through, hoping, in his next life, to return as a human.

"Enzo narrates his life story, beginning with his impending death. Enzo's not afraid of dying, as he's seen a television documentary on the Mongolian belief that a good dog will reincarnate as a man. Yes, Enzo is a dog. And he belongs to Denny: husband, father, customer service technician. Denny's dream is to be a professional race-car driver, and Enzo recounts the triumphs and tragedies-medical, financial, and legal-they share in this quest, the dangers of the racetrack being the least of their obstacles.... [Stein] creates a patient, wise, and doggish narrator that is more than just fluff and collar." —*Library Journal*

Stein, Gertrude

★ **Three** lives. Vintage Books, 1936. 279 p.

ISBN 9780394701530

1. Women 2. Short stories

A kindly housekeeper, a German servant, and a young black girl seek happiness within the strict confines of their lives.

First published : 1909.

Steinbeck, John

Cannery Row. John Steinbeck. Penguin Books, 1994. Xxx, 185 p.

ISBN 9780140187373

1. Community life 2. Loneliness 3. Homeless persons 4. Misfits (Persons) 5. Marine biologists 6. California 7. Monterey, California 8. Literary fiction 9. Books to movies 10. Modern classics

LC 93-11713

Vividly depicts the colorful, sometimes disreputable, inhabitants of a run-down area in Monterey, California.

Sequel : Sweet Thursday.

★ **East** of Eden. John Steinbeck. Viking, 1986. 778 p.

ISBN 9780670287383

1. Good and evil 2. Brothers 3. Sibling rivalry 4. Fathers and sons 5. World War I 6. California 7. Salinas Valley, California 8. Modern classics 9. Family sagas 10. Literary fiction

LC 86001526

California's fertile Salinas Valley is home to two families whose destinies and fruitfully, and fatally, intertwined. Over generations, between the beginning of the twentieth century and the end of the First World War, the Trasks and the Hamiltons with helplessly replay the fall of Adam and Eve and the murderous rivalry of Cain and Abel.

"The saga of more than half a century in the lives of two American familiesthe Trasks, a mixture of gentleness and brutality doled out in unequal measure and the Hamiltons, Steinbeck's own forebears, a well adjusted, lovable group who provide a tranquil background for the turbulent careers of the Trasks. The scene is chiefly Salinas, California from the turn of the century through the first World War, and thanks to a great wealth of fascinating detail woven through the plot, we are given a complete and unforgettable picture of country and small town life during the period." —*Library Journal*

Book was adapted into an eight-hour miniseries by ABC in 1981, as well as inspiring a film in 1955.

Originally published: New York : Viking Press, 1952.

★ The **grapes** of wrath. John Steinbeck. Penguin Books, 2002. 455 p.

ISBN 9780142000663

1. Rural families 2. Depressions 3. Migrant agricultural laborers 4. Poor people 5. Labor camps 6. Dust Bowl (South Central United States) 7. California 8. Domestic fiction 9. Modern classics 10. Literary fiction

LC 2001056103

Pulitzer Prize for Fiction, 1940

Depicts the hardships and suffering endured by the Joads as they journey from Oklahoma to California during the Depression.

Originally published: New York : Viking, 1939.

The **long** valley. John Steinbeck; with an introduction and notes by John H. Timmerman. Penguin Books, 1995. 233 p.

ISBN 9780140187458

1. Growing up 2. Interpersonal relations 3. Aging 4. Salinas Valley, California 5. Short stories 6. Literary fiction 7. Modern classics

Presents a collection of short stories, including "The Murder," "The Chrysanthemums," "Flight," and "The Red Pony."

15 short stories.

Includes the O. Henry Prize winning story "The murder ... and the classic tales of The red pony.

First published in 1938.

★ **Of** mice and men. John Steinbeck. Penguin Books, 1994. Xxviii, 105 p.

ISBN 9780140186420

1. Men with developmental disabilities 2. Migrant workers 3. Ranch life 4. People with developmental disabilities 5. Male friendship 6. California 7. Salinas River Valley (Calif.) 8. Psychological fiction 9. Literary fiction 10. Modern classics

LC 93011712

The tragic story of two itinerant ranch hands on the run—one is the lifelong companion to the other, a developmentally disabled man.

Of mice and men has been closely adapted to film in 1939 and 1992 and to television movies in 1968 and 1981.

Includes bibliographical references (p. [xxvii]-xxviii).

Originally published: New York .: Covici, Friede, 1937.

The **pearl**. John Steinbeck. Penguin Books, 2002. 87 p.

ISBN 9780142000694

1. Husband and wife 2. Poor people 3. Greed 4. Fishers 5. Pearls 6. Mexico 7. Literary fiction 8. Modern classics

LC 2001056113

A poor fisherman dreams of wealth and happiness for his family when he finds a priceless pearl.

Originally published in Woman's home companion as 'The pearl of the world'—Title page verso.

Originally published in book form: New York : Viking Press, 1947.

Tortilla Flat. John Steinbeck. Penguin Books, 1986. 207 p.

ISBN 9780140042405

1. Gangs 2. Poor people 3. Loyalty 4. Misadventures 5. Rogues 6. California 7. Monterey, California 8. 1930s 9. Sassoon, Siegfried 10. Books to movies 11. Modern classics

In the shabby district called Tortilla Flat above Monterey, California lives a gang whose exploits compare to those of King Arthur's knights.

Steiner, Susie

Missing, presumed: a novel. Susie Steiner. Random House, 2016. 350 p. (DS Manon, 1)

ISBN 9780812998320

1. Women detectives 2. Missing persons investigation 3. Women college students 4. Missing persons 5. Online dating 6. England 7. Mysteries

LC 2015037112

LibraryReads Favorites, 2016

Assigned to the high-profile case of a missing graduate student, brilliant detective and lonelyheart Manon Bradshaw uncovers the abductee's erratic behavior, a close friend's secrets and the role of a sex offender while struggling to maintain a professional distance.

★ **Persons** unknown: a novel. Susie Steiner. Random House, 2017. 272 p. (DS Manon, 2)

ISBN 9780812998344

1. Women detectives 2. Pregnant women 3. Cold cases (Criminal investigation) 4. Murder 5. Murder investigation 6. England 7. Mysteries

LC 2016057332

Library Journal Best Books, 2017

Having left the Met police for Cambridgeshire in order to give her adopted 12-year-old son a new start, detective Manon Bradshaw finds things aren't going as planned. Her black son is being bullied, she's single and pregnant, and most troubling, someone close to her family has been murdered and the police think her son may be involved. The case pits her against colleagues, but Manon will do whatever she can to find the real killer and prove her son's innocence. Told from multiple points of view, this thought-provoking second book to feature Manon (after Missing, Presumed) slowly builds momentum and addresses timely topics.

"With its multiple viewpoints, this follow-up to the acclaimed Missing Presumed is another engrossing stunner, incorporating social justice issues into the narrative along with superb plotting, dark humor, and excellent characterizations." —*Library Journal*

Sequel to: Missing, Presumed

Steinhauer, Olen

★ **All** the old knives. Olen Steinhauer. Minotaur Books, 2015. Viii, 294 pages

ISBN 9781250045423

1. CIA Agents 2. Former lovers 3. Dinners and dining 4. Terrorists 5. Intelligence service 6. Spy fiction 7. Multiple perspectives

After a failed rescue attempt of a hijacked plane in Vienna, two retired spies, former lovers, can't help but relive the past and determine if the mission went wrong because of a compromised agent on the inside.

"It's an understatement to say that nothing is as it seems, but even readers well-versed in espionage fiction will be pleasantly surprised by Steinhauer's plot twists and double backs." —*Kirkus*

An **American** spy. Olen Steinhauer. Minotaur Books, 2012. 416 p. (Milo Weaver trilogy, 3)

ISBN 9780312622893

1. Elite operatives 2. Kidnapping 3. Secrecy 4. Loyalty in men 5. Intelligence service 6. Spy fiction 7. Thrillers and suspense

LC 2011040874

New York Times Notable Book, 2012

When the CIA's Department of Tourism is dismantled by an elaborate Chinese intelligence scheme that has caused numerous agent deaths, survivor Milo Weaver is placed at risk by his former boss, Alan Drummond, who uses one of Milo's aliases to exact revenge.

The **Bridge** of Sighs. Olen Steinhauer. St. Martin's Minotaur, 2003. 278 p; (Eastern European crime series, 1)

ISBN 9780312302450

1. Murder investigation 2. Political corruption 3. Police 4. Suspicion 5. Rookie police 6. Eastern Europe 7. Berlin, Germany 8. Second World War era (1939-1945) 9. 1940s 10. Psychological suspense 11. Historical thrillers 12. Political thrillers

LC 2002068127

Investigating murders for the post-World War II People's Militia, Emil Brod suspects political motives behind the killing of a state songwriter and finds himself accused of spying by his corrupt colleagues in the homicide department.

"This is an intelligent, finely polished debut, loaded with atmospheric detail that effortlessly re-creates the rubble-strewn streets of the postwar period in an Eastern state 'liberated' from German occupation by the Russians." —*Library Journal*

The **Cairo** affair. Olen Steinhauer. Minotaur Books, 2014. 400 p.

ISBN 9781250036131

1. Extramarital affairs 2. Diplomats 3. Marriage 4. Husband and wife 5. Former lovers 6. Cairo (Egypt) 7. Thrillers and suspense 8. Spy fiction

LC 2013033452

The assassination of an American diplomat in Hungary places a Cairo-based CIA agent in love with the victim's wife, an Egyptian intelligence agent and an American analyst at the mercy of a dangerous political game of shifting allegiances.

"A complex tale of the Arab Spring, WikiLeaks, the CIA, and a marriage, this leaves us with the unsettling feeling that, despite all the information won, lost, hoarded, and put to use, the world of intelligence is no stronger than the fragile, fallible humans who navigate it." —*Booklist*

The **last** tourist. Olen Steinhauer. Minotaur Books, 2020. 416 p. (Milo Weaver trilogy, 4)

ISBN 9781250036216

1. Former CIA agents 2. Intelligence service 3. Terrorists 4. Espionage 5. Intrigue 6. Spy fiction 7. Thrillers and suspense

LC 2019048501

Retired agent Milo Weaver has his hideout in the Western Sahara invaded by a young CIA analyst who questions him about suspicious deaths and the possible return of the Tourists.

"Steinhauer reinforces his position at the top of the espionage genre." —*Publishers Weekly*

The **middleman**. Olen Steinhauer. Minotaur Books, 2018. 416 pages

ISBN 9781250036179

1. Undercover operations 2. Domestic terrorism 3. Terrorists 4. FBI agents 5. Revolutionaries 6. United States 7. 2010s 8. Thrillers and suspense 9. Multiple perspectives

LC 2018004424

The rise and fall of a domestic left-wing terrorist group is traced from the perspectives of an FBI agent, an undercover agent, a convert and a writer on the sidelines.

The **nearest** exit. Olen Steinhauer. Minotaur Books, 2010. 416 p. (Milo Weaver trilogy, 2)

ISBN 9780312622879

1. Undercover operations 2. Elite operatives 3. Secrecy 4. Loyalty in men 5. Intelligence service 6. Spy fiction 7. Thrillers and suspense

LC 2009047486

RUSA Reading List, 2011; New York Times Notable Book, 2010

Now faced with the end of his quiet, settled life, reluctant spy Milo Weaver has no choice but to turn back to his old job as a 'tourist.' Before he can get back to the CIA's dirty work, he has to prove his loyalty to his new bosses, who know little of Milo's background and less about who is really pulling the strings in the government above the Department of Tourism—or in the outside world, which is beginning to believe the legend of its existence. Milo is suddenly in a dangerous position, between right and wrong, between powerful self-interested men, between patriots and traitors—especially as a man who has nothing left to lose.

The **tourist**. Olen Steinhauer. Minotaur Books, 2009. 416 p. (Milo Weaver trilogy, 1)

ISBN 9780312369729

1. Undercover operations 2. Innocence (Law) 3. Betrayal 4. Spies 5. Paranoia 6. Spy fiction 7. Thrillers and suspense

LC 2008033958

Milo Weaver is drawn into a conspiracy that links riots in the Sudan, an assassin committing suicide and an old friend who's been accused of selling secrets to the Chinese. Once the CIA and Homeland Security are after him, the only way for him to survive is to return, headfirst, into Tourism.

"As rich and intriguing as the best of Le Carre, Deighton or Graham Greene, Steinhauer's complex, moving spy novel is perfect for our uncertain, emotionally fraught times." —*Los Angeles Times Book Review*

Steinke, Rene

Holy skirts. Rene Steinke. William Morrow, 2005. 368 p.

ISBN 9780688176945

1. Freytag-Loringhoven, Elsa von 2. Germans in New York State 3. Women poets 4. Women artists 5. Women performance artists 6. Artists' models 7. New York City 8. Greenwich Village, New York City 9. 1910s 10. 1900s (Decade) 11. Biographical fiction 12. Historical fiction

LC 2004052783

National Book Award for Fiction finalist, 2005

"Steinke's writing is vivid and wonderful, and she can make even a sorrowful story entertaining because she never allows the character's melancholy to infect the prose. The baroness might have been sad, but not tragic. The heroism of her spirit is expressed in a way that transcends the shroud of misfortune." —*The Hudson Review*

Stephens, Alice

Famous adopted people. By Alice Stephens. Unnamed Press, 2018. N/a

ISBN 9781944700744

1. Best friends 2. Adoptees 3. Birthparents — Identification 4. Korean Americans 5. Quarreling 6. South Korea 7. North Korea 8. Mainstream fiction

LC 2018033188

Lisa Pearl and her best friend, Mindy, both Koreans adopted as children into white American families, are in Seoul where Mindy hopes to find her birthmother and tries to persuade Lisa to search for hers, until Lisa wakes up in captivity.

Stephenson, Neal

Anathem. Neal Stephenson. William Morrow, 2008. 928 p.

ISBN 9780061474095

1. Intellectual life 2. Life on other planets 3. Monasteries 4. Mathematics 5. Disasters 6. Hard science fiction 7. Science fiction

LC 2008013175

Locus Award for Best Science Fiction Novel, 2009

Having lived in a monastery since childhood, away from the violent upheavals of the outside world, Raz becomes one of a group of formerly cloistered scholars who are appointed by a fear-driven higher power to avert an impending catastrophe.

"The novel is beautifully written (fans of Adam Roberts' ornately written science fiction will see some similarities), and, even though it runs to nearly 1,000 pages, it feels somehow too short, as though we're made to leave this carefully constructed world and return to our own before we're quite ready. A magnificent achievement." —*Booklist*

★ **Cryptonomicon**. Neal Stephenson. Avon Press, 1999. 918 p.

ISBN 9780380973460

1. Conspiracies 2. Cryptographers 3. Deception 4. Secrecy 5. Drug addicts 6. United States 7. Hard science fiction 8. Science fiction

LC 99-11685

Library Journal Best Books, 1999; Locus Award for Best Science Fiction Novel, 2000; New York Times Notable Book, 1999

More than fifty years after Lawrence Pritchard Waterhouse and Sergeant Bobby Shaftoe are assigned to Detachment 2702, a secret cryptographic mission, their grandchildren—Randy and Amy—join forces to create a "data haven" in the South Pacific, only to uncover a massive conspiracy with roots in Detachment 2702

"This fast-paced, genre-transcending novel is full of absorbing action, witty dialogue and well-drawn characters. Amazingly, it is also, even at its tremendous length, only the first volume in what promises to be one of the most extravagant literary creations of the turn of the millenniumand beyond." —*Publishers Weekly*

Cryptonomicon features characters descended from those who appear in Stephenson's Baroque cycle series, and takes place about 300 years after the storyline of the cycle.

The **diamond** age,: or, a young lady's illustrated primer. Neal Stephenson. Bantam Books, 1995. 455 p.

ISBN 9780553096095

1. Girl heroes 2. Social classes 3. Nanotechnology 4. Far future 5. Computers 6. Shanghai, China 7. 21st century 8. Hard science fiction 9. Cyberpunk 10. Science fiction

LC 679416021

Hugo Award for Best Novel, 1996; Locus Award for Best Science Fiction Novel, 1996

The story of an engineer who creates a device to raise a girl capable of thinking for herself reveals what happens when a young girl of the poor underclass obtains the device.

"With breathtaking vision and insight, Stephenson establishes himself as not only a major voice in contemporary sf but also a prophet of technology's future." —*Booklist*

★ **Fall** or, Dodge in hell: a novel. Neal Stephenson. William Morrow, 2019. 883 p; (Dodge novels, 2)

ISBN 9780062458711

1. Life after death 2. High technology 3. Cyberspace 4. Soul 5. Cryonics 6. Science fiction

New York Times Notable Book, 2019

When a routine procedure gone wrong renders a gaming billionaire brain dead, his stunned family and friends cryopreserve and digitally transfer his consciousness into an immortal tech-driven existence.

"Best-selling Stephenson is cutting edge and his followers and all readers intrigued by shrewd speculative fiction will queue up." —*Booklist*

Reamde. Neal Stephenson. William Morrow, 2011. 1044 p; (Dodge novels, 1)

ISBN 9780061977961

1. Entrepreneurs 2. Computer games 3. Money laundering 4. Virtual reality 5. Technology 6. Cyber-thrillers 7. Science fiction 8. Science fiction thrillers

When his own high-tech start up turns into a Fortune 500 computer gaming group, Richard Forthrast, the black sheep of an Iowa family who has amassed an illegal fortune, finds the line between fantasy and reality becoming blurred when a virtual war for dominance is triggered.

"Stephenson's novels have always been a little nuts, but thoughtfully nuts. That he is even able to keep this big, careening, recreational-vehicular novel on the road during its hairpin narrative turns says a lot about him as a plot juggler and information wrangler." —*New York Times Book Review*

The **rise** and fall of D.O.D.O.: a novel. Neal Stephenson and Nicole Galland. William Morrow, 2017. 800 p. (D.O.D.O, 1)

ISBN 9780062409164

1. Time travel (Past) 2. Linguists 3. Intelligence officers 4. Magic 5. Language and languages 6. Contemporary fantasy 7. Fantasy fiction 8. Adult books for young adults

LC 2016043352

School Library Journal Best Books: Best Adult Books 4 Teens, 2017

A discreet translation assignment enmeshes a linguistics expert and a military intelligence operator in the world-shattering revelation that magic was once widely practiced and can be reactivated if they travel back in time to make historical changes that are complicated by human treachery.

"A departure for both authors and a pleasing combination of much appeal to fans of speculative fiction." —*Kirkus*

Seveneves. Neal Stephenson. William Morrow, 2015. 1056 p.

ISBN 9780062190376

1. Disasters 2. Survival 3. Space exploration 4. Space colonies 5. Far future 6. Earth 7. Moon 8. Hard science fiction 9. Apocalyptic fiction 10. Science fiction

LibraryReads Favorites, 2015; RUSA Reading List Short List, 2016

When a catastrophic event dooms the planet, nations around the world band together to devise an ambitious survival plan in outer space 5,000 years before their progeny organize an audacious return.

"Stephenson's remarkable novel is deceptively complex, a disaster story and transhumanism tale that serves as the delivery mechanism for a series of technical and sociological visions.... There's a ton to digest, but Stephensons lucid prose makes it worth the while." —*Publishers Weekly*

★ **Snow** crash. Neal Stephenson. Bantam Books, 1992. 440 p.

ISBN 9780553088533

1. Computer viruses 2. Virtual reality 3. Hackers 4. Dystopias 5. Technology 6. 21st century 7. Cyberpunk 8. Science fiction classics 9. Science fiction

LC 91045453

With the strange new designer drug, Snow Crash, making zombies of nearly everyone and a deadly computer virus striking down hackers, Hiro Protagonist, the last of the free-lance hackers, comes to the rescue.

Sterling, Bruce

Pirate Utopia. Bruce Sterling; art by John Coulthart; introduction by Warren Ellis. Tachyon Publications, 2016. 187 pages

ISBN 9781616962364

1. Political intrigue 2. Pirates 3. Ideology 4. Futurists 5. Revolutionaries 6. Alternate histories 7. Science fiction 8. Satirical fiction

At the end of the Great War, the Futurists, a group of utopian pirate warriors, rampage through Europe with the help of a sinister American to establish world domination.

Sterling, Erin

The **ex** hex. Erin Sterling. Avon, 2021. 352 p.

ISBN 9780063027473

1. Young women 2. Jilted women 3. Leonardo da Vinci 4. Witchcraft 5. Magic 6. Georgia 7. Romantic comedies 8. Paranormal romances 9. Holiday romances

Nine years ago, Vivienne Jones nursed her broken heart like any young witch would: vodka, weepy music, bubble baths—and a curse on the horrible boyfriend. Sure, Vivi knows she shouldn't use her magic this way, but with only a scented candle on hand, she isn't worried it will cause him anything more than a bad hair day or two. That is until Rhys Penhallow, descendent of the town's ancestors, breaker of hearts, and annoyingly just as gorgeous as he always was, returns to Graves Glen, Georgia. What should be a quick trip to recharge the town's ley lines and make an appearance at the annual fall festival turns disastrously wrong. Vivi and Rhys have to ignore their off the charts chemistry to work together to save the town and find a way to break the break-up curse before it's too late.

"A wickedly funny rom-com about the power of second chances, family, and love." —*Kirkus*

Sternbergh, Adam

The **blinds**. Adam Sternbergh. HarperCollins 2017. 304 p.

ISBN 9780062661340

1. Criminals 2. Memories 3. Sheriffs 4. Rural life 5. Communities 6. Texas 7. Crime fiction 8. Modern Westerns

Helping maintain an uneasy peace in The Blinds, a rural Texas community of criminal misfits who were given a chance at a new life after having their memories altered, sheriff Calvin Cooper struggles with personal secrets in the wake of a suicide and murder.

Stevens, Chevy

Never let you go. Chevy Stevens. St. Martin's Press, 2017. 406 p.
ISBN 9781250034564
1. Abused women 2. Life change events 3. Violence in men 4. Former convicts 5. Stalkers 6. British Columbia 7. Canada 8. Psychological suspense 9. Multiple perspectives 10. Canadian fiction 11. Adult books for young adults

When someone begins stalking her, intimidating her boyfriend, and shadowing her daughter, Lindsey Nash is convinced it's her abusive ex-husband, but his claims of innocence have her wondering if the threat is closer to home.

"Stevens's taut writing and chilling depiction of love twisted beyond recognition make this a compelling read from the first page to the last." —*Publishers Weekly*

Still missing. Chevy Stevens. St. Martin's Press, 2010. 352 p.
ISBN 9780312595678
1. Self-fulfillment in women 2. Captives 3. Identity (Psychology) 4. Survival 5. Real estate agents 6. British Columbia 7. Canada 8. Psychological suspense 9. First person narratives 10. Canadian fiction
LC 2009047037
Thriller Award for Best First Novel, 2011

Interwoven with the story of the year Annie spent captive in a remote mountain cabin, which unfolds through sessions with her psychiatrist, is a second narrative recounting the nightmare that follows her escape and her struggle to piece her shattered life back together.

"As Annie's experience as an abductee prompts her to explore hidden corners of her former life and dredge up old secrets, Still Missing risks sounding extremely generic. This, after all, is the template for countless current novels in which a single shattering event leads to shocking revelations about the past. But Still Missing runs deeper than that in the chills it delivers, the surprises it holds and the resilience of its main character." —*New York Times*

Stevens, Francis

The **heads** of Cerberus. Francis Stevens; introduction by Naomi Alderman. Modern Library, 2019. 208 p.
ISBN 9781984854209
1. Friendship 2. Time travel (Future) 3. Dictatorship 4. Women rulers 5. Competition 6. Philadelphia, Pennsylvania 7. 1910s 8. Fantasy classics 9. Dystopian fiction

Philadelphia, 1918: Three friends—brave, confident Viola Trenmore, clever but shy Robert Drayton, and Viola's strong and hot-tempered brother, Terry—discover a mysterious powder that transports them two hundred years into the future. The Philadelphia of 2118 is no longer a bustling metropolis but instead a completely isolated city recovering from an unknown disaster. Citizens are issued identification tags instead of having names, and society is split between a wealthy, powerful minority and a downtrodden lower class. The position of supreme authority is held by a woman, and once a year she oversees competitions to the death to determine who rules alongside her.

Originally published in serial form in The thrill book by Street & Smith Pulications, 1919.

Stevenson, Robert Louis

★ The **strange** case of Dr. Jekyll and Mr. Hyde. Robert Louis Stevenson; wood engravings by Barry Moser; foreword by Joyce Carol Oates. University of Nebraska Press, 1990. 157 p. : Illustration
ISBN 9780803242128

1. Physicians 2. Scientists 3. Jekyll, Henry (Fictitious character) 4. Dissociative identity disorder 5. Self medication 6. London, England 7. Horror 8. Gothic fiction 9. Classics
LC 90030544

Wood engravings accompany this edition of the story of Dr. Jekyll, who becomes transformed into the horrifying Mr. Hyde after conducting a scientific experiment.

First published in 1886.

This book has inspired movies called Dr. Jekyll and Mr. Hyde, Jekyll and Hyde, and Mary Reilly.

Stewart, Amy

★ **Dear** Miss Kopp. Amy Stewart. Houghton Mifflin Harcourt, 2020. 320 p. (Kopp sisters novels, 6)
ISBN 9780358093107
1. Spies 2. Military service 3. Secret identity 4. Sisters 5. World War I home front 6. First World War era (1914-1918) 7. Historical mysteries
LC 2019057826

While Constance pursues suspected German spies and Fleurette performs for the troops as America enters World War I, Army Signal Corps pigeon-project manager Norma investigates a theft of medical supplies to clear a field hospital nurse's name.

"Smart, fun, staunchly feminist entertainment." —*Kirkus*

★ **Girl** waits with gun. Amy Stewart. Houghton Mifflin Harcourt, 2015. 408 pages (Kopp sisters novels, 1)
ISBN 9780544409910
1. Policewomen 2. Organized crime 3. Silk Workers' Strike, Paterson, New Jersey, 1913 4. Black Hand (United States) 5. Extortion 6. New Jersey 7. 1910s 8. Historical fiction
LC 2014045223
LibraryReads Favorites, 2015; RUSA Reading List Short List, 2016

Living in virtual isolation years after the revelation of a painful family secret, Constance Kopp is terrorized by a belligerent silk factory owner and fights back in ways outside the norm for early twentieth-century women.

"A sheer delight to read and based on actual events, this debut historical mystery packs the unexpected, the unconventional, and a serendipitous humor into every chapter." —*Booklist*

Kopp sisters on the march. Amy Stewart. Houghton Mifflin Harcourt, 2019. 355 p. (Kopp sisters novels, 5)
ISBN 9781328736529
1. Sisters 2. Military service 3. World War I home front 4. Military training camps 5. Women murder suspects 6. Maryland 7. United States 8. First World War era (1914-1918) 9. Historical mysteries
LC 2019002553

In 1917, as the U.S. prepares to enter World War I, the Kopp sisters arrive at Camp Chevy Chase training camp where they are faced with scandal, betrayal, the skepticism of the War Department, the double standards of a scornful public and the very real perils of war.

"Told in Stewart's nimble, witty prose, this fifth in the popular series is based largely on fact and offers a paean to patriotism and the role women have played in war, even a century ago. Devoted fans will be pleased with the tantalizing hint Stewart provides about what lies ahead for Constance." —*Booklist*

Lady cop makes trouble. Amy Stewart. 2016. 272 p. (Kopp sisters novels, 2)
ISBN 9780544409941
1. Policewomen 2. Sisters 3. Swindlers and swindling 4. Germans in the United States 5. Sexism 6. New York City 7. First World War era (1914-1918) 8. Historical mysteries

LC 2016004634

The best-selling author of Girl Waits with Gun returns with another adventure featuring the fascinating, feisty, and unforgettable Kopp sisters..

"Stewart adeptly introduces details of early twentieth-century life in Hackensack, New Jersey, a burgeoning city on the outskirts of New York, and timely concerns such as jail reform and womens rights, rounding out this immensely satisfying mystery." —*Booklist*

★ **Miss** Kopp investigates. Amy Stewart. Houghton Mifflin Harcourt, 2021. 272 p. (Kopp sisters novels, 7)
ISBN 9780358093091
1. Sisters 2. Postwar life 3. Women amateur detectives 4. Widows 5. Families 6. New Jersey 7. Between the Wars (1918-1939) 8. Historical mysteries

Life after the war takes an unexpected turn for the Kopp sisters, but soon enough, they are putting their unique detective skills to use in new and daring ways.

"Stewart, gifted at bringing women's issues to life, illustrates the complex legal and financial challenges facing women after WWI, and concludes with an exciting development in the Kopp women's future. Another strong entry for this historically fact-based series." —*Booklist*

★ **Miss** Kopp just won't quit. Amy Stewart. Houghton Mifflin Harcourt, 2018. 336 p. (Kopp sisters novels, 4)
ISBN 9781328736512
1. Women sheriffs 2. Elections 3. Psychiatric hospitals 4. Deception 5. Criminal investigation 6. New Jersey 7. United States 8. First World War era (1914-1918) 9. Historical mysteries

LC 2017061492

In 1916, New Jersey's first female deputy, Constance Kopp, while trying to investigate two cases involving the same asylum, finds her controversial career on the line.

"This entry is more suspenseful than its predecessors and boasts a deeper emphasis on character, politics, and social issues. A must for Constance's growing fan base." —*Booklist*

Miss Kopp's midnight confessions. Amy Stewart. Houghton Mifflin Harcourt, 2017. 304 p. (Kopp sisters novels, 3)
ISBN 9780544409996
1. Policewomen 2. Sisters 3. Sexism 4. Prisoners 5. Sheriffs 6. New York City 7. United States 8. First World War era (1914-1918) 9. Historical mysteries

LC 2017007453

RUSA Reading List Short List, 2018

Deputy Sheriff Constance Kopp and her sister Fleurette defend the young women being brought into the 1916 Hackensack jail under dubious charges like waywardness and incorrigibility.

"Collectively, the story lines intersect to create an intriguing window into women's rights and the social mores that women challenged on the eve of World War I." —*Library Journal*

Stewart, Ann Marie

Stars in the grass. Ann Marie Stewart. Shiloh Run Press, 2017. 305 pages
ISBN 9781634099509
1. Loss (Psychology) 2. Nine-year-old girls 3. Families 4. Grief in families 5. Faith (Christianity) 6. 1970s 7. Christian fiction
Christy Award for First Novel Category, 2017

Set in 1970, a story told through the eyes of nine-year-old Abby relates how she, her older brother, her mother, and her father take very different paths to cope with the horrendous loss of her baby brother.

Stewart, George R.

Earth abides. George R. Stewart. Del Rey, 2006. Xiv, 345 p.
ISBN 9780345487131
1. Plague 2. Virus diseases 3. Epidemics 4. Survival (after environmental catastrophe) 5. Disasters 6. Apocalyptic fiction 7. Science fiction classics 8. Science fiction

Returning from a field trip, Isherwood Williams discovers that a mysterious plague has destroyed human civilization during his absence and makes his way to San Francisco, where he finds a few survivors who build a small community, living like their pioneer ancestors.

Originally published: New York : Random House, 1949.

Stewart, Mary

★ The **crystal** cave. Mary Stewart. Eos, 2003. 494 p. (Merlin, the enchanter series, 1)
ISBN 9780060548254
1. Misfits (Persons) 2. Illegitimate children of royalty 3. Prophecies 4. Merlin (Legendary character) 5. Wizards 6. Great Britain 7. 5th century 8. Arthurian fantasy 9. Historical fantasy
Mythopoeic Award for Adult Literature, 1971

Born the bastard son of a Welsh princess, Myridden Emrys—or as he would later be known, Merlin—leads a perilous childhood, haunted by portents and visions. But destiny has great plans for this no-man's-son, taking him from prophesying before the High King Vortigern to the crowning of Uther Pendragon...and the conception of Arthur—king for once and always.

Originally published: New York : Morrow, 1970.
Later collected in Mary Stewart's Merlin trilogy: New York : Morrow, 1980.

★ The **hollow** hills. Mary Stewart. Eos, 2003. 475 p. (Merlin, the enchanter series, 2)
ISBN 9780060548261
1. Arthur 2. Rulers 3. Swords 4. Fate and Fatalism 5. Merlin (Legendary character) 6. Wizards 7. Great Britain 8. 5th century 9. Arthurian fantasy 10. Historical fantasy
Mythopoeic Award for Adult Literature, 1974

Keeping watch over the young Arthur Pendragon, the prince and prophet Merlin Ambrosius is haunted by dreams of the magical sword Caliburn, which has been hidden for centuries. When Uther Pendragon is killed in battle, the time of destiny is at hand, and Arthur must claim the fabled sword to become the true High King of Britain.

Map on lining paper.
Originally published: New York : Morrow, 1973.
Later collected in Mary Stewart's Merlin trilogy: New York : Morrow, 1980.

The **last** enchantment. Mary Stewart. Eos, 2003. 513 p. (Merlin, the enchanter series, 3)
ISBN 9780060548278
1. Arthur 2. Enchantment 3. Witches 4. Lust 5. Merlin (Legendary character) 6. Wizards 7. Great Britain 8. 5th century 9. Arthurian fantasy 10. Historical fantasy

Merlin the Enchanter recounts the events of Arthur's formative years as he grew from young warrior to king and reveals the horrible consequences of Arthur's incestuous relationship with Morgause, his half-sister.

Originally published: New York : Morrow, 1979.
Later collected in Mary Stewart's Merlin trilogy: New York : Morrow, 1980.

Nine coaches waiting. Mary Stewart. HarperCollins, 2001. 391 p.
ISBN 9780380820764

1. Boy orphans 2. Governesses 3. Attempted murder 4. Uncles 5. Nobility 6. Paris, France 7. Gothic romances

Charmed in spite of herself, English governess Linda Martin is baffled by the increasingly strange behavior of the de Valmys.

"Intelligent, spirited Linda Martin comes to Valmy, an isolated chateau in the French Alps, as English governess to nine-year-old Philippe, the orphaned Comte de Valmy. After several frightening 'accidents' Linda discovers that her pupil is the object of a murder plot which apparently involves his crippled uncle and the latter's handsome son Raoul, with whom she is in love." —*Booklist*

Originally published: New York : M. S. Mill and W. Morrow, 1959.

The **wicked** day. Mary Stewart. Eos, 2003. 417 p. (Merlin, the enchanter series, 4)

ISBN 9780060548285

1. Arthur 2. Fate and fatalism 3. Family secrets 4. Incest 5. Illegitimacy 6. Children of incest victims 7. Great Britain 8. 5th century 9. Arthurian fantasy 10. Historical fantasy

Mordred, the son of King Arthur and his treacherous half-sister, the enchantress Morgause, unwittingly becomes caught up in a scheme to destroy Arthur and his kingdom.

"The author returns to the Arthurian world she portrayed...in her Merlin trilogy. The principal character is Mordred, born of the incestuous liaison between Arthur the High King and his half-sister, the evil sorceress and northern queen Morgause. Mordred is summoned to Camelot by the formidable warrior king, along with Morgause and her four legitimate but ungovernable sons, and told of his true parentage. After growing to manhood in Arthur's court...Mordred is left in charge of the kingdom, and of Queen Guinevere, while Arthur is off fighting the Romans in Brittany. Reported dead, the king returns to Britain and there ensues the fulfillment of the 'wicked day' that has been prophesied by Merlin." —*Publishers Weekly*

Originally published: New York : Morrow, 1983.

Sthers, Amanda

Holy lands: a novel. Amanda Sthers. Bloomsbury Publishing, 2019. 161 p.

ISBN 9781635572834

1. Physicians 2. Letter writing 3. Lifestyle change 4. Pig farming 5. Jewish men 6. Israel 7. Epistolary novels 8. Humorous stories 9. Translations

LC 2018015184

Leaving a thriving medical practice in Paris to raise pigs in Israel, a Jewish cardiologist disconnects himself from modern technology, forcing his gay playwright son, heartbroken daughter and cancer-stricken wife to correspond strictly through written letters.

"Her slim, swiftly moving novel describes the complicated relationships between siblings, a married couple, a man and his rabbi and still has room for a light critique of Israel's policies toward Palestine. This is a book you can read in an afternoon, but it'll stick with you for much longer than that. Comic, moving, and occasionally profound, Sthers' novel is a delight." —*Kirkus*

Translated from the French.

Stibbe, Nina

Reasons to be cheerful. Nina Stibbe. Little Brown & Co, 2019. 240 pages (Man at the helm novels (Nina Stibbe), 3)

ISBN 9780316309370

1. Eccentrics and eccentricities 2. Gender role 3. Crushes (Interpersonal relations) 4. Dentists 5. Dental assistants 6. England 7. 1980s

8. Coming-of-age stories 9. Satirical fiction 10. First person narratives 11. Adult books for young adults

Taking a job as an assistant to an eccentric dental surgeon, 18-year-old Lizzie pursues a fantasy relationship with her crush before realizing that he is not quite as imagined.

Stirling, S. M.

Dies the fire. S.M. Stirling. New American Library, 2004. 496 p. (Dies the fire trilogy, 1)

ISBN 9780451459794

1. Regression (Civilization) 2. Technology and civilization 3. Determination (Personal quality) 4. Collyer, Homer Lusk 5. Survival (after disaster) 6. Pacific Northwest 7. Oregon 8. Science fiction 9. Canadian fiction 10. Apocalyptic fiction 11. Adult books for young adults

LC 2004004363

Library Journal Best Books, 2004

The change occurred when an electrical storm centered over the island of Nantucket produced a blinding white flash that rendered all electronic devices and fuels inoperable. What follows is the most terrible global catastrophe in the history of the human race—and a Dark Age more universal and complete than could possibly be imagined.

Sequel: The protector's war.

Set in the world that was left behind in the author's book Island in the Sea of Time.

Includes bibliographical references and index.

A **meeting** at Corvallis. S.M. Stirling. Roc, 2006. 512 p. (Dies the fire trilogy, 3)

ISBN 9780451461117

1. Exiles 2. Communities 3. Kidnapping 4. Regression (Civilization) 5. Technology and civilization 6. Oregon 7. Pacific Northwest 8. Science fiction 9. Canadian fiction 10. Apocalyptic fiction 11. Adult books for young adults

LC 2006002080

Tensions continue among Mike Havel's Bearkillers and their allies, Clan Mackenzie under the leadership of Juniper Mackenzie and Norman Arminger, the warlord of Portland, after Arminger's daughter falls into the hands of Clan Mackenzie.

The **protector's** war. S. M. Stirling. ROC, 2005. 486 p. : Map (Dies the fire trilogy, 2)

ISBN 9780451460462

1. Civilization 2. Determination (Personal quality) 3. Imaginary wars and battles 4. Regression (Civilization) 5. Witches 6. Oregon 7. Great Britain 8. Science fiction 9. Canadian fiction 10. Apocalyptic fiction 11. Adult books for young adults

LC 2005008432

Ten years after all of Earth's technology had been rendered useless by the Change, two thriving communities in Oregon's Willamette Valley are confronted by a dangerous new challenge when the totalitarian Protectorate prepares to seek control over their priceless farmland.

Sequel to: Dies the fire.

Stivers, Carole

The **mother** code. Carole Stivers. Penguin Group USA 2020. 352 p.

ISBN 9781984806925

1. Artificial intelligence 2. Motherhood 3. Epidemics 4. Robots 5. Genetic engineering 6. United States 7. Apocalyptic fiction 8. Hard science fiction

LC 2019042643

Racing to protect human survival in the wake of a bio-warfare attack gone wrong, a team of scientists creates a generation of genetically engineered children who struggle to survive when their robot protectors are slated for demolition.

"Each story line is emotionally resonant, leading to a devastating gut punch when they eventually collide. Stivers's mythic vision and sound science will strike a chord with readers who fear for humanity's future. This dystopia is painful, provocative, and ultimately infused with hope." —*Publishers Weekly*

Stockett, Kathryn

★ The **help**. Kathryn Stockett. Amy Einhorn Books/G.P. Putnam's Sons, 2009. 464 p.

ISBN 9780399155345

1. Interracial friendship 2. Determination in women 3. African American women 4. Household employees 5. Unemployed persons 6. Jackson, Mississippi 7. 1960s 8. Relationship fiction 9. Historical fiction 10. Books to movies

LC 2008030185

Goodreads Choice Award, 2009; Indies' Choice Book Awards, Adult Debut, 2010; Amelia Bloomer List, 2010

Limited and persecuted by racial divides in 1962 Jackson, Mississippi, three women, including an African-American maid, her sassy and chronically unemployed friend, and a recently graduated white woman, team up for a clandestine project.

Stoker, Bram

★ **Dracula**. Bram Stoker; edited with an introduction and notes by Maurice Hindle; preface by Christopher Frayling. Penguin Books, 2003. Xlvii, 454 p.

ISBN 9780141439846

1. Dracula, Count (Fictitious character) 2. Vampires 3. British in Romania 4. Good and evil 5. Man-woman relationships 6. Transylvania, Romania 7. London, England 8. 19th century 9. Gothic fiction 10. Horror classics 11. Horror 12. Adult books for young adults

Having discovered the double identity of the wealthy Transylvanian nobleman, Count Dracula, a small group of people vow to rid the world of the evil vampire.

Inspired the movie entitled Nosferatu.

Includes bibliographical references (p. [xl]-xlv).

The **new** annotated Dracula. Bram Stoker; edited with a foreword and notes by Leslie S. Klinger; additional research by Janet Byrne; introduction by Neil Gaiman. W.W. Norton, 2008. 672 p.

ISBN 9780393064506

1. Stoker, Bram 2. Dracula, Count (Fictitious character) 3. Vampires 4. British in Romania 5. Good and evil 6. Man-woman relationships 7. Transylvania, Romania 8. London, England 9. 19th century 10. Gothic fiction 11. Horror 12. Books to movies

LC 2008025919

An illustrated tribute to Bram Stoker's classic shares additional insights into the historical plausibility of vampire lore, in an edition that surveys more than two centuries of popular culture and myth while providing a detailed examination of the book's original typescript and different ending.

"An introduction by Neil Gaiman, numerous illustrations, essays on topics ranging from Dracula in the movies to the academic response, and much more enhance the package." —*Publishers Weekly*

Inspired the movie entitled Nosferatu.

Includes bibliographical references.

Stoker, Dacre

Dracul. Putnam Pub Group, 2018. 512 p. : Illustration

ISBN 9780735219342

1. Stoker, Bram 2. Vampires 3. Siblings 4. Nannies 5. Secrets 6. Memories 7. Historical horror 8. Horror

Library Journal Best Books, 2018

A prequel to Dracula, based on original author notes and co-written by a family descendant, reveals the iconic vampire's origin story, the early years of Bram Stoker and the tale of the enigmatic woman who connected them.

Stone, Irving

★ The **agony** and the ecstasy: a biographical novel of Michelangelo. Irving Stone. Signet, 1987. 776 p.

ISBN 9780451171351

1. Michelangelo Buonarroti 2. Artists 3. Creativity in men 4. Men and success 5. European Renaissance 6. Sexuality 7. Italy 8. Florence, Italy 9. Renaissance (1300-1600) 10. Biographical fiction 11. Historical fiction 12. Books to movies

Dramatizes the life of the artistic genius Michelangelo, recalls his love affairs, his disputes with cardinals and popes, and his years of working on the Sistine Chapel BT

Originally published: Garden City, N.Y. : Doubleday, 1961.

The great best seller about Michelangelo.

Lust for life: a novel of Vincent van Gogh. Irving Stone. Penguin, 1989. X, 489 p.

ISBN 9780452262492

1. Gogh, Vincent van 2. Purpose in life 3. Artists — History 4. Determination in men 5. Painters 6. Brothers 7. Netherlands 8. London, England 9. Biographical fiction 10. Historical fiction 11. Books to movies

LC 83024666

A Novel of the life of the tormented genius who put so much of himself into his art that he found it difficult to maintain himself in ordinary society.

Lust for Life inspired the film Lust for Life in 1956.

Companion book: Dear Theo.

Originally published: New York : Longmans, Green, 1934.

Stone, Nick

The **verdict**. Nick Stone. Pegasus Crime, 2015. 499 pages

ISBN 9781605989235

1. Trials (Murder) 2. Former friends 3. Law firms 4. Law clerks 5. Conspiracies 6. London, England 7. Legal thrillers

Leaping at a chance to make his career by taking a high-profile murder case, Terry Flynt is forced to make a terrible choice and confront secrets from the past when he discovers that his millionaire client is a former friend who brutally betrayed him years earlier.

"The suspense never lets up in this terrific courtroom drama. Fans of John Grisham will love it. It's definitely movie material." —*Kirkus*

Stout, Dan

★ **Titanshade**. Dan Stout. DAW Books, 2019. 400 p. (Carter archives, 1)

ISBN 9780756414863

1. Detectives 2. Cities and towns 3. Energy resources 4. Oil executives 5. Diplomats 6. Fantasy mysteries 7. Urban fantasy

In Titanshade, a metropolis on the edge of disaster, homicide cop Carter is led into a conflict with the city's elite while investigating the brutal murder of a Squib diplomat and must solve the case quickly to protect those closest to him.

Stout, Rex

The **doorbell** rang. Rex Stout; introduction by Stuart M. Kaminsky. ImPress Mystery, 2000. 207 p; (Nero Wolfe mysteries, 41)
ISBN 9780762188574
1. Murder investigation 2. FBI agents 3. Secrecy in government 4. Rich women 5. Private investigators 6. New York City 7. Mysteries 8. First person narratives 9. Mystery classics

LC 61464
"Nero Wolfe tangles with the FBI, on behalf of a wealthy woman who has sent as gifts to prominent people 10,000 copies of Fred Cook's book criticizing the FBI.... She is being shadowed and spied on by the FBI. To the surprise of Wolfe and of Archie Goodwin, they have the good will of the New York Police Department. The New York Police believe that FBI agents have murdered a magazine writer who was doing an article on the FBI. The police are powerless to prove anything or to prosecute. Clever and ingenious, this ranks among the best Rex Stout mysteries." —*Publishers Weekly*

Originally published: New York : Viking Press, 1965.

★ **Gambit**. Rex Stout. Bantam Books, 1973. 155 p. (Nero Wolfe mysteries, 37)
ISBN 9780553251722
1. Murder investigation 2. Poisoning 3. Murder suspects 4. Chess 5. Private investigators 6. New York City 7. Mysteries 8. First person narratives 9. Mystery classics
Master sleuth Nero Wolfe and his confidential assistant Archie Goodwin match wits with a deadly adversary to solve a bizarre murder that takes place during a chess game at a private club.
"Nero Wolfe, with his usual witty, urbane, conversational approach, looks into a case of arsenic poisoning in a Manhattan chess club." —*Publishers Weekly*

Originally published: New York : Viking Press, 1962.

Stowe, Harriet Beecher

★ **Uncle** Tom's cabin. By Harriet Beecher Stowe; with a new introduction by Charles Johnson. Oxford University Press, 2002. Xv, 456 p.
ISBN 9780195158168
1. Slavery 2. Freedom seekers 3. African Americans 4. Master and servant 5. Plantation life 6. Southern States 7. United States 8. Books to movies 9. Classics

LC 2002068424
Uncle Tom's master sells him, separating him from his wife, and he becomes attached to the gentle daughter of his new owner, but after her death, he is sold to the evil Simon Legree.
First published in the National era at Washington from June 1851 to April 1852.
Originally published in two volumes: Boston : John P. Jewett & company; Cleveland : Jewett, Proctor & Worthington, 1852.
Originally published as Uncle Tom's cabin or, life among the lowly.

Stradal, J. Ryan

★ The **lager** queen of Minnesota. J. Ryan Stradal. Pamela Dorman Books / Viking, 2019. 384 p.
ISBN 9780399563058
1. Women-owned businesses 2. Breweries 3. Family businesses 4. Sisters 5. Inheritance and succession 6. Minnesota 7. Middle West 8. Relationship fiction

LC 2018057023
WILLA Literary Awards: Contemporary Fiction, 2020; LibraryReads Favorites, 2019
A talented baker running a business out of her nursing home reconnects with her master brewer sister at the same time her pregnant granddaughter launches an IPA brewpub.

Straight, Susan

A **million** nightingales. Susan Straight. Pantheon Books, 2006. 352 p.
ISBN 9780375423642
1. Enslaved women 2. Slavery 3. Plantations 4. Multiracial teenagers 5. Multiracial women 6. Louisiana 7. Antebellum America (1820-1861) 8. 1800s (Decade) 9. Historical fiction 10. Literary fiction 11. First person narratives 12. Adult books for young adults

LC 2005050052
When she is sold away from her family, Moinette begins to prepare herself for an escape to freedom, journeying through a world of brutality, sexual violence, loss, and struggle to find her way out of the bonds of slavery.
"Straight's book is a deep consideration of the servitude all women experienced then—and, in some ways and some places, continue to experience even now.... But her novel is, besides, a powerful and moving story, written in language so beautiful you can almost believe the words themselves are capable of salving history's wounds." —*New York Times Book Review*

Straley, John

The **big** both ways. John Straley. Alaska Northwest Books, 2008. 350 p. (Cold storage novels, 1)
ISBN 9780882407395
1. Women labor organizers 2. Revenge 3. Survival 4. Labor movement 5. Aunt and niece 6. Inside Passage (Pacific Northwest) 7. Alaska 8. 1930s 9. Mysteries 10. Historical mysteries

LC 2007051440
Fleeing a logging camp after an accident kills a coworker, Slip Wilson's life changes forever when he meets Ellie Hobbes, an anarchist from Seattle who is on the run with a dead body in the trunk of her car.

Stratford, Sarah-Jane

Red letter days. Sarah-Jane Stratford. Berkley, 2020. 384 pages
ISBN 9780451475572
1. McCarthy, Joseph 2. McCarthyism 3. Women screenwriters 4. Americans in England 5. Women television producers and directors 6. Female friendship 7. England 8. London, England 9. 1950s 10. Historical fiction

LC 2019022993
When two brave women flee from the Communist Red Scare, they soon discover that no future is free from the past.
"A...thoroughly fascinating and too-little-known story of Hannah Weinstein and her role in supporting blacklisted Americans, regardless of gender or race." —*Booklist*

Straub, Emma

★ **All** adults here. Emma Straub. Riverhead Books, 2020. 368 p.
ISBN 9781594634697
1. Mother and adult child 2. Widows 3. Family secrets 4. Families 5. Granddaughters 6. Hudson Valley 7. New York (State) 8. 21st century 9. Domestic fiction
LibraryReads Favorites, 2020

A warm, funny, and keenly perceptive novel about the life cycle of one family—as the kids become parents, grandchildren become teenagers, and a matriarch confronts the legacy of her mistakes.

"There are a lot of issues at play here (abortion, bullying, IVF, gender identity, sexual predators) that Straub easily juggles, and her strong and flawed characters carry the day. This affecting family saga packs plenty of punch." —*Publishers Weekly*

★ **Modern** lovers. Emma Straub. Riverhead Books, 2016. 320 p.
ISBN 9781594634673
1. Friendship 2. Growing up 3. Parenthood 4. Identity (Psychology) 5. Aging 6. Brooklyn, New York City 7. Coming-of-age stories 8. Relationship fiction

Three friends and former college bandmates struggle with the midlife difficulties of managing the sexuality, independence, and secrets of their young-adult children against painful memories of a friend who soared and fell without them.

"Straubs handful of characters, followed with alternating close third-person narratives, are honestly and devilishly observed with clarity and kindness." —*Booklist*

The **vacationers**. Emma Straub. Riverhead Books, a member of Penguin Group (USA), 2014. 304 pages
ISBN 9781594631573
1. Family vacations 2. Couples 3. Change (Psychology) 4. Americans in Spain 5. Friendship 6. Majorca, Spain 7. Spain 8. Mainstream fiction 9. Coming-of-age stories 10. Adult books for young adults

LC 2013037110

Celebrating their thirty-fifth anniversary and their daughter's high-school graduation during a two-week vacation in Mallorca, Franny and Jim Post confront old secrets, hurts, and rivalries that reveal sides of themselves they try to conceal.

"Spongy and dear, sharply observed and funny, Straub's domestic-drama-goes-abroad is a delightful study of the complexities of family and love, and the many distractions from both." —*Booklist*

Straub, Peter

★ A **dark** matter: a novel. By Peter Straub. Doubleday, 2010. 416 p.
ISBN 9780385516389
1. High school students 2. Rites and ceremonies 3. Supernatural 4. Teenagers 5. Psychic trauma 6. Madison, Wisconsin 7. 1960s 8. Horror 9. Psychological suspense 10. Multiple perspectives 11. Adult books for young adults

LC 2009020028

Bram Stoker Award for Best Novel, 2010

Old friends try to come to grips with the darkness of the past—a secret ritual that left behind a gruesomely dismembered body—and find themselves face-to-face with the evil they helped create.

"A multiple-perspective take on a murky collegiate misadventure in 1966. Spencer Mallon, campus-flitting intellectual and seducer of coeds, is compared in the early pages to a host of flattering figures: a god, a hero, a guru. What Mallon feels most like to us, though, is a Manson-like charmer who lures several young people out to a field, where one of them dies. How, though? Straub expertly weaves a Rashmon-crazy quilt of varying and sometimes conflicting recollections of the incident, left purposefully vague, as we shuttle through the intervening yearsunkind ones in which his characters are struck by blindness, become criminals and, in an especially sad case, go insane. A slight slackness in the story's middle game will have some readers exhorting, Get over it already! whatever it is. But ambitiously, the author mounts his referendum on a wild, unpredictable moment of the 1960s, saluting the era's competing urges of decadence and justice." —*Time Out New York*

★ **Ghost** story. Peter Straub. Pocket Books, 1980. 567 p.
ISBN 9780671826857
1. Ghosts 2. Secret societies 3. Seniors 4. Brothers 5. Authors 6. New York (State) 7. Horror 8. Ghost stories 9. Books to movies

Questions arise concerning the connections between a strangely detached young girl's captivity in a seedy Florida motel, a death that occurs at a party for a visiting actress, and a young California instructor's obsession with one of his students.

"With considerable technical skill, Peter Straub has constructed an extravagant entertainment which, though flawed, achieves in its second half some awesome effects." —*Newsweek*

Lost boy lost girl: a novel. Peter Straub. Random House, 2003. 320 p.
ISBN 9781400060924
1. Suicide victims 2. Haunted houses 3. Missing persons 4. Vietnam veterans 5. Underhill, Tim (Fictitious character) 6. Illinois 7. Horror 8. Multiple perspectives 9. First person narratives 10. Adult books for young adults

LC 2003046689

Bram Stoker Award for Best Novel, 2003; International Horror Guild Award for Best Novel, 2003

The suicide of a woman and the disappearance of her teenage son, Mark, draws the boy's uncle, Timothy Underhill, back to his hometown of Millhaven, where his investigation uncovers a neighborhood haunted by a serial killer.

"Inquisitive and open-minded as Tim is, he makes it easy for Mr. Straub to move from conventionally hair-raising effects...to the more happening teenage world of cyberscares. Strongly visual without resorting to secondhand cinematic imagery, the book is equally well equipped to play both kinds of tricks." —*New York Times*

Mr. X. Peter Straub. Random House, 1999. 482 p.
ISBN 9780679401384
1. Father-separated children 2. Serial murderers 3. Nightmares 4. Paranormal phenomena 5. Horror

LC 98047688

Bram Stoker Award for Best Novel, 1999

Every year on his birthday, Ned Dunstan experiences a seizure in which he is forced to witness scenes of ruthless slaughter perpetrated by a mysterious and malevolent figure in black whom Ned calls Mr. X. This year Ned learns from his mother, who is on her death bed, the name of his long-absent father and other disturbing information about his own identity and that of his entire fantastic family.

"[Straub's] evocative prose, a seamless splice of clipped hard-boiled banter and poetic reflection, contributes to the thick atmosphere of apprehension that makes this one of the most invigorating horror reads of the year." —*Publishers Weekly*

★ **Mystery**. Peter Straub. E. P. Dutton, 1990. 548 p. (Blue rose, 2)
ISBN 9780525248187
1. Cold cases (Criminal investigation) 2. Murder investigation 3. Murder 4. Deception 5. Upper class 6. Wisconsin 7. Caribbean Area 8. 1960s 9. Mysteries

LC 89007734

A near-fatal traffic accident and a resulting obsession with death drive Tom Pasmore to join his neighbor, famous retired detective Lamont von Heilitz, in investigating two very different murders.

"The remarkable depth of characterization make apparent the fact that Mystery is meant to be much more than a conventional shocker. For the most part, Straub delivers the goods." —*Booklist*

Stridsberg, Sara

Valerie: or the faculty of dreams : amendment to the theory of sexuality. Sara Stridsberg; translated from the Swedish by Deborah Bragan-Turner. Farrar, Straus and Giroux, 2019. 384 p.

ISBN 9780374151911

1. Solanas, Valerie 2. Feminists 3. Women with mental illnesses 4. Women radicals 5. Women — Psychology 6. Paranoid schizophrenia 7. United States 8. 20th century 9. Experimental fiction 10. Multiple perspectives 11. Biographical fiction

LC 2018060814

In April 1988, Valerie Solanas, the writer, radical feminist and would-be assassin of Andy Warhol, was discovered dead in her hotel room, in a grimy corner of San Francisco. She was only 52; alone, penniless and surrounded by the typed pages of her last writings. In The Faculty of Dreams, Sara Stridsberg revisits the hotel room where Solanas died, the courtroom where she was tried and convicted of attempting to murder Andy Warhol, the Georgia wastelands where she spent her childhood, and the mental hospitals where she was interned. Through imagined conversations and monologues, reminiscences and rantings, Stridsberg reconstructs this most intriguing and enigmatic of women, articulating the thoughts and fears that she struggled to express in life and giving a powerful, heartbreaking voice to the writer of the infamous SCUM Manifesto.

Translation of: Dromfakulteten, tillagg till sexualteorin.

Translated from the Swedish.

Stringer, Vickie M.

Dirty Red: a novel. Vickie M. Stringer. Atria Books, 2006. 238 p. (Dirty Red novels, 1)

ISBN 9780743493482

1. African American women 2. Swindlers and swindling 3. Pregnancy 4. Violence 5. Sexuality 6. African American fiction 7. Drama lit

Having tricked her boyfriend into believing she is pregnant, eighteen-year-old Red enjoys his lavish attentions until she becomes pregnant for real by an ex-boyfriend who is in jail, a situation that leads her into a successful new career.

★ **Let** that be the reason. Vickie M. Stringer. Upstream, 2002. 247 p; (Let that be the reason novels, 1)

ISBN 9781886433854

1. Women drug dealers 2. Street life 3. Prostitution 4. Drug traffic 5. African American women 6. New York City 7. Columbus, Ohio 8. African American fiction 9. Drama lit

Street Lit Book Award Medal: Adult Fiction, 2003

Abandoned by a drug-dealing boyfriend who leaves her with a stack of bills and nothing to her name, Pamela Xavier assumes a tough alter ego, Carmen, to survive on the streets as the head of a call-girl operation.

Prequel: The reason why.

Originally published: Columbus, Ohio : Triple Crown Publications, c1999.

Still dirty: a novel. Vickie M. Stringer. Atria Books, 2008. 226 p. (Dirty Red novels, 2)

ISBN 9781416563587

1. Manipulation by women 2. Street life 3. Former convicts 4. Former boyfriends 5. African American women 6. African American fiction 7. Drama lit

The hustler Red and her companions Bacon and Q face such challenges as a double-dealing boyfriend, a friend's betrayal, and an unscrupulous business partner.

Stroby, Wallace

Some die nameless. Wallace Stroby. Mulholland Books, 2018. 352 p. ISBN 9780316440202

1. Mercenaries 2. Journalists 3. Survival 4. Murder 5. Dictators 6. Florida 7. Pennsylvania 8. Thrillers and suspense

An ex-mercenary and an embattled journalist find themselves unlikely allies against a corrupt defense contractor.

Stross, Charles

Accelerando. Charles Stross. Ace Books, 2005. 390 p. ISBN 9780441012848

1. Entrepreneurs 2. Dysfunctional families 3. Family relationships 4. Parent and adult child 5. Artificial intelligence 6. Space 7. 21st century 8. Hard science fiction 9. Science fiction

LC 2005042815

Locus Award for Best Science Fiction Novel, 2006

Trying to cope with the unchecked technological innovations that have rendered humankind nearly obsolete, the members of the Macx family are confronted by an unknown enemy that is systematically attempting to annihilate all biological lifeforms.

"Expanded from several stories originally published in Asimov's Science Fiction,...[this] novel follows several generations of the Macx family through the rapidly transforming, Internet-enabled global economy of the early twenty-first century to the human and transhuman populated worlds of the outer solar system a half century later.... Stross has his thumb squarely on the pulse of technology's leading edge and exults in extrapolating mere glimmers of ideas out to their mind-bending limits." —*Booklist*

Empire Games. Charles Stross. Tor, 2017. 336 p. (Empire Games, 1) ISBN 9780765337566

1. Near future 2. Espionage 3. Drone aircraft 4. Spies 5. Political intrigue 6. United States 7. Science fiction 8. Spy fiction 9. Political thrillers

A tale set in an alternate world of the immediate future follows the efforts of the head of a paratime espionage agency to prepare for an upcoming drone war at the same time her estranged spy daughter attempts to protect national security during an ominous succession crisis.

Stross handles the story well enough that you dont need to have read the previous six books. Of course, those who have will be overjoyed to renew their acquaintance with Miriam and her associates...Booklist.

Empire Games is set after and in the same world as the author's Merchant Princes novels.

Includes main time lines, character profiles, cast list and glossary.

Glasshouse. Charles Stross. Ace Books, 2006. 335 p. ISBN 9780441014033

1. Men with amnesia 2. Volunteers 3. Identity (Psychology) 4. Resistance to government 5. Recovered memory 6. 27th century 7. Social science fiction 8. Science fiction

LC 2006004358

When Robin wakes up in a clinic with most of his memories missing, it doesn't take him long to discover that someone is trying to kill him. It's the 27th century, when interstellar travel is by teleport gate and conflicts are fought by network worms that censor refugees' personalities and target historians. The civil war is over and Robin has been demobilized, but someone wants him out of the picture because of something his earlier self knew. On the run from a ruthless pursuer, he volunteers to participate in a unique experimental polity, the Glasshouse, constructed to simulate a pre-accelerated culture. Participants are assigned anonymized identities: it looks like the ideal hiding place for a posthuman on the run. But in this escape-proof environment,Robin will undergo an even more radical change, placing him at the mercy of the experimenters—and the mercy of his own unbalanced psyche. —From publisher description.

Neptune's brood. Charles Stross. ACE BOOKS, 2013. 336 p.
ISBN 9780425256770
1. Androids 2. Assassins 3. Life on other planets 4. Space flight 5. Robots 6. Space opera 7. Science fiction
LC 2013002384
After being stalked across the galaxy by an assassin, post-human Krina Alzon-114 journeys to the water-world Shin-Tethys in search of her sister in this new space opera.

Saturn's children: a space opera. Charles Stross. Ace Books, 2008. 323 p.
ISBN 9780441015948
1. Androids 2. Space flight 3. Life on other planets 4. Robots 5. Sexuality 6. 23rd century 7. Space opera 8. Science fiction
LC 2008008228
Sometime in the twenty-third century, humanity went extinct leaving only androids behind. Freya Nakamichi 47 is a femmebot, one of the last of her kind still functioning. With no humans left to pay for the pleasures she provides, she agrees to transport a mysterious package from Mercury to Mars. Unfortunately for Freya, she has just made herself a moving target for some very powerful, very determined humanoids who will stop at nothing to possess the contents of the package.
"Stross tosses out ideas aplenty. Since his robots know they were created by humans, for example, they consider evolution heretical. It isn't a relaxing bedtime read, but it is the sort of mind-expanding adventure that made hard science fiction famous." —*The New Scientist*

Stroud, Carsten

The **shimmer**. Carsten Stroud. MIRA Books, 2018. 384 p.
ISBN 9780778331223
1. Serial murderers 2. Time travel 3. Widowers 4. Detectives 5. Serial murder investigation 6. Thrillers and suspense 7. Canadian fiction
Craving to bathe in the shimmering afterglow that sometimes emanates when the soul leaves the body, a traveling female serial killer finds a way to slip into the past to right a wrong, changing the lives of two families in two different time periods.

Strout, Elizabeth

Amy and Isabelle: a novel. Elizabeth Strout. Random House, 1998. 303 p.
ISBN 9780375501340
1. Mothers and daughters 2. Teacher-student relationships 3. Family secrets 4. Teenage girls 5. Extramarital affairs 6. New England 7. McGavock, Caroline E. Winder 8. Coming-of-age stories 9. Adult books for young adults
LC 9819995
Los Angeles Times Art Seidenbaum Award for First Fiction, 1999; New York Times Notable Book, 1999; Shortlisted for The Orange Prize for Fiction, 2000
When Amy Goodrow, a shy high school student, falls in love with her math teacher, the love affair threatens the intimate relationship between Amy and her mother, Isabelle, whose feelings are influenced by the shame of her own past.
"As the cacophony of disaster grows ever louder in contemporary culture, Strout has written an excellent novel about enduring the banalities of ordinary life." —*The New Yorker*

★ **Anything** is possible: fiction. Elizabeth Strout. Random House, 2017. 254 pages

ISBN 9780812989403
1. Mothers and daughters 2. Siblings 3. Families 4. Small town life 5. Interpersonal relations 6. Illinois 7. Domestic fiction 8. Literary fiction
LC 2016020620
LibraryReads Favorites, 2017; Librarians' Choice (Australia), 2017; New York Times Notable Book, 2017
Two sisters, one who trades self-respect for a wealthy husband and one who discovers a kindred spirit in the pages of a book, struggle with intimate human dramas at the sides of their community members and a returned Lucy Barton.
"A radiant collection of stories linked to Strout's previous novel, My Name Is Lucy Barton...but moving beyond its first-person narration to limn small-town life from multiple perspectives." —*Kirkus*
Featuring the setting and characters from Elizabeth Strout's 2016 novel My Name Is Lucy Barton.

★ The **Burgess** boys: a novel. Elizabeth Strout. Random House, 2013. 320 p.
ISBN 9781400067688
1. Homecomings 2. Brothers 3. Guilt in men 4. Fathers — Death 5. Deception 6. Maine 7. Literary fiction
LC 2012035132
Catalyzed by a nephew's thoughtless prank, a pair of brothers confront painful psychological issues surrounding the freak accident that killed their father when they were boys, a loss linked to a heartbreaking deception that shaped their personal and professional lives.

My name is Lucy Barton. Elizabeth Strout. Random House, 2016. 193 p.
ISBN 9781400067695
1. Mothers and daughters 2. Family relationships 3. Motherhood 4. Hospital care 5. Appendix (Anatomy) — Surgery 6. New York City 7. 1980s 8. Domestic fiction
LibraryReads Favorites, 2016; New York Times Notable Book, 2016; Longlisted for the Baileys Women's Prize for Fiction, 2016; Longlisted for the Man Booker Prize, 2016; Shortlisted for the International Dublin Literary Award, 2018
After an appendix operation puts her in the hospital, New York writer Lucy Barton reconnects with her estranged mother as the pair reminisce about the past.
"In a compact novel brimming with insight and emotion, Strout relays with great tenderness and sadness the way family relationships can both make and break us." —*Booklist*

★ **Oh** William! Elizabeth Strout. Random House, 2021. 256 p.
ISBN 9780812989434
1. Divorced women 2. Widows 3. Women authors 4. Former husbands 5. Friendship 6. New York City 7. Maine 8. Literary fiction 9. Domestic fiction
The iconic heroine of My Name is Lucy Barton recounts her complicated, compassionate relationship with William, her first husband—and longtime, on-again-off-again friend and confidant—and the lives they eventually built with other people.
"Loneliness and betrayal, themes to which the Pulitzer Prize-winning Strout has returned throughout her career, are ever present in this illuminating character-driven saga, the third in her Amgash series, after Anything Is Possible." —*Publishers Weekly*

Olive Kitteridge. Elizabeth Strout. Random House, 2007. 288 p. (Olive novels, 1)
ISBN 9781400062089
1. Teachers 2. Mothers and sons 3. Change (Psychology) 4. Coastal towns 5. Small town life 6. Maine 7. Literary fiction 8. Short stories 9. Books to TV

ALA Notable Book, 2009; Library Journal Best Books, 2008; Pulitzer Prize for Fiction, 2009; National Book Critics Circle Award for Fiction finalist, 2008

The world of Olive Kitteridge, a retired school teacher in a small coastal town in Maine, is revealed in stories that explore her diverse roles in many lives, including a lounge singer haunted by a past love, her stoic husband, and her own resentful son.

"These linked stories introduce the inhabitants of Crosby, Maine, where the pull of domestic tragedy is stronger for rarely being spoken of.... Strout makes us experience not only the terrors of change but also the terrifying hope that change can bring: she plunges us into these churning waters and we come up gasping for air." —*The New Yorker*

13 linked stories
Sequel: Olive, again
HBO TV series of the same name based on this book.

★ **Olive,** again: a novel. Elizabeth Strout. Random House, 2019. 304 p. (Olive novels, 2)
ISBN 9780812996548
1. Former teachers 2. Mothers and sons 3. Change (Psychology) 4. Coastal towns 5. Small town life 6. Maine 7. Literary fiction 8. Short stories

LC 2019004792

A sequel to Olive Kitteridge finds Olive struggling to understand herself while bonding with a teen suffering from loss, a woman who gives birth unexpectedly, a nurse harboring a longtime crush and a lawyer who resists an unwanted inheritance.
Sequel to: Olive Kitteridge

Stuart, Douglas

★ **Shuggie** Bain. Douglas Stuart. Grove Press, 2020. 448 p.
ISBN 9780802148049
1. Working class families 2. Alcoholism 3. Mothers 4. Family violence 5. Working class boys 6. Glasgow, Scotland 7. 1980s 8. Literary fiction 9. Coming-of-age stories 10. Adult books for young adults

LC 2019037882

ALA Notable Book, 2021; Man Booker Prize, 2020; New York Times Notable Book, 2020; National Book Award for Fiction finalist, 2020; Kirkus Prize for Fiction finalist, 2020

A young boy growing up in a rundown 1980s Glasgow public housing facility pursues some semblance of a normal life as his older siblings move on and his mother increasingly succumbs to alcoholism.

"Perfect for getting lost in, Stuart's richly wrought coming-of-age saga is a trenchant portrayal of poverty and addiction, true to life and steeped in its era, setting, and dialect." —*Booklist*

Styles, Toy

Black and ugly. T. Styles. Triple Crown Publications, 2006. Vi, 241 p; (Black and ugly novels, 1)
ISBN 9780977880416
1. African American women 2. Friendship 3. Self-esteem in women 4. Street life 5. Appearances 6. Hyattsville, Maryland 7. Maryland 8. African American fiction 9. Drama lit

LC 2006937037

The tale of four totally different friends from the same block, whose friendship is tested during a seemingly innocent game of Truth or Dare.
Sequel: Black and ugly as ever.

A **hustler's** son: a novel. By T. Styles. Triple Crown Publications, 2006. 210 p; (Hustler's son, 1)
ISBN 9780976789499

1. Mothers and sons 2. African American teenage boys 3. Street life 4. Violence 5. Drug traffic 6. Maryland 7. Bladensburg, Maryland 8. Urban fiction 9. African American fiction

Trying to shield her son, Kelsi, from the realities of life on the streets, Janet Stayley realizes it is too late after Kelsi murders a fellow high school student and he finds out about his mother's past.

Raunchy. T. Styles; [edited by] Advanced Editorial Services. Cartel Publications, 2010. 338 p. (Making of a mother monster, 1)
ISBN 9780982391372
1. Family secrets 2. Mothers and daughters 3. Child abuse victims 4. African American women 5. Sexuality 6. Maryland 7. Urban fiction 8. African American fiction

LC 2010936906

"Raunchy is a heartbreaking, explicit story of failed mother and daughter relationships." —Provided by publisher

Raunchy 2: Mad's love. T. Styles; [edited by] Advanced Editorial Services. Cartel Publications, 2011. 324 p. (Making of a mother monster, 2)
ISBN 9780984303069
1. Mothers and daughters 2. Revenge 3. Betrayal 4. African American women 5. Inheritance and succession 6. Maryland 7. Urban fiction 8. African American fiction

After escaping death at her own child's hands, you'd think Harmony Phillips would change. Instead she feels resentful believing her kids took the life from her she felt she deserved. In a bed in Concord Manor, she is nursed back to health by those she wrote off.

Redbone. T. Styles. Urban Books; 2012. 484 p; (Redbone novels, 1)
ISBN 9781601624932
1. Roommates 2. Obsession in women 3. African American women — Interpersonal relations 4. Privacy 5. Secrets 6. Washington, D.C. 7. Urban fiction 8. African American fiction

LC Bl2012009756

When her new roommate Farah Cotton becomes obsessed with her and her personal life, Lesa Carmine tries to sever ties immediately, but Farah has other ideas, forcing Lesa to investigate Farah's past, which leads to a shocking discovery that could end her life.

★ **War**. T. Styles. Cartel Pubs, 2018. 308 p.
ISBN 9781948373227
1. Childhood friends 2. Betrayal 3. Baltimore, Maryland 4. Urban fiction 5. African American fiction
Two families. Two egos. One war.

War 2: All hell breaks loose. T. Styles. Cartel Pubns, 2018. 322 p.
ISBN 9781948373241
1. Male friendship 2. Betrayal 3. Families 4. Love-hate relationships 5. Urban fiction 6. African American fiction
In the Wales and Louisville clans, love and hate mean the same.

Styron, William

The **confessions** of Nat Turner. William Styron. Random House, 1967. 428 p.
ISBN 9780679601012
1. Turner, Nat 2. African American clergy 3. Slavery 4. Enslaved people's resistance and revolts 5. Race relations 6. Turner's Slave Revolt, Southampton, Virginia, 1831 7. Virginia 8. Antebellum America (1820-1861) 9. Biographical fiction 10. Historical fiction 11. Literary fiction
Pulitzer Prize for Fiction, 1968

Gives an account, based on the true story of a slave rebellion in 1831, of a noble man's moral decline.

Lie down in darkness. William Styron. Vintage Books, 1992. 400 p.
ISBN 9780679735977
1. Dysfunctional families 2. Suicide 3. Fathers and daughters 4. Daughters — Death 5. Loss (Psychology) 6. Southern States 7. Domestic fiction 8. Psychological fiction 9. Southern Gothic

As Milton Loftis follows the hearse in which his beautiful daughter, Peyton, is being carried to the grave, a story unfolds about the degeneration of a tormented Southern family submerged in infidelity and vengeful love.

"The book is not bleakly written. On the contrary, it is richly and even (in the best sense) poetically written.... If the parts seem to succeed each other with no apparent logic or dialectic, each part is brilliantly made and lovingly accomplished." —*The Atlantic*
Originally published in 1951.

★ **Sophie's** choice. William Styron. Random House, 1979. 515 p.
ISBN 9780394461090
1. Authors, American 2. Concentration camp survivors 3. Women Holocaust survivors 4. Jewish men 5. Man-woman relationships 6. Historical fiction 7. Books to movies 8. Modern classics
LC 78021835
National Book Award for Fiction, 1980; National Book Critics Circle Award for Fiction finalist, 1979

As the fierce lovemaking and fights of Nathan, a paranoiac Jewish intellectual, and Sophie, a Polish-Catholic concentration-camp survivor, intensify, Stingo, a writer who lives below them in a cheap rooming house, becomes more and more involved in their lives.

Suarez, Daniel
Change agent: a novel. Daniel Suarez. Dutton, 2017. 416 p.
ISBN 9781101984666
1. Interpol agents 2. Human evolution 3. Genetic engineering 4. Identity (Psychology) 5. Human trafficking 6. Singapore 7. 21st century 8. Science fiction
LC 2016030244

Drugged and abducted while standing on a crowded train platform, Kenneth Durand, an Interpol agent working against black-market labs that perform illegal embryo augmentation, awakens to discover he has been genetically transformed into his most wanted suspect.

"This outstanding speculative thriller from bestseller Suarez (Kill Decision) imagines a future of 'living technology—a fourth industrial revolution of synthetic biology and genetic editing,' as the author puts it in an opening note to the reader." —*Publishers Weekly*

Sullivan, Emily
The **rebel** and the rake. Emily Sullivan. Forever, 2021. 368 p. (League of scoundrels, 2)
ISBN 9781538737347
1. Live-in companions 2. Spies 3. Independence in women 4. Secrets 5. Extortion 6. Scotland 7. Great Britain 8. Victorian era (1837-1901) 9. 1890s 10. Victorian romances series 11. Historical romances

Fans of Netflix's Bridgerton series will love this enchanting story of a spy who finds himself entangled with the most intriguing bluestocking.

"After wowing readers with her superb debut, A Rogue to Remember (2021), rising historical romance star Sullivan returns with another entrancing addition to her League of Scoundrels series that brilliantly showcases her mastery of deep characterization as well as her gift for crafting a wit-infused plot that effectively threads the needle between desire and danger without dropping a single stitch." —*Booklist*

Sullivan, J. Courtney
Friends and strangers. J. Courtney Sullivan. Alfred A. Knopf, 2020. 416 pages
ISBN 9780525520597
1. New mothers 2. Social classes 3. Babysitters 4. Social media 5. Women journalists 6. Literary fiction 7. Multiple perspectives

Struggling to adjust to small-town life after having a baby, an accomplished New York City journalist immerses herself in social media before bonding with a babysitter from a very different walk of life.

"Friends and Strangers is a deeply personal yet profound exploration of motherhood, friendships, and the role of privilege in determining how we shape our lives." —*Booklist*

Sullivan, Michael J.
Theft of swords. Michael J. Sullivan. Orbit, 2011. 688 (Riyria revelations, 1)
ISBN 9780316187749
1. Thieves 2. Swordplay 3. Adventure 4. Extortion 5. Rulers 6. Fantasy fiction 7. Sword and sorcery
LC 2011008814
Library Journal Best Books, 2011

Two thieves, Royce Melborn and Hadrian Blackwater, become the unwitting scapegoats in a plot to murder the king after taking on too many dangerous assignments for machinating and conspiring noble people.
Originally published as two books, under the titles, The Crown Conspiracy and Avempartha.

Sundaresan, Indu
The **splendor** of silence: a novel. Indu Sundaresan. Atria Books, 2006. 416 p.
ISBN 9780743283670
1. Nobility 2. Interracial romance 3. Intelligence service 4. Americans in India 5. Romantic love 6. India 7. Second World War era (1939-1945) 8. Love stories 9. Historical fiction
LC 2006042884

In 1942, Sam Hawthorne, a young U.S. Army captain, arrives in a tiny princely state in western India. He carries combat wounds and several secrets, one of which is the real reason behind his visit: to find his brother Mike, an idealistic American soldier who disappeared after joining the local struggle for independence from the British. But Sam's mission is soon threatened when he falls in love with Mila, daughter of the local political agent. Betrothed to the local prince, Mila draws Sam into a doomed affair that places them both in the path of dynastic intrigue, racial prejudice, and the explosive circumstances of a country torn between imperialism and nationalism.

"Flashbacks to 1940s India occur when Olivia receives a mysterious trunk that promises to explain who she is. The trunk arrives on the same day that her father, Sam, dies and contains information about her biological mother, Mila. Through a letter hidden among the keepsakes in the box, Olivia learns that her father spent time in India searching for his missing brother. While there, he fell in love with Mila, the daughter of the local political agent and fiance of a prince. It was also there that he got to know Mila's brothers, who knew the whereabouts of his own brother. A series of events leads to the arrival of the trunk for Olivia years later. Sundaresan's descriptive writing style makes for a colorful, engrossing read, and while the story does hop between time periods and locations, the reader is never lost along the way." —*Library Journal*

Sundin, Sarah

Through waters deep: a novel. Sarah Sundin. Revell, a division of Baker Publishing Group, 2015. 368 p. (Waves of freedom, 1)
ISBN 9780800723422

1. Secretaries 2. Destroyers (Warships) 3. Sabotage 4. Criminal investigation 5. Man-woman relationships 6. Second World War era (1939-1945) 7. Christian historical romances

LC 2015000435

A World War II naval officer and a Boston Navy Yard secretary investigate evidence on board the officer's destroyer that implicates someone in their personal lives.

"Providing readers with an immersive experience, Sundin (In Perfect Time) vividly re-creates the atmosphere of a country on the brink of entering World War II. The tender romance at the story's center keeps readers rooting for Jim and Mary to realize their true feelings for each other. In the wake of the popularity of Anita Diamant's The Boston Girl, this book holds local interest for those who have lived in or loved the city.." —*Library Journal*

When twilight breaks. Sarah Sundin. Revell, 2021. 384 p.
ISBN 9780800736361

1. Americans in Germany 2. Espionage 3. World War II 4. Nazis 5. Jews 6. Germany 7. Between the Wars (1918-1939) 8. Christian historical fiction

LC 2020024621

Two Americans meet in 1938 in the heart of Nazi Germany. Their efforts to expose oppression attract unwanted attention, pulling them deeper into danger as the world marches toward war.

"Sundin masterfully combines action and attraction to generate multilayered thrills while exploring such themes as individual freedom versus the common good, gender and racial discrimination, and the polarization of viewpoints, which all have deep relevance today." —*Booklist*

Sundstol, Vidar

The **land** of dreams. Vidar Sundstol; translated from the Norwegian by Tiina Nunnally. University of Minnesota Press, 2013. 284 pages (Minnesota trilogy, 1)
ISBN 9780816689408

1. Family secrets 2. Crimes against tourists 3. Norwegians in the United States 4. Brothers 5. Guilt 6. Lake Superior 7. Minnesota 8. Scandinavian crime fiction 9. Mysteries

Lance Hansen, forest service officer and grandson of Norwegian immigrants, lives a quiet life working and pursuing the hobby of genealogy, until he finds a Norwegian tourist's dead body near a stone cross on the shore of Lake Superior.

"The landscape is a big part of the story, as is the history of the area, making this a fascinating look at Minnesota as well as a suspenseful thriller." —*Booklist*

Translation from the Norwegian of: Drommenes Land.
Originally published: Oslo : Tiden Norsk Forlag, c2008.

Suri, Manil

The **age** of Shiva: a novel. Manil Suri. W.W. Norton, 2008. 448 p.
ISBN 9780393065695

1. Husband and wife 2. Conflict in families 3. Politics and culture 4. Man-woman relationships 5. Marital conflict 6. India 7. Domestic fiction 8. Historical fiction 9. Political fiction

LC 2007037322

Marrying in order to escape an overbearing father, Meera is further victimized by her physically demanding husband and lustful brother-in-law, a circumstance from which she finds fleeting escape through her relationships with her sister-in-law and young son.

"Suri's...novel is a sensuous, nuanced portrait of motherhood, but it also sparks with the frictions of being female in an India where television soaps and political slogans compete noisily with Hindu myth." —*The New Yorker*

Suri, Tasha

★ **Empire** of sand. Tasha Suri. Orbit, 2018. 480 p. (Books of Ambha, 1)
ISBN 9780316449717

1. Aristocracy 2. Rulers 3. Gods and goddesses 4. Imperialism 5. Young women 6. Asian-influenced fantasy 7. Fantasy fiction 8. Adult books for young adults

LC 2018027281

LibraryReads Favorites, 2018

The illegitimate daughter of an imperial governor and an Amrithi, an outcast nomad with magic in her blood, must fight the plans of the Emperor's mystics to use her ability to manipulate the dreams of gods to alter the shape of the world.

"The desert setting, complex characters, and epic mythology will captivate readers of Suri's debut fantasy." —*Booklist*

The **Jasmine** throne. Tasha Suri. Orbit, 2021. 512 p. (Burning kingdoms, 1)
ISBN 9780759554160

1. Exile (Punishment) 2. Princesses 3. Household employees 4. Imprisonment 5. Despotism 6. Fantasy fiction 7. LGBTQIA fiction 8. Multiple perspectives

LC 2020040047

Exiled by her despotic brother when he claimed their father's kingdom, Malini spends her days trapped in the Hirana: an ancient, cliffside temple that was once the source of the magical deathless waters, but is now little more than a decaying ruin. A servant in the regent's household, Priya makes the treacherous climb to the Hirana every night to clean Malini's chambers. She is happy to play the role of a drudge so long as it keeps anyone from discovering her ties to the temple and the dark secret of her past. But when Malini bears witness to Priya's true nature, their destinies become irrevocably tangled.

"Suri (Realm of Ash) has created this world with great deliberation, including details about clothing, cuisine, and architecture. Malini and Priya both have depth and nuance, and their attraction to each other is written with care and sensitivity. Changing viewpoints help move the action along, but this is the first book in a trilogy, which inevitably means that some of the plotting will set the stage for books to come." —*Library Journal*

★ **Realm** of ash. Tasha Suri. Orbit, 2019. 496 pages (Books of Ambha, 2)
ISBN 9780316449755

1. Young widows 2. Princes 3. Imaginary empires 4. Curses 5. Magic 6. Asian-influenced fantasy 7. Fantasy fiction 8. Adult books for young adults

LC 2019027766

The Ambhan Empire is crumbling. A terrible war of succession hovers on the horizon. The only hope for peace lies in the mysterious realm of ash, where mortals can find what they seek in the echoes of their ancestors' dreams. But to walk there requires a steep price.

"Those with a penchant for lyrical prose, intricate world building, beautifully imagined characters, compelling immersive folklore, and a fascinating look into a setting reminiscent of the Mughal Empire need look no further." —*Booklist*

Suskind, Patrick

★ **Perfume:** the story of a murderer. Patrick Suskind; translated from the German by John E. Woods. A.A. Knopf, 1986. 255 p.
ISBN 9780394550848

1. Perfumes 2. Murderers 3. Women murder victims 4. Serial murders 5. Smell 6. France 7. 18th century 8. 1730s 9. Horror 10. Translations 11. Books to movies

LC 86045419

World Fantasy Award, 1987

Survivor, genius, perfumer, killer: this is Jean-Baptiste Grenouille. He was abandoned on the filthy streets of Paris as a child, but grows up to discover he has an extraordinary gift: a sense of smell more powerful than any other human's. Soon, he is creating the most sublime fragrances in all the city. Yet there is one odour he cannot capture. It is exquisite, magical: the scent of a young virgin. And to get it he must kill.

"Those readers who feel they are wasting their time with novels unless they are picking up facts will welcome Siskind's encyclopedic overview of the methods of making perfume. Like the best scents, there is something fundamentally formulaic about this novel, but its effects will linger long after it has been stoppered." —*Time*

Translation from the German of: Das Parfum.

First published as Das Parfum: Diogenes Verlag A.G.: Zurich, 1985.

This translation first published: Great Britain: Hamish Hamilton, 1986.

Sutanto, Jesse Q.

Dial A for aunties. Jesse Q. Sutanto. Berkley, 2021. 320 p. (Aunties (Jesse Q Sutanto);, 1)
ISBN 9780593336731

1. Accidental death 2. Mothers and daughters 3. Aunts 4. Superstition 5. Asian American families 6. California 7. Relationship fiction

LC 2020050425

Loan Stars Favourites, 2021; LibraryReads Favorites, 2021

Accidentally causing the death of a blind date, Meddy is persuaded by her meddlesome Chinese-Indonesian mother and aunts to dispose of the body, which upends a billionaire's wedding and Meddy's reunion with a former flame.

"In Sutanto's rollicking debut, which she describes in a 'Dear reader' foreword as 'a love letter to my family—a ridiculously large bunch with a long history of immigration,' a fatal accident begets family reconciliation, true love at second sight, and happy beginnings all around." —*Booklist*

Sutcliff, Rosemary

Sword at sunset. Rosemary Sutcliff. Tom Doherty Associates, 1987. 498 p.
ISBN 9780812588521

1. Arthur 2. Rulers 3. Great Britain 4. Arthurian fantasy 5. Historical fantasy 6. Celtic fantasy

"A novel based on historical facts about the legendary Arthur. The time is the century after the last Roman legions leave Britain, and Arthur is desperately striving to hold Britain against the Saxons, Picts, and other invading savage tribes. [This is] the story of his tragic fate, his good times and bad." —*Publishers Weekly*

A Tor book.

Originally published: New York : Coward-McCann, 1963.

Sveistrup, Soren

★ The **chestnut** man: a novel. Soren Sveistrup; translated from the Danish by Caroline Waight. Harper, 2019. 516 pages
ISBN 9780062895363

1. Serial murder investigation 2. Detectives 3. Missing persons 4. Murder victims 5. Scandinavian crime fiction 6. Translations 7. Police procedurals

When a serial killer begins leaving handmade dolls at his murder scenes, two detectives struggle to put aside their differences and follow forensic clues linking the case to a politician's kidnapped daughter.

Svevo, Italo

Zeno's conscience. Italo Svevo; translated from the Italian by William Weaver. Alfred A. Knopf, 2001. Xlix, 437 p.
ISBN 9780375413308

1. Psychoanalysis 2. Married men 3. Psychiatric hospital patients 4. Guilt 5. Autobiography — Therapeutic use 6. Italy 7. Translations 8. Modern classics

LC 2001040821

After being advised by his doctor to write his memoirs as a form of therapy, Zeno sets out in search of truth, health, and happiness.

"This is a highly human story and its material is fundamentally as sound as its method.... The work of a man who wrote to please himself, it has an individuality and originality you cannot escape noticing, and it has, too, a fine and comprehensive knowledge of its character." —*New York Times Book Review*

Includes bibliographical references.

Swamy, Shruti

The **archer**. A novel by Shruti Anna Swamy. Algonquin Books of Chapel Hill, 2021. 320 p.
ISBN 9781616209902

1. Growing up 2. Dancers 3. Dancing 4. Interpersonal relations 5. Social classes 6. Mumbai, India 7. 1960s 8. Literary fiction 9. Historical fiction 10. Coming-of-age stories

LC 2021010464

Vidya, a rebellious young dancer and motherless daughter, comes of age in 1960s and 70s Bombay.

"Each segment challenges expectations and exposes the limitations of being female. Beyond adaptation, sacrifice, and even erasure, Swamy provides no easy answers to the search for fulfillment." —*Booklist*

A **house** is a body: stories. Shruti Swamy. Algonquin Books of Chapel Hill, 2020. 205 p.
ISBN 9781616209896

1. Women 2. Desire 3. Fear 4. Obsession 5. Motherhood 6. United States 7. India 8. Literary fiction 9. Short stories

LC 2019059046

Dreams collide with reality, modernity with antiquity, and myth with identity in the twelve arresting stories of A House Is a Body. Immersive and assured, provocative and probing, these are stories written with the edge and precision of a knife blade. Set in the United States and India, they reveal small but intense moments of beauty, pain, and power that contain the world.

"Spanning the geographical and social distance between India and the U.S., Swamy's 12 tales illuminate her characters' imperfections and struggles, ultimately forming an attuned and mystical exploration into the enigmas of being human." —*Booklist*

Swann, Stacey

Olympus Texas. Stacey Swann. Doubleday, 2021. 336 p.
ISBN 9780385545211

1. Homecomings 2. Interpersonal conflict 3. Marriage 4. Small towns 5. Family secrets 6. Texas 7. Family sagas

Weaving elements of classical mythology into a thoroughly modern family drama, this novel follows the Briscoe family as prodigal son March returns home and with his arrival, marriages are upended and even the strongest of alliances are shattered.

"Swann's debut is rich in Texas flavor and full of nods to classical mythology: quotes from Ovid, twins human and canine, and the kind of relentless bad luck that usually means you've offended a deity. A total page-turner." —*Kirkus*

Swanson, Peter

Eight perfect murders: a novel. Peter Swanson. William Morrow & Co, 2020. 270 p.
ISBN 9780062838209
1. Booksellers 2. Women FBI agents 3. Serial murderers 4. Murder suspects 5. Murder victims 6. Boston, Massachusetts 7. Psychological suspense

Years after establishing a literary career through his compilation of the mystery genre's most unsolvable classics, an unsuspecting bookseller is tapped by the FBI for help solving murders that eerily mimic the books on his list.

"The wintry New England setting and eerily cool narration, together with trust-no-one twists and garish murders, will satisfy thriller readers; fans of classic mysteries by Agatha Christie, Ira Levin, and John D. MacDonald will enjoy how Swanson (Before She Knew Him) repurposes the plots." —*Library Journal*

Her every fear: a novel. Peter Swanson. William Morrow, 2017. 304 p.
ISBN 9780062427021
1. Art students 2. Fear in women 3. Apartment dwellers 4. Murder 5. Cousins 6. Boston, Massachusetts 7. London, England 8. Psychological suspense
LC 2016007758
LibraryReads Favorites, 2017

A woman prone to panic attacks in the aftermath of a violent kidnapping relocates to a cousin's home in Boston, where a neighbor's murder embroils her in speculation about her cousin's nature and the intentions of an appealing stranger.

"Psychological thriller devotees should block time to read Swanson's (The Kind Worth Killing) novel in one sitting, preferably in the daylight. Readers can expect the hairs on their necks to stand straight up as they are consumed with a full-blown case of heebie-jeebies." —*Library Journal*

The kind worth killing: a novel. Peter Swanson. William Morrow, 2015. 352 p.
ISBN 9780062267528
1. Strangers 2. Married men 3. Women murderers 4. Wife-killing 5. Deception 6. Psychological suspense
LC 2014019249

Engaging in an intimate sharing of secrets with a mysterious woman on an airplane, an unhappily married businessman is tangled in a psychologically twisted game of cat-and-mouse involving a plot to kill the man's wife.

Swanwick, Michael

Bones of the Earth. Michael Swanwick. EOS, 2002. 335 p.
ISBN 9780380978366
1. Dinosaurs 2. Time travel 3. Paleontologists 4. Science fiction 5. Adult books for young adults
LC 2001040196

A paleontologist who discovers the secret of time travel is initially thrilled at the prospect of conducting research on live dinosaurs, but his frequent trips into the past soon begin to have negative consequences on the present.

Swarthout, Glendon

Bless the beasts and children. Glendon Swarthout. Pocket Books, 1970. 192 p.
ISBN 9780385033626
1. Misfits (Persons) 2. Summer camps 3. Animal liberation 4. Rejection (Psychology) 5. Children of rich people 6. Arizona 7. Southwest (United States) 8. 1960s 9. Coming-of-age stories 10. Books to movies 11. Adult books for young adults
LC 79094331

The neglected attendees of the Box Canyon Boys Camp find their lives turned around by Cotton, who, in a hot-wired pickup, challenges them to join efforts to save a herd of buffalo and rediscover themselves in the process.

★ The **shootist**. Glendon Swarthout. Berkley, 1998. Xvi, 215 p; (Shootist, 1)
ISBN 9780425164198
1. Gunfighters 2. Death 3. Cancer 4. The West (United States) 5. 1900s (Decade) 6. Westerns 7. Books to movies
Spur Award for Best Western Novel (Short Novel), 1976

John Bernard Books rides into El Paso in 1901 only to be told by a doctor that he will soon confront the greatest shootist of all: Death.

"This is definitely more than a Western; the characterization is flawless, the plot absorbing and convincing." —*Library Journal*
Sequel: The last shootist.
This novel was adapted into a film by the same name in 1976, starring John Wayne, Lauren Bacall, and Ron Howard and directed by Don Siegel.
Originally published: Garden City, N.Y. : Doubleday, 1975.

Swarup, Shubhangi

Latitudes of longing. Shubhangi Swarup. One World, 2020. 320 pages : Illustration
ISBN 9780593132555
1. Humans 2. Nature 3. Generation gap 4. Psychic ability 5. XXXXXXXX 6. South Asia 7. Magical realism 8. Literary fiction

An award-winning debut from India explores the love and longing between humanity and the earth through the stories of a botanist, a clairvoyant, a geologist, a revolutionary's mother, a shapeshifting turtle and other protagonists.

"Extraordinarily affecting, this work should be a priority acquisition for all libraries with astute, globally hungry patrons." —*Library Journal*

Sweeney, Cynthia D'Aprix

★ **Good** company: a novel. Cynthia D'Aprix Sweeney. Ecco, 2021. 320 p.
ISBN 9780062876003
1. Married women 2. Marriage 3. Actors and actresses 4. Secrets 5. Friendship 6. Relationship fiction
LC 2020041878

Flora Mancini has been happily married for more than twenty years. But everything she thought she knew about herself, her marriage, and her relationship with her best friend, Margot, is upended when she stumbles upon an envelope containing her husband's wedding ring, the one he claimed he lost one summer when their daughter, Ruby, was five.

"Readers of introspective, relational novels will devour this." —*Booklist*

Sweeney-Baird, Christina

The **end** of men. Christina Sweeney-Baird. Putnam, 2021. 400 p.
ISBN 9780593328132
1. Women physicians 2. Epidemics 3. Plague 4. Men — Death
5. Women 6. 2020s 7. Apocalyptic fiction 8. Science fiction 9. Multiple
perspectives

The year is 2025, and a mysterious virus has broken out in Scotland—a lethal illness that seems to effect only men. When Dr. Amanda MacLean reports this phenomenon, she is dismissed as hysterical. By the time her warning is heeded, it is too late. The virus becomes a global pandemic—and a political one. The victims are all men. The world becomes alien—a women's world.

"This may be just the novel you want to read right now or the last thing you'd want to pick up. Sweeney-Baird's dystopian debut novel, begun in 2018, is unsettlingly prescient." —*Kirkus*

Swift, Graham

★ **Here** we are. Graham Swift. Alfred A. Knopf, 2020. 192 p.
ISBN 9780525658054
1. Vaudeville performers 2. Magicians 3. Friendship 4. Engaged persons 5. Secrets 6. Brighton, England 7. Great Britain 8. 1950s 9. Literary fiction

It's the summer of 1959, and something magical can be witnessed at the end of the pier in beach town Brighton, England. Jack Robbins, Ronnie Deane, and Evie White are performing in a seaside variety show, starring as Jack Robinson the compere comedian, and The Great Pablo and Eve: a magic act. By the end of the summer, Evie's glinting engagement ring will be flung to the bottom of the ocean and one of the trifecta will vanish forever.

"Swift's brief, magical tale demonstrates one more brilliant example of his talent for pulling universal themes out of the hats of ordinary lives." —*Publishers Weekly*

★ **Last** orders: a novel. Graham Swift. Knopf, 1996. 294 p.
ISBN 9780679412243
1. World War II veterans 2. Senior men — Friendship 3. Betrayal
4. Austen, Jane 5. Parents of children with developmental disabilities
6. England 7. Psychological fiction 8. Literary fiction 9. Multiple perspectives
ALA Notable Book, 1997; Booker Prize, 1996; James Tait Black Memorial Prize for Fiction, 1996; Shortlisted for the International IMPAC Dublin Literary Award, 1998

In England three working-class buddies, united by pub-drinking and World War II experiences, drive the ashes of the fourth to the sea. In the process emerge the lives of four families and the reason no wife came.

"The narrative is parceled out among...four men, as well as Amy, the widow, Vince's wife, Mandy, and Jack, the dead man. The accent is flat London vernacular, and the tone varies between mordant humor, gentle regret, and deep sorrow. Swift carries off this feat of ventriloquism with admirable skill." —*The New York Review of Books*

★ **Mothering** Sunday: a romance. Graham Swift. Alfred A. Knopf, 2016. 208 p.
ISBN 9781101947524
1. Self-discovery in women 2. Social classes 3. Household employees
4. Lovers 5. Grief in women 6. Between the Wars (1918-1939) 7. 1920s
8. Historical fiction 9. Literary fiction 10. First person narratives
LC 2015033402
Hawthornden Prize, 2017; Shortlisted for the Walter Scott Prize for Historical Fiction, 2017

Sharing what she believes will be a last tryst with a longtime secret lover on the eve of his marriage, a woman reflects on the years they have spent together and her journey of self-discovery against a backdrop of 20th-century history.

"Swift has fun with language, with class conventions, and with narrative expectations in a novel where nothing is as simple or obvious as it seems at first." —*Kirkus*

Wish you were here. Graham Swift. Vintage Canada, 2011. 352 p.
ISBN 9780307360106
1. Brothers 2. Grief in men 3. Loss (Psychology) 4. Funerals 5. Soldiers
6. England 7. Iraq 8. Psychological fiction 9. Literary fiction

Jack must travel to bring the body of his brother, who has been killed in the Iraq War, home to England. The process of doing this has a terrible impact on Jack and on his relationship with his wife.
First published in 2011.
Originally published: London : Picador, 2011.

Swift, Jonathan

★ **Gulliver's** travels. Jonathan Swift. Dover Publications, 1996. Xiii, 226 p. : Illustration; Map
ISBN 9780486292731
1. Voyages and travels 2. Giants 3. Lilliputians (Fictitious characters)
4. Sailing 5. Miniature persons (Imaginary characters) 6. 19th century
7. Fantasy classics 8. Fantasy fiction 9. Satirical fiction

Gullible ship's doctor Lemuel Gulliver experiences extraordinary travels, in which he goes through a series of apparently child-like fantasy worlds of tiny people and giants, floating islands and talking horses.
Originally published: 1726.

Swinson, David

City on the edge. David Swinson. Mulholland Books, 2021. 336 p.
ISBN 9780316528542
1. Moving to a new city 2. Teenage boys 3. Family secrets 4. Death
5. Violence 6. Beirut, Lebanon 7. 1970s 8. Coming-of-age stories
9. Thrillers and suspense

In the wake of a baffling tragedy, 13-year-old Graham moves with his family to Beirut, Lebanon, a city on the edge of the sea and cataclysmic violence. Inquisitive and restless by nature, Graham suspects his State Department father is a CIA operative, and that their family's fragile domesticity is merely a front for American efforts along the nearby Israeli border. Over the course of one year, 1972, Graham's life will utterly change. Two men are murdered, his parent's marriage disintegrates, and Graham, along with his two ex-pat friends, run afoul of forces they cannot understand.

"Because Swinson's ('Frank Marr' series) father served in the U.S. Foreign Service and his family lived all over the world, this book has a particular realism and an almost autobiographical perspective. Readers who enjoy international intrigue, spies, and mystery, or coming-of-age stories, will enjoy this book." —*Library Journal*

Swinson, Kiki

A **gangster** and a gentleman. . Dafina, 2012. 295 p.
ISBN 9780758251824
1. African American women 2. Protectiveness in men 3. Extramarital affairs 4. Organized crime 5. Gunfights 6. African American fiction
7. Drama lit
LC Bl2012021793
Library Journal Best Books, 2012

Two stories about women and their bad men, featuring Melody, who hires Scotty to take care of her cheating husband, but winds up seeking revenge, and Blake, who turns to her kingpin father's enforcer for protection from his employer.

I'm New York's finest. Kiki Swinson. K S Publicatons, 2017. 238 p. ISBN 9780986203794

1. Drug dealers 2. Siblings 3. Families 4. Drug traffic 5. Suspicion 6. Urban fiction 7. African American fiction

Naomi is a hustler at heart. And she loves her family. Put the two together and you'll end up with a very profitable drug enterprise.

Lifestyles of the rich and shameless. . Dafina, 2012. 264 p. ISBN 9780758251800

1. Street life 2. Heirs and heiresses 3. African American women 4. Police 5. Wealth 6. Urban erotica 7. African American fiction

In "Shamelessly rich," heiress Megan Rich suddenly loses her inheritance and must make a life-changing choice; and in "Puttin' Shame In The Game," three women scheme to seduce New York police officer Noble for his riches.

The **safe** house. Kiki Swinson. Kensington Pub Corp, 2019. 256 p. (Black market (Kiki Swinson), 2) ISBN 9781496720023

1. Cartels 2. Fugitives 3. African American women 4. Drug enforcement agents 5. Missing persons investigation 6. Virginia 7. Urban fiction 8. African American fiction

With the local police closing in on her as the prime suspect in her abusive boyfriend's disappearance, a fierce, strong woman has no choice but to ditch the feds and take down a cartel leader on her own.

Who's wife extraordinaire now. Kiki Swinson. K. S. Publications, 2014. 240 p. (Wife extraordinaire, 4) ISBN 9780985349554

1. African-American women 2. Power (Social sciences) 3. Married women 4. Extramarital affairs 5. Secrets 6. African American fiction 7. Drama lit

Trice & her husband Troy are total enemies now. With Charlene dead, Troy has no one on the streets.

Wifey. By Kiki Swinson. Dafina, 2008. 294 p. (Wifey, 1) ISBN 9780758229014

1. African American women 2. Drug traffic 3. Street life 4. Husband and wife 5. Sexuality 6. Washington, D.C. 7. Urban fiction 8. African American fiction

Street Lit Book Award Medal: Adult Fiction, 2005

Tired of his hustling and cheating, Kira tries to leave her drug-dealing husband Ricky as federal charges mount against him, but she faces complications along the way.

Wifey's next sticky situation. Kiki Swinson. KS Publications, 2017. 238 p. (Wifey, 10) ISBN 9780986203756

1. African American women 2. Drug traffic 3. Revenge 4. Murderers 5. Street life 6. New Jersey 7. Washington, D.C. 8. Urban fiction 9. African American fiction

Kira is the on the homicide detectives' radar once again. Right now, she's clueless as to how she's going to fix this situation but with Dylan now dead, things are going to get even stickier.

Swyler, Erika

★ **Light** from other stars: a novel. Erika Swyler. Bloomsbury Publishing, 2019. 352 p. ISBN 9781635573169

1. Women astronauts 2. Space and time 3. Ambition 4. Inventions 5. Loss (Psychology) 6. Florida 7. Space 8. 1980s 9. 21st century

10. Coming-of-age stories 11. Science fiction 12. Parallel narratives 13. Adult books for young adults

LC 2018034280

Decades after her grieving father, a laid-off NASA scientist, triggers chaotic changes in his pursuit of life-extending technology, an astronaut confronts dangerous family secrets to stop a world-threatening crisis.

Sylvester, Natalia

Everyone knows you go home. Natalia Sylvester. Little A, 2018. 334 pages
ISBN 9781542046367

1. Mexican Americans 2. Fathers-in-law 3. Ghosts 4. Redemption 5. Immigrants 6. Texas 7. Mexican-American Border Region 8. Literary fiction 9. Family sagas

From the acclaimed author of Chasing the Sun comes a new novel about immigration and the depths to which one Mexican American family will go for forgiveness and redemption.

"A forceful record of migration within a family and the dangers and triumphs of our undocumented population." —*Kirkus*

Szabo, Magda

Abigail. By Magda Szabo; translated from Hungarian by Len Rix. New York Review Books, 2020. 360 p. ISBN 9781681374031

1. World War II 2. Boarding schools 3. Teenage girls 4. Spoiled children 5. Statues 6. Hungary 7. Second World War era (1939-1945) 8. Historical fiction 9. Coming-of-age stories 10. Translations

LC 2019025320

Fourteen-year-old Gina, the spoiled daughter of a Hungarian general, rails against being sent to boarding school far from Budapest when war breaks out, but finds help in a statue of Abigail and her new "sisters.

"This infectious coming-of-age novel from Szab (1917 2007), released in 1970 and translated into English for the first time, is a rollicking delight." —*Publishers Weekly*

Translation of: Abigel.

Originally published: Budapest : Europa, 1970.

Translated from the Hungarian

T

T. I.

Power & Beauty: a love story of life on the streets. T.I.. William Morrow, 2011. 352 p. ISBN 9780062067654

1. African American men 2. Fashion 3. Drug traffic 4. Man-woman relationships 5. Street life 6. Atlanta, Georgia 7. New York City 8. Urban fiction 9. African American fiction

After the death of his mother, Paul "Power" Clay allows himself to be guided by Slim, a local businessman. Power is sure that if he learns Slim's ways, he'll make something of himself— and perhaps be worthy of Tanya "Beauty" Long. From Chicago to Miami to New York, through drugs, women, and violence, Power makes the difficult transition from boy to man and, in doing so, begins to question if those who have taught him truly have his best interests at heart.

Sequel: Trouble & Triumph

Trouble & triumph: a novel of Power & Beauty. T.I.. HarperCollins, 2012. 288 p.

ISBN 9780062067685

1. African American men 2. Fashion 3. Drug traffic 4. Street life 5. Man-woman relationships 6. Atlanta, Georgia 7. Urban fiction 8. African American fiction

Leaving Power, the boy she's come to love, behind, Tanya "Beauty" Long makes a name for herself in New York City's fashion industry, while Power becomes trapped in a world of drugs, women and money where he makes a shocking discovery that brings Tanya back to him.

Sequel to: Power & Beauty.

Tademy, Lalita

Cane River. Lalita Tademy. Warner Books, 2001. 418 p. (Tademy family chronicles, 1)

ISBN 9780446527323

1. Tademy family 2. Race relations 3. Family relationships 4. Enslaved women 5. African American families 6. African American women 7. Cane River Region, Louisiana 8. Louisiana 9. 19th century 10. 20th century 11. African American fiction 12. Historical fiction 13. Family sagas 14. Adult books for young adults

LC 43682

Cane River is an isolated community that lies on a small river in central Louisiana. There in the early 19th century, slaves, free people of color, and Creole French planters lived and worked, loved and bore children. The author discovered her amazing heritage there and chronicles four generations of strong, determined black women.

"Five generations and a hundred years in the life of a matriarchal black Louisiana family are encapsulated in this...novel that is based in part upon the lives, as preserved in both historical record and oral tradition, of the author's ancestors.... Her frank observations about black racism add depth to the tale, and she demonstrates that although the practice of slavery fell most harshly upon blacks, and especially women, it also constricted the lives and choices of white men. Photos of and documents relating to Tademy's ancestors add authenticity to a fascinating story." —*Publishers Weekly*

Takamura, Kaoru

★ **Lady** Joker. Kaoru Takamura; translated from the Japanese by Marie Iida and Allison Markin Powell. Soho Crime, 2021. 600 pages

ISBN 9781616957018

1. Corporate greed 2. Factories 3. Business — Corrupt practices 4. Hostages 5. Identity (Psychology) 6. Japan 7. 1990s 8. Crime fiction 9. Thrillers and suspense

LC 2020032998

This tour-de-force is widely regarded as the quintessential post-WWII Japanese novel. A plan to kidnap a major corporation's CEO becomes an allegory for the alienation of the individual self, a mirror to modern-day Japanese identity.

"Readers open to delaying gratification will be hooked. Takamura shows why she's one of Japan's most prominent mystery novelists." —*Publishers Weekly*

Tallis, Frank

Vienna blood: a Max Liebermann mystery. Frank Tallis. Random House, 2007. 496 p. (Liebermann papers, 2)

ISBN 9780812977769

1. Secret societies 2. Mutilation 3. Prostitutes 4. Detectives 5. Serial murders 6. Vienna, Austria 7. Austria 8. Belle Epoque (1871-1914) 9. 1900s (Decade) 10. Historical mysteries 11. Mysteries

LC 2007019605

In the sequel to "A Death in Vienna," 1902 Vienna is terrorized by a serial killer targeting prostitutes and leaving strange crosslike symbols in his wake, and Detective Oscar Rheinhardt and Dr. Max Liebermann reunite to find a murderer.

Tallo, Katie

Dark August. Katie Tallo. HarperCollins, 2020. 448 p.

ISBN 9780062948045

1. Inheritance and succession 2. Twenties (Age) 3. Cold cases (Criminal investigation) 4. Obsession 5. Loss (Psychology) 6. Ottawa, Ontario 7. Canada 8. Mysteries 9. Canadian fiction

A young woman haunted by her tragic past returns to her hometown and discovers that there might be more to her police detective mother's death—and last case—than she ever could have imagined.

"Anyone who has read Faulkner's story A Rose for Emily will appreciate the singular grotesqueness that manifests itself in the closing chapters, which culminate in a frightening, yet moving, conclusion. Highly recommended for mystery fans, as well as devotees of Margaret Atwood and Alice Munro." —*Booklist*

Talton, Jon

City of dark corners. Jon Talton. Poisoned Pen Press, 2021. 256 p.

ISBN 9781464213250

1. Veterans 2. Private investigators 3. Women murder victims 4. Corruption 5. Secrets 6. Phoenix, Arizona 7. Arizona 8. 1930s 9. Mysteries 10. Historical mysteries

LC 2020036126

Phoenix, 1933: A young city with big dreams and dark corners Great War veteran and rising star Gene Hammons lost his job as a homicide detective when he tried to prove that a woman was wrongly convicted of murder to protect a well-connected man. Now a private investigator, Hammons makes his living looking for missing persons-a plentiful caseload during the Great Depression, when people seem to disappear all the time. But his routine is disrupted when his brother-another homicide detective, still on the force-enlists his help looking into the death of a young woman whose dismembered body is found beside the railroad tracks. The sheriff rules it an accident, but the carnage is too neat, and the staging of the body parts too ritual. Hammons suspects it's the work of a "lust murderer-similar to the serial strangler whose killing spree he had ended a few years earlier. But who was the poor girl, dressed demurely in pink? And why was his business card tucked into her small purse? As Hammons searches for the victim's identity, he discovers that the dead girl had some secrets of her own, and that the case is connected to some of Phoenix's most powerful citizens-on both sides of the law.

"Gene is an amiable and savvy protagonist, and Talton shines in weaving together the mystery elements of the plots with historical events from the Prohibition period. Fast-paced, gritty, and exciting, this one will have fans of both Depression-era and southwestern-set crime fiction begging for more!"—*Booklist*

Tamirat, Nafkote

The **parking** lot attendant: a novel. Nafkote Tamirat. Henry Holt & Company, 2018. 225 p.

ISBN 9781250128508

1. Ethiopians 2. Immigrants 3. Fathers and daughters 4. Teenage girls — Relations with older men 5. Swindlers and swindling 6. Boston, Massachusetts 7. Coming-of-age stories 8. Literary fiction 9. African American fiction 10. Adult books for young adults

LC 2017019274

Booklist Editors' Choice: Adult Books for Young Adults, 2018; New York Times Notable Book, 2018

A reviled member of a dysfunctional Ethiopian immigrant community in Boston reflects on the experiences that brought her and her introverted father to America and traces her growing bond with the community's charismatic con-man leader, whose schemes embroil her in a plot with unanticipated repercussions.

"Tamirat's razor-sharp prose fashions a magnificently dimensional and emotionally resonant narrator, herself a storyteller who frames her own tale with beguiling skill. This debut is remarkable in every way." —*Booklist*

Tan, Amy

The **bonesetter's** daughter. Amy Tan. G.P. Putnam's, 2001. 333 p. ISBN 9780399146435

1. Mothers and daughters 2. Generation gap 3. Chinese American families 4. Chinese American women 5. Women immigrants 6. China 7. San Francisco, California 8. Relationship fiction

LC 62673

New York Times Notable Book, 2001

Set in Contemporary San Francisco and in a Chinese village where Peking Man is being unearthed, The Bonesetter's Daughter is an excavation of the human spirit: the past, its deepest wounds, its most profound hopes. The story conjures the pain of broken dream, the power of myths, and the strength of love that enables us to recover in memory what we have lost in grief. Over the course of one fog-shrouded year, between one season of falling stars and the next, mother and daughter find what they share in their bones through heredity, history, and inexpressible qualities of love.

"A fine and highly readable novel, The Bonesetter's Daughter is essentially about writing and the act of writing, what fuels it and how it is created. More specifically still, it is about how we, as women creatively express ourselves via language." —*Women's Review of Books*

First published in Great Britain by Flamingo, 2001.

The **hundred** secret senses. Amy Tan. G.P. Putnam's Sons, 1995. 358 p. ISBN 9780399141140

1. Chinese American women 2. Sisters 3. Senses and sensation 4. Half-sisters 5. Chinese Americans in China 6. China 7. Ghost stories 8. Magical realism 9. Literary fiction

LC 95031791

Shortlisted for The Orange Prize for Fiction, 1996

Kwan, a seventeen-year-old half-sister from China, turns young Olivia's world upside-down with her stories of ghosts of another time, tales that have a profound impact on Olivia's life and imagination, until she discovers a way to reconcile the ghosts of the past with her dreams of the future.

"Nearing divorce from her husband, Simon, Olivia Yee is guided by her elder half-sister, the irrepressible Kwan, into the heart of China. Olivia was five when 18-year-old Kwan first joined her family in the United States, and though always irritated by Kwan's oddities, Olivia was entranced by her eerie dreams of the ghost World of Yin. Only when visiting Kwan's home in Changmian does Olivia realize the dreams are, in Kwan's mind, memories from past lives.... Tan tells a mysterious, believable story and delivers Kwan's clipped, immigrant voice and engaging personality with charming clarity." —*Library Journal*

★ The **Joy** Luck Club. Amy Tan. Putnam's, 1989. 288 p. ISBN 9780399134203

1. Chinese American women — Identity 2. Generation gap 3. Mothers and daughters 4. Friendship 5. Female friendship 6. San Francisco,

California 7. Relationship fiction 8. Historical fiction 9. Multiple perspectives

LC 88026492

ALA Notable Book, 1990; National Book Critics Circle Award for Fiction finalist, 1989; National Book Award for Fiction finalist, 1989

After being drawn together by the shadows of their past, four women start meeting every week in San Francisco to engage in hobbies they all enjoy. After one of the four members dies, her daughter takes her place to fulfill her mother's dying wish. After the revelation of a secret, the women are forced to think back to their pasts and remember the sometimes painful events of their lives.

★ The **kitchen** god's wife. Amy Tan. G. P. Putnam's Sons, 1991. 415 p. ISBN 9780399135781

1. Mothers and daughters 2. Generation gap 3. Chinese American women 4. Secrets 5. Family secrets 6. Los Angeles, California 7. China 8. Relationship fiction

LC 91007828

ALA Notable Book, 1992

For forty years, in China and in San Francisco, Winnie Louie and Helen Kwong have kept certian confidences. Suddenly, those shattering secrets are about to be revealed. So begins a series of comic misunderstandings and heartbreaking realizations about luck, loss, and trust; about the things a mother cannot tell her daughter, the secrets daughters keep, and the miraculous resiliency of love.

"Within the peculiar construction of Amy Tan's second novel is a harrowing, compelling and at times bitterly humorous tale in which an entire world unfolds in a Tolstoyan tide of event and detail." —*New York Times Book Review*

The **Valley** of Amazement. Amy Tan. Ecco Press, 2013. 608 p. ISBN 9780062107312

1. Mothers and daughters 2. Prostitution 3. Identity (Psychology) 4. Kidnapping 5. Art 6. Shanghai, China 7. San Francisco, California 8. Family sagas 9. Historical fiction

LibraryReads Favorites, 2013; New York Times Notable Book, 2013

Violet Minturn, a half-Chinese/half-American courtesan who deals in seduction and illusion in Shanghai, struggles to find her place in the world, while her mother, Lucia, tries to make sense of the choices she has made and the men who have shaped her.

Tan, Lucy

What we were promised. Lucy Tan. Little Brown & Co 2018. 336 p. ISBN 9780316437189

1. Rich families 2. Immigrants 3. Discontent 4. Secrets 5. Jewelry theft 6. Shanghai, China 7. Literary fiction

Returning home to Shanghai after years of chasing the American dream, Wei Zhen and his newly wealthy family, including his wife, Lina, and their daughter, Karen, must each confront painful secrets and unfulfilled promises.

Tan, Sue Lynn

★ **Daughter** of the Moon Goddess. Sue Lynn Tan. Harper Voyager, 2022. 448 p. (Celestial kingdom, 1) ISBN 9780063031302

1. Gods and goddesses, Chinese 2. Gods and goddesses 3. Mothers and daughters 4. Rescues 5. Magic 6. Moon 7. Epic fantasy 8. Asian-influenced fantasy

A debut fantasy inspired by the legend of the Chinese moon goddess, Chang'e, in which a young woman's quest to free her mother pits her against the most powerful immortal in the realm and sets her on a dangerous path—where choices come with deadly consequences, and she risks losing more than her heart.

"Tan's remarkable debut and duology launch transports readers into a stunning world built from Chinese legend and replete with mythical creatures, magical artifacts, and mortal entanglements." —*Publishers Weekly*

Tan, Twan Eng

The **garden** of evening mists. Tan Twan Eng. Weinstein Books, 2012. 352 p.

ISBN 9781602861800

1. Former prisoners of war 2. Loss (Psychology) 3. Survival (in concentration camps, prisons, etc.) 4. World War II 5. Tea plantations 6. Malaysia 7. Malaya 8. 1950s 9. Historical fiction 10. Literary fiction
Man Asian Literary Prize, 2012; Walter Scott Prize for Historical Fiction, 2013; Shortlisted for the Man Booker Prize, 2012; Shortlisted for the International IMPAC Dublin Literary Award, 2014

Seeking solace in the Malaysian plantations of her childhood after grueling World War II experiences, criminal prosecutor Yun Ling Teoh discovers a Japanese garden and its enigmatic tender, an exiled Japanese royal gardener who reluctantly accepts her as an apprentice.

Tanabe, Karin

A **hundred** suns. Karin Tanabe. St Martins Pr 2020. 400 p.
ISBN 9781250231475

1. Expatriates 2. Heirs and heiresses 3. Colonialism 4. Husband and wife 5. Rubber plantations 6. Vietnam 7. 1930s 8. Historical fiction
LC 2019047193

An evocative historical novel set in 1930's Indochine, about the American wife of a Michelin heir who journeys to the French colony in the name of family fortune, and the glamorous, tumultuous world she finds herself in—and the truth she may be running from.

"Stylish, with a dash of noir and heaps of the exotic and elegant setting, A Hundred Suns flips the script of bored society ladies into something altogether more devious and delicious." —*Booklist*

★ A **woman** of intelligence. Karin Tanabe. St. Martin's Press, 2021. 448 p.

ISBN 9781250231505

1. Informers 2. Stay-at-home mothers 3. Cold War 4. Espionage 5. Former lovers 6. New York City 7. 1950s 8. Historical thrillers 9. Spy fiction
LC 2021006924

A former translator at the United Nations who has become a bored 1950s housewife is asked to join the FBI as an informant after a man from her past has become a high-level Soviet spy.

"Perhaps the most subversive thing about the twinned stories is this: how well the masks and performances Rina puts on as wife and mother prepare her for the world of espionage. Being a traditional 1950s wife and mother turns out to be perfect training for spycraft." —*Kirkus*

Taneja, Preti

We that are young: a novel. Preti Taneja. Knopf, 2018. 512 p.
ISBN 9780525521525

1. Families 2. Family businesses 3. Power (Social sciences) 4. Inheritance and succession 5. Gender role 6. India 7. Delhi 8. 2010s 9. Literary fiction 10. Adaptations, retellings, and spin-offs 11. Multiple perspectives
LC 2018015399

Library Journal Best Books, 2018

A modern-day King Lear, set in contemporary India, traces the power struggles of a turbulent family that becomes painfully subject to the anti-corruption riots of 2011 and 2012, a father's advancing dementia and an unwanted arranged marriage.

A reissue of the 2017 edition published by Galley Beggar Press (Norwich, England).

Tanen, Sloane

There's a word for that. Sloane Tanen. Little, Brown and Company, 2019. 375 pages

ISBN 9780316437165

1. Dysfunctional families 2. Addiction 3. Rehabilitation 4. Rehabilitation centers 5. Celebrities 6. Los Angeles, California 7. California 8. Domestic fiction 9. Humorous stories

The wildly flawed and dysfunctional Kessler family—retired film producer Marty; his daughter Janine, a former child star; granddaughter Hailey; and long-forgotten first wife, Bunny—comes together in Malibu's most exclusive rehab center.

"With equal parts humor and empathy, Tanen's first novel for adults employs multiple narrators and a skillfully drawn cross-generational family to examine how relatives impact one another." —*Booklist*

Tarkington, Booth

★ **Alice** Adams. Booth Tarkington; illustrated by Arthur William Brown; introduction by Donald Gray. Indiana University Press, 2003. Xix, 434 p, [3] leaves of plates : Illustration

ISBN 9780253215932

1. Young women 2. Social classes 3. Middle-class families 4. Indiana 5. Coming-of-age stories 6. Books to movies 7. Modern classics
Pulitzer Prize for Fiction, 1922

This is the story of a middle-class family living in the industrialized "midland country" at the turn of the 20th century. It is against this dingy backdrop that Alice Adams seeks to distinguish herself. She goes to a dance in a used dress, which her mother attempts to renew by changing the lining and adding some lace. She adorns herself not with orchids sent by the florist but with a bouquet of violets she has picked herself. Because her family cannot afford to equip her with the social props or "background" so needed to shine in society. Alice is forced to make do. Ultimately, her ambitions for making a successful marriage must be tempered by the realities of her situation.

Originally published: New York : Grosset & Dunlap, 1921.

★ The **magnificent** Ambersons. By Booth Tarkington. Tor, 2001. 346 p.

ISBN 9780812590043

1. Rich families 2. Fathers and daughters 3. Mothers and sons 4. Social classes 5. Family relationships 6. Indiana 7. Family sagas 8. Books to movies 9. Modern classics
Pulitzer Prize for Fiction, 1919

The rise and fall of a prominent Hoosier family centers around the life and experiences of George Amberson Menafer, a spoiled young man.

Originally published: New York : Grosset & Dunlap, 1918.

Tartt, Donna

★ The **goldfinch**. Donna Tartt. Little Brown & Co, 2013. 771 p.
ISBN 9780316055437

1. Misfits (Persons) 2. Obsession 3. Loss (Psychology) 4. Art 5. Mothers — Death 6. Manhattan, New York City 7. New York City 8. Psychological fiction 9. Literary fiction 10. Coming-of-age stories 11. Adult books for young adults

ALA Notable Book, 2014; Andrew Carnegie Medal for Excellence in Fiction, 2014; Booklist Editors' Choice, 2013; LibraryReads Favorites, 2013; New York Times Notable Book, 2013; Pulitzer Prize for Fiction, 2014; Shortlisted for The Baileys Women's Prize for Fiction, 2014; National Book Critics Circle Award for Fiction finalist, 2013

Taken in by a wealthy family friend after surviving an accident that killed his mother, thirteen-year-old Theo Decker tries to adjust to life on Park Avenue.

"The novel is slow to build but eloquent and assured, with memorable characters.... A standout." —*Kirkus*

Adapted as a motion picture, 2019.

★ The **secret** history. Donna Tartt. Alfred A. Knopf, 1992. 523 p.
ISBN 9780679410324
1. College students 2. Guilt in men 3. Intellectuals 4. Cliques 5. Friendship 6. Vermont 7. Psychological suspense 8. Literary fiction 9. First person narratives
LC 92053053

A transfer student from a small town in California, Richard Papen is determined to affect the ways of his Hampden College peers, and he begins his intense studies under the tutelage of eccentric Julian Morrow.

"Tartt records the aftereffects of unpunished crime with great skill." —*The New Republic*

Taseer, Aatish

The **way** things were: a novel. Aatish Taseer. Faber & Faber, 2015. 496 p.
ISBN 9780865478244
1. Families 2. Fathers and sons 3. Scholars and academics 4. Voyages and travels 5. Family relationships 6. India 7. Domestic fiction 8. Historical fiction
LC 2014049064

"Authors often attempt to frame a given period of a country's history through a single family's story, but Taseer's book is a cut above the rest. Colonialism, racism, sectarian violence, class tension, and the rise of the Indian nouveau riche are all handled with a delicate touch. This is a difficult book to put down, and readers will enjoy every minute of it, as well as learning about contemporary Indian culture." —*Publishers Weekly*

Tata, A. J.

Dark winter. A. J. Tata. Kensington, 2018. 464 p. (Jake Mahegan thrillers, 5)
ISBN 9781496717900
1. National security 2. International intrigue 3. Hackers 4. Power (Social sciences) 5. Terrorism — Prevention 6. Political thrillers 7. Thrillers and suspense

In a blistering scenario almost too close to the headlines, former Brigadier General Anthony J. Tata delivers a chillingly authentic glimpse of tomorrow's wars—and the anonymous hackers who hold the fate of the world at their fingertips . . .

Tatlock, Ann

Promises to keep. Ann Tatlock. Bethany House, 2011. 368 p.
ISBN 9780764208096
1. Escapes 2. Senior women — Friendship 3. Mothers and daughters 4. Secrets 5. Courage in women 6. Illinois 7. Christian fiction 8. Gentle reads 9. Adult books for young adults
LC 2010037083

Christy Award for Contemporary (Stand Alone) Category, 2012

The Anthony family, on the run from their alcoholic husband and father, leaves Minneapolis for the small town of Mills River, Ill. But they've barely begun to acclimate when sassy old lady Tillie Monroe shows up at their doorstep explaining that the house once belonged to her and her late husband.

Tawada, Yoko

★ The **emissary**. Yoko Tawada; translated by Margaret Mitsutani. New Directions, 2018. 128 p.
ISBN 9780811227629
1. Dystopias 2. Post-apocalypse 3. Intergenerational relations 4. Aging 5. Longevity 6. Japan 7. Literary fiction 8. Apocalyptic fiction 9. Dystopian fiction
LC 2017041786

National Book Award for Translated Literature, 2018; Library Journal Best Books, 2018

In Japan, which has cut itself off from the world after suffering a massive irreparable disaster, Yoshiro cares for his grandson, Mumei, a strangely wonderful boy and ancient soul whom he believes is a beacon of hope for the world in this time of darkness.

"An ebullient meditation on language and time that feels strikingly significant in the present moment." —*Kirkus*

Originally published in Japanese as Kentoshi in 2014.

Also published as The last children of Tokyo.

Taylor, Brad

★ **Daughter** of war: a novel. Brad Taylor. Dutton, 2019. 416 p. (Pike Logan thrillers, 13)
ISBN 9781101984840
1. Weapons of mass destruction 2. Special forces 3. Military missions 4. International relations 5. Military intelligence 6. Thrillers and suspense
LC 2018031286

Pike Logan and the Taskforce uncover a Syrian plot to create a weapon of mass destruction against American and Kurdish forces, a situation that is complicated by a violent North Korean retaliation against western sanctions.

Ring of fire. Brad Taylor. E.P. Dutton, 2017. 416 p. (Pike Logan thrillers, 11)
ISBN 9781101984765
1. Special forces 2. Special operations (Military science) 3. Terrorism — Prevention 4. Secrets 5. News leaks 6. Thrillers and suspense

Learning of an imminent terrorist attack on the U.S, Pike Logan, Jennifer Cahill and the Taskforce race against time to stop catastrophic events in multiple locations.

"Taylors background in Special Forces gives his story lines authenticity, and his uncanny sense of tomorrows headlines makes him seem almost psychic. Fine work from a thriller writer at the very top of his game." —*Booklist*

Taylor, Brandon

★ **Filthy** animals. Brandon Taylor. Riverhead Books, 2021. 240 pages
ISBN 9780525538912
1. African Americans 2. LGBTQIA persons 3. Sexuality 4. Desire 5. Creativity 6. Middle West 7. African American fiction 8. Short stories 9. Literary fiction

The author of the Booker Prize finalist Real Life presents a group portrait of young adults enmeshed in desire and violence ATLAS.

"Taylor's language sparks with the tension of beauty and cruelty, conveying a sense of desire and the pleasures of food and sex complicated by capricious behavior. The author has an impressive range, and his depictions of complex characters trapped in untenable situations are hard to forget." —*Publishers Weekly*

★ **Real** life. Brandon Taylor. Riverhead Books, 2020. 288 p.
ISBN 9780525538882
1. Gay men 2. African American gay men 3. African American men 4. Austen, Jane 5. Graduate students 6. Middle West 7. Literary fiction 8. African American fiction
LC 2019022438
Shortlisted for the Booker Prize, 2020
Keeping his head down at a lakeside Midwestern university where the culture is in sharp contrast to his Alabama upbringing, an introverted African-American biochem student endures unexpected encounters that bring his orientation and defenses into question.
"He works a needle through Wallace's knots of race, class, and love, stopping after loosening their loops and making hidden intricacies visible, before neatly untying them." —*Booklist*

Temple, Emily

The **lightness**. Emily Temple. William Morrow & Co, 2020. 224 p.
ISBN 9780062905321
1. Summer 2. Buddhism 3. Levitation 4. Spiritual retreats 5. Teenage girls 6. Coming-of-age stories 7. First person narratives
One year after her father leaves home for a meditation retreat and never returns, Olivia, yearning to make sense of his departure and to escape her overbearing mother, runs away and retraces his path to a place known as the Levitation Center.
"Temple weaves Buddhist practice, rumor, philosophy, and teenage sexual longing into a story that is both deep and compelling. Her characters are complicated and conflicted, immersed in the throes of teenage angst and hormones." —*Library Journal*

Tenorio, Lysley A.

The **son** of good fortune: a novel. Lysley Tenorio. HarperCollins 2020. 290 pages
ISBN 9780062059574
1. Filipino Americans 2. Undocumented immigrants 3. Mothers and sons 4. Secrecy 5. Teenage boys 6. California 7. Literary fiction
LC 2019050685
An undocumented Filipino teenager redefines his relationships with his mother, his culture, and the place he calls home.
"Tenorio creates an unusual perspective on Filipino culture and inspires readers to reflect on what it means to be an undocumented American from birth. What it means, essentially, to not belong anywhere. A thoughtful and challenging first novel." —*Booklist*

Tepper, Sheri S.

The **gate** to Women's Country. Sheri S. Tepper. Foundation Books, 1988. 278 p.
ISBN 9780385247092
1. Dystopias 2. Man-woman relationships 3. Survival (after nuclear warfare) 4. Warriors 5. Men psychics 6. Social science fiction 7. Science fiction
LC 88000387
In a futuristic society where the sexes are separated, men are warriors, and women cultivate the arts, Stavia disobeys the group's prohibitions by loving a man forbidden to her, setting the stage for a momentous decision.
A feminist fable set somewhere in the Pacific Northwest 300 years after a nuclear holocaust. Men and women now live in separate but adjacent communities. Although the men are organized into military garrisons, the women appear to have the upper hand in government, deciding matters of trade and law and, most important, reproduction.... The elaborate society that the author takes such pains to describe is based on a big lie; the story she tells is part of the deception. Some will find this narrative strategy as distasteful as the secret it conceals. But Ms. Tepper is not afraid to ask hard questions, beginning with this: If biology is destiny, how can society hope to control its self-destructive tendencies without controlling biology as well? New York Times Book Review.

★ **Grass**. Sheri S. Tepper. Doubleday, 1989. 426 p. (Marjorie Westriding trilogy, 1)
ISBN 9780385260121
1. Interplanetary relations 2. Human/alien encounters 3. Plague 4. Space flight 5. Space vehicles 6. Science fiction classics 7. Social science fiction 8. Science fiction
LC 89030105
Sent to the land of Grass to find out how that planet has escaped the deadly plague that threatens the rest of the galaxy, a strong-willed woman makes some unexpected and frightening discoveries.
"This is a beautifully written novel with well-developed characters and a number of very interesting aliens." —*Anatomy of Wonder, 4th edition*
Sequel: Raising the stones.

Singer from the sea. Sheri S. Tepper. Eos, 1999. 426 p.
ISBN 9780380974801
1. Longevity 2. Mothers and daughters 3. Class conflict 4. Social classes 5. Heirs and heiresses 6. Social science fiction 7. Science fiction 8. Adult books for young adults
LC 99-10231
The heiress to a great title on the isolated planet of Haven, Genevieve is torn between the rigid teachings of the Covenants, inflexible laws that govern women of her class, and the secret knowledge learned from her late mother, only to discover that she alone holds the key to the salvation of her world.
"Despite her status as a young noblewoman of the planet Haven, Genevieve rebels against the strict regulations concerning highborn women. Defying her father's wishes, she seeks her own forbidden destiny and discovers the dark secrets that lie at the heart of her world and its forgotten history. Tepper...continues to explore the intricacies of human societal structures and the complex connections between humans and their environment, combining stylistic grace with imaginative insight." —*Library Journal*

The **visitor**. Sheri S. Tepper. EOS, 2002. 407 p.
ISBN 9780380979059
1. Dystopias 2. Asteroids — Collisions with Earth 3. Religious fanatics 4. Ancestors 5. Magic 6. Social science fiction 7. Science fiction 8. Science fantasy 9. Adult books for young adults
LC 2001040197
Civilization has survived—barely—in the wake of a twenty-first century collision with an asteroid, but when Disme, an orphan, begins to read a fascinating book by one of her ancestors from before the dark times, she is compelled to search out a mystery.

Tesh, Emily

Silver in the wood. Emily Tesh. Tom Doherty Associates, 2019. 112 p; (Greenhollow duology, 1)
ISBN 9781250229793
1. Forests 2. Men/men relations 3. Dryads 4. Cats 5. Gay men 6. Victorian era (1837-1901) 7. Fantasy fiction 8. Mythological fiction 9. LGBTQIA fiction

There is a Wild Man who lives in the deep quiet of Greenhollow, and he listens to the wood. Tobias, tethered to the forest, does not dwell on his past life, but he lives a perfectly unremarkable existence with his cottage, his cat, and his dryads. When Greenhollow Hall acquires a handsome, intensely curious new owner in Henry Silver, everything changes. Old secrets better left buried are dug up, and Tobias is forced to reckon with his troubled past, both the green magic of the woods, and the dark things that rest in its heart.

Thackeray, William Makepeace

★ **Vanity** fair: a novel without a hero. William Makepeace Thackeray; edited with an introduction and notes by John Carey. Penguin Books, 2001. Xl, 866 p.

ISBN 9780141439839

1. Young women — History 2. Upward mobility 3. Manipulation by women 4. Man-woman relationships 5. Social status 6. England 7. 19th century 8. Literary fiction 9. Satirical fiction 10. Books to movies

Chronicles the exploits of Becky Sharp, an unscrupulous young woman who is determined to achieve wealth and social success, and her sentimental companion, Amelia, who has fallen for a caddish soldier, in the classic novel set against the backdrop of English society in the early 1800s.

Originally serialized in Punch magazine, January 1847-July 1848.

Thammavongsa, Souvankham

How to pronounce knife: stories. Souvankham Thammavongsa. Little, Brown and Company, 2020. 304 pages

ISBN 9780316422130

1. Language and languages 2. Home (Concept) 3. Meaning (Psychology) 4. Belonging 5. Immigrants 6. Literary fiction 7. Short stories 8. Canadian fiction

LC 2019948532

Loan Stars Favourites, 2020; Scotiabank Giller Prize, 2020; Trillium Book Award, 2021; National Book Critics Circle Award for Fiction finalist, 2020

A young girl brings a book home from school and asks her father to help her pronounce a tricky word, a simple exchange with unforgettable consequences. A failed boxer discovers what it truly means to be a champion when he starts painting nails at his sister's salon. A young woman tries to discern the invisible but immutable social hierarchies at a chicken processing plant. Focusing on characters struggling to find their bearings in unfamiliar territory, the author pushes us right up against the limits of language.

"Cosmopolitan aficionados of pristine short fiction—think Paul Yoon, Jhumpa Lahiri, and Phil Klay—will want to read." —*Library Journal*

Stories about immigrants and refugees struggling to find their place.

Thayne, RaeAnne

The **cliff** house. RaeAnne Thayne. Hqn Books, 2019. 384 p.
ISBN 9781335004901

1. Aunt and niece 2. Sisters 3. Romantic love 4. Coastal towns 5. Family secrets 6. Relationship fiction

Growing up dependent on each other for everything, two orphaned sisters and their aunt reevaluate their choices at a crossroads in life.

Thelen, Albert Vigoleis

The **island** of second sight: from the applied recollections of Vigoleis. Albert Vigoleis Thelen; translated from the German by Donald O. White. Overlook Press, 2012. 730 pages

ISBN 9781468301168

1. Authors 2. Husband and wife 3. Fugitives 4. Civil War 5. Brothers 6. Majorca, Spain 7. Spain 8. 1930s 9. Literary fiction 10. Historical fiction 11. Translations

An English-language release of a German award-winner originally published in 1953 traces the largely autobiographical experiences of inventor Vigoleis, who with his wife scrapes out an existence in 1930s Mallorca and befriends literary figures and Jewish neighbors before making Nazi enemies and plotting a daring escape during the Spanish Civil War.

First published in German as Die Insel des zweiten Gesichts: Dusseldorf : Diederichs, 1953.

Theroux, Paul

★ The **Mosquito** Coast: a novel. By Paul Theroux; with woodcuts by David Frampton. Houghton Mifflin, 1982. 374 p.

ISBN 9780395318379

1. Americans in Honduras 2. Inventors 3. Fathers and sons 4. Ideology 5. Utopians 6. Honduras 7. Literary fiction 8. Books to movies 9. Books to TV

LC 81006787

James Tait Black Memorial Prize for Fiction, 1981; National Book Award for Fiction finalist, 1983

An eccentric American inventor moves his family to the jungles of Central America in hopes of finding a better life.

Made into a television show, 2021.

Originally published: London : Hamilton, 1981.

Thien, Madeleine

Do not say we have nothing. Madeleine Thien. W. W. Norton & Co, 2016. 473 p.

ISBN 9780393609882

1. Families — History 2. Social conflict 3. Social change 4. Family relationships 5. Politics and culture 6. Shanghai, China 7. China 8. 1960s 9. 1980s 10. Literary fiction 11. Canadian fiction

Governor General's Literary Award for English-Language Fiction, 2016; Loan Stars Favourites, 2016; New York Times Notable Book, 2016; Scotiabank Giller Prize, 2016; Shortlisted for the Man Booker Prize, 2016; Shortlisted for The Baileys Women's Prize for Fiction, 2017

Marie endeavors to piece together the story of her fractured family's past and its connection to her friend Ai-Ming, uncovering information about how both women's fathers were forced to reimagine their identities during Mao's Cultural Revolution.

"Mythic yet realistic, panoramic yet intimate, intellectual yet romantic—Thien has written a concerto dauntingly complex and deeply haunting." —*Kirkus*

First published in Canada in 2016 by Alfred A. Knopf Canada.

Thomas, Bev

A **good** enough mother: a novel. Bev Thomas. Pamela Dorman Books, 2019. 384 p.

ISBN 9780525561255

1. Mothers and sons 2. Missing men 3. Psychotherapist and patient 4. Women psychotherapists 5. Loss (Psychology) 6. London, England 7. Psychological suspense

LC 2018039700
When a new patient, Dan—unstable and traumatized— looks exactly like her missing son, psychotherapist Ruth Hartland is determined to help him, but soon, her own complicated feelings cloud her professional judgement, and she begins to cross some dangerous boundaries.

Thomas, Dylan
The **collected** stories. Dylan Thomas. New Directions Books, 1984. 362 p.
ISBN 9780811209984
1. Manners and customs 2. Wales 3. Short stories
LC 84006822
This edition of Dylan Thomas's collected stories is published to coincide with the 50th anniversary of his death.
Includes bibliographical references (pages 359-362).

Thomas, Elisabeth
Catherine House. Elisabeth Thomas. Custom House, 2020. 311 p.
ISBN 9780062905659
1. Universities and colleges 2. Secrets 3. Psychology — Experiments 4. Elite (Social sciences) 5. Power (Social sciences) 6. Pennsylvania 7. Gothic fiction
A dangerously curious, rebellious undergraduate uncovers a shocking secret about an exclusive circle of students and the dark truths beneath their school's promises of prestige.

Thomas, Russ
★ **Firewatching**. Russ Thomas. G. P. Putnam's Sons, 2020. 320 p. (Detective Sergeant Adam Tyler, 1)
ISBN 9780525542025
1. Detectives 2. Cold cases (Criminal investigation) 3. One-night stands (Interpersonal relations) 4. Murder investigation 5. Murder suspects 6. England 7. Great Britain 8. Mysteries 9. Police procedurals
LC 2019042363
A taut and ambitious police procedural debut introducing Detective Sergeant Adam Tyler, a cold case reviewer who lands a high-profile murder investigation only to find the main suspect is a recent one-night stand..
"Red herrings and uncovered family secrets abound. This stunning police procedural marks Thomas as an author to watch." —*Publishers Weekly*

Nighthawking. Russ Thomas. Putnam Pub Group, 2021. 384 p. (Detective Sergeant Adam Tyler, 2)
ISBN 9780525542056
1. Murder investigation 2. Detectives 3. Gay men 4. Cold cases (Criminal investigation) 5. Exchange students 6. England 7. Mysteries 8. Police procedurals
A sequel to Firewatching finds Detective Sergeant Adam Tyler and his protege, Detective Constable Amina Rabbani, investigating the suspicious death of a Chinese national whose demise threatens to trigger an international incident.
"Thomas adeptly develops his diverse cast, but the novel's real power lies in its intricate structure—the mystery surrounding the body is impressively deep, the various levels of tension are relentless, and every chapter ends with a narrative punch to the face. This police procedural is virtually unputdownable." —*Publishers Weekly*

Thomas, Scarlett
Oligarchy. Scarlett Thomas. Counterpoint, 2020. 208 p.

ISBN 9781640093065
1. Boarding schools 2. Conspiracies 3. Teenage girls 4. Eating disorders 5. Weight control 6. Literary fiction 7. Coming-of-age stories
Arriving at her English boarding school, the daughter of a Russian oligarch is enmeshed in her classmates' thin-obsessed world of pecking orders, eating disorders and online drama, before a friend goes missing amid rumors of a dormitory ghost.
"Though Thomas's characters get a lot of flak for being insufferable rich girls from outsiders in the novel—and they are—she's captured with an empathetic eye all the brutal, visceral, and surprisingly funny aspects of teenage girlhood." —*Publishers Weekly*

Thomas, Will
Dance with death. Will Thomas. Minotaur Books, 2021. 320 p. (Cyrus Barker and Thomas Llewelyn mysteries, 12)
ISBN 9781250624772
1. Attempted assassination 2. Weddings 3. Assassins 4. Espionage 5. International intrigue 6. London, England 7. Victorian era (1837-1901) 8. Mysteries 9. Historical mysteries 10. Victorian mysteries
LC 2020047620
When an attempt on the life of a future Nicholas II occurs at a British royal wedding, private enquiry agents Barker and Llewelyn consult with an assassin from Llewelyn's past before uncovering a killer's dangerous political agenda.
"The stakes are high here and will keep readers on edge: a royal wedding is fast approaching, and Queen Victoria's relatives from the European royal houses have converged on London...masterful depictions of jealousy and cunning also help drop readers right into the summer of 1893, along with the politics, danger, and romance that was the Romanovs' world. Recommend this to fans of the series and of Sherlock Holmes." —*Booklist*

Thompson, Jim
The **killer** inside me. Jim Thompson. Vintage Books/Black Lizard, 1991. 244 p.
ISBN 9780679733973
1. Sheriffs 2. Murderers 3. Teachers 4. Deception 5. Psychopaths 6. Texas 7. Psychological suspense 8. Books to movies 9. Modern classics
LC 90050472
Lou Ford, an easy-going deputy sheriff in Central City, hides his psychotic nature as he plans a double murder.

Thompson, Tade
Rosewater. Tade Thompson. Orbit, 2018. 423 pages; (Wormwood trilogy, 1)
ISBN 9780316449052
1. Aliens 2. Human/alien encounters 3. Government investigators 4. Secrecy in government 5. Aliens (Non-humanoid) 6. Nigeria 7. West Africa 8. Science fiction 9. Afrofuturism
Arthur C. Clarke Award, 2019
Rosewater is a town on the edge. A community formed around the edges of a mysterious alien biodome, its residents comprise the hopeful, the hungry and the helpless—people eager for a glimpse inside the dome or a taste of its rumored healing powers. Kaaro is a government agent with a criminal past. He has seen inside the biodome, and doesn't care to again—but when something begins killing off others like himself, Kaaro must defy his masters to search for an answer, facing his dark history and coming to a realization about a horrifying future.

"Never fails to intrigue and entertain. A captivating, cerebral work of science fiction that may very well signal a new definitive voice in the genre." —*Kirkus*

Originally published by Apex Publications in 2016.

The **Rosewater** insurrection. Tade Thompson. Orbit, 2019. 400 pages (Wormwood trilogy, 2)

ISBN 9780316449083

1. Aliens 2. Human/alien encounters 3. Government investigators 4. Secrecy in government 5. Aliens (Non-humanoid) 6. Nigeria 7. West Africa 8. Science fiction 9. Afrofuturism

Amidst a secret invasion, government agent Aminat must capture a woman who is the key to the survival of the human race but her mission is endangered by the Mayor of Rosewater and the emergence of an old enemy of Wormwood.

The **Rosewater** redemption. Tade Thompson. Orbit, 2019. 416 pages (Wormwood trilogy, 3)

ISBN 9780316449090

1. Aliens 2. Human/alien encounters 3. War 4. Undead 5. Aliens (Non-humanoid) 6. Nigeria 7. West Africa 8. Science fiction 9. Multiple perspectives 10. Afrofuturism

Operating across spacetime, the xenosphere, and international borders, it is up to a small group of hackers and criminals to prevent the extra-terrestrial advance. The fugitive known as Bicycle Girl, Kaaro, and his former handler Femi may be humanity's last line of defense.

Thompson, Victoria

Murder on Wall Street. Victoria Thompson. Berkley Prime Crime, 2021. 336 p. (Gaslight mysteries (Victoria Thompson), 24)

ISBN 9781984805775

1. Alfred, King of England, 849-899 2. Detectives 3. Midwives 4. Families 5. Pregnant women 6. New York City 7. Gilded Age (1865-1898) 8. 1900s (Decade) 9. Historical mysteries

LC 2020046439

Midwife Sarah Brandt Malloy and her detective husband, Frank, scour the upper echelons of society as well as Gilded Age New York City's highest-risk areas to prove a family man's innocence of a dangerous rival's murder.

"The charms and horrors of early-20th-century New York on full display." —*Kirkus*

Thompson-Spires, Nafissa

Heads of the colored people: stories. Nafissa Thompson-Spires. Atria/37 INK, 2018. 209 p.

ISBN 9781501167997

1. Borden, Lizzie 2. Race relations 3. Identity (Psychology) 4. Interpersonal relations 5. Human behavior 6. Short stories 7. African American fiction 8. Literary fiction

LC 2017050727

Hurston/Wright Legacy Award: Fiction, 2019; Los Angeles Times Art Seidenbaum Award for First Fiction, 2018; Shortlisted for the James Tait Black Memorial Prize for Fiction, 2018; Kirkus Prize for Fiction finalist, 2018

In a collection of boundary-pushing stories that are touching, contemporary and darkly humorous, the author illuminates the simmering tensions and precariousness of black citizenship and the concept of black identity in this so-called post-racial era.

Includes bibliographical references.

Thomson, E. S.

Beloved poison. E.S. Thomson. Pegasus Crime, 2016. 390 pages; (Jem Flockhart novels, 1)

ISBN 9781681772141

1. Hospitals 2. Medicine — History 3. Intrigue 4. Secrets 5. Pharmacists 6. London, England 7. Victorian era (1837-1901) 8. 1850s 9. Victorian mysteries 10. Historical mysteries

After the discovery of six tiny coffins filled with dried flowers and rags in the old chapel of a crumbling 1850s London infirmary, apothecary Jem Flockhart begins a quest to understand their meaning and is forced to make impossible choices.

"A debut mystery chock full of mysterious doings, riveting historical detail, and so many horrifying anecdotes about the state of medicine in the mid-1800s that you can almost feel the evil miasma rising from the pages." —*Kirkus*

The **blood**. E. S. Thomson. 2018. 384 p; (Jem Flockhart novels, 3)

ISBN 9781681778754

1. Hospitals 2. Amateur detectives 3. Medicine — History 4. Docks 5. Sailors 6. London, England 7. Victorian era (1837-1901) 8. 1850s 9. Victorian mysteries 10. Historical mysteries

In a hunt that takes Jem Flockhart and Will Quartermain through the harrowing streets of Victorian London to the dangers of the seamen's floating hospital, The Blood, they will endeavor to solve a dark and terrible new mystery.

Thorne, Sally

Second first impressions. Sally Thorne. William Morrow & Co, 2021. 384 p.

ISBN 9780063007130

1. Retirement communities 2. Personal assistants 3. Rich men 4. First impressions 5. Selfishness 6. Romantic comedies

LibraryReads Favorites, 2021

A spoiled, tattooed rich man reluctantly agrees to become an assistant to two casually exploitative nonagenarians before unexpectedly catching the eye of the property's serious-minded manager.

"Following 99 Percent Mine, Thorne's latest novel is a sweet story, merging a woman whose fears tend to overpower her dreams, and a slow-burn romance that turns her world upside down." —*Library Journal*

Thorpe, Rufi

★ The **knockout** queen. Rufi Thorpe. Alfred A. Knopf, 2020. 288 p.

ISBN 9780525656784

1. High school students 2. Misfits (Persons) 3. Gender role 4. Gay teenagers 5. Friendship 6. Southern California 7. California 8. 2010s 9. Coming-of-age stories

Pen/Faulkner Award Finalist, 2021

Privileged teen Bunny Lampert befriends in-the-closet rebel Michael, who lives on the other side of the tracks.

"Her novel is devastatingly honest, her characters vulnerable, and her readers will be spellbound." —*Booklist*

Tieu, Julie

The **donut** trap. Julie Tieu. Avon Books, 2021. 384 p.

ISBN 9780063069800

1. Women shopkeepers 2. Family businesses 3. Chinese American families 4. Expectation (Psychology) 5. Women college graduates 6. Los Angeles, California 7. California 8. Multicultural romances 9. Romantic comedies 10. Contemporary romances

LibraryReads Favorites, 2021

Stuck in a rut working at her parents' donut shop, Jasmine Tran finds help in the form of an old college crush, but when their relationship doesn't work out, she must scheme a solution to get herself out of the donut trap once and for all.

"The narrative gives ample time to the fraught relationship between Jas and her parents, but at the expense of developing the romance between Jas and Alex, who bond over their similar traumas, but share little else. Meanwhile, the friend ex-machina through which Jas eventually finds professional fulfilment strains credulity. Still, the diverse cast and deliciously described donuts make up for some of these flaws." —*Publishers Weekly*

Tinti, Hannah

The **twelve** lives of Samuel Hawley: a novel. Hannah Tinti. The Dial Press, 2017. 480 p.

ISBN 9780812989885

1. Former criminals 2. Twelve-year-old girls 3. Fathers and daughters 4. Fishers 5. Villages 6. New England 7. Coming-of-age stories 8. Crime fiction 9. Literary fiction 10. Adult books for young adults

LC 2016021409

Librarians' Choice (Australia), 2017; LibraryReads Favorites, 2017; Loan Stars Favourites, 2017

A once-professional killer protects his daughter from the legacy of his criminal past, an effort that is challenged by his daughter's struggles with the death of her mother and the reckoning of old enemies.

"An accomplished if overstuffed merger of coming-of-age tale and literary thriller." —*Kirkus*

Title, Sarah

The **undateable**. Sarah Title. Zebra Books, 2017. 352 p. (Librarians in love, 1)

ISBN 9781420141832

1. Women librarians 2. Single women 3. Journalists 4. Matchmaking 5. Dating (Social customs) 6. San Francisco, California 7. Contemporary romances

Rendered as a love-hating, undateable librarian after a video of her rolling her eyes at a marriage proposal goes viral, Melissa {34Bernie{34 Bernard, who doesn't believe in happily-ever-afters, but never backs down from a challenge, agrees to let reporter Colin Rodriguez find her the perfect match.

Tobar, Hector

The **last** great road bum. Hector Tobar. MCD/Farrar, Straus and Giroux, 2020. 432 p.

ISBN 9780374183424

1. Sanderson, Joe 2. Adventure 3. Wanderers and wandering 4. Hitchhiking 5. Writing 6. Ambition 7. 20th century 8. Biographical fiction 9. Historical fiction 10. Literary fiction

LC 2020003424

A novel inspired by true events follows the experiences of an Illinois adventurer who gives his life to fight beside other activists in 1960s El Salvador.

"Tobar brilliantly succeeds in capturing Joe's guileless yearning for adventure through high-velocity prose that is both relentless and wry. Tobar's wild ride achieves a version of Kerouac for a new age." —*Publishers Weekly*

Todd, Charles

★ A **hanging** at dawn. Charles Todd. Witness Impulse, 2020. 160 pages (Bess Crawford mysteries)

ISBN 9780063048577

1. Friendship 2. Soldiers 3. Family secrets 4. Consequences 5. Families 6. Historical mysteries

From the New York Times bestselling author of the Bess Crawford mystery series, a short story that unravels dark secrets from her close friend Simon Brandon's past.

"Unlike many origin stories, which exist because the authors have run out of fresh ideas, this one adds new and important history to the Crawford saga, fleshing out the existing novels and adding new depth to our reading of them. For series fans, it's a must-read." —*Booklist*

A Bess Crawford short story—Cover.

Toews, Miriam

Fight night. Miriam Toews. St Martins Press, 2021. 336 pages

ISBN 9781635578171

1. Nine-year-old girls 2. Grandmothers 3. Psychic trauma 4. Letter writing 5. People with mental illnesses 6. Toronto, Ontario 7. Literary fiction 8. Multiple perspectives 9. Canadian fiction

Shortlisted for the Scotiabank Giller Prize, 2021; Atwood Gibson Writers' Trust Fiction Prize finalist, 2021

"Despite the dark elements in the story, the humor and love between the characters shine through." —*Library Journal*

Longlisted for the Scotiabank Giller Prize, 2021.

★ **Women** talking: a novel. Miriam Toews. Bloomsbury Publishing, 2019. 216 pages

ISBN 9781635572582

1. Mennonite women 2. Rape victims 3. Patriarchy 4. Sex crimes 5. Mennonites 6. South America 7. Literary fiction 8. Canadian fiction

Library Journal Best Books, 2019; LibraryReads Favorites, 2019; Loan Stars Favourites, 2018; New York Times Notable Book, 2019

After learning the men in the community have been drugging and attacking more than a hundred women, eight Mennonite women meet in secret to decide whether they should escape to a place outside the colony or stay in the only world they've ever known.

"An exquisite critique of patriarchal culture...Stunningly original and altogether arresting." —*Kirkus*

Originally published: Toronto, Ont. : Knopf Canada, 2018.

Toibin, Colm

House of names. Colm Toibin. Scribner, 2017. 288 p.

ISBN 9781501140211

1. Revenge in women 2. Women murderers 3. Husband-killing 4. Human sacrifice 5. Family violence 6. Mycenae (Extinct city) 7. Ancient Greece 8. Ancient Greece (800 BCE-640 CE) 9. Adaptations, retellings, and spin-offs 10. Mythological fiction 11. Literary fiction

Librarians' Choice (Australia), 2017

A retelling of the Greek myth Agememnon, in which Clytemnestra and her children become involved in revenge schemes because of Agamemnon's actions.

"This extraordinary book reads like a pristine translation rather than a retelling, conveying both confounded strangeness and timeless truths about love's sometimes terrible and always exhilarating energies." —*Library Journal*

★ The **magician**: a novel. Colm Toibin. Scribner, 2021. 320 p.

ISBN 9781476785080

1. Mann, Thomas 2. Authors, German 3. Creativity in men 4. Closeted gay men 5. Desire 6. Men — Sexuality 7. Germany 8. Europe 9. 19th century 10. 20th century 11. Biographical fiction 12. Literary fiction 13. Historical fiction

LC 2021004476

An intimate, astonishingly complex portrait of writer Thomas Mann, a man profoundly flawed and unforgettable, his magnificent and complex wife Katia, and the times in which they lived—the first world war, the rise of Hitler, World War II, the Cold War, and exile.

"This vibrates with the strength of Mann's visions and the sublimity of Toibin's mellifluous prose. Toibin has surpassed himself." —*Publishers Weekly*

Tolkien, J. R. R.

Beren and Luthien. J. R. R. Tolkien; edited by Christopher Tolkien; illustrated by Alan Lee. Houghton Mifflin Harcourt, 2017. 304 p. : Illustration

ISBN 9781328791825

1. Elves 2. Immortalism 3. Heroes and heroines 4. Good and evil 5. Mortality 6. Epic fantasy

An important chapter in the saga of The Silmarillion, first conceived by Tolkien at the end of his service in World War I, follows the romance between an immortal elf and a mortal whose worthiness is put to an impossible test.

Originally written in 1917.

The **children** of Hurin. J.R.R. Tolkien; edited by Christopher Tolkien; illustrated by Alan Lee. Houghton Mifflin, 2007. 313 p, 8 leaves of plates, 1 fold-out leaf : Illustration; Color; Map

ISBN 9780618894642

1. Elves 2. Imaginary wars and battles 3. Good and evil 4. Dwarves (Fantasy characters) 5. Wizards 6. Epic fantasy 7. Adult books for young adults

Library Journal Best Books, 2007

A fantasy adventure saga set in the early days of Middle-Earth features humans and elves, dwarves and dragons, orcs and dark sorcerers clashing in an epic battle between good and evil.

"If anyone still labors under the delusion that J. R. R. Tolkien was a writer of twee fantasies for children, this novel should set them straight. A bleak, darkly beautiful tale played out against the background of the First Age of Tolkien's Middle Earth, The Children of Hurin possesses the mythic resonance and grim sense of inexorable fate found in Greek tragedy." —*Washington Post Book World.*

The **fall** of Gondolin. J. R. R. Tolkien; edited by Christopher Tolkien; illustrated by Alan Lee. Houghton Mifflin Harcourt, 2018. 320 p.

ISBN 9781328613042

1. Elves 2. Wizards 3. Rulers 4. Good and evil 5. Gods and goddesses 6. Epic fantasy

Following his presentation of Beren and Luthien, Christopher Tolkien has used the same 'history in sequence' mode in the writing of this edition of The Fall of Gondolin. In the words of J.R.R. Tolkien, it was 'the first real story of this imaginary world' and, together with Beren and Luthien and The Children of Hurin, he regarded it as one of the three 'Great Tales' of the Elder Days.

The **fellowship** of the ring: being the first part of The lord of the rings. By J.R.R. Tolkien. Houghton Mifflin, 2001. Viii, 423 p, [1] folded leaf of plates : Illustration; Map; Color (Lord of the rings, 1)

ISBN 9780618153985

1. Heroes and heroines 2. Magic rings 3. Quests 4. Middle Earth (Imaginary place) 5. Good and evil 6. Epic fantasy 7. Fantasy classics 8. Books to movies

LC 2001276576

Frodo the hobbit and his companions set out to deliver the One Ring of Power to the dark land of Mordor in order to destroy the ring in the forge of its creation.

"Elves, dwarfs, hobbits, men, and sundry evil beings, each as real as the other, populate an allegorical tale that shows how power corrupts." —*Booklist*

Sequel: The two towers.

Originally published: London : Allen & Unwin, 1954.

First published in the United States as part one of The Lord of the rings: Boston : Houghton Mifflin, 1965.

★ The **hobbit,** or, there and back again. J. R. R. Tolkien. Ballantine, 1996. 306 p. : Map (Lord of the rings)

ISBN 9780345339683

1. Adventurers 2. Quests 3. Dragons 4. Hobbits (Fictitious characters) 5. Wizards 6. Epic fantasy 7. Fantasy classics 8. Books to movies 9. Adult books for young adults

LC 77-8025

Books I Love Best Yearly (BILBY), Older Reader, 1997; Books I Love Best Yearly (BILBY), Older Reader, 2013

Bilbo Baggins, a respectable, well-to-do hobbit, lives comfortably in his hobbit-hole until the day the wandering wizard Gandalf chooses him to take part in an adventure from which he may never return.

Prelude to: The lord of the rings.

Book made into three feature motion pictures called The Hobbit: An unexpected journey; The Hobbit: There and back again; and The Hobbit: The battle of the Five Armies.

Originally published: London: Allen & Unwin, 1937.

★ The **lord** of the rings. J.R.R. Tolkien. Houghton Mifflin, 2004. Xxv, 1157 p, 3 p. of plates : Color illustration; Map

ISBN 9780618517657

1. Dwarves (Fantasy characters) 2. Magic rings 3. Quests 4. Good and evil 5. Elves 6. Hargreaves, Alice Pleasance Liddell 7. Fantasy classics 8. Books to movies

LC 2004275215

Presents the epic depicting the Great War of the Ring, a struggle between good and evil in Middle-earth, following the odyssey of Frodo the hobbit and his companions on a quest to destroy the Ring of Power.

The **return** of the king: being the third part of The lord of the rings. By J.R.R. Tolkien; illustrated by Alan Lee. Houghton Mifflin, 2004. Xii, [929]-1439 p. : Illustration; Color; Map (Lord of the rings, 3)

ISBN 9780618574971

1. Heroes and heroines 2. Magic rings 3. Quests 4. Middle Earth (Imaginary place) 5. Good and evil 6. Epic fantasy 7. Fantasy classics 8. Books to movies

LC 2005278030

In the concluding volume of the trilogy, Frodo and Sam make a terrible journey to the heart of the Land of the Shadow in a final reckoning with the power of Sauron.

Sequel to: The two towers.

Includes index.

Includes indexes.

Originally published: London: George Allen & Unwin, 1955. 2nd ed. originally published: 1966.

Originally published: Allen & Unwin, 1955. This large print edition first published by Clio Press 1990.

First published in the United States as part three of The Lord of the rings: Boston : Houghton Mifflin, 1965.

Originally published: London : Allen & Unwin, 1955.

The **Silmarillion**. J.R.R. Tolkien; edited by Christopher Tolkien. Houghton Mifflin, 1977. 365 p. : Map; Footnotes

ISBN 9780395257302

1. Elves 2. Middle Earth (Imaginary place) 3. Creation 4. Gems 5. Magic 6. Fantasy fiction 7. Fantasy classics

Locus Award for Fantasy Novel, 1978; Hugo Awards: Gandalf Award for Best Book-Length Fantasy, 1978

The Silmarillion tells of the Elder Days, or the First Age of the World, and is the history of the rebellion of Fëanor, the most gifted of the Elves, and his people against the gods, their exile in Middle-earth, and their war against the first Dark Lord, Morgoth, for the recovery of the Silmarils, the jewels containing the pure light of Valinor.

"Tolkien began writing these introductory legends in 1917 and, sporadically throughout his life, continued adding to them; his son Christopher has edited and compiled the various versions into a single cohesive work. Two brief tales, which outline the origin of the world and describe the gods who create and rule, precede the title story about the Silmarilsthree brilliant, jewel-like creatures who are desired and fought over, setting up a clash between good and evil." —*Booklist*

Includes index.

Some copies have folded map in rear.

The **two** towers: being the second part of The lord of the rings. J.R.R. Tolkien; illustrated by Alan Lee. Houghton, Mifflin, 2002. X, 415-750 p. : Color illustration; Map (Lord of the rings, 2)

ISBN 9780618260591

1. Heroes and heroines 2. Magic rings 3. Quests 4. Middle Earth (Imaginary place) 5. Good and evil 6. Epic fantasy 7. Fantasy classics 8. Books to movies

LC 2003542568

Tells of the quest to destroy Sauron's mighty Ring of Power and the struggle against the Darkness of Mordor.

"Here the Companions of the Ring, separated, meet Saruman the wizard, cross the Dead Marshes, and prepare for the Great War in which the power of the Ring will be undone." —*Library Journal*

Sequel to: The fellowship of the ring.

Sequel: The return of the king.

First published by George Allen & Unwin 1954; Second edition published 1966 — First published by Harper Collins in 1991 — This edition is based on the 50th anniversary edition published 2004.

This new edition published with the same ISBN as HarperCollins 1999 edition.

Originally published: Allen & Unwin, 1954. This large print edition first published by Clio Press 1990.

Originally published: London : Allen & Unwin, 1954.

First published in the United States as part two of The Lord of the rings: Boston : Houghton Mifflin, 1965.

Tolstaya, Tatyana

Aetherial worlds: stories. Tatyana Tolstaya; translated from the Russian by Anya Migdal. Alfred A. Knopf, 2018. 256 p.

ISBN 9781524732776

1. Love 2. Interpersonal relations 3. Human nature 4. Literary fiction 5. Short stories 6. Translations

LC 2017032042

"Tolstaya's daring, masterful stories, crisply translated, glint and whirl with extraordinary dimension and force." —*Booklist*

Borzoi book.

The **slynx**. Tatyana Tolstaya; translated by Jamey Gambrell. Houghton Mifflin, 2003. 288 p.

ISBN 9780618124978

1. Survival (after disaster) 2. Rulers 3. Banned books 4. Moscow, Russia 5. Dystopian fiction 6. Literary fiction 7. Translations

LC 2002027627

In the ruins of Moscow two centuries after the apocalypse, inhabitants dwell in primitive, frequently brutal conditions in which mice are a source of food, clothing, and commerce and books are banned by the ruling tyrant.

"It takes some time for a plot to develop, but Tolstaya sketches a vivid picture of life in this permanent winter.... In this extended fable, she captures the Russian yearning for culture, even in desperate circumstances. Gambrell ably translates the mix of neologisms and plain speech with which Tolstaya describes this devastated world." —*Publishers Weekly*

Translation of: Kys'.

Tolstoy, Leo

★ **Anna** Karenina. Leo Tolstoy; translated by Richard Pevear and Larissa Volokhonsky. Penguin Books, 2002. Xxi, 837 p.

ISBN 9780142000274

1. Married people 2. Extramarital affairs 3. Man-woman relationships 4. Russia 5. Romanov Dynasty (1613-1917) 6. Literary fiction 7. Classics 8. Multiple perspectives

A new translation of the classic nineteenth-century Russian novel in which a young woman is destroyed when she attempts to live outside the moral law of her society.

A movie called Love was inspired by the book.

Originally serialized in The Russian Messenger, 1873-1877.

Divine and human and other stories. Leo Tolstoy; translated from the Russian and with an introduction and notes by Gordon Spence. Northwestern University Press, 2000. Xxi, 112 p.

ISBN 9780810117624

1. Short stories 2. Christian fiction 3. Translations

"These 16 selections from Tolstoy's final eclectic collection of tales titled The Sunday Reading Stories represent the Russian novelist's turn away from the troubling human condition in Anna Karenina toward a growing preoccupation with moral issues." —*Publishers Weekly*

Includes bibliographical references (p. 97-112).

★ **War** and peace. Leo Tolstoy; translated by Constance Garnett. The Modern Library, 1994. Vii,1386 pages

ISBN 9780679600848

1. Napoleonic Wars, 1800-1815 2. Military campaigns 3. Aristocracy 4. Russia 5. Romanov Dynasty (1613-1917) 6. Literary fiction 7. Classics 8. Translations

The monumental Russian classic reflects the life and times of Russian society during the Napoleonic War.

War and peace. Leo Tolstoy; translated from the Russian by Richard Pevear and Larissa Volokhonsky. Alfred A. Knopf, 2007. Xviii, 1273 p.

ISBN 9780307266934

1. Napoleonic Wars, 1800-1815 2. Military campaigns 3. Aristocracy 4. Russia 5. Romanov Dynasty (1613-1917) 6. Literary fiction 7. Classics 8. War stories

Presents a new translation of the classic reflecting the life and times of Russian society during the Napoleonic Wars, in a book accompanied by an index of historical figures, textual annotation, a chapter summary, and an introduction.

"Stressing that their War and Peace sticks more closely to the Russian text than any other, including Louise and Aylmer Maude's semi-canonical 1923 version, Pevear and Volokhonsky retain the considerable amount of French used by Tolstoy's counts and princesses, preserve the author's penchant for word repetition and aim to match his tidy syntactic conciseness. The result certainly reads smoothly, its English being neither egregiously contemporary nor inappropriately old-fashioned." —*Washington Post Book World.*

Adapted into a 1956 theatrical film and television series.

Includes bibliographical references (p. [1223]-1247) and index.

Toole, John Kennedy

★ A **confederacy** of dunces. John Kennedy Toole; foreword by Walker Percy. Louisiana State University Press, 1980. Vii, 338 p.

ISBN 9780807106570

1. Alienation in men 2. Mothers and sons 3. Social reformers 4. Self-fulfillment in men 5. New Orleans, Louisiana 6. Satirical fiction 7. Literary fiction 8. Southern fiction

LC 79020190

Pulitzer Prize for Fiction, 1981

Ignatius J. Reilly of New Orleans, —selfish, domineering, deluded, tragic and larger than life— is a noble crusader against a world of dunces. He is a modern-day Quixote beset by giants of the modern age. In magnificent revolt against the twentieth century, Ignatius propels his monstrous bulk among the flesh posts of the fallen city, documenting life on his Big Chief tablets as he goes, until his maroon-haired mother decrees that Ignatius must work.

"At the heart of this splendid mock-heroic with its blundering and canniness, its falstaffian excesses and Alice in Wonderland wit, lies a profound sense of solitude. Like everything else in Ignatuis J. Reilly's world, the absence of love is larger than life." —*Newsweek*

Toro, Guillermo del

The **hollow** ones. Grand Central Pub, 2020. 400 pages

ISBN 9781538761748

1. Women FBI agents 2. Good and evil 3. Immortalism 4. Spirit possession 5. Violence in men 6. New York City 7. Horror

Forced to shoot her suddenly violent partner, a rookie FBI agent witnesses the escape of a shadowy form before embarking on a sanity-risking investigation into a centuries-old being..

"An inventive and macabre new spin on malevolent body snatchers." —*Kirkus*

Torre, A. R.

Every last secret. A. R. Torre. Thomas & Mercer, 2020. 301 pages

ISBN 9781542020190

1. Rich people 2. Neighbors 3. Competition 4. Married people 5. Ambition in women 6. California 7. Psychological suspense

Welcome to the neighborhood. Watch your husband, watch your friends, and watch your back.

"Torre raises the heat on the plotting and counterplotting with such delicate mastery that even readers who can see perfectly well where this is all going will race to watch it get there. Deliciously, sublimely nasty: Mean Girls for grown-ups." —*Kirkus*

Towles, Amor

★ A **gentleman** in Moscow. Amor Towles. Viking, 2016. 448 p.

ISBN 9780670026197

1. Aristocracy 2. Home confinement (Corrections) 3. Hotels 4. Counts and countesses 5. Interpersonal relations 6. Moscow, Russia 7. Russia 8. 1920s 9. Historical fiction 10. Literary fiction

Kirkus Prize for Fiction finalist, 2016

Deemed unrepentant by a Bolshevik tribunal in 1922, Count Alexander Rostov is sentenced to house arrest in a hotel across the street from the Kremlin, where he lives in an attic room while some of the most tumultuous decades in Russian history unfold.

"Count Rostovs long transformation occurs against a lightly sketched background of upheaval, repression, and war. Gently but dauntlessly, like his protagonist, Towles is determined to chart the course of the individual." —*Publishers Weekly*

Rules of civility: a novel. Amor Towles. Viking, 2011. 334 p.

ISBN 9780670022694

1. Young women 2. Fate and fatalism 3. Upper class 4. Ambition in women 5. Upward mobility 6. Wall Street, New York City 7. New York City 8. 1930s 9. Historical fiction 10. Literary fiction

LC 2011004118

A chance encounter with a handsome banker in a jazz bar on New Year's Eve 1938 catapults Wall Street secretary Katey Kontent into the upper echelons of New York society, where she befriends a shy multi-millionaire, an Upper East Side ne'er-do-well, and a single-minded widow.

"On New Year's Eve 1937, at a jazz bar in New York's Greenwich Village, Katey and Eve are charmed by the handsome and successful Tinker Grey. The three become fast friends and spend early 1938 exploring the town together, until a car accident permanently injures Eve. Feeling guilty, Tinker, the driver, takes care of Eve and unsuccessfully tries to love her. Despite the presence and initial impact of Tinker and Eve, though, this first novel is about Katey's 1938." —*Library Journal*

Tracy, P. J.

★ **Deep** into the dark. P.J. Tracy. Minotaur Books, 2021. 352 pages (Margaret Nolan mysteries, 1)

ISBN 9781250754943

1. Women detectives 2. Bartenders 3. Separated men (Marital relations) 4. Afghan War veterans 5. People with post-traumatic stress disorder 6. Los Angeles, California 7. Hardboiled fiction 8. Mysteries

LC 2020035305

Sam Easton—a true survivor—is home from Afghanistan, trying to rebuild a life in his hometown of LA. Separated from his wife, bartending and therapy sessions are what occupy his days and nights. When friend and colleague Melody Traeger is beaten by her boyfriend, she turns to Sam for help. When the boyfriend turns up dead the next day, a hard case like Sam is the perfect suspect. But LAPD Detective Margaret Nolan, whose brother recently died serving overseas, is sympathetic to Sam's troubles, and can't quite see him as a killer. She's more interested in the secrets Melody might be keeping and the developments in another murder case on the other side of town.

"The author of the award-winning 'Monkeewrench' novels launches a new L.A.-based series with an intense, unforgettable novel that focuses on the predators and prey that thrive in the city. The intricately plotted story handles Easton's PTSD with compassion while revealing his disturbing torment." —*Library Journal*

Ice cold heart. P. J. Tracy. Crooked Lane Books, 2019. 320 p. (Monkeewrench, 10)

ISBN 9781643851327

1. Computer software developers 2. Detectives 3. Conspiracies 4. Art 5. Murder investigation 6. Minnesota 7. Thrillers and suspense

With the help of Grace MacBride and her partners at Monkeewrench Software, Detectives Magazine and Rolseth investigate a grisly murder that exactly mirrors a previous homicide.

Tran, Vu

Dragonfish: a novel. Vu Tran. W. W. Norton & Company, 2015. 320 p.

ISBN 9780393077803

1. Missing women 2. Divorced persons 3. Loss (Psychology) 4. Vietnamese Americans 5. Violence in men 6. Las Vegas, Nevada 7. Vietnam 8. Noir fiction 9. Crime fiction 10. First person narratives

LC 2015005764

New York Times Notable Book, 2015

Unable to forget the mysterious Vietnamese wife who left him and blackmailed by her second husband into searching for her, a rugged Oakland cop infiltrates the sleazy gambling dens of Las Vegas to uncover his ex's painful past in a Malaysian refugee camp.

"This haunting and mesmerizing debut is filled with all the noir elements: a dark and seedy underworld, damsels in distress, tarnished heroes, and a blurring of moral boundaries. It examines such themes as culture, desperation, memory, mental illness, love, loss, and redemption. Highly recommended for mystery fans." —*Library Journal*

Traven, B.

★ The **treasure** of the Sierra Madre. B. Traven. Farrar, Straus and Giroux, 2010. 308 p.

ISBN 9780809092970

1. Americans in Mexico 2. Gold mines and mining 3. Mexico 4. Westerns 5. Translations 6. Books to movies

LC 6723519

Two hard-luck drifters and a grizzled prospector seek gold in the mountains in Mexico. They start off as friends, but after they discover the lode the greed and paranoia set in.

Tremblay, Paul

★ The **cabin** at the end of the world: a novel. Paul Tremblay. William Morrow, 2018. 272 p.

ISBN 9780062679109

1. End of the world 2. Home invasions 3. Strangers 4. Violence 5. Cabins 6. New Hampshire 7. Horror 8. Psychological suspense

LC 2017048369

Bram Stoker Award for Best Novel, 2018; Library Journal Best Books, 2018; Locus Award for Dark Fantasy-Horror Novel, 2019; RUSA Reading List Short List, 2019

A family vacationing at a remote cabin on a quiet New Hampshire lake faces a home invasion by four strangers carrying menacing but unidentifiable objects who claim to be acting to save the world.

"Alternating between unreliable narrators, Tremblay captures the intense emotional struggle, especially in flashbacks into the lives of the odds-defying family of Wen, Andrew, and Eric, while dread and terror permeate every sentence." —*Booklist*

Growing things and other stories. Paul Tremblay. William Morrow, 2019. 336 p.

ISBN 9780062679130

1. Short stories 2. Horror

LC 2018051852

Bram Stoker Award for Best Fiction Collection, 2019; Booklist Editors' Choice, 2019; Library Journal Best Books, 2019; New York Times Notable Book, 2019

An anthology of psychological suspense tales by the award-winning author of A Head Full of Ghosts includes such entries as "The Teacher," "The Getaway" and "Swim Wants to Know If It's as Bad as Swim Thinks."

"These are stories that live in the increasing popular space between literary fiction and horror, where speculative terrors and very real universal truths collide, much like the works of Stephen Graham Jones, John Langan, and Jac Jemc." —*Booklist*

Survivor song. Paul Tremblay. William Morrow & Co, 2020. 336 pages

ISBN 9780062679161

1. Epidemics 2. Viruses 3. Women pediatricians 4. Pregnant women 5. Rabies 6. Massachusetts 7. Horror

LibraryReads Favorites, 2020

When Massachusetts is overrun by a rabies-like virus that is incurable an hour after infection, a soft-spoken pediatrician navigates apocalyptic obstacles to get a vaccine to her eight-months pregnant friend.

"A prescient, insidious horror novel that takes sheer terror to a whole new level." —*Kirkus*

Trevor, William

Last stories. William Trevor. Viking, 2018. 212 p.

ISBN 9780525558101

1. Interpersonal relations 2. Short stories 3. Literary fiction

New York Times Notable Book, 2018; Library Journal Best Books, 2018

Collects ten short stories that illuminate the human condition

"The situations behind Trevor's (Selected Stories, 2010) beautifully composed stories revolve around themes of personal cruelty, romantic and marital heartbreak, lover betrayal, and even violent death, and he has long established himself as a writer of great charity for the ordinary person and sympathy for the hard knocks of unheralded lives." —*Booklist*

Trigiani, Adriana

Big Cherry Holler: a Big Stone Gap novel. Adriana Trigiani. Random House, 2001. 272 p; (Big Stone Gap novels, 2)

ISBN 9780375506178

1. Italian American women 2. Grief in women 3. Loss (Psychology) 4. Sons — Death 5. Women pharmacists 6. Virginia 7. Big Stone Gap, Virginia 8. 1980s 9. Gentle reads 10. Domestic fiction 11. Southern fiction

LC 2001018599

Revisits the marriage of Ave Maria and Jack MacChesney, eight years after their wedding, amid the eccentric inhabitants in the small Virginia mountain town of Big Stone Gap.

"Although readers of Big Stone Gap are going to find this novel more serious, they should rest assured that most of the old favorite small town characters are still there. Catching an earful, usually unsolicited, of their views and advice on life, marriage, and love is a part of the charm of both the predecessor and this follow-up." —*Booklist*

Sequel to: Big Stone Gap.

Big Stone Gap: a novel. Adriana Trigiani. Random House, 2000. 272 p; (Big Stone Gap novels, 1)

ISBN 9780375504037

1. Women pharmacists 2. Single women 3. Italian American women 4. Family secrets 5. Pharmacists 6. Virginia 7. Big Stone Gap, Virginia 8. 1970s 9. Romantic comedies 10. Gentle reads 11. Books to movies

LC 99043306

The 35-year-old self-proclaimed spinster of a small Virginia village discovers a skeleton in her family's formerly tidy closet that completely unravels her quiet, conventional life.

"One chapter, which is based on a real-life campaign visit from John Warner and his then-wife Elizabeth Taylor is a hoot. And you don't want to miss Ave Maria's friend, the sexy Iva Lou Wade, one of the best fictional librarians to come along in years." —*Library Journal*

Sequel: Big Cherry Holler.

The 2014 film Big Stone Gap is closely adapted from this book.

FICTION CORE COLLECTION
TWENTY-FIRST EDITION

Trollope, Anthony

★ **Barchester** Towers. Anthony Trollope. A.A. Knopf, 1992. 277 p. (Chronicles of Barsetshire, 2)

ISBN 9780679405870

1. Victoriana 2. Rural life 3. Small town life 4. Clergy 5. Barsetshire (England : Imaginary place) 6. England 7. Literary fiction 8. Classics

LC 91053197

Citizens enjoy their daily lives in Barchester, an English cathedral town, during the 19th century.

Originally published in 1857.

Doctor Thorne. Anthony Trollope; introduction by N. John Hall. A. A. Knopf, 1993. Various pagings. (Chronicles of Barsetshire, 3)

ISBN 9780679423041

1. Rural physicians 2. Heirs and heiresses 3. Rural life 4. Gentry 5. Nieces and nephews 6. England 7. 19th century 8. Psychological fiction 9. Classics

LC 93001853 //r94

Frank Gresham, son of the impoverished squire of Greshambury, has fallen in love with penniless Mary Thorne. Despite the promptings of his family to consider a Miss Dunstable, heiress to a fortune, Frank's affections persist and the humane Doctor Thorne, as Mary's protector, must confront the prejudices of the mid-Victorian society.

Includes chronology.

First published in 1858.

★ The **Eustace** diamonds. Anthony Trollope. Oxford University Press, 1998. 832 p. (The Palliser novels, 3)

ISBN 9780192834669

1. Widows 2. Greed in women 3. Diamonds 4. Jewelry 5. Politicians 6. England 7. Great Britain 8. Psychological fiction 9. Classics

Young and widowed, Lizzie Eustace makes bold to keep a family necklace given to her by her late husband. The in-laws consolidate against her.

First published in 1873.

Framley parsonage. Anthony Trollope; with an introduction by Graham Handley. A. A. Knopf, 1994. 587 p. (Chronicles of Barsetshire, 4)

ISBN 9780679431336

1. Clergy — History 2. Classism 3. Small town life 4. Barsetshire (England : Imaginary place) 5. Rural life 6. England 7. Psychological fiction 8. Classics

LC 93-81320

Mark Robarts the new vicar of Framley, with ambitions to further his career, seeks connections in the county's high society. He agrees guarantee a substantial loan for a local member of parliament which brings him to the brink of ruin. Lord Lufton has proposed to Mark's sister Lucy, but his mother Lady Lufton is against the marriage, preferring that her son choose the coldly beautiful Griselda Grantly.

Includes select bibliography and chronology.

Originally published in 1861.

The **last** chronicle of Barset. Anthony Trollope. Knopf, 1995. Xxix, 983 pages; (Chronicles of Barsetshire, 6)

ISBN 9780679443667

1. Courtship 2. Classism 3. Small town life 4. Rural life 5. Barsetshire (England : Imaginary place) 6. England 7. Psychological fiction 8. Classics

LC 68112673

Barsetshire's latest scandal involves Mr. Crawley, the impoverished curate of Hogglestock, accused of theft when he uses a large check to pay off his debts. Unables to remember how he came by the money, he feels himself shames in the eyes of the community and even begins question his own sanity. The scandal fiercely divides the citizens of Barsetshire and threatens to tear apart Mr. Crawley's family.

Originally published in 1867.

★ The **Prime** Minister. Anthony Trollope; edited with an introduction and notes by David Skilton. Penguin Books, 1996. 702 p. (The Palliser novels, 5)

ISBN 9780140433494

1. Prime Ministers 2. Politicians 3. Dukes and duchesses 4. Marriage 5. Victoriana 6. Great Britain 7. England 8. Political fiction 9. Psychological fiction 10. Classics

Plantaganet Palliser, Prime Minister of England—a man of power and prestige, with all the breeding and inherited wealth that goes with it—is appalled at the inexorable rise of Ferdinand Lopez. An exotic impostor, seemingly from nowhere, Lopez has society at his feet, while well-connected ladies vie with each other to exert influence on his behalf—even Palliser's own wife, Lady Glencora...

First published in eight monthly parts, from November 1875 to June 1876, reissued in four volumes in 1876.

The **warden**. Anthony Trollope. Oxford University Press, 2008. 294 p. (Chronicles of Barsetshire, 1)

ISBN 9780199537785

1. Small town life 2. Clergy 3. Social reformers 4. Charities 5. Barsetshire (England : Imaginary place) 6. England 7. 19th century 8. Psychological fiction 9. Classics

Set in the world of the Victorian professional and landed classes, the book centres on Mr. Harding, a clergyman of great personal integrity who is nevertheless in possession of an income from a charity far in excess of the sum devoted to the purposes of the foundation. On discovering such an apparent abuse of privilege, and despite the fact that he is in love with Mr. Harding's daughter, John Bold turns his reforming zeal to the matter. —Back cover.

Originally published in 1855.

Trollope, Joanna

Other people's children. Joanna Trollope. Viking, 1999. 294 p.

ISBN 9780670885138

1. Remarriage 2. Divorce 3. Blended families 4. Stepmothers 5. Stepchildren 6. England 7. Relationship fiction 8. Domestic fiction

LC 9840004

An exploration into that ever-expanding unit—the step-family—and how to cope with present and former husbands and wives, but most of all other people's children.

"Falling in love with a man does not mean falling in love with his children: that is the premise of this story of linked and sundered families. Josie's second marriage includes three stepchildren, whose loyalty to their inadequate mother makes them hate Josie for her very competence; Elizabeth's beloved fiance comes with a son she adores and a grown daughter determined to oust her. Trollope may not aim high, but she aims for the heart, and she hits it." —*The New Yorker*

Trumbo, Dalton

★ **Johnny** got his gun. Dalton Trumbo. L. Stuart 1970. 309 p.

ISBN 9780818401107

1. World War I 2. Veterans with disabilities 3. World War I veterans 4. War — Psychological aspects 5. Violence 6. Psychological fiction 7. Books to movies

LC 71115416

During World War I, an American soldier awakens in a hospital and realizes his arms, legs, ears, and face have been destroyed by an artillery shell. After nine years of lying in bed, he begins to tap messages in Morse code by moving his head. He communicates with a nurse and asks for someone to help him leave the hospital or die.

First published 1939.

Truong, Monique T. D.

The **sweetest** fruits. Monique Truong. Viking Press, 2019. 304 p.
ISBN 9780735221017
1. Hearn, Lafcadio 2. Life change events 3. Voyages and travels 4. Influence (literary, artistic, etc.) 5. Freed people 6. Authors 7. 19th century 8. Biographical fiction

A reimagining of Greek-Irish writer Lafcadio Hearn's migratory life through the voices of the women who knew him best, and who testify to their own remarkable journeys.

Truss, Lynne

The **man** that got away: a Constable Twitten mystery. Lynne Truss. Bloomsbury Pub Plc USA, 2019. 304 p. (Constable Twitten mysteries, 2)
ISBN 9781635570731
1. Detectives 2. Coastal towns 3. Witnesses 4. Nightlife 5. Murder investigation 6. Brighton, England 7. England 8. 1950s 9. Historical mysteries

A sequel to A Shot in the Dark finds the murder of a young man at a 1957 Brighton beach party challenging Constable Twitten to seek clues in a notorious nightspot.

Murder by milk bottle. Lynne Truss. Bloomsbury Pub Plc USA, 2020. 320 p. (Constable Twitten mysteries, 3)
ISBN 9781635575965
1. Detectives 2. Coastal towns 3. Mass media 4. Chekhov, Anton Pavlovich,, 1860-1904 5. Murder victims 6. Brighton, England 7. England 8. 1950s 9. Historical mysteries

Constable Twitten and his Brighton colleagues navigate regional uproar and media drama in the summer of 1957 to identify a common link among three murder victims who have been killed with an unusual weapon.

"Truss faithfully re-creates both the ingenious appeal and the formulaic limitations of golden-age puzzlers." —*Kirkus*

Tsao, Tiffany

The **majesties**. Tiffany Tsao. Atria Books, 2020. 256 pages
ISBN 9781982115500
1. Rich families 2. Poisoning 3. Family violence 4. Family problems 5. Family secrets 6. Indonesia 7. Paris, France 8. Literary fiction 9. Australian fiction

A sole survivor of a Chinese-Indonesian family struggles on the edge of a coma to regain consciousness while reexamining tragic elements in her family that may have driven a beloved sister to a shocking act of violence.

"This is a bold and dramatic portrayal of characters on the cusp of an impossible choice between complicit self-preservation and total annihilation." —*Publishers Weekly*

Tsukiyama, Gail

The **street** of a thousand blossoms. Gail Tsukiyama. St. Martin's Press, 2007. 432 p.
ISBN 9780312274825
1. Brothers 2. Orphans 3. World War II — Influence 4. Grandparents 5. Sumo wrestling 6. Japan 7. Historical fiction 8. Domestic fiction 9. Adult books for young adults

LC 2007021012

Raised by loving and traditionally minded grandparents, Japanese youths Hiroshi and Kenji are forced to put their dreams on hold in the wake of World War II and find their destinies intertwining with those of a famous sumo master's daughters.

"Set in Japan and spanning over 25 years (1939-66), the novel unravels the hardships and triumphs of two brothers raised by their loving maternal grandparents following the loss of their parents in a tragic accident. The dreams of older brother Hiroshi of becoming a sumotori (a sumo wrestler) and younger brother Kenji of becoming a Noh theater mask artisan are quelled by the onset of World War II. Passages describing the devastation wrought by the atomic bombings upon their lives and of those close to them, particularly the family of sisters Haru and Aki, who later becomes Hiroshi's wife, are well written and emotionally gripping." —*Library Journal*

Tudor, C. J.

The **burning** girls: a novel. C.J. Tudor. Ballantine Books, 2021. 352 p.
ISBN 9781984825025
1. Vicars 2. Secrecy 3. Single parents 4. Teenage girls 5. Robinson, Betty 6. Great Britain 7. Thrillers and suspense 8. Psychological suspense 9. Multiple perspectives

LC 2020044387

Loan Stars Favourites, 2021

Reverend Jack Brooks, a single parent with a fourteen-year-old daughter and a heavy conscience, arrives in the village hoping to make a fresh start and find some peace. Instead, Jack finds a town mired in secrecy and a strange welcome package: an old exorcism kit and a note quoting scripture. The more Jack and daughter Flo get acquainted with the town and its strange denizens, the deeper they are drawn into their rifts, mysteries, and suspicions. And when Flo is troubled by strange sightings in the old chapel, it becomes apparent that there are ghosts here that refuse to be laid to rest.

"Tudor expertly doles out the plot twists, some of them small, some sizable, and one so shocking that it turns the entire story inside out." —*Publishers Weekly*

The **chalk** man: a novel. C J Tudor. Crown Publishers, 2018. 288 p.
ISBN 9781524760984
1. Games 2. Childhood 3. Dismemberment 4. Friendship 5. Chalk drawing 6. England 7. 1980s 8. 2010s 9. Thrillers and suspense 10. First person narratives

LC 2016058866

Thriller Award for Best First Novel, 2019; Librarians' Choice (Australia), 2017

Three decades after his circle of friends is traumatized by the discovery of a murder victim while passing secret messages through a chalk-figure code of their invention, Eddie finds himself targeted by an unknown adversary who is using their former communication methods to torment and kill his friends.

A mystery set in 1986 and 2016—Publisher's note.
Includes bibliographical references and index.

The **other** people. C.J. Tudor. Ballantine Books, 2020. 288 pages
ISBN 9781984824998
1. Hockney, David 2. Fathers 3. Threat (Psychology) 4. Mothers and daughters 5. Kidnapping 6. Great Britain 7. Thrillers and suspense
Loan Stars Favourites, 2020

Gabe desperately looks for his missing daughter, who most people believe is dead. Fran and her daughter also put in a lot of miles on the road—running from the people who want to hurt them. Because Fran knows what really happened to Gabe's daughter.

"A breathless escape story with hints of the supernatural and the promise of redemption dangling just out of reach." —*Booklist*

Turansky, Carrie

No ocean too wide: a novel. Carrie Turansky. Multnomah, 2019. 320 p. (McAlister family novels, 1)
ISBN 9780525652939
1. Poor families 2. Siblings 3. Orphanages 4. Immigration and emigration 5. Interclass romance 6. England 7. Edwardian era (1901-1914) 8. Christian historical romances
LC 2018058174
When Edna McAlister falls gravely ill and is hospitalized, twins Katie and Garth and eight-year-old Grace are forced into an orphans' home before oldest daughter, Laura " who works at an estate more than an hour away "is notified about her family's unfortunate turn of events in 1908 London.

Turgenev, Ivan Sergeevich

★ **Fathers** and sons. Ivan Turgenev; a new translation by Michael R. Katz. W.W. Norton, 1994. 157 p.
ISBN 9780393035599
1. Fathers and sons 2. Generation gap 3. Russia 4. Romanov Dynasty (1613-1917) 5. Translations 6. Classics
LC 92040010
Bazarov, a nihilist, advocates a materialistic view of life and disappoints his adoring parents.
Translation of Otsy i deti (1862).
Includes bibliographical references (p. ix).

Turnbull, Cadwell

★ The **lesson**. Cadwell Turnbull. Blackstone Publishing, 2019. 290 pages
ISBN 9781538584644
1. Human/alien encounters 2. Aliens 3. Violence — Psychological aspects 4. Ambassadors 5. Research 6. Virgin Islands of the United States 7. Caribbean Area 8. Science fiction 9. Afrofuturism
The people of the U.S. Virgin Islands tensely coexist with an alien species on an undisclosed research mission on Earth, until the death of a boy plunges three families into a conflict that will touch everyone and teach a terrible lesson.

No gods, no monsters. Cadwell Turnbull. Blackstone Pub, 2021. 330 p. (Convergence saga, 1)
ISBN 9798200724239
1. Police misconduct 2. Monsters 3. Werewolves 4. Protests, demonstrations, vigils, etc. 5. Missing persons 6. Boston, Massachusetts 7. Urban fantasy 8. African American fiction
LibraryReads Favorites, 2021
One October morning, Laina gets the news that her brother has been shot and killed by Boston cops. But what looks like a case of police brutality soon reveals something much stranger. Monsters are real. And they want everyone to know it.
"The expert combination of immersive prose, strong characters, sharp social commentary, and well-woven speculative elements makes for an unforgettable experience." —*Publishers Weekly*

Turner, Bethany

The **secret** life of Sarah Hollenbeck. Bethany Turner. Revell, 2017. 296 pages

ISBN 9780800727666
1. Romance writers 2. Women — Religious life 3. Divorced women 4. Women authors 5. Christian life 6. Christian romances
LC 2017024938
Sarah Hollenbeck is torn between her Christian faith and her future as a writer of steamy romance novels and things become even more complicated when she finds herself falling in love with her pastor.

Wooing Cadie McCaffrey. Bethany Turner. Revell, 2019. 352 p.
ISBN 9780800736309
1. Jilted men 2. Former girlfriends 3. Breaking up (Interpersonal relations) 4. Romantic comedy films 5. Romantic love 6. Christian romances
LC 2018049157
When Cadie McCaffrey breaks up with her adorably oblivious boyfriend, he determines to win her back by pulling out every 'foolproof' romantic comedy tactic he's ever seen. What could go wrong?

Turow, Scott

The **last** trial. Scott Turow. Grand Central Publishing, 2020. 496 p. (Kindle County novels, 11)
ISBN 9781538748138
1. Octogenarians 2. Defense attorneys 3. Criminal justice system 4. Murder suspects 5. Trials, Murder 6. Legal thrillers
LC 2019049243
A brilliant octogenarian defense lawyer on the brink of retirement seeks to prove the innocence of a long-time friend, a former Nobel Prize winner who has been charged with murder.
"Turow has established the gold standard for legal thrillers for decades, and he delivers another bar-raising example of his talent here, with his signature absorbing legal details, cerebral suspense, and fascinatingly flawed characters all on full view." —*Booklist*

Presumed innocent. Scott Turow. Farrar, Straus, Giroux, 1987. 431 p. (Kindle County novels, 1)
ISBN 9780374237134
1. Public prosecutors 2. Extramarital affairs 3. Murder investigation 4. Former lovers 5. Innocence (Law) 6. Middle West 7. Legal thrillers 8. Books to movies
LC 87000368
Silver Dagger Award for Fiction, 1987
Rusty Sabich, a prosecuting attorney investigating the murder of Carolyn Polhemus, his former lover and a prominent member of his boss's staff, finds himself accused of the crime BT
"This novel contains high drama and suspense, as scenes in and out of the courtroom crackle with the amazing interactions of complex, fascinating characters. This is a great book." —*Library Journal*

Testimony. Scott Turow. Grand Central Pub, 2017. 416 p. (Kindle County novels, 10)
ISBN 9781455553549
1. Lawyers 2. Refugees 3. Refugee camps 4. Missing persons 5. Survival 6. Kosovo, Serbia 7. Bosnia and Hercegovina 8. Legal thrillers
Assigned to investigate the unsolved disappearance of an entire Gypsy refugee camp during the Bosnian War, a disillusioned American prosecutor navigates a host of suspects while uncovering disturbing alliances and betrayals.

Tursten, Helene

An **elderly** lady must not be crossed. Helene Tursten; translated from the Swedish by Marlaine Delargy. Soho Crime, 2021. 272 p.

ISBN 9781641291675

1. Octogenarians 2. Dead 3. Suspicion 4. Senior women 5. Manipulation (Social sciences) 6. Sweden 7. South Africa 8. Mainstream fiction 9. Translations 10. Short stories

LC 2021021905

Just when things have finally cooled down for 88-year-old Maud after the disturbing discovery of a dead body in her apartment in Gothenburg, a couple of detectives return to her doorstep, ruining a perfectly good afternoon. Though Maud deftly dodges their questions with the skill of an Olympic gymnast a fifth of her age, she wonders if suspicion has fallen on her, little old lady that she is. The truth is, ever since Maud was a girl, death has seemed to follow her. In these six interlocking stories, memories of unfortunate incidents from Maud's past keep bubbling to the surface, each triggered by something around her: an image, a word-even a taste. Meanwhile, certain Problems in the present require immediate attention. Luckily, Maud is no stranger to taking matters into her own hands...even if it means she has to get a little blood on them in the process.

"This absorbing dive into the mind of a ruthless pragmatist posing as a Swedish Miss Marple will please psychological-thriller fans, once they realize that Maud isn't nearly as cozy as she looks." —*Booklist*

Translated from the Swedish.

Hunting game. Helene Tursten; translated from the Swedish by Paul Norlen. Soho Crime, 2019. 288 pages (Embla Nystrom investigations, 1)

ISBN 9781616956509

1. Women detectives 2. Hunting 3. Vacations 4. Murder investigation 5. Anxiety in women 6. Sweden 7. Scandinavian crime fiction 8. Police procedurals 9. Translations

LC 2018016750

When an annual moose hunt leads to murder, 28-year-old Swedish Detective Inspector Embla Nystrom must delve into the dark pasts of her fellow hunters to expose a killer.

Translations of: Jaktmark.

Translated from the Swedish.

Turton, Stuart

The 7 1/2 deaths of Evelyn Hardcastle. Stuart Turton. Sourcebooks Landmark, 2018. 435 pages

ISBN 9781492657965

1. Women murder victims 2. Reincarnation 3. Consciousness transfer 4. Country homes 5. Murder investigation 6. England 7. Mysteries

Costa First Novel Award, 2018; Librarians' Choice (Australia), 2018; LibraryReads Favorites, 2018

Doomed to repeat the same day over and over, Aiden Bishop must solve the murder of Evelyn Hardcastle in order to escape the curse in a world filled with enemies where nothing and no one are quite what they seem.

★ The **devil** and the dark water. Stuart Turton. Sourcebooks Landmark, 2020. 448 pages

ISBN 9781728206028

1. Detectives 2. Prisoners 3. Ocean travel 4. Ships 5. Warnings 6. 17th century 7. Historical mysteries

LC 2020023597

RUSA Reading List Short List, 2021

Sailing back to Amsterdam as a prisoner accused of an unknown crime, Detective Pipps relies on his faithful sidekick to help solve an onboard mystery in the new novel from the author of The 7 1/2 Deaths of Evelyn Hardcastle.

"As Turton ratchets up the tension en route to the brilliant resolution of the plot, he keeps readers in doubt as to whether a rational explanation is possible. Fans of impossible crime fiction won't want to miss this one." —*Publishers Weekly*

Twain, Mark

★ **Adventures** of Huckleberry Finn: Tom Sawyer's comrade .... . University of California Press, 2001. 561 p. Illustration; Map

ISBN 9780520228061

1. Twain, Mark 2. Boys — Friendship 3. Freedom seekers 4. Boy adventurers 5. Slavery 6. Personal conduct 7. Mississippi River 8. Missouri 9. 19th century 10. Picaresque fiction 11. Coming-of-age stories 12. Books to movies

LC 2001027448

Rather than be 'sivilized' by the Widow Douglas, Huckleberry Finn sets off with Jim, an escaped slave, to find freedom on the Mississippi river. With the law on their tail, they navigate a world of robbers, slave hunters and con men, and Huck must choose between what society says is right and his own burgeoning understanding of Jim's friendship and humanity, in a razor-sharp satire of the antebellum South that is one of the most important of all American novels.

The book has been made into a movie calledTom and Huck, Huckleberry Finn, and one called Adventures of Huck Finn.

First published in 1885.

Complete and unabridged.

Includes a short biography of the author.

★ The **complete** short stories of Mark Twain. Edited with an introduction by Charles Neider. Bantam Books, 2005. Xxii, 814 pages

ISBN 9780553211955

1. Short stories 2. Anthologies

Gathers all sixty of Twains stories, including tall tales, mysteries, sketches, and tales of travel.

"The sixty pieces which are here hospitably called short stories illustrate both the weaknesses and the strengths of Mark Twain as a writer of fiction." —*New York Times Book Review*

★ A **Connecticut** Yankee in King Arthur's Court. . Modern Library, 2001. Xxx, 465 p. : Illustration

ISBN 9780375757808

1. Arthur 2. Time travel (Past) 3. Camelot (Legendary place) 4. Knights and knighthood 5. Feudalism 6. Merlin (Legendary character) 7. England 8. 6th century 9. 19th century 10. Satirical fiction 11. Classics 12. Books to movies

This satirical novel tells the story of Hank Morgan, the quintessential self-reliant New Englander, who brings to King Arthur's Age of Chivalry the "great and beneficent" miracles of nineteenth-century engineering and Yankee ingenuity.

The films A Kid in King Arthur's Court (1995) and Black Knight (2001) were inspired by A Connecticut Yankee in King Arthur's Court.

Originally published: New York : Charles L. Webster & Co, 1889

Personal recollections of Joan of Arc. Mark Twain. Dover Publications, 2002. Xvi, 329 p.

ISBN 9780486424590

1. Joan of Arc 2. Women saints 3. Courage in women 4. Leadership in women 5. Women — Spiritual life 6. Religious persecution 7. France 8. Biographical fiction 9. Historical fiction 10. Classics

LC 2002067628

Offers a fictional account of the 15th century saint as a paragon of honesty, unselfishness, and innocence.

Originally published: New York : Harper & Bros, 1896.

Pudd'nhead Wilson;: and, Those extraordinary twins. Mark Twain; introduction by Ron Powers; illustrations by F.M. Senior and C.H. Warren. Modern Library, 2002. Xvi, 263 p. : Illustration

ISBN 9780812966220

1. Passing (Identity) 2. Trials (Murder) 3. Impostors 4. Race relations 5. Mistaken identity 6. Missouri 7. Satirical fiction 8. Legal thrillers 9. Classics

LC 2002066002

David Wilson is called "Pudd'nhead" by the townspeople, who fail to understand his combination of wisdom and eccentricity. He redeems himself by simultaneously solving a murder mystery and a case of transposed identities. Two children, a white boy and a mulatto, are born on the same day. Roxy, mother of the mulatto, is given charge of the children; in fear that her son will be sold, she exchanges the babies. The mulatto, though he grows up as a white boy, turns out to be a scoundrel. He sells his mother and murders and robs his uncle. He accuses Luigi, one of a pair of twins, of the murder. Pudd'nhead, a lawyer, undertakes Luigi's defense. On the basis of fingerprint evidence, he exposes the real murderer, and the white boy takes his rightful place.

Twardoch, Szczepan

The **king** of Warsaw. Szczepan Twardoch; translated from the Polish by Sean Gasper Bye. Amazon Crossing, 2020. 384 p.

ISBN 9781542044462

1. Jews, Polish 2. Gangsters 3. Fascists 4. Antisemitism 5. Anti-fascism 6. Warsaw, Poland 7. Poland 8. 1930s 9. 1980s 10. Historical thrillers 11. Translations

"Twardoch's willingness to stare into the abyss elevates this racing work to sublime heights." —*Publishers Weekly*

Translated from the Polish.

Tyler, Anne

★ The **accidental** tourist: a novel. Anne Tyler. Ballantine Books, 2002. 329 p.

ISBN 9780345452009

1. Separated men (Marital relations) 2. Coping in men 3. Man-woman relationships 4. Women dog trainers 5. Separated women (Marital relations) 6. Baltimore, Maryland 7. Love stories 8. Books to movies 9. Mainstream fiction

National Book Critics Circle Award for Fiction, 1985; Pulitzer Prize for Fiction finalist, 1986

A travel writer who hates to travel, and to whom "things just happen," becomes involved with an unusual woman following the desertion of his wife.

"After 20 years of marriage, Macon and Sarah separate. Thus, a man used to intense order in his life finds his existence thrown into disorder; forced to create a new life for himself, Macon must overcome numerous obstacles—particularly his inability to communicate, to relate to other people's needs and problems." —*Booklist*

Originally published: New York : Knopf, 1985.

The **amateur** marriage: a novel. Anne Tyler. Knopf, 2004. 306 p.

ISBN 9781400042074

1. Marital conflict 2. Married people 3. Husband and wife 4. Runaway teenagers 5. Teenage mothers 6. Baltimore, Maryland 7. San Francisco, California 8. Mainstream fiction 9. Domestic fiction 10. Gentle reads

LC 2003059536

New York Times Notable Book, 2004

Marrying quickly during World War II after falling in love at first sight, a mismatched couple discovers that their very different personali-

ties and approaches to life are taking a toll on their lives, their relationship, and their family.

"Although Tyler's prose occasionally slips into banality, she never falters in creating vivid characters whose weaknesses are both credible and compelling." —*The New Yorker*

★ **Clock** dance: a novel. By Anne Tyler. Alfred A. Knopf, 2018. 288 p.

ISBN 9780525521228

1. Families 2. Senior women 3. Single mothers 4. Marriage 5. Married women 6. Baltimore, Maryland 7. Literary fiction 8. Gentle reads

LC 2017043200

LibraryReads Favorites, 2018; Librarians' Choice (Australia), 2018

A lifetime of painful milestones and fading grandchild prospects compel a woman to help her son's ex, whose 9-year-old daughter needs protection from violent local dynamics.

"Tyler's bedazzling yet fathoms-deep feel-good novel is wrought with nimble humor, intricate understanding of emotions and family, place and community—and bounteous pleasure in quirkiness, discovery, and renewal." —*Booklist*

A **patchwork** planet. Anne Tyler. A. A. Knopf, 1998. 287 p.

ISBN 9780375402562

1. Divorced men 2. Emotional maturity 3. Eccentrics and eccentricities 4. Poe, Edgar Allan 5. Mother and adult son 6. Baltimore, Maryland 7. Mainstream fiction 8. Gentle reads

New York Times Notable Book, 1998

A troubled boy with a compulsion to break into other people's houses to read their mail is not able to break free of it until he is almost thirty, when he meets Sophia, a woman of unshakeable goodness who little by little transforms him into the good man he wants to be.

"For some readers, the story may indeed be too quiltlikecozy and cute. But unlike the patchwork it depicts, it is a wonder of construction: everything fits; it's seamless." —*The New Yorker*

★ **Redhead** by the side of the road. Anne Tyler. Alfred A. Knopf, 2020. 192 pages

ISBN 9780525658412

1. Middle-aged men 2. Apartment house life 3. Everyday life 4. Self-discovery in men 5. Girlfriends 6. Baltimore, Maryland 7. Relationship fiction

LC 2019026099

Loan Stars Favourites, 2020

A tech expert and building superintendent finds his circumscribed routines upended by his significant other's eviction and the appearance of a teen at his doorstep who claims to be his son.

"Tyler's warmly comedic, quickly read tale, a perfect stress antidote, will delight her fans and provides an excellent {34first{34 for readers new to this master of subtle and sublime brilliance." —*Booklist*

★ **Saint** Maybe. Anne Tyler. A. A. Knopf, 1991. 337 p.

ISBN 9780679403616

1. SIngle fathers 2. Adoptive fathers 3. Teenage fathers 4. Seventeen-year-old boys 5. Baltimore, Maryland 6. Mainstream fiction 7. Domestic fiction 8. Gentle reads

LC 91052704

In 1965, the Bedloe family is living an ideal life in Baltimore. But an accident shatters their peace forever, and seventeen year-old Ian Bedloe is guilt-wracked over the accidental death of his brother. Unable to live under the weight of his self-punishment, he espies a second chance in a stereotypical, and therefore, unlikely, place.

"Tyler's remarkable novel pulls at the heart strings and jogs the memories of forgotten youth.... While the majority of YA readers lack enough life experiences to appreciate the pure joy of Tyler's descriptions and thoughts, not to steer them in her direction would be a shame." —*School Library Journal*

Vinegar girl: The taming of the shrew retold. Anne Tyler. Hogarth Shakespeare, 2016. 237 p. (Hogarth Shakespeare)
ISBN 9780804141260
1. Fathers and daughters 2. Independence in women 3. Women's role 4. Scientists 5. Gender role 6. Domestic fiction 7. Adaptations, retellings, and spin-offs 8. Gentle reads
LC 2015040137
LibraryReads Favorites, 2016; Loan Stars Favourites, 2016
A modern retelling of The Taming of the Shrew follows the experiences of a preschool teacher who alienates others by speaking her mind and who manages her family's home before she is expected by her eccentric father to marry his assistant to prevent the young man's deportation.
"The Taming of the Shrew meets Green Card in this delightful reinvention that owes as much to Tyler's quirky sensibilities as it does to its literary forebear. Come for the Shakespeare, stay for the wonderful Tyler." —*Library Journal*

Tyree, Omar
★ **Flyy** girl. Omar Tyree. Simon & Schuster, 1996. 415 p; (Tracy Ellison novels, 1)
ISBN 9780684829289
1. African American teenage girls 2. Casual sex 3. Street life 4. African American girls 5. Ellison, Tracy (Fictitious character) 6. Philadelphia, Pennsylvania 7. Germantown (Philadelphia, Pa.) 8. 1980s 9. African American fiction 10. Coming-of-age stories 11. Urban fiction
LC 96024834
As a young black woman motivated by material things, Tracey plunges into a world of violence, gratuitous sex, and lies, until heartbreak forces her to take a closer look at her own life, sexuality, and dreams.
Sequel: For the love of money.

For the love of money: a novel. Omar Tyree. Simon & Schuster, 2000. 416 p; (Tracy Ellison novels, 2)
ISBN 9780684872919
1. African American women screenwriters 2. Moving to a new state 3. Homecomings 4. Young women 5. African American actors and actresses 6. Philadelphia, Pennsylvania 7. California 8. African American fiction 9. Coming-of-age stories 10. Urban fiction
LC 37166
After making it in Hollywood, twenty-eight-year-old "Flyy Girl" Tracy Ellison returns to her old Philadelphia neighborhood, but her homecoming is bittersweet as she confronts the things and people she left behind.
Sequel to: Flyy girl.

Leslie: a novel. Omar Tyree. Simon & Schuster, 2002. 352 p.
ISBN 9780743228664
1. African American women college students 2. Murder suspects 3. Voodoo 4. African American universities and colleges 5. Haitian American families 6. New Orleans, Louisiana 7. Thrillers and suspense 8. African American fiction 9. Urban fiction 10. Adult books for young adults
LC 2002066790
Idolized by her family and admired by her peers and teachers at Dillard University, New Orleans native Leslie Beaudet becomes the center of a disturbing murder mystery that reveals her misunderstood personal struggles and craving for power.

U

Ugresic, Dubravka
Fox. Dubravka Ugresic; translated from the Croatian by Ellen Elias-Bursa and David Williams. Open Letter, 2018. 308 p.
ISBN 9781940953762
1. Writing 2. Women 3. Storytelling 4. Literature 5. Foxes 6. Literary fiction 7. Translations 8. First person narratives
LC 2017055368
Using the duplicitous and shape-shifting fox of Eastern folklore as a motif, Ugresic constructs a novel that reinvents itself over and over, blending nuggets of literary trivia (like how Nabokov named the Neonympha Dorothea Dorothea butterfly after the woman who drove him cross country), with the timeless story of a woman trying to escape her hometown and find love to magical effect." —Provided by publisher
Originally published by Nijgh & van Ditmar, 2017.

Ullmann, Linn
Unquiet: a novel. Linn Ullmann; translated from the Norwegian by Thilo Reinhard. W. W. Norton & Co, 2019. 392 p.
ISBN 9780393609943
1. Bergman, Ingmar 2. Memories 3. Family relationships 4. Fathers and daughters 5. Aging 6. Authors 7. Literary fiction 8. Autobiographical fiction 9. Translations
Presents a genre-bending novel about time, memory and the author's extraordinary childhood as the daughter of a genius filmmaker and his muse.
"To examine the soul of Ingmar Bergman, a man so private and so iconic, requires much deconstruction and reconstruction, not unlike the careful editing of a film. Ullman succeeds on every level, blending time, memory, and emotion into a fascinating and intimate portrait that easily evokes the universal sense of love and loss." —*Library Journal*
Originally published by Oktober forlag, 2015.
Translated from the Norwegian De urolige.

Umrigar, Thrity N.
Everybody's son. Thrity Umrigar. HarperCollins, 2017. 352 p.
ISBN 9780062442246
1. Race relations 2. Identity (Psychology) 3. Power (Social sciences) 4. Social classes 5. Politicians 6. Relationship fiction
The bestselling, critically acclaimed author of The Space Between Us and The World We Found deftly explores issues of race, class, privilege, and power and asks us to consider uncomfortable moral questions in this probing, ambitious, emotionally wrenching novel of two families—one black, one white.

★ **Honor**. Thrity Umrigar. Algonquin Books of Chapel Hill, 2022. 304 p.
ISBN 9781616209957
1. East Indian American women 2. Immigrants 3. Women journalists 4. Americans in India 5. Trials 6. India 7. Relationship fiction
LC 2021026242
Indian American journalist Smita has returned to India to cover a story, but reluctantly: long ago she and her family left the country with no intention of ever coming back. As she follows the case of Meena—a Hindu woman attacked by members of her own village and her own family for marrying a Muslim man—Smita comes face to face with a society where tradition carries more weight than one's own heart, and a story that threatens to unearth the painful secrets of Smita's own past.

"Umrigar is a library favorite and readers will be talking about this intense, incisive, and timely drama." —*Booklist*

The **secrets** between us. Thrity Umrigar. HarperCollins, 2018. 352 p. ISBN 9780062442208
1. Female friendship 2. Inequality 3. Poor women 4. Senior women 5. Women business owners 6. India 7. Mumbai, India 8. Relationship fiction

After being fired from her job as a servant, Bhima forms a partnership with Parvati to sell produce at the local market and makes her first true friend, in a follow up to The Space Between Us.

Features the character Bhima who previously appeared in "The Space Between Us."

Unger, Lisa

★ The **stranger** inside. Lisa Unger. Park Row Books, 2019. 374 pages ISBN 9780778308720
1. Women journalists 2. Recovered memory 3. Vigilantes 4. Psychic trauma 5. Suburban life 6. New York state 7. Psychological suspense 8. Multiple perspectives

A woman is forced to confront the dark secrets of her past when a serial killer strikes too close to home.

Under my skin. Lisa Unger. Park Row, 2018. 368 p. ISBN 9780778308409
1. Widows 2. Loss of consciousness 3. Married men — Death 4. Loss (Psychology) 5. Murder 6. New York City 7. Psychological suspense

Emerging from grief a year after her beloved husband's unsolved murder, a haunted widow has nightmares and blackouts before realizing she is trapped in a surreal game of cat and mouse.

Unsworth, Emma Jane

Grown ups. Emma Jane Unsworth. Scout Press, 2020. 338 p. ISBN 9781982141936
1. Women 2. Social media 3. Thirties (Age) 4. Friendship 5. Lifestyles 6. Mainstream fiction 7. Satirical fiction

In a novel told through prose, texts, emails, script dialogue and social media messages, a woman goes through a break-up—but is really having more of a breakdown.

"Though directed squarely at millennials, Jenny's stumbling journey toward authenticity will resonate with anyone who's taken the bold, hard step of assessing their life without any filters." —*Publishers Weekly*

Originally published in London by Borough Press as "Adults," 2020.

Updike, John

The **afterlife** and other stories. John Updike. A. A. Knopf, 1994. 316 p. ISBN 9780679435839
1. Middle-aged persons 2. Marriage 3. Mortality 4. Married people 5. Literary fiction 6. Short stories

LC 949818

Booklist Editors' Choice, 1994

An anthology of short fiction features twenty-two tales that explore the magical fragility, memory, nostalgia, and translucent quality of life beyond middle age BT

"In these mellow, reflective stories, where parents die and grandchildren are born, Updike's heroes are acutely aware of lost glory yet discover the strength to persevere." —*Library Journal*

22 short stories.

Brazil: a novel. John Updike. Knopf, 1994. 260 p. ISBN 9780679430711

1. Interracial romance 2. Interclass romance 3. Racism 4. African Brazilians 5. Classism 6. Brazil 7. Love stories 8. Magical realism 9. Literary fiction

LC 9328632

Tristao, an African-Brazilian street kid, and Isabel, an upper-class teen fresh from convent school, fall in love and flee from her rich father and the toughs he has sent in pursuit of them BT

"This novel, for all its political incorrectness, seems good-natured and bent on self-parody.... If the book's surface is sometimes a little sticky, its allegorical underpinnings are graceful and firm." —*New York Times Book Review*

Gertrude and Claudius. John Updike. A.A. Knopf, 2000. 212 p. ISBN 9780375409080
1. Brothers 2. Betrayal 3. Remarriage 4. Fratricide 5. Rulers 6. Denmark 7. Historical fiction 8. Literary fiction 9. Adaptations, retellings, and spin-offs 10. Adult books for young adults

LC 99033436

School Library Journal Best Books: Best Adult Books 4 Teens, 2000

Set before the action begins in Shakespeare's "Hamlet," this speculative novel follows the lives of Gertrude and Claudius, King and Queen of Denmark, as they wend their way towards adultery and treachery to ascend the throne

"Updike turns to Shakespeare's 'Hamlet,' exploring the origin of Gertrude and Claudius' 'reechy kisses.' When the sixteen-year-old Gertrude is unwillingly betrothed to the elder Hamlet, Horwendil, by her father...she quickly falls for his brother, Claudius. The two honorably resist their feelings until they are beset by the anxieties of aging; as it turns out, the murder of Horwendil is an act of emotional (and political) desperation rather than cold calculation. Likewise, Updike's portrayal of Gertrude and Claudius' thwarted affections is not just a deft literary exercise but an affecting—and funny—invocation of the abundant desires of what Hamlet called 'this too too solid flesh." —*The New Yorker*

In the beauty of the lilies. John Updike. A.A. Knopf, 1996. 491 p. ISBN 9780679446408
1. God 2. Belief and doubt 3. Faith 4. Families 5. Family relationships 6. United States 7. Family sagas

LC 95-23467

Booklist Editors' Choice, 1996

Through four generations—from Clarence Wilmot, a lapsed minister-turned-encyclopedia salesman, in 1910, to the present day—one family pursues the American obsession with God and the unreal world of the motion picture BT

"The novel opens in Paterson, New Jersey, in 1910. 'At the moment Mary Pickford fainted' while making a movie close by, Presbyterian minister Clarence Wilmot loses his faith. That loss precipitates another loss: his job. Since 'now he was freefree to sink,' he turns to selling encyclopedias door to door and to an addictive habit of watching the fabulous new medium, moving pictures. Updike then tells of the following three generations of Clarence's family.... Updike's soaring novel becomes an extended yet taut metaphor for the secularization of religion and the concomitant infatuation with movies as a substitute for religion." —*Booklist*

Licks of love: short stories and a sequel. John Updike. Alfred A. Knopf, 2000. 359 p. ISBN 9780375411137
1. Aging 2. Regret 3. Married men 4. Man-woman relationships 5. Extramarital affairs 6. United States 7. Literary fiction 8. Short stories

LC 34906

New York Times Notable Book, 2000

Twelve short stories revisit the locales of the author's previous works of fiction and focus on a theme of love, in an anthology that is complemented by a novella-length sequel, "Rabbit Remembered," to his Harry Angstrom series.

Twelve short stories and a sequel, "Rabbit remembered."

Memories of the Ford administration: a novel. John Updike. Alfred A. Knopf, 1992. 371 p.
ISBN 9780679416814
1. Ford, Gerald R. 2. Historians 3. Presidents 4. Extramarital affairs 5. Separated men (Marital relations) 6. Man-woman relationships 7. United States 8. 1970s 9. Political fiction 10. Satirical fiction
LC 92052955
Alfred Clayton, a history instructor at Wayward Junior College in New Hampshire, juxtaposes his memories of Gerald Ford's administration with pages from his unpublished biography of James Buchanan BT

"Updike's elegant, yet slangy portrait of the Ford era demonstrates considerable finesse. Even more impressive is his authentic, yet unstilted, evocation of Buchanan's era." —*Christian Science Monitor*
Includes bibliographical references (p. 371).

My father's tears and other stories. By John Updike. Alfred A. Knopf, 2009. 304 p.
ISBN 9780307271563
1. Men — Identity 2. Senior men 3. Small town life 4. Aging 5. Voyages and travels 6. Pennsylvania 7. Literary fiction 8. Short stories
LC 2008054376
Booklist Editors' Choice, 2009; New York Times Notable Book, 2009
A collection of short fiction includes tales set in the author's native Pennsylvania, the New England suburbs, and foreign countries, all depicting different facets of the American experience from the Depression through the aftermath of 9/11.

"A perfect bookend to Pigeon Feathers, the precocious collection of stories that nearly five decades ago announced their 30-year-old writer's discovery of his own inimitable voice.... Mr. Updike writes in these stories...with the quiet assurance of someone in complete control of his craft." —*New York Times*

★ **Rabbit** is rich: a novel. John Updike. A. A. Knopf, 1981. 467 p. (Rabbit Angstrom novels, 3)
ISBN 9780394520872
1. Middle-aged men 2. Small town life 3. Father and child 4. Man-woman relationships 5. Married men 6. Pennsylvania 7. 1970s 8. Literary fiction 9. Modern classics
LC 81001287
National Book Award for Fiction, 1982; National Book Critics Circle Award for Fiction, 1981; Pulitzer Prize for Fiction, 1982.

Harry Angstrom, now middle-aged and the chief sales representative of a Toyota dealership, attempts to cope with such problems as inflation, governmental ineffectiveness, the return of his prodigal son, and a chance encounter with an old girlfriend BT

"A superlative comic novel that is also an American romance." —*Time*

★ **Rabbit,** run. John Updike. A. A. Knopf, 1960. 308 p. (Rabbit Angstrom novels, 1)
ISBN 9780394442068
1. Self-perception in men 2. Runaway wives, husbands, etc. 3. Disillusionment in men 4. Small town life 5. Married men 6. Pennsylvania 7. 1950s 8. Literary fiction 9. Modern classics 10. Books to movies
LC 60012552
Tired of the responsibility of married life, Harry Angstrom leaves his wife and home

Seek my face. John Updike. Alfred A. Knopf, 2002. 276 p.
ISBN 9780375414909

1. Reminiscing in old age 2. Women painters 3. Art appreciation 4. Interviewing 5. Autobiographical memory 6. Vermont 7. Psychological fiction 8. Literary fiction
LC 2002018442
Booklist Editors' Choice, 2002; New York Times Notable Book, 2002
During an interview with a New York writer, seventy-nine-year-old artist Hope Chafetz describes her eventful life and her integral place in the saga of postwar American art, as the evolving relationship between the interviewer and subject subtly evolves in and out of the roles of mother and daughter, patient and therapist, prey and predator.

"Despite its uncomplicated premise, the novel achieves a remarkable depth of characterization and a glowing beauty in its articulation of the artistic sensibility." —*Booklist*

The **widows** of Eastwick. By John Updike. Alfred A. Knopf, 2008. 308 p.
ISBN 9780307269607
1. Widows 2. Supernatural 3. Guilt 4. Voyages and travels 5. Consequences 6. Rhode Island 7. Satirical fiction 8. Contemporary fantasy
LC 2008018513
Booklist Editors' Choice, 2008; New York Times Notable Book, 2008
Alexandra, Jane, and Sukie, all now widowed, return to the Rhode Island seaside town of Eastwick after many years away and find themselves dealing with the legacy of their evil deeds, the shocks of a mysterious counterspell, and the inroads of aging.

"One wonders whether anybody has ever described the small physical indignities of the aging process with as much tenderness and good humor as Updike.... Now the witches' sex lives are over, but their lives aren't, and you sense Updike's twinkly eyes peering cautiously into the darkness, beyond the glow of the merely fleshly, trying to make out what the world beyond might look like." —*Time*
Sequel to: The witches of Eastwick.

★ The **witches** of Eastwick. John Updike. A. A. Knopf, 1984. 307 p.
ISBN 9780394537603
1. Witches 2. Suburban life 3. Divorced women 4. Female friendship 5. Devil 6. Rhode Island 7. 1960s 8. Satirical fiction 9. Contemporary fantasy 10. Books to movies
LC 83049048
Alexandra, Jane, and Sukie ply their individual witcheries in contemporary Eastwick, Rhode Island, and are themselves bewitched by a dark, wealthy, decadent stranger BT

"While not a typical Updike narrative, the author's glittering wit, pungent observations, and fabled legerdemain at tabulating mundane particulars reach their peaks in the first half of the novel. Only in the last sections does the reader's attention flag." —*Booklist*
Sequel : The widows of Eastwick.

Uris, Leon

Armageddon: a novel of Berlin. Leon Uris. Doubleday, 1964. 632 p.
ISBN 9780385003568
1. Cold War 2. East-West relations 3. Man-woman relationships 4. Communism 5. World War II — Influence 6. Berlin, Germany 7. War stories 8. Historical fiction
LC 64016837
The struggle to limit Communist control in Berlin underlies this story of the romances and personal conflicts of American, British, and Russian officers

"The author provides a broad and moving panorama of the rebuilding of postwar Germany at the time when the Allies and the Russians first came to clash over Berlin and its routes of access." —*The Atlantic*

★ **Exodus**. Leon Uris. Doubleday, 1958. 626 p.
ISBN 9780385050821
1. Jews 2. Israel-Arab War, 1948-1949 3. Americans in Israel 4. Zionism 5. Holocaust survivors 6. Israel 7. Palestine 8. Historical fiction 9. Books to movies

LC 58011328

National Jewish Book Award for Fiction, 1959
Describes the flight of Jews from areas such as the ghettos of Russia and Poland to find haven and a homeland in Israel
Sequel: The Haj.

Redemption: a novel. Leon Uris. HarperCollins, 1995. 827 p.
ISBN 9780060183332
1. Churchill, Winston 2. Families 3. Tragedy 4. Interpersonal relations 5. Loss (Psychology) 6. Grief in women 7. Gallipoli, Turkey 8. Ireland 9. 20th century 10. Family sagas 11. Historical fiction

LC 95010834

From the magnificence of New Zealand's green mountains, to the bloody beaches and cliffs of Gallipoli, to the streets of Dublin and the shipyards of Belfast, Redemption follows three Irish patriots on their odysseys of freedom and passion—in a monumental tale of the men and women who loved, fought, and died for the chance to live free.
"The focus of this sequel is the conflict between two of the three dominant families of Trinity, the tempestuous Larkins and their staid British counterparts, the Hubbles.... Uris begins by tracing the Larkin legacy from patriarch Liam's exile to New Zealand, where he becomes squire of a sheep farm; his brother, Conor, becomes a legendary Irish revolutionary. Another Larkin progeny, Liam's son Rory, is acclaimed as a war hero after fighting with the British at Gallipoli, while Rory's brother Dary takes Catholic clerical vows, only to have a powerful love drive him to question both celibacy and his calling. Uris balances the struggles of the Larkins with the more repressed travails of Caroline Hubble, who battles the efforts of her husband to oppress the Irish after losing a pair of sons in the disastrous British battle against the Turks." —*Publishers Weekly*
Sequel to: Trinity (1976)

★ **Trinity**. Leon Uris. Doubleday, 1976. 751 p.
ISBN 9780385034586
1. Famines 2. Rob Roy 3. Families 4. Tragedy 5. Irish resistance and revolts 6. Ireland 7. Irish Potato Famine (1845-1852) 8. 19th century 9. Historical fiction 10. Family sagas

LC 75014844

Recounts the interrelationships, clashes, and common concerns of the Catholic, hill-farming Larkins of Donegal, the aristocratic and British Hubbles, and the Scottish-Presbyterian MacLeods of Belfast during the years from the 1840's famine to the 1916 Easter Rising.
"The story has a kind of relentless power, based on the real tragedy of Ireland, and Uris's achievement is that he has neither cheapened nor trivialized that tragedy." —*New York Times Book Review*
Sequel: Redemption (1995)

Urquhart, Jane
The **night** stages: a novel. Jane Urquhart. Farrar, Straus and Giroux, 2015. 401 pages
ISBN 9780374222192
1. Women pilots 2. City life 3. Man-woman relationships 4. Bicycle racing 5. Extramarital affairs 6. Ireland 7. 1950s 8. Historical fiction 9. Canadian fiction

LC 2015010123

Leaving Ireland behind after being abandoned by her lover, Tamara, an auxiliary pilot in World War II, during a layover in Gander, Newfoundland, takes stock of her life and the events that forced her into exile while searching to find the truth about the man who betrayed her.

"Canadian author Urquhart's (Sanctuary Line, 2013) elegiac prose evokes metaphors of arrivals and departures as she weaves together Tam and Niall's love story, Kieran's history, and a fictionalized account of Lochhead's creation of the enigmatic mural that serves as the narrative centerpiece." —*Booklist*

Urquhart, Rachel
The **visionist**. Rachel Urquhart. Little, Brown & Co, 2014. 345 p.
ISBN 9780316228114
1. Deception 2. Secrets 3. Teenage girls 4. Suspicion 5. Indentured servants 6. New England 7. Antebellum America (1820-1861) 8. 19th century 9. Historical fiction

After killing her abusive father in an intentionally-set fire, Polly Kimball and her younger brother seek refuge in a Shaker community in 1840s Massachusetts and unexpectedly become involved in a wave of mystical visions sweeping the Northeast religious communities.
"For historical fiction fans wanting to immerse themselves in a setting they may know little about, this novel fits the bill." —*Library Journal*

Urrea, Luis Alberto
★ The **house** of broken angels. Luis Alberto Urrea. Little Brown & Co 2018. 326 p.
ISBN 9780316154888
1. Mexican American families 2. Families — History 3. Birthday parties 4. Weekends 5. Hispanic American families 6. San Diego, California 7. Mexican-American Border Region 8. Literary fiction
New York Times Notable Book, 2018; ALA Notable Book, 2019; National Book Critics Circle Award for Fiction finalist, 2018
Across one bittersweet weekend in their San Diego neighborhood, revelers mingle among the palm trees and cacti, celebrating the lives of family patriarch Miguel "Big Angel" De La Cruz and his mother, and recounting the many tales that have passed into family lore.

The **hummingbird's** daughter: a novel. Luis Alberto Urrea. Little, Brown, 2005. 499 p.
ISBN 9780316745468
1. Teenage girls 2. Young women 3. Women healers 4. Women saints 5. Ranchers 6. Mexico 7. 19th century 8. Historical fiction 9. Coming-of-age stories 10. Magical realism

LC 2004027849

ALA Notable Book, 2006; Kiriyama Prize for Fiction, 2006
When sixteen-year-old Teresita, the illegitimate daughter of a late-nineteenth-century rancher, arises from death possessing the power to heal, she is declared a saint and finds her faith tested by the impending Mexican civil war.
Sequel: Queen of America

Into the beautiful North: a novel. Luis Alberto Urrrea. Little, Brown and Company, 2009. 352 p.
ISBN 9780316025270
1. Fitzgerald, Zelda 2. City life 3. Thieves 4. Return migration 5. Undocumented immigrants 6. Mexico 7. LGBTQIA fiction 8. Mainstream fiction 9. Adult books for young adults

LC 2008039962

Booklist Editors' Choice: Adult Books for Young Adults, 2009; Rainbow List, 2010
In recent years, the tiny Mexican village of Tres Camarones has been losing its men to the lure of good jobs in the U.S. Inspired by the film The Magnificent Seven, beautiful 19-year-old Nayeli decides to leave her home for "el Norte," where she plans to find and ultimately bring home seven men to repopulate and protect Tres Camarones. With encouragement from the women left behind and accompanied by three friends,

Nayeli marches north, where she finds far more than she'd been looking for.

Queen of America: a novel. Luis Alberto Urrea. Little, Brown, 2011. 384 p.
ISBN 9780316154864
1. Women healers 2. Women saints 3. Mexicans in the United States 4. Fathers and daughters 5. Assassins 6. Arizona 7. United States 8. 1890s 9. 19th century 10. Historical fiction 11. Magical realism 12. Literary fiction
LC 2011023065
The sequel to The Hummingbird's Daughter finds Teresita Urrea fleeing to Arizona with her father after the Tomochic Rebellion but is inundated with visits from pilgrims seeking her skills as a healer until she is chased to New York by assassins.
Sequel to: The Hummingbird's Daughter

The **water** museum: stories. Luis Alberto Urrea. Little, Brown & Co, 2015. 258 p.
ISBN 9780316334372
1. Hispanic Americans 2. Culture shock 3. Small towns 4. Short stories
"Urrea's well-recommended collection leads readers to feel empathy for each character, deserving or not, and provides a gut-wrenching view of life along the sidelines." —*Library Journal*

V

Vachss, Andrew H.
Two trains running. Andrew Vachss. Pantheon Books, 2005. 464 p.
ISBN 9781400043811
1. Mafia 2. Illegal arms transfers 3. Gangs 4. Racism 5. Strategic alliances (Military) 6. Southern States 7. 1950s 8. Crime fiction 9. Political thrillers 10. Historical thrillers
LC 2004060127
"Locke City, a Southern mill town turned tourist mecca, is controlled by the firm but benevolent hand of local crime tsar Royal Beaumont. When the New York mafia arrives, he hires former undercover FBI agent Walker Dett to protect his interests. In short snippets of action and dialog, Vachss...creates a broad picture of crime in Locke City, from teenage street gangs to crooked national politicians, with the Ku Klux Klan, militant African Americans, and other factions woven into a shocking climax. A riveting page-turner that marks a definite change of direction from the author's dark Burke thrillers." —*Library Journal*

Valdes, Alisa
Dirty Girls on top. Alisa Valdes-Rodriguez. St. Martin's Press, 2008. 336 p. (Dirty Girls Social Club, 2)
ISBN 9780312349677
1. Hispanic American women 2. Friendship 3. Self-acceptance in women 4. Thirties (Age) 5. Man-woman relationships 6. Boston, Massachusetts 7. New Mexico 8. Relationship fiction
LC 2008012930
A follow-up to The Dirty Girls Social Club takes place five years after the first tale and finds Lauren still struggling to find love in spite of her career successes, Usnavys seeking fun away from her husband and baby daughter, and Rebecca facing the prospect of a life without children.
"The six sucias (dirty girls) return with hilarious and raunchy tales of Latina-tinged love, marriage, and sex told from each character's point of view. Pop star Cuicatl likens the touch of one of her groupie lovers to uncooked tofu from the refrigerator, while man-izer Usnavys describes her husband's wardrobe style as like a college student on welfare cheese. Despite a plot full of guilty-pleasure material, Dirty Girls admirably dives into darker areas like infidelity, mortality, addiction, and abuse. Hey, life can't be a fiesta 24/7." —*Entertainment Weekly*
Sequel to: : The Dirty Girls Social Club.

Valente, Catherynne M.
Radiance. Catherynne M. Valente. Tor, 2015. 352 p.
ISBN 9780765335296
1. Filmmaking 2. Space flight 3. Aliens 4. Documentary films 5. Colonies 6. Venus (Planet) 7. Science fiction 8. Space opera
Romantic Times Reviewer's Choice Award, 2015
In the shadow of her father's movie-directing fame, Severin Unck blazes her own artistic trail making documentaries about obscure and overlooked cultures within the solar system. However, her latest project, a film about a lost colony on Venus, becomes her controversial final work when she disappears during the shoot. In a "found footage" narrative style that compiles transcripts, news items, eyewitness accounts, and more, Radiance is a must-read for SF fans seeking a lush, lyrical outer space adventure.
"The splendiferous prose swirls and twirls in a manic, vocabulary-enhancing dance in a world where silent black-and-white movies have never gone out of vogue. Expect Valentes hugely imaginative, retro adventure on multiple science-fiction- and fantasy-award short lists." —*Booklist*

Space opera. Catherynne M. Valente. Saga Press, 2018. 304 pages
ISBN 9781481497497
1. Music — Competitions 2. Interplanetary relations 3. Human/alien encounters 4. Singing contests 5. Aliens 6. Space opera 7. Science fiction 8. Humorous stories 9. Adult books for young adults
LC 2017028788
Booklist Editors' Choice: Adult Books for Young Adults, 2018
A band of human musicians, dancers, and roadies have been chosen to represent Earth on the greatest stage in the galaxy. And the fate of their species lies in their ability to rock.

Valentine, Genevieve
Mechanique: a tale of the Circus Tresaulti. Genevieve Valentine. Prime Books, 2011. 320 p.
ISBN 9781607012535
1. Circus 2. Circus performers 3. Dystopias 4. Imaginary wars and battles 5. Steampunk 6. Dystopian fiction 7. Multiple perspectives
As a circus of performers recreated with mechanical parts treks across a chaotic world, a government man asks for the ringmaster's help in building a world of order, while two performers desire a pair of cursed magical wings.
The author raises the novel above the ordinary through her ability to convey the richness of the circus performers' emotional lives, coupled with impressive writing—as in a description of Alec's surgically attached wings, 'every bone-and-brass feather jigsawed and hammered and smoothed so thin that when it strikes another feather it rings out a clear note.' New York Times Book Review.

Van Booy, Simon
The **illusion** of separateness. Simon Van Booy. HarperCollins, 2013. 224 p.
ISBN 9780062112248

1. World War II 2. War wounds 3. Friendship 4. Nazis 5. Aging 6. France 7. Second World War era (1939-1945) 8. 1940s 9. Historical fiction

One by one, through seemingly random acts of selflessness, the lives of several individuals, including a deformed German infantryman, a lonely British film director, and a young, blind museum curator, become intertwined, shattering the illusion of their separateness.

Van der Vliet Oloomi, Azareen

Call me Zebra. Azareen Van der Vliet Oloomi. Houghton Mifflin Harcourt, 2018. 292 p.
ISBN 9780544944602
1. Self-discovery in women 2. Identity (Psychology) 3. Young women 4. Exiles 5. Refugees 6. New York City 7. Spain 8. Literary fiction 9. Picaresque fiction
LC 2017044915
PEN-Faulkner Award, 2019

The last surviving member of a line of exiled, bookish anarchists, atheists and autodidacts leaves her New York home for Barcelona to retrace the journey she made years earlier with her father, only to forge an unexpected connection with a man with very different perspectives.

Van Dyken, Rachel

Risky play. Rachel Van Dyken. Skyscape, 2019. 274 pages (Red card, 1)
ISBN 9781542043724
1. Jilted brides 2. Professional soccer players 3. Personal assistants 4. Virgins 5. One-night stands (Interpersonal relations) 6. Seattle, Washington 7. Washington (State) 8. Contemporary romances 9. Sports romances

"Some of Slade's locker-room banter with his teammates is a little too macho, but that misstep does not detract from an uncomplicated story about a guy getting over himself to stand up for the woman he loves." —*Booklist*

van Heemstra, Marjolijn

In search of a name. Marjolijn van Heemstra. Atria Books, 2020. 224 pages
ISBN 9781982100483
1. Family lore 2. Family history 3. Great uncles 4. Pregnant women 5. World War II veterans 6. Literary fiction

Inspired by the stories of her great-uncle's World War II heroism, an expectant mother researching family history uncovers disturbing clues about her ancestor's actual wartime activities. By the award-winning author of The Last of the Aedemas.

"In this fictionalized account of her own family's history, van Heemstra offers a taut cat-and-mouse mystery made deceptively poignant by a mother's desire to offer her unborn child the best possible start in life." —*Booklist*

Van Meter, Crissy

Creatures: a novel. Crissy Van Meter. Algonquin Books of Chapel Hill, 2020. 256 p.
ISBN 9781616208592
1. Island life 2. Brides 3. Fathers and daughters 4. Memories 5. Nature 6. Southern California 7. California 8. Literary fiction
LC 2019010469

A bride explores the complexities of love, abandonment and forgiveness when her California wedding is upended by a trapped whale carcass, the groom's disappearance at sea and the unexpected return of her long-absent mother.

"Heavily influenced by the weather and wildlife of this ruggedly beautiful place, Van Meter's wonderfully un-ordinary debut is rather like the ocean itself: layered, deep, and happening all at once." —*Booklist*

Van Vogt, A. E.

★ **Slan.** A.E. Van Vogt. Tom Doherty, 2007. 255 pages
ISBN 9780312852368
1. Genocide 2. Human evolution 3. Psychic ability 4. Adaptation (Biology) 5. Mutation (Biology) 6. Pulp fiction 7. Science fiction classics 8. Canadian fiction
LC 97-38438

After escaping extermination by the humans, young Jommy Cross searches for the meaning of the Slans' great mental superiority.

"One of the landmark novels of the genre, Van Vogt's 1940 tale follows the Slan, a new breed of telepathic humans and their search for a society free from persecution. Essential for all libraries." —*Library Journal*
Sequel: Slan hunter.

Vandelly, T. Marie

Theme music. T. Marie Vandelly. Dutton, 2019. 384 pages
ISBN 9781524744700
1. Family-killing 2. Moving, Household 3. Nightmares 4. Murder investigation 5. Demons 6. Virginia 7. Psychological suspense 8. Horror
LC 2018048002

An only survivor of her family's massacre, Dixie impulsively moves into her early childhood home, where she begins to question her sanity and the haunted shadows of the past that threaten her future.

"Vandelly shows a deft touch at creating characters and spinning plots, leading to an almost unbearably terrifying and bloody climax in this gripping debut." —*Booklist*

VanderMeer, Jeff

Acceptance: a novel. Jeff VanderMeer. FSG Originals, 2014. 240 p. (Southern Reach novels, 3)
ISBN 9780374104115
1. Scientists 2. Expeditions 3. Psychic ability 4. Threat (Psychology) 5. Missing persons 6. Science fiction

It is winter in Area X. A new team embarks across the border on a mission to find a member of a previous expedition who may have been left behind. As they press deeper into the unknown, navigating new terrain and new challenges, the threat to the outside world becomes more daunting. In Acceptance, the last installment of Jeff VanderMeer's Southern Reach Trilogy, the mysteries of Area X may have been solved, but their consequences and implications are no less profound or terrifying.

"The series is less about a straight throughline of plot and more about constructing a fully realized portrait of peculiar, often alienated people and the odd landscapes they inhabit, both inside and outside of their skulls; and this the author has decidedly achieved." —*Kirkus*
Sequel to: Authority.

★ **Annihilation:** a novel. Jeff VanderMeer. Farrar, Straus & Giroux, 2014. 195 pages; (Southern Reach novels, 1)
ISBN 9780374104092
1. Scientists 2. Expeditions 3. Survival 4. Women scientists 5. Psychic ability 6. Science fiction 7. First person narratives 8. Books to movies 9. Adult books for young adults

Nebula Award for Best Novel, 2014; School Library Journal Best Books: Best Adult Books 4 Teens, 2014; Shirley Jackson Awards, Novel, 2014

Four women—a biologist, a psychologist, a surveyor, and an anthropologist—set out on a scientific expedition to Area X, a quarantined zone that defies all attempts to map its terrain or understand its nature. Eleven previous missions have failed; is the twelfth time the charm, or will these intrepid explorers join their predecessors as casualties of Area X?

"A gripping fantasy thriller.... VanderMeer weaves together an otherworldly tale of the supernatural and the half-human." —*Booklist*

Title adapted into a film in 2018.

Authority: a novel. Jeff VanderMeer. Farrar, Straus and Giroux, 2014. 341 pages; (Southern Reach novels, 2)

ISBN 9780374104108

1. Scientists 2. Expeditions 3. Psychic ability 4. Threat (Psychology) 5. Secrecy in government 6. Science fiction

LC 2013041337

John Rodriguez, the new head of a secret agency tasked to monitor Area X—a lush and remote terrain mysteriously sequestered from civilization—is faced with disturbing truths about himself and the agency he has sworn to serve when the secrets of Area X begin to reveal themselves.

"The new director of the Southern Reach is in over his head. His predecessor disappeared on the last mission that the agency sent across the border into Area X, and all that John Rodriguez, aka 'Control,' has to go on to understand the mysterious zone are cryptic notes, disturbing videos, unreliable colleagues, and the interviews he conducts with one of the survivors who made it out.... [VanderMeer] carefully ladles out just enough information to keep readers hooked and the truth shadowed." —*Library Journal*

★ **Borne:** a novel. Jeff VanderMeer. Farrar, Straus and Giroux, 2017. 323 pages; (Borne novels, 1)

ISBN 9780374115241

1. Biotechnology 2. Post-apocalypse 3. Genetically engineered organisms 4. Couples 5. Survival 6. Apocalyptic fiction 7. Science fiction 8. Mayakovsky, Vladimir

LC 2016033244

School Library Journal Best Books: Best Adult Books 4 Teens, 2017

Animal, mineral, or vegetable? When scavenger Rachel rescues Borne, the discarded creation of a defunct biotech company, she has no idea what she's discovered. That doesn't stop her from taking it home and raising it. To her surprise, the shapeshifting Borne is not only sentient, but intelligent. But Rachel's partner, Wick, is not enchanted with the new arrival. With its dark dystopian setting and non-human(oid) characters, author Jeff VanderMeer's latest novel has more in common with his Ambergris series than his more recent Southern Reach novels.

"VanderMeer marries bildungsroman, domestic drama, love story, and survival thriller into one compelling, intelligent story centered not around the gee-whiz novelty of a flying bear but around complex, vulnerable characters struggling with what it means to be a person." —*Booklist*

Dead astronauts: a novel. Jeff VanderMeer. MCD/Farrar, Straus and Giroux, 2019. 224 p. (Borne novels, 2)

ISBN 9780374276805

1. Biotechnology 2. Genetically engineered organisms 3. Near future 4. Creation 5. Post-apocalypse 6. Literary fiction 7. Dystopian fiction 8. Science fiction

LC 2019022186

Centers around a City with no name of its own where, in the shadow of the all-powerful Company, dwells humans and other creatures who come together in terrifying and miraculous ways.

"The varied points of view and stylistic shifts of the narrative allow the reader to experience reality through the eyes of different characters,

human and otherwise, and the struggle of different forms of life trying to survive unites the vignettes that form the bulk of the novel. Highly recommended for those interested in sf invested in ecological concerns and speculative fiction that plays with narrative form." —*Booklist*

Finch. Jeff VanderMeer. Underland Press, 2009. 339 p.

ISBN 9780980226010

1. Martial law 2. Counterculture 3. Murder 4. Murder investigation 5. Brown, John, 1800-1859 6. Fantasy fiction

Ruled by sentient fungi, the human inhabitants of the city of Ambergris spend their days constructing a tower for their "gray cap" overlords—or, in the case of detective Finch, keeping societal disruption to a minimum. When Finch is tasked with investigating a double homicide involving a human and a gray cap, his life gets infinitely more complicated and dangerous.

"Surreal and at times intoxicating, Finch is ambitious in a way that few genre novels ever are. VanderMeer has tried and, often, succeeded in blending fantasy, science fiction, and crime fiction into something delightfully evil and strange. He's converted the traditional hard edges of noir fiction into the foggy, fungal shapes of magical science realism." —*io9*

A single-volume anthology of the Ambergris Trilogy was published by MCD/Farrar, Straus and Giroux, 2020.

The **third** bear. Jeff VanderMeer. Tachyon, 2010. 273 p.

ISBN 9781892391988

1. Fantasy fiction 2. Short stories

"These 15 elegantly crafted stories ably demonstrate VanderMeer's skill at telling tales of wonder in language that enhances the reading experience. Fans of imaginative literature and true speculative fiction should appreciate this groundbreaking collection by a World Fantasy Award winner that calls to mind the works of Borges, Kafka, and Stanislaw Lem." —*Library Journal*

Vann, David

Aquarium. David Vann. Atlantic Monthly Press, 2015. 266 pages : Color; Illustration

ISBN 9780802123527

1. Mothers and daughters 2. Fishes 3. Senior men 4. Aquariums 5. Twelve-year-old girls 6. Seattle, Washington 7. 1990s 8. Coming-of-age stories 9. Literary fiction 10. First person narratives

Immersing herself in a fantasy life inspired by the Seattle aquarium, a preadolescent girl living in subsidized housing befriends an elderly fellow enthusiast before making a shattering discovery about a family secret.

"By pulling no punches in this explicit exploration of family, forgiveness, duty, acceptance, parent-child relationships, and what constitutes abuse, Vann has outdone himself." —*Booklist*

First published: London: William Heinemann, 2015.

Vargas Llosa, Mario

Aunt Julia and the scriptwriter. Mario Vargas Llosa; translated from the Spanish by Helen R. Lane. Farrar/Straus/Giroux, 1982. 374 p.

ISBN 9780571130214

1. Aunt and nephew 2. Scandals 3. Divorced women 4. Man-woman relationships 5. Radio playwriting 6. Lima, Peru 7. 1950s 8. Literary fiction 9. Parallel narratives 10. First person narratives

LC 82005159

Mario falls in love with and and embarks on a secret love affair with his recently divorced Aunt Julia, scandalizing the town of Lima, Peru, while Mario's friend Pedro Camacho becomes more and more obsessed with the soap operas he writes.

Translation of La Tia Julia y el escribidor (1977).

The **bad** girl. Mario Vargas Llosa; translated from the Spanish by Edith Grossman. Farrar, Straus and Giroux, 2007. 304 p.

ISBN 9780374182434

1. Expatriates 2. Crushes (Interpersonal relations) 3. Lovers 4. Man-woman relationships 5. Interpersonal attraction 6. France 7. Peru 8. Literary fiction 9. Translations

LC 2007004941

New York Times Notable Book, 2007

Presents the story of a love affair between a Peruvian translator and an adventurous and independent woman, "the bad girl," as it unfolds over the course of forty years, from Lima to London, Paris, Tokyo, and Madrid.

"Each chapter in Ricardo's life, in Edith Grossman's tart, fluent translation, is a small novel unto itself with its own amiable or striking protagonists, offering a whole fabric of reality waiting to be shredded to pieces by the reappearance of the bad girl. In this way, Vargas Llosa lures us into the world of Latin American revolutionaries; the tony equestrian crowd of Norfolk, England; the denizens of sex clubs in Tokyo; and much more.... Vargas Llosa, pulling back one illusory screen after another, eventually reveals the bad girl's true story in a manner that couldn't be more satisfying." —*Seattle Times*

★ The **discreet** hero. Mario Vargas Llosa; translated from the Spanish by Edith Grossman. Farrar, Straus and Giroux, 2015. 288 p.

ISBN 9780374146740

1. Fathers and sons 2. Personal conduct 3. Businesspeople 4. Men — Psychology 5. Extortion 6. Peru 7. Literary fiction 8. Translations

LC 2014031209

A successful insurance company owner whose two lazy sons want him permanently out of the way crosses paths with a blackmail victim in Peru.

"Vargas Llosa, a soaring storyteller, mixes humor with solemnity, farce with seriousness, to arrive at novels that maintain a perfect balance between rigorous literary standards and free-for-all fun." —*Booklist*

Translation from the Spanish of: El heroe discreto.

Originally published: Lima, Peru : Alfaguara, 2013.

The **dream** of the Celt. Mario Vargas Llosa; translated from the Spanish by Edith Grossman. Farrar Straus & Giroux, 2012. 480 p.

ISBN 9780374143466

1. Casement, Roger 2. Class conflict 3. Treason 4. Nationalism 5. Nationalism and social classes 6. Capital punishment 7. Biographical fiction 8. Literary fiction 9. Historical fiction

Booklist Editors' Choice, 2012

A Nobel Prize-winning author offers a work of historical fiction that centers around real-life Irish nationalist Roger Casement, who was hanged for treason after he challenged the British authority in Northern Ireland.

Originally published in Spanish in 2010 by Alfaguara Ediciones, Spain, as El sueno del Celta

The **feast** of the Goat. Mario Vargas Llosa; translated from the Spanish by Edith Grossman. Farrar, Straus, and Giroux, 2001. 404 p.

ISBN 9780374154769

1. Trujillo Molina, Rafael Leonidas 2. Presidents 3. Fathers and daughters 4. Women lawyers 5. Dictators 6. Assassination 7. Dominican Republic 8. 1960s 9. Literary fiction 10. Political fiction 11. Multiple perspectives

LC 2001033480

Booklist Editors' Choice, 2001; Library Journal Best Books, 2001; New York Times Notable Book, 2001

Returning to her native Domincan Republic, forty-nine-year-old Urania Cabral, discovers that Rafael Trujillo, the depraved dictator called the Goat by the Domincans, still reigns over his inner circle, which includes Urania's father, with brutality and blackmail, but soon an uprising against him will result in a revolution that will have profound consequences.

Green house. Mario Vargas Llosa; translated from the Spanish by Gregory Rabassa. Harper Perennial, 2005. 416 p.

ISBN 9780060732790

1. Brothels 2. Prostitution 3. Small towns 4. Jungles 5. Prostitutes 6. Peru 7. Literary fiction 8. Translations

Known as the Green House, the brothel founded by the enigmatic stranger Don Anselmo on the outskirts of Puira affects both the Latin American city and the mission deep in the jungle.

Originally published under the title La Casa Verde. Copyright 1965 by Editorial Seix Barral, S.A, Barcelona, Spain.

The **time** of the hero. Mario Vargas Llosa. Faber and Faber, 2004. 379 p.

ISBN 9780571173204

1. Military cadets 2. Students — Personal conduct 3. Hazing 4. Armed forces and society 5. Peru 6. Satirical fiction 7. Literary fiction 8. Translations

At a military academy in Peru in which savage initiation ceremonies, lewdness, and bullying take place, one of the most put-upon cadets reveals the name of the perpetrator of a minor crime and is shot during maneuvers shortly afterward.

"This novel is a remarkably mature (and, one imagines, highly autobiographical) account.... In a sense Llosa is too clever a writer, for his novel gets swamped in places with unnecessary attempts at literary sophistication, repeated flashbacks, multiple viewpoints, and so on. The first hundred pages or so are inordinately prolix, but it is worth making an effort.... If [the] novel had been severely edited at an early stage its dramatic core would, I think, have emerged more effectively: despite its prolixity, it is still a harsh and honest piece of fiction." —*New York Review of Books*

Translation of: La ciudad y los perros.

Originally published in English: New York : Grove Press, 1967.

Translated from the Spanish.

The **war** of the end of the world. Mario Vargas Llosa; translated from the Spanish by Helen R. Lane. Farrar Straus Giroux, 1984. 568 p.

ISBN 9780374286514

1. Utopias 2. Prophets 3. Religious fanaticism 4. Revolutionaries 5. Brazil 6. 19th century 7. Literary fiction 8. Epic fiction 9. Historical fiction

LC 84010187

In nineteenth-century Brazil, just after the establishment of the Republic, an apocalyptic movement, led by a mysterious prophet, establishes another republic of prostitutes, bandits, and beggars, who reject every aspect of the modern state.

"Vargas Llosa depicts a clash not only between two opposing factions but also between two societies inhabiting the same nation, who share only one thing in common: their ignorance of one another. This work represents his most ambitious novel to date in terms of the vastness of the world it portrays and the intensity of its epic action. Helen R. Lane's superb translation now makes this novel available to the English-speaking reader who will find the book to be a memorable literary experience." —*Choice*

Originally published in Spanish under the title: La guerra del fin del mundo.

★ The **way** to paradise. Mario Vargas Llosa; translated from the Spanish by Natasha Wimmer. Farrar Straus and Giroux, 2003. 373 p.

ISBN 9780374228033

1. Tristan, Flora 2. Independence (Personal quality) 3. Painters 4. Feminists 5. Women labor organizers 6. Travelers 7. France 8. Oceania 9. 19th century 10. Literary fiction 11. Biographical fiction 12. Historical fiction

LC 2003056379

New York Times Notable Book, 2003

Recounts the stories of civil rights campaigner Flora Tristan and Paul Gauguin, the artist grandson who was born after her death, in a tale that follows Flora's struggles with class imbalances and her grandson's effort to escape civilization.

"A whiff of the lecture hall is detectable all through this book. (Some passages have more dates than an almanac.) But the juxtaposition of Tristan's and Gauguin's stories is fascinating all the same. In their different ways, both were moralists and proselytizers." —*New York Times Book Review*

Varley, John

Dark lightning. John Varley. Ace Books, 2014. 344 pages; (Thunder and lightning (John Varley), 4)

ISBN 9780425274071

1. Space vehicles 2. Mutiny 3. Twins 4. Suspended animation 5. Eccentrics and eccentricities 6. Science fiction 7. Space opera

LC 2014009515

Awakening from his cryogenic sleep, Jubal Broussard, the inventor of a strange energy that powers his starship, announces that the current mission must stop or everyone on board will die.

Demon. John Varley. Ace Books, 1987. 464 p. (Gaea trilogy, 3)
ISBN 9781101623299

1. Aliens (Non-humanoid) 2. Human-alien encounters 3. Nuclear warfare 4. Sexuality 5. Aliens 6. Science fiction

LC 84004814

"The author concludes his trilogy about Gaea, the sentient asteroid circling Titan. Cirocco Jones and her allies, including various Titanides and a Terran bodybuilder, struggle to provide the last refuge for fugitives from an Earth devastated by nuclear war." —*Booklist*

Previously published: New York : G. P. Putnam's Sons, 1984.

★ **Titan**. John Varley; illustrated by Freff. Berkley, 1979. 302 p. : Illustration (Gaea trilogy, 1)

ISBN 9780441813049

1. Space flight 2. Aliens (Non-humanoid) 3. Human-alien encounters 4. Sexuality 5. Aliens 6. Science fiction

LC 78023865

Locus Award for Best Science Fiction Novel, 1980

When Cirocco Jones, captain of the spaceship Ringmaster, and his crew are captured by Gaea, a planet-sized creature that orbits around Saturn, they find themselves inside a bizarre world inhabited by centaurs, harpies, and constantly shifting environment.

"Conscientiously nonsexist action-adventure SF." —*Anatomy of Wonder, 3rd edition*

Sequel: Wizard (1980).

Vasquez, Juan Gabriel

★ The **shape** of the ruins. Juan Gabriel Vasquez; translated by Anne McLean. Riverhead Books, 2018. 560 p.

ISBN 9780735211148

1. Assassination 2. Political violence 3. Conspiracy theories 4. Memories 5. Secrecy in government 6. Colombia 7. Political fiction 8. Metafiction 9. Literary fiction

A sweeping tale of conspiracy theories, assassinations, and twisted obsessions—the much anticipated masterpiece from Juan Gabriel Vasquez.

Translation of: Forma de las ruinas.

Originally published: 2015.

Translated from the Spanish.

Vatner, Jonathan

Carnegie Hill: a novel. Jonathan Vatner. Thomas Dunne Books/St. Martin's Press, 2019. 352 p.

ISBN 9781250174765

1. Apartment house life 2. Marital conflict 3. Rich people 4. Upper class 5. Marriage 6. Upper East Side, New York City 7. New York City 8. Mainstream fiction

LC 2018055679

Urged by her overprotective parents to call off her wedding at the same time she discovers suspicious texts, an aimless woman in her early 30s turns for advice to her neighbors, who reveal their own marital crises.

Vaughan, Sarah

★ **Anatomy** of a scandal: a novel. Sarah Vaughan. Atria/Emily Bestler Books, 2018. 256 p.

ISBN 9781501172168

1. Women lawyers 2. Elite (Social sciences) 3. Trials (Rape) 4. Politicians 5. Married women 6. England 7. Legal thrillers 8. Multiple perspectives

LC 2017010834

Librarians' Choice (Australia), 2017

Desperate to clear the name of her loving and charismatic public figure husband in the wake of scandalous accusations, Sophie clashes with a determined prosecution lawyer, Kate, who resolves to uncover the truth and bring Sophie's husband to justice.

"Vaughan, a former political correspondent, offers gripping insight into a political scandal's hidden machinations and the tension between justice and privilege. An absorbing, polished debut mystery." —*Booklist*

Vaughn, Carrie

Bannerless. Carrie Vaughn. Houghton Mifflin Harcourt, 2017. 352 p. (Bannerless novels (Carrie Vaughn), 1)

ISBN 9780544947306

1. Dystopias 2. Post-apocalypse 3. Survival (after environmental catastrophe) 4. Sustainability 5. Near future 6. Apocalyptic fiction 7. Science fiction mysteries

LC 2017000816

Philip K. Dick Award for Science Fiction, 2018

An investigator must discover the truth behind a mysterious death in a world where small communities struggle to maintain a ravaged civilization decades after environmental and economic collapse.

A John Joseph Adams Book.

Vayden, Kristin

Fortune favors the duke. Kristin Vayden. Sourcebooks Casablanca, 2021. 312 p. (Cambridge brotherhood, 1)

ISBN 9781728234311

1. Dukes and duchesses 2. College teachers 3. Inheritance and succession 4. Mate selection 5. Aristocracy 6. England 7. Regency period (1811-1820) 8. Regency romances 9. Historical romances

The new Duke has a proper scandal brewing.

"The historical setting is rich, and the conflicts are driven by the way of life specific to the time period, particularly in regard to lack of women's rights and courtship customs." —*Kirkus*

Veletzos, Roxanne

The **girl** they left behind. Roxanne Veletzos. Atria Books, 2018. 368 p.
ISBN 9781501187681

1. Adopted girls 2. Jewish girls 3. Rich families 4. Young men 5. Communism 6. Bucharest, Romania 7. Romania 8. Historical fiction 9. Love stories

LC 2018005009

On a freezing night in January 1941, a little Jewish girl is found on the steps of an apartment building in Bucharest. The girl is placed in an orphanage and eventually adopted by a wealthy childless couple who name her Natalia. As she assimilates into her new life, she all but forgets the parents who were forced to leave her behind. Yet, as Natalia comes of age in a bleak and hopeless world, traces of her identity pierce the surface of her everyday life, leading gradually to a discovery that will change her destiny.

Verble, Margaret

★ **Cherokee** America. Margaret Verble. Houghton Mifflin Harcourt, 2019. 384 p.
ISBN 9781328494221

1. Native American women 2. Missing persons 3. Culture conflict 4. Crimes against Native Americans 5. Cherokee Indians — History 6. 1870s 7. 19th century 8. Historical fiction 9. Literary fiction

LC 2018006352

Spur Awards, Best Western Traditional Novel, 2020; New York Times Notable Book, 2019

In the Spring of 1875 in the Cherokee Nation, Check, a wealthy farmer and mother of five boys, must protect her mixed-race family and tight-knit community at all costs when violence erupts.

"This complicated, engrossing story of the post-Civil War West is a prequel to Verble's Pulitzer Prize finalist, Maud's Line (2016), but stands on its own." —*Booklist*

★ **When** Two Feathers fell from the sky. Margaret Verble. Houghton Mifflin Harcourt, 2021. 352 p.
ISBN 9780358554837

1. Cherokee women 2. African American men 3. Amusement park employees 4. Amusement parks 5. Horses 6. Nashville, Tennessee 7. Tennessee 8. 1920s 9. 20th century 10. Historical fiction 11. Multiple perspectives

LC 2021004083

After disaster strikes during one of her shows, Two Feathers, a young Cherokee horse-diver on loan to Glendale Park Zoo from a Wild West show, must get to the bottom of a mystery that spans centuries with the help of an eclectic cast of characters.

"Verble beautifully weaves period details with the cast's histories, and enthralls with the supernatural elements, which are made as real for the reader as they are for the characters. This lands perfectly." —*Publishers Weekly*

Verdon, John

On Harrow Hill. John Verdon. Counterpoint, 2021. 400 p. (Dave Gurney novels, 7)
ISBN 9781640093102

1. Retirees 2. Former police 3. Former detectives 4. Undead 5. Murder suspects 6. New York (State) 7. Police procedurals 8. Thrillers and suspense

Approached by a former colleague for help solving the death of a prominent community resident, retired NYPD detective Dave Gurney finds the limits of his analytic skills tested by a murderer who may be working from beyond the grave.

"The surprises keep coming as the plot builds to an impressive reveal. Verdon has never been better at crafting a bizarre setup and resolving it in a satisfactory way." —*Publishers Weekly*

Verghese, A.

Cutting for stone: a novel. Abraham Verghese. Alfred A. Knopf, 2009. 560 p.
ISBN 9780375414497

1. Physicians 2. Brothers 3. Adoption 4. Fathers and sons 5. Medicine — Practice 6. Ethiopia 7. Bronx, New York City 8. Family sagas

LC 2008028252

Indies' Choice Book Awards, Adult Fiction, 2010

Marion and Shiva Stone, twin brothers born from a secret love affair between an Indian nun and a British surgeon in Addis Ababa, come of age in an Ethiopia on the brink of revolution, where their love for the same woman drives them apart.

"A novel about identical twin boys born in Addis Ababa in 1954 and instantly orphaned—their mother dies, their father flees. Raised by doctors at the hospital, Shiva and Marion soon begin practicing medicine themselves, but their lives unhappily diverge.... Verghese, a doctor, has an affinity for unstinting detail and unscientific intuition. The exhaustive gore of the medical procedures is matched by a poetic perception of the outside world: arriving in New York, Marion misses the cacophony of Addis Ababa's roads, observing that in America the cars were near silent, like a school of fish. Verghese bends history and coincidence to his narrative needs—characters cross paths when they should and find the information they seek—creating a story much like the human bodies Marion painstakingly describes: beautiful, amazing, and a bit of a mess." —*The New Yorker*

Verne, Jules

★ **Around** the world in eighty days. Jules Verne; translated with an introduction and notes by William Butcher. Oxford University Press, 2008. Xlv, 247 p.
ISBN 9780199552511

1. Bets 2. Trips around the world 3. Travelers 4. Fogg, Phileas (Fictitious character) 5. Voyages and travels 6. 19th century 7. Adventure stories 8. Translations 9. Classics

LC 2008482138

Jules Verne's classic, a bestseller for over a century, has never appeared in a critical edition before. William Butcher's stylish new translation moves as fast and as brilliantly as Fogg's own journey.

Includes bibliographical references.

Translated from the French.

★ **Journey** to the centre of the Earth. . Penguin, 2009. 252 p.
ISBN 9780141441979

1. Adventurers 2. Volcanoes 3. Scientific expeditions 4. Imaginary journeys 5. Adventure 6. Iceland 7. Earth 8. Science fiction 9. Classics 10. Translations

Follows Professor Lidenbrock, his nephew Axel, and their guide Hans as they venture deep into a volcanic crater in Iceland on a journey that leads them to the center of the earth and to incredible and horrifying discoveries.

"More than half the book is given to the preliminaries before the actual descent begins, the first two chapters relying on a standard point of departure, the discovery of a manuscript giving the location of the caverns in Iceland. The narrative shows Verne's intense care in presenting the latest scientific thought of his age, while the sighting of the plesiosaurus and the giant humanoid shepherding mammoths indicates how well he incorporated lengthy imaginary episodes to flesh out the factual report." —*Anatomy of Wonder, 4th edition*

First published in Paris in 1864 as Voyage au centre de la terre.
First published in the United Kingdom in 1871 by Griffith and Farran.
Translated from the French.

The **mysterious** island. Jules Verne; pictures by N. C. Wyeth. Scribner's, 1988. Viii, 493 p, 14 leaves of plates : Illustration; Color
ISBN 9780684189574
1. Castaways 2. Escapes 3. Islands 4. Survival 5. Adventurers 6. Islands of the Pacific 7. Adventure stories 8. Sea stories 9. Translations 10. Adult books for young adults
After using a helium-filled balloon to escape from the Confederate Army, five men find themselves being swept across the ocean by hurricane winds.
The book The mysterious island was the inspiration for the movie "Journey 2 : the mysterious island."
Text originally published : Paris : Hetzel, 1874.

Vernon, P. J.

Bath haus: a thriller. P.J. Vernon. Doubleday, 2021. 320 p.
ISBN 9780385546737
1. Gay men 2. Married people 3. Cheating (Interpersonal relations) 4. Public baths 5. Gay culture 6. Washington, D.C. 7. Thrillers and suspense 8. Psychological suspense 9. LGBTQIA fiction
LC 2020051998
Oliver shouldn't be visiting Haus, a gay bathhouse. He shouldn't be looking for an encounter with a stranger. He shouldn't even be looking. That's not the way his life works anymore. But Oliver just wants one last jolt from his old, transgressive life, a life marked by dangerous secrets and toxic relationships. One new secret to remind him of the good life he has created with Nathan. What he finds is a nightmare encounter and a searing moment of violence that threatens to shatter the new life he's embraced, and resurrect the past he's tried to bury.
"A sleek, sexy queer thriller for fans of B.A. Paris's Behind Closed Doors." —*Library Journal*

Vestal, Shawn

Daredevils. Shawn Vestal. Penguin Press, 2016. 320 p.
ISBN 9781101979891
1. Mormons 2. Teenage girls 3. Mormon polygamy 4. Polygamy 5. Runaway wives, husbands, etc. 6. Idaho 7. Arizona 8. 1970s 9. Coming-of-age stories 10. Adult books for young adults
Booklist Editors' Choice: Adult Books for Young Adults, 2016
1974: Fifteen-year-old Loretta slips out of her bedroom window to meet her "Gentile" boyfriend. This time, however, her strict Mormon parents catch her returning at dawn and quickly arrange for her to marry the upstanding Dean Harder, a devout yet materialistic fundamentalist who already has a wife and a brood of kids, some not much younger than Loretta herself. Trapped in her role as a "sister wife," Loretta dreams of another, better future, of a world glimpsed in magazines and ads. Her chance comes when Dean uproots the family to Idaho, and she meets Jason, Dean's teenage nephew, who worships Evel Knievel and longs to leave his small town—and the Mormon faith—behind. As Jason's parents clash with Dean and struggle to come to terms with his unconventional

family living next door, Loretta and Jason make their plans to escape. Vestal delivers a dizzying jolt of teenage freedom as the two drive off into the starry night, with hopes of recovering Dean's cache of "Mormon gold." But someone Loretta left behind is on their trail.
"Vestal has created a riveting, rollicking thrill ride about throwing caution to the wind." —*Publishers Weekly*

Vidal, Gore

★ **Lincoln:** a novel. Gore Vidal. Random House, 1984. 657 p. (American chronicle (Gore Vidal), 2)
ISBN 9780394528953
1. Lincoln, Abraham 2. Presidents — History 3. Character in men 4. Politics and culture 5. Slavery 6. United States 7. Biographical fiction 8. Historical fiction 9. Political fiction
LC 83043185
The character of President Lincoln, unremittingly tested by the trials of the war years, is reflected through the eyes of the diverse and colorful denizens of Washington, including his wife Mary and his political rivals and disciples.
"This novel is not so much an imaginative reconstruction of an era as an intelligent, lucid and highly informative transcript of it, never less than workmanlike in its blocking out of scenes and often extremely compelling." —*New York Times Book Review*

Washington, D. C.: a novel. Gore Vidal. Vintage International, 2000. 374 p. (American chronicle (Gore Vidal), 6)
ISBN 9780375708770
1. Ambition in men 2. Political corruption 3. Journalists 4. Washington, D.C. 5. United States 6. 1940s 7. Historical fiction 8. Political fiction 9. Literary fiction
A new age of media politics emerges when conservative senator Clay Overbury begins his quest for the Presidency during World War II, and receives help from liberal newspaper tycoon Blaise Sanford.
"Set from the New Deal to the McCarthy years this political novel features the ambitions of both a senator and his young secretary for the Presidency. The senator loses his chance for the Democratic nomination when Roosevelt decides to run for a third term. The secretary, mapping his course to the top, with the help of a journalist invents a non-happening which makes him a national hero. He then blackmails the senator into withdrawing from the race and wins the senatorial seat for himself." —*Booklist*

Vidich, Paul

The **coldest** warrior. Paul Vidich. Pegasus Books, 2020. 256 p.
ISBN 9781643133355
1. Espionage 2. Government cover-ups 3. CIA agents 4. Experiments 5. Criminal investigation 6. Thrillers and suspense
When the release of the Rockefeller Commission report implicates the CIA in the death of a bioweapons scientist decades earlier, agent Jack Gabriel confronts a life-threatening cover-up at the highest levels of government.
"With this outing, Vidich enters the upper ranks of espionage thriller writers." —*Publishers Weekly*

Vine, Barbara

The **minotaur:** a novel. Barbara Vine. Shaye Areheart Books, 2006. 352 p.
ISBN 9780307237606

1. Murder 2. Dysfunctional families 3. People with autism 4. Nurses 5. People with schizophrenia 6. England 7. Essex, England 8. 1960s 9. Psychological suspense

LC 2005010837

Swedish nurse Kirsten Kvist has no idea what to expect when she takes a job with the Cosway family at their estate deep in the Essex countryside, but she discovers a divided family in which secrets, sexual obsession, and betrayal lead to murder.

"This is very satisfying reading, a sort of blend of Edgar Allan Poe and Anthony Trollope." —*Booklist*

Ruth Rendell writing as Barbara Vine.

Vinge, Joan D.

The **snow** queen. Joan D. Vinge. Dial Press, 1980. 536 p.
ISBN 9780803777392

1. Women rulers 2. Clones and cloning 3. Oracles 4. Interstellar relations 5. Environmental degradation 6. Science fiction classics 7. Science fiction

LC 79020555

Hugo Award for Best Novel, 1981; Locus Award for Best Science Fiction Novel, 1981

"An amalgam of SF and heroic fantasy borrowing the structure of Hans Christian Andersen's famous story, set on a barbarian world exploited by technologically superior outworlders, against the background of a fallen galactic empire." —*Anatomy of Wonder, 4th edition*

A Quantum novel

Sequel: The Summer Queen.

Vinge, Vernor

The **children** of the sky. Vernor Vinge. Tor Books, 2011. 448 p. (Zones of thought, 2)
ISBN 9780312875626

1. Life on other planets 2. Survival (after disaster) 3. Librarians 4. Teenagers 5. Greed 6. Space opera 7. Hard science fiction 8. Science fiction

LC 2011024210

Library Journal Best Books, 2011

Ten years after a disaster that nearly obliterated humankind throughout the galaxy, Ravna Bergnsdot must try to prevent power-seeking humans and intelligent pack animals called Tines from dragging the fledgling civilization on Tines World into chaos.

"Vinge has crafted a tale that should captivate his fans and win for him a larger and well-deserved audience. Libraries should anticipate demand." —*Library Journal*

A **fire** upon the deep. Vernor Vinge. TOR, 1992. 391 p. (Zones of thought, 1)
ISBN 9780312851828

1. Space warfare 2. Aliens (Non-humanoid) 3. Space flight 4. Refugees 5. Knowledge 6. Space opera 7. Hard science fiction 8. Science fiction classics

LC 91039020

Hugo Award for Best Novel, 1993

When scientists of the Straumli realm use an ancient Transcendent artifact as a weapon, they unwittingly unleash an awesome power that destroys thousands of worlds and enslaves all natural and artificial intelligence.

"Thoughtful space opera at its best, this book delivers everything it promises in terms of galactic scope, audacious concepts and believable characters both human and nonhuman." —*New York Times Book Review*

Prequel: A deepness in the sky

Vlautin, Willy

Don't skip out on me. Willy Vlautin. Perennial, 2018. 288 p.
ISBN 9780062684455

1. Identity (Psychology) 2. Abandonment (Psychology) 3. Boxers (Sports) 4. Orphans 5. Ranches 6. Mexico 7. Las Vegas, Nevada 8. Literary fiction

ALA Notable Book, 2019; Booklist Editors' Choice, 2018; Pen/Faulkner Award Finalist, 2019

Determined to prove his worth as a son abandoned by his biological parents, a half-Paiute, half-Irish ranch hand leaves his aging caregivers to become a champion boxer before matches organized in Mexico and Las Vegas lead to his realization that he cannot change his identity or outrun his destiny.

★ The **night** always comes. Willy Vlautin. Harper, 2021. 224 p.
ISBN 9780063035089

1. Families 2. Mother and adult daughter 3. Brothers 4. Men with developmental disabilities 5. Waitresses 6. Portland, Oregon 7. Literary fiction

LibraryReads Favorites, 2021

Working multiple jobs to buy a home that will give her family much-needed stability, Lynette is sidelined by a betrayal that forces her to consider dangerous options among the hustlers and wealthy elite controlling her booming city. As her desperation builds and her pleas for help go unanswered, Lynette makes a dangerous choice that sets her on a precarious, frenzied spiral. In trying to save her family's future, she is plunged into the darkness of her past, and forced to confront the reality of her life.

"This gritty page-turner sings with pitch-perfect prose, and Lynette's desperation is palpable. Vlautin has achieved a brilliant synthesis of Raymond Carver and Jim Thompson." —*Publishers Weekly*

Vo, Nghi

★ The **chosen** and the beautiful. Nghi Vo. Tor.com, 2021. 272 p.
ISBN 9781250784780

1. Asian American women 2. Bisexual women 3. Lesbians 4. Immigrants 5. Racism 6. 1920s 7. Historical fantasy 8. Adaptations, retellings, and spin-offs 9. Coming-of-age stories

LC 2021008744

Treated as an exotic attraction by her peers, Jordan Baker, queer and Asian, has the world of illusion, magic and mystery at her fingertips but the most important doors remain closed to her until she can figure out a way to open them.

"Vo's extraordinary full-length debut (after the novella When the Tiger Came Down the Mountain) draws readers into a fantastical reimagining of the world of The Great Gatsby." —*Publishers Weekly*

A Tom Doherty Associates book.

Vollmann, William T.

Last stories and other stories. William T. Vollmann. Viking, 2014. Xvii, 677 pages
ISBN 9780670015979

1. Sexuality 2. Death 3. Love 4. Life after death 5. Ghosts 6. Fantasy fiction 7. Short stories

LC 2013047856

A collection of connected ghost stories includes tales about a farmer's deceased wife who returns, a geisha who becomes a cherry tree, and a man who romances the ghost of his high school girlfriend.

"The writing is atmospheric, otherworldly, and highly accessible." —*Library Journal*

Includes bibliographical references (pages 653-674).

Voltaire

Candide and other stories. . A. A. Knopf, 1990. 307 p.
ISBN 9780679417460

1. Happiness 2. Rationalism 3. Optimism 4. Short stories 5. Satirical fiction 6. Translations

LC 92522911

A classic, satiric novel by the eighteenth century author and philosopher chronicles the misadventures of Candide, who continues to manifest his belief that "all is for the best" despite life's injustice, despair, and suffering.

Includes chronology of Voltaire's life and works.

Candide also published as: Candide, or Optimism.

Originally published in French: Geneve : Cramer, 1759.

Von Ziegesar, Cecily

Cobble Hill. Cecily Von Ziegesar. Atria Books, 2020. 320 p.
ISBN 9781982147037

1. Married people 2. Secrets 3. Marital conflict 4. Neighbors 5. Misfits (Persons) 6. Brooklyn, New York City 7. Relationship fiction

Navigating private spats and embarrassing secrets in their upscale Brooklyn neighborhood, four families seek purpose and meaningful relationships until a raucous party combusts in a maelstrom of ego clashes, taboo desires and hidden cameras.

"Von Ziegesar's adult debut gently satirizes the excesses of Brooklyn's self-consciously privileged characters." —*Booklist*

Vonnegut, Kurt

Armageddon in retrospect: and other new and unpublished writings on war and peace. Kurt Vonnegut. G. P. Putnams Sons, 2008. 232 p. : Illustration
ISBN 9780399155086

1. Popular culture 2. Peace 3. War 4. Violence 5. World War II 6. United States 7. Essays 8. Arts and Entertainment — Writing and Publishing

LC 2008921969

Twelve previously unpublished writings on war and peace include such pieces as an essay on the destruction of Dresden, a story about the first-meal fantasies of three soldiers, and a meditation on the impossibility of shielding children from the temptations of violence.

"Only a few of the...stories rely on the twists of reality and narrative present in Vonnegut's novels; the majority are carried by the characters' struggle with the absurdities of war and peace. Vonnegut's World War II experience as a prisoner of war in Dresden haunts the work, with multiple stories featuring American POWs in Germany.... Readers of Vonnegut's books won't find any surprises here, but because he is at his sardonic best when working in short form, they won't be let down by his humor and poignancy, either." —*Library Journal*

Includes non-fiction and short stories.

Bagombo snuff box: uncollected short fiction. Kurt Vonnegut. G.P. Putnam's Sons, 1999. 295 p.
ISBN 9780399145056

1. United States 2. Short stories

LC 99013665

This is vintage Vonnegut: short stories never-before collected or published in book form. They are from the era of the Golden Age of magazines: a pre-television time when publications such as The Saturday Evening Post, Collier's, Argosy and others reigned supreme as Americans' entertainment choice.

"The 23 stories in this collection were published in magazines...during the Fifties and are collected here for the first time. The topics covered include space travel ("Thanasphere"), which describes the first manned orbit of Earth; finding the American dream ("The package"), about a new home full of the latest accessories; and an attempt to impress an old girlfriend (the title story).... Although many of the stories are topically dated, the ironic insights and illumination of character are timeless, and no one does it better than Vonnegut." —*Library Journal*

★ **Breakfast** of champions: or, Goodbye blue Monday!. . Delacorte Press, 1973. 295 p. : Illustration
ISBN 9780224008884

1. Purpose in life 2. Human nature 3. Reality 4. Automobile dealers 5. Men with mental illnesses 6. 1970s 7. Satirical fiction 8. Literary fiction 9. Books to movies

LC 72013086

The author questions the condition of modern man in this novel depicting a science fiction writer's struggle to find peace and sanity in the world.

"In this novel Vonnegut is...clearing his head by throwing out acquired ideas, and also liberating some of the characters from his previous books.... This explosive meditation ranks with Vonnegut's best." —*New York Times Book Review*

★ **Cat's** cradle. Kurt Vonnegut. Delta Trade Paperbacks, 1998. Xiii, 287 p.
ISBN 9780385333481

1. Human nature 2. Fate and fatalism 3. End of the world 4. Disasters 5. Scientists 6. Satirical fiction 7. Literary fiction 8. Modern classics

LC 2004557124

A young writer decides to interview the children of a scientist primarily responsible for the creation of the atomic bomb.

Complete stories. Kurt Vonnegut; collected and introduced by Jerome Klinkowitz and Dan Wakefield; foreword by Dave Eggers. Seven Stories Press, 2017. 1024 p.
ISBN 9781609808082

1. Short stories 2. Literary fiction

LC 2017013594

A complete volume of the 20th century literary master's short fiction is organized thematically under such headers as "War," "Women" and "Fortune" and includes five previously unpublished stories as well as several that were published only online.

★ **Galapagos:** a novel. By Kurt Vonnegut. Delacorte Press/Seymour Lawrence, 1985. 295 p.
ISBN 9780385294164

1. Human evolution 2. Adaptation (Biology) 3. Purpose in life 4. Ghosts 5. Voyages and travels 6. Galapagos Islands 7. 1980s 8. Satirical fiction 9. Roth, Philip 10. Science fiction

LC 85004581

Observed by a ghost of the Vietnam War for one million years, the descendants of survivors of a cruise to the Galapagos Archipelago prove Darwin's Theory of Evolution.

Also published in omnibus titled Kurt Vonnegut : novels 1976-1985.

Hocus pocus. Kurt Vonnegut. G. P. Putnam's Sons, 1990. 302 p.
ISBN 9780425130216

1. Fate and fatalism 2. Veterans 3. Vietnam veterans 4. Prisoners 5. 21st century 6. Satirical fiction

LC 90034535

Tarkington College, a small, exclusive college in upstate New York, is turned upside down when ten thousand prisoners from the maximum security prison across Lake Mohiga break out and head for the college.

"Vonnegut remains an effectual stylist, combining deadpan irony and faux naivet. As usual, his central narrative winds through a mosaic of aphorisms, verbal tics, digressions, homilies, obscure facts.... This compendium of devices and concerns may have hardened into a formula, but it has not yet ceased to be a diverting one." —*Times Literary Supplement*

Jailbird: a novel. Kurt Vonnegut. Doubleday, 1979. 246 p.
ISBN 9780385286275
1. Political corruption 2. Bureaucracy 3. Selfishness 4. Watergate Scandal 5. Trout, Kilgore (Fictitious character) 6. 1970s 7. Satirical fiction

LC 79012881

Recently released from a prison for white-collar criminals, Walter Starbuck tries to rebuild the life that was ruined during the Communist witchhunt of the 1950s.

Also published in omnibus titled Kurt Vonnegut : novels 1976-1985 (2014).

★ **Player** piano. Kurt Vonnegut. Delacorte Press, 1952. 295 p.
ISBN 9780385333788
1. Far future 2. Conformity 3. Dystopias 4. Rebels 5. Machines and labor 6. Satirical fiction 7. Dystopian fiction 8. Science fiction classics

LC 73154037

Kurt Vonnegut's first novel spins the chilling tale of engineer Paul Proteus, who must find a way to live in a world dominated by a supercomputer and run completely by machines. Paul's rebellion is vintage Vonnegut: wildly funny, deadly serious, and terrifyingly close to reality.

"Incisive satire; a classic modern dystopia." —*Anatomy of Wonder, 3rd edition*

A Seymour Lawrence book.

★ The **sirens** of Titan. . Houghton Mifflin, 1961. 319 p.
ISBN 9780385289238
1. Rich men 2. Space flight to Mars 3. Space vehicles 4. Life on other planets 5. Martians 6. Satirical fiction 7. Science fiction classics 8. Science fiction

LC 61006895

America's wealthiest man succumbs to the irresistible charms of a lunar siren.

Slapstick: or, Lonesome no more! a novel. Kurt Vonnegut. Delacorte/S. Lawrence, 1976. 243 p.
ISBN 9780385334235
1. Loneliness 2. Presidents 3. Near future 4. End of the world 5. Diseases 6. New York City 7. Fantasy fiction 8. Black humor 9. Books to movies

LC 76015605

Flying to a favorite uncle's funeral, a middle-aged Kurt Vonnegut daydreams of one-hundred-year-old Wilbur Oriole-11 Swain, pediatrician and past United States President, who wrote history's most popular child-rearing manual and sold the original Louisiana Purchase

"Slapstick is a deceptively short and simple book. Its readability should not distract one from the fact that Vonnegut has found a fictional situation which considers serious human problems." —*The New Republic*

Book inspired a 1980's film called: Slapstick of another kind.

Also published in omnibus titled Kurt Vonnegut : novels 1976-1985 (2014).

★ **Slaughterhouse-five:** or, The children's crusade : a duty-dance with death. . Delacorte Press/Seymour Lawrence, 1994. Xiii, 205 p. : Illustration
ISBN 9780099800200

1. Life on other planets 2. Space flight 3. Prisoners of war, American 4. World War II 5. Time travel 6. Germany 7. Dresden, Germany 8. Second World War era (1939-1945) 9. Literary fiction 10. Books to movies 11. Modern classics

LC 94171120

Billy Pilgrim, a chaplain's assistant during the Second World War, returns home only to be kidnapped by aliens from the planet Tralfamadore, who teach him that time is an eternal present.

Timequake. Kurt Vonnegut. G. P. Putnam's Sons, 1997. 219 p.
ISBN 9780399137372
1. Deja vu 2. Free will and determinism 3. Time 4. Trout, Kilgore (Fictitious character) 5. 1990s 6. Satirical fiction 7. Literary fiction 8. Metafiction

LC 9714508

New York Times Notable Book, 1997

After the universe decides to back up ten years and all humans must live through the 1990s again, author Kurt Vonnegut finds himself trying to write a book called Timequake, which he knows he will never finish since he already did not finish it.

"The cataclysm of the title—in 2001, time undergoes a tremor, and everyone must relive the nineties—provides an excuse for Vonnegut and his longtime alter ego, Kilgore Trout, to trade rants: on desert camouflage, thirties socialism, the joys of waiting in line at the post office, the traitorousness of Dillinger's Hungarian girlfriend, semicolons. The resulting quilt of snippets is equal parts memoir, literary charm, self-congratulation, humanist sermon, randy geriatric fantasy, and toastmasterly jokefest." —*The New Yorker*

Welcome to the monkey house. Kurt Vonnegut. Delta 1998. 352 p.
ISBN 9780385333504
1. Near future 2. Religion 3. Birth control 4. Censorship 5. Human nature 6. Short stories 7. Satirical fiction 8. Science fiction

Tender stories of love, incisive esays on human greed and misery, and imaginative tales of futuristic happenings reveal Vonnegut's versatility and vision.

Originally published: New York : Delacorte, 1968.

While mortals sleep: unpublished short fiction. Kurt Vonnegut. Delacorte Press, 2011. Xii, 253 p.
ISBN 9780385343732
1. Social isolation 2. Technology 3. Ethics 4. Short stories 5. Adult books for young adults

LC 2010033817

An anthology of sixteen previously unpublished works includes selections from the iconic writer's early literary career and is complemented by more than a dozen of his original works of art.

"In well over a dozen novels and hundreds of short stories, Vonnegut wrote about the madness of war and about alienation in the modern machine age. When he died in 2007, he was acclaimed as a great American writer with a signature style. [This] is the second collection of his previously unpublished short stories. Written early in his career, they are concerned less with war and corporate malfeasance than with the pursuit of success, happiness and love. Vintage Vonnegut, for better and worse, they put characters, settings and stories in the service of moral messages. At their best, these messages achieve a simple and powerful eloquence." —*Pittsburgh Post-Gazette*

Vreeland, Susan

Girl in hyacinth blue. Susan Vreeland. MacMurray & Beck, 1999. 242 p.
ISBN 9781878448903

1. Vermeer, Johannes 2. Artists — History 3. Jewish girls 4. Art thefts 5. Children of artists 6. College teachers 7. Netherlands 8. Amsterdam, Netherlands 9. 20th century 10. 19th century 11. Biographical fiction 12. Literary fiction

LC 99027405

Chronicles the history of a painting and the lives with which it intersects, from the artist's inspiration to its admiration by two art scholars three hundred years later.

"Vreeland strikes a pleasing balance between the timeless world of the painting as a work of art and the finite worlds of its possessors and admirersnot to mention the world of its subject and its creator. Intelligent, searching and unusual, the novel is filled with luminous moments; like the painting it describes so well, it has a way of lingering in the reader's mind." —*New York Times Book Review*

Vuong, Ocean

★ **On** Earth we're briefly gorgeous: a novel. Ocean Vuong. Penguin Press, 2019. 246 pages

ISBN 9780525562023

1. Mothers and sons 2. Immigration and emigration 3. Vietnamese Americans 4. Teenage boy/boy relations 5. Single mothers 6. Literary fiction 7. Coming-of-age stories 8. Epistolary novels 9. Adult books for young adults

LC 2018046290

ALA Notable Book, 2020; Library Journal Best Books, 2019; Pen/Faulkner Award Finalist, 2020; Kirkus Prize for Fiction finalist, 2019; Longlisted for the National Book Award for Fiction, 2019; Shortlisted for the International Dublin Literary Award, 2021

A letter from a son to a mother who cannot read reveals the impact of the Vietnam War on their family history and provides a view into parts of the son's life that his mother has never known.

Vyleta, Dan

Smoke: a novel. Dan Vyleta. Doubleday, 2016. 431 p. (Smoke, 1)

ISBN 9780385540162

1. Social classes 2. Power (Social sciences) 3. Friendship 4. Political intrigue 5. Good and evil 6. England 7. Victorian era (1837-1901) 8. Historical fantasy 9. Canadian fiction 10. Multiple perspectives 11. Adult books for young adults

LC 2015037301

LibraryReads Favorites, 2016

A tale set in an alternate 19th-century England where the lower classes emit smoke from their bodies that is believed to reflect wicked natures, three students at an elite boarding school for future leaders make discoveries that could cost them their lives.

"Vyleta imagines an alternative turn-of-the-century England where the proletariat and aristocratic classes are further divided by the relationship to Smoke, the manifestation of sin that flows from the body as blackened breath or ashen sweat whenever someone thinks or acts immorally." —*Booklist*

W

Wade, Becky

Falling for you. Becky Wade. Bethany House, 2018. 368 p. (Bradford sisters, 2)

ISBN 9780764219375

1. Mate selection 2. Innkeepers 3. Missing persons investigation 4. Fashion models 5. Quarterbacks (Football) 6. Christian romances 7. Contemporary romances

LC 2017963578

Christy Award for Contemporary Romance Category, 2019

Willow Bradford is content taking a break from modeling to run her family's inn until she comes face-to-face with NFL quarterback Corbin Stewart, the man who broke her heart—and wants to win her back. When a decades-old family mystery brings them together, they're forced to decide whether they can risk falling for one another all over again.

★ **True** to you. Becky Wade. Bethany House, 2017. 368 p. (Bradford sisters, 1)

ISBN 9780764219368

1. Single women 2. Genealogy 3. Former Navy SEALs 4. Veterans 5. Birthparents 6. Christian romances

LC 2016050049

Christy Award for Book of the Year, 2018; Christy Award for Contemporary Romance Category, 2018

Genealogist and historical village owner Nora Bradford throws herself into her work following a heartbreak, until she meets former Navy SEAL John Lawson, who seeks her out when he suddenly needs to find his birth parents.

Wagers, K. B.

After the crown. K.B. Wagers. Orbit, 2016. 432 p. (Indranan war, 2)

ISBN 9780316308632

1. Smugglers 2. Space vehicles 3. Conspiracies 4. Alliances 5. Betrayal 6. Space opera 7. Science fiction

Former gunrunner-turned-Empress Hail Bristol discovers the work of a traitor when peaceful alliance efforts with neighboring worlds turn violent.

Hold fast through the fire. K. B. Wagers. HarperVoyager, 2021. 336 p. (Neog, 2)

ISBN 9780062887818

1. Space stations 2. Competition 3. Conspiracies 4. Space colonies 5. Women spaceship captains 6. Military science fiction

While protecting the solar system, the crew of Zuma's Ghost deals with personnel changes and a powerful, untouchable cabal that attempts to take over the Trappist colonies and start a war with the Near-Earth Orbital Guard.

"Wagers's second NeoG novel (following A Pale Light in the Black) serves up buffet-size portions of everything their fans have come to expect: dug-in friendships, action, impossible odds, and clever dialogue that always hits home." —*Publishers Weekly*

A **pale** light in the black: a Neog novel. K. B. Wagers. Harper Voyager, 2020. 421 pages; (Neog, 1)

ISBN 9780062887788

1. Space stations 2. Astronauts 3. Space exploration 4. Space flight 5. Trust 6. Military science fiction

RUSA Reading List Short List, 2021

Max and her Jupiter Station team must learn to work together when their routine mission to retrieve a missing ship turns dangerous.

"The U.S. Coast Guard in space! Wagers (Indranan War trilogy) launches an exciting new military sf series filled with smart characters and taut action sequences that will keep readers engaged." —*Library Journal*

There before the chaos. K. B. Wagers. Orbit, 2018. 465 p. (Farian war, 1)

ISBN 9780316411219

1. Women rulers 2. Political intrigue 3. Imaginary empires 4. Aliens 5. Rulers 6. Space opera 7. Science fiction

LC 2018026314

Retiring her gun to rebuild her Empire, former runaway princess and infamous galactic gunrunner Hail Bristol finds her hard-won peace short-lived when she is asked to intervene in an interstellar military crisis between two alien civilizations.

"This series launch provides an exciting dose of space opera and political intrigue peppered with hard choices. Highly recommended for fans of science fiction with assertive female characters." —*Booklist*

Waite, Jen

Survival instincts. Jen Waite. E.P. Dutton, 2020. 368 p.

ISBN 9781524745837

1. Cabins 2. Captives 3. Violence against women 4. Mothers and daughters 5. Grandmothers 6. New Hampshire 7. Vermont 8. Thrillers and suspense

Dragged at gunpoint into an abandoned cabin in the woods, a therapist, her 12-year-old daughter and her mother find themselves fighting to survive in the face of their captor's mysterious agenda.

"Give this to fans of psychological thrillers and of strong female characters." —*Booklist*

Waite, Olivia

The **care** and feeding of waspish widows. Olivia Waite. Avon Books, 2020. 336 p. (Feminine pursuits, 2)

ISBN 9780062931825

1. Widows 2. Married women 3. Women business owners 4. Women beekeepers 5. Middle-aged women 6. Great Britain 7. England 8. Regency period (1811-1820) 9. Regency romances 10. LGBTQIA romances 11. Historical romances

"Waite set the literary bar high for herself with the exceptional start to her Feminine Pursuits series, The Lady's Guide to Celestial Mechanics (2019), but she easily matches it with this brilliantly conceived, breathtakingly romantic Regency historical. Waite's poetically polished prose is infused with just the right measure of sly wit and perfectly complemented by a marvelously inventive plot involving not only the art and science of beekeeping but also a village queen bee's attempt to use censorship to wield control over her fellow citizens, and the political turmoil surrounding George IV and his wife, Caroline." —*Booklist*

★ The **lady's** guide to celestial mechanics. Olivia Waite. Avon Impulse, 2019. 322 p. (Feminine pursuits, 1)

ISBN 9780062931795

1. Widows 2. Women scientists 3. Interpersonal attraction 4. Astronomy 5. Celestial mechanics 6. Great Britain 7. England 8. Regency period (1811-1820) 9. Regency romances 10. LGBTQIA romances 11. Historical romances

Hired to translate a French treatise on celestial mechanics, aspiring astronomer Lucy Muchelney finds herself drawn to her employer, the widowed Catherine St. Day, Countess of Moth.

Walbert, Kate

She was like that: new and selected stories. Kate Walbert. Scribner, 2019. 288 p.

ISBN 9781476799421

1. Maternal love 2. Motherhood 3. Anxiety in women 4. Female friendship 5. Single mothers 6. Short stories 7. Literary fiction

New York Times Notable Book, 2019

From the National Book Award finalist and national best-selling author of A Short History of Women and His Favorites comes a career-spanning collection of new and selected stories.

Waldman, Amy

A **door** in the earth. Amy Waldman. Little Brown & Company, 2019. 400 pages

ISBN 9780316451574

1. Women college graduates 2. War and society 3. Deception 4. Clinics 5. Voyages and travels 6. Afghanistan 7. Political fiction 8. Literary fiction 9. Multiple perspectives

An Afghan-American college student in California travels to a remote village in Afghanistan to work for a professor's charitable foundation and after surviving a horrific bombing must side with either the villagers or the American soldiers.

Walker, Alice

★ The **color** purple: a novel. Alice Walker. Harcourt Brace Jovanovich, 1982. 245 p.

ISBN 9780151191536

1. African American women 2. Separated friends, relatives, etc. 3. Loyalty in women 4. African American lesbians 5. Sisters 6. Southern States 7. Epistolary novels 8. African American fiction 9. Literary fiction

LC 81048242

National Book Award for Fiction, 1983; Pulitzer Prize for Fiction, 1983; National Book Critics Circle Award for Fiction finalist, 1982

The lives of two sisters—Nettie, a missionary in Africa, and Celie, a southern woman married to a man she hates—are revealed in a series of letters exchanged over thirty years.

Possessing the secret of joy. Alice Walker. Harcourt Brace Jovanovich, 1992. 286 p.

ISBN 9780151731527

1. African American women — Psychotherapy 2. Clitoridectomy 3. Grief in women 4. African American women with mental illnesses 5. Revenge 6. African American fiction 7. Literary fiction

LC 92006883

Severely traumatized after suffering genital mutilation in her native Africa, Tashi Johnson spends much of her adult life in North America seeking help through psychoanalysis and desperate to regain the ability to feel BT

"The people in Ms. Walker's book are archetypes rather than characters as we have come to expect them in the 20th-century novel, and this is by defiant intention.... When the novel is operating genuinely on this archetypal level, it has a mythic strength. Its many voices are not rendered as stream-of-consciousness monologues, nor are they made to belong to distinct individuals. Instead, they are highly stylized, operatic, prophetic—and powerfully poetic." —*New York Times Book Review*

The **temple** of my familiar. Alice Walker. Washington Square Press, 1997. 417 p. : Illustration

ISBN 9780671003760

1. African American women 2. Ethnic identity 3. Self-discovery 4. African Americans 5. Man-woman relationships 6. Africa 7. England 8. Epic fiction 9. African American fiction 10. Literary fiction

LC 96042427

In a story that moves through America, England, and Africa, men, women, and animals share a spiritual world and learn the intricacies of their connecting lives BT

"This is a novel only in a loose sense. Rather, it is a mixture of mythic fantasy, revisionary history, exemplary biography and sermon. It is short on narrative tension, long on inspirational message." —*New York Times Book Review*

Originally published: San Diego : Harcourt Brace Jovanovich, 1989.

The **third** life of Grange Copeland. Alice Walker. Pocket Books, 1988. 346 p.

ISBN 9780671745882

1. Family violence 2. African American families 3. Fathers and sons 4. African-American tenant farmers 5. African American men 6. Georgia 7. Family sagas 8. Literary fiction 9. African American fiction

LC 79117577

In Georgia during the 1920s, Grange Copeland creates and sustains a dream for his granddaughter in the midst of African American dehumanization.

You can't keep a good woman down: stories. Alice Walker. Harcourt Brace Jovanovich, 1981. 167 p.

ISBN 9780151997541

1. Women 2. African American women 3. African American fiction 4. Short stories

LC 80008761

Thirteen short stories, including a political dialogue between two young black women as they meet over the years, explore the African-American experience in contemporary America, probing into relations between races and between sexes.

Walker, Caroline Louise

Man of the year. Caroline Louise Walker. Gallery Books, 2019. 256 pages

ISBN 9781982100452

1. Married people 2. Fathers and sons 3. Jealousy 4. Physicians 5. Suspicion 6. New York (State) 7. Sag Harbor, New York 8. Psychological suspense

LC 2018049693

Offering shelter to a former college roommate, a doctor who has just been named Sag Harbor's Man of the Year reveals a dark inner nature when he develops paranoid suspicions about his wife's fidelity.

Walker, Karen Thompson

The **age** of miracles: a novel. Karen Thompson Walker. Random House, 2012. 320 p.

ISBN 9780812992977

1. Teenage girls 2. Climate change 3. Environmental disasters 4. Teenage boy/girl relations 5. Family problems 6. California 7. Earth 8. Coming-of-age stories 9. Apocalyptic fiction 10. Science fiction 11. Adult books for young adults

LC 2011040664

Booklist Editors' Choice: Adult Books for Young Adults, 2012; School Library Journal Best Books: Best Adult Books 4 Teens, 2012

Julia's world is thrown into upheaval when it is discovered that the Earth's rotation has suddenly begun to slow, posing a catastrophic threat to all life.

The **dreamers**. Karen Thompson Walker. Random House, 2019. 303 p.

ISBN 9780812994162

1. Epidemics 2. Sleep disorders 3. College students 4. Universities and colleges 5. Interpersonal relations 6. California 7. Southern California 8. Apocalyptic fiction 9. Literary fiction

LibraryReads Favorites, 2019

Presents the story of a student in an isolated Southern California college town who witnesses a strange sleeping illness that subjects patients to life-altering, heightened dreams.

"Walker jolts the narrative with surprising twists, ensuring it keeps its energy until the end. This is a skillful, complex, and thoroughly satisfying novel about a community in peril." —*Publishers Weekly*

Walker, Martin

The **coldest** case. Martin Walker. Alfred A. Knopf, 2021. 336 p. (Bruno Courreges mysteries, 14)

ISBN 9780525656678

1. Police chiefs 2. Rural life 3. Cold cases (Criminal investigation) 4. Murder investigation 5. Skull 6. France 7. Southern France 8. Mysteries

Reopening a 31-year-old cold case due to new technology on the facial recognition of ancient skulls, Bruno finds himself immersed in an investigation that gets stranger by the minute as sinister rumors from the Cold War era of espionage swirl about.

"Walker has the rare ability in a series writer of orienting old and new readers alike. A feast." —*Booklist*

The **shooting** at Chateau Rock. Martin Walker. Random House Inc 2020. 320 p. (Bruno Courreges mysteries, 13)

ISBN 9780525656654

1. Police chiefs 2. Rural life 3. International businesses 4. Disinheritance 5. Families 6. France 7. Southern France 8. Mysteries

LC 2019045578

When a wealthy farmer is found dead amid revelations about his disinherited family, Bruno follows leads to a Russian oligarch and a shadowy multinational conglomerate in a case involving the chief suspect's daughter and an aging rock star.

"Francophiles will relish the evocative descriptions of the Perigord region and its cuisine. Distinctive characters complement the intricate mystery." —*Publishers Weekly*

Walker, Nico

★ **Cherry**: a novel. Nico Walker. Knopf, 2018. 272 p.

ISBN 9780525520139

1. Veterans 2. Drug addicts 3. Lamarr, Hedy 4. Iraq War veterans 5. Iraq War, 2003-2011 6. Ohio 7. Literary fiction 8. Autobiographical fiction 9. First person narratives

LC 2017056634

New York Times Notable Book, 2018

Rashly marrying his college girlfriend to keep their relationship active during his tour of duty, a college dropout turned army soldier is overwhelmed by the realities of war, PTSD and opioid addiction before forging a desperate plan.

"A raging, agonized scream of a novel and a tremendously powerful debut." —*Library Journal*

Walker, Sarai

Dietland. Sarai Walker. Houghton Mifflin Harcourt, 2015. 272 p.

ISBN 9780544373433

1. Overweight women 2. Self-esteem in women 3. Women radicals 4. Nonconformists 5. Revenge 6. Satirical fiction

LC 2014026803

Biding her time alone until she can have weight-loss surgery, Plum joins an underground community of empowered women and agrees to a series of challenges, including work with a group that stages anti-misogyny terrorist acts.

"Through her protagonist, debut novelist Walker gives a plaintive yet powerful voice to anyone who has struggled with body image, feelings of marginalization, and sexual manipulation. Her robust satire also vibrantly redefines what it means to be a woman in contemporary society." —*Booklist*

Walker, Wendy

Emma in the night. Wendy Walker. St Martin's Press, 2017. 320 p.
ISBN 9781250141439
1. Sisters 2. Missing teenage girls 3. Missing persons investigation 4. Dysfunctional families 5. Kidnapping victims 6. Psychological suspense 7. Multiple perspectives 8. Adult books for young adults
LibraryReads Favorites, 2017

One night three years ago, the Tanner sisters disappeared: fifteen-year-old Cass and seventeen-year-old Emma. Three years later, Cass returns, without her sister Emma. Her story is one of kidnapping and betrayal, of a mysterious island where the two were held. But to forensic psychiatrist Dr. Abby Winter, something doesn't add up. Looking deep within this dysfunctional family Dr. Winter uncovers a life where boundaries were violated and a narcissistic parent held sway. And where one sister's return might just be the beginning of the crime.

"Walkers second thriller (following All Is Not Forgotten, 2016) delves into dark territory, pitting a fully dimensional cast of clever, damaged characters against each other in high-stakes mind games." —*Booklist*

Wall, Cara

The **dearly** beloved: a novel. Cara Wall. Simon & Schuster, 2019. 342 pages
ISBN 9781982104528
1. Clergy 2. Husband and wife 3. Individual differences 4. Social change 5. Faith (Christianity) 6. Greenwich Village, New York City 7. New York City 8. 20th century 9. Historical fiction 10. Literary fiction
LC 2019000251

In a novel that spans decades, two young couples' lives become intertwined when the husbands are appointed co-ministers of a venerable New York City church in the 1960s.

Wallace, Carol

Our kind of people. Carol Wallace. G.P. Putnam's Sons, 2022. 368 p.
ISBN 9780525540021
1. Wealth 2. Social status 3. Socialites 4. Married people 5. Default (Finance) 6. New York City 7. Gilded Age (1865-1898) 8. Historical fiction
LC 2021040575

Among New York City's Gilded Age elite, one family will defy convention.

"Wallace does full justice to the era's conventions, and her characters' attempts to navigate meteoric social and technological change are recognizably and deliciously modern. Fans of Daisy Goodwin and Curtis Sittenfeld will relish this." —*Publishers Weekly*

Wallace, Daniel

★ **Big** fish: a novel of mythic proportions. Daniel Wallace. Algonquin Books Of Chapel Hill, 1998. 180 p.
ISBN 9781565122178
1. Father and adult son 2. Family storytelling 3. Eccentrics and eccentricities 4. Men with terminal illnesses 5. Joking relationships 6. Alabama 7. Picaresque fiction 8. Books to movies

LC 9826216

When his attempts to get to know his dying father fail, William Bloom makes up stories that recreate his father's life in heroic proportions.

"In a plainspoken style dotted with transcendent passages, Wallace mixes the mundane and the mythical. His chapters have the transformative quality of fable and fairy tale, and the novel's roomy structure allows the mystery and lyricism of the story to coalesce." —*Publishers Weekly*

Wallace, David Foster

★ **Brief** interviews with hideous men. David Foster Wallace. Little, Brown, 1999. 273 p.
ISBN 9780316925419
1. Man-woman relationships 2. Men — Sexuality 3. Sexuality 4. Short stories 5. Literary fiction 6. Books to movies
LC 9850944
New York Times Notable Book, 1999

Twenty-two stories tell of a frightened boy frozen on a diving board, a depressed woman trying to find help, and a group of men who try to rationalize their relationships with women
23 short stories.

★ **Infinite** jest: a novel. David Foster Wallace. Little, Brown, 1996. Xv, 1079 p.
ISBN 9780316920049
1. Ataturk, Kemal 2. Addiction 3. Pleasure 4. Fathers — Suicide 5. Dysfunctional families 6. Boston, Massachusetts 7. Quebec (Province) 8. Satirical fiction
LC 2006934927

The story of an intelligent but zany dysfunctional family is set in a drug-and-alcohol addicts' halfway house and a tennis academy and follows such themes as heartbreak, philosophy, and advertising BT

"This novel is set sometime in the next century, on the grounds of a New England tennis academy and in a rehab clinic. Among other things, the book contains perhaps the most moving and hypnotic writing on the psychology of addiction and recovery to be found in modern fiction. There are obsessive riffs on sports, on drugs, and on the hidden horrors of entertainment: the title of the novel refers to the title of a movie that is said to be so 'terminally compelling' that viewers will watch it passively and repeatedly to the point of death. Comparisons with Pynchon are inevitable, and in this case they are fully justified." —*The New Yorker*

Oblivion: stories. David Foster Wallace. Little, Brown, 2004. 384 p.
ISBN 9780316919814
1. Self-consciousness 2. Interpersonal relations 3. Short stories
LC 2003027135
New York Times Notable Book, 2004

A collection of short stories includes "The Soul Is Not a Smithy," in which a father distracts his son from noticing a teacher's breakdown; and "The Suffering Channel," in which a sculpture artist's profile is influenced by office politics.

"Unpacking our inner lives with empathy and care, Oblivion showcases the incredibly rich textures and crystalline clarity of Wallace's prose, confirming the singular genius of his expansive imagination and resonating with the complexities of minds in motion." —*American Book Review*
8 short stories

★ The **pale** king: an unfinished novel. David Foster Wallace. Little, Brown and Co, 2011. 432 p.
ISBN 9780316074230
1. Boredom 2. Meaning (Psychology) 3. Happiness 4. Interpersonal relations 5. Occupations 6. Illinois 7. Satirical fiction 8. Literary fiction

LC 2010045489

New York Times Notable Book, 2011; Library Journal Best Books, 2011; Pulitzer Prize for Fiction finalist, 2012

Partially written before his death, author David Foster Wallace presents a fictitious version of himself as the protagonist in his final novel. When Wallace arrives for training at the IRS Regional Examination Center in Peoria, Illinois, everything appears normal. However, as Wallace quickly learns, normal just isn't the case. From the bizarre boredom-survival training to the wild personalities among his co-workers, Wallace is convinced the IRS is determined to dehumanize and humiliate him.

Wallace, Lew

★ **Ben-Hur**. By Lew Wallace; edited and with an introduction and notes by David Mayer. Oxford University Press, 1998. 530 p.
ISBN 9780192831996
1. Jesus Christ 2. Jews — History 3. Enslaved people 4. Chariot-racing 5. Revenge 6. Judaea (Region) 7. Palestine 8. Roman Empire (27 BCE-476 CE) 9. 1st century 10. Historical fiction 11. Bible novels 12. Books to movies

Details how a wealthy young Jewish man and his family, who are all experiencing changing fortunes under Roman tyranny, are affected by the life and teachings of a Nazarene named Jesus Christ.

First published 1880.

Includes chronology.

Wallace, Melanie

The **girl** in the garden. Melanie Wallace. Houghton Mifflin Harcourt, 2017. 240 p.
ISBN 9780544784666
1. Abandoned women 2. De Quincey, Thomas 3. Coastal towns 4. Small town life 5. Motels 6. New England 7. 1970s 8. Mainstream fiction

LC 2015043036

Abandoned in a seaside motel and offered shelter in the home of the manager's friend, a young woman with an infant son is integrated into the lives of long-time locals and starts over amid revelations of loves and crimes from the past.

"Wallace's (The Housekeeper, 2006) poignant novel is, at once, a portrait of a small, coastal, New England town; a bit of a mystery; and a completely engaging study of an odd mix of characters whose lives become intricately intertwined." —*Booklist*

Waller, Robert James

★ The **bridges** of Madison County. Robert James Waller. Warner Books, 1992. 171 p.
ISBN 9780446516525
1. Extramarital affairs 2. Lovers 3. Romantic love 4. Photographers 5. Middle-aged women 6. Iowa 7. 1960s 8. Love stories 9. Books to movies 10. Mainstream fiction

LC 91050416

Book Sense Book of the Year Adult Trade, 1993

A novel about the profound love between a photographer and an Iowa farmer's wife. They spend only four days together while he is on location to photograph covered bridges for National Geographic magazine, yet they never lose their feelings for each other.

"An erotic, bittersweet tale of lingering memories and forsaken possibilities." —*Publishers Weekly*

Sequel: A thousand country roads.

Walls, Jeannette

The **silver** star: a novel. Jeannette Walls. Scribner, 2013. 288 p.
ISBN 9781451661507
1. Mother-deserted children 2. Sisters 3. Self-discovery in teenagers 4. Small towns 5. Mothers and daughters 6. Virginia 7. 1970s 8. Coming-of-age stories 9. Mainstream fiction 10. Adult books for young adults

LC 2012050790

School Library Journal Best Books: Best Adult Books 4 Teens, 2013

Abandoned by their artist mother at the age of 12, Bean and her older sister, Liz, are sent to live in the decaying antebellum mansion of their widowed uncle, where they learn the truth about their parents and take odd jobs to earn extra money before an increasingly withdrawn Liz has a life-shattering experience.

"[A] captivating, read-in-one-sitting, coming-of-age adventure." —*Booklist*

First published: Great Britain: Simon & Schuster UK Ltd, 2013.

Walschots, Natalie Zina

Hench: a novel. 2020. William Morrow, 2020. 403 p.
ISBN 9780062978578
1. Supervillains 2. Superheroes 3. Office workers 4. Data processing 5. Wounds and injuries 6. Superhero stories 7. Canadian fiction

RUSA Reading List Short List, 2021

Temping for people on the wrong side of the law, Anna becomes unfairly unemployed before using her talents for manipulating data to expose how the heroes of her world do more harm than good.

"Evocative prose, acerbic wit, and patient yet propulsive pacing complement Walschots' sophisticated plot, which juxtaposes philosophic profundity with brutal, meticulously choreographed action. Boldly drawn characters of sundry ethnicities, sexualities, and gender identities engage in realistically complex relationships that evolve (and devolve) over the course of the tale, illustrating the relativity of good and evil, the corrupting influence of power, and the necrotic nature of revenge." —*Kirkus*

Walser, Robert

The **assistant**. Robert Walser; translated from the German by Susan Bernofsky; with an afterword by the translator. New Directions, 2007. 320 p.
ISBN 9780811215909
1. Coworkers 2. Business partners 3. Inventors 4. Interpersonal relations 5. Helpfulness in men 6. Psychological fiction 7. Translations

LC 2007006865

Joseph, hired to become an inventor's new assistant, arrives one rainy Monday morning at Technical Engineer Karl Tobler's splendid hilltop villa: he is at once pleased and terribly worried, a state soon followed by even stickier psychological complexities. He enjoys the beautiful view over Lake Zurich, in the company of the proud wife, Frau Tobler, and the delicious savory meals. But does he deserve any of these pleasures?

Originally published in 1908.

Walsh, M. O.

★ The **big** door prize: a novel. M.O. Walsh. G.P. Putnam's Sons, 2020. 370 pages
ISBN 9780735218482
1. Self-fulfillment 2. Purpose in life 3. Husband and wife 4. Ambition 5. Life change events 6. Louisiana 7. Southern fiction 8. Relationship fiction

LC 2020010820

When an unassuming DNA machine is installed at their local grocery store, Douglas and his wife, Cherilyn, are swept up by their community's efforts to transform lives by reconnecting with their ancestry.

"It's hard to believe that Walsh (My Sunshine Away, 2015) wrote this moving novel long before the COVID-19 pandemic, for there is eerie prescience in its soulful message that gratitude and grace are not to be taken for granted and that life can be upended in an instant." —*Booklist*

Walsh, S. Kirk

The **elephant** of Belfast: a novel. S. Kirk Walsh. Counterpoint, 2021. 336 p.
ISBN 9781640094000
1. Zoo keepers 2. Elephants 3. World War II home front 4. War and society 5. Determination in women 6. Belfast, Northern Ireland 7. Northern Ireland 8. Second World War era (1939-1945) 9. Historical fiction

In a story inspired by true events, a young woman zookeeper is compelled to protect an elephant during the German blitz of Belfast during World War II.

"Overall, fans of WWII fiction and historical fiction will enjoy this fresh take on the era, and it is recommended for all collections." —*Booklist*

Walters, Minette

The **last** hours: a novel. Minette Walters. MIRA 2018. 608 p. (Last hours, 1)
ISBN 9780778369318
1. Civilization, Medieval 2. Black death 3. Plague 4. Women rulers 5. Independence in women 6. England 7. Medieval period (476-1492) 8. Historical fiction 9. Australian fiction

When the Black Death enters England in June of 1348, Lady Anne decides to quarantine her estate of Develish, including two hundred bonded serfs she must bring inside the walls. But with this sudden overturning of the accepted social order, where serfs exist only to serve their lords, conflicts soon arise and a dreadful event threatens the safety of everyone inside the walls.

Originally published: Sydney : Allen & Unwin, 2017.

Walton, Dawnie

★ The **final** revival of Opal & Nev. Dawnie Walton. 37 Ink/Simon & Schuster, 2021. 368 p.
ISBN 9781982140168
1. Women rock musicians 2. Rock musicians 3. African American women 4. Secrets 5. Social advocates 6. New York City 7. New York (State) 8. 1970s 9. 2010s 10. African American fiction 11. Literary fiction

LC 2020046657
Accepting a contract from a fledgling record company, a talented music artist in early 1970s New York endures racist responses to her activism, before a reunion interview decades later reveals explosive secrets.

"An intelligently executed love letter to Black female empowerment and the world of rock music." —*Kirkus*

Walton, Jo

★ **Lent**. By Jo Walton. Tor Book, 2019. 320 p.
ISBN 9780765379061
1. Savonarola, Girolamo 2. Priests 3. Demons 4. Prophecy 5. God (Christianity) 6. Spirituality 7. Florence, Italy 8. Italy 9. Renaissance (1300-1600) 10. Historical fantasy

LC 2019006678
Possessing the supernatural ability to see and cast out demons, Girolamo Savanarola of 15th-century Florence organizes seemingly miraculous peace initiatives and delivers soul-transforming sermons before enthralled crowds, inciting the wrath of the pope.

A Tom Doherty Associates Book.

★ **Necessity**. Jo Walton. Tor, 2016. 320 p. (Just city novels, 3)
ISBN 9780765379023
1. Gods and goddesses, Greek 2. Fathers and daughters 3. Social conflict 4. Voyages and travels 5. Civilization, Ancient 6. Thera (Islands) 7. Ancient Greece 8. Mythological fiction 9. Science fiction 10. Multiple perspectives 11. Adult books for young adults

The conclusion to The Just City and The Philosopher Kings."

"As before, Walton has done a superb job of world building and character development, giving readers a novel that both stimulates and satisfies." —*Booklist*

Or what you will. Jo Walton. Tor Books, 2020. 320 pages
ISBN 9781250308993
1. Women authors 2. Characters and characteristics in literature 3. Sick women 4. Heroes and heroines 5. Writing 6. Florence, Italy 7. Canadian fiction 8. Metafiction 9. Contemporary fantasy

A fictional hero who has assumed the roles of gods, warriors, scholars and lovers in award-winning novels discovers that his author is dying and orchestrates a daring plan to catapult writer and character into immortality.

"Hugo and Nebula Award?winner Walton (Among Others) brilliantly braids somber realism, fanciful metafiction, and Shakespearean-influenced fantasy into a moving paean to the power of storytelling." —*Publishers Weekly*

Wambaugh, Joseph

The **new** centurions. Joseph Wambaugh. Dell, 1987. 358 p.
ISBN 9780440164173
1. Police 2. Crime 3. Criminals 4. Justice 5. Los Angeles, California 6. 1960s 7. Thrillers and suspense 8. Police procedurals

Depicts the brutal experiences and rigorous training endured by three Los Angeles policemen.

"The author shows us the excitement, danger and sordidness found in the daily work of three young Los Angeles policemen. From the police academy to the first foot patrol, from the first patrol-car duty to the first promotion, Wambaugh follows his three main characters in their professional and personal lives, and shows us that police work, like the ministry, medicine or the military, is a profession demanding 24-hour dedication, determination, discipline and often a frustrating acceptance of defeat." —*The National Review*

Wang, Kathy

Family trust: a novel. Kathy Wang. William Morrow, 2018. 400 p.
ISBN 9780062855251
1. Chinese Americans 2. Rich families 3. Inheritance and succession 4. Ambition 5. Sick men 6. Silicon Valley, California 7. California 8. 21st century 9. Domestic fiction

LC 2018029406
Struggling to fulfill a terminally ill father's final bequest, a privileged Chinese-American family in Silicon Valley is forced to contend with the realities of their ambitions and actual desires.

Impostor syndrome: a novel. Kathy Wang. Custom House, 2021. 384 p.
ISBN 9780062855282

1. Corporations 2. Children of immigrants 3. Spies 4. Business intelligence 5. Assimilation (Sociology) 6. Silicon Valley, California 7. Satirical fiction 8. Thrillers and suspense

LC 2021006379

This Silicon Valley satire follows Alice, a first generation Chinese American who discovers suspicious activity in her company's servers that violate their privacy policies and may lead back to the chief operating officer.

"Wang (Family Trust) leavens this glossy tale of corporate espionage with savvy takes on cultural assimilation in contemporary America." —*Publishers Weekly*

Ward, Catriona

The **last** house on Needless Street. Catriona Ward. Nightfire, 2021. 352 p.
ISBN 9781250812629
1. Abandoned houses 2. Neighbors 3. Recluses 4. Memory 5. Amnesia 6. Horror 7. Psychological suspense 8. Multiple perspectives

LC 2021028494

LibraryReads Favorites, 2021

When a neighbor moves in next door, a family of three—a teenage girl who isn't allowed outside, a man with memory loss and a house cat who reads the bible—are terrified that the unspeakable secret that binds them together will be exposed.

"Recommended for anyone interested in horror with well-realized characters and a claustrophobic, intense setting." —*Booklist*

A Tom Doherty Associates book.

Ward, Jesmyn

★ **Sing**, unburied, sing. Jesmyn Ward. Scribner, 2017. 288 p.
ISBN 9781501126062
1. Multiracial children 2. Extended families 3. Automobile travel 4. Women drug abusers 5. Former convicts 6. Mississippi 7. Gulf Coast, Mississippi 8. Literary fiction 9. Southern fiction 10. Multiple perspectives
ALA Notable Book, 2018; Indies' Choice Book Awards, Adult Fiction, 2018; Librarians' Choice (Australia), 2017; National Book Award for Fiction, 2017; New York Times Notable Book, 2017; Finalist for the Hurston/Wright Legacy Awards for Fiction, 2018; Kirkus Prize for Fiction finalist, 2017; Andrew Carnegie Medal for Excellence in Fiction finalist, 2018; Shortlisted for The Women's Prize for Fiction, 2018; National Book Critics Circle Award for Fiction finalist, 2017; Pen/Faulkner Award Finalist, 2018

A story of how the past affects the present, and of deeply entrenched racism, Sing Unburied Sing describes the life of a biracial boy, his addicted, grieving black mother, and his incarcerated white father. A road trip to Dad's prison kick-starts the novel, which offers deeply affecting characters, a strong sense of place (rural Mississippi), and a touch of magical realism in appearances by the dead.

"Lyrical yet tough, Ward's distilled language effectively captures the hard lives, fraught relationships, and spiritual depth of her characters." —*Library Journal*

Ware, Ruth

The **death** of Mrs. Westaway. Ruth Ware. Gallery/Scout Press, 2018. 384 pages
ISBN 9781501156212
1. Inheritance and succession 2. False personation 3. Young women 4. Wills 5. Tarot 6. Brighton, England 7. Penzance, England 8.

Psychological suspense 9. Gothic fiction 10. Adult books for young adults

LC 2018004355

Loan Stars Favourites, 2018; LibraryReads Favorites, 2018; Librarians' Choice (Australia), 2018

Harriet Westaway—better known as Hal—makes ends meet as a tarot reader, but she doesn't believe in the power of her trade. On a day that begins like any other, she receives a mysterious and unexpected letter bequeathing her a substantial inheritance. She realizes quickly that the letter was sent to the wrong person—but she also knows that she can use her cold-reading skills to potentially claim the money. Hal attends the funeral of the deceased and meets the family... but it dawns on her that there is something very, very wrong about this strange situation and the inheritance at the center of it.

In a dark, dark wood. By Ruth Ware. Scout Press, 2015. 310 p.
ISBN 9781501112317
1. Women authors 2. Female friendship 3. Hospital patients 4. Recluses 5. Country homes 6. England 7. Psychological suspense

LC 2015005077

LibraryReads Favorites, 2015; Romantic Times Reviewer's Choice Award, 2015

Reluctantly accepting an old friend's invitation to spend a weekend on the English countryside, reclusive writer Leonora awakens in a hospital badly injured, unable to recall what happened and confronting a growing certainty that someone involved has died.

The **lying** game. Ruth Ware. Gallery Books, 2017. 320 p.
ISBN 9781501156007
1. Dishonesty 2. Consequences 3. Boarding school students 4. Dead 5. Cliques 6. Great Britain 7. England 8. Psychological suspense
LibraryReads Favorites, 2017; Loan Stars Favourites, 2017

On a cool June morning, a woman walking her dog in the idyllic coastal village of Salten finds something sinister in the water. The next day, three women—Fatima, Thea, and Isabel—receive the text they had always hoped would never come, from the fourth in their former clique, Kate. The four girls were inseparable best friends at the boarding school in Salten who loved playing the Lying Game, telling lies at every turn. But their game had consequences, and the girls were all expelled in their final year of school under mysterious circumstances surrounding the death of a teacher.

"Alternating between the past and present, Ware builds up a rock-solid cast of intriguing characters and spins a mystery that will keep readers turning pages to the end." —*Publishers Weekly*

Four friends. One promise. But someone isn't telling the truth"—Cover.

★ **One** by one. Ruth Ware. Scout Press, 2020. 352 pages
ISBN 9781501188817
1. Ski resorts 2. Avalanches 3. Deception 4. Coworkers 5. Disagreement 6. French Alps 7. Thrillers and suspense 8. Adaptations, retellings, and spin-offs

LC 2020008544

When an offsite company retreat is upended by an avalanche that strands them in a remote mountain chalet, eight coworkers are forced to set aside their corporate rankings and mutual distrust in order to survive.

This is And Then There Were None rendered for the twenty-first century, and David Baldacci is spot-on in calling Ware 'The Agatha Christie of our generation.' Booklist

★ The **turn** of the key. Ruth Ware. Scout Press, 2019. 352 pages
ISBN 9781501188770
1. Nannies 2. Technology 3. Child murder victims 4. Women murder suspects 5. Women prisoners 6. Highlands, Scotland 7. Scotland 8. 21st

century 9. Gothic fiction 10. Psychological suspense 11. Epistolary novels

LC 2019021733

Loan Stars Favourites, 2019

When a high-paying nanny job at a luxurious Scottish Highlands home ends with her imprisonment for a child's murder, a young woman struggles to explain to her lawyer the unravelling events that led to her incarceration.

"Ware's [Henry] James-like embroidery of the strange and sinister produces a Turn of the Screw with cellphones and Teslas that will enthrall today's readers." —*Booklist*

The **woman** in cabin ten. Ruth Ware. Gallery, 2016. 288 p.
ISBN 9781501132933
1. Journalists 2. Pleasure cruises 3. Murder witnesses 4. Murder 5. Missing persons 6. North Sea 7. Psychological suspense
LibraryReads Favorites, 2016

Assigned to review an exclusive North Sea luxury cruise, travel journalist Lo Blacklock witnesses a woman being thrown overboard and is baffled when all passengers remain unruffled and accounted for, a nightmare that unravels as Lo struggles to convince everyone that what she saw was real.

"Ware's follow-up to her best-selling debut, In a Dark, Dark Wood, is a gripping maritime psychological thriller that will keep readers spellbound. The intense final chapters just might induce heart palpitations." —*Library Journal*

Warren, Robert Penn

All the king's men. Robert Penn Warren. Harcourt, 2005. 661 p.
ISBN 9780151011636
1. Political corruption 2. Journalists 3. Politicians 4. Personal conduct 5. Race relations 6. Southern States 7. 1930s 8. Literary fiction 9. Political fiction 10. Modern classics

LC 2005004239

Pulitzer Prize for Fiction, 1947

Louisiana governor Willie Stark's obsession with political power leads to the ultimate corruption of his gubernatorial administration, in the story of the rise and fall of a Southern politician and demagogue in the 1930s.

Originally published: New York : Harcourt, Brace, 1946.

Band of angels. Robert Penn Warren. Louisiana State University Press, 1994. 375 p.
ISBN 9780807119464
1. Multiracial women 2. Identity (Psychology) 3. Freedom 4. Slavery 5. Multiracial persons — Identity 6. Kentucky 7. New Orleans, Louisiana 8. American Civil War era (1861-1865) 9. Historical fiction 10. First person narratives 11. Southern fiction

LC 94213598

Returning to Kentucky upon her father's sudden death, sixteen-year-old Amantha Starr learns that she is to be sold into slavery to appease her father's creditors BT

Originally published: New York : Random House, 1955.

World enough and time: a romantic novel. Robert Penn Warren. Louisiana State University Press, 1999. 465 p.
ISBN 9780807124789
1. Married people 2. Betrayal 3. Love triangles 4. Frontier and pioneer life 5. Murder 6. Kentucky 7. 1820s 8. 19th century 9. Historical fiction 10. Literary fiction 11. Southern fiction

LC 99015675

Jeremiah Beaumont, accused of murder, tries to justify the murder before he repents of it.

Originally published: New York : Random House, 1950.

Warren, Susan May

Rescue me. Susan May Warren. Baker Pub Group 2017. 336 p. (Montana rescue, 2)
ISBN 9780800727444
1. Search and rescue operations 2. Small towns 3. Sisters 4. Rescues 5. Montana 6. Christian romantic suspense

LC 2016036310

Deputy Sam Brooks, a member of the PEAK rescue team, faces a life-and-death situation, causing him to spill his heart to his girlfriend. Except the room was dark and it was actually Sierra's sister, flower child Willow, he talked to...and kissed. Willow, who's hoping to be named her church's youth pastor, has loved Sam for years, but wants her sister to be happy, and they agree to never mention what happened. But when the two of them lead a youth group trip in Glacier National Park, disaster strikes and they must work together to save themselves and the teens in their care—and they might just find a way to understand their feelings for each other. Buckle up for outdoor adventures, suspense, and a fast-paced plot.

Washington, Bryan

Lot: stories. Bryan Washington. Riverhead Books, 2019. 240 p.
ISBN 9780525533672
1. Multiracial boys 2. City life 3. Neighborhoods 4. Working class 5. Identity (Psychology) 6. Houston, Texas 7. Short stories 8. Literary fiction 9. King, Martin Luther, 1929-1968 10. Adult books for young adults
Lambda Literary Award for Gay Fiction, 2020; Library Journal Best Books, 2019; New York Times Notable Book, 2019

In the city of Houston—a sprawling, diverse microcosm of America—the son of a black mother and a Latino father is coming of age. He's working at his family's restaurant, weathering his brother's blows, resenting his older sister's absence. And discovering he likes boys.

"Washington debuts with a stellar collection in which he turns his gaze onto Houston, mapping the sprawl of both the city and the relationships within it, especially those between young black and brown boys." —*Publishers Weekly*

★ **Memorial**. Bryan Washington. Riverhead Books, 2020. 320 p.
ISBN 9780593087275
1. Japanese Americans 2. African Americans 3. Gay couples 4. Parent and child 5. Identity (Psychology) 6. Houston, Texas 7. Osaka, Japan 8. Literary fiction 9. Multiple perspectives 10. LGBTQIA fiction
New York Times Notable Book, 2020; National Book Critics Circle Award for Fiction finalist, 2020

A Japanese-American chef and a Black daycare teacher begin reevaluating their stale relationship in the wake of a father's death and the arrival of an acerbic mother-in-law who becomes an unconventional roommate.

"Washington deftly strings together the ordinary moments that make and can break a relationship, resulting in an alternately told heart-on-sleeve narrative probing racial and gay identity, the ties between lovers and between parents and children, and the resonant idea that in the midst of that hot mess called human relationships we just have to figure things out." —*Library Journal*

Wasserman, Robin

Mother daughter widow wife. Robin Wasserman. Scribner, 2020. 288 pages

ISBN 9781982139490

1. Women with amnesia 2. Women — Identity 3. Identity (Psychology) 4. Memory 5. Women — Psychology 6. Literary fiction 7. Multiple perspectives

Pen/Faulkner Award Finalist, 2021

Left with no memory of who she is, Wendy Doe arrives at the Meadowlark Institute of Memory Research, where she falls under the control of a doctor and his ambitious student, while the daughter she left behind tries to make sense of it all.

"In addition to meditating on personhood and recollection, Wasserman deftly explores power dynamics, ambition, and the lingering scars of trauma. A beautifully written exploration of identity, memory, power, and agency." —*Kirkus*

Waters, Martha

★ **To** have and to hoax: a novel. Martha Waters. Simon & Schuster 2020. 352 p. (Regency vows, 1)

ISBN 9781982136116

1. Husband and wife 2. Marital conflict 3. Deception 4. Misunderstanding 5. Separation (Marital relations) 6. England 7. Regency period (1811-1820) 8. Regency romances 9. Romantic comedies 10. Historical romances

LC 2019031862

After their marriage has become cold and detached, a Lady and Lord in Regency England each fake accidents and illness in an escalating game of manipulation that includes sanitariums, fake affairs and possibly a rekindled flirtation.

"Waters gently lampoons genre tropes without sacrificing genuine feeling. Self-aware and brimming with well-timed epiphanies, this joyful, elegant romp is sure to enchant." —*Publishers Weekly*

To love and to loathe: a novel. Martha Waters. Atria Paperback, 2021. 384 p. (Regency vows, 2)

ISBN 9781982160876

1. Bets 2. Aristocracy 3. Widows 4. Casual sex 5. Competition 6. England 7. Great Britain 8. Regency period (1811-1820) 9. Regency romances 10. Romantic comedies 11. Historical romances

LC 2020035440

LibraryReads Favorites, 2021

To Love and to Loathe is another clever and delightful historical rom-com that is perfect for fans of Christina Lauren and Evie Dunmore.

"In her second superbly entertaining Regency-set historical, following To Have and to Hoax (2020), Waters once again rewards readers with a comically clever love story that blithely blends engaging writing spiked with deliciously dry wit and a beguiling cast of characters." —*Booklist*

Watkins, Claire Vaye

★ **Gold** fame citrus. Claire Vaye Watkins. Riverhead Books, 2015. 352 p.

ISBN 9781594634239

1. Squatters 2. Near future 3. Water supply 4. Cults 5. Surfers 6. Southern California 7. Dystopian fiction 8. Literary fiction

LC 2015013564

In the wake of a devastating Southern California drought, two idealistic holdouts fall in love and scavenge for their needs before taking charge of a mysterious child and embarking on a perilous journey in search of water. —Publisher's description.

"In Margaret Atwood mode, Watkins spikes this fast-moving, high-tension, sexy, ecocrisis saga with caustic parodies and resounding al-

lusions that cohere into a knowing and elegiac tale of scrappy adaptation and epic loss." —*Booklist*

First published: [New York] : Riverhead Books, 2015.

I love you but I've chosen darkness. Claire Vaye Watkins. Riverhead Books, 2021. 320 p.

ISBN 9780593330210

1. Watkins, Claire Vaye 2. Women authors 3. New mothers 4. Married women 5. Postpartum depression 6. Family history 7. Nevada 8. Mojave Desert 9. Literary fiction 10. Autobiographical fiction

LC 2021009728

The furious, hilarious, soul-rending story of one woman's reckoning with marriage, work, sex, and motherhood.

"In her second novel after the speculative Gold Fame Citrus (2015), Watkins' angry, grieving, wild-at-heart narrator shares Watkins' name, home ground, parentage, and literary calling, creating a wily fusion of autobiography and imagination." —*Booklist*

Watson, Brad

Miss Jane: a novel. Brad Watson. W. W. Norton & Co, 2016. 224 p.

ISBN 9780393241730

1. Birth defects 2. Gender role 3. Misfits (Persons) 4. Women and nature 5. Loneliness in women 6. Mississippi 7. Southern gothic 8. Historical fiction 9. Southern fiction

LC 2016011032

Booklist Editors' Choice, 2016

A tale inspired by the story of the author's great-aunt explores the life of a woman in early 20th-century rural Mississippi whose genital birth defect prevents her marriageability as she endures the hardships of farm life, observes the erotic qualities of nature and shares a relationship with a boy who loves but is forced to leave her.

"As Watson arcs through the story of Jane's life in sensitive, beautifully precise prose, we are both absorbed and humbled. Highly recommended." —*Library Journal*

Watson, Martine Fournier

The **dream** peddler. Martine Fournier Watson. Penguin Books, 2019. 336 p.

ISBN 9780143133179

1. Dreams 2. Missing children 3. Loss (Psychology) 4. Sales personnel 5. Grief 6. Psychological fiction

In early 20th-century America, traveling salesman Robert Owens arrives to sell dreams to a rural town rocked by a child's disappearance.

Watson, S. J.

Final cut. S. J. Watson. HarperCollins, 2020. 368 pages

ISBN 9780062382153

1. Documentary filmmakers 2. Missing teenage girls 3. Secrets 4. Villages 5. Coastal towns 6. Northern England 7. England 8. Psychological suspense

Explores themes of memory and identity in the story of a documentary filmmaker who investigates the disappearance of a girl from a quiet fishing village.

"A tight, brisk plot drives this sharp character study. Watson perfectly capture small town ennui while illustrating how corruption can hide in plain sight." —*Publishers Weekly*

Watt, Holly

To the lions. Holly Watt. Dutton, 2019. 400 p.

ISBN 9781524745455

1. Women investigative journalists 2. Hunting 3. International intrigue 4. Undercover operations 5. Journalism 6. North Africa 7. Thrillers and suspense

Ian Fleming Steel Dagger Award, 2019; Loan Stars Favourites, 2019

After she stumbles upon a dark conspiracy having to do with an extreme and secret hunt in North Africa, journalist Casey Benedict is determined to follow the clues, no matter how far it takes her.

Waugh, Evelyn

★ **Brideshead** revisited. Evelyn Waugh; with an introduction by Frank Kermode. A. A. Knopf, 1993. 315 p.

ISBN 9780679423003

1. Gould, William Buelow 2. Catholics 3. Male friendship 4. Man-woman relationships 5. Religion — Social aspects 6. England 7. Great Britain 8. 1920s 9. Literary fiction 10. Modern classics 11. Books to movies

LC 93-1854

Set in 1920's England, the story examines the wealthy Flyte family through the eyes of Sebastian Flyte's less wealthy school friend Charles Ryder, who is eventually tempted into an extramarital affair with Sebastian's sister, Lady Julia. The novel is a story of faith and disillusionment in a glamorous upper-class world.

Originally published: London: Chapman & Hall, 1945.

★ The **complete** stories of Evelyn Waugh. Evelyn Waugh. Little, Brown & Company, 1999. 535 p.

ISBN 9780316925464

1. Manners and customs 2. England 3. Short stories 4. Literary fiction 5. Modern classics

A brilliant collection of thirty-nine stories spans the entire career of the literary master and comic genius, from his earliest character sketches and barbed portraits of the British upper class to Brideshead Revisited and Black Mischief.

"These 39 stories span Waugh's writing career, and to a one they demonstrate his trademark wit and sophistication." —*Booklist*

Decline and fall. Evelyn Waugh. Back Bay Books, 1999. 293 p. : Illustration

ISBN 9780316926072

1. Young men 2. Upper class 3. Manners and customs 4. Misadventures 5. Boarding schools 6. England 7. Satirical fiction 8. Modern classics

Sent down from Oxford in outrageous circumstances, Paul Pennyfeather is oddly unsurprised to find himself qualifying for the position of schoolmaster at Llanabba Castle, where his colleagues turn out to be an assortment of misfits, rascals and fools.

Originally published: London : Chapman & Hall, 1928.

The **loved** one: an Anglo-American tragedy. Evelyn Waugh. Back Bay Books, 1999. 164 p.

ISBN 9780316926089

1. Expatriates 2. Undertakers 3. Film industry and trade 4. Funeral homes 5. Poets, English 6. Hollywood, California 7. Satirical fiction 8. Modern classics 9. Books to movies

Mr. Joyboy, the embalmer at a full-service funeral home for Hollywood's departed greats, and Aimee Thanatogenos, the crematorium cosmetician, find their romance complicated with the appearance of a young English poet.

Originally published: Boston : Little, Brown, 1948.

★ **Vile** bodies. Evelyn Waugh. Back Bay Books, 1999. 321 p.

ISBN 9780316926119

1. Young men 2. Socialites 3. Rich people 4. Parties 5. Man-woman relationships 6. England 7. London, England 8. 1920s 9. Satirical fiction 10. Modern classics

The comic aspects of London society during the thirties are presented in Waugh's early novel.

Originally published: Boston : Little, Brown, 1930.

Waxman, Abbi

The **bookish** life of Nina Hill. Abbi Waxman. Berkley, 2019. 320 p.

ISBN 9780451491879

1. Women — Family relationships 2. Life change events 3. Introverts 4. Families 5. Bookstores 6. Southern California 7. California 8. Chick lit 9. Relationship fiction

LC 2018057848

LibraryReads Favorites, 2019; Loan Stars Favourites, 2019

A confirmed introvert finds her simple life upended when the father she never knew passes away, revealing an enormous extended family that overwhelms her budding relationship with a fellow trivia buff.

Wayne, Teddy

Apartment: a novel. Teddy Wayne. Bloomsbury Publishing, 2020. 240 p.

ISBN 9781635574005

1. Male friendship 2. Apartments 3. Social isolation 4. Authors 5. Insecurity (Psychology) 6. New York City 7. 1990s 8. Literary fiction 9. Satirical fiction 10. First person narratives

LC 2019024893

A man who offers a rent-free spare bedroom in his illegal sublet of a rent-stabilized NYC apartment to a working-class, Midwestern student on scholarship at Columbia develop a friendship that eventually clashes over politics, socioeconomic identity and privilege in 1996.

"A near-anthropological study of male insecurity." —*Kirkus*

Weatherspoon, Rebekah

A **cowboy** to remember. Rebekah Weatherspoon. Dafina, 2020. 320 pages (Cowboys of California, 1)

ISBN 9781496725400

1. Cowboys 2. Women cooks 3. Amnesia 4. Dude ranches 5. Former rodeo performers 6. Contemporary romances 7. Western romances 8. Multicultural romances

When an accident leaves her with no memory, chef Evie Buchanan gets her own happily-ever-after when former rodeo champion Zach Pleasant walks into her hospital and awakens feelings long dormant.

"The amnesia trope gets a pop culture-infused update in this second-chance romance featuring reality-star chefs, ranch resorts, Instagram feuds, and Hollywood royalty." —*Publishers Weekly*

If the boot fits. Rebekah Weatherspoon. Dafina, 2020. 320 p. (Cowboys of California, 2)

ISBN 9781496725417

1. Actors and actresses 2. Personal assistants 3. One night stands (Interpersonal relations) 4. Cowboys 5. Ranches 6. California 7. Western romances 8. Contemporary romances 9. African American fiction

Determined to sell her screenplay and gain independence from her boss, one of Hollywood's cruelest divas, Amanda Queen decides to have a one-night stand with an Oscar-winning actor, which gives her an unexpected chance to turn that magical night into forever.

"Although her vindictive boss has damaged her confidence and belief in herself, Amanda is surrounded by supportive friends and a steady, sexy, and respectful love interest in Sam. The sexual tension and flirty banter between the two will have readers rooting them on and anticipating Dru's comeuppance. Another winner from rising star Weatherspoon." —*Library Journal*

Rafe: a buff male nanny. Rebekah Weatherspoon. Rebekah Weatherspoon, 2018. 252 p; (Loose ends, 1)
ISBN 9781724106506
1. Divorced women 2. Single mothers 3. Nannies 4. Women physicians 5. African American women 6. California 7. Los Angeles, California 8. Contemporary romances 9. Multicultural romances

After a nasty divorce and a thousand mile move, Dr. Sloan Copeland and her twin daughters are adjusting to their new life in Los Angeles. When their live-in nanny suddenly quits, Sloan is left scrambling to find a competent replacement. Enter Rafe Whitcomb. He's good with the girls, not to mention good-natured and a whiz in the kitchen. He's also tall, handsome, bearded, ripped, and tatted...Sloan and Rafe quickly find themselves succumbing to a heady mutual attraction neither of them wants to deny.

A **thorn** in the saddle. Rebekah Weatherspoon. Dafina, 2021. 320 p. (Cowboys of California, 3)
ISBN 9781496725424
1. African Americans 2. Cowboys 3. Ranchers 4. Women consultants 5. Personal conduct 6. California 7. Western romances 8. Multicultural romances 9. Contemporary romances

When she discovers that big-headed rancher Jesse Pleasant has a softer side during a painfully awkward showing at a community date auction, former tech consultant Lily-Grace Leroux warms to the sparks flying between them, never dreaming that she could have her own happily ever after.

"Jesse's trajectory is more fully realized than Lily-Grace's career struggles, but it's so refreshing to see a romance hero in therapy that many readers won't mind the imbalance. The focus on mental health and emotional support makes this cute western rom-com sing." —*Publishers Weekly*

★ **Xeni:** a marriage of inconvenience. Rebekah Weatherspoon. Rebekah Weatherspoon Presents, 2019. 275 p; (Loose ends, 2)
ISBN 9780578592077
1. Inheritance and succession 2. Musicians 3. African American women 4. Married people 5. Interracial romance 6. Contemporary romances 7. Multicultural romances

When Sable Everly passes away, she leaves her estate to her niece, Xeni Everly-Wilkins, with one condition: Xeni must marry before she can inherit. And Sable had just the groom in mind: her friend, the ruggedly handsome Scotsman Mason McInroy. Neither Mason nor Xeni imagined that Sable would use her dying breaths to play match-maker, trapping them in a marriage scheme that comes with more complications than either of them need. With no choice but to say I do, the unlikely pair try to make the best of a messy situation—with no plans to actually fall in love.

Weaver, Ashley
★ A **peculiar** combination. Ashley Weaver. Minotaur Books, 2021. 304 p. (Electra McDonnell novels, 1)
ISBN 9781250780485
1. World War II 2. Young women 3. Uncle and niece 4. Family businesses 5. Locks and keys 6. London, England 7. Second World War era (1939-1945) 8. Historical mysteries
LC 2020053225

Electra McDonnell has always known that the way she and her family earn their living is slightly outside of the law. Breaking into the homes of the rich and picking the locks on their safes may not be condoned by Brit-ish law enforcement, but World War II is in full swing, and Uncle Mick's more honorable business as a locksmith can't pay the bills any more. After Ellie and Mick are caught following a tip about a safe full of jewels, Ellie expects them to be taken straight to prison. Instead, they are delivered to a large townhouse, where government official Major Ramsey is waiting with an offer: either Ellie agrees to help him break into a safe and retrieve blueprints that will be critical to the British war effort, before they can be delivered to a German spy, or he turns her over to the police.

"Louisiana librarian Weaver (Murder at Brightwell) launches an engaging new series that sparkles. Infused with witty romantic conflict, this historical mystery with convincing period details concludes with enticing story threads for future entries." —*Library Journal*

Webb, Brandon
★ **Steel** fear. . Bantam Dell Pub Group, 2021. 448 pages (Finn novels, 1)
ISBN 9780593356289
1. Aircraft carriers 2. Navy SEALs 3. Snipers 4. Serial murderers 5. Men with amnesia 6. Techno-thrillers

Discovering that there is a serial killer onboard the U.S.S. Abraham Lincoln, disgraced Navy SEAL sniper Finn finds suspicion falling on him as a newcomer and must expose the real killer while searching for redemption.

"Former SEAL Webb and coauthor Mann (they've paired on several best-selling nonfiction books) hit all the right notes in their fiction debut, which blends the high-tech trappings of a military thriller with the crushing claustrophobia of a locked-room mystery (if that locked room was home to more than 5,000 people, along with 90 aircraft and a handful of nuclear reactors)." —*Booklist*

Wecker, Helene
The **golem** and the jinni. Helene Wecker. Harper, 2013. 486 p. (Golem and the jinni, 1)
ISBN 9780062110831
1. Golem 2. Genies 3. Magicians 4. Immigrants 5. Power (Social sciences) 6. New York City 7. Gilded Age (1865-1898) 8. 1890s 9. Historical fantasy 10. Middle Eastern-influenced fantasy
Mythopoeic Award for Adult Literature, 2014

After her creator dies en route to America, Chava, a golem from a Polish shtetl, must navigate the streets of 1899 New York City by herself—her only ally is a rabbi unsure whether to destroy her, or allow her to fulfill her destiny as the harbinger of destruction. Ahmad, a jinni from Syria's deserts has been released from his thousand-year-old glass bottle by a tinsmith but has little intention of remaining a metalworker, despite his uncanny talent for it. Chava and Ahmad meet and discover that they're soul mates, but a dangerous adversary threatens their future. This vibrant blend of myth, adventure, and romance will enchant fans of stories based on folklore.

★ The **hidden** palace. Helene Wecker. HarperCollins, 2021. 448 p. (Golem and the jinni, 2)
ISBN 9780062468710
1. Golem 2. Genies 3. Immigrants 4. Mythical creatures 5. Consequences 6. New York City 7. Middle East 8. 20th century 9. Historical fantasy 10. Middle Eastern-influenced fantasy

Pretending to be human, magical beings Chava, a golem, and Ahmad, a jinni, find their lives intertwined as they try to make sense of the world around them and the people whose lives they have unwittingly affected.

"Whereas the first installment was a propulsive battle of good versus evil, this delightful entry is more serialized storytelling la Dickens. Throughout, Wecker pulls off an impressive juggling act with the many characters, all of whom are well positioned for another sequel." —*Publishers Weekly*

Weiden, David L.

★ **Winter** counts. David Heska Wanbli Weiden. Ecco Press, 2020. 336 p.

ISBN 9780062968944

1. Enforcers (Criminals) 2. Indian reservations 3. Drug traffic 4. Multiracial men 5. Lakota Indians 6. South Dakota 7. Colorado 8. Crime fiction 9. First person narratives

Anthony Award for Best First Novel, 2021; Macavity Award for Best First Mystery Novel, 2021; Spur Awards, Best Western First Novel, 2021; Spur Awards, Best Western Contemporary Novel, 2021; Thriller Award for Best First Novel, 2021

A vigilante enforcer on South Dakota's Rosebud Indian Reservation enlists the help of an ex to investigate the activities of an expanding drug cartel, while a new tribal council initiative raises controversial questions.

Weinberg, Kate

The **truants**. Kate Weinberg. G. P. Putnam & Sons, 2020. 320 p.
ISBN 9780525541967

1. Christie, Agatha 2. Women college students 3. Women college teachers 4. Creativity 5. Hedonism 6. Obsession 7. England 8. Charlot, Edmond

LC 2019021290

Jess Walker has come to a concrete campus under the flat grey skies of East Anglia for one reason: To be taught by the mesmerizing and rebellious Dr Lorna Clay, whose seminars soon transform Jess' thinking on life, love and Agatha Christie.

"With intrigue sparking throughout, Weinberg's immensely compelling debut novel explores the years-long reverberations of a fractured friend group and echoes Donna Tartt's The Secret History." —*Booklist*
Originally published in Great Britain, 2019.

Weiner, Jennifer

★ **Big** summer. Jennifer Weiner. Atria Books, 2020. 416 pages
ISBN 9781501133510

1. Maid of honor (Weddings) 2. Overweight women 3. Influencers 4. Social media 5. Weddings 6. Cape Cod, Massachusetts 7. Massachusetts 8. Chick lit

LibraryReads Favorites, 2020; Loan Stars Favourites, 2020

A woman confronts the dynamics of friendship and forgiveness while visiting Cape Cod to attend an old friend's increasingly disastrous wedding.

"Weiner's story of female friendships (after Mrs. Everything) mixes a splash of romance, a dash of humor, and a pinch of mystery to create a deliciously bloody poolside cocktail." —*Publishers Weekly*

In her shoes: a novel. Jennifer Weiner. Atria Books, 2002. 424 p.
ISBN 9780743418195

1. Retirement communities 2. Self-fulfillment in women 3. Sibling rivalry 4. Grandmothers 5. Sisters 6. Florida 7. Philadelphia, Pennsylvania 8. Relationship fiction 9. Books to movies

Meet Rose Feller. She's thirty years old and a high-powered attorney with a secret passion for romance novels. She dreams of a man who will slide off her glasses, gaze into her eyes, and tell her that she's beautiful. She also dreams of getting her fantastically screwed-up little sister to get her life together. Meet Rose's sister, Maggie. Twenty-eight years old, drop-dead gorgeous and only occasionally employed.

Little earthquakes. Jennifer Weiner. Atria, 2004. 432 p.

ISBN 9780743470094

1. Pregnant women 2. Infant death 3. Husband and wife 4. Mothers-in-law 5. Mothers and daughters 6. Pennsylvania 7. Philadelphia, Pennsylvania 8. Multiple perspectives 9. Relationship fiction

A chef, an event planner, and a basketball player's wife find their marriages and careers in Philadelphia challenged by new motherhood, difficult schedules, and infidelity.

"This is the story of four women in Philadelphia who bond over pregnancy and motherhood. Becky, Kelly, and Ayinde meet in yoga class, and the three become friends when Ayinde's water breaks one day after class and they take her to the hospital. Becky is a chef with an adoring husband and an annoying mother-in-law; Kelly is frustrated when her husband loses his job and drags his feet looking for another; Ayinde's husband is a famous basketball player whom she suspects of infidelity. What brings the women together is their love for their newborns. The fourth woman, Lia, watches the group from afar; she's an actress who walked out on her husband after a devastating tragedy. Weiner seamlessly and gracefully weaves the four women's stories together." —*Booklist*

★ **Mrs.** Everything: a novel. Jennifer Weiner. Atria Books, 2019. 416 pages
ISBN 9781501133480

1. Sisters 2. Family relationships 3. Identity (Psychology) 4. Jewish families 5. Women's role 6. Michigan 7. Detroit, Michigan 8. 20th century 9. Relationship fiction 10. Historical fiction

LC 2018056036

LibraryReads Favorites, 2019; New York Times Notable Book, 2019

Two sisters struggle to find their place, be true to themselves and adapt to rapid changes happening throughout the latter half of 20th-century America.

"It's been a while since Weiner explored the complicated terrain of sisterhood, and readers will flock to this ambitious, nearly flawless novel." —*Booklist*

Weinstein, Alexander

Children of the new world: stories. Alexander Weinstein. Picador, 2016. 272 p.
ISBN 9781250098993

1. Social media 2. Memories 3. Virtual reality 4. Robots 5. Artificial intelligence 6. Science fiction 7. Short stories

LC 2016019224

New York Times Notable Book, 2016

A collection of short stories explores the near-future world of social-media implants, immersive virtual reality games, and frighteningly intuitive robots.

"Complete with footnotes from fictional future publications and technology that is just one leap away, this is mind-bending stuff. Weinsteins collection is full of spot-on prose, wicked humor, and heart." —*Publishers Weekly*

Weir, Alison

Anna of Kleve: the princess in the portrait. Alison Weir. Ballantine Books, 2019. 288 p. (Six Tudor queens, 4)
ISBN 9781101966570

1. Anne, of Cleves, Queen, consort of Henry VIII, King of England, 1515-1557 2. Marriages of royalty and nobility 3. Courts and courtiers 4. Germans in Great Britain 5. Marital conflict 6. Nobility 7. Great Britain 8. England 9. Tudor period (1485-1603) 10. Biographical fiction 11. Historical fiction

Arranged in a doomed marriage to England's infamous Henry VIII, a princess from a small German duchy hides a desperate secret in a hostile foreign court.

Katharine Parr, the sixth wife. Alison Weir. Random House Inc 2021. 544 p. (Six Tudor queens, 6)
ISBN 9781101966631
1. Catharine Parr 2. Women rulers 3. Widows 4. Royal houses 5. Heirs and heiresses 6. Courts and courtiers 7. Great Britain 8. England 9. Biographical fiction 10. Historical fiction
LC 2020057085
Author and historian Alison Weir brings her Tudor Queens series to a close with the remarkable story of Katharine Parr, Henry VIII's sixth and final wife, who manages to survive him and remarry, only to be thrown into a romantic intrigue that threatens the very throne of England.

"Weir handles Katharine's relations with her stepchildren with realistic nuance as well as how Henry's death leads Katharine into intense romantic intrigue. This wide-ranging novel expertly showcases Katharine's courageous, eventful life and many noteworthy accomplishments." —*Booklist*

Series complete in six volumes.

Weir, Andy

Artemis. Andy Weir. Crown Publishing, 2017. 384 p.
ISBN 9780553448122
1. Smugglers 2. Near future 3. Conspiracies 4. Space colonies 5. Organized crime 6. Moon 7. Crime fiction 8. Science fiction 9. Hard science fiction 10. Adult books for young adults
Goodreads Choice Award, 2017; Loan Stars Favourites, 2017; LibraryReads Favorites, 2017; Librarians' Choice (Australia), 2017

Augmenting his limited income by smuggling contraband to survive on the moon's wealthy city of Artemis, Jazz agrees to commit what seems to be a perfect, lucrative crime, only to find herself embroiled in a conspiracy for control of the city.

The **Martian**. Andy Weir. Crown Publishers, 2014. 368 p.
ISBN 9780804139021
1. Survival 2. Astronauts 3. Space flight to Mars 4. Extreme environments 5. Planets — Exploration 6. Mars (Planet) 7. Hard science fiction 8. Science fiction 9. Diary novels 10. Adult books for young adults
Alex Award, 2015; Goodreads Choice Award, 2014; Green Mountain Book Award (Vermont), 2016; Indies' Choice Book Awards, Adult Debut, 2015; Library Journal Best Books 2014; LibraryReads Favorites, 2014; RUSA Reading List, 2015; School Library Journal Best Books: Best Adult Books 4 Teens, 2014

Stranded on Mars by a duststorm that compromised his space suit and forced his crew to leave him behind, astronaut Mark Watney struggles to survive in spite of minimal supplies and harsh environmental challenges that test his ingenuity in unique ways.

"[A] tightly constructed and completely believable story of a man's ingenuity and strength in the face of seemingly insurmountable odds." —*Booklist*

This book was adapted into film of the same name in 2015, directed by Ridley Scott, and starring Matt Damon, Jessica Chastain, Jeff Daniels, Kristen Wiig, Chiwetel Ejiofor and Donald Glover.
Originally self-published as an ebook in 2011—Title page verso.

Project Hail Mary. Andy Weir. Ballantine Books, 2021. 496 p.
ISBN 9780593135204
1. Space flight 2. Amnesia 3. Solitude 4. Alliances 5. Astronauts 6. Space 7. Science fiction thrillers 8. Hard science fiction
LibraryReads Favorites Top Ten, 2021; Loan Stars Favourites, 2021

Ryland Grace is the sole survivor on a desperate, last-chance mission—and if he fails, humanity and the earth itself will perish. Except that right now, he doesn't know that. He can't even remember his own name, let alone the nature of his assignment or how to complete it. His crewmates dead, his memories fuzzily returning, he realizes that an impossible task now confronts him. Alone on this tiny ship that's been cobbled together by every government and space agency on the planet and hurled into the depths of space, it's up to him to conquer an extinction-level threat to our species. And thanks to an unexpected ally, he just might have a chance.

"Although hard scientific speculation fuels the storyline, the real power lies in the many jaw-dropping plot twists, the relentless tension, and the extraordinary dynamic between Ryland and the alien (whom he nicknames Rocky because of its carapace of oxidized minerals and metallic alloy bones). Readers may find themselves consuming this emotionally intense and thematically profound novel in one stay-up-all-night-until-your-eyes-bleed sitting." —*Kirkus*

Weiss, Elizabeth

The **sisters** Sweet. Elizabeth Weiss. Dial Press, 2021. 416 p.
ISBN 9781984801548
1. Vaudeville 2. Vaudeville performers 3. Conjoined twins 4. Impersonation 5. Sisters 6. Chicago, Illinois 7. 20th century 8. Historical fiction 9. Coming-of-age stories 10. First person narratives

After her sister exposes the family's fraud and runs away to Hollywood, Harriet, who has only ever known life onstage posing as a conjoined twin in a vaudeville act, begins to form her first relationships outside her family, which forces her to make a difficult decision.

"Harriet's astute and descriptive narration is interspersed with flashbacks of Maude and Lenny's own ill-fated careers in show business. Readers who enjoy bittersweet, coming-of-age stories like Anna Quindlen's Miller's Valley (2016) or The Distance Home by Paula Saunders (2018) will root for Harriet." —*Booklist*

Weiss, Leah

If the creek don't rise: a novel. Leah Weiss. Sourcebooks Landmark, 2017. 320 p.
ISBN 9781492647454
1. Rural life 2. Mountain life 3. Abused women 4. Teachers 5. Abusive men 6. North Carolina 7. Appalachian Region 8. 1970s 9. Southern gothic 10. Southern fiction 11. Relationship fiction
LibraryReads Favorites, 2017

In a North Carolina mountain town filled with moonshine and rotten husbands, Sadie Blue is only the latest girl to face a dead-end future at the mercy of a dangerous drunk. She's been married to Roy Tupkin for fifteen days, and she knows now that she should have listened to the folks who said he was trouble. But when a stranger sweeps in and knocks the world off-kilter for everyone in town, Sadie begins to think there might be more to life than being Roy's wife. As stark and magnificent as Appalachia itself, If the Creek Don't Rise is a bold and beautifully layered debut about a dusty, desperate town finding the inner strength it needs to outrun its demons. The folks of Baines Creek will take you deep into the mountains with heart, honesty, and homegrown grit..

"In this tender but powerful debut, Weiss paints both the bright and the dark in the lives of her fictional Appalachian communitys denizens." —*Publishers Weekly*

Weldon, Fay

The **life** and loves of a she-devil. Fay Weldon. Pantheon Books, 1983. 241 p.

ISBN 9780394539201

1. Anger in women 2. Revenge 3. Homemakers 4. Beauty 5. Mistresses 6. Literary fiction 7. Books to movies

LC 84007070

Humble and unassuming Ruth, long-suffering wife and mother is ditched by her husband and decides to get what she wants—power, money, sex, and revenge.

Book made into a movie called She-devil.

Wellington, David

Positive. David Wellington. HarperCollins, 2015. 416 p.

ISBN 9780062315373

1. Zombies 2. Exiles 3. Post-apocalypse 4. Concentration camps 5. Infection 6. Horror 7. Adult books for young adults

Anyone can be positive. Acclaimed author David Wellington delivers his most ambitious, breakout novel yet a huge zombie novel in the best-selling vein of Guillermo Del Toro and Justin Cronin.

"Like The Walking Dead, the book uses the zombie apocalypse as a backdrop for a gripping story about the shattering of human society—the real villains here aren't the zombies but rather the road pirates, looters, religious cultists, and other groups that have sprung up in the 20 years since the "crisis." Wellington's most ambitious book is also his best, written with a maturity and compassion indicative of a writer who's found the story he was made to tell. Zombie groupies will eat this one up, but it should also be recommended to readers of all epic-scale fantasy, including Justin Cronins best-selling epic vampire novel The Passage (2010)." —*Booklist*

Wells, Benedict

The **end** of loneliness: a novel. Benedict Wells; translated from the German by Charlotte Collins. Penguin Books, 2019. 240 p.

ISBN 9780143134008

1. Grief 2. Orphans 3. Siblings 4. Memories 5. Life change events 6. Germany 7. Translations 8. Literary fiction 9. First person narratives 10. Adult books for young adults

LC 2018033281

Follows the struggles of a directionless young man who, after a childhood overshadowed by the loss of his family, seeks to reconnect with a boarding-school friend and his own literary ambitions

Translation of: Vom Ende der Einsamkeit.

Originally published in German: Diogenes Verlag, Zurich 2016.

Translated from the German.

Wells, H. G.

The **complete** short stories of H. G. Wells. Edited by John Hammond. Phoenix Giant, 1999. 883 p.

ISBN 9780753808726

1. Science fiction 2. Short stories

A fat, heavy volume packed with humour, strangeness, horror and imaginative stimulus. Telegraph (London, UK).

★ The **invisible** man. By H. G. Wells. Signet Classic, 2002. Xvi, 176 p.

ISBN 9780451528520

1. Invisibility 2. Human experimentation in medicine 3. Mad scientist (Concept) 4. Scientists 5. Men with mental illnesses 6. Books to movies 7. Classics 8. Science fiction classics

A scientist who has discovered a way to make himself invisible unleashes his growing madness and frustrations by terrorizing a small town.

First published 1897.

First published by C.A. Pearson, 1897.

★ The **island** of Dr. Moreau. H. G. Wells. Signet Classics, 2005. Vi, 224 p.

ISBN 9780451529893

1. Survival (after airplane accidents, shipwrecks, etc.) 2. Animal experimentation 3. Mad scientist (Concept) 4. Islands 5. Shipwrecks 6. Horror 7. Books to movies 8. Classics

LC 2005008127

The sole survivor of a shipwreck, Edward Prendick, a young naturalist, finds himself stranded on a remote Pacific island run by the sinister Dr. Moreau, a mad scientist intent on creating a strain of beast men.

Includes bibliographical references (p. 223-224).

Originally published: 1896.

★ The **time** machine. H.G. Wells; with a new introduction by Greg Bear. Signet Classic, 2014. Xix, 123 p.

ISBN 9780451470706

1. Time travel 2. Far future 3. Scientists 4. Inventions 5. Class conflict 6. Books to movies 7. Classics 8. Dystopian fiction

LC 2002066963

A classic novel of the future follows the Time Traveller as he hurtles one million years into the future and encounters a world populated by two distinct races, the childlike Eloi and the disgusting Morlocks who prey on the Eloi.

The time machine was closely adapted into a film of the same name in 1960 and loosely adapted into a film of the same name in 2002.

Includes bibliographical references (p. [119]-123).

Originally published: London : Heinemann, 1895. First American edition: New York : H. Holt and company, 1895.

★ The **war** of the worlds. H.G. Wells; introduction by Arthur C. Clarke. Modern Library, 2002. 190 p.

ISBN 9780375759239

1. Aliens (Non-humanoid) — Sightings and encounters 2. Human/alien encounters 3. Martians 4. Life on other planets 5. Space vehicles 6. Earth 7. Books to TV 8. Books to movies 9. Classics

The ultimate tale of Earth's invasion, written by one of the fathers of the science fiction genre. They came from a depleted, dying planet. Their target: the riches of a moist, green Earth. With horrifyingly advanced machines of destruction, they began their inexorable conquest. The war for Earth seemed destined to be...but was it?

War of the Worlds has been loosely adapted into a movies of the same name (1953, 2005), loosely adapted into a television series of the same name (1988), and closely adapted into a movie of the same name (2005).

First serialized in Pearson's Magazine, 1897.

Originally published: London : Heninemann, 1898.

Wells, Martha

All systems red. Martha Wells. Tor, 2017. 144 p. (Murderbot diaries, 1)

ISBN 9780765397539

1. Androids 2. Artificial intelligence 3. Scientists 4. High technology 5. Robots 6. Science fiction 7. First person narratives 8. Adult books for young adults

Alex Award, 2018

As a heartless killing machine, I was a terrible failure," confesses the AI narrator of this fast-paced SF adventure. After hacking its own governor module and overriding its programming, security droid "Murderbot" ends up saving lives instead of ending them—but only because letting all the humans die would interfere with its favorite activity: binge-watching some 35,000 hours' worth of entertainment media. All Systems Red's snarky protagonist and suspenseful, action-packed plot should have readers eagerly anticipating future installments of the Murderbot Diaries.

"Wells gives depth to a rousing but basically familiar action plot by turning it into the vehicle by which SecUnit engages with its own rigorously denied humanity. The creepy panopticon of SecUnits multiple interfaces allows a hybrid first-person/omniscient perspective that contextualizes its experience without ever giving center stage to the humans." —*Publishers Weekly*

Network effect. Martha Wells. Tor.com, 2020. 352 p. (Murderbot diaries, 5)
  ISBN 9781250229861
  1. Androids 2. Artificial intelligence 3. Identity (Psychology) 4. Caring 5. Security consultants 6. Science fiction 7. First person narratives 8. Adult books for young adults
  Hugo Award for Best Novel, 2021; LibraryReads Favorites, 2020; Loan Stars Favourites, 2020; Locus Award for Best Science Fiction Novel, 2021; Nebula Award for Best Novel, 2020
  When Murderbot's human associates are captured and need its help, it must choose between inertia and drastic action, in this first, full-length standalone novel about a sentient murder machine programmed for destruction.
  "It's a welcome expansion of this universe and lays the groundwork for more stories to come in a series that continues to grow and impress." —*Booklist*

Wells, Rebecca
Divine secrets of the Ya-Ya Sisterhood: a novel. Rebecca Wells. Harper Collins, 1996. 400 p. (Ya-Yas, 2)
  ISBN 9780060173289
  1. Forgiveness 2. Mother and adult daughter 3. Small town life 4. Middle-aged women — Friendship 5. Girls — Friendship 6. Louisiana 7. Relationship fiction 8. Multiple perspectives 9. First person narratives
                  LC 964151
  Book Sense Book of the Year Adult Trade, 1999
  When Siddi inadvertently reveals some revealing things about her Southern childhood in a newspaper interview, her mother, Vivi, virtually disowns her. Vivi's lifelong friends, the Ya-Ya's, set in motion a plan to bring the mother and daughter back together using a scrapbook of childhood memories that they ask Vivi to put together.
  "She has written an entertaining and engrossing novel filled with humor and heartbreak." —*Library Journal*
  Sequel to: Little Altars Everywhere.
  Sequel: Ya-Yas in Bloom.

Welsh, Irvine
Dead men's trousers. Irvine Welsh. Melville House, 2019. 419 pages; (Trainspotting, 3)
  ISBN 9781612197555
  1. Human body parts industry and trade 2. Men and success 3. Art 4. Drug addicts 5. Sexuality 6. Edinburgh, Scotland 7. Black humor 8. Multiple perspectives 9. First person narratives
  Somewhat matured, international jet-setter Mark Renton and psychotic artist Frank Begbie accidentally reunite with Sick Boy and Spud in Scotland for one last scheme involving organ harvesting.
  "Raunchy, profane, violent, and frequently hilarious in its epic descriptions of drug and alcohol abuse, the continued saga is remarkable for the way it delivers the anarchic goods to Trainspotting fans while touching on the ultimate obsessions of middle age: death and the purpose of life. The zenith of these books may well be the powerful prequel, Skagboys (2012), and nothing will match the intensity with which Welsh announced himself, but Dead Men's Trousers delivers a strangely life-affirming dose

of dark absurdity, ensuring that, if this is the last we see of these characters, they won't soon be forgotten." —*Booklist*
  Originally published: London : Jonathan Cape, 2018.

Trainspotting. Irvine Welsh. W. W. Norton, 1996. 348 p. (Trainspotting, 1)
  ISBN 9780393314809
  1. Drug addicts 2. Working class 3. Young men 4. Young women 5. Heroin addicts 6. Edinburgh, Scotland 7. Great Britain 8. Black humor 9. Multiple perspectives 10. First person narratives
                  LC 9615044
  The story of a group of working-class junkies in Edinburgh, Rents, Sick Boy, Mother Superior, Swanney, Spuds, and Begbie. Violent, rude, sexually explicit, and very, very black.
  "This novel is set in a working class neighborhood in Edinburgh. Narrator Mark Renton tells the story of young junkies in their 20s living on the dole, fending off adulthood and trying to escape from a world of AIDS, death and national despair." —*The New Republic*
  Sequel: Porno.
  Originally published: London: Secker & Warburg, 1993.

Welsh, Kaite
The **unquiet** heart. Kaite Welsh. Pegasus Crime, 2019. 281 p. (Sarah Gilchrist series, 2)
  ISBN 9781681777498
  1. Women medical students 2. Ambition in women 3. Autopsy 4. College teachers 5. Murder suspects 6. Edinburgh, Scotland 7. Scotland 8. Victorian era (1837-1901) 9. 1890s 10. Historical mysteries
  In this sequel to the acclaimed The Wages of Sin—and once again set in moody fin de siecle Edinburgh—Sarah Gilchrist finds herself trying to prove her fiance's innocence in the midst of his murder trial.
  This excellent mix of historical mystery and romance should be recommended to fans of Deanna Raybourn's Lady Julia Grey's Victorian mysteries. Bookist.

The **wages** of sin. Kaite Welsh. Pegasus Crime, 2017. 290 p. (Sarah Gilchrist series, 1)
  ISBN 9781681773322
  1. Women medical students 2. Pariahs 3. Public hospitals 4. Murder investigation 5. Rape victims 6. Edinburgh, Scotland 7. Scotland 8. Victorian era (1837-1901) 9. Historical mysteries 10. Adult books for young adults
  Despite numerous barriers, Sarah Gilchrist is determined to become a doctor in 1882, the first year the University of Edinburgh admitted women, but is drawn into a murder mystery when a former acquaintance turns up as a corpse in the dissecting room.
  "Welshs deeply feminist novel is an engaging, fast-paced tale full of twists and turns." —*Booklist*

Welty, Eudora
  ★ The **collected** stories of Eudora Welty. Eudora Welty. Harcourt Brace Jovanovich, 1980. Xvi, 622 p.
  ISBN 9780151189946
  1. Southern States 2. Short stories 3. Modern classics 4. Southern fiction
                  LC 80007947
  National Book Award for Fiction finalist, 1981
  All forty-one stories published by the distinguished writer are brought together, displaying her insights into the American South and including her most famous work, "Death of a Traveling Salesman" BT

  ★ **Delta** wedding. Eudora Welty. Harcourt, 1946. 247 p.

ISBN 9781784971670
1. Orphans 2. Weddings 3. Family relationships 4. Girls 5. Cousins 6. Southern States 7. Mississippi 8. 1920s 9. Domestic fiction 10. Modern classics 11. Southern fiction
Set in 1923, on the Mississippi Delta, this story captures the mind and manners of a large aristocratic family.

The **optimist's** daughter. Eudora Welty. Random House, 1972. 180 p.
ISBN 9780394480176
1. Funerals 2. Reunions 3. Young women 4. Families 5. Middle-aged women 6. Mississippi 7. Psychological fiction 8. Domestic fiction 9. Modern classics
LC 76039769
Pulitzer Prize for Fiction, 1973
Laurel Hand is forced to face her Southern past when she returns to Mississippi for her father's funeral.

★ The **ponder** heart. Eudora Welty; drawings by Joe Krush. Harcourt Brace Jovanovich, 1954. 156 p.
ISBN 9780860683650
1. Husband and wife 2. Small town life 3. Rich men 4. Marriage 5. Seventeen-year-old girls 6. Modern classics 7. Southern fiction
Edna Earle, a person of large distinction in Clay County, and the talkative owner of the Beulah Hotel, tells the story of her Uncle Daniel Ponder, a local hero whose over-affection for society compels him to give everything he owns away. The disappearance of Uncle Daniel's second wife, the waifish and willowy Bonnie Dee Peacock, leads to his arrest for murder. The trial, which comprises the second half of the novel, is a masterpiece of courtroom anarchy.

★ The **robber** bridegroom. Eudora Welty; designed and illustrated by Barry Moser. Harcourt Brace Jovanovich, 1987. 134 p. : Illustration; Color
ISBN 9780151783182
1. Thieves 2. Merchants 3. Frontier and pioneer life 4. Mississippi 5. Historical fiction 6. Modern classics 7. Southern Gothic
LC 87021195
This surrealistic tale about a Mississippi planter's family and their encounters with assorted bandits and Indians recaptures the innocence, energy, and easy carelessness of our lost frontier.

Stories, essays & memoir. Eudora Welty. Library of America, 1998. X, 976 p. : Illustration
ISBN 9781883011550
1. Welty, Eudora 2. Authors, American 3. Racism 4. Violence 5. Family reunions 6. Southern States 7. Mississippi 8. Short stories 9. Essays 10. Modern classics
LC 97046691
Gathers all of the short stories, published between 1941 and 1954, by the influential Southern writer, along with two nonfiction pieces from the 1960s and a perennially popular memoir, One Writer's Beginnings, from 1984.
Includes bibliographical references (p. 960-976).

Wendig, Chuck

The **book** of accidents. Chuck Wendig. Del Rey, 2021. 528 p.
ISBN 9780399182136
1. Husband and wife 2. Families 3. Former police 4. Women artists 5. Sons 6. Pennsylvania 7. Horror
Haunted by their tragic pasts, Nate and Maddie Graves move back to their hometown with their son, Oliver, who becomes involved with a strange boy who has a taste for dark magic that puts them at the heart of a battle of good vs. evil.

"A grade-A, weirdly comforting, and familiar stew of domestic drama, slasher horror, and primeval evil." —*Kirkus*

★ **Wanderers:** a novel. Chuck Wendig. Del Rey, 2019. Xii, 782 pages
ISBN 9780399182105
1. Epidemics 2. Sleep walkers 3. Wanderers and wandering 4. Rock musicians 5. Radio personalities 6. Science fiction 7. Apocalyptic fiction
Library Journal Best Books, 2019; LibraryReads Favorites, 2019
When her little sister is afflicted by a bizarre sleepwalking disorder that begins to affect people all across the country, Shana is embroiled in an apocalyptic epidemic involving a decadent rock star, a religious radio host and a disgraced scientist.
"Wendig is clearly wrestling with some of the demons of our time, resulting in a story that is ambitious, bold, and worthy of attention." —*Kirkus*

Werfel, Franz

★ The **forty** days of Musa Dagh. Franz Werfel. Carroll & Graf, 1990. Xviii, 824 p.
ISBN 9780881846683
1. Armenian genocide, 1915-1923 2. Armenians in Turkey — History 3. Persecution 4. Musa Dagh, Defense of, Turkey, 1915 5. Revolutions 6. Turkey 7. Historical fiction 8. Translations
Wealthy Armenian Gabriel Bagradian returns to Syria from Paris in 1915 and becomes caught in the Turkish campaign against the Armenians of Musa Dagh.
Translation of: Vierzig Tage des Musa Dagh.
Originally published: London : Jarrolds, Ltd, 1934.

West, Dorothy

The **wedding**. Dorothy West. Doubleday, 1995. 240 p.
ISBN 9780385471435
1. African American families 2. Weddings 3. African American intellectuals 4. Family relationships 5. Middle class African Americans 6. Martha's Vineyard, Massachusetts 7. 1950s 8. African American fiction 9. Family sagas 10. Adult books for young adults
LC 9427285
School Library Journal Best Books: Best Adult Books 4 Teens, 1995
Shelby Coles' marriage to a white jazz musician sends shockwaves through her upper class African American community on Martha's Vineyard in the 1950s.
"Through the ancestral histories of the Coles family, West...subtly reveals the ways in which color can burden and codify behavior. The author makes her points with a delicate hand, maneuvering with confidence and ease through a sometimes incendiary subject." —*Publishers Weekly*

West, Jessamyn

The **friendly** persuasion. Jessamyn West. Harcourt Brace Jovanovich, 1991. 214 p.
ISBN 9780156336062
1. Quaker families 2. Families 3. Quakers 4. United States Civil War, 1861-1865 5. Indiana 6. United States 7. American Civil War era (1861-1865) 8. Historical fiction 9. War stories 10. Books to movies
LC 91006468
Jess Birdwell, a Quaker with a fondness for fast horses, his wife Eliza, and their children struggle to deal with the turmoil, violence, and challenges of the Civil War in their own way.

West, Kathleen

Minor dramas & other catastrophes. Kathleen West. Berkley, 2020. 377 pages.

ISBN 9780593098400

1. Overprotectiveness in parents 2. Women teachers 3. Obsession 4. High schools 5. Gossiping and gossips 6. Minnesota 7. Literary fiction

Targeted by privileged families for her progressive educational approaches, a beloved teacher discovers unexpected common ground with a meddling parent whose inadvertent encounter with a drama student has had dangerous consequences for her family.

"An excellent, nuanced exploration of the world of high school and the students and adults who live within it." —*Kirkus*

West, Monica

Revival season: a novel. Monica West. Simon & Schuster, 2021. 304 p.

ISBN 9781982133306

1. Baptists 2. Fathers and daughters 3. Small towns 4. Faith 5. African American teenage girls 6. Coming-of-age stories 7. Literary fiction

LC 2020040328

Every summer, fifteen-year-old Miriam Horton and her family pack themselves tight in their old minivan and travel through small southern towns for revival season: the time when Miriam's father—one of the South's most famous preachers—holds massive healing services for people desperate to be cured of ailments and disease. This summer, the revival season doesn't go as planned, and after one service in which Reverend Horton's healing powers are tested like never before, Miriam witnesses a shocking act of violence that shakes her belief in her father—and in her faith.

"West does a fantastic job illuminating the struggles faced by women and girls in the Southern Baptist evangelical movement, and the change in Miriam is palpable and moving." —*Publishers Weekly*

West, Nathanael

Novels and other writings. Nathanael West. Library of America 1997. 829 p.

ISBN 9781883011284

1. Advice columnists 2. Film industry and trade 3. Los Angeles, California 4. Satirical fiction 5. Short stories 6. Letters

The first comprehensive, authoritative edition of the work of America's prince of black humor and social satire includes his most famous novels of the thirties, along with his poetry, essays, plays, film scripts, and letters.

Westheimer, David

★ **Von** Ryan's express. David Westheimer. Doubleday, 1964. 327 p.

ISBN 9780385025478

1. Escapes 2. World War II 3. Prisoners of war, American 4. Italy 5. War stories

LC 63020513

An Air Force colonel unwittingly delivers a group of British and American officers into the hands of the Germans and then plans an escape. Sequel: Von Ryan's return.

Westlake, Donald E.

★ **Bank** shot. Donald E. Westlake. Simon and Schuster, 1972. 224 p. (Dortmunder novels, 2)

ISBN 9780671211806

1. Swindlers and swindling 2. Criminals 3. Bank robberies 4. Burglary 5. Banks and banking 6. Caper novels 7. Farcical fiction

LC 72183763

When John Dortmunder sets out to rob a bank, he really means it. He steals the whole thing. With the help of a sophomoric ex-FBI man, a militant safe-cracker, and old standbys Andy Kelp, Stan Murch, and Murch's Mom, Dortmunder puts a set of wheels under a trailer that just happens to be the temporary site of the Capitalists' & Immigrants' Trust (Just Watch Us Grow!). But when the safe won't open and the cops get close, Dortmunder realizes he's got a bigger problem than robbing a bank. He's got to find a place—somewhere in the suburban wasteland of Long Island—to put it.

"It is Westlake's triumph that whereas on one hand the reader knows he simply can't take the characters and situations seriously, those characters are so deftly drawn that they are eminently believable." —*New York Times Book Review*

Forever and a death. Donald E. Westlake. Hard Case Crime, 2017. 463 p.

ISBN 9781785654237

1. Revenge in men 2. Businesspeople 3. Bank robberies 4. Inventors 5. Espionage 6. Hong Kong 7. 1990s 8. Thrillers and suspense 9. Pulp fiction

A formerly wealthy businessman who loses everything to Hong Kong's new Chinese authorities vengefully plots to use a construction technology to destroy the city and steal its gold, a heist that is countered by the technology's developer and a beautiful young environmental activist.

Get real. Donald E. Westlake. Grand Central Pub, 2009. 288 p. (Dortmunder novels, 14)

ISBN 9780446178600

1. Thieves 2. Reality television programs 3. Organized crime 4. Criminals 5. Rich men 6. New York City 7. Caper novels

LC Bl2009012454

Reluctantly agreeing to allow his gang to appear in a reality television cop show that promises a lucrative payout and legal protection, luckless thief John Dortmunder and his partner, Kelp, devise a secondary plot to deceive case-cracking television viewers.

"A rollicking crime caper that pulls the pants right off the reality TV industry." —*New York Times Book Review*

The **hot** rock. Donald E. Westlake. Mysterious Press, 2001. 287 p. (Dortmunder novels, 1)

ISBN 9780671205416

1. Jewelry theft 2. Jewel thieves 3. Former convicts 4. Criminals 5. Emeralds 6. Caper novels 7. Books to movies

LC 70107263

John Dortmunder proves he has what it takes to be an habitual offender. Dortmunder steals the same jewel not just once, not twice, but again, and again, and again. Dortmunder didn't want to steal the Balabomo Emerald, but when one of two competing African countries—the nation of Talabwo—finances the scheme, he can be persuaded. Talabwo has purchased a fiasco. As Dortmunder's gang strikes by car, helicopter, and train, one heist after another goes wrong. The gem keeps slipping away, fast becoming an emerald with a sense of humor.

"This novel comes awesomely close to the ultimate in comic, big-caper novels; it's...filled with mocking style and action and imagination." —*New York Times Book Review*

Memory. Donald E. Westlake. Leisure Books, 2010. 336 p.

ISBN 9780843963755

1. Life change events 2. Memory 3. Amnesia 4. Actors and actresses 5. Extramarital affairs 6. Psychological fiction

Hospitalized after a liaison with another man's wife ends in violence, Paul Cole has just one goal: to rebuild his shattered life. But with his memory damaged, the police hounding him, and no way even to get home, Paul's facing steep odds—and a bleak fate if he fails.

"In this novel that Westlake wrote in the early 1960s and never published, Paul Cole suffers from partial amnesia his past is just beyond the reach of his mind. He keeps moving, like a fugitive, through a succession of working-class jobs; he falls in love; he gets in trouble with the law. Westlake never again dabbled in social realism, which is a shame: Memory is terse and bleak and low-key emotional, and as indelible as Westlake's other books." —*Entertainment Weekly*

The **road** to ruin. Donald E. Westlake. Mysterious Press, 2004. 342 p. (Dortmunder novels, 11)
ISBN 9780892968015
1. Criminals 2. Swindlers and swindling 3. Kidnapping 4. Dortmunder Gang (Fictitious characters) 5. Impostors 6. Caper novels
LC 2003065007
"Ingenuity fuels the plot, but what puts the match to the comedy is the moral outrage of the furiously funny characters." —*New York Times Book Review*

Wetmore, Elizabeth
★ **Valentine**. Elizabeth Wetmore. Harper360, 2020. 320 p.
ISBN 9780062913265
1. Small towns 2. Violence against women 3. Hispanic American teenage girls 4. Oil industry and trade 5. Mexican American teenage girls 6. Texas 7. 1970s 8. Literary fiction
In the early hours of the morning after Valentine's Day, fourteen-year-old Gloria Ramirez appears on the front porch of Mary Rose Whitehead's ranch house, broken and barely alive. The teenager had been viciously attacked in a nearby oil field—an act of brutality that is tried in the churches and barrooms of Odessa before it can reach a court of law. When justice is evasive, one of the town's women decides to take matters into her own hands, setting the stage for a showdown with potentially devastating consequences.
"This moving portrait of West Texas oil country evokes the work of Larry McMurtry and John Sayles with strong, memorable female voices." —*Publishers Weekly*

Wexler, Django
Ashes of the sun. Django Wexler. Orbit, 2020. 640 p. (Burningblade & Silvereye novels, 1)
ISBN 9780316519540
1. Siblings 2. Imaginary wars and battles 3. Post-apocalypse 4. Epidemics 5. Magic 6. Epic fantasy
LC 2019044375
Torn apart in a magical war, Gyre comes face-to-face with his long-lost sister, Maya, who has become a magic-wielding warrior in the twelve intervening years in the first novel of a new series.
"Wexler's (City of Stone and Silence, 2020) post-apocalyptic world is rich with history and fascinating in its inventive combination of magic, alchemy, and technology. This standout series opener is a winner: intricate, immersive, and irresistible."—*Booklist*, starred review

Wharton, Edith
The **children**. Edith Wharton; with an introduction by Marilyn French. Virago, 2006. 368 p.
ISBN 9781844082926
1. Stepsiblings 2. Eccentric families 3. Single men and children 4. Children of divorced parents 5. Loss (Psychology) 6. Domestic fiction 7. Books to movies 8. Modern classics

On a cruise ship between Algiers and Venice Martin Boyne, a bachelor in his forties, befriends a band of ebullient, precocious children. With humour and drama, the author portrays a world of intrigues and infidelities, skewering the manners and mores of Americans abroad.
The Children inspired the film The Marriage Playground,/i in 1929, and was more closely adapted into a film titled The Children in 1990.
Originally published: New York : D. Appleton & Co, 1928.

Collected stories, 1891-1910. Edith Wharton; selected and with notes by Maureen Howard. Library of America; 2001. X, 928 p.
ISBN 9781883011932
1. Manners and customs 2. United States 3. Short stories 4. Modern classics
LC 57596
Contains thirty-eight short stories exploring the author's themes of relations between the sexes, satire of social class, character, and morality.
Includes bibliographical references (p. 921-923).

★ **Ethan** Frome. Edith Wharton. Scribner, 1997. 150 p.
ISBN 9780684825915
1. Farmers 2. Married men 3. Single women 4. Farm life 5. Accident victims 6. Massachusetts 7. New England 8. Literary fiction 9. Books to movies 10. Modern classics
Ethan Frome works his unproductive farm and struggles to maintain a bearable existence with his difficult, suspicious, and hypochondriac wife, Zeenie. But when Zeenie's vivacious cousin enters their household as a "hired girl, Ethan finds himself obsessed with her and with the possibilities for happiness she comes to represent.
Originally published: New York : C. Scribner's Sons, 1911.

Whelan, Julia
My Oxford year. Julia Whelan. William Morrow & Co, 2018. 329 p.
ISBN 9780062740649
1. Women graduate students 2. College teachers 3. Studying abroad 4. People with cancer 5. Nash, Richard 6. England 7. Oxford, England 8. Contemporary romances
Offered a fantastic job in a rising star's political campaign on condition that she will work abroad and return to Washington after spending a dream year at Oxford, Ella clashes with, and then falls for, an outspoken literature professor with a life-changing secret that forces her to rethink her ambitions.

Whitaker, Chris
★ **We** begin at the end. Chris Whitaker. Henry Holt & Company, 2021. 464 p.
ISBN 9781250759665
1. Former convicts 2. Single mothers 3. Sisters of murder victims 4. Homecomings 5. Police chiefs 6. California 7. Literary fiction 8. Thrillers and suspense
LC 2020010399
Gold Dagger Award for Best Crime Novel of the Year, 2021; LibraryReads Favorites, 2021; Theakston Old Peculier Crime Novel of the Year Award, 2021
Thirty years ago, a teenage Vincent King was sent to prison. But now, he's served his sentence and is returning to his hometown. The hometown where his childhood best friend, Walk, is now the chief of police. The town where his childhood sweetheart, Star Radley, still lives. The same Star Radley whose sister he killed. Duchess, Star's daughter, is a self-proclaimed outlaw. She needs to be. Who else is going to take care of her and her five-year-old brother? Star is still dazzling, still beautiful, but she hasn't shined as bright since Vincent was sent away. Too often it's Duchess and Walk who are the ones taking care of her. But when Duchess exacts

her own vigilante revenge, she will set into motion a series of events that threatens not only her own family, but everyone she grows close to.

"Powered by extraordinarily deep character development and an impressively intricate plot, this novel is simultaneously a murder mystery, a love story, and a heartbreaking tragedy. The existential agony is palpable throughout, but so, too, is the hope at the end. Whitaker has upped his game with this emotionally charged page-turner." —*Publishers Weekly*

Originally published: London : Zaffre, 2020.

White, Edmund

A **boy's** own story. Edmund White. Penguin, 2009. 217 p.
ISBN 9780143114840
1. Owen, Wilfred 2. Homosexuality 3. Identity (Psychology) 4. Growing up 5. Coming-of-age stories 6. LGBTQIA fiction 7. First person narratives

At home, in school, and on the streets, a homosexual teenager moves through comic sexual experiments, isolation, fear, and exciting expectations toward an escape from childhood and a firm sense of self.

This first-person novel is written with the flourish of a master stylist.... It is an endearing portrait of a child's longing to be charming, popular, powerful, and loved, and of his struggles with adults...[told with] sensitivity and elegance. Harper's..

Sequel: The beautiful room is empty.

Originally published: New York : Dutton, 1982.

White, Elle Katharine

Dragonshadow. Elle Katharine White. Harper Voyager, 2018. 352 p. (Heartstone, 2)
ISBN 9780062747969
1. Quests 2. Dragons 3. Married people 4. Monsters 5. Newlyweds 6. Epic fantasy 7. Adaptations, retellings, and spin-offs

A second Austen-inspired romantic fantasy continues of the story of warrior newlyweds Aliza and Alastair, who journey through the Tekari-infested Old Wilds of Arle to assist the mysterious Lord Selwyn amid rumors of an unseen monster.

White, Randy Wayne

Salt river. Randy Wayne White. G. P. Putnam's Sons, 2020. 384 p. (Doc Ford novels, 26)
ISBN 9780735212725
1. Marine biologists 2. Male friendship 3. Sperm donors 4. Single men 5. Adult children 6. Florida 7. Gulf Coast, Florida 8. Thrillers and suspense

LC 2019050880

When his reckless bachelor friend reveals that he has fathered numerous children through sperm-bank donations, Doc Ford races to prevent his friend's past misdeeds from turning deadly during an impromptu family reunion.

White, T. H.

★ The **once** and future king. T.H. White. G. P. Putnam's Sons, 1958. 677 p. (Once and future king, 4)
ISBN 9780399105975
1. Arthur 2. Knights and knighthood 3. Grail 4. Merlin (Legendary character) 5. Wizards 6. Magic 7. Great Britain 8. Arthurian fantasy 9. Historical fantasy 10. Books to movies

LC 58010760

Merlyn instructs Arthur and his brother Sir Kay in the ways of the world. One of them will need it— the king has died leaving no heir, and a rightful one must be found by pulling a sword from an anvil resting on a stone. In the second and third parts of the novel, Arthur has become king and the kingdom is threatened from the north. In the final two books, the aging king faces his greatest challenge, when his own son threatens to overthrow him. In The Book of Merlyn, Arthur's tutor Merlyn reappears, and teaches him that, even in the face of apparent ruin, there is hope.

Part 1 was the inspiration for the movie The sword in the stone.

Part 2, The Queen of air and darkness, also known as The witch in the wood.

The once and future king (comprising four books) first published by Collins, 1958. The book of Merlyn first published by Voyager, 1996.

Whitehead, Colson

Apex hides the hurt. Colson Whitehead. Doubleday : 2006. 224 p.
ISBN 9780385507950
1. Consultants 2. Identity (Psychology) 3. Marketing 4. Name-brand products — Marketing 5. City life 6. Satirical fiction 7. African American fiction

LC 2005049391

New York Times Notable Book, 2006

A small Midwestern town is having an identity crisis—should they have a new techno-savvy name or a name honoring the freedmen who founded the town? Or is the current name just fine? They call in a professional naming consultant, famous for naming Apex bandages—guaranteed to match any skin color. But even he is losing his faith in monikers.

"A secretive narrator often means the story is weak and has to be puffed up with mystery, but Whitehead's gorgeous, expertly crafted sentences help the reader past the novel's slow start.... We are slowly filled in on the limp, the misfortune, the meaning of the title and we're treated to an eloquent novel about racial identity in America.... What could have been an academic exercise becomes a smart tale about who we are under our labels." —*Newsweek*

★ **Harlem** shuffle. Colson Whitehead. Doubleday, 2021. 336 p.
ISBN 9780385545136
1. Fences (Persons) 2. City life 3. Crime 4. Cousins 5. Personal conduct 6. Harlem, New York City 7. New York City 8. 1960s 9. Crime fiction 10. Historical fiction 11. Literary fiction

LibraryReads Favorites, 2021; Kirkus Prize for Fiction finalist, 2021

A furniture salesman in 1960s Harlem becomes a fence for shady cops, local gangsters and low-life pornographers after his cousin involves him in a failed heist in the new novel from the two-time Pulitzer Prize-winning author of The Underground Railroad.

"Whitehead delivers a portrait of Harlem in the early '60s, culminating with the Harlem Riot of 1964, that is brushed with lovingly etched detail and features a wonderful panoply of characters who spring to full-bodied life, blending joy, humor, and tragedy. A triumph on every level." —*Booklist*

The **intuitionist**. Colson Whitehead. Anchor Books, 1999. 255 p.
ISBN 9780385492997
1. African American women — Identity 2. Race relations 3. Intrigue 4. City life 5. Sects 6. Literary fiction 7. Contemporary fantasy 8. African American fiction

LC 986756

New York Times Notable Book, 1999

A black female elevator inspector must prove that her method of inspection by intuition, as opposed to visual observation, is not at fault when an elevator in a new city building crashes.

"Whitehead's prose is graceful and often lyrical and his elevator underworld is a complex, lovingly realized creation." —*The New Yorker*

John Henry Days: a novel. Colson Whitehead. Doubleday, 2001. 389 p.

ISBN 9780385498197

1. John Henry 2. African American journalists 3. Michelangelo Buonarroti 4. Festivals 5. West Virginia 6. Psychological fiction 7. African American fiction

LC 43143

Booklist Editors' Choice, 2001; National Book Critics Circle Award for Fiction finalist, 2001; Pulitzer Prize for Fiction finalist, 2002

An assignment for a travel Web site takes J. Sutter, a young black journalist, to West Virginia for the first annual "John Henry Days" festival, where history and popular culture are juxtaposed as the real story of John Henry unfolds.

"Whitehead relishes slashing through the mindlessness of the age in a voice so intelligent and an idiom so imaginative that it can lift a reader right out of his chair. But he is not remorseless. He likes these people and respects their longings. They have no moral compass, but he has, so we can laugh at them but still grieve for the loss of so much possiblility." —*New York Times Book Review*

★ The **Nickel** boys: a novel. Colson Whitehead. Doubleday, 2019. 213 pages

ISBN 9780385537070

1. King, Martin Luther 2. African American teenage boys 3. Juvenile correctional institutions 4. Racism 5. Corruption 6. Teenage abuse victims 7. Florida 8. Southern States 9. 1960s 10. Historical fiction 11. African American fiction 12. Adult books for young adults

ALA Notable Book, 2020; Alex Award, 2020; BCALA Literary Award for Fiction, 2020; Booklist Editors' Choice, 2019; Kirkus Prize for Fiction, 2019; Library Journal Best Books, 2019; LibraryReads Favorites, 2019; New York Times Notable Book, 2019; Orwell Prize, 2020; Pulitzer Prize for Fiction, 2020; National Book Critics Circle Award for Fiction finalist, 2019; Longlisted for the National Book Award for Fiction, 2019; Shortlisted for the International Dublin Literary Award, 2021

Follows the harrowing experiences of two African-American teens at an abusive reform school in Jim Crow-era Florida.

"Whitehead's magnetic characters exemplify stoicism and courage, and each supremely crafted scene smolders and flares with injustice and resistance, building to a staggering revelation. Inspired by an actual school, Whitehead's potently concentrated drama pinpoints the brutality and insidiousness of Jim Crow racism with compassion and protest." —*Booklist*

Sag Harbor: a novel. Colson Whitehead. Doubleday, 2009. 288 p.

ISBN 9780385527651

1. African American teenage boys 2. Prep schools 3. Teenagers 4. Identity (Psychology) 5. Misfits (Persons) 6. Manhattan, New York City 7. Sag Harbor, New York 8. 1980s 9. Coming-of-age stories 10. First person narratives 11. African American fiction 12. Adult books for young adults

Booklist Editors' Choice: Adult Books for Young Adults, 2009; New York Times Notable Book, 2009

Benji, one of the only black kids at an elite prep school in Manhattan, tries desperately to fit in, but every summer, he and his brother, Reggie, escape to the East End of Sag Harbor, where a small community of African American professionals has built a world of their own.

"The author serves up whole sundaes worth of riffs on the quotidian, all hung on the skinny frame of a 15-year-old everyman virgin and his marginally less distinct friends, give or take a repressive father and a particularly evocative shoreline landscape." —*Village Voice*

★ The **underground** railroad: a novel. Colson Whitehead. Doubleday, 2016. 304 p.

ISBN 9780385542364

1. Underground Railroad 2. Freedom seekers 3. Race (Social sciences) 4. Racism 5. African Americans — Social conditions 6. Southern States 7. United States 8. Antebellum America (1820-1861) 9. Literary fiction 10. Historical fiction 11. African American fiction

LC 2016000643

ALA Notable Book, 2017; Andrew Carnegie Medal for Excellence in Fiction, 2017; Arthur C. Clarke Award, 2017; Booklist Editors' Choice, 2016; Goodreads Choice Award, 2016; Hurston/Wright Legacy Award: Fiction, 2017; Indies' Choice Book Awards, Adult Fiction, 2017; Library Journal Best Books, 2016; National Book Award for Fiction, 2016; New York Times Notable Book, 2016; Pulitzer Prize for Fiction, 2017; Longlisted for the Man Booker Prize, 2017; Kirkus Prize for Fiction finalist, 2016

After Cora, a pre-Civil War Georgia slave, escapes with another slave, Caesar, they seek the help of the Underground Railroad as they flee from state to state and try to evade a slave catcher, Ridgeway, who is determined to return them to the South.

"Everything Whitehead describes is vividly, often joltingly realistic, even the novels most fantastic element, his vision of this secret transport network as an actual railroad running through tunnels dug beneath the blood-soaked fields of the South, a jolting and resounding embodiment of heroic efforts and colossal risks." —*Booklist*

Includes extract from: The Intuitionist.

Made into a television show, 2021.

Zone one: a novel. Colson Whitehead. Doubleday, 2011. 240 p.

ISBN 9780385528078

1. End of the world 2. Zombies 3. Coping 4. Virus diseases 5. Loneliness in men 6. New York City 7. Manhattan, New York City 8. Satirical fiction 9. Horror 10. African American fiction 11. Adult books for young adults

LC 2011008339

Library Journal Best Books, 2011

In a post-apocalyptic world decimated by zombies, the U.S. government has retreated to Buffalo, New York, and survivor efforts to rebuild are focused on lower Manhattan. With several others, Mark Spitz works as a "sweeper"—eliminating zombie stragglers as he struggles with PASD (Post-Apocalyptic Stress Disorder) and recalls humanity before the apocalypse.

"It's a book you want to read rather than one you should read. Sure, there are familiar paradigms: the pandemic subsides behind a foreground of chase scenes, us-or-them admonitions, even the occasional bite sequence. But Zone One is mercilessly free of cookie-cutter social commentariesoffice culture is for mindless drones; technology destroys our ability to connectwhile still providing the chilling, fleshy pleasures of zombies who lurch, pursue, hunger." —*Esquire*

Whiteley, Aliya

From the neck up and other stories. Aliya Whiteley. Titan Books, 2021. 368 p.

ISBN 9781789094756

1. High technology 2. Imaginary creatures 3. Aliens 4. Interpersonal relations 5. Utopias 6. Science fiction 7. Fantasy fiction 8. Short stories

In 16 stories Aliya Whiteley deftly unpeels the strangeness of everyday life through beguiling gardens, rebellious bodies and journeys across familiar worlds, with her trademark wit and compassion. Witness the future of farming in a new Ice Age, or the artist bringing life to glass; the many-eyed monsters we carry and the secret cities inside our bodies; the alien invasion through our language to the Chantress and her twists on the fairy tale. Fascinating and always unexpected, Whiteley is unlike any other writer working today.

"This beguiling and beautiful, yet undeniably unnerving collection, with its tales of the ordinary made strange, will captivate readers." —*Library Journal*

Whitfield, Clare

People of abandoned character. Clare Whitfield. Head of Zeus, 2021. 432 p.
ISBN 9781838932732
1. Jack 2. Newlyweds 3. Suspicion 4. Violence in men 5. Surgeons 6. Secrets 7. London, England 8. 1880s 9. First person narratives 10. Historical thrillers

London, 1888: Susannah rushes into marriage to a young and wealthy surgeon. After a passionate honeymoon, she returns home with her new husband wrapped around her little finger. But then everything changes. Thomas's behavior becomes increasingly volatile and violent. He stays out all night, returning home bloodied and full of secrets. The gentle caresses she enjoyed on her wedding night are now just a honeyed memory. When the first woman is murdered in Whitechapel, Susannah's interest is piqued. But as she follows the reports of the ongoing hunt for the killer, her mind takes her down the darkest path imaginable. Every time Thomas stays out late, another victim is found dead. Is it coincidence? Or is her husband the man they call Jack the Ripper?

"This debut historical mystery contains echoes of Daphne du Maurier's Rebecca and Jack the Ripper. The unreliable narrator combines with richly detailed writing in a mystery with a shocking conclusion." —*Library Journal*

Whitlow, Robert

A time to stand. Robert Whitlow. Harpercollins Christian Pub 2017. 400 p.
ISBN 9780718083038
1. African American women lawyers 2. Race relations 3. Police brutality 4. Trials (Murder) 5. Defense attorneys 6. Christian fiction 7. Legal stories
LC 2017012470
Library Journal Best Books, 2017

Adisa Johnson, a young African American attorney, is living her dream of practicing law with a prestigious firm in downtown Atlanta. Then a split-second mistake changes the course of her career. Left with no other options, Adisa returns to her hometown where a few days earlier a white police officer shot an unarmed black teen who is now lying comatose in the hospital. Adisa is itching to jump into the fight as a special prosecutor, but feels pulled to do what she considers unthinkable—defend the officer. As the court case unfolds, everyone in the small community must confront their own prejudices.

Whittall, Zoe

The spectacular: a novel. Zoe Whittall. Ballantine Books, 2021. 288 p.
ISBN 9781524799410
1. Mothers and daughters 2. Grandmothers 3. Expectation (Psychology) 4. Women — Sexuality 5. Independence in women 6. 1990s 7. 2010s 8. Literary fiction 9. Canadian fiction
LC 2021003312

In 1997, three generations of women—Missy, a cellist in an indie rock band; her mother Carola, who is just surfacing from a sex scandal; and her grandmother Ruth—each struggle to build an authentic life as they try to find a way to understand one another again.

Whitten, Hannah

For the wolf. Hannah Whitten. Orbit, 2021. 448 p. (Wilderwood novels, 1)
ISBN 9780316592789
1. Wolves 2. Magic 3. Forests 4. Twins 5. Young women 6. Epic fantasy 7. Fairy tale and folklore-inspired fiction
LC 2020044439
Loan Stars Favourites, 2021

As the only Second Daughter born in centuries, Red has one purpose-to be sacrificed to the Wolf in the Wood in the hope he'll return the world's captured gods. Red is almost relieved to go. Plagued by a dangerous power she can't control, at least she knows that in the Wilderwood, she can't hurt those she loves. Again. But the legends lie. The Wolf is a man, not a monster. Her magic is a calling, not a curse. And if she doesn't learn how to use it, the monsters the gods have become will swallow the Wilderwood-and her world-whole.

"This hauntingly beautiful, fractured retelling of Little Red Riding Hood is dark, emotional, and filled with tense action." —*Library Journal*

Wideman, John Edgar

★ **American** histories: stories. John Edgar Wideman. Scribner, 2018. 227 p.
ISBN 9781501178344
1. Putin, Vladimir Vladimirovich 2. Interpersonal relations 3. Family relationships 4. African Americans 5. Abolitionists 6. Race relations 7. United States 8. Literary fiction 9. Short stories 10. African American fiction
Booklist Editors' Choice, 2018

Collects short stories about love, death, and struggle.

Look for me and I'll be gone: stories. John Edgar Wideman. Simon & Schuster, 2021. 192 p.
ISBN 9781982148942
1. Families 2. Loss (Psychology) 3. Imprisonment 4. Identity (Psychology) 5. Poverty 6. Pittsburgh, Pennsylvania 7. Short stories 8. African American fiction

Here, in John Edgar Wideman's sixth story collection, he revisits themes that have infused his work for the duration of his career: family, loss, the penal system, Pittsburgh, physical and emotional life, art, and memory.

"Short-story virtuoso Wideman follows the substantial You Made Me Love You: Selected Stories, 1981?2018 (2021) with a collection of new stories, another compelling contribution to his expansive oeuvre." —*Booklist*

Wieland, Liza

Paris, 7 a.m. Liza Wieland. Simon & Schuster, 2019. 352 pages
ISBN 9781501197215
1. Bishop, Elizabeth 2. Women poets 3. Americans in France 4. Mothers and daughters 5. Women/women relations 6. Loss (Psychology) 7. Paris, France 8. Normandy 9. Between the Wars (1918-1939) 10. 1930s 11. Historical fiction 12. Biographical fiction

The award-winning author of A Watch of Nightingales reimagines the experiences of pre-fame poet Elizabeth Bishop during three life-changing weeks spent in Paris on the eve of World War II.

Wiesel, Elie

★ **Dawn**. Elie Wiesel; translated from the French by Frances Frenaye. Bantam Books, 1982. 102 p.
ISBN 9780553225365

1. Holocaust survivors 2. Executions and executioners 3. Murder 4. Ethics 5. Jewish men 6. Israel 7. Autobiographical fiction 8. Translations

Deals with the conflicts and thoughts of a young Jewish concentration-camp veteran as he prepares to assassinate a British hostage in occupied Palestine

Translation of L'Aube.

First published in 1960 in French.

Sequel to: Night.

Sequel: The accident, which is also known as Day.

Hostage. Elie Wiesel; translated from the French by Catherine Temerson. Alfred A. Knopf, 2012. 224 p.

ISBN 9780307599582

1. Hostages 2. Hostage taking 3. Jewish men 4. Storytelling 5. 1970s 6. Thrillers and suspense 7. Political thrillers 8. Translations 9. Adult books for young adults

LC 2011050747

Traces the experiences of an innocent Jewish writer from Brooklyn who endures a nightmarish abduction by Arab and Italian captors by sharing poignant stories from the time he spent hiding from the Nazis.

This is a Borzoi book.

Translated from the French.

A **mad** desire to dance: a novel. Elie Wiesel; translated from the French by Catherine Temerson. Alfred A. Knopf, 2009. 288 p.

ISBN 9780307266507

1. Men with depression 2. Holocaust survivors 3. Death 4. Loneliness 5. Orphans 6. Literary fiction 7. Translations

LC 2008038951

A European orphan transplanted to New York, Doriel is shaped by the pain of the deaths of his parents following World War II and the horrors of the Holocaust, and seeks solace in an intense study of Judaism and a search for the secrets of his mother's life.

Translated from the French

★ **Night,** Dawn, The accident: three tales. By Elie Wiesel. Hill and Wang 1972. 318 p.

ISBN 9780809073528

1. Wiesel, Elie 2. God (Judaism) 3. Jews — Identity 4. Holocaust survivors 5. Jewish men 6. Holocaust (1933-1945) 7. Autobiographies and memoirs 8. Translations 9. History writing — Wars and conflicts — Holocaust — World War II 10. Life stories — Facing adversity — War and oppression — War survivors 11. Antiracist literature

LC 72081290

A terrifying account of Auschwitz that turns a young Jewish boy into an agonized witness to the death of his family, a member of the Israeli underground has to face the prospect of murder, and a near-fatal auto accident changes a man's outlook on life.

Translations of: Un di velt hot geshvign, L'aube, and Le jour, respectively.

Later editions published under the title: Night, Dawn, Day.

Wiggs, Susan

★ The **Oysterville** sewing circle. Susan Wiggs. William Morrow & Co, 2019. 320 pages

ISBN 9780062425584

1. Homecomings 2. Guardian and ward 3. Sewing 4. Family violence victims 5. Undocumented immigrants 6. Washington (State) 7. Relationship fiction

Forced by scandal to return to her Pacific coast childhood home, a Manhattan fashionista assumes guardianship over two orphans and bonds with a circle of fellow seamstresses before an unexpected challenge tests her courage and heart.

Wilde, Oscar

★ The **picture** of Dorian Gray. Oscar Wilde. Modern Library, 1998. Xii, 254 p.

ISBN 9780375751516

1. Portraits 2. Personal conduct 3. Immortality 4. Aging 5. Great Britain 6. London, England 7. Victorian era (1837-1901) 8. Gothic fiction 9. Classics 10. Books to movies

An exquisitely beautiful young man in Victorian England retains his youthful and innocent appearance over the years while his portrait reflects both his age and evil soul as he pursues a life of decadence and corruption.

Originally published as a story in Lippincott's Monthly Magazine (Philadelphia, Pa.) on June 20, 1890. A revised and expanded version was published as a novel in April 1891 by Ward and Lock (London).

Wilder, Thornton

★ **Theophilus** North. Thornton Wilder. Harper & Row, 1973. 374 p.

ISBN 9780060146368

1. Former teachers 2. Tutors 3. Cities and towns 4. City life 5. Octogenarians 6. Newport, Rhode Island 7. Rhode Island 8. 1920s 9. Coming-of-age stories 10. Books to movies

LC 73004165

Banta Award (Wisconsin), 1974

A twenty-nine-year-old teacher attempts to achieve his nine life ambitions while passing the summer in Newport, Rhode Island.

Book adapted into the 1988 film Mr. North.

Later published as: Mr. North. New York : Carroll & Graf, 1988.

Wilhelm, Kate

Where late the sweet birds sang. Kate Wilhelm. Harper & Row, 1976. 251 p.

ISBN 9780060146542

1. Clones and cloning 2. Survivalism 3. Individuality 4. Disasters 5. Catastrophism 6. Virginia 7. Apocalyptic fiction 8. Science fiction classics 9. Science fiction

LC 75006379

Hugo Award for Best Novel, 1977; Locus Award for Best Science Fiction Novel, 1977

Having foreseen and planned for the worldwide devastation of war and pestilence, the landed Sumner family of Virginia have assured themselves physical survival but are hard-put to provide for a meaningful human future.

Wilkinson, Lauren

★ **American** spy: a novel. Lauren Wilkinson. Random House, 2019. 292 pages

ISBN 9780812998955

1. Sankara, Thomas 2. Cold War 3. Undercover operations 4. Spies 5. Espionage 6. Loyalty 7. Burkina Faso 8. 1980s 9. Literary fiction 10. African American fiction 11. Spy fiction

New York Times Notable Book, 2019

A Cold War FBI intelligence officer joins an undercover task force to seduce a revolutionary African Communist president she secretly admires and comes to love.

"Written in the form of a lengthy missive from a mother to her young sons, this intriguing first novel blends literary fiction with a Cold War-era spy story." —*Library Journal*

Willett, Marcia

The **garden** house. Marcia Willett. St. Martin's Press, 2021. 256 p.
ISBN 9781250760265
1. Death 2. Fathers and daughters 3. Homecomings 4. Family secrets
5. Memories 6. Contemporary romances

LC 2021006995

After her father dies, El moves into his house where she uncovers more about his life, and the secrets he had been keeping from her and her family, while his lover Julie holds on to the memories of their time spent at The Garden House.

"Willett's atmospheric writing successfully conjures the idyllic English countryside while delivering multifaceted relationship dynamics and well-shaded characters." —*Publishers Weekly*

Originally published by Transworld Publishers Limited, 2020.

Williams, Beatriz

All the ways we said goodbye: a novel of the Ritz Paris. . William Morrow & Co, 2020. 368 pages
ISBN 9780062931092
1. Hotels 2. Family history 3. Family secrets 4. Romantic love
5. Women and war 6. Paris, France 7. First World War era (1914-1918)
8. Second World War era (1939-1945) 9. Parallel narratives
10. Historical fiction
LibraryReads Favorites, 2020

An heiress, a Resistance fighter and a widow find their lives intertwined by their wartime experiences and the turbulent 1960s when they seek refuge at Paris' legendary Ritz hotel.

"Full of heart and intrigue, the authors' latest collaboration captures women's perseverance and how history connects us all." —*Booklist*

The **golden** hour. Beatriz Williams. William Morrow, 2019. 384 pages
ISBN 9780062834751
1. Windsor, Edward J. 2. Dukes and duchesses 3. Women journalists 4. Scientists 5. Social classes 6. Race relations 7. Bahamas 8. Nassau, Bahamas 9. Second World War era (1939-1945) 10. Historical fiction
11. Parallel narratives

Traveling to World War II Nassau to interview the infamous Duke and Duchess of Windsor, an investigator for a New York society magazine uncovers a treasonous plot that is complicated by her romance with an unscrupulous scientist.

The **summer** wives. Beatriz Williams. William Morrow, 2018. 367 p.
ISBN 9780062660343
1. Secrecy 2. Upper class 3. Judicial error 4. Interclass romance
5. Murder suspects 6. New England 7. 1950s 8. Historical fiction 9. Love stories

LC Bl2018072167

Drawn into and then banished from exclusive Winthrop Island when a complex relationship between her stepsister and a working-class college youth ends in violence, a Shakespearean actress returns after 20 years to pursue justice.

Williams, Denise

The **fastest** way to fall. Denise Williams. Jove, 2021. 336 p.
ISBN 9780593101926
1. Single women 2. Bloggers 3. Body image 4. Personal trainers
5. Chief executive officers 6. Romantic comedies 7. Multicultural romances

LC 2021010370

LibraryReads Favorites, 2021

Britta didn't plan on falling for her personal trainer, and Wes didn't plan on Britta. Plans change and it's unclear if love, career, or both will meet them at the finish line. Britta Colby works for a lifestyle website, and when tasked to write about her experience with a hot new body-positive fitness app that includes personal coaching, she knows it's a major opportunity to prove she should write for the site full-time. As CEO of the FitMe app, Wes Lawson finally has the financial security he grew up without, but despite his success, his floundering love life and complicated family situation leaves him feeling isolated and unfulfilled. He decides to get back to what he loves-coaching. Britta's his first new client and they click immediately. As weeks pass, she's surprised at how much she enjoys experimenting with her exercise routine. He's surprised at how much he looks forward to talking to her every day. They convince themselves their attraction is harmless, but when they start working out in person, Wes and Britta find it increasingly challenging to deny their chemistry and maintain a professional distance.

"Williams has mastered writing cinnamon-roll heroes, and expertly balances Wes's sweetness with Britta's admirable strength. The plot is emotionally weighty, but the romance is just as cute as in her debut." —*Publishers Weekly*

How to fail at flirting. Denise Williams. Jove, 2020. 336 p.
ISBN 9780593101902
1. College teachers 2. Overachievers 3. Dating (Social customs)
4. Self-fulfillment in women 5. Universities and colleges 6. Romantic comedies

LC 2020012255

LibraryReads Favorites, 2020

Challenged by her friends to start enjoying her life when her university department is cut, a Type-A overachiever embarks on a daring to-do list that involves leaving an abusive ex and pursuing a career-risking fling with a charming stranger.

"Naya and Jake's relationship is both sexy and sweet as these two people, who love their work but are not skilled at socializing or romance, find their way forward. Academia is vividly portrayed, and readers will await the next book from Williams, a talented debut author and a PhD herself." —*Booklist*

Williams, Drew

The **stars** now unclaimed. Drew Williams. Tor Books, 2018. 447 pages; (Universe after, 1)
ISBN 9781250186119
1. Child psychics 2. Psychokinesis 3. Disasters — Prevention 4. Cults
5. Aliens 6. Space opera 7. Science fiction

Recruiting supernaturally gifted kids to help stop a cataclysmic force from decimating countless worlds, agent Jane Kamali teams up with a telekinetic teen to navigate the madcap schemes of a power-hungry fascist cult.

"This cast of memorable characters, particularly Jane, who wears her heart on her sleeve, and the sacrifices they make to save the universe is not to be missed." —*Booklist*

Williams, Eley

The **liar's** dictionary. Eley Williams. Doubleday, 2021. 288 p.
ISBN 9780385546775
1. Deception 2. Lexicographers 3. Dictionaries 4. Words 5. Closeted lesbians 6. Farcical fiction 7. Literary fiction 8. LGBTQIA fiction

Tasked with identifying false entries in an encyclopedic dictionary before it is digitized, a young intern questioning her sexuality and place in the world uncovers the laugh-out-loud mountweazels of a disaffected Victorian lexicographer.

"The Liar's Dictionary, while prone to detours through esoteric linguistic explorations, will nonetheless amuse word lovers intrigued by the pair's unusual exploits." —*Booklist*

Williams, Joy

Harrow. Joy Williams. Alfred A Knopf, 2021. 240 p.
ISBN 9780525657569
1. Post-apocalypse 2. Near future 3. Eco-terrorists 4. Deserts 5. Resorts 6. The West (United States) 7. United States 8. Apocalyptic fiction 9. Literary fiction
Kirkus Prize for Fiction, 2021

With her mother missing and her boarding school closed, Khristen searches the post-apocalyptic landscape until she reaches a "resort" on the shores of a putrid lake in the author's first novel since The Quick and the Dead.

"Pulitzer finalist Williams (The Quick and the Dead) returns with a dystopian saga of environmental cataclysm that is by turns triumphant, damning, and beguiling." —*Publishers Weekly*

Ninety-nine stories of God. Joy Williams. Tin House Books, 2016. 220 p.
ISBN 9781941040355
1. God 2. Spirituality 3. Short stories
LC 2016006741
New York Times Notable Book, 2016

A collection from the Pulitzer Prize and National Book Award finalist author feature stories about humans' daily, random interactions with the divine in the most unlikely of places.

"Each story is brief, with some less than a paragraph. Some amaze, some are quietly powerful, some gracefully absurd. Much like the divine, Williams prose is simple and brutal, thoughtful and haunting." —*Booklist*

Williams, Katie

Tell the machine goodnight. Katie Williams. Riverhead Books, 2018. 287 p.
ISBN 9780525533122
1. Women professional employees 2. Happiness 3. Mothers and sons 4. Near future 5. Teenage boys 6. Domestic fiction 7. Mainstream fiction 8. Multiple perspectives 9. Adult books for young adults
Kirkus Prize for Fiction finalist, 2018

A woman whose job it is to help people find happiness finds a challenge in her own son, who seems to get the most joy out of being unhappy.

"Following the trajectory of today's preoccupation with self-help and our perhaps not-entirely-justified faith that technology can fix everything, Williams explores the way machines and screens can both disconnect us, launching us into loneliness, and connect us, bringing us closer to one another. In this imaginative, engaging, emotionally resonant story, she reveals how the devices we depend on can both deprive us of our humanity and deliver us back to it. With its clever, compelling vision of the future, deeply human characters, and delightfully unpredictable story, this novel is itself a recipe for contentment." —*Kirkus*
Republished in 2019 as "The happiness machine."

Williams, Lara

A **selfie** as big as the Ritz: stories. Lara Williams. Flatiron Books, 2017. 160 p.
ISBN 9781250126627
1. Short stories 2. Literary fiction
LC 2017025683

A collection of short stories focuses on women trying to navigate their lives, including a woman whose relationship goes sour in the most romantic city on earth and another woman who supports her best friend through an abortion.

"Williams can limn huge swaths of a character's life in a handful of pages by zeroing in on details that communicate everything about everything, all in an instant. Williams' painstakingly, pointillistically composed portraits capture the small moments that can change the trajectory of a life." —*Kirkus*

Supper club: a novel. Lara Williams. G. P. Putnams Sons, 2019. 304 pages
ISBN 9780525539582
1. Young women 2. Clubs 3. Dinners and dining 4. Women's organizations 5. Secret societies 6. Literary fiction 7. Adult books for young adults
LC 2018046714

A woman confronts her personal limits and repressed past after forming a nighttime collective of women who gorge themselves passionately and embrace their bodies.

Williams, Niall

This is happiness. Niall Williams. Bloomsbury, 2019. 368 pages
ISBN 9781635574203
1. Reminiscing in old age 2. Villages 3. Electricity 4. Boarders 5. Jilted women 6. Ireland 7. 1950s 8. Literary fiction

A young man's first experiences of falling in and out of love are shaped by the arrival of electricity in his small western seaboard village, an enigmatic woman and a mysterious drought.

"Warm and whimsical, sometimes sorrowful, but always expressed in curlicues of Irish lyricism, this charming book makes varied use of its electrical metaphor, not least to express the flickering pulse of humanity. A story both little and large and one that pulls out all the Irish stops." —*Kirkus*

Williams, Pip

The **dictionary** of lost words. Pip Williams. Ballantine Books, 2021. 400 p.
ISBN 9780593160190
1. Women's role 2. Language and culture 3. Words 4. English language 5. History 6. England 7. Oxford, England 8. Edwardian era (1901-1914) 9. 20th century 10. Historical fiction 11. Australian fiction
Australian Book Industry Awards, General Fiction Book of the Year, 2021; Nielsen BookData Australian Booksellers' Choice Award, 2021; NSW Premier's Literary Awards, People's Choice Award for Fiction, 2021; Shortlisted for the Walter Scott Prize for Historical Fiction, 2021

As a team of male scholars compiles the first Oxford English Dictionary, one of their daughters decides to collect the "objectionable" words they omit.

"Enchanting, sorrowful, and wonderfully written, the book is a one-of-a-kind celebration of language and its importance in our lives. A must-have for every library collection." —*Library Journal*
Originally published: South Melbourne, VIC : Affirm Press, 2020.

Williams, Preslaysa

A **lowcountry** bride. Preslaysa Williams. Avon Books, 2021. 320 p.
ISBN 9780063040298
1. Women fashion designers 2. Homecomings 3. Bridal shops 4. Widowers 5. Single fathers 6. Charleston, South Carolina 7. South

Carolina 8. Multicultural romances 9. Contemporary romances 10. African American fiction

A talented dress designer leaves New York to care for her father in Charleston, South Carolina and accepts a job at a local wedding gown shop only to find herself falling for the store's owner.

"With superb character development and great emotional depth, Afro Filipina writer Williams stitches together a quietly powerful love story that is beautifully enriched by the deft and insightful incorporation of weighty issues such as grief and medical conditions into the compelling plot and brightly enhanced by glimpses into the vibrant culture and history of Charleston." —*Booklist*

Williams, Synithia

Forbidden promises. Synithia Williams. HQN Books, 2020. 368 pages (Jackson Falls, 1)

ISBN 9781335013248

1. Women violinists 2. Divorced men 3. Campaigning 4. Families 5. Siblings 6. Multicultural romances 7. Contemporary romances 8. African American fiction

Recruited by her politician brother to work with her older sister's ex-husband, with whom she is in love, violinist India Robidoux and Travis Strickland have a secret affair that neither of them wants to stop until family loyalties and desperate enemies threaten to tear them apart.

"With skillful characterization and sizzling chemistry, Williams succeeds at capturing the allure of this taboo connection. Even skeptical readers will be hard-pressed not to root for India and Travis." —*Publishers Weekly*

Williams, Tennessee

★ **Collected** stories. Tennessee Williams; with an introduction by Gore Vidal. New Directions, 1985. 57p.

ISBN 9780811209526

1. Manners and customs 2. Short stories

LC 85010642

A chronological arrangement of the noted American playwright's complete stories, published and unpublished, provides a veiled look at his life and concerns.

49 short stories.

★ The **Roman** spring of Mrs. Stone. Tennessee Williams. New Directions, 1993. 111 p.

ISBN 9780811212496

1. Middle-aged women 2. Young men — Relations with older women 3. Man-woman relationships 4. Resentfulness 5. Female friendship 6. Rome, Italy 7. Italy 8. 1950s

This is the story of a 50-ish wealthy American widow who was most recently a famous stage beauty but is now drifting after the death of her husband. With poignant wit and his own particular brand of relish, Williams charts her drift into an affair with a cruel young gigolo.

"There are many superb moments, scenes which move with a dramatist's ease. There is a hard candor about Mrs. Stone, about all people who fail at real living and attempt a life of fantasy and fail at that, leaving them vulnerable to annihilation.... This different version of Mr. Williams' repeated theme has resulted in a sharp, witty and moving novel." —*Chicago Tribune*

Williams, Tia

★ **Seven** days in June: a novel. Tia Williams. Grand Central Publishing, 2021. 304 p.

ISBN 9781538719107

1. African American authors 2. Romance writing 3. Literary prizes 4. African American women 5. African American men 6. New York City 7. Contemporary romances 8. African American fiction

LC 2020054050

Eva Mercy is a single mom and bestselling writer; Shane Hall is a reclusive, award-winning literary author. As high school seniors, teenage Eva and Shane spent one crazy, torrid week madly in love before Shane disappeared from Eva's life—but they've been secretly writing to each other in their books ever since. When Eva and Shane meet unexpectedly at a literary event, sparks fly once again. Eva's not sure how she can trust the man who broke her heart; but before Shane disappears again, there are a few questions she needs answered...

"With funny, snappy writing and a strong eye for detail, Williams (The Perfect Find) builds a compelling, glamorous Black literary world for the protagonists to inhabit. The book balances a second-chance romance with themes of motherhood, childhood trauma, and life with chronic pain." —*Library Journal*

Willig, Lauren

The **summer** country: a novel. Lauren Willig. William Morrow, 2019. 384 pages

ISBN 9780062839022

1. Inheritance and succession 2. Family secrets 3. Sugar plantations 4. Race relations 5. Interracial romance 6. West Indies 7. Barbados 8. Victorian era (1837-1901) 9. Regency period (1811-1820) 10. Family sagas 11. Historical fiction 12. Parallel narratives

LC 2018044474

Inheriting the ruins of a Barbados sugar plantation, a young woman from Victorian Bristol is seduced by the region's dark tropical beauty at the same time her new neighbors take steps to acquire the property for themselves.

Willink, Jocko

Final spin. Jocko Willink. St. Martin's Press, 2021. 176 p.

ISBN 9781250276858

1. Brothers 2. People with developmental disabilities 3. Fugitives 4. Robbery 5. Alcoholics 6. Crime fiction

LC 2021027560

A novel about brotherhood and the search for happiness, from a #1 New York Times best-selling author.

"Told with a gritty simplicity, this retains a hold on the reader right through to the inevitable tragic climax." —*Publishers Weekly*

Willis, Connie

Crosstalk. Connie Willis. Del Rey, 2016. 384 p.

ISBN 9780345540676

1. Near future 2. Young women 3. Interpersonal communication 4. Couples 5. Empathy 6. Satirical fiction 7. Science fiction

LibraryReads Favorites, 2016; RUSA Reading List Short List, 2017

One of science fiction's premiere humorists turns her eagle eye to the crushing societal implications of telepathy. In a not-too-distant future, a simple outpatient procedure that has been promised to increase empathy between romantic partners has become all the rage. So when Briddey Flannigan's fiancé proposes that he and Briddey undergo the procedure, she is delighted! Only...the results aren't quite as expected. Instead of gaining an increased empathetic link with her fiancé Briddey finds herself hearing the actual thoughts of one of the nerdiest techs in her office. And that's the least of her problems.

"In other hands this novel could have been mere cliche, but Willis exuberant humor and warmhearted, fast-paced plotting transform it into a satisfying, if old-fashioned, romantic comedy." —*Kirkus*

★ **Doomsday** book. Connie Willis. Bantam Books, 1992. 445 p. (Oxford time travel novels, 2)
ISBN 9780553081312
1. Time travel (Past) 2. Plague — History 3. Civilization, Medieval 4. Women college students 5. Historians 6. Europe 7. Medieval period (476-1492) 8. 14th century 9. Science fiction classics 10. Science fiction 11. Multiple perspectives 12. Adult books for young adults
LC 91042819
Hugo Award for Best Novel, 1993; Locus Award for Best Science Fiction Novel, 1993; Nebula Award for Best Novel, 1992
A crisis linking the past and future, strands an Oxford student in the most dangerous year of the Middle Ages.

Willocks, Tim

Memo from Turner. Tim Willocks. Blackstone Pub 2019. 334 pages
ISBN 9781538519615
1. Traffic accidents 2. Police corruption 3. Murder investigation 4. Secrets 5. Classism 6. South Africa 7. Cape Town, South Africa 8. Thrillers and suspense
During a weekend spree in Cape Town a young, rich Afrikaner fatally injures a teenage street girl with his Range Rover but is too drunk to know that he has hit her. His companions-who do know-leave the girl to die. The driver's mother, a self-made mining magnate named Margot Le Roux, intends to keep her son in ignorance of his crime. By chance the case falls to the relentless Warrant Officer Turner of Cape Town Homicide.
Originally published: London : Jonathan Cape, 2018.

Wilsner, Meryl

★ **Something** to talk about. Meryl Wilsner. Jove, 2020. 304 pages
ISBN 9780593102527
1. Women television producers and directors 2. Former child actors and actresses 3. Personal assistants 4. Rumor 5. Scandals 6. Contemporary romances 7. LGBTQIA romances
LC 2019052279
LibraryReads Favorites, 2020
When her career is threatened by a red-carpet photo that appears to have romantic undertones, a Hollywood showrunner and her female assistant are targeted by paparazzi before realizing their actual feelings for each other.
"The novel is populated with strong secondary characters who bring Jo and Emma to life. Emma's Judaism in particular is thoughtfully integrated into her character. Wilsner's writing is matter-of-fact but effective, lending the novel a believable Hollywood insider vibe with a deftly handled #MeToo subplot. A sparkling debut with vibrant characters, a compelling Hollywood studio setting, and a sweet slow-burn romance." —*Kirkus*

Wilson, Carter

Dead girl in 2A. Carter Wilson. Sourcebooks Landmark, 2019. 384 p.
ISBN 9781492686033
1. Amnesia 2. Experiments 3. Change (Psychology) 4. Memory 5. Flights 6. Colorado 7. Psychological suspense 8. Multiple perspectives
LC 2019000366
This flight will take them somewhere they never expected to go...

Wilson, Daniel H.

The **Andromeda** evolution: a novel. Daniel H. Wilson. Harper, 2019. 448 pages (Andromeda novels, 2)
ISBN 9780062473271
1. Human/alien encounters 2. Microorganisms 3. Evolution 4. Pathogenic microorganisms 5. Molecular evolution 6. Washington (State) 7. Brazil 8. Bio-thrillers 9. Science fiction 10. Science fiction thrillers
LC 2019023408
A 50th-anniversary sequel to The Andromeda Strain finds a Brazilian drone detecting a bizarre anomaly in the middle of the jungle with the same chemical signature of the microparticle that nearly ended all life on Earth.
"Wilson takes one of Crichton's most durable story structures a group of specialists ventures into the unknown and works numerous variations, some small, some devastatingly large, on the theme." —*Booklist*

The **clockwork** dynasty: a novel. Daniel H. Wilson. Doubleday, 2017. 352 p.
ISBN 9780385541787
1. Automata 2. Immortalism 3. Secret societies 4. Robots 5. Secrets 6. Europe 7. Russia 8. 18th century 9. 21st century 10. Steampunk 11. Science fiction 12. Parallel narratives 13. Adult books for young adults
LC 2016053069
Alex Award, 2018; LibraryReads Favorites, 2017; Loan Stars Favourites, 2017
A young anthropologist specializing in ancient technology makes the astonishing discovery that a race of human-like machines has been hiding among people for untold centuries.
"This is science fiction at its bestthoughtful, challenging, beautifully written, and astonishing." —*Booklist*

Robogenesis: a novel. Daniel H. Wilson. Random, 2014. 361 pages; (Robopocalypse novels, 2)
ISBN 9780385537094
1. Robots 2. Artificial intelligence 3. Technology and civilization 4. Revolutions 5. Science fiction 6. Apocalyptic fiction 7. Science fiction thrillers
A sequel to Robopocalypse is told through a series of narratives that finds new and former characters fighting to rebuild a war-stricken world under threat of the surviving Archos machine code.
"This Hollywood-ready techno-thriller is packed to the brim with enough tough characters and brutal conflict to satisfy the most hardcore video gamers and action movie fans." —*Publishers Weekly*

Wilson, G. Willow

Alif the unseen. G. Willow Wilson. Grove Press, 2012. 433 p.
ISBN 9780802120205
1. Hackers 2. Computer technology 3. Death threats 4. Magic 5. Surveillance 6. Middle East 7. Urban fantasy 8. Middle Eastern-influenced fantasy 9. Adult books for young adults
Booklist Editors' Choice: Adult Books for Young Adults, 2012; New York Times Notable Book, 2012; School Library Journal Best Books: Best Adult Books 4 Teens, 2012; World Fantasy Award, 2013; Middle East Book Award, Youth Literature Winner, 2012
Forced underground when his ex-lover's new fiance breaches his computer, putting him and his clients in jeopardy, young Arab-Indian hacker and shielder Alif discovers the secret book of the jinn and uses its insights to enable life-threatening developments in information technology.

"Wilson skillfully weaves a story linking modern-day technologies and computer languages to the folklore and religion of the Middle East." —*Library Journal*

★ The **bird** king. G. Willow Wilson. Grove Press, 2019. 403 pages : Map
ISBN 9780802129031
1. Inquisition 2. Cartographers 3. Concubinage 4. Malicious accusation 5. Muslims 6. Spain 7. 15th century 8. Historical fantasy 9. Literary fiction 10. Middle Eastern-influenced fantasy 11. Adult books for young adults
LC 2018045952
LibraryReads Favorites, 2019
A concubine in the royal court of Granada at the height of the Spanish Inquisition and her mapmaker friend risk their lives to escape when the latter is accused of sorcery.

Wilson, Kevin
Nothing to see here. Kevin Wilson. Ecco, 2019. 288 p.
ISBN 9780062913463
1. Women caregivers 2. Child care 3. Spontaneous human combustion 4. Twins 5. Familial love 6. Mainstream fiction 7. Domestic fiction 8. Humorous stories
LC 2019008256
LibraryReads Favorites, 2019; New York Times Notable Book, 2019
Agreeing to help her former college roommate care for two stepchildren who possess the ability to spontaneously combust when agitated, Lillian endeavors to keep her young charges cool in the face of an astonishing revelation.

Wilson, Sloan
★ The **man** in the gray flannel suit. Sloan Wilson. Four Walls Eight Windows, 2002. 276 p.
ISBN 9781568582467
1. World War II veterans 2. Suburban life 3. Corporate culture 4. Marriage 5. Businesspeople 6. Connecticut 7. 1950s 8. Psychological fiction 9. Domestic fiction 10. Modern classics
LC 2002-69297
After returning from World War II, Tom Rath enters the corporate world to face the pressures and demands of the rat race.
Originally published: New York : Simon and Schuster, 1955.

Winch, Tara June
The **yield**. Tara June Winch. HarperVia, 2020. 352 p.
ISBN 9780063003460
1. Aboriginal Australians 2. Identity (Psychology) 3. Grief 4. Language and languages 5. Race relations 6. Literary fiction 7. Australian fiction 8. Multiple perspectives
LC 2020000143
Nielsen BookData Australian Booksellers' Choice Award, 2020; NSW Premier's Literary Awards, People's Choice Award for Fiction, 2020; Miles Franklin Award, 2020; Prime Minister's Literary Awards: Fiction, 2020; NSW Premier's Literary Awards, Book of the Year, 2020; NSW Premier's Literary Awards, Christina Stead Prize for Fiction, 2020; Shortlisted for the Stella Prize, 2020
Knowing that he will soon die, Albert 'Poppy' Gondiwindi takes pen to paper. His life has been spent on the banks of the Murrumby River at Prosperous House, on Massacre Plains. Albert is determined to pass on the language of his people and everything that was ever remembered. He finds the words on the wind. August Gondiwindi has been living on the other side of the world for ten years when she learns of her grandfather's death. She returns home for his burial, wracked with grief and burdened with all she tried to leave behind.
"Already a best-seller in Australia, Winch's second novel is a clear-eyed look at the experiences of native people and the ways in which history is inherited through generations." —*Booklist*

Winer, Jeanne
Her kind of case. Jeanne Winer. Bancroft Press, 2018. 308 pages; (Lee Isaacs, Esq. novels, 1)
ISBN 9781610882286
1. Lawyers 2. Hate crimes 3. Public defenders 4. Crimes against gay men and lesbians 5. Teenage murder suspects 6. Boulder, Colorado 7. Legal stories
A legal drama that centers on Lee Isaacs, a female defense attorney on the cusp of turning 60, who, out of curiosity, determination, and desire for a big, even impossible, professional challenge, chooses to take on a tough murder case in which a largely uncooperative young man is accused of helping kill a gay gang member.
"Winer...who was a criminal defense attorney for decades, brings vivid, insider knowledge of all things legal, from lawyers' black humor to the importance of details to a jury. Unlike many dull legal novels, though, this is filled with witty dialogue, believable characters, and quick pacing." —*Kirkus*

Winfrey, Kerry
Not like the movies. Kerry Winfrey. Jove, 2020. 320 p. (Waiting for Tom Hanks, 2)
ISBN 9781984804044
1. Coworkers 2. Coffee shops 3. Responsibility 4. Women caregivers 5. Father and adult daughter 6. Columbus, Ohio 7. Ohio 8. Romantic comedies
LC 2020004900
Avoiding relationships to focus on caring for her ailing father, Chloe is challenged to resolve the disparity between fiction and truth when her friend writes a screenplay about Chloe's romantically charged relationship with her too-good-to-be-true boss.
"Winfrey excels at upending typical romantic comedy tropes, and Chloe is a complicated, realistic, believable character. Sitcoms, movies, and music are all heavily referenced in the story; fans of the TV series New Girl will no doubt love this book. A quirky novel perfect for rom-com fans and readers looking for a little sweet escapism." —*Kirkus*

Waiting for Tom Hanks: a novel. Kerry Winfrey. Jove, 2019. Viii, 274 pages; (Waiting for Tom Hanks, 1)
ISBN 9781984804020
1. Screenplay writing 2. Single women 3. Obsession 4. Film industry and trade 5. Bishop, Elizabeth 6. Ohio 7. Romantic comedies
A rom-com-obsessed romantic waiting for her perfect leading man learns that life doesn't always go according to a script.
"The chemistry between Annie and Drew is irresistible, and the plots many moving pieces add complexity. Chloe, lovable Uncle Don, and the local coffee shops colorful characters provide humor and heart in just the right places." —*Publishers Weekly*

Winslow, De'Shawn Charles
★ **In** West Mills. De'Shawn Charles Winslow. Bloomsbury Publishing, 2019. 272 pages
ISBN 9781635573404

1. African American women 2. Independence in women 3. African American communities 4. Small town life 5. Eccentric women 6. North Carolina 7. 20th century 8. Literary fiction 9. Historical fiction 10. African American fiction

LC 2018034737

A woman in mid-20th-century rural North Carolina, determined to live on her own terms in spite of community gossip, finds unexpected support from a veteran fixer who struggles with an inability to correct his own troubled past.

Winslow, Don

The **border**. Don Winslow. William Morrow, 2019. 750 p. (Art Keller novels, 3)

ISBN 9780062664488

1. Drug enforcement agents 2. Drug cartels 3. Organized crime 4. Redemption 5. Heroin addiction 6. New Mexico 7. Mexico 8. Crime fiction

LC 2018037648

Booklist Editors' Choice, 2019

Promoted by the DEA after a crucial victory, Art Keller is targeted by the power-hungry traffickers behind an American heroin epidemic.

"An action-filled, sometimes even instructive look at the world of the narcos and their discontents." —*Kirkus*

Broken: six short novels. Don Winslow. William Morrow & Co, 2020. 338 pages

ISBN 9780062988904

1. Crime 2. Corruption 3. Loss (Psychology) 4. Revenge 5. Crime fiction 6. Short stories

Drug dealers, bounty hunters, fugitives, struggling cops and lost souls rob, steal, kill, corrupt and betray their way through five intense novellas in this collection from the internationally best-selling author of The Border.

"Bookending several novellas that reunite fans with characters from previous Winslow novels are two hard-hitting tales that evoke the tragedy-soaked worlds of The Force and The Border." —*Booklist*

Winspear, Jacqueline

The **American** agent. Jacqueline Winspear. Harper, 2019. 352 pages (Maisie Dobbs novels, 15)

ISBN 9780062436665

1. World War II 2. Women private investigators 3. Women journalists 4. Americans in England 5. Organized crime 6. Great Britain 7. Second World War era (1939-1945) 8. 1930s 9. Historical mysteries 10. Mysteries

When Catherine Saxon, an American correspondent reporting on the war in Europe, is found murdered in her London digs, news of her death is concealed by British authorities. Serving as a linchpin between Scotland Yard and the Secret Service, Robert MacFarlane pays a visit to Maisie Dobbs, seeking her help. Accompanied by an agent from the US Department of Justice-Mark Scott, the American who helped Maisie escape Hitler's Munich in 1938-he asks Maisie to work with Scott to uncover the truth about Saxon's death. As the Germans unleash the full terror of their blitzkrieg upon the citizens of London, raining death and destruction from the skies, Maisie must balance the demands of solving this dangerous case with her need to protect the young evacuee she has grown to love. Entangled in an investigation linked to the power of wartime propaganda and American political intrigue being played out in Britain, Maisie will face losing her dearest friend-and the possibility that she might be falling in love again.

★ The **consequences** of fear: a Maisie Dobbs novel. Jacqueline Winspear. HarperCollins, 2021. 352 p. (Maisie Dobbs novels, 16)

ISBN 9780062868022

1. World War II 2. Women private investigators 3. Boys 4. Murder investigation 5. Murderers 6. Great Britain 7. Second World War era (1939-1945) 8. 1940s 9. Historical mysteries 10. Mysteries

Entreated by a witness nobody believes to investigate a murder, Maisie Dobbs uncovers a conspiracy with devastating implications for Britain's war effort during the Nazi occupation of Europe.

"Fans of the series will need no encouragement to try this, and they'll be thrilled with the ending; also recommend it as a less-weighty read-alike for Anthony Doerr's All the Light We Cannot See (2014)." —*Booklist*

Winter, Evan

The **fires** of vengeance. Evan Winter. Orbit, 2020. 544 p; Map (The burning, 2)

ISBN 9780316489805

1. Warriors 2. Imaginary wars and battles 3. Women rulers 4. Anger in men 5. Class conflict 6. Sword and sorcery 7. Afrofantasy

LC 2020009321

Loan Stars Favourites, 2020

To reclaim her throne, Queen Tsiora joins forces with Tau, a young warrior, to assemble her forces and launch an all-out assault on her own capital city and reunite her people.

"Winter's beautifully descriptive, South African-inspired, military fantasy of war, revenge, and loss culminates with an impending battle against tremendous odds and the delivery of an unexpected plea heralding the arrival of an ancient, fearsome foe." —*Booklist*

★ The **rage** of dragons. Evan Winter. Orbit, 2019. 544 pages (The burning, 1)

ISBN 9780316489768

1. Warriors 2. Revenge 3. Determination in men 4. Class conflict 5. Social classes 6. Sword and sorcery 7. Afrofantasy

Born into a never ceasing war dominated by women who summon dragons and magically strong men, Tau has no gifts, but pledges to do all in his power to avenge his murdered family members.

"Winter's secondary characters support his heros story and amplify its themes of brotherhood, but it is Tau himself, far more nuanced than a simple underdog, who will move readers to eagerly seek the next volume." —*Publishers Weekly*

Winters, Ben H.

The **quiet** boy. Ben H. Winters. Mulholland Books, 2021. 336 p.

ISBN 9780316505444

1. Teenage boys 2. Time 3. People in comas 4. Accidents 5. Lawyers 6. Legal thrillers 7. Science fiction

A sweeping legal thriller follows a sixteen-year-old who suffers from a neurological condition that has frozen him in time, the team of lawyers, doctors, and detectives who are desperate to wake him up, and—more than a decade later—the trial of the teenager's father for murder.

"Winters, who got his start writing parodies (Android Karenina, 2010), has proved himself to be one of of our most fascinating genre benders of crime and speculative fiction, a writer who never fails to challenge his readers to embrace new ideas and new forms of reality. A wonderful, thoughtful book." —*Booklist*

Winterson, Jeanette

★ **Frankissstein**. Jeanette Winterson. Grove Press, 2019. 340 p.

ISBN 9780802129499

1. Shelley, Mary Wollstonecraft 2. Posthumanism 3. Artificial intelligence 4. Trans men 5. Cryonics 6. Sexuality 7. 19th century 8. 21st century 9. Multiple perspectives 10. Science fiction 11. Literary fiction

Longlisted for the Booker Prize, 2019

A transgender doctor falls in love with a celebrated professor who is leading the debate about artificial intelligence and conducting controversial experiments impacting cryogenics and the sex trade.

The **passion**. Jeanette Winterson. Atlantic Monthly Press, 1988. 160p.
ISBN 9780802135223
1. Soldiers 2. Married women 3. Bisexuality 4. Gambling 5. Man-woman relationships 6. Venice, Italy 7. Moscow, Russia 8. Stalin, Joseph 9. LGBTQIA fiction

LC 88003427

Passion consumes Henri, a chef with Napoleon's army, and Villanelle, who has lost her heart to a married noblewoman, until the two meet at the gates of Moscow and form a bond based on bitter loss.

Winthrop, Elizabeth Hartley

The **mercy** seat: a novel. Elizabeth Hartley Winthrop. Grove Press, 2018. 240 p.
ISBN 9780802128188
1. Racism 2. Race relations 3. Small town life 4. Trials (Rape) 5. Judicial error 6. Louisiana 7. 1940s 8. Literary fiction 9. Historical fiction 10. Multiple perspectives

LC 2017051039

Set during the hours leading up to the scheduled execution of a black teen for the alleged rape of a white woman in 1943 Louisiana, a meticulous portrait of race, racism and injustice in the Jim Crow era South traces the experiences of the convicted boy; his father, the District Attorney; the convict truck driver delivering the executioner's chair and a couple grappling with grief and secrets.

"This potent novel about prejudice and the constraints of challenging the status quo will move and captivate readers, especially those looking for socially conscious historical fiction." —*Publishers Weekly*

★ The **why** of things. Elizabeth Hartley Winthrop. Simon & Schuster, 2013. 256 p.
ISBN 9781451695755
1. Murder investigation 2. Family and suicide 3. Family relationships 4. Dog adoption 5. Grief in families 6. Mainstream fiction 7. Adult books for young adults

LC 2012041122

Arriving in their summer home less than a year after the suicide of a teenage daughter, Joan and her family stumble on the death of a local young man and adopt his homeless dog before bonding with his grieving mother and learning that the victim's death was not accidental.

Winton, Tim

The **shepherd's** hut. Tim Winton. Farrar, Straus and Giroux, 2018. 272 p.
ISBN 9780374262327
1. Hermits 2. Deserts 3. Teenage boys 4. Accidental death 5. Survival 6. Western Australia 7. Australia 8. Literary fiction 9. Australian fiction

Librarians' Choice (Australia), 2018

A brutalized rural youth flees his father's violent death to live in exile in Australia's harsh saltlands, where his life comes to depend on a ruined priest he is not sure he trusts.

Wiseman, Beth

Listening to love. Beth Wiseman. Zondervan, 2019. 320 p. (Amish journey, 2)
ISBN 9780529118714
1. Amish 2. Faith (Christianity) 3. Interfaith romance 4. Expectation (Psychology) 5. Man-woman relationships 6. Indiana 7. Christian romances

LC 2019013783

Lucas, a member of the Old Order Amish, falls in love with Natalie, a woman pursuing a veterinary medicine career, and both of their families are against their relationship, making it hard for the couple to stay true to themselves.

Wiseman, Ellen Marie

The **orphan** collector. Ellen Marie Wiseman. Kensington Pub Corp, 2020. 304 p.
ISBN 9781496715869
1. Influenza Epidemic, 1918-1919 2. Immigrants, German 3. Prejudice 4. Loss (Psychology) 5. Neighbors 6. Philadelphia, Pennsylvania 7. Pennsylvania 8. First World War era (1914-1918) 9. Historical fiction

Powerful, harrowing, and ultimately exultant, The Orphan Collector is a story of love, resilience, and the lengths we will go to protect those who need us most.

"Wiseman has written a touching tale of loss, survival, and perseverance with some light fantastical elements. Highly recommended for all collections." —*Booklist*

Wodehouse, P. G.

★ The **inimitable** Jeeves. P.G. Wodehouse. Overlook Hardcover, 2007. 272 p. (Jeeves and Wooster, 3)
ISBN 9781585679225
1. Single men 2. Butlers 3. Marriage 4. Upper class 5. Jeeves (Fictitious character) 6. England 7. Farcical fiction 8. Short stories 9. Gentle reads

Typical, just when Bertie thinks that God's in his heaven and all's right with the world, things start to go wrong again. There's young Bingo Little, who's in love for the umpteenth time and needs Bertie to put in a good word for him with his uncle. Aunt Agatha, who forces Bertie to get engaged to the formidable Honoria Glossop, and the troublesome twins, Claude and Eustace, whose antics when let loose in London knows no bounds. Add to that some friction in the Wooster home over a red cummerbund, purple socks and some snazzy old Etonian spats, and poor Bertie's really in the soup. Only one man can save the day, the inimitable Jeeves.

My man Jeeves. P. G. Wodehouse. Overlook Press, 2006. 185 p; (Jeeves and Wooster, 2)
ISBN 9781585678754
1. Rich people 2. Single men 3. Misadventures 4. Butlers 5. Valets 6. England 7. Humorous stories 8. Short stories 9. Gentle reads

LC 2006938089

The story of the relationship between Bertie Wooster and his valet Jeeves.

Originally published in the U.K. in 1919.

Wojtas, Olga

Miss Blaine's prefect and the golden samovar. Olga Wojtas. Felony & Mayhem Press, 2018. 264 p. (Miss Blaine's prefect, 1)
ISBN 9781631941702
1. Spark, Muriel 2. Librarians 3. Time travel (Past) 4. Murder investigation 5. Aristocracy 6. Middle-aged women 7. Edinburgh,

Scotland 8. Russia 9. 19th century 10. Historical mysteries
11. Humorous stories

LC 2018025061

Skills in everything from martial arts to quantum physics make Shona McMonagle the perfect recruit for a new and interesting project: Time-travel to Tzarist Russia, prevent a gross miscarriage of romance, and—in any spare time—see to it that only the right people get murdered.

"Firmly set in Russia with fascinating details of the life and times of the people, from princesses to serfs, woven through the story, and with Shona cleverly using historical clues gained from conversations to piece together facts about her new environment, this humorous romp includes plot twists and well-delineated, quirky, characters." —*Booklist*

Wolf, Dick

The **ultimatum**. Dick Wolf. William Morrow, 2015. 341 pages; (Jeremy Fisk novels, 3)
ISBN 9780062286833
1. Assassins 2. International intrigue 3. Snipers 4. Detectives 5. Fisk, Jeremy (Fictitious character) 6. New York City 7. Thrillers and suspense

When sensitive NYPD intelligence including his home address is released to WikiLeaks, Detective Jeremy Fisk is attacked by mysterious assailants linked to a serial sniper who is using cutting edge drone technology to murder innocent civilians.

Wolfe, Gene

★ The **best** of Gene Wolfe: a definitive retrospective of his finest short fiction. Gene Wolfe. St. Martins Press, 2009. 480 p.
ISBN 9780765321350
1. Short stories 2. Science fiction 3. Fantasy fiction
Locus Award for Best Collection, 2010

An anthology of thirty-one signature short works by the winner of the World Fantasy Award for Life Achievement includes "Petting Zoo," "The Tree Is My Hat," and "The Island of Dr. Death and Other Stories."

"This is a highly flattering career retrospective of a postmodern fabulist disguised as a mild-mannered SF writer." —*Publishers Weekly*

The **citadel** of the Autarch. Gene Wolfe. Timescape Books, 1983. 317 p. (Book of the new sun, 4)
ISBN 9780671452513
1. Exiles 2. Gems 3. Torturers 4. Parallel universes 5. Time travel 6. First person narratives 7. Science fiction classics 8. Science fantasy

LC 82005964

John W. Campbell Memorial Award for Best Science Fiction Novel, 1984

Severian the Torturer, possessor of the miracle-producing gem, the Claw of the Conciliator, experiences strange adventures as he journeys across the savage land of Urth BT

The **claw** of the conciliator. Gene Wolfe. Timescape Books, 1981. 301 p. (Book of the new sun, 2)
ISBN 9780671413705
1. Exiles 2. Gems 3. Monsters 4. Torturers 5. Executions and executioners 6. First person narratives 7. Science fiction classics 8. Science fantasy
Locus Award for Fantasy Novel, 1982; Nebula Award for Best Novel, 1981

Continues the tale of an Earth one million years in the future, following the cross-continent journey of Severian, owner of the Claw of the Conciliator, a miracle-producing gem BT
Sequel to: The shadow of the torturer.
Sequel: The sword of the Lictor.

The **land** across. Gene Wolfe. Tor Books, 2013. 286 p.
ISBN 9780765335951
1. Travel writers 2. Espionage 3. Supernatural 4. Political corruption 5. Spies 6. Eastern Europe 7. Noir fiction 8. Horror 9. First person narratives

LC 2013022126

In need of a new location, an American writer of travel guides journeys to a small and obscure Eastern European country where it soon becomes evident that there are supernatural forces at work, but they are not as threatening as the country's corruption and brute forces of bureaucracy.

"Mirroring the absurdist novels of Franz Kafka and the surreal stories of Stanislaw Lem and Jorge Luis Borges, Wolfe's latest novel begins quietly and grows stranger and more whimsical by the page. In the end, the author's creative genius brings everything together with twists and turns that are both surprising and immensely satisfying." —*Library Journal*

Wolfe, Paul

The **lost** diary of M. Paul Wolfe. HarperCollins, 2020. 304 p.
ISBN 9780062910660
1. Kennedy, John F. 2. Conspiracy theories 3. Presidents 4. Mistresses 5. Murder 6. Political intrigue 7. 1960s 8. Historical fiction 9. Biographical fiction 10. Literary fiction

aNavigating her attraction to a married customer who has brought her a 16th-century treatise, a book restorer uncovers the story of a forbidden romance between a courtesan and a Renaissance artist who is losing his sight.

"Wolfe's inspired study of a cryptic woman is credible and haunting." —*Booklist*

Wolfe, Suzanne M.

The **course** of all treasons. Suzanne M. Wolfe. Crooked Lane Books, 2019. 272 p. (Elizabethan spy novels, 2)
ISBN 9781643851785
1. Elizabeth 2. Spies 3. Political intrigue 4. Treason 5. Catholic families 6. Undercover operations 7. Tudor period (1485-1603) 8. Elizabethan era (1558-1603) 9. Historical mysteries

Working directly for Sir Francis Walsingham in 1586 England, Nicholas Holt, a spy for Queen Elizabeth I, tries to figure out who is attacking his loved ones.

"Wolfe vividly brings London to life, from the raunchy taverns to the stages offering plays by Will Shakespeare. But the book's greatest strength is its characters, starting with the clever but flawed Holt, and including a twin brother and sister team of Jewish healers and a young Irish woman with a talent for disguise." —*Publishers Weekly*

Wolfe, Thomas

★ **Look** homeward, angel: a story of a buried life. Thomas Wolfe. Scribner's, 2006. 512 p.
ISBN 9780743297318
1. Authors, American 2. Small town life 3. Dysfunctional families 4. Children of alcoholic fathers 5. Small town families 6. North Carolina 7. Coming-of-age stories 8. Autobiographical fiction 9. Books to movies

Wolfe's largely autobiographical novel features Eugene Gant, who pines for a more expansive life after being born to a father whose bouts of maniacal raving are fueled by a prodigious appetite for drink.

First published in the United States of America, 1929.

★ **Of** time and the river: a legend of man's hunger in his youth. Thomas Wolfe. C. Scribner's Sons, 1935. 912 p.
ISBN 9780241215760
1. Authors, American 2. Coming-of-age stories

LC 35027095

It is 1920 and Eugene Gant leaves the American South for Harvard, New York and Europe, determined to make his way as a writer. On the boat home, he meets Esther Jack, the woman who is to dominate his life. Autobiographical, vital and passionate, this novel blazes with energy and life.

Wolfe, Tom

Back to blood: a novel. Tom Wolfe. Little, Brown, 2012. 608 p.
ISBN 9780316036313
1. Police 2. Mayors 3. Journalists 4. Immigration and emigration 5. Ambition in men 6. Miami, Florida 7. Satirical fiction

LC 2012019545

A colorful cast of residents and visitors to Miami go about their daily activities, both legal and illegal.

"Wolfe is back to some old tricks, including an ever-shifting, sometimes untrustworthy point of view, dizzying pans from one actor to another and rat-a-tat prose...a welcome pleasure from an old master and the best from his pen in a long while." —*Kirkus*

The **bonfire** of the vanities. Tom Wolfe. Farrar, Straus Giroux, 1987. 659 p.
ISBN 9780374115340
1. City life 2. Social classes 3. Traffic accidents 4. Brokers 5. District attorneys 6. New York City 7. 1980s 8. Satirical fiction 9. Books to movies 10. Modern classics

LC 87017691

National Book Critics Circle Award for Fiction finalist, 1987

Sherman McCoy, a young investment banker in Manhattan, finds himself arrested following a freak accident and becomes involved with prosecutors, politicians, the press, and assorted hustlers.

Wolff, Tobias

Old school: a novel. Tobias Wolff. Knopf, 2003. 208 p.
ISBN 9780375401466
1. Prep schools 2. Social classes 3. Belonging 4. Teenage boys 5. Prep school students 6. New England 7. New England 8. Psychological fiction 9. Literary fiction 10. First person narratives 11. Adult books for young adults

LC 2003052930

ALA Notable Book, 2005; Booklist Editors' Choice: Adult Books for Young Adults, 2003; New York Times Notable Book, 2003; National Book Critics Circle Award for Fiction finalist, 2003

During his senior year at an elite New England prep school, a young man who had struggled to fit in with his contemporaries finds his life unraveling due to the school's obsession with literary figures and their work.

Our story begins: new and selected stories. Tobias Wolff. Alfred A. Knopf, 2008. Xii, 379 p.
ISBN 9781400044597
1. Short stories
New York Times Notable Book, 2008

Ten potent new stories that, along with twenty-one classics, display Wolff's mastery over a quarter century.

"It does not seem coincidental that Wolff's most protean narratives draw heavily upon his autobiographical experiences. Wolff, at his best, is truly a novelist of himself. His feats of self-invention offer a compelling rebuttal both to the fabulists whose stories fall so short of reality that they have to borrow the truth guarantee of memoir—if the lies rang truer, they could be published as fiction—and to those who denounce the faking of memoir as some sort of heinous crime, rather than the failed act of literature it is." —*Slate*

Wolitzer, Meg

The **female** persuasion. Meg Wolitzer. Riverhead Books, 2018. 456 p.
ISBN 9781594488405
1. Ambition in women 2. Feminists 3. Mentors 4. Couples 5. Self-fulfillment in women 6. Coming-of-age stories 7. Adult books for young adults

LC 2017031394

LibraryReads Favorites, 2018; Loan Stars Favourites, 2018; New York Times Notable Book, 2018

A shy college freshman finds her perspectives transformed by a mentor activist at the center of the women's movement who challenges her to discover herself in ways that take her far from the traditional life she envisioned at the side of her boyfriend.

The **Interestings**. Meg Wolitzer. Riverhead Books, 2013. 468 p.
ISBN 9781594488399
1. Marriage 2. Friendship 3. Success (Concept) 4. Actors and actresses 5. Jealousy in women 6. Mainstream fiction
New York Times Notable Book, 2013

Forging a powerful bond in the mid-1970s that lasts throughout subsequent decades, six individuals pursue respective challenges into their midlife years, including an aspiring actress who harbors jealousy toward friends who achieve successful creative careers.

Wong, David

Futuristic violence and fancy suits. David Wong. Thomas Dunne Books, 2015. 374 pages; (Zoey Ashe novels, 1)
ISBN 9781250040190
1. Near future 2. Superheroes 3. Supervillains 4. Young women 5. Secrets 6. Superhero stories 7. Science fiction 8. Satirical fiction 9. Adult books for young adults

LC 2015025817

Alex Award, 2016; RUSA Reading List Short List, 2016

The pseudonymous author of John Dies at the End forays into science fiction with this fast-paced, darkly humorous novel. After barista Zoey Ashe survives a live-streamed assassination attempt, she discovers that her deceased biological father was not the deadbeat she always assumed; he's actually the billionaire founder of Tabula Ra$a, a Mob-ruled metropolis in the Utah desert. Her dead dad's associates, the Suits, offer to protect her from future attacks in exchange for help defeating cyborg crime boss Molech. Staying alive is Zoey's top priority, so she has no choice but to take their deal.

"Well-timed humor and explosive thrills, a smart backbone, and witty wordsmithing make this new release by Cracked.com's pseudonym-wielding Jason Pargin (John Dies at the End, 2009) as fun as it gets. Steer this one toward readers of sf with a sense of humor, and fans of Max Barry's satirical futuristic novels." —*Booklist*

This book is full of spiders: seriously, dude, don't touch it. David Wong. St. Martin's Press, 2012. 384 p. (John dies at the end, 2)
ISBN 9780312546342

1. Paranormal phenomena 2. Zombies 3. Quakers 4. Slackers 5. Shapeshifters 6. Horror 7. Humorous stories

A sequel to John Dies at the End finds heroes David and John embroiled in a new set of horrific but absurd challenges when movie-induced zombie phobia enables a nefarious shape-shifter race to take over the world.

Sequel to: John Dies At the End

Woo, Sung J.

Love love: a novel. Sung J. Woo. Soft Skull Press, 2015. 256 p.
ISBN 9781593766177
1. Siblings 2. Divorced persons 3. Parent and adult child 4. Identity (Psychology) 5. Adopted children 6. Mainstream fiction 7. Adult books for young adults

LC 2015009333

Booklist Editors' Choice, 2015

Two siblings try to deal with the disappointments they have encountered in their lives, as Judy Lee tries to find love and her brother Kevin, hoping to help his father by donating a kidney, discovers that he was adopted.

"Woo's narrative takes serendipitous turns—he has a knack for making these twists seem organic, like things that would happen in life. Scenes recounting memories of family and lost love are also skillfully interspersed." —*Publishers Weekly*

Wood, James

Upstate. James Wood. Farrar, Straus & Giroux, 2018. 214 p.
ISBN 9780374279530
1. Widowers 2. Real estate developers 3. Family relationships 4. Fathers and daughters 5. Sisters 6. Saratoga Springs, New York 7. New York (State) 8. Domestic fiction

A British property developer faces philosophical questions about family and suffering when one of his estranged daughters falls into a severe depression.

Wood, Shelley

The **Quintland** sisters. Shelley Wood. William Morrow & Co, 2019. 384 pages
ISBN 9780062839091
1. Dionne quintuplets 2. Quintuplets 3. Child custody 4. Midwives 5. Nurses 6. Exploitation 7. Ontario 8. Canada 9. 1930s 10. Depression era (1929-1941) 11. Coming-of-age stories 12. Historical fiction 13. Canadian fiction 14. Adult books for young adults

Attending the birth of the Dionne quintuplets in 1934 Ontario, a teen midwife witnesses an explosive custody dispute between the government and family members involving the quintuplets' exploitation as curiosities.

"Blending historical fact with a fictional coming-of-age story, Wood has crafted an ambitious, meticulously researched, and imaginative debut novel that is engrossing and compelling." —*Booklist*

Wood, Tracey Enerson

The **engineer's** wife: a novel. Tracey Enerson Wood. Sourcebooks Landmark, 2020. 352 p.
ISBN 9781492698135
1. Roebling, Emily Warren 2. Bridges 3. Husband and wife 4. Married women — Identity 5. Helpfulness in women 6. Life change events 7. New York City 8. Brooklyn Bridge, New York City 9. 1870s 10. Historical fiction 11. Biographical fiction

LC 2019032996

When her happy domestic life is turned upside-down by her husband's work as the chief engineer on an under-construction Brooklyn Bridge, Emily Warren Roebling gradually takes over the project to advocate on behalf of worker safety.

"This important work of historical fiction brings to life the strength and resolve of a nineteenth-century woman overshadowed by men and overlooked by history books." —*Booklist*

Woodrell, Daniel

The **Maid's** Version: a novel. Daniel Woodrell. Little, Brown and Company, 2013. 164 pages
ISBN 9780316205856
1. Grandmother and grandson 2. Housekeepers 3. Justice 4. Explosions 5. Death 6. Missouri 7. Literary fiction 8. Historical fiction 9. Southern fiction

In 1929, Alma DeGeer Dunahew, the maid for a prominent family in Missouri, chases down justice after her younger sister is one of forty-two people killed in a mysterious explosion at a local dance hall.

Woods, Chavisa

Things to do when you're goth in the country: and other stories. Chavisa Woods. Seven Stories Press, 2017. 221 p.
ISBN 9781609807450
1. Misfits (Persons) 2. United States 3. 21st century 4. Short stories 5. Literary fiction

LC 2016043180

Things to Do When You're Goth in the Country introduces us to Chavisa Woods's people. They are smart and poor, lost and hoping not to be found, a people of faith who have no god, and of high hopes but few if any expectations—inhabitants, mostly young, of a third world country without a name that exists within America, mostly hidden.

"This book is tight, intelligent, and important, and sure to secure Woods a seat in the pantheon of critical twenty-first-century voices." —*Booklist*

Woods, Rita

★ **Remembrance**. Rita Woods. Forge, 2020. 352 p.
ISBN 9781250298454
1. Slavery 2. Racism 3. Supernatural 4. Protectiveness 5. Freedom 6. Haiti 7. New Orleans, Louisiana 8. 1790s 9. 1850s 10. Historical fantasy 11. Literary fiction

LC 2019041000

Hurston/Wright Legacy Award: Fiction, 2021

Looks at present-day Ohio, 1791 Haiti, and 1857 New Orleans, in which house girl Margot is sold just before her 18th birthday and her promised freedom, and, desperate, she escapes and tries to find Remembrance, a rumored stop on the Underground Railroad.

"This book deserves to be a breakout hit. Woods's magical realist take on the black female experience will have huge appeal to readers of Marlon James and Tara Conklin." —*Library Journal*

Woods, Stuart

Below the belt. Stuart Woods. G.P. Putnam's Sons, 2017. 320 p. (Stone Barrington novels, 40)
ISBN 9780399573972
1. Former police 2. Law firms 3. Power (Social sciences) 4. Ambition 5. Intrigue 6. Santa Fe, New Mexico 7. Thrillers and suspense

Stone Barrington and the gang are back in the line of fire, but with his usual unflappable aplomb, Stone always comes out on top.

"Woods brings back several recurring characters in this political novel in which art comes to imitate life.... Woods is compulsively readable, even as he churns out three novels a year, so a slip on the last page is easy to forgive and doesnt really lessen the pleasure of the journey in this easy-reading page-turner." —*Booklist*

★ **Bombshell**. Stuart Woods and Parnell Hall. Penguin Group USA 2020. 320 p. (Teddy Fay novels, 4)
ISBN 9780593083253
1. Former CIA agents 2. Film producers and directors 3. Criminals 4. Actors and actresses 5. Undercover operations 6. Hollywood, California 7. California 8. Thrillers and suspense
LC 2019057176
Former CIA operative-turned-movie producer Teddy Fay becomes embroiled in two sticky situations involving a vengeful criminal thug and malicious gossip that is overshadowing the career of a rising Centurion star.
"Woods and Parnell mix crime with Hollywood glitz for a winning combination. Nonstop action and brisk prose, plus the senior Barrington in a cameo role, make for amiable summer reading." —*Booklist*

Chiefs. By Stuart Woods. W. W. Norton, 1981. 427 p. (Lee family saga, 1)
ISBN 9780039014612
1. Small towns 2. Political corruption 3. Secrets 4. Missing persons 5. Arthur, King 6. Georgia 7. 1920s 8. Thrillers and suspense
LC 80027350
Edgar Allan Poe Award for Best First Mystery Novel, 1982
Beginning in 1920, the experiences of three Georgia police chiefs, who watch the world, their town, and their jobs change. At the heart of this is a 40-year-old mystery each chief must try to crack.

A **delicate** touch. Stuart Woods. G. P. Putnam's Sons, 2018. 320 p. (Stone Barrington novels, 48)
ISBN 9780735219250
1. Private investigators 2. Law firms 3. Scandals 4. Upper class 5. Secrets 6. New York City 7. Thrillers and suspense
LC 2018041585
Asked by an old acquaintance with help solving a tricky puzzle, Stone Barrington unwittingly stirs up a decades-old scandal in high-society New York and must risk his life to protect innocent lives.

Fast & loose. Stuart Woods. G.P. Putnam's Sons, 2017. 357 p. (Stone Barrington novels, 41)
ISBN 9780399574191
1. Former police 2. Law firms 3. Power (Social sciences) 4. Ambition 5. Intrigue 6. Manhattan, New York City 7. Thrillers and suspense
Stone Barrington, a New York City cop turned rainmaker for a white-shoe Manhattan law firm, tackles a formidable case that challenges the boundaries of his talents.
"In Barrington, Woods has created a rich man who could walk through the needles eye into heaven and then have St. Peter waiting for him with Stone's favorite drink on the bar. Pure fantasy, to be sure, but a thoroughly entertaining escapist read." —*Booklist*

Hit list. Stuart Woods. Putnam Publishing Group, 2020. 336 pages (Stone Barrington novels, 53)
ISBN 9780593083222
1. Private investigators 2. Assassins 3. Threat (Psychology) 4. Intrigue 5. Former police 6. Thrillers and suspense
Former New York City cop turned Manhattan law firm rainmaker finds himself in rather hot water in a high-suspense latest entry in the best-selling series.
"Fast-moving easy reading in the familiar Woods style." —*Booklist*

The **money** shot. . G.P. Putnam's Sons, 2018. 320 p. (Teddy Fay novels, 2)
ISBN 9780735218598
1. Extortion 2. Actors and actresses 3. Criminal investigation 4. Disguises 5. Stunt performers 6. Hollywood, California 7. Thrillers and suspense
LC 2018000922
Disguising himself as a stuntman to investigate blackmail threats against an actress starring in a new production, Teddy Fay discovers that the perpetrators are looking for something other than money, in a novel that also features fan-favorite Stone Barrington.

New York dead. Stuart Woods. HarperCollins Publishers, 1991. 303 p. (Stone Barrington novels, 1)
ISBN 9780060179250
1. Murder 2. Police 3. Sexuality 4. Women television newscasters and commentators 5. Barrington, Stone (Fictitious character) 6. New York City 7. Thrillers and suspense
LC 90056374
On disability leave from the New York City Police Department, Detective Sergeant Stone Barrington witnesses the murder of network news star Sasha Nijinsky, who is pushed from her penthouse terrace.
"A mystery set in Manhattan's Upper East Side, the stomping ground of Stone Barrington, a well-bred but unpretentious detective.... Late one evening, as Stone trudges home from Elaine's Restaurant, popular TV newscaster Sasha Nijinsky plummets 12 stories from her terrace and lands on a heap of dirt 20 yards away from himremarkably, still alive. Stone fails to apprehend the person who flees Sasha's penthouse and, after the ambulance carrying her collides with a fire truck, Sasha herself disappears. Despite the fact that no corpse is in evidence, the baffled NYPD eagerly pins a murder rap on Sasha's distraught lesbian lover. Stone refuses to accept his colleagues' pat solution." —*Publishers Weekly*

Orchid beach. Stuart Woods. Harper Collins, 1998. 325 p. (Holly Barker novels, 1)
ISBN 9780060191818
1. Murder 2. Conspiracies 3. Drug smuggling 4. Small town life 5. Women deputy police chiefs 6. Florida 7. Thrillers and suspense 8. Adult books for young adults
Military policewoman Holly Barker lost a harassment case against her superior and quit the army. On arriving for a new job as deputy of a Florida town she finds the chief shot, a case which will lead to an assault by the FBI on a compound of the very rich.
"The story gets extra bite from Holly's intriguing relationship with an inherited canine named Daisy, the clairvoyant Doberman that belonged to her mentor." —*Publishers Weekly*

Palindrome. Stuart Woods. Harper Collins Publishers, 1991. 344 p.
ISBN 9780060179113
1. Abused women 2. Solitude 3. Revenge 4. Women photographers 5. Man-woman relationships 6. Cumberland Island, Georgia 7. Atlanta, Georgia 8. Thrillers and suspense
LC 90055587
For years, Liz Barwick, a talented photographer, has been battered by her husband, a pro football player. This time, it takes an emergency room to keep her from death. Liz retreats to an island off Georgia's coast to find solitude and herself. She becomes involved with the strange and handsome Drummond twins and begins to leave her past behind. Then, a series of gruesome murders occur, and Liz realizes that there's no place to hide.
"When Liz Barwick is beaten nearly to death by her steroid-crazed husband, Baker Ramsey, a star NFL running back, she quickly divorces him, takes a large cash settlement and disappears from public view. Liz, whose book of sports photographs has just been released, takes advantage of her publisher's offer to live in his cottage on an isolated private island

off the Georgia coast. But when Ramsey goes on a murderous rampage, Liz's lawyer and publisher and his wife are among his victims. Meanwhile other events are unfolding on Cumberland Island, where Liz becomes involved with the Drummond family." —*Publishers Weekly*

Santa Fe rules. Stuart Woods. Harper Collins Publishers, 1992. 303 p; (Ed Eagle novels, 1)
ISBN 9780060179632
1. Husband and wife 2. Innocence (Law) 3. Secrets 4. Native American lawyers 5. Film producers and directors 6. Santa Fe, New Mexico 7. Thrillers and suspense
LC 91058476
Learning that his wife and partner have died suspiciously while he was away, successful Hollywood producer Wolf Willett returns home and hires ace criminal defense lawyer Ed Eagle to clear his name of the murder charge.
Sequel: Short straw.

Skin game. Stuart Woods and Parnell Hall. Penguin Group USA 2019. 320 p. (Teddy Fay novels, 3)
ISBN 9780735219168
1. Treason 2. Rare and endangered animals 3. Double agents 4. Espionage 5. Undercover operations 6. Paris, France 7. Thrillers and suspense
LC 2018049556
When former CIA operative Teddy Fay travels to Paris in search of a treasonous criminal, his trail of clues leads to complicated secrets, evildoers making power grabs, and a global threat.

Smooth operator. G.P. Putnam's Sons, 2016. 320 p. (Teddy Fay novels, 1)
ISBN 9780399185267
1. Assassination 2. Former assassins 3. Intelligence officers 4. Intrigue 5. Snipers 6. Washington, D.C. 7. Thrillers and suspense
LC 2016008414
"When President Kate Lee calls Stone Barrington to Washington on an urgent matter, it's soon clear that a potentially disastrous situation requires the kind of help more delicate than even he can provide. and he knows just the right man for the job. Teddy Fay: ex-CIA, master of disguise, and a gentleman not known for abiding by legal niceties in the pursuit of his own brand of justice." —Provided by publisher.

Stealth. Stuart Woods. Putnam Pub Group, 2019. 320 p. (Stone Barrington novels, 51)
ISBN 9780593083161
1. Private investigators 2. Lawyers 3. Sabotage 4. Attempted murder 5. Intelligence service 6. Great Britain 7. Scotland 8. Thrillers and suspense
Abruptly dispatched to a remote region of the U.K, Stone Barrington teams up with two brilliant colleagues only to land in a trap that reveals a rival power's lethal agenda and the larger conspiracy of a criminal mastermind.

Woodson, Jacqueline
★ **Another** Brooklyn. Jacqueline Woodson. Amistad, 2016. 192 pages
ISBN 9780062359988
1. Female friendship 2. African Americans — Identity 3. Memories 4. Violence in men 5. Sexual violence 6. Brooklyn, New York City 7. New York City 8. 1970s 9. Coming-of-age stories 10. Literary fiction 11. First person narratives 12. Adult books for young adults
BCALA Literary Award for Fiction, 2017; Booklist Editors' Choice: Adult Books for Young Adults, 2016; New York Times Notable Book, 2016; School Library Journal Best Books: Best Adult Books 4

Teens, 2016; Finalist for the Hurston/Wright Legacy Awards for Fiction, 2017
August is 35 the year she returns to Brooklyn to bury her father, and a chance encounter with a friend in her old neighborhood prompts a flood of memories from her youth. Having moved to Brooklyn at eight, August's coming of age was marked by a search for belonging, close friendships, freedom, and the little-understood absence of her mother. Her memories explore what it was like to be an African-American girl (and teen) in the 1970s, what possibilities existed—and what challenges. This tale of friendship, love, and loss cuts back and forth through time.
"Woodson draws on all the senses to trace the milestones in a woman's life and how her early experiences shaped her identity." —*Publishers Weekly*

★ **Red** at the bone. Jacqueline Woodson. Riverhead Books, 2019. 176 p.
ISBN 9780525535270
1. Family celebrations 2. Social classes 3. Unplanned pregnancy 4. Mothers and daughters 5. Gentrification of cities 6. Brooklyn, New York City 7. New York City 8. 20th century 9. African American fiction 10. Coming-of-age stories 11. Literary fiction
Library Journal Best Books, 2019; LibraryReads Favorites, 2019; New York Times Notable Book, 2019
As Melody celebrates a coming of age ceremony at her grandparents' house in 2001 Brooklyn, her family remembers 1985, when Melody's own mother prepared for a similar party that never took place in this novel about different social classes.

Woolf, Virginia
Between the acts. Virginia Woolf. Harcourt Brace Jovanovich, 1969. 219 p.
ISBN 9780156118705
1. Husband and wife 2. Villages 3. Pageants 4. Manors 5. Women dramatists 6. 1930s 7. Psychological fiction 8. Modern classics
LC 41017876
Isa and her husband must confront each other after a day of pageantry and emotional tension

Jacob's room. Virginia Woolf. Harcourt Brace Jovanovich, 1978. 176 p.
ISBN 9780156457422
1. Young men 2. Soldiers 3. Man-woman relationships 4. Growing up 5. Social classes 6. Experimental fiction 7. Psychological fiction 8. Modern classics
An extraordinary departure from traditional forms of the novel, Jacob's Room is both an elegiac and experimental tale told in pieces and fragments and a paean to the slaughter and loss of the First World War.

★ **Mrs.** Dalloway. Virginia Woolf. Harcourt Brace & Company, 1997. 212 p.
ISBN 9780156005555
1. Middle-aged women 2. Social classes 3. Feminism 4. Politicians' spouses 5. Social conflict 6. England 7. Psychological fiction 8. Multiple perspectives 9. Books to movies
LC 97-13622
During one day of arranging for her party Mrs. Dalloway remembers her youth, considers the crushing effects of the Great War, and reexamines her marriage.
First published in Great Britain: Hogarth, 1925.

Orlando: a biography. By Virginia Woolf. Harcourt Brace Jovanovich, 1973. Ix, 333 p. : Illustration
ISBN 9780156701600

1. Young men 2. Nobility — History 3. Sex (Psychology) 4. Metamorphosis 5. Transgender persons 6. Satirical fiction 7. Books to movies 8. Modern classics

Orlando emerges as a young man at the court of Queen Elizabeth I and progresses, with breathtaking ease, through three centuries until, by now a woman, she arrives in the bustle and diversions of the 1920s...Orlando's journey, from wondrous youth barbed by love, to feted writer, settled in her femininity, is a wild and curiously relevant fable.

Originally published: London : Hogarth Press, 1928.

★ **To** the lighthouse. Virginia Woolf. Harcourt Brace Jovanovich, 1981. Xii, 209 p.
ISBN 9780151907366
1. Women 2. Human behavior 3. Man-woman relationships 4. Nature 5. Husband and wife 6. 1920s 7. Psychological fiction 8. Modern classics

The Ramsay family and the one summer spent with their friends in their holiday home in Scotland. Offshore stands the lighthouse; remote, inaccessible, and an external presence in a changing world.

The text of this edition is based on that of the original Hogarth Press edition, published by Leonard and Virginia Woolf on 5 May 1927—Page facing colophon.

Originally published: London : Hogarth, 1927.

The **voyage** out. . Penguin Books, 1992. 382 p.
ISBN 9780140185638
1. Young women 2. Self-discovery in women 3. Women travelers 4. Man-woman relationships 5. Ocean travel 6. Coming-of-age stories 7. Modern classics

Disillusioned with her life, Rachel Vinrace embarks on a journey to South American aboard her father's vessel. During the long voyage, Rachel discovers the true plight of women during the early 20th century and becomes determined to reinvent herself.

Standard print edition originally published: London : Duckworth, 1915.

The **waves**. Harcourt, 2006. Lxvii, 270 p.
ISBN 9780156031578
1. Identity (Psychology) 2. Friendship 3. Aging 4. Growing up 5. Purpose in life 6. Psychological fiction 7. Experimental fiction 8. Literary fiction
LC 2005037770

As they move from childhood to maturity, the personalities of six friends are revealed through interior monologues. Elliptical, but deeply poetic, the strands of their experiences emerge gently and reflectively in a stream of consciousness, illuminating the meaning of life itself.

Includes bibliographical references (p. [265]-270).

First published in the U.K. : Hogarth Press, 1931.

★ The **years**. Virginia Woolf. Harcourt Brace Jovanovich, 1965. 435 p.
ISBN 9780156997010
1. Rich families 2. Family relationships 3. Death 4. Families 5. England 6. Domestic fiction 7. Modern classics
LC 37027268

Three generations of the Pargiters, an upper-class English family, are caught up in the changes, burdens, and promises of life from 1880 to the 1930's.

Originally published: The Hogarth Press, 1937.

Wouk, Herman

★ The **Caine** mutiny: a novel of World War II. By Herman Wouk. Back Bay Books, 2003. Xii, 537 p. : Map
ISBN 9780316955102

1. Mutiny 2. Courts-martial and courts of inquiry 3. Leadership in men 4. World War II — Naval operations, American 5. Sailors 6. Pacific Ocean 7. Second World War era (1939-1945) 8. War stories 9. Sea stories 10. Historical fiction
LC 2003109473

Pulitzer Prize for Fiction, 1952

When Lieutenant Commander Philip Queeg becomes captain of the destroyer-minesweeper USS Caine, Ensign Willie Keith believes that the tough Naval Academy graduate will bring much needed discipline to the Caine's rough crew. But Queeg soon reveals himslef to be a cowardly, paranoid man. When his actions begin to endanger not just the crew but the war effort itself, Keith finds himself faced with a terrible choice: obey Queeg, and risk the lives of his shipmates and allies—or mutiny.

Originally published: Garden City, N.Y. : Doubleday, 1951.

★ **War** and remembrance: a novel. Herman Wouk. Little, Brown, 1978. 1042 p.
ISBN 9781444779288
1. Hitler, Adolf 2. Family relationships 3. World War II 4. Jews 5. Holocaust (1933-1945) 6. Man-woman relationships 7. Second World War era (1939-1945) 8. 1940s 9. War stories 10. Historical fiction
LC 78017746

"Wouk's work is a journey of extraordinary emotional riches. Quantity in time becomes quality, movement becomes scope, and history becomes human yearning." —*New York Times Book Review*

Sequel to: The winds of war.

America at war, from Pearl Harbor to Hiroshima.

★ The **winds** of war: a novel. Herman Wouk. Little, Brown, 1971. 885 p.
ISBN 9781444779264
1. Hitler, Adolf 2. Family relationships 3. World War II. 4. Holocaust (1933-1945) 5. Atrocities 6. Jews 7. Second World War era (1939-1945) 8. 1940s 9. War stories 10. Historical fiction
LC 72161857

As the war escalates in Europe, the Henry clan, a family of American naval heroes, finds itself drawn into the center of the conflict and must send its patriarch and several sons into the fray.

"On the broadest of tapestries, Wouk weaves the effect of the preparation and the actual outbreak of World War II upon the family of Commander Pug Henry. The affairs of the Henry family became intertwined with those of others, in such varying scenes as Washington, Berlin, Rome, London, and Moscow.... Despite the novel's breadth, the development of Henry's character as the middle-class military leader America needed in the 1940's is surprisingly credible." —*Choice*

Sequel: War and remembrance.

Wright, Jaime Jo

The **haunting** at Bonaventure Circus. Jaime Jo Wright. Bethany House, 2020. 390 p.
ISBN 9780764233890
1. Circus 2. Women circus performers 3. Abandoned children 4. Birth defects 5. Identity (Psychology) 6. Wisconsin 7. 1920s 8. Christian suspense 9. Historical fiction 10. Parallel narratives

In 1928, Bonaventure Circus outcast Pippa Ripley must decide if uncovering her roots is worth putting herself directly in the path of a killer preying on the troupe. Decades later, while determining if an old circus train depot will be torn down or preserved, Chandler Faulk is pulled into a story far darker and more haunting than she imagined.

"Drawing from the author's personal connection to Wisconsin's circus history, the tantalizing plot and immersive rendition of place are masterful. As Wright alternates between Chandler's present-day story and interludes set in 1928, she captivates with compassion, eerie eloquence, and astounding intensity." —*Booklist*

Wright, Lawrence

The **end** of October. Lawrence Wright. Alfred A Knopf, 2020. 352 pages

ISBN 9780525658658

1. Epidemics 2. Viruses 3. Physicians 4. Diseases 5. International relations 6. Medical thrillers

Investigating dozens of mysterious deaths in an Indonesian internment camp, a World Health Organization doctor finds himself on a race to uncover the origins of a mysterious killer virus and find a cure before it decimates world populations.

"Wright pulls few punches and imbues even walk-on characters with enough humanity that their fate will matter to readers. This timely literary page-turner shows Wright is on a par with the best writers in the genre." —*Publishers Weekly*

Wright, Richard

The **man** who lived underground. Richard Wright. Penguin Group USA 2021. 250 p.

ISBN 9781598536768

1. African American men 2. Racism 3. Innocence (Law) 4. Murder investigation 5. Malicious accusation 6. Chicago, Illinois 7. Literary fiction 8. African American fiction

Fred Daniels, a black man, is picked up randomly by the police after a brutal murder in a Chicago neighborhood and taken to the local precinct where he is tortured until he confesses to a crime he didn't commit. After signing a confession, he escapes from the precinct and takes up residence in the sewers below the streets of Chicago. This is the simple, horrible premise of Richard Wright's scorching novel, The Man Who Lived Underground, a masterpiece written in the same period as his landmark books Native Son (1940) and Black Boy (1945) that he was unable to publish in his lifetime. Now, for the first time, this incendiary novel about race and violence in America, the work that meant more to Wright than any other is published in full, in the form that he intended.

"Now, finally, this devastating inquiry into oppression and delusion, this timeless tour de force, emerges in full, the work Wright was most passionate about, as he explains in the profoundly illuminating essay, 'Memories of My Grandmother,' also published here for the first time." —*Booklist*

★ **Native** son. Richard Wright; with an introduction by Arnold Rampersad. Harper Perennial Modern Classics, 2005. Xxii, 504, 16 p.

ISBN 9780060837563

1. Murderers 2. Racism 3. Poverty 4. African Americans 5. Ghettoes, African American 6. Chicago, Illinois 7. 1930s 8. Literary fiction 9. Modern classics 10. African American fiction

LC 79086654

Right from the start, Bigger Thomas had been headed for jail. It could have been for assault or petty larceny; by chance, it was for murder and rape. Native Son tells the story of this young black man caught in a downward spiral after he kills a young white woman in a brief moment of panic. Set in Chicago in the 1930s, Richard Wright's novel is just as powerful today as when it was written—in its reflection of poverty and hopelessness, and what it means to be black in America.

The restored text, established by the Library of America.

Wrobel, Stephanie

Darling Rose Gold. Stephanie Wrobel. Berkley, 2020. 320 pages

ISBN 9780593100066

1. Munchausen syndrome by proxy 2. Mothers and daughters 3. Deception 4. Child abuse 5. Former convicts 6. Psychological suspense 7. First person narratives 8. Multiple perspectives

LibraryReads Favorites, 2020

Enduring decades of serious illness as a victim of Munchausen Syndrome by Proxy before exposing her mother's behavior, Rose Gold invites her unrepentant mother back into her life to secretly settle the score.

"Propulsive pacing, a claustrophobic setting, and vividly sketched characters who are equal parts victim and villain conspire to create an anxious, unsettling narrative. Psychological suspense fans will be well satisfied." —*Publishers Weekly*

Wynne, Phoebe

Madam. Phoebe Wynne. St. Martin's Press, 2021. 352 p.

ISBN 9781250272041

1. Boarding schools 2. Teachers 3. Secrets 4. Castles 5. Tradition (Philosophy) 6. Scotland 7. Gothic fiction

LC 2020053426

While working at Caldonbrae, a prestigious boarding school high above the rocky Scottish cliffs, 26-year-old Rose Christie discovers the true extent of the school's nefarious purpose when she tries to find out what really happened to her predecessor.

"Fans of dark academia will fall hard for this gothic tale powered by bold heroines who refuse to submit." —*Booklist*

First published in the UK by Quercus Books.

Y

Yanagihara, Hanya

A **little** life: a novel. Hanya Yanagihara. Doubleday, 2015. 728 p.

ISBN 9780385539258

1. Male friendship 2. Psychic trauma 3. Ambition 4. City life 5. Self-destructive behavior 6. New York City 7. 21st century 8. Literary fiction 9. Psychological fiction

LC 2014027379

ALA Notable Book, 2016; Booklist Editors' Choice, 2015; Kirkus Prize for Fiction, 2015; New York Times Notable Book, 2015; Andrew Carnegie Medal for Excellence in Fiction finalist, 2016; National Book Award for Fiction finalist, 2015; Shortlisted for The Baileys Women's Prize for Fiction, 2016; Shortlisted for the International Dublin Literary Award, 2017; Shortlisted for the Man Booker Prize, 2015

Moving to New York to pursue creative ambitions, four former classmates share decades marked by love, loss, addiction and haunting elements from a brutal childhood.

"This is a novel that values the everyday over the extraordinary, the push and pull of human relationshipsand the book's effect is cumulative. There is real pleasure in following characters over such a long period, as they react to setbacks and successes, and, in some cases, change." —*Publishers Weekly*

Yang, JY

The **ascent** to godhood. J. Y. Yang. St Martins Press, 2019. 112 p. (Tensorate novellas, 4)

ISBN 9781250165886

1. Women rulers 2. Resistance to government 3. Power (Social sciences) 4. Psychic ability 5. Loss (Psychology) 6. Asian-influenced fantasy 7. Steampunk 8. Fantasy fiction

The Protector is dead. For fifty years, the world turned around her as she built her armies, trained her Tensors, and grasped at the reins of fate itself. Now she is dead. Her followers will quiver, her enemies rejoice. But in one tavern, deep in rebel territory, her greatest enemy drowns her sorrows. Lady Han raised a movement that sought the Protector's head, yet now she can only mourn her loss. She remembers how it all began, when the Protector was young, not yet crowned, and a desperate dancing girl dared to fall in love with her.

The **black** tides of heaven. J. Y. Yang. Tor.com, 2017. 160 p. (Tensorate novellas, 1)
ISBN 9780765395412
1. Twins 2. Psychic ability 3. Resistance to government 4. Power (Social sciences) 5. Secrets 6. Steampunk 7. Asian-influenced fantasy 8. Fantasy fiction

The Black Tides of Heaven is one of a pair of unique, standalone introductions to JY Yang's Tensorate Series, which Kate Elliott calls "effortlessly fascinating." For more of the story you can read its twin novella The Red Threads of Fortune, available simultaneously.

"Yang's world is imbued with magic, yet a burgeoning rebellion eschews that magic for technology. The other striking bit of worldbuilding is that children in this world do not have gender until they choose which sex they wish to be, and the stories are full of fascinating gender explorations." —*Library Journal*

The **descent** of monsters. J. Y. Yang. St Martins Pr 2018. 160 p. (Tensorate novellas, 3)
ISBN 9781250165855
1. Criminal investigation 2. Political corruption 3. Secrets 4. Experiments 5. Monsters 6. Fantasy mysteries 7. Asian-influenced fantasy 8. Steampunk

An investigation into atrocities committed at a classified research facility threaten to expose secrets that the Protectorate will do anything to keep hidden.

The **red** threads of fortune. J. Y. Yang. Tor.com, 2017. 160 p. (Tensorate novellas, 2)
ISBN 9780765395399
1. Psychic ability 2. Loss (Psychology) 3. Women psychics 4. Women hunters 5. Monsters 6. Steampunk 7. Asian-influenced fantasy 8. Fantasy fiction

The Red Threads of Fortune is one of a pair of unique, standalone introductions to JY Yang's Tensorate Series, which Kate Elliott calls "effortlessly fascinating." For more of the story you can read its twin novella The Black Tides of Heaven, available simultaneously.

Yang, Susie

White Ivy: a novel. Susie Yang. Simon & Schuster, 2020. 368 p.
ISBN 9781982100599
1. Chinese American women 2. Women thieves 3. Upper class 4. Ambition in women 5. Assimilation (Sociology) 6. Boston, Massachusetts 7. Massachusetts 8. Coming-of-age stories 9. Literary fiction
LC 2020002254
LibraryReads Favorites, 2020

Years after she is sent away from Boston to China for shoplifting, a conflicted Chinese-American woman reconnects with her golden-boy childhood crush before a ghost from the past threatens her ambitions.

"Yang's dark, spellbinding debut gives insight into the immigrant experience and life in the upper class, challenging the stereotypes and per-

ceptions associated with both. The surprising twists, elegant prose, and complex characters in this coming-of-age story make this a captivating read." —*Booklist*

Yates, Christopher J.

Grist Mill Road: a novel. Christopher J. Yates. Picador, 2018. 342 pages
ISBN 9781250150288
1. Violence against teenage girls 2. Crime 3. Witnesses 4. Life change events 5. Married people 6. New York City 7. New York (State) 8. 1980s 9. 2000s (Decade) 10. Psychological suspense 11. Literary fiction 12. Multiple perspectives
LC 2017028306

Years after three friends from an idyllic hamlet 90 miles north of New York City are bound and then separated by a devastating, seemingly senseless crime, the trio revisits their painful pasts in even more traumatizing ways.

"Mesmerizing and impossible to put down, this novel demands full attention, full empathy, and full responsibility; in return it offers poignant insight into h u man fragility and resilience." —*Kirkus*

Yates, Richard

★ The **collected** stories of Richard Yates. Richard Yates; introduction by Richard Russo. Henry Holt and Co, 2001. Xx, 472 p.
ISBN 9780805066937
1. United States 2. Short stories
LC 61400
Library Journal Best Books, 2001; New York Times Notable Book, 2001

Collects the stories of Richard Yates, featuring nine new stories as well as works from the anthologies "Eleven Kinds of Loneliness" and "Liars in Love."

"Bitterness, loneliness and lack of fulfillment are the central themes of this grim posthumous collection." —*Publishers Weekly*

Yellin, Jessica

Savage news. Jessica Yellin. Mira Books, 2019. 384 p.
ISBN 9780778308423
1. Women journalists 2. Competition 3. Television industry and trade 4. Sexism 5. Politicians 6. Washington, D.C. 7. Satirical fiction

A first novel by the award-winning former CNN chief White House correspondent follows the career of a woman cable news journalist who navigates ratings wars, sexual harassment and impossible standards throughout a precarious diplomatic and political incident.

Yocum, Robin

A **welcome** murder. Robin Yocum. Seventh Street Books, 2017. 280 pages
ISBN 9781633882638
1. Murder investigation 2. Small towns 3. Drug dealers 4. Murder suspects 5. Former convicts 6. Ohio 7. Mysteries 8. Multiple perspectives 9. First person narratives
LC 2016051813

Meet Johnny Earl, a washed-up former professional baseball player and ex-con who is the best athlete Steubenville, Ohio has ever produced. He'd like to find the drug money he's hidden there and get out of town, but a Neo Nazi also wants the money... and the high-school friend and FBI informant who sent Johnny up the river has been murdered. Johnny's a suspect, of course, but he's not the only one. Turns out plenty of people are happy Rayce Daubner is dead, including Johnny Earl's high-school girlfriend, her current husband, the local sheriff, and his unhappy wife. Told from the first-person point of view of several people, this lively, violent, funny novel provides an intimate look at an eccentric cast of memorable characters.

"Yocum (A Brilliant Death) has produced a rollicking tale sure to appeal to Donald Westlake and Elmore Leonard fans." —*Publishers Weekly*

Yoder, Rachel

Nightbitch. Rachel Yoder. Doubleday, 2021. 256 p.
ISBN 9780385546812
1. Motherhood 2. Stay-at-home mothers 3. Women artists 4. Metamorphosis 5. Anger in women 6. Satirical fiction

An artist turned stay-at-home mom becomes convinced that she is turning into a dog and, as her symptoms intensify, struggles to keep her alter-canine-identity a secret, until she meets a group of mothers who may also be more than what they seem.

"Yoder's guttural and luminous debut blends absurdism, humor, and myth to lay bare the feral, violent realities underlying a new mother's existence." —*Publishers Weekly*

Yoon, David

Version zero. David Yoon. G. P. Putnam's Sons, 2021. 368 p.
ISBN 9780593190357
1. Technology 2. Social media 3. Revenge 4. Near future 5. Hacking 6. United States 7. Dystopian fiction 8. Cyber-thrillers
LC 2020057329

"Digitally agile readers will recognize plenty of the ills of our time, and some will empathize with the counterintuitive way our heroes interpret the modern adage 'Move fast and break things.' A fast-paced, contemporary take on The Monkey Wrench Gang, blowing up digital infrastructure instead of dams." —*Kirkus*

Yoon, Paul

★ **Run** me to earth: a novel. Paul Yoon. Simon & Schuster, 2020. 259 pages
ISBN 9781501154041
1. Orphans 2. Children and war 3. Physicians 4. Friendship 5. War — Psychological aspects 6. Laos 7. 1960s 8. 2010s 9. Historical fiction 10. Literary fiction
LC 2019013516
ALA Notable Book, 2021

Three children orphaned in 1960s Laos meet a dedicated doctor who enlists them as motorcycle couriers in his effort to rescue civilians and find medical supplies.

"Yoon again exemplifies his unparalleled ability to create a quietly spectacular narrative that reveals the unfathomable worst and unwavering best of humanity; the result here provides mesmerizing gratification." —*Booklist*

Yoshimoto, Banana

The **lake**. Banana Yoshimoto; translated from the Japanese by Michael Emmerich. Melville House, 2011. 128 pages
ISBN 9781933633770
1. Friendship 2. Growing up 3. Man-woman relationships 4. Mothers — Death 5. Artists 6. Tokyo, Japan 7. Japan 8. First person narratives 9. Translations 10. Psychological fiction 11. Adult books for young adults
LC 2011006711

"Chihiro, an artist, and Nakajima, a graduate student in genetics, finally meet after watching and waving to each other from their respective apartment windows across a Tokyo street. They're both unconventional and seemingly untethered souls; they've both lost their beloved mothers. They meander into a sweet, simple life together, although past secrets involving a mysterious brother and sister who live by an ethereal lake threaten to create an emotional divide.... Yoshimoto aficionados...will recognize her signature crisp, clipped style (thanks to exacting translator Emmerich's constancy) and revel in her latest cast of quirky characters." —*Library Journal*
Originally published: Mizuumi (2010).
Translated from the Japanese.

Moshi-moshi. Banana Yoshimoto; translated from the Japanese by Asa Yoneda. Counterpoint Press, 2016. 206 pages
ISBN 9781619027862
1. Survivors of suicide victims 2. Loss (Psychology) 3. Fathers — Death 4. Grief 5. Spirits 6. Tokyo, Japan 7. Coming-of-age stories 8. Mainstream fiction 9. Translations

In Moshi-Moshi, Yoshie's much-loved musician father has died in a suicide pact with an unknown woman. It is only when Yoshie and her mother move to Shimo-kitazawa, a traditional Tokyo neighborhood of narrow streets, quirky shops, and friendly residents that they can finally start to put their painful past behind them. However, despite their attempts to move forward, Yoshie is haunted by nightmares in which her father is looking for the phone he left behind on the day he died, or on which she is trying-unsuccessfully-to call him. Is her dead father trying to communicate a message to her through these dreams? With the lightness of touch and surreal detachment that are the hallmarks of her writing, Banana Yoshimoto turns a potential tragedy into a poignant coming-of-age ghost story and a life-affirming homage to the healing powers of community, food, and family. Published in 2010 in Japanese in Tokyo, it has sold over 29,000 copies there so far..

"Prolific novelist Yoshimoto (The Lake, 2011, etc.) offers another story of youth, grief, and redemption in this ephemeral yet lovely portrait of an unformed woman." —*Kirkus*
Originally published as Moshi moshi Shimokitazawa, 2010.
Translated from the Japanese.

Youers, Rio

Lola on fire. Rio Youers. William Morrow & Company, 2021. 352 p.
ISBN 9780063001008
1. Siblings 2. Robbery 3. Gangsters 4. Extortion 5. Revenge 6. Crime fiction 7. Thrillers and suspense 8. Psychological suspense

Blackmailed by a witness after robbing a convenience store, a desperate man is forced to commit a burglary before realizing that a young woman and he have been rendered pawns in an organized crime dispute.

"Fans of full-throttled cinematic action-fests of the Long Kiss Goodnight variety are in for a treat." —*Publishers Weekly*

Young, Heather

The **distant** dead. Heather Young. William Morrow & Co, 2020. 400 p.
ISBN 9780062690814
1. Murder victims 2. Misfits (Persons) 3. Teachers 4. Orphans 5. Secrets 6. Nevada 7. Psychological suspense

When a young boy finds himself at the center of a murder mystery, several members of an American small town must deal with the fallout.

"Electrifying, ambitious, and crushingly beautiful." —*Kirkus*

Youngson, Anne

Meet me at the museum. Anne Youngson. Flatiron Books, 2018. 224 p.
ISBN 9781250295163
1. Heaney, Seamus 2. Friendship 3. Museum curators 4. Farmers' spouses 5. Seniors 6. Widowers 7. Denmark 8. England 9. Literary fiction 10. Epistolary novels
LibraryReads Favorites, 2018; RUSA Reading List Short List, 2019
A disenchanted farmer's wife and a widowed museum curator begin a correspondence over their mutual fascination with poet Seamus Heaney's "The Tollund Man" and gradually share details from their lives, forging an unexpected bond along the way.

Yourcenar, Marguerite

★ **Memoirs** of Hadrian: and reflections on the composition of memoirs of Hadrian. Marguerite Yourcenar; translated from the French by Grace Frick in collaboration with the author. Modern Library, 1984. 393 p. : Illustration
ISBN 9780394605050
1. Hadrian 2. Rulers 3. Personal conduct 4. Letter writing 5. Roman emperors 6. Humanists 7. Rome 8. Roman Empire (27 BCE-476 CE) 9. Modern classics 10. Psychological fiction 11. Biographical fiction
LC 83022065 //r93
In a letter to his adopted grandson (later Marcus Aurelius), Hadrian tells about his life.
Illustrated with black-and-white unpaged photos.
Originally published in French: Paris : Plon, 1951.
Translated from the French.

Yu, Charles

How to live safely in a science fictional universe: a novel. Charles Yu. Pantheon Books, 2010. 240 p.
ISBN 9780307379207
1. Time travel 2. Missing persons 3. Fathers and sons 4. Time machines 5. Science fiction 6. Humorous stories 7. Adult books for young adults
LC 2010001837
New York Times Notable Book, 2010
In a world transformed by time-travel technology, counselor Charles Yu searches for the father who invented time travel and vanished, a quest marked by quirky pseudo-companions.
"Yu is fond of meta-narrative, and packs the novel with adventures that take place entirely in theoretical universes, nostalgia-altered pasts, fictional worlds, and inside the protagonist's own time-looped mind." —io9

★ **Interior** Chinatown. Charles Yu. Pantheon Books, 2020. 240 p.
ISBN 9780307907196
1. Actors and actresses 2. Asian-Americans 3. Stereotypes (Social psychology) 4. Families 5. Kung fu 6. Literary fiction 7. Family sagas
National Book Award for Fiction, 2020
A stereotyped character actor stumbles into the spotlight before uncovering surprising links between his family and the secret history of Chinatown.
"An acid indictment of Asian stereotypes and a parable for outcasts feeling invisible in this fast-moving world." —Kirkus

Yu, E. Lily

★ **On** fragile waves. E. Lily Yu. Erewhon Trading Company, 2021. 224 pages
ISBN 9781645660095

1. Political refugees 2. Refugees 3. Storytelling 4. Imagination 5. Families 6. Literary fiction 7. Magical realism
Growing up on their parents' mythical stories about the opportunities of Australia, a girl and her brother travel from war-torn Pakistan through temporary homes in Indonesia and Nauru, before government indifference challenges their dreams.
"While Yu's exactingly detailed story is told in the third person, the voices of the children predominate, which makes this wrenching portrait of the immigrant experience especially affecting." —Library Journal

Yu, Miri

Tokyo Ueno station. Yu Miri; translated from the Japanese by Morgan Giles. Riverhead Books, 2020. 192 p.
ISBN 9780593088029
1. Ghosts 2. Inequality 3. City life 4. Loss (Psychology) 5. History 6. Japan 7. Literary fiction 8. Translations 9. First person narratives
LC 2019052105
National Book Award for Translated Literature, 2020; New York Times Notable Book, 2020
Haunting the park near Tokyo's Uneo Station, the ghost of a man whose life eerily paralleled the Emperor's reflects on the milestones that impacted his existence, from his homelessness and the 2011 tsunami to the 1964 and 2020 Olympics.
"Her anglophoned latest (gratitude to translator Giles for providing fluent accessibility) is a surreal fable of splintered families, disintegrating relationships, and the casual devaluation of humanity." —Booklist
First published in Japan by Kawade Shob Shinsha as JR Ueno-eki Koen-guchi, Tokyo, 2014. First published in Great Britain in paperback in English by Tilted Axis Press, London, 2019.
Translated from the Japanese.

Yun, Jung

O beautiful: a novel. Jung Yun. St. Martin's Press, 2021. 336 p.
ISBN 9781250274328
1. Korean American women 2. Multiracial women 3. Oil industry and trade 4. Forties (Age) 5. Homecomings 6. North Dakota 7. New York City 8. Literary fiction
LC 2021027557
A forty-something former model trying to reinvent herself, Elinor Hanson is offered a chance to write for a prestigious magazine that forces her to come to terms with the ghosts of her past and the tortured realities of a deeply divided America.
"Yun's sprawling second novel, after her brilliantly honed Shelter (2016), ambitiously confronts the multilayered mutations of the male gaze—modeling, catcalling, porn, #MeToo, sexual violence—magnified by socioeconomic disparities and, most affectingly, the cutting divides of race." —Booklist

Z

Zaman, Nadeem

Up in the main house & other stories. Nadeem Zaman. Unnamed Press, 2019. 176 p.
ISBN 9781944700980

1. Social classes 2. Class conflict 3. City dwellers 4. Working class 5. City life 6. Dhaka, Bangladesh 7. Bangladesh 8. Short stories 9. Literary fiction

LC 2019030045

Set in modern Dhaka, a brand-new collection of eight stories explores the inner lives of the cooks and butlers, nightwatchmen and peons who have spent decades working for the same family.

Zamyatin, Yevgeny Ivanovich

★ **We**. Yevgeny Zamyatin; translated by Bela Shayevich with an introduction by Margaret Atwood. Ecco Press, 2021. Xxxii, 221 p.
ISBN 9780063068445

1. Men — Identity 2. Totalitarianism 3. Freedom 4. Isolationism 5. Man-woman relationships 6. 26th century 7. Dystopian fiction 8. Social science fiction 9. Modern classics

LC 92044187

In a glass-enclosed city of perfectly straight lines, ruled over by an all-powerful 'Benefactor,' the citizens of the totalitarian society of OneState are regulated by spies and secret police; wear identical clothing; and are distinguished only by a number assigned to them at birth. That is, until D-503, a mathematician who dreams in numbers, makes a discovery: he has an individual soul. He can feel things. He can fall in love. And, in doing so, he begins to dangerously veer from the norms of his society, becoming embroiled in a plot to destroy OneState and liberate the city.

Includes bibliographical references (p. [xxxi]-xxxii).

Originally published: New York : Dutton, 1924.

Zapata, Mike

The **lost** book of Adana Moreau. Michael Zapata. Hanover Square Press, 2020. 336 p.
ISBN 9781335010124

1. Women authors 2. Manuscripts 3. Voyages and travels 4. Immigrants 5. Lawyers 6. New Orleans, Louisiana 7. Literary fiction 8. Multiple perspectives

Decades after a 1929 Dominican immigrant writer passes away believing her final manuscript was destroyed, a Chicago lawyer discovers the book and endeavors to learn the woman's remarkable story against a backdrop of Hurricane Katrina.

"In a lyrical tale spanning a century and veering from the colonized Caribbean to revolutionary Russia, from mid-twentieth-century Chicago to Katrina-besieged New Orleans, Zapata spins an iridescent web of grief, loss, and memory." —*Booklist*

Zettel, Sarah

A **mother's** lie. Sarah Zettel. Grand Central Pub, 2020. 400 p.
ISBN 9781538760925

1. Single mothers 2. Businesspeople 3. Swindlers and swindling 4. Parent and adult child 5. Grandparents 6. Chicago, Illinois 7. Psychological suspense

A compulsive family drama about a mother's desperate search to reclaim her daughter from the horrors of her own past, perfect for fans of Then She Was Gone.

"Zettel creates a realistic, infuriatingly dysfunctional family, with which many readers will be all too familiar. A highlight is the portrayal of Dana and Beth's relationship, with love and aggravation entwining to make a mother-daughter bond to remember." —*Booklist*

Zhou, Haohui

Death notice: a novel. Zhou Haohui; translated from the Chinese by Zac Haluza. Doubleday, 2018. 301 p. (Death notice, 1)
ISBN 9780385543323

1. Police 2. Revenge 3. Vigilantes 4. Justice 5. Murderers 6. China 7. Chengdu (China) 8. Thrillers and suspense 9. Translations

LC 2017048812

An elite police squad hunts a manipulative mastermind out to publically execute criminals the law cannot reach.

Originally published in Chinese as "Si wang tong zhi dan: an hei zhe" in 2014.

Translated from the Chinese.

Zola, Emile

★ **Germinal**. Emile Zola; translated from the French with an introduction by Havelock Ellis. Dutton, 1946. Viii, 404 p. (Rougon-Macquart, 13)
ISBN 9780460008976

1. Coal miners 2. Revolutionaries 3. Strikes — Coal miners 4. Working class 5. Class struggle 6. France 7. Political fiction 8. Translations 9. Classics

LC 37018102

Étienne Lenier works in the mines and leads an ultimately unsuccessful strike against the low wages and fines.

Translation of Germinal.

Originally published in French: Paris : G. Charpentier, 1885; originally translated by Havelock Ellis, 1894; first published in this edition, 1933. Revised and reset 1946.

Translated from the French.

★ **Nana**. Emile Zola; translated from the French with an introduction by Douglas Parmee. Oxford University Press 1992. 430 pages. (Rougon-Macquart, 9)
ISBN 9780192826749

1. Prostitutes 2. Brothels 3. Actors and actresses — History 4. Pornography 5. Women — Social conditions 6. Paris, France 7. 19th century 8. Classics 9. Historical fiction 10. Translations

LC 91022416

Nana, daughter of Gervaise and Coupeau, is beautiful enough to attract the attention of a theatrical producer of pornography.

AUTHOR, TITLE, AND SUBJECT INDEX

Numeric

★*10 Minutes 38 Seconds in This Strange World*. Shafak, Elif

10TH CENTURY
Follett, Ken. ★*The Evening and the Morning*
Seton, Anya. *Avalon*

11TH CENTURY
Hertmans, Stefan. ★*The Convert: A Novel*
11/22/63. King, Stephen

12TH CENTURY
Eco, Umberto. *Baudolino*
Groff, Lauren. ★*Matrix*
Holland, Cecelia. *Jerusalem*
Sharratt, Mary. *Illuminations: A Novel of Hildegard Von Bingen*
★*13 Ways of Looking at a Fat Girl*. Awad, Mona

13TH CENTURY
Jones, Sherry. *Four Sisters, All Queens*
The 13th Valley: A Novel. Del Vecchio, John M.
142 Ostriches. Davila, April

14TH CENTURY
Arden, Katherine. ★*The Bear and the Nightingale*
Arden, Katherine. ★*The Girl in the Tower*
Arden, Katherine. ★*The Winter of the Witch*
Druon, Maurice. *The Iron King*
Eco, Umberto. ★*The Name of the Rose*
Flynn, Michael. *Eifelheim*
Follett, Ken. *World Without End*
Kadare, Ismail. ★*The Three-Arched Bridge*
Parker-Chan, Shelley. ★*She Who Became the Sun*
Robinson, Kim Stanley. *The Years of Rice and Salt*
Seton, Anya. *Katherine*
Willis, Connie. ★*Doomsday Book*

15TH CENTURY
Doerr, Anthony. ★*Cloud Cuckoo Land: A Novel*
Dunant, Sarah. *The Birth of Venus: A Novel*
Dunnett, Dorothy. *Niccolo Rising*
Poole, Sara. *The Borgia Mistress*
Wilson, G. Willow. ★*The Bird King*

1660S
Potzsch, Oliver. *The Beggar King*
Potzsch, Oliver. *The Dark Monk: A Hangman's Daughter Tale*
Potzsch, Oliver. *The Hangman's Daughter: A Historical Novel*
Potzsch, Oliver. *The Poisoned Pilgrim: A Hangman's Daughter Tale*
Potzsch, Oliver. *The Werewolf of Bamberg*

16TH CENTURY
Amirrezvani, Anita. *Equal of the Sun*
Andersen, Laura. *The Boleyn Deceit*
Andersen, Laura. ★*The Boleyn King*
Andersen, Laura. *The Boleyn Reckoning*
Baker, Kage. *In the Garden of Iden: A Novel of the Company*
Black, Benjamin. *Wolf on a String: A Novel*
Brandreth, Benet. *The Spy of Venice*
Buckley, Fiona. *The Siren Queen: An Ursula Blanchard Mystery at Queen Elizabeth I's Court*

Cervantes Saavedra, Miguel de. ★*Don Quixote*
DeRoux, Margaux. *The Lost Diary of Venice*
Dunant, Sarah. *Blood and Beauty: A Novel*
Dunant, Sarah. *In the Company of the Courtesan: A Novel*
Dunant, Sarah. *Sacred Hearts: A Novel*
George, Margaret. *Elizabeth I: A Novel*
Gregory, Philippa. *The Boleyn Inheritance*
Gregory, Philippa. *The Constant Princess*
Gregory, Philippa. *The Last Tudor*
Gregory, Philippa. *The Taming of the Queen*
Harkness, Deborah E. *Shadow of Night*
Mantel, Hilary. ★*Wolf Hall*
Marston, Edward. *The Roaring Boy: A Novel*
Marston, Edward. *The Wanton Angel: A Novel*
Mina, Denise. ★*Rizzio*
Mosse, Kate. *The City of Tears*
Newman, Sandra. *The Heavens*
O'Farrell, Maggie. *Hamnet*
Parris, S. J. ★*The Dead of Winter*
Parris, S. J. *Sacrilege*
Parris, S. J. *Treachery*
Sansom, C. J. ★*Lamentation*
Sansom, C. J. *Revelation*
Sansom, C. J. ★*Sovereign*
Sansom, C. J. *Tombland*
Saramago, Jose. ★*The Elephant's Journey*
Spann, Susan. *Blade of the Samurai: A Shinobi Mystery*
Spann, Susan. ★*Claws of the Cat: A Shinobi Mystery*
Spann, Susan. *Trial on Mount Koya: A Hiro Hattori Novel*

1700S (DECADE)
Hart, Elsa. *City of Ink: A Mystery*
Scott, Walter. *The Bride of Lammermoor*

1710S
Scott, Walter. ★*Rob Roy*

1720S
Green, Jocelyn. *The Mark of the King*
Hodgson, Antonia. *The Last Confession of Thomas Hawkins*

1730S
Nickson, Chris. *Come the Fear*
Suskind, Patrick. ★*Perfume: The Story of a Murderer*

1740S
Spufford, Francis. ★*Golden Hill*

1760S
Beverley, Jo. *My Lady Notorious*
Beverley, Jo. *Tempting Fortune*

1770S
Gabaldon, Diana. ★*A Breath of Snow and Ashes*
Gabaldon, Diana. *An Echo in the Bone*
Gabaldon, Diana. ★*The Fiery Cross*
Gabaldon, Diana. *Written in My Own Heart's Blood*
Heyer, Georgette. *These Old Shades*

1780S
Robertson, Imogen. *Anatomy of Murder*
Robertson, Imogen. *Instruments of Darkness: A Novel*

Sabatini, Rafael. *Scaramouche: A Romance of the French Revolution*

1790S

Orczy, Emmuska Orczy. ★*The Scarlet Pimpernel*

Woods, Rita. ★*Remembrance*

17TH CENTURY

Amirrezvani, Anita. *The Blood of Flowers: A Novel*

Brom. *Slewfoot: A Tale of Bewitchery*

Burton, Jessie. *The Miniaturist*

Chevalier, Tracy. ★*Girl with a Pearl Earring*

Conde, Maryse. *I, Tituba, Black Witch of Salem*

Crichton, Michael. *Pirate Latitudes*

Dumas, Alexandre. ★*The Man in the Iron Mask*

Dumas, Alexandre. *Twenty Years After*

Eco, Umberto. *The Island of the Day Before*

Endo, Shusaku. *Silence*

Galchen, Rivka. *Everyone Knows Your Mother Is a Witch*

Hargrave, Kiran Millwood. *The Mercies: A Novel*

Jones, Gayl. ★*Palmares*

L'Amour, Louis. *To the Far Blue Mountains*

Morrison, Toni. *A Mercy: A Novel*

Parry, H. G. *A Declaration of the Rights of Magicians*

Pears, Iain. *An Instance of the Fingerpost*

Phillips, Christi. *The Rossetti Letter: A Novel*

Potzsch, Oliver. *The Beggar King*

Potzsch, Oliver. *The Dark Monk: A Hangman's Daughter Tale*

Potzsch, Oliver. *The Hangman's Daughter: A Historical Novel*

Potzsch, Oliver. *The Play of Death*

Potzsch, Oliver. *The Poisoned Pilgrim: A Hangman's Daughter Tale*

Potzsch, Oliver. *The Werewolf of Bamberg*

Proulx, Annie. ★*Barkskins: A Novel*

Purcell, Laura. *The Silent Companions: A Ghost Story*

Rowland, Laura Joh. *The Snow Empress*

Sabatini, Rafael. *Captain Blood*

See, Lisa. *Peony in Love: A Novel*

Seton, Anya. ★*The Winthrop Woman*

Smith, Dominic. ★*The Last Painting of Sara De Vos*

Smith, Gregory Blake. ★*The Maze at Windermere: A Novel*

Smith, Wilbur A. *Birds of Prey*

Turton, Stuart. ★*The Devil and the Dark Water*

1800S (DECADE)

Charles, KJ. *Wanted, a Gentleman: Or, Virtue Over-Rated*

Gelernter, J. H. *Hold Fast*

James, Eloisa. ★*Seven Minutes in Heaven*

Straight, Susan. *A Million Nightingales*

1810S

Bayard, Louis. *The Black Tower: A Novel*

Golding, William. *Close Quarters*

Golding, William. *Fire Down Below*

Golding, William. *Rites of Passage*

Quincy, D. M. *Murder at the Opera*

Quincy, D. M. *Murder in Mayfair: An Atlas Catesby Mystery*

Shupe, Joanna. *The Courtesan Duchess*

1820S

Warren, Robert Penn. *World Enough and Time: A Romantic Novel*

1830S

Bayard, Louis. *The Pale Blue Eye: A Novel*

Brink, Andre P. *Philida: A Novel*

Carter, Miranda. *The Strangler Vine*

Chase, Loretta Lynda. *A Duke in Shining Armor*

Edugyan, Esi. ★*Washington Black: A Novel*

Eliot, George. ★*Middlemarch: A Study of Provincial Life*

Gaynor, Hazel. *The Lighthouse Keeper's Daughter*

Gerritsen, Tess. *The Bone Garden*

Ghosh, Amitav. *Flood of Fire*

Ghosh, Amitav. *River of Smoke*

Ghosh, Amitav. *Sea of Poppies*

Putnam, Jonathan F. *These Honored Dead*

Rhys, Jean. ★*Wide Sargasso Sea*

1840S

Adams, Hope. *Dangerous Women*

Allende, Isabel. *Daughter of Fortune: A Novel*

Atwood, Margaret. *Alias Grace*

Austin, Finola. *Bronte's Mistress*

Ellis, Bella. *The Vanished Bride*

Faye, Lyndsay. *The Gods of Gotham*

Faye, Lyndsay. *Seven for a Secret*

Frampton, Megan. *The Duke's Guide to Correct Behavior*

Hambly, Barbara. *House of the Patriarch*

Katsu, Alma. *The Hunger: A Novel*

Kirkpatrick, Jane. *One More River to Cross*

McCann, Colum. ★*Transatlantic: A Novel*

Parry, Ambrose. *The Way of All Flesh*

Pearl, Matthew. *The Poe Shadow: A Novel*

Pipkin, John. *Woodsburner: A Novel*

Simmons, Dan. ★*The Terror: A Novel*

1850S

Ashley, Jennifer. *Death at the Crystal Palace*

Cather, Willa. ★*Death Comes for the Archbishop*

Chevalier, Tracy. *The Last Runaway*

Dallas, Sandra. *Westering Women: A Novel*

Donoghue, Emma. ★*The Wonder*

Evison, Jonathan. ★*Small World*

Finch, Charles. *The Last Passenger*

Finch, Charles. *The Vanishing Man*

Goodwin, S. M. *Absence of Mercy*

McCarthy, Cormac. ★*Blood Meridian, Or, the Evening Redness in the West*

Pulley, Natasha. *The Bedlam Stacks*

Rivers, Francine. ★*Redeeming Love*

Saunders, Kate. *The Case of the Wandering Scholar*

Schanbacher, Gary Lester. *Crossing Purgatory*

Thomson, E. S. *Beloved Poison*

Thomson, E. S. *The Blood*

Woods, Rita. ★*Remembrance*

1860S

Burnet, Graeme Macrae. *His Bloody Project: Documents Relating to the Case of Roderick Macrae*

Cobbs Hoffman, Elizabeth. *The Tubman Command: A Novel*

Collins, Manda. ★*A Lady's Guide to Mischief and Mayhem*

Doctorow, E. L. *The March: A Novel*

Finch, Charles. *The September Society*

Fowles, John. ★*The French Lieutenant's Woman*

Frazier, Charles. ★*Cold Mountain*

Garcia, Gabriela. *Of Women and Salt*

Gleason, Colleen. *Murder at the Capitol*

Greenidge, Kaitlyn. ★*Libertie: A Novel*

Haldane, Sean. *The Devil's Making*
Harris, Nathan. *The Sweetness of Water*
Harte, Bret. ★*The Best Short Stories of Bret Harte*
Hicks, Robert. *The Widow of the South*
Jakes, John. *Love and War*
Jenkins, Beverly. *Rebel*
Jenkins, Beverly. *Wild Rain*
Kelton, Elmer. ★*The Way of the Coyote*
Mason, Timothy. *The Darwin Affair*
McGuire, Ian. *The Abstainer: A Novel*
Milan, Courtney. *The Duchess War*
Pearl, Matthew. *The Dante Club: A Novel*
Pearl, Matthew. *The Technologists: A Novel*
Perry, Anne. *Dark Tide Rising: A William Monk Novel*
Powning, Beth. *The Sea Captain's Wife: A Novel*
Saunders, George. ★*Lincoln in the Bardo: A Novel*
Shaara, Jeff. *Gods and Generals: A Novel of the Civil War*
Shaara, Jeff. *The Last Full Measure*
Simmons, Dan. *Drood: A Novel*
Smith, Lee. *On Agate Hill: A Novel*

1870S
Abdul-Jabbar, Kareem. *The Empty Birdcage*
Abdul-Jabbar, Kareem. *Mycroft and Sherlock*
Abdul-Jabbar, Kareem. ★*Mycroft Holmes*
Beams, Clare. *The Illness Lesson*
Brooks, Bill. *Blood Storm*
Buchanan, Cathy Marie. ★*The Painted Girls*
Chiaverini, Jennifer. *Mrs. Lincoln's Sisters*
Clark, P. Djeli. *The Black God's Drums*
Deluca, Marjorie. *The Savage Instinct*
Donoghue, Emma. ★*Frog Music*
Estleman, Loren D. *The Adventures of Johnny Vermillion: A Novel*
Everett, Percival L. *God's Country*
Green, Jocelyn. *Veiled in Smoke*
Greenidge, Kaitlyn. ★*Libertie: A Novel*
Jenkins, Beverly. *Forbidden*
Jiles, Paulette. *News of the World: A Novel*
Pearl, Matthew. *The Dante Chamber*
Portis, Charles. ★*True Grit: A Novel*
Setterfield, Diane. ★*Once Upon a River*
Singer, Isaac Bashevis. ★*The Magician of Lublin*
Smith, Martin Cruz. *Rose*
Sontag, Susan. ★*In America*
Verble, Margaret. ★*Cherokee America*
Wood, Tracey Enerson. *The Engineer's Wife: A Novel*

1880S
Anderson, Alison. *The Summer Guest*
Ashley, Jennifer. *Lady Isabella's Scandalous Marriage*
Ashley, Jennifer. *The Madness of Lord Ian Mackenzie*
Benton, Janet. *Lilli De Jong: A Novel*
Clare, Alys. *The Woman Who Spoke to Spirits*
Dallas, Sandra. *The Last Midwife*
Enger, Lin. *The High Divide: A Novel*
Evison, Jonathan. *West of Here: A Novel*
Faye, Lyndsay. *The Whole Art of Detection: Lost Mysteries of Sherlock Holmes*
Ghosh, Amitav. *The Glass Palace*
Gibbon, Maureen. *The Lost Notebook of Edouard Manet: A Novel*

Guinn, Matthew. *The Scribe: A Novel*
Howarth, Paul. *Only Killers and Thieves: A Novel*
Llewellyn, Richard. ★*How Green Was My Valley*
Mas, Victoria. *The Mad Women's Ball*
Priest, Cherie. *Clementine*
Priest, Cherie. *Ganymede*
Pulley, Natasha. *The Lost Future of Pepperharrow*
Pulley, Natasha. *The Watchmaker of Filigree Street*
Raybourn, Deanna. *A Curious Beginning: A Veronica Speedwell Mystery*
Raybourn, Deanna. *A Dangerous Collaboration*
Raybourn, Deanna. ★*A Murderous Relation*
Raybourn, Deanna. *A Perilous Undertaking: A Veronica Speedwell Mystery*
Raybourn, Deanna. *A Treacherous Curse: A Veronica Speedwell Mystery*
Russell, Mary Doria. *Epitaph: A Novel of the O.K. Corral*
Whitfield, Clare. *People of Abandoned Character*

1890S
Carr, Caleb. ★*The Alienist*
Carr, Caleb. *The Angel of Darkness*
Cather, Willa. *A Lost Lady*
Choo, Yangsze. *The Ghost Bride: A Novel*
Couto, Mia. *The Sword and the Spear*
Finlay, Mick. *The Murder Pit*
Freeman, Dianne. *A Fiancee's Guide to First Wives and Murder*
Goodman, Jo. *In Want of a Wife*
Goodwin, Daisy. *The American Heiress*
Gunning, Sally. *Painting the Light*
Horowitz, Anthony. *The House of Silk: A Sherlock Holmes Novel*
Howarth, Paul. *Dust off the Bones*
Lewis, Beverly. *The Preacher's Daughter*
Llewellyn, Richard. ★*How Green Was My Valley*
Morrison, Toni. *Paradise*
O'Donnell, Paraic. *The House on Vesper Sands: A Novel*
Patterson, Molly. *Rebellion*
Pronzini, Bill. *The Stolen Gold Affair*
Pynchon, Thomas. *Against the Day: A Novel*
Sayles, John. *A Moment in the Sun*
Schmidt, Sarah. *See What I Have Done*
Schwarz, Christina. *The Edge of the Earth*
Sedgwick, Marcus. *Mister Memory: A Novel*
Simmons, Dan. *The Fifth Heart*
Simpson, Rosemary. *Let the Dead Keep Their Secrets*
Simpson, Rosemary. ★*What the Dead Leave Behind*
Sullivan, Emily. *The Rebel and the Rake*
Urrea, Luis Alberto. *Queen of America: A Novel*
Wecker, Helene. *The Golem and the Jinni*
Welsh, Kaite. *The Unquiet Heart*

18TH CENTURY
Barth, John. ★*The Sot-Weed Factor*
Brown, Dee. *Creek Mary's Blood: A Novel*
Chakraborty, S. A. *The Empire of Gold*
Cobbs Hoffman, Elizabeth. *The Hamilton Affair*
Collins, Sara. *The Confessions of Frannie Langton*
Cooper, James Fenimore. *The Last of the Mohicans: A Narrative of 1757*
Donoghue, Emma. *Slammerkin*

Francis-Sharma, Lauren. ★*Book of the Little Axe*
Gabaldon, Diana. ★*Dragonfly in Amber*
Gabaldon, Diana. ★*Drums of Autumn*
Gabaldon, Diana. ★*Outlander*
Gabaldon, Diana. ★*Voyager*
Gilbert, Elizabeth. ★*The Signature of All Things: A Novel*
Gyasi, Yaa. ★*Homegoing: A Novel*
Hill, Lawrence. *Someone Knows My Name: A Novel*
Hill, Ruth Beebe. *Hanta Yo*
Levine, David D. *Arabella of Mars*
Miller, Rebecca. ★*Jacob's Folly: A Novel*
Palmer, Dexter Clarence. ★*Mary Toft; Or, the Rabbit Queen: A Novel*
Richardson, Samuel. ★*Clarissa, Or, the History of a Young Lady*
Richardson, Samuel. ★*Pamela: Or, Virtue Rewarded*
Riley, Vanessa. ★*Island Queen*
Robertson, Imogen. *Island of Bones*
Rowland, Laura Joh. *The Incense Game: A Novel of Feudal Japan*
Rowland, Laura Joh. *The Shogun's Daughter: A Novel of Feudal Japan*
Smith, Gregory Blake. ★*The Maze at Windermere: A Novel*
Smith, Wilbur A. *Monsoon*
Sontag, Susan. *The Volcano Lover: A Romance*
Stachniak, Eva. *The Winter Palace: A Novel of Catherine the Great*
Suskind, Patrick. ★*Perfume: The Story of a Murderer*
Wilson, Daniel H. *The Clockwork Dynasty: A Novel*

1900S (DECADE)

Adamson, Gil. *The Outlander*
Agee, Jonis. *The Bones of Paradise*
Burns, Olive Ann. ★*Cold Sassy Tree*
Cussler, Clive. *The Cutthroat*
Cussler, Clive. *The Wrecker*
Doctorow, E. L. ★*Ragtime*
Faulkner, William. *The Reivers: A Reminiscence*
Goldstone, Lawrence. *Assassin of Shadows*
Goodman, Jo. *A Touch of Forever*
Hoffman, Alice. *The Museum of Extraordinary Things: A Novel*
Kibler, Julie. *Home for Erring and Outcast Girls*
Kimani, Peter. *Dance of the Jakaranda*
Lawrence, D. H. *Women in Love*
Lee, Jonathan. *The Great Mistake*
Marlantes, Karl. *Deep River*
Meyer, Nicholas. *The Adventure of the Peculiar Protocols: Adapted from the Journals of John H. Watson, M.D.*
Parmar, Priya. *Vanessa and Her Sister*
Peterson, Tracie. *What Comes My Way*
Phillips, Caryl. *Dancing in the Dark*
Rindell, Suzanne. ★*The Two Mrs. Carlyles*
Sayles, John. *A Moment in the Sun*
Sinclair, Upton. ★*The Jungle*
Smith, Betty. ★*A Tree Grows in Brooklyn*
Steinke, Rene. *Holy Skirts*
Swarthout, Glendon. ★*The Shootist*
Tallis, Frank. *Vienna Blood: A Max Liebermann Mystery*
Thompson, Victoria. *Murder on Wall Street*

1910S

Bainbridge, Beryl. *Every Man for Himself*
Barker, Pat. ★*The Eye in the Door*
Barnett, LaShonda K. *Jam on the Vine*

Bohjalian, Chris. *The Sandcastle Girls*
Buchan, John. *The Thirty-Nine Steps*
Burdick, Serena. *The Girls with No Names*
Cussler, Clive. ★*The Chase*
Cussler, Clive. ★*The Titanic Secret*
Davis, Fiona. *The Lions of Fifth Avenue: A Novel*
Diop, David. ★*At Night All Blood Is Black*
Endicott, Marina. *The Voyage of the Morning Light*
Fredericks, Mariah. *Death of a New American: A Mystery*
Gallagher, Stephen. *The Bedlam Detective: A Novel*
Gilman, Charlotte Perkins. *Herland*
Groom, Winston. *El Paso: A Novel*
Hammad, Isabella. ★*The Parisian, Or, Al-Barisi: A Novel*
Hand, Elizabeth. *Curious Toys*
Huber, Anna Lee. *Penny for Your Secrets*
Katsu, Alma. *The Deep*
Lee, Min Jin. ★*Pachinko*
Lehane, Dennis. ★*The Given Day*
Marshall, Catherine. *Christy*
McCann, Colum. ★*Transatlantic: A Novel*
Moyes, Jojo. *The Girl You Left Behind*
Perry, Anne. ★*Death with a Double Edge: A Daniel Pitt Novel*
Perry, Anne. *One Fatal Flaw: A Daniel Pitt Novel*
Portis, Charles. ★*Masters of Atlantis: A Novel*
Rash, Ron. ★*The Cove*
Remarque, Erich Maria. *The Road Back*
Robertson, Imogen. *The Paris Winter*
Rose, M. J. ★*Cartier's Hope*
Roth, Henry. ★*Call It Sleep*
Roth, Henry. *A Star Shines Over Mt. Morris Park*
Russell, Mary Doria. *The Women of the Copper Country: A Novel*
Smith, B. J. *The Return of Kid Cooper: A Novel*
Steinke, Rene. *Holy Skirts*
Stevens, Francis. *The Heads of Cerberus*
Stewart, Amy. ★*Girl Waits with Gun*

1919. Dos Passos, John

1920S

Armstrong, Addison. *The Light of Luna Park*
Avery, Ellis. *The Last Nude*
Baker, Dorothy. ★*Young Man with a Horn*
Bennett, Jenn. *Bitter Spirits*
Bilenchi, Romano. ★*The Chill*
Bradbury, Ray. ★*Dandelion Wine: A Novel*
Brown, Sandra. ★*Blind Tiger*
Bulgakov, Mikhail. ★*The Master and Margarita*
Cash, Wiley. *The Last Ballad: A Novel*
Cheng, Bill. *Southern Cross the Dog*
Clark, P. Djeli. *Ring Shout*
Cleary, Jon. *The Sundowners*
Cook, Thomas H. *The Chatham School Affair*
Dann, Patty. *The Wright Sister*
Darznik, Jasmin. *The Bohemians*
Davis, Fiona. *The Masterpiece*
Dos Passos, John. *Manhattan Transfer*
Dunmore, Helen. *The Lie*
Faulkner, William. ★*The Sound and the Fury*
Faye, Lyndsay. ★*The Paragon Hotel*
Fitzgerald, F. Scott. *Novels and Stories, 1920-1922*

Fitzgerald, F. Scott. *Six Tales of the Jazz Age and Other Stories*

Fowler, Therese. ★*Z: A Novel of Zelda Fitzgerald*

Greenwood, Kerry. *Unnatural Habits*

Grossman, Paul. *Children of Wrath*

Hambly, Barbara. *Scandal in Babylon*

Hammett, Dashiell. ★*The Maltese Falcon*

Hannah, Sophie. *The Mystery of Three Quarters: The New Hercule Poirot Mystery*

Harrison, Cora. *Beyond Absolution: A Mystery Set in 1920s Ireland*

Hemingway, Ernest. ★*The Sun Also Rises*

Hesse, Hermann. ★*Steppenwolf*

Hunt, Laird. *The Evening Road*

Kaplan, Mitchell James. *Rhapsody*

Kerr, Philip. ★*Metropolis: A Bernie Gunther Novel*

King, Laurie R. *Castle Shade*

Larsen, Nella. *Passing*

Lehane, Dennis. *Live by Night*

Lewis, Sinclair. *Babbitt*

Lewis, Sinclair. ★*Main Street: The Story of Carol Kennicott*

Mamet, David. *Chicago: A Novel*

Massey, Sujata. ★*The Bombay Prince*

Massey, Sujata. *The Satapur Moonstone*

Massey, Sujata. ★*The Widows of Malabar Hill: A Mystery of 1920s Bombay*

McLain, Paula. *Circling the Sun*

McLain, Paula. *The Paris Wife: A Novel*

Miller, Henry. ★*Tropic of Capricorn*

Montgomery, Jess. *The Stills*

Montgomery, Jess. *The Widows*

Moreno-Garcia, Silvia. ★*Gods of Jade and Shadow: A Novel*

Morrison, Toni. *Jazz*

Morton, Kate. *The House at Riverton: A Novel*

Mukherjee, Abir. *Death in the East*

Mukherjee, Abir. *The Shadows of Men*

Mukherjee, Abir. *Smoke and Ashes: A Novel*

Nabokov, Vladimir Vladimirovich. *King, Queen, Knave: A Novel*

Perez-Reverte, Arturo. *What We Become*

Preston, Caroline. *The Scrapbook of Frankie Pratt*

Ramsay, Frederick. *Countdown*

Reed, Ishmael. ★*Mumbo Jumbo*

Rindell, Suzanne. *The Other Typist*

Rose, M. J. *Tiffany Blues: A Novel*

Rosen, Renee. *Dollface: A Novel of the Roaring Twenties*

Roth, Henry. *A Diving Rock on the Hudson*

Roth, Henry. *From Bondage*

Roth, Henry. *Requiem for Harlem*

Ruiz Zafon, Carlos. *The Angel's Game*

Sayers, Dorothy L. ★*Clouds of Witness*

Sayers, Dorothy L. ★*The Documents in the Case*

Sayers, Dorothy L. *The Unpleasantness at the Bellona Club*

Sayers, Dorothy L. ★*Whose Body?: A Lord Peter Wimsey Novel*

Shreve, Anita. *Sea Glass: A Novel*

Simmons, Dan. *The Abominable: A Novel*

Smiley, Jane. *Some Luck*

Solomon, Anna. *Leaving Lucy Pear*

Speller, Elizabeth. *The Return of Captain John Emmett*

Speller, Elizabeth. *The Strange Fate of Kitty Easton*

St. James, Simone. *The Haunting of Maddy Clare*

Swift, Graham. ★*Mothering Sunday: A Romance*

Towles, Amor. ★*A Gentleman in Moscow*

Verble, Margaret. ★*When Two Feathers Fell from the Sky*

Vo, Nghi. ★*The Chosen and the Beautiful*

Waugh, Evelyn. ★*Brideshead Revisited*

Waugh, Evelyn. ★*Vile Bodies*

Welty, Eudora. ★*Delta Wedding*

Wilder, Thornton. ★*Theophilus North*

Woods, Stuart. *Chiefs*

Woolf, Virginia. ★*To the Lighthouse*

Wright, Jaime Jo. *The Haunting at Bonaventure Circus*

1930S

Abbott, Megan E. *Bury Me Deep*

Adams, Alina. *The Nesting Dolls*

Algren, Nelson. *A Walk on the Wild Side*

Allen, Jane. *I Lost My Girlish Laughter*

Baldwin, James. ★*Go Tell It on the Mountain*

Barr, Mark. *Watershed*

Blake, Sarah. *The Guest Book: A Novel*

Bloom, Amy. ★*White Houses: A Novel*

Bolano, Roberto. *Monsieur Pain*

Boschwitz, Ulrich Alexander. *The Passenger: A Novel*

Chandler, Raymond. ★*The Big Sleep*

Chevalier, Tracy. *A Single Thread*

Chiaverini, Jennifer. *Resistance Women: A Novel*

Choo, Yangsze. ★*The Night Tiger: A Novel*

Clayton, Meg Waite. *The Last Train to London*

Deaver, Jeffery. *Garden of Beasts: A Novel of Berlin 1936*

Deon, Natashia. *The Perishing: A Novel*

Depestre, Rene. *Hadriana in All My Dreams*

Doctorow, E. L. ★*Billy Bathgate: A Novel*

Doctorow, E. L. *World's Fair*

Duenas, Maria. *The Time in Between: A Novel*

Fitzgerald, F. Scott. ★*The Last Tycoon: An Unfinished Novel*

Flagg, Fannie. ★*Fried Green Tomatoes at the Whistle Stop Cafe*

Flagg, Fannie. ★*The Wonder Boy of Whistle Stop: A Novel*

French, Albert. *Billy*

Furst, Alan. *The Foreign Correspondent: A Novel*

Furst, Alan. ★*Mission to Paris*

Furst, Alan. *The Spies of Warsaw*

Gardam, Jane. *God on the Rocks*

Gaynor, Hazel. *The Lighthouse Keeper's Daughter*

Gaynor, Hazel. *Three Words for Goodbye*

Golden, Arthur. ★*Memoirs of a Geisha: A Novel*

Greene, Graham. *The Power and the Glory*

Gross, Andrew. *Button Man*

Hannah, Sophie. *The Killings at Kingfisher Hill*

Harman, Patricia. *The Midwife of Hope River: A Novel*

Harrison, Nicola. *Montauk*

Hegi, Ursula. *Children and Fire: A Novel*

Hemingway, Ernest. *To Have and Have Not*

Hooper, Elise. *Fast Girls: A Novel of the 1936 Women's Olympic Team*

Hurston, Zora Neale. ★*Their Eyes Were Watching God*

Isherwood, Christopher. ★*The Berlin Stories: The Last of Mr. Norris, Goodbye to Berlin*

Ishiguro, Kazuo. *When We Were Orphans*

Jackson-Brown, Angela. ★*When Stars Rain Down: A Novel*

Kaplan, Mitchell James. *Rhapsody*
Kennedy, William. ★*Ironweed: A Novel*
Koestler, Arthur. *Darkness at Noon*
Krueger, William Kent. *This Tender Land: A Novel*
Lansdale, Joe R. *The Bottoms*
Lansdale, Joe R. *Edge of Dark Water*
Lansdale, Joe R. *The Thicket*
Leonard, Elmore. *The Hot Kid*
Lessing, Doris May. *A Proper Marriage*
Lewis, Sinclair. ★*It Can't Happen Here*
McCarthy, Cormac. *The Crossing*
McCullers, Carson. *Reflections in a Golden Eye*
McEwan, Ian. ★*Atonement: A Novel*
McLain, Paula. *Love and Ruin*
McPherson, Catriona. ★*A Step so Grave*
Meadows, Rae. *I Will Send Rain: A Novel*
Mengiste, Maaza. ★*The Shadow King: A Novel*
Miller, Henry. ★*Tropic of Cancer*
Moyes, Jojo. ★*The Giver of Stars: A Novel*
O'Farrell, Maggie. *The Vanishing Act of Esme Lennox*
O'Hara, John. *Appointment in Samarra*
Oates, Joyce Carol. *A Garden of Earthly Delights*
Orringer, Julie. ★*The Invisible Bridge: A Novel*
Ozick, Cynthia. *Heir to the Glimmering World*
Pawel, Rebecca. *Death of a Nationalist*
Peebles, Frances de Pontes. *The Air You Breathe*
Perez-Reverte, Arturo. *What We Become*
Perry, Anne. ★*A Darker Reality*
Perry, Anne. ★*Death in Focus: An Elena Standish Novel*
Perry, Anne. *A Question of Betrayal*
Phillips, Jayne Anne. *Quiet Dell: A Novel*
Pilcher, Rosamunde. *Coming Home*
Porter, Katherine Anne. *Ship of Fools*
Quick, Amanda. *Close Up*
Quick, Amanda. *The Girl Who Knew Too Much*
Quick, Amanda. ★*The Lady Has a Past*
Quick, Amanda. *The Other Lady Vanishes*
Rash, Ron. ★*Serena: A Novel*
Roosevelt, Elliott. ★*Murder and the First Lady*
Roosevelt, Elliott. *Murder in the Oval Office*
Saint-Exupery, Antoine de. *Night Flight*
Sartre, Jean Paul. *The Age of Reason*
Sayers, Dorothy L. ★*The Five Red Herrings*
Sayers, Dorothy L. ★*Gaudy Night*
Sayers, Dorothy L. *Have His Carcase*
Sayers, Dorothy L. *Murder Must Advertise*
Sayers, Dorothy L. *The Nine Tailors*
Sayers, Dorothy L. *Thrones, Dominations*
See, Lisa. *Shanghai Girls: A Novel*
Shan, Sa. *The Girl Who Played Go*
Smith, Dodie. ★*I Capture the Castle*
Snow, C. P. ★*Strangers and Brothers*
Spark, Muriel. ★*The Prime of Miss Jean Brodie*
Steinbeck, John. *Tortilla Flat*
Straley, John. *The Big Both Ways*
Talton, Jon. *City of Dark Corners*
Tanabe, Karin. *A Hundred Suns*

Thelen, Albert Vigoleis. *The Island of Second Sight: From the Applied Recollections of Vigoleis*
Towles, Amor. *Rules of Civility: A Novel*
Twardoch, Szczepan. *The King of Warsaw*
Warren, Robert Penn. *All the King's Men*
Wieland, Liza. *Paris, 7 A.M.*
Winspear, Jacqueline. *The American Agent*
Wood, Shelley. *The Quintland Sisters*
Woolf, Virginia. *Between the Acts*
Wright, Richard. ★*Native Son*

1940S

Albahari, David. *Gotz and Meyer*
Atwood, Margaret. ★*The Blind Assassin*
Baldacci, David. ★*One Good Deed*
Bausch, Richard. *Peace*
Beauvoir, Simone de. ★*The Mandarins: A Novel*
Benn, James R. *Billy Boyle: A World War Two Mystery*
Bloom, Amy. *Lucky Us: A Novel*
Bloom, Amy. ★*White Houses: A Novel*
Bohjalian, Chris. *Skeletons at the Feast: A Novel*
Burke, James Lee. *Wayfaring Stranger: A Novel*
Chabon, Michael. *The Yiddish Policemen's Union*
Chakrabarti, Jai. *A Play for the End of the World*
Chandler, Raymond. *The Lady in the Lake*
Chiaverini, Jennifer. *Resistance Women: A Novel*
Copenhaver, John. *The Savage Kind*
Cramer, W. Dale. *Levi's Will: A Novel*
Dallas, Sandra. *Tallgrass*
Dean, Debra. *The Madonnas of Leningrad: A Novel*
Deane, Seamus. *Reading in the Dark*
Dexter, Pete. *Paris Trout*
Edugyan, Esi. *Half-Blood Blues*
Ellroy, James. *Perfidia*
Ellroy, James. *This Storm: A Novel*
Faulks, Sebastian. *Charlotte Gray: A Novel*
Flagg, Fannie. *Standing in the Rainbow: A Novel*
Flanagan, Richard. ★*The Narrow Road to the Deep North*
Fleischmann, Raymond. *How Quickly She Disappears*
Follett, Ken. *Eye of the Needle*
Follett, Ken. *Hornet Flight*
Follett, Ken. *Jackdaws*
Furst, Alan. *Blood of Victory: A Novel*
Furst, Alan. *Dark Voyage: A Novel*
Furst, Alan. ★*A Hero of France*
Furst, Alan. *Spies of the Balkans: A Novel*
Gardam, Jane. *The Flight of the Maidens*
Gendry-Kim, Keum Suk. ★*The Waiting*
Gilbert, Elizabeth. ★*City of Girls*
Gillham, David R. *City of Women*
Godwin, Gail. *Flora: A Novel*
Golden, Arthur. ★*Memoirs of a Geisha: A Novel*
Goonan, Kathleen Ann. *In War Times*
Greene, Graham. *The Tenth Man*
Greenwood, T. *Rust & Stardust*
Groot, Tracy. *Flame of Resistance*
Hart, Carolyn G. *Letter from Home*
Hazzard, Shirley. ★*The Great Fire*
Heggen, Thomas. *Mister Roberts*

Heller, Joseph. ★*Catch-22*
Helprin, Mark. *In Sunlight and in Shadow*
Hewson, David. *The Garden of Angels*
Higgins, Jack. *The Eagle Has Flown*
Higgins, Jack. *The Eagle Has Landed*
Indriðason, Arnaldur. *The Shadow District: A Thriller*
Jakes, John. ★*North and South*
Jenner, Natalie. *The Jane Austen Society*
Jenoff, Pam. *The Lost Girls of Paris*
Jones, James. ★*The Thin Red Line*
Jordan, Hillary. *Mudbound: A Novel*
Kaminsky, Stuart M. *Dancing in the Dark*
Kaminsky, Stuart M. *To Catch a Spy: A Toby Peters Mystery*
Kelly, Stephen. *The Wages of Desire: A World War II Mystery*
Knowles, John. ★*A Separate Peace*
Kutsukake, Lynne. *The Translation of Love: A Novel*
Kuznetsov, Anatolii Petrovich. *Babi Yar: A Document in the Form of a Novel*
Landau, Alexis. *Those Who Are Saved*
Leavitt, David. *The Two Hotel Francforts: A Novel*
Levy, Andrea. *Small Island*
Luesse, Valerie Fraser. *Under the Bayou Moon: A Novel*
Mankell, Henning. ★*The Return of the Dancing Master*
McCarthy, Cormac. ★*All the Pretty Horses*
McCullers, Carson. ★*The Heart Is a Lonely Hunter*
McLain, Paula. *Love and Ruin*
Momaday, N. Scott. *House Made of Dawn*
Montclair, Allison. *The Right Sort of Man*
Montclair, Allison. *A Rogue's Company*
Montclair, Allison. *A Royal Affair*
Mosley, Walter. *Devil in a Blue Dress*
Moss, Tara. *The War Widow*
Mullen, Thomas. *Darktown: A Novel*
Munro, Alice. *Lives of Girls and Women*
Otsuka, Julie. *When the Emperor Was Divine: A Novel*
Paton, Alan. ★*Cry, the Beloved Country*
Peace, David. *Occupied City*
Pelecanos, George P. *The Big Blowdown*
Petry, Ann. ★*The Street*
Petterson, Per. *Out Stealing Horses: A Novel*
Rabb, Jonathan. *Among the Living*
Rhys, Rachel. *Fatal Inheritance*
Robertson, Robin. *The Long Take: A Noir Narrative*
Roth, Philip. *I Married a Communist*
Roth, Philip. ★*Nemesis*
Roth, Philip. ★*The Plot Against America*
Roth, Philip. ★*Portnoy's Complaint*
Ruiz Zafon, Carlos. ★*The Shadow of the Wind*
Russell, Mary Doria. *A Thread of Grace: A Novel*
Saroyan, William. ★*The Human Comedy*
Shaara, Jeff. *The Rising Tide: A Novel of World War II*
Shaara, Jeff. *The Steel Wave: A Novel of World War II*
Shapiro, Barbara A. *The Muralist*
Singer, Isaac Bashevis. *Enemies, a Love Story*
Smith, Martin Cruz. *December 6*
Solzhenitsyn, Aleksandr Isaevich. *In the First Circle: A Novel : The Restored Text*
Spark, Muriel. ★*The Girls of Slender Means*

Steinhauer, Olen. *The Bridge of Sighs*
Van Booy, Simon. *The Illusion of Separateness*
Vidal, Gore. *Washington, D. C.: A Novel*
Winspear, Jacqueline. ★*The Consequences of Fear: A Maisie Dobbs Novel*
Winthrop, Elizabeth Hartley. *The Mercy Seat: A Novel*
Wouk, Herman. ★*War and Remembrance: A Novel*
Wouk, Herman. ★*The Winds of War: A Novel*

1950S
Allison, Dorothy. ★*Bastard Out of Carolina*
Amis, Kingsley. ★*Lucky Jim*
Armstrong, Addison. *The Light of Luna Park*
Atkins, Ace. *Wicked City*
Baldacci, David. ★*A Gambling Man*
Baldwin, James. ★*Giovanni's Room*
Baldwin, James. *Just Above My Head*
Bartlett, Neil. *The Disappearance Boy*
Bates, Judy Fong. ★*Midnight at the Dragon Cafe*
Bauer, Carlene. ★*Frances and Bernard*
Berg, Gretchen. *The Operator*
Black, Benjamin. ★*Christine Falls: A Novel*
Blake, Sarah. *The Guest Book: A Novel*
Blume, Judy. *In the Unlikely Event*
Bowman, David. *Big Bang: A Nonfiction Novel*
Bradley, C. Alan. *The Golden Tresses of the Dead: A Flavia De Luce Novel*
Bradley, C. Alan. *The Grave's a Fine and Private Place: A Flavia De Luce Novel*
Bradley, C. Alan. ★*The Sweetness at the Bottom of the Pie*
Bradley, C. Alan. *The Weed That Strings the Hangman's Bag: A Flavia De Luce Mystery*
Brown, Taylor. ★*Gods of Howl Mountain: A Novel*
Burke, James Lee. *The Jealous Kind*
Campbell, Bebe Moore. *Your Blues Ain't Like Mine*
Carey, Peter. *A Long Way from Home*
Castellani, Christopher. *Leading Men: A Novel*
Chambers, Clare. *Small Pleasures*
Cheek, Chip. *Cape May*
Cleeton, Chanel. *Next Year in Havana*
Cussler, Clive. ★*Golden Buddha*
Deane, Seamus. *Reading in the Dark*
Delany, Vicki. *Deadly Summer Nights*
DeLillo, Don. *Underworld*
Doctorow, E. L. ★*The Book of Daniel: A Novel*
Dybek, Nick. *The Verdun Affair: A Novel*
Dybek, Stuart. *I Sailed with Magellan*
Ellroy, James. ★*L.A. Confidential*
Ellroy, James. ★*Widespread Panic: A Novel*
Erdrich, Louise. ★*The Night Watchman: A Novel*
Feldman, Ellen. *Paris Never Leaves You*
Ferrante, Elena. *My Brilliant Friend*
Francis, Patry. *All the Children Are Home*
Garcia Marquez, Gabriel. *Memories of My Melancholy Whores*
Gaynor, Hazel. *Meet Me in Monaco: A Novel*
Glynn, Alan. *Receptor*
Greene, Graham. ★*The Quiet American*
Guterson, David. ★*Snow Falling on Cedars*
Harrigan, Stephen. *The Leopard Is Loose: A Novel*

Hijuelos, Oscar. *Beautiful Maria of My Soul*
Hijuelos, Oscar. ★*The Mambo Kings Play Songs of Love: A Novel*
Hoffman, Alice. *The Rules of Magic: A Novel*
Horowitz, Anthony. ★*Magpie Murders*
Howard, Ravi. *Driving the King: A Novel*
Hozar, Nazanine. *Aria*
Irving, John. ★*A Prayer for Owen Meany: A Novel*
Janowitz, Brenda. *The Grace Kelly Dress*
Johnson, Keith Lee. ★*Little Black Girl Lost*
Joshi, Alka. *The Henna Artist*
Joyce, Rachel. *Miss Benson's Beetle*
Kamali, Marjan. ★*The Stationery Shop*
Kelly, Julia. *The Last Dance of the Debutante*
Kerouac, Jack. ★*On the Road*
Kerouac, Jack. ★*Road Novels 1957-1960*
Kerr, Philip. ★*Greeks Bearing Gifts: A Bernie Gunther Novel*
Kerr, Philip. ★*Prussian Blue*
Kim, Crystal Hana. *If You Leave Me*
King, Stephen. *11/22/63*
Kowal, Mary Robinette. *The Calculating Stars: A Lady Astronaut Novel*
Lee, Harper. ★*Go Set a Watchman*
Lee, Ji-Min. *The Starlet and the Spy*
Lehane, Dennis. *Shutter Island*
London, Joan. *The Golden Age*
Mendez, Paul. *Rainbow Milk*
Michener, James A. ★*The Bridges at Toko-Ri*
Momaday, N. Scott. *House Made of Dawn*
Moreno-Garcia, Silvia. *Mexican Gothic*
Mullen, Thomas. *Lightning Men: A Novel*
Murr, Naeem. *The Perfect Man: A Novel*
Naipaul, V. S. *Magic Seeds*
Oates, Joyce Carol. *Because It Is Bitter, and Because It Is My Heart*
Oyeyemi, Helen. *Boy, Snow, Bird: A Novel*
Ozick, Cynthia. *Foreign Bodies*
Paton, Alan. *Ah, but Your Land Is Beautiful*
Patterson, Molly. *Rebellion*
Pelecanos, George P. *The Big Blowdown*
Phillips, Jayne Anne. *Lark and Termite: A Novel*
Porter, Regina. *The Travelers*
Prescott, Lara. *The Secrets We Kept*
Prose, Francine. ★*The Vixen*
Pufahl, Shannon. *On Swift Horses*
Reid, Taylor Jenkins. ★*Malibu Rising*
Rimmer, Kelly. *Truths I Never Told You*
Robertson, Robin. *The Long Take: A Noir Narrative*
Robinson, Marilynne. ★*Gilead*
Robinson, Marilynne. *Home*
Roth, Philip. *The Ghost Writer*
Roth, Philip. ★*Goodbye, Columbus, and Five Short Stories*
Roth, Philip. *Indignation*
Roth, Philip. ★*Portnoy's Complaint*
Ruff, Matt. *Lovecraft Country: A Novel*
Ruiz Zafon, Carlos. *The Labyrinth of the Spirits*
Ruiz Zafon, Carlos. *The Prisoner of Heaven*
Runcie, James. *Canvey Island*
Runcie, James. *Sidney Chambers and the Forgiveness of Sins*
Runcie, James. *Sidney Chambers and the Perils of the Night*

Runcie, James. *Sidney Chambers and the Problem of Evil*
Runcie, James. *Sidney Chambers and the Shadow of Death*
Schell, Orville. *My Old Home: A Novel of Exile*
Scott, A. D. ★*Beneath the Abbey Wall: A Novel*
Scott, A. D. *A Double Death on the Black Isle: A Novel*
Scott, A. D. *A Kind of Grief: A Novel*
Scott, A. D. ★*The Low Road*
See, Lisa. *Dreams of Joy: A Novel*
Sepetys, Ruta. ★*Out of the Easy*
Seth, Vikram. ★*A Suitable Boy: A Novel*
Slimani, Leïla. *In the Country of Others*
Smith, Dominic. ★*The Last Painting of Sara De Vos*
Smith, Tom Rob. *Agent 6*
Smith, Tom Rob. *Child 44*
Smith, Tom Rob. *The Secret Speech*
Solzhenitsyn, Aleksandr Isaevich. ★*Cancer Ward*
Spark, Muriel. ★*A Far Cry from Kensington*
Spark, Muriel. ★*Memento Mori*
Sparks, Nicholas. *A Walk to Remember*
Stratford, Sarah-Jane. *Red Letter Days*
Swift, Graham. ★*Here We Are*
Tan, Twan Eng. *The Garden of Evening Mists*
Tanabe, Karin. ★*A Woman of Intelligence*
Truss, Lynne. *The Man That Got Away: A Constable Twitten Mystery*
Truss, Lynne. *Murder by Milk Bottle*
Updike, John. ★*Rabbit, Run*
Urquhart, Jane. *The Night Stages: A Novel*
Vachss, Andrew H. *Two Trains Running*
Vargas Llosa, Mario. *Aunt Julia and the Scriptwriter*
West, Dorothy. *The Wedding*
Williams, Beatriz. *The Summer Wives*
Williams, Niall. *This Is Happiness*
Williams, Tennessee. ★*The Roman Spring of Mrs. Stone*
Wilson, Sloan. ★*The Man in the Gray Flannel Suit*

1960S

Acevedo, Chantel. *The Distant Marvels*
Adichie, Chimamanda Ngozi. *Half of a Yellow Sun*
Adjapon, Bisi. *The Teller of Secrets: A Novel*
Alexander, V. S. *The Magdalen Girls*
Alvarez, Julia. *How the Garcia Girls Lost Their Accents*
Auster, Paul. *Invisible*
Ausubel, Ramona. *Sons and Daughters of Ease and Plenty*
Baldwin, James. ★*Another Country*
Baldwin, James. *Just Above My Head*
Barth, John. ★*Giles Goat-Boy ;: Or, the Revised New Syllabus*
Bausch, Richard. ★*Rebel Powers*
Bellow, Saul. ★*Mr. Sammler's Planet*
Binchy, Maeve. *Firefly Summer*
Bird, Sarah. *The Yokota Officers Club: A Novel*
Bisson, Terry. *Any Day Now*
Block, Lawrence. *Killing Castro*
Blum, Jenna. *The Lost Family*
Bolano, Roberto. *Amulet*
Bowman, David. *Big Bang: A Nonfiction Novel*
Boyd, William. *Trio*
Boyle, T. Coraghessan. *Outside Looking In: A Novel*
Brodie, Emma. *Songs in Ursa Major*
Buckley, William F. ★*Mongoose, R.I.P.: A Blackford Oakes Novel*

Burke, James Lee. *Another Kind of Eden*

Butler, Nickolas. ★*The Hearts of Men*

Byatt, A. S. *Babel Tower*

Byatt, A. S. *A Whistling Woman*

Carter, Stephen L. *Back Channel*

Castellani, Christopher. *Leading Men: A Novel*

Cheever, John. *Bullet Park: A Novel*

Childress, Mark. *Crazy in Alabama*

Chung, Catherine. *The Tenth Muse: A Novel*

Cline, Emma. *The Girls: A Novel*

Cruz, Angie. *Dominicana: A Novel*

DeLillo, Don. *Libra*

Dick, Philip K. ★*The Man in the High Castle*

Didion, Joan. ★*Play It as It Lays: A Novel*

Doyle, Roddy. *Paddy Clarke, Ha-Ha-Ha*

Dunmore, Helen. *Exposure*

Dybek, Stuart. *I Sailed with Magellan*

Ellroy, James. *American Tabloid: A Novel*

Ellroy, James. *Blood's a Rover*

Ellroy, James. *The Cold Six Thousand: A Novel*

Faulks, Sebastian. *On Green Dolphin Street: A Novel*

Flint, Emma. ★*Little Deaths: A Novel*

Foster, Brooke Lea. *Summer Darlings*

Fowler, Christopher. *Bryant & May: Hall of Mirrors : A Peculiar Crimes Unit Mystery*

Francis, Patry. *All the Children Are Home*

Frazier, Charles. *Nightwoods: A Novel*

Fuller, Claire. ★*Bitter Orange*

Groff, Lauren. ★*Arcadia: A Novel*

Gunesekera, Romesh. ★*Suncatcher: A Novel*

Harrison, Jamie. *The Center of Everything: A Novel*

Hilderbrand, Elin. ★*Summer of '69*

Hill, Donna. ★*Confessions in B-Flat*

Hill, Nathan. *The Nix: A Novel*

Kaufman, Sue. *Diary of a Mad Housewife*

Kidd, Sue Monk. ★*The Secret Life of Bees*

Kim, Crystal Hana. *If You Leave Me*

Kimani, Peter. *Dance of the Jakaranda*

Kowal, Mary Robinette. *The Fated Sky: A Lady Astronaut Novel*

Krueger, William Kent. ★*Lightning Strike*

Kundera, Milan. ★*The Unbearable Lightness of Being*

Lansdale, Joe R. *More Better Deals*

Lawton, John. *Hammer to Fall*

Lawton, John. *Then We Take Berlin*

Laymon, Kiese. *Long Division*

Lessing, Doris May. *The Sweetest Dream*

Lippman, Laura. ★*Lady in the Lake: A Novel*

Luesse, Valerie Fraser. *Missing Isaac*

MacDonald, John D. *A Purple Place for Dying*

Mangan, Christine. *Palace of the Drowned*

Marlantes, Karl. ★*Matterhorn: A Novel of the Vietnam War*

Mason, Bobbie Ann. *Dear Ann: A Novel*

McBride, James. ★*Deacon King Kong: A Novel*

McCammon, Robert R. *Boy's Life*

McDermott, Alice. *After This*

McDermott, Alice. *At Weddings and Wakes*

McDermott, Alice. *Child of My Heart*

McDermott, Alice. ★*That Night*

McEwan, Ian. ★*On Chesil Beach*

McKinney-Whetstone, Diane. *Leaving Cecil Street: A Novel*

Means, David. ★*Hystopia: A Novel*

Meuleman, Sarah. *Find Me Gone*

Mitchell, David. ★*Utopia Avenue: A Novel*

Moshfegh, Ottessa. *Eileen*

Mosley, Walter. *Black Betty: An Easy Rawlins Mystery*

Mosley, Walter. ★*Blood Grove*

Mosley, Walter. *Charcoal Joe: An Easy Rawlins Mystery*

Mosley, Walter. *Little Scarlet: An Easy Rawlins Mystery*

Mukherjee, Neel. *The Lives of Others*

Oates, Joyce Carol. *The Gravedigger's Daughter: A Novel*

Oates, Joyce Carol. ★*Them*

Onuzo, Chibundu. *Sankofa: A Novel*

Owens, Delia. *Where the Crawdads Sing*

Oyeyemi, Helen. *Boy, Snow, Bird: A Novel*

Paton, Alan. *Ah, but Your Land Is Beautiful*

Piercy, Marge. *Vida: A Novel*

Prescott, Lara. *The Secrets We Kept*

Pynchon, Thomas. ★*The Crying of Lot 49*

Pynchon, Thomas. *Inherent Vice*

Pynchon, Thomas. *Vineland*

Randisi, Robert J. *Hey There (You with the Gun in Your Hand): A Rat Pack Mystery*

Reed, Ishmael. *Flight to Canada*

Ripley, Mike. *Mr Campion's Fault*

Roth, Philip. ★*American Pastoral*

Rowland, Russell. *Cold Country: A Novel*

Roy, Lori. *Bent Road*

Scerbanenco, Giorgio. *A Private Venus*

Scerbanenco, Giorgio. *Traitors to All*

Schell, Orville. *My Old Home: A Novel of Exile*

Sjowall, Maj. ★*Cop Killer: The Story of a Crime*

Sjowall, Maj. ★*The Laughing Policeman*

Sjowall, Maj. ★*The Locked Room: The Story of a Crime*

Sjowall, Maj. *The Man on the Balcony: The Story of a Crime*

Sjowall, Maj. ★*Murder at the Savoy*

Smith, Dominic. ★*The Electric Hotel*

Spark, Muriel. ★*The Mandelbaum Gate*

Spencer, Sally. ★*A Dying Fall*

Spencer, Scott. ★*Endless Love*

Spillane, Mickey. *The Consummata*

Stockett, Kathryn. ★*The Help*

Straub, Peter. ★*A Dark Matter: A Novel*

Straub, Peter. ★*Mystery*

Swamy, Shruti. *The Archer*

Swarthout, Glendon. *Bless the Beasts and Children*

Thien, Madeleine. *Do Not Say We Have Nothing*

Updike, John. ★*The Witches of Eastwick*

Vargas Llosa, Mario. *The Feast of the Goat*

Vine, Barbara. *The Minotaur: A Novel*

Waller, Robert James. ★*The Bridges of Madison County*

Wambaugh, Joseph. *The New Centurions*

Whitehead, Colson. ★*Harlem Shuffle*

Whitehead, Colson. ★*The Nickel Boys: A Novel*

Wolfe, Paul. *The Lost Diary of M*

Yoon, Paul. ★*Run Me to Earth: A Novel*

1970S

Abbott, Patricia. *Concrete Angel*

Aciman, Andre. *Harvard Square*

Adams, Alina. *The Nesting Dolls*

Adjapon, Bisi. *The Teller of Secrets: A Novel*

Aguilar Camin, Hector. *Death in Veracruz*

Aimaq, Jasmine. *The Opium Prince*

Allende, Isabel. *In the Midst of Winter: A Novel*

Allio, Kirstin. *Buddhism for Western Children: A Novel*

Amis, Martin. ★*The Pregnant Widow*

Ammaniti, Niccolo. *I'm Not Scared*

Ausubel, Ramona. *Sons and Daughters of Ease and Plenty*

Baldwin, James. ★*If Beale Street Could Talk*

Beattie, Ann. *Chilly Scenes of Winter*

Bender, Tony. *The Last Ghost Dancer*

Benedetti, Mario. *Springtime in a Broken Mirror*

Blau, Jessica Anya. *Mary Jane: A Novel*

Block, Lawrence. ★*When the Sacred Ginmill Closes*

Bolano, Roberto. ★*The Savage Detectives*

Brodie, Emma. *Songs in Ursa Major*

Brundage, Elizabeth. ★*All Things Cease to Appear*

Burns, Anna. *Milkman: A Novel*

Burns, Charles. ★*Black Hole*

Campbell, Bonnie Jo. *Once Upon a River*

Chakrabarti, Jai. *A Play for the End of the World*

Clark, Mary Higgins. *Death Wears a Beauty Mask and Other Stories*

Coe, Jonathan. *The Rotters' Club*

Coetzee, J. M. *Summertime: Scenes from a Provincial Life*

Conner, M. Shelly. *Everyman*

Cotterill, Colin. *The Coroner's Lunch*

Cotterill, Colin. *Disco for the Departed*

Cotterill, Colin. *The Second Biggest Nothing*

Cotterill, Colin. *Slash and Burn: A Dr. Siri Mystery Set in Laos*

Couto, Mia. *Sleepwalking Land*

Crow, Sarah McCraw. *The Wrong Kind of Woman*

Cumming, Charles. *A Colder War*

Cumming, Charles. *A Foreign Country*

D'Souza, Tony. *The Konkans*

Daughters, Amy Weinland. *You Cannot Mess This Up: A True Story That Never Happened*

Davidson, Ash. ★*Damnation Spring*

Davis, Fiona. *The Masterpiece*

Dean, Pamela. *Tam Lin*

Deb, Siddhartha. *The Point of Return: A Novel*

DePoy, Phillip. *Sidewalk Saint*

Diehl, Heidi. *Lifelines*

Eskens, Allen. *Nothing More Dangerous: A Novel*

Eugenides, Jeffrey. ★*The Virgin Suicides*

Ferrante, Elena. *The Story of the Lost Child*

Fesperman, Dan. *Safe Houses: A Novel*

Franzen, Jonathan. ★*Crossroads*

French, Marilyn. ★*The Women's Room*

Fu, Kim. *For Today I Am a Boy*

Fuqua, Jonathon Scott. *Gone and Back Again*

Gaines, Ernest J. ★*A Gathering of Old Men*

Ghaffari, Rabeah. ★*To Keep the Sun Alive*

Gordimer, Nadine. *The Conservationist*

Gordon, Jaimy. ★*Lord of Misrule: A Novel*

Gorman, Edward. *Riders on the Storm : A Sam McCain Mystery*

Greer, Robert O. *First of State*

Grisham, John. *The Last Juror*

Hage, Rawi. *Beirut Hellfire Society: A Novel*

Hallberg, Garth Risk. ★*City on Fire*

Hannah, Kristin. *The Great Alone*

Harding Thornton, Christina. *Pickard County Atlas*

Harvey, Michael T. *Pulse*

Hay, Elizabeth. *Late Nights on Air*

Heller, Joseph. *Good as Gold*

Ishiguro, Kazuo. ★*Never Let Me Go*

Kennedy, Randy. *Presidio*

Le Carre, John. ★*The Honourable Schoolboy*

Li, Yiyun. *The Vagrants: A Novel*

Limon, Martin. *The Line*

Limon, Martin. *War Women*

Loedel, Daniel. *Hades, Argentina*

MacDonald, John D. ★*The Lonely Silver Rain*

MacDonald, John D. *The Scarlet Ruse*

Matar, Hisham. *In the Country of Men*

Matheson, Richard. ★*I Am Legend*

McClure, James. *The Steam Pig*

McDermott, Alice. *After This*

Moreno-Garcia, Silvia. ★*Velvet Was the Night*

Morrison, Toni. *Paradise*

Murphy, Devin. *Tiny Americans*

Ng, Celeste. ★*Everything I Never Told You: A Novel*

Nguyen, Viet Thanh. ★*The Sympathizer*

Pamuk, Orhan. *The Museum of Innocence*

Piercy, Marge. *Vida: A Novel*

Reid, Taylor Jenkins. ★*Daisy Jones & The Six: A Novel*

Ripley, Mike. *Mr Campion's Coven*

Ripley, Mike. *Mr. Campion's War*

Rizzuto, Rahna R. *Shadow Child*

Roth, Philip. ★*The Anatomy Lesson*

Runcie, James. *Sidney Chambers and the Persistence of Love*

Schwarz, Liese O'Halloran. *What Could Be Saved*

Shafak, Elif. *Honor: A Novel*

Slaughter, Karin. *Cop Town: A Novel*

Smith, Michael F. *Blackwood*

Smith, Zadie. ★*White Teeth: A Novel*

Spencer, Sally. *Backlash*

Spencer, Sally. *Best Served Cold*

Spencer, Sally. *Dead End*

Spencer, Sally. *The Dead Hand of History*

Spencer, Sally. *Death's Dark Shadow*

Spencer, Sally. ★*Echoes of the Dead*

Spencer, Sally. *Lambs to the Slaughter*

Spencer, Sally. *The Ring of Death*

Spencer, Sally. *The Shivering Turn*

Spencer, Sally. *A Walk with the Dead*

Spencer, Scott. ★*Endless Love*

Stewart, Ann Marie. *Stars in the Grass*

Swinson, David. *City on the Edge*

Trigiani, Adriana. *Big Stone Gap: A Novel*

Updike, John. *Memories of the Ford Administration: A Novel*

Updike, John. ★*Rabbit Is Rich: A Novel*

Vestal, Shawn. *Daredevils*

Vonnegut, Kurt. ★*Breakfast of Champions: Or, Goodbye Blue Monday!*

Vonnegut, Kurt. *Jailbird: A Novel*

Wallace, Melanie. *The Girl in the Garden*

Walls, Jeannette. *The Silver Star: A Novel*

Walton, Dawnie. ★*The Final Revival of Opal & Nev*

Weiss, Leah. *If the Creek Don't Rise: A Novel*

Wetmore, Elizabeth. ★*Valentine*

Wiesel, Elie. *Hostage*

Woodson, Jacqueline. ★*Another Brooklyn*

1980S

Ali, Monica. ★*Brick Lane: A Novel*

Allio, Kirstin. *Buddhism for Western Children: A Novel*

Anderson, Kent. *Green Sun: A Novel*

Apostol, Gina. *Bibliolepsy*

Aramburu, Fernando. *Homeland*

Auster, Paul. *Oracle Night*

Bambara, Toni Cade. *Those Bones Are Not My Child*

Beatty, Paul. *Slumberland: A Novel*

Blau, Jessica Anya. *The Wonder Bread Summer*

Block, Lawrence. *A Drop of the Hard Stuff: A Matthew Scudder Novel*

Boyne, John. ★*A Ladder to the Sky*

Brown, Rita Mae. *Six of One*

Brunt, Carol Rifka. ★*Tell the Wolves I'm Home: A Novel*

Byatt, A. S. ★*Possession: A Romance*

Cash, Wiley. *When Ghosts Come Home: A Novel*

Cassara, Joseph. *The House of Impossible Beauties*

Castillo, Elaine. *America Is Not the Heart*

Choi, Ann Y. K. *Kay's Lucky Coin Variety*

Cooper, Tom. *Florida Man*

Cotterill, Colin. *Don't Eat Me*

Couto, Mia. *Sleepwalking Land*

Cruse, Howard. *The Complete Wendel*

Dalton, Trent. *Boy Swallows Universe*

Deb, Siddhartha. *The Point of Return: A Novel*

Desai, Kiran. *The Inheritance of Loss*

Dunne, Dominick. *People Like Us: A Novel*

Eugenides, Jeffrey. ★*The Marriage Plot*

Ferrante, Elena. *The Story of the Lost Child*

Fforde, Jasper. *The Eyre Affair: A Novel*

Fforde, Jasper. *Lost in a Good Book: A Thursday Next Novel*

Fitch, Janet. *Paint It Black: A Novel*

Flagg, Fannie. ★*Fried Green Tomatoes at the Whistle Stop Cafe*

Ford, Richard. ★*Independence Day*

Fuller, Claire. ★*Bitter Orange*

Gaitskill, Mary. *Veronica*

Garey, Juliann. *Too Bright to Hear Too Loud to See*

Grafton, Sue. *X*

Grafton, Sue. *Y Is for Yesterday*

Hage, Rawi. *De Niro's Game*

Hajdu, David. *Adrianne Geffel: A Fiction*

Harvey, John. *Darkness, Darkness*

Henderson, Smith. *Fourth of July Creek*

Hendrix, Grady. *My Best Friend's Exorcism*

Jedrowski, Tomasz. *Swimming in the Dark*

Jónasson, Ragnar. ★*The Girl Who Died*

Jónasson, Ragnar. *The Mist*

Jones, Tayari. *Silver Sparrow: A Novel*

Laymon, Kiese. *Long Division*

Le Carre, John. *The Tailor of Panama*

Levin, Adam. *Bubblegum*

Loedel, Daniel. *Hades, Argentina*

Ma, Jian. *Beijing Coma*

Makkai, Rebecca. ★*The Great Believers*

Mallon, Thomas. *Finale: A Novel*

Marias, Javier. *Thus Bad Begins: A Novel*

McCarthy, Cormac. ★*No Country for Old Men*

McKevett, G. A. *Murder at Mabel's Motel*

McKinty, Adrian. *In the Morning I'll Be Gone: A Detective Sean Duffy Novel*

Mehta, Rahul. *No Other World: A Novel*

Mitchell, David. *Black Swan Green: A Novel*

Mohamed, Nadifa. *The Orchard of Lost Souls: A Novel*

Moore, Liz. *The Unseen World*

Murakami, Haruki. ★*1q84*

Nava, Michael. ★*Carved in Bone*

Nguyen, Viet Thanh. ★*The Committed*

Osborne, Lawrence. *Only to Sleep: A Philip Marlowe Novel*

Pamuk, Orhan. *Silent House*

Petterson, Per. *I Curse the River of Time*

Pynchon, Thomas. *Vineland*

Reid, Taylor Jenkins. ★*Malibu Rising*

Restrepo, Laura. ★*Delirium: A Novel*

Restrepo, Laura. *No Place for Heroes: A Novel*

Rooney, Kathleen. ★*Lillian Boxfish Takes a Walk*

Rous, Emma. *The Perfect Guests*

Sapphire. ★*Push: A Novel*

Schlink, Bernhard. *Self's Punishment*

Skeslien Charles, Janet. *The Paris Library: A Novel*

Slaughter, Karin. ★*Pieces of Her*

Sofer, Dalia. *The Septembers of Shiraz*

Solomon, Asali. *Disgruntled: A Novel*

Stibbe, Nina. *Reasons to Be Cheerful*

Strout, Elizabeth. *My Name Is Lucy Barton*

Stuart, Douglas. ★*Shuggie Bain*

Swyler, Erika. ★*Light from Other Stars: A Novel*

Thien, Madeleine. *Do Not Say We Have Nothing*

Trigiani, Adriana. *Big Cherry Holler: A Big Stone Gap Novel*

Tudor, C. J. *The Chalk Man: A Novel*

Twardoch, Szczepan. *The King of Warsaw*

Tyree, Omar. ★*Flyy Girl*

Vonnegut, Kurt. ★*Galapagos: A Novel*

Whitehead, Colson. *Sag Harbor: A Novel*

Wilkinson, Lauren. ★*American Spy: A Novel*

Wolfe, Tom. *The Bonfire of the Vanities*

Yates, Christopher J. *Grist Mill Road: A Novel*

★*1984: a Novel*. Orwell, George

1990S

Abraham, Tola Rotimi. *Black Sunday*

Al Rawi, Shahad. *The Baghdad Clock*

Alenyikov, Michael. *Ivan and Misha: Stories*

Ali, Monica. ★*Brick Lane: A Novel*

Aliu, Xhenet. ★*Brass: A Novel*

Amis, Martin. *London Fields: A Novel*

Aramburu, Fernando. *Homeland*

Bacon, Charlotte. *There Is Room for You*

Bandi. *The Accusation: Forbidden Stories from Inside North Korea*

Barr, Nevada. *The Rope: An Anna Pigeon Novel*

Batuman, Elif. ★*The Idiot*

Benaron, Naomi. *Running the Rift: A Novel*

Black, Cara. *Murder in the Bastille*

Black, Cara. *Murder in the Rue De Paradis: An Aimee Leduc Investigation*

Bock, Charles. *Alice & Oliver: A Novel*

Boyle, T. Coraghessan. *The Terranauts*

Boyle, William. *City of Margins: A Novel*

Cassara, Joseph. *The House of Impossible Beauties*

Castillo, Elaine. *America Is Not the Heart*

Chariandy, David John. *Brother: A Novel*

Child, Lee. *The Enemy: A Jack Reacher Novel*

Cleage, Pearl. *What Looks Like Crazy on an Ordinary Day: A Novel*

Connolly, John. *The Dirty South*

Dahl, Arne. *Bad Blood*

Dahl, Arne. *Misterioso: A Crime Novel*

Darnielle, John. *Universal Harvester*

Davis, Fiona. *The Lions of Fifth Avenue: A Novel*

Dennis-Benn, Nicole. *Here Comes the Sun*

Eco, Umberto. *Numero Zero*

Edugyan, Esi. *Half-Blood Blues*

Faye, Gael. ★*Small Country: A Novel*

Ferrante, Elena. *The Lying Life of Adults*

Ferrell, Carolyn. *Dear Miss Metropolitan*

Flagg, Fannie. ★*The Wonder Boy of Whistle Stop: A Novel*

Frear, Caz. *Sweet Little Lies*

Gabel, Aja. *The Ensemble: A Novel*

Gilligan, Ruth. *The Butchers' Blessing*

Gosling, Victoria. *Before the Ruins: A Novel*

Graff, Andrew J. *Raft of Stars*

Harrison, M. John. *Light*

Heller, Zoe. *What Was She Thinking?: Notes on a Scandal*

Hendrix, Grady. *The Southern Book Club's Guide to Slaying Vampires*

Higashino, Keigo. *Malice*

Higashino, Keigo. *Newcomer*

Holbert, Bruce. *Whiskey*

Ishiguro, Kazuo. ★*Never Let Me Go*

King, Lily. *Writers & Lovers: A Novel*

Larkin, Allie. *The People We Keep*

Lattari, Katie. *Dark Things I Adore*

Lerner, Ben. ★*The Topeka School*

Levy, Deborah. *Swimming Home: A Novel*

Lippman, Laura. ★*Sunburn*

Lowe, Kathryn A. *The Furies*

Mankell, Henning. *The Dogs of Riga*

Mankell, Henning. ★*The Return of the Dancing Master*

Masood, Syed M. *The Bad Muslim Discount*

McLean, Felicity. *The Van Apfel Girls Are Gone*

Mehta, Rahul. *No Other World: A Novel*

Murakami, Haruki. *After the Quake: Stories*

Novic, Sara. *Girl at War*

O'Nan, Stewart. *Henry, Himself*

O'Rawe, Richard. *Northern Heist*

Obioma, Chigozie. ★*The Fishermen: A Novel*

Park, Ishle Yi. *Angel & Hannah: A Novel in Verse*

Persson, Leif G. W. *Another Time, Another Life: The Story of a Crime*

Prcic, Ismet. *Shards: A Novel*

Racculia, Kate. ★*Bellweather Rhapsody*

Restrepo, Laura. *No Place for Heroes: A Novel*

Rimmer, Kelly. *Truths I Never Told You*

Riordan, Kate. *The Heatwave*

Rivero, Melissa. *The Affairs of the Falcons*

Robertson, Michael. *The Baker Street Letters*

Robertson, Michael. *The Baker Street Translation: A Mystery*

Robertson, Michael. *The Brothers of Baker Street*

Robertson, Michael. *Moriarty Returns a Letter: A Baker Street Mystery*

Rojas Contreras, Ingrid. ★*Fruit of the Drunken Tree: A Novel*

Roth, Philip. ★*The Human Stain*

Russo, Richard. ★*Everybody's Fool*

Senna, Danzy. *New People*

Shafak, Elif. *Honor: A Novel*

Shteyngart, Gary. *The Russian Debutante's Handbook*

Spencer, Scott. *An Ocean Without a Shore*

Takamura, Kaoru. ★*Lady Joker*

Vann, David. *Aquarium*

Vonnegut, Kurt. *Timequake*

Wayne, Teddy. *Apartment: A Novel*

Westlake, Donald E. *Forever and a Death*

Whittall, Zoe. *The Spectacular: A Novel*

19TH CENTURY

Aalborg, Gordon. *River of Porcupines*

Akunin, B. *The Coronation: The Further Adventures of Erast Fandorin*

Akunin, B. *Sister Pelagia and the White Bulldog: A Mystery*

Alexie, Sherman. *Flight*

Allende, Isabel. *Portrait in Sepia: A Novel*

Atakora, Afia. ★*Conjure Women*

Austen, Jane. *Mansfield Park*

Austen, Jane. ★*Pride and Prejudice*

Balogh, Mary. *The Arrangement*

Balogh, Mary. *The Escape*

Balogh, Mary. *Only Enchanting*

Banks, Russell. *Cloudsplitter: A Novel*

Barry, Sebastian. *Days Without End: A Novel*

Barry, Sebastian. ★*A Thousand Moons: A Novel*

Bayard, Louis. *The Black Tower: A Novel*

Bear, Elizabeth. *Stone Mad*

Bell, Lenora. ★*What a Difference a Duke Makes*

Benjamin, Melanie. *Alice I Have Been*

Blake, Audrey. *The Girl in His Shadow: A Novel*

Brink, Andre P. *Philida: A Novel*

Brockway, Connie. *The Golden Season*

Brockway, Connie. *So Enchanting*

Bronte, Charlotte. ★*Jane Eyre*

Brooks, Bill. *Blood Storm*

Brown, Dee. *Creek Mary's Blood: A Novel*

Burrowes, Grace. *Tremaine's True Love*

Byatt, A. S. ★*Possession: A Romance*

Callihan, Kristen. ★*Firelight*

Cantor, Jillian. *Half Life*

Cather, Willa. ★*My Antonia*
Cather, Willa. *O Pioneers!*
Chase, Loretta Lynda. *Miss Wonderful*
Chiaverini, Jennifer. *Mrs. Lincoln's Dressmaker: A Novel*
Cho, Zen. *Sorcerer to the Crown*
Ciotta, Beth. *Her Sky Cowboy*
Clarke, Susanna. ★*Jonathan Strange & Mr. Norrell*
Clinch, Jon. *Marley: A Novel*
Collins, Wilkie. ★*The Moonstone*
Couto, Mia. *The Sword and the Spear*
Crummey, Michael. *The Innocents*
Cunningham, Michael. *Specimen Days*
Dare, Tessa. *A Week to Be Wicked*
Deon, Natashia. *Grace*
Dexter, Pete. ★*Deadwood*
Diaz, Hernan. ★*In the Distance*
Dickens, Charles. ★*Bleak House*
Dickens, Charles. ★*David Copperfield*
Dickens, Charles. *Dombey and Son*
Dickens, Charles. ★*Great Expectations*
Dickens, Charles. ★*Nicholas Nickleby*
Dickens, Charles. *The Old Curiosity Shop*
Dickens, Charles. *Oliver Twist, or the Parish Boy's Progress*
Dickens, Charles. *Our Mutual Friend*
Dickens, Charles. *The Pickwick Papers*
Dostoyevsky, Fyodor. ★*Crime and Punishment*
Doyle, Arthur Conan. ★*The Complete Sherlock Holmes*
Doyle, Arthur Conan. ★*The Hound of the Baskervilles*
Dreiser, Theodore. ★*Sister Carrie*
Dumas, Alexandre. ★*Camille*
Dumas, Alexandre. ★*The Count of Monte Cristo*
Ebershoff, David. *The 19th Wife: A Novel*
Edugyan, Esi. ★*Washington Black: A Novel*
Eliot, George. ★*The Mill on the Floss*
Eliot, George. ★*Silas Marner: The Weaver of Raveloe*
Estleman, Loren D. ★*The Master Executioner*
Faber, Michel. *The Crimson Petal and the White*
Faye, Lyndsay. *Jane Steele*
Finch, Charles. *A Beautiful Blue Death*
Finch, Charles. *The Last Passenger*
Finch, Charles. *The Vanishing Man*
Flaubert, Gustave. *Sentimental Education*
Forester, C. S. *Beat to Quarters*
Forester, C. S. *Commodore Hornblower*
Forester, C. S. *Flying Colours*
Forester, C. S. *Hornblower and the Atropos*
Forester, C. S. *Hornblower and the Hotspur*
Forester, C. S. *Lieutenant Hornblower*
Forester, C. S. *Lord Hornblower*
Forester, C. S. *Ship of the Line*
Frampton, Megan. *The Duke's Guide to Correct Behavior*
Francis-Sharma, Lauren. ★*Book of the Little Axe*
Franklin, Miles. *My Brilliant Career*
Frazier, Charles. *Thirteen Moons: A Novel*
Gaines, Ernest J. ★*The Autobiography of Miss Jane Pittman*
Gallagher, Stephen. *The Kingdom of Bones: A Novel*
Gappah, Petina. ★*Out of Darkness, Shining Light*
Garcia Marquez, Gabriel. *The General in His Labyrinth*

Gerritsen, Tess. *The Bone Garden*
Ghosh, Amitav. *Flood of Fire*
Ghosh, Amitav. *River of Smoke*
Gibbon, Maureen. *The Lost Notebook of Edouard Manet: A Novel*
Gortner, C. W. *The First Actress: A Novel of Sarah Bernhardt*
Guthrie, A. B. ★*The Big Sky*
Gyasi, Yaa. ★*Homegoing: A Novel*
Harris, Nathan. *The Sweetness of Water*
Harris, Robert. *An Officer and a Spy*
Hijuelos, Oscar. *Twain & Stanley Enter Paradise*
Hill, Ruth Beebe. *Hanta Yo*
Hoffman, Alice. *The Marriage of Opposites: A Novel Based on the Life of Rachel Pizzarro*
Hornby, Gill. *Miss Austen*
James, Henry. *Complete Stories, 1874-1884*
James, Henry. *Complete Stories, 1884-1891*
James, Henry. *Complete Stories, 1892-1898*
Johnson, Charles Richard. ★*Middle Passage*
Jones, Douglas C. *The Court-Martial of George Armstrong Custer*
Kidd, Sue Monk. ★*The Invention of Wings: A Novel*
Kingsolver, Barbara. ★*Unsheltered*
Labatut, Benjamin. *When We Cease to Understand the World*
Laurens, Stephanie. *The Pursuits of Lord Kit Cavanaugh*
Lee, Jonathan. *The Great Mistake*
Leonard, Elmore. ★*The Complete Western Stories of Elmore Leonard.*
Malerman, Josh. *Unbury Carol*
Mann, Thomas. *Buddenbrooks*
Mas, Victoria. *The Mad Women's Ball*
McCarthy, Cormac. ★*Blood Meridian, Or, the Evening Redness in the West*
McMurtry, Larry. ★*Lonesome Dove: A Novel*
Mitchell, David. *The Thousand Autumns of Jacob De Zoet: A Novel*
Morgenstern, Erin. ★*The Night Circus: A Novel*
Morrison, Toni. ★*Beloved: A Novel*
North, Claire. *The Pursuit of William Abbey*
Novik, Naomi. *His Majesty's Dragon*
O'Connor, Joseph. *Star of the Sea*
Palliser, Charles. *The Quincunx*
Pearl, Matthew. *The Last Dickens: A Novel*
Pearl, Matthew. *The Technologists: A Novel*
Pears, Iain. *Stone's Fall*
Perry, Anne. *A Dangerous Mourning*
Perry, Anne. *The Face of a Stranger*
Pesci, David. *Amistad: A Novel*
Pirie, David. *The Patient's Eyes*
Powning, Beth. *The Sea Captain's Wife: A Novel*
Priest, Cherie. *Boneshaker*
Priest, Cherie. *Clementine*
Pulley, Natasha. ★*The Kingdoms*
Purcell, Laura. *The Silent Companions: A Ghost Story*
Putney, Mary Jo. *Loving a Lost Lord*
Quick, Amanda. *Garden of Lies*
Rawles, Nancy. *My Jim: A Novel*
Rhys, Jean. ★*Wide Sargasso Sea*
Ridley, Erica. *The Duke Heist*
Ridley, Erica. ★*The Perks of Loving a Wallflower*
Romano-Lax, Andromeda. *The Spanish Bow*
Rowland, Laura Joh. *The Hangman's Secret*

Sand, George. *Marianne*
Santiago, Esmeralda. *Conquistadora: A Novel*
Schaefer, Jack. ★*Shane*
Seton, Anya. ★*Dragonwyck*
Shaara, Jeff. *Gone for Soldiers*
Shelley, Mary Wollstonecraft. ★*Frankenstein: Or, the Modern Prometheus*
Shreve, Anita. *Fortune's Rocks: A Novel*
Silko, Leslie Marmon. *Gardens in the Dunes: A Novel*
Sjón. *The Blue Fox*
Smith, Lee. *On Agate Hill: A Novel*
Smith, Martin Cruz. *Rose*
Sontag, Susan. ★*In America*
Stoker, Bram. ★*Dracula*
Stoker, Bram. *The New Annotated Dracula*
Swift, Jonathan. ★*Gulliver's Travels*
Tademy, Lalita. *Cane River*
Thackeray, William Makepeace. ★*Vanity Fair: A Novel Without a Hero*
Toibin, Colm. ★*The Magician: A Novel*
Trollope, Anthony. *Doctor Thorne*
Trollope, Anthony. *The Warden*
Truong, Monique T. D. *The Sweetest Fruits*
Twain, Mark. ★*Adventures of Huckleberry Finn: Tom Sawyer's Comrade ...*
Twain, Mark. ★*A Connecticut Yankee in King Arthur's Court*
Uris, Leon. ★*Trinity*
Urquhart, Rachel. *The Visionist*
Urrea, Luis Alberto. *The Hummingbird's Daughter: A Novel*
Urrea, Luis Alberto. *Queen of America: A Novel*
Vargas Llosa, Mario. *The War of the End of the World*
Vargas Llosa, Mario. ★*The Way to Paradise*
Verble, Margaret. ★*Cherokee America*
Verne, Jules. ★*Around the World in Eighty Days*
Vreeland, Susan. *Girl in Hyacinth Blue*
Warren, Robert Penn. *World Enough and Time: A Romantic Novel*
Winterson, Jeanette. ★*Frankissstein*
Wojtas, Olga. *Miss Blaine's Prefect and the Golden Samovar*
Zola, Emile. ★*Nana*
The 19th Wife: A Novel. Ebershoff, David
★*1q84.* Murakami, Haruki

1ST CENTURY
Davis, Lindsey. *A Body in the Bathhouse*
Davis, Lindsey. *A Comedy of Terrors: A Flavia Albia Novel*
Davis, Lindsey. *The Ides of April: A Flavia Albia Mystery*
Davis, Lindsey. *One Virgin Too Many*
Harris, Robert. *Pompeii: A Novel*
Parini, Jay. *The Damascus Road: A Novel of Saint Paul*
Wallace, Lew. ★*Ben-Hur*

1ST CENTURY BCE
Saylor, Steven. *The House of the Vestals: The Investigations of Gordianus the Finder*
Saylor, Steven. *A Mist of Prophecies*
Saylor, Steven. *Rubicon*
Saylor, Steven. *The Triumph of Caesar: A Novel of Ancient Rome*
1st to Die: A Novel. Patterson, James
2000S (DECADE)
Auster, Paul. *The Brooklyn Follies*

Bolton, S. J. *A Dark and Twisted Tide*
Bolton, S. J. *Now You See Me*
Cussler, Clive. ★*Golden Buddha*
DeMille, Nelson. *Wild Fire*
Diehl, Heidi. *Lifelines*
Evison, Jonathan. *West of Here: A Novel*
Florio, Gwen. *Silent Hearts*
Ford, Richard. *The Lay of the Land*
Gessen, Keith. *A Terrible Country*
Harrison, Jamie. *The Center of Everything: A Novel*
Hughes, Caoilinn. *Orchid and the Wasp*
Jin, Ha. *The Boat Rocker: A Novel*
Johnson, Nancy. *The Kindest Lie*
Kohnstamm, Thomas B. *Lake City*
Kushner, Rachel. *The Mars Room*
Lutz, Lisa. *The Swallows: A Novel*
Mallon, Thomas. *Landfall: A Novel*
Marra, Anthony. ★*A Constellation of Vital Phenomena: A Novel*
Masood, Syed M. *The Bad Muslim Discount*
Morton, Brian. *Florence Gordon*
Moshfegh, Ottessa. *My Year of Rest and Relaxation*
Newman, Sandra. *The Heavens*
O'Farrell, Maggie. *The Vanishing Act of Esme Lennox*
Porter, Regina. *The Travelers*
Pynchon, Thomas. ★*Bleeding Edge*
Sathian, Sanjena. *Gold Diggers*
Yates, Christopher J. *Grist Mill Road: A Novel*
★*2001: a Space Odyssey.* Clarke, Arthur C.
2010S
Ackerman, Elliot. *Red Dress in Black and White*
Aliu, Xhenet. ★*Brass: A Novel*
Allende, Isabel. *In the Midst of Winter: A Novel*
Bartz, Andrea. *The Lost Night*
Benjamin, Ali. *The Smash-Up: A Novel*
Camp, Bryan. *The City of Lost Fortunes*
Daughters, Amy Weinland. *You Cannot Mess This Up: A True Story That Never Happened*
Erdrich, Louise. ★*The Sentence*
Garcia, Gabriela. *Of Women and Salt*
Gilligan, Ruth. *The Butchers' Blessing*
Glynn, Alan. *Receptor*
Gosling, Victoria. *Before the Ruins: A Novel*
Gray, Anissa. *The Care and Feeding of Ravenously Hungry Girls*
Hill, Nathan. *The Nix: A Novel*
Janowitz, Brenda. *The Grace Kelly Dress*
Kamali, Marjan. ★*The Stationery Shop*
Kunzru, Hari. *Red Pill: A Novel*
Lasdun, James. *Afternoon of a Faun: A Novel*
Lattari, Katie. *Dark Things I Adore*
Le Carre, John. *Agent Running in the Field*
Leavitt, David. ★*Shelter in Place*
Levin, Adam. *Bubblegum*
Ma, Ling. *Severance*
Makkai, Rebecca. ★*The Great Believers*
Markley, Stephen. *Ohio*
Mason, Bobbie Ann. *Dear Ann: A Novel*
Meuleman, Sarah. *Find Me Gone*
Murphy, Devin. *Tiny Americans*

Powell, Mark. *Firebird*
Rous, Emma. *The Perfect Guests*
Schwarz, Liese O'Halloran. *What Could Be Saved*
Slaughter, Karin. ★*Pieces of Her*
Smith, Ali. ★*Spring*
Smith, Ali. ★*Winter*
Spiotta, Dana. *Wayward*
Steinhauer, Olen. *The Middleman*
Taneja, Preti. *We That Are Young: A Novel*
Thorpe, Rufi. ★*The Knockout Queen*
Tudor, C. J. *The Chalk Man: A Novel*
Walton, Dawnie. ★*The Final Revival of Opal & Nev*
Whittall, Zoe. *The Spectacular: A Novel*
Yoon, Paul. ★*Run Me to Earth: A Novel*

2020S
Brown, Dale. *Eagle Station: A Novel*
Connelly, Michael. ★*The Dark Hours*
DeLillo, Don. *The Silence*
Erdrich, Louise. ★*The Sentence*
Monroe, Mary Alice. ★*The Summer of Lost and Found*
Penny, Louise. ★*The Madness of Crowds*
Picoult, Jodi. ★*Wish You Were Here: A Novel*
Sweeney-Baird, Christina. *The End of Men*

206 Bones. Reichs, Kathy

20TH CENTURY
Abbott, Megan E. *Queenpin: A Novel*
Airth, Rennie. *The Decent Inn of Death*
Akhtar, Ayad. ★*Homeland Elegies: A Novel*
Alharthi, Jokha. *Celestial Bodies: A Novel*
Allende, Isabel. *A Long Petal of the Sea: A Novel*
Altan, Ahmet. ★*Love in the Days of Rebellion*
Anstruther, Eleanor. *A Perfect Explanation*
Araghi, Alireza Taheri. ★*The Immortals of Tehran*
Archer, Jeffrey. *Nothing Ventured*
Artson, Barbara. *Odessa, Odessa*
Atkinson, Kate. ★*Transcription*
Auster, Paul. *4 3 2 1: A Novel*
Bailey, Paul. *Uncle Rudolf*
Ballard, J. G. *The Kindness of Women*
Banks, Russell. *Foregone*
Banner, Catherine. *The House at the Edge of Night: A Novel*
Bauman, Bruce. ★*Broken Sleep: An American Dream*
Belfer, Lauren. *And After the Fire: A Novel*
Benedict, Marie. ★*Lady Clementine*
Benedict, Marie. *The Only Woman in the Room*
Benjamin, Melanie. ★*The Aviator's Wife: A Novel*
Bennett, Brit. ★*The Vanishing Half*
Boyle, T. Coraghessan. *The Women: A Novel*
Boyne, John. *The Heart's Invisible Furies*
Butler, Robert Olen. *Late City*
Cantor, Jillian. *Half Life*
Chen, Da. *Brothers: A Novel*
Colvin, Jeffrey. ★*Africaville: A Novel*
Craig, Charmaine. *Miss Burma*
Danforth, Emily M. *Plain Bad Heroines*
Dangarembga, Tsitsi. *This Mournable Body*
Darznik, Jasmin. *Song of a Captive Bird: A Novel*
Davis, Fiona. *The Chelsea Girls*

De Robertis, Carolina. *Cantoras*
Del Amo, Jean-Baptiste. *Animalia*
Diamant, Anita. *The Boston Girl: A Novel*
Dupont, Eric. *The American Fiancee: A Novel*
Epstein, Jennifer Cody. ★*Wunderland: A Novel*
Feng, Linda Rui. *Swimming Back to Trout River*
Fernandez, Nona. *The Twilight Zone*
Follett, Ken. *Edge of Eternity*
Follett, Ken. *Fall of Giants*
Follett, Ken. *Winter of the World*
Forbes, Curdella. *A Tall History of Sugar*
Gaines, Ernest J. ★*The Autobiography of Miss Jane Pittman*
Ghosh, Amitav. *The Glass Palace*
Gilman, Susan Jane. *The Ice Cream Queen of Orchard Street: A Novel*
Giordano, Paolo. *Heaven and Earth*
Goldberg, Myla. *Feast Your Eyes*
Grames, Juliet. *The Seven or Eight Deaths of Stella Fortuna*
Hahn, Sumi. *The Mermaid from Jeju: A Novel*
Han, Kang. ★*Human Acts: A Novel*
Haratischvili, Nino. *The Eighth Life: (For Brilka)*
Hegi, Ursula. *Stones from the River*
Hilderbrand, Elin. ★*28 Summers*
Hozar, Nazanine. *Aria*
Hunt, Laird. *Zorrie*
James, Marlon. ★*A Brief History of Seven Killings: A Novel*
Joukhadar, Zeyn. ★*The Thirty Names of Night: A Novel*
Kim, Eugenia. *The Kinship of Secrets*
Krivak, Andrew. *The Signal Flame: A Novel*
Kuang, R. F. ★*The Dragon Republic*
Kuang, R. F. *The Poppy War*
Labatut, Benjamin. *When We Cease to Understand the World*
Lahiri, Jhumpa. ★*The Namesake*
Lebrecht, Norman. *The Song of Names*
Lee, Min Jin. ★*Pachinko*
Liardet, Frances. *We Must Be Brave*
MacLeod, Alison. *Tenderness*
McCracken, Elizabeth. ★*Bowlaway: A Novel*
McDermott, Alice. ★*The Ninth Hour*
McEwan, Ian. ★*On Chesil Beach*
Miller, Derek B. *How to Find Your Way in the Dark*
Miller, Kei. ★*Augustown*
Mitchell, David. *The Bone Clocks: A Novel*
Monroe, Mary. ★*Mrs. Wiggins*
Morris, Heather. *Cilka's Journey*
Nguyen, Phan Que Mai. ★*The Mountains Sing: A Novel*
Nguyen, Viet Thanh. ★*The Sympathizer*
North, Claire. *The Pursuit of William Abbey*
Oates, Joyce Carol. *The Falls: A Novel*
Oates, Joyce Carol. ★*We Were the Mulvaneys*
Offutt, Chris. *Country Dark*
Ondaatje, Michael. ★*Warlight*
Onyebuchi, Tochi. ★*Riot Baby*
Pamuk, Orhan. ★*A Strangeness in My Mind: A Novel*
Paul, Gill. ★*The Lost Daughter*
Phillips, Caryl. *A View of the Empire at Sunset*
Pollock, Donald Ray. *The Devil All the Time*
Pontoppidan, Henrik. *Lucky Per*
Pynchon, Thomas. ★*V: A Novel*

Rachman, Tom. *The Italian Teacher*

Reddi, Rishi. *Passage West: A Novel*

Ritter, Josh. *The Great Glorious Goddamn of It All*

Roberts, Bethan. ★*My Policeman*

Robinson, Marilynne. ★*Jack*

Rooney, Kathleen. ★*Lillian Boxfish Takes a Walk*

Roy, Anuradha. *All the Lives We Never Lived: A Novel*

Runcie, James. *The Road to Grantchester*

Scharer, Whitney. *The Age of Light*

Schlink, Bernhard. *Olga*

See, Lisa. *The Island of Sea Women*

Serpell, Namwali. ★*The Old Drift*

Shields, Carol. ★*The Stone Diaries*

Shriver, Lionel. *Should We Stay or Should We Go*

Sittenfeld, Curtis. *Rodham: A Novel*

Smiley, Jane. *Early Warning*

Smiley, Jane. *Golden Age*

Smiley, Jane. *Some Luck*

Solomons, Natasha. *House of Gold*

Stridsberg, Sara. *Valerie: Or the Faculty of Dreams : Amendment to the Theory of Sexuality*

Tademy, Lalita. *Cane River*

Tobar, Hector. *The Last Great Road Bum*

Toibin, Colm. ★*The Magician: A Novel*

Uris, Leon. *Redemption: A Novel*

Verble, Margaret. ★*When Two Feathers Fell from the Sky*

Vreeland, Susan. *Girl in Hyacinth Blue*

Wall, Cara. *The Dearly Beloved: A Novel*

Wecker, Helene. ★*The Hidden Palace*

Weiner, Jennifer. ★*Mrs. Everything: A Novel*

Weiss, Elizabeth. *The Sisters Sweet*

Williams, Pip. *The Dictionary of Lost Words*

Winslow, De'Shawn Charles. ★*In West Mills*

Woodson, Jacqueline. ★*Red at the Bone*

21ST CENTURY

Adebayo, Ayobami. ★*Stay with Me*

Akhtar, Ayad. ★*Homeland Elegies: A Novel*

Alexie, Sherman. *Flight*

Anam, Tahmima. *The Startup Wife*

Anderson, Alison. *The Summer Guest*

Angelo, Megan. *Followers*

Atwood, Margaret. ★*The Handmaid's Tale*

Atwood, Margaret. ★*The Testaments: A Novel*

Bandi. *The Accusation: Forbidden Stories from Inside North Korea*

Banks, Russell. *Foregone*

Banner, Catherine. *The House at the Edge of Night: A Novel*

Bauman, Bruce. ★*Broken Sleep: An American Dream*

Belfer, Lauren. *And After the Fire: A Novel*

Broun, Bill. *Night of the Animals*

Butler, Octavia E. ★*Parable of the Sower*

Butler, Octavia E. *Parable of the Talents: A Novel*

Butler, Robert Olen. *Late City*

Clarke, Arthur C. ★*2001: A Space Odyssey*

Cline, Ernest. *Ready Player One: A Novel*

Crouch, Blake. *Recursion*

Cunningham, Michael. *Specimen Days*

Danforth, Emily M. *Plain Bad Heroines*

De Robertis, Carolina. *Cantoras*

Doctorow, Cory. *Rapture of the Nerds*

Donoghue, Emma. *Akin*

Ebershoff, David. *The 19th Wife: A Novel*

El Akkad, Omar. *American War*

Ellmann, Lucy. *Ducks, Newburyport*

Fernandez, Nona. *The Twilight Zone*

Ferrell, Carolyn. *Dear Miss Metropolitan*

Foer, Jonathan Safran. *Extremely Loud and Incredibly Close*

Fowler, Karen Joy. *The Jane Austen Book Club*

Gibson, William. ★*Agency*

Gibson, William. *Pattern Recognition*

Giordano, Paolo. *Heaven and Earth*

Grames, Juliet. *The Seven or Eight Deaths of Stella Fortuna*

Hamya, Jo. *Three Rooms*

Han, Kang. ★*Human Acts: A Novel*

Harvey, John. *Darkness, Darkness*

Heiny, Katherine. ★*Early Morning Riser*

Hilderbrand, Elin. ★*28 Summers*

Jayatissa, Amanda. ★*My Sweet Girl*

Joukhadar, Zeyn. ★*The Thirty Names of Night: A Novel*

Khadra, Yasmina. ★*Khalil: A Novel*

Kingsolver, Barbara. ★*Unsheltered*

Kress, Nancy. *Beggars in Spain*

Kroese, Robert. *The Last Iota*

Lunde, Maja. *The End of the Ocean: A Novel*

Miles, Jonathan. *Anatomy of a Miracle*

Miller, Rebecca. ★*Jacob's Folly: A Novel*

Mitchell, David. *The Bone Clocks: A Novel*

Onyebuchi, Tochi. ★*Riot Baby*

Pamuk, Orhan. ★*A Strangeness in My Mind: A Novel*

Porter, Max. ★*Lanny: A Novel*

Rachman, Tom. *The Italian Teacher*

Rao, Shobha. ★*Girls Burn Brighter*

Robb, J. D. *Connections in Death: An Eve Dallas Novel*

Robb, J. D. *Fantasy in Death*

Robb, J. D. *Innocent in Death*

Robb, J. D. *Leverage in Death: An Eve Dallas Novel*

Robb, J. D. *Naked in Death*

Robinson, Kim Stanley. *Antarctica*

Robinson, Kim Stanley. ★*Red Mars*

Rushdie, Salman. ★*Quichotte: A Novel*

Russell, Mary Doria. ★*Children of God: A Novel*

Russell, Mary Doria. ★*The Sparrow*

Sakey, Marcus. *A Better World*

Sakey, Marcus. *Brilliance*

Schlink, Bernhard. *Olga*

Self, Will. *The Book of Dave: A Revelation of the Recent Past and the Distant Future*

Serpell, Namwali. ★*The Old Drift*

Shannon, Samantha. *The Bone Season*

Shannon, Samantha. *The Mime Order*

Shriver, Lionel. *Should We Stay or Should We Go*

Sittenfeld, Curtis. *Rodham: A Novel*

Smiley, Jane. *Golden Age*

Steele, Allen M. *Coyote: A Novel of Interstellar Exploration*

Stephenson, Neal. *The Diamond Age,: Or, a Young Lady's Illustrated Primer*

Stephenson, Neal. ★*Snow Crash*

Straub, Emma. ★*All Adults Here*
Stross, Charles. *Accelerando*
Suarez, Daniel. *Change Agent: A Novel*
Swyler, Erika. ★*Light from Other Stars: A Novel*
Vonnegut, Kurt. *Hocus Pocus*
Wang, Kathy. *Family Trust: A Novel*
Ware, Ruth. ★*The Turn of the Key*
Wilson, Daniel H. *The Clockwork Dynasty: A Novel*
Winterson, Jeanette. ★*Frankissstein*
Woods, Chavisa. *Things to Do When You're Goth in the Country: And Other Stories*
Yanagihara, Hanya. *A Little Life: A Novel*

22ND CENTURY
Clarke, Arthur C. *Rendezvous with Rama*
Gibson, William. ★*Agency*
Hamilton, Peter F. *Great North Road*
Lai, Larissa. *The Tiger Flu*
McKinney, Chris. *Midnight, Water City*
Robinson, Kim Stanley. ★*Green Mars*
Robinson, Kim Stanley. *New York 2140*

23RD CENTURY
Stross, Charles. *Saturn's Children: A Space Opera*

24TH CENTURY
Baker, Kage. *In the Garden of Iden: A Novel of the Company*
Hamilton, Peter F. *Pandora's Star*

25TH CENTURY
Harrison, M. John. *Light*
Lafferty, Mur. *Six Wakes*
Palmer, Ada. *Too Like the Lightning*
★*2666*. Bolano, Roberto

26TH CENTURY
Huxley, Aldous. ★*Brave New World*
Reynolds, Alastair. *Revelation Space*
Zamyatin, Yevgeny Ivanovich. ★*We*

27TH CENTURY
Stross, Charles. *Glasshouse*
★*28 Summers*. Hilderbrand, Elin

28TH CENTURY
Simmons, Dan. *The Fall of Hyperion*
Simmons, Dan. ★*Hyperion*

32ND CENTURY
Simmons, Dan. *Endymion*

34TH CENTURY
Hamilton, Peter F. *The Dreaming Void*
36 Arguments for the Existence of God: A Work of Fiction. Goldstein, Rebecca
36 Righteous Men: A Novel. Pressfield, Steven
4 3 2 1: A Novel. Auster, Paul
The 42nd Parallel. Dos Passos, John
44901. Smith, Martin Cruz
The 47th Samurai. Hunter, Stephen
500 Miles from You. Colgan, Jenny

5TH CENTURY
Stewart, Mary. ★*The Crystal Cave*
Stewart, Mary. ★*The Hollow Hills*
Stewart, Mary. *The Last Enchantment*
Stewart, Mary. *The Wicked Day*

5TH CENTURY BCE
Andrews, Mesu. *Of Fire and Lions: A Novel*
61 Hours: A Reacher Novel. Child, Lee

6TH CENTURY
Pike, Signe. *The Forgotten Kingdom: A Novel*
Pike, Signe. *The Lost Queen*
Twain, Mark. ★*A Connecticut Yankee in King Arthur's Court*
The 7 1/2 Deaths of Evelyn Hardcastle. Turton, Stuart

7TH CENTURY
Griffith, Nicola. *Hild: A Novel*
82 Desire: A Skip Langdon Novel. Smith, Julie
★*88 Names*. Ruff, Matt

A

★*The A B C Murders*. Christie, Agatha
Aalborg, Gordon
River of Porcupines
Aaron Falk novels [Series]. Harper, Jane
Aaronovitch, Ben
Broken Homes
Midnight Riot
Moon Over Soho
Whispers Under Ground
Abaddon's Gate. Corey, James S. A.
ABANDONED BOYS
Greene, Graham. *The Captain and the Enemy*
Murr, Naeem. *The Perfect Man: A Novel*
ABANDONED CHILDREN
Bloom, Amy. *Lucky Us: A Novel*
Bronte, Charlotte. ★*Emma*
Chen, Da. *Brothers: A Novel*
Cleeves, Ann. *The Darkest Evening*
Edwards, Kim. *The Memory Keeper's Daughter*
Eliot, George. ★*Silas Marner: The Weaver of Raveloe*
Fielding, Henry. ★*The History of Tom Jones, a Foundling*
Franck, Julia. *Blindness of the Heart*
Holt, Victoria. *The Black Opal*
Hozar, Nazanine. *Aria*
Kingsolver, Barbara. ★*The Bean Trees: A Novel*
Kosinski, Jerzy. ★*The Painted Bird*
Livesey, Margot. *Criminals: A Novel*
Lovesey, Peter. *Diamond Solitaire*
McCaffrey, Anne. ★*Acorna: The Unicorn Girl*
Solomon, Anna. *Leaving Lucy Pear*
Wright, Jaime Jo. *The Haunting at Bonaventure Circus*
ABANDONED DOGS
Cameron, W. Bruce. *The Dogs of Christmas*
ABANDONED GIRLS
Durrow, Heidi W. *The Girl Who Fell from the Sky: A Novel*
Gilman, Susan Jane. *The Ice Cream Queen of Orchard Street: A Novel*
Grey, Zane. *Woman of the Frontier: A Western Story*
ABANDONED HOUSES
Ward, Catriona. *The Last House on Needless Street*
ABANDONED INFANTS
Carr, Robyn. ★*Virgin River*

Rivers, Francine. *Bridge to Haven*
Spencer-Fleming, Julia. *In the Bleak Midwinter*

ABANDONED TEENAGERS

Butler, Season. ★*Cygnet*
Heaberlin, Julia. *We Are All the Same in the Dark: A Novel*

ABANDONED WIVES

Starnone, Domenico. *Ties*

ABANDONED WOMEN

Wallace, Melanie. *The Girl in the Garden*

ABANDONMENT (PSYCHOLOGY)

Erdrich, Louise. *The Beet Queen: A Novel*
Igharo, Jane. *The Sweetest Remedy*
Ko, Lisa. *The Leavers*
Lundrigan, Nicole. *Glass Boys: A Novel*
Makumbi, Jennifer Nansubuga. ★*A Girl Is a Body of Water*
Moore, Alison. *The Lighthouse*
Reid, Iain. *I'm Thinking of Ending Things*
Vlautin, Willy. *Don't Skip Out on Me*

ABBESSES

Groff, Lauren. ★*Matrix*
The Abbot's Tale. Iggulden, Conn

Abbott, Jeff

Blame
The Three Beths

Abbott, Megan E.

Bury Me Deep
The Fever
★*Give Me Your Hand*
Queenpin: A Novel
★*The Turnout: A Novel*
You Will Know Me: A Novel

Abbott, Patricia

Concrete Angel

ABDUCTION

Allen, Susanna. *A Wolf in Duke's Clothing*
James, Eloisa. ★*Seven Minutes in Heaven*

Abdul-Jabbar, Kareem

The Empty Birdcage
Mycroft and Sherlock
★*Mycroft Holmes*

Abe, Kobo

The Woman in the Dunes

ABERDEEN, SCOTLAND

MacBride, Stuart. *Cold Granite*
Rankin, Ian. ★*Black and Blue: An Inspector Rebus Novel*
Abigail. Szabo, Magda

ABOLITIONISTS

Johnson, Tara. *Engraved on the Heart*
McBride, James. ★*The Good Lord Bird*
Wideman, John Edgar. ★*American Histories: Stories*

ABOLITIONISTS — HISTORY

Banks, Russell. *Cloudsplitter: A Novel*
Jakes, John. *Love and War*
Jakes, John. ★*North and South*
The Abominable: a Novel. Simmons, Dan

ABORIGINAL AUSTRALIANS

Howarth, Paul. *Only Killers and Thieves: A Novel*
Lucashenko, Melissa. *Too Much Lip*

Malouf, David. *Remembering Babylon*
Winch, Tara June. *The Yield*

ABORTION

Bennett, Brit. *The Mothers*
Davies, Peter Ho. *A Lie Someone Told You About Yourself*
Didion, Joan. ★*Play It as It Lays: A Novel*
Donati, Sara. *Where the Light Enters*
McKinney-Whetstone, Diane. *Leaving Cecil Street: A Novel*
Patterson, Richard North. *Protect and Defend*

Aboulela, Leila

Elsewhere, Home
About Schmidt. Begley, Louis
Above the Waterfall. Rash, Ron

Abraham, Tola Rotimi

Black Sunday

ABRAMOVIC, MARINA

Rose, Heather. *The Museum of Modern Love*

Abrams, David

Fobbit

Abrams, Melanie

Meadowlark

Abrams, Stacey

While Justice Sleeps: A Novel
★*Absalom, Absalom!* Faulkner, William

ABSENCE AND PRESUMPTION OF DEATH

Brundage, Elizabeth. *The Vanishing Point*
Gunning, Sally. *Painting the Light*
Oakley, Colleen. *The Invisible Husband of Frick Island*
Absence of Mercy. Goodwin, S. M.
The Absent One. Adler-Olsen, Jussi

ABSENT WITHOUT LEAVE

O'Brien, Perry Edmond. *Fire in the Blood*
Absolutely remarkable thing novels [Series]. Green, Hank
An Absolutely Remarkable Thing: A Novel. Green, Hank
Absolution: a Novel. Flanery, Patrick
The Abstainer: a Novel. McGuire, Ian
The Abstinence Teacher. Perrotta, Tom

ABSTRACT EXPRESSIONISM

Heller, Peter. *The Painter: A Novel*

Abu-Jaber, Diana

Birds of Paradise: A Novel
Crescent
Origin: A Novel

Abulhawa, Susan

The Blue Between Sky and Water

ABUSE OF ADMINISTRATIVE POWER

Soyinka, Wole. *Chronicles from the Land of the Happiest People on Earth*

ABUSED WOMEN

Adler-Olsen, Jussi. *A Conspiracy of Faith*
Anders, Adriana. *Under Her Skin*
Beck, Haylen. *Here and Gone*
Belle, Kimberly. *Dear Wife*
Carey, M. R. *Someone Like Me*
Clark, Julie. *Last Flight*
Dallas, Sandra. *Westering Women: A Novel*
Dodd, Christina. *Dead Girl Running*
Doyle, Roddy. ★*The Woman Who Walked into Doors*

Durst, Sarah Beth. *Race the Sands*
Gardner, Lisa. *Love You More: A Detective D.D. Warren Novel*
Hall, Rachel Howzell. *And Now She's Gone*
Higashino, Keigo. ★*The Devotion of Suspect X*
Hyde, Catherine Ryan. *My Name Is Anton*
Kandasamy, Meena. *When I Hit You, Or, a Portrait of the Writer as a Young Wife*
McCrumb, Sharyn. ★*The Ballad of Frankie Silver*
Pronzini, Bill. *Fever: A Nameless Detective Novel*
Roberts, Nora. ★*Under Currents*
Ryan, Kennedy. ★*Long Shot*
Shalvis, Jill. *Simply Irresistible*
Stevens, Chevy. *Never Let You Go*
Weiss, Leah. *If the Creek Don't Rise: A Novel*
Woods, Stuart. *Palindrome*

ABUSIVE MEN
Attenberg, Jami. ★*All This Could Be Yours*
Beattie, Ann. *The Doctor's House: A Novel*
Beck, Haylen. *Here and Gone*
Clark, Julie. *Last Flight*
Gailey, Sarah. *The Echo Wife*
Joshi, Alka. *The Henna Artist*
Mihalic, Susan. *Dark Horses*
Moss, Sarah. *Ghost Wall: A Novel*
Quincy, D. M. *Murder in Mayfair: An Atlas Catesby Mystery*
Weiss, Leah. *If the Creek Don't Rise: A Novel*

ACADEMIC RIVALRY
Abbott, Megan E. ★*Give Me Your Hand*
Amis, Kingsley. ★*Lucky Jim*

Acampora, Lauren
The Paper Wasp: A Novel
The Wonder Garden
Accelerando. Stross, Charles
Acceptance: a Novel. VanderMeer, Jeff

ACCIDENT INVESTIGATION
Johnston, Tim. *The Current: A Novel*
Koryta, Michael. *If She Wakes*
Lalami, Laila. *The Other Americans: A Novel*

ACCIDENT VICTIMS
Albom, Mitch. *The Next Person You Meet in Heaven*
Brown, Rosellen. *Tender Mercies*
Center, Katherine. *How to Walk Away: A Novel*
Delaney, J. P. *The Perfect Wife: A Novel*
Ellison, J. T. *Tear Me Apart*
Ganshert, Katie. *Life After*
Hawley, Noah. *Before the Fall*
Johnson, Craig. *Spirit of Steamboat: A Walt Longmire Story*
Lippman, Laura. ★*Dream Girl*
Sinha, Indra. *Animal's People*
Wharton, Edith. ★*Ethan Frome*
The Accidental. Smith, Ali
The Accidental Countess. Bowman, Valerie

ACCIDENTAL DEATH
Clarke, Brock. *An Arsonist's Guide to Writers' Homes in New England: A Novel*
Horowitz, Anthony. ★*Magpie Murders*
Mankell, Henning. *The Man Who Smiled: A Kurt Wallander Mystery*
Minato, Kanae. *Confessions*

Sutanto, Jesse Q. *Dial a for Aunties*
Winton, Tim. *The Shepherd's Hut*

ACCIDENTAL DEATH INVESTIGATION
Scerbanenco, Giorgio. *Traitors to All*
An Accidental Light. Diamond, Elizabeth
An Accidental Man. Murdoch, Iris
★*The Accidental Tourist: A Novel*. Tyler, Anne
Accidentally Engaged. Heron, Farah

ACCIDENTS
Evans, Nicholas. ★*The Horse Whisperer: A Novel*
Harrison, Jamie. *The Center of Everything: A Novel*
Hibbert, Talia. ★*Act Your Age, Eve Brown*
Kennedy, James. *Dare to Know*
Maynard, Joyce. *Count the Ways*
Oates, Joyce Carol. *Pursuit*
Simmons, Dan. *Drood: A Novel*
Slaughter, Karin. ★*Undone: A Novel*
Winters, Ben H. *The Quiet Boy*

ACCRA, GHANA
Quartey, Kwei. *The Missing American*
Quartey, Kwei. ★*Sleep Well, My Lady*
Accursed kings [Series]. Druon, Maurice
The Accusation: Forbidden Stories from Inside North Korea. Bandi

Acevedo, Chantel
The Distant Marvels

Achebe, Chinua
★*Things Fall Apart*

ACHILLES (GREEK MYTHOLOGY)
Malouf, David. *Ransom*

Aciman, Andre
Call Me by Your Name
Enigma Variations: A Novel
Find Me
Harvard Square

Acker, Jennifer
★*The Limits of the World*

Ackerman, Elliot
Dark at the Crossing
Red Dress in Black and White
★*Waiting for Eden: A Novel*
Acorna series [Series]. McCaffrey, Anne
★*Acorna: the Unicorn Girl*. McCaffrey, Anne
★*Act Your Age, Eve Brown*. Hibbert, Talia
★*Acting on Impulse*. Sosa, Mia

ACTORS AND ACTRESSES
Alarcon, Daniel. *At Night We Walk in Circles: A Novel*
Alexander, Jennet. *I Kissed a Girl*
Allen, Jane. *I Lost My Girlish Laughter*
Antopol, Molly. *The Unamericans*
Armstrong, Richard. *The Don Con*
Bagshawe, Tilly. *Adored*
Banville, John. *Ancient Light*
Banville, John. ★*Eclipse: A Novel*
Barnes, Jonathan. *The Somnambulist*
Baxter, Charles. ★*The Sun Collective*
Benedict, Marie. *The Only Woman in the Room*
Bradley, C. Alan. *I Am Half-Sick of Shadows: A Flavia De Luce Novel*

Bram, Christopher. *Lives of the Circus Animals: A Novel*
Brandreth, Benet. *The Spy of Venice*
Brett, Simon. *Murder Unprompted*
Brunkhorst, Alex. *The Gilded Life of Matilda Duplaine*
Byrne, Kerrigan. *The Hunter*
Copperman, E. J. *Judgment at Santa Monica*
Dalton, Trent. *All Our Shimmering Skies*
Davis, Fiona. *The Chelsea Girls*
Delaney, J. P. *Believe Me: A Novel*
DeLuca, Jen. ★*Well Met*
Dev, Sonali. *The Bollywood Bride*
Downes, Anna. *The Safe Place: A Novel*
Dreiser, Theodore. ★*Sister Carrie*
Estleman, Loren D. ★*Indigo: A Valentino Mystery*
Feeney, Alice. ★*I Know Who You Are: A Novel*
Francis, Dick. *Smokescreen*
Garrett, Kellye. ★*Hollywood Homicide*
Goldberg, Lee. *Fake Truth*
Gortner, C. W. *The First Actress: A Novel of Sarah Bernhardt*
Guillory, Jasmine. ★*While We Were Dating*
Haddam, Jane. *Cheating at Solitaire: A Gregor Demarkian Novel*
Hambly, Barbara. *Scandal in Babylon*
Hawke, Ethan. *A Bright Ray of Darkness*
James, P. D. *The Skull Beneath the Skin*
Kleeman, Alexandra. *Something New Under the Sun*
Lane, Byron. ★*A Star Is Bored*
Lau, Jackie. *Donut Fall in Love*
Lee, Ji-Min. *The Starlet and the Spy*
Mandel, Emily St. John. ★*Station Eleven*
Marston, Edward. *The Roaring Boy: A Novel*
Marston, Edward. *The Wanton Angel: A Novel*
Miller, Andrew. *Oxygen*
Pamuk, Orhan. ★*Snow*
Parker, Lucy. *The Austen Playbook*
Parker, Robert B. *Sixkill*
Phillips, Susan Elizabeth. *Heroes Are My Weakness*
Phillips, Susan Elizabeth. *What I Did for Love*
Rivers, Francine. *Bridge to Haven*
Rous, Emma. *The Perfect Guests*
Sabatini, Rafael. *Scaramouche: A Romance of the French Revolution*
Shepard, Sam. *The One Inside*
Smith, B. J. *Shoot the Dog: A Virgil Cain Mystery*
Sontag, Susan. ★*In America*
Sosa, Mia. ★*Acting on Impulse*
Spencer, Sally. *Best Served Cold*
Steadman, Catherine. *The Disappearing Act*
Sweeney, Cynthia D'Aprix. ★*Good Company: A Novel*
Weatherspoon, Rebekah. *If the Boot Fits*
Westlake, Donald E. *Memory*
Wolitzer, Meg. *The Interestings*
Woods, Stuart. ★*Bombshell*
Woods, Stuart. *The Money Shot*
Yu, Charles. ★*Interior Chinatown*

ACTORS AND ACTRESSES — HISTORY
Zola, Emile. ★*Nana*
Actress: a Novel. Enright, Anne
★*Adam Bede*. Eliot, George
Adam Dalgliesh mysteries [Series]. James, P. D.

Adam, Claire
  Golden Child: A Novel
Adams, Alina
  The Nesting Dolls
Adams, Douglas
  Dirk Gently's Holistic Detective Agency
  ★*The Hitchhiker's Guide to the Galaxy*
  The Restaurant at the End of the Universe
Adams, Henry
  ★*Democracy: An American Novel*
Adams, Hope
  Dangerous Women
ADAMS, JOHN QUINCY
  Penman, Sharon Kay. *The Sunne in Splendour*
  Pesci, David. *Amistad: A Novel*
Adams, Lyssa Kay
  The Bromance Book Club
ADAMS, NICK (FICTITIOUS CHARACTER)
  Hemingway, Ernest. *The Nick Adams Stories*
Adams, Richard
  Watership Down
Adams, Sara Nisha
  ★*The Reading List*
Adams, Taylor
  Hairpin Bridge
Adamson, Gil
  The Outlander
ADAPTATION (BIOLOGY)
  Van Vogt, A. E. ★*Slan*
  Vonnegut, Kurt. ★*Galapagos: A Novel*
ADAPTATIONS, RETELLINGS, AND SPIN-OFFS
  Abdul-Jabbar, Kareem. *The Empty Birdcage*
  Abdul-Jabbar, Kareem. *Mycroft and Sherlock*
  Abdul-Jabbar, Kareem. ★*Mycroft Holmes*
  Baker, Jo. *Longbourn*
  Balaskovits, A. A. *Magic for Unlucky Girls: Stories*
  Barker, Pat. ★*The Silence of the Girls: A Novel*
  Barker, Pat. *The Women of Troy*
  Benjamin, Ali. *The Smash-Up: A Novel*
  Carter, Angela. ★*Burning Your Boats: The Collected Short Stories*
  Clinch, Jon. *Finn: A Novel*
  Clinch, Jon. *Marley: A Novel*
  Daoud, Kamel. *The Meursault Investigation*
  Dean, Pamela. *Tam Lin*
  Dev, Sonali. ★*Pride, Prejudice, and Other Flavors: A Novel*
  Dorn, L. R. *The Anatomy of Desire*
  Faye, Lyndsay. *Jane Steele*
  Faye, Lyndsay. ★*The King of Infinite Space*
  Faye, Lyndsay. *The Whole Art of Detection: Lost Mysteries of Sherlock Holmes*
  Golding, Melanie. *The Hidden: A Novel*
  Goss, Theodora. *The Sinister Mystery of the Mesmerizing Girl*
  Goss, Theodora. *The Strange Case of the Alchemist's Daughter*
  Gratton, Tessa. *The Queens of Innis Lear*
  Greeley, Molly. *The Clergyman's Wife*
  Headley, Maria Dahvana. *The Mere Wife*
  Horowitz, Anthony. *The House of Silk: A Sherlock Holmes Novel*
  Huang, S. L. *Burning Roses*

Kamal, Soniah. *Unmarriageable: A Novel*
Kantra, Virginia. ★*Meg and Jo*
King, Laurie R. *Castle Shade*
Kwan, Kevin. *Sex and Vanity: A Novel*
Lansdale, Joe R. *More Better Deals*
Lippman, Laura. ★*Sunburn*
MacLaughlin, Nina. *Wake, Siren: Ovid Resung*
Maguire, Gregory. *Son of a Witch: A Novel*
Maguire, Gregory. ★*Wicked: The Life and Times of the Wicked Witch of the West : A Novel*
Novik, Naomi. ★*Spinning Silver*
Novik, Naomi. ★*Uprooted*
O'Dell, Claire. *A Study in Honor: A Novel*
Obioma, Chigozie. ★*An Orchestra of Minorities*
Ogden, Aimee. *Sun-Daughters, Sea-Daughters*
Oyeyemi, Helen. *Boy, Snow, Bird: A Novel*
Oyeyemi, Helen. *Gingerbread: A Novel*
Rawles, Nancy. *My Jim: A Novel*
Rhys, Jean. ★*Wide Sargasso Sea*
Rubart, James L. ★*The Man He Never Was*
Rushdie, Salman. ★*Quichotte: A Novel*
Saint, Jennifer. *Ariadne*
Shaykh, Hanan. ★*One Thousand and One Nights: A Sparkling Retelling of the Beloved Classic*
Simmons, Dan. *The Fifth Heart*
Sittenfeld, Curtis. *Eligible: A Novel*
Smiley, Jane. ★*A Thousand Acres*
Taneja, Preti. *We That Are Young: A Novel*
Toibin, Colm. *House of Names*
Tyler, Anne. *Vinegar Girl: The Taming of the Shrew Retold*
Updike, John. *Gertrude and Claudius*
Vo, Nghi. ★*The Chosen and the Beautiful*
Ware, Ruth. ★*One by One*
White, Elle Katharine. *Dragonshadow*

ADDICTION
Alexie, Sherman. *Blasphemy: New and Selected Stories*
Bohjalian, Chris. *The Flight Attendant: A Novel*
Divya, S. B. *Machinehood*
Glynn, Alan. *Receptor*
Goodwin, Bobi Gentry. *Revelation*
Harding, Lisa. *Bright Burning Things*
K'wan. *The Fix*
Lane, Byron. ★*A Star Is Bored*
Moore, Liz. *Long Bright River*
Reid, Taylor Jenkins. ★*Daisy Jones & The Six: A Novel*
Robb, J. D. *Connections in Death: An Eve Dallas Novel*
Tanen, Sloane. *There's a Word for That*
Wallace, David Foster. ★*Infinite Jest: A Novel*

Addison, Katherine
★*The Goblin Emperor*

Adebayo, Ayobami
★*Stay with Me*

Adelia Aguilar series [Series]. Franklin, Ariana

Adichie, Chimamanda Ngozi
★*Americanah: A Novel*
Half of a Yellow Sun
The Thing Around Your Neck

Adiga, Aravind
★*Amnesty*
Last Man in Tower: A Novel
Selection Day
★*The White Tiger: A Novel*

Adimi, Kaouther
Our Riches

ADIRONDACK MOUNTAINS, NEW YORK
Banks, Russell. ★*The Sweet Hereafter*
DeMille, Nelson. *Wild Fire*
Miller, Derek B. ★*American by Day*
Spencer-Fleming, Julia. *All Mortal Flesh*
Spencer-Fleming, Julia. *Hid from Our Eyes*
Spencer-Fleming, Julia. *I Shall Not Want: A Clare Fergusson/Russ Van Alstyne Mystery*
Spencer-Fleming, Julia. *In the Bleak Midwinter*
Spencer-Fleming, Julia. *Through the Evil Days: A Clare Fergusson/Russ Van Alstyne Mystery*

Adjapon, Bisi
The Teller of Secrets: A Novel

Adjei-Brenyah, Nana Kwame
Friday Black: Stories

Adkins, Mary
When You Read This

Adlakha, Sarah
She Wouldn't Change a Thing

Adler-Olsen, Jussi
The Absent One
A Conspiracy of Faith
The Hanging Girl
The Keeper of Lost Causes
The Marco Effect: A Department Q Novel
The Purity of Vengeance: A Department Q Novel
The Scarred Woman
★*Victim 2117*

ADMINISTRATION OF ESTATES
Pynchon, Thomas. ★*The Crying of Lot 49*
Admiral Hornblower in the West Indies. Forester, C. S.

ADMIRALS
Poyer, David. *Violent Peace: The War with China - Aftermath of Armageddon*

ADOPTED CHILDREN
Eco, Umberto. *Baudolino*
Forbes, Curdella. *A Tall History of Sugar*
Leilani, Raven. ★*Luster*
Patchett, Ann. *Run*
Woo, Sung J. *Love Love: A Novel*

ADOPTED GIRLS
Fabry, Chris. *Looking into You*
See, Lisa. *The Tea Girl of Hummingbird Lane*
Veletzos, Roxanne. *The Girl They Left Behind*

ADOPTEES
Patchett, Ann. *Run*
Shaw, William. *Salt Lane*
Stephens, Alice. *Famous Adopted People*

ADOPTEES — IDENTITY
Pronzini, Bill. *Hardcase*

ADOPTION

Erdrich, Louise. *Future Home of the Living God*
Halls, Stacey. *The Lost Orphan*
Hoffmann, R. J. *Other People's Children: A Novel*
James, Rebecca. *The Woman in the Mirror*
Jayatissa, Amanda. ★*My Sweet Girl*
Johnson, Nancy. *The Kindest Lie*
Ludwig, Benjamin. *Ginny Moon*
Moore, Lorrie. *A Gate at the Stairs: A Novel*
Ng, Celeste. ★*Little Fires Everywhere: A Novel*
Verghese, A. *Cutting for Stone: A Novel*

ADOPTION RACKET

Atkins, Ace. *The Lost Ones*
Endicott, Marina. *The Voyage of the Morning Light*

ADOPTIVE FAMILIES

Barry, Sebastian. ★*A Thousand Moons: A Novel*

ADOPTIVE FATHERS

Tyler, Anne. ★*Saint Maybe*

ADOPTIVE PARENTS

Hozar, Nazanine. *Aria*

Adored. Bagshawe, Tilly

Adrianne Geffel: A Fiction. Hajdu, David

ADULT BOOKS FOR YOUNG ADULTS

Abbott, Jeff. *Blame*
Abbott, Megan E. *Bury Me Deep*
Abbott, Megan E. *The Fever*
Abbott, Megan E. ★*Give Me Your Hand*
Abbott, Megan E. *You Will Know Me: A Novel*
Abu-Jaber, Diana. *Birds of Paradise: A Novel*
Abu-Jaber, Diana. *Crescent*
Abu-Jaber, Diana. *Origin: A Novel*
Aciman, Andre. *Call Me by Your Name*
Aciman, Andre. *Find Me*
Adam, Claire. *Golden Child: A Novel*
Adams, Douglas. ★*The Hitchhiker's Guide to the Galaxy*
Adiga, Aravind. *Selection Day*
Adler-Olsen, Jussi. *The Hanging Girl*
Adler-Olsen, Jussi. *The Marco Effect: A Department Q Novel*
Adler-Olsen, Jussi. *The Scarred Woman*
Adler-Olsen, Jussi. ★*Victim 2117*
Ahern, Cecelia. *Roar*
Ahlborn, Ania. *The Devil Crept In*
Ajvide Lindqvist, John. *Let the Right One In*
Akhtar, Ayad. *American Dervish: A Novel*
Akpan, Uwem. *Say You're One of Them*
Al Rawi, Shahad. *The Baghdad Clock*
Albahari, David. *Gotz and Meyer*
Alderman, Naomi. ★*The Power: A Novel*
Alexander, Tamera. ★*A Note yet Unsung*
Alexander, V. S. *The Magdalen Girls*
Alexie, Sherman. *Flight*
Aliu, Xhenet. ★*Brass: A Novel*
Allende, Isabel. *Ripper: A Novel*
Alvarez, Julia. ★*Afterlife: A Novel*
Amirrezvani, Anita. *The Blood of Flowers: A Novel*
Anappara, Deepa. *Djinn Patrol on the Purple Line: A Novel*
Anaya, Rudolfo A. *The Man Who Could Fly and Other Stories*
Anders, Charlie Jane. ★*All the Birds in the Sky*

Anders, Charlie Jane. ★*The City in the Middle of the Night*
Anderson, Kevin J. *The Last Days of Krypton*
Arden, Katherine. ★*The Bear and the Nightingale*
Arden, Katherine. ★*The Girl in the Tower*
Arimah, Lesley Nneka. ★*What It Means When a Man Falls from the Sky: Stories*
Atwood, Margaret. ★*Maddaddam: A Novel*
Atwood, Margaret. ★*The Year of the Flood: A Novel*
Auel, Jean M. ★*The Clan of the Cave Bear: A Novel*
Awad, Mona. ★*13 Ways of Looking at a Fat Girl*
Awad, Mona. *Bunny*
Ayatsuji, Yukito. *The Decagon House Murders*
Bacigalupi, Paolo. ★*The Water Knife*
Bacigalupi, Paolo. ★*The Windup Girl*
Backman, Fredrik. ★*Beartown: A Novel*
Backman, Fredrik. ★*My Grandmother Asked Me to Tell You She's Sorry: A Novel*
Backman, Fredrik. *Us Against You: A Novel*
Baker, Kage. *The Bird of the River*
Baker, Kage. *The House of the Stag*
Balogh, Mary. *Someone to Hold*
Balogh, Mary. ★*Someone to Love*
Banks, Iain. *The Crow Road*
Bardugo, Leigh. ★*Ninth House*
Barnes, Jonathan. *The Somnambulist*
Barnhill, Kelly Regan. *Dreadful Young Ladies and Other Stories*
Barr, Nevada. *The Rope: An Anna Pigeon Novel*
Barr, Nevada. *Track of the Cat*
Barry, Sebastian. *Days Without End: A Novel*
Bartlett, Neil. *The Disappearance Boy*
Barzak, Christopher. *One for Sorrow*
Bates, Judy Fong. ★*Midnight at the Dragon Cafe*
Baxter, Charles. *Saul and Patsy*
Beagle, Peter S. ★*The Last Unicorn*
Beams, Clare. *The Illness Lesson*
Bear, Greg. *The Collected Stories of Greg Bear*
Beattie, Ann. *A Wonderful Stroke of Luck: A Novel*
Benaron, Naomi. *Running the Rift: A Novel*
Bender, Tony. *The Last Ghost Dancer*
Benioff, David. *City of Thieves: A Novel*
Benjamin, Melanie. *Alice I Have Been*
Bergstrom, Heather Brittain. *Steal the North: A Novel*
Beverly, William. *Dodgers: A Novel*
Bieker, Chelsea Jean. *Godshot: A Novel*
Bilenchi, Romano. ★*The Chill*
Birch, Carol. *Jamrach's Menagerie*
Bird, Sarah. *The Yokota Officers Club: A Novel*
Block, Stefan Merrill. *Oliver Loving: A Novel*
Bloom, Amy. *Lucky Us: A Novel*
Blume, Judy. *In the Unlikely Event*
Bohjalian, Chris. *The Buffalo Soldier: A Novel*
Bohjalian, Chris. *The Double Bind: A Novel*
Bouchet, Amanda. ★*A Promise of Fire*
Bourdeaut, Olivier. *Waiting for Bojangles: A Novel*
Boyle, T. Coraghessan. *The Relive Box: And Other Stories*
Boyle, T. Coraghessan. *When the Killing's Done: A Novel*
Boyne, John. *The Heart's Invisible Furies*
Bradbury, Jamey. *The Wild Inside: A Novel*

Bradbury, Ray. *Bradbury Stories: 100 of His Most Celebrated Tales*

Bradley, C. Alan. *As Chimney Sweepers Come to Dust: A Flavia De Luce Novel*

Bradley, C. Alan. *The Golden Tresses of the Dead: A Flavia De Luce Novel*

Bradley, C. Alan. *The Grave's a Fine and Private Place: A Flavia De Luce Novel*

Bradley, C. Alan. *I Am Half-Sick of Shadows: A Flavia De Luce Novel*

Bradley, C. Alan. *A Red Herring Without Mustard*

Bradley, C. Alan. *Speaking from Among the Bones: A Flavia De Luce Novel*

Bradley, C. Alan. ★*The Sweetness at the Bottom of the Pie*

Bradley, C. Alan. *Thrice the Brinded Cat Hath Mew'd: A Flavia De Luce Novel*

Bradley, C. Alan. *The Weed That Strings the Hangman's Bag: A Flavia De Luce Mystery*

Brandreth, Benet. *The Spy of Venice*

Braun, Lilian Jackson. *The Cat Who Ate Danish Modern*

Brink, Andre P. *Philida: A Novel*

Bronte, Emily. ★*Wuthering Heights*

Brown, Pierce. *Golden Son*

Brown, Pierce. *Morning Star*

Brown, Pierce. *Red Rising*

Brown, Rita Mae. *Wish You Were Here*

Bruni, Sarah. *The Night Gwen Stacy Died*

Brunkhorst, Alex. *The Gilded Life of Matilda Duplaine*

Brunt, Carol Rifka. ★*Tell the Wolves I'm Home: A Novel*

Buchanan, Cathy Marie. ★*The Painted Girls*

Bulawayo, NoViolet. *We Need New Names: A Novel*

Bump, Gabriel. ★*Everywhere You Don't Belong: A Novel*

Buntin, Julie. ★*Marlena: A Novel*

Burke, James Lee. *The Jealous Kind*

Butler, Nickolas. ★*The Hearts of Men*

Butler, Octavia E. *Bloodchild: And Other Stories*

Buxton, Kira Jane. ★*Hollow Kingdom*

Cameron, W. Bruce. *A Dog's Promise*

Camp, Bryan. *Gather the Fortunes*

Campbell, Bebe Moore. *Brothers and Sisters*

Campbell, Bonnie Jo. *Once Upon a River*

Campisi, Megan. *Sin Eater*

Card, Orson Scott. ★*Ender's Game*

Carey, Jacqueline. *Starless*

Carey, M. R. *Someone Like Me*

Center, Katherine. *Things You Save in a Fire*

Chai, May-Lee. *Useful Phrases for Immigrants: Stories*

Chakraborty, S. A. *The City of Brass*

Chakraborty, S. A. *The Empire of Gold*

Chakraborty, S. A. *The Kingdom of Copper: A Novel*

Chancellor, Bryn. *Sycamore: A Novel*

Chariandy, David John. *Brother: A Novel*

Chen, Da. *Brothers: A Novel*

Chevalier, Tracy. ★*Girl with a Pearl Earring*

Chiang, Ted. ★*Stories of Your Life and Others*

Cho, Nam-Ju. ★*Kim Jiyoung, Born 1982*

Choi, Ann Y. K. *Kay's Lucky Coin Variety*

Choi, Susan. *My Education*

Choo, Yangsze. ★*The Night Tiger: A Novel*

Christie, Agatha. ★*And Then There Were None*

Clare, Alys. *The Woman Who Spoke to Spirits*

Clark, P. Djeli. *The Black God's Drums*

Clarke, Susanna. ★*Jonathan Strange & Mr. Norrell*

Cleeves, Ann. *Raven Black*

Clement, Jennifer. *Gun Love*

Clinch, Jon. *Finn: A Novel*

Cline, Ernest. *Ready Player One: A Novel*

Coben, Harlan. *Hold Tight*

Coben, Harlan. *Long Lost*

Coe, Jonathan. *The Rotters' Club*

Coetzee, J. M. *Summertime: Scenes from a Provincial Life*

Collins, Ciaran. *The Gamal*

Connelly, Michael. *The Scarecrow: A Novel*

Cooney, Ellen. *The Mountaintop School for Dogs and Other Second Chances*

Coonts, Stephen. ★*Flight of the Intruder*

Cooper, Tom. *The Marauders*

Coster, Naima. *Halsey Street*

Cotterill, Colin. *Disco for the Departed*

Cotterill, Colin. *Slash and Burn: A Dr. Siri Mystery Set in Laos*

Cramer, W. Dale. *Levi's Will: A Novel*

Crichton, Michael. *Prey: A Novel*

Crowell, Jenn. *Etched on Me: A Novel*

Crucet, Jennine Capo. *Make Your Home Among Strangers*

Crummey, Michael. *The Innocents*

Cruz, Angie. *Dominicana: A Novel*

Cunningham, Michael. *Specimen Days*

Cush, Jean Love. *Endangered*

Czerneda, Julie. *A Turn of Light*

Dallas, Sandra. *Tallgrass*

Dalton, Trent. *Boy Swallows Universe*

Danforth, Emily M. *Plain Bad Heroines*

Danielewski, Mark Z. *Only Revolutions*

Dare, Abi. *The Girl with the Louding Voice*

Darnielle, John. *Wolf in White Van: A Novel*

Davidson, Andrew. *The Gargoyle*

Davies, Peter Ho. *The Fortunes*

Davis, Lindsey. *The Ides of April: A Flavia Albia Mystery*

De la Motte, Anders. *MemoRandom: A Thriller*

De los Santos, Marisa. *The Precious One*

De Robertis, Carolina. *The Gods of Tango*

Dean, Margaret Lazarus. *The Time It Takes to Fall*

Deaver, Jeffery. *The Empty Chair*

Deaver, Jeffery. *Garden of Beasts: A Novel of Berlin 1936*

Deaver, Jeffery. *The Stone Monkey: A Lincoln Rhyme Novel*

Deb, Siddhartha. *The Point of Return: A Novel*

Dee, Jonathan. *The Privileges: A Novel*

Dektar, Molly. *The Ash Family*

Delaney, J. P. *The Girl Before: A Novel*

deWitt, Patrick. *The Sisters Brothers: A Novel*

deWitt, Patrick. *Undermajordomo Minor*

DeWoskin, Rachel. *Big Girl Small: A Novel*

Dexter, Pete. *Spooner*

Diachenko, Serhii. *Vita Nostra*

Diamant, Anita. *The Boston Girl: A Novel*

Diaz, Junot. ★*The Brief Wondrous Life of Oscar Wao*

Diaz, Junot. ★*This Is How You Lose Her*

Diffenbaugh, Vanessa. *The Language of Flowers: A Novel*
Dimechkie, Karim. *Lifted by the Great Nothing*
Doctorow, E. L. *The March: A Novel*
Doerr, Anthony. ★*All the Light We Cannot See: A Novel*
Dolan-Leach, Caite. *We Went to the Woods: A Novel*
Donoghue, Emma. ★*Room: A Novel*
Donohue, Keith. *The Stolen Child*
Doyle, Roddy. *Paddy Clarke, Ha-Ha-Ha*
Dunant, Sarah. *The Birth of Venus: A Novel*
Dunn, Mark. *Ella Minnow Pea: A Progressively Lipogrammatic Epistolary Fable*
Durham, David Anthony. ★*Gabriel's Story*
Durrow, Heidi W. *The Girl Who Fell from the Sky: A Novel*
Durst, Sarah Beth. *The Queen of Blood*
Dybek, Stuart. *I Sailed with Magellan*
Edghill, India. *Queenmaker: A Novel of King David's Queen*
Edugyan, Esi. ★*Washington Black: A Novel*
Edwards, Rachel. *Darling*
Egan, Jennifer. *The Keep*
Eggers, Dave. *What Is the What: The Autobiography of Valentino Achak Deng*
Ehirim, Nnamdi. *Prince of Monkeys*
El Akkad, Omar. *American War*
Emezi, Akwaeke. *Freshwater*
Enger, Lin. *Undiscovered Country: A Novel*
Erdrich, Louise. ★*The Round House: A Novel*
Eskens, Allen. *Nothing More Dangerous: A Novel*
Estleman, Loren D. *Infernal Angels*
Evison, Jonathan. ★*Lawn Boy: A Novel*
Extence, Gavin. *The Universe Versus Alex Woods*
Faye, Lyndsay. *The Gods of Gotham*
Faye, Lyndsay. *Jane Steele*
Faye, Lyndsay. *Seven for a Secret*
Ferencik, Erica. *Into the Jungle*
Ferrante, Elena. *My Brilliant Friend*
Ferraris, Zoe. *Finding Nouf*
Ferraris, Zoe. *Kingdom of Strangers: A Novel*
Fforde, Jasper. *The Eyre Affair: A Novel*
Fforde, Jasper. *Lost in a Good Book: A Thursday Next Novel*
Fforde, Jasper. *Shades of Grey: A Novel*
Finch, Charles. *The September Society*
Finder, Joseph. *The Fixer*
Finder, Joseph. *Guilty Minds*
Finder, Joseph. *The Switch: A Novel*
Fine, Julia. *What Should Be Wild*
Fitch, Janet. *Paint It Black: A Novel*
Fitzpatrick, Lydia. *Lights All Night Long: A Novel*
Flagg, Fannie. *Standing in the Rainbow: A Novel*
Flynn, Gillian. ★*Gone Girl: A Novel*
Foer, Jonathan Safran. *Extremely Loud and Incredibly Close*
Follett, Ken. *Hornet Flight*
Fountain, Ben. ★*Billy Lynn's Long Halftime Walk*
Fowler, Karen Joy. ★*We Are All Completely Beside Ourselves*
Fowler, Therese. ★*A Good Neighborhood*
Francis, Patry. *The Orphans of Race Point: A Novel*
Frankel, Laurie. *This Is How It Always Is*
Franklin, Ariana. *The Serpent's Tale*
Franklin, Ariana. *The Siege Winter*

Franzen, Jonathan. *Purity*
Frayn, Michael. *Spies: A Novel*
Frazier, Charles. ★*Cold Mountain*
Freeman, Brian. *The Night Bird*
French, Tana. ★*The Secret Place*
Fridlund, Emily. ★*History of Wolves: A Novel*
Fu, Kim. *For Today I Am a Boy*
Fuller, Claire. *Our Endless Numbered Days: A Novel*
Fuqua, Jonathon Scott. *Gone and Back Again*
Gabel, Aja. *The Ensemble: A Novel*
Gailey, Sarah. *Magic for Liars*
Gaiman, Neil. ★*Anansi Boys: A Novel*
Gaiman, Neil. ★*Fragile Things: Short Fictions and Wonders*
Gaiman, Neil. ★*Good Omens: The Nice and Accurate Prophecies of Agnes Nutter, Witch*
Gaiman, Neil. ★*Norse Mythology*
Gaiman, Neil. ★*The Ocean at the End of the Lane*
Gaiman, Neil. ★*Stardust*
Gaitskill, Mary. *The Mare: A Novel*
Galloway, Gregory. *As Simple as Snow*
Gardam, Jane. *The Flight of the Maidens*
Garrett, Kellye. ★*Hollywood Homicide*
Garriott, Leah. *Promised*
Gaynor, Hazel. *The Lighthouse Keeper's Daughter*
George, Elizabeth. *What Came Before He Shot Her*
Gibbons, Kaye. *The Life All Around Me by Ellen Foster*
Gibson, William. *Pattern Recognition*
Gilb, Dagoberto. *The Flowers: A Novel*
Gilman, Laura Anne. *Silver on the Road*
Godwin, Gail. *Grief Cottage: A Novel*
Godwin, Gail. *Unfinished Desires*
Golding, William. ★*Lord of the Flies: A Novel*
Goonan, Kathleen Ann. *In War Times*
Goss, Theodora. *The Sinister Mystery of the Mesmerizing Girl*
Goss, Theodora. *The Strange Case of the Alchemist's Daughter*
Grafton, Sue. *X*
Grafton, Sue. *Y Is for Yesterday*
Grant, Helen. *The Glass Demon*
Grant, Helen. *The Vanishing of Katharina Linden*
Gratton, Tessa. *The Queens of Innis Lear*
Green, Hank. *An Absolutely Remarkable Thing: A Novel*
Greenidge, Kaitlyn. ★*Libertie: A Novel*
Greenidge, Kaitlyn. *We Love You, Charlie Freeman: A Novel*
Greenwood, Kerry. *Death in Daylesford*
Greenwood, Kerry. *Unnatural Habits*
Grenville, Kate. *The Secret River*
Griffiths, Elly. *The Postscript Murders*
Griffiths, Elly. *The Stranger Diaries*
Grisham, John. *The Client*
Grossman, Lev. *The Magician King: A Novel*
Grossman, Lev. *The Magician's Land: A Novel*
Grossman, Lev. ★*The Magicians: A Novel*
Gruen, Sara. *The Ape House*
Gruen, Sara. ★*Water for Elephants: A Novel*
Gunesekera, Romesh. ★*Suncatcher: A Novel*
Guterson, David. *Our Lady of the Forest*
Gyasi, Yaa. ★*Homegoing: A Novel*

Haddon, Mark. ★*The Curious Incident of the Dog in the Night-Time: A Novel*

Haig, Francesca. *The Fire Sermon: A Novel*

Haig, Matt. *The Humans: A Novel*

Haigh, Jennifer. *Baker Towers: A Novel*

Hale, Shannon. *Austenland: A Novel*

Hall, Tarquin. *The Case of the Deadly Butter Chicken: A Vish Puri Mystery*

Hamer, Kate. *The Girl in the Red Coat*

Hamid, Mohsin. ★*Exit West: A Novel*

Hamill, Pete. *Forever*

Hamilton, Peter F. *Pandora's Star*

Hamilton, Steve. ★*The Lock Artist*

Hand, Elizabeth. *Curious Toys*

Hannah, Kristin. *The Great Alone*

Hannah, Kristin. *The Nightingale*

Hannah, Sophie. *The Killings at Kingfisher Hill*

Hannah, Sophie. *The Mystery of Three Quarters: The New Hercule Poirot Mystery*

Harkness, Deborah E. *Time's Convert*

Harris, C. S. *Good Time Coming*

Harris, Robert. *Enigma*

Harris, Robert. *Pompeii: A Novel*

Harrison, Rachel. *The Return*

Hart, John. *The King of Lies*

Hart, John. *The Last Child*

Haruf, Kent. *Eventide*

Haruf, Kent. ★*Plainsong*

Hauck, Rachel. *Once Upon a Prince*

Hawkins, Paula. ★*The Girl on the Train: A Novel*

Hawkins, Scott. ★*The Library at Mount Char*

Hawthorne, Nathaniel. ★*The Scarlet Letter: A Romance*

Haydon, Elizabeth. *The Merchant Emperor*

Hendrix, Grady. *My Best Friend's Exorcism*

Herbert, Frank. ★*Dune*

Hiaasen, Carl. *Star Island*

Higashino, Keigo. *The Miracles of the Namiya General Store*

Hill, Joe. *The Fireman: A Novel*

Hill, Joe. *Heart-Shaped Box*

Hill, Joe. ★*Nos4a2*

Hill, Lawrence. *Someone Knows My Name: A Novel*

Hillerman, Tony. *The Sinister Pig*

Hillerman, Tony. *The Wailing Wind*

Hoffman, Alice. *The Museum of Extraordinary Things: A Novel*

Hoffman, Alice. *The River King*

Hoffman, Alice. *The Rules of Magic: A Novel*

Hosseini, Khaled. ★*The Kite Runner*

Hosseini, Khaled. ★*Sea Prayer*

Howarth, Paul. *Only Killers and Thieves: A Novel*

Ishiguro, Kazuo. ★*Never Let Me Go*

Iweala, Uzodinma. ★*Speak No Evil*

Jalaluddin, Uzma. ★*Ayesha at Last*

Jemisin, N. K. *How Long 'Til Black Future Month?*

Jiles, Paulette. *News of the World: A Novel*

Jones, Stephen Graham. ★*The Only Good Indians: A Novel*

Jones, Tayari. *Silver Sparrow: A Novel*

Jordan, Hillary. *Mudbound: A Novel*

Katsu, Alma. *The Deep*

Katsu, Alma. *The Hunger: A Novel*

Keesey, Anna. *Little Century: A Novel*

Kellerman, Jonathan. *Bones: An Alex Delaware Novel*

Kellerman, Jonathan. *Gone*

Khadivi, Laleh. ★*A Good Country: A Novel*

Kidd, Jess. ★*Things in Jars*

Kidd, Sue Monk. ★*The Secret Life of Bees*

Kim, Eugenia. *The Kinship of Secrets*

King, Stephen. *Doctor Sleep: A Novel*

King, Stephen. *End of Watch: A Novel*

King, Stephen. *The Girl Who Loved Tom Gordon*

King, Stephen. *It*

King, Stephen. *Mr. Mercedes: A Novel*

King, Stephen. *Pet Sematary*

Klune, TJ. *The House in the Cerulean Sea*

Ko, Lisa. *The Leavers*

Konar, Affinity. *Mischling: A Novel*

Koontz, Dean R. *The Darkest Evening of the Year*

Koontz, Dean R. *The Husband*

Koontz, Dean R. *Velocity*

Kuang, R. F. *The Poppy War*

Kutsukake, Lynne. *The Translation of Love: A Novel*

Lahiri, Jhumpa. ★*The Namesake*

Landvik, Lorna. *Chronicles of a Radical Hag: With Recipes*

Lansdale, Joe R. *The Bottoms*

Lansdale, Joe R. *Edge of Dark Water*

Lansdale, Joe R. *The Thicket*

Larison, John. *Whiskey When We're Dry*

Larkwood, A. K. *The Unspoken Name*

Lawson, Mary. *Crow Lake*

Laymon, Kiese. *Long Division*

Le Guin, Ursula K. *The Birthday of the World: And Other Stories*

Le Guin, Ursula K. *The Telling*

Lee, Fonda. ★*Jade City*

Lee, Fonda. *Jade War*

Lessing, Doris May. *The Sweetest Dream*

Levine, David D. *Arabella of Mars*

Levy, Andrea. *Small Island*

Lippman, Laura. *What the Dead Know*

Lippman, Laura. *Wilde Lake*

Locke, Attica. ★*Bluebird, Bluebird*

Lodato, Victor. *Mathilda Savitch*

Louis, Edouard. *The End of Eddy: A Novel*

Lowe, Kathryn A. *The Furies*

Ludwig, Benjamin. *Ginny Moon*

Lutz, Lisa. *The Spellman Files: A Novel*

Lutz, Lisa. *The Swallows: A Novel*

Maaren, Kari. ★*Weave a Circle Round*

Mabanckou, Alain. ★*Black Moses*

MacNeal, Susan Elia. *The King's Justice*

Maguire, Gregory. *Son of a Witch: A Novel*

Makkai, Rebecca. *The Borrower: A Novel*

Mandel, Emily St. John. ★*Station Eleven*

Marillier, Juliet. *Daughter of the Forest*

Martin, George R. R. ★*A Dance with Dragons*

Martine, Arkady. ★*A Desolation Called Peace*

Martine, Arkady. ★*A Memory Called Empire*

Massey, Sujata. *The Satapur Moonstone*

Massey, Sujata. ★*The Widows of Malabar Hill: A Mystery of 1920s Bombay*

Matar, Hisham. *In the Country of Men*

McBride, James. ★*The Good Lord Bird*

McCaffrey, Anne. *Dragonflight*

McCall Smith, Alexander. *The Full Cupboard of Life*

McCall Smith, Alexander. *The Good Husband of Zebra Drive*

McCarthy, Cormac. ★*All the Pretty Horses*

McCarthy, Cormac. *The Crossing*

McCrumb, Sharyn. ★*If Ever I Return, Pretty Peggy-O*

McDermid, Val. *The Distant Echo*

McDermott, Alice. *After This*

McDermott, Alice. *Child of My Heart*

McDevitt, Jack. *The Engines of God*

McEwan, Ian. ★*Atonement: A Novel*

McFadden, Bernice L. *The Book of Harlan*

McGhee, Alison. *The Opposite of Fate*

McGregor, Jon. *The Reservoir Tapes*

McGuire, Seanan. ★*Beneath the Sugar Sky*

McGuire, Seanan. ★*Down Among the Sticks and Bones*

McGuire, Seanan. ★*Every Heart a Doorway*

McGuire, Seanan. ★*In an Absent Dream*

McGuire, Seanan. ★*Middlegame*

McKenzie, Elizabeth. *The Portable Veblen*

McKinlay, Jenn. *The Good Ones*

McKinney-Whetstone, Diane. *Leaving Cecil Street: A Novel*

McLaughlin, Emma. *The Nanny Diaries: A Novel*

McLean, Felicity. *The Van Apfel Girls Are Gone*

McMurtry, Larry. *Boone's Lick: A Novel*

McQuiston, Casey. ★*Red, White & Royal Blue: A Novel*

Mehta, Rahul. *No Other World: A Novel*

Meltzer, Brad. *The Inner Circle*

Merullo, Roland. *The Talk-Funny Girl: A Novel*

Mieville, China. ★*The City & The City*

Mieville, China. ★*Perdido Street Station*

Miller, Madeline. ★*Circe*

Miller, Madeline. *The Song of Achilles*

Minato, Kanae. *Confessions*

Mitchell, David. *Black Swan Green: A Novel*

Mohamed, Nadifa. *The Orchard of Lost Souls: A Novel*

Moore, Liz. *The Unseen World*

Moore, Lorrie. *A Gate at the Stairs: A Novel*

Morgenstern, Erin. ★*The Night Circus: A Novel*

Mosley, Walter. *Fortunate Son: A Novel*

Moss, Sarah. *Ghost Wall: A Novel*

Moyes, Jojo. *Me Before You: A Novel*

Mozley, Fiona. ★*Elmet*

Murr, Naeem. *The Perfect Man: A Novel*

Murray, Paul. *Skippy Dies*

Napolitano, Ann. *Dear Edward*

Ng, Celeste. ★*Everything I Never Told You: A Novel*

Ng, Celeste. ★*Little Fires Everywhere: A Novel*

Nguyen, Kevin. ★*New Waves*

Niffenegger, Audrey. *The Time Traveler's Wife: A Novel*

Novic, Sara. *Girl at War*

Novik, Naomi. *His Majesty's Dragon*

Novik, Naomi. ★*Spinning Silver*

Novik, Naomi. ★*Uprooted*

Nunez, Sigrid. *The Last of Her Kind: A Novel*

Nunez, Sigrid. *Salvation City*

Nussbaum, Susan. *Good Kings, Bad Kings: A Novel*

O'Donnell, Lisa. *The Death of Bees: A Novel*

Oates, Joyce Carol. *The Gravedigger's Daughter: A Novel*

Oates, Joyce Carol. ★*My Life as a Rat*

Obreht, Tea. *The Tiger's Wife: A Novel*

Okparanta, Chinelo. ★*Under the Udala Trees*

Olmstead, Robert. ★*Coal Black Horse*

Ondaatje, Michael. ★*Warlight*

Onyebuchi, Tochi. ★*Riot Baby*

Orange, Tommy. ★*There There*

Otsuka, Julie. *When the Emperor Was Divine: A Novel*

Owens, Delia. *Where the Crawdads Sing*

Oyeyemi, Helen. *Gingerbread: A Novel*

Oyeyemi, Helen. *What Is Not Yours Is Not Yours: Stories*

Ozick, Cynthia. *Heir to the Glimmering World*

Packer, Ann. *The Dive from Clausen's Pier*

Packer, Ann. *Songs Without Words*

Palahniuk, Chuck. *Pygmy*

Palmer, Dexter Clarence. *Version Control*

Paretsky, Sara. ★*Dead Land*

Paretsky, Sara. *Shell Game*

Paris, B. A. *Behind Closed Doors*

Parks, Brad. *Say Nothing: A Novel*

Patterson, Richard North. *Balance of Power*

Patterson, Richard North. *Protect and Defend*

Pearl, Matthew. *The Last Dickens: A Novel*

Penelope, L. *Song of Blood and Stone*

Perrotta, Tom. *The Leftovers*

Pesci, David. *Amistad: A Novel*

Pessl, Marisha. *Special Topics in Calamity Physics*

Petterson, Per. *Out Stealing Horses: A Novel*

Pickard, Nancy. *The Scent of Rain and Lightning: A Novel*

Picoult, Jodi. *House Rules: A Novel*

Picoult, Jodi. *Leaving Time: A Novel*

Picoult, Jodi. ★*My Sister's Keeper*

Picoult, Jodi. *Nineteen Minutes: A Novel*

Picoult, Jodi. *Sing You Home: A Novel*

Picoult, Jodi. *A Spark of Light: A Novel*

Pintoff, Stefanie. *Hostage Taker: A Novel*

Pitoniak, Anna. *Necessary People*

Pochoda, Ivy. *Visitation Street: A Novel*

Power, Susan. *The Grass Dancer*

Powers, Kevin. ★*The Yellow Birds: A Novel*

Pratchett, Terry. ★*The Color of Magic*

Pratchett, Terry. *Equal Rites*

Pratchett, Terry. *The Fifth Elephant: A Novel of Discworld*

Pratchett, Terry. *Going Postal: A Novel of Discworld*

Pratchett, Terry. *Guards! Guards!*

Pratchett, Terry. *The Last Hero: A Discworld Fable*

Pratchett, Terry. *Lords and Ladies: A Novel of Discworld*

Pratchett, Terry. *Men at Arms: A Novel of Discworld*

Pratchett, Terry. *Monstrous Regiment*

Pratchett, Terry. *Pyramids: The Book of Going Forth*

Pratchett, Terry. *Reaper Man*

Pratchett, Terry. *Small Gods: A Novel of Discworld*

Pratchett, Terry. *Thief of Time*

Pratchett, Terry. *Thud!: A Novel of Discworld*
Pratchett, Terry. *The Truth: A Novel of Discworld*
Pratchett, Terry. *Witches Abroad*
Pratchett, Terry. *Wyrd Sisters*
Preston, Caroline. *The Scrapbook of Frankie Pratt*
Preston, Douglas J. *City of Endless Night*
Preston, Douglas J. *The Obsidian Chamber*
Preston, Douglas J. *Thunderhead*
Priest, Cherie. *Clementine*
Prose, Francine. *Blue Angel: A Novel*
Prose, Francine. *Goldengrove: A Novel*
Proust, Marcel. ★*Remembrance of Things Past*
Pryor, Mark. *Hollow Man*
Pulley, Natasha. *The Watchmaker of Filigree Street*
Putney, Mary Jo. *The Marriage Spell: A Novel*
Quade, Kirstin Valdez. *Night at the Fiestas: Stories*
Quinonez, Ernesto. *Bodega Dreams*
Rabb, Jonathan. *Among the Living*
Racculia, Kate. ★*Bellweather Rhapsody*
Racculia, Kate. ★*Tuesday Mooney Talks to Ghosts: A Novel*
Rajaniemi, Hannu. *The Fractal Prince*
Rajaniemi, Hannu. *The Quantum Thief*
Rao, Shobha. ★*Girls Burn Brighter*
Rash, Ron. *Above the Waterfall*
Rash, Ron. ★*The Cove*
Rawles, Nancy. *My Jim: A Novel*
Reay, Katherine. *The Bronte Plot*
Reichs, Kathy. *Deadly Decisions*
Remarque, Erich Maria. ★*All Quiet on the Western Front*
Reynolds, Alastair. ★*Revenger*
Rhodes, Jewell Parker. *Yellow Moon: A Novel*
Ricciardi, David. *Warning Light*
Rice, Anne. *Blackwood Farm*
Rice, Anne. *Christ the Lord: Out of Egypt: A Novel*
Rice, Anne. *Prince Lestat: The Vampire Chronicles*
Rice, Luanne. *Little Night*
Richler, Nancy. *Your Mouth Is Lovely: A Novel*
Richmond, Michelle. *No One You Know*
Roanhorse, Rebecca. ★*Black Sun*
Roanhorse, Rebecca. *Storm of Locusts*
Roanhorse, Rebecca. ★*Trail of Lightning*
Robertson, Michael. *The Baker Street Letters*
Robertson, Michael. *The Baker Street Translation: A Mystery*
Robertson, Michael. *The Brothers of Baker Street*
Robinson, Kim Stanley. *Antarctica*
Robinson, Kim Stanley. *Aurora*
Robinson, Kim Stanley. ★*Blue Mars*
Robinson, Kim Stanley. ★*Green Mars*
Robinson, Kim Stanley. *The Martians*
Robinson, Kim Stanley. ★*Red Mars*
Robinson, Kim Stanley. *The Years of Rice and Salt*
Robinson, Peter. *Playing with Fire*
Robotham, Michael. ★*Good Girl, Bad Girl: A Novel*
Rodrigues Fowler, Yara. *Stubborn Archivist*
Rojas Contreras, Ingrid. ★*Fruit of the Drunken Tree: A Novel*
Rollins, James. *The Devil Colony*
Rollins, James. *The Eye of God*
Rooney, Sally. ★*Conversations with Friends*

Rooney, Sally. *Normal People: A Novel*
Roorbach, Bill. *Life Among Giants: A Novel*
Roth, Philip. ★*The Plot Against America*
Rothfuss, Patrick. ★*The Name of the Wind*
Rothfuss, Patrick. ★*The Wise Man's Fear*
Rowland, Laura Joh. *The Incense Game: A Novel of Feudal Japan*
Rowland, Laura Joh. *The Snow Empress*
Roy, Anuradha. *All the Lives We Never Lived: A Novel*
Roy, Anuradha. *An Atlas of Impossible Longing*
Ruiz Zafon, Carlos. *The Prisoner of Heaven*
Ruiz Zafon, Carlos. ★*The Shadow of the Wind*
Rushdie, Salman. *Haroun and the Sea of Stories*
Russell, Karen. ★*Swamplandia!*
Russell, Kate Elizabeth. ★*My Dark Vanessa*
Sager, Riley. *The Last Time I Lied: A Novel*
Salinger, J. D. ★*The Catcher in the Rye*
Sathian, Sanjena. *Gold Diggers*
Saul, John. *Midnight Voices*
Sayers, Dorothy L. *Thrones, Dominations*
Scalzi, John. *Head On*
Scalzi, John. ★*Lock In*
Schlink, Bernhard. *The Reader: A Novel*
Schwab, Victoria. *A Conjuring of Light*
Schwab, Victoria. *A Darker Shade of Magic*
Schwab, Victoria. *A Gathering of Shadows*
Schwarz, Christina. *Drowning Ruth*
Scottoline, Lisa. *One Perfect Lie*
Searles, John. *Help for the Haunted*
Sebold, Alice. ★*The Lovely Bones*
Sedgwick, Marcus. *Mister Memory: A Novel*
See, Lisa. *Dragon Bones: A Novel*
See, Lisa. *Shanghai Girls: A Novel*
Semple, Maria. *Where'd You Go, Bernadette: A Novel*
Setterfield, Diane. *The Thirteenth Tale: A Novel*
Shan, Sa. *The Girl Who Played Go*
Shannon, Samantha. *The Bone Season*
Shannon, Samantha. *The Mime Order*
Shepard, Jim. ★*The Book of Aron*
Shreve, Anita. *Testimony: A Novel*
Shriver, Lionel. *We Need to Talk About Kevin*
Siegel, Jan. *Prospero's Children*
Simmons, Dan. *Drood: A Novel*
Simmons, Dan. ★*The Terror: A Novel*
Simonson, Helen. *The Summer Before the War: A Novel*
Simpson, Rosemary. ★*What the Dead Leave Behind*
Simsion, Graeme C. *The Rosie Effect*
Simsion, Graeme C. ★*The Rosie Project*
Simsion, Graeme C. *The Rosie Result*
Sittenfeld, Curtis. *Eligible: A Novel*
Sittenfeld, Curtis. *Prep: A Novel*
Sittenfeld, Curtis. ★*You Think It, I'll Say It: Stories*
Sloan, Robin. *Mr. Penumbra's 24-Hour Bookstore*
Smiley, Jane. *Horse Heaven*
Smith, Ali. *The Accidental*
Smith, Dodie. ★*I Capture the Castle*
Smith, Martin Cruz. *December 6*
Smith, Scott. *The Ruins: A Novel*
Smith, Scott. *A Simple Plan: A Novel*

Smith, Zadie. *On Beauty*

Soli, Tatjana. *The Lotus Eaters*

Solomon, Asali. *Disgruntled: A Novel*

Sparks, Nicholas. *The Guardian*

Sparks, Nicholas. *A Walk to Remember*

St. James, Simone. *The Broken Girls*

St. James, Simone. *The Haunting of Maddy Clare*

Stabenow, Dana. ★*A Deeper Sleep: A Kate Shugak Novel*

Stabenow, Dana. ★*A Fine and Bitter Snow: A Kate Shugak Novel*

Stabenow, Dana. ★*A Grave Denied*

Stabenow, Dana. ★*Hunter's Moon*

Stabenow, Dana. *Killing Grounds: A Kate Shugak Mystery*

Stabenow, Dana. *A Night Too Dark: A Kate Shugak Novel*

Stabenow, Dana. *The Singing of the Dead*

Stabenow, Dana. *So Sure of Death: A Liam Campbell Mystery*

Stabenow, Dana. *Spoils of the Dead*

Stabenow, Dana. ★*A Taint in the Blood*

Stabenow, Dana. *Though Not Dead: A Kate Shugak Novel*

Stabenow, Dana. *Whisper to the Blood: A Kate Shugak Novel*

Steadman, Catherine. *Something in the Water*

Steele, Allen M. *Coyote: A Novel of Interstellar Exploration*

Stein, Garth. *The Art of Racing in the Rain: A Novel*

Stephenson, Neal. *The Rise and Fall of D.O.D.O.: A Novel*

Stevens, Chevy. *Never Let You Go*

Stibbe, Nina. *Reasons to Be Cheerful*

Stirling, S. M. *Dies the Fire*

Stirling, S. M. *A Meeting at Corvallis*

Stirling, S. M. *The Protector's War*

Stoker, Bram. ★*Dracula*

Straight, Susan. *A Million Nightingales*

Straub, Emma. *The Vacationers*

Straub, Peter. ★*A Dark Matter: A Novel*

Straub, Peter. *Lost Boy Lost Girl: A Novel*

Strout, Elizabeth. *Amy and Isabelle: A Novel*

Stuart, Douglas. ★*Shuggie Bain*

Suri, Tasha. ★*Empire of Sand*

Suri, Tasha. ★*Realm of Ash*

Swanwick, Michael. *Bones of the Earth*

Swarthout, Glendon. *Bless the Beasts and Children*

Swyler, Erika. ★*Light from Other Stars: A Novel*

Tademy, Lalita. *Cane River*

Tamirat, Nafkote. *The Parking Lot Attendant: A Novel*

Tartt, Donna. ★*The Goldfinch*

Tatlock, Ann. *Promises to Keep*

Tepper, Sheri S. *Singer from the Sea*

Tepper, Sheri S. *The Visitor*

Tinti, Hannah. *The Twelve Lives of Samuel Hawley: A Novel*

Tolkien, J. R. R. *The Children of Hurin*

Tolkien, J. R. R. ★*The Hobbit, Or, There and Back Again*

Tsukiyama, Gail. *The Street of a Thousand Blossoms*

Tyree, Omar. *Leslie: A Novel*

Updike, John. *Gertrude and Claudius*

Urrea, Luis Alberto. *Into the Beautiful North: A Novel*

Valente, Catherynne M. *Space Opera*

Vandermeer, Jeff. ★*Annihilation: A Novel*

Verne, Jules. *The Mysterious Island*

Vestal, Shawn. *Daredevils*

Vonnegut, Kurt. *While Mortals Sleep: Unpublished Short Fiction*

Vuong, Ocean. ★*On Earth We're Briefly Gorgeous: A Novel*

Vyleta, Dan. *Smoke: A Novel*

Walker, Karen Thompson. *The Age of Miracles: A Novel*

Walker, Wendy. *Emma in the Night*

Walls, Jeannette. *The Silver Star: A Novel*

Walton, Jo. ★*Necessity*

Ware, Ruth. *The Death of Mrs. Westaway*

Washington, Bryan. *Lot: Stories*

Weir, Andy. *Artemis*

Weir, Andy. *The Martian*

Wellington, David. *Positive*

Wells, Benedict. *The End of Loneliness: A Novel*

Wells, Martha. *All Systems Red*

Wells, Martha. *Network Effect*

Welsh, Kaite. *The Wages of Sin*

West, Dorothy. *The Wedding*

Whitehead, Colson. ★*The Nickel Boys: A Novel*

Whitehead, Colson. *Sag Harbor: A Novel*

Whitehead, Colson. *Zone One: A Novel*

Wiesel, Elie. *Hostage*

Williams, Katie. *Tell the Machine Goodnight*

Williams, Lara. *Supper Club: A Novel*

Willis, Connie. ★*Doomsday Book*

Wilson, Daniel H. *The Clockwork Dynasty: A Novel*

Wilson, G. Willow. *Alif the Unseen*

Wilson, G. Willow. ★*The Bird King*

Winthrop, Elizabeth Hartley. ★*The Why of Things*

Wolff, Tobias. *Old School: A Novel*

Wolitzer, Meg. *The Female Persuasion*

Wong, David. *Futuristic Violence and Fancy Suits*

Woo, Sung J. *Love Love: A Novel*

Wood, Shelley. *The Quintland Sisters*

Woods, Stuart. *Orchid Beach*

Woodson, Jacqueline. ★*Another Brooklyn*

Yoshimoto, Banana. *The Lake*

Yu, Charles. *How to Live Safely in a Science Fictional Universe: A Novel*

ADULT CHILD ABUSE VICTIMS

Bausch, Richard. *Hello to the Cannibals: A Novel*

Conroy, Pat. *The Prince of Tides*

Gunday, Hakan. *The Few*

Harris, Thomas. *Red Dragon*

Johnstone, Carole. *Mirrorland*

Koontz, Dean R. *Intensity: A Novel*

Oates, Joyce Carol. *Blonde: A Novel*

Roberts, Nora. *Chesapeake Blue*

Roberts, Nora. ★*Under Currents*

Robinson, Marilynne. ★*Lila*

ADULT CHILD SEXUAL ABUSE VICTIMS

Crowell, Jenn. *Etched on Me: A Novel*

Lehane, Dennis. ★*Mystic River*

ADULT CHILDREN

Hilderbrand, Elin. ★*Troubles in Paradise*

Hilderbrand, Elin. ★*What Happens in Paradise: A Novel*

White, Randy Wayne. *Salt River*

ADULT CHILDREN OF ALCOHOLICS

Murphy, Devin. *Tiny Americans*

ADULT CHILDREN OF CELEBRITIES

Hall, Alexis. ★*Boyfriend Material*

ADULT CHILDREN OF DIVORCED PARENTS

Picoult, Jodi. *Vanishing Acts: A Novel*

ADULT CHILDREN OF DYSFUNCTIONAL FAMILIES

Hadley, Tessa. *The Past*

Hoover, Colleen. *It Ends with Us*

Miller, Sue. *The Senator's Wife*

Packer, Ann. *The Children's Crusade*

Petterson, Per. *I Refuse*

ADULT CHILDREN OF MURDER VICTIMS

Callender, Kacen. *Queen of the Conquered*

Daugherty, Christi. *A Beautiful Corpse*

ADULT CHILDREN OF MURDERERS

Roberts, Nora. *The Obsession*

ADULT CHILDREN OF POLICE

Rader-Day, Lori. ★*The Lucky One*

ADULT CHILDREN OF POLITICIANS

Cole, Alyssa. ★*A Prince on Paper*

Liu, Ken. *The Wall of Storms*

ADULTHOOD

Smith, Zadie. ★*Nw: A Novel*

Adulthood Rites. Butler, Octavia E.

ADVENTURE

Pulley, Natasha. *The Bedlam Stacks*

Ryan, Anthony. *The Waking Fire*

Saberhagen, Fred. *Sightblinder's Story*

Saberhagen, Fred. *Stonecutter's Story*

Saramago, Jose. ★*The Elephant's Journey*

Sullivan, Michael J. *Theft of Swords*

Tobar, Hector. *The Last Great Road Bum*

Verne, Jules. ★*Journey to the Centre of the Earth*

The Adventure of the Peculiar Protocols: Adapted from the Journals of John H. Watson, M.D.. Meyer, Nicholas

ADVENTURE STORIES

Alten, Steve. *Meg: Generations*

Ballard, J. G. ★*The Day of Creation*

Bell, Ted. *Overkill: An Alex Hawke Novel*

Birch, Carol. *Jamrach's Menagerie*

Carter, Miranda. *The Strangler Vine*

Clinch, Jon. *Finn: A Novel*

Cooper, James Fenimore. *The Last of the Mohicans: A Narrative of 1757*

Crichton, Michael. *Pirate Latitudes*

Cussler, Clive. *Blue Gold: A Novel from the Numa Files*

Cussler, Clive. *Celtic Empire*

Cussler, Clive. ★*The Chase*

Cussler, Clive. *The Cutthroat*

Cussler, Clive. ★*Final Option*

Cussler, Clive. *Ghost Ship*

Cussler, Clive. ★*Golden Buddha*

Cussler, Clive. ★*The Gray Ghost*

Cussler, Clive. *Havana Storm*

Cussler, Clive. *The Mediterranean Caper*

Cussler, Clive. *Nighthawk: A Novel from the Numa Files*

Cussler, Clive. *Odessa Sea*

Cussler, Clive. ★*The Oracle*

Cussler, Clive. *Pacific Vortex!*

Cussler, Clive. *The Pharaoh's Secret*

Cussler, Clive. ★*Raise the Titanic!*

Cussler, Clive. ★*The Rising Sea: A Novel from the Numa Files*

Cussler, Clive. *The Romanov Ransom*

Cussler, Clive. *Sacred Stone*

Cussler, Clive. *Sahara: A Novel*

Cussler, Clive. ★*Sea of Greed: A Novel from the Numa Files*

Cussler, Clive. *Serpent: A Novel from the Numa Files*

Cussler, Clive. *Shadow Tyrants*

Cussler, Clive. ★*The Titanic Secret*

Cussler, Clive. *Typhoon Fury*

Cussler, Clive. *The Wrecker*

Defoe, Daniel. ★*Robinson Crusoe*

Diaz, Hernan. ★*In the Distance*

Dickens, Charles. *Martin Chuzzlewit*

Dumas, Alexandre. ★*The Count of Monte Cristo*

Dumas, Alexandre. ★*The Man in the Iron Mask*

Dumas, Alexandre. ★*The Three Musketeers*

Dumas, Alexandre. *Twenty Years After*

Dunnett, Dorothy. *Niccolo Rising*

Fleming, Ian. ★*Casino Royale: A James Bond Novel*

Fleming, Ian. *Doctor No*

Fleming, Ian. *From Russia with Love*

Fleming, Ian. ★*Goldfinger*

Fleming, Ian. *The Man with the Golden Gun*

Fleming, Ian. *On Her Majesty's Secret Service*

Fleming, Ian. *You Only Live Twice*

Forester, C. S. *Admiral Hornblower in the West Indies*

Forester, C. S. *The African Queen*

Forester, C. S. *Beat to Quarters*

Forester, C. S. *Commodore Hornblower*

Forester, C. S. *Flying Colours*

Forester, C. S. *Hornblower and the Atropos*

Forester, C. S. *Hornblower and the Hotspur*

Forester, C. S. *Lieutenant Hornblower*

Forester, C. S. *Lord Hornblower*

Forester, C. S. *Mr. Midshipman Hornblower*

Forester, C. S. *Ship of the Line*

Hackwith, A. J. *The Library of the Unwritten*

Hall, Adam. *The Quiller Memorandum*

Heacox, Kim. *Jimmy Bluefeather: A Novel*

Hemingway, Ernest. *The Snows of Kilimanjaro and Other Stories*

Hilton, James. ★*Lost Horizon: A Novel*

Johnson, Charles Richard. ★*Middle Passage*

Krueger, William Kent. *This Tender Land: A Novel*

L'Amour, Louis. *The Last of the Breed*

Lansdale, Joe R. *The Thicket*

London, Jack. ★*The Call of the Wild*

London, Jack. ★*White Fang*

Monsarrat, Nicholas. *The Cruel Sea*

O'Brian, Patrick. *Master and Commander*

Orczy, Emmuska Orczy. ★*The Scarlet Pimpernel*

Pearson, Ridley. *The Risk Agent*

Perez-Reverte, Arturo. *The Club Dumas*

Preston, Douglas J. *Thunderhead*

Racculia, Kate. ★*Tuesday Mooney Talks to Ghosts: A Novel*

Redfield, James. *The Celestine Prophecy: An Adventure*

Rollins, James. *Crucible*

Rollins, James. *The Demon Crown: A Sigma Force Novel*
Rollins, James. *The Devil Colony*
Rollins, James. *The Eye of God*
Rollins, James. ★*The Last Odyssey*
Rollins, James. *The Sixth Extinction: A Sigma Force Novel*
Sabatini, Rafael. *Captain Blood*
Sabatini, Rafael. *Scaramouche: A Romance of the French Revolution*
Saint-Exupery, Antoine de. *Night Flight*
Scott, Walter. ★*Ivanhoe*
Smith, Wilbur A. *Birds of Prey*
Smith, Wilbur A. *Monsoon*
Verne, Jules. ★*Around the World in Eighty Days*
Verne, Jules. *The Mysterious Island*

ADVENTURERS
Cervantes Saavedra, Miguel de. ★*Don Quixote*
Delany, Samuel R. *Dhalgren*
Guthrie, A. B. ★*The Big Sky*
James, Eloisa. *Wilde in Love*
Lebbon, Tim. *Eden*
Schlink, Bernhard. *Olga*
Tolkien, J. R. R. ★*The Hobbit, Or, There and Back Again*
Verne, Jules. ★*Journey to the Centre of the Earth*
Verne, Jules. *The Mysterious Island*

Adventures of Arabella Ashby [Series]. Levine, David D.
★*The **Adventures** of Augie March*. Bellow, Saul
★***Adventures** of Huckleberry Finn: Tom Sawyer's Comrade* .... Twain, Mark
*The **Adventures** of Johnny Vermillion: A Novel*. Estleman, Loren D.

ADVERTISING
Saunders, George. *In Persuasion Nation: Stories*

ADVERTISING AGENCIES
Sayers, Dorothy L. *Murder Must Advertise*

ADVERTISING COPYWRITERS
Berger, Thomas. *Being Invisible: A Novel*

ADVERTISING EXECUTIVES
Ballard, J. G. *Kingdom Come*
Guillory, Jasmine. ★*While We Were Dating*
Hauck, Rachel. *The Wedding Chapel*

ADVICE COLUMNISTS
Andrew, Sally. *The Satanic Mechanic: A Tannie Maria Mystery*
Guhrke, Laura Lee. *The Trouble with True Love*
Guhrke, Laura Lee. *The Truth About Love and Dukes*
West, Nathanael. *Novels and Other Writings*

Aector McAvoy novels [Series]. Mark, David John
Aerialists: Stories. Mayer, Mark

AEROSPACE INDUSTRY AND TRADE
Knopf, Chris. *You're Dead*

AEROSPACE TECHNOLOGY
Clarke, Arthur C. *Rendezvous with Rama*

AESTHETICS
Barbery, Muriel. *The Elegance of the Hedgehog*

Aetherial Worlds: Stories. Tolstaya, Tatyana
*The **Affair**: a Reacher Novel*. Child, Lee
*The **Affairs** of the Falcons*. Rivero, Melissa
★*Affliction*. Banks, Russell

AFGHAN AMERICANS
Aimaq, Jasmine. *The Opium Prince*

AFGHAN WAR VETERANS
Laukkanen, Owen. *Deception Cove*
Tracy, P. J. ★*Deep into the Dark*

AFGHAN WAR, 2001-2021
Giordano, Paolo. *The Human Body*
Hosseini, Khaled. ★*The Kite Runner*

AFGHANISTAN
Ahmad, Jamil. *The Wandering Falcon*
Aimaq, Jasmine. *The Opium Prince*
Aslam, Nadeem. ★*The Blind Man's Garden*
Coughlin, Jack. *In the Crosshairs: A Sniper Novel*
Florio, Gwen. *Silent Hearts*
Hosseini, Khaled. ★*The Kite Runner*
Khadra, Yasmina. *The Swallows of Kabul: A Novel*
Waldman, Amy. *A Door in the Earth*

Afifi, Nadia
The Sentient

AFRICA
Akpan, Uwem. *Say You're One of Them*
Beah, Ishmael. *Little Family*
Bellow, Saul. ★*Henderson the Rain King: A Novel*
Cole, Alyssa. ★*How to Catch a Queen*
Cole, Alyssa. ★*A Prince on Paper*
Couto, Mia. *Rain: And Other Stories*
Forester, C. S. *The African Queen*
Gappah, Petina. ★*Out of Darkness, Shining Light*
Gruber, Michael. *Valley of Bones: A Novel*
Gyasi, Yaa. ★*Homegoing: A Novel*
Lessing, Doris May. *A Proper Marriage*
Lessing, Doris May. *The Sweetest Dream*
McCall Smith, Alexander. *The Double Comfort Safari Club*
McCall Smith, Alexander. *The Full Cupboard of Life*
McCall Smith, Alexander. *In the Company of Cheerful Ladies*
McCall Smith, Alexander. *The Joy and Light Bus Company*
McCall Smith, Alexander. *The Kalahari Typing School for Men*
McCall Smith, Alexander. *The Limpopo Academy of Private Detection*
McCall Smith, Alexander. ★*The No. 1 Ladies' Detective Agency*
McCall Smith, Alexander. *The Saturday Big Tent Wedding Party*
Mengestu, Dinaw. ★*All Our Names*
Naipaul, V. S. *A Bend in the River*
Okorafor, Nnedi. ★*Who Fears Death*
Osondu, E. C. *This House Is Not for Sale: A Novel*
Phillips, Caryl. *A Distant Shore*
Serpell, Namwali. ★*The Old Drift*
Smith, Wilbur A. *Monsoon*
Stanley, Michael. *A Carrion Death*
Stanley, Michael. *Deadly Harvest*
Stanley, Michael. *A Death in the Family*
Stanley, Michael. *Death of the Mantis*
Stanley, Michael. *Dying to Live*
Walker, Alice. *The Temple of My Familiar*

AFRICAN AMERICAN ACTORS AND ACTRESSES
Harris, E. Lynn. *Not a Day Goes By: A Novel*
Tyree, Omar. *For the Love of Money: A Novel*

AFRICAN AMERICAN AUTHORS
Everett, Percival L. *Erasure: A Novel*
Iles, Greg. *Mississippi Blood: A Novel*

K'wan. *Gangsta*
Miller, Karen E. Quinones. *An Angry-Ass Black Woman*
Williams, Tia. ★*Seven Days in June: A Novel*

AFRICAN AMERICAN BOYS
Brinkley, Jamel. *A Lucky Man: Stories*
French, Albert. *Billy*
Hughes, Langston. *Not Without Laughter*

AFRICAN AMERICAN BOYS — IDENTITY
Sapphire. ★*The Kid: A Novel*

AFRICAN AMERICAN BROTHERS
K'wan. *Hoodlum*

AFRICAN AMERICAN CELEBRITIES
Lovely, Lutishia. *Blind Ambition*

AFRICAN AMERICAN CHURCHES
Harris, E. Lynn. *I Say a Little Prayer: A Novel*

AFRICAN AMERICAN CLERGY
Ellison, Ralph. ★*Juneteenth*
Styron, William. *The Confessions of Nat Turner*

AFRICAN AMERICAN COLLEGE TEACHERS
Carter, Stephen L. *New England White: A Novel*

AFRICAN AMERICAN COMEDIANS
Phillips, Caryl. *Dancing in the Dark*

AFRICAN AMERICAN COMMUNITIES
Bambara, Toni Cade. ★*The Salt Eaters*
Bennett, Brit. *The Mothers*
Morrison, Toni. *Paradise*
Scott, Rion Amilcar. ★*The World Doesn't Require You: Stories*
Winslow, De'Shawn Charles. ★*In West Mills*

AFRICAN AMERICAN COMMUNITY LIFE
McKinney-Whetstone, Diane. *Leaving Cecil Street: A Novel*

AFRICAN AMERICAN COWBOYS
Durham, David Anthony. ★*Gabriel's Story*
Lansdale, Joe R. ★*Paradise Sky*

AFRICAN AMERICAN DEFENDANTS
Faulkner, William. *Intruder in the Dust*
Grisham, John. *A Time to Kill*

AFRICAN AMERICAN ENGINEERS
Johnson, Nancy. *The Kindest Lie*

AFRICAN AMERICAN ENTERTAINERS
Phillips, Caryl. *Dancing in the Dark*

AFRICAN AMERICAN FAMILIES
Baldwin, James. *Just Above My Head*
Bennett, Brit. ★*The Vanishing Half*
Cha, Steph. ★*Your House Will Pay*
Collins, Kathleen. *Notes from a Black Woman's Diary: Selected Works of Kathleen Collins*
Collins, Kathleen. ★*Whatever Happened to Interracial Love?: Stories*
Cross-Smith, Leesa. *Whiskey & Ribbons*
Dickey, Eric Jerome. *The Business of Lovers*
Durham, David Anthony. ★*Gabriel's Story*
Flournoy, Angela. *The Turner House*
Gray, Anissa. *The Care and Feeding of Ravenously Hungry Girls*
Greenidge, Kaitlyn. *We Love You, Charlie Freeman: A Novel*
Holmes, Shannon. ★*B-More Careful: A Novel*
Jeffers, Honoree Fanonne. ★*The Love Songs of W. E. B. Du Bois*
Johnson, Jocelyn Nicole. ★*My Monticello: Fiction*
Jones, Tayari. ★*An American Marriage: A Novel*

Jones, Tayari. *Silver Sparrow: A Novel*
Lovely, Lutishia. *Blind Ambition*
Mathis, Ayana. *The Twelve Tribes of Hattie*
Monroe, Mary. ★*Mrs. Wiggins*
Onyebuchi, Tochi. ★*Riot Baby*
Porter, Regina. *The Travelers*
Ruff, Matt. *Lovecraft Country: A Novel*
Sexton, Margaret Wilkerson. *A Kind of Freedom*
Sexton, Margaret Wilkerson. *The Revisioners: A Novel*
Tademy, Lalita. *Cane River*
Walker, Alice. *The Third Life of Grange Copeland*
West, Dorothy. *The Wedding*

AFRICAN AMERICAN FATHERS AND SONS
Morrison, Toni. ★*Song of Solomon*

AFRICAN AMERICAN FICTION
Abrams, Stacey. *While Justice Sleeps: A Novel*
Akinmade-Akerstrom, Lola. *In Every Mirror She's Black*
Alderson, Kaia. *Sisters in Arms*
Allen, Jayne. *Black Girls Must Die Exhausted*
Antoinette, Ashley. *Butterfly*
Antoinette, Ashley. *Butterfly.; Vol 2*
Antoinette, Ashley. *Butterfly.; Vol 3*
Ashley & JaQuavis. *The Cartel*
Ashley & JaQuavis. *Murderville*
Asim, Jabari. ★*Yonder*
Askaripour, Mateo. ★*Black Buck*
Atakora, Afia. ★*Conjure Women*
Baldwin, James. ★*Another Country*
Baldwin, James. ★*Going to Meet the Man*
Baldwin, James. ★*If Beale Street Could Talk*
Baldwin, James. *Tell Me How Long the Train's Been Gone: A Novel*
Bambara, Toni Cade. *Gorilla, My Love*
Bambara, Toni Cade. ★*The Salt Eaters*
Bambara, Toni Cade. *Those Bones Are Not My Child*
Barnett, LaShonda K. *Jam on the Vine*
Beatty, Paul. ★*The Sellout: A Novel*
Beatty, Paul. *Slumberland: A Novel*
Bennett, Brit. ★*The Vanishing Half*
Billingsley, ReShonda Tate. *A Little Bit of Karma: A Novel*
Billingsley, ReShonda Tate. ★*The Secret She Kept*
Bond, Cynthia. *Ruby: A Novel*
Booth, Coe. ★*Bronxwood*
Brinkley, Jamel. *A Lucky Man: Stories*
Bryant, Niobia. *Madam, May I*
Bryant, Niobia. *Message from a Mistress*
Bump, Gabriel. ★*Everywhere You Don't Belong: A Novel*
Burke, Marcus. *Team Seven*
Burns, V. M. *Killer Words*
Bush, Keisha. *No Heaven for Good Boys: A Novel*
Butler, Octavia E. *Adulthood Rites*
Butler, Octavia E. *Bloodchild: And Other Stories*
Butler, Octavia E. ★*Dawn: Xenogenesis*
Butler, Octavia E. ★*Kindred*
Butler, Octavia E. ★*Parable of the Sower*
Ca$h. *Thugs Cry: A Novel*
Ca$h. ★*Trust No Bitch*
Campbell, Bebe Moore. *Brothers and Sisters*
Campbell, Bebe Moore. *Your Blues Ain't Like Mine*

Capri, NeNe. *The Pussy Trap*
Capri, NeNe. *The Pussy Trap.; Part 3,*
Clark, Cherae. ★*The Unbroken*
Clark, Tracy P. *Runner*
Clark, Tracy P. *What You Don't See*
Clark, Wahida. *Blood, Sweat and Payback*
Clark, Wahida. *Honor Thy Thug*
Clark, Wahida. *Justify My Thug: A Novel*
Clark, Wahida. *Payback Ain't Enough*
Clark, Wahida. ★*Payback Is a Mutha*
Clark, Wahida. *Payback with Ya Life*
Clark, Wahida. *Thug Lovin'*
Clark, Wahida. *Thug Matrimony*
Clark, Wahida. *Thugs*
Clark, Wahida. ★*Thugs and the Women Who Love Them*
Cleage, Pearl. *Some Things I Never Thought I'd Do*
Cleage, Pearl. *What Looks Like Crazy on an Ordinary Day: A Novel*
Clemmons, Zinzi. *What We Lose*
Cole, Alyssa. ★*A Duke by Default*
Cole, Alyssa. ★*An Extraordinary Union*
Cole, Alyssa. ★*A Hope Divided*
Cole, Alyssa. ★*How to Catch a Queen*
Cole, Alyssa. ★*A Prince on Paper*
Cole, Alyssa. ★*A Princess in Theory*
Cole, Alyssa. ★*An Unconditional Freedom*
Collins, Kathleen. *Notes from a Black Woman's Diary: Selected Works of Kathleen Collins*
Collins, Kathleen. ★*Whatever Happened to Interracial Love?: Stories*
Cosby, S. A. ★*Blacktop Wasteland*
Cosby, S. A. ★*Razorblade Tears*
Coster, Naima. *What's Mine and Yours: A Novel*
Crafts, Hannah. *The Bondwoman's Narrative*
Cross-Smith, Leesa. *Whiskey & Ribbons*
De Leon, Aya. *Side Chick Nation*
De Leon, Aya. ★*A Spy in the Struggle*
Delany, Samuel R. *Dhalgren*
Delany, Samuel R. *Stars in My Pocket Like Grains of Sand*
Dickey, Eric Jerome. ★*Bad Men and Wicked Women*
Dickey, Eric Jerome. *Before We Were Wicked*
Dickey, Eric Jerome. *The Blackbirds*
Dickey, Eric Jerome. *The Business of Lovers*
Dickey, Eric Jerome. *Finding Gideon*
Dickey, Eric Jerome. ★*The Son of Mr. Suleman*
Draper, Sharon M. ★*Forged by Fire*
Dumas, Henry. *Echo Tree: The Collected Short Fiction of Henry Dumas*
Durham, David Anthony. ★*Gabriel's Story*
Ellison, Ralph. ★*Invisible Man*
Ellison, Ralph. ★*Juneteenth*
Ellison, Ralph. *Three Days Before the Shooting . . .*
Evans, Danielle. ★*The Office of Historical Corrections: A Novella and Stories*
Everett, Percival L. *I Am Not Sidney Poitier*
Ferrell, Carolyn. *Dear Miss Metropolitan*
Flournoy, Angela. *The Turner House*
Frank, Alli. *Tiny Imperfections*
French, Albert. *Billy*

Gaines, Ernest J. ★*The Autobiography of Miss Jane Pittman*
Gaines, Ernest J. ★*A Gathering of Old Men*
Garrett, Kellye. ★*Hollywood Homicide*
Gay, Roxane. ★*Ayiti*
Goodwin, Bobi Gentry. *Revelation*
Gray, Erick S. *Love & a Gangsta: A Novel*
Greenidge, Kaitlyn. *We Love You, Charlie Freeman: A Novel*
Greer, Robert O. *First of State*
Guillory, Jasmine. *The Proposal*
Guillory, Jasmine. ★*The Wedding Date*
Guillory, Jasmine. *The Wedding Party*
Guillory, Jasmine. ★*While We Were Dating*
Gyasi, Yaa. ★*Homegoing: A Novel*
Gyasi, Yaa. ★*Transcendent Kingdom*
Hairston, Andrea. *Master of Poisons*
Hall, Rachel Howzell. *These Toxic Things*
Hampton, Brenda. *Stalker*
Hannaham, James. ★*Delicious Foods*
Harris, E. Lynn. *Basketball Jones: A Novel*
Harris, E. Lynn. *I Say a Little Prayer: A Novel*
Harris, E. Lynn. *Invisible Life: A Novel*
Harris, E. Lynn. *Not a Day Goes By: A Novel*
Harris, Nathan. *The Sweetness of Water*
Harris, Zakiya Dalila. *The Other Black Girl: A Novel*
Haywood, Gar Anthony. *Cemetery Road*
Hill, Donna. ★*Confessions in B-Flat*
Hodges, Cheris F. *Rumor Has It*
Holmes, Shannon. ★*B-More Careful: A Novel*
Hostin, Sunny. ★*Summer on the Bluffs*
Howard, Ravi. *Driving the King: A Novel*
Hughes, Langston. *Not Without Laughter*
Hughes, Langston. ★*Short Stories*
Hurston, Zora Neale. *Hitting a Straight Lick with a Crooked Stick: Stories from the Harlem Renaissance*
Jackson, Brenda. *Forged in Desire*
Jackson-Brown, Angela. ★*When Stars Rain Down: A Novel*
Jeffers, Honoree Fanonne. ★*The Love Songs of W. E. B. Du Bois*
Jemisin, N. K. ★*The City We Became*
Jemisin, N. K. *The Fifth Season*
Jemisin, N. K. *The Obelisk Gate*
Jemisin, N. K. *The Stone Sky*
Jenkins, Beverly. *Rebel*
Jenkins, Beverly. *Wild Rain*
Johnson, Alaya Dawn. *Trouble the Saints*
Johnson, Jocelyn Nicole. ★*My Monticello: Fiction*
Johnson, Nancy. *The Kindest Lie*
Johnson, Sadeqa. ★*Yellow Wife*
Jones, Stephen Mack. *Dead of Winter*
Joseph, Fabiola. *Niya: Rainbow Dreams*
K'wan. *Animal*
K'wan. *Animal II: The Omen*
K'wan. *The Diamond Empire*
K'wan. *Gangsta*
K'wan. *Hoodlum*
K'wan. *Lawless*
K'wan. *Revelations*
K'wan. *Street Dreams*
Laymon, Kiese. *Long Division*

Lee, Andrea. *Red Island House*
Leilani, Raven. ★*Luster*
Livesay, Tracey. *Like Lovers Do*
Locke, Attica. ★*Bluebird, Bluebird*
Locke, Attica. ★*Heaven, My Home*
McBride, James. ★*Deacon King Kong: A Novel*
McBride, James. *Five-Carat Soul*
McBride, James. ★*The Good Lord Bird*
McCarthy, Jesse. *The Fugitivities*
McFarland, Jeni. *The House of Deep Water*
McKinney-Whetstone, Diane. *Leaving Cecil Street: A Novel*
McMillan, Terry. ★*How Stella Got Her Groove Back*
McMillan, Terry. ★*It's Not All Downhill from Here: A Novel*
McMillan, Terry. ★*Waiting to Exhale*
Miller, Karen E. Quinones. *An Angry-Ass Black Woman*
Monroe, Mary. ★*God Don't Like Ugly*
Monroe, Mary. *God Still Don't Like Ugly*
Monroe, Mary. ★*Mrs. Wiggins*
Morrison, Toni. ★*The Bluest Eye: A Novel*
Morrison, Toni. ★*God Help the Child*
Morrison, Toni. *Home*
Morrison, Toni. *Love*
Morrison, Toni. *A Mercy: A Novel*
Morrison, Toni. ★*Song of Solomon*
Morrison, Toni. *Sula*
Morrison, Toni. *Tar Baby*
Mosley, Walter. *All I Did Was Shoot My Man: A Leonid McGill Mystery*
Mosley, Walter. *And Sometimes I Wonder About You: A Leonid McGill Mystery*
Mosley, Walter. *Black Betty: An Easy Rawlins Mystery*
Mosley, Walter. ★*Blood Grove*
Mosley, Walter. *Charcoal Joe: An Easy Rawlins Mystery*
Mosley, Walter. *Devil in a Blue Dress*
Mosley, Walter. *Down the River Unto the Sea*
Mosley, Walter. *Fortunate Son: A Novel*
Mosley, Walter. ★*John Woman*
Mosley, Walter. *Little Scarlet: An Easy Rawlins Mystery*
Mosley, Walter. *The Right Mistake: The Further Philosophical Investigations of Socrates Fortlow*
Mosley, Walter. *Trouble Is What I Do: A Leonid McGill Mystery*
Mott, Jason. *Hell of a Book*
Naylor, Gloria. *Mama Day*
Okorafor, Nnedi. ★*Binti*
Okorafor, Nnedi. *Binti: Home*
Okorafor, Nnedi. *Binti: The Night Masquerade*
Okorafor, Nnedi. ★*Remote Control*
Parks, Gordon. ★*The Learning Tree*
Pearson, Robin W. *A Long Time Comin'*
Penelope, L. *Cry of Metal & Bone: Earthsinger Chronicles, Book 3*
Penelope, L. *Song of Blood and Stone*
Penelope, L. *Whispers of Shadow & Flame*
Petry, Ann. ★*The Street*
Philyaw, Deesha. *The Secret Lives of Church Ladies*
Porter, Regina. *The Travelers*
Pride, Christine. ★*We Are Not Like Them*
Quartey, Kwei. ★*Sleep Well, My Lady*
Randall, Alice. ★*Black Bottom Saints*

Reed, Ishmael. *Flight to Canada*
Reed, Ishmael. ★*Mumbo Jumbo*
Reid, Kiley. ★*Such a Fun Age*
Rhodes, Jewell Parker. *Voodoo Dreams: A Novel of Marie Laveau*
Rhodes, Jewell Parker. *Yellow Moon: A Novel*
Riley, Vanessa. ★*Island Queen*
Rochon, Farrah. *The Boyfriend Project*
Rochon, Farrah. *The Dating Playbook*
Roy, Lucinda. *The Freedom Race*
Sapphire. *American Dreams*
Sapphire. ★*The Kid: A Novel*
Sapphire. ★*Push: A Novel*
Senna, Danzy. *New People*
Sexton, Margaret Wilkerson. *A Kind of Freedom*
Sexton, Margaret Wilkerson. *The Revisioners: A Novel*
Sister Souljah. ★*The Coldest Winter Ever: A Novel*
Sister Souljah. ★*A Deeper Love Inside: The Porsche Santiaga Story*
Sister Souljah. *Midnight and the Meaning of Love*
Smith, Ian. *The Unspoken*
Smith, Ian. *Wolf Point*
Snipes, Wesley. *Talon of God*
Solomon, Asali. *The Days of Afrekete*
Solomon, Rivers. *The Deep*
Speight, Shameek A. ★*A Child of a Crack Head*
Speight, Shameek A. *The Pleasure of Pain*
Stringer, Vickie M. *Dirty Red: A Novel*
Stringer, Vickie M. ★*Let That Be the Reason*
Stringer, Vickie M. *Still Dirty: A Novel*
Styles, Toy. *Black and Ugly*
Styles, Toy. *A Hustler's Son: A Novel*
Styles, Toy. *Raunchy*
Styles, Toy. *Raunchy 2: Mad's Love*
Styles, Toy. *Redbone*
Styles, Toy. ★*War*
Styles, Toy. *War 2: All Hell Breaks Loose*
Swinson, Kiki. *A Gangster and a Gentleman*
Swinson, Kiki. *I'm New York's Finest*
Swinson, Kiki. *Lifestyles of the Rich and Shameless*
Swinson, Kiki. *The Safe House*
Swinson, Kiki. *Who's Wife Extraordinaire Now*
Swinson, Kiki. *Wifey*
Swinson, Kiki. *Wifey's Next Sticky Situation*
T. I. *Power & Beauty: A Love Story of Life on the Streets*
T. I. *Trouble & Triumph: A Novel of Power & Beauty*
Tademy, Lalita. *Cane River*
Tamirat, Nafkote. *The Parking Lot Attendant: A Novel*
Taylor, Brandon. ★*Filthy Animals*
Taylor, Brandon. ★*Real Life*
Thompson-Spires, Nafissa. *Heads of the Colored People: Stories*
Turnbull, Cadwell. *No Gods, No Monsters*
Tyree, Omar. ★*Flyy Girl*
Tyree, Omar. *For the Love of Money: A Novel*
Tyree, Omar. *Leslie: A Novel*
Walker, Alice. ★*The Color Purple: A Novel*
Walker, Alice. *Possessing the Secret of Joy*
Walker, Alice. *The Temple of My Familiar*
Walker, Alice. *The Third Life of Grange Copeland*
Walker, Alice. *You Can't Keep a Good Woman Down: Stories*

Walton, Dawnie. ★*The Final Revival of Opal & Nev*
Weatherspoon, Rebekah. *If the Boot Fits*
West, Dorothy. *The Wedding*
Whitehead, Colson. *Apex Hides the Hurt*
Whitehead, Colson. *The Intuitionist*
Whitehead, Colson. *John Henry Days: A Novel*
Whitehead, Colson. ★*The Nickel Boys: A Novel*
Whitehead, Colson. *Sag Harbor: A Novel*
Whitehead, Colson. ★*The Underground Railroad: A Novel*
Whitehead, Colson. *Zone One: A Novel*
Wideman, John Edgar. ★*American Histories: Stories*
Wideman, John Edgar. *Look for Me and I'll Be Gone: Stories*
Wilkinson, Lauren. ★*American Spy: A Novel*
Williams, Preslaysa. *A Lowcountry Bride*
Williams, Synithia. *Forbidden Promises*
Williams, Tia. ★*Seven Days in June: A Novel*
Winslow, De'Shawn Charles. ★*In West Mills*
Woodson, Jacqueline. ★*Red at the Bone*
Wright, Richard. *The Man Who Lived Underground*
Wright, Richard. ★*Native Son*

AFRICAN AMERICAN FOSTER CHILDREN
Bohjalian, Chris. *The Buffalo Soldier: A Novel*

AFRICAN AMERICAN GAY MEN
Baldwin, James. ★*Early Novels and Stories*
Harris, E. Lynn. *Basketball Jones: A Novel*
Harris, E. Lynn. *I Say a Little Prayer: A Novel*
Mathis, Ayana. *The Twelve Tribes of Hattie*
Roberts, Nora. ★*The Becoming*
Taylor, Brandon. ★*Real Life*

AFRICAN AMERICAN GIRLS
Monroe, Mary. ★*God Don't Like Ugly*
Morrison, Toni. *A Mercy: A Novel*
Solomon, Asali. *Disgruntled: A Novel*
Tyree, Omar. ★*Flyy Girl*

AFRICAN AMERICAN HUSBAND AND WIFE
Pitts, Leonard. *Freeman*

AFRICAN AMERICAN INTELLECTUALS
West, Dorothy. *The Wedding*

AFRICAN AMERICAN JOURNALISTS
Whitehead, Colson. *John Henry Days: A Novel*

AFRICAN AMERICAN LESBIANS
Sapphire. *American Dreams*
Walker, Alice. ★*The Color Purple: A Novel*

AFRICAN AMERICAN LOYALISTS (UNITED STATES HISTORY)
Hill, Lawrence. *Someone Knows My Name: A Novel*

AFRICAN AMERICAN MEN
Baldwin, James. ★*Go Tell It on the Mountain*
Baldwin, James. *Tell Me How Long the Train's Been Gone: A Novel*
Beatty, Paul. *Slumberland: A Novel*
Brinkley, Jamel. *A Lucky Man: Stories*
Cole, Alyssa. ★*An Unconditional Freedom*
Cosby, S. A. ★*Blacktop Wasteland*
Dickey, Eric Jerome. *Finding Gideon*
Dickey, Eric Jerome. ★*The Son of Mr. Suleman*
Ellison, Ralph. ★*Invisible Man*
Everett, Percival L. *Erasure: A Novel*
Everett, Percival L. *God's Country*

Faulkner, William. *The Reivers: A Reminiscence*
Gaines, Ernest J. ★*A Gathering of Old Men*
Greer, Robert O. *First of State*
Hambly, Barbara. *Lady of Perdition*
Holmes, J. M. *How Are You Going to Save Yourself*
K'wan. *Gangsta*
K'wan. *Gutter*
K'wan. *Street Dreams*
Locke, Attica. ★*Bluebird, Bluebird*
Locke, Attica. ★*Heaven, My Home*
McCarthy, Jesse. *The Fugitivities*
Moore, Graham. *The Holdout: A Novel*
Morgan, C. E. ★*The Sport of Kings*
Morrison, Toni. *Love*
Mosley, Walter. ★*The Awkward Black Man: Stories*
Mosley, Walter. *Black Betty: An Easy Rawlins Mystery*
Mosley, Walter. *Charcoal Joe: An Easy Rawlins Mystery*
Mosley, Walter. *Devil in a Blue Dress*
Mosley, Walter. *The Right Mistake: The Further Philosophical Investigations of Socrates Fortlow*
Patterson, James. ★*Along Came a Spider: A Novel*
Patterson, James. *Kiss the Girls: A Novel*
Reed, Ishmael. ★*Mumbo Jumbo*
Roth, Philip. ★*The Human Stain*
Souljah. *Midnight and the Meaning of Love*
T. I. *Power & Beauty: A Love Story of Life on the Streets*
T. I. *Trouble & Triumph: A Novel of Power & Beauty*
Taylor, Brandon. ★*Real Life*
Verble, Margaret. ★*When Two Feathers Fell from the Sky*
Walker, Alice. *The Third Life of Grange Copeland*
Williams, Tia. ★*Seven Days in June: A Novel*
Wright, Richard. *The Man Who Lived Underground*

AFRICAN AMERICAN MEN — IDENTITY
Everett, Percival L. *I Am Not Sidney Poitier*
Phillips, Caryl. *Dancing in the Dark*

AFRICAN AMERICAN MEN — SEXUALITY
Harris, E. Lynn. *Invisible Life: A Novel*

AFRICAN AMERICAN MEN/WOMEN RELATIONS
Ashley & JaQuavis. *Murderville*
Harris, E. Lynn. *Not a Day Goes By: A Novel*
McMillan, Terry. ★*Waiting to Exhale*
Monroe, Mary. *God Still Don't Like Ugly*
Morrison, Toni. *Jazz*
Morrison, Toni. *Love*
Morrison, Toni. *Paradise*

AFRICAN AMERICAN MOTHERS AND DAUGHTERS
Butler, Octavia E. ★*Parable of the Sower*
Butler, Octavia E. *Parable of the Talents: A Novel*

AFRICAN AMERICAN MURDER SUSPECTS
Brooks, Bill. *Frontier Justice*

AFRICAN AMERICAN MUSICIANS
McKinney-Whetstone, Diane. *Leaving Cecil Street: A Novel*

AFRICAN AMERICAN NEIGHBORHOODS
Anderson, Kent. *Green Sun: A Novel*

AFRICAN AMERICAN POETRY
Sapphire. *American Dreams*

AFRICAN AMERICAN POLICE
Ball, John Dudley. *In the Heat of the Night*

AUTHOR, TITLE, AND SUBJECT INDEX

AFRICAN AMERICAN POLITICAL ACTIVISTS
De Leon, Aya. ★*A Spy in the Struggle*
AFRICAN AMERICAN PRISONERS
Grisham, John. ★*The Guardians*
AFRICAN AMERICAN PSYCHOLOGISTS
Patterson, James. *Kiss the Girls: A Novel*
AFRICAN AMERICAN SENIOR WOMEN
Naylor, Gloria. *Mama Day*
AFRICAN AMERICAN SINGERS
Harris, E. Lynn. *I Say a Little Prayer: A Novel*
AFRICAN AMERICAN SISTERS
Lovely, Lutishia. *Blind Ambition*
AFRICAN AMERICAN SOLDIERS
Burdett, John. *Bangkok 8*
Cobbs Hoffman, Elizabeth. *The Tubman Command: A Novel*
AFRICAN AMERICAN TEENAGE BOYS
Booth, Coe. ★*Bronxwood*
Bump, Gabriel. ★*Everywhere You Don't Belong: A Novel*
Campbell, Bebe Moore. *Your Blues Ain't Like Mine*
Cash, Wiley. *When Ghosts Come Home: A Novel*
DeLillo, Don. *Underworld*
Draper, Sharon M. ★*Forged by Fire*
Styles, Toy. *A Hustler's Son: A Novel*
Whitehead, Colson. ★*The Nickel Boys: A Novel*
Whitehead, Colson. *Sag Harbor: A Novel*
AFRICAN AMERICAN TEENAGE GIRLS
Jones, Tayari. *Silver Sparrow: A Novel*
McKinney-Whetstone, Diane. *Leaving Cecil Street: A Novel*
Morrison, Toni. *Jazz*
Tyree, Omar. ★*Flyy Girl*
West, Monica. *Revival Season: A Novel*
AFRICAN AMERICAN TEENAGERS
Burke, Marcus. *Team Seven*
Price, Richard. *Clockers*
Souljah. ★*A Deeper Love Inside: The Porsche Santiaga Story*
AFRICAN AMERICAN UNIVERSITIES AND COLLEGES
Tyree, Omar. *Leslie: A Novel*
AFRICAN AMERICAN VETERANS
Jordan, Hillary. *Mudbound: A Novel*
Morrison, Toni. *Home*
AFRICAN AMERICAN WIDOWS
Cross-Smith, Leesa. *Whiskey & Ribbons*
AFRICAN AMERICAN WOMEN
Akinmade-Akerstrom, Lola. *In Every Mirror She's Black*
Alam, Rumaan. *That Kind of Mother: A Novel*
Alderson, Kaia. *Sisters in Arms*
Bambara, Toni Cade. *Gorilla, My Love*
Bambara, Toni Cade. ★*The Salt Eaters*
Bambara, Toni Cade. *Those Bones Are Not My Child*
Barnett, LaShonda K. *Jam on the Vine*
Bird, Sarah. *Daughter of a Daughter of a Queen*
Bryant, Niobia. *Madam, May I*
Butler, Octavia E. ★*Parable of the Sower*
Butler, Octavia E. *Parable of the Talents: A Novel*
Campbell, Bebe Moore. *Brothers and Sisters*
Capri, NeNe. *The Pussy Trap.; Part 3,*
Chiaverini, Jennifer. *Mrs. Lincoln's Dressmaker: A Novel*
Clark, Tracy P. *Runner*

Clark, Tracy P. *What You Don't See*
Clark, Wahida. *Thug Lovin'*
Clark, Wahida. *Thug Matrimony*
Clark, Wahida. ★*Thugs and the Women Who Love Them*
Cleage, Pearl. *Some Things I Never Thought I'd Do*
Cleage, Pearl. *What Looks Like Crazy on an Ordinary Day: A Novel*
Cobbs Hoffman, Elizabeth. *The Tubman Command: A Novel*
Cole, Alyssa. ★*A Hope Divided*
Cole, Alyssa. *How to Find a Princess*
Conner, M. Shelly. *Everyman*
Crafts, Hannah. *The Bondwoman's Narrative*
Deon, Natashia. *The Perishing: A Novel*
Dickey, Eric Jerome. *The Blackbirds*
Faulkner, William. *Requiem for a Nun*
Frank, Alli. *Tiny Imperfections*
Gaines, Ernest J. ★*The Autobiography of Miss Jane Pittman*
Glass, Seressia. ★*The Love Con*
Guillory, Jasmine. ★*The Wedding Date*
Hall, Rachel Howzell. *And Now She's Gone*
Harris, Zakiya Dalila. *The Other Black Girl: A Novel*
Hostin, Sunny. ★*Summer on the Bluffs*
Hunt, Laird. *The Evening Road*
Hurston, Zora Neale. ★*Their Eyes Were Watching God*
Igharo, Jane. *The Sweetest Remedy*
Jackson-Brown, Angela. ★*When Stars Rain Down: A Novel*
Johnson, Keith Lee. ★*Little Black Girl Lost*
Johnson, Nancy. *The Kindest Lie*
K'wan. *Lawless*
Kidd, Sue Monk. ★*The Secret Life of Bees*
Lee, Andrea. *Red Island House*
Leilani, Raven. ★*Luster*
Livesay, Tracey. *Like Lovers Do*
Martin, Alexa. ★*Intercepted*
Mathis, Ayana. *The Twelve Tribes of Hattie*
Morrison, Toni. ★*Beloved: A Novel*
Morrison, Toni. *Love*
Morrison, Toni. *Sula*
Nguyen, Kevin. ★*New Waves*
Petry, Ann. ★*The Street*
Philyaw, Deesha. *The Secret Lives of Church Ladies*
Pronzini, Bill. *Nightcrawlers*
Rhodes, Jewell Parker. *Voodoo Dreams: A Novel of Marie Laveau*
Rogers, Morgan Callan. ★*Honey Girl*
Smith, Julie. *Louisiana Hotshot*
Solomon, Asali. *The Days of Afrekete*
Souljah. ★*The Coldest Winter Ever: A Novel*
Speight, Shameek A. *The Pleasure of Pain*
Stockett, Kathryn. ★*The Help*
Stringer, Vickie M. *Dirty Red: A Novel*
Stringer, Vickie M. ★*Let That Be the Reason*
Stringer, Vickie M. *Still Dirty: A Novel*
Styles, Toy. *Black and Ugly*
Styles, Toy. *Raunchy*
Styles, Toy. *Raunchy 2: Mad's Love*
Swinson, Kiki. *A Gangster and a Gentleman*
Swinson, Kiki. *Lifestyles of the Rich and Shameless*
Swinson, Kiki. *The Safe House*
Swinson, Kiki. *Who's Wife Extraordinaire Now*

Swinson, Kiki. *Wifey*
Swinson, Kiki. *Wifey's Next Sticky Situation*
Tademy, Lalita. *Cane River*
Walker, Alice. ★*The Color Purple: A Novel*
Walker, Alice. *The Temple of My Familiar*
Walker, Alice. *You Can't Keep a Good Woman Down: Stories*
Walton, Dawnie. ★*The Final Revival of Opal & Nev*
Weatherspoon, Rebekah. *Rafe: A Buff Male Nanny*
Weatherspoon, Rebekah. ★*Xeni: A Marriage of Inconvenience*
Williams, Tia. *Seven Days in June: A Novel*
Winslow, De'Shawn Charles. ★*In West Mills*

AFRICAN AMERICAN WOMEN — FRIENDSHIP
Clark, Wahida. *Blood, Sweat and Payback*
Clark, Wahida. *Payback Ain't Enough*
Clark, Wahida. ★*Payback Is a Mutha*
Clark, Wahida. *Payback with Ya Life*
McMillan, Terry. ★*How Stella Got Her Groove Back*
McMillan, Terry. ★*Waiting to Exhale*
Morrison, Toni. *Sula*

AFRICAN AMERICAN WOMEN — IDENTITY
Jeffers, Honoree Fanonne. ★*The Love Songs of W. E. B. Du Bois*
Larsen, Nella. *Passing*
Reid, Kiley. ★*Such a Fun Age*
Whitehead, Colson. *The Intuitionist*

AFRICAN AMERICAN WOMEN — INTERPERSONAL RELATIONS
Styles, Toy. *Redbone*

AFRICAN AMERICAN WOMEN — PSYCHOLOGY
Deon, Natashia. *Grace*

AFRICAN AMERICAN WOMEN — PSYCHOTHERAPY
Walker, Alice. *Possessing the Secret of Joy*

AFRICAN AMERICAN WOMEN COLLEGE STUDENTS
Tyree, Omar. *Leslie: A Novel*

AFRICAN AMERICAN WOMEN INVESTMENT ADVISERS
McMillan, Terry. ★*How Stella Got Her Groove Back*

AFRICAN AMERICAN WOMEN JOURNALISTS
Barnett, LaShonda K. *Jam on the Vine*
Pride, Christine. ★*We Are Not Like Them*

AFRICAN AMERICAN WOMEN LAWYERS
Clark, Wahida. *Thug Matrimony*
De Leon, Aya. ★*A Spy in the Struggle*
Whitlow, Robert. *A Time to Stand*

AFRICAN AMERICAN WOMEN SCREENWRITERS
Tyree, Omar. *For the Love of Money: A Novel*

AFRICAN AMERICAN WOMEN SINGERS
Lovely, Lutishia. *Blind Ambition*

AFRICAN AMERICAN WOMEN WITH HIV
Cleage, Pearl. *What Looks Like Crazy on an Ordinary Day: A Novel*

AFRICAN AMERICAN WOMEN WITH MENTAL ILLNESSES
Walker, Alice. *Possessing the Secret of Joy*

AFRICAN AMERICAN WORLD WAR II VETERANS
Mosley, Walter. *Devil in a Blue Dress*

AFRICAN AMERICAN YOUNG MEN
K'wan. *Hoodlum*
K'wan. *Street Dreams*

AFRICAN AMERICAN YOUNG WOMEN
Holmes, Shannon. ★*B-More Careful: A Novel*
Monroe, Mary. *God Still Don't Like Ugly*

AFRICAN AMERICANS
Adjei-Brenyah, Nana Kwame. *Friday Black: Stories*
Allen, Jayne. *Black Girls Must Die Exhausted*
Baldwin, James. ★*Early Novels and Stories*
Baldwin, James. ★*Going to Meet the Man*
Bambara, Toni Cade. *Gorilla, My Love*
Bambara, Toni Cade. *Those Bones Are Not My Child*
Beatty, Paul. ★*The Sellout: A Novel*
Beatty, Paul. *Slumberland: A Novel*
Benz, Chanelle. ★*The Gone Dead*
Billingsley, ReShonda Tate. *A Little Bit of Karma: A Novel*
Bond, Cynthia. *Ruby: A Novel*
Bryant, Niobia. *Message from a Mistress*
Ca$h. *Thugs Cry: A Novel*
Carter, Stephen L. *Back Channel*
Clark, P. Djeli. *Ring Shout*
Clark, Wahida. *Blood, Sweat and Payback*
Clark, Wahida. *Payback Ain't Enough*
Collins, Kathleen. ★*Whatever Happened to Interracial Love?: Stories*
Cush, Jean Love. *Endangered*
DeLillo, Don. *Underworld*
Dumas, Henry. *Echo Tree: The Collected Short Fiction of Henry Dumas*
Ellison, Ralph. ★*Invisible Man*
Faulkner, William. ★*The Sound and the Fury*
Glover, Nicole. ★*The Conductors*
Glover, Nicole. *The Undertakers*
Harris, E. Lynn. *I Say a Little Prayer: A Novel*
Harris, Nathan. *The Sweetness of Water*
Holmes, Shannon. ★*B-More Careful: A Novel*
Hurston, Zora Neale. *Hitting a Straight Lick with a Crooked Stick: Stories from the Harlem Renaissance*
Ide, Joe. ★*Hi Five: An IQ Novel*
Jackson, K. M. *How to Marry Keanu Reeves in 90 Days*
Jemisin, N. K. *How Long 'Til Black Future Month?*
Jenkins, Beverly. *Tempest*
K'wan. *The Diamond Empire*
K'wan. ★*Diamonds and Pearl*
K'wan. *The Fix*
K'wan. *Gangsta*
K'wan. *Lawless*
Luesse, Valerie Fraser. *Missing Isaac*
McFadden, Bernice L. *The Book of Harlan*
Morrison, Toni. ★*The Bluest Eye: A Novel*
Morrison, Toni. *Paradise*
Mott, Jason. *Hell of a Book*
Mullen, Thomas. *Darktown: A Novel*
Naylor, Gloria. *Mama Day*
Oates, Joyce Carol. *Because It Is Bitter, and Because It Is My Heart*
Reed, Ishmael. *Flight to Canada*
Reed, Ishmael. ★*Mumbo Jumbo*
Rochon, Farrah. *The Dating Playbook*
Sapphire. ★*Push: A Novel*
Scott, Rion Amilcar. ★*The World Doesn't Require You: Stories*
Smith, Ian. *Wolf Point*
Solomon, Rivers. *Sorrowland*
Stowe, Harriet Beecher. ★*Uncle Tom's Cabin*

Taylor, Brandon. ★*Filthy Animals*
Walker, Alice. *The Temple of My Familiar*
Washington, Bryan. ★*Memorial*
Weatherspoon, Rebekah. *A Thorn in the Saddle*
Wideman, John Edgar. ★*American Histories: Stories*
Wright, Richard. ★*Native Son*

AFRICAN AMERICANS — CIVIL RIGHTS
Gaines, Ernest J. ★*The Autobiography of Miss Jane Pittman*
Hill, Donna. ★*Confessions in B-Flat*

AFRICAN AMERICANS — IDENTITY
Ellison, Ralph. *Three Days Before the Shooting . . .*
Morrison, Toni. ★*Song of Solomon*
Roth, Philip. ★*The Human Stain*
Woodson, Jacqueline. ★*Another Brooklyn*

AFRICAN AMERICANS — MIGRATIONS
Colvin, Jeffrey. ★*Africaville: A Novel*
Mathis, Ayana. *The Twelve Tribes of Hattie*

AFRICAN AMERICANS — SOCIAL CONDITIONS
Collins, Kathleen. *Notes from a Black Woman's Diary: Selected Works of Kathleen Collins*
Howard, Ravi. *Driving the King: A Novel*
Lansdale, Joe R. ★*Paradise Sky*
Porter, Regina. *The Travelers*
Whitehead, Colson. ★*The Underground Railroad: A Novel*

AFRICAN AMERICANS — SOCIAL LIFE AND CUSTOMS
Hughes, Langston. ★*Short Stories*
Reed, Ishmael. ★*Mumbo Jumbo*

AFRICAN AMERICANS IN GERMANY
Beatty, Paul. *Slumberland: A Novel*

AFRICAN BRAZILIANS
Updike, John. *Brazil: A Novel*

AFRICAN DIASPORA
Gay, Roxane. ★*Ayiti*
The **African** Queen. Forester, C. S.

AFRICAN WEST INDIAN WOMEN
Conde, Maryse. *I, Tituba, Black Witch of Salem*

AFRICAN-AMERICAN MOTIVATIONAL SPEAKERS
Cleage, Pearl. *Some Things I Never Thought I'd Do*

AFRICAN-AMERICAN SPORTS AGENTS
Harris, E. Lynn. *Not a Day Goes By: A Novel*

AFRICAN-AMERICAN TENANT FARMERS
Walker, Alice. *The Third Life of Grange Copeland*

AFRICANS IN EUROPE
Dongala, Emmanuel Boundzeki. *The Bridgetower Sonata: Sonata Mulattica*

AFRICANS IN GREAT BRITAIN
Phillips, Caryl. *Foreigners*

AFRICANS IN THE UNITED STATES
Bulawayo, NoViolet. *We Need New Names: A Novel*
★*Africaville: a Novel*. Colvin, Jeffrey

AFRICVILLE (HALIFAX, N.S.)
Colvin, Jeffrey. ★*Africaville: A Novel*

AFROFANTASY
Beukes, Lauren. *Zoo City*
Hairston, Andrea. *Master of Poisons*
James, Marlon. ★*Black Leopard, Red Wolf*
Makumbi, Jennifer Nansubuga. *Kintu*
Solomon, Rivers. *The Deep*

Winter, Evan. *The Fires of Vengeance*
Winter, Evan. ★*The Rage of Dragons*

AFROFUTURISM
Delany, Samuel R. *Stars in My Pocket Like Grains of Sand*
Okorafor, Nnedi. ★*Noor*
Okorafor, Nnedi. ★*Remote Control*
Thompson, Tade. *Rosewater*
Thompson, Tade. *The Rosewater Insurrection*
Thompson, Tade. *The Rosewater Redemption*
Turnbull, Cadwell. ★*The Lesson*

Afshar, Tessa
Jewel of the Nile
Thief of Corinth

After Anna. Scottoline, Lisa
After Dark. Murakami, Haruki
★*After I'm Gone*. Lippman, Laura
After She's Gone: A Novel. Grebe, Camilla
After the Bloom. Shimotakahara, Leslie
After the Crown. Wagers, K. B.
After the End. Mackintosh, Clare
After the Flood: A Novel. Montag, Kassandra
After the Quake: Stories. Murakami, Haruki
After This. McDermott, Alice
Afterland. Beukes, Lauren
The *Afterlife and Other Stories*. Updike, John
★*Afterlife: a Novel*. Alvarez, Julia
Afternoon of a Faun: A Novel. Lasdun, James
Afterparties: Stories. So, Anthony Veasna
Afterparty. Gregory, Daryl
Aftershock. Sorenson, Jill
Aftershock (Jill Sorenson) [Series]. Sorenson, Jill
Against the Day: A Novel. Pynchon, Thomas
Agape Agape. Gaddis, William
Agatha Arch Is Afraid of Everything. Bair, Kristin
Agatha of Little Neon. Luchette, Claire
Agatha Raisin and the Quiche of Death. Beaton, M. C.
Agatha Raisin and the Witch of Wyckhadden. Beaton, M. C.
Agatha Raisin mysteries [Series]. Beaton, M. C.
Age of Iron. Coetzee, J. M.
The *Age of Light*. Scharer, Whitney
The *Age of Miracles: A Novel*. Walker, Karen Thompson
The *Age of Reason*. Sartre, Jean Paul
The *Age of Shiva: A Novel*. Suri, Manil

Agee, James
★*A Death in the Family*

Agee, Jonis
The Bones of Paradise
★*Agency*. Gibson, William
Agent 6. Smith, Tom Rob
Agent Running in the Field. Le Carre, John
Agent Sayer Altair novels [Series]. Cooper, Ellison
Agents of the crown (Clements) [Series]. Clements, Oliver

AGGRESSION (INTERNATIONAL RELATIONS)
Liu, Ken. *The Wall of Storms*

AGGRESSIVENESS IN CHILDREN
Arnett, Kristen N. *With Teeth: A Novel*

AGING
Allende, Isabel. *The Japanese Lover*

Atkinson, Kate. ★*A God in Ruins*
Atwood, Margaret. *Moral Disorder*
Drabble, Margaret. ★*The Dark Flood Rises*
Ford, Richard. *The Lay of the Land*
Ford, Richard. *Let Me Be Frank with You*
Garcia Marquez, Gabriel. *Memories of My Melancholy Whores*
Groen, Hendrik. *On the Bright Side: The New Secret Diary of Hendrik Groen, 85 Years Old*
Haldeman, Joe W. ★*The Forever War*
Hannah, Sophie. *Perfect Little Children*
Irving, John. *Avenue of Mysteries: A Novel*
Johnson, Denis. *The Largesse of the Sea Maiden: Stories*
McMillan, Terry. ★*It's Not All Downhill from Here: A Novel*
O'Nan, Stewart. *Henry, Himself*
Rooney, Kathleen. ★*Lillian Boxfish Takes a Walk*
Roth, Philip. ★*Everyman*
Roth, Philip. *Exit Ghost*
Roth, Philip. *Sabbath's Theater*
Shriver, Lionel. *Should We Stay or Should We Go*
Smith, Ali. ★*Autumn*
Steinbeck, John. *The Long Valley*
Straub, Emma. ★*Modern Lovers*
Tawada, Yoko. ★*The Emissary*
Ullmann, Linn. *Unquiet: A Novel*
Updike, John. *Licks of Love: Short Stories and a Sequel*
Updike, John. *My Father's Tears and Other Stories*
Van Booy, Simon. *The Illusion of Separateness*
Wilde, Oscar. ★*The Picture of Dorian Gray*
Woolf, Virginia. *The Waves*

AGING — PSYCHOLOGICAL ASPECTS
McMurtry, Larry. *The Evening Star: A Novel*

Agnon, Shmuel Yosef
★*Only Yesterday*

★*The Agony and the Ecstasy: A Biographical Novel of Michelangelo.* Stone, Irving

AGORAPHOBIA
Colgan, Jenny. *Sunrise by the Sea*
Finn, A. J. ★*The Woman in the Window*

AGORAPHOBIA IN WOMEN
Lehane, Dennis. *Since We Fell*
Semple, Maria. *Where'd You Go, Bernadette: A Novel*

AGRIBUSINESS
Bacigalupi, Paolo. ★*The Windup Girl*

AGRICULTURAL LABORERS
Goldman, William. ★*The Princess Bride: S. Morgenstern's Classic Tale of True Love and High Adventure : The*

AGRICULTURE
Reddi, Rishi. *Passage West: A Novel*

The Aguero Sisters. Garcia, Cristina

Aguilar Camin, Hector
Death in Veracruz

Ah, but Your Land Is Beautiful. Paton, Alan

AHAB, CAPTAIN (FICTITIOUS CHARACTER)
Melville, Herman. ★*Moby-Dick; Or, the Whale*

Ahern, Cecelia
Roar

Ahlborn, Ania
The Devil Crept In

Ahmad, Jamil
The Wandering Falcon

Aiding & Abetting. Spark, Muriel

AIDS (DISEASE)
Brunt, Carol Rifka. ★*Tell the Wolves I'm Home: A Novel*
Makkai, Rebecca. ★*The Great Believers*

Aimaq, Jasmine
The Opium Prince

Aimee Leduc investigations [Series]. Black, Cara

AIR BASES
Cussler, Clive. *The Mediterranean Caper*

AIR MAIL SERVICE
Saint-Exupery, Antoine de. *Night Flight*

The Air You Breathe. Peebles, Frances de Pontes

AIRCRAFT CARRIERS
Webb, Brandon. ★*Steel Fear*

AIRPLANE ACCIDENTS
Blume, Judy. *In the Unlikely Event*
Bohjalian, Chris. *The Night Strangers: A Novel*
Cash, Wiley. *When Ghosts Come Home: A Novel*
Clark, Julie. *Last Flight*
Hawley, Noah. *Before the Fall*
L'Amour, Louis. *The Last of the Breed*
MacDonald, Philip. *The List of Adrian Messenger*
Napolitano, Ann. *Dear Edward*
Paris, B. A. ★*The Dilemma*
Parrish, Christa. *Still Life*
Richler, Mordecai. *Solomon Gursky Was Here*
Smith, Scott. *A Simple Plan: A Novel*
Stabenow, Dana. *No Fixed Line*

AIRSHIPS
Ciotta, Beth. *Her Sky Cowboy*
Clark, P. Djeli. *The Black God's Drums*
Edugyan, Esi. ★*Washington Black: A Novel*

Airth, Rennie
The Decent Inn of Death

Ajvide Lindqvist, John
Let the Right One In

Akhtar, Ayad
American Dervish: A Novel
★*Homeland Elegies: A Novel*

AKHTAR, AYAD
Akhtar, Ayad. ★*Homeland Elegies: A Novel*

Akin. Donoghue, Emma

Akinmade-Akerstrom, Lola
In Every Mirror She's Black

Akpan, Uwem
Say You're One of Them

Akunin, B.
The Coronation: The Further Adventures of Erast Fandorin
Sister Pelagia and the White Bulldog: A Mystery

Al Rawi, Shahad
The Baghdad Clock

Al-Ramli, Muhsin
The President's Gardens

ALABAMA
Atkins, Ace. *Wicked City*
Childress, Mark. *Crazy in Alabama*

Everett, Percival L. *I Am Not Sidney Poitier*
Flagg, Fannie. ★*Fried Green Tomatoes at the Whistle Stop Cafe*
Flagg, Fannie. ★*The Wonder Boy of Whistle Stop: A Novel*
Gyasi, Yaa. ★*Transcendent Kingdom*
Johnson, Caleb. *Treeborne*
Kerley, Jack. ★*The Death Collectors*
Lee, Harper. ★*Go Set a Watchman*
Lee, Harper. ★*To Kill a Mockingbird*
Luesse, Valerie Fraser. *Missing Isaac*
McCammon, Robert R. *Boy's Life*
Monroe, Mary. ★*Mrs. Wiggins*
Saums, Mary. *Thistle & Twigg*
Wallace, Daniel. ★*Big Fish: A Novel of Mythic Proportions*
Alam, Rumaan
　★*Leave the World Behind: A Novel*
　That Kind of Mother: A Novel
ALAMEDA, CALIFORNIA
　Carr, Robyn. *The View from Alameda Island: A Novel*
Alameddine, Rabih
　An Unnecessary Woman
　The Wrong End of the Telescope
Alarcon, Daniel
　At Night We Walk in Circles: A Novel
　The King Is Always Above the People: Stories
ALASKA
　Bradbury, Jamey. *The Wild Inside: A Novel*
　Chabon, Michael. *The Yiddish Policemen's Union*
　Fleischmann, Raymond. *How Quickly She Disappears*
　Hannah, Kristin. *The Great Alone*
　Heacox, Kim. *Jimmy Bluefeather: A Novel*
　Laukkanen, Owen. *Gale Force*
　London, Jack. ★*The Call of the Wild*
　Shelton, Paige. *Thin Ice: A Mystery*
　Snow, Jennifer. *An Alaskan Christmas*
　Stabenow, Dana. ★*A Deeper Sleep: A Kate Shugak Novel*
　Stabenow, Dana. ★*A Fine and Bitter Snow: A Kate Shugak Novel*
　Stabenow, Dana. ★*A Grave Denied*
　Stabenow, Dana. ★*Hunter's Moon*
　Stabenow, Dana. *Killing Grounds: A Kate Shugak Mystery*
　Stabenow, Dana. ★*Less Than a Treason*
　Stabenow, Dana. *A Night Too Dark: A Kate Shugak Novel*
　Stabenow, Dana. *No Fixed Line*
　Stabenow, Dana. *Restless in the Grave*
　Stabenow, Dana. *The Singing of the Dead*
　Stabenow, Dana. *So Sure of Death: A Liam Campbell Mystery*
　Stabenow, Dana. *Spoils of the Dead*
　Stabenow, Dana. ★*A Taint in the Blood*
　Stabenow, Dana. *Though Not Dead: A Kate Shugak Novel*
　Stabenow, Dana. *Whisper to the Blood: A Kate Shugak Novel*
　Straley, John. *The Big Both Ways*
Alaska mysteries (Paige Shelton) [Series]. Shelton, Paige
*An **Alaskan** Christmas*. Snow, Jennifer
Albahari, David
　Gotz and Meyer
Albany cycle [Series]. Kennedy, William
ALBANY, NEW YORK
　Kennedy, William. ★*Ironweed: A Novel*
Albert Campion mysteries [Series]. Ripley, Mike

Albert Schmidt novels [Series]. Begley, Louis
ALBERTA
　Adamson, Gil. *The Outlander*
ALBINOS AND ALBINISM
　Dugoni, Robert. ★*The Extraordinary Life of Sam Hell*
　Solomon, Rivers. *Sorrowland*
Albom, Mitch
　The Five People You Meet in Heaven
　The Next Person You Meet in Heaven
　The Stranger in the Lifeboat
ALBUQUERQUE, NEW MEXICO
　Bird, Sarah. ★*The Flamenco Academy: A Novel*
★*The **Alchemist**. Coelho, Paulo
ALCHEMISTS
　Goss, Theodora. *The Strange Case of the Alchemist's Daughter*
ALCHEMY
　Harkness, Deborah E. *The Book of Life*
　Harkness, Deborah E. *A Discovery of Witches: A Novel*
　Harkness, Deborah E. *Shadow of Night*
　Harkness, Deborah E. *The World of All Souls: The Complete Guide to a Discovery of Witches, Shadow of Night, and the Book*
　McGuire, Seanan. ★*Middlegame*
　Sathian, Sanjena. *Gold Diggers*
ALCOHOLIC FATHERS
　Banks, Russell. ★*Affliction*
ALCOHOLIC MEN
　Block, Lawrence. *A Drop of the Hard Stuff: A Matthew Scudder Novel*
　Block, Lawrence. ★*When the Sacred Ginmill Closes*
　Breslin, Jimmy. *Table Money*
　Bronte, Anne. *The Tenant of Wildfell Hall*
　Bruen, Ken. *The Guards*
　Dovlatov, Sergei. *Pushkin Hills*
　Kennedy, William. ★*Ironweed: A Novel*
　King, Stephen. *Cujo*
　McDermott, Alice. ★*Charming Billy*
　Parker, Robert B. *Night Passage*
　Quade, Kirstin Valdez. ★*The Five Wounds: A Novel*
　Richler, Mordecai. *Solomon Gursky Was Here*
ALCOHOLIC MOTHERS
　Crane, Stephen. *Maggie: A Girl of the Streets*
　Lodato, Victor. *Mathilda Savitch*
ALCOHOLIC PRIESTS
　Greene, Graham. *The Power and the Glory*
ALCOHOLIC WOMEN
　Bohjalian, Chris. *The Flight Attendant: A Novel*
　Doyle, Roddy. ★*The Woman Who Walked into Doors*
　Giordano, Mario. ★*Auntie Poldi and the Lost Madonna*
ALCOHOLICS
　Crumley, James. *The Last Good Kiss: A Novel*
　Crumley, James. ★*The Wrong Case*
　Fitzgerald, F. Scott. ★*The Beautiful and Damned*
　Jackson, Charles. *The Lost Weekend*
　McDermott, Alice. ★*Charming Billy*
　Robinson, Marilynne. ★*Jack*
　Willink, Jocko. *Final Spin*
ALCOHOLISM
　Fowler, Therese. ★*Z: A Novel of Zelda Fitzgerald*

Harding, Lisa. *Bright Burning Things*
Jackson, Charles. *The Lost Weekend*
Parini, Jay. *The Passages of H.M.: A Novel of Herman Melville*
Peterson, Tracie. *What Comes My Way*
Stuart, Douglas. ★*Shuggie Bain*

Alcott, Kate
A Touch of Stardust

Alderman, Naomi
★*The Power: A Novel*

Alderson, Kaia
Sisters in Arms

Alderton, Dolly
★*Ghosts: A Novel*

Aleichem, Sholem
Tevye the Dairyman and the Railroad Stories
Tevye's Daughters

Alenyikov, Michael
Ivan and Misha: Stories

ALEUT WOMEN
Stabenow, Dana. ★*Less Than a Treason*
Stabenow, Dana. *No Fixed Line*
Stabenow, Dana. *The Singing of the Dead*
Stabenow, Dana. *Whisper to the Blood: A Kate Shugak Novel*

ALEUTS
Stabenow, Dana. ★*Less Than a Treason*

Alex Cross novels [Series]. Patterson, James
Alex Delaware novels [Series]. Kellerman, Jonathan

ALEXANDER
Renault, Mary. *Funeral Games*
Renault, Mary. *The Persian Boy*

Alexander Cleave trilogy [Series]. Banville, John
Alexander Hawke thrillers [Series]. Bell, Ted
Alexander the Great trilogy (Mary Renault) [Series]. Renault, Mary

Alexander, Jennet
I Kissed a Girl

Alexander, Tamera
★*A Note yet Unsung*
With This Pledge

ALEXANDER, THE GREAT, 356 B.C.-323 B.C.
Bohjalian, Chris. *The Sandcastle Girls*
Eliot, George. ★*The Mill on the Floss*

Alexander, V. S.
The Magdalen Girls

Alexander, Victoria
The Lady Travelers Guide to Larceny with a Dashing Stranger
The Lady Travelers Guide to Scoundrels and Other Gentlemen

Alexandra Cooper novels [Series]. Fairstein, Linda A.
Alexandra Cupidi novels [Series]. Shaw, William
Alexandria quartet [Series]. Durrell, Lawrence

ALEXANDRIA, EGYPT
Durrell, Lawrence. ★*Justine*

ALEXANDRIA, VIRGINIA
Cornwell, Patricia Daniels. *Autopsy*

Alexie, Sherman
Blasphemy: New and Selected Stories
Flight
Reservation Blues

Alexis, Andre
Fifteen Dogs
The Hidden Keys

Alfon, Dov
A Long Night in Paris

ALFRED
Cornwell, Bernard. *The Last Kingdom: A Novel*
Iggulden, Conn. *The Abbot's Tale*

ALFRED, KING OF ENGLAND, 849-899
Beaton, M. C. *Death of a Macho Man*
Thompson, Victoria. *Murder on Wall Street*

ALGAE
Bunn, T. Davis. *Outbreak*

ALGERIA
Adimi, Kaouther. *Our Riches*
Boudjedra, Rachid. *The Barbary Figs*
Camus, Albert. *The Plague*
Camus, Albert. ★*The Stranger*
Daoud, Kamel. *The Meursault Investigation*

ALGIERS, ALGERIA
Adimi, Kaouther. *Our Riches*

Algren, Nelson
★*The Man with the Golden Arm: A Novel*
A Walk on the Wild Side

Alharthi, Jokha
Celestial Bodies: A Novel

Ali, Monica
★*Brick Lane: A Novel*

Alias Grace. Atwood, Margaret

ALIBI
Harper, Jane. *The Dry*

Alice & Oliver: A Novel. Bock, Charles
★*Alice Adams.* Tarkington, Booth
Alice I Have Been. Benjamin, Melanie
Alice in Jeopardy. McBain, Ed
Alice Vega novels [Series]. Luna, Louisa

ALIEN ARTIFACTS
Brin, David. *Existence*
Clarke, Arthur C. ★*The Collected Stories of Arthur C. Clarke*
Paolini, Christopher. ★*To Sleep in a Sea of Stars*
Pohl, Frederik. *Gateway*

ALIEN CHILDREN (HUMANOID)
McCaffrey, Anne. ★*Acorna: The Unicorn Girl*

ALIENATION (SOCIAL PSYCHOLOGY)
Aboulela, Leila. *Elsewhere, Home*
Baldwin, James. ★*Giovanni's Room*
Castel-Bloom, Orly. *Textile*
Dos Passos, John. *Manhattan Transfer*
Hemingway, Ernest. ★*The Sun Also Rises*
Joyce, James. ★*Ulysses*
Kafka, Franz. ★*The Trial*
Levin, Adam. *Bubblegum*
Mengestu, Dinaw. ★*All Our Names*
Moshfegh, Ottessa. *My Year of Rest and Relaxation*
Murakami, Haruki. *After Dark*
Murakami, Haruki. *The Wind-Up Bird Chronicle*
Murata, Sayaka. *Earthlings: A Novel*
Schulman, Alex. *The Survivors: A Novel*

Sherrill, Steven. *The Minotaur Takes His Own Sweet Time: A Novel*

ALIENATION IN FAMILIES
Burke, Alafair. *The Better Sister: A Novel*

ALIENATION IN MEN
Begley, Louis. *About Schmidt*
Bellow, Saul. ★*Herzog*
Conrad, Joseph. *Victory: An Island Tale*
Cooley, Martha. *The Archivist: A Novel*
Darnielle, John. *Wolf in White Van: A Novel*
Flaubert, Gustave. *Sentimental Education*
Hesse, Hermann. ★*Steppenwolf*
Savage, Sam. *The Way of the Dog: A Novel*
Toole, John Kennedy. ★*A Confederacy of Dunces*

ALIENATION IN TEENAGERS
Salinger, J. D. ★*The Catcher in the Rye*

ALIENATION IN WOMEN
Didion, Joan. ★*Play It as It Lays: A Novel*

★*The Alienist*. Carr, Caleb

ALIENS
Anders, Charlie Jane. ★*The City in the Middle of the Night*
Chambers, Becky. ★*The Galaxy, and the Ground Within*
Cho, Zen. *Spirits Abroad and Other Stories*
Delany, Samuel R. *Aye, and Gomorrah: Stories*
Dewes, J. S. *The Last Watch*
Foster, Alan Dean. *Relic*
Gilman, Carolyn Ives. *Dark Orbit*
Haig, Matt. *The Humans: A Novel*
Haldeman, Joe W. ★*The Forever War*
Harrison, M. John. *Light*
Harrison, M. John. *Nova Swing*
Kress, Nancy. *If Tomorrow Comes*
Kress, Nancy. *Tomorrow's Kin*
Leckie, Ann. *Ancillary Justice*
Leckie, Ann. *Ancillary Mercy*
Leckie, Ann. *Ancillary Sword*
Lem, Stanislaw. *His Master's Voice*
Liu, Cixin. ★*The Dark Forest*
Liu, Cixin. ★*Death's End*
Liu, Cixin. ★*The Three-Body Problem*
Okorafor, Nnedi. ★*Binti*
Okorafor, Nnedi. *Binti: Home*
Okorafor, Nnedi. *Binti: The Night Masquerade*
Paolini, Christopher. ★*To Sleep in a Sea of Stars*
Porter, Chana. *The Seep: A Novel*
Reynolds, Alastair. *Revelation Space*
Sagan, Carl. *Contact: A Novel*
Thompson, Tade. *Rosewater*
Thompson, Tade. *The Rosewater Insurrection*
Thompson, Tade. *The Rosewater Redemption*
Turnbull, Cadwell. ★*The Lesson*
Valente, Catherynne M. *Radiance*
Valente, Catherynne M. *Space Opera*
Varley, John. *Demon*
Varley, John. ★*Titan*
Wagers, K. B. *There Before the Chaos*
Whiteley, Aliya. *From the Neck up and Other Stories*
Williams, Drew. *The Stars Now Unclaimed*

ALIENS (HUMANOID)
Adams, Douglas. ★*The Hitchhiker's Guide to the Galaxy*
Adams, Douglas. *The Restaurant at the End of the Universe*
Banks, Iain. *Matter*
Card, Orson Scott. ★*Ender's Game*
Egan, Greg. *Phoresis*
Le Guin, Ursula K. *The Birthday of the World: And Other Stories*
Le Guin, Ursula K. *The Telling*
Scalzi, John. *Redshirts: A Novel with Three Codas*

ALIENS (HUMANOID) — SIGHTINGS AND ENCOUNTERS
Cherryh, C. J. *Foreigner: A Novel of First Contact*

ALIENS (NON-HUMANOID)
Bear, Greg. *The Forge of God*
Burke, Sue. *Semiosis*
Butler, Octavia E. *Adulthood Rites*
Butler, Octavia E. *Bloodchild: And Other Stories*
Butler, Octavia E. ★*Dawn: Xenogenesis*
Chambers, Becky. *A Closed and Common Orbit*
Chambers, Becky. ★*The Long Way to a Small, Angry Planet*
Clarke, Arthur C. ★*Childhood's End*
Gilman, Carolyn Ives. *Dark Orbit*
Hamilton, Peter F. *Pandora's Star*
Heinlein, Robert A. ★*Starship Troopers*
Lem, Stanislaw. ★*Solaris*
McDevitt, Jack. *The Engines of God*
Thompson, Tade. *Rosewater*
Thompson, Tade. *The Rosewater Insurrection*
Thompson, Tade. *The Rosewater Redemption*
Varley, John. *Demon*
Varley, John. ★*Titan*
Vinge, Vernor. *A Fire Upon the Deep*

ALIENS (NON-HUMANOID) — SIGHTINGS AND ENCOUNTERS
Wells, H. G. ★*The War of the Worlds*

Alif the Unseen. Wilson, G. Willow

Aliu, Xhenet
★*Brass: A Novel*

All About Lulu: A Novel. Evison, Jonathan
★*All Adults Here*. Straub, Emma
All Girls. Layden, Emily
All Hat: A Novel. Smith, B. J.
All I Did Was Shoot My Man: A Leonid McGill Mystery. Mosley, Walter
All Mortal Flesh. Spencer-Fleming, Julia
All My Mother's Lovers: A Novel. Masad, Ilana
★*All Our Names*. Mengestu, Dinaw
All Our Shimmering Skies. Dalton, Trent
All Passion Spent. Sackville-West, V.
★*All Quiet on the Western Front*. Remarque, Erich Maria
All souls trilogy [Series]. Harkness, Deborah E.
All souls universe [Series]. Harkness, Deborah E.
All Systems Red. Wells, Martha
All That I Have: A Novel. Freeman, Castle
★*All the Birds in the Sky*. Anders, Charlie Jane
All the Children Are Home. Francis, Patry
All the Colors of Darkness. Robinson, Peter
★*All the Colors of Night*. Krentz, Jayne Ann
All the Devils. Eisler, Barry
★*All the Devils Are Here*. Penny, Louise

All the Feels. Dade, Olivia
All the Flowers Are Dying. Block, Lawrence
All the King's Men. Warren, Robert Penn
★*All* the Light We Cannot See: A Novel. Doerr, Anthony
All the Lives We Never Lived: A Novel. Roy, Anuradha
All the Names. Saramago, Jose
★*All* the Old Knives. Steinhauer, Olen
★*All* the Pretty Horses. McCarthy, Cormac
All the Time in the World: New and Selected Stories. Doctorow, E. L.
All the Water I've Seen Is Running: A Novel. Rodrigues, Elias
All the Ways We Said Goodbye: A Novel of the Ritz Paris. Williams, Beatriz
All the Windwracked Stars. Bear, Elizabeth
All the Wrong Places: A Novel. Fielding, Joy
★*All* Things Cease to Appear. Brundage, Elizabeth
★*All* This Could Be Yours. Attenberg, Jami
All Your Perfects. Hoover, Colleen
Allain, Suzanne
   Miss Lattimore's Letter
ALLEGORIES
   Abe, Kobo. *The Woman in the Dunes*
   Agnon, Shmuel Yosef. ★*Only Yesterday*
   Ahern, Cecelia. *Roar*
   Alomar, Osama. *The Teeth of the Comb & Other Stories*
   Balzac, Honore de. *Eugenie Grandet*
   Barth, John. ★*Giles Goat-Boy ;: Or, the Revised New Syllabus*
   Bauman, Bruce. ★*Broken Sleep: An American Dream*
   Bulgakov, Mikhail. ★*The Master and Margarita*
   Coelho, Paulo. ★*The Alchemist*
   Coetzee, J. M. ★*Foe*
   Gao, XIngjian. *Soul Mountain*
   Hemingway, Ernest. ★*The Old Man and the Sea*
   Hesse, Hermann. *The Fairy Tales of Hermann Hesse*
   Kadare, Ismail. ★*The Three-Arched Bridge*
   Kafka, Franz. ★*The Metamorphosis*
   Kafka, Franz. ★*The Trial*
   Mann, Thomas. *The Magic Mountain*
   Melville, Herman. ★*Moby-Dick; Or, the Whale*
   Orwell, George. ★*Animal Farm*
   Pelevin, Viktor. *The Hall of Singing Caryatids*
   Porter, Katherine Anne. *Ship of Fools*
   Rawlings, David. *The Baggage Handler: A Novel*
   Rushdie, Salman. *Haroun and the Sea of Stories*
   Saint-Exupery, Antoine de. ★*The Little Prince*
Allen, Jane
   I Lost My Girlish Laughter
Allen, Jayne
   Black Girls Must Die Exhausted
Allen, Sarah Addison
   Garden Spells
   The Girl Who Chased the Moon: A Novel
Allen, Susanna
   A Wolf in Duke's Clothing
Allende, Isabel
   Daughter of Fortune: A Novel
   ★*Eva Luna*
   ★*The House of the Spirits*
   In the Midst of Winter: A Novel

   The Japanese Lover
   A Long Petal of the Sea: A Novel
   Of Love and Shadows
   Portrait in Sepia: A Novel
   Ripper: A Novel
   The Stories of Eva Luna
ALLIANCES
   Bear, Elizabeth. *Range of Ghosts*
   Bear, Elizabeth. *Shattered Pillars*
   Benn, James R. *Road of Bones: A Billy Boyle World War II Mystery*
   Brown, Dale. *Eagle Station: A Novel*
   Carrick, M. A. *The Mask of Mirrors*
   Chambers, Becky. ★*A Psalm for the Wild-Built*
   Connelly, Michael. *The Night Fire*
   French, Jonathan. *The Free Bastards*
   French, Jonathan. *The True Bastards*
   Kuhn, M. J. *Among Thieves*
   Poole, Sara. *The Borgia Mistress*
   Rollins, James. *The Devil Colony*
   Wagers, K. B. *After the Crown*
   Weir, Andy. *Project Hail Mary*
Allio, Kirstin
   Buddhism for Western Children: A Novel
Allison, Dorothy
   ★*Bastard Out of Carolina*
Almanac of the Dead. Silko, Leslie Marmon
Almost Famous Women: Stories. Bergman, Megan Mayhew
Almost Midnight. Doiron, Paul
The *Almost* Moon: A Novel. Sebold, Alice
Alomar, Osama
   The Teeth of the Comb & Other Stories
Alone. Gardner, Lisa
Alone in the Crowd: An Inspector Espinosa Mystery. Garcia-Roza, L. A.
Alone in the Wild. Armstrong, Kelley
Along Came a Duke. Boyle, Elizabeth
★*Along* Came a Spider: A Novel. Patterson, James
Aloysius Archer novels [Series]. Baldacci, David
ALPS
   Reynolds, Allie. ★*Shiver*
Alpsten, Ellen
   Tsarina
Alsterdal, Tove
   We Know You Remember
Altan, Ahmet
   ★*Love in the Days of Rebellion*
Alten, Steve
   Meg: Generations
ALTERED STATES OF CONSCIOUSNESS
   Chayefsky, Paddy. *Altered States: A Novel*
Altered States: A Novel. Chayefsky, Paddy
ALTERNATE HISTORIES
   Andersen, Laura. *The Boleyn Deceit*
   Andersen, Laura. ★*The Boleyn King*
   Andersen, Laura. *The Boleyn Reckoning*
   Atkinson, Kate. ★*Life After Life: A Novel*
   Binet, Laurent. *Civilizations*
   Bisson, Terry. *Any Day Now*
   Cantor, Jillian. *Half Life*

Chabon, Michael. *The Yiddish Policemen's Union*
Clark, P. Djeli. *The Black God's Drums*
Dick, Philip K. ★*The Man in the High Castle*
Flynn, Michael. *Eifelheim*
Goonan, Kathleen Ann. *In War Times*
Harris, Robert. ★*Fatherland*
Khoury, Raymond. *Empire of Lies*
King, Stephen. *11/22/63*
Kowal, Mary Robinette. *The Calculating Stars: A Lady Astronaut Novel*
Kowal, Mary Robinette. *The Fated Sky: A Lady Astronaut Novel*
Kowal, Mary Robinette. *The Relentless Moon*
Levin, Adam. *Bubblegum*
Levine, David D. *Arabella of Mars*
Means, David. ★*Hystopia: A Novel*
Newland, Courttia. *A River Called Time*
Parry, H. G. *A Declaration of the Rights of Magicians*
Priest, Cherie. *Boneshaker*
Priest, Cherie. *Clementine*
Priest, Cherie. *Dreadnought*
Priest, Cherie. *Ganymede*
Priest, Cherie. *The Inexplicables*
Pulley, Natasha. ★*The Kingdoms*
Robinson, Kim Stanley. *The Years of Rice and Salt*
Roth, Philip. ★*The Plot Against America*
Sittenfeld, Curtis. *Rodham: A Novel*
Sterling, Bruce. *Pirate Utopia*

ALTERNATE REALITY GAMES
Miles, Terry. *Rabbits*

ALTERNATIVE COMICS
Cruse, Howard. *The Complete Wendel*

ALTERNATIVE LIFESTYLES
ffitch, Madeline. *Stay and Fight*

ALTRUISM
Butler, Nickolas. ★*The Hearts of Men*

Alvar, Mia
In the Country: Stories

Alvarez, Julia
★*Afterlife: A Novel*
How the Garcia Girls Lost Their Accents

Always the Last to Know. Higgins, Kristan

Alyan, Hala
Salt Houses

ALZHEIMER'S DISEASE
Henkin, Joshua. *Morningside Heights*
Moore, Liz. *The Unseen World*

Amado, Jorge
★*Dona Flor and Her Two Husbands: A Moral and Amorous Tale*
Gabriela, Clove and Cinnamon

AMATEUR DETECTIVES
Cantero, Edgar. *Meddling Kids: A Novel*
Coben, Harlan. *Long Lost*
DePoy, Phillip. *Sidewalk Saint*
Deveraux, Jude. *A Willing Murder*
Donoghue, Emma. ★*Frog Music*
Doyle, Arthur Conan. ★*The Complete Sherlock Holmes*
Doyle, Arthur Conan. ★*The Hound of the Baskervilles*
Estleman, Loren D. ★*Indigo: A Valentino Mystery*

Finch, Charles. *A Beautiful Blue Death*
Finch, Charles. *The September Society*
Francis, Felix. *Guilty Not Guilty*
Friedman, Daniel. *Riot Most Uncouth: A Lord Byron Mystery*
Gaylin, Alison. *Never Look Back*
Griffiths, Elly. *The Postscript Murders*
Hallinan, Timothy. *Fools' River*
Hambly, Barbara. *House of the Patriarch*
Hambly, Barbara. *Lady of Perdition*
Harris, C. S. *What the Devil Knows: A Sebastian St. Cyr Mystery*
Iles, Greg. *Cemetery Road: A Novel*
James, Miranda. *What the Cat Dragged In*
Lloyd, Catherine. *Death Comes to the Nursery*
Lloyd, Catherine. *Death Comes to the Rectory*
Malliet, G. M. *A Demon Summer: A Max Tudor Mystery*
Malliet, G. M. *Pagan Spring: A Mystery*
Orczy, Emmuska Orczy. *The Old Man in the Corner*
Osman, Richard. *The Man Who Died Twice: A Thursday Murder Club Mystery*
Osman, Richard. ★*The Thursday Murder Club*
Pearl, Matthew. *The Dante Chamber*
Peters, Ellis. *Brother Cadfael's Penance*
Peters, Ellis. *The Holy Thief*
Pirie, David. *The Patient's Eyes*
Quick, Amanda. *Garden of Lies*
Quincy, D. M. *Murder at the Opera*
Ramsay, Frederick. *Countdown*
Rice, Craig. *Home Sweet Homicide*
Ripley, Mike. *Mr Campion's Coven*
Ripley, Mike. *Mr Campion's Fault*
Ripley, Mike. *Mr. Campion's War*
Runcie, James. *Sidney Chambers and the Forgiveness of Sins*
Runcie, James. *Sidney Chambers and the Perils of the Night*
Runcie, James. *Sidney Chambers and the Persistence of Love*
Runcie, James. *Sidney Chambers and the Problem of Evil*
Runcie, James. *Sidney Chambers and the Shadow of Death*
Sayers, Dorothy L. ★*Clouds of Witness*
Sayers, Dorothy L. ★*The Five Red Herrings*
Sayers, Dorothy L. ★*Gaudy Night*
Sayers, Dorothy L. *Hangman's Holiday*
Sayers, Dorothy L. *In the Teeth of the Evidence*
Sayers, Dorothy L. ★*Lord Peter*
Sayers, Dorothy L. *Murder Must Advertise*
Sayers, Dorothy L. *The Nine Tailors*
Sayers, Dorothy L. *Thrones, Dominations*
Sayers, Dorothy L. *The Unpleasantness at the Bellona Club*
Sayers, Dorothy L. ★*Whose Body?: A Lord Peter Wimsey Novel*
Scerbanenco, Giorgio. *Traitors to All*
Simpson, Rosemary. *Let the Dead Keep Their Secrets*
Starr, Melvin R. *Unhallowed Ground*
Thomson, E. S. *The Blood*

The *Amateur* Marriage: A Novel. Tyler, Anne
The *Amazing* Adventures of Kavalier & Clay: A Novel. Chabon, Michael

AMAZON VALLEY
Patchett, Ann. ★*State of Wonder: A Novel*

AMBASSADORS
Clancy, Tom. *Clear and Present Danger*
Hao, Jingfang. *Vagabonds: A Novel*

Martine, Arkady. ★*A Memory Called Empire*
Turnbull, Cadwell. ★*The Lesson*
Amberville. Davys, Tim
AMBITION
  Askaripour, Mateo. ★*Black Buck*
  Auci, Stefania. *The Florios of Sicily: A Novel*
  Benedict, Marie. ★*Lady Clementine*
  Castellani, Christopher. *Leading Men: A Novel*
  Diofebi, Dario. *Paradise, Nevada*
  Dobmeier, Tracy. ★*Girls with Bright Futures: A Novel*
  Dunant, Sarah. *Blood and Beauty: A Novel*
  Faye, Lyndsay. ★*The King of Infinite Space*
  Follett, Ken. *A Column of Fire*
  Follett, Ken. *World Without End*
  Gabel, Aja. *The Ensemble: A Novel*
  Gregory, Philippa. *The Boleyn Inheritance*
  Gregory, Philippa. *The Lady of the Rivers*
  Gregory, Philippa. *The Other Boleyn Girl: A Novel*
  Gregory, Philippa. *The Red Queen: A Novel*
  Gregory, Philippa. *The White Princess*
  Haigh, Jennifer. *Baker Towers: A Novel*
  Harvey, Michael T. *The Governor's Wife*
  Howrey, Meg. *The Wanderers*
  Kadrey, Richard. *The Grand Dark*
  Lattari, Katie. *Dark Things I Adore*
  Lewis, Sinclair. ★*Elmer Gantry*
  Lindsay, Jeffry P. *Just Watch Me*
  Martin, George R. R. ★*A Clash of Kings*
  Martin, George R. R. ★*A Dance with Dragons*
  Martin, George R. R. ★*A Feast for Crows*
  Martin, George R. R. ★*A Game of Thrones*
  Martin, George R. R. ★*A Storm of Swords*
  Maugham, W. Somerset. *The Moon and Sixpence*
  McKenzie, Elizabeth. *The Portable Veblen*
  Parker-Chan, Shelley. ★*She Who Became the Sun*
  Pomerantz, Sharon. *Rich Boy*
  Rachman, Tom. *The Italian Teacher*
  Rushdie, Salman. ★*The Golden House*
  Sathian, Sanjena. *Gold Diggers*
  Serle, Rebecca. *In Five Years: A Novel*
  Shepard, Jim. *The World to Come: Stories*
  Simpson, Mona. *Anywhere but Here*
  Smith, Gregory Blake. ★*The Maze at Windermere: A Novel*
  Swyler, Erika. ★*Light from Other Stars: A Novel*
  Tobar, Hector. *The Last Great Road Bum*
  Walsh, M. O. ★*The Big Door Prize: A Novel*
  Wang, Kathy. *Family Trust: A Novel*
  Woods, Stuart. *Below the Belt*
  Woods, Stuart. *Fast & Loose*
  Yanagihara, Hanya. *A Little Life: A Novel*
AMBITION IN BOYS
  Box, C. J. *Badlands*
AMBITION IN GIRLS
  Hoffman, Alice. *The Marriage of Opposites: A Novel Based on the Life of Rachel Pizzarro*
AMBITION IN MEN
  Boyne, John. ★*A Ladder to the Sky*
  Burrowes, Grace. ★*A Rogue of Her Own*

Clinch, Jon. *Marley: A Novel*
Cronin, A. J. *Citadel*
Dee, Jonathan. *The Privileges: A Novel*
Dreiser, Theodore. ★*An American Tragedy*
Gray, Erick S. *Love & a Gangsta: A Novel*
Gregory, Philippa. *The Kingmaker's Daughter*
Hegi, Ursula. *The Vision of Emma Blau*
Iggulden, Conn. *The Abbot's Tale*
K'wan. *Street Dreams*
Kohnstamm, Thomas B. *Lake City*
Levin, Ira. *A Kiss Before Dying*
Mantel, Hilary. ★*Bring up the Bodies: A Novel*
Mantel, Hilary. ★*Wolf Hall*
McCullough, Colleen. *The First Man in Rome*
McEwan, Ian. ★*Amsterdam*
McQuiston, Casey. ★*Red, White & Royal Blue: A Novel*
Meyer, Philipp. ★*The Son: A Novel*
Pontoppidan, Henrik. *Lucky Per*
Schwarz, Christina. *The Edge of the Earth*
Vidal, Gore. *Washington, D. C.: A Novel*
Wolfe, Tom. *Back to Blood: A Novel*
AMBITION IN TEENAGE GIRLS
  Mihalic, Susan. *Dark Horses*
AMBITION IN WOMEN
  Abrams, Stacey. *While Justice Sleeps: A Novel*
  Acampora, Lauren. *The Paper Wasp: A Novel*
  Allen, Jayne. *Black Girls Must Die Exhausted*
  Bauer, Belinda. *The Beautiful Dead*
  Blumberg, Chandra. *Digging up Love*
  Bourland, Barbara. ★*Fake Like Me*
  Brockway, Connie. *No Place for a Dame*
  Christopher, Andie J. *Not the Girl You Marry*
  Daria, Alexis. ★*You Had Me at Hola*
  Drake, Olivia. *When a Duke Loves a Governess*
  Fowler, Therese. *A Well-Behaved Woman: A Novel of the Vanderbilts*
  Francis-Sharma, Lauren. ★*Book of the Little Axe*
  George, Margaret. *The Confessions of Young Nero*
  Glass, Seressia. ★*The Love Con*
  Gortner, C. W. *The First Actress: A Novel of Sarah Bernhardt*
  Gyasi, Yaa. ★*Transcendent Kingdom*
  Hostin, Sunny. ★*Summer on the Bluffs*
  Hughes, Caoilinn. *Orchid and the Wasp*
  Jenkins, Beverly. *Rebel*
  Jin, Meng. *Little Gods*
  Kantra, Virginia. ★*Meg and Jo*
  Kelly, Erin. *Watch Her Fall*
  Kidd, Sue Monk. ★*The Book of Longings*
  Laureano, C. E. ★*The Saturday Night Supper Club*
  Leckie, Ann. *Provenance*
  Mackintosh, Anneliese. *Bright and Dangerous Objects*
  Messud, Claire. ★*The Woman Upstairs: A Novel*
  Peebles, Frances de Pontes. *The Air You Breathe*
  Pitoniak, Anna. *Necessary People*
  Polk, C. L. *The Midnight Bargain*
  Quincy, Diana. *The Viscount Made Me Do It*
  Rao, Shobha. ★*Girls Burn Brighter*
  Scharer, Whitney. *The Age of Light*
  Sittenfeld, Curtis. *Rodham: A Novel*

Steadman, Catherine. *The Disappearing Act*
Torre, A. R. *Every Last Secret*
Towles, Amor. *Rules of Civility: A Novel*
Welsh, Kaite. *The Unquiet Heart*
Wolitzer, Meg. *The Female Persuasion*
Yang, Susie. *White Ivy: A Novel*

AMBULANCE DRIVERS — HISTORY
Hemingway, Ernest. ★*A Farewell to Arms*

Amdahl, Gary
I Am Death: Two Novellas

America Is Not the Heart. Castillo, Elaine
The American Agent. Winspear, Jacqueline
★*American by Day*. Miller, Derek B.
American chronicle (Gore Vidal) [Series]. Vidal, Gore

AMERICAN CIVIL WAR ERA (1861-1865)
Alexander, Tamera. *With This Pledge*
Brown, Taylor. *Fallen Land*
Cobbs Hoffman, Elizabeth. *The Tubman Command: A Novel*
Cole, Alyssa. ★*An Extraordinary Union*
Cole, Alyssa. ★*A Hope Divided*
Corthron, Kia. *Moon and the Mars*
Crane, Stephen. ★*The Red Badge of Courage: An Episode of the American Civil War*
Doctorow, E. L. *The March: A Novel*
Frazier, Charles. ★*Cold Mountain*
Frazier, Charles. *Varina*
Gleason, Colleen. *Murder at the Capitol*
Harris, C. S. *Good Time Coming*
Hicks, Robert. *The Widow of the South*
Jakes, John. *Love and War*
Johnson, Tara. *Engraved on the Heart*
Kantor, MacKinlay. ★*Andersonville*
Mitchell, Margaret. ★*Gone with the Wind*
Olmstead, Robert. ★*Coal Black Horse*
Piercy, Marge. *Sex Wars*
Shaara, Jeff. *Gods and Generals: A Novel of the Civil War*
Shaara, Jeff. *The Last Full Measure*
Shaara, Michael. ★*The Killer Angels: A Novel*
Warren, Robert Penn. *Band of Angels*
West, Jessamyn. *The Friendly Persuasion*

American Dervish: A Novel. Akhtar, Ayad

AMERICAN DREAM
Evison, Jonathan. ★*Lawn Boy: A Novel*
Evison, Jonathan. ★*Small World*
Fitzgerald, F. Scott. ★*The Last Tycoon: An Unfinished Novel*
Ramos, Joanne. *The Farm: A Novel*
Roth, Philip. ★*American Pastoral*
Skyhorse, Brando. *Madonnas of Echo Park: A Novel*

★*American Dreamer*. Herrera, Adriana
American Dreams. Sapphire
American Fairytale. Herrera, Adriana
American fantastic tales [Series].
The American Fiancee: A Novel. Dupont, Eric
★*American Gods: A Novel*. Gaiman, Neil
The American Heiress. Goodwin, Daisy
An **American** heiress in London [Series]. Guhrke, Laura Lee
★*American Histories: Stories*. Wideman, John Edgar
American Housewife: Stories. Ellis, Helen

American Innovations: Stories. Galchen, Rivka
American Love Story. Herrera, Adriana
★*An American Marriage: A Novel*. Jones, Tayari
★*American Pastoral*. Roth, Philip

AMERICAN REVOLUTION, 1775-1783
Cobbs Hoffman, Elizabeth. *The Hamilton Affair*
Harkness, Deborah E. *Time's Convert*

AMERICAN SIGN LANGUAGE
Gruen, Sara. *The Ape House*

An American Spy. Steinhauer, Olen
★*American Spy: A Novel*. Wilkinson, Lauren
American Tabloid: A Novel. Ellroy, James
★*An American Tragedy*. Dreiser, Theodore
American War. El Akkad, Omar

AMERICAN WESTWARD EXPANSION (1803-1899)
Bird, Sarah. *Daughter of a Daughter of a Queen*
Bittner, Rosanne. *Logan's Lady*
Dallas, Sandra. *The Last Midwife*
Dallas, Sandra. *Westering Women: A Novel*
Davies, Carys. *West*
Diaz, Hernan. ★*In the Distance*
Gilman, Laura Anne. *The Cold Eye*
Gilman, Laura Anne. *Silver on the Road*
Guthrie, A. B. ★*The Big Sky*
Harmon, Amy. *Where the Lost Wander*
Jenkins, Beverly. *Tempest*
Jenkins, Beverly. *Wild Rain*
Jiles, Paulette. *News of the World: A Novel*
Katsu, Alma. *The Hunger: A Novel*
Kirkpatrick, Jane. *One More River to Cross*
Larison, John. *Whiskey When We're Dry*
Malerman, Josh. *Unbury Carol*
Michener, James A. ★*Centennial*
Obreht, Tea. *Inland: A Novel*
Priest, Cherie. *Boneshaker*
Priest, Cherie. *Dreadnought*
Punke, Michael. *Ridgeline: A Novel*
Rivers, Francine. ★*Redeeming Love*
Russell, Mary Doria. ★*Doc: A Novel*
Russell, Mary Doria. *Epitaph: A Novel of the O.K. Corral*
Schanbacher, Gary Lester. *Crossing Purgatory*

★*Americanah: a Novel*. Adichie, Chimamanda Ngozi

AMERICANS IN AFGHANISTAN
Florio, Gwen. *Silent Hearts*

AMERICANS IN AFRICA
Bellow, Saul. ★*Henderson the Rain King: A Novel*
Crouch, Katie. *Embassy Wife*
Kingsolver, Barbara. ★*The Poisonwood Bible: A Novel*
Rush, Norman. ★*Mating*

AMERICANS IN AUSTRALIA
London, Stefanie. *The Aussie Next Door*

AMERICANS IN BULGARIA
Greenwell, Garth. *What Belongs to You: A Novel*

AMERICANS IN CONGO (DEMOCRATIC REPUBLIC)
Kingsolver, Barbara. ★*The Poisonwood Bible: A Novel*

AMERICANS IN CUBA
Hemingway, Ernest. *To Have and Have Not*

AMERICANS IN EASTERN EUROPE
  Greenwell, Garth. *Cleanness*
AMERICANS IN EGYPT
  Neubauer, Erica Ruth. *Murder at the Mena House*
AMERICANS IN ENGLAND
  Aaronovitch, Ben. *Whispers Under Ground*
  Cocks, Heather. *The Royal We*
  Goodwin, Daisy. *The American Heiress*
  James, Henry. *The Portrait of a Lady*
  Murdoch, Iris. *An Accidental Man*
  Stratford, Sarah-Jane. *Red Letter Days*
  Winspear, Jacqueline. *The American Agent*
AMERICANS IN EUROPE
  Hemingway, Ernest. ★*The Sun Also Rises*
  James, Henry. *Complete Stories, 1874-1884*
  James, Henry. *Complete Stories, 1884-1891*
  James, Henry. *Complete Stories, 1892-1898*
  James, Henry. *Complete Stories, 1898-1910*
  James, Henry. *Daisy Miller*
  James, Henry. *The Wings of the Dove*
  Meacham, Leila. *Dragonfly: A Novel*
  Pynchon, Thomas. ★*Gravity's Rainbow*
AMERICANS IN FOREIGN COUNTRIES
  Greer, Andrew Sean. ★*Less*
  Isaac, Kara. *Then There Was You*
  Leithauser, Brad. *The Promise of Elsewhere*
AMERICANS IN FRANCE
  Baldwin, James. ★*Giovanni's Room*
  Bellow, Saul. *Ravelstein*
  Child, Lee. *The Enemy: A Jack Reacher Novel*
  McLain, Paula. *The Paris Wife: A Novel*
  Miller, Henry. ★*Tropic of Cancer*
  Ozick, Cynthia. *Foreign Bodies*
  Portis, Charles. ★*Masters of Atlantis: A Novel*
  Rosnay, Tatiana de. ★*Sarah's Key*
  Sedaris, David. *Holidays on Ice*
  Wieland, Liza. *Paris, 7 A.M.*
AMERICANS IN GERMANY
  Belfer, Lauren. *And After the Fire: A Novel*
  Chiaverini, Jennifer. *Resistance Women: A Novel*
  Ford, Ford Madox. ★*The Good Soldier: A Tale of Passion*
  Kunzru, Hari. *Red Pill: A Novel*
  Sundin, Sarah. *When Twilight Breaks*
AMERICANS IN GREAT BRITAIN
  Berry, Connie. *A Legacy of Murder*
  Freeman, Dianne. *A Fiancée's Guide to First Wives and Murder*
  Freeman, Dianne. *A Lady's Guide to Etiquette and Murder*
AMERICANS IN GREECE
  DeLillo, Don. *The Names*
AMERICANS IN HONDURAS
  Theroux, Paul. ★*The Mosquito Coast: A Novel*
AMERICANS IN INDIA
  Bacon, Charlotte. *There Is Room for You*
  Sundaresan, Indu. *The Splendor of Silence: A Novel*
  Umrigar, Thrity N. ★*Honor*
AMERICANS IN IRELAND
  Binchy, Maeve. *Firefly Summer*
  Connolly, Sheila. *The Lost Traveller*

French, Tana. ★*The Searcher*
  O'Farrell, Maggie. *This Must Be the Place*
AMERICANS IN ISRAEL
  Kemelman, Harry. *Monday the Rabbi Took Off*
  Uris, Leon. ★*Exodus*
AMERICANS IN ITALY
  Hemingway, Ernest. ★*A Farewell to Arms*
  Hersey, John. ★*A Bell for Adano*
  Highsmith, Patricia. ★*The Talented Mr. Ripley*
  Rachman, Tom. *The Imperfectionists: A Novel*
AMERICANS IN JAPAN
  Murakami, Ryu. *In the Miso Soup*
  Smith, Martin Cruz. *December 6*
AMERICANS IN KOREA
  Limon, Martin. *War Women*
AMERICANS IN LONDON, ENGLAND
  Lurie, Alison. *Foreign Affairs*
AMERICANS IN MEXICO
  Doerr, Harriet. ★*Stones for Ibarra*
  Fuentes, Carlos. ★*The Old Gringo*
  Gaspar de Alba, Alicia. *Desert Blood: The Juarez Murders*
  McCarthy, Cormac. ★*All the Pretty Horses*
  McCarthy, Cormac. *The Crossing*
  Smith, Scott. *The Ruins: A Novel*
  Traven, B. ★*The Treasure of the Sierra Madre*
AMERICANS IN MOROCCO
  Bowles, Paul. ★*The Sheltering Sky*
AMERICANS IN MOSCOW, RUSSIA
  Harris, Robert. *Archangel: A Novel*
AMERICANS IN PARIS, FRANCE
  Barnes, Djuna. ★*Nightwood*
  Faulks, Sebastian. *Paris Echo: A Novel*
  Miller, Henry. ★*Tropic of Cancer*
AMERICANS IN RUSSIA
  Robbins, David L. *War of the Rats: A Novel*
AMERICANS IN RWANDA
  Leonard, Elmore. *Pagan Babies*
AMERICANS IN SAUDI ARABIA
  Eggers, Dave. *A Hologram for the King: A Novel*
AMERICANS IN SCOTLAND
  McCall Smith, Alexander. *The Comforts of a Muddy Saturday: An Isabel Dalhousie Novel*
AMERICANS IN SINGAPORE
  Kwan, Kevin. *Crazy Rich Asians*
AMERICANS IN SOMALIA
  Farah, Nuruddin. *Crossbones*
  Farah, Nuruddin. *Knots*
AMERICANS IN SOUTH AMERICA
  Klay, Phil. ★*Missionaries*
AMERICANS IN SPAIN
  Hemingway, Ernest. *For Whom the Bell Tolls*
  Straub, Emma. *The Vacationers*
AMERICANS IN SUNDARBANS (BANGLADESH AND INDIA)
  Ghosh, Amitav. *The Hungry Tide*
AMERICANS IN SWEDEN
  Dahl, Arne. *Bad Blood*
AMERICANS IN SWITZERLAND
  Essbaum, Jill Alexander. *Hausfrau: A Novel*

AMERICANS IN THAILAND
Osborne, Lawrence. *The Glass Kingdom: A Novel*
Schwarz, Liese O'Halloran. *What Could Be Saved*
AMERICANS IN THE MIDDLE EAST
Bohjalian, Chris. *The Sandcastle Girls*
AMERICANS IN THE SOVIET UNION
Benn, James R. *Road of Bones: A Billy Boyle World War II Mystery*
AMERICANS IN TOKYO, JAPAN
Murakami, Ryu. *In the Miso Soup*
AMERICANS IN TURKEY
Ackerman, Elliot. *Dark at the Crossing*
Ackerman, Elliot. *Red Dress in Black and White*
AMERICANS IN URUGUAY
Cameron, Peter. *The City of Your Final Destination*
AMERICANS IN VIETNAM
Greene, Graham. ★*The Quiet American*
Kupersmith, Violet. ★*Build Your House Around My Body*
Soli, Tatjana. *The Lotus Eaters*
AMERICANS IN WEST AFRICA
D'Souza, Tony. *Whiteman*
Ames, Jonathan
A Man Named Doll
Amidon, Stephen
Security: A Novel
Amirrezvani, Anita
The Blood of Flowers: A Novel
Equal of the Sun
Amis, Kingsley
★*Lucky Jim*
Amis, Martin
★*Inside Story*
Lionel Asbo: State of England
London Fields: A Novel
★*The Pregnant Widow*
★*Time's Arrow, or the Nature of the Offense*
★*The Zone of Interest: A Novel*
AMIS, MARTIN
Amis, Martin. ★*Inside Story*
AMISH
Castillo, Linda. ★*Fallen*
Castillo, Linda. *Outsider*
Cramer, W. Dale. *Levi's Will: A Novel*
Lewis, Beverly. *The Ebb Tide*
Lewis, Beverly. *The Missing*
Wiseman, Beth. *Listening to Love*
AMISH — SOCIAL LIFE AND CUSTOMS
Lewis, Beverly. *The Brethren*
AMISH FAMILIES
Cramer, W. Dale. *Levi's Will: A Novel*
Lewis, Beverly. *The Brethren*
Amish journey [Series]. Wiseman, Beth
AMISH WOMEN
Lewis, Beverly. *The Ebb Tide*
Lewis, Beverly. *The Preacher's Daughter*
AMISTAD CASE, 1839-1841
Pesci, David. *Amistad: A Novel*
Amistad: a Novel. Pesci, David

Ammaniti, Niccolo
I'm Not Scared
AMNESIA
Abbott, Jeff. *Blame*
Barr, Nevada. *What Rose Forgot*
Chen, Mike. *Here and Now and Then*
Cussler, Clive. *Ghost Ship*
Dodd, Christina. *Dead Girl Running*
Dundas, Chad. *The Blaze*
Eco, Umberto. *The Mysterious Flame of Queen Loana: An Illustrated Novel*
Enger, Leif. *Virgil Wander*
Grant, Mira. *Parasite*
Lee, Patrick. *Runner*
Lightman, Alan P. *The Diagnosis*
Ludlum, Robert. ★*The Bourne Identity*
Machado, Carmen Maria. ★*The Low, Low Woods*
McDonald, Christina. *Behind Every Lie*
Rosenfelt, David. *Blackout*
Ward, Catriona. *The Last House on Needless Street*
Weatherspoon, Rebekah. *A Cowboy to Remember*
Weir, Andy. *Project Hail Mary*
Westlake, Donald E. *Memory*
Wilson, Carter. *Dead Girl in 2a*
★*Amnesty*. Adiga, Aravind
Among the Living. Rabb, Jonathan
Among the Ruins. Khan, Ausma Zehanat
Among Thieves. Kuhn, M. J.
Amos Decker novels [Series]. Baldacci, David
Amos Walker novels [Series]. Estleman, Loren D.
★*Amos Walker: The Complete Story Collection*. Estleman, Loren D.
AMPUTATION
Potzsch, Oliver. *The Werewolf of Bamberg*
Amreekiya: a Novel. Mahmoud, Lena
★*Amsterdam*. McEwan, Ian
AMSTERDAM, NETHERLANDS
Burton, Jessie. *The Miniaturist*
Camus, Albert. ★*The Fall*
Groen, Hendrik. *On the Bright Side: The New Secret Diary of Hendrik Groen, 85 Years Old*
McEwan, Ian. ★*Amsterdam*
Vreeland, Susan. *Girl in Hyacinth Blue*
Amulet. Bolano, Roberto
AMUSEMENT PARK EMPLOYEES
Verble, Margaret. ★*When Two Feathers Fell from the Sky*
AMUSEMENT PARKS
Albom, Mitch. *The Next Person You Meet in Heaven*
Barnes, Julian. ★*England, England*
Hand, Elizabeth. *Curious Toys*
Russell, Karen. ★*Swamplandia!*
Verble, Margaret. ★*When Two Feathers Fell from the Sky*
AMUSEMENT RIDES
Albom, Mitch. *The Next Person You Meet in Heaven*
Amy and Isabelle: A Novel. Strout, Elizabeth
AMYOTROPHIC LATERAL SCLEROSIS — PATIENTS
Genova, Lisa. *Every Note Played*
Anam, Tahmima
The Bones of Grace

FICTION CORE COLLECTION
TWENTY-FIRST EDITION

The Startup Wife

ANANSI (LEGENDARY CHARACTER)
Gaiman, Neil. ★*Anansi Boys: A Novel*

★*Anansi Boys: A Novel*. Gaiman, Neil

Anappara, Deepa
Djinn Patrol on the Purple Line: A Novel

ANARCHISM
Sainz Borgo, Karina. ★*It Would Be Night in Caracas*

ANARCHISTS
Auster, Paul. ★*Leviathan*
Barthelme, Frederick. *Painted Desert: A Novel*
Baxter, Charles. ★*The Sun Collective*
Goldstone, Lawrence. *Assassin of Shadows*
Le Guin, Ursula K. ★*The Dispossessed: An Ambiguous Utopia*

ANASAZI CULTURE
Preston, Douglas J. *Thunderhead*

Anathem. Stephenson, Neal

ANATOMISTS
Robertson, Imogen. *Circle of Shadows*
Robertson, Imogen. *Instruments of Darkness: A Novel*
Robertson, Imogen. *Island of Bones*

ANATOMISTS — HISTORY
Robertson, Imogen. *Anatomy of Murder*

ANATOMY
Kidd, Jess. ★*Things in Jars*

★*The Anatomy Lesson*. Roth, Philip

★*Anatomy of a Killer ;: A Shroud for Jesso*. Rabe, Peter

Anatomy of a Miracle. Miles, Jonathan

★*Anatomy of a Scandal: A Novel*. Vaughan, Sarah

The Anatomy of Desire. Dorn, L. R.

Anatomy of Murder. Robertson, Imogen

Anaya, Rudolfo A.
The Man Who Could Fly and Other Stories

ANCESTORS
Butler, Octavia E. ★*Kindred*
Evison, Jonathan. ★*Small World*
Gyasi, Yaa. ★*Homegoing: A Novel*
Jeffers, Honoree Fanonne. ★*The Love Songs of W. E. B. Du Bois*
Lukas, Michael David. *The Last Watchman of Old Cairo: A Novel*
Perkins, S. C. *Murder Once Removed*
Tepper, Sheri S. *The Visitor*

Ancestry detective novels [Series]. Perkins, S. C.

ANCHORAGE, ALASKA
Stabenow, Dana. ★*A Deeper Sleep: A Kate Shugak Novel*
Stabenow, Dana. ★*A Taint in the Blood*

Anchored Hearts. Oliveras, Priscilla

ANCIENT AEGEAN CIVILIZATIONS (3000?1000 BCE)
Barker, Pat. ★*The Silence of the Girls: A Novel*
Barker, Pat. *The Women of Troy*
Haynes, Natalie. *A Thousand Ships*
Miller, Madeline. ★*Circe*
Miller, Madeline. *The Song of Achilles*

The Ancient Child: A Novel. Momaday, N. Scott

ANCIENT EGYPT
Greenwood, Kerry. *Out of the Black Land*
Saylor, Steven. *Raiders of the Nile: A Novel of the Ancient World*
Saylor, Steven. *Wrath of the Furies: A Novel of the Ancient World*

ANCIENT EGYPT (3100 BCE-640 CE)
Greenwood, Kerry. *Out of the Black Land*
Saylor, Steven. *The Judgment of Caesar: A Novel of Ancient Rome*
Saylor, Steven. *Raiders of the Nile: A Novel of the Ancient World*
Saylor, Steven. *Wrath of the Furies: A Novel of the Ancient World*

ANCIENT GREECE
Corby, Gary. *The Marathon Conspiracy*
Haynes, Natalie. *A Thousand Ships*
Malouf, David. *Ransom*
Miller, Madeline. ★*Circe*
Miller, Madeline. *The Song of Achilles*
Renault, Mary. *Funeral Games*
Renault, Mary. *The Last of the Wine*
Saint, Jennifer. *Ariadne*
Toibin, Colm. *House of Names*
Walton, Jo. ★*Necessity*

ANCIENT GREECE (800 BCE-640 CE)
Afshar, Tessa. *Thief of Corinth*
Corby, Gary. *The Marathon Conspiracy*
Malouf, David. *Ransom*
Renault, Mary. *Funeral Games*
Renault, Mary. *The Last of the Wine*
Rice, Anne. *Blackwood Farm*
Toibin, Colm. *House of Names*

Ancient Light. Banville, John

Ancillary Justice. Leckie, Ann

Ancillary Mercy. Leckie, Ann

Ancillary Sword. Leckie, Ann

And After the Fire: A Novel. Belfer, Lauren

And Now She's Gone. Hall, Rachel Howzell

And Sometimes I Wonder About You: A Leonid McGill Mystery. Mosley, Walter

And the Miss Ran Away with the Rake. Boyle, Elizabeth

★*And Then There Were None*. Christie, Agatha

★*And When She Was Good*. Lippman, Laura

Anders, Adriana
Under Her Skin

Anders, Charlie Jane
★*All the Birds in the Sky*
★*The City in the Middle of the Night*
Rock Manning Goes for Broke

Andersen, Laura
The Boleyn Deceit
★*The Boleyn King*
The Boleyn Reckoning

Anderson, Alison
The Summer Guest

Anderson, Kent
Green Sun: A Novel

Anderson, Kevin J.
Death Warmed Over
The Last Days of Krypton

★*Andersonville*. Kantor, MacKinlay

Anderton, Jo
Debris

Andreades, Daphne Palasi
Brown Girls

Andrew Yancy novels [Series]. Hiaasen, Carl

Andrew's Brain. Doctorow, E. L.

Andrew, Sally
   The Satanic Mechanic: A Tannie Maria Mystery

Andrews, Donna
   Murder Most Fowl: A Meg Langslow Mystery
   Owl Be Home for Christmas: A Meg Langslow Mystery
   The Twelve Jays of Christmas: A Meg Langslow Mystery

Andrews, Mary Kay
   Sunset Beach

Andrews, Mesu
   Isaiah's Daughter: A Novel of Prophets and Kings
   Of Fire and Lions: A Novel

Andric, Ivo
   The Bridge on the Drina

ANDROGYNY (PSYCHOLOGY)
   Le Guin, Ursula K. ★*The Left Hand of Darkness*

ANDROIDS
   Asimov, Isaac. ★*I, Robot*
   Delaney, J. P. *The Perfect Wife: A Novel*
   Dick, Philip K. ★*Do Androids Dream of Electric Sheep?*
   Nguyen, Lena. *We Have Always Been Here*
   Simmons, Dan. *Endymion*
   Simmons, Dan. *The Rise of Endymion*
   Stross, Charles. *Neptune's Brood*
   Stross, Charles. *Saturn's Children: A Space Opera*
   Wells, Martha. *All Systems Red*
   Wells, Martha. *Network Effect*

The Andromeda Evolution: A Novel. Wilson, Daniel H.

Andromeda novels [Series]. Wilson, Daniel H.

Andy Carpenter novels [Series]. Rosenfelt, David

ANESTHESIOLOGISTS
   Cook, Robin. *Charlatans*

Angel & Hannah: A Novel in Verse. Park, Ishle Yi

Angel in a Devil's Arms. Long, Julie Anne

The Angel of Darkness. Carr, Caleb

The Angel's Game. Ruiz Zafon, Carlos

Angelmaker. Harkaway, Nick

Angelo, Megan
   Followers

ANGELS
   Gaiman, Neil. ★*Good Omens: The Nice and Accurate Prophecies of Agnes Nutter, Witch*
   Hackwith, A. J. *The Library of the Unwritten*
   Mandanipour, Shahriar. *Moon Brow*
   Polk, C. L. *Witchmark*

ANGER IN MEN
   Boyle, T. Coraghessan. *The Harder They Come*
   Rubart, James L. ★*The Man He Never Was*
   Winter, Evan. *The Fires of Vengeance*

ANGER IN WOMEN
   Dang, Catherine. *Nice Girls*
   Ellis, Helen. *American Housewife: Stories*
   Giordano, Paolo. ★*The Solitude of Prime Numbers: A Novel*
   Kincaid, Jamaica. *See Now Then*
   Weldon, Fay. *The Life and Loves of a She-Devil*
   Yoder, Rachel. *Nightbitch*

★*Angle* of Repose. Stegner, Wallace

ANGLO-SAXON PERIOD (449-1066)
   Cornwell, Bernard. *The Last Kingdom: A Novel*
   Cornwell, Bernard. *Sword of Kings*
   Follett, Ken. ★*The Evening and the Morning*
   Griffith, Nicola. *Hild: A Novel*
   Iggulden, Conn. *The Abbot's Tale*
   Ishiguro, Kazuo. *The Buried Giant: A Novel*
   Rutherfurd, Edward. *London*
   Seton, Anya. *Avalon*

An Angry-Ass Black Woman. Miller, Karen E. Quinones

Animal. K'wan

Animal II: The Omen. K'wan

ANIMAL ATTACKS
   King, Stephen. *Cujo*

ANIMAL BEHAVIOR
   Duncan, Glen. *By Blood We Live*
   Duncan, Glen. *The Last Werewolf*
   Duncan, Glen. *Talulla Rising*

ANIMAL DETECTIVES
   Brown, Rita Mae. *Wish You Were Here*

ANIMAL EXPERIMENTATION
   Wells, H. G. ★*The Island of Dr. Moreau*

★*Animal* Farm. Orwell, George

Animal liberation
   Swarthout, Glendon. *Bless the Beasts and Children*

ANIMAL MUTILATIONS
   Box, C. J. *Trophy Hunt: A Joe Pickett Novel*

Animal novels (K'wan) [Series]. K'wan

ANIMAL RESCUE
   Cameron, W. Bruce. *The Dogs of Christmas*
   Cooney, Ellen. *The Mountaintop School for Dogs and Other Second Chances*
   Kerr, Laurel. *Wild on My Mind*

ANIMAL RIGHTS
   Fowler, Karen Joy. ★*We Are All Completely Beside Ourselves*
   Geni, Abby. *The Wildlands: A Novel*
   Leon, Donna. *Beastly Things: A Commissario Guido Brunetti Mystery*

ANIMAL RIGHTS ADVOCATES
   Follett, Ken. ★*Whiteout*
   Geni, Abby. *The Wildlands: A Novel*
   Scottoline, Lisa. *Legal Tender*

ANIMAL SHELTER WORKERS
   Cameron, W. Bruce. *The Dogs of Christmas*

ANIMAL WELFARE
   Cooney, Ellen. *The Mountaintop School for Dogs and Other Second Chances*
   Del Amo, Jean-Baptiste. *Animalia*
   Picoult, Jodi. *Leaving Time: A Novel*
   Rosenfelt, David. ★*Dog Eat Dog*
   Spencer, Scott. *Man in the Woods*

Animal's People. Sinha, Indra

Animalia. Del Amo, Jean-Baptiste

ANIMALS
   Alomar, Osama. *The Teeth of the Comb & Other Stories*
   Kerr, Laurel. *Wild on My Mind*

The Animals at Lockwood Manor. Healey, Jane

ANKH-MORPORK (IMAGINARY PLACE)

Pratchett, Terry. *Going Postal: A Novel of Discworld*
Pratchett, Terry. *Guards! Guards!*
Pratchett, Terry. *Men at Arms: A Novel of Discworld*
Pratchett, Terry. *Pyramids: The Book of Going Forth*
Pratchett, Terry. *Thud!: A Novel of Discworld*

ANN ARBOR, MICHIGAN

Baxter, Charles. *The Feast of Love*
Ann Lindell novels [Series]. Eriksson, Kjell
★*Anna Karenina*. Tolstoy, Leo
Anna of Kleve: The Princess in the Portrait. Weir, Alison
Anna Pigeon mysteries [Series]. Barr, Nevada

ANNE

Weir, Alison. *Anna of Kleve: The Princess in the Portrait*

ANNE BOLEYN

Adler-Olsen, Jussi. *The Keeper of Lost Causes*
Andersen, Laura. *The Boleyn Deceit*
Andersen, Laura. ★*The Boleyn King*
Andersen, Laura. *The Boleyn Reckoning*
Banks, Maya. *Never Seduce a Scot*
Mayor, Archer. *Red Herring: A Joe Gunther Novel*
Anne Boleyn trilogy [Series]. Andersen, Laura

ANNE, OF CLEVES, QUEEN, CONSORT OF HENRY VIII, KING OF ENGLAND, 1515-1557

Carty-Williams, Candice. ★*Queenie*
★*Annie John*. Kincaid, Jamaica
Annie's people [Series]. Lewis, Beverly
★*Annihilation: a Novel*. Vandermeer, Jeff
*An **Anonymous** Girl*. Hendricks, Greer

ANONYMOUS LETTERS

Allain, Suzanne. *Miss Lattimore's Letter*
Glass, Seraphina Nova. *Someone's Listening*
James, P. D. *The Skull Beneath the Skin*
Koontz, Dean R. *Velocity*

ANONYMOUS PERSONS

Davies, Peter Ho. *A Lie Someone Told You About Yourself*

ANONYMS AND PSEUDONYMS

Mosley, Walter. ★*John Woman*

ANOREXIA NERVOSA

Giordano, Paolo. ★*The Solitude of Prime Numbers: A Novel*
★*Another Brooklyn*. Woodson, Jacqueline
★*Another Country*. Baldwin, James
Another day [Series]. Maguire, Gregory
Another Kind of Eden. Burke, James Lee
Another Time, Another Life: The Story of a Crime. Persson, Leif G. W.
Another World. Barker, Pat

ANSCHLUSS MOVEMENT, 1918-1938

Clayton, Meg Waite. *The Last Train to London*

Anshaw, Carol

Carry the One

Anstruther, Eleanor

A Perfect Explanation
Antarctica. Robinson, Kim Stanley

ANTARCTICA

Bledsoe, Lucy Jane. *The Big Bang Symphony: A Novel of Antarctica*
Bolton, S. J. *The Split*
McGregor, Jon. *Lean Fall Stand*
Robinson, Kim Stanley. *Antarctica*

Robinson, Kim Stanley. *The Martians*
Semple, Maria. *Where'd You Go, Bernadette: A Novel*

ANTEBELLUM AMERICA (1820-1861)

Asim, Jabari. ★*Yonder*
Chevalier, Tracy. *The Last Runaway*
Coates, Ta-Nehisi. ★*The Water Dancer: A Novel*
Corthron, Kia. *Moon and the Mars*
Evison, Jonathan. ★*Small World*
Faye, Lyndsay. *Seven for a Secret*
Hambly, Barbara. *House of the Patriarch*
Hambly, Barbara. *Lady of Perdition*
Johnson, Sadeqa. ★*Yellow Wife*
Jones, Robert. ★*The Prophets: A Novel*
Kidd, Sue Monk. ★*The Invention of Wings: A Novel*
McBride, James. ★*The Good Lord Bird*
Pesci, David. *Amistad: A Novel*
Rawles, Nancy. *My Jim: A Novel*
Straight, Susan. *A Million Nightingales*
Styron, William. *The Confessions of Nat Turner*
Urquhart, Rachel. *The Visionist*
Whitehead, Colson. ★*The Underground Railroad: A Novel*

ANTHOLOGIES

Barthelme, Donald. *Sixty Stories*
Bear, Greg. *The Collected Stories of Greg Bear*
Clarke, Arthur C. ★*The Collected Stories of Arthur C. Clarke*
Colette. *The Collected Stories of Colette*
Coover, Robert. *Going for a Beer: Selected Short Fictions*
Dahl, Roald. *Collected Stories*
Gogol, Nikolai Vasilievich. *The Collected Tales of Nikolai Gogol*
Henry, O. ★*The Complete Works of O. Henry*
Henry, O. *O. Henry: 101 Stories*
Hesse, Hermann. *The Fairy Tales of Hermann Hesse*
James, Henry. *Complete Stories, 1864-1874*
Kafka, Franz. ★*Collected Stories*
Kiernan, Caitlin R. *The Very Best of Caitlin R. Kiernan*
Nabokov, Vladimir Vladimirovich. *Novels and Memoirs, 1941-51*
Nin, Anais. *Cities of the Interior*
Orczy, Emmuska Orczy. *The Old Man in the Corner*
Poe, Edgar Allan. ★*Complete Stories and Poems of Edgar Allan Poe*
Twain, Mark. ★*The Complete Short Stories of Mark Twain*
Anthony Gethryn mysteries [Series]. MacDonald, Philip

ANTI-APARTHEID MOVEMENTS

Paton, Alan. *Ah, but Your Land Is Beautiful*

ANTI-FASCISM

Hemingway, Ernest. *For Whom the Bell Tolls*
Twardoch, Szczepan. *The King of Warsaw*

ANTI-NAZI MOVEMENT

Black, Cara. ★*Three Hours in Paris*
Chiaverini, Jennifer. *Resistance Women: A Novel*
Ramzipoor, E. R. *The Ventriloquists*

ANTI-SLAVERY MOVEMENTS

Kidd, Sue Monk. ★*The Invention of Wings: A Novel*

ANTIAIRCRAFT GUNS

Kelly, Julia. *The Light Over London*

ANTICHRIST

Levin, Ira. ★*Rosemary's Baby: A Novel*

ANTIETAM, BATTLE OF, MD., 1862

Gurganus, Allan. *Oldest Living Confederate Widow Tells All*

ANTIGUA AND BARBUDA
Kincaid, Jamaica. ★*Annie John*
Le Carre, John. ★*Our Kind of Traitor: A Novel*

ANTIHEROES AND ANTIHEROINES
Scerbanenco, Giorgio. *Traitors to All*

ANTIQUARIAN BOOKSELLERS
Eco, Umberto. *The Mysterious Flame of Queen Loana: An Illustrated Novel*
Ghosh, Amitav. ★*Gun Island*
Grossman, David. *Be My Knife*
Hand, Elizabeth. *The Book of Lamps and Banners: A Novel*
Perez-Reverte, Arturo. *The Club Dumas*
Ruiz Zafon, Carlos. *The Angel's Game*

ANTIQUE AND CLASSIC CARS
Cussler, Clive. ★*The Gray Ghost*

ANTIQUE DEALERS
Berry, Connie. *A Legacy of Murder*
Black, Cara. *Murder in the Bastille*
Dickens, Charles. *The Old Curiosity Shop*
Kelly, Julia. *The Light Over London*

ANTIQUES
Harrison, Cora. *Beyond Absolution: A Mystery Set in 1920s Ireland*
Krentz, Jayne Ann. ★*All the Colors of Night*

ANTIQUITIES
Gruber, Michael. *The Book of Air and Shadows*
Rollins, James. *The Demon Crown: A Sigma Force Novel*
Rollins, James. *The Eye of God*
Rollins, James. ★*The Last Odyssey*
Rollins, James. *The Sixth Extinction: A Sigma Force Novel*

ANTIQUITIES — COLLECTION AND PRESERVATION
See, Lisa. *Dragon Bones: A Novel*

ANTIQUITIES THEFTS
Raybourn, Deanna. *A Treacherous Curse: A Veronica Speedwell Mystery*

ANTIQUITIES, PREHISTORIC
Flynn, Michael. *The January Dancer*

ANTIRACIST LITERATURE
Wiesel, Elie. ★*Night, Dawn, the Accident: Three Tales*

ANTISEMITISM
Adams, Alina. *The Nesting Dolls*
Artson, Barbara. *Odessa, Odessa*
Blake, Sarah. *The Guest Book: A Novel*
Bohjalian, Chris. *Skeletons at the Feast: A Novel*
Burke, James Lee. *Wayfaring Stranger: A Novel*
Harris, Robert. *An Officer and a Spy*
Levin, Ira. *The Boys from Brazil: A Novel*
Malamud, Bernard. ★*The Fixer*
Meyer, Nicholas. *The Adventure of the Peculiar Protocols: Adapted from the Journals of John H. Watson, M.D.*
Miller, Derek B. *How to Find Your Way in the Dark*
Rosnay, Tatiana de. ★*Sarah's Key*
Roth, Henry. *A Star Shines Over Mt. Morris Park*
Roth, Philip. ★*The Plot Against America*
Singer, Isaac Bashevis. *The Family Moskat*
Twardoch, Szczepan. *The King of Warsaw*

ANTISOCIAL PERSONALITY DISORDERS
Donoghue, Emma. ★*Room: A Novel*
Levin, Ira. *A Kiss Before Dying*

ANTITERRORISTS
Hayes, Terry. *I Am Pilgrim*
Sakey, Marcus. *A Better World*
Sakey, Marcus. *Brilliance*

Antkind: a Novel. Kaufman, Charlie
Antoinette, Ashley
Butterfly
Butterfly.; Vol 2
Butterfly.; Vol 3
Antopol, Molly
The Unamericans
Anvil of Stars. Bear, Greg

ANXIETY
Backman, Fredrik. ★*Anxious People: A Novel*
Ellmann, Lucy. *Ducks, Newburyport*
Hunt, Samantha. *The Dark Dark: Stories*
Kawabata, Yasunari. *The Sound of the Mountain*
Perrotta, Tom. *The Leftovers*
Ripper, Kris. *The Hate Project*

ANXIETY DISORDERS
Brazier, Eliza Jane. *If I Disappear*

ANXIETY IN WOMEN
Bair, Kristin. *Agatha Arch Is Afraid of Everything*
Offill, Jenny. ★*Weather*
Rai, Alisha. ★*Girl Gone Viral*
Tursten, Helene. *Hunting Game*
Walbert, Kate. *She Was Like That: New and Selected Stories*

★*Anxious People: A Novel*. Backman, Fredrik
Any Day Now. Bisson, Terry
★*Anyone*. Soule, Charles
Anything for You. Black, Saul
★*Anything Is Possible: Fiction*. Strout, Elizabeth
Anywhere but Here. Simpson, Mona
Aoki, Ryka
Light from Uncommon Stars

APACHE INDIANS
Grey, Zane. *Woman of the Frontier: A Western Story*
Leonard, Elmore. ★*The Complete Western Stories of Elmore Leonard.*
Luiselli, Valeria. ★*Lost Children Archive: A Novel*
McCarthy, Cormac. ★*Blood Meridian, Or, the Evening Redness in the West*

APARTHEID
Coetzee, J. M. *Age of Iron*
Flanery, Patrick. *Absolution: A Novel*
McClure, James. *The Steam Pig*
Paton, Alan. ★*Cry, the Beloved Country*
Paton, Alan. *Too Late the Phalarope*

APARTMENT DWELLERS
Swanson, Peter. *Her Every Fear: A Novel*

APARTMENT HOUSE LIFE
DeLillo, Don. *The Silence*
Gilb, Dagoberto. *The Flowers: A Novel*
O'Leary, Beth. *The Flatshare: A Novel*
Osborne, Lawrence. *The Glass Kingdom: A Novel*
Sager, Riley. *Lock Every Door: A Novel*
Saul, John. *Midnight Voices*
Tyler, Anne. ★*Redhead by the Side of the Road*
Vatner, Jonathan. *Carnegie Hill: A Novel*

APARTMENT HOUSES

Adiga, Aravind. *Last Man in Tower: A Novel*

Levin, Ira. ★*Rosemary's Baby: A Novel*

Rosnay, Tatiana de. ★*Flowers of Darkness*

Apartment: a Novel. Wayne, Teddy

APARTMENTS

Wayne, Teddy. *Apartment: A Novel*

APATHY

Garcia Marquez, Gabriel. *Chronicle of a Death Foretold*

The Ape House. Gruen, Sara

★*Apeirogon: a Novel*. McCann, Colum

APES

Gruen, Sara. *The Ape House*

Apex Hides the Hurt. Whitehead, Colson

APOCALYPTIC FICTION

Anders, Charlie Jane. ★*All the Birds in the Sky*

Anders, Charlie Jane. *Rock Manning Goes for Broke*

Atwood, Margaret. ★*Maddaddam: A Novel*

Atwood, Margaret. ★*Oryx and Crake*

Atwood, Margaret. ★*The Year of the Flood: A Novel*

Auster, Paul. ★*In the Country of Last Things*

Brooks, Max. ★*World War Z: An Oral History of the Zombie War*

Buxton, Kira Jane. ★*Hollow Kingdom*

Chambers, Becky. ★*A Psalm for the Wild-Built*

Cronin, Justin. *The City of Mirrors*

Cronin, Justin. *The Passage*

Cronin, Justin. *The Twelve*

Delany, Samuel R. *Dhalgren*

Egan, Greg. *Perihelion Summer*

Elison, Meg. *The Book of Etta*

Elison, Meg. *The Book of Flora*

Elison, Meg. *The Book of the Unnamed Midwife*

Erdrich, Louise. *Future Home of the Living God*

French, Jonathan. ★*The Grey Bastards*

French, Jonathan. *The True Bastards*

Grant, Mira. *Blackout*

Grant, Mira. *Deadline*

Grant, Mira. *Feed*

Grant, Mira. *Feedback*

Harkaway, Nick. *The Gone-Away World*

Harkaway, Nick. *Tigerman*

Harris, Robert. *The Second Sleep: A Novel*

Heller, Peter. ★*The Dog Stars: A Novel*

Hill, Joe. *The Fireman: A Novel*

Holroyde, Claire. *The Effort*

Jemisin, N. K. *The Fifth Season*

Jemisin, N. K. *The Obelisk Gate*

Jemisin, N. K. *The Stone Sky*

Jones, Cynan. *Stillicide*

King, Stephen. *Sleeping Beauties: A Novel*

King, Stephen. ★*The Stand*

Krivak, Andrew. *The Bear*

Lai, Larissa. *The Tiger Flu*

Lunde, Maja. *The End of the Ocean: A Novel*

Ma, Ling. *Severance*

Malerman, Josh. *Bird Box: A Novel*

Malerman, Josh. *Malorie: A Bird Box Novel*

Mandel, Emily St. John. ★*Station Eleven*

Matheson, Richard. ★*I Am Legend*

McCarthy, Cormac. ★*The Road*

Miller, Walter M. ★*A Canticle for Leibowitz*

Montag, Kassandra. *After the Flood: A Novel*

Nagamatsu, Sequoia. *How High We Go in the Dark*

Okorafor, Nnedi. ★*Who Fears Death*

Rice, Waubgeshig. *Moon of the Crusted Snow: A Novel*

Roanhorse, Rebecca. *Storm of Locusts*

Roanhorse, Rebecca. ★*Trail of Lightning*

Robinson, Kim Stanley. *New York 2140*

Romero, George A. *The Living Dead*

Shepherd, Peng. *The Book of M: A Novel*

Stephenson, Neal. *Seveneves*

Stewart, George R. *Earth Abides*

Stirling, S. M. *Dies the Fire*

Stirling, S. M. *A Meeting at Corvallis*

Stirling, S. M. *The Protector's War*

Stivers, Carole. *The Mother Code*

Sweeney-Baird, Christina. *The End of Men*

Tawada, Yoko. ★*The Emissary*

VanderMeer, Jeff. ★*Borne: A Novel*

Vaughn, Carrie. *Bannerless*

Walker, Karen Thompson. *The Age of Miracles: A Novel*

Walker, Karen Thompson. *The Dreamers*

Wendig, Chuck. ★*Wanderers: A Novel*

Wilhelm, Kate. *Where Late the Sweet Birds Sang*

Williams, Joy. *Harrow*

Wilson, Daniel H. *Robogenesis: A Novel*

APOSTLES

Parini, Jay. *The Damascus Road: A Novel of Saint Paul*

Apostol, Gina

Bibliolepsy

Gun Dealers' Daughter: A Novel

Insurrecto

APPALACHIAN REGION

ffitch, Madeline. *Stay and Fight*

Frazier, Charles. *Nightwoods: A Novel*

Graley, Lisa. *The Current That Carries: Stories*

Harman, Patricia. *The Midwife of Hope River: A Novel*

King, Stephen. *Sleeping Beauties: A Novel*

Marshall, Catherine. *Christy*

McCrumb, Sharyn. ★*If Ever I Return, Pretty Peggy-O*

McLaughlin, James A. *Bearskin*

Montgomery, Jess. *The Stills*

Montgomery, Jess. *The Widows*

Panowich, Brian. *Bull Mountain*

Panowich, Brian. *Like Lions*

Rash, Ron. *Above the Waterfall*

Rash, Ron. *Burning Bright: Stories*

Rash, Ron. ★*The Cove*

Rash, Ron. ★*In the Valley: Stories and a Novella Based on Serena*

Rash, Ron. *Nothing Gold Can Stay: Stories*

Rash, Ron. *Something Rich and Strange: Selected Stories*

Weiss, Leah. *If the Creek Don't Rise: A Novel*

APPALACHIAN REGION, SOUTHERN

Kingsolver, Barbara. ★*Flight Behavior*

APPALACHIAN TRAIL

King, Stephen. *The Girl Who Loved Tom Gordon*

Appaloosa. Parker, Robert B.
Appanah-Mouriquand, Nathacha
　Tropic of Violence: A Novel
APPARITIONS
　Sandford, John. *Holy Ghost*
APPEARANCES
　Styles, Toy. *Black and Ugly*
APPENDIX (ANATOMY) — SURGERY
　Strout, Elizabeth. *My Name Is Lucy Barton*
APPLICATION SOFTWARE
　Anam, Tahmima. *The Startup Wife*
　Bellefleur, Alexandria. *Hang the Moon*
　Lauren, Christina. *The Soulmate Equation*
　Menon, Lily. *Make up Break Up: A Novel*
Appointment in Samarra. O'Hara, John
The Apprentice: a Novel. Gerritsen, Tess
APPRENTICES
　Dunnett, Dorothy. *Niccolo Rising*
　Franklin, Ariana. *The Siege Winter*
　Kuang, R. F. *The Poppy War*
　Palmer, Dexter Clarence. ★*Mary Toft; Or, the Rabbit Queen: A Novel*
　Pamuk, Orhan. *The Red-Haired Woman*
APPRENTICESHIP
　Cole, Alyssa. ★*A Duke by Default*
　Dean, Michael. *I, Hogarth*
Aquarium. Vann, David
AQUARIUMS
　Vann, David. *Aquarium*
AQUEDUCTS
　Harris, Robert. *Pompeii: A Novel*
ARAB AMERICAN WOMEN
　Abu-Jaber, Diana. *Crescent*
ARAB AMERICANS
　Ackerman, Elliot. *Dark at the Crossing*
ARAB COUNTRIES
　Gordimer, Nadine. *The Pickup*
　Ramadan, Ahmad Danny. *The Clothesline Swing*
ARAB-ISRAELI RELATIONS
　McCann, Colum. ★*Apeirogon: A Novel*
Arabella of Mars. Levine, David D.
ARABIAN SEA
　Alten, Steve. *Meg: Generations*
Araghi, Alireza Taheri
　★*The Immortals of Tehran*
Aramburu, Fernando
　Homeland
ARAPAHO INDIANS
　Michener, James A. ★*Centennial*
Ararat. Golden, Christopher
Arbol, Victor del
　Breathing Through the Wound
★*Arcadia: a Novel*. Groff, Lauren
ARCHAEOLOGICAL EXPEDITIONS
　Cussler, Clive. *Serpent: A Novel from the Numa Files*
　Golden, Christopher. *Ararat*
ARCHAEOLOGICAL SITES
　Griffiths, Elly. *The Stone Circle*

Pattison, Eliot. *Bones of the Earth: An Inspector Shan Tao Yun Mystery*
See, Lisa. *Dragon Bones: A Novel*
ARCHAEOLOGICAL THEFTS
　Portis, Charles. ★*Gringos: A Novel*
　Spillane, Mickey. *The Goliath Bone*
ARCHAEOLOGISTS
　Garcia Saenz, Eva. *The Silence of the White City*
　Golden, Christopher. *Ararat*
　Golden, Christopher. *The Pandora Room: A Novel*
　Hart, Erin. *The Book of Killowen*
　Hart, Erin. *Haunted Ground: A Crime Novel*
　Picoult, Jodi. ★*The Book of Two Ways*
　Preston, Douglas J. *Thunderhead*
ARCHAEOLOGY
　Cussler, Clive. *Celtic Empire*
　Griffiths, Elly. *The Dark Angel*
　Moss, Sarah. *Ghost Wall: A Novel*
　Stabenow, Dana. *Spoils of the Dead*
Archangel: a Novel. Harris, Robert
ARCHBISHOPS
　Robb, Candace M. ★*A Choir of Crows*
The Archer. Swamy, Shruti
The Archer's Tale. Cornwell, Bernard
Archer, Jeffrey
　Nothing Ventured
ARCHER, LEW (FICTITIOUS CHARACTER)
　Macdonald, Ross. *The Drowning Pool*
　Macdonald, Ross. *The Far Side of the Dollar*
　Macdonald, Ross. *The Galton Case*
　Macdonald, Ross. *The Goodbye Look*
ARCHER, OWEN (FICTITIOUS CHARACTER)
　Robb, Candace M. *A Gift of Sanctuary: An Owen Archer Mystery*
　Robb, Candace M. *The Riddle of St. Leonard's: An Owen Archer Mystery.*
ARCHERS
　Cornwell, Bernard. *The Archer's Tale*
　Huang, S. L. *Burning Roses*
ARCHETYPE (PSYCHOLOGY)
　Kincaid, Jamaica. *See Now Then*
ARCHITECTS
　Barbash, Tom. *The Last Good Chance*
　Barthelme, Frederick. *Bob the Gambler*
　Belfoure, Charles. *The Paris Architect: A Novel*
　Boyle, T. Coraghessan. *The Women: A Novel*
　Delaney, J. P. *The Girl Before: A Novel*
　Holahan, Cate. *Her Three Lives*
　Horan, Nancy. *Loving Frank: A Novel*
　Jenkins, Beverly. *Rebel*
　McKinlay, Jenn. *The Good Ones*
　Rand, Ayn. ★*The Fountainhead*
ARCHITECTURE
　Clarke, Susanna. ★*Piranesi*
　Kilalea, Katharine. *Ok, Mr. Field: A Novel*
ARCHIVES
　Adimi, Kaouther. *Our Riches*
　Ross, Ann B. *Miss Julia Delivers the Goods: A Novel*
The Archivist: a Novel. Cooley, Martha

ARCHIVISTS
  Estleman, Loren D. *Frames*
  Meltzer, Brad. *The Inner Circle*
Archy McNally mysteries [Series]. Sanders, Lawrence
★*The **Arctic** Fury.* Macallister, Greer
ARCTIC REGIONS
  Macallister, Greer. ★*The Arctic Fury*
  McEwan, Ian. *Solar: A Novel*
  Reynolds, Alastair. *Permafrost*
  Simmons, Dan. ★*The Terror: A Novel*
Arden, Katherine
  ★*The Bear and the Nightingale*
  ★*The Girl in the Tower*
  ★*The Winter of the Witch*
ARGENTINA
  De Robertis, Carolina. *Perla*
  Englander, Nathan. *The Ministry of Special Cases*
  Greene, Graham. *The Honorary Consul*
  Loedel, Daniel. *Hades, Argentina*
  Restrepo, Laura. *No Place for Heroes: A Novel*
  Reyes, Dolores. *Eartheater*
  Saint-Exupery, Antoine de. *Night Flight*
  Schweblin, Samanta. *Fever Dream: A Novel*
  Schweblin, Samanta. *Mouthful of Birds: Stories*
ARGYLL, JONATHAN (FICTITIOUS CHARACTER)
  Pears, Iain. *Death and Restoration*
  Pears, Iain. *The Immaculate Deception*
  Pears, Iain. *The Last Judgement*
Aria. Hozar, Nazanine
Ariadne. Saint, Jennifer
ARIADNE (GREEK DEITY)
  Saint, Jennifer. *Ariadne*
Aridjis, Chloe
  Asunder
Arikawa, Hiro
  The Travelling Cat Chronicles
Arimah, Lesley Nneka
  ★*What It Means When a Man Falls from the Sky: Stories*
ARISTOCRACY
  Anstruther, Eleanor. *A Perfect Explanation*
  Auci, Stefania. *The Florios of Sicily: A Novel*
  Balogh, Mary. *The Arrangement*
  Balogh, Mary. ★*Someone to Remember: A Westcott Story*
  Balogh, Mary. *Someone to Trust*
  Bennett, Anna. *First Earl I See Tonight*
  Bennett, Bethany. *West End Earl*
  Bittner, Rosanne. *Logan's Lady*
  Bowen, Kelly. *A Rogue by Night*
  Bowman, Valerie. *A Duke Like No Other*
  Bowman, Valerie. *No Other Duke but You*
  Bowman, Valerie. *The Unexpected Duchess*
  Clarke, Susanna. ★*Jonathan Strange & Mr. Norrell*
  Collins, Manda. *One for the Rogue*
  Dare, Tessa. ★*The Governess Game*
  Dare, Tessa. ★*The Wallflower Wager*
  Finch, Charles. *The Vanishing Man*
  Guhrke, Laura Lee. *Governess Gone Rogue*
  Guhrke, Laura Lee. *The Trouble with True Love*

  Huber, Anna Lee. *Penny for Your Secrets*
  James, Eloisa. *Three Weeks with Lady X*
  James, Eloisa. *Wilde in Love*
  James, P. D. *A Taste for Death*
  Kidd, Jess. ★*Things in Jars*
  Kleypas, Lisa. ★*Devil in Disguise*
  London, Julia. *Wild Wicked Scot*
  MacLean, Sarah. ★*Bombshell*
  Macmillan, Gilly. *The Nanny*
  Mishima, Yukio. *Spring Snow*
  Mitford, Nancy. *Love in a Cold Climate*
  Mitford, Nancy. ★*The Pursuit of Love: A Novel*
  Pears, Iain. *The Dream of Scipio*
  Polk, C. L. *Witchmark*
  Putney, Mary Jo. *Not Quite a Wife*
  Putney, Mary Jo. *Once a Scoundrel*
  Quincy, D. M. *Murder at the Opera*
  Sackville-West, V. *The Edwardians*
  Sebastian, Cat. *Unmasked by the Marquess*
  Spencer, Minerva. *Barbarous*
  Spencer, Minerva. *Dangerous*
  Suri, Tasha. ★*Empire of Sand*
  Tolstoy, Leo. ★*War and Peace*
  Towles, Amor. ★*A Gentleman in Moscow*
  Vayden, Kristin. *Fortune Favors the Duke*
  Waters, Martha. *To Love and to Loathe: A Novel*
  Wojtas, Olga. *Miss Blaine's Prefect and the Golden Samovar*
ARISTOCRACY — HISTORY
  Goodwin, Daisy. *The American Heiress*
ARIZONA
  Baldacci, David. *Long Road to Mercy*
  Beck, Haylen. *Here and Gone*
  Boyle, T. Coraghessan. *The Terranauts*
  Chancellor, Bryn. *Sycamore: A Novel*
  Dimberg, Kelsey Rae. *Girl in the Rearview Mirror*
  Harrison, Jim. *The Great Leader*
  Leonard, Elmore. ★*The Complete Western Stories of Elmore Leonard.*
  Picoult, Jodi. *Vanishing Acts: A Novel*
  Sallis, James. *Drive*
  Swarthout, Glendon. *Bless the Beasts and Children*
  Talton, Jon. *City of Dark Corners*
  Urrea, Luis Alberto. *Queen of America: A Novel*
  Vestal, Shawn. *Daredevils*
ARIZONA (TERRITORY)
  Grey, Zane. *Woman of the Frontier: A Western Story*
  Obreht, Tea. *Inland: A Novel*
  Russell, Mary Doria. *Epitaph: A Novel of the O.K. Corral*
Arkady Renko novels [Series]. Smith, Martin Cruz
ARKANSAS
  Belle, Kimberly. *Dear Wife*
  Connolly, John. *The Dirty South*
  Davidson, Andy. *The Boatman's Daughter: A Novel*
*The **Armageddon** File.* Coonts, Stephen
Armageddon in Retrospect: And Other New and Unpublished Writings on War and Peace. Vonnegut, Kurt
Armageddon: a Novel of Berlin. Uris, Leon
ARMED FORCES
  Campbell, Rick. *Treason*

Fuentes, Carlos. *The Eagle's Throne: A Novel*

ARMED FORCES — OFFICERS
Benn, James R. ★*The Red Horse: A Billy Boyle World War II Mystery*
Deutermann, Peter T. *The Iceman*
Eliasberg, Jan. ★*Hannah's War*

ARMED FORCES AND SOCIETY
Vargas Llosa, Mario. *The Time of the Hero*

ARMENIAN AMERICAN MEN
Haddam, Jane. *Cheating at Solitaire: A Gregor Demarkian Novel*

ARMENIAN AMERICANS
Shafak, Elif. *The Bastard of Istanbul*

ARMENIAN GENOCIDE, 1915-1923
Bohjalian, Chris. *The Sandcastle Girls*
Werfel, Franz. ★*The Forty Days of Musa Dagh*

ARMENIANS IN TURKEY
Shafak, Elif. *The Bastard of Istanbul*

ARMENIANS IN TURKEY — HISTORY
Werfel, Franz. ★*The Forty Days of Musa Dagh*

Armfield, Julia
Salt Slow: Stories

ARMIES
Kelly, Greta. *The Frozen Crown*

ARMISTICES
Hurley, Kameron. *The Stars Are Legion*

ARMORERS
Cole, Alyssa. ★*A Duke by Default*

ARMS DEALERS
Burke, James Lee. *House of the Rising Sun: A Novel*
Child, Lee. *The Hard Way: A Jack Reacher Novel*
Le Carre, John. ★*A Delicate Truth*
Sjowall, Maj. ★*Murder at the Savoy*

ARMS TRANSFERS
Pears, Iain. *Stone's Fall*

Armstrong, Addison
The Light of Luna Park

Armstrong, Kelley
Alone in the Wild
Watcher in the Woods
Wherever She Goes

Armstrong, Richard
The Don Con

ARMY SPOUSES
Marcelo, Tif. *In a Book Club Far Away*

Arnett, Kristen N.
Mostly Dead Things
With Teeth: A Novel

★*Around the World in Eighty Days*. Verne, Jules

ARRANGED MARRIAGE
Auci, Stefania. *The Florios of Sicily: A Novel*
Banks, Maya. *Never Seduce a Scot*
Boyle, Elizabeth. *Along Came a Duke*
Callihan, Kristen. ★*Firelight*
Cruz, Angie. *Dominicana: A Novel*
Dev, Sonali. ★*A Bollywood Affair*
Frampton, Megan. *Put up Your Duke*
Freudenberger, Nell. *The Newlyweds*
Garriott, Leah. *Promised*
Garwood, Julie. *The Bride*

Gregory, Philippa. *The White Princess*
Heron, Farah. *Accidentally Engaged*
Hoang, Helen. ★*The Bride Test*
Hoyt, Elizabeth. *When a Rogue Meets His Match*
Jin, Ha. ★*Waiting*
Joshi, Alka. *The Henna Artist*
Medie, Peace A. *His Only Wife: A Novel*
Raheem, Zara. *The Marriage Clock: A Novel*
Rao, Shobha. ★*Girls Burn Brighter*
Scott, Walter. *The Bride of Lammermoor*
Sharratt, Mary. *Revelations*
Shupe, Joanna. *The Heiress Hunt*
St. George, Harper. *The Heiress Gets a Duke*
Stachniak, Eva. *The Winter Palace: A Novel of Catherine the Great*
Starling, Caitlin. *The Death of Jane Lawrence*

The Arrangement. Balogh, Mary

ARREST
Benioff, David. *City of Thieves: A Novel*

ARROGANCE IN MEN
Jeffries, Sabrina. *Project Duchess*

Arrowood novels (Mick Finlay) [Series]. Finlay, Mick

★*Arsenic and Adobo*. Manansala, Mia P.

ARSON
Barnard, Robert. *Death of a Literary Widow*
Crace, Jim. *Harvest*
DeSilva, Bruce. *Rogue Island*
Francis, Felix. *Crisis*
Nickson, Chris. *Come the Fear*
Ritter, Todd. *Devil's Night*
Robinson, Peter. *Playing with Fire*
Runcie, James. *Sidney Chambers and the Perils of the Night*
Spencer, Scott. ★*Endless Love*
Stabenow, Dana. ★*A Grave Denied*

ARSON INVESTIGATION
Adler-Olsen, Jussi. *A Conspiracy of Faith*
Stabenow, Dana. ★*A Taint in the Blood*

An Arsonist's Guide to Writers' Homes in New England: A Novel. Clarke, Brock

ARSONISTS
Auslander, Shalom. *Hope: A Tragedy*
Clarke, Brock. *An Arsonist's Guide to Writers' Homes in New England: A Novel*

ART
Aridjis, Chloe. *Asunder*
Campbell, Ramsey. *The Wise Friend*
Clark, Clare. *In the Full Light of the Sun*
Cusk, Rachel. *Kudos*
Davis, Fiona. *The Masterpiece*
Gainza, Maria. *The Optic Nerve*
Gibbon, Maureen. *The Lost Notebook of Edouard Manet: A Novel*
Halliday, Lisa. ★*Asymmetry*
Hewson, David. *The Garden of Evil*
Hughes, Caoilinn. *Orchid and the Wasp*
Marra, Anthony. *The Tsar of Love and Techno: Stories*
Potok, Chaim. ★*My Name Is Asher Lev*
Tan, Amy. *The Valley of Amazement*
Tartt, Donna. ★*The Goldfinch*
Tracy, P. J. *Ice Cold Heart*

Welsh, Irvine. *Dead Men's Trousers*

ART — COLLECTORS AND COLLECTING

Alexander, Victoria. *The Lady Travelers Guide to Larceny with a Dashing Stranger*

ART — EXHIBITIONS

Bauer, Belinda. *The Beautiful Dead*

McLaughlin, Danielle. *The Art of Falling*

ART AND SOCIETY

Smith, Ali. ★*How to Be Both*

ART APPRECIATION

Updike, John. *Seek My Face*

ART CRITICISM

DeRoux, Margaux. *The Lost Diary of Venice*

ART DEALERS

Bialosky, Jill. *The Prize: A Novel*

Clark, Clare. *In the Full Light of the Sun*

Gruber, Michael. *The Forgery of Venus: A Novel*

Rothschild, Hannah. *The Improbability of Love: A Novel*

ART FORGERIES

Clark, Clare. *In the Full Light of the Sun*

Gaddis, William. ★*The Recognitions*

Goddard, Robert. ★*Long Time Coming: A Novel*

Gruber, Michael. *The Forgery of Venus: A Novel*

McDermid, Val. ★*Still Life*

Phillips, Arthur. *The Tragedy of Arthur: A Novel*

Robinson, Peter. *Playing with Fire*

Smith, Dominic. ★*The Last Painting of Sara De Vos*

ART FORGERS

Smith, Dominic. ★*The Last Painting of Sara De Vos*

ART HISTORIANS

Pears, Iain. *Death and Restoration*

Pears, Iain. *The Immaculate Deception*

Pears, Iain. *The Last Judgement*

Smith, Dominic. ★*The Last Painting of Sara De Vos*

ART HISTORY TEACHERS

Sandford, John. *Chosen Prey*

ART INDUSTRY AND TRADE

Hilton, L. S. *Maestra*

Art Keller novels [Series]. Winslow, Don

ART MOVEMENTS

Carter, Michaela. *Leonora in the Morning Light*

ART MUSEUMS

Gainza, Maria. *The Optic Nerve*

The Art of Crash Landing: A Novel. DeCarlo, Melissa

The Art of Falling. McLaughlin, Danielle

The Art of Racing in the Rain: A Novel. Stein, Garth

★*The Art of Violence*. Rozan, S. J.

The Art of War: A Novel. Coonts, Stephen

ART RESTORERS

Silva, Daniel. ★*The Kill Artist: A Novel*

ART SCHOOLS

Davis, Fiona. *The Masterpiece*

ART STUDENTS

Fitch, Janet. *Paint It Black: A Novel*

Hummel, Maria. *Lesson in Red*

Kellerman, Jonathan. *Gone*

Swanson, Peter. *Her Every Fear: A Novel*

ART TEACHERS

Barthelme, Frederick. *Elroy Nights*

Cook, Thomas H. *The Chatham School Affair*

ART THEFTS

Archer, Jeffrey. *Nothing Ventured*

Banville, John. *The Book of Evidence*

Bell, Lenora. *For the Duke's Eyes Only*

Bilal, Parker. *The Burning Gates: A Makana Investigation*

Braun, Lilian Jackson. *The Cat Who Ate Danish Modern*

Finch, Charles. *The Vanishing Man*

Johnson, Craig. *Next to Last Stand*

Mason, Jamie. *The Hidden Things*

Parker, Robert B. *Painted Ladies*

Pears, Iain. *Death and Restoration*

Pears, Iain. *The Immaculate Deception*

Rademacher, Cay. *Deadly Camargue: A Provence Mystery*

Rice, Luanne. ★*Last Day*

Ridley, Erica. *The Duke Heist*

Vreeland, Susan. *Girl in Hyacinth Blue*

Artemis. Weir, Andy

ARTHUR

Cornwell, Bernard. *The Winter King: A Novel of Arthur*

Griffiths, Elly. *A Dying Fall: A Ruth Galloway Mystery*

Stewart, Mary. ★*The Hollow Hills*

Stewart, Mary. *The Last Enchantment*

Stewart, Mary. *The Wicked Day*

Sutcliff, Rosemary. *Sword at Sunset*

Twain, Mark. ★*A Connecticut Yankee in King Arthur's Court*

White, T. H. ★*The Once and Future King*

ARTHUR, KING

Austen, Jane. *Northanger Abbey*

Beukes, Lauren. *The Shining Girls*

Hadley, Tessa. *Clever Girl*

Haslett, Adam. *Union Atlantic*

Lessing, Doris May. *A Proper Marriage*

Riley, Lucinda. *The Girl on the Cliff: A Novel*

Stedman, M. L. ★*The Light Between Oceans: A Novel*

Woods, Stuart. *Chiefs*

ARTHURIAN FANTASY

Cornwell, Bernard. *The Winter King: A Novel of Arthur*

Ishiguro, Kazuo. *The Buried Giant: A Novel*

Pike, Signe. *The Forgotten Kingdom: A Novel*

Pike, Signe. *The Lost Queen*

Stewart, Mary. ★*The Crystal Cave*

Stewart, Mary. ★*The Hollow Hills*

Stewart, Mary. *The Last Enchantment*

Stewart, Mary. *The Wicked Day*

Sutcliff, Rosemary. *Sword at Sunset*

White, T. H. ★*The Once and Future King*

ARTIFICIAL INTELLIGENCE

Asimov, Isaac. ★*I, Robot*

Clarke, Arthur C. ★*2001: A Space Odyssey*

Gibson, William. ★*Agency*

Gladstone, Max. ★*Empress of Forever*

Hall, Louisa. *Speak*

Heinlein, Robert A. *The Moon Is a Harsh Mistress*

Ishiguro, Kazuo. ★*Klara and the Sun*

Jen, Gish. ★*The Resisters*

O'Keefe, Megan E. *Velocity Weapon*
Petrie, Nicholas. *Burning Bright*
Reynolds, Alastair. *Revelation Space*
Simmons, Dan. *Endymion*
Simmons, Dan. *The Rise of Endymion*
Stivers, Carole. *The Mother Code*
Stross, Charles. *Accelerando*
Weinstein, Alexander. *Children of the New World: Stories*
Wells, Martha. *All Systems Red*
Wells, Martha. *Network Effect*
Wilson, Daniel H. *Robogenesis: A Novel*
Winterson, Jeanette. ★*Frankissstein*

ARTIFICIAL LIFE
Crichton, Michael. *Prey: A Novel*

ARTIFICIAL LIMBS
O'Dell, Claire. *A Study in Honor: A Novel*

ARTISANS
Golden, Arthur. ★*Memoirs of a Geisha: A Novel*

An Artist of the Floating World. Ishiguro, Kazuo

ARTISTS
Allende, Isabel. *The Japanese Lover*
Ashley, Jennifer. *Lady Isabella's Scandalous Marriage*
Banville, John. *The Blue Guitar*
Bialosky, Jill. *The Prize: A Novel*
Brenner, Jamie. *Drawing Home*
Brown, Dan. *The Da Vinci Code*
Carter, Michaela. *Leonora in the Morning Light*
Chabon, Michael. *The Amazing Adventures of Kavalier & Clay: A Novel*
Cusk, Rachel. *Second Place*
Cusset, Catherine. *Life of David Hockney: A Novel*
Darznik, Jasmin. *The Bohemians*
Diehl, Heidi. *Lifelines*
Erdrich, Louise. ★*Shadow Tag: A Novel*
Forbes, Curdella. *A Tall History of Sugar*
Gibbon, Maureen. *The Lost Notebook of Edouard Manet: A Novel*
Hesse, Hermann. *Narcissus and Goldmund*
Hibbert, Talia. ★*Get a Life, Chloe Brown*
Hummel, Maria. *Lesson in Red*
Ishiguro, Kazuo. *An Artist of the Floating World*
Joyce, James. ★*A Portrait of the Artist as a Young Man*
Lipsyte, Sam. *The Ask*
Maugham, W. Somerset. *The Moon and Sixpence*
Maugham, W. Somerset. ★*Of Human Bondage*
McKenzie, Alecia. *A Million Aunties*
Murakami, Haruki. *Killing Commendatore: A Novel*
Parmar, Priya. *Vanessa and Her Sister*
Phillips, Susan Elizabeth. ★*Dance Away with Me*
Pilcher, Rosamunde. ★*The Shell Seekers*
Potok, Chaim. ★*The Gift of Asher Lev*
Rachman, Tom. *The Italian Teacher*
Rivers, Francine. *The Masterpiece*
Rose, M. J. *Tiffany Blues: A Novel*
Roy, Anuradha. *All the Lives We Never Lived: A Novel*
Rozan, S. J. ★*The Art of Violence*
Sager, Riley. *The Last Time I Lied: A Novel*
Saramago, Jose. *The Manual of Painting and Calligraphy*
Savage, Sam. *The Way of the Dog: A Novel*

Sayers, Dorothy L. ★*The Five Red Herrings*
Scharer, Whitney. *The Age of Light*
Shapiro, Barbara A. *The Muralist*
Shaw, M. B. *Murder at the Mill: A Mystery*
Smith, Michael F. *Blackwood*
Stone, Irving. ★*The Agony and the Ecstasy: A Biographical Novel of Michelangelo*
Yoshimoto, Banana. *The Lake*

ARTISTS — HISTORY
Chevalier, Tracy. ★*Girl with a Pearl Earring*
Dean, Michael. *I, Hogarth*
Stone, Irving. *Lust for Life: A Novel of Vincent Van Gogh*
Vreeland, Susan. *Girl in Hyacinth Blue*

ARTISTS — SOCIAL RESPONSIBILITY
Roth, Philip. *Zuckerman Bound*

ARTISTS' COLONIES
Rose, M. J. *Tiffany Blues: A Novel*

ARTISTS' MODELS
Avery, Ellis. *The Last Nude*
Buchanan, Cathy Marie. ★*The Painted Girls*
Chevalier, Tracy. ★*Girl with a Pearl Earring*
Macneal, Elizabeth. *The Doll Factory*
Steinke, Rene. *Holy Skirts*

ARTISTS' RETREATS
Bourland, Barbara. ★*Fake Like Me*

ARTS AND ENTERTAINMENT — WRITING AND PUBLISHING
Coetzee, J. M. *Summertime: Scenes from a Provincial Life*
Harkness, Deborah E. *The World of All Souls: The Complete Guide to a Discovery of Witches, Shadow of Night, and the Book*
Nabokov, Vladimir Vladimirovich. *Novels and Memoirs, 1941-51*
Vonnegut, Kurt. *Armageddon in Retrospect: And Other New and Unpublished Writings on War and Peace*

Artson, Barbara
Odessa, Odessa

Arturo's Island: A Novel. Morante, Elsa

ARUBA
Sosa, Mia. ★*Acting on Impulse*

Arudpragasam, Anuk
The Story of a Brief Marriage

Arvin, Reed
Blood of Angels: A Novel

As Chimney Sweepers Come to Dust: A Flavia De Luce Novel. Bradley, C. Alan
★*As I Lay Dying: The Corrected Text.* Faulkner, William
As Simple as Snow. Galloway, Gregory
Ascension of Larks. Linden, Rachel
The Ascent to Godhood. Yang, JY

Asch, Sholem
The Nazarene

The Ash Family. Dektar, Molly
Ashe Cayne novels [Series]. Smith, Ian
Ashes of the Sun. Wexler, Django

Ashley & JaQuavis
The Cartel
Murderville

Ashley, Jennifer
Death at the Crystal Palace
Lady Isabella's Scandalous Marriage

The Madness of Lord Ian Mackenzie

ASIA

Church, James. ★*A Corpse in the Koryo*

Church, James. *Hidden Moon: An Inspector O Novel*

Harkaway, Nick. *Tigerman*

Robinson, Kim Stanley. *The Years of Rice and Salt*

ASIAN AMERICAN FAMILIES

Sutanto, Jesse Q. *Dial a for Aunties*

ASIAN AMERICAN MEN

Nguyen, Kevin. ★*New Waves*

ASIAN AMERICAN WOMEN

Chang, Alexandra. ★*Days of Distraction*

Vo, Nghi. ★*The Chosen and the Beautiful*

ASIAN AMERICANS

Chai, May-Lee. *Useful Phrases for Immigrants: Stories*

Jin, Ha. *The Boat Rocker: A Novel*

Yu, Charles. ★*Interior Chinatown*

Asian saga [Series]. Clavell, James

ASIAN-INFLUENCED FANTASY

Bear, Elizabeth. *Range of Ghosts*

Bear, Elizabeth. *Shattered Pillars*

Bear, Elizabeth. *Steles of the Sky*

Choo, Yangsze. *The Ghost Bride: A Novel*

Choo, Yangsze. ★*The Night Tiger: A Novel*

Krueger, Paul. *Steel Crow Saga*

Kuang, R. F. ★*The Dragon Republic*

Kuang, R. F. *The Poppy War*

Lee, Fonda. ★*Jade City*

Lee, Fonda. *Jade War*

Liu, Ken. ★*The Grace of Kings*

Liu, Ken. ★*The Veiled Throne*

Liu, Ken. *The Wall of Storms*

Lu, S. Qiouyi. *In the Watchful City*

Parker-Chan, Shelley. ★*She Who Became the Sun*

Suri, Tasha. ★*Empire of Sand*

Suri, Tasha. ★*Realm of Ash*

Tan, Sue Lynn. ★*Daughter of the Moon Goddess*

Yang, JY. *The Ascent to Godhood*

Yang, JY. *The Black Tides of Heaven*

Yang, JY. *The Descent of Monsters*

Yang, JY. *The Red Threads of Fortune*

Asim, Jabari

★*Yonder*

Asimov, Isaac

★*Foundation*

Foundation and Empire

★*I, Robot*

Second Foundation

The Ask. Lipsyte, Sam

Ask the Parrot: A Parker Novel. Stark, Richard

Askaripour, Mateo

★*Black Buck*

Aslam, Nadeem

★*The Blind Man's Garden*

★*The Golden Legend: A Novel*

ASPERGER'S SYNDROME

Picoult, Jodi. *House Rules: A Novel*

Assassin of Shadows. Goldstone, Lawrence

ASSASSINATION

Bell, Ted. *Overkill: An Alex Hawke Novel*

Berry, Steve. ★*The Bishop's Pawn*

Bolano, Roberto. *Monsieur Pain*

Church, James. *Hidden Moon: An Inspector O Novel*

Clancy, Tom. *Clear and Present Danger*

Coonts, Stephen. *The Art of War: A Novel*

Costello, Mark. *Big If*

Coulter, Catherine. *The Sixth Day*

DeLillo, Don. *Libra*

deWitt, Patrick. *The Sisters Brothers: A Novel*

Ellroy, James. *Blood's a Rover*

Fleming, Ian. *You Only Live Twice*

Follett, Ken. *Edge of Eternity*

Garcia Marquez, Gabriel. *The General in His Labyrinth*

Goldstone, Lawrence. *Assassin of Shadows*

Grisham, John. ★*The Pelican Brief*

Hawley, Noah. *The Good Father*

Hurwitz, Gregg Andrew. ★*Out of the Dark: The Return of Orphan X*

Polk, C. L. *Soulstar*

Sayles, John. *A Moment in the Sun*

Saylor, Steven. *The Triumph of Caesar: A Novel of Ancient Rome*

Silva, Daniel. ★*The Black Widow*

Sjowall, Maj. ★*Murder at the Savoy*

Smith, Julie. *Crescent City Kill: A Skip Langdon Novel*

Spann, Susan. *Blade of the Samurai: A Shinobi Mystery*

Vargas Llosa, Mario. *The Feast of the Goat*

Vasquez, Juan Gabriel. ★*The Shape of the Ruins*

Woods, Stuart. *Smooth Operator*

ASSASSINATION INVESTIGATION

Persson, Leif G. W. *Free Falling, as If in a Dream: The Story of a Crime*

★*The **Assassination** of Jesse James by the Coward Robert Ford*. Hansen, Ron

ASSASSINATION PLOTS

Child, Lee. *Without Fail*

Perry, Anne. ★*Death in Focus: An Elena Standish Novel*

Putney, Mary Jo. *Nowhere Near Respectable*

Singh, Nalini. ★*Silver Silence*

ASSASSINS

Baker, Kage. *The Bird of the River*

Binet, Laurent. ★*HHhH*

Black, Cara. *Murder in the Rue De Paradis: An Aimee Leduc Investigation*

Block, Lawrence. *Killing Castro*

Box, C. J. ★*Long Range*

Box, C. J. ★*Wolf Pack*

Brandreth, Benet. *The Spy of Venice*

Burke, James Lee. ★*A Private Cathedral*

Byrne, Kerrigan. *The Hunter*

Child, Lee. *61 Hours*

Child, Lee. *Echo Burning*

Child, Lee. *Make Me*

Child, Lee. *Night School*

Child, Lee. *No Middle Name: The Complete Collected Jack Reacher Short Stories*

Child, Lee. *Personal*

Child, Lee. *Without Fail*

Coes, Ben. *The Russian: A Thriller*
Connolly, John. *The Nameless Ones*
Coonts, Stephen. ★*The Russia Account*
Costello, Mark. *Big If*
Cussler, Clive. *Serpent: A Novel from the Numa Files*
Deaver, Jeffery. *Garden of Beasts: A Novel of Berlin 1936*
DeLillo, Don. *Libra*
DeMille, Nelson. ★*The Deserter: A Novel*
Dickey, Eric Jerome. *Finding Gideon*
Dugoni, Robert. *The Eighth Sister: A Thriller*
Ellison, Ralph. ★*Juneteenth*
Ellroy, James. *The Cold Six Thousand: A Novel*
Estleman, Loren D. ★*Something Borrowed, Something Black*
Fleming, Ian. *The Man with the Golden Gun*
Forsyth, Frederick. *The Kill List*
Goldberg, Tod. *Gangsterland: A Novel*
Goldstone, Lawrence. *Assassin of Shadows*
Hagberg, David. *Gambit*
Higgins, George V. *The Friends of Eddie Coyle*
Higgins, Jack. *Confessional*
Holton, India. *The Wisteria Society of Lady Scoundrels*
Hunter, Stephen. *Game of Snipers: A Bob Lee Swagger Novel*
Hurwitz, Gregg Andrew. ★*Out of the Dark: The Return of Orphan X*
James, Marlon. ★*A Brief History of Seven Killings: A Novel*
King, Stephen. ★*Billy Summers*
Kuhn, M. J. *Among Thieves*
Leonard, Elmore. ★*Killshot*
Ludlum, Robert. ★*The Bourne Identity*
Ludlum, Robert. *The Bourne Supremacy*
Ludlum, Robert. *The Bourne Ultimatum*
Martineau, Maxym M. *Kingdom of Exiles*
Mayor, Archer. *Tag Man: A Joe Gunther Novel*
Mina, Denise. ★*Rizzio*
Mosley, Walter. *Trouble Is What I Do: A Leonid McGill Mystery*
Penelope, L. *Whispers of Shadow & Flame*
Perry, Thomas. *Fidelity*
Perry, Thomas. *The Old Man*
Pratchett, Terry. *Men at Arms: A Novel of Discworld*
Quirk, Matthew. *Dead Man Switch*
Rabe, Peter. ★*Anatomy of a Killer ;: A Shroud for Jesso*
Spann, Susan. ★*Claws of the Cat: A Shinobi Mystery*
Stross, Charles. *Neptune's Brood*
Thomas, Will. *Dance with Death*
Urrea, Luis Alberto. *Queen of America: A Novel*
Wolf, Dick. *The Ultimatum*
Woods, Stuart. *Hit List*

ASSAULT AND BATTERY
French, Tana. ★*The Witch Elm: A Novel*

ASSAULTS ON POLICE
Cross-Smith, Leesa. *Whiskey & Ribbons*

ASSIMILATION (SOCIOLOGY)
Aciman, Andre. *Harvard Square*
Davies, Peter Ho. *The Fortunes*
Ko, Lisa. *The Leavers*
Liu, Ken. ★*The Veiled Throne*
Otsuka, Julie. *The Buddha in the Attic*
Roth, Philip. ★*Goodbye, Columbus, and Five Short Stories*
Silko, Leslie Marmon. *Gardens in the Dunes: A Novel*

Wang, Kathy. *Impostor Syndrome: A Novel*
Yang, Susie. *White Ivy: A Novel*
The Assistant. Malamud, Bernard
The Assistant. Walser, Robert

ASSISTED LIVING FOR SENIORS
Fossey, Brooke. *The Big Finish*

ASSISTED SUICIDE
Lyons, Annie. *The Brilliant Life of Eudora Honeysett*
Nunez, Sigrid. *What Are You Going Through*

ASSOCIATIONS, INSTITUTIONS, ETC.
Everett, Elizabeth. ★*A Lady's Formula for Love*

ASTAIRE, FRED
Kaminsky, Stuart M. *Dancing in the Dark*
Paton, Alan. *Ah, but Your Land Is Beautiful*

ASTEROIDS — COLLISIONS WITH EARTH
Tepper, Sheri S. *The Visitor*

ASTRAL PROJECTION
Newland, Courttia. *A River Called Time*

ASTROLOGY
Catton, Eleanor. *The Luminaries: A Novel*

ASTRONAUTICS
Michener, James A. *Space*

ASTRONAUTS
Barnett, David. *Calling Major Tom*
Chambers, Becky. *A Closed and Common Orbit*
Chambers, Becky. ★*The Long Way to a Small, Angry Planet*
Chambers, Becky. *Record of a Spaceborn Few*
Clarke, Arthur C. ★*2001: A Space Odyssey*
Clarke, Arthur C. *Rendezvous with Rama*
Howrey, Meg. *The Wanderers*
Wagers, K. B. *A Pale Light in the Black: A Neog Novel*
Weir, Andy. *The Martian*
Weir, Andy. *Project Hail Mary*

ASTRONOMERS
Holroyde, Claire. *The Effort*

ASTRONOMY
Waite, Olivia. ★*The Lady's Guide to Celestial Mechanics*

ASTROPHYSICISTS
Pobi, Robert. *City of Windows*
Pobi, Robert. *Under Pressure*

Asunder. Aridjis, Chloe

Aswani, Alaa
Chicago: A Modern Arabic Novel
Asylum City: A Novel. Shoham, Liad

ASYLUM, RIGHT OF
Bala, Sharon. *The Boat People: A Novel*
Clarke, Maxine Beneba. ★*Foreign Soil*
★*Asymmetry*. Halliday, Lisa
At His Mercy. Bell, Shelly
At Last. St. Aubyn, Edward
★*At Night All Blood Is Black*. Diop, David
At Night We Walk in Circles: A Novel. Alarcon, Daniel
At the End of the Century: The Stories of Ruth Prawer Jhabvala..
    Jhabvala, Ruth Prawer
At the shore novels [Series]. Pineiro, Caridad
At Weddings and Wakes. McDermott, Alice

Atakora, Afia
★*Conjure Women*

ATATURK, KEMAL

De Bernieres, Louis. *Birds Without Wings*

Wallace, David Foster. ★*Infinite Jest: A Novel*

ATCHAFALAYA RIVER

Luesse, Valerie Fraser. *Under the Bayou Moon: A Novel*

ATHEISTS

Austin, Emily. *Everyone in This Room Will Someday Be Dead*

Rivers, Francine. *The Masterpiece*

Athenian mysteries [Series]. Corby, Gary

ATHENS, GREECE

Corby, Gary. *The Marathon Conspiracy*

Cusk, Rachel. *Outline: A Novel*

ATHLETES

Benaron, Naomi. *Running the Rift: A Novel*

ATHLETIC CLUBS

Pandya, Sameer. *Members Only*

ATHLETIC TRAINERS

Loren, Roni. *The One You Fight For*

Atilgan, Yusuf

Motherland Hotel

Atkins, Ace

The Broken Places

The Fallen

The Forsaken

★*The Heathens*

The Innocents

The Lost Ones

The Ranger

The Redeemers

The Revelators

The Shameless

The Sinners

Wicked City

Atkinson, Kate

★*Big Sky*

★*Case Histories*

★*A God in Ruins*

Human Croquet

★*Life After Life: A Novel*

One Good Turn: A Novel

Started Early, Took My Dog

★*Transcription*

★*When Will There Be Good News?: A Novel*

ATLANTA, GEORGIA

Bambara, Toni Cade. *Those Bones Are Not My Child*

Cleage, Pearl. *Some Things I Never Thought I'd Do*

Enjeti, Anjali. ★*The Parted Earth*

Guinn, Matthew. *The Scribe: A Novel*

Harris, E. Lynn. *I Say a Little Prayer: A Novel*

Jones, Tayari. ★*An American Marriage: A Novel*

Jones, Tayari. *Silver Sparrow: A Novel*

K'wan. *Lawless*

Mullen, Thomas. *Darktown: A Novel*

Mullen, Thomas. *Lightning Men: A Novel*

Slaughter, Karin. *Cop Town: A Novel*

Slaughter, Karin. *Criminal: A Novel*

Slaughter, Karin. ★*Fallen: A Novel*

Slaughter, Karin. *The Kept Woman*

Slaughter, Karin. ★*The Last Widow*

Slaughter, Karin. ★*The Silent Wife*

Slaughter, Karin. ★*Undone: A Novel*

T. I. *Power & Beauty: A Love Story of Life on the Streets*

T. I. *Trouble & Triumph: A Novel of Power & Beauty*

Woods, Stuart. *Palindrome*

ATLANTIC CITY, NEW JERSEY

Leonard, Elmore. *Glitz*

ATLANTIC COAST (SOUTH CAROLINA)

Powell, Padgett. ★*Edisto: A Novel*

ATLANTIC OCEAN

Albom, Mitch. *The Stranger in the Lifeboat*

Child, Lincoln. *Deep Storm: A Novel*

Clancy, Tom. ★*The Hunt for Red October*

Golding, William. *Close Quarters*

Golding, William. *Rites of Passage*

Johnson, Charles Richard. ★*Middle Passage*

Porter, Katherine Anne. *Ship of Fools*

ATLANTIS (LEGENDARY PLACE)

Child, Lincoln. *Deep Storm: A Novel*

Portis, Charles. ★*Masters of Atlantis: A Novel*

Siegel, Jan. *Prospero's Children*

Atlas Catesby mysteries [Series]. Quincy, D. M.

*An **Atlas** of Impossible Longing*. Roy, Anuradha

Atlee Pine novels [Series]. Baldacci, David

*The **Atmospherians***. McElroy, Alex

ATOMIC BOMB

Follett, Ken. *Winter of the World*

Kiernan, Stephen P. *Universe of Two*

ATOMIC BOMB — TESTING

Smith, Martin Cruz. *Stallion Gate*

ATONEMENT

Diop, David. ★*At Night All Blood Is Black*

Erdrich, Louise. ★*Larose*

McCracken, Elizabeth. *The Souvenir Museum: Stories*

★*Atonement: a Novel*. McEwan, Ian

ATROCITIES

Howarth, Paul. *Only Killers and Thieves: A Novel*

Kuznetsov, Anatolii Petrovich. *Babi Yar: A Document in the Form of a Novel*

Solomon, Rivers. *Sorrowland*

Wouk, Herman. ★*The Winds of War: A Novel*

ATTEMPTED ASSASSINATION

Black, Cara. ★*Three Hours in Paris*

Block, Lawrence. *Killing Castro*

Clancy, Tom. *Patriot Games*

Ellison, Ralph. *Three Days Before the Shooting . . .*

Higgins, Jack. *Eye of the Storm*

Mason, Timothy. *The Darwin Affair*

Porter, Henry. *The Old Enemy*

Thomas, Will. *Dance with Death*

ATTEMPTED MURDER

Barr, Nevada. *The Rope: An Anna Pigeon Novel*

Box, C. J. ★*Long Range*

Deaver, Jeffery. *The Stone Monkey: A Lincoln Rhyme Novel*

Francis, Dick. *Smokescreen*

Francis, Felix. *Pulse*

Furst, Alan. *The Foreign Correspondent: A Novel*

Hiaasen, Carl. *Skin Tight*
James, Marlon. ★*A Brief History of Seven Killings: A Novel*
Johnson, D. E. *Detroit Shuffle*
K'wan. *Animal*
Koryta, Michael. *If She Wakes*
MacDonald, John D. *The Turquoise Lament*
Saylor, Steven. *The Triumph of Caesar: A Novel of Ancient Rome*
Smith, Julie. ★*Mean Woman Blues*
Stabenow, Dana. *Though Not Dead: A Kate Shugak Novel*
Stewart, Mary. *Nine Coaches Waiting*
Woods, Stuart. *Stealth*

Attenberg, Jami
★*All This Could Be Yours*
The Middlesteins

ATTITUDE (PSYCHOLOGY)
Rawlings, David. *The Baggage Handler: A Novel*

ATTORNEY AND CLIENT
Connelly, Michael. *The Fifth Witness*
Connelly, Michael. *The Gods of Guilt*
Connelly, Michael. *The Lincoln Lawyer: A Novel*
Silver, Elizabeth L. *The Execution of Noa P. Singleton: A Novel*

Atwood, Margaret
Alias Grace
★*The Blind Assassin*
Bluebeard's Egg and Other Stories
★*Cat's Eye*
★*The Handmaid's Tale*
Life Before Man
★*Maddaddam: A Novel*
Moral Disorder
★*Oryx and Crake*
★*Stone Mattress: Nine Tales*
★*The Testaments: A Novel*
★*The Year of the Flood: A Novel*

AU PAIRS
Kincaid, Jamaica. ★*Lucy*

Auci, Stefania
The Florios of Sicily: A Novel

AUDITIONS
Steadman, Catherine. *The Disappearing Act*

AUDITORY HALLUCINATIONS
Cameron, W. Bruce. *Repo Madness*
Ozeki, Ruth L. *The Book of Form and Emptiness: A Novel*

Audrain, Ashley
The Push

Auel, Jean M.
★*The Clan of the Cave Bear: A Novel*

August Snow novels [Series]. Jones, Stephen Mack
★*Augustown*. Miller, Kei

AUNT AND NEPHEW
Vargas Llosa, Mario. *Aunt Julia and the Scriptwriter*

AUNT AND NIECE
Bergstrom, Heather Brittain. *Steal the North: A Novel*
Cleage, Pearl. *Some Things I Never Thought I'd Do*
Deveraux, Jude. *A Willing Murder*
Gray, Anissa. *The Care and Feeding of Ravenously Hungry Girls*
McCall Smith, Alexander. *The Forgotten Affairs of Youth*
Monroe, Mary Alice. *Beach House Reunion*

Rice, Luanne. *Little Night*
Straley, John. *The Big Both Ways*
Thayne, RaeAnne. *The Cliff House*

Aunt Julia and the Scriptwriter. Vargas Llosa, Mario
★*Auntie Poldi and the Lost Madonna*. Giordano, Mario
Auntie Poldi and the Vineyards of Etna. Giordano, Mario
Auntie Poldi novels [Series]. Giordano, Mario
Aunties (Jesse Q Sutanto); [Series]. Sutanto, Jesse Q.

AUNTS
Frazier, Charles. *Nightwoods: A Novel*
Heyer, Georgette. *Black Sheep*
Phillips, Jayne Anne. *Lark and Termite: A Novel*
Rinehart, Mary Roberts. *Miss Pinkerton*
Shapiro, Barbara A. *The Muralist*
St. James, Simone. *The Sun Down Motel*
Sutanto, Jesse Q. *Dial a for Aunties*

Aurelio Zen mysteries [Series]. Dibdin, Michael
Aurora. Robinson, Kim Stanley

Auslander, Shalom
Hope: A Tragedy

The Aussie Next Door. London, Stefanie
The Austen Playbook. Parker, Lucy

AUSTEN, CASSANDRA
Hornby, Gill. *Miss Austen*
Lane, Byron. ★*A Star Is Bored*

Austen, Jane
★*Emma*
Mansfield Park
Northanger Abbey
★*Persuasion*
★*Pride and Prejudice*
★*Sense and Sensibility*

AUSTEN, JANE
Fowler, Karen Joy. *The Jane Austen Book Club*
Jenner, Natalie. *The Jane Austen Society*
Swift, Graham. ★*Last Orders: A Novel*
Taylor, Brandon. ★*Real Life*

Austenland novels [Series]. Hale, Shannon
Austenland: a Novel. Hale, Shannon

Auster, Paul
4 3 2 1: A Novel
★*The Book of Illusions: A Novel*
The Brooklyn Follies
★*In the Country of Last Things*
Invisible
★*Leviathan*
Oracle Night
Sunset Park
Timbuktu: A Novel
Travels in the Scriptorium: A Novel

★*Austerlitz*. Sebald, Winfried Georg

Austin, Emily
Everyone in This Room Will Someday Be Dead

Austin, Finola
Bronte's Mistress

AUSTIN, KURT (FICTITIOUS CHARACTER)
Cussler, Clive. *Ghost Ship*
Cussler, Clive. *Nighthawk: A Novel from the Numa Files*

Cussler, Clive. *The Pharaoh's Secret*

Austin, Lynn N.
Chasing Shadows

AUSTIN, TEXAS
Abbott, Jeff. *Blame*
Loren, Roni. *The One You Fight For*
Perkins, S. C. *Murder Once Removed*
Pryor, Mark. *Hollow Man*
Rochon, Farrah. *The Boyfriend Project*

AUSTRALIA
Adams, Hope. *Dangerous Women*
Carey, Peter. *A Long Way from Home*
Christian, Claire. *It's Been a Pleasure, Noni Blake*
Cleary, Jon. *The Sundowners*
Coetzee, J. M. *Elizabeth Costello*
Dalton, Trent. *All Our Shimmering Skies*
Dalton, Trent. *Boy Swallows Universe*
Disher, Garry. *Under the Cold Bright Lights*
Egan, Greg. *Perihelion Summer*
Flanagan, Richard. *Gould's Book of Fish: A Novel in Twelve Fish*
Flanagan, Richard. *The Living Sea of Waking Dreams*
Flanagan, Richard. ★*The Narrow Road to the Deep North*
Flanagan, Richard. *The Unknown Terrorist*
Fox, Candice. *Crimson Lake*
Fox, Candice. *Gone by Midnight*
Fox, Candice. *Redemption Point*
Franklin, Miles. *My Brilliant Career*
Golding, William. *Fire Down Below*
Greenwood, Kerry. *Death in Daylesford*
Greenwood, Kerry. *Unnatural Habits*
Grenville, Kate. *Sarah Thornhill*
Grenville, Kate. *The Secret River*
Harper, Jane. *The Dry*
Harper, Jane. *The Lost Man*
Howarth, Paul. *Dust off the Bones*
Howarth, Paul. *Only Killers and Thieves: A Novel*
James, Wendy. *A Little Bird*
Jimenez, Abby. ★*The Happy Ever After Playlist*
Kate, Jessica. *A Girl's Guide to the Outback: A Novel*
Keneally, Thomas. *Shame and the Captives: A Novel*
Keneally, Thomas. *Woman of the Inner Sea*
London, Joan. *The Golden Age*
London, Stefanie. *The Aussie Next Door*
Malouf, David. *Remembering Babylon*
Marsh, Nicola. *The Boy Toy*
McLean, Felicity. *The Van Apfel Girls Are Gone*
Moriarty, Jaclyn. *Gravity Is the Thing*
Moriarty, Liane. *The Husband's Secret*
Moriarty, Liane. *Nine Perfect Strangers*
Moriarty, Liane. *Truly Madly Guilty*
Moss, Tara. *The War Widow*
Rimmer, Kelly. *Before I Let You Go*
Simsion, Graeme C. ★*The Rosie Project*
Stedman, M. L. ★*The Light Between Oceans: A Novel*
Winton, Tim. *The Shepherd's Hut*

AUSTRALIAN FICTION
Aalborg, Gordon. *River of Porcupines*
Adiga, Aravind. ★*Amnesty*

Anderton, Jo. *Debris*
Carey, Peter. *A Long Way from Home*
Christian, Claire. *It's Been a Pleasure, Noni Blake*
Clarke, Maxine Beneba. ★*Foreign Soil*
Coetzee, J. M. *Elizabeth Costello*
De Kretser, Michelle. *The Life to Come*
Disher, Garry. *Under the Cold Bright Lights*
Drayson, Nicholas. *A Guide to the Birds of East Africa*
Flanagan, Richard. *Gould's Book of Fish: A Novel in Twelve Fish*
Flanagan, Richard. *The Living Sea of Waking Dreams*
Flanagan, Richard. *The Unknown Terrorist*
Fox, Candice. *Crimson Lake*
Fox, Candice. *Gone by Midnight*
Fox, Candice. *Redemption Point*
Franklin, Miles. *My Brilliant Career*
Garner, Helen. *The Spare Room*
Goldin, Megan. *The Escape Room*
Goldin, Megan. *The Night Swim*
Gracie, Anne. *Marry in Scandal*
Greenwood, Kerry. *Death in Daylesford*
Greenwood, Kerry. *Out of the Black Land*
Greenwood, Kerry. *Unnatural Habits*
Grenville, Kate. *Sarah Thornhill*
Grenville, Kate. *The Secret River*
Harper, Jane. *The Dry*
Harper, Jane. *The Lost Man*
Harper, Jane. *The Survivors*
Hazzard, Shirley. ★*The Great Fire*
Hazzard, Shirley. ★*The Transit of Venus*
Hepworth, Sally. *The Secrets of Midwives*
Irwin, Stephen M. *The Broken Ones: A Novel*
James, Wendy. *A Little Bird*
Kate, Jessica. *A Girl's Guide to the Outback: A Novel*
Keneally, Thomas. *Woman of the Inner Sea*
Landragin, Alex. ★*Crossings: Consisting of Three Manuscripts : The Education of a Monster : City of Ghosts : Tales Of*
Laurens, Stephanie. *The Pursuits of Lord Kit Cavanaugh*
London, Joan. *The Golden Age*
London, Stefanie. *The Aussie Next Door*
Lucashenko, Melissa. *Too Much Lip*
Malouf, David. *Remembering Babylon*
Marsh, Nicola. *The Boy Toy*
McConaghy, Charlotte. *Migrations*
McConaghy, Charlotte. *Once There Were Wolves: A Novel*
McCullough, Colleen. *The First Man in Rome*
McCullough, Colleen. *An Indecent Obsession*
McLean, Felicity. *The Van Apfel Girls Are Gone*
Moriarty, Jaclyn. *Gravity Is the Thing*
Moriarty, Liane. *Big Little Lies*
Moriarty, Liane. *The Husband's Secret*
Moriarty, Liane. *Nine Perfect Strangers*
Moriarty, Liane. *Truly Madly Guilty*
Morris, Heather. *Cilka's Journey*
Morton, Kate. *The House at Riverton: A Novel*
Moss, Tara. *The War Widow*
Rawlings, David. *The Baggage Handler: A Novel*
Reynolds, Allie. ★*Shiver*
Rimmer, Kelly. *Before I Let You Go*

Rimmer, Kelly. *Truths I Never Told You*
Robotham, Michael. ★*Close Your Eyes*
Robotham, Michael. ★*Good Girl, Bad Girl: A Novel*
Robotham, Michael. *Life or Death*
Robotham, Michael. ★*The Other Wife*
Robotham, Michael. ★*Say You're Sorry*
Robotham, Michael. ★*When She Was Good*
Robotham, Michael. ★*The Wreckage*
Rose, Heather. *The Museum of Modern Love*
Schmidt, Sarah. *See What I Have Done*
Simsion, Graeme C. *The Rosie Effect*
Simsion, Graeme C. ★*The Rosie Project*
Simsion, Graeme C. *The Rosie Result*
Smith, Dominic. *Bright and Distant Shores*
Smith, Dominic. ★*The Electric Hotel*
Stead, Christina. ★*The Man Who Loved Children*
Tsao, Tiffany. *The Majesties*
Walters, Minette. *The Last Hours: A Novel*
Williams, Pip. *The Dictionary of Lost Words*
Winch, Tara June. *The Yield*
Winton, Tim. *The Shepherd's Hut*

AUSTRALIANS IN FOREIGN COUNTRIES
Hazzard, Shirley. ★*The Transit of Venus*

AUSTRIA
Balzano, Marco. *I'm Staying Here*
Bernhard, Thomas. *Frost: A Novel*
Bernhard, Thomas. *Wittgenstein's Nephew: A Friendship*
Clayton, Meg Waite. *The Last Train to London*
Musil, Robert. *The Man Without Qualities*
Sem-Sandberg, Steve. *The Chosen Ones: A Novel*
Solomons, Natasha. *House of Gold*
Tallis, Frank. *Vienna Blood: A Max Liebermann Mystery*

Ausubel, Ramona
Sons and Daughters of Ease and Plenty

Authority: a Novel. VanderMeer, Jeff

AUTHORS
Amis, Martin. ★*Inside Story*
Apostol, Gina. *Bibliolepsy*
Auster, Paul. *Oracle Night*
Baldwin, Joshua. *The Wilshire Sun*
Barclay, Linwood. *A Noise Downstairs: A Novel*
Barth, John. *The Last Voyage of Somebody the Sailor*
Bauer, Carlene. ★*Frances and Bernard*
Benjamin, Melanie. *Alice I Have Been*
Bernhard, Thomas. *Wittgenstein's Nephew: A Friendship*
Bolano, Roberto. ★*2666*
Bolano, Roberto. ★*Nazi Literature in the Americas*
Boyne, John. ★*A Ladder to the Sky*
Bryant, Niobia. *Christmas with the Billionaire*
Burke, James Lee. *Another Kind of Eden*
Cameron, Peter. *The City of Your Final Destination*
Castellani, Christopher. *Leading Men: A Novel*
Cleave, Paul. *Trust No One: A Thriller*
Cohen, Joshua. *Book of Numbers: A Novel*
Cumming, Charles. *The Moroccan Girl*
Currie, Ron. *Flimsy Little Plastic Miracles: A True Story*
Cusk, Rachel. *Kudos*
Daly, Paula. *Open Your Eyes*

Dekker, Ted. *Black: The Birth of Evil*
Dekker, Ted. *Red: The Heroic Rescue*
Dekker, Ted. *White: The Great Pursuit*
Doyle, Rob. *Threshold*
Dunne, Dominick. *Too Much Money*
Durrell, Lawrence. ★*Justine*
Ferris, Joshua. *A Calling for Charlie Barnes*
Fuentes, Carlos. ★*The Old Gringo*
Furst, Alan. ★*Under Occupation: A Novel*
Gentill, Sulari. *Crossing the Lines*
Ginzburg, Natalia. *A Family Lexicon*
Goldberg, Lee. *Fake Truth*
Greer, Andrew Sean. ★*Less*
Gunday, Hakan. *The Few*
Hall, Steven. *Maxwell's Demon*
Henry, Emily. *Beach Read*
Henry, Patti Callahan. ★*Becoming Mrs. Lewis: The Improbable Love Story of Joy Davidman and C. S. Lewis*
Horowitz, Anthony. ★*The Sentence Is Death*
Horowitz, Anthony. ★*The Word Is Murder*
King, Stephen. *Finders Keepers*
King, Stephen. *Salem's Lot*
Kleeman, Alexandra. *Something New Under the Sun*
Korelitz, Jean Hanff. ★*The Plot*
Kotzwinkle, William. *The Bear Went Over the Mountain*
Kunzru, Hari. *Red Pill: A Novel*
Lippman, Laura. ★*Dream Girl*
Mann, Thomas. *Death in Venice and Seven Other Stories*
McCall Smith, Alexander. *The Limpopo Academy of Private Detection*
McLain, Paula. *Love and Ruin*
Means, David. ★*Hystopia: A Novel*
Miller, Henry. ★*Tropic of Cancer*
Morton, Brian. *Florence Gordon*
Mott, Jason. *Hell of a Book*
Nabokov, Vladimir Vladimirovich. *Look at the Harlequins!*
O'Connor, Carlene. *Murder in an Irish Bookshop*
Oe, Kenzaburo. ★*Death by Water*
Ogawa, Yoko. ★*The Memory Police: A Novel*
Oyeyemi, Helen. *Mr. Fox*
Palmer, Lindsey J. *Otherwise Engaged*
Parmar, Priya. *Vanessa and Her Sister*
Pearl, Matthew. *The Dante Club: A Novel*
Phillips, Susan Elizabeth. *Heroes Are My Weakness*
Powers, Richard. *Generosity: An Enhancement*
Prose, Francine. *Blue Angel: A Novel*
Richler, Mordecai. *Solomon Gursky Was Here*
Ruiz Zafon, Carlos. *The Angel's Game*
Saramago, Jose. *The History of the Siege of Lisbon*
Sartre, Jean Paul. ★*Nausea*
Straub, Peter. ★*Ghost Story*
Thelen, Albert Vigoleis. *The Island of Second Sight: From the Applied Recollections of Vigoleis*
Truong, Monique T. D. *The Sweetest Fruits*
Ullmann, Linn. *Unquiet: A Novel*
Wayne, Teddy. *Apartment: A Novel*

AUTHORS — DEATH
Galbraith, Robert. *The Silkworm*

Pearl, Matthew. *The Last Dickens: A Novel*

AUTHORS' SPOUSES
Fowler, Therese. ★*Z: A Novel of Zelda Fitzgerald*
McLain, Paula. *The Paris Wife: A Novel*

AUTHORS, AMERICAN
Bellow, Saul. ★*Humboldt's Gift*
Bellow, Saul. *Ravelstein*
Berger, Thomas. *Being Invisible: A Novel*
Chabon, Michael. ★*Wonder Boys*
Gilbert, David. *& Sons: A Novel*
Irving, John. ★*The World According to Garp: A Novel*
McLain, Paula. *The Paris Wife: A Novel*
Nabokov, Vladimir Vladimirovich. *Novels and Memoirs, 1941-51*
Parini, Jay. *The Passages of H.M.: A Novel of Herman Melville*
Pearl, Matthew. *The Poe Shadow: A Novel*
Simmons, Dan. *The Fifth Heart*
Styron, William. ★*Sophie's Choice*
Welty, Eudora. *Stories, Essays & Memoir*
Wolfe, Thomas. ★*Look Homeward, Angel: A Story of a Buried Life*
Wolfe, Thomas. ★*Of Time and the River: A Legend of Man's Hunger in His Youth*

AUTHORS, AMERICAN — HOMES AND HAUNTS
Clarke, Brock. *An Arsonist's Guide to Writers' Homes in New England: A Novel*

AUTHORS, BRITISH
MacLeod, Alison. *Tenderness*
Savas, Aysegul. *Walking on the Ceiling*

AUTHORS, ENGLISH
Barnard, Robert. *Death of a Literary Widow*
Greene, Graham. ★*The End of the Affair*
Griffiths, Elly. *The Stranger Diaries*
Pearl, Matthew. *The Dante Chamber*
Simmons, Dan. *Drood: A Novel*

AUTHORS, GERMAN
Toibin, Colm. ★*The Magician: A Novel*

AUTHORS, JAPANESE
Higashino, Keigo. *Malice*
Murakami, Haruki. ★*1q84*

AUTHORS, RUSSIAN
Dovlatov, Sergei. *Pushkin Hills*
Nabokov, Vladimir Vladimirovich. *Novels and Memoirs, 1941-51*
Prescott, Lara. *The Secrets We Kept*

AUTHORS, SOUTH AFRICAN
Coetzee, J. M. *Summertime: Scenes from a Provincial Life*

AUTHORS, SOVIET
Bulgakov, Mikhail. ★*The Master and Margarita*

AUTISM
Haddon, Mark. ★*The Curious Incident of the Dog in the Night-Time: A Novel*
Hoang, Helen. ★*The Kiss Quotient*
Ludwig, Benjamin. *Ginny Moon*

AUTOBIOGRAPHICAL FICTION
Akhtar, Ayad. ★*Homeland Elegies: A Novel*
Amis, Martin. ★*Inside Story*
Atwood, Margaret. *Moral Disorder*
Baldwin, James. ★*Early Novels and Stories*
Ballard, J. G. *The Kindness of Women*
Batuman, Elif. ★*The Idiot*

Bernhard, Thomas. ★*The Loser*
Crafts, Hannah. *The Bondwoman's Narrative*
D'Eramo, Luce. *Deviation*
Dalton, Trent. *Boy Swallows Universe*
Daughters, Amy Weinland. *You Cannot Mess This Up: A True Story That Never Happened*
Ellis, Bret Easton. *Lunar Park*
Emezi, Akwaeke. *Freshwater*
Franklin, Miles. *My Brilliant Career*
Ginzburg, Natalia. *A Family Lexicon*
Greenberg, Joanne. *I Never Promised You a Rose Garden: A Novel*
Han, Kang. *The White Book*
Howland, Bette. *Calm Sea and Prosperous Voyage*
Hughes, Langston. ★*Short Stories*
Huisman, Violaine. *The Book of Mother*
Isherwood, Christopher. ★*The Berlin Stories: The Last of Mr. Norris, Goodbye to Berlin*
Joyce, James. ★*A Portrait of the Artist as a Young Man*
Kandasamy, Meena. *When I Hit You, Or, a Portrait of the Writer as a Young Wife*
Kerouac, Jack. *The Dharma Bums*
Kerouac, Jack. ★*On the Road*
Kerouac, Jack. ★*Road Novels 1957-1960*
Kosinski, Jerzy. ★*The Painted Bird*
London, Jack. *Martin Eden*
Louis, Edouard. *The End of Eddy: A Novel*
Miller, Karen E. Quinones. *An Angry-Ass Black Woman*
Plath, Sylvia. ★*The Bell Jar*
Proust, Marcel. ★*Remembrance of Things Past*
Proust, Marcel. *Swann's Way*
Proust, Marcel. *Time Regained*
Proust, Marcel. *Within a Budding Grove*
Rodrigues Fowler, Yara. *Stubborn Archivist*
Roth, Philip. ★*American Pastoral*
Roth, Philip. ★*Everyman*
Roth, Philip. *Exit Ghost*
Roth, Philip. *The Ghost Writer*
Roth, Philip. ★*The Human Stain*
Roth, Philip. *I Married a Communist*
Roth, Philip. *Zuckerman Unbound*
Stegner, Wallace. ★*The Big Rock Candy Mountain*
Ullmann, Linn. *Unquiet: A Novel*
Walker, Nico. ★*Cherry: A Novel*
Watkins, Claire Vaye. *I Love You but I've Chosen Darkness*
Wiesel, Elie. ★*Dawn*
Wolfe, Thomas. ★*Look Homeward, Angel: A Story of a Buried Life*

AUTOBIOGRAPHICAL MEMORY
Updike, John. *Seek My Face*

AUTOBIOGRAPHIES AND MEMOIRS
Coetzee, J. M. *Summertime: Scenes from a Provincial Life*
Nabokov, Vladimir Vladimirovich. *Novels and Memoirs, 1941-51*
Wiesel, Elie. ★*Night, Dawn, the Accident: Three Tales*

AUTOBIOGRAPHY
Cohen, Joshua. *Book of Numbers: A Novel*
Grossman, David. ★*A Horse Walks into a Bar*

AUTOBIOGRAPHY — THERAPEUTIC USE
Svevo, Italo. *Zeno's Conscience*

★*The **Autobiography** of Miss Jane Pittman*. Gaines, Ernest J.

The *Autobiography* of My Mother. Kincaid, Jamaica
The *Autograph* Man: A Novel. Smith, Zadie
AUTOGRAPHS — COLLECTORS AND COLLECTING
  Smith, Zadie. *The Autograph Man: A Novel*
AUTOMATA
  Wilson, Daniel H. *The Clockwork Dynasty: A Novel*
AUTOMOBILE DEALERS
  Vonnegut, Kurt. ★*Breakfast of Champions: Or, Goodbye Blue
    Monday!*
AUTOMOBILE DRIVERS
  Adiga, Aravind. ★*The White Tiger: A Novel*
AUTOMOBILE DRIVING
  Sallis, James. *Drive*
AUTOMOBILE INDUSTRY AND TRADE
  Lewis, Sinclair. *Dodsworth*
AUTOMOBILE LICENSE PLATES
  Greer, Robert O. *First of State*
AUTOMOBILE MECHANICS
  Cosby, S. A. ★*Blacktop Wasteland*
  Roberts, Nora. *The Obsession*
AUTOMOBILE RACING
  Carey, Peter. *A Long Way from Home*
  Stein, Garth. *The Art of Racing in the Rain: A Novel*
AUTOMOBILE RACING DRIVERS
  Stein, Garth. *The Art of Racing in the Rain: A Novel*
AUTOMOBILE THEFTS
  Faulkner, William. *The Reivers: A Reminiscence*
  Kennedy, Randy. *Presidio*
AUTOMOBILE THIEVES
  Cussler, Clive. ★*The Gray Ghost*
AUTOMOBILE TRAVEL
  Barthelme, Frederick. *Painted Desert: A Novel*
  Danielewski, Mark Z. *Only Revolutions*
  Downing, Samantha. *He Started It*
  Evison, Jonathan. *The Revised Fundamentals of Caregiving: A Novel*
  Faulkner, William. *The Reivers: A Reminiscence*
  Gilman, Susan Jane. *Donna Has Left the Building*
  Makkai, Rebecca. *The Borrower: A Novel*
  Ólafsdóttir, Auður A. *Butterflies in November*
  Phillips, Susan Elizabeth. ★*Natural Born Charmer*
  Reid, Iain. *I'm Thinking of Ending Things*
  Ruff, Matt. *Lovecraft Country: A Novel*
  Rushdie, Salman. ★*Quichotte: A Novel*
  Spillane, Mickey. *Kill Me, Darling*
  Ward, Jesmyn. ★*Sing, Unburied, Sing*
Autonomous. Newitz, Annalee
AUTONOMY
  McGhee, Alison. *The Opposite of Fate*
Autopsy. Cornwell, Patricia Daniels
AUTOPSY
  Parris, S. J. ★*The Dead of Winter*
  Welsh, Kaite. *The Unquiet Heart*
★*Autumn*. Smith, Ali
★*The Autumn* of the Patriarch. Garcia Marquez, Gabriel
The *Autumnal*: the Complete Series. Kraus, Daniel
Available Dark: A Thriller. Hand, Elizabeth
AVALANCHES
  Ware, Ruth. ★*One by One*

Avalon. Seton, Anya
AVALON (LEGENDARY PLACE)
  Seton, Anya. *Avalon*
AVATARS (VIRTUAL REALITY)
  Ruff, Matt. ★*88 Names*
Avenue of Mysteries: A Novel. Irving, John
AVERSION
  Guillory, Jasmine. *The Wedding Party*
AVERSION THERAPY
  Burgess, Anthony. ★*A Clockwork Orange*
Avery & Blake novels [Series]. Carter, Miranda
Avery, Ellis
  The Last Nude
AVIATION
  Saint-Exupery, Antoine de. *Night Flight*
★*The Aviator's Wife*: A Novel. Benjamin, Melanie
Avon, Joy
  In Peppermint Peril: A Book Tea Shop Mystery
Aw, Tash
  We, the Survivors
Awad, Mona
  ★*13 Ways of Looking at a Fat Girl*
  Bunny
★*The Awakening*. Roberts, Nora
AWARDS, PRIZES, HONORS, ETC.
  Coetzee, J. M. *Elizabeth Costello*
★*The Awkward* Black Man: Stories. Mosley, Walter
AYATOLLAHS
  Dowlatabadi, Mahmoud. *The Colonel*
Ayatsuji, Yukito
  The Decagon House Murders
Aye, and Gomorrah: Stories. Delany, Samuel R.
★*Ayesha* at Last. Jalaluddin, Uzma
★*Ayiti*. Gay, Roxane
AYLA (FICTITIOUS CHARACTER)
  Auel, Jean M. ★*The Clan of the Cave Bear: A Novel*
AZTECS — RELIGION
  Bowles, David. *Feathered Serpent, Dark Heart of Sky: Myths of
    Mexico*

B

★*B-More* Careful: A Novel. Holmes, Shannon
BAALBERGEN, SARAH VAN
  Schwab, Victoria. *The Invisible Life of Addie Larue*
  Smith, Dominic. ★*The Last Painting of Sara De Vos*
Babalola, Bolu
  Love in Color: Mythical Tales from Around the World, Retold
Babbitt. Lewis, Sinclair
Babel Tower. Byatt, A. S.
The *Babes* in the Wood: A Chief Inspector Wexford Mystery. Rendell,
Ruth
BABI YAR MASSACRE, 1941
  Kuznetsov, Anatolii Petrovich. *Babi Yar: A Document in the Form of
    a Novel*

Babi Yar: A Document in the Form of a Novel. Kuznetsov, Anatolii Petrovich

Baby Ganesh Agency investigations [Series]. Khan, Vaseem

BABY STEALING
    Barton, Fiona. *The Child*
★*Baby Teeth: A Novel.* Stage, Zoje

BABYLON (EXTINCT CITY)
    Andrews, Mesu. *Of Fire and Lions: A Novel*
Babylon's Ashes. Corey, James S. A.

BABYSITTERS
    McDermott, Alice. *Child of My Heart*
    Reid, Kiley. ★*Such a Fun Age*
    Sullivan, J. Courtney. *Friends and Strangers*

BABYSITTING
    Starnone, Domenico. *Trick*

BACH, JOHANN SEBASTIAN
    Belfer, Lauren. *And After the Fire: A Novel*
    Cumming, Charles. *A Divided Spy*

Bacigalupi, Paolo
    ★*The Water Knife*
    ★*The Windup Girl*

BACK BAY, BOSTON, MASSACHUSETTS
    Lehane, Dennis. ★*Mystic River*
Back Channel. Carter, Stephen L.
Back to Blood: A Novel. Wolfe, Tom
Backlash. Spencer, Sally

Backman, Fredrik
    ★*Anxious People: A Novel*
    ★*Beartown: A Novel*
    Britt-Marie Was Here
    A Man Called Ove
    ★*My Grandmother Asked Me to Tell You She's Sorry: A Novel*
    Us Against You: A Novel

Bacon, Charlotte
    There Is Room for You
Bad Axe County novels [Series]. Galligan, John
Bad Blood. Dahl, Arne
Bad Blood. Malone, Minx
The Bad Daughter: A Novel. Fielding, Joy
A Bad Day for Sunshine. Jones, Darynda

BAD DAYS
    Barry, Dave. *Lunatics*
Bad Dirt: Wyoming Stories 2. Proulx, Annie
Bad Dreams and Other Stories. Hadley, Tessa
The Bad Girl. Vargas Llosa, Mario
Bad Girl Creek trilogy [Series]. Mapson, Jo-Ann
Bad Girl Creek: A Novel. Mapson, Jo-Ann
Bad Little Falls: A Novel. Doiron, Paul

BAD LUCK
    Amirrezvani, Anita. *The Blood of Flowers: A Novel*
    Cooper, Tom. *Florida Man*
    Dexter, Pete. *Spooner*
    Russo, Richard. ★*Nobody's Fool*
Bad Luck and Trouble. Child, Lee
★*Bad Men and Wicked Women.* Dickey, Eric Jerome
Bad Monkey. Hiaasen, Carl
Bad Moon Rising. Galligan, John
The Bad Muslim Discount. Masood, Syed M.

BAD NAUHEIM, GERMANY
    Ford, Ford Madox. ★*The Good Soldier: A Tale of Passion*
The Bad Seed: A Novel. March, William
Badlands. Bowen, Peter
Badlands. Box, C. J.
The Baggage Handler: A Novel. Rawlings, David
The Baghdad Clock. Al Rawi, Shahad

BAGHDAD, IRAQ
    Barth, John. *The Last Voyage of Somebody the Sailor*
Bagombo Snuff Box: Uncollected Short Fiction. Vonnegut, Kurt

Bagshawe, Tilly
    Adored

BAHAMAS
    Williams, Beatriz. *The Golden Hour*

BAHAMIAN AMERICANS
    Phillips, Caryl. *Dancing in the Dark*

BAHIA, BRAZIL
    Amado, Jorge. ★*Dona Flor and Her Two Husbands: A Moral and Amorous Tale*

BAIL BOND AGENTS
    Leonard, Elmore. *Rum Punch*
Bailey Ruth mysteries [Series]. Hart, Carolyn G.

Bailey, Paul
    Chapman's Odyssey
    Uncle Rudolf

Bailey, Tessa
    Fix Her Up

Bainbridge, Beryl
    Every Man for Himself

Bair, Kristin
    Agatha Arch Is Afraid of Everything
Baked. Smith, Mark Haskell
Baker Street brothers [Series]. Robertson, Michael
The Baker Street Letters. Robertson, Michael
The Baker Street Translation: A Mystery. Robertson, Michael
Baker Towers: A Novel. Haigh, Jennifer

Baker, Chandler
    Whisper Network: A Novel

Baker, Dorothy
    ★*Young Man with a Horn*

Baker, Jo
    The Body Lies
    Longbourn

Baker, Kage
    The Bird of the River
    The House of the Stag
    In the Garden of Iden: A Novel of the Company

BAKERIES
    Colgan, Jenny. *Sunrise by the Sea*

BAKERS
    Allen, Sarah Addison. *The Girl Who Chased the Moon: A Novel*
    Parker, Lucy. *Battle Royal*

BAKING
    Berg, Elizabeth. *Night of Miracles*
    Fluke, Joanne. ★*Christmas Cupcake Murder*
    Lau, Jackie. *Donut Fall in Love*
    Parker, Lucy. *Battle Royal*

Bala, Sharon
  The Boat People: A Novel
***Balance** of Power.* Patterson, Richard North
Balaskovits, A. A.
  Magic for Unlucky Girls: Stories
Balasubramanyam, Rajeev
  Professor Chandra Follows His Bliss: A Novel
Baldacci, David
  The Fallen
  ★*A Gambling Man*
  Hell's Corner
  Long Road to Mercy
  A Minute to Midnight
  ★*One Good Deed*
  One Summer
  Redemption
Baldwin, James
  ★*Another Country*
  ★*Early Novels and Stories*
  ★*Giovanni's Room*
  ★*Go Tell It on the Mountain*
  ★*Going to Meet the Man*
  ★*If Beale Street Could Talk*
  Just Above My Head
  Tell Me How Long the Train's Been Gone: A Novel
Baldwin, Joshua
  The Wilshire Sun
BALKAN PENINSULA
  Furst, Alan. *Spies of the Balkans: A Novel*
  Kadare, Ismail. ★*The Three-Arched Bridge*
  Obreht, Tea. *The Tiger's Wife: A Novel*
***Ball** Lightning.* Liu, Cixin
Ball, Jesse
  Census
Ball, John Dudley
  In the Heat of the Night
Ballad novels [Series]. McCrumb, Sharyn
★*The **Ballad** of Frankie Silver.* McCrumb, Sharyn
Ballard, J. G.
  ★*The Complete Stories of J.G. Ballard.*
  ★*The Day of Creation*
  Empire of the Sun: A Novel
  The Kindness of Women
  Kingdom Come
  Millennium People
BALLARD, J. G.
  Ballard, J. G. *Empire of the Sun: A Novel*
  Ballard, J. G. *The Kindness of Women*
  Leckie, Ann. *Ancillary Sword*
  Renault, Mary. *The Last of the Wine*
BALLET
  Kelly, Erin. *Watch Her Fall*
BALLET DANCERS
  Abbott, Megan E. ★*The Turnout: A Novel*
  Brayden, Melissa. *First Position*
  Buchanan, Cathy Marie. ★*The Painted Girls*
  Kelly, Erin. *Watch Her Fall*
  Stachniak, Eva. *The Chosen Maiden: A Novel*

BALLS (PARTIES)
  Baker, Jo. *Longbourn*
  Mas, Victoria. *The Mad Women's Ball*
Balogh, Mary
  The Arrangement
  The Escape
  More Than a Mistress
  Only Enchanting
  The Secret Mistress
  Simply Love
  ★*Someone to Care*
  ★*Someone to Cherish*
  Someone to Hold
  ★*Someone to Love*
  ★*Someone to Remember: A Westcott Story*
  Someone to Trust
  Someone to Wed
BALTIMORE, MARYLAND
  Blau, Jessica Anya. *Mary Jane: A Novel*
  Constantine, Liv. *The Last Time I Saw You*
  Holmes, Shannon. ★*B-More Careful: A Novel*
  Lippman, Laura. ★*After I'm Gone*
  Lippman, Laura. ★*Dream Girl*
  Lippman, Laura. ★*Hush Hush*
  Lippman, Laura. ★*Lady in the Lake: A Novel*
  Lippman, Laura. *No Good Deeds*
  Lippman, Laura. *What the Dead Know*
  Pearl, Matthew. *The Poe Shadow: A Novel*
  Row, Jess. *Your Face in Mine: A Novel*
  Styles, Toy. ★*War*
  Tyler, Anne. ★*The Accidental Tourist: A Novel*
  Tyler, Anne. *The Amateur Marriage: A Novel*
  Tyler, Anne. ★*Clock Dance: A Novel*
  Tyler, Anne. *A Patchwork Planet*
  Tyler, Anne. ★*Redhead by the Side of the Road*
  Tyler, Anne. ★*Saint Maybe*
Balzac, Honore de
  Eugenie Grandet
Balzano, Marco
  I'm Staying Here
Bambara, Toni Cade
  Gorilla, My Love
  ★*The Salt Eaters*
  Those Bones Are Not My Child
***Bamboo** and Blood: An Inspector O Novel.* Church, James
Banasky, Carmiel
  The Suicide of Claire Bishop
***Band** of Angels.* Warren, Robert Penn
Bandi
  The Accusation: Forbidden Stories from Inside North Korea
BANDS (MUSIC)
  Mitchell, David. ★*Utopia Avenue: A Novel*
BANGALORE, INDIA
  Adiga, Aravind. ★*The White Tiger: A Novel*
***Bangkok** 8.* Burdett, John
BANGKOK, THAILAND
  Bacigalupi, Paolo. ★*The Windup Girl*
  Burdett, John. *Bangkok 8*

Hallinan, Timothy. *Fools' River*
Osborne, Lawrence. *The Glass Kingdom: A Novel*
Schwarz, Liese O'Halloran. *What Could Be Saved*
Silber, Joan. *Secrets of Happiness*

BANGLADESH

Ali, Monica. ★*Brick Lane: A Novel*
Anam, Tahmima. *The Bones of Grace*
Hensher, Philip. *Scenes from Early Life: A Novel*
Hossain, Saad Z. *Cyber Mage: A Novel*
Zaman, Nadeem. *Up in the Main House & Other Stories*

BANGLADESHI AMERICANS

Anam, Tahmima. *The Startup Wife*

BANGLADESHI FAMILIES

Hensher, Philip. *Scenes from Early Life: A Novel*

BANK ROBBERIES

Atkins, Ace. *The Fallen*
Church, James. *Hidden Moon: An Inspector O Novel*
Cussler, Clive. ★*The Chase*
O'Rawe, Richard. *Northern Heist*
Peace, David. *Occupied City*
Sjowall, Maj. ★*The Locked Room: The Story of a Crime*
Stark, Richard. *Ask the Parrot: A Parker Novel*
Stark, Richard. *Dirty Money*
Westlake, Donald E. ★*Bank Shot*
Westlake, Donald E. *Forever and a Death*

BANK ROBBERS

Backman, Fredrik. ★*Anxious People: A Novel*
Estleman, Loren D. *The Adventures of Johnny Vermillion: A Novel*
O'Rawe, Richard. *Northern Heist*

★*Bank Shot*. Westlake, Donald E.

BANKERS

Bowman, Conor. ★*Horace Winter Says Goodbye*
Box, C. J. *Blue Heaven*
Livesey, Margot. *Criminals: A Novel*

BANKS AND BANKING

Bowman, Conor. ★*Horace Winter Says Goodbye*
Faulks, Sebastian. *A Week in December*
Haslett, Adam. *Union Atlantic*
Robotham, Michael. ★*The Wreckage*
Schlink, Bernhard. *Self's Murder*
Westlake, Donald E. ★*Bank Shot*

BANKS, ALAN (FICTITIOUS CHARACTER)

Robinson, Peter. *Children of the Revolution*
Robinson, Peter. *Cold Is the Grave*
Robinson, Peter. *In the Dark Places*
Robinson, Peter. *Innocent Graves: An Inspector Banks Mystery*

Banks, Iain

Consider Phlebas
The Crow Road
The Hydrogen Sonata
Matter
The Player of Games
Use of Weapons

Banks, Maya

Never Seduce a Scot

Banks, Russell

★*Affliction*
Cloudsplitter: A Novel

Continental Drift
Foregone
Lost Memory of Skin
★*The Sweet Hereafter*

Bannalec, Jean-Luc

Death in Brittany
The Granite Coast Murders
The Killing Tide: A Brittany Mystery

BANNED BOOKS

Bradbury, Ray. ★*Fahrenheit 451*
Pearl, Matthew. *The Dante Club: A Novel*
Prescott, Lara. *The Secrets We Kept*
Tolstaya, Tatyana. *The Slynx*

Banner, Catherine

The House at the Edge of Night: A Novel

Bannerless. Vaughn, Carrie

Bannerless novels (Carrie Vaughn) [Series]. Vaughn, Carrie

Bannister, Ilona

When I Ran Away

Bannister, Jo

Kindred Spirits
Silent Footsteps

*A **Banquet** of Consequences*. George, Elizabeth

Banville, John

Ancient Light
The Blue Guitar
The Book of Evidence
★*Eclipse: A Novel*
The Infinities
★*The Sea*

Bao, Ninh

The Sorrow of War: A Novel of North Vietnam

BAPTISM

Lloyd, Catherine. *Death Comes to the Rectory*

BAPTISTS

West, Monica. *Revival Season: A Novel*

BAR OWNERS

Carr, Robyn. ★*Virgin River*
Dell, Kari Lynn. *Fearless in Texas*
Murakami, Haruki. *South of the Border, West of the Sun*
Shalvis, Jill. *Sweet Little Lies*

BARBADOS

Edugyan, Esi. ★*Washington Black: A Novel*
Jones, Cherie. *How the One-Armed Sister Sweeps Her House*
Willig, Lauren. *The Summer Country: A Novel*

Barbarous. Spencer, Minerva

*The **Barbary** Figs*. Boudjedra, Rachid

Barbash, Tom

The Last Good Chance

BARBECUES

Moriarty, Liane. *Truly Madly Guilty*

Barbed Wire Heart. Sharpe, Tess

BARBER, FRANK

Phillips, Caryl. *Foreigners*
Stark, Richard. *Breakout*

Barber, Lizzy

A Girl Named Anna

BARBERS
Berry, Wendell. *Jayber Crow: A Novel*
Danticat, Edwidge. *The Dew Breaker*
Barbery, Muriel
The Elegance of the Hedgehog
BARCELONA, SPAIN
Hill Gumbao, Toni. *The Good Suicides: A Thriller*
Hill Gumbao, Toni. *The Summer of Dead Toys*
Ruiz Zafon, Carlos. *The Angel's Game*
Ruiz Zafon, Carlos. *The Labyrinth of the Spirits*
Ruiz Zafon, Carlos. *The Prisoner of Heaven*
Ruiz Zafon, Carlos. ★*The Shadow of the Wind*
★*Barchester Towers*. Trollope, Anthony
Barclay, Linwood
Broken Promise
★*Elevator Pitch: A Novel*
Far from True: A Novel
No Safe House
A Noise Downstairs: A Novel
Parting Shot
A Tap on the Window
Trust Your Eyes: A Thriller
The Twenty-Three: A Promise Falls Novel
Bardugo, Leigh
★*Ninth House*
Bare Bones. Reichs, Kathy
BARE KNUCKLE BOXING
Smith, Michael F. *The Fighter: A Novel*
Bareknuckle bastards [Series]. MacLean, Sarah
Barker, Clive
★*Weaveworld*
Barker, Nicola
Darkmans
Barker, Pat
Another World
★*The Eye in the Door*
★*The Ghost Road*
★*Regeneration*
★*The Silence of the Girls: A Novel*
The Women of Troy
Barker, Susan
★*The Incarnations: A Novel*
★*Barkskins: a Novel*. Proulx, Annie
BARNARD'S CROSSING, MASSACHUSETTS
Kemelman, Harry. *Monday the Rabbi Took Off*
Kemelman, Harry. *One Fine Day the Rabbi Bought a Cross*
Barnard, Robert
Death of a Literary Widow
Barnes, Djuna
★*Nightwood*
Barnes, Jonathan
The Somnambulist
Barnes, Julian
★*England, England*
★*Flaubert's Parrot*
★*A History of the World in 10 1/2 Chapters*
The Noise of Time
The Only Story

★*The Sense of an Ending*
Barnett, David
Calling Major Tom
Barnett, Karen
Ever Faithful
Barnett, LaShonda K.
Jam on the Vine
Barnett, S. K.
Safe
Barney's Version: A Novel. Richler, Mordecai
Barnhill, Kelly Regan
Dreadful Young Ladies and Other Stories
Baroness Pontalba novels [Series]. Smith, Julie
BARONS AND BARONESSES
deWitt, Patrick. *Undermajordomo Minor*
Barr, Mark
Watershed
Barr, Nevada
Destroyer Angel: An Anna Pigeon Novel
The Rope: An Anna Pigeon Novel
Track of the Cat
What Rose Forgot
BARRINGTON, STONE (FICTITIOUS CHARACTER)
Woods, Stuart. *New York Dead*
Barry, Ava
Windhall
Barry, Brunonia
The Map of True Places
Barry, Dave
Insane City
Lunatics
Barry, Jessica
★*Don't Turn Around*
Barry, Sebastian
Days Without End: A Novel
The Secret Scripture: A Novel
★*A Thousand Moons: A Novel*
Barrytown novels [Series]. Doyle, Roddy
BARS (DRINKING ESTABLISHMENTS)
Banner, Catherine. *The House at the Edge of Night: A Novel*
Bruno, Anna. *Ordinary Hazards: A Novel*
BARSETSHIRE (ENGLAND : IMAGINARY PLACE)
Trollope, Anthony. ★*Barchester Towers*
Trollope, Anthony. *Framley Parsonage*
Trollope, Anthony. *The Last Chronicle of Barset*
Trollope, Anthony. *The Warden*
Bartels, Erin
We Hope for Better Things
BARTENDERS
Koontz, Dean R. *Velocity*
Mandel, Emily St. John. ★*The Glass Hotel: A Novel*
Tracy, P. J. ★*Deep into the Dark*
Barth, John
Chimera
★*The Floating Opera*
★*Giles Goat-Boy ;: Or, the Revised New Syllabus*
The Last Voyage of Somebody the Sailor
★*The Sot-Weed Factor*

Barthelme, Donald
Sixty Stories
Barthelme, Frederick
Bob the Gambler
Elroy Nights
Painted Desert: A Novel
Bartlett, Neil
The Disappearance Boy
Barton, Fiona
The Child
The Suspect
Bartz, Andrea
The Herd: A Novel
The Lost Night
Barzak, Christopher
One for Sorrow
BASEBALL
Malamud, Bernard. *The Natural*
Murakami, Haruki. ★*First Person Singular: Stories*
Roth, Philip. *The Great American Novel*
BASEBALL — HISTORY
DeLillo, Don. *Underworld*
BASEBALL PLAYERS
Holmes, Linda. ★*Evvie Drake Starts Over: A Novel*
Roth, Philip. *The Great American Novel*
BASEBALL TEAMS
Roth, Philip. *The Great American Novel*
Basket Case. Hiaasen, Carl
BASKETBALL COACHES
McCarthy, Jesse. *The Fugitivities*
Basketball Jones: A Novel. Harris, E. Lynn
BASQUE FAMILIES
Aramburu, Fernando. *Homeland*
BASQUE PROVINCES
Garcia Saenz, Eva. *The Silence of the White City*
Redondo, Dolores. *The Invisible Guardian*
The Bastard of Istanbul. Shafak, Elif
★*Bastard Out of Carolina*. Allison, Dorothy
The Bastards of Pizzofalcone. De Giovanni, Maurizio
Bateman, Kate
A Reckless Match
This Earl of Mine
Bates, Judy Fong
★*Midnight at the Dragon Cafe*
Bath Haus: A Thriller. Vernon, P. J.
BATH, ENGLAND
Austen, Jane. *Northanger Abbey*
Balogh, Mary. *Someone to Hold*
Hayder, Mo. *Hanging Hill*
Heyer, Georgette. *Black Sheep*
Lovesey, Peter. *Beau Death*
Lovesey, Peter. ★*The Last Detective*
Lovesey, Peter. *The Tooth Tattoo*
BATTLE CASUALTIES
Keneally, Thomas. ★*The Daughters of Mars*
Battle Royal. Parker, Lucy
BATTLE, SUPERINTENDENT (FICTITIOUS CHARACTER)
Christie, Agatha. *Towards Zero*

BATTLES
Iggulden, Conn. *The Abbot's Tale*
Penman, Sharon Kay. *When Christ and His Saints Slept*
Pike, Signe. *The Forgotten Kingdom: A Novel*
Punke, Michael. *Ridgeline: A Novel*
Renault, Mary. *The Persian Boy*
Robbins, David L. *Last Citadel: A Novel of the Battle of Kursk*
Saylor, Steven. *The Judgment of Caesar: A Novel of Ancient Rome*
Scott, Walter. ★*Rob Roy*
Shaara, Jeff. *Gods and Generals: A Novel of the Civil War*
Shaara, Jeff. *The Last Full Measure*
Batuman, Elif
★*The Idiot*
BAUDELAIRE, CHARLES
Delaney, J. P. *Believe Me: A Novel*
Kelly, Julia. *The Light Over London*
Baudolino. Eco, Umberto
Bauer, Belinda
The Beautiful Dead
Snap
Bauer, Carlene
★*Frances and Bernard*
Bauermeister, Erica
The Scent Keeper
Bauman, Bruce
★*Broken Sleep: An American Dream*
Bausch, Richard
Hello to the Cannibals: A Novel
Peace
★*Rebel Powers*
The Stories of Richard Bausch
BAVARIA
Sebald, Winfried Georg. *Vertigo*
Bawden, Nina
Family Money
Baxter, Charles
The Feast of Love
Saul and Patsy
★*The Sun Collective*
There's Something I Want You to Do: Stories
Bayard, Louis
The Black Tower: A Novel
The Pale Blue Eye: A Novel
Baztan trilogy [Series]. Redondo, Dolores
★*Be Cool: Everyone Is Looking for the Next Big Hit*. Leonard, Elmore
Be My Knife. Grossman, David
Beach House Reunion. Monroe, Mary Alice
Beach Read. Henry, Emily
Beach, Edward L.
Run Silent, Run Deep
BEACHES
Andrews, Mary Kay. *Sunset Beach*
Baldacci, David. *One Summer*
Bannalec, Jean-Luc. *The Granite Coast Murders*
Sparks, Nicholas. *Every Breath*
Beagin, Jen
★*Vacuum in the Dark: A Novel*

Beagle, Peter S.
A Fine and Private Place
In Calabria
★*The Last Unicorn*
Summerlong
The Unicorn Sonata
Beah, Ishmael
Little Family
Beams, Clare
The Illness Lesson
★*The Bean Trees: A Novel*. Kingsolver, Barbara
The Bear. Krivak, Andrew
★*The Bear and the Nightingale*. Arden, Katherine
The Bear Went Over the Mountain. Kotzwinkle, William
Bear, Elizabeth
All the Windwracked Stars
Blood and Iron: A Novel of the Promethean Age
Ink and Steel: A Novel of the Promethean Age
Range of Ghosts
The Red-Stained Wings
Shattered Pillars
Steles of the Sky
The Stone in the Skull
Stone Mad
Bear, Greg
Anvil of Stars
The Collected Stories of Greg Bear
The Forge of God
BEARS
Kotzwinkle, William. *The Bear Went Over the Mountain*
McLaughlin, James A. *Bearskin*
Bearskin. McLaughlin, James A.
Beartown [Series]. Backman, Fredrik
★*Beartown: a Novel*. Backman, Fredrik
Beast Charmer [Series]. Martineau, Maxym M.
Beastly Things: A Commissario Guido Brunetti Mystery. Leon, Donna
BEAT CULTURE
Bisson, Terry. *Any Day Now*
Kerouac, Jack. ★*Road Novels 1957-1960*
BEAT GENERATION
Kerouac, Jack. ★*Road Novels 1957-1960*
Beat to Quarters. Forester, C. S.
Beaton, M. C.
Agatha Raisin and the Quiche of Death
Agatha Raisin and the Witch of Wyckhadden
Death of a Macho Man
★*Hot to Trot*
Pushing up Daisies: An Agatha Raisin Mystery
Beattie, Ann
Chilly Scenes of Winter
The Doctor's House: A Novel
★*Picturing Will*
The State We're In: Maine Stories
A Wonderful Stroke of Luck: A Novel
Beatty, Paul
★*The Sellout: A Novel*
Slumberland: A Novel
Beau Death. Lovesey, Peter

BEAUFORT, MARGARET
Gregory, Philippa. *The Red Queen: A Novel*
Putney, Mary Jo. *The Marriage Spell: A Novel*
★*The Beautiful and Damned*. Fitzgerald, F. Scott
A Beautiful Blue Death. Finch, Charles
The Beautiful Bureaucrat: A Novel. Phillips, Helen
Beautiful Children: A Novel. Bock, Charles
A Beautiful Corpse. Daugherty, Christi
The Beautiful Dead. Bauer, Belinda
Beautiful Maria of My Soul. Hijuelos, Oscar
★*Beautiful World, Where Are You*. Rooney, Sally
BEAUTY
McDermott, Alice. *Child of My Heart*
Morris, Heather. *Cilka's Journey*
Oyeyemi, Helen. *Boy, Snow, Bird: A Novel*
Weldon, Fay. *The Life and Loves of a She-Devil*
BEAUTY CARE
Rai, Alisha. ★*First Comes Like*
Beauvoir, Simone de
★*The Mandarins: A Novel*
The Woman Destroyed
Because I'm Watching. Dodd, Christina
Because It Is Bitter, and Because It Is My Heart. Oates, Joyce Carol
Beck, Haylen
Here and Gone
Lost You
BECK, MARTIN (FICTITIOUS CHARACTER)
Sjowall, Maj. ★*The Laughing Policeman*
Sjowall, Maj. ★*The Locked Room: The Story of a Crime*
Beckerman, Hannah
If Only I Could Tell You
BECKETT, JO (FICTITIOUS CHARACTER)
Gardiner, Meg. *The Dirty Secrets Club*
Beckett, L. X.
Gamechanger
Beckett, Samuel
★*Murphy*
★*The Becoming*. Roberts, Nora
★*Becoming Mrs. Lewis: The Improbable Love Story of Joy Davidman and C. S. Lewis*. Henry, Patti Callahan
BED AND BREAKFAST
Block, Lawrence. ★*The Burglar in the Library*
Delany, Vicki. *Tea & Treachery*
Hibbert, Talia. ★*Act Your Age, Eve Brown*
The Bedlam Detective: A Novel. Gallagher, Stephen
The Bedlam Stacks. Pulley, Natasha
The Beekeeper of Aleppo: A Novel. Lefteri, Christy
BEEKEEPERS
Frank, Dorothea Benton. *Queen Bee*
Kidd, Sue Monk. ★*The Secret Life of Bees*
Lefteri, Christy. *The Beekeeper of Aleppo: A Novel*
BEEKEEPING
Garvin, Eileen. *The Music of Bees*
The Beet Queen: A Novel. Erdrich, Louise
BEETLES
Joyce, Rachel. *Miss Benson's Beetle*
★*Before and After*. Brown, Rosellen
Before I Let You Go. Rimmer, Kelly

★*Before* She Disappeared: A Novel. Gardner, Lisa

Before the Coffee Gets Cold. Kawaguchi, Toshikazu

Before the coffee gets cold [Series]. Kawaguchi, Toshikazu

Before the Devil Fell. Olson, Neil

Before the Fall. Hawley, Noah

Before the Frost: A Linda Wallander Mystery. Mankell, Henning

Before the Ruins: A Novel. Gosling, Victoria

Before We Were Wicked. Dickey, Eric Jerome

The *Beggar* King. Potzsch, Oliver

Beggarman, Thief. Shaw, Irwin

BEGGARS

> Bush, Keisha. *No Heaven for Good Boys: A Novel*

Beggars in Spain. Kress, Nancy

Beggars trilogy [Series]. Kress, Nancy

The *Beginning* Place. Le Guin, Ursula K.

Begley, Louis

> *About Schmidt*

BEHEADING

> Fuentes, Carlos. *Destiny and Desire: A Novel*

> Preston, Douglas J. *City of Endless Night*

> Quartey, Kwei. *Murder at Cape Three Points*

> Rees, Matt. *The Fourth Assassin*

Behind Closed Doors. Paris, B. A.

Behind Every Lie. McDonald, Christina

★*Behind* Her Eyes: A Novel. Pinborough, Sarah

Beijing Coma. Ma, Jian

Being Invisible: A Novel. Berger, Thomas

★*Being* There. Kosinski, Jerzy

Beirut Hellfire Society: A Novel. Hage, Rawi

BEIRUT, LEBANON

> Hage, Rawi. *Beirut Hellfire Society: A Novel*

> Hage, Rawi. *De Niro's Game*

> Swinson, David. *City on the Edge*

★*Bel* Canto: A Novel. Patchett, Ann

BELFAST, NORTHERN IRELAND

> McKinty, Adrian. *In the Morning I'll Be Gone: A Detective Sean Duffy Novel*

> O'Rawe, Richard. *Northern Heist*

> Walsh, S. Kirk. *The Elephant of Belfast: A Novel*

Belfer, Lauren

> *And After the Fire: A Novel*

Belfoure, Charles

> *The Paris Architect: A Novel*

BELGIANS IN ENGLAND

> Christie, Agatha. *Curtain*

> Christie, Agatha. *Mrs. McGinty's Dead*

> Christie, Agatha. ★*Murder on the Orient Express*

BELGIUM

> Khadra, Yasmina. ★*Khalil: A Novel*

> Meuleman, Sarah. *Find Me Gone*

> Ramzipoor, E. R. *The Ventriloquists*

BELIEF AND DOUBT

> Dekker, Ted. *The Girl Behind the Red Rope*

> Donoghue, Emma. ★*The Wonder*

> Elison, Meg. *The Book of Flora*

> Masood, Syed M. *The Bad Muslim Discount*

> Miles, Jonathan. *Anatomy of a Miracle*

> Perry, Sarah. *The Essex Serpent*

> Rawlings, David. *The Baggage Handler: A Novel*

> Rivers, Francine. ★*Redeeming Love*

> Runcie, James. *The Road to Grantchester*

> Updike, John. *In the Beauty of the Lilies*

Believe Me: A Novel. Delaney, J. P.

Believing the Lie. George, Elizabeth

Bell Elkins mysteries [Series]. Keller, Julia

★*A* **Bell** *for Adano*. Hersey, John

★*The* **Bell** *Jar*. Plath, Sylvia

The **Bell** Ringers. Porter, Henry

Bell, Darcey

> *Something She's Not Telling Us*

BELL, ISAAC (FICTITIOUS CHARACTER)

> Cussler, Clive. ★*The Chase*

Bell, Lenora

> *For the Duke's Eyes Only*

> ★*How the Duke Was Won*

> *One Fine Duke*

> ★*What a Difference a Duke Makes*

Bell, Shelly

> *At His Mercy*

> *For His Pleasure*

Bell, Ted

> *Overkill: An Alex Hawke Novel*

BELL, VANESSA

> Clark, Wahida. ★*Thugs and the Women Who Love Them*

> Parmar, Priya. *Vanessa and Her Sister*

The *Bellarosa* Connection. Bellow, Saul

BELLE EPOQUE (1871-1914)

> Buchanan, Cathy Marie. ★*The Painted Girls*

> Chee, Alexander. *The Queen of the Night*

> Harris, Robert. *An Officer and a Spy*

> Horrocks, Caitlin. *The Vexations*

> Robertson, Imogen. *The Paris Winter*

> Sedgwick, Marcus. *Mister Memory: A Novel*

> Tallis, Frank. *Vienna Blood: A Max Liebermann Mystery*

Belle, Kimberly

> *Dear Wife*

Bellefleur, Alexandria

> *Hang the Moon*

> *Written in the Stars*

Belles of London [Series]. Matthews, Mimi

Belli, Kate

> *Deception by Gaslight: A Gilded Gotham Mystery*

Bellow, Saul

> ★*The Adventures of Augie March*

> *The Bellarosa Connection*

> *Dangling Man*

> *The Dean's December: A Novel*

> ★*Henderson the Rain King: A Novel*

> ★*Herzog*

> ★*Humboldt's Gift*

> *More Die of Heartbreak*

> ★*Mr. Sammler's Planet*

> *Novels, 1944-1953*

> *Ravelstein*

> ★*Seize the Day*

★*Bellweather* Rhapsody. Racculia, Kate

Belmont mansion novels [Series]. Alexander, Tamera
BELMONT, ALVA
    Bell, Lenora. *For the Duke's Eyes Only*
    Fowler, Therese. *A Well-Behaved Woman: A Novel of the Vanderbilts*
    Pineiro, Caridad. *South Beach Love: A Feel-Good Romance from Hallmark Publishing*
    Rosen, Renee. *The Social Graces*
BELONGING
    Ahmad, Jamil. *The Wandering Falcon*
    Awad, Mona. *Bunny*
    Chai, May-Lee. *Useful Phrases for Immigrants: Stories*
    Clemmons, Zinzi. *What We Lose*
    Cusset, Catherine. *Life of David Hockney: A Novel*
    Fridlund, Emily. ★*History of Wolves: A Novel*
    Hesse, Hermann. *The Fairy Tales of Hermann Hesse*
    Kafka, Franz. ★*Collected Stories*
    Larkin, Allie. *The People We Keep*
    McCullers, Carson. *The Member of the Wedding*
    Mozley, Fiona. ★*Elmet*
    Onuzo, Chibundu. *Sankofa: A Novel*
    Rivers, Francine. *Bridge to Haven*
    Row, Jess. *Your Face in Mine: A Novel*
    Savas, Aysegul. *Walking on the Ceiling*
    Singer, Isaac Bashevis. *Collected Stories: A Friend of Kafka to Passions*
    Singer, Isaac Bashevis. *Collected Stories: Gimpel the Fool to the Letter Writer*
    Thammavongsa, Souvankham. *How to Pronounce Knife: Stories*
    Wolff, Tobias. *Old School: A Novel*
Beloved Poison. Thomson, E. S.
★*Beloved: a Novel*. Morrison, Toni
Below stairs mysteries [Series]. Ashley, Jennifer
Below the Belt. Woods, Stuart
Ben Walker novels [Series]. Golden, Christopher
Ben Webster novels [Series]. Morgan Jones, Chris
★*Ben-Hur*. Wallace, Lew
Benaron, Naomi
    Running the Rift: A Novel
A *Bend* in the River. Naipaul, V. S.
Bender, Aimee
    The Butterfly Lampshade
Bender, Tony
    The Last Ghost Dancer
★*Bendigo* Shafter. L'Amour, Louis
★*Beneath* the Abbey Wall: A Novel. Scott, A. D.
★*Beneath* the Sugar Sky. McGuire, Seanan
Benedetti, Mario
    Springtime in a Broken Mirror
Benedict, Helen
    Wolf Season
Benedict, Marie
    ★*Lady Clementine*
    The Only Woman in the Room
BENEDICTINE NUNS
    Sharratt, Mary. *Illuminations: A Novel of Hildegard Von Bingen*
Benediction. Haruf, Kent
BENEFACTORS
    Ozick, Cynthia. *Heir to the Glimmering World*

BENGU, DAVID (FICTITIOUS CHARACTER)
    Stanley, Michael. *Death of the Mantis*
Benioff, David
    City of Thieves: A Novel
Benjamin January mysteries [Series]. Hambly, Barbara
Benjamin, Ali
    The Smash-Up: A Novel
Benjamin, Chloe
    ★*The Immortalists: A Novel*
Benjamin, Melanie
    Alice I Have Been
    ★*The Aviator's Wife: A Novel*
Benn, James R.
    Billy Boyle: A World War Two Mystery
    ★*The Red Horse: A Billy Boyle World War II Mystery*
    Road of Bones: A Billy Boyle World War II Mystery
Bennett, Alan
    ★*The Uncommon Reader*
Bennett, Anna
    First Earl I See Tonight
Bennett, Bethany
    West End Earl
Bennett, Brit
    The Mothers
    ★*The Vanishing Half*
Bennett, Jenn
    Bitter Spirits
Bennett, Robert Jackson
    Foundryside
    Shorefall
Benny Griessel novels [Series]. Meyer, Deon
Bent Road. Roy, Lori
Benton, Janet
    Lilli De Jong: A Novel
Benz, Chanelle
    ★*The Gone Dead*
BEREAVEMENT
    Adkins, Mary. *When You Read This*
    Bilenchi, Romano. ★*The Chill*
    Brockmeier, Kevin. *The Illumination*
    Byrne, Trevor. *Ghosts and Lightning*
    Grossman, David. *Falling Out of Time*
    Hemmings, Kaui Hart. *The Possibilities: A Novel*
BEREAVEMENT — PSYCHOLOGICAL ASPECTS
    Banks, Russell. ★*The Sweet Hereafter*
BEREAVEMENT IN FAMILIES
    Haruf, Kent. *Benediction*
    Kelly, Erin. *The Burning Air: A Novel*
BEREAVEMENT IN PARENTS
    Bohjalian, Chris. *The Buffalo Soldier: A Novel*
BEREAVEMENT IN WOMEN
    Butler, Marcia. *Pickle's Progress*
    Garvin, Eileen. *The Music of Bees*
Beren and Luthien. Tolkien, J. R. R.
Berenson, Alex
    The Deceivers
    The Faithful Spy: A Novel
    The Prisoner

Berg, Elizabeth
  The Confession Club: A Novel
  Night of Miracles
  The Story of Arthur Truluv: A Novel
Berg, Gretchen
  The Operator
Berger, Thomas
  Being Invisible: A Novel
  ★*Neighbors: A Novel*
BERGMAN, INGMAR
  Golding, Melanie. *Little Darlings*
  Ullmann, Linn. *Unquiet: A Novel*
Bergman, Megan Mayhew
  Almost Famous Women: Stories
Bergstrom, Heather Brittain
  Steal the North: A Novel
BERKELEY, CALIFORNIA
  Kellerman, Jonathan. ★*Half Moon Bay: A Novel*
  Sekaran, Shanthi. ★*Lucky Boy*
Berkowitz, Ira
  Old Flame: A Jackson Steeg Novel
BERKSHIRE HILLS, MASSACHUSETTS
  Benjamin, Ali. *The Smash-Up: A Novel*
  Dee, Jonathan. *The Locals: A Novel*
  Roth, Philip. *The Ghost Writer*
Berlin Game. Deighton, Len
★*The Berlin Stories: The Last of Mr. Norris, Goodbye to Berlin.*
  Isherwood, Christopher
BERLIN WALL — DISMANTLING, 1989
  McEwan, Ian. *Black Dogs*
BERLIN, GERMANY
  Beatty, Paul. *Slumberland: A Novel*
  Chiaverini, Jennifer. *Resistance Women: A Novel*
  Clark, Clare. *In the Full Light of the Sun*
  Deaver, Jeffery. *Garden of Beasts: A Novel of Berlin 1936*
  Deighton, Len. *Berlin Game*
  Edugyan, Esi. *Half-Blood Blues*
  Eliasberg, Jan. ★*Hannah's War*
  Epstein, Jennifer Cody. ★*Wunderland: A Novel*
  Erpenbeck, Jenny. *Go, Went, Gone: A Novel*
  Fesperman, Dan. *Safe Houses: A Novel*
  Gillham, David R. *City of Women*
  Grass, Gunter. *Too Far Afield*
  Grossman, Paul. *Children of Wrath*
  Hall, Adam. *The Quiller Memorandum*
  Hoffman, Alice. ★*The World That We Knew*
  Hooper, Elise. *Fast Girls: A Novel of the 1936 Women's Olympic Team*
  Isherwood, Christopher. ★*The Berlin Stories: The Last of Mr. Norris, Goodbye to Berlin*
  Kerr, Philip. ★*Metropolis: A Bernie Gunther Novel*
  Lawton, John. *Then We Take Berlin*
  Le Carre, John. *The Spy Who Came in from the Cold*
  Steinhauer, Olen. *The Bridge of Sighs*
  Uris, Leon. *Armageddon: A Novel of Berlin*
Berlin, Lucia
  ★*Evening in Paradise: More Stories*
  ★*A Manual for Cleaning Women: Selected Stories*

Bernard Samson novels [Series]. Deighton, Len
Berne, Lisa
  You May Kiss the Bride
Bernhard Gunther mysteries [Series]. Kerr, Philip
Bernhard, Emilia
  The Books of the Dead
Bernhard, Thomas
  Frost: A Novel
  ★*The Loser*
  Wittgenstein's Nephew: A Friendship
  ★*Woodcutters*
BERNHARD, THOMAS
  Bernhard, Thomas. *Wittgenstein's Nephew: A Friendship*
BERNHARDT, SARAH
  Austin, Finola. *Bronte's Mistress*
  Gortner, C. W. *The First Actress: A Novel of Sarah Bernhardt*
Bernie Rhodenbarr mysteries [Series]. Block, Lawrence
Berry, Connie
  A Legacy of Murder
Berry, Steve
  ★*The Bishop's Pawn*
  The Lost Order
  ★*The Malta Exchange: A Novel*
  ★*The Templar Legacy: A Novel of Suspense*
  ★*The Warsaw Protocol*
Berry, Wendell
  Jayber Crow: A Novel
  ★*That Distant Land: The Collected Stories of Wendell Berry*
Bess Crawford mysteries [Series]. Todd, Charles
Best American mystery stories [Series].
Best American science fiction and fantasy [Series].
Best American short stories [Series].
Best Boy: A Novel. Gottlieb, Eli
Best Day Ever: A Novel. Rouda, Kaira Sturdivant
BEST FRIENDS
  Bowman, Valerie. *No Other Duke but You*
  Bradbury, Ray. ★*Something Wicked This Way Comes*
  Chung, Maxine Mei-Fung. *The Eighth Girl*
  Doan, Amy Mason. *The Summer List*
  Hage, Rawi. *De Niro's Game*
  Harrington, Anna. *An Inconvenient Duke*
  Hendrix, Grady. *My Best Friend's Exorcism*
  Henry, Emily. *People We Meet on Vacation*
  Henson, Pene. *Into the Blue*
  Hodges, Cheris F. *Rumor Has It*
  K'wan. *Gutter*
  Loren, Roni. ★*The One for You*
  Machado, Carmen Maria. ★*The Low, Low Woods*
  Monroe, Mary. ★*God Don't Like Ugly*
  Pride, Christine. ★*We Are Not Like Them*
  Rader-Day, Lori. *Little Pretty Things*
  Rooney, Sally. ★*Conversations with Friends*
  Shupe, Joanna. *The Heiress Hunt*
  Snow, Jennifer. *An Alaskan Christmas*
  Stephens, Alice. *Famous Adopted People*
BEST FRIENDS — DEATH
  Bellow, Saul. ★*Humboldt's Gift*
Best horror of the year (Ellen Datlow) [Series].

***Best** Laid Plans*. Florio, Gwen

★*The **Best** Man*. Higgins, Kristan

★*The **Best** of Gene Wolfe: A Definitive Retrospective of His Finest Short Fiction*. Wolfe, Gene

***Best** of My Love*. Mallery, Susan

BEST SELLERS (BOOKS)

    Kotzwinkle, William. *The Bear Went Over the Mountain*

***Best** Served Cold*. Spencer, Sally

★*The **Best** Short Stories of Bret Harte*. Harte, Bret

*The **Best** Short Stories of Dostoevsky*. Dostoyevsky, Fyodor

***Beth** & Amy*. Kantra, Virginia

BETRAYAL

    Akunin, B. *Sister Pelagia and the White Bulldog: A Mystery*

    Allende, Isabel. *Portrait in Sepia: A Novel*

    Banville, John. *The Blue Guitar*

    Bezmozgis, David. *The Betrayers: A Novel*

    Binchy, Maeve. *Circle of Friends*

    Boyle, T. Coraghessan. *World's End: A Novel*

    Brink, Andre P. *Philida: A Novel*

    Bryant, Niobia. *Message from a Mistress*

    Ca$h. ★*Trust No Bitch*

    Center, Katherine. *Things You Save in a Fire*

    Cheek, Chip. *Cape May*

    Clark, Wahida. ★*Payback Is a Mutha*

    Cleeves, Ann. *The Crow Trap*

    Cobbs Hoffman, Elizabeth. *The Hamilton Affair*

    Cook, Thomas H. *Instruments of Night*

    Coulter, Catherine. *The Sixth Day*

    Deane, Seamus. *Reading in the Dark*

    Diamant, Anita. ★*The Red Tent*

    Doan, Amy Mason. *The Summer List*

    Doshi, Avni. *Burnt Sugar: A Novel*

    Edugyan, Esi. *Half-Blood Blues*

    Edugyan, Esi. ★*Washington Black: A Novel*

    Edwards, Louis. *Ramadan Ramsey: A Novel*

    Feeney, Alice. ★*Sometimes I Lie*

    Fleming, Ian. *From Russia with Love*

    Follett, Ken. ★*The Pillars of the Earth*

    Follett, Ken. ★*Whiteout*

    Gentry, Amy. *Last Woman Standing*

    George, Margaret. *The Splendor Before the Dark: A Novel of the Emperor Nero*

    Gibson, William. ★*Neuromancer*

    Goddard, Robert. ★*Into the Blue*

    Gross, Andrew. *Button Man*

    Hallberg, Garth Risk. ★*City on Fire*

    Hamilton, Karen. *The Last Wife*

    Higgins, Jack. *The Eagle Has Flown*

    Hilderbrand, Elin. ★*Winter in Paradise: A Novel*

    Hill, Reginald. *The Woodcutter: A Novel*

    Hunter, Megan. *The Harpy*

    Jones, Robert. ★*The Prophets: A Novel*

    Jones, Tayari. *Silver Sparrow: A Novel*

    Knowles, John. ★*A Separate Peace*

    Kuang, R. F. ★*The Dragon Republic*

    Lackberg, Camilla. *The Golden Cage*

    Lehane, Dennis. *Live by Night*

    Lehane, Dennis. *Since We Fell*

Leonard, Elmore. *Rum Punch*

Marcelo, Tif. *In a Book Club Far Away*

Martell, Nick. *The Kingdom of Liars*

Maturin, Charles Robert. *Melmoth the Wanderer: A Tale*

Mayor, Archer. *Red Herring: A Joe Gunther Novel*

McLaughlin, Danielle. *The Art of Falling*

Meltzer, Brad. *The Tenth Justice*

Offutt, Chris. ★*The Killing Hills*

Penelope, L. *Cry of Metal & Bone: Earthsinger Chronicles, Book 3*

Perry, Anne. *Dark Tide Rising: A William Monk Novel*

Petterson, Per. *I Refuse*

Pinborough, Sarah. ★*Cross Her Heart: A Novel*

Renault, Mary. *Funeral Games*

Rosnay, Tatiana de. ★*Flowers of Darkness*

Roth, Philip. *I Married a Communist*

Runcie, James. *Sidney Chambers and the Forgiveness of Sins*

Sallis, James. *Drive*

Saylor, Steven. *The Triumph of Caesar: A Novel of Ancient Rome*

Scalzi, John. *Redshirts: A Novel with Three Codas*

Scott, A. D. *A Double Death on the Black Isle: A Novel*

Sebastian, Tim. *Fatal Ally*

Smith, Wilbur A. *Birds of Prey*

Spencer-Fleming, Julia. *All Mortal Flesh*

Stark, Richard. *Comeback*

Steinhauer, Olen. *The Tourist*

Styles, Toy. *Raunchy 2: Mad's Love*

Styles, Toy. ★*War*

Styles, Toy. *War 2: All Hell Breaks Loose*

Swift, Graham. ★*Last Orders: A Novel*

Updike, John. *Gertrude and Claudius*

Wagers, K. B. *After the Crown*

Warren, Robert Penn. *World Enough and Time: A Romantic Novel*

*The **Betrayers**: a Novel*. Bezmozgis, David

BETS

    Verne, Jules. ★*Around the World in Eighty Days*

    Waters, Martha. *To Love and to Loathe: A Novel*

*The **Better** Liar: A Novel*. Jones, Tanen

***Better** Luck Next Time: A Novel*. Johnson, Julia Claiborne

★*A **Better** Man: A Chief Inspector Gamache Novel*. Penny, Louise

*The **Better** Sister: A Novel*. Burke, Alafair

***Better** Than People*. Parrish, Roan

*A **Better** World*. Sakey, Marcus

Betts, Doris

    Souls Raised from the Dead: A Novel

***Between** earth and sky* [Series]. Roanhorse, Rebecca

***Between** My Father and the King: New and Uncollected Stories*. Frame, Janet

***Between** the Acts*. Woolf, Virginia

★***Between** the Devil and the Duke*. Bowen, Kelly

BETWEEN THE WARS (1918-1939)

    Balzano, Marco. *I'm Staying Here*

    Boschwitz, Ulrich Alexander. *The Passenger: A Novel*

    Brown, Sandra. ★*Blind Tiger*

    Chevalier, Tracy. *A Single Thread*

    Clark, Clare. *In the Full Light of the Sun*

    Clayton, Meg Waite. *The Last Train to London*

    Dunmore, Helen. *The Lie*

    Durrell, Lawrence. ★*Justine*

Dybek, Nick. *The Verdun Affair: A Novel*
Gaynor, Hazel. *Three Words for Goodbye*
George, Alex. *The Paris Hours: A Novel*
Gross, Andrew. *Button Man*
Hambly, Barbara. *Scandal in Babylon*
Hannah, Sophie. *The Killings at Kingfisher Hill*
Hannah, Sophie. *The Mystery of Three Quarters: The New Hercule Poirot Mystery*
Huber, Anna Lee. *Penny for Your Secrets*
Johnson, Julia Claiborne. *Better Luck Next Time: A Novel*
Kerr, Philip. ★*Metropolis: A Bernie Gunther Novel*
King, Laurie R. *Castle Shade*
Mamet, David. *Chicago: A Novel*
McPherson, Catriona. ★*A Step so Grave*
Morante, Elsa. *Arturo's Island: A Novel*
Neubauer, Erica Ruth. *Murder at the Mena House*
Perry, Anne. ★*A Darker Reality*
Perry, Anne. ★*Death in Focus: An Elena Standish Novel*
Perry, Anne. *A Question of Betrayal*
Solomon, Anna. *Leaving Lucy Pear*
Stachniak, Eva. *The Chosen Maiden: A Novel*
Stewart, Amy. ★*Miss Kopp Investigates*
Sundin, Sarah. *When Twilight Breaks*
Swift, Graham. ★*Mothering Sunday: A Romance*
Wieland, Liza. *Paris, 7 A.M.*

Beukes, Lauren
Afterland
Broken Monsters
The Shining Girls
Slipping: Stories, Essays, & Other Writing
Zoo City

Beverley, Jo
My Lady Notorious
Tempting Fortune

BEVERLY HILLS, CALIFORNIA
Connelly, Michael. *The Lincoln Lawyer: A Novel*
Martin, Steve. *Shopgirl*

Beverly, William
Dodgers: A Novel

★*Bewilderment: a Novel*. Powers, Richard

Beyda, Emily
The Body Double

Beyond Absolution: A Mystery Set in 1920s Ireland. Harrison, Cora
Beyond All Reasonable Doubt: A Novel. Persson Giolito, Malin
Beyond Recall: A Novel. Goddard, Robert
Beyond the Point: A Novel. Gibson, Claire

Bezmozgis, David
The Betrayers: A Novel

BHOPAL UNION CARBIDE PLANT DISASTER, BHOPAL, INDIA, 1984
Sinha, Indra. *Animal's People*

Bhuvaneswar, Chaya
White Dancing Elephants: Stories

BIAFRA (1967-1970)
Adichie, Chimamanda Ngozi. *Half of a Yellow Sun*

Bialosky, Jill
House Under Snow
The Prize: A Novel

BIBLE NOVELS
Andrews, Mesu. *Isaiah's Daughter: A Novel of Prophets and Kings*
Andrews, Mesu. *Of Fire and Lions: A Novel*
Asch, Sholem. *The Nazarene*
Cossette, Connilyn. ★*Shelter of the Most High*
Crace, Jim. *Quarantine*
Diamant, Anita. ★*The Red Tent*
Edghill, India. *Queenmaker: A Novel of King David's Queen*
Parini, Jay. *The Damascus Road: A Novel of Saint Paul*
Rice, Anne. *Christ the Lord: Out of Egypt: A Novel*
Rice, Anne. *Christ the Lord: The Road to Cana: A Novel*
Saramago, Jose. *Cain*
Smith, Jill Eileen. *Star of Persia: Esther's Story*
Wallace, Lew. ★*Ben-Hur*

Biblical series (Sholem Asch) [Series]. Asch, Sholem
Bibliolepsy. Apostol, Gina

BICYCLE MESSENGERS
Kadrey, Richard. *The Grand Dark*

BICYCLE RACING
Urquhart, Jane. *The Night Stages: A Novel*

BICYCLING
Bohjalian, Chris. ★*The Red Lotus*

Bieker, Chelsea Jean
Godshot: A Novel

BIERCE, AMBROSE
Fuentes, Carlos. ★*The Old Gringo*

Big Bad Wolf. Snyder, Suleikha
The Big Bang Symphony: A Novel of Antarctica. Bledsoe, Lucy Jane
Big Bang: A Nonfiction Novel. Bowman, David
The Big Blowdown. Pelecanos, George P.
The Big Both Ways. Straley, John
Big Cherry Holler: A Big Stone Gap Novel. Trigiani, Adriana

BIG CHURCHES
Isaac, Kara. *Then There Was You*

★*The Big Door Prize: A Novel*. Walsh, M. O.
Big Familia. Moniz, Tomas
The Big Finish. Fossey, Brooke
★*Big Fish: A Novel of Mythic Proportions*. Wallace, Daniel

BIG GAME HUNTERS
Stabenow, Dana. ★*Hunter's Moon*

Big Girl Small: A Novel. DeWoskin, Rachel
Big Girl, Small Town: A Novel. Gallen, Michelle
Big If. Costello, Mark
Big Little Lies. Moriarty, Liane
★*The Big Rock Candy Mountain*. Stegner, Wallace
★*Big Sky*. Atkinson, Kate
★*The Big Sky*. Guthrie, A. B.
★*The Big Sleep*. Chandler, Raymond
Big Stone Gap novels [Series]. Trigiani, Adriana

BIG STONE GAP, VIRGINIA
Trigiani, Adriana. *Big Cherry Holler: A Big Stone Gap Novel*
Trigiani, Adriana. *Big Stone Gap: A Novel*

Big Stone Gap: A Novel. Trigiani, Adriana
★*Big Summer*. Weiner, Jennifer

BIGAMY
Balogh, Mary. ★*Someone to Care*

Bijan, Donia
The Last Days of Cafe Leila

Bilal, Parker
  The Burning Gates: A Makana Investigation
  The Ghost Runner
Bilenchi, Romano
  ★*The Chill*
BILINGUAL MATERIALS
  Cisneros, Sandra. *Martita, I Remember You: Martita, Te Recuerdo*
BILL COLLECTING
  Baldacci, David. ★*One Good Deed*
Bill Hodges novels [Series]. King, Stephen
BILLIARDS
  Boll, Heinrich. *Billiards at Half-Past Nine*
***Billiards** at Half-Past Nine*. Boll, Heinrich
Billie Walker mysteries [Series]. Moss, Tara
Billingham, Mark
  ★*Their Little Secret*
Billingsley, ReShonda Tate
  A Little Bit of Karma: A Novel
  ★*The Secret She Kept*
Billionaire wolf (Terry Spear) [Series]. Spear, Terry
*A **Billionaire** Wolf for Christmas*. Spear, Terry
BILLIONAIRES
  Albom, Mitch. *The Stranger in the Lifeboat*
  Connelly, Michael. *The Wrong Side of Goodbye*
  Cussler, Clive. *Sahara: A Novel*
  Cussler, Clive. ★*Sea of Greed: A Novel from the Numa Files*
  Dee, Jonathan. *The Locals: A Novel*
  DeLillo, Don. *Zero K: A Novel*
  Hagberg, David. *Gambit*
  Jones, Stephen Mack. *Dead of Winter*
  Pelevin, Viktor. *The Hall of Singing Caryatids*
  Powell, Mark. *Firebird*
  Pynchon, Thomas. ★*Bleeding Edge*
  Racculia, Kate. ★*Tuesday Mooney Talks to Ghosts: A Novel*
  Spear, Terry. *A Billionaire Wolf for Christmas*
Billy. French, Albert
BILLY
  Momaday, N. Scott. *The Ancient Child: A Novel*
★***Billy** Bathgate: A Novel*. Doctorow, E. L.
Billy Boyle World War II mysteries [Series]. Benn, James R.
***Billy** Boyle: A World War Two Mystery*. Benn, James R.
★***Billy** Lynn's Long Halftime Walk*. Fountain, Ben
★***Billy** Summers*. King, Stephen
***Billy,** Come Home*. Callaghan, Mary Rose
BILLY, THE KID
  Bowles, Paul. ★*The Sheltering Sky*
BILOXI, MISSISSIPPI
  Barthelme, Frederick. *Bob the Gambler*
  Miles, Jonathan. *Anatomy of a Miracle*
  Miller, Mary. *Biloxi: A Novel*
***Biloxi:** a Novel*. Miller, Mary
BIN LADEN, OSAMA
  Berenson, Alex. *The Faithful Spy: A Novel*
  Cunningham, Michael. ★*The Hours*
Binchy, Maeve
  Circle of Friends
  Firefly Summer
  ★*Whitethorn Woods*

Binder, L. Annette
  The Vanishing Sky
Binet, Laurent
  Civilizations
  ★*HHhH*
BINGE-DRINKING
  Bohjalian, Chris. *The Flight Attendant: A Novel*
***Binocular** Vision: New & Selected Stories*. Pearlman, Edith
★***Binti***. Okorafor, Nnedi
Binti [Series]. Okorafor, Nnedi
***Binti:** Home*. Okorafor, Nnedi
***Binti:** the Night Masquerade*. Okorafor, Nnedi
BIO-THRILLERS
  Grant, Mira. *Parasite*
  Koepp, David. *Cold Storage: A Novel*
  Mooney, Chris. *Blood World*
  Wilson, Daniel H. *The Andromeda Evolution: A Novel*
BIODIVERSITY
  Powers, Richard. ★*Bewilderment: A Novel*
BIOFEEDBACK
  Powers, Richard. ★*Bewilderment: A Novel*
BIOGRAPHERS
  Barnes, Julian. ★*Flaubert's Parrot*
  Cameron, Peter. *The City of Your Final Destination*
  Coetzee, J. M. *Summertime: Scenes from a Provincial Life*
  Flanery, Patrick. *Absolution: A Novel*
BIOGRAPHICAL FICTION
  Adimi, Kaouther. *Our Riches*
  Alcott, Kate. *A Touch of Stardust*
  Alpsten, Ellen. *Tsarina*
  Anstruther, Eleanor. *A Perfect Explanation*
  Banks, Russell. *Cloudsplitter: A Novel*
  Barnes, Julian. ★*Flaubert's Parrot*
  Barnes, Julian. *The Noise of Time*
  Benedict, Marie. ★*Lady Clementine*
  Benedict, Marie. *The Only Woman in the Room*
  Benioff, David. *City of Thieves: A Novel*
  Benjamin, Melanie. *Alice I Have Been*
  Benjamin, Melanie. ★*The Aviator's Wife: A Novel*
  Bergman, Megan Mayhew. *Almost Famous Women: Stories*
  Bernhard, Thomas. *Wittgenstein's Nephew: A Friendship*
  Bird, Sarah. *Daughter of a Daughter of a Queen*
  Bloom, Amy. ★*White Houses: A Novel*
  Boyle, T. Coraghessan. *The Women: A Novel*
  Brown, Amy Belding. *Emily's House*
  Burdick, Serena. *Find Me in Havana*
  Calvi, Mary. *Dear George, Dear Mary: A Novel of George Washington's First Love*
  Cantor, Jillian. *Half Life*
  Carey, Edward. *Little: A Novel*
  Chiaverini, Jennifer. *Mrs. Lincoln's Sisters*
  Chiaverini, Jennifer. *Resistance Women: A Novel*
  Cobbs Hoffman, Elizabeth. *The Hamilton Affair*
  Cobbs Hoffman, Elizabeth. *The Tubman Command: A Novel*
  Cusset, Catherine. *Life of David Hockney: A Novel*
  Dann, Patty. *The Wright Sister*
  Darznik, Jasmin. *The Bohemians*
  Darznik, Jasmin. *Song of a Captive Bird: A Novel*

Dean, Michael. *I, Hogarth*

DeLillo, Don. *Libra*

Doctorow, E. L. *Homer and Langley: A Novel*

Dongala, Emmanuel Boundzeki. *The Bridgetower Sonata: Sonata Mulattica*

Donoghue, Emma. *Slammerkin*

Druon, Maurice. *The Iron King*

Dunant, Sarah. *Blood and Beauty: A Novel*

Ebershoff, David. *The Danish Girl: A Novel*

Eggers, Dave. *What Is the What: The Autobiography of Valentino Achak Deng*

Ellroy, James. ★*Widespread Panic: A Novel*

Fallada, Hans. *Every Man Dies Alone*

Fowler, Therese. *A Well-Behaved Woman: A Novel of the Vanderbilts*

Fowler, Therese. ★*Z: A Novel of Zelda Fitzgerald*

Frazier, Charles. *Varina*

Freedman, Benedict. *Mrs. Mike: The Story of Katherine Mary Flannigan*

Fuentes, Carlos. ★*The Old Gringo*

Garcia Marquez, Gabriel. *The General in His Labyrinth*

George, Margaret. *The Confessions of Young Nero*

George, Margaret. *Elizabeth I: A Novel*

George, Margaret. *Helen of Troy*

George, Margaret. *The Splendor Before the Dark: A Novel of the Emperor Nero*

Gibbon, Maureen. *The Lost Notebook of Edouard Manet: A Novel*

Gortner, C. W. *The First Actress: A Novel of Sarah Bernhardt*

Graves, Robert. ★*I, Claudius: From the Autobiography of Tiberius Claudius, Born 10 B.C., Murdered and Deified A.D. 54*

Gregory, Philippa. *The Boleyn Inheritance*

Gregory, Philippa. *The Constant Princess*

Gregory, Philippa. *The Kingmaker's Daughter*

Gregory, Philippa. *The Lady of the Rivers*

Gregory, Philippa. *The Last Tudor*

Gregory, Philippa. *The Other Boleyn Girl: A Novel*

Gregory, Philippa. *The Red Queen: A Novel*

Gregory, Philippa. *The Taming of the Queen*

Gregory, Philippa. *The White Princess*

Griffith, Nicola. *Hild: A Novel*

Hansen, Ron. ★*The Assassination of Jesse James by the Coward Robert Ford*

Henry, Patti Callahan. ★*Becoming Mrs. Lewis: The Improbable Love Story of Joy Davidman and C. S. Lewis*

Hensher, Philip. *Scenes from Early Life: A Novel*

Hicks, Robert. *The Widow of the South*

Hijuelos, Oscar. *Twain & Stanley Enter Paradise*

Hooper, Elise. *Fast Girls: A Novel of the 1936 Women's Olympic Team*

Horan, Nancy. *Loving Frank: A Novel*

Hornby, Gill. *Miss Austen*

Horrocks, Caitlin. *The Vexations*

Howard, Ravi. *Driving the King: A Novel*

Jones, Sherry. *Four Sisters, All Queens*

Kaplan, Mitchell James. *Rhapsody*

Kidd, Sue Monk. ★*The Invention of Wings: A Novel*

Kiernan, Stephen P. *Universe of Two*

Labatut, Benjamin. *When We Cease to Understand the World*

Lansdale, Joe R. ★*Paradise Sky*

Lee, Jonathan. *The Great Mistake*

Littell, Robert. *The Mayakovsky Tapes: A Novel*

Mailer, Norman. ★*The Executioner's Song*

McCann, Colum. ★*Apeirogon: A Novel*

McLain, Paula. *Circling the Sun*

McLain, Paula. *Love and Ruin*

McLain, Paula. *The Paris Wife: A Novel*

Oates, Joyce Carol. *Blonde: A Novel*

Orringer, Julie. ★*The Flight Portfolio: A Novel*

Parini, Jay. *The Passages of H.M.: A Novel of Herman Melville*

Parmar, Priya. *Vanessa and Her Sister*

Parris, S. J. ★*The Dead of Winter*

Parris, S. J. *Sacrilege*

Parris, S. J. *Treachery*

Paul, Gill. ★*The Lost Daughter*

Penman, Sharon Kay. *Here Be Dragons*

Penman, Sharon Kay. *When Christ and His Saints Slept*

Phillips, Caryl. *Dancing in the Dark*

Phillips, Caryl. *Foreigners*

Phillips, Caryl. *A View of the Empire at Sunset*

Pipkin, John. *Woodsburner: A Novel*

Puzo, Mario. *The Family: A Novel*

Pynchon, Thomas. *Mason & Dixon*

Randall, Alice. ★*Black Bottom Saints*

Renault, Mary. *Funeral Games*

Renault, Mary. *The Persian Boy*

Rhodes, Jewell Parker. *Voodoo Dreams: A Novel of Marie Laveau*

Riley, Vanessa. ★*Island Queen*

Rosen, Renee. *The Social Graces*

Russell, Mary Doria. ★*Doc: A Novel*

Russell, Mary Doria. *Epitaph: A Novel of the O.K. Corral*

Russell, Mary Doria. *The Women of the Copper Country: A Novel*

Saunders, George. ★*Lincoln in the Bardo: A Novel*

Scharer, Whitney. *The Age of Light*

Seton, Anya. *Katherine*

Seton, Anya. ★*The Winthrop Woman*

Shaara, Jeff. *Gods and Generals: A Novel of the Civil War*

Shaara, Jeff. *The Last Full Measure*

Shaara, Jeff. *The Rising Tide: A Novel of World War II*

Shaara, Jeff. *The Steel Wave: A Novel of World War II*

Sharratt, Mary. *Illuminations: A Novel of Hildegard Von Bingen*

Sharratt, Mary. *Revelations*

Simmons, Dan. *Drood: A Novel*

Smith, Dominic. ★*The Last Painting of Sara De Vos*

Sontag, Susan. ★*In America*

Sontag, Susan. *The Volcano Lover: A Romance*

Stachniak, Eva. *The Winter Palace: A Novel of Catherine the Great*

Steinke, Rene. *Holy Skirts*

Stone, Irving. ★*The Agony and the Ecstasy: A Biographical Novel of Michelangelo*

Stone, Irving. *Lust for Life: A Novel of Vincent Van Gogh*

Stridsberg, Sara. *Valerie: Or the Faculty of Dreams : Amendment to the Theory of Sexuality*

Styron, William. *The Confessions of Nat Turner*

Tobar, Hector. *The Last Great Road Bum*

Toibin, Colm. ★*The Magician: A Novel*

Truong, Monique T. D. *The Sweetest Fruits*

Twain, Mark. *Personal Recollections of Joan of Arc*

Vargas Llosa, Mario. *The Dream of the Celt*
Vargas Llosa, Mario. ★*The Way to Paradise*
Vidal, Gore. ★*Lincoln: A Novel*
Vreeland, Susan. *Girl in Hyacinth Blue*
Weir, Alison. *Anna of Kleve: The Princess in the Portrait*
Weir, Alison. *Katharine Parr, the Sixth Wife*
Wieland, Liza. *Paris, 7 A.M.*
Wolfe, Paul. *The Lost Diary of M*
Wood, Tracey Enerson. *The Engineer's Wife: A Novel*
Yourcenar, Marguerite. ★*Memoirs of Hadrian: And Reflections on the Composition of Memoirs of Hadrian*

BIOGRAPHICAL FILMS
Hall, Parnell. *Lights! Camera! Puzzles!*

BIOLOGICAL INVASIONS
McCaffrey, Anne. *Dragonflight*

BIOLOGICAL TERRORISM
Bacigalupi, Paolo. ★*The Windup Girl*
Dekker, Ted. *Red: The Heroic Rescue*
Follett, Ken. ★*Whiteout*
Harvey, Michael T. *We All Fall Down*
Koepp, David. *Cold Storage: A Novel*
Parnell, Sean. *Left for Dead*

BIOLOGICAL WARFARE
Peace, David. *Occupied City*

BIOLOGICAL WEAPONS
Golden, Christopher. *Red Hands*
Parnell, Sean. *Left for Dead*

BIOMEDICAL ENGINEERING
Fairstein, Linda A. *Blood Oath*

BIOTECHNOLOGY
Abrams, Stacey. *While Justice Sleeps: A Novel*
Okorafor, Nnedi. ★*Noor*
VanderMeer, Jeff. ★*Borne: A Novel*
VanderMeer, Jeff. *Dead Astronauts: A Novel*

BIOTIC COMMUNITIES
Boyle, T. Coraghessan. *The Terranauts*

BIPOLAR DISORDER
Garey, Juliann. *Too Bright to Hear Too Loud to See*

Birch, Carol
    Jamrach's Menagerie
Bird Box novels [Series]. Malerman, Josh
Bird Box: A Novel. Malerman, Josh
★*The **Bird** King*. Wilson, G. Willow
The **Bird** of the River. Baker, Kage

BIRD WATCHERS
Shaw, William. *The Birdwatcher*

BIRD WATCHING
Drayson, Nicholas. *A Guide to the Birds of East Africa*

Bird, Sarah
    Daughter of a Daughter of a Queen
    ★*The Flamenco Academy: A Novel*
    The Gap Year: A Novel
    The Yokota Officers Club: A Novel

BIRDS
Andrews, Donna. *The Twelve Jays of Christmas: A Meg Langslow Mystery*

BIRDS — MIGRATION
McConaghy, Charlotte. *Migrations*

BIRDS AS PETS
Bourdeaut, Olivier. *Waiting for Bojangles: A Novel*
Birds of Paradise: A Novel. Abu-Jaber, Diana
Birds of Prey. Smith, Wilbur A.
Birds Without Wings. De Bernieres, Louis
★*Birdsong*. Faulks, Sebastian
The *Birdwatcher*. Shaw, William

BIRMINGHAM, ALABAMA
Carpenter, Emily. *Until the Day I Die*

BIRMINGHAM, ENGLAND
Coe, Jonathan. *The Rotters' Club*

BIRTH AND DEATH RECORDS
Saramago, Jose. *All the Names*

BIRTH CONTROL
Vonnegut, Kurt. *Welcome to the Monkey House*

BIRTH DEFECTS
Dunn, Katherine. *Geek Love*
Watson, Brad. *Miss Jane: A Novel*
Wright, Jaime Jo. *The Haunting at Bonaventure Circus*
The *Birth* of Venus: A Novel. Dunant, Sarah
The *Birthday* of the World: And Other Stories. Le Guin, Ursula K.

BIRTHDAY PARTIES
Carter, Mary Dixie. *The Photographer*
McCall Smith, Alexander. *The Lost Art of Gratitude*
McKevett, G. A. *A Few Drops of Bitters*
Paris, B. A. ★*The Dilemma*
Urrea, Luis Alberto. ★*The House of Broken Angels*

BIRTHDAYS
Greer, Andrew Sean. ★*Less*
Jackson-Brown, Angela. ★*When Stars Rain Down: A Novel*

BIRTHFATHERS
Cook, Robin. ★*Genesis*
Kwan, Kevin. *China Rich Girlfriend*
Onuzo, Chibundu. *Sankofa: A Novel*
See, Lisa. *Dreams of Joy: A Novel*

BIRTHFATHERS — IDENTIFICATION
Simsion, Graeme C. ★*The Rosie Project*

BIRTHMOTHERS
Bauman, Bruce. ★*Broken Sleep: An American Dream*
Hoffmann, R. J. *Other People's Children: A Novel*
Kohnstamm, Thomas B. *Lake City*
Ludwig, Benjamin. *Ginny Moon*
Mina, Denise. *The Less Dead*

BIRTHMOTHERS — IDENTIFICATION
Fabry, Chris. *Looking into You*

BIRTHPARENTS
Jewell, Lisa. *The Family Upstairs*
Sparks, Nicholas. *Every Breath*
Wade, Becky. ★*True to You*

BIRTHPARENTS — IDENTIFICATION
McCall Smith, Alexander. *The Forgotten Affairs of Youth*
Stephens, Alice. *Famous Adopted People*

BISEXUAL AFRICAN AMERICAN MEN
Harris, E. Lynn. *I Say a Little Prayer: A Novel*
Harris, E. Lynn. *Invisible Life: A Novel*
Harris, E. Lynn. *Not a Day Goes By: A Novel*

BISEXUAL MEN
Aciman, Andre. *Enigma Variations: A Novel*

Gonzalez, Christopher. *I'm Not Hungry but I Could Eat*

Moniz, Tomas. *Big Familia*

BISEXUAL WOMEN

Alexander, Jennet. *I Kissed a Girl*

Bloom, Amy. ★*White Houses: A Novel*

Christian, Claire. *It's Been a Pleasure, Noni Blake*

Gilman, Laura Anne. *Hard Magic*

Griffith, Nicola. *Hild: A Novel*

Hall, Alexis. *Rosaline Palmer Takes the Cake*

McQuiston, Casey. ★*One Last Stop*

Vo, Nghi. ★*The Chosen and the Beautiful*

BISEXUALITY

Winterson, Jeanette. *The Passion*

BISEXUALS

Barker, Pat. ★*The Eye in the Door*

★*The Bishop's* Pawn. Berry, Steve

The Bishop's Wife. Harrison, Mette Ivie

BISHOP, ELIZABETH

Wieland, Liza. *Paris, 7 A.M.*

Winfrey, Kerry. *Waiting for Tom Hanks: A Novel*

BISHOPS

Camilleri, Andrea. *Riccardino*

Robb, Candace M. *The Cross-Legged Knight: An Owen Archer Mystery*

BISHOPS' SPOUSES

Harrison, Mette Ivie. *The Prodigal Daughter*

Bisson, Terry

Any Day Now

A Bitter Feast. Crombie, Deborah

★*Bitter Orange.* Fuller, Claire

Bitter Spirits. Bennett, Jenn

★*The Bitterroots: a Novel.* Box, C. J.

Bittner, Rosanne

Logan's Lady

Bivald, Katarina

The Readers of Broken Wheel Recommend

Black and Blue: A Doug Brock Thriller. Rosenfelt, David

★*Black and Blue: An Inspector Rebus Novel.* Rankin, Ian

Black and Ugly. Styles, Toy

Black and ugly novels [Series]. Styles, Toy

Black Betty: An Easy Rawlins Mystery. Mosley, Walter

The Black Book. Rankin, Ian

★*Black Bottom Saints.* Randall, Alice

BLACK BRITISH

Carty-Williams, Candice. ★*Queenie*

Charles, KJ. *Wanted, a Gentleman: Or, Virtue Over-Rated*

Evaristo, Bernardine. ★*Girl, Woman, Other*

Hibbert, Talia. ★*Take a Hint, Dani Brown*

Riley, Vanessa. ★*An Earl, the Girl, and a Toddler*

BLACK BRITISH MEN

Hornby, Nick. *Just Like You*

BLACK BRITISH WOMEN

Onuzo, Chibundu. *Sankofa: A Novel*

★*Black Buck.* Askaripour, Mateo

BLACK CANADIAN FICTION

Alexis, Andre. *Fifteen Dogs*

Alexis, Andre. *The Hidden Keys*

Edugyan, Esi. ★*Washington Black: A Novel*

Hill, Lawrence. *Someone Knows My Name: A Novel*

BLACK CANADIAN WOMEN

Hill, Lawrence. *Someone Knows My Name: A Novel*

BLACK CANADIANS

Colvin, Jeffrey. ★*Africaville: A Novel*

★*The Black Cathedral.* Gala, Marcial

Black Cherry Blues. Burke, James Lee

BLACK DEATH

Pears, Iain. *The Dream of Scipio*

Robinson, Kim Stanley. *The Years of Rice and Salt*

Rutherfurd, Edward. *London*

Walters, Minette. *The Last Hours: A Novel*

Black Dogs. McEwan, Ian

Black Fridays. Sears, Michael

Black Girls Must Die Exhausted. Allen, Jayne

Black girls must die exhausted [Series]. Allen, Jayne

The Black God's Drums. Clark, P. Djeli

BLACK HAND (UNITED STATES)

Stewart, Amy. ★*Girl Waits with Gun*

The Black Hawk. Bourne, Joanna

★*Black Hole.* Burns, Charles

BLACK HOLES (ASTRONOMY)

Egan, Greg. *Perihelion Summer*

The Black Hour. Rader-Day, Lori

BLACK HUMOR

Amdahl, Gary. *I Am Death: Two Novellas*

Awad, Mona. *Bunny*

Braithwaite, Oyinkan. *My Sister, the Serial Killer: A Novel*

Clarke, Brock. *An Arsonist's Guide to Writers' Homes in New England: A Novel*

Crews, Harry. *A Feast of Snakes: A Novel*

DeLillo, Don. ★*White Noise*

Dermansky, Marcy. *Very Nice*

Dostoyevsky, Fyodor. *Notes from Underground*

Dunn, Katherine. *Geek Love*

Gass, William H. *Middle C*

Harrison, Jim. *The Great Leader*

Heller, Joseph. ★*Catch-22*

Hiaasen, Carl. *Skin Tight*

Jin, Ha. *The Boat Rocker: A Novel*

Lucashenko, Melissa. *Too Much Lip*

Lutz, Lisa. *The Swallows: A Novel*

McMurtry, Larry. *The Evening Star: A Novel*

O'Donnell, Lisa. *The Death of Bees: A Novel*

Smith, B. J. *Crow's Landing: A Novel*

Smith, B. J. *Shoot the Dog: A Virgil Cain Mystery*

Vonnegut, Kurt. *Slapstick: Or, Lonesome No More! a Novel*

Welsh, Irvine. *Dead Men's Trousers*

Welsh, Irvine. *Trainspotting*

The Black Ice. Connelly, Michael

★*Black Leopard, Red Wolf.* James, Marlon

BLACK MAGIC

Garcia, Cristina. *Dreaming in Cuban*

Pratchett, Terry. *Wyrd Sisters*

Saberhagen, Fred. *Stonecutter's Story*

Black Maps. Spiegelman, Peter

BLACK MARKET

Corey, James S. A. *Babylon's Ashes*

Black market (Kiki Swinson) [Series]. Swinson, Kiki
The **Black** Minutes. Solares, Martin
★**Black** Moses. Mabanckou, Alain
The **Black** Opal. Holt, Victoria
★**Black** River. Hulse, S. M.
Black Sheep. Heyer, Georgette
BLACK SHEEP
    Heyer, Georgette. *Black Sheep*
★**Black** Sun. Roanhorse, Rebecca
Black Sunday. Abraham, Tola Rotimi
Black Swan Green: A Novel. Mitchell, David
The **Black** Tides of Heaven. Yang, JY
The **Black** Tower: A Novel. Bayard, Louis
★The **Black** Widow. Silva, Daniel
Black, Benjamin
    ★*Christine Falls: A Novel*
    ★*The Secret Guests: A Novel*
    Wolf on a String: A Novel
Black, Cara
    Murder in the Bastille
    Murder in the Marais
    Murder in the Rue De Paradis: An Aimee Leduc Investigation
    ★*Three Hours in Paris*
Black, Lisa
    Let Justice Descend
    Suffer the Children
    That Darkness
Black, Saul
    Anything for You
    ★*The Killing Lessons*
    ★*Lovemurder*
Black: the Birth of Evil. Dekker, Ted
The **Blackbirds**. Dickey, Eric Jerome
BLACKFACE ENTERTAINERS
    Phillips, Caryl. *Dancing in the Dark*
BLACKFEET INDIAN RESERVATION, MONTANA
    Jones, Stephen Graham. ★*The Only Good Indians: A Novel*
Blackford Oakes novels [Series]. Buckley, William F.
The **Blackhouse**. May, Peter
Blackmore, R. D.
    Lorna Doone: A Romance of Exmoor
Blackout. Grant, Mira
Blackout. Rosenfelt, David
Blackstock, Terri
    Catching Christmas
    Smoke Screen
★**Blacktop** Wasteland. Cosby, S. A.
Blackwell, Juliet
    Letters from Paris
Blackwood. Smith, Michael F.
Blackwood Farm. Rice, Anne
Blade of the Samurai: A Shinobi Mystery. Spann, Susan
BLADENSBURG, MARYLAND
    Styles, Toy. *A Hustler's Son: A Novel*
Blake, Audrey
    The Girl in His Shadow: A Novel
Blake, James Carlos
    The House of Wolfe

Blake, Sarah
    The Guest Book: A Novel
    The Postmistress
BLAKE, WILLIAM
    Barnes, Jonathan. *The Somnambulist*
    Ford, Richard. *A Multitude of Sins: Stories*
Blakemore, A. K.
    The Manningtree Witches
Blame. Abbott, Jeff
BLAME
    Cook, Robin. *Charlatans*
    Franklin, Ariana. *Mistress of the Art of Death*
    Hiaasen, Carl. ★*Squeeze Me: A Novel*
    McAllister, Tom. *How to Be Safe: A Novel*
    McGregor, Jon. *Lean Fall Stand*
BLANCHARD, URSULA (FICTITIOUS CHARACTER)
    Buckley, Fiona. *The Siren Queen: An Ursula Blanchard Mystery at Queen Elizabeth I's Court*
Blank canvas series [Series]. Anders, Adriana
★**Blank** Pages: And Other Stories. MacLaverty, Bernard
Blasphemy: New and Selected Stories. Alexie, Sherman
Blatty, William Peter
    ★*The Exorcist*
Blau, Jessica Anya
    Mary Jane: A Novel
    The Wonder Bread Summer
The **Blaze**. Dundas, Chad
★**Bleak** House. Dickens, Charles
Bledsoe, Alex
    Gather Her Round: A Novel of the Tufa
    The Hum and the Shiver
    Long Black Curl
    Wisp of a Thing
Bledsoe, Lucy Jane
    The Big Bang Symphony: A Novel of Antarctica
★**Bleeding** Edge. Pynchon, Thomas
BLENDED FAMILIES
    Barker, Pat. *Another World*
    Evison, Jonathan. *All About Lulu: A Novel*
    Fielding, Joy. *The Bad Daughter: A Novel*
    Gilb, Dagoberto. *The Flowers: A Novel*
    Mallery, Susan. ★*When We Found Home*
    Patchett, Ann. ★*Commonwealth*
    Scottoline, Lisa. *After Anna*
    Trollope, Joanna. *Other People's Children*
Bless the Beasts and Children. Swarthout, Glendon
Blind Ambition. Lovely, Lutishia
★The **Blind** Assassin. Atwood, Margaret
★The **Blind** Man's Garden. Aslam, Nadeem
★**Blind** Tiger. Brown, Sandra
Blind Willow, Sleeping Woman: 24 Stories. Murakami, Haruki
★**Blindness**. Saramago, Jose
BLINDNESS
    Anderson, Alison. *The Summer Guest*
    Lefteri, Christy. *The Beekeeper of Aleppo: A Novel*
Blindness of the Heart. Franck, Julia
The **Blinds**. Sternbergh, Adam

BLIZZARDS

Andrews, Donna. *The Twelve Jays of Christmas: A Meg Langslow Mystery*

Block, Lawrence. ★*The Burglar in the Library*

Cleeves, Ann. *The Darkest Evening*

Doiron, Paul. *Bad Little Falls: A Novel*

Farrow, John. *The Storm Murders: A Thriller*

Foley, Lucy. *The Hunting Party*

Indriðason, Arnaldur. *Strange Shores: An Inspector Erlendur Novel*

Jónasson, Ragnar. *The Mist*

Knott, Robert. *Robert B. Parker's Buckskin*

Nelson, Christina Suzann. *If We Make It Home: A Novel of Faith and Survival in the Oregon Wilderness*

Simpson, Rosemary. ★*What the Dead Leave Behind*

Stabenow, Dana. *No Fixed Line*

BLOCK ISLAND, RHODE ISLAND

Moore, Meg Mitchell. *The Islanders*

Block, Lawrence

All the Flowers Are Dying

The Burglar in the Closet

★*The Burglar in the Library*

A Drop of the Hard Stuff

Eight Million Ways to Die

Hit Me: A Keller Novel

Killing Castro

The Sins of the Fathers

A Ticket to the Boneyard

★*When the Sacred Ginmill Closes*

Block, Stefan Merrill

Oliver Loving: A Novel

BLOGGERS

Williams, Denise. *The Fastest Way to Fall*

BLOGS

Pellegrino, Amanda. *Smile and Look Pretty*

Blonde: a Novel. Oates, Joyce Carol

The Blood. Thomson, E. S.

BLOOD

Mooney, Chris. *Blood World*

Ryan, Anthony. *The Waking Fire*

Blood and Beauty: A Novel. Dunant, Sarah

Blood and Gold: Or, the Story of Marius. Rice, Anne

Blood and Iron: A Novel of the Promethean Age. Bear, Elizabeth

Blood Canticle. Rice, Anne

Blood Communion: A Tale of Prince Lestat. Rice, Anne

★*Blood Grove*. Mosley, Walter

Blood Hunt: A Novel. Rankin, Ian

★*Blood Meridian, Or, the Evening Redness in the West*. McCarthy, Cormac

Blood Oath. Fairstein, Linda A.

Blood of Angels: A Novel. Arvin, Reed

The Blood of Flowers: A Novel. Amirrezvani, Anita

Blood of Victory: A Novel. Furst, Alan

Blood Storm. Brooks, Bill

Blood Victory. Rice, Christopher

Blood World. Mooney, Chris

Blood's a Rover. Ellroy, James

Blood, Sweat and Payback. Clark, Wahida

Bloodchild: and Other Stories. Butler, Octavia E.

BLOODHOUNDS

Buxton, Kira Jane. ★*Hollow Kingdom*

Bloody Genius. Sandford, John

Bloom, Amy

Lucky Us: A Novel

★*White Houses: A Novel*

BLOOM, LEOPOLD (FICTITIOUS CHARACTER)

Joyce, James. ★*Ulysses*

BLOOMSBURY GROUP

Parmar, Priya. *Vanessa and Her Sister*

Blue Angel: A Novel. Prose, Francine

Blue Ant trilogy [Series]. Gibson, William

The Blue Between Sky and Water. Abulhawa, Susan

BLUE COLLAR FAMILIES

Lehane, Dennis. ★*Mystic River*

BLUE COLLAR WORKERS

Bolano, Roberto. ★*2666*

Breslin, Jimmy. *Table Money*

Pamuk, Orhan. *The Red-Haired Woman*

Russo, Richard. ★*Nobody's Fool*

The Blue Fox. Sjón

Blue Gold: A Novel from the Numa Files. Cussler, Clive

The Blue Guitar. Banville, John

Blue Heaven. Box, C. J.

Blue Heron romances [Series]. Higgins, Kristan

The Blue Hour. Parker, T. Jefferson

Blue Light Yokohama. Obregon, Nicolas

★*Blue Mars*. Robinson, Kim Stanley

★*Blue Monday*. French, Nicci

★*Blue Moon*. Child, Lee

BLUE RIDGE MOUNTAINS

L'Amour, Louis. *To the Far Blue Mountains*

Roberts, Nora. ★*Under Currents*

BLUE RIDGE MOUNTAINS REGION

Brown, Taylor. *Fallen Land*

Blue rose [Series]. Straub, Peter

Blue Shoes and Happiness. McCall Smith, Alexander

Blue-Eyed Devil. Parker, Robert B.

Bluebeard's Egg and Other Stories. Atwood, Margaret

★*Bluebird, Bluebird*. Locke, Attica

BLUES MUSIC

Cheng, Bill. *Southern Cross the Dog*

Kunzru, Hari. *White Tears*

BLUES MUSICIANS

Mosley, Walter. *Trouble Is What I Do: A Leonid McGill Mystery*

★*The Bluest Eye: A Novel*. Morrison, Toni

Blum, Jenna

The Lost Family

Blumberg, Chandra

Digging up Love

Blume, Judy

In the Unlikely Event

Blumenfeld, Amy

The Cast

Blundell, Judy

The High Season: A Novel

Blush: a Novel. Brenner, Jamie

BOARD GAMES
Shan, Sa. *The Girl Who Played Go*
BOARDERS
Deveraux, Jude. *A Willing Murder*
Persaud, Ingrid. *Love After Love: A Novel*
Williams, Niall. *This Is Happiness*
BOARDING HOUSES
Disher, Garry. *Under the Cold Bright Lights*
Long, Julie Anne. ★*Lady Derring Takes a Lover*
Mapson, Jo-Ann. *Bad Girl Creek: A Novel*
Spark, Muriel. ★*A Far Cry from Kensington*
BOARDING HOUSES FOR WOMEN
Spark, Muriel. ★*The Girls of Slender Means*
BOARDING SCHOOL STUDENTS
Lutz, Lisa. *The Swallows: A Novel*
McGuire, Seanan. ★*Beneath the Sugar Sky*
Sittenfeld, Curtis. *Prep: A Novel*
Ware, Ruth. *The Lying Game*
BOARDING SCHOOLS
Bradley, C. Alan. *As Chimney Sweepers Come to Dust: A Flavia De Luce Novel*
Bronte, Charlotte. ★*Emma*
French, Tana. ★*The Secret Place*
Goodman, Carol. *The Sea of Lost Girls*
Hilton, James. ★*Good-Bye, Mr. Chips*
Hogan, Ruth. *Queenie Malone's Paradise Hotel*
Lowe, Kathryn A. *The Furies*
McGuire, Seanan. ★*Beneath the Sugar Sky*
McGuire, Seanan. ★*Down Among the Sticks and Bones*
McGuire, Seanan. ★*Every Heart a Doorway*
Murray, Paul. *Skippy Dies*
Shreve, Anita. *Testimony: A Novel*
St. James, Simone. *The Broken Girls*
Szabo, Magda. *Abigail*
Thomas, Scarlett. *Oligarchy*
Waugh, Evelyn. *Decline and Fall*
Wynne, Phoebe. *Madam*
BOAT LIVING
Shreve, Anita. *The Weight of Water*
*The **Boat** People: A Novel*. Bala, Sharon
*The **Boat** Rocker: A Novel*. Jin, Ha
BOATING
Bradley, C. Alan. *The Grave's a Fine and Private Place: A Flavia De Luce Novel*
BOATING ACCIDENTS
Brown, Rosellen. *Tender Mercies*
Leon, Donna. ★*Transient Desires*
*The **Boatman's** Daughter: A Novel*. Davidson, Andy
BOATS
Baker, Kage. *The Bird of the River*
Bob Lee Swagger novels [Series]. Hunter, Stephen
***Bob** the Gambler*. Barthelme, Frederick
Bobotis, Andrea
The Last List of Miss Judith Kratt
Bock, Charles
Alice & Oliver: A Novel
Beautiful Children: A Novel
***Bodega** Dreams*. Quinonez, Ernesto

*The **Body** Double*. Beyda, Emily
BODY IMAGE
Awad, Mona. ★*13 Ways of Looking at a Fat Girl*
Clark, Georgia. *The Bucket List*
Murphy, Julie. *If the Shoe Fits*
Williams, Denise. *The Fastest Way to Fall*
*A **Body** in the Bathhouse*. Davis, Lindsey
*The **Body** in the Library: A Miss Marple Mystery*. Christie, Agatha
*The **Body** Lies*. Baker, Jo
BODY WEIGHT
King, Stephen. *Elevation*
BODYGUARDS
Carey, Jacqueline. *Starless*
Everett, Elizabeth. ★*A Lady's Formula for Love*
Fowler, Christopher. *Bryant & May: Hall of Mirrors : A Peculiar Crimes Unit Mystery*
Gaiman, Neil. ★*American Gods: A Novel*
Jackson, Brenda. *Forged in Desire*
Malpas, Jodi Ellen. *Leave Me Breathless*
Parker, Robert B. *Sixkill*
Pope, Jamie. *One Warm Winter*
Rai, Alisha. ★*Girl Gone Viral*
Sharp, Zoe. *Second Shot: A Charlie Fox Thriller*
BOGOTA, COLOMBIA
Engel, Patricia. ★*Infinite Country*
Restrepo, Laura. ★*Delirium: A Novel*
Rojas Contreras, Ingrid. ★*Fruit of the Drunken Tree: A Novel*
BOGS
Griffiths, Elly. *The Crossing Places*
Hart, Erin. *Haunted Ground: A Crime Novel*
BOHEMIANISM
Miller, Henry. ★*Tropic of Capricorn*
Richler, Mordecai. *Barney's Version: A Novel*
*The **Bohemians***. Darznik, Jasmin
Bohjalian, Chris
The Buffalo Soldier: A Novel
The Double Bind: A Novel
The Flight Attendant: A Novel
The Night Strangers: A Novel
★*The Red Lotus*
The Sandcastle Girls
Secrets of Eden: A Novel
Skeletons at the Feast: A Novel
The Sleepwalker
Boianjiu, Shani
The People of Forever Are Not Afraid: A Novel
Bolano, Roberto
★*2666*
Amulet
★*By Night in Chile*
★*Distant Star*
Last Evenings on Earth
Monsieur Pain
★*Nazi Literature in the Americas*
★*The Savage Detectives*
★*The Third Reich*
BOLANO, ROBERTO
Bolano, Roberto. *Last Evenings on Earth*

James, Henry. *Complete Stories, 1864-1874*
Bold novels [Series]. Cherezinska, Elzbieta
*The **Boleyn** Deceit*. Andersen, Laura
*The **Boleyn** Inheritance*. Gregory, Philippa
★*The **Boleyn** King*. Andersen, Laura
*The **Boleyn** Reckoning*. Andersen, Laura
BOLEYN, JANE
   Gaiman, Neil. ★*Stardust*
   Gregory, Philippa. *The Boleyn Inheritance*
BOLEYN, MARY
   Gibbons, Kaye. *Charms for the Easy Life*
   Gregory, Philippa. *The Other Boleyn Girl: A Novel*
BOLIVAR, SIMON
   Garcia Marquez, Gabriel. *The General in His Labyrinth*
BOLIVIA
   Ferencik, Erica. *Into the Jungle*
Boll, Heinrich
   Billiards at Half-Past Nine
   The Clown
Bolla. Statovci, Pajtim
★*A **Bollywood** Affair*. Dev, Sonali
*The **Bollywood** Bride*. Dev, Sonali
Bolton, S. J.
   The Craftsman
   A Dark and Twisted Tide
   Now You See Me
   The Split
*The **Bomb** Maker*. Perry, Thomas
BOMB SQUADS
   Crais, Robert. *Demolition Angel: A Novel.*
BOMB THREATS
   Perry, Thomas. *The Bomb Maker*
★*The **Bombay** Prince*. Massey, Sujata
BOMBER PILOTS
   Atkinson, Kate. ★*A God in Ruins*
   Robbins, David L. *Last Citadel: A Novel of the Battle of Kursk*
BOMBING
   Hulse, S. M. *Eden Mine*
   Michener, James A. ★*The Bridges at Toko-Ri*
   Parker, Robert B. *Painted Ladies*
   Reichs, Kathy. *Deadly Decisions*
   Sandford, John. *Shock Wave*
BOMBING VICTIMS
   Remarque, Erich Maria. *A Time to Love and a Time to Die*
BOMBINGS
   Bisson, Terry. *Any Day Now*
   Coughlin, Jack. *In the Crosshairs: A Sniper Novel*
   Crais, Robert. *Demolition Angel: A Novel.*
   Diofebi, Dario. *Paradise, Nevada*
   Freeman, Brian. *Marathon*
   MacDonald, John D. *Cinnamon Skin: The Twentieth Adventure of Travis McGee*
   Perry, Thomas. *The Bomb Maker*
   Robotham, Michael. ★*The Wreckage*
   Roth, Philip. ★*American Pastoral*
   Rutherfurd, Edward. *London*
   Silva, Daniel. ★*The Black Widow*
   Spufford, Francis. ★*Light Perpetual*

BOMBS
   Pobi, Robert. *Under Pressure*
   Pulley, Natasha. *The Watchmaker of Filigree Street*
★*Bombshell*. MacLean, Sarah
★*Bombshell*. Woods, Stuart
Bond, Cynthia
   Ruby: A Novel
BOND, JAMES (FICTIONAL CHARACTER)
   Fleming, Ian. *From Russia with Love*
   Fleming, Ian. ★*Goldfinger*
BONDING (HUMAN/ANIMAL)
   Fowler, Karen Joy. ★*We Are All Completely Beside Ourselves*
*The **Bondwoman's** Narrative*. Crafts, Hannah
Bone Canyon. Goldberg, Lee
*The **Bone** Clocks: A Novel*. Mitchell, David
*The **Bone** Garden*. Gerritsen, Tess
★*Bone on Bone*. Keller, Julia
★*The **Bone** People: A Novel*. Hulme, Keri
*The **Bone** Season*. Shannon, Samantha
Bone season [Series]. Shannon, Samantha
*The **Bone** Tree: A Novel*. Iles, Greg
BONES
   Coulter, Catherine. *Paradox*
   Harrod-Eagles, Cynthia. *Old Bones*
   Reichs, Kathy. *206 Bones*
   Reichs, Kathy. *Bones of the Lost: A Temperance Brennan Novel*
   Spillane, Mickey. *The Goliath Bone*
*The **Bones** of Grace*. Anam, Tahmima
*The **Bones** of Paradise*. Agee, Jonis
Bones of the Earth. Swanwick, Michael
Bones of the Earth: An Inspector Shan Tao Yun Mystery. Pattison, Eliot
Bones of the Lost: A Temperance Brennan Novel. Reichs, Kathy
Bones to Ashes. Reichs, Kathy
Bones: an Alex Delaware Novel. Kellerman, Jonathan
*The **Bonesetter's** Daughter*. Tan, Amy
Boneshaker. Priest, Cherie
*The **Bonfire** of the Vanities*. Wolfe, Tom
Bonita Avenue: A Novel. Buwalda, Peter
★*Bonjour Tristesse*. Sagan, Francoise
Bonnaffons, Amy
   The Regrets
   The Wrong Heaven: Stories
BONOBOS
   Gruen, Sara. *The Ape House*
*The **Book** and the Brotherhood*. Murdoch, Iris
BOOK CLUBS
   Adams, Lyssa Kay. *The Bromance Book Club*
   Fowler, Karen Joy. *The Jane Austen Book Club*
   Heller, L. Alison. *The Neighbor's Secret*
   Hendrix, Grady. *The Southern Book Club's Guide to Slaying Vampires*
   Jackson, Joshilyn. *Never Have I Ever*
   Marcelo, Tif. *In a Book Club Far Away*
   Pearl, Matthew. *The Dante Club: A Novel*
   Shaffer, Mary Ann. *The Guernsey Literary and Potato Peel Pie Society*
BOOK COLLECTORS
   Perez-Reverte, Arturo. *The Club Dumas*

The **Book** of Accidents. Wendig, Chuck
The **Book** of Air and Shadows. Gruber, Michael
★The **Book** of Aron. Shepard, Jim
A **Book** of Bones. Connolly, John
A **Book** of Common Prayer. Didion, Joan
★The **Book** of Daniel: A Novel. Doctorow, E. L.
The **Book** of Dave: A Revelation of the Recent Past and the Distant Future. Self, Will
The **Book** of Dreams. George, Nina
The **Book** of Etta. Elison, Meg
The **Book** of Evidence. Banville, John
The **Book** of Flora. Elison, Meg
The **Book** of Form and Emptiness: A Novel. Ozeki, Ruth L.
The **Book** of Harlan. McFadden, Bernice L.
The **Book** of Hidden Things. Dimitri, Francesco
★The **Book** of Illusions: A Novel. Auster, Paul
The **Book** of Killowen. Hart, Erin
The **Book** of Lamps and Banners: A Novel. Hand, Elizabeth
The **Book** of Life. Harkness, Deborah E.
★The **Book** of Longings. Kidd, Sue Monk
Book of Lost Swords [Series]. Saberhagen, Fred
The **Book** of M: A Novel. Shepherd, Peng
The **Book** of Magic. Hoffman, Alice
The **Book** of Mother. Huisman, Violaine
Book of Numbers: A Novel. Cohen, Joshua
The **Book** of Strange New Things. Faber, Michel
★**Book** of the Little Axe. Francis-Sharma, Lauren
Book of the new sun [Series]. Wolfe, Gene
The **Book** of the Unnamed Midwife. Elison, Meg
★The **Book** of Two Ways. Picoult, Jodi
The **Book** of Words. Erpenbeck, Jenny
Book Tea Shop novel [Series]. Avon, Joy
BOOK THEFTS
    Block, Lawrence. ★The Burglar in the Library
BOOKBINDING
    DeRoux, Margaux. The Lost Diary of Venice
The **Bookish** Life of Nina Hill. Waxman, Abbi
BOOKS
    Apostol, Gina. Bibliolepsy
    George, Nina. The Little Paris Bookshop
    Gruber, Michael. The Book of Air and Shadows
    Laymon, Kiese. Long Division
    Natsukawa, Sosuke. The Cat Who Saved Books
    Self, Will. The Book of Dave: A Revelation of the Recent Past and the Distant Future
BOOKS — CONSERVATION AND RESTORATION
    DeRoux, Margaux. The Lost Diary of Venice
BOOKS AND READING
    Adams, Sara Nisha. ★The Reading List
    Alameddine, Rabih. An Unnecessary Woman
    Avon, Joy. In Peppermint Peril: A Book Tea Shop Mystery
    Bennett, Alan. ★The Uncommon Reader
    Bivald, Katarina. The Readers of Broken Wheel Recommend
    Calvino, Italo. ★If on a Winter's Night a Traveler
    Doerr, Anthony. ★Cloud Cuckoo Land: A Novel
    Extence, Gavin. The Universe Versus Alex Woods
    Fowler, Karen Joy. The Jane Austen Book Club
    Griffiths, Elly. The Postscript Murders

    Hall, Steven. Maxwell's Demon
    Horowitz, Anthony. ★Moonflower Murders
    Jaswal, Balli Kaur. Erotic Stories for Punjabi Widows
    King, Stephen. Finders Keepers
    Landragin, Alex. ★Crossings: Consisting of Three Manuscripts : The Education of a Monster : City of Ghosts : Tales Of
    Lelchuk, Saul. Save Me from Dangerous Men: A Novel
    MacLeod, Alison. Tenderness
    Makkai, Rebecca. The Borrower: A Novel
    Ozeki, Ruth L. The Book of Form and Emptiness: A Novel
    Parry, H. G. The Unlikely Escape of Uriah Heep
    Ruiz Zafon, Carlos. The Labyrinth of the Spirits
    Ruiz Zafon, Carlos. ★The Shadow of the Wind
    Savage, Sam. Firmin: Adventures of a Metropolitan Lowlife
    Setterfield, Diane. The Thirteenth Tale: A Novel
    Skeslien Charles, Janet. The Paris Library: A Novel
BOOKS FOR RELUCTANT READERS
    Booth, Coe. ★Bronxwood
    Draper, Sharon M. ★Forged by Fire
Books of Ambha [Series]. Suri, Tasha
Books of history chronicles. [Series]. Dekker, Ted
The **Books** of the Dead. Bernhard, Emilia
BOOKS TO MOVIES
    Adams, Douglas. ★The Hitchhiker's Guide to the Galaxy
    Adams, Richard. Watership Down
    Ajvide Lindqvist, John. Let the Right One In
    Albom, Mitch. The Five People You Meet in Heaven
    Allison, Dorothy. ★Bastard Out of Carolina
    Amis, Martin. London Fields: A Novel
    Asimov, Isaac. ★I, Robot
    Auel, Jean M. ★The Clan of the Cave Bear: A Novel
    Austen, Jane. ★Emma
    Austen, Jane. Mansfield Park
    Austen, Jane. ★Persuasion
    Backman, Fredrik. A Man Called Ove
    Ball, John Dudley. In the Heat of the Night
    Banks, Russell. ★Affliction
    Barnes, Julian. ★The Sense of an Ending
    Barzak, Christopher. One for Sorrow
    Baxter, Charles. The Feast of Love
    Beagle, Peter S. ★The Last Unicorn
    Begley, Louis. About Schmidt
    Bellow, Saul. ★Seize the Day
    Berger, Thomas. ★Neighbors: A Novel
    Binchy, Maeve. Circle of Friends
    Blatty, William Peter. ★The Exorcist
    Block, Lawrence. The Burglar in the Closet
    Boulle, Pierre. The Bridge Over the River Kwai: A Novel
    Bowles, Paul. ★The Sheltering Sky
    Bradbury, Ray. The Illustrated Man
    Bradbury, Ray. ★Something Wicked This Way Comes
    Bradford, Barbara Taylor. ★A Woman of Substance
    Brown, Dan. The Da Vinci Code
    Brown, Rosellen. ★Before and After
    Brundage, Elizabeth. ★All Things Cease to Appear
    Buchan, John. The Thirty-Nine Steps
    Burgess, Anthony. ★A Clockwork Orange
    Burns, Olive Ann. ★Cold Sassy Tree

Cameron, Peter. *The City of Your Final Destination*

Capote, Truman. ★*Breakfast at Tiffany's*

Capote, Truman. ★*The Complete Stories of Truman Capote*

Carver, Raymond. *What We Talk About When We Talk About Love: Stories*

Chabon, Michael. *The Amazing Adventures of Kavalier & Clay: A Novel*

Chayefsky, Paddy. *Altered States: A Novel*

Chevalier, Tracy. ★*Girl with a Pearl Earring*

Child, Lee. *One Shot*

Childress, Mark. *Crazy in Alabama*

Christie, Agatha. ★*And Then There Were None*

Christie, Agatha. *Mrs. McGinty's Dead*

Christie, Agatha. *A Murder Is Announced: A Miss Marple Mystery*

Christie, Agatha. ★*Murder on the Orient Express*

Christie, Agatha. *The Pale Horse*

Clancy, Tom. *Patriot Games*

Clarke, Arthur C. ★*2001: A Space Odyssey*

Connelly, Michael. *The Lincoln Lawyer: A Novel*

Conroy, Pat. *The Prince of Tides*

Cook, Robin. *Coma: A Novel*

Coonts, Stephen. ★*Flight of the Intruder*

Crane, Stephen. ★*The Red Badge of Courage: An Episode of the American Civil War*

Cronin, A. J. *Citadel*

Cronin, A. J. *The Keys of the Kingdom*

Cussler, Clive. *Sahara: A Novel*

Defoe, Daniel. ★*Moll Flanders*

Defoe, Daniel. ★*Robinson Crusoe*

Dexter, Pete. ★*Deadwood*

Dick, Philip K. *The Minority Report*

Dickens, Charles. ★*David Copperfield*

Dickens, Charles. ★*Nicholas Nickleby*

Dickens, Charles. *The Old Curiosity Shop*

Dickens, Charles. *Oliver Twist, or the Parish Boy's Progress*

Dickens, Charles. ★*A Tale of Two Cities*

Doctorow, E. L. ★*The Book of Daniel: A Novel*

Doyle, Arthur Conan. ★*The Hound of the Baskervilles*

Dreiser, Theodore. ★*An American Tragedy*

Dreiser, Theodore. ★*Sister Carrie*

Du Maurier, Daphne. *Frenchman's Creek*

Du Maurier, Daphne. ★*Rebecca*

Edgerton, Clyde. ★*Walking Across Egypt: A Novel*

Edwards, Kim. *The Memory Keeper's Daughter*

Eggers, Dave. *The Circle*

Eggers, Dave. *A Hologram for the King: A Novel*

Eliot, George. ★*Silas Marner: The Weaver of Raveloe*

Ellroy, James. ★*L.A. Confidential*

Evans, Nicholas. ★*The Horse Whisperer: A Novel*

Fallada, Hans. *Every Man Dies Alone*

Farrell, Henry. ★*What Ever Happened to Baby Jane?*

Faulkner, William. *The Hamlet*

Faulkner, William. *Intruder in the Dust*

Faulkner, William. *The Reivers: A Reminiscence*

Ferrante, Elena. *The Lost Daughter*

Fielding, Helen. ★*Bridget Jones's Diary: A Novel*

Finn, A. J. ★*The Woman in the Window*

Fitch, Janet. *White Oleander: A Novel*

Fitzgerald, F. Scott. ★*The Last Tycoon: An Unfinished Novel*

Fitzgerald, F. Scott. *Novels and Stories, 1920-1922*

Fitzgerald, F. Scott. ★*The Short Stories of F. Scott Fitzgerald: A New Collection*

Fitzgerald, F. Scott. *Six Tales of the Jazz Age and Other Stories*

Flaubert, Gustave. ★*Madame Bovary: Provincial Ways*

Fleming, Ian. ★*Casino Royale: A James Bond Novel*

Fleming, Ian. *Doctor No*

Fleming, Ian. *From Russia with Love*

Fleming, Ian. ★*Goldfinger*

Fleming, Ian. *The Man with the Golden Gun*

Fleming, Ian. *On Her Majesty's Secret Service*

Fleming, Ian. *You Only Live Twice*

Flynn, Gillian. *Dark Places*

Foer, Jonathan Safran. *Extremely Loud and Incredibly Close*

Follett, Ken. *Eye of the Needle*

Forester, C. S. *The African Queen*

Forster, E. M. ★*A Passage to India*

Fountain, Ben. ★*Billy Lynn's Long Halftime Walk*

Franklin, Miles. *My Brilliant Career*

Fuentes, Carlos. ★*The Old Gringo*

Golden, Arthur. ★*Memoirs of a Geisha: A Novel*

Golding, William. ★*Lord of the Flies: A Novel*

Greenberg, Joanne. *I Never Promised You a Rose Garden: A Novel*

Greene, Graham. *The Honorary Consul*

Greene, Graham. *The Human Factor*

Greene, Graham. *Our Man in Havana*

Greene, Graham. *The Power and the Glory*

Gregory, Philippa. *The Other Boleyn Girl: A Novel*

Grisham, John. *The Client*

Grisham, John. ★*The Firm*

Grisham, John. ★*The Pelican Brief*

Grisham, John. *A Time to Kill*

Guterson, David. ★*Snow Falling on Cedars*

Hale, Shannon. *Austenland: A Novel*

Hamilton, Jane. *A Map of the World*

Hammett, Dashiell. ★*The Maltese Falcon*

Hammett, Dashiell. ★*The Thin Man*

Hansen, Ron. ★*The Assassination of Jesse James by the Coward Robert Ford*

Hansen, Ron. *Mariette in Ecstasy*

Hardy, Thomas. ★*Jude the Obscure*

Hardy, Thomas. ★*Tess of the D'urbervilles: A Pure Woman Faithfully Presented*

Harper, Jane. *The Dry*

Harris, Joanne. ★*Chocolat: A Novel*

Harris, Robert. ★*Fatherland*

Harris, Robert. *The Ghost: A Novel*

Harris, Thomas. *Red Dragon*

Harris, Thomas. ★*The Silence of the Lambs*

Hart, Josephine. *Damage: A Novel*

Hawkins, Paula. ★*The Girl on the Train: A Novel*

Hawthorne, Nathaniel. ★*The House of the Seven Gables*

Hawthorne, Nathaniel. ★*The Scarlet Letter: A Romance*

Heinlein, Robert A. ★*Starship Troopers*

Heller, Zoe. *What Was She Thinking?: Notes on a Scandal*

Helprin, Mark. ★*Winter's Tale*

Hemingway, Ernest. *For Whom the Bell Tolls*

Hemingway, Ernest. ★*The Old Man and the Sea*
Hemingway, Ernest. ★*The Sun Also Rises*
Hemingway, Ernest. *To Have and Have Not*
Hiaasen, Carl. *Strip Tease: A Novel*
Higgins, Jack. *The Eagle Has Landed*
Hijuelos, Oscar. ★*The Mambo Kings Play Songs of Love: A Novel*
Hill, Joe. *Horns*
Hilton, James. ★*Good-Bye, Mr. Chips*
Hilton, James. ★*Lost Horizon: A Novel*
Hilton, James. *Random Harvest*
Hoeg, Peter. ★*Smilla's Sense of Snow*
Hoffman, Alice. *The River King*
Hoffman, Alice. *The Rules of Magic: A Novel*
Hornby, Nick. *High Fidelity*
Irving, John. ★*The Cider House Rules: A Novel*
Irving, John. ★*A Prayer for Owen Meany: A Novel*
Irving, John. ★*The World According to Garp: A Novel*
Ishiguro, Kazuo. ★*Never Let Me Go*
Ishiguro, Kazuo. ★*The Remains of the Day*
Jackson, Charles. *The Lost Weekend*
Jackson, Shirley. ★*The Haunting of Hill House*
James, Henry. *Daisy Miller*
James, Henry. *The Golden Bowl*
James, Henry. *The Portrait of a Lady*
James, Henry. *The Wings of the Dove*
Jhabvala, Ruth Prawer. ★*Heat and Dust*
Jiles, Paulette. *News of the World: A Novel*
Jones, James. ★*The Thin Red Line*
Joyce, James. ★*Dubliners*
Joyce, James. ★*A Portrait of the Artist as a Young Man*
Joyce, James. ★*Ulysses*
Kaufman, Sue. *Diary of a Mad Housewife*
Kazantzakis, Nikos. *The Last Temptation of Christ*
Kerouac, Jack. ★*On the Road*
Kidd, Sue Monk. ★*The Secret Life of Bees*
King, Stephen. ★*Carrie*
King, Stephen. *Cujo*
King, Stephen. *Doctor Sleep: A Novel*
King, Stephen. *Dolores Claiborne*
King, Stephen. *Firestarter*
King, Stephen. *It*
King, Stephen. ★*Misery*
King, Stephen. *Night Shift*
King, Stephen. *Pet Sematary*
King, Stephen. *Salem's Lot*
King, Stephen. ★*The Shining*
King, Stephen. ★*The Stand*
Kosinski, Jerzy. ★*The Painted Bird*
Kundera, Milan. ★*The Unbearable Lightness of Being*
Kwan, Kevin. *Crazy Rich Asians*
Lahiri, Jhumpa. ★*The Namesake*
Larsen, Nella. *Passing*
Larsson, Stieg. ★*The Girl Who Kicked the Hornet's Nest*
Larsson, Stieg. *The Girl Who Played with Fire*
Lawrence, D. H. *Sons and Lovers*
Lawrence, D. H. *Women in Love*
Le Carre, John. *The Constant Gardener: A Novel*
Le Carre, John. *A Most Wanted Man: A Novel*

Le Carre, John. *The Spy Who Came in from the Cold*
Le Carre, John. *The Tailor of Panama*
Le Carre, John. ★*Tinker, Tailor, Soldier, Spy*
Le Guin, Ursula K. *The Lathe of Heaven*
Lebrecht, Norman. *The Song of Names*
Lehane, Dennis. *Live by Night*
Lehane, Dennis. *Shutter Island*
Lem, Stanislaw. ★*Solaris*
Leonard, Elmore. ★*Be Cool: Everyone Is Looking for the Next Big Hit*
Leonard, Elmore. ★*The Complete Western Stories of Elmore Leonard.*
Leonard, Elmore. ★*Get Shorty*
Leonard, Elmore. *Glitz*
Leonard, Elmore. ★*Killshot*
Leonard, Elmore. *Rum Punch*
Lethem, Jonathan. ★*Motherless Brooklyn*
Levin, Ira. *The Boys from Brazil: A Novel*
Levin, Ira. *A Kiss Before Dying*
Levin, Ira. ★*Rosemary's Baby: A Novel*
Levin, Ira. ★*The Stepford Wives: A Novel*
Lewis, Sinclair. *Babbitt*
Lewis, Sinclair. *Dodsworth*
Lewis, Sinclair. ★*Elmer Gantry*
Lockridge, Ross Franklin. *Raintree County*
London, Jack. ★*The Call of the Wild*
London, Jack. ★*White Fang*
Ludlum, Robert. ★*The Bourne Identity*
Ludlum, Robert. *The Bourne Supremacy*
Ludlum, Robert. *The Bourne Ultimatum*
Mailer, Norman. ★*The Executioner's Song*
Malamud, Bernard. ★*The Fixer*
Malamud, Bernard. *The Natural*
Malerman, Josh. *Bird Box: A Novel*
Martin, Steve. *Shopgirl*
Matheson, Richard. ★*I Am Legend*
Matthews, Jason. *Red Sparrow: A Novel*
McCarthy, Cormac. ★*All the Pretty Horses*
McCarthy, Cormac. ★*The Road*
McCullers, Carson. ★*The Heart Is a Lonely Hunter*
McDermid, Val. *A Place of Execution*
McDermott, Alice. ★*That Night*
McEwan, Ian. ★*On Chesil Beach*
McLaughlin, Emma. *The Nanny Diaries: A Novel*
McMillan, Terry. ★*How Stella Got Her Groove Back*
McMillan, Terry. ★*Waiting to Exhale*
McMurtry, Larry. *The Evening Star: A Novel*
McMurtry, Larry. ★*Terms of Endearment: A Novel : With a New Preface*
Melville, Herman. ★*Moby-Dick; Or, the Whale*
Michener, James A. ★*The Bridges at Toko-Ri*
Michener, James A. ★*Tales of the South Pacific*
Momaday, N. Scott. *House Made of Dawn*
Mosley, Walter. *Devil in a Blue Dress*
Moyes, Jojo. *Me Before You: A Novel*
Nabokov, Vladimir Vladimirovich. ★*Lolita*
O'Connor, Flannery. ★*Wise Blood*
Oates, Joyce Carol. ★*We Were the Mulvaneys*
Orczy, Emmuska Orczy. ★*The Scarlet Pimpernel*

Packer, Ann. *The Dive from Clausen's Pier*
Palahniuk, Chuck. *Choke: A Novel*
Palahniuk, Chuck. *Fight Club*
Parker, Robert B. *Appaloosa*
Parks, Gordon. ★*The Learning Tree*
Pasternak, Boris Leonidovich. ★*Doctor Zhivago*
Patchett, Ann. ★*Bel Canto: A Novel*
Paton, Alan. ★*Cry, the Beloved Country*
Patterson, James. *1st to Die: A Novel*
Patterson, James. ★*Along Came a Spider: A Novel*
Patterson, James. *Kiss the Girls: A Novel*
Pava, Sergio de la. *A Naked Singularity*
Perrotta, Tom. *Little Children*
Plath, Sylvia. ★*The Bell Jar*
Porter, Katherine Anne. *Ship of Fools*
Portis, Charles. ★*True Grit: A Novel*
Powers, Kevin. ★*The Yellow Birds: A Novel*
Price, Richard. *Clockers*
Proulx, Annie. ★*The Shipping News*
Puzo, Mario. ★*The Godfather*
Puzo, Mario. *The Sicilian: A Novel*
Rand, Ayn. ★*The Fountainhead*
Rash, Ron. ★*Serena: A Novel*
Redfield, James. *The Celestine Prophecy: An Adventure*
Reid, Iain. *I'm Thinking of Ending Things*
Rendell, Ruth. ★*A Judgement in Stone*
Rice, Anne. *Christ the Lord: Out of Egypt: A Novel*
Rice, Anne. ★*Interview with the Vampire*
Rice, Anne. ★*The Queen of the Damned*
Rivers, Francine. ★*Redeeming Love*
Roth, Philip. ★*Goodbye, Columbus, and Five Short Stories*
Roth, Philip. ★*Portnoy's Complaint*
Rushdie, Salman. ★*Midnight's Children: A Novel*
Russo, Richard. ★*Nobody's Fool*
Sabatini, Rafael. *Scaramouche: A Romance of the French Revolution*
Sagan, Carl. *Contact: A Novel*
Saint-Exupery, Antoine de. ★*The Little Prince*
Sallis, James. *Drive*
Sanders, Lawrence. ★*The First Deadly Sin*
Sandford, John. *Certain Prey*
Sandford, John. ★*Mind Prey*
Sapphire. ★*Push: A Novel*
Schaefer, Jack. ★*Shane*
Scott, Walter. ★*Rob Roy*
Sebold, Alice. ★*The Lovely Bones*
Segal, Erich. ★*Love Story*
Semple, Maria. *Where'd You Go, Bernadette: A Novel*
Shelley, Mary Wollstonecraft. ★*Frankenstein: Or, the Modern Prometheus*
Shreve, Anita. *The Pilot's Wife: A Novel*
Shreve, Anita. *The Weight of Water*
Shriver, Lionel. *We Need to Talk About Kevin*
Simpson, Mona. *Anywhere but Here*
Singer, Isaac Bashevis. *Enemies, a Love Story*
Smith, Dodie. ★*I Capture the Castle*
Smith, Martin Cruz. ★*Gorky Park*
Smith, Scott. *A Simple Plan: A Novel*
Smith, Tom Rob. *Child 44*

Spark, Muriel. ★*The Prime of Miss Jean Brodie*
Sparks, Nicholas. ★*The Notebook*
Sparks, Nicholas. *A Walk to Remember*
Spencer, Scott. ★*Endless Love*
Stark, Richard. *The Hunter: A Parker Novel*
Stein, Garth. *The Art of Racing in the Rain: A Novel*
Steinbeck, John. *Cannery Row*
Steinbeck, John. *Tortilla Flat*
Stockett, Kathryn. ★*The Help*
Stoker, Bram. *The New Annotated Dracula*
Stone, Irving. ★*The Agony and the Ecstasy: A Biographical Novel of Michelangelo*
Stone, Irving. *Lust for Life: A Novel of Vincent Van Gogh*
Stowe, Harriet Beecher. ★*Uncle Tom's Cabin*
Straub, Peter. ★*Ghost Story*
Styron, William. ★*Sophie's Choice*
Suskind, Patrick. ★*Perfume: The Story of a Murderer*
Swarthout, Glendon. *Bless the Beasts and Children*
Swarthout, Glendon. ★*The Shootist*
Tarkington, Booth. ★*Alice Adams*
Tarkington, Booth. ★*The Magnificent Ambersons*
Thackeray, William Makepeace. ★*Vanity Fair: A Novel Without a Hero*
Theroux, Paul. ★*The Mosquito Coast: A Novel*
Thompson, Jim. *The Killer Inside Me*
Tolkien, J. R. R. *The Fellowship of the Ring: Being the First Part of the Lord of the Rings*
Tolkien, J. R. R. ★*The Hobbit, Or, There and Back Again*
Tolkien, J. R. R. ★*The Lord of the Rings*
Tolkien, J. R. R. *The Return of the King: Being the Third Part of the Lord of the Rings*
Tolkien, J. R. R. *The Two Towers: Being the Second Part of the Lord of the Rings*
Traven, B. ★*The Treasure of the Sierra Madre*
Trigiani, Adriana. *Big Stone Gap: A Novel*
Trumbo, Dalton. ★*Johnny Got His Gun*
Turow, Scott. *Presumed Innocent*
Twain, Mark. ★*Adventures of Huckleberry Finn: Tom Sawyer's Comrade ...*
Twain, Mark. ★*A Connecticut Yankee in King Arthur's Court*
Tyler, Anne. ★*The Accidental Tourist: A Novel*
Updike, John. ★*Rabbit, Run*
Updike, John. ★*The Witches of Eastwick*
Uris, Leon. ★*Exodus*
Vandermeer, Jeff. ★*Annihilation: A Novel*
Vonnegut, Kurt. ★*Breakfast of Champions: Or, Goodbye Blue Monday!*
Vonnegut, Kurt. *Slapstick: Or, Lonesome No More! a Novel*
Vonnegut, Kurt. ★*Slaughterhouse-Five: Or, the Children's Crusade : A Duty-Dance with Death*
Wallace, Daniel. ★*Big Fish: A Novel of Mythic Proportions*
Wallace, David Foster. ★*Brief Interviews with Hideous Men*
Wallace, Lew. ★*Ben-Hur*
Waller, Robert James. ★*The Bridges of Madison County*
Waugh, Evelyn. ★*Brideshead Revisited*
Waugh, Evelyn. *The Loved One: An Anglo-American Tragedy*
Weiner, Jennifer. *In Her Shoes: A Novel*
Weldon, Fay. *The Life and Loves of a She-Devil*

Wells, H. G. ★*The Invisible Man*
Wells, H. G. ★*The Island of Dr. Moreau*
Wells, H. G. ★*The Time Machine*
Wells, H. G. ★*The War of the Worlds*
West, Jessamyn. *The Friendly Persuasion*
Westlake, Donald E. *The Hot Rock*
Wharton, Edith. *The Children*
Wharton, Edith. ★*Ethan Frome*
White, T. H. ★*The Once and Future King*
Wilde, Oscar. ★*The Picture of Dorian Gray*
Wilder, Thornton. ★*Theophilus North*
Wolfe, Thomas. ★*Look Homeward, Angel: A Story of a Buried Life*
Wolfe, Tom. *The Bonfire of the Vanities*
Woolf, Virginia. ★*Mrs. Dalloway*
Woolf, Virginia. *Orlando: A Biography*

BOOKS TO TV
Adams, Douglas. ★*The Hitchhiker's Guide to the Galaxy*
Austen, Jane. ★*Pride and Prejudice*
Austen, Jane. ★*Sense and Sensibility*
Backman, Fredrik. ★*Beartown: A Novel*
Beaton, M. C. *Agatha Raisin and the Quiche of Death*
Beaton, M. C. *Agatha Raisin and the Witch of Wyckhadden*
Clavell, James. *Shogun*
Cleeves, Ann. *The Crow Trap*
Coben, Harlan. *The Stranger*
Connelly, Michael. *The Burning Room*
Connelly, Michael. *Dark Sacred Night*
Corey, James S. A. ★*Leviathan Wakes*
Cornwell, Bernard. *The Last Kingdom: A Novel*
Cronin, A. J. *Citadel*
Cronin, Justin. *The Passage*
Danler, Stephanie. *Sweetbitter*
Diamant, Anita. ★*The Red Tent*
Dibdin, Michael. *Ratking*
Dickens, Charles. ★*David Copperfield*
Dickens, Charles. ★*Great Expectations*
Dickens, Charles. ★*Nicholas Nickleby*
Dumas, Alexandre. ★*The Count of Monte Cristo*
Eliot, George. ★*The Mill on the Floss*
Flynn, Gillian. ★*Sharp Objects: A Novel*
Follett, Ken. ★*The Pillars of the Earth*
Furst, Alan. *The Spies of Warsaw*
Gaiman, Neil. ★*American Gods: A Novel*
Gaiman, Neil. ★*Good Omens: The Nice and Accurate Prophecies of Agnes Nutter, Witch*
Galbraith, Robert. *Career of Evil*
Galbraith, Robert. *The Cuckoo's Calling*
Galbraith, Robert. *Lethal White*
Galbraith, Robert. *The Silkworm*
Gaskell, Elizabeth Cleghorn. ★*Cranford*
Gaskell, Elizabeth Cleghorn. ★*North and South*
Grossman, Lev. ★*The Magicians: A Novel*
Hardy, Thomas. ★*Tess of the D'urbervilles: A Pure Woman Faithfully Presented*
Harkness, Deborah E. *The Book of Life*
Harkness, Deborah E. *A Discovery of Witches: A Novel*
Harkness, Deborah E. *Shadow of Night*
Harris, Robert. *Archangel: A Novel*

Hill, Joe. ★*Nos4a2*
Hilton, James. ★*Good-Bye, Mr. Chips*
Hugo, Victor. ★*The Hunchback of Notre Dame*
King, Stephen. *It*
Le Carre, John. *Smiley's People*
Levin, Ira. ★*Rosemary's Baby: A Novel*
Littell, Robert. *The Company: A Novel of the Cia*
London, Jack. ★*White Fang*
Mantel, Hilary. ★*Bring up the Bodies: A Novel*
Mantel, Hilary. ★*Wolf Hall*
Martin, George R. R. ★*A Clash of Kings*
Martin, George R. R. ★*A Game of Thrones*
Martin, George R. R. ★*A Storm of Swords*
Michener, James A. ★*Centennial*
Michener, James A. *Space*
Mitford, Nancy. ★*The Pursuit of Love: A Novel*
Moriarty, Liane. *Big Little Lies*
Moriarty, Liane. *Nine Perfect Strangers*
Ng, Celeste. ★*Little Fires Everywhere: A Novel*
Orczy, Emmuska Orczy. ★*The Scarlet Pimpernel*
Perrotta, Tom. *The Leftovers*
Pratchett, Terry. ★*The Color of Magic*
Pratchett, Terry. *Going Postal: A Novel of Discworld*
Pratchett, Terry. *Wyrd Sisters*
Reid, Taylor Jenkins. ★*Daisy Jones & The Six: A Novel*
Rooney, Sally. *Normal People: A Novel*
Rowling, J. K. *The Casual Vacancy*
Runcie, James. *Sidney Chambers and the Shadow of Death*
St. Aubyn, Edward. *At Last*
Strout, Elizabeth. *Olive Kitteridge*
Theroux, Paul. ★*The Mosquito Coast: A Novel*
Wells, H. G. ★*The War of the Worlds*

BOOKSELLERS
Berry, Steve. ★*The Templar Legacy: A Novel of Suspense*
Block, Lawrence. *The Burglar in the Closet*
George, Nina. *The Little Paris Bookshop*
Gruber, Michael. *The Book of Air and Shadows*
Landragin, Alex. ★*Crossings: Consisting of Three Manuscripts : The Education of a Monster : City of Ghosts : Tales Of*
Natsukawa, Sosuke. *The Cat Who Saved Books*
Quick, Amanda. ★*The Lady Has a Past*
Reay, Katherine. *The Bronte Plot*
Ruiz Zafon, Carlos. *The Prisoner of Heaven*
Setterfield, Diane. *The Thirteenth Tale: A Novel*
Swanson, Peter. *Eight Perfect Murders: A Novel*

BOOKSTORES
Adimi, Kaouther. *Our Riches*
Butland, Stephanie. *The Lost for Words Bookshop: A Novel*
Erdrich, Louise. ★*The Sentence*
Lelchuk, Saul. *Save Me from Dangerous Men: A Novel*
McKinlay, Jenn. *The Good Ones*
McPherson, Catriona. *Quiet Neighbors: A Novel*
O'Connor, Carlene. *Murder in an Irish Bookshop*
Savage, Sam. *Firmin: Adventures of a Metropolitan Lowlife*
Sloan, Robin. *Mr. Penumbra's 24-Hour Bookstore*
Waxman, Abbi. *The Bookish Life of Nina Hill*
Boone's Lick: A Novel. McMurtry, Larry

Booth, Coe

  ★*Bronxwood*

***Bootlegger's** Daughter*. Maron, Margaret

BOOTLEGGERS

  Algren, Nelson. *A Walk on the Wild Side*

  Bennett, Jenn. *Bitter Spirits*

  Brown, Taylor. ★*Gods of Howl Mountain: A Novel*

  Lehane, Dennis. *Live by Night*

  Montgomery, Jess. *The Stills*

  Offutt, Chris. *Country Dark*

BORA-BORA (FRENCH POLYNESIA)

  Steadman, Catherine. *Something in the Water*

Bordas, Camille

  How to Behave in a Crowd

BORDEAUX (NOUVELLE-AQUITAINE, FRANCE)

  Forester, C. S. *Lord Hornblower*

BORDEN, LIZZIE

  Schmidt, Sarah. *See What I Have Done*

  Thompson-Spires, Nafissa. *Heads of the Colored People: Stories*

*The **Border***. Winslow, Don

Border trilogy (Cormac McCarthy) [Series]. McCarthy, Cormac

BORDERLANDS

  Ahmad, Jamil. *The Wandering Falcon*

BOREDOM

  Aridjis, Chloe. *Asunder*

  Lee, Chang-Rae. ★*My Year Abroad*

  Wallace, David Foster. ★*The Pale King: An Unfinished Novel*

BOREDOM IN WOMEN

  Enright, Anne. *The Forgotten Waltz*

  Flaubert, Gustave. ★*Madame Bovary: Provincial Ways*

  Gideon, Melanie. *Wife 22*

  Shriver, Lionel. *The Post-Birthday World*

Borges, Jorge Luis

  ★*Collected Fictions*

  Ficciones

BORGIA FAMILY

  Poole, Sara. *The Borgia Mistress*

  Puzo, Mario. *The Family: A Novel*

*The **Borgia** Mistress*. Poole, Sara

BORGIA, LUCREZIA

  Child, Lee. *61 Hours*

  Dunant, Sarah. *Blood and Beauty: A Novel*

Borne novels [Series]. VanderMeer, Jeff

★***Borne:** a Novel*. VanderMeer, Jeff

*The **Borrower:** a Novel*. Makkai, Rebecca

BORTHWICK, MAMAH BOUTON

  Horan, Nancy. *Loving Frank: A Novel*

  Munro, Alice. *Hateship, Friendship, Courtship, Loveship, Marriage: Stories*

BOSCH, HARRY (FICTITIOUS CHARACTER)

  Connelly, Michael. *The Black Ice*

  Connelly, Michael. *The Burning Room*

Boschwitz, Ulrich Alexander

  The Passenger: A Novel

BOSNIA AND HERCEGOVINA

  Andric, Ivo. *The Bridge on the Drina*

  Prcic, Ismet. *Shards: A Novel*

  Turow, Scott. *Testimony*

BOSNIANS IN THE UNITED STATES

  Prcic, Ismet. *Shards: A Novel*

*The **Boston** Girl: A Novel*. Diamant, Anita

BOSTON TERRIERS

  Avon, Joy. *In Peppermint Peril: A Book Tea Shop Mystery*

BOSTON, MASSACHUSETTS

  Black, Benjamin. ★*Christine Falls: A Novel*

  Center, Katherine. *Things You Save in a Fire*

  Child, Lee. *Persuader*

  Cook, Robin. *Charlatans*

  Cook, Robin. *Coma: A Novel*

  Daniel, Ray. *Hacked: A Tucker Mystery*

  Diamant, Anita. *The Boston Girl: A Novel*

  Finder, Joseph. *Buried Secrets*

  Finder, Joseph. ★*Judgment*

  Finder, Joseph. *Suspicion*

  Finder, Joseph. *The Switch: A Novel*

  Gardner, Lisa. *Alone*

  Gardner, Lisa. ★*Before She Disappeared: A Novel*

  Gardner, Lisa. *Fear Nothing: A Detective D. D. Warren Novel*

  Gardner, Lisa. *Find Her*

  Gardner, Lisa. ★*Look for Me: A Novel*

  Gardner, Lisa. *Love You More: A Detective D.D. Warren Novel*

  Gardner, Lisa. *The Neighbor*

  Gardner, Lisa. ★*Never Tell: A Novel*

  Garwood, Julie. *Wired*

  Gerritsen, Tess. *The Apprentice: A Novel*

  Gerritsen, Tess. *The Bone Garden*

  Gerritsen, Tess. *Choose Me*

  Gerritsen, Tess. *The Surgeon*

  Harvey, Michael T. *Brighton*

  Harvey, Michael T. *Pulse*

  Higgins, George V. *The Friends of Eddie Coyle*

  Higgins, Kristan. *Now That You Mention It*

  Hill, Edwin J. *Little Comfort*

  Hoover, Colleen. *It Ends with Us*

  Horowitz, Anthony. *The House of Silk: A Sherlock Holmes Novel*

  Lehane, Dennis. ★*The Given Day*

  Lehane, Dennis. ★*Mystic River*

  Lehane, Dennis. *Since We Fell*

  Lightman, Alan P. *The Diagnosis*

  Lipman, Elinor. *The Pursuit of Alice Thrift: A Novel*

  Moore, Liz. *The Unseen World*

  Mosley, Walter. *Fortunate Son: A Novel*

  Olson, Neil. *Before the Devil Fell*

  Parker, Robert B. *Painted Ladies*

  Parker, Robert B. *Sixkill*

  Patchett, Ann. *Run*

  Pearl, Matthew. *The Dante Club: A Novel*

  Pearl, Matthew. *The Technologists: A Novel*

  Picoult, Jodi. ★*The Book of Two Ways*

  Racculia, Kate. ★*Tuesday Mooney Talks to Ghosts: A Novel*

  Rosenfield, Kat. *No One Will Miss Her*

  Savage, Sam. *Firmin: Adventures of a Metropolitan Lowlife*

  Segal, Erich. ★*Love Story*

  Swanson, Peter. *Eight Perfect Murders: A Novel*

  Swanson, Peter. *Her Every Fear: A Novel*

  Tamirat, Nafkote. *The Parking Lot Attendant: A Novel*

Turnbull, Cadwell. *No Gods, No Monsters*
Valdes, Alisa. *Dirty Girls on Top*
Wallace, David Foster. ★*Infinite Jest: A Novel*
Yang, Susie. *White Ivy: A Novel*

BOTANISTS
Bellow, Saul. *More Die of Heartbreak*

BOTSWANA
McCall Smith, Alexander. *Blue Shoes and Happiness*
McCall Smith, Alexander. *The Double Comfort Safari Club*
McCall Smith, Alexander. *The Full Cupboard of Life*
McCall Smith, Alexander. *The Good Husband of Zebra Drive*
McCall Smith, Alexander. *In the Company of Cheerful Ladies*
McCall Smith, Alexander. *The Joy and Light Bus Company*
McCall Smith, Alexander. *The Kalahari Typing School for Men*
McCall Smith, Alexander. *The Limpopo Academy of Private Detection*
McCall Smith, Alexander. ★*The No. 1 Ladies' Detective Agency*
McCall Smith, Alexander. *The Saturday Big Tent Wedding Party*
Rush, Norman. ★*Mating*
Stanley, Michael. *A Carrion Death*
Stanley, Michael. *Deadly Harvest*
Stanley, Michael. *A Death in the Family*
Stanley, Michael. *Death of the Mantis*
Stanley, Michael. *Dying to Live*
*The **Bottoms**. Lansdale, Joe R.*

Bouchet, Amanda
Breath of Fire
Nightchaser
★*A Promise of Fire*

Boudjedra, Rachid
The Barbary Figs

BOULDER, COLORADO
Winer, Jeanne. *Her Kind of Case*

Boulle, Pierre
The Bridge Over the River Kwai: A Novel

*The **bounceback** [Series]. Beckett, L. X.*

BOUNTY HUNTERS
Bittner, Rosanne. *Logan's Lady*
Brooks, Bill. *Frontier Justice*
Dick, Philip K. ★*Do Androids Dream of Electric Sheep?*
Evanovich, Janet. ★*Game On: Tempting Twenty-Eight*
Evanovich, Janet. *Look Alive Twenty-Five*
Evanovich, Janet. *Turbo Twenty-Three*
Lansdale, Joe R. *The Thicket*
McMurtry, Larry. ★*Streets of Laredo: A Novel*

Bourdeaut, Olivier
Waiting for Bojangles: A Novel

Bourland, Barbara
★*Fake Like Me*

★*The **Bourne** Identity. Ludlum, Robert.*
*The **Bourne** Supremacy. Ludlum, Robert.*
*The **Bourne** Ultimatum. Ludlum, Robert.*

BOURNE, JASON (FICTITIOUS CHARACTER)
Ludlum, Robert. ★*The Bourne Identity*
Ludlum, Robert. *The Bourne Supremacy*
Ludlum, Robert. *The Bourne Ultimatum*

Bourne, Joanna
The Black Hawk

The Forbidden Rose
★*My Lord and Spymaster*
Rogue Spy
★*The Spymaster's Lady*

Bow Street bachelors [Series]. Bateman, Kate

Bowen, Elizabeth
The Heat of the Day

Bowen, Kelly
★*Between the Devil and the Duke*
A Rogue by Night

Bowen, Peter
Badlands

Bowen, Rhys
The Victory Garden

BOWERY, NEW YORK CITY
Crane, Stephen. *Maggie: A Girl of the Streets*
★*Bowlaway: a Novel*. McCracken, Elizabeth

Bowles, David
Feathered Serpent, Dark Heart of Sky: Myths of Mexico

Bowles, Paul
★*The Sheltering Sky*

BOWLING ALLEYS
McCracken, Elizabeth. ★*Bowlaway: A Novel*

Bowman, Conor
★*Horace Winter Says Goodbye*

Bowman, David
Big Bang: A Nonfiction Novel

Bowman, Valerie
The Accidental Countess
A Duke Like No Other
No Other Duke but You
Secrets of a Wedding Night
The Unexpected Duchess

Box, C. J.
Badlands
★*The Bitterroots: A Novel*
Blue Heaven
★*Dark Sky: A Joe Pickett Novel*
The Disappeared
The Highway
★*Long Range*
★*Open Season*
Paradise Valley
Savage Run
Trophy Hunt: A Joe Pickett Novel
Vicious Circle
Winterkill: A Novel
★*Wolf Pack*

*The **Box**: Tales from the Darkroom. Grass, Gunter*

BOXERS (SPORTS)
Dare, Tessa. ★*Say Yes to the Marquess*
Mendez, Paul. *Rainbow Milk*
Mosley, Walter. *Charcoal Joe: An Easy Rawlins Mystery*
Phillips, Caryl. *Foreigners*
Smith, Michael F. *The Fighter: A Novel*
Vlautin, Willy. *Don't Skip Out on Me*

BOXES
Fisher, Helen. *Space Hopper*

BOXING
Freeman, Anna. *The Fair Fight: A Novel*
BOY ADVENTURERS
Saint-Exupery, Antoine de. ★*The Little Prince*
Twain, Mark. ★*Adventures of Huckleberry Finn: Tom Sawyer's Comrade ...*
★*The **Boy** from the Woods.* Coben, Harlan
★*The **Boy** in the Field.* Livesey, Margot
BOY KIDNAPPING VICTIMS
Donohue, Keith. *The Stolen Child*
Hill, Joe. ★*Nos4a2*
Lodato, Victor. *Edgar and Lucy: A Novel*
Rowland, Laura Joh. *The Snow Empress*
BOY MURDER VICTIMS
Harding Thornton, Christina. *Pickard County Atlas*
Russell, Mary Doria. ★*Doc: A Novel*
BOY MURDERERS
George, Elizabeth. *What Came Before He Shot Her*
BOY ORPHANS
Gardam, Jane. *Old Filth*
Kelton, Elmer. ★*The Way of the Coyote*
Mabanckou, Alain. ★*Black Moses*
Stewart, Mary. *Nine Coaches Waiting*
BOY PRODIGIES
Dongala, Emmanuel Boundzeki. *The Bridgetower Sonata: Sonata Mulattica*
BOY PSYCHICS
King, Stephen. ★*The Shining*
BOY SCOUTS
Butler, Nickolas. ★*The Hearts of Men*
BOY SHEPHERDS
Coelho, Paulo. ★*The Alchemist*
***Boy** Swallows Universe.* Dalton, Trent
*The **Boy** Toy.* Marsh, Nicola
***Boy's** Life.* McCammon, Robert R.
*A **Boy's** Own Story.* White, Edmund
***Boy,** Snow, Bird: A Novel.* Oyeyemi, Helen
BOY/GIRL RELATIONS
London, Joan. *The Golden Age*
Boyd, William
Trio
★***Boyfriend** Material.* Hall, Alexis
*The **Boyfriend** Project.* Rochon, Farrah
Boyfriend project [Series]. Rochon, Farrah
BOYFRIENDS
Beagin, Jen. ★*Vacuum in the Dark: A Novel*
Frazier, Jean Kyoung. *Pizza Girl*
Smith, Ian. *The Unspoken*
St. Aubyn, Edward. *Double Blind*
Boyle, Elizabeth
Along Came a Duke
And the Miss Ran Away with the Rake
Boyle, T. Coraghessan
The Harder They Come
Outside Looking In: A Novel
The Relive Box: And Other Stories
The Terranauts
★*The Tortilla Curtain*

When the Killing's Done: A Novel
The Women: A Novel
World's End: A Novel
Boyle, William
City of Margins: A Novel
The Lonely Witness
Boyne, John
The Heart's Invisible Furies
★*A Ladder to the Sky*
BOYS
Ahlborn, Ania. *The Devil Crept In*
Ballard, J. G. *Empire of the Sun: A Novel*
Bock, Charles. *Beautiful Children: A Novel*
Cargill, C. Robert. *Day Zero*
Couto, Mia. *Sleepwalking Land*
Cunningham, Michael. *Specimen Days*
Deane, Seamus. *Reading in the Dark*
Donoghue, Emma. ★*Room: A Novel*
Earley, Tony. *Jim the Boy: A Novel*
Faye, Gael. ★*Small Country: A Novel*
Foer, Jonathan Safran. *Extremely Loud and Incredibly Close*
Golding, William. ★*Lord of the Flies: A Novel*
Harrigan, Stephen. *The Leopard Is Loose: A Novel*
Hart, John. *Redemption Road*
Haruf, Kent. *Eventide*
Holdstock, Pauline. *Here I Am!*
Llewellyn, Richard. ★*How Green Was My Valley*
Makkai, Rebecca. *The Borrower: A Novel*
McCammon, Robert R. *Boy's Life*
Napolitano, Ann. *Dear Edward*
Powell, Padgett. ★*Edisto: A Novel*
Proust, Marcel. *Within a Budding Grove*
Roberts, Nora. *Sea Swept*
Smiley, Jane. ★*Perestroika in Paris: A Novel*
Winspear, Jacqueline. ★*The Consequences of Fear: A Maisie Dobbs Novel*
BOYS — FRIENDSHIP
Bradbury, Ray. ★*Something Wicked This Way Comes*
Frayn, Michael. *Spies: A Novel*
Hosseini, Khaled. ★*The Kite Runner*
Lebrecht, Norman. *The Song of Names*
Petterson, Per. *Out Stealing Horses: A Novel*
Twain, Mark. ★*Adventures of Huckleberry Finn: Tom Sawyer's Comrade ...*
BOYS AND HORSES
McCarthy, Cormac. ★*All the Pretty Horses*
BOYS AND MEN
Faulkner, William. *The Reivers: A Reminiscence*
BOYS AND WOLVES
McCarthy, Cormac. *The Crossing*
*The **Boys** from Brazil: A Novel.* Levin, Ira
BOYS WHO ARE MUTE
Dalton, Trent. *Boy Swallows Universe*
Jimenez, Simon. ★*The Vanished Birds*
BOYS WITH AUTISM
Dazieri, Sandrone. *Kill the King*
Picoult, Jodi. *House Rules: A Novel*

BOYS WITH DISABILITIES
　Mosley, Walter. *Fortunate Son: A Novel*
BOYS WITH LEARNING DISABILITIES
　Box, C. J. *Paradise Valley*
BOYS' BOARDING SCHOOLS
　Dickens, Charles. ★*Nicholas Nickleby*
The Boys' Club. Katz, Erica
BOYS' SCHOOLS
　Hilton, James. ★*Good-Bye, Mr. Chips*
　Ripley, Mike. *Mr Campion's Fault*
Bradbury Stories: 100 of His Most Celebrated Tales. Bradbury, Ray
Bradbury, Jamey
　The Wild Inside: A Novel
Bradbury, Ray
　Bradbury Stories: 100 of His Most Celebrated Tales
　★*Dandelion Wine: A Novel*
　★*Fahrenheit 451*
　The Illustrated Man
　★*The Martian Chronicles: The Fortieth Anniversary Edition*
　★*Something Wicked This Way Comes*
Bradby, Tom
　Double Agent
Bradford sisters [Series]. Wade, Becky
Bradford, Barbara Taylor
　★*A Woman of Substance*
Bradley, Anna
　A Season of Ruin
　A Wicked Way to Win an Earl
Bradley, C. Alan
　As Chimney Sweepers Come to Dust: A Flavia De Luce Novel
　The Golden Tresses of the Dead: A Flavia De Luce Novel
　The Grave's a Fine and Private Place: A Flavia De Luce Novel
　I Am Half-Sick of Shadows: A Flavia De Luce Novel
　A Red Herring Without Mustard
　Speaking from Among the Bones: A Flavia De Luce Novel
　★*The Sweetness at the Bottom of the Pie*
　Thrice the Brinded Cat Hath Mew'd: A Flavia De Luce Novel
　The Weed That Strings the Hangman's Bag: A Flavia De Luce Mystery
BRADLEY, OMAR N.
　Perrotta, Tom. *Little Children*
　Shaara, Jeff. *The Steel Wave: A Novel of World War II*
Braffet, Kelly
　★*Last Seen Leaving: A Novel*
BRAIN
　Doctorow, E. L. *Andrew's Brain*
BRAIN ANEURYSMS
　Reichs, Kathy. ★*A Conspiracy of Bones*
BRAIN INJURY
　Anderton, Jo. *Debris*
BRAINWASHING
　Ballard, J. G. *Millennium People*
Braithwaite, Oyinkan
　My Sister, the Serial Killer: A Novel
Bram, Christopher
　Lives of the Circus Animals: A Novel
Brand, Max
　★*The Collected Stories of Max Brand*

　Max Brand's Best Western Stories
　The Stingaree
Brandreth, Benet
　The Spy of Venice
Brandt, Harry
　The Whites: A Novel
The Brass Verdict: A Novel. Connelly, Michael
★*Brass: a Novel*. Aliu, Xhenet
BRATTLEBORO, VERMONT
　Mayor, Archer. *Red Herring: A Joe Gunther Novel*
　Mayor, Archer. *Tag Man: A Joe Gunther Novel*
Braun, Lilian Jackson
　The Cat Who Ate Danish Modern
Brautigan, Richard
　An Unfortunate Woman: A Journey
★*Brave New World*. Huxley, Aldous
Brayden, Melissa
　First Position
★*Brazen and the Beast*. MacLean, Sarah
Brazier, Eliza Jane
　If I Disappear
BRAZIL
　Amado, Jorge. ★*Dona Flor and Her Two Husbands: A Moral and Amorous Tale*
　Amado, Jorge. *Gabriela, Clove and Cinnamon*
　Jones, Gayl. ★*Palmares*
　Peebles, Frances de Pontes. *The Air You Breathe*
　Rodrigues Fowler, Yara. *Stubborn Archivist*
　Rollins, James. *The Demon Crown: A Sigma Force Novel*
　Updike, John. *Brazil: A Novel*
　Vargas Llosa, Mario. *The War of the End of the World*
　Wilson, Daniel H. *The Andromeda Evolution: A Novel*
Brazil: a Novel. Updike, John
BRAZILIANS
　Rodrigues Fowler, Yara. *Stubborn Archivist*
Break No Bones. Reichs, Kathy
The Breakdown. Paris, B. A.
The Breaker. Petrie, Nicholas
★*Breakfast at Tiffany's*. Capote, Truman
★*Breakfast of Champions: Or, Goodbye Blue Monday!* Vonnegut, Kurt
BREAKING UP (INTERPERSONAL RELATIONS)
　Broder, Melissa. *The Pisces: A Novel*
　Garriott, Leah. *Promised*
　Gerritsen, Tess. *Choose Me*
　Linden, Rachel. *The Enlightenment of Bees*
　Mallery, Susan. *California Girls*
　McFarlane, Mhairi. *If I Never Met You: A Novel*
　Nicholls, Owen. *Love, Unscripted: A Novel*
　Riley, Lucinda. *The Girl on the Cliff: A Novel*
　Rooney, Sally. ★*Beautiful World, Where Are You*
　Turner, Bethany. *Wooing Cadie McCaffrey*
Breakout. Stark, Richard
BREAST CANCER — GENETIC ASPECTS
　Clark, Georgia. *The Bucket List*
Breath of Fire. Bouchet, Amanda
★*A Breath of Snow and Ashes*. Gabaldon, Diana
Breathe. Oates, Joyce Carol
Breathing Through the Wound. Arbol, Victor del

BRECKENRIDGE, COLORADO
Hemmings, Kaui Hart. *The Possibilities: A Novel*
Breen and Tozer novels [Series]. Shaw, William
Brennan, Marie
Driftwood
Within the Sanctuary of Wings: A Memoir by Lady Trent
BRENNAN, TEMPERANCE (FICTITIOUS CHARACTER)
Reichs, Kathy. *Bare Bones*
Reichs, Kathy. *Bones to Ashes*
Reichs, Kathy. *Break No Bones*
Reichs, Kathy. *Deadly Decisions*
Reichs, Kathy. *Death Du Jour*
Reichs, Kathy. ★*Deja Dead*
Reichs, Kathy. *Grave Secrets*
Reichs, Kathy. *Monday Mourning*
Brenner, Jamie
Blush: A Novel
Drawing Home
Breslin, Jimmy
Table Money
The **Brethren**. Lewis, Beverly
Brett, Simon
Guilt at the Garage
Mrs Pargeter's Principle
Murder Unprompted
BREWERIES
Stradal, J. Ryan. ★*The Lager Queen of Minnesota*
BREXIT, 2016-2020
Hamya, Jo. *Three Rooms*
Smith, Ali. ★*Summer*
★*Brick Lane: A Novel*. Ali, Monica
BRIDAL SHOPS
Williams, Preslaysa. *A Lowcountry Bride*
The **Bride**. Garwood, Julie
The **Bride** of Lammermoor. Scott, Walter
★*Bride of the Sea: A Novel*. Quotah, Eman
★*The Bride Test*. Hoang, Helen
BRIDES
Khaw, Cassandra. *Nothing but Blackened Teeth*
Phillips, Susan Elizabeth. *The Great Escape*
Van Meter, Crissy. *Creatures: A Novel*
The **Brides** of Maracoor. Maguire, Gregory
★*Brideshead Revisited*. Waugh, Evelyn
★*The Bridesmaid*. Rendell, Ruth
BRIDESMAIDS
Rendell, Ruth. ★*The Bridesmaid*
Bridge of Sighs. Russo, Richard
The **Bridge** of Sighs. Steinhauer, Olen
The **Bridge** on the Drina. Andric, Ivo
The **Bridge** Over the River Kwai: A Novel. Boulle, Pierre
Bridge to Haven. Rivers, Francine
Bridgerton series [Series]. Quinn, Julia
BRIDGES
Boulle, Pierre. *The Bridge Over the River Kwai: A Novel*
Michener, James A. ★*The Bridges at Toko-Ri*
Patrick, Phaedra. ★*The Secrets of Love Story Bridge*
Wood, Tracey Enerson. *The Engineer's Wife: A Novel*

BRIDGES — DESIGN AND CONSTRUCTION
Andric, Ivo. *The Bridge on the Drina*
Kadare, Ismail. ★*The Three-Arched Bridge*
★*The Bridges at Toko-Ri*. Michener, James A.
★*The Bridges of Madison County*. Waller, Robert James
★*Bridget Jones's Diary: A Novel*. Fielding, Helen
Bridget Jones [Series]. Fielding, Helen
The **Bridgetower** Sonata: Sonata Mulattica. Dongala, Emmanuel Boundzeki
BRIDGETOWER, GEORGE AUGUSTUS POLGREEN
Dongala, Emmanuel Boundzeki. *The Bridgetower Sonata: Sonata Mulattica*
★*A Brief History of Seven Killings: A Novel*. James, Marlon
★*Brief Interviews with Hideous Men*. Wallace, David Foster
★*The Brief Wondrous Life of Oscar Wao*. Diaz, Junot
Bright and Dangerous Objects. Mackintosh, Anneliese
Bright and Distant Shores. Smith, Dominic
Bright Burning Things. Harding, Lisa
A **Bright** Ray of Darkness. Hawke, Ethan
★*A Brightness Long Ago*. Kay, Guy Gavriel
Brighton. Harvey, Michael T.
★*Brighton Rock*. Greene, Graham
BRIGHTON, ENGLAND
Boyd, William. *Trio*
Greene, Graham. ★*Brighton Rock*
Roberts, Bethan. ★*My Policeman*
Swift, Graham. ★*Here We Are*
Truss, Lynne. *The Man That Got Away: A Constable Twitten Mystery*
Truss, Lynne. *Murder by Milk Bottle*
Ware, Ruth. *The Death of Mrs. Westaway*
Brilliance. Sakey, Marcus
Brilliance saga [Series]. Sakey, Marcus
The **Brilliant** Life of Eudora Honeysett. Lyons, Annie
Brin, David
Existence
Bring Me Back: A Novel. Paris, B. A.
Bring Me the Head of Quentin Tarantino: Stories. Herbert, Julian
★*Bring up the Bodies: A Novel*. Mantel, Hilary
★*Bringing Down the Duke*. Dunmore, Evie
Brink, Andre P.
Philida: A Novel
Brinkley, Jamel
A Lucky Man: Stories
BRISBANE, QUEENSLAND
Dalton, Trent. *Boy Swallows Universe*
Briscoe, Joanna
The Seduction
BRISTOL, ENGLAND
Freeman, Anna. *The Fair Fight: A Novel*
Hayder, Mo. *Gone*
Hayder, Mo. *Poppet*
Brit in the FBI [Series]. Coulter, Catherine
BRITISH COLUMBIA
Haldane, Sean. *The Devil's Making*
Kamal, Sheena. *It All Falls Down*
Munro, Alice. *Runaway: Stories*
Stevens, Chevy. *Never Let You Go*
Stevens, Chevy. *Still Missing*

BRITISH IN AFRICA
Forester, C. S. *The African Queen*
McLain, Paula. *Circling the Sun*
BRITISH IN BRAZIL
Rodrigues Fowler, Yara. *Stubborn Archivist*
BRITISH IN BURMA
Mason, Daniel. *The Piano Tuner*
BRITISH IN CANADA
Haldane, Sean. *The Devil's Making*
BRITISH IN CHINA
Ishiguro, Kazuo. *When We Were Orphans*
Rendell, Ruth. *Speaker of Mandarin*
BRITISH IN CUBA
Greene, Graham. *Our Man in Havana*
BRITISH IN ETHIOPIA
Gibb, Camilla. *Sweetness in the Belly*
BRITISH IN FRANCE
Faulks, Sebastian. ★*Birdsong*
Faulks, Sebastian. *Charlotte Gray: A Novel*
Godden, Rumer. *The Greengage Summer: A Novel*
Ripley, Mike. *Mr. Campion's War*
BRITISH IN GERMANY
Ford, Ford Madox. ★*The Good Soldier: A Tale of Passion*
Hall, Adam. *The Quiller Memorandum*
Isherwood, Christopher. ★*The Berlin Stories: The Last of Mr. Norris, Goodbye to Berlin*
BRITISH IN GREECE
Goddard, Robert. ★*Into the Blue*
BRITISH IN INDIA
Bacon, Charlotte. *There Is Room for You*
Carter, Miranda. *The Strangler Vine*
Dyer, Geoff. *Jeff in Venice, Death in Varanasi*
Forster, E. M. ★*A Passage to India*
Scott, Paul. ★*Staying On: A Novel*
BRITISH IN IRELAND
Black, Benjamin. ★*The Secret Guests: A Novel*
Rutherfurd, Edward. *The Rebels of Ireland: The Dublin Saga*
BRITISH IN ISRAEL
Spark, Muriel. ★*The Mandelbaum Gate*
BRITISH IN ITALY
Amis, Martin. ★*The Pregnant Widow*
Forster, E. M. ★*A Room with a View*
George, Elizabeth. *Just One Evil Act*
Mangan, Christine. *Palace of the Drowned*
BRITISH IN JAPAN
Clavell, James. *Shogun*
BRITISH IN PANAMA
Le Carre, John. *The Tailor of Panama*
BRITISH IN ROMANIA
Stoker, Bram. ★*Dracula*
Stoker, Bram. *The New Annotated Dracula*
BRITISH IN SOUTH AFRICA
Lessing, Doris May. *A Proper Marriage*
BRITISH IN SOUTH AMERICA
Pulley, Natasha. *The Bedlam Stacks*
BRITISH IN TAHITI
Maugham, W. Somerset. *The Moon and Sixpence*

BRITISH IN THAILAND
Barton, Fiona. *The Suspect*
BRITISH IN THE CARIBBEAN AREA
Sabatini, Rafael. *Captain Blood*
BRITISH IN THE UNITED STATES
Bittner, Rosanne. *Logan's Lady*
Coulter, Catherine. *The Devil's Triangle*
Coulter, Catherine. *The End Game*
Coulter, Catherine. *The Final Cut*
Coulter, Catherine. *The Lost Key*
Delaney, J. P. *Believe Me: A Novel*
Dickens, Charles. *Martin Chuzzlewit*
Faulks, Sebastian. *On Green Dolphin Street: A Novel*
Goodwin, S. M. *Absence of Mercy*
L'Amour, Louis. *To the Far Blue Mountains*
Pynchon, Thomas. ★*V: A Novel*
Steadman, Catherine. *The Disappearing Act*
BRITISH IN THE WEST INDIES
Forester, C. S. *Admiral Hornblower in the West Indies*
Naipaul, V. S. *Guerrillas*
BRITISH IN VIETNAM
Greene, Graham. ★*The Quiet American*
BRITISH IN WEST AFRICA
Greene, Graham. ★*The Heart of the Matter*
BRITISH RAJ (1858-1947)
Enjeti, Anjali. ★*The Parted Earth*
Forster, E. M. ★*A Passage to India*
March, Nev. *Murder in Old Bombay*
Massey, Sujata. ★*The Bombay Prince*
Massey, Sujata. *The Satapur Moonstone*
Mukherjee, Abir. *Death in the East*
Mukherjee, Abir. *The Shadows of Men*
Mukherjee, Abir. *Smoke and Ashes: A Novel*
BRITISH WOMEN IN ITALY
Hemingway, Ernest. ★*A Farewell to Arms*
Britt Montero novels [Series]. Buchanan, Edna
Britt-Marie Was Here. Backman, Fredrik
BRITTANY, FRANCE
Bannalec, Jean-Luc. *Death in Brittany*
Bannalec, Jean-Luc. *The Granite Coast Murders*
Bannalec, Jean-Luc. *The Killing Tide: A Brittany Mystery*
Broadchurch: a Novel. Kelly, Erin
BROADWAY, NEW YORK CITY
Bram, Christopher. *Lives of the Circus Animals: A Novel*
Phillips, Caryl. *Dancing in the Dark*
Brockmeier, Kevin
The Illumination
Brockway, Connie
The Golden Season
No Place for a Dame
So Enchanting
Broder, Melissa
Milk Fed
The Pisces: A Novel
Brodesser-Akner, Taffy
Fleishman Is in Trouble: A Novel
Brodie, Emma
Songs in Ursa Major

Broken Earth novels [Series]. Jemisin, N. K.

*The **Broken** Girls*. St. James, Simone

★***Broken** Harbor*. French, Tana

*Broken** Homes*. Aaronovitch, Ben

*Broken** Monsters*. Beukes, Lauren

*The **Broken** Ones: A Novel*. Irwin, Stephen M.

*The **Broken** Places*. Atkins, Ace

*Broken** Prey*. Sandford, John

*Broken** Promise*. Barclay, Linwood

★*Broken** Sleep: An American Dream*. Bauman, Bruce

Broken: Six Short Novels. Winslow, Don

BROKERS

Wolfe, Tom. *The Bonfire of the Vanities*

Brom

Slewfoot: A Tale of Bewitchery

*The **Bromance** Book Club*. Adams, Lyssa Kay

Bromance book club [Series]. Adams, Lyssa Kay

Bronsky, Alina

The Hottest Dishes of the Tartar Cuisine

*The **Bronte** Plot*. Reay, Katherine

Bronte sisters mystery [Series]. Ellis, Bella

*Bronte's** Mistress*. Austin, Finola

Bronte, Anne

The Tenant of Wildfell Hall

Bronte, Charlotte

★*Emma*

★*Jane Eyre*

BRONTE, CHARLOTTE

Ellis, Bella. *The Vanished Bride*

Sofer, Dalia. *Man of My Time*

Bronte, Emily

★*Wuthering Heights*

BRONTE, EMILY

Beaton, M. C. *Pushing up Daisies: An Agatha Raisin Mystery*

Reay, Katherine. *The Bronte Plot*

BRONTE, PATRICK BRANWELL

Austin, Finola. *Bronte's Mistress*

Engel, Patricia. ★*Infinite Country*

BRONX, NEW YORK CITY

Alvarez, Julia. *How the Garcia Girls Lost Their Accents*

Booth, Coe. ★*Bronxwood*

Doctorow, E. L. *World's Fair*

O'Brien, Perry Edmond. *Fire in the Blood*

Ozick, Cynthia. *Heir to the Glimmering World*

Rice-Gonzalez, Charles. *Chulito*

Verghese, A. *Cutting for Stone: A Novel*

★*Bronxwood*. Booth, Coe

BROOKLYN BRIDGE, NEW YORK CITY

Wood, Tracey Enerson. *The Engineer's Wife: A Novel*

*The **Brooklyn** Follies*. Auster, Paul

BROOKLYN, NEW YORK CITY

Auster, Paul. *Oracle Night*

Auster, Paul. *Sunset Park*

Bartz, Andrea. *The Lost Night*

Boyle, William. *City of Margins: A Novel*

Boyle, William. *The Lonely Witness*

Carter, Mary Dixie. *The Photographer*

Coster, Naima. *Halsey Street*

Danticat, Edwidge. *The Dew Breaker*

Gaitskill, Mary. *The Mare: A Novel*

Garcia, Cristina. *Dreaming in Cuban*

Goldbloom, Goldie. *On Division*

Gran, Sara. *Claire Dewitt and the City of the Dead*

Greenidge, Kaitlyn. ★*Libertie: A Novel*

Lethem, Jonathan. ★*Motherless Brooklyn*

Loigman, Lynda Cohen. *The Wartime Sisters: A Novel*

Malamud, Bernard. *The Assistant*

McBride, James. ★*Deacon King Kong: A Novel*

McDermott, Alice. ★*The Ninth Hour*

McDermott, Alice. *Someone*

Miller, Henry. ★*Tropic of Capricorn*

Molloy, Aimee. *The Perfect Mother: A Novel*

Orenstein, Hannah. *Love at First Like*

Pochoda, Ivy. *Visitation Street: A Novel*

Potok, Chaim. ★*The Gift of Asher Lev*

Rees, Matt. *The Fourth Assassin*

Senna, Danzy. *New People*

Sister Souljah. ★*The Coldest Winter Ever: A Novel*

Sister Souljah. ★*A Deeper Love Inside: The Porsche Santiaga Story*

Sister Souljah. *Midnight and the Meaning of Love*

Smith, Betty. ★*A Tree Grows in Brooklyn*

Smith, Dominic. ★*The Last Painting of Sara De Vos*

Straub, Emma. ★*Modern Lovers*

Von Ziegesar, Cecily. *Cobble Hill*

Woodson, Jacqueline. ★*Another Brooklyn*

Woodson, Jacqueline. ★*Red at the Bone*

Brookner, Anita

Hotel Du Lac

Brooks, Bill

Blood Storm

Frontier Justice

Winter Kill

Brooks, Max

Devolution: A Firsthand Account of the Rainier Sasquatch Massacre

★*World War Z: An Oral History of the Zombie War*

Brooks, Terry

Child of Light

Brookstone brides [Series]. Peterson, Tracie

BROTHELS

Priest, Cherie. *Ganymede*

Vargas Llosa, Mario. *Green House*

Zola, Emile. ★*Nana*

Brother Cadfael medieval mysteries [Series]. Peters, Ellis

*Brother** Cadfael's Penance*. Peters, Ellis

Brother: a Novel. Chariandy, David John

BROTHERS

Adamson, Gil. *The Outlander*

Adiga, Aravind. *Selection Day*

Adler-Olsen, Jussi. *A Conspiracy of Faith*

Aslam, Nadeem. ★*The Blind Man's Garden*

Baldwin, James. *Just Above My Head*

Barbash, Tom. *The Last Good Chance*

Bell, Lenora. *One Fine Duke*

Bernhard, Thomas. *Frost: A Novel*

Chariandy, David John. *Brother: A Novel*

Clinch, Jon. *Finn: A Novel*

Coben, Harlan. *Don't Let Go*
Dalton, Trent. *Boy Swallows Universe*
Dickey, Eric Jerome. *The Business of Lovers*
Doctorow, E. L. *Homer and Langley: A Novel*
Dostoyevsky, Fyodor. ★*The Brothers Karamazov*
Finder, Joseph. *Vanished*
Fitzpatrick, Lydia. *Lights All Night Long: A Novel*
Gregory, Philippa. *The Constant Princess*
Gross, Andrew. *Button Man*
Harper, Jane. *The Lost Man*
Harris, Nathan. *The Sweetness of Water*
Hart, John. *Iron House*
Hart, John. *The Unwilling*
Haruf, Kent. *Eventide*
Holbert, Bruce. *Whiskey*
Kerley, Jack. ★*The Death Collectors*
L'Amour, Louis. ★*Bendigo Shafter*
L'Amour, Louis. *The Californios*
Lahiri, Jhumpa. *The Lowland: A Novel*
Lauren, Christina. *In a Holidaze*
Leonard, Elmore. ★*Raylan*
MacLean, Sarah. ★*Brazen and the Beast*
McCarthy, Cormac. *The Crossing*
Murdoch, Iris. *The Green Knight*
Obioma, Chigozie. ★*The Fishermen: A Novel*
Orringer, Julie. ★*The Invisible Bridge: A Novel*
Panowich, Brian. *Bull Mountain*
Parry, H. G. *The Unlikely Escape of Uriah Heep*
Piccirilli, Tom. *The Last Kind Words*
Piccirilli, Tom. *The Last Whisper in the Dark: A Novel*
Pufahl, Shannon. *On Swift Horses*
Roberts, Nora. *Sea Swept*
Robertson, Michael. *The Baker Street Letters*
Robertson, Michael. *Moriarty Returns a Letter: A Baker Street
    Mystery*
Roth, Philip. ★*Everyman*
Salinger, J. D. *Raise High the Roof Beam, Carpenters,: And
    Seymour—An Introduction.*
Saramago, Jose. *Cain*
Saroyan, William. ★*The Human Comedy*
Schulman, Alex. *The Survivors: A Novel*
Singer, I. J. *The Brothers Ashkenazi*
Smith, Scott. *A Simple Plan: A Novel*
Sosa, Mia. ★*The Worst Best Man*
Stansel, Ian. *The Last Cowboys of San Geronimo*
Steinbeck, John. ★*East of Eden*
Stone, Irving. *Lust for Life: A Novel of Vincent Van Gogh*
Straub, Peter. ★*Ghost Story*
Strout, Elizabeth. ★*The Burgess Boys: A Novel*
Sundstol, Vidar. *The Land of Dreams*
Swift, Graham. *Wish You Were Here*
Thelen, Albert Vigoleis. *The Island of Second Sight: From the
    Applied Recollections of Vigoleis*
Tsukiyama, Gail. *The Street of a Thousand Blossoms*
Updike, John. *Gertrude and Claudius*
Verghese, A. *Cutting for Stone: A Novel*
Vlautin, Willy. ★*The Night Always Comes*
Willink, Jocko. *Final Spin*

BROTHERS — DEATH
    Child, Lee. ★*Killing Floor*
    Collins, Manda. *A Good Rake Is Hard to Find*
    Daoud, Kamel. *The Meursault Investigation*
    Enright, Anne. ★*The Gathering*
    Harper, Jane. *The Survivors*
    McHugh, Laura. *The Wolf Wants In: A Novel*
Brothers and Sisters. Campbell, Bebe Moore
The **Brothers** Ashkenazi. Singer, I. J.
★The **Brothers** Karamazov. Dostoyevsky, Fyodor
The **Brothers** of Baker Street. Robertson, Michael
The **Brothers** Sinister [Series]. Milan, Courtney
BROTHERS-IN-LAW
    Oe, Kenzaburo. *The Changeling*
Brothers: a Novel. Chen, Da
Broun, Bill
    Night of the Animals
Brouwer, Sigmund
    Thief of Glory: A Novel
Brown Girls. Andreades, Daphne Palasi
The **Brown** sisters [Series]. Hibbert, Talia
Brown, Amy Belding
    Emily's House
Brown, Dale
    Eagle Station: A Novel
    The Moscow Offensive: A Novel
Brown, Dan
    The Da Vinci Code
Brown, Dee
    Creek Mary's Blood: A Novel
Brown, Eleanor
    The Weird Sisters
BROWN, JOHN, 1800-1859
    Banks, Russell. *Cloudsplitter: A Novel*
    Ishiguro, Kazuo. *An Artist of the Floating World*
    McBride, James. ★*The Good Lord Bird*
    Vandermeer, Jeff. *Finch*
Brown, Karen
    The Clairvoyants: A Novel
Brown, Larry
    Joe: A Novel
    ★*Tiny Love: The Complete Stories of Larry Brown*
BROWN, MARGARET WISE
    Fine, Julia. *The Upstairs House*
    Mason, Meg. *Sorrow and Bliss*
Brown, Pierce
    Golden Son
    Morning Star
    Red Rising
Brown, Rita Mae
    ★*Rubyfruit Jungle*
    Six of One
    Wish You Were Here
Brown, Rosellen
    ★*Before and After*
    Tender Mercies
Brown, Sandra
    ★*Blind Tiger*

★*Ricochet*
Tailspin
The Witness
Brown, Taylor
Fallen Land
★*Gods of Howl Mountain: A Novel*
Browne, S. G.
Less Than Hero: A Novel
Brownrigg, Sylvia
★*The Delivery Room: A Novel*
Bruen, Ken
Galway Girl: A Jack Taylor Novel
The Guards
Brundage, Elizabeth
★*All Things Cease to Appear*
The Vanishing Point
BRUNETTI, GUIDO (FICTITIOUS CHARACTER)
Leon, Donna. *Beastly Things: A Commissario Guido Brunetti Mystery*
Leon, Donna. *Uniform Justice*
Bruni, Sarah
The Night Gwen Stacy Died
Brunkhorst, Alex
The Gilded Life of Matilda Duplaine
Bruno Courreges mysteries [Series]. Walker, Martin
Bruno, Anna
Ordinary Hazards: A Novel
BRUNO, GIORDANO
Clark, Mary Higgins. *Death Wears a Beauty Mask and Other Stories*
Franzen, Jonathan. ★*Crossroads*
Parris, S. J. ★*The Dead of Winter*
Parris, S. J. *Sacrilege*
Parris, S. J. *Treachery*
Rowland, Laura Joh. *The Snow Empress*
Brunt, Carol Rifka
★*Tell the Wolves I'm Home: A Novel*
BRUSSELS, BELGIUM
Ramzipoor, E. R. *The Ventriloquists*
Bryant & May: Hall of Mirrors : A Peculiar Crimes Unit Mystery. Fowler, Christopher
Bryant & May: Oranges and Lemons. Fowler, Christopher
Bryant & May: Strange Tide. Fowler, Christopher
Bryant & May: The Lonely Hour. Fowler, Christopher
Bryant and May mysteries [Series]. Fowler, Christopher
Bryant, Niobia
Christmas with the Billionaire
Madam, May I
Message from a Mistress
Bubblegum. Levin, Adam
Buchan, John
The Thirty-Nine Steps
Buchanan novels (Julie Garwood) [Series]. Garwood, Julie
Buchanan, Cathy Marie
★*The Painted Girls*
Buchanan, Edna
You Only Die Twice: A Britt Montero Mystery
BUCHAREST, ROMANIA
Veletzos, Roxanne. *The Girl They Left Behind*

Buchman, M. L.
Pure Heat
Buck Schatz mysteries [Series]. Friedman, Daniel
Buck, Pearl S.
The Good Earth
The Bucket List. Clark, Georgia
Buckley, Fiona
The Doublet Affair: A Mystery at Queen Elizabeth I's Court
The Siren Queen: An Ursula Blanchard Mystery at Queen Elizabeth I's Court
Buckley, William F.
★*Mongoose, R.I.P.: A Blackford Oakes Novel*
BUDAPEST, HUNGARY
Orringer, Julie. ★*The Invisible Bridge: A Novel*
Buddenbrooks. Mann, Thomas
The Buddha in the Attic. Otsuka, Julie
BUDDHISM
Hesse, Hermann. ★*Siddhartha: A New Translation*
Spann, Susan. *Trial on Mount Koya: A Hiro Hattori Novel*
Temple, Emily. *The Lightness*
Buddhism for Western Children: A Novel. Allio, Kirstin
BUDDHISTS
Burdett, John. *Bangkok 8*
Robinson, Kim Stanley. *The Years of Rice and Salt*
Buehlman, Christopher
The Suicide Motor Club
BUENOS AIRES, ARGENTINA
Benedetti, Mario. *Springtime in a Broken Mirror*
De Robertis, Carolina. *The Gods of Tango*
De Robertis, Carolina. *Perla*
Dickey, Eric Jerome. *Finding Gideon*
Gainza, Maria. *The Optic Nerve*
Loedel, Daniel. *Hades, Argentina*
Perez-Reverte, Arturo. *What We Become*
Restrepo, Laura. *No Place for Heroes: A Novel*
The Buffalo Soldier: A Novel. Bohjalian, Chris
★*Build Your House Around My Body*. Kupersmith, Violet
BUILDING
Davis, Lindsey. *A Body in the Bathhouse*
Sandford, John. *Shock Wave*
BUILDING SITES
Lovesey, Peter. *Beau Death*
Slaughter, Karin. *The Kept Woman*
Bujold, Lois McMaster
★*Shards of Honor*
★*The Warrior's Apprentice*
Bulawayo, NoViolet
We Need New Names: A Novel
Bulgakov, Mikhail
★*The Master and Margarita*
BULGARIA
Greenwell, Garth. *Cleanness*
Greenwell, Garth. *What Belongs to You: A Novel*
The Bull from the Sea. Renault, Mary
Bull Mountain. Panowich, Brian
Bull Mountain [Series]. Panowich, Brian
Bullet Park: A Novel. Cheever, John

BULLFIGHTERS
Dell, Kari Lynn. *Mistletoe in Texas*
Dell, Kari Lynn. *Reckless in Texas*
BULLFIGHTS
Hemingway, Ernest. ★*The Sun Also Rises*
BULLYING AND BULLIES
Grant, Helen. *The Vanishing of Katharina Linden*
King, Stephen. ★*Carrie*
Minato, Kanae. *Confessions*
Picoult, Jodi. *Nineteen Minutes: A Novel*
Solomon, Asali. *Disgruntled: A Novel*
Bump, Gabriel
★*Everywhere You Don't Belong: A Novel*
BUMPPO, NATTY (FICTITIOUS CHARACTER)
Cooper, James Fenimore. *The Last of the Mohicans: A Narrative of 1757*
Bunn, T. Davis
Outbreak
Bunny. Awad, Mona
Buntin, Julie
★*Marlena: A Novel*
Burdett, John
Bangkok 8
Burdick, Serena
Find Me in Havana
The Girls with No Names
BUREAUCRACY
Kafka, Franz. ★*The Trial*
Phillips, Helen. *The Beautiful Bureaucrat: A Novel*
Vonnegut, Kurt. *Jailbird: A Novel*
★*The **Burgess** Boys: A Novel*. Strout, Elizabeth
Burgess, Anthony
★*A Clockwork Orange*
*The **Burglar** in the Closet*. Block, Lawrence
★*The **Burglar** in the Library*. Block, Lawrence
BURGLARY
Bauer, Belinda. *Snap*
McCall Smith, Alexander. *In the Company of Cheerful Ladies*
Westlake, Donald E. ★*Bank Shot*
BURIAL
Hage, Rawi. *Beirut Hellfire Society: A Novel*
Buried. Cooper, Ellison
Buried Deep. Ragan, Theresa
*The **Buried** Giant: A Novel*. Ishiguro, Kazuo
Buried Prey. Sandford, John
Buried Secrets. Finder, Joseph
Burke, Alafair
The Better Sister: A Novel
Burke, James Lee
Another Kind of Eden
Black Cherry Blues
House of the Rising Sun: A Novel
The Jealous Kind
★*The New Iberia Blues*
★*A Private Cathedral*
Robicheaux
Wayfaring Stranger: A Novel

Burke, Marcus
Team Seven
Burke, Sue
Semiosis
BURKINA FASO
Wilkinson, Lauren. ★*American Spy: A Novel*
BURMA
Craig, Charmaine. *Miss Burma*
Ghosh, Amitav. *The Glass Palace*
Mason, Daniel. *The Piano Tuner*
*The **Burn***. Kent, Kathleen
BURN OUT (PSYCHOLOGY)
Hoang, Helen. ★*The Heart Principle*
BURN VICTIMS
Ackerman, Elliot. ★*Waiting for Eden: A Novel*
Golding, William. ★*Darkness Visible*
Reichs, Kathy. *Death Du Jour*
Burnet, Graeme Macrae
His Bloody Project: Documents Relating to the Case of Roderick Macrae
*A **Burning***. Majumdar, Megha
*The **Burning** Air: A Novel*. Kelly, Erin
Burning Bright. Petrie, Nicholas
Burning Bright: Stories. Rash, Ron
Burning chambers [Series]. Mosse, Kate
Burning Cove [Series]. Quick, Amanda
*The **Burning** Gates: A Makana Investigation*. Bilal, Parker
Burning girl novels [Series]. Rice, Christopher
Burning Girls and Other Stories. Schanoes, Veronica L.
*The **Burning** Girls: A Novel*. Tudor, C. J.
Burning kingdoms [Series]. Suri, Tasha
*The **Burning** Room*. Connelly, Michael
Burning Roses. Huang, S. L.
★*Burning Your Boats: The Collected Short Stories*. Carter, Angela
The **burning** [Series]. Winter, Evan
Burningblade & Silvereye novels [Series]. Wexler, Django
BURNS AND SCALDS
Davidson, Andrew. *The Gargoyle*
Burns, Anna
Milkman: A Novel
Burns, Charles
★*Black Hole*
Burns, Olive Ann
★*Cold Sassy Tree*
Burns, V. M.
Killer Words
Burnt Sugar: A Novel. Doshi, Avni
Burroughs, William S.
★*Naked Lunch: The Restored Text*
Burrowes, Grace
The Captive
My One and Only Duke
★*A Rogue of Her Own*
Tremaine's True Love
The Trouble with Dukes
Burton, Jeffrey B.
★*The Finders: A Mace Reid K-9 Mystery*
The Keepers: A Mace Reid K-9 Mystery

Burton, Jessie
The Miniaturist
Burton, Tara Isabella
Social Creature
BURUNDI
Faye, Gael. ★*Small Country: A Novel*
Bury Me Deep. Abbott, Megan E.
BUSH PILOTS
Stabenow, Dana. *Spoils of the Dead*
BUSH, GEORGE W.
Mallon, Thomas. *Landfall: A Novel*
Bush, Keisha
No Heaven for Good Boys: A Novel
Bushnell, Candace
Is There Still Sex in the City?
BUSINESS — CORRUPT PRACTICES
Deaver, Jeffery. ★*The Never Game*
Dee, Jonathan. *A Thousand Pardons: A Novel*
Hawley, Noah. *Before the Fall*
Hill Gumbao, Toni. *The Good Suicides: A Thriller*
Le Carre, John. *The Constant Gardener: A Novel*
Sanders, Lawrence. *McNally's Trial*
Takamura, Kaoru. ★*Lady Joker*
BUSINESS COMPETITION
K'wan. *The Diamond Empire*
Laurens, Stephanie. *The Pursuits of Lord Kit Cavanaugh*
Sosa, Mia. ★*The Worst Best Man*
BUSINESS ETHICS
Reay, Katherine. *The Bronte Plot*
BUSINESS INTELLIGENCE
Morgan Jones, Chris. *The Silent Oligarch*
Wang, Kathy. *Impostor Syndrome: A Novel*
The Business of Lovers. Dickey, Eric Jerome
BUSINESS PARTNERS
Danan, Rosie. *The Intimacy Experiment*
Friedland, Elyssa. *Last Summer at the Golden Hotel*
Hammett, Dashiell. ★*The Maltese Falcon*
Schlink, Bernhard. *Self's Murder*
Walser, Robert. *The Assistant*
BUSINESS SABOTAGE
Muller, Marcia. *Dead Midnight*
BUSINESSPEOPLE
Balogh, Mary. *Someone to Wed*
Bellefleur, Alexandria. *Hang the Moon*
Benjamin, Ali. *The Smash-Up: A Novel*
Billingsley, ReShonda Tate. ★*The Secret She Kept*
Bradford, Barbara Taylor. ★*A Woman of Substance*
Bruno, Anna. *Ordinary Hazards: A Novel*
Clark, Marcia. *Final Judgment*
Cosby, S. A. ★*Blacktop Wasteland*
Cussler, Clive. ★*Golden Buddha*
Cussler, Clive. *Sacred Stone*
Dee, Jonathan. *A Thousand Pardons: A Novel*
Dickens, Charles. *Our Mutual Friend*
Eggers, Dave. *A Hologram for the King: A Novel*
Foster, Lori. *Sisters of Summer's End*
Fuentes, Carlos. *The Death of Artemio Cruz*
Garcia, Cristina. *The Aguero Sisters*

Herrera, Adriana. *American Fairytale*
Lee, Chang-Rae. ★*My Year Abroad*
Livesay, Tracey. *Like Lovers Do*
Martin, Alexa. ★*Intercepted*
Meyer, Deon. *Icarus*
Pynchon, Thomas. ★*Bleeding Edge*
Robb, J. D. *Leverage in Death: An Eve Dallas Novel*
Vargas Llosa, Mario. ★*The Discreet Hero*
Westlake, Donald E. *Forever and a Death*
Wilson, Sloan. ★*The Man in the Gray Flannel Suit*
Zettel, Sarah. *A Mother's Lie*
★*Busman's Honeymoon*. Sayers, Dorothy L.
BUTCHERS
Gilligan, Ruth. *The Butchers' Blessing*
The Butchers' Blessing. Gilligan, Ruth
Butland, Stephanie
The Lost for Words Bookshop: A Novel
Butler, Gwendoline
Death Lives Next Door
Butler, Halle
The New Me: A Novel
Butler, Marcia
Pickle's Progress
Butler, Nickolas
Godspeed
★*The Hearts of Men*
Little Faith: A Novel
Butler, Octavia E.
Adulthood Rites
Bloodchild: And Other Stories
★*Dawn: Xenogenesis*
★*Kindred*
★*Parable of the Sower*
Parable of the Talents: A Novel
Butler, Robert Olen
A Good Scent from a Strange Mountain: Stories
Hell: A Novel
Late City
Perfume River
Butler, Sarah
Ten Things I've Learnt About Love: A Novel
Butler, Season
★*Cygnet*
BUTLERS
Faulks, Sebastian. *Jeeves and the Wedding Bells*
Finch, Charles. *A Beautiful Blue Death*
Ishiguro, Kazuo. ★*The Remains of the Day*
Wodehouse, P. G. ★*The Inimitable Jeeves*
Wodehouse, P. G. *My Man Jeeves*
Butter Honey Pig Bread: A Novel. Ekwuyasi, Francesca
BUTTERFLIES
Raybourn, Deanna. *A Dangerous Collaboration*
Butterflies in November. Ólafsdóttir, Auður A.
Butterfly. Antoinette, Ashley
The Butterfly Lampshade. Bender, Aimee
Butterfly novels [Series]. Antoinette, Ashley
Butterfly.; Vol 2. Antoinette, Ashley
Butterfly.; Vol 3. Antoinette, Ashley

Button Man. Gross, Andrew
Buwalda, Peter
  Bonita Avenue: A Novel
Buxton, Kira Jane
  ★*Hollow Kingdom*
By Blood We Live. Duncan, Glen
★*By Night in Chile*. Bolano, Roberto
Byatt, A. S.
  Babel Tower
  Medusa's Ankles: Selected Stories
  ★*Possession: A Romance*
  ★*Ragnarok: The End of the Gods*
  A Whistling Woman
Bynum, Sarah Shun-Lien
  Ms. Hempel Chronicles
Byrne, Kerrigan
  The Duke with the Dragon Tattoo
  How to Love a Duke in Ten Days
  The Hunter
Byrne, Trevor
  Ghosts and Lightning
BYRON, GEORGE GORDON BYRON
  Crowley, John. *Lord Byron's Novel: The Evening Land*
  Friedman, Daniel. *Riot Most Uncouth: A Lord Byron Mystery*
  Patchett, Ann. ★*Commonwealth*
  Rushdie, Salman. *The Moor's Last Sigh*
BYZANTINE EMPIRE (330-1453)
  Doerr, Anthony. ★*Cloud Cuckoo Land: A Novel*

C

C. J. Floyd mysteries [Series]. Greer, Robert O.
C. W. Sughrue mysteries [Series]. Crumley, James
Ca$h
  Thugs Cry: A Novel
  ★*Trust No Bitch*
★*The Cabin at the End of the World: A Novel*. Tremblay, Paul
The Cabinets of Barnaby Mayne. Hart, Elsa
CABINS
  Cohen, Tish. *The Summer We Lost Her: A Novel*
  Malpas, Jodi Ellen. *Leave Me Breathless*
  Moss, Sarah. *Summerwater*
  Tremblay, Paul. ★*The Cabin at the End of the World: A Novel*
  Waite, Jen. *Survival Instincts*
Cackleberry Club mysteries [Series]. Childs, Laura
The Cactus. Haywood, Sarah
CAESAR, JULIUS
  Erdrich, Louise. *The Master Butchers Singing Club: A Novel*
  Oates, Joyce Carol. ★*Them*
  Saylor, Steven. *Roma: The Novel of Ancient Rome*
  Saylor, Steven. *The Triumph of Caesar: A Novel of Ancient Rome*
Cage. Sigurðardóttir, Lilja
Cain. Saramago, Jose
CAIN
  Saramago, Jose. *Cain*

Cain, Chelsea
  One Kick: A Novel
★*The Caine Mutiny: A Novel of World War II*. Wouk, Herman
The Cairo Affair. Steinhauer, Olen
Cairo trilogy [Series]. Mahfuz, Najib
CAIRO, EGYPT
  Bilal, Parker. *The Burning Gates: A Makana Investigation*
  Bilal, Parker. *The Ghost Runner*
  Chakraborty, S. A. *The City of Brass*
  Chakraborty, S. A. *The Empire of Gold*
  Chakraborty, S. A. *The Kingdom of Copper: A Novel*
  Hassib, Rajia. *A Pure Heart: A Novel*
  Lukas, Michael David. *The Last Watchman of Old Cairo: A Novel*
  Mahfuz, Najib. ★*Palace Walk*
  Neubauer, Erica Ruth. *Murder at the Mena House*
  Russell, Mary Doria. *Dreamers of the Day: A Novel*
  Steinhauer, Olen. *The Cairo Affair*
CAJUN MEN
  Luesse, Valerie Fraser. *Under the Bayou Moon: A Novel*
The Calculating Stars: A Lady Astronaut Novel. Kowal, Mary Robinette
CALCUTTA, INDIA
  Carter, Miranda. *The Strangler Vine*
  Mukherjee, Abir. *Smoke and Ashes: A Novel*
  Mukherjee, Neel. *The Lives of Others*
Caldwell, Erskine
  Tobacco Road
Caliban's War. Corey, James S. A.
CALIFORNIA
  Alexander, Jennet. *I Kissed a Girl*
  Allen, Jayne. *Black Girls Must Die Exhausted*
  Allende, Isabel. *Daughter of Fortune: A Novel*
  Ames, Jonathan. *A Man Named Doll*
  Anderson, Kent. *Green Sun: A Novel*
  Aoki, Ryka. *Light from Uncommon Stars*
  Baldacci, David. ★*A Gambling Man*
  Barry, Ava. *Windhall*
  Bender, Aimee. *The Butterfly Lampshade*
  Bieker, Chelsea Jean. *Godshot: A Novel*
  Blau, Jessica Anya. *The Wonder Bread Summer*
  Boyle, T. Coraghessan. *The Harder They Come*
  Butler, Octavia E. ★*Parable of the Sower*
  Cander, Chris. *The Weight of a Piano: A Novel*
  Castillo, Elaine. *America Is Not the Heart*
  Chavez, Heather. *No Bad Deed*
  Clark, Marcia. *Final Judgment*
  Clark, Wahida. *Thug Lovin'*
  Cline, Emma. *The Girls: A Novel*
  Connelly, Michael. ★*The Dark Hours*
  Connelly, Michael. *The Night Fire*
  Copperman, E. J. *Judgment at Santa Monica*
  Crichton, Michael. *Prey: A Novel*
  Cronin, Justin. *The Passage*
  Cussler, Clive. ★*The Chase*
  Darnielle, John. *Wolf in White Van: A Novel*
  Davila, April. *142 Ostriches*
  De Leon, Aya. ★*A Spy in the Struggle*
  Dev, Sonali. ★*Incense and Sensibility*
  Dev, Sonali. ★*Recipe for Persuasion*

Didion, Joan. *A Book of Common Prayer*
Didion, Joan. ★*Play It as It Lays: A Novel*
Dodd, Christina. *Strangers She Knows*
Estleman, Loren D. *Frames*
Estleman, Loren D. ★*Indigo: A Valentino Mystery*
Fielding, Joy. *The Bad Daughter: A Novel*
Fitch, Janet. *White Oleander: A Novel*
Fowler, Karen Joy. *The Jane Austen Book Club*
Frank, Alli. *Tiny Imperfections*
Gailey, Sarah. *Magic for Liars*
Gardiner, Meg. *The Dirty Secrets Club*
Gardiner, Meg. *Phantom Instinct*
Garrett, Kellye. ★*Hollywood Homicide*
Goodman, Allegra. *The Cookbook Collector: A Novel*
Grafton, Sue. *X*
Grafton, Sue. *Y Is for Yesterday*
Guillory, Jasmine. *Party of Two*
Guillory, Jasmine. *The Proposal*
Guillory, Jasmine. ★*The Wedding Date*
Guillory, Jasmine. *The Wedding Party*
Guillory, Jasmine. ★*While We Were Dating*
Hall, Rachel Howzell. *And Now She's Gone*
Hambly, Barbara. *Scandal in Babylon*
Harte, Bret. ★*The Best Short Stories of Bret Harte*
Heger, Amanda. *Crazy Cupid Love*
Hoang, Helen. ★*The Bride Test*
Hollis, Lee. *Poppy Harmon Investigates*
K'wan. *Gangsta*
Kellerman, Jonathan. *Bones: An Alex Delaware Novel*
Kellerman, Jonathan. *Gone*
Kells, Claire. *Vanishing Edge*
Koontz, Dean R. *Intensity: A Novel*
Kushner, Rachel. *The Mars Room*
L'Amour, Louis. *The Californios*
Lalami, Laila. *The Other Americans: A Novel*
Lane, Byron. ★*A Star Is Bored*
Lauren, Christina. *The Soulmate Equation*
Lee, Patrick. *Runner*
Lelchuk, Saul. *Save Me from Dangerous Men: A Novel*
Lukas, Michael David. *The Last Watchman of Old Cairo: A Novel*
MacDonald, John D. *The Green Ripper*
Macdonald, Ross. *The Galton Case*
Macdonald, Ross. *The Goodbye Look*
Macdonald, Ross. *Sleeping Beauty*
Macdonald, Ross. *The Underground Man*
Macmillan, Gilly. *The Nanny*
Mahmoud, Lena. *Amreekiya: A Novel*
Mallery, Susan. *Best of My Love*
Mallery, Susan. *California Girls*
Mapson, Jo-Ann. *Bad Girl Creek: A Novel*
Marcom, Micheline Aharonian. *The New American*
Masood, Syed M. *The Bad Muslim Discount*
McKevett, G. A. *A Few Drops of Bitters*
McLain, Paula. ★*When the Stars Go Dark: A Novel*
McMillan, Terry. ★*It's Not All Downhill from Here: A Novel*
McPherson, Catriona. *Scot & Soda*
Mitchell, David. ★*Cloud Atlas: A Novel*
Mooney, Chris. *Blood World*

Mosley, Walter. ★*Blood Grove*
Nguyen, Viet Thanh. ★*The Refugees*
Orange, Tommy. ★*There There*
Osborne, Lawrence. *Only to Sleep: A Philip Marlowe Novel*
Otsuka, Julie. *When the Emperor Was Divine: A Novel*
Packer, Ann. *The Children's Crusade*
Packer, Ann. *Songs Without Words*
Palahniuk, Chuck. *The Invention of Sound*
Pandya, Sameer. *Members Only*
Parker, T. Jefferson. *The Blue Hour*
Parker, T. Jefferson. *L.A. Outlaws: A Novel*
Patterson, James. ★*Private*
Patterson, Richard North. *No Safe Place*
Petrie, Nicholas. *Burning Bright*
Prcic, Ismet. *Shards: A Novel*
Preston, Douglas J. *Old Bones*
Pronzini, Bill. *Crazybone*
Pronzini, Bill. *Fever*
Pronzini, Bill. *Mourners*
Pronzini, Bill. *Nemesis*
Pronzini, Bill. *Savages*
Pronzini, Bill. *Spook*
Pronzini, Bill. *The Stolen Gold Affair*
Pronzini, Bill. *The Violated*
Quick, Amanda. *Close Up*
Quick, Amanda. ★*The Lady Has a Past*
Ragan, Theresa. *Buried Deep*
Ragan, Theresa. *Deadly Recall*
Ragan, Theresa. *Deranged*
Ragan, Theresa. *Her Last Day*
Rai, Alisha. ★*Girl Gone Viral*
Reddi, Rishi. *Passage West: A Novel*
Rice, Luanne. *The Lemon Orchard*
Rindell, Suzanne. ★*The Two Mrs. Carlyles*
Rivers, Francine. *Bridge to Haven*
Rouda, Kaira Sturdivant. *The Favorite Daughter*
Saroyan, William. ★*The Human Comedy*
Schulman, Helen. *Come with Me*
Schwarz, Christina. *The Edge of the Earth*
See, Lisa. *The Tea Girl of Hummingbird Lane*
Shalvis, Jill. *Sweet Little Lies*
Sharpe, Tess. *Barbed Wire Heart*
Shimotakahara, Leslie. *After the Bloom*
Sloan, Robin. *Mr. Penumbra's 24-Hour Bookstore*
So, Anthony Veasna. *Afterparties: Stories*
Stansel, Ian. *The Last Cowboys of San Geronimo*
Stegner, Wallace. ★*Angle of Repose*
Steinbeck, John. *Cannery Row*
Steinbeck, John. ★*East of Eden*
Steinbeck, John. ★*The Grapes of Wrath*
Steinbeck, John. ★*Of Mice and Men*
Steinbeck, John. *Tortilla Flat*
Sutanto, Jesse Q. *Dial a for Aunties*
Tanen, Sloane. *There's a Word for That*
Tenorio, Lysley A. *The Son of Good Fortune: A Novel*
Thorpe, Rufi. ★*The Knockout Queen*
Tieu, Julie. *The Donut Trap*
Torre, A. R. *Every Last Secret*

Tyree, Omar. *For the Love of Money: A Novel*
Van Meter, Crissy. *Creatures: A Novel*
Walker, Karen Thompson. *The Age of Miracles: A Novel*
Walker, Karen Thompson. *The Dreamers*
Wang, Kathy. *Family Trust: A Novel*
Waxman, Abbi. *The Bookish Life of Nina Hill*
Weatherspoon, Rebekah. *If the Boot Fits*
Weatherspoon, Rebekah. *Rafe: A Buff Male Nanny*
Weatherspoon, Rebekah. *A Thorn in the Saddle*
Whitaker, Chris. ★*We Begin at the End*
Woods, Stuart. ★*Bombshell*
California Girls. Mallery, Susan
The *Californios*. L'Amour, Louis
CALIPHATE
    Khoury, Raymond. *Empire of Lies*
★*Call It Sleep*. Roth, Henry
Call Me by Your Name. Aciman, Andre
Call me by your name novels [Series]. Aciman, Andre
Call Me Irresistible. Phillips, Susan Elizabeth
Call Me Zebra. Van der Vliet Oloomi, Azareen
★The *Call* of the Wild. London, Jack
Callaghan, Mary Rose
    Billy, Come Home
Callender, Kacen
    King of the Rising
    Queen of the Conquered
Callihan, Kristen
    ★*Firelight*
A *Calling* for Charlie Barnes. Ferris, Joshua
Calling Major Tom. Barnett, David
Calm Sea and Prosperous Voyage. Howland, Bette
Calvi, Mary
    Dear George, Dear Mary: A Novel of George Washington's First Love
CALVINISM
    Robinson, Marilynne. ★*Lila*
Calvino, Italo
    ★*If on a Winter's Night a Traveler*
    Invisible Cities
Cambias, James L.
    A Darkling Sea
CAMBODIA
    Ratner, Vaddey. *Music of the Ghosts*
CAMBODIAN AMERICANS
    So, Anthony Veasna. *Afterparties: Stories*
Cambridge brotherhood [Series]. Vayden, Kristin
CAMBRIDGE, ENGLAND
    Atkinson, Kate. ★*Case Histories*
    Cumming, Charles. ★*The Trinity Six*
    Franklin, Ariana. *Mistress of the Art of Death*
    Friedman, Daniel. *Riot Most Uncouth: A Lord Byron Mystery*
    Hannah, Sophie. *Perfect Little Children*
    James, P. D. *An Unsuitable Job for a Woman*
CAMBRIDGE, MASSACHUSETTS
    Aciman, Andre. *Harvard Square*
    Batuman, Elif. ★*The Idiot*
    Goodman, Allegra. *The Cookbook Collector: A Novel*
    Lahiri, Jhumpa. ★*The Namesake*

Messud, Claire. ★*The Woman Upstairs: A Novel*
Pearl, Matthew. *The Dante Club: A Novel*
Pearl, Matthew. *The Technologists: A Novel*
Camel Club novels [Series]. Baldacci, David
CAMELOT (LEGENDARY PLACE)
    Twain, Mark. ★*A Connecticut Yankee in King Arthur's Court*
Cameron, Lindsay
    Just One Look
Cameron, Marc
    ★*Code of Honor*
    Power and Empire
Cameron, Peter
    The City of Your Final Destination
Cameron, W. Bruce
    A Dog's Promise
    The Dogs of Christmas
    Repo Madness
★*Camille*. Dumas, Alexandre
Camilleri, Andrea
    Riccardino
CAMP SITES, FACILITIES, ETC.
    Carr, Robyn. *The Family Gathering*
Camp, Bryan
    The City of Lost Fortunes
    Gather the Fortunes
CAMPAIGNING
    Smith, Julie. *The Kindness of Strangers: A Skip Langdon Novel*
    Williams, Synithia. *Forbidden Promises*
Campbell, Bebe Moore
    Brothers and Sisters
    Your Blues Ain't Like Mine
Campbell, Bonnie Jo
    Once Upon a River
CAMPBELL, ENID
    Anstruther, Eleanor. *A Perfect Explanation*
    Johnson, Alaya Dawn. *Trouble the Saints*
CAMPBELL, LIAM (FICTITIOUS CHARACTER)
    Stabenow, Dana. *So Sure of Death: A Liam Campbell Mystery*
Campbell, Lisbeth
    The Vanished Queen
Campbell, Ramsey
    The Wise Friend
Campbell, Rick
    Treason
CAMPION, ALBERT (FICTITIOUS CHARACTER)
    Ripley, Mike. *Mr. Campion's War*
Campisi, Megan
    Sin Eater
CAMPUS LIFE
    Auster, Paul. *Invisible*
    Barth, John. ★*Giles Goat-Boy ;: Or, the Revised New Syllabus*
    Cartwright, Justin. *To Heaven by Water*
    Nugent, Benjamin. *Fraternity: Stories*
CAMPUS MURDERS
    Sandford, John. *Bloody Genius*
Camus, Albert
    ★*The Fall*
    The Plague

★*The Stranger*

Canada. Ford, Richard

CANADA

Aalborg, Gordon. *River of Porcupines*

Alexis, Andre. *Fifteen Dogs*

Armstrong, Kelley. *Alone in the Wild*

Armstrong, Kelley. *Watcher in the Woods*

Atwood, Margaret. *Alias Grace*

Atwood, Margaret. ★*The Blind Assassin*

Atwood, Margaret. ★*Cat's Eye*

Atwood, Margaret. *Moral Disorder*

Atwood, Margaret. ★*Oryx and Crake*

Banks, Russell. *Foregone*

Bates, Judy Fong. ★*Midnight at the Dragon Cafe*

Bradley, C. Alan. *As Chimney Sweepers Come to Dust: A Flavia De Luce Novel*

Choi, Ann Y. K. *Kay's Lucky Coin Variety*

Colvin, Jeffrey. ★*Africaville: A Novel*

Crummey, Michael. *Galore*

Doctorow, Cory. *Walkaway*

Freedman, Benedict. *Mrs. Mike: The Story of Katherine Mary Flannigan*

Fu, Kim. *For Today I Am a Boy*

Heller, Peter. *The River: A Novel*

Hooper, Emma. *Etta and Otto and Russell and James: A Novel*

Jalaluddin, Uzma. ★*Ayesha at Last*

Khan, Ausma Zehanat. *The Unquiet Dead*

Kimmel, Fran. *No Good Asking: A Novel*

Lalli, Sonya. *The Matchmaker's List*

Mandel, Emily St. John. ★*Station Eleven*

Munro, Alice. *Dear Life: Stories*

Munro, Alice. *Family Furnishings: Selected Stories, 1995-2014*

Munro, Alice. *Hateship, Friendship, Courtship, Loveship, Marriage: Stories*

Munro, Alice. *Lives of Girls and Women*

Munro, Alice. *Open Secrets: Stories*

Munro, Alice. *Runaway: Stories*

Munro, Alice. *Selected Stories*

Munro, Alice. *Too Much Happiness: Stories*

Munro, Alice. *The View from Castle Rock: Stories*

Penny, Louise. *The Cruelest Month: A Three Pines Mystery*

Penny, Louise. *Still Life*

Reichs, Kathy. *Bones to Ashes*

Rice, Waubgeshig. *Moon of the Crusted Snow: A Novel*

Shields, Carol. *The Republic of Love*

Smith, B. J. *All Hat: A Novel*

Stevens, Chevy. *Never Let You Go*

Stevens, Chevy. *Still Missing*

Tallo, Katie. *Dark August*

Wood, Shelley. *The Quintland Sisters*

CANADIAN FICTION

Aalborg, Gordon. *River of Porcupines*

Adamson, Gil. *The Outlander*

Alexis, Andre. *Fifteen Dogs*

Alexis, Andre. *The Hidden Keys*

Armstrong, Kelley. *Alone in the Wild*

Armstrong, Kelley. *Watcher in the Woods*

Armstrong, Kelley. *Wherever She Goes*

Atwood, Margaret. ★*The Blind Assassin*

Atwood, Margaret. *Bluebeard's Egg and Other Stories*

Atwood, Margaret. ★*Cat's Eye*

Atwood, Margaret. *Life Before Man*

Atwood, Margaret. ★*Stone Mattress: Nine Tales*

Audrain, Ashley. *The Push*

Austin, Emily. *Everyone in This Room Will Someday Be Dead*

Awad, Mona. ★*13 Ways of Looking at a Fat Girl*

Awad, Mona. *Bunny*

Bala, Sharon. *The Boat People: A Novel*

Balogh, Mary. *The Arrangement*

Balogh, Mary. *The Escape*

Balogh, Mary. *More Than a Mistress*

Balogh, Mary. *Only Enchanting*

Balogh, Mary. *The Secret Mistress*

Balogh, Mary. *Simply Love*

Barclay, Linwood. *Broken Promise*

Barclay, Linwood. ★*Elevator Pitch: A Novel*

Barclay, Linwood. *Far from True: A Novel*

Barclay, Linwood. *No Safe House*

Barclay, Linwood. *Parting Shot*

Barclay, Linwood. *A Tap on the Window*

Barclay, Linwood. *Trust Your Eyes: A Thriller*

Barclay, Linwood. *The Twenty-Three: A Promise Falls Novel*

Bates, Judy Fong. ★*Midnight at the Dragon Cafe*

Beverley, Jo. *My Lady Notorious*

Beverley, Jo. *Tempting Fortune*

Bezmozgis, David. *The Betrayers: A Novel*

Bowen, Kelly. ★*Between the Devil and the Duke*

Bowen, Kelly. *A Rogue by Night*

Bradley, C. Alan. *As Chimney Sweepers Come to Dust: A Flavia De Luce Novel*

Bradley, C. Alan. *The Golden Tresses of the Dead: A Flavia De Luce Novel*

Bradley, C. Alan. *The Grave's a Fine and Private Place: A Flavia De Luce Novel*

Bradley, C. Alan. *I Am Half-Sick of Shadows: A Flavia De Luce Novel*

Bradley, C. Alan. *A Red Herring Without Mustard*

Bradley, C. Alan. *Speaking from Among the Bones: A Flavia De Luce Novel*

Bradley, C. Alan. ★*The Sweetness at the Bottom of the Pie*

Bradley, C. Alan. *Thrice the Brinded Cat Hath Mew'd: A Flavia De Luce Novel*

Bradley, C. Alan. *The Weed That Strings the Hangman's Bag: A Flavia De Luce Mystery*

Buchanan, Cathy Marie. ★*The Painted Girls*

Chariandy, David John. *Brother: A Novel*

Christie, Michael. ★*Greenwood: A Novel*

Crummey, Michael. *Galore*

Crummey, Michael. *The Innocents*

Crummey, Michael. *Sweetland*

Cumyn, Alan. *Losing It*

Cusk, Rachel. *Kudos*

Cusk, Rachel. *Outline: A Novel*

Cusk, Rachel. *Transit*

Czerneda, Julie. *A Turn of Light*

Davidson, Andrew. *The Gargoyle*

Davis, Fiona. *The Chelsea Girls*
deWitt, Patrick. *The Sisters Brothers: A Novel*
deWitt, Patrick. *Undermajordomo Minor*
Dimaline, Cherie. *Empire of Wild*
Doctorow, Cory. *Rapture of the Nerds*
Doctorow, Cory. *Walkaway*
Donoghue, Emma. *Akin*
Donoghue, Emma. ★*Frog Music*
Donoghue, Emma. ★*Room: A Novel*
Donoghue, Emma. ★*The Wonder*
Edugyan, Esi. *Half-Blood Blues*
Edugyan, Esi. ★*Washington Black: A Novel*
Ekwuyasi, Francesca. *Butter Honey Pig Bread: A Novel*
El Akkad, Omar. *What Strange Paradise*
Endicott, Marina. *The Voyage of the Morning Light*
Farrow, John. *The Storm Murders: A Thriller*
Feng, Linda Rui. *Swimming Back to Trout River*
Fielding, Joy. *The Bad Daughter: A Novel*
Fu, Kim. *For Today I Am a Boy*
Galchen, Rivka. *American Innovations: Stories*
Galchen, Rivka. *Everyone Knows Your Mother Is a Witch*
Gibb, Camilla. *Sweetness in the Belly*
Gibson, William. ★*Neuromancer*
Gowdy, Barbara. *Helpless: A Novel*
Gruen, Sara. *The Ape House*
Gruen, Sara. ★*Water for Elephants: A Novel*
Hage, Rawi. *Beirut Hellfire Society: A Novel*
Haldane, Sean. *The Devil's Making*
Hay, Elizabeth. *Late Nights on Air*
Holdstock, Pauline. *Here I Am!*
Hooper, Emma. *Etta and Otto and Russell and James: A Novel*
Hosking, Jay. *Three Years with the Rat: A Novel*
Hozar, Nazanine. *Aria*
Igharo, Jane. *The Sweetest Remedy*
Jalaluddin, Uzma. ★*Ayesha at Last*
Jalaluddin, Uzma. *Hana Khan Carries On*
Jenner, Natalie. *The Jane Austen Society*
Kamal, Sheena. *It All Falls Down*
Kay, Guy Gavriel. ★*A Brightness Long Ago*
Kay, Guy Gavriel. ★*Children of Earth and Sky*
Kay, Guy Gavriel. *The Summer Tree*
Kay, Guy Gavriel. *Tigana*
Khan, Ausma Zehanat. *Among the Ruins*
Khan, Ausma Zehanat. *The Unquiet Dead*
Kimmel, Fran. *No Good Asking: A Novel*
Kutsukake, Lynne. *The Translation of Love: A Novel*
Lai, Larissa. *The Tiger Flu*
Lalli, Sonya. *The Matchmaker's List*
Lalli, Sonya. *Serena Singh Flips the Script*
Laukkanen, Owen. *Lone Jack Trail*
Lawson, Mary. *Crow Lake*
Lee, Fonda. ★*Jade City*
Lee, Fonda. *Jade War*
Lim, Roselle. *Vanessa Yu's Magical Paris Tea Shop*
Livesey, Margot. ★*The Boy in the Field*
Lundrigan, Nicole. *Glass Boys: A Novel*
Maaren, Kari. ★*Weave a Circle Round*
MacDonald, Andrew. *When We Were Vikings*

MacLeod, Alison. *Tenderness*
Mandel, Emily St. John. *The Singer's Gun: A Novel*
Messud, Claire. ★*The Woman Upstairs: A Novel*
Moreno-Garcia, Silvia. ★*Gods of Jade and Shadow: A Novel*
Moreno-Garcia, Silvia. *Mexican Gothic*
Moreno-Garcia, Silvia. ★*Velvet Was the Night*
Moss, Tara. *The War Widow*
Munro, Alice. *Dear Life: Stories*
Munro, Alice. *Family Furnishings: Selected Stories, 1995-2014*
Munro, Alice. *Hateship, Friendship, Courtship, Loveship, Marriage: Stories*
Munro, Alice. *Lives of Girls and Women*
Munro, Alice. *Open Secrets: Stories*
Munro, Alice. *Runaway: Stories*
Munro, Alice. *Selected Stories*
Munro, Alice. *Too Much Happiness: Stories*
O'Neill, Heather. *The Lonely Hearts Hotel: A Novel*
Ondaatje, Michael. ★*Warlight*
Penny, Louise. ★*All the Devils Are Here*
Penny, Louise. ★*A Better Man: A Chief Inspector Gamache Novel*
Penny, Louise. *The Cruelest Month: A Three Pines Mystery*
Penny, Louise. ★*The Madness of Crowds*
Penny, Louise. *Still Life*
Polk, C. L. *The Midnight Bargain*
Powning, Beth. *The Sea Captain's Wife: A Novel*
Pyper, Andrew. *The Damned: A Novel*
Pyper, Andrew. *The Homecoming: A Novel*
Rachman, Tom. *The Imperfectionists: A Novel*
Rachman, Tom. *The Italian Teacher*
Ramadan, Ahmad Danny. *The Clothesline Swing*
Rice, Waubgeshig. *Moon of the Crusted Snow: A Novel*
Richardson, C. S. *The End of the Alphabet*
Richler, Mordecai. *Barney's Version: A Novel*
Richler, Mordecai. *Solomon Gursky Was Here*
Richler, Nancy. *Your Mouth Is Lovely: A Novel*
Robinson, Peter. *All the Colors of Darkness*
Robinson, Peter. ★*Careless Love*
Robinson, Peter. *Children of the Revolution*
Robinson, Peter. *Close to Home*
Robinson, Peter. *Cold Is the Grave*
Robinson, Peter. *The First Cut*
Robinson, Peter. *Friend of the Devil*
Robinson, Peter. *In the Dark Places*
Robinson, Peter. *Innocent Graves: An Inspector Banks Mystery*
Robinson, Peter. *Piece of My Heart*
Robinson, Peter. *Playing with Fire*
Robinson, Peter. *Strange Affair*
Shields, Carol. *The Republic of Love*
Shields, Carol. ★*The Stone Diaries*
Shields, Carol. *Unless*
Shimotakahara, Leslie. *After the Bloom*
Smith, B. J. *All Hat: A Novel*
Smith, B. J. *Crow's Landing: A Novel*
Smith, B. J. *Shoot the Dog: A Virgil Cain Mystery*
Snow, Jennifer. *An Alaskan Christmas*
Spencer, Minerva. *Scandalous*
St. James, Simone. *The Haunting of Maddy Clare*
Stachniak, Eva. *The Chosen Maiden: A Novel*

Stachniak, Eva. *The Winter Palace: A Novel of Catherine the Great*
Stevens, Chevy. *Never Let You Go*
Stevens, Chevy. *Still Missing*
Stirling, S. M. *Dies the Fire*
Stirling, S. M. *A Meeting at Corvallis*
Stirling, S. M. *The Protector's War*
Stroud, Carsten. *The Shimmer*
Tallo, Katie. *Dark August*
Thammavongsa, Souvankham. *How to Pronounce Knife: Stories*
Thien, Madeleine. *Do Not Say We Have Nothing*
Toews, Miriam. *Fight Night*
Toews, Miriam. ★*Women Talking: A Novel*
Urquhart, Jane. *The Night Stages: A Novel*
Van Vogt, A. E. ★*Slan*
Vyleta, Dan. *Smoke: A Novel*
Walschots, Natalie Zina. *Hench: A Novel*
Walton, Jo. *Or What You Will*
Whittall, Zoe. *The Spectacular: A Novel*
Wood, Shelley. *The Quintland Sisters*

CANADIANS IN THE UNITED STATES
Child, Lee. ★*Past Tense*

CANALS
Johnson, Daisy. *Everything Under*

CANALS — DESIGN AND CONSTRUCTION
Chase, Loretta Lynda. *Miss Wonderful*

CANARY ISLANDS
Drabble, Margaret. ★*The Dark Flood Rises*

CANCER
Swarthout, Glendon. ★*The Shootist*

CANCER RESEARCH
Sanders, Lawrence. *The Sixth Commandment: A Novel*
★*Cancer Ward*. Solzhenitsyn, Aleksandr Isaevich

CANCUN, MEXICO
Smith, Scott. *The Ruins: A Novel*

Cander, Chris
The Weight of a Piano: A Novel

CANDIDATES FOR PUBLIC OFFICE
Bauman, Bruce. ★*Broken Sleep: An American Dream*
Candide and Other Stories. Voltaire

Candlish, Louise
Our House
Cane River. Tademy, Lalita

CANE RIVER REGION, LOUISIANA
Tademy, Lalita. *Cane River*
Cannery Row. Steinbeck, John

CANNIBALISM
Katsu, Alma. *The Hunger: A Novel*
McCarthy, Cormac. ★*The Road*

Cannon, Joanna
Three Things About Elsie: A Novel

CANOEING
Barr, Nevada. *Destroyer Angel: An Anna Pigeon Novel*
Heller, Peter. *The River: A Novel*

CANOES
Heacox, Kim. *Jimmy Bluefeather: A Novel*

Cantero, Edgar
Meddling Kids: A Novel
★*A Canticle* for Leibowitz. Miller, Walter M.

Cantor, Jillian
Half Life
Cantoras. De Robertis, Carolina

Cantrell, Christian
Scorpion
Canvey Island. Runcie, James

CANVEY ISLAND, ENGLAND
Runcie, James. *Canvey Island*

Cape Charade [Series]. Dodd, Christina

CAPE COD, MASSACHUSETTS
Cook, Thomas H. *The Chatham School Affair*
Delany, Vicki. *Murder in a Teacup*
Delany, Vicki. *Tea & Treachery*
Weiner, Jennifer. ★*Big Summer*
Cape May. Cheek, Chip

CAPE MAY, NEW JERSEY
Lewis, Beverly. *The Ebb Tide*

CAPE TOWN, SOUTH AFRICA
Coetzee, J. M. *Summertime: Scenes from a Provincial Life*
Flanery, Patrick. *Absolution: A Novel*
Kilalea, Katharine. *Ok, Mr. Field: A Novel*
Willocks, Tim. *Memo from Turner*

CAPER NOVELS
Armstrong, Richard. *The Don Con*
Blau, Jessica Anya. *The Wonder Bread Summer*
Block, Lawrence. *The Burglar in the Closet*
Block, Lawrence. ★*The Burglar in the Library*
Cosimano, Elle. *Finlay Donovan Is Killing It*
Leonard, Elmore. ★*Be Cool: Everyone Is Looking for the Next Big Hit*
Leonard, Elmore. ★*Get Shorty*
Lindsay, Jeffry P. *Just Watch Me*
Petersen, Todd Robert. *Picnic in the Ruins*
Smith, B. J. *All Hat: A Novel*
Westlake, Donald E. ★*Bank Shot*
Westlake, Donald E. *Get Real*
Westlake, Donald E. *The Hot Rock*
Westlake, Donald E. *The Road to Ruin*

CAPITAL PUNISHMENT
Arvin, Reed. *Blood of Angels: A Novel*
Estleman, Loren D. ★*The Master Executioner*
Mailer, Norman. ★*The Executioner's Song*
Roslund, Anders. *Cell 8*
Vargas Llosa, Mario. *The Dream of the Celt*

CAPITALISM
Gessen, Keith. *A Terrible Country*
Ma, Ling. *Severance*
Sinclair, Upton. ★*The Jungle*

CAPITALISTS AND FINANCIERS
Chandler, Raymond. ★*The Big Sleep*
Gaddis, William. ★*J R: A Novel*
Groom, Winston. *El Paso: A Novel*
Pears, Iain. *Stone's Fall*
Rai, Alisha. ★*Girl Gone Viral*
Spiegelman, Peter. *Black Maps*

CAPITOL HILL (WASHINGTON, D.C.)
Meltzer, Brad. *The Zero Game*

CAPITOL PAGES
  Meltzer, Brad. *The Zero Game*
Capote, Truman
  ★*Breakfast at Tiffany's*
  ★*The Complete Stories of Truman Capote*
Capri, NeNe
  The Pussy Trap
  The Pussy Trap: Part 3
*The **Captain** and the Enemy*. Greene, Graham
***Captain** Blood*. Sabatini, Rafael
*The **Captive***. Burrowes, Grace
Captive hearts (Grace Burrowes) [Series]. Burrowes, Grace
*The **Captive**: a Novel*. Foster, Fiona King
CAPTIVES
  Barker, Pat. ★*The Silence of the Girls: A Novel*
  Barker, Pat. *The Women of Troy*
  Dazieri, Sandrone. *Kill the Angel*
  Donoghue, Emma. ★*Room: A Novel*
  Ferrell, Carolyn. *Dear Miss Metropolitan*
  French, Nicci. ★*Blue Monday*
  Gowar, Imogen Hermes. *The Mermaid and Mrs. Hancock*
  Hamer, Kate. *The Girl in the Red Coat*
  King, Stephen. ★*Misery*
  Miller, Derek B. ★*The Girl in Green*
  Richardson, Samuel. ★*Clarissa, Or, the History of a Young Lady*
  Roy, Lori. ★*Gone Too Long: A Novel*
  Stevens, Chevy. *Still Missing*
  Waite, Jen. *Survival Instincts*
CAPTIVITY
  Chakraborty, S. A. *The Kingdom of Copper: A Novel*
  Donoghue, Emma. ★*Room: A Novel*
  Hamer, Kate. *The Girl in the Red Coat*
  Hannaham, James. ★*Delicious Foods*
  Hausmann, Romy. ★*Dear Child*
  King, Stephen. *The Institute*
  King, Stephen. ★*Misery*
CARACAS (VENEZUELA)
  Sainz Borgo, Karina. ★*It Would Be Night in Caracas*
CARAVAGGIO, MICHELANGELO MERISI DA
  Doctorow, E. L. *World's Fair*
  Pears, Iain. *Death and Restoration*
CARD DEALERS
  Bowen, Kelly. ★*Between the Devil and the Duke*
Card, Maisy
  ★*These Ghosts Are Family: A Novel*
Card, Orson Scott
  ★*Ender's Game*
CARDINALS
  Pears, Iain. *The Dream of Scipio*
CARDSHARPING
  Bowen, Kelly. ★*Between the Devil and the Duke*
*The **Care** and Feeding of Ravenously Hungry Girls*. Gray, Anissa
*The **Care** and Feeding of Waspish Widows*. Waite, Olivia
***Career** of Evil*. Galbraith, Robert
CAREGIVERS
  Cooney, Caroline B. *The Grandmother Plot*
  Doshi, Avni. *Burnt Sugar: A Novel*
  Drabble, Margaret. ★*The Dark Flood Rises*

  Evison, Jonathan. *The Revised Fundamentals of Caregiving: A Novel*
  Moyes, Jojo. *Me Before You: A Novel*
***Careless** in Red*. George, Elizabeth
★***Careless** Love*. Robinson, Peter
CARETAKERS
  Dillard, Annie. *The Maytrees: A Novel*
  Ellison, Ralph. *Three Days Before the Shooting . . .*
  Genova, Lisa. *Left Neglected: A Novel*
  King, Stephen. ★*The Shining*
Carey, Edward
  Little: A Novel
Carey, Jacqueline
  Starless
Carey, M. R.
  Someone Like Me
Carey, Peter
  A Long Way from Home
Cargill, C. Robert
  Day Zero
Caribbean. Michener, James A.
CARIBBEAN AMERICANS
  Herrera, Adriana. ★*American Dreamer*
  Holahan, Cate. *Her Three Lives*
CARIBBEAN AREA
  Albom, Mitch. *The Stranger in the Lifeboat*
  Carpenter, Emily. *Until the Day I Die*
  Crichton, Michael. *Pirate Latitudes*
  Doller, Trish. *Float Plan*
  Michener, James A. *Caribbean*
  Morrison, Toni. *Tar Baby*
  Riley, Vanessa. ★*Island Queen*
  Sabatini, Rafael. *Captain Blood*
  Schaitkin, Alexis. *Saint X*
  Sosa, Mia. ★*Acting on Impulse*
  Straub, Peter. ★*Mystery*
  Turnbull, Cadwell. ★*The Lesson*
CARING
  Wells, Martha. *Network Effect*
CARJACKING
  Hayder, Mo. *Gone*
  Manning, Max. *The Victim: A Novel*
CARLOS
  Ludlum, Robert. *The Bourne Ultimatum*
CARLOS AVERY STATE WILDLIFE MANAGEMENT AREA, MINNESOTA
  Sandford, John. ★*Night Prey*
Carlos Tejada Alonso y Leon investigations [Series]. Pawel, Rebecca
Carlyle, Christy
  Duke Gone Rogue
***Carnegie** Hill: A Novel*. Vatner, Jonathan
CARNIVALS
  Bradbury, Ray. ★*Something Wicked This Way Comes*
  Dunn, Katherine. *Geek Love*
Carnton novels [Series]. Alexander, Tamera
Caroline Ferriday [Series]. Kelly, Martha Hall
CARPATHIAN MOUNTAINS
  Feehan, Christine. *Dark Illusion*
Carpenter and Quincannon novels [Series]. Pronzini, Bill

Carpenter, Emily
    Until the Day I Die
CARPENTERS
    Eliot, George. ★*Adam Bede*
    Picoult, Jodi. *Change of Heart: A Novel*
    Spencer, Scott. *Man in the Woods*
Carr, Brian Allen
    ★*Opioid, Indiana*
Carr, Caleb
    ★*The Alienist*
    The Angel of Darkness
Carr, Robyn
    The Family Gathering
    The View from Alameda Island: A Novel
    ★*Virgin River*
    ★*The Wanderer*
    What We Find
Carrick, M. A.
    The Mask of Mirrors
★*Carrie*. King, Stephen
CARRIER PILOTS
    Coonts, Stephen. ★*Flight of the Intruder*
CARRINGTON, LEONORA
    Carter, Michaela. *Leonora in the Morning Light*
    Doiron, Paul. ★*Dead by Dawn*
A Carrion Death. Stanley, Michael
Carry the One. Anshaw, Carol
Carsington brothers series [Series]. Chase, Loretta Lynda
Carson Ryder and Harry Nautilus mysteries [Series]. Kerley, Jack
The Cartel. Ashley& JaQuavis
Cartel novels [Series]. Ashley & JaQuavis
CARTELS
    Flores, Fernando A. *Tears of the Trufflepig*
    Solares, Martin. *Don't Send Flowers*
    Swinson, Kiki. *The Safe House*
Carter archives [Series]. Stout, Dan
Carter Ross mysteries [Series]. Parks, Brad
Carter, Angela
    ★*Burning Your Boats: The Collected Short Stories*
Carter, Mary Dixie
    The Photographer
Carter, Michaela
    Leonora in the Morning Light
Carter, Miranda
    The Strangler Vine
Carter, Stephen L.
    Back Channel
    New England White: A Novel
★*Cartier's Hope*. Rose, M. J.
CARTOGRAPHERS
    Wilson, G. Willow. ★*The Bird King*
Cartwright, Justin
    To Heaven by Water
Carty-Williams, Candice
    ★*Queenie*
★*Carved in Bone*. Nava, Michael
Carver, Raymond
    What We Talk About When We Talk About Love: Stories

Cas Russell novels [Series]. Huang, S. L.
★*Case Histories*. Atkinson, Kate
The Case of the Deadly Butter Chicken: A Vish Puri Mystery. Hall, Tarquin
The Case of the Love Commandos: From the Files of Vish Puri, India's Most Private Investigator. Hall, Tarquin
The Case of the Wandering Scholar. Saunders, Kate
Caselli and Torre novels [Series]. Dazieri, Sandrone
CASEMENT, ROGER
    Matthiessen, Peter. *Shadow Country: A New Rendering of the Watson Legend*
    Vargas Llosa, Mario. *The Dream of the Celt*
Casey Duncan novels [Series]. Armstrong, Kelley
Cash, Wiley
    The Last Ballad: A Novel
    When Ghosts Come Home: A Novel
CASINO EMPLOYEES
    Randisi, Robert J. *Hey There (You with the Gun in Your Hand): A Rat Pack Mystery*
★*Casino Royale: A James Bond Novel*. Fleming, Ian
CASINOS
    Barthelme, Frederick. *Bob the Gambler*
    Bowen, Kelly. ★*Between the Devil and the Duke*
    Diofebi, Dario. *Paradise, Nevada*
    Leonard, Elmore. *Tishomingo Blues: A Novel*
    MacLean, Sarah. *No Good Duke Goes Unpunished*
    Shupe, Joanna. *The Prince of Broadway*
Cass Neary novels [Series]. Hand, Elizabeth
Cassara, Joseph
    The House of Impossible Beauties
Cassie Dewell novels [Series]. Box, C. J.
The Cast. Blumenfeld, Amy
CASTAWAYS
    Albom, Mitch. *The Stranger in the Lifeboat*
    Maguire, Gregory. *The Brides of Maracoor*
    Verne, Jules. *The Mysterious Island*
CASTE
    Addison, Katherine. ★*The Goblin Emperor*
    Atwood, Margaret. ★*The Handmaid's Tale*
    Mukherjee, Neel. ★*A State of Freedom*
Castel-Bloom, Orly
    Textile
Castellani, Christopher
    Leading Men: A Novel
Castillo, Elaine
    America Is Not the Heart
Castillo, Linda
    ★*Fallen*
    Outsider
Castle Shade. King, Laurie R.
Castle, Jayne
    Illusion Town
CASTLES
    Dare, Tessa. *Romancing the Duke*
    Dare, Tessa. ★*Say Yes to the Marquess*
    deWitt, Patrick. *Undermajordomo Minor*
    Egan, Jennifer. *The Keep*
    King, Laurie R. *Castle Shade*

Morton, Kate. *The Distant Hours: A Novel*
Radcliffe, Ann Ward. ★*The Mysteries of Udolpho*
Wynne, Phoebe. *Madam*
Castles ever after [Series]. Dare, Tessa
CASTRO, FIDEL
    Block, Lawrence. *Killing Castro*
    Buckley, William F. ★*Mongoose, R.I.P.: A Blackford Oakes Novel*
    Davies, Valentine. *Miracle on 34th Street*
    See, Lisa. *Dragon Bones: A Novel*
Castro, V.
    Goddess of Filth
    The Queen of the Cicadas
CASUAL SEX
    Marsh, Nicola. *The Boy Toy*
    Ripper, Kris. *The Hate Project*
    Tyree, Omar. ★*Flyy Girl*
    Waters, Martha. *To Love and to Loathe: A Novel*
*The **Casual** Vacancy*. Rowling, J. K.
CAT DETECTIVES
    Braun, Lilian Jackson. *The Cat Who Ate Danish Modern*
    Brown, Rita Mae. *Wish You Were Here*
Cat in the stacks mysteries [Series]. James, Miranda
Cat Kinsella [Series]. Frear, Caz
*The **Cat** Who Ate Danish Modern*. Braun, Lilian Jackson
Cat Who mysteries [Series]. Braun, Lilian Jackson
*The **Cat** Who Saved Books*. Natsukawa, Sosuke
★***Cat's** Cradle*. Vonnegut, Kurt
★***Cat's** Eye*. Atwood, Margaret
CAT/DOG RELATIONS
    Gates, Eva. *Deadly Ever After*
CATASTROPHISM
    Wilhelm, Kate. *Where Late the Sweet Birds Sang*
★***Catch-22***. Heller, Joseph
★*The **Catcher** in the Rye*. Salinger, J. D.
***Catching** Christmas*. Blackstock, Terri
CATEGORY ROMANCES
    Sorenson, Jill. *Aftershock*
CATERERS AND CATERING
    Davidson, Diane Mott. *Killer Pancake*
    Davidson, Diane Mott. *The Last Suppers*
CATERPILLARS
    Mieville, China. ★*Perdido Street Station*
CATHARINE PARR, QUEEN, CONSORT OF HENRY VIII, KING OF ENGLAND
    Daly, Paula. *Clear My Name*
    Gregory, Philippa. *The Constant Princess*
    Gregory, Philippa. *The Taming of the Queen*
    Panowich, Brian. *Like Lions*
    Weir, Alison. *Katharine Parr, the Sixth Wife*
CATHEDRALS
    Chevalier, Tracy. *A Single Thread*
    Follett, Ken. ★*The Pillars of the Earth*
    Gala, Marcial. ★*The Black Cathedral*
Cather, Willa
    ★*Death Comes for the Archbishop*
    A Lost Lady
    ★*My Antonia*
    O Pioneers!

The Song of the Lark
CATHERINE II, EMPRESS OF RUSSIA, 1729-1796
    Alpsten, Ellen. *Tsarina*
    Stachniak, Eva. *The Winter Palace: A Novel of Catherine the Great*
Catherine House. Thomas, Elisabeth
CATHOLIC BOYS
    Doyle, Roddy. *Paddy Clarke, Ha-Ha-Ha*
CATHOLIC FAMILIES
    Lange, Tracey. ★*We Are the Brennans*
    McDermott, Alice. *At Weddings and Wakes*
    Quade, Kirstin Valdez. ★*The Five Wounds: A Novel*
    Wolfe, Suzanne M. *The Course of All Treasons*
CATHOLIC MEN
    Greene, Graham. ★*The Heart of the Matter*
    McKinty, Adrian. *In the Morning I'll Be Gone: A Detective Sean Duffy Novel*
CATHOLIC SCHOOLS
    Ólafsson, Ólafur Jóhann. *The Sacrament: A Novel*
CATHOLIC WOMEN
    Gregory, Philippa. *The Constant Princess*
    McDermott, Alice. *Someone*
CATHOLICS
    Bauer, Carlene. ★*Frances and Bernard*
    Black, Benjamin. ★*Christine Falls: A Novel*
    Enright, Anne. ★*The Gathering*
    Joyce, James. ★*A Portrait of the Artist as a Young Man*
    Percy, Walker. ★*The Moviegoer*
    Percy, Walker. *The Second Coming*
    Quade, Kirstin Valdez. *Night at the Fiestas: Stories*
    Russell, Mary Doria. *A Thread of Grace: A Novel*
    Waugh, Evelyn. ★*Brideshead Revisited*
CATS
    Arikawa, Hiro. *The Travelling Cat Chronicles*
    James, Miranda. *What the Cat Dragged In*
    McCall Smith, Alexander. *Tiny Tales: Stories of Romance, Ambition, Kindness, and Happiness*
    Murakami, Haruki. ★*Kafka on the Shore*
    Tesh, Emily. *Silver in the Wood*
CATSKILL MOUNTAINS REGION, NEW YORK
    Delany, Vicki. *Deadly Summer Nights*
    Friedland, Elyssa. *Last Summer at the Golden Hotel*
    Harrison, Rachel. *The Return*
    McCreight, Kimberly. *Friends Like These*
Catskill summer resort mysteries [Series]. Delany, Vicki
CATTLE
    Gilligan, Ruth. *The Butchers' Blessing*
    McCall Smith, Alexander. *The Saturday Big Tent Wedding Party*
CATTLE DRIVES
    McMurtry, Larry. ★*Lonesome Dove: A Novel*
CATTLE INDUSTRY AND TRADE
    Howarth, Paul. *Dust off the Bones*
CATTLE RANCHES
    Harper, Jane. *The Lost Man*
Catton, Eleanor
    The Luminaries: A Novel
CAULFIELD, HOLDEN (FICTITIOUS CHARACTER)
    Salinger, J. D. ★*The Catcher in the Rye*

Cavanagh, Steve
Thirteen
Cavanaughs (Stephanie Laurens) [Series]. Laurens, Stephanie
★*The Cave*. Saramago, Jose
CAVE DWELLERS
Auel, Jean M. ★*The Clan of the Cave Bear: A Novel*
Golding, William. *The Inheritors*
The Cave Dwellers: A Novel. McDowell, Christina
CAVES
Evison, Jonathan. *Legends of the North Cascades: A Novel*
Golden, Christopher. *Ararat*
Starling, Caitlin. *The Luminous Dead*
CAVING
Starling, Caitlin. *The Luminous Dead*
Cedar Ridge novels [Series]. Shalvis, Jill
CELEBRITIES
Angelo, Megan. *Followers*
Bagshawe, Tilly. *Adored*
Beyda, Emily. *The Body Double*
Bowman, David. *Big Bang: A Nonfiction Novel*
Copperman, E. J. *Judgment at Santa Monica*
Dev, Sonali. ★*Recipe for Persuasion*
Ellroy, James. ★*Widespread Panic: A Novel*
Enright, Anne. *Actress: A Novel*
Foley, Lucy. *The Guest List*
Galbraith, Robert. *The Cuckoo's Calling*
Haddam, Jane. *Cheating at Solitaire: A Gregor Demarkian Novel*
Hiaasen, Carl. *Star Island*
Ishiguro, Kazuo. *The Unconsoled*
James, Eloisa. *Wilde in Love*
Knight, Renee. *The Secretary: A Novel*
Lethem, Jonathan. *Chronic City*
McKevett, G. A. *A Few Drops of Bitters*
Randall, Alice. ★*Black Bottom Saints*
Tanen, Sloane. *There's a Word for That*
CELEBRITIES — PRESS COVERAGE
Phillips, Susan Elizabeth. *What I Did for Love*
Celestial Bodies: A Novel. Alharthi, Jokha
Celestial kingdom [Series]. Tan, Sue Lynn
CELESTIAL MECHANICS
Waite, Olivia. ★*The Lady's Guide to Celestial Mechanics*
The Celestine Prophecy: An Adventure. Redfield, James
Celestine series (James Redfield) [Series]. Redfield, James
Celine: a Novel. Heller, Peter
Cell 8. Roslund, Anders
CELLISTS
Helprin, Mark. *Paris in the Present Tense*
Romano-Lax, Andromeda. *The Spanish Bow*
Celtic Empire. Cussler, Clive
CELTIC FANTASY
Bear, Elizabeth. *Blood and Iron: A Novel of the Promethean Age*
Marillier, Juliet. *Daughter of the Forest*
Sutcliff, Rosemary. *Sword at Sunset*
CEMETERIES
Beagle, Peter S. *A Fine and Private Place*
Khalfah, Khlid. *Death Is Hard Work: A Novel*
King, Stephen. *Pet Sematary*
Reichs, Kathy. *Break No Bones*

CEMETERY MANAGERS
Hicks, Robert. *The Widow of the South*
Cemetery of forgotten books [Series]. Ruiz Zafon, Carlos
Cemetery Road. Haywood, Gar Anthony
Cemetery Road: A Novel. Iles, Greg
CENSORSHIP
Bandi. *The Accusation: Forbidden Stories from Inside North Korea*
Bradbury, Ray. ★*Fahrenheit 451*
Fforde, Jasper. *The Eyre Affair: A Novel*
MacLeod, Alison. *Tenderness*
Pearl, Matthew. *The Dante Club: A Novel*
Vonnegut, Kurt. *Welcome to the Monkey House*
CENSORSHIP — HISTORY
Byatt, A. S. *Babel Tower*
Census. Ball, Jesse
CENSUS
Ball, Jesse. *Census*
CENTENARIANS
Butler, Robert Olen. *Late City*
Shocklee, Michelle. *Under the Tulip Tree*
★*Centennial*. Michener, James A.
The Center of Everything: A Novel. Harrison, Jamie
Center, Katherine
How to Walk Away: A Novel
Things You Save in a Fire
What You Wish For
CENTRAL AFRICA
Ballard, J. G. ★*The Day of Creation*
Central Park pact [Series]. Layne, Lauren
Century trilogy [Series]. Follett, Ken
★*Ceremony*. Silko, Leslie Marmon
Certain Prey. Sandford, John
Cervantes Saavedra, Miguel de
★*Don Quixote*
Cha, Steph
★*Your House Will Pay*
Chabon, Michael
The Amazing Adventures of Kavalier & Clay: A Novel
★*Wonder Boys*
The Yiddish Policemen's Union
Chai, May-Lee
Useful Phrases for Immigrants: Stories
★*The Chain*. McKinty, Adrian
Chakrabarti, Jai
A Play for the End of the World
Chakraborty, S. A.
The City of Brass
The Empire of Gold
The Kingdom of Copper: A Novel
CHALK DRAWING
Tudor, C. J. *The Chalk Man: A Novel*
The Chalk Man: A Novel. Tudor, C. J.
CHAMBERLAIN, JOSHUA LAWRENCE
Breslin, Jimmy. *Table Money*
Shaara, Jeff. *The Last Full Measure*
Chambers, Becky
A Closed and Common Orbit
★*The Galaxy, and the Ground Within*

★*The Long Way to a Small, Angry Planet*
★*A Psalm for the Wild-Built*
Record of a Spaceborn Few
To Be Taught, If Fortunate
Chambers, Clare
　Small Pleasures
Chan, Jessamine
　The School for Good Mothers
Chancellor, Bryn
　Sycamore: A Novel
CHANCELLORSVILLE, BATTLE OF, 1863
　Shaara, Jeff. *Gods and Generals: A Novel of the Civil War*
★*Chances Are...: A Novel*. Russo, Richard
Chancy, Myriam J. A.
　★*What Storm, What Thunder*
Chandler, Raymond
　★*The Big Sleep*
　The Lady in the Lake
　The Long Goodbye
Chang, Alexandra
　★*Days of Distraction*
CHANGE
　Egan, Jennifer. ★*A Visit from the Goon Squad*
　Flournoy, Angela. *The Turner House*
　Johnson, Caleb. *Treeborne*
CHANGE (PSYCHOLOGY)
　Berg, Elizabeth. *The Confession Club: A Novel*
　Center, Katherine. *What You Wish For*
　Chee, Alexander. *The Queen of the Night*
　Clegg, Bill. *Did You Ever Have a Family*
　Conell, Lee. *The Party Upstairs*
　D'Erasmo, Stacey. *The Sky Below*
　Gerritsen, Tess. *Playing with Fire*
　Harrison, Rachel. *The Return*
　Henderson, Susan. *The Flicker of Old Dreams*
　Ma, Jian. *Beijing Coma*
　Patchett, Ann. ★*State of Wonder: A Novel*
　Rash, Ron. *Nothing Gold Can Stay: Stories*
　Rawlings, David. *The Baggage Handler: A Novel*
　Russell, Mary Doria. ★*The Sparrow*
　Sofer, Dalia. *Man of My Time*
　Straub, Emma. *The Vacationers*
　Strout, Elizabeth. *Olive Kitteridge*
　Strout, Elizabeth. ★*Olive, Again: A Novel*
　Wilson, Carter. *Dead Girl in 2a*
CHANGE — PSYCHOLOGICAL ASPECTS
　Enright, Anne. *Yesterday's Weather: Stories*
Change Agent: A Novel. Suarez, Daniel
Change of Heart: A Novel. Picoult, Jodi
The Changeling. Oe, Kenzaburo
CHANGELINGS
　Bear, Elizabeth. *Blood and Iron: A Novel of the Promethean Age*
　Donohue, Keith. *The Stolen Child*
　Golding, Melanie. *Little Darlings*
CHANNEL ISLANDS, CALIFORNIA
　Boyle, T. Coraghessan. *When the Killing's Done: A Novel*
Chanter, Catherine
　The Well

Chaon, Dan
　Ill Will
CHAOS
　Maaren, Kari. ★*Weave a Circle Round*
★*Chaos of Crime*. Shannon, Dell
Chapman's Odyssey. Bailey, Paul
CHARACTER
　Musil, Robert. *The Man Without Qualities*
CHARACTER IN MEN
　Musil, Robert. *The Man Without Qualities*
　Vidal, Gore. ★*Lincoln: A Novel*
CHARACTERS AND CHARACTERISTICS IN FAIRY TALES
　Balaskovits, A. A. *Magic for Unlucky Girls: Stories*
　Okri, Ben. *Prayer for the Living*
　Oyeyemi, Helen. *Gingerbread: A Novel*
　Perry, Sarah. *Melmoth: A Novel*
CHARACTERS AND CHARACTERISTICS IN LITERATURE
　Bailey, Paul. *Chapman's Odyssey*
　Fforde, Jasper. *Lost in a Good Book: A Thursday Next Novel*
　Gaiman, Neil. *Trigger Warning: Short Fictions and Disturbances*
　Gentill, Sulari. *Crossing the Lines*
　Goss, Theodora. *The Sinister Mystery of the Mesmerizing Girl*
　Goss, Theodora. *The Strange Case of the Alchemist's Daughter*
　Ishiguro, Kazuo. *The Buried Giant: A Novel*
　Parry, H. G. *The Unlikely Escape of Uriah Heep*
　Rawles, Nancy. *My Jim: A Novel*
　Simmons, Dan. *The Fifth Heart*
　Walton, Jo. *Or What You Will*
CHARACTERS AND CHARACTERISTICS IN MYTHOLOGY
　Heger, Amanda. *Crazy Cupid Love*
　Okri, Ben. *Prayer for the Living*
Charcoal Joe: An Easy Rawlins Mystery. Mosley, Walter
Chariandy, David John
　Brother: A Novel
CHARIOT-RACING
　Wallace, Lew. ★*Ben-Hur*
CHARISMA
　Oe, Kenzaburo. *Somersault: A Novel*
CHARITIES
　Daly, Paula. *Clear My Name*
　Trollope, Anthony. *The Warden*
Charlatans. Cook, Robin
CHARLES II, KING OF ENGLAND, 1630-1685
　Gabaldon, Diana. ★*Dragonfly in Amber*
　Parks, Gordon. ★*The Learning Tree*
Charles Jenkins novels [Series]. Dugoni, Robert
Charles Lenox chronicles [Series]. Finch, Charles
Charles Paris mysteries [Series]. Brett, Simon
Charles, KJ
　Wanted, a Gentleman: Or, Virtue Over-Rated
CHARLES, NICK (FICTITIOUS CHARACTER)
　Hammett, Dashiell. ★*The Thin Man*
CHARLESTON, SOUTH CAROLINA
　Gabaldon, Diana. ★*Drums of Autumn*
　Hendrix, Grady. *My Best Friend's Exorcism*
　Kidd, Sue Monk. ★*The Invention of Wings: A Novel*
　Reichs, Kathy. *Break No Bones*
　Williams, Preslaysa. *A Lowcountry Bride*

Charlie [Series]. Connolly, John
Charlie Bradshaw mysteries [Series]. Dobyns, Stephen
Charlie Fox novels [Series]. Sharp, Zoe
Charlie Hood thrillers [Series]. Parker, T. Jefferson
Charlie Martz and Other Stories: The Unpublished Stories. Leonard, Elmore
Charlie Resnick mysteries [Series]. Harvey, John
CHARLOT, EDMOND
    Adimi, Kaouther. *Our Riches*
    Weinberg, Kate. *The Truants*
Charlotte Gray: A Novel. Faulks, Sebastian
CHARLOTTE, NORTH CAROLINA
    Barr, Nevada. *What Rose Forgot*
    Reichs, Kathy. *Bare Bones*
    Reichs, Kathy. ★*A Conspiracy of Bones*
The Charm Offensive. Cochrun, Alison
The Charmer in Chaps. London, Julia
★*Charming Billy*. McDermott, Alice
Charms for the Easy Life. Gibbons, Kaye
★*The Chase*. Cussler, Clive
Chase, Loretta Lynda
    Don't Tempt Me
    A Duke in Shining Armor
    Miss Wonderful
CHASES
    Dekker, Ted. *White: The Great Pursuit*
    Dodd, Christina. *What Doesn't Kill Her*
    Fleming, Ian. *On Her Majesty's Secret Service*
    Goodis, David. *Nightfall*
    MacDonald, John D. *Cinnamon Skin: The Twentieth Adventure of Travis McGee*
    MacDonald, John D. *The Green Ripper*
    Portis, Charles. ★*The Dog of the South*
Chasing Shadows. Austin, Lynn N.
Chasing the Boogeyman. Chizmar, Richard T.
The Chatham School Affair. Cook, Thomas H.
Chatterjee, Upamanyu
    English, August: An Indian Story
CHAUCER, GEOFFREY
    Deighton, Len. *London Match*
    Robb, Candace M. *A Gift of Sanctuary: An Owen Archer Mystery*
CHAUFFEURS
    Hanson, Hart. *The Driver*
    Howard, Ravi. *Driving the King: A Novel*
Chavez, Heather
    No Bad Deed
Chayefsky, Paddy
    Altered States: A Novel
CHEATING (INTERPERSONAL RELATIONS)
    Antoinette, Ashley. *Butterfly*
    Antoinette, Ashley. *Butterfly.; Vol 2*
    Antoinette, Ashley. *Butterfly.; Vol 3*
    De Leon, Aya. *Side Chick Nation*
    Florio, Gwen. *Best Laid Plans*
    Hodges, Cheris F. *Rumor Has It*
    Hunter, Megan. *The Harpy*
    Pinborough, Sarah. ★*Dead to Her: A Novel*
    Starnone, Domenico. *Ties*

    Vernon, P. J. *Bath Haus: A Thriller*
Cheating at Solitaire: A Gregor Demarkian Novel. Haddam, Jane
CHECHNYA, RUSSIA
    Marra, Anthony. ★*A Constellation of Vital Phenomena: A Novel*
Chee, Alexander
    The Queen of the Night
Cheek, Chip
    Cape May
Cheever, John
    Bullet Park: A Novel
    Falconer
Chekhov, Anton Pavlovich
    Early Short Stories, 1883-1888
    Later Short Stories, 1888-1903
CHEKHOV, ANTON PAVLOVICH
    Anderson, Alison. *The Summer Guest*
    Truss, Lynne. *Murder by Milk Bottle*
The Chelsea Girls. Davis, Fiona
CHEMICAL SPILLS
    Frankel, Laurie. *One Two Three: A Novel*
    Sinha, Indra. *Animal's People*
Chen, Da
    Brothers: A Novel
Chen, Mike
    Here and Now and Then
    We Could Be Heroes
Chen, Qiufan
    Waste Tide
Cheng, Bill
    Southern Cross the Dog
CHENGDU (CHINA)
    Zhou, Haohui. *Death Notice: A Novel*
★*Cher Ami and Major Whittlesey*. Rooney, Kathleen
Cherezinska, Elzbieta
    The Widow Queen
CHERNOBYL NUCLEAR ACCIDENT, 1986
    Pohl, Frederik. *Chernobyl: A Novel*
Chernobyl: a Novel. Pohl, Frederik
★*Cherokee America*. Verble, Margaret
CHEROKEE GIRLS
    Kingsolver, Barbara. ★*The Bean Trees: A Novel*
    Kingsolver, Barbara. *Pigs in Heaven*
CHEROKEE INDIANS
    Brown, Dee. *Creek Mary's Blood: A Novel*
    Ford, Kelli Jo. ★*Crooked Hallelujah*
    Frazier, Charles. *Thirteen Moons: A Novel*
    Hobson, Brandon. ★*The Removed: A Novel*
    Kingsolver, Barbara. *Pigs in Heaven*
CHEROKEE INDIANS — HISTORY
    Verble, Margaret. ★*Cherokee America*
CHEROKEE WOMEN
    Ford, Kelli Jo. ★*Crooked Hallelujah*
    Verble, Margaret. ★*When Two Feathers Fell from the Sky*
★*Cherry: a Novel*. Walker, Nico
Cherryh, C. J.
    Foreigner: A Novel of First Contact
Chesapeake. Michener, James A.

CHESAPEAKE BAY
Michener, James A. *Chesapeake*
CHESAPEAKE BAY REGION
Michener, James A. *Chesapeake*
Oakley, Colleen. *The Invisible Husband of Frick Island*
Roberts, Nora. *Chesapeake Blue*
Roberts, Nora. *Sea Swept*
Chesapeake Bay saga [Series]. Roberts, Nora
Chesapeake Blue. Roberts, Nora
CHESS
Stout, Rex. ★*Gambit*
★*The **Chestnut** Man: A Novel.* Sveistrup, Soren
Chet and Bernie mysteries [Series]. Quinn, Spencer
Chevalier, Tracy
★*Girl with a Pearl Earring*
The Last Runaway
A Single Thread
CHEYENNE INDIANS
Brown, Dee. *Creek Mary's Blood: A Novel*
Chiang, Ted
★*Exhalation: Stories*
★*Stories of Your Life and Others*
Chiaverini, Jennifer
Mrs. Lincoln's Dressmaker: A Novel
Mrs. Lincoln's Sisters
Resistance Women: A Novel
Chicago mysteries (Tracy Clark) [Series]. Clark, Tracy P.
Chicago Stars [Series]. Phillips, Susan Elizabeth
*The **Chicago** Way.* Harvey, Michael T.
CHICAGO, ILLINOIS
Algren, Nelson. ★*The Man with the Golden Arm: A Novel*
Aswani, Alaa. *Chicago: A Modern Arabic Novel*
Bellow, Saul. ★*The Adventures of Augie March*
Bellow, Saul. *The Dean's December: A Novel*
Bellow, Saul. ★*Herzog*
Beukes, Lauren. *The Shining Girls*
Blackwell, Juliet. *Letters from Paris*
Blumberg, Chandra. *Digging up Love*
Bump, Gabriel. ★*Everywhere You Don't Belong: A Novel*
Burton, Jeffrey B. ★*The Finders: A Mace Reid K-9 Mystery*
Burton, Jeffrey B. *The Keepers: A Mace Reid K-9 Mystery*
Cather, Willa. *The Song of the Lark*
Child, Lee. ★*Die Trying*
Child, Lee. *A Wanted Man*
Cisneros, Sandra. ★*The House on Mango Street*
Clark, Tracy P. *Runner*
Clark, Tracy P. *What You Don't See*
Conner, M. Shelly. *Everyman*
Crouch, Blake. *Dark Matter: A Novel*
Dev, Sonali. *The Bollywood Bride*
Dybek, Stuart. *I Sailed with Magellan*
Epstein, Joseph. *The Love Song of A. Jerome Minkoff, and Other Stories*
Feehan, Christine. *Shadow Rider*
Ferber, Edna. *So Big*
Finder, Joseph. ★*Judgment*
Franzen, Jonathan. ★*Crossroads*
Ganshert, Katie. *Life After*

Goldberg, Tod. *Gangsterland: A Novel*
Hamilton, Steve. *The Second Life of Nick Mason: A Novel*
Hand, Elizabeth. *Curious Toys*
Harvey, Michael T. *The Chicago Way*
Harvey, Michael T. *The Fifth Floor*
Harvey, Michael T. *The Governor's Wife*
Harvey, Michael T. *We All Fall Down*
Hirahara, Naomi. ★*Clark and Division*
Hoffmann, R. J. *Other People's Children: A Novel*
Lombardo, Claire. *The Most Fun We Ever Had: A Novel*
Macomber, Debbie. *If Not for You: A Novel*
Makkai, Rebecca. ★*The Great Believers*
Mamet, David. *Chicago: A Novel*
Martinson, T. J. *The Reign of the Kingfisher: A Novel*
Meader, Kate. *Playing with Fire*
Moreno, Gus. *This Thing Between US: A Novel*
Niffenegger, Audrey. *The Time Traveler's Wife: A Novel*
Nussbaum, Susan. *Good Kings, Bad Kings: A Novel*
Paretsky, Sara. ★*Dead Land*
Paretsky, Sara. *Indemnity Only: A Novel*
Paretsky, Sara. *Shell Game*
Phillips, Jayne Anne. *Quiet Dell: A Novel*
Rader-Day, Lori. *The Black Hour*
Raimondo, Lynne. *Dante's Dilemma: A Mark Angelotti Novel*
Raimondo, Lynne. *Dante's Poison: A Mark Angelotti Novel*
Raimondo, Lynne. *Dante's Wood: A Mark Angelotti Novel*
Reay, Katherine. *The Bronte Plot*
Reichs, Kathy. *206 Bones*
Rosen, Renee. *Dollface: A Novel of the Roaring Twenties*
Ruff, Matt. *Lovecraft Country: A Novel*
Schaffhausen, Joanna. *Gone for Good*
Sinclair, Upton. ★*The Jungle*
Smith, Dominic. *Bright and Distant Shores*
Smith, Ian. *The Unspoken*
Smith, Ian. *Wolf Point*
Snipes, Wesley. *Talon of God*
Weiss, Elizabeth. *The Sisters Sweet*
Wright, Richard. *The Man Who Lived Underground*
Wright, Richard. ★*Native Son*
Zettel, Sarah. *A Mother's Lie*
Chicago: a Modern Arabic Novel. Aswani, Alaa
Chicago: a Novel. Mamet, David
CHICK LIT
Alderton, Dolly. ★*Ghosts: A Novel*
Bushnell, Candace. *Is There Still Sex in the City?*
Carr, Robyn. *What We Find*
Christian, Claire. *It's Been a Pleasure, Noni Blake*
Clark, Georgia. *The Bucket List*
Evanovich, Janet. ★*Game On: Tempting Twenty-Eight*
Evanovich, Janet. *Look Alive Twenty-Five*
Evanovich, Janet. *One for the Money*
Evanovich, Janet. *Turbo Twenty-Three*
Evanovich, Stephanie. *Under the Table*
Fielding, Helen. ★*Bridget Jones's Diary: A Novel*
Hale, Shannon. *Austenland: A Novel*
Ho, Lauren. *Last Tang Standing*
Jalaluddin, Uzma. ★*Ayesha at Last*
Kamal, Soniah. *Unmarriageable: A Novel*

McLaughlin, Emma. *The Nanny Diaries: A Novel*
Palmer, Lindsey J. *Otherwise Engaged*
Pearson, Allison. ★*How Hard Can It Be?*
Raheem, Zara. *The Marriage Clock: A Novel*
Rockaway, Kristin. *How to Hack a Heartbreak*
Shumway, Charity. *Ten Girls to Watch: A Novel*
Sittenfeld, Curtis. *Prep: A Novel*
Waxman, Abbi. *The Bookish Life of Nina Hill*
Weiner, Jennifer. ★*Big Summer*
The **Chicken** *Sisters*. Dell'Antonia, K. J.

CHIEF EXECUTIVE OFFICERS
Hunting, Helena. *Handle with Care*
Williams, Denise. *The Fastest Way to Fall*

Chief Inspector Wexford mysteries [Series]. Rendell, Ruth
Chief Inspector Woodend mysteries [Series]. Spencer, Sally
Chiefs. Woods, Stuart
The **Child**. Barton, Fiona
Child 44. Smith, Tom Rob

CHILD ABUSE
McCaffrey, Anne. ★*Acorna: The Unicorn Girl*
Morrison, Toni. ★*God Help the Child*
Wrobel, Stephanie. *Darling Rose Gold*

CHILD ABUSE AND CRIME
Price, Richard. *Lush Life*

CHILD ABUSE VICTIMS
Atkins, Ace. *The Lost Ones*
Francis, Patry. *All the Children Are Home*
Gibbons, Kaye. ★*Ellen Foster: A Novel*
Graff, Andrew J. *Raft of Stars*
Harris, Thomas. *Hannibal Rising*
Monroe, Mary. ★*God Don't Like Ugly*
Styles, Toy. *Raunchy*

CHILD ABUSERS
Greenwood, T. *Rust & Stardust*

CHILD CARE
Wilson, Kevin. *Nothing to See Here*

CHILD CASTAWAYS
Golding, William. ★*Lord of the Flies: A Novel*

CHILD CUSTODY
Anstruther, Eleanor. *A Perfect Explanation*
Armstrong, Kelley. *Wherever She Goes*
Beck, Haylen. *Here and Gone*
Crowell, Jenn. *Etched on Me: A Novel*
Gaige, Amity. *Schroder*
Jimenez, Abby. *Life's Too Short*
Lippman, Laura. ★*Hush Hush*
Miller, Sue. *The Good Mother*
Montclair, Allison. *A Rogue's Company*
Picoult, Jodi. *Keeping Faith: A Novel*
Rosen, Leonard J. *The Kortelisy Escape*
Wood, Shelley. *The Quintland Sisters*

CHILD IMMIGRANTS
Luiselli, Valeria. ★*Lost Children Archive: A Novel*
Shafak, Elif. *Honor: A Novel*
The **Child** *in Time*. McEwan, Ian

CHILD KIDNAPPING VICTIMS
Armstrong, Kelley. *Wherever She Goes*
Bambara, Toni Cade. *Those Bones Are Not My Child*

Barber, Lizzy. *A Girl Named Anna*
Barnett, S. K. *Safe*
Bell, Darcey. *Something She's Not Telling Us*
Dugoni, Robert. *In Her Tracks*
George, Elizabeth. *Just One Evil Act*
Hausmann, Romy. ★*Dear Child*
Hill, Lawrence. *Someone Knows My Name: A Novel*
Mooney, Chris. *Blood World*
Parks, Brad. *Say Nothing: A Novel*
Petrie, Nicholas. *The Wild One*

CHILD LABOR
Dickens, Charles. ★*David Copperfield*

CHILD MURDER INVESTIGATION
Roslund, Anders. *Pen 33*

CHILD MURDER VICTIMS
Bambara, Toni Cade. *Those Bones Are Not My Child*
Dixon, Stephen. *Interstate: A Novel*
Flint, Emma. ★*Little Deaths: A Novel*
Franklin, Ariana. *Mistress of the Art of Death*
Griffiths, Elly. *The Janus Stone*
Kelly, Erin. *Broadchurch: A Novel*
Ware, Ruth. ★*The Turn of the Key*

CHILD MURDERS
Faulkner, William. *Requiem for a Nun*
MacBride, Stuart. *Cold Granite*

CHILD NEGLECT
Gardam, Jane. *God on the Rocks*
★*A* **Child** *of a Crack Head*. Speight, Shameek A.
Child of Light. Brooks, Terry
Child of light [Series]. Brooks, Terry
Child of My Heart. McDermott, Alice

CHILD PORNOGRAPHY VICTIMS
Cain, Chelsea. *One Kick: A Novel*

CHILD PRODIGIES
O'Neill, Heather. ★*The Lonely Hearts Hotel: A Novel*
Romano-Lax, Andromeda. *The Spanish Bow*

CHILD PROTECTIVE SERVICES
Chan, Jessamine. *The School for Good Mothers*

CHILD PSYCHICS
Williams, Drew. *The Stars Now Unclaimed*

CHILD REFUGEES
Byatt, A. S. ★*Ragnarok: The End of the Gods*
El Akkad, Omar. *American War*
Hosseini, Khaled. ★*Sea Prayer*

CHILD SEXUAL ABUSE
Ólafsson, Ólafur Jóhann. *The Sacrament: A Novel*
Raimondo, Lynne. *Dante's Wood: A Mark Angelotti Novel*

CHILD SEXUAL ABUSERS
Rendell, Ruth. *Harm Done*

CHILD SOLDIERS
El Akkad, Omar. *American War*

CHILD WAR VICTIMS
Akpan, Uwem. *Say You're One of Them*

CHILD WELFARE
Rimmer, Kelly. *Before I Let You Go*

CHILD WITNESSES
Box, C. J. *Blue Heaven*
Freeman, Brian. *Thief River Falls*

Child, Lee
61 Hours
The Affair
Bad Luck and Trouble
★*Blue Moon*
★*Die Trying*
Echo Burning
The Enemy
The Hard Way
★*Killing Floor*
Make Me
The Midnight Line
Never Go Back
Night School
No Middle Name: The Complete Collected Jack Reacher Short Stories
Nothing to Lose
One Shot
★*Past Tense*
Personal
Persuader
★*The Sentinel*
A Wanted Man
Without Fail
Worth Dying For
Child, Lincoln
Deep Storm: A Novel
CHILD-REARING
Beattie, Ann. ★*Picturing Will*
CHILD-SEPARATED FATHERS
Priest, Cherie. *Dreadnought*
CHILD-SEPARATED MOTHERS
Hozar, Nazanine. *Aria*
Lippman, Laura. ★*Hush Hush*
CHILDBIRTH
Palmer, Dexter Clarence. ★*Mary Toft; Or, the Rabbit Queen: A Novel*
Sharratt, Mary. *Revelations*
CHILDHOOD
Atwood, Margaret. ★*Cat's Eye*
Bender, Aimee. *The Butterfly Lampshade*
Daughters, Amy Weinland. *You Cannot Mess This Up: A True Story That Never Happened*
Doyle, Roddy. *Paddy Clarke, Ha-Ha-Ha*
Grass, Gunter. *The Box: Tales from the Darkroom*
Harris, Thomas. *Hannibal Rising*
Matar, Hisham. *In the Country of Men*
Tudor, C. J. *The Chalk Man: A Novel*
CHILDHOOD FRIENDS
Abrams, Melanie. *Meadowlark*
Acampora, Lauren. *The Paper Wasp: A Novel*
Doyle, Roddy. *Love*
Ferrante, Elena. *The Story of a New Name*
Ferrante, Elena. *The Story of the Lost Child*
Forbes, Curdella. *A Tall History of Sugar*
Franklin, Tom. *Crooked Letter, Crooked Letter: A Novel*
Loedel, Daniel. *Hades, Argentina*
McElroy, Alex. *The Atmospherians*
Styles, Toy. ★*War*

CHILDHOOD INNOCENCE (CONCEPT)
Faye, Gael. ★*Small Country: A Novel*
★*Childhood's End*. Clarke, Arthur C.
CHILDLESSNESS
Allen, Jayne. *Black Girls Must Die Exhausted*
Liardet, Frances. *We Must Be Brave*
*The **Children**. Wharton, Edith
CHILDREN
Bush, Keisha. *No Heaven for Good Boys: A Novel*
Clarke, Arthur C. ★*Childhood's End*
Hannah, Sophie. *Perfect Little Children*
Heley, Veronica. *Murder in Law*
King, Stephen. *The Institute*
King, Stephen. *It*
Ray, Eleanor. *The Missing Treasures of Amy Ashton*
Reid, Kiley. ★*Such a Fun Age*
Rushdie, Salman. ★*Midnight's Children: A Novel*
Shepard, Jim. ★*The Book of Aron*
CHILDREN — DEATH
Banks, Russell. ★*The Sweet Hereafter*
Betts, Doris. *Souls Raised from the Dead: A Novel*
Black, Lisa. *Suffer the Children*
Cantrell, Christian. *Scorpion*
Drake, Laura. *The Sweet Spot*
Morrison, Toni. ★*Beloved: A Novel*
O'Farrell, Maggie. *Hamnet*
Spufford, Francis. ★*Light Perpetual*
CHILDREN — FRIENDSHIP
Murr, Naeem. *The Perfect Man: A Novel*
CHILDREN AND ADULTS
McBride, James. ★*The Good Lord Bird*
Children and Fire: A Novel. Hegi, Ursula
CHILDREN AND WAR
Couto, Mia. *Sleepwalking Land*
Hosseini, Khaled. ★*Sea Prayer*
Yoon, Paul. ★*Run Me to Earth: A Novel*
CHILDREN OF ACTORS AND ACTRESSES
Enright, Anne. *Actress: A Novel*
CHILDREN OF AGING PARENTS
Olson, Neil. *Before the Devil Fell*
CHILDREN OF ALCOHOLIC FATHERS
Smith, Betty. ★*A Tree Grows in Brooklyn*
Wolfe, Thomas. ★*Look Homeward, Angel: A Story of a Buried Life*
CHILDREN OF ARTISTS
Vreeland, Susan. *Girl in Hyacinth Blue*
CHILDREN OF AUTHORS
Ozick, Cynthia. *Heir to the Glimmering World*
Rice, Craig. *Home Sweet Homicide*
CHILDREN OF CLERGY
Baldwin, James. ★*Go Tell It on the Mountain*
Cather, Willa. *The Song of the Lark*
Fabry, Chris. *The Promise of Jesse Woods*
Jordan, Sophie. *The Duke Goes Down*
Lewis, Beverly. *The Brethren*
Lewis, Beverly. *The Preacher's Daughter*
Monroe, Mary. ★*Mrs. Wiggins*
Pontoppidan, Henrik. *Lucky Per*
Price, Reynolds. *The Good Priest's Son*

Robinson, Marilynne. ★*Jack*

CHILDREN OF CRIMINALS

DePoy, Phillip. *Sidewalk Saint*

CHILDREN OF DIVORCED PARENTS

Allende, Isabel. *Ripper: A Novel*

Hawley, Noah. *The Good Father*

King, Stephen. *The Girl Who Loved Tom Gordon*

Moniz, Tomas. *Big Familia*

Wharton, Edith. *The Children*

★***Children*** of Earth and Sky. Kay, Guy Gavriel

CHILDREN OF FORMER CONVICTS

Booth, Coe. ★*Bronxwood*

CHILDREN OF GAMBLERS

Ferber, Edna. *So Big*

CHILDREN OF GANGSTERS

Harkaway, Nick. *Angelmaker*

★***Children*** of God: A Novel. Russell, Mary Doria

*The **Children** of Hurin.* Tolkien, J. R. R.

CHILDREN OF IMMIGRANTS

Batuman, Elif. ★*The Idiot*

Chariandy, David John. *Brother: A Novel*

Diamant, Anita. *The Boston Girl: A Novel*

Edwards, Louis. *Ramadan Ramsey: A Novel*

Kwok, Jean. *Searching for Sylvie Lee*

Ma, Ling. *Severance*

Oates, Joyce Carol. *The Gravedigger's Daughter: A Novel*

Pava, Sergio de la. *A Naked Singularity*

Richman, Alyson. *The Secret of Clouds*

Rodrigues Fowler, Yara. *Stubborn Archivist*

Smith, Betty. ★*A Tree Grows in Brooklyn*

Wang, Kathy. *Impostor Syndrome: A Novel*

CHILDREN OF INCEST VICTIMS

Stewart, Mary. *The Wicked Day*

CHILDREN OF MIGRANT WORKERS

Oates, Joyce Carol. *A Garden of Earthly Delights*

CHILDREN OF MURDER VICTIMS

Black, Saul. ★*The Killing Lessons*

Black, Saul. ★*Lovemurder*

Bohjalian, Chris. *Secrets of Eden: A Novel*

Fesperman, Dan. *Safe Houses: A Novel*

Flynn, Gillian. *Dark Places*

Miller, Derek B. *How to Find Your Way in the Dark*

Roorbach, Bill. *Life Among Giants: A Novel*

CHILDREN OF PEOPLE WITH MENTAL ILLNESSES

Abbott, Patricia. *Concrete Angel*

Huisman, Violaine. *The Book of Mother*

CHILDREN OF PEOPLE WITH TERMINAL ILLNESSES

Genova, Lisa. *Inside the O'Briens: A Novel*

CHILDREN OF PRESIDENTS

McQuiston, Casey. ★*Red, White & Royal Blue: A Novel*

Phillips, Susan Elizabeth. *The Great Escape*

CHILDREN OF PRISONERS

Dickens, Charles. *Little Dorrit*

Fitch, Janet. *White Oleander: A Novel*

Ford, Richard. *Canada*

CHILDREN OF PROSTITUTES

Monroe, Mary. ★*Mrs. Wiggins*

Sepetys, Ruta. ★*Out of the Easy*

CHILDREN OF RICH PEOPLE

Gardam, Jane. *God on the Rocks*

Swarthout, Glendon. *Bless the Beasts and Children*

CHILDREN OF SHIP CAPTAINS

Powning, Beth. *The Sea Captain's Wife: A Novel*

CHILDREN OF SINGLE PARENTS

Irving, John. ★*The World According to Garp: A Novel*

CHILDREN OF SUICIDE VICTIMS

Durrow, Heidi W. *The Girl Who Fell from the Sky: A Novel*

McDermott, Alice. ★*The Ninth Hour*

Children of the New World: Stories. Weinstein, Alexander

Children of the Revolution. Robinson, Peter

*The **Children** of the Sky.* Vinge, Vernor

Children of the Street: A Novel. Quartey, Kwei

CHILDREN OF VETERINARIANS

Deb, Siddhartha. *The Point of Return: A Novel*

Children of violence series [Series]. Lessing, Doris May

CHILDREN OF WIDOWS

Bialosky, Jill. *House Under Snow*

CHILDREN OF WOMEN COCAINE ADDICTS

Cleage, Pearl. *What Looks Like Crazy on an Ordinary Day: A Novel*

Children of Wrath. Grossman, Paul

CHILDREN WHO ARE DEAF AND MUTE

Ólafsdóttir, Auður A. *Butterflies in November*

CHILDREN WHO ARE MUTE

Frazier, Charles. *Nightwoods: A Novel*

CHILDREN WITH AUTISM

Lovesey, Peter. *Diamond Solitaire*

Picoult, Jodi. *House Rules: A Novel*

CHILDREN WITH BEHAVIORAL DISORDERS

Seo, Mi-Ae. *The Only Child*

CHILDREN WITH CANCER

Cleave, Chris. *Gold*

CHILDREN WITH CHRONIC ILLNESSES

Sem-Sandberg, Steve. *The Chosen Ones: A Novel*

CHILDREN WITH DEPRESSION

Fuqua, Jonathon Scott. *Gone and Back Again*

CHILDREN WITH DEVELOPMENTAL DISABILITIES

Nussbaum, Susan. *Good Kings, Bad Kings: A Novel*

CHILDREN WITH DISABILITIES

Drabble, Margaret. *The Pure Gold Baby*

Nussbaum, Susan. *Good Kings, Bad Kings: A Novel*

CHILDREN WITH DOWN SYNDROME

Edwards, Kim. *The Memory Keeper's Daughter*

O'Connor, Flannery. ★*The Violent Bear It Away*

CHILDREN WITH TERMINAL ILLNESSES

Hazzard, Shirley. ★*The Great Fire*

CHILDREN'S BOOK ILLUSTRATORS

Parrish, Roan. *Better Than People*

*The **Children's** Crusade.* Packer, Ann

CHILDREN'S SECRETS

Ammaniti, Niccolo. *I'm Not Scared*

Childress, Mark

Crazy in Alabama

Childs, Laura

Egg Shooters

Haunted Hibiscus

Lavender Blue Murder

Twisted Tea Christmas
CHILE
    Allende, Isabel. ★*The House of the Spirits*
    Allende, Isabel. *A Long Petal of the Sea: A Novel*
    Allende, Isabel. *Portrait in Sepia: A Novel*
    Berlin, Lucia. ★*Evening in Paradise: More Stories*
    Bolano, Roberto. ★*By Night in Chile*
    Bolano, Roberto. ★*Distant Star*
    Fernandez, Nona. *The Twilight Zone*
    McGregor, Jon. *Lean Fall Stand*
    Skarmeta, Antonio. *The Dancer and the Thief: A Novel*
★*The **Chill***. Bilenchi, Romano
Chilly Scenes of Winter. Beattie, Ann
Chimera. Barth, John
Chimes at Midnight: An October Daye Novel. McGuire, Seanan
CHIMPANZEES
    Greenidge, Kaitlyn. *We Love You, Charlie Freeman: A Novel*
CHINA
    Ballard, J. G. *Empire of the Sun: A Novel*
    Barker, Susan. ★*The Incarnations: A Novel*
    Buck, Pearl S. *The Good Earth*
    Cameron, Marc. *Power and Empire*
    Chai, May-Lee. *Useful Phrases for Immigrants: Stories*
    Chen, Da. *Brothers: A Novel*
    Chen, Qiufan. *Waste Tide*
    Church, James. *A Drop of Chinese Blood*
    Cronin, A. J. *The Keys of the Kingdom*
    Feng, Linda Rui. *Swimming Back to Trout River*
    Freudenberger, Nell. *The Dissident*
    Gao, XIngjian. *Soul Mountain*
    Ghosh, Amitav. *Flood of Fire*
    Ghosh, Amitav. *River of Smoke*
    Hart, Elsa. *City of Ink: A Mystery*
    Jen, Gish. ★*Thank You, Mr. Nixon: Stories*
    Jin, Ha. *A Map of Betrayal: A Novel*
    Jin, Ha. ★*Waiting*
    Jin, Meng. *Little Gods*
    Jin, Yong. *A Hero Born: A Novel*
    Ko, Lisa. *The Leavers*
    Kwan, Kevin. *China Rich Girlfriend*
    Li, Yiyun. *The Vagrants: A Novel*
    Lin, Jeannie. *The Lotus Palace*
    Liu, Cixin. *Ball Lightning*
    Liu, Cixin. ★*The Dark Forest*
    Liu, Cixin. ★*Death's End*
    Liu, Cixin. ★*The Three-Body Problem*
    Ludlum, Robert. *The Bourne Supremacy*
    Ma, Jian. *Beijing Coma*
    Ma, Jian. *China Dream*
    Parker-Chan, Shelley. ★*She Who Became the Sun*
    Patterson, Molly. *Rebellion*
    Pattison, Eliot. *Bones of the Earth: An Inspector Shan Tao Yun Mystery*
    Pearson, Ridley. *The Risk Agent*
    Poyer, David. *Overthrow: The War with China and North Korea—Fall of an Empire*
    Poyer, David. *Violent Peace: The War with China - Aftermath of Armageddon*

    Qiu, Xiaolong. *Death of a Red Heroine*
    Qiu, Xiaolong. *Don't Cry Tai Lake: An Inspector Chen Novel*
    Qiu, Xiaolong. *Enigma of China*
    Qiu, Xiaolong. *Hold Your Breath, China*
    Qiu, Xiaolong. *Red Mandarin Dress: An Inspector Chen Novel*
    Qiu, Xiaolong. *Shanghai Redemption: An Inspector Chen Novel*
    Qiu, Xiaolong. *When Red Is Black*
    Rendell, Ruth. *Speaker of Mandarin*
    Robinson, Kim Stanley. *The Years of Rice and Salt*
    Schell, Orville. *My Old Home: A Novel of Exile*
    See, Lisa. *Dragon Bones: A Novel*
    See, Lisa. *Dreams of Joy: A Novel*
    See, Lisa. *Peony in Love: A Novel*
    See, Lisa. *Shanghai Girls: A Novel*
    See, Lisa. *The Tea Girl of Hummingbird Lane*
    Tan, Amy. *The Bonesetter's Daughter*
    Tan, Amy. *The Hundred Secret Senses*
    Tan, Amy. ★*The Kitchen God's Wife*
    Thien, Madeleine. *Do Not Say We Have Nothing*
    Zhou, Haohui. *Death Notice: A Novel*
China Dream. Ma, Jian
China Rich Girlfriend. Kwan, Kevin
CHINATOWN, NEW YORK CITY
    Deaver, Jeffery. *The Stone Monkey: A Lincoln Rhyme Novel*
CHINATOWN, SAN FRANCISCO, CALIFORNIA
    Lim, Roselle. *Natalie Tan's Book of Luck and Fortune*
CHINESE AMERICAN FAMILIES
    Jen, Gish. ★*Thank You, Mr. Nixon: Stories*
    Lim, Roselle. *Vanessa Yu's Magical Paris Tea Shop*
    Tan, Amy. *The Bonesetter's Daughter*
    Tieu, Julie. *The Donut Trap*
CHINESE AMERICAN GIRLS
    See, Lisa. *The Tea Girl of Hummingbird Lane*
CHINESE AMERICAN MEN
    Lee, Chang-Rae. ★*My Year Abroad*
CHINESE AMERICAN WOMEN
    Chan, Jessamine. *The School for Good Mothers*
    Darznik, Jasmin. *The Bohemians*
    Jin, Ha. *A Map of Betrayal: A Novel*
    Jin, Meng. *Little Gods*
    Kwan, Kevin. *Crazy Rich Asians*
    Kwan, Kevin. *Sex and Vanity: A Novel*
    Rozan, S. J. ★*The Art of Violence*
    Rozan, S. J. ★*Paper Son*
    Rozan, S. J. *Winter and Night*
    See, Lisa. *Shanghai Girls: A Novel*
    Tan, Amy. *The Bonesetter's Daughter*
    Tan, Amy. *The Hundred Secret Senses*
    Tan, Amy. ★*The Kitchen God's Wife*
    Yang, Susie. *White Ivy: A Novel*
CHINESE AMERICAN WOMEN — IDENTITY
    Tan, Amy. ★*The Joy Luck Club*
CHINESE AMERICANS
    Allende, Isabel. *Daughter of Fortune: A Novel*
    Chai, May-Lee. *Useful Phrases for Immigrants: Stories*
    Davies, Peter Ho. *The Fortunes*
    Jen, Gish. ★*Thank You, Mr. Nixon: Stories*
    Lim, Roselle. *Natalie Tan's Book of Luck and Fortune*

Ma, Ling. *Severance*
Ng, Celeste. ★*Everything I Never Told You: A Novel*
Wang, Kathy. *Family Trust: A Novel*
CHINESE AMERICANS IN CHINA
Tan, Amy. *The Hundred Secret Senses*
CHINESE CANADIAN GIRLS
Bates, Judy Fong. ★*Midnight at the Dragon Cafe*
CHINESE CANADIANS
Fu, Kim. *For Today I Am a Boy*
CHINESE CULTURAL REVOLUTION (1966-1976)
Chen, Da. *Brothers: A Novel*
Feng, Linda Rui. *Swimming Back to Trout River*
Li, Yiyun. *The Vagrants: A Novel*
Liu, Cixin. ★*The Three-Body Problem*
CHINESE IN CANADA
Bates, Judy Fong. ★*Midnight at the Dragon Cafe*
Fu, Kim. *For Today I Am a Boy*
CHINESE IN ONTARIO
Bates, Judy Fong. ★*Midnight at the Dragon Cafe*
CHINESE IN THE UNITED STATES
Jin, Ha. *The Boat Rocker: A Novel*
CHINESE IN WASHINGTON, D.C.
Roosevelt, Elliott. *Murder in the Map Room: An Eleanor Roosevelt Mystery*
CHIVALRY
Scott, Walter. ★*Ivanhoe*
Chizmar, Richard T.
Chasing the Boogeyman
A Long December
Cho, Nam-Ju
★*Kim Jiyoung, Born 1982*
Cho, Zen
Sorcerer to the Crown
Spirits Abroad and Other Stories
Chocolat novels (Joanne Harris) [Series]. Harris, Joanne
★*Chocolat: a Novel*. Harris, Joanne
CHOCOLATE
Haratischvili, Nino. *The Eighth Life: (For Brilka)*
Harris, Joanne. ★*Chocolat: A Novel*
Choi, Ann Y. K.
Kay's Lucky Coin Variety
Choi, Susan
My Education
★*Trust Exercise: A Novel*
Choi, Yoon
Skinship: Stories
★*A **Choir** of Crows*. Robb, Candace M.
Choke Hold. Faust, Christa
Choke: a Novel. Palahniuk, Chuck
Choo, Yangsze
The Ghost Bride: A Novel
★*The Night Tiger: A Novel*
Choose Me. Gerritsen, Tess
Chorus of dragons [Series]. Lyons, Jenn
★*The **Chosen** and the Beautiful*. Vo, Nghi
*The **Chosen** Maiden: A Novel*. Stachniak, Eva
*The **Chosen** Ones: A Novel*. Sem-Sandberg, Steve
Chosen Prey. Sandford, John

Christ the Lord [Series]. Rice, Anne
Christ the Lord: Out of Egypt: A Novel. Rice, Anne
Christ the Lord: The Road to Cana: A Novel. Rice, Anne
CHRISTIAN CHURCH CONTROVERSIES
Hansen, Ron. *Mariette in Ecstasy*
CHRISTIAN FAMILIES
Kingsolver, Barbara. ★*The Poisonwood Bible: A Novel*
CHRISTIAN FANTASY
Dekker, Ted. *Black: The Birth of Evil*
Dekker, Ted. *Red: The Heroic Rescue*
Dekker, Ted. *White: The Great Pursuit*
Locke, Thomas. *Emissary*
Snipes, Wesley. *Talon of God*
CHRISTIAN FICTION
Bartels, Erin. *We Hope for Better Things*
Cramer, W. Dale. *Levi's Will: A Novel*
Cronin, A. J. *The Keys of the Kingdom*
Endo, Shusaku. *Silence*
Fabry, Chris. *Looking into You*
Fabry, Chris. *The Promise of Jesse Woods*
Fabry, Chris. *War Room: Prayer Is a Powerful Weapon*
Ganshert, Katie. *Life After*
Ganshert, Katie. ★*No One Ever Asked: A Novel*
Lewis, Beverly. *The Brethren*
Lewis, Beverly. *The Missing*
Linden, Rachel. *The Enlightenment of Bees*
Parrish, Christa. *Still Life*
Pearson, Robin W. *A Long Time Comin'*
Rawlings, David. *The Baggage Handler: A Novel*
Reay, Katherine. *The Bronte Plot*
Rice, Anne. *Christ the Lord: The Road to Cana: A Novel*
Smith, Jill Eileen. *Star of Persia: Esther's Story*
Stewart, Ann Marie. *Stars in the Grass*
Tatlock, Ann. *Promises to Keep*
Tolstoy, Leo. *Divine and Human and Other Stories*
Whitlow, Robert. *A Time to Stand*
CHRISTIAN HISTORICAL FICTION
Afshar, Tessa. *Thief of Corinth*
Andrews, Mesu. *Of Fire and Lions: A Novel*
Austin, Lynn N. *Chasing Shadows*
Brouwer, Sigmund. *Thief of Glory: A Novel*
Dykes, Amanda. *Whose Waves These Are*
Endo, Shusaku. *Silence*
Green, Amy Lynn. *Things We Didn't Say*
Green, Jocelyn. *The Mark of the King*
Green, Jocelyn. *Veiled in Smoke*
Groot, Tracy. *Flame of Resistance*
Johnson, Tara. *Engraved on the Heart*
Kirkpatrick, Jane. *One More River to Cross*
Lewis, Beverly. *The Preacher's Daughter*
Luesse, Valerie Fraser. *Missing Isaac*
Luesse, Valerie Fraser. *Under the Bayou Moon: A Novel*
Parini, Jay. *The Damascus Road: A Novel of Saint Paul*
Phoenix, Michele. *The Space Between Words*
Rivers, Francine. *Bridge to Haven*
Shocklee, Michelle. *Under the Tulip Tree*
Sundin, Sarah. *When Twilight Breaks*

CHRISTIAN HISTORICAL ROMANCES
Afshar, Tessa. *Jewel of the Nile*
Alexander, Tamera. ★*A Note yet Unsung*
Alexander, Tamera. *With This Pledge*
Barnett, Karen. *Ever Faithful*
Cossette, Connilyn. ★*Shelter of the Most High*
Frantz, Laura. *The Lacemaker*
Gohlke, Cathy. *Promise Me This*
Marshall, Catherine. *Christy*
Peterson, Tracie. *What Comes My Way*
Rivers, Francine. ★*Redeeming Love*
Sundin, Sarah. *Through Waters Deep: A Novel*
Turansky, Carrie. *No Ocean Too Wide: A Novel*
CHRISTIAN LIFE
Philyaw, Deesha. *The Secret Lives of Church Ladies*
Reay, Katherine. *The Bronte Plot*
Rivers, Francine. *Bridge to Haven*
Turner, Bethany. *The Secret Life of Sarah Hollenbeck*
CHRISTIAN MEN
Searles, John. *Help for the Haunted*
CHRISTIAN MISSIONARIES
Cather, Willa. ★*Death Comes for the Archbishop*
Endo, Shusaku. *Silence*
Kingsolver, Barbara. ★*The Poisonwood Bible: A Novel*
CHRISTIAN MISSIONS
Cronin, A. J. *The Keys of the Kingdom*
CHRISTIAN MYSTERIES
Green, Jocelyn. *Veiled in Smoke*
CHRISTIAN RELIC THEFTS
Peters, Ellis. *The Holy Thief*
CHRISTIAN RELICS
Berry, Steve. ★*The Warsaw Protocol*
CHRISTIAN ROMANCES
Blackstock, Terri. *Catching Christmas*
Hatcher, Robin Lee. *Cross My Heart*
Hatcher, Robin Lee. *Who I Am with You*
Hauck, Rachel. *How to Catch a Prince*
Hauck, Rachel. *Once Upon a Prince*
Hauck, Rachel. *The Wedding Chapel*
Isaac, Kara. *Then There Was You*
Kate, Jessica. *A Girl's Guide to the Outback: A Novel*
Laureano, C. E. ★*The Saturday Night Supper Club*
Lewis, Beverly. *The Ebb Tide*
Rivers, Francine. *The Masterpiece*
Turner, Bethany. *The Secret Life of Sarah Hollenbeck*
Turner, Bethany. *Wooing Cadie McCaffrey*
Wade, Becky. *Falling for You*
Wade, Becky. ★*True to You*
Wiseman, Beth. *Listening to Love*
CHRISTIAN ROMANTIC SUSPENSE
Irvin, Kelly. *Tell Her No Lies*
Warren, Susan May. *Rescue Me*
CHRISTIAN SAINTS
Griffith, Nicola. *Hild: A Novel*
CHRISTIAN SUSPENSE
Blackstock, Terri. *Smoke Screen*
Bunn, T. Davis. *Outbreak*
Dekker, Ted. *Black: The Birth of Evil*

Dekker, Ted. *The Girl Behind the Red Rope*
Dekker, Ted. *Red: The Heroic Rescue*
Dekker, Ted. *White: The Great Pursuit*
Martin, Charles. *The Water Keeper*
Nelson, Christina Suzann. *If We Make It Home: A Novel of Faith and Survival in the Oregon Wilderness*
Rubart, James L. ★*The Man He Never Was*
Wright, Jaime Jo. *The Haunting at Bonaventure Circus*
CHRISTIAN TEACHERS
Marshall, Catherine. *Christy*
CHRISTIAN WOMEN
Austin, Lynn N. *Chasing Shadows*
Clayton, Meg Waite. *The Last Train to London*
Ganshert, Katie. ★*No One Ever Asked: A Novel*
Griffith, Nicola. *Hild: A Novel*
Marshall, Catherine. *Christy*
Rivers, Francine. *The Masterpiece*
Christian, Claire
It's Been a Pleasure, Noni Blake
CHRISTIANITY
Cather, Willa. ★*Death Comes for the Archbishop*
Greene, Graham. *The Last Word and Other Stories*
O'Connor, Flannery. ★*Wise Blood*
Parini, Jay. *The Damascus Road: A Novel of Saint Paul*
Sharratt, Mary. *Illuminations: A Novel of Hildegard Von Bingen*
CHRISTIANS
Irving, John. ★*A Prayer for Owen Meany: A Novel*
Lacey, Catherine. ★*Pew: A Novel*
Sienkiewicz, Henryk. ★*Quo Vadis: A Story of Faith in the Last Days of the Roman Empire*
Christie, Agatha
★*The A B C Murders*
★*And Then There Were None*
The Body in the Library: A Miss Marple Mystery
Curtain
Endless Night
The Hollow
Mrs. McGinty's Dead
★*The Murder at the Vicarage*
A Murder Is Announced: A Miss Marple Mystery
★*The Murder of Roger Ackroyd: A Hercule Poirot Mystery*
★*Murder on the Orient Express*
The Pale Horse
Three Blind Mice, and Other Stories
Towards Zero
CHRISTIE, AGATHA
Kunsken, Derek. *The House of Styx*
Weinberg, Kate. *The Truants*
Christie, Michael
★*Greenwood: A Novel*
★*Christine* *Falls: A Novel*. Black, Benjamin
CHRISTMAS
Andrews, Donna. *Owl Be Home for Christmas: A Meg Langslow Mystery*
Andrews, Donna. *The Twelve Jays of Christmas: A Meg Langslow Mystery*
Avon, Joy. *In Peppermint Peril: A Book Tea Shop Mystery*
Balogh, Mary. *Someone to Trust*

Berry, Connie. *A Legacy of Murder*
Blackstock, Terri. *Catching Christmas*
Bryant, Niobia. *Christmas with the Billionaire*
Childs, Laura. *Twisted Tea Christmas*
Dickens, Charles. ★*A Christmas Carol*
Fluke, Joanne. ★*Christmas Cupcake Murder*
Guillory, Jasmine. *Royal Holiday*
Hallinan, Timothy. *Fields Where They Lay*
Hill, Joe. ★*Nos4a2*
Johnson, Craig. *Spirit of Steamboat: A Walt Longmire Story*
Rowell, Rainbow. *Landline*
Smith, Ali. ★*Winter*
Snow, Jennifer. *An Alaskan Christmas*
★*A Christmas Carol*. Dickens, Charles
★*Christmas Cupcake Murder*. Fluke, Joanne
CHRISTMAS STORIES
Bradley, C. Alan. *I Am Half-Sick of Shadows: A Flavia De Luce Novel*
Cameron, W. Bruce. *The Dogs of Christmas*
Davies, Valentine. *Miracle on 34th Street*
Dickens, Charles. ★*A Christmas Carol*
Henry, O. ★*The Complete Works of O. Henry*
Sedaris, David. *Holidays on Ice*
Christmas with the Billionaire. Bryant, Niobia
Christopher, Andie J.
Not the Girl You Marry
Christy. Marshall, Catherine
Christy, Bryan
In the Company of Killers
Chromatacia novels [Series]. Fforde, Jasper
Chronic City. Lethem, Jonathan
CHRONIC FATIGUE SYNDROME
Meltzer, Jean. ★*The Matzah Ball*
Chronicle of a Death Foretold. Garcia Marquez, Gabriel
Chronicle of Hugh de Singleton [Series]. Starr, Melvin R.
Chronicles from the Land of the Happiest People on Earth. Soyinka, Wole
Chronicles of a Radical Hag: With Recipes. Landvik, Lorna
Chronicles of Barsetshire [Series]. Trollope, Anthony
Chulito. Rice-Gonzalez, Charles
Chung, Catherine
The Tenth Muse: A Novel
Chung, Maxine Mei-Fung
The Eighth Girl
CHURCH AND STATE
Dunant, Sarah. *Blood and Beauty: A Novel*
Follett, Ken. *A Column of Fire*
Follett, Ken. ★*The Pillars of the Earth*
Follett, Ken. *World Without End*
CHURCH HISTORY
Parini, Jay. *The Damascus Road: A Novel of Saint Paul*
Sienkiewicz, Henryk. ★*Quo Vadis: A Story of Faith in the Last Days of the Roman Empire*
CHURCH MANAGEMENT
Isaac, Kara. *Then There Was You*
CHURCH WORK
Kate, Jessica. *A Girl's Guide to the Outback: A Novel*

Church, James
Bamboo and Blood: An Inspector O Novel
★*A Corpse in the Koryo*
A Drop of Chinese Blood
Hidden Moon: An Inspector O Novel
CHURCHES
Lacey, Catherine. ★*Pew: A Novel*
Parris, S. J. ★*The Dead of Winter*
Philyaw, Deesha. *The Secret Lives of Church Ladies*
Sayers, Dorothy L. *The Nine Tailors*
Stark, Richard. *Dirty Money*
CHURCHILL, CLEMENTINE
Benedict, Marie. ★*Lady Clementine*
McDermid, Val. *How the Dead Speak: A Tony Hill and Carol Jordan Novel*
CHURCHILL, WINSTON
Fleming, Ian. *Doctor No*
Higgins, Jack. *The Eagle Has Flown*
Higgins, Jack. *The Eagle Has Landed*
McCaffrey, Anne. *Dragonflight*
Pasternak, Boris Leonidovich. ★*Doctor Zhivago*
Uris, Leon. *Redemption: A Novel*
CIA AGENTS
Berenson, Alex. *The Deceivers*
Berenson, Alex. *The Faithful Spy: A Novel*
Berenson, Alex. *The Prisoner*
Coes, Ben. *The Russian: A Thriller*
Coonts, Stephen. *The Armageddon File*
Coonts, Stephen. *The Art of War: A Novel*
Coonts, Stephen. ★*The Russia Account*
Dugoni, Robert. *The Eighth Sister: A Thriller*
Littell, Robert. *The Company: A Novel of the Cia*
Matthews, Jason. ★*The Kremlin's Candidate*
Matthews, Jason. *Red Sparrow: A Novel*
Ricciardi, David. *Warning Light*
Steinhauer, Olen. ★*All the Old Knives*
Vidich, Paul. *The Coldest Warrior*
Cibola Burn. Corey, James S. A.
★*The **Cider** House Rules: A Novel*. Irving, John
Cilka's Journey. Morris, Heather
CINCINNATI, OHIO
Draper, Sharon M. ★*Forged by Fire*
Sittenfeld, Curtis. *Eligible: A Novel*
CINEMATOGRAPHERS
Smith, Dominic. ★*The Electric Hotel*
Cinnamon Skin: The Twentieth Adventure of Travis McGee. MacDonald, John D.
Ciotta, Beth
Her Sky Cowboy
Cipri, Nino
Defekt
★*Circe*. Miller, Madeline
*The **Circle***. Eggers, Dave
Circle of Friends. Binchy, Maeve
Circle of Shadows. Robertson, Imogen
Circling the Sun. McLain, Paula
*The **Circular** Staircase*. Rinehart, Mary Roberts

CIRCUS

Littlejohn, Emily. *Inherit the Bones*
Mayer, Mark. *Aerialists: Stories*
Morgenstern, Erin. ★*The Night Circus: A Novel*
Sayers, Constance. *The Ladies of the Secret Circus*
Valentine, Genevieve. *Mechanique: A Tale of the Circus Tresaulti*
Wright, Jaime Jo. *The Haunting at Bonaventure Circus*

CIRCUS PERFORMERS

Gruen, Sara. ★*Water for Elephants: A Novel*
Smith, Michael F. *The Fighter: A Novel*
Valentine, Genevieve. *Mechanique: A Tale of the Circus Tresaulti*

Cisneros, Sandra

★*The House on Mango Street*
Martita, I Remember You: Martita, Te Recuerdo

Citadel. Cronin, A. J.
The Citadel of the Autarch. Wolfe, Gene

CITIES AND TOWNS

Calvino, Italo. *Invisible Cities*
Cole, Teju. *Every Day Is for the Thief*
Jemisin, N. K. ★*The City We Became*
Lee, Fonda. ★*Jade City*
Lu, S. Qiouyi. *In the Watchful City*
Patterson, Richard North. *Dark Lady*
Rutherfurd, Edward. *Paris*
Smith, Gregory Blake. ★*The Maze at Windermere: A Novel*
Stout, Dan. ★*Titanshade*
Wilder, Thornton. ★*Theophilus North*

Cities of refuge [Series]. Cossette, Connilyn
Cities of the Interior. Nin, Anais
★*The City & The City*. Mieville, China

CITY COUNCIL MEMBERS

Rowling, J. K. *The Casual Vacancy*

CITY DWELLERS

Lahiri, Jhumpa. ★*Whereabouts*
Zaman, Nadeem. *Up in the Main House & Other Stories*

★*The City in the Middle of the Night*. Anders, Charlie Jane

CITY LIFE

Algren, Nelson. ★*The Man with the Golden Arm: A Novel*
Algren, Nelson. *A Walk on the Wild Side*
Andreades, Daphne Palasi. *Brown Girls*
Belli, Kate. *Deception by Gaslight: A Gilded Gotham Mystery*
Bellow, Saul. ★*Mr. Sammler's Planet*
Bennett, Robert Jackson. *Foundryside*
Bennett, Robert Jackson. *Shorefall*
Beukes, Lauren. *Broken Monsters*
Boyle, William. *City of Margins: A Novel*
Brandt, Harry. *The Whites: A Novel*
Braun, Lilian Jackson. *The Cat Who Ate Danish Modern*
Burke, Marcus. *Team Seven*
Chatterjee, Upamanyu. *English, August: An Indian Story*
Chung, Maxine Mei-Fung. *The Eighth Girl*
Clark, Clare. *In the Full Light of the Sun*
Clark, Wahida. *Honor Thy Thug*
Clark, Wahida. *Justify My Thug: A Novel*
Clark, Wahida. *Thugs*
Cole, Teju. *Every Day Is for the Thief*
Crane, Stephen. *Maggie: A Girl of the Streets*
Cunningham, Michael. *Specimen Days*

Danler, Stephanie. *Sweetbitter*
Dickens, Charles. *Our Mutual Friend*
Dos Passos, John. *Manhattan Transfer*
Ellis, Bret Easton. *Imperial Bedrooms*
Eugenides, Jeffrey. ★*Middlesex*
Gunaratne, Guy. *In Our Mad and Furious City*
Hand, Elizabeth. *Curious Toys*
Isherwood, Christopher. ★*The Berlin Stories: The Last of Mr. Norris, Goodbye to Berlin*
Johnson, Alaya Dawn. *Trouble the Saints*
Joyce, James. ★*Ulysses*
Lahiri, Jhumpa. ★*Whereabouts*
Lee, Jonathan. *The Great Mistake*
Macneal, Elizabeth. *The Doll Factory*
Mieville, China. ★*The City & The City*
Pamuk, Orhan. ★*A Strangeness in My Mind: A Novel*
Park, Ishle Yi. *Angel & Hannah: A Novel in Verse*
Park, Sang Young. ★*Love in the Big City: A Novel*
Perry, Anne. ★*Death with a Double Edge: A Daniel Pitt Novel*
Rash, Ron. *Something Rich and Strange: Selected Stories*
Robinson, Kim Stanley. *New York 2140*
Rooney, Kathleen. ★*Lillian Boxfish Takes a Walk*
Rutherfurd, Edward. *London*
Rutherfurd, Edward. *Paris*
Sapphire. *American Dreams*
Sears, Michael. *Tower of Babel*
Senna, Danzy. *New People*
Shoham, Liad. *Asylum City: A Novel*
Shupe, Joanna. *The Rogue of Fifth Avenue*
Sister Souljah. ★*The Coldest Winter Ever: A Novel*
Smith, Betty. ★*A Tree Grows in Brooklyn*
Smith, Zadie. ★*Nw: A Novel*
Urquhart, Jane. *The Night Stages: A Novel*
Urrea, Luis Alberto. *Into the Beautiful North: A Novel*
Washington, Bryan. *Lot: Stories*
Whitehead, Colson. *Apex Hides the Hurt*
Whitehead, Colson. ★*Harlem Shuffle*
Whitehead, Colson. *The Intuitionist*
Wilder, Thornton. ★*Theophilus North*
Wolfe, Tom. *The Bonfire of the Vanities*
Yanagihara, Hanya. *A Little Life: A Novel*
Yu, Miri. *Tokyo Ueno Station*
Zaman, Nadeem. *Up in the Main House & Other Stories*

The City of Brass. Chakraborty, S. A.
City of Dark Corners. Talton, Jon
City of dark magic [Series]. Flyte, Magnus
City of Dark Magic: A Novel. Flyte, Magnus
City of Endless Night. Preston, Douglas J.
★*City of Girls*. Gilbert, Elizabeth
City of Ink: A Mystery. Hart, Elsa
City of Lost Dreams: A Novel. Flyte, Magnus
The City of Lost Fortunes. Camp, Bryan
City of Margins: A Novel. Boyle, William
The City of Mirrors. Cronin, Justin
The City of Tears. Mosse, Kate
City of Thieves: A Novel. Benioff, David
City of Windows. Pobi, Robert
City of Women. Gillham, David R.

The **City** of Your Final Destination. Cameron, Peter
★**City** on Fire. Hallberg, Garth Risk
City on the Edge. Swinson, David
★The **City** We Became. Jemisin, N. K.

CIVIL DISOBEDIENCE
    Fallada, Hans. *Every Man Dies Alone*

CIVIL ENGINEERS
    Harris, Robert. *Pompeii: A Novel*

CIVIL RIGHTS
    Lehane, Dennis. ★*The Given Day*

CIVIL RIGHTS MOVEMENT
    Campbell, Bebe Moore. *Your Blues Ain't Like Mine*
    Collins, Kathleen. *Notes from a Black Woman's Diary: Selected Works of Kathleen Collins*
    Collins, Kathleen. ★*Whatever Happened to Interracial Love?: Stories*
    Follett, Ken. *Edge of Eternity*
    Hill, Donna. ★*Confessions in B-Flat*
    Kowal, Mary Robinette. *The Fated Sky: A Lady Astronaut Novel*

CIVIL RIGHTS WORKERS
    Hill, Donna. ★*Confessions in B-Flat*

CIVIL SERVICE
    Chatterjee, Upamanyu. *English, August: An Indian Story*

CIVIL SERVICE WORKERS
    Deb, Siddhartha. *The Point of Return: A Novel*
    Fforde, Jasper. ★*Early Riser: A Novel*
    Marske, Freya. *A Marvellous Light*

CIVIL WAR
    Ackerman, Elliot. *Dark at the Crossing*
    Adichie, Chimamanda Ngozi. *Half of a Yellow Sun*
    Al Rawi, Shahad. *The Baghdad Clock*
    Arudpragasam, Anuk. *The Story of a Brief Marriage*
    Bacigalupi, Paolo. ★*The Windup Girl*
    Bear, Elizabeth. *Range of Ghosts*
    Bear, Elizabeth. *Shattered Pillars*
    Clark, P. Djeli. *The Black God's Drums*
    Cole, Alyssa. ★*A Hope Divided*
    Couto, Mia. *Rain: And Other Stories*
    Couto, Mia. *Sleepwalking Land*
    Craig, Charmaine. *Miss Burma*
    Crane, Stephen. ★*The Red Badge of Courage: An Episode of the American Civil War*
    Eggers, Dave. *What Is the What: The Autobiography of Valentino Achak Deng*
    El Akkad, Omar. *American War*
    Faye, Gael. ★*Small Country: A Novel*
    Frazier, Charles. *Varina*
    Hage, Rawi. *De Niro's Game*
    Hamid, Mohsin. ★*Exit West: A Novel*
    Harris, C. S. *Good Time Coming*
    Kantor, MacKinlay. ★*Andersonville*
    Khalfah, Khlid. *Death Is Hard Work: A Novel*
    Lockridge, Ross Franklin. *Raintree County*
    Marias, Javier. *Thus Bad Begins: A Novel*
    Marra, Anthony. ★*A Constellation of Vital Phenomena: A Novel*
    Mohamed, Nadifa. *The Orchard of Lost Souls: A Novel*
    O'Dell, Claire. *A Study in Honor: A Novel*
    Okparanta, Chinelo. ★*Under the Udala Trees*

    Olmstead, Robert. ★*Coal Black Horse*
    Pasternak, Boris Leonidovich. ★*Doctor Zhivago*
    Reed, Ishmael. *Flight to Canada*
    Roy, Lucinda. *The Freedom Race*
    Saylor, Steven. *A Mist of Prophecies*
    Saylor, Steven. *Rubicon*
    Shaara, Jeff. *The Last Full Measure*
    Shaara, Michael. ★*The Killer Angels: A Novel*
    Thelen, Albert Vigoleis. *The Island of Second Sight: From the Applied Recollections of Vigoleis*

CIVIL WAR — POST-WAR ASPECTS
    Alarcon, Daniel. *At Night We Walk in Circles: A Novel*
Civil War trilogy (Jeff Shaara) [Series]. Shaara, Jeff

CIVIL WAR VETERANS
    Barry, Sebastian. ★*A Thousand Moons: A Novel*
    Estleman, Loren D. ★*The Master Executioner*
    Green, Jocelyn. *Veiled in Smoke*
    Jenkins, Beverly. *Forbidden*
    McGuire, Ian. *The Abstainer: A Novel*
    Pearl, Matthew. *The Technologists: A Novel*

CIVILIAN CONSERVATION CORPS
    Barnett, Karen. *Ever Faithful*

CIVILIANS IN WAR
    Spufford, Francis. ★*Light Perpetual*

CIVILIZATION
    Khoury, Raymond. *Empire of Lies*
    McCormack, Mike. ★*Solar Bones*
    Stirling, S. M. *The Protector's War*

CIVILIZATION, ANCIENT
    Corby, Gary. *The Marathon Conspiracy*
    Harris, Robert. *Pompeii: A Novel*
    Saylor, Steven. *Wrath of the Furies: A Novel of the Ancient World*
    Walton, Jo. ★*Necessity*

CIVILIZATION, CELTIC
    Pike, Signe. *The Forgotten Kingdom: A Novel*
    Pike, Signe. *The Lost Queen*

CIVILIZATION, MEDIEVAL
    Follett, Ken. ★*The Evening and the Morning*
    Griffith, Nicola. *Hild: A Novel*
    Harris, Robert. *The Second Sleep: A Novel*
    Hesse, Hermann. *Narcissus and Goldmund*
    Lin, Jeannie. *The Lotus Palace*
    Penman, Sharon Kay. *Here Be Dragons*
    Penman, Sharon Kay. *When Christ and His Saints Slept*
    Robb, Candace M. *The Cross-Legged Knight: An Owen Archer Mystery*
    Robb, Candace M. *A Gift of Sanctuary: An Owen Archer Mystery*
    Robb, Candace M. *The Riddle of St. Leonard's: An Owen Archer Mystery.*
    Sharratt, Mary. *Illuminations: A Novel of Hildegard Von Bingen*
    Walters, Minette. *The Last Hours: A Novel*
    Willis, Connie. ★*Doomsday Book*

CIVILIZATION, WESTERN
    Mann, Thomas. *The Magic Mountain*
Civilizations. Binet, Laurent
Claire Dewitt and the City of the Dead. Gran, Sara
Claire DeWitt mysteries [Series]. Gran, Sara
Claire of the Sea Light. Danticat, Edwidge

CLAIRVOYANCE
Lim, Roselle. *Vanessa Yu's Magical Paris Tea Shop*
Shannon, Samantha. *The Bone Season*
Shannon, Samantha. *The Mime Order*
*The **Clairvoyants**: a Novel*. Brown, Karen
★*The **Clan** of the Cave Bear: A Novel*. Auel, Jean M.
Clancy, Tom
Clear and Present Danger
★*The Hunt for Red October*
Patriot Games
Clandestine affairs [Series]. Quincy, Diana
CLANS
Chen, Qiufan. *Waste Tide*
Gabaldon, Diana. ★*Outlander*
Jordan, Sophie. *This Scot of Mine*
Makumbi, Jennifer Nansubuga. *Kintu*
Roanhorse, Rebecca. ★*Black Sun*
Clare, Alys
The Woman Who Spoke to Spirits
★*Clarissa, Or, the History of a Young Lady*. Richardson, Samuel
★*Clark and Division*. Hirahara, Naomi
Clark, Cherae
★*The Unbroken*
Clark, Clare
In the Full Light of the Sun
Clark, Georgia
The Bucket List
Clark, Julie
Last Flight
Clark, Marcia
Final Judgment
Clark, Martin
The Substitution Order
Clark, Mary Higgins
Death Wears a Beauty Mask and Other Stories
★*Kiss the Girls and Make Them Cry*
The Melody Lingers On
Clark, P. Djeli
The Black God's Drums
Ring Shout
Clark, Tracy P.
Runner
What You Don't See
Clark, Wahida
Blood, Sweat and Payback
Honor Thy Thug
Justify My Thug: A Novel
Payback Ain't Enough
★*Payback Is a Mutha*
Payback with Ya Life
Thug Lovin'
Thug Matrimony
Thugs
★*Thugs and the Women Who Love Them*
Clarke, Arthur C.
★*2001: A Space Odyssey*
★*Childhood's End*
★*The Collected Stories of Arthur C. Clarke*
Rendezvous with Rama
Clarke, Brock
An Arsonist's Guide to Writers' Homes in New England: A Novel
Clarke, Diana
Thin Girls
Clarke, Maxine Beneba
★*Foreign Soil*
Clarke, Susanna
★*Jonathan Strange & Mr. Norrell*
★*Piranesi*
★*A **Clash** of Kings*. Martin, George R. R.
CLASS CONFLICT
Adiga, Aravind. ★*The White Tiger: A Novel*
Brown, Pierce. *Morning Star*
Burke, James Lee. *The Jealous Kind*
Cho, Zen. *Sorcerer to the Crown*
Everett, Percival L. *I Am Not Sidney Poitier*
Ganshert, Katie. ★*No One Ever Asked: A Novel*
Gaskell, Elizabeth Cleghorn. ★*North and South*
Guterson, David. *The Other*
Holsinger, Bruce W. *The Gifted School: A Novel*
Hoyt, Elizabeth. *When a Rogue Meets His Match*
Kadrey, Richard. *The Grand Dark*
Kohnstamm, Thomas B. *Lake City*
Naipaul, V. S. *Guerrillas*
Pitoniak, Anna. *Necessary People*
Ripley, Mike. *Mr Campion's Fault*
Schwartz, John Burnham. *The Commoner: A Novel*
Tepper, Sheri S. *Singer from the Sea*
Vargas Llosa, Mario. *The Dream of the Celt*
Wells, H. G. ★*The Time Machine*
Winter, Evan. *The Fires of Vengeance*
Winter, Evan. ★*The Rage of Dragons*
Zaman, Nadeem. *Up in the Main House & Other Stories*
CLASS CONSCIOUSNESS
Gunesekera, Romesh. ★*Suncatcher: A Novel*
Class Mom [Series]. Gelman, Laurie
Class Mom: A Novel. Gelman, Laurie
CLASS REUNIONS
Lipman, Elinor. *Good Riddance*
McCrumb, Sharyn. ★*If Ever I Return, Pretty Peggy-O*
Sayers, Dorothy L. ★*Gaudy Night*
CLASS STRUGGLE
Boyle, T. Coraghessan. *World's End: A Novel*
Shin, Ann. *The Last Exiles*
Zola, Emile. ★*Germinal*
CLASSICAL MUSIC INDUSTRY AND TRADE
Lovesey, Peter. *The Tooth Tattoo*
CLASSICS
Adams, Richard. *Watership Down*
Allen, Jane. *I Lost My Girlish Laughter*
Austen, Jane. ★*Emma*
Austen, Jane. *Mansfield Park*
Austen, Jane. *Northanger Abbey*
Austen, Jane. ★*Persuasion*
Austen, Jane. ★*Pride and Prejudice*
Austen, Jane. ★*Sense and Sensibility*
Balzac, Honore de. *Eugenie Grandet*

Blackmore, R. D. *Lorna Doone: A Romance of Exmoor*
Bronte, Anne. *The Tenant of Wildfell Hall*
Bronte, Charlotte. ★*Emma*
Bronte, Charlotte. ★*Jane Eyre*
Bronte, Emily. ★*Wuthering Heights*
Buchan, John. *The Thirty-Nine Steps*
Camus, Albert. ★*The Fall*
Cather, Willa. ★*Death Comes for the Archbishop*
Cather, Willa. *O Pioneers!*
Cervantes Saavedra, Miguel de. ★*Don Quixote*
Cisneros, Sandra. ★*The House on Mango Street*
Conrad, Joseph. *Complete Short Fiction of Joseph Conrad: The Stories: Volume 1*
Conrad, Joseph. ★*Heart of Darkness*
Conrad, Joseph. ★*Lord Jim*
Conrad, Joseph. *Nostromo: A Tale of the Seaboard*
Conrad, Joseph. *Victory: An Island Tale*
Defoe, Daniel. ★*Moll Flanders*
Dickens, Charles. ★*Bleak House*
Dickens, Charles. ★*A Christmas Carol*
Dickens, Charles. *Dombey and Son*
Dickens, Charles. *Little Dorrit*
Dickens, Charles. *The Old Curiosity Shop*
Dickens, Charles. *Oliver Twist, or the Parish Boy's Progress*
Dickens, Charles. *The Pickwick Papers*
Dickens, Charles. ★*A Tale of Two Cities*
Dostoyevsky, Fyodor. *The Best Short Stories of Dostoevsky*
Dostoyevsky, Fyodor. ★*The Brothers Karamazov*
Dostoyevsky, Fyodor. ★*Crime and Punishment*
Doyle, Arthur Conan. ★*The Complete Sherlock Holmes*
Doyle, Arthur Conan. ★*The Hound of the Baskervilles*
Dreiser, Theodore. ★*An American Tragedy*
Dreiser, Theodore. ★*Sister Carrie*
Dumas, Alexandre. ★*Camille*
Eliot, George. ★*Adam Bede*
Eliot, George. ★*Middlemarch: A Study of Provincial Life*
Fielding, Henry. ★*The History of Tom Jones, a Foundling*
Flaubert, Gustave. *Sentimental Education*
Ford, Ford Madox. ★*The Good Soldier: A Tale of Passion*
Gaskell, Elizabeth Cleghorn. ★*Cranford*
Gilman, Charlotte Perkins. ★*The Yellow Wallpaper and Selected Writings*
Godden, Rumer. *The Greengage Summer: A Novel*
Gogol, Nikolai Vasilievich. ★*Dead Souls*
Hardy, Thomas. ★*Far from the Madding Crowd*
Hardy, Thomas. ★*Jude the Obscure*
Hardy, Thomas. ★*The Return of the Native*
Hawthorne, Nathaniel. ★*The Scarlet Letter: A Romance*
Hilton, James. ★*Good-Bye, Mr. Chips*
Hilton, James. ★*Lost Horizon: A Novel*
Hugo, Victor. ★*Les Miserables*
Jackson, Shirley. ★*The Lottery: And Other Stories*
James, Henry. *Complete Stories, 1874-1884*
James, Henry. *Complete Stories, 1884-1891*
James, Henry. *Complete Stories, 1892-1898*
James, Henry. *Complete Stories, 1898-1910*
James, Henry. *Daisy Miller*
James, Henry. *The Golden Bowl*

James, Henry. *The Wings of the Dove*
London, Jack. ★*The Call of the Wild*
London, Jack. *Martin Eden*
Maturin, Charles Robert. *Melmoth the Wanderer: A Tale*
Melville, Herman. *The Complete Shorter Fiction*
Melville, Herman. *The Confidence-Man: His Masquerade*
Poe, Edgar Allan. *The Narrative of Arthur Gordon Pym of Nantucket*
Pontoppidan, Henrik. *Lucky Per*
Proust, Marcel. ★*Remembrance of Things Past*
Proust, Marcel. *Time Regained*
Pym, Barbara. ★*Excellent Women*
Radcliffe, ANN Ward. ★*The Mysteries of Udolpho*
Richardson, Samuel. ★*Clarissa, Or, the History of a Young Lady*
Richardson, Samuel. ★*Pamela: Or, Virtue Rewarded*
Scott, Walter. *The Bride of Lammermoor*
Scott, Walter. ★*Rob Roy*
Sinclair, Upton. ★*The Jungle*
Stevenson, Robert Louis. ★*The Strange Case of Dr. Jekyll and Mr. Hyde*
Stowe, Harriet Beecher. ★*Uncle Tom's Cabin*
Tolstoy, Leo. ★*Anna Karenina*
Tolstoy, Leo. ★*War and Peace*
Trollope, Anthony. ★*Barchester Towers*
Trollope, Anthony. *Doctor Thorne*
Trollope, Anthony. ★*The Eustace Diamonds*
Trollope, Anthony. *Framley Parsonage*
Trollope, Anthony. *The Last Chronicle of Barset*
Trollope, Anthony. ★*The Prime Minister*
Trollope, Anthony. *The Warden*
Turgenev, Ivan Sergeevich. ★*Fathers and Sons*
Twain, Mark. ★*A Connecticut Yankee in King Arthur's Court*
Twain, Mark. *Personal Recollections of Joan of Arc*
Twain, Mark. *Pudd'nhead Wilson ;: And, Those Extraordinary Twins*
Verne, Jules. ★*Around the World in Eighty Days*
Verne, Jules. ★*Journey to the Centre of the Earth*
Wells, H. G. ★*The Invisible Man*
Wells, H. G. ★*The Island of Dr. Moreau*
Wells, H. G. ★*The Time Machine*
Wells, H. G. ★*The War of the Worlds*
Wilde, Oscar. ★*The Picture of Dorian Gray*
Zola, Emile. ★*Germinal*
Zola, Emile. ★*Nana*

CLASSISM
Austen, Jane. ★*Persuasion*
Dev, Sonali. ★*Pride, Prejudice, and Other Flavors: A Novel*
Dickens, Charles. ★*A Tale of Two Cities*
Fitzgerald, F. Scott. ★*This Side of Paradise*
Forster, E. M. ★*Howards End*
Forster, E. M. ★*A Room with a View*
Golding, William. *Close Quarters*
Golding, William. *Fire Down Below*
Hardy, Thomas. ★*Far from the Madding Crowd*
Lipsyte, Sam. *The Ask*
Rendell, Ruth. ★*A Judgement in Stone*
Trollope, Anthony. *Framley Parsonage*
Trollope, Anthony. *The Last Chronicle of Barset*
Updike, John. *Brazil: A Novel*
Willocks, Tim. *Memo from Turner*

CLASSISM — HISTORY
Dickens, Charles. ★*Great Expectations*
CLAUDINE (FICTITIOUS CHARACTER : COLETTE)
Colette. *The Complete Claudine*
CLAUDIUS
Graves, Robert. *Claudius the God and His Wife Messalina: The Troublesome Reign of Tiberius Claudius Caesar, Emperor*
Graves, Robert. ★*I, Claudius: From the Autobiography of Tiberius Claudius, Born 10 B.C., Murdered and Deified A.D. 54*
Claudius the God and His Wife Messalina: The Troublesome Reign of Tiberius Claudius Caesar, Emperor. Graves, Robert
CLAUSTROPHOBIA
Petrie, Nicholas. *The Drifter*
Clavell, James
Shogun
*The **Claw** of the Conciliator*. Wolfe, Gene
★***Claws** of the Cat: A Shinobi Mystery*. Spann, Susan
Clay Edison novels [Series]. Kellerman, Jonathan
CLAY, MARCUS (FICTITIOUS CHARACTER)
Pelecanos, George P. *The Big Blowdown*
Clayborn, Kate
Love Lettering
Clayton, Meg Waite
The Last Train to London
Cleage, Pearl
Some Things I Never Thought I'd Do
What Looks Like Crazy on an Ordinary Day: A Novel
Cleanness. Greenwell, Garth
Clear and Present Danger. Clancy, Tom
Clear Light of Day. Desai, Anita
Clear My Name. Daly, Paula
Cleary, Jon
The Sundowners
Cleave, Chris
Gold
Cleave, Paul
A Killer Harvest: A Thriller
Trust No One: A Thriller
Cleeton, Chanel
The Most Beautiful Girl in Cuba
Next Year in Havana
Cleeves, Ann
The Crow Trap
The Darkest Evening
★*The Heron's Cry*
The Long Call
Raven Black
Thin Air
Wild Fire
CLEFT PALATE
Harris, Thomas. *Red Dragon*
Clegg, Bill
Did You Ever Have a Family
The End of the Day
Cleland, Jane K.
Hidden Treasure
CLEMENC, ANA K.
Fisher, Tarryn. *The Wives*

Russell, Mary Doria. *The Women of the Copper Country: A Novel*
Clement, Jennifer
Gun Love
Clementine. Priest, Cherie
Clements, Oliver
The Eyes of the Queen
The Queen's Men
Clemmons, Zinzi
What We Lose
CLEOPATRA
Saylor, Steven. *The Judgment of Caesar: A Novel of Ancient Rome*
CLERGY
Akunin, B. *Sister Pelagia and the White Bulldog: A Mystery*
Alexander, V. S. *The Magdalen Girls*
Cronin, Marianne. *The One Hundred Years of Lenni and Margot*
Davidson, Andy. *The Boatman's Daughter: A Novel*
Faber, Michel. *The Book of Strange New Things*
Franzen, Jonathan. ★*Crossroads*
Golding, William. *Rites of Passage*
Harrison, Cora. *Beyond Absolution: A Mystery Set in 1920s Ireland*
Harrison, Mette Ivie. *The Prodigal Daughter*
Iggulden, Conn. *The Abbot's Tale*
Jones, Robert. ★*The Prophets: A Novel*
Kate, Jessica. *A Girl's Guide to the Outback: A Novel*
Lloyd, Catherine. *Death Comes to the Rectory*
Malliet, G. M. *A Demon Summer: A Max Tudor Mystery*
Malliet, G. M. *Pagan Spring: A Mystery*
Penrose, Andrea. *Murder on Black Swan Lane*
Perry, Sarah. *The Essex Serpent*
Robinson, Marilynne. *Home*
Robinson, Marilynne. ★*Lila*
Sebastian, Cat. *It Takes Two to Tumble*
Trollope, Anthony. ★*Barchester Towers*
Trollope, Anthony. *The Warden*
Wall, Cara. *The Dearly Beloved: A Novel*
CLERGY — HISTORY
Trollope, Anthony. *Framley Parsonage*
*The **Clergyman's** Wife*. Greeley, Molly
CLERGYMEN
Block, Lawrence. *The Sins of the Fathers*
Bohjalian, Chris. *Secrets of Eden: A Novel*
Leigh, Eva. *Temptations of a Wallflower*
Paton, Alan. ★*Cry, the Beloved Country*
Runcie, James. *Sidney Chambers and the Forgiveness of Sins*
Runcie, James. *Sidney Chambers and the Perils of the Night*
Runcie, James. *Sidney Chambers and the Persistence of Love*
Runcie, James. *Sidney Chambers and the Problem of Evil*
Runcie, James. *Sidney Chambers and the Shadow of Death*
CLERGYMEN CHILD SEXUAL ABUSERS
Ólafsson, Ólafur Jóhann. *The Sacrament: A Novel*
CLERGYWOMEN
Eliot, George. ★*Adam Bede*
McPherson, Catriona. *Strangers at the Gate*
Spencer-Fleming, Julia. *Hid from Our Eyes*
Spencer-Fleming, Julia. *In the Bleak Midwinter*
Spencer-Fleming, Julia. *Through the Evil Days: A Clare Fergusson/Russ Van Alstyne Mystery*

CLERKS (RETAIL INDUSTRY AND TRADE)
Cipri, Nino. *Defekt*
Martin, Steve. *Shopgirl*
CLEVELAND, OHIO
Black, Lisa. *Let Justice Descend*
Black, Lisa. *Suffer the Children*
Black, Lisa. *That Darkness*
Logan, Kylie. *The Secrets of Bones: A Mystery*
Ng, Celeste. ★*Little Fires Everywhere: A Novel*
Satyal, Rakesh. *No One Can Pronounce My Name: A Novel*
Clever Girl. Hadley, Tessa
The *Client*. Grisham, John
The *Cliff* House. Thayne, RaeAnne
CLIMACTERIC, MALE
Lewis, Sinclair. *Dodsworth*
CLIMATE CHANGE
Cook, Diane. ★*The New Wilderness: A Novel*
Egan, Greg. *Perihelion Summer*
Flanagan, Richard. *The Living Sea of Waking Dreams*
Ghosh, Amitav. ★*Gun Island*
Jones, Cynan. *Stillicide*
Lebbon, Tim. *Eden*
Lunde, Maja. *The End of the Ocean: A Novel*
McConaghy, Charlotte. *Migrations*
Reynolds, Alastair. *Permafrost*
Robinson, Kim Stanley. ★*The Ministry for the Future*
Robinson, Kim Stanley. *New York 2140*
Walker, Karen Thompson. *The Age of Miracles: A Novel*
Climate novels [Series]. Lunde, Maja
Clinch, Jon
Finn: A Novel
Marley: A Novel
Cline, Emma
Daddy: Stories
The Girls: A Novel
Cline, Ernest
Ready Player One: A Novel
Cline, Rachel
My Liar: A Novel
CLINICAL PSYCHOLOGISTS
Robotham, Michael. ★*Close Your Eyes*
Robotham, Michael. ★*The Other Wife*
Robotham, Michael. ★*Say You're Sorry*
CLINICAL TRIALS
Kurian, Vera. *Never Saw Me Coming*
CLINICS
Waldman, Amy. *A Door in the Earth*
CLINTON, HILLARY RODHAM
Sittenfeld, Curtis. *Rodham: A Novel*
CLIQUES
French, Tana. ★*The Secret Place*
Laskowski, Tara. *The Mother Next Door*
Tartt, Donna. ★*The Secret History*
Ware, Ruth. *The Lying Game*
CLITORIDECTOMY
Walker, Alice. *Possessing the Secret of Joy*
★*Clock Dance: A Novel*. Tyler, Anne
Clockers. Price, Richard

CLOCKS AND WATCHES
Pulley, Natasha. *The Lost Future of Pepperharrow*
Pulley, Natasha. *The Watchmaker of Filigree Street*
CLOCKS AND WATCHES — REPAIRING AND ADJUSTING
Harkaway, Nick. *Angelmaker*
Clockwork century [Series]. Priest, Cherie
The *Clockwork* Dynasty: A Novel. Wilson, Daniel H.
★*A Clockwork Orange*. Burgess, Anthony
CLONES AND CLONING
Afifi, Nadia. *The Sentient*
Hamilton, Peter F. *Great North Road*
Ishiguro, Kazuo. ★*Never Let Me Go*
Lafferty, Mur. *Six Wakes*
Levin, Ira. *The Boys from Brazil: A Novel*
Vinge, Joan D. *The Snow Queen*
Wilhelm, Kate. *Where Late the Sweet Birds Sang*
CLONES AND CLONING — MORAL AND ETHICAL ASPECTS
Gailey, Sarah. *The Echo Wife*
Close Quarters. Golding, William
Close to Home. Robinson, Peter
Close Up. Quick, Amanda
★*Close Your Eyes*. Robotham, Michael
A *Closed and Common Orbit*. Chambers, Becky
Closer Than You Know. Parks, Brad
CLOSETED GAY MEN
Persaud, Ingrid. *Love After Love: A Novel*
Pufahl, Shannon. *On Swift Horses*
Roberts, Bethan. ★*My Policeman*
Spencer, Scott. *An Ocean Without a Shore*
Statovci, Pajtim. *Bolla*
Toibin, Colm. ★*The Magician: A Novel*
CLOSETED LESBIANS
Williams, Eley. *The Liar's Dictionary*
The *Clothesline* Swing. Ramadan, Ahmad Danny
CLOTHING
Donoghue, Emma. *Slammerkin*
CLOTHING INDUSTRY AND TRADE
Steel, Danielle. *First Sight*
★*Cloud Atlas: A Novel*. Mitchell, David
★*Cloud Cuckoo Land: A Novel*. Doerr, Anthony
★*Cloudbursts: Collected and New Stories*. McGuane, Thomas
★*Clouds of Witness*. Sayers, Dorothy L.
Cloudsplitter: a Novel. Banks, Russell
The *Clover Girls*. Shipman, Viola
The *Clown*. Boll, Heinrich
CLOWNS
Bailey, Tessa. *Fix Her Up*
King, Stephen. *It*
Rushdie, Salman. *Shalimar the Clown: A Novel*
The *Club* Dumas. Perez-Reverte, Arturo
CLUBFOOT MEN
Maugham, W. Somerset. ★*Of Human Bondage*
CLUBS
Berg, Elizabeth. *The Confession Club: A Novel*
Groen, Hendrik. *On the Bright Side: The New Secret Diary of Hendrik Groen, 85 Years Old*
Harbison, Beth. *The Cookbook Club*
Osman, Richard. ★*The Thursday Murder Club*

Williams, Lara. *Supper Club: A Novel*

CLUES

Barclay, Linwood. *Parting Shot*

Barclay, Linwood. *The Twenty-Three: A Promise Falls Novel*

Harris, Sarah J. *The Color of Bee Larkham's Murder: A Novel*

Preston, Douglas J. *City of Endless Night*

Preston, Douglas J. *The Obsidian Chamber*

Pulley, Natasha. ★*The Kingdoms*

Racculia, Kate. ★*Tuesday Mooney Talks to Ghosts: A Novel*

★*Coal Black Horse*. Olmstead, Robert

COAL MINE ACCIDENTS

Coover, Robert. *The Origin of the Brunists: A Novel*

Cussler, Clive. ★*The Titanic Secret*

Smith, Martin Cruz. *Rose*

COAL MINERS

Llewellyn, Richard. ★*How Green Was My Valley*

Montgomery, Jess. *The Widows*

Smith, Martin Cruz. *Rose*

Zola, Emile. ★*Germinal*

COAL MINERS' FAMILIES

Llewellyn, Richard. ★*How Green Was My Valley*

COAL MINES AND MINING

Cussler, Clive. ★*The Titanic Secret*

Russell, Mary Doria. *The Women of the Copper Country: A Novel*

COAL MINING TOWNS

Haigh, Jennifer. *Baker Towers: A Novel*

COASTAL TOWNS

Andrews, Mary Kay. *Sunset Beach*

Atkinson, Kate. ★*Big Sky*

Bannalec, Jean-Luc. *The Killing Tide: A Brittany Mystery*

Beattie, Ann. *The State We're In: Maine Stories*

Carr, Robyn. ★*The Wanderer*

Colgan, Jenny. *Sunrise by the Sea*

Danticat, Edwidge. *Claire of the Sea Light*

Dare, Tessa. ★*A Night to Surrender*

Delinsky, Barbara. *A Week at the Shore*

Doerr, Anthony. ★*All the Light We Cannot See: A Novel*

Donoghue, Emma. *Akin*

Dorey-Stein, Beck. *Rock the Boat: A Novel*

Gates, Eva. *Deadly Ever After*

Harris, Robert. *Pompeii: A Novel*

Holmes, Linda. ★*Evvie Drake Starts Over: A Novel*

Kubica, Mary. ★*The Other Mrs.*

Monroe, Mary Alice. ★*The Summer of Lost and Found*

Nichols, Peter. *The Rocks*

Ono, Masatsugu. *Echo on the Bay*

Pineiro, Caridad. *What Happens in Summer*

Quick, Amanda. *The Other Lady Vanishes*

Shalvis, Jill. *The Sweetest Thing*

Strout, Elizabeth. *Olive Kitteridge*

Strout, Elizabeth. ★*Olive, Again: A Novel*

Thayne, RaeAnne. *The Cliff House*

Truss, Lynne. *The Man That Got Away: A Constable Twitten Mystery*

Truss, Lynne. *Murder by Milk Bottle*

Wallace, Melanie. *The Girl in the Garden*

Watson, S. J. *Final Cut*

COASTS

Owens, Delia. *Where the Crawdads Sing*

Coates, Ta-Nehisi

★*The Water Dancer: A Novel*

Cobb, May K.

The Hunting Wives

Cobble Hill. Von Ziegesar, Cecily

Cobbs Hoffman, Elizabeth

The Hamilton Affair

The Tubman Command: A Novel

Coben, Harlan

★*The Boy from the Woods*

Don't Let Go

Fool Me Once

Hold Tight

Long Lost

Run Away

The Stranger

COCAINE

Blau, Jessica Anya. *The Wonder Bread Summer*

Parks, Brad. *Closer Than You Know*

COCAINE SMUGGLING

MacDonald, John D. ★*The Lonely Silver Rain*

Cochrun, Alison

The Charm Offensive

Cocks, Heather

The Heir Affair

The Royal We

★*Code of Honor*. Cameron, Marc

CODEPENDENCY

Spencer, Scott. *An Ocean Without a Shore*

CODES (COMMUNICATION)

Crowley, John. *Lord Byron's Novel: The Evening Land*

Fleming, Ian. *You Only Live Twice*

Ignatius, David. *The Increment: A Novel*

Rollins, James. *The Eye of God*

Rollins, James. *The Sixth Extinction: A Sigma Force Novel*

Sloan, Robin. *Mr. Penumbra's 24-Hour Bookstore*

Cody Hoyt novels [Series]. Box, C. J.

Coe, Jonathan

The Rotters' Club

Coelho, Paulo

★*The Alchemist*

COERCION

Diachenko, Serhii. *Vita Nostra*

Kerr, Philip. ★*Prussian Blue*

Coes, Ben

The Russian: A Thriller

Coetzee, J. M.

Age of Iron

Disgrace

Elizabeth Costello

★*Foe*

★*Life & Times of Michael K*

Summertime: Scenes from a Provincial Life

COETZEE, J. M.

Coetzee, J. M. *Summertime: Scenes from a Provincial Life*

Mosley, Walter. *Little Scarlet: An Easy Rawlins Mystery*

COFFEE SHOPS

Kawaguchi, Toshikazu. *Before the Coffee Gets Cold*

Moyes, Jojo. *The Peacock Emporium*
Winfrey, Kerry. *Not Like the Movies*
★*The Coffin Dancer.* Deaver, Jeffery

COFFIN, JOHN (FICTITIOUS CHARACTER)

Butler, Gwendoline. *Death Lives Next Door*

Cogman, Genevieve

The Invisible Library
The Masked City

COGNITIVE DISORDERS

Powers, Richard. *The Echo Maker*

COGNITIVE SCIENCE

Doctorow, E. L. *Andrew's Brain*

Cohen, Joshua

Book of Numbers: A Novel

Cohen, Tish

The Summer We Lost Her: A Novel
Coinspinner's Story. Saberhagen, Fred
Cold Barrel Zero. Quirk, Matthew

COLD CASES (CRIMINAL INVESTIGATION)

Adler-Olsen, Jussi. *The Absent One*
Adler-Olsen, Jussi. *A Conspiracy of Faith*
Adler-Olsen, Jussi. *The Hanging Girl*
Adler-Olsen, Jussi. *The Keeper of Lost Causes*
Adler-Olsen, Jussi. *The Purity of Vengeance: A Department Q Novel*
Adler-Olsen, Jussi. *The Scarred Woman*
Atkins, Ace. *The Shameless*
Bannister, Jo. *Kindred Spirits*
Barclay, Linwood. *Far from True: A Novel*
Brundage, Elizabeth. ★*All Things Cease to Appear*
Cantero, Edgar. *Meddling Kids: A Novel*
Child, Lee. *Never Go Back*
Child, Lee. *Worth Dying For*
Clark, Mary Higgins. *The Melody Lingers On*
Connelly, Michael. *The Burning Room*
Connelly, Michael. *Dark Sacred Night*
Connelly, Michael. *The Night Fire*
Cook, Thomas H. *The Fate of Katherine Carr*
Cook, Thomas H. *Instruments of Night*
Cooper, Ellison. *Buried*
Dahl, Julia. *Conviction*
Daugherty, Christi. *The Echo Killing*
Davidson, MaryJanice. *Truth, Lies, and Second Dates*
Dexter, Colin. *The Remorseful Day*
Disher, Garry. *Under the Cold Bright Lights*
Doiron, Paul. *One Last Lie*
Dugoni, Robert. *In Her Tracks*
Dugoni, Robert. *My Sister's Grave*
French, Nicci. *Dark Saturday*
French, Tana. *In the Woods*
Galbraith, Robert. *Lethal White*
Gardner, Lisa. ★*Before She Disappeared: A Novel*
Gardner, Lisa. ★*When You See Me: A Novel*
Goddard, Robert. *Beyond Recall: A Novel*
Goldberg, Lee. *Bone Canyon*
Goldin, Megan. *The Night Swim*
Grebe, Camilla. *After She's Gone: A Novel*
Griffiths, Elly. *The Lantern Men: A Dr. Ruth Galloway Mystery*
Griffiths, Elly. *The Stone Circle*

Harrod-Eagles, Cynthia. *Old Bones*
Hart, Erin. *The Book of Killowen*
Harvey, Michael T. *The Chicago Way*
Harvey, Michael T. *The Fifth Floor*
Heller, Peter. *Celine: A Novel*
Hill Gumbao, Toni. *The Good Suicides: A Thriller*
Iles, Greg. *Natchez Burning: A Novel*
Indriðason, Arnaldur. *The Darkness Knows*
Indriðason, Arnaldur. *Outrage*
Indriðason, Arnaldur. *The Shadow District: A Thriller*
Indriðason, Arnaldur. *Strange Shores: An Inspector Erlendur Novel*
Ishiguro, Kazuo. *When We Were Orphans*
Jewell, Lisa. *Then She Was Gone: A Novel*
Johnston, Tim. *The Current: A Novel*
Kellerman, Jonathan. ★*Half Moon Bay: A Novel*
Kelly, Stephen. *The Wages of Desire: A World War II Mystery*
Kepler, Lars. *The Sandman*
Kwon, Yo-Son. *Lemon*
Lansdale, Joe R. *Devil Red*
Lansdale, Joe R. *Honky Tonk Samurai*
Larsson, Stieg. *The Girl with the Dragon Tattoo*
Lippman, Laura. ★*After I'm Gone*
Lippman, Laura. *What the Dead Know*
Lippman, Laura. *Wilde Lake*
Lovesey, Peter. *Beau Death*
Lutz, Lisa. *The Spellman Files: A Novel*
Mayor, Archer. ★*Marked Man*
McDermid, Val. *The Distant Echo*
McDermid, Val. ★*Still Life*
McPherson, Catriona. *Scot & Soda*
Patterson, James. ★*Private*
Persson, Leif G. W. *The Dying Detective: A Mystery*
Persson, Leif G. W. *Free Falling, as If in a Dream: The Story of a Crime*
Rademacher, Cay. *Deadly Camargue: A Provence Mystery*
Rankin, Ian. *The Black Book*
Rankin, Ian. ★*Rather Be the Devil*
Robertson, Michael. *The Baker Street Letters*
Rosenfelt, David. *Black and Blue: A Doug Brock Thriller*
Roslund, Anders. ★*Knock Knock*
Roy, Lori. *Bent Road*
Sandford, John. *Buried Prey*
Scoppettone, Sandra. *My Sweet Untraceable You*
Shaw, William. *A Song for the Brokenhearted*
Slaughter, Karin. *The Good Daughter*
Slaughter, Karin. ★*The Silent Wife*
Spencer, Sally. *Dead End*
Spencer, Sally. ★*Echoes of the Dead*
Steiner, Susie. ★*Persons Unknown: A Novel*
Straub, Peter. ★*Mystery*
Tallo, Katie. *Dark August*
Thomas, Russ. ★*Firewatching*
Thomas, Russ. *Nighthawking*
Walker, Martin. *The Coldest Case*
Cold Country: A Novel. Rowland, Russell
The Cold Eye. Gilman, Laura Anne
Cold Granite. MacBride, Stuart
Cold in Hand. Harvey, John

Cold Is the Grave. Robinson, Peter
★*Cold Mountain.* Frazier, Charles
Cold Sassy series [Series]. Burns, Olive Ann
★*Cold Sassy Tree.* Burns, Olive Ann
*The **Cold** Six Thousand: A Novel.* Ellroy, James
Cold storage novels [Series]. Straley, John
Cold Storage: A Novel. Koepp, David
COLD WAR
    Deighton, Len. *Berlin Game*
    DeLillo, Don. *Underworld*
    Dunmore, Helen. *Exposure*
    Fesperman, Dan. *Safe Houses: A Novel*
    Le Carre, John. ★*The Honourable Schoolboy*
    Le Carre, John. *The Spy Who Came in from the Cold*
    Lem, Stanislaw. *His Master's Voice*
    Littell, Robert. *The Company: A Novel of the Cia*
    Mallon, Thomas. *Finale: A Novel*
    Mankell, Henning. *The Troubled Man*
    Pitoniak, Anna. ★*Our American Friend*
    Tanabe, Karin. ★*A Woman of Intelligence*
    Uris, Leon. *Armageddon: A Novel of Berlin*
    Wilkinson, Lauren. ★*American Spy: A Novel*
Cold-Hearted Rake. Kleypas, Lisa
*A **Colder** War.* Cumming, Charles
*The **Coldest** Case.* Walker, Martin
*The **Coldest** Warrior.* Vidich, Paul
Coldest winter ever [Series]. Sister Souljah
★*The **Coldest** Winter Ever: A Novel.* Sister Souljah
Coldsmith, Don
    Tallgrass: A Novel of the Great Plains
Cole, Alyssa
    ★*A Duke by Default*
    ★*An Extraordinary Union*
    ★*A Hope Divided*
    ★*How to Catch a Queen*
    How to Find a Princess
    ★*A Prince on Paper*
    ★*A Princess in Theory*
    ★*An Unconditional Freedom*
COLE, NAT
    Howard, Ravi. *Driving the King: A Novel*
Cole, Teju
    Every Day Is for the Thief
    ★*Open City: A Novel*
Coleman, Reed Farrel
    Where It Hurts: A Gus Murphy Novel
Colette
    The Collected Stories of Colette
    The Complete Claudine
Colgan, Jenny
    500 Miles from You
    ★*The Endless Beach*
    Sunrise by the Sea
*The **Collapsing** Empire.* Scalzi, John
★*Collected Fictions.* Borges, Jorge Luis
Collected Novellas. Garcia Marquez, Gabriel
Collected Stories. Dahl, Roald
★*Collected Stories.* Gilchrist, Ellen

★*Collected Stories.* Kafka, Franz
Collected Stories. O'Connor, Frank
★*The **Collected** Stories.* Paley, Grace
Collected Stories. Rendell, Ruth
*The **Collected** Stories.* Thomas, Dylan
★*Collected Stories.* Williams, Tennessee
★*The **Collected** Stories of Arthur C. Clarke.* Clarke, Arthur C.
*The **Collected** Stories of Colette.* Colette
★*The **Collected** Stories of Eudora Welty.* Welty, Eudora
*The **Collected** Stories of Greg Bear.* Bear, Greg
*The **Collected** Stories of Joseph Roth.* Roth, Joseph
★*The **Collected** Stories of Katherine Anne Porter.* Porter, Katherine Anne
*The **Collected** Stories of Lydia Davis.* Davis, Lydia
★*The **Collected** Stories of Max Brand.* Brand, Max
★*The **Collected** Stories of Richard Yates.* Yates, Richard
Collected Stories, 1891-1910. Wharton, Edith
Collected Stories: A Friend of Kafka to Passions. Singer, Isaac Bashevis
Collected Stories: Gimpel the Fool to the Letter Writer. Singer, Isaac Bashevis
Collected Stories: Including May We Borrow Your Husband? a Sense of Reality, Twenty-One Stories. Greene, Graham
*The **Collected** Tales of Nikolai Gogol.* Gogol, Nikolai Vasilievich
★*Collected Works.* O'Connor, Flannery
COLLECTIVE MEMORY
    Alsterdal, Tove. *We Know You Remember*
    Gordimer, Nadine. *No Time Like the Present: A Novel*
COLLECTIVISM
    Solzhenitsyn, Aleksandr Isaevich. ★*Cancer Ward*
COLLECTORS AND COLLECTING
    Flynn, Michael. *The January Dancer*
    Hart, Elsa. *The Cabinets of Barnaby Mayne*
    Kerley, Jack. ★*The Death Collectors*
    Ray, Eleanor. *The Missing Treasures of Amy Ashton*
    Smith, Dominic. *Bright and Distant Shores*
COLLEGE ATHLETES
    Ryan, Kennedy. ★*Long Shot*
COLLEGE BASKETBALL PLAYERS
    North, Anna. *The Life and Death of Sophie Stark*
COLLEGE DEANS
    Bellow, Saul. *The Dean's December: A Novel*
COLLEGE FOOTBALL PLAYERS
    Harvey, Michael T. *Pulse*
COLLEGE FRIENDS
    Gates, Eva. *A Death Long Overdue*
    McCreight, Kimberly. *Friends Like These*
    St. Aubyn, Edward. *Double Blind*
COLLEGE GRADUATES
    Askaripour, Mateo. ★*Black Buck*
COLLEGE SENIORS
    Salinger, J. D. ★*Franny and Zooey*
COLLEGE STUDENTS
    Auster, Paul. *Invisible*
    Ayatsuji, Yukito. *The Decagon House Murders*
    Barth, John. ★*Giles Goat-Boy ;: Or, the Revised New Syllabus*
    Bolano, Roberto. *Amulet*
    Carter, Stephen L. *Back Channel*
    Cho, Zen. *Spirits Abroad and Other Stories*

Crucet, Jennine Capo. *Make Your Home Among Strangers*
Cumyn, Alan. *Losing It*
Dickey, Eric Jerome. *Before We Were Wicked*
Faulkner, William. ★*Sanctuary*
Finch, Charles. *The September Society*
Fitzgerald, F. Scott. *Novels and Stories, 1920-1922*
Friedman, Daniel. *Riot Most Uncouth: A Lord Byron Mystery*
Goenawan, Clarissa. *The Perfect World of Miwako Sumida*
James, P. D. *An Unsuitable Job for a Woman*
Johnston, Tim. *The Current: A Novel*
Kay, Guy Gavriel. *The Summer Tree*
Kayode, Femi. ★*Lightseekers*
Koryta, Michael. *If She Wakes*
Lahiri, Jhumpa. ★*The Namesake*
Lee, Chang-Rae. ★*My Year Abroad*
Lewis, Beverly. *The Ebb Tide*
Lukas, Michael David. *The Last Watchman of Old Cairo: A Novel*
Mankell, Henning. ★*One Step Behind*
Marcom, Micheline Aharonian. *The New American*
McDermid, Val. *The Distant Echo*
Moore, Lorrie. *A Gate at the Stairs: A Novel*
Nugent, Benjamin. *Fraternity: Stories*
O'Donnell, Paraic. *The House on Vesper Sands: A Novel*
Pastan, Rachel. *In the Field*
Pearl, Matthew. *The Technologists: A Novel*
Ripley, Mike. *Mr Campion's Coven*
Rooney, Sally. *Normal People: A Novel*
Roth, Henry. *Requiem for Harlem*
Roth, Philip. *Indignation*
Segal, Erich. ★*Love Story*
Shin, Ann. *The Last Exiles*
Statovci, Pajtim. *Bolla*
Tartt, Donna. ★*The Secret History*
Walker, Karen Thompson. *The Dreamers*

COLLEGE STUDENTS — SEXUALITY
Amis, Martin. ★*The Pregnant Widow*

COLLEGE TEACHERS
Abu-Jaber, Diana. *Crescent*
Allende, Isabel. *In the Midst of Winter: A Novel*
Amis, Kingsley. ★*Lucky Jim*
Balasubramanyam, Rajeev. *Professor Chandra Follows His Bliss: A Novel*
Banks, Russell. *Lost Memory of Skin*
Barclay, Linwood. *A Noise Downstairs: A Novel*
Barthelme, Frederick. *Elroy Nights*
Bell, Shelly. *At His Mercy*
Bellow, Saul. ★*Herzog*
Bellow, Saul. *Ravelstein*
Buwalda, Peter. *Bonita Avenue: A Novel*
Byatt, A. S. ★*Possession: A Romance*
Choi, Susan. *My Education*
Cook, Thomas H. *Sandrine's Case*
Crouch, Blake. *Dark Matter: A Novel*
Crow, Sarah McCraw. *The Wrong Kind of Woman*
Dean, Pamela. *Tam Lin*
Delaney, J. P. *Believe Me: A Novel*
DeLillo, Don. ★*White Noise*
Dermansky, Marcy. *Very Nice*

Dexter, Colin. *The Daughters of Cain*
Dickey, Eric Jerome. ★*The Son of Mr. Suleman*
Doiron, Paul. ★*Dead by Dawn*
Fabry, Chris. *Looking into You*
Farah, Nuruddin. *Crossbones*
Freudenberger, Nell. ★*Lost and Wanted: A Novel*
Gaddis, William. *A Frolic of His Own: A Novel*
Gass, William H. *Middle C*
Hazelwood, Ali. *The Love Hypothesis*
Henry, Patti Callahan. ★*Becoming Mrs. Lewis: The Improbable Love Story of Joy Davidman and C. S. Lewis*
Herrera, Adriana. *American Love Story*
Houellebecq, Michel. *Submission*
Kotzwinkle, William. *The Bear Went Over the Mountain*
Lahiri, Jhumpa. ★*Whereabouts*
Lattari, Katie. *Dark Things I Adore*
Lovett, Charles C. *The Lost Book of the Grail: Or a Visitor's Guide to Barchester Cathedral*
Lurie, Alison. *Foreign Affairs*
Mosley, Walter. ★*John Woman*
Nabokov, Vladimir Vladimirovich. *Pale Fire*
Nabokov, Vladimir Vladimirovich. *Pnin*
O'Farrell, Maggie. *This Must Be the Place*
Offill, Jenny. *Dept. Of Speculation*
Ogawa, Yoko. *The Housekeeper and the Professor*
Olson, Neil. *Before the Devil Fell*
Pandya, Sameer. *Members Only*
Pava, Sergio de la. *Personae: A Novel*
Phillips, Christi. *The Devlin Diary*
Pobi, Robert. *City of Windows*
Powers, Richard. *Generosity: An Enhancement*
Prose, Francine. *Blue Angel: A Novel*
Raimondo, Lynne. *Dante's Dilemma: A Mark Angelotti Novel*
Robinson, Peter. *Children of the Revolution*
Russo, Richard. *Straight Man*
Sartre, Jean Paul. *The Age of Reason*
Schell, Orville. *My Old Home: A Novel of Exile*
Smith, Ali. *The Accidental*
Smith, Zadie. *On Beauty*
Vayden, Kristin. *Fortune Favors the Duke*
Vreeland, Susan. *Girl in Hyacinth Blue*
Welsh, Kaite. *The Unquiet Heart*
Whelan, Julia. *My Oxford Year*
Williams, Denise. *How to Fail at Flirting*

COLLEGE TOWNS
Shepard, Sara. ★*Reputation*

Collins, Ciaran
The Gamal

Collins, Kathleen
Notes from a Black Woman's Diary: Selected Works of Kathleen Collins
★*Whatever Happened to Interracial Love?: Stories*

Collins, Manda
A Good Rake Is Hard to Find
★*A Lady's Guide to Mischief and Mayhem*
One for the Rogue
Ready Set Rogue

Collins, Sara
The Confessions of Frannie Langton
Collins, Wilkie
★*The Moonstone*
★*The Woman in White*
COLLYER, HOMER LUSK
Doctorow, E. L. *Homer and Langley: A Novel*
Stirling, S. M. *Dies the Fire*
COLOMBIA
Garcia Marquez, Gabriel. *Chronicle of a Death Foretold*
Garcia Marquez, Gabriel. *Memories of My Melancholy Whores*
Klay, Phil. ★*Missionaries*
Restrepo, Laura. ★*Delirium: A Novel*
Rojas Contreras, Ingrid. ★*Fruit of the Drunken Tree: A Novel*
Vasquez, Juan Gabriel. ★*The Shape of the Ruins*
The Colonel. Dowlatabadi, Mahmoud
COLONIAL AMERICA (1600-1775)
Barth, John. ★*The Sot-Weed Factor*
Brom. *Slewfoot: A Tale of Bewitchery*
Calvi, Mary. *Dear George, Dear Mary: A Novel of George Washington's First Love*
Gabaldon, Diana. ★*Drums of Autumn*
Gabaldon, Diana. ★*The Fiery Cross*
Green, Jocelyn. *The Mark of the King*
Hawthorne, Nathaniel. ★*The Scarlet Letter: A Romance*
L'Amour, Louis. *To the Far Blue Mountains*
Pynchon, Thomas. *Mason & Dixon*
Seton, Anya. ★*The Winthrop Woman*
Spufford, Francis. ★*Golden Hill*
COLONIAL AUSTRALIA (1788-1901)
Flanagan, Richard. *Gould's Book of Fish: A Novel in Twelve Fish*
Grenville, Kate. *Sarah Thornhill*
Grenville, Kate. *The Secret River*
Malouf, David. *Remembering Babylon*
COLONIAL NEW ZEALAND (1841-1907)
Catton, Eleanor. *The Luminaries: A Novel*
COLONIALISM
Achebe, Chinua. ★*Things Fall Apart*
Binet, Laurent. *Civilizations*
Choo, Yangsze. ★*The Night Tiger: A Novel*
Conrad, Joseph. ★*Heart of Darkness*
Conrad, Joseph. *Victory: An Island Tale*
Couto, Mia. *Rain: And Other Stories*
Couto, Mia. *The Sword and the Spear*
Francis-Sharma, Lauren. ★*Book of the Little Axe*
Gappah, Petina. ★*Out of Darkness, Shining Light*
Ghosh, Amitav. *The Glass Palace*
Hammad, Isabella. ★*The Parisian, Or, Al-Barisi: A Novel*
Mason, Daniel. *The Piano Tuner*
Massey, Sujata. ★*The Bombay Prince*
Mitchell, David. ★*Cloud Atlas: A Novel*
Mukherjee, Abir. *Smoke and Ashes: A Novel*
Naipaul, V. S. *A Bend in the River*
Phillips, Caryl. *A View of the Empire at Sunset*
Proulx, Annie. ★*Barkskins: A Novel*
Sayles, John. *A Moment in the Sun*
Tanabe, Karin. *A Hundred Suns*

COLONIES
Robinson, Kim Stanley. ★*Red Mars*
Valente, Catherynne M. *Radiance*
COLONISTS
Green, Jocelyn. *The Mark of the King*
Haldane, Sean. *The Devil's Making*
Slimani, Leïla. *In the Country of Others*
COLONIZED PEOPLES
Boudjedra, Rachid. *The Barbary Figs*
Gappah, Petina. ★*Out of Darkness, Shining Light*
COLOR BLINDNESS
Fforde, Jasper. *Shades of Grey: A Novel*
COLOR OF AFRICAN AMERICANS
Greenidge, Kaitlyn. ★*Libertie: A Novel*
Morrison, Toni. ★*God Help the Child*
The Color of Bee Larkham's Murder: A Novel. Harris, Sarah J.
★*The Color of Magic*. Pratchett, Terry
★*The Color Purple: A Novel*. Walker, Alice
COLORADO
Black, Saul. ★*The Killing Lessons*
Black, Saul. ★*Lovemurder*
Burke, James Lee. *Another Kind of Eden*
Cameron, W. Bruce. *The Dogs of Christmas*
Carr, Robyn. *The Family Gathering*
Carr, Robyn. *What We Find*
Cather, Willa. *The Song of the Lark*
Child, Lee. *Nothing to Lose*
Cussler, Clive. ★*The Titanic Secret*
Dallas, Sandra. *The Last Midwife*
Dallas, Sandra. *Tallgrass*
Davidson, Diane Mott. *Killer Pancake*
Ellison, J. T. *Tear Me Apart*
Goodman, Jo. *A Touch of Forever*
Haruf, Kent. *Benediction*
Haruf, Kent. *Eventide*
Haruf, Kent. ★*Our Souls at Night*
Haruf, Kent. ★*Plainsong*
Heller, L. Alison. *The Neighbor's Secret*
Hemmings, Kaui Hart. *The Possibilities: A Novel*
Holsinger, Bruce W. *The Gifted School: A Novel*
King, Stephen. ★*The Shining*
Littlejohn, Emily. *Inherit the Bones*
Littlejohn, Emily. *Lost Lake: A Detective Gemma Monroe Mystery*
Michener, James A. ★*Centennial*
Mizushima, Margaret. *Killing Trail*
Phillips, Susan Elizabeth. ★*Natural Born Charmer*
Shalvis, Jill. *Second Chance Summer*
Weiden, David L. ★*Winter Counts*
Wilson, Carter. *Dead Girl in 2a*
Colorless Tsukuru Tazaki and His Years of Pilgrimage. Murakami, Haruki
COLSON, QUINN (FICTITIOUS CHARACTER)
Atkins, Ace. *The Innocents*
Atkins, Ace. *The Revelators*
Colter Shaw novels [Series]. Deaver, Jeffery
COLUMBUS, OHIO
Lepionka, Kristen. *Once You Go This Far: A Mystery*
Stringer, Vickie M. ★*Let That Be the Reason*

Winfrey, Kerry. *Not Like the Movies*

A **Column** of Fire. Follett, Ken

COLUMNISTS

Landvik, Lorna. *Chronicles of a Radical Hag: With Recipes*

Colvin, Jeffrey

★*Africaville: A Novel*

Colwin, Laurie

Goodbye Without Leaving

Happy All the Time: A Novel

COMA

Krentz, Jayne Ann. ★*All the Colors of Night*

Malerman, Josh. *Unbury Carol*

COMA — PATIENTS

Feeney, Alice. ★*Sometimes I Lie*

Coma: a Novel. Cook, Robin

**COMANCHE INDIANS — RELATIONS WITH
    EUROPEAN-AMERICANS**

McMurtry, Larry. *Comanche Moon: A Novel*

McMurtry, Larry. ★*Lonesome Dove: A Novel*

McMurtry, Larry. ★*Streets of Laredo: A Novel*

Comanche Moon: A Novel. McMurtry, Larry

★**Come** Home. Scottoline, Lisa

Come Sundown. Roberts, Nora

Come the Fear. Nickson, Chris

Come with Me. Schulman, Helen

Comeback. Stark, Richard

COMEDIANS

Grossman, David. ★*A Horse Walks into a Bar*

A **Comedy** of Terrors: A Flavia Albia Novel. Davis, Lindsey

COMET COLLISIONS

Holroyde, Claire. *The Effort*

COMETS

Amirrezvani, Anita. *The Blood of Flowers: A Novel*

Holroyde, Claire. *The Effort*

COMFORT WOMEN

Lewis, Linden A. *The First Sister: A Novel*

The **Comforts** of a Muddy Saturday: An Isabel Dalhousie Novel. McCall Smith, Alexander

COMIC BOOK FANS

Harkaway, Nick. *Tigerman*

COMIC BOOK WRITING

Chabon, Michael. *The Amazing Adventures of Kavalier & Clay: A Novel*

COMICS AND GRAPHIC NOVELS

Burns, Charles. ★*Black Hole*

Cruse, Howard. *The Complete Wendel*

Gendry-Kim, Keum Suk. ★*The Waiting*

Kraus, Daniel. *The Autumnal: The Complete Series*

Machado, Carmen Maria. ★*The Low, Low Woods*

Coming Home. Pilcher, Rosamunde

COMING OUT (SEXUAL OR GENDER IDENTITY)

Rice-Gonzalez, Charles. *Chulito*

COMING OF AGE STORIES

Aciman, Andre. *Call Me by Your Name*

Agee, James. ★*A Death in the Family*

Akhtar, Ayad. *American Dervish: A Novel*

Ali, Monica. ★*Brick Lane: A Novel*

Allio, Kirstin. *Buddhism for Western Children: A Novel*

Allison, Dorothy. ★*Bastard Out of Carolina*

Anappara, Deepa. *Djinn Patrol on the Purple Line: A Novel*

Andreades, Daphne Palasi. *Brown Girls*

Apostol, Gina. *Gun Dealers' Daughter: A Novel*

Askaripour, Mateo. ★*Black Buck*

Atkinson, Kate. *Human Croquet*

Auster, Paul. *4 3 2 1: A Novel*

Auster, Paul. *Invisible*

Bainbridge, Beryl. *Every Man for Himself*

Baker, Kage. *The House of the Stag*

Baldwin, James. ★*Go Tell It on the Mountain*

Ballard, J. G. *Empire of the Sun: A Novel*

Ballard, J. G. *The Kindness of Women*

Banks, Iain. *The Crow Road*

Bartlett, Neil. *The Disappearance Boy*

Barzak, Christopher. *One for Sorrow*

Batuman, Elif. ★*The Idiot*

Bauermeister, Erica. *The Scent Keeper*

Bellow, Saul. ★*The Adventures of Augie March*

Benaron, Naomi. *Running the Rift: A Novel*

Bender, Tony. *The Last Ghost Dancer*

Benioff, David. *City of Thieves: A Novel*

Bennett, Brit. *The Mothers*

Berg, Elizabeth. *The Story of Arthur Truluv: A Novel*

Bergstrom, Heather Brittain. *Steal the North: A Novel*

Beverly, William. *Dodgers: A Novel*

Bieker, Chelsea Jean. *Godshot: A Novel*

Bijan, Donia. *The Last Days of Cafe Leila*

Bisson, Terry. *Any Day Now*

Blau, Jessica Anya. *Mary Jane: A Novel*

Blau, Jessica Anya. *The Wonder Bread Summer*

Boianjiu, Shani. *The People of Forever Are Not Afraid: A Novel*

Bordas, Camille. *How to Behave in a Crowd*

Boyne, John. *The Heart's Invisible Furies*

Bradbury, Jamey. *The Wild Inside: A Novel*

Bradbury, Ray. ★*Dandelion Wine: A Novel*

Bradbury, Ray. ★*Something Wicked This Way Comes*

Broder, Melissa. *Milk Fed*

Brown, Rita Mae. ★*Rubyfruit Jungle*

Brunt, Carol Rifka. ★*Tell the Wolves I'm Home: A Novel*

Bump, Gabriel. ★*Everywhere You Don't Belong: A Novel*

Burke, James Lee. *The Jealous Kind*

Burke, Marcus. *Team Seven*

Burns, Olive Ann. ★*Cold Sassy Tree*

Bush, Keisha. *No Heaven for Good Boys: A Novel*

Butler, Nickolas. ★*The Hearts of Men*

Butler, Season. ★*Cygnet*

Bynum, Sarah Shun-Lien. *Ms. Hempel Chronicles*

Campbell, Bebe Moore. *Your Blues Ain't Like Mine*

Campbell, Bonnie Jo. *Once Upon a River*

Carr, Brian Allen. ★*Opioid, Indiana*

Cather, Willa. ★*My Antonia*

Cather, Willa. *The Song of the Lark*

Chang, Alexandra. ★*Days of Distraction*

Chatterjee, Upamanyu. *English, August: An Indian Story*

Chevalier, Tracy. ★*Girl with a Pearl Earring*

Childress, Mark. *Crazy in Alabama*

Choi, Ann Y. K. *Kay's Lucky Coin Variety*

Cisneros, Sandra. ★*The House on Mango Street*
Cleary, Jon. *The Sundowners*
Clement, Jennifer. *Gun Love*
Clinch, Jon. *Finn: A Novel*
Cline, Emma. *The Girls: A Novel*
Cline, Ernest. *Ready Player One: A Novel*
Coe, Jonathan. *The Rotters' Club*
Colette. *The Complete Claudine*
Corthron, Kia. *Moon and the Mars*
Coster, Naima. *What's Mine and Yours: A Novel*
Crowell, Jenn. *Etched on Me: A Novel*
Crucet, Jennine Capo. *Make Your Home Among Strangers*
Cruz, Angie. *Dominicana: A Novel*
Dalton, Trent. *Boy Swallows Universe*
Danler, Stephanie. *Sweetbitter*
Dare, Abi. *The Girl with the Louding Voice*
De Robertis, Carolina. *The Gods of Tango*
De Robertis, Carolina. *Perla*
Dean, Margaret Lazarus. *The Time It Takes to Fall*
Deane, Seamus. *Reading in the Dark*
Dennis-Benn, Nicole. *Here Comes the Sun*
deWitt, Patrick. *Undermajordomo Minor*
DeWoskin, Rachel. *Big Girl Small: A Novel*
Diachenko, Serhii. *Vita Nostra*
Dickens, Charles. ★*David Copperfield*
Dickens, Charles. ★*Great Expectations*
Dickens, Charles. *Martin Chuzzlewit*
Dickens, Charles. ★*Nicholas Nickleby*
Dickens, Charles. *Oliver Twist, or the Parish Boy's Progress*
Dimechkie, Karim. *Lifted by the Great Nothing*
Divakaruni, Chitra Banerjee. *Oleander Girl: A Novel*
Doctorow, E. L. ★*Billy Bathgate: A Novel*
Dorey-Stein, Beck. *Rock the Boat: A Novel*
Doyle, Roddy. *Paddy Clarke, Ha-Ha-Ha*
Dreiser, Theodore. ★*Sister Carrie*
Dugoni, Robert. ★*The Extraordinary Life of Sam Hell*
Durham, David Anthony. ★*Gabriel's Story*
Durrow, Heidi W. *The Girl Who Fell from the Sky: A Novel*
Earley, Tony. *Jim the Boy: A Novel*
Ehirim, Nnamdi. *Prince of Monkeys*
El Akkad, Omar. *What Strange Paradise*
Erdrich, Louise. *The Beet Queen: A Novel*
Erdrich, Louise. ★*The Round House: A Novel*
Eskens, Allen. *Nothing More Dangerous: A Novel*
Eugenides, Jeffrey. ★*Middlesex*
Eugenides, Jeffrey. ★*The Virgin Suicides*
Evison, Jonathan. *All About Lulu: A Novel*
Evison, Jonathan. ★*Lawn Boy: A Novel*
Extence, Gavin. *The Universe Versus Alex Woods*
Fabry, Chris. *The Promise of Jesse Woods*
Faulkner, William. *The Reivers: A Reminiscence*
Faye, Gael. ★*Small Country: A Novel*
Ferber, Edna. *So Big*
Ferrante, Elena. *The Lying Life of Adults*
Fine, Julia. *What Should Be Wild*
Fitzgerald, F. Scott. ★*This Side of Paradise*
Fitzpatrick, Lydia. *Lights All Night Long: A Novel*
Francis, Patry. *All the Children Are Home*

Frankel, Laurie. *One Two Three: A Novel*
Frazier, Charles. *Thirteen Moons: A Novel*
Fridlund, Emily. ★*History of Wolves: A Novel*
Fu, Kim. *For Today I Am a Boy*
Fuller, Claire. *Our Endless Numbered Days: A Novel*
Fuqua, Jonathon Scott. *Gone and Back Again*
Gabel, Aja. *The Ensemble: A Novel*
Gaitskill, Mary. *The Mare: A Novel*
Gallen, Michelle. *Big Girl, Small Town: A Novel*
Galloway, Gregory. *As Simple as Snow*
Gardam, Jane. *The Flight of the Maidens*
Gardam, Jane. *God on the Rocks*
Gibbons, Kaye. ★*Ellen Foster: A Novel*
Gibbons, Kaye. *The Life All Around Me by Ellen Foster*
Gilb, Dagoberto. *The Flowers: A Novel*
Gilligan, Ruth. *The Butchers' Blessing*
Gilman, Laura Anne. *Flesh and Fire*
Giordano, Paolo. *Heaven and Earth*
Gnuse, A. J. *Girl in the Walls: A Novel*
Godwin, Gail. *Flora: A Novel*
Godwin, Gail. *Grief Cottage: A Novel*
Graff, Andrew J. *Raft of Stars*
Grames, Juliet. *The Seven or Eight Deaths of Stella Fortuna*
Grant, Helen. *The Vanishing of Katharina Linden*
Green, Hank. *An Absolutely Remarkable Thing: A Novel*
Greenidge, Kaitlyn. ★*Libertie: A Novel*
Greenidge, Kaitlyn. *We Love You, Charlie Freeman: A Novel*
Groff, Lauren. ★*Arcadia: A Novel*
Gunday, Hakan. *The Few*
Gunesekera, Romesh. ★*Suncatcher: A Novel*
Hahn, Sumi. *The Mermaid from Jeju: A Novel*
Hamill, Shaun. *A Cosmology of Monsters*
Harris, Thomas. *Hannibal Rising*
Hemingway, Ernest. *The Nick Adams Stories*
Hemingway, Ernest. ★*The Old Man and the Sea*
Herbert, Frank. ★*Dune*
Hesse, Hermann. *Narcissus and Goldmund*
Hewson, David. *The Garden of Angels*
Holmes, J. M. *How Are You Going to Save Yourself*
Hosseini, Khaled. ★*The Kite Runner*
Howarth, Paul. *Only Killers and Thieves: A Novel*
Hughes, Caoilinn. *Orchid and the Wasp*
Hughes, Langston. *Not Without Laughter*
Hyde, Catherine Ryan. *My Name Is Anton*
Irving, John. ★*The World According to Garp: A Novel*
Jackson-Brown, Angela. ★*When Stars Rain Down: A Novel*
James, Henry. *The Portrait of a Lady*
Jedrowski, Tomasz. *Swimming in the Dark*
Jeffers, Honoree Fanonne. ★*The Love Songs of W. E. B. Du Bois*
Jones, Gayl. ★*Palmares*
Jones, Tayari. *Silver Sparrow: A Novel*
Joukhadar, Zeyn. ★*The Thirty Names of Night: A Novel*
Joyce, James. ★*A Portrait of the Artist as a Young Man*
K'wan. *Street Dreams*
Kagen, Lesley. *Every Now and Then*
Kawakami, Mieko. *Ms. Ice Sandwich*
Khadivi, Laleh. ★*A Good Country: A Novel*
Kidd, Sue Monk. ★*The Secret Life of Bees*

Kincaid, Jamaica. ★*Annie John*
Kincaid, Jamaica. ★*Lucy*
King, Lily. *Writers & Lovers: A Novel*
Knowles, John. ★*A Separate Peace*
Ko, Lisa. *The Leavers*
Krivak, Andrew. *The Bear*
Krueger, William Kent. *This Tender Land: A Novel*
Kunzru, Hari. *White Tears*
Lansdale, Joe R. *The Bottoms*
Larison, John. *Whiskey When We're Dry*
Larkin, Allie. *The People We Keep*
Lawrence, D. H. *Sons and Lovers*
Layden, Emily. *All Girls*
Laymon, Kiese. *Long Division*
Le Guin, Ursula K. *The Beginning Place*
Lee, Harper. ★*To Kill a Mockingbird*
Lewis, Beverly. *The Preacher's Daughter*
Livesey, Margot. ★*The Boy in the Field*
Llewellyn, Richard. ★*How Green Was My Valley*
Louis, Edouard. *The End of Eddy: A Novel*
Lowe, Kathryn A. *The Furies*
MacDonald, Andrew. *When We Were Vikings*
Makumbi, Jennifer Nansubuga. ★*A Girl Is a Body of Water*
Mann, Thomas. *The Magic Mountain*
Marcom, Micheline Aharonian. *The New American*
Matar, Hisham. *In the Country of Men*
Maugham, W. Somerset. ★*Of Human Bondage*
McCammon, Robert R. *Boy's Life*
McCarthy, Cormac. ★*All the Pretty Horses*
McCarthy, Cormac. *The Crossing*
McCullers, Carson. *The Member of the Wedding*
McDermott, Alice. *Child of My Heart*
Mehta, Rahul. *No Other World: A Novel*
Mendez, Paul. *Rainbow Milk*
Miller, Derek B. *How to Find Your Way in the Dark*
Mitchell, David. *Black Swan Green: A Novel*
Monroe, Mary. ★*God Don't Like Ugly*
Moore, Liz. *The Unseen World*
Moore, Lorrie. *A Gate at the Stairs: A Novel*
Morante, Elsa. *Arturo's Island: A Novel*
Morrison, Toni. ★*The Bluest Eye: A Novel*
Moss, Sarah. *Ghost Wall: A Novel*
Munro, Alice. *Lives of Girls and Women*
Murata, Sayaka. *Earthlings: A Novel*
Murr, Naeem. *The Perfect Man: A Novel*
Murray, Paul. *Skippy Dies*
Novic, Sara. *Girl at War*
Novik, Naomi. ★*Uprooted*
Nunez, Sigrid. *The Last of Her Kind: A Novel*
Nunez, Sigrid. *Salvation City*
O'Donnell, Lisa. *The Death of Bees: A Novel*
Okorafor, Nnedi. ★*Who Fears Death*
Okparanta, Chinelo. ★*Under the Udala Trees*
Ondaatje, Michael. ★*Warlight*
Owens, Delia. *Where the Crawdads Sing*
Ozeki, Ruth L. *The Book of Form and Emptiness: A Novel*
Packer, Ann. *The Dive from Clausen's Pier*
Pamuk, Orhan. ★*A Strangeness in My Mind: A Novel*

Park, Ishle Yi. *Angel & Hannah: A Novel in Verse*
Parks, Gordon. ★*The Learning Tree*
Patchett, Ann. ★*The Dutch House: A Novel*
Peebles, Frances de Pontes. *The Air You Breathe*
Persson Giolito, Malin. *Quicksand*
Pessl, Marisha. *Special Topics in Calamity Physics*
Petterson, Per. *Out Stealing Horses: A Novel*
Pilcher, Rosamunde. *Coming Home*
Pontoppidan, Henrik. *Lucky Per*
Potok, Chaim. ★*My Name Is Asher Lev*
Powell, Padgett. ★*Edisto: A Novel*
Prose, Francine. *Goldengrove: A Novel*
Proust, Marcel. *Swann's Way*
Proust, Marcel. *Within a Budding Grove*
Quindlen, Anna. *Miller's Valley*
Quotah, Eman. ★*Bride of the Sea: A Novel*
Reyes, Dolores. *Eartheater*
Rice-Gonzalez, Charles. *Chulito*
Rodriques, Elias. *All the Water I've Seen Is Running: A Novel*
Rojas Contreras, Ingrid. ★*Fruit of the Drunken Tree: A Novel*
Roth, Henry. ★*Call It Sleep*
Roth, Henry. *A Diving Rock on the Hudson*
Roth, Henry. *From Bondage*
Roth, Henry. *Requiem for Harlem*
Roth, Henry. *A Star Shines Over Mt. Morris Park*
Roth, Philip. *Indignation*
Russell, Karen. ★*Swamplandia!*
Sagan, Francoise. ★*Bonjour Tristesse*
Salinger, J. D. ★*The Catcher in the Rye*
Sapphire. ★*The Kid: A Novel*
Saroyan, William. ★*The Human Comedy*
Sathian, Sanjena. *Gold Diggers*
Savage, Sam. *Firmin: Adventures of a Metropolitan Lowlife*
Savas, Aysegul. *Walking on the Ceiling*
Schlink, Bernhard. *The Reader: A Novel*
Schulman, Alex. *The Survivors: A Novel*
Shreve, Anita. *Fortune's Rocks: A Novel*
Shteyngart, Gary. *The Russian Debutante's Handbook*
Sister Souljah. ★*A Deeper Love Inside: The Porsche Santiaga Story*
Sittenfeld, Curtis. *Prep: A Novel*
Smith, Dodie. ★*I Capture the Castle*
Smith, Lee. *On Agate Hill: A Novel*
Smith, Zadie. ★*Nw: A Novel*
Solomon, Asali. *Disgruntled: A Novel*
Stibbe, Nina. *Reasons to Be Cheerful*
Straub, Emma. ★*Modern Lovers*
Straub, Emma. *The Vacationers*
Strout, Elizabeth. *Amy and Isabelle: A Novel*
Stuart, Douglas. ★*Shuggie Bain*
Swamy, Shruti. *The Archer*
Swarthout, Glendon. *Bless the Beasts and Children*
Swinson, David. *City on the Edge*
Swyler, Erika. ★*Light from Other Stars: A Novel*
Szabo, Magda. *Abigail*
Tamirat, Nafkote. *The Parking Lot Attendant: A Novel*
Tarkington, Booth. ★*Alice Adams*
Tartt, Donna. ★*The Goldfinch*
Temple, Emily. *The Lightness*

Thomas, Scarlett. *Oligarchy*
Thorpe, Rufi. ★*The Knockout Queen*
Tinti, Hannah. *The Twelve Lives of Samuel Hawley: A Novel*
Twain, Mark. ★*Adventures of Huckleberry Finn: Tom Sawyer's Comrade ...*
Tyree, Omar. ★*Flyy Girl*
Tyree, Omar. *For the Love of Money: A Novel*
Urrea, Luis Alberto. *The Hummingbird's Daughter: A Novel*
Vann, David. *Aquarium*
Vestal, Shawn. *Daredevils*
Vo, Nghi. ★*The Chosen and the Beautiful*
Vuong, Ocean. ★*On Earth We're Briefly Gorgeous: A Novel*
Walker, Karen Thompson. *The Age of Miracles: A Novel*
Walls, Jeannette. *The Silver Star: A Novel*
Weiss, Elizabeth. *The Sisters Sweet*
West, Monica. *Revival Season: A Novel*
White, Edmund. *A Boy's Own Story*
Whitehead, Colson. *Sag Harbor: A Novel*
Wilder, Thornton. ★*Theophilus North*
Wolfe, Thomas. ★*Look Homeward, Angel: A Story of a Buried Life*
Wolfe, Thomas. ★*Of Time and the River: A Legend of Man's Hunger in His Youth*
Wolitzer, Meg. *The Female Persuasion*
Wood, Shelley. *The Quintland Sisters*
Woodson, Jacqueline. ★*Another Brooklyn*
Woodson, Jacqueline. ★*Red at the Bone*
Woolf, Virginia. *The Voyage Out*
Yang, Susie. *White Ivy: A Novel*
Yoshimoto, Banana. *Moshi-Moshi*

COMMAND OF TROOPS
Shaara, Jeff. *Gods and Generals: A Novel of the Civil War*
Shaara, Jeff. *Gone for Soldiers*
Shaara, Jeff. *The Last Full Measure*

COMMANDO OPERATIONS
Shaara, Jeff. *The Rising Tide: A Novel of World War II*

COMMITMENT (PSYCHOLOGY)
Hijuelos, Oscar. ★*The Mambo Kings Play Songs of Love: A Novel*
Moniz, Tomas. *Big Familia*
Ripper, Kris. *The Love Study*
★*The Committed*. Nguyen, Viet Thanh

COMMITTEES
Carlyle, Christy. *Duke Gone Rogue*
Commodore Hornblower. Forester, C. S.
The Commoner: a Novel. Schwartz, John Burnham
★*Commonwealth*. Patchett, Ann
Commonwealth saga [Series]. Hamilton, Peter F.

COMMUNES
Bisson, Terry. *Any Day Now*
Cline, Emma. *The Girls: A Novel*
Dalcher, Christina. *Femlandia*
Dektar, Molly. *The Ash Family*
Dolan-Leach, Caite. *We Went to the Woods: A Novel*
Dunn, Mark. *Ella Minnow Pea: A Progressively Lipogrammatic Epistolary Fable*
Groff, Lauren. ★*Arcadia: A Novel*

COMMUNICABLE DISEASES
Abbott, Megan E. *The Fever*
Golden, Christopher. *Red Hands*

COMMUNICATION
Burke, Sue. *Semiosis*
Hall, Louisa. *Speak*
Hoover, Colleen. *All Your Perfects*

COMMUNICATION IN FAMILIES
Runcie, James. *Canvey Island*

COMMUNICATION TECHNOLOGY
Fuentes, Carlos. *The Eagle's Throne: A Novel*

COMMUNISM
Bandi. *The Accusation: Forbidden Stories from Inside North Korea*
Barnes, Julian. *The Noise of Time*
Gessen, Keith. *A Terrible Country*
Jedrowski, Tomasz. *Swimming in the Dark*
Jin, Ha. *The Boat Rocker: A Novel*
Lessing, Doris May. ★*The Golden Notebook*
Lethem, Jonathan. *Dissident Gardens*
Li, Yiyun. *The Vagrants: A Novel*
McEwan, Ian. *Black Dogs*
Schell, Orville. *My Old Home: A Novel of Exile*
See, Lisa. *Dreams of Joy: A Novel*
Smith, Tom Rob. *Agent 6*
Solzhenitsyn, Aleksandr Isaevich. ★*Cancer Ward*
Solzhenitsyn, Aleksandr Isaevich. *One Day in the Life of Ivan Denisovich*
Uris, Leon. *Armageddon: A Novel of Berlin*
Veletzos, Roxanne. *The Girl They Left Behind*

COMMUNIST COUNTRIES
Cleeton, Chanel. *Next Year in Havana*

COMMUNISTS
Roth, Philip. *I Married a Communist*

COMMUNITIES
Abbott, Megan E. *The Fever*
Allio, Kirstin. *Buddhism for Western Children: A Novel*
Backman, Fredrik. ★*Beartown: A Novel*
Backman, Fredrik. *A Man Called Ove*
Bambara, Toni Cade. ★*The Salt Eaters*
Banner, Catherine. *The House at the Edge of Night: A Novel*
Bolton, S. J. *A Dark and Twisted Tide*
Brooks, Max. *Devolution: A Firsthand Account of the Rainier Sasquatch Massacre*
Cha, Steph. ★*Your House Will Pay*
Chevalier, Tracy. *A Single Thread*
Colgan, Jenny. ★*The Endless Beach*
Colgan, Jenny. *Sunrise by the Sea*
Dallas, Sandra. *The Last Midwife*
De Bernieres, Louis. *Birds Without Wings*
De Robertis, Carolina. *Cantoras*
Doiron, Paul. *Stay Hidden*
Galchen, Rivka. *Everyone Knows Your Mother Is a Witch*
Hannah, Kristin. *The Great Alone*
Hunt, Laird. *Zorrie*
Jaswal, Balli Kaur. *Erotic Stories for Punjabi Widows*
McBride, James. ★*Deacon King Kong: A Novel*
McCall Smith, Alexander. *The Joy and Light Bus Company*
Montgomery, Jess. *The Widows*
Phillips, Julia. ★*Disappearing Earth*
Quade, Kirstin Valdez. ★*The Five Wounds: A Novel*
Rabb, Jonathan. *Among the Living*

Robinson, Kim Stanley. *Aurora*
Russo, Richard. *Straight Man*
Sahota, Sunjeev. *The Year of the Runaways*
Sampson, Freya. *The Last Chance Library*
Scott, Rion Amilcar. ★*The World Doesn't Require You: Stories*
Sternbergh, Adam. *The Blinds*
Stirling, S. M. *A Meeting at Corvallis*

COMMUNITY LIFE
Baxter, Charles. *The Feast of Love*
Berg, Elizabeth. *Night of Miracles*
Danticat, Edwidge. *Claire of the Sea Light*
Morrison, Toni. *Love*
Morrison, Toni. *Paradise*
Morrison, Toni. *Tar Baby*
Oates, Joyce Carol. *The Falls: A Novel*
Russo, Richard. *Bridge of Sighs*
Steinbeck, John. *Cannery Row*

COMMUNITY POLICING
Anderson, Kent. *Green Sun: A Novel*

COMPANIONSHIP
Diaz, Junot. ★*This Is How You Lose Her*
Ishiguro, Kazuo. ★*Klara and the Sun*
Kerouac, Jack. ★*On the Road*
The **Company** [Series]. Baker, Kage
*The **Company**: a Novel of the Cia*. Littell, Robert
Compass. Enard, Mathias

COMPASSION
Ozeki, Ruth L. ★*A Tale for the Time Being*

COMPASSION IN TEENAGERS
Lodato, Victor. *Mathilda Savitch*

COMPETITION
Aalborg, Gordon. *River of Porcupines*
Abbott, Megan E. ★*Give Me Your Hand*
Brundage, Elizabeth. *The Vanishing Point*
Clements, Oliver. *The Eyes of the Queen*
De la Motte, Anders. *MemoRandom: A Thriller*
Dell'Antonia, K. J. *The Chicken Sisters*
Dobmeier, Tracy. ★*Girls with Bright Futures: A Novel*
Follett, Ken. ★*Whiteout*
Gardam, Jane. *Last Friends*
Gelman, Laurie. *Class Mom: A Novel*
Holsinger, Bruce W. *The Gifted School: A Novel*
Jalaluddin, Uzma. *Hana Khan Carries On*
Katz, Erica. *The Boys' Club*
Lauren, Christina. *Dating You / Hating You*
McDonald, Ian. *New Moon*
Menon, Lily. *Make up Break Up: A Novel*
Miles, Terry. *Rabbits*
Morgenstern, Erin. ★*The Night Circus: A Novel*
Quincy, D. M. *Murder at the Opera*
Russell, Mary Doria. *Epitaph: A Novel of the O.K. Corral*
Smith, Zadie. ★*Swing Time*
Steadman, Catherine. *The Disappearing Act*
Stevens, Francis. *The Heads of Cerberus*
Torre, A. R. *Every Last Secret*
Wagers, K. B. *Hold Fast Through the Fire*
Waters, Martha. *To Love and to Loathe: A Novel*
Yellin, Jessica. *Savage News*

COMPETITION IN GIRLS
Godwin, Gail. *Unfinished Desires*

COMPETITION IN MEN
Banks, Iain. *The Player of Games*
Romano-Lax, Andromeda. *The Spanish Bow*

COMPETITION IN WOMEN
Golden, Arthur. ★*Memoirs of a Geisha: A Novel*
Pitoniak, Anna. *Necessary People*

COMPETITIVE SNOWBOARDING
Reynolds, Allie. ★*Shiver*
The **Complaints**. Rankin, Ian
The **Complete** *Claudine*. Colette
★The **Complete** *Sherlock Holmes*. Doyle, Arthur Conan
Complete *Short Fiction of Joseph Conrad: The Stories: Volume 1*. Conrad, Joseph
The **Complete** *Short Stories of H. G. Wells*. Wells, H. G.
★The **Complete** *Short Stories of Mark Twain*. Twain, Mark
The **Complete** *Shorter Fiction*. Melville, Herman
★The **Complete** *Stories*. Malamud, Bernard
The **Complete** *Stories*. O'Connor, Flannery
Complete *Stories*. Vonnegut, Kurt
★**Complete** *Stories and Poems of Edgar Allan Poe*. Poe, Edgar Allan
★The **Complete** *Stories of Evelyn Waugh*. Waugh, Evelyn
★The **Complete** *Stories of J.G. Ballard.*. Ballard, J. G.
★The **Complete** *Stories of Truman Capote*. Capote, Truman
Complete *Stories, 1864-1874*. James, Henry
Complete *Stories, 1874-1884*. James, Henry
Complete *Stories, 1884-1891*. James, Henry
Complete *Stories, 1892-1898*. James, Henry
Complete *Stories, 1898-1910*. James, Henry
The **Complete** *Wendel*. Cruse, Howard
★The **Complete** *Western Stories of Elmore Leonard.*. Leonard, Elmore
★The **Complete** *Works of O. Henry*. Henry, O.

COMPOSERS
Barnes, Julian. *The Noise of Time*
Dongala, Emmanuel Boundzeki. *The Bridgetower Sonata: Sonata Mulattica*
Horrocks, Caitlin. *The Vexations*
Kaplan, Mitchell James. *Rhapsody*
Mann, Thomas. *Doctor Faustus*
McEwan, Ian. ★*Amsterdam*
Powers, Richard. *Orfeo: A Novel*
Rose, Heather. *The Museum of Modern Love*

COMPULSIVE BEHAVIOR
Abbott, Patricia. *Concrete Angel*
Burton, Tara Isabella. *Social Creature*
Ferris, Joshua. *The Unnamed*
McCullers, Carson. *Reflections in a Golden Eye*

COMPULSIVE BEHAVIOR IN MEN
Doctorow, E. L. *Homer and Langley: A Novel*
Eugenides, Jeffrey. ★*The Marriage Plot*
Ferris, Joshua. *To Rise Again at a Decent Hour: A Novel*
Moore, Alison. *The Lighthouse*
Roth, Philip. ★*Portnoy's Complaint*
Roth, Philip. *Sabbath's Theater*

COMPULSIVE BEHAVIOR IN WOMEN
Attenberg, Jami. *The Middlesteins*
Reyes, Dolores. *Eartheater*

Salinger, J. D. ★*Franny and Zooey*

COMPULSIVE GAMBLERS
Barthelme, Frederick. *Bob the Gambler*

COMPUTER ALGORITHMS
Schulman, Helen. *Come with Me*

COMPUTER CRIME INVESTIGATION
Evanovich, Janet. ★*Game On: Tempting Twenty-Eight*

COMPUTER CRIMES
Evanovich, Janet. ★*Game On: Tempting Twenty-Eight*
Quartey, Kwei. *The Missing American*

COMPUTER GAMES
Stephenson, Neal. *Reamde*

COMPUTER INDUSTRY AND TRADE
Connelly, Michael. *The Scarecrow: A Novel*

COMPUTER PROGRAMMERS
Evanovich, Stephanie. *Under the Table*
Frankel, Laurie. *Goodbye for Now: A Novel*
Garwood, Julie. *Wired*
Gentry, Amy. *Last Woman Standing*

COMPUTER PROGRAMMING
Anam, Tahmima. *The Startup Wife*

COMPUTER PROGRAMS
Menon, Lily. *Make up Break Up: A Novel*

COMPUTER SCIENTISTS
Moore, Liz. *The Unseen World*

COMPUTER SOFTWARE — TESTING
Gibson, William. *The Peripheral*

COMPUTER SOFTWARE DEVELOPERS
Tracy, P. J. *Ice Cold Heart*

COMPUTER TECHNOLOGY
Wilson, G. Willow. *Alif the Unseen*

COMPUTER VIRUSES
Stephenson, Neal. ★*Snow Crash*

COMPUTERIZED MAPPING SYSTEMS
Barclay, Linwood. *Trust Your Eyes: A Thriller*

COMPUTERS
Gibson, William. ★*Neuromancer*
Heinlein, Robert A. *The Moon Is a Harsh Mistress*
Stephenson, Neal. *The Diamond Age,: Or, a Young Lady's Illustrated Primer*

CONCENTRATION CAMP INMATES
Gross, Andrew. *The One Man*
Grossman, David. ★*More Than I Love My Life: A Novel*

CONCENTRATION CAMP SURVIVORS
Konar, Affinity. *Mischling: A Novel*
Rothschild, Hannah. *The Improbability of Love: A Novel*
Singer, Isaac Bashevis. *Enemies, a Love Story*
Styron, William. ★*Sophie's Choice*

CONCENTRATION CAMPS
Amis, Martin. ★*The Zone of Interest: A Novel*
Bolano, Roberto. ★*Distant Star*
Brouwer, Sigmund. *Thief of Glory: A Novel*
Green, Amy Lynn. *Things We Didn't Say*
Jensen, Nancy. *In Our Midst*
McFadden, Bernice L. *The Book of Harlan*
Otsuka, Julie. *When the Emperor Was Divine: A Novel*
Solzhenitsyn, Aleksandr Isaevich. *One Day in the Life of Ivan Denisovich*

Wellington, David. *Positive*

Concrete Angel. Abbott, Patricia

CONCUBINAGE
Barker, Pat. *The Women of Troy*
Wilson, G. Willow. ★*The Bird King*

Conde, Maryse
I, Tituba, Black Witch of Salem

CONDITIONED RESPONSE
Pynchon, Thomas. ★*Gravity's Rainbow*

★*The **Conductors**. Glover, Nicole

CONDUCTORS (MUSIC)
Alexander, Tamera. ★*A Note yet Unsung*
Elias, Gerald. ★*Death and Transfiguration: A Daniel Jacobus Novel*

Conell, Lee
The Party Upstairs

CONEY ISLAND, NEW YORK CITY
Hoffman, Alice. *The Museum of Extraordinary Things: A Novel*

★*A **Confederacy** of Dunces*. Toole, John Kennedy

CONFEDERATE SOLDIERS
Alexander, Tamera. *With This Pledge*
Doctorow, E. L. *The March: A Novel*
Frazier, Charles. ★*Cold Mountain*
Harris, C. S. *Good Time Coming*
Shaara, Michael. ★*The Killer Angels: A Novel*

CONFEDERATE STATES OF AMERICA
Brown, Taylor. *Fallen Land*
Frazier, Charles. *Varina*
Jakes, John. *Love and War*
Jakes, John. ★*North and South*
Shaara, Jeff. *Gods and Generals: A Novel of the Civil War*
Shaara, Jeff. *The Last Full Measure*

CONFESSION (LAW)
Bolton, S. J. *The Craftsman*

*The **Confession** Club: A Novel*. Berg, Elizabeth

Confessional. Higgins, Jack

Confessions. Minato, Kanae

★*Confessions in B-Flat*. Hill, Donna

Confessions of an Innocent Man. Dow, David R.

*The **Confessions** of Frannie Langton*. Collins, Sara

*The **Confessions** of Nat Turner*. Styron, William

*The **Confessions** of Young Nero*. George, Margaret

*The **Confidence-Man**: His Masquerade*. Melville, Herman

CONFIDENTIAL COMMUNICATIONS
Meltzer, Brad. *The Tenth Justice*

CONFLICT IN FAMILIES
Gardam, Jane. *God on the Rocks*
Mandel, Emily St. John. *The Singer's Gun: A Novel*
Mosley, Walter. *All I Did Was Shoot My Man: A Leonid McGill Mystery*
Perrotta, Tom. *The Leftovers*
Suri, Manil. *The Age of Shiva: A Novel*

CONFLICT RESOLUTION
Okorafor, Nnedi. ★*Binti*
Ross, Ann B. *Miss Julia Delivers the Goods: A Novel*

CONFORMITY
Bellow, Saul. *Dangling Man*
Bellow, Saul. *Novels, 1944-1953*
Bradbury, Ray. ★*Fahrenheit 451*

Camus, Albert. ★*The Stranger*
Lewis, Sinclair. *Babbitt*
Vonnegut, Kurt. ★*Player Piano*
CONFRONTATION (INTERPERSONAL RELATIONS)
Hulse, S. M. ★*Black River*
CONGO (BRAZZAVILLE)
Mabanckou, Alain. ★*Black Moses*
CONGO (DEMOCRATIC REPUBLIC)
Conrad, Joseph. ★*Heart of Darkness*
Kingsolver, Barbara. ★*The Poisonwood Bible: A Novel*
CONGRESSIONAL AIDES
Meltzer, Brad. *The Zero Game*
CONJOINED TWINS
Weiss, Elizabeth. *The Sisters Sweet*
★*Conjure Women*. Atakora, Afia
A Conjuring of Light. Schwab, Victoria
CONNECTICUT
Acampora, Lauren. *The Wonder Garden*
Aliu, Xhenet. ★*Brass: A Novel*
Bardugo, Leigh. ★*Ninth House*
Brom. *Slewfoot: A Tale of Bewitchery*
Brown, Karen. *The Clairvoyants: A Novel*
Cooney, Caroline B. *The Grandmother Plot*
Grames, Juliet. *The Seven or Eight Deaths of Stella Fortuna*
Higgins, Kristan. *Always the Last to Know*
Knopf, Chris. *You're Dead*
Layden, Emily. *All Girls*
McKinlay, Jenn. *Killer Research*
Pesci, David. *Amistad: A Novel*
Poeppel, Amy. *Musical Chairs: A Novel*
Rice, Luanne. ★*Last Day*
Roorbach, Bill. *Life Among Giants: A Novel*
Wilson, Sloan. ★*The Man in the Gray Flannel Suit*
★*A Connecticut Yankee in King Arthur's Court*. Twain, Mark
Connections in Death: An Eve Dallas Novel. Robb, J. D.
Connelly, Michael
The Black Ice
The Brass Verdict: A Novel
The Burning Room
The Crossing
★*The Dark Hours*
Dark Sacred Night
★*Fair Warning*
The Fifth Witness
The Gods of Guilt
The Late Show
★*The Law of Innocence: A Novel*
The Lincoln Lawyer: A Novel
The Night Fire
The Scarecrow: A Novel
The Wrong Side of Goodbye
Conner, M. Shelly
Everyman
Connolly, John
A Book of Bones
The Dirty South
The Nameless Ones

Connolly, Sheila
The Lost Traveller
Conquistadora: a Novel. Santiago, Esmeralda
Conrad, Joseph
Complete Short Fiction of Joseph Conrad: The Stories: Volume 1
★*Heart of Darkness*
★*Lord Jim*
Nostromo: A Tale of the Seaboard
Victory: An Island Tale
Conroy, Pat
The Prince of Tides
CONSCIENCE
Amis, Martin. ★*Time's Arrow, or the Nature of the Offense*
Camus, Albert. ★*The Fall*
Dostoyevsky, Fyodor. ★*Crime and Punishment*
CONSCIENTIOUS OBJECTORS
Kelly, Stephen. *The Wages of Desire: A World War II Mystery*
MacNeal, Susan Elia. *The King's Justice*
CONSCIOUSNESS
Ackerman, Elliot. ★*Waiting for Eden: A Novel*
Alexis, Andre. *Fifteen Dogs*
Chambers, Becky. ★*A Psalm for the Wild-Built*
Kasulke, Calvin. *Several People Are Typing*
Lem, Stanislaw. ★*Solaris*
Soule, Charles. ★*Anyone*
CONSCIOUSNESS TRANSFER
Reynolds, Alastair. *Permafrost*
Turton, Stuart. *The 7 1/2 Deaths of Evelyn Hardcastle*
CONSEQUENCES
Attenberg, Jami. ★*All This Could Be Yours*
Barnes, Julian. *The Only Story*
Bezmozgis, David. *The Betrayers: A Novel*
Brandt, Harry. *The Whites: A Novel*
Cantero, Edgar. *Meddling Kids: A Novel*
Cantor, Jillian. *Half Life*
Dennis-Benn, Nicole. ★*Patsy: A Novel*
Evison, Jonathan. *West of Here: A Novel*
Freitas, Donna. *The Nine Lives of Rose Napolitano*
Gibson, William. ★*Agency*
Han, Kang. ★*Human Acts: A Novel*
Livesey, Margot. ★*The Boy in the Field*
McGuire, Seanan. ★*In an Absent Dream*
McKinty, Adrian. ★*The Chain*
Moriarty, Liane. *Truly Madly Guilty*
Morris, Heather. *Cilka's Journey*
Newman, Sandra. *The Heavens*
Ng, Celeste. ★*Little Fires Everywhere: A Novel*
Palmer, Dexter Clarence. *Version Control*
Reay, Katherine. *The Bronte Plot*
Rindell, Suzanne. ★*The Two Mrs. Carlyles*
Silber, Joan. *Improvement*
Todd, Charles. ★*A Hanging at Dawn*
Updike, John. *The Widows of Eastwick*
Ware, Ruth. *The Lying Game*
Wecker, Helene. ★*The Hidden Palace*
★*The Consequences of Fear: A Maisie Dobbs Novel*. Winspear, Jacqueline

CONSERVATION OF NATURAL RESOURCES

Gordimer, Nadine. *The Conservationist*
Robinson, Kim Stanley. *Antarctica*
Robinson, Kim Stanley. ★*Green Mars*
The Conservationist. Gordimer, Nadine

CONSERVATORIES OF MUSIC

Schell, Orville. *My Old Home: A Novel of Exile*
Consider Phlebas. Banks, Iain

CONSPIRACIES

Abrams, Stacey. *While Justice Sleeps: A Novel*
Adams, Douglas. *The Restaurant at the End of the Universe*
Addison, Katherine. ★*The Goblin Emperor*
Adler-Olsen, Jussi. *The Keeper of Lost Causes*
Afifi, Nadia. *The Sentient*
Andersen, Laura. *The Boleyn Deceit*
Andersen, Laura. ★*The Boleyn King*
Andersen, Laura. *The Boleyn Reckoning*
Anderton, Jo. *Debris*
Ashley, Jennifer. *Death at the Crystal Palace*
Berenson, Alex. *The Deceivers*
Berry, Steve. ★*The Bishop's Pawn*
Berry, Steve. ★*The Templar Legacy: A Novel of Suspense*
Box, C. J. *Savage Run*
Brown, Dan. *The Da Vinci Code*
Brown, Sandra. *The Witness*
Buchan, John. *The Thirty-Nine Steps*
Buckley, Fiona. *The Doublet Affair: A Mystery at Queen Elizabeth I's Court*
Butler, Nickolas. *Godspeed*
Chen, Mike. *We Could Be Heroes*
Child, Lee. *The Affair*
Child, Lee. *Bad Luck and Trouble*
Child, Lee. *The Enemy*
Child, Lee. ★*Killing Floor*
Child, Lee. *Make Me*
Child, Lee. *Never Go Back*
Child, Lee. *Night School*
Child, Lee. *Nothing to Lose*
Child, Lee. ★*The Sentinel*
Child, Lee. *A Wanted Man*
Christy, Bryan. *In the Company of Killers*
Church, James. *Bamboo and Blood: An Inspector O Novel*
Coben, Harlan. *The Stranger*
Coonts, Stephen. *The Armageddon File*
Coonts, Stephen. ★*The Russia Account*
Corey, James S. A. *Abaddon's Gate*
Corey, James S. A. *Caliban's War*
Corey, James S. A. ★*Leviathan Wakes*
Crompton, Richard. *Hour of the Red God*
Cumming, Charles. *A Foreign Country*
Cussler, Clive. *The Mediterranean Caper*
Doctorow, Cory. *Rapture of the Nerds*
Dodd, Christina. *Because I'm Watching*
Doetsch, Richard. *Half-Past Dawn*
Doiron, Paul. *Almost Midnight*
Eisler, Barry. *The Killer Collective*
Eisler, Barry. *The Night Trade*
Elliott, Kate. *Servant Mage*

Ellis, Bret Easton. *Imperial Bedrooms*
Ellroy, James. *Blood's a Rover*
Ellroy, James. *The Cold Six Thousand: A Novel*
Ellroy, James. ★*Widespread Panic: A Novel*
Fesperman, Dan. *Safe Houses: A Novel*
Finder, Joseph. *Guilty Minds*
Fleming, Ian. *On Her Majesty's Secret Service*
Flores, Fernando A. *Tears of the Trufflepig*
Goss, Theodora. *The Sinister Mystery of the Mesmerizing Girl*
Grant, Mira. *Blackout*
Grant, Mira. *Deadline*
Grant, Mira. *Feed*
Gregory, Philippa. *The Kingmaker's Daughter*
Gregory, Philippa. *The Red Queen: A Novel*
Harkaway, Nick. *The Gone-Away World*
Harris, Robert. ★*Fatherland*
Hoeg, Peter. ★*Smilla's Sense of Snow*
Horowitz, Anthony. *The House of Silk: A Sherlock Holmes Novel*
Huang, S. L. *Zero Sum Game*
Johnson, D. E. *Detroit Shuffle*
Krentz, Jayne Ann. *When All the Girls Have Gone*
Larsson, Stieg. ★*The Girl Who Kicked the Hornet's Nest*
Le Carre, John. *The Constant Gardener: A Novel*
Le Carre, John. ★*A Delicate Truth*
Le Carre, John. *The Tailor of Panama*
Lepionka, Kristen. *Once You Go This Far: A Mystery*
Levin, Ira. *The Boys from Brazil: A Novel*
Mantel, Hilary. ★*Bring up the Bodies: A Novel*
Mason, Timothy. *The Darwin Affair*
Maxwell, Everina. *Winter's Orbit*
McKinney, Chris. *Midnight, Water City*
Meltzer, Brad. *The Escape Artist*
Meltzer, Brad. *The Inner Circle*
Merbeth, K. S. ★*Fortuna*
Meyer, Nicholas. *The Adventure of the Peculiar Protocols: Adapted from the Journals of John H. Watson, M.D.*
Miles, Terry. *Rabbits*
Mina, Denise. ★*Rizzio*
Parris, S. J. ★*The Dead of Winter*
Parris, S. J. *Treachery*
Pattison, Eliot. *The Skull Mantra*
Persson, Leif G. W. *Another Time, Another Life: The Story of a Crime*
Petrie, Nicholas. *The Drifter*
Phillips, Christi. *The Rossetti Letter: A Novel*
Phillips, Helen. *The Beautiful Bureaucrat: A Novel*
Pickard, Nancy. *The Scent of Rain and Lightning: A Novel*
Poole, Sara. *The Borgia Mistress*
Porter, Henry. *The Bell Ringers*
Priest, Cherie. *Clementine*
Pynchon, Thomas. ★*The Crying of Lot 49*
Raybourn, Deanna. *A Treacherous Curse: A Veronica Speedwell Mystery*
Renault, Mary. *Funeral Games*
Rice, Christopher. *Blood Victory*
Ridpath, Michael. *Far North*
Robb, Candace M. ★*A Choir of Crows*
Rollins, James. *The Devil Colony*
Sansom, C. J. ★*Sovereign*

Slaughter, Karin. ★*The Last Widow*
Smith, Tom Rob. *Agent 6*
Stabenow, Dana. *Restless in the Grave*
Stephenson, Neal. ★*Cryptonomicon*
Stone, Nick. *The Verdict*
Thomas, Scarlett. *Oligarchy*
Tracy, P. J. *Ice Cold Heart*
Wagers, K. B. *After the Crown*
Wagers, K. B. *Hold Fast Through the Fire*
Weir, Andy. *Artemis*
Woods, Stuart. *Orchid Beach*
★*A Conspiracy* of Bones. Reichs, Kathy
A Conspiracy of Faith. Adler-Olsen, Jussi
CONSPIRACY THEORIES
Eco, Umberto. ★*Foucault's Pendulum*
Goldstone, Lawrence. *Assassin of Shadows*
Rankin, Ian. *Exit Music*
Rankin, Ian. *Set in Darkness: An Inspector Rebus Novel*
Vasquez, Juan Gabriel. ★*The Shape of the Ruins*
Wolfe, Paul. *The Lost Diary of M*
Constable Twitten mysteries [Series]. Truss, Lynne
The Constant Gardener: A Novel. Le Carre, John
The Constant Princess. Gregory, Philippa
Constantine, Liv
The Last Time I Saw You
★*A Constellation* of Vital Phenomena: A Novel. Marra, Anthony
CONSTRUCTION WORKERS
Butler, Nickolas. *Godspeed*
CONSULTANTS
Whitehead, Colson. *Apex Hides the Hurt*
CONSUMERISM
Ballard, J. G. *Kingdom Come*
Saunders, George. *In Persuasion Nation: Stories*
The Consummata. Spillane, Mickey
Contact: a Novel. Sagan, Carl
CONTEMPORARY CHRISTIAN MUSIC
Isaac, Kara. *Then There Was You*
CONTEMPORARY FANTASY
Beagle, Peter S. *A Fine and Private Place*
Beagle, Peter S. *In Calabria*
Beagle, Peter S. *Summerlong*
Bear, Elizabeth. *Blood and Iron: A Novel of the Promethean Age*
Broder, Melissa. *The Pisces: A Novel*
Dean, Pamela. *Tam Lin*
Donohue, Keith. *The Stolen Child*
Faye, Lyndsay. ★*The King of Infinite Space*
Gaiman, Neil. ★*American Gods: A Novel*
Gaiman, Neil. ★*The Ocean at the End of the Lane*
Grant, Mira. *Into the Drowning Deep*
Grossman, Lev. *The Magician King: A Novel*
Grossman, Lev. *The Magician's Land: A Novel*
Grossman, Lev. ★*The Magicians: A Novel*
Harkness, Deborah E. *The Book of Life*
Harkness, Deborah E. *A Discovery of Witches: A Novel*
Harkness, Deborah E. *The World of All Souls: The Complete Guide to a Discovery of Witches, Shadow of Night, and the Book*
King, Stephen. *Elevation*
Klune, TJ. *The House in the Cerulean Sea*

Klune, TJ. ★*Under the Whispering Door*
Mitchell, David. *The Bone Clocks: A Novel*
Murphy, Sara Flannery. *The Possessions*
Natsukawa, Sosuke. *The Cat Who Saved Books*
Parry, H. G. *The Unlikely Escape of Uriah Heep*
Poore, Michael. *Reincarnation Blues*
Power, Susan. *The Grass Dancer*
Sherrill, Steven. *The Minotaur Takes His Own Sweet Time: A Novel*
Stephenson, Neal. *The Rise and Fall of D.O.D.O.: A Novel*
Updike, John. *The Widows of Eastwick*
Updike, John. ★*The Witches of Eastwick*
Walton, Jo. *Or What You Will*
Whitehead, Colson. *The Intuitionist*
CONTEMPORARY ROMANCES
Adams, Lyssa Kay. *The Bromance Book Club*
Anders, Adriana. *Under Her Skin*
Bailey, Tessa. *Fix Her Up*
Bellefleur, Alexandria. *Hang the Moon*
Bellefleur, Alexandria. *Written in the Stars*
Billingsley, ReShonda Tate. ★*The Secret She Kept*
Blumberg, Chandra. *Digging up Love*
Brayden, Melissa. *First Position*
Bryant, Niobia. *Christmas with the Billionaire*
Carr, Robyn. *The Family Gathering*
Carr, Robyn. ★*Virgin River*
Carr, Robyn. ★*The Wanderer*
Carr, Robyn. *What We Find*
Christopher, Andie J. *Not the Girl You Marry*
Cleage, Pearl. *Some Things I Never Thought I'd Do*
Cole, Alyssa. ★*A Duke by Default*
Cole, Alyssa. ★*How to Catch a Queen*
Cole, Alyssa. *How to Find a Princess*
Cole, Alyssa. ★*A Prince on Paper*
Cole, Alyssa. ★*A Princess in Theory*
Danan, Rosie. *The Intimacy Experiment*
Davidson, MaryJanice. *Truth, Lies, and Second Dates*
Dell, Kari Lynn. *Fearless in Texas*
Dell, Kari Lynn. *Mistletoe in Texas*
Dell, Kari Lynn. *Reckless in Texas*
DeLuca, Jen. ★*Well Met*
Dev, Sonali. ★*A Bollywood Affair*
Dev, Sonali. *The Bollywood Bride*
Dev, Sonali. *A Distant Heart*
Dev, Sonali. ★*Incense and Sensibility*
Dev, Sonali. ★*Pride, Prejudice, and Other Flavors: A Novel*
Dev, Sonali. ★*Recipe for Persuasion*
Deveraux, Jude. *Someone to Love*
Dimon, HelenKay. *Her Other Secret*
Doller, Trish. *Float Plan*
Drake, Laura. *The Sweet Spot*
Force, Marie. *Five Years Gone*
Foster, Lori. *Sisters of Summer's End*
Glass, Seressia. ★*The Love Con*
Guillory, Jasmine. *Party of Two*
Guillory, Jasmine. *The Proposal*
Guillory, Jasmine. *Royal Holiday*
Guillory, Jasmine. ★*The Wedding Date*
Guillory, Jasmine. *The Wedding Party*

Guillory, Jasmine. ★*While We Were Dating*
Hall, Alexis. *For Real*
Hazelwood, Ali. *The Love Hypothesis*
Henry, Emily. *Beach Read*
Henson, Pene. *Into the Blue*
Herrera, Adriana. ★*American Dreamer*
Herrera, Adriana. *American Fairytale*
Herrera, Adriana. *American Love Story*
Hibbert, Talia. ★*Act Your Age, Eve Brown*
Hibbert, Talia. ★*Get a Life, Chloe Brown*
Hibbert, Talia. *A Girl Like Her*
Hibbert, Talia. ★*Take a Hint, Dani Brown*
Higgins, Kristan. ★*The Best Man*
Hoang, Helen. ★*The Heart Principle*
Hoang, Helen. ★*The Kiss Quotient*
Hockman, Angie. *Shipped*
Hodges, Cheris F. *Rumor Has It*
Hoover, Colleen. *All Your Perfects*
Hoover, Colleen. *It Ends with Us*
Humphreys, Sara Taney. *Trouble Walks In*
Hunting, Helena. *Handle with Care*
Jackson, K. M. *How to Marry Keanu Reeves in 90 Days*
Jalaluddin, Uzma. *Hana Khan Carries On*
James, Lorelei. *I Want You Back*
Jimenez, Abby. *The Friend Zone*
Jimenez, Abby. ★*The Happy Ever After Playlist*
Jimenez, Abby. *Life's Too Short*
Kantra, Virginia. *Beth & Amy*
Kate, Jessica. *A Girl's Guide to the Outback: A Novel*
Kerr, Laurel. *Wild on My Mind*
Landon, Sydney. *Wishing for Us*
Lau, Jackie. *Donut Fall in Love*
Lauren, Christina. *Dating You / Hating You*
Lauren, Christina. *Roomies*
Lauren, Christina. *The Soulmate Equation*
Layne, Lauren. *Passion on Park Avenue*
Livesay, Tracey. *Like Lovers Do*
London, Julia. *The Charmer in Chaps*
London, Stefanie. *The Aussie Next Door*
Loren, Roni. ★*The One for You*
Loren, Roni. *The One You Can't Forget*
Loren, Roni. *The One You Fight For*
Macomber, Debbie. *If Not for You: A Novel*
Mallery, Susan. *Best of My Love*
Mallery, Susan. ★*When We Found Home*
Malone, Minx. *Bad Blood*
March, Emily. *Jackson*
Martin, Alexa. *Fumbled*
Martin, Alexa. ★*Intercepted*
McFarlane, Mhairi. *If I Never Met You: A Novel*
McKinlay, Jenn. *The Good Ones*
McQuiston, Casey. ★*One Last Stop*
Meader, Kate. *Playing with Fire*
Meltzer, Jean. ★*The Matzah Ball*
Menon, Lily. *Make up Break Up: A Novel*
Murphy, Julie. *If the Shoe Fits*
Oliveras, Priscilla. *Anchored Hearts*
Parker, Lucy. *The Austen Playbook*

Parker, Lucy. *Battle Royal*
Parrish, Roan. *Better Than People*
Phillips, Susan Elizabeth. *Call Me Irresistible*
Phillips, Susan Elizabeth. ★*Dance Away with Me*
Phillips, Susan Elizabeth. *First Star I See Tonight*
Phillips, Susan Elizabeth. *The Great Escape*
Phillips, Susan Elizabeth. *Heroes Are My Weakness*
Phillips, Susan Elizabeth. ★*Natural Born Charmer*
Phillips, Susan Elizabeth. *What I Did for Love*
Phillips, Susan Elizabeth. ★*When Stars Collide*
Pineiro, Caridad. *One Summer Night*
Pineiro, Caridad. *South Beach Love: A Feel-Good Romance from Hallmark Publishing*
Pineiro, Caridad. *What Happens in Summer*
Pope, Jamie. *One Warm Winter*
Rai, Alisha. ★*First Comes Like*
Rai, Alisha. ★*Girl Gone Viral*
Rai, Alisha. ★*The Right Swipe*
Ramsay, Hope. *Summer on Moonlight Bay*
Roberts, Nora. *Chesapeake Blue*
Roberts, Nora. *Sea Swept*
Rochon, Farrah. *The Boyfriend Project*
Rochon, Farrah. *The Dating Playbook*
Rogers, Morgan Callan. ★*Honey Girl*
Ruiz, Sarah Grunder. *Love, Lists, and Fancy Ships*
Ryan, Kennedy. ★*Long Shot*
Shalvis, Jill. *Second Chance Summer*
Shalvis, Jill. *Simply Irresistible*
Shalvis, Jill. *Sweet Little Lies*
Shalvis, Jill. *The Sweetest Thing*
Snow, Jennifer. *An Alaskan Christmas*
Solomon, Rachel Lynn. ★*The Ex Talk*
Solomon, Rachel Lynn. *Weather Girl*
Sosa, Mia. ★*Acting on Impulse*
Steel, Danielle. *First Sight*
Tieu, Julie. *The Donut Trap*
Title, Sarah. *The Undateable*
Van Dyken, Rachel. *Risky Play*
Wade, Becky. *Falling for You*
Weatherspoon, Rebekah. *A Cowboy to Remember*
Weatherspoon, Rebekah. *If the Boot Fits*
Weatherspoon, Rebekah. *Rafe: A Buff Male Nanny*
Weatherspoon, Rebekah. *A Thorn in the Saddle*
Weatherspoon, Rebekah. ★*Xeni: A Marriage of Inconvenience*
Whelan, Julia. *My Oxford Year*
Willett, Marcia. *The Garden House*
Williams, Preslaysa. *A Lowcountry Bride*
Williams, Synithia. *Forbidden Promises*
Williams, Tia. ★*Seven Days in June: A Novel*
Wilsner, Meryl. ★*Something to Talk About*

CONTEMPT
Stead, Christina. ★*The Man Who Loved Children*
CONTESTS
Banks, Iain. *The Player of Games*
Heron, Farah. *Accidentally Engaged*
Laymon, Kiese. *Long Division*
Schwab, Victoria. *A Gathering of Shadows*
Continental Drift. Banks, Russell

CONTRACTORS
Davis, Lindsey. *A Body in the Bathhouse*
Dee, Jonathan. *The Locals: A Novel*
CONTROL (PSYCHOLOGY)
Carey, M. R. *Someone Like Me*
Delaney, J. P. *The Girl Before: A Novel*
Gilman, Charlotte Perkins. ★*The Yellow Wallpaper and Selected Writings*
Hamilton, Steve. *The Second Life of Nick Mason: A Novel*
Palmer, Daniel. *The New Husband*
Pinborough, Sarah. ★*Behind Her Eyes: A Novel*
CONVALESCENCE
Genova, Lisa. *Left Neglected: A Novel*
Lippman, Laura. ★*Dream Girl*
CONVENTS
Dunant, Sarah. *Sacred Hearts: A Novel*
Spain, Jo. *With Our Blessing: An Inspector Tom Reynolds Mystery*
Convergence saga [Series]. Turnbull, Cadwell
CONVERSATION
Bailey, Paul. *Chapman's Odyssey*
Boudjedra, Rachid. *The Barbary Figs*
Cusk, Rachel. *Outline: A Novel*
DeLillo, Don. *The Silence*
★**Conversations** with Friends. Rooney, Sally
CONVERSION TO CHRISTIANITY
Parini, Jay. *The Damascus Road: A Novel of Saint Paul*
CONVERSION TO ISLAM
Berenson, Alex. *The Faithful Spy: A Novel*
CONVERSION TO JUDAISM
Hertmans, Stefan. ★*The Convert: A Novel*
★*The* **Convert***: a Novel.* Hertmans, Stefan
CONVICT SHIPS
Adams, Hope. *Dangerous Women*
Conviction. Dahl, Julia
The **Conviction**. Dugoni, Robert
Conviction. Mina, Denise
Cook, Diane
★*The New Wilderness: A Novel*
Cook, Robin
Charlatans
Coma: A Novel
★*Genesis*
Cook, Thomas H.
The Chatham School Affair
The Fate of Katherine Carr
Instruments of Night
Sandrine's Case
The **Cookbook** *Club.* Harbison, Beth
The **Cookbook** *Collector: A Novel.* Goodman, Allegra
COOKBOOKS
Harbison, Beth. *The Cookbook Club*
COOKING
Harbison, Beth. *The Cookbook Club*
COOKING CONTESTS
Beaton, M. C. *Agatha Raisin and the Quiche of Death*
COOKING, CHINESE
Lim, Roselle. *Natalie Tan's Book of Luck and Fortune*

COOKING, CUBAN
Pineiro, Caridad. *South Beach Love: A Feel-Good Romance from Hallmark Publishing*
COOKING, LEBANESE
Abu-Jaber, Diana. *Crescent*
COOKING, MEXICAN
Esquivel, Laura. ★*Like Water for Chocolate: A Novel in Monthly Installments, with Recipes, Romances, and Home Remedies*
COOKS
Blum, Jenna. *The Lost Family*
Fuentes, Carlos. *The Crystal Frontier: A Novel in Nine Stories*
Handke, Peter. *Don Juan: His Own Version*
Mukherjee, Neel. ★*A State of Freedom*
Ruiz, Sarah Grunder. *Love, Lists, and Fancy Ships*
COOL (PERSONAL QUALITY)
Leonard, Elmore. ★*Be Cool: Everyone Is Looking for the Next Big Hit*
Cooley, Martha
The Archivist: A Novel
Cooney, Caroline B.
The Grandmother Plot
Cooney, Ellen
The Mountaintop School for Dogs and Other Second Chances
Coonts, Stephen
The Armageddon File
The Art of War: A Novel
★*Flight of the Intruder*
★*The Russia Account*
Cooper, Ellison
Buried
Cooper, James Fenimore
The Last of the Mohicans: A Narrative of 1757
Cooper, Tom
Florida Man
The Marauders
COOPERATION
K'wan. *Animal II: The Omen*
Robinson, Kim Stanley. ★*Red Mars*
COOPERATIVES
Conell, Lee. *The Party Upstairs*
Coover, Robert
Going for a Beer: Selected Short Fictions
The Origin of the Brunists: A Novel
★**Cop** *Killer: The Story of a Crime.* Sjowall, Maj
Cop *Town: A Novel.* Slaughter, Karin
COPARENTING
Candlish, Louise. *Our House*
James, Lorelei. *I Want You Back*
COPENHAGEN, DENMARK
Adler-Olsen, Jussi. *The Absent One*
Adler-Olsen, Jussi. *A Conspiracy of Faith*
Adler-Olsen, Jussi. *The Keeper of Lost Causes*
Adler-Olsen, Jussi. *The Purity of Vengeance: A Department Q Novel*
Hoeg, Peter. ★*Smilla's Sense of Snow*
Pontoppidan, Henrik. *Lucky Per*
Copenhaver, John
The Savage Kind

COPING
Adams, Sara Nisha. ★*The Reading List*
Anders, Adriana. *Under Her Skin*
Bynum, Sarah Shun-Lien. *Ms. Hempel Chronicles*
Carr, Robyn. *What We Find*
Chaon, Dan. *Ill Will*
De Kretser, Michelle. *The Life to Come*
Grossman, David. ★*More Than I Love My Life: A Novel*
Haslett, Adam. ★*Imagine Me Gone: A Novel*
Haywood, Sarah. *The Cactus*
Joseph, Fabiola. *Niya: Rainbow Dreams*
Kafka, Franz. ★*The Metamorphosis*
Lippman, Laura. ★*After I'm Gone*
Moriarty, Jaclyn. *Gravity Is the Thing*
Phoenix, Michele. *The Space Between Words*
Porter, Max. ★*Grief Is the Thing with Feathers*
Whitehead, Colson. *Zone One: A Novel*
COPING IN CHILDREN
Fuqua, Jonathon Scott. *Gone and Back Again*
COPING IN MEN
Tyler, Anne. ★*The Accidental Tourist: A Novel*
COPING IN TEENAGE BOYS
Ford, Richard. *Canada*
COPING IN WOMEN
Bohjalian, Chris. *The Double Bind: A Novel*
Fallon, Siobhan. *You Know When the Men Are Gone*
Grossman, David. ★*To the End of the Land*
Hilderbrand, Elin. ★*Troubles in Paradise*
Hilderbrand, Elin. ★*What Happens in Paradise: A Novel*
Hilderbrand, Elin. ★*Winter in Paradise: A Novel*
McFarlane, Mhairi. *Don't You Forget About Me*
Morrison, Toni. ★*Beloved: A Novel*
Sager, Riley. *Final Girls: A Novel*
Shreve, Anita. *Eden Close: A Novel*
Coplin, Amanda
The Orchardist
COPPER MINERS' STRIKE, MICH., 1913-1914
Russell, Mary Doria. *The Women of the Copper Country: A Novel*
COPPER MINES AND MINING
Doerr, Harriet. ★*Stones for Ibarra*
Copperman, E. J.
Judgment at Santa Monica
COPTS
Durrell, Lawrence. ★*Justine*
COPYCAT MURDERERS
Bolton, S. J. *Now You See Me*
Spencer-Fleming, Julia. *Hid from Our Eyes*
COPYCAT MURDERS
Barry, Ava. *Windhall*
North, Alex. *The Shadows*
COPYRIGHT
Gaddis, William. *A Frolic of His Own: A Novel*
Corby, Gary
The Marathon Conspiracy
Cordelia Gray mysteries [Series]. James, P. D.
Cordova, Zoraida
The Inheritance of Orquidea Divina

COREY, DORIAN
Cassara, Joseph. *The House of Impossible Beauties*
Scottoline, Lisa. *Feared*
Corey, James S. A.
Abaddon's Gate
Babylon's Ashes
Caliban's War
Cibola Burn
★*Leviathan Wakes*
Nemesis Games
Persepolis Rising
Tiamat's Wrath
COREY, JOHN (FICTITIOUS CHARACTER)
DeMille, Nelson. *Wild Fire*
CORINTH, GREECE
Afshar, Tessa. *Thief of Corinth*
CORK COUNTY, IRELAND
Connolly, Sheila. *The Lost Traveller*
O'Connor, Carlene. *Murder in an Irish Bookshop*
Cork O'Connor mysteries [Series]. Krueger, William Kent
CORK, IRELAND
Harrison, Cora. *Beyond Absolution: A Mystery Set in 1920s Ireland*
Corleone, Douglas
Good as Gone
Corman, Avery
Prized Possessions
Cormoran Strike novels [Series]. Galbraith, Robert
CORN
Pastan, Rachel. *In the Field*
CORNWALL, ENGLAND
Carlyle, Christy. *Duke Gone Rogue*
Colgan, Jenny. *Sunrise by the Sea*
Du Maurier, Daphne. *Frenchman's Creek*
Du Maurier, Daphne. *Jamaica Inn*
Du Maurier, Daphne. ★*Rebecca*
George, Elizabeth. *Careless in Red*
Goddard, Robert. *Beyond Recall: A Novel*
James, Rebecca. *The Woman in the Mirror*
Kelly, Julia. *The Light Over London*
Pilcher, Rosamunde. ★*The Shell Seekers*
Purcell, Laura. *The House of Whispers*
Smith, Ali. ★*Winter*
Cornwell, Bernard
The Archer's Tale
The Last Kingdom: A Novel
Sword of Kings
The Winter King: A Novel of Arthur
Cornwell, Patricia Daniels
Autopsy
Postmortem
*The **Coronation**: the Further Adventures of Erast Fandorin*. Akunin, B.
CORONATIONS
Akunin, B. *The Coronation: The Further Adventures of Erast Fandorin*
CORONAVIRUSES
Parnell, Sean. *Left for Dead*
*The **Coroner's** Lunch*. Cotterill, Colin

CORONERS

Cook, Robin. ★*Genesis*

Cornwell, Patricia Daniels. *Autopsy*

Cotterill, Colin. *The Coroner's Lunch*

Cotterill, Colin. *Disco for the Departed*

Cotterill, Colin. *Don't Eat Me*

Cotterill, Colin. *The Second Biggest Nothing*

Davidson, MaryJanice. *Truth, Lies, and Second Dates*

Kellerman, Jonathan. ★*Half Moon Bay: A Novel*

CORPORATE ACCOUNTABILITY

Sinclair, Upton. ★*The Jungle*

CORPORATE CRIME

Sears, Michael. *Black Fridays*

CORPORATE CULTURE

Baker, Chandler. *Whisper Network: A Novel*

Finder, Joseph. *Vanished*

Kasulke, Calvin. *Several People Are Typing*

Wilson, Sloan. ★*The Man in the Gray Flannel Suit*

CORPORATE GREED

Cipri, Nino. *Defekt*

Doctorow, Cory. *Radicalized*

Takamura, Kaoru. ★*Lady Joker*

CORPORATE MERGERS

Robb, J. D. *Leverage in Death: An Eve Dallas Novel*

CORPORATE POWER

Doctorow, Cory. *Radicalized*

CORPORATIONS

Aalborg, Gordon. *River of Porcupines*

Bacigalupi, Paolo. ★*The Windup Girl*

Carpenter, Emily. *Until the Day I Die*

Hart, Rob. *The Warehouse: A Novel*

Huang, S. L. *Zero Sum Game*

Kennedy, James. *Dare to Know*

Pohl, Frederik. *Gateway*

Powell, Mark. *Firebird*

Wang, Kathy. *Impostor Syndrome: A Novel*

★*A Corpse in the Koryo*. Church, James

CORRECTIONAL PERSONNEL

Hulse, S. M. ★*Black River*

★*The Corrections*. Franzen, Jonathan

CORRUPTION

Afshar, Tessa. *Thief of Corinth*

Atkins, Ace. *The Shameless*

Belli, Kate. *Deception by Gaslight: A Gilded Gotham Mystery*

Davidson, Andy. *The Boatman's Daughter: A Novel*

DeSilva, Bruce. *A Scourge of Vipers*

Eco, Umberto. *Numero Zero*

Egan, Jennifer. ★*Manhattan Beach: A Novel*

Ehirim, Nnamdi. *Prince of Monkeys*

Finder, Joseph. *Guilty Minds*

Hill Gumbao, Toni. *The Summer of Dead Toys*

McDermid, Val. *How the Dead Speak: A Tony Hill and Carol Jordan Novel*

Paretsky, Sara. ★*Dead Land*

Pattison, Eliot. *Bones of the Earth: An Inspector Shan Tao Yun Mystery*

Quartey, Kwei. *Gold of Our Fathers*

Rushdie, Salman. ★*The Golden House*

Slaughter, Karin. ★*Pretty Girls: A Novel*

Smith, Ian. *Wolf Point*

Solares, Martin. *Don't Send Flowers*

Stanley, Michael. *A Death in the Family*

Talton, Jon. *City of Dark Corners*

Whitehead, Colson. ★*The Nickel Boys: A Novel*

Winslow, Don. *Broken: Six Short Novels*

CORRUPTION INVESTIGATION

Grisham, John. ★*The Firm*

Qiu, Xiaolong. *Red Mandarin Dress: An Inspector Chen Novel*

Stanley, Michael. *A Carrion Death*

Corry, Jane

The Dead Ex

Corthron, Kia

Moon and the Mars

Cosby, S. A.

★*Blacktop Wasteland*

★*Razorblade Tears*

Cosimano, Elle

Finlay Donovan Is Killing It

COSMIC BACKGROUND RADIATION

Lem, Stanislaw. *His Master's Voice*

A Cosmology of Monsters. Hamill, Shaun

COSPLAY

Glass, Seressia. ★*The Love Con*

COSSA, FRANCESCO DEL

Sandford, John. *Mad River*

Smith, Ali. ★*How to Be Both*

COSSACKS

Rutherfurd, Edward. *Russka: The Novel of Russia*

Cossette, Connilyn

★*Shelter of the Most High*

COSSIO Y CISNEROS, EVANGELINA

Cleeton, Chanel. *The Most Beautiful Girl in Cuba*

Dev, Sonali. ★*Incense and Sensibility*

COSTA, NIC (FICTITIOUS CHARACTER)

Hewson, David. *The Garden of Evil*

Costello, Mark

Big If

Coster, Naima

Halsey Street

What's Mine and Yours: A Novel

COSTUME

Glass, Seressia. ★*The Love Con*

COTE D'IVOIRE

D'Souza, Tony. *Whiteman*

COTSWOLDS, ENGLAND

Beaton, M. C. *Agatha Raisin and the Quiche of Death*

Beaton, M. C. ★*Hot to Trot*

Beaton, M. C. *Pushing up Daisies: An Agatha Raisin Mystery*

COTTAGES

Andrews, Mary Kay. *Sunset Beach*

Godwin, Gail. *Grief Cottage: A Novel*

Cotterill, Colin

The Coroner's Lunch

Disco for the Departed

Don't Eat Me

Killed at the Whim of a Hat

The Second Biggest Nothing
Slash and Burn: A Dr. Siri Mystery Set in Laos
Cotton Malone novels [Series]. Berry, Steve
COTTON, MARY ANN
    Deluca, Marjorie. *The Savage Instinct*
    Hamer, Kate. *The Girl in the Red Coat*
Coughlin novels [Series]. Lehane, Dennis
Coughlin, Jack
    In the Crosshairs: A Sniper Novel
    Long Shot: A Sniper Novel
Coulter, Catherine
    The Devil's Triangle
    The End Game
    The Final Cut
    Labyrinth
    The Last Second
    The Lost Key
    Paradox
    The Sixth Day
★*The **Count** of Monte Cristo*. Dumas, Alexandre
Count the Ways. Maynard, Joyce
Countdown. Ramsay, Frederick
COUNTERCULTURE
    Byatt, A. S. *A Whistling Woman*
    Cline, Emma. *The Girls: A Novel*
    Darznik, Jasmin. *The Bohemians*
    Dektar, Molly. *The Ash Family*
    ffitch, Madeline. *Stay and Fight*
    Kerouac, Jack. *The Dharma Bums*
    Kerouac, Jack. ★*On the Road*
    Kerouac, Jack. ★*Road Novels 1957-1960*
    Pynchon, Thomas. ★*The Crying of Lot 49*
    Pynchon, Thomas. *Vineland*
    Vandermeer, Jeff. *Finch*
COUNTERFEITS AND COUNTERFEITING
    MacDonald, John D. *The Scarlet Ruse*
Countess of Harleigh mysteries [Series]. Freeman, Dianne
Country Dark. Offutt, Chris
COUNTRY HOMES
    Foley, Lucy. *The Hunting Party*
    Fowler, Christopher. *Bryant & May: Hall of Mirrors : A Peculiar Crimes Unit Mystery*
    Ishiguro, Kazuo. ★*The Remains of the Day*
    Kelly, Erin. *The Burning Air: A Novel*
    Leigh, Eva. *Scandal Takes the Stage*
    Purcell, Laura. *The House of Whispers*
    Turton, Stuart. *The 7 1/2 Deaths of Evelyn Hardcastle*
    Ware, Ruth. *In a Dark, Dark Wood*
COUNTRY MUSICIANS
    Creech, Sarah. *The Whole Way Home*
COUNTS AND COUNTESSES
    Bowman, Valerie. *Secrets of a Wedding Night*
    Dumas, Alexandre. ★*Camille*
    Freeman, Dianne. *A Fiancee's Guide to First Wives and Murder*
    Freeman, Dianne. *A Lady's Guide to Etiquette and Murder*
    Kay, Guy Gavriel. ★*A Brightness Long Ago*
    Long, Julie Anne. ★*Lady Derring Takes a Lover*
    Maxwell, Everina. *Winter's Orbit*

Towles, Amor. ★*A Gentleman in Moscow*
County Cork mysteries [Series]. Connolly, Sheila
COUPLES
    Archer, Jeffrey. *Nothing Ventured*
    Atwood, Margaret. ★*Stone Mattress: Nine Tales*
    Beagle, Peter S. *Summerlong*
    Bohjalian, Chris. ★*The Red Lotus*
    Bolano, Roberto. ★*The Third Reich*
    Cameron, Lindsay. *Just One Look*
    Chakrabarti, Jai. *A Play for the End of the World*
    Clark, Marcia. *Final Judgment*
    Davis, Kathryn. *Duplex*
    Earley, Tony. *Mr. Tall: A Novella and Stories*
    Hamid, Mohsin. ★*Exit West: A Novel*
    Heiny, Katherine. ★*Early Morning Riser*
    Hilderbrand, Elin. *The Perfect Couple*
    Hoang, Helen. ★*The Heart Principle*
    Jones, Sandie. *The Other Woman*
    Krauss, Nicole. ★*To Be a Man: Stories*
    Laukkanen, Owen. *Lone Jack Trail*
    McMahon, Jennifer. *The Invited: A Novel*
    O'Hara, John. *Appointment in Samarra*
    Palmer, Lindsey J. *Otherwise Engaged*
    Reid, Iain. *I'm Thinking of Ending Things*
    Shriver, Lionel. *The Post-Birthday World*
    Slaughter, Karin. ★*The Last Widow*
    Stegner, Wallace. *Crossing to Safety*
    Straub, Emma. *The Vacationers*
    VanderMeer, Jeff. ★*Borne: A Novel*
    Willis, Connie. *Crosstalk*
    Wolitzer, Meg. *The Female Persuasion*
COUPS D'ETAT
    Campbell, Rick. *Treason*
    Pamuk, Orhan. *Silent House*
    Scott, Walter. ★*Ivanhoe*
COURAGE
    O'Brien, Tim. *Going After Cacciato: A Novel*
    Putney, Mary Jo. *Once a Soldier*
COURAGE IN MEN
    Box, C. J. ★*Open Season*
    Crane, Stephen. ★*The Red Badge of Courage: An Episode of the American Civil War*
    Frazier, Charles. *Thirteen Moons: A Novel*
    Hemingway, Ernest. ★*The Old Man and the Sea*
COURAGE IN WOMEN
    Acevedo, Chantel. *The Distant Marvels*
    Alderson, Kaia. *Sisters in Arms*
    Bird, Sarah. *Daughter of a Daughter of a Queen*
    Duenas, Maria. *The Time in Between: A Novel*
    Kandasamy, Meena. *When I Hit You, Or, a Portrait of the Writer as a Young Wife*
    Macallister, Greer. ★*The Arctic Fury*
    McHugh, Laura. *What's Done in Darkness: A Novel*
    Sharratt, Mary. *Illuminations: A Novel of Hildegard Von Bingen*
    Smith, Jill Eileen. *Star of Persia: Esther's Story*
    Tatlock, Ann. *Promises to Keep*
    Twain, Mark. *Personal Recollections of Joan of Arc*

COURAGE IN YOUNG MEN
Forester, C. S. *Lieutenant Hornblower*
COURAGE IN YOUNG WOMEN
Merullo, Roland. *The Talk-Funny Girl: A Novel*
*The **Course** of All Treasons.* Wolfe, Suzanne M.
*The **Court-Martial** of George Armstrong Custer.* Jones, Douglas C.
*The **Courtesan** Duchess.* Shupe, Joanna
COURTESANS
Bell, Lenora. ★*How the Duke Was Won*
Dumas, Alexandre. ★*Camille*
Dunant, Sarah. *In the Company of the Courtesan: A Novel*
Gowar, Imogen Hermes. *The Mermaid and Mrs. Hancock*
Hesse, Hermann. ★*Siddhartha: A New Translation*
Phillips, Christi. *The Rossetti Letter: A Novel*
Romain, Theresa. *Fortune Favors the Wicked*
Shupe, Joanna. *The Courtesan Duchess*
COURTNEY FAMILY (FICTITIOUS CHARACTERS)
Smith, Wilbur A. *Monsoon*
Courtney novels [Series]. Smith, Wilbur A.
COURTS AND COURTIERS
Alpsten, Ellen. *Tsarina*
Amirrezvani, Anita. *Equal of the Sun*
Andersen, Laura. *The Boleyn Deceit*
Andersen, Laura. ★*The Boleyn King*
Andersen, Laura. *The Boleyn Reckoning*
Black, Benjamin. *Wolf on a String: A Novel*
Clements, Oliver. *The Eyes of the Queen*
Clements, Oliver. *The Queen's Men*
Dunant, Sarah. *In the Company of the Courtesan: A Novel*
Eco, Umberto. *Baudolino*
George, Margaret. *Elizabeth I: A Novel*
Ghosh, Amitav. *The Glass Palace*
Gregory, Philippa. *The Boleyn Inheritance*
Gregory, Philippa. *The Last Tudor*
Jones, Sherry. *Four Sisters, All Queens*
Kay, Guy Gavriel. ★*A Brightness Long Ago*
Massey, Sujata. *The Satapur Moonstone*
Mina, Denise. ★*Rizzio*
Stachniak, Eva. *The Winter Palace: A Novel of Catherine the Great*
Weir, Alison. *Anna of Kleve: The Princess in the Portrait*
Weir, Alison. *Katharine Parr, the Sixth Wife*
COURTS AND COURTIERS — HISTORY
Mantel, Hilary. ★*Bring up the Bodies: A Novel*
Mantel, Hilary. ★*Wolf Hall*
COURTS-MARTIAL AND COURTS OF INQUIRY
Jones, Douglas C. *The Court-Martial of George Armstrong Custer*
Wouk, Herman. ★*The Caine Mutiny: A Novel of World War II*
COURTSHIP
Amis, Martin. ★*The Zone of Interest: A Novel*
Austen, Jane. ★*Emma*
Austen, Jane. ★*Pride and Prejudice*
Austen, Jane. ★*Sense and Sensibility*
Balogh, Mary. *The Arrangement*
Balogh, Mary. *The Escape*
Balogh, Mary. ★*Someone to Remember: A Westcott Story*
Bowman, Valerie. *The Unexpected Duchess*
Calvi, Mary. *Dear George, Dear Mary: A Novel of George Washington's First Love*

Franklin, Ariana. ★*Death and the Maiden*
Garcia Marquez, Gabriel. ★*Love in the Time of Cholera*
Hardy, Thomas. ★*Far from the Madding Crowd*
Helprin, Mark. *In Sunlight and in Shadow*
Lipman, Elinor. *The Pursuit of Alice Thrift: A Novel*
Long, Julie Anne. *Angel in a Devil's Arms*
Luesse, Valerie Fraser. *Under the Bayou Moon: A Novel*
McCall Smith, Alexander. *The Full Cupboard of Life*
Rush, Norman. ★*Mating*
Simenon, Georges. *Maigret's Memoirs*
Sparks, Nicholas. *The Guardian*
Trollope, Anthony. *The Last Chronicle of Barset*
COUSINS
Austen, Jane. *Mansfield Park*
Boudjedra, Rachid. *The Barbary Figs*
Bowman, Valerie. *The Accidental Countess*
Bush, Keisha. *No Heaven for Good Boys: A Novel*
Daniel, Ray. *Hacked: A Tucker Mystery*
Egan, Jennifer. *The Keep*
Evanovich, Janet. *One for the Money*
George, Margaret. *Elizabeth I: A Novel*
Hardy, Thomas. ★*Jude the Obscure*
Heyer, Georgette. *The Grand Sophy*
Moreno-Garcia, Silvia. ★*Gods of Jade and Shadow: A Novel*
Moreno-Garcia, Silvia. *Mexican Gothic*
Murata, Sayaka. *Earthlings: A Novel*
Penman, Sharon Kay. *When Christ and His Saints Slept*
Puzo, Mario. *The Last Don*
Roy, Arundhati. ★*The God of Small Things*
Rozan, S. J. ★*Paper Son*
Swanson, Peter. *Her Every Fear: A Novel*
Welty, Eudora. ★*Delta Wedding*
Whitehead, Colson. ★*Harlem Shuffle*
Cousins' war [Series]. Gregory, Philippa
Couto, Mia
Rain: And Other Stories
Sleepwalking Land
The Sword and the Spear
★*The **Cove**.* Rash, Ron
COVID-19 (DISEASE)
Picoult, Jodi. ★*Wish You Were Here: A Novel*
COVID-19 PANDEMIC, 2019-
Monroe, Mary Alice. ★*The Summer of Lost and Found*
COWARDICE
Conrad, Joseph. ★*Lord Jim*
COWARDICE IN MEN
Crane, Stephen. ★*The Red Badge of Courage: An Episode of the American Civil War*
Greene, Graham. *The Tenth Man*
*A **Cowboy** to Remember.* Weatherspoon, Rebekah
COWBOYS
Brown, Sandra. ★*Blind Tiger*
Ciotta, Beth. *Her Sky Cowboy*
Dexter, Pete. ★*Deadwood*
Drake, Laura. *The Sweet Spot*
Fields, Hilary. *Last Chance Llama Ranch*
McMurtry, Larry. ★*Lonesome Dove: A Novel*
Proulx, Annie. *Bad Dirt: Wyoming Stories 2*

Schaefer, Jack. *Monte Walsh*
Smith, B. J. *All Hat: A Novel*
Smith, B. J. *The Return of Kid Cooper: A Novel*
Weatherspoon, Rebekah. *A Cowboy to Remember*
Weatherspoon, Rebekah. *If the Boot Fits*
Weatherspoon, Rebekah. *A Thorn in the Saddle*
Cowboys of California [Series]. Weatherspoon, Rebekah
Cowboys of Colorado [Series]. Goodman, Jo
COWGIRLS
Peterson, Tracie. *What Comes My Way*
COWORKERS
Dazieri, Sandrone. *Kill the King*
Dickey, Eric Jerome. ★*The Son of Mr. Suleman*
French, Tana. *In the Woods*
Ho, Lauren. *Last Tang Standing*
Kasulke, Calvin. *Several People Are Typing*
Lauren, Christina. *Dating You / Hating You*
Solomon, Rachel Lynn. ★*The Ex Talk*
Walser, Robert. *The Assistant*
Ware, Ruth. ★*One by One*
Winfrey, Kerry. *Not Like the Movies*
Coyote novels [Series]. Steele, Allen M.
Coyote: *a Novel of Interstellar Exploration*. Steele, Allen M.
COZY MYSTERIES
Andrew, Sally. *The Satanic Mechanic: A Tannie Maria Mystery*
Andrews, Donna. *Murder Most Fowl: A Meg Langslow Mystery*
Andrews, Donna. *Owl Be Home for Christmas: A Meg Langslow Mystery*
Andrews, Donna. *The Twelve Jays of Christmas: A Meg Langslow Mystery*
Avon, Joy. *In Peppermint Peril: A Book Tea Shop Mystery*
Beaton, M. C. *Agatha Raisin and the Quiche of Death*
Beaton, M. C. *Death of a Macho Man*
Beaton, M. C. ★*Hot to Trot*
Beaton, M. C. *Pushing up Daisies: An Agatha Raisin Mystery*
Bernhard, Emilia. *The Books of the Dead*
Berry, Connie. *A Legacy of Murder*
Block, Lawrence. *The Burglar in the Closet*
Block, Lawrence. ★*The Burglar in the Library*
Braun, Lilian Jackson. *The Cat Who Ate Danish Modern*
Brett, Simon. *Guilt at the Garage*
Brett, Simon. *Mrs Pargeter's Principle*
Brown, Rita Mae. *Wish You Were Here*
Burns, V. M. *Killer Words*
Childs, Laura. *Egg Shooters*
Childs, Laura. *Haunted Hibiscus*
Childs, Laura. *Lavender Blue Murder*
Childs, Laura. *Twisted Tea Christmas*
Cleland, Jane K. *Hidden Treasure*
Connolly, Sheila. *The Lost Traveller*
Davidson, Diane Mott. *Killer Pancake*
Davidson, Diane Mott. *The Last Suppers*
Delany, Vicki. *Murder in a Teacup*
Delany, Vicki. *Tea & Treachery*
Estleman, Loren D. *Frames*
Fluke, Joanne. ★*Christmas Cupcake Murder*
Gates, Eva. *Deadly Ever After*
Gates, Eva. *A Death Long Overdue*

Gates, Eva. *Read and Buried*
Hall, Parnell. *Lights! Camera! Puzzles!*
Hart, Carolyn G. *Ghost Blows a Kiss*
Heley, Veronica. *Murder in Law*
Hollis, Lee. *Poppy Harmon Investigates*
James, Miranda. *What the Cat Dragged In*
Malliet, G. M. *A Demon Summer: A Max Tudor Mystery*
Malliet, G. M. *Pagan Spring: A Mystery*
Manansala, Mia P. ★*Arsenic and Adobo*
McCall Smith, Alexander. *Blue Shoes and Happiness*
McCall Smith, Alexander. *The Double Comfort Safari Club*
McCall Smith, Alexander. *The Full Cupboard of Life*
McCall Smith, Alexander. *The Good Husband of Zebra Drive*
McCall Smith, Alexander. *In the Company of Cheerful Ladies*
McCall Smith, Alexander. *The Joy and Light Bus Company*
McCall Smith, Alexander. *The Kalahari Typing School for Men*
McCall Smith, Alexander. *The Limpopo Academy of Private Detection*
McCall Smith, Alexander. ★*The No. 1 Ladies' Detective Agency*
McCall Smith, Alexander. *The Saturday Big Tent Wedding Party*
McKevett, G. A. *A Few Drops of Bitters*
McKevett, G. A. *Murder at Mabel's Motel*
McKevett, G. A. *Murder in the Corn Maze*
McKinlay, Jenn. *Killer Research*
Meier, Leslie. *Silver Anniversary Murder*
O'Connor, Carlene. *Murder in an Irish Bookshop*
O'Donohue, Clare. *The Lover's Knot: A Someday Quilts Mystery*
Perkins, S. C. *Murder Once Removed*
Roosevelt, Elliott. ★*Murder and the First Lady*
Roosevelt, Elliott. *Murder at Midnight*
Roosevelt, Elliott. *Murder in the Map Room: An Eleanor Roosevelt Mystery*
Roosevelt, Elliott. *Murder in the Oval Office*
Ross, Ann B. *Miss Julia Delivers the Goods: A Novel*
Ross, Ann B. ★*Miss Julia Happily Ever After*
Ross, Ann B. *Miss Julia Knows a Thing or Two*
Ross, Ann B. *Miss Julia Takes the Wheel*
Ross, Ann B. *Miss Julia Throws a Wedding*
Saums, Mary. *Thistle & Twigg*
Shaw, M. B. *Murder at the Mill: A Mystery*
Crabwalk. Grass, Gunter
Crace, Jim
Harvest
Quarantine
CRACK ADDICTS
Speight, Shameek A. ★*A Child of a Crack Head*
CRACK TRAFFIC
Price, Richard. *Clockers*
Crafts, Hannah
The Bondwoman's Narrative
CRAFTS, HANNAH
Crafts, Hannah. *The Bondwoman's Narrative*
The Craftsman. Bolton, S. J.
Craig, Charmaine
Miss Burma
Crais, Robert
A Dangerous Man
Demolition Angel: A Novel.

The First Rule
Suspect
Cramer, W. Dale
   Levi's Will: A Novel
Crane, Stephen
   Maggie: A Girl of the Streets
   ★*The Red Badge of Courage: An Episode of the American Civil War*
★*Cranford*. Gaskell, Elizabeth Cleghorn
Crave all [Series]. Gray, Erick S.
Crazy Cupid Love. Heger, Amanda
CRAZY HORSE
   Punke, Michael. *Ridgeline: A Novel*
CRAZY HORSE, APPROXIMATELY 1842-1877
   Perry, Anne. ★*A Darker Reality*
Crazy in Alabama. Childress, Mark
Crazy Rich Asians. Kwan, Kevin
Crazybone: A. Pronzini, Bill
CREATION
   Tolkien, J. R. R. *The Silmarillion*
   VanderMeer, Jeff. *Dead Astronauts: A Novel*
CREATION (LITERARY, ARTISTIC, ETC.)
   Gentill, Sulari. *Crossing the Lines*
CREATIVE WRITING
   Baker, Jo. *The Body Lies*
   Dermansky, Marcy. *Very Nice*
CREATIVE WRITING TEACHERS
   Chabon, Michael. ★*Wonder Boys*
   Korelitz, Jean Hanff. ★*The Plot*
   Lutz, Lisa. *The Swallows: A Novel*
   Schumacher, Julie. *Dear Committee Members*
CREATIVITY
   Brundage, Elizabeth. *The Vanishing Point*
   Hajdu, David. *Adrianne Geffel: A Fiction*
   Hughes, Caoilinn. *Orchid and the Wasp*
   Jaswal, Balli Kaur. *Erotic Stories for Punjabi Widows*
   Kaufman, Charlie. *Antkind: A Novel*
   Rand, Ayn. ★*The Fountainhead*
   Rose, Heather. *The Museum of Modern Love*
   Roth, Henry. *From Bondage*
   Taylor, Brandon. ★*Filthy Animals*
   Weinberg, Kate. *The Truants*
CREATIVITY IN MEN
   Banville, John. *The Blue Guitar*
   Barnes, Julian. *The Noise of Time*
   Castellani, Christopher. *Leading Men: A Novel*
   Chabon, Michael. ★*Wonder Boys*
   Doyle, Rob. *Threshold*
   Littell, Robert. *The Mayakovsky Tapes: A Novel*
   Saramago, Jose. *The Manual of Painting and Calligraphy*
   Stone, Irving. ★*The Agony and the Ecstasy: A Biographical Novel of Michelangelo*
   Toibin, Colm. ★*The Magician: A Novel*
CREATIVITY IN WOMEN
   Acampora, Lauren. *The Paper Wasp: A Novel*
   Bourland, Barbara. ★*Fake Like Me*
   Ferrante, Elena. *Those Who Leave and Those Who Stay*
   Goldberg, Myla. *Feast Your Eyes*
Creatures: a Novel. Van Meter, Crissy

Creech, Sarah
   The Whole Way Home
CREEK INDIANS
   Brown, Dee. *Creek Mary's Blood: A Novel*
Creek Mary's Blood: A Novel. Brown, Dee
CREOLE WOMEN
   Depestre, Rene. *Hadriana in All My Dreams*
Crescent. Abu-Jaber, Diana
Crescent City Kill: A Skip Langdon Novel. Smith, Julie
Crescent City novels (Bryan Camp) [Series]. Camp, Bryan
CRETE
   Horowitz, Anthony. ★*Moonflower Murders*
   Renault, Mary. *The King Must Die*
   Saint, Jennifer. *Ariadne*
Crews, Harry
   A Feast of Snakes: A Novel
Crichton, Michael
   Pirate Latitudes
   Prey: A Novel
CRICKET (SPORTS)
   Adiga, Aravind. *Selection Day*
   Hall, Tarquin. *The Case of the Deadly Butter Chicken: A Vish Puri Mystery*
CRIME
   Atkins, Ace. *The Sinners*
   Burgess, Anthony. ★*A Clockwork Orange*
   Burke, James Lee. *The Jealous Kind*
   Carr, Caleb. ★*The Alienist*
   Catton, Eleanor. *The Luminaries: A Novel*
   Crace, Jim. *Harvest*
   Cussler, Clive. ★*The Chase*
   Doctorow, E. L. ★*Billy Bathgate: A Novel*
   Estleman, Loren D. ★*Amos Walker: The Complete Story Collection*
   Evanovich, Janet. ★*Game On: Tempting Twenty-Eight*
   Faye, Lyndsay. *The Whole Art of Detection: Lost Mysteries of Sherlock Holmes*
   Goldberg, Tod. *Gangsterland: A Novel*
   Hawkins, Paula. ★*The Girl on the Train: A Novel*
   Herron, Mick. *Dolphin Junction: Collected Stories*
   Indriðason, Arnaldur. *Reykjavik Nights: An Inspector Erlendur Novel*
   Leon, Donna. ★*Transient Desires*
   Leonard, Elmore. *Charlie Martz and Other Stories: The Unpublished Stories*
   Leonard, Elmore. *Tishomingo Blues: A Novel*
   McCall Smith, Alexander. ★*The Man with the Silver Saab: A Detective Varg Novel*
   Mina, Denise. *Conviction*
   Moshfegh, Ottessa. *Eileen*
   Panowich, Brian. *Like Lions*
   Paretsky, Sara. *Love & Other Crimes: Stories*
   Rindell, Suzanne. *The Other Typist*
   Rinehart, Mary Roberts. *The Circular Staircase*
   Robotham, Michael. ★*Good Girl, Bad Girl: A Novel*
   Russo, Richard. ★*Everybody's Fool*
   Sharpe, Tess. *Barbed Wire Heart*
   Spillane, Mickey. *A Long Time Dead: A Mike Hammer Casebook*
   Wambaugh, Joseph. *The New Centurions*
   Whitehead, Colson. ★*Harlem Shuffle*

Winslow, Don. *Broken: Six Short Novels*
Yates, Christopher J. *Grist Mill Road: A Novel*
★*Crime and Punishment*. Dostoyevsky, Fyodor
CRIME BOSSES
Pelecanos, George P. *The Cut: A Novel*
CRIME FICTION
Abbott, Megan E. *Queenpin: A Novel*
Beverly, William. *Dodgers: A Novel*
Blake, James Carlos. *The House of Wolfe*
Block, Lawrence. *Hit Me: A Keller Novel*
Burke, James Lee. *The Jealous Kind*
Cooper, Tom. *Florida Man*
Cooper, Tom. *The Marauders*
Cosby, S. A. ★*Blacktop Wasteland*
Cosby, S. A. ★*Razorblade Tears*
Ellroy, James. ★*L.A. Confidential*
Estleman, Loren D. ★*Gas City*
Faust, Christa. *Choke Hold*
Faust, Christa. *Money Shot*
Goldberg, Tod. *Gangsterland: A Novel*
Goodis, David. *Nightfall*
Greene, Graham. ★*Brighton Rock*
Hamilton, Steve. ★*The Lock Artist*
Hamilton, Steve. *The Second Life of Nick Mason: A Novel*
Hart, John. *Iron House*
Harvey, Michael T. *Brighton*
Hiaasen, Carl. *Bad Monkey*
Hiaasen, Carl. ★*Squeeze Me: A Novel*
Hilton, L. S. *Maestra*
Hoeg, Peter. ★*Smilla's Sense of Snow*
Kennedy, Randy. *Presidio*
Lawton, John. *Then We Take Berlin*
Lehane, Dennis. *Live by Night*
Lehane, Dennis. *World Gone By: A Novel*
Leonard, Elmore. ★*Be Cool: Everyone Is Looking for the Next Big Hit*
Leonard, Elmore. ★*Get Shorty*
Leonard, Elmore. ★*Killshot*
Leonard, Elmore. *Pagan Babies*
Leonard, Elmore. ★*Raylan*
Leonard, Elmore. *Tishomingo Blues: A Novel*
Leonard, Elmore. *When the Women Come Out to Dance: Stories*
Mamet, David. *Chicago: A Novel*
Martinson, T. J. *The Reign of the Kingfisher: A Novel*
McCarthy, Cormac. ★*No Country for Old Men*
O'Rawe, Richard. *Northern Heist*
Panowich, Brian. *Hard Cash Valley*
Petersen, Todd Robert. *Picnic in the Ruins*
Piccirilli, Tom. *The Last Kind Words*
Piccirilli, Tom. *The Last Whisper in the Dark: A Novel*
Pollock, Donald Ray. *The Devil All the Time*
Price, Richard. *Lush Life*
Pryor, Mark. *Hollow Man*
Puzo, Mario. ★*The Godfather*
Puzo, Mario. *The Last Don*
Puzo, Mario. *The Sicilian: A Novel*
Robotham, Michael. *Life or Death*
Rosen, Leonard J. *The Kortelisy Escape*

Rosen, Renee. *Dollface: A Novel of the Roaring Twenties*
Sharpe, Tess. *Barbed Wire Heart*
Sigurðardóttir, Lilja. *Cage*
Skarmeta, Antonio. *The Dancer and the Thief: A Novel*
Smith, B. J. *All Hat: A Novel*
Smith, Mark Haskell. *Baked*
Soderberg, Alexander. *The Other Son: A Sophie Brinkmann Novel*
Stansel, Ian. *The Last Cowboys of San Geronimo*
Stark, Richard. *Ask the Parrot: A Parker Novel*
Stark, Richard. *Breakout*
Stark, Richard. *Comeback*
Stark, Richard. *Dirty Money*
Stark, Richard. *The Hunter: A Parker Novel*
Stark, Richard. *The Jugger: A Parker Novel*
Sternbergh, Adam. *The Blinds*
Takamura, Kaoru. ★*Lady Joker*
Tinti, Hannah. *The Twelve Lives of Samuel Hawley: A Novel*
Tran, Vu. *Dragonfish: A Novel*
Vachss, Andrew H. *Two Trains Running*
Weiden, David L. ★*Winter Counts*
Weir, Andy. *Artemis*
Whitehead, Colson. ★*Harlem Shuffle*
Willink, Jocko. *Final Spin*
Winslow, Don. *The Border*
Winslow, Don. *Broken: Six Short Novels*
Youers, Rio. *Lola on Fire*
CRIME LABORATORIES
James, P. D. *Death of an Expert Witness*
CRIME PREVENTION
Dick, Philip K. *The Minority Report*
Hayes, Terry. *I Am Pilgrim*
CRIME SCENES
Black, Saul. ★*Lovemurder*
Burton, Jeffrey B. ★*The Finders: A Mace Reid K-9 Mystery*
Coben, Harlan. *Long Lost*
Cornwell, Patricia Daniels. *Autopsy*
Goldberg, Lee. *Bone Canyon*
Hunt, April. *Deadly Obsession*
Kellerman, Jonathan. ★*Half Moon Bay: A Novel*
McPherson, Catriona. *Strangers at the Gate*
Pobi, Robert. *City of Windows*
Quick, Amanda. *Close Up*
Rice, Craig. *Home Sweet Homicide*
Robinson, Peter. ★*Careless Love*
Robinson, Peter. *In the Dark Places*
Rowland, Laura Joh. *The Hangman's Secret*
CRIMEAN TATARS
Rutherfurd, Edward. *Russka: The Novel of Russia*
CRIMEAN WAR VETERANS
Goodwin, S. M. *Absence of Mercy*
CRIMEAN WAR, 1853-1856
Fforde, Jasper. *The Eyre Affair: A Novel*
CRIMES ABOARD TRAINS
Christie, Agatha. ★*Murder on the Orient Express*
CRIMES AGAINST AFRICAN AMERICANS
Guinn, Matthew. *The Scribe: A Novel*
Shames, Terry. ★*An Unsettling Crime for Samuel Craddock*

CRIMES AGAINST BOYS
Carr, Caleb. ★*The Alienist*
CRIMES AGAINST CHILDREN
Abdul-Jabbar, Kareem. ★*Mycroft Holmes*
Bolton, S. J. *The Craftsman*
Carr, Caleb. *The Angel of Darkness*
Corby, Gary. *The Marathon Conspiracy*
Faye, Lyndsay. *The Gods of Gotham*
Fox, Candice. *Gone by Midnight*
Grossman, Paul. *Children of Wrath*
King, Stephen. *It*
MacBride, Stuart. *Cold Granite*
CRIMES AGAINST FAMILY
Flynn, Gillian. *Dark Places*
CRIMES AGAINST GAY MEN AND LESBIANS
Winer, Jeanne. *Her Kind of Case*
CRIMES AGAINST GENERALS
Child, Lee. *The Enemy*
CRIMES AGAINST GIRLS
Danticat, Edwidge. *Claire of the Sea Light*
Krentz, Jayne Ann. *Secret Sisters*
McLean, Felicity. *The Van Apfel Girls Are Gone*
Patterson, James. ★*Private*
Roy, Lori. *Bent Road*
Spencer, Sally. *A Walk with the Dead*
CRIMES AGAINST JOURNALISTS
Rankin, Ian. *Blood Hunt: A Novel*
Solares, Martin. *The Black Minutes*
CRIMES AGAINST JUDGES
Grisham, John. ★*The Pelican Brief*
CRIMES AGAINST LAWYERS
Connelly, Michael. *The Brass Verdict: A Novel*
CRIMES AGAINST MARRIED PEOPLE
Robotham, Michael. ★*Say You're Sorry*
CRIMES AGAINST MEN
Qiu, Xiaolong. *Don't Cry Tai Lake: An Inspector Chen Novel*
Qiu, Xiaolong. *Enigma of China*
CRIMES AGAINST NATIVE AMERICANS
Verble, Margaret. ★*Cherokee America*
CRIMES AGAINST POLICE
Sjowall, Maj. ★*Cop Killer: The Story of a Crime*
Spillane, Mickey. *Kill Me, Darling*
CRIMES AGAINST POLITICIANS
Ridpath, Michael. *Far North*
CRIMES AGAINST PROSTITUTES
Block, Lawrence. *Eight Million Ways to Die*
Brooks, Bill. *Blood Storm*
Connelly, Michael. *The Gods of Guilt*
Crompton, Richard. *Hour of the Red God*
Hill, Susan. *The Shadows in the Street: A Simon Serrailler Mystery*
Lippman, Laura. ★*And When She Was Good*
Shannon, Dell. ★*Chaos of Crime*
CRIMES AGAINST RICH PEOPLE
Dahl, Arne. *Misterioso: A Crime Novel*
Quartey, Kwei. *Murder at Cape Three Points*
CRIMES AGAINST SECRETARIES
Quick, Amanda. *Garden of Lies*

CRIMES AGAINST SENIORS
Barclay, Linwood. *No Safe House*
Keller, Julia. *A Killing in the Hills*
Penny, Louise. ★*All the Devils Are Here*
Sandford, John. ★*Invisible Prey*
CRIMES AGAINST TEENAGE GIRLS
Connelly, Michael. *Dark Sacred Night*
Rendell, Ruth. *End in Tears*
Robinson, Peter. *Innocent Graves*
Sebold, Alice. ★*The Lovely Bones*
Smith, Julie. *Louisiana Hotshot*
CRIMES AGAINST TOURISTS
Robertson, Michael. *The Brothers of Baker Street*
Sundstol, Vidar. *The Land of Dreams*
CRIMES AGAINST WOMEN
Bolton, S. J. *Now You See Me*
Church, James. *Bamboo and Blood: An Inspector O Novel*
Connelly, Michael. *The Late Show*
Faulkner, William. ★*Sanctuary*
Ferraris, Zoe. *Kingdom of Strangers: A Novel*
Fielding, Joy. *All the Wrong Places: A Novel*
Fleischmann, Raymond. *How Quickly She Disappears*
George, Elizabeth. *This Body of Death: An Inspector Lynley Novel*
Greenwood, Kerry. *Death in Daylesford*
Hart, Carolyn G. *Letter from Home*
Kellerman, Jonathan. *Bones: An Alex Delaware Novel*
Lovesey, Peter. *The Tooth Tattoo*
Nesbo, Jo. *The Leopard*
Qiu, Xiaolong. *When Red Is Black*
Reichs, Kathy. *206 Bones*
Ross, Adam. *Mr. Peanut*
Sandford, John. ★*Rules of Prey*
Sjowall, Maj. ★*Cop Killer: The Story of a Crime*
Spencer, Sally. *Death's Dark Shadow*
CRIMES OF PASSION
Simenon, Georges. ★*Maigret and the Saturday Caller*
CRIMINAL EVIDENCE
Edwards, Yvvette. *The Mother*
Kane, Darby. *Pretty Little Wife*
Robinson, Peter. ★*Careless Love*
Rosen, Leonard J. *The Kortelisy Escape*
Roslund, Anders. *Cell 8*
CRIMINAL EVIDENCE TAMPERING
Brown, Rosellen. ★*Before and After*
CRIMINAL INVESTIGATION
Box, C. J. *Savage Run*
Christie, Agatha. *Three Blind Mice, and Other Stories*
Crombie, Deborah. *A Bitter Feast*
Crumley, James. *The Last Good Kiss: A Novel*
De Leon, Aya. ★*A Spy in the Struggle*
Doyle, Arthur Conan. ★*The Complete Sherlock Holmes*
Faye, Lyndsay. *The Whole Art of Detection: Lost Mysteries of Sherlock Holmes*
Finder, Joseph. *Buried Secrets*
Finder, Joseph. *Guilty Minds*
Fowler, Christopher. *Bryant & May: Oranges and Lemons*
Freeman, Brian. *Marathon*
George, Elizabeth. *A Banquet of Consequences*

Golding, Melanie. *The Hidden: A Novel*
Griffiths, Elly. *The Crossing Places*
Griffiths, Elly. *The Janus Stone*
Harvey, John. *A Darker Shade of Blue: Stories*
Herron, Mick. *Dolphin Junction: Collected Stories*
Hillerman, Tony. *The Shape Shifter*
Kemelman, Harry. *Monday the Rabbi Took Off*
Kemelman, Harry. *One Fine Day the Rabbi Bought a Cross*
Leon, Donna. *Trace Elements*
Leon, Donna. ★*Transient Desires*
Leon, Donna. *Unto Us a Son Is Given*
Leonard, Elmore. ★*Raylan*
Mandel, Emily St. John. *The Singer's Gun: A Novel*
McCall Smith, Alexander. ★*The Department of Sensitive Crimes: A Detective Varg Novel*
McCall Smith, Alexander. ★*The Man with the Silver Saab: A Detective Varg Novel*
Nava, Michael. ★*Carved in Bone*
Paretsky, Sara. *Indemnity Only: A Novel*
Preston, Douglas J. *Crooked River*
Price, Richard. *Samaritan*
Pronzini, Bill. *The Stolen Gold Affair*
Rollins, James. *The Devil Colony*
Sansom, C. J. ★*Lamentation*
Saylor, Steven. *The House of the Vestals: The Investigations of Gordianus the Finder*
Simenon, Georges. ★*Maigret and the Killer*
Simenon, Georges. *Maigret and the Madwoman*
Simenon, Georges. *Maigret and the Wine Merchant*
Spillane, Mickey. *A Long Time Dead: A Mike Hammer Casebook*
Stewart, Amy. ★*Miss Kopp Just Won't Quit*
Sundin, Sarah. *Through Waters Deep: A Novel*
Vidich, Paul. *The Coldest Warrior*
Woods, Stuart. *The Money Shot*
Yang, JY. *The Descent of Monsters*

CRIMINAL JUSTICE SYSTEM
Dow, David R. *Confessions of an Innocent Man*
Pava, Sergio de la. *Lost Empress: A Novel*
Persson Giolito, Malin. *Beyond All Reasonable Doubt: A Novel*
Turow, Scott. *The Last Trial*

CRIMINAL PROFILERS
Gardiner, Meg. *The Dark Corners of the Night*
Gardiner, Meg. *Into the Black Nowhere*
Grebe, Camilla. *After She's Gone: A Novel*
Grebe, Camilla. *The Ice Beneath Her: A Novel*

CRIMINAL PROFILING
Rader-Day, Lori. *The Day I Died*

CRIMINAL PSYCHOLOGY
Garcia-Roza, L. A. *Alone in the Crowd: An Inspector Espinosa Mystery*
Robotham, Michael. ★*When She Was Good*

Criminal: a Novel. Slaughter, Karin

CRIMINALS
Adler-Olsen, Jussi. *The Marco Effect: A Department Q Novel*
Algren, Nelson. ★*The Man with the Golden Arm: A Novel*
Amis, Martin. *Lionel Asbo: State of England*
Amis, Martin. *London Fields: A Novel*
Archer, Jeffrey. *Nothing Ventured*

Atkins, Ace. *The Fallen*
Atkins, Ace. *The Sinners*
Auster, Paul. *Travels in the Scriptorium: A Novel*
Banville, John. *The Book of Evidence*
Beukes, Lauren. *Zoo City*
Child, Lee. ★*The Sentinel*
Child, Lee. *Worth Dying For*
Crais, Robert. *The First Rule*
Cussler, Clive. ★*The Oracle*
Deaver, Jeffery. *Edge: A Novel*
Deaver, Jeffery. *Garden of Beasts: A Novel of Berlin 1936*
Dickens, Charles. *Oliver Twist, or the Parish Boy's Progress*
Dostoyevsky, Fyodor. ★*Crime and Punishment*
Ellroy, James. *American Tabloid: A Novel*
Estleman, Loren D. *The Adventures of Johnny Vermillion: A Novel*
Estleman, Loren D. ★*Amos Walker: The Complete Story Collection*
Estleman, Loren D. *Infernal Angels*
Flores, Fernando A. *Tears of the Trufflepig*
Freeman, Castle. *All That I Have: A Novel*
Grafton, Sue. *Y Is for Yesterday*
Gray, Erick S. *Love & a Gangsta: A Novel*
Grenville, Kate. *The Secret River*
Hamilton, Steve. ★*The Lock Artist*
Hiaasen, Carl. *Skin Tight*
Higgins, George V. *The Friends of Eddie Coyle*
Jones, Cherie. *How the One-Armed Sister Sweeps Her House*
K'wan. ★*Diamonds and Pearl*
Lehane, Dennis. *World Gone By: A Novel*
Leonard, Elmore. *The Hot Kid*
Leonard, Elmore. *Pagan Babies*
Leonard, Elmore. *When the Women Come Out to Dance: Stories*
Manning, Max. *The Victim: A Novel*
Montgomery, Jess. *The Stills*
Mosley, Walter. *Trouble Is What I Do: A Leonid McGill Mystery*
Palmer, Ada. *Too Like the Lightning*
Panowich, Brian. *Hard Cash Valley*
Panowich, Brian. *Like Lions*
Parker, T. Jefferson. *L.A. Outlaws: A Novel*
Petersen, Todd Robert. *Picnic in the Ruins*
Piccirilli, Tom. *The Last Kind Words*
Piccirilli, Tom. *The Last Whisper in the Dark: A Novel*
Pintoff, Stefanie. *Hostage Taker: A Novel*
Pynchon, Thomas. *Inherent Vice*
Rabe, Peter. ★*Anatomy of a Killer ;: A Shroud for Jesso*
Rajaniemi, Hannu. *The Fractal Prince*
Rajaniemi, Hannu. *The Quantum Thief*
Rankin, Ian. ★*A Song for the Dark Times*
Sallis, James. *Drive*
Sandford, John. *Storm Prey*
Sears, Michael. *Tower of Babel*
Shannon, Dell. ★*Chaos of Crime*
Shelton, Paige. *Thin Ice: A Mystery*
Shoham, Liad. *Asylum City: A Novel*
Spillane, Mickey. *The Consummata*
Stark, Richard. *Ask the Parrot: A Parker Novel*
Stark, Richard. *Dirty Money*
Stark, Richard. *The Hunter: A Parker Novel*
Stark, Richard. *The Jugger: A Parker Novel*

Sternbergh, Adam. *The Blinds*
Wambaugh, Joseph. *The New Centurions*
Westlake, Donald E. ★*Bank Shot*
Westlake, Donald E. *Get Real*
Westlake, Donald E. *The Hot Rock*
Westlake, Donald E. *The Road to Ruin*
Woods, Stuart. ★*Bombshell*
CRIMINALS WITH MENTAL ILLNESSES
    Lehane, Dennis. *Shutter Island*
Criminals: a Novel. Livesey, Margot
Crimson Lake. Fox, Candice
Crimson Lake [Series]. Fox, Candice
The Crimson Petal and the White. Faber, Michel
Crisis. Francis, Felix
CRITICISM
    Nabokov, Vladimir Vladimirovich. *Pale Fire*
CRITICS
    Lethem, Jonathan. *Chronic City*
CROATIA
    Grossman, David. ★*More Than I Love My Life: A Novel*
    Novic, Sara. *Girl at War*
The Crocodile. De Giovanni, Maurizio
Crombie, Deborah
    A Bitter Feast
Crompton, Richard
    Hell's Gate: A Novel
    Hour of the Red God
CROMWELL, THOMAS
    Child, Lee. *The Enemy*
    Mantel, Hilary. ★*Bring up the Bodies: A Novel*
    Mantel, Hilary. ★*Wolf Hall*
    Pynchon, Thomas. ★*Bleeding Edge*
Cronin, A. J.
    Citadel
    The Keys of the Kingdom
Cronin, Justin
    The City of Mirrors
    The Passage
    The Twelve
Cronin, Marianne
    The One Hundred Years of Lenni and Margot
★*Crooked Hallelujah*. Ford, Kelli Jo
Crooked Letter, Crooked Letter: A Novel. Franklin, Tom
Crooked Numbers. O'Mara, Tim
Crooked River. Preston, Douglas J.
★*Cross Her Heart: A Novel*. Pinborough, Sarah
Cross My Heart. Hatcher, Robin Lee
CROSS-COUNTRY AUTOMOBILE TRIPS
    Bloom, Amy. *Lucky Us: A Novel*
    Luiselli, Valeria. ★*Lost Children Archive: A Novel*
CROSS-DRESSERS
    Grebe, Camilla. *After She's Gone: A Novel*
The Cross-Legged Knight: An Owen Archer Mystery. Robb, Candace M.
Cross-Smith, Leesa
    Whiskey & Ribbons
Crossan, Sarah
    Here Is the Beehive
Crossbones. Farah, Nuruddin

The Crossing. Connelly, Michael
The Crossing. McCarthy, Cormac
The Crossing Places. Griffiths, Elly
Crossing Purgatory. Schanbacher, Gary Lester
Crossing the Lines. Gentill, Sulari
Crossing to Safety. Stegner, Wallace
★*Crossings: Consisting of Three Manuscripts : The Education of a Monster : City of Ghosts : Tales Of.* Landragin, Alex
★*Crossroads*. Franzen, Jonathan
Crosstalk. Willis, Connie
CROSSWORD PUZZLE MAKERS
    Hall, Parnell. *Lights! Camera! Puzzles!*
CROSSWORD PUZZLES
    Hall, Parnell. *Lights! Camera! Puzzles!*
Crouch, Blake
    Dark Matter: A Novel
    Recursion
Crouch, Katie
    Embassy Wife
Crow Fair: Stories. McGuane, Thomas
Crow Lake. Lawson, Mary
The Crow Road. Banks, Iain
The Crow Trap. Cleeves, Ann
Crow's Landing: A Novel. Smith, B. J.
Crow, Sarah McCraw
    The Wrong Kind of Woman
Crowell, Jenn
    Etched on Me: A Novel
Crowley, John
    Lord Byron's Novel: The Evening Land
CROWN HEIGHTS, NEW YORK CITY
    Potok, Chaim. ★*My Name Is Asher Lev*
CROWN JEWELS
    Khan, Vaseem. *The Perplexing Theft of the Jewel in the Crown*
CROWS
    Buxton, Kira Jane. ★*Hollow Kingdom*
Crowther and Westerman mysteries [Series]. Robertson, Imogen
CROZET, VIRGINIA
    Brown, Rita Mae. *Wish You Were Here*
Crucet, Jennine Capo
    Make Your Home Among Strangers
Crucible. Rollins, James
CRUCIFIXION
    Potzsch, Oliver. *The Play of Death*
Cruel as the Grave. Harrod-Eagles, Cynthia
Cruel Mercy. Mark, David John
The Cruel Sea. Monsarrat, Nicholas
The Cruelest Month: A Three Pines Mystery. Penny, Louise
CRUELTY IN MEN
    Dickens, Charles. ★*Nicholas Nickleby*
CRUELTY IN WOMEN
    Bronsky, Alina. *The Hottest Dishes of the Tartar Cuisine*
CRUISE SHIPS
    Hockman, Angie. *Shipped*
Crumley, James
    The Last Good Kiss: A Novel
    ★*The Wrong Case*

Crummey, Michael
Galore
The Innocents
Sweetland
CRUSADERS (MIDDLE AGES)
Holland, Cecelia. *Jerusalem*
CRUSADES
Eco, Umberto. *Baudolino*
Holland, Cecelia. *Jerusalem*
Cruse, Howard
The Complete Wendel
CRUSHES (INTERPERSONAL RELATIONS)
Jones, Darynda. *A Good Day for Chardonnay*
Lauren, Christina. *In a Holidaze*
Loedel, Daniel. *Hades, Argentina*
McQuiston, Casey. ★*One Last Stop*
Ridley, Erica. ★*The Perks of Loving a Wallflower*
Stibbe, Nina. *Reasons to Be Cheerful*
Vargas Llosa, Mario. *The Bad Girl*
CRUSHES IN BOYS
Kawakami, Mieko. *Ms. Ice Sandwich*
CRUSHES IN MEN
Bellow, Saul. ★*Humboldt's Gift*
CRUSOE, ROBINSON (FICTITIOUS CHARACTER)
Defoe, Daniel. ★*Robinson Crusoe*
Cruz, Angie
Dominicana: A Novel
Cry of Metal & Bone: Earthsinger Chronicles, Book 3. Penelope, L.
★*Cry, the Beloved Country*. Paton, Alan
★*The Crying of Lot 49*. Pynchon, Thomas
CRYONICS
DeLillo, Don. *Zero K: A Novel*
Stephenson, Neal. ★*Fall Or, Dodge in Hell: A Novel*
Winterson, Jeanette. ★*Frankissstein*
CRYPTOGRAPHERS
Harris, Robert. *Enigma*
Stephenson, Neal. ★*Cryptonomicon*
CRYPTOGRAPHY
Harris, Robert. *Enigma*
★*Cryptonomicon*. Stephenson, Neal
★*The Crystal Cave*. Stewart, Mary
The Crystal Frontier: A Novel in Nine Stories. Fuentes, Carlos
CTHULHU (FICTITIOUS CHARACTER)
Lovecraft, H. P. ★*Tales*
CUBA
Acevedo, Chantel. *The Distant Marvels*
Block, Lawrence. *Killing Castro*
Burdick, Serena. *Find Me in Havana*
Cussler, Clive. ★*Golden Buddha*
Cussler, Clive. *Havana Storm*
DeMille, Nelson. ★*The Cuban Affair: A Novel*
Gala, Marcial. ★*The Black Cathedral*
Garcia, Cristina. *The Aguero Sisters*
Garcia, Cristina. *Dreaming in Cuban*
Garcia, Gabriela. *Of Women and Salt*
Hemingway, Ernest. ★*The Old Man and the Sea*
Hijuelos, Oscar. *Twain & Stanley Enter Paradise*
Lehane, Dennis. *World Gone By: A Novel*

★*The Cuban Affair: A Novel*. DeMille, Nelson
CUBAN AMERICAN MEN
Gruber, Michael. *Valley of Bones: A Novel*
CUBAN AMERICAN WOMEN
Cleeton, Chanel. *Next Year in Havana*
Garcia, Cristina. *The Aguero Sisters*
Garcia, Cristina. *Dreaming in Cuban*
Garcia, Gabriela. *Of Women and Salt*
Hijuelos, Oscar. *Beautiful Maria of My Soul*
CUBAN AMERICANS
Burdick, Serena. *Find Me in Havana*
CUBAN RESISTANCE AND REVOLTS
Michener, James A. *Caribbean*
CUBANS
Garcia, Cristina. *Dreaming in Cuban*
CUBANS IN GREAT BRITAIN
Oyeyemi, Helen. *The Opposite House*
CUBANS IN THE UNITED STATES
Garcia, Cristina. *King of Cuba: A Novel*
Hijuelos, Oscar. *Beautiful Maria of My Soul*
Hijuelos, Oscar. ★*The Mambo Kings Play Songs of Love: A Novel*
The Cuckoo's Calling. Galbraith, Robert
Cujo. King, Stephen
CULINARY MYSTERIES
Andrew, Sally. *The Satanic Mechanic: A Tannie Maria Mystery*
Childs, Laura. *Egg Shooters*
Childs, Laura. *Lavender Blue Murder*
Childs, Laura. *Twisted Tea Christmas*
Davidson, Diane Mott. *Killer Pancake*
Davidson, Diane Mott. *The Last Suppers*
Delany, Vicki. *Murder in a Teacup*
Delany, Vicki. *Tea & Treachery*
Fluke, Joanne. ★*Christmas Cupcake Murder*
Manansala, Mia P. ★*Arsenic and Adobo*
Cullen, Helen
The Dazzling Truth
CULLODEN, BATTLE OF, 1746
Gabaldon, Diana. ★*Voyager*
Culper Ring novels (Brad Meltzer) [Series]. Meltzer, Brad
CULT LEADERS
Dektar, Molly. *The Ash Family*
Merullo, Roland. *The Talk-Funny Girl: A Novel*
CULTS
Adler-Olsen, Jussi. *The Hanging Girl*
Allio, Kirstin. *Buddhism for Western Children: A Novel*
Bieker, Chelsea Jean. *Godshot: A Novel*
Bowen, Peter. *Badlands*
Box, C. J. *Winterkill: A Novel*
Broun, Bill. *Night of the Animals*
Burke, James Lee. *Another Kind of Eden*
Carter, Miranda. *The Strangler Vine*
Chanter, Catherine. *The Well*
Clarke, Diana. *Thin Girls*
Coover, Robert. *The Origin of the Brunists: A Novel*
Davis, Lindsey. *One Virgin Too Many*
Deaver, Jeffery. ★*The Goodbye Man*
Dekker, Ted. *The Girl Behind the Red Rope*
DeLillo, Don. *The Names*

Harrison, Jim. *The Great Leader*
Kent, Kathleen. *The Pledge*
Lansdale, Joe R. *Devil Red*
MacDonald, John D. *The Green Ripper*
Murakami, Haruki. ★*1q84*
Parris, S. J. *Sacrilege*
Portis, Charles. ★*Gringos: A Novel*
Reichs, Kathy. *Death Du Jour*
Roanhorse, Rebecca. *Storm of Locusts*
Ruff, Matt. *Lovecraft Country: A Novel*
See, Lisa. *Dragon Bones: A Novel*
Watkins, Claire Vaye. ★*Gold Fame Citrus*
Williams, Drew. *The Stars Now Unclaimed*

CULTURAL APPROPRIATION
Kunzru, Hari. *White Tears*

CULTURAL DIFFERENCES
Aboulela, Leila. *Elsewhere, Home*
Florio, Gwen. *Silent Hearts*
Goodwin, Daisy. *The American Heiress*
Lalli, Sonya. *A Holly Jolly Diwali*
Martine, Arkady. ★*A Desolation Called Peace*
Martine, Arkady. ★*A Memory Called Empire*
Mitchell, David. *The Thousand Autumns of Jacob De Zoet: A Novel*
Phillips, Caryl. *A View of the Empire at Sunset*
Potok, Chaim. ★*The Gift of Asher Lev*

CULTURE
Khoury, Raymond. *Empire of Lies*

CULTURE CONFLICT
Achebe, Chinua. ★*Things Fall Apart*
Adichie, Chimamanda Ngozi. *The Thing Around Your Neck*
Allende, Isabel. ★*The House of the Spirits*
Alyan, Hala. *Salt Houses*
Andric, Ivo. *The Bridge on the Drina*
Aslam, Nadeem. ★*The Golden Legend: A Novel*
Baldwin, James. ★*Go Tell It on the Mountain*
Castillo, Elaine. *America Is Not the Heart*
Chatterjee, Upamanyu. *English, August: An Indian Story*
Cherryh, C. J. *Foreigner: A Novel of First Contact*
D'Souza, Tony. *The Konkans*
Davies, Peter Ho. *The Fortunes*
Gay, Roxane. ★*Ayiti*
Gilman, Charlotte Perkins. *Herland*
Hamid, Mohsin. ★*Exit West: A Novel*
Hensher, Philip. *Scenes from Early Life: A Novel*
Jen, Gish. ★*Thank You, Mr. Nixon: Stories*
Kingsolver, Barbara. ★*The Poisonwood Bible: A Novel*
Kutsukake, Lynne. *The Translation of Love: A Novel*
Lahiri, Jhumpa. ★*The Namesake*
Lalli, Sonya. *The Matchmaker's List*
Le Guin, Ursula K. ★*The Left Hand of Darkness*
Michener, James A. *Caribbean*
Momaday, N. Scott. *House Made of Dawn*
Orange, Tommy. ★*There There*
Potok, Chaim. ★*My Name Is Asher Lev*
Scott, Paul. ★*Staying On: A Novel*
Shafak, Elif. *Honor: A Novel*
Silko, Leslie Marmon. ★*Ceremony*
Verble, Margaret. ★*Cherokee America*

CULTURE SHOCK
Bowles, Paul. ★*The Sheltering Sky*
Fitzpatrick, Lydia. *Lights All Night Long: A Novel*
Kincaid, Jamaica. ★*Lucy*
Miller, Derek B. ★*American by Day*
Satyal, Rakesh. *No One Can Pronounce My Name: A Novel*
Urrea, Luis Alberto. *The Water Museum: Stories*
Culture Universe series [Series]. Banks, Iain

CULTURE WARS
Sandford, John. *Bloody Genius*

CUMBERLAND ISLAND, GEORGIA
Woods, Stuart. *Palindrome*

CUMBRIA, ENGLAND
Hill, Reginald. *The Woodcutter: A Novel*

Cumming, Charles
A Colder War
A Divided Spy
A Foreign Country
The Moroccan Girl
★*The Trinity Six*

Cumyn, Alan
Losing It

Cunningham, Michael
★*The Hours*
Specimen Days

CUPCAKES
Fluke, Joanne. ★*Christmas Cupcake Murder*

CUPID (ROMAN DEITY)
Lewis, C. S. *Till We Have Faces: A Myth Retold*

CURIE, MARIE
Cantor, Jillian. *Half Life*
Gunning, Sally. *Painting the Light*

CURIOSITIES AND WONDERS
Borges, Jorge Luis. ★*Collected Fictions*
Knausgaard, Karl Ove. *The Morning Star*
Palmer, Dexter Clarence. ★*Mary Toft; Or, the Rabbit Queen: A Novel*
*A **Curious** Beginning: A Veronica Speedwell Mystery*. Raybourn, Deanna
★*The **Curious** Incident of the Dog in the Night-Time: A Novel*. Haddon, Mark
***Curious** Toys*. Hand, Elizabeth
*The **Current** That Carries: Stories*. Graley, Lisa
*The **Current**: a Novel*. Johnston, Tim

Currie, Ron
Flimsy Little Plastic Miracles: A True Story

CURSES
Aoki, Ryka. *Light from Uncommon Stars*
Atakora, Afia. ★*Conjure Women*
Bennett, Jenn. *Bitter Spirits*
Bledsoe, Alex. *Wisp of a Thing*
Callihan, Kristen. ★*Firelight*
Cheng, Bill. *Southern Cross the Dog*
Christie, Agatha. *Endless Night*
Danforth, Emily M. *Plain Bad Heroines*
Doyle, Arthur Conan. ★*The Hound of the Baskervilles*
Druon, Maurice. *The Iron King*
Hawthorne, Nathaniel. ★*The House of the Seven Gables*
Lackberg, Camilla. *The Golden Cage*
Lopez Barrio, Cristina. *The House of the Impossible Loves*

Marske, Freya. *A Marvellous Light*
North, Claire. *The Pursuit of William Abbey*
Novik, Naomi. ★*Uprooted*
Schwab, Victoria. *The Invisible Life of Addie Larue*
Suri, Tasha. ★*Realm of Ash*
Curtain. Christie, Agatha
Cush, Jean Love
   Endangered
Cusk, Rachel
   Kudos
   Outline: A Novel
   Second Place
   Transit
Cusset, Catherine
   Life of David Hockney: A Novel
Cussler, Clive
   Blue Gold: A Novel from the Numa Files
   Celtic Empire
   ★*The Chase*
   The Cutthroat
   ★*Final Option*
   Ghost Ship
   ★*Golden Buddha*
   ★*The Gray Ghost*
   Havana Storm
   The Mediterranean Caper
   Nighthawk: A Novel from the Numa Files
   Odessa Sea
   ★*The Oracle*
   Pacific Vortex!
   The Pharaoh's Secret
   ★*Raise the Titanic!*
   ★*The Rising Sea: A Novel from the Numa Files*
   The Romanov Ransom
   Sacred Stone
   Sahara: A Novel
   ★*Sea of Greed: A Novel from the Numa Files*
   Serpent: A Novel from the Numa Files
   Shadow Tyrants
   ★*The Titanic Secret*
   Typhoon Fury
   The Wrecker
CUSTER, GEORGE A.
   Jones, Douglas C. *The Court-Martial of George Armstrong Custer*
*The **Cut**: a Novel*. Pelecanos, George P.
Cutler [Series]. Krentz, Jayne Ann
*The **Cutthroat***. Cussler, Clive
***Cutting** for Stone: A Novel*. Verghese, A.
*The **Cutting** Season*. Locke, Attica
***Cyber** Mage: A Novel*. Hossain, Saad Z.
CYBER-THRILLERS
   Cohen, Joshua. *Book of Numbers: A Novel*
   Daniel, Ray. *Hacked: A Tucker Mystery*
   Deaver, Jeffery. ★*The Never Game*
   Forsyth, Frederick. *The Fox*
   Ruff, Matt. ★*88 Names*
   Stephenson, Neal. *Reamde*
   Yoon, David. *Version Zero*

CYBERBULLYING
   Daniel, Ray. *Hacked: A Tucker Mystery*
CYBERPUNK
   Dick, Philip K. ★*Do Androids Dream of Electric Sheep?*
   Doctorow, Cory. *Rapture of the Nerds*
   Gibson, William. ★*Agency*
   Gibson, William. ★*Neuromancer*
   Gibson, William. *Pattern Recognition*
   Harrison, M. John. *Nova Swing*
   Lu, S. Qiouyi. *In the Watchful City*
   McDonald, Ian. *New Moon*
   Minh, Drew. *Neon Empire*
   Stephenson, Neal. *The Diamond Age,: Or, a Young Lady's Illustrated Primer*
   Stephenson, Neal. ★*Snow Crash*
CYBERSPACE
   Gibson, William. ★*Neuromancer*
   Stephenson, Neal. ★*Fall Or, Dodge in Hell: A Novel*
CYBERTERRORISM
   Child, Lee. ★*The Sentinel*
   Mankell, Henning. *Firewall*
CYBORGS
   Banks, Iain. *Matter*
   Okorafor, Nnedi. ★*Noor*
CYCLONES
   Ghosh, Amitav. *River of Smoke*
★*Cygnet*. Butler, Season
CYNICISM
   Banks, Russell. ★*Affliction*
   Barth, John. ★*The Floating Opera*
   McQuiston, Casey. ★*One Last Stop*
CYPRUS
   Obioma, Chigozie. ★*An Orchestra of Minorities*
Cyrus Barker and Thomas Llewelyn mysteries [Series]. Thomas, Will
Cyrus Haven novels [Series]. Robotham, Michael
CZECH AMERICAN WOMEN
   Bird, Sarah. ★*The Flamenco Academy: A Novel*
   Cather, Willa. ★*My Antonia*
CZECH AMERICANS
   Chabon, Michael. *The Amazing Adventures of Kavalier & Clay: A Novel*
CZECH REPUBLIC
   Perry, Sarah. *Melmoth: A Novel*
CZECHOSLOVAKIA
   Binet, Laurent. ★*HHhH*
   Kundera, Milan. ★*The Unbearable Lightness of Being*
Czerneda, Julie
   A Turn of Light

D

D'Eramo, Luce
   Deviation
D'Erasmo, Stacey
   The Sky Below

D'Souza, Tony
The Konkans
Whiteman
D.O.D.O [Series]. Stephenson, Neal
The **Da** *Vinci Code*. Brown, Dan
Daddy: *Stories*. Cline, Emma
Dade, Olivia
All the Feels
Spoiler Alert
Daevabad trilogy [Series]. Chakraborty, S. A.
Dahl, Arne
Bad Blood
Misterioso: A Crime Novel
Dahl, Julia
Conviction
The Missing Hours
Dahl, Roald
Collected Stories
DAIRY FARMS
Kate, Jessica. *A Girl's Guide to the Outback: A Novel*
★**Daisy** *Jones & The Six: A Novel*. Reid, Taylor Jenkins
Daisy *Miller*. James, Henry
DAKAR, SENEGAL
Bush, Keisha. *No Heaven for Good Boys: A Novel*
DAKOTA INDIANS
Hill, Ruth Beebe. *Hanta Yo*
Power, Susan. *The Grass Dancer*
DAKOTA MEN
Hill, Ruth Beebe. *Hanta Yo*
DAKOTA TERRITORY
Brooks, Bill. *Blood Storm*
DALAI LAMAS
Cussler, Clive. ★*Golden Buddha*
Dalcher, Christina
Femlandia
DALGLIESH, ADAM (FICTITIOUS CHARACTER)
James, P. D. *Death of an Expert Witness*
James, P. D. *Original Sin*
James, P. D. *An Unsuitable Job for a Woman*
DALLAS, EVE (FICTITIOUS CHARACTER)
Robb, J. D. *Innocent in Death*
Robb, J. D. *Naked in Death*
Dallas, Sandra
The Last Midwife
Tallgrass
Westering Women: A Novel
DALLAS, TEXAS
Baker, Chandler. *Whisper Network: A Novel*
DeLillo, Don. *Libra*
Fountain, Ben. ★*Billy Lynn's Long Halftime Walk*
Kent, Kathleen. *The Burn*
Kent, Kathleen. *The Pledge*
King, Stephen. *11/22/63*
Dalton, Trent
All Our Shimmering Skies
Boy Swallows Universe
Daly, Paula
Clear My Name

Open Your Eyes
Damage: *a Novel*. Hart, Josephine
The **Damascus** *Road: A Novel of Saint Paul*. Parini, Jay
DAMASCUS, SYRIA
Schami, Rafik. *Sophia: Or the Beginning of All Tales*
★**Damnation** *Spring*. Davidson, Ash
DAMNED PERSONS
Butler, Robert Olen. *Hell: A Novel*
The **Damned:** *a Novel*. Pyper, Andrew
DAMS
Evison, Jonathan. *West of Here: A Novel*
Greene, Amy. *Long Man*
DAMS — DESIGN AND CONSTRUCTION
Barr, Mark. *Watershed*
Danan, Rosie
The Intimacy Experiment
The Roommate
★**Dance** *Away with Me*. Phillips, Susan Elizabeth
Dance *of the Jakaranda*. Kimani, Peter
DANCE SCHOOLS
Abbott, Megan E. ★*The Turnout: A Novel*
Dance *with Death*. Thomas, Will
★*A* **Dance** *with Dragons*. Martin, George R. R.
The **Dancer** *and the Thief: A Novel*. Skarmeta, Antonio
DANCERS
Sedgwick, Marcus. *Mister Memory: A Novel*
Skarmeta, Antonio. *The Dancer and the Thief: A Novel*
Swamy, Shruti. *The Archer*
DANCING
Kaminsky, Stuart M. *Dancing in the Dark*
Sapphire. ★*The Kid: A Novel*
Smith, Zadie. ★*Swing Time*
Swamy, Shruti. *The Archer*
DANCING — STUDY AND TEACHING
McCall Smith, Alexander. *In the Company of Cheerful Ladies*
Dancing *in the Dark*. Kaminsky, Stuart M.
Dancing *in the Dark*. Phillips, Caryl
Dandelion dynasty [Series]. Liu, Ken
★**Dandelion** *Wine: A Novel*. Bradbury, Ray
DANDIES
Orczy, Emmuska Orczy. ★*The Scarlet Pimpernel*
Dandy Gilver murder mysteries [Series]. McPherson, Catriona
Danforth, Emily M.
Plain Bad Heroines
Dang, Catherine
Nice Girls
Dangarembga, Tsitsi
This Mournable Body
Dangerous. Spencer, Minerva
A **Dangerous** *Collaboration*. Raybourn, Deanna
Dangerous damsels [Series]. Holton, India
A **Dangerous** *Man*. Crais, Robert
A **Dangerous** *Mourning*. Perry, Anne
Dangerous *Women*. Adams, Hope
Dangling *Man*. Bellow, Saul
DANIEL
Andrews, Mesu. *Of Fire and Lions: A Novel*
Daniel Hawthorne novels [Series]. Horowitz, Anthony

Daniel Jacobus mysteries [Series]. Elias, Gerald
Daniel Pitt novels (Anne Perry) [Series]. Perry, Anne
Daniel, Ray
    Hacked: A Tucker Mystery
Danielewski, Mark Z.
    ★*The Familiar.; Volume 4,*
    ★*House of Leaves: A Novel*
    Only Revolutions
Daniels, Natalie
    Too Close
The **Danish** Girl: A Novel. Ebershoff, David
Danler, Stephanie
    Sweetbitter
Dann, Patty
    The Wright Sister
Danse Macabre. Elias, Gerald
DANTE ALIGHIERI
    Davis, Fiona. *The Masterpiece*
    Hamilton, Jane. *A Map of the World*
    Pearl, Matthew. *The Dante Chamber*
    Pearl, Matthew. *The Dante Club: A Novel*
*The **Dante** Chamber*. Pearl, Matthew
Dante Club novels (Matthew Pearl) [Series]. Pearl, Matthew
*The **Dante** Club: A Novel*. Pearl, Matthew
Dante's Dilemma: A Mark Angelotti Novel. Raimondo, Lynne
Dante's Poison: A Mark Angelotti Novel. Raimondo, Lynne
Dante's Wood: A Mark Angelotti Novel. Raimondo, Lynne
Danticat, Edwidge
    Claire of the Sea Light
    The Dew Breaker
    ★*Everything Inside: Stories*
    ★*Krik? Krak!*
Danvers novels [Series]. Landon, Sydney
Daoud, Kamel
    The Meursault Investigation
Dare to Know. Kennedy, James
Dare, Abi
    The Girl with the Louding Voice
Dare, Tessa
    Do You Want to Start a Scandal
    ★*The Duchess Deal*
    ★*The Governess Game*
    ★*A Night to Surrender*
    Romancing the Duke
    ★*Say Yes to the Marquess*
    ★*The Wallflower Wager*
    A Week to Be Wicked
    When a Scot Ties the Knot
Daredevils. Vestal, Shawn
DAREDEVILS (STUNT PERFORMERS)
    Leonard, Elmore. *Tishomingo Blues: A Novel*
DARGER, HENRY
    Beah, Ishmael. *Little Family*
    Hand, Elizabeth. *Curious Toys*
Daria, Alexis
    ★*A Lot Like Adios*
    ★*You Had Me at Hola*
*A **Dark** and Twisted Tide*. Bolton, S. J.

*The **Dark** Angel*. Griffiths, Elly
Dark at the Crossing. Ackerman, Elliot
Dark August. Tallo, Katie
Dark beginnings of Sherlock Holmes [Series]. Pirie, David
*The **Dark** Corners of the Night*. Gardiner, Meg
*The **Dark** Dark: Stories*. Hunt, Samantha
★*The **Dark** Flood Rises*. Drabble, Margaret
★*The **Dark** Forest*. Liu, Cixin
Dark Horses. Mihalic, Susan
★*The **Dark** Hours*. Connelly, Michael
Dark Illusion. Feehan, Christine
Dark Lady. Patterson, Richard North
Dark Lightning. Varley, John
Dark Matter: A Novel. Crouch, Blake
★*A **Dark** Matter: A Novel*. Straub, Peter
*The **Dark** Monk: A Hangman's Daughter Tale*. Potzsch, Oliver
Dark Orbit. Gilman, Carolyn Ives
Dark Places. Flynn, Gillian
*The **Dark** Remains: Laidlaw's First Case*. McIlvanney, William
Dark Sacred Night. Connelly, Michael
Dark Saturday. French, Nicci
Dark series [Series]. Feehan, Christine
★*Dark Sky: A Joe Pickett Novel*. Box, C. J.
Dark star trilogy (Marlon James) [Series]. James, Marlon
Dark Things I Adore. Lattari, Katie
Dark Tide Rising: A William Monk Novel. Perry, Anne
Dark Voyage: A Novel. Furst, Alan
Dark Winter. Tata, A. J.
★*A **Darker** Reality*. Perry, Anne
*A **Darker** Shade of Blue: Stories*. Harvey, John
*A **Darker** Shade of Magic*. Schwab, Victoria
Darker shade of magic [Series]. Schwab, Victoria
*The **Darkest** Evening*. Cleeves, Ann
*The **Darkest** Evening of the Year*. Koontz, Dean R.
Darkest London [Series]. Callihan, Kristen
*A **Darkling** Sea*. Cambias, James L.
Darkmans. Barker, Nicola
Darkness at Noon. Koestler, Arthur
*The **Darkness** Knows*. Indriðason, Arnaldur
★*Darkness Visible*. Golding, William
Darkness, Darkness. Harvey, John
Darktown novels [Series]. Mullen, Thomas
Darktown: a Novel. Mullen, Thomas
Darling. Edwards, Rachel
Darling Rose Gold. Wrobel, Stephanie
Darnielle, John
    Universal Harvester
    Wolf in White Van: A Novel
DARROW, CLARENCE
    Carr, Caleb. *The Angel of Darkness*
    Kennedy, William. ★*Ironweed: A Novel*
DARTMOOR, ENGLAND
    Doyle, Arthur Conan. ★*The Hound of the Baskervilles*
*The **Darwin** Affair*. Mason, Timothy
DARWIN, CHARLES
    Jeffries, Sabrina. *Project Duchess*
    Mason, Timothy. *The Darwin Affair*

DARWIN, NORTHERN TERRITORY
Dalton, Trent. *All Our Shimmering Skies*

Darznik, Jasmin
The Bohemians
Song of a Captive Bird: A Novel

DATA ENCRYPTION (COMPUTER SCIENCE)
Harris, Oliver. *A Shadow Intelligence*

DATA PROCESSING
Walschots, Natalie Zina. *Hench: A Novel*

DATA PROCESSING — DATA ENTRY
Phillips, Helen. *The Beautiful Bureaucrat: A Novel*

DATE RAPE
DeWoskin, Rachel. *Big Girl Small: A Novel*
Oates, Joyce Carol. ★*We Were the Mulvaneys*

DATING (SOCIAL CUSTOMS)
Alderton, Dolly. ★*Ghosts: A Novel*
Bellefleur, Alexandria. *Hang the Moon*
Bellefleur, Alexandria. *Written in the Stars*
Bushnell, Candace. *Is There Still Sex in the City?*
Carty-Williams, Candice. ★*Queenie*
Christopher, Andie J. *Not the Girl You Marry*
Cochrun, Alison. *The Charm Offensive*
Colwin, Laurie. *Happy All the Time: A Novel*
Fielding, Helen. ★*Bridget Jones's Diary: A Novel*
Fielding, Joy. *All the Wrong Places: A Novel*
Guillory, Jasmine. *Party of Two*
Guillory, Jasmine. *The Proposal*
Guillory, Jasmine. *Royal Holiday*
Hazelwood, Ali. *The Love Hypothesis*
Hoang, Helen. ★*The Kiss Quotient*
McMillan, Terry. ★*Waiting to Exhale*
Nicholls, Owen. *Love, Unscripted: A Novel*
Raheem, Zara. *The Marriage Clock: A Novel*
Ripper, Kris. *The Love Study*
Rochon, Farrah. *The Boyfriend Project*
Rockaway, Kristin. *How to Hack a Heartbreak*
Simsion, Graeme C. ★*The Rosie Project*
Solomon, Rachel Lynn. *Weather Girl*
Title, Sarah. *The Undateable*
Williams, Denise. *How to Fail at Flirting*
The Dating Playbook. Rochon, Farrah

DATING SHOWS (TELEVISION PROGRAMS)
Cochrun, Alison. *The Charm Offensive*
Dating You / Hating You. Lauren, Christina

Daugherty, Christi
A Beautiful Corpse
The Echo Killing
Revolver Road: A Harper McClain Mystery

Daughter of a Daughter of a Queen. Bird, Sarah
Daughter of Fortune: A Novel. Allende, Isabel
Daughter of the Forest. Marillier, Juliet
★*Daughter of the Moon Goddess*. Tan, Sue Lynn
Daughter of the Morning Star. Johnson, Craig
★*Daughter of War: A Novel*. Taylor, Brad

DAUGHTERS
Corman, Avery. *Prized Possessions*
Dobmeier, Tracy. ★*Girls with Bright Futures: A Novel*
Ellison, J. T. *Tear Me Apart*

Franklin, Ariana. ★*Death and the Maiden*
Lombardo, Claire. *The Most Fun We Ever Had: A Novel*
Riley, Vanessa. ★*An Earl, the Girl, and a Toddler*
Scott, Stephanie. *What's Left of Me Is Yours: A Novel*

DAUGHTERS — DEATH
Bohjalian, Chris. *The Buffalo Soldier: A Novel*
Diamond, Elizabeth. *An Accidental Light*
Dixon, Stephen. *Interstate: A Novel*
Ng, Celeste. ★*Everything I Never Told You: A Novel*
Riordan, Kate. *The Heatwave*
Rouda, Kaira Sturdivant. *The Favorite Daughter*
Smith, Tom Rob. *Agent 6*
Styron, William. *Lie Down in Darkness*
The Daughters of Cain. Dexter, Colin
The Daughters of Erietown. Schultz, Connie
★*The Daughters of Mars*. Keneally, Thomas
Daughters of the Witching Hill. Sharratt, Mary

Daughters, Amy Weinland
You Cannot Mess This Up: A True Story That Never Happened

DAUGHTERS-IN-LAW
Lessing, Doris May. *The Sweetest Dream*

Dave Gurney novels [Series]. Verdon, John
Dave Robicheaux novels [Series]. Burke, James Lee

DAVENPORT, LUCAS (FICTITIOUS CHARACTER)
Sandford, John. *Chosen Prey*
Sandford, John. *Field of Prey*
Sandford, John. ★*Mind Prey*
Sandford, John. ★*Night Prey*
Sandford, John. ★*Rules of Prey*
Sandford, John. ★*Silent Prey*
Sandford, John. *Sudden Prey*

★*David Copperfield*. Dickens, Charles
David Sloane thrillers [Series]. Dugoni, Robert

DAVIDMAN, JOY
Finch, Charles. *The Vanishing Man*
Henry, Patti Callahan. ★*Becoming Mrs. Lewis: The Improbable Love Story of Joy Davidman and C. S. Lewis*

Davidson, Andrew
The Gargoyle

Davidson, Andy
The Boatman's Daughter: A Novel

Davidson, Ash
★*Damnation Spring*

Davidson, Diane Mott
Killer Pancake
The Last Suppers

Davidson, MaryJanice
Truth, Lies, and Second Dates

Davies, Carys
The Mission House
West

Davies, Peter Ho
The Fortunes
A Lie Someone Told You About Yourself

Davies, Valentine
Miracle on 34th Street

Davila, April
142 Ostriches

Davis, Fiona
The Chelsea Girls
The Lions of Fifth Avenue: A Novel
The Masterpiece
Davis, Kathryn
Duplex
Davis, Lindsey
A Body in the Bathhouse
A Comedy of Terrors: A Flavia Albia Novel
The Ides of April: A Flavia Albia Mystery
One Virgin Too Many
Davis, Lydia
The Collected Stories of Lydia Davis
DAVIS, VARINA
Atkinson, Kate. ★*Transcription*
Frazier, Charles. *Varina*
Davys, Tim
Amberville
★*Dawn*. Wiesel, Elie
Dawn: Stories. Demirtas, Selahattin
★*Dawn: Xenogenesis*. Butler, Octavia E.
*The **Day** I Died*. Rader-Day, Lori
*A **Day** in the Life of a Smiling Woman: Complete Short Stories*. Drabble, Margaret
★*The **Day** of Creation*. Ballard, J. G.
★*The **Day** of the Dead: A Novel*. French, Nicci
Day Zero. Cargill, C. Robert
*The **Days** of Afrekete*. Solomon, Asali
★*Days of Distraction*. Chang, Alexandra
Days Without End: A Novel. Barry, Sebastian
DAYTON, OHIO
Daughters, Amy Weinland. *You Cannot Mess This Up: A True Story That Never Happened*
Dazieri, Sandrone
Kill the Angel
Kill the Father
Kill the King
*The **Dazzling** Truth*. Cullen, Helen
De Bernieres, Louis
Birds Without Wings
De Giovanni, Maurizio
The Bastards of Pizzofalcone
The Crocodile
De Kretser, Michelle
The Life to Come
De la Motte, Anders
MemoRandom: A Thriller
Ultimatum: A Thriller
De Leon, Aya
Side Chick Nation
★*A Spy in the Struggle*
De los Santos, Marisa
The Precious One
DE LUCE, FLAVIA (FICTITIOUS CHARACTER)
Bradley, C. Alan. ★*The Sweetness at the Bottom of the Pie*
De Niro's Game. Hage, Rawi
DE QUINCEY, THOMAS
Morrell, David. *Ruler of the Night*

Wallace, Melanie. *The Girl in the Garden*
De Robertis, Carolina
Cantoras
The Gods of Tango
Perla
★*Deacon King Kong: A Novel*. McBride, James
DEAD
Ackerman, Elliot. ★*Waiting for Eden: A Novel*
Beukes, Lauren. *Broken Monsters*
Bonnaffons, Amy. *The Regrets*
Bradley, C. Alan. *The Grave's a Fine and Private Place: A Flavia De Luce Novel*
Burton, Jeffrey B. ★*The Finders: A Mace Reid K-9 Mystery*
Burton, Jeffrey B. *The Keepers: A Mace Reid K-9 Mystery*
Chancellor, Bryn. *Sycamore: A Novel*
Choo, Yangsze. *The Ghost Bride: A Novel*
Cooper, Ellison. *Buried*
Cotterill, Colin. *Don't Eat Me*
Emezi, Akwaeke. ★*The Death of Vivek Oji*
Harvey, John. *Darkness, Darkness*
Indriðason, Arnaldur. *The Darkness Knows*
Logan, Kylie. *The Secrets of Bones: A Mystery*
Lovesey, Peter. *Beau Death*
McDermid, Val. ★*Still Life*
Rendell, Ruth. *Not in the Flesh: A Wexford Novel*
Robertson, Imogen. *Island of Bones*
Tursten, Helene. *An Elderly Lady Must Not Be Crossed*
Ware, Ruth. *The Lying Game*
DEAD — IDENTIFICATION
Macmillan, Gilly. *The Nanny*
Dead and Gone: An Inspector Luke Thanet Novel.. Simpson, Dorothy
Dead Astronauts: A Novel. VanderMeer, Jeff
★*Dead by Dawn*. Doiron, Paul
Dead by Morning. Simpson, Dorothy
Dead End. Spencer, Sally
The Dead Ex. Corry, Jane
Dead Girl in 2a. Wilson, Carter
Dead Girl Running. Dodd, Christina
The Dead Hand of History. Spencer, Sally
★*Dead Land*. Paretsky, Sara
Dead Man Switch. Quirk, Matthew
Dead Men's Trousers. Welsh, Irvine
Dead Midnight. Muller, Marcia
Dead of Winter. Jones, Stephen Mack
★*The Dead of Winter*. Parris, S. J.
The Dead Sit Round in a Ring. Lawrence, David
★*Dead Souls*. Gogol, Nikolai Vasilievich
Dead Souls: An Inspector Rebus Novel. Rankin, Ian
★*Dead to Her: A Novel*. Pinborough, Sarah
Dead West. Goldman, Matt
Deadline. Grant, Mira
★*Deadline*. Sandford, John
Deadly Camargue: A Provence Mystery. Rademacher, Cay
Deadly Decisions. Reichs, Kathy
A Deadly Education: A Novel. Novik, Naomi
Deadly Ever After. Gates, Eva
Deadly Harvest. Stanley, Michael
Deadly Obsession. Hunt, April

Deadly *Recall*. Ragan, Theresa
Deadly *Summer Nights*. Delany, Vicki
★**Deadwood**. Dexter, Pete
DEADWOOD, SOUTH DAKOTA
    Dexter, Pete. ★*Deadwood*
DEALS
    Brom. *Slewfoot: A Tale of Bewitchery*
    Egan, Jennifer. ★*Manhattan Beach: A Novel*
    Gilman, Laura Anne. *Silver on the Road*
    McGuire, Seanan. ★*In an Absent Dream*
The **Dean's** *December: A Novel*. Bellow, Saul
Dean, Debra
    The Madonnas of Leningrad: A Novel
Dean, Margaret Lazarus
    The Time It Takes to Fall
Dean, Michael
    I, Hogarth
Dean, Pamela
    Tam Lin
Deane, Seamus
    Reading in the Dark
Dear *Ann: A Novel*. Mason, Bobbie Ann
★**Dear** *Child*. Hausmann, Romy
Dear *Committee Members*. Schumacher, Julie
Dear committee members [Series]. Schumacher, Julie
Dear *Edward*. Napolitano, Ann
Dear *George, Dear Mary: A Novel of George Washington's First Love*.
    Calvi, Mary
Dear Lady Truelove [Series]. Guhrke, Laura Lee
Dear *Life: Stories*. Munro, Alice
★**Dear** *Miss Kopp*. Stewart, Amy
Dear *Miss Metropolitan*. Ferrell, Carolyn
Dear *Wife*. Belle, Kimberly
The **Dearly** *Beloved: A Novel*. Wall, Cara
The **Dearly** *Departed*. Lipman, Elinor
DEATH
    Alarcon, Daniel. *The King Is Always Above the People: Stories*
    Albom, Mitch. *The Five People You Meet in Heaven*
    Amis, Martin. ★*Inside Story*
    Auster, Paul. ★*In the Country of Last Things*
    Banks, Iain. *The Crow Road*
    Bannister, Ilona. *When I Ran Away*
    Banville, John. ★*The Sea*
    Bellow, Saul. *The Dean's December: A Novel*
    Bilenchi, Romano. ★*The Chill*
    Brockmeier, Kevin. *The Illumination*
    Castro, V. *The Queen of the Cicadas*
    Cleeves, Ann. *Raven Black*
    Clegg, Bill. *Did You Ever Have a Family*
    Danforth, Emily M. *Plain Bad Heroines*
    DeLillo, Don. *Zero K: A Novel*
    Doiron, Paul. ★*Dead by Dawn*
    Faulkner, William. ★*As I Lay Dying: The Corrected Text*
    Fuentes, Carlos. *The Death of Artemio Cruz*
    Gaiman, Neil. *Trigger Warning: Short Fictions and Disturbances*
    Garcia Marquez, Gabriel. ★*The Autumn of the Patriarch*
    Golden, Christopher. *Red Hands*
    Grossman, David. *Falling Out of Time*

    Hage, Rawi. *Beirut Hellfire Society: A Novel*
    Han, Kang. *The White Book*
    Hand, Elizabeth. *Available Dark: A Thriller*
    Hand, Elizabeth. *Hard Light*
    Haruf, Kent. *Benediction*
    Helprin, Mark. ★*Winter's Tale*
    Horn, Dara. *Eternal Life: A Novel*
    Horrocks, Caitlin. *Life Among the Terranauts*
    Kennedy, James. *Dare to Know*
    Klune, TJ. ★*Under the Whispering Door*
    MacLaverty, Bernard. ★*Blank Pages: And Other Stories*
    McDermott, Alice. ★*Charming Billy*
    Okorafor, Nnedi. ★*Remote Control*
    Oyeyemi, Helen. *Mr. Fox*
    Pearl, Matthew. *The Poe Shadow: A Novel*
    Pears, Iain. *Stone's Fall*
    Ramadan, Ahmad Danny. *The Clothesline Swing*
    Rodriques, Elias. *All the Water I've Seen Is Running: A Novel*
    Rowland, Laura Joh. *The Shogun's Daughter: A Novel of Feudal*
        Japan
    Sandford, John. *Sudden Prey*
    Saramago, Jose. *Death with Interruptions*
    Sarton, May. *A Reckoning: A Novel*
    Shteyngart, Gary. ★*Super Sad True Love Story: A Novel*
    Smith, Lee. ★*Fair and Tender Ladies*
    Smith, Lee. *Family Linen*
    Swarthout, Glendon. ★*The Shootist*
    Swinson, David. *City on the Edge*
    Vollmann, William T. *Last Stories and Other Stories*
    Wiesel, Elie. *A Mad Desire to Dance: A Novel*
    Willett, Marcia. *The Garden House*
    Woodrell, Daniel. *The Maid's Version: A Novel*
    Woolf, Virginia. ★*The Years*
DEATH (FICTITIOUS CHARACTER : PRATCHETT)
    Pratchett, Terry. *Equal Rites*
    Pratchett, Terry. *Reaper Man*
DEATH (PERSONIFICATION)
    Poore, Michael. *Reincarnation Blues*
DEATH — PSYCHOLOGICAL ASPECTS
    Brautigan, Richard. *An Unfortunate Woman: A Journey*
    Garcia Marquez, Gabriel. *The General in His Labyrinth*
    Garner, Helen. *The Spare Room*
    Hemingway, Ernest. *The Snows of Kilimanjaro and Other Stories*
    Robotham, Michael. ★*Close Your Eyes*
Death *and Restoration*. Pears, Iain
★**Death** *and the Maiden*. Franklin, Ariana
★**Death** *and Transfiguration: A Daniel Jacobus Novel*. Elias, Gerald
Death *at the Crystal Palace*. Ashley, Jennifer
Death *Benefits: A Novel*. Perry, Thomas
★**Death** *by Water*. Oe, Kenzaburo
★The **Death** *Collectors*. Kerley, Jack
★**Death** *Comes for the Archbishop*. Cather, Willa
Death *Comes to the Nursery*. Lloyd, Catherine
Death *Comes to the Rectory*. Lloyd, Catherine
DEATH CONTROL
    Shriver, Lionel. *Should We Stay or Should We Go*
Death *Du Jour*. Reichs, Kathy
Death *in Brittany*. Bannalec, Jean-Luc

Death in Daylesford. Greenwood, Kerry

★**Death** in Focus: An Elena Standish Novel. Perry, Anne

★**Death** in Her Hands: A Novel. Moshfegh, Ottessa

Death in Paradise. Parker, Robert B.

Death in Paris mysteries [Series]. Bernhard, Emilia

Death in the East. Mukherjee, Abir

★A **Death** in the Family. Agee, James

A **Death** in the Family. Stanley, Michael

Death in Venice and Seven Other Stories. Mann, Thomas

Death in Veracruz. Aguilar Camin, Hector

Death Is Hard Work: A Novel. Khalfah, Khlid

Death Lives Next Door. Butler, Gwendoline

A **Death** Long Overdue. Gates, Eva

Death notice [Series]. Zhou, Haohui

Death Notice: A Novel. Zhou, Haohui

Death of a Literary Widow. Barnard, Robert

Death of a Macho Man. Beaton, M. C.

Death of a Nationalist. Pawel, Rebecca

Death of a New American: A Mystery. Fredericks, Mariah

Death of a Red Heroine. Qiu, Xiaolong

Death of a Showman. Fredericks, Mariah

Death of an Expert Witness. James, P. D.

The **Death** of Artemio Cruz. Fuentes, Carlos

The **Death** of Bees: A Novel. O'Donnell, Lisa

The **Death** of Jane Lawrence. Starling, Caitlin

The **Death** of Mrs. Westaway. Ware, Ruth

Death of the Mantis. Stanley, Michael

★The **Death** of Vivek Oji. Emezi, Akwaeke

DEATH ROW PRISONERS

  Block, Lawrence. All the Flowers Are Dying

  Dow, David R. Confessions of an Innocent Man

  Friedman, Daniel. Running Out of Road

  Lepionka, Kristen. The Last Place You Look

  McCrumb, Sharyn. ★The Ballad of Frankie Silver

  Picoult, Jodi. Change of Heart: A Novel

  Roslund, Anders. Cell 8

  Silver, Elizabeth L. The Execution of Noa P. Singleton: A Novel

DEATH THREATS

  Bauer, Belinda. Snap

  Brockway, Connie. So Enchanting

  Cotterill, Colin. The Second Biggest Nothing

  Johnson, Alaya Dawn. Trouble the Saints

  Johnson, Craig. Daughter of the Morning Star

  Jones, Stephen Mack. Dead of Winter

  Lippman, Laura. ★And When She Was Good

  McKinty, Adrian. ★The Chain

  Petrie, Nicholas. Tear It Down

  Sanders, Lawrence. McNally's Puzzle

  Slaughter, Karin. Criminal: A Novel

  Somer, Mehmet Murat. The Serenity Murders

  Wilson, G. Willow. Alif the Unseen

DEATH VALLEY

  Cander, Chris. The Weight of a Piano: A Novel

Death Warmed Over. Anderson, Kevin J.

Death Wears a Beauty Mask and Other Stories. Clark, Mary Higgins

★**Death** with a Double Edge: A Daniel Pitt Novel. Perry, Anne

Death with Interruptions. Saramago, Jose

Death's Dark Shadow. Spencer, Sally

★**Death**'s End. Liu, Cixin

The **Deathwatch** Beetle: A Mystery. Eriksson, Kjell

Deaver, Jeffery

  ★The Coffin Dancer

  Edge: A Novel

  The Empty Chair

  Garden of Beasts: A Novel of Berlin 1936

  ★The Goodbye Man

  ★The Never Game

  The October List

  The Stone Monkey: A Lincoln Rhyme Novel

Deb, Siddhartha

  The Point of Return: A Novel

DEBATES AND DEBATING

  Lerner, Ben. ★The Topeka School

Deborah Knott mysteries [Series]. Maron, Margaret

Debris. Anderton, Jo

DEBT

  Child, Lee. ★Blue Moon

  Lloyd, Catherine. Death Comes to the Rectory

  Long, Julie Anne. ★Lady Derring Takes a Lover

  Novik, Naomi. ★Spinning Silver

DEBTOR AND CREDITOR

  Dickens, Charles. Little Dorrit

Debutante diaries [Series]. Bennett, Anna

DEBUTANTES

  Bradley, Anna. A Season of Ruin

  Fitzgerald, F. Scott. ★This Side of Paradise

  Jeffries, Sabrina. Project Duchess

  Johnson, Tara. Engraved on the Heart

  Kelly, Julia. The Last Dance of the Debutante

The **Decagon** House Murders. Ayatsuji, Yukito

DeCarlo, Melissa

  The Art of Crash Landing: A Novel

Deceived by Desire. Force, Marie

The **Deceivers**. Berenson, Alex

December Heat. Garcia-Roza, L. A.

The **Decent** Inn of Death. Airth, Rennie

DECEPTION

  Abbott, Patricia. Concrete Angel

  Angelo, Megan. Followers

  Arden, Katherine. ★The Girl in the Tower

  Arden, Katherine. ★The Winter of the Witch

  Atkinson, Kate. ★Big Sky

  Barber, Lizzy. A Girl Named Anna

  Bear, Greg. The Forge of God

  Bennett, Bethany. West End Earl

  Beverley, Jo. Tempting Fortune

  Beyda, Emily. The Body Double

  Block, Lawrence. Hit Me: A Keller Novel

  Bohjalian, Chris. The Flight Attendant: A Novel

  Bowman, Valerie. The Accidental Countess

  Bruni, Sarah. The Night Gwen Stacy Died

  Ca$h. ★Trust No Bitch

  Campbell, Ramsey. The Wise Friend

  Camus, Albert. ★The Fall

  Carter, Stephen L. New England White: A Novel

  Child, Lee. ★Past Tense

Chizmar, Richard T. *A Long December*
Clinch, Jon. *Marley: A Novel*
Coben, Harlan. *Fool Me Once*
Cole, Alyssa. ★*A Princess in Theory*
Collins, Wilkie. ★*The Woman in White*
Coulter, Catherine. *Labyrinth*
Crais, Robert. *The First Rule*
Crouch, Blake. *Recursion*
Dare, Tessa. *A Week to Be Wicked*
Delaney, J. P. *The Perfect Wife: A Novel*
Delaney, J. P. *Playing Nice*
Dorey-Stein, Beck. *Rock the Boat: A Novel*
Finch, Charles. *A Beautiful Blue Death*
French, Nicci. ★*The Lying Room*
Fuller, Claire. ★*Bitter Orange*
Gardner, Lisa. *Fear Nothing: A Detective D. D. Warren Novel*
Gass, William H. *Middle C*
Goldberg, Tod. *Gangsterland: A Novel*
Gordon, Jaimy. ★*Lord of Misrule: A Novel*
Grecian, Alex. *The Saint of Wolves and Butchers*
Greenwood, T. *Rust & Stardust*
Gregory, Philippa. *The Red Queen: A Novel*
Guhrke, Laura Lee. *Governess Gone Rogue*
Halls, Stacey. *The Lost Orphan*
Hannah, Sophie. *Keep Her Safe*
Harper, Jane. *The Dry*
Harris, Robert. *The Ghost: A Novel*
Harvey, Michael T. *The Chicago Way*
Hegi, Ursula. *The Vision of Emma Blau*
Hendricks, Greer. ★*You Are Not Alone*
Horowitz, Anthony. ★*The Sentence Is Death*
Horowitz, Anthony. ★*The Word Is Murder*
James, Henry. *The Golden Bowl*
Jordan, Sophie. *This Scot of Mine*
Khan, Ausma Zehanat. *The Unquiet Dead*
Kwan, Kevin. *Sex and Vanity: A Novel*
Lehane, Dennis. *Since We Fell*
Leigh, Eva. *Forever Your Earl*
Levin, Ira. *A Kiss Before Dying*
Lin, Jeannie. *The Lotus Palace*
Lloyd, Catherine. *Death Comes to the Nursery*
Mayor, Archer. *Red Herring: A Joe Gunther Novel*
Meltzer, Brad. *The Inner Circle*
O'Rawe, Richard. *Northern Heist*
Orenstein, Hannah. *Love at First Like*
Palmer, Daniel. *The New Husband*
Paris, B. A. *Behind Closed Doors*
Paris, B. A. *Bring Me Back: A Novel*
Paris, B. A. ★*The Dilemma*
Pavone, Chris. ★*The Expats: A Novel*
Pavone, Chris. *The Paris Diversion: A Novel*
Penny, Louise. ★*The Madness of Crowds*
Perry, Thomas. *Vanishing Act*
Putney, Mary Jo. *Loving a Lost Lord*
Qiu, Xiaolong. *Hold Your Breath, China*
Qiu, Xiaolong. *Shanghai Redemption: An Inspector Chen Novel*
Richardson, Samuel. ★*Clarissa, Or, the History of a Young Lady*
Rimmer, Kelly. ★*The Warsaw Orphan: A Wwii Novel*

Rindell, Suzanne. ★*The Two Mrs. Carlyles*
Robotham, Michael. ★*Good Girl, Bad Girl: A Novel*
Robotham, Michael. ★*The Other Wife*
Rochon, Farrah. *The Boyfriend Project*
Rollins, James. *The Devil Colony*
Rowling, J. K. *The Casual Vacancy*
Runcie, James. *Sidney Chambers and the Forgiveness of Sins*
Sanders, Lawrence. ★*The Fourth Deadly Sin*
Sanders, Lawrence. *McNally's Secret*
Sanders, Lawrence. *McNally's Trial*
Sanders, Lawrence. *The Sixth Commandment: A Novel*
Sandford, John. *Broken Prey*
Scottoline, Lisa. *One Perfect Lie*
Smith, Wilbur A. *Birds of Prey*
Spark, Muriel. *Aiding & Abetting*
Spark, Muriel. *The Driver's Seat*
Spufford, Francis. ★*Golden Hill*
Stark, Richard. *Dirty Money*
Stephenson, Neal. ★*Cryptonomicon*
Stewart, Amy. ★*Miss Kopp Just Won't Quit*
Straub, Peter. ★*Mystery*
Strout, Elizabeth. ★*The Burgess Boys: A Novel*
Swanson, Peter. *The Kind Worth Killing: A Novel*
Thompson, Jim. *The Killer Inside Me*
Urquhart, Rachel. *The Visionist*
Waldman, Amy. *A Door in the Earth*
Ware, Ruth. ★*One by One*
Waters, Martha. ★*To Have and to Hoax: A Novel*
Williams, Eley. *The Liar's Dictionary*
Wrobel, Stephanie. *Darling Rose Gold*

***Deception** by Gaslight: A Gilded Gotham Mystery*. Belli, Kate
***Deception** Cove*. Laukkanen, Owen
DECEPTION IN MEN
    Matar, Hisham. *In the Country of Men*
    Perry, Thomas. *Death Benefits: A Novel*
    Rouda, Kaira Sturdivant. *Best Day Ever: A Novel*
DECISION-MAKING
    Freitas, Donna. *The Nine Lives of Rose Napolitano*
    Gilman, Susan Jane. *Donna Has Left the Building*
    Jimenez, Simon. ★*The Vanished Birds*
    Mackintosh, Clare. *After the End*
*A **Declaration** of the Rights of Magicians*. Parry, H. G.
***Decline** and Fall*. Waugh, Evelyn
DEE, JOHN
    Clements, Oliver. *The Eyes of the Queen*
    Raybourn, Deanna. ★*A Murderous Relation*
Dee, Jonathan
    The Locals: A Novel
    The Privileges: A Novel
    A Thousand Pardons: A Novel
*The **Deep***. Katsu, Alma
*The **Deep***. Solomon, Rivers
DEEP DIVING
    Hahn, Sumi. *The Mermaid from Jeju: A Novel*
***Deep** Freeze*. Sandford, John
★***Deep** into the Dark*. Tracy, P. J.
***Deep** River*. Endo, Shusaku
***Deep** River*. Marlantes, Karl

Deep Storm: A Novel. Child, Lincoln
DEEP-SEA SOUNDING
  Laukkanen, Owen. *Gale Force*
★*A Deeper* Love Inside: The Porsche Santiaga Story. Sister Souljah
★*A Deeper* Sleep: A Kate Shugak Novel. Stabenow, Dana
DEFAULT (FINANCE)
  Rinehart, Mary Roberts. *The Circular Staircase*
  Wallace, Carol. *Our Kind of People*
DEFECTORS
  Coughlin, Jack. *Long Shot: A Sniper Novel*
  Deighton, Len. *London Match*
  DeLillo, Don. *Libra*
  Greene, Graham. *The Human Factor*
  Le Carre, John. ★*Our Kind of Traitor: A Novel*
  Limon, Martin. *War Women*
  Sebastian, Tim. *Fatal Ally*
Defekt. Cipri, Nino
DEFENSE ATTORNEYS
  Connelly, Michael. *The Brass Verdict: A Novel*
  Connelly, Michael. *The Gods of Guilt*
  Connelly, Michael. ★*The Law of Innocence: A Novel*
  Connelly, Michael. *The Lincoln Lawyer: A Novel*
  Grisham, John. *A Time to Kill*
  Hannah, Kristin. *Home Front*
  Hart, John. *The King of Lies*
  Perry, Anne. *One Fatal Flaw: A Daniel Pitt Novel*
  Turow, Scott. *The Last Trial*
  Whitlow, Robert. *A Time to Stand*
DEFIANCE
  Benton, Janet. *Lilli De Jong: A Novel*
Defoe, Daniel
  ★*Moll Flanders*
  ★*Robinson Crusoe*
DEGAS, EDGAR
  Buchanan, Cathy Marie. ★*The Painted Girls*
  Gabaldon, Diana. *An Echo in the Bone*
DEGENERATION (PATHOLOGY)
  Genova, Lisa. *Every Note Played*
Deighton, Len
  Berlin Game
  London Match
★*Deja* Dead. Reichs, Kathy
DEJA VU
  Vonnegut, Kurt. *Timequake*
Dekker, Ted
  Black: The Birth of Evil
  The Girl Behind the Red Rope
  Red: The Heroic Rescue
  White: The Great Pursuit
Dektar, Molly
  The Ash Family
Del Amo, Jean-Baptiste
  Animalia
Del Tribute series [Series]. Barthelme, Frederick
Del Vecchio, John M.
  The 13th Valley: A Novel
DELANEY, EDWARD X. (FICTITIOUS CHARACTER)
  Sanders, Lawrence. ★*The First Deadly Sin*

  Sanders, Lawrence. ★*The Fourth Deadly Sin*
  Sanders, Lawrence. *The Second Deadly Sin*
Delaney, J. P.
  Believe Me: A Novel
  The Girl Before: A Novel
  The Perfect Wife: A Novel
  Playing Nice
Delany, Samuel R.
  Aye, and Gomorrah: Stories
  Dhalgren
  Stars in My Pocket Like Grains of Sand
Delany, Vicki
  Deadly Summer Nights
  Murder in a Teacup
  Tea & Treachery
DELAWARE
  Lippman, Laura. ★*Sunburn*
DELAWARE, ALEX (FICTITIOUS CHARACTER)
  Kellerman, Jonathan. *Bones: An Alex Delaware Novel*
DELHI
  Desai, Anita. *Clear Light of Day*
  Roy, Arundhati. ★*The Ministry of Utmost Happiness: A Novel*
  Taneja, Preti. *We That Are Young: A Novel*
Delicate Edible Birds and Other Stories. Groff, Lauren
A *Delicate* Touch. Woods, Stuart
★*A Delicate* Truth. Le Carre, John
★*Delicious* Foods. Hannaham, James
DeLillo, Don
  Falling Man: A Novel
  Libra
  The Names
  The Silence
  Underworld
  ★*White Noise*
  Zero K: A Novel
Delinsky, Barbara
  Lake News: A Novel
  A Week at the Shore
★*Delirium: a Novel*. Restrepo, Laura
DELIVERY DRIVERS
  Frazier, Jean Kyoung. *Pizza Girl*
★*The Delivery* Room: A Novel. Brownrigg, Sylvia
Dell'Antonia, K. J.
  The Chicken Sisters
Dell, Kari Lynn
  Fearless in Texas
  Mistletoe in Texas
  Reckless in Texas
DELTA REGION, MISSISSIPPI
  Rozan, S. J. ★*Paper Son*
  Smith, Michael F. *The Fighter: A Novel*
★*Delta* Wedding. Welty, Eudora
DeLuca, Jen
  Well Matched
  ★*Well Met*
Deluca, Marjorie
  The Savage Instinct

DELUSIONS

Gruber, Michael. *The Forgery of Venus: A Novel*

Portis, Charles. ★*Masters of Atlantis: A Novel*

DEMARKIAN, GREGOR (FICTITIOUS CHARACTER)

Haddam, Jane. *Cheating at Solitaire: A Gregor Demarkian Novel*

DEMENTIA

Blackstock, Terri. *Catching Christmas*

Cooney, Caroline B. *The Grandmother Plot*

Doshi, Avni. *Burnt Sugar: A Novel*

Grebe, Camilla. *The Ice Beneath Her: A Novel*

Ruskovich, Emily. *Idaho: A Novel*

DEMIGODS

Camp, Bryan. *The City of Lost Fortunes*

DeMille, Nelson

★*The Cuban Affair: A Novel*

★*The Deserter: A Novel*

Wild Fire

Demirtas, Selahattin

Dawn: Stories

★***Democracy:** an American Novel*. Adams, Henry

***Demolition** Angel: A Novel.*. Crais, Robert

Demon. Varley, John

*The **Demon** Crown: A Sigma Force Novel*. Rollins, James

*A **Demon** Summer: A Max Tudor Mystery*. Malliet, G. M.

DEMONIC POSSESSION

Blatty, William Peter. ★*The Exorcist*

Hendrix, Grady. *My Best Friend's Exorcism*

Snipes, Wesley. *Talon of God*

DEMONS

Barker, Clive. ★*Weaveworld*

Blatty, William Peter. ★*The Exorcist*

Gaiman, Neil. ★*Good Omens: The Nice and Accurate Prophecies of Agnes Nutter, Witch*

Grant, Helen. *The Glass Demon*

Hackwith, A. J. *The Library of the Unwritten*

Haydon, Elizabeth. *The Merchant Emperor*

Perez-Reverte, Arturo. *The Club Dumas*

Rice, Anne. *Blood Communion: A Tale of Prince Lestat*

Rothfuss, Patrick. ★*The Name of the Wind*

Saberhagen, Fred. *Shieldbreaker's Story*

Saul, John. *Midnight Voices*

Searles, John. *Help for the Haunted*

Snipes, Wesley. *Talon of God*

Vandelly, T. Marie. *Theme Music*

Walton, Jo. ★*Lent*

DENG, VALENTINO ACHAK

Eggers, Dave. *What Is the What: The Autobiography of Valentino Achak Deng*

DENMARK

Adler-Olsen, Jussi. *The Absent One*

Adler-Olsen, Jussi. *A Conspiracy of Faith*

Adler-Olsen, Jussi. *The Hanging Girl*

Adler-Olsen, Jussi. *The Keeper of Lost Causes*

Adler-Olsen, Jussi. *The Marco Effect: A Department Q Novel*

Adler-Olsen, Jussi. *The Purity of Vengeance: A Department Q Novel*

Adler-Olsen, Jussi. *The Scarred Woman*

Adler-Olsen, Jussi. ★*Victim 2117*

Follett, Ken. *Hornet Flight*

Pontoppidan, Henrik. *Lucky Per*

Updike, John. *Gertrude and Claudius*

Youngson, Anne. *Meet Me at the Museum*

Dennis-Benn, Nicole

Here Comes the Sun

★*Patsy: A Novel*

DENTAL ASSISTANTS

Stibbe, Nina. *Reasons to Be Cheerful*

DENTISTS

Block, Lawrence. *The Burglar in the Closet*

Ferris, Joshua. *To Rise Again at a Decent Hour: A Novel*

Russell, Mary Doria. ★*Doc: A Novel*

Stibbe, Nina. *Reasons to Be Cheerful*

DENVER, COLORADO

Dekker, Ted. *Black: The Birth of Evil*

Fajardo-Antine, Kali. ★*Sabrina & Corina: Stories*

Greer, Robert O. *First of State*

Laureano, C. E. ★*The Saturday Night Supper Club*

Martin, Alexa. *Fumbled*

Deon, Natashia

Grace

The Perishing: A Novel

★*The **Department** of Sensitive Crimes: A Detective Varg Novel*. McCall Smith, Alexander

Department Q [Series]. Adler-Olsen, Jussi

DEPARTMENT STORE EMPLOYEES

Martin, Steve. *Shopgirl*

DEPARTMENT STORES

Martin, Steve. *Shopgirl*

Depestre, Rene

Hadriana in All My Dreams

DEPORTATION

Engel, Patricia. ★*Infinite Country*

Grippando, James. *The Girl in the Glass Box*

Kutsukake, Lynne. *The Translation of Love: A Novel*

Marcom, Micheline Aharonian. *The New American*

DePoy, Phillip

Sidewalk Saint

DEPRESSION

Haig, Matt. *The Midnight Library*

Haslett, Adam. ★*Imagine Me Gone: A Novel*

Jackson, Charles. *The Lost Weekend*

Nicholls, Owen. *Love, Unscripted: A Novel*

DEPRESSION ERA (1929-1941)

Barnett, Karen. *Ever Faithful*

Barr, Mark. *Watershed*

Earley, Tony. *Jim the Boy: A Novel*

Harman, Patricia. *The Midwife of Hope River: A Novel*

Krueger, William Kent. *This Tender Land: A Novel*

Lansdale, Joe R. *Edge of Dark Water*

Lansdale, Joe R. *Sunset and Sawdust*

Leonard, Elmore. *The Hot Kid*

Moyes, Jojo. ★*The Giver of Stars: A Novel*

O'Neill, Heather. ★*The Lonely Hearts Hotel: A Novel*

Ozick, Cynthia. *Heir to the Glimmering World*

Shocklee, Michelle. *Under the Tulip Tree*

Shreve, Anita. *Sea Glass: A Novel*

Silver, Marisa. *Mary Coin: A Novel*

Wood, Shelley. *The Quintland Sisters*

DEPRESSIONS
Barr, Mark. *Watershed*
Bellow, Saul. ★*The Adventures of Augie March*
Bellow, Saul. *Novels, 1944-1953*
Caldwell, Erskine. *Tobacco Road*
Doctorow, E. L. *World's Fair*
Gruen, Sara. ★*Water for Elephants: A Novel*
Harman, Patricia. *The Midwife of Hope River: A Novel*
Lansdale, Joe R. *The Bottoms*
Lansdale, Joe R. *Sunset and Sawdust*
Shreve, Anita. *Sea Glass: A Novel*
Silver, Marisa. *Mary Coin: A Novel*
Steinbeck, John. ★*The Grapes of Wrath*

Dept. of Speculation. Offill, Jenny
Deranged. Ragan, Theresa

DERBYSHIRE, ENGLAND
Romain, Theresa. *Fortune Favors the Wicked*

Dermansky, Marcy
Very Nice

DeRoux, Margaux
The Lost Diary of Venice

Desai, Anita
Clear Light of Day
Fire on the Mountain

Desai, Kiran
The Inheritance of Loss

DESALTING OF WATER
Cussler, Clive. *Blue Gold: A Novel from the Numa Files*

The Descent of Monsters. Yang, JY
Desert Blood: The Juarez Murders. Gaspar de Alba, Alicia
Desert Flowers mysteries [Series]. Hollis, Lee

DESERT SURVIVAL
Diaz, Hernan. ★*In the Distance*

★*The Deserter: a Novel*. DeMille, Nelson

DESERTERS
Frazier, Charles. ★*Cold Mountain*
O'Brien, Tim. *Going After Cacciato: A Novel*

DESERTS
Barr, Nevada. *The Rope: An Anna Pigeon Novel*
Bock, Charles. *Beautiful Children: A Novel*
Hairston, Andrea. *Master of Poisons*
MacDonald, John D. *A Purple Place for Dying*
Williams, Joy. *Harrow*
Winton, Tim. *The Shepherd's Hut*

DESHIMA (NAGASAKI-SHI, JAPAN)
Mitchell, David. *The Thousand Autumns of Jacob De Zoet: A Novel*

DESIGNER DRUGS
Divya, S. B. *Machinehood*

DeSilva, Bruce
Providence Rag
Rogue Island
A Scourge of Vipers

DESIRE
Beauvoir, Simone de. ★*The Mandarins: A Novel*
Bolano, Roberto. *Last Evenings on Earth*
Broder, Melissa. *Milk Fed*
Cline, Emma. *Daddy: Stories*

Cusk, Rachel. *Second Place*
Dubus, Andre. *Dirty Love*
Enright, Anne. *The Forgotten Waltz*
Garcia, Cristina. *The Lady Matador's Hotel: A Novel*
Means, David. ★*Instructions for a Funeral: Stories*
Rivers, Francine. ★*Redeeming Love*
Swamy, Shruti. *A House Is a Body: Stories*
Taylor, Brandon. ★*Filthy Animals*
Toibin, Colm. ★*The Magician: A Novel*

DESIRE (PHILOSOPHY)
Aciman, Andre. *Enigma Variations: A Novel*

DESIRE IN MEN
Dyer, Geoff. *Jeff in Venice, Death in Varanasi*

★*A Desolation* Called Peace. Martine, Arkady

DESPAIR
Ramqvist, Karolina. *The White City*
Silko, Leslie Marmon. ★*Ceremony*

Desperate duchesses by the numbers [Series]. James, Eloisa

DESPOTISM
Garcia Marquez, Gabriel. ★*The Autumn of the Patriarch*
Suri, Tasha. *The Jasmine Throne*

Destiny and Desire: A Novel. Fuentes, Carlos
Destroyer Angel: An Anna Pigeon Novel. Barr, Nevada

DESTROYERS (WARSHIPS)
Sundin, Sarah. *Through Waters Deep: A Novel*

Detective Annalisa Vega novels [Series]. Schaffhausen, Joanna
Detective Betty novels [Series]. Kent, Kathleen
Detective by day novels [Series]. Garrett, Kellye
Detective D. D. Warren novels [Series]. Gardner, Lisa
Detective Galileo mysteries [Series]. Higashino, Keigo
Detective Gemma Monroe novels [Series]. Littlejohn, Emily
Detective Harry Hole [Series]. Nesbo, Jo
Detective Inspector Jack Caffery mysteries [Series]. Hayder, Mo
Detective Inspector Joona Linna mysteries [Series]. Kepler, Lars
Detective Konrad novels [Series]. Indriðason, Arnaldur
Detective Kubu mysteries [Series]. Stanley, Michael
Detective Mollel mysteries [Series]. Crompton, Richard
Detective Sergeant Adam Tyler [Series]. Thomas, Russ
Detective Sunderson novels [Series]. Harrison, Jim
Detective Varg novels [Series]. McCall Smith, Alexander

DETECTIVES
Aaronovitch, Ben. *Broken Homes*
Aaronovitch, Ben. *Moon Over Soho*
Aaronovitch, Ben. *Whispers Under Ground*
Alfon, Dov. *A Long Night in Paris*
Ames, Jonathan. *A Man Named Doll*
Archer, Jeffrey. *Nothing Ventured*
Ball, John Dudley. *In the Heat of the Night*
Bannalec, Jean-Luc. *Death in Brittany*
Bannalec, Jean-Luc. *The Granite Coast Murders*
Bannalec, Jean-Luc. *The Killing Tide: A Brittany Mystery*
Bannister, Jo. *Kindred Spirits*
Bateman, Kate. *This Earl of Mine*
Bauer, Belinda. *Snap*
Bayard, Louis. *The Black Tower: A Novel*
Belle, Kimberly. *Dear Wife*
Billingham, Mark. ★*Their Little Secret*
Black, Lisa. *Let Justice Descend*

Box, C. J. *Badlands*
Brett, Simon. *Murder Unprompted*
Brooks, Bill. *Blood Storm*
Brooks, Bill. *Winter Kill*
Brown, Sandra. ★*Ricochet*
Burke, James Lee. ★*A Private Cathedral*
Camilleri, Andrea. *Riccardino*
Church, James. ★*A Corpse in the Koryo*
Cleeves, Ann. ★*The Heron's Cry*
Cleeves, Ann. *The Long Call*
Cleeves, Ann. *Raven Black*
Cleeves, Ann. *Thin Air*
Cole, Alyssa. ★*An Extraordinary Union*
Collins, Manda. ★*A Lady's Guide to Mischief and Mayhem*
Collins, Wilkie. ★*The Moonstone*
Connelly, Michael. *The Burning Room*
Connelly, Michael. *The Crossing*
Connelly, Michael. *The Night Fire*
Connolly, John. *A Book of Bones*
Corey, James S. A. ★*Leviathan Wakes*
Crompton, Richard. *Hell's Gate: A Novel*
Cussler, Clive. ★*The Chase*
Cussler, Clive. *The Cutthroat*
Cussler, Clive. ★*The Titanic Secret*
Cussler, Clive. *The Wrecker*
De Giovanni, Maurizio. *The Bastards of Pizzofalcone*
De Giovanni, Maurizio. *The Crocodile*
Deaver, Jeffery. *Edge: A Novel*
DeMille, Nelson. *Wild Fire*
Dibdin, Michael. *Ratking*
Dick, Philip K. ★*Do Androids Dream of Electric Sheep?*
Dickens, Charles. ★*Bleak House*
Eisler, Barry. *Livia Lone*
Ellroy, James. ★*L.A. Confidential*
Fairstein, Linda A. *Blood Oath*
Fowler, Christopher. *Bryant & May: Hall of Mirrors : A Peculiar
    Crimes Unit Mystery*
Fowler, Christopher. *Bryant & May: Oranges and Lemons*
Fowler, Christopher. *Bryant & May: Strange Tide*
Fowler, Christopher. *Bryant & May: The Lonely Hour*
French, Nicci. *Tuesday's Gone*
French, Tana. *In the Woods*
Gallagher, Stephen. *The Bedlam Detective: A Novel*
Gallagher, Stephen. *The Kingdom of Bones: A Novel*
Garcia-Roza, L. A. *Alone in the Crowd: An Inspector Espinosa
    Mystery*
Garcia-Roza, L. A. *December Heat*
George, Elizabeth. *A Banquet of Consequences*
Gilbers, Harald. *Germania: A Novel of Nazi Berlin*
Gilman, Laura Anne. *Hard Magic*
Glover, Nicole. ★*The Conductors*
Glover, Nicole. *The Undertakers*
Goodwin, S. M. *Absence of Mercy*
Griffiths, Elly. *The Crossing Places*
Griffiths, Elly. *The Night Hawks*
Grossman, Paul. *Children of Wrath*
Hall, Tarquin. *The Case of the Deadly Butter Chicken: A Vish Puri
    Mystery*

Hallberg, Garth Risk. ★*City on Fire*
Harrison, M. John. *Nova Swing*
Harrod-Eagles, Cynthia. *Cruel as the Grave*
Harrod-Eagles, Cynthia. *Headlong*
Harrod-Eagles, Cynthia. *Old Bones*
Hart, John. *The Last Child*
Harvey, John. *A Darker Shade of Blue: Stories*
Hayder, Mo. *Gone*
Hayder, Mo. *Poppet*
Higashino, Keigo. *Malice*
Higashino, Keigo. *Newcomer*
Hill Gumbao, Toni. *The Good Suicides: A Thriller*
Hill, Susan. *The Pure in Heart: A Simon Serrailler Crime Novel*
Hillerman, Tony. *The Sinister Pig*
Horowitz, Anthony. *The House of Silk: A Sherlock Holmes Novel*
Horowitz, Anthony. ★*Magpie Murders*
Horowitz, Anthony. ★*The Sentence Is Death*
Indriðason, Arnaldur. *Strange Shores: An Inspector Erlendur Novel*
Irwin, Stephen M. *The Broken Ones: A Novel*
Ishiguro, Kazuo. *When We Were Orphans*
Johnson, D. E. *Detroit Shuffle*
Kelly, Stephen. *The Wages of Desire: A World War II Mystery*
Kepler, Lars. *The Sandman*
Khan, Ausma Zehanat. *Among the Ruins*
Khan, Ausma Zehanat. *The Unquiet Dead*
Kidd, Jess. ★*Things in Jars*
Leon, Donna. *Trace Elements*
Leon, Donna. ★*Transient Desires*
Leon, Donna. *Uniform Justice*
Leon, Donna. *Unto Us a Son Is Given*
Lippman, Laura. *No Good Deeds*
Lippman, Laura. *What the Dead Know*
Locke, Attica. ★*Bluebird, Bluebird*
Locke, Attica. ★*Heaven, My Home*
Lovesey, Peter. *Beau Death*
Lovesey, Peter. *The Tooth Tattoo*
MacBride, Stuart. *Cold Granite*
MacDonald, Philip. *The List of Adrian Messenger*
Mankell, Henning. *The Dogs of Riga*
Mankell, Henning. *The Man Who Smiled: A Kurt Wallander Mystery*
Mark, David John. *Cruel Mercy*
Mason, Timothy. *The Darwin Affair*
May, Peter. *The Blackhouse*
McCall Smith, Alexander. ★*The Department of Sensitive Crimes: A
    Detective Varg Novel*
McCall Smith, Alexander. ★*The Man with the Silver Saab: A
    Detective Varg Novel*
McClure, James. *The Steam Pig*
McIlvanney, William. *The Dark Remains: Laidlaw's First Case*
McKinty, Adrian. *In the Morning I'll Be Gone: A Detective Sean
    Duffy Novel*
Meyer, Deon. *Icarus*
Mosley, Walter. ★*Blood Grove*
Mosley, Walter. *Little Scarlet: An Easy Rawlins Mystery*
Mukherjee, Abir. *The Shadows of Men*
Mukherjee, Abir. *Smoke and Ashes: A Novel*
Nesbo, Jo. *The Redeemer*
North, Alex. *The Whisper Man*

Obregon, Nicolas. *Blue Light Yokohama*
Pava, Sergio de la. *Personae: A Novel*
Penny, Louise. ★*All the Devils Are Here*
Penny, Louise. *Still Life*
Perry, Anne. ★*Death with a Double Edge: A Daniel Pitt Novel*
Perry, Thomas. *Fidelity*
Pressfield, Steven. *36 Righteous Men: A Novel*
Price, Richard. *Clockers*
Price, Richard. *Samaritan*
Qiu, Xiaolong. *Death of a Red Heroine*
Quartey, Kwei. *Children of the Street: A Novel*
Quartey, Kwei. *Gold of Our Fathers*
Quartey, Kwei. *Wife of the Gods: A Novel*
Rademacher, Cay. *Deadly Camargue: A Provence Mystery*
Rankin, Ian. ★*Black and Blue: An Inspector Rebus Novel*
Rankin, Ian. *The Black Book*
Rankin, Ian. *The Complaints*
Rankin, Ian. *Dead Souls: An Inspector Rebus Novel*
Rankin, Ian. *Exit Music*
Rankin, Ian. *The Falls: An Inspector Rebus Novel*
Rankin, Ian. *The Hanging Garden: An Inspector Rebus Novel*
Rankin, Ian. *The Naming of the Dead: An Inspector Rebus Novel*
Rankin, Ian. *A Question of Blood: An Inspector Rebus Novel*
Rankin, Ian. *Resurrection Men: An Inspector Rebus Novel*
Rankin, Ian. *Set in Darkness: An Inspector Rebus Novel*
Rice, Luanne. ★*Last Day*
Ridpath, Michael. *Far North*
Rinehart, Mary Roberts. *Miss Pinkerton*
Robinson, Peter. *All the Colors of Darkness*
Robotham, Michael. *The Night Ferry: A Novel*
Rodriguez, Linda. *Every Broken Trust: A Mystery*
Rodriguez, Linda. *Every Hidden Fear: A Skeet Bannion Mystery*
Roslund, Anders. *Cell 8*
Roslund, Anders. ★*Knock Knock*
Roslund, Anders. *Pen 33*
Rowland, Laura Joh. *The Incense Game: A Novel of Feudal Japan*
Rowland, Laura Joh. *The Shogun's Daughter: A Novel of Feudal Japan*
Runcie, James. *Sidney Chambers and the Problem of Evil*
Runcie, James. *Sidney Chambers and the Shadow of Death*
Sandford, John. *Broken Prey*
Sandford, John. *Buried Prey*
Sandford, John. ★*Deadline*
Sandford, John. *Deep Freeze*
Sandford, John. *Field of Prey*
Sandford, John. *Heat Lightning*
Sandford, John. *Hidden Prey*
Sandford, John. *Mad River*
Sandford, John. ★*Phantom Prey*
Sandford, John. *Storm Front*
Sandford, John. *Storm Prey*
Shaw, William. *The Birdwatcher*
Shaw, William. *A Song for the Brokenhearted*
Simenon, Georges. ★*Maigret and the Killer*
Simenon, Georges. *Maigret and the Madwoman*
Simenon, Georges. ★*Maigret and the Saturday Caller*
Simenon, Georges. *Maigret and the Wine Merchant*
Simenon, Georges. *Maigret in Holland*

Simenon, Georges. *Maigret's Memoirs*
Simenon, Georges. *My Friend Maigret*
Simmons, Dan. *The Fall of Hyperion*
Simpson, Dorothy. *Dead and Gone: An Inspector Luke Thanet Novel.*
Simpson, Dorothy. *Dead by Morning*
Simpson, Dorothy. *Doomed to Die*
Simpson, Dorothy. *Last Seen Alive: A Luke Thanet Mystery*
Simpson, Dorothy. *No Laughing Matter*
Simpson, Dorothy. *Once Too Often: An Inspector Luke Thanet Novel*
Sjowall, Maj. ★*Cop Killer: The Story of a Crime*
Sjowall, Maj. ★*The Laughing Policeman*
Sjowall, Maj. ★*The Locked Room: The Story of a Crime*
Sjowall, Maj. *The Man on the Balcony: The Story of a Crime*
Sjowall, Maj. ★*Murder at the Savoy*
Slaughter, Karin. *Criminal: A Novel*
Smith, B. J. *Shoot the Dog: A Virgil Cain Mystery*
Smith, Martin Cruz. ★*Gorky Park*
Smith, Martin Cruz. *Havana Bay*
Smith, Martin Cruz. *Polar Star*
Smith, Martin Cruz. *The Siberian Dilemma*
Smith, Martin Cruz. *Stalin's Ghost*
Smith, Martin Cruz. ★*Tatiana: An Arkady Renko Novel*
Smith, Martin Cruz. *Three Stations: An Arkady Renko Novel*
Smith, Martin Cruz. *Wolves Eat Dogs: A Novel*
Solares, Martin. *The Black Minutes*
Spain, Jo. *With Our Blessing: An Inspector Tom Reynolds Mystery*
Spencer, Sally. ★*A Dying Fall*
Stanley, Michael. *A Carrion Death*
Stanley, Michael. *Deadly Harvest*
Stanley, Michael. *A Death in the Family*
Stanley, Michael. *Death of the Mantis*
Stanley, Michael. *Dying to Live*
Stout, Dan. ★*Titanshade*
Stroud, Carsten. *The Shimmer*
Sveistrup, Soren. ★*The Chestnut Man: A Novel*
Tallis, Frank. *Vienna Blood: A Max Liebermann Mystery*
Thomas, Russ. ★*Firewatching*
Thomas, Russ. *Nighthawking*
Thompson, Victoria. *Murder on Wall Street*
Tracy, P. J. *Ice Cold Heart*
Truss, Lynne. *The Man That Got Away: A Constable Twitten Mystery*
Truss, Lynne. *Murder by Milk Bottle*
Turton, Stuart. ★*The Devil and the Dark Water*
Wolf, Dick. *The Ultimatum*

DETERMINATION (PERSONAL QUALITY)

Ferencik, Erica. *Into the Jungle*
Parker-Chan, Shelley. ★*She Who Became the Sun*
Stachniak, Eva. *The Chosen Maiden: A Novel*
Stirling, S. M. *Dies the Fire*
Stirling, S. M. *The Protector's War*

DETERMINATION IN MEN

Bellefleur, Alexandria. *Hang the Moon*
Clark, Wahida. *Payback with Ya Life*
Feehan, Christine. *Shadow Rider*
Obioma, Chigozie. ★*An Orchestra of Minorities*
Stone, Irving. *Lust for Life: A Novel of Vincent Van Gogh*
Winter, Evan. ★*The Rage of Dragons*

FICTION CORE COLLECTION
TWENTY-FIRST EDITION

DETERMINATION IN WOMEN

Alderson, Kaia. *Sisters in Arms*

Alpsten, Ellen. *Tsarina*

Barr, Nevada. *The Rope: An Anna Pigeon Novel*

Bird, Sarah. *Daughter of a Daughter of a Queen*

Cather, Willa. *The Song of the Lark*

Cole, Alyssa. ★*How to Catch a Queen*

Goodman, Jo. *In Want of a Wife*

Gortner, C. W. *The First Actress: A Novel of Sarah Bernhardt*

Gregory, Philippa. *The Constant Princess*

Harper, Karen. *The Queen's Secret: A Novel of England's World War II Queen*

Jenkins, Beverly. *Rebel*

Jenkins, Beverly. *Wild Rain*

Mallery, Susan. *The Summer of Sunshine and Margot*

McHugh, Laura. *What's Done in Darkness: A Novel*

Okorafor, Nnedi. ★*Noor*

Sekaran, Shanthi. ★*Lucky Boy*

Stockett, Kathryn. ★*The Help*

Walsh, S. Kirk. *The Elephant of Belfast: A Novel*

★*Detransition, Baby*. Peters, Torrey

Detroit Shuffle. Johnson, D. E.

DETROIT, MICHIGAN

Ashley & JaQuavis. *Murderville*

Beukes, Lauren. *Broken Monsters*

Clark, Wahida. *Blood, Sweat and Payback*

Clark, Wahida. *Payback Ain't Enough*

Clark, Wahida. *Payback with Ya Life*

Estleman, Loren D. ★*Amos Walker: The Complete Story Collection*

Estleman, Loren D. *Infernal Angels*

Estleman, Loren D. *A Smile on the Face of the Tiger*

Eugenides, Jeffrey. ★*Middlesex*

Eugenides, Jeffrey. ★*The Virgin Suicides*

Flournoy, Angela. *The Turner House*

Johnson, D. E. *Detroit Shuffle*

Kamal, Sheena. *It All Falls Down*

Leonard, Elmore. *Charlie Martz and Other Stories: The Unpublished Stories*

Leonard, Elmore. *Pagan Babies*

Morrison, Toni. ★*Song of Solomon*

Oates, Joyce Carol. ★*Them*

Pyper, Andrew. *The Damned: A Novel*

Randall, Alice. ★*Black Bottom Saints*

Weiner, Jennifer. ★*Mrs. Everything: A Novel*

Deutermann, Peter T.

The Iceman

The Nugget: A Novel

Pacific Glory: A Novel

Dev, Sonali

★*A Bollywood Affair*

The Bollywood Bride

A Distant Heart

★*Incense and Sensibility*

★*Pride, Prejudice, and Other Flavors: A Novel*

★*Recipe for Persuasion*

Deveraux, Jude

Someone to Love

A Willing Murder

Deviation. D'Eramo, Luce

DEVIL

Bulgakov, Mikhail. ★*The Master and Margarita*

Gilman, Laura Anne. *The Cold Eye*

Gilman, Laura Anne. *Silver on the Road*

Hill, Joe. *Horns*

Hurley, Andrew Michael. *Devil's Day*

Mann, Thomas. *Doctor Faustus*

Rice, Anne. *Memnoch the Devil*

Updike, John. ★*The Witches of Eastwick*

The Devil All the Time. Pollock, Donald Ray

★*The Devil and the Dark Water*. Turton, Stuart

The Devil Colony. Rollins, James

The Devil Crept In. Ahlborn, Ania

Devil in a Blue Dress. Mosley, Walter

★*Devil in Disguise*. Kleypas, Lisa

Devil Red. Lansdale, Joe R.

The Devil Tree. Kosinski, Jerzy

Devil you know [Series]. Byrne, Kerrigan

The Devil's Alphabet. Gregory, Daryl

Devil's Day. Hurley, Andrew Michael

The Devil's Making. Haldane, Sean

Devil's Night. Ritter, Todd

The Devil's Triangle. Coulter, Catherine

Devil's West [Series]. Gilman, Laura Anne

Devils of Dover [Series]. Bowen, Kelly

The Devlin Diary. Phillips, Christi

DEVLIN, LIAM (FICTITIOUS CHARACTER)

Higgins, Jack. *The Eagle Has Landed*

Devolution: a Firsthand Account of the Rainier Sasquatch Massacre. Brooks, Max

DEVON, ENGLAND

Bowen, Rhys. *The Victory Garden*

Christie, Agatha. ★*And Then There Were None*

Cleeves, Ann. ★*The Heron's Cry*

Cleeves, Ann. *The Long Call*

Doyle, Arthur Conan. ★*The Hound of the Baskervilles*

★*The Devotion of Suspect X*. Higashino, Keigo

The Dew Breaker. Danticat, Edwidge

Dewes, J. S.

The Last Watch

deWitt, Patrick

The Sisters Brothers: A Novel

Undermajordomo Minor

DeWoskin, Rachel

Big Girl Small: A Novel

Dexter, Colin

The Daughters of Cain

The Remorseful Day

The Way Through the Woods

Dexter, Pete

★*Deadwood*

Paris Trout

Spooner

DHAKA, BANGLADESH

Zaman, Nadeem. *Up in the Main House & Other Stories*

Dhalgren. Delany, Samuel R.

DHARMA (BUDDHISM)
Kerouac, Jack. *The Dharma Bums*
*The **Dharma** Bums*. Kerouac, Jack
DI STEFANO, FLAVIA (FICTITIOUS CHARACTER)
Pears, Iain. *Death and Restoration*
Pears, Iain. *The Immaculate Deception*
Pears, Iain. *The Last Judgement*
Diachenko, Serhii
Vita Nostra
*The **Diagnosis***. Lightman, Alan P.
Dial a for Aunties. Sutanto, Jesse Q.
Diamant, Anita
The Boston Girl: A Novel
★*The Red Tent*
*The **Diamond** Age,: Or, a Young Lady's Illustrated Primer*. Stephenson, Neal
*The **Diamond** Empire*. K'wan
DIAMOND INDUSTRY AND TRADE
Goddard, Robert. ★*Long Time Coming: A Novel*
DIAMOND MINES AND MINING
Stanley, Michael. *A Carrion Death*
Diamond Solitaire. Lovesey, Peter
Diamond, Elizabeth
An Accidental Light
DIAMOND, PETER (FICTITIOUS CHARACTER)
Lovesey, Peter. *Diamond Solitaire*
Lovesey, Peter. ★*The Last Detective*
DIAMONDS
Khan, Vaseem. *The Perplexing Theft of the Jewel in the Crown*
Lindsay, Jeffry P. *Just Watch Me*
Meyerson, Amy. *The Imperfects*
Osman, Richard. *The Man Who Died Twice: A Thursday Murder Club Mystery*
Trollope, Anthony. ★*The Eustace Diamonds*
★*Diamonds and Pearl*. K'wan
Diamonds and Pearl [Series]. K'wan
DIANA
Clancy, Tom. *Patriot Games*
DIARIES
Collins, Kathleen. *Notes from a Black Woman's Diary: Selected Works of Kathleen Collins*
Mankell, Henning. *The Man from Beijing*
DIARY NOVELS
Bellow, Saul. *Dangling Man*
Bernhard, Thomas. *Frost: A Novel*
Brautigan, Richard. *An Unfortunate Woman: A Journey*
Butler, Octavia E. ★*Parable of the Sower*
Colette. *The Complete Claudine*
Copenhaver, John. *The Savage Kind*
Downing, David. *Diary of a Dead Man on Leave*
Erdrich, Louise. ★*Shadow Tag: A Novel*
Fielding, Helen. ★*Bridget Jones's Diary: A Novel*
Gibbon, Maureen. *The Lost Notebook of Edouard Manet: A Novel*
Groen, Hendrik. *On the Bright Side: The New Secret Diary of Hendrik Groen, 85 Years Old*
Hijuelos, Oscar. *Twain & Stanley Enter Paradise*
Johnson, Charles Richard. ★*Middle Passage*
Kaufman, Sue. *Diary of a Mad Housewife*

Lem, Stanislaw. *His Master's Voice*
Lessing, Doris May. ★*The Golden Notebook*
Meyer, Nicholas. *The Adventure of the Peculiar Protocols: Adapted from the Journals of John H. Watson, M.D.*
Parmar, Priya. *Vanessa and Her Sister*
Pearson, Allison. ★*How Hard Can It Be?*
Preston, Caroline. *The Scrapbook of Frankie Pratt*
Richler, Nancy. *Your Mouth Is Lovely: A Novel*
Sartre, Jean Paul. ★*Nausea*
Smith, Dodie. ★*I Capture the Castle*
Weir, Andy. *The Martian*
Diary of a Dead Man on Leave. Downing, David
Diary of a Mad Housewife. Kaufman, Sue
Diary of a Murderer: And Other Stories. Kim, Young-Ha
DIARY WRITING
Anderson, Alison. *The Summer Guest*
Clarke, Susanna. ★*Piranesi*
DeRoux, Margaux. *The Lost Diary of Venice*
Jin, Ha. *A Map of Betrayal: A Novel*
Ozeki, Ruth L. ★*A Tale for the Time Being*
Rimmer, Kelly. *Truths I Never Told You*
Diaz, Hernan
★*In the Distance*
Diaz, Junot
★*The Brief Wondrous Life of Oscar Wao*
★*This Is How You Lose Her*
Dibdin, Michael
Ratking
Dick Francis novels [Series]. Francis, Felix
Dick, Philip K.
★*Do Androids Dream of Electric Sheep?*
★*The Man in the High Castle*
The Minority Report
Dickens, Charles
★*Bleak House*
★*A Christmas Carol*
★*David Copperfield*
Dombey and Son
★*Great Expectations*
Little Dorrit
Martin Chuzzlewit
★*Nicholas Nickleby*
The Old Curiosity Shop
Oliver Twist, or the Parish Boy's Progress
Our Mutual Friend
The Pickwick Papers
★*A Tale of Two Cities*
DICKENS, CHARLES
Hillerman, Tony. *The Sinister Pig*
Simmons, Dan. *Drood: A Novel*
Dickey, Eric Jerome
★*Bad Men and Wicked Women*
Before We Were Wicked
The Blackbirds
The Business of Lovers
Finding Gideon
★*The Son of Mr. Suleman*

DICKINSON, EMILY
    Brown, Amy Belding. *Emily's House*
    Clarke, Brock. *An Arsonist's Guide to Writers' Homes in New England: A Novel*
    Cline, Emma. *The Girls: A Novel*
    Kelton, Elmer. ★*The Way of the Coyote*
DICTATORS
    Bandi. *The Accusation: Forbidden Stories from Inside North Korea*
    Block, Lawrence. *Killing Castro*
    Elison, Meg. *The Book of Etta*
    Garcia Marquez, Gabriel. ★*The Autumn of the Patriarch*
    Garcia, Cristina. *King of Cuba: A Novel*
    Lewis, Sinclair. ★*It Can't Happen Here*
    Ruff, Matt. ★*88 Names*
    Stroby, Wallace. *Some Die Nameless*
    Vargas Llosa, Mario. *The Feast of the Goat*
DICTATORSHIP
    Allende, Isabel. *Of Love and Shadows*
    Apostol, Gina. *Bibliolepsy*
    Balzano, Marco. *I'm Staying Here*
    Bolano, Roberto. ★*Distant Star*
    Danticat, Edwidge. ★*Krik? Krak!*
    De Robertis, Carolina. *Perla*
    Stevens, Francis. *The Heads of Cerberus*
DICTIONARIES
    Williams, Eley. *The Liar's Dictionary*
*The **Dictionary** of Lost Words*. Williams, Pip
Did You Ever Have a Family. Clegg, Bill
Didion, Joan
    A Book of Common Prayer
    ★*Play It as It Lays: A Novel*
★*Die Trying*. Child, Lee
Diehl, Heidi
    Lifelines
Dies the Fire. Stirling, S. M.
Dies the fire trilogy [Series]. Stirling, S. M.
DIETING
    Awad, Mona. ★*13 Ways of Looking at a Fat Girl*
    Broder, Melissa. *Milk Fed*
    Clarke, Diana. *Thin Girls*
DIETING FOR WOMEN
    Fielding, Helen. ★*Bridget Jones's Diary: A Novel*
Dietland. Walker, Sarai
Diffenbaugh, Vanessa
    The Language of Flowers: A Novel
DIFFERENCE (PSYCHOLOGY)
    Malouf, David. *Remembering Babylon*
    McCaffrey, Anne. ★*Acorna: The Unicorn Girl*
    Rodrigues Fowler, Yara. *Stubborn Archivist*
Difficult dukes [Series]. Chase, Loretta Lynda
★*Difficult Women*. Gay, Roxane
Digging up Love. Blumberg, Chandra
DIGITAL COMMUNICATIONS
    DeLillo, Don. *The Silence*
★*The **Dilemma***. Paris, B. A.
DILEMMAS
    Gabaldon, Diana. ★*A Breath of Snow and Ashes*
    Gabaldon, Diana. *An Echo in the Bone*

    Gabaldon, Diana. *Written in My Own Heart's Blood*
    Miller, Sue. *The Senator's Wife*
Dillard, Annie
    The Maytrees: A Novel
Dimaline, Cherie
    Empire of Wild
Dimberg, Kelsey Rae
    Girl in the Rearview Mirror
Dimechkie, Karim
    Lifted by the Great Nothing
Dimitri, Francesco
    The Book of Hidden Things
Dimon, HelenKay
    Her Other Secret
DINAH (BIBLICAL FIGURE)
    Diamant, Anita. ★*The Red Tent*
DINERS (RESTAURANTS)
    Russo, Richard. ★*Empire Falls*
DINNERS AND DINING
    Berg, Elizabeth. *The Confession Club: A Novel*
    Bernhard, Thomas. ★*Woodcutters*
    Faulks, Sebastian. *A Week in December*
    Laureano, C. E. ★*The Saturday Night Supper Club*
    Malliet, G. M. *A Demon Summer: A Max Tudor Mystery*
    Malliet, G. M. *Pagan Spring: A Mystery*
    Steinhauer, Olen. ★*All the Old Knives*
    Williams, Lara. *Supper Club: A Novel*
DINOSAURS
    Swanwick, Michael. *Bones of the Earth*
Diofebi, Dario
    Paradise, Nevada
DIONNE QUINTUPLETS
    Wood, Shelley. *The Quintland Sisters*
Dionne, Karen
    The Wicked Sister
Diop, David
    ★*At Night All Blood Is Black*
DIPLOMACY
    Okorafor, Nnedi. *Binti: Home*
    Okorafor, Nnedi. *Binti: The Night Masquerade*
DIPLOMATS
    Crouch, Katie. *Embassy Wife*
    Greene, Graham. *The Honorary Consul*
    Le Carre, John. *The Constant Gardener: A Novel*
    Mason, Daniel. *The Piano Tuner*
    Patchett, Ann. ★*Bel Canto: A Novel*
    Steinhauer, Olen. *The Cairo Affair*
    Stout, Dan. ★*Titanshade*
DIPLOMATS' SPOUSES
    Faulks, Sebastian. *On Green Dolphin Street: A Novel*
Dirk Gently's Holistic Detective Agency. Adams, Douglas
Dirk Gently [Series]. Adams, Douglas
Dirk Pitt adventures [Series]. Cussler, Clive
Dirty Girls on Top. Valdes, Alisa
Dirty Girls Social Club [Series]. Valdes, Alisa
Dirty Love. Dubus, Andre
Dirty Money. Stark, Richard
Dirty Red novels [Series]. Stringer, Vickie M.

Dirty Red: A Novel. Stringer, Vickie M.
The *Dirty* Secrets Club. Gardiner, Meg
The *Dirty* South. Connolly, John
DISAGREEMENT
    Ware, Ruth. ★*One by One*
The *Disappearance* Boy. Bartlett, Neil
The *Disappeared*. Box, C. J.
DISAPPEARED PERSONS
    Fernandez, Nona. *The Twilight Zone*
    Perrotta, Tom. *The Leftovers*
The *Disappearing* Act. Steadman, Catherine
★*Disappearing* Earth. Phillips, Julia
The *Disaster* Tourist. Ko-Eun, Yun
DISASTER VICTIMS
    Kirkpatrick, Jane. *One More River to Cross*
DISASTERS
    Atwood, Margaret. ★*Oryx and Crake*
    Barclay, Linwood. ★*Elevator Pitch: A Novel*
    DeLillo, Don. *The Silence*
    Egan, Greg. *Perihelion Summer*
    Kowal, Mary Robinette. *The Calculating Stars: A Lady Astronaut Novel*
    Stephenson, Neal. *Anathem*
    Stephenson, Neal. *Seveneves*
    Stewart, George R. *Earth Abides*
    Vonnegut, Kurt. ★*Cat's Cradle*
    Wilhelm, Kate. *Where Late the Sweet Birds Sang*
DISASTERS — PREVENTION
    Kress, Nancy. *If Tomorrow Comes*
    Kress, Nancy. *Tomorrow's Kin*
    Williams, Drew. *The Stars Now Unclaimed*
DISBARRED LAWYERS
    Clark, Martin. *The Substitution Order*
Disco for the Departed. Cotterill, Colin
DISCONTENT
    Beagin, Jen. ★*Vacuum in the Dark: A Novel*
    Kenney, John. *Talk to Me*
    Schweblin, Samanta. *Mouthful of Birds: Stories*
    Tan, Lucy. *What We Were Promised*
DISCONTENT IN MEN
    Crews, Harry. *A Feast of Snakes: A Novel*
A *Discovery* of Witches: A Novel. Harkness, Deborah E.
★The *Discreet* Hero. Vargas Llosa, Mario
DISCRIMINATION
    Bond, Cynthia. *Ruby: A Novel*
    Boyne, John. *The Heart's Invisible Furies*
    Hooper, Elise. *Fast Girls: A Novel of the 1936 Women's Olympic Team*
DISCWORLD (IMAGINARY PLACE)
    Pratchett, Terry. ★*The Color of Magic*
    Pratchett, Terry. *Equal Rites*
    Pratchett, Terry. *The Fifth Elephant: A Novel of Discworld*
    Pratchett, Terry. *Going Postal: A Novel of Discworld*
    Pratchett, Terry. *Guards! Guards!*
    Pratchett, Terry. *The Last Hero: A Discworld Fable*
    Pratchett, Terry. *Lords and Ladies: A Novel of Discworld*
    Pratchett, Terry. *Men at Arms: A Novel of Discworld*
    Pratchett, Terry. *Monstrous Regiment*

    Pratchett, Terry. *Pyramids: The Book of Going Forth*
    Pratchett, Terry. *Reaper Man*
    Pratchett, Terry. *Small Gods: A Novel of Discworld*
    Pratchett, Terry. *Thief of Time*
    Pratchett, Terry. *Thud!: A Novel of Discworld*
    Pratchett, Terry. *The Truth: A Novel of Discworld*
    Pratchett, Terry. *Witches Abroad*
    Pratchett, Terry. *Wyrd Sisters*
Discworld [Series]. Pratchett, Terry
DISEASES
    Brooks, Max. ★*World War Z: An Oral History of the Zombie War*
    Cussler, Clive. *Celtic Empire*
    Ferris, Joshua. *The Unnamed*
    King, Stephen. *Elevation*
    Parks, Brad. *The Player: A Mystery*
    Vonnegut, Kurt. *Slapstick: Or, Lonesome No More! a Novel*
    Wright, Lawrence. *The End of October*
Disgrace. Coetzee, J. M.
Disgraceful dukes [Series]. Bell, Lenora
Disgruntled: a Novel. Solomon, Asali
DISGUISES
    Bayard, Louis. *The Black Tower: A Novel*
    Bennett, Bethany. *West End Earl*
    Beverley, Jo. *My Lady Notorious*
    Bourne, Joanna. *The Forbidden Rose*
    Brockway, Connie. *No Place for a Dame*
    Haig, Matt. *The Humans: A Novel*
    Hawks, Arlem. *Georgana's Secret*
    Orczy, Emmuska Orczy. ★*The Scarlet Pimpernel*
    Ridley, Erica. ★*The Perks of Loving a Wallflower*
    Riley, Vanessa. ★*A Duke, the Lady, and a Baby*
    Sabatini, Rafael. *Scaramouche: A Romance of the French Revolution*
    Sosa, Mia. ★*Acting on Impulse*
    Woods, Stuart. *The Money Shot*
Disher, Garry
    Under the Cold Bright Lights
DISHONESTY
    Beattie, Ann. *A Wonderful Stroke of Luck: A Novel*
    Buwalda, Peter. *Bonita Avenue: A Novel*
    deWitt, Patrick. *Undermajordomo Minor*
    Eco, Umberto. *Baudolino*
    Frear, Caz. *Stone Cold Heart*
    MacLean, Sarah. ★*Wicked and the Wallflower*
    Ware, Ruth. *The Lying Game*
DISILLUSIONMENT
    Hemingway, Ernest. ★*The Sun Also Rises*
    Remarque, Erich Maria. *A Time to Love and a Time to Die*
DISILLUSIONMENT IN MEN
    Flaubert, Gustave. *Sentimental Education*
    Hemingway, Ernest. *For Whom the Bell Tolls*
    Naipaul, V. S. *A Bend in the River*
    Updike, John. ★*Rabbit, Run*
DISINHERITANCE
    Walker, Martin. *The Shooting at Chateau Rock*
DISMEMBERMENT
    Brown, Rita Mae. *Wish You Were Here*
    Tudor, C. J. *The Chalk Man: A Novel*
Disoriental. Djavadi, Negar

DISORIENTATION

Garcia Marquez, Gabriel. ★*Strange Pilgrims: Twelve Stories*

Saramago, Jose. ★*Blindness*

DISPLACED WORKERS

Sloan, Robin. *Mr. Penumbra's 24-Hour Bookstore*

★The **Dispossessed**: *an Ambiguous Utopia*. Le Guin, Ursula K.

DISSENTERS

Bandi. *The Accusation: Forbidden Stories from Inside North Korea*

Goldberg, Lee. *Fake Truth*

Han, Kang. ★*Human Acts: A Novel*

Harkaway, Nick. *Gnomon: A Novel*

Ramzipoor, E. R. *The Ventriloquists*

Steele, Allen M. *Coyote: A Novel of Interstellar Exploration*

DISSERTATION WRITING

Phillips, Christi. *The Rossetti Letter: A Novel*

The **Dissident**. Freudenberger, Nell

Dissident *Gardens*. Lethem, Jonathan

DISSOCIATIVE IDENTITY DISORDER

Carey, M. R. *Someone Like Me*

Chung, Maxine Mei-Fung. *The Eighth Girl*

Ide, Joe. ★*Hi Five: An IQ Novel*

Stevenson, Robert Louis. ★*The Strange Case of Dr. Jekyll and Mr. Hyde*

The **Distant** *Dead*. Young, Heather

The **Distant** *Echo*. McDermid, Val

A **Distant** *Heart*. Dev, Sonali

The **Distant** *Hours: A Novel*. Morton, Kate

The **Distant** *Marvels*. Acevedo, Chantel

A **Distant** *Shore*. Phillips, Caryl

★**Distant** *Star*. Bolano, Roberto

DISTILLING INDUSTRY AND TRADE

Kleypas, Lisa. ★*Devil in Disguise*

DISTRESS (PSYCHOLOGY)

Demirtas, Selahattin. *Dawn: Stories*

DISTRICT ATTORNEYS

Doetsch, Richard. *Half-Past Dawn*

Lippman, Laura. *Wilde Lake*

Stabenow, Dana. ★*A Deeper Sleep: A Kate Shugak Novel*

Wolfe, Tom. *The Bonfire of the Vanities*

Divakaruni, Chitra Banerjee

Oleander Girl: A Novel

DIVALI

Lalli, Sonya. *A Holly Jolly Diwali*

The **Dive** *from Clausen's Pier*. Packer, Ann

DIVERS

Egan, Jennifer. ★*Manhattan Beach: A Novel*

Hahn, Sumi. *The Mermaid from Jeju: A Novel*

Leonard, Elmore. *Tishomingo Blues: A Novel*

Mackintosh, Anneliese. *Bright and Dangerous Objects*

Divide (Dewes) [Series]. Dewes, J. S.

A **Divided** *Spy*. Cumming, Charles

DIVINATION

Saylor, Steven. *The Seven Wonders: A Novel of the Ancient World*

Divine *and Human and Other Stories*. Tolstoy, Leo

Divine *Secrets of the Ya-Ya Sisterhood: A Novel*. Wells, Rebecca

DIVING

Jackson, Joshilyn. *Never Have I Ever*

A **Diving** *Rock on the Hudson*. Roth, Henry

DIVORCE

Anstruther, Eleanor. *A Perfect Explanation*

Bellow, Saul. ★*Herzog*

Bellow, Saul. ★*Humboldt's Gift*

Byatt, A. S. *Babel Tower*

Crucet, Jennine Capo. *Make Your Home Among Strangers*

Danticat, Edwidge. ★*Everything Inside: Stories*

Escandon, Maria Amparo. ★*L.A. Weather*

Fuqua, Jonathon Scott. *Gone and Back Again*

Johnson, Julia Claiborne. *Better Luck Next Time: A Novel*

Moore, Meg Mitchell. *The Islanders*

Petterson, Per. *I Curse the River of Time*

Phillips, Susan Elizabeth. *What I Did for Love*

Quotah, Eman. ★*Bride of the Sea: A Novel*

Rosnay, Tatiana de. ★*Flowers of Darkness*

Russo, Richard. ★*Empire Falls*

Scott, Stephanie. *What's Left of Me Is Yours: A Novel*

Trollope, Joanna. *Other People's Children*

DIVORCED COUPLES

Drake, Laura. *The Sweet Spot*

Heiny, Katherine. ★*Early Morning Riser*

DIVORCED FATHERS

Brodesser-Akner, Taffy. *Fleishman Is in Trouble: A Novel*

DIVORCED MEN

Atkinson, Kate. ★*Case Histories*

Auster, Paul. *The Brooklyn Follies*

Balasubramanyam, Rajeev. *Professor Chandra Follows His Bliss: A Novel*

Banks, Russell. ★*Affliction*

Dickey, Eric Jerome. ★*Bad Men and Wicked Women*

Disher, Garry. *Under the Cold Bright Lights*

Dovlatov, Sergei. *Pushkin Hills*

Dunne, Dominick. *People Like Us: A Novel*

Ford, Richard. ★*Independence Day*

French, Tana. ★*The Searcher*

Goldman, Matt. *Dead West*

Goldman, Matt. *The Shallows*

King, Stephen. *Elevation*

Loren, Roni. *The One You Can't Forget*

March, Emily. *Jackson*

Miller, Mary. *Biloxi: A Novel*

Moniz, Tomas. *Big Familia*

O'Farrell, Maggie. *This Must Be the Place*

Parker, Robert B. *Night Passage*

Patterson, Richard North. *Eclipse*

Shields, Carol. *The Republic of Love*

Tyler, Anne. *A Patchwork Planet*

Williams, Synithia. *Forbidden Promises*

DIVORCED MOTHERS

McMillan, Terry. ★*How Stella Got Her Groove Back*

DIVORCED PARENTS

Candlish, Louise. *Our House*

Perrotta, Tom. *The Abstinence Teacher*

DIVORCED PERSONS

Ellis, David. *In the Company of Liars*

Kwan, Kevin. *Rich People Problems*

Tran, Vu. *Dragonfish: A Novel*

Woo, Sung J. *Love Love: A Novel*

DIVORCED WOMEN
Bacon, Charlotte. *There Is Room for You*
Brazier, Eliza Jane. *If I Disappear*
Bruno, Anna. *Ordinary Hazards: A Novel*
Byatt, A. S. *Babel Tower*
Byatt, A. S. *A Whistling Woman*
Chan, Jessamine. *The School for Good Mothers*
Corry, Jane. *The Dead Ex*
Dee, Jonathan. *A Thousand Pardons: A Novel*
DeLuca, Jen. *Well Matched*
Didion, Joan. ★*Play It as It Lays: A Novel*
Erdrich, Louise. *The Painted Drum: A Novel*
Ferrante, Elena. *The Lost Daughter*
Gerritsen, Tess. *The Bone Garden*
Hampton, Brenda. *Stalker*
Hawkins, Paula. ★*The Girl on the Train: A Novel*
Henry, Patti Callahan. ★*Becoming Mrs. Lewis: The Improbable Love Story of Joy Davidman and C. S. Lewis*
Jewell, Lisa. *Then She Was Gone: A Novel*
Lackberg, Camilla. *Silver Tears*
Majors, Inman. *Penelope Lemon: Game On!*
Marsh, Nicola. *The Boy Toy*
McFarland, Jeni. *The House of Deep Water*
Meier, Leslie. *Silver Anniversary Murder*
Ozick, Cynthia. *Foreign Bodies*
Scottoline, Lisa. ★*Come Home*
Sebold, Alice. *The Almost Moon: A Novel*
Shalvis, Jill. *The Sweetest Thing*
Strout, Elizabeth. ★*Oh William!*
Turner, Bethany. *The Secret Life of Sarah Hollenbeck*
Updike, John. ★*The Witches of Eastwick*
Vargas Llosa, Mario. *Aunt Julia and the Scriptwriter*
Weatherspoon, Rebekah. *Rafe: A Buff Male Nanny*
Divya, S. B.
Machinehood
Dixon, Stephen
Interstate: A Novel
Djavadi, Negar
Disoriental
Djinn Patrol on the Purple Line: A Novel. Anappara, Deepa
DNA
Chaon, Dan. *Ill Will*
Cook, Robin. ★*Genesis*
★*Do Androids Dream of Electric Sheep?*. Dick, Philip K.
Do Not Say We Have Nothing. Thien, Madeleine
Do You Want to Start a Scandal. Dare, Tessa
Doan, Amy Mason
The Summer List
Dobmeier, Tracy
★*Girls with Bright Futures: A Novel*
Dobyns, Stephen
Saratoga Payback
Doc Ford novels [Series]. White, Randy Wayne
Doc novels (Mary Doria Russell) [Series]. Russell, Mary Doria
★*Doc: a Novel*. Russell, Mary Doria
DOCKS
Thomson, E. S. *The Blood*
Doctor Faustus. Mann, Thomas

Doctor No. Fleming, Ian
Doctor Sleep: A Novel. King, Stephen
Doctor Thorne. Trollope, Anthony
★*Doctor Zhivago*. Pasternak, Boris Leonidovich
The Doctor's House: A Novel. Beattie, Ann
DOCTORAL STUDENTS
Hazelwood, Ali. *The Love Hypothesis*
Senna, Danzy. *New People*
Doctorow, Cory
Radicalized
Rapture of the Nerds
Walkaway
Doctorow, E. L.
All the Time in the World: New and Selected Stories
Andrew's Brain
★*Billy Bathgate: A Novel*
★*The Book of Daniel: A Novel*
Doctorow: Collected Stories
Homer and Langley: A Novel
The March: A Novel
★*Ragtime*
World's Fair
Doctorow: Collected Stories. Doctorow, E. L.
DOCUMENTARY FILMMAKERS
Andrews, Donna. *Murder Most Fowl: A Meg Langslow Mystery*
Banks, Russell. *Foregone*
Watson, S. J. *Final Cut*
DOCUMENTARY FILMS
Valente, Catherynne M. *Radiance*
DOCUMENTARY FILMS — PRODUCTION AND DIRECTION
North, Anna. *The Life and Death of Sophie Stark*
★*The Documents in the Case*. Sayers, Dorothy L.
Dodd, Christina
Because I'm Watching
Dead Girl Running
Obsession Falls
Strangers She Knows
Virtue Falls
What Doesn't Kill Her
The Woman Who Couldn't Scream
DODGE CITY, KANSAS
Russell, Mary Doria. ★*Doc: A Novel*
Dodge novels [Series]. Stephenson, Neal
Dodgers: a Novel. Beverly, William
Dodsworth. Lewis, Sinclair
Doerr, Anthony
★*All the Light We Cannot See: A Novel*
★*Cloud Cuckoo Land: A Novel*
Doerr, Harriet
★*Stones for Ibarra*
Doetsch, Richard
Half-Past Dawn
DOG ADOPTION
Winthrop, Elizabeth Hartley. ★*The Why of Things*
DOG BABY SITTERS
Broder, Melissa. *The Pisces: A Novel*
★*Dog Eat Dog*. Rosenfelt, David
★*The Dog of the South*. Portis, Charles

Dog on It: *A Chet and Bernie Mystery*. Quinn, Spencer

DOG OWNERS

Quinn, Spencer. *Dog on It: A Chet and Bernie Mystery*

DOG RESCUE

Cooney, Ellen. *The Mountaintop School for Dogs and Other Second Chances*

★*The Dog Stars: A Novel*. Heller, Peter

DOG TRAINERS

Burton, Jeffrey B. ★*The Finders: A Mace Reid K-9 Mystery*

Burton, Jeffrey B. *The Keepers: A Mace Reid K-9 Mystery*

Logan, Kylie. *The Secrets of Bones: A Mystery*

A Dog's Promise. Cameron, W. Bruce

Dog's purpose [Series]. Cameron, W. Bruce

DOGS

Alexis, Andre. *Fifteen Dogs*

Auster, Paul. *Timbuktu: A Novel*

Buxton, Kira Jane. ★*Hollow Kingdom*

Cameron, W. Bruce. *The Dogs of Christmas*

Doyle, Arthur Conan. ★*The Hound of the Baskervilles*

King, Stephen. *Cujo*

Koontz, Dean R. *The Darkest Evening of the Year*

London, Jack. ★*The Call of the Wild*

Quinn, Spencer. *Dog on It: A Chet and Bernie Mystery*

Quinn, Spencer. ★*It's a Wonderful Woof*

Ramsay, Hope. *Summer on Moonlight Bay*

Ripley, Mike. *Mr Campion's Coven*

Smiley, Jane. ★*Perestroika in Paris: A Novel*

Stein, Garth. *The Art of Racing in the Rain: A Novel*

DOGS — DEATH

Haddon, Mark. ★*The Curious Incident of the Dog in the Night-Time: A Novel*

DOGS — TRAINING

Cooney, Ellen. *The Mountaintop School for Dogs and Other Second Chances*

DOGS AS PETS

Avon, Joy. *In Peppermint Peril: A Book Tea Shop Mystery*

The Dogs of Christmas. Cameron, W. Bruce

The Dogs of Riga. Mankell, Henning

Doiron, Paul

Almost Midnight

Bad Little Falls: A Novel

★*Dead by Dawn*

One Last Lie

The Poacher's Son

The Precipice

Stay Hidden

Dolan-Leach, Caite

We Went to the Woods: A Novel

The Doll Factory. Macneal, Elizabeth

Doller, Trish

Float Plan

Dollface: a Novel of the Roaring Twenties. Rosen, Renee

Dolores Claiborne. King, Stephen

Dolphin Junction: *Collected Stories*. Herron, Mick

DOLPHINS

Ghosh, Amitav. *The Hungry Tide*

Dombey and Son. Dickens, Charles

DOMESTIC ANIMALS

Orwell, George. ★*Animal Farm*

DOMESTIC FICTION

Abraham, Tola Rotimi. *Black Sunday*

Abu-Jaber, Diana. *Birds of Paradise: A Novel*

Adebayo, Ayobami. ★*Stay with Me*

Adlakha, Sarah. *She Wouldn't Change a Thing*

Alam, Rumaan. *That Kind of Mother: A Novel*

Alvarez, Julia. ★*Afterlife: A Novel*

Arikawa, Hiro. *The Travelling Cat Chronicles*

Arnett, Kristen N. *With Teeth: A Novel*

Attenberg, Jami. ★*All This Could Be Yours*

Attenberg, Jami. *The Middlesteins*

Atwood, Margaret. *Life Before Man*

Ausubel, Ramona. *Sons and Daughters of Ease and Plenty*

Bacon, Charlotte. *There Is Room for You*

Bates, Judy Fong. ★*Midnight at the Dragon Cafe*

Baxter, Charles. *Saul and Patsy*

Beckerman, Hannah. *If Only I Could Tell You*

Benjamin, Ali. *The Smash-Up: A Novel*

Berry, Wendell. *Jayber Crow: A Novel*

Berry, Wendell. ★*That Distant Land: The Collected Stories of Wendell Berry*

Betts, Doris. *Souls Raised from the Dead: A Novel*

Binder, L. Annette. *The Vanishing Sky*

Bird, Sarah. *The Gap Year: A Novel*

Bird, Sarah. *The Yokota Officers Club: A Novel*

Bock, Charles. *Alice & Oliver: A Novel*

Bohjalian, Chris. *The Buffalo Soldier: A Novel*

Bronte, Anne. *The Tenant of Wildfell Hall*

Brown, Eleanor. *The Weird Sisters*

Butler, Nickolas. *Little Faith: A Novel*

Callaghan, Mary Rose. *Billy, Come Home*

Cather, Willa. *A Lost Lady*

Cather, Willa. ★*My Antonia*

Cather, Willa. *O Pioneers!*

Cather, Willa. *The Song of the Lark*

Cleary, Jon. *The Sundowners*

Cline, Rachel. *My Liar: A Novel*

Cohen, Tish. *The Summer We Lost Her: A Novel*

Colwin, Laurie. *Goodbye Without Leaving*

Corman, Avery. *Prized Possessions*

Cross-Smith, Leesa. *Whiskey & Ribbons*

Crummey, Michael. *Sweetland*

D'Souza, Tony. *The Konkans*

De los Santos, Marisa. *The Precious One*

DeCarlo, Melissa. *The Art of Crash Landing: A Novel*

Dickens, Charles. *The Old Curiosity Shop*

Diehl, Heidi. *Lifelines*

Dillard, Annie. *The Maytrees: A Novel*

Doerr, Harriet. ★*Stones for Ibarra*

Eliot, George. ★*Middlemarch: A Study of Provincial Life*

Eliot, George. ★*Silas Marner: The Weaver of Raveloe*

Ellis, Bret Easton. *Lunar Park*

Enger, Lin. *Undiscovered Country: A Novel*

Erdrich, Louise. ★*Larose*

Erdrich, Louise. *The Painted Drum: A Novel*

Erdrich, Louise. *The Plague of Doves*

Escandon, Maria Amparo. ★*L.A. Weather*
Fabry, Chris. *War Room: Prayer Is a Powerful Weapon*
Ferber, Edna. *So Big*
Ferrante, Elena. *The Lost Daughter*
Ferris, Joshua. *The Unnamed*
Flaubert, Gustave. ★*Madame Bovary: Provincial Ways*
Flournoy, Angela. *The Turner House*
Foer, Jonathan Safran. *Here I Am: A Novel*
Forster, E. M. ★*Howards End*
Frank, Dorothea Benton. *Queen Bee*
Frankel, Laurie. *This Is How It Always Is*
Friedland, Elyssa. *The Floating Feldmans*
Friedland, Elyssa. *The Intermission*
Fuller, Claire. ★*Bitter Orange*
Fuller, Claire. *Unsettled Ground*
Gelman, Laurie. *Class Mom: A Novel*
Genova, Lisa. *Inside the O'Briens: A Novel*
Gibbons, Kaye. ★*Ellen Foster: A Novel*
Gibbons, Kaye. *The Life All Around Me by Ellen Foster*
Gilb, Dagoberto. *The Flowers: A Novel*
Ginzburg, Natalia. *A Family Lexicon*
Glass, Julia. *The Whole World Over*
Gordimer, Nadine. *Get a Life*
Grames, Juliet. *The Seven or Eight Deaths of Stella Fortuna*
Gray, Anissa. *The Care and Feeding of Ravenously Hungry Girls*
Grodstein, Lauren. *Our Short History*
Groff, Lauren. ★*Fates and Furies*
Hadley, Tessa. *The Past*
Hannah, Kristin. *The Great Alone*
Hannah, Kristin. *Home Front*
Hardiman, Rebecca. *Good Eggs*
Haruf, Kent. *Eventide*
Haruf, Kent. ★*Plainsong*
Hashemzadeh Bonde, Golnaz. *What We Owe*
Heller, Joseph. *Good as Gold*
Holsinger, Bruce W. *The Gifted School: A Novel*
Jones, Tayari. ★*An American Marriage: A Novel*
Kantra, Virginia. *Beth & Amy*
Kantra, Virginia. ★*Meg and Jo*
Kenney, John. *Talk to Me*
Kim, Nancy Jooyoun. *The Last Story of Mina Lee*
Kimmel, Fran. *No Good Asking: A Novel*
Kincaid, Jamaica. ★*Annie John*
Lange, Tracey. ★*We Are the Brennans*
Lessing, Doris May. *A Proper Marriage*
Lewis, Beverly. *The Brethren*
Lewis, Beverly. *The Preacher's Daughter*
Lewis, Sinclair. *Dodsworth*
Lodato, Victor. *Edgar and Lucy: A Novel*
Mahmoud, Lena. *Amreekiya: A Novel*
Mason, Bobbie Ann. *Patchwork*
Maynard, Joyce. *Count the Ways*
McDermott, Alice. *After This*
McDermott, Alice. *At Weddings and Wakes*
McFarland, Jeni. *The House of Deep Water*
McKinney-Whetstone, Diane. *Leaving Cecil Street: A Novel*
Meadows, Rae. *I Will Send Rain: A Novel*
Murphy, Devin. *Tiny Americans*

Nicholls, David. *US: A Novel*
Oates, Joyce Carol. *The Falls: A Novel*
Oates, Joyce Carol. *A Garden of Earthly Delights*
Oates, Joyce Carol. *Night. Sleep. Death. The Stars*
Osondu, E. C. *This House Is Not for Sale: A Novel*
Ozick, Cynthia. *Heir to the Glimmering World*
Packer, Ann. *Songs Without Words*
Patchett, Ann. *Run*
Phillips, Jayne Anne. *Lark and Termite: A Novel*
Picoult, Jodi. ★*My Sister's Keeper*
Poissant, David James. *Lake Life*
Potok, Chaim. ★*The Gift of Asher Lev*
Price, Reynolds. *The Good Priest's Son*
Proulx, Annie. *Postcards*
Quade, Kirstin Valdez. ★*The Five Wounds: A Novel*
Quindlen, Anna. *Miller's Valley*
Richmond, Michelle. *No One You Know*
Robinson, Marilynne. *Home*
Rojas Contreras, Ingrid. ★*Fruit of the Drunken Tree: A Novel*
Roth, Philip. *I Married a Communist*
Russo, Richard. *The Risk Pool*
Schwartz, John Burnham. *The Commoner: A Novel*
Sekaran, Shanthi. ★*Lucky Boy*
Shafak, Elif. *The Bastard of Istanbul*
Shanbhag, Vivek. *Ghachar Ghochar*
Silber, Joan. *Secrets of Happiness*
Simpson, Mona. *Anywhere but Here*
Smiley, Jane. ★*A Thousand Acres*
Smith, Ali. *The Accidental*
Smith, Zadie. *On Beauty*
Sofer, Dalia. *The Septembers of Shiraz*
Starnone, Domenico. *Ties*
Stead, Christina. ★*The Man Who Loved Children*
Stegner, Wallace. ★*The Big Rock Candy Mountain*
Stegner, Wallace. *Crossing to Safety*
Steinbeck, John. ★*The Grapes of Wrath*
Straub, Emma. ★*All Adults Here*
Strout, Elizabeth. ★*Anything Is Possible: Fiction*
Strout, Elizabeth. *My Name Is Lucy Barton*
Strout, Elizabeth. ★*Oh William!*
Styron, William. *Lie Down in Darkness*
Suri, Manil. *The Age of Shiva: A Novel*
Tanen, Sloane. *There's a Word for That*
Taseer, Aatish. *The Way Things Were: A Novel*
Trigiani, Adriana. *Big Cherry Holler: A Big Stone Gap Novel*
Trollope, Joanna. *Other People's Children*
Tsukiyama, Gail. *The Street of a Thousand Blossoms*
Tyler, Anne. *The Amateur Marriage: A Novel*
Tyler, Anne. ★*Saint Maybe*
Tyler, Anne. *Vinegar Girl: The Taming of the Shrew Retold*
Wang, Kathy. *Family Trust: A Novel*
Welty, Eudora. ★*Delta Wedding*
Welty, Eudora. *The Optimist's Daughter*
Wharton, Edith. *The Children*
Williams, Katie. *Tell the Machine Goodnight*
Wilson, Kevin. *Nothing to See Here*
Wilson, Sloan. ★*The Man in the Gray Flannel Suit*
Wood, James. *Upstate*

Woolf, Virginia. ★*The Years*

DOMESTIC TERRORISM

Geni, Abby. *The Wildlands: A Novel*

Hulse, S. M. *Eden Mine*

Slaughter, Karin. ★*Pieces of Her*

Steinhauer, Olen. *The Middleman*

DOMINICA

Kincaid, Jamaica. *The Autobiography of My Mother*

DOMINICAN AMERICAN FAMILIES

Alvarez, Julia. *How the Garcia Girls Lost Their Accents*

DOMINICAN REPUBLIC

Coster, Naima. *Halsey Street*

Cruz, Angie. *Dominicana: A Novel*

Vargas Llosa, Mario. *The Feast of the Goat*

Dominicana: a Novel. Cruz, Angie

Dominika Egorova and Nathaniel Nash novels [Series]. Matthews, Jason

*The **Don** Con.* Armstrong, Richard

DON JUAN (LEGENDARY CHARACTER)

Handke, Peter. *Don Juan: His Own Version*

Don Juan: His Own Version. Handke, Peter

★*Don Quixote.* Cervantes Saavedra, Miguel de

DON QUIXOTE (FICTITIOUS CHARACTER)

Cervantes Saavedra, Miguel de. ★*Don Quixote*

Don't Cry Tai Lake: An Inspector Chen Novel. Qiu, Xiaolong

Don't Cry: Stories. Gaitskill, Mary

Don't Eat Me. Cotterill, Colin

★*Don't Ever Get Old.* Friedman, Daniel

Don't Go. Scottoline, Lisa

Don't Let Go. Coben, Harlan

Don't Send Flowers. Solares, Martin

Don't Skip Out on Me. Vlautin, Willy

Don't Tempt Me. Chase, Loretta Lynda

★*Don't Turn Around.* Barry, Jessica

Don't Wake Up. Lawler, Liz

Don't You Forget About Me. McFarlane, Mhairi

★*Dona* Flor and Her Two Husbands: A Moral and Amorous Tale. Amado, Jorge

Donati, Sara

Where the Light Enters

DONATION OF ORGANS, TISSUES, ETC.

Cleave, Paul. *A Killer Harvest: A Thriller*

Picoult, Jodi. ★*My Sister's Keeper*

Dongala, Emmanuel Boundzeki

The Bridgetower Sonata: Sonata Mulattica

Donna Has Left the Building. Gilman, Susan Jane

DONNER PARTY

Katsu, Alma. *The Hunger: A Novel*

Preston, Douglas J. *Old Bones*

Donoghue, Emma

Akin

★*Frog Music*

★*Room: A Novel*

Slammerkin

★*The Wonder*

Donohue, Keith

The Stolen Child

Donut Fall in Love. Lau, Jackie

*The **Donut** Trap.* Tieu, Julie

Doomed to Die. Simpson, Dorothy

★*Doomsday* Book. Willis, Connie

*A **Door** in the Earth.* Waldman, Amy

*The **Doorbell** Rang.* Stout, Rex

DOORWAYS

Roberts, Nora. ★*The Becoming*

DOPPELGANGERS

Donohue, Keith. *The Stolen Child*

Herbert, Julian. *Bring Me the Head of Quentin Tarantino: Stories*

Johnson, Micaiah. *The Space Between Worlds*

Dorey-Stein, Beck

Rock the Boat: A Novel

Dorn, L. R.

The Anatomy of Desire

DORSET, ENGLAND

James, P. D. *The Private Patient*

Kelly, Erin. *Broadchurch: A Novel*

DORTMUNDER GANG (FICTITIOUS CHARACTERS)

Westlake, Donald E. *The Road to Ruin*

Dortmunder novels [Series]. Westlake, Donald E.

Dos Passos, John

1919

The 42nd Parallel

Manhattan Transfer

Doshi, Avni

Burnt Sugar: A Novel

Dostoyevsky, Fyodor

The Best Short Stories of Dostoevsky

★*The Brothers Karamazov*

★*Crime and Punishment*

Notes from Underground

Double Agent. Bradby, Tom

DOUBLE AGENTS

Bourne, Joanna. *Rogue Spy*

Coughlin, Jack. *Long Shot: A Sniper Novel*

Furst, Alan. *The Spies of Warsaw*

Greene, Graham. *The Human Factor*

Le Carre, John. *The Spy Who Came in from the Cold*

Matthews, Jason. ★*The Kremlin's Candidate*

Nguyen, Viet Thanh. ★*The Sympathizer*

Sebastian, Tim. *Fatal Ally*

Spillane, Mickey. *The Consummata*

Woods, Stuart. *Skin Game*

*The **Double** Bind: A Novel.* Bohjalian, Chris

Double Blind. St. Aubyn, Edward

*The **Double** Comfort Safari Club.* McCall Smith, Alexander

*A **Double** Death on the Black Isle: A Novel.* Scott, A. D.

*The **Doublet** Affair: A Mystery at Queen Elizabeth I's Court.* Buckley, Fiona

Doug Brock novels [Series]. Rosenfelt, David

DOUGLASS, FREDERICK

Banville, John. *The Infinities*

Loren, Roni. *The One You Can't Forget*

McCann, Colum. ★*Transatlantic: A Novel*

Dovlatov, Sergei

Pushkin Hills

Dow, David R.

Confessions of an Innocent Man

Dowlatabadi, Mahmoud
  The Colonel
★*Down* Among the Sticks and Bones. McGuire, Seanan
Down River. Hart, John
Down the River Unto the Sea. Mosley, Walter
Downes, Anna
  The Safe Place: A Novel
Downing, David
  Diary of a Dead Man on Leave
Downing, Samantha
  He Started It
  My Lovely Wife
Doyle, Arthur Conan
  ★*The Complete Sherlock Holmes*
  ★*The Hound of the Baskervilles*
DOYLE, ARTHUR CONAN
  Dallas, Sandra. *The Last Midwife*
  Pirie, David. *The Patient's Eyes*
  Rhodes, Jewell Parker. *Voodoo Dreams: A Novel of Marie Laveau*
Doyle, Brian
  The Plover: A Novel
Doyle, Rob
  Threshold
Doyle, Roddy
  The Guts
  Love
  Paddy Clarke, Ha-Ha-Ha
  Smile
  A Star Called Henry
  ★*The Woman Who Walked into Doors*
Dr Lucas Page novels [Series]. Pobi, Robert
Dr. Paiboun novels [Series]. Cotterill, Colin
Drabble, Margaret
  ★*The Dark Flood Rises*
  A Day in the Life of a Smiling Woman: Complete Short Stories
  The Pure Gold Baby
  The Sea Lady
  The Witch of Exmoor
Draconis memoria [Series]. Ryan, Anthony
Dracul. Stoker, Dacre
★*Dracula*. Stoker, Bram
DRACULA, COUNT (FICTITIOUS CHARACTER)
  Stoker, Bram. ★*Dracula*
  Stoker, Bram. *The New Annotated Dracula*
DRAFT
  Bellow, Saul. *Dangling Man*
  Boianjiu, Shani. *The People of Forever Are Not Afraid: A Novel*
  Clark, Cherae. ★*The Unbroken*
DRAFT RESISTERS
  Banks, Russell. *Foregone*
  Murdoch, Iris. *An Accidental Man*
Dragon Bones: A Novel. See, Lisa
Dragon Bound. Harrison, Thea
Dragon heart legacy [Series]. Roberts, Nora
★*The Dragon* Republic. Kuang, R. F.
Dragonfish: a Novel. Tran, Vu
Dragonflight. McCaffrey, Anne
The Dragonfly. Dunn, Kate

★*Dragonfly* in Amber. Gabaldon, Diana
Dragonfly: a Novel. Meacham, Leila
Dragonriders of Pern [Series]. McCaffrey, Anne
DRAGONS
  Brennan, Marie. *Within the Sanctuary of Wings: A Memoir by Lady Trent*
  Harrison, Thea. *Dragon Bound*
  Le Guin, Ursula K. *The Other Wind*
  Lyons, Jenn. *The Name of All Things*
  Martin, George R. R. ★*A Clash of Kings*
  Martin, George R. R. ★*A Dance with Dragons*
  Martin, George R. R. *Fire & Blood: 300 Years Before a Game of Thrones (A Targaryen History)*
  McCaffrey, Anne. *Dragonflight*
  Novik, Naomi. *His Majesty's Dragon*
  Pratchett, Terry. ★*The Color of Magic*
  Pratchett, Terry. *Guards! Guards!*
  Ryan, Anthony. *The Waking Fire*
  Shannon, Samantha. *The Priory of the Orange Tree*
  Tolkien, J. R. R. ★*The Hobbit, Or, There and Back Again*
  White, Elle Katharine. *Dragonshadow*
Dragonshadow. White, Elle Katharine
★*Dragonwyck*. Seton, Anya
Drake, Laura
  The Sweet Spot
Drake, Olivia
  When a Duke Loves a Governess
DRAMA
  Alarcon, Daniel. *At Night We Walk in Circles: A Novel*
  Chakrabarti, Jai. *A Play for the End of the World*
DRAMA LIT
  Antoinette, Ashley. *Butterfly*
  Antoinette, Ashley. *Butterfly.; Vol 2*
  Antoinette, Ashley. *Butterfly.; Vol 3*
  Ashley & JaQuavis. *The Cartel*
  Bryant, Niobia. *Madam, May I*
  Bryant, Niobia. *Message from a Mistress*
  Dickey, Eric Jerome. ★*Bad Men and Wicked Women*
  Dickey, Eric Jerome. *Before We Were Wicked*
  Dickey, Eric Jerome. *The Blackbirds*
  Dickey, Eric Jerome. *Finding Gideon*
  Dickey, Eric Jerome. ★*The Son of Mr. Suleman*
  Hampton, Brenda. *Stalker*
  Harris, E. Lynn. *Basketball Jones: A Novel*
  Harris, E. Lynn. *Not a Day Goes By: A Novel*
  Lovely, Lutishia. *Blind Ambition*
  Monroe, Mary. ★*God Don't Like Ugly*
  Monroe, Mary. *God Still Don't Like Ugly*
  Stringer, Vickie M. *Dirty Red: A Novel*
  Stringer, Vickie M. ★*Let That Be the Reason*
  Stringer, Vickie M. *Still Dirty: A Novel*
  Styles, Toy. *Black and Ugly*
  Swinson, Kiki. *A Gangster and a Gentleman*
  Swinson, Kiki. *Who's Wife Extraordinaire Now*
DRAMATISTS
  Miller, Andrew. *Oxygen*
  O'Farrell, Maggie. *Hamnet*
  Phillips, Arthur. *The Tragedy of Arthur: A Novel*

DRAMATISTS, AMERICAN
Bram, Christopher. *Lives of the Circus Animals: A Novel*
Gaddis, William. *A Frolic of His Own: A Novel*
Draper, Sharon M.
★*Forged by Fire*
Draven, Grace
Phoenix Unbound
Drawing Conclusions: A Commissario Guido Brunetti Mystery. Leon, Donna
Drawing Home. Brenner, Jamie
Drayson, Nicholas
A Guide to the Birds of East Africa
★*Dreadful Company*. Shaw, Vivian
Dreadful Young Ladies and Other Stories. Barnhill, Kelly Regan
Dreadnought. Priest, Cherie
★*Dream Girl*. Lippman, Laura
The Dream of Scipio. Pears, Iain
The Dream of the Celt. Vargas Llosa, Mario
The Dream Peddler. Watson, Martine Fournier
★*The Dream-Quest of Vellitt Boe*. Johnson, Kij
Dreambird chronicles [Series]. Roy, Lucinda
The Dreamers. Walker, Karen Thompson
Dreamers (Adriana Herrera) [Series]. Herrera, Adriana
Dreamers of the Day: A Novel. Russell, Mary Doria
Dreaming in Cuban. Garcia, Cristina
The Dreaming Void. Hamilton, Peter F.
DREAMS
Bailey, Paul. *Chapman's Odyssey*
Chariandy, David John. *Brother: A Novel*
Coelho, Paulo. ★*The Alchemist*
Irving, John. *Avenue of Mysteries: A Novel*
Johnson, Kij. ★*The Dream-Quest of Vellitt Boe*
Joyce, James. ★*Finnegans Wake*
Le Guin, Ursula K. *The Lathe of Heaven*
Lightman, Alan P. ★*Einstein's Dreams*
Ma, Jian. *China Dream*
Newman, Sandra. *The Heavens*
North, Alex. *The Shadows*
Oakley, Colleen. *You Were There Too*
Pickard, Nancy. *The Scent of Rain and Lightning: A Novel*
Watson, Martine Fournier. *The Dream Peddler*
Dreams of Joy: A Novel. See, Lisa
Dreiser, Theodore
★*An American Tragedy*
★*Sister Carrie*
DRESDEN, GERMANY
Foer, Jonathan Safran. *Extremely Loud and Incredibly Close*
Vonnegut, Kurt. ★*Slaughterhouse-Five: Or, the Children's Crusade : A Duty-Dance with Death*
DRESSMAKERS
Chiaverini, Jennifer. *Mrs. Lincoln's Dressmaker: A Novel*
Janowitz, Brenda. *The Grace Kelly Dress*
DREYFUS AFFAIR, 1894-1906
Harris, Robert. *An Officer and a Spy*
DREYFUS, ALFRED
Cumming, Charles. ★*The Trinity Six*
Harris, Robert. *An Officer and a Spy*
The Drifter. Petrie, Nicholas

DRIFTERS
Brown, Sandra. ★*Blind Tiger*
Cleary, Jon. *The Sundowners*
Faulkner, William. ★*Light in August*
Kennedy, Randy. *Presidio*
Robinson, Marilynne. ★*Lila*
Russo, Richard. *The Risk Pool*
Driftwood. Brennan, Marie
DRINKING
Amis, Kingsley. ★*Lucky Jim*
Carver, Raymond. *What We Talk About When We Talk About Love: Stories*
Doyle, Roddy. *Love*
Gamboa, Santiago. *Necropolis*
Scerbanenco, Giorgio. *A Private Venus*
Drive. Sallis, James
Drive novels [Series]. Sallis, James
DRIVE-BY SHOOTINGS
Dixon, Stephen. *Interstate: A Novel*
The Driver. Hanson, Hart
The Driver's Seat. Spark, Muriel
Driving the King: A Novel. Howard, Ravi
Drndic, Dasa
Trieste
DRONE AIRCRAFT
Box, C. J. ★*Wolf Pack*
Stross, Charles. *Empire Games*
Drood: a Novel. Simmons, Dan
A Drop of Chinese Blood. Church, James
A Drop of the Hard Stuff: A Matthew Scudder Novel. Block, Lawrence
DROUGHTS
Bacigalupi, Paolo. ★*The Water Knife*
Bieker, Chelsea Jean. *Godshot: A Novel*
Chanter, Catherine. *The Well*
Hairston, Andrea. *Master of Poisons*
Harper, Jane. *The Dry*
Lunde, Maja. *The End of the Ocean: A Novel*
Meadows, Rae. *I Will Send Rain: A Novel*
Obreht, Tea. *Inland: A Novel*
DROWNING
George, Elizabeth. *Believing the Lie*
Hamilton, Jane. *A Map of the World*
Ng, Celeste. ★*Everything I Never Told You: A Novel*
The Drowning Pool. Macdonald, Ross
Drowning Ruth. Schwarz, Christina
DROWNING VICTIMS
Doiron, Paul. ★*Dead by Dawn*
Fowler, Christopher. *Bryant & May: Strange Tide*
Indriðason, Arnaldur. *Reykjavik Nights: An Inspector Erlendur Novel*
March, William. *The Bad Seed: A Novel*
Robertson, Imogen. *Anatomy of Murder*
Scerbanenco, Giorgio. *Traitors to All*
Schwarz, Christina. *Drowning Ruth*
Setterfield, Diane. ★*Once Upon a River*
DRUG ABUSE
Carr, Brian Allen. ★*Opioid, Indiana*
Chatterjee, Upamanyu. *English, August: An Indian Story*
Ellis, Bret Easton. *Lunar Park*

DRUG ABUSERS

Koryta, Michael. ★*How It Happened*

DRUG ADDICTION

Hannaham, James. ★*Delicious Foods*

Keller, Julia. ★*Bone on Bone*

Markley, Stephen. *Ohio*

Sanders, Lawrence. *The Timothy Files*

DRUG ADDICTS

Algren, Nelson. ★*The Man with the Golden Arm: A Novel*

Beagin, Jen. ★*Vacuum in the Dark: A Novel*

Burroughs, William S. ★*Naked Lunch: The Restored Text*

Cheever, John. *Falconer*

Rimmer, Kelly. *Before I Let You Go*

Stephenson, Neal. ★*Cryptonomicon*

Walker, Nico. ★*Cherry: A Novel*

Welsh, Irvine. *Dead Men's Trousers*

Welsh, Irvine. *Trainspotting*

DRUG CARTELS

Atkins, Ace. *The Lost Ones*

Kent, Kathleen. *The Burn*

McLaughlin, James A. *Bearskin*

Sandford, John. ★*Golden Prey*

Winslow, Don. *The Border*

DRUG CONTROL

Gregory, Daryl. *Afterparty*

DRUG DEALERS

Atkins, Ace. *The Sinners*

Barker, Nicola. *Darkmans*

Capri, NeNe. *The Pussy Trap*

Capri, NeNe. *The Pussy Trap.; Part 3,*

Connelly, Michael. *The Scarecrow: A Novel*

Dalton, Trent. *Boy Swallows Universe*

Doiron, Paul. *Bad Little Falls: A Novel*

Haywood, Gar Anthony. *Cemetery Road*

Leonard, Elmore. ★*Raylan*

Price, Richard. *Clockers*

Priest, Cherie. *The Inexplicables*

Speight, Shameek A. *The Pleasure of Pain*

Swinson, Kiki. *I'm New York's Finest*

Yocum, Robin. *A Welcome Murder*

DRUG ENFORCEMENT AGENTS

Finder, Joseph. *Suspicion*

Swinson, Kiki. *The Safe House*

Winslow, Don. *The Border*

DRUG INDUSTRY AND TRADE

Cussler, Clive. *Typhoon Fury*

Follett, Ken. ★*Whiteout*

DRUG INDUSTRY AND TRADE — CORRUPT PRACTICES

Finder, Joseph. ★*House on Fire: A Novel*

DRUG LORDS

Brown, Sandra. ★*Ricochet*

Clancy, Tom. *Clear and Present Danger*

Coughlin, Jack. *In the Crosshairs: A Sniper Novel*

K'wan. *The Diamond Empire*

Quinonez, Ernesto. *Bodega Dreams*

Sandford, John. *Mortal Prey*

DRUG SMUGGLERS

Clancy, Tom. *Clear and Present Danger*

Ellroy, James. *The Cold Six Thousand: A Novel*

DRUG SMUGGLING

Connelly, Michael. *The Black Ice*

Cussler, Clive. *The Mediterranean Caper*

Estleman, Loren D. *Infernal Angels*

Reichs, Kathy. *Bare Bones*

Sigurðardóttir, Lilja. *Cage*

Woods, Stuart. *Orchid Beach*

DRUG TRAFFIC

Ashley & JaQuavis. *The Cartel*

Atkins, Ace. *The Ranger*

Barclay, Linwood. *A Tap on the Window*

Burke, Marcus. *Team Seven*

Ca$h. *Thugs Cry: A Novel*

Capri, NeNe. *The Pussy Trap*

Child, Lee. *Persuader*

Clark, Wahida. *Blood, Sweat and Payback*

Clark, Wahida. *Payback Ain't Enough*

Clark, Wahida. *Payback with Ya Life*

Cooper, Tom. *The Marauders*

Crais, Robert. *The First Rule*

Dalton, Trent. *Boy Swallows Universe*

Dugoni, Robert. *Murder One*

Finder, Joseph. *Suspicion*

Franzen, Jonathan. ★*Crossroads*

George, Elizabeth. *What Came Before He Shot Her*

Gray, Erick S. *Love & a Gangsta: A Novel*

Indriðason, Arnaldur. *Outrage*

James, Marlon. ★*A Brief History of Seven Killings: A Novel*

K'wan. *The Diamond Empire*

Kamal, Sheena. *It All Falls Down*

McBride, James. ★*Deacon King Kong: A Novel*

Nesbo, Jo. *Phantom*

Nguyen, Viet Thanh. ★*The Committed*

Panowich, Brian. *Bull Mountain*

Price, Richard. *Clockers*

Rash, Ron. *Above the Waterfall*

Sayers, Dorothy L. *Murder Must Advertise*

Sharpe, Tess. *Barbed Wire Heart*

Sister Souljah. ★*The Coldest Winter Ever: A Novel*

Smith, B. J. *Crow's Landing: A Novel*

Spencer-Fleming, Julia. *I Shall Not Want: A Clare Fergusson/Russ Van Alstyne Mystery*

Stabenow, Dana. *Spoils of the Dead*

Stringer, Vickie M. ★*Let That Be the Reason*

Styles, Toy. *A Hustler's Son: A Novel*

Swinson, Kiki. *I'm New York's Finest*

Swinson, Kiki. *Wifey*

Swinson, Kiki. *Wifey's Next Sticky Situation*

T. I. *Power & Beauty: A Love Story of Life on the Streets*

T. I. *Trouble & Triumph: A Novel of Power & Beauty*

Weiden, David L. ★*Winter Counts*

DRUG USE

Baxter, Charles. ★*The Sun Collective*

Blau, Jessica Anya. *Mary Jane: A Novel*

Blau, Jessica Anya. *The Wonder Bread Summer*

Byrne, Trevor. *Ghosts and Lightning*

Cooper, Tom. *Florida Man*

Cooper, Tom. *The Marauders*
Gran, Sara. *Claire Dewitt and the City of the Dead*
K'wan. *The Fix*
Mitchell, David. ★*Utopia Avenue: A Novel*
Reid, Taylor Jenkins. ★*Daisy Jones & The Six: A Novel*

DRUGS

Clark, Wahida. *Honor Thy Thug*
Clark, Wahida. *Justify My Thug: A Novel*
Clark, Wahida. *Thug Lovin'*
Clark, Wahida. *Thugs*
Mooney, Chris. *Blood World*
Moshfegh, Ottessa. *My Year of Rest and Relaxation*

DRUGS — OVERDOSE

Dugoni, Robert. *Murder One*

DRUGS — SIDE EFFECTS

Browne, S. G. *Less Than Hero: A Novel*

DRUGS — TESTING

Browne, S. G. *Less Than Hero: A Novel*

DRUIDS AND DRUIDISM

Pike, Signe. *The Lost Queen*

★*Drums of Autumn*. Gabaldon, Diana

DRUNK DRIVERS

Barclay, Linwood. *Parting Shot*
Lange, Tracey. ★*We Are the Brennans*

DRUNK DRIVING VICTIMS

Arbol, Victor del. *Breathing Through the Wound*

Druon, Maurice

The Iron King

*The **Dry***. Harper, Jane

DRYADS

Tesh, Emily. *Silver in the Wood*

DS Manon [Series]. Steiner, Susie

DU BOIS, W. E. B.

Jeffers, Honoree Fanonne. ★*The Love Songs of W. E. B. Du Bois*

Du Maurier, Daphne

Frenchman's Creek
Jamaica Inn
★*Rebecca*

DUBAI

Alten, Steve. *Meg: Generations*

Dublin Murder Squad novels [Series]. French, Tana

Dublin saga [Series]. Rutherfurd, Edward

DUBLIN, IRELAND

Alexander, V. S. *The Magdalen Girls*
Beckett, Samuel. ★*Murphy*
Binchy, Maeve. *Circle of Friends*
Black, Benjamin. ★*Christine Falls: A Novel*
Bowman, Conor. ★*Horace Winter Says Goodbye*
Byrne, Trevor. *Ghosts and Lightning*
Doyle, Roddy. *The Guts*
Doyle, Roddy. *Love*
Doyle, Roddy. *Paddy Clarke, Ha-Ha-Ha*
Doyle, Roddy. *A Star Called Henry*
Enright, Anne. ★*The Gathering*
French, Tana. ★*Broken Harbor*
French, Tana. *Faithful Place: A Novel*
French, Tana. *In the Woods*
French, Tana. ★*The Secret Place*

Joyce, James. ★*Dubliners*
Joyce, James. ★*Finnegans Wake*
Joyce, James. ★*A Portrait of the Artist as a Young Man*
Joyce, James. ★*Ulysses*
Murray, Paul. *Skippy Dies*
Rooney, Sally. ★*Conversations with Friends*
Rooney, Sally. *Normal People: A Novel*
Rutherfurd, Edward. *The Princes of Ireland: The Dublin Saga*
Rutherfurd, Edward. *The Rebels of Ireland: The Dublin Saga*

★***Dubliners***. Joyce, James

Dubus, Andre

Dirty Love

★*The **Duchess** Deal*. Dare, Tessa

*The **Duchess** War*. Milan, Courtney

Ducks, *Newburyport*. Ellmann, Lucy

DUDE RANCHES

Weatherspoon, Rebekah. *A Cowboy to Remember*

Due, Tananarive

Ghost Summer: Stories

DUELING

Gabaldon, Diana. ★*Dragonfly in Amber*

Duenas, Maria

The Time in Between: A Novel

Duffy, Brendan

House of Echoes: A Novel

Dugoni, Robert

The Conviction
The Eighth Sister: A Thriller
★*The Extraordinary Life of Sam Hell*
In Her Tracks
Murder One
My Sister's Grave

★*A **Duke** by Default*. Cole, Alyssa

Duke dynasty [Series]. Jeffries, Sabrina

*The **Duke** Goes Down*. Jordan, Sophie

***Duke** Gone Rogue*. Carlyle, Christy

*The **Duke** Heist*. Ridley, Erica

Duke hunt novels [Series]. Jordan, Sophie

*A **Duke** in Shining Armor*. Chase, Loretta Lynda

*A **Duke** Like No Other*. Bowman, Valerie

*The **Duke** with the Dragon Tattoo*. Byrne, Kerrigan

The **Duke's** daughters [Series]. Frampton, Megan

*The **Duke's** Guide to Correct Behavior*. Frampton, Megan

★*A **Duke**, the Lady, and a Baby*. Riley, Vanessa

DUKES AND DUCHESSES

Allen, Susanna. *A Wolf in Duke's Clothing*
Balogh, Mary. *More Than a Mistress*
Balogh, Mary. ★*Someone to Love*
Bell, Lenora. *For the Duke's Eyes Only*
Bell, Lenora. ★*How the Duke Was Won*
Bell, Lenora. *One Fine Duke*
Bell, Lenora. ★*What a Difference a Duke Makes*
Bowman, Valerie. *No Other Duke but You*
Burrowes, Grace. *The Captive*
Burrowes, Grace. *The Trouble with Dukes*
Byrne, Kerrigan. *The Duke with the Dragon Tattoo*
Byrne, Kerrigan. *How to Love a Duke in Ten Days*
Carlyle, Christy. *Duke Gone Rogue*

Chase, Loretta Lynda. *A Duke in Shining Armor*
Cocks, Heather. *The Heir Affair*
Cole, Alyssa. ★*A Duke by Default*
Cole, Alyssa. ★*A Prince on Paper*
Dare, Tessa. ★*The Duchess Deal*
Dare, Tessa. ★*The Governess Game*
Dare, Tessa. ★*The Wallflower Wager*
Drake, Olivia. *When a Duke Loves a Governess*
Force, Marie. *Deceived by Desire*
Frampton, Megan. *The Duke's Guide to Correct Behavior*
Frampton, Megan. *Never a Bride*
Frampton, Megan. *Put up Your Duke*
Galen, Shana. *Third Son's a Charm*
Goodwin, Daisy. *The American Heiress*
Guhrke, Laura Lee. *How to Lose a Duke in Ten Days*
Guhrke, Laura Lee. *The Truth About Love and Dukes*
Harrington, Anna. *An Inconvenient Duke*
Heath, Lorraine. *Falling into Bed with a Duke*
Herbert, Frank. ★*Dune*
Heyer, Georgette. *These Old Shades*
Hoyt, Elizabeth. *Not the Duke's Darling*
Hoyt, Elizabeth. *When a Rogue Meets His Match*
James, Eloisa. *The Ugly Duchess*
Jeffries, Sabrina. *Project Duchess*
MacLean, Sarah. *No Good Duke Goes Unpunished*
MacLean, Sarah. ★*Wicked and the Wallflower*
Pratchett, Terry. *Monstrous Regiment*
Quincy, Diana. *Her Night with the Duke*
Ridley, Erica. *The Duke Heist*
Riley, Vanessa. ★*A Duke, the Lady, and a Baby*
Shupe, Joanna. *The Courtesan Duchess*
Shupe, Joanna. *The Heiress Hunt*
St. George, Harper. *The Heiress Gets a Duke*
Trollope, Anthony. ★*The Prime Minister*
Vayden, Kristin. *Fortune Favors the Duke*
Williams, Beatriz. *The Golden Hour*
Dukes behaving badly [Series]. Frampton, Megan
DULUTH, MINNESOTA
Freeman, Brian. *Goodbye to the Dead*
Freeman, Brian. *Marathon*
DUMAS, ALEXANDER
Perez-Reverte, Arturo. *The Club Dumas*
Dumas, Alexandre
★*Camille*
★*The Count of Monte Cristo*
★*The Man in the Iron Mask*
★*The Three Musketeers*
Twenty Years After
Dumas, Henry
Echo Tree: The Collected Short Fiction of Henry Dumas
Dunant, Sarah
The Birth of Venus: A Novel
Blood and Beauty: A Novel
In the Company of the Courtesan: A Novel
Sacred Hearts: A Novel
Duncan Kincaid and Gemma James mysteries [Series]. Crombie, Deborah

Duncan, Glen
By Blood We Live
The Last Werewolf
Talulla Rising
Dundas, Chad
The Blaze
★*Dune*. Herbert, Frank
Dune novels. [Series]. Herbert, Frank
Dunmore, Evie
★*Bringing Down the Duke*
Dunmore, Helen
Exposure
The Lie
Dunn, Kate
The Dragonfly
Dunn, Katherine
Geek Love
Dunn, Mark
Ella Minnow Pea: A Progressively Lipogrammatic Epistolary Fable
Dunne, Dominick
People Like Us: A Novel
Too Much Money
Dunnett, Dorothy
Niccolo Rising
Duplex. Davis, Kathryn
Dupont, Eric
The American Fiancee: A Novel
Durham, David Anthony
★*Gabriel's Story*
Durrell, Lawrence
★*Justine*
Durrow, Heidi W.
The Girl Who Fell from the Sky: A Novel
Durst, Sarah Beth
The Queen of Blood
Race the Sands
DUST BOWL (SOUTH CENTRAL UNITED STATES)
Steinbeck, John. ★*The Grapes of Wrath*
DUST BOWL ERA, 1931-1939
Meadows, Rae. *I Will Send Rain: A Novel*
Dust off the Bones. Howarth, Paul
DUTCH AMERICANS
Boyle, T. Coraghessan. *World's End: A Novel*
★*The Dutch House: A Novel*. Patchett, Ann
DUTCH IN SWEDEN
Furst, Alan. *Dark Voyage: A Novel*
DUTY
Balogh, Mary. *The Secret Mistress*
Bausch, Richard. *Peace*
Cornwell, Bernard. *Sword of Kings*
McCullough, Colleen. *An Indecent Obsession*
DWARVES (FANTASY CHARACTERS)
Pratchett, Terry. *The Fifth Elephant: A Novel of Discworld*
Pratchett, Terry. *Guards! Guards!*
Pratchett, Terry. *Lords and Ladies: A Novel of Discworld*
Tolkien, J. R. R. *The Children of Hurin*
Tolkien, J. R. R. ★*The Lord of the Rings*

Dybek, Nick
The Verdun Affair: A Novel
Dybek, Stuart
I Sailed with Magellan
Dyer, Geoff
Jeff in Venice, Death in Varanasi
*The **Dying** Detective: A Mystery*. Persson, Leif G. W.
★*A **Dying** Fall*. Spencer, Sally
*A **Dying** Fall: A Ruth Galloway Mystery*. Griffiths, Elly
Dying to Live. Stanley, Michael
Dykes, Amanda
Whose Waves These Are

DYSFUNCTIONAL FAMILIES
Abu-Jaber, Diana. *Birds of Paradise: A Novel*
Arnett, Kristen N. *Mostly Dead Things*
Attenberg, Jami. ★*All This Could Be Yours*
Beattie, Ann. *The Doctor's House: A Novel*
Bird, Sarah. *The Yokota Officers Club: A Novel*
Bronsky, Alina. *The Hottest Dishes of the Tartar Cuisine*
Burke, Alafair. *The Better Sister: A Novel*
Buwalda, Peter. *Bonita Avenue: A Novel*
Davila, April. *142 Ostriches*
Dean, Michael. *I, Hogarth*
Downes, Anna. *The Safe Place: A Novel*
Dunn, Kate. *The Dragonfly*
Faulkner, William. ★*As I Lay Dying: The Corrected Text*
Faulkner, William. ★*The Sound and the Fury*
Ferris, Joshua. *A Calling for Charlie Barnes*
Foer, Jonathan Safran. *Here I Am: A Novel*
Franzen, Jonathan. ★*The Corrections*
Franzen, Jonathan. ★*Freedom*
Frazier, Jean Kyoung. *Pizza Girl*
French, Tana. *Faithful Place: A Novel*
Freudenberger, Nell. *The Dissident*
Friedland, Elyssa. *The Floating Feldmans*
Friedland, Elyssa. *Last Summer at the Golden Hotel*
George, Elizabeth. *What Came Before He Shot Her*
Gilbert, David. *& Sons: A Novel*
Harding Thornton, Christina. *Pickard County Atlas*
Hart, John. *The Last Child*
Holbert, Bruce. *Whiskey*
Kelly, Cathy. *Secrets of a Happy Marriage*
Lethem, Jonathan. *Dissident Gardens*
McKenzie, Elizabeth. *The Portable Veblen*
Oates, Joyce Carol. ★*My Life as a Rat*
Oates, Joyce Carol. *Night. Sleep. Death. The Stars*
Oates, Joyce Carol. ★*Them*
Reid, Taylor Jenkins. ★*Malibu Rising*
Rendell, Ruth. *The Babes in the Wood*
Sapphire. *American Dreams*
Schulman, Alex. *The Survivors: A Novel*
Sittenfeld, Curtis. *Eligible: A Novel*
St. Aubyn, Edward. *At Last*
Stross, Charles. *Accelerando*
Styron, William. *Lie Down in Darkness*
Tanen, Sloane. *There's a Word for That*
Vine, Barbara. *The Minotaur: A Novel*
Walker, Wendy. *Emma in the Night*

Wallace, David Foster. ★*Infinite Jest: A Novel*
Wolfe, Thomas. ★*Look Homeward, Angel: A Story of a Buried Life*

DYSTOPIAN FICTION
Angelo, Megan. *Followers*
Atwood, Margaret. ★*The Handmaid's Tale*
Atwood, Margaret. ★*The Testaments: A Novel*
Bacigalupi, Paolo. ★*The Water Knife*
Bacigalupi, Paolo. ★*The Windup Girl*
Beukes, Lauren. *Afterland*
Bradbury, Ray. ★*Fahrenheit 451*
Brennan, Marie. *Driftwood*
Broun, Bill. *Night of the Animals*
Brown, Pierce. *Golden Son*
Brown, Pierce. *Morning Star*
Brown, Pierce. *Red Rising*
Butler, Octavia E. ★*Parable of the Sower*
Butler, Octavia E. *Parable of the Talents: A Novel*
Cargill, C. Robert. *Day Zero*
Chan, Jessamine. *The School for Good Mothers*
Chanter, Catherine. *The Well*
Chen, Qiufan. *Waste Tide*
Cook, Diane. ★*The New Wilderness: A Novel*
Dalcher, Christina. *Femlandia*
Doctorow, Cory. *Radicalized*
El Akkad, Omar. *American War*
Erdrich, Louise. *Future Home of the Living God*
Fforde, Jasper. ★*Early Riser: A Novel*
Graedon, Alena. *The Word Exchange: A Novel*
Haig, Francesca. *The Fire Sermon: A Novel*
Harkaway, Nick. *Gnomon: A Novel*
Hart, Rob. *The Warehouse: A Novel*
Heinlein, Robert A. *The Moon Is a Harsh Mistress*
Hossain, Saad Z. *Cyber Mage: A Novel*
Huxley, Aldous. ★*Brave New World*
Jen, Gish. ★*The Resisters*
Kleeman, Alexandra. *Something New Under the Sun*
Le Guin, Ursula K. ★*The Dispossessed: An Ambiguous Utopia*
Lee, Chang-Rae. ★*On Such a Full Sea*
Newland, Courttia. *A River Called Time*
North, Claire. *Notes from the Burning Age*
Ogawa, Yoko. ★*The Memory Police: A Novel*
Onyebuchi, Tochi. ★*Riot Baby*
Orwell, George. ★*1984: A Novel*
Rosnay, Tatiana de. ★*Flowers of Darkness*
Roy, Lucinda. *The Freedom Race*
Sakey, Marcus. *A Better World*
Sakey, Marcus. *Brilliance*
Shannon, Samantha. *The Bone Season*
Shannon, Samantha. *The Mime Order*
Stevens, Francis. *The Heads of Cerberus*
Tawada, Yoko. ★*The Emissary*
Tolstaya, Tatyana. *The Slynx*
Valentine, Genevieve. *Mechanique: A Tale of the Circus Tresaulti*
VanderMeer, Jeff. *Dead Astronauts: A Novel*
Vonnegut, Kurt. ★*Player Piano*
Watkins, Claire Vaye. ★*Gold Fame Citrus*
Wells, H. G. ★*The Time Machine*
Yoon, David. *Version Zero*

Zamyatin, Yevgeny Ivanovich. ★*We*

DYSTOPIAS

Atwood, Margaret. ★*The Handmaid's Tale*
Atwood, Margaret. ★*Maddaddam: A Novel*
Atwood, Margaret. ★*Oryx and Crake*
Atwood, Margaret. ★*The Year of the Flood: A Novel*
Auster, Paul. ★*In the Country of Last Things*
Banks, Iain. *The Hydrogen Sonata*
Bradbury, Ray. ★*Fahrenheit 451*
Broun, Bill. *Night of the Animals*
Brown, Pierce. *Golden Son*
Brown, Pierce. *Morning Star*
Brown, Pierce. *Red Rising*
Burgess, Anthony. ★*A Clockwork Orange*
Butler, Octavia E. *Adulthood Rites*
Butler, Octavia E. ★*Parable of the Sower*
Butler, Octavia E. *Parable of the Talents: A Novel*
Dick, Philip K. ★*Do Androids Dream of Electric Sheep?*
Fforde, Jasper. *Shades of Grey: A Novel*
Gibson, William. *The Peripheral*
Gilman, Felix. *The Half-Made World*
Gladstone, Max. ★*Empress of Forever*
Graedon, Alena. *The Word Exchange: A Novel*
Grant, Mira. *Blackout*
Grant, Mira. *Deadline*
Grant, Mira. *Feedback*
Haig, Francesca. *The Fire Sermon: A Novel*
Harkaway, Nick. *Gnomon: A Novel*
Hart, Rob. *The Warehouse: A Novel*
Hossain, Saad Z. *Cyber Mage: A Novel*
Huxley, Aldous. ★*Brave New World*
Johnson, Micaiah. *The Space Between Worlds*
Le Guin, Ursula K. ★*The Dispossessed: An Ambiguous Utopia*
Lee, Chang-Rae. ★*On Such a Full Sea*
Liu, Ken. *Invisible Planets: Contemporary Chinese Science Fiction in Translation*
Malerman, Josh. *Malorie: A Bird Box Novel*
Mieville, China. ★*Perdido Street Station*
Minh, Drew. *Neon Empire*
North, Claire. *Notes from the Burning Age*
Orwell, George. ★*1984: A Novel*
Orwell, George. ★*Animal Farm*
Roy, Lucinda. *The Freedom Race*
Self, Will. *The Book of Dave: A Revelation of the Recent Past and the Distant Future*
Stephenson, Neal. ★*Snow Crash*
Tawada, Yoko. ★*The Emissary*
Tepper, Sheri S. *The Gate to Women's Country*
Tepper, Sheri S. *The Visitor*
Valentine, Genevieve. *Mechanique: A Tale of the Circus Tresaulti*
Vaughn, Carrie. *Bannerless*
Vonnegut, Kurt. ★*Player Piano*

E

E-ZINES

Muller, Marcia. *Dead Midnight*
The *Eagle* Has Flown. Higgins, Jack
The *Eagle* Has Landed. Higgins, Jack
Eagle Station: A Novel. Brown, Dale
The *Eagle's* Throne: A Novel. Fuentes, Carlos
★*An **Earl**, the Girl, and a Toddler.* Riley, Vanessa

Earley, Tony

Jim the Boy: A Novel
Mr. Tall: A Novella and Stories

EARLS AND COUNTESSES

Balogh, Mary. *Someone to Wed*
Bateman, Kate. *A Reckless Match*
Bennett, Bethany. *West End Earl*
Bradley, Anna. *A Wicked Way to Win an Earl*
Dare, Tessa. ★*A Night to Surrender*
Hamill, Pete. *Forever*
Kleypas, Lisa. *Cold-Hearted Rake*
Leigh, Eva. *Forever Your Earl*
Pembrooke, Kate. *Not the Kind of Earl You Marry*
Penrose, Andrea. ★*Murder at Kensington Palace*
Quinn, Julia. ★*An Offer from a Gentleman*
Sebastian, Cat. *The Lawrence Browne Affair*

★*Early Morning Riser.* Heiny, Katherine
★*Early Novels and Stories.* Baldwin, James
★*Early Riser: A Novel.* Fforde, Jasper
Early Short Stories, 1883-1888. Chekhov, Anton Pavlovich
Early Warning. Smiley, Jane

EARP, WYATT

Quade, Kirstin Valdez. *Night at the Fiestas: Stories*
Russell, Mary Doria. *Epitaph: A Novel of the O.K. Corral*

EARTH

Bear, Greg. *The Forge of God*
Bradbury, Ray. *The Illustrated Man*
Chambers, Becky. *To Be Taught, If Fortunate*
Egan, Greg. *Perihelion Summer*
Flynn, Michael. *Eifelheim*
Hao, Jingfang. *Vagabonds: A Novel*
Stephenson, Neal. *Seveneves*
Verne, Jules. ★*Journey to the Centre of the Earth*
Walker, Karen Thompson. *The Age of Miracles: A Novel*
Wells, H. G. ★*The War of the Worlds*

Earth Abides. Stewart, George R.
Earth's children [Series]. Auel, Jean M.
Eartheater. Reyes, Dolores
Earthlings: a Novel. Murata, Sayaka

EARTHQUAKES

Chancy, Myriam J. A. ★*What Storm, What Thunder*
Foley, Bridget. *Just Get Home*
Murakami, Haruki. *After the Quake: Stories*
Sittenfeld, Curtis. *Sisterland: A Novel*
Sorenson, Jill. *Aftershock*

Earthsea series [Series]. Le Guin, Ursula K.
Earthsinger chronicles [Series]. Penelope, L.

Eason, K.

How Rory Thorne Destroyed the Multiverse

EAST AFRICA
McLain, Paula. *Circling the Sun*
EAST AND WEST
Mitchell, David. *The Thousand Autumns of Jacob De Zoet: A Novel*
EAST GERMANY
Grass, Gunter. *Too Far Afield*
EAST HAMPTON, NEW YORK
Kwan, Kevin. *Sex and Vanity: A Novel*
EAST INDIAN AMERICAN TEENAGERS
Sathian, Sanjena. *Gold Diggers*
EAST INDIAN AMERICAN WOMEN
Lalli, Sonya. *A Holly Jolly Diwali*
Umrigar, Thrity N. ★*Honor*
EAST INDIAN AMERICANS
Cochrun, Alison. *The Charm Offensive*
Dev, Sonali. *The Bollywood Bride*
Dev, Sonali. ★*Incense and Sensibility*
Dev, Sonali. ★*Pride, Prejudice, and Other Flavors: A Novel*
Enjeti, Anjali. ★*The Parted Earth*
Ghosh, Amitav. ★*Gun Island*
Mehta, Rahul. *No Other World: A Novel*
Pandya, Sameer. *Members Only*
Raheem, Zara. *The Marriage Clock: A Novel*
Roisin, Fariha. *Like a Bird*
Satyal, Rakesh. *No One Can Pronounce My Name: A Novel*
EAST INDIAN AMERICANS — SOCIAL LIFE AND CUSTOMS
Lahiri, Jhumpa. ★*The Namesake*
EAST INDIAN BRITISH MEN
Balasubramanyam, Rajeev. *Professor Chandra Follows His Bliss: A Novel*
EAST INDIANS
Anappara, Deepa. *Djinn Patrol on the Purple Line: A Novel*
Enjeti, Anjali. ★*The Parted Earth*
Naipaul, V. S. *A House for Mr. Biswas*
Rushdie, Salman. ★*The Satanic Verses*
EAST INDIANS IN AFRICA
Naipaul, V. S. *A Bend in the River*
EAST INDIANS IN ENGLAND
Collins, Wilkie. ★*The Moonstone*
Naipaul, V. S. *Magic Seeds*
Sahota, Sunjeev. *The Year of the Runaways*
EAST INDIANS IN THE UNITED STATES
D'Souza, Tony. *The Konkans*
Dev, Sonali. ★*A Bollywood Affair*
Divakaruni, Chitra Banerjee. *Oleander Girl: A Novel*
Murr, Naeem. *The Perfect Man: A Novel*
★*East of Eden*. Steinbeck, John
EAST TENNESSEE
Bledsoe, Alex. *The Hum and the Shiver*
EAST TEXAS
Lansdale, Joe R. *The Bottoms*
Lansdale, Joe R. *More Better Deals*
Lansdale, Joe R. *Sunset and Sawdust*
Lansdale, Joe R. *The Thicket*
EAST-WEST RELATIONS
Uris, Leon. *Armageddon: A Novel of Berlin*
EASTER RISING, 1916
Doyle, Roddy. *A Star Called Henry*

EASTERN EUROPE
Egan, Jennifer. *The Keep*
Le Guin, Ursula K. *Orsinian Tales*
Mieville, China. ★*The City & The City*
Steinhauer, Olen. *The Bridge of Sighs*
Wolfe, Gene. *The Land Across*
Eastern European crime series [Series]. Steinhauer, Olen
EASTERN RELIGIONS
Robinson, Kim Stanley. *The Years of Rice and Salt*
EASTERN SHORE, MARYLAND
Roberts, Nora. *Chesapeake Blue*
Easy Prey. Sandford, John
Easy Rawlins mysteries [Series]. Mosley, Walter
EATING DISORDERS
Thomas, Scarlett. *Oligarchy*
EAVESDROPPING
Berg, Gretchen. *The Operator*
The Ebb Tide. Lewis, Beverly
Ebershoff, David
The 19th Wife: A Novel
The Danish Girl: A Novel
ECCENTRIC BOYS
Porter, Max. ★*Lanny: A Novel*
ECCENTRIC FAMILIES
Atkinson, Kate. *Human Croquet*
Jackson, Shirley. *We Have Always Lived in the Castle*
Proulx, Annie. *Postcards*
Smith, Dodie. ★*I Capture the Castle*
Wharton, Edith. *The Children*
ECCENTRIC MEN
Beagle, Peter S. *A Fine and Private Place*
Cervantes Saavedra, Miguel de. ★*Don Quixote*
Cheever, John. *Bullet Park: A Novel*
Munro, Alice. *Lives of Girls and Women*
Shteyngart, Gary. ★*Super Sad True Love Story: A Novel*
ECCENTRIC WOMEN
Childress, Mark. *Crazy in Alabama*
Drabble, Margaret. *The Witch of Exmoor*
Simpson, Mona. *Anywhere but Here*
Winslow, De'Shawn Charles. ★*In West Mills*
ECCENTRICS AND ECCENTRICITIES
Arnett, Kristen N. *Mostly Dead Things*
Auster, Paul. *The Brooklyn Follies*
Backman, Fredrik. ★*My Grandmother Asked Me to Tell You She's Sorry: A Novel*
Bellow, Saul. ★*The Adventures of Augie March*
Boyle, T. Coraghessan. *The Relive Box: And Other Stories*
Brown, Amy Belding. *Emily's House*
Crummey, Michael. *Sweetland*
Diaz, Junot. ★*The Brief Wondrous Life of Oscar Wao*
Doctorow, E. L. *Homer and Langley: A Novel*
Evison, Jonathan. *West of Here: A Novel*
Fowler, Christopher. *Bryant & May: Hall of Mirrors : A Peculiar Crimes Unit Mystery*
Gallagher, Stephen. *The Bedlam Detective: A Novel*
Herbert, Julian. *Bring Me the Head of Quentin Tarantino: Stories*
Hogan, Ruth. *Queenie Malone's Paradise Hotel*
Irving, John. ★*The World According to Garp: A Novel*

Kidd, Jess. ★*Things in Jars*

Kroese, Robert. *The Last Iota*

Mason, Meg. *Sorrow and Bliss*

McCall Smith, Alexander. ★*The Department of Sensitive Crimes: A Detective Varg Novel*

McCall Smith, Alexander. ★*The Man with the Silver Saab: A Detective Varg Novel*

McCracken, Elizabeth. ★*Bowlaway: A Novel*

Murakami, Haruki. ★*Kafka on the Shore*

O'Connor, Flannery. ★*Wise Blood*

Ondaatje, Michael. ★*Warlight*

Robbins, Tom. *Fierce Invalids Home from Hot Climates*

Robbins, Tom. ★*Jitterbug Perfume*

Saums, Mary. *Thistle & Twigg*

Spark, Muriel. ★*A Far Cry from Kensington*

Stibbe, Nina. *Reasons to Be Cheerful*

Tyler, Anne. *A Patchwork Planet*

Varley, John. *Dark Lightning*

Wallace, Daniel. ★*Big Fish: A Novel of Mythic Proportions*

Echo Burning. Child, Lee

An *Echo* in the Bone. Gabaldon, Diana

The *Echo* Killing. Daugherty, Christi

The *Echo* Maker. Powers, Richard

Echo on the Bay. Ono, Masatsugu

ECHO PARK, LOS ANGELES, CALIFORNIA

Skyhorse, Brando. *Madonnas of Echo Park: A Novel*

Echo Tree: The Collected Short Fiction of Henry Dumas. Dumas, Henry

The *Echo* Wife. Gailey, Sarah

★*Echoes* of the Dead. Spencer, Sally

Eclipse. Patterson, Richard North

★*Eclipse: a Novel*. Banville, John

Eco, Umberto

Baudolino

★*Foucault's Pendulum*

The Island of the Day Before

The Mysterious Flame of Queen Loana: An Illustrated Novel

★*The Name of the Rose*

Numero Zero

ECO-TERRORISTS

Box, C. J. *Savage Run*

Williams, Joy. *Harrow*

ECOLOGISTS

Gordimer, Nadine. *Get a Life*

St. Aubyn, Edward. *Double Blind*

ECOLOGY

Atwood, Margaret. ★*Oryx and Crake*

Fowler, Therese. ★*A Good Neighborhood*

ECSTASY

Haratischvili, Nino. *The Eighth Life: (For Brilka)*

ECUADOR

Cordova, Zoraida. *The Inheritance of Orquidea Divina*

Ed Eagle novels [Series]. Woods, Stuart

Edda of burdens [Series]. Bear, Elizabeth

Eddie Flynn novels [Series]. Cavanagh, Steve

Eden. Lebbon, Tim

Eden Close: A Novel. Shreve, Anita

Eden Mine. Hulse, S. M.

Edgar and Lucy: A Novel. Lodato, Victor

Edge of Dark Water. Lansdale, Joe R.

Edge of Eternity. Follett, Ken

The *Edge* of the Earth. Schwarz, Christina

Edge: a Novel. Deaver, Jeffery

Edgerton, Clyde

★*Walking Across Egypt: A Novel*

Edghill, India

Queenmaker: A Novel of King David's Queen

Edinburgh nights [Series]. Huchu, Tendai

EDINBURGH, SCOTLAND

Atkinson, Kate. *One Good Turn: A Novel*

Atkinson, Kate. ★*When Will There Be Good News?: A Novel*

Huchu, Tendai. *The Library of the Dead*

Johnstone, Carole. *Mirrorland*

McCall Smith, Alexander. *The Forgotten Affairs of Youth*

McCall Smith, Alexander. ★*The Geometry of Holding Hands*

McCall Smith, Alexander. *The Lost Art of Gratitude*

Parry, Ambrose. *The Way of All Flesh*

Pirie, David. *The Patient's Eyes*

Rankin, Ian. ★*Black and Blue: An Inspector Rebus Novel*

Rankin, Ian. *The Black Book*

Rankin, Ian. *The Complaints*

Rankin, Ian. *Dead Souls: An Inspector Rebus Novel*

Rankin, Ian. *Exit Music*

Rankin, Ian. *The Falls: An Inspector Rebus Novel*

Rankin, Ian. *The Hanging Garden: An Inspector Rebus Novel*

Rankin, Ian. *The Impossible Dead*

Rankin, Ian. *The Naming of the Dead: An Inspector Rebus Novel*

Rankin, Ian. *A Question of Blood: An Inspector Rebus Novel*

Rankin, Ian. ★*Rather Be the Devil*

Rankin, Ian. *Resurrection Men: An Inspector Rebus Novel*

Rankin, Ian. *Set in Darkness: An Inspector Rebus Novel*

Rankin, Ian. ★*A Song for the Dark Times*

Spark, Muriel. ★*The Prime of Miss Jean Brodie*

Welsh, Irvine. *Dead Men's Trousers*

Welsh, Irvine. *Trainspotting*

Welsh, Kaite. *The Unquiet Heart*

Welsh, Kaite. *The Wages of Sin*

Wojtas, Olga. *Miss Blaine's Prefect and the Golden Samovar*

EDISON, THOMAS A.

Dos Passos, John. *1919*

★*Edisto: a Novel*. Powell, Padgett

EDITORS

Gruber, Michael. *The Return: A Novel*

Harris, Zakiya Dalila. *The Other Black Girl: A Novel*

Horowitz, Anthony. ★*Magpie Murders*

Prose, Francine. ★*The Vixen*

EDUCATION

Cantor, Jillian. *Half Life*

Dare, Abi. *The Girl with the Louding Voice*

Edugyan, Esi

Half-Blood Blues

★*Washington Black: A Novel*

EDWARD IV, KING OF ENGLAND 1442-1483

Gregory, Philippa. *The Kingmaker's Daughter*

EDWARD SEYMOUR, DUKE OF SOMERSET 1500-1552

Sansom, C. J. *Tombland*

Edward X. Delaney mysteries [Series]. Sanders, Lawrence

EDWARDIAN ERA (1901-1914)
    Gallagher, Stephen. *The Bedlam Detective: A Novel*
    Marske, Freya. *A Marvellous Light*
    Orczy, Emmuska Orczy. *The Old Man in the Corner*
    Parmar, Priya. *Vanessa and Her Sister*
    Perry, Anne. ★*Death with a Double Edge: A Daniel Pitt Novel*
    Perry, Anne. *One Fatal Flaw: A Daniel Pitt Novel*
    Sackville-West, V. *The Edwardians*
    Simonson, Helen. *The Summer Before the War: A Novel*
    Turansky, Carrie. *No Ocean Too Wide: A Novel*
    Williams, Pip. *The Dictionary of Lost Words*
The Edwardians. Sackville-West, V.
Edwards, Kim
    The Memory Keeper's Daughter
Edwards, Louis
    Ramadan Ramsey: A Novel
Edwards, Rachel
    Darling
Edwards, Yvvette
    The Mother
*The **Effort***. Holroyde, Claire
Egan, Greg
    Perihelion Summer
    Phoresis
    Schild's Ladder
Egan, Jennifer
    The Keep
    ★*Manhattan Beach: A Novel*
    ★*A Visit from the Goon Squad*
Egg Shooters. Childs, Laura
Eggers, Dave
    The Circle
    A Hologram for the King: A Novel
    How We Are Hungry: Stories
    What Is the What: The Autobiography of Valentino Achak Deng
EGGS
    Davila, April. *142 Ostriches*
EGOTISM
    Rand, Ayn. ★*The Fountainhead*
EGOTISM IN MEN
    Bolano, Roberto. ★*The Third Reich*
    McEwan, Ian. *Solar: A Novel*
EGYPT
    Bilal, Parker. *The Burning Gates: A Makana Investigation*
    Bilal, Parker. *The Ghost Runner*
    Chakraborty, S. A. *The City of Brass*
    Chakraborty, S. A. *The Empire of Gold*
    Chakraborty, S. A. *The Kingdom of Copper: A Novel*
    Durrell, Lawrence. ★*Justine*
    Hertmans, Stefan. ★*The Convert: A Novel*
    Neubauer, Erica Ruth. *Murder at the Mena House*
    Picoult, Jodi. ★*The Book of Two Ways*
    Rice, Anne. *Christ the Lord: Out of Egypt: A Novel*
    Saylor, Steven. *The Judgment of Caesar: A Novel of Ancient Rome*
EGYPTIAN-AMERICANS
    Hassib, Rajia. *A Pure Heart: A Novel*
EGYPTIANS IN THE UNITED STATES
    Aswani, Alaa. *Chicago: A Modern Arabic Novel*

Ehirim, Nnamdi
    Prince of Monkeys
Eifelheim. Flynn, Michael
EIFFEL TOWER, PARIS, FRANCE
    Rutherfurd, Edward. *Paris*
Eight Million Ways to Die. Block, Lawrence
Eight Perfect Murders: A Novel. Swanson, Peter
EIGHT-YEAR-OLD GIRLS
    Hamer, Kate. *The Girl in the Red Coat*
    March, William. *The Bad Seed: A Novel*
    Marra, Anthony. ★*A Constellation of Vital Phenomena: A Novel*
EIGHTEEN-YEAR-OLD MEN
    L'Amour, Louis. ★*Bendigo Shafter*
    Saylor, Steven. *The Seven Wonders: A Novel of the Ancient World*
EIGHTEEN-YEAR-OLD WOMEN
    Keesey, Anna. *Little Century: A Novel*
EIGHTEEN-YEAR-OLDS
    Bird, Sarah. *The Yokota Officers Club: A Novel*
The Eighth Girl. Chung, Maxine Mei-Fung
The Eighth Life: (For Brilka). Haratischvili, Nino
The Eighth Sister: A Thriller. Dugoni, Robert
Eileen. Moshfegh, Ottessa
★*Einstein's Dreams*. Lightman, Alan P.
EINSTEIN, ALBERT
    Lightman, Alan P. ★*Einstein's Dreams*
Eisenberg, Deborah
    The Twilight of the Superheroes
EISENHOWER, DWIGHT D.
    Shaara, Jeff. *The Rising Tide: A Novel of World War II*
Eisler, Barry
    All the Devils
    The God's Eye View
    The Killer Collective
    Livia Lone
    The Night Trade
Ekwuyasi, Francesca
    Butter Honey Pig Bread: A Novel
El Akkad, Omar
    American War
    What Strange Paradise
EL PASO, TEXAS
    Gaspar de Alba, Alicia. *Desert Blood: The Juarez Murders*
El Paso: A Novel. Groom, Winston
EL SALVADOR
    Didion, Joan. *A Book of Common Prayer*
El-Mohtar, Amal
    ★*This Is How You Lose the Time War*
ELBE, LILI
    Ebershoff, David. *The Danish Girl: A Novel*
    Eco, Umberto. ★*Foucault's Pendulum*
Elder races [Series]. Harrison, Thea
*An **Elderly** Lady Must Not Be Crossed*. Tursten, Helene
ELEANOR
    Penman, Sharon Kay. *The Queen's Man: A Medieval Mystery*
Eleanor Roosevelt mysteries [Series]. Roosevelt, Elliott
ELECTIONS
    Black, Lisa. *Let Justice Descend*
    Houellebecq, Michel. *Submission*

Maron, Margaret. *Bootlegger's Daughter*
Ono, Masatsugu. *Echo on the Bay*
Rowling, J. K. *The Casual Vacancy*
Stewart, Amy. ★*Miss Kopp Just Won't Quit*
Electra McDonnell novels [Series]. Weaver, Ashley
ELECTRIC ALARMS
Amidon, Stephen. *Security: A Novel*
★*The **Electric** Hotel*. Smith, Dominic
ELECTRIC SHOCK THERAPY
Greer, Andrew Sean. *The Impossible Lives of Greta Wells*
ELECTRICITY
Barr, Mark. *Watershed*
Williams, Niall. *This Is Happiness*
ELECTRONIC BULLETIN BOARDS
Smith, Julie. *New Orleans Beat*
ELECTRONIC SURVEILLANCE
Beckett, L. X. *Gamechanger*
Schweblin, Samanta. *Little Eyes*
*The **Elegance** of the Hedgehog*. Barbery, Muriel
ELEMENTARY SCHOOL TEACHERS
Messud, Claire. ★*The Woman Upstairs: A Novel*
ELEMENTARY SCHOOLS
Center, Katherine. *What You Wish For*
Gelman, Laurie. *Yoga Pant Nation: A Novel*
Elena Standish [Series]. Perry, Anne
*The **Elephant** of Belfast: A Novel*. Walsh, S. Kirk
★*The **Elephant's** Journey*. Saramago, Jose
ELEPHANTS
Khan, Vaseem. *The Perplexing Theft of the Jewel in the Crown*
Saramago, Jose. ★*The Elephant's Journey*
Walsh, S. Kirk. *The Elephant of Belfast: A Novel*
Elevation. King, Stephen
★*Elevator Pitch: A Novel*. Barclay, Linwood
ELEVATORS
Barclay, Linwood. ★*Elevator Pitch: A Novel*
ELEVEN-YEAR-OLD BOYS
Faulkner, William. *The Reivers: A Reminiscence*
Fuqua, Jonathon Scott. *Gone and Back Again*
Gaddis, William. ★*J R: A Novel*
Godwin, Gail. *Grief Cottage: A Novel*
Grisham, John. *The Client*
Henderson, Smith. *Fourth of July Creek*
Lansdale, Joe R. *The Bottoms*
Shepard, Jim. *Phase Six*
ELEVEN-YEAR-OLD GIRLS
Blatty, William Peter. ★*The Exorcist*
Bradley, C. Alan. *The Weed That Strings the Hangman's Bag: A Flavia De Luce Mystery*
Carter, Mary Dixie. *The Photographer*
Gibbons, Kaye. ★*Ellen Foster: A Novel*
Greenwood, T. *Rust & Stardust*
Hayder, Mo. *Gone*
ELEVEN-YEAR-OLDS
Gunday, Hakan. *The Few*
Elias, Gerald
Danse Macabre
★*Death and Transfiguration: A Daniel Jacobus Novel*

Eliasberg, Jan
★*Hannah's War*
Eligible: a Novel. Sittenfeld, Curtis
Eliot, George
★*Adam Bede*
★*Middlemarch: A Study of Provincial Life*
★*The Mill on the Floss*
★*Silas Marner: The Weaver of Raveloe*
ELIOT, T. S.
Block, Lawrence. ★*When the Sacred Ginmill Closes*
Cooley, Martha. *The Archivist: A Novel*
Elison, Meg
The Book of Etta
The Book of Flora
The Book of the Unnamed Midwife
ELITE (SOCIAL SCIENCES)
Beah, Ishmael. *Little Family*
Hill Gumbao, Toni. *The Summer of Dead Toys*
Layne, Lauren. *Passion on Park Avenue*
Leavitt, David. ★*Shelter in Place*
Pelevin, Viktor. *The Hall of Singing Caryatids*
Thomas, Elisabeth. *Catherine House*
Vaughan, Sarah. ★*Anatomy of a Scandal: A Novel*
ELITE OPERATIVES
Cameron, Marc. ★*Code of Honor*
Clancy, Tom. ★*The Hunt for Red October*
Eisler, Barry. *The Killer Collective*
Golden, Christopher. *Red Hands*
Parnell, Sean. *Left for Dead*
Rollins, James. *Crucible*
Rollins, James. ★*The Last Odyssey*
Steinhauer, Olen. *An American Spy*
Steinhauer, Olen. *The Nearest Exit*
ELITISM
Glynn, Alan. *Receptor*
Rosen, Renee. *The Social Graces*
ELIZABETH I, QUEEN OF ENGLAND, 1533-1603
Buckley, Fiona. *The Doublet Affair: A Mystery at Queen Elizabeth I's Court*
Buckley, Fiona. *The Siren Queen: An Ursula Blanchard Mystery at Queen Elizabeth I's Court*
Clements, Oliver. *The Queen's Men*
George, Margaret. *Elizabeth I: A Novel*
Phillips, Arthur. ★*The King at the Edge of the World: Novel*
Wolfe, Suzanne M. *The Course of All Treasons*
ELIZABETH II, QUEEN OF GREAT BRITAIN, 1926-
Bennett, Alan. ★*The Uncommon Reader*
Black, Benjamin. ★*The Secret Guests: A Novel*
Harper, Karen. *The Queen's Secret: A Novel of England's World War II Queen*
Elizabeth Costello. Coetzee, J. M.
Elizabeth I: A Novel. George, Margaret
★*Elizabeth Is Missing*. Healey, Emma
ELIZABETH, QUEEN, CONSORT OF HENRY VII, KING OF ENGLAND, 1465-1503
Gregory, Philippa. *The White Princess*
McCall Smith, Alexander. ★*The Geometry of Holding Hands*

ELIZABETHAN ERA (1558-1603)

Bear, Elizabeth. *Ink and Steel: A Novel of the Promethean Age*

Buckley, Fiona. *The Doublet Affair: A Mystery at Queen Elizabeth I's Court*

Buckley, Fiona. *The Siren Queen: An Ursula Blanchard Mystery at Queen Elizabeth I's Court*

Campisi, Megan. *Sin Eater*

Clements, Oliver. *The Eyes of the Queen*

Clements, Oliver. *The Queen's Men*

Follett, Ken. *A Column of Fire*

George, Margaret. *Elizabeth I: A Novel*

Marston, Edward. *The Roaring Boy: A Novel*

Marston, Edward. *The Wanton Angel: A Novel*

O'Farrell, Maggie. *Hamnet*

Phillips, Arthur. ★*The King at the Edge of the World: Novel*

Wolfe, Suzanne M. *The Course of All Treasons*

Elizabethan spy novels [Series]. Wolfe, Suzanne M.

ELK

Jones, Stephen Graham. ★*The Only Good Indians: A Novel*

Ella Minnow Pea: A Progressively Lipogrammatic Epistolary Fable. Dunn, Mark

Ellen Foster duology [Series]. Gibbons, Kaye

★*Ellen Foster: A Novel.* Gibbons, Kaye

Ellie Quicke mysteries [Series]. Heley, Veronica

Elliot Kane novels [Series]. Harris, Oliver

Elliott, Kate

Servant Mage

Unconquerable Sun

Elliott, Lexie

The Missing Years

Ellis, Bella

The Vanished Bride

Ellis, Bret Easton

Imperial Bedrooms

Lunar Park

ELLIS, BRET EASTON

Ellis, Bret Easton. *Lunar Park*

Ellis, David

In the Company of Liars

Ellis, Helen

American Housewife: Stories

Ellison, J. T.

Good Girls Lie

Tear Me Apart

Ellison, Ralph

★*Invisible Man*

★*Juneteenth*

Three Days Before the Shooting . . .

ELLISON, TRACY (FICTITIOUS CHARACTER)

Tyree, Omar. ★*Flyy Girl*

Ellmann, Lucy

Ducks, Newburyport

Ellroy, James

American Tabloid: A Novel

Blood's a Rover

The Cold Six Thousand: A Novel

★*L.A. Confidential*

Perfidia

This Storm: A Novel

★*Widespread Panic: A Novel*

★*Elmer Gantry.* Lewis, Sinclair

★*Elmet.* Mozley, Fiona

ELOPEMENT

Burns, Olive Ann. ★*Cold Sassy Tree*

Fielding, Henry. ★*The History of Tom Jones, a Foundling*

Elroy Nights. Barthelme, Frederick

Elsewhere, Home. Aboulela, Leila

ELVES

Addison, Katherine. ★*The Goblin Emperor*

Novik, Naomi. ★*Spinning Silver*

Tolkien, J. R. R. *Beren and Luthien*

Tolkien, J. R. R. *The Children of Hurin*

Tolkien, J. R. R. *The Fall of Gondolin*

Tolkien, J. R. R. ★*The Lord of the Rings*

Tolkien, J. R. R. *The Silmarillion*

Elvis Cole/Joe Pike novels [Series]. Crais, Robert

EMAIL CORRESPONDENCE

Cameron, Lindsay. *Just One Look*

EMANCIPATION OF MINORS

Robotham, Michael. ★*Good Girl, Bad Girl: A Novel*

Embassy Wife. Crouch, Katie

Embassytown. Mieville, China

EMBEZZLERS

Eugenides, Jeffrey. *Fresh Complaint: Stories*

Embla Nystrom investigations [Series]. Tursten, Helene

EMBRYO TRANSFER — MORAL AND ETHICAL ASPECTS

Picoult, Jodi. *Sing You Home: A Novel*

EMERALDS

Westlake, Donald E. *The Hot Rock*

Emezi, Akwaeke

★*The Death of Vivek Oji*

Freshwater

EMEZI, AKWAEKE

Emezi, Akwaeke. *Freshwater*

The Emigrants. Sebald, Winfried Georg

Emile Cinq-Mars mysteries [Series]. Farrow, John

Emily's House. Brown, Amy Belding

EMINENT DOMAIN

Crummey, Michael. *Sweetland*

Emissary. Locke, Thomas

★*The Emissary.* Tawada, Yoko

★*Emma.* Austen, Jane

★*Emma.* Bronte, Charlotte

Emma Djan novels [Series]. Quartey, Kwei

Emma in the Night. Walker, Wendy

EMOTIONAL ABUSE

Rooney, Sally. *Normal People: A Novel*

EMOTIONAL MATURITY

Tyler, Anne. *A Patchwork Planet*

EMOTIONS

Kawabata, Yasunari. *The Sound of the Mountain*

Sartre, Jean Paul. ★*Nausea*

EMPATHY

Willis, Connie. *Crosstalk*

★*Empire Falls.* Russo, Richard

Empire Games. Stross, Charles

Empire Games [Series]. Stross, Charles
The **Empire** of Gold. Chakraborty, S. A.
Empire of Lies. Khoury, Raymond
★**Empire** of Sand. Suri, Tasha
Empire of the Sun: A Novel. Ballard, J. G.
Empire of Wild. Dimaline, Cherie
EMPLOYEES — DISMISSAL
    Child, Lee. ★The Sentinel
    Lalli, Sonya. A Holly Jolly Diwali
    McAllister, Tom. How to Be Safe: A Novel
EMPLOYEES — INTERPERSONAL RELATIONS
    Amdahl, Gary. I Am Death: Two Novellas
EMPLOYMENT REFERENCES
    Schumacher, Julie. Dear Committee Members
EMPOWERMENT (SOCIAL SCIENCES)
    Pellegrino, Amanda. Smile and Look Pretty
★**Empress** of Forever. Gladstone, Max
The **Empty** Birdcage. Abdul-Jabbar, Kareem
The **Empty** Chair. Deaver, Jeffery
Enard, Mathias
    Compass
ENCHANTMENT
    Allen, Sarah Addison. Garden Spells
    Heger, Amanda. Crazy Cupid Love
    Stewart, Mary. The Last Enchantment
The **Enchantress** of Florence: A Novel. Rushdie, Salman
ENCODING MACHINES
    Fleming, Ian. From Russia with Love
The **End** Game. Coulter, Catherine
End in Tears. Rendell, Ruth
The **End** of Eddy: A Novel. Louis, Edouard
The **End** of Loneliness: A Novel. Wells, Benedict
The **End** of Men. Sweeney-Baird, Christina
The **End** of October. Wright, Lawrence
★The **End** of the Affair. Greene, Graham
The **End** of the Alphabet. Richardson, C. S.
The **End** of the Day. Clegg, Bill
End of the Drive. L'Amour, Louis
The **End** of the Ocean: A Novel. Lunde, Maja
END OF THE UNIVERSE
    Dewes, J. S. The Last Watch
END OF THE WORLD
    Anders, Charlie Jane. ★All the Birds in the Sky
    Anders, Charlie Jane. Rock Manning Goes for Broke
    Atwood, Margaret. ★The Year of the Flood: A Novel
    Bear, Elizabeth. All the Windwracked Stars
    Byatt, A. S. ★Ragnarok: The End of the Gods
    Gaiman, Neil. ★Good Omens: The Nice and Accurate Prophecies of Agnes Nutter, Witch
    Gaiman, Neil. ★Norse Mythology
    Gibson, William. ★Agency
    Harkaway, Nick. Angelmaker
    Harkaway, Nick. The Gone-Away World
    Heller, Peter. ★The Dog Stars: A Novel
    Hill, Joe. The Fireman: A Novel
    Jemisin, N. K. The Fifth Season
    Jemisin, N. K. The Obelisk Gate
    Jemisin, N. K. The Stone Sky

    Ma, Ling. Severance
    Mandel, Emily St. John. ★Station Eleven
    Miller, Walter M. ★A Canticle for Leibowitz
    Newland, Courttia. A River Called Time
    North, Claire. Notes from the Burning Age
    Percy, Walker. The Second Coming
    Pressfield, Steven. 36 Righteous Men: A Novel
    Romero, George A. The Living Dead
    Tremblay, Paul. ★The Cabin at the End of the World: A Novel
    Vonnegut, Kurt. ★Cat's Cradle
    Vonnegut, Kurt. Slapstick: Or, Lonesome No More! a Novel
    Whitehead, Colson. Zone One: A Novel
End of Watch: A Novel. King, Stephen
Endangered. Cush, Jean Love
Ender Wiggin [Series]. Card, Orson Scott
★**Ender's** Game. Card, Orson Scott
Endicott, Marina
    The Voyage of the Morning Light
★The **Endless** Beach. Colgan, Jenny
★**Endless** Love. Spencer, Scott
Endless Night. Christie, Agatha
Endo, Shusaku
    Deep River
    Silence
Endymion. Simmons, Dan
ENEMIES
    Bateman, Kate. A Reckless Match
    Bradley, Anna. A Wicked Way to Win an Earl
    Burke, James Lee. House of the Rising Sun: A Novel
    Child, Lee. Persuader
    Corey, James S. A. Persepolis Rising
    Cussler, Clive. ★Final Option
    Cussler, Clive. Shadow Tyrants
    Daly, Paula. Open Your Eyes
    Dickey, Eric Jerome. Finding Gideon
    El-Mohtar, Amal. ★This Is How You Lose the Time War
    Flyte, Magnus. City of Lost Dreams: A Novel
    Frankel, Laurie. One Two Three: A Novel
    French, Jonathan. The Free Bastards
    Galbraith, Robert. Career of Evil
    Goss, Theodora. The Sinister Mystery of the Mesmerizing Girl
    Hansen, Ron. ★The Assassination of Jesse James by the Coward Robert Ford
    Higashino, Keigo. Malice
    Hockman, Angie. Shipped
    K'wan. Animal II: The Omen
    K'wan. Revelations
    Mosse, Kate. The City of Tears
    Mukherjee, Abir. Death in the East
    Piccirilli, Tom. The Last Whisper in the Dark: A Novel
    Robertson, Michael. Moriarty Returns a Letter: A Baker Street Mystery
    Rollins, James. The Demon Crown: A Sigma Force Novel
    Ruiz Zafon, Carlos. The Prisoner of Heaven
    Schwab, Victoria. A Conjuring of Light
    Schwab, Victoria. A Darker Shade of Magic
    Schwab, Victoria. A Gathering of Shadows
    Schwab, Victoria. Vengeful

Schwab, Victoria. *Vicious*
Scottoline, Lisa. *Feared*
Shannon, Samantha. *The Bone Season*
Silva, Daniel. *The New Girl*
Enemies, *a Love Story*. Singer, Isaac Bashevis
*The **Enemy***. Child, Lee
ENERGY RESOURCES
Stout, Dan. ★*Titanshade*
ENFORCERS (CRIMINALS)
Dickey, Eric Jerome. ★*Bad Men and Wicked Women*
Dickey, Eric Jerome. *Before We Were Wicked*
Weiden, David L. ★*Winter Counts*
ENGAGED PERSONS
Antoinette, Ashley. *Butterfly*
Antoinette, Ashley. *Butterfly.; Vol 2*
Antoinette, Ashley. *Butterfly.; Vol 3*
Barry, Dave. *Insane City*
Bowen, Rhys. *The Victory Garden*
Center, Katherine. *How to Walk Away: A Novel*
Childs, Laura. *Egg Shooters*
Cole, Alyssa. ★*A Princess in Theory*
Dare, Tessa. ★*Say Yes to the Marquess*
Divakaruni, Chitra Banerjee. *Oleander Girl: A Novel*
Freeman, Dianne. *A Fiancee's Guide to First Wives and Murder*
Hannah, Sophie. *The Killings at Kingfisher Hill*
Hodges, Cheris F. *Rumor Has It*
Holahan, Cate. *Her Three Lives*
Kwan, Kevin. *Crazy Rich Asians*
Kwan, Kevin. *Sex and Vanity: A Novel*
McKenzie, Elizabeth. *The Portable Veblen*
McPherson, Catriona. ★*A Step so Grave*
Packer, Ann. *The Dive from Clausen's Pier*
Palmer, Lindsey J. *Otherwise Engaged*
Paolini, Christopher. ★*To Sleep in a Sea of Stars*
Phillips, Susan Elizabeth. *Call Me Irresistible*
Ryan, Kennedy. ★*Long Shot*
Simpson, Rosemary. ★*What the Dead Leave Behind*
Swift, Graham. ★*Here We Are*
ENGAGEMENT
Helprin, Mark. *In Sunlight and in Shadow*
Heyer, Georgette. *The Grand Sophy*
Kamali, Marjan. ★*The Stationery Shop*
McCall Smith, Alexander. *The Forgotten Affairs of Youth*
Palmer, Lindsey J. *Otherwise Engaged*
ENGAGEMENT RINGS
Orenstein, Hannah. *Love at First Like*
Engel, Patricia
★*Infinite Country*
Enger, Leif
Virgil Wander
Enger, Lin
The High Divide: A Novel
Undiscovered Country: A Novel
*The **Engineer's** Wife: A Novel*. Wood, Tracey Enerson
ENGINEERS
Anders, Charlie Jane. ★*All the Birds in the Sky*
Barr, Mark. *Watershed*
Bohjalian, Chris. *The Sandcastle Girls*

Furst, Alan. *The Spies of Warsaw*
Harris, Robert. *Pompeii: A Novel*
Pontoppidan, Henrik. *Lucky Per*
*The **Engines** of God*. McDevitt, Jack
ENGLAND
Adams, Sara Nisha. ★*The Reading List*
Adichie, Chimamanda Ngozi. ★*Americanah: A Novel*
Airth, Rennie. *The Decent Inn of Death*
Alexander, Victoria. *The Lady Travelers Guide to Larceny with a Dashing Stranger*
Alexander, Victoria. *The Lady Travelers Guide to Scoundrels and Other Gentlemen*
Amis, Martin. *Lionel Asbo: State of England*
Andersen, Laura. ★*The Boleyn King*
Ashley, Jennifer. *Death at the Crystal Palace*
Ashley, Jennifer. *Lady Isabella's Scandalous Marriage*
Ashley, Jennifer. *The Madness of Lord Ian Mackenzie*
Atkinson, Kate. ★*Big Sky*
Atkinson, Kate. ★*Case Histories*
Atkinson, Kate. *Human Croquet*
Austen, Jane. ★*Emma*
Austen, Jane. *Mansfield Park*
Austen, Jane. *Northanger Abbey*
Austen, Jane. ★*Persuasion*
Austen, Jane. ★*Pride and Prejudice*
Austen, Jane. ★*Sense and Sensibility*
Bagshawe, Tilly. *Adored*
Baker, Kage. *In the Garden of Iden: A Novel of the Company*
Balasubramanyam, Rajeev. *Professor Chandra Follows His Bliss: A Novel*
Balogh, Mary. *The Arrangement*
Balogh, Mary. *The Escape*
Balogh, Mary. *More Than a Mistress*
Balogh, Mary. *Only Enchanting*
Balogh, Mary. *The Secret Mistress*
Balogh, Mary. *Simply Love*
Balogh, Mary. ★*Someone to Cherish*
Balogh, Mary. ★*Someone to Love*
Balogh, Mary. ★*Someone to Remember: A Westcott Story*
Balogh, Mary. *Someone to Trust*
Banville, John. ★*The Sea*
Barber, Lizzy. *A Girl Named Anna*
Barker, Pat. *Another World*
Barnes, Jonathan. *The Somnambulist*
Barnes, Julian. ★*England, England*
Barnes, Julian. *The Only Story*
Barnes, Julian. ★*The Sense of an Ending*
Bartlett, Neil. *The Disappearance Boy*
Bateman, Kate. *A Reckless Match*
Bauer, Belinda. *Snap*
Beaton, M. C. *Agatha Raisin and the Quiche of Death*
Beaton, M. C. *Agatha Raisin and the Witch of Wyckhadden*
Beaton, M. C. ★*Hot to Trot*
Beaton, M. C. *Pushing up Daisies: An Agatha Raisin Mystery*
Bell, Lenora. ★*How the Duke Was Won*
Benjamin, Melanie. *Alice I Have Been*
Berne, Lisa. *You May Kiss the Bride*
Berry, Connie. *A Legacy of Murder*

Billingham, Mark. ★*Their Little Secret*
Birch, Carol. *Jamrach's Menagerie*
Blakemore, A. K. *The Manningtree Witches*
Bolton, S. J. *The Craftsman*
Bourne, Joanna. *Rogue Spy*
Bourne, Joanna. ★*The Spymaster's Lady*
Bowen, Kelly. ★*Between the Devil and the Duke*
Bowen, Kelly. *A Rogue by Night*
Bowen, Rhys. *The Victory Garden*
Bowman, Valerie. *The Accidental Countess*
Bowman, Valerie. *A Duke Like No Other*
Boyd, William. *Trio*
Boyle, Elizabeth. *Along Came a Duke*
Boyle, Elizabeth. *And the Miss Ran Away with the Rake*
Bradley, Anna. *A Season of Ruin*
Bradley, Anna. *A Wicked Way to Win an Earl*
Bradley, C. Alan. *The Golden Tresses of the Dead: A Flavia De Luce Novel*
Bradley, C. Alan. *The Grave's a Fine and Private Place: A Flavia De Luce Novel*
Bradley, C. Alan. *I Am Half-Sick of Shadows: A Flavia De Luce Novel*
Bradley, C. Alan. *A Red Herring Without Mustard*
Bradley, C. Alan. *Speaking from Among the Bones: A Flavia De Luce Novel*
Bradley, C. Alan. ★*The Sweetness at the Bottom of the Pie*
Bradley, C. Alan. *Thrice the Brinded Cat Hath Mew'd: A Flavia De Luce Novel*
Bradley, C. Alan. *The Weed That Strings the Hangman's Bag: A Flavia De Luce Mystery*
Brett, Simon. *Guilt at the Garage*
Brett, Simon. *Mrs Pargeter's Principle*
Brett, Simon. *Murder Unprompted*
Brockway, Connie. *The Golden Season*
Bronte, Anne. *The Tenant of Wildfell Hall*
Bronte, Charlotte. ★*Emma*
Bronte, Charlotte. ★*Jane Eyre*
Bronte, Emily. ★*Wuthering Heights*
Burns, V. M. *Killer Words*
Burrowes, Grace. *The Captive*
Burrowes, Grace. *The Trouble with Dukes*
Butland, Stephanie. *The Lost for Words Bookshop: A Novel*
Byatt, A. S. *Babel Tower*
Byatt, A. S. ★*Ragnarok: The End of the Gods*
Byatt, A. S. *A Whistling Woman*
Campisi, Megan. *Sin Eater*
Cannon, Joanna. *Three Things About Elsie: A Novel*
Chambers, Clare. *Small Pleasures*
Chase, Loretta Lynda. *Don't Tempt Me*
Chase, Loretta Lynda. *A Duke in Shining Armor*
Chase, Loretta Lynda. *Miss Wonderful*
Chevalier, Tracy. *A Single Thread*
Cho, Zen. *Sorcerer to the Crown*
Christie, Agatha. ★*And Then There Were None*
Christie, Agatha. *The Body in the Library: A Miss Marple Mystery*
Christie, Agatha. *Curtain*
Christie, Agatha. *Endless Night*
Christie, Agatha. ★*The Murder at the Vicarage*

Christie, Agatha. *A Murder Is Announced: A Miss Marple Mystery*
Christie, Agatha. *The Pale Horse*
Ciotta, Beth. *Her Sky Cowboy*
Clarke, Susanna. ★*Jonathan Strange & Mr. Norrell*
Cleeves, Ann. ★*The Heron's Cry*
Cleeves, Ann. *The Long Call*
Clinch, Jon. *Marley: A Novel*
Cocks, Heather. *The Heir Affair*
Cocks, Heather. *The Royal We*
Colgan, Jenny. *Sunrise by the Sea*
Collins, Manda. *A Good Rake Is Hard to Find*
Collins, Manda. *One for the Rogue*
Collins, Manda. *Ready Set Rogue*
Collins, Sara. *The Confessions of Frannie Langton*
Collins, Wilkie. ★*The Moonstone*
Collins, Wilkie. ★*The Woman in White*
Crace, Jim. *Harvest*
Crombie, Deborah. *A Bitter Feast*
Cumming, Charles. ★*The Trinity Six*
Cusset, Catherine. *Life of David Hockney: A Novel*
Daly, Paula. *Open Your Eyes*
Daniels, Natalie. *Too Close*
Dare, Tessa. *Do You Want to Start a Scandal*
Dare, Tessa. ★*The Duchess Deal*
Dare, Tessa. ★*The Governess Game*
Dare, Tessa. ★*A Night to Surrender*
Dare, Tessa. *Romancing the Duke*
Dare, Tessa. ★*Say Yes to the Marquess*
Dare, Tessa. ★*The Wallflower Wager*
Dare, Tessa. *A Week to Be Wicked*
Deighton, Len. *London Match*
Delaney, J. P. *The Girl Before: A Novel*
Deveraux, Jude. *Someone to Love*
Dexter, Colin. *The Daughters of Cain*
Dexter, Colin. *The Way Through the Woods*
Dickens, Charles. ★*Bleak House*
Dickens, Charles. ★*David Copperfield*
Dickens, Charles. *Dombey and Son*
Dickens, Charles. *Little Dorrit*
Dickens, Charles. *Martin Chuzzlewit*
Dickens, Charles. ★*Nicholas Nickleby*
Dickens, Charles. *The Old Curiosity Shop*
Dickens, Charles. *The Pickwick Papers*
Drabble, Margaret. ★*The Dark Flood Rises*
Drabble, Margaret. *The Sea Lady*
Drabble, Margaret. *The Witch of Exmoor*
Dunmore, Evie. ★*Bringing Down the Duke*
Dunmore, Helen. *Exposure*
Dunmore, Helen. *The Lie*
Edwards, Rachel. *Darling*
Eliot, George. ★*Adam Bede*
Eliot, George. ★*Middlemarch: A Study of Provincial Life*
Ellis, Bella. *The Vanished Bride*
Evaristo, Bernardine. ★*Girl, Woman, Other*
Faulks, Sebastian. *Charlotte Gray: A Novel*
Faye, Lyndsay. *Jane Steele*
Faye, Lyndsay. *The Whole Art of Detection: Lost Mysteries of Sherlock Holmes*

Fforde, Jasper. *The Eyre Affair: A Novel*
Fforde, Jasper. *Lost in a Good Book: A Thursday Next Novel*
Fforde, Jasper. *Shades of Grey: A Novel*
Fielding, Henry. ★*The History of Tom Jones, a Foundling*
Finch, Charles. *A Beautiful Blue Death*
Finch, Charles. *The Last Passenger*
Finch, Charles. *The September Society*
Finch, Charles. *The Vanishing Man*
Follett, Ken. ★*The Evening and the Morning*
Forbes, Curdella. *A Tall History of Sugar*
Forster, E. M. ★*Howards End*
Forster, E. M. ★*A Room with a View*
Fowler, Christopher. *Bryant & May: Hall of Mirrors : A Peculiar Crimes Unit Mystery*
Fowler, Christopher. *Bryant & May: Oranges and Lemons*
Fowler, Christopher. *Bryant & May: The Lonely Hour*
Fowles, John. ★*The French Lieutenant's Woman*
Frampton, Megan. *Never a Bride*
Frampton, Megan. *Put up Your Duke*
Franklin, Ariana. ★*Death and the Maiden*
Franklin, Ariana. *Mistress of the Art of Death*
Frear, Caz. *Stone Cold Heart*
Frear, Caz. *Sweet Little Lies*
Freeman, Anna. *The Fair Fight: A Novel*
French, Nicci. ★*House of Correction*
French, Nicci. ★*The Lying Room*
Friedman, Daniel. *Riot Most Uncouth: A Lord Byron Mystery*
Fuller, Claire. ★*Bitter Orange*
Fuller, Claire. *Our Endless Numbered Days: A Novel*
Fuller, Claire. *Unsettled Ground*
Gaiman, Neil. ★*Anansi Boys: A Novel*
Gaiman, Neil. ★*The Ocean at the End of the Lane*
Galen, Shana. *Third Son's a Charm*
Gallagher, Stephen. *The Bedlam Detective: A Novel*
Gardam, Jane. *The Flight of the Maidens*
Gardam, Jane. *God on the Rocks*
Gardam, Jane. *Last Friends*
Gardam, Jane. *The People on Privilege Hill and Other Stories*
Garriott, Leah. *Promised*
Garwood, Julie. *The Bride*
Gaskell, Elizabeth Cleghorn. ★*Cranford*
Gaskell, Elizabeth Cleghorn. ★*North and South*
George, Elizabeth. *A Banquet of Consequences*
George, Elizabeth. *Believing the Lie*
George, Elizabeth. *Careless in Red*
George, Elizabeth. *Just One Evil Act*
George, Elizabeth. *The Punishment She Deserves*
George, Elizabeth. *This Body of Death: An Inspector Lynley Novel*
George, Elizabeth. *What Came Before He Shot Her*
Goddard, Robert. *Beyond Recall: A Novel*
Goddard, Robert. ★*Into the Blue*
Goddard, Robert. ★*Long Time Coming: A Novel*
Golding, Melanie. *The Hidden: A Novel*
Golding, Melanie. *Little Darlings*
Golding, William. *Rites of Passage*
Goodwin, Daisy. *The American Heiress*
Gosling, Victoria. *Before the Ruins: A Novel*
Gowar, Imogen Hermes. *The Mermaid and Mrs. Hancock*

Gracie, Anne. *Marry in Scandal*
Graves, Stephanie. *Olive Bright, Pigeoneer*
Greeley, Molly. *The Clergyman's Wife*
Greene, Graham. ★*Brighton Rock*
Greene, Graham. *The Captain and the Enemy*
Gregory, Philippa. *The Last Tudor*
Gregory, Philippa. *Tidelands*
Griffith, Nicola. *Hild: A Novel*
Griffiths, Elly. *A Dying Fall: A Ruth Galloway Mystery*
Griffiths, Elly. *The Lantern Men: A Dr. Ruth Galloway Mystery*
Griffiths, Elly. *The Postscript Murders*
Griffiths, Elly. *The Stone Circle*
Griffiths, Elly. *The Stranger Diaries*
Groff, Lauren. ★*Matrix*
Gruber, Michael. *The Book of Air and Shadows*
Guhrke, Laura Lee. *Governess Gone Rogue*
Guhrke, Laura Lee. *How to Lose a Duke in Ten Days*
Guhrke, Laura Lee. *The Trouble with True Love*
Guhrke, Laura Lee. *The Truth About Love and Dukes*
Guhrke, Laura Lee. *When the Marquess Met His Match*
Guillory, Jasmine. *Royal Holiday*
Haddon, Mark. ★*The Curious Incident of the Dog in the Night-Time: A Novel*
Hadley, Tessa. *Clever Girl*
Hale, Shannon. *Austenland: A Novel*
Hall, Alexis. ★*Boyfriend Material*
Hamer, Kate. *The Girl in the Red Coat*
Hamya, Jo. *Three Rooms*
Hannah, Sophie. *The Killings at Kingfisher Hill*
Hannah, Sophie. *Perfect Little Children*
Hardy, Thomas. ★*Far from the Madding Crowd*
Hardy, Thomas. ★*Jude the Obscure*
Hardy, Thomas. ★*The Return of the Native*
Hardy, Thomas. ★*Tess of the D'urbervilles: A Pure Woman Faithfully Presented*
Harrington, Anna. *An Inconvenient Duke*
Harris, C. S. *What the Devil Knows: A Sebastian St. Cyr Mystery*
Harris, Robert. *Enigma*
Harris, Robert. *The Ghost: A Novel*
Harris, Robert. *The Second Sleep: A Novel*
Harris, Sarah J. *The Color of Bee Larkham's Murder: A Novel*
Harrod-Eagles, Cynthia. *Cruel as the Grave*
Harrod-Eagles, Cynthia. *Old Bones*
Hart, Josephine. *Damage: A Novel*
Harvey, John. *Cold in Hand*
Harvey, John. *A Darker Shade of Blue: Stories*
Harvey, John. *Darkness, Darkness*
Hayder, Mo. *Gone*
Hayder, Mo. *Hanging Hill*
Hayder, Mo. *Poppet*
Hazzard, Shirley. ★*The Great Fire*
Healey, Emma. ★*Elizabeth Is Missing*
Healey, Jane. *The Animals at Lockwood Manor*
Heath, Lorraine. *Falling into Bed with a Duke*
Heley, Veronica. *Murder in Law*
Heyer, Georgette. *The Grand Sophy*
Hibbert, Talia. ★*Act Your Age, Eve Brown*
Hibbert, Talia. ★*Get a Life, Chloe Brown*

Hibbert, Talia. *A Girl Like Her*
Hibbert, Talia. ★*Take a Hint, Dani Brown*
Hill, Reginald. *The Woodcutter: A Novel*
Hill, Susan. *The Pure in Heart: A Simon Serrailler Crime Novel*
Hill, Susan. *The Shadows in the Street: A Simon Serrailler Mystery*
Hilton, James. ★*Good-Bye, Mr. Chips*
Hilton, James. *Random Harvest*
Hogan, Ruth. *Queenie Malone's Paradise Hotel*
Holdstock, Pauline. *Here I Am!*
Holt, Victoria. *The Black Opal*
Hornby, Gill. *Miss Austen*
Horowitz, Anthony. ★*Magpie Murders*
Horowitz, Anthony. ★*Moonflower Murders*
Horowitz, Anthony. ★*The Sentence Is Death*
Horowitz, Anthony. ★*The Word Is Murder*
Huber, Anna Lee. *Penny for Your Secrets*
Hurley, Andrew Michael. *Devil's Day*
Ishiguro, Kazuo. ★*Never Let Me Go*
Ishiguro, Kazuo. ★*The Remains of the Day*
James, Eloisa. ★*Seven Minutes in Heaven*
James, Eloisa. *The Ugly Duchess*
James, Eloisa. *Wilde in Love*
James, Henry. ★*The Turn of the Screw*
James, P. D. *The Skull Beneath the Skin*
James, Rebecca. *The Woman in the Mirror*
Jaswal, Balli Kaur. *Erotic Stories for Punjabi Widows*
Jeffries, Sabrina. *Project Duchess*
Jenner, Natalie. *The Jane Austen Society*
Jewell, Lisa. *Watching You*
Johnson, Daisy. *Sisters*
Jordan, Sophie. *The Duke Goes Down*
Kantaria, Annabel. *I Know You: A Novel of Suspense*
Kelly, Erin. *Broadchurch: A Novel*
Kelly, Erin. *The Burning Air: A Novel*
Kelly, Erin. *Watch Her Fall*
Kelly, Stephen. *The Wages of Desire: A World War II Mystery*
Kleypas, Lisa. *Cold-Hearted Rake*
Kleypas, Lisa. ★*Devil in Disguise*
Knight, Renee. *The Secretary: A Novel*
Laurens, Stephanie. *The Pursuits of Lord Kit Cavanaugh*
Lawler, Liz. *Don't Wake Up*
Lawrence, D. H. ★*Lady Chatterley's Lover*
Lawrence, D. H. *Sons and Lovers*
Leigh, Eva. *Forever Your Earl*
Leigh, Eva. *Scandal Takes the Stage*
Leigh, Eva. *Temptations of a Wallflower*
Levy, Andrea. *Small Island*
Liardet, Frances. *We Must Be Brave*
Livesey, Margot. ★*The Boy in the Field*
Long, Julie Anne. *Angel in a Devil's Arms*
Long, Julie Anne. ★*Lady Derring Takes a Lover*
Lovesey, Peter. *Beau Death*
Lovesey, Peter. *Diamond Solitaire*
Lovesey, Peter. ★*The Last Detective*
Lovett, Charles C. *The Lost Book of the Grail: Or a Visitor's Guide to Barchester Cathedral*
Lowe, Kathryn A. *The Furies*
Lurie, Alison. *Foreign Affairs*

Lyons, Annie. *The Brilliant Life of Eudora Honeysett*
MacDonald, Philip. *The List of Adrian Messenger*
Mackintosh, Clare. *After the End*
MacLean, Sarah. ★*Brazen and the Beast*
MacLean, Sarah. *No Good Duke Goes Unpunished*
MacLean, Sarah. *The Rogue Not Taken*
MacLean, Sarah. ★*Wicked and the Wallflower*
Macmillan, Gilly. *The Nanny*
MacNeal, Susan Elia. *The King's Justice*
Malliet, G. M. *A Demon Summer: A Max Tudor Mystery*
Malliet, G. M. *Pagan Spring: A Mystery*
Malpas, Jodi Ellen. *Leave Me Breathless*
Marsh, Ngaio. *A Man Lay Dead*
Mason, Meg. *Sorrow and Bliss*
Maugham, W. Somerset. ★*Of Human Bondage*
McDermid, Val. *How the Dead Speak: A Tony Hill and Carol Jordan Novel*
McDermid, Val. *A Place of Execution*
McEwan, Ian. ★*Atonement: A Novel*
McEwan, Ian. *Black Dogs*
McEwan, Ian. *The Child in Time*
McEwan, Ian. ★*On Chesil Beach*
McGregor, Jon. *The Reservoir Tapes*
McGuire, Ian. *The Abstainer: A Novel*
Milan, Courtney. *The Duchess War*
Miller, Andrew. *Oxygen*
Mitchell, David. *Black Swan Green: A Novel*
Mitford, Nancy. *Love in a Cold Climate*
Mitford, Nancy. ★*The Pursuit of Love: A Novel*
Montclair, Allison. *A Royal Affair*
Moor, Jessica. *The Keeper*
Moore, Alan. *Jerusalem: A Novel*
Morton, Kate. *The Distant Hours: A Novel*
Moss, Sarah. *Ghost Wall: A Novel*
Moyes, Jojo. *Me Before You: A Novel*
Moyes, Jojo. *The Peacock Emporium*
Mozley, Fiona. ★*Elmet*
Murdoch, Iris. *An Accidental Man*
Murdoch, Iris. *The Book and the Brotherhood*
Murdoch, Iris. *The Philosopher's Pupil*
Murdoch, Iris. *The Sea, the Sea*
Naipaul, V. S. *Magic Seeds*
Newman, Sandra. *The Heavens*
Nicholls, David. *US: A Novel*
Nicholls, Owen. *Love, Unscripted: A Novel*
Nickson, Chris. *Come the Fear*
North, Alex. *The Shadows*
North, Alex. *The Whisper Man*
Novik, Naomi. *His Majesty's Dragon*
O'Connor, Joseph. *Star of the Sea*
O'Farrell, Maggie. *Hamnet*
O'Leary, Beth. *The Flatshare: A Novel*
Orczy, Emmuska Orczy. ★*The Scarlet Pimpernel*
Osman, Richard. *The Man Who Died Twice: A Thursday Murder Club Mystery*
Osman, Richard. ★*The Thursday Murder Club*
Palliser, Charles. *The Quincunx*
Paris, B. A. ★*The Dilemma*

Parker, Lucy. *The Austen Playbook*
Parmar, Priya. *Vanessa and Her Sister*
Parris, S. J. ★*The Dead of Winter*
Parris, S. J. *Sacrilege*
Parris, S. J. *Treachery*
Patrick, Phaedra. ★*The Secrets of Love Story Bridge*
Penman, Sharon Kay. *The Queen's Man: A Medieval Mystery*
Penman, Sharon Kay. *When Christ and His Saints Slept*
Penrose, Andrea. *Murder at Half Moon Gate*
Penrose, Andrea. ★*Murder at Kensington Palace*
Penrose, Andrea. *Murder on Black Swan Lane*
Perry, Anne. ★*Death in Focus: An Elena Standish Novel*
Perry, Anne. ★*Death with a Double Edge: A Daniel Pitt Novel*
Perry, Anne. *One Fatal Flaw: A Daniel Pitt Novel*
Perry, Anne. *A Question of Betrayal*
Perry, Sarah. *The Essex Serpent*
Phillips, Arthur. ★*The King at the Edge of the World: Novel*
Phillips, Caryl. *A Distant Shore*
Phillips, Caryl. *Foreigners*
Polk, C. L. *The Midnight Bargain*
Porter, Henry. *The Bell Ringers*
Porter, Max. ★*Lanny: A Novel*
Pulley, Natasha. *The Bedlam Stacks*
Pulley, Natasha. *The Lost Future of Pepperharrow*
Pulley, Natasha. *The Watchmaker of Filigree Street*
Purcell, Laura. *The Silent Companions: A Ghost Story*
Putney, Mary Jo. *The Marriage Spell: A Novel*
Putney, Mary Jo. *No Longer a Gentleman*
Putney, Mary Jo. *Not Quite a Wife*
Pym, Barbara. ★*Excellent Women*
Quick, Amanda. *'til Death Do Us Part*
Quincy, Diana. *Her Night with the Duke*
Quincy, Diana. *The Viscount Made Me Do It*
Quinn, Julia. ★*An Offer from a Gentleman*
Raybourn, Deanna. *A Curious Beginning: A Veronica Speedwell Mystery*
Raybourn, Deanna. *A Dangerous Collaboration*
Raybourn, Deanna. ★*A Murderous Relation*
Raybourn, Deanna. *A Perilous Undertaking: A Veronica Speedwell Mystery*
Raybourn, Deanna. *A Treacherous Curse: A Veronica Speedwell Mystery*
Rendell, Ruth. *The Babes in the Wood*
Rendell, Ruth. *End in Tears*
Rendell, Ruth. *Harm Done*
Rendell, Ruth. *Kissing the Gunner's Daughter*
Rendell, Ruth. *Not in the Flesh*
Rendell, Ruth. *Road Rage*
Rendell, Ruth. *Simisola*
Rendell, Ruth. *A Sleeping Life*
Rendell, Ruth. *The Tree of Hands*
Richardson, Samuel. ★*Clarissa, Or, the History of a Young Lady*
Richardson, Samuel. ★*Pamela: Or, Virtue Rewarded*
Ridley, Erica. *The Duke Heist*
Ridley, Erica. ★*The Perks of Loving a Wallflower*
Riley, Vanessa. ★*An Earl, the Girl, and a Toddler*
Ripley, Mike. *Mr Campion's Coven*
Ripley, Mike. *Mr Campion's Fault*

Ripley, Mike. *Mr. Campion's War*
Roberts, Bethan. ★*My Policeman*
Robertson, Imogen. *Anatomy of Murder*
Robertson, Imogen. *Circle of Shadows*
Robertson, Imogen. *Instruments of Darkness: A Novel*
Robertson, Imogen. *Island of Bones*
Robertson, Michael. *The Baker Street Translation: A Mystery*
Robertson, Michael. *The Brothers of Baker Street*
Robinson, Peter. *Children of the Revolution*
Robinson, Peter. *Close to Home*
Robinson, Peter. *Cold Is the Grave*
Robinson, Peter. *The First Cut*
Robinson, Peter. *Friend of the Devil*
Robinson, Peter. *Innocent Graves: An Inspector Banks Mystery*
Robinson, Peter. *Piece of My Heart*
Robinson, Peter. *Playing with Fire*
Robinson, Peter. *Strange Affair*
Robotham, Michael. *The Night Ferry: A Novel*
Robotham, Michael. ★*When She Was Good*
Romain, Theresa. *Fortune Favors the Wicked*
Rowling, J. K. *The Casual Vacancy*
Runcie, James. *Canvey Island*
Runcie, James. *The Road to Grantchester*
Runcie, James. *Sidney Chambers and the Forgiveness of Sins*
Runcie, James. *Sidney Chambers and the Perils of the Night*
Runcie, James. *Sidney Chambers and the Persistence of Love*
Runcie, James. *Sidney Chambers and the Problem of Evil*
Runcie, James. *Sidney Chambers and the Shadow of Death*
Rutherfurd, Edward. *Sarum: The Novel of England*
Ryan, Jennifer. *The Spies of Shilling Lane: A Novel*
Sackville-West, V. *All Passion Spent*
Sackville-West, V. *The Edwardians*
Sahota, Sunjeev. *The Year of the Runaways*
Sampson, Freya. *The Last Chance Library*
Saunders, Kate. *The Case of the Wandering Scholar*
Sayers, Dorothy L. ★*Busman's Honeymoon*
Sayers, Dorothy L. ★*Gaudy Night*
Sayers, Dorothy L. *Have His Carcase*
Sayers, Dorothy L. *Murder Must Advertise*
Sayers, Dorothy L. *The Nine Tailors*
Sayers, Dorothy L. *Thrones, Dominations*
Sayers, Dorothy L. ★*Whose Body?: A Lord Peter Wimsey Novel*
Sebastian, Cat. *It Takes Two to Tumble*
Sebastian, Cat. *Unmasked by the Marquess*
Shaffer, Mary Ann. *The Guernsey Literary and Potato Peel Pie Society*
Sharratt, Mary. *Daughters of the Witching Hill*
Shaw, Vivian. ★*Strange Practice*
Shaw, William. *Salt Lane*
Simonson, Helen. *Major Pettigrew's Last Stand: A Novel*
Simonson, Helen. *The Summer Before the War: A Novel*
Simpson, Dorothy. *Dead and Gone: An Inspector Luke Thanet Novel.*
Smith, Ali. *There but for The: A Novel*
Smith, Dodie. ★*I Capture the Castle*
Smith, Martin Cruz. *Rose*
Snow, C. P. ★*Strangers and Brothers*
Solomons, Natasha. *House of Gold*
Spark, Muriel. *Aiding & Abetting*

Spark, Muriel. ★*A Far Cry from Kensington*
Spark, Muriel. ★*Memento Mori*
Speller, Elizabeth. *The Return of Captain John Emmett*
Speller, Elizabeth. *The Strange Fate of Kitty Easton*
Spencer, Minerva. *Barbarous*
Spencer, Minerva. *Dangerous*
Spencer, Sally. *Backlash*
Spencer, Sally. *Best Served Cold*
Spencer, Sally. *Dead End*
Spencer, Sally. *The Dead Hand of History*
Spencer, Sally. *Death's Dark Shadow*
Spencer, Sally. ★*A Dying Fall*
Spencer, Sally. ★*Echoes of the Dead*
Spencer, Sally. ★*The Hidden*
Spencer, Sally. *Lambs to the Slaughter*
Spencer, Sally. *The Ring of Death*
Spencer, Sally. *Thicker Than Water: A Monika Paniatowski British Police Procedural*
Spencer, Sally. *A Walk with the Dead*
St. James, Simone. *The Haunting of Maddy Clare*
Starr, Melvin R. *Unhallowed Ground*
Steadman, Catherine. *Mr. Nobody: A Novel*
Steiner, Susie. *Missing, Presumed: A Novel*
Steiner, Susie. ★*Persons Unknown: A Novel*
Stibbe, Nina. *Reasons to Be Cheerful*
Stratford, Sarah-Jane. *Red Letter Days*
Swift, Graham. ★*Last Orders: A Novel*
Swift, Graham. *Wish You Were Here*
Thackeray, William Makepeace. ★*Vanity Fair: A Novel Without a Hero*
Thomas, Russ. ★*Firewatching*
Thomas, Russ. *Nighthawking*
Trollope, Anthony. ★*Barchester Towers*
Trollope, Anthony. *Doctor Thorne*
Trollope, Anthony. ★*The Eustace Diamonds*
Trollope, Anthony. *Framley Parsonage*
Trollope, Anthony. *The Last Chronicle of Barset*
Trollope, Anthony. ★*The Prime Minister*
Trollope, Anthony. *The Warden*
Trollope, Joanna. *Other People's Children*
Truss, Lynne. *The Man That Got Away: A Constable Twitten Mystery*
Truss, Lynne. *Murder by Milk Bottle*
Tudor, C. J. *The Chalk Man: A Novel*
Turansky, Carrie. *No Ocean Too Wide: A Novel*
Turton, Stuart. *The 7 1/2 Deaths of Evelyn Hardcastle*
Twain, Mark. ★*A Connecticut Yankee in King Arthur's Court*
Vaughan, Sarah. ★*Anatomy of a Scandal: A Novel*
Vayden, Kristin. *Fortune Favors the Duke*
Vine, Barbara. *The Minotaur: A Novel*
Vyleta, Dan. *Smoke: A Novel*
Waite, Olivia. *The Care and Feeding of Waspish Widows*
Waite, Olivia. ★*The Lady's Guide to Celestial Mechanics*
Walker, Alice. *The Temple of My Familiar*
Walters, Minette. *The Last Hours: A Novel*
Ware, Ruth. *In a Dark, Dark Wood*
Ware, Ruth. *The Lying Game*
Waters, Martha. ★*To Have and to Hoax: A Novel*
Waters, Martha. *To Love and to Loathe: A Novel*

Watson, S. J. *Final Cut*
Waugh, Evelyn. ★*Brideshead Revisited*
Waugh, Evelyn. ★*The Complete Stories of Evelyn Waugh*
Waugh, Evelyn. *Decline and Fall*
Waugh, Evelyn. ★*Vile Bodies*
Weinberg, Kate. *The Truants*
Weir, Alison. *Anna of Kleve: The Princess in the Portrait*
Weir, Alison. *Katharine Parr, the Sixth Wife*
Whelan, Julia. *My Oxford Year*
Williams, Pip. *The Dictionary of Lost Words*
Wodehouse, P. G. ★*The Inimitable Jeeves*
Wodehouse, P. G. *My Man Jeeves*
Woolf, Virginia. ★*Mrs. Dalloway*
Woolf, Virginia. ★*The Years*
Youngson, Anne. *Meet Me at the Museum*
★*England, England*. Barnes, Julian
Englander, Nathan
   The Ministry of Special Cases
   What We Talk About When We Talk About Anne Frank: Stories
ENGLISH CIVIL WAR, 1642-1649
   Blakemore, A. K. *The Manningtree Witches*
   Gregory, Philippa. *Tidelands*
ENGLISH IN SCOTLAND
   London, Julia. *Wild Wicked Scot*
ENGLISH LANGUAGE
   Graedon, Alena. *The Word Exchange: A Novel*
   Schine, Cathleen. *The Grammarians*
   Williams, Pip. *The Dictionary of Lost Words*
ENGLISH LANGUAGE TEACHERS
   Cusk, Rachel. *Outline: A Novel*
   Cusk, Rachel. *Transit*
   Kupersmith, Violet. ★*Build Your House Around My Body*
English, *August: An Indian Story*. Chatterjee, Upamanyu
Engraved *on the Heart*. Johnson, Tara
Enigma. Harris, Robert
ENIGMA MACHINE
   Harris, Robert. *Enigma*
Enigma *of China*. Qiu, Xiaolong
Enigma *Variations: A Novel*. Aciman, Andre
Enjeti, Anjali
   ★*The Parted Earth*
ENLIGHTENMENT (BUDDHISM)
   Hesse, Hermann. ★*Siddhartha: A New Translation*
ENLIGHTENMENT (EUROPEAN INTELLECTUAL MOVEMENT)
   Parry, H. G. *A Declaration of the Rights of Magicians*
The **Enlightenment** *of Bees*. Linden, Rachel
Enright, Anne
   Actress: A Novel
   The Forgotten Waltz
   ★*The Gathering*
   The Green Road: A Novel
   Yesterday's Weather: Stories
The **Ensemble**: *a Novel*. Gabel, Aja
ENSLAVED BOYS
   Coates, Ta-Nehisi. ★*The Water Dancer: A Novel*
ENSLAVED FAMILIES
   Coates, Ta-Nehisi. ★*The Water Dancer: A Novel*

ENSLAVED GIRLS

Hill, Lawrence. *Someone Knows My Name: A Novel*

Johnson, Keith Lee. ★*Little Black Girl Lost*

ENSLAVED PEOPLE

Asim, Jabari. ★*Yonder*

Edugyan, Esi. ★*Washington Black: A Novel*

Jones, Gayl. ★*Palmares*

Jones, Robert. ★*The Prophets: A Novel*

Lalami, Laila. ★*The Moor's Account: A Novel*

Le Guin, Ursula K. *Four Ways to Forgiveness*

Pesci, David. *Amistad: A Novel*

Phillips, Caryl. *Foreigners*

Rawles, Nancy. *My Jim: A Novel*

Roy, Lucinda. *The Freedom Race*

Saylor, Steven. *The House of the Vestals: The Investigations of Gordianus the Finder*

Saylor, Steven. *A Mist of Prophecies*

Saylor, Steven. *Raiders of the Nile: A Novel of the Ancient World*

Wallace, Lew. ★*Ben-Hur*

ENSLAVED PEOPLE'S RESISTANCE AND REVOLTS

Le Guin, Ursula K. *Four Ways to Forgiveness*

Styron, William. *The Confessions of Nat Turner*

ENSLAVED WOMEN

Barker, Pat. *The Women of Troy*

Brink, Andre P. *Philida: A Novel*

Conde, Maryse. *I, Tituba, Black Witch of Salem*

Crafts, Hannah. *The Bondwoman's Narrative*

Gaines, Ernest J. ★*The Autobiography of Miss Jane Pittman*

Johnson, Sadeqa. ★*Yellow Wife*

Levy, Andrea. *The Long Song*

Straight, Susan. *A Million Nightingales*

Tademy, Lalita. *Cane River*

ENTERTAINERS

Randisi, Robert J. *Hey There (You with the Gun in Your Hand): A Rat Pack Mystery*

Skarmeta, Antonio. *The Dancer and the Thief: A Novel*

ENTERTAINMENT INDUSTRY AND TRADE

Cline, Rachel. *My Liar: A Novel*

Davis, Fiona. *The Chelsea Girls*

Leonard, Elmore. ★*Be Cool: Everyone Is Looking for the Next Big Hit*

Pellegrino, Amanda. *Smile and Look Pretty*

ENTITLEMENT ATTITUDES

Gunesekera, Romesh. ★*Suncatcher: A Novel*

Lutz, Lisa. *The Swallows: A Novel*

Entombed. Fairstein, Linda A.

ENTOMOLOGISTS

Abe, Kobo. *The Woman in the Dunes*

ENTREPRENEURS

Fuentes, Carlos. *The Crystal Frontier: A Novel in Nine Stories*

Gilman, Susan Jane. *The Ice Cream Queen of Orchard Street: A Novel*

Millhauser, Steven. *Martin Dressler: The Tale of an American Dreamer*

Soyinka, Wole. *Chronicles from the Land of the Happiest People on Earth*

Stephenson, Neal. *Reamde*

Stross, Charles. *Accelerando*

ENTROPY

Pynchon, Thomas. ★*The Crying of Lot 49*

ENVIRONMENTAL CRIMES

Deaver, Jeffery. *The Empty Chair*

Robinson, Kim Stanley. *Antarctica*

ENVIRONMENTAL DEGRADATION

Atwood, Margaret. ★*Oryx and Crake*

Flanagan, Richard. *The Living Sea of Waking Dreams*

Mbue, Imbolo. *How Beautiful We Were*

Robinson, Kim Stanley. ★*The Ministry for the Future*

Vinge, Joan D. *The Snow Queen*

ENVIRONMENTAL DISASTERS

Faber, Michel. *The Book of Strange New Things*

Kowal, Mary Robinette. *The Relentless Moon*

Walker, Karen Thompson. *The Age of Miracles: A Novel*

ENVIRONMENTAL PROTECTION

Parks, Brad. *The Player: A Mystery*

ENVIRONMENTAL SURVEYS

Cleeves, Ann. *The Crow Trap*

ENVIRONMENTALISM

McConaghy, Charlotte. *Once There Were Wolves: A Novel*

Rash, Ron. ★*Serena: A Novel*

ENVIRONMENTALISTS

Box, C. J. *Savage Run*

Boyle, T. Coraghessan. *When the Killing's Done: A Novel*

Dektar, Molly. *The Ash Family*

Qiu, Xiaolong. *Hold Your Breath, China*

Robinson, Kim Stanley. *Antarctica*

ENVY

Burton, Tara Isabella. *Social Creature*

Kress, Nancy. *Beggars in Spain*

EPIC FANTASY

Bear, Elizabeth. *Range of Ghosts*

Bear, Elizabeth. *The Red-Stained Wings*

Bear, Elizabeth. *Shattered Pillars*

Bear, Elizabeth. *Steles of the Sky*

Bear, Elizabeth. *The Stone in the Skull*

Brooks, Terry. *Child of Light*

Callender, Kacen. *King of the Rising*

Callender, Kacen. *Queen of the Conquered*

Campbell, Lisbeth. *The Vanished Queen*

Carrick, M. A. *The Mask of Mirrors*

Durst, Sarah Beth. *The Queen of Blood*

Durst, Sarah Beth. *Race the Sands*

French, Jonathan. *The Free Bastards*

Glass, Jenna. *The Women's War*

Gratton, Tessa. *The Queens of Innis Lear*

Hairston, Andrea. *Master of Poisons*

Haydon, Elizabeth. *The Merchant Emperor*

James, Marlon. ★*Black Leopard, Red Wolf*

Jin, Yong. *A Hero Born: A Novel*

Kay, Guy Gavriel. ★*A Brightness Long Ago*

Kay, Guy Gavriel. *The Summer Tree*

Kay, Guy Gavriel. *Tigana*

Kuhn, M. J. *Among Thieves*

Leckie, Ann. ★*The Raven Tower*

Lee, Fonda. ★*Jade City*

Lee, Fonda. *Jade War*

Liu, Ken. ★*The Grace of Kings*
Liu, Ken. ★*The Veiled Throne*
Liu, Ken. *The Wall of Storms*
Lyons, Jenn. *The Name of All Things*
Lyons, Jenn. *The Ruin of Kings*
Martin, George R. R. ★*A Clash of Kings*
Martin, George R. R. ★*A Dance with Dragons*
Martin, George R. R. ★*A Feast for Crows*
Martin, George R. R. *Fire & Blood: 300 Years Before a Game of Thrones (A Targaryen History)*
Martin, George R. R. ★*A Game of Thrones*
Martin, George R. R. ★*A Storm of Swords*
Penelope, L. *Cry of Metal & Bone: Earthsinger Chronicles, Book 3*
Penelope, L. *Song of Blood and Stone*
Penelope, L. *Whispers of Shadow & Flame*
Roanhorse, Rebecca. ★*Black Sun*
Rothfuss, Patrick. ★*The Name of the Wind*
Rothfuss, Patrick. ★*The Wise Man's Fear*
Shannon, Samantha. *The Priory of the Orange Tree*
Tan, Sue Lynn. ★*Daughter of the Moon Goddess*
Tolkien, J. R. R. *Beren and Luthien*
Tolkien, J. R. R. *The Children of Hurin*
Tolkien, J. R. R. *The Fall of Gondolin*
Tolkien, J. R. R. *The Fellowship of the Ring: Being the First Part of the Lord of the Rings*
Tolkien, J. R. R. ★*The Hobbit, Or, There and Back Again*
Tolkien, J. R. R. *The Return of the King: Being the Third Part of the Lord of the Rings*
Tolkien, J. R. R. *The Two Towers: Being the Second Part of the Lord of the Rings*
Wexler, Django. *Ashes of the Sun*
White, Elle Katharine. *Dragonshadow*
Whitten, Hannah. *For the Wolf*

EPIC FICTION

Follett, Ken. *Edge of Eternity*
Follett, Ken. *Fall of Giants*
Follett, Ken. *Winter of the World*
Gilbert, Elizabeth. ★*The Signature of All Things: A Novel*
Lee, Chang-Rae. ★*The Surrendered*
Malouf, David. *Ransom*
McMurtry, Larry. *Comanche Moon: A Novel*
McMurtry, Larry. ★*Lonesome Dove: A Novel*
McMurtry, Larry. ★*Streets of Laredo: A Novel*
Meyer, Philipp. *The Son: A Novel*
Mitchell, Margaret. ★*Gone with the Wind*
Rutherfurd, Edward. *London*
Rutherfurd, Edward. *Paris*
Rutherfurd, Edward. *The Princes of Ireland: The Dublin Saga*
Rutherfurd, Edward. *The Rebels of Ireland: The Dublin Saga*
Rutherfurd, Edward. *Russka: The Novel of Russia*
Rutherfurd, Edward. *Sarum: The Novel of England*
Sayles, John. *A Moment in the Sun*
Saylor, Steven. *Roma: The Novel of Ancient Rome*
Scott, Walter. ★*Ivanhoe*
Serpell, Namwali. ★*The Old Drift*
Vargas Llosa, Mario. *The War of the End of the World*
Walker, Alice. *The Temple of My Familiar*

EPIDEMICS

Barclay, Linwood. *The Twenty-Three: A Promise Falls Novel*
Beukes, Lauren. *Afterland*
Bunn, T. Davis. *Outbreak*
Camus, Albert. *The Plague*
Foster, Alan Dean. *Relic*
Groff, Lauren. ★*Arcadia: A Novel*
Groff, Lauren. *Delicate Edible Birds and Other Stories*
Heller, Peter. ★*The Dog Stars: A Novel*
King, Stephen. *Sleeping Beauties: A Novel*
King, Stephen. ★*The Stand*
Koepp, David. *Cold Storage: A Novel*
Kress, Nancy. *If Tomorrow Comes*
Lai, Larissa. *The Tiger Flu*
Makkai, Rebecca. ★*The Great Believers*
Mandel, Emily St. John. ★*Station Eleven*
Nagamatsu, Sequoia. *How High We Go in the Dark*
Nunez, Sigrid. *Salvation City*
Pinsker, Sarah. *A Song for a New Day*
Reed, Ishmael. ★*Mumbo Jumbo*
Romero, George A. *The Living Dead*
Roth, Philip. ★*Nemesis*
Saramago, Jose. ★*Blindness*
Scalzi, John. ★*Lock In*
Shepard, Jim. *Phase Six*
Shepherd, Peng. *The Book of M: A Novel*
Slaughter, Karin. ★*The Last Widow*
Smith, Ali. ★*Summer*
Stewart, George R. *Earth Abides*
Stivers, Carole. *The Mother Code*
Sweeney-Baird, Christina. *The End of Men*
Tremblay, Paul. *Survivor Song*
Walker, Karen Thompson. *The Dreamers*
Wendig, Chuck. ★*Wanderers: A Novel*
Wexler, Django. *Ashes of the Sun*
Wright, Lawrence. *The End of October*

EPISTOLARY NOVELS

Adiga, Aravind. ★*The White Tiger: A Novel*
Adkins, Mary. *When You Read This*
Banks, Russell. *Cloudsplitter: A Novel*
Bauer, Carlene. ★*Frances and Bernard*
Bivald, Katarina. *The Readers of Broken Wheel Recommend*
Burdick, Serena. *Find Me in Havana*
Clarke, Susanna. ★*Piranesi*
Coetzee, J. M. *Age of Iron*
Cooley, Martha. *The Archivist: A Novel*
Crowley, John. *Lord Byron's Novel: The Evening Land*
Dann, Patty. *The Wright Sister*
Doyle, Rob. *Threshold*
Dunn, Mark. *Ella Minnow Pea: A Progressively Lipogrammatic Epistolary Fable*
El-Mohtar, Amal. ★*This Is How You Lose the Time War*
Foer, Jonathan Safran. *Everything Is Illuminated: A Novel*
Green, Amy Lynn. *Things We Didn't Say*
Hosseini, Khaled. ★*Sea Prayer*
Kasulke, Calvin. *Several People Are Typing*
Richardson, Samuel. ★*Clarissa, Or, the History of a Young Lady*
Richardson, Samuel. ★*Pamela: Or, Virtue Rewarded*

Rimmer, Kelly. *Truths I Never Told You*
Robinson, Marilynne. ★*Gilead*
Schlink, Bernhard. *Olga*
Schumacher, Julie. *Dear Committee Members*
Shaffer, Mary Ann. *The Guernsey Literary and Potato Peel Pie Society*
Smith, Lee. ★*Fair and Tender Ladies*
Sthers, Amanda. *Holy Lands: A Novel*
Vuong, Ocean. ★*On Earth We're Briefly Gorgeous: A Novel*
Walker, Alice. ★*The Color Purple: A Novel*
Ware, Ruth. ★*The Turn of the Key*
Youngson, Anne. *Meet Me at the Museum*
Epitaph: a Novel of the O.K. Corral. Russell, Mary Doria
Epstein, Jennifer Cody
  ★*Wunderland: A Novel*
Epstein, Joseph
  The Love Song of A. Jerome Minkoff, and Other Stories
Equal of the Sun. Amirrezvani, Anita
Equal Rites. Pratchett, Terry
EQUALITY
  Shteyngart, Gary. ★*Super Sad True Love Story: A Novel*
EQUESTRIANS
  Beaton, M. C. ★*Hot to Trot*
  Smiley, Jane. *Horse Heaven*
Erasmus Keane novels [Series]. Kroese, Robert
Erast Fandorin mysteries [Series]. Akunin, B.
Erasure: a Novel. Everett, Percival L.
Erdrich, Louise
  The Beet Queen: A Novel
  Four Souls: A Novel
  Future Home of the Living God
  ★*Larose*
  The Last Report on the Miracles at Little No Horse
  Love Medicine: A Novel
  The Master Butchers Singing Club: A Novel
  ★*The Night Watchman: A Novel*
  The Painted Drum: A Novel
  The Plague of Doves
  The Red Convertible: Selected and New Stories, 1978-2008
  ★*The Round House: A Novel*
  ★*The Sentence*
  ★*Shadow Tag: A Novel*
  Tracks: A Novel
Eric Steele novels [Series]. Parnell, Sean
Eriksson, Kjell
  The Deathwatch Beetle: A Mystery
Erlendur Sveinsson mysteries [Series]. Arnaldur Indridason
EROTIC FICTION
  Cumyn, Alan. *Losing It*
  Dickey, Eric Jerome. *The Business of Lovers*
  Hilton, L. S. *Maestra*
  Jong, Erica. ★*Fear of Flying: A Novel*
  Lawrence, D. H. ★*Lady Chatterley's Lover*
  Miller, Henry. ★*Tropic of Cancer*
  Miller, Henry. ★*Tropic of Capricorn*
EROTIC PHOTOGRAPHS
  Rowland, Laura Joh. *The Ripper's Shadow*

EROTIC ROMANCES
  Bell, Shelly. *At His Mercy*
  Bell, Shelly. *For His Pleasure*
  Hoang, Helen. ★*The Kiss Quotient*
Erotic Stories for Punjabi Widows. Jaswal, Balli Kaur
Erpenbeck, Jenny
  The Book of Words
  Go, Went, Gone: A Novel
ERRORS
  Bowman, Valerie. *No Other Duke but You*
Escandon, Maria Amparo
  ★*L.A. Weather*
The Escape. Balogh, Mary
ESCAPE (PSYCHOLOGY)
  Dimon, HelenKay. *Her Other Secret*
The Escape Artist. Meltzer, Brad
ESCAPE ARTISTS
  Singer, Isaac Bashevis. ★*The Magician of Lublin*
The Escape Room. Goldin, Megan
ESCAPED CONVICTS
  Burke, James Lee. ★*The New Iberia Blues*
  Foster, Fiona King. *The Captive: A Novel*
  Gerritsen, Tess. *The Apprentice: A Novel*
  Lehane, Dennis. *Shutter Island*
  Robotham, Michael. *Life or Death*
  Roslund, Anders. *Pen 33*
ESCAPES
  Barr, Nevada. *The Rope: An Anna Pigeon Novel*
  Barr, Nevada. *What Rose Forgot*
  Beagle, Peter S. ★*The Last Unicorn*
  Beukes, Lauren. *Afterland*
  Brooks, Terry. *Child of Light*
  Brown, Taylor. *Fallen Land*
  Coates, Ta-Nehisi. ★*The Water Dancer: A Novel*
  Dallas, Sandra. *Westering Women: A Novel*
  Davys, Tim. *Amberville*
  DeLillo, Don. *Falling Man: A Novel*
  Dumas, Alexandre. ★*The Count of Monte Cristo*
  Foster, Fiona King. *The Captive: A Novel*
  Gottlieb, Eli. *Best Boy: A Novel*
  Hayder, Mo. *Poppet*
  Jones, Gayl. ★*Palmares*
  Kane, Ben. *Spartacus: The Gladiator*
  Keneally, Thomas. *Shame and the Captives: A Novel*
  Lee, Patrick. *Runner*
  Mabanckou, Alain. ★*Black Moses*
  O'Brien, Edna. ★*Girl*
  Quick, Amanda. *The Other Lady Vanishes*
  Rajaniemi, Hannu. *The Fractal Prince*
  Rajaniemi, Hannu. *The Quantum Thief*
  Reed, Ishmael. *Flight to Canada*
  Spufford, Francis. ★*Golden Hill*
  Stark, Richard. *Breakout*
  Tatlock, Ann. *Promises to Keep*
  Verne, Jules. *The Mysterious Island*
  Westheimer, David. ★*Von Ryan's Express*
Escobar, Mario
  The Librarian of Saint-Malo: A Novel

ESCORT SERVICES (PROSTITUTION)
Bryant, Niobia. *Madam, May I*
Hoang, Helen. ★*The Kiss Quotient*
Eskens, Allen
Nothing More Dangerous: A Novel
ESPINOSA, INSPECTOR (FICTITIOUS CHARACTER)
Garcia-Roza, L. A. *Alone in the Crowd: An Inspector Espinosa Mystery*
Garcia-Roza, L. A. *December Heat*
ESPIONAGE
Atkinson, Kate. ★*Transcription*
Berenson, Alex. *The Prisoner*
Brandreth, Benet. *The Spy of Venice*
Clements, Oliver. *The Eyes of the Queen*
Cumming, Charles. *A Colder War*
Cumming, Charles. *A Divided Spy*
Cumming, Charles. *The Moroccan Girl*
Cumming, Charles. ★*The Trinity Six*
Downing, David. *Diary of a Dead Man on Leave*
Duenas, Maria. *The Time in Between: A Novel*
Dugoni, Robert. *The Eighth Sister: A Thriller*
Dunmore, Helen. *Exposure*
Forsyth, Frederick. *The Fox*
Gleason, Colleen. *Murder at the Capitol*
Harris, Robert. *An Officer and a Spy*
Lawton, John. *Hammer to Fall*
London, Julia. *Wild Wicked Scot*
Matthews, Jason. ★*The Kremlin's Candidate*
Meacham, Leila. *Dragonfly: A Novel*
Reich, Christopher. ★*The Take*
Steinhauer, Olen. *The Last Tourist*
Stross, Charles. *Empire Games*
Sundin, Sarah. *When Twilight Breaks*
Tanabe, Karin. ★*A Woman of Intelligence*
Thomas, Will. *Dance with Death*
Vidich, Paul. *The Coldest Warrior*
Westlake, Donald E. *Forever and a Death*
Wilkinson, Lauren. ★*American Spy: A Novel*
Wolfe, Gene. *The Land Across*
Woods, Stuart. *Skin Game*
Esquivel, Laura
★*Like Water for Chocolate: A Novel in Monthly Installments, with Recipes, Romances, and Home Remedies*
ESSAYS
O'Connor, Flannery. ★*Collected Works*
Sedaris, David. *Holidays on Ice*
Vonnegut, Kurt. *Armageddon in Retrospect: And Other New and Unpublished Writings on War and Peace*
Welty, Eudora. *Stories, Essays & Memoir*
Essbaum, Jill Alexander
Hausfrau: A Novel
The Essex Serpent. Perry, Sarah
ESSEX, ENGLAND
Morton, Kate. *The House at Riverton: A Novel*
Vine, Barbara. *The Minotaur: A Novel*
ESTHER
Smith, Jill Eileen. *Star of Persia: Esther's Story*

Estleman, Loren D.
The Adventures of Johnny Vermillion: A Novel
★*Amos Walker: The Complete Story Collection*
Frames
★*Gas City*
★*Indigo: A Valentino Mystery*
Infernal Angels
★*The Master Executioner*
A Smile on the Face of the Tiger
★*Something Borrowed, Something Black*
ESTONIA
Porter, Henry. *The Old Enemy*
Etched on Me: A Novel. Crowell, Jenn
Eternal Life: A Novel. Horn, Dara
Eternal sky trilogy [Series]. Bear, Elizabeth
ETERNITY
Moore, Alan. *Jerusalem: A Novel*
Eternity Springs: McBrides of Texas [Series]. March, Emily
★*Ethan Frome*. Wharton, Edith
ETHICAL PROBLEMS
Bialosky, Jill. *The Prize: A Novel*
ETHICS
Bausch, Richard. *Peace*
Gruber, Michael. *The Return: A Novel*
Hendricks, Greer. *An Anonymous Girl*
Ishiguro, Kazuo. ★*Never Let Me Go*
Kidd, Sue Monk. ★*The Book of Longings*
King, Stephen. ★*Billy Summers*
Kingsolver, Barbara. ★*Unsheltered*
Lescroart, John T. *Guilt*
McCall Smith, Alexander. *The Kalahari Typing School for Men*
Murdoch, Iris. *The Philosopher's Pupil*
Penny, Louise. ★*The Madness of Crowds*
Shelley, Mary Wollstonecraft. ★*Frankenstein: Or, the Modern Prometheus*
Vonnegut, Kurt. *While Mortals Sleep: Unpublished Short Fiction*
Wiesel, Elie. ★*Dawn*
ETHIOPIA
Mengiste, Maaza. ★*The Shadow King: A Novel*
Verghese, A. *Cutting for Stone: A Novel*
ETHIOPIANS
Tamirat, Nafkote. *The Parking Lot Attendant: A Novel*
ETHNIC GROUPS
Bledsoe, Alex. *Gather Her Round: A Novel of the Tufa*
Bledsoe, Alex. *The Hum and the Shiver*
Bledsoe, Alex. *Long Black Curl*
Bledsoe, Alex. *Wisp of a Thing*
ETHNIC IDENTITY
Brinkley, Jamel. *A Lucky Man: Stories*
Gay, Roxane. ★*Ayiti*
Smith, Zadie. *On Beauty*
Solomon, Asali. *Disgruntled: A Novel*
Walker, Alice. *The Temple of My Familiar*
ETHNICITY
Smith, Zadie. *The Autograph Man: A Novel*
ETHNOLOGICAL MUSEUMS
Smith, Dominic. *Bright and Distant Shores*

FICTION CORE COLLECTION
TWENTY-FIRST EDITION

ETHNOLOGISTS
 Le Guin, Ursula K. ★*The Left Hand of Darkness*
Etta and Otto and Russell and James: A Novel. Hooper, Emma
EUGENICS
 Butler, Octavia E. ★*Dawn: Xenogenesis*
Eugenides, Jeffrey
 Fresh Complaint: Stories
 ★*The Marriage Plot*
 ★*Middlesex*
 ★*The Virgin Suicides*
Eugenie Grandet. Balzac, Honore de
EUNUCHS
 Amirrezvani, Anita. *Equal of the Sun*
 Renault, Mary. *The Persian Boy*
EUROPE
 Auel, Jean M. ★*The Clan of the Cave Bear: A Novel*
 Bailey, Paul. *Uncle Rudolf*
 Bell, Ted. *Overkill: An Alex Hawke Novel*
 Cherezinska, Elzbieta. *The Widow Queen*
 Connolly, John. *The Nameless Ones*
 Cusk, Rachel. *Kudos*
 Dunnett, Dorothy. *Niccolo Rising*
 Eco, Umberto. *Baudolino*
 Eco, Umberto. *The Island of the Day Before*
 Fleming, Ian. *From Russia with Love*
 Furst, Alan. *The Foreign Correspondent: A Novel*
 Gaynor, Hazel. *Three Words for Goodbye*
 Hemingway, Ernest. ★*The Sun Also Rises*
 Ishiguro, Kazuo. *The Unconsoled*
 James, Henry. *Complete Stories, 1864-1874*
 James, Henry. *Complete Stories, 1874-1884*
 James, Henry. *Complete Stories, 1884-1891*
 James, Henry. *Complete Stories, 1892-1898*
 James, Henry. *Complete Stories, 1898-1910*
 James, Henry. *Daisy Miller*
 Jones, Sherry. *Four Sisters, All Queens*
 Khadra, Yasmina. ★*Khalil: A Novel*
 Khoury, Raymond. *Empire of Lies*
 Lunde, Maja. *The End of the Ocean: A Novel*
 McFadden, Bernice L. *The Book of Harlan*
 Mina, Denise. *Conviction*
 Murakami, Haruki. *Colorless Tsukuru Tazaki and His Years of Pilgrimage*
 Nicholls, David. *US: A Novel*
 Orringer, Julie. ★*The Invisible Bridge: A Novel*
 Pears, Iain. *Stone's Fall*
 Porter, Henry. *The Old Enemy*
 Putney, Mary Jo. *Once a Soldier*
 Rachman, Tom. *The Italian Teacher*
 Rooney, Kathleen. ★*Cher Ami and Major Whittlesey*
 Saylor, Steven. *The Seven Wonders: A Novel of the Ancient World*
 Saylor, Steven. *The Triumph of Caesar: A Novel of Ancient Rome*
 Sebald, Winfried Georg. ★*Austerlitz*
 Shaara, Jeff. *The Rising Tide: A Novel of World War II*
 Shaara, Jeff. *The Steel Wave: A Novel of World War II*
 Sharratt, Mary. *Revelations*
 Soderberg, Alexander. *The Other Son: A Sophie Brinkmann Novel*
 Toibin, Colm. ★*The Magician: A Novel*

 Willis, Connie. ★*Doomsday Book*
 Wilson, Daniel H. *The Clockwork Dynasty: A Novel*
EUROPEAN AFRICANS
 Coetzee, J. M. *Summertime: Scenes from a Provincial Life*
 Naipaul, V. S. *Guerrillas*
EUROPEAN AMERICAN WOMEN
 Alam, Rumaan. *That Kind of Mother: A Novel*
EUROPEAN AMERICANS
 Gurganus, Allan. *White People: Stories and Novellas*
EUROPEAN RENAISSANCE
 Eco, Umberto. ★*The Name of the Rose*
 Follett, Ken. *World Without End*
 Rice, Anne. *The Vampire Armand*
 Stone, Irving. ★*The Agony and the Ecstasy: A Biographical Novel of Michelangelo*
EUROPEANS IN AFRICA
 Couto, Mia. *The Sword and the Spear*
EUROPEANS IN INDIA
 Jhabvala, Ruth Prawer. *At the End of the Century: The Stories of Ruth Prawer Jhabvala.*
EUROPEANS IN INDONESIA
 Conrad, Joseph. *Victory: An Island Tale*
★*The **Eustace** Diamonds*. Trollope, Anthony
EUTHANASIA
 Sem-Sandberg, Steve. *The Chosen Ones: A Novel*
★***Eva** Luna*. Allende, Isabel
EVACUATION OF CIVILIANS
 Morton, Kate. *The Distant Hours: A Novel*
Evan Smoak thrillers [Series]. Hurwitz, Gregg Andrew
EVANGELISTS
 Cleeves, Ann. *The Long Call*
 Lewis, Sinclair. ★*Elmer Gantry*
 Smith, Julie. ★*Mean Woman Blues*
 Stark, Richard. *Comeback*
Evanovich, Janet
 ★*Game On: Tempting Twenty-Eight*
 Look Alive Twenty-Five
 One for the Money
 Turbo Twenty-Three
Evanovich, Stephanie
 Under the Table
Evans, Danielle
 ★*The Office of Historical Corrections: A Novella and Stories*
Evans, Diana
 Ordinary People: A Novel
Evans, Nicholas
 ★*The Horse Whisperer: A Novel*
Evaristo, Bernardine
 ★*Girl, Woman, Other*
Eve Ronin novels [Series]. Goldberg, Lee
Eve Rossi novels [Series]. Pintoff, Stefanie
★*The **Evening** and the Morning*. Follett, Ken
★***Evening** in Paradise: More Stories*. Berlin, Lucia
*The **Evening** Road*. Hunt, Laird
*The **Evening** Star: A Novel*. McMurtry, Larry
Eventide. Haruf, Kent
***Ever** Faithful*. Barnett, Karen

Everett, Elizabeth
  ★*A Lady's Formula for Love*
Everett, Percival L.
  Erasure: A Novel
  God's Country
  I Am Not Sidney Poitier
EVERGLADES, FLORIDA
  Hiaasen, Carl. *Nature Girl*
  Hiaasen, Carl. *Skinny Dip: A Novel*
  MacDonald, John D. *The Long Lavender Look*
  Matthiessen, Peter. *Shadow Country: A New Rendering of the Watson Legend*
  Russell, Karen. ★*Swamplandia!*
Every Breath. Sparks, Nicholas
Every Broken Trust: A Mystery. Rodriguez, Linda
Every Day Is for the Thief. Cole, Teju
★*Every Fifteen Minutes.* Scottoline, Lisa
★*Every Heart a Doorway.* McGuire, Seanan
Every Hidden Fear: A Skeet Bannion Mystery. Rodriguez, Linda
Every Last Secret. Torre, A. R.
Every Last Secret: A Mystery. Rodriguez, Linda
Every Man Dies Alone. Fallada, Hans
Every Man for Himself. Bainbridge, Beryl
Every Note Played. Genova, Lisa
Every Now and Then. Kagen, Lesley
★*Everybody's Fool.* Russo, Richard
Everybody's Son. Umrigar, Thrity N.
EVERYDAY LIFE
  Gallen, Michelle. *Big Girl, Small Town: A Novel*
  Herbert, Julian. *Bring Me the Head of Quentin Tarantino: Stories*
  Horrocks, Caitlin. *Life Among the Terranauts*
  Knausgaard, Karl Ove. *The Morning Star*
  Tyler, Anne. ★*Redhead by the Side of the Road*
Everyman. Conner, M. Shelly
★*Everyman.* Roth, Philip
Everyone in This Room Will Someday Be Dead. Austin, Emily
Everyone Knows You Go Home. Sylvester, Natalia
Everyone Knows Your Mother Is a Witch. Galchen, Rivka
★*Everything I Never Told You: A Novel.* Ng, Celeste
★*Everything Inside: Stories.* Danticat, Edwidge
Everything Is Illuminated: A Novel. Foer, Jonathan Safran
Everything Under. Johnson, Daisy
Everything You Have Is Mine. Scoppettone, Sandra
★*Everywhere You Don't Belong: A Novel.* Bump, Gabriel
EVIDENCE (LAW)
  Smith, B. J. *Crow's Landing: A Novel*
Evidence trilogy [Series]. Banville, John
Evison, Jonathan
  All About Lulu: A Novel
  ★*Lawn Boy: A Novel*
  Legends of the North Cascades: A Novel
  The Revised Fundamentals of Caregiving: A Novel
  ★*Small World*
  West of Here: A Novel
EVOLUTION
  Clarke, Arthur C. ★*Childhood's End*
  Crichton, Michael. *Prey: A Novel*
  Wilson, Daniel H. *The Andromeda Evolution: A Novel*

★*Evvie Drake Starts Over: A Novel.* Holmes, Linda
Ewert Grens thrillers [Series]. Roslund, Anders
The Ex Hex. Sterling, Erin
★*The Ex Talk.* Solomon, Rachel Lynn
EXCAVATION
  Cotterill, Colin. *Slash and Burn: A Dr. Siri Mystery Set in Laos*
EXCAVATIONS (ARCHAEOLOGY)
  Stabenow, Dana. *So Sure of Death: A Liam Campbell Mystery*
★*Excellent Women.* Pym, Barbara
EXCHANGE STUDENTS
  Fitzpatrick, Lydia. *Lights All Night Long: A Novel*
  Thomas, Russ. *Nighthawking*
The Execution of Noa P. Singleton: A Novel. Silver, Elizabeth L.
★*The Executioner's Song.* Mailer, Norman
EXECUTIONS AND EXECUTIONERS
  Block, Lawrence. *All the Flowers Are Dying*
  Dickens, Charles. ★*A Tale of Two Cities*
  Draven, Grace. *Phoenix Unbound*
  Estleman, Loren D. ★*The Master Executioner*
  Gregory, Philippa. *The Last Tudor*
  Li, Yiyun. *The Vagrants: A Novel*
  Potzsch, Oliver. *The Beggar King*
  Potzsch, Oliver. *The Hangman's Daughter: A Historical Novel*
  Potzsch, Oliver. *The Play of Death*
  Wiesel, Elie. ★*Dawn*
  Wolfe, Gene. *The Claw of the Conciliator*
EXECUTIVES
  Chancy, Myriam J. A. ★*What Storm, What Thunder*
  Landon, Sydney. *Wishing for Us*
  Lewis, Sinclair. *Dodsworth*
  Lightman, Alan P. *The Diagnosis*
★*Exhalation: Stories.* Chiang, Ted
EXHIBITIONS
  Gates, Eva. *A Death Long Overdue*
EXILE (PUNISHMENT)
  Adams, Hope. *Dangerous Women*
  Ahmad, Jamil. *The Wandering Falcon*
  Brockway, Connie. *So Enchanting*
  Paul, Gill. ★*The Lost Daughter*
  Suri, Tasha. *The Jasmine Throne*
EXILES
  Achebe, Chinua. ★*Things Fall Apart*
  Anders, Charlie Jane. ★*The City in the Middle of the Night*
  Bailey, Paul. *Uncle Rudolf*
  Bear, Elizabeth. *Range of Ghosts*
  Benedetti, Mario. *Springtime in a Broken Mirror*
  Dewes, J. S. *The Last Watch*
  Ghosh, Amitav. *The Glass Palace*
  Gilman, Carolyn Ives. *Dark Orbit*
  Green, Jocelyn. *The Mark of the King*
  Grenville, Kate. *The Secret River*
  Hairston, Andrea. *Master of Poisons*
  Harris, Robert. *An Officer and a Spy*
  Matar, Hisham. *In the Country of Men*
  Miller, Madeline. ★*Circe*
  Miller, Madeline. *The Song of Achilles*
  Nabokov, Vladimir Vladimirovich. *Look at the Harlequins!*
  Nabokov, Vladimir Vladimirovich. *Pnin*

Penelope, L. *Song of Blood and Stone*
Schami, Rafik. *Sophia: Or the Beginning of All Tales*
Sebald, Winfried Georg. ★*Austerlitz*
Sebald, Winfried Georg. *The Emigrants*
Sofer, Dalia. *Man of My Time*
Stirling, S. M. *A Meeting at Corvallis*
Van der Vliet Oloomi, Azareen. *Call Me Zebra*
Wellington, David. *Positive*
Wolfe, Gene. *The Citadel of the Autarch*
Wolfe, Gene. *The Claw of the Conciliator*
Existence. Brin, David

EXISTENTIALISM
Camus, Albert. ★*The Fall*
Hage, Rawi. *Beirut Hellfire Society: A Novel*
Pava, Sergio de la. *A Naked Singularity*
Sartre, Jean Paul. *The Age of Reason*
Sartre, Jean Paul. ★*Nausea*
Exit Ghost. Roth, Philip
Exit Music. Rankin, Ian
★*Exit West: A Novel*. Hamid, Mohsin

EXMOOR, ENGLAND
Blackmore, R. D. *Lorna Doone: A Romance of Exmoor*

EXOBIOLOGY
Powers, Richard. ★*Bewilderment: A Novel*
★*Exodus*. Uris, Leon

EXORCISM
Blatty, William Peter. ★*The Exorcist*
Hendrix, Grady. *My Best Friend's Exorcism*
★*The Exorcist*. Blatty, William Peter

EXORCISTS
Hendrix, Grady. *My Best Friend's Exorcism*
Expanse [Series]. Corey, James S. A.

EXPATRIATE AUTHORS
McLain, Paula. *The Paris Wife: A Novel*

EXPATRIATE WOMEN
Giordano, Mario. ★*Auntie Poldi and the Lost Madonna*

EXPATRIATES
Baldwin, James. ★*Giovanni's Room*
Bernhard, Emilia. *The Books of the Dead*
Crouch, Katie. *Embassy Wife*
Furst, Alan. *The Foreign Correspondent: A Novel*
Garcia Marquez, Gabriel. ★*Strange Pilgrims: Twelve Stories*
Hemingway, Ernest. ★*The Sun Also Rises*
Jones, Cherie. *How the One-Armed Sister Sweeps Her House*
Kupersmith, Violet. ★*Build Your House Around My Body*
Leavitt, David. *The Two Hotel Francforts: A Novel*
Miller, Henry. ★*Tropic of Cancer*
Osborne, Lawrence. *The Glass Kingdom: A Novel*
Portis, Charles. ★*Gringos: A Novel*
Shteyngart, Gary. *The Russian Debutante's Handbook*
Tanabe, Karin. *A Hundred Suns*
Vargas Llosa, Mario. *The Bad Girl*
Waugh, Evelyn. *The Loved One: An Anglo-American Tragedy*
★*The Expats: a Novel*. Pavone, Chris

EXPECTATION (PSYCHOLOGY)
Andreades, Daphne Palasi. *Brown Girls*
Crace, Jim. *Quarantine*
Dang, Catherine. *Nice Girls*

Daria, Alexis. ★*A Lot Like Adios*
Ho, Lauren. *Last Tang Standing*
Hoang, Helen. ★*The Heart Principle*
Ishiguro, Kazuo. *The Unconsoled*
Jalaluddin, Uzma. ★*Ayesha at Last*
Lalli, Sonya. *Serena Singh Flips the Script*
Murata, Sayaka. *Earthlings: A Novel*
Rogers, Morgan Callan. ★*Honey Girl*
Roth, Philip. ★*Portnoy's Complaint*
Tieu, Julie. *The Donut Trap*
Whittall, Zoe. *The Spectacular: A Novel*
Wiseman, Beth. *Listening to Love*

EXPEDITIONS
Preston, Douglas J. *Old Bones*
Pulley, Natasha. *The Bedlam Stacks*
VanderMeer, Jeff. *Acceptance: A Novel*
Vandermeer, Jeff. ★*Annihilation: A Novel*
VanderMeer, Jeff. *Authority: A Novel*

EXPERIMENTAL DRUGS
Glynn, Alan. *Receptor*

EXPERIMENTAL FICTION
Barth, John. *Chimera*
Barth, John. ★*The Floating Opera*
Barth, John. *The Last Voyage of Somebody the Sailor*
Barth, John. ★*The Sot-Weed Factor*
Barthelme, Donald. *Sixty Stories*
Coover, Robert. *Going for a Beer: Selected Short Fictions*
Danielewski, Mark Z. ★*The Familiar.; Volume 4,*
Danielewski, Mark Z. ★*House of Leaves: A Novel*
Danielewski, Mark Z. *Only Revolutions*
Dos Passos, John. *Manhattan Transfer*
Ellmann, Lucy. *Ducks, Newburyport*
Gentill, Sulari. *Crossing the Lines*
Hall, Steven. *Maxwell's Demon*
Joyce, James. ★*Finnegans Wake*
Levin, Adam. *Bubblegum*
Mitchell, David. ★*Cloud Atlas: A Novel*
Pava, Sergio de la. *A Naked Singularity*
Pava, Sergio de la. *Personae: A Novel*
Pynchon, Thomas. *Inherent Vice*
Stridsberg, Sara. *Valerie: Or the Faculty of Dreams : Amendment to the Theory of Sexuality*
Woolf, Virginia. *Jacob's Room*
Woolf, Virginia. *The Waves*

EXPERIMENTAL MUSIC
Hajdu, David. *Adrianne Geffel: A Fiction*

EXPERIMENTS
Boyle, T. Coraghessan. *The Terranauts*
Horrocks, Caitlin. *Life Among the Terranauts*
Vidich, Paul. *The Coldest Warrior*
Wilson, Carter. *Dead Girl in 2a*
Yang, JY. *The Descent of Monsters*

EXPLOITATION
Brown, Pierce. *Morning Star*
Wood, Shelley. *The Quintland Sisters*

EXPLORATION
Chiang, Ted. ★*Exhalation: Stories*
Gappah, Petina. ★*Out of Darkness, Shining Light*

Starling, Caitlin. *The Luminous Dead*

EXPLORERS
Gilman, Charlotte Perkins. *Herland*
Lalami, Laila. ★*The Moor's Account: A Novel*

EXPLOSIONS
Albom, Mitch. *The Stranger in the Lifeboat*
Box, C. J. *Savage Run*
Woodrell, Daniel. *The Maid's Version: A Novel*

EXPLOSIVES
Pobi, Robert. *Under Pressure*

Exposure. Dunmore, Helen

Extence, Gavin
The Universe Versus Alex Woods

EXTENDED FAMILIES
Araghi, Alireza Taheri. ★*The Immortals of Tehran*
Castillo, Elaine. *America Is Not the Heart*
Erdrich, Louise. *Love Medicine: A Novel*
Ghaffari, Rabeah. ★*To Keep the Sun Alive*
Goldbloom, Goldie. *On Division*
Joukhadar, Zeyn. ★*The Thirty Names of Night: A Novel*
Lessing, Doris May. *The Sweetest Dream*
Seth, Vikram. ★*A Suitable Boy: A Novel*
Ward, Jesmyn. ★*Sing, Unburied, Sing*

EXTINCT CITIES
Delany, Samuel R. *Dhalgren*
Golden, Christopher. *The Pandora Room: A Novel*

EXTINCTION (BIOLOGY)
Saramago, Jose. ★*The Cave*

EXTORTION
Baldacci, David. ★*A Gambling Man*
Bourne, Joanna. *Rogue Spy*
Chandler, Raymond. ★*The Big Sleep*
Christie, Agatha. ★*The Murder of Roger Ackroyd: A Hercule Poirot Mystery*
Clinch, Jon. *Marley: A Novel*
Dare, Tessa. *When a Scot Ties the Knot*
Dickey, Eric Jerome. ★*Bad Men and Wicked Women*
Goddard, Robert. ★*Into the Blue*
Grafton, Sue. *Y Is for Yesterday*
Gruber, Michael. *The Forgery of Venus: A Novel*
Gundar-Goshen, Ayelet. *Waking Lions*
Harris, E. Lynn. *Basketball Jones: A Novel*
Harrison, Thea. *Dragon Bound*
Hiaasen, Carl. *Strip Tease: A Novel*
Jones, Stephen Mack. *Dead of Winter*
Lansdale, Joe R. *Honky Tonk Samurai*
Leon, Donna. *The Golden Egg*
Macdonald, Ross. *Sleeping Beauty*
Meltzer, Brad. *The Tenth Justice*
Murdoch, Iris. *The Nice and the Good*
Parks, Brad. *Say Nothing: A Novel*
Pronzini, Bill. *Nemesis*
Randisi, Robert J. *Hey There (You with the Gun in Your Hand): A Rat Pack Mystery*
Roberts, Nora. *Chesapeake Blue*
Rose, M. J. ★*Cartier's Hope*
Sanders, Lawrence. *McNally's Dilemma*
Sanders, Lawrence. *McNally's Secret*

Sandford, John. ★*Silken Prey*
Shepard, Sam. *The One Inside*
Spark, Muriel. *Aiding & Abetting*
Spark, Muriel. ★*A Far Cry from Kensington*
Spark, Muriel. ★*Memento Mori*
Spiegelman, Peter. *Black Maps*
Stewart, Amy. ★*Girl Waits with Gun*
Sullivan, Emily. *The Rebel and the Rake*
Sullivan, Michael J. *Theft of Swords*
Vargas Llosa, Mario. ★*The Discreet Hero*
Woods, Stuart. *The Money Shot*
Youers, Rio. *Lola on Fire*

EXTRAMARITAL AFFAIRS
Abbott, Megan E. *Bury Me Deep*
Ackerman, Elliot. *Red Dress in Black and White*
Alcott, Kate. *A Touch of Stardust*
Atkinson, Kate. *One Good Turn: A Novel*
Atwood, Margaret. *Life Before Man*
Austin, Finola. *Bronte's Mistress*
Ausubel, Ramona. *Sons and Daughters of Ease and Plenty*
Bair, Kristin. *Agatha Arch Is Afraid of Everything*
Banks, Russell. *Continental Drift*
Barnes, Djuna. ★*Nightwood*
Beagin, Jen. ★*Vacuum in the Dark: A Novel*
Bhuvaneswar, Chaya. *White Dancing Elephants: Stories*
Bilal, Parker. *The Ghost Runner*
Bryant, Niobia. *Message from a Mistress*
Cheek, Chip. *Cape May*
Cobbs Hoffman, Elizabeth. *The Hamilton Affair*
Cook, Thomas H. *The Chatham School Affair*
Crossan, Sarah. *Here Is the Beehive*
Dreiser, Theodore. ★*Sister Carrie*
Dubus, Andre. *Dirty Love*
Durrell, Lawrence. ★*Justine*
Enright, Anne. *The Forgotten Waltz*
Essbaum, Jill Alexander. *Hausfrau: A Novel*
Evans, Diana. *Ordinary People: A Novel*
Faulks, Sebastian. ★*Birdsong*
Faulks, Sebastian. *On Green Dolphin Street: A Novel*
Ferraris, Zoe. *Kingdom of Strangers: A Novel*
Finder, Joseph. ★*Judgment*
Flaubert, Gustave. ★*Madame Bovary: Provincial Ways*
Ford, Ford Madox. ★*The Good Soldier: A Tale of Passion*
French, Nicci. ★*The Lying Room*
Gailey, Sarah. *The Echo Wife*
Gordimer, Nadine. ★*My Son's Story*
Greene, Graham. ★*The End of the Affair*
Greene, Graham. ★*The Heart of the Matter*
Grossman, David. *Be My Knife*
Hardy, Thomas. ★*Jude the Obscure*
Hart, Josephine. *Damage: A Novel*
Hawke, Ethan. *A Bright Ray of Darkness*
Hilderbrand, Elin. ★*28 Summers*
Hilderbrand, Elin. ★*Winter in Paradise: A Novel*
Horan, Nancy. *Loving Frank: A Novel*
Itami, Emily. *Fault Lines: A Novel*
James, Henry. *The Golden Bowl*
Jhabvala, Ruth Prawer. ★*Heat and Dust*

Jong, Erica. ★*Fear of Flying: A Novel*
Kaplan, Mitchell James. *Rhapsody*
Lansdale, Joe R. *More Better Deals*
Lawrence, D. H. ★*Lady Chatterley's Lover*
Le Carre, John. ★*Tinker, Tailor, Soldier, Spy*
Leavitt, David. *The Two Hotel Francforts: A Novel*
Lescroart, John T. *Guilt*
Lessing, Doris May. *A Proper Marriage*
Logan, T. M. *The Vacation*
Lurie, Alison. *Foreign Affairs*
MacLeod, Alison. *Tenderness*
Mandel, Emily St. John. *The Singer's Gun: A Novel*
Mantel, Hilary. ★*Bring up the Bodies: A Novel*
Masad, Ilana. *All My Mother's Lovers: A Novel*
McCall Smith, Alexander. *In the Company of Cheerful Ladies*
McLaughlin, Danielle. *The Art of Falling*
Meyer, Deon. *Icarus*
Miller, Sue. ★*Monogamy*
Morrison, Toni. *Jazz*
Mosley, Walter. *And Sometimes I Wonder About You: A Leonid McGill Mystery*
Murakami, Haruki. *South of the Border, West of the Sun*
Nabokov, Vladimir Vladimirovich. *King, Queen, Knave: A Novel*
Naipaul, V. S. *A Bend in the River*
Osondu, E. C. *This House Is Not for Sale: A Novel*
Patchett, Ann. ★*Commonwealth*
Patterson, Molly. *Rebellion*
Perez-Reverte, Arturo. *What We Become*
Sanders, Lawrence. ★*The Fourth Deadly Sin*
Scott, Stephanie. *What's Left of Me Is Yours: A Novel*
Seton, Anya. *Katherine*
Shreve, Anita. *Fortune's Rocks: A Novel*
Shriver, Lionel. *The Post-Birthday World*
Simenon, Georges. *Maigret and the Black Sheep*
Simenon, Georges. ★*Maigret and the Saturday Caller*
Singer, Isaac Bashevis. ★*The Magician of Lublin*
Smith, Zadie. *On Beauty*
Sontag, Susan. *The Volcano Lover: A Romance*
Spark, Muriel. ★*Memento Mori*
Spencer, Sally. *The Dead Hand of History*
Stegner, Wallace. ★*Angle of Repose*
Steinhauer, Olen. *The Cairo Affair*
Strout, Elizabeth. *Amy and Isabelle: A Novel*
Swinson, Kiki. *A Gangster and a Gentleman*
Swinson, Kiki. *Who's Wife Extraordinaire Now*
Tolstoy, Leo. ★*Anna Karenina*
Turow, Scott. *Presumed Innocent*
Updike, John. *Licks of Love: Short Stories and a Sequel*
Updike, John. *Memories of the Ford Administration: A Novel*
Urquhart, Jane. *The Night Stages: A Novel*
Waller, Robert James. ★*The Bridges of Madison County*
Westlake, Donald E. *Memory*
Extraordinary adventures of the Athena Club [Series]. Goss, Theodora
★*The **Extraordinary** Life of Sam Hell*. Dugoni, Robert
*An **Extraordinary** Lord*. Harrington, Anna
★*An **Extraordinary** Union*. Cole, Alyssa
EXTREME ENVIRONMENTS
Weir, Andy. *The Martian*

Extremely Loud and Incredibly Close. Foer, Jonathan Safran
EXTREMISM
Lewis, Sinclair. ★*It Can't Happen Here*
Richler, Mordecai. *Barney's Version: A Novel*
Rushdie, Salman. *Shalimar the Clown: A Novel*
EXTREMISTS
Hunter, Stephen. *Game of Snipers: A Bob Lee Swagger Novel*
EYE
Cleave, Paul. *A Killer Harvest: A Thriller*
★*The **Eye** in the Door*. Barker, Pat
*The **Eye** of God*. Rollins, James
Eye of the Needle. Follett, Ken
Eye of the Storm. Higgins, Jack
*The **Eyes** of the Queen*. Clements, Oliver
*The **Eyre** Affair: A Novel*. Fforde, Jasper

F

Faber, Michel
The Book of Strange New Things
The Crimson Petal and the White
Fabry, Chris
Looking into You
The Promise of Jesse Woods
War Room: Prayer Is a Powerful Weapon
*The **Face** of a Stranger*. Perry, Anne
FACTORIES
Bolano, Roberto. ★*2666*
Erdrich, Louise. ★*The Night Watchman: A Novel*
Gaskell, Elizabeth Cleghorn. ★*North and South*
Takamura, Kaoru. ★*Lady Joker*
FACTORY OWNERS
Gaskell, Elizabeth Cleghorn. ★*North and South*
★*Fahrenheit 451*. Bradbury, Ray
FAILURE (PSYCHOLOGY)
Carver, Raymond. *What We Talk About When We Talk About Love: Stories*
Ferris, Joshua. *A Calling for Charlie Barnes*
Fitzgerald, F. Scott. ★*The Last Tycoon: An Unfinished Novel*
Ford, Richard. *A Multitude of Sins: Stories*
Korelitz, Jean Hanff. ★*The Plot*
Lipsyte, Sam. *The Ask*
★*Fair and Tender Ladies*. Smith, Lee
*The **Fair** Fight: A Novel*. Freeman, Anna
★*Fair Warning*. Connelly, Michael
FAIRIES
Bear, Elizabeth. *Blood and Iron: A Novel of the Promethean Age*
Bear, Elizabeth. *Ink and Steel: A Novel of the Promethean Age*
Brooks, Terry. *Child of Light*
Clarke, Susanna. ★*Jonathan Strange & Mr. Norrell*
Gaiman, Neil. ★*Stardust*
McGuire, Seanan. *Chimes at Midnight: An October Daye Novel*
Roberts, Nora. ★*The Awakening*
Rothfuss, Patrick. ★*The Wise Man's Fear*
Fairmile novels [Series]. Gregory, Philippa

Fairstein, Linda A.
Blood Oath
Entombed
FAIRY TALE AND FOLKLORE-INSPIRED FICTION
Murphy, Julie. *If the Shoe Fits*
Whitten, Hannah. *For the Wolf*
FAIRY TALES
Backman, Fredrik. ★*My Grandmother Asked Me to Tell You She's Sorry: A Novel*
The *Fairy* Tales of Hermann Hesse. Hesse, Hermann
Fairy tales: A series of fantasy novels retelling classic tales [Series]. Dean, Pamela
FAITH
Akhtar, Ayad. *American Dervish: A Novel*
Benjamin, Chloe. ★*The Immortalists: A Novel*
Cossette, Connilyn. ★*Shelter of the Most High*
Gunn, James E. *Transcendental*
Harrison, Mette Ivie. *The Bishop's Wife*
Moniz, Dantiel W. *Milk Blood Heat*
Oe, Kenzaburo. *Somersault: A Novel*
Oyeyemi, Helen. *The Opposite House*
Picoult, Jodi. *Keeping Faith: A Novel*
Smith, Jill Eileen. *Star of Persia: Esther's Story*
Updike, John. *In the Beauty of the Lilies*
West, Monica. *Revival Season: A Novel*
FAITH (CHRISTIANITY)
Brouwer, Sigmund. *Thief of Glory: A Novel*
Butler, Nickolas. *Little Faith: A Novel*
Cather, Willa. ★*Death Comes for the Archbishop*
Donoghue, Emma. ★*The Wonder*
Fabry, Chris. *War Room: Prayer Is a Powerful Weapon*
Goodwin, Bobi Gentry. *Revelation*
Greene, Graham. *The Power and the Glory*
Hatcher, Robin Lee. *Cross My Heart*
Hauck, Rachel. *Once Upon a Prince*
Henry, Patti Callahan. ★*Becoming Mrs. Lewis: The Improbable Love Story of Joy Davidman and C. S. Lewis*
Pearson, Robin W. *A Long Time Comin'*
Rawlings, David. *The Baggage Handler: A Novel*
Robinson, Marilynne. ★*Gilead*
Stewart, Ann Marie. *Stars in the Grass*
Wall, Cara. *The Dearly Beloved: A Novel*
Wiseman, Beth. *Listening to Love*
FAITH (JUDAISM)
Andrews, Mesu. *Of Fire and Lions: A Novel*
FAITH AND REASON
Goldstein, Rebecca. *36 Arguments for the Existence of God: A Work of Fiction*
FAITH HEALING
Bergstrom, Heather Brittain. *Steal the North: A Novel*
FAITH IN MEN
Bohjalian, Chris. *Secrets of Eden: A Novel*
Greene, Graham. *The Power and the Glory*
Reimringer, John. *Vestments*
FAITH IN WOMEN
Austin, Lynn N. *Chasing Shadows*
Faithful Place: A Novel. French, Tana
The *Faithful* Spy: A Novel. Berenson, Alex

Fajardo-Anstine, Kali
★*Sabrina & Corina: Stories*
★*Fake Like Me.* Bourland, Barbara
FAKE NEWS
Goldberg, Lee. *Fake Truth*
Fake Truth. Goldberg, Lee
Falconer. Cheever, John
FALCONERS
Box, C. J. *The Disappeared*
★*The Fall.* Camus, Albert
Fall of Giants. Follett, Ken
The *Fall* of Gondolin. Tolkien, J. R. R.
The *Fall* of Hyperion. Simmons, Dan
★*Fall* Or, Dodge in Hell: A Novel. Stephenson, Neal
Fallada, Hans
Every Man Dies Alone
The *Fallen.* Atkins, Ace
The *Fallen.* Baldacci, David
★*Fallen.* Castillo, Linda
Fallen empire [Series]. Draven, Grace
Fallen Land. Brown, Taylor
Fallen women [Series]. Chase, Loretta Lynda
★*Fallen: a Novel.* Slaughter, Karin
Falling for You. Wade, Becky
Falling in Love: A Commissario Guido Brunetti Mystery. Leon, Donna
Falling into Bed with a Duke. Heath, Lorraine
Falling Man: A Novel. DeLillo, Don
Falling Out of Time. Grossman, David
Fallon, Siobhan
You Know When the Men Are Gone
FALLS (ACCIDENTS)
Gerritsen, Tess. *Choose Me*
Hill Gumbao, Toni. *The Summer of Dead Toys*
The *Falls: a Novel.* Oates, Joyce Carol
The *Falls: an Inspector Rebus Novel.* Rankin, Ian
FALSE CONFESSIONS (LAW)
Koryta, Michael. ★*How It Happened*
FALSE IMPRISONMENT
Baldacci, David. *Redemption*
Baldwin, James. ★*If Beale Street Could Talk*
Dodd, Christina. *Virtue Falls*
Jones, Tayari. ★*An American Marriage: A Novel*
Spencer, Sally. ★*Echoes of the Dead*
FALSE MEMORY SYNDROME
Crouch, Blake. *Recursion*
FALSE PERSONATION
Ferris, Joshua. *To Rise Again at a Decent Hour: A Novel*
French, Nicci. *Tuesday's Gone*
Gass, William H. *Middle C*
Mengiste, Maaza. ★*The Shadow King: A Novel*
Ware, Ruth. *The Death of Mrs. Westaway*
FAME
Angelo, Megan. *Followers*
Benaron, Naomi. *Running the Rift: A Novel*
Bergman, Megan Mayhew. *Almost Famous Women: Stories*
Boyd, William. *Trio*
Boyne, John. ★*A Ladder to the Sky*
Brodie, Emma. *Songs in Ursa Major*

Castellani, Christopher. *Leading Men: A Novel*
Cleeves, Ann. *Wild Fire*
Currie, Ron. *Flimsy Little Plastic Miracles: A True Story*
Enright, Anne. *Actress: A Novel*
Green, Hank. *An Absolutely Remarkable Thing: A Novel*
Guillory, Jasmine. ★*While We Were Dating*
Hall, Alexis. ★*Boyfriend Material*
Lane, Byron. ★*A Star Is Bored*
Leonard, Elmore. *The Hot Kid*
Mandel, Emily St. John. ★*Station Eleven*
Mitchell, David. ★*Utopia Avenue: A Novel*
North, Anna. *The Life and Death of Sophie Stark*
Parker, Lucy. *Battle Royal*
Phillips, Susan Elizabeth. *First Star I See Tonight*
Reid, Taylor Jenkins. ★*Daisy Jones & The Six: A Novel*
Roth, Philip. *Zuckerman Unbound*

FAMILIAL LOVE

Alenyikov, Michael. *Ivan and Misha: Stories*
Bourdeaut, Olivier. *Waiting for Bojangles: A Novel*
Emezi, Akwaeke. ★*The Death of Vivek Oji*
Fowler, Karen Joy. ★*We Are All Completely Beside Ourselves*
Glass, Julia. ★*Three Junes*
Lutz, Lisa. *The Spellman Files: A Novel*
McCarthy, Cormac. ★*The Road*
Roy, Anuradha. *An Atlas of Impossible Longing*
Wilson, Kevin. *Nothing to See Here*

Familiar novels [Series]. Danielewski, Mark Z.
★*The **Familiar**; Volume 4.* Danielewski, Mark Z.

FAMILIES

Abulhawa, Susan. *The Blue Between Sky and Water*
Adlakha, Sarah. *She Wouldn't Change a Thing*
Agee, Jonis. *The Bones of Paradise*
Akunin, B. *Sister Pelagia and the White Bulldog: A Mystery*
Alarcon, Daniel. *The King Is Always Above the People: Stories*
Alvar, Mia. *In the Country: Stories*
Alvarez, Julia. ★*Afterlife: A Novel*
Apostol, Gina. *Gun Dealers' Daughter: A Novel*
Atkinson, Kate. *Human Croquet*
Attenberg, Jami. *The Middlesteins*
Austen, Jane. *Mansfield Park*
Austen, Jane. ★*Pride and Prejudice*
Baker, Jo. *Longbourn*
Balzano, Marco. *I'm Staying Here*
Banks, Iain. *The Crow Road*
Banner, Catherine. *The House at the Edge of Night: A Novel*
Barthelme, Frederick. *Bob the Gambler*
Bauman, Bruce. ★*Broken Sleep: An American Dream*
Beckerman, Hannah. *If Only I Could Tell You*
Benjamin, Chloe. ★*The Immortalists: A Novel*
Berry, Wendell. ★*That Distant Land: The Collected Stories of Wendell Berry*
Betts, Doris. *Souls Raised from the Dead: A Novel*
Binder, L. Annette. *The Vanishing Sky*
Blume, Judy. *In the Unlikely Event*
Bohjalian, Chris. *The Night Strangers: A Novel*
Bordas, Camille. *How to Behave in a Crowd*
Box, C. J. *Trophy Hunt: A Joe Pickett Novel*
Box, C. J. *Winterkill: A Novel*

Bradbury, Jamey. *The Wild Inside: A Novel*
Bradbury, Ray. ★*Dandelion Wine: A Novel*
Brown, Rosellen. ★*Before and After*
Buck, Pearl S. *The Good Earth*
Bulawayo, NoViolet. *We Need New Names: A Novel*
Butler, Sarah. *Ten Things I've Learnt About Love: A Novel*
Byrne, Trevor. *Ghosts and Lightning*
Cash, Wiley. *The Last Ballad: A Novel*
Chen, Mike. *Here and Now and Then*
Choi, Ann Y. K. *Kay's Lucky Coin Variety*
Choi, Yoon. *Skinship: Stories*
Cleary, Jon. *The Sundowners*
Clegg, Bill. *The End of the Day*
Conner, M. Shelly. *Everyman*
Coplin, Amanda. *The Orchardist*
Cordova, Zoraida. *The Inheritance of Orquidea Divina*
Crane, Stephen. *Maggie: A Girl of the Streets*
Cruz, Angie. *Dominicana: A Novel*
Danielewski, Mark Z. ★*House of Leaves: A Novel*
Daria, Alexis. ★*A Lot Like Adios*
Davis, Lindsey. *A Body in the Bathhouse*
Dean, Margaret Lazarus. *The Time It Takes to Fall*
Dee, Jonathan. *The Privileges: A Novel*
Dibdin, Michael. *Ratking*
Doctorow, E. L. ★*Ragtime*
Dodd, Christina. *Strangers She Knows*
Drabble, Margaret. *The Witch of Exmoor*
Dupont, Eric. *The American Fiancee: A Novel*
Earley, Tony. *Jim the Boy: A Novel*
Ebershoff, David. *The 19th Wife: A Novel*
Eisenberg, Deborah. *The Twilight of the Superheroes*
Engel, Patricia. ★*Infinite Country*
Enger, Lin. *The High Divide: A Novel*
Enjeti, Anjali. ★*The Parted Earth*
Erdrich, Louise. ★*Larose*
Esquivel, Laura. ★*Like Water for Chocolate: A Novel in Monthly Installments, with Recipes, Romances, and Home Remedies*
Feng, Linda Rui. *Swimming Back to Trout River*
Ferber, Edna. *So Big*
Flanagan, Richard. *The Living Sea of Waking Dreams*
Flournoy, Angela. *The Turner House*
Follett, Ken. *Fall of Giants*
Follett, Ken. *Winter of the World*
Ford, Richard. ★*Independence Day*
Frankel, Laurie. *This Is How It Always Is*
Franzen, Jonathan. ★*Crossroads*
Fuentes, Carlos. *The Crystal Frontier: A Novel in Nine Stories*
Garcia Marquez, Gabriel. ★*One Hundred Years of Solitude*
Garcia, Cristina. *The Aguero Sisters*
Ginzburg, Natalia. *A Family Lexicon*
Giordano, Paolo. *Like Family*
Gnuse, A. J. *Girl in the Walls: A Novel*
Godwin, Gail. *Old Lovegood Girls*
Gordimer, Nadine. ★*July's People*
Greenidge, Kaitlyn. *We Love You, Charlie Freeman: A Novel*
Grey, Zane. *Woman of the Frontier: A Western Story*
Groff, Lauren. ★*Fates and Furies*
Gunesekera, Romesh. ★*Suncatcher: A Novel*

Hadley, Tessa. *Bad Dreams and Other Stories*

Hall, Tarquin. *The Case of the Love Commandos: From the Files of Vish Puri, India's Most Private Investigator*

Haratischvili, Nino. *The Eighth Life: (For Brilka)*

Hardiman, Rebecca. *Good Eggs*

Harding Thornton, Christina. *Pickard County Atlas*

Harris, C. S. *Good Time Coming*

Harrison, Mette Ivie. *The Bishop's Wife*

Hart, John. *Down River*

Hawthorne, Nathaniel. ★*The House of the Seven Gables*

Hemmings, Kaui Hart. *The Possibilities: A Novel*

Henkin, Joshua. *Morningside Heights*

Hilderbrand, Elin. ★*Summer of '69*

Horn, Dara. *Eternal Life: A Novel*

Hunting, Helena. *Handle with Care*

Jackson, Joshilyn. *Never Have I Ever*

Jackson-Brown, Angela. ★*When Stars Rain Down: A Novel*

Jen, Gish. ★*The Resisters*

Jiles, Paulette. *News of the World: A Novel*

Joyce, James. ★*A Portrait of the Artist as a Young Man*

Kamal, Soniah. *Unmarriageable: A Novel*

Kantra, Virginia. *Beth & Amy*

Kawaguchi, Toshikazu. *Before the Coffee Gets Cold*

Kenney, John. *Talk to Me*

King, Stephen. *Cujo*

Krivak, Andrew. *The Signal Flame: A Novel*

Kwan, Kevin. *Rich People Problems*

Lee, Min Jin. ★*Pachinko*

Lim, Roselle. *Natalie Tan's Book of Luck and Fortune*

Llewellyn, Richard. ★*How Green Was My Valley*

Lucashenko, Melissa. *Too Much Lip*

MacLaverty, Bernard. ★*Blank Pages: And Other Stories*

Makumbi, Jennifer Nansubuga. *Kintu*

Malamud, Bernard. *The Assistant*

Marillier, Juliet. *Daughter of the Forest*

Marra, Anthony. *The Tsar of Love and Techno: Stories*

Massey, Sujata. ★*The Bombay Prince*

Maynard, Joyce. *Count the Ways*

McCracken, Elizabeth. *The Souvenir Museum: Stories*

McCullough, Colleen. *The First Man in Rome*

McDowell, Christina. *The Cave Dwellers: A Novel*

Meyer, Philipp. ★*The Son: A Novel*

Moniz, Dantiel W. *Milk Blood Heat*

Moreno-Garcia, Silvia. ★*Gods of Jade and Shadow: A Novel*

Munro, Alice. *The View from Castle Rock: Stories*

Nguyen, Phan Que Mai. ★*The Mountains Sing: A Novel*

Nguyen, Viet Thanh. ★*The Refugees*

Nicholls, David. *US: A Novel*

O'Connor, Flannery. ★*The Violent Bear It Away*

Oates, Joyce Carol. *Because It Is Bitter, and Because It Is My Heart*

Oe, Kenzaburo. ★*A Quiet Life*

Offill, Jenny. *Dept. Of Speculation*

Offill, Jenny. ★*Weather*

Pamuk, Orhan. *Silent House*

Patchett, Ann. *Run*

Perry, Anne. ★*Death in Focus: An Elena Standish Novel*

Piccirilli, Tom. *The Last Kind Words*

Pilcher, Rosamunde. *Coming Home*

Potzsch, Oliver. *The Poisoned Pilgrim: A Hangman's Daughter Tale*

Proulx, Annie. ★*Barkskins: A Novel*

Proulx, Annie. ★*The Shipping News*

Puzo, Mario. *The Last Don*

Quade, Kirstin Valdez. *Night at the Fiestas: Stories*

Quindlen, Anna. *Miller's Valley*

Richardson, Samuel. ★*Pamela: Or, Virtue Rewarded*

Robinson, Marilynne. *Home*

Rojas Contreras, Ingrid. ★*Fruit of the Drunken Tree: A Novel*

Rowell, Rainbow. *Landline*

Roy, Anuradha. *An Atlas of Impossible Longing*

Roy, Arundhati. ★*The God of Small Things*

Rushdie, Salman. *The Moor's Last Sigh*

Rutherfurd, Edward. *London*

Rutherfurd, Edward. *The Rebels of Ireland: The Dublin Saga*

Rutherfurd, Edward. *Russka: The Novel of Russia*

Rutherfurd, Edward. *Sarum: The Novel of England*

Sakey, Marcus. *A Better World*

Sakey, Marcus. *Brilliance*

Saroyan, William. ★*The Human Comedy*

Sayers, Constance. *The Ladies of the Secret Circus*

Saylor, Steven. *Roma: The Novel of Ancient Rome*

Sedaris, David. *Holidays on Ice*

See, Lisa. *The Tea Girl of Hummingbird Lane*

Serpell, Namwali. ★*The Old Drift*

Shanbhag, Vivek. *Ghachar Ghochar*

Shaw, Irwin. *Beggarman, Thief*

Shields, Carol. ★*The Stone Diaries*

Shimotakahara, Leslie. *After the Bloom*

Shin, Ann. *The Last Exiles*

Simpson, Dorothy. *Dead and Gone: An Inspector Luke Thanet Novel.*

Simpson, Mona. *Anywhere but Here*

Singer, Isaac Bashevis. *Collected Stories: A Friend of Kafka to Passions*

Singer, Isaac Bashevis. *Collected Stories: Gimpel the Fool to the Letter Writer*

Smiley, Jane. *Early Warning*

Smith, Lee. *Family Linen*

Smith, Zadie. ★*White Teeth: A Novel*

Snow, C. P. ★*Strangers and Brothers*

Stewart, Amy. ★*Miss Kopp Investigates*

Stewart, Ann Marie. *Stars in the Grass*

Straub, Emma. ★*All Adults Here*

Strout, Elizabeth. ★*Anything Is Possible: Fiction*

Styles, Toy. *War 2: All Hell Breaks Loose*

Swinson, Kiki. *I'm New York's Finest*

Taneja, Preti. *We That Are Young: A Novel*

Taseer, Aatish. *The Way Things Were: A Novel*

Thompson, Victoria. *Murder on Wall Street*

Todd, Charles. ★*A Hanging at Dawn*

Tyler, Anne. ★*Clock Dance: A Novel*

Updike, John. *In the Beauty of the Lilies*

Uris, Leon. *Redemption: A Novel*

Uris, Leon. ★*Trinity*

Vlautin, Willy. ★*The Night Always Comes*

Walker, Martin. *The Shooting at Chateau Rock*

Waxman, Abbi. *The Bookish Life of Nina Hill*

Welty, Eudora. *The Optimist's Daughter*

Wendig, Chuck. *The Book of Accidents*
West, Jessamyn. *The Friendly Persuasion*
Wideman, John Edgar. *Look for Me and I'll Be Gone: Stories*
Williams, Synithia. *Forbidden Promises*
Woolf, Virginia. ★*The Years*
Yu, Charles. ★*Interior Chinatown*
Yu, E. Lily. ★*On Fragile Waves*

FAMILIES — DEATH
Schanbacher, Gary Lester. *Crossing Purgatory*

FAMILIES — HISTORY
Boyle, T. Coraghessan. *World's End: A Novel*
Djavadi, Negar. *Disoriental*
Grenville, Kate. *Sarah Thornhill*
Hensher, Philip. *Scenes from Early Life: A Novel*
Locke, Attica. *The Cutting Season*
Porter, Regina. *The Travelers*
Rizzuto, Rahna R. *Shadow Child*
Serpell, Namwali. ★*The Old Drift*
Thien, Madeleine. *Do Not Say We Have Nothing*
Urrea, Luis Alberto. ★*The House of Broken Angels*

FAMILIES OF AIRPLANE ACCIDENT VICTIMS
Auster, Paul. ★*The Book of Illusions: A Novel*

FAMILIES OF KIDNAPPING VICTIMS
Parks, Brad. *Say Nothing: A Novel*

FAMILIES OF MILITARY PERSONNEL
Fallon, Siobhan. *You Know When the Men Are Gone*

FAMILIES OF MISSING PERSONS
Heller, Peter. *Celine: A Novel*
Robinson, Peter. *Strange Affair*

FAMILIES OF MURDER VICTIMS
Baldacci, David. *A Minute to Midnight*
Blackmore, R. D. *Lorna Doone: A Romance of Exmoor*
Constantine, Liv. *The Last Time I Saw You*
Daugherty, Christi. *The Echo Killing*
French, Tana. ★*Broken Harbor*
Gaylin, Alison. *Never Look Back*
Hart, John. *The King of Lies*
Pickard, Nancy. *The Scent of Rain and Lightning: A Novel*
Pinter, Jason. *A Stranger at the Door*
Schaitkin, Alexis. *Saint X*
Sebold, Alice. ★*The Lovely Bones*
Stabenow, Dana. ★*A Taint in the Blood*

FAMILY AND ALCOHOLISM
Breslin, Jimmy. *Table Money*

FAMILY AND DEATH
Agee, James. ★*A Death in the Family*
Alarcon, Daniel. *The King Is Always Above the People: Stories*

FAMILY AND MENTAL ILLNESS
Haslett, Adam. ★*Imagine Me Gone: A Novel*

FAMILY AND SUICIDE
Arnett, Kristen N. *Mostly Dead Things*
Kamal, Sheena. *It All Falls Down*
McDermott, Alice. ★*The Ninth Hour*
Winthrop, Elizabeth Hartley. ★*The Why of Things*

FAMILY AND WAR
Aramburu, Fernando. *Homeland*
Benedict, Helen. *Wolf Season*
Hosseini, Khaled. ★*Sea Prayer*

Landau, Alexis. *Those Who Are Saved*
Loigman, Lynda Cohen. *The Wartime Sisters: A Novel*
Moyes, Jojo. *The Girl You Left Behind*

FAMILY BUSINESSES
Abbott, Megan E. ★*The Turnout: A Novel*
Arnett, Kristen N. *Mostly Dead Things*
Banner, Catherine. *The House at the Edge of Night: A Novel*
Bijan, Donia. *The Last Days of Cafe Leila*
Bradford, Barbara Taylor. ★*A Woman of Substance*
Carlyle, Christy. *Duke Gone Rogue*
Christie, Michael. ★*Greenwood: A Novel*
Cole, Alyssa. *How to Find a Princess*
Dickens, Charles. *Dombey and Son*
Dorey-Stein, Beck. *Rock the Boat: A Novel*
Evanovich, Janet. *One for the Money*
Heger, Amanda. *Crazy Cupid Love*
Hunting, Helena. *Handle with Care*
Malamud, Bernard. *The Assistant*
Manansala, Mia P. ★*Arsenic and Adobo*
Merbeth, K. S. ★*Fortuna*
Phillips, Susan Elizabeth. *First Star I See Tonight*
Pineiro, Caridad. *One Summer Night*
Roberts, Nora. *Come Sundown*
Russo, Richard. ★*Empire Falls*
Stradal, J. Ryan. ★*The Lager Queen of Minnesota*
Taneja, Preti. *We That Are Young: A Novel*
Tieu, Julie. *The Donut Trap*
Weaver, Ashley. ★*A Peculiar Combination*

FAMILY CELEBRATIONS
Woodson, Jacqueline. ★*Red at the Bone*

Family chronicles [Series]. Singer, Isaac Bashevis

FAMILY CURSES
Dalton, Trent. *All Our Shimmering Skies*
Diaz, Junot. ★*The Brief Wondrous Life of Oscar Wao*
Fine, Julia. *What Should Be Wild*
Jordan, Sophie. *This Scot of Mine*
Makumbi, Jennifer Nansubuga. *Kintu*
Serpell, Namwali. ★*The Old Drift*

FAMILY ESTATES
Austen, Jane. *Northanger Abbey*
Bennett, Anna. *First Earl I See Tonight*
Blake, Sarah. *The Guest Book: A Novel*
Cleeves, Ann. *The Darkest Evening*
Crombie, Deborah. *A Bitter Feast*
Du Maurier, Daphne. ★*Rebecca*
Fine, Julia. *What Should Be Wild*
Forster, E. M. ★*Howards End*
Ghaffari, Rabeah. ★*To Keep the Sun Alive*
Giordano, Paolo. *Heaven and Earth*
Hannah, Sophie. *The Killings at Kingfisher Hill*
Hart, Erin. *Haunted Ground: A Crime Novel*
Jackson, Shirley. *We Have Always Lived in the Castle*
Johnson, Daisy. *Sisters*
Kleypas, Lisa. *Cold-Hearted Rake*
Marsh, Ngaio. *A Man Lay Dead*
McPherson, Catriona. ★*A Step so Grave*
Moreno-Garcia, Silvia. *Mexican Gothic*
Morton, Kate. *The House at Riverton: A Novel*

Seton, Anya. ★*Dragonwyck*

FAMILY FARMS

Smiley, Jane. ★*A Thousand Acres*

FAMILY FEUDS

Aramburu, Fernando. *Homeland*

Bateman, Kate. *A Reckless Match*

Bradley, Anna. *A Wicked Way to Win an Earl*

Burke, James Lee. ★*A Private Cathedral*

Dell'Antonia, K. J. *The Chicken Sisters*

Pineiro, Caridad. *One Summer Night*

Saberhagen, Fred. *Farslayer's Story*

FAMILY FORTUNES

Sister Souljah. *Midnight and the Meaning of Love*

Family Furnishings: Selected Stories, 1995-2014. Munro, Alice

The Family Gathering. Carr, Robyn

FAMILY HISTORY

Bartels, Erin. *We Hope for Better Things*

Cander, Chris. *The Weight of a Piano: A Novel*

Card, Maisy. ★*These Ghosts Are Family: A Novel*

Chung, Catherine. *The Tenth Muse: A Novel*

Evison, Jonathan. ★*Small World*

Halfon, Eduardo. *Mourning*

Jeffers, Honoree Fanonne. ★*The Love Songs of W. E. B. Du Bois*

Oyeyemi, Helen. *Gingerbread: A Novel*

Patchett, Ann. ★*Commonwealth*

Shalev, Meir. *Two She-Bears: A Novel*

Smith, Michael F. *Blackwood*

So, Anthony Veasna. *Afterparties: Stories*

van Heemstra, Marjolijn. *In Search of a Name*

Watkins, Claire Vaye. *I Love You but I've Chosen Darkness*

Williams, Beatriz. *All the Ways We Said Goodbye: A Novel of the Ritz Paris*

FAMILY KILLING

Gardiner, Meg. *The Dark Corners of the Night*

Gardner, Lisa. ★*Look for Me: A Novel*

Mina, Denise. *Conviction*

Obregon, Nicolas. *Blue Light Yokohama*

Vandelly, T. Marie. *Theme Music*

Silvis, Randall. *Two Days Gone: A Novel*

A Family Lexicon. Ginzburg, Natalia

Family Linen. Smith, Lee

FAMILY LORE

McCracken, Elizabeth. ★*Bowlaway: A Novel*

van Heemstra, Marjolijn. *In Search of a Name*

Family Money. Bawden, Nina

The Family Moskat. Singer, Isaac Bashevis

FAMILY PROBLEMS

Abraham, Tola Rotimi. *Black Sunday*

Abu-Jaber, Diana. *Birds of Paradise: A Novel*

Booth, Coe. ★*Bronxwood*

Conroy, Pat. *The Prince of Tides*

Cullen, Helen. *The Dazzling Truth*

Goodwin, Bobi Gentry. *Revelation*

Gordimer, Nadine. *None to Accompany Me*

Hamill, Shaun. *A Cosmology of Monsters*

Harper, Jane. *The Lost Man*

Higgins, Kristan. *Now That You Mention It*

Kimmel, Fran. *No Good Asking: A Novel*

Lessing, Doris May. ★*The Fifth Child*

Lundrigan, Nicole. *Glass Boys: A Novel*

Mitchell, David. *Black Swan Green: A Novel*

Morrison, Toni. ★*The Bluest Eye: A Novel*

Oates, Joyce Carol. ★*We Were the Mulvaneys*

Osondu, E. C. *This House Is Not for Sale: A Novel*

Petterson, Per. *I Refuse*

Roberts, Nora. ★*Under Currents*

Shields, Carol. *Unless*

Smiley, Jane. ★*A Thousand Acres*

Tsao, Tiffany. *The Majesties*

Walker, Karen Thompson. *The Age of Miracles: A Novel*

FAMILY RECIPES

Oyeyemi, Helen. *Gingerbread: A Novel*

FAMILY RELATIONSHIPS

Acker, Jennifer. ★*The Limits of the World*

Alexie, Sherman. *Flight*

Allende, Isabel. ★*The House of the Spirits*

Antopol, Molly. *The Unamericans*

Arimah, Lesley Nneka. ★*What It Means When a Man Falls from the Sky: Stories*

Ashley & JaQuavis. *The Cartel*

Atkinson, Kate. ★*A God in Ruins*

Atkinson, Kate. *Human Croquet*

Atwood, Margaret. *Bluebeard's Egg and Other Stories*

Atwood, Margaret. *Moral Disorder*

Audrain, Ashley. *The Push*

Baldacci, David. *One Summer*

Bambara, Toni Cade. *Gorilla, My Love*

Banville, John. ★*Eclipse: A Novel*

Banville, John. *The Infinities*

Barker, Pat. *Another World*

Barnett, S. K. *Safe*

Beckerman, Hannah. *If Only I Could Tell You*

Bellow, Saul. *More Die of Heartbreak*

Benedict, Helen. *Wolf Season*

Berger, Thomas. ★*Neighbors: A Novel*

Berlin, Lucia. ★*Evening in Paradise: More Stories*

Berlin, Lucia. ★*A Manual for Cleaning Women: Selected Stories*

Bezmozgis, David. *The Betrayers: A Novel*

Bohjalian, Chris. *The Sleepwalker*

Bordas, Camille. *How to Behave in a Crowd*

Bourdeaut, Olivier. *Waiting for Bojangles: A Novel*

Bradbury, Ray. ★*Dandelion Wine: A Novel*

Bradford, Barbara Taylor. ★*A Woman of Substance*

Braffet, Kelly. ★*Last Seen Leaving: A Novel*

Braithwaite, Oyinkan. *My Sister, the Serial Killer: A Novel*

Bronsky, Alina. *The Hottest Dishes of the Tartar Cuisine*

Brown, Eleanor. *The Weird Sisters*

Brown, Rosellen. *Tender Mercies*

Butler, Nickolas. *Little Faith: A Novel*

Buwalda, Peter. *Bonita Avenue: A Novel*

Castel-Bloom, Orly. *Textile*

Chaon, Dan. *Ill Will*

Chizmar, Richard T. *A Long December*

Cho, Zen. *Spirits Abroad and Other Stories*

Choi, Ann Y. K. *Kay's Lucky Coin Variety*

Cisneros, Sandra. ★*The House on Mango Street*

Collins, Kathleen. ★*Whatever Happened to Interracial Love?: Stories*

Corman, Avery. *Prized Possessions*

Crucet, Jennine Capo. *Make Your Home Among Strangers*

Crummey, Michael. *Galore*

Cruse, Howard. *The Complete Wendel*

Dann, Patty. *The Wright Sister*

Daughters, Amy Weinland. *You Cannot Mess This Up: A True Story That Never Happened*

Deane, Seamus. *Reading in the Dark*

DeCarlo, Melissa. *The Art of Crash Landing: A Novel*

Dickens, Charles. *Dombey and Son*

Diehl, Heidi. *Lifelines*

Doctorow, E. L. ★*Ragtime*

Doctorow, E. L. *World's Fair*

Doshi, Avni. *Burnt Sugar: A Novel*

Doyle, Roddy. *Paddy Clarke, Ha-Ha-Ha*

Eggers, Dave. *How We Are Hungry: Stories*

Eliot, George. ★*The Mill on the Floss*

Ellmann, Lucy. *Ducks, Newburyport*

Epstein, Joseph. *The Love Song of A. Jerome Minkoff, and Other Stories*

Erdrich, Louise. ★*Shadow Tag: A Novel*

Faulkner, William. *The Hamlet*

Faulkner, William. *Uncollected Stories of William Faulkner*

Fay, Juliette. *The Shortest Way Home*

Foer, Jonathan Safran. *Here I Am: A Novel*

Ford, Kelli Jo. ★*Crooked Hallelujah*

Foster, Lori. *Sisters of Summer's End*

Frank, Dorothea Benton. *Folly Beach: A Lowcountry Tale*

Franzen, Jonathan. ★*The Corrections*

Franzen, Jonathan. ★*Freedom*

French, Tana. *Faithful Place: A Novel*

Gaige, Amity. *Schroder*

Garcia, Gabriela. *Of Women and Salt*

Gardam, Jane. *God on the Rocks*

Gideon, Melanie. *Wife 22*

Gilbert, David. *& Sons: A Novel*

Ginzburg, Natalia. *A Family Lexicon*

Glass, Julia. ★*Three Junes*

Glass, Julia. *The Widower's Tale*

Grossman, David. ★*To the End of the Land*

Gustine, Amy. *You Should Pity Us Instead: Stories*

Hadley, Tessa. *Bad Dreams and Other Stories*

Hadley, Tessa. *The Past*

Haruf, Kent. *Benediction*

Hegi, Ursula. *The Vision of Emma Blau*

Hempel, Amy. *Sing to It: New Stories*

Higgins, Kristan. ★*Life and Other Inconveniences*

Holbert, Bruce. *Whiskey*

Howland, Bette. *Calm Sea and Prosperous Voyage*

Howrey, Meg. *The Wanderers*

Irvin, Kelly. *Tell Her No Lies*

Jackson, Charles. *The Lost Weekend*

Jakes, John. *Love and War*

Jakes, John. ★*North and South*

Jen, Gish. ★*Thank You, Mr. Nixon: Stories*

Kantra, Virginia. ★*Meg and Jo*

Kimmel, Fran. *No Good Asking: A Novel*

Kincaid, Jamaica. ★*Annie John*

Kincaid, Jamaica. *See Now Then*

Kwan, Kevin. *Rich People Problems*

Lalami, Laila. *The Other Americans: A Novel*

Lawrence, D. H. *Sons and Lovers*

Leon, Donna. *Unto Us a Son Is Given*

Lippman, Laura. ★*After I'm Gone*

Lipsyte, Sam. *The Ask*

Loigman, Lynda Cohen. *The Wartime Sisters: A Novel*

Lombardo, Claire. *The Most Fun We Ever Had: A Novel*

Mallery, Susan. *The Summer of Sunshine and Margot*

Mallery, Susan. ★*When We Found Home*

Mann, Thomas. *Buddenbrooks*

Mason, Bobbie Ann. *Patchwork*

Mathis, Ayana. *The Twelve Tribes of Hattie*

McCracken, Elizabeth. *The Souvenir Museum: Stories*

McDermott, Alice. *After This*

McDermott, Alice. *At Weddings and Wakes*

McGuane, Thomas. *Crow Fair: Stories*

McKenzie, Elizabeth. *The Portable Veblen*

McMurtry, Larry. *Boone's Lick: A Novel*

Moriarty, Liane. *Big Little Lies*

Mosley, Walter. *And Sometimes I Wonder About You: A Leonid McGill Mystery*

Mukherjee, Neel. *The Lives of Others*

Munro, Alice. *Runaway: Stories*

Oates, Joyce Carol. ★*We Were the Mulvaneys*

Obioma, Chigozie. ★*The Fishermen: A Novel*

Osondu, E. C. *This House Is Not for Sale: A Novel*

Otsuka, Julie. *When the Emperor Was Divine: A Novel*

Panowich, Brian. *Like Lions*

Patchett, Ann. ★*The Dutch House: A Novel*

Paul, Gill. ★*The Lost Daughter*

Petterson, Per. *I Curse the River of Time*

Phillips, Arthur. *The Tragedy of Arthur: A Novel*

Phillips, Jayne Anne. *Lark and Termite: A Novel*

Philyaw, Deesha. *The Secret Lives of Church Ladies*

Pilcher, Rosamunde. ★*The Shell Seekers*

Price, Reynolds. *Roxanna Slade*

Proulx, Annie. *Bad Dirt: Wyoming Stories 2*

Proulx, Annie. *Fine Just the Way It Is: Wyoming Stories 3*

Proulx, Annie. *Postcards*

Pyper, Andrew. *The Homecoming: A Novel*

Quindlen, Anna. *Miller's Valley*

Rendell, Ruth. *Kissing the Gunner's Daughter*

Rice, Luanne. *Little Night*

Richmond, Michelle. *No One You Know*

Rimmer, Kelly. *Truths I Never Told You*

Roberts, Nora. *Come Sundown*

Roth, Philip. ★*The Anatomy Lesson*

Roth, Philip. ★*Portnoy's Complaint*

Roth, Philip. *Zuckerman Unbound*

Roy, Anuradha. *An Atlas of Impossible Longing*

Russell, Karen. ★*Swamplandia!*

Rutherfurd, Edward. *The Rebels of Ireland: The Dublin Saga*

Saunders, George. ★*Lincoln in the Bardo: A Novel*

Schmidt, Sarah. *See What I Have Done*

Schulman, Helen. *Come with Me*
Schultz, Connie. *The Daughters of Erietown*
Sedaris, David. *Holidays on Ice*
See, Lisa. *Dreams of Joy: A Novel*
Seth, Vikram. ★*A Suitable Boy: A Novel*
Singer, Isaac Bashevis. *The Family Moskat*
Sister Souljah. *Midnight and the Meaning of Love*
Sittenfeld, Curtis. *Eligible: A Novel*
Smiley, Jane. *Early Warning*
Smiley, Jane. *Golden Age*
Smiley, Jane. *Some Luck*
Smith, Julie. *Louisiana Hotshot*
Smith, Lee. *Oral History*
Smith, Zadie. *On Beauty*
Stegner, Wallace. ★*The Big Rock Candy Mountain*
Stross, Charles. *Accelerando*
Strout, Elizabeth. *My Name Is Lucy Barton*
Tademy, Lalita. *Cane River*
Tarkington, Booth. ★*The Magnificent Ambersons*
Taseer, Aatish. *The Way Things Were: A Novel*
Thien, Madeleine. *Do Not Say We Have Nothing*
Ullmann, Linn. *Unquiet: A Novel*
Updike, John. *In the Beauty of the Lilies*
Weiner, Jennifer. ★*Mrs. Everything: A Novel*
Welty, Eudora. ★*Delta Wedding*
West, Dorothy. *The Wedding*
Wideman, John Edgar. ★*American Histories: Stories*
Winthrop, Elizabeth Hartley. ★*The Why of Things*
Wood, James. *Upstate*
Woolf, Virginia. ★*The Years*
Wouk, Herman. ★*War and Remembrance: A Novel*
Wouk, Herman. ★*The Winds of War: A Novel*

FAMILY REUNIONS
Harrison, Jamie. *The Center of Everything: A Novel*
Welty, Eudora. *Stories, Essays & Memoir*

FAMILY SAGAS
Abulhawa, Susan. *The Blue Between Sky and Water*
Acker, Jennifer. ★*The Limits of the World*
Adams, Alina. *The Nesting Dolls*
Alharthi, Jokha. *Celestial Bodies: A Novel*
Allen, Sarah Addison. *The Girl Who Chased the Moon: A Novel*
Allende, Isabel. ★*The House of the Spirits*
Allende, Isabel. *Portrait in Sepia: A Novel*
Alyan, Hala. *Salt Houses*
Araghi, Alireza Taheri. ★*The Immortals of Tehran*
Archer, Jeffrey. *Nothing Ventured*
Artson, Barbara. *Odessa, Odessa*
Atkinson, Kate. *Human Croquet*
Auci, Stefania. *The Florios of Sicily: A Novel*
Banner, Catherine. *The House at the Edge of Night: A Novel*
Bauman, Bruce. ★*Broken Sleep: An American Dream*
Benjamin, Chloe. ★*The Immortalists: A Novel*
Blake, Sarah. *The Guest Book: A Novel*
Blume, Judy. *In the Unlikely Event*
Boyle, T. Coraghessan. *World's End: A Novel*
Bradford, Barbara Taylor. ★*A Woman of Substance*
Brown, Dee. *Creek Mary's Blood: A Novel*
Brown, Rita Mae. *Six of One*

Buck, Pearl S. *The Good Earth*
Burke, James Lee. *Another Kind of Eden*
Card, Maisy. ★*These Ghosts Are Family: A Novel*
Castillo, Elaine. *America Is Not the Heart*
Chen, Da. *Brothers: A Novel*
Christie, Michael. ★*Greenwood: A Novel*
Colvin, Jeffrey. ★*Africaville: A Novel*
Coster, Naima. *Halsey Street*
Coster, Naima. *What's Mine and Yours: A Novel*
Cramer, W. Dale. *Levi's Will: A Novel*
Crummey, Michael. *Galore*
Cullen, Helen. *The Dazzling Truth*
Deb, Siddhartha. *The Point of Return: A Novel*
Deon, Natashia. *Grace*
Djavadi, Negar. *Disoriental*
Dunnett, Dorothy. *Niccolo Rising*
Dupont, Eric. *The American Fiancee: A Novel*
Dykes, Amanda. *Whose Waves These Are*
Ekwuyasi, Francesca. *Butter Honey Pig Bread: A Novel*
Enjeti, Anjali. ★*The Parted Earth*
Enright, Anne. *Actress: A Novel*
Enright, Anne. *The Green Road: A Novel*
Faulkner, William. ★*Absalom, Absalom!*
Faulkner, William. *The Hamlet*
Follett, Ken. *Edge of Eternity*
Follett, Ken. *Fall of Giants*
Follett, Ken. *Winter of the World*
Ford, Kelli Jo. ★*Crooked Hallelujah*
Francis-Sharma, Lauren. ★*Book of the Little Axe*
Gaines, Ernest J. ★*The Autobiography of Miss Jane Pittman*
Galsworthy, John. ★*The Forsyte Saga*
Garcia Marquez, Gabriel. ★*One Hundred Years of Solitude*
Garcia, Cristina. *The Aguero Sisters*
Garcia, Gabriela. *Of Women and Salt*
Ghaffari, Rabeah. ★*To Keep the Sun Alive*
Ghosh, Amitav. *The Glass Palace*
Gibbons, Kaye. *Charms for the Easy Life*
Gilbert, Elizabeth. ★*The Signature of All Things: A Novel*
Ginzburg, Natalia. *A Family Lexicon*
Gregory, Philippa. *Tidelands*
Gyasi, Yaa. ★*Homegoing: A Novel*
Haigh, Jennifer. *Baker Towers: A Novel*
Haratischvili, Nino. *The Eighth Life: (For Brilka)*
Hawthorne, Nathaniel. ★*The House of the Seven Gables*
Hegi, Ursula. *The Vision of Emma Blau*
Hill, Ruth Beebe. *Hanta Yo*
Jakes, John. *Love and War*
Jakes, John. ★*North and South*
Janowitz, Brenda. *The Grace Kelly Dress*
Jeffers, Honoree Fanonne. ★*The Love Songs of W. E. B. Du Bois*
Johnson, Caleb. *Treeborne*
Kim, Crystal Hana. *If You Leave Me*
Kim, Eugenia. *The Kinship of Secrets*
Krivak, Andrew. *The Signal Flame: A Novel*
L'Amour, Louis. *To the Far Blue Mountains*
Lahiri, Jhumpa. *The Lowland: A Novel*
Lee, Min Jin. ★*Pachinko*
Lessing, Doris May. *The Sweetest Dream*

Lethem, Jonathan. *Dissident Gardens*

Llewellyn, Richard. ★*How Green Was My Valley*

Lombardo, Claire. *The Most Fun We Ever Had: A Novel*

Lopez Barrio, Cristina. *The House of the Impossible Loves*

Lukas, Michael David. *The Last Watchman of Old Cairo: A Novel*

Mahfuz, Najib. ★*Palace Walk*

Makumbi, Jennifer Nansubuga. *Kintu*

Mann, Thomas. *Buddenbrooks*

Mathis, Ayana. *The Twelve Tribes of Hattie*

Matthiessen, Peter. *Shadow Country: A New Rendering of the Watson Legend*

McCann, Colum. ★*Transatlantic: A Novel*

McCracken, Elizabeth. ★*Bowlaway: A Novel*

McDermott, Alice. ★*The Ninth Hour*

Meyer, Philipp. ★*The Son: A Novel*

Meyerson, Amy. *The Imperfects*

Michener, James A. *Chesapeake*

Morrison, Toni. ★*Song of Solomon*

Nguyen, Phan Que Mai. ★*The Mountains Sing: A Novel*

Packer, Ann. *The Children's Crusade*

Patchett, Ann. ★*Commonwealth*

Patchett, Ann. ★*The Dutch House: A Novel*

Patterson, Molly. *Rebellion*

Persaud, Ingrid. *Love After Love: A Novel*

Pilcher, Rosamunde. ★*The Shell Seekers*

Proulx, Annie. ★*Barkskins: A Novel*

Puzo, Mario. *The Family: A Novel*

Puzo, Mario. ★*The Godfather*

Puzo, Mario. *The Sicilian: A Novel*

Richler, Mordecai. *Solomon Gursky Was Here*

Riley, Lucinda. *The Girl on the Cliff: A Novel*

Roy, Anuradha. *An Atlas of Impossible Longing*

Rushdie, Salman. *The Moor's Last Sigh*

Rutherfurd, Edward. *London*

Rutherfurd, Edward. *Paris*

Rutherfurd, Edward. *The Princes of Ireland: The Dublin Saga*

Rutherfurd, Edward. *The Rebels of Ireland: The Dublin Saga*

Rutherfurd, Edward. *Russka: The Novel of Russia*

Rutherfurd, Edward. *Sarum: The Novel of England*

Serpell, Namwali. ★*The Old Drift*

Sexton, Margaret Wilkerson. *A Kind of Freedom*

Sexton, Margaret Wilkerson. *The Revisioners: A Novel*

Shaw, Irwin. *Beggarman, Thief*

Shaw, Irwin. ★*Rich Man, Poor Man*

Singer, I. J. *The Brothers Ashkenazi*

Singer, Isaac Bashevis. *The Family Moskat*

Smiley, Jane. *Early Warning*

Smiley, Jane. *Golden Age*

Smiley, Jane. *Some Luck*

Smith, Lee. *Oral History*

Stegner, Wallace. ★*Angle of Repose*

Steinbeck, John. ★*East of Eden*

Swann, Stacey. *Olympus Texas*

Sylvester, Natalia. *Everyone Knows You Go Home*

Tademy, Lalita. *Cane River*

Tan, Amy. *The Valley of Amazement*

Tarkington, Booth. ★*The Magnificent Ambersons*

Updike, John. *In the Beauty of the Lilies*

Uris, Leon. *Redemption: A Novel*

Uris, Leon. ★*Trinity*

Verghese, A. *Cutting for Stone: A Novel*

Walker, Alice. *The Third Life of Grange Copeland*

West, Dorothy. *The Wedding*

Willig, Lauren. *The Summer Country: A Novel*

Yu, Charles. ★*Interior Chinatown*

FAMILY SECRETS

Abu-Jaber, Diana. *Birds of Paradise: A Novel*

Acker, Jennifer. ★*The Limits of the World*

Afshar, Tessa. *Jewel of the Nile*

Allen, Sarah Addison. *The Girl Who Chased the Moon: A Novel*

Allende, Isabel. *Portrait in Sepia: A Novel*

Attenberg, Jami. ★*All This Could Be Yours*

Atwood, Margaret. ★*The Blind Assassin*

Barclay, Linwood. *Broken Promise*

Barclay, Linwood. *Far from True: A Novel*

Barker, Pat. *Another World*

Barry, Brunonia. *The Map of True Places*

Bartels, Erin. *We Hope for Better Things*

Bauermeister, Erica. *The Scent Keeper*

Bauman, Bruce. ★*Broken Sleep: An American Dream*

Beattie, Ann. *The Doctor's House: A Novel*

Beckerman, Hannah. *If Only I Could Tell You*

Belfer, Lauren. *And After the Fire: A Novel*

Blackwell, Juliet. *Letters from Paris*

Bobotis, Andrea. *The Last List of Miss Judith Kratt*

Briscoe, Joanna. *The Seduction*

Brouwer, Sigmund. *Thief of Glory: A Novel*

Burdick, Serena. *The Girls with No Names*

Capri, NeNe. *The Pussy Trap.; Part 3,*

Card, Maisy. ★*These Ghosts Are Family: A Novel*

Carter, Stephen L. *New England White: A Novel*

Cartwright, Justin. *To Heaven by Water*

Chavez, Heather. *No Bad Deed*

Child, Lee. ★*Past Tense*

Christie, Michael. ★*Greenwood: A Novel*

Clark, Mary Higgins. *The Melody Lingers On*

Cleeton, Chanel. *Next Year in Havana*

Cocks, Heather. *The Heir Affair*

Davis, Fiona. *The Lions of Fifth Avenue: A Novel*

De Robertis, Carolina. *Perla*

Deane, Seamus. *Reading in the Dark*

DeCarlo, Melissa. *The Art of Crash Landing: A Novel*

Delaney, J. P. *Playing Nice*

Delinsky, Barbara. *A Week at the Shore*

Dimechkie, Karim. *Lifted by the Great Nothing*

Divakaruni, Chitra Banerjee. *Oleander Girl: A Novel*

Downes, Anna. *The Safe Place: A Novel*

Downing, Samantha. *He Started It*

Edwards, Kim. *The Memory Keeper's Daughter*

Enger, Lin. *Undiscovered Country: A Novel*

Erdrich, Louise. *Love Medicine: A Novel*

Fabry, Chris. *The Promise of Jesse Woods*

Feng, Linda Rui. *Swimming Back to Trout River*

Fielding, Joy. *The Bad Daughter: A Novel*

Finder, Joseph. *The Fixer*

Frankel, Laurie. *This Is How It Always Is*

French, Tana. ★*The Witch Elm: A Novel*
Fuller, Claire. *Our Endless Numbered Days: A Novel*
Gabaldon, Diana. *Written in My Own Heart's Blood*
Garcia, Cristina. *The Aguero Sisters*
Garcia, Gabriela. *Of Women and Salt*
Gardner, Lisa. *Love You More: A Detective D.D. Warren Novel*
Gaynor, Hazel. *Three Words for Goodbye*
George, Elizabeth. *Believing the Lie*
Godwin, Gail. *Flora: A Novel*
Goodwin, Bobi Gentry. *Revelation*
Grenville, Kate. *Sarah Thornhill*
Hadley, Tessa. *The Past*
Halfon, Eduardo. *Mourning*
Hart, John. *Down River*
Hegi, Ursula. *Children and Fire: A Novel*
Hepworth, Sally. *The Secrets of Midwives*
Hewson, David. *The Garden of Angels*
Hilderbrand, Elin. ★*28 Summers*
Hilderbrand, Elin. ★*Summer of '69*
Hill, Nathan. *The Nix: A Novel*
Hill, Reginald. *The Woodcutter: A Novel*
Holt, Victoria. *The Black Opal*
James, Rebecca. *The Woman in the Mirror*
James, Wendy. *A Little Bird*
Johnson, Nancy. *The Kindest Lie*
Jones, Tayari. *Silver Sparrow: A Novel*
Kelly, Erin. *The Burning Air: A Novel*
Kelly, Julia. *The Last Dance of the Debutante*
Kim, Nancy Jooyoun. *The Last Story of Mina Lee*
Kwok, Jean. *Searching for Sylvie Lee*
Lewis, Beverly. *The Brethren*
Linden, Rachel. *Ascension of Larks*
Lipman, Elinor. *The Dearly Departed*
Lipman, Elinor. *Good Riddance*
Lukas, Michael David. *The Last Watchman of Old Cairo: A Novel*
Lyons, Jenn. *The Ruin of Kings*
Mallery, Susan. ★*When We Found Home*
Marias, Javier. *Thus Bad Begins: A Novel*
Masad, Ilana. *All My Mother's Lovers: A Novel*
McCorkle, Jill. ★*Hieroglyphics: A Novel*
McCracken, Elizabeth. ★*Bowlaway: A Novel*
Meyerson, Amy. *The Imperfects*
Moreno-Garcia, Silvia. *Mexican Gothic*
Morton, Kate. *The Distant Hours: A Novel*
Mosley, Walter. *Trouble Is What I Do: A Leonid McGill Mystery*
Nichols, Peter. *The Rocks*
O'Donnell, Lisa. *The Death of Bees: A Novel*
O'Farrell, Maggie. *The Hand That First Held Mine: A Novel*
O'Farrell, Maggie. *The Vanishing Act of Esme Lennox*
Oates, Joyce Carol. ★*My Life as a Rat*
Obreht, Tea. *The Tiger's Wife: A Novel*
Paris, B. A. ★*The Dilemma*
Parry, H. G. *The Unlikely Escape of Uriah Heep*
Patchett, Ann. ★*Commonwealth*
Paul, Gill. ★*The Lost Daughter*
Pearson, Robin W. *A Long Time Comin'*
Perkins, S. C. *Murder Once Removed*
Perry, Anne. ★*A Darker Reality*

Phillips, Jayne Anne. *Lark and Termite: A Novel*
Pickard, Nancy. *The Scent of Rain and Lightning: A Novel*
Poissant, David James. *Lake Life*
Pope, Jamie. *One Warm Winter*
Pronzini, Bill. *Hardcase*
Prose, Francine. ★*The Vixen*
Putney, Mary Jo. *The Marriage Spell: A Novel*
Pyper, Andrew. *The Homecoming: A Novel*
Rendell, Ruth. *The Babes in the Wood*
Restrepo, Laura. ★*Delirium: A Novel*
Rhodes, Jewell Parker. *Voodoo Dreams: A Novel of Marie Laveau*
Rhys, Rachel. *Fatal Inheritance*
Riley, Lucinda. *The Girl on the Cliff: A Novel*
Rimmer, Kelly. *Truths I Never Told You*
Riordan, Kate. *The Heatwave*
Roberts, Nora. *The Obsession*
Robertson, Imogen. *Instruments of Darkness: A Novel*
Robotham, Michael. ★*The Other Wife*
Rosnay, Tatiana de. ★*Sarah's Key*
Roy, Lori. ★*Gone Too Long: A Novel*
Rushdie, Salman. ★*The Golden House*
Ryan, Jennifer. *The Spies of Shilling Lane: A Novel*
Sayers, Constance. *The Ladies of the Secret Circus*
Schwarz, Christina. *Drowning Ruth*
Schwarz, Liese O'Halloran. *What Could Be Saved*
Scottoline, Lisa. *Don't Go*
Searles, John. *Help for the Haunted*
See, Lisa. *Dreams of Joy: A Novel*
See, Lisa. *The Island of Sea Women*
Silber, Joan. *Secrets of Happiness*
Slaughter, Karin. ★*Pieces of Her*
Smiley, Jane. *Golden Age*
Smith, Lee. ★*Fair and Tender Ladies*
Stabenow, Dana. *Though Not Dead: A Kate Shugak Novel*
Stewart, Mary. *The Wicked Day*
Straub, Emma. ★*All Adults Here*
Strout, Elizabeth. *Amy and Isabelle: A Novel*
Styles, Toy. *Raunchy*
Sundstol, Vidar. *The Land of Dreams*
Swann, Stacey. *Olympus Texas*
Swinson, David. *City on the Edge*
Tan, Amy. ★*The Kitchen God's Wife*
Thayne, RaeAnne. *The Cliff House*
Todd, Charles. ★*A Hanging at Dawn*
Trigiani, Adriana. *Big Stone Gap: A Novel*
Tsao, Tiffany. *The Majesties*
Willett, Marcia. *The Garden House*
Williams, Beatriz. *All the Ways We Said Goodbye: A Novel of the Ritz Paris*
Willig, Lauren. *The Summer Country: A Novel*

FAMILY STORYTELLING
Wallace, Daniel. ★*Big Fish: A Novel of Mythic Proportions*
FAMILY TRADITIONS
Gilligan, Ruth. *The Butchers' Blessing*
Singer, Isaac Bashevis. *The Family Moskat*
Family Trust: A Novel. Wang, Kathy
*The **Family** Upstairs*. Jewell, Lisa

FAMILY VACATIONS

Friedland, Elyssa. *The Floating Feldmans*
Levy, Deborah. *Swimming Home: A Novel*
Nicholls, David. *US: A Novel*
Straub, Emma. *The Vacationers*

FAMILY VIOLENCE

Byatt, A. S. *Babel Tower*
Hall, Rachel Howzell. *And Now She's Gone*
Hoover, Colleen. *It Ends with Us*
Hyde, Catherine Ryan. *My Name Is Anton*
King, Stephen. *Dolores Claiborne*
McCammon, Robert R. *Boy's Life*
Mihalic, Susan. *Dark Horses*
Moor, Jessica. *The Keeper*
Patterson, Richard North. *Balance of Power*
Rader-Day, Lori. *The Day I Died*
Speight, Shameek A. ★*A Child of a Crack Head*
Stuart, Douglas. ★*Shuggie Bain*
Toibin, Colm. *House of Names*
Tsao, Tiffany. *The Majesties*
Walker, Alice. *The Third Life of Grange Copeland*

FAMILY VIOLENCE VICTIMS

Wiggs, Susan. ★*The Oysterville Sewing Circle*

FAMILY VISITS

Roy, Arundhati. ★*The God of Small Things*
The *Family: a Novel*. Puzo, Mario

FAMINES

Rutherfurd, Edward. *The Rebels of Ireland: The Dublin Saga*
Uris, Leon. ★*Trinity*
Famous Adopted People. Stephens, Alice
Famous All Over Town. Santiago, Danny

FAN CONVENTIONS

Armstrong, Richard. *The Don Con*

FAN FICTION

Dade, Olivia. *Spoiler Alert*

FANATICISM

Aswani, Alaa. *Chicago: A Modern Arabic Novel*
Pearl, Matthew. *The Poe Shadow: A Novel*
Reid, Ava. *The Wolf and the Woodsman*

FANDORIN, ERAST (FICTITIOUS CHARACTER)

Akunin, B. *The Coronation: The Further Adventures of Erast Fandorin*

FANS

Gerritsen, Tess. *I Know a Secret*
Leon, Donna. *Falling in Love: A Commissario Guido Brunetti Mystery*
Phillips, Susan Elizabeth. ★*When Stars Collide*

FANS (PERSONS)

Brazier, Eliza Jane. *If I Disappear*
Dade, Olivia. *Spoiler Alert*
Jenner, Natalie. *The Jane Austen Society*
King, Stephen. *Finders Keepers*
King, Stephen. ★*Misery*

FANTASY CLASSICS

Pratchett, Terry. ★*The Color of Magic*
Stevens, Francis. *The Heads of Cerberus*
Swift, Jonathan. ★*Gulliver's Travels*

Tolkien, J. R. R. *The Fellowship of the Ring: Being the First Part of the Lord of the Rings*
Tolkien, J. R. R. ★*The Hobbit, Or, There and Back Again*
Tolkien, J. R. R. ★*The Lord of the Rings*
Tolkien, J. R. R. *The Return of the King: Being the Third Part of the Lord of the Rings*
Tolkien, J. R. R. *The Silmarillion*
Tolkien, J. R. R. *The Two Towers: Being the Second Part of the Lord of the Rings*

FANTASY FICTION

Adams, Richard. *Watership Down*
Addison, Katherine. ★*The Goblin Emperor*
Baker, Kage. *The Bird of the River*
Baker, Kage. *The House of the Stag*
Balaskovits, A. A. *Magic for Unlucky Girls: Stories*
Barker, Clive. ★*Weaveworld*
Barnhill, Kelly Regan. *Dreadful Young Ladies and Other Stories*
Beagle, Peter S. ★*The Last Unicorn*
Beagle, Peter S. *The Unicorn Sonata*
Bear, Elizabeth. *All the Windwracked Stars*
Bear, Elizabeth. *The Red-Stained Wings*
Bear, Elizabeth. *The Stone in the Skull*
Bennett, Robert Jackson. *Foundryside*
Bennett, Robert Jackson. *Shorefall*
Brennan, Marie. *Within the Sanctuary of Wings: A Memoir by Lady Trent*
Brooks, Terry. *Child of Light*
Campbell, Lisbeth. *The Vanished Queen*
Carey, Jacqueline. *Starless*
Carrick, M. A. *The Mask of Mirrors*
Carter, Angela. ★*Burning Your Boats: The Collected Short Stories*
Cho, Zen. *Sorcerer to the Crown*
Clarke, Susanna. ★*Piranesi*
Cogman, Genevieve. *The Invisible Library*
Cogman, Genevieve. *The Masked City*
Czerneda, Julie. *A Turn of Light*
Dean, Pamela. *Tam Lin*
Delany, Samuel R. *Aye, and Gomorrah: Stories*
Diachenko, Serhii. *Vita Nostra*
Due, Tananarive. *Ghost Summer: Stories*
Elliott, Kate. *Servant Mage*
Fforde, Jasper. *Shades of Grey: A Novel*
Gaiman, Neil. ★*Anansi Boys: A Novel*
Gaiman, Neil. ★*Fragile Things: Short Fictions and Wonders*
Gaiman, Neil. ★*Good Omens: The Nice and Accurate Prophecies of Agnes Nutter, Witch*
Gaiman, Neil. ★*The Ocean at the End of the Lane*
Gaiman, Neil. *Trigger Warning: Short Fictions and Disturbances*
Gilman, Laura Anne. *Flesh and Fire*
Glover, Nicole. ★*The Conductors*
Glover, Nicole. *The Undertakers*
Goldman, William. ★*The Princess Bride: S. Morgenstern's Classic Tale of True Love and High Adventure : The*
Hackwith, A. J. *The Library of the Unwritten*
Hawkins, Scott. ★*The Library at Mount Char*
Huang, S. L. *Burning Roses*
Jemisin, N. K. *How Long 'Til Black Future Month?*
Johnson, Kij. ★*The Dream-Quest of Vellitt Boe*

Kay, Guy Gavriel. ★*Children of Earth and Sky*
Kelly, Greta. *The Frozen Crown*
Kiernan, Caitlin R. *The Very Best of Caitlin R. Kiernan*
Krueger, Paul. *Steel Crow Saga*
Larkwood, A. K. *The Unspoken Name*
Le Guin, Ursula K. *The Beginning Place*
Le Guin, Ursula K. *The Other Wind*
Lewis, C. S. *Till We Have Faces: A Myth Retold*
Maaren, Kari. ★*Weave a Circle Round*
Maguire, Gregory. *The Brides of Maracoor*
Maguire, Gregory. *Son of a Witch: A Novel*
Maguire, Gregory. ★*Wicked: The Life and Times of the Wicked Witch of the West : A Novel*
Marillier, Juliet. *Daughter of the Forest*
Martell, Nick. *The Kingdom of Liars*
McGuire, Seanan. ★*Beneath the Sugar Sky*
McGuire, Seanan. ★*Down Among the Sticks and Bones*
McGuire, Seanan. ★*Every Heart a Doorway*
McGuire, Seanan. ★*In an Absent Dream*
McGuire, Seanan. ★*Middlegame*
Moore, Alan. *Jerusalem: A Novel*
Morgenstern, Erin. ★*The Starless Sea*
Novik, Naomi. *A Deadly Education: A Novel*
Novik, Naomi. *His Majesty's Dragon*
Novik, Naomi. *The Last Graduate: A Novel*
Novik, Naomi. ★*Spinning Silver*
Novik, Naomi. ★*Uprooted*
Parry, H. G. *The Unlikely Escape of Uriah Heep*
Penelope, L. *Cry of Metal & Bone: Earthsinger Chronicles, Book 3*
Penelope, L. *Song of Blood and Stone*
Penelope, L. *Whispers of Shadow & Flame*
Polk, C. L. *Soulstar*
Poore, Michael. *Reincarnation Blues*
Pratchett, Terry. ★*The Color of Magic*
Pratchett, Terry. *Equal Rites*
Pratchett, Terry. *The Fifth Elephant: A Novel of Discworld*
Pratchett, Terry. *Going Postal: A Novel of Discworld*
Pratchett, Terry. *Guards! Guards!*
Pratchett, Terry. *The Last Hero: A Discworld Fable*
Pratchett, Terry. *Lords and Ladies: A Novel of Discworld*
Pratchett, Terry. *Men at Arms: A Novel of Discworld*
Pratchett, Terry. *Monstrous Regiment*
Pratchett, Terry. *Pyramids: The Book of Going Forth*
Pratchett, Terry. *Reaper Man*
Pratchett, Terry. *Small Gods: A Novel of Discworld*
Pratchett, Terry. *Thief of Time*
Pratchett, Terry. *Thud!: A Novel of Discworld*
Pratchett, Terry. *The Truth: A Novel of Discworld*
Pratchett, Terry. *Witches Abroad*
Pratchett, Terry. *Wyrd Sisters*
Reid, Ava. *The Wolf and the Woodsman*
Roanhorse, Rebecca. *Storm of Locusts*
Roanhorse, Rebecca. ★*Trail of Lightning*
Rushdie, Salman. *Two Years Eight Months and Twenty-Eight Nights: A Novel*
Ryan, Anthony. *The Waking Fire*
Saberhagen, Fred. *Coinspinner's Story*
Saberhagen, Fred. *Farslayer's Story*

Saberhagen, Fred. *Mindsword's Story*
Saberhagen, Fred. *Shieldbreaker's Story*
Saberhagen, Fred. *Sightblinder's Story*
Saberhagen, Fred. *Stonecutter's Story*
Saberhagen, Fred. *Wayfinder's Story*
Saberhagen, Fred. *Woundhealer's Story*
Savage, Sam. *Firmin: Adventures of a Metropolitan Lowlife*
Schanoes, Veronica L. *Burning Girls and Other Stories*
Schwab, Victoria. *A Conjuring of Light*
Schwab, Victoria. *A Darker Shade of Magic*
Schwab, Victoria. *A Gathering of Shadows*
Siegel, Jan. *Prospero's Children*
Solomon, Rivers. *The Deep*
Stephenson, Neal. *The Rise and Fall of D.O.D.O.: A Novel*
Sullivan, Michael J. *Theft of Swords*
Suri, Tasha. ★*Empire of Sand*
Suri, Tasha. *The Jasmine Throne*
Suri, Tasha. ★*Realm of Ash*
Swift, Jonathan. ★*Gulliver's Travels*
Tesh, Emily. *Silver in the Wood*
Tolkien, J. R. R. *The Silmarillion*
Vandermeer, Jeff. *Finch*
Vandermeer, Jeff. *The Third Bear*
Vollmann, William T. *Last Stories and Other Stories*
Vonnegut, Kurt. *Slapstick: Or, Lonesome No More! a Novel*
Whiteley, Aliya. *From the Neck up and Other Stories*
Wolfe, Gene. ★*The Best of Gene Wolfe: A Definitive Retrospective of His Finest Short Fiction*
Yang, JY. *The Ascent to Godhood*
Yang, JY. *The Black Tides of Heaven*
Yang, JY. *The Red Threads of Fortune*
***Fantasy** in Death*. Robb, J. D.
FANTASY MYSTERIES
Aaronovitch, Ben. *Broken Homes*
Aaronovitch, Ben. *Midnight Riot*
Aaronovitch, Ben. *Moon Over Soho*
Aaronovitch, Ben. *Whispers Under Ground*
Fforde, Jasper. *The Eyre Affair: A Novel*
Fforde, Jasper. *Lost in a Good Book: A Thursday Next Novel*
Glover, Nicole. *The Undertakers*
Mieville, China. ★*The City & The City*
Polansky, Daniel. *The Seventh Perfection*
Stout, Dan. ★*Titanshade*
Yang, JY. *The Descent of Monsters*
FANTASY ROMANCES
Bouchet, Amanda. *Breath of Fire*
Bouchet, Amanda. ★*A Promise of Fire*
Draven, Grace. *Phoenix Unbound*
Martineau, Maxym M. *Kingdom of Exiles*
★*A **Far** Cry from Kensington*. Spark, Muriel
★***Far** from the Madding Crowd*. Hardy, Thomas
***Far** from True: A Novel*. Barclay, Linwood
FAR FUTURE
Asimov, Isaac. ★*Foundation*
Delany, Samuel R. *Aye, and Gomorrah: Stories*
Egan, Greg. *Schild's Ladder*
Elison, Meg. *The Book of Etta*
Elison, Meg. *The Book of Flora*

Gunn, James E. *Transcendental*
Huxley, Aldous. ★*Brave New World*
Le Guin, Ursula K. ★*The Dispossessed: An Ambiguous Utopia*
Le Guin, Ursula K. *Four Ways to Forgiveness*
Le Guin, Ursula K. ★*The Left Hand of Darkness*
Le Guin, Ursula K. *The Telling*
Mieville, China. *Embassytown*
Newitz, Annalee. *Autonomous*
Okorafor, Nnedi. ★*Who Fears Death*
Palmer, Ada. *Too Like the Lightning*
Pohl, Frederik. *Gateway*
Reynolds, Alastair. *Revelation Space*
Reynolds, Alastair. ★*Revenger*
Robinson, Kim Stanley. *Aurora*
Stephenson, Neal. *The Diamond Age,: Or, a Young Lady's Illustrated Primer*
Stephenson, Neal. *Seveneves*
Vonnegut, Kurt. ★*Player Piano*
Wells, H. G. ★*The Time Machine*
Far North. Ridpath, Michael
The *Far* Side of the Dollar. Macdonald, Ross
Farah, Nuruddin
 Crossbones
 Knots
FARCICAL FICTION
 Anders, Charlie Jane. *Rock Manning Goes for Broke*
 Bloom, Amy. *Lucky Us: A Novel*
 Cosimano, Elle. *Finlay Donovan Is Killing It*
 McBride, James. ★*Deacon King Kong: A Novel*
 Westlake, Donald E. ★*Bank Shot*
 Williams, Eley. *The Liar's Dictionary*
 Wodehouse, P. G. ★*The Inimitable Jeeves*
★*A **Farewell** to Arms.* Hemingway, Ernest
Fargo adventures [Series]. Cussler, Clive
Farian war [Series]. Wagers, K. B.
FARM ANIMALS
 Orwell, George. ★*Animal Farm*
FARM LIFE
 Berry, Wendell. *Jayber Crow: A Novel*
 Burke, James Lee. *Another Kind of Eden*
 Coetzee, J. M. *Disgrace*
 Del Amo, Jean-Baptiste. *Animalia*
 Dolan-Leach, Caite. *We Went to the Woods: A Novel*
 Faulkner, William. ★*As I Lay Dying: The Corrected Text*
 Frazier, Charles. ★*Cold Mountain*
 Gunning, Sally. *Painting the Light*
 Jordan, Hillary. *Mudbound: A Novel*
 Kate, Jessica. *A Girl's Guide to the Outback: A Novel*
 Lawson, Mary. *Crow Lake*
 Meadows, Rae. *I Will Send Rain: A Novel*
 Proulx, Annie. *Postcards*
 Quindlen, Anna. *Miller's Valley*
 Reddi, Rishi. *Passage West: A Novel*
 Rutherfurd, Edward. *Russka: The Novel of Russia*
 Schwarz, Christina. *Drowning Ruth*
 Smiley, Jane. *Early Warning*
 Smiley, Jane. *Some Luck*
 Smiley, Jane. ★*A Thousand Acres*

Wharton, Edith. ★*Ethan Frome*
The **Farm:** a Novel. Ramos, Joanne
FARMERS
 Beagle, Peter S. *In Calabria*
 Berry, Wendell. ★*That Distant Land: The Collected Stories of Wendell Berry*
 Buck, Pearl S. *The Good Earth*
 Dallas, Sandra. *Tallgrass*
 Harris, Nathan. *The Sweetness of Water*
 Hunt, Laird. *Zorrie*
 Obioma, Chigozie. ★*An Orchestra of Minorities*
 Smiley, Jane. *Golden Age*
 Smiley, Jane. ★*A Thousand Acres*
 Wharton, Edith. ★*Ethan Frome*
FARMERS' SPOUSES
 Youngson, Anne. *Meet Me at the Museum*
FARMHOUSES
 Auslander, Shalom. *Hope: A Tragedy*
 Bartels, Erin. *We Hope for Better Things*
 Jónasson, Ragnar. *The Mist*
FARMS
 Brundage, Elizabeth. ★*All Things Cease to Appear*
 Chanter, Catherine. *The Well*
 Davies, Carys. *West*
 Farrow, John. *The Storm Murders: A Thriller*
 Gaiman, Neil. ★*The Ocean at the End of the Lane*
 Garvin, Eileen. *The Music of Bees*
 Gordimer, Nadine. *The Conservationist*
 Greene, Amy. *Long Man*
 Hannaham, James. ★*Delicious Foods*
 Locke, Attica. *The Cutting Season*
 Smiley, Jane. *Early Warning*
 Smith, B. J. *All Hat: A Novel*
Farrell, Henry
 ★*What Ever Happened to Baby Jane?*
Farrow, John
 The Storm Murders: A Thriller
FARRUKHZAD, FURUGH
 Darznik, Jasmin. *Song of a Captive Bird: A Novel*
Farslayer's Story. Saberhagen, Fred
FASCISM
 Balzano, Marco. *I'm Staying Here*
 Bolano, Roberto. ★*Nazi Literature in the Americas*
 Lewis, Sinclair. ★*It Can't Happen Here*
 Musil, Robert. *The Man Without Qualities*
FASCISM — HISTORY
 Furst, Alan. ★*A Hero of France*
 Furst, Alan. ★*Mission to Paris*
FASCISTS
 D'Eramo, Luce. *Deviation*
 Twardoch, Szczepan. *The King of Warsaw*
FASHION
 Clark, Mary Higgins. *Death Wears a Beauty Mask and Other Stories*
 Murphy, Julie. *If the Shoe Fits*
 Steel, Danielle. *First Sight*
 T. I. *Power & Beauty: A Love Story of Life on the Streets*
 T. I. *Trouble & Triumph: A Novel of Power & Beauty*

FASHION DESIGN
Matthews, Mimi. ★*The Siren of Sussex*
FASHION DESIGNERS
Cleeves, Ann. *Wild Fire*
Ripper, Kris. *The Life Revamp*
FASHION MODELS
Akinmade-Akerstrom, Lola. *In Every Mirror She's Black*
Gaitskill, Mary. *Veronica*
Galbraith, Robert. *The Cuckoo's Calling*
Sandford, John. *Easy Prey*
Scharer, Whitney. *The Age of Light*
Silva, Daniel. ★*The Kill Artist: A Novel*
Wade, Becky. *Falling for You*
Fast & Loose. Woods, Stuart
Fast Girls: A Novel of the 1936 Women's Olympic Team. Hooper, Elise
The Fastest Way to Fall. Williams, Denise
FASTING
Donoghue, Emma. ★*The Wonder*
FASTING — RELIGIOUS ASPECTS
Crace, Jim. *Quarantine*
Fatal Ally. Sebastian, Tim
Fatal Inheritance. Rhys, Rachel
FATAL TRAFFIC ACCIDENTS
Aimaq, Jasmine. *The Opium Prince*
Anshaw, Carol. *Carry the One*
Baldacci, David. *One Summer*
Garcia-Roza, L. A. *Alone in the Crowd: An Inspector Espinosa Mystery*
FATE AND FATALISM
Baker, Kage. *The House of the Stag*
Banks, Russell. ★*The Sweet Hereafter*
Beagle, Peter S. *Summerlong*
Benjamin, Chloe. ★*The Immortalists: A Novel*
Bouchet, Amanda. *Breath of Fire*
Bouchet, Amanda. ★*A Promise of Fire*
Deon, Natashia. *The Perishing: A Novel*
Dexter, Pete. ★*Deadwood*
Dos Passos, John. *Manhattan Transfer*
Gabaldon, Diana. ★*A Breath of Snow and Ashes*
Hugo, Victor. ★*Les Miserables*
Irving, John. *Avenue of Mysteries: A Novel*
Kamali, Marjan. ★*The Stationery Shop*
Locke, Thomas. *Emissary*
Mitchell, David. ★*Cloud Atlas: A Novel*
Munro, Alice. *Dear Life: Stories*
Murakami, Haruki. ★*Kafka on the Shore*
Newman, Sandra. *The Heavens*
Niffenegger, Audrey. *The Time Traveler's Wife: A Novel*
Oates, Joyce Carol. *The (Other) You: Stories*
Obioma, Chigozie. ★*An Orchestra of Minorities*
Parker-Chan, Shelley. ★*She Who Became the Sun*
Pava, Sergio de la. *Personae: A Novel*
Roanhorse, Rebecca. ★*Black Sun*
Roberts, Nora. ★*The Awakening*
Schwartz, Lynne Sharon. *Truthtelling: Stories, Fables, Glimpses*
Serle, Rebecca. *In Five Years: A Novel*
Stewart, Mary. ★*The Hollow Hills*
Stewart, Mary. *The Wicked Day*

Towles, Amor. *Rules of Civility: A Novel*
Vonnegut, Kurt. ★*Cat's Cradle*
Vonnegut, Kurt. *Hocus Pocus*
The Fate of Katherine Carr. Cook, Thomas H.
The Fated Sky: A Lady Astronaut Novel. Kowal, Mary Robinette
★*Fates and Furies*. Groff, Lauren
FATHER AND ADULT CHILD
Glass, Julia. *The Widower's Tale*
Mosley, Walter. *All I Did Was Shoot My Man: A Leonid McGill Mystery*
Murphy, Devin. *Tiny Americans*
Sanders, Lawrence. *McNally's Puzzle*
FATHER AND ADULT DAUGHTER
Barry, Brunonia. *The Map of True Places*
Begley, Louis. *About Schmidt*
Cash, Wiley. *When Ghosts Come Home: A Novel*
Coben, Harlan. *Run Away*
Coetzee, J. M. *Disgrace*
Conell, Lee. *The Party Upstairs*
Dickey, Eric Jerome. ★*Bad Men and Wicked Women*
James, Henry. *The Golden Bowl*
James, Wendy. *A Little Bird*
Mankell, Henning. *Before the Frost: A Linda Wallander Mystery*
Rankin, Ian. ★*A Song for the Dark Times*
Rendell, Ruth. *Kissing the Gunner's Daughter*
Winfrey, Kerry. *Not Like the Movies*
FATHER AND ADULT SON
Ball, Jesse. *Census*
Bellow, Saul. ★*Seize the Day*
Boyle, T. Coraghessan. *The Harder They Come*
Hall, Steven. *Maxwell's Demon*
Hawley, Noah. *The Good Father*
Iles, Greg. *The Bone Tree: A Novel*
Iles, Greg. *Mississippi Blood: A Novel*
Iles, Greg. *Natchez Burning: A Novel*
K'wan. *Animal II: The Omen*
Perry, Anne. ★*Death with a Double Edge: A Daniel Pitt Novel*
Savage, Sam. *The Way of the Dog: A Novel*
Wallace, Daniel. ★*Big Fish: A Novel of Mythic Proportions*
FATHER AND CHILD
Dowlatabadi, Mahmoud. *The Colonel*
Grass, Gunter. *The Box: Tales from the Darkroom*
Khalfah, Khlid. *Death Is Hard Work: A Novel*
Mozley, Fiona. ★*Elmet*
Stead, Christina. ★*The Man Who Loved Children*
Updike, John. ★*Rabbit Is Rich: A Novel*
FATHER-DESERTED CHILDREN
Lopez Barrio, Cristina. *The House of the Impossible Loves*
Murphy, Devin. *Tiny Americans*
FATHER-DESERTED FAMILIES
Enger, Lin. *The High Divide: A Novel*
Rachman, Tom. *The Italian Teacher*
Shafak, Elif. *Honor: A Novel*
FATHER-SEPARATED BOYS
Earley, Tony. *Jim the Boy: A Novel*
Eggers, Dave. *What Is the What: The Autobiography of Valentino Achak Deng*
Greene, Graham. *The Captain and the Enemy*

FATHER-SEPARATED CHILDREN

Marra, Anthony. ★*A Constellation of Vital Phenomena: A Novel*
Straub, Peter. *Mr. X*

FATHER-SEPARATED FAMILIES

Benedetti, Mario. *Springtime in a Broken Mirror*
De los Santos, Marisa. *The Precious One*
Kwan, Kevin. *China Rich Girlfriend*

FATHER-SEPARATED GIRLS

Braffet, Kelly. ★*Last Seen Leaving: A Novel*

FATHER-SEPARATED TEENAGE BOYS

Restrepo, Laura. *No Place for Heroes: A Novel*

FATHERHOOD

Atkinson, Kate. ★*A God in Ruins*
Ballard, J. G. *The Kindness of Women*
Hawke, Ethan. *A Bright Ray of Darkness*
Simsion, Graeme C. *The Rosie Effect*
Simsion, Graeme C. *The Rosie Result*
★*Fatherland*. Harris, Robert

FATHERS

Blackstock, Terri. *Smoke Screen*
Cramer, W. Dale. *Levi's Will: A Novel*
Edwards, Louis. *Ramadan Ramsey: A Novel*
Gurganus, Allan. *The Practical Heart: Four Novellas*
Haslett, Adam. ★*Imagine Me Gone: A Novel*
Palahniuk, Chuck. *The Invention of Sound*
Penny, Louise. ★*A Better Man: A Chief Inspector Gamache Novel*
Perrotta, Tom. *The Abstinence Teacher*
Smith, Scott. *A Simple Plan: A Novel*
Tudor, C. J. *The Other People*

FATHERS — DEATH

Aleichem, Sholem. *Tevye's Daughters*
Amirrezvani, Anita. *The Blood of Flowers: A Novel*
Attenberg, Jami. ★*All This Could Be Yours*
Benaron, Naomi. *Running the Rift: A Novel*
Benz, Chanelle. ★*The Gone Dead*
Bialosky, Jill. *House Under Snow*
Campbell, Bonnie Jo. *Once Upon a River*
Faye, Lyndsay. ★*The King of Infinite Space*
Foer, Jonathan Safran. *Extremely Loud and Incredibly Close*
Forsyth, Frederick. *The Kill List*
Frazier, Jean Kyoung. *Pizza Girl*
Hall, Steven. *Maxwell's Demon*
Hunting, Helena. *Handle with Care*
Igharo, Jane. *The Sweetest Remedy*
Jones, Tanen. *The Better Liar: A Novel*
Khalfah, Khlid. *Death Is Hard Work: A Novel*
Oe, Kenzaburo. ★*Death by Water*
Ozeki, Ruth L. *The Book of Form and Emptiness: A Novel*
Portis, Charles. ★*True Grit: A Novel*
Pyper, Andrew. *The Homecoming: A Novel*
Quinn, Julia. ★*An Offer from a Gentleman*
Ramsay, Frederick. *Countdown*
Smith, Wilbur A. *Birds of Prey*
Strout, Elizabeth. ★*The Burgess Boys: A Novel*
Yoshimoto, Banana. *Moshi-Moshi*

FATHERS — SUICIDE

Wallace, David Foster. ★*Infinite Jest: A Novel*

FATHERS AND DAUGHTERS

Afshar, Tessa. *Thief of Corinth*
Antopol, Molly. *The Unamericans*
Atkinson, Kate. ★*Case Histories*
Banks, Russell. ★*Affliction*
Banville, John. ★*Eclipse: A Novel*
Bauermeister, Erica. *The Scent Keeper*
Berger, Thomas. ★*Neighbors: A Novel*
Betts, Doris. *Souls Raised from the Dead: A Novel*
Bloom, Amy. *Lucky Us: A Novel*
Bourne, Joanna. ★*My Lord and Spymaster*
Box, C. J. *Vicious Circle*
Butler, Sarah. *Ten Things I've Learnt About Love: A Novel*
Chen, Mike. *Here and Now and Then*
Crowley, John. *Lord Byron's Novel: The Evening Land*
De los Santos, Marisa. *The Precious One*
De Robertis, Carolina. *Perla*
Dickens, Charles. *Dombey and Son*
Dickens, Charles. ★*A Tale of Two Cities*
Divakaruni, Chitra Banerjee. *Oleander Girl: A Novel*
Dixon, Stephen. *Interstate: A Novel*
Enright, Anne. *The Forgotten Waltz*
Evison, Jonathan. *Legends of the North Cascades: A Novel*
Ferber, Edna. *So Big*
Fforde, Jasper. *The Eyre Affair: A Novel*
Frear, Caz. *Sweet Little Lies*
Fuller, Claire. *Our Endless Numbered Days: A Novel*
Gaddis, William. *Agape Agape*
Gaige, Amity. *Schroder*
Garey, Juliann. *Too Bright to Hear Too Loud to See*
Gibson, William. *Pattern Recognition*
Grant, Helen. *The Glass Demon*
Greene, Graham. *Our Man in Havana*
Gregory, Philippa. *The Kingmaker's Daughter*
Ishiguro, Kazuo. *An Artist of the Floating World*
Jenkins, Beverly. *Tempest*
Kamal, Sheena. *It All Falls Down*
Krivak, Andrew. *The Bear*
Lee, Harper. ★*Go Set a Watchman*
Lee, Harper. ★*To Kill a Mockingbird*
Maizes, R. L. *Other People's Pets*
Marillier, Juliet. *Daughter of the Forest*
Maron, Margaret. *Bootlegger's Daughter*
McCann, Colum. ★*Apeirogon: A Novel*
Miller, Xander. *Zo: A Novel*
Mishima, Yukio. *The Sound of Waves*
Monroe, Mary. *God Still Don't Like Ugly*
Moore, Liz. *The Unseen World*
Morgan, C. E. ★*The Sport of Kings*
Morrell, David. *Ruler of the Night*
Niffenegger, Audrey. *The Time Traveler's Wife: A Novel*
Oates, Joyce Carol. *A Garden of Earthly Delights*
Penny, Louise. ★*A Better Man: A Chief Inspector Gamache Novel*
Perrotta, Tom. *The Abstinence Teacher*
Pessl, Marisha. *Night Film: A Novel*
Pessl, Marisha. *Special Topics in Calamity Physics*
Purcell, Laura. *The House of Whispers*
Robards, Karen. *The Ultimatum*

Robinson, Peter. *Piece of My Heart*
Rossner, Rena. *The Light of the Midnight Stars*
Roth, Philip. ★*American Pastoral*
Sagan, Francoise. ★*Bonjour Tristesse*
Scottoline, Lisa. *Don't Go*
See, Lisa. *Shanghai Girls: A Novel*
Simpson, Dorothy. *Once Too Often: An Inspector Luke Thanet Novel*
Styron, William. *Lie Down in Darkness*
Tamirat, Nafkote. *The Parking Lot Attendant: A Novel*
Tarkington, Booth. ★*The Magnificent Ambersons*
Tinti, Hannah. *The Twelve Lives of Samuel Hawley: A Novel*
Tyler, Anne. *Vinegar Girl: The Taming of the Shrew Retold*
Ullmann, Linn. *Unquiet: A Novel*
Urrea, Luis Alberto. *Queen of America: A Novel*
Van Meter, Crissy. *Creatures: A Novel*
Vargas Llosa, Mario. *The Feast of the Goat*
Walton, Jo. ★*Necessity*
West, Monica. *Revival Season: A Novel*
Willett, Marcia. *The Garden House*
Wood, James. *Upstate*
★*Fathers and Sons*. Turgenev, Ivan Sergeevich

FATHERS AND SONS
Adam, Claire. *Golden Child: A Novel*
Adiga, Aravind. *Selection Day*
Agee, James. ★*A Death in the Family*
Alenyikov, Michael. *Ivan and Misha: Stories*
Atkinson, Kate. ★*Big Sky*
Bala, Sharon. *The Boat People: A Novel*
Banks, Russell. *Cloudsplitter: A Novel*
Banville, John. *The Infinities*
Barker, Nicola. *Darkmans*
Bausch, Richard. ★*Rebel Powers*
Block, Lawrence. *The Sins of the Fathers*
Burke, James Lee. *House of the Rising Sun: A Novel*
Butler, Robert Olen. *Perfume River*
Campbell, Ramsey. *The Wise Friend*
Child, Lee. ★*Past Tense*
Cleave, Paul. *A Killer Harvest: A Thriller*
Clinch, Jon. *Finn: A Novel*
Cosby, S. A. ★*Razorblade Tears*
DeLillo, Don. *Zero K: A Novel*
Dexter, Pete. *Spooner*
Dimechkie, Karim. *Lifted by the Great Nothing*
Doiron, Paul. *The Poacher's Son*
Dostoyevsky, Fyodor. ★*The Brothers Karamazov*
Doyle, Roddy. *The Guts*
Dugoni, Robert. *The Conviction*
Dunn, Kate. *The Dragonfly*
Ellis, Bret Easton. *Lunar Park*
Enger, Lin. *Undiscovered Country: A Novel*
Ferris, Joshua. *A Calling for Charlie Barnes*
Finder, Joseph. *The Fixer*
Ford, Richard. ★*Independence Day*
Ford, Richard. *The Lay of the Land*
Fu, Kim. *For Today I Am a Boy*
Gaiman, Neil. ★*Anansi Boys: A Novel*
George, Nina. *The Book of Dreams*
Gilbert, David. *& Sons: A Novel*

Glass, Julia. ★*Three Junes*
Gordimer, Nadine. ★*My Son's Story*
Grass, Gunter. *Crabwalk*
Harding, Paul. *Tinkers*
Hart, John. *The King of Lies*
Hart, Josephine. *Damage: A Novel*
Heller, Joseph. *Good as Gold*
Hosseini, Khaled. ★*Sea Prayer*
Kayode, Femi. ★*Lightseekers*
Krueger, William Kent. ★*Lightning Strike*
Lehane, Dennis. *World Gone By: A Novel*
Levin, Adam. *Bubblegum*
McCammon, Robert R. *Boy's Life*
McCarthy, Cormac. ★*The Road*
Miller, Rebecca. ★*Jacob's Folly: A Novel*
Morante, Elsa. *Arturo's Island: A Novel*
North, Alex. *The Whisper Man*
Paton, Alan. ★*Cry, the Beloved Country*
Peters, Ellis. *Brother Cadfael's Penance*
Petterson, Per. *Out Stealing Horses: A Novel*
Phillips, Arthur. *The Tragedy of Arthur: A Novel*
Porter, Max. ★*Grief Is the Thing with Feathers*
Powers, Richard. ★*Bewilderment: A Novel*
Puzo, Mario. ★*The Godfather*
Puzo, Mario. *The Sicilian: A Novel*
Rachman, Tom. *The Italian Teacher*
Ragan, Theresa. *Deranged*
Rees, Matt. *The Fourth Assassin*
Robinson, Marilynne. ★*Gilead*
Robinson, Peter. *Piece of My Heart*
Rowland, Laura Joh. *The Snow Empress*
Ruiz Zafon, Carlos. *The Prisoner of Heaven*
Ruiz Zafon, Carlos. ★*The Shadow of the Wind*
Rushdie, Salman. *Haroun and the Sea of Stories*
Rushdie, Salman. ★*Quichotte: A Novel*
Russo, Richard. *The Risk Pool*
Schell, Orville. *My Old Home: A Novel of Exile*
Silber, Joan. *Secrets of Happiness*
Smith, Wilbur A. *Birds of Prey*
Smith, Wilbur A. *Monsoon*
Speight, Shameek A. ★*A Child of a Crack Head*
Stabenow, Dana. *Though Not Dead: A Kate Shugak Novel*
Steinbeck, John. ★*East of Eden*
Taseer, Aatish. *The Way Things Were: A Novel*
Theroux, Paul. ★*The Mosquito Coast: A Novel*
Turgenev, Ivan Sergeevich. ★*Fathers and Sons*
Vargas Llosa, Mario. ★*The Discreet Hero*
Verghese, A. *Cutting for Stone: A Novel*
Walker, Alice. *The Third Life of Grange Copeland*
Walker, Caroline Louise. *Man of the Year*
Yu, Charles. *How to Live Safely in a Science Fictional Universe: A Novel*

FATHERS-IN-LAW
Sylvester, Natalia. *Everyone Knows You Go Home*
FATIGUE
Cosimano, Elle. *Finlay Donovan Is Killing It*
Faulkner, William
★*Absalom, Absalom!*

★*As I Lay Dying: The Corrected Text*
★*Go Down, Moses*
The Hamlet
Intruder in the Dust
★*Light in August*
The Reivers: A Reminiscence
Requiem for a Nun
★*Sanctuary*
★*The Sound and the Fury*
Uncollected Stories of William Faulkner
Faulks, Sebastian
  ★*Birdsong*
  Charlotte Gray: A Novel
  Jeeves and the Wedding Bells
  On Green Dolphin Street: A Novel
  Paris Echo: A Novel
  A Week in December
Fault Lines: A Novel. Itami, Emily
Faust, Christa
  Choke Hold
  Money Shot
FAUSTIAN BARGAINS
  Aoki, Ryka. *Light from Uncommon Stars*
  Bulgakov, Mikhail. ★*The Master and Margarita*
  Gilman, Laura Anne. *Silver on the Road*
  Horn, Dara. *Eternal Life: A Novel*
  Mann, Thomas. *Doctor Faustus*
  Schwab, Victoria. *The Invisible Life of Addie Larue*
The **Favorite** *Daughter.* Rouda, Kaira Sturdivant
Fay, Juliette
  The Shortest Way Home
Faye, Gael
  ★*Small Country: A Novel*
Faye, Lyndsay
  The Gods of Gotham
  Jane Steele
  ★*The King of Infinite Space*
  ★*The Paragon Hotel*
  Seven for a Secret
  The Whole Art of Detection: Lost Mysteries of Sherlock Holmes
FBI AGENTS
  Baldacci, David. *Long Road to Mercy*
  Coulter, Catherine. *The End Game*
  Coulter, Catherine. *The Final Cut*
  Coulter, Catherine. *Labyrinth*
  Coulter, Catherine. *The Last Second*
  Coulter, Catherine. *The Lost Key*
  Coulter, Catherine. *Paradox*
  Coulter, Catherine. *The Sixth Day*
  De Leon, Aya. ★*A Spy in the Struggle*
  Dodd, Christina. *Virtue Falls*
  Gardiner, Meg. *The Dark Corners of the Night*
  Jones, Darynda. *A Bad Day for Sunshine*
  Koryta, Michael. ★*How It Happened*
  Pavone, Chris. ★*The Expats: A Novel*
  Preston, Douglas J. *City of Endless Night*
  Preston, Douglas J. *Crooked River*
  Preston, Douglas J. *Verses for the Dead*

Redondo, Dolores. *The North Face of the Heart*
Scalzi, John. *Head On*
Scalzi, John. ★*Lock In*
Smith, Martin Cruz. ★*Gorky Park*
Steinhauer, Olen. *The Middleman*
Stout, Rex. *The Doorbell Rang*
FBI INFORMANTS
  Grisham, John. ★*The Firm*
FBI suspense thriller series [Series]. Coulter, Catherine
FEAR
  Barclay, Linwood. ★*Elevator Pitch: A Novel*
  Bolton, S. J. *The Split*
  Chizmar, Richard T. *Chasing the Boogeyman*
  Garcia Marquez, Gabriel. ★*Strange Pilgrims: Twelve Stories*
  Harrigan, Stephen. *The Leopard Is Loose: A Novel*
  Racculia, Kate. ★*Bellweather Rhapsody*
  Swamy, Shruti. *A House Is a Body: Stories*
FEAR IN CHILDREN
  King, Stephen. *It*
FEAR IN MEN
  Amdahl, Gary. *I Am Death: Two Novellas*
  Barnes, Julian. *The Noise of Time*
FEAR IN WOMEN
  Hegi, Ursula. *Children and Fire: A Novel*
  MacDonald, John D. *The Turquoise Lament*
  Seton, Anya. *Green Darkness*
  Swanson, Peter. *Her Every Fear: A Novel*
Fear Nothing: A Detective D. D. Warren Novel. Gardner, Lisa
★*Fear* of Flying: A Novel. Jong, Erica
Feared. Scottoline, Lisa
Fearless in Texas. Dell, Kari Lynn
★*A* **Feast** *for Crows.* Martin, George R. R.
The **Feast** *of Love.* Baxter, Charles
A **Feast** *of Snakes: A Novel.* Crews, Harry
The **Feast** *of the Goat.* Vargas Llosa, Mario
Feast Your Eyes. Goldberg, Myla
Feathered Serpent, Dark Heart of Sky: Myths of Mexico. Bowles, David
FEDERAL WITNESS PROTECTION PROGRAM
  Faust, Christa. *Choke Hold*
  Leonard, Elmore. ★*Killshot*
Feed. Grant, Mira
Feedback. Grant, Mira
Feehan, Christine
  Dark Illusion
  Shadow Rider
Feeney, Alice
  ★*I Know Who You Are: A Novel*
  ★*Sometimes I Lie*
Feldman, Ellen
  Paris Never Leaves You
The **Fellowship** *of the Ring: Being the First Part of the Lord of the Rings.* Tolkien, J. R. R.
FEMALE FRIENDSHIP
  Alameddine, Rabih. *An Unnecessary Woman*
  Alcott, Kate. *A Touch of Stardust*
  Andreades, Daphne Palasi. *Brown Girls*
  Atwood, Margaret. ★*Cat's Eye*
  Awad, Mona. ★*13 Ways of Looking at a Fat Girl*

Awad, Mona. *Bunny*
Berg, Elizabeth. *The Confession Club: A Novel*
Bledsoe, Lucy Jane. *The Big Bang Symphony: A Novel of Antarctica*
Boianjiu, Shani. *The People of Forever Are Not Afraid: A Novel*
Bowman, Valerie. *The Unexpected Duchess*
Brockway, Connie. *So Enchanting*
Buntin, Julie. ★*Marlena: A Novel*
Burton, Tara Isabella. *Social Creature*
Bushnell, Candace. *Is There Still Sex in the City?*
Carty-Williams, Candice. ★*Queenie*
Chiaverini, Jennifer. *Mrs. Lincoln's Dressmaker: A Novel*
Childs, Laura. *Egg Shooters*
Clark, Georgia. *The Bucket List*
Cleave, Chris. *Gold*
Cline, Rachel. *My Liar: A Novel*
Crouch, Katie. *Embassy Wife*
Daniels, Natalie. *Too Close*
Darznik, Jasmin. *The Bohemians*
Davis, Fiona. *The Chelsea Girls*
Diamant, Anita. *The Boston Girl: A Novel*
Dickey, Eric Jerome. *The Blackbirds*
Doan, Amy Mason. *The Summer List*
Drabble, Margaret. *A Day in the Life of a Smiling Woman: Complete Short Stories*
Drabble, Margaret. *The Pure Gold Baby*
Ferrante, Elena. *The Story of a New Name*
Ferrante, Elena. *The Story of the Lost Child*
Ferrante, Elena. *Those Who Leave and Those Who Stay*
Fielding, Helen. ★*Bridget Jones's Diary: A Novel*
Flagg, Fannie. ★*Fried Green Tomatoes at the Whistle Stop Cafe*
Florio, Gwen. *Silent Hearts*
Foster, Lori. *Sisters of Summer's End*
Freudenberger, Nell. ★*Lost and Wanted: A Novel*
Gaitskill, Mary. *Veronica*
Garner, Helen. *The Spare Room*
Gibson, Claire. *Beyond the Point: A Novel*
Gilbert, Elizabeth. ★*City of Girls*
Godwin, Gail. *Old Lovegood Girls*
Hall, Araminta. *Imperfect Women: A Novel*
Hamilton, Karen. *The Last Wife*
Harbison, Beth. *The Cookbook Club*
Harrison, Rachel. *The Return*
Healey, Emma. ★*Elizabeth Is Missing*
Heller, Zoe. *What Was She Thinking?: Notes on a Scandal*
Hendricks, Greer. ★*You Are Not Alone*
Hendrix, Grady. *My Best Friend's Exorcism*
Huber, Anna Lee. *Penny for Your Secrets*
Jaswal, Balli Kaur. *Erotic Stories for Punjabi Widows*
Kane, Jessica Francis. *Rules for Visiting*
Kelly, Julia. *The Last Dance of the Debutante*
Kelly, Martha Hall. *Lost Roses: A Novel*
Kibler, Julie. *Home for Erring and Outcast Girls*
Kingsolver, Barbara. ★*The Bean Trees: A Novel*
Krentz, Jayne Ann. *Secret Sisters*
Kutsukake, Lynne. *The Translation of Love: A Novel*
Langan, Sarah. *Good Neighbors*
Lansdale, Joe R. *Edge of Dark Water*
Lewis, Beverly. *The Missing*

Luchette, Claire. *Agatha of Little Neon*
McCall Smith, Alexander. *The Joy and Light Bus Company*
McMillan, Terry. ★*It's Not All Downhill from Here: A Novel*
McMurtry, Larry. *The Evening Star: A Novel*
Molloy, Aimee. *The Perfect Mother: A Novel*
Morrison, Toni. *Sula*
Moshfegh, Ottessa. *Eileen*
Nunez, Sigrid. *What Are You Going Through*
Parrish, Christa. *Still Life*
Patterson, James. *1st to Die: A Novel*
Peebles, Frances de Pontes. *The Air You Breathe*
Pride, Christine. ★*We Are Not Like Them*
Rao, Shobha. ★*Girls Burn Brighter*
Rochon, Farrah. *The Boyfriend Project*
Rooney, Sally. ★*Conversations with Friends*
Ross, Ann B. ★*Miss Julia Happily Ever After*
Ross, Ann B. *Miss Julia Knows a Thing or Two*
Ross, Ann B. *Miss Julia Takes the Wheel*
Saums, Mary. *Thistle & Twigg*
See, Lisa. *The Island of Sea Women*
Shipman, Viola. *The Clover Girls*
Shipman, Viola. *The Heirloom Garden*
Smith, Zadie. ★*Swing Time*
Solomon, Asali. *The Days of Afrekete*
Stratford, Sarah-Jane. *Red Letter Days*
Tan, Amy. ★*The Joy Luck Club*
Umrigar, Thrity N. *The Secrets Between Us*
Updike, John. ★*The Witches of Eastwick*
Walbert, Kate. *She Was Like That: New and Selected Stories*
Ware, Ruth. *In a Dark, Dark Wood*
Williams, Tennessee. ★*The Roman Spring of Mrs. Stone*
Woodson, Jacqueline. ★*Another Brooklyn*

FEMALE GANG LEADERS
De Leon, Aya. *Side Chick Nation*

FEMALE IMPERSONATORS
McBride, James. ★*The Good Lord Bird*
*The **Female** Persuasion*. Wolitzer, Meg

FEMININE BEAUTY (AESTHETICS)
James, Eloisa. *The Ugly Duchess*

Feminine pursuits [Series]. Waite, Olivia

FEMININITY
Ellis, Helen. *American Housewife: Stories*
Krauss, Nicole. ★*To Be a Man: Stories*
Moniz, Dantiel W. *Milk Blood Heat*

FEMINISM
Ahern, Cecelia. *Roar*
Armfield, Julia. *Salt Slow: Stories*
Farah, Nuruddin. *Knots*
Irving, John. ★*The World According to Garp: A Novel*
Shields, Carol. *Unless*
Woolf, Virginia. ★*Mrs. Dalloway*

FEMINISTS
Darznik, Jasmin. *Song of a Captive Bird: A Novel*
French, Marilyn. ★*The Women's Room*
Kidd, Sue Monk. ★*The Invention of Wings: A Novel*
Lessing, Doris May. ★*The Golden Notebook*
Scoppettone, Sandra. *Everything You Have Is Mine*
Scoppettone, Sandra. *My Sweet Untraceable You*

Stridsberg, Sara. *Valerie: Or the Faculty of Dreams : Amendment to the Theory of Sexuality*

Vargas Llosa, Mario. ★*The Way to Paradise*

Wolitzer, Meg. *The Female Persuasion*

Femlandia. Dalcher, Christina

FEMMES FATALES

Hammett, Dashiell. ★*The Maltese Falcon*

Hilton, L. S. *Maestra*

Lansdale, Joe R. *More Better Deals*

Lippman, Laura. ★*Sunburn*

FENCES (PERSONS)

Whitehead, Colson. ★*Harlem Shuffle*

Feng, Linda Rui

Swimming Back to Trout River

FENS

Griffiths, Elly. *The Lantern Men: A Dr. Ruth Galloway Mystery*

Ferber, Edna

So Big

Ferencik, Erica

Into the Jungle

FERGUSSON, CLARE (FICTITIOUS CHARACTER)

Spencer-Fleming, Julia. *I Shall Not Want: A Clare Fergusson/Russ Van Alstyne Mystery*

Fernandez, Nona

The Twilight Zone

Ferrante, Elena

The Lost Daughter

The Lying Life of Adults

My Brilliant Friend

The Story of a New Name

The Story of the Lost Child

Those Who Leave and Those Who Stay

FERRARA, ITALY

Dunant, Sarah. *Sacred Hearts: A Novel*

Ferraris, Zoe

Finding Nouf

Kingdom of Strangers: A Novel

Ferrell, Carolyn

Dear Miss Metropolitan

Ferris, Joshua

A Calling for Charlie Barnes

To Rise Again at a Decent Hour: A Novel

The Unnamed

FERTILITY DRUGS

Patchett, Ann. ★*State of Wonder: A Novel*

Fesperman, Dan

Safe Houses: A Novel

FESTIVALS

Crews, Harry. *A Feast of Snakes: A Novel*

Davis, Lindsey. *A Comedy of Terrors: A Flavia Albia Novel*

Whitehead, Colson. *John Henry Days: A Novel*

FETAL ALCOHOL SYNDROME

MacDonald, Andrew. *When We Were Vikings*

Fethering mysteries [Series]. Brett, Simon

FETISHISM (SEXUALITY)

Cumyn, Alan. *Losing It*

FEUDALISM

Druon, Maurice. *The Iron King*

Twain, Mark. ★*A Connecticut Yankee in King Arthur's Court*

FEUDS

Berger, Thomas. ★*Neighbors: A Novel*

Goldin, Megan. *The Escape Room*

Riley, Lucinda. *The Girl on the Cliff: A Novel*

The Fever. Abbott, Megan E.

Fever Dream: A Novel. Schweblin, Samanta

Fever. Pronzini, Bill

The Few. Gunday, Hakan

A Few Drops of Bitters. McKevett, G. A.

ffitch, Madeline

Stay and Fight

Fforde, Jasper

★*Early Riser: A Novel*

The Eyre Affair: A Novel

Lost in a Good Book: A Thursday Next Novel

Shades of Grey: A Novel

A Fiancee's Guide to First Wives and Murder. Freeman, Dianne

FIANCES

Bialosky, Jill. *House Under Snow*

FIANCES — DEATH

Deveraux, Jude. *Someone to Love*

Jimenez, Abby. ★*The Happy Ever After Playlist*

Landon, Sydney. *Wishing for Us*

Ficciones. Borges, Jorge Luis

FICTION — APPRECIATION

Fowler, Karen Joy. *The Jane Austen Book Club*

FICTION WRITING

Auster, Paul. *Oracle Night*

Crowley, John. *Lord Byron's Novel: The Evening Land*

Everett, Percival L. *Erasure: A Novel*

Fidelity. Perry, Thomas

Field of Prey. Sandford, John

Fielding, Helen

★*Bridget Jones's Diary: A Novel*

Fielding, Henry

★*The History of Tom Jones, a Foundling*

Fielding, Joy

All the Wrong Places: A Novel

The Bad Daughter: A Novel

Fields Where They Lay. Hallinan, Timothy

Fields, Hilary

Last Chance Llama Ranch

Fierce Invalids Home from Hot Climates. Robbins, Tom

Fierce Kingdom: A Novel. Phillips, Gin

★*The Fiery Cross*. Gabaldon, Diana

Fifteen Dogs. Alexis, Andre

FIFTEEN-YEAR-OLD BOYS

Brown, Larry. *Joe: A Novel*

Doctorow, E. L. ★*Billy Bathgate: A Novel*

Ford, Richard. *Canada*

Haddon, Mark. ★*The Curious Incident of the Dog in the Night-Time: A Novel*

McMurtry, Larry. *Boone's Lick: A Novel*

Schaefer, Jack. ★*Shane*

FIFTEEN-YEAR-OLD GIRLS

Gibbons, Kaye. *The Life All Around Me by Ellen Foster*

Shreve, Anita. *The Pilot's Wife: A Novel*

Fifth Avenue rebels [Series]. Shupe, Joanna
★*The Fifth Child*. Lessing, Doris May
The Fifth Elephant: A Novel of Discworld. Pratchett, Terry
The Fifth Floor. Harvey, Michael T.
The Fifth Heart. Simmons, Dan
The Fifth Season. Jemisin, N. K.
The Fifth Witness. Connelly, Michael
FIFTIES (AGE)
    Dann, Patty. *The Wright Sister*
    Fuller, Claire. *Unsettled Ground*
    Ozick, Cynthia. *Foreign Bodies*
    Porter, Chana. *The Seep: A Novel*
Fight Club. Palahniuk, Chuck
Fight Night. Toews, Miriam
FIGHTER PILOTS
    Dalton, Trent. *All Our Shimmering Skies*
    Deutermann, Peter T. *The Nugget: A Novel*
    Groot, Tracy. *Flame of Resistance*
    Michener, James A. ★*The Bridges at Toko-Ri*
FIGHTER PLANE COMBAT
    Benn, James R. *Road of Bones: A Billy Boyle World War II Mystery*
The Fighter: a Novel. Smith, Michael F.
FILIPINO AMERICAN WOMEN
    Manansala, Mia P. ★*Arsenic and Adobo*
FILIPINO AMERICANS
    Tenorio, Lysley A. *The Son of Good Fortune: A Novel*
FILIPINOS
    Alvar, Mia. *In the Country: Stories*
FILM — PRESERVATION
    Estleman, Loren D. *Frames*
FILM ACTORS AND ACTRESSES
    Alcott, Kate. *A Touch of Stardust*
    Auster, Paul. ★*The Book of Illusions: A Novel*
    Bagshawe, Tilly. *Adored*
    Barry, Ava. *Windhall*
    Burdick, Serena. *Find Me in Havana*
    Furst, Alan. ★*Mission to Paris*
    Gaynor, Hazel. *Meet Me in Monaco: A Novel*
    Kaminsky, Stuart M. *Dancing in the Dark*
    Kaminsky, Stuart M. *To Catch a Spy: A Toby Peters Mystery*
    Leonard, Elmore. *Labrava*
    Oates, Joyce Carol. *Blonde: A Novel*
    Randisi, Robert J. *Hey There (You with the Gun in Your Hand): A Rat Pack Mystery*
FILM COLLECTORS AND COLLECTING
    Estleman, Loren D. ★*Indigo: A Valentino Mystery*
FILM CRITICS
    Kaufman, Charlie. *Antkind: A Novel*
FILM INDUSTRY AND TRADE
    Alexander, Jennet. *I Kissed a Girl*
    Allen, Jane. *I Lost My Girlish Laughter*
    Bagshawe, Tilly. *Adored*
    Boyd, William. *Trio*
    Bradley, C. Alan. *I Am Half-Sick of Shadows: A Flavia De Luce Novel*
    Burke, James Lee. ★*The New Iberia Blues*
    Cline, Rachel. *My Liar: A Novel*
    Dev, Sonali. ★*A Bollywood Affair*

Didion, Joan. ★*Play It as It Lays: A Novel*
Hambly, Barbara. *Scandal in Babylon*
Leonard, Elmore. ★*Be Cool: Everyone Is Looking for the Next Big Hit*
Puzo, Mario. *The Last Don*
Quick, Amanda. *The Girl Who Knew Too Much*
Smith, Dominic. ★*The Electric Hotel*
Waugh, Evelyn. *The Loved One: An Anglo-American Tragedy*
West, Nathanael. *Novels and Other Writings*
Winfrey, Kerry. *Waiting for Tom Hanks: A Novel*
FILM INDUSTRY AND TRADE — CORRUPT PRACTICES
    Leonard, Elmore. ★*Get Shorty*
FILM INDUSTRY AND TRADE — HISTORY
    Estleman, Loren D. *Frames*
FILM INDUSTRY AND TRADE EXECUTIVES
    Fitzgerald, F. Scott. ★*The Last Tycoon: An Unfinished Novel*
    Garey, Juliann. *Too Bright to Hear Too Loud to See*
    Kroese, Robert. *The Last Iota*
FILM PRODUCERS AND DIRECTORS
    Allen, Jane. *I Lost My Girlish Laughter*
    Barry, Ava. *Windhall*
    Dev, Sonali. ★*A Bollywood Affair*
    Leonard, Elmore. ★*Be Cool: Everyone Is Looking for the Next Big Hit*
    Woods, Stuart. ★*Bombshell*
    Woods, Stuart. *Santa Fe Rules*
FILM PROJECTIONISTS
    Nicholls, Owen. *Love, Unscripted: A Novel*
FILM STUDIOS
    Allen, Jane. *I Lost My Girlish Laughter*
FILM THEATER MANAGERS
    Enger, Leif. *Virgil Wander*
FILMMAKERS
    Anders, Charlie Jane. *Rock Manning Goes for Broke*
    Gerritsen, Tess. *I Know a Secret*
    Minh, Drew. *Neon Empire*
    North, Anna. *The Life and Death of Sophie Stark*
    Rushdie, Salman. ★*The Golden House*
FILMMAKING
    Auster, Paul. ★*The Book of Illusions: A Novel*
    Bradley, C. Alan. *I Am Half-Sick of Shadows: A Flavia De Luce Novel*
    Cotterill, Colin. *Don't Eat Me*
    Hall, Parnell. *Lights! Camera! Puzzles!*
    Scoppettone, Sandra. *My Sweet Untraceable You*
    Valente, Catherynne M. *Radiance*
FILMS
    Kaufman, Charlie. *Antkind: A Novel*
FILMS — HISTORY
    Smith, Dominic. ★*The Electric Hotel*
FILMS — PRODUCTION AND DIRECTION
    Furst, Alan. ★*Mission to Paris*
    Kleeman, Alexandra. *Something New Under the Sun*
★*Filthy Animals*. Taylor, Brandon
Fima. Oz, Amos
The Final Cut. Coulter, Catherine
Final Cut. Watson, S. J.
The Final Girl Support Group. Hendrix, Grady

Final Girls: A Novel. Sager, Riley

Final Judgment. Clark, Marcia

★*Final Option*. Cussler, Clive

★The *Final Revival of Opal & Nev.* Walton, Dawnie

Final Spin. Willink, Jocko

Finale: a Novel. Mallon, Thomas

FINANCIAL CRISES
    Brockway, Connie. *The Golden Season*

FINANCIAL INTRIGUE
    Porter, Henry. *White Hot Silence*
    Spiegelman, Peter. *Black Maps*

FINANCIAL PLANNERS
    Pronzini, Bill. *Mourners*

FINANCIAL SERVICES INDUSTRY AND TRADE — CORRUPT PRACTICES
    Sears, Michael. *Black Fridays*

FINANCIAL THRILLERS
    Finder, Joseph. *Buried Secrets*
    Finder, Joseph. *The Fixer*
    Finder, Joseph. *Suspicion*
    Finder, Joseph. *Vanished*
    McDonald, Ian. *New Moon*
    Sears, Michael. *Black Fridays*
    Spiegelman, Peter. *Black Maps*

Finch. Vandermeer, Jeff

Finch, Charles
    A Beautiful Blue Death
    The Last Passenger
    The September Society
    The Vanishing Man

Find Her. Gardner, Lisa

Find Me. Aciman, Andre

Find Me Gone. Meuleman, Sarah

Find Me in Havana. Burdick, Serena

Finder, Joseph
    Buried Secrets
    The Fixer
    Guilty Minds
    ★*House on Fire: A Novel*
    ★*Judgment*
    Suspicion
    The Switch: A Novel
    Vanished

Finders Keepers. King, Stephen

★The *Finders: a Mace Reid K-9 Mystery*. Burton, Jeffrey B.

Finding Gideon. Dickey, Eric Jerome

Finding Nouf. Ferraris, Zoe

★*A Fine and Bitter Snow: A Kate Shugak Novel*. Stabenow, Dana

A Fine and Private Place. Beagle, Peter S.

Fine Just the Way It Is: Wyoming Stories 3. Proulx, Annie

Fine, Julia
    The Upstairs House
    What Should Be Wild

FINLAND
    Hand, Elizabeth. *Available Dark: A Thriller*
    Lawton, John. *Hammer to Fall*
    Marlantes, Karl. *Deep River*

Finlay Donovan Is Killing It. Cosimano, Elle

Finlay Donovan novels [Series]. Cosimano, Elle

Finlay, Mick
    The Murder Pit

Finn novels [Series]. Webb, Brandon

Finn, A. J.
    ★*The Woman in the Window*

FINN, HUCKLEBERRY (FICTITIOUS CHARACTER)
    Clinch, Jon. *Finn: A Novel*

Finn: a Novel. Clinch, Jon

Finna novels (Nino Cipri) [Series]. Cipri, Nino

★*Finnegans Wake*. Joyce, James

Fionavar tapestry [Series]. Kay, Guy Gavriel

FIRE
    Andrews, Mesu. *Of Fire and Lions: A Novel*
    George, Margaret. *The Splendor Before the Dark: A Novel of the Emperor Nero*

Fire & Blood: 300 Years Before a Game of Thrones (A Targaryen History). Martin, George R. R.

Fire and ice [Series]. Ridpath, Michael

Fire Down Below. Golding, William

FIRE FIGHTERS
    Blackstock, Terri. *Smoke Screen*
    Buchman, M. L. *Pure Heat*
    Jimenez, Abby. *The Friend Zone*

Fire in the Blood. O'Brien, Perry Edmond

Fire on the Mountain. Desai, Anita

Fire sermon [Series]. Haig, Francesca

The Fire Sermon: A Novel. Haig, Francesca

A Fire Upon the Deep. Vinge, Vernor

Firebird. Powell, Mark

Firefly. Porter, Henry

Firefly Summer. Binchy, Maeve

Firehawks [Series]. Buchman, M. L.

★*Firelight*. Callihan, Kristen

The Fireman: a Novel. Hill, Joe

FIRES
    Francis, Felix. *Crisis*
    Hill, Joe. *The Fireman: A Novel*
    Hoffman, Alice. *The Museum of Extraordinary Things: A Novel*
    King, Stephen. *Firestarter*
    Macdonald, Ross. *The Underground Man*
    Reid, Taylor Jenkins. ★*Malibu Rising*
    Spencer-Fleming, Julia. *Through the Evil Days: A Clare Fergusson/Russ Van Alstyne Mystery*

The Fires of Vengeance. Winter, Evan

Firestarter. King, Stephen

Firewall. Mankell, Henning

★*Firewatching*. Thomas, Russ

★*The Firm*. Grisham, John

Firmin: Adventures of a Metropolitan Lowlife. Savage, Sam

The First Actress: A Novel of Sarah Bernhardt. Gortner, C. W.

★*First Comes Like*. Rai, Alisha

The First Cut. Robinson, Peter

★*The First Deadly Sin*. Sanders, Lawrence

First Earl I See Tonight. Bennett, Anna

FIRST EDITIONS
    Block, Lawrence. ★*The Burglar in the Library*

FIRST IMPRESSIONS

Ohlsson, Kristina. *Unwanted: A Novel*

Thorne, Sally. *Second First Impressions*

FIRST LOVES

Aciman, Andre. *Call Me by Your Name*

Aciman, Andre. *Enigma Variations: A Novel*

Banville, John. *Ancient Light*

Calvi, Mary. *Dear George, Dear Mary: A Novel of George Washington's First Love*

Dev, Sonali. *The Bollywood Bride*

Fitch, Janet. *Paint It Black: A Novel*

Francis, Patry. *The Orphans of Race Point: A Novel*

French, Tana. *Faithful Place: A Novel*

Giordano, Paolo. *Heaven and Earth*

Hijuelos, Oscar. *Beautiful Maria of My Soul*

Hijuelos, Oscar. ★*The Mambo Kings Play Songs of Love: A Novel*

McFarlane, Mhairi. *Don't You Forget About Me*

Murakami, Haruki. *South of the Border, West of the Sun*

O'Neill, Heather. ★*The Lonely Hearts Hotel: A Novel*

Park, Ishle Yi. *Angel & Hannah: A Novel in Verse*

Rooney, Sally. *Normal People: A Novel*

Roth, Philip. *Indignation*

Schami, Rafik. *Sophia: Or the Beginning of All Tales*

Sparks, Nicholas. *A Walk to Remember*

*The **First** Man in Rome*. McCullough, Colleen

FIRST NATIONS (CANADA)

Kamal, Sheena. *It All Falls Down*

Rice, Waubgeshig. *Moon of the Crusted Snow: A Novel*

First of State. Greer, Robert O.

FIRST PERSON NARRATIVES

Abbott, Megan E. *Queenpin: A Novel*

Abu-Jaber, Diana. *Origin: A Novel*

Aciman, Andre. *Harvard Square*

Ackerman, Elliot. ★*Waiting for Eden: A Novel*

Alameddine, Rabih. *An Unnecessary Woman*

Alarcon, Daniel. *At Night We Walk in Circles: A Novel*

Albahari, David. *Gotz and Meyer*

Amis, Martin. ★*The Zone of Interest: A Novel*

Anderton, Jo. *Debris*

Andrews, Mesu. *Of Fire and Lions: A Novel*

Atwood, Margaret. ★*The Testaments: A Novel*

Austin, Finola. *Bronte's Mistress*

Baker, Jo. *The Body Lies*

Baldwin, Joshua. *The Wilshire Sun*

Ball, Jesse. *Census*

Banks, Russell. ★*The Sweet Hereafter*

Banville, John. *The Blue Guitar*

Banville, John. *The Book of Evidence*

Banville, John. ★*Eclipse: A Novel*

Banville, John. ★*The Sea*

Barbery, Muriel. *The Elegance of the Hedgehog*

Barnes, Jonathan. *The Somnambulist*

Barnett, S. K. *Safe*

Barry, Sebastian. ★*A Thousand Moons: A Novel*

Barth, John. ★*The Floating Opera*

Bates, Judy Fong. ★*Midnight at the Dragon Cafe*

Bauermeister, Erica. *The Scent Keeper*

Beattie, Ann. *The Doctor's House: A Novel*

Beattie, Ann. *A Wonderful Stroke of Luck: A Novel*

Bellow, Saul. *The Bellarosa Connection*

Bellow, Saul. ★*Henderson the Rain King: A Novel*

Bellow, Saul. ★*Humboldt's Gift*

Benn, James R. ★*The Red Horse: A Billy Boyle World War II Mystery*

Benn, James R. *Road of Bones: A Billy Boyle World War II Mystery*

Bernhard, Thomas. *Frost: A Novel*

Beukes, Lauren. *Zoo City*

Binchy, Maeve. ★*Whitethorn Woods*

Bolano, Roberto. *Amulet*

Bolano, Roberto. ★*Distant Star*

Booth, Coe. ★*Bronxwood*

Bordas, Camille. *How to Behave in a Crowd*

Bouchet, Amanda. *Breath of Fire*

Bouchet, Amanda. ★*A Promise of Fire*

Bourland, Barbara. ★*Fake Like Me*

Boyle, T. Coraghessan. *The Terranauts*

Bronte, Charlotte. ★*Jane Eyre*

Burke, James Lee. *Black Cherry Blues*

Butland, Stephanie. *The Lost for Words Bookshop: A Novel*

Butler, Robert Olen. *A Good Scent from a Strange Mountain: Stories*

Byrne, Trevor. *Ghosts and Lightning*

Cameron, W. Bruce. *A Dog's Promise*

Cameron, W. Bruce. *Repo Madness*

Carr, Brian Allen. ★*Opioid, Indiana*

Carr, Caleb. ★*The Alienist*

Carr, Caleb. *The Angel of Darkness*

Carter, Mary Dixie. *The Photographer*

Carty-Williams, Candice. ★*Queenie*

Chandler, Raymond. ★*The Big Sleep*

Chandler, Raymond. *The Lady in the Lake*

Chandler, Raymond. *The Long Goodbye*

Chang, Alexandra. ★*Days of Distraction*

Chavez, Heather. *No Bad Deed*

Cherryh, C. J. *Foreigner: A Novel of First Contact*

Child, Lee. ★*The Sentinel*

Choi, Susan. *My Education*

Chung, Catherine. *The Tenth Muse: A Novel*

Church, James. *A Drop of Chinese Blood*

Clark, Martin. *The Substitution Order*

Clark, P. Djeli. *Ring Shout*

Clegg, Bill. *Did You Ever Have a Family*

Cline, Ernest. *Ready Player One: A Novel*

Cobb, May K. *The Hunting Wives*

Cocks, Heather. *The Heir Affair*

Cocks, Heather. *The Royal We*

Cole, Teju. *Every Day Is for the Thief*

Cole, Teju. ★*Open City: A Novel*

Colette. *The Complete Claudine*

Collins, Ciaran. *The Gamal*

Collins, Sara. *The Confessions of Frannie Langton*

Cooley, Martha. *The Archivist: A Novel*

Cornwell, Patricia Daniels. *Autopsy*

Cornwell, Patricia Daniels. *Postmortem*

Corthron, Kia. *Moon and the Mars*

Crossan, Sarah. *Here Is the Beehive*

Danler, Stephanie. *Sweetbitter*

Deaver, Jeffery. *Edge: A Novel*

Delinsky, Barbara. *A Week at the Shore*
Diop, David. ★*At Night All Blood Is Black*
Doctorow, E. L. *Homer and Langley: A Novel*
Doctorow, E. L. ★*Ragtime*
Doctorow, E. L. *World's Fair*
Dolan-Leach, Caite. *We Went to the Woods: A Novel*
Dostoyevsky, Fyodor. *Notes from Underground*
Dovlatov, Sergei. *Pushkin Hills*
Downing, Samantha. *My Lovely Wife*
Drabble, Margaret. *The Pure Gold Baby*
Duenas, Maria. *The Time in Between: A Novel*
Dunant, Sarah. *In the Company of the Courtesan: A Novel*
Duncan, Glen. *By Blood We Live*
Duncan, Glen. *The Last Werewolf*
Duncan, Glen. *Talulla Rising*
Eggers, Dave. *What Is the What: The Autobiography of Valentino Achak Deng*
Ellmann, Lucy. *Ducks, Newburyport*
Emezi, Akwaeke. ★*The Death of Vivek Oji*
Enger, Leif. *Virgil Wander*
Erpenbeck, Jenny. *The Book of Words*
Estleman, Loren D. *Infernal Angels*
Estleman, Loren D. *A Smile on the Face of the Tiger*
Evanovich, Janet. ★*Game On: Tempting Twenty-Eight*
Evanovich, Janet. *Look Alive Twenty-Five*
Evanovich, Janet. *One for the Money*
Evanovich, Janet. *Turbo Twenty-Three*
Fabry, Chris. *The Promise of Jesse Woods*
Faye, Lyndsay. ★*The Paragon Hotel*
Fernandez, Nona. *The Twilight Zone*
Fforde, Jasper. ★*Early Riser: A Novel*
Fforde, Jasper. *The Eyre Affair: A Novel*
Fforde, Jasper. *Lost in a Good Book: A Thursday Next Novel*
Flynn, Gillian. ★*Gone Girl: A Novel*
Flynn, Gillian. ★*Sharp Objects: A Novel*
Foer, Jonathan Safran. *Extremely Loud and Incredibly Close*
Force, Marie. *Five Years Gone*
Ford, Richard. ★*Independence Day*
Ford, Richard. *The Lay of the Land*
Ford, Richard. *Let Me Be Frank with You*
Fowler, Karen Joy. ★*We Are All Completely Beside Ourselves*
Francis, Dick. *Smokescreen*
Francis, Felix. *Guilty Not Guilty*
Frank, Dorothea Benton. *Folly Beach: A Lowcountry Tale*
Frazier, Jean Kyoung. *Pizza Girl*
Freeman, Anna. *The Fair Fight: A Novel*
French, Tana. *In the Woods*
French, Tana. *The Likeness*
Friedman, Daniel. *Running Out of Road*
Fuller, Claire. *Our Endless Numbered Days: A Novel*
Gabaldon, Diana. ★*A Breath of Snow and Ashes*
Gabaldon, Diana. ★*Dragonfly in Amber*
Gabaldon, Diana. ★*Drums of Autumn*
Gabaldon, Diana. *An Echo in the Bone*
Gabaldon, Diana. ★*The Fiery Cross*
Gabaldon, Diana. ★*Outlander*
Gabaldon, Diana. ★*Voyager*
Gabaldon, Diana. *Written in My Own Heart's Blood*

Gaige, Amity. *Schroder*
Gaige, Amity. *Sea Wife*
Gailey, Sarah. *Magic for Liars*
Gaiman, Neil. ★*The Ocean at the End of the Lane*
Galloway, Gregory. *As Simple as Snow*
Garcia Marquez, Gabriel. *Memories of My Melancholy Whores*
Gardner, Lisa. *The Neighbor*
Garey, Juliann. *Too Bright to Hear Too Loud to See*
Garner, Helen. *The Spare Room*
Garrett, Kellye. ★*Hollywood Homicide*
Gates, Eva. *Deadly Ever After*
Gates, Eva. *A Death Long Overdue*
Gates, Eva. *Read and Buried*
Genova, Lisa. *Left Neglected: A Novel*
George, Margaret. *Elizabeth I: A Novel*
Gibbons, Kaye. *Charms for the Easy Life*
Gideon, Melanie. *Wife 22*
Gilman, Laura Anne. *Hard Magic*
Giordano, Mario. ★*Auntie Poldi and the Lost Madonna*
Giordano, Mario. *Auntie Poldi and the Vineyards of Etna*
Giordano, Paolo. *Like Family*
Glass, Julia. ★*Three Junes*
Goddard, Robert. *Beyond Recall: A Novel*
Godwin, Gail. *Unfinished Desires*
Golding, William. *Rites of Passage*
Gordimer, Nadine. *The Conservationist*
Gortner, C. W. *The First Actress: A Novel of Sarah Bernhardt*
Gottlieb, Eli. *Best Boy: A Novel*
Grass, Gunter. *Crabwalk*
Greengrass, Jessie. *Sight: A Novel*
Gruen, Sara. ★*Water for Elephants: A Novel*
Haddon, Mark. ★*The Curious Incident of the Dog in the Night-Time: A Novel*
Hall, Alexis. ★*Boyfriend Material*
Hall, Rachel Howzell. *These Toxic Things*
Han, Kang. *The White Book*
Harris, Sarah J. *The Color of Bee Larkham's Murder: A Novel*
Harrison, Rachel. *The Return*
Hart, John. *The King of Lies*
Hart, Josephine. *Damage: A Novel*
Haslett, Adam. ★*Imagine Me Gone: A Novel*
Heacox, Kim. *Jimmy Bluefeather: A Novel*
Healey, Emma. ★*Elizabeth Is Missing*
Heinlein, Robert A. ★*Starship Troopers*
Heller, Peter. *The Painter: A Novel*
Hemmings, Kaui Hart. *The Possibilities: A Novel*
Hensher, Philip. *Scenes from Early Life: A Novel*
Hiaasen, Carl. *Basket Case*
Hoffman, Alice. *The Ice Queen: A Novel*
Holt, Victoria. *The Black Opal*
Hoover, Colleen. *It Ends with Us*
Horowitz, Anthony. *The House of Silk: A Sherlock Holmes Novel*
Horowitz, Anthony. ★*The Sentence Is Death*
Horowitz, Anthony. ★*The Word Is Murder*
Hosking, Jay. *Three Years with the Rat: A Novel*
Hosseini, Khaled. ★*The Kite Runner*
Jordan, Hillary. *Mudbound: A Novel*
Kadare, Ismail. ★*The Three-Arched Bridge*

Kaminsky, Stuart M. *Dancing in the Dark*
Kaminsky, Stuart M. *To Catch a Spy: A Toby Peters Mystery*
Khadivi, Laleh. ★*A Good Country: A Novel*
Khadra, Yasmina. ★*Khalil: A Novel*
Kidd, Sue Monk. ★*The Book of Longings*
Kilalea, Katharine. *Ok, Mr. Field: A Novel*
Kirshenbaum, Binnie. *Rabbits for Food*
Knight, Renee. *The Secretary: A Novel*
Knott, Robert. *Robert B. Parker's Buckskin*
Kundera, Milan. ★*Immortality*
Kurian, Vera. *Never Saw Me Coming*
Kushner, Rachel. *The Mars Room*
Lasdun, James. *Afternoon of a Faun: A Novel*
Lattari, Katie. *Dark Things I Adore*
Leckie, Ann. ★*The Raven Tower*
Leilani, Raven. ★*Luster*
Limon, Martin. *The Line*
Limon, Martin. *War Women*
Liu, Cixin. *Ball Lightning*
Lodato, Victor. *Mathilda Savitch*
MacDonald, John D. *Cinnamon Skin: The Twentieth Adventure of Travis McGee*
MacDonald, John D. *The Green Ripper*
MacDonald, John D. ★*The Lonely Silver Rain*
MacDonald, John D. *The Long Lavender Look*
MacDonald, John D. *A Purple Place for Dying*
MacDonald, John D. *The Scarlet Ruse*
MacDonald, John D. *The Turquoise Lament*
March, Nev. *Murder in Old Bombay*
Marias, Javier. *The Infatuations*
Mason, Meg. *Sorrow and Bliss*
Maugham, W. Somerset. *The Moon and Sixpence*
McCarthy, Cormac. ★*No Country for Old Men*
McHugh, Laura. *What's Done in Darkness: A Novel*
McKinney, Chris. *Midnight, Water City*
McMurtry, Larry. *Boone's Lick: A Novel*
McPherson, Catriona. ★*A Step so Grave*
Medie, Peace A. *His Only Wife: A Novel*
Mihalic, Susan. *Dark Horses*
Miller, Sue. *The Good Mother*
Minato, Kanae. *Confessions*
Mitchell, David. *Black Swan Green: A Novel*
Moniz, Tomas. *Big Familia*
Moore, Lorrie. *A Gate at the Stairs: A Novel*
Morante, Elsa. *Arturo's Island: A Novel*
Moreno, Gus. *This Thing Between US: A Novel*
Morrison, Toni. *Jazz*
Moshfegh, Ottessa. *Eileen*
Moshfegh, Ottessa. *My Year of Rest and Relaxation*
Mosley, Walter. ★*The Awkward Black Man: Stories*
Moyes, Jojo. *Me Before You: A Novel*
Mozley, Fiona. ★*Elmet*
Muller, Marcia. *Dead Midnight*
Nabokov, Vladimir Vladimirovich. ★*Lolita*
Nicholls, David. *US: A Novel*
Niffenegger, Audrey. *The Time Traveler's Wife: A Novel*
Novik, Naomi. *A Deadly Education: A Novel*
Novik, Naomi. *The Last Graduate: A Novel*

Nunez, Sigrid. *What Are You Going Through*
Nussbaum, Susan. *Good Kings, Bad Kings: A Novel*
Oates, Joyce Carol. *The Gravedigger's Daughter: A Novel*
Obioma, Chigozie. ★*The Fishermen: A Novel*
Oe, Kenzaburo. *Nip the Buds, Shoot the Kids*
Ólafsdóttir, Auður A. *Butterflies in November*
Osborne, Lawrence. *Only to Sleep: A Philip Marlowe Novel*
Otsuka, Julie. *The Buddha in the Attic*
Parker, Robert B. *Appaloosa*
Parker, Robert B. *Blue-Eyed Devil*
Parks, Brad. *Say Nothing: A Novel*
Pears, Iain. *An Instance of the Fingerpost*
Pearson, Allison. ★*How Hard Can It Be?*
Percy, Walker. ★*The Moviegoer*
Pike, Signe. *The Forgotten Kingdom: A Novel*
Pike, Signe. *The Lost Queen*
Poole, Sara. *The Borgia Mistress*
Portis, Charles. ★*The Dog of the South*
Portis, Charles. ★*Gringos: A Novel*
Price, Reynolds. *Roxanna Slade*
Pronzini, Bill. *Nightcrawlers*
Pronzini, Bill. *The Violated*
Raheem, Zara. *The Marriage Clock: A Novel*
Rawles, Nancy. *My Jim: A Novel*
Raybourn, Deanna. *A Curious Beginning: A Veronica Speedwell Mystery*
Raybourn, Deanna. *A Dangerous Collaboration*
Raybourn, Deanna. ★*A Murderous Relation*
Raybourn, Deanna. *A Perilous Undertaking: A Veronica Speedwell Mystery*
Raybourn, Deanna. *A Treacherous Curse: A Veronica Speedwell Mystery*
Reid, Iain. *I'm Thinking of Ending Things*
Remarque, Erich Maria. *The Road Back*
Rindell, Suzanne. ★*The Two Mrs. Carlyles*
Rooney, Sally. ★*Conversations with Friends*
Rose, M. J. *Tiffany Blues: A Novel*
Roth, Philip. ★*American Pastoral*
Rouda, Kaira Sturdivant. *Best Day Ever: A Novel*
Rowland, Laura Joh. *The Hangman's Secret*
Russell, Mary Doria. *Dreamers of the Day: A Novel*
Sager, Riley. *The Last Time I Lied: A Novel*
Sapphire. ★*The Kid: A Novel*
Sapphire. ★*Push: A Novel*
Savage, Sam. *The Way of the Dog: A Novel*
Schlink, Bernhard. *Self's Deception*
Schlink, Bernhard. *Self's Murder*
Schlink, Bernhard. *Self's Punishment*
Searles, John. *Help for the Haunted*
Sebald, Winfried Georg. ★*Austerlitz*
Sebald, Winfried Georg. *Vertigo*
See, Lisa. *The Island of Sea Women*
Shalev, Meir. *Two She-Bears: A Novel*
Shanbhag, Vivek. *Ghachar Ghochar*
Shannon, Samantha. *The Bone Season*
Shannon, Samantha. *The Mime Order*
Shapiro, Barbara A. *The Muralist*
Shepard, Jim. ★*The Book of Aron*

Simmons, Dan. *Drood: A Novel*
Smith, Scott. *A Simple Plan: A Novel*
Smith, Zadie. ★*Swing Time*
Solomon, Asali. *Disgruntled: A Novel*
Spencer, Scott. ★*Endless Love*
Spencer, Scott. *An Ocean Without a Shore*
Steadman, Catherine. *The Disappearing Act*
Stevens, Chevy. *Still Missing*
Stibbe, Nina. *Reasons to Be Cheerful*
Stout, Rex. *The Doorbell Rang*
Stout, Rex. ★*Gambit*
Straight, Susan. *A Million Nightingales*
Straub, Peter. *Lost Boy Lost Girl: A Novel*
Swift, Graham. ★*Mothering Sunday: A Romance*
Tartt, Donna. ★*The Secret History*
Temple, Emily. *The Lightness*
Tran, Vu. *Dragonfish: A Novel*
Tudor, C. J. *The Chalk Man: A Novel*
Ugresic, Dubravka. *Fox*
Vandermeer, Jeff. ★*Annihilation: A Novel*
Vann, David. *Aquarium*
Vargas Llosa, Mario. *Aunt Julia and the Scriptwriter*
Walker, Nico. ★*Cherry: A Novel*
Warren, Robert Penn. *Band of Angels*
Wayne, Teddy. *Apartment: A Novel*
Weiden, David L. ★*Winter Counts*
Weiss, Elizabeth. *The Sisters Sweet*
Wells, Benedict. *The End of Loneliness: A Novel*
Wells, Martha. *All Systems Red*
Wells, Martha. *Network Effect*
Wells, Rebecca. *Divine Secrets of the Ya-Ya Sisterhood: A Novel*
Welsh, Irvine. *Dead Men's Trousers*
Welsh, Irvine. *Trainspotting*
White, Edmund. *A Boy's Own Story*
Whitehead, Colson. *Sag Harbor: A Novel*
Whitfield, Clare. *People of Abandoned Character*
Wolfe, Gene. *The Citadel of the Autarch*
Wolfe, Gene. *The Claw of the Conciliator*
Wolfe, Gene. *The Land Across*
Wolff, Tobias. *Old School: A Novel*
Woodson, Jacqueline. ★*Another Brooklyn*
Wrobel, Stephanie. *Darling Rose Gold*
Yocum, Robin. *A Welcome Murder*
Yoshimoto, Banana. *The Lake*
Yu, Miri. *Tokyo Ueno Station*
★*First Person Singular: Stories*. Murakami, Haruki
First Position. Brayden, Melissa
The First Rule. Crais, Robert
First Sight. Steel, Danielle
First Sister novels [Series]. Lewis, Linden A.
The First Sister: A Novel. Lewis, Linden A.
First Star I See Tonight. Phillips, Susan Elizabeth
FIRST WORLD WAR ERA (1914-1918)
   Barker, Pat. ★*Regeneration*
   Bowen, Rhys. *The Victory Garden*
   Burke, James Lee. *House of the Rising Sun: A Novel*
   Dos Passos, John. *1919*
   Faulks, Sebastian. ★*Birdsong*

   Follett, Ken. *Fall of Giants*
   Forester, C. S. *The African Queen*
   Gohlke, Cathy. *Promise Me This*
   Hammad, Isabella. ★*The Parisian, Or, Al-Barisi: A Novel*
   Kelly, Martha Hall. *Lost Roses: A Novel*
   Keneally, Thomas. ★*The Daughters of Mars*
   Moyes, Jojo. *The Girl You Left Behind*
   Rash, Ron. ★*The Cove*
   Remarque, Erich Maria. ★*All Quiet on the Western Front*
   Riley, Lucinda. *The Girl on the Cliff: A Novel*
   Rooney, Kathleen. ★*Cher Ami and Major Whittlesey*
   Stewart, Amy. ★*Dear Miss Kopp*
   Stewart, Amy. *Kopp Sisters on the March*
   Stewart, Amy. *Lady Cop Makes Trouble*
   Stewart, Amy. ★*Miss Kopp Just Won't Quit*
   Stewart, Amy. *Miss Kopp's Midnight Confessions*
   Williams, Beatriz. *All the Ways We Said Goodbye: A Novel of the Ritz Paris*
   Wiseman, Ellen Marie. *The Orphan Collector*
Fisher, Helen
   Space Hopper
FISHER, PHRYNE (FICTITIOUS CHARACTER)
   Greenwood, Kerry. *Death in Daylesford*
Fisher, Tarryn
   The Wives
FISHERIES
   Stabenow, Dana. *Killing Grounds: A Kate Shugak Mystery*
★*The **Fishermen**: a Novel*. Obioma, Chigozie
FISHERS
   Ghosh, Amitav. *The Hungry Tide*
   Hemingway, Ernest. ★*The Old Man and the Sea*
   Mishima, Yukio. *The Sound of Waves*
   See, Lisa. *The Island of Sea Women*
   Shreve, Anita. *The Weight of Water*
   Stabenow, Dana. *Killing Grounds: A Kate Shugak Mystery*
   Steinbeck, John. *The Pearl*
   Tinti, Hannah. *The Twelve Lives of Samuel Hawley: A Novel*
FISHES
   Vann, David. *Aquarium*
FISHES IN ART
   Flanagan, Richard. *Gould's Book of Fish: A Novel in Twelve Fish*
FISHING
   DeMille, Nelson. ★*The Cuban Affair: A Novel*
   Smith, B. J. *Crow's Landing: A Novel*
FISHING BOAT CAPTAINS
   DeMille, Nelson. ★*The Cuban Affair: A Novel*
   Hemingway, Ernest. *To Have and Have Not*
FISHING BOATS
   McConaghy, Charlotte. *Migrations*
FISHING GUIDES
   Heller, Peter. *The Guide*
FISHING VILLAGES
   Crummey, Michael. *Galore*
   Hargrave, Kiran Millwood. *The Mercies: A Novel*
   Ono, Masatsugu. *Echo on the Bay*
   Stabenow, Dana. *So Sure of Death: A Liam Campbell Mystery*
FISK, CHARLES B.
   Angelo, Megan. *Followers*

Kiernan, Stephen P. *Universe of Two*
FISK, JEREMY (FICTITIOUS CHARACTER)
    Wolf, Dick. *The Ultimatum*
Fitch, Janet
    Paint It Black: A Novel
    White Oleander: A Novel
Fitzgerald, F. Scott
    ★*The Beautiful and Damned*
    ★*The Last Tycoon: An Unfinished Novel*
    Novels and Stories, 1920-1922
    ★*The Short Stories of F. Scott Fitzgerald: A New Collection*
    Six Tales of the Jazz Age and Other Stories
    ★*This Side of Paradise*
Fitzgerald, Penelope
    The Means of Escape: Stories
FITZGERALD, ZELDA
    Fowler, Therese. ★*Z: A Novel of Zelda Fitzgerald*
    Urrea, Luis Alberto. *Into the Beautiful North: A Novel*
Fitzpatrick, Lydia
    Lights All Night Long: A Novel
*The **Five** People You Meet in Heaven*. Albom, Mitch
Five people you meet in Heaven [Series]. Albom, Mitch
★*The **Five** Red Herrings*. Sayers, Dorothy L.
★*The **Five** Wounds: A Novel*. Quade, Kirstin Valdez
Five Years Gone. Force, Marie
Five-Carat Soul. McBride, James
FIVE-YEAR-OLD BOYS
    Beattie, Ann. ★*Picturing Will*
*The **Fix***. K'wan
Fix Her Up. Bailey, Tessa
Fix novels [Series]. K'wan
*The **Fixer***. Finder, Joseph
★*The **Fixer***. Malamud, Bernard
Flagg, Fannie
    ★*Fried Green Tomatoes at the Whistle Stop Cafe*
    Standing in the Rainbow: A Novel
    ★*The Wonder Boy of Whistle Stop: A Novel*
Flame of Resistance. Groot, Tracy
★*The **Flamenco** Academy: A Novel*. Bird, Sarah
FLAMENCO DANCERS
    Bird, Sarah. ★*The Flamenco Academy: A Novel*
Flanagan, Richard
    Gould's Book of Fish: A Novel in Twelve Fish
    The Living Sea of Waking Dreams
    ★*The Narrow Road to the Deep North*
    The Unknown Terrorist
Flanery, Patrick
    Absolution: A Novel
FLANNIGAN, KATHERINE MARY
    Freedman, Benedict. *Mrs. Mike: The Story of Katherine Mary*
        Flannigan
FLAPPERS
    Rosen, Renee. *Dollface: A Novel of the Roaring Twenties*
FLASHBACKS
    Black, Saul. *Anything for You*
    Eco, Umberto. *The Island of the Day Before*
    Foley, Lucy. *The Hunting Party*
    Robotham, Michael. *Life or Death*

*The **Flatshare**: a Novel*. O'Leary, Beth
★*Flaubert's Parrot*. Barnes, Julian
Flaubert, Gustave
    ★*Madame Bovary: Provincial Ways*
    Sentimental Education
FLAUBERT, GUSTAVE
    Barnes, Julian. ★*Flaubert's Parrot*
    Flaubert, Gustave. *Sentimental Education*
    Iles, Greg. *The Bone Tree: A Novel*
    Mengestu, Dinaw. ★*All Our Names*
Flavia Albia mysteries [Series]. Davis, Lindsey
Flavia De Luce mysteries [Series]. Bradley, C. Alan
Fleischmann, Raymond
    How Quickly She Disappears
Fleishman Is in Trouble: A Novel. Brodesser-Akner, Taffy
Fleming, Ian
    ★*Casino Royale: A James Bond Novel*
    Doctor No
    From Russia with Love
    ★*Goldfinger*
    The Man with the Golden Gun
    On Her Majesty's Secret Service
    You Only Live Twice
Flesh and Fire. Gilman, Laura Anne
*The **Flicker** of Old Dreams*. Henderson, Susan
Flight. Alexie, Sherman
FLIGHT
    Mieville, China. ★*Perdido Street Station*
    Saint-Exupery, Antoine de. *Night Flight*
*The **Flight** Attendant: A Novel*. Bohjalian, Chris
FLIGHT ATTENDANTS
    Bohjalian, Chris. *The Flight Attendant: A Novel*
    Leonard, Elmore. *Rum Punch*
★*Flight Behavior*. Kingsolver, Barbara
★*Flight of the Intruder*. Coonts, Stephen
*The **Flight** of the Maidens*. Gardam, Jane
★*The **Flight** Portfolio: A Novel*. Orringer, Julie
Flight to Canada. Reed, Ishmael
FLIGHTS
    Wilson, Carter. *Dead Girl in 2a*
Flimsy Little Plastic Miracles: A True Story. Currie, Ron
Flint, Emma
    ★*Little Deaths: A Novel*
FLINT, MICHIGAN
    Antoinette, Ashley. *Butterfly*
    Antoinette, Ashley. *Butterfly.; Vol 2*
    Antoinette, Ashley. *Butterfly.; Vol 3*
FLIRTATION
    Guillory, Jasmine. ★*While We Were Dating*
Float Plan. Doller, Trish
*The **Floating** Feldmans*. Friedland, Elyssa
★*The **Floating** Opera*. Barth, John
Flood of Fire. Ghosh, Amitav
FLOODS
    Cheng, Bill. *Southern Cross the Dog*
    Montag, Kassandra. *After the Flood: A Novel*
    Runcie, James. *Canvey Island*
Flora: a Novel. Godwin, Gail

Florence Gordon. Morton, Brian
FLORENCE, ITALY
    Dunant, Sarah. *The Birth of Venus: A Novel*
    Stone, Irving. ★*The Agony and the Ecstasy: A Biographical Novel of Michelangelo*
    Walton, Jo. ★*Lent*
    Walton, Jo. *Or What You Will*
Flores, Fernando A.
    Tears of the Trufflepig
★*Florida*. Groff, Lauren
FLORIDA
    Arnett, Kristen N. *Mostly Dead Things*
    Arnett, Kristen N. *With Teeth: A Novel*
    Banks, Russell. *Continental Drift*
    Barber, Lizzy. *A Girl Named Anna*
    Butler, Robert Olen. *Perfume River*
    Clement, Jennifer. *Gun Love*
    Cooper, Tom. *Florida Man*
    Cramer, W. Dale. *Levi's Will: A Novel*
    Dean, Margaret Lazarus. *The Time It Takes to Fall*
    DePoy, Phillip. *Sidewalk Saint*
    Deveraux, Jude. *A Willing Murder*
    Fuqua, Jonathon Scott. *Gone and Back Again*
    Gaiman, Neil. ★*Anansi Boys: A Novel*
    Garcia, Cristina. *The Aguero Sisters*
    Grippando, James. *The Girl in the Glass Box*
    Groff, Lauren. ★*Florida*
    Hauck, Rachel. *How to Catch a Prince*
    Hiaasen, Carl. *Bad Monkey*
    Hiaasen, Carl. *Basket Case*
    Hiaasen, Carl. *Lucky You: A Novel*
    Hiaasen, Carl. *Nature Girl*
    Hiaasen, Carl. *Skin Tight*
    Hiaasen, Carl. *Skinny Dip: A Novel*
    Hiaasen, Carl. ★*Squeeze Me: A Novel*
    Hiaasen, Carl. *Star Island*
    Hiaasen, Carl. *Strip Tease: A Novel*
    Hurston, Zora Neale. ★*Their Eyes Were Watching God*
    Kaufman, Charlie. *Antkind: A Novel*
    Martin, Charles. *The Water Keeper*
    Matthiessen, Peter. *Shadow Country: A New Rendering of the Watson Legend*
    McBain, Ed. *Alice in Jeopardy*
    Moniz, Dantiel W. *Milk Blood Heat*
    Morrison, Toni. *Love*
    Oliveras, Priscilla. *Anchored Hearts*
    Panowich, Brian. *Hard Cash Valley*
    Pineiro, Caridad. *South Beach Love: A Feel-Good Romance from Hallmark Publishing*
    Rodriques, Elias. *All the Water I've Seen Is Running: A Novel*
    Ruiz, Sarah Grunder. *Love, Lists, and Fancy Ships*
    Stroby, Wallace. *Some Die Nameless*
    Swyler, Erika. ★*Light from Other Stars: A Novel*
    Weiner, Jennifer. *In Her Shoes: A Novel*
    White, Randy Wayne. *Salt River*
    Whitehead, Colson. ★*The Nickel Boys: A Novel*
    Woods, Stuart. *Orchid Beach*
Florida Man. Cooper, Tom

Florio, Gwen
    Best Laid Plans
    Silent Hearts
The *Florios* of Sicily: A Novel. Auci, Stefania
Flournoy, Angela
    The Turner House
FLOWER GARDENING
    Mapson, Jo-Ann. *Bad Girl Creek: A Novel*
FLOWER LANGUAGE
    Diffenbaugh, Vanessa. *The Language of Flowers: A Novel*
★*Flowers of Darkness*. Rosnay, Tatiana de
The *Flowers*: a Novel. Gilb, Dagoberto
Fluke, Joanne
    ★*Christmas Cupcake Murder*
Flying Colours. Forester, C. S.
Flynn, Gillian
    Dark Places
    ★*Gone Girl: A Novel*
    ★*Sharp Objects: A Novel*
Flynn, Michael
    Eifelheim
    The January Dancer
Flyte, Magnus
    City of Dark Magic: A Novel
    City of Lost Dreams: A Novel
★*Flyy* Girl. Tyree, Omar
Fobbit. Abrams, David
★*Foe*. Coetzee, J. M.
Foer, Jonathan Safran
    Everything Is Illuminated: A Novel
    Extremely Loud and Incredibly Close
    Here I Am: A Novel
Fogg Lake novels [Series]. Krentz, Jayne Ann
FOGG, PHILEAS (FICTITIOUS CHARACTER)
    Verne, Jules. ★*Around the World in Eighty Days*
Foggy Moskowitz novels [Series]. DePoy, Phillip
Foley, Bridget
    Just Get Home
Foley, Lucy
    The Guest List
    The Hunting Party
FOLKLORE — GENERAL
    Tesh, Emily. *Silver in the Wood*
FOLKTALES, RUSSIAN
    Arden, Katherine. ★*The Girl in the Tower*
    Arden, Katherine. ★*The Winter of the Witch*
Follett, Ken
    A Column of Fire
    Edge of Eternity
    ★*The Evening and the Morning*
    Eye of the Needle
    Fall of Giants
    Hornet Flight
    Jackdaws
    ★*The Pillars of the Earth*
    ★*Whiteout*
    Winter of the World
    World Without End

Followers. Angelo, Megan

FOLLY BEACH, SOUTH CAROLINA
Frank, Dorothea Benton. *Folly Beach: A Lowcountry Tale*
Folly Beach: A Lowcountry Tale. Frank, Dorothea Benton

FOOD
Gonzalez, Christopher. *I'm Not Hungry but I Could Eat*

FOOD COLUMNISTS
Manansala, Mia P. ★*Arsenic and Adobo*

FOOD HABITS
Attenberg, Jami. *The Middlesteins*

FOOD PROCESSING PLANTS
Smith, Martin Cruz. *Polar Star*

FOOD RELIEF
Linden, Rachel. *The Enlightenment of Bees*

FOOD SUPPLY
Remarque, Erich Maria. *The Road Back*

FOOD TRUCKS
Herrera, Adriana. ★*American Dreamer*
Fool Me Once. Coben, Harlan
Fools Gold series (Susan Mallery) [Series]. Mallery, Susan
Fools' River. Hallinan, Timothy

FOOT
Preston, Douglas J. *Crooked River*

FOOTBALL INJURIES
Rochon, Farrah. *The Dating Playbook*

FOOTBALL PLAYERS
Rochon, Farrah. *The Dating Playbook*

FOOTBALL TEAM OWNERS
Pava, Sergio de la. *Lost Empress: A Novel*

FOOTBALL TEAMS
Pava, Sergio de la. *Lost Empress: A Novel*
For His Pleasure. Bell, Shelly
For Real. Hall, Alexis
For the Duke's Eyes Only. Bell, Lenora
For the Love of Money: A Novel. Tyree, Omar
For the Wolf. Whitten, Hannah
For Today I Am a Boy. Fu, Kim
For Whom the Bell Tolls. Hemingway, Ernest
Forbes, Curdella
A Tall History of Sugar
Forbidden. Jenkins, Beverly

FORBIDDEN LOVE
Bledsoe, Alex. *Long Black Curl*
Rose, M. J. *Tiffany Blues: A Novel*
Forbidden lovers novels [Series]. Bell, Shelly
Forbidden Promises. Williams, Synithia
The *Forbidden Rose*. Bourne, Joanna
Force, Marie
Deceived by Desire
Five Years Gone

FORCED LABOR
Alexander, V. S. *The Magdalen Girls*
Boulle, Pierre. *The Bridge Over the River Kwai: A Novel*
Flanagan, Richard. ★*The Narrow Road to the Deep North*
Pattison, Eliot. *The Skull Mantra*
Solzhenitsyn, Aleksandr Isaevich. *One Day in the Life of Ivan Denisovich*

FORCED MARRIAGE
Amirrezvani, Anita. *The Blood of Flowers: A Novel*
Anam, Tahmima. *The Bones of Grace*
Dare, Abi. *The Girl with the Louding Voice*
Gregory, Philippa. *The Taming of the Queen*
Rhys, Jean. ★*Wide Sargasso Sea*

FORCED RELOCATIONS
Ellroy, James. *Perfidia*
Pitts, Leonard. *Freeman*

Ford, Ford Madox
★*The Good Soldier: A Tale of Passion*

FORD, GERALD R.
Portis, Charles. ★*True Grit: A Novel*
Updike, John. *Memories of the Ford Administration: A Novel*

Ford, Kelli Jo
★*Crooked Hallelujah*

Ford, Richard
Canada
★*Independence Day*
The Lay of the Land
Let Me Be Frank with You
A Multitude of Sins: Stories
Sorry for Your Trouble: Stories

FORD, ROBERT
Dumas, Alexandre. ★*Camille*
Hansen, Ron. ★*The Assassination of Jesse James by the Coward Robert Ford*

FORECLOSURE
Connelly, Michael. *The Fifth Witness*
Foregone. Banks, Russell
Foreign Affairs. Lurie, Alison
Foreign Bodies. Ozick, Cynthia
The *Foreign Correspondent: A Novel*. Furst, Alan
A *Foreign Country*. Cumming, Charles
★*Foreign Soil*. Clarke, Maxine Beneba

FOREIGN STUDENTS
Palahniuk, Chuck. *Pygmy*
Foreigner. [Series]. Cherryh, C. J.
Foreigner: a Novel of First Contact. Cherryh, C. J.
Foreigners. Phillips, Caryl

FORENSIC MEDICINE
Cornwell, Patricia Daniels. *Postmortem*

FORENSIC PATHOLOGISTS
Deaver, Jeffery. *The Empty Chair*

FORENSIC PHOTOGRAPHERS
Quick, Amanda. *Close Up*

FORENSIC PSYCHOLOGISTS
Robotham, Michael. ★*Good Girl, Bad Girl: A Novel*

FORENSIC PSYCHOLOGY
Carr, Caleb. *The Angel of Darkness*

FORENSIC SCIENCES
Abu-Jaber, Diana. *Origin: A Novel*
Gardiner, Meg. *The Dirty Secrets Club*
Gerritsen, Tess. *The Bone Garden*
Griffiths, Elly. *The Dark Angel*
Griffiths, Elly. *A Dying Fall: A Ruth Galloway Mystery*
Griffiths, Elly. *The House at Sea's End: A Ruth Galloway Mystery*
Griffiths, Elly. *The Lantern Men: A Dr. Ruth Galloway Mystery*

Griffiths, Elly. *The Night Hawks*
Griffiths, Elly. *The Stone Circle*
Lovesey, Peter. ★*The Last Detective*
Picoult, Jodi. *House Rules: A Novel*
Reichs, Kathy. *Bare Bones*
Reichs, Kathy. *Bones of the Lost: A Temperance Brennan Novel*
Reichs, Kathy. *Bones to Ashes*
Reichs, Kathy. ★*A Conspiracy of Bones*
Reichs, Kathy. *Grave Secrets*
Reichs, Kathy. *Monday Mourning*

FORENSIC SCIENTISTS
Black, Lisa. *That Darkness*
Deaver, Jeffery. ★*The Coffin Dancer*
James, P. D. *Death of an Expert Witness*
Pirie, David. *The Patient's Eyes*

FOREST CONSERVATION
McLaughlin, James A. *Bearskin*
Forest Dark. Krauss, Nicole

FOREST FIRES
Barnett, Karen. *Ever Faithful*
Pipkin, John. *Woodsburner: A Novel*
Riordan, Kate. *The Heatwave*

Forester, C. S.
Admiral Hornblower in the West Indies
The African Queen
Beat to Quarters
Commodore Hornblower
Flying Colours
Hornblower and the Atropos
Hornblower and the Hotspur
Lieutenant Hornblower
Lord Hornblower
Mr. Midshipman Hornblower
Ship of the Line

FORESTS
Christie, Michael. ★*Greenwood: A Novel*
Fine, Julia. *What Should Be Wild*
Moshfegh, Ottessa. ★*Death in Her Hands: A Novel*
Powers, Richard. ★*The Overstory: A Novel*
Proulx, Annie. ★*Barkskins: A Novel*
Pulley, Natasha. *The Bedlam Stacks*
Tesh, Emily. *Silver in the Wood*
Whitten, Hannah. *For the Wolf*
Forever. Hamill, Pete
Forever and a Death. Westlake, Donald E.
Forever series (Joe W. Haldeman) [Series]. Haldeman, Joe W.
★*The Forever War*. Haldeman, Joe W.
Forever Your Earl. Leigh, Eva
Forever, Interrupted: A Novel. Reid, Taylor Jenkins
The Forge of God. Bear, Greg
Forge of God [Series]. Bear, Greg
★*Forged by Fire*. Draper, Sharon M.
Forged in Desire. Jackson, Brenda

FORGERY
Auster, Paul. *The Brooklyn Follies*
Mandel, Emily St. John. *The Singer's Gun: A Novel*
The Forgery of Venus: A Novel. Gruber, Michael
The Forgetting Time. Guskin, Sharon

FORGIVENESS
Afshar, Tessa. *Thief of Corinth*
Aslam, Nadeem. ★*The Golden Legend: A Novel*
Crummey, Michael. *The Innocents*
DeCarlo, Melissa. *The Art of Crash Landing: A Novel*
Diffenbaugh, Vanessa. *The Language of Flowers: A Novel*
Flanery, Patrick. *Absolution: A Novel*
Hart, John. *Down River*
Lundrigan, Nicole. *Glass Boys: A Novel*
Moniz, Dantiel W. *Milk Blood Heat*
Nunez, Sigrid. *Salvation City*
Rice, Luanne. *Little Night*
Rivers, Francine. ★*Redeeming Love*
Runcie, James. *Sidney Chambers and the Forgiveness of Sins*
Shreve, Anita. *The Last Time They Met: A Novel*
Starnone, Domenico. *Ties*
Wells, Rebecca. *Divine Secrets of the Ya-Ya Sisterhood: A Novel*
The Forgotten Affairs of Youth. McCall Smith, Alexander
The Forgotten Kingdom: A Novel. Pike, Signe
The Forgotten Waltz. Enright, Anne

Forman, Gayle
Leave Me: A Novel

FORMER ACTORS AND ACTRESSES
O'Farrell, Maggie. *This Must Be the Place*
Rowley, Steven. ★*The Guncle: A Novel*

FORMER AMISH
Castillo, Linda. ★*Fallen*
Cramer, W. Dale. *Levi's Will: A Novel*

FORMER ARMY RANGERS
Hunt, April. *Deadly Obsession*

FORMER ASSASSINS
Hurwitz, Gregg Andrew. ★*Into the Fire*
Hurwitz, Gregg Andrew. ★*Out of the Dark: The Return of Orphan X*
Woods, Stuart. *Smooth Operator*

FORMER ATHLETES
Fields, Hilary. *Last Chance Llama Ranch*

FORMER BASEBALL PLAYERS
Kennedy, William. ★*Ironweed: A Novel*
Parker, Robert B. *Death in Paradise*

FORMER BOYFRIENDS
French, Nicci. *Friday on My Mind: A Frieda Klein Mystery*
Hoover, Colleen. *It Ends with Us*
Rader-Day, Lori. *The Black Hour*
Stringer, Vickie M. *Still Dirty: A Novel*

FORMER CAPTIVES
Barnett, S. K. *Safe*
McHugh, Laura. *What's Done in Darkness: A Novel*
Roy, Lori. ★*Gone Too Long: A Novel*
Spencer, Minerva. *Dangerous*

FORMER CHILD ACTORS AND ACTRESSES
Wilsner, Meryl. ★*Something to Talk About*

FORMER CIA AGENTS
DeLillo, Don. *Libra*
Hagberg, David. *Gambit*
Jin, Ha. *A Map of Betrayal: A Novel*
Pavone, Chris. ★*The Expats: A Novel*
Pavone, Chris. *The Paris Diversion: A Novel*
Robbins, Tom. *Fierce Invalids Home from Hot Climates*

Steinhauer, Olen. *The Last Tourist*
Woods, Stuart. ★*Bombshell*

FORMER CLERGY
Martin, Charles. *The Water Keeper*

FORMER COLLEGE TEACHERS
Erpenbeck, Jenny. *Go, Went, Gone: A Novel*

FORMER CONVICTS
Armstrong, Richard. *The Don Con*
Atkins, Ace. *The Broken Places*
Baldacci, David. ★*One Good Deed*
Baldacci, David. *Redemption*
Bell, Shelly. *For His Pleasure*
Block, Lawrence. *A Ticket to the Boneyard: A Matthew Scudder Novel*
Clarke, Brock. *An Arsonist's Guide to Writers' Homes in New England: A Novel*
Coleman, Reed Farrel. *Where It Hurts: A Gus Murphy Novel*
Cosby, S. A. ★*Razorblade Tears*
Erdrich, Louise. ★*The Sentence*
Gaiman, Neil. ★*American Gods: A Novel*
Gamboa, Santiago. *Necropolis*
Gardner, Lisa. *Alone*
Goddard, Robert. ★*Long Time Coming: A Novel*
Greenwood, T. *Rust & Stardust*
Grisham, John. *The Last Juror*
Hamilton, Steve. ★*The Lock Artist*
Hamilton, Steve. *The Second Life of Nick Mason: A Novel*
Hart, John. *Redemption Road*
Heller, Peter. *The Painter: A Novel*
Hill, Reginald. *The Woodcutter: A Novel*
Keller, Julia. ★*Bone on Bone*
Kelman, James. *How Late It Was, How Late*
Lackberg, Camilla. *Silver Tears*
Laukkanen, Owen. *Lone Jack Trail*
Leonard, Elmore. *Glitz*
Leonard, Elmore. *The Hot Kid*
Macmillan, Gilly. *The Perfect Girl*
Mosley, Walter. *The Right Mistake: The Further Philosophical Investigations of Socrates Fortlow*
Parker, Robert B. *Trouble in Paradise*
Rendell, Ruth. *Live Flesh*
Sears, Michael. *Black Fridays*
Smith, B. J. *All Hat: A Novel*
Smith, B. J. *The Return of Kid Cooper: A Novel*
Stark, Richard. *Ask the Parrot: A Parker Novel*
Stevens, Chevy. *Never Let You Go*
Stringer, Vickie M. *Still Dirty: A Novel*
Ward, Jesmyn. ★*Sing, Unburied, Sing*
Westlake, Donald E. *The Hot Rock*
Whitaker, Chris. ★*We Begin at the End*
Wrobel, Stephanie. *Darling Rose Gold*
Yocum, Robin. *A Welcome Murder*

FORMER CRIMINALS
Mandel, Emily St. John. *The Singer's Gun: A Novel*
Tinti, Hannah. *The Twelve Lives of Samuel Hawley: A Novel*

FORMER DETECTIVES
Airth, Rennie. *The Decent Inn of Death*
Connelly, Michael. ★*The Dark Hours*

Eriksson, Kjell. *The Deathwatch Beetle: A Mystery*
Indriðason, Arnaldur. *The Darkness Knows*
Indriðason, Arnaldur. *The Shadow District: A Thriller*
Kerr, Philip. ★*Greeks Bearing Gifts: A Bernie Gunther Novel*
Kerr, Philip. ★*Prussian Blue*
Nesbo, Jo. *Phantom*
Panowich, Brian. *Hard Cash Valley*
Smith, Ian. *The Unspoken*
Verdon, John. *On Harrow Hill*

FORMER EROTIC FILM ACTORS AND ACTRESSES
Faust, Christa. *Choke Hold*
Faust, Christa. *Money Shot*

FORMER FASHION MODELS
Frank, Alli. *Tiny Imperfections*
Pitoniak, Anna. ★*Our American Friend*
Rai, Alisha. ★*Girl Gone Viral*

FORMER FBI AGENTS
Pobi, Robert. *City of Windows*

FORMER FIANCES
Collins, Manda. *A Good Rake Is Hard to Find*

FORMER FILM ACTORS AND ACTRESSES
Farrell, Henry. ★*What Ever Happened to Baby Jane?*

FORMER FOOTBALL PLAYERS
Phillips, Susan Elizabeth. *First Star I See Tonight*
Rubart, James L. ★*The Man He Never Was*

FORMER FOSTER CHILDREN
London, Stefanie. *The Aussie Next Door*
Meader, Kate. *Playing with Fire*

FORMER FRIENDS
Doyle, Roddy. *Smile*
Hannah, Sophie. *Perfect Little Children*
Marcelo, Tif. *In a Book Club Far Away*
Schwab, Victoria. *Vengeful*
Schwab, Victoria. *Vicious*
Stone, Nick. *The Verdict*

FORMER GIRLFRIENDS
James, Lorelei. *I Want You Back*
Pynchon, Thomas. *Inherent Vice*
Turner, Bethany. *Wooing Cadie McCaffrey*

FORMER HOCKEY PLAYERS
James, Lorelei. *I Want You Back*

FORMER HUSBANDS
Beaton, M. C. *Death of a Macho Man*
Bird, Sarah. *The Gap Year: A Novel*
Corry, Jane. *The Dead Ex*
Diehl, Heidi. *Lifelines*
Ellis, David. *In the Company of Liars*
Higashino, Keigo. ★*The Devotion of Suspect X*
Lackberg, Camilla. *Silver Tears*
Maron, Margaret. *Up Jumps the Devil*
Portis, Charles. ★*The Dog of the South*
Strout, Elizabeth. ★*Oh William!*

FORMER HUSBANDS — DEATH
Scottoline, Lisa. ★*Come Home*

FORMER INTELLIGENCE OFFICERS
Ripley, Mike. *Mr. Campion's War*

FORMER JOURNALISTS
Portis, Charles. ★*The Dog of the South*

FORMER LAWYERS

Keller, Julia. ★*Bone on Bone*
Sears, Michael. *Tower of Babel*
Stabenow, Dana. ★*A Deeper Sleep: A Kate Shugak Novel*
Stabenow, Dana. ★*A Grave Denied*
Stabenow, Dana. *Killing Grounds: A Kate Shugak Mystery*
Stabenow, Dana. *The Singing of the Dead*

FORMER LIBRARIANS

Glass, Julia. *The Widower's Tale*
Hart, Elsa. *City of Ink: A Mystery*

FORMER LOVERS

Balogh, Mary. *Only Enchanting*
Balogh, Mary. ★*Someone to Remember: A Westcott Story*
Beaton, M. C. ★*Hot to Trot*
Blackstock, Terri. *Smoke Screen*
Coben, Harlan. *Don't Let Go*
Creech, Sarah. *The Whole Way Home*
Dickey, Eric Jerome. *Finding Gideon*
Dodd, Christina. *The Woman Who Couldn't Scream*
Fredericks, Mariah. *Death of a Showman*
George, Nina. *The Book of Dreams*
Greene, Graham. ★*The End of the Affair*
Hauck, Rachel. *How to Catch a Prince*
Hewson, David. *A Season for the Dead*
K'wan. *Revelations*
Lippman, Laura. ★*And When She Was Good*
Littell, Robert. *The Mayakovsky Tapes: A Novel*
Nichols, Peter. *The Rocks*
Oliveras, Priscilla. *Anchored Hearts*
Paris, B. A. *Bring Me Back: A Novel*
Perry, Anne. *A Question of Betrayal*
Pineiro, Caridad. *What Happens in Summer*
Porter, Henry. *White Hot Silence*
Rai, Alisha. ★*The Right Swipe*
Robinson, Peter. *Playing with Fire*
Shalvis, Jill. *Second Chance Summer*
Sparks, Nicholas. ★*The Notebook*
Steinhauer, Olen. ★*All the Old Knives*
Steinhauer, Olen. *The Cairo Affair*
Tanabe, Karin. ★*A Woman of Intelligence*
Turow, Scott. *Presumed Innocent*

FORMER LOVERS — DEATH

McEwan, Ian. ★*Amsterdam*

FORMER MARINES

Carr, Robyn. ★*Virgin River*
Eisler, Barry. *The Night Trade*
Hunter, Stephen. *Soft Target: A Thriller*
Petrie, Nicholas. *Burning Bright*

FORMER MARSHALS

Corleone, Douglas. *Good as Gone*

FORMER MILITARY POLICE

Child, Lee. *61 Hours*
Child, Lee. *The Affair*
Child, Lee. *Bad Luck and Trouble*
Child, Lee. ★*Die Trying*
Child, Lee. *Echo Burning*
Child, Lee. *The Hard Way*
Child, Lee. ★*Killing Floor*
Child, Lee. *Never Go Back*
Child, Lee. *Nothing to Lose*
Child, Lee. *One Shot*
Child, Lee. *Persuader*
Child, Lee. *A Wanted Man*
Child, Lee. *Without Fail*
Child, Lee. *Worth Dying For*

FORMER NAVY SEALS

Kells, Claire. *Vanishing Edge*
Wade, Becky. ★*True to You*

FORMER NAZIS

Picoult, Jodi. *The Storyteller*
Schlink, Bernhard. *The Reader: A Novel*

FORMER PHYSICIANS

Scerbanenco, Giorgio. *Traitors to All*

FORMER POLICE

Ames, Jonathan. *A Man Named Doll*
Atkinson, Kate. *Started Early, Took My Dog*
Bayard, Louis. *The Pale Blue Eye: A Novel*
Berkowitz, Ira. *Old Flame: A Jackson Steeg Novel*
Block, Lawrence. ★*When the Sacred Ginmill Closes*
Box, C. J. ★*The Bitterroots: A Novel*
Box, C. J. *Blue Heaven*
Bruen, Ken. *Galway Girl: A Jack Taylor Novel*
Bruen, Ken. *The Guards*
Coleman, Reed Farrel. *Where It Hurts: A Gus Murphy Novel*
Connolly, John. *The Dirty South*
Disher, Garry. *Under the Cold Bright Lights*
Dobyns, Stephen. *Saratoga Payback*
Fox, Candice. *Crimson Lake*
Fox, Candice. *Redemption Point*
French, Tana. ★*The Searcher*
Friedman, Daniel. ★*Don't Ever Get Old*
Friedman, Daniel. *Running Out of Road*
Garcia-Roza, L. A. *December Heat*
Gardiner, Meg. *Phantom Instinct*
Harvey, John. *A Darker Shade of Blue: Stories*
Harvey, Michael T. *We All Fall Down*
Hiaasen, Carl. *Skinny Dip: A Novel*
Hillerman, Tony. *The Shape Shifter*
Hillerman, Tony. *The Sinister Pig*
Jones, Stephen Mack. *Dead of Winter*
Khan, Vaseem. *The Perplexing Theft of the Jewel in the Crown*
Kimmel, Fran. *No Good Asking: A Novel*
King, Stephen. *Mr. Mercedes: A Novel*
Lovesey, Peter. *Diamond Solitaire*
Nesbo, Jo. *Phantom*
O'Mara, Tim. *Crooked Numbers*
Parker, T. Jefferson. *The Blue Hour*
Pattison, Eliot. *The Skull Mantra*
Perrotta, Tom. *Little Children*
Perry, Thomas. *The Bomb Maker*
Persson, Leif G. W. *The Dying Detective: A Mystery*
Rankin, Ian. ★*A Song for the Dark Times*
Robotham, Michael. ★*The Wreckage*
Sanders, Lawrence. *The Second Deadly Sin*
Sanders, Lawrence. ★*The Third Deadly Sin*
Sandford, John. ★*Winter Prey*

Slaughter, Karin. *The Kept Woman*
Solares, Martin. *Don't Send Flowers*
Verdon, John. *On Harrow Hill*
Wendig, Chuck. *The Book of Accidents*
Woods, Stuart. *Below the Belt*
Woods, Stuart. *Fast & Loose*
Woods, Stuart. *Hit List*

FORMER POLICEWOMEN
McDermid, Val. *How the Dead Speak: A Tony Hill and Carol Jordan Novel*

FORMER PRIME MINISTERS
Harris, Robert. *The Ghost: A Novel*

FORMER PRISONERS OF WAR
Friedman, Daniel. ★*Don't Ever Get Old*
Tan, Twan Eng. *The Garden of Evening Mists*

FORMER PRIVATE INVESTIGATORS
Dobyns, Stephen. *Saratoga Payback*

FORMER PROFESSIONAL ATHLETES
Bailey, Tessa. *Fix Her Up*

FORMER PROSTITUTES
Rendell, Ruth. ★*A Judgement in Stone*

FORMER RODEO PERFORMERS
Weatherspoon, Rebekah. *A Cowboy to Remember*

FORMER SHERIFFS
Atkins, Ace. *The Redeemers*
Harrison, Jim. *The Great Leader*
Keller, Julia. ★*Bone on Bone*

FORMER SPECIAL FORCES MEMBERS
Coben, Harlan. *Fool Me Once*
Finder, Joseph. *Vanished*
Quirk, Matthew. *Cold Barrel Zero*
Quirk, Matthew. *Dead Man Switch*
Rankin, Ian. *Blood Hunt: A Novel*
Sharp, Zoe. *Second Shot: A Charlie Fox Thriller*

FORMER SPIES
Cumming, Charles. *A Colder War*
Cumming, Charles. *A Divided Spy*
Cumming, Charles. *A Foreign Country*
Gelernter, J. H. *Hold Fast*
Hayes, Terry. *I Am Pilgrim*
Lawton, John. *Then We Take Berlin*
Montclair, Allison. *The Right Sort of Man*
Osman, Richard. *The Man Who Died Twice: A Thursday Murder Club Mystery*
Porter, Henry. *The Old Enemy*
Putney, Mary Jo. *No Longer a Gentleman*
Smith, Tom Rob. *Agent 6*

FORMER TEACHERS
Beattie, Ann. *A Wonderful Stroke of Luck: A Novel*
Strout, Elizabeth. ★*Olive, Again: A Novel*
Wilder, Thornton. ★*Theophilus North*

FORMER WIVES
Berkowitz, Ira. *Old Flame: A Jackson Steeg Novel*
Robinson, Peter. *Playing with Fire*

The Forsaken. Atkins, Ace

Forster, E. M.
★*Howards End*
★*A Passage to India*

★*A Room with a View*
★*The Forsyte Saga*. Galsworthy, John

Forsyte saga [Series]. Galsworthy, John

Forsyth, Frederick
The Fox
The Kill List

FORT LAUDERDALE, FLORIDA
MacDonald, John D. *Cinnamon Skin: The Twentieth Adventure of Travis McGee*
MacDonald, John D. *The Green Ripper*
MacDonald, John D. ★*The Lonely Silver Rain*
MacDonald, John D. *The Long Lavender Look*
MacDonald, John D. *A Purple Place for Dying*
MacDonald, John D. *The Scarlet Ruse*
MacDonald, John D. *The Turquoise Lament*

FORTIES (AGE)
Brandt, Harry. *The Whites: A Novel*
Dyer, Geoff. *Jeff in Venice, Death in Varanasi*
Mason, Meg. *Sorrow and Bliss*
Miller, Karen E. Quinones. *An Angry-Ass Black Woman*
Yun, Jung. *O Beautiful: A Novel*

FORTS
Punke, Michael. *Ridgeline: A Novel*
★*Fortuna*. Merbeth, K. S.
Fortunate Son: A Novel. Mosley, Walter
Fortune Favors the Duke. Vayden, Kristin
Fortune Favors the Wicked. Romain, Theresa

FORTUNE HUNTERS
Heyer, Georgette. *Black Sheep*
Fortune's Rocks: A Novel. Shreve, Anita

FORTUNE-TELLERS
Benjamin, Chloe. ★*The Immortalists: A Novel*
Camilleri, Andrea. *Riccardino*
Simenon, Georges. *Maigret and the Fortuneteller*
The Fortunes. Davies, Peter Ho
★*The Forty Days of Musa Dagh*. Werfel, Franz

Fossey, Brooke
The Big Finish

FOSSIL DINOSAURS
Blumberg, Chandra. *Digging up Love*

FOSSILS
Collins, Manda. *One for the Rogue*
Davies, Carys. *West*

FOSTER CARE
Diffenbaugh, Vanessa. *The Language of Flowers: A Novel*
Gardner, Lisa. ★*Look for Me: A Novel*
Parks, Brad. *Closer Than You Know*

FOSTER CHILD ABUSE
Hulme, Keri. ★*The Bone People: A Novel*

FOSTER CHILDREN
Bronte, Emily. ★*Wuthering Heights*
Foley, Bridget. *Just Get Home*
Francis, Patry. *All the Children Are Home*
Gibbons, Kaye. ★*Ellen Foster: A Novel*
Hobson, Brandon. ★*The Removed: A Novel*
Ludwig, Benjamin. *Ginny Moon*
McKevett, G. A. *A Few Drops of Bitters*

FOSTER FAMILY

Francis, Patry. *All the Children Are Home*

Stabenow, Dana. *Whisper to the Blood: A Kate Shugak Novel*

FOSTER FATHERS

Greene, Graham. *The Captain and the Enemy*

FOSTER MOTHERS

Overton, Hollie. *The Runaway*

Sekaran, Shanthi. ★*Lucky Boy*

Smith, Michael F. *The Fighter: A Novel*

FOSTER PARENTS

Box, C. J. *Winterkill: A Novel*

Francis, Patry. *All the Children Are Home*

FOSTER TEENAGERS

Carr, Brian Allen. ★*Opioid, Indiana*

Ferencik, Erica. *Into the Jungle*

Foster, Alan Dean

Relic

Foster, Brooke Lea

Summer Darlings

Foster, Fiona King

The Captive: A Novel

Foster, Lori

Sisters of Summer's End

★*Foucault's* Pendulum. Eco, Umberto

★*Foundation*. Asimov, Isaac

Foundation and Empire. Asimov, Isaac

Foundation series [Series]. Asimov, Isaac

The **founders** [Series]. Bennett, Robert Jackson

Foundryside. Bennett, Robert Jackson

Founds, Kathleen

When Mystical Creatures Attack!

Fountain, Ben

★*Billy Lynn's Long Halftime Walk*

★The **Fountainhead**. Rand, Ayn

Four Sisters, All Queens. Jones, Sherry

Four Souls: A Novel. Erdrich, Louise

Four Ways to Forgiveness. Le Guin, Ursula K.

FOUR-YEAR-OLD BOYS

Hawley, Noah. *Before the Fall*

McLaughlin, Emma. *The Nanny Diaries: A Novel*

Starnone, Domenico. *Trick*

FOURTEEN-YEAR-OLD GIRLS

Fridlund, Emily. ★*History of Wolves: A Novel*

Mason, Jamie. *The Hidden Things*

Sittenfeld, Curtis. *Prep: A Novel*

FOURTEEN-YEAR-OLDS

Cleary, Jon. *The Sundowners*

The **Fourth** Assassin. Rees, Matt

★The **Fourth** Deadly Sin. Sanders, Lawrence

FOURTH OF JULY

Blumenfeld, Amy. *The Cast*

Fourth of July Creek. Henderson, Smith

Fowler, Christopher

Bryant & May: Hall of Mirrors : A Peculiar Crimes Unit Mystery

Bryant & May: Oranges and Lemons

Bryant & May: Strange Tide

Bryant & May: The Lonely Hour

Fowler, Karen Joy

The Jane Austen Book Club

★*We Are All Completely Beside Ourselves*

Fowler, Therese

★*A Good Neighborhood*

A Well-Behaved Woman: A Novel of the Vanderbilts

★*Z: A Novel of Zelda Fitzgerald*

Fowles, John

★*The French Lieutenant's Woman*

The Magus

The **Fox**. Forsyth, Frederick

Fox. Ugresic, Dubravka

Fox Hunter. Sharp, Zoe

Fox, Candice

Crimson Lake

Gone by Midnight

Redemption Point

FOX, MALCOLM (FICTITIOUS CHARACTER)

Rankin, Ian. *The Complaints*

FOXES

Ugresic, Dubravka. *Fox*

The *Fractal* Prince. Rajaniemi, Hannu

★*Fragile* Things: Short Fictions and Wonders. Gaiman, Neil

Frame, Janet

Between My Father and the King: New and Uncollected Stories

Frames. Estleman, Loren D.

FRAMEUPS

Banks, Iain. *The Hydrogen Sonata*

Bourne, Joanna. *The Black Hawk*

Burrowes, Grace. *My One and Only Duke*

Cavanagh, Steve. *Thirteen*

Child, Lee. *One Shot*

Connelly, Michael. *The Crossing*

Connelly, Michael. ★*The Law of Innocence: A Novel*

Dodd, Christina. *Obsession Falls*

Goddard, Robert. ★*Into the Blue*

Grisham, John. ★*The Guardians*

Hammett, Dashiell. *The Glass Key*

Hannah, Sophie. *Keep Her Safe*

Harvey, Michael T. *The Fifth Floor*

Hugo, Victor. ★*The Hunchback of Notre Dame*

Knopf, Chris. *You're Dead*

Mayor, Archer. *Tag Man: A Joe Gunther Novel*

Moore, Graham. *The Holdout: A Novel*

Mosley, Walter. *All I Did Was Shoot My Man: A Leonid McGill Mystery*

Mosley, Walter. *Down the River Unto the Sea*

Parks, Brad. *Closer Than You Know*

Patterson, Richard North. *Eclipse*

Pronzini, Bill. *Nemesis*

Quincy, D. M. *Murder in Mayfair: An Atlas Catesby Mystery*

Raimondo, Lynne. *Dante's Dilemma: A Mark Angelotti Novel*

Scottoline, Lisa. ★*Every Fifteen Minutes*

Framley Parsonage. Trollope, Anthony

Frampton, Megan

The Duke's Guide to Correct Behavior

Never a Bride

Put up Your Duke

FRANCE

Balzac, Honore de. *Eugenie Grandet*
Bannalec, Jean-Luc. *The Granite Coast Murders*
Bannalec, Jean-Luc. *The Killing Tide: A Brittany Mystery*
Bayard, Louis. *The Black Tower: A Novel*
Beauvoir, Simone de. ★*The Mandarins: A Novel*
Belfoure, Charles. *The Paris Architect: A Novel*
Berry, Steve. ★*The Templar Legacy: A Novel of Suspense*
Black, Cara. *Murder in the Marais*
Black, Cara. ★*Three Hours in Paris*
Bordas, Camille. *How to Behave in a Crowd*
Bourne, Joanna. *The Forbidden Rose*
Bourne, Joanna. ★*The Spymaster's Lady*
Cantor, Jillian. *Half Life*
Carey, Edward. *Little: A Novel*
Chee, Alexander. *The Queen of the Night*
Child, Lee. *The Enemy*
Cisneros, Sandra. *Martita, I Remember You: Martita, Te Recuerdo*
Colette. *The Collected Stories of Colette*
Colette. *The Complete Claudine*
Cornwell, Bernard. *The Archer's Tale*
Cumming, Charles. *A Foreign Country*
Del Amo, Jean-Baptiste. *Animalia*
Dickens, Charles. ★*A Tale of Two Cities*
Doerr, Anthony. ★*All the Light We Cannot See: A Novel*
Donoghue, Emma. *Akin*
Downes, Anna. *The Safe Place: A Novel*
Druon, Maurice. *The Iron King*
Dumas, Alexandre. ★*The Count of Monte Cristo*
Dumas, Alexandre. ★*The Man in the Iron Mask*
Dumas, Alexandre. ★*The Three Musketeers*
Dumas, Alexandre. *Twenty Years After*
Dunmore, Helen. *The Lie*
Dybek, Nick. *The Verdun Affair: A Novel*
Escobar, Mario. *The Librarian of Saint-Malo: A Novel*
Faulks, Sebastian. ★*Birdsong*
Faulks, Sebastian. *Charlotte Gray: A Novel*
Faulks, Sebastian. *Paris Echo: A Novel*
Flaubert, Gustave. ★*Madame Bovary: Provincial Ways*
Flaubert, Gustave. *Sentimental Education*
Fleming, Ian. ★*Casino Royale: A James Bond Novel*
Follett, Ken. *Jackdaws*
Furst, Alan. ★*A Hero of France*
Furst, Alan. ★*Mission to Paris*
Furst, Alan. ★*Under Occupation: A Novel*
Gabaldon, Diana. ★*Dragonfly in Amber*
Gaynor, Hazel. *Meet Me in Monaco: A Novel*
George, Alex. *The Paris Hours: A Novel*
George, Nina. *The Little Paris Bookshop*
Godden, Rumer. *The Greengage Summer: A Novel*
Gortner, C. W. *The First Actress: A Novel of Sarah Bernhardt*
Greene, Graham. *The Tenth Man*
Handke, Peter. *Don Juan: His Own Version*
Hannah, Kristin. *The Nightingale*
Harris, Joanne. ★*Chocolat: A Novel*
Harris, Robert. *An Officer and a Spy*
Harris, Thomas. *Hannibal Rising*
Helprin, Mark. *Paris in the Present Tense*

Hertmans, Stefan. ★*The Convert: A Novel*
Hoffman, Alice. *The Marriage of Opposites: A Novel Based on the Life of Rachel Pizzarro*
Hoffman, Alice. ★*The World That We Knew*
Holdstock, Pauline. *Here I Am!*
Houellebecq, Michel. *Submission*
Hugo, Victor. ★*The Hunchback of Notre Dame*
Hugo, Victor. ★*Les Miserables*
Keneally, Thomas. ★*The Daughters of Mars*
Kerangal, Maylis de. *The Heart: A Novel*
Kerr, Philip. ★*Prussian Blue*
Landau, Alexis. *Those Who Are Saved*
Landragin, Alex. ★*Crossings: Consisting of Three Manuscripts : The Education of a Monster : City of Ghosts : Tales Of*
Lim, Roselle. *Vanessa Yu's Magical Paris Tea Shop*
Logan, T. M. *The Vacation*
Longworth, M. L. *Murder on the Ile Sordou: A Verlaque and Bonnet Provencal Mystery*
Lopez Barrio, Cristina. *The House of the Impossible Loves*
Louis, Edouard. *The End of Eddy: A Novel*
Mas, Victoria. *The Mad Women's Ball*
Meyer, Nicholas. *The Adventure of the Peculiar Protocols: Adapted from the Journals of John H. Watson, M.D.*
Miller, Henry. ★*Tropic of Cancer*
Mosse, Kate. *The City of Tears*
Moyes, Jojo. *The Girl You Left Behind*
Ólafsson, Ólafur Jóhann. *The Sacrament: A Novel*
Orczy, Emmuska Orczy. ★*The Scarlet Pimpernel*
Orringer, Julie. ★*The Flight Portfolio: A Novel*
Phoenix, Michele. *The Space Between Words*
Portis, Charles. ★*Masters of Atlantis: A Novel*
Proust, Marcel. ★*Remembrance of Things Past*
Proust, Marcel. *Swann's Way*
Proust, Marcel. *Time Regained*
Proust, Marcel. *Within a Budding Grove*
Rademacher, Cay. *Deadly Camargue: A Provence Mystery*
Reynolds, Allie. ★*Shiver*
Rhys, Rachel. *Fatal Inheritance*
Riordan, Kate. *The Heatwave*
Ripley, Mike. *Mr. Campion's War*
Rosnay, Tatiana de. ★*Sarah's Key*
Rutherfurd, Edward. *Paris*
Sabatini, Rafael. *Scaramouche: A Romance of the French Revolution*
Sand, George. *Marianne*
Sartre, Jean Paul. *The Age of Reason*
Sartre, Jean Paul. *Troubled Sleep*
Schwarz-Bart, Andre. *The Last of the Just: A Novel*
Sedgwick, Marcus. *Mister Memory: A Novel*
Shaw, Vivian. ★*Dreadful Company*
Simenon, Georges. *Maigret and the Black Sheep*
Simenon, Georges. *Maigret and the Fortuneteller*
Simenon, Georges. ★*Maigret and the Killer*
Simenon, Georges. *Maigret and the Madwoman*
Simenon, Georges. ★*Maigret and the Saturday Caller*
Simenon, Georges. ★*Maigret and the Toy Village*
Simenon, Georges. *Maigret and the Wine Merchant*
Simenon, Georges. ★*Maigret Bides His Time*
Simenon, Georges. ★*Maigret Goes Home*

Simenon, Georges. *Maigret's Memoirs*
Simenon, Georges. *My Friend Maigret*
Suskind, Patrick. ★*Perfume: The Story of a Murderer*
Twain, Mark. *Personal Recollections of Joan of Arc*
Van Booy, Simon. *The Illusion of Separateness*
Vargas Llosa, Mario. *The Bad Girl*
Vargas Llosa, Mario. ★*The Way to Paradise*
Walker, Martin. *The Coldest Case*
Walker, Martin. *The Shooting at Chateau Rock*
Zola, Emile. ★*Germinal*
★*Frances and Bernard*. Bauer, Carlene
FRANCHISE BOOKS
Anderson, Kevin J. *The Last Days of Krypton*
Holland, Cecelia. *Jerusalem*
Francis, Dick
Smokescreen
Francis, Felix
Crisis
Guilty Not Guilty
Pulse
Francis, Patry
All the Children Are Home
The Orphans of Race Point: A Novel
Francis-Sharma, Lauren
★*Book of the Little Axe*
Franck, Julia
Blindness of the Heart
Frank Bascombe novels [Series]. Ford, Richard
FRANK, ALBERTA
Adamson, Gil. *The Outlander*
Frank, Alli
Tiny Imperfections
Frank, Dorothea Benton
Folly Beach: A Lowcountry Tale
Queen Bee
Frankel, Laurie
Goodbye for Now: A Novel
One Two Three: A Novel
This Is How It Always Is
FRANKENSTEIN'S MONSTER (FICTITIOUS CHARACTER)
Shelley, Mary Wollstonecraft. ★*Frankenstein: Or, the Modern Prometheus*
★*Frankenstein: Or, the Modern Prometheus*. Shelley, Mary Wollstonecraft
Frankie Elkin novels [Series]. Gardner, Lisa
★*Frankissstein*. Winterson, Jeanette
Franklin, Ariana
★*Death and the Maiden*
Mistress of the Art of Death
The Serpent's Tale
The Siege Winter
FRANKLIN, BATTLE OF, 1864
Hicks, Robert. *The Widow of the South*
FRANKLIN, JANE
Kupersmith, Violet. ★*Build Your House Around My Body*
Macallister, Greer. ★*The Arctic Fury*
Franklin, Miles
My Brilliant Career

FRANKLIN, MILES
Austen, Jane. ★*Emma*
Franklin, Miles. *My Brilliant Career*
FRANKLIN, TENNESSEE
Alexander, Tamera. *With This Pledge*
Franklin, Tom
Crooked Letter, Crooked Letter: A Novel
★*Franny* and Zooey. Salinger, J. D.
Frantz, Laura
The Lacemaker
Franzen, Jonathan
★*The Corrections*
★*Crossroads*
★*Freedom*
Purity
FRATERNAL TWINS
Edwards, Kim. *The Memory Keeper's Daughter*
FRATERNITIES
Nugent, Benjamin. *Fraternity: Stories*
Fraternity: Stories. Nugent, Benjamin
FRATRICIDE
Stansel, Ian. *The Last Cowboys of San Geronimo*
Updike, John. *Gertrude and Claudius*
FRAUD
French, Nicci. *Tuesday's Gone*
McCall Smith, Alexander. *The Lost Art of Gratitude*
Sandford, John. *Holy Ghost*
Sigurðardóttir, Lilja. *Cage*
Snow, C. P. ★*Strangers and Brothers*
FRAUD INVESTIGATION
Greaves, Chuck. *Hush Money: A Mystery*
Perry, Thomas. *Death Benefits: A Novel*
Frayn, Michael
Spies: A Novel
Frazier, Charles
★*Cold Mountain*
Nightwoods: A Novel
Thirteen Moons: A Novel
Varina
Frazier, Jean Kyoung
Pizza Girl
FREAK SHOWS
Hoffman, Alice. *The Museum of Extraordinary Things: A Novel*
Frear, Caz
Stone Cold Heart
Sweet Little Lies
Frederica Potter series [Series]. Byatt, A. S.
Fredericks, Mariah
Death of a New American: A Mystery
Death of a Showman
FREDERICKSBURG, BATTLE OF, 1862
Shaara, Jeff. *Gods and Generals: A Novel of the Civil War*
Fredrika Bergman mysteries [Series]. Ohlsson, Kristina
FREE AFRICAN AMERICANS
Faye, Lyndsay. *Seven for a Secret*
The Free Bastards. French, Jonathan
FREE ENTERPRISE
Gaddis, William. ★*J R: A Novel*

Free Falling, as If in a Dream: The Story of a Crime. Persson, Leif G. W.
FREE WILL AND DETERMINISM
    Butler, Robert Olen. *Hell: A Novel*
    Obioma, Chigozie. ★*An Orchestra of Minorities*
    Vonnegut, Kurt. *Timequake*
FREED PEOPLE
    Cho, Zen. *Sorcerer to the Crown*
    Cole, Alyssa. ★*An Extraordinary Union*
    Cole, Alyssa. ★*An Unconditional Freedom*
    Colvin, Jeffrey. ★*Africaville: A Novel*
    Doctorow, E. L. *The March: A Novel*
    Hambly, Barbara. *House of the Patriarch*
    Hambly, Barbara. *Lady of Perdition*
    Harris, Nathan. *The Sweetness of Water*
    Johnson, Charles Richard. ★*Middle Passage*
    McCann, Colum. ★*Transatlantic: A Novel*
    Morrison, Toni. ★*Beloved: A Novel*
    Riley, Vanessa. ★*Island Queen*
    Sexton, Margaret Wilkerson. *The Revisioners: A Novel*
    Truong, Monique T. D. *The Sweetest Fruits*
Freedman, Benedict
    Mrs. Mike: The Story of Katherine Mary Flannigan
★*Freedom*. Franzen, Jonathan
FREEDOM
    Altan, Ahmet. ★*Love in the Days of Rebellion*
    Clarke, Arthur C. ★*Childhood's End*
    Cusk, Rachel. *Kudos*
    Fowles, John. *The Magus*
    Le Guin, Ursula K. *Orsinian Tales*
    Ma, Jian. *Beijing Coma*
    Parry, H. G. *A Declaration of the Rights of Magicians*
    Sackville-West, V. *The Edwardians*
    Sartre, Jean Paul. *The Age of Reason*
    Warren, Robert Penn. *Band of Angels*
    Woods, Rita. ★*Remembrance*
    Zamyatin, Yevgeny Ivanovich. ★*We*
The Freedom Race. Roy, Lucinda
FREEDOM SEEKERS
    Chevalier, Tracy. *The Last Runaway*
    Clinch, Jon. *Finn: A Novel*
    Crafts, Hannah. *The Bondwoman's Narrative*
    Jones, Gayl. ★*Palmares*
    McBride, James. ★*The Good Lord Bird*
    Priest, Cherie. *Clementine*
    Rawles, Nancy. *My Jim: A Novel*
    Reed, Ishmael. *Flight to Canada*
    Stowe, Harriet Beecher. ★*Uncle Tom's Cabin*
    Twain, Mark. ★*Adventures of Huckleberry Finn: Tom Sawyer's Comrade ...*
    Whitehead, Colson. ★*The Underground Railroad: A Novel*
Freeman. Pitts, Leonard
Freeman, Anna
    The Fair Fight: A Novel
Freeman, Brian
    Goodbye to the Dead
    Marathon
    The Night Bird
    Thief River Falls

Freeman, Castle
    All That I Have: A Novel
Freeman, Dianne
    A Fiancee's Guide to First Wives and Murder
    A Lady's Guide to Etiquette and Murder
FREIGHT TRAINS
    Brown, Sandra. ★*Blind Tiger*
Freitas, Donna
    The Nine Lives of Rose Napolitano
FRENCH ALPS
    Ware, Ruth. ★*One by One*
FRENCH AMERICANS
    Donoghue, Emma. *Akin*
FRENCH IN ENGLAND
    Dickens, Charles. ★*A Tale of Two Cities*
★*The French Lieutenant's Woman*. Fowles, John
FRENCH QUARTER (NEW ORLEANS, LA.)
    Algren, Nelson. *A Walk on the Wild Side*
    Sepetys, Ruta. ★*Out of the Easy*
FRENCH RESISTANCE (WORLD WAR II)
    Furst, Alan. ★*A Hero of France*
    Furst, Alan. ★*Under Occupation: A Novel*
    Groot, Tracy. *Flame of Resistance*
    Meacham, Leila. *Dragonfly: A Novel*
    Pears, Iain. *The Last Judgement*
    Skeslien Charles, Janet. *The Paris Library: A Novel*
FRENCH REVOLUTION, 1789-1799
    Hugo, Victor. ★*Les Miserables*
    Sabatini, Rafael. *Scaramouche: A Romance of the French Revolution*
FRENCH RIVIERA
    Kerr, Philip. ★*Prussian Blue*
    Levy, Deborah. *Swimming Home: A Novel*
    Rhys, Rachel. *Fatal Inheritance*
    Sagan, Francoise. ★*Bonjour Tristesse*
French trilogy [Series]. Faulks, Sebastian
French, Albert
    Billy
French, Jonathan
    The Free Bastards
    ★*The Grey Bastards*
    The True Bastards
French, Marilyn
    ★*The Women's Room*
French, Nicci
    ★*Blue Monday*
    Dark Saturday
    ★*The Day of the Dead: A Novel*
    Friday on My Mind: A Frieda Klein Mystery
    ★*House of Correction*
    ★*The Lying Room*
    Sunday Silence
    Thursday's Children
    Tuesday's Gone
    Waiting for Wednesday: A Frieda Klein Mystery
French, Tana
    ★*Broken Harbor*
    Faithful Place: A Novel
    In the Woods

The Likeness

★*The Searcher*

★*The Secret Place*

★*The Witch Elm: A Novel*

Frenchman's Creek. Du Maurier, Daphne

Fresh Complaint: Stories. Eugenides, Jeffrey

Freshwater. Emezi, Akwaeke

Freudenberger, Nell

The Dissident

★*Lost and Wanted: A Novel*

The Newlyweds

FREYTAG-LORINGHOVEN, ELSA VON

Perez-Reverte, Arturo. *The Club Dumas*

Steinke, Rene. *Holy Skirts*

FRIDAY (FICTITIOUS CHARACTER)

Defoe, Daniel. ★*Robinson Crusoe*

Friday Black: Stories. Adjei-Brenyah, Nana Kwame

Friday on My Mind: A Frieda Klein Mystery. French, Nicci

Fridlund, Emily

★*History of Wolves: A Novel*

★*Fried Green Tomatoes at the Whistle Stop Cafe*. Flagg, Fannie

Frieda Klein novels [Series]. French, Nicci

Friedland, Elyssa

The Floating Feldmans

The Intermission

Last Summer at the Golden Hotel

Friedman, Daniel

★*Don't Ever Get Old*

Riot Most Uncouth: A Lord Byron Mystery

Running Out of Road

★*The Friend*. Nunez, Sigrid

Friend of the Devil. Robinson, Peter

The Friend Zone. Jimenez, Abby

The Friendly Persuasion. West, Jessamyn

Friends and Strangers. Sullivan, J. Courtney

Friends Like These. McCreight, Kimberly

The Friends of Eddie Coyle. Higgins, George V.

FRIENDS' DEATH

Adkins, Mary. *When You Read This*

Aguilar Camin, Hector. *Death in Veracruz*

Bartz, Andrea. *The Lost Night*

Brenner, Jamie. *Drawing Home*

Chakrabarti, Jai. *A Play for the End of the World*

Deutermann, Peter T. *The Nugget: A Novel*

Goenawan, Clarissa. *The Perfect World of Miwako Sumida*

Hauck, Rachel. *How to Catch a Prince*

Lansdale, Joe R. *Edge of Dark Water*

Nunez, Sigrid. ★*The Friend*

Rader-Day, Lori. *Little Pretty Things*

Rodriques, Elias. *All the Water I've Seen Is Running: A Novel*

Sansom, C. J. *Revelation*

Shipman, Viola. *The Clover Girls*

FRIENDSHIP

Al Rawi, Shahad. *The Baghdad Clock*

Alderton, Dolly. ★*Ghosts: A Novel*

Amis, Martin. ★*Inside Story*

Anappara, Deepa. *Djinn Patrol on the Purple Line: A Novel*

Anders, Charlie Jane. ★*All the Birds in the Sky*

Anderson, Alison. *The Summer Guest*

Asim, Jabari. ★*Yonder*

Ballard, J. G. *The Kindness of Women*

Barbery, Muriel. *The Elegance of the Hedgehog*

Barnett, David. *Calling Major Tom*

Bartlett, Neil. *The Disappearance Boy*

Bauer, Carlene. ★*Frances and Bernard*

Bellow, Saul. *Ravelstein*

Benjamin, Melanie. *Alice I Have Been*

Berg, Elizabeth. *Night of Miracles*

Binchy, Maeve. *Circle of Friends*

Bivald, Katarina. *The Readers of Broken Wheel Recommend*

Blume, Judy. *In the Unlikely Event*

Blumenfeld, Amy. *The Cast*

Brandt, Harry. *The Whites: A Novel*

Bronte, Charlotte. ★*Jane Eyre*

Brookner, Anita. *Hotel Du Lac*

Brown, Amy Belding. *Emily's House*

Brunt, Carol Rifka. ★*Tell the Wolves I'm Home: A Novel*

Bryant, Niobia. *Message from a Mistress*

Cameron, Marc. ★*Code of Honor*

Cannon, Joanna. *Three Things About Elsie: A Novel*

Capote, Truman. ★*Breakfast at Tiffany's*

Chambers, Clare. *Small Pleasures*

Cisneros, Sandra. ★*The House on Mango Street*

Cisneros, Sandra. *Martita, I Remember You: Martita, Te Recuerdo*

Clegg, Bill. *The End of the Day*

Collins, Ciaran. *The Gamal*

Colwin, Laurie. *Happy All the Time: A Novel*

Cotterill, Colin. *Don't Eat Me*

Danticat, Edwidge. ★*Everything Inside: Stories*

Donoghue, Emma. ★*Frog Music*

Dorey-Stein, Beck. *Rock the Boat: A Novel*

Eggers, Dave. *How We Are Hungry: Stories*

Ehirim, Nnamdi. *Prince of Monkeys*

Eisenberg, Deborah. *The Twilight of the Superheroes*

Ellis, Bret Easton. *Imperial Bedrooms*

Fabry, Chris. *The Promise of Jesse Woods*

Ford, Ford Madox. ★*The Good Soldier: A Tale of Passion*

Fowler, Karen Joy. *The Jane Austen Book Club*

Frayn, Michael. *Spies: A Novel*

Fuentes, Carlos. *Destiny and Desire: A Novel*

Fuller, Claire. ★*Bitter Orange*

Gabel, Aja. *The Ensemble: A Novel*

Gaynor, Hazel. *Meet Me in Monaco: A Novel*

Ghosh, Amitav. *The Glass Palace*

Ginzburg, Natalia. *A Family Lexicon*

Godwin, Gail. *Unfinished Desires*

Goenawan, Clarissa. *The Perfect World of Miwako Sumida*

Gosling, Victoria. *Before the Ruins: A Novel*

Grushin, Olga. *The Line*

Guillory, Jasmine. *The Wedding Party*

Gunesekera, Romesh. ★*Suncatcher: A Novel*

Harkaway, Nick. *The Gone-Away World*

Haruf, Kent. ★*Our Souls at Night*

Haywood, Gar Anthony. *Cemetery Road*

Heller, Peter. *The River: A Novel*

Jiles, Paulette. *News of the World: A Novel*

Jimenez, Abby. *The Friend Zone*
Joseph, Fabiola. *Niya: Rainbow Dreams*
K'wan. *Gangsta*
Kantaria, Annabel. *I Know You: A Novel of Suspense*
Kawakami, Mieko. *Ms. Ice Sandwich*
Kelly, Martha Hall. *Lost Roses: A Novel*
Kerouac, Jack. ★*On the Road*
Khadivi, Laleh. ★*A Good Country: A Novel*
Kibler, Julie. *Home for Erring and Outcast Girls*
Kingsolver, Barbara. ★*The Bean Trees: A Novel*
Knowles, John. ★*A Separate Peace*
Lee, Ji-Min. *The Starlet and the Spy*
Li, Yiyun. *The Vagrants: A Novel*
Littlejohn, Emily. *Lost Lake: A Detective Gemma Monroe Mystery*
Liu, Ken. ★*The Grace of Kings*
Logan, T. M. *The Vacation*
Lowe, Kathryn A. *The Furies*
Mallery, Susan. *Best of My Love*
McCreight, Kimberly. *Friends Like These*
McDermid, Val. *The Distant Echo*
McGuane, Thomas. *Crow Fair: Stories*
McMillan, Terry. ★*Waiting to Exhale*
Meuleman, Sarah. *Find Me Gone*
Moore, Meg Mitchell. *The Islanders*
Moriarty, Liane. *Truly Madly Guilty*
Morrison, Toni. *Sula*
Munro, Alice. *Hateship, Friendship, Courtship, Loveship, Marriage: Stories*
Murakami, Haruki. *Colorless Tsukuru Tazaki and His Years of Pilgrimage*
Murdoch, Iris. *The Book and the Brotherhood*
O'Donohue, Clare. *The Lover's Knot: A Someday Quilts Mystery*
Packer, Ann. *Songs Without Words*
Park, Sang Young. ★*Love in the Big City: A Novel*
Peebles, Frances de Pontes. *The Air You Breathe*
Phillips, Susan Elizabeth. *Call Me Irresistible*
Reddi, Rishi. *Passage West: A Novel*
Reid, Taylor Jenkins. *Forever, Interrupted: A Novel*
Reynolds, Allie. ★*Shiver*
Robb, Candace M. *A Murdered Peace*
Roberts, Nora. ★*The Becoming*
Rooney, Sally. ★*Beautiful World, Where Are You*
Sampson, Freya. *The Last Chance Library*
Saramago, Jose. ★*The Elephant's Journey*
Saunders, Kate. *The Case of the Wandering Scholar*
Savas, Aysegul. *Walking on the Ceiling*
Shreve, Anita. *Eden Close: A Novel*
Silvis, Randall. *Two Days Gone: A Novel*
Simmons, Dan. *The Abominable: A Novel*
Smiley, Jane. ★*Perestroika in Paris: A Novel*
Smith, Zadie. *The Autograph Man: A Novel*
Stegner, Wallace. *Crossing to Safety*
Stevens, Francis. *The Heads of Cerberus*
Straub, Emma. ★*Modern Lovers*
Straub, Emma. *The Vacationers*
Strout, Elizabeth. ★*Oh William!*
Styles, Toy. *Black and Ugly*
Sweeney, Cynthia D'Aprix. ★*Good Company: A Novel*

Swift, Graham. ★*Here We Are*
Tan, Amy. ★*The Joy Luck Club*
Tartt, Donna. ★*The Secret History*
Thorpe, Rufi. ★*The Knockout Queen*
Todd, Charles. ★*A Hanging at Dawn*
Tudor, C. J. *The Chalk Man: A Novel*
Unsworth, Emma Jane. *Grown Ups*
Valdes, Alisa. *Dirty Girls on Top*
Van Booy, Simon. *The Illusion of Separateness*
Vyleta, Dan. *Smoke: A Novel*
Wolitzer, Meg. *The Interestings*
Woolf, Virginia. *The Waves*
Yoon, Paul. ★*Run Me to Earth: A Novel*
Yoshimoto, Banana. *The Lake*
Youngson, Anne. *Meet Me at the Museum*

FRIGHTFUL SOUNDS

Palahniuk, Chuck. *The Invention of Sound*
★*Frog Music*. Donoghue, Emma
A Frolic of His Own: A Novel. Gaddis, William
From Bondage. Roth, Henry
★*From Here to Eternity*. Jones, James
From Russia with Love. Fleming, Ian
From sea to sea [Series]. Haldane, Sean
From the Neck up and Other Stories. Whiteley, Aliya

FRONTIER AND PIONEER LIFE

Barry, Sebastian. *Days Without End: A Novel*
Brand, Max. *Max Brand's Best Western Stories*
Brooks, Bill. *Blood Storm*
Brooks, Bill. *Frontier Justice*
Brooks, Bill. *Winter Kill*
Cather, Willa. *A Lost Lady*
Cather, Willa. ★*My Antonia*
Cather, Willa. *O Pioneers!*
Coldsmith, Don. *Tallgrass: A Novel of the Great Plains*
Cooper, James Fenimore. *The Last of the Mohicans: A Narrative of 1757*
Czerneda, Julie. *A Turn of Light*
Davies, Carys. *West*
Diaz, Hernan. ★*In the Distance*
Enger, Lin. *The High Divide: A Novel*
Estleman, Loren D. ★*The Master Executioner*
Everett, Percival L. *God's Country*
Freedman, Benedict. *Mrs. Mike: The Story of Katherine Mary Flannigan*
Gilman, Laura Anne. *The Cold Eye*
Goodman, Jo. *In Want of a Wife*
Goodman, Jo. *A Touch of Forever*
Grey, Zane. *Woman of the Frontier: A Western Story*
Groom, Winston. *El Paso: A Novel*
Guthrie, A. B. ★*The Big Sky*
Haldane, Sean. *The Devil's Making*
Harte, Bret. ★*The Best Short Stories of Bret Harte*
Howarth, Paul. *Dust off the Bones*
Howarth, Paul. *Only Killers and Thieves: A Novel*
L'Amour, Louis. ★*Bendigo Shafter*
L'Amour, Louis. *End of the Drive*
L'Amour, Louis. *To the Far Blue Mountains*
Lansdale, Joe R. ★*Paradise Sky*

Leonard, Elmore. ★*The Complete Western Stories of Elmore Leonard.*
Levine, David D. *Arabella of Mars*
Malouf, David. *Remembering Babylon*
Matthiessen, Peter. *Shadow Country: A New Rendering of the Watson Legend*
McMurtry, Larry. *Comanche Moon: A Novel*
McMurtry, Larry. ★*Lonesome Dove: A Novel*
McMurtry, Larry. ★*Streets of Laredo: A Novel*
Meyer, Philipp. ★*The Son: A Novel*
Michener, James A. ★*Centennial*
Munro, Alice. *The View from Castle Rock: Stories*
Punke, Michael. *Ridgeline: A Novel*
Pynchon, Thomas. *Mason & Dixon*
Russell, Mary Doria. ★*Doc: A Novel*
Russell, Mary Doria. *Epitaph: A Novel of the O.K. Corral*
Rølvaag, O. E. ★*Giants in the Earth: A Saga of the Prairie*
Schanbacher, Gary Lester. *Crossing Purgatory*
Sontag, Susan. ★*In America*
Warren, Robert Penn. *World Enough and Time: A Romantic Novel*
Welty, Eudora. ★*The Robber Bridegroom*
Frontier Justice. Brooks, Bill
Frost Easton novels [Series]. Freeman, Brian
Frost: a Novel. Bernhard, Thomas
The **Frozen** *Crown.* Kelly, Greta
FRUIT GROWERS
    Coplin, Amanda. *The Orchardist*
★**Fruit** *of the Drunken Tree: A Novel.* Rojas Contreras, Ingrid
FRUSTRATION
    Cusk, Rachel. *Second Place*
FRY, VARIAN
    Jimenez, Abby. *The Friend Zone*
    Orringer, Julie. ★*The Flight Portfolio: A Novel*
Fu, Kim
    For Today I Am a Boy
FUEL INDUSTRY AND TRADE
    Hay, Elizabeth. *Late Nights on Air*
Fuentes, Carlos
    The Crystal Frontier: A Novel in Nine Stories
    The Death of Artemio Cruz
    Destiny and Desire: A Novel
    The Eagle's Throne: A Novel
    ★*The Old Gringo*
    The Years with Laura Diaz
FUGITIVES
    Auster, Paul. *Sunset Park*
    Child, Lee. *Make Me*
    Child, Lee. *Night School*
    Child, Lee. *No Middle Name: The Complete Collected Jack Reacher Short Stories*
    Child, Lee. *Personal*
    Dodd, Christina. *Obsession Falls*
    Doiron, Paul. *The Poacher's Son*
    Edugyan, Esi. ★*Washington Black: A Novel*
    Erdrich, Louise. *Future Home of the Living God*
    Evanovich, Janet. *One for the Money*
    Freeman, Brian. *Marathon*
    French, Nicci. *Friday on My Mind: A Frieda Klein Mystery*
    Goodis, David. *Nightfall*

Goss, Theodora. *The Strange Case of the Alchemist's Daughter*
K'wan. *Animal*
L'Amour, Louis. *To the Far Blue Mountains*
Lyons, Jenn. *The Name of All Things*
Perry, Thomas. *The Old Man*
Petrie, Nicholas. *The Breaker*
Petrie, Nicholas. *The Wild One*
Pollock, Donald Ray. *The Devil All the Time*
Rajaniemi, Hannu. *The Fractal Prince*
Rajaniemi, Hannu. *The Quantum Thief*
Robotham, Michael. *Life or Death*
Sallis, James. *Drive*
Saramago, Jose. *Cain*
Spark, Muriel. *Aiding & Abetting*
Swinson, Kiki. *The Safe House*
Thelen, Albert Vigoleis. *The Island of Second Sight: From the Applied Recollections of Vigoleis*
Willink, Jocko. *Final Spin*
The **Fugitives**. McCarthy, Jesse
The **Full** *Cupboard of Life.* McCall Smith, Alexander
★**Full** *Throttle: Stories.* Hill, Joe
Fuller, Claire
    ★*Bitter Orange*
    Our Endless Numbered Days: A Novel
    Unsettled Ground
Fumbled. Martin, Alexa
FUNDAMENTALISM
    Forsyth, Frederick. *The Kill List*
    Rushdie, Salman. *Two Years Eight Months and Twenty-Eight Nights: A Novel*
FUNDAMENTALISTS
    Ebershoff, David. *The 19th Wife: A Novel*
Funeral Games. Renault, Mary
FUNERAL HOMES
    Henderson, Susan. *The Flicker of Old Dreams*
    Ross, Ann B. *Miss Julia Takes the Wheel*
    Sanders, Lawrence. *McNally's Trial*
    Waugh, Evelyn. *The Loved One: An Anglo-American Tragedy*
FUNERALS
    Cordova, Zoraida. *The Inheritance of Orquidea Divina*
    Diehl, Heidi. *Lifelines*
    Downing, Samantha. *He Started It*
    Gaiman, Neil. ★*The Ocean at the End of the Lane*
    Harris, Robert. *The Second Sleep: A Novel*
    Igharo, Jane. *The Sweetest Remedy*
    Jeffries, Sabrina. *Project Duchess*
    Lipman, Elinor. *The Dearly Departed*
    St. Aubyn, Edward. *At Last*
    Swift, Graham. *Wish You Were Here*
    Welty, Eudora. *The Optimist's Daughter*
Fuqua, Jonathon Scott
    Gone and Back Again
FUR INDUSTRY AND TRADE
    Aalborg, Gordon. *River of Porcupines*
The **Furies**. Lowe, Kathryn A.
FURNITURE INDUSTRY AND TRADE
    Cipri, Nino. *Defekt*

Furst, Alan
  Blood of Victory: A Novel
  Dark Voyage: A Novel
  The Foreign Correspondent: A Novel
  ★*A Hero of France*
  ★*Mission to Paris*
  Spies of the Balkans: A Novel
  The Spies of Warsaw
  ★*Under Occupation: A Novel*
Future Home of the Living God. Erdrich, Louise
FUTURE PUNISHMENT
  Butler, Robert Olen. *Hell: A Novel*
FUTURISTIC ROMANCES
  Bouchet, Amanda. *Nightchaser*
  Castle, Jayne. *Illusion Town*
Futuristic Violence and Fancy Suits. Wong, David
FUTURISTS
  Sterling, Bruce. *Pirate Utopia*

G

G I RESISTANCE AND REVOLTS
  Barker, Pat. ★*Regeneration*
Gabaldon, Diana
  ★*A Breath of Snow and Ashes*
  ★*Dragonfly in Amber*
  ★*Drums of Autumn*
  An Echo in the Bone
  ★*The Fiery Cross*
  ★*Outlander*
  ★*Voyager*
  Written in My Own Heart's Blood
Gabel, Aja
  The Ensemble: A Novel
GABLE, CLARK
  Alcott, Kate. *A Touch of Stardust*
  Monroe, Mary. *God Still Don't Like Ugly*
Gabriel Allon novels [Series]. Silva, Daniel
Gabriel Ash and Hazel Best mysteries [Series]. Bannister, Jo
Gabriel Du Pre mysteries [Series]. Bowen, Peter
★*Gabriel's Story*. Durham, David Anthony
Gabriela, Clove and Cinnamon. Amado, Jorge
Gaddis, William
  Agape Agape
  A Frolic of His Own: A Novel
  ★*J R: A Novel*
  ★*The Recognitions*
GADGETS
  Bauermeister, Erica. *The Scent Keeper*
Gaea trilogy [Series]. Varley, John
Gaige, Amity
  Schroder
  Sea Wife
Gailey, Sarah
  The Echo Wife
  Magic for Liars

Gaiman, Neil
  ★*American Gods: A Novel*
  ★*Anansi Boys: A Novel*
  ★*Fragile Things: Short Fictions and Wonders*
  ★*Good Omens: The Nice and Accurate Prophecies of Agnes Nutter, Witch*
  ★*Norse Mythology*
  ★*The Ocean at the End of the Lane*
  ★*Stardust*
  Trigger Warning: Short Fictions and Disturbances
Gaines, Ernest J.
  ★*The Autobiography of Miss Jane Pittman*
  ★*A Gathering of Old Men*
Gainza, Maria
  The Optic Nerve
Gaitskill, Mary
  Don't Cry: Stories
  The Mare: A Novel
  Veronica
Gala, Marcial
  ★*The Black Cathedral*
GALAPAGOS ISLANDS
  Hockman, Angie. *Shipped*
  Picoult, Jodi. ★*Wish You Were Here: A Novel*
  Vonnegut, Kurt. ★*Galapagos: A Novel*
★*Galapagos: a Novel*. Vonnegut, Kurt
★*The Galaxy, and the Ground Within*. Chambers, Becky
Galbraith, Robert
  Career of Evil
  The Cuckoo's Calling
  Lethal White
  The Silkworm
Galchen, Rivka
  American Innovations: Stories
  Everyone Knows Your Mother Is a Witch
Gale Force. Laukkanen, Owen
Galen, Shana
  Third Son's a Charm
Gallagher, Stephen
  The Bedlam Detective: A Novel
  The Kingdom of Bones: A Novel
Gallen, Michelle
  Big Girl, Small Town: A Novel
Galligan, John
  Bad Moon Rising
GALLIPOLI PENINSULA, TURKEY
  De Bernieres, Louis. *Birds Without Wings*
GALLIPOLI, TURKEY
  Keneally, Thomas. ★*The Daughters of Mars*
  Uris, Leon. *Redemption: A Novel*
Galloway, Gregory
  As Simple as Snow
GALLOWAY, RUTH (FICTITIOUS CHARACTER)
  Griffiths, Elly. *The House at Sea's End: A Ruth Galloway Mystery*
  Griffiths, Elly. *The Janus Stone*
Galore. Crummey, Michael
Galsworthy, John
  ★*The Forsyte Saga*

*The **Galton** Case*. Macdonald, Ross
***Galway** Girl: A Jack Taylor Novel*. Bruen, Ken
GALWAY, IRELAND
    Bruen, Ken. *Galway Girl: A Jack Taylor Novel*
    Bruen, Ken. *The Guards*
GAMACHE, ARMAND (FICTITIOUS CHARACTER)
    Penny, Louise. *The Cruelest Month: A Three Pines Mystery*
*The **Gamal***. Collins, Ciaran
Gambit. Hagberg, David
★***Gambit***. Stout, Rex
GAMBLERS
    Dickens, Charles. *The Old Curiosity Shop*
    Ferber, Edna. *So Big*
    Hammett, Dashiell. *The Glass Key*
    Leonard, Elmore. ★*Get Shorty*
    Putney, Mary Jo. *Nowhere Near Respectable*
GAMBLING
    Algren, Nelson. ★*The Man with the Golden Arm: A Novel*
    Barthelme, Frederick. *Bob the Gambler*
    DeSilva, Bruce. *A Scourge of Vipers*
    Dickens, Charles. *The Old Curiosity Shop*
    Fleming, Ian. ★*Casino Royale: A James Bond Novel*
    Freeman, Anna. *The Fair Fight: A Novel*
    Meltzer, Brad. *The Zero Game*
    Winterson, Jeanette. *The Passion*
★*A **Gambling** Man*. Baldacci, David
Gamboa, Santiago
    Necropolis
***Game** of Snipers: A Bob Lee Swagger Novel*. Hunter, Stephen
★*A **Game** of Thrones*. Martin, George R. R.
★***Game** On: Tempting Twenty-Eight*. Evanovich, Janet
GAME WARDENS
    Box, C. J. ★*Dark Sky: A Joe Pickett Novel*
    Box, C. J. *The Disappeared*
    Box, C. J. ★*Long Range*
    Box, C. J. *Vicious Circle*
    Box, C. J. ★*Wolf Pack*
    Doiron, Paul. *Almost Midnight*
    Doiron, Paul. *Bad Little Falls: A Novel*
    Doiron, Paul. ★*Dead by Dawn*
    Doiron, Paul. *One Last Lie*
    Doiron, Paul. *The Poacher's Son*
    Doiron, Paul. *The Precipice*
    Doiron, Paul. *Stay Hidden*
Gamechanger. Beckett, L. X.
GAMES
    Gosling, Victoria. *Before the Ruins: A Novel*
    Morgenstern, Erin. ★*The Night Circus: A Novel*
    Tudor, C. J. *The Chalk Man: A Novel*
GANG MEMBERS
    Beverly, William. *Dodgers: A Novel*
    K'wan. *Gangsta*
    K'wan. *Gutter*
GANGES RIVER
    Endo, Shusaku. *Deep River*
GANGS
    Atkins, Ace. *The Lost Ones*
    Blake, James Carlos. *The House of Wolfe*

    Burke, Marcus. *Team Seven*
    Ca$h. *Thugs Cry: A Novel*
    Child, Lee. ★*Blue Moon*
    Harvey, Michael T. *We All Fall Down*
    Mabanckou, Alain. ★*Black Moses*
    McIlvanney, William. *The Dark Remains: Laidlaw's First Case*
    McKevett, G. A. *Murder at Mabel's Motel*
    Mosley, Walter. *The Right Mistake: The Further Philosophical Investigations of Socrates Fortlow*
    O'Mara, Tim. *Crooked Numbers*
    Sandford, John. ★*Golden Prey*
    Scott, A. D. ★*The Low Road*
    Steinbeck, John. *Tortilla Flat*
    Vachss, Andrew H. *Two Trains Running*
Gangsta. K'wan
***Gangsta** novels [Series]*. K'wan
*A **Gangster** and a Gentleman*. Swinson, Kiki
***Gangsterland**: a Novel*. Goldberg, Tod
GANGSTERS
    Abbott, Megan E. *Queenpin: A Novel*
    Amdahl, Gary. *I Am Death: Two Novellas*
    Berkowitz, Ira. *Old Flame: A Jackson Steeg Novel*
    Chandler, Raymond. *The Long Goodbye*
    Clark, Wahida. ★*Thugs and the Women Who Love Them*
    Doctorow, E. L. ★*Billy Bathgate: A Novel*
    Goldberg, Tod. *Gangsterland: A Novel*
    Goodis, David. *Nightfall*
    Gray, Erick S. *Love & a Gangsta: A Novel*
    Greene, Graham. ★*Brighton Rock*
    Hallinan, Timothy. *Fields Where They Lay*
    Kaminsky, Stuart M. *Dancing in the Dark*
    Lehane, Dennis. *Live by Night*
    Leonard, Elmore. *Charlie Martz and Other Stories: The Unpublished Stories*
    Leonard, Elmore. *The Hot Kid*
    McBride, James. ★*Deacon King Kong: A Novel*
    Moss, Tara. *The War Widow*
    Pelecanos, George P. *The Big Blowdown*
    Puzo, Mario. ★*The Godfather*
    Puzo, Mario. *The Sicilian: A Novel*
    Rabe, Peter. ★*Anatomy of a Killer ;: A Shroud for Jesso*
    Rankin, Ian. *The Hanging Garden: An Inspector Rebus Novel*
    Reich, Christopher. ★*The Take*
    Rosen, Renee. *Dollface: A Novel of the Roaring Twenties*
    Snyder, Suleikha. *Big Bad Wolf*
    Twardoch, Szczepan. *The King of Warsaw*
    Youers, Rio. *Lola on Fire*
Ganshert, Katie
    Life After
    ★*No One Ever Asked: A Novel*
Ganymede. Priest, Cherie
Gao, XIngjian
    Soul Mountain
*The **Gap** Year: A Novel*. Bird, Sarah
Gappah, Petina
    ★*Out of Darkness, Shining Light*
Garcia Marquez, Gabriel
    ★*The Autumn of the Patriarch*

Chronicle of a Death Foretold
Collected Novellas
The General in His Labyrinth
In Evil Hour
Leaf Storm, and Other Stories
★*Love in the Time of Cholera*
Memories of My Melancholy Whores
★*One Hundred Years of Solitude*
★*Strange Pilgrims: Twelve Stories*

Garcia Saenz, Eva
The Silence of the White City

Garcia, Cristina
The Aguero Sisters
Dreaming in Cuban
King of Cuba: A Novel
The Lady Matador's Hotel: A Novel

Garcia, Gabriela
Of Women and Salt

Garcia-Roza, L. A.
Alone in the Crowd: An Inspector Espinosa Mystery
December Heat

Gardam, Jane
The Flight of the Maidens
God on the Rocks
Last Friends
Old Filth
The People on Privilege Hill and Other Stories

*The **Garden** House*. Willett, Marcia
*The **Garden** of Angels*. Hewson, David
***Garden** of Beasts: A Novel of Berlin 1936*. Deaver, Jeffery
*A **Garden** of Earthly Delights*. Oates, Joyce Carol
*The **Garden** of Evening Mists*. Tan, Twan Eng
*The **Garden** of Evil*. Hewson, David
***Garden** of Lies*. Quick, Amanda
***Garden** Spells*. Allen, Sarah Addison

GARDENERS
Coetzee, J. M. ★*Life & Times of Michael K*
Hale, Shannon. *Austenland: A Novel*
Koontz, Dean R. *The Husband*

GARDENS
Allen, Sarah Addison. *Garden Spells*
Bowen, Rhys. *The Victory Garden*
Shipman, Viola. *The Heirloom Garden*

***Gardens** in the Dunes: A Novel*. Silko, Leslie Marmon

Gardiner, Meg
The Dark Corners of the Night
The Dirty Secrets Club
Into the Black Nowhere
Phantom Instinct
Unsub: A Novel

Gardner, Lisa
Alone
★*Before She Disappeared: A Novel*
Fear Nothing: A Detective D. D. Warren Novel
Find Her
★*Look for Me: A Novel*
Love You More: A Detective D.D. Warren Novel
The Neighbor

★*Never Tell: A Novel*
★*When You See Me: A Novel*

Garey, Juliann
Too Bright to Hear Too Loud to See

*The **Gargoyle***. Davidson, Andrew

Garner, Helen
The Spare Room

Garnet Run [Series]. Parrish, Roan

Garrett, Kellye
★*Hollywood Homicide*

Garriott, Leah
Promised

GARUDA (MYTHICAL BIRD)
Mieville, China. ★*Perdido Street Station*

Garvin, Eileen
The Music of Bees

Garwood, Julie
The Bride
Wired

★***Gas** City*. Estleman, Loren D.

Gaskell, Elizabeth Cleghorn
★*Cranford*
★*North and South*

Gaslight mysteries (Victoria Thompson) [Series]. Thompson, Victoria

Gaspar de Alba, Alicia
Desert Blood: The Juarez Murders

Gass, William H.
Middle C

*A **Gate** at the Stairs: A Novel*. Moore, Lorrie
*The **Gate** to Women's Country*. Tepper, Sheri S.

GATED COMMUNITIES
Headley, Maria Dahvana. *The Mere Wife*
Rojas Contreras, Ingrid. ★*Fruit of the Drunken Tree: A Novel*
Rouda, Kaira Sturdivant. *The Favorite Daughter*

Gates, Eva
Deadly Ever After
A Death Long Overdue
Read and Buried

Gateway. Pohl, Frederik

GATEWAY FANTASY
Beagle, Peter S. *The Unicorn Sonata*
Dekker, Ted. *Black: The Birth of Evil*
Dekker, Ted. *Red: The Heroic Rescue*
Dekker, Ted. *White: The Great Pursuit*
Gaiman, Neil. ★*Stardust*
Grossman, Lev. *The Magician King: A Novel*
Kay, Guy Gavriel. *The Summer Tree*
Maaren, Kari. ★*Weave a Circle Round*
McGuire, Seanan. ★*Beneath the Sugar Sky*
McGuire, Seanan. ★*Down Among the Sticks and Bones*
McGuire, Seanan. ★*Every Heart a Doorway*
McGuire, Seanan. ★*In an Absent Dream*
Schwab, Victoria. *A Conjuring of Light*
Schwab, Victoria. *A Darker Shade of Magic*
Schwab, Victoria. *A Gathering of Shadows*

***Gather** Her Round: A Novel of the Tufa*. Bledsoe, Alex
***Gather** the Fortunes*. Camp, Bryan
★*The **Gathering***. Enright, Anne

★*A **Gathering** of Old Men.* Gaines, Ernest J.

*A **Gathering** of Shadows.* Schwab, Victoria

GAUCHOS

    Borges, Jorge Luis. ★*Collected Fictions*

★*Gaudy Night.* Sayers, Dorothy L.

GAUGUIN, PAUL

    Maugham, W. Somerset. *The Moon and Sixpence*

GAUTAMA BUDDHA

    Hesse, Hermann. ★*Siddhartha: A New Translation*

GAY ACTORS

    Bram, Christopher. *Lives of the Circus Animals: A Novel*

GAY COUPLES

    Castellani, Christopher. *Leading Men: A Novel*

    Cruse, Howard. *The Complete Wendel*

    Oyeyemi, Helen. *Peaces*

    Ramadan, Ahmad Danny. *The Clothesline Swing*

    Washington, Bryan. ★*Memorial*

GAY CULTURE

    Cassara, Joseph. *The House of Impossible Beauties*

    Cruse, Howard. *The Complete Wendel*

    Vernon, P. J. *Bath Haus: A Thriller*

GAY MEN

    Baldwin, James. ★*Early Novels and Stories*

    Baldwin, James. ★*Giovanni's Room*

    Barry, Sebastian. *Days Without End: A Novel*

    Barry, Sebastian. ★*A Thousand Moons: A Novel*

    Bartlett, Neil. *The Disappearance Boy*

    Burroughs, William S. ★*Naked Lunch: The Restored Text*

    Charles, KJ. *Wanted, a Gentleman: Or, Virtue Over-Rated*

    Cruse, Howard. *The Complete Wendel*

    Cusset, Catherine. *Life of David Hockney: A Novel*

    D'Erasmo, Stacey. *The Sky Below*

    Ebershoff, David. *The 19th Wife: A Novel*

    Gonzalez, Christopher. *I'm Not Hungry but I Could Eat*

    Greene, Graham. *Collected Stories: Including May We Borrow Your Husband? a Sense of Reality, Twenty-One Stories*

    Greenwell, Garth. *What Belongs to You: A Novel*

    Greer, Andrew Sean. ★*Less*

    Hall, Alexis. ★*Boyfriend Material*

    Hall, Alexis. *For Real*

    Herrera, Adriana. ★*American Dreamer*

    Herrera, Adriana. *American Fairytale*

    Herrera, Adriana. *American Love Story*

    Isherwood, Christopher. ★*The Berlin Stories: The Last of Mr. Norris, Goodbye to Berlin*

    Jedrowski, Tomasz. *Swimming in the Dark*

    Jones, Robert. ★*The Prophets: A Novel*

    Leavitt, David. *The Two Hotel Francforts: A Novel*

    Manning, Corinne. *We Had No Rules: Stories*

    Marske, Freya. *A Marvellous Light*

    Nava, Michael. ★*Carved in Bone*

    Park, Sang Young. ★*Love in the Big City: A Novel*

    Parrish, Roan. *Better Than People*

    Renault, Mary. *The Last of the Wine*

    Renault, Mary. *The Persian Boy*

    Ripper, Kris. *The Hate Project*

    Rooney, Kathleen. ★*Cher Ami and Major Whittlesey*

    Rowley, Steven. ★*The Guncle: A Novel*

    Sebastian, Cat. *It Takes Two to Tumble*

    Sebastian, Cat. *The Lawrence Browne Affair*

    Staples, Dennis E. *This Town Sleeps*

    Taylor, Brandon. ★*Real Life*

    Tesh, Emily. *Silver in the Wood*

    Thomas, Russ. *Nighthawking*

    Vernon, P. J. *Bath Haus: A Thriller*

GAY MEN — RELATIONS WITH WOMEN

    Gide, Andre. ★*The Immoralist*

GAY MEN — SEXUALITY

    Gide, Andre. ★*The Immoralist*

    Greenwell, Garth. *Cleanness*

GAY MEN — SOCIAL CONDITIONS

    Roberts, Bethan. ★*My Policeman*

GAY MEN'S WIVES

    Gide, Andre. ★*The Immoralist*

GAY TEENAGERS

    Aciman, Andre. *Call Me by Your Name*

    Cassara, Joseph. *The House of Impossible Beauties*

    Iweala, Uzodinma. ★*Speak No Evil*

    Louis, Edouard. *The End of Eddy: A Novel*

    Mehta, Rahul. *No Other World: A Novel*

    Thorpe, Rufi. ★*The Knockout Queen*

Gay, Roxane

    ★*Ayiti*

    ★*Difficult Women*

    ★*An Untamed State*

Gaylin, Alison

    Never Look Back

Gaynor, Hazel

    The Lighthouse Keeper's Daughter

    Meet Me in Monaco: A Novel

    Three Words for Goodbye

GED (FICTITIOUS CHARACTER)

    Le Guin, Ursula K. *The Other Wind*

Geek Love. Dunn, Katherine

GEEKS (COMPUTER ENTHUSIASTS)

    Hibbert, Talia. ★*Get a Life, Chloe Brown*

GEESE

    Davis, Lindsey. *One Virgin Too Many*

GEISHAS

    Golden, Arthur. ★*Memoirs of a Geisha: A Novel*

Gelernter, J. H.

    Hold Fast

GELLHORN, MARTHA

    Fuller, Claire. ★*Bitter Orange*

    McLain, Paula. *Love and Ruin*

Gelman, Laurie

    Class Mom: A Novel

    Yoga Pant Nation: A Novel

    You've Been Volunteered: A Class Mom Novel

GEMS

    Gaiman, Neil. ★*Stardust*

    Tolkien, J. R. R. *The Silmarillion*

    Wolfe, Gene. *The Citadel of the Autarch*

    Wolfe, Gene. *The Claw of the Conciliator*

GENDER FLUID

    Emezi, Akwaeke. ★*The Death of Vivek Oji*

Ripper, Kris. *The Love Study*
GENDER IDENTITY
  Barry, Sebastian. *Days Without End: A Novel*
  De Robertis, Carolina. *The Gods of Tango*
  Elison, Meg. *The Book of Flora*
  Manning, Corinne. *We Had No Rules: Stories*
  Parker-Chan, Shelley. ★*She Who Became the Sun*
GENDER ROLE
  Abbott, Megan E. *Bury Me Deep*
  Abbott, Megan E. *Queenpin: A Novel*
  Adjapon, Bisi. *The Teller of Secrets: A Novel*
  Alderman, Naomi. ★*The Power: A Novel*
  Atwood, Margaret. ★*The Testaments: A Novel*
  Barker, Pat. ★*The Silence of the Girls: A Novel*
  Cho, Nam-Ju. ★*Kim Jiyoung, Born 1982*
  Delany, Samuel R. *Stars in My Pocket Like Grains of Sand*
  Diamant, Anita. *The Boston Girl: A Novel*
  Diamant, Anita. ★*The Red Tent*
  Dunmore, Evie. ★*Bringing Down the Duke*
  Ellis, Bella. *The Vanished Bride*
  Everett, Elizabeth. ★*A Lady's Formula for Love*
  Ferraris, Zoe. *Finding Nouf*
  Gilman, Charlotte Perkins. ★*The Yellow Wallpaper and Selected Writings*
  Greenidge, Kaitlyn. ★*Libertie: A Novel*
  Hoffman, Alice. *The Marriage of Opposites: A Novel Based on the Life of Rachel Pizzarro*
  Kaufman, Sue. *Diary of a Mad Housewife*
  Krauss, Nicole. ★*To Be a Man: Stories*
  Le Guin, Ursula K. *The Birthday of the World: And Other Stories*
  Levin, Ira. ★*The Stepford Wives: A Novel*
  Mas, Victoria. *The Mad Women's Ball*
  Polk, C. L. *The Midnight Bargain*
  Richardson, Samuel. ★*Pamela: Or, Virtue Rewarded*
  Schlink, Bernhard. *Olga*
  Smith, Zadie. ★*White Teeth: A Novel*
  Solomon, Anna. *Leaving Lucy Pear*
  Spencer, Sally. *The Dead Hand of History*
  Stibbe, Nina. *Reasons to Be Cheerful*
  Taneja, Preti. *We That Are Young: A Novel*
  Thorpe, Rufi. ★*The Knockout Queen*
  Tyler, Anne. *Vinegar Girl: The Taming of the Shrew Retold*
  Watson, Brad. *Miss Jane: A Novel*
GENDERQUEER
  Sebastian, Cat. *Unmasked by the Marquess*
Gendry-Kim, Keum Suk
  ★*The Waiting*
GENEALOGY
  Conner, M. Shelly. *Everyman*
  Wade, Becky. ★*True to You*
*The **General** in His Labyrinth*. Garcia Marquez, Gabriel
GENERAL RELATIVITY (PHYSICS)
  Lightman, Alan P. ★*Einstein's Dreams*
GENERALS
  Ballard, J. G. ★*The Day of Creation*
  Bowman, Valerie. *A Duke Like No Other*
  Dekker, Ted. *Black: The Birth of Evil*
  Dekker, Ted. *Red: The Heroic Rescue*

  Dekker, Ted. *White: The Great Pursuit*
  Shaara, Jeff. *Gods and Generals: A Novel of the Civil War*
  Shaara, Jeff. *Gone for Soldiers*
  Shaara, Jeff. *The Last Full Measure*
GENERATION GAP
  Hardiman, Rebecca. *Good Eggs*
  Mukherjee, Neel. *The Lives of Others*
  Robinson, Marilynne. *Home*
  Sackville-West, V. *The Edwardians*
  Swarup, Shubhangi. *Latitudes of Longing*
  Tan, Amy. *The Bonesetter's Daughter*
  Tan, Amy. ★*The Joy Luck Club*
  Tan, Amy. ★*The Kitchen God's Wife*
  Turgenev, Ivan Sergeevich. ★*Fathers and Sons*
★*Generation Loss: A Novel*. Hand, Elizabeth
GENERATION X
  Ellis, Bret Easton. *Imperial Bedrooms*
GENERATIONS
  Dupont, Eric. *The American Fiancee: A Novel*
  Saylor, Steven. *Roma: The Novel of Ancient Rome*
GENEROSITY
  Adimi, Kaouther. *Our Riches*
Generosity: an Enhancement. Powers, Richard
★*Genesis*. Cook, Robin
GENETIC ENGINEERING
  Butler, Octavia E. *Adulthood Rites*
  Butler, Octavia E. ★*Dawn: Xenogenesis*
  Grant, Mira. *Parasite*
  Huxley, Aldous. ★*Brave New World*
  Kress, Nancy. *Beggars in Spain*
  Mieville, China. *Embassytown*
  Stivers, Carole. *The Mother Code*
  Suarez, Daniel. *Change Agent: A Novel*
GENETIC GENEALOGY
  Cook, Robin. ★*Genesis*
GENETIC RESEARCH
  Powers, Richard. *Generosity: An Enhancement*
GENETICALLY ENGINEERED ANIMALS
  Atwood, Margaret. ★*Maddaddam: A Novel*
GENETICALLY ENGINEERED ORGANISMS
  VanderMeer, Jeff. ★*Borne: A Novel*
  VanderMeer, Jeff. *Dead Astronauts: A Novel*
GENETICALLY ENGINEERED WOMEN
  Bacigalupi, Paolo. ★*The Windup Girl*
  Chambers, Becky. *To Be Taught, If Fortunate*
GENETICISTS
  Lauren, Christina. *The Soulmate Equation*
  Simsion, Graeme C. *The Rosie Effect*
  Simsion, Graeme C. ★*The Rosie Project*
  Simsion, Graeme C. *The Rosie Result*
GENETICS
  Pastan, Rachel. *In the Field*
  Powers, Richard. *Generosity: An Enhancement*
GENGHIS KHAN
  Jin, Yong. *A Hero Born: A Novel*
  Porter, Henry. *The Bell Ringers*
Geni, Abby
  The Lightkeepers: A Novel

The Wildlands: A Novel

GENIES

Chakraborty, S. A. *The City of Brass*

Chakraborty, S. A. *The Empire of Gold*

Chakraborty, S. A. *The Kingdom of Copper: A Novel*

Rushdie, Salman. *Two Years Eight Months and Twenty-Eight Nights: A Novel*

Wecker, Helene. *The Golem and the Jinni*

Wecker, Helene. ★*The Hidden Palace*

GENIUS

Hayes, Terry. *I Am Pilgrim*

Horrocks, Caitlin. *The Vexations*

Rachman, Tom. *The Italian Teacher*

Sakey, Marcus. *A Better World*

Sakey, Marcus. *Brilliance*

GENOCIDE

Akpan, Uwem. *Say You're One of Them*

Benaron, Naomi. *Running the Rift: A Novel*

Faye, Gael. ★*Small Country: A Novel*

Hensher, Philip. *Scenes from Early Life: A Novel*

Okorafor, Nnedi. ★*Who Fears Death*

Ratner, Vaddey. *Music of the Ghosts*

Van Vogt, A. E. ★*Slan*

Genova, Lisa

Every Note Played

Inside the O'Briens: A Novel

Left Neglected: A Novel

Gentill, Sulari

Crossing the Lines

GENTLE READS

Allen, Sarah Addison. *Garden Spells*

Allen, Sarah Addison. *The Girl Who Chased the Moon: A Novel*

Andrew, Sally. *The Satanic Mechanic: A Tannie Maria Mystery*

Andrews, Donna. *Murder Most Fowl: A Meg Langslow Mystery*

Andrews, Donna. *Owl Be Home for Christmas: A Meg Langslow Mystery*

Andrews, Donna. *The Twelve Jays of Christmas: A Meg Langslow Mystery*

Andrews, Mary Kay. *Sunset Beach*

Beaton, M. C. *Agatha Raisin and the Quiche of Death*

Beaton, M. C. *Agatha Raisin and the Witch of Wyckhadden*

Beaton, M. C. *Death of a Macho Man*

Beaton, M. C. ★*Hot to Trot*

Beaton, M. C. *Pushing up Daisies: An Agatha Raisin Mystery*

Berg, Elizabeth. *The Confession Club: A Novel*

Berg, Elizabeth. *Night of Miracles*

Berg, Elizabeth. *The Story of Arthur Truluv: A Novel*

Berry, Wendell. *Jayber Crow: A Novel*

Binchy, Maeve. *Circle of Friends*

Binchy, Maeve. *Firefly Summer*

Bowen, Rhys. *The Victory Garden*

Braun, Lilian Jackson. *The Cat Who Ate Danish Modern*

Brett, Simon. *Guilt at the Garage*

Brett, Simon. *Mrs Pargeter's Principle*

Brown, Eleanor. *The Weird Sisters*

Brown, Rita Mae. *Wish You Were Here*

Burns, V. M. *Killer Words*

Chiaverini, Jennifer. *Mrs. Lincoln's Dressmaker: A Novel*

Childs, Laura. *Egg Shooters*

Childs, Laura. *Haunted Hibiscus*

Childs, Laura. *Lavender Blue Murder*

Colgan, Jenny. *Sunrise by the Sea*

Connolly, Sheila. *The Lost Traveller*

Dallas, Sandra. *The Last Midwife*

Dallas, Sandra. *Tallgrass*

Davidson, Diane Mott. *Killer Pancake*

Davidson, Diane Mott. *The Last Suppers*

Delany, Vicki. *Murder in a Teacup*

Delany, Vicki. *Tea & Treachery*

Edgerton, Clyde. ★*Walking Across Egypt: A Novel*

Estleman, Loren D. *Frames*

Faulks, Sebastian. *Jeeves and the Wedding Bells*

Flagg, Fannie. *Standing in the Rainbow: A Novel*

Frank, Dorothea Benton. *Folly Beach: A Lowcountry Tale*

Gates, Eva. *Deadly Ever After*

Gates, Eva. *A Death Long Overdue*

Gates, Eva. *Read and Buried*

Heyer, Georgette. *The Grand Sophy*

Hollis, Lee. *Poppy Harmon Investigates*

James, Miranda. *What the Cat Dragged In*

Landvik, Lorna. *Chronicles of a Radical Hag: With Recipes*

Malliet, G. M. *A Demon Summer: A Max Tudor Mystery*

Malliet, G. M. *Pagan Spring: A Mystery*

Manansala, Mia P. ★*Arsenic and Adobo*

McCall Smith, Alexander. *Blue Shoes and Happiness*

McCall Smith, Alexander. *The Comforts of a Muddy Saturday: An Isabel Dalhousie Novel*

McCall Smith, Alexander. ★*The Department of Sensitive Crimes: A Detective Varg Novel*

McCall Smith, Alexander. *The Double Comfort Safari Club*

McCall Smith, Alexander. *The Forgotten Affairs of Youth*

McCall Smith, Alexander. *The Full Cupboard of Life*

McCall Smith, Alexander. ★*The Geometry of Holding Hands*

McCall Smith, Alexander. *The Good Husband of Zebra Drive*

McCall Smith, Alexander. *In the Company of Cheerful Ladies*

McCall Smith, Alexander. *The Joy and Light Bus Company*

McCall Smith, Alexander. *The Kalahari Typing School for Men*

McCall Smith, Alexander. *The Limpopo Academy of Private Detection*

McCall Smith, Alexander. *The Lost Art of Gratitude*

McCall Smith, Alexander. ★*The Man with the Silver Saab: A Detective Varg Novel*

McCall Smith, Alexander. ★*The No. 1 Ladies' Detective Agency*

McCall Smith, Alexander. *The Saturday Big Tent Wedding Party*

McKevett, G. A. *A Few Drops of Bitters*

McKevett, G. A. *Murder at Mabel's Motel*

McKevett, G. A. *Murder in the Corn Maze*

McKinlay, Jenn. *Killer Research*

Meier, Leslie. *Silver Anniversary Murder*

O'Connor, Carlene. *Murder in an Irish Bookshop*

O'Donohue, Clare. *The Lover's Knot: A Someday Quilts Mystery*

Perkins, S. C. *Murder Once Removed*

Pilcher, Rosamunde. ★*The Shell Seekers*

Pym, Barbara. ★*Excellent Women*

Robinson, Marilynne. *Home*

Robinson, Marilynne. ★*Jack*

Robinson, Marilynne. ★*Lila*
Roosevelt, Elliott. ★*Murder and the First Lady*
Roosevelt, Elliott. *Murder at Midnight*
Roosevelt, Elliott. *Murder in the Map Room: An Eleanor Roosevelt Mystery*
Roosevelt, Elliott. *Murder in the Oval Office*
Ross, Ann B. *Miss Julia Delivers the Goods: A Novel*
Ross, Ann B. ★*Miss Julia Happily Ever After*
Ross, Ann B. *Miss Julia Knows a Thing or Two*
Ross, Ann B. *Miss Julia Takes the Wheel*
Ross, Ann B. *Miss Julia Throws a Wedding*
Saums, Mary. *Thistle & Twigg*
Simonson, Helen. *Major Pettigrew's Last Stand: A Novel*
Tatlock, Ann. *Promises to Keep*
Trigiani, Adriana. *Big Cherry Holler: A Big Stone Gap Novel*
Trigiani, Adriana. *Big Stone Gap: A Novel*
Tyler, Anne. *The Amateur Marriage: A Novel*
Tyler, Anne. ★*Clock Dance: A Novel*
Tyler, Anne. *A Patchwork Planet*
Tyler, Anne. ★*Saint Maybe*
Tyler, Anne. *Vinegar Girl: The Taming of the Shrew Retold*
Wodehouse, P. G. ★*The Inimitable Jeeves*
Wodehouse, P. G. *My Man Jeeves*
★*A Gentleman in Moscow*. Towles, Amor
GENTLY, DIRK (FICTITIOUS CHARACTER)
Adams, Douglas. *Dirk Gently's Holistic Detective Agency*
GENTRIFICATION OF CITIES
Jemisin, N. K. ★*The City We Became*
Kohnstamm, Thomas B. *Lake City*
Woodson, Jacqueline. ★*Red at the Bone*
GENTRY
Trollope, Anthony. *Doctor Thorne*
Gentry, Amy
Last Woman Standing
GEOLOGICAL RESEARCH
McGregor, Jon. *Lean Fall Stand*
GEOLOGISTS
Okuizumi, Hikaru. *The Stones Cry Out*
★*The Geometry of Holding Hands*. McCall Smith, Alexander
Georgana's Secret. Hawks, Arlem
George Smiley novels [Series]. Le Carre, John
George Sueno and Ernie Bascom mysteries [Series]. Limon, Martin
George, Alex
The Paris Hours: A Novel
George, Elizabeth
A Banquet of Consequences
Believing the Lie
Careless in Red
Just One Evil Act
The Punishment She Deserves
This Body of Death: An Inspector Lynley Novel
What Came Before He Shot Her
George, Margaret
The Confessions of Young Nero
Elizabeth I: A Novel
Helen of Troy
The Splendor Before the Dark: A Novel of the Emperor Nero

George, Nina
The Book of Dreams
The Little Paris Bookshop
Georges Dupin novels [Series]. Bannalec, Jean-Luc
GEORGIA
Baldacci, David. *A Minute to Midnight*
Bambara, Toni Cade. ★*The Salt Eaters*
Brown, Sandra. *Tailspin*
Burns, Olive Ann. ★*Cold Sassy Tree*
Caldwell, Erskine. *Tobacco Road*
Child, Lee. ★*Killing Floor*
Clark, P. Djeli. *Ring Shout*
Conner, M. Shelly. *Everyman*
Crews, Harry. *A Feast of Snakes: A Novel*
Daugherty, Christi. *Revolver Road: A Harper McClain Mystery*
Dexter, Pete. *Paris Trout*
Doctorow, E. L. *The March: A Novel*
Everett, Percival L. *I Am Not Sidney Poitier*
Gardner, Lisa. ★*When You See Me: A Novel*
Harris, E. Lynn. *I Say a Little Prayer: A Novel*
Harris, Nathan. *The Sweetness of Water*
Hauck, Rachel. *Once Upon a Prince*
Jackson-Brown, Angela. ★*When Stars Rain Down: A Novel*
McCullers, Carson. *The Member of the Wedding*
McKevett, G. A. *Murder at Mabel's Motel*
McKevett, G. A. *Murder in the Corn Maze*
Mitchell, Margaret. ★*Gone with the Wind*
Morrison, Toni. *Home*
Panowich, Brian. *Bull Mountain*
Panowich, Brian. *Hard Cash Valley*
Rabb, Jonathan. *Among the Living*
Roy, Lori. ★*Gone Too Long: A Novel*
Sathian, Sanjena. *Gold Diggers*
Slaughter, Karin. *Cop Town: A Novel*
Slaughter, Karin. *Criminal: A Novel*
Slaughter, Karin. ★*Fallen: A Novel*
Slaughter, Karin. *The Good Daughter*
Slaughter, Karin. ★*Pieces of Her*
Sterling, Erin. *The Ex Hex*
Walker, Alice. *The Third Life of Grange Copeland*
Woods, Stuart. *Chiefs*
Georgia series (Karin Slaughter) [Series]. Slaughter, Karin
GEORGIAN ERA (1714-1837)
Beverley, Jo. *My Lady Notorious*
Beverley, Jo. *Tempting Fortune*
Bronte, Anne. *The Tenant of Wildfell Hall*
Chase, Loretta Lynda. *A Duke in Shining Armor*
Clarke, Susanna. ★*Jonathan Strange & Mr. Norrell*
Dickens, Charles. ★*A Tale of Two Cities*
Dongala, Emmanuel Boundzeki. *The Bridgetower Sonata: Sonata Mulattica*
Donoghue, Emma. *Slammerkin*
Freeman, Anna. *The Fair Fight: A Novel*
Friedman, Daniel. *Riot Most Uncouth: A Lord Byron Mystery*
Gelernter, J. H. *Hold Fast*
Gowar, Imogen Hermes. *The Mermaid and Mrs. Hancock*
Halls, Stacey. *The Lost Orphan*
Heyer, Georgette. *These Old Shades*

Hoyt, Elizabeth. *Not the Duke's Darling*
Hoyt, Elizabeth. *When a Rogue Meets His Match*
James, Eloisa. ★*Seven Minutes in Heaven*
James, Eloisa. *Three Weeks with Lady X*
James, Eloisa. *Wilde in Love*
MacLean, Sarah. ★*Brazen and the Beast*
Putney, Mary Jo. *Once a Scoundrel*
Putney, Mary Jo. *Once a Soldier*
Robertson, Imogen. *Anatomy of Murder*
Robertson, Imogen. *Circle of Shadows*
Robertson, Imogen. *Instruments of Darkness: A Novel*
Robertson, Imogen. *Island of Bones*
GEORGIAN ROMANCES
Beverley, Jo. *My Lady Notorious*
Beverley, Jo. *Tempting Fortune*
Chase, Loretta Lynda. *A Duke in Shining Armor*
Heyer, Georgette. *These Old Shades*
Hoyt, Elizabeth. *Not the Duke's Darling*
Hoyt, Elizabeth. *When a Rogue Meets His Match*
James, Eloisa. ★*Seven Minutes in Heaven*
James, Eloisa. *Three Weeks with Lady X*
James, Eloisa. *Wilde in Love*
MacLean, Sarah. ★*Brazen and the Beast*
Putney, Mary Jo. *Once a Soldier*
Gerhard Self mysteries [Series]. Schlink, Bernhard
GERMAN AMERICANS
Deaver, Jeffery. *Garden of Beasts: A Novel of Berlin 1936*
GERMAN REUNIFICATION
Grass, Gunter. *Too Far Afield*
Germania: a Novel of Nazi Berlin. Gilbers, Harald
GERMANS IN GREAT BRITAIN
Follett, Ken. *Eye of the Needle*
Weir, Alison. *Anna of Kleve: The Princess in the Portrait*
GERMANS IN NEW YORK STATE
Steinke, Rene. *Holy Skirts*
GERMANS IN SPAIN
Bolano, Roberto. ★*The Third Reich*
GERMANS IN THE UNITED STATES
Stewart, Amy. *Lady Cop Makes Trouble*
GERMANTOWN (PHILADELPHIA, PA.)
Tyree, Omar. ★*Flyy Girl*
GERMANY
Amis, Martin. ★*The Zone of Interest: A Novel*
Belfer, Lauren. *And After the Fire: A Novel*
Bernhard, Thomas. *Wittgenstein's Nephew: A Friendship*
Binder, L. Annette. *The Vanishing Sky*
Bohjalian, Chris. *Skeletons at the Feast: A Novel*
Boll, Heinrich. *Billiards at Half-Past Nine*
Boll, Heinrich. *The Clown*
Boschwitz, Ulrich Alexander. *The Passenger: A Novel*
Chiaverini, Jennifer. *Resistance Women: A Novel*
Deaver, Jeffery. *Garden of Beasts: A Novel of Berlin 1936*
Diehl, Heidi. *Lifelines*
Diop, David. ★*At Night All Blood Is Black*
Doerr, Anthony. ★*All the Light We Cannot See: A Novel*
Downing, David. *Diary of a Dead Man on Leave*
Eliasberg, Jan. ★*Hannah's War*
Epstein, Jennifer Cody. ★*Wunderland: A Novel*

Fallada, Hans. *Every Man Dies Alone*
Flynn, Michael. *Eifelheim*
Ford, Ford Madox. ★*The Good Soldier: A Tale of Passion*
Franck, Julia. *Blindness of the Heart*
Fuller, Claire. *Our Endless Numbered Days: A Novel*
Galchen, Rivka. *Everyone Knows Your Mother Is a Witch*
Gillham, David R. *City of Women*
Grant, Helen. *The Glass Demon*
Grant, Helen. *The Vanishing of Katharina Linden*
Grossman, Paul. *Children of Wrath*
Harris, Robert. ★*Fatherland*
Hausmann, Romy. ★*Dear Child*
Hegi, Ursula. *Children and Fire: A Novel*
Hesse, Hermann. *Narcissus and Goldmund*
Hesse, Hermann. ★*Steppenwolf*
Kelly, Martha Hall. *Lilac Girls*
Keneally, Thomas. ★*Schindler's List*
Kerr, Philip. ★*Greeks Bearing Gifts: A Bernie Gunther Novel*
Kerr, Philip. ★*Metropolis: A Bernie Gunther Novel*
Kunzru, Hari. *Red Pill: A Novel*
Le Carre, John. *A Most Wanted Man: A Novel*
Mann, Thomas. *Buddenbrooks*
Moore, Alison. *The Lighthouse*
Potzsch, Oliver. *The Beggar King*
Potzsch, Oliver. *The Dark Monk: A Hangman's Daughter Tale*
Potzsch, Oliver. *The Hangman's Daughter: A Historical Novel*
Potzsch, Oliver. *The Play of Death*
Potzsch, Oliver. *The Poisoned Pilgrim: A Hangman's Daughter Tale*
Potzsch, Oliver. *The Werewolf of Bamberg*
Pynchon, Thomas. ★*Gravity's Rainbow*
Rabe, Peter. ★*Anatomy of a Killer ;: A Shroud for Jesso*
Remarque, Erich Maria. ★*All Quiet on the Western Front*
Remarque, Erich Maria. *The Road Back*
Schlink, Bernhard. *Self's Deception*
Schlink, Bernhard. *Self's Murder*
Schlink, Bernhard. *Self's Punishment*
Sebald, Winfried Georg. *The Emigrants*
Sharratt, Mary. *Illuminations: A Novel of Hildegard Von Bingen*
Sundin, Sarah. *When Twilight Breaks*
Toibin, Colm. ★*The Magician: A Novel*
Vonnegut, Kurt. ★*Slaughterhouse-Five: Or, the Children's Crusade : A Duty-Dance with Death*
Wells, Benedict. *The End of Loneliness: A Novel*
★*Germinal*. Zola, Emile
Gerritsen, Tess
The Apprentice: A Novel
The Bone Garden
Choose Me
I Know a Secret
Playing with Fire
★*The Shape of Night: A Novel*
The Surgeon
Gertrude and *Claudius*. Updike, John
Gessen, Keith
A Terrible Country
Get a Life. Gordimer, Nadine
★*Get a Life, Chloe Brown*. Hibbert, Talia
Get Real. Westlake, Donald E.

★*Get Shorty*. Leonard, Elmore
GET-RICH-QUICK VENTURES
    Palahniuk, Chuck. *Choke: A Novel*
Getaway. Stage, Zoje
GETTYSBURG, BATTLE OF, 1863
    Shaara, Michael. ★*The Killer Angels: A Novel*
Ghachar Ghochar. Shanbhag, Vivek
Ghaffari, Rabeah
    ★*To Keep the Sun Alive*
GHANA
    Adjapon, Bisi. *The Teller of Secrets: A Novel*
    Gyasi, Yaa. ★*Homegoing: A Novel*
    Gyasi, Yaa. ★*Transcendent Kingdom*
    Medie, Peace A. *His Only Wife: A Novel*
    Okorafor, Nnedi. ★*Remote Control*
    Quartey, Kwei. *Children of the Street: A Novel*
    Quartey, Kwei. *Gold of Our Fathers*
    Quartey, Kwei. *The Missing American*
    Quartey, Kwei. *Murder at Cape Three Points*
    Quartey, Kwei. ★*Sleep Well, My Lady*
    Quartey, Kwei. *Wife of the Gods: A Novel*
GHETTOES, AFRICAN AMERICAN
    K'wan. *Street Dreams*
    Petry, Ann. ★*The Street*
    Wright, Richard. ★*Native Son*
GHETTOES, JEWISH
    Keneally, Thomas. ★*Schindler's List*
    Schwarz-Bart, Andre. *The Last of the Just: A Novel*
    Shepard, Jim. ★*The Book of Aron*
Ghosh, Amitav
    Flood of Fire
    The Glass Palace
    ★*Gun Island*
    The Hungry Tide
    River of Smoke
    Sea of Poppies
Ghost Blows a Kiss. Hart, Carolyn G.
The Ghost Bride: A Novel. Choo, Yangsze
★*The Ghost Road*. Barker, Pat
The Ghost Runner. Bilal, Parker
Ghost Ship. Cussler, Clive
GHOST STORIES
    Bohjalian, Chris. *The Night Strangers: A Novel*
    Erdrich, Louise. ★*The Sentence*
    Hill, Joe. *Heart-Shaped Box*
    James, Henry. ★*The Turn of the Screw*
    Jónasson, Ragnar. ★*The Girl Who Died*
    McMahon, Jennifer. *The Invited: A Novel*
    Murdoch, Iris. *The Sea, the Sea*
    Pyper, Andrew. *The Residence: A Novel*
    St. James, Simone. *The Broken Girls*
    St. James, Simone. *The Haunting of Maddy Clare*
    Straub, Peter. ★*Ghost Story*
    Tan, Amy. *The Hundred Secret Senses*
★*Ghost Story*. Straub, Peter
Ghost Summer: Stories. Due, Tananarive
Ghost Wall: A Novel. Moss, Sarah
The Ghost Writer. Roth, Philip

The Ghost: a Novel. Harris, Robert
GHOSTS
    Aaronovitch, Ben. *Midnight Riot*
    Barzak, Christopher. *One for Sorrow*
    Beagle, Peter S. *A Fine and Private Place*
    Bennett, Jenn. *Bitter Spirits*
    Bohjalian, Chris. *The Night Strangers: A Novel*
    Brown, Karen. *The Clairvoyants: A Novel*
    Camp, Bryan. *Gather the Fortunes*
    Choo, Yangsze. *The Ghost Bride: A Novel*
    Cotterill, Colin. *The Coroner's Lunch*
    Dickens, Charles. ★*A Christmas Carol*
    Fine, Julia. *The Upstairs House*
    Freudenberger, Nell. ★*Lost and Wanted: A Novel*
    Gaiman, Neil. *Trigger Warning: Short Fictions and Disturbances*
    Garcia Marquez, Gabriel. ★*One Hundred Years of Solitude*
    Gerritsen, Tess. ★*The Shape of Night: A Novel*
    Godwin, Gail. *Grief Cottage: A Novel*
    Hart, Carolyn G. *Ghost Blows a Kiss*
    Hill, Joe. *Heart-Shaped Box*
    Huchu, Tendai. *The Library of the Dead*
    Irwin, Stephen M. *The Broken Ones: A Novel*
    Jackson, Shirley. ★*The Haunting of Hill House*
    James, Henry. ★*The Turn of the Screw*
    Jónasson, Ragnar. ★*The Girl Who Died*
    Khaw, Cassandra. *Nothing but Blackened Teeth*
    Lippman, Laura. *Lady in the Lake: A Novel*
    McCormack, Mike. ★*Solar Bones*
    McMahon, Jennifer. *The Invited: A Novel*
    Pulley, Natasha. *The Lost Future of Pepperharrow*
    Pyper, Andrew. *The Damned: A Novel*
    Pyper, Andrew. *The Residence: A Novel*
    Rhodes, Jewell Parker. *Yellow Moon: A Novel*
    St. James, Simone. *The Broken Girls*
    St. James, Simone. *The Haunting of Maddy Clare*
    Straub, Peter. ★*Ghost Story*
    Sylvester, Natalia. *Everyone Knows You Go Home*
    Vollmann, William T. *Last Stories and Other Stories*
    Vonnegut, Kurt. ★*Galapagos: A Novel*
    Yu, Miri. *Tokyo Ueno Station*
Ghosts and Lightning. Byrne, Trevor
★*Ghosts: a Novel*. Alderton, Dolly
GHOSTWRITERS
    Amdahl, Gary. *I Am Death: Two Novellas*
    Eco, Umberto. *Numero Zero*
    Harris, Robert. *The Ghost: A Novel*
GIANTS
    Swift, Jonathan. ★*Gulliver's Travels*
★*Giants in the Earth: A Saga of the Prairie*. Rølvaag, O. E.
Gibb, Camilla
    Sweetness in the Belly
Gibbon, Maureen
    The Lost Notebook of Edouard Manet: A Novel
Gibbons, Kaye
    Charms for the Easy Life
    ★*Ellen Foster: A Novel*
    The Life All Around Me by Ellen Foster

Gibson, Claire
  Beyond the Point: A Novel
Gibson, William
  ★*Agency*
  ★*Neuromancer*
  Pattern Recognition
  The Peripheral
Gide, Andre
  ★*The Immoralist*
Gideon, Melanie
  Wife 22
★*The **Gift** of Asher Lev.* Potok, Chaim
*A **Gift** of Sanctuary: An Owen Archer Mystery.* Robb, Candace M.
GIFTED CHILDREN
  Card, Orson Scott. ★*Ender's Game*
GIFTED GIRLS
  Gardam, Jane. *God on the Rocks*
*The **Gifted** School: A Novel.* Holsinger, Bruce W.
GIFTED TEENAGERS
  Gibbons, Kaye. *The Life All Around Me by Ellen Foster*
  Macmillan, Gilly. *The Perfect Girl*
GIFTS
  Solomon, Rachel Lynn. *Weather Girl*
Gilb, Dagoberto
  The Flowers: A Novel
Gilbers, Harald
  Germania: A Novel of Nazi Berlin
Gilbert, David
  & Sons: A Novel
Gilbert, Elizabeth
  ★*City of Girls*
  ★*The Signature of All Things: A Novel*
Gilchrist, Ellen
  ★*Collected Stories*
GILDED AGE (1865-1898)
  Alexander, Tamera. ★*A Note yet Unsung*
  Beams, Clare. *The Illness Lesson*
  Belli, Kate. *Deception by Gaslight: A Gilded Gotham Mystery*
  Brown, Amy Belding. *Emily's House*
  Carr, Caleb. ★*The Alienist*
  Carr, Caleb. *The Angel of Darkness*
  Cleeton, Chanel. *The Most Beautiful Girl in Cuba*
  Crane, Stephen. *Maggie: A Girl of the Streets*
  Donati, Sara. *Where the Light Enters*
  Donoghue, Emma. ★*Frog Music*
  Fowler, Therese. *A Well-Behaved Woman: A Novel of the Vanderbilts*
  Goodwin, Daisy. *The American Heiress*
  Guinn, Matthew. *The Scribe: A Novel*
  Gunning, Sally. *Painting the Light*
  Helprin, Mark. ★*Winter's Tale*
  Millhauser, Steven. *Martin Dressler: The Tale of an American Dreamer*
  Piercy, Marge. *Sex Wars*
  Rosen, Renee. *The Social Graces*
  Shupe, Joanna. *The Prince of Broadway*
  Shupe, Joanna. *The Rogue of Fifth Avenue*
  Simmons, Dan. *The Fifth Heart*
  Simpson, Rosemary. *Let the Dead Keep Their Secrets*

  Simpson, Rosemary. ★*What the Dead Leave Behind*
  Smith, Dominic. *Bright and Distant Shores*
  Thompson, Victoria. *Murder on Wall Street*
  Wallace, Carol. *Our Kind of People*
  Wecker, Helene. *The Golem and the Jinni*
Gilded Age heiresses [Series]. St. George, Harper
Gilded Age mysteries (Rosemary Simpson) [Series]. Simpson, Rosemary
Gilded Gotham mysteries [Series]. Belli, Kate
Gilded hour novels [Series]. Donati, Sara
*The **Gilded** Life of Matilda Duplaine.* Brunkhorst, Alex
Gilded novels [Series]. Force, Marie
★*Gilead*. Robinson, Marilynne
Gilead novels [Series]. Robinson, Marilynne
★*Giles* Goat-Boy; Or, the Revised New Syllabus.* Barth, John
Gillham, David R.
  City of Women
Gilligan, Ruth
  The Butchers' Blessing
Gilman, Carolyn Ives
  Dark Orbit
Gilman, Charlotte Perkins
  Herland
  ★*The Yellow Wallpaper and Selected Writings*
GILMAN, CHARLOTTE PERKINS
  Gilman, Charlotte Perkins. ★*The Yellow Wallpaper and Selected Writings*
Gilman, Felix
  The Half-Made World
Gilman, Laura Anne
  The Cold Eye
  Flesh and Fire
  Hard Magic
  Silver on the Road
Gilman, Susan Jane
  Donna Has Left the Building
  The Ice Cream Queen of Orchard Street: A Novel
GILMORE, GARY MARK
  Mailer, Norman. ★*The Executioner's Song*
GINGERBREAD
  Oyeyemi, Helen. *Gingerbread: A Novel*
Gingerbread: a Novel. Oyeyemi, Helen
Ginny Moon. Ludwig, Benjamin
Ginzburg, Natalia
  A Family Lexicon
  Voices in the Evening
GINZBURG, NATALIA
  Block, Stefan Merrill. *Oliver Loving: A Novel*
  Ginzburg, Natalia. *A Family Lexicon*
Giordano Bruno novels [Series]. Parris, S. J.
Giordano, Mario
  ★*Auntie Poldi and the Lost Madonna*
  Auntie Poldi and the Vineyards of Etna
Giordano, Paolo
  Heaven and Earth
  The Human Body
  Like Family
  ★*The Solitude of Prime Numbers: A Novel*
★*Giovanni's Room.* Baldwin, James

★*Girl*. O'Brien, Edna
Girl at War. Novic, Sara
The Girl Before: A Novel. Delaney, J. P.
The Girl Behind the Red Rope. Dekker, Ted
GIRL BOARDING SCHOOL STUDENTS
  French, Tana. ★*The Secret Place*
  Layden, Emily. *All Girls*
GIRL DETECTIVES
  Bradley, C. Alan. *As Chimney Sweepers Come to Dust: A Flavia De Luce Novel*
  Bradley, C. Alan. *The Golden Tresses of the Dead: A Flavia De Luce Novel*
  Bradley, C. Alan. *The Grave's a Fine and Private Place: A Flavia De Luce Novel*
  Bradley, C. Alan. *I Am Half-Sick of Shadows: A Flavia De Luce Novel*
  Bradley, C. Alan. *A Red Herring Without Mustard*
  Bradley, C. Alan. *Speaking from Among the Bones: A Flavia De Luce Novel*
  Bradley, C. Alan. ★*The Sweetness at the Bottom of the Pie*
  Bradley, C. Alan. *Thrice the Brinded Cat Hath Mew'd: A Flavia De Luce Novel*
  Bradley, C. Alan. *The Weed That Strings the Hangman's Bag: A Flavia De Luce Mystery*
★*Girl Gone Viral*. Rai, Alisha
GIRL HEROES
  Stephenson, Neal. *The Diamond Age,: Or, a Young Lady's Illustrated Primer*
GIRL HIKERS
  King, Stephen. *The Girl Who Loved Tom Gordon*
GIRL IMMIGRANTS
  Bulawayo, NoViolet. *We Need New Names: A Novel*
★*The Girl in Green*. Miller, Derek B.
The Girl in His Shadow: A Novel. Blake, Audrey
Girl in Hyacinth Blue. Vreeland, Susan
The Girl in the Garden. Wallace, Melanie
The Girl in the Glass Box. Grippando, James
Girl in the Rearview Mirror. Dimberg, Kelsey Rae
The Girl in the Red Coat. Hamer, Kate
★*The Girl in the Tower*. Arden, Katherine
Girl in the Walls: A Novel. Gnuse, A. J.
★*A Girl Is a Body of Water*. Makumbi, Jennifer Nansubuga
GIRL KIDNAPPING VICTIMS
  Gardner, Lisa. *Alone*
  Greenwood, T. *Rust & Stardust*
  Kennedy, Randy. *Presidio*
  Lippman, Laura. *What the Dead Know*
  O'Brien, Edna. ★*Girl*
  Phillips, Julia. ★*Disappearing Earth*
  Picoult, Jodi. *Vanishing Acts: A Novel*
  Ragan, Theresa. *Deadly Recall*
A Girl Like Her. Hibbert, Talia
Girl meets duke [Series]. Dare, Tessa
GIRL MURDER VICTIMS
  Chizmar, Richard T. *Chasing the Boogeyman*
  Connolly, John. *The Dirty South*
  Flynn, Gillian. ★*Sharp Objects: A Novel*
  French, Tana. *In the Woods*

Mizushima, Margaret. *Killing Trail*
Persson, Leif G. W. *The Dying Detective: A Mystery*
Sandford, John. *Deep Freeze*
A Girl Named Anna. Barber, Lizzy
The Girl on the Cliff: A Novel. Riley, Lucinda
★*The Girl on the Train: A Novel*. Hawkins, Paula
GIRL ORPHANS
  Atkinson, Kate. *Started Early, Took My Dog*
GIRL PRODIGIES
  Moore, Liz. *The Unseen World*
  Rosner, Jennifer. ★*The Yellow Bird Sings*
GIRL REBELS
  Kincaid, Jamaica. ★*Annie John*
GIRL SCIENTISTS
  Bradley, C. Alan. *As Chimney Sweepers Come to Dust: A Flavia De Luce Novel*
  Bradley, C. Alan. *The Golden Tresses of the Dead: A Flavia De Luce Novel*
  Bradley, C. Alan. *The Grave's a Fine and Private Place: A Flavia De Luce Novel*
  Bradley, C. Alan. *A Red Herring Without Mustard*
  Bradley, C. Alan. *Speaking from Among the Bones: A Flavia De Luce Novel*
  Bradley, C. Alan. ★*The Sweetness at the Bottom of the Pie*
  Bradley, C. Alan. *Thrice the Brinded Cat Hath Mew'd: A Flavia De Luce Novel*
The Girl They Left Behind. Veletzos, Roxanne
★*Girl Waits with Gun*. Stewart, Amy
The Girl Who Chased the Moon: A Novel. Allen, Sarah Addison
★*The Girl Who Died*. Jónasson, Ragnar
The Girl Who Fell from the Sky: A Novel. Durrow, Heidi W.
★*The Girl Who Kicked the Hornet's Nest*. Larsson, Stieg
The Girl Who Knew Too Much. Quick, Amanda
The Girl Who Lived Twice: A Lisbeth Salander Novel. Lagercrantz, David
The Girl Who Loved Tom Gordon. King, Stephen
The Girl Who Played Go. Shan, Sa
The Girl Who Played with Fire. Larsson, Stieg
The Girl Who Takes an Eye for an Eye. Lagercrantz, David
★*Girl with a Pearl Earring*. Chevalier, Tracy
The Girl with the Dragon Tattoo. Larsson, Stieg
The Girl with the Louding Voice. Dare, Abi
The Girl You Left Behind. Moyes, Jojo
A Girl's Guide to the Outback: A Novel. Kate, Jessica
★*Girl, Woman, Other*. Evaristo, Bernardine
GIRLFRIENDS
  Bell, Darcey. *Something She's Not Telling Us*
  Tyler, Anne. ★*Redhead by the Side of the Road*
GIRLS
  Al Rawi, Shahad. *The Baghdad Clock*
  Balaskovits, A. A. *Magic for Unlucky Girls: Stories*
  Bates, Judy Fong. ★*Midnight at the Dragon Cafe*
  Byatt, A. S. ★*Ragnarok: The End of the Gods*
  Choi, Ann Y. K. *Kay's Lucky Coin Variety*
  Dalton, Trent. *All Our Shimmering Skies*
  Godwin, Gail. *Flora: A Novel*
  Hazzard, Shirley. ★*The Great Fire*
  Lee, Patrick. *Runner*

Lyons, Annie. *The Brilliant Life of Eudora Honeysett*
Murakami, Haruki. *Killing Commendatore: A Novel*
Proust, Marcel. *Within a Budding Grove*
Quindlen, Anna. *Miller's Valley*
Smith, Betty. ★*A Tree Grows in Brooklyn*
Welty, Eudora. ★*Delta Wedding*

GIRLS — CAREER ASPIRATIONS
Dean, Margaret Lazarus. *The Time It Takes to Fall*

GIRLS — FRIENDSHIP
Monroe, Mary. ★*God Don't Like Ugly*
Wells, Rebecca. *Divine Secrets of the Ya-Ya Sisterhood: A Novel*

GIRLS AND CATS
Danielewski, Mark Z. ★*The Familiar; Volume 4*

GIRLS AND HORSES
Gaitskill, Mary. *The Mare: A Novel*
★*Girls Burn Brighter*. Rao, Shobha
★*The Girls of Slender Means*. Spark, Muriel
Girls trip [Series]. Livesay, Tracey

GIRLS WITH AMNESIA
Maguire, Gregory. *The Brides of Maracoor*

GIRLS WITH AUTISM
Ludwig, Benjamin. *Ginny Moon*
★*Girls with Bright Futures: A Novel*. Dobmeier, Tracy
The Girls with No Names. Burdick, Serena

GIRLS' BOARDING SCHOOLS
Danforth, Emily M. *Plain Bad Heroines*
Ellison, J. T. *Good Girls Lie*

GIRLS' SCHOOLS
Beams, Clare. *The Illness Lesson*
Godwin, Gail. *Unfinished Desires*
The Girls: a Novel. Cline, Emma

Giuseppe Lojacono mysteries [Series]. De Giovanni, Maurizio
★*Give Me Your Hand*. Abbott, Megan E.
★*The Given Day*. Lehane, Dennis
★*The Giver of Stars: A Novel*. Moyes, Jojo

GLACIERS
Indriðason, Arnaldur. *The Darkness Knows*
Stabenow, Dana. ★*A Grave Denied*

GLADIATORS
Kane, Ben. *Spartacus: The Gladiator*

Gladstone, Max
★*Empress of Forever*

GLASGOW, SCOTLAND
Cronin, Marianne. *The One Hundred Years of Lenni and Margot*
Kelman, James. *How Late It Was, How Late*
McIlvanney, William. *The Dark Remains: Laidlaw's First Case*
Mina, Denise. *The Less Dead*
O'Donnell, Lisa. *The Death of Bees: A Novel*
Stuart, Douglas. ★*Shuggie Bain*

Glass Boys: A Novel. Lundrigan, Nicole
The Glass Demon. Grant, Helen

GLASS FAMILY (FICTITIOUS CHARACTERS)
Salinger, J. D. *Raise High the Roof Beam, Carpenters,: And Seymour—An Introduction.*
★*The Glass Hotel: A Novel*. Mandel, Emily St. John
The Glass Key. Hammett, Dashiell
The Glass Kingdom: A Novel. Osborne, Lawrence
The Glass Palace. Ghosh, Amitav

Glass, Jenna
The Women's War

Glass, Julia
★*Three Junes*
The Whole World Over
The Widower's Tale

Glass, Seraphina Nova
Someone's Listening

Glass, Seressia
★*The Love Con*

Glasshouse. Stross, Charles

Gleason, Colleen
Murder at the Capitol

GLEN CANYON
Barr, Nevada. *The Rope: An Anna Pigeon Novel*

Glitz. Leonard, Elmore

GLITZ AND GLAMOUR NOVELS
Bagshawe, Tilly. *Adored*
Burton, Tara Isabella. *Social Creature*

GLOBAL ENVIRONMENTAL CHANGE
Egan, Greg. *Perihelion Summer*

GLOBAL WARMING
Kingsolver, Barbara. ★*Flight Behavior*
Nagamatsu, Sequoia. *How High We Go in the Dark*
Reynolds, Alastair. *Permafrost*

Glorious victorious Darcys [Series]. Ciotta, Beth

Glover, Nicole
★*The Conductors*
The Undertakers

Glynn, Alan
Receptor

Gnomon: a Novel. Harkaway, Nick

Gnuse, A. J.
Girl in the Walls: A Novel

GO (GAME)
Shan, Sa. *The Girl Who Played Go*
★*Go Down, Moses*. Faulkner, William
★*Go Set a Watchman*. Lee, Harper
★*Go Tell It on the Mountain*. Baldwin, James
Go, Went, Gone: A Novel. Erpenbeck, Jenny

GOALS AND OBJECTIVES
Aliu, Xhenet. ★*Brass: A Novel*

GOATS
Barth, John. ★*Giles Goat-Boy ;: Or, the Revised New Syllabus*
★*The Goblin Emperor*. Addison, Katherine

Goblin emperor novels [Series]. Addison, Katherine
Goblin: a Novel in Six Novellas. Malerman, Josh

GOBLINS
Addison, Katherine. ★*The Goblin Emperor*
Donohue, Keith. *The Stolen Child*
French, Jonathan. ★*The Grey Bastards*

GOD
Butler, Robert Olen. *Late City*
Saramago, Jose. *Cain*
Updike, John. *In the Beauty of the Lilies*
Williams, Joy. *Ninety-Nine Stories of God*

GOD (CHRISTIANITY)
Walton, Jo. ★*Lent*

GOD (CHRISTIANITY) — WILL
Hauck, Rachel. *Once Upon a Prince*
GOD (JUDAISM)
Wiesel, Elie. ★*Night, Dawn, the Accident: Three Tales*
★*God Don't Like Ugly*. Monroe, Mary
God don't novels [Series]. Monroe, Mary
★*God Help the Child*. Morrison, Toni
★*A God in Ruins*. Atkinson, Kate
★*The God of Small Things*. Roy, Arundhati
God on the Rocks. Gardam, Jane
God Still Don't Like Ugly. Monroe, Mary
God's Country. Everett, Percival L.
The **God's** Eye View. Eisler, Barry
Goddard, Robert
  Beyond Recall: A Novel
  ★*Into the Blue*
  ★*Long Time Coming: A Novel*
  Never Go Back
Godden, Rumer
  The Greengage Summer: A Novel
Goddess of Filth. Castro, V.
★*The Godfather*. Puzo, Mario
Godfather series (Mario Puzo) [Series]. Puzo, Mario
GODFATHERS
  Penny, Louise. ★*All the Devils Are Here*
GODMOTHERS
  Hostin, Sunny. ★*Summer on the Bluffs*
Gods and Generals: A Novel of the Civil War. Shaara, Jeff
GODS AND GODDESSES
  Babalola, Bolu. *Love in Color: Mythical Tales from Around the World, Retold*
  Banville, John. *The Infinities*
  Camp, Bryan. *The City of Lost Fortunes*
  Camp, Bryan. *Gather the Fortunes*
  Carey, Jacqueline. *Starless*
  Gaiman, Neil. ★*American Gods: A Novel*
  Hawkins, Scott. ★*The Library at Mount Char*
  Johnson, Kij. ★*The Dream-Quest of Vellitt Boe*
  Kim, Bo Young. ★*I'm Waiting for You: And Other Stories*
  Kuang, R. F. ★*The Dragon Republic*
  Kuang, R. F. *The Poppy War*
  Larkwood, A. K. *The Unspoken Name*
  Leckie, Ann. ★*The Raven Tower*
  Liu, Ken. ★*The Grace of Kings*
  Polansky, Daniel. *The Seventh Perfection*
  Pratchett, Terry. *Small Gods: A Novel of Discworld*
  Robbins, Tom. ★*Jitterbug Perfume*
  Showalter, Gena. *Shadow and Ice*
  Suri, Tasha. ★*Empire of Sand*
  Tan, Sue Lynn. ★*Daughter of the Moon Goddess*
  Tolkien, J. R. R. *The Fall of Gondolin*
GODS AND GODDESSES, AFRICAN
  Gaiman, Neil. ★*Anansi Boys: A Novel*
GODS AND GODDESSES, AZTEC
  Castro, V. *Goddess of Filth*
GODS AND GODDESSES, CHINESE
  Tan, Sue Lynn. ★*Daughter of the Moon Goddess*

GODS AND GODDESSES, GREEK
  Alexis, Andre. *Fifteen Dogs*
  Barth, John. *Chimera*
  Haynes, Natalie. *A Thousand Ships*
  McCall Smith, Alexander. *Tiny Tales: Stories of Romance, Ambition, Kindness, and Happiness*
  Miller, Madeline. ★*Circe*
  Walton, Jo. ★*Necessity*
GODS AND GODDESSES, MAYAN
  Moreno-Garcia, Silvia. ★*Gods of Jade and Shadow: A Novel*
GODS AND GODDESSES, NORSE
  Byatt, A. S. ★*Ragnarok: The End of the Gods*
  Gaiman, Neil. ★*Norse Mythology*
  McCall Smith, Alexander. *Tiny Tales: Stories of Romance, Ambition, Kindness, and Happiness*
The **Gods** of Gotham. Faye, Lyndsay
Gods of Gotham [Series]. Faye, Lyndsay
The **Gods** of Guilt. Connelly, Michael
★*Gods of Howl Mountain: A Novel*. Brown, Taylor
★*Gods of Jade and Shadow: A Novel*. Moreno-Garcia, Silvia
The **Gods** of Tango. De Robertis, Carolina
Gods of war [Series]. Showalter, Gena
Godshot: a Novel. Bieker, Chelsea Jean
Godspeed. Butler, Nickolas
Godwin, Gail
  Flora: A Novel
  Grief Cottage: A Novel
  Old Lovegood Girls
  Unfinished Desires
Goenawan, Clarissa
  The Perfect World of Miwako Sumida
  Rainbirds
GOGH, VINCENT VAN
  Racculia, Kate. ★*Bellweather Rhapsody*
  Stone, Irving. *Lust for Life: A Novel of Vincent Van Gogh*
Gogol, Nikolai Vasilievich
  The Collected Tales of Nikolai Gogol
  ★*Dead Souls*
Gohlke, Cathy
  Promise Me This
Going After Cacciato: A Novel. O'Brien, Tim
Going for a Beer: Selected Short Fictions. Coover, Robert
Going Postal: A Novel of Discworld. Pratchett, Terry
★*Going to Meet the Man*. Baldwin, James
Gold. Cleave, Chris
GOLD
  Crichton, Michael. *Pirate Latitudes*
Gold Diggers. Sathian, Sanjena
★*Gold Fame Citrus*. Watkins, Claire Vaye
GOLD MINERS
  Catton, Eleanor. *The Luminaries: A Novel*
GOLD MINES AND MINING
  Allende, Isabel. *Daughter of Fortune: A Novel*
  Francis, Dick. *Smokescreen*
  Quartey, Kwei. *Gold of Our Fathers*
  Stabenow, Dana. *A Night Too Dark: A Kate Shugak Novel*
  Traven, B. ★*The Treasure of the Sierra Madre*
Gold of Our Fathers. Quartey, Kwei

GOLD PROSPECTING
L'Amour, Louis. *The Californios*

GOLD RUSH
Allende, Isabel. *Daughter of Fortune: A Novel*
deWitt, Patrick. *The Sisters Brothers: A Novel*
Harte, Bret. ★*The Best Short Stories of Bret Harte*
London, Jack. ★*White Fang*
Sayles, John. *A Moment in the Sun*

GOLD THEFTS
Fleming, Ian. ★*Goldfinger*

Goldberg, Lee
Bone Canyon
Fake Truth

Goldberg, Myla
Feast Your Eyes

Goldberg, Tod
Gangsterland: A Novel

Goldbloom, Goldie
On Division

The *Golden Age*. London, Joan
Golden Age. Smiley, Jane
The *Golden Bowl*. James, Henry
★*Golden Buddha*. Cussler, Clive
The *Golden Cage*. Lackberg, Camilla
Golden Child: A Novel. Adam, Claire
The *Golden Egg*. Leon, Donna
★*Golden Hill*. Spufford, Francis
The *Golden Hour*. Williams, Beatriz
★*The Golden House*. Rushdie, Salman
★*The Golden Legend: A Novel*. Aslam, Nadeem
★*The Golden Notebook*. Lessing, Doris May
★*Golden Prey*. Sandford, John

GOLDEN RETRIEVERS
Koontz, Dean R. *The Darkest Evening of the Year*
The *Golden Season*. Brockway, Connie
Golden Son. Brown, Pierce
The *Golden Tresses of the Dead: A Flavia De Luce Novel*. Bradley, C. Alan

Golden, Arthur
★*Memoirs of a Geisha: A Novel*

Golden, Christopher
Ararat
The Pandora Room: A Novel
Red Hands

Goldengrove: a Novel. Prose, Francine
★*The Goldfinch*. Tartt, Donna
★*Goldfinger*. Fleming, Ian

Goldin, Megan
The Escape Room
The Night Swim

Golding, Melanie
The Hidden: A Novel
Little Darlings

Golding, William
Close Quarters
★*Darkness Visible*
Fire Down Below
The Inheritors

★*Lord of the Flies: A Novel*
Rites of Passage

Goldman, Matt
Dead West
The Shallows

Goldman, William
★*The Princess Bride: S. Morgenstern's Classic Tale of True Love and High Adventure : The*

GOLDSMITHS
Penman, Sharon Kay. *The Queen's Man: A Medieval Mystery*

Goldstein, Rebecca
36 Arguments for the Existence of God: A Work of Fiction

Goldstone, Lawrence
Assassin of Shadows

Goldy Bear mysteries [Series]. Davidson, Diane Mott

GOLEM
Hoffman, Alice. ★*The World That We Knew*
Ozick, Cynthia. *The Puttermesser Papers*
Wecker, Helene. *The Golem and the Jinni*
Wecker, Helene. ★*The Hidden Palace*

The *Golem and the Jinni*. Wecker, Helene
Golem and the jinni [Series]. Wecker, Helene

GOLIATH
Spillane, Mickey. *The Goliath Bone*

The *Goliath Bone*. Spillane, Mickey
Gone. Hayder, Mo
Gone. Kellerman, Jonathan
Gone and Back Again. Fuqua, Jonathon Scott
Gone by Midnight. Fox, Candice
★*The Gone Dead*. Benz, Chanelle
Gone for Good. Schaffhausen, Joanna
Gone for Soldiers. Shaara, Jeff
★*Gone Girl: A Novel*. Flynn, Gillian
Gone to Soldiers: A Novel. Piercy, Marge
★*Gone Too Long: A Novel*. Roy, Lori
★*Gone with the Wind*. Mitchell, Margaret
The *Gone-Away World*. Harkaway, Nick

Gonzalez, Christopher
I'm Not Hungry but I Could Eat

GOOD AND EVIL
Arden, Katherine. ★*The Bear and the Nightingale*
Baker, Kage. *The House of the Stag*
Banks, Iain. *The Player of Games*
Banks, Iain. *Use of Weapons*
Banks, Russell. *Continental Drift*
Banville, John. *The Book of Evidence*
Barth, John. ★*The Sot-Weed Factor*
Bear, Greg. *The Forge of God*
Blatty, William Peter. ★*The Exorcist*
Bradbury, Ray. ★*Something Wicked This Way Comes*
Brown, Larry. *Joe: A Novel*
Burke, James Lee. *Wayfaring Stranger: A Novel*
Cheever, John. *Bullet Park: A Novel*
Cronin, Justin. *The City of Mirrors*
Cronin, Justin. *The Passage*
Cronin, Justin. *The Twelve*
Davys, Tim. *Amberville*
Dekker, Ted. *The Girl Behind the Red Rope*

Feehan, Christine. *Dark Illusion*
Gaiman, Neil. ★*The Ocean at the End of the Lane*
Garcia Marquez, Gabriel. *In Evil Hour*
Garcia Marquez, Gabriel. ★*One Hundred Years of Solitude*
Greene, Graham. *The Tenth Man*
Gregory, Daryl. *We Are All Completely Fine*
Grossman, Lev. ★*The Magicians: A Novel*
Jemisin, N. K. ★*The City We Became*
Katsu, Alma. *The Hunger: A Novel*
Kay, Guy Gavriel. *The Summer Tree*
King, Stephen. *Doctor Sleep: A Novel*
King, Stephen. *Salem's Lot*
King, Stephen. ★*The Stand*
Koontz, Dean R. *Velocity*
Maguire, Gregory. *Son of a Witch: A Novel*
Moreno, Gus. *This Thing Between US: A Novel*
Novik, Naomi. *A Deadly Education: A Novel*
Novik, Naomi. *The Last Graduate: A Novel*
Pratchett, Terry. *The Last Hero: A Discworld Fable*
Pratchett, Terry. *Lords and Ladies: A Novel of Discworld*
Pratchett, Terry. *Men at Arms: A Novel of Discworld*
Pynchon, Thomas. *Against the Day: A Novel*
Pyper, Andrew. *The Damned: A Novel*
Rhodes, Jewell Parker. *Yellow Moon: A Novel*
Rice, Anne. *Blackwood Farm*
Rice, Anne. *Blood and Gold: Or, the Story of Marius*
Rice, Anne. *Blood Canticle*
Rice, Anne. ★*Interview with the Vampire*
Rice, Anne. *Memnoch the Devil*
Rice, Anne. *Merrick: A Novel*
Rice, Anne. *Prince Lestat: The Vampire Chronicles*
Rice, Anne. ★*The Queen of the Damned*
Rice, Anne. *The Tale of the Body Thief*
Rice, Anne. *The Vampire Armand*
Rice, Anne. ★*The Vampire Lestat*
Rushdie, Salman. ★*The Satanic Verses*
Saberhagen, Fred. *Farslayer's Story*
Saberhagen, Fred. *Mindsword's Story*
Saberhagen, Fred. *Shieldbreaker's Story*
Saberhagen, Fred. *Woundhealer's Story*
Snipes, Wesley. *Talon of God*
Stage, Zoje. *Wonderland*
Steinbeck, John. ★*East of Eden*
Stoker, Bram. ★*Dracula*
Stoker, Bram. *The New Annotated Dracula*
Tolkien, J. R. R. *Beren and Luthien*
Tolkien, J. R. R. *The Children of Hurin*
Tolkien, J. R. R. *The Fall of Gondolin*
Tolkien, J. R. R. *The Fellowship of the Ring: Being the First Part of the Lord of the Rings*
Tolkien, J. R. R. ★*The Lord of the Rings*
Tolkien, J. R. R. *The Return of the King: Being the Third Part of the Lord of the Rings*
Tolkien, J. R. R. *The Two Towers: Being the Second Part of the Lord of the Rings*
Toro, Guillermo del. *The Hollow Ones*
Vyleta, Dan. *Smoke: A Novel*
Good as Gold. Heller, Joseph

Good as Gone. Corleone, Douglas
★*Good Company: A Novel*. Sweeney, Cynthia D'Aprix
★*A Good Country: A Novel*. Khadivi, Laleh
The Good Daughter. Slaughter, Karin
A Good Day for Chardonnay. Jones, Darynda
The Good Earth. Buck, Pearl S.
Good Eggs. Hardiman, Rebecca
A Good Enough Mother: A Novel. Thomas, Bev
The Good Father. Hawley, Noah
★*Good Girl, Bad Girl: A Novel*. Robotham, Michael
Good Girls Lie. Ellison, J. T.
The Good Husband of Zebra Drive. McCall Smith, Alexander
Good Kings, Bad Kings: A Novel. Nussbaum, Susan
★*The Good Lord Bird*. McBride, James
The Good Mother. Miller, Sue
★*A Good Neighborhood*. Fowler, Therese
Good Neighbors. Langan, Sarah
★*Good Omens: The Nice and Accurate Prophecies of Agnes Nutter, Witch*. Gaiman, Neil
The Good Ones. McKinlay, Jenn
The Good Priest's Son. Price, Reynolds
A Good Rake Is Hard to Find. Collins, Manda
Good Riddance. Lipman, Elinor
A Good Scent from a Strange Mountain: Stories. Butler, Robert Olen
★*The Good Soldier: A Tale of Passion*. Ford, Ford Madox
The Good Suicides: A Thriller. Hill Gumbao, Toni
Good Time Coming. Harris, C. S.
★*Good-Bye, Mr. Chips*. Hilton, James
Goodbye for Now: A Novel. Frankel, Laurie
The Goodbye Look. Macdonald, Ross
★*The Goodbye Man*. Deaver, Jeffery
Goodbye to the Dead. Freeman, Brian
Goodbye Without Leaving. Colwin, Laurie
★*Goodbye, Columbus, and Five Short Stories*. Roth, Philip
Goodis, David
   Nightfall
Goodman, Allegra
   The Cookbook Collector: A Novel
Goodman, Carol
   The Sea of Lost Girls
Goodman, Jo
   In Want of a Wife
   A Touch of Forever
Goodwin, Bobi Gentry
   Revelation
Goodwin, Daisy
   The American Heiress
Goodwin, S. M.
   Absence of Mercy
Goonan, Kathleen Ann
   In War Times
GORDIANUS THE FINDER (FICTITIOUS CHARACTER)
   Saylor, Steven. *The House of the Vestals: The Investigations of Gordianus the Finder*
   Saylor, Steven. *The Judgment of Caesar: A Novel of Ancient Rome*
   Saylor, Steven. *The Seven Wonders: A Novel of the Ancient World*
   Saylor, Steven. *The Triumph of Caesar: A Novel of Ancient Rome*
   Saylor, Steven. *Wrath of the Furies: A Novel of the Ancient World*

Gordimer, Nadine

The Conservationist

Get a Life

★*July's People*

Life Times: Stories, 1952-2007

★*My Son's Story*

No Time Like the Present: A Novel

None to Accompany Me

The Pickup

Gordon, Jaimy

★*Lord of Misrule: A Novel*

***Gorilla**, My Love*. Bambara, Toni Cade

★*Gorky Park*. Smith, Martin Cruz

Gorman, Edward

Riders on the Storm : A Sam McCain Mystery

Gornichec, Genevieve

★*The Witch's Heart*

Gortner, C. W.

The First Actress: A Novel of Sarah Bernhardt

Gosling, Victoria

Before the Ruins: A Novel

GOSPEL SINGERS

Flagg, Fannie. *Standing in the Rainbow: A Novel*

Goss, Theodora

The Sinister Mystery of the Mesmerizing Girl

The Strange Case of the Alchemist's Daughter

GOSSIP COLUMNISTS

Leigh, Eva. *Forever Your Earl*

GOSSIPING AND GOSSIPS

Balogh, Mary. ★*Someone to Cherish*

Berg, Gretchen. *The Operator*

Bradley, Anna. *A Season of Ruin*

Garcia Marquez, Gabriel. *In Evil Hour*

Gogol, Nikolai Vasilievich. ★*Dead Souls*

Leigh, Eva. *Forever Your Earl*

Lewis, Sinclair. ★*Main Street: The Story of Carol Kennicott*

Martin, Alexa. ★*Intercepted*

Quick, Amanda. *The Girl Who Knew Too Much*

Spencer-Fleming, Julia. *All Mortal Flesh*

West, Kathleen. *Minor Dramas & Other Catastrophes*

GOTH CULTURE

Sandford, John. ★*Phantom Prey*

GOTHIC FICTION

Bolton, S. J. *The Craftsman*

Bronte, Charlotte. ★*Emma*

Bronte, Charlotte. ★*Jane Eyre*

Bronte, Emily. ★*Wuthering Heights*

Brown, Karen. *The Clairvoyants: A Novel*

Collins, Wilkie. ★*The Woman in White*

Crowley, John. *Lord Byron's Novel: The Evening Land*

Danforth, Emily M. *Plain Bad Heroines*

Downes, Anna. *The Safe Place: A Novel*

Du Maurier, Daphne. ★*Rebecca*

Duffy, Brendan. *House of Echoes: A Novel*

Egan, Jennifer. *The Keep*

Elliott, Lexie. *The Missing Years*

Faye, Lyndsay. *Jane Steele*

Fine, Julia. *The Upstairs House*

Fine, Julia. *What Should Be Wild*

Fuller, Claire. ★*Bitter Orange*

Gerritsen, Tess. ★*The Shape of Night: A Novel*

Griffiths, Elly. *The Stranger Diaries*

Harrison, Rachel. *The Return*

Hawthorne, Nathaniel. ★*The House of the Seven Gables*

Healey, Jane. *The Animals at Lockwood Manor*

Hurley, Andrew Michael. *Devil's Day*

Jackson, Shirley. ★*The Haunting of Hill House*

Jackson, Shirley. *We Have Always Lived in the Castle*

James, Henry. ★*The Turn of the Screw*

James, Rebecca. *The Woman in the Mirror*

Johnson, Daisy. *Sisters*

Johnstone, Carole. *Mirrorland*

Mas, Victoria. *The Mad Women's Ball*

Maturin, Charles Robert. *Melmoth the Wanderer: A Tale*

Moreno-Garcia, Silvia. *Mexican Gothic*

Morton, Kate. *The Distant Hours: A Novel*

O'Donnell, Paraic. *The House on Vesper Sands: A Novel*

Perry, Sarah. *Melmoth: A Novel*

Poe, Edgar Allan. *The Narrative of Arthur Gordon Pym of Nantucket*

Purcell, Laura. *The House of Whispers*

Purcell, Laura. *The Silent Companions: A Ghost Story*

Radcliffe, Ann Ward. ★*The Mysteries of Udolpho*

Rice, Anne. *Blackwood Farm*

Rice, Anne. *Blood Canticle*

Rice, Anne. *Blood Communion: A Tale of Prince Lestat*

Rice, Anne. ★*Interview with the Vampire*

Rice, Anne. *Memnoch the Devil*

Rice, Anne. *Merrick: A Novel*

Rice, Anne. *Prince Lestat: The Vampire Chronicles*

Rice, Anne. ★*The Queen of the Damned*

Rice, Anne. *The Tale of the Body Thief*

Rice, Anne. *The Vampire Armand*

Rice, Anne. ★*The Vampire Lestat*

Rindell, Suzanne. ★*The Two Mrs. Carlyles*

Rous, Emma. *The Perfect Guests*

Seton, Anya. ★*Dragonwyck*

Seton, Anya. *Green Darkness*

Setterfield, Diane. *The Thirteenth Tale: A Novel*

Shelley, Mary Wollstonecraft. ★*Frankenstein: Or, the Modern Prometheus*

Starling, Caitlin. *The Death of Jane Lawrence*

Stevenson, Robert Louis. ★*The Strange Case of Dr. Jekyll and Mr. Hyde*

Stoker, Bram. ★*Dracula*

Stoker, Bram. *The New Annotated Dracula*

Thomas, Elisabeth. *Catherine House*

Ware, Ruth. *The Death of Mrs. Westaway*

Ware, Ruth. ★*The Turn of the Key*

Wilde, Oscar. ★*The Picture of Dorian Gray*

Wynne, Phoebe. *Madam*

GOTHIC ROMANCES

Stewart, Mary. *Nine Coaches Waiting*

Gottlieb, Eli

Best Boy: A Novel

***Gotz** and Meyer*. Albahari, David

***Gould's** Book of Fish: A Novel in Twelve Fish*. Flanagan, Richard

GOULD, GLENN
Bernhard, Thomas. ★*The Loser*
GOULD, WILLIAM BUELOW
Flanagan, Richard. *Gould's Book of Fish: A Novel in Twelve Fish*
Waugh, Evelyn. ★*Brideshead Revisited*
★*The Governess Game*. Dare, Tessa
Governess Gone Rogue. Guhrke, Laura Lee
GOVERNESSES
Alexander, Tamera. *With This Pledge*
Bell, Lenora. ★*What a Difference a Duke Makes*
Bronte, Charlotte. ★*Jane Eyre*
Dare, Tessa. ★*The Governess Game*
Drake, Olivia. *When a Duke Loves a Governess*
Faye, Lyndsay. *Jane Steele*
Frampton, Megan. *The Duke's Guide to Correct Behavior*
James, Eloisa. ★*Seven Minutes in Heaven*
James, Henry. ★*The Turn of the Screw*
Seton, Anya. ★*Dragonwyck*
Stewart, Mary. *Nine Coaches Waiting*
GOVERNMENT COVER-UPS
Finder, Joseph. *The Switch: A Novel*
Grisham, John. ★*The Pelican Brief*
Le Carre, John. ★*A Delicate Truth*
Meltzer, Brad. *The Escape Artist*
Smith, Martin Cruz. ★*Gorky Park*
Smith, Martin Cruz. ★*Tatiana: An Arkady Renko Novel*
Vidich, Paul. *The Coldest Warrior*
GOVERNMENT INVESTIGATORS
Box, C. J. *Winterkill: A Novel*
Child, Lee. *Persuader*
DeMille, Nelson. *Wild Fire*
Eisler, Barry. *All the Devils*
Furst, Alan. *Blood of Victory: A Novel*
Harkaway, Nick. *Gnomon: A Novel*
Harper, Jane. *The Dry*
Kells, Claire. *Vanishing Edge*
Koepp, David. *Cold Storage: A Novel*
Mayor, Archer. ★*Marked Man*
Robb, Candace M. *The Cross-Legged Knight: An Owen Archer Mystery*
Sandford, John. ★*Deadline*
Sandford, John. *Mad River*
Sandford, John. *Shock Wave*
Sandford, John. *Storm Front*
Slaughter, Karin. *The Kept Woman*
Slaughter, Karin. ★*The Last Widow*
Slaughter, Karin. ★*The Silent Wife*
Thompson, Tade. *Rosewater*
Thompson, Tade. *The Rosewater Insurrection*
GOVERNMENT MISSIONS
Forsyth, Frederick. *The Kill List*
The Governor's Wife. Harvey, Michael T.
GOVERNORS' SPOUSES
Seton, Anya. ★*The Winthrop Woman*
Gowar, Imogen Hermes
The Mermaid and Mrs. Hancock
Gowdy, Barbara
Helpless: A Novel

Grace. Deon, Natashia
GRACE
Gaynor, Hazel. *Meet Me in Monaco: A Novel*
Janowitz, Brenda. *The Grace Kelly Dress*
GRACE (THEOLOGY)
O'Connor, Flannery. ★*Wise Blood*
Grace Chu and John Knox novels [Series]. Pearson, Ridley
The Grace Kelly Dress. Janowitz, Brenda
★*The Grace of Kings*. Liu, Ken
Gracie, Anne
Marry in Scandal
GRADUATE STUDENTS
Aciman, Andre. *Call Me by Your Name*
Aciman, Andre. *Harvard Square*
Boyle, T. Coraghessan. *Outside Looking In: A Novel*
Choi, Susan. *My Education*
French, Tana. *The Likeness*
Hosking, Jay. *Three Years with the Rat: A Novel*
Korelitz, Jean Hanff. ★*The Plot*
Lattari, Katie. *Dark Things I Adore*
Morgenstern, Erin. ★*The Starless Sea*
Rader-Day, Lori. *The Black Hour*
Taylor, Brandon. ★*Real Life*
GRADUATION (SCHOOL)
Novik, Naomi. *The Last Graduate: A Novel*
Graedon, Alena
The Word Exchange: A Novel
Graff, Andrew J.
Raft of Stars
GRAFTON, JAKE (FICTITIOUS CHARACTER)
Coonts, Stephen. ★*Flight of the Intruder*
Grafton, Sue
X
Y Is for Yesterday
GRAIL
Burke, James Lee. *House of the Rising Sun: A Novel*
Cornwell, Bernard. *The Archer's Tale*
Lovett, Charles C. *The Lost Book of the Grail: Or a Visitor's Guide to Barchester Cathedral*
White, T. H. ★*The Once and Future King*
Grail Quest (Bernard Cornwell) [Series]. Cornwell, Bernard
Graley, Lisa
The Current That Carries: Stories
Grames, Juliet
The Seven or Eight Deaths of Stella Fortuna
The Grammarians. Schine, Cathleen
Gran, Sara
Claire Dewitt and the City of the Dead
The Infinite Blacktop: A Novel
GRAND CANYON
Baldacci, David. *Long Road to Mercy*
Ford, Richard. *A Multitude of Sins: Stories*
The Grand Dark. Kadrey, Richard
The Grand Sophy. Heyer, Georgette
★*Grand Union: Stories*. Smith, Zadie
GRANDCHILDREN
McKevett, G. A. *Murder in the Corn Maze*
Ross, Ann B. *Miss Julia Knows a Thing or Two*

GRANDDAUGHTERS
    Fossey, Brooke. *The Big Finish*
    Hepworth, Sally. *The Secrets of Midwives*
    Straub, Emma. ★*All Adults Here*

GRANDFATHER AND CHILD
    Foer, Jonathan Safran. *Everything Is Illuminated: A Novel*

GRANDFATHER AND GRANDDAUGHTER
    Desai, Kiran. *The Inheritance of Loss*
    Dunn, Kate. *The Dragonfly*
    Erdrich, Louise. *The Plague of Doves*
    Rosen, Leonard J. *The Kortelisy Escape*

GRANDFATHER AND GRANDSON
    Heacox, Kim. *Jimmy Bluefeather: A Novel*
    Hewson, David. *The Garden of Angels*
    Starnone, Domenico. *Trick*

GRANDFATHERS
    Allen, Sarah Addison. *The Girl Who Chased the Moon: A Novel*
    Bilenchi, Romano. ★*The Chill*
    Dickens, Charles. *Martin Chuzzlewit*
    Harding, Paul. *Tinkers*
    James, Miranda. *What the Cat Dragged In*

GRANDFATHERS — DEATH
    Hurley, Andrew Michael. *Devil's Day*

GRANDMOTHER AND ADULT CHILD
    Cole, Alyssa. *How to Find a Princess*
    Higgins, Kristan. ★*Life and Other Inconveniences*
    McMurtry, Larry. *The Evening Star: A Novel*

GRANDMOTHER AND CHILD
    Allende, Isabel. *Portrait in Sepia: A Novel*

GRANDMOTHER AND GRANDDAUGHTER
    Blackwell, Juliet. *Letters from Paris*
    Delany, Vicki. *Murder in a Teacup*
    Delany, Vicki. *Tea & Treachery*
    Gibbons, Kaye. *Charms for the Easy Life*
    Lalli, Sonya. *The Matchmaker's List*
    O'Leary, Beth. *The Switch*
    Paretsky, Sara. ★*Dead Land*
    Pearson, Robin W. *A Long Time Comin'*

GRANDMOTHER AND GRANDSON
    Brown, Taylor. ★*Gods of Howl Mountain: A Novel*
    Cooney, Caroline B. *The Grandmother Plot*
    Gessen, Keith. *A Terrible Country*
    Woodrell, Daniel. *The Maid's Version: A Novel*
*The **Grandmother** Plot*. Cooney, Caroline B.

GRANDMOTHERS
    Barr, Nevada. *What Rose Forgot*
    Blackstock, Terri. *Catching Christmas*
    Brenner, Jamie. *Blush: A Novel*
    Corthron, Kia. *Moon and the Mars*
    Drabble, Margaret. *The Witch of Exmoor*
    Friedland, Elyssa. *The Floating Feldmans*
    Grossman, David. ★*More Than I Love My Life: A Novel*
    Stegner, Wallace. ★*Angle of Repose*
    Toews, Miriam. *Fight Night*
    Waite, Jen. *Survival Instincts*
    Weiner, Jennifer. *In Her Shoes: A Novel*
    Whittall, Zoe. *The Spectacular: A Novel*

GRANDMOTHERS — DEATH
    Backman, Fredrik. ★*My Grandmother Asked Me to Tell You She's Sorry: A Novel*
    Meyerson, Amy. *The Imperfects*

GRANDPARENT AND CHILD
    Backman, Fredrik. ★*My Grandmother Asked Me to Tell You She's Sorry: A Novel*
    Dickens, Charles. *The Old Curiosity Shop*
    Obreht, Tea. *The Tiger's Wife: A Novel*

GRANDPARENTS
    Blumberg, Chandra. *Digging up Love*
    Erdrich, Louise. *Love Medicine: A Novel*
    Tsukiyama, Gail. *The Street of a Thousand Blossoms*
    Zettel, Sarah. *A Mother's Lie*

GRANDPARENTS — DEATH
    Davila, April. *142 Ostriches*
    Mankell, Henning. *The Man from Beijing*

GRANDSONS
    Stegner, Wallace. ★*Angle of Repose*
*The **Granite** Coast Murders*. Bannalec, Jean-Luc
Granny Reid mysteries [Series]. McKevett, G. A.

GRANT, CARY
    Allison, Dorothy. ★*Bastard Out of Carolina*
    Kaminsky, Stuart M. *To Catch a Spy: A Toby Peters Mystery*

Grant, Helen
    The Glass Demon
    The Vanishing of Katharina Linden

Grant, Mira
    Blackout
    Deadline
    Feed
    Feedback
    Into the Drowning Deep
    Parasite

Grantchester mysteries [Series]. Runcie, James

GRANTCHESTER, ENGLAND
    Runcie, James. *Sidney Chambers and the Forgiveness of Sins*
    Runcie, James. *Sidney Chambers and the Perils of the Night*
    Runcie, James. *Sidney Chambers and the Persistence of Love*
    Runcie, James. *Sidney Chambers and the Problem of Evil*
    Runcie, James. *Sidney Chambers and the Shadow of Death*
★*The **Grapes** of Wrath*. Steinbeck, John

GRAPHIC DESIGNERS
    Daria, Alexis. ★*A Lot Like Adios*
    Parrish, Roan. *Better Than People*

GRAPHOLOGISTS
    Rader-Day, Lori. *The Day I Died*
★*Grass*. Tepper, Sheri S.
*The **Grass** Dancer*. Power, Susan

Grass, Gunter
    The Box: Tales from the Darkroom
    Crabwalk
    Too Far Afield

Gratton, Tessa
    The Queens of Innis Lear

Grau, Shirley Ann
    The Keepers of the House
★*A **Grave** Denied*. Stabenow, Dana

GRAVE ROBBING

Preston, Douglas J. *Old Bones*

Grave Secrets. Reichs, Kathy

The *Grave's* a Fine and Private Place: A Flavia De Luce Novel. Bradley, C. Alan

The *Gravedigger's* Daughter: A Novel. Oates, Joyce Carol

GRAVEDIGGERS

Oates, Joyce Carol. *The Gravedigger's Daughter: A Novel*

Graves, Robert

Claudius the God and His Wife Messalina: The Troublesome Reign of Tiberius Claudius Caesar, Emperor

★*I, Claudius: From the Autobiography of Tiberius Claudius, Born 10 B.C., Murdered and Deified A.D. 54*

Graves, Stephanie

Olive Bright, Pigeoneer

Gravity Is the Thing. Moriarty, Jaclyn

★*Gravity's Rainbow*. Pynchon, Thomas

★The *Gray* Ghost. Cussler, Clive

Gray, Anissa

The Care and Feeding of Ravenously Hungry Girls

Gray, Erick S.

Love & a Gangsta: A Novel

The *Great* Alone. Hannah, Kristin

The *Great* American Novel. Roth, Philip

★The *Great* Believers. Makkai, Rebecca

GREAT BRITAIN

Aboulela, Leila. *Elsewhere, Home*

Allain, Suzanne. *Miss Lattimore's Letter*

Amis, Kingsley. ★*Lucky Jim*

Andersen, Laura. *The Boleyn Deceit*

Andersen, Laura. ★*The Boleyn King*

Andersen, Laura. *The Boleyn Reckoning*

Archer, Jeffrey. *Nothing Ventured*

Ashley, Jennifer. *Death at the Crystal Palace*

Atkinson, Kate. ★*A God in Ruins*

Atkinson, Kate. ★*Life After Life: A Novel*

Atkinson, Kate. ★*Transcription*

Austen, Jane. ★*Sense and Sensibility*

Austin, Finola. *Bronte's Mistress*

Baker, Jo. *Longbourn*

Ballard, J. G. ★*The Complete Stories of J.G. Ballard.*

Ballard, J. G. *Millennium People*

Balogh, Mary. ★*Someone to Care*

Balogh, Mary. ★*Someone to Cherish*

Balogh, Mary. ★*Someone to Remember: A Westcott Story*

Balogh, Mary. *Someone to Trust*

Balogh, Mary. *Someone to Wed*

Bannister, Jo. *Kindred Spirits*

Bannister, Jo. *Silent Footsteps*

Barnett, David. *Calling Major Tom*

Barth, John. ★*The Sot-Weed Factor*

Bear, Elizabeth. *Ink and Steel: A Novel of the Promethean Age*

Bell, Lenora. *For the Duke's Eyes Only*

Bell, Lenora. ★*How the Duke Was Won*

Bell, Lenora. *One Fine Duke*

Bell, Lenora. ★*What a Difference a Duke Makes*

Benedict, Marie. ★*Lady Clementine*

Benn, James R. ★*The Red Horse: A Billy Boyle World War II Mystery*

Bennett, Alan. ★*The Uncommon Reader*

Bennett, Anna. *First Earl I See Tonight*

Bennett, Bethany. *West End Earl*

Berne, Lisa. *You May Kiss the Bride*

Beverley, Jo. *My Lady Notorious*

Beverley, Jo. *Tempting Fortune*

Birch, Carol. *Jamrach's Menagerie*

Blackmore, R. D. *Lorna Doone: A Romance of Exmoor*

Blakemore, A. K. *The Manningtree Witches*

Bowen, Kelly. ★*Between the Devil and the Duke*

Bowen, Kelly. *A Rogue by Night*

Bowman, Valerie. *A Duke Like No Other*

Bowman, Valerie. *No Other Duke but You*

Brockway, Connie. *No Place for a Dame*

Bronte, Anne. *The Tenant of Wildfell Hall*

Buchan, John. *The Thirty-Nine Steps*

Buckley, Fiona. *The Doublet Affair: A Mystery at Queen Elizabeth I's Court*

Buckley, Fiona. *The Siren Queen: An Ursula Blanchard Mystery at Queen Elizabeth I's Court*

Burrowes, Grace. *Tremaine's True Love*

Byrne, Kerrigan. *The Duke with the Dragon Tattoo*

Byrne, Kerrigan. *The Hunter*

Callihan, Kristen. ★*Firelight*

Chanter, Catherine. *The Well*

Chase, Loretta Lynda. *Miss Wonderful*

Cho, Zen. *Spirits Abroad and Other Stories*

Christian, Claire. *It's Been a Pleasure, Noni Blake*

Clare, Alys. *The Woman Who Spoke to Spirits*

Cleave, Chris. *Gold*

Clements, Oliver. *The Eyes of the Queen*

Clements, Oliver. *The Queen's Men*

Cocks, Heather. *The Heir Affair*

Collins, Manda. *A Good Rake Is Hard to Find*

Collins, Manda. ★*A Lady's Guide to Mischief and Mayhem*

Collins, Manda. *One for the Rogue*

Collins, Manda. *Ready Set Rogue*

Cornwell, Bernard. *The Archer's Tale*

Cornwell, Bernard. *The Last Kingdom: A Novel*

Cornwell, Bernard. *Sword of Kings*

Cornwell, Bernard. *The Winter King: A Novel of Arthur*

Corry, Jane. *The Dead Ex*

Crowley, John. *Lord Byron's Novel: The Evening Land*

Daly, Paula. *Clear My Name*

Dare, Tessa. *Do You Want to Start a Scandal*

Davis, Lindsey. *A Body in the Bathhouse*

Dean, Michael. *I, Hogarth*

Defoe, Daniel. ★*Moll Flanders*

Deluca, Marjorie. *The Savage Instinct*

Donoghue, Emma. *Slammerkin*

Du Maurier, Daphne. *Frenchman's Creek*

Evaristo, Bernardine. ★*Girl, Woman, Other*

Faber, Michel. *The Crimson Petal and the White*

Fforde, Jasper. *Lost in a Good Book: A Thursday Next Novel*

Follett, Ken. *A Column of Fire*

Follett, Ken. ★*The Evening and the Morning*

Follett, Ken. *Hornet Flight*

Follett, Ken. ★*The Pillars of the Earth*

Follett, Ken. *World Without End*

Forester, C. S. *Admiral Hornblower in the West Indies*

Forester, C. S. *Beat to Quarters*

Forester, C. S. *Commodore Hornblower*

Forester, C. S. *Flying Colours*

Forester, C. S. *Hornblower and the Atropos*

Forester, C. S. *Hornblower and the Hotspur*

Forester, C. S. *Lieutenant Hornblower*

Forester, C. S. *Lord Hornblower*

Forester, C. S. *Mr. Midshipman Hornblower*

Forester, C. S. *Ship of the Line*

Fowles, John. ★*The French Lieutenant's Woman*

Franklin, Ariana. *The Serpent's Tale*

Franklin, Ariana. *The Siege Winter*

Freeman, Dianne. *A Fiancee's Guide to First Wives and Murder*

French, Nicci. *Dark Saturday*

French, Nicci. ★*The Day of the Dead: A Novel*

French, Nicci. ★*House of Correction*

French, Nicci. *Sunday Silence*

Galsworthy, John. ★*The Forsyte Saga*

Gardam, Jane. *Old Filth*

Gelernter, J. H. *Hold Fast*

George, Margaret. *Elizabeth I: A Novel*

Golding, William. ★*Darkness Visible*

Goodwin, Daisy. *The American Heiress*

Goss, Theodora. *The Sinister Mystery of the Mesmerizing Girl*

Goss, Theodora. *The Strange Case of the Alchemist's Daughter*

Gracie, Anne. *Marry in Scandal*

Greeley, Molly. *The Clergyman's Wife*

Greene, Graham. *Collected Stories: Including May We Borrow Your Husband? a Sense of Reality, Twenty-One Stories*

Greene, Graham. *The Last Word and Other Stories*

Gregory, Philippa. *The Boleyn Inheritance*

Gregory, Philippa. *The Constant Princess*

Gregory, Philippa. *The Kingmaker's Daughter*

Gregory, Philippa. *The Lady of the Rivers*

Gregory, Philippa. *The Last Tudor*

Gregory, Philippa. *The Other Boleyn Girl: A Novel*

Gregory, Philippa. *The Red Queen: A Novel*

Gregory, Philippa. *The Taming of the Queen*

Gregory, Philippa. *Tidelands*

Gregory, Philippa. *The White Princess*

Griffith, Nicola. *Hild: A Novel*

Griffiths, Elly. *The Lantern Men: A Dr. Ruth Galloway Mystery*

Griffiths, Elly. *The Night Hawks*

Griffiths, Elly. *The Stone Circle*

Guhrke, Laura Lee. *Governess Gone Rogue*

Guhrke, Laura Lee. *The Trouble with True Love*

Guhrke, Laura Lee. *The Truth About Love and Dukes*

Hall, Adam. *The Quiller Memorandum*

Hall, Alexis. *Rosaline Palmer Takes the Cake*

Hamer, Kate. *The Girl in the Red Coat*

Hamya, Jo. *Three Rooms*

Harper, Karen. *The Queen's Secret: A Novel of England's World War II Queen*

Harrington, Anna. *An Extraordinary Lord*

Harrington, Anna. *An Inconvenient Duke*

Heath, Lorraine. *Falling into Bed with a Duke*

Holton, India. *The Wisteria Society of Lady Scoundrels*

Hoyt, Elizabeth. *Not the Duke's Darling*

Hoyt, Elizabeth. *When a Rogue Meets His Match*

Huber, Anna Lee. *Penny for Your Secrets*

Iggulden, Conn. *The Abbot's Tale*

Ishiguro, Kazuo. *The Buried Giant: A Novel*

James, Eloisa. ★*Seven Minutes in Heaven*

James, Eloisa. *Three Weeks with Lady X*

James, Eloisa. *Wilde in Love*

Jeffries, Sabrina. *Project Duchess*

Jewell, Lisa. *The Family Upstairs*

Johnson, Daisy. *Everything Under*

Jordan, Sophie. *The Duke Goes Down*

Kleypas, Lisa. *Cold-Hearted Rake*

Kleypas, Lisa. ★*Devil in Disguise*

Lefteri, Christy. *The Beekeeper of Aleppo: A Novel*

Llewellyn, Richard. ★*How Green Was My Valley*

Lloyd, Catherine. *Death Comes to the Nursery*

MacLean, Sarah. ★*Bombshell*

MacLean, Sarah. *The Rogue Not Taken*

MacLeod, Alison. *Tenderness*

Mantel, Hilary. ★*Bring up the Bodies: A Novel*

Mantel, Hilary. ★*Wolf Hall*

Marske, Freya. *A Marvellous Light*

Marston, Edward. *The Roaring Boy: A Novel*

Marston, Edward. *The Wanton Angel: A Novel*

Mason, Timothy. *The Darwin Affair*

Matthews, Mimi. ★*The Siren of Sussex*

McQuiston, Casey. ★*Red, White & Royal Blue: A Novel*

Milan, Courtney. *The Duchess War*

Mitchell, David. ★*Cloud Atlas: A Novel*

Mitchell, David. ★*Utopia Avenue: A Novel*

Morton, Kate. *The House at Riverton: A Novel*

Moyes, Jojo. *The Peacock Emporium*

Novik, Naomi. *A Deadly Education: A Novel*

Novik, Naomi. *The Last Graduate: A Novel*

O'Brian, Patrick. *Master and Commander*

Orczy, Emmuska Orczy. *The Old Man in the Corner*

Parker, Lucy. *Battle Royal*

Pears, Iain. *An Instance of the Fingerpost*

Penman, Sharon Kay. *Here Be Dragons*

Penman, Sharon Kay. *The Sunne in Splendour*

Peters, Ellis. *Brother Cadfael's Penance*

Peters, Ellis. *The Holy Thief*

Phillips, Caryl. *A View of the Empire at Sunset*

Phillips, Christi. *The Devlin Diary*

Pilcher, Rosamunde. *Coming Home*

Quincy, Diana. *Her Night with the Duke*

Quincy, Diana. *The Viscount Made Me Do It*

Reay, Katherine. *The Bronte Plot*

Ridley, Erica. *The Duke Heist*

Ridley, Erica. ★*The Perks of Loving a Wallflower*

Riley, Vanessa. ★*A Duke, the Lady, and a Baby*

Riley, Vanessa. ★*An Earl, the Girl, and a Toddler*

Robb, Candace M. *The Cross-Legged Knight: An Owen Archer Mystery*

Robb, Candace M. *A Gift of Sanctuary: An Owen Archer Mystery*

Robb, Candace M. *A Murdered Peace*

Robb, Candace M. *The Riddle of St. Leonard's: An Owen Archer Mystery.*
Robb, Candace M. *A Twisted Vengeance*
Sackville-West, V. *The Edwardians*
Sansom, C. J. ★*Lamentation*
Sansom, C. J. *Revelation*
Sansom, C. J. ★*Sovereign*
Sansom, C. J. *Tombland*
Schellman, Katharine. *Silence in the Library*
Scott, Walter. ★*Ivanhoe*
Seton, Anya. *Avalon*
Seton, Anya. *Green Darkness*
Seton, Anya. *Katherine*
Shamsie, Kamila. *Home Fire: A Novel*
Shriver, Lionel. *Should We Stay or Should We Go*
Smith, Ali. ★*Autumn*
Smith, Ali. ★*Spring*
Smith, Ali. ★*Summer*
Smith, Ali. ★*Winter*
Smith, Zadie. ★*White Teeth: A Novel*
St. Aubyn, Edward. *Double Blind*
Stewart, Mary. ★*The Crystal Cave*
Stewart, Mary. ★*The Hollow Hills*
Stewart, Mary. *The Last Enchantment*
Stewart, Mary. *The Wicked Day*
Stirling, S. M. *The Protector's War*
Sullivan, Emily. *The Rebel and the Rake*
Sutcliff, Rosemary. *Sword at Sunset*
Swift, Graham. ★*Here We Are*
Thomas, Russ. ★*Firewatching*
Trollope, Anthony. ★*The Eustace Diamonds*
Trollope, Anthony. ★*The Prime Minister*
Tudor, C. J. *The Burning Girls: A Novel*
Tudor, C. J. *The Other People*
Waite, Olivia. *The Care and Feeding of Waspish Widows*
Waite, Olivia. ★*The Lady's Guide to Celestial Mechanics*
Ware, Ruth. *The Lying Game*
Waters, Martha. *To Love and to Loathe: A Novel*
Waugh, Evelyn. ★*Brideshead Revisited*
Weir, Alison. *Anna of Kleve: The Princess in the Portrait*
Weir, Alison. *Katharine Parr, the Sixth Wife*
Welsh, Irvine. *Trainspotting*
White, T. H. ★*The Once and Future King*
Wilde, Oscar. ★*The Picture of Dorian Gray*
Winspear, Jacqueline. *The American Agent*
Winspear, Jacqueline. ★*The Consequences of Fear: A Maisie Dobbs Novel*
Woods, Stuart. *Stealth*
Great cities trilogy [Series]. Jemisin, N. K.
*The **Great** Escape.* Phillips, Susan Elizabeth
★***Great** Expectations.* Dickens, Charles
★*The **Great** Fire.* Hazzard, Shirley
*The **Great** Glorious Goddamn of It All.* Ritter, Josh
GREAT LAKES
Phillips, Susan Elizabeth. *The Great Escape*
*The **Great** Leader.* Harrison, Jim
*The **Great** Mistake.* Lee, Jonathan
***Great** North Road.* Hamilton, Peter F.

GREAT PLAINS (UNITED STATES)
Brown, Dee. *Creek Mary's Blood: A Novel*
Coldsmith, Don. *Tallgrass: A Novel of the Great Plains*
Great Plains saga [Series]. Coldsmith, Don
GREAT SMOKY MOUNTAINS (N.C. AND TENN.)
Bledsoe, Alex. *Gather Her Round: A Novel of the Tufa*
Bledsoe, Alex. *Long Black Curl*
Bledsoe, Alex. *Wisp of a Thing*
Dektar, Molly. *The Ash Family*
Marshall, Catherine. *Christy*
GREAT-AUNTS
Hardy, Thomas. ★*Jude the Obscure*
Holton, India. *The Wisteria Society of Lady Scoundrels*
GREAT-GRANDMOTHERS
Desai, Anita. *Fire on the Mountain*
GREAT-UNCLES
Dykes, Amanda. *Whose Waves These Are*
van Heemstra, Marjolijn. *In Search of a Name*
Greaves, Chuck
Hush Money: A Mystery
Grebe, Camilla
After She's Gone: A Novel
The Ice Beneath Her: A Novel
Grecian, Alex
The Saint of Wolves and Butchers
GREECE
Alameddine, Rabih. *The Wrong End of the Telescope*
Cussler, Clive. *The Mediterranean Caper*
Fowles, John. *The Magus*
Furst, Alan. *Spies of the Balkans: A Novel*
Goddard, Robert. ★*Into the Blue*
Siger, Jeffrey. *Mykonos After Midnight: A Chief Inspector Kaldis Mystery*
Siger, Jeffrey. *Target Tinos: An Inspector Kaldis Mystery*
GREED
Abdul-Jabbar, Kareem. *The Empty Birdcage*
Andrew, Sally. *The Satanic Mechanic: A Tannie Maria Mystery*
Bawden, Nina. *Family Money*
Bialosky, Jill. *The Prize: A Novel*
Box, C. J. *Badlands*
Clinch, Jon. *Marley: A Novel*
Conrad, Joseph. *Nostromo: A Tale of the Seaboard*
Cussler, Clive. ★*The Gray Ghost*
Dickens, Charles. *Martin Chuzzlewit*
Faulks, Sebastian. *A Week in December*
Finder, Joseph. *Buried Secrets*
Follett, Ken. *World Without End*
Gaddis, William. *A Frolic of His Own: A Novel*
Goodman, Allegra. *The Cookbook Collector: A Novel*
Gregory, Philippa. *The Lady of the Rivers*
Harkaway, Nick. *The Gone-Away World*
Hunter, Stephen. *The 47th Samurai*
Jones, Cherie. *How the One-Armed Sister Sweeps Her House*
Lewis, Sinclair. ★*Main Street: The Story of Carol Kennicott*
Mandel, Emily St. John. ★*The Glass Hotel: A Novel*
Mayor, Archer. ★*Marked Man*
McDonald, Ian. *New Moon*
Paretsky, Sara. *Shell Game*

Patterson, Richard North. *Dark Lady*
Pickard, Nancy. *The Scent of Rain and Lightning: A Novel*
Pilcher, Rosamunde. ★*The Shell Seekers*
Priest, Cherie. *The Inexplicables*
Puzo, Mario. *The Family: A Novel*
Rash, Ron. ★*Serena: A Novel*
Robinson, Kim Stanley. *Antarctica*
Robotham, Michael. *Life or Death*
Russell, Mary Doria. *Epitaph: A Novel of the O.K. Corral*
Sanders, Lawrence. ★*McNally's Gamble*
Sanders, Lawrence. *The Second Deadly Sin*
Steadman, Catherine. *Something in the Water*
Steinbeck, John. *The Pearl*
Vinge, Vernor. *The Children of the Sky*

GREED IN MEN
Anderson, Kevin J. *The Last Days of Krypton*
Aswani, Alaa. *Chicago: A Modern Arabic Novel*
deWitt, Patrick. *The Sisters Brothers: A Novel*
Goddard, Robert. *Beyond Recall: A Novel*
Hawthorne, Nathaniel. ★*The House of the Seven Gables*
Smith, Scott. *A Simple Plan: A Novel*

GREED IN WOMEN
Trollope, Anthony. ★*The Eustace Diamonds*

GREEK AMERICANS
Eugenides, Jeffrey. ★*Middlesex*

GREEK FIRE
Clements, Oliver. *The Queen's Men*
Greek mysteries (Jeffrey Siger) [Series]. Siger, Jeffrey
★***Greeks** Bearing Gifts: A Bernie Gunther Novel*. Kerr, Philip
Greeley, Molly
 The Clergyman's Wife
Green Bone saga [Series]. Lee, Fonda
Green Darkness. Seton, Anya
Green House. Vargas Llosa, Mario
*The **Green** Knight*. Murdoch, Iris
★***Green** Mars*. Robinson, Kim Stanley

GREEN MOVEMENT
Rendell, Ruth. *Road Rage*
*The **Green** Ripper*. MacDonald, John D.
*The **Green** Road: A Novel*. Enright, Anne
Green Sun: A Novel. Anderson, Kent
Green, Amy Lynn
 Things We Didn't Say

GREEN, ANDREW HASWELL
Lee, Jonathan. *The Great Mistake*
Green, Hank
 An Absolutely Remarkable Thing: A Novel
Green, Jocelyn
 The Mark of the King
 Veiled in Smoke
Greenberg, Joanne
 I Never Promised You a Rose Garden: A Novel

GREENBERG, JOANNE
Bohjalian, Chris. *The Double Bind: A Novel*
Greenberg, Joanne. *I Never Promised You a Rose Garden: A Novel*
Greene, Amy
 Long Man

Greene, Graham
 ★*Brighton Rock*
 The Captain and the Enemy
 Collected Stories: Including May We Borrow Your Husband? a Sense of Reality, Twenty-One Stories
 ★*The End of the Affair*
 ★*The Heart of the Matter*
 The Honorary Consul
 The Human Factor
 The Last Word and Other Stories
 Our Man in Havana
 The Power and the Glory
 ★*The Quiet American*
 The Tenth Man
*The **Greengage** Summer: A Novel*. Godden, Rumer
Greengrass, Jessie
 Sight: A Novel
Greenhollow duology [Series]. Tesh, Emily
Greenidge, Kaitlyn
 ★*Libertie: A Novel*
 We Love You, Charlie Freeman: A Novel

GREENLAND
Cussler, Clive. *Sacred Stone*
Hoeg, Peter. ★*Smilla's Sense of Snow*
Greenwell, Garth
 Cleanness
 What Belongs to You: A Novel

GREENWICH VILLAGE, NEW YORK CITY
Scoppettone, Sandra. *Everything You Have Is Mine*
Scoppettone, Sandra. *My Sweet Untraceable You*
Steinke, Rene. *Holy Skirts*
Wall, Cara. *The Dearly Beloved: A Novel*

GREENWICH, ENGLAND
Smith, Ali. *There but for The: A Novel*
Greenwood, Kerry
 Death in Daylesford
 Out of the Black Land
 Unnatural Habits
Greenwood, T.
 Rust & Stardust
★***Greenwood**: a Novel*. Christie, Michael
Greer, Andrew Sean
 The Impossible Lives of Greta Wells
 ★*Less*
Greer, Robert O.
 First of State
Gregor Demarkian mysteries [Series]. Haddam, Jane
Gregory, Daryl
 Afterparty
 The Devil's Alphabet
 We Are All Completely Fine
Gregory, Philippa
 The Boleyn Inheritance
 The Constant Princess
 The Kingmaker's Daughter
 The Lady of the Rivers
 The Last Tudor
 The Other Boleyn Girl: A Novel

The Red Queen: A Novel
The Taming of the Queen
Tidelands
The White Princess
Grenville, Kate
  Sarah Thornhill
  The Secret River
Greta Helsing novels [Series]. Shaw, Vivian
★*The Grey Bastards*. French, Jonathan
GREY, JANE
  Gregory, Philippa. *The Last Tudor*
  Horowitz, Anthony. ★*The Word Is Murder*
Grey, Zane
  ★*Riders of the Purple Sage*
  Woman of the Frontier: A Western Story
Greycourt novels [Series]. Hoyt, Elizabeth
GRIEF
  Agee, James. ★*A Death in the Family*
  Alvarez, Julia. ★*Afterlife: A Novel*
  Barclay, Linwood. *A Tap on the Window*
  Bhuvaneswar, Chaya. *White Dancing Elephants: Stories*
  Bialosky, Jill. *House Under Snow*
  Bruno, Anna. *Ordinary Hazards: A Novel*
  Cook, Thomas H. *The Fate of Katherine Carr*
  Dexter, Pete. *Spooner*
  Erdrich, Louise. ★*Larose*
  Erdrich, Louise. *The Painted Drum: A Novel*
  Evison, Jonathan. *All About Lulu: A Novel*
  Fallada, Hans. *Every Man Dies Alone*
  Freudenberger, Nell. ★*Lost and Wanted: A Novel*
  Garvin, Eileen. *The Music of Bees*
  Gibson, William. *Pattern Recognition*
  Goldman, Matt. *Dead West*
  Greengrass, Jessie. *Sight: A Novel*
  Grossman, David. *Falling Out of Time*
  Hall, Araminta. *Imperfect Women: A Novel*
  Han, Kang. *The White Book*
  Harmon, Amy. *Where the Lost Wander*
  Heller, Peter. *The Guide*
  Hemmings, Kaui Hart. *The Possibilities: A Novel*
  Higgins, Kristan. ★*Pack up the Moon*
  Hobson, Brandon. ★*The Removed: A Novel*
  Jones, Cherie. *How the One-Armed Sister Sweeps Her House*
  Kerangal, Maylis de. *The Heart: A Novel*
  King, Lily. *Writers & Lovers: A Novel*
  Kraus, Daniel. *The Autumnal: The Complete Series*
  Krivak, Andrew. *The Signal Flame: A Novel*
  MacLaverty, Bernard. ★*Blank Pages: And Other Stories*
  McCann, Colum. ★*Apeirogon: A Novel*
  Miller, Holly. ★*The Sight of You*
  Moriarty, Jaclyn. *Gravity Is the Thing*
  Murphy, Sara Flannery. *The Possessions*
  O'Farrell, Maggie. *Hamnet*
  O'Leary, Beth. *The Switch*
  Packer, Ann. *Songs Without Words*
  Porter, Max. ★*Grief Is the Thing with Feathers*
  Prose, Francine. *Goldengrove: A Novel*
  Proust, Marcel. *Time Regained*

Reid, Taylor Jenkins. *Forever, Interrupted: A Novel*
Rodriques, Elias. *All the Water I've Seen Is Running: A Novel*
Ruiz, Sarah Grunder. *Love, Lists, and Fancy Ships*
Saunders, George. ★*Lincoln in the Bardo: A Novel*
Watson, Martine Fournier. *The Dream Peddler*
Wells, Benedict. *The End of Loneliness: A Novel*
Winch, Tara June. *The Yield*
Yoshimoto, Banana. *Moshi-Moshi*
Grief Cottage: A Novel. Godwin, Gail
GRIEF IN ANIMALS
  Nunez, Sigrid. ★*The Friend*
GRIEF IN BOYS
  Lodato, Victor. *Edgar and Lucy: A Novel*
GRIEF IN FAMILIES
  Bird, Sarah. ★*The Flamenco Academy: A Novel*
  Diamond, Elizabeth. *An Accidental Light*
  Lodato, Victor. *Mathilda Savitch*
  Oates, Joyce Carol. *Night. Sleep. Death. The Stars*
  Stewart, Ann Marie. *Stars in the Grass*
  Winthrop, Elizabeth Hartley. ★*The Why of Things*
GRIEF IN MEN
  Auster, Paul. ★*The Book of Illusions: A Novel*
  Baldwin, James. *Just Above My Head*
  Banville, John. ★*The Sea*
  Block, Lawrence. *A Drop of the Hard Stuff: A Matthew Scudder Novel*
  Burke, James Lee. *Black Cherry Blues*
  Connolly, John. *The Dirty South*
  Deveraux, Jude. *Someone to Love*
  Dickens, Charles. *Dombey and Son*
  Hill, Joe. *Horns*
  Malouf, David. *Ransom*
  May, Peter. *The Blackhouse*
  McEwan, Ian. *The Child in Time*
  Moreno, Gus. *This Thing Between US: A Novel*
  Oe, Kenzaburo. *The Changeling*
  Scottoline, Lisa. *Don't Go*
  Swift, Graham. *Wish You Were Here*
GRIEF IN MOTHERS
  Peikoff, Kira. *Mother Knows Best*
GRIEF IN WOMEN
  Adamson, Gil. *The Outlander*
  Audrain, Ashley. *The Push*
  Austin, Finola. *Bronte's Mistress*
  Bynum, Sarah Shun-Lien. *Ms. Hempel Chronicles*
  Carpenter, Emily. *Until the Day I Die*
  Clegg, Bill. *Did You Ever Have a Family*
  Clemmons, Zinzi. *What We Lose*
  Coben, Harlan. *Hold Tight*
  Crossan, Sarah. *Here Is the Beehive*
  Doller, Trish. *Float Plan*
  Edwards, Yvvette. *The Mother*
  Keneally, Thomas. *Woman of the Inner Sea*
  Oates, Joyce Carol. *Breathe*
  Rice, Luanne. *The Lemon Orchard*
  Rouda, Kaira Sturdivant. *The Favorite Daughter*
  Stedman, M. L. ★*The Light Between Oceans: A Novel*
  Swift, Graham. ★*Mothering Sunday: A Romance*

Trigiani, Adriana. *Big Cherry Holler: A Big Stone Gap Novel*
Uris, Leon. *Redemption: A Novel*
Walker, Alice. *Possessing the Secret of Joy*
★*Grief Is the Thing with Feathers*. Porter, Max

Griffin, Anne
When All Is Said: A Novel

Griffith, Nicola
Hild: A Novel

Griffiths, Elly
The Crossing Places
The Dark Angel
A Dying Fall: A Ruth Galloway Mystery
The House at Sea's End: A Ruth Galloway Mystery
The Janus Stone
The Lantern Men: A Dr. Ruth Galloway Mystery
The Night Hawks
The Postscript Murders
The Stone Circle
The Stranger Diaries

GRIM REAPER (SYMBOLIC CHARACTER)
Klune, TJ. ★*Under the Whispering Door*

GRIMKE, SARAH MOORE
DeSilva, Bruce. *Rogue Island*
Kidd, Sue Monk. ★*The Invention of Wings: A Novel*

★*Gringos: a Novel*. Portis, Charles
★*The Grip of It*. Jemc, Jac

Grippando, James
The Girl in the Glass Box

Grisham, John
The Client
★*The Firm*
★*The Guardians*
The Last Juror
★*The Pelican Brief*
A Time to Kill

Grist Mill Road: A Novel. Yates, Christopher J.

Grodstein, Lauren
Our Short History

Groen, Hendrik
On the Bright Side: The New Secret Diary of Hendrik Groen, 85 Years Old

Groff, Lauren
★*Arcadia: A Novel*
Delicate Edible Birds and Other Stories
★*Fates and Furies*
★*Florida*
★*Matrix*

Groom, Winston
El Paso: A Novel

Groot, Tracy
Flame of Resistance

Gross, Andrew
Button Man
The One Man

Gross, Max
The Lost Shtetl

Grossman, David
Be My Knife
Falling Out of Time
★*A Horse Walks into a Bar*
★*More Than I Love My Life: A Novel*
★*To the End of the Land*

Grossman, Lev
The Magician King: A Novel
The Magician's Land: A Novel
★*The Magicians: A Novel*

Grossman, Paul
Children of Wrath

GROUCHES
Backman, Fredrik. *A Man Called Ove*
Dickens, Charles. ★*A Christmas Carol*
Fossey, Brooke. *The Big Finish*
Parrish, Roan. *Better Than People*

GROUP HOMES
Luchette, Claire. *Agatha of Little Neon*

Growing Things and Other Stories. Tremblay, Paul

GROWING UP
Adjapon, Bisi. *The Teller of Secrets: A Novel*
Al Rawi, Shahad. *The Baghdad Clock*
Anappara, Deepa. *Djinn Patrol on the Purple Line: A Novel*
Andreades, Daphne Palasi. *Brown Girls*
Atwood, Margaret. *Moral Disorder*
Auster, Paul. *4 3 2 1: A Novel*
Boyne, John. *The Heart's Invisible Furies*
Bradbury, Ray. ★*Dandelion Wine: A Novel*
Brown, Rita Mae. ★*Rubyfruit Jungle*
Bump, Gabriel. ★*Everywhere You Don't Belong: A Novel*
Choi, Ann Y. K. *Kay's Lucky Coin Variety*
Cisneros, Sandra. ★*The House on Mango Street*
Cleary, Jon. *The Sundowners*
Corthron, Kia. *Moon and the Mars*
Dalton, Trent. *Boy Swallows Universe*
Doctorow, E. L. *World's Fair*
Doerr, Anthony. ★*Cloud Cuckoo Land: A Novel*
Doyle, Roddy. *Paddy Clarke, Ha-Ha-Ha*
Dugoni, Robert. ★*The Extraordinary Life of Sam Hell*
Eliot, George. ★*The Mill on the Floss*
Enright, Anne. *The Green Road: A Novel*
Ferrante, Elena. *The Lying Life of Adults*
Ferrante, Elena. *My Brilliant Friend*
Grass, Gunter. *The Box: Tales from the Darkroom*
Groff, Lauren. ★*Arcadia: A Novel*
Hadley, Tessa. *Clever Girl*
Hahn, Sumi. *The Mermaid from Jeju: A Novel*
Harrigan, Stephen. *The Leopard Is Loose: A Novel*
Hughes, Langston. *Not Without Laughter*
Huisman, Violaine. *The Book of Mother*
Khadivi, Laleh. ★*A Good Country: A Novel*
Larkin, Allie. *The People We Keep*
Le Guin, Ursula K. *The Beginning Place*
McDermott, Alice. *Someone*
Miller, Karen E. Quinones. *An Angry-Ass Black Woman*
Morante, Elsa. *Arturo's Island: A Novel*
Pamuk, Orhan. ★*A Strangeness in My Mind: A Novel*
Pilcher, Rosamunde. *Coming Home*
Preston, Caroline. *The Scrapbook of Frankie Pratt*

Prose, Francine. *Goldengrove: A Novel*
Proust, Marcel. *Swann's Way*
Proust, Marcel. *Within a Budding Grove*
Quindlen, Anna. *Miller's Valley*
Shields, Carol. ★*The Stone Diaries*
Sister Souljah. ★*A Deeper Love Inside: The Porsche Santiaga Story*
Smiley, Jane. *Golden Age*
Steinbeck, John. *The Long Valley*
Straub, Emma. ★*Modern Lovers*
Swamy, Shruti. *The Archer*
White, Edmund. *A Boy's Own Story*
Woolf, Virginia. *Jacob's Room*
Woolf, Virginia. *The Waves*
Yoshimoto, Banana. *The Lake*
Grown Ups. Unsworth, Emma Jane

GROWTH (PSYCHOLOGY)
Butler, Halle. *The New Me: A Novel*
Parks, Gordon. ★*The Learning Tree*

Gruber, Michael
The Book of Air and Shadows
The Forgery of Venus: A Novel
Night of the Jaguar: A Novel
The Return: A Novel
Valley of Bones: A Novel

Gruen, Sara
The Ape House
★*Water for Elephants: A Novel*

Grushin, Olga
The Line

GUADALCANAL, BATTLE OF, 1942-1943
Jones, James. ★*The Thin Red Line*

GUADALUPE MOUNTAINS NATIONAL PARK
Barr, Nevada. *Track of the Cat*
The Guardian. Sparks, Nicholas
Guardian (Karen Robards) [Series]. Robards, Karen

GUARDIAN AND WARD
Amis, Martin. *Lionel Asbo: State of England*
Dare, Tessa. ★*The Governess Game*
Donoghue, Emma. *Akin*
Godwin, Gail. *Flora: A Novel*
Heyer, Georgette. *These Old Shades*
James, Eloisa. ★*Seven Minutes in Heaven*
Ondaatje, Michael. ★*Warlight*
Radcliffe, Ann Ward. ★*The Mysteries of Udolpho*
Sjón. *The Blue Fox*
Stabenow, Dana. ★*A Grave Denied*
Wiggs, Susan. ★*The Oysterville Sewing Circle*
★*The Guardians*. Grisham, John
The Guards. Bruen, Ken

GUARDS
Aridjis, Chloe. *Asunder*
Erdrich, Louise. ★*The Night Watchman: A Novel*
Lovesey, Peter. *Diamond Solitaire*
Guards! Guards! Pratchett, Terry

GUATEMALA
Allende, Isabel. *In the Midst of Winter: A Novel*
Reichs, Kathy. *Grave Secrets*

GUATEMALANS IN THE UNITED STATES
Marcom, Micheline Aharonian. *The New American*

GUERNSEY (CHANNEL ISLANDS)
Shaffer, Mary Ann. *The Guernsey Literary and Potato Peel Pie Society*
The Guernsey Literary and Potato Peel Pie Society. Shaffer, Mary Ann
Guerrillas. Naipaul, V. S.

GUERRILLAS
Hemingway, Ernest. *For Whom the Bell Tolls*
Loedel, Daniel. *Hades, Argentina*
Naipaul, V. S. *Guerrillas*
The Guest Book: A Novel. Blake, Sarah
The Guest List. Foley, Lucy

Guhrke, Laura Lee
Governess Gone Rogue
How to Lose a Duke in Ten Days
The Trouble with True Love
The Truth About Love and Dukes
When the Marquess Met His Match
The Guide. Heller, Peter
A Guide to the Birds of East Africa. Drayson, Nicholas
Guido Brunetti mysteries [Series]. Leon, Donna

Guillory, Jasmine
Party of Two
The Proposal
Royal Holiday
★*The Wedding Date*
The Wedding Party
★*While We Were Dating*
Guilt. Lescroart, John T.

GUILT
Ganshert, Katie. *Life After*
Gerritsen, Tess. ★*The Shape of Night: A Novel*
Grass, Gunter. *Crabwalk*
Harper, Jane. *The Survivors*
Kafka, Franz. ★*The Trial*
Kay, Guy Gavriel. *Tigana*
Lescroart, John T. *Guilt*
McEwan, Ian. *The Child in Time*
Murdoch, Iris. *The Book and the Brotherhood*
North, Claire. *The Pursuit of William Abbey*
Paris, B. A. *The Breakdown*
Paris, B. A. ★*The Dilemma*
Perry, Sarah. *Melmoth: A Novel*
Pintoff, Stefanie. *Hostage Taker: A Novel*
Ramsay, Hope. *Summer on Moonlight Bay*
Rushdie, Salman. *Shalimar the Clown: A Novel*
Schanbacher, Gary Lester. *Crossing Purgatory*
Shepard, Jim. *Phase Six*
Sundstol, Vidar. *The Land of Dreams*
Svevo, Italo. *Zeno's Conscience*
Updike, John. *The Widows of Eastwick*

GUILT (LAW)
Burnet, Graeme Macrae. *His Bloody Project: Documents Relating to the Case of Roderick Macrae*
Guilt at the Garage. Brett, Simon

GUILT IN MEN
Amis, Martin. ★*Time's Arrow, or the Nature of the Offense*

Auster, Paul. *Sunset Park*

Banville, John. *The Book of Evidence*

Bohjalian, Chris. *Secrets of Eden: A Novel*

Dostoyevsky, Fyodor. ★*Crime and Punishment*

Flanagan, Richard. ★*The Narrow Road to the Deep North*

Foer, Jonathan Safran. *Everything Is Illuminated: A Novel*

Murdoch, Iris. *The Green Knight*

Okuizumi, Hikaru. *The Stones Cry Out*

Petterson, Per. *I Curse the River of Time*

Picoult, Jodi. *The Storyteller*

Prcic, Ismet. *Shards: A Novel*

Schlink, Bernhard. *Self's Punishment*

Singer, Isaac Bashevis. *Enemies, a Love Story*

Spencer, Scott. *Man in the Woods*

Strout, Elizabeth. ★*The Burgess Boys: A Novel*

Tartt, Donna. ★*The Secret History*

GUILT IN WOMEN

Hardy, Thomas. ★*Tess of the D'urbervilles: A Pure Woman Faithfully Presented*

McEwan, Ian. ★*Atonement: A Novel*

Spencer, Sally. *A Walk with the Dead*

Guilty Minds. Finder, Joseph

Guilty Not Guilty. Francis, Felix

Guinn, Matthew

The Scribe: A Novel

GULF COAST, FLORIDA

White, Randy Wayne. *Salt River*

GULF COAST, MISSISSIPPI

Barthelme, Frederick. *Elroy Nights*

Ward, Jesmyn. ★*Sing, Unburied, Sing*

GULF OF MEXICO

Cussler, Clive. ★*Sea of Greed: A Novel from the Numa Files*

★*Gulliver's* Travels. Swift, Jonathan

GUN CONTROL

Patterson, Richard North. *Balance of Power*

Gun Dealers' Daughter: A Novel. Apostol, Gina

★*Gun* Island. Ghosh, Amitav

Gun Love. Clement, Jennifer

GUN SMUGGLERS

Greene, Graham. *The Captain and the Enemy*

Leonard, Elmore. *Rum Punch*

Gunaratne, Guy

In Our Mad and Furious City

★*The* **Guncle:** *a Novel*. Rowley, Steven

Gundar-Goshen, Ayelet

Waking Lions

Gunday, Hakan

The Few

Gunesekera, Romesh

★*Suncatcher: A Novel*

GUNFIGHTERS

Brand, Max. *Max Brand's Best Western Stories*

Brooks, Bill. *Blood Storm*

deWitt, Patrick. *The Sisters Brothers: A Novel*

Dexter, Pete. ★*Deadwood*

Grey, Zane. ★*Riders of the Purple Sage*

Knott, Robert. *Robert B. Parker's Buckskin*

Parker, Robert B. *Blue-Eyed Devil*

Russell, Mary Doria. *Epitaph: A Novel of the O.K. Corral*

Schaefer, Jack. ★*Shane*

Swarthout, Glendon. ★*The Shootist*

GUNFIGHTS

Kelton, Elmer. *Hard Ride*

Russell, Mary Doria. *Epitaph: A Novel of the O.K. Corral*

Swinson, Kiki. *A Gangster and a Gentleman*

Gunn, James E.

Transcendental

Gunning, Sally

Painting the Light

GUNS

Clement, Jennifer. *Gun Love*

Hunter, Stephen. *Game of Snipers: A Bob Lee Swagger Novel*

GUNSHOT VICTIMS

Christie, Agatha. ★*The Murder at the Vicarage*

Christie, Agatha. *A Murder Is Announced: A Miss Marple Mystery*

Faye, Lyndsay. ★*The Paragon Hotel*

Petrie, Nicholas. *The Breaker*

Rader-Day, Lori. *The Black Hour*

Rinehart, Mary Roberts. *Miss Pinkerton*

Roberts, Nora. *Shelter in Place*

Sjowall, Maj. ★*The Laughing Policeman*

Smith, Mark Haskell. *Baked*

GUNSHOT WOUNDS

Larsson, Stieg. ★*The Girl Who Kicked the Hornet's Nest*

Rosenfelt, David. *Blackout*

Gurganus, Allan

★*Local Souls: Novellas*

Oldest Living Confederate Widow Tells All

The Practical Heart: Four Novellas

White People: Stories and Novellas

GURUS

Allio, Kirstin. *Buddhism for Western Children: A Novel*

Gus Murphy novels [Series]. Coleman, Reed Farrel

Guskin, Sharon

The Forgetting Time

Gustine, Amy

You Should Pity Us Instead: Stories

Guterson, David

The Other

Our Lady of the Forest

★*Snow Falling on Cedars*

Guthrie, A. B.

★*The Big Sky*

The **Guts**. Doyle, Roddy

Gutter. K'wan

Gyasi, Yaa

★*Homegoing: A Novel*

★*Transcendent Kingdom*

GYMNASTICS

Abbott, Megan E. *You Will Know Me: A Novel*

GYMNASTS

Abbott, Megan E. *You Will Know Me: A Novel*

H

HABER, FRITZ
Gay, Roxane. ★*Ayiti*
Labatut, Benjamin. *When We Cease to Understand the World*
HABSBURG, HOUSE OF
Phillips, Christi. *The Rossetti Letter: A Novel*
Hacked: a Tucker Mystery. Daniel, Ray
HACKERS
Daniel, Ray. *Hacked: A Tucker Mystery*
Doctorow, Cory. *Radicalized*
Evanovich, Janet. ★*Game On: Tempting Twenty-Eight*
Forsyth, Frederick. *The Fox*
Gibson, William. ★*Neuromancer*
Gibson, William. *Pattern Recognition*
Hossain, Saad Z. *Cyber Mage: A Novel*
Lagercrantz, David. *The Girl Who Lived Twice: A Lisbeth Salander Novel*
Lagercrantz, David. *The Girl Who Takes an Eye for an Eye*
Mankell, Henning. *Firewall*
Schlink, Bernhard. *Self's Punishment*
Stephenson, Neal. ★*Snow Crash*
Tata, A. J. *Dark Winter*
Wilson, G. Willow. *Alif the Unseen*
HACKING
Doctorow, Cory. *Radicalized*
Shepard, Sara. ★*Reputation*
Yoon, David. *Version Zero*
Hackwith, A. J.
The Library of the Unwritten
Haddam, Jane
Cheating at Solitaire: A Gregor Demarkian Novel
Hardscrabble Road
Haddon, Mark
★*The Curious Incident of the Dog in the Night-Time: A Novel*
Hades, Argentina. Loedel, Daniel
Hadley, Tessa
Bad Dreams and Other Stories
Clever Girl
The Past
HADRIAN, EMPEROR OF ROME, 76-138
Raimondo, Lynne. *Dante's Poison: A Mark Angelotti Novel*
Yourcenar, Marguerite. ★*Memoirs of Hadrian: And Reflections on the Composition of Memoirs of Hadrian*
Hadriana in All My Dreams. Depestre, Rene
Hagberg, David
Gambit
Hage, Rawi
Beirut Hellfire Society: A Novel
De Niro's Game
Hahn, Sumi
The Mermaid from Jeju: A Novel
Haig, Francesca
The Fire Sermon: A Novel
Haig, Matt
The Humans: A Novel
The Midnight Library

Haigh, Jennifer
Baker Towers: A Novel
Mrs. Kimble: A Novel
HAIGHT-ASHBURY DISTRICT, SAN FRANCISCO, CALIFORNIA
Crumley, James. *The Last Good Kiss: A Novel*
Hainish series [Series]. Le Guin, Ursula K.
HAIR
Beaton, M. C. *Agatha Raisin and the Witch of Wyckhadden*
HAIRDRESSERS
Cleage, Pearl. *What Looks Like Crazy on an Ordinary Day: A Novel*
Hairpin Bridge. Adams, Taylor
Hairston, Andrea
Master of Poisons
HAITI
Chancy, Myriam J. A. ★*What Storm, What Thunder*
Danticat, Edwidge. *Claire of the Sea Light*
Danticat, Edwidge. *The Dew Breaker*
Danticat, Edwidge. ★*Everything Inside: Stories*
Danticat, Edwidge. ★*Krik? Krak!*
Depestre, Rene. *Hadriana in All My Dreams*
Gay, Roxane. ★*An Untamed State*
Miller, Xander. *Zo: A Novel*
Woods, Rita. ★*Remembrance*
HAITI EARTHQUAKE, HAITI, 2010
Chancy, Myriam J. A. ★*What Storm, What Thunder*
Miller, Xander. *Zo: A Novel*
HAITIAN AMERICAN FAMILIES
Tyree, Omar. *Leslie: A Novel*
HAITIAN AMERICANS
Danticat, Edwidge. *The Dew Breaker*
HAITIAN AMERICANS — SOCIAL LIFE AND CUSTOMS
Danticat, Edwidge. ★*Krik? Krak!*
Hajdu, David
Adrianne Geffel: A Fiction
Haldane, Sean
The Devil's Making
Haldeman, Joe W.
★*The Forever War*
Hale, Shannon
Austenland: A Novel
Half Life. Cantor, Jillian
★*Half Moon Bay: A Novel*. Kellerman, Jonathan
Half of a Yellow Sun. Adichie, Chimamanda Ngozi
Half-Blood Blues. Edugyan, Esi
HALF-BROTHERS
Beverley, Jo. *Tempting Fortune*
Nabokov, Vladimir Vladimirovich. *Novels and Memoirs, 1941-51*
HALF-HUMAN HYBRIDS
French, Jonathan. *The Free Bastards*
French, Jonathan. ★*The Grey Bastards*
French, Jonathan. *The True Bastards*
Rushdie, Salman. *Two Years Eight Months and Twenty-Eight Nights: A Novel*
The Half-Made World. Gilman, Felix
Half-Made world novels [Series]. Gilman, Felix
Half-Past Dawn. Doetsch, Richard

HALF-SISTERS
    Bloom, Amy. *Lucky Us: A Novel*
    Elliott, Lexie. *The Missing Years*
    Gyasi, Yaa. ★*Homegoing: A Novel*
    Tan, Amy. *The Hundred Secret Senses*
Halfon, Eduardo
    Mourning
*The **Hall** of Singing Caryatids*. Pelevin, Viktor
Hall, Adam
    The Quiller Memorandum
Hall, Alexis
    ★*Boyfriend Material*
    For Real
    Rosaline Palmer Takes the Cake
Hall, Araminta
    Imperfect Women: A Novel
Hall, Louisa
    Speak
Hall, Parnell
    Lights! Camera! Puzzles!
Hall, Rachel Howzell
    And Now She's Gone
    These Toxic Things
Hall, Steven
    Maxwell's Demon
Hall, Tarquin
    The Case of the Deadly Butter Chicken: A Vish Puri Mystery
    *The Case of the Love Commandos: From the Files of Vish Puri,
        India's Most Private Investigator*
Hallberg, Garth Risk
    ★*City on Fire*
HALLER, MICKEY (FICTITIOUS CHARACTER)
    Connelly, Michael. *The Lincoln Lawyer: A Novel*
Halliday, Lisa
    ★*Asymmetry*
Hallinan, Timothy
    Fields Where They Lay
    Fools' River
HALLOWEEN
    Childs, Laura. *Haunted Hibiscus*
    McKevett, G. A. *Murder in the Corn Maze*
Halls, Stacey
    The Lost Orphan
HALLUCINATIONS AND ILLUSIONS
    Burns, Charles. ★*Black Hole*
    Burroughs, William S. ★*Naked Lunch: The Restored Text*
    Fowles, John. *The Magus*
    Jayatissa, Amanda. ★*My Sweet Girl*
    Mieville, China. ★*The City & The City*
HALLUCINOGENIC DRUGS
    Boyle, T. Coraghessan. *Outside Looking In: A Novel*
Halsey Street. Coster, Naima
Hambly, Barbara
    House of the Patriarch
    Lady of Perdition
    Scandal in Babylon
Hamer, Kate
    The Girl in the Red Coat

Hamid, Mohsin
    ★*Exit West: A Novel*
Hamill, Pete
    Forever
Hamill, Shaun
    A Cosmology of Monsters
*The **Hamilton** Affair*. Cobbs Hoffman, Elizabeth
HAMILTON, ALEXANDER
    Cobbs Hoffman, Elizabeth. *The Hamilton Affair*
    Kerr, Philip. ★*Prussian Blue*
Hamilton, Jane
    A Map of the World
Hamilton, Karen
    The Last Wife
Hamilton, Peter F.
    The Dreaming Void
    Great North Road
    Pandora's Star
Hamilton, Steve
    ★*The Lock Artist*
    The Second Life of Nick Mason: A Novel
Hamish Macbeth mysteries [Series]. Beaton, M. C.
*The **Hamlet***. Faulkner, William
Hammad, Isabella
    ★*The Parisian, Or, Al-Barisi: A Novel*
Hammer to Fall. Lawton, John
HAMMER, MIKE (FICTITIOUS CHARACTER)
    Spillane, Mickey. *A Long Time Dead: A Mike Hammer Casebook*
Hammett, Dashiell
    The Glass Key
    ★*The Maltese Falcon*
    ★*The Thin Man*
Hamnet. O'Farrell, Maggie
HAMPEL, OTTO HERMANN
    Fallada, Hans. *Every Man Dies Alone*
    Pratchett, Terry. *Monstrous Regiment*
Hampton, Brenda
    Stalker
HAMPTONS, NEW YORK
    Bushnell, Candace. *Is There Still Sex in the City?*
Hamya, Jo
    Three Rooms
Han, Kang
    ★*Human Acts: A Novel*
    The White Book
HAN, KANG
    Chen, Qiufan. *Waste Tide*
    Han, Kang. *The White Book*
Hana Khan Carries On. Jalaluddin, Uzma
*The **Hand** That First Held Mine: A Novel*. O'Farrell, Maggie
Hand, Elizabeth
    Available Dark: A Thriller
    The Book of Lamps and Banners: A Novel
    Curious Toys
    ★*Generation Loss: A Novel*
    Hard Light
HANDICRAFT SHOPS
    Malpas, Jodi Ellen. *Leave Me Breathless*

Handke, Peter
  Don Juan: His Own Version
Handle with Care. Hunting, Helena
★*The Handmaid's Tale*. Atwood, Margaret
Handmaid's tale [Series]. Atwood, Margaret
Hang the Moon. Bellefleur, Alexandria
★*A Hanging at Dawn*. Todd, Charles
The Hanging Garden: An Inspector Rebus Novel. Rankin, Ian
The Hanging Girl. Adler-Olsen, Jussi
Hanging Hill. Hayder, Mo
Hangman's daughter tales [Series]. Potzsch, Oliver
The Hangman's Daughter: A Historical Novel. Potzsch, Oliver
Hangman's Holiday. Sayers, Dorothy L.
The Hangman's Secret. Rowland, Laura Joh
Hankin, Laura
  Happy & You Know It
Hannah Swensen mysteries [Series]. Fluke, Joanne
★*Hannah's War*. Eliasberg, Jan
Hannah, Kristin
  The Great Alone
  Home Front
  The Nightingale
Hannah, Sophie
  Keep Her Safe
  The Killings at Kingfisher Hill
  The Mystery of Three Quarters: The New Hercule Poirot Mystery
  Perfect Little Children
Hannaham, James
  ★*Delicious Foods*
Hannibal. Harris, Thomas
Hannibal Lecter novels [Series]. Harris, Thomas
Hannibal Rising. Harris, Thomas
Hansen, Ron
  ★*The Assassination of Jesse James by the Coward Robert Ford*
  Mariette in Ecstasy
Hanson, Hart
  The Driver
Hanta Yo. Hill, Ruth Beebe
HANUKKAH
  Meltzer, Jean. ★*The Matzah Ball*
Hao, Jingfang
  Vagabonds: A Novel
Hap Collins and Leonard Pine novels [Series]. Lansdale, Joe R.
Happily ever after (Jenn McKinlay) [Series]. McKinlay, Jenn
Happily ever afters (Eloisa James) [Series]. James, Eloisa
HAPPINESS
  Alexis, Andre. *Fifteen Dogs*
  Le Guin, Ursula K. *The Beginning Place*
  Romano-Lax, Andromeda. *The Spanish Bow*
  Voltaire. *Candide and Other Stories*
  Wallace, David Foster. ★*The Pale King: An Unfinished Novel*
  Williams, Katie. *Tell the Machine Goodnight*
HAPPINESS IN TEENAGE BOYS
  Barzak, Christopher. *One for Sorrow*
HAPPINESS IN WOMEN
  Bennett, Alan. ★*The Uncommon Reader*
Happy & You Know It. Hankin, Laura
Happy All the Time: A Novel. Colwin, Laurie

★*The Happy Ever After Playlist*. Jimenez, Abby
Haque family trilogy [Series]. Anam, Tahmima
HARASSMENT
  Hazelwood, Ali. *The Love Hypothesis*
Haratischvili, Nino
  The Eighth Life: (For Brilka)
Harbinder Kaur novels : [Series]. Griffiths, Elly
Harbison, Beth
  The Cookbook Club
HARBORS
  Barbash, Tom. *The Last Good Chance*
Hard Cash Valley. Panowich, Brian
Hard Light. Hand, Elizabeth
Hard Magic. Gilman, Laura Anne
Hard Ride. Kelton, Elmer
HARD SCIENCE FICTION
  Asimov, Isaac. ★*Foundation*
  Asimov, Isaac. *Foundation and Empire*
  Asimov, Isaac. ★*I, Robot*
  Asimov, Isaac. *Second Foundation*
  Banks, Iain. *Consider Phlebas*
  Banks, Iain. *The Hydrogen Sonata*
  Banks, Iain. *Matter*
  Banks, Iain. *The Player of Games*
  Banks, Iain. *Use of Weapons*
  Bear, Greg. *Anvil of Stars*
  Bear, Greg. *The Forge of God*
  Brin, David. *Existence*
  Burke, Sue. *Semiosis*
  Butler, Octavia E. *Adulthood Rites*
  Butler, Octavia E. ★*Dawn: Xenogenesis*
  Cambias, James L. *A Darkling Sea*
  Card, Orson Scott. ★*Ender's Game*
  Chambers, Becky. *To Be Taught, If Fortunate*
  Chiang, Ted. ★*Exhalation: Stories*
  Chiang, Ted. ★*Stories of Your Life and Others*
  Clarke, Arthur C. ★*2001: A Space Odyssey*
  Clarke, Arthur C. ★*Childhood's End*
  Clarke, Arthur C. *Rendezvous with Rama*
  Egan, Greg. *Perihelion Summer*
  Egan, Greg. *Phoresis*
  Egan, Greg. *Schild's Ladder*
  Flynn, Michael. *Eifelheim*
  Gunn, James E. *Transcendental*
  Haldeman, Joe W. ★*The Forever War*
  Heinlein, Robert A. *The Moon Is a Harsh Mistress*
  Higgins, C. A. *Lightless*
  Kress, Nancy. *Beggars in Spain*
  Kress, Nancy. *If Tomorrow Comes*
  Kress, Nancy. *Tomorrow's Kin*
  Lem, Stanislaw. *His Master's Voice*
  Lem, Stanislaw. ★*Solaris*
  Liu, Cixin. ★*The Dark Forest*
  Liu, Cixin. ★*Death's End*
  Liu, Cixin. ★*The Three-Body Problem*
  McDevitt, Jack. *The Engines of God*
  Newitz, Annalee. *Autonomous*
  Palmer, Dexter Clarence. *Version Control*

Rajaniemi, Hannu. *The Fractal Prince*
Rajaniemi, Hannu. *The Quantum Thief*
Reynolds, Alastair. *Revelation Space*
Robinson, Kim Stanley. *Aurora*
Robinson, Kim Stanley. ★*Blue Mars*
Robinson, Kim Stanley. ★*Green Mars*
Robinson, Kim Stanley. *The Martians*
Robinson, Kim Stanley. ★*The Ministry for the Future*
Robinson, Kim Stanley. *New York 2140*
Robinson, Kim Stanley. ★*Red Mars*
Sagan, Carl. *Contact: A Novel*
Stephenson, Neal. *Anathem*
Stephenson, Neal. ★*Cryptonomicon*
Stephenson, Neal. *The Diamond Age,: Or, a Young Lady's Illustrated Primer*
Stephenson, Neal. *Seveneves*
Stivers, Carole. *The Mother Code*
Stross, Charles. *Accelerando*
Vinge, Vernor. *The Children of the Sky*
Vinge, Vernor. *A Fire Upon the Deep*
Weir, Andy. *Artemis*
Weir, Andy. *The Martian*
Weir, Andy. *Project Hail Mary*
The **Hard** Way. Child, Lee

HARDBOILED FICTION

Berkowitz, Ira. *Old Flame: A Jackson Steeg Novel*
Block, Lawrence. *All the Flowers Are Dying*
Block, Lawrence. *A Drop of the Hard Stuff: A Matthew Scudder Novel*
Block, Lawrence. *Eight Million Ways to Die*
Block, Lawrence. *The Sins of the Fathers*
Block, Lawrence. *A Ticket to the Boneyard: A Matthew Scudder Novel*
Block, Lawrence. ★*When the Sacred Ginmill Closes*
Brandt, Harry. *The Whites: A Novel*
Bruen, Ken. *Galway Girl: A Jack Taylor Novel*
Bruen, Ken. *The Guards*
Burke, James Lee. *Black Cherry Blues*
Burke, James Lee. ★*The New Iberia Blues*
Burke, James Lee. ★*A Private Cathedral*
Burke, James Lee. *Robicheaux*
Chabon, Michael. *The Yiddish Policemen's Union*
Chandler, Raymond. ★*The Big Sleep*
Chandler, Raymond. *The Lady in the Lake*
Chandler, Raymond. *The Long Goodbye*
Coben, Harlan. *Long Lost*
Coleman, Reed Farrel. *Where It Hurts: A Gus Murphy Novel*
Copenhaver, John. *The Savage Kind*
Crais, Robert. *A Dangerous Man*
Crais, Robert. *The First Rule*
Crumley, James. *The Last Good Kiss: A Novel*
Crumley, James. ★*The Wrong Case*
Davys, Tim. *Amberville*
De Giovanni, Maurizio. *The Crocodile*
Ellroy, James. ★*Widespread Panic: A Novel*
Estleman, Loren D. ★*Amos Walker: The Complete Story Collection*
Estleman, Loren D. *Infernal Angels*
Estleman, Loren D. *A Smile on the Face of the Tiger*

Finlay, Mick. *The Murder Pit*
Garcia-Roza, L. A. *Alone in the Crowd: An Inspector Espinosa Mystery*
Garcia-Roza, L. A. *December Heat*
Goldman, Matt. *Dead West*
Goldman, Matt. *The Shallows*
Gran, Sara. *Claire Dewitt and the City of the Dead*
Gran, Sara. *The Infinite Blacktop: A Novel*
Hammett, Dashiell. *The Glass Key*
Hammett, Dashiell. ★*The Maltese Falcon*
Hanson, Hart. *The Driver*
Harvey, Michael T. *The Chicago Way*
Harvey, Michael T. *The Fifth Floor*
Harvey, Michael T. *The Governor's Wife*
Harvey, Michael T. *We All Fall Down*
Jones, Stephen Mack. *Dead of Winter*
Kaminsky, Stuart M. *Dancing in the Dark*
Kaminsky, Stuart M. *Murder on the Trans-Siberian Express*
Kaminsky, Stuart M. *To Catch a Spy: A Toby Peters Mystery*
Kerr, Philip. ★*Greeks Bearing Gifts: A Bernie Gunther Novel*
Kerr, Philip. ★*Metropolis: A Bernie Gunther Novel*
Kerr, Philip. ★*Prussian Blue*
Lethem, Jonathan. ★*Motherless Brooklyn*
Mieville, China. ★*The City & The City*
Mosley, Walter. *Trouble Is What I Do: A Leonid McGill Mystery*
Muller, Marcia. *Dead Midnight*
Muller, Marcia. *Ice and Stone*
Osborne, Lawrence. *Only to Sleep: A Philip Marlowe Novel*
Parker, Robert B. *Death in Paradise*
Parker, Robert B. *Night Passage*
Parker, Robert B. *Painted Ladies*
Parker, Robert B. *Sixkill*
Parker, Robert B. *Trouble in Paradise*
Pelecanos, George P. *The Big Blowdown*
Pelecanos, George P. *The Cut: A Novel*
Pronzini, Bill. *Crazybone*
Pronzini, Bill. *Fever*
Pronzini, Bill. *Hardcase*
Pronzini, Bill. *Hellbox*
Pronzini, Bill. *Illusions*
Pronzini, Bill. *Mourners*
Pronzini, Bill. *Nemesis*
Pronzini, Bill. *Savages*
Pronzini, Bill. *Spook*
Sears, Michael. *Tower of Babel*
Shannon, Dell. ★*Chaos of Crime*
Smith, Ian. *Wolf Point*
Spiegelman, Peter. *Black Maps*
Spillane, Mickey. *The Consummata*
Spillane, Mickey. *The Goliath Bone*
Spillane, Mickey. *Kill Me, Darling*
Spillane, Mickey. *A Long Time Dead: A Mike Hammer Casebook*
Tracy, P. J. ★*Deep into the Dark*
Hardcase. Pronzini, Bill
The **Harder** They Come. Boyle, T. Coraghessan
Hardiman, Rebecca
Good Eggs

Harding Thornton, Christina
   Pickard County Atlas
Harding, Lisa
   Bright Burning Things
Harding, Paul
   Tinkers
Hardscrabble Road. Haddam, Jane
Hardy, Thomas
   ★*Far from the Madding Crowd*
   ★*Jude the Obscure*
   ★*The Return of the Native*
   ★*Tess of the D'urbervilles: A Pure Woman Faithfully Presented*
HAREMS
   Chase, Loretta Lynda. *Don't Tempt Me*
HARER, ETHIOPIA
   Gibb, Camilla. *Sweetness in the Belly*
Hargrave, Kiran Millwood
   The Mercies: A Novel
HARGREAVES, ALICE PLEASANCE LIDDELL
   Benjamin, Melanie. *Alice I Have Been*
   Tolkien, J. R. R. ★*The Lord of the Rings*
Harkaway, Nick
   Angelmaker
   Gnomon: A Novel
   The Gone-Away World
   Tigerman
Harkness, Deborah E.
   The Book of Life
   A Discovery of Witches: A Novel
   Shadow of Night
   Time's Convert
   The World of All Souls: The Complete Guide to a Discovery of Witches, Shadow of Night, and the Book
HARLAN COUNTY, KENTUCKY
   Leonard, Elmore. ★*Raylan*
HARLEM RENAISSANCE
   Reed, Ishmael. ★*Mumbo Jumbo*
★*Harlem* Shuffle. Whitehead, Colson
HARLEM, NEW YORK CITY
   Alderson, Kaia. *Sisters in Arms*
   Baldwin, James. ★*Go Tell It on the Mountain*
   Baldwin, James. ★*If Beale Street Could Talk*
   Baldwin, James. *Tell Me How Long the Train's Been Gone: A Novel*
   Cassara, Joseph. *The House of Impossible Beauties*
   Ellison, Ralph. ★*Invisible Man*
   Hill, Donna. ★*Confessions in B-Flat*
   Hughes, Langston. ★*Short Stories*
   Johnson, Alaya Dawn. *Trouble the Saints*
   K'wan. *Animal*
   K'wan. *Animal II: The Omen*
   K'wan. *The Fix*
   K'wan. *Gutter*
   K'wan. *Hoodlum*
   K'wan. *Revelations*
   K'wan. *Street Dreams*
   Larsen, Nella. *Passing*
   Miller, Karen E. Quinones. *An Angry-Ass Black Woman*
   Morrison, Toni. *Jazz*

   Petry, Ann. ★*The Street*
   Phillips, Caryl. *Dancing in the Dark*
   Reed, Ishmael. ★*Mumbo Jumbo*
   Roth, Henry. *Requiem for Harlem*
   Roth, Henry. *A Star Shines Over Mt. Morris Park*
   Sapphire. ★*The Kid: A Novel*
   Whitehead, Colson. ★*Harlem Shuffle*
Harm Done. Rendell, Ruth
Harman, Patricia
   The Midwife of Hope River: A Novel
Harmel, Kristin
   The Room on Rue Amelie
Harmon, Amy
   Where the Lost Wander
HARNACK-FISH, MILDRED
   Chiaverini, Jennifer. *Resistance Women: A Novel*
   Lalli, Sonya. *The Matchmaker's List*
Haroun and the Sea of Stories. Rushdie, Salman
Harper McClain novels [Series]. Daugherty, Christi
HARPER'S FERRY, WEST VIRGINIA
   McBride, James. ★*The Good Lord Bird*
Harper, Jane
   The Dry
   The Lost Man
   The Survivors
Harper, Karen
   The Queen's Secret: A Novel of England's World War II Queen
The **Harpy**. Hunter, Megan
Harrigan, Stephen
   The Leopard Is Loose: A Novel
Harrington, Anna
   An Extraordinary Lord
   An Inconvenient Duke
Harris, C. S.
   Good Time Coming
   What the Devil Knows: A Sebastian St. Cyr Mystery
Harris, E. Lynn
   Basketball Jones: A Novel
   I Say a Little Prayer: A Novel
   Invisible Life: A Novel
   Not a Day Goes By: A Novel
Harris, Joanne
   ★*Chocolat: A Novel*
Harris, Nathan
   The Sweetness of Water
Harris, Oliver
   A Shadow Intelligence
Harris, Robert
   Archangel: A Novel
   Enigma
   ★*Fatherland*
   The Ghost: A Novel
   An Officer and a Spy
   Pompeii: A Novel
   The Second Sleep: A Novel
Harris, Sarah J.
   The Color of Bee Larkham's Murder: A Novel

Harris, Thomas
Hannibal
Hannibal Rising
Red Dragon
★*The Silence of the Lambs*
Harris, Zakiya Dalila
The Other Black Girl: A Novel
Harrison, Cora
Beyond Absolution: A Mystery Set in 1920s Ireland
Harrison, Jamie
The Center of Everything: A Novel
Harrison, Jim
The Great Leader
Harrison, M. John
Light
Nova Swing
Harrison, Mette Ivie
The Bishop's Wife
The Prodigal Daughter
Harrison, Nicola
Montauk
Harrison, Rachel
The Return
Harrison, Thea
Dragon Bound
Harrod-Eagles, Cynthia
Cruel as the Grave
Headlong
Old Bones
Harrow. Williams, Joy
Harrow the Ninth. Muir, Tamsyn
Harry Barnett series [Series]. Goddard, Robert
Harry Bosch mysteries [Series]. Connelly, Michael
Hart, Carolyn G.
Ghost Blows a Kiss
Letter from Home
Hart, Elsa
The Cabinets of Barnaby Mayne
City of Ink: A Mystery
Hart, Erin
The Book of Killowen
Haunted Ground: A Crime Novel
Hart, John
Down River
Iron House
The King of Lies
The Last Child
Redemption Road
The Unwilling
Hart, Josephine
Damage: A Novel
Hart, Rob
The Warehouse: A Novel
Harte Family [Series]. Bradford, Barbara Taylor
Harte, Bret
★*The Best Short Stories of Bret Harte*
Haruf, Kent
Benediction

Eventide
★*Our Souls at Night*
★*Plainsong*
Harvard Square. Aciman, Andre
Harvest. Crace, Jim
Harvey, John
Cold in Hand
A Darker Shade of Blue: Stories
Darkness, Darkness
Harvey, Michael T.
Brighton
The Chicago Way
The Fifth Floor
The Governor's Wife
Pulse
We All Fall Down
Hashemzadeh Bonde, Golnaz
What We Owe
HASIDIM
Potok, Chaim. ★*The Gift of Asher Lev*
HASIDISM
Goldbloom, Goldie. *On Division*
HASKELL, KATHARINE WRIGHT
Dann, Patty. *The Wright Sister*
Gardner, Lisa. ★*Before She Disappeared: A Novel*
Haslett, Adam
★*Imagine Me Gone: A Novel*
Union Atlantic
Hassib, Rajia
A Pure Heart: A Novel
Hatcher, Robin Lee
Cross My Heart
Who I Am with You
HATE
Barry, Dave. *Lunatics*
HATE CRIMES
Atkins, Ace. *The Forsaken*
Campbell, Bebe Moore. *Your Blues Ain't Like Mine*
Deaver, Jeffery. ★*The Goodbye Man*
Jackson-Brown, Angela. ★*When Stars Rain Down: A Novel*
Jalaluddin, Uzma. *Hana Khan Carries On*
Mullen, Thomas. *Lightning Men: A Novel*
Shames, Terry. ★*An Unsettling Crime for Samuel Craddock*
Siger, Jeffrey. *Target Tinos: An Inspector Kaldis Mystery*
Winer, Jeanne. *Her Kind of Case*
HATE GROUPS
Iles, Greg. *Mississippi Blood: A Novel*
Mullen, Thomas. *Lightning Men: A Novel*
Roy, Lori. ★*Gone Too Long: A Novel*
The **Hate** *Project*. Ripper, Kris
Hateship, Friendship, Courtship, Loveship, Marriage: Stories. Munro, Alice
Hauck, Rachel
How to Catch a Prince
Once Upon a Prince
The Wedding Chapel
Haunted Ground: A Crime Novel. Hart, Erin
Haunted Hibiscus. Childs, Laura

HAUNTED HOTELS
King, Stephen. ★*The Shining*
HAUNTED HOUSES
Deveraux, Jude. *Someone to Love*
Gerritsen, Tess. ★*The Shape of Night: A Novel*
Hawthorne, Nathaniel. ★*The House of the Seven Gables*
Jackson, Shirley. ★*The Haunting of Hill House*
Purcell, Laura. *The Silent Companions: A Ghost Story*
Pyper, Andrew. *The Residence: A Novel*
Straub, Peter. *Lost Boy Lost Girl: A Novel*
HAUNTED PLACES
Erdrich, Louise. ★*The Sentence*
St. James, Simone. *The Haunting of Maddy Clare*
The **Haunting** at Bonaventure Circus. Wright, Jaime Jo
★*The **Haunting** of Hill House*. Jackson, Shirley
*The **Haunting** of Maddy Clare*. St. James, Simone
Hausfrau: a Novel. Essbaum, Jill Alexander
Hausmann, Romy
★*Dear Child*
Havana Bay. Smith, Martin Cruz
Havana Storm. Cussler, Clive
HAVANA, CUBA
Cleeton, Chanel. *The Most Beautiful Girl in Cuba*
Cleeton, Chanel. *Next Year in Havana*
Garcia, Cristina. *King of Cuba: A Novel*
Greene, Graham. *Our Man in Havana*
Hemingway, Ernest. *To Have and Have Not*
Smith, Martin Cruz. *Havana Bay*
Have His Carcase. Sayers, Dorothy L.
HAVERS, BARBARA (FICTITIOUS CHARACTER)
George, Elizabeth. *A Banquet of Consequences*
HAWAII
Henson, Pene. *Into the Blue*
MacDonald, John D. *The Turquoise Lament*
Rizzuto, Rahna R. *Shadow Child*
Hawke, Ethan
A Bright Ray of Darkness
Hawkins, Paula
★*The Girl on the Train: A Novel*
Hawkins, Scott
★*The Library at Mount Char*
Hawks, Arlem
Georgana's Secret
Hawley, Noah
Before the Fall
The Good Father
Hawthorne, Nathaniel
★*The House of the Seven Gables*
★*The Scarlet Letter: A Romance*
Hay, Elizabeth
Late Nights on Air
Hayder, Mo
Gone
Hanging Hill
Poppet
Haydon, Elizabeth
The Merchant Emperor

Hayes, Terry
I Am Pilgrim
Haynes, Natalie
A Thousand Ships
Haywood, Gar Anthony
Cemetery Road
Haywood, Sarah
The Cactus
HAZARDOUS WASTE
Schweblin, Samanta. *Fever Dream: A Novel*
HAZARDOUS WASTE SITES
Barbash, Tom. *The Last Good Chance*
Hazelwood High trilogy [Series]. Draper, Sharon M.
Hazelwood, Ali
The Love Hypothesis
HAZING
Muller, Marcia. *Dead Midnight*
Vargas Llosa, Mario. *The Time of the Hero*
Hazzard, Shirley
★*The Great Fire*
★*The Transit of Venus*
He Started It. Downing, Samantha
Heaberlin, Julia
We Are All the Same in the Dark: A Novel
Heacox, Kim
Jimmy Bluefeather: A Novel
HEAD INJURY SURVIVORS
Harrison, Jamie. *The Center of Everything: A Novel*
Head On. Scalzi, John
Headley, Maria Dahvana
The Mere Wife
Headlong. Harrod-Eagles, Cynthia
HEADMASTERS
Jewell, Lisa. *Watching You*
*The **Heads** of Cerberus*. Stevens, Francis
Heads of the Colored People: Stories. Thompson-Spires, Nafissa
HEALERS
Barker, Nicola. *Darkmans*
Rice, Anne. *Christ the Lord: Out of Egypt: A Novel*
Rice, Anne. *Christ the Lord: The Road to Cana: A Novel*
Healey, Emma
★*Elizabeth Is Missing*
Healey, Jane
The Animals at Lockwood Manor
HEALING
Carr, Robyn. *What We Find*
Clegg, Bill. *Did You Ever Have a Family*
Harrison, Jamie. *The Center of Everything: A Novel*
Rice, Luanne. *The Lemon Orchard*
Saberhagen, Fred. *Woundhealer's Story*
HEALTH RESORTS
Greenwood, Kerry. *Death in Daylesford*
Moriarty, Liane. *Nine Perfect Strangers*
Murdoch, Iris. *The Philosopher's Pupil*
Quick, Amanda. ★*The Lady Has a Past*
HEANEY, SEAMUS
Draven, Grace. *Phoenix Unbound*
Youngson, Anne. *Meet Me at the Museum*

HEARN, LAFCADIO

Truong, Monique T. D. *The Sweetest Fruits*

HEART ATTACK

Leon, Donna. *Drawing Conclusions: A Commissario Guido Brunetti Mystery*

★*The Heart Is a Lonely Hunter*. McCullers, Carson

★*Heart of Darkness*. Conrad, Joseph

★*The Heart of the Matter*. Greene, Graham

★*The Heart Principle*. Hoang, Helen

The Heart's Invisible Furies. Boyne, John

Heart-Shaped Box. Hill, Joe

The Heart: a Novel. Kerangal, Maylis de

Heartbreaker Bay novels [Series]. Shalvis, Jill

★*The Hearts of Men*. Butler, Nickolas

Hearts of the Missing. Potenza, Carol

Heartstone [Series]. White, Elle Katharine

★*Heat and Dust*. Jhabvala, Ruth Prawer

Heat Lightning. Sandford, John

The Heat of the Day. Bowen, Elizabeth

HEAT WAVES (METEOROLOGY)

Galligan, John. *Bad Moon Rising*

Shannon, Dell. ★*Chaos of Crime*

Heath, Lorraine

Falling into Bed with a Duke

★*The Heathens*. Atkins, Ace

The Heatwave. Riordan, Kate

HEAVEN

Albom, Mitch. *The Five People You Meet in Heaven*

Albom, Mitch. *The Next Person You Meet in Heaven*

Heaven and Earth. Giordano, Paolo

★*Heaven, My Home*. Locke, Attica

The Heavens. Newman, Sandra

HEBRIDES

May, Peter. *The Blackhouse*

HEDONISM

Kerouac, Jack. *The Dharma Bums*

Weinberg, Kate. *The Truants*

Heechee saga [Series]. Pohl, Frederik

Heger, Amanda

Crazy Cupid Love

Heggen, Thomas

Mister Roberts

Hegi, Ursula

Children and Fire: A Novel

Stones from the River

The Vision of Emma Blau

Heinlein, Robert A.

The Moon Is a Harsh Mistress

★*Starship Troopers*

★*Stranger in a Strange Land*

Heiny, Katherine

★*Early Morning Riser*

The Heir Affair. Cocks, Heather

Heir to the Glimmering World. Ozick, Cynthia

The Heiress Gets a Duke. St. George, Harper

The Heiress Hunt. Shupe, Joanna

The Heirloom Garden. Shipman, Viola

HEIRLOOMS

Bobotis, Andrea. *The Last List of Miss Judith Kratt*

HEIRS AND HEIRESSES

Alexander, Victoria. *The Lady Travelers Guide to Scoundrels and Other Gentlemen*

Andersen, Laura. *The Boleyn Deceit*

Andersen, Laura. ★*The Boleyn King*

Andersen, Laura. *The Boleyn Reckoning*

Balogh, Mary. *Someone to Wed*

Bateman, Kate. *This Earl of Mine*

Bear, Elizabeth. *Shattered Pillars*

Boyle, Elizabeth. *Along Came a Duke*

Burrowes, Grace. *My One and Only Duke*

Castle, Jayne. *Illusion Town*

Chandler, Raymond. ★*The Big Sleep*

Christie, Agatha. *Endless Night*

Collins, Manda. *Ready Set Rogue*

Dare, Tessa. ★*The Duchess Deal*

Dare, Tessa. *When a Scot Ties the Knot*

Dunnett, Dorothy. *Niccolo Rising*

Goodwin, Daisy. *The American Heiress*

Gracie, Anne. *Marry in Scandal*

Guhrke, Laura Lee. *How to Lose a Duke in Ten Days*

Guhrke, Laura Lee. *When the Marquess Met His Match*

Hammett, Dashiell. *The Glass Key*

Hauck, Rachel. *How to Catch a Prince*

Heath, Lorraine. *Falling into Bed with a Duke*

Helprin, Mark. *In Sunlight and in Shadow*

Jackson, Brenda. *Forged in Desire*

James, Henry. *The Portrait of a Lady*

James, Henry. *The Wings of the Dove*

Jordan, Sophie. *The Duke Goes Down*

Kelly, Greta. *The Frozen Crown*

Kwan, Kevin. *China Rich Girlfriend*

McDonald, Ian. *New Moon*

Pirie, David. *The Patient's Eyes*

Pope, Jamie. *One Warm Winter*

Putney, Mary Jo. *Once a Soldier*

Ragan, Theresa. *Buried Deep*

Renault, Mary. *Funeral Games*

Robertson, Michael. *The Baker Street Translation: A Mystery*

Rowland, Laura Joh. *The Iris Fan: A Novel of Feudal Japan*

Rowland, Laura Joh. *The Shogun's Daughter: A Novel of Feudal Japan*

Sanders, Lawrence. *McNally's Puzzle*

Sandford, John. ★*Phantom Prey*

Sandford, John. ★*Silken Prey*

Scott, Walter. *The Bride of Lammermoor*

Simpson, Rosemary. *Let the Dead Keep Their Secrets*

Simpson, Rosemary. ★*What the Dead Leave Behind*

Solomons, Natasha. *House of Gold*

St. George, Harper. *The Heiress Gets a Duke*

Stachniak, Eva. *The Winter Palace: A Novel of Catherine the Great*

Swinson, Kiki. *Lifestyles of the Rich and Shameless*

Tanabe, Karin. *A Hundred Suns*

Tepper, Sheri S. *Singer from the Sea*

Trollope, Anthony. *Doctor Thorne*

Weir, Alison. *Katharine Parr, the Sixth Wife*

HEISENBERG UNCERTAINTY PRINCIPLE
Labatut, Benjamin. *When We Cease to Understand the World*
Helen of Troy. George, Margaret
HELEN OF TROY (GREEK MYTHOLOGY)
George, Margaret. *Helen of Troy*
Heley, Veronica
Murder in Law
HELICOPTER PILOTS
Hannah, Kristin. *Home Front*
HELICOPTERS — ACCIDENTS
Cotterill, Colin. *Slash and Burn: A Dr. Siri Mystery Set in Laos*
HELL
Butler, Robert Olen. *Hell: A Novel*
Hackwith, A. J. *The Library of the Unwritten*
Hell of a Book. Mott, Jason
Hell's belles [Series]. MacLean, Sarah
Hell's Corner. Baldacci, David
Hell's Gate: A Novel. Crompton, Richard
Hell's library novels [Series]. Hackwith, A. J.
Hell: a Novel. Butler, Robert Olen
Hellbox. Pronzini, Bill
Heller, Joseph
★*Catch-22*
Good as Gold
Heller, L. Alison
The Neighbor's Secret
Heller, Peter
Celine: A Novel
★*The Dog Stars: A Novel*
The Guide
The Painter: A Novel
The River: A Novel
Heller, Zoe
What Was She Thinking?: Notes on a Scandal
Hellions of Havisham [Series]. Heath, Lorraine
Hello to the Cannibals: A Novel. Bausch, Richard
★*The Help.* Stockett, Kathryn
Help for the Haunted. Searles, John
HELPFULNESS
Backman, Fredrik. ★*Anxious People: A Novel*
HELPFULNESS IN MEN
Barnett, David. *Calling Major Tom*
Martin, Charles. *The Water Keeper*
Walser, Robert. *The Assistant*
HELPFULNESS IN WOMEN
Green, Amy Lynn. *Things We Didn't Say*
Heyer, Georgette. *The Grand Sophy*
Kerr, Laurel. *Wild on My Mind*
Ross, Ann B. *Miss Julia Knows a Thing or Two*
Shupe, Joanna. *The Rogue of Fifth Avenue*
Wood, Tracey Enerson. *The Engineer's Wife: A Novel*
Helpless: a Novel. Gowdy, Barbara
Helprin, Mark
In Sunlight and in Shadow
Paris in the Present Tense
★*Winter's Tale*
Hemingway, Ernest
★*A Farewell to Arms*

For Whom the Bell Tolls
The Nick Adams Stories
★*The Old Man and the Sea*
The Short Stories
The Snows of Kilimanjaro and Other Stories
★*The Sun Also Rises*
To Have and Have Not
HEMINGWAY, ERNEST
Atkinson, Kate. *One Good Turn: A Novel*
McLain, Paula. *The Paris Wife: A Novel*
Hemmings, Kaui Hart
The Possibilities: A Novel
Hempel, Amy
Sing to It: New Stories
Hench: a Novel. Walschots, Natalie Zina
HENCHMEN
Hoyt, Elizabeth. *When a Rogue Meets His Match*
★*Henderson* the Rain King: A Novel. Bellow, Saul
Henderson, Smith
Fourth of July Creek
Henderson, Susan
The Flicker of Old Dreams
Hendricks, Greer
An Anonymous Girl
★*You Are Not Alone*
Hendrix, Grady
The Final Girl Support Group
My Best Friend's Exorcism
The Southern Book Club's Guide to Slaying Vampires
Henkin, Joshua
Morningside Heights
The Henna Artist. Joshi, Alka
Henna artist [Series]. Joshi, Alka
HENRY
Franklin, Ariana. ★*Death and the Maiden*
Franklin, Ariana. *Mistress of the Art of Death*
Franklin, Ariana. *The Serpent's Tale*
Gregory, Philippa. *The Lady of the Rivers*
Rutherfurd, Edward. *The Princes of Ireland: The Dublin Saga*
Sansom, C. J. ★*Sovereign*
Henry II novels [Series]. Penman, Sharon Kay
Henry Rios mysteries [Series]. Nava, Michael
Henry, Emily
Beach Read
People We Meet on Vacation
Henry, Himself. O'Nan, Stewart
Henry, O.
★*The Complete Works of O. Henry*
O. Henry: 101 Stories
Henry, Patti Callahan
★*Becoming Mrs. Lewis: The Improbable Love Story of Joy Davidman and C. S. Lewis*
Hensher, Philip
Scenes from Early Life: A Novel
Henson, Pene
Into the Blue
Hepworth, Sally
The Secrets of Midwives

Her Body and Other Parties: Stories. Machado, Carmen Maria

Her Every Fear: A Novel. Swanson, Peter

Her Kind of Case. Winer, Jeanne

Her Last Day. Ragan, Theresa

Her Night with the Duke. Quincy, Diana

Her Other Secret. Dimon, HelenKay

Her Sky Cowboy. Ciotta, Beth

Her Three Lives. Holahan, Cate

HERBALISTS

Bohjalian, Chris. *The Night Strangers: A Novel*

Bowen, Rhys. *The Victory Garden*

Hart, Elsa. *The Cabinets of Barnaby Mayne*

O'Farrell, Maggie. *Hamnet*

Herbert, Frank

★*Dune*

Herbert, Julian

Bring Me the Head of Quentin Tarantino: Stories

Hercule Poirot mysteries [Series]. Christie, Agatha

The Herd: a Novel. Bartz, Andrea

Here and Gone. Beck, Haylen

Here and Now and Then. Chen, Mike

Here Be Dragons. Penman, Sharon Kay

Here Comes the Sun. Dennis-Benn, Nicole

Here I Am! Holdstock, Pauline

Here I Am: A Novel. Foer, Jonathan Safran

Here Is the Beehive. Crossan, Sarah

★*Here* We Are. Swift, Graham

HEREDITY

Makumbi, Jennifer Nansubuga. *Kintu*

HERETICS

Harris, Robert. *The Second Sleep: A Novel*

Herland. Gilman, Charlotte Perkins

HERMITS

Owens, Delia. *Where the Crawdads Sing*

Winton, Tim. *The Shepherd's Hut*

A Hero Born: A Novel. Jin, Yong

★*A Hero of France.* Furst, Alan

HEROES AND HEROINES

Auel, Jean M. ★*The Clan of the Cave Bear: A Novel*

Blackmore, R. D. *Lorna Doone: A Romance of Exmoor*

Brennan, Marie. *Driftwood*

Conrad, Joseph. *Nostromo: A Tale of the Seaboard*

Cussler, Clive. *Pacific Vortex!*

Jin, Yong. *A Hero Born: A Novel*

MacLaughlin, Nina. *Wake, Siren: Ovid Resung*

Oyeyemi, Helen. *Mr. Fox*

Pratchett, Terry. *The Last Hero: A Discworld Fable*

Rothfuss, Patrick. ★*The Wise Man's Fear*

Tolkien, J. R. R. *Beren and Luthien*

Tolkien, J. R. R. *The Fellowship of the Ring: Being the First Part of the Lord of the Rings*

Tolkien, J. R. R. *The Return of the King: Being the Third Part of the Lord of the Rings*

Tolkien, J. R. R. *The Two Towers: Being the Second Part of the Lord of the Rings*

Walton, Jo. *Or What You Will*

HEROES AND HEROINES IN MASS MEDIA

Chabon, Michael. *The Amazing Adventures of Kavalier & Clay: A Novel*

HEROES AND HEROINES, ENGLISH

Orczy, Emmuska Orczy. ★*The Scarlet Pimpernel*

HEROES AND HEROINES, GREEK

Haynes, Natalie. *A Thousand Ships*

Renault, Mary. *The Bull from the Sea*

Renault, Mary. *The King Must Die*

HEROES AND HEROINES, NORSE

Gaiman, Neil. ★*Norse Mythology*

Heroes Are My Weakness. Phillips, Susan Elizabeth

HEROIN ADDICTION

Winslow, Don. *The Border*

HEROIN ADDICTS

Welsh, Irvine. *Trainspotting*

HEROIN TRAFFIC

McCarthy, Cormac. ★*No Country for Old Men*

★*The Heron's Cry.* Cleeves, Ann

Heron, Farah

Accidentally Engaged

Herrera, Adriana

★*American Dreamer*

American Fairytale

American Love Story

Herron, Mick

Dolphin Junction: Collected Stories

Hersey, John

★*A Bell for Adano*

Hertmans, Stefan

★*The Convert: A Novel*

HERTMANS, STEFAN

Hertmans, Stefan. ★*The Convert: A Novel*

★*Herzog.* Bellow, Saul

Hesse, Hermann

The Fairy Tales of Hermann Hesse

Narcissus and Goldmund

★*Siddhartha: A New Translation*

★*Steppenwolf*

Hession, Ronan

Leonard and Hungry Paul

Hester Thursby novels [Series]. Hill, Edwin J.

HETEROSEXUAL MEN

Spencer, Scott. *An Ocean Without a Shore*

Hewson, David

The Garden of Angels

The Garden of Evil

A Season for the Dead

Hey There (You with the Gun in Your Hand): A Rat Pack Mystery. Randisi, Robert J.

HEYDRICH, REINHARD

Binet, Laurent. ★*HHhH*

Goddard, Robert. *Never Go Back*

Heyer, Georgette

Black Sheep

The Grand Sophy

These Old Shades

★*HHhH.* Binet, Laurent

★*Hi Five: An IQ Novel*. Ide, Joe
Hiaasen, Carl
  Bad Monkey
  Basket Case
  Lucky You: A Novel
  Nature Girl
  Skin Tight
  Skinny Dip: A Novel
  ★*Squeeze Me: A Novel*
  Star Island
  Strip Tease: A Novel
Hibbert, Talia
  ★*Act Your Age, Eve Brown*
  ★*Get a Life, Chloe Brown*
  A Girl Like Her
  ★*Take a Hint, Dani Brown*
HIBERNATION
  Fforde, Jasper. ★*Early Riser: A Novel*
HICKOK, WILD BILL
  Bellow, Saul. *The Bellarosa Connection*
  Dexter, Pete. ★*Deadwood*
  McMurtry, Larry. *Boone's Lick: A Novel*
  Saint-Exupery, Antoine de. *Night Flight*
Hicks, Robert
  The Widow of the South
Hid from Our Eyes. Spencer-Fleming, Julia
★*The Hidden*. Spencer, Sally
The Hidden Keys. Alexis, Andre
Hidden Moon: An Inspector O Novel. Church, James
★*The Hidden Palace*. Wecker, Helene
Hidden Prey. Sandford, John
The Hidden Things. Mason, Jamie
Hidden Treasure. Cleland, Jane K.
The Hidden: a Novel. Golding, Melanie
Hide Away. Pinter, Jason
HIDING
  Brown, Taylor. *Fallen Land*
  Castillo, Linda. *Outsider*
  Dodd, Christina. *Obsession Falls*
  Foster, Fiona King. *The Captive: A Novel*
  Gnuse, A. J. *Girl in the Walls: A Novel*
  Rosner, Jennifer. ★*The Yellow Bird Sings*
HIDING-PLACES (SECRET CHAMBERS, ETC.)
  Belfoure, Charles. *The Paris Architect: A Novel*
  Finder, Joseph. *The Fixer*
HIERARCHY (SOCIAL SCIENCES)
  Doctorow, Cory. *Walkaway*
★*Hieroglyphics: a Novel*. McCorkle, Jill
Higashino, Keigo
  ★*The Devotion of Suspect X*
  Malice
  The Miracles of the Namiya General Store
  Newcomer
Higgins, C. A.
  Lightless
Higgins, George V.
  The Friends of Eddie Coyle

Higgins, Jack
  Confessional
  The Eagle Has Flown
  The Eagle Has Landed
  Eye of the Storm
  Touch the Devil
Higgins, Kristan
  Always the Last to Know
  ★*The Best Man*
  ★*Life and Other Inconveniences*
  Now That You Mention It
  ★*Pack up the Moon*
High coast novels [Series]. Alsterdal, Tove
*The **High** Divide: A Novel*. Enger, Lin
HIGH FANTASY
  Brooks, Terry. *Child of Light*
  Kelly, Greta. *The Frozen Crown*
  Le Guin, Ursula K. *The Other Wind*
***High** Fidelity*. Hornby, Nick
HIGH SCHOOL GIRLS
  Persson Giolito, Malin. *Quicksand*
HIGH SCHOOL STUDENTS
  Abbott, Megan E. *The Fever*
  Burke, James Lee. *The Jealous Kind*
  Copenhaver, John. *The Savage Kind*
  Coster, Naima. *What's Mine and Yours: A Novel*
  DeWoskin, Rachel. *Big Girl Small: A Novel*
  Galloway, Gregory. *As Simple as Snow*
  King, Stephen. ★*Carrie*
  Lerner, Ben. ★*The Topeka School*
  Maaren, Kari. ★*Weave a Circle Round*
  Natsukawa, Sosuke. *The Cat Who Saved Books*
  Picoult, Jodi. *Nineteen Minutes: A Novel*
  Pinter, Jason. *A Stranger at the Door*
  Rodriques, Elias. *All the Water I've Seen Is Running: A Novel*
  Straub, Peter. ★*A Dark Matter: A Novel*
  Thorpe, Rufi. ★*The Knockout Queen*
HIGH SCHOOL TEACHERS
  DeLuca, Jen. *Well Matched*
  Founds, Kathleen. *When Mystical Creatures Attack!*
  Haruf, Kent. ★*Plainsong*
  Kaufman, Bel. *Up the Down Staircase*
  King, Stephen. *11/22/63*
  McAllister, Tom. *How to Be Safe: A Novel*
  McCarthy, Jesse. *The Fugitivities*
  Perrotta, Tom. *The Abstinence Teacher*
  Russell, Kate Elizabeth. ★*My Dark Vanessa*
HIGH SCHOOLS
  Bump, Gabriel. ★*Everywhere You Don't Belong: A Novel*
  Frankel, Laurie. *One Two Three: A Novel*
  Kaufman, Bel. *Up the Down Staircase*
  West, Kathleen. *Minor Dramas & Other Catastrophes*
*The **High** Season: A Novel*. Blundell, Judy
HIGH TECHNOLOGY
  Brown, Dale. *The Moscow Offensive: A Novel*
  Chiang, Ted. ★*Exhalation: Stories*
  Crouch, Blake. *Recursion*
  Cussler, Clive. ★*The Rising Sea: A Novel from the Numa Files*

Gibson, William. ★*Agency*
McKinney, Chris. *Midnight, Water City*
Moreno, Gus. *This Thing Between US: A Novel*
Pynchon, Thomas. ★*Bleeding Edge*
Robinson, Kim Stanley. *Aurora*
Rosnay, Tatiana de. ★*Flowers of Darkness*
Soule, Charles. ★*Anyone*
Stephenson, Neal. ★*Fall Or, Dodge in Hell: A Novel*
Wells, Martha. *All Systems Red*
Whiteley, Aliya. *From the Neck up and Other Stories*

HIGH TECHNOLOGY INDUSTRY AND TRADE
Chang, Alexandra. ★*Days of Distraction*
Cohen, Joshua. *Book of Numbers: A Novel*
Crichton, Michael. *Prey: A Novel*

HIGH TECHNOLOGY WEAPONS
Bell, Ted. *Overkill: An Alex Hawke Novel*

Highland grooms [Series]. London, Julia
Highland pleasures [Series]. Ashley, Jennifer

HIGHLAND ROMANCES
Ashley, Jennifer. *Lady Isabella's Scandalous Marriage*
Ashley, Jennifer. *The Madness of Lord Ian Mackenzie*
Banks, Maya. *Never Seduce a Scot*
Burrowes, Grace. *The Trouble with Dukes*
Garwood, Julie. *The Bride*
Jordan, Sophie. *This Scot of Mine*
London, Julia. *Wild Wicked Scot*

HIGHLANDS, SCOTLAND
Banks, Maya. *Never Seduce a Scot*
Burnet, Graeme Macrae. *His Bloody Project: Documents Relating to the Case of Roderick Macrae*
Colgan, Jenny. *500 Miles from You*
Elliott, Lexie. *The Missing Years*
Foley, Lucy. *The Hunting Party*
London, Julia. *Wild Wicked Scot*
Moss, Sarah. *Summerwater*
Scott, A. D. ★*Beneath the Abbey Wall: A Novel*
Scott, A. D. *A Double Death on the Black Isle: A Novel*
Scott, A. D. *A Kind of Grief: A Novel*
Scott, A. D. ★*The Low Road*
Ware, Ruth. ★*The Turn of the Key*

The **Highsmith** Reader: Selected Novels and Short Stories. Highsmith, Patricia

Highsmith, Patricia
The Highsmith Reader: Selected Novels and Short Stories
★*The Talented Mr. Ripley*

The **Highway**. Box, C. J.

Highway 59 [Series]. Locke, Attica

Hijuelos, Oscar
Beautiful Maria of My Soul
★*The Mambo Kings Play Songs of Love: A Novel*
Twain & Stanley Enter Paradise

HIKERS
Carr, Robyn. *What We Find*
Doiron, Paul. *The Precipice*

HIKING
Grossman, David. ★*To the End of the Land*
Nelson, Christina Suzann. *If We Make It Home: A Novel of Faith and Survival in the Oregon Wilderness*

Stage, Zoje. *Getaway*

Hild: a Novel. Griffith, Nicola

HILDA
Griffith, Nicola. *Hild: A Novel*

HILDEGARD VON BINGEN
McCall Smith, Alexander. *The Comforts of a Muddy Saturday: An Isabel Dalhousie Novel*
Sharratt, Mary. *Illuminations: A Novel of Hildegard Von Bingen*

Hilderbrand, Elin
★*28 Summers*
The Perfect Couple
★*Summer of '69*
★*Troubles in Paradise*
★*What Happens in Paradise: A Novel*
★*Winter in Paradise: A Novel*

Hill Gumbao, Toni
The Good Suicides: A Thriller
The Summer of Dead Toys

Hill, Donna
★*Confessions in B-Flat*

Hill, Edwin J.
Little Comfort

Hill, Joe
The Fireman: A Novel
★*Full Throttle: Stories*
Heart-Shaped Box
Horns
★*Nos4a2*
Strange Weather: Four Short Novels

Hill, Lawrence
Someone Knows My Name: A Novel

Hill, Nathan
The Nix: A Novel

Hill, Reginald
The Woodcutter: A Novel

Hill, Ruth Beebe
Hanta Yo

Hill, Susan
The Pure in Heart: A Simon Serrailler Crime Novel
The Shadows in the Street: A Simon Serrailler Mystery

Hillerman, Tony
The Shape Shifter
The Sinister Pig
The Wailing Wind

Hilton, James
★*Good-Bye, Mr. Chips*
★*Lost Horizon: A Novel*
Random Harvest

Hilton, L. S.
Maestra

HIMALAYA MOUNTAINS REGION
Hilton, James. ★*Lost Horizon: A Novel*
Pattison, Eliot. *The Skull Mantra*

HINDUISM — RELATIONS
Rushdie, Salman. ★*Midnight's Children: A Novel*

HIPPIES
Cotterill, Colin. *Killed at the Whim of a Hat*
Groff, Lauren. ★*Arcadia: A Novel*

Runcie, James. *Sidney Chambers and the Persistence of Love*

HIPPIES — INFLUENCE

Pynchon, Thomas. *Vineland*

Hirahara, Naomi

★*Clark and Division*

His Bloody Project: Documents Relating to the Case of Roderick Macrae. Burnet, Graeme Macrae

His Majesty's Dragon. Novik, Naomi

His Master's Voice. Lem, Stanislaw

His Only Wife: A Novel. Medie, Peace A.

HISPANIC AMERICAN FAMILIES

Oliveras, Priscilla. *Anchored Hearts*

Pineiro, Caridad. *South Beach Love: A Feel-Good Romance from Hallmark Publishing*

Quade, Kirstin Valdez. ★*The Five Wounds: A Novel*

Urrea, Luis Alberto. ★*The House of Broken Angels*

HISPANIC AMERICAN GIRLS

Gaitskill, Mary. *The Mare: A Novel*

HISPANIC AMERICAN TEENAGE GIRLS

Wetmore, Elizabeth. ★*Valentine*

HISPANIC AMERICAN WOMEN

Allende, Isabel. *Daughter of Fortune: A Novel*

Fajardo-Anstine, Kali. ★*Sabrina & Corina: Stories*

Valdes, Alisa. *Dirty Girls on Top*

HISPANIC AMERICANS

Alvarez, Julia. *How the Garcia Girls Lost Their Accents*

Daria, Alexis. ★*A Lot Like Adios*

Daria, Alexis. ★*You Had Me at Hola*

Moreno, Gus. *This Thing Between US: A Novel*

Rice-Gonzalez, Charles. *Chulito*

Urrea, Luis Alberto. *The Water Museum: Stories*

HISTORIANS

Flynn, Michael. *Eifelheim*

Updike, John. *Memories of the Ford Administration: A Novel*

Willis, Connie. ★*Doomsday Book*

HISTORIC BUILDINGS

McMahon, Jennifer. *The Invited: A Novel*

HISTORIC DOCUMENTS

Phoenix, Michele. *The Space Between Words*

HISTORIC PRESERVATION

Petersen, Todd Robert. *Picnic in the Ruins*

HISTORICAL COMICS

Gendry-Kim, Keum Suk. ★*The Waiting*

HISTORICAL FANTASY

Arden, Katherine. ★*The Bear and the Nightingale*

Arden, Katherine. ★*The Girl in the Tower*

Arden, Katherine. ★*The Winter of the Witch*

Barnes, Jonathan. *The Somnambulist*

Bear, Elizabeth. *Ink and Steel: A Novel of the Promethean Age*

Callender, Kacen. *King of the Rising*

Campisi, Megan. *Sin Eater*

Chakraborty, S. A. *The City of Brass*

Chakraborty, S. A. *The Empire of Gold*

Chakraborty, S. A. *The Kingdom of Copper: A Novel*

Cho, Zen. *Sorcerer to the Crown*

Choo, Yangsze. *The Ghost Bride: A Novel*

Choo, Yangsze. ★*The Night Tiger: A Novel*

Clarke, Susanna. ★*Jonathan Strange & Mr. Norrell*

Cornwell, Bernard. *The Winter King: A Novel of Arthur*

Gaiman, Neil. ★*Stardust*

Gilman, Felix. *The Half-Made World*

Gilman, Laura Anne. *The Cold Eye*

Gilman, Laura Anne. *Silver on the Road*

Glover, Nicole. ★*The Conductors*

Glover, Nicole. *The Undertakers*

Goss, Theodora. *The Sinister Mystery of the Mesmerizing Girl*

Goss, Theodora. *The Strange Case of the Alchemist's Daughter*

Gowar, Imogen Hermes. *The Mermaid and Mrs. Hancock*

Harkness, Deborah E. *Shadow of Night*

Harkness, Deborah E. *Time's Convert*

Holton, India. *The Wisteria Society of Lady Scoundrels*

Ishiguro, Kazuo. *The Buried Giant: A Novel*

Jin, Yong. *A Hero Born: A Novel*

Johnson, Alaya Dawn. *Trouble the Saints*

Kay, Guy Gavriel. ★*Children of Earth and Sky*

Kidd, Jess. ★*Things in Jars*

Kuang, R. F. ★*The Dragon Republic*

Kuang, R. F. *The Poppy War*

Marske, Freya. *A Marvellous Light*

Miller, Madeline. ★*Circe*

Moreno-Garcia, Silvia. ★*Gods of Jade and Shadow: A Novel*

Moreno-Garcia, Silvia. *Mexican Gothic*

Morgenstern, Erin. ★*The Night Circus: A Novel*

North, Claire. *The Pursuit of William Abbey*

Novik, Naomi. *His Majesty's Dragon*

Parker-Chan, Shelley. ★*She Who Became the Sun*

Parry, H. G. *A Declaration of the Rights of Magicians*

Pike, Signe. *The Forgotten Kingdom: A Novel*

Pike, Signe. *The Lost Queen*

Polk, C. L. *The Midnight Bargain*

Polk, C. L. *Stormsong*

Polk, C. L. *Witchmark*

Pulley, Natasha. *The Bedlam Stacks*

Pulley, Natasha. *The Lost Future of Pepperharrow*

Pulley, Natasha. *The Watchmaker of Filigree Street*

Rossner, Rena. *The Light of the Midnight Stars*

Sayers, Constance. *The Ladies of the Secret Circus*

Schwab, Victoria. *A Conjuring of Light*

Schwab, Victoria. *A Darker Shade of Magic*

Schwab, Victoria. *A Gathering of Shadows*

Schwab, Victoria. *The Invisible Life of Addie Larue*

Stewart, Mary. ★*The Crystal Cave*

Stewart, Mary. ★*The Hollow Hills*

Stewart, Mary. *The Last Enchantment*

Stewart, Mary. *The Wicked Day*

Sutcliff, Rosemary. *Sword at Sunset*

Vo, Nghi. ★*The Chosen and the Beautiful*

Vyleta, Dan. *Smoke: A Novel*

Walton, Jo. ★*Lent*

Wecker, Helene. *The Golem and the Jinni*

Wecker, Helene. ★*The Hidden Palace*

White, T. H. ★*The Once and Future King*

Wilson, G. Willow. ★*The Bird King*

Woods, Rita. ★*Remembrance*

HISTORICAL FICTION

Aalborg, Gordon. *River of Porcupines*

Abbott, Megan E. *Bury Me Deep*

Achebe, Chinua. ★*Things Fall Apart*

Adams, Alina. *The Nesting Dolls*

Adams, Hope. *Dangerous Women*

Adamson, Gil. *The Outlander*

Adichie, Chimamanda Ngozi. *Half of a Yellow Sun*

Adimi, Kaouther. *Our Riches*

Agee, Jonis. *The Bones of Paradise*

Alcott, Kate. *A Touch of Stardust*

Alderson, Kaia. *Sisters in Arms*

Alexander, V. S. *The Magdalen Girls*

Allende, Isabel. *Daughter of Fortune: A Novel*

Allende, Isabel. *A Long Petal of the Sea: A Novel*

Alpsten, Ellen. *Tsarina*

Altan, Ahmet. ★*Love in the Days of Rebellion*

Amirrezvani, Anita. *The Blood of Flowers: A Novel*

Amirrezvani, Anita. *Equal of the Sun*

Amis, Martin. ★*The Zone of Interest: A Novel*

Anderson, Alison. *The Summer Guest*

Anstruther, Eleanor. *A Perfect Explanation*

Apostol, Gina. *Bibliolepsy*

Araghi, Alireza Taheri. ★*The Immortals of Tehran*

Armstrong, Addison. *The Light of Luna Park*

Asim, Jabari. ★*Yonder*

Atakora, Afia. ★*Conjure Women*

Atkinson, Kate. ★*A God in Ruins*

Atkinson, Kate. ★*Transcription*

Auci, Stefania. *The Florios of Sicily: A Novel*

Auel, Jean M. ★*The Clan of the Cave Bear: A Novel*

Austin, Finola. *Bronte's Mistress*

Avery, Ellis. *The Last Nude*

Bainbridge, Beryl. *Every Man for Himself*

Baker, Jo. *Longbourn*

Ballard, J. G. *Empire of the Sun: A Novel*

Balzano, Marco. *I'm Staying Here*

Banner, Catherine. *The House at the Edge of Night: A Novel*

Barker, Pat. ★*The Eye in the Door*

Barker, Pat. ★*The Ghost Road*

Barker, Pat. ★*Regeneration*

Barker, Susan. ★*The Incarnations: A Novel*

Barnes, Julian. *The Noise of Time*

Barnett, LaShonda K. *Jam on the Vine*

Barr, Mark. *Watershed*

Barry, Sebastian. *Days Without End: A Novel*

Barry, Sebastian. ★*A Thousand Moons: A Novel*

Bausch, Richard. *Peace*

Beach, Edward L. *Run Silent, Run Deep*

Beams, Clare. *The Illness Lesson*

Belfer, Lauren. *And After the Fire: A Novel*

Belfoure, Charles. *The Paris Architect: A Novel*

Benedict, Marie. ★*Lady Clementine*

Benedict, Marie. *The Only Woman in the Room*

Benioff, David. *City of Thieves: A Novel*

Benjamin, Melanie. *Alice I Have Been*

Benjamin, Melanie. ★*The Aviator's Wife: A Novel*

Bennett, Brit. ★*The Vanishing Half*

Benton, Janet. *Lilli De Jong: A Novel*

Berg, Gretchen. *The Operator*

Binder, L. Annette. *The Vanishing Sky*

Binet, Laurent. ★*HHhH*

Birch, Carol. *Jamrach's Menagerie*

Bird, Sarah. *Daughter of a Daughter of a Queen*

Black, Cara. ★*Three Hours in Paris*

Blackmore, R. D. *Lorna Doone: A Romance of Exmoor*

Blake, Audrey. *The Girl in His Shadow: A Novel*

Blake, Sarah. *The Guest Book: A Novel*

Blake, Sarah. *The Postmistress*

Blakemore, A. K. *The Manningtree Witches*

Bloom, Amy. *Lucky Us: A Novel*

Bloom, Amy. ★*White Houses: A Novel*

Blum, Jenna. *The Lost Family*

Blume, Judy. *In the Unlikely Event*

Bohjalian, Chris. *The Sandcastle Girls*

Bohjalian, Chris. *Skeletons at the Feast: A Novel*

Boulle, Pierre. *The Bridge Over the River Kwai: A Novel*

Bowen, Rhys. *The Victory Garden*

Bowman, David. *Big Bang: A Nonfiction Novel*

Boyle, T. Coraghessan. *The Women: A Novel*

Brink, Andre P. *Philida: A Novel*

Brodie, Emma. *Songs in Ursa Major*

Brown, Amy Belding. *Emily's House*

Brown, Dee. *Creek Mary's Blood: A Novel*

Brown, Taylor. *Fallen Land*

Buchanan, Cathy Marie. ★*The Painted Girls*

Buck, Pearl S. *The Good Earth*

Burdick, Serena. *The Girls with No Names*

Burke, James Lee. *Wayfaring Stranger: A Novel*

Burton, Jessie. *The Miniaturist*

Butler, Robert Olen. *Late City*

Calvi, Mary. *Dear George, Dear Mary: A Novel of George Washington's First Love*

Carey, Edward. *Little: A Novel*

Carey, Peter. *A Long Way from Home*

Carter, Michaela. *Leonora in the Morning Light*

Carter, Stephen L. *Back Channel*

Cash, Wiley. *The Last Ballad: A Novel*

Castellani, Christopher. *Leading Men: A Novel*

Cather, Willa. ★*Death Comes for the Archbishop*

Cather, Willa. ★*My Antonia*

Cather, Willa. *O Pioneers!*

Catton, Eleanor. *The Luminaries: A Novel*

Chabon, Michael. *The Amazing Adventures of Kavalier & Clay: A Novel*

Chakrabarti, Jai. *A Play for the End of the World*

Chambers, Clare. *Small Pleasures*

Chee, Alexander. *The Queen of the Night*

Cheek, Chip. *Cape May*

Chen, Da. *Brothers: A Novel*

Cheng, Bill. *Southern Cross the Dog*

Cherezinska, Elzbieta. *The Widow Queen*

Chevalier, Tracy. ★*Girl with a Pearl Earring*

Chevalier, Tracy. *The Last Runaway*

Chevalier, Tracy. *A Single Thread*

Chiaverini, Jennifer. *Mrs. Lincoln's Dressmaker: A Novel*

Chiaverini, Jennifer. *Mrs. Lincoln's Sisters*

Chiaverini, Jennifer. *Resistance Women: A Novel*

Chung, Catherine. *The Tenth Muse: A Novel*
Clark, Clare. *In the Full Light of the Sun*
Clavell, James. *Shogun*
Clayton, Meg Waite. *The Last Train to London*
Cleeton, Chanel. *The Most Beautiful Girl in Cuba*
Cleeton, Chanel. *Next Year in Havana*
Clinch, Jon. *Marley: A Novel*
Coates, Ta-Nehisi. ★*The Water Dancer: A Novel*
Cobbs Hoffman, Elizabeth. *The Hamilton Affair*
Cobbs Hoffman, Elizabeth. *The Tubman Command: A Novel*
Collins, Sara. *The Confessions of Frannie Langton*
Conde, Maryse. *I, Tituba, Black Witch of Salem*
Cooper, James Fenimore. *The Last of the Mohicans: A Narrative of 1757*
Coplin, Amanda. *The Orchardist*
Cornwell, Bernard. *The Archer's Tale*
Cornwell, Bernard. *The Last Kingdom: A Novel*
Cornwell, Bernard. *Sword of Kings*
Corthron, Kia. *Moon and the Mars*
Couto, Mia. *The Sword and the Spear*
Crace, Jim. *Harvest*
Crace, Jim. *Quarantine*
Craig, Charmaine. *Miss Burma*
Crane, Stephen. ★*The Red Badge of Courage: An Episode of the American Civil War*
Crummey, Michael. *Galore*
Crummey, Michael. *The Innocents*
Cruz, Angie. *Dominicana: A Novel*
D'Eramo, Luce. *Deviation*
Dallas, Sandra. *The Last Midwife*
Dallas, Sandra. *Tallgrass*
Dallas, Sandra. *Westering Women: A Novel*
Dalton, Trent. *All Our Shimmering Skies*
Dann, Patty. *The Wright Sister*
Darznik, Jasmin. *The Bohemians*
Darznik, Jasmin. *Song of a Captive Bird: A Novel*
Davies, Carys. *West*
Davis, Fiona. *The Chelsea Girls*
Davis, Fiona. *The Lions of Fifth Avenue: A Novel*
Davis, Fiona. *The Masterpiece*
De Bernieres, Louis. *Birds Without Wings*
Dean, Debra. *The Madonnas of Leningrad: A Novel*
Dean, Michael. *I, Hogarth*
Deluca, Marjorie. *The Savage Instinct*
Deon, Natashia. *Grace*
DeRoux, Margaux. *The Lost Diary of Venice*
Deutermann, Peter T. *Pacific Glory: A Novel*
Dexter, Pete. *Paris Trout*
Diamant, Anita. *The Boston Girl: A Novel*
Diamant, Anita. ★*The Red Tent*
Dickens, Charles. ★*A Tale of Two Cities*
Diop, David. ★*At Night All Blood Is Black*
Doctorow, E. L. ★*Billy Bathgate: A Novel*
Doctorow, E. L. *The March: A Novel*
Doctorow, E. L. ★*Ragtime*
Doctorow, E. L. *World's Fair*
Doerr, Anthony. ★*All the Light We Cannot See: A Novel*
Donati, Sara. *Where the Light Enters*

Dongala, Emmanuel Boundzeki. *The Bridgetower Sonata: Sonata Mulattica*
Donoghue, Emma. *Slammerkin*
Donoghue, Emma. ★*The Wonder*
Doyle, Roddy. *A Star Called Henry*
Druon, Maurice. *The Iron King*
Du Maurier, Daphne. *Frenchman's Creek*
Duenas, Maria. *The Time in Between: A Novel*
Dumas, Alexandre. ★*The Man in the Iron Mask*
Dumas, Alexandre. ★*The Three Musketeers*
Dumas, Alexandre. *Twenty Years After*
Dunant, Sarah. *The Birth of Venus: A Novel*
Dunant, Sarah. *Blood and Beauty: A Novel*
Dunant, Sarah. *In the Company of the Courtesan: A Novel*
Dunant, Sarah. *Sacred Hearts: A Novel*
Dunmore, Helen. *The Lie*
Dunnett, Dorothy. *Niccolo Rising*
Dybek, Nick. *The Verdun Affair: A Novel*
Earley, Tony. *Jim the Boy: A Novel*
Ebershoff, David. *The 19th Wife: A Novel*
Ebershoff, David. *The Danish Girl: A Novel*
Eco, Umberto. *Baudolino*
Edugyan, Esi. *Half-Blood Blues*
Edugyan, Esi. ★*Washington Black: A Novel*
Edwards, Louis. *Ramadan Ramsey: A Novel*
Egan, Jennifer. ★*Manhattan Beach: A Novel*
Eliasberg, Jan. ★*Hannah's War*
Endicott, Marina. *The Voyage of the Morning Light*
Enjeti, Anjali. ★*The Parted Earth*
Epstein, Jennifer Cody. ★*Wunderland: A Novel*
Erdrich, Louise. *The Master Butchers Singing Club: A Novel*
Erdrich, Louise. ★*The Night Watchman: A Novel*
Escobar, Mario. *The Librarian of Saint-Malo: A Novel*
Evison, Jonathan. *Legends of the North Cascades: A Novel*
Evison, Jonathan. ★*Small World*
Faber, Michel. *The Crimson Petal and the White*
Fallada, Hans. *Every Man Dies Alone*
Faulkner, William. ★*Absalom, Absalom!*
Faulks, Sebastian. ★*Birdsong*
Faulks, Sebastian. *Charlotte Gray: A Novel*
Feldman, Ellen. *Paris Never Leaves You*
Flanagan, Richard. *Gould's Book of Fish: A Novel in Twelve Fish*
Flanagan, Richard. ★*The Narrow Road to the Deep North*
Follett, Ken. *A Column of Fire*
Follett, Ken. *Edge of Eternity*
Follett, Ken. ★*The Evening and the Morning*
Follett, Ken. *Fall of Giants*
Follett, Ken. ★*The Pillars of the Earth*
Follett, Ken. *Winter of the World*
Follett, Ken. *World Without End*
Forester, C. S. *Admiral Hornblower in the West Indies*
Forester, C. S. *The African Queen*
Forester, C. S. *Beat to Quarters*
Forester, C. S. *Commodore Hornblower*
Forester, C. S. *Flying Colours*
Forester, C. S. *Hornblower and the Atropos*
Forester, C. S. *Hornblower and the Hotspur*
Forester, C. S. *Lieutenant Hornblower*

Forester, C. S. *Lord Hornblower*

Forester, C. S. *Mr. Midshipman Hornblower*

Forester, C. S. *Ship of the Line*

Foster, Brooke Lea. *Summer Darlings*

Fowler, Therese. *A Well-Behaved Woman: A Novel of the Vanderbilts*

Fowler, Therese. ★*Z: A Novel of Zelda Fitzgerald*

Fowles, John. ★*The French Lieutenant's Woman*

Francis-Sharma, Lauren. ★*Book of the Little Axe*

Franck, Julia. *Blindness of the Heart*

Franklin, Ariana. *The Siege Winter*

Franzen, Jonathan. ★*Crossroads*

Frazier, Charles. ★*Cold Mountain*

Frazier, Charles. *Thirteen Moons: A Novel*

Frazier, Charles. *Varina*

Freedman, Benedict. *Mrs. Mike: The Story of Katherine Mary Flannigan*

Freeman, Anna. *The Fair Fight: A Novel*

French, Albert. *Billy*

Fuentes, Carlos. *The Death of Artemio Cruz*

Gabaldon, Diana. ★*A Breath of Snow and Ashes*

Gabaldon, Diana. ★*Drums of Autumn*

Gabaldon, Diana. ★*The Fiery Cross*

Gabaldon, Diana. ★*Outlander*

Gabaldon, Diana. ★*Voyager*

Gabaldon, Diana. *Written in My Own Heart's Blood*

Gaines, Ernest J. ★*The Autobiography of Miss Jane Pittman*

Galchen, Rivka. *Everyone Knows Your Mother Is a Witch*

Gappah, Petina. ★*Out of Darkness, Shining Light*

Gass, William H. *Middle C*

Gaynor, Hazel. *The Lighthouse Keeper's Daughter*

Gaynor, Hazel. *Meet Me in Monaco: A Novel*

Gaynor, Hazel. *Three Words for Goodbye*

Gelernter, J. H. *Hold Fast*

George, Alex. *The Paris Hours: A Novel*

George, Margaret. *The Confessions of Young Nero*

George, Margaret. *Elizabeth I: A Novel*

George, Margaret. *Helen of Troy*

George, Margaret. *The Splendor Before the Dark: A Novel of the Emperor Nero*

Ghosh, Amitav. *Flood of Fire*

Ghosh, Amitav. *The Glass Palace*

Ghosh, Amitav. *River of Smoke*

Ghosh, Amitav. *Sea of Poppies*

Gibbon, Maureen. *The Lost Notebook of Edouard Manet: A Novel*

Gilbert, Elizabeth. ★*City of Girls*

Gilbert, Elizabeth. ★*The Signature of All Things: A Novel*

Gillham, David R. *City of Women*

Godwin, Gail. *Flora: A Novel*

Golden, Arthur. ★*Memoirs of a Geisha: A Novel*

Golding, William. *Close Quarters*

Golding, William. *Fire Down Below*

Golding, William. *The Inheritors*

Golding, William. *Rites of Passage*

Goodwin, Daisy. *The American Heiress*

Gortner, C. W. *The First Actress: A Novel of Sarah Bernhardt*

Grames, Juliet. *The Seven or Eight Deaths of Stella Fortuna*

Graves, Robert. *Claudius the God and His Wife Messalina: The Troublesome Reign of Tiberius Claudius Caesar, Emperor*

Graves, Robert. ★*I, Claudius: From the Autobiography of Tiberius Claudius, Born 10 B.C., Murdered and Deified A.D. 54*

Greeley, Molly. *The Clergyman's Wife*

Greene, Amy. *Long Man*

Greenidge, Kaitlyn. ★*Libertie: A Novel*

Greenwood, T. *Rust & Stardust*

Gregory, Philippa. *The Boleyn Inheritance*

Gregory, Philippa. *The Constant Princess*

Gregory, Philippa. *The Kingmaker's Daughter*

Gregory, Philippa. *The Lady of the Rivers*

Gregory, Philippa. *The Last Tudor*

Gregory, Philippa. *The Other Boleyn Girl: A Novel*

Gregory, Philippa. *The Red Queen: A Novel*

Gregory, Philippa. *The Taming of the Queen*

Gregory, Philippa. *Tidelands*

Gregory, Philippa. *The White Princess*

Grenville, Kate. *Sarah Thornhill*

Grenville, Kate. *The Secret River*

Griffith, Nicola. *Hild: A Novel*

Groff, Lauren. ★*Matrix*

Gross, Andrew. *Button Man*

Gross, Max. *The Lost Shtetl*

Gunesekera, Romesh. ★*Suncatcher: A Novel*

Gunning, Sally. *Painting the Light*

Gurganus, Allan. *Oldest Living Confederate Widow Tells All*

Gyasi, Yaa. ★*Homegoing: A Novel*

Hahn, Sumi. *The Mermaid from Jeju: A Novel*

Haigh, Jennifer. *Baker Towers: A Novel*

Halls, Stacey. *The Lost Orphan*

Hammad, Isabella. ★*The Parisian, Or, Al-Barisi: A Novel*

Hannah, Kristin. *The Nightingale*

Hansen, Ron. *Mariette in Ecstasy*

Haratischvili, Nino. *The Eighth Life: (For Brilka)*

Hargrave, Kiran Millwood. *The Mercies: A Novel*

Harman, Patricia. *The Midwife of Hope River: A Novel*

Harmel, Kristin. *The Room on Rue Amelie*

Harmon, Amy. *Where the Lost Wander*

Harper, Karen. *The Queen's Secret: A Novel of England's World War II Queen*

Harrigan, Stephen. *The Leopard Is Loose: A Novel*

Harris, C. S. *Good Time Coming*

Harris, Nathan. *The Sweetness of Water*

Harris, Robert. *Pompeii: A Novel*

Harrison, Jamie. *The Center of Everything: A Novel*

Harrison, Nicola. *Montauk*

Hart, John. *The Unwilling*

Hawthorne, Nathaniel. ★*The Scarlet Letter: A Romance*

Haynes, Natalie. *A Thousand Ships*

Healey, Jane. *The Animals at Lockwood Manor*

Heggen, Thomas. *Mister Roberts*

Hegi, Ursula. *Children and Fire: A Novel*

Helprin, Mark. *In Sunlight and in Shadow*

Hemingway, Ernest. ★*A Farewell to Arms*

Hemingway, Ernest. *For Whom the Bell Tolls*

Henry, Patti Callahan. ★*Becoming Mrs. Lewis: The Improbable Love Story of Joy Davidman and C. S. Lewis*

Hersey, John. ★*A Bell for Adano*

Hertmans, Stefan. ★*The Convert: A Novel*

Hesse, Hermann. *Narcissus and Goldmund*
Hicks, Robert. *The Widow of the South*
Hijuelos, Oscar. *Twain & Stanley Enter Paradise*
Hilderbrand, Elin. ★*Summer of '69*
Hill, Lawrence. *Someone Knows My Name: A Novel*
Hill, Ruth Beebe. *Hanta Yo*
Hoffman, Alice. *The Marriage of Opposites: A Novel Based on the Life of Rachel Pizzarro*
Hoffman, Alice. *The Museum of Extraordinary Things: A Novel*
Hoffman, Alice. ★*The World That We Knew*
Holland, Cecelia. *Jerusalem*
Hooper, Elise. *Fast Girls: A Novel of the 1936 Women's Olympic Team*
Horan, Nancy. *Loving Frank: A Novel*
Hornby, Gill. *Miss Austen*
Horrocks, Caitlin. *The Vexations*
Howard, Ravi. *Driving the King: A Novel*
Howarth, Paul. *Dust off the Bones*
Howarth, Paul. *Only Killers and Thieves: A Novel*
Hozar, Nazanine. *Aria*
Hugo, Victor. ★*The Hunchback of Notre Dame*
Hunt, Laird. *The Evening Road*
Hunt, Laird. *Zorrie*
Iggulden, Conn. *The Abbot's Tale*
Isherwood, Christopher. ★*The Berlin Stories: The Last of Mr. Norris, Goodbye to Berlin*
Ishiguro, Kazuo. *An Artist of the Floating World*
Jackson-Brown, Angela. ★*When Stars Rain Down: A Novel*
Jakes, John. *Love and War*
Jakes, John. ★*North and South*
James, Marlon. ★*A Brief History of Seven Killings: A Novel*
Jenner, Natalie. *The Jane Austen Society*
Jenoff, Pam. *The Lost Girls of Paris*
Jensen, Nancy. *In Our Midst*
Jiles, Paulette. *News of the World: A Novel*
Johnson, Julia Claiborne. *Better Luck Next Time: A Novel*
Johnson, Sadeqa. ★*Yellow Wife*
Jones, Gayl. ★*Palmares*
Jones, James. ★*The Thin Red Line*
Jones, Robert. ★*The Prophets: A Novel*
Jones, Sherry. *Four Sisters, All Queens*
Jordan, Hillary. *Mudbound: A Novel*
Joshi, Alka. *The Henna Artist*
Joyce, Rachel. *Miss Benson's Beetle*
Kamali, Marjan. ★*The Stationery Shop*
Kane, Ben. *Spartacus: The Gladiator*
Kantor, MacKinlay. ★*Andersonville*
Kaplan, Mitchell James. *Rhapsody*
Kawabata, Yasunari. *The Sound of the Mountain*
Kazantzakis, Nikos. *The Last Temptation of Christ*
Kelly, Julia. *The Last Dance of the Debutante*
Kelly, Julia. *The Light Over London*
Kelly, Martha Hall. *Lilac Girls*
Kelly, Martha Hall. *Lost Roses: A Novel*
Keneally, Thomas. ★*The Daughters of Mars*
Keneally, Thomas. ★*Schindler's List*
Keneally, Thomas. *Shame and the Captives: A Novel*
Kennedy, William. ★*Ironweed: A Novel*

Kibler, Julie. *Home for Erring and Outcast Girls*
Kidd, Sue Monk. ★*The Book of Longings*
Kidd, Sue Monk. ★*The Invention of Wings: A Novel*
Kiernan, Stephen P. *Universe of Two*
Kim, Crystal Hana. *If You Leave Me*
Kim, Eugenia. *The Kinship of Secrets*
Kimani, Peter. *Dance of the Jakaranda*
Kingsolver, Barbara. ★*The Poisonwood Bible: A Novel*
Koestler, Arthur. *Darkness at Noon*
Konar, Affinity. *Mischling: A Novel*
Krivak, Andrew. *The Signal Flame: A Novel*
Krueger, William Kent. *This Tender Land: A Novel*
Kutsukake, Lynne. *The Translation of Love: A Novel*
Kuznetsov, Anatolii Petrovich. *Babi Yar: A Document in the Form of a Novel*
Lalami, Laila. ★*The Moor's Account: A Novel*
Landau, Alexis. *Those Who Are Saved*
Landragin, Alex. ★*Crossings: Consisting of Three Manuscripts : The Education of a Monster : City of Ghosts : Tales Of*
Lansdale, Joe R. *Edge of Dark Water*
Lawton, John. *Then We Take Berlin*
Le Guin, Ursula K. *Orsinian Tales*
Leavitt, David. *The Two Hotel Francforts: A Novel*
Lebrecht, Norman. *The Song of Names*
Lee, Ji-Min. *The Starlet and the Spy*
Lee, Jonathan. *The Great Mistake*
Lee, Min Jin. ★*Pachinko*
Lehane, Dennis. ★*The Given Day*
Lehane, Dennis. *Live by Night*
Levy, Andrea. *The Long Song*
Levy, Andrea. *Small Island*
Li, Yiyun. *The Vagrants: A Novel*
Liardet, Frances. *We Must Be Brave*
Littell, Robert. *The Mayakovsky Tapes: A Novel*
Llewellyn, Richard. ★*How Green Was My Valley*
Loigman, Lynda Cohen. *The Wartime Sisters: A Novel*
London, Joan. *The Golden Age*
Ma, Jian. *Beijing Coma*
Macallister, Greer. ★*The Arctic Fury*
MacLeod, Alison. *Tenderness*
Macneal, Elizabeth. *The Doll Factory*
Malouf, David. *Ransom*
Malouf, David. *Remembering Babylon*
Mamet, David. *Chicago: A Novel*
Mantel, Hilary. ★*Bring up the Bodies: A Novel*
Mantel, Hilary. ★*Wolf Hall*
Marlantes, Karl. *Deep River*
Marlantes, Karl. ★*Matterhorn: A Novel of the Vietnam War*
Mas, Victoria. *The Mad Women's Ball*
Mason, Daniel. *The Piano Tuner*
Mason, Daniel. *A Registry of My Passage Upon the Earth: Stories*
Mathis, Ayana. *The Twelve Tribes of Hattie*
Matthiessen, Peter. *Shadow Country: A New Rendering of the Watson Legend*
McBride, James. ★*Deacon King Kong: A Novel*
McBride, James. ★*The Good Lord Bird*
McCann, Colum. ★*Transatlantic: A Novel*
McCracken, Elizabeth. ★*Bowlaway: A Novel*

McCullough, Colleen. *The First Man in Rome*
McCullough, Colleen. *An Indecent Obsession*
McDermott, Alice. ★*The Ninth Hour*
McEwan, Ian. ★*Atonement: A Novel*
McFadden, Bernice L. *The Book of Harlan*
McKinney-Whetstone, Diane. *Leaving Cecil Street: A Novel*
McLain, Paula. *Circling the Sun*
McLain, Paula. *Love and Ruin*
McLain, Paula. *The Paris Wife: A Novel*
Meacham, Leila. *Dragonfly: A Novel*
Meadows, Rae. *I Will Send Rain: A Novel*
Mengiste, Maaza. ★*The Shadow King: A Novel*
Michener, James A. ★*The Bridges at Toko-Ri*
Michener, James A. *Caribbean*
Michener, James A. *Chesapeake*
Michener, James A. *Space*
Michener, James A. ★*Tales of the South Pacific*
Miller, Derek B. *How to Find Your Way in the Dark*
Miller, Kei. ★*Augustown*
Miller, Madeline. *The Song of Achilles*
Miller, Rebecca. ★*Jacob's Folly: A Novel*
Millhauser, Steven. *Martin Dressler: The Tale of an American Dreamer*
Mitchell, David. *The Thousand Autumns of Jacob De Zoet: A Novel*
Mitchell, David. ★*Utopia Avenue: A Novel*
Mitchell, Margaret. ★*Gone with the Wind*
Monroe, Mary. ★*Mrs. Wiggins*
Montgomery, Jess. *The Stills*
Montgomery, Jess. *The Widows*
Morelli, Laura. *The Stolen Lady*
Moreno-Garcia, Silvia. ★*Velvet Was the Night*
Morris, Heather. *Cilka's Journey*
Morrison, Toni. ★*Beloved: A Novel*
Morrison, Toni. *A Mercy: A Novel*
Morton, Kate. *The House at Riverton: A Novel*
Mosse, Kate. *The City of Tears*
Moyes, Jojo. *The Girl You Left Behind*
Moyes, Jojo. ★*The Giver of Stars: A Novel*
Nguyen, Viet Thanh. ★*The Sympathizer*
O'Brian, Patrick. *Master and Commander*
O'Farrell, Maggie. *Hamnet*
O'Farrell, Maggie. *The Vanishing Act of Esme Lennox*
O'Neill, Heather. ★*The Lonely Hearts Hotel: A Novel*
Obreht, Tea. *Inland: A Novel*
Offutt, Chris. *Country Dark*
Olmstead, Robert. ★*Coal Black Horse*
Orringer, Julie. ★*The Flight Portfolio: A Novel*
Orringer, Julie. ★*The Invisible Bridge: A Novel*
Otsuka, Julie. *The Buddha in the Attic*
Otsuka, Julie. *When the Emperor Was Divine: A Novel*
Ozick, Cynthia. *Heir to the Glimmering World*
Palmer, Dexter Clarence. ★*Mary Toft; Or, the Rabbit Queen: A Novel*
Parini, Jay. *The Passages of H.M.: A Novel of Herman Melville*
Parmar, Priya. *Vanessa and Her Sister*
Pastan, Rachel. *In the Field*
Paton, Alan. *Ah, but Your Land Is Beautiful*
Patterson, Molly. *Rebellion*
Paul, Gill. ★*The Lost Daughter*

Pears, Iain. *The Dream of Scipio*
Peebles, Frances de Pontes. *The Air You Breathe*
Penman, Sharon Kay. *Here Be Dragons*
Penman, Sharon Kay. *The Sunne in Splendour*
Penman, Sharon Kay. *When Christ and His Saints Slept*
Perez-Reverte, Arturo. *What We Become*
Perry, Sarah. *The Essex Serpent*
Pesci, David. *Amistad: A Novel*
Phillips, Caryl. *Dancing in the Dark*
Phillips, Caryl. *Foreigners*
Phillips, Caryl. *A View of the Empire at Sunset*
Phillips, Jayne Anne. *Lark and Termite: A Novel*
Phillips, Jayne Anne. *Quiet Dell: A Novel*
Piercy, Marge. *Gone to Soldiers: A Novel*
Piercy, Marge. *Sex Wars*
Pilcher, Rosamunde. *Coming Home*
Pipkin, John. *Woodsburner: A Novel*
Pitts, Leonard. *Freeman*
Powning, Beth. *The Sea Captain's Wife: A Novel*
Prescott, Lara. *The Secrets We Kept*
Preston, Caroline. *The Scrapbook of Frankie Pratt*
Prose, Francine. ★*The Vixen*
Proulx, Annie. ★*Barkskins: A Novel*
Punke, Michael. *Ridgeline: A Novel*
Purcell, Laura. *The House of Whispers*
Purcell, Laura. *The Silent Companions: A Ghost Story*
Puzo, Mario. *The Family: A Novel*
Pynchon, Thomas. *Against the Day: A Novel*
Pynchon, Thomas. *Mason & Dixon*
Pyper, Andrew. *The Residence: A Novel*
Rabb, Jonathan. *Among the Living*
Rachman, Tom. *The Italian Teacher*
Ramzipoor, E. R. *The Ventriloquists*
Rash, Ron. ★*The Cove*
Rash, Ron. ★*Serena: A Novel*
Rawles, Nancy. *My Jim: A Novel*
Reddi, Rishi. *Passage West: A Novel*
Reed, Ishmael. ★*Mumbo Jumbo*
Reid, Taylor Jenkins. ★*Malibu Rising*
Remarque, Erich Maria. *A Time to Love and a Time to Die*
Renault, Mary. *The Bull from the Sea*
Renault, Mary. *Funeral Games*
Renault, Mary. *The King Must Die*
Renault, Mary. *The Last of the Wine*
Renault, Mary. *The Persian Boy*
Rhys, Jean. ★*Wide Sargasso Sea*
Richler, Nancy. *Your Mouth Is Lovely: A Novel*
Riley, Vanessa. ★*Island Queen*
Rimmer, Kelly. ★*The Warsaw Orphan: A Wwii Novel*
Rindell, Suzanne. ★*The Two Mrs. Carlyles*
Ritter, Josh. *The Great Glorious Goddamn of It All*
Rizzuto, Rahna R. *Shadow Child*
Robbins, David L. *Last Citadel: A Novel of the Battle of Kursk*
Robbins, David L. *War of the Rats: A Novel*
Roberts, Bethan. ★*My Policeman*
Robertson, Imogen. *The Paris Winter*
Robinson, Marilynne. ★*Gilead*
Romano-Lax, Andromeda. *The Spanish Bow*

Rooney, Kathleen. ★*Cher Ami and Major Whittlesey*
Rooney, Kathleen. ★*Lillian Boxfish Takes a Walk*
Rose, M. J. ★*Cartier's Hope*
Rose, M. J. *Tiffany Blues: A Novel*
Rosen, Renee. *Dollface: A Novel of the Roaring Twenties*
Rosen, Renee. *The Social Graces*
Rosnay, Tatiana de. ★*Sarah's Key*
Rosner, Jennifer. ★*The Yellow Bird Sings*
Roth, Philip. ★*Nemesis*
Roy, Anuradha. *All the Lives We Never Lived: A Novel*
Ruiz Zafon, Carlos. *The Angel's Game*
Ruiz Zafon, Carlos. *The Labyrinth of the Spirits*
Ruiz Zafon, Carlos. *The Prisoner of Heaven*
Ruiz Zafon, Carlos. ★*The Shadow of the Wind*
Runcie, James. *Canvey Island*
Rushdie, Salman. *The Enchantress of Florence: A Novel*
Russell, Mary Doria. *Dreamers of the Day: A Novel*
Russell, Mary Doria. *A Thread of Grace: A Novel*
Russell, Mary Doria. *The Women of the Copper Country: A Novel*
Rutherfurd, Edward. *London*
Rutherfurd, Edward. *Paris*
Rutherfurd, Edward. *The Princes of Ireland: The Dublin Saga*
Rutherfurd, Edward. *The Rebels of Ireland: The Dublin Saga*
Rutherfurd, Edward. *Russka: The Novel of Russia*
Rutherfurd, Edward. *Sarum: The Novel of England*
Ryan, Jennifer. *The Spies of Shilling Lane: A Novel*
Rølvaag, O. E. ★*Giants in the Earth: A Saga of the Prairie*
Sabatini, Rafael. *Scaramouche: A Romance of the French Revolution*
Santiago, Esmeralda. *Conquistadora: A Novel*
Saramago, Jose. ★*The Elephant's Journey*
Saroyan, William. ★*The Human Comedy*
Sartre, Jean Paul. *The Age of Reason*
Sartre, Jean Paul. *Troubled Sleep*
Saunders, George. ★*Lincoln in the Bardo: A Novel*
Sayles, John. *A Moment in the Sun*
Saylor, Steven. *Roma: The Novel of Ancient Rome*
Scharer, Whitney. *The Age of Light*
Schell, Orville. *My Old Home: A Novel of Exile*
Schlink, Bernhard. *Olga*
Schmidt, Sarah. *See What I Have Done*
Schultz, Connie. *The Daughters of Erietown*
Schwartz, John Burnham. *The Commoner: A Novel*
Schwarz, Christina. *The Edge of the Earth*
Schwarz-Bart, Andre. *The Last of the Just: A Novel*
Scott, Paul. ★*Staying On: A Novel*
Scott, Walter. *The Bride of Lammermoor*
Scott, Walter. ★*Ivanhoe*
Scott, Walter. ★*Rob Roy*
See, Lisa. *Dreams of Joy: A Novel*
See, Lisa. *The Island of Sea Women*
See, Lisa. *Peony in Love: A Novel*
See, Lisa. *Shanghai Girls: A Novel*
Sem-Sandberg, Steve. *The Chosen Ones: A Novel*
Seton, Anya. *Avalon*
Seton, Anya. *Katherine*
Seton, Anya. ★*The Winthrop Woman*
Setterfield, Diane. ★*Once Upon a River*
Shaara, Jeff. *Gods and Generals: A Novel of the Civil War*

Shaara, Jeff. *Gone for Soldiers*
Shaara, Jeff. *The Last Full Measure*
Shaara, Jeff. *The Rising Tide: A Novel of World War II*
Shaara, Jeff. *The Steel Wave: A Novel of World War II*
Shaara, Michael. ★*The Killer Angels: A Novel*
Shaffer, Mary Ann. *The Guernsey Literary and Potato Peel Pie Society*
Shan, Sa. *The Girl Who Played Go*
Shapiro, Barbara A. *The Muralist*
Sharratt, Mary. *Daughters of the Witching Hill*
Sharratt, Mary. *Illuminations: A Novel of Hildegard Von Bingen*
Sharratt, Mary. *Revelations*
Shepard, Jim. ★*The Book of Aron*
Shimotakahara, Leslie. *After the Bloom*
Shreve, Anita. *Fortune's Rocks: A Novel*
Shreve, Anita. *Sea Glass: A Novel*
Sienkiewicz, Henryk. ★*Quo Vadis: A Story of Faith in the Last Days of the Roman Empire*
Silko, Leslie Marmon. ★*Ceremony*
Silko, Leslie Marmon. *Gardens in the Dunes: A Novel*
Silver, Marisa. *Mary Coin: A Novel*
Simonson, Helen. *The Summer Before the War: A Novel*
Singer, Isaac Bashevis. ★*The Magician of Lublin*
Skeslien Charles, Janet. *The Paris Library: A Novel*
Smith, Dominic. *Bright and Distant Shores*
Smith, Dominic. ★*The Electric Hotel*
Smith, Dominic. ★*The Last Painting of Sara De Vos*
Smith, Gregory Blake. ★*The Maze at Windermere: A Novel*
Smith, Lee. *On Agate Hill: A Novel*
Smith, Martin Cruz. *Rose*
Smith, Wilbur A. *Birds of Prey*
Smith, Wilbur A. *Monsoon*
Snow, C. P. ★*Strangers and Brothers*
Sofer, Dalia. *The Septembers of Shiraz*
Soli, Tatjana. *The Lotus Eaters*
Solomon, Anna. *Leaving Lucy Pear*
Solomons, Natasha. *House of Gold*
Sontag, Susan. ★*In America*
Sontag, Susan. *The Volcano Lover: A Romance*
Spufford, Francis. ★*Golden Hill*
St. James, Simone. *The Haunting of Maddy Clare*
Stachniak, Eva. *The Chosen Maiden: A Novel*
Stachniak, Eva. *The Winter Palace: A Novel of Catherine the Great*
Stedman, M. L. ★*The Light Between Oceans: A Novel*
Steinke, Rene. *Holy Skirts*
Stewart, Amy. ★*Girl Waits with Gun*
Stockett, Kathryn. ★*The Help*
Stone, Irving. ★*The Agony and the Ecstasy: A Biographical Novel of Michelangelo*
Stone, Irving. *Lust for Life: A Novel of Vincent Van Gogh*
Straight, Susan. *A Million Nightingales*
Stratford, Sarah-Jane. *Red Letter Days*
Styron, William. *The Confessions of Nat Turner*
Styron, William. ★*Sophie's Choice*
Sundaresan, Indu. *The Splendor of Silence: A Novel*
Suri, Manil. *The Age of Shiva: A Novel*
Swamy, Shruti. *The Archer*
Swift, Graham. ★*Mothering Sunday: A Romance*

Szabo, Magda. *Abigail*
Tademy, Lalita. *Cane River*
Tan, Amy. ★*The Joy Luck Club*
Tan, Amy. *The Valley of Amazement*
Tan, Twan Eng. *The Garden of Evening Mists*
Tanabe, Karin. *A Hundred Suns*
Taseer, Aatish. *The Way Things Were: A Novel*
Thelen, Albert Vigoleis. *The Island of Second Sight: From the Applied Recollections of Vigoleis*
Tobar, Hector. *The Last Great Road Bum*
Toibin, Colm. ★*The Magician: A Novel*
Towles, Amor. ★*A Gentleman in Moscow*
Towles, Amor. *Rules of Civility: A Novel*
Tsukiyama, Gail. *The Street of a Thousand Blossoms*
Twain, Mark. *Personal Recollections of Joan of Arc*
Updike, John. *Gertrude and Claudius*
Uris, Leon. *Armageddon: A Novel of Berlin*
Uris, Leon. ★*Exodus*
Uris, Leon. *Redemption: A Novel*
Uris, Leon. ★*Trinity*
Urquhart, Jane. *The Night Stages: A Novel*
Urquhart, Rachel. *The Visionist*
Urrea, Luis Alberto. *The Hummingbird's Daughter: A Novel*
Urrea, Luis Alberto. *Queen of America: A Novel*
Van Booy, Simon. *The Illusion of Separateness*
Vargas Llosa, Mario. *The Dream of the Celt*
Vargas Llosa, Mario. *The War of the End of the World*
Vargas Llosa, Mario. ★*The Way to Paradise*
Veletzos, Roxanne. *The Girl They Left Behind*
Verble, Margaret. ★*Cherokee America*
Verble, Margaret. ★*When Two Feathers Fell from the Sky*
Vidal, Gore. ★*Lincoln: A Novel*
Vidal, Gore. *Washington, D. C.: A Novel*
Wall, Cara. *The Dearly Beloved: A Novel*
Wallace, Carol. *Our Kind of People*
Wallace, Lew. ★*Ben-Hur*
Walsh, S. Kirk. *The Elephant of Belfast: A Novel*
Walters, Minette. *The Last Hours: A Novel*
Warren, Robert Penn. *Band of Angels*
Warren, Robert Penn. *World Enough and Time: A Romantic Novel*
Watson, Brad. *Miss Jane: A Novel*
Weiner, Jennifer. ★*Mrs. Everything: A Novel*
Weir, Alison. *Anna of Kleve: The Princess in the Portrait*
Weir, Alison. *Katharine Parr, the Sixth Wife*
Weiss, Elizabeth. *The Sisters Sweet*
Welty, Eudora. ★*The Robber Bridegroom*
Werfel, Franz. ★*The Forty Days of Musa Dagh*
West, Jessamyn. *The Friendly Persuasion*
Whitehead, Colson. ★*Harlem Shuffle*
Whitehead, Colson. ★*The Nickel Boys: A Novel*
Whitehead, Colson. ★*The Underground Railroad: A Novel*
Wieland, Liza. *Paris, 7 A.M.*
Williams, Beatriz. *All the Ways We Said Goodbye: A Novel of the Ritz Paris*
Williams, Beatriz. *The Golden Hour*
Williams, Beatriz. *The Summer Wives*
Williams, Pip. *The Dictionary of Lost Words*
Willig, Lauren. *The Summer Country: A Novel*

Winslow, De'Shawn Charles. ★*In West Mills*
Winthrop, Elizabeth Hartley. *The Mercy Seat: A Novel*
Wiseman, Ellen Marie. *The Orphan Collector*
Wolfe, Paul. *The Lost Diary of M*
Wood, Shelley. *The Quintland Sisters*
Wood, Tracey Enerson. *The Engineer's Wife: A Novel*
Woodrell, Daniel. *The Maid's Version: A Novel*
Wouk, Herman. ★*The Caine Mutiny: A Novel of World War II*
Wouk, Herman. ★*War and Remembrance: A Novel*
Wouk, Herman. ★*The Winds of War: A Novel*
Wright, Jaime Jo. *The Haunting at Bonaventure Circus*
Yoon, Paul. ★*Run Me to Earth: A Novel*
Zola, Emile. ★*Nana*

HISTORICAL HORROR

Brom. *Slewfoot: A Tale of Bewitchery*
Clark, P. Djeli. *Ring Shout*
Katsu, Alma. *The Deep*
Katsu, Alma. *The Hunger: A Novel*
Ruff, Matt. *Lovecraft Country: A Novel*
Simmons, Dan. *The Abominable: A Novel*
Stoker, Dacre. *Dracul*

HISTORICAL MYSTERIES

Abdul-Jabbar, Kareem. *The Empty Birdcage*
Abdul-Jabbar, Kareem. *Mycroft and Sherlock*
Abdul-Jabbar, Kareem. ★*Mycroft Holmes*
Airth, Rennie. *The Decent Inn of Death*
Akunin, B. *The Coronation: The Further Adventures of Erast Fandorin*
Akunin, B. *Sister Pelagia and the White Bulldog: A Mystery*
Ashley, Jennifer. *Death at the Crystal Palace*
Atwood, Margaret. *Alias Grace*
Baldacci, David. ★*A Gambling Man*
Baldacci, David. ★*One Good Deed*
Bayard, Louis. *The Black Tower: A Novel*
Bayard, Louis. *The Pale Blue Eye: A Novel*
Belli, Kate. *Deception by Gaslight: A Gilded Gotham Mystery*
Benn, James R. *Billy Boyle: A World War Two Mystery*
Benn, James R. ★*The Red Horse: A Billy Boyle World War II Mystery*
Benn, James R. *Road of Bones: A Billy Boyle World War II Mystery*
Black, Benjamin. *Wolf on a String: A Novel*
Bradley, C. Alan. *The Golden Tresses of the Dead: A Flavia De Luce Novel*
Bradley, C. Alan. *The Grave's a Fine and Private Place: A Flavia De Luce Novel*
Brandreth, Benet. *The Spy of Venice*
Buckley, Fiona. *The Doublet Affair: A Mystery at Queen Elizabeth I's Court*
Buckley, Fiona. *The Siren Queen: An Ursula Blanchard Mystery at Queen Elizabeth I's Court*
Carr, Caleb. ★*The Alienist*
Carter, Miranda. *The Strangler Vine*
Clare, Alys. *The Woman Who Spoke to Spirits*
Copenhaver, John. *The Savage Kind*
Corby, Gary. *The Marathon Conspiracy*
Davis, Lindsey. *A Body in the Bathhouse*
Davis, Lindsey. *A Comedy of Terrors: A Flavia Albia Novel*
Davis, Lindsey. *The Ides of April: A Flavia Albia Mystery*
Davis, Lindsey. *One Virgin Too Many*

Deaver, Jeffery. *Garden of Beasts: A Novel of Berlin 1936*
Delany, Vicki. *Deadly Summer Nights*
Donoghue, Emma. ★*Frog Music*
Eco, Umberto. ★*The Name of the Rose*
Ellis, Bella. *The Vanished Bride*
Ellroy, James. *Perfidia*
Ellroy, James. *This Storm: A Novel*
Ellroy, James. ★*Widespread Panic: A Novel*
Faye, Lyndsay. *The Gods of Gotham*
Faye, Lyndsay. ★*The Paragon Hotel*
Faye, Lyndsay. *Seven for a Secret*
Finch, Charles. *A Beautiful Blue Death*
Finch, Charles. *The Last Passenger*
Finch, Charles. *The September Society*
Finch, Charles. *The Vanishing Man*
Finlay, Mick. *The Murder Pit*
Franklin, Ariana. ★*Death and the Maiden*
Franklin, Ariana. *Mistress of the Art of Death*
Franklin, Ariana. *The Serpent's Tale*
Fredericks, Mariah. *Death of a New American: A Mystery*
Fredericks, Mariah. *Death of a Showman*
Freeman, Dianne. *A Fiancee's Guide to First Wives and Murder*
Freeman, Dianne. *A Lady's Guide to Etiquette and Murder*
Friedman, Daniel. *Riot Most Uncouth: A Lord Byron Mystery*
Gilbers, Harald. *Germania: A Novel of Nazi Berlin*
Gleason, Colleen. *Murder at the Capitol*
Goodwin, S. M. *Absence of Mercy*
Graves, Stephanie. *Olive Bright, Pigeoneer*
Greenwood, Kerry. *Death in Daylesford*
Greenwood, Kerry. *Out of the Black Land*
Greenwood, Kerry. *Unnatural Habits*
Grossman, Paul. *Children of Wrath*
Guinn, Matthew. *The Scribe: A Novel*
Haldane, Sean. *The Devil's Making*
Hambly, Barbara. *House of the Patriarch*
Hambly, Barbara. *Lady of Perdition*
Hambly, Barbara. *Scandal in Babylon*
Hand, Elizabeth. *Curious Toys*
Hannah, Sophie. *The Killings at Kingfisher Hill*
Hannah, Sophie. *The Mystery of Three Quarters: The New Hercule Poirot Mystery*
Harris, C. S. *What the Devil Knows: A Sebastian St. Cyr Mystery*
Harrison, Cora. *Beyond Absolution: A Mystery Set in 1920s Ireland*
Hart, Carolyn G. *Letter from Home*
Hart, Elsa. *The Cabinets of Barnaby Mayne*
Hart, Elsa. *City of Ink: A Mystery*
Hirahara, Naomi. ★*Clark and Division*
Hodgson, Antonia. *The Last Confession of Thomas Hawkins*
Horowitz, Anthony. *The House of Silk: A Sherlock Holmes Novel*
Huber, Anna Lee. *Penny for Your Secrets*
Indriðason, Arnaldur. *The Shadow District: A Thriller*
Johnson, D. E. *Detroit Shuffle*
Kaminsky, Stuart M. *Dancing in the Dark*
Kaminsky, Stuart M. *To Catch a Spy: A Toby Peters Mystery*
Kelly, Stephen. *The Wages of Desire: A World War II Mystery*
Kerr, Philip. ★*Greeks Bearing Gifts: A Bernie Gunther Novel*
Kerr, Philip. ★*Metropolis: A Bernie Gunther Novel*
Kerr, Philip. ★*Prussian Blue*

King, Laurie R. *Castle Shade*
Lansdale, Joe R. *Sunset and Sawdust*
Lansdale, Joe R. *The Thicket*
Lloyd, Catherine. *Death Comes to the Nursery*
Lloyd, Catherine. *Death Comes to the Rectory*
MacNeal, Susan Elia. *The King's Justice*
March, Nev. *Murder in Old Bombay*
Marston, Edward. *The Roaring Boy: A Novel*
Marston, Edward. *The Wanton Angel: A Novel*
Mason, Timothy. *The Darwin Affair*
Massey, Sujata. ★*The Bombay Prince*
Massey, Sujata. *The Satapur Moonstone*
Massey, Sujata. ★*The Widows of Malabar Hill: A Mystery of 1920s Bombay*
McCrumb, Sharyn. ★*The Ballad of Frankie Silver*
McPherson, Catriona. ★*A Step so Grave*
Meyer, Nicholas. *The Adventure of the Peculiar Protocols: Adapted from the Journals of John H. Watson, M.D.*
Montclair, Allison. *The Right Sort of Man*
Montclair, Allison. *A Rogue's Company*
Montclair, Allison. *A Royal Affair*
Morrell, David. *Ruler of the Night*
Mosley, Walter. *Black Betty: An Easy Rawlins Mystery*
Mosley, Walter. ★*Blood Grove*
Mosley, Walter. *Charcoal Joe: An Easy Rawlins Mystery*
Mosley, Walter. *Devil in a Blue Dress*
Mosley, Walter. *Little Scarlet: An Easy Rawlins Mystery*
Moss, Tara. *The War Widow*
Mukherjee, Abir. *Death in the East*
Mukherjee, Abir. *The Shadows of Men*
Mukherjee, Abir. *Smoke and Ashes: A Novel*
Mullen, Thomas. *Darktown: A Novel*
Mullen, Thomas. *Lightning Men: A Novel*
Neubauer, Erica Ruth. *Murder at the Mena House*
Nickson, Chris. *Come the Fear*
O'Connor, Joseph. *Star of the Sea*
O'Donnell, Paraic. *The House on Vesper Sands: A Novel*
Palliser, Charles. *The Quincunx*
Parris, S. J. ★*The Dead of Winter*
Parris, S. J. *Sacrilege*
Parris, S. J. *Treachery*
Parry, Ambrose. *The Way of All Flesh*
Pawel, Rebecca. *Death of a Nationalist*
Pearl, Matthew. *The Dante Chamber*
Pearl, Matthew. *The Dante Club: A Novel*
Pearl, Matthew. *The Last Dickens: A Novel*
Pearl, Matthew. *The Poe Shadow: A Novel*
Pearl, Matthew. *The Technologists: A Novel*
Pears, Iain. *An Instance of the Fingerpost*
Pears, Iain. *Stone's Fall*
Penman, Sharon Kay. *The Queen's Man: A Medieval Mystery*
Penrose, Andrea. *Murder at Half Moon Gate*
Penrose, Andrea. ★*Murder at Kensington Palace*
Penrose, Andrea. *Murder on Black Swan Lane*
Perry, Anne. *A Dangerous Mourning*
Perry, Anne. *Dark Tide Rising: A William Monk Novel*
Perry, Anne. ★*Death in Focus: An Elena Standish Novel*
Perry, Anne. ★*Death with a Double Edge: A Daniel Pitt Novel*

Perry, Anne. *The Face of a Stranger*
Perry, Anne. *One Fatal Flaw: A Daniel Pitt Novel*
Peters, Ellis. *Brother Cadfael's Penance*
Peters, Ellis. *The Holy Thief*
Phillips, Christi. *The Rossetti Letter: A Novel*
Pirie, David. *The Patient's Eyes*
Poole, Sara. *The Borgia Mistress*
Potzsch, Oliver. *The Beggar King*
Potzsch, Oliver. *The Dark Monk: A Hangman's Daughter Tale*
Potzsch, Oliver. *The Hangman's Daughter: A Historical Novel*
Potzsch, Oliver. *The Play of Death*
Potzsch, Oliver. *The Poisoned Pilgrim: A Hangman's Daughter Tale*
Potzsch, Oliver. *The Werewolf of Bamberg*
Pronzini, Bill. *The Stolen Gold Affair*
Putnam, Jonathan F. *These Honored Dead*
Quick, Amanda. *Garden of Lies*
Quincy, D. M. *Murder at the Opera*
Quincy, D. M. *Murder in Mayfair: An Atlas Catesby Mystery*
Ramsay, Frederick. *Countdown*
Raybourn, Deanna. *A Curious Beginning: A Veronica Speedwell Mystery*
Raybourn, Deanna. *A Dangerous Collaboration*
Raybourn, Deanna. *A Perilous Undertaking: A Veronica Speedwell Mystery*
Raybourn, Deanna. *A Treacherous Curse: A Veronica Speedwell Mystery*
Rhys, Rachel. *Fatal Inheritance*
Ripley, Mike. *Mr Campion's Coven*
Robb, Candace M. ★*A Choir of Crows*
Robb, Candace M. *The Cross-Legged Knight: An Owen Archer Mystery*
Robb, Candace M. *A Gift of Sanctuary: An Owen Archer Mystery*
Robb, Candace M. *A Murdered Peace*
Robb, Candace M. *The Riddle of St. Leonard's: An Owen Archer Mystery.*
Robb, Candace M. *A Twisted Vengeance*
Robertson, Imogen. *Anatomy of Murder*
Robertson, Imogen. *Circle of Shadows*
Robertson, Imogen. *Instruments of Darkness: A Novel*
Robertson, Imogen. *Island of Bones*
Roosevelt, Elliott. ★*Murder and the First Lady*
Roosevelt, Elliott. *Murder at Midnight*
Roosevelt, Elliott. *Murder in the Map Room: An Eleanor Roosevelt Mystery*
Roosevelt, Elliott. *Murder in the Oval Office*
Rowland, Laura Joh. *The Hangman's Secret*
Rowland, Laura Joh. *The Incense Game: A Novel of Feudal Japan*
Rowland, Laura Joh. *The Iris Fan: A Novel of Feudal Japan*
Rowland, Laura Joh. *The Ripper's Shadow*
Rowland, Laura Joh. *The Shogun's Daughter: A Novel of Feudal Japan*
Rowland, Laura Joh. *The Snow Empress*
Runcie, James. *The Road to Grantchester*
Sansom, C. J. ★*Lamentation*
Sansom, C. J. *Revelation*
Sansom, C. J. ★*Sovereign*
Sansom, C. J. *Tombland*
Saunders, Kate. *The Case of the Wandering Scholar*

Saunders, Kate. *The Secrets of Wishtide*
Saylor, Steven. *The House of the Vestals: The Investigations of Gordianus the Finder*
Saylor, Steven. *The Judgment of Caesar: A Novel of Ancient Rome*
Saylor, Steven. *A Mist of Prophecies*
Saylor, Steven. *Raiders of the Nile: A Novel of the Ancient World*
Saylor, Steven. *Rubicon*
Saylor, Steven. *The Seven Wonders: A Novel of the Ancient World*
Saylor, Steven. *The Triumph of Caesar: A Novel of Ancient Rome*
Saylor, Steven. *Wrath of the Furies: A Novel of the Ancient World*
Schellman, Katharine. *Silence in the Library*
Sedgwick, Marcus. *Mister Memory: A Novel*
Sepetys, Ruta. ★*Out of the Easy*
Shaw, William. *A Song for the Brokenhearted*
Simmons, Dan. *Drood: A Novel*
Simmons, Dan. *The Fifth Heart*
Simpson, Rosemary. *Let the Dead Keep Their Secrets*
Simpson, Rosemary. ★*What the Dead Leave Behind*
Smith, Martin Cruz. *Stallion Gate*
Spann, Susan. *Blade of the Samurai: A Shinobi Mystery*
Spann, Susan. ★*Claws of the Cat: A Shinobi Mystery*
Spann, Susan. *Trial on Mount Koya: A Hiro Hattori Novel*
Speller, Elizabeth. *The Return of Captain John Emmett*
Speller, Elizabeth. *The Strange Fate of Kitty Easton*
Starr, Melvin R. *Unhallowed Ground*
Stewart, Amy. ★*Dear Miss Kopp*
Stewart, Amy. *Kopp Sisters on the March*
Stewart, Amy. *Lady Cop Makes Trouble*
Stewart, Amy. ★*Miss Kopp Investigates*
Stewart, Amy. ★*Miss Kopp Just Won't Quit*
Stewart, Amy. *Miss Kopp's Midnight Confessions*
Straley, John. *The Big Both Ways*
Tallis, Frank. *Vienna Blood: A Max Liebermann Mystery*
Talton, Jon. *City of Dark Corners*
Thomas, Will. *Dance with Death*
Thompson, Victoria. *Murder on Wall Street*
Thomson, E. S. *Beloved Poison*
Thomson, E. S. *The Blood*
Todd, Charles. ★*A Hanging at Dawn*
Truss, Lynne. *The Man That Got Away: A Constable Twitten Mystery*
Truss, Lynne. *Murder by Milk Bottle*
Turton, Stuart. ★*The Devil and the Dark Water*
Weaver, Ashley. ★*A Peculiar Combination*
Welsh, Kaite. *The Unquiet Heart*
Welsh, Kaite. *The Wages of Sin*
Winspear, Jacqueline. *The American Agent*
Winspear, Jacqueline. ★*The Consequences of Fear: A Maisie Dobbs Novel*
Wojtas, Olga. *Miss Blaine's Prefect and the Golden Samovar*
Wolfe, Suzanne M. *The Course of All Treasons*

HISTORICAL REENACTMENTS
Andrews, Donna. *Murder Most Fowl: A Meg Langslow Mystery*
Moss, Sarah. *Ghost Wall: A Novel*
HISTORICAL ROMANCES
Afshar, Tessa. *Jewel of the Nile*
Alexander, Victoria. *The Lady Travelers Guide to Larceny with a Dashing Stranger*

Alexander, Victoria. *The Lady Travelers Guide to Scoundrels and Other Gentlemen*
Allain, Suzanne. *Miss Lattimore's Letter*
Allen, Susanna. *A Wolf in Duke's Clothing*
Ashley, Jennifer. *Lady Isabella's Scandalous Marriage*
Ashley, Jennifer. *The Madness of Lord Ian Mackenzie*
Balogh, Mary. *The Arrangement*
Balogh, Mary. *The Escape*
Balogh, Mary. *More Than a Mistress*
Balogh, Mary. *Only Enchanting*
Balogh, Mary. *The Secret Mistress*
Balogh, Mary. *Simply Love*
Balogh, Mary. ★*Someone to Care*
Balogh, Mary. ★*Someone to Cherish*
Balogh, Mary. *Someone to Hold*
Balogh, Mary. ★*Someone to Love*
Balogh, Mary. ★*Someone to Remember: A Westcott Story*
Balogh, Mary. *Someone to Trust*
Balogh, Mary. *Someone to Wed*
Banks, Maya. *Never Seduce a Scot*
Bateman, Kate. *A Reckless Match*
Bateman, Kate. *This Earl of Mine*
Bell, Lenora. *For the Duke's Eyes Only*
Bell, Lenora. ★*How the Duke Was Won*
Bell, Lenora. *One Fine Duke*
Bell, Lenora. ★*What a Difference a Duke Makes*
Bennett, Bethany. *West End Earl*
Berne, Lisa. *You May Kiss the Bride*
Beverley, Jo. *My Lady Notorious*
Beverley, Jo. *Tempting Fortune*
Bittner, Rosanne. *Logan's Lady*
Bourne, Joanna. *The Black Hawk*
Bourne, Joanna. *The Forbidden Rose*
Bourne, Joanna. ★*My Lord and Spymaster*
Bourne, Joanna. *Rogue Spy*
Bourne, Joanna. ★*The Spymaster's Lady*
Bowen, Kelly. ★*Between the Devil and the Duke*
Bowen, Kelly. *A Rogue by Night*
Bowman, Valerie. *The Accidental Countess*
Bowman, Valerie. *A Duke Like No Other*
Bowman, Valerie. *No Other Duke but You*
Bowman, Valerie. *Secrets of a Wedding Night*
Bowman, Valerie. *The Unexpected Duchess*
Boyle, Elizabeth. *Along Came a Duke*
Boyle, Elizabeth. *And the Miss Ran Away with the Rake*
Bradley, Anna. *A Season of Ruin*
Bradley, Anna. *A Wicked Way to Win an Earl*
Brockway, Connie. *The Golden Season*
Brockway, Connie. *No Place for a Dame*
Brockway, Connie. *So Enchanting*
Brown, Sandra. ★*Blind Tiger*
Burrowes, Grace. *The Captive*
Burrowes, Grace. *My One and Only Duke*
Burrowes, Grace. ★*A Rogue of Her Own*
Burrowes, Grace. *Tremaine's True Love*
Burrowes, Grace. *The Trouble with Dukes*
Byrne, Kerrigan. *The Duke with the Dragon Tattoo*
Byrne, Kerrigan. *How to Love a Duke in Ten Days*

Byrne, Kerrigan. *The Hunter*
Callihan, Kristen. ★*Firelight*
Carlyle, Christy. *Duke Gone Rogue*
Charles, KJ. *Wanted, a Gentleman: Or, Virtue Over-Rated*
Chase, Loretta Lynda. *Don't Tempt Me*
Chase, Loretta Lynda. *A Duke in Shining Armor*
Chase, Loretta Lynda. *Miss Wonderful*
Cole, Alyssa. ★*An Extraordinary Union*
Cole, Alyssa. ★*A Hope Divided*
Cole, Alyssa. ★*An Unconditional Freedom*
Collins, Manda. *A Good Rake Is Hard to Find*
Collins, Manda. ★*A Lady's Guide to Mischief and Mayhem*
Collins, Manda. *One for the Rogue*
Collins, Manda. *Ready Set Rogue*
Dare, Tessa. *Do You Want to Start a Scandal*
Dare, Tessa. ★*The Duchess Deal*
Dare, Tessa. ★*The Governess Game*
Dare, Tessa. ★*A Night to Surrender*
Dare, Tessa. *Romancing the Duke*
Dare, Tessa. ★*Say Yes to the Marquess*
Dare, Tessa. ★*The Wallflower Wager*
Dare, Tessa. *A Week to Be Wicked*
Dare, Tessa. *When a Scot Ties the Knot*
Drake, Olivia. *When a Duke Loves a Governess*
Du Maurier, Daphne. *Jamaica Inn*
Dunmore, Evie. ★*Bringing Down the Duke*
Everett, Elizabeth. ★*A Lady's Formula for Love*
Force, Marie. *Deceived by Desire*
Frampton, Megan. *The Duke's Guide to Correct Behavior*
Frampton, Megan. *Never a Bride*
Frampton, Megan. *Put up Your Duke*
Frantz, Laura. *The Lacemaker*
Galen, Shana. *Third Son's a Charm*
Garriott, Leah. *Promised*
Garwood, Julie. *The Bride*
Goodman, Jo. *In Want of a Wife*
Goodman, Jo. *A Touch of Forever*
Gracie, Anne. *Marry in Scandal*
Guhrke, Laura Lee. *Governess Gone Rogue*
Guhrke, Laura Lee. *How to Lose a Duke in Ten Days*
Guhrke, Laura Lee. *The Trouble with True Love*
Guhrke, Laura Lee. *The Truth About Love and Dukes*
Guhrke, Laura Lee. *When the Marquess Met His Match*
Harrington, Anna. *An Extraordinary Lord*
Harrington, Anna. *An Inconvenient Duke*
Hawks, Arlem. *Georgana's Secret*
Heath, Lorraine. *Falling into Bed with a Duke*
Heyer, Georgette. *Black Sheep*
Heyer, Georgette. *The Grand Sophy*
Heyer, Georgette. *These Old Shades*
Hill, Donna. ★*Confessions in B-Flat*
Hoyt, Elizabeth. *Not the Duke's Darling*
Hoyt, Elizabeth. *When a Rogue Meets His Match*
James, Eloisa. ★*Seven Minutes in Heaven*
James, Eloisa. *Three Weeks with Lady X*
James, Eloisa. *The Ugly Duchess*
James, Eloisa. *Wilde in Love*
Jeffries, Sabrina. *Project Duchess*

Jenkins, Beverly. *Forbidden*
Jenkins, Beverly. *Rebel*
Jenkins, Beverly. *Tempest*
Jenkins, Beverly. *Wild Rain*
Jordan, Sophie. *The Duke Goes Down*
Jordan, Sophie. *This Scot of Mine*
Kleypas, Lisa. *Cold-Hearted Rake*
Kleypas, Lisa. ★*Devil in Disguise*
Laurens, Stephanie. *The Pursuits of Lord Kit Cavanaugh*
Leigh, Eva. *Forever Your Earl*
Leigh, Eva. *Scandal Takes the Stage*
Leigh, Eva. *Temptations of a Wallflower*
Lin, Jeannie. *The Lotus Palace*
London, Julia. *Wild Wicked Scot*
Long, Julie Anne. *Angel in a Devil's Arms*
Long, Julie Anne. ★*Lady Derring Takes a Lover*
MacLean, Sarah. ★*Bombshell*
MacLean, Sarah. ★*Brazen and the Beast*
MacLean, Sarah. *No Good Duke Goes Unpunished*
MacLean, Sarah. *The Rogue Not Taken*
MacLean, Sarah. ★*Wicked and the Wallflower*
Matthews, Mimi. ★*The Siren of Sussex*
Milan, Courtney. *The Duchess War*
Putney, Mary Jo. *Loving a Lost Lord*
Putney, Mary Jo. *The Marriage Spell: A Novel*
Putney, Mary Jo. *No Longer a Gentleman*
Putney, Mary Jo. *Not Quite a Wife*
Putney, Mary Jo. *Nowhere Near Respectable*
Putney, Mary Jo. *Once a Scoundrel*
Putney, Mary Jo. *Once a Soldier*
Quick, Amanda. *'til Death Do Us Part*
Quick, Amanda. *Close Up*
Quick, Amanda. *The Girl Who Knew Too Much*
Quick, Amanda. ★*The Lady Has a Past*
Quick, Amanda. *The Other Lady Vanishes*
Quincy, Diana. *Her Night with the Duke*
Quincy, Diana. *The Viscount Made Me Do It*
Quinn, Julia. ★*An Offer from a Gentleman*
Ridley, Erica. *The Duke Heist*
Ridley, Erica. ★*The Perks of Loving a Wallflower*
Riley, Vanessa. ★*A Duke, the Lady, and a Baby*
Riley, Vanessa. ★*An Earl, the Girl, and a Toddler*
Romain, Theresa. *Fortune Favors the Wicked*
Sebastian, Cat. *It Takes Two to Tumble*
Sebastian, Cat. *The Lawrence Browne Affair*
Sebastian, Cat. *Unmasked by the Marquess*
Shupe, Joanna. *The Courtesan Duchess*
Shupe, Joanna. *The Heiress Hunt*
Shupe, Joanna. *The Prince of Broadway*
Shupe, Joanna. *The Rogue of Fifth Avenue*
Spencer, Minerva. *Barbarous*
Spencer, Minerva. *Dangerous*
Spencer, Minerva. *Scandalous*
St. George, Harper. *The Heiress Gets a Duke*
Sullivan, Emily. *The Rebel and the Rake*
Vayden, Kristin. *Fortune Favors the Duke*
Waite, Olivia. *The Care and Feeding of Waspish Widows*
Waite, Olivia. ★*The Lady's Guide to Celestial Mechanics*

Waters, Martha. ★*To Have and to Hoax: A Novel*
Waters, Martha. *To Love and to Loathe: A Novel*

HISTORICAL THRILLERS
Black, Benjamin. ★*The Secret Guests: A Novel*
Black, Cara. ★*Three Hours in Paris*
Burke, James Lee. *House of the Rising Sun: A Novel*
Burnet, Graeme Macrae. *His Bloody Project: Documents Relating to the Case of Roderick Macrae*
Clements, Oliver. *The Eyes of the Queen*
Clements, Oliver. *The Queen's Men*
Cussler, Clive. ★*The Chase*
Cussler, Clive. *The Cutthroat*
Cussler, Clive. ★*The Titanic Secret*
Cussler, Clive. *The Wrecker*
Deutermann, Peter T. *The Iceman*
Deutermann, Peter T. *The Nugget: A Novel*
Downing, David. *Diary of a Dead Man on Leave*
Dunmore, Helen. *Exposure*
Fleischmann, Raymond. *How Quickly She Disappears*
Follett, Ken. *Eye of the Needle*
Follett, Ken. *Jackdaws*
Furst, Alan. *Blood of Victory: A Novel*
Furst, Alan. *The Foreign Correspondent: A Novel*
Furst, Alan. ★*A Hero of France*
Furst, Alan. ★*Mission to Paris*
Furst, Alan. *Spies of the Balkans: A Novel*
Furst, Alan. *The Spies of Warsaw*
Furst, Alan. ★*Under Occupation: A Novel*
Goldstone, Lawrence. *Assassin of Shadows*
Gross, Andrew. *The One Man*
Harris, Robert. *Enigma*
Harris, Robert. *An Officer and a Spy*
Hewson, David. *The Garden of Angels*
Higgins, Jack. *The Eagle Has Flown*
Higgins, Jack. *The Eagle Has Landed*
Lehane, Dennis. *World Gone By: A Novel*
Lippman, Laura. ★*Lady in the Lake: A Novel*
McGuire, Ian. *The Abstainer: A Novel*
Mina, Denise. ★*Rizzio*
Perry, Anne. ★*A Darker Reality*
Perry, Anne. *A Question of Betrayal*
Phillips, Arthur. ★*The King at the Edge of the World: Novel*
Quinn, Kate. ★*The Huntress*
Rindell, Suzanne. *The Other Typist*
Smith, Martin Cruz. *December 6*
Smith, Tom Rob. *Agent 6*
Smith, Tom Rob. *Child 44*
Smith, Tom Rob. *The Secret Speech*
Steinhauer, Olen. *The Bridge of Sighs*
Tanabe, Karin. ★*A Woman of Intelligence*
Twardoch, Szczepan. *The King of Warsaw*
Vachss, Andrew H. *Two Trains Running*
Whitfield, Clare. *People of Abandoned Character*

HISTORY
Barnes, Julian. ★*A History of the World in 10 1/2 Chapters*
Faulks, Sebastian. *Paris Echo: A Novel*
Khoury, Raymond. *Empire of Lies*
McMahon, Jennifer. *The Invited: A Novel*

Williams, Pip. *The Dictionary of Lost Words*
Yu, Miri. *Tokyo Ueno Station*
The **History** of the Siege of Lisbon. Saramago, Jose
★*A **History** of the World in 10 1/2 Chapters*. Barnes, Julian
★*The **History** of Tom Jones, a Foundling*. Fielding, Henry
★***History** of Wolves: A Novel*. Fridlund, Emily
HISTORY WRITING — WARS AND CONFLICTS — HOLOCAUST — WORLD WAR II
   Wiesel, Elie. ★*Night, Dawn, the Accident: Three Tales*
Hit List. Woods, Stuart
Hit Me: A Keller Novel. Block, Lawrence
HIT-AND-RUN ACCIDENTS
   Gran, Sara. *The Infinite Blacktop: A Novel*
   Gundar-Goshen, Ayelet. *Waking Lions*
   Lalami, Laila. *The Other Americans: A Novel*
   O'Brien, Perry Edmond. *Fire in the Blood*
HIT-AND-RUN DRIVERS
   Gundar-Goshen, Ayelet. *Waking Lions*
HIT-AND-RUN VICTIMS
   Abbott, Megan E. *You Will Know Me: A Novel*
Hitchhiker series [Series]. Adams, Douglas
★*The **Hitchhiker's** Guide to the Galaxy*. Adams, Douglas
HITCHHIKING
   Kerouac, Jack. ★*On the Road*
   Tobar, Hector. *The Last Great Road Bum*
HITLER, ADOLF
   Amis, Martin. *Lionel Asbo: State of England*
   Black, Cara. ★*Three Hours in Paris*
   Brown, Pierce. *Golden Son*
   Harris, Robert. ★*Fatherland*
   Jimenez, Abby. ★*The Happy Ever After Playlist*
   Levin, Ira. *The Boys from Brazil: A Novel*
   Wouk, Herman. ★*War and Remembrance: A Novel*
   Wouk, Herman. ★*The Winds of War: A Novel*
Hitting a Straight Lick with a Crooked Stick: Stories from the Harlem Renaissance. Hurston, Zora Neale
HO CHI MINH CITY (VIETNAM)
   Soli, Tatjana. *The Lotus Eaters*
Ho, Lauren
   Last Tang Standing
Hoang, Helen
   ★*The Bride Test*
   ★*The Heart Principle*
   ★*The Kiss Quotient*
HOAXES
   Kellerman, Jonathan. *Gone*
   Kunzru, Hari. *White Tears*
   Palmer, Dexter Clarence. ★*Mary Toft; Or, the Rabbit Queen: A Novel*
★*The **Hobbit**, Or, There and Back Again*. Tolkien, J. R. R.
HOBBITS (FICTITIOUS CHARACTERS)
   Tolkien, J. R. R. ★*The Hobbit, Or, There and Back Again*
HOBBY MYSTERIES
   Cleland, Jane K. *Hidden Treasure*
   Hall, Parnell. *Lights! Camera! Puzzles!*
   O'Donohue, Clare. *The Lover's Knot: A Someday Quilts Mystery*
HOBOES
   James, P. D. *A Taste for Death*

Hobson, Brandon
   ★*The Removed: A Novel*
HOCKEY
   Backman, Fredrik. ★*Beartown: A Novel*
   Backman, Fredrik. *Us Against You: A Novel*
Hockman, Angie
   Shipped
HOCKNEY, DAVID
   Cusset, Catherine. *Life of David Hockney: A Novel*
   Tudor, C. J. *The Other People*
Hocus Pocus. Vonnegut, Kurt
Hodges, Cheris F.
   Rumor Has It
Hodgson, Antonia
   The Last Confession of Thomas Hawkins
Hoeg, Peter
   ★*Smilla's Sense of Snow*
Hoffman, Alice
   The Book of Magic
   The Ice Queen: A Novel
   The Marriage of Opposites: A Novel Based on the Life of Rachel Pizzarro
   The Museum of Extraordinary Things: A Novel
   The River King
   The Rules of Magic: A Novel
   ★*The World That We Knew*
Hoffmann, R. J.
   Other People's Children: A Novel
Hogan, Ruth
   Queenie Malone's Paradise Hotel
Hogarth Shakespeare [Series]. Tyler, Anne
HOGARTH, WILLIAM
   Dean, Michael. *I, Hogarth*
Holahan, Cate
   Her Three Lives
Holbert, Bruce
   Whiskey
Hold Fast. Gelernter, J. H.
Hold Fast Through the Fire. Wagers, K. B.
Hold Tight. Coben, Harlan
Hold Your Breath, China. Qiu, Xiaolong
*The **Holdout**: a Novel*. Moore, Graham
Holdstock, Pauline
   Here I Am!
HOLE, HARRY (FICTITIOUS CHARACTER)
   Nesbo, Jo. *The Leopard*
   Nesbo, Jo. *The Redeemer*
HOLIDAY MYSTERIES
   Andrews, Donna. *Owl Be Home for Christmas: A Meg Langslow Mystery*
   Andrews, Donna. *The Twelve Jays of Christmas: A Meg Langslow Mystery*
   Avon, Joy. *In Peppermint Peril: A Book Tea Shop Mystery*
   Berry, Connie. *A Legacy of Murder*
   Childs, Laura. *Haunted Hibiscus*
   Childs, Laura. *Twisted Tea Christmas*
   Fluke, Joanne. ★*Christmas Cupcake Murder*
   Shaw, M. B. *Murder at the Mill: A Mystery*

HOLIDAY ROMANCES
    Balogh, Mary. *Someone to Trust*
    Blackstock, Terri. *Catching Christmas*
    Bryant, Niobia. *Christmas with the Billionaire*
    Guillory, Jasmine. *Royal Holiday*
    Lalli, Sonya. *A Holly Jolly Diwali*
    Lauren, Christina. *In a Holidaze*
    Meltzer, Jean. ★*The Matzah Ball*
    Snow, Jennifer. *An Alaskan Christmas*
    Sterling, Erin. *The Ex Hex*
HOLIDAYS
    Hobson, Brandon. ★*The Removed: A Novel*
    Quinn, Spencer. ★*It's a Wonderful Woof*
    Sedaris, David. *Holidays on Ice*
Holidays on Ice. Sedaris, David
Holland family saga [Series]. Burke, James Lee
Holland, Cecelia
    Jerusalem
HOLLIDAY, JOHN H.
    Russell, Mary Doria. ★*Doc: A Novel*
    Smith, Scott. *The Ruins: A Novel*
Hollis, Lee
    Poppy Harmon Investigates
The **Hollow**. Christie, Agatha
★*The* **Hollow** *Hills*. Stewart, Mary
★*Hollow Kingdom*. Buxton, Kira Jane
Hollow kingdom [Series]. Buxton, Kira Jane
Hollow Man. Pryor, Mark
Hollow man [Series]. Pryor, Mark
The **Hollow** *Ones*. Toro, Guillermo del
Holly Barker novels [Series]. Woods, Stuart
A **Holly** *Jolly Diwali*. Lalli, Sonya
HOLLYWOOD CALIFORNIA
    Quick, Amanda. *Close Up*
    Quick, Amanda. ★*The Lady Has a Past*
★*Hollywood Homicide*. Garrett, Kellye
HOLLYWOOD, CALIFORNIA
    Alcott, Kate. *A Touch of Stardust*
    Alexander, Jennet. *I Kissed a Girl*
    Allen, Jane. *I Lost My Girlish Laughter*
    Bagshawe, Tilly. *Adored*
    Benedict, Marie. *The Only Woman in the Room*
    Bloom, Amy. *Lucky Us: A Novel*
    Brunkhorst, Alex. *The Gilded Life of Matilda Duplaine*
    Childress, Mark. *Crazy in Alabama*
    Connelly, Michael. *Dark Sacred Night*
    Connelly, Michael. *The Late Show*
    Estleman, Loren D. *Frames*
    Estleman, Loren D. ★*Indigo: A Valentino Mystery*
    Fitzgerald, F. Scott. ★*The Last Tycoon: An Unfinished Novel*
    Garrett, Kellye. ★*Hollywood Homicide*
    Goldman, Matt. *Dead West*
    Guillory, Jasmine. ★*While We Were Dating*
    Hallinan, Timothy. *Fields Where They Lay*
    Hambly, Barbara. *Scandal in Babylon*
    Kaminsky, Stuart M. *Dancing in the Dark*
    Kaminsky, Stuart M. *To Catch a Spy: A Toby Peters Mystery*
    Kleeman, Alexandra. *Something New Under the Sun*

    Lane, Byron. ★*A Star Is Bored*
    Lauren, Christina. *Dating You / Hating You*
    Leonard, Elmore. ★*Be Cool: Everyone Is Looking for the Next Big Hit*
    Leonard, Elmore. ★*Get Shorty*
    Oates, Joyce Carol. *Blonde: A Novel*
    Palahniuk, Chuck. *The Invention of Sound*
    Phillips, Susan Elizabeth. *What I Did for Love*
    Puzo, Mario. *The Last Don*
    Quick, Amanda. *The Girl Who Knew Too Much*
    Quick, Amanda. *The Other Lady Vanishes*
    Smith, Dominic. ★*The Electric Hotel*
    Steadman, Catherine. *The Disappearing Act*
    Waugh, Evelyn. *The Loved One: An Anglo-American Tragedy*
    Woods, Stuart. ★*Bombshell*
    Woods, Stuart. *The Money Shot*
Holmes, J. M.
    How Are You Going to Save Yourself
Holmes, Linda
    ★*Evvie Drake Starts Over: A Novel*
Holmes, Shannon
    ★*B-More Careful: A Novel*
HOLMES, SHERLOCK (FICTITIOUS CHARACTER)
    Doyle, Arthur Conan. ★*The Complete Sherlock Holmes*
    Faye, Lyndsay. *The Whole Art of Detection: Lost Mysteries of Sherlock Holmes*
    Simmons, Dan. *The Fifth Heart*
HOLOCAUST (1933-1945)
    Amis, Martin. ★*Time's Arrow, or the Nature of the Offense*
    Amis, Martin. ★*The Zone of Interest: A Novel*
    D'Eramo, Luce. *Deviation*
    Englander, Nathan. *What We Talk About When We Talk About Anne Frank: Stories*
    Faulks, Sebastian. *Charlotte Gray: A Novel*
    Foer, Jonathan Safran. *Everything Is Illuminated: A Novel*
    Gross, Andrew. *The One Man*
    Harris, Robert. ★*Fatherland*
    Hoffman, Alice. ★*The World That We Knew*
    Keneally, Thomas. ★*Schindler's List*
    Konar, Affinity. *Mischling: A Novel*
    Kosinski, Jerzy. ★*The Painted Bird*
    Picoult, Jodi. *The Storyteller*
    Russell, Mary Doria. *A Thread of Grace: A Novel*
    Sebald, Winfried Georg. ★*Austerlitz*
    Sebald, Winfried Georg. *The Emigrants ;*
    Shepard, Jim. ★*The Book of Aron*
    Wiesel, Elie. ★*Night, Dawn, the Accident: Three Tales*
    Wouk, Herman. ★*War and Remembrance: A Novel*
    Wouk, Herman. ★*The Winds of War: A Novel*
HOLOCAUST SURVIVORS
    Bellow, Saul. ★*Mr. Sammler's Planet*
    Blum, Jenna. *The Lost Family*
    Chakrabarti, Jai. *A Play for the End of the World*
    Englander, Nathan. *What We Talk About When We Talk About Anne Frank: Stories*
    Helprin, Mark. *Paris in the Present Tense*
    Horowitz, Anthony. ★*Magpie Murders*
    Keneally, Thomas. ★*Schindler's List*

Morris, Heather. *Cilka's Journey*
Rabb, Jonathan. *Among the Living*
Singer, Isaac Bashevis. *Enemies, a Love Story*
Uris, Leon. ★*Exodus*
Wiesel, Elie. ★*Dawn*
Wiesel, Elie. *A Mad Desire to Dance: A Novel*
Wiesel, Elie. ★*Night, Dawn, the Accident: Three Tales*
A **Hologram** for the King: A Novel. Eggers, Dave
Holroyde, Claire
   The Effort
Holsinger, Bruce W.
   The Gifted School: A Novel
Holt, Victoria
   The Black Opal
Holton, India
   The Wisteria Society of Lady Scoundrels
Holy Ghost. Sandford, John
Holy Lands: A Novel. Sthers, Amanda
HOLY ROMAN EMPIRE
   Galchen, Rivka. *Everyone Knows Your Mother Is a Witch*
Holy Skirts. Steinke, Rene
The *Holy* Thief. Peters, Ellis
Home. Morrison, Toni
Home. Robinson, Marilynne
HOME (CONCEPT)
   Alvar, Mia. *In the Country: Stories*
   Alyan, Hala. *Salt Houses*
   Carr, Robyn. ★*The Wanderer*
   Chambers, Becky. *Record of a Spaceborn Few*
   Chambers, Becky. *To Be Taught, If Fortunate*
   Cisneros, Sandra. ★*The House on Mango Street*
   Crummey, Michael. *Sweetland*
   Ekwuyasi, Francesca. *Butter Honey Pig Bread: A Novel*
   Enright, Anne. *The Green Road: A Novel*
   Garcia, Cristina. *Dreaming in Cuban*
   Johnson, Caleb. *Treeborne*
   Kingsolver, Barbara. ★*Unsheltered*
   Larkin, Allie. *The People We Keep*
   Lucashenko, Melissa. *Too Much Lip*
   Naipaul, V. S. *A House for Mr. Biswas*
   Nguyen, Viet Thanh. ★*The Refugees*
   Thammavongsa, Souvankham. *How to Pronounce Knife: Stories*
HOME BIRTH
   Harman, Patricia. *The Midwife of Hope River: A Novel*
HOME CONFINEMENT (CORRECTIONS)
   Towles, Amor. ★*A Gentleman in Moscow*
HOME EXCHANGES
   Colgan, Jenny. *500 Miles from You*
Home Fire: A Novel. Shamsie, Kamila
Home for Erring and Outcast Girls. Kibler, Julie
Home Front. Hannah, Kristin
HOME INVASIONS
   Crais, Robert. *The First Rule*
   Fielding, Joy. *The Bad Daughter: A Novel*
   Heley, Veronica. *Murder in Law*
   Phillips, Helen. *The Need: A Novel*
   Slaughter, Karin. *The Good Daughter*
   Tremblay, Paul. ★*The Cabin at the End of the World: A Novel*

HOME OWNERSHIP
   Hamya, Jo. *Three Rooms*
Home Sweet Homicide. Rice, Craig
The **Homecoming**: a Novel. Pyper, Andrew
HOMECOMINGS
   Barnett, S. K. *Safe*
   Bijan, Donia. *The Last Days of Cafe Leila*
   Blackstock, Terri. *Smoke Screen*
   Bond, Cynthia. *Ruby: A Novel*
   Bradley, C. Alan. *Thrice the Brinded Cat Hath Mew'd: A Flavia De Luce Novel*
   Butler, Sarah. *Ten Things I've Learnt About Love: A Novel*
   Byrne, Trevor. *Ghosts and Lightning*
   Cleage, Pearl. *What Looks Like Crazy on an Ordinary Day: A Novel*
   Cole, Teju. *Every Day Is for the Thief*
   Cornwell, Patricia Daniels. *Autopsy*
   Coster, Naima. *Halsey Street*
   Dang, Catherine. *Nice Girls*
   Delinsky, Barbara. *A Week at the Shore*
   Dorey-Stein, Beck. *Rock the Boat: A Novel*
   Fielding, Joy. *The Bad Daughter: A Novel*
   Frank, Dorothea Benton. *Folly Beach: A Lowcountry Tale*
   French, Nicci. ★*House of Correction*
   Guhrke, Laura Lee. *How to Lose a Duke in Ten Days*
   Harper, Jane. *The Survivors*
   Hart, Elsa. *City of Ink: A Mystery*
   Higgins, Kristan. ★*The Best Man*
   Higgins, Kristan. *Now That You Mention It*
   Hogan, Ruth. *Queenie Malone's Paradise Hotel*
   James, Wendy. *A Little Bird*
   Jordan, Sophie. *The Duke Goes Down*
   Kraus, Daniel. *The Autumnal: The Complete Series*
   Lee, Harper. ★*Go Set a Watchman*
   London, Julia. *The Charmer in Chaps*
   Markley, Stephen. *Ohio*
   Marsh, Nicola. *The Boy Toy*
   Mason, Meg. *Sorrow and Bliss*
   McFarland, Jeni. *The House of Deep Water*
   McHugh, Laura. *What's Done in Darkness: A Novel*
   North, Alex. *The Shadows*
   Okorafor, Nnedi. *Binti: The Night Masquerade*
   Pineiro, Caridad. *South Beach Love: A Feel-Good Romance from Hallmark Publishing*
   Price, Reynolds. *The Good Priest's Son*
   Ratner, Vaddey. *Music of the Ghosts*
   Redondo, Dolores. *The Invisible Guardian*
   Robinson, Marilynne. *Home*
   Rodriques, Elias. *All the Water I've Seen Is Running: A Novel*
   Shalvis, Jill. *Second Chance Summer*
   Singh, Nalini. *A Madness of Sunshine*
   Smith, Michael F. *Blackwood*
   Strout, Elizabeth. ★*The Burgess Boys: A Novel*
   Swann, Stacey. *Olympus Texas*
   Tyree, Omar. *For the Love of Money: A Novel*
   Whitaker, Chris. ★*We Begin at the End*
   Wiggs, Susan. ★*The Oysterville Sewing Circle*
   Willett, Marcia. *The Garden House*
   Williams, Preslaysa. *A Lowcountry Bride*

Yun, Jung. *O Beautiful: A Novel*
★*Homegoing: a Novel*. Gyasi, Yaa
Homeland. Aramburu, Fernando
★*Homeland Elegies: A Novel*. Akhtar, Ayad
HOMELESS FAMILIES
Clement, Jennifer. *Gun Love*
HOMELESS MEN
Coetzee, J. M. *Age of Iron*
Galligan, John. *Bad Moon Rising*
Haddam, Jane. *Hardscrabble Road*
Pronzini, Bill. *Spook*
HOMELESS PEOPLE WITH MENTAL ILLNESSES
Pronzini, Bill. *Spook*
HOMELESS PERSONS
Green, Jocelyn. *Veiled in Smoke*
Steinbeck, John. *Cannery Row*
HOMELESS TEENAGERS
Burns, Charles. ★*Black Hole*
Guterson, David. *Our Lady of the Forest*
Lippman, Laura. *No Good Deeds*
HOMELESSNESS
Robertson, Robin. *The Long Take: A Noir Narrative*
HOMEMAKERS
Barr, Mark. *Watershed*
Hendrix, Grady. *The Southern Book Club's Guide to Slaying Vampires*
Itami, Emily. *Fault Lines: A Novel*
Kaufman, Sue. *Diary of a Mad Housewife*
Levin, Ira. ★*The Stepford Wives: A Novel*
Weldon, Fay. *The Life and Loves of a She-Devil*
HOMEOWNERS
Jemc, Jac. ★*The Grip of It*
HOMER
Rollins, James. ★*The Last Odyssey*
Homer and Langley: A Novel. Doctorow, E. L.
HOMESTEADERS
Durham, David Anthony. ★*Gabriel's Story*
Grey, Zane. *Woman of the Frontier: A Western Story*
Michener, James A. ★*Centennial*
HOMESTEADING
ffitch, Madeline. *Stay and Fight*
Keesey, Anna. *Little Century: A Novel*
HOMETOWNS
Dimitri, Francesco. *The Book of Hidden Things*
French, Nicci. *Thursday's Children*
Higgins, Kristan. *Now That You Mention It*
James, Wendy. *A Little Bird*
Simenon, Georges. ★*Maigret Goes Home*
Singh, Nalini. *A Madness of Sunshine*
HOMING PIGEONS
Rooney, Kathleen. ★*Cher Ami and Major Whittlesey*
HOMOPHOBIA
De Robertis, Carolina. *Cantoras*
Iweala, Uzodinma. ★*Speak No Evil*
Makkai, Rebecca. ★*The Great Believers*
Rice-Gonzalez, Charles. *Chulito*
HOMOSEXUALITY
Aciman, Andre. *Find Me*

Burroughs, William S. ★*Naked Lunch: The Restored Text*
D'Erasmo, Stacey. *The Sky Below*
Harris, E. Lynn. *Basketball Jones: A Novel*
Mann, Thomas. *Death in Venice and Seven Other Stories*
White, Edmund. *A Boy's Own Story*
HONDURAS
Theroux, Paul. ★*The Mosquito Coast: A Novel*
HONESTY
Camus, Albert. ★*The Stranger*
★*Honey Girl*. Rogers, Morgan Callan
Honeydew: Stories. Pearlman, Edith
HONEYMOONS
Cheek, Chip. *Cape May*
Estleman, Loren D. ★*Something Borrowed, Something Black*
Greene, Graham. *Collected Stories: Including May We Borrow Your Husband? a Sense of Reality, Twenty-One Stories*
Oyeyemi, Helen. *Peaces*
Sayers, Dorothy L. ★*Busman's Honeymoon*
Steadman, Catherine. *Something in the Water*
HONG KONG
Westlake, Donald E. *Forever and a Death*
Honky Tonk Samurai. Lansdale, Joe R.
★*Honor*. Umrigar, Thrity N.
HONOR
Clavell, James. *Shogun*
HONOR IN MEN
Parker, Robert B. *Appaloosa*
Parker, Robert B. *Blue-Eyed Devil*
HONOR KILLINGS
Bilal, Parker. *The Ghost Runner*
Honor Thy Thug. Clark, Wahida
Honor: a Novel. Shafak, Elif
The Honorary Consul. Greene, Graham
★*The Honourable Schoolboy*. Le Carre, John
Hoodlum. K'wan
Hooper, Elise
Fast Girls: A Novel of the 1936 Women's Olympic Team
Hooper, Emma
Etta and Otto and Russell and James: A Novel
Hoops [Series]. Ryan, Kennedy
Hoover, Colleen
All Your Perfects
It Ends with Us
Hop-Ciki-Yaya mysteries [Series]. Somer, Mehmet Murat
HOPE
Couto, Mia. *Rain: And Other Stories*
Grushin, Olga. *The Line*
Lopez Barrio, Cristina. *The House of the Impossible Loves*
Singer, Isaac Bashevis. *Collected Stories: A Friend of Kafka to Passions*
Singer, Isaac Bashevis. *Collected Stories: Gimpel the Fool to the Letter Writer*
HOPE DIAMOND
Rose, M. J. ★*Cartier's Hope*
★*A Hope Divided*. Cole, Alyssa
Hope River novels [Series]. Harman, Patricia
Hope: a Tragedy. Auslander, Shalom
★*Horace Winter Says Goodbye*. Bowman, Conor

Horan, Nancy
Loving Frank: A Novel
Horatio Hornblower saga [Series]. Forester, C. S.
Horn, Dara
Eternal Life: A Novel
Hornblower and the Atropos. Forester, C. S.
Hornblower and the Hotspur. Forester, C. S.
HORNBLOWER, HORATIO (FICTITIOUS CHARACTER)
Forester, C. S. *Admiral Hornblower in the West Indies*
Forester, C. S. *Beat to Quarters*
Forester, C. S. *Flying Colours*
Forester, C. S. *Hornblower and the Hotspur*
Forester, C. S. *Lord Hornblower*
Forester, C. S. *Mr. Midshipman Hornblower*
Forester, C. S. *Ship of the Line*
Hornby, Gill
Miss Austen
Hornby, Nick
High Fidelity
Just Like You
HORNER, SALLY
Greenwood, T. *Rust & Stardust*
Hornet Flight. Follett, Ken
Horns. Hill, Joe
Horowitz, Anthony
The House of Silk: A Sherlock Holmes Novel
★*Magpie Murders*
★*Moonflower Murders*
★*The Sentence Is Death*
★*The Word Is Murder*
Horrocks, Caitlin
Life Among the Terranauts
The Vexations
HORROR
Ahlborn, Ania. *The Devil Crept In*
Ajvide Lindqvist, John. *Let the Right One In*
Alten, Steve. *Meg: Generations*
Blatty, William Peter. ★*The Exorcist*
Bohjalian, Chris. *The Night Strangers: A Novel*
Bradbury, Ray. *The Illustrated Man*
Bradbury, Ray. ★*Something Wicked This Way Comes*
Brooks, Max. *Devolution: A Firsthand Account of the Rainier Sasquatch Massacre*
Brooks, Max. ★*World War Z: An Oral History of the Zombie War*
Buehlman, Christopher. *The Suicide Motor Club*
Burton, Tara Isabella. *Social Creature*
Campbell, Ramsey. *The Wise Friend*
Cantero, Edgar. *Meddling Kids: A Novel*
Castro, V. *Goddess of Filth*
Castro, V. *The Queen of the Cicadas*
Chizmar, Richard T. *A Long December*
Cronin, Justin. *The City of Mirrors*
Cronin, Justin. *The Passage*
Cronin, Justin. *The Twelve*
Danielewski, Mark Z. ★*House of Leaves: A Novel*
Davidson, Andy. *The Boatman's Daughter: A Novel*
Duncan, Glen. *By Blood We Live*
Duncan, Glen. *The Last Werewolf*

Duncan, Glen. *Talulla Rising*
French, Jonathan. ★*The Grey Bastards*
Gaiman, Neil. ★*Fragile Things: Short Fictions and Wonders*
Gaiman, Neil. *Trigger Warning: Short Fictions and Disturbances*
Golden, Christopher. *Ararat*
Golden, Christopher. *The Pandora Room: A Novel*
Golden, Christopher. *Red Hands*
Grant, Helen. *The Glass Demon*
Grant, Mira. *Blackout*
Grant, Mira. *Deadline*
Grant, Mira. *Feed*
Grant, Mira. *Feedback*
Grant, Mira. *Into the Drowning Deep*
Gregory, Daryl. *The Devil's Alphabet*
Gregory, Daryl. *We Are All Completely Fine*
Hamill, Shaun. *A Cosmology of Monsters*
Harris, Thomas. *Hannibal*
Harris, Thomas. *Hannibal Rising*
Harrison, Rachel. *The Return*
Hendrix, Grady. *The Final Girl Support Group*
Hendrix, Grady. *My Best Friend's Exorcism*
Hendrix, Grady. *The Southern Book Club's Guide to Slaying Vampires*
Hill, Joe. *The Fireman: A Novel*
Hill, Joe. ★*Full Throttle: Stories*
Hill, Joe. *Heart-Shaped Box*
Hill, Joe. *Horns*
Hill, Joe. ★*Nos4a2*
Hill, Joe. *Strange Weather: Four Short Novels*
Hurley, Andrew Michael. *Devil's Day*
Jackson, Shirley. ★*The Haunting of Hill House*
Jackson, Shirley. ★*The Lottery: And Other Stories*
Jackson, Shirley. *We Have Always Lived in the Castle*
Jemc, Jac. ★*The Grip of It*
Johnson, Daisy. *Everything Under*
Jones, Stephen Graham. *My Heart Is a Chainsaw*
Jones, Stephen Graham. ★*The Only Good Indians: A Novel*
Katsu, Alma. *The Hunger: A Novel*
Khaw, Cassandra. *Nothing but Blackened Teeth*
Kiernan, Caitlin R. *The Very Best of Caitlin R. Kiernan*
King, Stephen. ★*Carrie*
King, Stephen. *Cujo*
King, Stephen. *Doctor Sleep: A Novel*
King, Stephen. *Firestarter*
King, Stephen. *If It Bleeds*
King, Stephen. *The Institute*
King, Stephen. *It*
King, Stephen. ★*Misery*
King, Stephen. *Night Shift*
King, Stephen. *Pet Sematary*
King, Stephen. *Salem's Lot*
King, Stephen. ★*The Shining*
King, Stephen. *Sleeping Beauties: A Novel*
King, Stephen. ★*The Stand*
Lebbon, Tim. *Eden*
Levin, Ira. ★*Rosemary's Baby: A Novel*
Levin, Ira. ★*The Stepford Wives: A Novel*
Lovecraft, H. P. ★*Tales*

Machado, Carmen Maria. *Her Body and Other Parties: Stories*
Malerman, Josh. *Bird Box: A Novel*
Malerman, Josh. *Goblin: A Novel in Six Novellas*
Malerman, Josh. *Malorie: A Bird Box Novel*
Malerman, Josh. *Unbury Carol*
Matheson, Richard. ★*I Am Legend*
McMahon, Jennifer. *The Invited: A Novel*
Moreno, Gus. *This Thing Between US: A Novel*
Palahniuk, Chuck. *Lullaby: A Novel*
Perry, Sarah. *Melmoth: A Novel*
Poe, Edgar Allan. ★*Complete Stories and Poems of Edgar Allan Poe*
Priest, Cherie. *Boneshaker*
Priest, Cherie. *Dreadnought*
Priest, Cherie. *Ganymede*
Priest, Cherie. *The Inexplicables*
Pyper, Andrew. *The Damned: A Novel*
Romero, George A. *The Living Dead*
Ruff, Matt. *Lovecraft Country: A Novel*
Saul, John. *Midnight Voices*
Schweblin, Samanta. *Mouthful of Birds: Stories*
Shelley, Mary Wollstonecraft. ★*Frankenstein: Or, the Modern Prometheus*
Simmons, Dan. *The Abominable: A Novel*
Simmons, Dan. ★*The Terror: A Novel*
Smith, Scott. *The Ruins: A Novel*
Solomon, Rivers. *Sorrowland*
St. James, Simone. *The Broken Girls*
St. James, Simone. *The Sun Down Motel*
Stage, Zoje. *Wonderland*
Starling, Caitlin. *The Death of Jane Lawrence*
Stevenson, Robert Louis. ★*The Strange Case of Dr. Jekyll and Mr. Hyde*
Stoker, Bram. ★*Dracula*
Stoker, Bram. *The New Annotated Dracula*
Stoker, Dacre. *Dracul*
Straub, Peter. ★*A Dark Matter: A Novel*
Straub, Peter. ★*Ghost Story*
Straub, Peter. *Lost Boy Lost Girl: A Novel*
Straub, Peter. *Mr. X*
Suskind, Patrick. ★*Perfume: The Story of a Murderer*
Toro, Guillermo del. *The Hollow Ones*
Tremblay, Paul. ★*The Cabin at the End of the World: A Novel*
Tremblay, Paul. *Growing Things and Other Stories*
Tremblay, Paul. *Survivor Song*
Vandelly, T. Marie. *Theme Music*
Ward, Catriona. *The Last House on Needless Street*
Wellington, David. *Positive*
Wells, H. G. ★*The Island of Dr. Moreau*
Wendig, Chuck. *The Book of Accidents*
Whitehead, Colson. *Zone One: A Novel*
Wolfe, Gene. *The Land Across*
Wong, David. *This Book Is Full of Spiders: Seriously, Dude, Don't Touch It*

HORROR CLASSICS
Blatty, William Peter. ★*The Exorcist*
Lovecraft, H. P. ★*Tales*
Stoker, Bram. ★*Dracula*

HORROR COMICS
Kraus, Daniel. *The Autumnal: The Complete Series*
Machado, Carmen Maria. ★*The Low, Low Woods*
HORROR FILM PRODUCERS AND DIRECTORS
Leonard, Elmore. ★*Get Shorty*
HORROR FILMS
Danforth, Emily M. *Plain Bad Heroines*
Gerritsen, Tess. *I Know a Secret*
Jones, Stephen Graham. *My Heart Is a Chainsaw*
Palahniuk, Chuck. *The Invention of Sound*
HORROR STORY AUTHORS
King, Stephen. ★*Misery*
Phillips, Susan Elizabeth. *Heroes Are My Weakness*
HORSE BREEDERS
McLain, Paula. *Circling the Sun*
HORSE BREEDING
Morgan, C. E. ★*The Sport of Kings*
HORSE FARMS
Hatcher, Robin Lee. *Cross My Heart*
Smith, B. J. *Shoot the Dog: A Virgil Cain Mystery*
Horse Heaven. Smiley, Jane
HORSE RACING
Francis, Dick. *Smokescreen*
Francis, Felix. *Crisis*
Francis, Felix. *Guilty Not Guilty*
Francis, Felix. *Pulse*
Gordon, Jaimy. ★*Lord of Misrule: A Novel*
Morgan, C. E. ★*The Sport of Kings*
Smiley, Jane. *Horse Heaven*
HORSE STEALING
McMurtry, Larry. *Comanche Moon: A Novel*
HORSE THEFTS
Dobyns, Stephen. *Saratoga Payback*
HORSE TRAINERS
Gordon, Jaimy. ★*Lord of Misrule: A Novel*
Stansel, Ian. *The Last Cowboys of San Geronimo*
HORSE TRAINING
McCarthy, Cormac. ★*All the Pretty Horses*
★*A **Horse** Walks into a Bar*. Grossman, David
★*The **Horse** Whisperer: A Novel*. Evans, Nicholas
HORSE WHISPERERS
Evans, Nicholas. ★*The Horse Whisperer: A Novel*
HORSES
Gaitskill, Mary. *The Mare: A Novel*
Greaves, Chuck. *Hush Money: A Mystery*
McCarthy, Cormac. ★*All the Pretty Horses*
Smith, B. J. *Shoot the Dog: A Virgil Cain Mystery*
Verble, Margaret. ★*When Two Feathers Fell from the Sky*
Hosking, Jay
Three Years with the Rat: A Novel
HOSPITAL CARE
Strout, Elizabeth. *My Name Is Lucy Barton*
HOSPITAL PATIENTS
Bailey, Paul. *Chapman's Odyssey*
Cook, Robin. *Coma: A Novel*
Cronin, Marianne. *The One Hundred Years of Lenni and Margot*
London, Joan. *The Golden Age*
Miller, Rebecca. ★*Jacob's Folly: A Novel*

Ware, Ruth. *In a Dark, Dark Wood*
HOSPITAL WARDS
Davidson, Andrew. *The Gargoyle*
HOSPITALS
Alexander, Tamera. *With This Pledge*
Benn, James R. ★*The Red Horse: A Billy Boyle World War II Mystery*
Delaney, J. P. *Playing Nice*
George, Nina. *The Book of Dreams*
Marra, Anthony. ★*A Constellation of Vital Phenomena: A Novel*
Robb, Candace M. *The Riddle of St. Leonard's: An Owen Archer Mystery.*
Scottoline, Lisa. ★*Every Fifteen Minutes*
Soyinka, Wole. *Chronicles from the Land of the Happiest People on Earth*
Thomson, E. S. *Beloved Poison*
Thomson, E. S. *The Blood*
HOSPITALS — EMERGENCY SERVICE
Bohjalian, Chris. ★*The Red Lotus*
Hossain, Saad Z.
Cyber Mage: A Novel
Hosseini, Khaled
★*The Kite Runner*
★*Sea Prayer*
HOST FAMILIES OF FOREIGN STUDENTS
Freudenberger, Nell. *The Dissident*
Hostage. Wiesel, Elie
HOSTAGE NEGOTIATIONS
Pearson, Ridley. *The Risk Agent*
Picoult, Jodi. *A Spark of Light: A Novel*
Hostage Taker: A Novel. Pintoff, Stefanie
HOSTAGE TAKING
Cussler, Clive. ★*The Oracle*
Greene, Graham. *The Honorary Consul*
Higgins, Jack. *The Eagle Has Flown*
Higgins, Jack. *The Eagle Has Landed*
Pintoff, Stefanie. *Hostage Taker: A Novel*
Wiesel, Elie. *Hostage*
HOSTAGES
Backman, Fredrik. ★*Anxious People: A Novel*
Child, Lee. ★*Die Trying*
Hunter, Stephen. *Soft Target: A Thriller*
Martinson, T. J. *The Reign of the Kingfisher: A Novel*
Mosley, Walter. *Charcoal Joe: An Easy Rawlins Mystery*
Patchett, Ann. ★*Bel Canto: A Novel*
Pearson, Ridley. *The Risk Agent*
Picoult, Jodi. *A Spark of Light: A Novel*
Pintoff, Stefanie. *Hostage Taker: A Novel*
Rendell, Ruth. *Road Rage*
Robb, J. D. *Leverage in Death: An Eve Dallas Novel*
Takamura, Kaoru. ★*Lady Joker*
Wiesel, Elie. *Hostage*
HOSTILITY (PSYCHOLOGY)
Butler, Season. ★*Cygnet*
Hostin, Sunny
★*Summer on the Bluffs*
Hot and hammered [Series]. Bailey, Tessa
Hot in Chicago novels [Series]. Meader, Kate
The Hot Kid. Leonard, Elmore

Hot Milk: A Novel. Levy, Deborah
The Hot Rock. Westlake, Donald E.
★*Hot to Trot*. Beaton, M. C.
Hotel Du Lac. Brookner, Anita
HOTEL MANAGEMENT
Delany, Vicki. *Deadly Summer Nights*
Millhauser, Steven. *Martin Dressler: The Tale of an American Dreamer*
HOTEL OWNERS
Atilgan, Yusuf. *Motherland Hotel*
Mandel, Emily St. John. ★*The Glass Hotel: A Novel*
Morrison, Toni. *Love*
Quick, Amanda. *The Girl Who Knew Too Much*
HOTEL WORKERS
Imamura, Natsuko. *The Woman in the Purple Skirt: A Novel*
HOTELS
Brookner, Anita. *Hotel Du Lac*
Diofebi, Dario. *Paradise, Nevada*
Faye, Lyndsay. ★*The Paragon Hotel*
Friedland, Elyssa. *Last Summer at the Golden Hotel*
Garcia, Cristina. *The Lady Matador's Hotel: A Novel*
Heller, Peter. *The Guide*
Krentz, Jayne Ann. *Secret Sisters*
Longworth, M. L. *Murder on the Ile Sordou: A Verlaque and Bonnet Provencal Mystery*
Racculia, Kate. ★*Bellweather Rhapsody*
Rader-Day, Lori. *Little Pretty Things*
Towles, Amor. ★*A Gentleman in Moscow*
Williams, Beatriz. *All the Ways We Said Goodbye: A Novel of the Ritz Paris*
The Hottest Dishes of the Tartar Cuisine. Bronsky, Alina
Houellebecq, Michel
Submission
★*The Hound of the Baskervilles*. Doyle, Arthur Conan
Hour of the Red God. Crompton, Richard
★*The Hours*. Cunningham, Michael
The House at Riverton: A Novel. Morton, Kate
The House at Sea's End: A Ruth Galloway Mystery. Griffiths, Elly
The House at the Edge of Night: A Novel. Banner, Catherine
HOUSE CLEANING
Ripper, Kris. *The Hate Project*
HOUSE CONSTRUCTION
Butler, Nickolas. *Godspeed*
A House for Mr. Biswas. Naipaul, V. S.
The House in the Cerulean Sea. Klune, TJ
A House Is a Body: Stories. Swamy, Shruti
House Made of Dawn. Momaday, N. Scott
House of Blues. Smith, Julie
★*The House of Broken Angels*. Urrea, Luis Alberto
★*House of Correction*. French, Nicci
The House of Deep Water. McFarland, Jeni
House of Earth trilogy [Series]. Buck, Pearl S.
House of Echoes: A Novel. Duffy, Brendan
House of Gold. Solomons, Natasha
The House of Impossible Beauties. Cassara, Joseph
★*House of Leaves: A Novel*. Danielewski, Mark Z.
House of Names. Toibin, Colm
House of Niccolo [Series]. Dunnett, Dorothy

*The **House** of Silk: A Sherlock Holmes Novel*. Horowitz, Anthony
*The **House** of Styx*. Kunsken, Derek
*The **House** of the Impossible Loves*. Lopez Barrio, Cristina
***House** of the Patriarch*. Hambly, Barbara
***House** of the Rising Sun: A Novel*. Burke, James Lee
★*The **House** of the Seven Gables*. Hawthorne, Nathaniel
★*The **House** of the Spirits*. Allende, Isabel
*The **House** of the Stag*. Baker, Kage
*The **House** of the Vestals: The Investigations of Gordianus the Finder*.
   Saylor, Steven
*The **House** of Whispers*. Purcell, Laura
*The **House** of Wolfe*. Blake, James Carlos
★***House** on Fire: A Novel*. Finder, Joseph
★*The **House** on Mango Street*. Cisneros, Sandra
*The **House** on Vesper Sands: A Novel*. O'Donnell, Paraic
***House** Rules: A Novel*. Picoult, Jodi
***House** Under Snow*. Bialosky, Jill
HOUSEBOATS
   Johnson, Daisy. *Everything Under*
HOUSEGUESTS
   Smith, Ali. *There but for The: A Novel*
HOUSEHOLD ACTIVITIES
   Boll, Heinrich. *Billiards at Half-Past Nine*
HOUSEHOLD EMPLOYEES
   Adiga, Aravind. ★*Amnesty*
   Ashley, Jennifer. *Death at the Crystal Palace*
   Baker, Jo. *Longbourn*
   Brown, Amy Belding. *Emily's House*
   Christie, Agatha. *Mrs. McGinty's Dead*
   Collins, Sara. *The Confessions of Frannie Langton*
   deWitt, Patrick. *Undermajordomo Minor*
   Dexter, Colin. *The Daughters of Cain*
   Du Maurier, Daphne. ★*Rebecca*
   Faulkner, William. *Requiem for a Nun*
   Fredericks, Mariah. *Death of a New American: A Mystery*
   Fredericks, Mariah. *Death of a Showman*
   George, Alex. *The Paris Hours: A Novel*
   Gordimer, Nadine. ★*July's People*
   Hosseini, Khaled. ★*The Kite Runner*
   King, Stephen. *Dolores Claiborne*
   McBain, Ed. *Alice in Jeopardy*
   McCaffrey, Anne. *Dragonflight*
   McCall Smith, Alexander. *The Forgotten Affairs of Youth*
   Morelli, Laura. *The Stolen Lady*
   Morton, Kate. *The House at Riverton: A Novel*
   O'Connor, Joseph. *Star of the Sea*
   Ogawa, Yoko. *The Housekeeper and the Professor*
   Okparanta, Chinelo. ★*Under the Udala Trees*
   Pamuk, Orhan. *Silent House*
   Quinn, Julia. ★*An Offer from a Gentleman*
   Rendell, Ruth. ★*A Judgement in Stone*
   Richardson, Samuel. ★*Pamela: Or, Virtue Rewarded*
   Rojas Contreras, Ingrid. ★*Fruit of the Drunken Tree: A Novel*
   Seton, Anya. *Green Darkness*
   Simenon, Georges. ★*Maigret and the Toy Village*
   Stachniak, Eva. *The Winter Palace: A Novel of Catherine the Great*
   Stockett, Kathryn. ★*The Help*
   Suri, Tasha. *The Jasmine Throne*

   Swift, Graham. ★*Mothering Sunday: A Romance*
HOUSEHOLD FINANCES
   Eggers, Dave. *A Hologram for the King: A Novel*
*The **Housekeeper** and the Professor*. Ogawa, Yoko
HOUSEKEEPERS
   Downes, Anna. *The Safe Place: A Novel*
   Force, Marie. *Deceived by Desire*
   Giordano, Paolo. *Like Family*
   Parry, Ambrose. *The Way of All Flesh*
   Woodrell, Daniel. *The Maid's Version: A Novel*
HOUSES
   Blundell, Judy. *The High Season: A Novel*
   Candlish, Louise. *Our House*
   Danielewski, Mark Z. ★*House of Leaves: A Novel*
   Duffy, Brendan. *House of Echoes: A Novel*
   Flournoy, Angela. *The Turner House*
   Gnuse, A. J. *Girl in the Walls: A Novel*
   Johnstone, Carole. *Mirrorland*
   Kilalea, Katharine. *Ok, Mr. Field: A Novel*
   Leavitt, David. ★*Shelter in Place*
   Osondu, E. C. *This House Is Not for Sale: A Novel*
   Patchett, Ann. ★*The Dutch House: A Novel*
HOUSES — CONSERVATION AND RESTORATION
   Block, Lawrence. *Hit Me: A Keller Novel*
HOUSES — HISTORY
   Kingsolver, Barbara. ★*Unsheltered*
HOUSES — REMODELING
   Gurganus, Allan. *The Practical Heart: Four Novellas*
HOUSESITTING
   Sager, Riley. *Lock Every Door: A Novel*
HOUSING
   Gottlieb, Eli. *Best Boy: A Novel*
***Houston** series* [Series]. McMurtry, Larry
HOUSTON, TEXAS
   Burke, James Lee. *The Jealous Kind*
   Daughters, Amy Weinland. *You Cannot Mess This Up: A True Story*
      That Never Happened
   Dow, David R. *Confessions of an Innocent Man*
   McMurtry, Larry. ★*Terms of Endearment: A Novel : With a New*
      Preface
   Washington, Bryan. *Lot: Stories*
   Washington, Bryan. ★*Memorial*
***How** Are You Going to Save Yourself*. Holmes, J. M.
***How** Beautiful We Were*. Mbue, Imbolo
★***How** Green Was My Valley*. Llewellyn, Richard
★***How** Hard Can It Be?*. Pearson, Allison
***How** High We Go in the Dark*. Nagamatsu, Sequoia
★***How** It Happened*. Koryta, Michael
***How** Late It Was, How Late*. Kelman, James
***How** Long 'Til Black Future Month?*. Jemisin, N. K.
★***How** Lucky*. Leitch, Will
***How** Quickly She Disappears*. Fleischmann, Raymond
***How** Rory Thorne Destroyed the Multiverse*. Eason, K.
★***How** Stella Got Her Groove Back*. McMillan, Terry
***How** the Dead Speak: A Tony Hill and Carol Jordan Novel*. McDermid,
   Val
★***How** the Duke Was Won*. Bell, Lenora
***How** the Garcia Girls Lost Their Accents*. Alvarez, Julia

How the One-Armed Sister Sweeps Her House. Jones, Cherie
★*How to Be Both*. Smith, Ali
How to Be Safe: A Novel. McAllister, Tom
How to Behave in a Crowd. Bordas, Camille
How to Catch a Prince. Hauck, Rachel
★*How to Catch a Queen*. Cole, Alyssa
How to Fail at Flirting. Williams, Denise
How to Find a Princess. Cole, Alyssa
How to Find Your Way in the Dark. Miller, Derek B.
How to Hack a Heartbreak. Rockaway, Kristin
How to Live Safely in a Science Fictional Universe: A Novel. Yu, Charles
How to Lose a Duke in Ten Days. Guhrke, Laura Lee
How to Love a Duke in Ten Days. Byrne, Kerrigan
How to Marry Keanu Reeves in 90 Days. Jackson, K. M.
How to Pronounce Knife: Stories. Thammavongsa, Souvankham
How to Walk Away: A Novel. Center, Katherine
How We Are Hungry: Stories. Eggers, Dave
Howard, Ravi
 Driving the King: A Novel
★*Howards End*. Forster, E. M.
Howarth, Paul
 Dust off the Bones
 Only Killers and Thieves: A Novel
Howland, Bette
 Calm Sea and Prosperous Voyage
Howrey, Meg
 The Wanderers
Hoyt, Elizabeth
 Not the Duke's Darling
 When a Rogue Meets His Match
Hozar, Nazanine
 Aria
Huang, S. L.
 Burning Roses
 Zero Sum Game
Huber, Anna Lee
 Penny for Your Secrets
Huchu, Tendai
 The Library of the Dead
HUDSON RIVER
 Seton, Anya. ★*Dragonwyck*
HUDSON VALLEY
 Boyle, T. Coraghessan. *World's End: A Novel*
 Spencer, Scott. *An Ocean Without a Shore*
 Straub, Emma. ★*All Adults Here*
Hughes, Caoilinn
 Orchid and the Wasp
Hughes, Langston
 Not Without Laughter
 ★*Short Stories*
Hugo, Victor
 ★*The Hunchback of Notre Dame*
 ★*Les Miserables*
HUGUENOTS
 Phoenix, Michele. *The Space Between Words*
Huisman, Violaine
 The Book of Mother

Hulme, Keri
 ★*The Bone People: A Novel*
Hulse, S. M.
 ★*Black River*
 Eden Mine
The Hum and the Shiver. Bledsoe, Alex
★*Human Acts: A Novel*. Han, Kang
HUMAN BEHAVIOR
 Barnhill, Kelly Regan. *Dreadful Young Ladies and Other Stories*
 Birch, Carol. *Jamrach's Menagerie*
 Chiang, Ted. ★*Exhalation: Stories*
 Duncan, Glen. *The Last Werewolf*
 Murakami, Haruki. *Blind Willow, Sleeping Woman: 24 Stories*
 Murakami, Haruki. *Men Without Women: Stories*
 Pynchon, Thomas. *Against the Day: A Novel*
 Schweblin, Samanta. *Mouthful of Birds: Stories*
 Thompson-Spires, Nafissa. *Heads of the Colored People: Stories*
 Woolf, Virginia. ★*To the Lighthouse*
The Human Body. Giordano, Paolo
HUMAN BODY
 Soule, Charles. ★*Anyone*
HUMAN BODY PARTS INDUSTRY AND TRADE
 Ames, Jonathan. *A Man Named Doll*
 Leonard, Elmore. ★*Raylan*
 Li, Yiyun. *The Vagrants: A Novel*
 Welsh, Irvine. *Dead Men's Trousers*
★*The Human Comedy*. Saroyan, William
The **Human** Comedy [Series]. Balzac, Honore de
Human Croquet. Atkinson, Kate
HUMAN EVOLUTION
 Butler, Octavia E. *Adulthood Rites*
 Erdrich, Louise. *Future Home of the Living God*
 Gregory, Daryl. *The Devil's Alphabet*
 Rutherfurd, Edward. *Sarum: The Novel of England*
 Suarez, Daniel. *Change Agent: A Novel*
 Van Vogt, A. E. ★*Slan*
 Vonnegut, Kurt. ★*Galapagos: A Novel*
HUMAN EXPERIMENTATION IN MEDICINE
 Browne, S. G. *Less Than Hero: A Novel*
 Goddard, Robert. *Never Go Back*
 Kim, Angie. *Miracle Creek*
 Konar, Affinity. *Mischling: A Novel*
 Sanders, Lawrence. *The Sixth Commandment: A Novel*
 Wells, H. G. ★*The Invisible Man*
The Human Factor. Greene, Graham
HUMAN NATURE
 Alarcon, Daniel. *The King Is Always Above the People: Stories*
 Arimah, Lesley Nneka. ★*What It Means When a Man Falls from the Sky: Stories*
 Berlin, Lucia. ★*Evening in Paradise: More Stories*
 Boyle, T. Coraghessan. *The Relive Box: And Other Stories*
 Danielewski, Mark Z. ★*The Familiar.; Volume 4,*
 Danticat, Edwidge. ★*Everything Inside: Stories*
 Eugenides, Jeffrey. *Fresh Complaint: Stories*
 Gass, William H. *Middle C*
 Gilchrist, Ellen. ★*Collected Stories*
 Golding, William. ★*Lord of the Flies: A Novel*
 Greene, Graham. *The Last Word and Other Stories*

Hadley, Tessa. *Bad Dreams and Other Stories*

Jhabvala, Ruth Prawer. *At the End of the Century: The Stories of Ruth Prawer Jhabvala.*

Liu, Cixin. ★*The Dark Forest*

Liu, Cixin. ★*Death's End*

Liu, Cixin. ★*The Three-Body Problem*

Mason, Bobbie Ann. *Patchwork*

Means, David. ★*Instructions for a Funeral: Stories*

Nguyen, Viet Thanh. ★*The Refugees*

Tolstaya, Tatyana. *Aetherial Worlds: Stories*

Vonnegut, Kurt. ★*Breakfast of Champions: Or, Goodbye Blue Monday!*

Vonnegut, Kurt. ★*Cat's Cradle*

Vonnegut, Kurt. *Welcome to the Monkey House*

HUMAN REMAINS (ARCHAEOLOGY)

Barton, Fiona. *The Child*

HUMAN REPRODUCTION

Ramos, Joanne. *The Farm: A Novel*

HUMAN RIGHTS

Allende, Isabel. *In the Midst of Winter: A Novel*

Englander, Nathan. *The Ministry of Special Cases*

HUMAN RIGHTS ACTIVISTS

Gordimer, Nadine. ★*My Son's Story*

HUMAN SACRIFICE

Khaw, Cassandra. *Nothing but Blackened Teeth*

Toibin, Colm. *House of Names*

HUMAN SETTLEMENTS

Michener, James A. *Chesapeake*

Robinson, Kim Stanley. ★*Blue Mars*

Robinson, Kim Stanley. ★*Green Mars*

Robinson, Kim Stanley. ★*Red Mars*

Rutherfurd, Edward. *Sarum: The Novel of England*

HUMAN SKIN COLOR

Larsen, Reif. *I Am Radar: A Novel*

Morrison, Toni. ★*God Help the Child*

HUMAN SMUGGLING

Deaver, Jeffery. *The Stone Monkey: A Lincoln Rhyme Novel*

★*The **Human** Stain.* Roth, Philip

HUMAN TRAFFICKING

Cussler, Clive. *Ghost Ship*

Eisler, Barry. *Livia Lone*

Eisler, Barry. *The Night Trade*

Freeman, Brian. *Goodbye to the Dead*

Greenwood, Kerry. *Unnatural Habits*

Gunday, Hakan. *The Few*

Harvey, John. *Cold in Hand*

Hill Gumbao, Toni. *The Summer of Dead Toys*

Luna, Louisa. *The Janes*

Martin, Charles. *The Water Keeper*

Rao, Shobha. ★*Girls Burn Brighter*

Suarez, Daniel. *Change Agent: A Novel*

HUMAN-ALIEN HYBRIDS

Butler, Octavia E. ★*Dawn: Xenogenesis*

HUMAN-ANIMAL RELATIONSHIPS

Arikawa, Hiro. *The Travelling Cat Chronicles*

Auster, Paul. *Timbuktu: A Novel*

Bear, Elizabeth. *Steles of the Sky*

Burton, Jeffrey B. *The Keepers: A Mace Reid K-9 Mystery*

Buxton, Kira Jane. ★*Hollow Kingdom*

Cameron, W. Bruce. *A Dog's Promise*

Crais, Robert. *Suspect*

Greenidge, Kaitlyn. *We Love You, Charlie Freeman: A Novel*

Gruen, Sara. *The Ape House*

Gruen, Sara. ★*Water for Elephants: A Novel*

Krivak, Andrew. *The Bear*

London, Jack. ★*White Fang*

Maizes, R. L. *Other People's Pets*

Martel, Yann. ★*Life of Pi: A Novel*

Miller, Mary. *Biloxi: A Novel*

Nunez, Sigrid. ★*The Friend*

HUMAN/ALIEN ENCOUNTERS

Anders, Charlie Jane. ★*The City in the Middle of the Night*

Box, C. J. *Trophy Hunt: A Joe Pickett Novel*

Bradbury, Ray. ★*The Martian Chronicles: The Fortieth Anniversary Edition*

Brin, David. *Existence*

Burke, Sue. *Semiosis*

Cambias, James L. *A Darkling Sea*

Cherryh, C. J. *Foreigner: A Novel of First Contact*

Haig, Matt. *The Humans: A Novel*

Hamilton, Peter F. *Great North Road*

Heinlein, Robert A. ★*Starship Troopers*

Kress, Nancy. *If Tomorrow Comes*

Kress, Nancy. *Tomorrow's Kin*

Le Guin, Ursula K. *The Birthday of the World: And Other Stories*

Mieville, China. *Embassytown*

Tepper, Sheri S. ★*Grass*

Thompson, Tade. *Rosewater*

Thompson, Tade. *The Rosewater Insurrection*

Thompson, Tade. *The Rosewater Redemption*

Turnbull, Cadwell. ★*The Lesson*

Valente, Catherynne M. *Space Opera*

Varley, John. *Demon*

Varley, John. ★*Titan*

Wells, H. G. ★*The War of the Worlds*

Wilson, Daniel H. *The Andromeda Evolution: A Novel*

HUMAN/ANIMAL COMMUNICATION

Danielewski, Mark Z. ★*The Familiar.; Volume 4,*

Evans, Nicholas. ★*The Horse Whisperer: A Novel*

Gruen, Sara. *The Ape House*

Maizes, R. L. *Other People's Pets*

Martineau, Maxym M. *Kingdom of Exiles*

Okorafor, Nnedi. ★*Remote Control*

Smiley, Jane. ★*Perestroika in Paris: A Novel*

HUMAN/ANIMAL TELEPATHY

Martineau, Maxym M. *Kingdom of Exiles*

HUMAN/COMPUTER INTERACTION

Clarke, Arthur C. ★*2001: A Space Odyssey*

HUMANISM (14TH-16TH CENTURIES)

Follett, Ken. *A Column of Fire*

Follett, Ken. *World Without End*

HUMANISTS

Yourcenar, Marguerite. ★*Memoirs of Hadrian: And Reflections on the Composition of Memoirs of Hadrian*

HUMANITARIAN ASSISTANCE

Florio, Gwen. *Silent Hearts*

Linden, Rachel. *The Enlightenment of Bees*

HUMANS

Foster, Alan Dean. *Relic*

Hamilton, Peter F. *Pandora's Star*

Kim, Bo Young. ★*I'm Waiting for You: And Other Stories*

Kunsken, Derek. *The House of Styx*

Swarup, Shubhangi. *Latitudes of Longing*

HUMANS — EFFECT OF ENVIRONMENT ON

Powers, Richard. ★*The Overstory: A Novel*

HUMANS AND CHIMPANZEES

Fowler, Karen Joy. ★*We Are All Completely Beside Ourselves*

HUMANS AND DOGS

Alexis, Andre. *Fifteen Dogs*

Cameron, W. Bruce. *A Dog's Promise*

Stein, Garth. *The Art of Racing in the Rain: A Novel*

HUMANS AND HORSES

Evans, Nicholas. ★*The Horse Whisperer: A Novel*

Smiley, Jane. *Horse Heaven*

HUMANS AND SHARKS

Alten, Steve. *Meg: Generations*

HUMANS AND WHALES

Melville, Herman. ★*Moby-Dick; Or, the Whale*

HUMANS AND WOLVES

Bear, Elizabeth. *Steles of the Sky*

The **Humans**: *a Novel*. Haig, Matt

★**Humboldt's** *Gift*. Bellow, Saul

HUMILIATION

DeWoskin, Rachel. *Big Girl Small: A Novel*

Dostoyevsky, Fyodor. *Notes from Underground*

McElroy, Alex. *The Atmospherians*

North, Anna. *The Life and Death of Sophie Stark*

Hummel, Maria

Lesson in Red

The **Hummingbird's** *Daughter: A Novel*. Urrea, Luis Alberto

HUMOROUS STORIES

Adams, Douglas. *Dirk Gently's Holistic Detective Agency*

Adams, Douglas. *The Restaurant at the End of the Universe*

Anderson, Kevin J. *Death Warmed Over*

Barker, Nicola. *Darkmans*

Barry, Dave. *Insane City*

Barry, Dave. *Lunatics*

Bennett, Alan. ★*The Uncommon Reader*

Bird, Sarah. *The Gap Year: A Novel*

Boyle, T. Coraghessan. *The Relive Box: And Other Stories*

Burns, Olive Ann. ★*Cold Sassy Tree*

Cantero, Edgar. *Meddling Kids: A Novel*

Chabon, Michael. ★*Wonder Boys*

Chatterjee, Upamanyu. *English, August: An Indian Story*

Costello, Mark. *Big If*

Doyle, Roddy. *The Guts*

Faulks, Sebastian. *Jeeves and the Wedding Bells*

Flagg, Fannie. ★*Fried Green Tomatoes at the Whistle Stop Cafe*

Flagg, Fannie. *Standing in the Rainbow: A Novel*

Flagg, Fannie. ★*The Wonder Boy of Whistle Stop: A Novel*

Fossey, Brooke. *The Big Finish*

Fowler, Karen Joy. *The Jane Austen Book Club*

Friedland, Elyssa. *The Floating Feldmans*

Gaiman, Neil. ★*Good Omens: The Nice and Accurate Prophecies of Agnes Nutter, Witch*

Goldman, William. ★*The Princess Bride: S. Morgenstern's Classic Tale of True Love and High Adventure : The*

Goldstein, Rebecca. *36 Arguments for the Existence of God: A Work of Fiction*

Groen, Hendrik. *On the Bright Side: The New Secret Diary of Hendrik Groen, 85 Years Old*

Hardiman, Rebecca. *Good Eggs*

Harkaway, Nick. *The Gone-Away World*

Hiaasen, Carl. *Bad Monkey*

Hiaasen, Carl. *Basket Case*

Hiaasen, Carl. *Lucky You: A Novel*

Hiaasen, Carl. *Nature Girl*

Hiaasen, Carl. *Star Island*

Hiaasen, Carl. *Strip Tease: A Novel*

Hornby, Nick. *High Fidelity*

Kohnstamm, Thomas B. *Lake City*

Landvik, Lorna. *Chronicles of a Radical Hag: With Recipes*

Leithauser, Brad. *The Promise of Elsewhere*

Lutz, Lisa. *The Spellman Files: A Novel*

Majors, Inman. *Penelope Lemon: Game On!*

McCall Smith, Alexander. ★*The Department of Sensitive Crimes: A Detective Varg Novel*

McCall Smith, Alexander. ★*The Man with the Silver Saab: A Detective Varg Novel*

McCall Smith, Alexander. *Tiny Tales: Stories of Romance, Ambition, Kindness, and Happiness*

Portis, Charles. ★*The Dog of the South*

Portis, Charles. ★*Gringos: A Novel*

Portis, Charles. ★*Masters of Atlantis: A Novel*

Pratchett, Terry. *Equal Rites*

Pratchett, Terry. *The Fifth Elephant: A Novel of Discworld*

Pratchett, Terry. *Going Postal: A Novel of Discworld*

Pratchett, Terry. *Guards! Guards!*

Pratchett, Terry. *The Last Hero: A Discworld Fable*

Pratchett, Terry. *Lords and Ladies: A Novel of Discworld*

Pratchett, Terry. *Men at Arms: A Novel of Discworld*

Pratchett, Terry. *Monstrous Regiment*

Pratchett, Terry. *Pyramids: The Book of Going Forth*

Pratchett, Terry. *Reaper Man*

Pratchett, Terry. *Small Gods: A Novel of Discworld*

Pratchett, Terry. *Thief of Time*

Pratchett, Terry. *Thud!: A Novel of Discworld*

Pratchett, Terry. *The Truth: A Novel of Discworld*

Pratchett, Terry. *Witches Abroad*

Pratchett, Terry. *Wyrd Sisters*

Robbins, Tom. *Fierce Invalids Home from Hot Climates*

Robbins, Tom. ★*Jitterbug Perfume*

Rojstaczer, Stuart. *The Mathematician's Shiva: A Novel*

Roth, Philip. ★*The Anatomy Lesson*

Roth, Philip. *The Ghost Writer*

Roth, Philip. *The Great American Novel*

Roth, Philip. *Sabbath's Theater*

Roth, Philip. *Zuckerman Bound*

Roth, Philip. *Zuckerman Unbound*

Russo, Richard. *Straight Man*

Scalzi, John. *Redshirts: A Novel with Three Codas*

Semple, Maria. *Where'd You Go, Bernadette: A Novel*
Sinha, Indra. *Animal's People*
Sthers, Amanda. *Holy Lands: A Novel*
Tanen, Sloane. *There's a Word for That*
Valente, Catherynne M. *Space Opera*
Wilson, Kevin. *Nothing to See Here*
Wodehouse, P. G. *My Man Jeeves*
Wojtas, Olga. *Miss Blaine's Prefect and the Golden Samovar*
Wong, David. *This Book Is Full of Spiders: Seriously, Dude, Don't Touch It*
Yu, Charles. *How to Live Safely in a Science Fictional Universe: A Novel*

Humphreys, Sara Taney
  Trouble Walks In
★*The **Hunchback** of Notre Dame*. Hugo, Victor
*The **Hundred** Secret Senses*. Tan, Amy
*A **Hundred** Suns*. Tanabe, Karin

HUNDRED YEARS' WAR, 1339-1453
  Cornwell, Bernard. *The Archer's Tale*
  Rutherfurd, Edward. *Paris*

HUNGARY
  Linden, Rachel. *The Enlightenment of Bees*
  Rossner, Rena. *The Light of the Midnight Stars*
  Szabo, Magda. *Abigail*

HUNGER
  Benioff, David. *City of Thieves: A Novel*
  Gonzalez, Christopher. *I'm Not Hungry but I Could Eat*
  McCarthy, Cormac. ★*The Road*
*The **Hunger**: a Novel*. Katsu, Alma
*The **Hungry** Tide*. Ghosh, Amitav

HUNSENMEIR SISTERS (FICTITIOUS CHARACTERS)
  Brown, Rita Mae. *Six of One*
★*The **Hunt** for Red October*. Clancy, Tom

Hunt, April
  Deadly Obsession

Hunt, Laird
  The Evening Road
  Zorrie

Hunt, Samantha
  The Dark Dark: Stories
*The **Hunter***. Byrne, Kerrigan
★*Hunter's Moon*. Stabenow, Dana

Hunter, Megan
  The Harpy

Hunter, Stephen
  The 47th Samurai
  Game of Snipers: A Bob Lee Swagger Novel
  Soft Target: A Thriller
*The **Hunter**: a Parker Novel*. Stark, Richard

HUNTERS
  Bledsoe, Alex. *Gather Her Round: A Novel of the Tufa*
  Box, C. J. ★*Open Season*
  Rutherfurd, Edward. *Sarum: The Novel of England*

HUNTING
  Bledsoe, Alex. *Gather Her Round: A Novel of the Tufa*
  Box, C. J. ★*Dark Sky: A Joe Pickett Novel*
  Childs, Laura. *Lavender Blue Murder*
  Jones, Stephen Graham. ★*The Only Good Indians: A Novel*

Sjón. *The Blue Fox*
Stabenow, Dana. ★*Hunter's Moon*
Tursten, Helene. *Hunting Game*
Watt, Holly. *To the Lions*

HUNTING ACCIDENTS
  Erdrich, Louise. ★*Larose*
Hunting Game. Tursten, Helene

HUNTING LODGES
  Jónasson, Ragnar. *The Island*
*The **Hunting** Party*. Foley, Lucy
*The **Hunting** Wives*. Cobb, May K.

Hunting, Helena
  Handle with Care

HUNTINGTON'S DISEASE
  Fay, Juliette. *The Shortest Way Home*
★*The **Huntress***. Quinn, Kate

Hurley, Andrew Michael
  Devil's Day

Hurley, Kameron
  ★*The Light Brigade*
  The Stars Are Legion

HURRICANE KATRINA, 2005
  Mallon, Thomas. *Landfall: A Novel*

HURRICANES
  Acevedo, Chantel. *The Distant Marvels*
  Ford, Richard. *Let Me Be Frank with You*
  Gaynor, Hazel. *The Lighthouse Keeper's Daughter*
  Stapley, Marissa. *The Last Resort*

Hurston, Zora Neale
  Hitting a Straight Lick with a Crooked Stick: Stories from the Harlem Renaissance
  ★*Their Eyes Were Watching God*

Hurwitz, Gregg Andrew
  ★*Into the Fire*
  ★*Out of the Dark: The Return of Orphan X*
*The **Husband***. Koontz, Dean R.

HUSBAND AND WIFE
  Adebayo, Ayobami. ★*Stay with Me*
  Amado, Jorge. ★*Dona Flor and Her Two Husbands: A Moral and Amorous Tale*
  Atwood, Margaret. *Bluebeard's Egg and Other Stories*
  Atwood, Margaret. *Life Before Man*
  Auster, Paul. *Oracle Night*
  Ausubel, Ramona. *Sons and Daughters of Ease and Plenty*
  Barnes, Djuna. ★*Nightwood*
  Bellow, Saul. *The Dean's December: A Novel*
  Benedict, Marie. ★*Lady Clementine*
  Benjamin, Ali. *The Smash-Up: A Novel*
  Benjamin, Melanie. ★*The Aviator's Wife: A Novel*
  Block, Lawrence. *All the Flowers Are Dying*
  Bock, Charles. *Alice & Oliver: A Novel*
  Boyle, T. Coraghessan. *Outside Looking In: A Novel*
  Boyle, T. Coraghessan. *The Women: A Novel*
  Bradbury, Ray. *The Illustrated Man*
  Bronte, Anne. *The Tenant of Wildfell Hall*
  Brown, Rosellen. *Tender Mercies*
  Buck, Pearl S. *The Good Earth*
  Burton, Jessie. *The Miniaturist*

Butler, Marcia. *Pickle's Progress*
Carey, Peter. *A Long Way from Home*
Carr, Robyn. *The View from Alameda Island: A Novel*
Carter, Mary Dixie. *The Photographer*
Chanter, Catherine. *The Well*
Chevalier, Tracy. ★*Girl with a Pearl Earring*
Choi, Susan. *My Education*
Christie, Agatha. *Endless Night*
Cobbs Hoffman, Elizabeth. *The Hamilton Affair*
Coben, Harlan. *Fool Me Once*
Coben, Harlan. *The Stranger*
Cocks, Heather. *The Heir Affair*
Cohen, Tish. *The Summer We Lost Her: A Novel*
Cornwell, Patricia Daniels. *Autopsy*
Crace, Jim. *Quarantine*
Cronin, A. J. *Citadel*
Cumyn, Alan. *Losing It*
Dee, Jonathan. *The Privileges: A Novel*
DeLillo, Don. ★*White Noise*
Dillard, Annie. *The Maytrees: A Novel*
Doerr, Harriet. ★*Stones for Ibarra*
Downing, Samantha. *My Lovely Wife*
Erdrich, Louise. ★*Shadow Tag: A Novel*
Estleman, Loren D. ★*Gas City*
Evans, Diana. *Ordinary People: A Novel*
Faber, Michel. *The Book of Strange New Things*
Ferris, Joshua. *The Unnamed*
Flynn, Gillian. ★*Gone Girl: A Novel*
Franzen, Jonathan. ★*Freedom*
Friedland, Elyssa. *The Intermission*
Gabaldon, Diana. ★*Drums of Autumn*
Gaige, Amity. *Sea Wife*
Galsworthy, John. ★*The Forsyte Saga*
Gardner, Lisa. *The Neighbor*
Gideon, Melanie. *Wife 22*
Glass, Julia. *The Whole World Over*
Glover, Nicole. ★*The Conductors*
Glover, Nicole. *The Undertakers*
Greene, Graham. ★*The Quiet American*
Groff, Lauren. ★*Fates and Furies*
Guhrke, Laura Lee. *How to Lose a Duke in Ten Days*
Gurganus, Allan. *Oldest Living Confederate Widow Tells All*
Hannah, Kristin. *Home Front*
Hardy, Thomas. ★*Jude the Obscure*
Harper, Karen. *The Queen's Secret: A Novel of England's World War II Queen*
Harrod-Eagles, Cynthia. *Cruel as the Grave*
Hauck, Rachel. *The Wedding Chapel*
Hawthorne, Nathaniel. ★*The Scarlet Letter: A Romance*
Higgins, Kristan. *Always the Last to Know*
Higgins, Kristan. ★*Pack up the Moon*
Hoover, Colleen. *All Your Perfects*
Ishiguro, Kazuo. *The Buried Giant: A Novel*
Jones, Tayari. ★*An American Marriage: A Novel*
Kaufman, Sue. *Diary of a Mad Housewife*
Kelly, Cathy. *Secrets of a Happy Marriage*
Kiernan, Stephen P. *Universe of Two*
Koontz, Dean R. *The Husband*

Le Carre, John. ★*Tinker, Tailor, Soldier, Spy*
Lee, Andrea. *Red Island House*
Leigh, Eva. *Temptations of a Wallflower*
Levin, Ira. ★*Rosemary's Baby: A Novel*
Levy, Andrea. *Small Island*
Lloyd, Catherine. *Death Comes to the Nursery*
Longworth, M. L. *Murder on the Ile Sordou: A Verlaque and Bonnet Provencal Mystery*
Mackintosh, Clare. *After the End*
Maynard, Joyce. *Count the Ways*
McCall Smith, Alexander. *The Double Comfort Safari Club*
McCall Smith, Alexander. *The Good Husband of Zebra Drive*
McCorkle, Jill. ★*Hieroglyphics: A Novel*
McCullers, Carson. *Reflections in a Golden Eye*
McEwan, Ian. *Black Dogs*
McLain, Paula. *Love and Ruin*
McLain, Paula. *The Paris Wife: A Novel*
McMurtry, Larry. ★*Terms of Endearment: A Novel : With a New Preface*
McPherson, Catriona. *Strangers at the Gate*
Moriarty, Liane. *The Husband's Secret*
Mosley, Walter. *And Sometimes I Wonder About You: A Leonid McGill Mystery*
Mosse, Kate. *The City of Tears*
Murakami, Haruki. *The Wind-Up Bird Chronicle*
Nabokov, Vladimir Vladimirovich. *King, Queen, Knave: A Novel*
Nicholls, David. *US: A Novel*
Niffenegger, Audrey. *The Time Traveler's Wife: A Novel*
Oates, Joyce Carol. *The Falls: A Novel*
Oates, Joyce Carol. *The Gravedigger's Daughter: A Novel*
Oates, Joyce Carol. *Pursuit*
Parini, Jay. *The Passages of H.M.: A Novel of Herman Melville*
Paris, B. A. *Behind Closed Doors*
Pearson, Allison. ★*How Hard Can It Be?*
Phillips, Helen. *The Beautiful Bureaucrat: A Novel*
Pinborough, Sarah. ★*Behind Her Eyes: A Novel*
Pronzini, Bill. *Fever*
Pronzini, Bill. *Mourners*
Pronzini, Bill. *Savages*
Proulx, Annie. *Bad Dirt: Wyoming Stories 2*
Rash, Ron. ★*Serena: A Novel*
Reid, Taylor Jenkins. *Forever, Interrupted: A Novel*
Restrepo, Laura. ★*Delirium: A Novel*
Richardson, C. S. *The End of the Alphabet*
Rivero, Melissa. *The Affairs of the Falcons*
Robb, Candace M. *The Cross-Legged Knight: An Owen Archer Mystery*
Robotham, Michael. ★*The Other Wife*
Rosenfelt, David. ★*Dog Eat Dog*
Roth, Philip. *I Married a Communist*
Rouda, Kaira Sturdivant. *Best Day Ever: A Novel*
Rubart, James L. ★*The Man He Never Was*
Runcie, James. *Sidney Chambers and the Persistence of Love*
Ruskovich, Emily. *Idaho: A Novel*
Sayers, Dorothy L. *Thrones, Dominations*
Schwarz, Christina. *The Edge of the Earth*
Scott, Paul. ★*Staying On: A Novel*
Scott, Walter. *The Bride of Lammermoor*

Shepherd, Peng. *The Book of M: A Novel*
Shreve, Anita. *Sea Glass: A Novel*
Shriver, Lionel. *Should We Stay or Should We Go*
Shriver, Lionel. *So Much for That*
Simsion, Graeme C. *The Rosie Effect*
Simsion, Graeme C. *The Rosie Result*
Solomons, Natasha. *House of Gold*
Spencer-Fleming, Julia. *Hid from Our Eyes*
Steinbeck, John. *The Pearl*
Steinhauer, Olen. *The Cairo Affair*
Suri, Manil. *The Age of Shiva: A Novel*
Swinson, Kiki. *Wifey*
Tanabe, Karin. *A Hundred Suns*
Thelen, Albert Vigoleis. *The Island of Second Sight: From the Applied Recollections of Vigoleis*
Tyler, Anne. *The Amateur Marriage: A Novel*
Wall, Cara. *The Dearly Beloved: A Novel*
Walsh, M. O. ★*The Big Door Prize: A Novel*
Waters, Martha. ★*To Have and to Hoax: A Novel*
Weiner, Jennifer. *Little Earthquakes*
Welty, Eudora. ★*The Ponder Heart*
Wendig, Chuck. *The Book of Accidents*
Wood, Tracey Enerson. *The Engineer's Wife: A Novel*
Woods, Stuart. *Santa Fe Rules*
Woolf, Virginia. *Between the Acts*
Woolf, Virginia. ★*To the Lighthouse*
The **Husband's** Secret. Moriarty, Liane

HUSBAND-AND-WIFE DETECTIVES
Crombie, Deborah. *A Bitter Feast*
DeMille, Nelson. *Wild Fire*
Hammett, Dashiell. ★*The Thin Man*
King, Laurie R. *Castle Shade*

HUSBAND-KILLING
King, Stephen. *Dolores Claiborne*
Sanders, Lawrence. *McNally's Dilemma*
Toibin, Colm. *House of Names*
★**Hush** Hush. Lippman, Laura
Hush Money: A Mystery. Greaves, Chuck
Hustler's son [Series]. Styles, Toy
A **Hustler's** Son: A Novel. Styles, Toy

Huxley, Aldous
★*Brave New World*

HYATTSVILLE, MARYLAND
Styles, Toy. *Black and Ugly*

Hyde, Catherine Ryan
My Name Is Anton
The **Hydrogen** Sonata. Banks, Iain
★**Hyperion**. Simmons, Dan
Hyperion series [Series]. Simmons, Dan

HYPERSPACE
Chambers, Becky. *A Closed and Common Orbit*
Chambers, Becky. ★*The Long Way to a Small, Angry Planet*

HYPNOTISM
Bolano, Roberto. *Monsieur Pain*

HYPNOTISTS
Bolano, Roberto. *Monsieur Pain*

HYPOCRISY
Aswani, Alaa. *Chicago: A Modern Arabic Novel*

Doctorow, E. L. ★*The Book of Daniel: A Novel*
Lewis, Sinclair. *Babbitt*
Lewis, Sinclair. ★*Elmer Gantry*
Lewis, Sinclair. ★*Main Street: The Story of Carol Kennicott*
Pomerantz, Sharon. *Rich Boy*

HYSTERIA (SOCIAL PSYCHOLOGY)
Flanagan, Richard. *The Unknown Terrorist*
Galchen, Rivka. *Everyone Knows Your Mother Is a Witch*
Malerman, Josh. *Bird Box: A Novel*
★**Hystopia**: a Novel. Means, David

I

I Am Death: Two Novellas. Amdahl, Gary
I Am Half-Sick of Shadows: A Flavia De Luce Novel. Bradley, C. Alan
★*I Am Legend*. Matheson, Richard
I Am Not Sidney Poitier. Everett, Percival L.
I Am Pilgrim. Hayes, Terry
I Am Radar: A Novel. Larsen, Reif
★*I Capture the Castle*. Smith, Dodie
I Curse the River of Time. Petterson, Per
I Kissed a Girl. Alexander, Jennet
I Know a Secret. Gerritsen, Tess
★*I Know Who You Are: A Novel*. Feeney, Alice
I Know You: A Novel of Suspense. Kantaria, Annabel
I Lost My Girlish Laughter. Allen, Jane
I Love You but I've Chosen Darkness. Watkins, Claire Vaye
I Married a Communist. Roth, Philip
I Never Promised You a Rose Garden: A Novel. Greenberg, Joanne
I Refuse. Petterson, Per
I Sailed with Magellan. Dybek, Stuart
I Say a Little Prayer: A Novel. Harris, E. Lynn
I Shall Not Want: A Clare Fergusson/Russ Van Alstyne Mystery. Spencer-Fleming, Julia
I Want You Back. James, Lorelei
I Will Send Rain: A Novel. Meadows, Rae
I'm New York's Finest. Swinson, Kiki
I'm Not Hungry but I Could Eat. Gonzalez, Christopher
I'm Not Scared. Ammaniti, Niccolo
I'm Staying Here. Balzano, Marco
I'm Thinking of Ending Things. Reid, Iain
★*I'm Waiting for You: And Other Stories*. Kim, Bo Young
★*I, Claudius: From the Autobiography of Tiberius Claudius, Born 10 B.C., Murdered and Deified A.D. 54*. Graves, Robert
I, Hogarth. Dean, Michael
★*I, Robot*. Asimov, Isaac
I, Tituba, Black Witch of Salem. Conde, Maryse
Ian Ludlow novels [Series]. Goldberg, Lee
Ibis trilogy [Series]. Ghosh, Amitav
Icarus. Meyer, Deon

ICE AGE (GEOLOGY)
Auel, Jean M. ★*The Clan of the Cave Bear: A Novel*
Ice and Stone. Muller, Marcia
The **Ice** Beneath Her: A Novel. Grebe, Camilla
Ice Cold Heart. Tracy, P. J.
The **Ice** Cream Queen of Orchard Street: A Novel. Gilman, Susan Jane

*The **Ice** Queen: A Novel.* Hoffman, Alice
ICELAND
  Hand, Elizabeth. *Available Dark: A Thriller*
  Indriðason, Arnaldur. *The Darkness Knows*
  Indriðason, Arnaldur. *Outrage*
  Indriðason, Arnaldur. *Reykjavik Nights: An Inspector Erlendur Novel*
  Indriðason, Arnaldur. *The Shadow District: A Thriller*
  Indriðason, Arnaldur. *Strange Shores: An Inspector Erlendur Novel*
  Jónasson, Ragnar. ★*The Girl Who Died*
  Jónasson, Ragnar. *The Island*
  Jónasson, Ragnar. *The Mist*
  Mallon, Thomas. *Finale: A Novel*
  Ólafsdóttir, Auður A. *Butterflies in November*
  Ólafsson, Ólafur Jóhann. *The Sacrament: A Novel*
  Petrie, Nicholas. *The Wild One*
  Ridpath, Michael. *Far North*
  Sigurðardóttir, Lilja. *Cage*
  Verne, Jules. ★*Journey to the Centre of the Earth*
*The **Iceman**.* Deutermann, Peter T.
IDAHO
  Box, C. J. *Blue Heaven*
  Dodd, Christina. *Obsession Falls*
  Doerr, Anthony. ★*Cloud Cuckoo Land: A Novel*
  Hatcher, Robin Lee. *Cross My Heart*
  Hatcher, Robin Lee. *Who I Am with You*
  Hunter, Stephen. *Game of Snipers: A Bob Lee Swagger Novel*
  Jones, Stephen Graham. *My Heart Is a Chainsaw*
  Ritter, Josh. *The Great Glorious Goddamn of It All*
  Ruskovich, Emily. *Idaho: A Novel*
  Vestal, Shawn. *Daredevils*
Idaho: a Novel. Ruskovich, Emily
Ide, Joe
  ★*Hi Five: An IQ Novel*
IDEALISM
  Ackerman, Elliot. *Dark at the Crossing*
  Dolan-Leach, Caite. *We Went to the Woods: A Novel*
  Flaubert, Gustave. *Sentimental Education*
IDEALISM IN MEN
  Pasternak, Boris Leonidovich. ★*Doctor Zhivago*
  Stead, Christina. ★*The Man Who Loved Children*
IDEALISM IN WOMEN
  Hale, Shannon. *Austenland: A Novel*
  Nunez, Sigrid. *The Last of Her Kind: A Novel*
IDEAS (PHILOSOPHY)
  Lawrence, D. H. *Women in Love*
  Pava, Sergio de la. *Personae: A Novel*
IDENTICAL TWIN BROTHERS
  Butler, Marcia. *Pickle's Progress*
IDENTICAL TWINS
  Schine, Cathleen. *The Grammarians*
  Sittenfeld, Curtis. *Sisterland: A Novel*
IDENTITY (PHILOSOPHICAL CONCEPT)
  Halfon, Eduardo. *Mourning*
IDENTITY (PSYCHOLOGY)
  Aboulela, Leila. *Elsewhere, Home*
  Abu-Jaber, Diana. *Origin: A Novel*
  Akhtar, Ayad. ★*Homeland Elegies: A Novel*
  Alexie, Sherman. *Flight*

  Andreades, Daphne Palasi. *Brown Girls*
  Askaripour, Mateo. ★*Black Buck*
  Atkinson, Kate. ★*Life After Life: A Novel*
  Auster, Paul. *4 3 2 1: A Novel*
  Auster, Paul. *Invisible*
  Auster, Paul. *Travels in the Scriptorium: A Novel*
  Baldwin, James. ★*Another Country*
  Baldwin, James. ★*Early Novels and Stories*
  Baldwin, James. ★*Giovanni's Room*
  Baldwin, James. ★*Go Tell It on the Mountain*
  Banks, Iain. *The Crow Road*
  Banville, John. ★*Eclipse: A Novel*
  Banville, John. ★*The Sea*
  Barker, Susan. ★*The Incarnations: A Novel*
  Batuman, Elif. ★*The Idiot*
  Bellow, Saul. *Dangling Man*
  Bellow, Saul. *Novels, 1944-1953*
  Bender, Aimee. *The Butterfly Lampshade*
  Bolano, Roberto. ★*By Night in Chile*
  Bourland, Barbara. ★*Fake Like Me*
  Carey, Peter. *A Long Way from Home*
  Castillo, Elaine. *America Is Not the Heart*
  Chang, Alexandra. ★*Days of Distraction*
  Chung, Catherine. *The Tenth Muse: A Novel*
  Clemmons, Zinzi. *What We Lose*
  Cline, Emma. *Daddy: Stories*
  Cole, Teju. *Every Day Is for the Thief*
  Cole, Teju. ★*Open City: A Novel*
  Coster, Naima. *What's Mine and Yours: A Novel*
  Cunningham, Michael. ★*The Hours*
  Cunningham, Michael. *Specimen Days*
  Cusk, Rachel. *Kudos*
  D'Souza, Tony. *The Konkans*
  Daoud, Kamel. *The Meursault Investigation*
  Davies, Peter Ho. *The Fortunes*
  Delany, Samuel R. *Dhalgren*
  Dimechkie, Karim. *Lifted by the Great Nothing*
  Doctorow, Cory. *Walkaway*
  Doctorow, E. L. *Andrew's Brain*
  Donoghue, Emma. ★*Frog Music*
  Donohue, Keith. *The Stolen Child*
  Durrow, Heidi W. *The Girl Who Fell from the Sky: A Novel*
  Ellison, Ralph. ★*Invisible Man*
  Ellison, Ralph. ★*Juneteenth*
  Emezi, Akwaeke. ★*The Death of Vivek Oji*
  Emezi, Akwaeke. *Freshwater*
  Erdrich, Louise. ★*Shadow Tag: A Novel*
  Eugenides, Jeffrey. ★*Middlesex*
  Evans, Diana. *Ordinary People: A Novel*
  Evaristo, Bernardine. ★*Girl, Woman, Other*
  Everett, Percival L. *Erasure: A Novel*
  Everett, Percival L. *I Am Not Sidney Poitier*
  Faulks, Sebastian. *Paris Echo: A Novel*
  Feldman, Ellen. *Paris Never Leaves You*
  Ferris, Joshua. *To Rise Again at a Decent Hour: A Novel*
  Ferris, Joshua. *The Unnamed*
  Fitch, Janet. *White Oleander: A Novel*
  Ford, Richard. *Sorry for Your Trouble: Stories*

Frank, Dorothea Benton. *Folly Beach: A Lowcountry Tale*
Frankel, Laurie. *This Is How It Always Is*
Franzen, Jonathan. *Purity*
Freitas, Donna. *The Nine Lives of Rose Napolitano*
Gaige, Amity. *Schroder*
Gibbons, Kaye. ★*Ellen Foster: A Novel*
Greengrass, Jessie. *Sight: A Novel*
Greer, Andrew Sean. *The Impossible Lives of Greta Wells*
Hamya, Jo. *Three Rooms*
Harris, E. Lynn. *Basketball Jones: A Novel*
Harris, E. Lynn. *Invisible Life: A Novel*
Johnson, Jocelyn Nicole. ★*My Monticello: Fiction*
Kafka, Franz. ★*Collected Stories*
Kaufman, Sue. *Diary of a Mad Housewife*
Khadra, Yasmina. ★*Khalil: A Novel*
Krauss, Nicole. *Forest Dark*
Kundera, Milan. ★*Immortality*
Lacey, Catherine. ★*Pew: A Novel*
Larsen, Nella. *Passing*
Lee, Min Jin. ★*Pachinko*
Lerner, Ben. ★*The Topeka School*
Lessing, Doris May. ★*The Golden Notebook*
Lewis, C. S. *Till We Have Faces: A Myth Retold*
Lightman, Alan P. *The Diagnosis*
Liu, Ken. ★*The Veiled Throne*
Masood, Syed M. *The Bad Muslim Discount*
Mehta, Rahul. *No Other World: A Novel*
Mengestu, Dinaw. ★*All Our Names*
Monroe, Mary. ★*Mrs. Wiggins*
Moore, Liz. *The Unseen World*
Mosley, Walter. ★*John Woman*
Murakami, Haruki. *Blind Willow, Sleeping Woman: 24 Stories*
Murakami, Haruki. *Colorless Tsukuru Tazaki and His Years of Pilgrimage*
Murakami, Haruki. ★*First Person Singular: Stories*
Naipaul, V. S. *A House for Mr. Biswas*
Nguyen, Viet Thanh. ★*The Sympathizer*
Oates, Joyce Carol. *Breathe*
Orwell, George. ★*1984: A Novel*
Otsuka, Julie. *The Buddha in the Attic*
Oyeyemi, Helen. *Boy, Snow, Bird: A Novel*
Oyeyemi, Helen. *The Opposite House*
Palliser, Charles. *The Quincunx*
Pandya, Sameer. *Members Only*
Pearlman, Edith. *Honeydew: Stories*
Potok, Chaim. ★*My Name Is Asher Lev*
Pronzini, Bill. *Spook*
Pulley, Natasha. ★*The Kingdoms*
Rice, Anne. *Christ the Lord: Out of Egypt: A Novel*
Rice, Anne. *Christ the Lord: The Road to Cana: A Novel*
Rimmer, Kelly. ★*The Warsaw Orphan: A Wwii Novel*
Robinson, Peter. *Friend of the Devil*
Rodrigues Fowler, Yara. *Stubborn Archivist*
Roth, Henry. *A Star Shines Over Mt. Morris Park*
Roth, Philip. ★*Goodbye, Columbus, and Five Short Stories*
Row, Jess. *Your Face in Mine: A Novel*
Satyal, Rakesh. *No One Can Pronounce My Name: A Novel*
Savage, Sam. *Firmin: Adventures of a Metropolitan Lowlife*

Setterfield, Diane. ★*Once Upon a River*
Shepherd, Peng. *The Book of M: A Novel*
Sherrill, Steven. *The Minotaur Takes His Own Sweet Time: A Novel*
Silko, Leslie Marmon. *Gardens in the Dunes: A Novel*
Skyhorse, Brando. *Madonnas of Echo Park: A Novel*
Smith, Ali. *There but for The: A Novel*
Smith, Zadie. ★*Grand Union: Stories*
Solomon, Anna. *Leaving Lucy Pear*
Stevens, Chevy. *Still Missing*
Straub, Emma. ★*Modern Lovers*
Stross, Charles. *Glasshouse*
Suarez, Daniel. *Change Agent: A Novel*
Takamura, Kaoru. ★*Lady Joker*
Tan, Amy. *The Valley of Amazement*
Thompson-Spires, Nafissa. *Heads of the Colored People: Stories*
Umrigar, Thrity N. *Everybody's Son*
Van der Vliet Oloomi, Azareen. *Call Me Zebra*
Vlautin, Willy. *Don't Skip Out on Me*
Warren, Robert Penn. *Band of Angels*
Washington, Bryan. *Lot: Stories*
Washington, Bryan. ★*Memorial*
Wasserman, Robin. *Mother Daughter Widow Wife*
Weiner, Jennifer. ★*Mrs. Everything: A Novel*
Wells, Martha. *Network Effect*
White, Edmund. *A Boy's Own Story*
Whitehead, Colson. *Apex Hides the Hurt*
Whitehead, Colson. *Sag Harbor: A Novel*
Wideman, John Edgar. *Look for Me and I'll Be Gone: Stories*
Winch, Tara June. *The Yield*
Woo, Sung J. *Love Love: A Novel*
Woolf, Virginia. *The Waves*
Wright, Jaime Jo. *The Haunting at Bonaventure Circus*

IDENTITY (RELIGION)
Chabon, Michael. *The Yiddish Policemen's Union*
D'Souza, Tony. *The Konkans*

IDEOLOGY
Hill, Donna. ★*Confessions in B-Flat*
Sterling, Bruce. *Pirate Utopia*
Theroux, Paul. ★*The Mosquito Coast: A Novel*
The Ides of April: A Flavia Albia Mystery. Davis, Lindsey
★*The Idiot*. Batuman, Elif

IDLEWILD, MICHIGAN
Cleage, Pearl. *What Looks Like Crazy on an Ordinary Day: A Novel*
★*If Beale Street Could Talk*. Baldwin, James
★*If Ever I Return, Pretty Peggy-O*. McCrumb, Sharyn
If I Disappear. Brazier, Eliza Jane
If I Never Met You: A Novel. McFarlane, Mhairi
If It Bleeds. King, Stephen
If Not for You: A Novel. Macomber, Debbie
★*If on a Winter's Night a Traveler*. Calvino, Italo
If Only I Could Tell You. Beckerman, Hannah
If She Wakes. Koryta, Michael
If the Boot Fits. Weatherspoon, Rebekah
If the Creek Don't Rise: A Novel. Weiss, Leah
If the Shoe Fits. Murphy, Julie
If Tomorrow Comes. Kress, Nancy
If We Make It Home: A Novel of Faith and Survival in the Oregon Wilderness. Nelson, Christina Suzann

If You Leave Me. Kim, Crystal Hana
IGBO (AFRICAN PEOPLE)
    Achebe, Chinua. ★*Things Fall Apart*
    Adichie, Chimamanda Ngozi. *Half of a Yellow Sun*
    Emezi, Akwaeke. *Freshwater*
Iggulden, Conn
    The Abbot's Tale
Igharo, Jane
    The Sweetest Remedy
Ignatius, David
    The Increment: A Novel
Iles, Greg
    The Bone Tree: A Novel
    Cemetery Road: A Novel
    Mississippi Blood: A Novel
    Natchez Burning: A Novel
Ill Will. Chaon, Dan
ILLEGAL ARMS TRANSFERS
    Brett, Simon. *Mrs Pargeter's Principle*
    Higgins, George V. *The Friends of Eddie Coyle*
    Kemelman, Harry. *One Fine Day the Rabbi Bought a Cross*
    Vachss, Andrew H. *Two Trains Running*
ILLEGITIMACY
    Balogh, Mary. *Someone to Hold*
    Chen, Da. *Brothers: A Novel*
    Fielding, Henry. ★*The History of Tom Jones, a Foundling*
    Halls, Stacey. *The Lost Orphan*
    Holt, Victoria. *The Black Opal*
    Jordan, Sophie. *The Duke Goes Down*
    Stewart, Mary. *The Wicked Day*
ILLEGITIMATE CHILDREN OF ROYALTY
    Rushdie, Salman. *The Enchantress of Florence: A Novel*
    Stewart, Mary. ★*The Crystal Cave*
ILLINOIS
    Armstrong, Kelley. *Wherever She Goes*
    Aswani, Alaa. *Chicago: A Modern Arabic Novel*
    Blumberg, Chandra. *Digging up Love*
    Bradbury, Ray. ★*Dandelion Wine: A Novel*
    Bradbury, Ray. ★*Something Wicked This Way Comes*
    Cisneros, Sandra. ★*The House on Mango Street*
    Horan, Nancy. *Loving Frank: A Novel*
    Lombardo, Claire. *The Most Fun We Ever Had: A Novel*
    Manansala, Mia P. ★*Arsenic and Adobo*
    Moreno, Gus. *This Thing Between US: A Novel*
    Phillips, Jayne Anne. *Quiet Dell: A Novel*
    Pinter, Jason. *Hide Away*
    Pinter, Jason. *A Stranger at the Door*
    Putnam, Jonathan F. *These Honored Dead*
    Straub, Peter. *Lost Boy Lost Girl: A Novel*
    Strout, Elizabeth. ★*Anything Is Possible: Fiction*
    Tatlock, Ann. *Promises to Keep*
    Wallace, David Foster. ★*The Pale King: An Unfinished Novel*
ILLITERATE MEN
    Barnett, Karen. *Ever Faithful*
The Illness Lesson. Beams, Clare
The Illumination. Brockmeier, Kevin
Illuminations: a Novel of Hildegard Von Bingen. Sharratt, Mary
The Illusion of Separateness. Van Booy, Simon

Illusion Town. Castle, Jayne
Illusion Town novels [Series]. Castle, Jayne
Illusions. Pronzini, Bill
ILLUSTRATED BOOKS
    Brom. *Slewfoot: A Tale of Bewitchery*
    Hosseini, Khaled. ★*Sea Prayer*
    Pessl, Marisha. *Night Film: A Novel*
    Preston, Caroline. *The Scrapbook of Frankie Pratt*
The Illustrated Man. Bradbury, Ray
IMAGINARY CREATURES
    Bear, Elizabeth. *Stone Mad*
    James, Marlon. ★*Black Leopard, Red Wolf*
    Jemisin, N. K. ★*The City We Became*
    Shaw, Vivian. ★*Dreadful Company*
    Shaw, Vivian. ★*Strange Practice*
    Whiteley, Aliya. *From the Neck up and Other Stories*
IMAGINARY EMPIRES
    Banks, Iain. *Consider Phlebas*
    Clark, Cherae. ★*The Unbroken*
    Corey, James S. A. *Tiamat's Wrath*
    Draven, Grace. *Phoenix Unbound*
    Elliott, Kate. *Servant Mage*
    Jemisin, N. K. *The Fifth Season*
    Jemisin, N. K. *The Obelisk Gate*
    Jemisin, N. K. *The Stone Sky*
    Krueger, Paul. *Steel Crow Saga*
    Lee, Yoon Ha. *Ninefox Gambit*
    Lee, Yoon Ha. *Raven Stratagem*
    Lee, Yoon Ha. *Revenant Gun*
    Liu, Ken. *The Wall of Storms*
    Martine, Arkady. ★*A Desolation Called Peace*
    Martine, Arkady. ★*A Memory Called Empire*
    Maxwell, Everina. *Winter's Orbit*
    Muir, Tamsyn. *Harrow the Ninth*
    Ryan, Anthony. *The Waking Fire*
    Scalzi, John. *The Collapsing Empire*
    Simmons, Dan. *The Fall of Hyperion*
    Simmons, Dan. ★*Hyperion*
    Suri, Tasha. ★*Realm of Ash*
    Wagers, K. B. *There Before the Chaos*
IMAGINARY JOURNEYS
    Verne, Jules. ★*Journey to the Centre of the Earth*
IMAGINARY KINGDOMS
    Bear, Elizabeth. *Ink and Steel: A Novel of the Promethean Age*
    Brennan, Marie. *Within the Sanctuary of Wings: A Memoir by Lady Trent*
    Campbell, Lisbeth. *The Vanished Queen*
    Chakraborty, S. A. *The Kingdom of Copper: A Novel*
    Goldman, William. ★*The Princess Bride: S. Morgenstern's Classic Tale of True Love and High Adventure : The*
    Kelly, Greta. *The Frozen Crown*
    Kuhn, M. J. *Among Thieves*
    Leckie, Ann. ★*The Raven Tower*
    Maguire, Gregory. *The Brides of Maracoor*
    Martin, George R. R. *Fire & Blood: 300 Years Before a Game of Thrones (A Targaryen History)*
IMAGINARY MACHINES
    Bauermeister, Erica. *The Scent Keeper*

IMAGINARY PLACES

Borges, Jorge Luis. *Ficciones*
Czerneda, Julie. *A Turn of Light*
deWitt, Patrick. *Undermajordomo Minor*
Durst, Sarah Beth. *Race the Sands*
Johnstone, Carole. *Mirrorland*
Le Guin, Ursula K. *The Beginning Place*
McGuire, Seanan. ★*Every Heart a Doorway*
McGuire, Seanan. ★*In an Absent Dream*
Morgenstern, Erin. ★*The Starless Sea*
Roberts, Nora. ★*The Awakening*

IMAGINARY WARS AND BATTLES

Banks, Iain. *Consider Phlebas*
Banks, Iain. *The Player of Games*
Banks, Iain. *Use of Weapons*
Bear, Elizabeth. *All the Windwracked Stars*
Bear, Elizabeth. *Ink and Steel: A Novel of the Promethean Age*
Corey, James S. A. *Tiamat's Wrath*
El-Mohtar, Amal. ★*This Is How You Lose the Time War*
French, Jonathan. *The Free Bastards*
Hao, Jingfang. *Vagabonds: A Novel*
Haydon, Elizabeth. *The Merchant Emperor*
Hurley, Kameron. ★*The Light Brigade*
Hurley, Kameron. *The Stars Are Legion*
Kay, Guy Gavriel. ★*Children of Earth and Sky*
Kay, Guy Gavriel. *The Summer Tree*
Lee, Fonda. ★*Jade City*
Lee, Fonda. *Jade War*
Lee, Yoon Ha. *Revenant Gun*
Liu, Ken. ★*The Grace of Kings*
Liu, Ken. *The Wall of Storms*
Martin, George R. R. *Fire & Blood: 300 Years Before a Game of Thrones (A Targaryen History)*
Mitchell, David. *The Bone Clocks: A Novel*
North, Claire. *Notes from the Burning Age*
Rushdie, Salman. *Two Years Eight Months and Twenty-Eight Nights: A Novel*
Showalter, Gena. *Shadow and Ice*
Singh, Nalini. ★*Silver Silence*
Stirling, S. M. *The Protector's War*
Tolkien, J. R. R. *The Children of Hurin*
Valentine, Genevieve. *Mechanique: A Tale of the Circus Tresaulti*
Wexler, Django. *Ashes of the Sun*
Winter, Evan. *The Fires of Vengeance*

IMAGINATION

Doerr, Anthony. ★*Cloud Cuckoo Land: A Novel*
Yu, E. Lily. ★*On Fragile Waves*

IMAGINATION IN MEN

Cervantes Saavedra, Miguel de. ★*Don Quixote*

IMAGINATION IN TEENAGE GIRLS

Austen, Jane. *Northanger Abbey*
★*Imagine Me Gone: A Novel*. Haslett, Adam
Imamura, Natsuko
  The Woman in the Purple Skirt: A Novel

IMITATION

Gerritsen, Tess. *The Apprentice: A Novel*
Janowitz, Brenda. *The Grace Kelly Dress*
The **Immaculate** Deception. Pears, Iain

IMMIGRANT FAMILIES

Acker, Jennifer. ★*The Limits of the World*
Alvarez, Julia. *How the Garcia Girls Lost Their Accents*
Artson, Barbara. *Odessa, Odessa*
Dev, Sonali. ★*Pride, Prejudice, and Other Flavors: A Novel*
Erpenbeck, Jenny. *The Book of Words*
Gross, Andrew. *Button Man*
Halfon, Eduardo. *Mourning*
Kim, Eugenia. *The Kinship of Secrets*
Lahiri, Jhumpa. ★*The Namesake*
Lalami, Laila. *The Other Americans: A Novel*
Lalli, Sonya. *The Matchmaker's List*
Lee, Min Jin. ★*Pachinko*
Masood, Syed M. *The Bad Muslim Discount*
Mehta, Rahul. *No Other World: A Novel*
Rivero, Melissa. *The Affairs of the Falcons*
Roth, Henry. *A Diving Rock on the Hudson*
Roth, Henry. *From Bondage*
Roth, Henry. *Requiem for Harlem*
Roth, Henry. *A Star Shines Over Mt. Morris Park*
Satyal, Rakesh. *No One Can Pronounce My Name: A Novel*
Shaw, Irwin. ★*Rich Man, Poor Man*

IMMIGRANTS

Aciman, Andre. *Harvard Square*
Adichie, Chimamanda Ngozi. ★*Americanah: A Novel*
Adichie, Chimamanda Ngozi. *The Thing Around Your Neck*
Alenyikov, Michael. *Ivan and Misha: Stories*
Ali, Monica. ★*Brick Lane: A Novel*
Aliu, Xhenet. ★*Brass: A Novel*
Allende, Isabel. *In the Midst of Winter: A Novel*
Alvarez, Julia. ★*Afterlife: A Novel*
Ashley & JaQuavis. *Murderville*
Brett, Simon. *Guilt at the Garage*
Burdick, Serena. *Find Me in Havana*
Castillo, Elaine. *America Is Not the Heart*
Cather, Willa. ★*My Antonia*
Cather, Willa. *O Pioneers!*
Cole, Teju. ★*Open City: A Novel*
Cordova, Zoraida. *The Inheritance of Orquidea Divina*
Crucet, Jennine Capo. *Make Your Home Among Strangers*
Davies, Peter Ho. *The Fortunes*
Diaz, Hernan. ★*In the Distance*
Erdrich, Louise. *The Master Butchers Singing Club: A Novel*
Faulks, Sebastian. *Paris Echo: A Novel*
Gaige, Amity. *Schroder*
Garcia, Gabriela. *Of Women and Salt*
Gay, Roxane. ★*Ayiti*
Gibb, Camilla. *Sweetness in the Belly*
Gilman, Susan Jane. *The Ice Cream Queen of Orchard Street: A Novel*
Golding, William. *Rites of Passage*
Gunaratne, Guy. *In Our Mad and Furious City*
Gyasi, Yaa. ★*Transcendent Kingdom*
Hashemzadeh Bonde, Golnaz. *What We Owe*
Iweala, Uzodinma. ★*Speak No Evil*
Lauren, Christina. *Roomies*
Malamud, Bernard. *The Assistant*
McDermott, Alice. ★*The Ninth Hour*
Munro, Alice. *The View from Castle Rock: Stories*

Nabokov, Vladimir Vladimirovich. *Pale Fire*
Nabokov, Vladimir Vladimirovich. *Pnin*
O'Connor, Joseph. *Star of the Sea*
Pelecanos, George P. *The Big Blowdown*
Piercy, Marge. *Sex Wars*
Robotham, Michael. *The Night Ferry: A Novel*
See, Lisa. *Shanghai Girls: A Novel*
Shteyngart, Gary. *The Russian Debutante's Handbook*
Sinclair, Upton. ★*The Jungle*
Smith, Zadie. ★*White Teeth: A Novel*
So, Anthony Veasna. *Afterparties: Stories*
Sylvester, Natalia. *Everyone Knows You Go Home*
Tamirat, Nafkote. *The Parking Lot Attendant: A Novel*
Tan, Lucy. *What We Were Promised*
Thammavongsa, Souvankham. *How to Pronounce Knife: Stories*
Umrigar, Thrity N. ★*Honor*
Vo, Nghi. ★*The Chosen and the Beautiful*
Wecker, Helene. *The Golem and the Jinni*
Wecker, Helene. ★*The Hidden Palace*
Zapata, Mike. *The Lost Book of Adana Moreau*

IMMIGRANTS — HISTORY
Rølvaag, O. E. ★*Giants in the Earth: A Saga of the Prairie*

IMMIGRANTS — IDENTITY
Chai, May-Lee. *Useful Phrases for Immigrants: Stories*
Djavadi, Negar. *Disoriental*
Mehta, Rahul. *No Other World: A Novel*

IMMIGRANTS, ARAB
Gordimer, Nadine. *The Pickup*
Hammad, Isabella. ★*The Parisian, Or, Al-Barisi: A Novel*

IMMIGRANTS, CHINESE
Bates, Judy Fong. ★*Midnight at the Dragon Cafe*
Chai, May-Lee. *Useful Phrases for Immigrants: Stories*
Feng, Linda Rui. *Swimming Back to Trout River*
Kwok, Jean. *Searching for Sylvie Lee*
See, Lisa. *Shanghai Girls: A Novel*

IMMIGRANTS, EAST INDIAN
Reddi, Rishi. *Passage West: A Novel*

IMMIGRANTS, FINNISH
Marlantes, Karl. *Deep River*

IMMIGRANTS, FRENCH
Proulx, Annie. ★*Barkskins: A Novel*

IMMIGRANTS, GERMAN
Jensen, Nancy. *In Our Midst*
Wiseman, Ellen Marie. *The Orphan Collector*

IMMIGRANTS, HISPANIC AMERICAN
Alvarez, Julia. *How the Garcia Girls Lost Their Accents*

IMMIGRANTS, IRISH
Barry, Sebastian. *Days Without End: A Novel*
Faye, Lyndsay. *The Gods of Gotham*

IMMIGRANTS, JEWISH
Chabon, Michael. *The Yiddish Policemen's Union*
Richler, Mordecai. *Barney's Version: A Novel*
Roth, Henry. ★*Call It Sleep*

IMMIGRANTS, RUSSIAN
Piercy, Marge. *Sex Wars*
Shteyngart, Gary. *The Russian Debutante's Handbook*

IMMIGRANTS, TURKISH
Gunday, Hakan. *The Few*

IMMIGRATION AND EMIGRATION
Acker, Jennifer. ★*The Limits of the World*
Alvar, Mia. *In the Country: Stories*
Bulawayo, NoViolet. *We Need New Names: A Novel*
Cruz, Angie. *Dominicana: A Novel*
Erpenbeck, Jenny. *Go, Went, Gone: A Novel*
Grames, Juliet. *The Seven or Eight Deaths of Stella Fortuna*
Jen, Gish. ★*Thank You, Mr. Nixon: Stories*
Lalami, Laila. *The Other Americans: A Novel*
Michener, James A. *Chesapeake*
Peynado, Brenda. *The Rock Eaters: Stories*
Rutherfurd, Edward. *The Rebels of Ireland: The Dublin Saga*
Sahota, Sunjeev. *The Year of the Runaways*
Smith, Ali. ★*Summer*
Turansky, Carrie. *No Ocean Too Wide: A Novel*
Vuong, Ocean. ★*On Earth We're Briefly Gorgeous: A Novel*
Wolfe, Tom. *Back to Blood: A Novel*

IMMIGRATION PRISONS
Clarke, Maxine Beneba. ★*Foreign Soil*
★*The **Immoralist***. Gide, Andre

IMMORTALISM
Arden, Katherine. ★*The Bear and the Nightingale*
Borges, Jorge Luis. ★*Collected Fictions*
Leckie, Ann. *Ancillary Justice*
Leckie, Ann. *Ancillary Mercy*
Leckie, Ann. *Ancillary Sword*
Robbins, Tom. ★*Jitterbug Perfume*
Tolkien, J. R. R. *Beren and Luthien*
Toro, Guillermo del. *The Hollow Ones*
Wilson, Daniel H. *The Clockwork Dynasty: A Novel*
★*The **Immortalists**: a Novel*. Benjamin, Chloe
★***Immortality***. Kundera, Milan

IMMORTALITY
Baker, Kage. *In the Garden of Iden: A Novel of the Company*
Brennan, Marie. *Driftwood*
Cronin, Justin. *The Passage*
Cronin, Justin. *The Twelve*
Deon, Natashia. *The Perishing: A Novel*
Haig, Matt. *The Humans: A Novel*
Hamill, Pete. *Forever*
Horn, Dara. *Eternal Life: A Novel*
Kundera, Milan. ★*Immortality*
Maturin, Charles Robert. *Melmoth the Wanderer: A Tale*
Rice, Anne. *Blackwood Farm*
Rice, Anne. *Blood and Gold: Or, the Story of Marius*
Rice, Anne. *Blood Canticle*
Rice, Anne. ★*Interview with the Vampire*
Rice, Anne. *Merrick: A Novel*
Rice, Anne. *Prince Lestat: The Vampire Chronicles*
Rice, Anne. ★*The Queen of the Damned*
Rice, Anne. *The Tale of the Body Thief*
Rice, Anne. *The Vampire Armand*
Rice, Anne. ★*The Vampire Lestat*
Saramago, Jose. *Death with Interruptions*
Schwab, Victoria. *The Invisible Life of Addie Larue*
Shteyngart, Gary. ★*Super Sad True Love Story: A Novel*
Wilde, Oscar. ★*The Picture of Dorian Gray*
★*The **Immortals** of Tehran*. Araghi, Alireza Taheri

IMMUNITY
Grant, Mira. *Parasite*

Imperfect Women: A Novel. Hall, Araminta

The *Imperfectionists: a Novel.* Rachman, Tom

The *Imperfects.* Meyerson, Amy

Imperial Bedrooms. Ellis, Bret Easton

Imperial Radch [Series]. Leckie, Ann

IMPERIALISM
Martine, Arkady. ★*A Memory Called Empire*
North, Claire. *The Pursuit of William Abbey*
Pynchon, Thomas. ★*V: A Novel*
Suri, Tasha. ★*Empire of Sand*

IMPERIALISM, AMERICAN
Apostol, Gina. *Insurrecto*

IMPERIALISM, BRITISH
Forster, E. M. ★*A Passage to India*

IMPERIALISM, RUSSIAN
Marlantes, Karl. *Deep River*

IMPERSONATION
Beyda, Emily. *The Body Double*
Bryant, Niobia. *Christmas with the Billionaire*
Jones, Tanen. *The Better Liar: A Novel*
Weiss, Elizabeth. *The Sisters Sweet*

IMPERSONATORS
Beverley, Jo. *My Lady Notorious*

The *Impossible* Dead. Rankin, Ian

The *Impossible* Lives of Greta Wells. Greer, Andrew Sean

Impostor Syndrome: A Novel. Wang, Kathy

IMPOSTORS
Austin, Emily. *Everyone in This Room Will Someday Be Dead*
Bell, Lenora. ★*How the Duke Was Won*
Erdrich, Louise. *The Last Report on the Miracles at Little No Horse*
Finch, Charles. *The Last Passenger*
Greene, Graham. *The Captain and the Enemy*
Higgins, Jack. *Confessional*
Highsmith, Patricia. ★*The Talented Mr. Ripley*
Ludlum, Robert. *The Bourne Supremacy*
Melville, Herman. *The Confidence-Man: His Masquerade*
Pearl, Matthew. *The Poe Shadow: A Novel*
Twain, Mark. *Pudd'nhead Wilson ;: And, Those Extraordinary Twins*
Westlake, Donald E. *The Road to Ruin*

IMPRISONMENT
Abe, Kobo. *The Woman in the Dunes*
Amis, Martin. ★*The Zone of Interest: A Novel*
Barr, Nevada. *The Rope: An Anna Pigeon Novel*
Dunant, Sarah. *Sacred Hearts: A Novel*
Hawkins, Scott. ★*The Library at Mount Char*
Sofer, Dalia. *The Septembers of Shiraz*
Suri, Tasha. *The Jasmine Throne*
Wideman, John Edgar. *Look for Me and I'll Be Gone: Stories*

The *Improbability* of Love: A Novel. Rothschild, Hannah

Improvement. Silber, Joan

In a Book Club Far Away. Marcelo, Tif

In a Dark, Dark Wood. Ware, Ruth

In a Holidaze. Lauren, Christina

★*In America.* Sontag, Susan

★*In an Absent Dream.* McGuire, Seanan

In Calabria. Beagle, Peter S.

In Death series [Series]. Robb, J. D.

In Every Mirror She's Black. Akinmade-Akerstrom, Lola

In Evil Hour. Garcia Marquez, Gabriel

In Five Years: A Novel. Serle, Rebecca

In Her Shoes: A Novel. Weiner, Jennifer

In Her Tracks. Dugoni, Robert

In Other Rooms, Other Wonders: Connected Stories. Mueenuddin, Daniyal

In Our Mad and Furious City. Gunaratne, Guy

In Our Midst. Jensen, Nancy

In Peppermint Peril: A Book Tea Shop Mystery. Avon, Joy

In Persuasion Nation: Stories. Saunders, George

In Search of a Name. van Heemstra, Marjolijn

In search of lost time [Series]. Proust, Marcel

In Sunlight and in Shadow. Helprin, Mark

In the Beauty of the Lilies. Updike, John

In the Bleak Midwinter. Spencer-Fleming, Julia

In the Company of Cheerful Ladies. McCall Smith, Alexander

In the Company of Killers. Christy, Bryan

In the Company of Liars. Ellis, David

In the Company of the Courtesan: A Novel. Dunant, Sarah

★*In the Country of Last Things.* Auster, Paul

In the Country of Men. Matar, Hisham

In the Country of Others. Slimani, Leïla

In the Country: Stories. Alvar, Mia

In the Crosshairs: A Sniper Novel. Coughlin, Jack

In the Dark Places. Robinson, Peter

★*In the Distance.* Diaz, Hernan

In the Field. Pastan, Rachel

In the First Circle: A Novel : The Restored Text. Solzhenitsyn, Aleksandr Isaevich

In the Full Light of the Sun. Clark, Clare

In the Garden of Iden: A Novel of the Company. Baker, Kage

In the Heat of the Night. Ball, John Dudley

In the Midst of Winter: A Novel. Allende, Isabel

In the Miso Soup. Murakami, Ryu

In the Morning I'll Be Gone: A Detective Sean Duffy Novel. McKinty, Adrian

In the Teeth of the Evidence. Sayers, Dorothy L.

In the Unlikely Event. Blume, Judy

★*In the Valley: Stories and a Novella Based on Serena.* Rash, Ron

In the Watchful City. Lu, S. Qiouyi

In the Woods. French, Tana

In Want of a Wife. Goodman, Jo

In War Times. Goonan, Kathleen Ann

★*In West Mills.* Winslow, De'Shawn Charles

INCA SHAMANS
Robbins, Tom. *Fierce Invalids Home from Hot Climates*

INCANTATIONS
Palahniuk, Chuck. *Lullaby: A Novel*

★The *Incarnations: a Novel.* Barker, Susan

INCAS
Binet, Laurent. *Civilizations*

★*Incense and Sensibility.* Dev, Sonali

The *Incense* Game: A Novel of Feudal Japan. Rowland, Laura Joh

INCEST
Faulkner, William. ★*The Sound and the Fury*
King, Stephen. *Dolores Claiborne*

Sapphire. ★*Push: A Novel*
Stewart, Mary. *The Wicked Day*

INCEST VICTIMS

Draper, Sharon M. ★*Forged by Fire*

INCOME INEQUALITY

Ganshert, Katie. ★*No One Ever Asked: A Novel*
An Inconvenient Duke. Harrington, Anna
The Increment: a Novel. Ignatius, David

INCUBATORS (PEDIATRICS)

Armstrong, Addison. *The Light of Luna Park*

INDECENT ASSAULT

Amidon, Stephen. *Security: A Novel*
An Indecent Obsession. McCullough, Colleen
Indemnity Only: A Novel. Paretsky, Sara

INDENTURED SERVANTS

Pulley, Natasha. ★*The Kingdoms*
Urquhart, Rachel. *The Visionist*

INDEPENDENCE (PERSONAL QUALITY)

Archer, Jeffrey. *Nothing Ventured*
Beagle, Peter S. *Summerlong*
Gibbons, Kaye. *The Life All Around Me by Ellen Foster*
Vargas Llosa, Mario. ★*The Way to Paradise*
★*Independence Day*. Ford, Richard

INDEPENDENCE IN AFRICAN AMERICAN WOMEN

Hurston, Zora Neale. ★*Their Eyes Were Watching God*

INDEPENDENCE IN SINGLE WOMEN

Balogh, Mary. ★*Someone to Remember: A Westcott Story*
Bell, Lenora. *One Fine Duke*

INDEPENDENCE IN TEENAGE GIRLS

Franklin, Miles. *My Brilliant Career*
Portis, Charles. ★*True Grit: A Novel*

INDEPENDENCE IN WOMEN

Balogh, Mary. ★*Someone to Cherish*
Bateman, Kate. *This Earl of Mine*
Benjamin, Melanie. ★*The Aviator's Wife: A Novel*
Bittner, Rosanne. *Logan's Lady*
Brockway, Connie. *No Place for a Dame*
Burrowes, Grace. ★*A Rogue of Her Own*
Burrowes, Grace. *Tremaine's True Love*
Carlyle, Christy. *Duke Gone Rogue*
Cather, Willa. *A Lost Lady*
Cather, Willa. ★*My Antonia*
Chase, Loretta Lynda. *Miss Wonderful*
Chee, Alexander. *The Queen of the Night*
Cherezinska, Elzbieta. *The Widow Queen*
Collins, Manda. ★*A Lady's Guide to Mischief and Mayhem*
Davis, Fiona. *The Masterpiece*
De Robertis, Carolina. *Cantoras*
Ferrante, Elena. *The Story of the Lost Child*
Francis-Sharma, Lauren. ★*Book of the Little Axe*
Freeman, Dianne. *A Lady's Guide to Etiquette and Murder*
Gay, Roxane. ★*Difficult Women*
Gibbons, Kaye. *Charms for the Easy Life*
Goodman, Jo. *A Touch of Forever*
Gortner, C. W. *The First Actress: A Novel of Sarah Bernhardt*
Greenidge, Kaitlyn. ★*Libertie: A Novel*
Gregory, Philippa. *The Taming of the Queen*
Gregory, Philippa. *Tidelands*

Hargrave, Kiran Millwood. *The Mercies: A Novel*
Heyer, Georgette. *The Grand Sophy*
Hoyt, Elizabeth. *Not the Duke's Darling*
Hughes, Caoilinn. *Orchid and the Wasp*
Jalaluddin, Uzma. ★*Ayesha at Last*
James, Eloisa. *Wilde in Love*
Jenkins, Beverly. *Wild Rain*
Kleypas, Lisa. ★*Devil in Disguise*
Lalli, Sonya. *Serena Singh Flips the Script*
Lee, Harper. ★*Go Set a Watchman*
MacLean, Sarah. ★*Brazen and the Beast*
McLain, Paula. *Circling the Sun*
McLain, Paula. *Love and Ruin*
Morton, Brian. *Florence Gordon*
Moyes, Jojo. ★*The Giver of Stars: A Novel*
Naylor, Gloria. *Mama Day*
Neubauer, Erica Ruth. *Murder at the Mena House*
Oates, Joyce Carol. *A Garden of Earthly Delights*
Peterson, Tracie. *What Comes My Way*
Pufahl, Shannon. *On Swift Horses*
Putney, Mary Jo. *Once a Soldier*
Raybourn, Deanna. *A Curious Beginning: A Veronica Speedwell Mystery*
Robb, Candace M. *A Murdered Peace*
Robb, Candace M. *A Twisted Vengeance*
Russell, Mary Doria. *Dreamers of the Day: A Novel*
Sand, George. *Marianne*
Santiago, Esmeralda. *Conquistadora: A Novel*
Seton, Anya. ★*The Winthrop Woman*
Shupe, Joanna. *The Rogue of Fifth Avenue*
Sittenfeld, Curtis. *Rodham: A Novel*
Spencer, Minerva. *Barbarous*
Spencer, Minerva. *Dangerous*
Sullivan, Emily. *The Rebel and the Rake*
Tyler, Anne. *Vinegar Girl: The Taming of the Shrew Retold*
Walters, Minette. *The Last Hours: A Novel*
Whittall, Zoe. *The Spectacular: A Novel*
Winslow, De'Shawn Charles. ★*In West Mills*

INDIA

Adiga, Aravind. *Last Man in Tower: A Novel*
Adiga, Aravind. *Selection Day*
Adiga, Aravind. ★*The White Tiger: A Novel*
Anappara, Deepa. *Djinn Patrol on the Purple Line: A Novel*
Bacon, Charlotte. *There Is Room for You*
Carter, Miranda. *The Strangler Vine*
Chakrabarti, Jai. *A Play for the End of the World*
Chatterjee, Upamanyu. *English, August: An Indian Story*
D'Souza, Tony. *The Konkans*
Davies, Carys. *The Mission House*
Deb, Siddhartha. *The Point of Return: A Novel*
Desai, Anita. *Clear Light of Day*
Desai, Anita. *Fire on the Mountain*
Desai, Kiran. *The Inheritance of Loss*
Dev, Sonali. ★*A Bollywood Affair*
Dev, Sonali. *The Bollywood Bride*
Dev, Sonali. *A Distant Heart*
Divakaruni, Chitra Banerjee. *Oleander Girl: A Novel*
Doshi, Avni. *Burnt Sugar: A Novel*

Dyer, Geoff. *Jeff in Venice, Death in Varanasi*

Enjeti, Anjali. ★*The Parted Earth*

Ghosh, Amitav. *Flood of Fire*

Ghosh, Amitav. *The Glass Palace*

Ghosh, Amitav. *The Hungry Tide*

Ghosh, Amitav. *Sea of Poppies*

Hall, Tarquin. *The Case of the Deadly Butter Chicken: A Vish Puri Mystery*

Hall, Tarquin. *The Case of the Love Commandos: From the Files of Vish Puri, India's Most Private Investigator*

Hesse, Hermann. ★*Siddhartha: A New Translation*

Jhabvala, Ruth Prawer. *At the End of the Century: The Stories of Ruth Prawer Jhabvala.*

Jhabvala, Ruth Prawer. ★*Heat and Dust*

Joshi, Alka. *The Henna Artist*

Kandasamy, Meena. *When I Hit You, Or, a Portrait of the Writer as a Young Wife*

Khan, Vaseem. *The Perplexing Theft of the Jewel in the Crown*

Lahiri, Jhumpa. *The Lowland: A Novel*

Majumdar, Megha. *A Burning*

March, Nev. *Murder in Old Bombay*

Massey, Sujata. ★*The Bombay Prince*

Massey, Sujata. *The Satapur Moonstone*

Massey, Sujata. ★*The Widows of Malabar Hill: A Mystery of 1920s Bombay*

Mehta, Rahul. *No Other World: A Novel*

Mukherjee, Abir. *Death in the East*

Mukherjee, Abir. *The Shadows of Men*

Mukherjee, Abir. *Smoke and Ashes: A Novel*

Mukherjee, Neel. *The Lives of Others*

Mukherjee, Neel. ★*A State of Freedom*

Naipaul, V. S. *Magic Seeds*

Narayan, R. K. *Malgudi Days*

Raheem, Zara. *The Marriage Clock: A Novel*

Rao, Shobha. ★*Girls Burn Brighter*

Roy, Anuradha. *All the Lives We Never Lived: A Novel*

Roy, Anuradha. *An Atlas of Impossible Longing*

Roy, Arundhati. ★*The God of Small Things*

Rushdie, Salman. ★*Midnight's Children: A Novel*

Rushdie, Salman. *The Moor's Last Sigh*

Scott, Paul. ★*Staying On: A Novel*

Seth, Vikram. ★*A Suitable Boy: A Novel*

Shanbhag, Vivek. *Ghachar Ghochar*

Sinha, Indra. *Animal's People*

Sundaresan, Indu. *The Splendor of Silence: A Novel*

Suri, Manil. *The Age of Shiva: A Novel*

Swamy, Shruti. *A House Is a Body: Stories*

Taneja, Preti. *We That Are Young: A Novel*

Taseer, Aatish. *The Way Things Were: A Novel*

Umrigar, Thrity N. ★*Honor*

Umrigar, Thrity N. *The Secrets Between Us*

INDIAN CAPTIVITIES

Meyer, Philipp. ★*The Son: A Novel*

INDIAN OCEAN

Golding, William. *Close Quarters*

Golding, William. *Fire Down Below*

Smith, Wilbur A. *Birds of Prey*

INDIAN RESERVATIONS

Erdrich, Louise. *Four Souls: A Novel*

Erdrich, Louise. *The Last Report on the Miracles at Little No Horse*

Erdrich, Louise. *Love Medicine: A Novel*

Erdrich, Louise. *The Plague of Doves*

Erdrich, Louise. ★*The Round House: A Novel*

Jones, Stephen Graham. ★*The Only Good Indians: A Novel*

Momaday, N. Scott. *House Made of Dawn*

Weiden, David L. ★*Winter Counts*

INDIANA

Carr, Brian Allen. ★*Opioid, Indiana*

Child, Lee. *One Shot*

Hunt, Laird. *The Evening Road*

Hunt, Laird. *Zorrie*

Lockridge, Ross Franklin. *Raintree County*

Nunez, Sigrid. *Salvation City*

Rader-Day, Lori. *The Day I Died*

Sittenfeld, Curtis. *Prep: A Novel*

Tarkington, Booth. ★*Alice Adams*

Tarkington, Booth. ★*The Magnificent Ambersons*

West, Jessamyn. *The Friendly Persuasion*

Wiseman, Beth. *Listening to Love*

INDIANS OF CENTRAL AMERICA — RELIGION

Bowles, David. *Feathered Serpent, Dark Heart of Sky: Myths of Mexico*

INDIANS OF NORTH AMERICA

Agee, Jonis. *The Bones of Paradise*

Alexie, Sherman. *Blasphemy: New and Selected Stories*

Alexie, Sherman. *Flight*

Alexie, Sherman. *Reservation Blues*

Coldsmith, Don. *Tallgrass: A Novel of the Great Plains*

Cooper, James Fenimore. *The Last of the Mohicans: A Narrative of 1757*

Frazier, Charles. *Thirteen Moons: A Novel*

Heacox, Kim. *Jimmy Bluefeather: A Novel*

Hill, Ruth Beebe. *Hanta Yo*

Jones, Douglas C. *The Court-Martial of George Armstrong Custer*

Leonard, Elmore. ★*The Complete Western Stories of Elmore Leonard.*

Michener, James A. *Chesapeake*

Momaday, N. Scott. *House Made of Dawn*

Orange, Tommy. ★*There There*

Perry, Thomas. ★*The Left-Handed Twin*

Potenza, Carol. *Hearts of the Missing*

Rice, Waubgeshig. *Moon of the Crusted Snow: A Novel*

Rodriguez, Linda. *Every Hidden Fear: A Skeet Bannion Mystery*

INDIANS OF NORTH AMERICA — ALCOHOLISM

Alexie, Sherman. *Reservation Blues*

INDIANS OF NORTH AMERICA — MATERIAL CULTURE

Petersen, Todd Robert. *Picnic in the Ruins*

INDIANS OF NORTH AMERICA — RELATIONS WITH EUROPEAN-AMERICANS

Coldsmith, Don. *Tallgrass: A Novel of the Great Plains*

Erdrich, Louise. *Tracks: A Novel*

INDIANS OF NORTH AMERICA — RELATIONS WITH MISSIONARIES, TRADERS, ETC.

Guthrie, A. B. ★*The Big Sky*

Michener, James A. ★*Centennial*

Silko, Leslie Marmon. *Almanac of the Dead*

Silko, Leslie Marmon. *Gardens in the Dunes: A Novel*

INDIANS OF SOUTH AMERICA

Ferencik, Erica. *Into the Jungle*

INDIGENOUS PEOPLES

Stanley, Michael. *Dying to Live*

INDIGENOUS WOMEN

Muller, Marcia. *Ice and Stone*

Indignation. Roth, Philip

★*Indigo: a Valentino Mystery*. Estleman, Loren D.

INDIVIDUAL DIFFERENCES

Wall, Cara. *The Dearly Beloved: A Novel*

INDIVIDUALISM

Rand, Ayn. ★*The Fountainhead*

INDIVIDUALISM IN MEN

London, Jack. *Martin Eden*

INDIVIDUALITY

Dostoyevsky, Fyodor. *Notes from Underground*

Hesse, Hermann. *The Fairy Tales of Hermann Hesse*

Wilhelm, Kate. *Where Late the Sweet Birds Sang*

INDOCHINA

Greene, Graham. ★*The Quiet American*

INDONESIA

Brouwer, Sigmund. *Thief of Glory: A Novel*

Conrad, Joseph. *Victory: An Island Tale*

Tsao, Tiffany. *The Majesties*

Indranan war [Series]. Wagers, K. B.

Indriðason, Arnaldur

The Darkness Knows

Outrage

Reykjavik Nights: An Inspector Erlendur Novel

The Shadow District: A Thriller

Strange Shores: An Inspector Erlendur Novel

INDUSTRIAL ACCIDENTS

DeLillo, Don. ★*White Noise*

INDUSTRIALISTS

Force, Marie. *Deceived by Desire*

Gordimer, Nadine. *The Conservationist*

Sjowall, Maj. ★*Murder at the Savoy*

INDUSTRIES

Gilman, Felix. *The Half-Made World*

INEQUALITY

Doctorow, Cory. *Walkaway*

Halliday, Lisa. ★*Asymmetry*

Majumdar, Megha. *A Burning*

Umrigar, Thrity N. *The Secrets Between Us*

Yu, Miri. *Tokyo Ueno Station*

The Inexplicables. Priest, Cherie

INFANT DEATH

Han, Kang. *The White Book*

Weiner, Jennifer. *Little Earthquakes*

INFANT KIDNAPPING VICTIMS

Molloy, Aimee. *The Perfect Mother: A Novel*

INFANTICIDE

Abu-Jaber, Diana. *Origin: A Novel*

Dallas, Sandra. *The Last Midwife*

Lippman, Laura. ★*Hush Hush*

INFANTS

Armstrong, Kelley. *Alone in the Wild*

Fine, Julia. *The Upstairs House*

Jimenez, Abby. *Life's Too Short*

Rimmer, Kelly. *Before I Let You Go*

INFANTS SWITCHED AT BIRTH

Delaney, J. P. *Playing Nice*

Ellison, J. T. *Tear Me Apart*

Rushdie, Salman. ★*Midnight's Children: A Novel*

The Infatuations. Marias, Javier

INFECTION

Wellington, David. *Positive*

Infernal Angels. Estleman, Loren D.

INFERTILITY

Adebayo, Ayobami. ★*Stay with Me*

Atwood, Margaret. ★*The Handmaid's Tale*

Beck, Haylen. *Lost You*

Bergstrom, Heather Brittain. *Steal the North: A Novel*

Hoover, Colleen. *All Your Perfects*

Rash, Ron. ★*Serena: A Novel*

The Infinite Blacktop: A Novel. Gran, Sara

★*Infinite Country*. Engel, Patricia

★*Infinite Jest: A Novel*. Wallace, David Foster

The Infinities. Banville, John

INFINITY

Borges, Jorge Luis. *Ficciones*

INFLUENCE (LITERARY, ARTISTIC, ETC.)

Truong, Monique T. D. *The Sweetest Fruits*

INFLUENCE (PSYCHOLOGY)

Buntin, Julie. ★*Marlena: A Novel*

INFLUENCERS

Dorn, L. R. *The Anatomy of Desire*

Holahan, Cate. *Her Three Lives*

McElroy, Alex. *The Atmospherians*

Rai, Alisha. ★*First Comes Like*

Weiner, Jennifer. ★*Big Summer*

INFLUENZA

King, Stephen. ★*The Stand*

INFLUENZA EPIDEMIC, 1918-1919

Wiseman, Ellen Marie. *The Orphan Collector*

INFORMERS

De la Motte, Anders. *Ultimatum: A Thriller*

Higgins, George V. *The Friends of Eddie Coyle*

Rinehart, Mary Roberts. *Miss Pinkerton*

Tanabe, Karin. ★*A Woman of Intelligence*

Inherent Vice. Pynchon, Thomas

Inherit the Bones. Littlejohn, Emily

INHERITANCE AND SUCCESSION

Alexis, Andre. *The Hidden Keys*

Alpsten, Ellen. *Tsarina*

Andrews, Mary Kay. *Sunset Beach*

Ashley, Jennifer. *The Madness of Lord Ian Mackenzie*

Balogh, Mary. ★*Someone to Love*

Benz, Chanelle. ★*The Gone Dead*

Boyle, Elizabeth. *Along Came a Duke*

Brenner, Jamie. *Drawing Home*

Bronte, Emily. ★*Wuthering Heights*

Carr, Robyn. ★*The Wanderer*

Cline, Ernest. *Ready Player One: A Novel*

Cocks, Heather. *The Heir Affair*

Collins, Manda. *Ready Set Rogue*
Collins, Wilkie. ★*The Woman in White*
Cordova, Zoraida. *The Inheritance of Orquidea Divina*
Dare, Tessa. *Romancing the Duke*
Dickens, Charles. *Our Mutual Friend*
Downing, Samantha. *He Started It*
Eason, K. *How Rory Thorne Destroyed the Multiverse*
Eliot, George. ★*Middlemarch: A Study of Provincial Life*
Faye, Lyndsay. *Jane Steele*
Fitzgerald, F. Scott. ★*The Beautiful and Damned*
Frampton, Megan. *Never a Bride*
Frampton, Megan. *Put up Your Duke*
Gaddis, William. *Agape Agape*
George, Margaret. *The Confessions of Young Nero*
Gracie, Anne. *Marry in Scandal*
Gratton, Tessa. *The Queens of Innis Lear*
Gregory, Philippa. *The Last Tudor*
James, Miranda. *What the Cat Dragged In*
Jewell, Lisa. *The Family Upstairs*
Kleypas, Lisa. *Cold-Hearted Rake*
Kubica, Mary. ★*The Other Mrs.*
Kwan, Kevin. *Rich People Problems*
Lansdale, Joe R. *Devil Red*
Leon, Donna. *Unto Us a Son Is Given*
Long, Julie Anne. *Angel in a Devil's Arms*
Mosley, Walter. *And Sometimes I Wonder About You: A Leonid McGill Mystery*
Palliser, Charles. *The Quincunx*
Pava, Sergio de la. *Lost Empress: A Novel*
Penman, Sharon Kay. *The Sunne in Splendour*
Phillips, Arthur. ★*The King at the Edge of the World: Novel*
Porter, Henry. *The Bell Ringers*
Pratchett, Terry. *The Fifth Elephant: A Novel of Discworld*
Pratchett, Terry. *Pyramids: The Book of Going Forth*
Putney, Mary Jo. *Loving a Lost Lord*
Rhys, Rachel. *Fatal Inheritance*
Riley, Vanessa. ★*A Duke, the Lady, and a Baby*
Robertson, Michael. *The Baker Street Translation: A Mystery*
Russell, Mary Doria. *Dreamers of the Day: A Novel*
Sayers, Dorothy L. *The Unpleasantness at the Bellona Club*
Shalvis, Jill. *Simply Irresistible*
Shipman, Viola. *The Clover Girls*
Shupe, Joanna. *The Heiress Hunt*
Stark, Richard. *The Jugger: A Parker Novel*
Stradal, J. Ryan. ★*The Lager Queen of Minnesota*
Styles, Toy. *Raunchy 2: Mad's Love*
Tallo, Katie. *Dark August*
Taneja, Preti. *We That Are Young: A Novel*
Vayden, Kristin. *Fortune Favors the Duke*
Wang, Kathy. *Family Trust: A Novel*
Ware, Ruth. *The Death of Mrs. Westaway*
Weatherspoon, Rebekah. ★*Xeni: A Marriage of Inconvenience*
Willig, Lauren. *The Summer Country: A Novel*
The **Inheritance** of Loss. Desai, Kiran
The **Inheritance** of Orquidea Divina. Cordova, Zoraida
The **Inheritors**. Golding, William
★The **Inimitable** Jeeves. Wodehouse, P. G.

INJUSTICE
Al-Ramli, Muhsin. *The President's Gardens*
Baldwin, James. ★*If Beale Street Could Talk*
Benz, Chanelle. ★*The Gone Dead*
Gordimer, Nadine. *The Conservationist*
Mosley, Walter. *Down the River Unto the Sea*
Smith, Ali. ★*How to Be Both*
Ink and Steel: A Novel of the Promethean Age. Bear, Elizabeth
Inland: a Novel. Obreht, Tea
The **Inner** Circle. Meltzer, Brad
INNER CITY
Beatty, Paul. ★*The Sellout: A Novel*
Burke, Marcus. *Team Seven*
Clark, Wahida. *Honor Thy Thug*
Clark, Wahida. *Justify My Thug: A Novel*
Clark, Wahida. ★*Payback Is a Mutha*
Clark, Wahida. *Thugs*
Ferrante, Elena. *My Brilliant Friend*
Gunaratne, Guy. *In Our Mad and Furious City*
Holmes, Shannon. ★*B-More Careful: A Novel*
Petry, Ann. ★*The Street*
Sister Souljah. ★*The Coldest Winter Ever: A Novel*
Sister Souljah. ★*A Deeper Love Inside: The Porsche Santiaga Story*
INNKEEPERS
Handke, Peter. *Don Juan: His Own Version*
Hibbert, Talia. ★*Act Your Age, Eve Brown*
Wade, Becky. *Falling for You*
INNOCENCE (LAW)
Adler-Olsen, Jussi. *The Absent One*
Baldwin, James. ★*If Beale Street Could Talk*
Banks, Iain. *The Hydrogen Sonata*
Cavanagh, Steve. *Thirteen*
Clark, Martin. *The Substitution Order*
Connelly, Michael. *The Crossing*
Connelly, Michael. *The Lincoln Lawyer: A Novel*
Dahl, Julia. *Conviction*
Daly, Paula. *Clear My Name*
Deaver, Jeffery. *The Empty Chair*
Dow, David R. *Confessions of an Innocent Man*
Fox, Candice. *Crimson Lake*
Fox, Candice. *Redemption Point*
Freeman, Brian. *Goodbye to the Dead*
French, Nicci. *Waiting for Wednesday: A Frieda Klein Mystery*
Goddard, Robert. *Beyond Recall: A Novel*
Grisham, John. ★*The Guardians*
Hill, Reginald. *The Woodcutter: A Novel*
Hodgson, Antonia. *The Last Confession of Thomas Hawkins*
Horowitz, Anthony. ★*Moonflower Murders*
Limon, Martin. *The Line*
Potzsch, Oliver. *The Beggar King*
Rozan, S. J. ★*Paper Son*
Saylor, Steven. *The Judgment of Caesar: A Novel of Ancient Rome*
Scott, A. D. ★*Beneath the Abbey Wall: A Novel*
Smith, B. J. *The Return of Kid Cooper: A Novel*
Spencer-Fleming, Julia. *All Mortal Flesh*
Stanley, Michael. *Death of the Mantis*
Steinhauer, Olen. *The Tourist*
Turow, Scott. *Presumed Innocent*

Woods, Stuart. *Santa Fe Rules*
Wright, Richard. *The Man Who Lived Underground*
INNOCENCE (PERSONAL QUALITY)
   Ammaniti, Niccolo. *I'm Not Scared*
   Barth, John. ★*The Sot-Weed Factor*
Innocent Graves: An Inspector Banks Mystery. Robinson, Peter
Innocent in Death. Robb, J. D.
The Innocents. Atkins, Ace
The Innocents. Crummey, Michael
INNS
   Andrews, Donna. *Owl Be Home for Christmas: A Meg Langslow Mystery*
INQUISITION
   Rollins, James. *Crucible*
   Wilson, G. Willow. ★*The Bird King*
Insane City. Barry, Dave
INSANITY (LAW)
   Burnet, Graeme Macrae. *His Bloody Project: Documents Relating to the Case of Roderick Macrae*
INSCRIPTIONS
   Ruiz Zafon, Carlos. *The Prisoner of Heaven*
INSECTS
   Kafka, Franz. ★*The Metamorphosis*
INSECURITY (PSYCHOLOGY)
   Backman, Fredrik. ★*Anxious People: A Novel*
   Wayne, Teddy. *Apartment: A Novel*
INSECURITY IN MEN
   Cole, Alyssa. ★*How to Catch a Queen*
   DeLuca, Jen. *Well Matched*
INSIDE PASSAGE (PACIFIC NORTHWEST)
   Straley, John. *The Big Both Ways*
★*Inside Story*. Amis, Martin
Inside the O'Briens: A Novel. Genova, Lisa
INSOMNIACS
   Dekker, Ted. *Black: The Birth of Evil*
   Dekker, Ted. *Red: The Heroic Rescue*
   Dekker, Ted. *White: The Great Pursuit*
Inspector Alan Banks mysteries [Series]. Robinson, Peter
Inspector Armand Gamache mysteries [Series]. Penny, Louise
Inspector Bill Slider mysteries [Series]. Harrod-Eagles, Cynthia
Inspector Chen Cao mysteries [Series]. Qiu, Xiaolong
Inspector Darko Dawson mysteries [Series]. Quartey, Kwei
Inspector Espinosa mysteries [Series]. Garcia-Roza, L. A.
Inspector Hector Salgado mysteries [Series]. Hill Gumbao, Toni
Inspector Hulda Hermannsdottir [Series]. Jónasson, Ragnar
Inspector Iwata novels [Series]. Obregon, Nicolas
Inspector John Rebus mysteries [Series]. Rankin, Ian
Inspector Lamb novels [Series]. Kelly, Stephen
Inspector Luke Thanet mysteries [Series]. Simpson, Dorothy
Inspector Morse mysteries [Series]. Dexter, Colin
Inspector O novels [Series]. Church, James
Inspector Porfiry Rostnikov mysteries [Series]. Kaminsky, Stuart M.
Inspector Tom Reynolds novels [Series]. Spain, Jo
INSPIRATION
   Korelitz, Jean Hanff. ★*The Plot*
An Instance of the Fingerpost. Pears, Iain
The Institute. King, Stephen

INSTITUTIONAL CARE — EMPLOYEES
   Nussbaum, Susan. *Good Kings, Bad Kings: A Novel*
INSTITUTIONALIZED PERSONS
   O'Farrell, Maggie. *The Vanishing Act of Esme Lennox*
★*Instructions for a Funeral: Stories*. Means, David
Instruments of Darkness: A Novel. Robertson, Imogen
Instruments of Night. Cook, Thomas H.
INSURANCE COMPANIES
   Kerr, Philip. ★*Greeks Bearing Gifts: A Bernie Gunther Novel*
INSURANCE FRAUD
   Greaves, Chuck. *Hush Money: A Mystery*
   Perry, Thomas. *Death Benefits: A Novel*
INSURANCE INVESTIGATORS
   Koryta, Michael. *If She Wakes*
   Perry, Thomas. *Death Benefits: A Novel*
INSURGENCY
   Desai, Kiran. *The Inheritance of Loss*
   Gabaldon, Diana. ★*The Fiery Cross*
   Gordimer, Nadine. ★*July's People*
   Lahiri, Jhumpa. *The Lowland: A Novel*
   Liu, Ken. ★*The Grace of Kings*
   Parry, H. G. *A Declaration of the Rights of Magicians*
   Saylor, Steven. *A Mist of Prophecies*
   Saylor, Steven. *Roma: The Novel of Ancient Rome*
   Saylor, Steven. *Rubicon*
Insurrecto. Apostol, Gina
INTELLECTUAL LIFE
   Beauvoir, Simone de. ★*The Mandarins: A Novel*
   Hijuelos, Oscar. *Twain & Stanley Enter Paradise*
   Morton, Brian. *Florence Gordon*
   Parmar, Priya. *Vanessa and Her Sister*
   Scharer, Whitney. *The Age of Light*
   Stephenson, Neal. *Anathem*
INTELLECTUAL PROPERTY
   McEwan, Ian. *Solar: A Novel*
INTELLECTUALS
   Bellow, Saul. ★*Herzog*
   Bellow, Saul. ★*Mr. Sammler's Planet*
   Chiaverini, Jennifer. *Resistance Women: A Novel*
   Chung, Catherine. *The Tenth Muse: A Novel*
   Hesse, Hermann. ★*Steppenwolf*
   Mosley, Walter. ★*John Woman*
   Tartt, Donna. ★*The Secret History*
INTELLIGENCE
   Bradley, C. Alan. *As Chimney Sweepers Come to Dust: A Flavia De Luce Novel*
   Bradley, C. Alan. ★*The Sweetness at the Bottom of the Pie*
   Bradley, C. Alan. *Thrice the Brinded Cat Hath Mew'd: A Flavia De Luce Novel*
INTELLIGENCE OFFICERS
   Alfon, Dov. *A Long Night in Paris*
   Berenson, Alex. *The Faithful Spy: A Novel*
   Church, James. *A Drop of Chinese Blood*
   De la Motte, Anders. *Ultimatum: A Thriller*
   Fleming, Ian. *From Russia with Love*
   Hall, Adam. *The Quiller Memorandum*
   Ignatius, David. *The Increment: A Novel*
   Le Carre, John. *A Most Wanted Man: A Novel*

Littell, Robert. *The Company: A Novel of the Cia*
Parnell, Sean. *Man of War: An Eric Steele Novel*
Silva, Daniel. ★*The Black Widow*
Silva, Daniel. ★*The Kill Artist: A Novel*
Silva, Daniel. *The New Girl*
Silva, Daniel. *The Other Woman*
Stephenson, Neal. *The Rise and Fall of D.O.D.O.: A Novel*
Woods, Stuart. *Smooth Operator*

INTELLIGENCE SERVICE
Baldacci, David. *Hell's Corner*
Bell, Ted. *Overkill: An Alex Hawke Novel*
Benn, James R. *Road of Bones: A Billy Boyle World War II Mystery*
Berenson, Alex. *The Deceivers*
Berenson, Alex. *The Prisoner*
Berry, Steve. ★*The Malta Exchange: A Novel*
Berry, Steve. ★*The Warsaw Protocol*
Black, Benjamin. ★*The Secret Guests: A Novel*
Bradby, Tom. *Double Agent*
Cantrell, Christian. *Scorpion*
Carter, Stephen L. *Back Channel*
Clancy, Tom. *Clear and Present Danger*
Clements, Oliver. *The Eyes of the Queen*
Clements, Oliver. *The Queen's Men*
Coonts, Stephen. *The Armageddon File*
Cumming, Charles. *The Moroccan Girl*
Cumming, Charles. ★*The Trinity Six*
Cussler, Clive. ★*Final Option*
Cussler, Clive. *Shadow Tyrants*
Cussler, Clive. *Typhoon Fury*
De la Motte, Anders. *MemoRandom: A Thriller*
De la Motte, Anders. *Ultimatum: A Thriller*
Deighton, Len. *Berlin Game*
Deighton, Len. *London Match*
Dugoni, Robert. *The Eighth Sister: A Thriller*
Eisler, Barry. *The God's Eye View*
Eisler, Barry. *The Night Trade*
Fesperman, Dan. *Safe Houses: A Novel*
Finder, Joseph. *The Switch: A Novel*
Fleming, Ian. *Doctor No*
Fleming, Ian. *You Only Live Twice*
Follett, Ken. *Eye of the Needle*
Gelernter, J. H. *Hold Fast*
Greene, Graham. *The Human Factor*
Greene, Graham. *Our Man in Havana*
Gross, Andrew. *The One Man*
Harris, Oliver. *A Shadow Intelligence*
Higgins, Jack. *Confessional*
Lawton, John. *Hammer to Fall*
Le Carre, John. *Agent Running in the Field*
Le Carre, John. ★*The Honourable Schoolboy*
Le Carre, John. *Smiley's People*
Le Carre, John. *The Spy Who Came in from the Cold*
Le Carre, John. ★*Tinker, Tailor, Soldier, Spy*
MacNeal, Susan Elia. *The King's Justice*
Parnell, Sean. *Man of War: An Eric Steele Novel*
Perry, Thomas. *The Old Man*
Porter, Henry. *Firefly*
Porter, Henry. *The Old Enemy*

Robbins, David L. *Last Citadel: A Novel of the Battle of Kursk*
Sandford, John. ★*Deadline*
Sandford, John. *Storm Front*
Schwarz, Liese O'Halloran. *What Could Be Saved*
Steinhauer, Olen. ★*All the Old Knives*
Steinhauer, Olen. *An American Spy*
Steinhauer, Olen. *The Last Tourist*
Steinhauer, Olen. *The Nearest Exit*
Sundaresan, Indu. *The Splendor of Silence: A Novel*
Woods, Stuart. *Stealth*

INTELLIGENCE SERVICE — HISTORY
Priest, Cherie. *Clementine*
Intensity: a Novel. Koontz, Dean R.
★*Intercepted*. Martin, Alexa

INTERCLASS FRIENDSHIP
Conell, Lee. *The Party Upstairs*
Greeley, Molly. *The Clergyman's Wife*
Nunez, Sigrid. *The Last of Her Kind: A Novel*
Peebles, Frances de Pontes. *The Air You Breathe*

INTERCLASS ROMANCE
Allain, Suzanne. *Miss Lattimore's Letter*
Austen, Jane. ★*Persuasion*
Bell, Lenora. ★*What a Difference a Duke Makes*
Bronte, Emily. ★*Wuthering Heights*
Dare, Tessa. ★*The Duchess Deal*
Dev, Sonali. *A Distant Heart*
Drake, Olivia. *When a Duke Loves a Governess*
Fielding, Henry. ★*The History of Tom Jones, a Foundling*
Fitzgerald, F. Scott. ★*This Side of Paradise*
Herrera, Adriana. *American Fairytale*
Lawrence, D. H. ★*Lady Chatterley's Lover*
Lin, Jeannie. *The Lotus Palace*
London, Jack. *Martin Eden*
Obioma, Chigozie. ★*An Orchestra of Minorities*
Roth, Philip. *Indignation*
Segal, Erich. ★*Love Story*
Turansky, Carrie. *No Ocean Too Wide: A Novel*
Updike, John. *Brazil: A Novel*
Williams, Beatriz. *The Summer Wives*

INTERCONTINENTAL BALLISTIC MISSILES
Church, James. *Bamboo and Blood: An Inspector O Novel*
Intercrime [Series]. Dahl, Arne
Interdependency novels [Series]. Scalzi, John
INTERDIMENSIONAL TRAVEL
Beagle, Peter S. *The Unicorn Sonata*
Cipri, Nino. *Defekt*
Czerneda, Julie. *A Turn of Light*
Davis, Kathryn. *Duplex*
Larkwood, A. K. *The Unspoken Name*
McGuire, Seanan. ★*Beneath the Sugar Sky*
McGuire, Seanan. ★*Down Among the Sticks and Bones*
McGuire, Seanan. ★*Every Heart a Doorway*
*The **Interestings***. Wolitzer, Meg
INTERETHNIC CONFLICT
Craig, Charmaine. *Miss Burma*
Okorafor, Nnedi. ★*Who Fears Death*
Spark, Muriel. ★*The Mandelbaum Gate*

INTERETHNIC FRIENDSHIP
Iweala, Uzodinma. ★*Speak No Evil*
INTERETHNIC MARRIAGE
Craig, Charmaine. *Miss Burma*
Freudenberger, Nell. *The Newlyweds*
INTERETHNIC RELATIONS
Desai, Kiran. *The Inheritance of Loss*
Gaitskill, Mary. *The Mare: A Novel*
Gordimer, Nadine. *The Pickup*
Kimani, Peter. *Dance of the Jakaranda*
Michener, James A. ★*Tales of the South Pacific*
INTERETHNIC ROMANCE
Freudenberger, Nell. *The Newlyweds*
McMillan, Terry. ★*How Stella Got Her Groove Back*
Michener, James A. ★*Tales of the South Pacific*
Okparanta, Chinelo. ★*Under the Udala Trees*
INTERFAITH FAMILIES
Escandon, Maria Amparo. ★*L.A. Weather*
INTERFAITH FRIENDSHIP
Hewson, David. *The Garden of Angels*
INTERFAITH ROMANCE
De Bernieres, Louis. *Birds Without Wings*
Malamud, Bernard. *The Assistant*
Wiseman, Beth. *Listening to Love*
INTERGENERATIONAL COMMUNICATION
Acker, Jennifer. ★*The Limits of the World*
Kimani, Peter. *Dance of the Jakaranda*
INTERGENERATIONAL FRIENDSHIP
Berg, Elizabeth. *The Story of Arthur Truluv: A Novel*
Bohjalian, Chris. *The Buffalo Soldier: A Novel*
Extence, Gavin. *The Universe Versus Alex Woods*
Lyons, Annie. *The Brilliant Life of Eudora Honeysett*
Makkai, Rebecca. *The Borrower: A Novel*
Pamuk, Orhan. *The Red-Haired Woman*
Picoult, Jodi. *The Storyteller*
Shipman, Viola. *The Heirloom Garden*
Skeslien Charles, Janet. *The Paris Library: A Novel*
Smith, Ali. ★*Autumn*
INTERGENERATIONAL RELATIONS
Auster, Paul. *Sunset Park*
Blume, Judy. *In the Unlikely Event*
Djavadi, Negar. *Disoriental*
Durrow, Heidi W. *The Girl Who Fell from the Sky: A Novel*
Edgerton, Clyde. ★*Walking Across Egypt: A Novel*
Egan, Greg. *Phoresis*
Flournoy, Angela. *The Turner House*
Hadley, Tessa. *The Past*
Holdstock, Pauline. *Here I Am!*
Hozar, Nazanine. *Aria*
Lee, Min Jin. ★*Pachinko*
McCracken, Elizabeth. *The Souvenir Museum: Stories*
Porter, Regina. *The Travelers*
Schweblin, Samanta. *Fever Dream: A Novel*
Tawada, Yoko. ★*The Emissary*
★*Interior* Chinatown. Yu, Charles
The Intermission. Friedland, Elyssa
INTERNATIONAL ADOPTION
See, Lisa. *The Tea Girl of Hummingbird Lane*

INTERNATIONAL BUSINESSES
Walker, Martin. *The Shooting at Chateau Rock*
INTERNATIONAL BUSINESSES — CORRUPT PRACTICES
Le Carre, John. *The Constant Gardener: A Novel*
INTERNATIONAL CRIME
Powell, Mark. *Firebird*
INTERNATIONAL FINANCE
Pears, Iain. *Stone's Fall*
INTERNATIONAL INTRIGUE
Adler-Olsen, Jussi. ★*Victim 2117*
Bell, Ted. *Overkill: An Alex Hawke Novel*
Berenson, Alex. *The Deceivers*
Berry, Steve. ★*The Warsaw Protocol*
Block, Lawrence. *Killing Castro*
Bradby, Tom. *Double Agent*
Brown, Dale. *Eagle Station: A Novel*
Cameron, Marc. ★*Code of Honor*
Cameron, Marc. *Power and Empire*
Campbell, Rick. *Treason*
Church, James. *Bamboo and Blood: An Inspector O Novel*
Church, James. *A Drop of Chinese Blood*
Church, James. *Hidden Moon: An Inspector O Novel*
Clancy, Tom. *Patriot Games*
Coonts, Stephen. *The Art of War: A Novel*
Coonts, Stephen. ★*The Russia Account*
Coulter, Catherine. *The Last Second*
Coulter, Catherine. *The Sixth Day*
Cumming, Charles. *The Moroccan Girl*
Cussler, Clive. *Celtic Empire*
Cussler, Clive. *Ghost Ship*
Cussler, Clive. *Havana Storm*
Cussler, Clive. *Nighthawk: A Novel from the Numa Files*
Cussler, Clive. *Odessa Sea*
Cussler, Clive. *Pacific Vortex!*
Cussler, Clive. *The Pharaoh's Secret*
Cussler, Clive. ★*Raise the Titanic!*
Cussler, Clive. ★*The Rising Sea: A Novel from the Numa Files*
Cussler, Clive. *Sahara: A Novel*
Cussler, Clive. ★*Sea of Greed: A Novel from the Numa Files*
Cussler, Clive. ★*The Titanic Secret*
Deighton, Len. *Berlin Game*
Dick, Philip K. ★*The Man in the High Castle*
Dugoni, Robert. *The Eighth Sister: A Thriller*
Fleming, Ian. ★*Casino Royale: A James Bond Novel*
Forsyth, Frederick. *The Fox*
Golden, Christopher. *The Pandora Room: A Novel*
Greene, Graham. *The Honorary Consul*
Harkaway, Nick. *Angelmaker*
Higgins, Jack. *Eye of the Storm*
Higgins, Jack. *Touch the Devil*
Lawton, John. *Hammer to Fall*
Le Carre, John. *Smiley's People*
Littell, Robert. *The Company: A Novel of the Cia*
Ludlum, Robert. ★*The Bourne Identity*
Ludlum, Robert. *The Bourne Supremacy*
Ludlum, Robert. *The Bourne Ultimatum*
Mankell, Henning. *The Troubled Man*
Paretsky, Sara. *Shell Game*

Pearson, Ridley. *The Risk Agent*
Perry, Anne. ★*Death in Focus: An Elena Standish Novel*
Perry, Anne. *A Question of Betrayal*
Porter, Henry. *Firefly*
Porter, Henry. *The Old Enemy*
Porter, Henry. *White Hot Silence*
Prescott, Lara. *The Secrets We Kept*
Reich, Christopher. ★*The Take*
Robbins, Tom. *Fierce Invalids Home from Hot Climates*
Rollins, James. ★*The Last Odyssey*
Rozan, S. J. *The Shanghai Moon: A Lydia Chin/Bill Smith Novel*
Sebastian, Tim. *Fatal Ally*
Silva, Daniel. ★*The Black Widow*
Silva, Daniel. ★*The Kill Artist: A Novel*
Silva, Daniel. *The New Girl*
Silva, Daniel. *The Other Woman*
Smith, Martin Cruz. *Havana Bay*
Smith, Martin Cruz. *Polar Star*
Tata, A. J. *Dark Winter*
Thomas, Will. *Dance with Death*
Watt, Holly. *To the Lions*
Wolf, Dick. *The Ultimatum*

INTERNATIONAL RELATIONS
Aimaq, Jasmine. *The Opium Prince*
Carter, Stephen L. *Back Channel*
Cussler, Clive. ★*Golden Buddha*
Klay, Phil. ★*Missionaries*
Lee, Fonda. *Jade War*
Littell, Robert. *The Company: A Novel of the Cia*
Liu, Ken. ★*The Veiled Throne*
McQuiston, Casey. ★*Red, White & Royal Blue: A Novel*
Palahniuk, Chuck. *Pygmy*
Poyer, David. *Overthrow: The War with China and North Korea—Fall of an Empire*
Saylor, Steven. *Wrath of the Furies: A Novel of the Ancient World*
Taylor, Brad. ★*Daughter of War: A Novel*
Wright, Lawrence. *The End of October*

INTERNATIONAL RELIEF
D'Souza, Tony. *Whiteman*

INTERNET
Cohen, Joshua. *Book of Numbers: A Novel*
Franzen, Jonathan. *Purity*
Katzenbach, John. *What Comes Next*

INTERNET — SOCIAL ASPECTS
Meyer, Deon. *Icarus*

INTERNET BROADCASTING
Laymon, Kiese. *Long Division*

INTERNET GAMES
Allende, Isabel. *Ripper: A Novel*
Rankin, Ian. *The Falls: An Inspector Rebus Novel*

INTERNET INDUSTRY AND TRADE
Eggers, Dave. *The Circle*

INTERPERSONAL ATTRACTION
Alexander, Victoria. *The Lady Travelers Guide to Larceny with a Dashing Stranger*
Balogh, Mary. *Someone to Trust*
Balogh, Mary. *Someone to Wed*
Bonnaffons, Amy. *The Regrets*

Bowen, Kelly. *A Rogue by Night*
Brockway, Connie. *The Golden Season*
Burrowes, Grace. *Tremaine's True Love*
Carr, Robyn. *The Family Gathering*
Chase, Loretta Lynda. *A Duke in Shining Armor*
Ciotta, Beth. *Her Sky Cowboy*
Dare, Tessa. ★*A Night to Surrender*
De Kretser, Michelle. *The Life to Come*
Dell, Kari Lynn. *Fearless in Texas*
Dell, Kari Lynn. *Mistletoe in Texas*
Dell, Kari Lynn. *Reckless in Texas*
Draven, Grace. *Phoenix Unbound*
Follett, Ken. *A Column of Fire*
Fowles, John. ★*The French Lieutenant's Woman*
Frampton, Megan. *The Duke's Guide to Correct Behavior*
Gilbert, Elizabeth. ★*The Signature of All Things: A Novel*
Gohlke, Cathy. *Promise Me This*
Goodman, Jo. *In Want of a Wife*
Guhrke, Laura Lee. *The Trouble with True Love*
Hampton, Brenda. *Stalker*
Higgins, Kristan. ★*The Best Man*
Hornby, Nick. *Just Like You*
Landon, Sydney. *Wishing for Us*
Lau, Jackie. *Donut Fall in Love*
Layne, Lauren. *Passion on Park Avenue*
Parker, Lucy. *The Austen Playbook*
Pilcher, Rosamunde. *A Place Like Home: Short Stories*
Putney, Mary Jo. *Loving a Lost Lord*
Renault, Mary. *The Bull from the Sea*
Ridley, Erica. *The Duke Heist*
Roberts, Nora. *Sea Swept*
See, Lisa. *Peony in Love: A Novel*
Shalvis, Jill. *Simply Irresistible*
Shalvis, Jill. *The Sweetest Thing*
Simsion, Graeme C. ★*The Rosie Project*
Sosa, Mia. ★*The Worst Best Man*
Vargas Llosa, Mario. *The Bad Girl*
Waite, Olivia. ★*The Lady's Guide to Celestial Mechanics*

INTERPERSONAL COMMUNICATION
Enger, Leif. *Virgil Wander*
Nunez, Sigrid. *What Are You Going Through*
Willis, Connie. *Crosstalk*

INTERPERSONAL CONFLICT
Dunant, Sarah. *Sacred Hearts: A Novel*
Gross, Max. *The Lost Shtetl*
Guillory, Jasmine. *The Wedding Party*
Henry, Emily. *People We Meet on Vacation*
McBride, James. *Five-Carat Soul*
Ng, Celeste. ★*Little Fires Everywhere: A Novel*
Roth, Philip. *Indignation*
Rowling, J. K. *The Casual Vacancy*
Schweblin, Samanta. *Mouthful of Birds: Stories*
Swann, Stacey. *Olympus Texas*

INTERPERSONAL RELATIONS
Anaya, Rudolfo A. *The Man Who Could Fly and Other Stories*
Andric, Ivo. *The Bridge on the Drina*
Anshaw, Carol. *Carry the One*

Arimah, Lesley Nneka. ★*What It Means When a Man Falls from the Sky: Stories*
Armfield, Julia. *Salt Slow: Stories*
Atwood, Margaret. *Bluebeard's Egg and Other Stories*
Atwood, Margaret. ★*Stone Mattress: Nine Tales*
Avery, Ellis. *The Last Nude*
Awad, Mona. ★*13 Ways of Looking at a Fat Girl*
Baxter, Charles. *The Feast of Love*
Beauvoir, Simone de. ★*The Mandarins: A Novel*
Berg, Elizabeth. *The Story of Arthur Truluv: A Novel*
Berlin, Lucia. ★*Evening in Paradise: More Stories*
Berlin, Lucia. ★*A Manual for Cleaning Women: Selected Stories*
Boyle, T. Coraghessan. *The Relive Box: And Other Stories*
Brinkley, Jamel. *A Lucky Man: Stories*
Brownrigg, Sylvia. ★*The Delivery Room: A Novel*
Choi, Yoon. *Skinship: Stories*
Clegg, Bill. *The End of the Day*
Cline, Emma. *Daddy: Stories*
Crummey, Michael. *Galore*
Cruse, Howard. *The Complete Wendel*
Danticat, Edwidge. ★*Everything Inside: Stories*
Davies, Carys. *The Mission House*
De Kretser, Michelle. *The Life to Come*
Diffenbaugh, Vanessa. *The Language of Flowers: A Novel*
Doyle, Brian. *The Plover: A Novel*
Drabble, Margaret. *A Day in the Life of a Smiling Woman: Complete Short Stories*
Earley, Tony. *Mr. Tall: A Novella and Stories*
Eggers, Dave. *How We Are Hungry: Stories*
Enard, Mathias. *Compass*
Evans, Danielle. ★*The Office of Historical Corrections: A Novella and Stories*
Fay, Juliette. *The Shortest Way Home*
Fitzgerald, Penelope. *The Means of Escape: Stories*
Ford, Richard. *A Multitude of Sins: Stories*
Ford, Richard. *Sorry for Your Trouble: Stories*
Franklin, Ariana. *The Serpent's Tale*
Franzen, Jonathan. *Purity*
Gaitskill, Mary. *Don't Cry: Stories*
Gay, Roxane. ★*Ayiti*
Geni, Abby. *The Lightkeepers: A Novel*
Graley, Lisa. *The Current That Carries: Stories*
Groff, Lauren. *Delicate Edible Birds and Other Stories*
Grushin, Olga. *The Line*
Gurganus, Allan. ★*Local Souls: Novellas*
Gustine, Amy. *You Should Pity Us Instead: Stories*
Hadley, Tessa. *Bad Dreams and Other Stories*
Hallberg, Garth Risk. ★*City on Fire*
Halliday, Lisa. ★*Asymmetry*
Haratischvili, Nino. *The Eighth Life: (For Brilka)*
Haslett, Adam. *Union Atlantic*
Hempel, Amy. *Sing to It: New Stories*
Horrocks, Caitlin. *Life Among the Terranauts*
Howland, Bette. *Calm Sea and Prosperous Voyage*
Hulme, Keri. ★*The Bone People: A Novel*
Ishiguro, Kazuo. *The Unconsoled*
Jones, Cynan. *Stillicide*
Kantra, Virginia. *Beth & Amy*

Kawaguchi, Toshikazu. *Before the Coffee Gets Cold*
Kay, Guy Gavriel. ★*Children of Earth and Sky*
Kim, Bo Young. ★*I'm Waiting for You: And Other Stories*
Knausgaard, Karl Ove. *The Morning Star*
Levy, Deborah. *Swimming Home: A Novel*
Marra, Anthony. *The Tsar of Love and Techno: Stories*
Mason, Bobbie Ann. *Patchwork*
McBride, James. *Five-Carat Soul*
McCracken, Elizabeth. *The Souvenir Museum: Stories*
McCullers, Carson. ★*The Heart Is a Lonely Hunter*
McGuane, Thomas. *Crow Fair: Stories*
Means, David. ★*Instructions for a Funeral: Stories*
Mukherjee, Neel. ★*A State of Freedom*
Munro, Alice. *Dear Life: Stories*
Munro, Alice. *Family Furnishings: Selected Stories, 1995-2014*
Munro, Alice. *Too Much Happiness: Stories*
Murakami, Haruki. *South of the Border, West of the Sun*
Murdoch, Iris. *The Book and the Brotherhood*
Offill, Jenny. *Dept. Of Speculation*
Ozick, Cynthia. *The Puttermesser Papers*
Packer, Ann. *Songs Without Words*
Pearlman, Edith. *Honeydew: Stories*
Pilcher, Rosamunde. *A Place Like Home: Short Stories*
Pipkin, John. *Woodsburner: A Novel*
Porter, Regina. *The Travelers*
Quade, Kirstin Valdez. *Night at the Fiestas: Stories*
Rash, Ron. ★*In the Valley: Stories and a Novella Based on Serena*
Renault, Mary. *The Last of the Wine*
Rooney, Sally. ★*Beautiful World, Where Are You*
Russo, Richard. *Bridge of Sighs*
Salinger, J. D. ★*Nine Stories*
Salter, James. *Last Night*
Schweblin, Samanta. *Mouthful of Birds: Stories*
Setterfield, Diane. ★*Once Upon a River*
Shaffer, Mary Ann. *The Guernsey Literary and Potato Peel Pie Society*
Shepard, Jim. *The World to Come: Stories*
Silber, Joan. *Improvement*
Smith, Ali. ★*Autumn*
Smith, Lee. *Oral History*
Smith, Zadie. ★*Grand Union: Stories*
Starnone, Domenico. *Trick*
Steinbeck, John. *The Long Valley*
Strout, Elizabeth. ★*Anything Is Possible: Fiction*
Swamy, Shruti. *The Archer*
Thompson-Spires, Nafissa. *Heads of the Colored People: Stories*
Tolstaya, Tatyana. *Aetherial Worlds: Stories*
Towles, Amor. ★*A Gentleman in Moscow*
Trevor, William. *Last Stories*
Uris, Leon. *Redemption: A Novel*
Walker, Karen Thompson. *The Dreamers*
Wallace, David Foster. *Oblivion: Stories*
Wallace, David Foster. ★*The Pale King: An Unfinished Novel*
Walser, Robert. *The Assistant*
Whiteley, Aliya. *From the Neck up and Other Stories*
Wideman, John Edgar. ★*American Histories: Stories*
INTERPLANETARY RELATIONS
Banks, Iain. *Consider Phlebas*

Banks, Iain. *The Player of Games*
Banks, Iain. *Use of Weapons*
Brown, Pierce. *Morning Star*
Cambias, James L. *A Darkling Sea*
Chambers, Becky. *A Closed and Common Orbit*
Chambers, Becky. ★*The Long Way to a Small, Angry Planet*
Doctorow, Cory. *Rapture of the Nerds*
Scalzi, John. *The Collapsing Empire*
Scalzi, John. *Redshirts: A Novel with Three Codas*
Tepper, Sheri S. ★*Grass*
Valente, Catherynne M. *Space Opera*

INTERPOL AGENTS
Suarez, Daniel. *Change Agent: A Novel*

INTERPRETERS
Lee, Ji-Min. *The Starlet and the Spy*

INTERRACIAL ADOPTION
Morrison, Toni. *A Mercy: A Novel*

INTERRACIAL COUPLES
Butler, Octavia E. ★*Kindred*
Holahan, Cate. *Her Three Lives*

INTERRACIAL DATING
Baldwin, James. *Tell Me How Long the Train's Been Gone: A Novel*
Dev, Sonali. ★*Pride, Prejudice, and Other Flavors: A Novel*

INTERRACIAL FAMILIES
Gordimer, Nadine. ★*My Son's Story*
Grau, Shirley Ann. *The Keepers of the House*
Lee, Andrea. *Red Island House*
Ng, Celeste. ★*Everything I Never Told You: A Novel*
Roisin, Fariha. *Like a Bird*
Smith, Zadie. *On Beauty*

INTERRACIAL FRIENDSHIP
Baldwin, James. *Tell Me How Long the Train's Been Gone: A Novel*
Campbell, Bebe Moore. *Brothers and Sisters*
Chiaverini, Jennifer. *Mrs. Lincoln's Dressmaker: A Novel*
Cooper, James Fenimore. *The Last of the Mohicans: A Narrative of 1757*
Eggers, Dave. *A Hologram for the King: A Novel*
Kidd, Sue Monk. ★*The Secret Life of Bees*
Lansdale, Joe R. *Honky Tonk Samurai*
Levy, Andrea. *Small Island*
Pride, Christine. ★*We Are Not Like Them*
Sexton, Margaret Wilkerson. *The Revisioners: A Novel*
Simonson, Helen. *Major Pettigrew's Last Stand: A Novel*
Smith, Zadie. ★*White Teeth: A Novel*
Stockett, Kathryn. ★*The Help*

INTERRACIAL MARRIAGE
Gordimer, Nadine. *No Time Like the Present: A Novel*
Grau, Shirley Ann. *The Keepers of the House*
Greene, Graham. *The Human Factor*

INTERRACIAL ROMANCE
Allende, Isabel. *The Japanese Lover*
Chang, Alexandra. ★*Days of Distraction*
Charles, KJ. *Wanted, a Gentleman: Or, Virtue Over-Rated*
Cole, Alyssa. ★*A Duke by Default*
Cole, Alyssa. ★*An Extraordinary Union*
Cole, Alyssa. ★*A Prince on Paper*
Cole, Alyssa. ★*An Unconditional Freedom*
Couto, Mia. *The Sword and the Spear*

Frazier, Charles. *Thirteen Moons: A Novel*
Glass, Seressia. ★*The Love Con*
Gordimer, Nadine. ★*My Son's Story*
Guillory, Jasmine. *Party of Two*
Guillory, Jasmine. *The Proposal*
Guillory, Jasmine. ★*The Wedding Date*
Lethem, Jonathan. *Dissident Gardens*
Livesay, Tracey. *Like Lovers Do*
Loren, Roni. *The One You Fight For*
Marsh, Nicola. *The Boy Toy*
McFarlane, Mhairi. *If I Never Met You: A Novel*
Oates, Joyce Carol. *Because It Is Bitter, and Because It Is My Heart*
Rice, Luanne. *The Lemon Orchard*
Robinson, Marilynne. ★*Jack*
Smith, Martin Cruz. *Stallion Gate*
Sundaresan, Indu. *The Splendor of Silence: A Novel*
Updike, John. *Brazil: A Novel*
Weatherspoon, Rebekah. ★*Xeni: A Marriage of Inconvenience*
Willig, Lauren. *The Summer Country: A Novel*

INTERRACIAL SEX
Jhabvala, Ruth Prawer. ★*Heat and Dust*

INTERSPECIES ROMANCE
Feehan, Christine. *Dark Illusion*

Interstate: a Novel. Dixon, Stephen

INTERSTELLAR COMMUNICATION
Lem, Stanislaw. *His Master's Voice*
Sagan, Carl. *Contact: A Novel*

INTERSTELLAR RELATIONS
Bujold, Lois McMaster. ★*Shards of Honor*
Bujold, Lois McMaster. ★*The Warrior's Apprentice*
Martine, Arkady. ★*A Desolation Called Peace*
Scalzi, John. *Redshirts: A Novel with Three Codas*
Vinge, Joan D. *The Snow Queen*

★*Interview with the Vampire*. Rice, Anne

INTERVIEWING
McGregor, Jon. *The Reservoir Tapes*
Updike, John. *Seek My Face*

INTERVIEWS
Banks, Russell. *Foregone*

Intimacies. Kitamura, Katie M.

INTIMACY (PSYCHOLOGY)
Choi, Yoon. *Skinship: Stories*
Diaz, Junot. ★*This Is How You Lose Her*
Ford, Richard. *A Multitude of Sins: Stories*
Ginzburg, Natalia. *A Family Lexicon*
Greenwell, Garth. *Cleanness*
McEwan, Ian. ★*On Chesil Beach*

*The **Intimacy** Experiment*. Danan, Rosie
Into the Beautiful North: A Novel. Urrea, Luis Alberto
Into the Black Nowhere. Gardiner, Meg
★*Into the Blue*. Goddard, Robert
Into the Blue. Henson, Pene
Into the Drowning Deep. Grant, Mira
Into the drowning deep [Series]. Grant, Mira
★*Into the Fire*. Hurwitz, Gregg Andrew
Into the Jungle. Ferencik, Erica

INTRIGUE
Baker, Jo. *Longbourn*

Bell, Lenora. *For the Duke's Eyes Only*
Black, Benjamin. ★*The Secret Guests: A Novel*
Brandreth, Benet. *The Spy of Venice*
Brown, Sandra. *Tailspin*
Carter, Miranda. *The Strangler Vine*
Child, Lee. ★*The Sentinel*
Dimberg, Kelsey Rae. *Girl in the Rearview Mirror*
Eisler, Barry. *The God's Eye View*
Finder, Joseph. *Guilty Minds*
Gibson, William. *The Peripheral*
Hagberg, David. *Gambit*
Hart, Elsa. *City of Ink: A Mystery*
Haydon, Elizabeth. *The Merchant Emperor*
Hurley, Kameron. *The Stars Are Legion*
Kay, Guy Gavriel. ★*Children of Earth and Sky*
McKinney, Chris. *Midnight, Water City*
Mina, Denise. *Conviction*
Moreno-Garcia, Silvia. ★*Velvet Was the Night*
Morrell, David. *Ruler of the Night*
Okorafor, Nnedi. ★*Noor*
Quirk, Matthew. *Cold Barrel Zero*
Quirk, Matthew. *Dead Man Switch*
Ricciardi, David. *Warning Light*
Rochon, Farrah. *The Boyfriend Project*
Rose, M. J. ★*Cartier's Hope*
Schwab, Victoria. *A Darker Shade of Magic*
Shannon, Samantha. *The Mime Order*
Steinhauer, Olen. *The Last Tourist*
Thomson, E. S. *Beloved Poison*
Whitehead, Colson. *The Intuitionist*
Woods, Stuart. *Below the Belt*
Woods, Stuart. *Fast & Loose*
Woods, Stuart. *Hit List*
Woods, Stuart. *Smooth Operator*

INTROSPECTION
Groff, Lauren. ★*Arcadia: A Novel*
Howrey, Meg. *The Wanderers*
McCormack, Mike. ★*Solar Bones*
Proust, Marcel. ★*Remembrance of Things Past*
Proust, Marcel. *Time Regained*

INTROVERTS
Waxman, Abbi. *The Bookish Life of Nina Hill*
Intruder in the Dust. Faulkner, William

INTUITION
Hanson, Hart. *The Driver*
The Intuitionist. Whitehead, Colson

INUIT CHILDREN
Hoeg, Peter. ★*Smilla's Sense of Snow*

INUIT WOMEN
Hoeg, Peter. ★*Smilla's Sense of Snow*
Simmons, Dan. ★*The Terror: A Novel*

INVASIVE SPECIES — CONTROL
Boyle, T. Coraghessan. *When the Killing's Done: A Novel*
The Invention of Sound. Palahniuk, Chuck
★*The Invention of Wings: A Novel*. Kidd, Sue Monk

INVENTIONS
Smith, Mark Haskell. *Baked*
Swyler, Erika. ★*Light from Other Stars: A Novel*

Wells, H. G. ★*The Time Machine*
INVENTORS
James, Eloisa. ★*Seven Minutes in Heaven*
Penrose, Andrea. *Murder at Half Moon Gate*
Priest, Cherie. *Boneshaker*
Theroux, Paul. ★*The Mosquito Coast: A Novel*
Walser, Robert. *The Assistant*
Westlake, Donald E. *Forever and a Death*

INVESTIGATIONS
Bannalec, Jean-Luc. *The Granite Coast Murders*
Cotterill, Colin. *The Second Biggest Nothing*
Daly, Paula. *Clear My Name*
Dugoni, Robert. *In Her Tracks*
Ellroy, James. ★*Widespread Panic: A Novel*
Gardiner, Meg. *Phantom Instinct*
Mason, Timothy. *The Darwin Affair*
McCall Smith, Alexander. ★*The Geometry of Holding Hands*
Qiu, Xiaolong. *Hold Your Breath, China*
Qiu, Xiaolong. *Shanghai Redemption: An Inspector Chen Novel*
Robertson, Imogen. *Island of Bones*
Roslund, Anders. ★*Knock Knock*
Runcie, James. *Sidney Chambers and the Perils of the Night*
Runcie, James. *Sidney Chambers and the Problem of Evil*

INVESTIGATIVE JOURNALISM
Parks, Brad. *The Player: A Mystery*
Pessl, Marisha. *Night Film: A Novel*
Pratchett, Terry. *The Truth: A Novel of Discworld*

INVESTIGATIVE JOURNALISM — MORAL AND ETHICAL ASPECTS
DeSilva, Bruce. *Providence Rag*

INVESTIGATIVE JOURNALISTS
Christy, Bryan. *In the Company of Killers*
DeSilva, Bruce. *Providence Rag*
DeSilva, Bruce. *Rogue Island*
DeSilva, Bruce. *A Scourge of Vipers*
Fredericks, Mariah. *Death of a Showman*
Harvey, Michael T. *Brighton*
Hiaasen, Carl. *Basket Case*
Iles, Greg. *Cemetery Road: A Novel*
Lagercrantz, David. *The Girl Who Lived Twice: A Lisbeth Salander Novel*
Lagercrantz, David. *The Girl Who Takes an Eye for an Eye*
Larsson, Stieg. *The Girl with the Dragon Tattoo*

INVESTMENT BANKERS
McCall Smith, Alexander. *The Lost Art of Gratitude*

INVESTMENT CLUBS
Krentz, Jayne Ann. *When All the Girls Have Gone*

INVISIBILITY
Berger, Thomas. *Being Invisible: A Novel*
Wells, H. G. ★*The Invisible Man*
Invisible. Auster, Paul
★*The Invisible Bridge: A Novel*. Orringer, Julie
Invisible Cities. Calvino, Italo
The Invisible Guardian. Redondo, Dolores
The Invisible Husband of Frick Island. Oakley, Colleen
The Invisible Library. Cogman, Genevieve
Invisible library [Series]. Cogman, Genevieve
The Invisible Life of Addie Larue. Schwab, Victoria

Invisible life trilogy [Series]. Harris, E. Lynn

Invisible Life: A Novel. Harris, E. Lynn

★*Invisible Man*. Ellison, Ralph

★*The Invisible Man*. Wells, H. G.

Invisible Planets: Contemporary Chinese Science Fiction in Translation. Liu, Ken

★*Invisible Prey*. Sandford, John

The Invited: a Novel. McMahon, Jennifer

IOWA

Bivald, Katarina. *The Readers of Broken Wheel Recommend*

Bruni, Sarah. *The Night Gwen Stacy Died*

Darnielle, John. *Universal Harvester*

Gorman, Edward. *Riders on the Storm : A Sam McCain Mystery*

Robinson, Marilynne. ★*Gilead*

Robinson, Marilynne. *Home*

Robinson, Marilynne. ★*Lila*

Smiley, Jane. *Early Warning*

Smiley, Jane. *Golden Age*

Smiley, Jane. *Some Luck*

Smiley, Jane. ★*A Thousand Acres*

Waller, Robert James. ★*The Bridges of Madison County*

IQ novels [Series]. Ide, Joe

IRAN

Amirrezvani, Anita. *The Blood of Flowers: A Novel*

Amirrezvani, Anita. *Equal of the Sun*

Araghi, Alireza Taheri. ★*The Immortals of Tehran*

Bijan, Donia. *The Last Days of Cafe Leila*

Darznik, Jasmin. *Song of a Captive Bird: A Novel*

Djavadi, Negar. *Disoriental*

Dowlatabadi, Mahmoud. *The Colonel*

Ghaffari, Rabeah. ★*To Keep the Sun Alive*

Hashemzadeh Bonde, Golnaz. *What We Owe*

Hozar, Nazanine. *Aria*

Kamali, Marjan. ★*The Stationery Shop*

Khan, Ausma Zehanat. *Among the Ruins*

Mandanipour, Shahriar. *Moon Brow*

Renault, Mary. *The Persian Boy*

Sofer, Dalia. *Man of My Time*

Sofer, Dalia. *The Septembers of Shiraz*

IRANIAN AMERICAN WOMEN

Bijan, Donia. *The Last Days of Cafe Leila*

IRANIAN AMERICANS

Khadivi, Laleh. ★*A Good Country: A Novel*

IRAQ

Abrams, David. *Fobbit*

Al Rawi, Shahad. *The Baghdad Clock*

Al-Ramli, Muhsin. *The President's Gardens*

Miller, Derek B. ★*The Girl in Green*

Powers, Kevin. ★*The Yellow Birds: A Novel*

Sharp, Zoe. *Fox Hunter*

Swift, Graham. *Wish You Were Here*

IRAQ WAR VETERANS

King, Stephen. ★*Billy Summers*

Petrie, Nicholas. *The Breaker*

Petrie, Nicholas. *Burning Bright*

Petrie, Nicholas. *The Drifter*

Petrie, Nicholas. *Tear It Down*

Petrie, Nicholas. *The Wild One*

Walker, Nico. ★*Cherry: A Novel*

IRAQ WAR, 2003-2011

Abrams, David. *Fobbit*

Benedict, Helen. *Wolf Season*

Fallon, Siobhan. *You Know When the Men Are Gone*

Fountain, Ben. ★*Billy Lynn's Long Halftime Walk*

Mallon, Thomas. *Landfall: A Novel*

Powers, Kevin. ★*The Yellow Birds: A Novel*

Walker, Nico. ★*Cherry: A Novel*

IRELAND

Barry, Sebastian. *The Secret Scripture: A Novel*

Binchy, Maeve. *Circle of Friends*

Binchy, Maeve. *Firefly Summer*

Binchy, Maeve. ★*Whitethorn Woods*

Black, Benjamin. ★*The Secret Guests: A Novel*

Boyne, John. *The Heart's Invisible Furies*

Bruen, Ken. *Galway Girl: A Jack Taylor Novel*

Bruen, Ken. *The Guards*

Burns, Anna. *Milkman: A Novel*

Byrne, Trevor. *Ghosts and Lightning*

Callaghan, Mary Rose. *Billy, Come Home*

Collins, Ciaran. *The Gamal*

Connolly, Sheila. *The Lost Traveller*

Cullen, Helen. *The Dazzling Truth*

Donoghue, Emma. ★*The Wonder*

Doyle, Roddy. *The Guts*

Doyle, Roddy. *Love*

Doyle, Roddy. *Smile*

Doyle, Roddy. *A Star Called Henry*

Doyle, Roddy. ★*The Woman Who Walked into Doors*

Enright, Anne. *Actress: A Novel*

Enright, Anne. *The Forgotten Waltz*

Enright, Anne. ★*The Gathering*

Enright, Anne. *The Green Road: A Novel*

Enright, Anne. *Yesterday's Weather: Stories*

Foley, Lucy. *The Guest List*

French, Tana. ★*The Searcher*

French, Tana. ★*The Witch Elm: A Novel*

Gilligan, Ruth. *The Butchers' Blessing*

Griffin, Anne. *When All Is Said: A Novel*

Hamill, Pete. *Forever*

Hardiman, Rebecca. *Good Eggs*

Harrison, Cora. *Beyond Absolution: A Mystery Set in 1920s Ireland*

Hart, Erin. *The Book of Killowen*

Hart, Erin. *Haunted Ground: A Crime Novel*

Higgins, Jack. *Touch the Devil*

Joyce, James. ★*Dubliners*

Joyce, James. ★*Finnegans Wake*

Joyce, James. ★*A Portrait of the Artist as a Young Man*

Joyce, James. ★*Ulysses*

Kelly, Cathy. *Secrets of a Happy Marriage*

Marillier, Juliet. *Daughter of the Forest*

Maturin, Charles Robert. *Melmoth the Wanderer: A Tale*

McCann, Colum. ★*Transatlantic: A Novel*

McCormack, Mike. ★*Solar Bones*

Murray, Paul. *Skippy Dies*

O'Connor, Carlene. *Murder in an Irish Bookshop*

O'Connor, Joseph. *Star of the Sea*

O'Farrell, Maggie. *This Must Be the Place*
Riley, Lucinda. *The Girl on the Cliff: A Novel*
Roberts, Nora. ★*The Becoming*
Rooney, Sally. ★*Conversations with Friends*
Rooney, Sally. *Normal People: A Novel*
Rutherfurd, Edward. *The Princes of Ireland: The Dublin Saga*
Rutherfurd, Edward. *The Rebels of Ireland: The Dublin Saga*
Spain, Jo. *With Our Blessing: An Inspector Tom Reynolds Mystery*
Uris, Leon. *Redemption: A Novel*
Uris, Leon. ★*Trinity*
Urquhart, Jane. *The Night Stages: A Novel*
Williams, Niall. *This Is Happiness*
The **Iris** Fan: A Novel of Feudal Japan. Rowland, Laura Joh
Iris Grey novels [Series]. Shaw, M. B.
IRISH AMERICAN FAMILIES
McDermott, Alice. *At Weddings and Wakes*
IRISH AMERICAN MEN
McGuire, Ian. *The Abstainer: A Novel*
IRISH AMERICAN WOMEN
Freedman, Benedict. *Mrs. Mike: The Story of Katherine Mary Flannigan*
IRISH AMERICANS
Helprin, Mark. ★*Winter's Tale*
Lange, Tracey. ★*We Are the Brennans*
McDermott, Alice. ★*Charming Billy*
McDermott, Alice. ★*The Ninth Hour*
McDermott, Alice. *Someone*
IRISH AMERICANS — DISCRIMINATION
Faye, Lyndsay. *The Gods of Gotham*
IRISH CANADIANS
Atwood, Margaret. *Alias Grace*
IRISH IN THE UNITED STATES
Lauren, Christina. *Roomies*
IRISH POTATO FAMINE (1845-1852)
O'Connor, Joseph. *Star of the Sea*
Uris, Leon. ★*Trinity*
IRISH RESISTANCE AND REVOLTS
Doyle, Roddy. *A Star Called Henry*
Uris, Leon. ★*Trinity*
Irish village mysteries [Series]. O'Connor, Carlene
IRON AGE
Moss, Sarah. *Ghost Wall: A Novel*
Iron House. Hart, John
The *Iron* King. Druon, Maurice
★*Ironweed: a Novel*. Kennedy, William
Irvin, Kelly
Tell Her No Lies
Irving, John
Avenue of Mysteries: A Novel
★*The Cider House Rules: A Novel*
★*A Prayer for Owen Meany: A Novel*
★*The World According to Garp: A Novel*
Irwin, Stephen M.
The Broken Ones: A Novel
Is There Still Sex in the City?. Bushnell, Candace
Isaac Bell thrillers [Series]. Cussler, Clive
Isaac, Kara
Then There Was You

Isabel Dalhousie mysteries [Series]. McCall Smith, Alexander
ISAIAH
Andrews, Mesu. *Isaiah's Daughter: A Novel of Prophets and Kings*
Isaiah's Daughter: A Novel of Prophets and Kings. Andrews, Mesu
Isherwood, Christopher
★*The Berlin Stories: The Last of Mr. Norris, Goodbye to Berlin*
ISHERWOOD, CHRISTOPHER
Flint, Emma. ★*Little Deaths: A Novel*
Isherwood, Christopher. ★*The Berlin Stories: The Last of Mr. Norris, Goodbye to Berlin*
Ishiguro, Kazuo
An Artist of the Floating World
The Buried Giant: A Novel
★*Klara and the Sun*
★*Never Let Me Go*
★*The Remains of the Day*
The Unconsoled
When We Were Orphans
ISLAM
Akhtar, Ayad. *American Dervish: A Novel*
Anam, Tahmima. *The Bones of Grace*
Robinson, Kim Stanley. *The Years of Rice and Salt*
Rushdie, Salman. ★*The Satanic Verses*
ISLAM — RELATIONS
Rushdie, Salman. ★*Midnight's Children: A Novel*
ISLAM AND STATE
Dowlatabadi, Mahmoud. *The Colonel*
ISLAM AND WOMEN
Pamuk, Orhan. ★*Snow*
The *Island*. Jónasson, Ragnar
ISLAND LIFE
Appanah-Mouriquand, Nathacha. *Tropic of Violence: A Novel*
Banner, Catherine. *The House at the Edge of Night: A Novel*
Boyle, T. Coraghessan. *When the Killing's Done: A Novel*
Colgan, Jenny. ★*The Endless Beach*
Conrad, Joseph. *Victory: An Island Tale*
Dennis-Benn, Nicole. *Here Comes the Sun*
Eriksson, Kjell. *The Deathwatch Beetle: A Mystery*
Frank, Dorothea Benton. *Queen Bee*
Godwin, Gail. *Grief Cottage: A Novel*
Hilderbrand, Elin. ★*Troubles in Paradise*
Kincaid, Jamaica. *The Autobiography of My Mother*
Lee, Andrea. *Red Island House*
Michener, James A. *Caribbean*
Oakley, Colleen. *The Invisible Husband of Frick Island*
Van Meter, Crissy. *Creatures: A Novel*
Island of Bones. Robertson, Imogen
★*The Island of Dr. Moreau*. Wells, H. G.
Island of Mure novels [Series]. Colgan, Jenny
The *Island* of Sea Women. See, Lisa
The *Island* of Second Sight: From the Applied Recollections of Vigoleis. Thelen, Albert Vigoleis
The *Island* of the Day Before. Eco, Umberto
★*Island* Queen. Riley, Vanessa
The *Islanders*. Moore, Meg Mitchell
ISLANDS
Adler-Olsen, Jussi. *The Hanging Girl*
Bannalec, Jean-Luc. *The Killing Tide: A Brittany Mystery*

Blake, Sarah. *The Guest Book: A Novel*
Bolton, S. J. *The Split*
Butler, Season. ★*Cygnet*
Callender, Kacen. *Queen of the Conquered*
Christie, Agatha. ★*And Then There Were None*
Cleeves, Ann. *Thin Air*
Coetzee, J. M. ★*Foe*
Dodd, Christina. *Strangers She Knows*
Doiron, Paul. *Stay Hidden*
Dunn, Mark. *Ella Minnow Pea: A Progressively Lipogrammatic Epistolary Fable*
El Akkad, Omar. *What Strange Paradise*
Foley, Lucy. *The Guest List*
Fowles, John. *The Magus*
Geni, Abby. *The Lightkeepers: A Novel*
Hand, Elizabeth. ★*Generation Loss: A Novel*
Harkaway, Nick. *Tigerman*
Harrison, Nicola. *Montauk*
James, P. D. *The Skull Beneath the Skin*
Jónasson, Ragnar. *The Island*
Ko-Eun, Yun. *The Disaster Tourist*
Lehane, Dennis. *Shutter Island*
Maguire, Gregory. *The Brides of Maracoor*
Mitchell, David. *The Thousand Autumns of Jacob De Zoet: A Novel*
Moore, Meg Mitchell. *The Islanders*
Naylor, Gloria. *Mama Day*
Nichols, Peter. *The Rocks*
See, Lisa. *The Island of Sea Women*
Verne, Jules. *The Mysterious Island*
Wells, H. G. ★*The Island of Dr. Moreau*
Islands of blood and storm [Series]. Callender, Kacen

ISLANDS OF THE AEGEAN
Fowles, John. *The Magus*

ISLANDS OF THE INDIAN OCEAN
Appanah-Mouriquand, Nathacha. *Tropic of Violence: A Novel*

ISLANDS OF THE PACIFIC
Mailer, Norman. ★*The Naked and the Dead*
Verne, Jules. *The Mysterious Island*
Isle of Palms novels [Series]. Monroe, Mary Alice

ISLE OF PALMS, SOUTH CAROLINA
Monroe, Mary Alice. *Beach House Reunion*
Monroe, Mary Alice. ★*The Summer of Lost and Found*

ISLE OF WIGHT (ENGLAND)
Barnes, Julian. ★*England, England*

ISOLATIONISM
Anderson, Kevin J. *The Last Days of Krypton*
Merullo, Roland. *The Talk-Funny Girl: A Novel*
Roth, Philip. ★*The Plot Against America*
Zamyatin, Yevgeny Ivanovich. ★*We*

ISRAEL
Abulhawa, Susan. *The Blue Between Sky and Water*
Agnon, Shmuel Yosef. ★*Only Yesterday*
Bezmozgis, David. *The Betrayers: A Novel*
Castel-Bloom, Orly. *Textile*
Foer, Jonathan Safran. *Here I Am: A Novel*
Gamboa, Santiago. *Necropolis*
Grossman, David. ★*A Horse Walks into a Bar*
Grossman, David. ★*To the End of the Land*

Gundar-Goshen, Ayelet. *Waking Lions*
Kemelman, Harry. *Monday the Rabbi Took Off*
Krauss, Nicole. *Forest Dark*
Rice, Anne. *Christ the Lord: Out of Egypt: A Novel*
Rice, Anne. *Christ the Lord: The Road to Cana: A Novel*
Shalev, Meir. *Two She-Bears: A Novel*
Shoham, Liad. *Asylum City: A Novel*
Silva, Daniel. ★*The Kill Artist: A Novel*
Sthers, Amanda. *Holy Lands: A Novel*
Uris, Leon. ★*Exodus*
Wiesel, Elie. ★*Dawn*

ISRAEL-ARAB WAR, 1948-1949
Uris, Leon. ★*Exodus*

ISRAELIS
Alfon, Dov. *A Long Night in Paris*

ISTANBUL, TURKEY
Doerr, Anthony. ★*Cloud Cuckoo Land: A Novel*
Fleming, Ian. *From Russia with Love*
Pamuk, Orhan. *The Museum of Innocence*
Pamuk, Orhan. *The Red-Haired Woman*
Pamuk, Orhan. ★*A Strangeness in My Mind: A Novel*
Savas, Aysegul. *Walking on the Ceiling*
Shafak, Elif. ★*10 Minutes 38 Seconds in This Strange World*
Shafak, Elif. *The Bastard of Istanbul*
Somer, Mehmet Murat. *The Serenity Murders*
It. King, Stephen
It All Falls Down. Kamal, Sheena
★*It Can't Happen Here*. Lewis, Sinclair
It Ends with Us. Hoover, Colleen
It Takes Two to Tumble. Sebastian, Cat
★*It Would Be Night in Caracas*. Sainz Borgo, Karina
★*It's a Wonderful Woof*. Quinn, Spencer
It's Been a Pleasure, Noni Blake. Christian, Claire
★*It's Not All Downhill from Here: A Novel*. McMillan, Terry

ITALIAN AMERICAN MEN
Malamud, Bernard. *The Assistant*

ITALIAN AMERICAN WOMEN
Grames, Juliet. *The Seven or Eight Deaths of Stella Fortuna*
Trigiani, Adriana. *Big Cherry Holler: A Big Stone Gap Novel*
Trigiani, Adriana. *Big Stone Gap: A Novel*

ITALIAN AMERICANS
Hersey, John. ★*A Bell for Adano*
*The **Italian** Teacher*. Rachman, Tom

ITALIANS IN ENGLAND
Pears, Iain. *An Instance of the Fingerpost*

ITALY
Aciman, Andre. *Call Me by Your Name*
Aciman, Andre. *Enigma Variations: A Novel*
Amis, Martin. ★*The Pregnant Widow*
Ammaniti, Niccolo. *I'm Not Scared*
Banner, Catherine. *The House at the Edge of Night: A Novel*
Bausch, Richard. *Peace*
Beagle, Peter S. *In Calabria*
Berry, Steve. ★*The Malta Exchange: A Novel*
Camilleri, Andrea. *Riccardino*
Castellani, Christopher. *Leading Men: A Novel*
Dazieri, Sandrone. *Kill the Angel*
Dazieri, Sandrone. *Kill the Father*

Dazieri, Sandrone. *Kill the King*
De Giovanni, Maurizio. *The Bastards of Pizzofalcone*
De Giovanni, Maurizio. *The Crocodile*
Dibdin, Michael. *Ratking*
Dimitri, Francesco. *The Book of Hidden Things*
Drndic, Dasa. *Trieste*
Dunant, Sarah. *Blood and Beauty: A Novel*
Dunant, Sarah. *Sacred Hearts: A Novel*
Eco, Umberto. *The Mysterious Flame of Queen Loana: An Illustrated Novel*
Eco, Umberto. ★*The Name of the Rose*
Eco, Umberto. *Numero Zero*
Ferrante, Elena. *The Lost Daughter*
Ferrante, Elena. *The Lying Life of Adults*
Ferrante, Elena. *My Brilliant Friend*
Ferrante, Elena. *The Story of a New Name*
Ferrante, Elena. *The Story of the Lost Child*
Ferrante, Elena. *Those Who Leave and Those Who Stay*
Ginzburg, Natalia. *A Family Lexicon*
Ginzburg, Natalia. *Voices in the Evening*
Giordano, Mario. ★*Auntie Poldi and the Lost Madonna*
Giordano, Mario. *Auntie Poldi and the Vineyards of Etna*
Giordano, Paolo. *Heaven and Earth*
Giordano, Paolo. ★*The Solitude of Prime Numbers: A Novel*
Grames, Juliet. *The Seven or Eight Deaths of Stella Fortuna*
Griffiths, Elly. *The Dark Angel*
Harris, Robert. *Pompeii: A Novel*
Harris, Thomas. *Hannibal*
Heller, Joseph. ★*Catch-22*
Hemingway, Ernest. ★*A Farewell to Arms*
Hewson, David. *The Garden of Angels*
Hewson, David. *The Garden of Evil*
Highsmith, Patricia. ★*The Talented Mr. Ripley*
James, Henry. *The Portrait of a Lady*
Lahiri, Jhumpa. ★*Whereabouts*
Lee, Andrea. *Red Island House*
Leon, Donna. *Beastly Things: A Commissario Guido Brunetti Mystery*
Leon, Donna. *Drawing Conclusions: A Commissario Guido Brunetti Mystery*
Leon, Donna. *Falling in Love: A Commissario Guido Brunetti Mystery*
Leon, Donna. *The Golden Egg*
Leon, Donna. *A Question of Belief: A Commissario Guido Brunetti Mystery*
Leon, Donna. *Trace Elements*
Leon, Donna. ★*Transient Desires*
Leon, Donna. *Uniform Justice*
Leon, Donna. *Unto Us a Son Is Given*
Mangan, Christine. *Palace of the Drowned*
Morante, Elsa. *Arturo's Island: A Novel*
Pears, Iain. *The Immaculate Deception*
Perry, Anne. ★*Death in Focus: An Elena Standish Novel*
Perry, Anne. *A Question of Betrayal*
Phillips, Christi. *The Rossetti Letter: A Novel*
Poole, Sara. *The Borgia Mistress*
Porter, Henry. *White Hot Silence*
Puzo, Mario. *The Family: A Novel*

Rachman, Tom. *The Imperfectionists: A Novel*
Russell, Mary Doria. *A Thread of Grace: A Novel*
Spark, Muriel. *The Driver's Seat*
Spencer, Elizabeth. *The Southern Woman: New and Selected Fiction*
Starnone, Domenico. *Ties*
Stone, Irving. ★*The Agony and the Ecstasy: A Biographical Novel of Michelangelo*
Svevo, Italo. *Zeno's Conscience*
Walton, Jo. ★*Lent*
Westheimer, David. ★*Von Ryan's Express*
Williams, Tennessee. ★*The Roman Spring of Mrs. Stone*
Itami, Emily
  Fault Lines: A Novel
ITHACA, NEW YORK
  Chang, Alexandra. ★*Days of Distraction*
  Herrera, Adriana. ★*American Dreamer*
  Herrera, Adriana. *American Love Story*
ITINERANT PREACHERS
  Lewis, Sinclair. ★*Elmer Gantry*
IVAN IV, THE TERRIBLE, CZAR OF RUSSIA, 1530-1584
  Rutherfurd, Edward. *Russka: The Novel of Russia*
Ivan and Misha: Stories. Alenyikov, Michael
★*Ivanhoe*. Scott, Walter
Iweala, Uzodinma
  ★*Speak No Evil*

J

★*J R: A Novel*. Gaddis, William
★*Jack*. Robinson, Marilynne
Jack Aubrey and Stephen Maturin novels [Series]. O'Brian, Patrick
Jack Brigance novels [Series]. Grisham, John
Jack Laidlaw [Series]. McIlvanney, William
Jack MacTaggart mysteries [Series]. Greaves, Chuck
Jack McEvoy novels [Series]. Connelly, Michael
Jack Reacher novels [Series]. Child, Lee
JACK RUSSELL TERRIERS
  Smiley, Jane. *Horse Heaven*
Jack Ryan and John Clark novels [Series]. Cameron, Marc
Jack Swyteck novels [Series]. Grippando, James
Jack Taylor series [Series]. Bruen, Ken
JACK, THE RIPPER
  Bolton, S. J. *Now You See Me*
  Child, Lincoln. *Deep Storm: A Novel*
  Milan, Courtney. *The Duchess War*
  Pamuk, Orhan. *The Red-Haired Woman*
  Raybourn, Deanna. ★*A Murderous Relation*
  Rowland, Laura Joh. *The Ripper's Shadow*
  Shaw, William. *A Song for the Brokenhearted*
  Whitfield, Clare. *People of Abandoned Character*
Jackdaws. Follett, Ken
Jackson. March, Emily
Jackson Brodie mysteries [Series]. Atkinson, Kate
Jackson Falls [Series]. Williams, Synithia
Jackson Steeg mysteries [Series]. Berkowitz, Ira

Jackson, Brenda
Forged in Desire
Jackson, Charles
The Lost Weekend
Jackson, Joshilyn
Never Have I Ever
Jackson, K. M.
How to Marry Keanu Reeves in 90 Days
JACKSON, MISSISSIPPI
Stockett, Kathryn. ★*The Help*
Jackson, Shirley
★*The Haunting of Hill House*
★*The Lottery: And Other Stories*
We Have Always Lived in the Castle
JACKSON, STONEWALL
Shaara, Jeff. *Gods and Generals: A Novel of the Civil War*
Jackson-Brown, Angela
★*When Stars Rain Down: A Novel*
★*Jacob's Folly: A Novel*. Miller, Rebecca
Jacob's Room. Woolf, Virginia
JACOBITE REBELLIONS (1689-1746)
Gabaldon, Diana. ★*Dragonfly in Amber*
Gabaldon, Diana. ★*Outlander*
London, Julia. *Wild Wicked Scot*
Scott, Walter. ★*Rob Roy*
JACOBITES
Gabaldon, Diana. ★*Dragonfly in Amber*
Gabaldon, Diana. ★*Outlander*
Scott, Walter. ★*Rob Roy*
JACOBUS, DANIEL (FICTITIOUS CHARACTER)
Elias, Gerald. ★*Death and Transfiguration: A Daniel Jacobus Novel*
JADE
Lee, Fonda. ★*Jade City*
Lee, Fonda. *Jade War*
★*Jade City*. Lee, Fonda
Jade War. Lee, Fonda
Jailbird: a Novel. Vonnegut, Kurt
Jake Grafton novels [Series]. Coonts, Stephen
Jake Keller novels [Series]. Ricciardi, David
Jake Mahegan thrillers [Series]. Tata, A. J.
Jakes, John
Love and War
★*North and South*
Jalaluddin, Uzma
★*Ayesha at Last*
Hana Khan Carries On
Jam on the Vine. Barnett, LaShonda K.
JAMAICA
Card, Maisy. ★*These Ghosts Are Family: A Novel*
Collins, Sara. *The Confessions of Frannie Langton*
Dennis-Benn, Nicole. *Here Comes the Sun*
Dennis-Benn, Nicole. ★*Patsy: A Novel*
Fleming, Ian. *Doctor No*
Fleming, Ian. *The Man with the Golden Gun*
Forbes, Curdella. *A Tall History of Sugar*
James, Marlon. ★*A Brief History of Seven Killings: A Novel*
Levy, Andrea. *The Long Song*
McKenzie, Alecia. *A Million Aunties*

McMillan, Terry. ★*How Stella Got Her Groove Back*
Miller, Kei. ★*Augustown*
Jamaica Inn. Du Maurier, Daphne
JAMAICAN AMERICANS
Dennis-Benn, Nicole. ★*Patsy: A Novel*
McKenzie, Alecia. *A Million Aunties*
JAMAICANS IN THE UNITED STATES
Card, Maisy. ★*These Ghosts Are Family: A Novel*
James Bond series [Series]. Fleming, Ian
James, Eloisa
★*Seven Minutes in Heaven*
Three Weeks with Lady X
The Ugly Duchess
Wilde in Love
James, Henry
Complete Stories, 1864-1874
Complete Stories, 1874-1884
Complete Stories, 1884-1891
Complete Stories, 1892-1898
Complete Stories, 1898-1910
Daisy Miller
The Golden Bowl
The Portrait of a Lady
★*The Turn of the Screw*
The Wings of the Dove
JAMES, HENRY
Blum, Jenna. *The Lost Family*
K'wan. *Gutter*
Simmons, Dan. *The Fifth Heart*
Smith, Gregory Blake. ★*The Maze at Windermere: A Novel*
James, Lorelei
I Want You Back
James, Marlon
★*Black Leopard, Red Wolf*
★*A Brief History of Seven Killings: A Novel*
James, Miranda
What the Cat Dragged In
James, P. D.
Death of an Expert Witness
The Lighthouse
Original Sin
The Private Patient
The Skull Beneath the Skin
A Taste for Death
An Unsuitable Job for a Woman
James, Rebecca
The Woman in the Mirror
James, Wendy
A Little Bird
JAMMU AND KASHMIR, INDIA
Roy, Arundhati. ★*The Ministry of Utmost Happiness: A Novel*
Rushdie, Salman. *Shalimar the Clown: A Novel*
Jamrach's Menagerie. Birch, Carol
The Jane Austen Book Club. Fowler, Karen Joy
The Jane Austen Society. Jenner, Natalie
★*Jane Eyre*. Bronte, Charlotte
Jane Marple murder mysteries [Series]. Christie, Agatha
Jane Prescott novels [Series]. Fredericks, Mariah

Jane Rizzoli and Maura Isles series [Series]. Gerritsen, Tess
Jane Steele. Faye, Lyndsay
Jane Whitefield novels ; [Series]. Perry, Thomas
Jane Whitefield novels [Series]. Perry, Thomas
Jane Wunderly novels [Series]. Neubauer, Erica Ruth
The Janes. Luna, Louisa
Janet Watson chronicles [Series]. O'Dell, Claire
Janowitz, Brenda
    The Grace Kelly Dress
The January Dancer. Flynn, Michael
January dancer [Series]. Flynn, Michael
★*January Thaw: A Murder-By-Month Mystery*. Lourey, Jess
The Janus Stone. Griffiths, Elly
JAPAN
    Arikawa, Hiro. *The Travelling Cat Chronicles*
    Ayatsuji, Yukito. *The Decagon House Murders*
    Bird, Sarah. *The Yokota Officers Club: A Novel*
    Clavell, James. *Shogun*
    Endo, Shusaku. *Silence*
    Fleming, Ian. *You Only Live Twice*
    Goenawan, Clarissa. *The Perfect World of Miwako Sumida*
    Goenawan, Clarissa. *Rainbirds*
    Hazzard, Shirley. ★*The Great Fire*
    Higashino, Keigo. ★*The Devotion of Suspect X*
    Higashino, Keigo. *Malice*
    Higashino, Keigo. *The Miracles of the Namiya General Store*
    Higashino, Keigo. *Newcomer*
    Hunter, Stephen. *The 47th Samurai*
    Ishiguro, Kazuo. *An Artist of the Floating World*
    Kawabata, Yasunari. *The Sound of the Mountain*
    Khaw, Cassandra. *Nothing but Blackened Teeth*
    Kutsukake, Lynne. *The Translation of Love: A Novel*
    Lee, Min Jin. ★*Pachinko*
    Minato, Kanae. *Confessions*
    Mishima, Yukio. *The Sound of Waves*
    Mishima, Yukio. *Spring Snow*
    Mitchell, David. *The Thousand Autumns of Jacob De Zoet: A Novel*
    Murakami, Haruki. *After Dark*
    Murakami, Haruki. *After the Quake: Stories*
    Murakami, Haruki. *Colorless Tsukuru Tazaki and His Years of Pilgrimage*
    Murakami, Haruki. ★*Kafka on the Shore*
    Murakami, Haruki. *Killing Commendatore: A Novel*
    Murakami, Haruki. *South of the Border, West of the Sun*
    Murakami, Haruki. *The Wind-Up Bird Chronicle*
    Murakami, Ryu. *In the Miso Soup*
    Murata, Sayaka. *Earthlings: A Novel*
    Obregon, Nicolas. *Blue Light Yokohama*
    Oe, Kenzaburo. ★*Death by Water*
    Oe, Kenzaburo. *Nip the Buds, Shoot the Kids*
    Oe, Kenzaburo. ★*A Quiet Life*
    Okuizumi, Hikaru. *The Stones Cry Out*
    Ono, Masatsugu. *Echo on the Bay*
    Peace, David. *Occupied City*
    Rizzuto, Rahna R. *Shadow Child*
    Rowland, Laura Joh. *The Incense Game: A Novel of Feudal Japan*
    Rowland, Laura Joh. *The Iris Fan: A Novel of Feudal Japan*
    Rowland, Laura Joh. *The Shogun's Daughter: A Novel of Feudal Japan*
    Rowland, Laura Joh. *The Snow Empress*
    Schwartz, John Burnham. *The Commoner: A Novel*
    Scott, Stephanie. *What's Left of Me Is Yours: A Novel*
    Spann, Susan. *Blade of the Samurai: A Shinobi Mystery*
    Spann, Susan. ★*Claws of the Cat: A Shinobi Mystery*
    Spann, Susan. *Trial on Mount Koya: A Hiro Hattori Novel*
    Takamura, Kaoru. ★*Lady Joker*
    Tawada, Yoko. ★*The Emissary*
    Tsukiyama, Gail. *The Street of a Thousand Blossoms*
    Yoshimoto, Banana. *The Lake*
    Yu, Miri. *Tokyo Ueno Station*
JAPANESE AMERICAN FAMILIES
    Hirahara, Naomi. ★*Clark and Division*
    Otsuka, Julie. *When the Emperor Was Divine: A Novel*
JAPANESE AMERICANS
    Guterson, David. ★*Snow Falling on Cedars*
    Washington, Bryan. ★*Memorial*
JAPANESE AMERICANS — FORCED REMOVAL AND INCARCERATION, 1942-1945
    Dallas, Sandra. *Tallgrass*
    Ellroy, James. *Perfidia*
    Hirahara, Naomi. ★*Clark and Division*
    Otsuka, Julie. *When the Emperor Was Divine: A Novel*
    Rizzuto, Rahna R. *Shadow Child*
JAPANESE CANADIANS
    Kutsukake, Lynne. *The Translation of Love: A Novel*
    Shimotakahara, Leslie. *After the Bloom*
JAPANESE IN INDIA
    Endo, Shusaku. *Deep River*
JAPANESE IN THE UNITED STATES
    Otsuka, Julie. *The Buddha in the Attic*
The Japanese Lover. Allende, Isabel
The Jasmine Throne. Suri, Tasha
Jason Bourne series [Series]. Ludlum, Robert
Jason Stafford novels [Series]. Sears, Michael
Jaswal, Balli Kaur
    Erotic Stories for Punjabi Widows
Jayatissa, Amanda
    ★*My Sweet Girl*
Jayber Crow: A Novel. Berry, Wendell
Jazz. Morrison, Toni
Jazz Funeral. Smith, Julie
JAZZ MUSIC
    Baldwin, James. ★*Going to Meet the Man*
    Goonan, Kathleen Ann. *In War Times*
    Kaplan, Mitchell James. *Rhapsody*
JAZZ MUSICIANS
    Aaronovitch, Ben. *Moon Over Soho*
    Baker, Dorothy. ★*Young Man with a Horn*
    Baldwin, James. ★*Another Country*
    Baldwin, James. ★*Going to Meet the Man*
    Edugyan, Esi. *Half-Blood Blues*
Jazz Ramsey novels [Series]. Logan, Kylie
JAZZ TRUMPETERS
    Baker, Dorothy. ★*Young Man with a Horn*
The Jealous Kind. Burke, James Lee

JEALOUSY

Bronte, Emily. ★*Wuthering Heights*

Clark, Wahida. ★*Thugs and the Women Who Love Them*

Erdrich, Louise. *The Beet Queen: A Novel*

Hall, Steven. *Maxwell's Demon*

Hamilton, Karen. *The Last Wife*

Kundera, Milan. ★*The Unbearable Lightness of Being*

McCullough, Colleen. *An Indecent Obsession*

Pinborough, Sarah. ★*Dead to Her: A Novel*

Rachman, Tom. *The Imperfectionists: A Novel*

Stage, Zoje. *Getaway*

Walker, Caroline Louise. *Man of the Year*

JEALOUSY IN MEN

Hugo, Victor. ★*The Hunchback of Notre Dame*

Kane, Ben. *Spartacus: The Gladiator*

JEALOUSY IN TEENAGE GIRLS

Sagan, Francoise. ★*Bonjour Tristesse*

JEALOUSY IN WOMEN

Wolitzer, Meg. *The Interestings*

Jedrowski, Tomasz

Swimming in the Dark

JEEVES (FICTITIOUS CHARACTER)

Wodehouse, P. G. ★*The Inimitable Jeeves*

Jeeves and the Wedding Bells. Faulks, Sebastian

Jeeves and Wooster [Series]. Wodehouse, P. G.

Jeff in Venice, Death in Varanasi. Dyer, Geoff

Jeffers, Honoree Fanonne

★*The Love Songs of W. E. B. Du Bois*

Jeffries, Sabrina

Project Duchess

JEJU ISLAND, SOUTH KOREA

See, Lisa. *The Island of Sea Women*

JEKYLL, HENRY (FICTITIOUS CHARACTER)

Stevenson, Robert Louis. ★*The Strange Case of Dr. Jekyll and Mr. Hyde*

Jem Flockhart novels [Series]. Thomson, E. S.

Jemc, Jac

★*The Grip of It*

Jemisin, N. K.

★*The City We Became*

The Fifth Season

How Long 'Til Black Future Month?

The Obelisk Gate

The Stone Sky

Jen, Gish

★*The Resisters*

★*Thank You, Mr. Nixon: Stories*

Jenkins, Beverly

Forbidden

Rebel

Tempest

Wild Rain

Jenner, Natalie

The Jane Austen Society

Jennie Redhead novels [Series]. Spencer, Sally

Jenoff, Pam

The Lost Girls of Paris

Jensen, Nancy

In Our Midst

Jeremy Fisk novels [Series]. Wolf, Dick

Jeremy Logan novels [Series]. Child, Lincoln

Jersey girl legal novels [Series]. Copperman, E. J.

Jerusalem. Holland, Cecelia

JERUSALEM, ISRAEL

Holland, Cecelia. *Jerusalem*

Horn, Dara. *Eternal Life: A Novel*

Kemelman, Harry. *One Fine Day the Rabbi Bought a Cross*

Oz, Amos. *Fima*

Spark, Muriel. ★*The Mandelbaum Gate*

Jerusalem: a Novel. Moore, Alan

Jesse Stone mysteries [Series]. Parker, Robert B.

Jesse Sutherlin mysteries [Series]. Ramsay, Frederick

Jessie Cole novels [Series]. Ragan, Theresa

JESUS CHRIST

Asch, Sholem. *The Nazarene*

Bulgakov, Mikhail. ★*The Master and Margarita*

Crace, Jim. *Quarantine*

Kazantzakis, Nikos. *The Last Temptation of Christ*

Kidd, Sue Monk. ★*The Book of Longings*

Percy, Walker. *The Second Coming*

Rice, Anne. *Christ the Lord: Out of Egypt: A Novel*

Rice, Anne. *Christ the Lord: The Road to Cana: A Novel*

Wallace, Lew. ★*Ben-Hur*

Jewel of the Nile. Afshar, Tessa

JEWEL THIEVES

Collins, Wilkie. ★*The Moonstone*

Coulter, Catherine. *The Final Cut*

Westlake, Donald E. *The Hot Rock*

Jewell, Lisa

The Family Upstairs

Then She Was Gone: A Novel

Watching You

JEWELRY

Meyerson, Amy. *The Imperfects*

Trollope, Anthony. ★*The Eustace Diamonds*

JEWELRY THEFT

Block, Lawrence. *The Burglar in the Closet*

Collins, Wilkie. ★*The Moonstone*

Cosby, S. A. ★*Blacktop Wasteland*

Coulter, Catherine. *The Final Cut*

Hollis, Lee. *Poppy Harmon Investigates*

Khan, Vaseem. *The Perplexing Theft of the Jewel in the Crown*

Lindsay, Jeffry P. *Just Watch Me*

Rozan, S. J. *The Shanghai Moon: A Lydia Chin/Bill Smith Novel*

Sayers, Dorothy L. *The Nine Tailors*

Simenon, Georges. ★*Maigret Bides His Time*

Tan, Lucy. *What We Were Promised*

Westlake, Donald E. *The Hot Rock*

JEWISH AMERICAN AUTHORS

Roth, Philip. ★*The Anatomy Lesson*

Roth, Philip. *Exit Ghost*

Roth, Philip. *The Ghost Writer*

Roth, Philip. *Zuckerman Bound*

Roth, Philip. *Zuckerman Unbound*

JEWISH AMERICAN BOYS
Roth, Henry. ★*Call It Sleep*
Roth, Henry. *A Star Shines Over Mt. Morris Park*
JEWISH AMERICAN FAMILIES
Doctorow, E. L. ★*Ragtime*
Heller, Joseph. *Good as Gold*
Oates, Joyce Carol. *The Gravedigger's Daughter: A Novel*
Roth, Philip. ★*American Pastoral*
Roth, Philip. ★*The Plot Against America*
JEWISH AMERICAN MEN
Bellow, Saul. ★*Herzog*
Bellow, Saul. ★*Mr. Sammler's Planet*
Bellow, Saul. *Novels, 1944-1953*
Chabon, Michael. *The Yiddish Policemen's Union*
Epstein, Joseph. *The Love Song of A. Jerome Minkoff, and Other Stories*
Pomerantz, Sharon. *Rich Boy*
Roth, Henry. *From Bondage*
Roth, Henry. *Requiem for Harlem*
Roth, Philip. ★*Everyman*
Roth, Philip. ★*Portnoy's Complaint*
JEWISH AMERICAN MEN — IDENTITY
Roth, Philip. *Exit Ghost*
Roth, Philip. *The Ghost Writer*
Roth, Philip. ★*Goodbye, Columbus, and Five Short Stories*
Roth, Philip. *I Married a Communist*
Roth, Philip. *Zuckerman Bound*
JEWISH AMERICAN TEENAGE BOYS
Roth, Henry. *A Diving Rock on the Hudson*
JEWISH AMERICAN WOMEN
Smith, Martin Cruz. *Stallion Gate*
JEWISH AMERICANS
Bellow, Saul. ★*The Adventures of Augie March*
Bellow, Saul. *The Bellarosa Connection*
Bellow, Saul. *Novels, 1944-1953*
Doctorow, E. L. ★*The Book of Daniel: A Novel*
Dos Passos, John. *1919*
Epstein, Joseph. *The Love Song of A. Jerome Minkoff, and Other Stories*
Foer, Jonathan Safran. *Here I Am: A Novel*
Potok, Chaim. ★*The Gift of Asher Lev*
Roth, Henry. *A Star Shines Over Mt. Morris Park*
Roth, Philip. ★*The Plot Against America*
Salinger, J. D. *Raise High the Roof Beam, Carpenters,: And Seymour—An Introduction.*
Singer, Isaac Bashevis. *Enemies, a Love Story*
JEWISH BOYS
Bailey, Paul. *Uncle Rudolf*
JEWISH FAMILIES
Artson, Barbara. *Odessa, Odessa*
Attenberg, Jami. *The Middlesteins*
Auslander, Shalom. *Hope: A Tragedy*
Castel-Bloom, Orly. *Textile*
Chabon, Michael. *The Yiddish Policemen's Union*
Foer, Jonathan Safran. *Here I Am: A Novel*
Friedland, Elyssa. *Last Summer at the Golden Hotel*
Goldbloom, Goldie. *On Division*
Gross, Andrew. *Button Man*

Meltzer, Jean. ★*The Matzah Ball*
Miller, Derek B. *How to Find Your Way in the Dark*
Ozick, Cynthia. *Heir to the Glimmering World*
Potok, Chaim. ★*My Name Is Asher Lev*
Rabb, Jonathan. *Among the Living*
Rice, Anne. *Christ the Lord: Out of Egypt: A Novel*
Rice, Anne. *Christ the Lord: The Road to Cana: A Novel*
Roth, Henry. ★*Call It Sleep*
Schwarz-Bart, Andre. *The Last of the Just: A Novel*
Singer, I. J. *The Brothers Ashkenazi*
Sofer, Dalia. *The Septembers of Shiraz*
Solomons, Natasha. *House of Gold*
Weiner, Jennifer. ★*Mrs. Everything: A Novel*
JEWISH FICTION
Henkin, Joshua. *Morningside Heights*
JEWISH GIRLS
Hoffman, Alice. ★*The World That We Knew*
Veletzos, Roxanne. *The Girl They Left Behind*
Vreeland, Susan. *Girl in Hyacinth Blue*
JEWISH MEN
Auster, Paul. *4 3 2 1: A Novel*
Baxter, Charles. *Saul and Patsy*
Bezmozgis, David. *The Betrayers: A Novel*
Danan, Rosie. *The Intimacy Experiment*
DePoy, Phillip. *Sidewalk Saint*
Friedman, Daniel. *Running Out of Road*
Gilbers, Harald. *Germania: A Novel of Nazi Berlin*
Heller, Joseph. *Good as Gold*
Hertmans, Stefan. ★*The Convert: A Novel*
Prose, Francine. ★*The Vixen*
Sthers, Amanda. *Holy Lands: A Novel*
Styron, William. ★*Sophie's Choice*
Wiesel, Elie. ★*Dawn*
Wiesel, Elie. *Hostage*
Wiesel, Elie. ★*Night, Dawn, the Accident: Three Tales*
JEWISH MEN — IDENTITY
Smith, Zadie. *The Autograph Man: A Novel*
JEWISH MOURNING CUSTOMS
Rojstaczer, Stuart. *The Mathematician's Shiva: A Novel*
JEWISH RESISTANCE AND REVOLTS
Rimmer, Kelly. ★*The Warsaw Orphan: A Wwii Novel*
JEWISH TEENAGE GIRLS
Rossner, Rena. *The Light of the Midnight Stars*
JEWISH TEENAGERS
Clayton, Meg Waite. *The Last Train to London*
JEWISH WAY OF LIFE
Englander, Nathan. *What We Talk About When We Talk About Anne Frank: Stories*
Roth, Henry. ★*Call It Sleep*
Singer, Isaac Bashevis. *Collected Stories: A Friend of Kafka to Passions*
Singer, Isaac Bashevis. *Collected Stories: Gimpel the Fool to the Letter Writer*
Singer, Isaac Bashevis. *The Family Moskat*
Singer, Isaac Bashevis. ★*The Magician of Lublin*
JEWISH WOMEN
Adams, Alina. *The Nesting Dolls*
Alexander, Jennet. *I Kissed a Girl*

Benedict, Marie. *The Only Woman in the Room*
Black, Cara. *Murder in the Marais*
Broder, Melissa. *Milk Fed*
Burke, James Lee. *Wayfaring Stranger: A Novel*
Diamant, Anita. *The Boston Girl: A Novel*
Drndic, Dasa. *Trieste*
Durrell, Lawrence. ★*Justine*
Eliasberg, Jan. ★*Hannah's War*
Feldman, Ellen. *Paris Never Leaves You*
Franck, Julia. *Blindness of the Heart*
Henkin, Joshua. *Morningside Heights*
Horn, Dara. *Eternal Life: A Novel*
Kowal, Mary Robinette. *The Fated Sky: A Lady Astronaut Novel*
Lethem, Jonathan. *Dissident Gardens*
Ozick, Cynthia. *The Puttermesser Papers*
Piercy, Marge. *Gone to Soldiers: A Novel*
Pontoppidan, Henrik. *Lucky Per*
Shapiro, Barbara A. *The Muralist*
Smith, Jill Eileen. *Star of Persia: Esther's Story*
Spark, Muriel. ★*The Mandelbaum Gate*

JEWS
Albahari, David. *Gotz and Meyer*
Antopol, Molly. *The Unamericans*
Cossette, Connilyn. ★*Shelter of the Most High*
Dahl, Julia. *Conviction*
Englander, Nathan. *The Ministry of Special Cases*
Englander, Nathan. *What We Talk About When We Talk About Anne Frank: Stories*
Halfon, Eduardo. *Mourning*
Krauss, Nicole. *Forest Dark*
Lebrecht, Norman. *The Song of Names*
Malamud, Bernard. ★*The Complete Stories*
Orringer, Julie. ★*The Invisible Bridge: A Novel*
Piercy, Marge. *Gone to Soldiers: A Novel*
Rice, Anne. *Christ the Lord: Out of Egypt: A Novel*
Rice, Anne. *Christ the Lord: The Road to Cana: A Novel*
Rosner, Jennifer. ★*The Yellow Bird Sings*
Shepard, Jim. ★*The Book of Aron*
Singer, Isaac Bashevis. *Collected Stories: A Friend of Kafka to Passions*
Singer, Isaac Bashevis. *Collected Stories: Gimpel the Fool to the Letter Writer*
Singer, Isaac Bashevis. *The Family Moskat*
Singer, Isaac Bashevis. ★*The Magician of Lublin*
Sundin, Sarah. *When Twilight Breaks*
Uris, Leon. ★*Exodus*
Wouk, Herman. ★*War and Remembrance: A Novel*
Wouk, Herman. ★*The Winds of War: A Novel*

JEWS — HISTORY
Wallace, Lew. ★*Ben-Hur*

JEWS — IDENTITY
Wiesel, Elie. ★*Night, Dawn, the Accident: Three Tales*

JEWS — PERSECUTIONS
Hertmans, Stefan. ★*The Convert: A Novel*
Orringer, Julie. ★*The Invisible Bridge: A Novel*
Schwarz-Bart, Andre. *The Last of the Just: A Novel*

JEWS, EASTERN EUROPEAN
Aleichem, Sholem. *Tevye the Dairyman and the Railroad Stories*

Aleichem, Sholem. *Tevye's Daughters*
Kosinski, Jerzy. ★*The Painted Bird*
Malamud, Bernard. ★*The Fixer*
Schwarz-Bart, Andre. *The Last of the Just: A Novel*

JEWS, ENGLISH
Scott, Walter. ★*Ivanhoe*

JEWS, FRENCH
Belfoure, Charles. *The Paris Architect: A Novel*
Orringer, Julie. ★*The Flight Portfolio: A Novel*

JEWS, GERMAN
Grossman, Paul. *Children of Wrath*
Schwarz-Bart, Andre. *The Last of the Just: A Novel*

JEWS, GERMAN — HISTORY
Bohjalian, Chris. *Skeletons at the Feast: A Novel*
Boschwitz, Ulrich Alexander. *The Passenger: A Novel*

JEWS, POLISH
Singer, I. J. *The Brothers Ashkenazi*
Twardoch, Szczepan. *The King of Warsaw*

JEWS, ROMANIAN
Bailey, Paul. *Uncle Rudolf*

JEWS, RUSSIAN
Landau, Alexis. *Those Who Are Saved*

JEWS, SERBIAN
Albahari, David. *Gotz and Meyer*

JEWS, SPANISH
Maturin, Charles Robert. *Melmoth the Wanderer: A Tale*

Jhabvala, Ruth Prawer
At the End of the Century: The Stories of Ruth Prawer Jhabvala.
★*Heat and Dust*

JIHAD
Khadivi, Laleh. ★*A Good Country: A Novel*

Jiles, Paulette
News of the World: A Novel

JILTED BRIDES
Cleage, Pearl. *Some Things I Never Thought I'd Do*
Van Dyken, Rachel. *Risky Play*

JILTED MEN
Balogh, Mary. *Only Enchanting*
Bennett, Anna. *First Earl I See Tonight*
Chase, Loretta Lynda. *A Duke in Shining Armor*
Dare, Tessa. ★*The Duchess Deal*
Portis, Charles. ★*The Dog of the South*
Turner, Bethany. *Wooing Cadie McCaffrey*

JILTED WOMEN
Cole, Alyssa. *How to Find a Princess*
Frantz, Laura. *The Lacemaker*
Higgins, Kristan. ★*The Best Man*
Kamali, Marjan. ★*The Stationery Shop*
Lopez Barrio, Cristina. *The House of the Impossible Loves*
Mallery, Susan. *California Girls*
Sosa, Mia. ★*The Worst Best Man*
Sterling, Erin. *The Ex Hex*
Williams, Niall. *This Is Happiness*

Jim the Boy: A Novel. Earley, Tony

Jimenez, Abby
The Friend Zone
★*The Happy Ever After Playlist*
Life's Too Short

Jimenez, Simon
  ★*The Vanished Birds*
Jimm Juree mysteries [Series]. Cotterill, Colin
Jimmy Bluefeather: A Novel. Heacox, Kim
Jimmy Paz series [Series]. Gruber, Michael
Jin, Ha
  The Boat Rocker: A Novel
  A Map of Betrayal: A Novel
  ★*Waiting*
Jin, Meng
  Little Gods
Jin, Yong
  A Hero Born: A Novel
★*Jitterbug Perfume*. Robbins, Tom
Jo Beckett series [Series]. Gardiner, Meg
JOAN OF ARC
  Grossman, David. *Falling Out of Time*
  Twain, Mark. *Personal Recollections of Joan of Arc*
Joanne Ross novels [Series]. Scott, A. D.
JOB OFFERS
  Jackson, K. M. *How to Marry Keanu Reeves in 90 Days*
JOCKEYS
  Francis, Felix. *Pulse*
Joe Gunther mysteries [Series]. Mayor, Archer
Joe Leaphorn and Jim Chee mysteries [Series]. Hillerman, Tony
Joe Pickett novels [Series]. Box, C. J.
Joe Wilderness novels [Series]. Lawton, John
Joe: a Novel. Brown, Larry
JOHANNESBURG, SOUTH AFRICA
  Beukes, Lauren. *Afterland*
  Beukes, Lauren. *Slipping: Stories, Essays, & Other Writing*
  Beukes, Lauren. *Zoo City*
  Clemmons, Zinzi. *What We Lose*
John Coffin mysteries [Series]. Butler, Gwendoline
John Corey novels [Series]. DeMille, Nelson
John dies at the end [Series]. Wong, David
John Hayes novels [Series]. Quirk, Matthew
JOHN HENRY
  Whitehead, Colson. *John Henry Days: A Novel*
John Henry Cole novels [Series]. Brooks, Bill
John Henry Days: A Novel. Whitehead, Colson
John Keller novels [Series]. Block, Lawrence
John Madden novels [Series]. Airth, Rennie
John March novels [Series]. Spiegelman, Peter
JOHN PAUL II, POPE, 1920-2005
  Higgins, Jack. *Confessional*
John Rain novels [Series]. Eisler, Barry
John Wells novels [Series]. Berenson, Alex
★*John Woman*. Mosley, Walter
★*Johnny Got His Gun*. Trumbo, Dalton
Johnson, Alaya Dawn
  Trouble the Saints
Johnson, Caleb
  Treeborne
Johnson, Charles Richard
  ★*Middle Passage*
Johnson, Craig
  Daughter of the Morning Star

  Land of Wolves
  Next to Last Stand
  Spirit of Steamboat: A Walt Longmire Story
Johnson, D. E.
  Detroit Shuffle
Johnson, Daisy
  Everything Under
  Sisters
Johnson, Denis
  The Largesse of the Sea Maiden: Stories
Johnson, Jocelyn Nicole
  ★*My Monticello: Fiction*
Johnson, Julia Claiborne
  Better Luck Next Time: A Novel
Johnson, Keith Lee
  ★*Little Black Girl Lost*
Johnson, Kij
  ★*The Dream-Quest of Vellitt Boe*
Johnson, Micaiah
  The Space Between Worlds
Johnson, Nancy
  The Kindest Lie
JOHNSON, ROBERT, 1911-1938
  Alexie, Sherman. *Reservation Blues*
  Sjowall, Maj. ★*Cop Killer: The Story of a Crime*
Johnson, Sadeqa
  ★*Yellow Wife*
Johnson, Tara
  Engraved on the Heart
JOHNSON, ZIGGY
  Dell'Antonia, K. J. *The Chicken Sisters*
  Randall, Alice. ★*Black Bottom Saints*
Johnston, Tim
  The Current: A Novel
Johnstone, Carole
  Mirrorland
JOKES
  Grossman, David. ★*A Horse Walks into a Bar*
JOKING RELATIONSHIPS
  Wallace, Daniel. ★*Big Fish: A Novel of Mythic Proportions*
Ragnar Jonasson
  ★*The Girl Who Died*
  The Island
  The Mist
Jonathan Argyll and Flavia DiStefano mysteries [Series]. Pears, Iain
★*Jonathan Strange & Mr. Norrell*. Clarke, Susanna
Jonathan Stride novels [Series]. Freeman, Brian
JONES
Jones, Cherie
  How the One-Armed Sister Sweeps Her House
Jones, Cynan
  Stillicide
Jones, Darynda
  A Bad Day for Sunshine
  A Good Day for Chardonnay
Jones, Douglas C.
  The Court-Martial of George Armstrong Custer

Jones, Gayl
  ★*Palmares*
Jones, James
  ★*From Here to Eternity*
  ★*The Thin Red Line*
JONES, MOTHER, 1837-1930
  Akunin, B. *The Coronation: The Further Adventures of Erast Fandorin*
  Montgomery, Jess. *The Widows*
Jones, Robert
  ★*The Prophets: A Novel*
Jones, Sandie
  The Other Woman
Jones, Sherry
  Four Sisters, All Queens
Jones, Stephen Graham
  My Heart Is a Chainsaw
  ★*The Only Good Indians: A Novel*
Jones, Stephen Mack
  Dead of Winter
Jones, Tanen
  The Better Liar: A Novel
Jones, Tayari
  ★*An American Marriage: A Novel*
  Silver Sparrow: A Novel
Jong, Erica
  ★*Fear of Flying: A Novel*
Jordan, Hillary
  Mudbound: A Novel
Jordan, Sophie
  The Duke Goes Down
  This Scot of Mine
Joseph O'Loughlin and Vincent Ruiz novels [Series]. Robotham, Michael
Joseph, Fabiola
  Niya: Rainbow Dreams
Joshi, Alka
  The Henna Artist
Josie Prescott mysteries [Series]. Cleland, Jane K.
Joukhadar, Zeyn
  ★*The Thirty Names of Night: A Novel*
JOURNALISM
  Delinsky, Barbara. *Lake News: A Novel*
  Eco, Umberto. *Numero Zero*
  Watt, Holly. *To the Lions*
JOURNALISM — POLITICAL ASPECTS
  Allende, Isabel. *Of Love and Shadows*
JOURNALISTS
  Allende, Isabel. *Of Love and Shadows*
  Baldacci, David. *The Fallen*
  Belli, Kate. *Deception by Gaslight: A Gilded Gotham Mystery*
  Brunkhorst, Alex. *The Gilded Life of Matilda Duplaine*
  Carr, Caleb. ★*The Alienist*
  Christopher, Andie J. *Not the Girl You Marry*
  Connelly, Michael. ★*Fair Warning*
  Connelly, Michael. *The Scarecrow: A Novel*
  Delinsky, Barbara. *Lake News: A Novel*
  Deon, Natashia. *The Perishing: A Novel*

Dunne, Dominick. *People Like Us: A Novel*
Dunne, Dominick. *Too Much Money*
Dyer, Geoff. *Jeff in Venice, Death in Varanasi*
Eco, Umberto. *Numero Zero*
Farah, Nuruddin. *Crossbones*
Flint, Emma. ★*Little Deaths: A Novel*
Furst, Alan. *Blood of Victory: A Novel*
Grant, Mira. *Feedback*
Grass, Gunter. *Crabwalk*
Greene, Graham. ★*Brighton Rock*
Guterson, David. ★*Snow Falling on Cedars*
Hiaasen, Carl. *Lucky You: A Novel*
Hijuelos, Oscar. *Twain & Stanley Enter Paradise*
Jenkins, Beverly. *Wild Rain*
Jin, Ha. *The Boat Rocker: A Novel*
Landvik, Lorna. *Chronicles of a Radical Hag: With Recipes*
Lasdun, James. *Afternoon of a Faun: A Novel*
Laureano, C. E. ★*The Saturday Night Supper Club*
Lippman, Laura. ★*Lady in the Lake: A Novel*
Mamet, David. *Chicago: A Novel*
Miller, Derek B. ★*The Girl in Green*
Nicieza, Fabian. *Suburban Dicks*
Oakley, Colleen. *The Invisible Husband of Frick Island*
Orringer, Julie. ★*The Flight Portfolio: A Novel*
Palahniuk, Chuck. *Lullaby: A Novel*
Petrie, Nicholas. *Burning Bright*
Pratchett, Terry. *The Truth: A Novel of Discworld*
Rachman, Tom. *The Imperfectionists: A Novel*
Rademacher, Cay. *Deadly Camargue: A Provence Mystery*
Ragan, Theresa. *Deadly Recall*
Ragan, Theresa. *Her Last Day*
Ramzipoor, E. R. *The Ventriloquists*
Restrepo, Laura. *No Place for Heroes: A Novel*
Robertson, Robin. *The Long Take: A Noir Narrative*
Ruiz Zafon, Carlos. *The Angel's Game*
Sandford, John. ★*Deadline*
Scott, A. D. ★*Beneath the Abbey Wall: A Novel*
Scott, A. D. *A Double Death on the Black Isle: A Novel*
Scott, A. D. *A Kind of Grief: A Novel*
Scott, A. D. ★*The Low Road*
Stroby, Wallace. *Some Die Nameless*
Title, Sarah. *The Undateable*
Vidal, Gore. *Washington, D. C.: A Novel*
Ware, Ruth. *The Woman in Cabin Ten*
Warren, Robert Penn. *All the King's Men*
Wolfe, Tom. *Back to Blood: A Novel*
★*Journey* to the Centre of the Earth. Verne, Jules
The Joy and Light Bus Company. McCall Smith, Alexander
JOY AND SORROW
  Pilcher, Rosamunde. *A Place Like Home: Short Stories*
  Smiley, Jane. *Early Warning*
  Smiley, Jane. *Golden Age*
  Smiley, Jane. *Some Luck*
JOY AND SORROW IN WOMEN
  Cunningham, Michael. ★*The Hours*
★*The Joy Luck Club*. Tan, Amy
Joyce, James
  ★*Dubliners*

★*Finnegans Wake*

★*A Portrait of the Artist as a Young Man*

★*Ulysses*

JOYCE, JAMES

Greene, Amy. *Long Man*

Joyce, James. ★*A Portrait of the Artist as a Young Man*

Joyce, Rachel

Miss Benson's Beetle

JUDAEA (REGION)

Wallace, Lew. ★*Ben-Hur*

JUDAISM

Miller, Rebecca. ★*Jacob's Folly: A Novel*

★*Jude the Obscure*. Hardy, Thomas

★*A Judgement in Stone*. Rendell, Ruth

JUDGES

Box, C. J. ★*Long Range*

Brown, Sandra. ★*Ricochet*

Grossman, David. ★*A Horse Walks into a Bar*

Parks, Brad. *Say Nothing: A Novel*

★*Judgment*. Finder, Joseph

Judgment at Santa Monica. Copperman, E. J.

The *Judgment* of Caesar: A Novel of Ancient Rome. Saylor, Steven

JUDICIAL CORRUPTION

Brown, Sandra. ★*Ricochet*

Dugoni, Robert. *The Conviction*

JUDICIAL ERROR

Arvin, Reed. *Blood of Angels: A Novel*

Baldacci, David. *Redemption*

Bell, Shelly. *For His Pleasure*

Buchanan, Edna. *You Only Die Twice: A Britt Montero Mystery*

Dow, David R. *Confessions of an Innocent Man*

Harris, C. S. *What the Devil Knows: A Sebastian St. Cyr Mystery*

Lepionka, Kristen. *The Last Place You Look*

Persson Giolito, Malin. *Beyond All Reasonable Doubt: A Novel*

Slaughter, Karin. ★*The Silent Wife*

Williams, Beatriz. *The Summer Wives*

Winthrop, Elizabeth Hartley. *The Mercy Seat: A Novel*

JUDICIAL SYSTEM

Pava, Sergio de la. *A Naked Singularity*

JUDICIAL SYSTEM — HISTORY

Dickens, Charles. ★*Bleak House*

The *Jugger: a Parker Novel*. Stark, Richard

Jules Maigret mysteries [Series]. Simenon, Georges

Julia and Louise novels [Series]. Brown, Rita Mae

★*July's People*. Gordimer, Nadine

★*Juneteenth*. Ellison, Ralph

★*The Jungle*. Sinclair, Upton

JUNGLE SURVIVAL

Smith, Scott. *The Ruins: A Novel*

JUNGLES

Ferencik, Erica. *Into the Jungle*

Marlantes, Karl. ★*Matterhorn: A Novel of the Vietnam War*

Smith, Scott. *The Ruins: A Novel*

Vargas Llosa, Mario. *Green House*

Junior Bender mysteries [Series]. Hallinan, Timothy

JURORS

Cavanagh, Steve. *Thirteen*

Grisham, John. *The Last Juror*

Moore, Graham. *The Holdout: A Novel*

JURY

Doctorow, Cory. *Rapture of the Nerds*

Just Above My Head. Baldwin, James

Just city novels [Series]. Walton, Jo

Just Get Home. Foley, Bridget

Just Like You. Hornby, Nick

Just One Evil Act. George, Elizabeth

Just One Look. Cameron, Lindsay

Just Watch Me. Lindsay, Jeffry P.

JUSTICE

Gruber, Michael. *The Return: A Novel*

Iles, Greg. *The Bone Tree: A Novel*

Iles, Greg. *Natchez Burning: A Novel*

Kelton, Elmer. *Hard Ride*

Leon, Donna. *A Question of Belief: A Commissario Guido Brunetti Mystery*

Pattison, Eliot. *Bones of the Earth: An Inspector Shan Tao Yun Mystery*

Quinn, Kate. ★*The Huntress*

Remarque, Erich Maria. *The Road Back*

Schlink, Bernhard. *Self's Punishment*

Wambaugh, Joseph. *The New Centurions*

Woodrell, Daniel. *The Maid's Version: A Novel*

Zhou, Haohui. *Death Notice: A Novel*

Justice hustlers [Series]. De Leon, Aya

Justify My Thug: A Novel. Clark, Wahida

Justin de Quincy mysteries [Series]. Penman, Sharon Kay

★*Justine*. Durrell, Lawrence

JUVENILE CORRECTIONAL INSTITUTIONS

Whitehead, Colson. ★*The Nickel Boys: A Novel*

JUVENILE CORRECTIONS

Dugoni, Robert. *The Conviction*

JUVENILE DELINQUENTS

Alsterdal, Tove. *We Know You Remember*

Atkins, Ace. ★*The Heathens*

Higashino, Keigo. *The Miracles of the Namiya General Store*

Oe, Kenzaburo. *Nip the Buds, Shoot the Kids*

JUVENILE DELINQUENTS (BOYS)

Edgerton, Clyde. ★*Walking Across Egypt: A Novel*

JUVENILE DETENTION

Black, Lisa. *Suffer the Children*

JUVENILE JAILS

Engel, Patricia. ★*Infinite Country*

K

K'wan

Animal

Animal II: The Omen

The Diamond Empire

★*Diamonds and Pearl*

The Fix

Gangsta

Gutter

Hoodlum

Lawless
Revelations
Street Dreams

KABUL, AFGHANISTAN
Florio, Gwen. *Silent Hearts*
Hosseini, Khaled. ★*The Kite Runner*
Khadra, Yasmina. *The Swallows of Kabul: A Novel*

Kadare, Ismail
★*The Three-Arched Bridge*

Kadrey, Richard
The Grand Dark
★*Kafka on the Shore*. Murakami, Haruki

Kafka, Franz
★*Collected Stories*
★*The Metamorphosis*
★*The Trial*

Kagen, Lesley
Every Now and Then

KAHLO, FRIDA
Fuentes, Carlos. *The Years with Laura Diaz*

KALAHARI DESERT
Rush, Norman. ★*Mating*
The Kalahari Typing School for Men. McCall Smith, Alexander

KALDIS, ANDREAS (FICTITIOUS CHARACTER)
Siger, Jeffrey. *Mykonos After Midnight: A Chief Inspector Kaldis Mystery*

Kamal, Sheena
It All Falls Down

Kamal, Soniah
Unmarriageable: A Novel

Kamali, Marjan
★*The Stationery Shop*

Kaminsky, Stuart M.
Dancing in the Dark
Murder on the Trans-Siberian Express
To Catch a Spy: A Toby Peters Mystery

Kandasamy, Meena
When I Hit You, Or, a Portrait of the Writer as a Young Wife

Kane, Ben
Spartacus: The Gladiator

Kane, Darby
Pretty Little Wife

Kane, Jessica Francis
Rules for Visiting

KANSAS
Cameron, Peter. *The City of Your Final Destination*
Coldsmith, Don. *Tallgrass: A Novel of the Great Plains*
Durham, David Anthony. ★*Gabriel's Story*
Grecian, Alex. *The Saint of Wolves and Butchers*
Hughes, Langston. *Not Without Laughter*
Lerner, Ben. ★*The Topeka School*
McHugh, Laura. *The Wolf Wants In: A Novel*
Paretsky, Sara. ★*Dead Land*
Parks, Gordon. ★*The Learning Tree*
Robinson, Marilynne. ★*Gilead*
Roy, Lori. *Bent Road*

KANSAS CITY, MISSOURI
Barnett, LaShonda K. *Jam on the Vine*

Flynn, Gillian. *Dark Places*
Gelman, Laurie. *Class Mom: A Novel*
Gelman, Laurie. *You've Been Volunteered: A Class Mom Novel*

Kantaria, Annabel
I Know You: A Novel of Suspense

Kantor, MacKinlay
★*Andersonville*

Kantra, Virginia
Beth & Amy
★*Meg and Jo*

Kaplan, Mitchell James
Rhapsody

Karen Pirie novels [Series]. McDermid, Val

KARRAS, DIMITRI (FICTITIOUS CHARACTER)
Pelecanos, George P. *The Big Blowdown*

KASRILEVKE (IMAGINARY PLACE)
Aleichem, Sholem. *Tevye the Dairyman and the Railroad Stories*
Aleichem, Sholem. *Tevye's Daughters*

Kasulke, Calvin
Several People Are Typing

Kat Campbell mysteries [Series]. Ritter, Todd
Kate Burkholder thrillers [Series]. Castillo, Linda
Kate Clifford novels [Series]. Robb, Candace M.
Kate Hamilton mystery [Series]. Berry, Connie
Kate Henderson novels [Series]. Bradby, Tom
Kate Moore novels [Series]. Pavone, Chris
Kate Reddy novels [Series]. Pearson, Allison
Kate Shugak mysteries [Series]. Stabenow, Dana
Kate Waters novels (Fiona Barton) [Series]. Barton, Fiona

Kate, Jessica
A Girl's Guide to the Outback: A Novel
Katharine Parr, the Sixth Wife. Weir, Alison

KATHARINE, DUCHESS OF LANCASTER
Robinson, Peter. *Children of the Revolution*
Seton, Anya. *Katherine*
Katherine. Seton, Anya

Katsu, Alma
The Deep
The Hunger: A Novel

Katya Hijazi novels [Series]. Ferraris, Zoe

Katz, Erica
The Boys' Club

Katzenbach, John
What Comes Next

Kaufman, Bel
Up the Down Staircase

Kaufman, Charlie
Antkind: A Novel

Kaufman, Sue
Diary of a Mad Housewife

Kawabata, Yasunari
The Sound of the Mountain

Kawaguchi, Toshikazu
Before the Coffee Gets Cold

Kawakami, Mieko
Ms. Ice Sandwich

Kay Scarpetta mysteries [Series]. Cornwell, Patricia Daniels
Kay's Lucky Coin Variety. Choi, Ann Y. K.

Kay, Guy Gavriel
★*A Brightness Long Ago*
★*Children of Earth and Sky*
The Summer Tree
Tigana
Kayode, Femi
★*Lightseekers*
KAZAKHSTAN
Harris, Oliver. *A Shadow Intelligence*
Kazantzakis, Nikos
The Last Temptation of Christ
KECKLEY, ELIZABETH, CA 1818-1907
Chiaverini, Jennifer. *Mrs. Lincoln's Dressmaker: A Novel*
Sandford, John. *Heat Lightning*
The Keep. Egan, Jennifer
Keep Her Safe. Hannah, Sophie
The Keeper. Moor, Jessica
The Keeper of Lost Causes. Adler-Olsen, Jussi
The Keepers of the House. Grau, Shirley Ann
The Keepers: a Mace Reid K-9 Mystery. Burton, Jeffrey B.
Keeping Faith: A Novel. Picoult, Jodi
Keesey, Anna
Little Century: A Novel
Keller, Julia
★*Bone on Bone*
A Killing in the Hills
Kellerman, Jonathan
Bones: An Alex Delaware Novel
Gone
★*Half Moon Bay: A Novel*
Kells, Claire
Vanishing Edge
Kelly, Cathy
Secrets of a Happy Marriage
Kelly, Erin
Broadchurch: A Novel
The Burning Air: A Novel
Watch Her Fall
Kelly, Greta
The Frozen Crown
Kelly, Julia
The Last Dance of the Debutante
The Light Over London
Kelly, Martha Hall
Lilac Girls
Lost Roses: A Novel
KELLY, MICHAEL (FICTITIOUS CHARACTER)
Harvey, Michael T. *The Fifth Floor*
Kelly, Stephen
The Wages of Desire: A World War II Mystery
Kelman, James
How Late It Was, How Late
Kelton, Elmer
Hard Ride
★*The Way of the Coyote*
Kemelman, Harry
Monday the Rabbi Took Off
One Fine Day the Rabbi Bought a Cross

KEMPE, MARGERY
Chancy, Myriam J. A. ★*What Storm, What Thunder*
Sharratt, Mary. *Revelations*
Ken Swift novels [Series]. Dickey, Eric Jerome
Keneally, Thomas
★*The Daughters of Mars*
★*Schindler's List*
Shame and the Captives: A Novel
Woman of the Inner Sea
Kennedy, James
Dare to Know
KENNEDY, JOHN F.
Ellroy, James. *American Tabloid: A Novel*
King, Stephen. *11/22/63*
Wolfe, Paul. *The Lost Diary of M*
Kennedy, Randy
Presidio
Kennedy, William
★*Ironweed: A Novel*
Kenney, John
Talk to Me
KENT, ENGLAND
Bradley, Anna. *A Wicked Way to Win an Earl*
Morton, Kate. *The Distant Hours: A Novel*
Shaw, William. *The Birdwatcher*
Simpson, Dorothy. *Dead by Morning*
Simpson, Dorothy. *Last Seen Alive: A Luke Thanet Mystery*
Simpson, Dorothy. *No Laughing Matter*
Simpson, Dorothy. *Once Too Often: An Inspector Luke Thanet Novel*
Kent, Kathleen
The Burn
The Pledge
KENTUCKY
Berry, Wendell. *Jayber Crow: A Novel*
Berry, Wendell. ★*That Distant Land: The Collected Stories of Wendell Berry*
Bisson, Terry. *Any Day Now*
Fleming, Ian. ★*Goldfinger*
Leonard, Elmore. ★*Raylan*
Mason, Bobbie Ann. *Patchwork*
Mason, Bobbie Ann. *Shiloh and Other Stories*
Morgan, C. E. ★*The Sport of Kings*
Moyes, Jojo. ★*The Giver of Stars: A Novel*
Offutt, Chris. *Country Dark*
Offutt, Chris. ★*The Killing Hills*
Warren, Robert Penn. *Band of Angels*
Warren, Robert Penn. *World Enough and Time: A Romantic Novel*
KENYA
Crompton, Richard. *Hell's Gate: A Novel*
Crompton, Richard. *Hour of the Red God*
Drayson, Nicholas. *A Guide to the Birds of East Africa*
Kimani, Peter. *Dance of the Jakaranda*
Le Carre, John. *The Constant Gardener: A Novel*
McLain, Paula. *Circling the Sun*
Shreve, Anita. *The Last Time They Met: A Novel*
KEPLER, JOHANNES
Freitas, Donna. *The Nine Lives of Rose Napolitano*
Galchen, Rivka. *Everyone Knows Your Mother Is a Witch*

Kepler, Lars
The Sandman
The Kept Woman. Slaughter, Karin
Kerangal, Maylis de
The Heart: A Novel
Kerley, Jack
★*The Death Collectors*
Kerouac, Jack
The Dharma Bums
★*On the Road*
★*Road Novels 1957-1960*
KEROUAC, JACK
Kerouac, Jack. *The Dharma Bums*
Kerouac, Jack. ★*On the Road*
Matthews, Jason. *Red Sparrow: A Novel*
Rice, Anne. *Blood and Gold: Or, the Story of Marius*
Kerr, Laurel
Wild on My Mind
Kerr, Philip
★*Greeks Bearing Gifts: A Bernie Gunther Novel*
★*Metropolis: A Bernie Gunther Novel*
★*Prussian Blue*
Kerry Kilcannon trilogy [Series]. Patterson, Richard North
Kesey, Ken
★*One Flew Over the Cuckoo's Nest*
Sometimes a Great Notion: A Novel
Key to all mythologies [Series]. Franzen, Jonathan
KEY WEST, FLORIDA
Hemingway, Ernest. *To Have and Have Not*
Oliveras, Priscilla. *Anchored Hearts*
The Keys of the Kingdom. Cronin, A. J.
Keys to love [Series]. Oliveras, Priscilla
KGB AGENTS
Lawton, John. *Hammer to Fall*
Smith, Martin Cruz. ★*Gorky Park*
Khadivi, Laleh
★*A Good Country: A Novel*
Khadra, Yasmina
★*Khalil: A Novel*
The Swallows of Kabul: A Novel
Khalfah, Khlid
Death Is Hard Work: A Novel
★*Khalil: a Novel.* Khadra, Yasmina
Khan, Ausma Zehanat
Among the Ruins
The Unquiet Dead
Khan, Vaseem
The Perplexing Theft of the Jewel in the Crown
KHARTOUM, SUDAN
Aboulela, Leila. *Elsewhere, Home*
Khaw, Cassandra
Nothing but Blackened Teeth
Khourdi trilogy [Series]. Khadivi, Laleh
Khoury, Raymond
Empire of Lies
Kibler, Julie
Home for Erring and Outcast Girls
Kick Lannigan [Series]. Cain, Chelsea

★*The Kid: a Novel.* Sapphire
Kidd, Jess
★*Things in Jars*
Kidd, Sue Monk
★*The Book of Longings*
★*The Invention of Wings: A Novel*
★*The Secret Life of Bees*
KIDNAPPERS
Dazieri, Sandrone. *Kill the Father*
Hausmann, Romy. ★*Dear Child*
Lodato, Victor. *Edgar and Lucy: A Novel*
Mosley, Walter. *Charcoal Joe: An Easy Rawlins Mystery*
O'Rawe, Richard. *Northern Heist*
Putney, Mary Jo. *Not Quite a Wife*
Quick, Amanda. *Otherwise Engaged*
Robertson, Michael. *The Baker Street Translation: A Mystery*
KIDNAPPING
Adler-Olsen, Jussi. *The Purity of Vengeance: A Department Q Novel*
Akunin, B. *The Coronation: The Further Adventures of Erast Fandorin*
Bambara, Toni Cade. *Those Bones Are Not My Child*
Bannister, Jo. *Kindred Spirits*
Barr, Nevada. *Destroyer Angel: An Anna Pigeon Novel*
Barton, Fiona. *The Child*
Bear, Elizabeth. *Stone Mad*
Beck, Haylen. *Lost You*
Beverley, Jo. *My Lady Notorious*
Blackmore, R. D. *Lorna Doone: A Romance of Exmoor*
Blake, James Carlos. *The House of Wolfe*
Bouchet, Amanda. ★*A Promise of Fire*
Brett, Simon. *Mrs Pargeter's Principle*
Chase, Loretta Lynda. *Don't Tempt Me*
Child, Lee. ★*Die Trying*
Child, Lee. *The Hard Way*
Cussler, Clive. *The Romanov Ransom*
Dazieri, Sandrone. *Kill the Father*
Deaver, Jeffery. *Edge: A Novel*
Deaver, Jeffery. *The October List*
Dibdin, Michael. *Ratking*
Everett, Percival L. *God's Country*
Faulkner, William. ★*Sanctuary*
Faye, Lyndsay. *Seven for a Secret*
Finder, Joseph. *Buried Secrets*
Fox, Candice. *Gone by Midnight*
Fox, Candice. *Redemption Point*
Galen, Shana. *Third Son's a Charm*
Gay, Roxane. ★*An Untamed State*
Goldman, William. ★*The Princess Bride: S. Morgenstern's Classic Tale of True Love and High Adventure : The*
Groom, Winston. *El Paso: A Novel*
Hart, John. *The Unwilling*
Hayder, Mo. *Gone*
Hiaasen, Carl. *Star Island*
Higgins, Jack. *Touch the Devil*
Jones, Darynda. *A Bad Day for Sunshine*
Kaminsky, Stuart M. *Murder on the Trans-Siberian Express*
Kelton, Elmer. ★*The Way of the Coyote*
Koontz, Dean R. *The Husband*

Lansdale, Joe R. *The Thicket*
Leitch, Will. ★*How Lucky*
Lippman, Laura. *What the Dead Know*
McBain, Ed. *Alice in Jeopardy*
McCall Smith, Alexander. ★*The No. 1 Ladies' Detective Agency*
McEwan, Ian. *The Child in Time*
McKinty, Adrian. ★*The Chain*
Montclair, Allison. *A Rogue's Company*
Ohlsson, Kristina. *Unwanted: A Novel*
Patterson, James. ★*Along Came a Spider: A Novel*
Petrie, Nicholas. *The Wild One*
Picoult, Jodi. *Vanishing Acts: A Novel*
Preston, Douglas J. *The Obsidian Chamber*
Pynchon, Thomas. *Inherent Vice*
Raybourn, Deanna. *A Curious Beginning: A Veronica Speedwell Mystery*
Rendell, Ruth. *The Tree of Hands*
Roanhorse, Rebecca. *Storm of Locusts*
Saunders, George. ★*Tenth of December: Stories*
Saylor, Steven. *Raiders of the Nile: A Novel of the Ancient World*
Scerbanenco, Giorgio. *A Private Venus*
Slaughter, Karin. ★*Undone: A Novel*
Smith, B. J. *Shoot the Dog: A Virgil Cain Mystery*
Smith, Wilbur A. *Monsoon*
Soderberg, Alexander. *The Other Son: A Sophie Brinkmann Novel*
Spencer-Fleming, Julia. *Through the Evil Days: A Clare Fergusson/Russ Van Alstyne Mystery*
Steinhauer, Olen. *An American Spy*
Stirling, S. M. *A Meeting at Corvallis*
Tan, Amy. *The Valley of Amazement*
Tudor, C. J. *The Other People*
Westlake, Donald E. *The Road to Ruin*

KIDNAPPING INVESTIGATION
Cumming, Charles. *A Foreign Country*
George, Elizabeth. *Just One Evil Act*
Hill, Susan. *The Pure in Heart: A Simon Serrailler Crime Novel*
Rader-Day, Lori. *The Day I Died*
Ragan, Theresa. *Deadly Recall*

KIDNAPPING VICTIMS
Cain, Chelsea. *One Kick: A Novel*
Crais, Robert. *A Dangerous Man*
Crouch, Blake. *Dark Matter: A Novel*
Deaver, Jeffery. *The Empty Chair*
Fox, Candice. *Gone by Midnight*
Franklin, Ariana. *The Siege Winter*
Goss, Theodora. *The Sinister Mystery of the Mesmerizing Girl*
Gowdy, Barbara. *Helpless: A Novel*
Hallinan, Timothy. *Fools' River*
Martin, Charles. *The Water Keeper*
McLain, Paula. ★*When the Stars Go Dark: A Novel*
Porter, Henry. *White Hot Silence*
Preston, Douglas J. *The Obsidian Chamber*
Slaughter, Karin. ★*The Last Widow*
Walker, Wendy. *Emma in the Night*

Kiernan, Caitlin R.
The Very Best of Caitlin R. Kiernan
Kiernan, Stephen P.
Universe of Two

KIEV, UKRAINE
Richler, Nancy. *Your Mouth Is Lovely: A Novel*
Stachniak, Eva. *The Chosen Maiden: A Novel*
KIEVAN RUS
Rice, Anne. *The Vampire Armand*
Kilalea, Katharine
Ok, Mr. Field: A Novel
KILCANNON, KERRY (FICTITIOUS CHARACTER)
Patterson, Richard North. *Balance of Power*
Patterson, Richard North. *No Safe Place*
Patterson, Richard North. *Protect and Defend*
KILIMANJARO
Hemingway, Ernest. *The Snows of Kilimanjaro and Other Stories*
★*The Kill Artist: A Novel*. Silva, Daniel
The Kill List. Forsyth, Frederick
Kill Me, Darling. Spillane, Mickey
Kill the Angel. Dazieri, Sandrone
Kill the Father. Dazieri, Sandrone
Kill the King. Dazieri, Sandrone
Killed at the Whim of a Hat. Cotterill, Colin
★*The Killer Angels: A Novel*. Shaara, Michael
The Killer Collective. Eisler, Barry
A Killer Harvest: A Thriller. Cleave, Paul
The Killer Inside Me. Thompson, Jim
Killer Pancake. Davidson, Diane Mott
Killer Research. McKinlay, Jenn
Killer Words. Burns, V. M.
KILLING (ETHICS)
Bausch, Richard. *Peace*
Killing Castro. Block, Lawrence
Killing Commendatore: A Novel. Murakami, Haruki
★*Killing Floor*. Child, Lee
Killing Grounds: A Kate Shugak Mystery. Stabenow, Dana
★*The Killing Hills*. Offutt, Chris
A Killing in the Hills. Keller, Julia
★*The Killing Lessons*. Black, Saul
The Killing Tide: A Brittany Mystery. Bannalec, Jean-Luc
Killing Trail. Mizushima, Margaret
The Killings at Kingfisher Hill. Hannah, Sophie
★*Killshot*. Leonard, Elmore
★*Kim Jiyoung, Born 1982*. Cho, Nam-Ju
Kim, Angie
Miracle Creek
Kim, Bo Young
★*I'm Waiting for You: And Other Stories*
KIM, CHONG-IL, 1942-2011
Aimaq, Jasmine. *The Opium Prince*
Bandi. *The Accusation: Forbidden Stories from Inside North Korea*
Kim, Crystal Hana
If You Leave Me
Kim, Eugenia
The Kinship of Secrets
Kim, Nancy Jooyoun
The Last Story of Mina Lee
Kim, Young-Ha
Diary of a Murderer: And Other Stories
Kimani, Peter
Dance of the Jakaranda

Kimmel, Fran
No Good Asking: A Novel
Kincaid, Jamaica
★*Annie John*
The Autobiography of My Mother
★*Lucy*
See Now Then
*A **Kind** of Freedom*. Sexton, Margaret Wilkerson
*A **Kind** of Grief: A Novel*. Scott, A. D.
*The **Kind** Worth Killing: A Novel*. Swanson, Peter
KINDERGARTEN
Frank, Alli. *Tiny Imperfections*
Gelman, Laurie. *Class Mom: A Novel*
KINDERTRANSPORTS (RESCUE OPERATIONS)
Clayton, Meg Waite. *The Last Train to London*
*The **Kindest** Lie*. Johnson, Nancy
Kindle County novels [Series]. Turow, Scott
KINDNESS
Hession, Ronan. *Leonard and Hungry Paul*
*The **Kindness** of Strangers: A Skip Langdon Novel*. Smith, Julie
*The **Kindness** of Women*. Ballard, J. G.
★*Kindred*. Butler, Octavia E.
Kindred Spirits. Bannister, Jo
★*The **King** at the Edge of the World: Novel*. Phillips, Arthur
*The **King** Is Always Above the People: Stories*. Alarcon, Daniel
*The **King** Must Die*. Renault, Mary
King of Cuba: A Novel. Garcia, Cristina
★*The **King** of Infinite Space*. Faye, Lyndsay
*The **King** of Lies*. Hart, John
King of the Rising. Callender, Kacen
*The **King** of Warsaw*. Twardoch, Szczepan
*The **King's** Justice*. MacNeal, Susan Elia
King, Laurie R.
Castle Shade
King, Lily
Writers & Lovers: A Novel
KING, MARTIN LUTHER, JR, 1929-1968
Barth, John. *The Last Voyage of Somebody the Sailor*
Berry, Steve. ★*The Bishop's Pawn*
Ellroy, James. *The Cold Six Thousand: A Novel*
Gran, Sara. *The Infinite Blacktop: A Novel*
Washington, Bryan. *Lot: Stories*
Whitehead, Colson. ★*The Nickel Boys: A Novel*
King, Queen, Knave: A Novel. Nabokov, Vladimir Vladimirovich
King, Stephen
11/22/63
★*Billy Summers*
★*Carrie*
Cujo
Doctor Sleep: A Novel
Dolores Claiborne
Elevation
End of Watch: A Novel
Finders Keepers
Firestarter
The Girl Who Loved Tom Gordon
If It Bleeds
The Institute

It
★*Misery*
Mr. Mercedes: A Novel
Night Shift
Pet Sematary
Salem's Lot
★*The Shining*
Sleeping Beauties: A Novel
★*The Stand*
Kingdom Come. Ballard, J. G.
*The **Kingdom** of Bones: A Novel*. Gallagher, Stephen
*The **Kingdom** of Copper: A Novel*. Chakraborty, S. A.
Kingdom of Exiles. Martineau, Maxym M.
*The **Kingdom** of Liars*. Martell, Nick
Kingdom of Strangers: A Novel. Ferraris, Zoe
★*The **Kingdoms***. Pulley, Natasha
Kingkiller chronicles [Series]. Rothfuss, Patrick
Kingmaker chronicles [Series]. Bouchet, Amanda
*The **Kingmaker's** Daughter*. Gregory, Philippa
KINGSLEY, MARY HENRIETTA
Bausch, Richard. *Hello to the Cannibals: A Novel*
Seth, Vikram. ★*A Suitable Boy: A Novel*
KINGSMARKHAM (ENGLAND : IMAGINARY PLACE)
Rendell, Ruth. *Simisola*
Rendell, Ruth. *A Sleeping Life*
Kingsolver, Barbara
★*The Bean Trees: A Novel*
★*Flight Behavior*
Pigs in Heaven
★*The Poisonwood Bible: A Novel*
★*Unsheltered*
Kingston cycle series [Series]. Polk, C. L.
Kinsey Millhone mysteries [Series]. Grafton, Sue
Kinship novels [Series]. Montgomery, Jess
*The **Kinship** of Secrets*. Kim, Eugenia
KINSHIP-BASED SOCIETY
Patchett, Ann. ★*State of Wonder: A Novel*
Kintu. Makumbi, Jennifer Nansubuga
KIOWA WOMEN SHAMANS
Momaday, N. Scott. *The Ancient Child: A Novel*
Kirk McGarvey adventures [Series]. Hagberg, David
Kirkpatrick, Jane
One More River to Cross
Kirshenbaum, Binnie
Rabbits for Food
*A **Kiss** Before Dying*. Levin, Ira
★*The **Kiss** Quotient*. Hoang, Helen
Kiss quotient novels [Series]. Hoang, Helen
★*Kiss the Girls and Make Them Cry*. Clark, Mary Higgins
Kiss the Girls: A Novel. Patterson, James
Kissing the Gunner's Daughter. Rendell, Ruth
Kitamura, Katie M.
Intimacies
★*The **Kitchen** God's Wife*. Tan, Amy
★*The **Kite** Runner*. Hosseini, Khaled
★*Klara and the Sun*. Ishiguro, Kazuo
Klay, Phil
★*Missionaries*

Kleeman, Alexandra
  Something New Under the Sun
Kleypas, Lisa
  Cold-Hearted Rake
  ★*Devil in Disguise*
KLONDIKE GOLD FIELDS
  London, Jack. ★*The Call of the Wild*
KLONDIKE RIVER VALLEY, YUKON TERRITORY
  London, Jack. ★*White Fang*
Klune, TJ
  The House in the Cerulean Sea
  ★*Under the Whispering Door*
Knausgaard, Karl Ove
  The Morning Star
Knight, Renee
  The Secretary: A Novel
KNIGHTS AND KNIGHTHOOD
  Cornwell, Bernard. *The Archer's Tale*
  Cornwell, Bernard. *The Winter King: A Novel of Arthur*
  Holland, Cecelia. *Jerusalem*
  Martin, George R. R. ★*A Game of Thrones*
  Martin, George R. R. ★*A Storm of Swords*
  Robb, Candace M. *A Twisted Vengeance*
  Scott, Walter. ★*Ivanhoe*
  Seton, Anya. *Katherine*
  Twain, Mark. ★*A Connecticut Yankee in King Arthur's Court*
  White, T. H. ★*The Once and Future King*
★***Knock** Knock*. Roslund, Anders
Knockemstiff. Pollock, Donald Ray
★*The **Knockout** Queen*. Thorpe, Rufi
Knopf, Chris
  You're Dead
Knots. Farah, Nuruddin
KNOTT, DEBORAH (FICTITIOUS CHARACTER)
  Maron, Margaret. *Up Jumps the Devil*
Knott, Robert
  Robert B. Parker's Buckskin
KNOWLEDGE
  Clarke, Susanna. ★*Piranesi*
  Vinge, Vernor. *A Fire Upon the Deep*
Knowles, John
  ★*A Separate Peace*
Ko, Lisa
  The Leavers
Ko-Eun, Yun
  The Disaster Tourist
Koepp, David
  Cold Storage: A Novel
Koestler, Arthur
  Darkness at Noon
Kohnstamm, Thomas B.
  Lake City
KOKNA (INDIC PEOPLE)
  D'Souza, Tony. *The Konkans*
KOLKATA, INDIA
  Divakaruni, Chitra Banerjee. *Oleander Girl: A Novel*
Konar, Affinity
  Mischling: A Novel

*The **Konkans***. D'Souza, Tony
Koontz, Dean R.
  The Darkest Evening of the Year
  The Husband
  Intensity: A Novel
  Velocity
Kopp sisters novels [Series]. Stewart, Amy
***Kopp** Sisters on the March*. Stewart, Amy
KOREA
  Gendry-Kim, Keum Suk. ★*The Waiting*
  Hahn, Sumi. *The Mermaid from Jeju: A Novel*
  Kim, Crystal Hana. *If You Leave Me*
  Lee, Chang-Rae. ★*The Surrendered*
  Lee, Min Jin. ★*Pachinko*
  Limon, Martin. *The Line*
  Limon, Martin. *War Women*
  Michener, James A. ★*The Bridges at Toko-Ri*
  Seo, Mi-Ae. *The Only Child*
KOREAN AMERICAN FAMILIES
  Cha, Steph. ★*Your House Will Pay*
  Choi, Yoon. *Skinship: Stories*
KOREAN AMERICAN TEENAGE GIRLS
  Park, Ishle Yi. *Angel & Hannah: A Novel in Verse*
KOREAN AMERICAN WOMEN
  Kim, Nancy Jooyoun. *The Last Story of Mina Lee*
  Yun, Jung. *O Beautiful: A Novel*
KOREAN AMERICANS
  Choi, Yoon. *Skinship: Stories*
  Kim, Nancy Jooyoun. *The Last Story of Mina Lee*
  Stephens, Alice. *Famous Adopted People*
KOREAN DEMILITARIZED ZONE
  Limon, Martin. *The Line*
  Limon, Martin. *War Women*
KOREAN WAR VETERANS
  Brown, Taylor. ★*Gods of Howl Mountain: A Novel*
  Burke, James Lee. *Another Kind of Eden*
  Morrison, Toni. *Home*
KOREAN WAR, 1950-1953
  Hahn, Sumi. *The Mermaid from Jeju: A Novel*
  Kim, Crystal Hana. *If You Leave Me*
  Lee, Chang-Rae. ★*The Surrendered*
  Phillips, Jayne Anne. *Lark and Termite: A Novel*
KOREAN WAR, 1950-1953 — AERIAL OPERATIONS, AMERICAN
  Michener, James A. ★*The Bridges at Toko-Ri*
KOREANS
  Choi, Ann Y. K. *Kay's Lucky Coin Variety*
  Seo, Mi-Ae. *The Only Child*
KOREANS IN THE UNITED STATES
  Kim, Eugenia. *The Kinship of Secrets*
KOREATOWN (LOS ANGELES, CALIF.)
  Kim, Nancy Jooyoun. *The Last Story of Mina Lee*
Korelitz, Jean Hanff
  ★*The Plot*
*The **Kortelisy** Escape*. Rosen, Leonard J.
Koryta, Michael
  ★*How It Happened*
  If She Wakes

Kosinski, Jerzy
  ★*Being There*
  The Devil Tree
  ★*The Painted Bird*
KOSINSKI, JERZY
  Clarke, Susanna. ★*Jonathan Strange & Mr. Norrell*
  Kosinski, Jerzy. ★*The Painted Bird*
KOSOVO (REPUBLIC)
  Statovci, Pajtim. *Bolla*
KOSOVO, SERBIA
  Statovci, Pajtim. *Bolla*
  Turow, Scott. *Testimony*
Kotzwinkle, William
  The Bear Went Over the Mountain
Kowal, Mary Robinette
  The Calculating Stars: A Lady Astronaut Novel
  The Fated Sky: A Lady Astronaut Novel
  The Relentless Moon
Kramer and Zondi mysteries [Series]. McClure, James
Kraus, Daniel
  The Autumnal: The Complete Series
Krauss, Nicole
  Forest Dark
  ★*To Be a Man: Stories*
★*The **Kremlin's** Candidate*. Matthews, Jason
Krentz, Jayne Ann
  ★*All the Colors of Night*
  Secret Sisters
  When All the Girls Have Gone
Kress, Nancy
  Beggars in Spain
  If Tomorrow Comes
  Tomorrow's Kin
★*Krik? Krak!* Danticat, Edwidge
KRISTALLNACHT, 1938
  Boschwitz, Ulrich Alexander. *The Passenger: A Novel*
  Epstein, Jennifer Cody. ★*Wunderland: A Novel*
Krivak, Andrew
  The Bear
  The Signal Flame: A Novel
Kroese, Robert
  The Last Iota
Krueger, Paul
  Steel Crow Saga
Krueger, William Kent
  ★*Lightning Strike*
  This Tender Land: A Novel
KRUGER NATIONAL PARK, SOUTH AFRICA
  Francis, Dick. *Smokescreen*
Kuang, R. F.
  ★*The Dragon Republic*
  The Poppy War
Kubica, Mary
  ★*The Other Mrs.*
Kudos. Cusk, Rachel
Kuhn, M. J.
  Among Thieves

Kundera, Milan
  ★*Immortality*
  ★*The Unbearable Lightness of Being*
KUNG FU
  Jin, Yong. *A Hero Born: A Novel*
  Yu, Charles. ★*Interior Chinatown*
Kunsken, Derek
  The House of Styx
Kunzru, Hari
  Red Pill: A Novel
  White Tears
Kupersmith, Violet
  ★*Build Your House Around My Body*
KURDS
  Black, Cara. *Murder in the Rue De Paradis: An Aimee Leduc Investigation*
Kurian, Vera
  Never Saw Me Coming
Kurland St. Mary mysteries [Series]. Lloyd, Catherine
KURSK, RUSSIA
  Robbins, David L. *Last Citadel: A Novel of the Battle of Kursk*
Kurt Wallander mysteries [Series]. Mankell, Henning
Kushner, Rachel
  The Mars Room
Kutsukake, Lynne
  The Translation of Love: A Novel
Kuznetsov, Anatolii Petrovich
  Babi Yar: A Document in the Form of a Novel
Kwan, Kevin
  China Rich Girlfriend
  Crazy Rich Asians
  Rich People Problems
  Sex and Vanity: A Novel
Kwok, Jean
  Searching for Sylvie Lee
Kwon, Yo-Son
  Lemon
Kyoichiro Kaga mysteries [Series]. Higashino, Keigo
KYOTO, JAPAN
  Golden, Arthur. ★*Memoirs of a Geisha: A Novel*
  Spann, Susan. *Blade of the Samurai: A Shinobi Mystery*
  Spann, Susan. ★*Claws of the Cat: A Shinobi Mystery*
  Spann, Susan. *Trial on Mount Koya: A Hiro Hattori Novel*
KYRGYZSTAN
  DeLillo, Don. *Zero K: A Novel*

L

L S D
  Boyle, T. Coraghessan. *Outside Looking In: A Novel*
L S D USE
  Boyle, T. Coraghessan. *Outside Looking In: A Novel*
L'Amour, Louis
  ★*Bendigo Shafter*
  The Californios
  End of the Drive

The Last of the Breed
To the Far Blue Mountains
L. A. quartet [Series]. Ellroy, James
★*L.A. Confidential*. Ellroy, James
L.A. Outlaws: A Novel. Parker, T. Jefferson
★*L.A. Weather*. Escandon, Maria Amparo
Labatut, Benjamin
   When We Cease to Understand the World
LABOR CAMPS
   Steinbeck, John. ★*The Grapes of Wrath*
LABOR DISPUTES — HISTORY
   Pynchon, Thomas. *Against the Day: A Novel*
LABOR MOVEMENT
   Cash, Wiley. *The Last Ballad: A Novel*
   Russell, Mary Doria. *The Women of the Copper Country: A Novel*
   Straley, John. *The Big Both Ways*
LABOR MOVEMENT — HISTORY
   Shreve, Anita. *Sea Glass: A Novel*
LABOR PRODUCTIVITY
   Kasulke, Calvin. *Several People Are Typing*
LABOR UNIONS
   Ellroy, James. *American Tabloid: A Novel*
   Marlantes, Karl. *Deep River*
LABOR UNIONS — CORRUPT PRACTICES
   Paretsky, Sara. *Indemnity Only: A Novel*
Labrava. Leonard, Elmore
Labyrinth. Coulter, Catherine
The Labyrinth of the Spirits. Ruiz Zafon, Carlos
LABYRINTHS
   Borges, Jorge Luis. ★*Collected Fictions*
   Borges, Jorge Luis. *Ficciones*
   Clarke, Susanna. ★*Piranesi*
The Lacemaker. Frantz, Laura
Lacey Flint novels [Series]. Bolton, S. J.
Lacey, Catherine
   ★*Pew: A Novel*
Lackberg, Camilla
   The Golden Cage
   Silver Tears
★*A Ladder to the Sky*. Boyne, John
Ladies of Lantern Street [Series]. Quick, Amanda
The Ladies of the Secret Circus. Sayers, Constance
LADIES-IN-WAITING
   Buckley, Fiona. *The Doublet Affair: A Mystery at Queen Elizabeth I's Court*
   Gregory, Philippa. *The Boleyn Inheritance*
Lady astronaut novels [Series]. Kowal, Mary Robinette
★*Lady Chatterley's Lover*. Lawrence, D. H.
★*Lady Clementine*. Benedict, Marie
Lady Cop Makes Trouble. Stewart, Amy
★*Lady Derring Takes a Lover*. Long, Julie Anne
★*The Lady Has a Past*. Quick, Amanda
The Lady in the Lake. Chandler, Raymond
★*Lady in the Lake: A Novel*. Lippman, Laura
Lady Isabella's Scandalous Marriage. Ashley, Jennifer
★*Lady Joker*. Takamura, Kaoru
The Lady Matador's Hotel: A Novel. Garcia, Cristina
Lady of Perdition. Hambly, Barbara

*The **Lady** of the Rivers*. Gregory, Philippa
*The **Lady** Travelers Guide to Larceny with a Dashing Stranger*. Alexander, Victoria
*The **Lady** Travelers Guide to Scoundrels and Other Gentlemen*. Alexander, Victoria
Lady Travelers Guide [Series]. Alexander, Victoria
★*A **Lady's** Formula for Love*. Everett, Elizabeth
Lady's guide novels [Series]. Collins, Manda
★*The **Lady's** Guide to Celestial Mechanics*. Waite, Olivia
*A **Lady's** Guide to Etiquette and Murder*. Freeman, Dianne
★*A **Lady's** Guide to Mischief and Mayhem*. Collins, Manda
Laetitia Rodd mysteries [Series]. Saunders, Kate
Lafferty, Mur
   Six Wakes
★*The **Lager** Queen of Minnesota*. Stradal, J. Ryan
Lagercrantz, David
   The Girl Who Lived Twice: A Lisbeth Salander Novel
   The Girl Who Takes an Eye for an Eye
LAGOS, NIGERIA
   Abraham, Tola Rotimi. *Black Sunday*
   Braithwaite, Oyinkan. *My Sister, the Serial Killer: A Novel*
   Ehirim, Nnamdi. *Prince of Monkeys*
   Ekwuyasi, Francesca. *Butter Honey Pig Bread: A Novel*
   Igharo, Jane. *The Sweetest Remedy*
LAGUNA PUEBLO RESERVATION, NEW MEXICO
   Silko, Leslie Marmon. ★*Ceremony*
Lahiri, Jhumpa
   The Lowland: A Novel
   ★*The Namesake*
   ★*Whereabouts*
Lai, Larissa
   The Tiger Flu
LAIDLAW, JACK (FICTITIOUS CHARACTER)
   McIlvanney, William. *The Dark Remains: Laidlaw's First Case*
The Lake. Yoshimoto, Banana
Lake City. Kohnstamm, Thomas B.
LAKE DISTRICT (ENGLAND)
   Robertson, Imogen. *Island of Bones*
LAKE HURON REGION
   Munro, Alice. *Dear Life: Stories*
Lake Life. Poissant, David James
Lake News: A Novel. Delinsky, Barbara
★*Lake Success: A Novel*. Shteyngart, Gary
LAKE SUPERIOR
   Sundstol, Vidar. *The Land of Dreams*
LAKES
   Cohen, Tish. *The Summer We Lost Her: A Novel*
   Littlejohn, Emily. *Lost Lake: A Detective Gemma Monroe Mystery*
   Poissant, David James. *Lake Life*
LAKOTA INDIANS
   Barry, Sebastian. ★*A Thousand Moons: A Novel*
   Punke, Michael. *Ridgeline: A Novel*
   Weiden, David L. ★*Winter Counts*
Lalami, Laila
   ★*The Moor's Account: A Novel*
   The Other Americans: A Novel
Lalli, Sonya
   A Holly Jolly Diwali

The Matchmaker's List
Serena Singh Flips the Script
LAMARR, HEDY
    Benedict, Marie. *The Only Woman in the Room*
    Walker, Nico. ★*Cherry: A Novel*
Lambs to the Slaughter. Spencer, Sally
★*Lamentation*. Sansom, C. J.
LANCASHIRE, ENGLAND
    Bolton, S. J. *The Craftsman*
    Griffiths, Elly. *A Dying Fall: A Ruth Galloway Mystery*
    Hurley, Andrew Michael. *Devil's Day*
    Sharratt, Mary. *Daughters of the Witching Hill*
    Smith, Martin Cruz. *Rose*
    Spencer, Sally. *Dead End*
The Land Across. Wolfe, Gene
LAND CLAIMS
    Andrew, Sally. *The Satanic Mechanic: A Tannie Maria Mystery*
    Hay, Elizabeth. *Late Nights on Air*
LAND DEVELOPMENT
    Carr, Robyn. ★*The Wanderer*
The Land of Dreams. Sundstol, Vidar
Land of Wolves. Johnson, Craig
LAND TENURE
    Erdrich, Louise. *Four Souls: A Novel*
LAND USE
    Petersen, Todd Robert. *Picnic in the Ruins*
Landau, Alexis
    Those Who Are Saved
Landfall: a Novel. Mallon, Thomas
LANDFORMS
    Ogden, Aimee. *Sun-Daughters, Sea-Daughters*
Landline. Rowell, Rainbow
LANDLORD AND TENANT
    Blundell, Judy. *The High Season: A Novel*
    Delaney, J. P. *The Girl Before: A Novel*
    Ng, Celeste. ★*Little Fires Everywhere: A Novel*
LANDLORDS
    Marston, Edward. *The Wanton Angel: A Novel*
Landon, Sydney
    Wishing for Us
LANDOWNERS
    Bryant, Niobia. *Christmas with the Billionaire*
    Hart, Erin. *Haunted Ground: A Crime Novel*
Landragin, Alex
    ★*Crossings: Consisting of Three Manuscripts : The Education of a Monster : City of Ghosts : Tales Of*
LANDSCAPE GARDENING
    Roberts, Nora. ★*Under Currents*
Landvik, Lorna
    Chronicles of a Radical Hag: With Recipes
Lane, Byron
    ★*A Star Is Bored*
Langan, Sarah
    Good Neighbors
LANGDON, SKIP (FICTITIOUS CHARACTER)
    Smith, Julie. *82 Desire: A Skip Langdon Novel*
    Smith, Julie. *Crescent City Kill: A Skip Langdon Novel*
    Smith, Julie. *House of Blues*

    Smith, Julie. *Jazz Funeral*
    Smith, Julie. *The Kindness of Strangers: A Skip Langdon Novel*
    Smith, Julie. *New Orleans Beat*
LANGE, DOROTHEA
    Darznik, Jasmin. *The Bohemians*
    Howarth, Paul. *Dust off the Bones*
Lange, Tracey
    ★*We Are the Brennans*
LANGUAGE AND CULTURE
    Asim, Jabari. ★*Yonder*
    Williams, Pip. *The Dictionary of Lost Words*
LANGUAGE AND LANGUAGES
    DeLillo, Don. *The Names*
    Stephenson, Neal. *The Rise and Fall of D.O.D.O.: A Novel*
    Thammavongsa, Souvankham. *How to Pronounce Knife: Stories*
    Winch, Tara June. *The Yield*
LANGUAGE AND LANGUAGES — GRAMMARS
    Schine, Cathleen. *The Grammarians*
LANGUAGE AND TECHNOLOGY
    Graedon, Alena. *The Word Exchange: A Novel*
The Language of Flowers: A Novel. Diffenbaugh, Vanessa
★*Lanny: a Novel*. Porter, Max
Lansdale, Joe R.
    The Bottoms
    Devil Red
    Edge of Dark Water
    Honky Tonk Samurai
    More Better Deals
    ★*Paradise Sky*
    Sunset and Sawdust
    The Thicket
The Lantern Men: A Dr. Ruth Galloway Mystery. Griffiths, Elly
LAOS
    Cotterill, Colin. *The Coroner's Lunch*
    Cotterill, Colin. *Disco for the Departed*
    Cotterill, Colin. *Don't Eat Me*
    Cotterill, Colin. *The Second Biggest Nothing*
    Cotterill, Colin. *Slash and Burn: A Dr. Siri Mystery Set in Laos*
    Yoon, Paul. ★*Run Me to Earth: A Novel*
LARGE FAMILIES
    Lessing, Doris May. ★*The Fifth Child*
    Osondu, E. C. *This House Is Not for Sale: A Novel*
The Largesse of the Sea Maiden: Stories. Johnson, Denis
Larison, John
    Whiskey When We're Dry
Lark and Termite: A Novel. Phillips, Jayne Anne
Larkin, Allie
    The People We Keep
Larkwood, A. K.
    The Unspoken Name
★*Larose*. Erdrich, Louise
Larsen, Nella
    Passing
Larsen, Reif
    I Am Radar: A Novel
Larsson, Stieg
    ★*The Girl Who Kicked the Hornet's Nest*
    The Girl Who Played with Fire

The Girl with the Dragon Tattoo
LAS VEGAS, NEVADA
 Bock, Charles. *Beautiful Children: A Novel*
 Diofebi, Dario. *Paradise, Nevada*
 Goldberg, Tod. *Gangsterland: A Novel*
 Pufahl, Shannon. *On Swift Horses*
 Puzo, Mario. *The Last Don*
 Randisi, Robert J. *Hey There (You with the Gun in Your Hand): A Rat Pack Mystery*
 Tran, Vu. *Dragonfish: A Novel*
 Vlautin, Willy. *Don't Skip Out on Me*
Lasdun, James
 Afternoon of a Faun: A Novel
Laskowski, Tara
 The Mother Next Door
*The **Last** Ballad: A Novel*. Cash, Wiley
Last binding [Series]. Marske, Freya
*The **Last** Chance Library*. Sampson, Freya
*The **Last** Chance Llama Ranch*. Fields, Hilary
*The **Last** Child*. Hart, John
*The **Last** Chronicle of Barset*. Trollope, Anthony
Last Citadel: A Novel of the Battle of Kursk. Robbins, David L.
*The **Last** Confession of Thomas Hawkins*. Hodgson, Antonia
*The **Last** Cowboys of San Geronimo*. Stansel, Ian
*The **Last** Dance of the Debutante*. Kelly, Julia
★*Last Day*. Rice, Luanne
*The **Last** Days of Cafe Leila*. Bijan, Donia
*The **Last** Days of Krypton*. Anderson, Kevin J.
★*The **Last** Detective*. Lovesey, Peter
*The **Last** Dickens: A Novel*. Pearl, Matthew
Last Ditch mysteries [Series]. McPherson, Catriona
*The **Last** Don*. Puzo, Mario
*The **Last** Enchantment*. Stewart, Mary
Last Evenings on Earth. Bolano, Roberto
*The **Last** Exiles*. Shin, Ann
Last Flight. Clark, Julie
Last Friends. Gardam, Jane
*The **Last** Full Measure*. Shaara, Jeff
*The **Last** Ghost Dancer*. Bender, Tony
*The **Last** Good Chance*. Barbash, Tom
*The **Last** Good Kiss: A Novel*. Crumley, James
*The **Last** Graduate: A Novel*. Novik, Naomi
*The **Last** Great Road Bum*. Tobar, Hector
*The **Last** Hero: A Discworld Fable*. Pratchett, Terry
Last hours [Series]. Walters, Minette
*The **Last** Hours: A Novel*. Walters, Minette
*The **Last** House on Needless Street*. Ward, Catriona
Last hundred years trilogy [Series]. Smiley, Jane
*The **Last** Iota*. Kroese, Robert
*The **Last** Judgement*. Pears, Iain
*The **Last** Juror*. Grisham, John
*The **Last** Kind Words*. Piccirilli, Tom
*The **Last** Kingdom: A Novel*. Cornwell, Bernard
*The **Last** List of Miss Judith Kratt*. Bobotis, Andrea
Last Man in Tower: A Novel. Adiga, Aravind
*The **Last** Midwife*. Dallas, Sandra
Last Night. Salter, James
*The **Last** Nude*. Avery, Ellis

★*The **Last** Odyssey*. Rollins, James
*The **Last** of Her Kind: A Novel*. Nunez, Sigrid
*The **Last** of the Breed*. L'Amour, Louis
*The **Last** of the Just: A Novel*. Schwarz-Bart, Andre
*The **Last** of the Mohicans: A Narrative of 1757*. Cooper, James Fenimore
*The **Last** of the Wine*. Renault, Mary
★*Last Orders: A Novel*. Swift, Graham
★*The **Last** Painting of Sara De Vos*. Smith, Dominic
*The **Last** Passenger*. Finch, Charles
*The **Last** Place You Look*. Lepionka, Kristen
*The **Last** Report on the Miracles at Little No Horse*. Erdrich, Louise
*The **Last** Resort*. Stapley, Marissa
The **last** roundup (Roddy Doyle) [Series]. Doyle, Roddy
*The **Last** Runaway*. Chevalier, Tracy
*The **Last** Second*. Coulter, Catherine
Last Seen Alive: A Luke Thanet Mystery. Simpson, Dorothy
★*Last Seen Leaving: A Novel*. Braffet, Kelly
Last Stories. Trevor, William
Last Stories and Other Stories. Vollmann, William T.
*The **Last** Story of Mina Lee*. Kim, Nancy Jooyoun
Last Summer at the Golden Hotel. Friedland, Elyssa
*The **Last** Suppers*. Davidson, Diane Mott
Last Tang Standing. Ho, Lauren
*The **Last** Temptation of Christ*. Kazantzakis, Nikos
*The **Last** Time I Lied: A Novel*. Sager, Riley
*The **Last** Time I Saw You*. Constantine, Liv
*The **Last** Time They Met: A Novel*. Shreve, Anita
*The **Last** Tourist*. Steinhauer, Olen
*The **Last** Train to London*. Clayton, Meg Waite
*The **Last** Trial*. Turow, Scott
*The **Last** Tudor*. Gregory, Philippa
★*The **Last** Tycoon: An Unfinished Novel*. Fitzgerald, F. Scott
★*The **Last** Unicorn*. Beagle, Peter S.
*The **Last** Voyage of Somebody the Sailor*. Barth, John
*The **Last** Watch*. Dewes, J. S.
*The **Last** Watchman of Old Cairo: A Novel*. Lukas, Michael David
*The **Last** Werewolf*. Duncan, Glen
The **last** werewolf trilogy [Series]. Duncan, Glen
*The **Last** Whisper in the Dark: A Novel*. Piccirilli, Tom
★*The **Last** Widow*. Slaughter, Karin
*The **Last** Wife*. Hamilton, Karen
Last Woman Standing. Gentry, Amy
*The **Last** Word and Other Stories*. Greene, Graham
LAST WORDS
 Adkins, Mary. *When You Read This*
 Gohlke, Cathy. *Promise Me This*
 Hamilton, Karen. *The Last Wife*
 Leon, Donna. *Trace Elements*
Laszlo Kreizler mysteries [Series]. Carr, Caleb
Late City. Butler, Robert Olen
Late Nights on Air. Hay, Elizabeth
*The **Late** Show*. Connelly, Michael
Later Short Stories, 1888-1903. Chekhov, Anton Pavlovich
*The **Lathe** of Heaven*. Le Guin, Ursula K.
LATIN AMERICA
 Allende, Isabel. *Of Love and Shadows*
 Bolano, Roberto. *Amulet*
 Garcia Marquez, Gabriel. ★*Love in the Time of Cholera*

Garcia Marquez, Gabriel. ★*One Hundred Years of Solitude*
Garcia, Cristina. *The Lady Matador's Hotel: A Novel*
LATIN AMERICANS
Bolano, Roberto. *Amulet*
LATIN AMERICANS IN EUROPE
Garcia Marquez, Gabriel. ★*Strange Pilgrims: Twelve Stories*
Latitudes of Longing. Swarup, Shubhangi
Lattari, Katie
Dark Things I Adore
LATVIA
Mankell, Henning. *The Dogs of Riga*
Lau, Jackie
Donut Fall in Love
★*The Laughing* Policeman. Sjowall, Maj
Laukkanen, Owen
Deception Cove
Gale Force
Lone Jack Trail
Laureano, C. E.
★*The Saturday Night Supper Club*
Lauren Laurano mysteries [Series]. Scoppettone, Sandra
Lauren, Christina
Dating You / Hating You
In a Holidaze
Roomies
The Soulmate Equation
Laurence Bartram novels [Series]. Speller, Elizabeth
Laurens, Stephanie
The Pursuits of Lord Kit Cavanaugh
LAVEAU, MARIE
Rhodes, Jewell Parker. *Voodoo Dreams: A Novel of Marie Laveau*
Lavender Blue Murder. Childs, Laura
LAW
Clark, Martin. *The Substitution Order*
LAW CLERKS
Abrams, Stacey. *While Justice Sleeps: A Novel*
Meltzer, Brad. *The Tenth Justice*
Stone, Nick. *The Verdict*
LAW ENFORCEMENT
Doiron, Paul. ★*Dead by Dawn*
Doiron, Paul. *One Last Lie*
Johnson, Craig. *Daughter of the Morning Star*
Johnson, Craig. *Next to Last Stand*
Leonard, Elmore. *Charlie Martz and Other Stories: The Unpublished Stories*
Leonard, Elmore. *When the Women Come Out to Dance: Stories*
LAW FIRMS
Andrews, Mary Kay. *Sunset Beach*
Goldman, Matt. *The Shallows*
Grisham, John. ★*The Firm*
Katz, Erica. *The Boys' Club*
Paretsky, Sara. *Shell Game*
Sanders, Lawrence. *The Tenth Commandment: A Novel*
Scottoline, Lisa. *Feared*
Stone, Nick. *The Verdict*
Woods, Stuart. *Below the Belt*
Woods, Stuart. *A Delicate Touch*
Woods, Stuart. *Fast & Loose*

★*The Law* of Innocence: A Novel. Connelly, Michael
LAW STUDENTS
Schlink, Bernhard. *The Reader: A Novel*
Lawler, Liz
Don't Wake Up
Lawless. K'wan
★*Lawn* Boy: A Novel. Evison, Jonathan
The Lawrence Browne Affair. Sebastian, Cat
Lawrence, D. H.
★*Lady Chatterley's Lover*
Sons and Lovers
Women in Love
LAWRENCE, D. H.
MacLeod, Alison. *Tenderness*
Lawrence, David
The Dead Sit Round in a Ring
LAWRENCE, T. E.
Russell, Mary Doria. *Dreamers of the Day: A Novel*
Lawson, Mary
Crow Lake
Lawton, John
Hammer to Fall
Then We Take Berlin
LAWYERS
Arvin, Reed. *Blood of Angels: A Novel*
Atkins, Ace. *Wicked City*
Atkinson, Kate. ★*Case Histories*
Barth, John. ★*The Floating Opera*
Begley, Louis. *About Schmidt*
Camus, Albert. ★*The Fall*
Connelly, Michael. *The Gods of Guilt*
Connelly, Michael. ★*The Law of Innocence: A Novel*
Dickens, Charles. ★*Bleak House*
Dugoni, Robert. *The Conviction*
Ferris, Joshua. *The Unnamed*
Gaddis, William. *A Frolic of His Own: A Novel*
Galsworthy, John. ★*The Forsyte Saga*
Gardam, Jane. *Last Friends*
Gardam, Jane. *Old Filth*
Greaves, Chuck. *Hush Money: A Mystery*
Grippando, James. *The Girl in the Glass Box*
Grisham, John. ★*The Firm*
Grisham, John. ★*The Guardians*
Hall, Alexis. ★*Boyfriend Material*
Harrington, Anna. *An Extraordinary Lord*
Hart, John. *The King of Lies*
Herrera, Adriana. *American Love Story*
Irvin, Kelly. *Tell Her No Lies*
Klune, TJ. ★*Under the Whispering Door*
McDermid, Val. *How the Dead Speak: A Tony Hill and Carol Jordan Novel*
McFarlane, Mhairi. *If I Never Met You: A Novel*
Morgan Jones, Chris. *The Silent Oligarch*
Nava, Michael. ★*Carved in Bone*
Oates, Joyce Carol. *The Falls: A Novel*
Patterson, Richard North. *Eclipse*
Pava, Sergio de la. *A Naked Singularity*
Pearl, Matthew. *The Poe Shadow: A Novel*

Perry, Anne. ★*Death with a Double Edge: A Daniel Pitt Novel*
Perry, Anne. *One Fatal Flaw: A Daniel Pitt Novel*
Pryor, Mark. *Hollow Man*
Putnam, Jonathan F. *These Honored Dead*
Riley, Vanessa. ★*An Earl, the Girl, and a Toddler*
Roberts, Nora. ★*Under Currents*
Robertson, Michael. *The Brothers of Baker Street*
Robertson, Michael. *Moriarty Returns a Letter: A Baker Street Mystery*
Rosenfelt, David. ★*Dog Eat Dog*
Sandford, John. ★*Rules of Prey*
Sansom, C. J. *Revelation*
Sansom, C. J. *Tombland*
Saunders, Kate. *The Secrets of Wishtide*
Shupe, Joanna. *The Rogue of Fifth Avenue*
Silber, Joan. *Secrets of Happiness*
Slaughter, Karin. ★*Pretty Girls: A Novel*
Snow, C. P. ★*Strangers and Brothers*
Turow, Scott. *Testimony*
Winer, Jeanne. *Her Kind of Case*
Winters, Ben H. *The Quiet Boy*
Woods, Stuart. *Stealth*
Zapata, Mike. *The Lost Book of Adana Moreau*
The **Lay** of the Land. Ford, Richard
Layden, Emily
   All Girls
Laymon, Kiese
   Long Division
Layne, Lauren
   Passion on Park Avenue
Le Carre, John
   Agent Running in the Field
   The Constant Gardener: A Novel
   ★*A Delicate Truth*
   ★*The Honourable Schoolboy*
   A Most Wanted Man: A Novel
   ★*Our Kind of Traitor: A Novel*
   Smiley's People
   The Spy Who Came in from the Cold
   The Tailor of Panama
   ★*Tinker, Tailor, Soldier, Spy*
Le Guin, Ursula K.
   The Beginning Place
   The Birthday of the World: And Other Stories
   ★*The Dispossessed: An Ambiguous Utopia*
   Four Ways to Forgiveness
   The Lathe of Heaven
   ★*The Left Hand of Darkness*
   Orsinian Tales
   The Other Wind
   The Telling
LEADERSHIP
   Rice, Anne. *Blood Communion: A Tale of Prince Lestat*
   Shaara, Jeff. *The Steel Wave: A Novel of World War II*
LEADERSHIP IN MEN
   Wouk, Herman. ★*The Caine Mutiny: A Novel of World War II*
LEADERSHIP IN WOMEN
   Gaines, Ernest J. ★*The Autobiography of Miss Jane Pittman*

Twain, Mark. *Personal Recollections of Joan of Arc*
Leading Men: A Novel. Castellani, Christopher
Leaf Storm, and Other Stories. Garc{@237}a M{@225}rquez, Gabriel
League of extraordinary women novels [Series]. Dunmore, Evie
League of scoundrels [Series]. Sullivan, Emily
Lean Fall Stand. McGregor, Jon
LEARNING AND SCHOLARSHIP
   Enard, Mathias. *Compass*
★*The **Learning** Tree*. Parks, Gordon
LEARY, TIMOTHY
   Boyle, T. Coraghessan. *Outside Looking In: A Novel*
   Sansom, C. J. *Tombland*
LEATHER LIFESTYLE (SEXUALITY)
   Hall, Alexis. *For Real*
Leatherstocking tales [Series]. Cooper, James Fenimore
Leave Me Breathless. Malpas, Jodi Ellen
Leave Me: A Novel. Forman, Gayle
★**Leave** the World Behind: A Novel. Alam, Rumaan
The **Leavers**. Ko, Lisa
Leaving Cecil Street: A Novel. McKinney-Whetstone, Diane
LEAVING HOME
   Persaud, Ingrid. *Love After Love: A Novel*
Leaving Lucy Pear. Solomon, Anna
Leaving Time: A Novel. Picoult, Jodi
Leavitt, David
   ★*Shelter in Place*
   The Two Hotel Francforts: A Novel
LEBANESE AMERICANS
   Dimechkie, Karim. *Lifted by the Great Nothing*
LEBANON
   Alameddine, Rabih. *An Unnecessary Woman*
   Dimechkie, Karim. *Lifted by the Great Nothing*
   Hage, Rawi. *Beirut Hellfire Society: A Novel*
   Hage, Rawi. *De Niro's Game*
Lebbon, Tim
   Eden
Lebrecht, Norman
   The Song of Names
Leckie, Ann
   Ancillary Justice
   Ancillary Mercy
   Ancillary Sword
   Provenance
   ★*The Raven Tower*
LEDUC, AIMEE (FICTITIOUS CHARACTER)
   Black, Cara. *Murder in the Bastille*
   Black, Cara. *Murder in the Marais*
   Black, Cara. *Murder in the Rue De Paradis: An Aimee Leduc Investigation*
Lee family saga [Series]. Woods, Stuart
Lee Isaacs [Series]. Winer, Jeanne
Lee, Andrea
   Red Island House
Lee, Chang-Rae
   ★*My Year Abroad*
   ★*On Such a Full Sea*
   ★*The Surrendered*

Lee, Fonda

★*Jade City*

Jade War

Lee, Harper

★*Go Set a Watchman*

★*To Kill a Mockingbird*

Lee, Ji-Min

The Starlet and the Spy

Lee, Jonathan

The Great Mistake

Lee, Min Jin

★*Pachinko*

Lee, Patrick

Runner

LEE, ROBERT E (ROBERT EDWARD), 1807-1870

Shaara, Jeff. *Gone for Soldiers*

Lee, Yoon Ha

Ninefox Gambit

Raven Stratagem

Revenant Gun

LEEDS, ENGLAND

Atkinson, Kate. *Started Early, Took My Dog*

Nickson, Chris. *Come the Fear*

Left at the altar [Series]. Malone, Minx

Left for Dead. Parnell, Sean

★*The Left Hand of Darkness*. Le Guin, Ursula K.

Left Neglected: A Novel. Genova, Lisa

★*The Left-Handed* Twin. Perry, Thomas

Lefteri, Christy

The Beekeeper of Aleppo: A Novel

The Leftovers. Perrotta, Tom

LEGACIES

Smith, Zadie. ★*Grand Union: Stories*

Legacy of faith novels [Series]. Hatcher, Robin Lee

A Legacy of Murder. Berry, Connie

Legacy of the mercenary king novels [Series]. Martell, Nick

LEGAL ASSISTANCE TO POOR PEOPLE

Grippando, James. *The Girl in the Glass Box*

LEGAL STORIES

Copperman, E. J. *Judgment at Santa Monica*

Kim, Angie. *Miracle Creek*

Nava, Michael. ★*Carved in Bone*

Whitlow, Robert. *A Time to Stand*

Winer, Jeanne. *Her Kind of Case*

Legal Tender. Scottoline, Lisa

LEGAL THRILLERS

Arvin, Reed. *Blood of Angels: A Novel*

Burnet, Graeme Macrae. *His Bloody Project: Documents Relating to the Case of Roderick Macrae*

Cavanagh, Steve. *Thirteen*

Clark, Marcia. *Final Judgment*

Clark, Martin. *The Substitution Order*

Connelly, Michael. *The Brass Verdict: A Novel*

Connelly, Michael. *The Fifth Witness*

Connelly, Michael. *The Gods of Guilt*

Connelly, Michael. ★*The Law of Innocence: A Novel*

Connelly, Michael. *The Lincoln Lawyer: A Novel*

Cook, Thomas H. *Sandrine's Case*

Dow, David R. *Confessions of an Innocent Man*

Dugoni, Robert. *The Conviction*

Dugoni, Robert. *Murder One*

Fairstein, Linda A. *Blood Oath*

Fairstein, Linda A. *Entombed*

Finder, Joseph. ★*Judgment*

French, Nicci. ★*House of Correction*

Grippando, James. *The Girl in the Glass Box*

Grisham, John. *The Client*

Grisham, John. ★*The Firm*

Grisham, John. ★*The Guardians*

Grisham, John. ★*The Pelican Brief*

Grisham, John. *A Time to Kill*

Hart, John. *The King of Lies*

Iles, Greg. *The Bone Tree: A Novel*

Iles, Greg. *Mississippi Blood: A Novel*

Iles, Greg. *Natchez Burning: A Novel*

Katz, Erica. *The Boys' Club*

Lescroart, John T. *Guilt*

Meltzer, Brad. *The Tenth Justice*

Meltzer, Brad. *The Zero Game*

Moore, Graham. *The Holdout: A Novel*

Parks, Brad. *Say Nothing: A Novel*

Patterson, Richard North. *Balance of Power*

Patterson, Richard North. *Dark Lady*

Patterson, Richard North. *Eclipse*

Persson Giolito, Malin. *Beyond All Reasonable Doubt: A Novel*

Scottoline, Lisa. *Feared*

Scottoline, Lisa. *Legal Tender*

Silver, Elizabeth L. *The Execution of Noa P. Singleton: A Novel*

Stone, Nick. *The Verdict*

Turow, Scott. *The Last Trial*

Turow, Scott. *Presumed Innocent*

Turow, Scott. *Testimony*

Twain, Mark. *Pudd'nhead Wilson ;: And, Those Extraordinary Twins*

Vaughan, Sarah. ★*Anatomy of a Scandal: A Novel*

Winters, Ben H. *The Quiet Boy*

Legends of the condor heroes [Series]. Jin, Yong

Legends of the North Cascades: A Novel. Evison, Jonathan

Legends of the realm [Series]. Locke, Thomas

LEGISLATORS

Patterson, Richard North. *No Safe Place*

Lehane, Dennis

★*The Given Day*

Live by Night

★*Mystic River*

Shutter Island

Since We Fell

World Gone By: A Novel

Leigh, Eva

Forever Your Earl

Scandal Takes the Stage

Temptations of a Wallflower

Leilani, Raven

★*Luster*

LEISURE CLASS

Ford, Ford Madox. ★*The Good Soldier: A Tale of Passion*

Leitch, Will
★*How Lucky*
Leithauser, Brad
The Promise of Elsewhere
Lelchuk, Saul
Save Me from Dangerous Men: A Novel
Lem, Stanislaw
His Master's Voice
★*Solaris*
Lemon. Kwon, Yo-Son
The *Lemon* Orchard. Rice, Luanne
LEMPICKA, TAMARA DE
Avery, Ellis. *The Last Nude*
Sofer, Dalia. *The Septembers of Shiraz*
★*Lent*. Walton, Jo
Leo Demidov thrillers [Series]. Smith, Tom Rob
Leon, Donna
Beastly Things: A Commissario Guido Brunetti Mystery
Drawing Conclusions: A Commissario Guido Brunetti Mystery
Falling in Love: A Commissario Guido Brunetti Mystery
The Golden Egg
A Question of Belief: A Commissario Guido Brunetti Mystery
Trace Elements
★*Transient Desires*
Uniform Justice
Unto Us a Son Is Given
Leonard and Hungry Paul. Hession, Ronan
Leonard, Elmore
★*Be Cool: Everyone Is Looking for the Next Big Hit*
Charlie Martz and Other Stories: The Unpublished Stories
★*The Complete Western Stories of Elmore Leonard.*
★*Get Shorty*
Glitz
The Hot Kid
★*Killshot*
Labrava
Pagan Babies
★*Raylan*
Rum Punch
Tishomingo Blues: A Novel
When the Women Come Out to Dance: Stories
LEONARDO DA VINCI
Brown, Dan. *The Da Vinci Code*
Endo, Shusaku. *Deep River*
Morelli, Laura. *The Stolen Lady*
Sterling, Erin. *The Ex Hex*
Leonid McGill mysteries [Series]. Mosley, Walter
Leonora in the Morning Light. Carter, Michaela
The *Leopard*. Nesbo, Jo
LEOPARD
Harrigan, Stephen. *The Leopard Is Loose: A Novel*
The *Leopard* Is Loose: A Novel. Harrigan, Stephen
Lepionka, Kristen
The Last Place You Look
Once You Go This Far: A Mystery
Lerner, Ben
★*The Topeka School*
★*Les* Miserables. Hugo, Victor

LESBIAN COUPLES
Picoult, Jodi. *Sing You Home: A Novel*
LESBIAN TEENAGERS
Brown, Rita Mae. ★*Rubyfruit Jungle*
Joseph, Fabiola. *Niya: Rainbow Dreams*
LESBIANS
Anshaw, Carol. *Carry the One*
Arnett, Kristen N. *With Teeth: A Novel*
Austin, Emily. *Everyone in This Room Will Someday Be Dead*
Avery, Ellis. *The Last Nude*
Barnes, Djuna. ★*Nightwood*
Barnett, LaShonda K. *Jam on the Vine*
Bellefleur, Alexandria. *Written in the Stars*
Bledsoe, Lucy Jane. *The Big Bang Symphony: A Novel of Antarctica*
Brayden, Melissa. *First Position*
Brown, Rita Mae. *Six of One*
Chambers, Clare. *Small Pleasures*
Cole, Alyssa. *How to Find a Princess*
Danforth, Emily M. *Plain Bad Heroines*
De Robertis, Carolina. *Cantoras*
De Robertis, Carolina. *The Gods of Tango*
Dennis-Benn, Nicole. *Here Comes the Sun*
Dennis-Benn, Nicole. ★*Patsy: A Novel*
Flagg, Fannie. ★*Fried Green Tomatoes at the Whistle Stop Cafe*
Gaspar de Alba, Alicia. *Desert Blood: The Juarez Murders*
Gregory, Daryl. *Afterparty*
Manning, Corinne. *We Had No Rules: Stories*
Masad, Ilana. *All My Mother's Lovers: A Novel*
Okparanta, Chinelo. ★*Under the Udala Trees*
Pastan, Rachel. *In the Field*
Piercy, Marge. *Gone to Soldiers: A Novel*
Rogers, Morgan Callan. ★*Honey Girl*
Sarton, May. *A Reckoning: A Novel*
Scoppettone, Sandra. *Everything You Have Is Mine*
Scoppettone, Sandra. *My Sweet Untraceable You*
Vo, Nghi. ★*The Chosen and the Beautiful*
LESBIANS — RIGHTS
Picoult, Jodi. *Sing You Home: A Novel*
LESBIANS — SEXUALITY
Brown, Rita Mae. ★*Rubyfruit Jungle*
Lescroart, John T.
Guilt
Leslie: a Novel. Tyree, Omar
★*Less*. Greer, Andrew Sean
The *Less* Dead. Mina, Denise
★*Less* Than a Treason. Stabenow, Dana
Less Than Hero: A Novel. Browne, S. G.
Lessing, Doris May
★*The Fifth Child*
★*The Golden Notebook*
A Proper Marriage
The Sweetest Dream
★*The Lesson*. Turnbull, Cadwell
Lesson in Red. Hummel, Maria
LESTAT (FICTITIOUS CHARACTER)
Rice, Anne. *Blackwood Farm*
Rice, Anne. *Blood and Gold: Or, the Story of Marius*
Rice, Anne. *Blood Canticle*

Rice, Anne. *Prince Lestat: The Vampire Chronicles*
Rice, Anne. ★*The Queen of the Damned*
Rice, Anne. *The Tale of the Body Thief*
Rice, Anne. ★*The Vampire Lestat*
Let Justice Descend. Black, Lisa
Let Me Be Frank with You. Ford, Richard
★*Let That Be the Reason*. Stringer, Vickie M.
Let that be the reason novels [Series]. Stringer, Vickie M.
Let the Dead Keep Their Secrets. Simpson, Rosemary
Let the Right One In. Ajvide Lindqvist, John
Let's get mythical [Series]. Heger, Amanda
Lethal White. Galbraith, Robert
Lethem, Jonathan
   Chronic City
   Dissident Gardens
   ★*Motherless Brooklyn*
LETTER CARRIERS
   Dykes, Amanda. *Whose Waves These Are*
Letter from Home. Hart, Carolyn G.
LETTER WRITING
   Bauer, Carlene. ★*Frances and Bernard*
   Boyle, Elizabeth. *And the Miss Ran Away with the Rake*
   Christie, Agatha. ★*The A B C Murders*
   Cisneros, Sandra. *Martita, I Remember You: Martita, Te Recuerdo*
   El-Mohtar, Amal. ★*This Is How You Lose the Time War*
   Escobar, Mario. *The Librarian of Saint-Malo: A Novel*
   Higashino, Keigo. *The Miracles of the Namiya General Store*
   Higgins, Kristan. ★*Pack up the Moon*
   Kutsukake, Lynne. *The Translation of Love: A Novel*
   Preston, Douglas J. *Verses for the Dead*
   Robertson, Michael. *The Baker Street Letters*
   Robertson, Michael. *Moriarty Returns a Letter: A Baker Street Mystery*
   Shaffer, Mary Ann. *The Guernsey Literary and Potato Peel Pie Society*
   Simenon, Georges. *Maigret and the Black Sheep*
   Sthers, Amanda. *Holy Lands: A Novel*
   Toews, Miriam. *Fight Night*
   Yourcenar, Marguerite. ★*Memoirs of Hadrian: And Reflections on the Composition of Memoirs of Hadrian*
LETTERING
   Clayborn, Kate. *Love Lettering*
LETTERS
   Berry, Steve. ★*The Malta Exchange: A Novel*
   Fuentes, Carlos. *The Eagle's Throne: A Novel*
   Gaynor, Hazel. *Three Words for Goodbye*
   Goldin, Megan. *The Night Swim*
   Hart, Carolyn G. *Letter from Home*
   Hornby, Gill. *Miss Austen*
   O'Connor, Flannery. ★*Collected Works*
   Phillips, Christi. *The Rossetti Letter: A Novel*
   Schumacher, Julie. *Dear Committee Members*
   West, Nathanael. *Novels and Other Writings*
Letters from Paris. Blackwell, Juliet
LETTING GO (PSYCHOLOGY)
   Bird, Sarah. *The Gap Year: A Novel*
LEUKEMIA
   Cleave, Chris. *Gold*

Leverage in Death: An Eve Dallas Novel. Robb, J. D.
Levi's Will: A Novel. Cramer, W. Dale
★*Leviathan*. Auster, Paul
★*Leviathan Wakes*. Corey, James S. A.
Levin, Adam
   Bubblegum
Levin, Ira
   The Boys from Brazil: A Novel
   A Kiss Before Dying
   ★*Rosemary's Baby: A Novel*
   ★*The Stepford Wives: A Novel*
Levine, David D.
   Arabella of Mars
LEVITATION
   Temple, Emily. *The Lightness*
Levy, Andrea
   The Long Song
   Small Island
Levy, Deborah
   Hot Milk: A Novel
   Swimming Home: A Novel
Lew Archer novels [Series]. Macdonald, Ross
Lewis trilogy [Series]. May, Peter
Lewis, Beverly
   The Brethren
   The Ebb Tide
   The Missing
   The Preacher's Daughter
Lewis, C. S.
   Till We Have Faces: A Myth Retold
LEWIS, ELIOT (FICTITIOUS CHARACTER)
   Snow, C. P. ★*Strangers and Brothers*
Lewis, Linden A.
   The First Sister: A Novel
Lewis, Sinclair
   Babbitt
   Dodsworth
   ★*Elmer Gantry*
   ★*It Can't Happen Here*
   ★*Main Street: The Story of Carol Kennicott*
LEXICOGRAPHERS
   Johnson, Daisy. *Everything Under*
   Williams, Eley. *The Liar's Dictionary*
LEXINGTON, KENTUCKY
   Edwards, Kim. *The Memory Keeper's Daughter*
LGBTQIA COMICS
   Cruse, Howard. *The Complete Wendel*
LGBTQIA FICTION
   Aciman, Andre. *Call Me by Your Name*
   Aciman, Andre. *Enigma Variations: A Novel*
   Aciman, Andre. *Find Me*
   Alameddine, Rabih. *The Wrong End of the Telescope*
   Arnett, Kristen N. *With Teeth: A Novel*
   Baldwin, James. ★*Another Country*
   Baldwin, James. ★*Early Novels and Stories*
   Baldwin, James. ★*Giovanni's Room*
   Barnett, LaShonda K. *Jam on the Vine*
   Barry, Sebastian. *Days Without End: A Novel*

Bartlett, Neil. *The Disappearance Boy*
Bledsoe, Lucy Jane. *The Big Bang Symphony: A Novel of Antarctica*
Bloom, Amy. ★*White Houses: A Novel*
Brayden, Melissa. *First Position*
Brown, Rita Mae. ★*Rubyfruit Jungle*
Cassara, Joseph. *The House of Impossible Beauties*
Castellani, Christopher. *Leading Men: A Novel*
Charles, KJ. *Wanted, a Gentleman: Or, Virtue Over-Rated*
Cheever, John. *Falconer*
Choi, Susan. *My Education*
Cusset, Catherine. *Life of David Hockney: A Novel*
Danforth, Emily M. *Plain Bad Heroines*
De Robertis, Carolina. *Cantoras*
De Robertis, Carolina. *The Gods of Tango*
Dennis-Benn, Nicole. *Here Comes the Sun*
Eugenides, Jeffrey. ★*Middlesex*
Fu, Kim. *For Today I Am a Boy*
Gaspar de Alba, Alicia. *Desert Blood: The Juarez Murders*
Greenwell, Garth. *Cleanness*
Greenwell, Garth. *What Belongs to You: A Novel*
Greer, Andrew Sean. ★*Less*
Hall, Alexis. *For Real*
Harris, E. Lynn. *Basketball Jones: A Novel*
Harris, E. Lynn. *I Say a Little Prayer: A Novel*
Harris, E. Lynn. *Invisible Life: A Novel*
Iweala, Uzodinma. ★*Speak No Evil*
Jedrowski, Tomasz. *Swimming in the Dark*
Jones, Robert. ★*The Prophets: A Novel*
Joseph, Fabiola. *Niya: Rainbow Dreams*
Kent, Kathleen. *The Burn*
Kent, Kathleen. *The Pledge*
Leavitt, David. *The Two Hotel Francforts: A Novel*
Louis, Edouard. *The End of Eddy: A Novel*
Makkai, Rebecca. ★*The Great Believers*
Manning, Corinne. *We Had No Rules: Stories*
Masad, Ilana. *All My Mother's Lovers: A Novel*
Maxwell, Everina. *Winter's Orbit*
Mehta, Rahul. *No Other World: A Novel*
Mendez, Paul. *Rainbow Milk*
Nava, Michael. ★*Carved in Bone*
Okparanta, Chinelo. ★*Under the Udala Trees*
Park, Sang Young. ★*Love in the Big City: A Novel*
Pastan, Rachel. *In the Field*
Peters, Torrey. ★*Detransition, Baby*
Pufahl, Shannon. *On Swift Horses*
Renault, Mary. *The Last of the Wine*
Renault, Mary. *The Persian Boy*
Rice-Gonzalez, Charles. *Chulito*
Rowley, Steven. ★*The Guncle: A Novel*
Scoppettone, Sandra. *Everything You Have Is Mine*
Scoppettone, Sandra. *My Sweet Untraceable You*
Somer, Mehmet Murat. *The Serenity Murders*
Staples, Dennis E. *This Town Sleeps*
Statovci, Pajtim. *Bolla*
Suri, Tasha. *The Jasmine Throne*
Tesh, Emily. *Silver in the Wood*
Urrea, Luis Alberto. *Into the Beautiful North: A Novel*
Vernon, P. J. *Bath Haus: A Thriller*

Washington, Bryan. ★*Memorial*
White, Edmund. *A Boy's Own Story*
Williams, Eley. *The Liar's Dictionary*
Winterson, Jeanette. *The Passion*

LGBTQIA PERSONS
Manning, Corinne. *We Had No Rules: Stories*
Ripper, Kris. *The Hate Project*
Ripper, Kris. *The Life Revamp*
Ripper, Kris. *The Love Study*
Roanhorse, Rebecca. ★*Black Sun*
Taylor, Brandon. ★*Filthy Animals*

LGBTQIA ROMANCES
Alexander, Jennet. *I Kissed a Girl*
Bellefleur, Alexandria. *Written in the Stars*
Brayden, Melissa. *First Position*
Charles, KJ. *Wanted, a Gentleman: Or, Virtue Over-Rated*
Cochrun, Alison. *The Charm Offensive*
Cole, Alyssa. *How to Find a Princess*
Hall, Alexis. ★*Boyfriend Material*
Hall, Alexis. *For Real*
Hall, Alexis. *Rosaline Palmer Takes the Cake*
Henson, Pene. *Into the Blue*
Herrera, Adriana. ★*American Dreamer*
Herrera, Adriana. *American Fairytale*
Herrera, Adriana. *American Love Story*
Klune, TJ. ★*Under the Whispering Door*
McQuiston, Casey. ★*One Last Stop*
McQuiston, Casey. ★*Red, White & Royal Blue: A Novel*
Parrish, Roan. *Better Than People*
Ridley, Erica. ★*The Perks of Loving a Wallflower*
Ripper, Kris. *The Hate Project*
Ripper, Kris. *The Life Revamp*
Ripper, Kris. *The Love Study*
Sebastian, Cat. *It Takes Two to Tumble*
Sebastian, Cat. *The Lawrence Browne Affair*
Sebastian, Cat. *Unmasked by the Marquess*
Waite, Olivia. *The Care and Feeding of Waspish Widows*
Waite, Olivia. ★*The Lady's Guide to Celestial Mechanics*
Wilsner, Meryl. ★*Something to Talk About*
Li Du novels [Series]. Hart, Elsa
Li, Yiyun
The Vagrants: A Novel
Liam Campbell mysteries [Series]. Stabenow, Dana
Liam Devlin thrillers [Series]. Higgins, Jack
Liam Mulligan mysteries [Series]. DeSilva, Bruce
*The **Liar's** Dictionary*. Williams, Eley
Liardet, Frances
We Must Be Brave
LIBERALS
Leavitt, David. ★*Shelter in Place*
★***Libertie**: a Novel*. Greenidge, Kaitlyn
Libra. DeLillo, Don
*The **Librarian** of Saint-Malo: A Novel*. Escobar, Mario
LIBRARIANS
Cogman, Genevieve. *The Invisible Library*
Cogman, Genevieve. *The Masked City*
Cooley, Martha. *The Archivist: A Novel*
Eco, Umberto. ★*The Name of the Rose*

Escobar, Mario. *The Librarian of Saint-Malo: A Novel*
Evison, Jonathan. ★*Lawn Boy: A Novel*
Gates, Eva. *Deadly Ever After*
Gates, Eva. *A Death Long Overdue*
Gates, Eva. *Read and Buried*
Hackwith, A. J. *The Library of the Unwritten*
Hegi, Ursula. *Stones from the River*
Herrera, Adriana. ★*American Dreamer*
Hill, Edwin J. *Little Comfort*
James, Miranda. *What the Cat Dragged In*
Kibler, Julie. *Home for Erring and Outcast Girls*
Makkai, Rebecca. *The Borrower: A Novel*
Offill, Jenny. ★*Weather*
Sampson, Freya. *The Last Chance Library*
Skeslien Charles, Janet. *The Paris Library: A Novel*
Vinge, Vernor. *The Children of the Sky*
Wojtas, Olga. *Miss Blaine's Prefect and the Golden Samovar*

Librarians in love [Series]. Title, Sarah
LIBRARIES
Adams, Sara Nisha. ★*The Reading List*
Bennett, Alan. ★*The Uncommon Reader*
Bernhard, Emilia. *The Books of the Dead*
Borges, Jorge Luis. *Ficciones*
Cogman, Genevieve. *The Invisible Library*
Cogman, Genevieve. *The Masked City*
Davis, Fiona. *The Lions of Fifth Avenue: A Novel*
Evison, Jonathan. ★*Lawn Boy: A Novel*
Haig, Matt. *The Midnight Library*
Hawkins, Scott. ★*The Library at Mount Char*
Huchu, Tendai. *The Library of the Dead*
Lovett, Charles C. *The Lost Book of the Grail: Or a Visitor's Guide to Barchester Cathedral*
McKinlay, Jenn. *Killer Research*
Morgenstern, Erin. ★*The Starless Sea*
Moyes, Jojo. ★*The Giver of Stars: A Novel*
Sampson, Freya. *The Last Chance Library*
Skeslien Charles, Janet. *The Paris Library: A Novel*
★*The **Library** at Mount Char.* Hawkins, Scott
Library lover's mysteries [Series]. McKinlay, Jenn
*The **Library** of the Dead.* Huchu, Tendai
*The **Library** of the Unwritten.* Hackwith, A. J.
LIBYA
Matar, Hisham. *In the Country of Men*
Licks of Love: Short Stories and a Sequel. Updike, John
*The **Lie**.* Dunmore, Helen
Lie Down in Darkness. Styron, William
*A **Lie** Someone Told You About Yourself.* Davies, Peter Ho
Liebermann papers [Series]. Tallis, Frank
Lieutenant Hornblower. Forester, C. S.
LIFE
Hadley, Tessa. *Bad Dreams and Other Stories*
★*Life & Times of Michael K.* Coetzee, J. M.
Life After. Ganshert, Katie
LIFE AFTER DEATH
Abulhawa, Susan. *The Blue Between Sky and Water*
Albom, Mitch. *The Five People You Meet in Heaven*
Albom, Mitch. *The Next Person You Meet in Heaven*
Bonnaffons, Amy. *The Regrets*

Choo, Yangsze. *The Ghost Bride: A Novel*
Flynn, Michael. *The January Dancer*
Irwin, Stephen M. *The Broken Ones: A Novel*
Pyper, Andrew. *The Damned: A Novel*
Stephenson, Neal. ★*Fall Or, Dodge in Hell: A Novel*
Vollmann, William T. *Last Stories and Other Stories*
★*Life After Life: A Novel.* Atkinson, Kate
*The **Life** All Around Me by Ellen Foster.* Gibbons, Kaye
Life Among Giants: A Novel. Roorbach, Bill
Life Among the Terranauts. Horrocks, Caitlin
*The **Life** and Death of Sophie Stark.* North, Anna
*The **Life** and Loves of a She-Devil.* Weldon, Fay
★*Life and Other Inconveniences.* Higgins, Kristan
Life Before Man. Atwood, Margaret
LIFE CHANGE EVENTS
Adams, Sara Nisha. ★*The Reading List*
Alarcon, Daniel. *At Night We Walk in Circles: A Novel*
Aliu, Xhenet. ★*Brass: A Novel*
Allio, Kirstin. *Buddhism for Western Children: A Novel*
Anshaw, Carol. *Carry the One*
Antoinette, Ashley. *Butterfly*
Artson, Barbara. *Odessa, Odessa*
Atkinson, Kate. *Started Early, Took My Dog*
Attenberg, Jami. *The Middlesteins*
Auster, Paul. *4 3 2 1: A Novel*
Ausubel, Ramona. *Sons and Daughters of Ease and Plenty*
Balogh, Mary. *Someone to Hold*
Balogh, Mary. ★*Someone to Love*
Barnes, Julian. *The Only Story*
Beagle, Peter S. *In Calabria*
Bennett, Brit. ★*The Vanishing Half*
Beyda, Emily. *The Body Double*
Bivald, Katarina. *The Readers of Broken Wheel Recommend*
Block, Stefan Merrill. *Oliver Loving: A Novel*
Butland, Stephanie. *The Lost for Words Bookshop: A Novel*
Cantor, Jillian. *Half Life*
Card, Maisy. ★*These Ghosts Are Family: A Novel*
Carr, Robyn. *What We Find*
Center, Katherine. *How to Walk Away: A Novel*
Clark, Martin. *The Substitution Order*
Colgan, Jenny. ★*The Endless Beach*
Corman, Avery. *Prized Possessions*
Crouch, Blake. *Dark Matter: A Novel*
Crow, Sarah McCraw. *The Wrong Kind of Woman*
D'Erasmo, Stacey. *The Sky Below*
Daniels, Natalie. *Too Close*
Davis, Kathryn. *Duplex*
Diamond, Elizabeth. *An Accidental Light*
Dickey, Eric Jerome. *The Business of Lovers*
Doller, Trish. *Float Plan*
Dubus, Andre. *Dirty Love*
Duffy, Brendan. *House of Echoes: A Novel*
Erdrich, Louise. ★*The Round House: A Novel*
Eugenides, Jeffrey. *Fresh Complaint: Stories*
Fabry, Chris. *The Promise of Jesse Woods*
Finder, Joseph. *The Fixer*
Francis-Sharma, Lauren. ★*Book of the Little Axe*
French, Tana. ★*The Witch Elm: A Novel*

Gaige, Amity. *Sea Wife*
Gaitskill, Mary. *Don't Cry: Stories*
Gaitskill, Mary. *The Mare: A Novel*
Ganshert, Katie. *Life After*
Gardam, Jane. *The Flight of the Maidens*
Genova, Lisa. *Inside the O'Briens: A Novel*
Genova, Lisa. *Left Neglected: A Novel*
Griffin, Anne. *When All Is Said: A Novel*
Han, Kang. ★*Human Acts: A Novel*
Hauck, Rachel. *Once Upon a Prince*
Heller, Peter. *The Painter: A Novel*
Hemmings, Kaui Hart. *The Possibilities: A Novel*
James, Lorelei. *I Want You Back*
Johnson, Jocelyn Nicole. ★*My Monticello: Fiction*
Jones, Tayari. ★*An American Marriage: A Novel*
K'wan. *The Fix*
Kelly, Martha Hall. *Lost Roses: A Novel*
Kenney, John. *Talk to Me*
Khadra, Yasmina. *The Swallows of Kabul: A Novel*
Kim, Crystal Hana. *If You Leave Me*
Kim, Eugenia. *The Kinship of Secrets*
King, Stephen. *11/22/63*
Krauss, Nicole. *Forest Dark*
Lauren, Christina. *In a Holidaze*
Leavitt, David. *The Two Hotel Francforts: A Novel*
Loren, Roni. ★*The One for You*
Macomber, Debbie. *If Not for You: A Novel*
Manning, Max. *The Victim: A Novel*
McKenzie, Alecia. *A Million Aunties*
Miller, Derek B. ★*The Girl in Green*
Monroe, Mary Alice. ★*The Summer of Lost and Found*
Moriarty, Liane. *The Husband's Secret*
Moriarty, Liane. *Truly Madly Guilty*
Napolitano, Ann. *Dear Edward*
O'Farrell, Maggie. *The Vanishing Act of Esme Lennox*
Oates, Joyce Carol. *The (Other) You: Stories*
Obioma, Chigozie. ★*The Fishermen: A Novel*
Ólafsdóttir, Auður A. *Butterflies in November*
Offutt, Chris. *Country Dark*
Ozick, Cynthia. *The Puttermesser Papers*
Parrish, Christa. *Still Life*
Perrotta, Tom. *The Leftovers*
Petterson, Per. *I Curse the River of Time*
Phillips, Gin. *Fierce Kingdom: A Novel*
Picoult, Jodi. ★*Wish You Were Here: A Novel*
Pochoda, Ivy. *Visitation Street: A Novel*
Ramqvist, Karolina. *The White City*
Robinson, Marilynne. ★*Lila*
Ross, Ann B. ★*Miss Julia Happily Ever After*
Sahota, Sunjeev. *The Year of the Runaways*
Schwartz, Lynne Sharon. *Truthtelling: Stories, Fables, Glimpses*
Shepard, Sam. *The One Inside*
Shreve, Anita. *Testimony: A Novel*
Simonson, Helen. *The Summer Before the War: A Novel*
Solomon, Anna. *Leaving Lucy Pear*
Stevens, Chevy. *Never Let You Go*
Truong, Monique T. D. *The Sweetest Fruits*
Walsh, M. O. ★*The Big Door Prize: A Novel*

Waxman, Abbi. *The Bookish Life of Nina Hill*
Wells, Benedict. *The End of Loneliness: A Novel*
Westlake, Donald E. *Memory*
Wood, Tracey Enerson. *The Engineer's Wife: A Novel*
Yates, Christopher J. *Grist Mill Road: A Novel*

LIFE CHANGE EVENTS — PSYCHOLOGICAL ASPECTS
Giordano, Paolo. ★*The Solitude of Prime Numbers: A Novel*
LIFE INSURANCE
McBain, Ed. *Alice in Jeopardy*
Life of David Hockney: A Novel. Cusset, Catherine
★*Life of Pi: A Novel*. Martel, Yann
LIFE ON OTHER PLANETS
Adams, Douglas. ★*The Hitchhiker's Guide to the Galaxy*
Adams, Douglas. *The Restaurant at the End of the Universe*
Asimov, Isaac. ★*Foundation*
Asimov, Isaac. *Foundation and Empire*
Asimov, Isaac. *Second Foundation*
Beukes, Lauren. *Slipping: Stories, Essays, & Other Writing*
Bradbury, Ray. ★*The Martian Chronicles: The Fortieth Anniversary Edition*
Brown, Pierce. *Golden Son*
Brown, Pierce. *Red Rising*
Chambers, Becky. *Record of a Spaceborn Few*
Corey, James S. A. *Abaddon's Gate*
Corey, James S. A. *Babylon's Ashes*
Corey, James S. A. *Caliban's War*
Corey, James S. A. *Cibola Burn*
Corey, James S. A. *Nemesis Games*
Corey, James S. A. *Persepolis Rising*
Corey, James S. A. *Tiamat's Wrath*
Delany, Samuel R. *Aye, and Gomorrah: Stories*
Faber, Michel. *The Book of Strange New Things*
Flynn, Michael. *The January Dancer*
Hamilton, Peter F. *The Dreaming Void*
Hamilton, Peter F. *Great North Road*
Heinlein, Robert A. ★*Starship Troopers*
Le Guin, Ursula K. *The Birthday of the World: And Other Stories*
Le Guin, Ursula K. ★*The Dispossessed: An Ambiguous Utopia*
Le Guin, Ursula K. *Four Ways to Forgiveness*
Le Guin, Ursula K. ★*The Left Hand of Darkness*
Le Guin, Ursula K. *The Telling*
Liu, Cixin. ★*The Dark Forest*
Liu, Cixin. ★*Death's End*
Mieville, China. *Embassytown*
Reynolds, Alastair. *Revelation Space*
Reynolds, Alastair. ★*Revenger*
Robinson, Kim Stanley. ★*Green Mars*
Robinson, Kim Stanley. *The Martians*
Russell, Mary Doria. ★*Children of God: A Novel*
Russell, Mary Doria. ★*The Sparrow*
Sagan, Carl. *Contact: A Novel*
Scalzi, John. *The Collapsing Empire*
Scalzi, John. ★*Old Man's War*
Steele, Allen M. *Coyote: A Novel of Interstellar Exploration*
Stephenson, Neal. *Anathem*
Stross, Charles. *Neptune's Brood*
Stross, Charles. *Saturn's Children: A Space Opera*
Vinge, Vernor. *The Children of the Sky*

Vonnegut, Kurt. ★*The Sirens of Titan*
Vonnegut, Kurt. ★*Slaughterhouse-Five: Or, the Children's Crusade : A Duty-Dance with Death*
Wells, H. G. ★*The War of the Worlds*
Life or Death. Robotham, Michael
The *Life* Revamp. Ripper, Kris
LIFE STORIES — ARTS AND CULTURE — WRITING — AUTHORS
    Coetzee, J. M. *Summertime: Scenes from a Provincial Life*
    Nabokov, Vladimir Vladimirovich. *Novels and Memoirs, 1941-51*
LIFE STORIES — FACING ADVERSITY — WAR AND OPPRESSION — WAR SURVIVORS
    Wiesel, Elie. ★*Night, Dawn, the Accident: Three Tales*
LIFE STORIES — GENERAL
    Sedaris, David. *Holidays on Ice*
Life Times: Stories, 1952-2007. Gordimer, Nadine
The *Life* to Come. De Kretser, Michelle
Life's Too Short. Jimenez, Abby
LIFEBOATS
    Albom, Mitch. *The Stranger in the Lifeboat*
Lifelines. Diehl, Heidi
LIFESTYLE CHANGE
    Butler, Halle. *The New Me: A Novel*
    Sthers, Amanda. *Holy Lands: A Novel*
LIFESTYLES
    Unsworth, Emma Jane. *Grown Ups*
Lifestyles of the Rich and Shameless. Swinson, Kiki
Lifted by the Great Nothing. Dimechkie, Karim
Light. Harrison, M. John
★*The Light* Between Oceans: A Novel. Stedman, M. L.
★*The Light* Brigade. Hurley, Kameron
★*Light* from Other Stars: A Novel. Swyler, Erika
Light from Uncommon Stars. Aoki, Ryka
★*Light* in August. Faulkner, William
The *Light* of Luna Park. Armstrong, Addison
The *Light* of the Midnight Stars. Rossner, Rena
The *Light* Over London. Kelly, Julia
★*Light* Perpetual. Spufford, Francis
The *Lighthouse*. James, P. D.
The *Lighthouse*. Moore, Alison
The *Lighthouse* Keeper's Daughter. Gaynor, Hazel
LIGHTHOUSE KEEPERS
    Gaynor, Hazel. *The Lighthouse Keeper's Daughter*
    Stedman, M. L. ★*The Light Between Oceans: A Novel*
Lighthouse library mysteries [Series]. Gates, Eva
LIGHTHOUSES
    Gaynor, Hazel. *The Lighthouse Keeper's Daughter*
    Schwarz, Christina. *The Edge of the Earth*
    Stedman, M. L. ★*The Light Between Oceans: A Novel*
The *Lightkeepers: a Novel*. Geni, Abby
Lightless. Higgins, C. A.
Lightless [Series]. Higgins, C. A.
Lightman, Alan P.
    The Diagnosis
    ★*Einstein's Dreams*
Lightner and Law novels [Series]. Goodwin, S. M.
The *Lightness*. Temple, Emily
Lightning Men: A Novel. Mullen, Thomas

★*Lightning* Strike. Krueger, William Kent
LIGHTNING STRIKE VICTIMS
    McDonald, Christina. *Behind Every Lie*
Lights All Night Long: A Novel. Fitzpatrick, Lydia
Lights! Camera! Puzzles! Hall, Parnell
★*Lightseekers*. Kayode, Femi
Like a Bird. Roisin, Fariha
Like Family. Giordano, Paolo
Like Lions. Panowich, Brian
Like Lovers Do. Livesay, Tracey
★*Like* Water for Chocolate: A Novel in Monthly Installments, with Recipes, Romances, and Home Remedies. Esquivel, Laura
The *Likeness*. French, Tana
★*Lila*. Robinson, Marilynne
Lilac Girls. Kelly, Martha Hall
Lilli De Jong: A Novel. Benton, Janet
★*Lillian* Boxfish Takes a Walk. Rooney, Kathleen
LILLIPUTIANS (FICTITIOUS CHARACTERS)
    Swift, Jonathan. ★*Gulliver's Travels*
Lily Adler mysteries [Series]. Schellman, Katharine
Lim, Roselle
    Natalie Tan's Book of Luck and Fortune
    Vanessa Yu's Magical Paris Tea Shop
LIMA, PERU
    Vargas Llosa, Mario. *Aunt Julia and the Scriptwriter*
Limitless novels [Series]. Glynn, Alan
★The *Limits* of the World. Acker, Jennifer
Limon, Martin
    The Line
    War Women
The *Limpopo* Academy of Private Detection. McCall Smith, Alexander
Lin, Jeannie
    The Lotus Palace
Lincoln and Speed novels [Series]. Putnam, Jonathan F.
★*Lincoln* in the Bardo: A Novel. Saunders, George
The *Lincoln* Lawyer: A Novel. Connelly, Michael
Lincoln Rhyme mysteries [Series]. Deaver, Jeffery
Lincoln's White House mysteries [Series]. Gleason, Colleen
LINCOLN, ABRAHAM
    El Akkad, Omar. *American War*
    Gleason, Colleen. *Murder at the Capitol*
    Masad, Ilana. *All My Mother's Lovers: A Novel*
    Putnam, Jonathan F. *These Honored Dead*
    Saunders, George. ★*Lincoln in the Bardo: A Novel*
    Sebastian, Cat. *The Lawrence Browne Affair*
    Vidal, Gore. ★*Lincoln: A Novel*
LINCOLN, MARY TODD
    Chiaverini, Jennifer. *Mrs. Lincoln's Sisters*
    Riordan, Kate. *The Heatwave*
★*Lincoln: a Novel*. Vidal, Gore
Linda Wallander mysteries [Series]. Mankell, Henning
Linda Wallheim mysteries [Series]. Harrison, Mette Ivie
LINDBERGH, ANNE MORROW
    Benjamin, Melanie. ★*The Aviator's Wife: A Novel*
    Pamuk, Orhan. *The Museum of Innocence*
LINDBERGH, CHARLES A.
    Roth, Philip. ★*The Plot Against America*

Linden, Rachel
Ascension of Larks
The Enlightenment of Bees
Lindsay, Jeffry P.
Just Watch Me
Lindsey, Odie
Some Go Home: A Novel
The Line. Grushin, Olga
The Line. Limon, Martin
LINGUISTS
Russell, Mary Doria. ★*Children of God: A Novel*
Russell, Mary Doria. ★*The Sparrow*
Stephenson, Neal. *The Rise and Fall of D.O.D.O.: A Novel*
Links trilogy [Series]. Farah, Nuruddin
LION
Andrews, Mesu. *Of Fire and Lions: A Novel*
Lionel Asbo: State of England. Amis, Martin
The Lions of Fifth Avenue: A Novel. Davis, Fiona
Lipman, Elinor
The Dearly Departed
Good Riddance
The Pursuit of Alice Thrift: A Novel
LIPOGRAMS
Dunn, Mark. *Ella Minnow Pea: A Progressively Lipogrammatic Epistolary Fable*
Lippman, Laura
★*After I'm Gone*
★*And When She Was Good*
★*Dream Girl*
★*Hush Hush*
★*Lady in the Lake: A Novel*
No Good Deeds
★*Sunburn*
What the Dead Know
Wilde Lake
Lipsyte, Sam
The Ask
LIQUOR SMUGGLING
Stegner, Wallace. ★*The Big Rock Candy Mountain*
LISBON, PORTUGAL
Leavitt, David. *The Two Hotel Francforts: A Novel*
Saramago, Jose. *All the Names*
Saramago, Jose. *The History of the Siege of Lisbon*
The List of Adrian Messenger. MacDonald, Philip
LISTENING
Nunez, Sigrid. *What Are You Going Through*
Listening to Love. Wiseman, Beth
LISTS
Hibbert, Talia. ★*Get a Life, Chloe Brown*
MacDonald, Philip. *The List of Adrian Messenger*
Ruiz, Sarah Grunder. *Love, Lists, and Fancy Ships*
LITERARY AGENTS
Harrod-Eagles, Cynthia. *Headlong*
LITERARY FICTION
Aboulela, Leila. *Elsewhere, Home*
Abraham, Tola Rotimi. *Black Sunday*
Abu-Jaber, Diana. *Crescent*
Abu-Jaber, Diana. *Origin: A Novel*

Acampora, Lauren. *The Paper Wasp: A Novel*
Acampora, Lauren. *The Wonder Garden*
Achebe, Chinua. ★*Things Fall Apart*
Aciman, Andre. *Call Me by Your Name*
Aciman, Andre. *Enigma Variations: A Novel*
Aciman, Andre. *Find Me*
Aciman, Andre. *Harvard Square*
Ackerman, Elliot. *Dark at the Crossing*
Ackerman, Elliot. *Red Dress in Black and White*
Ackerman, Elliot. ★*Waiting for Eden: A Novel*
Adam, Claire. *Golden Child: A Novel*
Adebayo, Ayobami. ★*Stay with Me*
Adichie, Chimamanda Ngozi. ★*Americanah: A Novel*
Adichie, Chimamanda Ngozi. *Half of a Yellow Sun*
Adichie, Chimamanda Ngozi. *The Thing Around Your Neck*
Adiga, Aravind. ★*Amnesty*
Adiga, Aravind. *Last Man in Tower: A Novel*
Adiga, Aravind. *Selection Day*
Adiga, Aravind. ★*The White Tiger: A Novel*
Adjei-Brenyah, Nana Kwame. *Friday Black: Stories*
Agee, James. ★*A Death in the Family*
Ahmad, Jamil. *The Wandering Falcon*
Aimaq, Jasmine. *The Opium Prince*
Akhtar, Ayad. ★*Homeland Elegies: A Novel*
Akinmade-Akerstrom, Lola. *In Every Mirror She's Black*
Akpan, Uwem. *Say You're One of Them*
Al Rawi, Shahad. *The Baghdad Clock*
Al-Ramli, Muhsin. *The President's Gardens*
Alam, Rumaan. *That Kind of Mother: A Novel*
Alameddine, Rabih. *An Unnecessary Woman*
Alameddine, Rabih. *The Wrong End of the Telescope*
Alarcon, Daniel. *The King Is Always Above the People: Stories*
Alderman, Naomi. ★*The Power: A Novel*
Aleichem, Sholem. *Tevye the Dairyman and the Railroad Stories*
Aleichem, Sholem. *Tevye's Daughters*
Alexie, Sherman. *Blasphemy: New and Selected Stories*
Alexie, Sherman. *Flight*
Alexie, Sherman. *Reservation Blues*
Alexis, Andre. *Fifteen Dogs*
Alexis, Andre. *The Hidden Keys*
Algren, Nelson. ★*The Man with the Golden Arm: A Novel*
Algren, Nelson. *A Walk on the Wild Side*
Alharthi, Jokha. *Celestial Bodies: A Novel*
Ali, Monica. ★*Brick Lane: A Novel*
Aliu, Xhenet. ★*Brass: A Novel*
Allende, Isabel. *Daughter of Fortune: A Novel*
Allende, Isabel. ★*Eva Luna*
Allende, Isabel. ★*The House of the Spirits*
Allende, Isabel. *In the Midst of Winter: A Novel*
Allende, Isabel. *The Japanese Lover*
Allende, Isabel. *Of Love and Shadows*
Allende, Isabel. *Portrait in Sepia: A Novel*
Allende, Isabel. *Ripper: A Novel*
Allende, Isabel. *The Stories of Eva Luna*
Altan, Ahmet. ★*Love in the Days of Rebellion*
Alvar, Mia. *In the Country: Stories*
Alvarez, Julia. ★*Afterlife: A Novel*
Alyan, Hala. *Salt Houses*

Amado, Jorge. ★*Dona Flor and Her Two Husbands: A Moral and Amorous Tale*

Amado, Jorge. *Gabriela, Clove and Cinnamon*

Amis, Kingsley. ★*Lucky Jim*

Amis, Martin. ★*Inside Story*

Amis, Martin. *London Fields: A Novel*

Amis, Martin. ★*The Pregnant Widow*

Amis, Martin. ★*Time's Arrow, or the Nature of the Offense*

Anam, Tahmima. *The Bones of Grace*

Anappara, Deepa. *Djinn Patrol on the Purple Line: A Novel*

Anderson, Alison. *The Summer Guest*

Andreades, Daphne Palasi. *Brown Girls*

Anshaw, Carol. *Carry the One*

Anstruther, Eleanor. *A Perfect Explanation*

Antopol, Molly. *The Unamericans*

Apostol, Gina. *Insurrecto*

Appanah-Mouriquand, Nathacha. *Tropic of Violence: A Novel*

Aramburu, Fernando. *Homeland*

Arden, Katherine. ★*The Bear and the Nightingale*

Arden, Katherine. ★*The Girl in the Tower*

Arden, Katherine. ★*The Winter of the Witch*

Arikawa, Hiro. *The Travelling Cat Chronicles*

Arimah, Lesley Nneka. ★*What It Means When a Man Falls from the Sky: Stories*

Armfield, Julia. *Salt Slow: Stories*

Arudpragasam, Anuk. *The Story of a Brief Marriage*

Asim, Jabari. ★*Yonder*

Aslam, Nadeem. ★*The Blind Man's Garden*

Aslam, Nadeem. ★*The Golden Legend: A Novel*

Atilgan, Yusuf. *Motherland Hotel*

Atkinson, Kate. ★*Big Sky*

Atkinson, Kate. ★*A God in Ruins*

Atkinson, Kate. ★*Life After Life: A Novel*

Atkinson, Kate. ★*Transcription*

Atwood, Margaret. *Alias Grace*

Atwood, Margaret. ★*The Blind Assassin*

Atwood, Margaret. *Bluebeard's Egg and Other Stories*

Atwood, Margaret. ★*Cat's Eye*

Atwood, Margaret. ★*The Handmaid's Tale*

Atwood, Margaret. *Life Before Man*

Atwood, Margaret. ★*Maddaddam: A Novel*

Atwood, Margaret. *Moral Disorder*

Atwood, Margaret. ★*Stone Mattress: Nine Tales*

Atwood, Margaret. ★*The Testaments: A Novel*

Atwood, Margaret. ★*The Year of the Flood: A Novel*

Auci, Stefania. *The Florios of Sicily: A Novel*

Auster, Paul. *4 3 2 1: A Novel*

Auster, Paul. ★*The Book of Illusions: A Novel*

Auster, Paul. *The Brooklyn Follies*

Auster, Paul. ★*In the Country of Last Things*

Auster, Paul. *Invisible*

Auster, Paul. ★*Leviathan*

Auster, Paul. *Oracle Night*

Auster, Paul. *Sunset Park*

Auster, Paul. *Timbuktu: A Novel*

Auster, Paul. *Travels in the Scriptorium: A Novel*

Austin, Emily. *Everyone in This Room Will Someday Be Dead*

Aw, Tash. *We, the Survivors*

Babalola, Bolu. *Love in Color: Mythical Tales from Around the World, Retold*

Baldwin, James. ★*Another Country*

Baldwin, James. ★*Early Novels and Stories*

Baldwin, James. ★*Giovanni's Room*

Baldwin, James. ★*Go Tell It on the Mountain*

Baldwin, James. ★*Going to Meet the Man*

Baldwin, James. ★*If Beale Street Could Talk*

Baldwin, James. *Just Above My Head*

Baldwin, James. *Tell Me How Long the Train's Been Gone: A Novel*

Ball, Jesse. *Census*

Bambara, Toni Cade. *Gorilla, My Love*

Bambara, Toni Cade. ★*The Salt Eaters*

Bambara, Toni Cade. *Those Bones Are Not My Child*

Bandi. *The Accusation: Forbidden Stories from Inside North Korea*

Banks, Russell. ★*Affliction*

Banks, Russell. *Cloudsplitter: A Novel*

Banks, Russell. *Continental Drift*

Banks, Russell. *Foregone*

Banks, Russell. *Lost Memory of Skin*

Banks, Russell. ★*The Sweet Hereafter*

Banville, John. *Ancient Light*

Banville, John. *The Blue Guitar*

Banville, John. *The Book of Evidence*

Banville, John. ★*Eclipse: A Novel*

Banville, John. *The Infinities*

Banville, John. ★*The Sea*

Barbery, Muriel. *The Elegance of the Hedgehog*

Barker, Nicola. *Darkmans*

Barker, Pat. ★*The Eye in the Door*

Barker, Pat. ★*The Ghost Road*

Barker, Susan. ★*The Incarnations: A Novel*

Barnes, Julian. ★*England, England*

Barnes, Julian. ★*Flaubert's Parrot*

Barnes, Julian. ★*A History of the World in 10 1/2 Chapters*

Barnes, Julian. *The Noise of Time*

Barnes, Julian. *The Only Story*

Barnes, Julian. ★*The Sense of an Ending*

Barry, Sebastian. *Days Without End: A Novel*

Barry, Sebastian. *The Secret Scripture: A Novel*

Barry, Sebastian. ★*A Thousand Moons: A Novel*

Barth, John. *Chimera*

Barth, John. ★*The Floating Opera*

Barth, John. ★*Giles Goat-Boy ;: Or, the Revised New Syllabus*

Barth, John. *The Last Voyage of Somebody the Sailor*

Barth, John. ★*The Sot-Weed Factor*

Batuman, Elif. ★*The Idiot*

Baxter, Charles. ★*The Sun Collective*

Beagin, Jen. ★*Vacuum in the Dark: A Novel*

Beah, Ishmael. *Little Family*

Beams, Clare. *The Illness Lesson*

Beattie, Ann. *A Wonderful Stroke of Luck: A Novel*

Beatty, Paul. ★*The Sellout: A Novel*

Beauvoir, Simone de. *The Woman Destroyed*

Beckett, Samuel. ★*Murphy*

Begley, Louis. *About Schmidt*

Bellow, Saul. ★*The Adventures of Augie March*

Bellow, Saul. *The Bellarosa Connection*

Bellow, Saul. *Dangling Man*
Bellow, Saul. *The Dean's December: A Novel*
Bellow, Saul. ★*Henderson the Rain King: A Novel*
Bellow, Saul. ★*Herzog*
Bellow, Saul. ★*Humboldt's Gift*
Bellow, Saul. *More Die of Heartbreak*
Bellow, Saul. ★*Mr. Sammler's Planet*
Bellow, Saul. *Novels, 1944-1953*
Bellow, Saul. *Ravelstein*
Bellow, Saul. ★*Seize the Day*
Bender, Aimee. *The Butterfly Lampshade*
Benedetti, Mario. *Springtime in a Broken Mirror*
Benjamin, Chloe. ★*The Immortalists: A Novel*
Benjamin, Melanie. ★*The Aviator's Wife: A Novel*
Bennett, Brit. *The Mothers*
Bennett, Brit. ★*The Vanishing Half*
Benz, Chanelle. ★*The Gone Dead*
Berry, Wendell. *Jayber Crow: A Novel*
Berry, Wendell. ★*That Distant Land: The Collected Stories of Wendell Berry*
Beukes, Lauren. *Slipping: Stories, Essays, & Other Writing*
Bezmozgis, David. *The Betrayers: A Novel*
Bieker, Chelsea Jean. *Godshot: A Novel*
Bijan, Donia. *The Last Days of Cafe Leila*
Binet, Laurent. *Civilizations*
Blau, Jessica Anya. *Mary Jane: A Novel*
Bloom, Amy. *Lucky Us: A Novel*
Blum, Jenna. *The Lost Family*
Bock, Charles. *Alice & Oliver: A Novel*
Bolano, Roberto. ★*2666*
Bolano, Roberto. *Amulet*
Bolano, Roberto. ★*By Night in Chile*
Bolano, Roberto. ★*Distant Star*
Bolano, Roberto. *Last Evenings on Earth*
Bolano, Roberto. *Monsieur Pain*
Bolano, Roberto. ★*The Savage Detectives*
Bolano, Roberto. ★*The Third Reich*
Boll, Heinrich. *Billiards at Half-Past Nine*
Boll, Heinrich. *The Clown*
Bond, Cynthia. *Ruby: A Novel*
Bonnaffons, Amy. *The Regrets*
Bonnaffons, Amy. *The Wrong Heaven: Stories*
Bordas, Camille. *How to Behave in a Crowd*
Borges, Jorge Luis. ★*Collected Fictions*
Borges, Jorge Luis. *Ficciones*
Bourdeaut, Olivier. *Waiting for Bojangles: A Novel*
Bowles, Paul. ★*The Sheltering Sky*
Bowman, David. *Big Bang: A Nonfiction Novel*
Boyd, William. *Trio*
Boyle, T. Coraghessan. *The Harder They Come*
Boyle, T. Coraghessan. *Outside Looking In: A Novel*
Boyle, T. Coraghessan. *The Women: A Novel*
Boyne, John. *The Heart's Invisible Furies*
Boyne, John. ★*A Ladder to the Sky*
Brinkley, Jamel. *A Lucky Man: Stories*
Brodesser-Akner, Taffy. *Fleishman Is in Trouble: A Novel*
Bronsky, Alina. *The Hottest Dishes of the Tartar Cuisine*
Brookner, Anita. *Hotel Du Lac*

Broun, Bill. *Night of the Animals*
Brown, Larry. *Joe: A Novel*
Brown, Larry. ★*Tiny Love: The Complete Stories of Larry Brown*
Brown, Taylor. ★*Gods of Howl Mountain: A Novel*
Brundage, Elizabeth. *The Vanishing Point*
Bruno, Anna. *Ordinary Hazards: A Novel*
Buck, Pearl S. *The Good Earth*
Bulawayo, NoViolet. *We Need New Names: A Novel*
Bulgakov, Mikhail. ★*The Master and Margarita*
Buntin, Julie. ★*Marlena: A Novel*
Burnet, Graeme Macrae. *His Bloody Project: Documents Relating to the Case of Roderick Macrae*
Burns, Anna. *Milkman: A Novel*
Butler, Nickolas. *Godspeed*
Butler, Nickolas. ★*The Hearts of Men*
Butler, Nickolas. *Little Faith: A Novel*
Butler, Robert Olen. *A Good Scent from a Strange Mountain: Stories*
Butler, Robert Olen. *Hell: A Novel*
Butler, Robert Olen. *Perfume River*
Buwalda, Peter. *Bonita Avenue: A Novel*
Byatt, A. S. *Babel Tower*
Byatt, A. S. *Medusa's Ankles: Selected Stories*
Byatt, A. S. ★*Possession: A Romance*
Byatt, A. S. ★*Ragnarok: The End of the Gods*
Byatt, A. S. *A Whistling Woman*
Caldwell, Erskine. *Tobacco Road*
Calvino, Italo. ★*If on a Winter's Night a Traveler*
Calvino, Italo. *Invisible Cities*
Cameron, Peter. *The City of Your Final Destination*
Campbell, Bonnie Jo. *Once Upon a River*
Camus, Albert. ★*The Fall*
Camus, Albert. *The Plague*
Camus, Albert. ★*The Stranger*
Cander, Chris. *The Weight of a Piano: A Novel*
Capote, Truman. ★*Breakfast at Tiffany's*
Capote, Truman. ★*The Complete Stories of Truman Capote*
Card, Maisy. ★*These Ghosts Are Family: A Novel*
Carey, Peter. *A Long Way from Home*
Carr, Brian Allen. ★*Opioid, Indiana*
Carver, Raymond. *What We Talk About When We Talk About Love: Stories*
Cash, Wiley. *When Ghosts Come Home: A Novel*
Cassara, Joseph. *The House of Impossible Beauties*
Cather, Willa. *A Lost Lady*
Cather, Willa. *The Song of the Lark*
Catton, Eleanor. *The Luminaries: A Novel*
Cha, Steph. ★*Your House Will Pay*
Chabon, Michael. *The Amazing Adventures of Kavalier & Clay: A Novel*
Chabon, Michael. ★*Wonder Boys*
Chai, May-Lee. *Useful Phrases for Immigrants: Stories*
Chan, Jessamine. *The School for Good Mothers*
Chancellor, Bryn. *Sycamore: A Novel*
Chancy, Myriam J. A. ★*What Storm, What Thunder*
Chang, Alexandra. ★*Days of Distraction*
Chariandy, David John. *Brother: A Novel*
Cheek, Chip. *Cape May*
Cheever, John. *Bullet Park: A Novel*

Cheever, John. *Falconer*

Cho, Nam-Ju. ★*Kim Jiyoung, Born 1982*

Choi, Susan. ★*Trust Exercise: A Novel*

Choi, Yoon. *Skinship: Stories*

Christie, Michael. ★*Greenwood: A Novel*

Cisneros, Sandra. *Martita, I Remember You: Martita, Te Recuerdo*

Clarke, Diana. *Thin Girls*

Clarke, Susanna. ★*Piranesi*

Clegg, Bill. *Did You Ever Have a Family*

Clegg, Bill. *The End of the Day*

Clement, Jennifer. *Gun Love*

Clemmons, Zinzi. *What We Lose*

Cline, Emma. *Daddy: Stories*

Coates, Ta-Nehisi. ★*The Water Dancer: A Novel*

Coelho, Paulo. ★*The Alchemist*

Coetzee, J. M. *Age of Iron*

Coetzee, J. M. *Disgrace*

Coetzee, J. M. *Elizabeth Costello*

Coetzee, J. M. ★*Foe*

Coetzee, J. M. ★*Life & Times of Michael K*

Cohen, Joshua. *Book of Numbers: A Novel*

Cole, Teju. *Every Day Is for the Thief*

Cole, Teju. ★*Open City: A Novel*

Collins, Kathleen. ★*Whatever Happened to Interracial Love?: Stories*

Conell, Lee. *The Party Upstairs*

Conrad, Joseph. *Complete Short Fiction of Joseph Conrad: The Stories: Volume 1*

Conrad, Joseph. ★*Heart of Darkness*

Conrad, Joseph. *Nostromo: A Tale of the Seaboard*

Conrad, Joseph. *Victory: An Island Tale*

Cook, Diane. ★*The New Wilderness: A Novel*

Coover, Robert. *The Origin of the Brunists: A Novel*

Coplin, Amanda. *The Orchardist*

Cordova, Zoraida. *The Inheritance of Orquidea Divina*

Coster, Naima. *Halsey Street*

Couto, Mia. *Rain: And Other Stories*

Couto, Mia. *The Sword and the Spear*

Crace, Jim. *Harvest*

Crace, Jim. *Quarantine*

Craig, Charmaine. *Miss Burma*

Crews, Harry. *A Feast of Snakes: A Novel*

Crossan, Sarah. *Here Is the Beehive*

Crouch, Katie. *Embassy Wife*

Crow, Sarah McCraw. *The Wrong Kind of Woman*

Crummey, Michael. *The Innocents*

Crummey, Michael. *Sweetland*

Cunningham, Michael. ★*The Hours*

Cunningham, Michael. *Specimen Days*

Cusk, Rachel. *Kudos*

Cusk, Rachel. *Outline: A Novel*

Cusk, Rachel. *Second Place*

Cusk, Rachel. *Transit*

Dalton, Trent. *All Our Shimmering Skies*

Dalton, Trent. *Boy Swallows Universe*

Dangarembga, Tsitsi. *This Mournable Body*

Danielewski, Mark Z. ★*The Familiar.; Volume 4,*

Danielewski, Mark Z. ★*House of Leaves: A Novel*

Danticat, Edwidge. *Claire of the Sea Light*

Danticat, Edwidge. ★*Everything Inside: Stories*

Dare, Abi. *The Girl with the Louding Voice*

Darnielle, John. *Universal Harvester*

Davidson, Andy. *The Boatman's Daughter: A Novel*

Davies, Carys. *The Mission House*

Davies, Carys. *West*

Davies, Peter Ho. *The Fortunes*

Davies, Peter Ho. *A Lie Someone Told You About Yourself*

Davila, April. *142 Ostriches*

Davis, Kathryn. *Duplex*

De Bernieres, Louis. *Birds Without Wings*

De Kretser, Michelle. *The Life to Come*

De Robertis, Carolina. *Cantoras*

Deane, Seamus. *Reading in the Dark*

Dektar, Molly. *The Ash Family*

Delany, Samuel R. *Dhalgren*

DeLillo, Don. *Falling Man: A Novel*

DeLillo, Don. *Libra*

DeLillo, Don. *The Names*

DeLillo, Don. *The Silence*

DeLillo, Don. *Underworld*

DeLillo, Don. ★*White Noise*

Dennis-Benn, Nicole. ★*Patsy: A Novel*

Deon, Natashia. *Grace*

Depestre, Rene. *Hadriana in All My Dreams*

Desai, Anita. *Clear Light of Day*

Desai, Anita. *Fire on the Mountain*

Desai, Kiran. *The Inheritance of Loss*

deWitt, Patrick. *The Sisters Brothers: A Novel*

Dexter, Pete. *Paris Trout*

Diaz, Junot. ★*The Brief Wondrous Life of Oscar Wao*

Diaz, Junot. ★*This Is How You Lose Her*

Dickens, Charles. *Dombey and Son*

Dickens, Charles. ★*Great Expectations*

Didion, Joan. *A Book of Common Prayer*

Didion, Joan. ★*Play It as It Lays: A Novel*

Dimitri, Francesco. *The Book of Hidden Things*

Diofebi, Dario. *Paradise, Nevada*

Djavadi, Negar. *Disoriental*

Doctorow, E. L. *All the Time in the World: New and Selected Stories*

Doctorow, E. L. *Andrew's Brain*

Doctorow, E. L. ★*Billy Bathgate: A Novel*

Doctorow, E. L. ★*The Book of Daniel: A Novel*

Doctorow, E. L. *Doctorow: Collected Stories*

Doctorow, E. L. *Homer and Langley: A Novel*

Doctorow, E. L. *The March: A Novel*

Doctorow, E. L. ★*Ragtime*

Doctorow, E. L. *World's Fair*

Doerr, Anthony. ★*All the Light We Cannot See: A Novel*

Doerr, Anthony. ★*Cloud Cuckoo Land: A Novel*

Dolan-Leach, Caite. *We Went to the Woods: A Novel*

Donoghue, Emma. *Akin*

Donoghue, Emma. ★*Frog Music*

Donoghue, Emma. ★*Room: A Novel*

Donoghue, Emma. *Slammerkin*

Donoghue, Emma. ★*The Wonder*

Dos Passos, John. *1919*

Dos Passos, John. *The 42nd Parallel*
Dos Passos, John. *Manhattan Transfer*
Doshi, Avni. *Burnt Sugar: A Novel*
Dovlatov, Sergei. *Pushkin Hills*
Doyle, Rob. *Threshold*
Doyle, Roddy. *Love*
Doyle, Roddy. *Paddy Clarke, Ha-Ha-Ha*
Drabble, Margaret. ★*The Dark Flood Rises*
Drabble, Margaret. *The Pure Gold Baby*
Drabble, Margaret. *The Sea Lady*
Dreiser, Theodore. ★*An American Tragedy*
Drndic, Dasa. *Trieste*
Duncan, Glen. *By Blood We Live*
Duncan, Glen. *The Last Werewolf*
Duncan, Glen. *Talulla Rising*
Dupont, Eric. *The American Fiancee: A Novel*
Durrell, Lawrence. ★*Justine*
Durrow, Heidi W. *The Girl Who Fell from the Sky: A Novel*
Dyer, Geoff. *Jeff in Venice, Death in Varanasi*
Earley, Tony. *Mr. Tall: A Novella and Stories*
Eco, Umberto. *Baudolino*
Eco, Umberto. ★*Foucault's Pendulum*
Eco, Umberto. *The Island of the Day Before*
Eco, Umberto. *The Mysterious Flame of Queen Loana: An Illustrated Novel*
Eco, Umberto. ★*The Name of the Rose*
Eco, Umberto. *Numero Zero*
Edugyan, Esi. *Half-Blood Blues*
Edwards, Louis. *Ramadan Ramsey: A Novel*
Egan, Jennifer. ★*Manhattan Beach: A Novel*
Egan, Jennifer. ★*A Visit from the Goon Squad*
Ehirim, Nnamdi. *Prince of Monkeys*
Eisenberg, Deborah. *The Twilight of the Superheroes*
Eliot, George. ★*Adam Bede*
Ellison, Ralph. ★*Invisible Man*
Ellison, Ralph. ★*Juneteenth*
Ellison, Ralph. *Three Days Before the Shooting . . .*
Ellmann, Lucy. *Ducks, Newburyport*
Emezi, Akwaeke. ★*The Death of Vivek Oji*
Emezi, Akwaeke. *Freshwater*
Enard, Mathias. *Compass*
Engel, Patricia. ★*Infinite Country*
Enger, Lin. *The High Divide: A Novel*
Englander, Nathan. *The Ministry of Special Cases*
Englander, Nathan. *What We Talk About When We Talk About Anne Frank: Stories*
Enright, Anne. *Actress: A Novel*
Enright, Anne. *The Forgotten Waltz*
Enright, Anne. ★*The Gathering*
Enright, Anne. *The Green Road: A Novel*
Erdrich, Louise. *The Beet Queen: A Novel*
Erdrich, Louise. *Four Souls: A Novel*
Erdrich, Louise. *Future Home of the Living God*
Erdrich, Louise. ★*Larose*
Erdrich, Louise. *The Last Report on the Miracles at Little No Horse*
Erdrich, Louise. *Love Medicine: A Novel*
Erdrich, Louise. *The Master Butchers Singing Club: A Novel*
Erdrich, Louise. ★*The Night Watchman: A Novel*

Erdrich, Louise. *The Painted Drum: A Novel*
Erdrich, Louise. *The Plague of Doves*
Erdrich, Louise. *The Red Convertible: Selected and New Stories, 1978-2008*
Erdrich, Louise. ★*The Round House: A Novel*
Erdrich, Louise. ★*The Sentence*
Erdrich, Louise. ★*Shadow Tag: A Novel*
Erdrich, Louise. *Tracks: A Novel*
Erpenbeck, Jenny. *The Book of Words*
Erpenbeck, Jenny. *Go, Went, Gone: A Novel*
Eugenides, Jeffrey. *Fresh Complaint: Stories*
Eugenides, Jeffrey. ★*The Marriage Plot*
Eugenides, Jeffrey. ★*Middlesex*
Eugenides, Jeffrey. ★*The Virgin Suicides*
Evans, Danielle. ★*The Office of Historical Corrections: A Novella and Stories*
Evaristo, Bernardine. ★*Girl, Woman, Other*
Everett, Percival L. *Erasure: A Novel*
Everett, Percival L. *God's Country*
Everett, Percival L. *I Am Not Sidney Poitier*
Evison, Jonathan. *Legends of the North Cascades: A Novel*
Evison, Jonathan. *West of Here: A Novel*
Faber, Michel. *The Book of Strange New Things*
Fajardo-Anstine, Kali. ★*Sabrina & Corina: Stories*
Farah, Nuruddin. *Crossbones*
Farah, Nuruddin. *Knots*
Faulkner, William. ★*Absalom, Absalom!*
Faulkner, William. ★*As I Lay Dying: The Corrected Text*
Faulkner, William. ★*Go Down, Moses*
Faulkner, William. *The Hamlet*
Faulkner, William. *Intruder in the Dust*
Faulkner, William. ★*Light in August*
Faulkner, William. *The Reivers: A Reminiscence*
Faulkner, William. *Requiem for a Nun*
Faulkner, William. ★*Sanctuary*
Faulkner, William. ★*The Sound and the Fury*
Faulkner, William. *Uncollected Stories of William Faulkner*
Faulks, Sebastian. ★*Birdsong*
Faulks, Sebastian. *Charlotte Gray: A Novel*
Faulks, Sebastian. *On Green Dolphin Street: A Novel*
Faulks, Sebastian. *Paris Echo: A Novel*
Faulks, Sebastian. *A Week in December*
Faye, Gael. ★*Small Country: A Novel*
Feng, Linda Rui. *Swimming Back to Trout River*
Fernandez, Nona. *The Twilight Zone*
Ferrante, Elena. *The Lying Life of Adults*
Ferrell, Carolyn. *Dear Miss Metropolitan*
Ferris, Joshua. *A Calling for Charlie Barnes*
Ferris, Joshua. *To Rise Again at a Decent Hour: A Novel*
Fforde, Jasper. *Shades of Grey: A Novel*
Fitch, Janet. *White Oleander: A Novel*
Fitzgerald, F. Scott. ★*This Side of Paradise*
Fitzgerald, Penelope. *The Means of Escape: Stories*
Flanagan, Richard. *Gould's Book of Fish: A Novel in Twelve Fish*
Flanagan, Richard. ★*The Narrow Road to the Deep North*
Flanery, Patrick. *Absolution: A Novel*
Flint, Emma. ★*Little Deaths: A Novel*
Florio, Gwen. *Silent Hearts*

Forbes, Curdella. *A Tall History of Sugar*
Ford, Ford Madox. ★*The Good Soldier: A Tale of Passion*
Ford, Kelli Jo. ★*Crooked Hallelujah*
Ford, Richard. *Canada*
Ford, Richard. ★*Independence Day*
Ford, Richard. *The Lay of the Land*
Ford, Richard. *Let Me Be Frank with You*
Ford, Richard. *Sorry for Your Trouble: Stories*
Forster, E. M. ★*Howards End*
Forster, E. M. ★*A Passage to India*
Forster, E. M. ★*A Room with a View*
Fountain, Ben. ★*Billy Lynn's Long Halftime Walk*
Fowler, Karen Joy. ★*We Are All Completely Beside Ourselves*
Fowles, John. ★*The French Lieutenant's Woman*
Fowles, John. *The Magus*
Frame, Janet. *Between My Father and the King: New and Uncollected Stories*
Francis, Patry. *The Orphans of Race Point: A Novel*
Franck, Julia. *Blindness of the Heart*
Franzen, Jonathan. ★*The Corrections*
Franzen, Jonathan. ★*Crossroads*
Franzen, Jonathan. ★*Freedom*
Franzen, Jonathan. *Purity*
Frazier, Charles. ★*Cold Mountain*
Frazier, Charles. *Nightwoods: A Novel*
Frazier, Jean Kyoung. *Pizza Girl*
French, Marilyn. ★*The Women's Room*
Freudenberger, Nell. ★*Lost and Wanted: A Novel*
Freudenberger, Nell. *The Newlyweds*
Fridlund, Emily. ★*History of Wolves: A Novel*
Fuentes, Carlos. *Destiny and Desire: A Novel*
Fuentes, Carlos. *The Years with Laura Diaz*
Fuller, Claire. *Our Endless Numbered Days: A Novel*
Gaddis, William. *Agape Agape*
Gaddis, William. *A Frolic of His Own: A Novel*
Gaddis, William. ★*J R: A Novel*
Gaddis, William. ★*The Recognitions*
Gaines, Ernest J. ★*A Gathering of Old Men*
Gainza, Maria. *The Optic Nerve*
Gaitskill, Mary. *Don't Cry: Stories*
Gaitskill, Mary. *Veronica*
Gala, Marcial. ★*The Black Cathedral*
Galchen, Rivka. *American Innovations: Stories*
Gallen, Michelle. *Big Girl, Small Town: A Novel*
Gamboa, Santiago. *Necropolis*
Gao, XIngjian. *Soul Mountain*
Garcia Marquez, Gabriel. ★*The Autumn of the Patriarch*
Garcia Marquez, Gabriel. *Chronicle of a Death Foretold*
Garcia Marquez, Gabriel. *Collected Novellas*
Garcia Marquez, Gabriel. *The General in His Labyrinth*
Garcia Marquez, Gabriel. *In Evil Hour*
Garcia Marquez, Gabriel. ★*Love in the Time of Cholera*
Garcia Marquez, Gabriel. *Memories of My Melancholy Whores*
Garcia Marquez, Gabriel. ★*One Hundred Years of Solitude*
Garcia Marquez, Gabriel. ★*Strange Pilgrims: Twelve Stories*
Gardam, Jane. *Last Friends*
Gardam, Jane. *Old Filth*
Garner, Helen. *The Spare Room*

Gaskell, Elizabeth Cleghorn. ★*Cranford*
Gaskell, Elizabeth Cleghorn. ★*North and South*
Gay, Roxane. ★*Ayiti*
Gay, Roxane. ★*Difficult Women*
Gay, Roxane. ★*An Untamed State*
Geni, Abby. *The Wildlands: A Novel*
Gessen, Keith. *A Terrible Country*
Ghosh, Amitav. *Flood of Fire*
Ghosh, Amitav. *The Glass Palace*
Ghosh, Amitav. ★*Gun Island*
Ghosh, Amitav. *The Hungry Tide*
Ghosh, Amitav. *River of Smoke*
Ghosh, Amitav. *Sea of Poppies*
Gide, Andre. ★*The Immoralist*
Gilbert, David. *& Sons: A Novel*
Gilligan, Ruth. *The Butchers' Blessing*
Ginzburg, Natalia. *Voices in the Evening*
Giordano, Paolo. *Heaven and Earth*
Giordano, Paolo. *The Human Body*
Giordano, Paolo. *Like Family*
Giordano, Paolo. ★*The Solitude of Prime Numbers: A Novel*
Glass, Julia. *The Whole World Over*
Glass, Julia. *The Widower's Tale*
Godden, Rumer. *The Greengage Summer: A Novel*
Godwin, Gail. *Flora: A Novel*
Godwin, Gail. *Grief Cottage: A Novel*
Godwin, Gail. *Old Lovegood Girls*
Godwin, Gail. *Unfinished Desires*
Goenawan, Clarissa. *Rainbirds*
Goldberg, Myla. *Feast Your Eyes*
Goldbloom, Goldie. *On Division*
Golding, William. *Close Quarters*
Golding, William. ★*Darkness Visible*
Golding, William. *The Inheritors*
Golding, William. ★*Lord of the Flies: A Novel*
Goldstein, Rebecca. *36 Arguments for the Existence of God: A Work of Fiction*
Gordimer, Nadine. *The Conservationist*
Gordimer, Nadine. *Get a Life*
Gordimer, Nadine. ★*July's People*
Gordimer, Nadine. ★*My Son's Story*
Gordimer, Nadine. *No Time Like the Present: A Novel*
Gordimer, Nadine. *None to Accompany Me*
Gordimer, Nadine. *The Pickup*
Gordon, Jaimy. ★*Lord of Misrule: A Novel*
Gosling, Victoria. *Before the Ruins: A Novel*
Gowar, Imogen Hermes. *The Mermaid and Mrs. Hancock*
Graedon, Alena. *The Word Exchange: A Novel*
Graley, Lisa. *The Current That Carries: Stories*
Grass, Gunter. *The Box: Tales from the Darkroom*
Grass, Gunter. *Crabwalk*
Grau, Shirley Ann. *The Keepers of the House*
Gray, Anissa. *The Care and Feeding of Ravenously Hungry Girls*
Greene, Amy. *Long Man*
Greene, Graham. ★*Brighton Rock*
Greene, Graham. *The Captain and the Enemy*
Greene, Graham. *Collected Stories: Including May We Borrow Your Husband? a Sense of Reality, Twenty-One Stories*

Greene, Graham. ★*The End of the Affair*
Greene, Graham. ★*The Heart of the Matter*
Greene, Graham. *The Honorary Consul*
Greene, Graham. *The Human Factor*
Greene, Graham. *The Last Word and Other Stories*
Greene, Graham. *The Power and the Glory*
Greene, Graham. *The Tenth Man*
Greengrass, Jessie. *Sight: A Novel*
Greenidge, Kaitlyn. ★*Libertie: A Novel*
Greenidge, Kaitlyn. *We Love You, Charlie Freeman: A Novel*
Greenwell, Garth. *Cleanness*
Greenwell, Garth. *What Belongs to You: A Novel*
Greer, Andrew Sean. *The Impossible Lives of Greta Wells*
Greer, Andrew Sean. ★*Less*
Grenville, Kate. *The Secret River*
Grodstein, Lauren. *Our Short History*
Groff, Lauren. ★*Arcadia: A Novel*
Groff, Lauren. *Delicate Edible Birds and Other Stories*
Groff, Lauren. ★*Fates and Furies*
Groff, Lauren. ★*Florida*
Groff, Lauren. ★*Matrix*
Gross, Max. *The Lost Shtetl*
Grossman, David. *Be My Knife*
Grossman, David. ★*A Horse Walks into a Bar*
Grossman, David. ★*More Than I Love My Life: A Novel*
Grossman, David. ★*To the End of the Land*
Gruen, Sara. *The Ape House*
Gruen, Sara. ★*Water for Elephants: A Novel*
Grushin, Olga. *The Line*
Gunaratne, Guy. *In Our Mad and Furious City*
Gunday, Hakan. *The Few*
Gunesekera, Romesh. ★*Suncatcher: A Novel*
Guskin, Sharon. *The Forgetting Time*
Gustine, Amy. *You Should Pity Us Instead: Stories*
Guterson, David. *The Other*
Guterson, David. *Our Lady of the Forest*
Guterson, David. ★*Snow Falling on Cedars*
Gyasi, Yaa. ★*Transcendent Kingdom*
Hadley, Tessa. *Bad Dreams and Other Stories*
Hadley, Tessa. *Clever Girl*
Hage, Rawi. *Beirut Hellfire Society: A Novel*
Hage, Rawi. *De Niro's Game*
Haigh, Jennifer. *Mrs. Kimble: A Novel*
Hajdu, David. *Adrianne Geffel: A Fiction*
Halfon, Eduardo. *Mourning*
Hall, Steven. *Maxwell's Demon*
Hallberg, Garth Risk. ★*City on Fire*
Halliday, Lisa. ★*Asymmetry*
Halls, Stacey. *The Lost Orphan*
Hamid, Mohsin. ★*Exit West: A Novel*
Hammad, Isabella. ★*The Parisian, Or, Al-Barisi: A Novel*
Hamya, Jo. *Three Rooms*
Han, Kang. ★*Human Acts: A Novel*
Han, Kang. *The White Book*
Handke, Peter. *Don Juan: His Own Version*
Hannaham, James. ★*Delicious Foods*
Harding, Paul. *Tinkers*
Harkaway, Nick. *Gnomon: A Novel*

Harrigan, Stephen. *The Leopard Is Loose: A Novel*
Harris, Joanne. ★*Chocolat: A Novel*
Harris, Sarah J. *The Color of Bee Larkham's Murder: A Novel*
Harrison, Jim. *The Great Leader*
Haruf, Kent. ★*Our Souls at Night*
Haruf, Kent. ★*Plainsong*
Hashemzadeh Bonde, Golnaz. *What We Owe*
Haslett, Adam. ★*Imagine Me Gone: A Novel*
Haslett, Adam. *Union Atlantic*
Hassib, Rajia. *A Pure Heart: A Novel*
Hawke, Ethan. *A Bright Ray of Darkness*
Hay, Elizabeth. *Late Nights on Air*
Hazzard, Shirley. ★*The Great Fire*
Hazzard, Shirley. ★*The Transit of Venus*
Heacox, Kim. *Jimmy Bluefeather: A Novel*
Headley, Maria Dahvana. *The Mere Wife*
Hegi, Ursula. *Stones from the River*
Hegi, Ursula. *The Vision of Emma Blau*
Helprin, Mark. *In Sunlight and in Shadow*
Helprin, Mark. *Paris in the Present Tense*
Helprin, Mark. ★*Winter's Tale*
Hemingway, Ernest. ★*The Sun Also Rises*
Hemingway, Ernest. *To Have and Have Not*
Hempel, Amy. *Sing to It: New Stories*
Henderson, Smith. *Fourth of July Creek*
Henkin, Joshua. *Morningside Heights*
Hensher, Philip. *Scenes from Early Life: A Novel*
Herbert, Julian. *Bring Me the Head of Quentin Tarantino: Stories*
Hersey, John. ★*A Bell for Adano*
Hesse, Hermann. *Narcissus and Goldmund*
Hesse, Hermann. ★*Steppenwolf*
Hession, Ronan. *Leonard and Hungry Paul*
Hijuelos, Oscar. *Beautiful Maria of My Soul*
Hijuelos, Oscar. ★*The Mambo Kings Play Songs of Love: A Novel*
Hill, Lawrence. *Someone Knows My Name: A Novel*
Hill, Nathan. *The Nix: A Novel*
Hobson, Brandon. ★*The Removed: A Novel*
Hoffman, Alice. *The Book of Magic*
Hoffman, Alice. *The Ice Queen: A Novel*
Hoffman, Alice. *The River King*
Hoffman, Alice. *The Rules of Magic: A Novel*
Hoffman, Alice. ★*The World That We Knew*
Holbert, Bruce. *Whiskey*
Holdstock, Pauline. *Here I Am!*
Holmes, J. M. *How Are You Going to Save Yourself*
Hooper, Emma. *Etta and Otto and Russell and James: A Novel*
Horn, Dara. *Eternal Life: A Novel*
Houellebecq, Michel. *Submission*
Howrey, Meg. *The Wanderers*
Hughes, Caoilinn. *Orchid and the Wasp*
Hugo, Victor. ★*Les Miserables*
Huisman, Violaine. *The Book of Mother*
Hulme, Keri. ★*The Bone People: A Novel*
Hulse, S. M. ★*Black River*
Hulse, S. M. *Eden Mine*
Hunt, Laird. *Zorrie*
Hunt, Samantha. *The Dark Dark: Stories*

Hurston, Zora Neale. *Hitting a Straight Lick with a Crooked Stick: Stories from the Harlem Renaissance*

Hurston, Zora Neale. ★*Their Eyes Were Watching God*

Irving, John. *Avenue of Mysteries: A Novel*

Irving, John. ★*The Cider House Rules: A Novel*

Isherwood, Christopher. ★*The Berlin Stories: The Last of Mr. Norris, Goodbye to Berlin*

Ishiguro, Kazuo. *An Artist of the Floating World*

Ishiguro, Kazuo. *The Buried Giant: A Novel*

Ishiguro, Kazuo. ★*Klara and the Sun*

Ishiguro, Kazuo. ★*Never Let Me Go*

Ishiguro, Kazuo. ★*The Remains of the Day*

Ishiguro, Kazuo. *The Unconsoled*

Ishiguro, Kazuo. *When We Were Orphans*

Iweala, Uzodinma. ★*Speak No Evil*

James, Marlon. ★*Black Leopard, Red Wolf*

James, Marlon. ★*A Brief History of Seven Killings: A Novel*

Jaswal, Balli Kaur. *Erotic Stories for Punjabi Widows*

Jen, Gish. ★*Thank You, Mr. Nixon: Stories*

Jhabvala, Ruth Prawer. *At the End of the Century: The Stories of Ruth Prawer Jhabvala.*

Jhabvala, Ruth Prawer. ★*Heat and Dust*

Jin, Ha. *The Boat Rocker: A Novel*

Jin, Ha. *A Map of Betrayal: A Novel*

Jin, Ha. ★*Waiting*

Jin, Meng. *Little Gods*

Johnson, Alaya Dawn. *Trouble the Saints*

Johnson, Daisy. *Everything Under*

Johnson, Daisy. *Sisters*

Johnson, Denis. *The Largesse of the Sea Maiden: Stories*

Jones, Cherie. *How the One-Armed Sister Sweeps Her House*

Jones, Cynan. *Stillicide*

Jones, James. ★*From Here to Eternity*

Jones, Robert. ★*The Prophets: A Novel*

Jones, Tayari. ★*An American Marriage: A Novel*

Jones, Tayari. *Silver Sparrow: A Novel*

Joukhadar, Zeyn. ★*The Thirty Names of Night: A Novel*

Kadare, Ismail. ★*The Three-Arched Bridge*

Kafka, Franz. ★*The Metamorphosis*

Kafka, Franz. ★*The Trial*

Kandasamy, Meena. *When I Hit You, Or, a Portrait of the Writer as a Young Wife*

Kantor, MacKinlay. ★*Andersonville*

Kawabata, Yasunari. *The Sound of the Mountain*

Kawaguchi, Toshikazu. *Before the Coffee Gets Cold*

Kawakami, Mieko. *Ms. Ice Sandwich*

Kelman, James. *How Late It Was, How Late*

Keneally, Thomas. ★*The Daughters of Mars*

Keneally, Thomas. ★*Schindler's List*

Keneally, Thomas. *Shame and the Captives: A Novel*

Kennedy, William. ★*Ironweed: A Novel*

Kerangal, Maylis de. *The Heart: A Novel*

Kerouac, Jack. *The Dharma Bums*

Kerouac, Jack. ★*Road Novels 1957-1960*

Kesey, Ken. ★*One Flew Over the Cuckoo's Nest*

Kesey, Ken. *Sometimes a Great Notion: A Novel*

Khadivi, Laleh. ★*A Good Country: A Novel*

Khadra, Yasmina. ★*Khalil: A Novel*

Khadra, Yasmina. *The Swallows of Kabul: A Novel*

Khalfah, Khlid. *Death Is Hard Work: A Novel*

Kilalea, Katharine. *Ok, Mr. Field: A Novel*

Kim, Young-Ha. *Diary of a Murderer: And Other Stories*

Kimani, Peter. *Dance of the Jakaranda*

Kincaid, Jamaica. ★*Annie John*

Kincaid, Jamaica. *The Autobiography of My Mother*

Kincaid, Jamaica. ★*Lucy*

Kincaid, Jamaica. *See Now Then*

King, Lily. *Writers & Lovers: A Novel*

Kingsolver, Barbara. ★*Flight Behavior*

Kingsolver, Barbara. ★*The Poisonwood Bible: A Novel*

Kingsolver, Barbara. ★*Unsheltered*

Kirshenbaum, Binnie. *Rabbits for Food*

Kitamura, Katie M. *Intimacies*

Klay, Phil. ★*Missionaries*

Kleeman, Alexandra. *Something New Under the Sun*

Knausgaard, Karl Ove. *The Morning Star*

Knowles, John. ★*A Separate Peace*

Ko, Lisa. *The Leavers*

Konar, Affinity. *Mischling: A Novel*

Krauss, Nicole. *Forest Dark*

Krauss, Nicole. ★*To Be a Man: Stories*

Kundera, Milan. ★*Immortality*

Kundera, Milan. ★*The Unbearable Lightness of Being*

Kunzru, Hari. *Red Pill: A Novel*

Kunzru, Hari. *White Tears*

Kupersmith, Violet. ★*Build Your House Around My Body*

Kushner, Rachel. *The Mars Room*

Kwok, Jean. *Searching for Sylvie Lee*

Labatut, Benjamin. *When We Cease to Understand the World*

Lacey, Catherine. ★*Pew: A Novel*

Lahiri, Jhumpa. *The Lowland: A Novel*

Lahiri, Jhumpa. ★*The Namesake*

Lahiri, Jhumpa. ★*Whereabouts*

Lalami, Laila. *The Other Americans: A Novel*

Langan, Sarah. *Good Neighbors*

Lange, Tracey. ★*We Are the Brennans*

Larison, John. *Whiskey When We're Dry*

Larsen, Nella. *Passing*

Larsen, Reif. *I Am Radar: A Novel*

Lasdun, James. *Afternoon of a Faun: A Novel*

Lawrence, D. H. ★*Lady Chatterley's Lover*

Lawrence, D. H. *Sons and Lovers*

Lawrence, D. H. *Women in Love*

Leavitt, David. ★*Shelter in Place*

Lebrecht, Norman. *The Song of Names*

Lee, Andrea. *Red Island House*

Lee, Chang-Rae. ★*My Year Abroad*

Lee, Chang-Rae. ★*On Such a Full Sea*

Lee, Chang-Rae. ★*The Surrendered*

Lee, Harper. ★*Go Set a Watchman*

Lee, Harper. ★*To Kill a Mockingbird*

Lehane, Dennis. *Since We Fell*

Leilani, Raven. ★*Luster*

Lem, Stanislaw. ★*Solaris*

Lerner, Ben. ★*The Topeka School*

Lessing, Doris May. ★*The Fifth Child*

Lessing, Doris May. ★*The Golden Notebook*
Lessing, Doris May. *A Proper Marriage*
Lessing, Doris May. *The Sweetest Dream*
Lethem, Jonathan. *Chronic City*
Lethem, Jonathan. *Dissident Gardens*
Lethem, Jonathan. ★*Motherless Brooklyn*
Levy, Andrea. *Small Island*
Levy, Deborah. *Hot Milk: A Novel*
Levy, Deborah. *Swimming Home: A Novel*
Lightman, Alan P. ★*Einstein's Dreams*
Lively, Penelope. ★*Moon Tiger*
Livesey, Margot. ★*The Boy in the Field*
Lodato, Victor. *Edgar and Lucy: A Novel*
Lodato, Victor. *Mathilda Savitch*
Loedel, Daniel. *Hades, Argentina*
Lombardo, Claire. *The Most Fun We Ever Had: A Novel*
Lopez Barrio, Cristina. *The House of the Impossible Loves*
Luchette, Claire. *Agatha of Little Neon*
Luiselli, Valeria. ★*Lost Children Archive: A Novel*
Lukas, Michael David. *The Last Watchman of Old Cairo: A Novel*
Lunde, Maja. *The End of the Ocean: A Novel*
Lurie, Alison. *Foreign Affairs*
Mabanckou, Alain. ★*Black Moses*
Machado, Carmen Maria. *Her Body and Other Parties: Stories*
MacLeod, Alison. *Tenderness*
Mahmoud, Lena. *Amreekiya: A Novel*
Mailer, Norman. ★*The Naked and the Dead*
Majumdar, Megha. *A Burning*
Makkai, Rebecca. ★*The Great Believers*
Makumbi, Jennifer Nansubuga. ★*A Girl Is a Body of Water*
Makumbi, Jennifer Nansubuga. *Kintu*
Malamud, Bernard. *The Assistant*
Malamud, Bernard. ★*The Fixer*
Malouf, David. *Ransom*
Malouf, David. *Remembering Babylon*
Mandanipour, Shahriar. *Moon Brow*
Mandel, Emily St. John. ★*The Glass Hotel: A Novel*
Mandel, Emily St. John. ★*Station Eleven*
Mann, Thomas. *Buddenbrooks*
Mann, Thomas. *Death in Venice and Seven Other Stories*
Mann, Thomas. *Doctor Faustus*
Manning, Corinne. *We Had No Rules: Stories*
Mantel, Hilary. ★*Bring up the Bodies: A Novel*
Mantel, Hilary. ★*Wolf Hall*
Marias, Javier. *The Infatuations*
Marias, Javier. *Thus Bad Begins: A Novel*
Markley, Stephen. *Ohio*
Marlantes, Karl. *Deep River*
Marlantes, Karl. ★*Matterhorn: A Novel of the Vietnam War*
Marra, Anthony. ★*A Constellation of Vital Phenomena: A Novel*
Marra, Anthony. *The Tsar of Love and Techno: Stories*
Martel, Yann. ★*Life of Pi: A Novel*
Masad, Ilana. *All My Mother's Lovers: A Novel*
Mason, Bobbie Ann. *Dear Ann: A Novel*
Mason, Bobbie Ann. *Patchwork*
Mason, Daniel. *A Registry of My Passage Upon the Earth: Stories*
Matthiessen, Peter. *Shadow Country: A New Rendering of the Watson Legend*

Maugham, W. Somerset. ★*Of Human Bondage*
Mayer, Mark. *Aerialists: Stories*
Mbue, Imbolo. *How Beautiful We Were*
McAllister, Tom. *How to Be Safe: A Novel*
McBride, James. *Five-Carat Soul*
McBride, James. ★*The Good Lord Bird*
McCann, Colum. ★*Apeirogon: A Novel*
McCann, Colum. ★*Transatlantic: A Novel*
McCarthy, Cormac. ★*All the Pretty Horses*
McCarthy, Cormac. ★*Blood Meridian, Or, the Evening Redness in the West*
McCarthy, Cormac. *The Crossing*
McCarthy, Cormac. ★*No Country for Old Men*
McCarthy, Cormac. ★*The Road*
McCarthy, Jesse. *The Fugitivities*
McConaghy, Charlotte. *Migrations*
McConaghy, Charlotte. *Once There Were Wolves: A Novel*
McCormack, Mike. ★*Solar Bones*
McCracken, Elizabeth. *The Souvenir Museum: Stories*
McCullers, Carson. ★*The Heart Is a Lonely Hunter*
McCullers, Carson. *The Member of the Wedding*
McCullers, Carson. *Reflections in a Golden Eye*
McDermott, Alice. *After This*
McDermott, Alice. *At Weddings and Wakes*
McDermott, Alice. ★*Charming Billy*
McDermott, Alice. *Child of My Heart*
McDermott, Alice. ★*The Ninth Hour*
McDermott, Alice. *Someone*
McDermott, Alice. ★*That Night*
McEwan, Ian. ★*Amsterdam*
McEwan, Ian. ★*Atonement: A Novel*
McEwan, Ian. *Black Dogs*
McEwan, Ian. *The Child in Time*
McEwan, Ian. ★*On Chesil Beach*
McEwan, Ian. *Solar: A Novel*
McFarland, Jeni. *The House of Deep Water*
McGregor, Jon. *The Reservoir Tapes*
McGuane, Thomas. ★*Cloudbursts: Collected and New Stories*
McKenzie, Alecia. *A Million Aunties*
McKenzie, Elizabeth. *The Portable Veblen*
McLain, Paula. ★*When the Stars Go Dark: A Novel*
McLaughlin, Danielle. *The Art of Falling*
McLean, Felicity. *The Van Apfel Girls Are Gone*
McMurtry, Larry. *Comanche Moon: A Novel*
McMurtry, Larry. *The Evening Star: A Novel*
McMurtry, Larry. ★*Lonesome Dove: A Novel*
McMurtry, Larry. ★*Streets of Laredo: A Novel*
McMurtry, Larry. ★*Terms of Endearment: A Novel : With a New Preface*
Means, David. ★*Instructions for a Funeral: Stories*
Mehta, Rahul. *No Other World: A Novel*
Mendez, Paul. *Rainbow Milk*
Mengiste, Maaza. ★*The Shadow King: A Novel*
Messud, Claire. ★*The Woman Upstairs: A Novel*
Miller, Kei. ★*Augustown*
Miller, Madeline. ★*Circe*
Miller, Madeline. *The Song of Achilles*
Miller, Mary. *Biloxi: A Novel*

Miller, Rebecca. ★*Jacob's Folly: A Novel*

Miller, Sue. ★*Monogamy*

Miller, Xander. *Zo: A Novel*

Millhauser, Steven. *Martin Dressler: The Tale of an American Dreamer*

Mitchell, David. *Black Swan Green: A Novel*

Mitchell, David. *The Bone Clocks: A Novel*

Mitchell, David. ★*Cloud Atlas: A Novel*

Mitchell, David. *The Thousand Autumns of Jacob De Zoet: A Novel*

Mitchell, David. ★*Utopia Avenue: A Novel*

Mohamed, Nadifa. *The Orchard of Lost Souls: A Novel*

Momaday, N. Scott. *The Ancient Child: A Novel*

Momaday, N. Scott. *House Made of Dawn*

Moniz, Dantiel W. *Milk Blood Heat*

Moore, Alan. *Jerusalem: A Novel*

Moore, Alison. *The Lighthouse*

Moore, Liz. *The Unseen World*

Moore, Lorrie. *A Gate at the Stairs: A Novel*

Morgan, C. E. ★*The Sport of Kings*

Morrison, Toni. ★*Beloved: A Novel*

Morrison, Toni. ★*The Bluest Eye: A Novel*

Morrison, Toni. ★*God Help the Child*

Morrison, Toni. *Home*

Morrison, Toni. *Jazz*

Morrison, Toni. *Love*

Morrison, Toni. *A Mercy: A Novel*

Morrison, Toni. *Paradise*

Morrison, Toni. ★*Song of Solomon*

Morrison, Toni. *Sula*

Morrison, Toni. *Tar Baby*

Morton, Brian. *Florence Gordon*

Moshfegh, Ottessa. ★*Death in Her Hands: A Novel*

Moshfegh, Ottessa. *Eileen*

Moshfegh, Ottessa. *My Year of Rest and Relaxation*

Mosley, Walter. ★*The Awkward Black Man: Stories*

Mosley, Walter. ★*John Woman*

Moss, Sarah. *Ghost Wall: A Novel*

Moss, Sarah. *Summerwater*

Mott, Jason. *Hell of a Book*

Mozley, Fiona. ★*Elmet*

Mukherjee, Neel. *The Lives of Others*

Mukherjee, Neel. ★*A State of Freedom*

Munro, Alice. *Dear Life: Stories*

Munro, Alice. *Family Furnishings: Selected Stories, 1995-2014*

Munro, Alice. *Hateship, Friendship, Courtship, Loveship, Marriage: Stories*

Munro, Alice. *Lives of Girls and Women*

Munro, Alice. *Open Secrets: Stories*

Munro, Alice. *Runaway: Stories*

Munro, Alice. *Selected Stories*

Munro, Alice. *Too Much Happiness: Stories*

Munro, Alice. *The View from Castle Rock: Stories*

Murakami, Haruki. ★*1q84*

Murakami, Haruki. *After Dark*

Murakami, Haruki. *Colorless Tsukuru Tazaki and His Years of Pilgrimage*

Murakami, Haruki. ★*First Person Singular: Stories*

Murakami, Haruki. *Killing Commendatore: A Novel*

Murakami, Haruki. *Men Without Women: Stories*

Murakami, Haruki. *South of the Border, West of the Sun*

Murakami, Haruki. *The Wind-Up Bird Chronicle*

Murata, Sayaka. *Earthlings: A Novel*

Murdoch, Iris. *An Accidental Man*

Murdoch, Iris. *The Book and the Brotherhood*

Murdoch, Iris. *The Green Knight*

Murdoch, Iris. *The Nice and the Good*

Murdoch, Iris. *The Philosopher's Pupil*

Murdoch, Iris. *The Sea, the Sea*

Murphy, Devin. *Tiny Americans*

Murray, Paul. *Skippy Dies*

Nabokov, Vladimir Vladimirovich. *King, Queen, Knave: A Novel*

Nabokov, Vladimir Vladimirovich. ★*Lolita*

Nabokov, Vladimir Vladimirovich. *Look at the Harlequins!*

Nabokov, Vladimir Vladimirovich. *Pale Fire*

Nabokov, Vladimir Vladimirovich. *Pnin*

Nabokov, Vladimir Vladimirovich. *The Stories of Vladimir Nabokov*

Naipaul, V. S. *A Bend in the River*

Naipaul, V. S. *Guerrillas*

Naipaul, V. S. *A House for Mr. Biswas*

Naipaul, V. S. *Magic Seeds*

Naylor, Gloria. *Mama Day*

Newman, Sandra. *The Heavens*

Ng, Celeste. ★*Little Fires Everywhere: A Novel*

Nguyen, Phan Que Mai. ★*The Mountains Sing: A Novel*

Nguyen, Viet Thanh. ★*The Committed*

Nguyen, Viet Thanh. ★*The Refugees*

Nguyen, Viet Thanh. ★*The Sympathizer*

Niffenegger, Audrey. *The Time Traveler's Wife: A Novel*

Nin, Anais. *Cities of the Interior*

North, Anna. *The Life and Death of Sophie Stark*

Nunez, Sigrid. ★*The Friend*

Nunez, Sigrid. *What Are You Going Through*

O'Brien, Edna. ★*Girl*

O'Brien, Tim. *Going After Cacciato: A Novel*

O'Connor, Flannery. *The Complete Stories*

O'Connor, Flannery. ★*The Violent Bear It Away*

O'Connor, Flannery. ★*Wise Blood*

O'Donnell, Lisa. *The Death of Bees: A Novel*

O'Farrell, Maggie. *Hamnet*

O'Farrell, Maggie. *This Must Be the Place*

O'Hara, John. *Appointment in Samarra*

Oates, Joyce Carol. *The (Other) You: Stories*

Oates, Joyce Carol. *Because It Is Bitter, and Because It Is My Heart*

Oates, Joyce Carol. *Blonde: A Novel*

Oates, Joyce Carol. *Breathe*

Oates, Joyce Carol. *The Falls: A Novel*

Oates, Joyce Carol. *A Garden of Earthly Delights*

Oates, Joyce Carol. *The Gravedigger's Daughter: A Novel*

Oates, Joyce Carol. ★*My Life as a Rat*

Oates, Joyce Carol. *Night. Sleep. Death. The Stars*

Oates, Joyce Carol. ★*We Were the Mulvaneys*

Obioma, Chigozie. ★*The Fishermen: A Novel*

Obioma, Chigozie. ★*An Orchestra of Minorities*

Obreht, Tea. *Inland: A Novel*

Obreht, Tea. *The Tiger's Wife: A Novel*

Oe, Kenzaburo. *The Changeling*

Oe, Kenzaburo. ★*Death by Water*
Oe, Kenzaburo. ★*A Quiet Life*
Oe, Kenzaburo. *Somersault: A Novel*
Offill, Jenny. *Dept. Of Speculation*
Offill, Jenny. ★*Weather*
Offutt, Chris. *Country Dark*
Okri, Ben. *Prayer for the Living*
Ólafsson, Ólafur Jóhann. *The Sacrament: A Novel*
Ondaatje, Michael. ★*Warlight*
Ono, Masatsugu. *Echo on the Bay*
Onuzo, Chibundu. *Sankofa: A Novel*
Onyebuchi, Tochi. ★*Riot Baby*
Orange, Tommy. ★*There There*
Orringer, Julie. ★*The Invisible Bridge: A Novel*
Osondu, E. C. *This House Is Not for Sale: A Novel*
Otsuka, Julie. *The Buddha in the Attic*
Owens, Delia. *Where the Crawdads Sing*
Oyeyemi, Helen. *Boy, Snow, Bird: A Novel*
Oyeyemi, Helen. *Gingerbread: A Novel*
Oyeyemi, Helen. *Peaces*
Oyeyemi, Helen. *What Is Not Yours Is Not Yours: Stories*
Ozeki, Ruth L. *The Book of Form and Emptiness: A Novel*
Ozeki, Ruth L. ★*A Tale for the Time Being*
Ozick, Cynthia. *Foreign Bodies*
Ozick, Cynthia. *The Puttermesser Papers*
Packer, Ann. *The Children's Crusade*
Paley, Grace. ★*The Collected Stories*
Palliser, Charles. *The Quincunx*
Pamuk, Orhan. *The Museum of Innocence*
Pamuk, Orhan. *The Red-Haired Woman*
Pamuk, Orhan. *Silent House*
Pamuk, Orhan. ★*Snow*
Pamuk, Orhan. ★*A Strangeness in My Mind: A Novel*
Pandya, Sameer. *Members Only*
Panowich, Brian. *Bull Mountain*
Panowich, Brian. *Like Lions*
Park, Sang Young. ★*Love in the Big City: A Novel*
Patchett, Ann. ★*Bel Canto: A Novel*
Patchett, Ann. ★*The Dutch House: A Novel*
Paton, Alan. ★*Cry, the Beloved Country*
Pava, Sergio de la. *Lost Empress: A Novel*
Pava, Sergio de la. *Personae: A Novel*
Peace, David. *Occupied City*
Pearlman, Edith. *Binocular Vision: New & Selected Stories*
Pearlman, Edith. *Honeydew: Stories*
Perez-Reverte, Arturo. *The Club Dumas*
Perry, Sarah. *Melmoth: A Novel*
Persaud, Ingrid. *Love After Love: A Novel*
Pessl, Marisha. *Night Film: A Novel*
Pessl, Marisha. *Special Topics in Calamity Physics*
Petry, Ann. ★*The Street*
Petterson, Per. *I Curse the River of Time*
Petterson, Per. *I Refuse*
Petterson, Per. *Out Stealing Horses: A Novel*
Peynado, Brenda. *The Rock Eaters: Stories*
Phillips, Caryl. *A Distant Shore*
Phillips, Helen. *The Beautiful Bureaucrat: A Novel*
Phillips, Helen. *The Need: A Novel*

Phillips, Julia. ★*Disappearing Earth*
Philyaw, Deesha. *The Secret Lives of Church Ladies*
Piercy, Marge. *Gone to Soldiers: A Novel*
Piercy, Marge. *Sex Wars*
Pochoda, Ivy. ★*These Women*
Poissant, David James. *Lake Life*
Pollock, Donald Ray. *The Devil All the Time*
Pollock, Donald Ray. *Knockemstiff*
Porter, Max. ★*Grief Is the Thing with Feathers*
Porter, Max. ★*Lanny: A Novel*
Porter, Regina. *The Travelers*
Powers, Kevin. ★*The Yellow Birds: A Novel*
Powers, Richard. ★*Bewilderment: A Novel*
Powers, Richard. *The Echo Maker*
Powers, Richard. *Generosity: An Enhancement*
Powers, Richard. ★*The Overstory: A Novel*
Powning, Beth. *The Sea Captain's Wife: A Novel*
Prcic, Ismet. *Shards: A Novel*
Price, Reynolds. *The Good Priest's Son*
Price, Reynolds. *Roxanna Slade*
Pride, Christine. ★*We Are Not Like Them*
Prose, Francine. *Blue Angel: A Novel*
Prose, Francine. *Goldengrove: A Novel*
Prose, Francine. ★*The Vixen*
Proulx, Annie. *Bad Dirt: Wyoming Stories 2*
Proulx, Annie. ★*Barkskins: A Novel*
Proulx, Annie. *Fine Just the Way It Is: Wyoming Stories 3*
Proulx, Annie. *Postcards*
Proulx, Annie. ★*The Shipping News*
Pufahl, Shannon. *On Swift Horses*
Pynchon, Thomas. ★*Bleeding Edge*
Pynchon, Thomas. ★*The Crying of Lot 49*
Pynchon, Thomas. ★*Gravity's Rainbow*
Pynchon, Thomas. *Inherent Vice*
Pynchon, Thomas. ★*V: A Novel*
Quade, Kirstin Valdez. ★*The Five Wounds: A Novel*
Quade, Kirstin Valdez. *Night at the Fiestas: Stories*
Quotah, Eman. ★*Bride of the Sea: A Novel*
Rachman, Tom. *The Imperfectionists: A Novel*
Rachman, Tom. *The Italian Teacher*
Ramadan, Ahmad Danny. *The Clothesline Swing*
Randall, Alice. ★*Black Bottom Saints*
Rao, Shobha. ★*Girls Burn Brighter*
Rash, Ron. *Above the Waterfall*
Rash, Ron. *Burning Bright: Stories*
Rash, Ron. ★*The Cove*
Rash, Ron. ★*In the Valley: Stories and a Novella Based on Serena*
Rash, Ron. *Nothing Gold Can Stay: Stories*
Rash, Ron. *Something Rich and Strange: Selected Stories*
Ratner, Vaddey. *Music of the Ghosts*
Reed, Ishmael. *Flight to Canada*
Reid, Kiley. ★*Such a Fun Age*
Reimringer, John. *Vestments*
Remarque, Erich Maria. ★*All Quiet on the Western Front*
Restrepo, Laura. ★*Delirium: A Novel*
Restrepo, Laura. *No Place for Heroes: A Novel*
Reyes, Dolores. *Eartheater*
Rhys, Jean. ★*Wide Sargasso Sea*

Richardson, C. S. *The End of the Alphabet*
Richardson, Samuel. ★*Clarissa, Or, the History of a Young Lady*
Richler, Mordecai. *Barney's Version: A Novel*
Richler, Mordecai. *Solomon Gursky Was Here*
Rivero, Melissa. *The Affairs of the Falcons*
Robertson, Robin. *The Long Take: A Noir Narrative*
Robinson, Marilynne. ★*Gilead*
Robinson, Marilynne. *Home*
Robinson, Marilynne. ★*Jack*
Robinson, Marilynne. ★*Lila*
Rodrigues Fowler, Yara. *Stubborn Archivist*
Roisin, Fariha. *Like a Bird*
Rojstaczer, Stuart. *The Mathematician's Shiva: A Novel*
Rooney, Sally. ★*Beautiful World, Where Are You*
Rooney, Sally. *Normal People: A Novel*
Rose, Heather. *The Museum of Modern Love*
Rosen, Leonard J. *The Kortelisy Escape*
Rosnay, Tatiana de. ★*Flowers of Darkness*
Roth, Philip. ★*American Pastoral*
Roth, Philip. ★*The Anatomy Lesson*
Roth, Philip. ★*Everyman*
Roth, Philip. *Exit Ghost*
Roth, Philip. *The Ghost Writer*
Roth, Philip. ★*Goodbye, Columbus, and Five Short Stories*
Roth, Philip. *The Great American Novel*
Roth, Philip. ★*The Human Stain*
Roth, Philip. *I Married a Communist*
Roth, Philip. *Indignation*
Roth, Philip. ★*The Plot Against America*
Roth, Philip. ★*Portnoy's Complaint*
Roth, Philip. *Sabbath's Theater*
Roth, Philip. *Zuckerman Bound*
Roth, Philip. *Zuckerman Unbound*
Rothschild, Hannah. *The Improbability of Love: A Novel*
Row, Jess. *Your Face in Mine: A Novel*
Rowley, Steven. ★*The Guncle: A Novel*
Roy, Anuradha. *All the Lives We Never Lived: A Novel*
Roy, Arundhati. ★*The God of Small Things*
Roy, Arundhati. ★*The Ministry of Utmost Happiness: A Novel*
Ruiz Zafon, Carlos. *The Angel's Game*
Ruiz Zafon, Carlos. *The Labyrinth of the Spirits*
Runcie, James. *Canvey Island*
Rush, Norman. ★*Mating*
Rushdie, Salman. *The Enchantress of Florence: A Novel*
Rushdie, Salman. ★*The Golden House*
Rushdie, Salman. *Haroun and the Sea of Stories*
Rushdie, Salman. ★*Midnight's Children: A Novel*
Rushdie, Salman. ★*Quichotte: A Novel*
Rushdie, Salman. ★*The Satanic Verses*
Rushdie, Salman. *Shalimar the Clown: A Novel*
Rushdie, Salman. *Two Years Eight Months and Twenty-Eight Nights: A Novel*
Ruskovich, Emily. *Idaho: A Novel*
Russell, Karen. *Orange World and Other Stories*
Russell, Karen. ★*Swamplandia!*
Russell, Karen. *Vampires in the Lemon Grove: Stories*
Russell, Mary Doria. ★*Children of God: A Novel*
Russell, Mary Doria. *Epitaph: A Novel of the O.K. Corral*

Russell, Mary Doria. ★*The Sparrow*
Russo, Richard. *Bridge of Sighs*
Russo, Richard. ★*Chances Are...: A Novel*
Russo, Richard. ★*Empire Falls*
Russo, Richard. ★*Everybody's Fool*
Russo, Richard. ★*Nobody's Fool*
Russo, Richard. *The Risk Pool*
Russo, Richard. *Straight Man*
Sackville-West, V. *The Edwardians*
Sahota, Sunjeev. *The Year of the Runaways*
Saint, Jennifer. *Ariadne*
Saramago, Jose. *All the Names*
Saramago, Jose. ★*Blindness*
Saramago, Jose. *Cain*
Saramago, Jose. ★*The Cave*
Saramago, Jose. *The History of the Siege of Lisbon*
Saramago, Jose. *The Manual of Painting and Calligraphy*
Sathian, Sanjena. *Gold Diggers*
Satyal, Rakesh. *No One Can Pronounce My Name: A Novel*
Saunders, George. *In Persuasion Nation: Stories*
Saunders, George. ★*Lincoln in the Bardo: A Novel*
Saunders, George. ★*Tenth of December: Stories*
Savage, Sam. *The Way of the Dog: A Novel*
Savas, Aysegul. *Walking on the Ceiling*
Schami, Rafik. *Sophia: Or the Beginning of All Tales*
Schlink, Bernhard. *The Reader: A Novel*
Schulman, Helen. *Come with Me*
Schultz, Connie. *The Daughters of Erietown*
Schwarz, Liese O'Halloran. *What Could Be Saved*
Schweblin, Samanta. *Fever Dream: A Novel*
Schweblin, Samanta. *Little Eyes*
Schweblin, Samanta. *Mouthful of Birds: Stories*
Scott, Paul. ★*Staying On: A Novel*
Scott, Rion Amilcar. ★*The World Doesn't Require You: Stories*
Sebald, Winfried Georg. ★*Austerlitz*
Sebald, Winfried Georg. *The Emigrants*
Sebald, Winfried Georg. *Vertigo*
Sebold, Alice. ★*The Lovely Bones*
See, Lisa. *The Tea Girl of Hummingbird Lane*
Sekaran, Shanthi. ★*Lucky Boy*
Sem-Sandberg, Steve. *The Chosen Ones: A Novel*
Senna, Danzy. *New People*
Setterfield, Diane. ★*Once Upon a River*
Sexton, Margaret Wilkerson. *A Kind of Freedom*
Sexton, Margaret Wilkerson. *The Revisioners: A Novel*
Shafak, Elif. ★*10 Minutes 38 Seconds in This Strange World*
Shafak, Elif. *Honor: A Novel*
Shalev, Meir. *Two She-Bears: A Novel*
Shamsie, Kamila. *Home Fire: A Novel*
Shepard, Jim. *The World to Come: Stories*
Shepard, Sam. *The One Inside*
Shepherd, Peng. *The Book of M: A Novel*
Shields, Carol. ★*The Stone Diaries*
Shields, Carol. *Unless*
Shin, Ann. *The Last Exiles*
Shreve, Anita. *Testimony: A Novel*
Shreve, Anita. *The Weight of Water*
Shriver, Lionel. *Should We Stay or Should We Go*

Silber, Joan. *Improvement*
Silber, Joan. *Secrets of Happiness*
Silko, Leslie Marmon. *Almanac of the Dead*
Silko, Leslie Marmon. ★*Ceremony*
Silko, Leslie Marmon. *Gardens in the Dunes: A Novel*
Singer, I. J. *The Brothers Ashkenazi*
Singer, Isaac Bashevis. *Enemies, a Love Story*
Singer, Isaac Bashevis. *The Family Moskat*
Singer, Isaac Bashevis. ★*The Magician of Lublin*
Sittenfeld, Curtis. ★*You Think It, I'll Say It: Stories*
Sloan, Robin. *Mr. Penumbra's 24-Hour Bookstore*
Smiley, Jane. ★*Perestroika in Paris: A Novel*
Smiley, Jane. ★*A Thousand Acres*
Smith, Ali. ★*Autumn*
Smith, Ali. ★*How to Be Both*
Smith, Ali. ★*Spring*
Smith, Ali. ★*Summer*
Smith, Ali. *There but for The: A Novel*
Smith, Ali. ★*Winter*
Smith, Betty. ★*A Tree Grows in Brooklyn*
Smith, Dominic. *Bright and Distant Shores*
Smith, Gregory Blake. ★*The Maze at Windermere: A Novel*
Smith, Michael F. *The Fighter: A Novel*
Smith, Zadie. ★*Grand Union: Stories*
Smith, Zadie. ★*Nw: A Novel*
Smith, Zadie. *On Beauty*
Smith, Zadie. ★*Swing Time*
Smith, Zadie. ★*White Teeth: A Novel*
So, Anthony Veasna. *Afterparties: Stories*
Sofer, Dalia. *Man of My Time*
Solares, Martin. *Don't Send Flowers*
Solomon, Rivers. *Sorrowland*
Solomon, Rivers. *An Unkindness of Ghosts*
Solzhenitsyn, Aleksandr Isaevich. *One Day in the Life of Ivan Denisovich*
Sontag, Susan. ★*In America*
Soyinka, Wole. *Chronicles from the Land of the Happiest People on Earth*
Spark, Muriel. *Aiding & Abetting*
Spark, Muriel. ★*The Girls of Slender Means*
Spark, Muriel. ★*The Mandelbaum Gate*
Spark, Muriel. ★*Memento Mori*
Spiotta, Dana. *Wayward*
Spufford, Francis. ★*Light Perpetual*
St. Aubyn, Edward. *Double Blind*
Staples, Dennis E. *This Town Sleeps*
Statovci, Pajtim. *Bolla*
Stedman, M. L. ★*The Light Between Oceans: A Novel*
Stegner, Wallace. ★*Angle of Repose*
Stegner, Wallace. *Crossing to Safety*
Stein, Garth. *The Art of Racing in the Rain: A Novel*
Steinbeck, John. *Cannery Row*
Steinbeck, John. ★*East of Eden*
Steinbeck, John. ★*The Grapes of Wrath*
Steinbeck, John. *The Long Valley*
Steinbeck, John. ★*Of Mice and Men*
Steinbeck, John. *The Pearl*
Straight, Susan. *A Million Nightingales*

Strout, Elizabeth. ★*Anything Is Possible: Fiction*
Strout, Elizabeth. ★*The Burgess Boys: A Novel*
Strout, Elizabeth. ★*Oh William!*
Strout, Elizabeth. *Olive Kitteridge*
Strout, Elizabeth. ★*Olive, Again: A Novel*
Stuart, Douglas. ★*Shuggie Bain*
Styron, William. *The Confessions of Nat Turner*
Sullivan, J. Courtney. *Friends and Strangers*
Swamy, Shruti. *The Archer*
Swamy, Shruti. *A House Is a Body: Stories*
Swarup, Shubhangi. *Latitudes of Longing*
Swift, Graham. ★*Here We Are*
Swift, Graham. ★*Last Orders: A Novel*
Swift, Graham. ★*Mothering Sunday: A Romance*
Swift, Graham. *Wish You Were Here*
Sylvester, Natalia. *Everyone Knows You Go Home*
Tamirat, Nafkote. *The Parking Lot Attendant: A Novel*
Tan, Amy. *The Hundred Secret Senses*
Tan, Lucy. *What We Were Promised*
Tan, Twan Eng. *The Garden of Evening Mists*
Taneja, Preti. *We That Are Young: A Novel*
Tartt, Donna. ★*The Goldfinch*
Tartt, Donna. ★*The Secret History*
Tawada, Yoko. ★*The Emissary*
Taylor, Brandon. ★*Filthy Animals*
Taylor, Brandon. ★*Real Life*
Tenorio, Lysley A. *The Son of Good Fortune: A Novel*
Thackeray, William Makepeace. ★*Vanity Fair: A Novel Without a Hero*
Thammavongsa, Souvankham. *How to Pronounce Knife: Stories*
Thelen, Albert Vigoleis. *The Island of Second Sight: From the Applied Recollections of Vigoleis*
Theroux, Paul. ★*The Mosquito Coast: A Novel*
Thien, Madeleine. *Do Not Say We Have Nothing*
Thomas, Scarlett. *Oligarchy*
Thompson-Spires, Nafissa. *Heads of the Colored People: Stories*
Tinti, Hannah. *The Twelve Lives of Samuel Hawley: A Novel*
Tobar, Hector. *The Last Great Road Bum*
Toews, Miriam. *Fight Night*
Toews, Miriam. ★*Women Talking: A Novel*
Toibin, Colm. *House of Names*
Toibin, Colm. ★*The Magician: A Novel*
Tolstaya, Tatyana. *Aetherial Worlds: Stories*
Tolstaya, Tatyana. *The Slynx*
Tolstoy, Leo. ★*Anna Karenina*
Tolstoy, Leo. ★*War and Peace*
Toole, John Kennedy. ★*A Confederacy of Dunces*
Towles, Amor. ★*A Gentleman in Moscow*
Towles, Amor. *Rules of Civility: A Novel*
Trevor, William. *Last Stories*
Trollope, Anthony. ★*Barchester Towers*
Tsao, Tiffany. *The Majesties*
Tyler, Anne. ★*Clock Dance: A Novel*
Ugresic, Dubravka. *Fox*
Ullmann, Linn. *Unquiet: A Novel*
Updike, John. *The Afterlife and Other Stories*
Updike, John. *Brazil: A Novel*
Updike, John. *Gertrude and Claudius*

Updike, John. *Licks of Love: Short Stories and a Sequel*
Updike, John. *My Father's Tears and Other Stories*
Updike, John. ★*Rabbit Is Rich: A Novel*
Updike, John. ★*Rabbit, Run*
Updike, John. *Seek My Face*
Urrea, Luis Alberto. ★*The House of Broken Angels*
Urrea, Luis Alberto. *Queen of America: A Novel*
Van der Vliet Oloomi, Azareen. *Call Me Zebra*
van Heemstra, Marjolijn. *In Search of a Name*
Van Meter, Crissy. *Creatures: A Novel*
VanderMeer, Jeff. *Dead Astronauts: A Novel*
Vann, David. *Aquarium*
Vargas Llosa, Mario. *Aunt Julia and the Scriptwriter*
Vargas Llosa, Mario. *The Bad Girl*
Vargas Llosa, Mario. ★*The Discreet Hero*
Vargas Llosa, Mario. *The Dream of the Celt*
Vargas Llosa, Mario. *The Feast of the Goat*
Vargas Llosa, Mario. *Green House*
Vargas Llosa, Mario. *The Time of the Hero*
Vargas Llosa, Mario. *The War of the End of the World*
Vargas Llosa, Mario. ★*The Way to Paradise*
Vasquez, Juan Gabriel. ★*The Shape of the Ruins*
Verble, Margaret. ★*Cherokee America*
Vidal, Gore. *Washington, D. C.: A Novel*
Vlautin, Willy. *Don't Skip Out on Me*
Vlautin, Willy. ★*The Night Always Comes*
Vonnegut, Kurt. ★*Breakfast of Champions: Or, Goodbye Blue Monday!*
Vonnegut, Kurt. ★*Cat's Cradle*
Vonnegut, Kurt. *Complete Stories*
Vonnegut, Kurt. ★*Slaughterhouse-Five: Or, the Children's Crusade : A Duty-Dance with Death*
Vonnegut, Kurt. *Timequake*
Vreeland, Susan. *Girl in Hyacinth Blue*
Vuong, Ocean. ★*On Earth We're Briefly Gorgeous: A Novel*
Walbert, Kate. *She Was Like That: New and Selected Stories*
Waldman, Amy. *A Door in the Earth*
Walker, Alice. ★*The Color Purple: A Novel*
Walker, Alice. *Possessing the Secret of Joy*
Walker, Alice. *The Temple of My Familiar*
Walker, Alice. *The Third Life of Grange Copeland*
Walker, Karen Thompson. *The Dreamers*
Walker, Nico. ★*Cherry: A Novel*
Wall, Cara. *The Dearly Beloved: A Novel*
Wallace, David Foster. ★*Brief Interviews with Hideous Men*
Wallace, David Foster. ★*The Pale King: An Unfinished Novel*
Walton, Dawnie. ★*The Final Revival of Opal & Nev*
Ward, Jesmyn. ★*Sing, Unburied, Sing*
Warren, Robert Penn. *All the King's Men*
Warren, Robert Penn. *World Enough and Time: A Romantic Novel*
Washington, Bryan. *Lot: Stories*
Washington, Bryan. ★*Memorial*
Wasserman, Robin. *Mother Daughter Widow Wife*
Watkins, Claire Vaye. ★*Gold Fame Citrus*
Watkins, Claire Vaye. *I Love You but I've Chosen Darkness*
Waugh, Evelyn. ★*Brideshead Revisited*
Waugh, Evelyn. ★*The Complete Stories of Evelyn Waugh*
Wayne, Teddy. *Apartment: A Novel*

Weldon, Fay. *The Life and Loves of a She-Devil*
Wells, Benedict. *The End of Loneliness: A Novel*
West, Kathleen. *Minor Dramas & Other Catastrophes*
West, Monica. *Revival Season: A Novel*
Wetmore, Elizabeth. ★*Valentine*
Wharton, Edith. ★*Ethan Frome*
Whitaker, Chris. ★*We Begin at the End*
Whitehead, Colson. ★*Harlem Shuffle*
Whitehead, Colson. *The Intuitionist*
Whitehead, Colson. ★*The Underground Railroad: A Novel*
Whittall, Zoe. *The Spectacular: A Novel*
Wideman, John Edgar. ★*American Histories: Stories*
Wiesel, Elie. *A Mad Desire to Dance: A Novel*
Wilkinson, Lauren. ★*American Spy: A Novel*
Williams, Eley. *The Liar's Dictionary*
Williams, Joy. *Harrow*
Williams, Lara. *A Selfie as Big as the Ritz: Stories*
Williams, Lara. *Supper Club: A Novel*
Williams, Niall. *This Is Happiness*
Wilson, G. Willow. ★*The Bird King*
Winch, Tara June. *The Yield*
Winslow, De'Shawn Charles. ★*In West Mills*
Winterson, Jeanette. ★*Frankissstein*
Winthrop, Elizabeth Hartley. *The Mercy Seat: A Novel*
Winton, Tim. *The Shepherd's Hut*
Wolfe, Paul. *The Lost Diary of M*
Wolff, Tobias. *Old School: A Novel*
Woodrell, Daniel. *The Maid's Version: A Novel*
Woods, Chavisa. *Things to Do When You're Goth in the Country: And Other Stories*
Woods, Rita. ★*Remembrance*
Woodson, Jacqueline. ★*Another Brooklyn*
Woodson, Jacqueline. ★*Red at the Bone*
Woolf, Virginia. *The Waves*
Wright, Richard. *The Man Who Lived Underground*
Wright, Richard. ★*Native Son*
Yanagihara, Hanya. *A Little Life: A Novel*
Yang, Susie. *White Ivy: A Novel*
Yates, Christopher J. *Grist Mill Road: A Novel*
Yoon, Paul. ★*Run Me to Earth: A Novel*
Youngson, Anne. *Meet Me at the Museum*
Yu, Charles. ★*Interior Chinatown*
Yu, E. Lily. ★*On Fragile Waves*
Yu, Miri. *Tokyo Ueno Station*
Yun, Jung. *O Beautiful: A Novel*
Zaman, Nadeem. *Up in the Main House & Other Stories*
Zapata, Mike. *The Lost Book of Adana Moreau*

LITERARY HISTORIANS
Barnes, Julian. ★*Flaubert's Parrot*
Byatt, A. S. ★*Possession: A Romance*
Fforde, Jasper. *Lost in a Good Book: A Thursday Next Novel*

LITERARY MOVEMENTS
Bolano, Roberto. ★*The Savage Detectives*

LITERARY PRIZES
Williams, Tia. ★*Seven Days in June: A Novel*

LITERARY SOCIETIES
Fairstein, Linda A. *Entombed*

LITERATURE
Henry, Patti Callahan. ★*Becoming Mrs. Lewis: The Improbable Love Story of Joy Davidman and C. S. Lewis*
Ugresic, Dubravka. *Fox*
LITERATURE TEACHERS
Griffiths, Elly. *The Stranger Diaries*
Littell, Robert
The Company: A Novel of the Cia
The Mayakovsky Tapes: A Novel
Little Beach Street Bakery [Series]. Colgan, Jenny
LITTLE BIG HORN, BATTLE OF THE, 1876
Jones, Douglas C. *The Court-Martial of George Armstrong Custer*
A *Little Bird*. James, Wendy
A *Little Bit of Karma: A Novel*. Billingsley, ReShonda Tate
★*Little Black Girl Lost*. Johnson, Keith Lee
Little black girl lost [Series]. Johnson, Keith Lee
Little Century: A Novel. Keesey, Anna
Little Children. Perrotta, Tom
Little Comfort. Hill, Edwin J.
Little Darlings. Golding, Melanie
★*Little Deaths: A Novel*. Flint, Emma
Little Dorrit. Dickens, Charles
Little Earthquakes. Weiner, Jennifer
Little Eyes. Schweblin, Samanta
Little Faith: A Novel. Butler, Nickolas
Little Family. Beah, Ishmael
★*Little Fires Everywhere: A Novel*. Ng, Celeste
Little Gods. Jin, Meng
A *Little Life: A Novel*. Yanagihara, Hanya
Little Night. Rice, Luanne
The *Little Paris Bookshop*. George, Nina
LITTLE PEOPLE
Black, Cara. *Murder in the Marais*
DeWoskin, Rachel. *Big Girl Small: A Novel*
Dunant, Sarah. *In the Company of the Courtesan: A Novel*
Dunn, Katherine. *Geek Love*
Little Pretty Things. Rader-Day, Lori
★*The Little Prince*. Saint-Exupery, Antoine de
LITTLE ROCK, ARKANSAS
Portis, Charles. ★*The Dog of the South*
Little Scarlet: An Easy Rawlins Mystery. Mosley, Walter
Little: a Novel. Carey, Edward
Littlejohn, Emily
Inherit the Bones
Lost Lake: A Detective Gemma Monroe Mystery
Liu, Cixin
Ball Lightning
★*The Dark Forest*
★*Death's End*
★*The Three-Body Problem*
Liu, Ken
★*The Grace of Kings*
Invisible Planets: Contemporary Chinese Science Fiction in Translation
★*The Veiled Throne*
The Wall of Storms
Live by Night. Lehane, Dennis
Live Flesh. Rendell, Ruth

LIVE-IN COMPANIONS
Sullivan, Emily. *The Rebel and the Rake*
Lively, Penelope
★*Moon Tiger*
LIVERPOOL, ENGLAND
Daly, Paula. *Open Your Eyes*
Lives of Girls and Women. Munro, Alice
The *Lives of Others*. Mukherjee, Neel
Lives of the Circus Animals: A Novel. Bram, Christopher
Livesay, Tracey
Like Lovers Do
Livesey, Margot
★*The Boy in the Field*
Criminals: A Novel
Livia Lone. Eisler, Barry
Livia Lone novels [Series]. Eisler, Barry
LIVING AND NON-LIVING THINGS
Levin, Adam. *Bubblegum*
The *Living Dead*. Romero, George A.
The *Living Sea of Waking Dreams*. Flanagan, Richard
LIVINGSTONE, DAVID
Chakraborty, S. A. *The Empire of Gold*
Gappah, Petina. ★*Out of Darkness, Shining Light*
LLAMAS
Fields, Hilary. *Last Chance Llama Ranch*
Llewellyn, Richard
★*How Green Was My Valley*
LLEWELYN AP IORWERTH, D 1240
Penman, Sharon Kay. *Here Be Dragons*
Roorbach, Bill. *Life Among Giants: A Novel*
Lloyd, Catherine
Death Comes to the Nursery
Death Comes to the Rectory
LOCAL GOVERNMENT
Dee, Jonathan. *The Locals: A Novel*
LOCAL HISTORY
Chancellor, Bryn. *Sycamore: A Novel*
Kunzru, Hari. *Red Pill: A Novel*
McMahon, Jennifer. *The Invited: A Novel*
Scott, Rion Amilcar. ★*The World Doesn't Require You: Stories*
Spiotta, Dana. *Wayward*
★*Local Souls: Novellas*. Gurganus, Allan
The *Locals: a Novel*. Dee, Jonathan
★*The Lock Artist*. Hamilton, Steve
Lock Every Door: A Novel. Sager, Riley
★*Lock In*. Scalzi, John
Lock in novels [Series]. Scalzi, John
Locke, Attica
★*Bluebird, Bluebird*
The Cutting Season
★*Heaven, My Home*
Locke, Thomas
Emissary
★*The Locked Room: The Story of a Crime*. Sjowall, Maj
LOCKED-IN SYNDROME
Koryta, Michael. *If She Wakes*
Lockridge, Ross Franklin
Raintree County

LOCKS AND KEYS
　　Foer, Jonathan Safran. *Extremely Loud and Incredibly Close*
　　Oyeyemi, Helen. *What Is Not Yours Is Not Yours: Stories*
　　Patrick, Phaedra. ★*The Secrets of Love Story Bridge*
　　Weaver, Ashley. ★*A Peculiar Combination*
LOCOMOTIVE ENGINEERS
　　Finch, Charles. *The Last Passenger*
Lodato, Victor
　　Edgar and Lucy: A Novel
　　Mathilda Savitch
LODZ, POLAND
　　Singer, I. J. *The Brothers Ashkenazi*
Loedel, Daniel
　　Hades, Argentina
Logan McRae mysteries [Series]. MacBride, Stuart
Logan's Lady. Bittner, Rosanne
Logan, Kylie
　　The Secrets of Bones: A Mystery
Logan, T. M.
　　The Vacation
LOGGING
　　Marlantes, Karl. *Deep River*
Loigman, Lynda Cohen
　　The Wartime Sisters: A Novel
LOKI (NORSE DEITY)
　　Gornichec, Genevieve. ★*The Witch's Heart*
Lola on Fire. Youers, Rio
★*Lolita*. Nabokov, Vladimir Vladimirovich
LOMAZZO, GIOVANNI PAOLO
　　DeRoux, Margaux. *The Lost Diary of Venice*
　　Doyle, Roddy. *Love*
Lombardo, Claire
　　The Most Fun We Ever Had: A Novel
London. Rutherfurd, Edward
London celebrities [Series]. Parker, Lucy
London Fields: A Novel. Amis, Martin
London Match. Deighton, Len
LONDON, ENGLAND
　　Aaronovitch, Ben. *Broken Homes*
　　Aaronovitch, Ben. *Midnight Riot*
　　Aaronovitch, Ben. *Moon Over Soho*
　　Abdul-Jabbar, Kareem. *The Empty Birdcage*
　　Abdul-Jabbar, Kareem. *Mycroft and Sherlock*
　　Abdul-Jabbar, Kareem. ★*Mycroft Holmes*
　　Adams, Sara Nisha. ★*The Reading List*
　　Alderton, Dolly. ★*Ghosts: A Novel*
　　Ali, Monica. ★*Brick Lane: A Novel*
　　Allain, Suzanne. *Miss Lattimore's Letter*
　　Allen, Susanna. *A Wolf in Duke's Clothing*
　　Amis, Martin. *London Fields: A Novel*
　　Amis, Martin. ★*The Pregnant Widow*
　　Anderson, Alison. *The Summer Guest*
　　Antoinette, Ashley. *Butterfly*
　　Archer, Jeffrey. *Nothing Ventured*
　　Aridjis, Chloe. *Asunder*
　　Bailey, Paul. *Uncle Rudolf*
　　Ballard, J. G. *Kingdom Come*
　　Balogh, Mary. ★*Someone to Care*

Balogh, Mary. *Someone to Hold*
Balogh, Mary. ★*Someone to Love*
Balogh, Mary. *Someone to Wed*
Barker, Pat. ★*The Eye in the Door*
Barnes, Jonathan. *The Somnambulist*
Barnes, Julian. *The Only Story*
Bauer, Belinda. *The Beautiful Dead*
Beckett, Samuel. ★*Murphy*
Benn, James R. *Billy Boyle: A World War Two Mystery*
Beverley, Jo. *My Lady Notorious*
Beverley, Jo. *Tempting Fortune*
Black, Benjamin. ★*The Secret Guests: A Novel*
Blake, Audrey. *The Girl in His Shadow: A Novel*
Blake, Sarah. *The Postmistress*
Bolton, S. J. *A Dark and Twisted Tide*
Bolton, S. J. *Now You See Me*
Bourne, Joanna. *The Black Hawk*
Bourne, Joanna. ★*My Lord and Spymaster*
Bourne, Joanna. *Rogue Spy*
Bowen, Elizabeth. *The Heat of the Day*
Bowman, Valerie. *No Other Duke but You*
Bowman, Valerie. *Secrets of a Wedding Night*
Bowman, Valerie. *The Unexpected Duchess*
Boyle, Elizabeth. *Along Came a Duke*
Boyle, Elizabeth. *And the Miss Ran Away with the Rake*
Bradley, Anna. *A Season of Ruin*
Brandreth, Benet. *The Spy of Venice*
Briscoe, Joanna. *The Seduction*
Broun, Bill. *Night of the Animals*
Brown, Dan. *The Da Vinci Code*
Brownrigg, Sylvia. ★*The Delivery Room: A Novel*
Burrowes, Grace. *My One and Only Duke*
Burrowes, Grace. *The Trouble with Dukes*
Butler, Sarah. *Ten Things I've Learnt About Love: A Novel*
Byatt, A. S. ★*Possession: A Romance*
Byrne, Kerrigan. *The Hunter*
Candlish, Louise. *Our House*
Carty-Williams, Candice. ★*Queenie*
Chambers, Clare. *Small Pleasures*
Charles, KJ. *Wanted, a Gentleman: Or, Virtue Over-Rated*
Chung, Maxine Mei-Fung. *The Eighth Girl*
Clare, Alys. *The Woman Who Spoke to Spirits*
Clarke, Susanna. ★*Jonathan Strange & Mr. Norrell*
Clinch, Jon. *Marley: A Novel*
Cogman, Genevieve. *The Invisible Library*
Cogman, Genevieve. *The Masked City*
Colgan, Jenny. *500 Miles from You*
Collins, Manda. ★*A Lady's Guide to Mischief and Mayhem*
Cronin, A. J. *Citadel*
Crossan, Sarah. *Here Is the Beehive*
Crowell, Jenn. *Etched on Me: A Novel*
Cusk, Rachel. *Transit*
Deighton, Len. *Berlin Game*
Delaney, J. P. *The Girl Before: A Novel*
Diamond, Elizabeth. *An Accidental Light*
Dickens, Charles. ★*A Christmas Carol*
Dickens, Charles. ★*David Copperfield*
Dickens, Charles. *Dombey and Son*

Dickens, Charles. ★*Great Expectations*
Dickens, Charles. *Little Dorrit*
Dickens, Charles. *Oliver Twist, or the Parish Boy's Progress*
Dickens, Charles. *Our Mutual Friend*
Dongala, Emmanuel Boundzeki. *The Bridgetower Sonata: Sonata Mulattica*
Donoghue, Emma. *Slammerkin*
Doyle, Arthur Conan. ★*The Complete Sherlock Holmes*
Drabble, Margaret. *The Pure Gold Baby*
Duncan, Glen. *By Blood We Live*
Duncan, Glen. *The Last Werewolf*
Duncan, Glen. *Talulla Rising*
Evans, Diana. *Ordinary People: A Novel*
Faber, Michel. *The Crimson Petal and the White*
Faulks, Sebastian. *A Week in December*
Faye, Lyndsay. *Jane Steele*
Faye, Lyndsay. *The Whole Art of Detection: Lost Mysteries of Sherlock Holmes*
Feeney, Alice. ★*Sometimes I Lie*
Fielding, Helen. ★*Bridget Jones's Diary: A Novel*
Finch, Charles. *A Beautiful Blue Death*
Finch, Charles. *The Last Passenger*
Finch, Charles. *The September Society*
Finch, Charles. *The Vanishing Man*
Finlay, Mick. *The Murder Pit*
Fisher, Helen. *Space Hopper*
Fowler, Christopher. *Bryant & May: Oranges and Lemons*
Fowler, Christopher. *Bryant & May: Strange Tide*
Fowler, Christopher. *Bryant & May: The Lonely Hour*
Frampton, Megan. *Put up Your Duke*
Frayn, Michael. *Spies: A Novel*
Frear, Caz. *Stone Cold Heart*
Frear, Caz. *Sweet Little Lies*
Freeman, Dianne. *A Fiancée's Guide to First Wives and Murder*
Freeman, Dianne. *A Lady's Guide to Etiquette and Murder*
French, Nicci. ★*Blue Monday*
French, Nicci. *Tuesday's Gone*
French, Nicci. *Waiting for Wednesday: A Frieda Klein Mystery*
Galsworthy, John. ★*The Forsyte Saga*
Gardam, Jane. *Old Filth*
George, Elizabeth. *A Banquet of Consequences*
George, Elizabeth. *Believing the Lie*
George, Elizabeth. *Just One Evil Act*
George, Elizabeth. *The Punishment She Deserves*
George, Elizabeth. *This Body of Death: An Inspector Lynley Novel*
George, Elizabeth. *What Came Before He Shot Her*
George, Nina. *The Book of Dreams*
Gibb, Camilla. *Sweetness in the Belly*
Gibson, William. *Pattern Recognition*
Goss, Theodora. *The Sinister Mystery of the Mesmerizing Girl*
Goss, Theodora. *The Strange Case of the Alchemist's Daughter*
Gowar, Imogen Hermes. *The Mermaid and Mrs. Hancock*
Greene, Graham. ★*The End of the Affair*
Guhrke, Laura Lee. *How to Lose a Duke in Ten Days*
Guhrke, Laura Lee. *When the Marquess Met His Match*
Gunaratne, Guy. *In Our Mad and Furious City*
Gunday, Hakan. *The Few*
Hall, Alexis. ★*Boyfriend Material*

Halls, Stacey. *The Lost Orphan*
Hand, Elizabeth. *The Book of Lamps and Banners: A Novel*
Hand, Elizabeth. *Hard Light*
Harkaway, Nick. *Angelmaker*
Harkness, Deborah E. *Time's Convert*
Harrington, Anna. *An Extraordinary Lord*
Harris, C. S. *What the Devil Knows: A Sebastian St. Cyr Mystery*
Harris, Robert. *The Ghost: A Novel*
Harris, Sarah J. *The Color of Bee Larkham's Murder: A Novel*
Harrod-Eagles, Cynthia. *Cruel as the Grave*
Harrod-Eagles, Cynthia. *Headlong*
Harrod-Eagles, Cynthia. *Old Bones*
Hawkins, Paula. ★*The Girl on the Train: A Novel*
Heller, Zoe. *What Was She Thinking?: Notes on a Scandal*
Heyer, Georgette. *The Grand Sophy*
Higgins, Jack. *Eye of the Storm*
Hilton, L. S. *Maestra*
Hodgson, Antonia. *The Last Confession of Thomas Hawkins*
Hornby, Nick. *High Fidelity*
Horowitz, Anthony. *The House of Silk: A Sherlock Holmes Novel*
James, Eloisa. *Three Weeks with Lady X*
James, Eloisa. *The Ugly Duchess*
James, Henry. *The Wings of the Dove*
James, P. D. *Original Sin*
James, P. D. *A Taste for Death*
Jaswal, Balli Kaur. *Erotic Stories for Punjabi Widows*
Jewell, Lisa. *The Family Upstairs*
Jewell, Lisa. *Then She Was Gone: A Novel*
Jones, Sandie. *The Other Woman*
Kelly, Erin. *Watch Her Fall*
Kelly, Julia. *The Light Over London*
Kidd, Jess. ★*Things in Jars*
Knight, Renee. *The Secretary: A Novel*
Lawrence, David. *The Dead Sit Round in a Ring*
Lawton, John. *Hammer to Fall*
Le Carre, John. *Agent Running in the Field*
Lebrecht, Norman. *The Song of Names*
Leigh, Eva. *Forever Your Earl*
Leigh, Eva. *Scandal Takes the Stage*
Leigh, Eva. *Temptations of a Wallflower*
Leithauser, Brad. *The Promise of Elsewhere*
Lessing, Doris May. ★*The Fifth Child*
Lessing, Doris May. ★*The Golden Notebook*
Lessing, Doris May. *The Sweetest Dream*
Livesey, Margot. *Criminals: A Novel*
Long, Julie Anne. *Angel in a Devil's Arms*
Long, Julie Anne. ★*Lady Derring Takes a Lover*
Lovesey, Peter. *Diamond Solitaire*
Lovesey, Peter. *The Tooth Tattoo*
Lurie, Alison. *Foreign Affairs*
MacLean, Sarah. ★*Bombshell*
MacLean, Sarah. *No Good Duke Goes Unpunished*
Manning, Max. *The Victim: A Novel*
Mason, Meg. *Sorrow and Bliss*
Mason, Timothy. *The Darwin Affair*
Matthews, Mimi. ★*The Siren of Sussex*
Maugham, W. Somerset. *The Moon and Sixpence*
Maugham, W. Somerset. ★*Of Human Bondage*

McEwan, Ian. ★*Amsterdam*
McEwan, Ian. ★*On Chesil Beach*
Montclair, Allison. *The Right Sort of Man*
Montclair, Allison. *A Rogue's Company*
Montclair, Allison. *A Royal Affair*
Morrell, David. *Ruler of the Night*
Murdoch, Iris. *The Green Knight*
Newland, Courttia. *A River Called Time*
Nicholls, Owen. *Love, Unscripted: A Novel*
O'Donnell, Paraic. *The House on Vesper Sands: A Novel*
O'Farrell, Maggie. *The Hand That First Held Mine: A Novel*
O'Leary, Beth. *The Flatshare: A Novel*
O'Leary, Beth. *The Switch*
Ondaatje, Michael. ★*Warlight*
Orczy, Emmuska Orczy. *The Old Man in the Corner*
Oyeyemi, Helen. *Gingerbread: A Novel*
Oyeyemi, Helen. *The Opposite House*
Palmer, Dexter Clarence. ★*Mary Toft; Or, the Rabbit Queen: A Novel*
Parker, Lucy. *Battle Royal*
Parmar, Priya. *Vanessa and Her Sister*
Pearl, Matthew. *The Dante Chamber*
Pearl, Matthew. *The Last Dickens: A Novel*
Pearson, Allison. ★*How Hard Can It Be?*
Pembrooke, Kate. *Not the Kind of Earl You Marry*
Penrose, Andrea. *Murder at Half Moon Gate*
Penrose, Andrea. ★*Murder at Kensington Palace*
Penrose, Andrea. *Murder on Black Swan Lane*
Perry, Anne. *A Dangerous Mourning*
Perry, Anne. *Dark Tide Rising: A William Monk Novel*
Perry, Anne. ★*Death with a Double Edge: A Daniel Pitt Novel*
Perry, Anne. *The Face of a Stranger*
Perry, Anne. *One Fatal Flaw: A Daniel Pitt Novel*
Pilcher, Rosamunde. ★*The Shell Seekers*
Pinborough, Sarah. ★*Behind Her Eyes: A Novel*
Porter, Max. ★*Grief Is the Thing with Feathers*
Pulley, Natasha. ★*The Kingdoms*
Purcell, Laura. *The Silent Companions: A Ghost Story*
Putney, Mary Jo. *No Longer a Gentleman*
Putney, Mary Jo. *Nowhere Near Respectable*
Quick, Amanda. *'til Death Do Us Part*
Quick, Amanda. *Garden of Lies*
Raybourn, Deanna. ★*A Murderous Relation*
Reich, Christopher. ★*The Take*
Robertson, Imogen. *Anatomy of Murder*
Robertson, Imogen. *Circle of Shadows*
Robertson, Michael. *The Baker Street Letters*
Robertson, Michael. *The Baker Street Translation: A Mystery*
Robertson, Michael. *The Brothers of Baker Street*
Robertson, Michael. *Moriarty Returns a Letter: A Baker Street Mystery*
Robinson, Peter. *All the Colors of Darkness*
Robotham, Michael. ★*Close Your Eyes*
Robotham, Michael. *The Night Ferry: A Novel*
Robotham, Michael. ★*The Other Wife*
Robotham, Michael. ★*Say You're Sorry*
Robotham, Michael. ★*Suspect*
Rodrigues Fowler, Yara. *Stubborn Archivist*
Rowland, Laura Joh. *The Hangman's Secret*

Rowland, Laura Joh. *The Ripper's Shadow*
Rushdie, Salman. ★*The Satanic Verses*
Rutherfurd, Edward. *London*
Ryan, Jennifer. *The Spies of Shilling Lane: A Novel*
Saunders, Kate. *The Secrets of Wishtide*
Sayers, Dorothy L. ★*The Documents in the Case*
Schellman, Katharine. *Silence in the Library*
Schwab, Victoria. *A Conjuring of Light*
Schwab, Victoria. *A Darker Shade of Magic*
Schwab, Victoria. *A Gathering of Shadows*
Self, Will. *The Book of Dave: A Revelation of the Recent Past and the Distant Future*
Shafak, Elif. *Honor: A Novel*
Shamsie, Kamila. *Home Fire: A Novel*
Shannon, Samantha. *The Bone Season*
Shannon, Samantha. *The Mime Order*
Shaw, Vivian. ★*Strange Practice*
Shaw, William. *A Song for the Brokenhearted*
Shreve, Anita. *The Pilot's Wife: A Novel*
Shriver, Lionel. *The Post-Birthday World*
Simmons, Dan. *Drood: A Novel*
Smith, Zadie. *The Autograph Man: A Novel*
Smith, Zadie. ★*Nw: A Novel*
Smith, Zadie. ★*Swing Time*
Smith, Zadie. ★*White Teeth: A Novel*
Spark, Muriel. ★*A Far Cry from Kensington*
Spark, Muriel. ★*The Girls of Slender Means*
Spark, Muriel. ★*Memento Mori*
Speller, Elizabeth. *The Return of Captain John Emmett*
Spufford, Francis. ★*Light Perpetual*
St. Aubyn, Edward. *At Last*
Stevenson, Robert Louis. ★*The Strange Case of Dr. Jekyll and Mr. Hyde*
Stoker, Bram. ★*Dracula*
Stoker, Bram. *The New Annotated Dracula*
Stone, Irving. *Lust for Life: A Novel of Vincent Van Gogh*
Stone, Nick. *The Verdict*
Stratford, Sarah-Jane. *Red Letter Days*
Swanson, Peter. *Her Every Fear: A Novel*
Thomas, Bev. *A Good Enough Mother: A Novel*
Thomas, Will. *Dance with Death*
Thomson, E. S. *Beloved Poison*
Thomson, E. S. *The Blood*
Waugh, Evelyn. ★*Vile Bodies*
Weaver, Ashley. ★*A Peculiar Combination*
Whitfield, Clare. *People of Abandoned Character*
Wilde, Oscar. ★*The Picture of Dorian Gray*

London, Jack
  ★*The Call of the Wild*
  Martin Eden
  ★*White Fang*
LONDON, JACK
  Gordimer, Nadine. *No Time Like the Present: A Novel*
  London, Jack. *Martin Eden*
London, Joan
  The Golden Age
London, Julia
  The Charmer in Chaps

Wild Wicked Scot
London, Stefanie
   The Aussie Next Door
Lone *Jack Trail*. Laukkanen, Owen
LONELINESS
   Atilgan, Yusuf. *Motherland Hotel*
   Awad, Mona. *Bunny*
   Bledsoe, Lucy Jane. *The Big Bang Symphony: A Novel of Antarctica*
   De Kretser, Michelle. *The Life to Come*
   Erdrich, Louise. *The Beet Queen: A Novel*
   George, Alex. *The Paris Hours: A Novel*
   Golding, William. ★*Darkness Visible*
   Haruf, Kent. ★*Our Souls at Night*
   Hunt, Samantha. *The Dark Dark: Stories*
   Imamura, Natsuko. *The Woman in the Purple Skirt: A Novel*
   McCullers, Carson. *The Member of the Wedding*
   Murakami, Haruki. *Blind Willow, Sleeping Woman: 24 Stories*
   Murakami, Haruki. *Men Without Women: Stories*
   Ozeki, Ruth L. ★*A Tale for the Time Being*
   Rash, Ron. ★*The Cove*
   Saramago, Jose. *All the Names*
   Steinbeck, John. *Cannery Row*
   Vonnegut, Kurt. *Slapstick: Or, Lonesome No More! a Novel*
   Wiesel, Elie. *A Mad Desire to Dance: A Novel*
LONELINESS IN MEN
   Daoud, Kamel. *The Meursault Investigation*
   Foster, Alan Dean. *Relic*
   Kafka, Franz. ★*The Metamorphosis*
   Malamud, Bernard. ★*The Fixer*
   Park, Sang Young. ★*Love in the Big City: A Novel*
   Whitehead, Colson. *Zone One: A Novel*
LONELINESS IN WOMEN
   Hendricks, Greer. ★*You Are Not Alone*
   Moshfegh, Ottessa. *Eileen*
   Schwab, Victoria. *The Invisible Life of Addie Larue*
   Watson, Brad. *Miss Jane: A Novel*
★*The **Lonely** Hearts Hotel: A Novel*. O'Neill, Heather
★*The **Lonely** Silver Rain*. MacDonald, John D.
*The **Lonely** Witness*. Boyle, William
LONERS
   Byrne, Kerrigan. *The Hunter*
   Eugenides, Jeffrey. ★*The Marriage Plot*
   Garcia-Roza, L. A. *Alone in the Crowd: An Inspector Espinosa Mystery*
   Jackson, Shirley. ★*The Haunting of Hill House*
   Kane, Jessica Francis. *Rules for Visiting*
   Matheson, Richard. ★*I Am Legend*
   Owens, Delia. *Where the Crawdads Sing*
Lonesome Dove saga [Series]. McMurtry, Larry
★***Lonesome*** *Dove: A Novel*. McMurtry, Larry
***Long** Black Curl*. Bledsoe, Alex
***Long** Bright River*. Moore, Liz
*The **Long** Call*. Cleeves, Ann
*A **Long** December*. Chizmar, Richard T.
***Long** Division*. Laymon, Kiese
*The **Long** Goodbye*. Chandler, Raymond
LONG ISLAND, NEW YORK
   Alam, Rumaan. ★*Leave the World Behind: A Novel*

Anam, Tahmima. *The Startup Wife*
Barnett, S. K. *Safe*
Blundell, Judy. *The High Season: A Novel*
Coleman, Reed Farrel. *Where It Hurts: A Gus Murphy Novel*
Fredericks, Mariah. *Death of a New American: A Mystery*
Glass, Julia. ★*Three Junes*
Harrison, Nicola. *Montauk*
McDermott, Alice. *At Weddings and Wakes*
McDermott, Alice. *Child of My Heart*
McDermott, Alice. ★*That Night*
Miller, Rebecca. ★*Jacob's Folly: A Novel*
Piccirilli, Tom. *The Last Kind Words*
Piccirilli, Tom. *The Last Whisper in the Dark: A Novel*
Richman, Alyson. *The Secret of Clouds*
Rose, M. J. *Tiffany Blues: A Novel*
Spillane, Mickey. *Kill ME, Darling*
*The **Long** Lavender Look*. MacDonald, John D.
***Long** Lost*. Coben, Harlan
***Long** Man*. Greene, Amy
*A **Long** Night in Paris*. Alfon, Dov
*A **Long** Petal of the Sea: A Novel*. Allende, Isabel
★***Long** Range*. Box, C. J.
***Long** Road to Mercy*. Baldacci, David
★***Long** Shot*. Ryan, Kennedy
***Long** Shot: A Sniper Novel*. Coughlin, Jack
*The **Long** Song*. Levy, Andrea
*The **Long** Take: A Noir Narrative*. Robertson, Robin
*A **Long** Time Comin'*. Pearson, Robin W.
★*A **Long** Time Coming: A Novel*. Goddard, Robert
*A **Long** Time Dead: A Mike Hammer Casebook*. Spillane, Mickey
*The **Long** Valley*. Steinbeck, John
*A **Long** Way from Home*. Carey, Peter
★*The **Long** Way to a Small, Angry Planet*. Chambers, Becky
Long, Julie Anne
   Angel in a Devil's Arms
   ★*Lady Derring Takes a Lover*
LONG-DISTANCE ROMANCE
   Gohlke, Cathy. *Promise Me This*
   Guillory, Jasmine. ★*The Wedding Date*
Longbourn. Baker, Jo
LONGEVITY
   Tawada, Yoko. ★*The Emissary*
   Tepper, Sheri S. *Singer from the Sea*
LONGSTREET, JAMES
   Shaara, Michael. ★*The Killer Angels: A Novel*
Longworth, M. L.
   Murder on the Ile Sordou: A Verlaque and Bonnet Provencal Mystery
***Look** Alive Twenty-Five*. Evanovich, Janet
***Look** at the Harlequins!* Nabokov, Vladimir Vladimirovich
***Look** for Me and I'll Be Gone: Stories*. Wideman, John Edgar
★***Look** for Me: A Novel*. Gardner, Lisa
★***Look** Homeward, Angel: A Story of a Buried Life*. Wolfe, Thomas
LOOK-ALIKES
   Dickens, Charles. ★*A Tale of Two Cities*
***Looking** into You*. Fabry, Chris
***Loose** ends [Series]. Weatherspoon, Rebekah
Lopez Barrio, Cristina
   The House of the Impossible Loves

Lord Byron mysteries [Series]. Friedman, Daniel

Lord Byron's Novel: The Evening Land. Crowley, John

Lord Hornblower. Forester, C. S.

★*Lord Jim.* Conrad, Joseph

★*Lord of Misrule: A Novel.* Gordon, Jaimy

★*Lord of the Flies: A Novel.* Golding, William

★*The Lord of the Rings.* Tolkien, J. R. R.

Lord of the rings [Series]. Tolkien, J. R. R.

★*Lord Peter.* Sayers, Dorothy L.

Lord Peter Wimsey mysteries [Series]. Sayers, Dorothy L.

LORD WESTFIELD'S MEN (FICTITIOUS CHARACTERS)

    Marston, Edward. *The Roaring Boy: A Novel*

    Marston, Edward. *The Wanton Angel: A Novel*

Lords and Ladies: A Novel of Discworld. Pratchett, Terry

Lords of Anarchy novels [Series]. Collins, Manda

Lords of the Armory [Series]. Harrington, Anna

Loren, Roni

    ★*The One for You*

    The One You Can't Forget

    The One You Fight For

Lorna Doone: A Romance of Exmoor. Blackmore, R. D.

LOS ALAMOS, NEW MEXICO

    Kiernan, Stephen P. *Universe of Two*

    Smith, Martin Cruz. *Stallion Gate*

LOS ANGELES COUNTY, CALIFORNIA

    Boyle, T. Coraghessan. ★*The Tortilla Curtain*

LOS ANGELES, CALIFORNIA

    Abu-Jaber, Diana. *Crescent*

    Acampora, Lauren. *The Paper Wasp: A Novel*

    Allen, Jayne. *Black Girls Must Die Exhausted*

    Ames, Jonathan. *A Man Named Doll*

    Aoki, Ryka. *Light from Uncommon Stars*

    Ashley & JaQuavis. *Murderville*

    Baldwin, Joshua. *The Wilshire Sun*

    Beatty, Paul. ★*The Sellout: A Novel*

    Bennett, Brit. ★*The Vanishing Half*

    Beyda, Emily. *The Body Double*

    Boyle, T. Coraghessan. ★*The Tortilla Curtain*

    Broder, Melissa. *The Pisces: A Novel*

    Campbell, Bebe Moore. *Brothers and Sisters*

    Cha, Steph. ★*Your House Will Pay*

    Chandler, Raymond. ★*The Big Sleep*

    Chandler, Raymond. *The Lady in the Lake*

    Chandler, Raymond. *The Long Goodbye*

    Clark, Marcia. *Final Judgment*

    Connelly, Michael. *The Black Ice*

    Connelly, Michael. *The Brass Verdict: A Novel*

    Connelly, Michael. *The Burning Room*

    Connelly, Michael. *The Crossing*

    Connelly, Michael. ★*The Dark Hours*

    Connelly, Michael. *Dark Sacred Night*

    Connelly, Michael. *The Fifth Witness*

    Connelly, Michael. *The Gods of Guilt*

    Connelly, Michael. *The Late Show*

    Connelly, Michael. ★*The Law of Innocence: A Novel*

    Connelly, Michael. *The Night Fire*

    Connelly, Michael. *The Scarecrow: A Novel*

    Connelly, Michael. *The Wrong Side of Goodbye*

    Copperman, E. J. *Judgment at Santa Monica*

    Crais, Robert. *A Dangerous Man*

    Crais, Robert. *Demolition Angel: A Novel.*

    Crais, Robert. *The First Rule*

    Crais, Robert. *Suspect*

    Danan, Rosie. *The Intimacy Experiment*

    Danan, Rosie. *The Roommate*

    Deon, Natashia. *The Perishing: A Novel*

    Dick, Philip K. ★*Do Androids Dream of Electric Sheep?*

    Dickey, Eric Jerome. ★*Bad Men and Wicked Women*

    Dickey, Eric Jerome. *The Business of Lovers*

    Dickey, Eric Jerome. ★*The Son of Mr. Suleman*

    Dorn, L. R. *The Anatomy of Desire*

    Ellis, Bret Easton. *Imperial Bedrooms*

    Ellroy, James. ★*L.A. Confidential*

    Ellroy, James. *Perfidia*

    Ellroy, James. *This Storm: A Novel*

    Ellroy, James. ★*Widespread Panic: A Novel*

    Escandon, Maria Amparo. ★*L.A. Weather*

    Estleman, Loren D. ★*Something Borrowed, Something Black*

    Evison, Jonathan. *All About Lulu: A Novel*

    Fitch, Janet. *Paint It Black: A Novel*

    Fitch, Janet. *White Oleander: A Novel*

    Foley, Bridget. *Just Get Home*

    Frazier, Jean Kyoung. *Pizza Girl*

    Freudenberger, Nell. *The Dissident*

    Friedland, Elyssa. *The Intermission*

    Gardiner, Meg. *The Dark Corners of the Night*

    Gardiner, Meg. *Phantom Instinct*

    Goldberg, Lee. *Bone Canyon*

    Guillory, Jasmine. *Party of Two*

    Guillory, Jasmine. *The Proposal*

    Hall, Rachel Howzell. *And Now She's Gone*

    Hanson, Hart. *The Driver*

    Haywood, Gar Anthony. *Cemetery Road*

    Hendrix, Grady. *The Final Girl Support Group*

    Hummel, Maria. *Lesson in Red*

    Ide, Joe. ★*Hi Five: An IQ Novel*

    Johnstone, Carole. *Mirrorland*

    Kim, Nancy Jooyoun. *The Last Story of Mina Lee*

    Kleeman, Alexandra. *Something New Under the Sun*

    Kroese, Robert. *The Last Iota*

    Lange, Tracey. ★*We Are the Brennans*

    Lovely, Lutishia. *Blind Ambition*

    Mooney, Chris. *Blood World*

    Mosley, Walter. *Black Betty: An Easy Rawlins Mystery*

    Mosley, Walter. ★*Blood Grove*

    Mosley, Walter. *Charcoal Joe: An Easy Rawlins Mystery*

    Mosley, Walter. *Devil in a Blue Dress*

    Mosley, Walter. *Little Scarlet: An Easy Rawlins Mystery*

    Mosley, Walter. *The Right Mistake: The Further Philosophical Investigations of Socrates Fortlow*

    Nava, Michael. ★*Carved in Bone*

    Overton, Hollie. *The Runaway*

    Parker, T. Jefferson. *L.A. Outlaws: A Novel*

    Perry, Thomas. *The Bomb Maker*

    Perry, Thomas. ★*The Left-Handed Twin*

    Pochoda, Ivy. ★*These Women*

Pynchon, Thomas. *Inherent Vice*
Raheem, Zara. *The Marriage Clock: A Novel*
Rivers, Francine. *The Masterpiece*
Robertson, Michael. *The Baker Street Letters*
Robertson, Michael. *Moriarty Returns a Letter: A Baker Street Mystery*
Robertson, Robin. *The Long Take: A Noir Narrative*
Rowell, Rainbow. *Landline*
Sallis, James. *Drive*
Santiago, Danny. *Famous All Over Town*
Shannon, Dell. ★*Chaos of Crime*
Simpson, Mona. *Anywhere but Here*
Skyhorse, Brando. *Madonnas of Echo Park: A Novel*
Smith, Mark Haskell. *Baked*
Tan, Amy. ★*The Kitchen God's Wife*
Tanen, Sloane. *There's a Word for That*
Tieu, Julie. *The Donut Trap*
Tracy, P. J. ★*Deep into the Dark*
Wambaugh, Joseph. *The New Centurions*
Weatherspoon, Rebekah. *Rafe: A Buff Male Nanny*
West, Nathanael. *Novels and Other Writings*
★*The **Loser**.* Bernhard, Thomas

LOSERS (PERSONS)
Pynchon, Thomas. ★*V: A Novel*
Losing It. Cumyn, Alan

LOSS (PSYCHOLOGY)
Alarcon, Daniel. *The King Is Always Above the People: Stories*
Andrews, Mesu. *Isaiah's Daughter: A Novel of Prophets and Kings*
Antoinette, Ashley. *Butterfly*
Antoinette, Ashley. *Butterfly.; Vol 3*
Aramburu, Fernando. *Homeland*
Arbol, Victor del. *Breathing Through the Wound*
Armfield, Julia. *Salt Slow: Stories*
Arudpragasam, Anuk. *The Story of a Brief Marriage*
Auster, Paul. ★*The Book of Illusions: A Novel*
Baldwin, James. *Just Above My Head*
Balogh, Mary. ★*Someone to Care*
Bannister, Ilona. *When I Ran Away*
Banville, John. *Ancient LightI*
Barber, Lizzy. *A Girl Named Anna*
Black, Cara. *Murder in the Rue De Paradis: An Aimee Leduc Investigation*
Block, Lawrence. *Hit Me: A Keller Novel*
Block, Stefan Merrill. *Oliver Loving: A Novel*
Bohjalian, Chris. *The Sandcastle Girls*
Boyle, William. *City of Margins: A Novel*
Bruen, Ken. *Galway Girl: A Jack Taylor Novel*
Bruno, Anna. *Ordinary Hazards: A Novel*
Brunt, Carol Rifka. ★*Tell the Wolves I'm Home: A Novel*
Burke, James Lee. *Robicheaux*
Butler, Sarah. *Ten Things I've Learnt About Love: A Novel*
Bynum, Sarah Shun-Lien. *Ms. Hempel Chronicles*
Cander, Chris. *The Weight of a Piano: A Novel*
Cha, Steph. ★*Your House Will Pay*
Chevalier, Tracy. *A Single Thread*
Clegg, Bill. *Did You Ever Have a Family*
Clemmons, Zinzi. *What We Lose*
Coates, Ta-Nehisi. ★*The Water Dancer: A Novel*

Connolly, John. *The Dirty South*
Cosby, S. A. ★*Razorblade Tears*
Couto, Mia. *Rain: And Other Stories*
Cullen, Helen. *The Dazzling Truth*
Cumming, Charles. *A Divided Spy*
Darnielle, John. *Universal Harvester*
Diaz, Junot. ★*The Brief Wondrous Life of Oscar Wao*
Diaz, Junot. ★*This Is How You Lose Her*
Dickens, Charles. *Dombey and Son*
Dimon, HelenKay. *Her Other Secret*
Dunmore, Helen. *The Lie*
Dykes, Amanda. *Whose Waves These Are*
Englander, Nathan. *The Ministry of Special Cases*
Evans, Danielle. ★*The Office of Historical Corrections: A Novella and Stories*
Evison, Jonathan. *The Revised Fundamentals of Caregiving: A Novel*
Foer, Jonathan Safran. *Extremely Loud and Incredibly Close*
Force, Marie. *Five Years Gone*
Ford, Richard. *Sorry for Your Trouble: Stories*
Frankel, Laurie. *Goodbye for Now: A Novel*
Frazier, Charles. *Thirteen Moons: A Novel*
Garcia Marquez, Gabriel. ★*Strange Pilgrims: Twelve Stories*
George, Alex. *The Paris Hours: A Novel*
George, Elizabeth. *Careless in Red*
Giordano, Paolo. ★*The Solitude of Prime Numbers: A Novel*
Glass, Julia. ★*Three Junes*
Godwin, Gail. *Flora: A Novel*
Godwin, Gail. *Old Lovegood Girls*
Graley, Lisa. *The Current That Carries: Stories*
Greene, Graham. ★*The End of the Affair*
Greengrass, Jessie. *Sight: A Novel*
Greer, Andrew Sean. *The Impossible Lives of Greta Wells*
Griffin, Anne. *When All Is Said: A Novel*
Han, Kang. *The White Book*
Hatcher, Robin Lee. *Who I Am with You*
Haywood, Sarah. *The Cactus*
Hill, Nathan. *The Nix: A Novel*
Hoffman, Alice. *The Ice Queen: A Novel*
Indriðason, Arnaldur. *Strange Shores: An Inspector Erlendur Novel*
Ishiguro, Kazuo. *The Buried Giant: A Novel*
Jenner, Natalie. *The Jane Austen Society*
Kaufman, Charlie. *Antkind: A Novel*
Kerangal, Maylis de. *The Heart: A Novel*
King, Stephen. *Pet Sematary*
Lahiri, Jhumpa. *The Lowland: A Novel*
Lau, Jackie. *Donut Fall in Love*
Liardet, Frances. *We Must Be Brave*
Linden, Rachel. *Ascension of Larks*
Liu, Cixin. ★*The Three-Body Problem*
Lodato, Victor. *Mathilda Savitch*
Lucashenko, Melissa. *Too Much Lip*
MacLaverty, Bernard. ★*Blank Pages: And Other Stories*
Malouf, David. *Ransom*
Martin, Charles. *The Water Keeper*
McEwan, Ian. *The Child in Time*
McLain, Paula. ★*When the Stars Go Dark: A Novel*
McMillan, Terry. ★*It's Not All Downhill from Here: A Novel*
Miller, Derek B. *How to Find Your Way in the Dark*

Moriarty, Jaclyn. *Gravity Is the Thing*
Moyes, Jojo. *The Girl You Left Behind*
Murphy, Sara Flannery. *The Possessions*
Napolitano, Ann. *Dear Edward*
Ng, Celeste. ★*Everything I Never Told You: A Novel*
Nguyen, Phan Que Mai. ★*The Mountains Sing: A Novel*
Novic, Sara. *Girl at War*
Nunez, Sigrid. ★*The Friend*
O'Leary, Beth. *The Switch*
Oates, Joyce Carol. *Breathe*
Obreht, Tea. *Inland: A Novel*
Oe, Kenzaburo. *The Changeling*
Oe, Kenzaburo. ★*Death by Water*
Ogawa, Yoko. ★*The Memory Police: A Novel*
Ozeki, Ruth L. *The Book of Form and Emptiness: A Novel*
Packer, Ann. *Songs Without Words*
Paris, B. A. *Bring Me Back: A Novel*
Pearlman, Edith. *Honeydew: Stories*
Peynado, Brenda. *The Rock Eaters: Stories*
Phillips, Julia. ★*Disappearing Earth*
Pinter, Jason. *Hide Away*
Porter, Chana. *The Seep: A Novel*
Porter, Max. ★*Grief Is the Thing with Feathers*
Prose, Francine. *Goldengrove: A Novel*
Reid, Taylor Jenkins. *Forever, Interrupted: A Novel*
Remarque, Erich Maria. *A Time to Love and a Time to Die*
Rice, Luanne. ★*Last Day*
Rice, Luanne. *The Lemon Orchard*
Rothfuss, Patrick. ★*The Name of the Wind*
Runcie, James. *Canvey Island*
Runcie, James. *The Road to Grantchester*
Salinger, J. D. ★*Nine Stories*
Saramago, Jose. ★*Blindness*
Saunders, George. ★*Lincoln in the Bardo: A Novel*
Schaitkin, Alexis. *Saint X*
Schanbacher, Gary Lester. *Crossing Purgatory*
Shalev, Meir. *Two She-Bears: A Novel*
Sherrill, Steven. *The Minotaur Takes His Own Sweet Time: A Novel*
Shipman, Viola. *The Heirloom Garden*
Stedman, M. L. ★*The Light Between Oceans: A Novel*
Stewart, Ann Marie. *Stars in the Grass*
Styron, William. *Lie Down in Darkness*
Swift, Graham. *Wish You Were Here*
Swyler, Erika. ★*Light from Other Stars: A Novel*
Tallo, Katie. *Dark August*
Tan, Twan Eng. *The Garden of Evening Mists*
Tartt, Donna. ★*The Goldfinch*
Thomas, Bev. *A Good Enough Mother: A Novel*
Tran, Vu. *Dragonfish: A Novel*
Trigiani, Adriana. *Big Cherry Holler: A Big Stone Gap Novel*
Unger, Lisa. *Under My Skin*
Uris, Leon. *Redemption: A Novel*
Watson, Martine Fournier. *The Dream Peddler*
Wharton, Edith. *The Children*
Wideman, John Edgar. *Look for Me and I'll Be Gone: Stories*
Wieland, Liza. *Paris, 7 A.M.*
Winslow, Don. *Broken: Six Short Novels*
Wiseman, Ellen Marie. *The Orphan Collector*

Yang, JY. *The Ascent to Godhood*
Yang, JY. *The Red Threads of Fortune*
Yoshimoto, Banana. *Moshi-Moshi*
Yu, Miri. *Tokyo Ueno Station*

LOSS OF CONSCIOUSNESS
Bartz, Andrea. *The Lost Night*
Bolton, S. J. *The Split*
Unger, Lisa. *Under My Skin*
★*Lost and Wanted: A Novel*. Freudenberger, Nell

LOST ANIMALS
Adams, Douglas. *Dirk Gently's Holistic Detective Agency*
The Lost Art of Gratitude. McCall Smith, Alexander

LOST ARTICLES
Barry, Dave. *Insane City*
Child, Lee. *The Midnight Line*
Goodis, David. *Nightfall*
Kroese, Robert. *The Last Iota*
Ogawa, Yoko. ★*The Memory Police: A Novel*
Sansom, C. J. ★*Lamentation*
The Lost Book of Adana Moreau. Zapata, Mike
The Lost Book of the Grail: Or a Visitor's Guide to Barchester Cathedral. Lovett, Charles C.

LOST BOOKS
Anderson, Alison. *The Summer Guest*
Doerr, Anthony. ★*Cloud Cuckoo Land: A Novel*
Gruber, Michael. *The Book of Air and Shadows*
Lost Boy Lost Girl: A Novel. Straub, Peter

LOST CHILDREN
Liardet, Frances. *We Must Be Brave*
★*Lost Children Archive: A Novel*. Luiselli, Valeria
The Lost Daughter. Ferrante, Elena
★*The Lost Daughter*. Paul, Gill
The Lost Diary of M. Wolfe, Paul
The Lost Diary of Venice. DeRoux, Margaux
Lost Empress: A Novel. Pava, Sergio de la
The Lost Family. Blum, Jenna
The Lost for Words Bookshop: A Novel. Butland, Stephanie
The Lost Future of Pepperharrow. Pulley, Natasha

LOST GIRLS
King, Stephen. *The Girl Who Loved Tom Gordon*
The Lost Girls of Paris. Jenoff, Pam
★*Lost Horizon: A Novel*. Hilton, James
Lost in a Good Book: A Thursday Next Novel. Fforde, Jasper
The Lost Key. Coulter, Catherine
A Lost Lady. Cather, Willa
Lost Lake: A Detective Gemma Monroe Mystery. Littlejohn, Emily
Lost lords (Mary Jo Putney) [Series]. Putney, Mary Jo

LOST LOVE
Bender, Tony. *The Last Ghost Dancer*
George, Nina. *The Little Paris Bookshop*
Hammad, Isabella. ★*The Parisian, Or, Al-Barisi: A Novel*
McFarlane, Mhairi. *Don't You Forget About Me*
The Lost Man. Harper, Jane
Lost Memory of Skin. Banks, Russell
The Lost Night. Bartz, Andrea
The Lost Notebook of Edouard Manet: A Novel. Gibbon, Maureen
The Lost Ones. Atkins, Ace
The Lost Order. Berry, Steve

The **Lost** Orphan. Halls, Stacey
The **Lost** Queen. Pike, Signe
Lost queen [Series]. Pike, Signe
Lost Roses: A Novel. Kelly, Martha Hall
The **Lost** Shtetl. Gross, Max
The **Lost** Traveller. Connolly, Sheila
The **Lost** Weekend. Jackson, Charles
Lost You. Beck, Haylen
Lot Lands [Series]. French, Jonathan
★*A Lot Like Adios*. Daria, Alexis
Lot: Stories. Washington, Bryan
LOTTERIES
    Jackson, Shirley. ★*The Lottery: And Other Stories*
LOTTERY WINNERS
    Amis, Martin. *Lionel Asbo: State of England*
★*The **Lottery**: and Other Stories*. Jackson, Shirley
The **Lotus** Eaters. Soli, Tatjana
Lotus Kingdoms [Series]. Bear, Elizabeth
The **Lotus** Palace. Lin, Jeannie
Lotus Palace [Series]. Lin, Jeannie
LOUIS
    Dumas, Alexandre. ★*The Three Musketeers*
Louis, Edouard
    The End of Eddy: A Novel
LOUISIANA
    Bennett, Brit. ★*The Vanishing Half*
    Burke, James Lee. ★*The New Iberia Blues*
    Burke, James Lee. ★*A Private Cathedral*
    Burke, James Lee. *Robicheaux*
    Butler, Robert Olen. *A Good Scent from a Strange Mountain: Stories*
    Cooper, Tom. *The Marauders*
    Fitzpatrick, Lydia. *Lights All Night Long: A Novel*
    Gaines, Ernest J. ★*The Autobiography of Miss Jane Pittman*
    Gaines, Ernest J. ★*A Gathering of Old Men*
    Grisham, John. ★*The Pelican Brief*
    Harris, C. S. *Good Time Coming*
    Jones, Tayari. ★*An American Marriage: A Novel*
    Locke, Attica. *The Cutting Season*
    Luesse, Valerie Fraser. *Under the Bayou Moon: A Novel*
    Percy, Walker. ★*The Moviegoer*
    Rhodes, Jewell Parker. *Yellow Moon: A Novel*
    Straight, Susan. *A Million Nightingales*
    Tademy, Lalita. *Cane River*
    Walsh, M. O. ★*The Big Door Prize: A Novel*
    Wells, Rebecca. *Divine Secrets of the Ya-Ya Sisterhood: A Novel*
    Winthrop, Elizabeth Hartley. *The Mercy Seat: A Novel*
Louisiana Hotshot. Smith, Julie
Lourey, Jess
    ★*January Thaw: A Murder-By-Month Mystery*
Love. Doyle, Roddy
Love. Morrison, Toni
LOVE
    Altan, Ahmet. ★*Love in the Days of Rebellion*
    Amis, Martin. ★*Inside Story*
    Apostol, Gina. *Bibliolepsy*
    Arnett, Kristen N. *With Teeth: A Novel*
    Ashley & JaQuavis. *Murderville*
    Asim, Jabari. ★*Yonder*

    Babalola, Bolu. *Love in Color: Mythical Tales from Around the World, Retold*
    Baldwin, James. ★*Another Country*
    Beagle, Peter S. *Summerlong*
    Bhuvaneswar, Chaya. *White Dancing Elephants: Stories*
    Cook, Thomas H. *Sandrine's Case*
    Danielewski, Mark Z. *Only Revolutions*
    Diaz, Junot. ★*This Is How You Lose Her*
    Duncan, Glen. *The Last Werewolf*
    Dupont, Eric. *The American Fiancee: A Novel*
    Ebershoff, David. *The Danish Girl: A Novel*
    Ford, Richard. *A Multitude of Sins: Stories*
    Gabaldon, Diana. *An Echo in the Bone*
    Gabaldon, Diana. ★*The Fiery Cross*
    Gabaldon, Diana. ★*Outlander*
    Gabaldon, Diana. *Written in My Own Heart's Blood*
    Groff, Lauren. ★*Fates and Furies*
    Helprin, Mark. ★*Winter's Tale*
    Hugo, Victor. ★*The Hunchback of Notre Dame*
    Ishiguro, Kazuo. ★*Klara and the Sun*
    Johnson, Alaya Dawn. *Trouble the Saints*
    Kundera, Milan. ★*Immortality*
    Lewis, C. S. *Till We Have Faces: A Myth Retold*
    MacLaverty, Bernard. ★*Blank Pages: And Other Stories*
    McCracken, Elizabeth. ★*Bowlaway: A Novel*
    Ogden, Aimee. *Sun-Daughters, Sea-Daughters*
    Peynado, Brenda. *The Rock Eaters: Stories*
    Pilcher, Rosamunde. *A Place Like Home: Short Stories*
    Proust, Marcel. *Time Regained*
    Proust, Marcel. *Within a Budding Grove*
    Russell, Mary Doria. *Dreamers of the Day: A Novel*
    Saramago, Jose. *Death with Interruptions*
    See, Lisa. *Peony in Love: A Novel*
    Shan, Sa. *The Girl Who Played Go*
    Shields, Carol. *The Republic of Love*
    Shin, Ann. *The Last Exiles*
    Tolstaya, Tatyana. *Aetherial Worlds: Stories*
    Vollmann, William T. *Last Stories and Other Stories*
Love & a Gangsta: A Novel. Gray, Erick S.
Love & Other Crimes: Stories. Paretsky, Sara
Love After Love: A Novel. Persaud, Ingrid
Love and Ruin. McLain, Paula
Love and War. Jakes, John
Love at First Like. Orenstein, Hannah
Love at the resort [Series]. Foster, Lori
★*The **Love** Con*. Glass, Seressia
*The **Love** Hypothesis*. Hazelwood, Ali
Love in a Cold Climate. Mitford, Nancy
Love in Color: Mythical Tales from Around the World, Retold. Babalola, Bolu
★*Love in the Big City: A Novel*. Park, Sang Young
★*Love in the Days of Rebellion*. Altan, Ahmet
★*Love in the Time of Cholera*. Garcia Marquez, Gabriel
LOVE LETTER WRITING
    Brockmeier, Kevin. *The Illumination*
Love Lettering. Clayborn, Kate
LOVE LETTERS
    Cooley, Martha. *The Archivist: A Novel*

Dare, Tessa. *When a Scot Ties the Knot*

Schaffhausen, Joanna. *Gone for Good*

Love Love: *A Novel*. Woo, Sung J.

Love Medicine: *A Novel*. Erdrich, Louise

Love on cue [Series]. Sosa, Mia

Love on holiday [Series]. Carlyle, Christy

LOVE POTIONS

Bowman, Valerie. *No Other Duke but You*

Erdrich, Louise. *Love Medicine: A Novel*

The **Love** *Song of A. Jerome Minkoff, and Other Stories*. Epstein, Joseph

★*The* **Love** *Songs of W. E. B. Du Bois*. Jeffers, Honoree Fanonne

LOVE STORIES

Adichie, Chimamanda Ngozi. ★*Americanah: A Novel*

Alcott, Kate. *A Touch of Stardust*

Allende, Isabel. *In the Midst of Winter: A Novel*

Allende, Isabel. *Of Love and Shadows*

Austen, Jane. ★*Emma*

Austen, Jane. *Mansfield Park*

Austen, Jane. ★*Persuasion*

Austen, Jane. ★*Pride and Prejudice*

Austen, Jane. ★*Sense and Sensibility*

Babalola, Bolu. *Love in Color: Mythical Tales from Around the World, Retold*

Baldwin, James. ★*If Beale Street Could Talk*

Bauer, Carlene. ★*Frances and Bernard*

Baxter, Charles. *The Feast of Love*

Beagle, Peter S. *A Fine and Private Place*

Beauvoir, Simone de. ★*The Mandarins: A Novel*

Benjamin, Melanie. *Alice I Have Been*

Blackmore, R. D. *Lorna Doone: A Romance of Exmoor*

Bohjalian, Chris. *The Sandcastle Girls*

Bonnaffons, Amy. *The Regrets*

Bourdeaut, Olivier. *Waiting for Bojangles: A Novel*

Brodie, Emma. *Songs in Ursa Major*

Bronte, Emily. ★*Wuthering Heights*

Bruni, Sarah. *The Night Gwen Stacy Died*

Byatt, A. S. ★*Possession: A Romance*

Cleeton, Chanel. *Next Year in Havana*

Davidson, Andrew. *The Gargoyle*

DeRoux, Margaux. *The Lost Diary of Venice*

Dickens, Charles. *Our Mutual Friend*

Dumas, Alexandre. ★*Camille*

El-Mohtar, Amal. ★*This Is How You Lose the Time War*

Erdrich, Louise. *The Master Butchers Singing Club: A Novel*

Esquivel, Laura. ★*Like Water for Chocolate: A Novel in Monthly Installments, with Recipes, Romances, and Home Remedies*

Evans, Nicholas. ★*The Horse Whisperer: A Novel*

Faulks, Sebastian. *On Green Dolphin Street: A Novel*

Fitzgerald, F. Scott. ★*The Last Tycoon: An Unfinished Novel*

Flanagan, Richard. ★*The Narrow Road to the Deep North*

Forbes, Curdella. *A Tall History of Sugar*

Forster, E. M. ★*A Room with a View*

Fowles, John. ★*The French Lieutenant's Woman*

Garcia Marquez, Gabriel. ★*Love in the Time of Cholera*

Gaskell, Elizabeth Cleghorn. ★*North and South*

Gaynor, Hazel. *Meet Me in Monaco: A Novel*

Ginzburg, Natalia. *Voices in the Evening*

Giordano, Paolo. ★*The Solitude of Prime Numbers: A Novel*

Greene, Graham. ★*The End of the Affair*

Greene, Graham. ★*The Heart of the Matter*

Grenville, Kate. *Sarah Thornhill*

Hamid, Mohsin. ★*Exit West: A Novel*

Hardy, Thomas. ★*Far from the Madding Crowd*

Hardy, Thomas. ★*Jude the Obscure*

Hardy, Thomas. ★*The Return of the Native*

Haruf, Kent. ★*Our Souls at Night*

Helprin, Mark. *In Sunlight and in Shadow*

Hemingway, Ernest. ★*A Farewell to Arms*

Henry, Patti Callahan. ★*Becoming Mrs. Lewis: The Improbable Love Story of Joy Davidman and C. S. Lewis*

Hilderbrand, Elin. ★*28 Summers*

Hilton, James. *Random Harvest*

Hoffman, Alice. *The Marriage of Opposites: A Novel Based on the Life of Rachel Pizzarro*

Horan, Nancy. *Loving Frank: A Novel*

King, Lily. *Writers & Lovers: A Novel*

Lawrence, D. H. *Women in Love*

London, Joan. *The Golden Age*

McEwan, Ian. ★*On Chesil Beach*

Miller, Holly. ★*The Sight of You*

Miller, Xander. *Zo: A Novel*

Mishima, Yukio. *The Sound of Waves*

Momaday, N. Scott. *The Ancient Child: A Novel*

Morrison, Toni. *Jazz*

Nicholls, Owen. *Love, Unscripted: A Novel*

Nichols, Peter. *The Rocks*

O'Farrell, Maggie. *The Hand That First Held Mine: A Novel*

O'Neill, Heather. ★*The Lonely Hearts Hotel: A Novel*

Oakley, Colleen. *You Were There Too*

Orringer, Julie. ★*The Invisible Bridge: A Novel*

Oyeyemi, Helen. *Mr. Fox*

Pasternak, Boris Leonidovich. ★*Doctor Zhivago*

Pears, Iain. *The Dream of Scipio*

Perez-Reverte, Arturo. *What We Become*

Pilcher, Rosamunde. *A Place Like Home: Short Stories*

Pitts, Leonard. *Freeman*

Reay, Katherine. *The Bronte Plot*

Reid, Taylor Jenkins. *Forever, Interrupted: A Novel*

Remarque, Erich Maria. *A Time to Love and a Time to Die*

Roy, Anuradha. *An Atlas of Impossible Longing*

Sand, George. *Marianne*

Schlink, Bernhard. *Olga*

See, Lisa. *Peony in Love: A Novel*

Segal, Erich. ★*Love Story*

Serle, Rebecca. *In Five Years: A Novel*

Seth, Vikram. ★*A Suitable Boy: A Novel*

Seton, Anya. *Katherine*

Shields, Carol. *The Republic of Love*

Shreve, Anita. *Eden Close: A Novel*

Shreve, Anita. *The Last Time They Met: A Novel*

Sister Souljah. *Midnight and the Meaning of Love*

Skarmeta, Antonio. *The Dancer and the Thief: A Novel*

Soli, Tatjana. *The Lotus Eaters*

Sontag, Susan. *The Volcano Lover: A Romance*

Sparks, Nicholas. *Every Breath*

Sparks, Nicholas. ★*The Notebook*

Sparks, Nicholas. *A Walk to Remember*
Spencer, Scott. ★*Endless Love*
Statovci, Pajtim. *Bolla*
Sundaresan, Indu. *The Splendor of Silence: A Novel*
Tyler, Anne. ★*The Accidental Tourist: A Novel*
Updike, John. *Brazil: A Novel*
Veletzos, Roxanne. *The Girl They Left Behind*
Waller, Robert James. ★*The Bridges of Madison County*
Williams, Beatriz. *The Summer Wives*
★*Love Story*. Segal, Erich
The Love Study. Ripper, Kris
Love study [Series]. Ripper, Kris
LOVE TRIANGLES
    Amis, Martin. *London Fields: A Novel*
    Amis, Martin. ★*The Pregnant Widow*
    Antoinette, Ashley. *Butterfly.; Vol 2 /*
    Auster, Paul. *Invisible*
    Auster, Paul. ★*Leviathan*
    Barth, John. ★*The Floating Opera*
    Bonnaffons, Amy. *The Regrets*
    Bowman, Valerie. *The Accidental Countess*
    Bowman, Valerie. *The Unexpected Duchess*
    Brundage, Elizabeth. *The Vanishing Point*
    Cameron, Peter. *The City of Your Final Destination*
    Choi, Susan. *My Education*
    Collins, Wilkie. ★*The Woman in White*
    Dare, Tessa. ★*Say Yes to the Marquess*
    Dermansky, Marcy. *Very Nice*
    Deutermann, Peter T. *Pacific Glory: A Novel*
    Drayson, Nicholas. *A Guide to the Birds of East Africa*
    Eliot, George. ★*Adam Bede*
    Erdrich, Louise. *The Master Butchers Singing Club: A Novel*
    Esquivel, Laura. ★*Like Water for Chocolate: A Novel in Monthly Installments, with Recipes, Romances, and Home Remedies*
    Eugenides, Jeffrey. ★*The Marriage Plot*
    Force, Marie. *Five Years Gone*
    Fowles, John. ★*The French Lieutenant's Woman*
    Franzen, Jonathan. ★*Freedom*
    Garcia Marquez, Gabriel. ★*Love in the Time of Cholera*
    George, Margaret. *Helen of Troy*
    Goldstein, Rebecca. *36 Arguments for the Existence of God: A Work of Fiction*
    Greene, Graham. ★*The End of the Affair*
    Greene, Graham. ★*The Quiet American*
    Harris, E. Lynn. *Invisible Life: A Novel*
    Hart, Josephine. *Damage: A Novel*
    Helprin, Mark. *In Sunlight and in Shadow*
    Hulme, Keri. ★*The Bone People: A Novel*
    Jin, Ha. ★*Waiting*
    Jin, Meng. *Little Gods*
    Joseph, Fabiola. *Niya: Rainbow Dreams*
    Kim, Crystal Hana. *If You Leave Me*
    King, Lily. *Writers & Lovers: A Novel*
    Kwan, Kevin. *Sex and Vanity: A Novel*
    Lahiri, Jhumpa. *The Lowland: A Novel*
    Marshall, Catherine. *Christy*
    McCullers, Carson. *Reflections in a Golden Eye*
    McLain, Paula. *Circling the Sun*

    Mitchell, Margaret. ★*Gone with the Wind*
    Nabokov, Vladimir Vladimirovich. *King, Queen, Knave: A Novel*
    Naipaul, V. S. *Guerrillas*
    Oakley, Colleen. *You Were There Too*
    Pamuk, Orhan. *The Museum of Innocence*
    Rendell, Ruth. *Live Flesh*
    Roberts, Bethan. ★*My Policeman*
    Ryan, Kennedy. ★*Long Shot*
    Sand, George. *Marianne*
    Santiago, Esmeralda. *Conquistadora: A Novel*
    Seton, Anya. *Katherine*
    Singer, Isaac Bashevis. *Enemies, a Love Story*
    Sontag, Susan. *The Volcano Lover: A Romance*
    Sparks, Nicholas. *The Guardian*
    Warren, Robert Penn. *World Enough and Time: A Romantic Novel*
Love You More: A Detective D.D. Warren Novel. Gardner, Lisa
Love, Lists, and Fancy Ships. Ruiz, Sarah Grunder
LOVE, NAT
    Crompton, Richard. *Hell's Gate: A Novel*
    Lansdale, Joe R. ★*Paradise Sky*
Love, Unscripted: A Novel. Nicholls, Owen
LOVE-HATE RELATIONSHIPS
    Lauren, Christina. *Dating You / Hating You*
    Menon, Lily. *Make up Break Up: A Novel*
    Styles, Toy. *War 2: All Hell Breaks Loose*
Lovecraft Country: A Novel. Ruff, Matt
Lovecraft, H. P.
    ★*Tales*
The Loved One: An Anglo-American Tragedy. Waugh, Evelyn
★*The Lovely Bones*. Sebold, Alice
Lovely, Lutishia
    Blind Ambition
★*Lovemurder*. Black, Saul
The Lover's Knot: A Someday Quilts Mystery. O'Donohue, Clare
LOVERS
    Aciman, Andre. *Enigma Variations: A Novel*
    Antoinette, Ashley. *Butterfly.; Vol 2*
    Antoinette, Ashley. *Butterfly.; Vol 3*
    Baxter, Charles. *The Feast of Love*
    Bulgakov, Mikhail. ★*The Master and Margarita*
    Cleeves, Ann. *Wild Fire*
    Collins, Ciaran. *The Gamal*
    Dickey, Eric Jerome. *The Blackbirds*
    Dunant, Sarah. *In the Company of the Courtesan: A Novel*
    Flanagan, Richard. ★*The Narrow Road to the Deep North*
    Force, Marie. *Five Years Gone*
    Gregory, Philippa. *The White Princess*
    Hardy, Thomas. ★*The Return of the Native*
    Heath, Lorraine. *Falling into Bed with a Duke*
    Kitamura, Katie M. *Intimacies*
    Lippman, Laura. ★*Sunburn*
    Monroe, Mary Alice. ★*The Summer of Lost and Found*
    Murakami, Haruki. *Killing Commendatore: A Novel*
    Nabokov, Vladimir Vladimirovich. *King, Queen, Knave: A Novel*
    Poole, Sara. *The Borgia Mistress*
    Pulley, Natasha. *The Lost Future of Pepperharrow*
    Renault, Mary. *The Persian Boy*
    Roberts, Bethan. ★*My Policeman*

Robinson, Peter. *Strange Affair*
Slaughter, Karin. ★*The Silent Wife*
Soli, Tatjana. *The Lotus Eaters*
Spencer, Scott. ★*Endless Love*
Swift, Graham. ★*Mothering Sunday: A Romance*
Vargas Llosa, Mario. *The Bad Girl*
Waller, Robert James. ★*The Bridges of Madison County*

LOVERS — DEATH
Atwood, Margaret. *Life Before Man*
Bledsoe, Alex. *Wisp of a Thing*
Crossan, Sarah. *Here Is the Beehive*
Gardiner, Meg. *Phantom Instinct*
Hill, Joe. *Horns*

LOVERS' REUNIONS
Dev, Sonali. *The Bollywood Bride*
Drake, Laura. *The Sweet Spot*
Frazier, Charles. ★*Cold Mountain*
Pineiro, Caridad. *What Happens in Summer*

Lovesey, Peter
Beau Death
Diamond Solitaire
★*The Last Detective*
The Tooth Tattoo

Lovett, Charles C.
The Lost Book of the Grail: Or a Visitor's Guide to Barchester Cathedral

Loving a Lost Lord. Putney, Mary Jo
Loving Frank: A Novel. Horan, Nancy
★*The Low Road*. Scott, A. D.
★*The Low, Low Woods*. Machado, Carmen Maria
A Lowcountry Bride. Williams, Preslaysa
Lowcountry tales [Series]. Frank, Dorothea Benton

Lowe, Kathryn A.
The Furies

LOWER EAST SIDE, NEW YORK CITY
Price, Richard. *Lush Life*
Roth, Henry. ★*Call It Sleep*

LOWER SWINSTEAD, ENGLAND
Dexter, Colin. *The Remorseful Day*

*The **Lowland**: a Novel*. Lahiri, Jhumpa
The **Loyal** League [Series]. Cole, Alyssa

LOYALTY
Anam, Tahmima. *The Bones of Grace*
Binchy, Maeve. *Circle of Friends*
Ca$h. ★*Trust No Bitch*
Cherryh, C. J. *Foreigner: A Novel of First Contact*
Crummey, Michael. *The Innocents*
Frantz, Laura. *The Lacemaker*
Gabaldon, Diana. ★*A Breath of Snow and Ashes*
Gregory, Philippa. *The Lady of the Rivers*
Gregory, Philippa. *The White Princess*
Horrocks, Caitlin. *The Vexations*
Ishiguro, Kazuo. ★*The Remains of the Day*
Jin, Ha. *A Map of Betrayal: A Novel*
Keesey, Anna. *Little Century: A Novel*
Kelton, Elmer. ★*The Way of the Coyote*
Knight, Renee. *The Secretary: A Novel*
Lasdun, James. *Afternoon of a Faun: A Novel*

Perry, Anne. *Dark Tide Rising: A William Monk Novel*
Pitts, Leonard. *Freeman*
Schami, Rafik. *Sophia: Or the Beginning of All Tales*
Shamsie, Kamila. *Home Fire: A Novel*
Steinbeck, John. *Tortilla Flat*
Wilkinson, Lauren. ★*American Spy: A Novel*

LOYALTY IN MEN
Steinhauer, Olen. *An American Spy*
Steinhauer, Olen. *The Nearest Exit*

LOYALTY IN WOMEN
Walker, Alice. ★*The Color Purple: A Novel*

Lu, S. Qiouyi
In the Watchful City

LUCAN, RICHARD JOHN BINGHAM
Brown, Rita Mae. *Wish You Were Here*
Spark, Muriel. *Aiding & Abetting*

Lucashenko, Melissa
Too Much Lip

Luchette, Claire
Agatha of Little Neon

LUCID DREAMS
North, Alex. *The Shadows*

★***Lucky** Boy*. Sekaran, Shanthi
Lucky Harbor novels [Series]. Shalvis, Jill
★***Lucky** Jim*. Amis, Kingsley
*A **Lucky** Man: Stories*. Brinkley, Jamel
★*The **Lucky** One*. Rader-Day, Lori
***Lucky** Per*. Pontoppidan, Henrik
***Lucky** Us: A Novel*. Bloom, Amy
***Lucky** You: A Novel*. Hiaasen, Carl
★***Lucy***. Kincaid, Jamaica
Lucy Stone mysteries [Series]. Meier, Leslie

LUDDITES
Brin, David. *Existence*

Ludlum, Robert
★*The Bourne Identity*
The Bourne Supremacy
The Bourne Ultimatum

Ludwig, Benjamin
Ginny Moon

Luesse, Valerie Fraser
Missing Isaac
Under the Bayou Moon: A Novel

Luis Mendoza mysteries [Series]. Shannon, Dell

Luiselli, Valeria
★*Lost Children Archive: A Novel*

Lukas, Michael David
The Last Watchman of Old Cairo: A Novel

Lullaby: a Novel. Palahniuk, Chuck

LUMBER INDUSTRY AND TRADE
Christie, Michael. ★*Greenwood: A Novel*
Kesey, Ken. *Sometimes a Great Notion: A Novel*
Rash, Ron. ★*Serena: A Novel*
Ritter, Josh. *The Great Glorious Goddamn of It All*

LUMBER WORKERS
Davidson, Ash. ★*Damnation Spring*
Kesey, Ken. *Sometimes a Great Notion: A Novel*
Ritter, Josh. *The Great Glorious Goddamn of It All*

*The **Luminaries:** a Novel*. Catton, Eleanor
*The **Luminous** Dead*. Starling, Caitlin
Luna novels (Ian McDonald) [Series]. McDonald, Ian
Luna, Louisa
  The Janes
Lunar Park. Ellis, Bret Easton
Lunatics. Barry, Dave
Lunde, Maja
  The End of the Ocean: A Novel
Lundrigan, Nicole
  Glass Boys: A Novel
Lurie, Alison
  Foreign Affairs
Lush Life. Price, Richard
LUST
  Brink, Andre P. *Philida: A Novel*
  Cheek, Chip. *Cape May*
  Dickey, Eric Jerome. *The Business of Lovers*
  Gamboa, Santiago. *Necropolis*
  Hunt, Samantha. *The Dark Dark: Stories*
  Sanders, Lawrence. ★*McNally's Gamble*
  Sanders, Lawrence. *McNally's Luck*
  Stewart, Mary. *The Last Enchantment*
Lust for Life: A Novel of Vincent Van Gogh. Stone, Irving
LUST IN MEN
  Dean, Michael. *I, Hogarth*
★*Luster*. Leilani, Raven
Lutz, Lisa
  The Spellman Files: A Novel
  The Swallows: A Novel
LUXEMBOURG
  Pavone, Chris. ★*The Expats: A Novel*
Lydia Chin and Bill Smith mysteries [Series]. Rozan, S. J.
*The **Lying** Game*. Ware, Ruth
*The **Lying** Life of Adults*. Ferrante, Elena
★*The **Lying** Room*. French, Nicci
LYNCHING
  Atkins, Ace. *The Forsaken*
  Erdrich, Louise. *The Plague of Doves*
  Faulkner, William. *Intruder in the Dust*
  Hunt, Laird. *The Evening Road*
  Sandford, John. ★*Naked Prey*
LYNLEY, THOMAS (FICTITIOUS CHARACTER)
  George, Elizabeth. *A Banquet of Consequences*
Lyons, Annie
  The Brilliant Life of Eudora Honeysett
Lyons, Jenn
  The Name of All Things
  The Ruin of Kings

M

Ma, Jian
  Beijing Coma
  China Dream

Ma, Ling
  Severance
Maaren, Kari
  ★*Weave a Circle Round*
Mabanckou, Alain
  ★*Black Moses*
MacAlister family [Series]. Garwood, Julie
Macallister, Greer
  ★*The Arctic Fury*
MACBETH, HAMISH (FICTITIOUS CHARACTER)
  Beaton, M. C. *Death of a Macho Man*
MacBride, Stuart
  Cold Granite
MacDonald, Andrew
  When We Were Vikings
MacDonald, John D.
  Cinnamon Skin: The Twentieth Adventure of Travis McGee
  The Green Ripper
  ★*The Lonely Silver Rain*
  The Long Lavender Look
  A Purple Place for Dying
  The Scarlet Ruse
  The Turquoise Lament
MacDonald, Philip
  The List of Adrian Messenger
Macdonald, Ross
  The Drowning Pool
  The Far Side of the Dollar
  The Galton Case
  The Goodbye Look
  Sleeping Beauty
  The Underground Man
Mace Reid K-9 novels [Series]. Burton, Jeffrey B.
Machado, Carmen Maria
  Her Body and Other Parties: Stories
  ★*The Low, Low Woods*
Machinehood. Divya, S. B.
Machineries of empire [Series]. Lee, Yoon Ha
MACHINERY
  Bear, Elizabeth. *The Red-Stained Wings*
  Bear, Elizabeth. *The Stone in the Skull*
  Gilman, Felix. *The Half-Made World*
MACHINES AND LABOR
  Vonnegut, Kurt. ★*Player Piano*
Mackintosh, Anneliese
  Bright and Dangerous Objects
Mackintosh, Clare
  After the End
MACKLIN, PETER (FICTITIOUS CHARACTER)
  Estleman, Loren D. ★*Something Borrowed, Something Black*
MacLaughlin, Nina
  Wake, Siren: Ovid Resung
MacLaverty, Bernard
  ★*Blank Pages: And Other Stories*
MacLean, Sarah
  ★*Bombshell*
  ★*Brazen and the Beast*
  No Good Duke Goes Unpunished

The Rogue Not Taken
★*Wicked and the Wallflower*
MacLeod, Alison
Tenderness
Macmillan, Gilly
The Nanny
The Perfect Girl
Macneal, Elizabeth
The Doll Factory
MacNeal, Susan Elia
The King's Justice
Macomber, Debbie
If Not for You: A Novel
A Mad Desire to Dance: A Novel. Wiesel, Elie
Mad River. Sandford, John
MAD SCIENTIST (CONCEPT)
Priest, Cherie. *Boneshaker*
Wells, H. G. ★*The Invisible Man*
Wells, H. G. ★*The Island of Dr. Moreau*
The Mad Women's Ball. Mas, Victoria
MADAGASCAR
Lee, Andrea. *Red Island House*
Madam. Wynne, Phoebe
Madam, May I. Bryant, Niobia
★*Madame Bovary: Provincial Ways.* Flaubert, Gustave
MADAMS (PROSTITUTION)
Bryant, Niobia. *Madam, May I*
Lippman, Laura. ★*And When She Was Good*
MaddAddam trilogy [Series]. Atwood, Margaret
★*Maddaddam: a Novel.* Atwood, Margaret
MADISON, WISCONSIN
Straub, Peter. ★*A Dark Matter: A Novel*
★*The Madness of Crowds.* Penny, Louise
The Madness of Lord Ian Mackenzie. Ashley, Jennifer
A Madness of Sunshine. Singh, Nalini
Madonnas of Echo Park: A Novel. Skyhorse, Brando
The Madonnas of Leningrad: A Novel. Dean, Debra
MADRID, SPAIN
Arbol, Victor del. *Breathing Through the Wound*
Marias, Javier. *The Infatuations*
Marias, Javier. *Thus Bad Begins: A Novel*
McLain, Paula. *Love and Ruin*
Pawel, Rebecca. *Death of a Nationalist*
Perez-Reverte, Arturo. *The Club Dumas*
Romano-Lax, Andromeda. *The Spanish Bow*
Maestra. Hilton, L. S.
Maestra novels [Series]. Hilton, L. S.
MAFIA
Armstrong, Richard. *The Don Con*
Bellow, Saul. ★*Humboldt's Gift*
Burke, James Lee. *Black Cherry Blues*
Burke, James Lee. *The Jealous Kind*
Burke, James Lee. ★*The New Iberia Blues*
Coes, Ben. *The Russian: A Thriller*
Coleman, Reed Farrel. *Where It Hurts: A Gus Murphy Novel*
Estleman, Loren D. ★*Gas City*
Faye, Lyndsay. ★*The Paragon Hotel*
Fleming, Ian. *On Her Majesty's Secret Service*

Fredericks, Mariah. *Death of a New American: A Mystery*
Grisham, John. *The Client*
Grisham, John. ★*The Firm*
Lawrence, David. *The Dead Sit Round in a Ring*
Le Carre, John. ★*Our Kind of Traitor: A Novel*
Mamet, David. *Chicago: A Novel*
Mayor, Archer. ★*Marked Man*
McBride, James. ★*Deacon King Kong: A Novel*
Pelecanos, George P. *The Big Blowdown*
Porter, Henry. *White Hot Silence*
Puzo, Mario. *The Last Don*
Vachss, Andrew H. *Two Trains Running*
The Magdalen Girls. Alexander, V. S.
Maggie Gardiner and Jack Renner novels [Series]. Black, Lisa
Maggie Hope mysteries [Series]. MacNeal, Susan Elia
Maggie: a Girl of the Streets. Crane, Stephen
MAGIC
Aaronovitch, Ben. *Moon Over Soho*
Allen, Sarah Addison. *Garden Spells*
Allen, Sarah Addison. *The Girl Who Chased the Moon: A Novel*
Anders, Charlie Jane. ★*All the Birds in the Sky*
Arden, Katherine. ★*The Girl in the Tower*
Babalola, Bolu. *Love in Color: Mythical Tales from Around the World, Retold*
Bardugo, Leigh. ★*Ninth House*
Barker, Clive. ★*Weaveworld*
Barnhill, Kelly Regan. *Dreadful Young Ladies and Other Stories*
Beagle, Peter S. ★*The Last Unicorn*
Bear, Elizabeth. *Range of Ghosts*
Bear, Elizabeth. *Shattered Pillars*
Bennett, Robert Jackson. *Foundryside*
Bennett, Robert Jackson. *Shorefall*
Bledsoe, Alex. *The Hum and the Shiver*
Bledsoe, Alex. *Long Black Curl*
Bolano, Roberto. *Monsieur Pain*
Bouchet, Amanda. *Breath of Fire*
Bradbury, Ray. *The Illustrated Man*
Brooks, Terry. *Child of Light*
Camp, Bryan. *The City of Lost Fortunes*
Carrick, M. A. *The Mask of Mirrors*
Castle, Jayne. *Illusion Town*
Chakraborty, S. A. *The City of Brass*
Chakraborty, S. A. *The Empire of Gold*
Cogman, Genevieve. *The Invisible Library*
Cogman, Genevieve. *The Masked City*
Cordova, Zoraida. *The Inheritance of Orquidea Divina*
Diachenko, Serhii. *Vita Nostra*
Draven, Grace. *Phoenix Unbound*
Eason, K. *How Rory Thorne Destroyed the Multiverse*
Elliott, Kate. *Servant Mage*
Flyte, Magnus. *City of Dark Magic: A Novel*
Flyte, Magnus. *City of Lost Dreams: A Novel*
Gaiman, Neil. ★*Anansi Boys: A Novel*
Gaiman, Neil. ★*Stardust*
Gaiman, Neil. *Trigger Warning: Short Fictions and Disturbances*
Gilman, Felix. *The Half-Made World*
Gilman, Laura Anne. *Hard Magic*
Glass, Jenna. *The Women's War*

Glover, Nicole. ★*The Conductors*
Glover, Nicole. *The Undertakers*
Gratton, Tessa. *The Queens of Innis Lear*
Grossman, Lev. *The Magician King: A Novel*
Grossman, Lev. *The Magician's Land: A Novel*
Harkness, Deborah E. *The World of All Souls: The Complete Guide to a Discovery of Witches, Shadow of Night, and the Book*
Huang, S. L. *Burning Roses*
Hunt, Samantha. *The Dark Dark: Stories*
Jemisin, N. K. *How Long 'Til Black Future Month?*
Jones, Gayl. ★*Palmares*
Kay, Guy Gavriel. *The Summer Tree*
Kay, Guy Gavriel. *Tigana*
Kelly, Greta. *The Frozen Crown*
Klune, TJ. *The House in the Cerulean Sea*
Klune, TJ. ★*Under the Whispering Door*
Krueger, Paul. *Steel Crow Saga*
Le Guin, Ursula K. *The Beginning Place*
Le Guin, Ursula K. *The Other Wind*
Locke, Thomas. *Emissary*
Malamud, Bernard. *The Natural*
Marske, Freya. *A Marvellous Light*
Martin, George R. R. ★*A Clash of Kings*
Martin, George R. R. ★*A Feast for Crows*
Martin, George R. R. ★*A Game of Thrones*
Martin, George R. R. ★*A Storm of Swords*
McCaffrey, Anne. ★*Acorna: The Unicorn Girl*
McGuire, Seanan. ★*Beneath the Sugar Sky*
McGuire, Seanan. *Chimes at Midnight: An October Daye Novel*
McGuire, Seanan. ★*Down Among the Sticks and Bones*
McGuire, Seanan. ★*Every Heart a Doorway*
McGuire, Seanan. ★*Middlegame*
Morgenstern, Erin. ★*The Starless Sea*
Novik, Naomi. *A Deadly Education: A Novel*
Novik, Naomi. *The Last Graduate: A Novel*
Novik, Naomi. ★*Spinning Silver*
Novik, Naomi. ★*Uprooted*
Okorafor, Nnedi. ★*Remote Control*
Oyeyemi, Helen. *The Opposite House*
Parry, H. G. *A Declaration of the Rights of Magicians*
Penelope, L. *Cry of Metal & Bone: Earthsinger Chronicles, Book 3*
Penelope, L. *Song of Blood and Stone*
Penelope, L. *Whispers of Shadow & Flame*
Polk, C. L. *The Midnight Bargain*
Polk, C. L. *Soulstar*
Polk, C. L. *Stormsong*
Polk, C. L. *Witchmark*
Pratchett, Terry. ★*The Color of Magic*
Pratchett, Terry. *Equal Rites*
Pratchett, Terry. *Going Postal: A Novel of Discworld*
Pratchett, Terry. *The Last Hero: A Discworld Fable*
Pratchett, Terry. *Reaper Man*
Pratchett, Terry. *Small Gods: A Novel of Discworld*
Pratchett, Terry. *Thud!: A Novel of Discworld*
Pratchett, Terry. *Witches Abroad*
Reid, Ava. *The Wolf and the Woodsman*
Rossner, Rena. *The Light of the Midnight Stars*
Rothfuss, Patrick. ★*The Name of the Wind*

Ruiz Zafon, Carlos. ★*The Shadow of the Wind*
Saberhagen, Fred. *Coinspinner's Story*
Saberhagen, Fred. *Mindsword's Story*
Saberhagen, Fred. *Sightblinder's Story*
Sathian, Sanjena. *Gold Diggers*
Sayers, Constance. *The Ladies of the Secret Circus*
Schwab, Victoria. *A Conjuring of Light*
Schwab, Victoria. *A Darker Shade of Magic*
Schwab, Victoria. *A Gathering of Shadows*
Stephenson, Neal. *The Rise and Fall of D.O.D.O.: A Novel*
Sterling, Erin. *The Ex Hex*
Suri, Tasha. ★*Realm of Ash*
Tan, Sue Lynn. ★*Daughter of the Moon Goddess*
Tepper, Sheri S. *The Visitor*
Tolkien, J. R. R. *The Silmarillion*
Wexler, Django. *Ashes of the Sun*
White, T. H. ★*The Once and Future King*
Whitten, Hannah. *For the Wolf*
Wilson, G. Willow. *Alif the Unseen*

MAGIC (OCCULTISM)
Beukes, Lauren. *Zoo City*
Rhodes, Jewell Parker. *Yellow Moon: A Novel*
Roanhorse, Rebecca. ★*Trail of Lightning*

MAGIC — STUDY AND TEACHING
Grossman, Lev. ★*The Magicians: A Novel*
Magic for Liars. Gailey, Sarah
Magic for Unlucky Girls: Stories. Balaskovits, A. A.
The Magic Mountain. Mann, Thomas
Magic of the lost [Series]. Clark, Cherae

MAGIC POTIONS
Gilman, Laura Anne. *Flesh and Fire*

MAGIC RINGS
Tolkien, J. R. R. *The Fellowship of the Ring: Being the First Part of the Lord of the Rings*
Tolkien, J. R. R. ★*The Lord of the Rings*
Tolkien, J. R. R. *The Return of the King: Being the Third Part of the Lord of the Rings*
Tolkien, J. R. R. *The Two Towers: Being the Second Part of the Lord of the Rings*
Magic Seeds. Naipaul, V. S.

MAGIC SWORDS
Saberhagen, Fred. *Coinspinner's Story*
Saberhagen, Fred. *Farslayer's Story*
Saberhagen, Fred. *Mindsword's Story*
Saberhagen, Fred. *Shieldbreaker's Story*
Saberhagen, Fred. *Sightblinder's Story*
Saberhagen, Fred. *Stonecutter's Story*
Saberhagen, Fred. *Wayfinder's Story*
Saberhagen, Fred. *Woundhealer's Story*

MAGIC TELEPHONES
Rowell, Rainbow. *Landline*

MAGIC TRICKS
Rosen, Leonard J. *The Kortelisy Escape*

MAGICAL BOOKS
Cogman, Genevieve. *The Invisible Library*
Cogman, Genevieve. *The Masked City*
Hackwith, A. J. *The Library of the Unwritten*

MAGICAL REALISM

Allende, Isabel. ★*Eva Luna*

Allende, Isabel. ★*The House of the Spirits*

Allende, Isabel. *The Stories of Eva Luna*

Amado, Jorge. ★*Dona Flor and Her Two Husbands: A Moral and Amorous Tale*

Araghi, Alireza Taheri. ★*The Immortals of Tehran*

Armfield, Julia. *Salt Slow: Stories*

Atkinson, Kate. *Human Croquet*

Bender, Aimee. *The Butterfly Lampshade*

Borges, Jorge Luis. *Ficciones*

Calvino, Italo. ★*If on a Winter's Night a Traveler*

Calvino, Italo. *Invisible Cities*

Coates, Ta-Nehisi. ★*The Water Dancer: A Novel*

Cordova, Zoraida. *The Inheritance of Orquidea Divina*

Couto, Mia. *Sleepwalking Land*

Dalton, Trent. *All Our Shimmering Skies*

Depestre, Rene. *Hadriana in All My Dreams*

Erdrich, Louise. ★*Larose*

Esquivel, Laura. ★*Like Water for Chocolate: A Novel in Monthly Installments, with Recipes, Romances, and Home Remedies*

Flanagan, Richard. *The Living Sea of Waking Dreams*

Flores, Fernando A. *Tears of the Trufflepig*

Foer, Jonathan Safran. *Everything Is Illuminated: A Novel*

Forbes, Curdella. *A Tall History of Sugar*

Fuentes, Carlos. *Destiny and Desire: A Novel*

Garcia Marquez, Gabriel. ★*The Autumn of the Patriarch*

Garcia Marquez, Gabriel. *Collected Novellas*

Garcia Marquez, Gabriel. *Leaf Storm, and Other Stories*

Garcia Marquez, Gabriel. ★*One Hundred Years of Solitude*

Garcia Marquez, Gabriel. ★*Strange Pilgrims: Twelve Stories*

Helprin, Mark. ★*Winter's Tale*

Higashino, Keigo. *The Miracles of the Namiya General Store*

Hoffman, Alice. *The Book of Magic*

Hoffman, Alice. *The Marriage of Opposites: A Novel Based on the Life of Rachel Pizzarro*

Hoffman, Alice. *The River King*

Hoffman, Alice. *The Rules of Magic: A Novel*

Hoffman, Alice. ★*The World That We Knew*

Hulme, Keri. ★*The Bone People: A Novel*

Hunt, Samantha. *The Dark Dark: Stories*

Jones, Gayl. ★*Palmares*

Kawaguchi, Toshikazu. *Before the Coffee Gets Cold*

Lopez Barrio, Cristina. *The House of the Impossible Loves*

Makumbi, Jennifer Nansubuga. ★*A Girl Is a Body of Water*

Mandanipour, Shahriar. *Moon Brow*

Mandel, Emily St. John. ★*The Glass Hotel: A Novel*

Miller, Xander. *Zo: A Novel*

Morrison, Toni. ★*Beloved: A Novel*

Murakami, Haruki. ★*First Person Singular: Stories*

Oyeyemi, Helen. *Boy, Snow, Bird: A Novel*

Oyeyemi, Helen. *Gingerbread: A Novel*

Oyeyemi, Helen. *Peaces*

Oyeyemi, Helen. *What Is Not Yours Is Not Yours: Stories*

Ozeki, Ruth L. *The Book of Form and Emptiness: A Novel*

Peynado, Brenda. *The Rock Eaters: Stories*

Reyes, Dolores. *Eartheater*

Ruiz Zafon, Carlos. *The Angel's Game*

Ruiz Zafon, Carlos. *The Labyrinth of the Spirits*

Ruiz Zafon, Carlos. *The Prisoner of Heaven*

Ruiz Zafon, Carlos. ★*The Shadow of the Wind*

Rushdie, Salman. ★*Midnight's Children: A Novel*

Rushdie, Salman. ★*The Satanic Verses*

Russell, Karen. ★*Swamplandia!*

Sathian, Sanjena. *Gold Diggers*

Serpell, Namwali. ★*The Old Drift*

Setterfield, Diane. ★*Once Upon a River*

Silko, Leslie Marmon. *Almanac of the Dead*

Solomon, Rivers. *Sorrowland*

Swarup, Shubhangi. *Latitudes of Longing*

Tan, Amy. *The Hundred Secret Senses*

Updike, John. *Brazil: A Novel*

Urrea, Luis Alberto. *The Hummingbird's Daughter: A Novel*

Urrea, Luis Alberto. *Queen of America: A Novel*

Yu, E. Lily. ★*On Fragile Waves*

*The **Magician** King: A Novel*. Grossman, Lev

Magician novels (Lev Grossman) [Series]. Grossman, Lev

★*The **Magician** of Lublin*. Singer, Isaac Bashevis

*The **Magician's** Land: A Novel*. Grossman, Lev

★*The **Magician**: a Novel*. Toibin, Colm

MAGICIANS

Barker, Clive. ★*Weaveworld*

Bartlett, Neil. *The Disappearance Boy*

Beagle, Peter S. ★*The Last Unicorn*

Bear, Elizabeth. *Ink and Steel: A Novel of the Promethean Age*

Clarke, Susanna. ★*Jonathan Strange & Mr. Norrell*

Morgenstern, Erin. ★*The Night Circus: A Novel*

Quick, Amanda. *The Girl Who Knew Too Much*

Rothfuss, Patrick. ★*The Wise Man's Fear*

Schwab, Victoria. *A Conjuring of Light*

Swift, Graham. ★*Here We Are*

Wecker, Helene. *The Golem and the Jinni*

MAGICIANS' APPRENTICES

Morgenstern, Erin. ★*The Night Circus: A Novel*

★*The **Magicians**: a Novel*. Grossman, Lev

★*The **Magnificent** Ambersons*. Tarkington, Booth

★***Magpie** Murders*. Horowitz, Anthony

Magpie murders [Series]. Horowitz, Anthony

Maguire, Gregory

The Brides of Maracoor

Son of a Witch: A Novel

★*Wicked: The Life and Times of the Wicked Witch of the West : A Novel*

*The **Magus***. Fowles, John

Mahfuz, Najib

★*Palace Walk*

MAHMOOD, ZAVED

Ferrante, Elena. *The Lost Daughter*

Hensher, Philip. *Scenes from Early Life: A Novel*

Mahmoud, Lena

Amreekiya: A Novel

MAID OF HONOR (WEDDINGS)

Weiner, Jennifer. ★*Big Summer*

*The **Maid's** Version: A Novel*. Woodrell, Daniel

***Maigret** and the Black Sheep*. Simenon, Georges

***Maigret** and the Fortuneteller*. Simenon, Georges

★*Maigret* and the Killer. Simenon, Georges
Maigret and the Madwoman. Simenon, Georges
★*Maigret* and the Saturday Caller. Simenon, Georges
★*Maigret* and the Toy Village. Simenon, Georges
Maigret and the Wine Merchant. Simenon, Georges
★*Maigret* Bides His Time. Simenon, Georges
★*Maigret* Goes Home. Simenon, Georges
Maigret in Holland. Simenon, Georges
Maigret's Memoirs. Simenon, Georges

MAIGRET, JULES (FICTITIOUS CHARACTER)
  Simenon, Georges. *Maigret and the Fortuneteller*
  Simenon, Georges. ★*Maigret Bides His Time*
  Simenon, Georges. ★*Maigret Goes Home*
  Simenon, Georges. *Maigret in Holland*
  Simenon, Georges. *Maigret's Memoirs*
  Simenon, Georges. *My Friend Maigret*

MAIL ORDER BRIDES
  Goodman, Jo. *In Want of a Wife*
  Jenkins, Beverly. *Tempest*
  Otsuka, Julie. *The Buddha in the Attic*

Mailer, Norman
  ★*The Executioner's Song*
  ★*The Naked and the Dead*

★*Main* Street: The Story of Carol Kennicott. Lewis, Sinclair

MAINE
  Allio, Kirstin. *Buddhism for Western Children: A Novel*
  Avon, Joy. *In Peppermint Peril: A Book Tea Shop Mystery*
  Beattie, Ann. *The State We're In: Maine Stories*
  Blake, Sarah. *The Guest Book: A Novel*
  Child, Lee. *Persuader*
  Connolly, John. *A Book of Bones*
  Connolly, John. *The Dirty South*
  Doiron, Paul. *Almost Midnight*
  Doiron, Paul. *Bad Little Falls: A Novel*
  Doiron, Paul. ★*Dead by Dawn*
  Doiron, Paul. *One Last Lie*
  Doiron, Paul. *The Poacher's Son*
  Doiron, Paul. *The Precipice*
  Doiron, Paul. *Stay Hidden*
  Dykes, Amanda. *Whose Waves These Are*
  Gerritsen, Tess. ★*The Shape of Night: A Novel*
  Goodman, Carol. *The Sea of Lost Girls*
  Groff, Lauren. ★*Fates and Furies*
  Hand, Elizabeth. ★*Generation Loss: A Novel*
  Higgins, Kristan. *Now That You Mention It*
  Holmes, Linda. ★*Evvie Drake Starts Over: A Novel*
  Irving, John. ★*The Cider House Rules: A Novel*
  King, Stephen. *11/22/63*
  King, Stephen. ★*Carrie*
  King, Stephen. *Cujo*
  King, Stephen. *Dolores Claiborne*
  King, Stephen. *Elevation*
  King, Stephen. *The Girl Who Loved Tom Gordon*
  King, Stephen. *It*
  King, Stephen. *Pet Sematary*
  King, Stephen. *Salem's Lot*
  Koryta, Michael. ★*How It Happened*
  Kotzwinkle, William. *The Bear Went Over the Mountain*

  Kubica, Mary. ★*The Other Mrs.*
  Lattari, Katie. *Dark Things I Adore*
  Meier, Leslie. *Silver Anniversary Murder*
  Perry, Thomas. ★*The Left-Handed Twin*
  Phillips, Susan Elizabeth. *Heroes Are My Weakness*
  Roberts, Nora. *Shelter in Place*
  Rosenfelt, David. ★*Dog Eat Dog*
  Rosenfield, Kat. *No One Will Miss Her*
  Russell, Kate Elizabeth. ★*My Dark Vanessa*
  Russo, Richard. ★*Empire Falls*
  Strout, Elizabeth. ★*The Burgess Boys: A Novel*
  Strout, Elizabeth. ★*Oh William!*
  Strout, Elizabeth. *Olive Kitteridge*
  Strout, Elizabeth. ★*Olive, Again: A Novel*

MAINSTREAM FICTION
  Adkins, Mary. *When You Read This*
  Albom, Mitch. *The Stranger in the Lifeboat*
  Alenyikov, Michael. *Ivan and Misha: Stories*
  Attenberg, Jami. *The Middlesteins*
  Bala, Sharon. *The Boat People: A Novel*
  Baldacci, David. *One Summer*
  Barthelme, Frederick. *Bob the Gambler*
  Barthelme, Frederick. *Elroy Nights*
  Barthelme, Frederick. *Painted Desert: A Novel*
  Bawden, Nina. *Family Money*
  Beattie, Ann. *Chilly Scenes of Winter*
  Beckerman, Hannah. *If Only I Could Tell You*
  Benedict, Helen. *Wolf Season*
  Bergstrom, Heather Brittain. *Steal the North: A Novel*
  Bhuvaneswar, Chaya. *White Dancing Elephants: Stories*
  Blackwell, Juliet. *Letters from Paris*
  Block, Stefan Merrill. *Oliver Loving: A Novel*
  Blumenfeld, Amy. *The Cast*
  Bohjalian, Chris. *The Buffalo Soldier: A Novel*
  Bowman, Conor. ★*Horace Winter Says Goodbye*
  Boyle, T. Coraghessan. ★*The Tortilla Curtain*
  Boyle, T. Coraghessan. *When the Killing's Done: A Novel*
  Brown, Rosellen. *Tender Mercies*
  Bruni, Sarah. *The Night Gwen Stacy Died*
  Brunkhorst, Alex. *The Gilded Life of Matilda Duplaine*
  Brunt, Carol Rifka. ★*Tell the Wolves I'm Home: A Novel*
  Butler, Sarah. *Ten Things I've Learnt About Love: A Novel*
  Cameron, W. Bruce. *The Dogs of Christmas*
  Cartwright, Justin. *To Heaven by Water*
  Chung, Catherine. *The Tenth Muse: A Novel*
  Colwin, Laurie. *Happy All the Time: A Novel*
  Conner, M. Shelly. *Everyman*
  Cooney, Ellen. *The Mountaintop School for Dogs and Other Second Chances*
  Creech, Sarah. *The Whole Way Home*
  Cronin, A. J. *Citadel*
  Crowell, Jenn. *Etched on Me: A Novel*
  Cush, Jean Love. *Endangered*
  Daughters, Amy Weinland. *You Cannot Mess This Up: A True Story That Never Happened*
  Davidson, Ash. ★*Damnation Spring*
  Dee, Jonathan. *The Locals: A Novel*
  Dee, Jonathan. *The Privileges: A Novel*

Dee, Jonathan. *A Thousand Pardons: A Novel*
DeMille, Nelson. ★*The Cuban Affair: A Novel*
Diamond, Elizabeth. *An Accidental Light*
Diehl, Heidi. *Lifelines*
Divakaruni, Chitra Banerjee. *Oleander Girl: A Novel*
Dixon, Stephen. *Interstate: A Novel*
Drayson, Nicholas. *A Guide to the Birds of East Africa*
Dunn, Kate. *The Dragonfly*
Edwards, Kim. *The Memory Keeper's Daughter*
Enger, Leif. *Virgil Wander*
Evans, Diana. *Ordinary People: A Novel*
Evans, Nicholas. ★*The Horse Whisperer: A Novel*
Evison, Jonathan. *All About Lulu: A Novel*
Evison, Jonathan. *The Revised Fundamentals of Caregiving: A Novel*
Extence, Gavin. *The Universe Versus Alex Woods*
Fay, Juliette. *The Shortest Way Home*
Ferrante, Elena. *My Brilliant Friend*
Ferrante, Elena. *The Story of a New Name*
Ferrante, Elena. *The Story of the Lost Child*
Ferrante, Elena. *Those Who Leave and Those Who Stay*
Ferris, Joshua. *The Unnamed*
Frankel, Laurie. *Goodbye for Now: A Novel*
Freudenberger, Nell. *The Dissident*
Friedland, Elyssa. *Last Summer at the Golden Hotel*
Garey, Juliann. *Too Bright to Hear Too Loud to See*
Genova, Lisa. *Every Note Played*
Genova, Lisa. *Left Neglected: A Novel*
George, Nina. *The Book of Dreams*
Gilman, Susan Jane. *The Ice Cream Queen of Orchard Street: A Novel*
Goodman, Allegra. *The Cookbook Collector: A Novel*
Goodwin, Bobi Gentry. *Revelation*
Hamilton, Jane. *A Map of the World*
Harding, Lisa. *Bright Burning Things*
Harris, E. Lynn. *I Say a Little Prayer: A Novel*
Harris, E. Lynn. *Invisible Life: A Novel*
Hemmings, Kaui Hart. *The Possibilities: A Novel*
Hogan, Ruth. *Queenie Malone's Paradise Hotel*
Holsinger, Bruce W. *The Gifted School: A Novel*
Itami, Emily. *Fault Lines: A Novel*
Jen, Gish. ★*The Resisters*
Kantra, Virginia. ★*Meg and Jo*
Kaufman, Bel. *Up the Down Staircase*
Kenney, John. *Talk to Me*
Kidd, Sue Monk. ★*The Secret Life of Bees*
Kosinski, Jerzy. *The Devil Tree*
Lefteri, Christy. *The Beekeeper of Aleppo: A Novel*
Ludwig, Benjamin. *Ginny Moon*
Mackintosh, Clare. *After the End*
Maizes, R. L. *Other People's Pets*
Makkai, Rebecca. *The Borrower: A Novel*
Martin, Steve. *Shopgirl*
Maynard, Joyce. *Count the Ways*
McCorkle, Jill. ★*Hieroglyphics: A Novel*
McGuane, Thomas. *Crow Fair: Stories*
Miller, Holly. ★*The Sight of You*
Moore, Meg Mitchell. *The Islanders*
Moriarty, Liane. *Big Little Lies*
Moriarty, Liane. *The Husband's Secret*

Moriarty, Liane. *Nine Perfect Strangers*
Moriarty, Liane. *Truly Madly Guilty*
Napolitano, Ann. *Dear Edward*
Nicholls, Owen. *Love, Unscripted: A Novel*
Nussbaum, Susan. *Good Kings, Bad Kings: A Novel*
Ólafsdóttir, Auður A. *Butterflies in November*
Pellegrino, Amanda. *Smile and Look Pretty*
Perrotta, Tom. *The Abstinence Teacher*
Perrotta, Tom. *Little Children*
Picoult, Jodi. *House Rules: A Novel*
Picoult, Jodi. *Keeping Faith: A Novel*
Picoult, Jodi. *Leaving Time: A Novel*
Picoult, Jodi. ★*My Sister's Keeper*
Picoult, Jodi. *Nineteen Minutes: A Novel*
Picoult, Jodi. *Sing You Home: A Novel*
Picoult, Jodi. *The Storyteller*
Picoult, Jodi. *Vanishing Acts: A Novel*
Powell, Padgett. ★*Edisto: A Novel*
Racculia, Kate. ★*Tuesday Mooney Talks to Ghosts: A Novel*
Ramos, Joanne. *The Farm: A Novel*
Rice, Luanne. *The Lemon Orchard*
Richman, Alyson. *The Secret of Clouds*
Rooney, Sally. ★*Conversations with Friends*
Rowling, J. K. *The Casual Vacancy*
Shreve, Anita. *The Last Time They Met: A Novel*
Shreve, Anita. *The Pilot's Wife: A Novel*
Shriver, Lionel. *So Much for That*
Shteyngart, Gary. ★*Lake Success: A Novel*
Sittenfeld, Curtis. *Sisterland: A Novel*
Smiley, Jane. *Horse Heaven*
Stephens, Alice. *Famous Adopted People*
Straub, Emma. *The Vacationers*
Tursten, Helene. *An Elderly Lady Must Not Be Crossed*
Tyler, Anne. ★*The Accidental Tourist: A Novel*
Tyler, Anne. *The Amateur Marriage: A Novel*
Tyler, Anne. *A Patchwork Planet*
Tyler, Anne. ★*Saint Maybe*
Unsworth, Emma Jane. *Grown Ups*
Urrea, Luis Alberto. *Into the Beautiful North: A Novel*
Vatner, Jonathan. *Carnegie Hill: A Novel*
Wallace, Melanie. *The Girl in the Garden*
Waller, Robert James. ★*The Bridges of Madison County*
Walls, Jeannette. *The Silver Star: A Novel*
Williams, Katie. *Tell the Machine Goodnight*
Wilson, Kevin. *Nothing to See Here*
Winthrop, Elizabeth Hartley. ★*The Why of Things*
Wolitzer, Meg. *The Interestings*
Woo, Sung J. *Love Love: A Novel*
Yoshimoto, Banana. *Moshi-Moshi*
Maisie Dobbs novels [Series]. Winspear, Jacqueline
Maizes, R. L.
 Other People's Pets
*The **Majesties**.* Tsao, Tiffany
__Major__ Pettigrew's Last Stand: A Novel. Simonson, Helen
MAJOR, JOHN
 Higgins, Jack. *Eye of the Storm*
 Nabokov, Vladimir Vladimirovich. *King, Queen, Knave: A Novel*

MAJORCA, SPAIN
  Nichols, Peter. *The Rocks*
  Straub, Emma. *The Vacationers*
  Thelen, Albert Vigoleis. *The Island of Second Sight: From the Applied Recollections of Vigoleis*
Majors, Inman
  Penelope Lemon: Game On!
Majumdar, Megha
  A Burning
Makana mysteries [Series]. Bilal, Parker
Make Me. Child, Lee
Make up Break Up: A Novel. Menon, Lily
Make Your Home Among Strangers. Crucet, Jennine Capo
MAKEUP ARTISTS
  Alexander, Jennet. *I Kissed a Girl*
  Hendricks, Greer. *An Anonymous Girl*
Making of a mother monster [Series]. Styles, Toy
Makkai, Rebecca
  The Borrower: A Novel
  ★*The Great Believers*
Makumbi, Jennifer Nansubuga
  ★*A Girl Is a Body of Water*
  Kintu
Malamud, Bernard
  The Assistant
  ★*The Complete Stories*
  ★*The Fixer*
  The Natural
MALAYA
  Tan, Twan Eng. *The Garden of Evening Mists*
MALAYSIA
  Aw, Tash. *We, the Survivors*
  Cho, Zen. *Spirits Abroad and Other Stories*
  Choo, Yangsze. *The Ghost Bride: A Novel*
  Choo, Yangsze. ★*The Night Tiger: A Novel*
  Tan, Twan Eng. *The Garden of Evening Mists*
Malcolm Fox mysteries [Series]. Rankin, Ian
MALE FRIENDSHIP
  Aciman, Andre. *Harvard Square*
  Adams, Lyssa Kay. *The Bromance Book Club*
  Al-Ramli, Muhsin. *The President's Gardens*
  Atwood, Margaret. ★*Oryx and Crake*
  Barnes, Julian. ★*The Sense of an Ending*
  Beattie, Ann. *Chilly Scenes of Winter*
  Bolano, Roberto. ★*The Savage Detectives*
  Coe, Jonathan. *The Rotters' Club*
  Dickens, Charles. *The Pickwick Papers*
  Dimitri, Francesco. *The Book of Hidden Things*
  Doyle, Roddy. *Love*
  Dumas, Alexandre. ★*The Three Musketeers*
  Eskens, Allen. *Nothing More Dangerous: A Novel*
  Faye, Lyndsay. ★*The King of Infinite Space*
  Franklin, Tom. *Crooked Letter, Crooked Letter: A Novel*
  Giordano, Paolo. *Heaven and Earth*
  Gorman, Edward. *Riders on the Storm : A Sam McCain Mystery*
  Guterson, David. *The Other*
  Hammett, Dashiell. *The Glass Key*
  Harvey, Michael T. *Brighton*

  Heller, Peter. *The River: A Novel*
  Hemingway, Ernest. ★*The Old Man and the Sea*
  Hijuelos, Oscar. *Twain & Stanley Enter Paradise*
  Hill, Ruth Beebe. *Hanta Yo*
  Holmes, J. M. *How Are You Going to Save Yourself*
  Irving, John. ★*A Prayer for Owen Meany: A Novel*
  McMurtry, Larry. *Comanche Moon: A Novel*
  McMurtry, Larry. ★*Lonesome Dove: A Novel*
  Oe, Kenzaburo. *The Changeling*
  Parker, Robert B. *Appaloosa*
  Petterson, Per. *I Refuse*
  Pulley, Natasha. *The Watchmaker of Filigree Street*
  Row, Jess. *Your Face in Mine: A Novel*
  Russell, Mary Doria. ★*Doc: A Novel*
  Russo, Richard. ★*Chances Are...: A Novel*
  Smith, B. J. *All Hat: A Novel*
  Spencer, Scott. *An Ocean Without a Shore*
  Steinbeck, John. ★*Of Mice and Men*
  Styles, Toy. *War 2: All Hell Breaks Loose*
  Waugh, Evelyn. ★*Brideshead Revisited*
  Wayne, Teddy. *Apartment: A Novel*
  White, Randy Wayne. *Salt River*
  Yanagihara, Hanya. *A Little Life: A Novel*
MALE FRIENDSHIP — HISTORY
  Parini, Jay. *The Passages of H.M.: A Novel of Herman Melville*
MALE IMPERSONATORS
  Allende, Isabel. *Daughter of Fortune: A Novel*
  Bird, Sarah. *Daughter of a Daughter of a Queen*
  De Robertis, Carolina. *The Gods of Tango*
  Elison, Meg. *The Book of the Unnamed Midwife*
  Erdrich, Louise. *The Last Report on the Miracles at Little No Horse*
  Guhrke, Laura Lee. *Governess Gone Rogue*
  Hand, Elizabeth. *Curious Toys*
  Larison, John. *Whiskey When We're Dry*
  Levine, David D. *Arabella of Mars*
Malerman, Josh
  Bird Box: A Novel
  Goblin: A Novel in Six Novellas
  Malorie: A Bird Box Novel
  Unbury Carol
MALGUDI (INDIA : IMAGINARY PLACE)
  Narayan, R. K. *Malgudi Days*
Malgudi Days. Narayan, R. K.
MALI
  Cussler, Clive. *Sahara: A Novel*
★*Malibu Rising*. Reid, Taylor Jenkins
MALIBU, CALIFORNIA
  Reid, Taylor Jenkins. ★*Malibu Rising*
Malice. Higashino, Keigo
MALICIOUS ACCUSATION
  Ashley, Jennifer. *The Madness of Lord Ian Mackenzie*
  Atkins, Ace. ★*The Heathens*
  Blakemore, A. K. *The Manningtree Witches*
  Callaghan, Mary Rose. *Billy, Come Home*
  Cameron, Marc. ★*Code of Honor*
  Campbell, Lisbeth. *The Vanished Queen*
  Crace, Jim. *Harvest*
  Cussler, Clive. ★*The Gray Ghost*

Davidson, MaryJanice. *Truth, Lies, and Second Dates*

De Giovanni, Maurizio. *The Crocodile*

Delinsky, Barbara. *Lake News: A Novel*

Eliot, George. ★*Silas Marner: The Weaver of Raveloe*

Flanagan, Richard. *The Unknown Terrorist*

Flint, Emma. ★*Little Deaths: A Novel*

Francis, Patry. *The Orphans of Race Point: A Novel*

Frantz, Laura. *The Lacemaker*

Galchen, Rivka. *Everyone Knows Your Mother Is a Witch*

Hannah, Sophie. *The Mystery of Three Quarters: The New Hercule Poirot Mystery*

Iles, Greg. *The Bone Tree: A Novel*

Iles, Greg. *Natchez Burning: A Novel*

Irvin, Kelly. *Tell Her No Lies*

MacDonald, John D. *The Long Lavender Look*

Malamud, Bernard. ★*The Fixer*

McAllister, Tom. *How to Be Safe: A Novel*

Parks, Brad. *Closer Than You Know*

Pronzini, Bill. *Nemesis*

Quirk, Matthew. *Cold Barrel Zero*

Quirk, Matthew. *Dead Man Switch*

Rankin, Ian. ★*Black and Blue: An Inspector Rebus Novel*

Raybourn, Deanna. *A Perilous Undertaking: A Veronica Speedwell Mystery*

Wilson, G. Willow. ★*The Bird King*

Wright, Richard. *The Man Who Lived Underground*

Mallery, Susan

Best of My Love

California Girls

The Summer of Sunshine and Margot

★*When We Found Home*

Malliet, G. M.

A Demon Summer: A Max Tudor Mystery

Pagan Spring: A Mystery

Mallon, Thomas

Finale: A Novel

Landfall: A Novel

Malloren chronicles [Series]. Beverley, Jo

MALLOREN FAMILY (FICTITIOUS CHARACTERS)

Beverley, Jo. *My Lady Notorious*

Beverley, Jo. *Tempting Fortune*

MALMO, SWEDEN

McCall Smith, Alexander. ★*The Department of Sensitive Crimes: A Detective Varg Novel*

McCall Smith, Alexander. ★*The Man with the Silver Saab: A Detective Varg Novel*

Malone, Minx

Bad Blood

Malorie: a Bird Box Novel. Malerman, Josh

Malouf, David

Ransom

Remembering Babylon

Malpas, Jodi Ellen

Leave Me Breathless

MALTA

Gelernter, J. H. *Hold Fast*

★*The Malta Exchange: A Novel*. Berry, Steve

★*The Maltese Falcon*. Hammett, Dashiell

Mama Day. Naylor, Gloria

★*The Mambo Kings Play Songs of Love: A Novel*. Hijuelos, Oscar

MAMBOS (VOODOOISM)

Rhodes, Jewell Parker. *Voodoo Dreams: A Novel of Marie Laveau*

Mamet, David

Chicago: A Novel

Man at the helm novels (Nina Stibbe) [Series]. Stibbe, Nina

A Man Called Ove. Backman, Fredrik

The Man from Beijing. Mankell, Henning

★*The Man He Never Was*. Rubart, James L.

★*The Man in the Gray Flannel Suit*. Wilson, Sloan

★*The Man in the High Castle*. Dick, Philip K.

★*The Man in the Iron Mask*. Dumas, Alexandre

MAN IN THE IRON MASK

Dumas, Alexandre. ★*The Man in the Iron Mask*

Man in the Woods. Spencer, Scott

A Man Lay Dead. Marsh, Ngaio

A Man Named Doll. Ames, Jonathan

Man of My Time. Sofer, Dalia

Man of the Year. Walker, Caroline Louise

Man of War: An Eric Steele Novel. Parnell, Sean

The Man on the Balcony: The Story of a Crime. Sjowall, Maj

The Man That Got Away: A Constable Twitten Mystery. Truss, Lynne

The Man Who Could Fly and Other Stories. Anaya, Rudolfo A.

The Man Who Died Twice: A Thursday Murder Club Mystery. Osman, Richard

The Man Who Lived Underground. Wright, Richard

★*The Man Who Loved Children*. Stead, Christina

The Man Who Smiled: A Kurt Wallander Mystery. Mankell, Henning

★*The Man with the Golden Arm: A Novel*. Algren, Nelson

The Man with the Golden Gun. Fleming, Ian

★*The Man with the Silver Saab: A Detective Varg Novel*. McCall Smith, Alexander

The Man Without Qualities. Musil, Robert

MAN-WOMAN RELATIONSHIPS

Abu-Jaber, Diana. *Crescent*

Adichie, Chimamanda Ngozi. ★*Americanah: A Novel*

Adichie, Chimamanda Ngozi. *The Thing Around Your Neck*

Aguilar Camin, Hector. *Death in Veracruz*

Algren, Nelson. *A Walk on the Wild Side*

Allende, Isabel. ★*The House of the Spirits*

Allende, Isabel. *Of Love and Shadows*

Allende, Isabel. *Portrait in Sepia: A Novel*

Amis, Martin. ★*The Pregnant Widow*

Atkinson, Kate. *One Good Turn: A Novel*

Atwood, Margaret. *Alias Grace*

Austen, Jane. ★*Persuasion*

Bailey, Tessa. *Fix Her Up*

Balogh, Mary. *More Than a Mistress*

Balogh, Mary. *Only Enchanting*

Balogh, Mary. *Someone to Wed*

Baxter, Charles. *The Feast of Love*

Beattie, Ann. *Chilly Scenes of Winter*

Bellow, Saul. ★*The Adventures of Augie March*

Benjamin, Melanie. *Alice I Have Been*

Billingsley, ReShonda Tate. ★*The Secret She Kept*

Blackwell, Juliet. *Letters from Paris*

Bohjalian, Chris. *The Sleepwalker*

Bolano, Roberto. *Last Evenings on Earth*

Bourne, Joanna. *The Black Hawk*

Bourne, Joanna. *The Forbidden Rose*

Boyle, T. Coraghessan. *The Women: A Novel*

Brockway, Connie. *The Golden Season*

Brockway, Connie. *So Enchanting*

Broder, Melissa. *The Pisces: A Novel*

Buck, Pearl S. *The Good Earth*

Burke, James Lee. *Wayfaring Stranger: A Novel*

Burrowes, Grace. *The Captive*

Burrowes, Grace. *Tremaine's True Love*

Bushnell, Candace. *Is There Still Sex in the City?*

Ca$h. *Thugs Cry: A Novel*

Ca$h. ★*Trust No Bitch*

Calvino, Italo. ★*If on a Winter's Night a Traveler*

Carr, Robyn. *The Family Gathering*

Carver, Raymond. *What We Talk About When We Talk About Love: Stories*

Center, Katherine. *Things You Save in a Fire*

Chase, Loretta Lynda. *Don't Tempt Me*

Chase, Loretta Lynda. *A Duke in Shining Armor*

Chase, Loretta Lynda. *Miss Wonderful*

Clark, Wahida. *Thug Matrimony*

Clark, Wahida. ★*Thugs and the Women Who Love Them*

Cleeton, Chanel. *Next Year in Havana*

Conrad, Joseph. *Complete Short Fiction of Joseph Conrad: The Stories: Volume 1*

Cooley, Martha. *The Archivist: A Novel*

Currie, Ron. *Flimsy Little Plastic Miracles: A True Story*

Dade, Olivia. *All the Feels*

Dare, Tessa. ★*A Night to Surrender*

Davidson, Andrew. *The Gargoyle*

Davidson, MaryJanice. *Truth, Lies, and Second Dates*

Dean, Pamela. *Tam Lin*

Dee, Jonathan. *A Thousand Pardons: A Novel*

Dell, Kari Lynn. *Fearless in Texas*

Dell, Kari Lynn. *Mistletoe in Texas*

Dell, Kari Lynn. *Reckless in Texas*

Deveraux, Jude. *Someone to Love*

Dickens, Charles. *Martin Chuzzlewit*

Dickey, Eric Jerome. *Before We Were Wicked*

Didion, Joan. ★*Play It as It Lays: A Novel*

Drabble, Margaret. ★*The Dark Flood Rises*

Dreiser, Theodore. ★*An American Tragedy*

Du Maurier, Daphne. *Frenchman's Creek*

Dunant, Sarah. *The Birth of Venus: A Novel*

Dyer, Geoff. *Jeff in Venice, Death in Varanasi*

Eggers, Dave. *How We Are Hungry: Stories*

Eisenberg, Deborah. *The Twilight of the Superheroes*

Ellroy, James. *Perfidia*

Epstein, Joseph. *The Love Song of A. Jerome Minkoff, and Other Stories*

Erdrich, Louise. *Tracks: A Novel*

Eugenides, Jeffrey. ★*The Marriage Plot*

Evanovich, Janet. *Turbo Twenty-Three*

Faulks, Sebastian. *Jeeves and the Wedding Bells*

Fitzgerald, F. Scott. ★*The Last Tycoon: An Unfinished Novel*

Follett, Ken. *A Column of Fire*

Ford, Richard. *The Lay of the Land*

Ford, Richard. *A Multitude of Sins: Stories*

Forester, C. S. *The African Queen*

Foster, Lori. *Sisters of Summer's End*

Fowles, John. ★*The French Lieutenant's Woman*

Frampton, Megan. *The Duke's Guide to Correct Behavior*

Frank, Dorothea Benton. *Queen Bee*

Franklin, Ariana. *The Serpent's Tale*

Freedman, Benedict. *Mrs. Mike: The Story of Katherine Mary Flannigan*

Fuentes, Carlos. *The Death of Artemio Cruz*

Garcia Marquez, Gabriel. ★*Love in the Time of Cholera*

Garwood, Julie. *The Bride*

Garwood, Julie. *Wired*

George, Margaret. *Elizabeth I: A Novel*

Gilbert, Elizabeth. ★*The Signature of All Things: A Novel*

Goldstein, Rebecca. *36 Arguments for the Existence of God: A Work of Fiction*

Goodman, Allegra. *The Cookbook Collector: A Novel*

Gordimer, Nadine. *None to Accompany Me*

Gordimer, Nadine. *The Pickup*

Gray, Erick S. *Love & a Gangsta: A Novel*

Greene, Graham. *Collected Stories: Including May We Borrow Your Husband? a Sense of Reality, Twenty-One Stories*

Grossman, David. ★*To the End of the Land*

Haigh, Jennifer. *Mrs. Kimble: A Novel*

Halliday, Lisa. ★*Asymmetry*

Hampton, Brenda. *Stalker*

Hardy, Thomas. ★*Far from the Madding Crowd*

Harmon, Amy. *Where the Lost Wander*

Hatcher, Robin Lee. *Cross My Heart*

Hauck, Rachel. *How to Catch a Prince*

Hazzard, Shirley. ★*The Transit of Venus*

Heyer, Georgette. *The Grand Sophy*

Heyer, Georgette. *These Old Shades*

Hijuelos, Oscar. *Beautiful Maria of My Soul*

Hijuelos, Oscar. ★*The Mambo Kings Play Songs of Love: A Novel*

Hill, Joe. *Heart-Shaped Box*

Hornby, Nick. *High Fidelity*

Hughes, Langston. ★*Short Stories*

James, Henry. ★*The Turn of the Screw*

Jewell, Lisa. *Then She Was Gone: A Novel*

Jhabvala, Ruth Prawer. *At the End of the Century: The Stories of Ruth Prawer Jhabvala.*

Jin, Ha. ★*Waiting*

Jong, Erica. ★*Fear of Flying: A Novel*

Kamal, Soniah. *Unmarriageable: A Novel*

Kelly, Julia. *The Light Over London*

King, Stephen. *11/22/63*

Krauss, Nicole. ★*To Be a Man: Stories*

Kundera, Milan. ★*Immortality*

Kundera, Milan. ★*The Unbearable Lightness of Being*

Lawrence, D. H. *Women in Love*

Leonard, Elmore. *Labrava*

Leonard, Elmore. *When the Women Come Out to Dance: Stories*

Lewis, Beverly. *The Ebb Tide*

Loren, Roni. *The One You Can't Forget*

Mailer, Norman. ★*The Executioner's Song*

Malone, Minx. *Bad Blood*

Martin, Alexa. *Fumbled*

McCall Smith, Alexander. *The Forgotten Affairs of Youth*

McDermott, Alice. ★*That Night*

McEwan, Ian. ★*On Chesil Beach*

Meltzer, Brad. *The Inner Circle*

Michener, James A. ★*Tales of the South Pacific*

Miller, Xander. *Zo: A Novel*

Mitchell, David. *The Thousand Autumns of Jacob De Zoet: A Novel*

Munro, Alice. *Selected Stories*

Murakami, Haruki. *After the Quake: Stories*

Murdoch, Iris. *The Nice and the Good*

Nicholls, David. *US: A Novel*

Nichols, Peter. *The Rocks*

O'Farrell, Maggie. *The Hand That First Held Mine: A Novel*

O'Leary, Beth. *The Flatshare: A Novel*

Oates, Joyce Carol. *Blonde: A Novel*

Palahniuk, Chuck. *Fight Club*

Pamuk, Orhan. *The Museum of Innocence*

Parker, Lucy. *The Austen Playbook*

Parker, Robert B. *Trouble in Paradise*

Paul, Gill. ★*The Lost Daughter*

Piercy, Marge. *Vida: A Novel*

Potzsch, Oliver. *The Beggar King*

Prescott, Lara. *The Secrets We Kept*

Preston, Caroline. *The Scrapbook of Frankie Pratt*

Price, Reynolds. *Roxanna Slade*

Putney, Mary Jo. *Nowhere Near Respectable*

Rash, Ron. ★*The Cove*

Rash, Ron. *Something Rich and Strange: Selected Stories*

Renault, Mary. *The Bull from the Sea*

Renault, Mary. *The King Must Die*

Rendell, Ruth. ★*The Bridesmaid*

Rice, Luanne. *The Lemon Orchard*

Richardson, C. S. *The End of the Alphabet*

Robards, Karen. *The Ultimatum*

Robbins, Tom. ★*Jitterbug Perfume*

Roberts, Nora. *Chesapeake Blue*

Roberts, Nora. *Sea Swept*

Rochon, Farrah. *The Dating Playbook*

Rockaway, Kristin. *How to Hack a Heartbreak*

Roth, Philip. *Sabbath's Theater*

Rothschild, Hannah. *The Improbability of Love: A Novel*

Rush, Norman. ★*Mating*

Salter, James. *Last Night*

Sand, George. *Marianne*

Sanders, Lawrence. *McNally's Secret*

Saramago, Jose. *The History of the Siege of Lisbon*

Schultz, Connie. *The Daughters of Erietown*

See, Lisa. *Peony in Love: A Novel*

Seton, Anya. *Avalon*

Seton, Anya. ★*Dragonwyck*

Shalvis, Jill. *Simply Irresistible*

Shreve, Anita. *The Last Time They Met: A Novel*

Sienkiewicz, Henryk. ★*Quo Vadis: A Story of Faith in the Last Days of the Roman Empire*

Simsion, Graeme C. ★*The Rosie Project*

Slaughter, Karin. *Criminal: A Novel*

Smith, Dodie. ★*I Capture the Castle*

Smith, Martin Cruz. *Rose*

Solzhenitsyn, Aleksandr Isaevich. ★*Cancer Ward*

Sontag, Susan. *The Volcano Lover: A Romance*

Sparks, Nicholas. *The Guardian*

Sparks, Nicholas. ★*The Notebook*

Speight, Shameek A. *The Pleasure of Pain*

Spencer, Scott. ★*Endless Love*

Stoker, Bram. ★*Dracula*

Stoker, Bram. *The New Annotated Dracula*

Styron, William. ★*Sophie's Choice*

Sundin, Sarah. *Through Waters Deep: A Novel*

Suri, Manil. *The Age of Shiva: A Novel*

T. I. *Power & Beauty: A Love Story of Life on the Streets*

T. I. *Trouble & Triumph: A Novel of Power & Beauty*

Tepper, Sheri S. *The Gate to Women's Country*

Thackeray, William Makepeace. ★*Vanity Fair: A Novel Without a Hero*

Tolstoy, Leo. ★*Anna Karenina*

Tyler, Anne. ★*The Accidental Tourist: A Novel*

Updike, John. *Licks of Love: Short Stories and a Sequel*

Updike, John. *Memories of the Ford Administration: A Novel*

Updike, John. ★*Rabbit Is Rich: A Novel*

Uris, Leon. *Armageddon: A Novel of Berlin*

Urquhart, Jane. *The Night Stages: A Novel*

Valdes, Alisa. *Dirty Girls on Top*

Vargas Llosa, Mario. *Aunt Julia and the Scriptwriter*

Vargas Llosa, Mario. *The Bad Girl*

Walker, Alice. *The Temple of My Familiar*

Wallace, David Foster. ★*Brief Interviews with Hideous Men*

Waugh, Evelyn. ★*Brideshead Revisited*

Waugh, Evelyn. ★*Vile Bodies*

Williams, Tennessee. ★*The Roman Spring of Mrs. Stone*

Winterson, Jeanette. *The Passion*

Wiseman, Beth. *Listening to Love*

Woods, Stuart. *Palindrome*

Woolf, Virginia. *Jacob's Room*

Woolf, Virginia. ★*To the Lighthouse*

Woolf, Virginia. *The Voyage Out*

Wouk, Herman. ★*War and Remembrance: A Novel*

Yoshimoto, Banana. *The Lake*

Zamyatin, Yevgeny Ivanovich. ★*We*

Manansala, Mia P.

  ★*Arsenic and Adobo*

MANCHESTER, ENGLAND

  McFarlane, Mhairi. *If I Never Met You: A Novel*

  McGuire, Ian. *The Abstainer: A Novel*

MANCHURIA

  Shan, Sa. *The Girl Who Played Go*

Mandanipour, Shahriar

  Moon Brow

★*The **Mandarins**: a Novel.* Beauvoir, Simone de

Mandel, Emily St. John

  ★*The Glass Hotel: A Novel*

  The Singer's Gun: A Novel

  ★*Station Eleven*

★*The **Mandelbaum** Gate.* Spark, Muriel

MANET, EDOUARD
Brom. *Slewfoot: A Tale of Bewitchery*
Gibbon, Maureen. *The Lost Notebook of Edouard Manet: A Novel*
Mangan, Christine
Palace of the Drowned
★*Manhattan Beach: A Novel.* Egan, Jennifer
Manhattan Transfer. Dos Passos, John
MANHATTAN, NEW YORK CITY
Bell, Darcey. *Something She's Not Telling Us*
Blum, Jenna. *The Lost Family*
Burton, Tara Isabella. *Social Creature*
Capote, Truman. ★*Breakfast at Tiffany's*
Conell, Lee. *The Party Upstairs*
D'Erasmo, Stacey. *The Sky Below*
Danler, Stephanie. *Sweetbitter*
Dee, Jonathan. *The Privileges: A Novel*
DeLillo, Don. *Falling Man: A Novel*
DeLillo, Don. *The Silence*
Dunne, Dominick. *People Like Us: A Novel*
Dunne, Dominick. *Too Much Money*
Gaitskill, Mary. *Veronica*
Glass, Julia. *The Whole World Over*
Hamill, Pete. *Forever*
Hendricks, Greer. *An Anonymous Girl*
Jemisin, N. K. ★*The City We Became*
Katz, Erica. *The Boys' Club*
Kaufman, Sue. *Diary of a Mad Housewife*
Lethem, Jonathan. *Chronic City*
Levin, Ira. ★*Rosemary's Baby: A Novel*
McLaughlin, Emma. *The Nanny Diaries: A Novel*
Pomerantz, Sharon. *Rich Boy*
Rooney, Kathleen. ★*Lillian Boxfish Takes a Walk*
Sager, Riley. *Final Girls: A Novel*
Sager, Riley. *Lock Every Door: A Novel*
Saul, John. *Midnight Voices*
Serle, Rebecca. *In Five Years: A Novel*
Spiegelman, Peter. *Black Maps*
Tartt, Donna. ★*The Goldfinch*
Whitehead, Colson. *Sag Harbor: A Novel*
Whitehead, Colson. *Zone One: A Novel*
Woods, Stuart. *Fast & Loose*
MANILA, PHILIPPINES
Apostol, Gina. *Gun Dealers' Daughter: A Novel*
Kwan, Kevin. *Rich People Problems*
MANIPULATION (SOCIAL SCIENCES)
Calvino, Italo. *Invisible Cities*
De los Santos, Marisa. *The Precious One*
Dodd, Christina. *Because I'm Watching*
Fowles, John. *The Magus*
Gilman, Laura Anne. *Silver on the Road*
Guterson, David. *Our Lady of the Forest*
Hamilton, Steve. *The Second Life of Nick Mason: A Novel*
Imamura, Natsuko. *The Woman in the Purple Skirt: A Novel*
James, Henry. *The Wings of the Dove*
King, Stephen. *The Institute*
Pinborough, Sarah. ★*Behind Her Eyes: A Novel*
Puzo, Mario. *The Family: A Novel*
Stage, Zoje. ★*Baby Teeth: A Novel*

Tursten, Helene. *An Elderly Lady Must Not Be Crossed*
MANIPULATION BY MEN
Boyne, John. ★*A Ladder to the Sky*
MANIPULATION BY TEENAGE GIRLS
Scottoline, Lisa. *After Anna*
MANIPULATION BY WOMEN
Amis, Martin. *London Fields: A Novel*
Jones, Sandie. *The Other Woman*
Overton, Hollie. *The Runaway*
Stringer, Vickie M. *Still Dirty: A Novel*
Thackeray, William Makepeace. ★*Vanity Fair: A Novel Without a Hero*
Mankell, Henning
Before the Frost: A Linda Wallander Mystery
The Dogs of Riga
Firewall
The Man from Beijing
The Man Who Smiled: A Kurt Wallander Mystery
★*One Step Behind*
★*The Return of the Dancing Master*
The Troubled Man
Mann, Thomas
Buddenbrooks
Death in Venice and Seven Other Stories
Doctor Faustus
The Magic Mountain
MANN, THOMAS
Meadows, Rae. *I Will Send Rain: A Novel*
Toibin, Colm. ★*The Magician: A Novel*
MANNERS AND CUSTOMS
Clark, P. Djeli. *Ring Shout*
Colette. *The Complete Claudine*
Colwin, Laurie. *Happy All the Time: A Novel*
Dos Passos, John. *1919*
Fitzgerald, F. Scott. *Novels and Stories, 1920-1922*
Fitzgerald, F. Scott. ★*The Short Stories of F. Scott Fitzgerald: A New Collection*
Fitzgerald, F. Scott. *Six Tales of the Jazz Age and Other Stories*
Gardam, Jane. *The People on Privilege Hill and Other Stories*
Gaskell, Elizabeth Cleghorn. ★*North and South*
Hemingway, Ernest. *The Short Stories*
Jackson, Shirley. ★*The Lottery: And Other Stories*
James, Henry. *Complete Stories, 1864-1874*
Thomas, Dylan. *The Collected Stories*
Waugh, Evelyn. ★*The Complete Stories of Evelyn Waugh*
Waugh, Evelyn. *Decline and Fall*
Wharton, Edith. *Collected Stories, 1891-1910*
Williams, Tennessee. ★*Collected Stories*
Manning, Corinne
We Had No Rules: Stories
Manning, Max
The Victim: A Novel
MANNING, RHODA KATHERINE (FICTITIOUS CHARACTER)
Gilchrist, Ellen. ★*Collected Stories*
The Manningtree Witches. Blakemore, A. K.
MANORS
Airth, Rennie. *The Decent Inn of Death*
Elliott, Lexie. *The Missing Years*

Fuller, Claire. ★*Bitter Orange*

Gosling, Victoria. *Before the Ruins: A Novel*

Healey, Jane. *The Animals at Lockwood Manor*

James, Henry. *The Portrait of a Lady*

Sebastian, Cat. *The Lawrence Browne Affair*

Starling, Caitlin. *The Death of Jane Lawrence*

Woolf, Virginia. *Between the Acts*

MANORS — RESTORATION

Carlyle, Christy. *Duke Gone Rogue*

Mansfield Park. Austen, Jane

MANSIONS

Brunkhorst, Alex. *The Gilded Life of Matilda Duplaine*

James, Rebecca. *The Woman in the Mirror*

Jewell, Lisa. *The Family Upstairs*

Khaw, Cassandra. *Nothing but Blackened Teeth*

Purcell, Laura. *The Silent Companions: A Ghost Story*

Rhys, Rachel. *Fatal Inheritance*

Roorbach, Bill. *Life Among Giants: A Novel*

MANSLAUGHTER

Cook, Robin. *Charlatans*

Mantel, Hilary

★*Bring up the Bodies: A Novel*

★*Wolf Hall*

★*A Manual for Cleaning Women: Selected Stories*. Berlin, Lucia

The Manual of Painting and Calligraphy. Saramago, Jose

MANUELITO, BERNADETTE (FICTITIOUS CHARACTER)

Hillerman, Tony. *The Wailing Wind*

MANUFACTURING INDUSTRY AND TRADE

Qiu, Xiaolong. *Don't Cry Tai Lake: An Inspector Chen Novel*

MANUSCRIPT THEFTS

Belfer, Lauren. *And After the Fire: A Novel*

MANUSCRIPTS

Belfer, Lauren. *And After the Fire: A Novel*

Danielewski, Mark Z. ★*House of Leaves: A Novel*

Dimitri, Francesco. *The Book of Hidden Things*

Hand, Elizabeth. *The Book of Lamps and Banners: A Novel*

Harkness, Deborah E. *The Book of Life*

Harkness, Deborah E. *A Discovery of Witches: A Novel*

Landragin, Alex. ★*Crossings: Consisting of Three Manuscripts : The Education of a Monster : City of Ghosts : Tales Of*

Sansom, C. J. ★*Lamentation*

Zapata, Mike. *The Lost Book of Adana Moreau*

MANUSCRIPTS — COLLECTORS AND COLLECTING

Crowley, John. *Lord Byron's Novel: The Evening Land*

MANUSCRIPTS, PERUVIAN

Redfield, James. *The Celestine Prophecy: An Adventure*

MAO, ZEDONG

Reid, Taylor Jenkins. ★*Malibu Rising*

Schell, Orville. *My Old Home: A Novel of Exile*

MAORI (NEW ZEALAND PEOPLE)

Hulme, Keri. ★*The Bone People: A Novel*

Singh, Nalini. *A Madness of Sunshine*

A Map of Betrayal: A Novel. Jin, Ha

A Map of the World. Hamilton, Jane

The Map of True Places. Barry, Brunonia

MAPS

Barclay, Linwood. *Trust Your Eyes: A Thriller*

Gates, Eva. *Read and Buried*

Mapson, Jo-Ann

Bad Girl Creek: A Novel

MAQUILADORAS

Fuentes, Carlos. *The Crystal Frontier: A Novel in Nine Stories*

Marathon. Freeman, Brian

The Marathon Conspiracy. Corby, Gary

MARATHONS

Freeman, Brian. *Marathon*

The Marauders. Cooper, Tom

Marcelo, Tif

In a Book Club Far Away

MARCH FAMILY (FICTITIOUS CHARACTERS)

Kantra, Virginia. *Beth & Amy*

March, Emily

Jackson

March, Nev

Murder in Old Bombay

March, William

The Bad Seed: A Novel

The March: a Novel. Doctorow, E. L.

The Marco Effect: A Department Q Novel. Adler-Olsen, Jussi

Marcom, Micheline Aharonian

The New American

Marcus Clay and Dimitri Karras novels [Series]. Pelecanos, George P.

Marcus Didius Falco mysteries [Series]. Davis, Lindsey

The Mare: a Novel. Gaitskill, Mary

Margaret Nolan mysteries [Series]. Tracy, P. J.

MARGATE, ENGLAND

Deveraux, Jude. *Someone to Love*

MARGINALIZED PEOPLE

Craig, Charmaine. *Miss Burma*

MARGUERITE, QUEEN, CONSORT OF LOUIS IX, KING OF FRANCE, 1221-1295

Barnes, Djuna. ★*Nightwood*

Jones, Sherry. *Four Sisters, All Queens*

MARIA NIKOLAEVNA, GRAND DUCHESS, DAUGHTER OF NICHOLAS II, EMPEROR OF RUSSIA, 1899-1918

Blakemore, A. K. *The Manningtree Witches*

Paul, Gill. ★*The Lost Daughter*

MARIANA TRENCH

Grant, Mira. *Into the Drowning Deep*

Marianne. Sand, George

Marias, Javier

The Infatuations

Thus Bad Begins: A Novel

MARIE, DE FRANCE, ACTIVE 12TH CENTURY

Groff, Lauren. ★*Matrix*

King, Laurie R. *Castle Shade*

Perez-Reverte, Arturo. *What We Become*

MARIE, QUEEN, CONSORT OF FERDINAND I, KING OF ROMANIA, 1875-1938.

Brenner, Jamie. *Blush: A Novel*

Mariette in Ecstasy. Hansen, Ron

MARIJUANA

Quartey, Kwei. *Children of the Street: A Novel*

Smith, Mark Haskell. *Baked*

Marillier, Juliet

Daughter of the Forest

MARINE ANIMALS IN ART
Flanagan, Richard. *Gould's Book of Fish: A Novel in Twelve Fish*
MARINE BIOLOGISTS
Alten, Steve. *Meg: Generations*
Drabble, Margaret. *The Sea Lady*
Hiaasen, Carl. *Skinny Dip: A Novel*
Steinbeck, John. *Cannery Row*
White, Randy Wayne. *Salt River*
MARINE PARKS AND RESERVES
Alten, Steve. *Meg: Generations*
MARINE SCIENTISTS
Hiaasen, Carl. *Skinny Dip: A Novel*
MARINES
Burdett, John. *Bangkok 8*
Marlantes, Karl. ★*Matterhorn: A Novel of the Vietnam War*
MARITAL CONFLICT
Ackerman, Elliot. *Red Dress in Black and White*
Adams, Lyssa Kay. *The Bromance Book Club*
Anstruther, Eleanor. *A Perfect Explanation*
Bellow, Saul. *More Die of Heartbreak*
Bialosky, Jill. *The Prize: A Novel*
Bijan, Donia. *The Last Days of Cafe Leila*
Bock, Charles. *Beautiful Children: A Novel*
Brodesser-Akner, Taffy. *Fleishman Is in Trouble: A Novel*
Carr, Robyn. *The View from Alameda Island: A Novel*
Choi, Susan. *My Education*
Clark, Wahida. *Honor Thy Thug*
Clark, Wahida. *Justify My Thug: A Novel*
Clark, Wahida. *Thugs*
De Giovanni, Maurizio. *The Crocodile*
Dean, Margaret Lazarus. *The Time It Takes to Fall*
Doyle, Roddy. *Smile*
Escandon, Maria Amparo. ★*L.A. Weather*
Essbaum, Jill Alexander. *Hausfrau: A Novel*
Evans, Diana. *Ordinary People: A Novel*
Fabry, Chris. *War Room: Prayer Is a Powerful Weapon*
Flynn, Gillian. ★*Gone Girl: A Novel*
Fowler, Therese. ★*Z: A Novel of Zelda Fitzgerald*
Franzen, Jonathan. ★*Crossroads*
Frear, Caz. *Stone Cold Heart*
Freitas, Donna. *The Nine Lives of Rose Napolitano*
Friedland, Elyssa. *The Intermission*
Gaige, Amity. *Sea Wife*
Gideon, Melanie. *Wife 22*
Glass, Julia. *The Whole World Over*
Hannah, Kristin. *Home Front*
Harrison, Mette Ivie. *The Prodigal Daughter*
Hauck, Rachel. *The Wedding Chapel*
Hoover, Colleen. *All Your Perfects*
Jong, Erica. ★*Fear of Flying: A Novel*
Leavitt, David. *The Two Hotel Francforts: A Novel*
Lessing, Doris May. *A Proper Marriage*
Luiselli, Valeria. ★*Lost Children Archive: A Novel*
Mallery, Susan. *California Girls*
Meadows, Rae. *I Will Send Rain: A Novel*
Offill, Jenny. *Dept. Of Speculation*
Offill, Jenny. ★*Weather*
Parini, Jay. *The Passages of H.M.: A Novel of Herman Melville*

Pronzini, Bill. *Fever*
Rivero, Melissa. *The Affairs of the Falcons*
Ross, Adam. *Mr. Peanut*
Rouda, Kaira Sturdivant. *Best Day Ever: A Novel*
Rouda, Kaira Sturdivant. *The Favorite Daughter*
Rowell, Rainbow. *Landline*
Shteyngart, Gary. ★*Lake Success: A Novel*
Simsion, Graeme C. *The Rosie Result*
Stapley, Marissa. *The Last Resort*
Starnone, Domenico. *Ties*
Stegner, Wallace. ★*Angle of Repose*
Suri, Manil. *The Age of Shiva: A Novel*
Tyler, Anne. *The Amateur Marriage: A Novel*
Vatner, Jonathan. *Carnegie Hill: A Novel*
Von Ziegesar, Cecily. *Cobble Hill*
Waters, Martha. ★*To Have and to Hoax: A Novel*
Weir, Alison. *Anna of Kleve: The Princess in the Portrait*
MARIUS, GAIUS
Beach, Edward L. *Run Silent, Run Deep*
McCullough, Colleen. *The First Man in Rome*
Marjorie Westriding trilogy [Series]. Tepper, Sheri S.
Mark Angelotti novels [Series]. Raimondo, Lynne
*The **Mark** of the King*. Green, Jocelyn
Mark, David John
Cruel Mercy
★***Marked** Man*. Mayor, Archer
MARKETING
Hockman, Angie. *Shipped*
Whitehead, Colson. *Apex Hides the Hurt*
MARKETING CONSULTANTS
K'wan. *Lawless*
MARKETING RESEARCH
Gibson, William. *Pattern Recognition*
MARKHAM, BERYL
Duffy, Brendan. *House of Echoes: A Novel*
McLain, Paula. *Circling the Sun*
Markley, Stephen
Ohio
MARKS, GRACE
Atwood, Margaret. *Alias Grace*
Roth, Philip. *Zuckerman Unbound*
Marlantes, Karl
Deep River
★*Matterhorn: A Novel of the Vietnam War*
★***Marlena**: a Novel*. Buntin, Julie
MARLEY, BOB
James, Marlon. ★*A Brief History of Seven Killings: A Novel*
***Marley**: a Novel*. Clinch, Jon
MARLIN FISHING
Hemingway, Ernest. ★*The Old Man and the Sea*
MARLOWE, PHILIP (FICTIONAL CHARACTER)
Chandler, Raymond. *The Lady in the Lake*
Maron, Margaret
Bootlegger's Daughter
Up Jumps the Devil
MARPLE, JANE (FICTITIOUS CHARACTER)
Christie, Agatha. *The Body in the Library: A Miss Marple Mystery*
Christie, Agatha. *Three Blind Mice, and Other Stories*

MARQUIS AND MARCHIONESSES
Collins, Manda. *Ready Set Rogue*
Dare, Tessa. *Do You Want to Start a Scandal*
Guhrke, Laura Lee. *When the Marquess Met His Match*
MacLean, Sarah. *The Rogue Not Taken*
Marquitta Skeet Bannion mysteries [Series]. Rodriguez, Linda
Marra, Anthony
★*A Constellation of Vital Phenomena: A Novel*
The Tsar of Love and Techno: Stories

MARRIAGE
Adebayo, Ayobami. ★*Stay with Me*
Alexie, Sherman. *Blasphemy: New and Selected Stories*
Allende, Isabel. *A Long Petal of the Sea: A Novel*
Atwood, Margaret. *Moral Disorder*
Ballard, J. G. *The Kindness of Women*
Blum, Jenna. *The Lost Family*
Bryant, Niobia. *Message from a Mistress*
Cantor, Jillian. *Half Life*
Capote, Truman. ★*Breakfast at Tiffany's*
Carr, Robyn. *The View from Alameda Island: A Novel*
Carver, Raymond. *What We Talk About When We Talk About Love: Stories*
Castle, Jayne. *Illusion Town*
Choo, Yangsze. *The Ghost Bride: A Novel*
Coben, Harlan. *The Stranger*
Cole, Alyssa. ★*How to Catch a Queen*
Colwin, Laurie. *Goodbye Without Leaving*
Dann, Patty. *The Wright Sister*
Dillard, Annie. *The Maytrees: A Novel*
Erdrich, Louise. ★*Shadow Tag: A Novel*
Ferrante, Elena. *The Story of a New Name*
Garey, Juliann. *Too Bright to Hear Too Loud to See*
Gordimer, Nadine. *None to Accompany Me*
Groff, Lauren. ★*Fates and Furies*
Gross, Max. *The Lost Shtetl*
James, Henry. *The Golden Bowl*
James, Henry. *The Portrait of a Lady*
Johnson, Julia Claiborne. *Better Luck Next Time: A Novel*
Jones, Tayari. ★*An American Marriage: A Novel*
Kamal, Soniah. *Unmarriageable: A Novel*
Kidd, Sue Monk. ★*The Book of Longings*
Kincaid, Jamaica. *See Now Then*
Lawrence, D. H. *Sons and Lovers*
Lipsyte, Sam. *The Ask*
Mahmoud, Lena. *Amreekiya: A Novel*
McCall Smith, Alexander. *The Double Comfort Safari Club*
McMurtry, Larry. ★*Terms of Endearment: A Novel : With a New Preface*
Miller, Sue. *The Senator's Wife*
Mitford, Nancy. *Love in a Cold Climate*
Niffenegger, Audrey. *The Time Traveler's Wife: A Novel*
Offill, Jenny. *Dept. Of Speculation*
Richardson, Samuel. ★*Clarissa, Or, the History of a Young Lady*
Richardson, Samuel. ★*Pamela: Or, Virtue Rewarded*
Rogers, Morgan Callan. ★*Honey Girl*
Rooney, Kathleen. ★*Lillian Boxfish Takes a Walk*
Sayers, Dorothy L. *Thrones, Dominations*
Simsion, Graeme C. *The Rosie Effect*
Simsion, Graeme C. *The Rosie Result*
Slimani, Leïla. *In the Country of Others*
Starnone, Domenico. *Ties*
Steinhauer, Olen. *The Cairo Affair*
Swann, Stacey. *Olympus Texas*
Sweeney, Cynthia D'Aprix. ★*Good Company: A Novel*
Trollope, Anthony. ★*The Prime Minister*
Tyler, Anne. ★*Clock Dance: A Novel*
Updike, John. *The Afterlife and Other Stories*
Vatner, Jonathan. *Carnegie Hill: A Novel*
Welty, Eudora. ★*The Ponder Heart*
Wilson, Sloan. ★*The Man in the Gray Flannel Suit*
Wodehouse, P. G. ★*The Inimitable Jeeves*
Wolitzer, Meg. *The Interestings*

MARRIAGE — PSYCHOLOGICAL ASPECTS
Stead, Christina. ★*The Man Who Loved Children*

MARRIAGE BURN OUT
Downing, Samantha. *My Lovely Wife*
*The **Marriage** Clock: A Novel*. Raheem, Zara

MARRIAGE COUNSELING
McPherson, Catriona. *Scot & Soda*
Stapley, Marissa. *The Last Resort*
Marriage of convenience romances [Series]. Gracie, Anne
*The **Marriage** of Opposites: A Novel Based on the Life of Rachel Pizzarro*. Hoffman, Alice
★*The **Marriage** Plot*. Eugenides, Jeffrey

MARRIAGE PROPOSALS
Bennett, Anna. *First Earl I See Tonight*
Ross, Ann B. ★*Miss Julia Happily Ever After*
Serle, Rebecca. *In Five Years: A Novel*
*The **Marriage** Spell: A Novel*. Putney, Mary Jo

MARRIAGES OF ROYALTY AND NOBILITY
Gregory, Philippa. *The Boleyn Inheritance*
Gregory, Philippa. *The Constant Princess*
Mosse, Kate. *The City of Tears*
Penman, Sharon Kay. *Here Be Dragons*
Weir, Alison. *Anna of Kleve: The Princess in the Portrait*

MARRIED MEN
Cramer, W. Dale. *Levi's Will: A Novel*
Faber, Michel. *The Book of Strange New Things*
Fisher, Tarryn. *The Wives*
Gide, Andre. ★*The Immoralist*
Haigh, Jennifer. *Mrs. Kimble: A Novel*
Kitamura, Katie M. *Intimacies*
Kleeman, Alexandra. *Something New Under the Sun*
Lescroart, John T. *Guilt*
Naipaul, V. S. *A House for Mr. Biswas*
Ripper, Kris. *The Life Revamp*
Roberts, Bethan. ★*My Policeman*
Statovci, Pajtim. *Bolla*
Steel, Danielle. *First Sight*
Svevo, Italo. *Zeno's Conscience*
Swanson, Peter. *The Kind Worth Killing: A Novel*
Updike, John. *Licks of Love: Short Stories and a Sequel*
Updike, John. ★*Rabbit Is Rich: A Novel*
Updike, John. ★*Rabbit, Run*
Wharton, Edith. ★*Ethan Frome*

MARRIED MEN — DEATH
Carpenter, Emily. *Until the Day I Die*
Unger, Lisa. *Under My Skin*
MARRIED MEN — RELATIONS WITH SINGLE WOMEN
Faber, Michel. *The Crimson Petal and the White*
MARRIED MEN — SEXUALITY
Ebershoff, David. *The Danish Girl: A Novel*
MARRIED PEOPLE
Abbott, Megan E. ★*The Turnout: A Novel*
Alam, Rumaan. ★*Leave the World Behind: A Novel*
Amado, Jorge. ★*Dona Flor and Her Two Husbands: A Moral and Amorous Tale*
Andrews, Mesu. *Of Fire and Lions: A Novel*
Atwood, Margaret. *Life Before Man*
Baxter, Charles. *Saul and Patsy*
Billingsley, ReShonda Tate. *A Little Bit of Karma: A Novel*
Bowman, Valerie. *A Duke Like No Other*
Brownrigg, Sylvia. ★*The Delivery Room: A Novel*
Cleland, Jane K. *Hidden Treasure*
Colwin, Laurie. *Happy All the Time: A Novel*
Dexter, Pete. *Paris Trout*
Doerr, Harriet. ★*Stones for Ibarra*
Edwards, Kim. *The Memory Keeper's Daughter*
Enger, Lin. *Undiscovered Country: A Novel*
Erdrich, Louise. *The Master Butchers Singing Club: A Novel*
Fitzgerald, F. Scott. ★*The Beautiful and Damned*
Flaubert, Gustave. ★*Madame Bovary: Provincial Ways*
Flynn, Gillian. ★*Gone Girl: A Novel*
Friedland, Elyssa. *The Intermission*
Gentill, Sulari. *Crossing the Lines*
Goodman, Carol. *The Sea of Lost Girls*
Hammett, Dashiell. ★*The Thin Man*
Hannah, Kristin. *Home Front*
Haslett, Adam. ★*Imagine Me Gone: A Novel*
Hauck, Rachel. *How to Catch a Prince*
Heley, Veronica. *Murder in Law*
Hemingway, Ernest. *To Have and Have Not*
Henkin, Joshua. *Morningside Heights*
Hiaasen, Carl. *Skinny Dip: A Novel*
Hunter, Megan. *The Harpy*
Jemc, Jac. ★*The Grip of It*
Jones, Cherie. *How the One-Armed Sister Sweeps Her House*
Joyce, James. ★*Ulysses*
Khadra, Yasmina. *The Swallows of Kabul: A Novel*
Logan, T. M. *The Vacation*
Lombardo, Claire. *The Most Fun We Ever Had: A Novel*
Mackintosh, Anneliese. *Bright and Dangerous Objects*
Marias, Javier. *Thus Bad Begins: A Novel*
Miller, Sue. *The Senator's Wife*
Moriarty, Liane. *Truly Madly Guilty*
Murdoch, Iris. *The Nice and the Good*
Naylor, Gloria. *Mama Day*
Oates, Joyce Carol. *Breathe*
Packer, Ann. *The Children's Crusade*
Palmer, Dexter Clarence. *Version Control*
Paris, B. A. *Behind Closed Doors*
Pavone, Chris. ★*The Expats: A Novel*
Perrotta, Tom. *Little Children*

Putney, Mary Jo. *Not Quite a Wife*
Quotah, Eman. ★*Bride of the Sea: A Novel*
Rhys, Jean. ★*Wide Sargasso Sea*
Robotham, Michael. ★*Suspect*
Ross, Adam. *Mr. Peanut*
Schulman, Helen. *Come with Me*
Schwartz, Lynne Sharon. *Truthtelling: Stories, Fables, Glimpses*
Shreve, Anita. *The Last Time They Met: A Novel*
Solomon, Asali. *The Days of Afrekete*
Sontag, Susan. *The Volcano Lover: A Romance*
Stabenow, Dana. *Spoils of the Dead*
Stapley, Marissa. *The Last Resort*
Steadman, Catherine. *Something in the Water*
Stegner, Wallace. *Crossing to Safety*
Tolstoy, Leo. ★*Anna Karenina*
Torre, A. R. *Every Last Secret*
Tyler, Anne. *The Amateur Marriage: A Novel*
Updike, John. *The Afterlife and Other Stories*
Vernon, P. J. *Bath Haus: A Thriller*
Von Ziegesar, Cecily. *Cobble Hill*
Walker, Caroline Louise. *Man of the Year*
Wallace, Carol. *Our Kind of People*
Warren, Robert Penn. *World Enough and Time: A Romantic Novel*
Weatherspoon, Rebekah. ★*Xeni: A Marriage of Inconvenience*
White, Elle Katharine. *Dragonshadow*
Yates, Christopher J. *Grist Mill Road: A Novel*
MARRIED PEOPLE — PSYCHOLOGY
Downing, Samantha. *My Lovely Wife*
MARRIED PEOPLE AND SECRETS
Daly, Paula. *Open Your Eyes*
Delaney, J. P. *The Perfect Wife: A Novel*
Downing, Samantha. *My Lovely Wife*
Friedland, Elyssa. *The Intermission*
Groff, Lauren. ★*Fates and Furies*
Hilderbrand, Elin. ★*Winter in Paradise: A Novel*
James, Eloisa. *The Ugly Duchess*
K'wan. *Lawless*
Shreve, Anita. *The Pilot's Wife: A Novel*
MARRIED WOMEN
Adebayo, Ayobami. ★*Stay with Me*
Adlakha, Sarah. *She Wouldn't Change a Thing*
Anam, Tahmima. *The Startup Wife*
Anstruther, Eleanor. *A Perfect Explanation*
Austin, Finola. *Bronte's Mistress*
Bair, Kristin. *Agatha Arch Is Afraid of Everything*
Bausch, Richard. *Hello to the Cannibals: A Novel*
Bernhard, Emilia. *The Books of the Dead*
Black, Saul. *Anything for You*
Bock, Charles. *Alice & Oliver: A Novel*
Bronte, Anne. *The Tenant of Wildfell Hall*
Chiaverini, Jennifer. *Mrs. Lincoln's Sisters*
Cho, Nam-Ju. ★*Kim Jiyoung, Born 1982*
Cobb, May K. *The Hunting Wives*
Crossan, Sarah. *Here Is the Beehive*
Crouch, Katie. *Embassy Wife*
Cusk, Rachel. *Second Place*
Delaney, J. P. *The Perfect Wife: A Novel*
Dimaline, Cherie. *Empire of Wild*

Dunant, Sarah. *The Birth of Venus: A Novel*
Durrell, Lawrence. ★*Justine*
Ellis, Helen. *American Housewife: Stories*
Essbaum, Jill Alexander. *Hausfrau: A Novel*
Faulks, Sebastian. *On Green Dolphin Street: A Novel*
Feeney, Alice. ★*I Know Who You Are: A Novel*
Feeney, Alice. ★*Sometimes I Lie*
Finder, Joseph. ★*Judgment*
Fisher, Helen. *Space Hopper*
Fisher, Tarryn. *The Wives*
Flaubert, Gustave. *Sentimental Education*
Follett, Ken. ★*The Evening and the Morning*
Follett, Ken. *Eye of the Needle*
Forman, Gayle. *Leave Me: A Novel*
Franzen, Jonathan. ★*The Corrections*
Frazier, Charles. *Varina*
French, Nicci. ★*The Lying Room*
Gillham, David R. *City of Women*
Gilman, Susan Jane. *Donna Has Left the Building*
Greeley, Molly. *The Clergyman's Wife*
Haigh, Jennifer. *Mrs. Kimble: A Novel*
Harrison, Mette Ivie. *The Bishop's Wife*
Harrison, Mette Ivie. *The Prodigal Daughter*
Harrison, Nicola. *Montauk*
Hawthorne, Nathaniel. ★*The Scarlet Letter: A Romance*
Heller, L. Alison. *The Neighbor's Secret*
Hiaasen, Carl. *Skinny Dip: A Novel*
Horan, Nancy. *Loving Frank: A Novel*
Hunt, Laird. *The Evening Road*
Hyde, Catherine Ryan. *My Name Is Anton*
Itami, Emily. *Fault Lines: A Novel*
Kandasamy, Meena. *When I Hit You, Or, a Portrait of the Writer as a Young Wife*
Kane, Darby. *Pretty Little Wife*
Kaplan, Mitchell James. *Rhapsody*
Larsen, Nella. *Passing*
Lawrence, D. H. ★*Lady Chatterley's Lover*
Lehane, Dennis. *Since We Fell*
Liardet, Frances. *We Must Be Brave*
Lippman, Laura. ★*Sunburn*
MacDonald, John D. *A Purple Place for Dying*
Maynard, Joyce. *Count the Ways*
McCall Smith, Alexander. ★*The Geometry of Holding Hands*
Moyes, Jojo. *The Peacock Emporium*
Munro, Alice. *Runaway: Stories*
Oakley, Colleen. *You Were There Too*
Pamuk, Orhan. ★*Snow*
Parrish, Christa. *Still Life*
Patterson, Molly. *Rebellion*
Perez-Reverte, Arturo. *What We Become*
Phillips, Helen. *The Beautiful Bureaucrat: A Novel*
Picoult, Jodi. ★*The Book of Two Ways*
Powning, Beth. *The Sea Captain's Wife: A Novel*
Restrepo, Laura. ★*Delirium: A Novel*
Rhys, Rachel. *Fatal Inheritance*
Rosenfield, Kat. *No One Will Miss Her*
Sweeney, Cynthia D'Aprix. ★*Good Company: A Novel*
Swinson, Kiki. *Who's Wife Extraordinaire Now*

Tyler, Anne. ★*Clock Dance: A Novel*
Vaughan, Sarah. ★*Anatomy of a Scandal: A Novel*
Waite, Olivia. *The Care and Feeding of Waspish Widows*
Watkins, Claire Vaye. *I Love You but I've Chosen Darkness*
Winterson, Jeanette. *The Passion*
MARRIED WOMEN — DEATH
Francis, Felix. *Guilty Not Guilty*
Scottoline, Lisa. *Don't Go*
MARRIED WOMEN — HISTORY
Flaubert, Gustave. ★*Madame Bovary: Provincial Ways*
MARRIED WOMEN — IDENTITY
Colwin, Laurie. *Goodbye Without Leaving*
Wood, Tracey Enerson. *The Engineer's Wife: A Novel*
MARRIED WOMEN — PSYCHOLOGY
Gilman, Charlotte Perkins. ★*The Yellow Wallpaper and Selected Writings*
Stead, Christina. ★*The Man Who Loved Children*
Marry in Scandal. Gracie, Anne
MARS (PLANET)
Bradbury, Ray. *Bradbury Stories: 100 of His Most Celebrated Tales*
Bradbury, Ray. *The Illustrated Man*
Bradbury, Ray. ★*The Martian Chronicles: The Fortieth Anniversary Edition*
Brown, Pierce. *Golden Son*
Brown, Pierce. *Morning Star*
Brown, Pierce. *Red Rising*
Hao, Jingfang. *Vagabonds: A Novel*
Heinlein, Robert A. ★*Stranger in a Strange Land*
Hurley, Kameron. ★*The Light Brigade*
Levine, David D. *Arabella of Mars*
Rajaniemi, Hannu. *The Fractal Prince*
Rajaniemi, Hannu. *The Quantum Thief*
Robinson, Kim Stanley. ★*Blue Mars*
Robinson, Kim Stanley. ★*Green Mars*
Robinson, Kim Stanley. *The Martians*
Robinson, Kim Stanley. ★*Red Mars*
Weir, Andy. *The Martian*
The Mars Room. Kushner, Rachel
Mars trilogy [Series]. Robinson, Kim Stanley
Marsh, Ngaio
A Man Lay Dead
Marsh, Nicola
The Boy Toy
Marshall, Catherine
Christy
MARSHES
Kellerman, Jonathan. *Bones: An Alex Delaware Novel*
Owens, Delia. *Where the Crawdads Sing*
Shaw, William. *Salt Lane*
Marske, Freya
A Marvellous Light
Marston, Edward
The Roaring Boy: A Novel
The Wanton Angel: A Novel
Martel, Yann
★*Life of Pi: A Novel*
Martell, Nick
The Kingdom of Liars

MARTHA'S VINEYARD, MASSACHUSETTS
Ausubel, Ramona. *Sons and Daughters of Ease and Plenty*
Foster, Brooke Lea. *Summer Darlings*
Gunning, Sally. *Painting the Light*
Hostin, Sunny. ★*Summer on the Bluffs*
Livesay, Tracey. *Like Lovers Do*
Russo, Richard. ★*Chances Are...: A Novel*
West, Dorothy. *The Wedding*
MARTIAL ARTISTS
Sister Souljah. *Midnight and the Meaning of Love*
MARTIAL ARTS
Jin, Yong. *A Hero Born: A Novel*
Kuang, R. F. *The Poppy War*
MARTIAL LAW
Vandermeer, Jeff. *Finch*
The **Martian**. Weir, Andy
★*The* **Martian** *Chronicles: The Fortieth Anniversary Edition*. Bradbury, Ray
The **Martians**. Robinson, Kim Stanley
MARTIANS
Bradbury, Ray. ★*The Martian Chronicles: The Fortieth Anniversary Edition*
Robinson, Kim Stanley. *The Martians*
Vonnegut, Kurt. ★*The Sirens of Titan*
Wells, H. G. ★*The War of the Worlds*
Martin Beck mysteries [Series]. Sjowall, Maj
Martin *Chuzzlewit*. Dickens, Charles
Martin *Dressler: The Tale of an American Dreamer*. Millhauser, Steven
Martin *Eden*. London, Jack
Martin, Alexa
Fumbled
★*Intercepted*
Martin, Charles
The Water Keeper
Martin, George R. R.
★*A Clash of Kings*
★*A Dance with Dragons*
★*A Feast for Crows*
Fire & Blood: 300 Years Before a Game of Thrones (A Targaryen History)
★*A Game of Thrones*
★*A Storm of Swords*
Martin, Steve
Shopgirl
Martine, Arkady
★*A Desolation Called Peace*
★*A Memory Called Empire*
Martineau, Maxym M.
Kingdom of Exiles
Martinson, T. J.
The Reign of the Kingfisher: A Novel
Martita, *I Remember You: Martita, Te Recuerdo*. Cisneros, Sandra
A **Marvellous** *Light*. Marske, Freya
MARXISM
Piercy, Marge. *Vida: A Novel*
Mary *Coin: A Novel*. Silver, Marisa
Mary *Jane: A Novel*. Blau, Jessica Anya
Mary Russell and Sherlock Holmes mysteries [Series]. King, Laurie R.

★**Mary** *Toft; Or, the Rabbit Queen: A Novel*. Palmer, Dexter Clarence
MARY, BLESSED VIRGIN, SAINT
Guterson, David. *Our Lady of the Forest*
Koontz, Dean R. *Intensity: A Novel*
MARYLAND
Barth, John. ★*The Sot-Weed Factor*
Butler, Octavia E. ★*Kindred*
Chizmar, Richard T. *Chasing the Boogeyman*
Coulter, Catherine. *Paradox*
DeLuca, Jen. *Well Matched*
DeLuca, Jen. ★*Well Met*
Holmes, Shannon. ★*B-More Careful: A Novel*
Lippman, Laura. *What the Dead Know*
Lippman, Laura. *Wilde Lake*
Oakley, Colleen. *The Invisible Husband of Frick Island*
Roberts, Nora. *Sea Swept*
Scott, Rion Amilcar. ★*The World Doesn't Require You: Stories*
Stewart, Amy. *Kopp Sisters on the March*
Styles, Toy. *Black and Ugly*
Styles, Toy. *A Hustler's Son: A Novel*
Styles, Toy. *Raunchy*
Styles, Toy. *Raunchy 2: Mad's Love*
Mas, Victoria
The Mad Women's Ball
Masad, Ilana
All My Mother's Lovers: A Novel
MASAI (AFRICAN PEOPLE)
Crompton, Richard. *Hell's Gate: A Novel*
Crompton, Richard. *Hour of the Red God*
MASCULINITY
Hawke, Ethan. *A Bright Ray of Darkness*
Krauss, Nicole. ★*To Be a Man: Stories*
Miller, Henry. ★*Tropic of Capricorn*
The **Mask** *of Mirrors*. Carrick, M. A.
The **Masked** *City*. Cogman, Genevieve
MASKS
Bradley, C. Alan. *Speaking from Among the Bones: A Flavia De Luce Novel*
Mason *& Dixon*. Pynchon, Thomas
Mason novels [Series]. Berg, Elizabeth
Mason, Bobbie Ann
Dear Ann: A Novel
Patchwork
Shiloh and Other Stories
MASON, CHARLES
Keneally, Thomas. ★*Schindler's List*
Pynchon, Thomas. *Mason & Dixon*
Mason, Daniel
The Piano Tuner
A Registry of My Passage Upon the Earth: Stories
Mason, Jamie
The Hidden Things
Mason, Meg
Sorrow and Bliss
Mason, Timothy
The Darwin Affair
MASON-DIXON LINE
Pynchon, Thomas. *Mason & Dixon*

Masood, Syed M.
The Bad Muslim Discount
MASS MEDIA
  Guillory, Jasmine. *Party of Two*
  Saunders, George. *In Persuasion Nation: Stories*
  Truss, Lynne. *Murder by Milk Bottle*
MASS MEDIA — SOCIAL ASPECTS
  Flanagan, Richard. *The Unknown Terrorist*
MASS MURDER
  Ellroy, James. ★*L.A. Confidential*
  King, Stephen. *Mr. Mercedes: A Novel*
  Rendell, Ruth. ★*A Judgement in Stone*
  Sandford, John. *Mad River*
  Sjowall, Maj. ★*The Laughing Policeman*
MASS MURDER INVESTIGATION
  Peace, David. *Occupied City*
MASS MURDERERS
  King, Stephen. *Mr. Mercedes: A Novel*
MASS SHOOTINGS
  Roberts, Nora. *Shelter in Place*
  Shriver, Lionel. *We Need to Talk About Kevin*
MASSACHUSETTS
  Amidon, Stephen. *Security: A Novel*
  Batuman, Elif. ★*The Idiot*
  Beams, Clare. *The Illness Lesson*
  Benjamin, Ali. *The Smash-Up: A Novel*
  Brown, Amy Belding. *Emily's House*
  Burke, Marcus. *Team Seven*
  Delany, Vicki. *Murder in a Teacup*
  Delany, Vicki. *Tea & Treachery*
  Dillard, Annie. *The Maytrees: A Novel*
  Dubus, Andre. *Dirty Love*
  Fay, Juliette. *The Shortest Way Home*
  Finder, Joseph. *The Fixer*
  Foster, Brooke Lea. *Summer Darlings*
  Francis, Patry. *All the Children Are Home*
  Gardner, Lisa. ★*Before She Disappeared: A Novel*
  Genova, Lisa. *Inside the O'Briens: A Novel*
  Genova, Lisa. *Left Neglected: A Novel*
  Greenidge, Kaitlyn. *We Love You, Charlie Freeman: A Novel*
  Grossman, Lev. *The Magician King: A Novel*
  Grossman, Lev. *The Magician's Land: A Novel*
  Gunning, Sally. *Painting the Light*
  Haddam, Jane. *Cheating at Solitaire: A Gregor Demarkian Novel*
  Haslett, Adam. *Union Atlantic*
  Hawley, Noah. *Before the Fall*
  Hawthorne, Nathaniel. ★*The Scarlet Letter: A Romance*
  Higgins, George V. *The Friends of Eddie Coyle*
  Hilderbrand, Elin. ★*28 Summers*
  Hilderbrand, Elin. *The Perfect Couple*
  Hilderbrand, Elin. ★*Summer of '69*
  Hoffman, Alice. *The River King*
  King, Lily. *Writers & Lovers: A Novel*
  Lahiri, Jhumpa. ★*The Namesake*
  Lehane, Dennis. *Shutter Island*
  Livesay, Tracey. *Like Lovers Do*
  Loigman, Lynda Cohen. *The Wartime Sisters: A Novel*
  McCracken, Elizabeth. ★*Bowlaway: A Novel*

  McKinty, Adrian. ★*The Chain*
  Messud, Claire. ★*The Woman Upstairs: A Novel*
  Miller, Sue. ★*Monogamy*
  Moshfegh, Ottessa. *Eileen*
  Nugent, Benjamin. *Fraternity: Stories*
  Parker, Robert B. *Death in Paradise*
  Parker, Robert B. *Night Passage*
  Parker, Robert B. *Painted Ladies*
  Parker, Robert B. *Sixkill*
  Parker, Robert B. *Trouble in Paradise*
  Patchett, Ann. *Run*
  Pipkin, John. *Woodsburner: A Novel*
  Preston, Douglas J. *City of Endless Night*
  Preston, Douglas J. *The Obsidian Chamber*
  Schmidt, Sarah. *See What I Have Done*
  Seton, Anya. ★*The Winthrop Woman*
  Shreve, Anita. *The Last Time They Met: A Novel*
  Sittenfeld, Curtis. *Prep: A Novel*
  Smith, Zadie. *On Beauty*
  Tremblay, Paul. *Survivor Song*
  Weiner, Jennifer. ★*Big Summer*
  Wharton, Edith. ★*Ethan Frome*
  Yang, Susie. *White Ivy: A Novel*
MASSACRES
  Apostol, Gina. *Insurrecto*
  Hendrix, Grady. *The Final Girl Support Group*
  McCarthy, Cormac. ★*Blood Meridian, Or, the Evening Redness in the West*
  Merbeth, K. S. ★*Fortuna*
  Peace, David. *Occupied City*
  Reichs, Kathy. *Grave Secrets*
MASSACRES — HISTORY
  Shreve, Anita. *Sea Glass: A Novel*
Massey, Sujata
  ★*The Bombay Prince*
  The Satapur Moonstone
  ★*The Widows of Malabar Hill: A Mystery of 1920s Bombay*
Master and Commander. O'Brian, Patrick
★*The Master and Margarita.* Bulgakov, Mikhail
MASTER AND SERVANT
  Levy, Andrea. *The Long Song*
  Stowe, Harriet Beecher. ★*Uncle Tom's Cabin*
The Master Butchers Singing Club: A Novel. Erdrich, Louise
★*The Master Executioner.* Estleman, Loren D.
Master of Poisons. Hairston, Andrea
The Masterpiece. Davis, Fiona
The Masterpiece. Rivers, Francine
★*Masters of Atlantis: A Novel.* Portis, Charles
Masters of Rome [Series]. McCullough, Colleen
MASTURBATION
  Roth, Philip. ★*Portnoy's Complaint*
Matar, Hisham
  In the Country of Men
The Matchmaker's List. Lalli, Sonya
MATCHMAKERS
  Austen, Jane. ★*Emma*
  Guhrke, Laura Lee. *When the Marquess Met His Match*
  Montclair, Allison. *The Right Sort of Man*

Quick, Amanda. *'til Death Do Us Part*
Sand, George. *Marianne*

MATCHMAKING
Allain, Suzanne. *Miss Lattimore's Letter*
Balogh, Mary. *The Arrangement*
Heger, Amanda. *Crazy Cupid Love*
Lalli, Sonya. *The Matchmaker's List*
Lauren, Christina. *The Soulmate Equation*
Montclair, Allison. *A Rogue's Company*
Montclair, Allison. *A Royal Affair*
Solomon, Rachel Lynn. *Weather Girl*
Title, Sarah. *The Undateable*

MATE SELECTION
Allen, Susanna. *A Wolf in Duke's Clothing*
Austen, Jane. ★*Sense and Sensibility*
Balogh, Mary. *The Escape*
Balogh, Mary. *Only Enchanting*
Bell, Lenora. ★*How the Duke Was Won*
Berne, Lisa. *You May Kiss the Bride*
Boyle, Elizabeth. *And the Miss Ran Away with the Rake*
Burrowes, Grace. ★*A Rogue of Her Own*
Byrne, Kerrigan. *The Duke with the Dragon Tattoo*
Dare, Tessa. ★*The Duchess Deal*
Feehan, Christine. *Dark Illusion*
Garriott, Leah. *Promised*
Guhrke, Laura Lee. *The Trouble with True Love*
Heath, Lorraine. *Falling into Bed with a Duke*
Heyer, Georgette. *Black Sheep*
James, Eloisa. *Wilde in Love*
Kamal, Soniah. *Unmarriageable: A Novel*
MacLean, Sarah. ★*Wicked and the Wallflower*
McCall Smith, Alexander. *The Full Cupboard of Life*
Sebastian, Cat. *Unmasked by the Marquess*
Showalter, Gena. *Shadow and Ice*
Sittenfeld, Curtis. *Eligible: A Novel*
Vayden, Kristin. *Fortune Favors the Duke*
Wade, Becky. *Falling for You*

MATE SELECTION FOR WOMEN
Austen, Jane. ★*Emma*
Austen, Jane. *Northanger Abbey*
Balogh, Mary. *The Secret Mistress*
Boyle, Elizabeth. *Along Came a Duke*
Mitford, Nancy. *Love in a Cold Climate*
Mitford, Nancy. ★*The Pursuit of Love: A Novel*

MATERIAL CULTURE
Brin, David. *Existence*
Cooper, Tom. *Florida Man*
Leckie, Ann. *Provenance*
McBride, James. *Five-Carat Soul*
Stabenow, Dana. *Though Not Dead: A Kate Shugak Novel*

MATERIALISM
Banks, Russell. *Continental Drift*
Saunders, George. *In Persuasion Nation: Stories*

MATERNAL LOVE
Phillips, Helen. *The Need: A Novel*
Walbert, Kate. *She Was Like That: New and Selected Stories*
*The **Mathematician's** Shiva: A Novel*. Rojstaczer, Stuart

MATHEMATICIANS
Asimov, Isaac. ★*Foundation*
Asimov, Isaac. *Second Foundation*
Banville, John. *The Infinities*
Haig, Matt. *The Humans: A Novel*
Kiernan, Stephen P. *Universe of Two*
Marston, Edward. *The Roaring Boy: A Novel*
Pears, Iain. *An Instance of the Fingerpost*
Rojstaczer, Stuart. *The Mathematician's Shiva: A Novel*
Solzhenitsyn, Aleksandr Isaevich. *In the First Circle: A Novel : The Restored Text*

MATHEMATICS
Huang, S. L. *Zero Sum Game*
McGuire, Seanan. ★*Middlegame*
Richmond, Michelle. *No One You Know*
Rojstaczer, Stuart. *The Mathematician's Shiva: A Novel*
Sagan, Carl. *Contact: A Novel*
Stephenson, Neal. *Anathem*

MATHEMATICS TEACHERS
Higashino, Keigo. ★*The Devotion of Suspect X*
Rojstaczer, Stuart. *The Mathematician's Shiva: A Novel*

Matheson, Richard
★*I Am Legend*

Mathilda Savitch. Lodato, Victor

Mathis, Ayana
The Twelve Tribes of Hattie

MATILDA, EMPRESS, CONSORT OF HENRY V, HOLY ROMAN EMPEROR, 1102-1167
Banks, Iain. *The Hydrogen Sonata*
Franklin, Ariana. *The Siege Winter*

★*Mating*. Rush, Norman

MATRIARCHS
Bobotis, Andrea. *The Last List of Miss Judith Kratt*
Sexton, Margaret Wilkerson. *A Kind of Freedom*

MATRIARCHY
Diamant, Anita. ★*The Red Tent*

★*Matrix*. Groff, Lauren

Matter. Banks, Iain

★*Matterhorn: a Novel of the Vietnam War*. Marlantes, Karl

Matthew Scudder mysteries [Series]. Block, Lawrence

Matthew Shardlake novels [Series]. Sansom, C. J.

Matthews, Jason
★*The Kremlin's Candidate*
Red Sparrow: A Novel

Matthews, Mimi
★*The Siren of Sussex*

Matthiessen, Peter
Shadow Country: A New Rendering of the Watson Legend

Maturin, Charles Robert
Melmoth the Wanderer: A Tale

★*The **Matzah** Ball*. Meltzer, Jean

MAUDE, PRINCESS OF ENGLAND, 1102-1167
Penman, Sharon Kay. *When Christ and His Saints Slept*

Maugham, W. Somerset
The Moon and Sixpence
★*Of Human Bondage*

MAURITIUS
Ghosh, Amitav. *River of Smoke*

Max Brand's Best Western Stories. Brand, Max
Max Tudor mysteries [Series]. Malliet, G. M.
Maxwell's Demon. Hall, Steven
Maxwell, Everina
Winter's Orbit
May, Peter
The Blackhouse
MAY-DECEMBER ROMANCES
Barnes, Julian. *The Only Story*
Begley, Louis. *About Schmidt*
Burns, Olive Ann. ★*Cold Sassy Tree*
Cather, Willa. *A Lost Lady*
Drabble, Margaret. ★*The Dark Flood Rises*
Hornby, Nick. *Just Like You*
Robinson, Marilynne. ★*Gilead*
The Mayakovsky Tapes: A Novel. Littell, Robert
MAYAKOVSKY, VLADIMIR
Littell, Robert. *The Mayakovsky Tapes: A Novel*
VanderMeer, Jeff. ★*Borne: A Novel*
MAYAS
Smith, Scott. *The Ruins: A Novel*
MAYAS — RELIGION
Bowles, David. *Feathered Serpent, Dark Heart of Sky: Myths of Mexico*
Mayer, Mark
Aerialists: Stories
Maynard, Joyce
Count the Ways
Mayor, Archer
★*Marked Man*
Red Herring: A Joe Gunther Novel
Tag Man: A Joe Gunther Novel
MAYORAL CANDIDATES
Smith, Julie. *The Kindness of Strangers: A Skip Langdon Novel*
MAYORS
Garcia Marquez, Gabriel. *In Evil Hour*
Meader, Kate. *Playing with Fire*
Perrotta, Tom. *The Leftovers*
Phillips, Susan Elizabeth. *Call Me Irresistible*
Sandford, John. *Holy Ghost*
Wolfe, Tom. *Back to Blood: A Novel*
The Maytrees: a Novel. Dillard, Annie
★*The Maze at Windermere: A Novel*. Smith, Gregory Blake
Mbue, Imbolo
How Beautiful We Were
McAlister family novels [Series]. Turansky, Carrie
McAllister, Tom
How to Be Safe: A Novel
McBain, Ed
Alice in Jeopardy
McBride, James
★*Deacon King Kong: A Novel*
Five-Carat Soul
★*The Good Lord Bird*
McCaffrey, Anne
★*Acorna: The Unicorn Girl*
Dragonflight

McCall Smith, Alexander
Blue Shoes and Happiness
The Comforts of a Muddy Saturday: An Isabel Dalhousie Novel
★*The Department of Sensitive Crimes: A Detective Varg Novel*
The Double Comfort Safari Club
The Forgotten Affairs of Youth
The Full Cupboard of Life
★*The Geometry of Holding Hands*
The Good Husband of Zebra Drive
In the Company of Cheerful Ladies
The Joy and Light Bus Company
The Kalahari Typing School for Men
The Limpopo Academy of Private Detection
The Lost Art of Gratitude
★*The Man with the Silver Saab: A Detective Varg Novel*
★*The No. 1 Ladies' Detective Agency*
The Saturday Big Tent Wedding Party
Tiny Tales: Stories of Romance, Ambition, Kindness, and Happiness
McCammon, Robert R.
Boy's Life
McCann, Colum
★*Apeirogon: A Novel*
★*Transatlantic: A Novel*
McCarthy, Cormac
★*All the Pretty Horses*
★*Blood Meridian, Or, the Evening Redness in the West*
The Crossing
★*No Country for Old Men*
★*The Road*
McCarthy, Jesse
The Fugitivities
MCCARTHY, JOSEPH
Malone, Minx. *Bad Blood*
Stratford, Sarah-Jane. *Red Letter Days*
MCCARTHYISM
Davis, Fiona. *The Chelsea Girls*
Roth, Philip. *I Married a Communist*
Stratford, Sarah-Jane. *Red Letter Days*
McClure, James
The Steam Pig
McConaghy, Charlotte
Migrations
Once There Were Wolves: A Novel
McCorkle, Jill
★*Hieroglyphics: A Novel*
McCormack, Mike
★*Solar Bones*
McCracken, Elizabeth
★*Bowlaway: A Novel*
The Souvenir Museum: Stories
McCreight, Kimberly
Friends Like These
McCrumb, Sharyn
★*The Ballad of Frankie Silver*
★*If Ever I Return, Pretty Peggy-O*
McCullers, Carson
★*The Heart Is a Lonely Hunter*
The Member of the Wedding

Reflections in a Golden Eye
McCullough, Colleen
  The First Man in Rome
  An Indecent Obsession
McDermid, Val
  The Distant Echo
  How the Dead Speak: A Tony Hill and Carol Jordan Novel
  A Place of Execution
  ★*Still Life*
McDermott, Alice
  After This
  At Weddings and Wakes
  ★*Charming Billy*
  Child of My Heart
  ★*The Ninth Hour*
  Someone
  ★*That Night*
McDevitt, Jack
  The Engines of God
McDonald, Christina
  Behind Every Lie
McDonald, Ian
  New Moon
McDowell, Christina
  The Cave Dwellers: A Novel
McElroy, Alex
  The Atmospherians
McEwan, Ian
  ★*Amsterdam*
  ★*Atonement: A Novel*
  Black Dogs
  The Child in Time
  ★*On Chesil Beach*
  Solar: A Novel
McFadden, Bernice L.
  The Book of Harlan
McFarland, Jeni
  The House of Deep Water
McFarlane, Mhairi
  Don't You Forget About Me
  If I Never Met You: A Novel
MCGAVOCK, CAROLINE E WINDER, 1829-1905
  Hicks, Robert. *The Widow of the South*
  Strout, Elizabeth. *Amy and Isabelle: A Novel*
McGhee, Alison
  The Opposite of Fate
McGregor, Jon
  Lean Fall Stand
  The Reservoir Tapes
McGuane, Thomas
  ★*Cloudbursts: Collected and New Stories*
  Crow Fair: Stories
McGuire brothers [Series]. Humphreys, Sara Taney
McGuire, Ian
  The Abstainer: A Novel
McGuire, Seanan
  ★*Beneath the Sugar Sky*
  Chimes at Midnight: An October Daye Novel

★*Down Among the Sticks and Bones*
★*Every Heart a Doorway*
★*In an Absent Dream*
★*Middlegame*
McHugh, Laura
  What's Done in Darkness: A Novel
  The Wolf Wants In: A Novel
McIlvanney, William
  The Dark Remains: Laidlaw's First Case
McKenzie, Alecia
  A Million Aunties
McKenzie, Elizabeth
  The Portable Veblen
McKevett, G. A.
  A Few Drops of Bitters
  Murder at Mabel's Motel
  Murder in the Corn Maze
McKinlay, Jenn
  The Good Ones
  Killer Research
MCKINLEY, WILLIAM
  Dunmore, Evie. ★*Bringing Down the Duke*
  Goldstone, Lawrence. *Assassin of Shadows*
McKinney, Chris
  Midnight, Water City
McKinney-Whetstone, Diane
  Leaving Cecil Street: A Novel
McKinty, Adrian
  ★*The Chain*
  In the Morning I'll Be Gone: A Detective Sean Duffy Novel
McLain, Paula
  Circling the Sun
  Love and Ruin
  The Paris Wife: A Novel
  ★*When the Stars Go Dark: A Novel*
McLaughlin, Danielle
  The Art of Falling
McLaughlin, Emma
  The Nanny Diaries: A Novel
McLaughlin, James A.
  Bearskin
McLean, Felicity
  The Van Apfel Girls Are Gone
McMahon, Jennifer
  The Invited: A Novel
McMillan, Terry
  ★*How Stella Got Her Groove Back*
  ★*It's Not All Downhill from Here: A Novel*
  ★*Waiting to Exhale*
McMurtry, Larry
  Boone's Lick: A Novel
  Comanche Moon: A Novel
  The Evening Star: A Novel
  ★*Lonesome Dove: A Novel*
  ★*Streets of Laredo: A Novel*
  ★*Terms of Endearment: A Novel : With a New Preface*
McNally's Dilemma. Sanders, Lawrence
★*McNally's Gamble.* Sanders, Lawrence

McNally's Luck. Sanders, Lawrence
McNally's Puzzle. Sanders, Lawrence
McNally's Secret. Sanders, Lawrence
McNally's Trial. Sanders, Lawrence
McPherson, Catriona
    Quiet Neighbors: A Novel
    Scot & Soda
    ★*A Step so Grave*
    Strangers at the Gate
McQuiston, Casey
    ★*One Last Stop*
    ★*Red, White & Royal Blue: A Novel*
Me before you [Series]. Moyes, Jojo
Me Before You: A Novel. Moyes, Jojo
ME TOO MOVEMENT
    Benjamin, Ali. *The Smash-Up: A Novel*
Meacham, Leila
    Dragonfly: A Novel
Meader, Kate
    Playing with Fire
Meadowlark. Abrams, Melanie
Meadows, Rae
    I Will Send Rain: A Novel
★*Mean Woman Blues*. Smith, Julie
MEANING (PSYCHOLOGY)
    Adams, Douglas. ★*The Hitchhiker's Guide to the Galaxy*
    Albom, Mitch. *The Five People You Meet in Heaven*
    Dick, Philip K. ★*The Man in the High Castle*
    Hesse, Hermann. *Narcissus and Goldmund*
    McCormack, Mike. ★*Solar Bones*
    Musil, Robert. *The Man Without Qualities*
    Thammavongsa, Souvankham. *How to Pronounce Knife: Stories*
    Wallace, David Foster. ★*The Pale King: An Unfinished Novel*
The Means of Escape: Stories. Fitzgerald, Penelope
Means, David
    ★*Hystopia: A Novel*
    ★*Instructions for a Funeral: Stories*
Meant to be [Series]. Murphy, Julie
MEAT INDUSTRY AND TRADE — CORRUPT PRACTICES
    Sinclair, Upton. ★*The Jungle*
MEAT WORKERS — HEALTH AND SAFETY
    Sinclair, Upton. ★*The Jungle*
MECHANICS
    Bender, Tony. *The Last Ghost Dancer*
    Bouchet, Amanda. *Nightchaser*
    Macomber, Debbie. *If Not for You: A Novel*
Mechanique: a Tale of the Circus Tresaulti. Valentine, Genevieve
Meddling Kids: A Novel. Cantero, Edgar
MEDIA TIE-INS
    Beaton, M. C. ★*Hot to Trot*
    Carr, Caleb. ★*The Alienist*
    Cleeves, Ann. *Wild Fire*
    Fabry, Chris. *War Room: Prayer Is a Powerful Weapon*
    Holland, Cecelia. *Jerusalem*
    Johnson, Craig. *Daughter of the Morning Star*
    Johnson, Craig. *Land of Wolves*
    Johnson, Craig. *Next to Last Stand*
    Kelly, Erin. *Broadchurch: A Novel*

    Miles, Terry. *Rabbits*
    Runcie, James. *The Road to Grantchester*
MEDICAL CARE
    Browne, S. G. *Less Than Hero: A Novel*
MEDICAL CARE — CORRUPT PRACTICES
    Solzhenitsyn, Aleksandr Isaevich. ★*Cancer Ward*
MEDICAL CARE — COSTS
    Shriver, Lionel. *So Much for That*
MEDICAL GENETICS
    Peikoff, Kira. *Mother Knows Best*
MEDICAL INNOVATIONS
    Armstrong, Addison. *The Light of Luna Park*
MEDICAL MALPRACTICE
    Cook, Robin. *Charlatans*
    McCall Smith, Alexander. *The Comforts of a Muddy Saturday: An Isabel Dalhousie Novel*
MEDICAL STUDENTS
    Bernhard, Thomas. *Frost: A Novel*
    Cook, Robin. *Coma: A Novel*
    Loedel, Daniel. *Hades, Argentina*
    Parry, Ambrose. *The Way of All Flesh*
MEDICAL THRILLERS
    Cook, Robin. *Charlatans*
    Cook, Robin. *Coma: A Novel*
    Cook, Robin. ★*Genesis*
    Gerritsen, Tess. *The Apprentice: A Novel*
    Gerritsen, Tess. *I Know a Secret*
    Gerritsen, Tess. *The Surgeon*
    Gregory, Daryl. *Afterparty*
    Peikoff, Kira. *Mother Knows Best*
    Shepard, Jim. *Phase Six*
    Wright, Lawrence. *The End of October*
MEDICINE
    Newitz, Annalee. *Autonomous*
    Powers, Richard. *The Echo Maker*
MEDICINE — HISTORY
    Thomson, E. S. *Beloved Poison*
    Thomson, E. S. *The Blood*
MEDICINE — PRACTICE
    Verghese, A. *Cutting for Stone: A Novel*
Medie, Peace A.
    His Only Wife: A Novel
MEDIEVAL MYSTERIES
    Eco, Umberto. ★*The Name of the Rose*
    Franklin, Ariana. ★*Death and the Maiden*
    Penman, Sharon Kay. *The Queen's Man: A Medieval Mystery*
    Peters, Ellis. *Brother Cadfael's Penance*
    Peters, Ellis. *The Holy Thief*
    Robb, Candace M. ★*A Choir of Crows*
    Robb, Candace M. *The Cross-Legged Knight: An Owen Archer Mystery*
    Robb, Candace M. *A Gift of Sanctuary: An Owen Archer Mystery*
    Robb, Candace M. *A Murdered Peace*
    Robb, Candace M. *The Riddle of St. Leonard's: An Owen Archer Mystery.*
    Robb, Candace M. *A Twisted Vengeance*
    Starr, Melvin R. *Unhallowed Ground*

MEDIEVAL PERIOD (476-1492)

Arden, Katherine. ★*The Bear and the Nightingale*
Banks, Maya. *Never Seduce a Scot*
Cherezinska, Elzbieta. *The Widow Queen*
Cornwell, Bernard. *The Archer's Tale*
Cornwell, Bernard. *The Last Kingdom: A Novel*
Cornwell, Bernard. *Sword of Kings*
Crace, Jim. *Harvest*
Druon, Maurice. *The Iron King*
Eco, Umberto. *Baudolino*
Eco, Umberto. ★*The Name of the Rose*
Follett, Ken. ★*The Pillars of the Earth*
Franklin, Ariana. ★*Death and the Maiden*
Franklin, Ariana. *Mistress of the Art of Death*
Franklin, Ariana. *The Serpent's Tale*
Franklin, Ariana. *The Siege Winter*
Garwood, Julie. *The Bride*
Gregory, Philippa. *The Kingmaker's Daughter*
Gregory, Philippa. *The Red Queen: A Novel*
Gregory, Philippa. *The White Princess*
Groff, Lauren. ★*Matrix*
Hesse, Hermann. *Narcissus and Goldmund*
Iggulden, Conn. *The Abbot's Tale*
Lin, Jeannie. *The Lotus Palace*
Pears, Iain. *The Dream of Scipio*
Penman, Sharon Kay. *Here Be Dragons*
Penman, Sharon Kay. *The Queen's Man: A Medieval Mystery*
Penman, Sharon Kay. *The Sunne in Splendour*
Penman, Sharon Kay. *When Christ and His Saints Slept*
Peters, Ellis. *Brother Cadfael's Penance*
Peters, Ellis. *The Holy Thief*
Pike, Signe. *The Forgotten Kingdom: A Novel*
Pike, Signe. *The Lost Queen*
Robb, Candace M. ★*A Choir of Crows*
Robb, Candace M. *The Cross-Legged Knight: An Owen Archer Mystery*
Robb, Candace M. *A Gift of Sanctuary: An Owen Archer Mystery*
Robb, Candace M. *A Murdered Peace*
Robb, Candace M. *The Riddle of St. Leonard's: An Owen Archer Mystery.*
Scott, Walter. ★*Ivanhoe*
Sharratt, Mary. *Illuminations: A Novel of Hildegard Von Bingen*
Sharratt, Mary. *Revelations*
Starr, Melvin R. *Unhallowed Ground*
Walters, Minette. *The Last Hours: A Novel*
Willis, Connie. ★*Doomsday Book*

MEDIEVAL ROMANCES

Banks, Maya. *Never Seduce a Scot*
Garwood, Julie. *The Bride*

MEDIOCRITY

Gass, William H. *Middle C*
The Mediterranean Caper. Cussler, Clive

MEDITERRANEAN REGION

El Akkad, Omar. *What Strange Paradise*
Rollins, James. ★*The Last Odyssey*

MEDITERRANEAN SEA

Cussler, Clive. ★*Sea of Greed: A Novel from the Numa Files*

MEDIUMS

Bennett, Jenn. *Bitter Spirits*
Hart, Carolyn G. *Ghost Blows a Kiss*
Murphy, Sara Flannery. *The Possessions*
Medlar mysteries [Series]. Deveraux, Jude
Medusa's Ankles: Selected Stories. Byatt, A. S.
Meet Me at the Museum. Youngson, Anne
Meet Me in Monaco: A Novel. Gaynor, Hazel
A Meeting at Corvallis. Stirling, S. M.

MEETINGS

Mosley, Walter. *The Right Mistake: The Further Philosophical Investigations of Socrates Fortlow*
★*Meg and Jo*. Kantra, Virginia
Meg Langslow mysteries [Series]. Andrews, Donna
Meg: Generations. Alten, Steve
Megalodon series [Series]. Alten, Steve

Mehta, Rahul

No Other World: A Novel

Meier, Leslie

Silver Anniversary Murder

MELBOURNE, VICTORIA

Clarke, Maxine Beneba. ★*Foreign Soil*
Garner, Helen. *The Spare Room*
Marsh, Nicola. *The Boy Toy*
Melmoth the Wanderer: A Tale. Maturin, Charles Robert
Melmoth: a Novel. Perry, Sarah
The Melody Lingers On. Clark, Mary Higgins

MELROSE, PATRICK (FICTITIOUS CHARACTER)

St. Aubyn, Edward. *At Last*

Meltzer, Brad

The Escape Artist
The Inner Circle
The Tenth Justice
The Zero Game

Meltzer, Jean

★*The Matzah Ball*

Melville, Herman

The Complete Shorter Fiction
The Confidence-Man: His Masquerade
★*Moby-Dick; Or, the Whale*

MELVILLE, HERMAN

Bird, Sarah. ★*The Flamenco Academy: A Novel*
Parini, Jay. *The Passages of H.M.: A Novel of Herman Melville*
The Member of the Wedding. McCullers, Carson
Members Only. Pandya, Sameer
★*Memento Mori*. Spark, Muriel
Memnoch the Devil. Rice, Anne
Memo from Turner. Willocks, Tim
Memoir trilogy [Series]. Coetzee, J. M.
★*Memoirs of a Geisha: A Novel*. Golden, Arthur
★*Memoirs of Hadrian: And Reflections on the Composition of Memoirs of Hadrian*. Yourcenar, Marguerite
Memoirs of John Watson [Series]. Meyer, Nicholas
Memoirs of Lady Trent [Series]. Brennan, Marie
MemoRandom [Series]. De la Motte, Anders
MemoRandom: a Thriller. De la Motte, Anders
★*Memorial*. Washington, Bryan

MEMORIALIZATION

Brennan, Marie. *Driftwood*

MEMORIES

Abrams, Melanie. *Meadowlark*

Allende, Isabel. *Portrait in Sepia: A Novel*

Apostol, Gina. *Gun Dealers' Daughter: A Novel*

Atwood, Margaret. ★*Cat's Eye*

Auster, Paul. *Travels in the Scriptorium: A Novel*

Banville, John. *The Blue Guitar*

Banville, John. ★*The Sea*

Bender, Aimee. *The Butterfly Lampshade*

Bobotis, Andrea. *The Last List of Miss Judith Kratt*

Bolano, Roberto. ★*By Night in Chile*

Boyle, T. Coraghessan. *The Relive Box: And Other Stories*

Brennan, Marie. *Driftwood*

Brooks, Terry. *Child of Light*

Cannon, Joanna. *Three Things About Elsie: A Novel*

Chancellor, Bryn. *Sycamore: A Novel*

Cisneros, Sandra. *Martita, I Remember You: Martita, Te Recuerdo*

Colwin, Laurie. *Goodbye Without Leaving*

Crouch, Blake. *Recursion*

Daughters, Amy Weinland. *You Cannot Mess This Up: A True Story That Never Happened*

Djavadi, Negar. *Disoriental*

Doan, Amy Mason. *The Summer List*

Dodd, Christina. *What Doesn't Kill Her*

Drabble, Margaret. *The Sea Lady*

Dunmore, Helen. *The Lie*

Eco, Umberto. *The Mysterious Flame of Queen Loana: An Illustrated Novel*

Enright, Anne. *The Forgotten Waltz*

Flagg, Fannie. ★*The Wonder Boy of Whistle Stop: A Novel*

French, Nicci. ★*House of Correction*

French, Tana. ★*Broken Harbor*

Fuentes, Carlos. *The Death of Artemio Cruz*

Gaiman, Neil. ★*The Ocean at the End of the Lane*

Gaitskill, Mary. *Veronica*

Gilbert, Elizabeth. ★*City of Girls*

Grass, Gunter. *The Box: Tales from the Darkroom*

Grass, Gunter. *Crabwalk*

Hall, Rachel Howzell. *These Toxic Things*

Hart, Elsa. *City of Ink: A Mystery*

Haruf, Kent. ★*Our Souls at Night*

Hooper, Emma. *Etta and Otto and Russell and James: A Novel*

Hornby, Gill. *Miss Austen*

Jayatissa, Amanda. ★*My Sweet Girl*

Kagen, Lesley. *Every Now and Then*

Lem, Stanislaw. ★*Solaris*

Littell, Robert. *The Mayakovsky Tapes: A Novel*

Machado, Carmen Maria. ★*The Low, Low Woods*

Markley, Stephen. *Ohio*

Mason, Bobbie Ann. *Dear Ann: A Novel*

McCorkle, Jill. ★*Hieroglyphics: A Novel*

McCormack, Mike. ★*Solar Bones*

McGregor, Jon. *The Reservoir Tapes*

Means, David. ★*Hystopia: A Novel*

Meuleman, Sarah. *Find Me Gone*

Montimore, Margarita. *Oona Out of Order*

Nicholls, Owen. *Love, Unscripted: A Novel*

Pamuk, Orhan. *Silent House*

Petterson, Per. *Out Stealing Horses: A Novel*

Picoult, Jodi. ★*The Book of Two Ways*

Proust, Marcel. ★*Remembrance of Things Past*

Proust, Marcel. *Swann's Way*

Proust, Marcel. *Time Regained*

Proust, Marcel. *Within a Budding Grove*

Ramadan, Ahmad Danny. *The Clothesline Swing*

Ratner, Vaddey. *Music of the Ghosts*

Ruskovich, Emily. *Idaho: A Novel*

Russell, Kate Elizabeth. ★*My Dark Vanessa*

Savas, Aysegul. *Walking on the Ceiling*

Schweblin, Samanta. *Fever Dream: A Novel*

Shafak, Elif. ★*10 Minutes 38 Seconds in This Strange World*

Shaffer, Mary Ann. *The Guernsey Literary and Potato Peel Pie Society*

Shepard, Sam. *The One Inside*

Simenon, Georges. *Maigret's Memoirs*

Solomon, Asali. *The Days of Afrekete*

Solomon, Rivers. *The Deep*

Sternbergh, Adam. *The Blinds*

Stoker, Dacre. *Dracul*

Ullmann, Linn. *Unquiet: A Novel*

Van Meter, Crissy. *Creatures: A Novel*

Vasquez, Juan Gabriel. ★*The Shape of the Ruins*

Weinstein, Alexander. *Children of the New World: Stories*

Wells, Benedict. *The End of Loneliness: A Novel*

Willett, Marcia. *The Garden House*

Woodson, Jacqueline. ★*Another Brooklyn*

MEMORIES — PSYCHOLOGICAL ASPECTS

Barnes, Julian. ★*The Sense of an Ending*

Moore, Alison. *The Lighthouse*

Prcic, Ismet. *Shards: A Novel*

Memories of My Melancholy Whores. Garcia Marquez, Gabriel

Memories of the Ford Administration: A Novel. Updike, John

Memory. Westlake, Donald E.

MEMORY

Acevedo, Chantel. *The Distant Marvels*

Afifi, Nadia. *The Sentient*

Amis, Martin. ★*The Pregnant Widow*

Banasky, Carmiel. *The Suicide of Claire Bishop*

Cleave, Paul. *Trust No One: A Thriller*

Dionne, Karen. *The Wicked Sister*

Doctorow, E. L. *Andrew's Brain*

Doyle, Roddy. *Smile*

Eco, Umberto. *The Mysterious Flame of Queen Loana: An Illustrated Novel*

Enger, Leif. *Virgil Wander*

Fernandez, Nona. *The Twilight Zone*

Freeman, Brian. *The Night Bird*

Gardner, Lisa. *Fear Nothing: A Detective D. D. Warren Novel*

Guskin, Sharon. *The Forgetting Time*

Hadley, Tessa. *Clever Girl*

Healey, Emma. ★*Elizabeth Is Missing*

Irving, John. *Avenue of Mysteries: A Novel*

Ishiguro, Kazuo. *The Buried Giant: A Novel*

Ishiguro, Kazuo. *The Unconsoled*

Kaufman, Charlie. *Antkind: A Novel*
Kawabata, Yasunari. *The Sound of the Mountain*
Lawler, Liz. *Don't Wake Up*
Martell, Nick. *The Kingdom of Liars*
Novic, Sara. *Girl at War*
O'Nan, Stewart. *Henry, Himself*
Ogawa, Yoko. ★*The Memory Police: A Novel*
Okorafor, Nnedi. ★*Remote Control*
Okuizumi, Hikaru. *The Stones Cry Out*
Ólafsson, Ólafur Jóhann. *The Sacrament: A Novel*
Paris, B. A. *The Breakdown*
Pulley, Natasha. *The Lost Future of Pepperharrow*
Schwab, Victoria. *The Invisible Life of Addie Larue*
Shepherd, Peng. *The Book of M: A Novel*
Smith, Ali. ★*Winter*
Ward, Catriona. *The Last House on Needless Street*
Wasserman, Robin. *Mother Daughter Widow Wife*
Westlake, Donald E. *Memory*
Wilson, Carter. *Dead Girl in 2a*
★*A Memory Called Empire*. Martine, Arkady
MEMORY DISORDERS
Healey, Emma. ★*Elizabeth Is Missing*
The *Memory Keeper's Daughter*. Edwards, Kim
★*The Memory Police: A Novel*. Ogawa, Yoko
MEMPHIS, TENNESSEE
Dickey, Eric Jerome. ★*The Son of Mr. Suleman*
Friedman, Daniel. ★*Don't Ever Get Old*
Friedman, Daniel. *Running Out of Road*
Grisham, John. ★*The Firm*
Petrie, Nicholas. *Tear It Down*
MEN
Atkinson, Kate. ★*A God in Ruins*
Bolano, Roberto. *Last Evenings on Earth*
Coe, Jonathan. *The Rotters' Club*
Davies, Carys. *The Mission House*
Goddard, Robert. *Beyond Recall: A Novel*
Gonzalez, Christopher. *I'm Not Hungry but I Could Eat*
Murakami, Ryu. *In the Miso Soup*
Musil, Robert. *The Man Without Qualities*
Pamuk, Orhan. *The Museum of Innocence*
Pawel, Rebecca. *Death of a Nationalist*
Peters, Torrey. ★*Detransition, Baby*
Poore, Michael. *Reincarnation Blues*
Richardson, C. S. *The End of the Alphabet*
Runcie, James. *Canvey Island*
Snow, C. P. ★*Strangers and Brothers*
MEN — DEATH
Hargrave, Kiran Millwood. *The Mercies: A Novel*
Sweeney-Baird, Christina. *The End of Men*
MEN — DECISION-MAKING
Block, Lawrence. *Hit Me: A Keller Novel*
MEN — EXTINCTION
Beukes, Lauren. *Afterland*
MEN — FAMILY RELATIONSHIPS
Bolano, Roberto. *Last Evenings on Earth*
MEN — IDENTITY
Palliser, Charles. *The Quincunx*
Updike, John. *My Father's Tears and Other Stories*

Zamyatin, Yevgeny Ivanovich. ★*We*
MEN — MORTALITY
D'Erasmo, Stacey. *The Sky Below*
MEN — PERSONAL CONDUCT
Harkness, Deborah E. *Time's Convert*
Joyce, James. ★*Ulysses*
MEN — PSYCHOLOGY
Auster, Paul. *4 3 2 1: A Novel*
Beattie, Ann. *A Wonderful Stroke of Luck: A Novel*
Doyle, Roddy. *Smile*
Ishiguro, Kazuo. ★*The Remains of the Day*
Joyce, James. ★*Finnegans Wake*
Lehane, Dennis. ★*Mystic River*
Murakami, Haruki. *Men Without Women: Stories*
Pamuk, Orhan. ★*A Strangeness in My Mind: A Novel*
Roth, Henry. *From Bondage*
Vargas Llosa, Mario. ★*The Discreet Hero*
MEN — RELIGIOUS LIFE
Goldstein, Rebecca. *36 Arguments for the Existence of God: A Work of Fiction*
MEN — SEXUALITY
McCullers, Carson. *Reflections in a Golden Eye*
Nabokov, Vladimir Vladimirovich. ★*Lolita*
Toibin, Colm. ★*The Magician: A Novel*
Wallace, David Foster. ★*Brief Interviews with Hideous Men*
MEN — SPIRITUAL LIFE
Berenson, Alex. *The Faithful Spy: A Novel*
Rubart, James L. ★*The Man He Never Was*
MEN AND BIRDS
Rooney, Kathleen. ★*Cher Ami and Major Whittlesey*
MEN AND DOGS
Auster, Paul. *Timbuktu: A Novel*
Cameron, W. Bruce. *Repo Madness*
London, Jack. ★*The Call of the Wild*
London, Jack. ★*White Fang*
McCall Smith, Alexander. ★*The Man with the Silver Saab: A Detective Varg Novel*
Miller, Mary. *Biloxi: A Novel*
Rosenfelt, David. ★*Dog Eat Dog*
MEN AND NATURE
Evison, Jonathan. *West of Here: A Novel*
Guterson, David. *The Other*
Rash, Ron. *Something Rich and Strange: Selected Stories*
MEN AND SUCCESS
Price, Richard. *Samaritan*
Stone, Irving. ★*The Agony and the Ecstasy: A Biographical Novel of Michelangelo*
Welsh, Irvine. *Dead Men's Trousers*
Men at Arms: A Novel of Discworld. Pratchett, Terry
MEN NURSES
Beckett, Samuel. ★*Murphy*
MEN PSYCHICS
Cotterill, Colin. *The Coroner's Lunch*
Heinlein, Robert A. ★*Stranger in a Strange Land*
Tepper, Sheri S. *The Gate to Women's Country*
MEN RECLUSES
Clarke, Susanna. ★*Jonathan Strange & Mr. Norrell*
Phillips, Susan Elizabeth. *Heroes Are My Weakness*

Quick, Amanda. *'til Death Do Us Part*
Robertson, Imogen. *Island of Bones*

MEN WHO ARE BLIND

Aslam, Nadeem. ★*The Blind Man's Garden*
Auster, Paul. *Oracle Night*
Doctorow, E. L. *Homer and Langley: A Novel*
Kelman, James. *How Late It Was, How Late*
Romain, Theresa. *Fortune Favors the Wicked*

MEN WHO ARE DEAF AND MUTE

McCullers, Carson. ★*The Heart Is a Lonely Hunter*

MEN WHO ARE MUTE

Araghi, Alireza Taheri. ★*The Immortals of Tehran*
Hamilton, Steve. ★*The Lock Artist*

MEN WITH AMNESIA

Byrne, Kerrigan. *The Duke with the Dragon Tattoo*
Coben, Harlan. ★*The Boy from the Woods*
De la Motte, Anders. *MemoRandom: A Thriller*
Dimaline, Cherie. *Empire of Wild*
Doetsch, Richard. *Half-Past Dawn*
Fluke, Joanne. ★*Christmas Cupcake Murder*
Hilton, James. *Random Harvest*
Lightman, Alan P. *The Diagnosis*
Pulley, Natasha. ★*The Kingdoms*
Ragan, Theresa. *Buried Deep*
Ragan, Theresa. *Deranged*
Ragan, Theresa. *Her Last Day*
Rosenfelt, David. *Black and Blue: A Doug Brock Thriller*
Steadman, Catherine. *Mr. Nobody: A Novel*
Stross, Charles. *Glasshouse*
Webb, Brandon. ★*Steel Fear*

MEN WITH BIPOLAR DISORDER

Leithauser, Brad. *The Promise of Elsewhere*

MEN WITH BRAIN INJURIES

Ogawa, Yoko. *The Housekeeper and the Professor*

MEN WITH DEPRESSION

Wiesel, Elie. *A Mad Desire to Dance: A Novel*

MEN WITH DEVELOPMENTAL DISABILITIES

Coetzee, J. M. ★*Life & Times of Michael K*
Faulkner, William. ★*The Sound and the Fury*
Leon, Donna. *The Golden Egg*
Oe, Kenzaburo. ★*A Quiet Life*
Steinbeck, John. ★*Of Mice and Men*
Vlautin, Willy. ★*The Night Always Comes*

MEN WITH DISABILITIES

Leitch, Will. ★*How Lucky*
Rendell, Ruth. *Live Flesh*

MEN WITH DISFIGUREMENTS

Balogh, Mary. *Simply Love*
Bujold, Lois McMaster. ★*The Warrior's Apprentice*
Callihan, Kristen. ★*Firelight*
Darnielle, John. *Wolf in White Van: A Novel*
Leon, Donna. *Beastly Things: A Commissario Guido Brunetti Mystery*
Sansom, C. J. *Revelation*
Sinha, Indra. *Animal's People*

MEN WITH DISSOCIATIVE IDENTITY DISORDER

Patterson, James. ★*Along Came a Spider: A Novel*

MEN WITH DYSLEXIA

London, Julia. *The Charmer in Chaps*

MEN WITH MENTAL ILLNESSES

Auster, Paul. *Timbuktu: A Novel*
Baldwin, Joshua. *The Wilshire Sun*
Block, Lawrence. *A Ticket to the Boneyard: A Matthew Scudder Novel*
Bohjalian, Chris. *The Double Bind: A Novel*
Broun, Bill. *Night of the Animals*
Callaghan, Mary Rose. *Billy, Come Home*
Harris, Thomas. *Hannibal*
Hesse, Hermann. ★*Steppenwolf*
Kadare, Ismail. ★*The Three-Arched Bridge*
Kilalea, Katharine. *Ok, Mr. Field: A Novel*
Vonnegut, Kurt. ★*Breakfast of Champions: Or, Goodbye Blue Monday!*
Wells, H. G. ★*The Invisible Man*

MEN WITH PARANOIA

Amdahl, Gary. *I Am Death: Two Novellas*

MEN WITH SCHIZOPHRENIA

Barclay, Linwood. *Trust Your Eyes: A Thriller*
Callaghan, Mary Rose. *Billy, Come Home*

MEN WITH TERMINAL ILLNESSES

Bailey, Paul. *Chapman's Odyssey*
Baldacci, David. *One Summer*
Gaddis, William. *Agape Agape*
Garcia Marquez, Gabriel. *The General in His Labyrinth*
Gibbon, Maureen. *The Lost Notebook of Edouard Manet: A Novel*
Guskin, Sharon. *The Forgetting Time*
Nabokov, Vladimir Vladimirovich. *Look at the Harlequins!*
Ramadan, Ahmad Danny. *The Clothesline Swing*
Wallace, Daniel. ★*Big Fish: A Novel of Mythic Proportions*

MEN WITH TERMINAL ILLNESSES — FAMILY RELATIONSHIPS

Haruf, Kent. *Benediction*

Men Without Women: Stories. Murakami, Haruki

MEN'S DREAMS

Dekker, Ted. *Black: The Birth of Evil*
Joyce, James. ★*Finnegans Wake*

MEN'S FANTASIES

Amis, Kingsley. ★*Lucky Jim*

MEN'S ORGANIZATIONS

Collins, Manda. *A Good Rake Is Hard to Find*
Dickens, Charles. *The Pickwick Papers*
Levin, Ira. ★*The Stepford Wives: A Novel*

MEN-HEADED FAMILIES

Porter, Max. ★*Grief Is the Thing with Feathers*
Puzo, Mario. ★*The Godfather*
Puzo, Mario. *The Sicilian: A Novel*

MEN/MEN RELATIONS

Greenwell, Garth. *What Belongs to You: A Novel*
Hall, Alexis. *For Real*
Renault, Mary. *The Last of the Wine*
Sebastian, Cat. *The Lawrence Browne Affair*
Tesh, Emily. *Silver in the Wood*

Mendez, Paul

Rainbow Milk

MENGELE, JOSEF, 1911-1979
Alyan, Hala. *Salt Houses*
Konar, Affinity. *Mischling: A Novel*
Mengestu, Dinaw
★*All Our Names*
Mengiste, Maaza
★*The Shadow King: A Novel*
MENNONITE WOMEN
Toews, Miriam. ★*Women Talking: A Novel*
MENNONITES
Toews, Miriam. ★*Women Talking: A Novel*
Menon, Lily
Make up Break Up: A Novel
MENOPAUSE
Pearson, Allison. ★*How Hard Can It Be?*
MENTAL HEALTH
Rooney, Sally. ★*Beautiful World, Where Are You*
MENTAL ILLNESS
Atilgan, Yusuf. *Motherland Hotel*
Bender, Aimee. *The Butterfly Lampshade*
Chiaverini, Jennifer. *Mrs. Lincoln's Sisters*
Deluca, Marjorie. *The Savage Instinct*
Gay, Roxane. ★*An Untamed State*
Golding, William. ★*Darkness Visible*
Gregory, Daryl. *Afterparty*
Heller, Joseph. ★*Catch-22*
Lippman, Laura. ★*Hush Hush*
Plath, Sylvia. ★*The Bell Jar*
Rendell, Ruth. *Collected Stories*
Rendell, Ruth. *The Tree of Hands*
Restrepo, Laura. ★*Delirium: A Novel*
Rogers, Morgan Callan. ★*Honey Girl*
MENTAL ILLNESS — TREATMENT
Freeman, Brian. *The Night Bird*
Kesey, Ken. ★*One Flew Over the Cuckoo's Nest*
MENTORING
Daly, Paula. *Clear My Name*
Shupe, Joanna. *The Prince of Broadway*
MENTORS
Backman, Fredrik. *Britt-Marie Was Here*
Connelly, Michael. *The Night Fire*
Flyte, Magnus. *City of Dark Magic: A Novel*
Flyte, Magnus. *City of Lost Dreams: A Novel*
Hart, Elsa. *City of Ink: A Mystery*
Heger, Amanda. *Crazy Cupid Love*
Ondaatje, Michael. ★*Warlight*
Shannon, Samantha. *The Bone Season*
Wolitzer, Meg. *The Female Persuasion*
Merbeth, K. S.
★*Fortuna*
MERCENARIES
Banks, Iain. *Consider Phlebas*
Bear, Elizabeth. *The Red-Stained Wings*
Bear, Elizabeth. *The Stone in the Skull*
Child, Lee. *Bad Luck and Trouble*
Child, Lee. *The Hard Way*
Child, Lee. *Nothing to Lose*
Christy, Bryan. *In the Company of Killers*

Cussler, Clive. ★*Final Option*
Cussler, Clive. *Sacred Stone*
Cussler, Clive. *Shadow Tyrants*
Cussler, Clive. *Typhoon Fury*
Dunnett, Dorothy. *Niccolo Rising*
Hossain, Saad Z. *Cyber Mage: A Novel*
Huang, S. L. *Zero Sum Game*
Kuhn, M. J. *Among Thieves*
Rothfuss, Patrick. ★*The Wise Man's Fear*
Stroby, Wallace. *Some Die Nameless*
The **Merchant** *Emperor*. Haydon, Elizabeth
MERCHANT SAILORS
Furst, Alan. *Dark Voyage: A Novel*
MERCHANT SHIPS
Endicott, Marina. *The Voyage of the Morning Light*
MERCHANTS
Gowar, Imogen Hermes. *The Mermaid and Mrs. Hancock*
Welty, Eudora. ★*The Robber Bridegroom*
Merci Rayborn mysteries [Series]. Parker, T. Jefferson
The **Mercies:** *a Novel*. Hargrave, Kiran Millwood
Mercy of a rude stream [Series]. Roth, Henry
The **Mercy** *Seat: A Novel*. Winthrop, Elizabeth Hartley
A **Mercy:** *a Novel*. Morrison, Toni
The **Mere** *Wife*. Headley, Maria Dahvana
MERLIN (LEGENDARY CHARACTER)
Pike, Signe. *The Lost Queen*
Stewart, Mary. ★*The Crystal Cave*
Stewart, Mary. ★*The Hollow Hills*
Stewart, Mary. *The Last Enchantment*
Twain, Mark. ★*A Connecticut Yankee in King Arthur's Court*
White, T. H. ★*The Once and Future King*
Merlin [Series]. Stewart, Mary
The **Mermaid** and Mrs. Hancock. Gowar, Imogen Hermes
The **Mermaid** *from Jeju: A Novel*. Hahn, Sumi
MERMAIDS
Gowar, Imogen Hermes. *The Mermaid and Mrs. Hancock*
Solomon, Rivers. *The Deep*
MERMEN
Broder, Melissa. *The Pisces: A Novel*
Merrick: *a Novel*. Rice, Anne
Merullo, Roland
The Talk-Funny Girl: A Novel
MESOTHELIOMA
Shriver, Lionel. *So Much for That*
Message *from a Mistress*. Bryant, Niobia
MESSIAHS
Heinlein, Robert A. ★*Stranger in a Strange Land*
Irving, John. ★*A Prayer for Owen Meany: A Novel*
Simmons, Dan. *Endymion*
Simmons, Dan. *The Rise of Endymion*
Messud, Claire
★*The Woman Upstairs: A Novel*
METAFICTION
Binet, Laurent. ★*HHhH*
Calvino, Italo. ★*If on a Winter's Night a Traveler*
Chizmar, Richard T. *Chasing the Boogeyman*
Currie, Ron. *Flimsy Little Plastic Miracles: A True Story*
Ferris, Joshua. *A Calling for Charlie Barnes*

Fforde, Jasper. *The Eyre Affair: A Novel*
Fforde, Jasper. *Lost in a Good Book: A Thursday Next Novel*
Goldman, William. ★*The Princess Bride: S. Morgenstern's Classic Tale of True Love and High Adventure : The*
Hall, Steven. *Maxwell's Demon*
Horowitz, Anthony. ★*Magpie Murders*
Horowitz, Anthony. ★*The Sentence Is Death*
Horowitz, Anthony. ★*The Word Is Murder*
Mott, Jason. *Hell of a Book*
O'Brien, Tim. *Going After Cacciato: A Novel*
Oyeyemi, Helen. *Mr. Fox*
Ozeki, Ruth L. ★*A Tale for the Time Being*
Phillips, Arthur. *The Tragedy of Arthur: A Novel*
Rushdie, Salman. ★*Quichotte: A Novel*
Scalzi, John. *Redshirts: A Novel with Three Codas*
Vasquez, Juan Gabriel. ★*The Shape of the Ruins*
Vonnegut, Kurt. *Timequake*
Walton, Jo. *Or What You Will*

METAL DETECTORS
Griffiths, Elly. *The Night Hawks*
★*The Metamorphosis*. Kafka, Franz

METAMORPHOSIS
Woolf, Virginia. *Orlando: A Biography*
Yoder, Rachel. *Nightbitch*

METAMORPHOSIS — MYTHOLOGY
MacLaughlin, Nina. *Wake, Siren: Ovid Resung*

METAPHYSICS
Borges, Jorge Luis. *Ficciones*
Poore, Michael. *Reincarnation Blues*

METEOROLOGISTS
Solomon, Rachel Lynn. *Weather Girl*

METEORS
Kowal, Mary Robinette. *The Calculating Stars: A Lady Astronaut Novel*

METHAMPHETAMINE
Rash, Ron. *Above the Waterfall*

METIS
Aalborg, Gordon. *River of Porcupines*
★*Metropolis: a Bernie Gunther Novel*. Kerr, Philip

Meuleman, Sarah
   Find Me Gone
The Meursault Investigation. Daoud, Kamel

MEXICAN AMERICAN BOYS
Santiago, Danny. *Famous All Over Town*

MEXICAN AMERICAN FAMILIES
Escandon, Maria Amparo. ★*L.A. Weather*
Santiago, Danny. *Famous All Over Town*
Urrea, Luis Alberto. ★*The House of Broken Angels*

MEXICAN AMERICAN GIRLS
Cisneros, Sandra. ★*The House on Mango Street*

MEXICAN AMERICAN MEN
Nava, Michael. ★*Carved in Bone*

MEXICAN AMERICAN TEENAGE BOYS
Gilb, Dagoberto. *The Flowers: A Novel*

MEXICAN AMERICAN TEENAGE GIRLS
Castro, V. *Goddess of Filth*
Wetmore, Elizabeth. ★*Valentine*

MEXICAN AMERICAN WOMEN
Anaya, Rudolfo A. *The Man Who Could Fly and Other Stories*

MEXICAN AMERICANS
Anaya, Rudolfo A. *The Man Who Could Fly and Other Stories*
Evison, Jonathan. ★*Lawn Boy: A Novel*
Flores, Fernando A. *Tears of the Trufflepig*
Fuentes, Carlos. *The Years with Laura Diaz*
Skyhorse, Brando. *Madonnas of Echo Park: A Novel*
Sylvester, Natalia. *Everyone Knows You Go Home*
Mexican Gothic. Moreno-Garcia, Silvia

MEXICAN REVOLUTION (1910-1920)
Fuentes, Carlos. ★*The Old Gringo*
Fuentes, Carlos. *The Years with Laura Diaz*
Groom, Winston. *El Paso: A Novel*
Pynchon, Thomas. *Against the Day: A Novel*

MEXICAN-AMERICAN BORDER REGION
Blake, James Carlos. *The House of Wolfe*
Bolano, Roberto. ★*2666*
Flores, Fernando A. *Tears of the Trufflepig*
Gaspar de Alba, Alicia. *Desert Blood: The Juarez Murders*
Moreno-Garcia, Silvia. ★*Gods of Jade and Shadow: A Novel*
Sylvester, Natalia. *Everyone Knows You Go Home*
Urrea, Luis Alberto. ★*The House of Broken Angels*

MEXICAN-AMERICAN WOMEN
Cisneros, Sandra. *Martita, I Remember You: Martita, Te Recuerdo*

MEXICANS IN THE UNITED STATES
Fuentes, Carlos. *The Crystal Frontier: A Novel in Nine Stories*
Urrea, Luis Alberto. *Queen of America: A Novel*

MEXICO
Aguilar Camin, Hector. *Death in Veracruz*
Anaya, Rudolfo A. *The Man Who Could Fly and Other Stories*
Bolano, Roberto. *Amulet*
Bowles, David. *Feathered Serpent, Dark Heart of Sky: Myths of Mexico*
D'Erasmo, Stacey. *The Sky Below*
Doerr, Harriet. ★*Stones for Ibarra*
Esquivel, Laura. ★*Like Water for Chocolate: A Novel in Monthly Installments, with Recipes, Romances, and Home Remedies*
Fuentes, Carlos. *The Crystal Frontier: A Novel in Nine Stories*
Fuentes, Carlos. *The Death of Artemio Cruz*
Fuentes, Carlos. *Destiny and Desire: A Novel*
Fuentes, Carlos. *The Eagle's Throne: A Novel*
Fuentes, Carlos. ★*The Old Gringo*
Fuentes, Carlos. *The Years with Laura Diaz*
Gordimer, Nadine. *Get a Life*
Greene, Graham. *The Power and the Glory*
Groom, Winston. *El Paso: A Novel*
Gruber, Michael. *The Return: A Novel*
Irving, John. *Avenue of Mysteries: A Novel*
McCarthy, Cormac. ★*Blood Meridian, Or, the Evening Redness in the West*
McCarthy, Cormac. ★*No Country for Old Men*
Moreno-Garcia, Silvia. ★*Gods of Jade and Shadow: A Novel*
Moreno-Garcia, Silvia. *Mexican Gothic*
Moreno-Garcia, Silvia. ★*Velvet Was the Night*
Pynchon, Thomas. *Against the Day: A Novel*
Shaara, Jeff. *Gone for Soldiers*
Solares, Martin. *The Black Minutes*

Solares, Martin. *Don't Send Flowers*
Stapley, Marissa. *The Last Resort*
Steinbeck, John. *The Pearl*
Traven, B. ★*The Treasure of the Sierra Madre*
Urrea, Luis Alberto. *The Hummingbird's Daughter: A Novel*
Urrea, Luis Alberto. *Into the Beautiful North: A Novel*
Vlautin, Willy. *Don't Skip Out on Me*
Winslow, Don. *The Border*

MEXICO CITY
Bolano, Roberto. ★*The Savage Detectives*
Moreno-Garcia, Silvia. ★*Velvet Was the Night*

Meyer, Deon
Icarus

Meyer, Nicholas
The Adventure of the Peculiar Protocols: Adapted from the Journals of John H. Watson, M.D.

Meyer, Philipp
★*The Son: A Novel*

Meyerson, Amy
The Imperfects

MIAMI BEACH, FLORIDA
Preston, Douglas J. *Verses for the Dead*

MIAMI, FLORIDA
Abu-Jaber, Diana. *Birds of Paradise: A Novel*
Ashley & JaQuavis. *The Cartel*
Banks, Russell. *Continental Drift*
Buchanan, Edna. *You Only Die Twice: A Britt Montero Mystery*
Cleeton, Chanel. *Next Year in Havana*
Crucet, Jennine Capo. *Make Your Home Among Strangers*
Danticat, Edwidge. ★*Everything Inside: Stories*
De Leon, Aya. *Side Chick Nation*
Garcia, Cristina. *King of Cuba: A Novel*
Garcia, Gabriela. *Of Women and Salt*
Grippando, James. *The Girl in the Glass Box*
Gruber, Michael. *Night of the Jaguar: A Novel*
Gruber, Michael. *Valley of Bones: A Novel*
Leonard, Elmore. *Glitz*
MacDonald, John D. ★*The Lonely Silver Rain*
Monroe, Mary. *God Still Don't Like Ugly*
Pineiro, Caridad. *South Beach Love: A Feel-Good Romance from Hallmark Publishing*
Spillane, Mickey. *The Consummata*
Spillane, Mickey. *Kill Me, Darling*
Wolfe, Tom. *Back to Blood: A Novel*

Michael Kelly mysteries [Series]. Harvey, Michael T.

MICHAL (BIBLICAL FIGURE)
Edghill, India. *Queenmaker: A Novel of King David's Queen*

MICHELANGELO BUONARROTI
Stone, Irving. ★*The Agony and the Ecstasy: A Biographical Novel of Michelangelo*
Whitehead, Colson. *John Henry Days: A Novel*

Michener, James A.
★*The Bridges at Toko-Ri*
Caribbean
★*Centennial*
Chesapeake
Space
★*Tales of the South Pacific*

MICHIGAN
Acampora, Lauren. *The Paper Wasp: A Novel*
Antoinette, Ashley. *Butterfly.; Vol 2*
Antoinette, Ashley. *Butterfly.; Vol 3*
Bartels, Erin. *We Hope for Better Things*
Baxter, Charles. *The Feast of Love*
Baxter, Charles. *Saul and Patsy*
Buntin, Julie. ★*Marlena: A Novel*
Cameron, W. Bruce. *Repo Madness*
Campbell, Bonnie Jo. *Once Upon a River*
Cleage, Pearl. *What Looks Like Crazy on an Ordinary Day: A Novel*
Dev, Sonali. ★*A Bollywood Affair*
Dionne, Karen. *The Wicked Sister*
Estleman, Loren D. ★*Amos Walker: The Complete Story Collection*
Estleman, Loren D. *Infernal Angels*
Eugenides, Jeffrey. ★*Middlesex*
Eugenides, Jeffrey. ★*The Virgin Suicides*
Gray, Anissa. *The Care and Feeding of Ravenously Hungry Girls*
Harrison, Jim. *The Great Leader*
Heiny, Katherine. ★*Early Morning Riser*
Malerman, Josh. *Malorie: A Bird Box Novel*
McFarland, Jeni. *The House of Deep Water*
Niffenegger, Audrey. *The Time Traveler's Wife: A Novel*
Oates, Joyce Carol. ★*Them*
Russell, Mary Doria. *The Women of the Copper Country: A Novel*
Shipman, Viola. *The Clover Girls*
Shipman, Viola. *The Heirloom Garden*
Weiner, Jennifer. ★*Mrs. Everything: A Novel*

Mickey Haller novels [Series]. Connelly, Michael

MICROAGGRESSIONS
Harris, Zakiya Dalila. *The Other Black Girl: A Novel*

MICRONESIA
Endicott, Marina. *The Voyage of the Morning Light*

MICROORGANISMS
Wilson, Daniel H. *The Andromeda Evolution: A Novel*

MIDDLE AGE
Doyle, Roddy. *The Guts*
Kane, Jessica Francis. *Rules for Visiting*

MIDDLE AGED WOMEN
Bushnell, Candace. *Is There Still Sex in the City?*

Middle C. Gass, William H.

MIDDLE CLASS
Austen, Jane. *Mansfield Park*
Desai, Anita. *Clear Light of Day*
Forster, E. M. ★*A Room with a View*
Mann, Thomas. *Buddenbrooks*
McFarland, Jeni. *The House of Deep Water*
Sexton, Margaret Wilkerson. *A Kind of Freedom*

MIDDLE CLASS AFRICAN AMERICANS
Randall, Alice. ★*Black Bottom Saints*
West, Dorothy. *The Wedding*

MIDDLE CLASS FAMILIES
Ferrante, Elena. *The Lying Life of Adults*
Galsworthy, John. ★*The Forsyte Saga*
Lerner, Ben. ★*The Topeka School*
Levy, Deborah. *Swimming Home: A Novel*
McDermott, Alice. *After This*
Shields, Carol. ★*The Stone Diaries*

Tarkington, Booth. ★*Alice Adams*

MIDDLE CLASS MEN

Lewis, Sinclair. *Babbitt*

MIDDLE CLASS TEENAGE GIRLS

Sittenfeld, Curtis. *Prep: A Novel*

MIDDLE CLASS WOMEN

Larsen, Nella. *Passing*

MIDDLE EARTH (IMAGINARY PLACE)

Tolkien, J. R. R. *The Fellowship of the Ring: Being the First Part of the Lord of the Rings*

Tolkien, J. R. R. *The Return of the King: Being the Third Part of the Lord of the Rings*

Tolkien, J. R. R. *The Silmarillion*

Tolkien, J. R. R. *The Two Towers: Being the Second Part of the Lord of the Rings*

MIDDLE EAST

Cumming, Charles. *A Colder War*

Demirtas, Selahattin. *Dawn: Stories*

Ferraris, Zoe. *Finding Nouf*

Ferraris, Zoe. *Kingdom of Strangers: A Novel*

Hayes, Terry. *I Am Pilgrim*

Hunter, Stephen. *Game of Snipers: A Bob Lee Swagger Novel*

Ricciardi, David. *Warning Light*

Robbins, Tom. *Fierce Invalids Home from Hot Climates*

Russell, Mary Doria. *Dreamers of the Day: A Novel*

Silva, Daniel. ★*The Kill Artist: A Novel*

Wecker, Helene. ★*The Hidden Palace*

Wilson, G. Willow. *Alif the Unseen*

MIDDLE EASTERN-INFLUENCED FANTASY

Bear, Elizabeth. *Range of Ghosts*

Bear, Elizabeth. *Shattered Pillars*

Bear, Elizabeth. *Steles of the Sky*

Chakraborty, S. A. *The City of Brass*

Chakraborty, S. A. *The Kingdom of Copper: A Novel*

Wecker, Helene. *The Golem and the Jinni*

Wecker, Helene. ★*The Hidden Palace*

Wilson, G. Willow. *Alif the Unseen*

Wilson, G. Willow. ★*The Bird King*

★*Middle* Passage. Johnson, Charles Richard

MIDDLE PASSAGE (ATLANTIC SLAVE TRADE)

Johnson, Charles Richard. ★*Middle Passage*

MIDDLE SCHOOL STUDENTS

Minato, Kanae. *Confessions*

MIDDLE SCHOOL TEACHERS

Bynum, Sarah Shun-Lien. *Ms. Hempel Chronicles*

MIDDLE SCHOOLS

Minato, Kanae. *Confessions*

MIDDLE WEST

Attenberg, Jami. *The Middlesteins*

Bellow, Saul. *Ravelstein*

Bender, Tony. *The Last Ghost Dancer*

Braun, Lilian Jackson. *The Cat Who Ate Danish Modern*

Child, Lee. *One Shot*

Childs, Laura. *Egg Shooters*

Dean, Pamela. *Tam Lin*

DeLillo, Don. ★*White Noise*

Franzen, Jonathan. ★*The Corrections*

Gass, William H. *Middle C*

Hamilton, Jane. *A Map of the World*

Hunt, Laird. *Zorrie*

King, Stephen. *End of Watch: A Novel*

King, Stephen. *Finders Keepers*

King, Stephen. *Mr. Mercedes: A Novel*

Lerner, Ben. ★*The Topeka School*

Markley, Stephen. *Ohio*

Palahniuk, Chuck. *Pygmy*

Patterson, Richard North. *Dark Lady*

Stradal, J. Ryan. ★*The Lager Queen of Minnesota*

Taylor, Brandon. ★*Filthy Animals*

Taylor, Brandon. ★*Real Life*

Turow, Scott. *Presumed Innocent*

MIDDLE-AGED COUPLES

Guillory, Jasmine. *Royal Holiday*

MIDDLE-AGED MEN

Barnes, Julian. ★*The Sense of an Ending*

Barthelme, Frederick. *Elroy Nights*

Bellow, Saul. ★*Henderson the Rain King: A Novel*

Bellow, Saul. ★*Seize the Day*

Brodesser-Akner, Taffy. *Fleishman Is in Trouble: A Novel*

Brown, Larry. *Joe: A Novel*

Coetzee, J. M. *Disgrace*

Cooper, Tom. *Florida Man*

Dostoyevsky, Fyodor. *Notes from Underground*

Doyle, Roddy. *The Guts*

Doyle, Roddy. *Love*

Ellis, Bret Easton. *Imperial Bedrooms*

Freeman, Castle. *All That I Have: A Novel*

Greer, Andrew Sean. ★*Less*

Grossman, David. *Be My Knife*

Heller, Joseph. *Good as Gold*

Hesse, Hermann. ★*Steppenwolf*

Jackson, Charles. *The Lost Weekend*

Lewis, Sinclair. *Dodsworth*

MacDonald, John D. ★*The Lonely Silver Rain*

Maugham, W. Somerset. *The Moon and Sixpence*

Moore, Alison. *The Lighthouse*

Naipaul, V. S. *A House for Mr. Biswas*

Naipaul, V. S. *Magic Seeds*

Nicholls, David. *US: A Novel*

Oz, Amos. *Fima*

Potok, Chaim. ★*The Gift of Asher Lev*

Price, Reynolds. *The Good Priest's Son*

Robotham, Michael. ★*Suspect*

Roth, Philip. ★*The Anatomy Lesson*

Russo, Richard. *Straight Man*

Smith, Ali. *There but for The: A Novel*

Smith, Michael F. *The Fighter: A Novel*

Sparks, Nicholas. *A Walk to Remember*

Tyler, Anne. ★*Redhead by the Side of the Road*

Updike, John. ★*Rabbit Is Rich: A Novel*

MIDDLE-AGED MEN — FAMILY RELATIONSHIPS

Auster, Paul. *The Brooklyn Follies*

MIDDLE-AGED MEN — RELATIONS WITH YOUNGER MEN

Hall, Alexis. *For Real*

MIDDLE-AGED MEN — RELATIONS WITH YOUNGER WOMEN
Momaday, N. Scott. *The Ancient Child: A Novel*
MIDDLE-AGED PERSONS
Benjamin, Ali. *The Smash-Up: A Novel*
Le Carre, John. *Agent Running in the Field*
Updike, John. *The Afterlife and Other Stories*
MIDDLE-AGED WOMEN
Atwood, Margaret. *Life Before Man*
Brown, Eleanor. *The Weird Sisters*
Doyle, Roddy. ★*The Woman Who Walked into Doors*
Enright, Anne. ★*The Gathering*
Ferrante, Elena. *The Story of the Lost Child*
French, Marilyn. ★*The Women's Room*
Gaitskill, Mary. *Veronica*
Gardner, Lisa. ★*Before She Disappeared: A Novel*
Gelman, Laurie. *Class Mom: A Novel*
Gelman, Laurie. *Yoga Pant Nation: A Novel*
Gelman, Laurie. *You've Been Volunteered: A Class Mom Novel*
Grossman, David. *Be My Knife*
Hadley, Tessa. *Clever Girl*
Heller, Zoe. *What Was She Thinking?: Notes on a Scandal*
Huang, S. L. *Burning Roses*
Joyce, Rachel. *Miss Benson's Beetle*
Lahiri, Jhumpa. ★*Whereabouts*
Mangan, Christine. *Palace of the Drowned*
McCall Smith, Alexander. *The Comforts of a Muddy Saturday: An Isabel Dalhousie Novel*
Pearson, Allison. ★*How Hard Can It Be?*
Porter, Katherine Anne. *Ship of Fools*
Rinehart, Mary Roberts. *The Circular Staircase*
Saunders, Kate. *The Case of the Wandering Scholar*
Saunders, Kate. *The Secrets of Wishtide*
Sebold, Alice. *The Almost Moon: A Novel*
Solomon, Asali. *The Days of Afrekete*
Spark, Muriel. ★*The Prime of Miss Jean Brodie*
Spiotta, Dana. *Wayward*
Waite, Olivia. *The Care and Feeding of Waspish Widows*
Waller, Robert James. ★*The Bridges of Madison County*
Welty, Eudora. *The Optimist's Daughter*
Williams, Tennessee. ★*The Roman Spring of Mrs. Stone*
Wojtas, Olga. *Miss Blaine's Prefect and the Golden Samovar*
Woolf, Virginia. ★*Mrs. Dalloway*
MIDDLE-AGED WOMEN — FRIENDSHIP
Wells, Rebecca. *Divine Secrets of the Ya-Ya Sisterhood: A Novel*
MIDDLE-AGED WOMEN — RELATIONS WITH YOUNGER MEN
Hornby, Nick. *Just Like You*
Lurie, Alison. *Foreign Affairs*
MIDDLE-AGED WOMEN — SEXUALITY
Goldbloom, Goldie. *On Division*
★*Middlegame*. McGuire, Seanan
The Middleman. Steinhauer, Olen
★*Middlemarch: a Study of Provincial Life*. Eliot, George
★*Middlesex*. Eugenides, Jeffrey
The Middlesteins. Attenberg, Jami
MIDLIFE CRISIS
Barthelme, Frederick. *Elroy Nights*

Bowman, Conor. ★*Horace Winter Says Goodbye*
Kunzru, Hari. *Red Pill: A Novel*
Leithauser, Brad. *The Promise of Elsewhere*
Shteyngart, Gary. ★*Lake Success: A Novel*
MIDLIFE CRISIS IN MEN
Banville, John. ★*Eclipse: A Novel*
Heller, Joseph. *Good as Gold*
Midnight and the Meaning of Love. Sister Souljah
★*Midnight at the Dragon Cafe*. Bates, Judy Fong
The Midnight Bargain. Polk, C. L.
The Midnight Library. Haig, Matt
The Midnight Line. Child, Lee
Midnight Riot. Aaronovitch, Ben
Midnight series [Series]. Sister Souljah
Midnight Voices. Saul, John
★*Midnight's Children: A Novel*. Rushdie, Salman
Midnight, Water City. McKinney, Chris
The Midwife of Hope River: A Novel. Harman, Patricia
MIDWIVES
Atakora, Afia. ★*Conjure Women*
Davidson, Ash. ★*Damnation Spring*
Elison, Meg. *The Book of Etta*
Elison, Meg. *The Book of the Unnamed Midwife*
Gibbons, Kaye. *Charms for the Easy Life*
Green, Jocelyn. *The Mark of the King*
Gregory, Philippa. *Tidelands*
Harman, Patricia. *The Midwife of Hope River: A Novel*
Hepworth, Sally. *The Secrets of Midwives*
Phillips, Susan Elizabeth. ★*Dance Away with Me*
Thompson, Victoria. *Murder on Wall Street*
Wood, Shelley. *The Quintland Sisters*
Mieville, China
★*The City & The City*
Embassytown
★*Perdido Street Station*
MIGRANT AGRICULTURAL LABORERS
Steinbeck, John. ★*The Grapes of Wrath*
MIGRANT WORKERS
Aw, Tash. *We, the Survivors*
Chen, Qiufan. *Waste Tide*
Locke, Attica. *The Cutting Season*
Spencer-Fleming, Julia. *I Shall Not Want: A Clare Fergusson/Russ Van Alstyne Mystery*
Steinbeck, John. ★*Of Mice and Men*
Migrations. McConaghy, Charlotte
Mihalic, Susan
Dark Horses
Mike Bowditch novels [Series]. Doiron, Paul
Mike Hammer mysteries [Series]. Spillane, Mickey
Milan, Courtney
The Duchess War
MILAN, ITALY
Eco, Umberto. *The Mysterious Flame of Queen Loana: An Illustrated Novel*
Scerbanenco, Giorgio. *A Private Venus*
Scerbanenco, Giorgio. *Traitors to All*
Milano quartet [Series]. Scerbanenco, Giorgio

Miles, Jonathan
Anatomy of a Miracle
Miles, Terry
Rabbits
MILITANTS
Bolano, Roberto. ★*The Savage Detectives*
Golden, Christopher. *The Pandora Room: A Novel*
MILITARY AIRCRAFT — HISTORY
Shaara, Jeff. *The Rising Tide: A Novel of World War II*
MILITARY BASES, AMERICAN
Abrams, David. *Fobbit*
Michener, James A. ★*Tales of the South Pacific*
MILITARY CADETS
Leon, Donna. *Uniform Justice*
Vargas Llosa, Mario. *The Time of the Hero*
MILITARY CAMPAIGNS
Forester, C. S. *Commodore Hornblower*
Jones, James. ★*The Thin Red Line*
Keneally, Thomas. ★*The Daughters of Mars*
Monsarrat, Nicholas. *The Cruel Sea*
Tolstoy, Leo. ★*War and Peace*
MILITARY DEPENDENTS
Bird, Sarah. *The Yokota Officers Club: A Novel*
MILITARY EDUCATION — ISRAEL
Boianjiu, Shani. *The People of Forever Are Not Afraid: A Novel*
MILITARY FANTASY
Clark, Cherae. ★*The Unbroken*
Kuang, R. F. ★*The Dragon Republic*
Kuang, R. F. *The Poppy War*
Novik, Naomi. *His Majesty's Dragon*
MILITARY HOSPITALS
Barker, Pat. ★*Regeneration*
MILITARY INTELLIGENCE
Coughlin, Jack. *Long Shot: A Sniper Novel*
Ellroy, James. *This Storm: A Novel*
Follett, Ken. *Jackdaws*
Taylor, Brad. ★*Daughter of War: A Novel*
MILITARY INTELLIGENCE — HISTORY
Follett, Ken. *Hornet Flight*
MILITARY INTERROGATION
Sofer, Dalia. *Man of My Time*
MILITARY JOURNALISM
Abrams, David. *Fobbit*
MILITARY LIFE
Boianjiu, Shani. *The People of Forever Are Not Afraid: A Novel*
Fallon, Siobhan. *You Know When the Men Are Gone*
McCullers, Carson. *Reflections in a Golden Eye*
Novik, Naomi. *His Majesty's Dragon*
Powers, Kevin. ★*The Yellow Birds: A Novel*
MILITARY MISSIONS
Cobbs Hoffman, Elizabeth. *The Tubman Command: A Novel*
Giordano, Paolo. *The Human Body*
Heller, Joseph. ★*Catch-22*
Lafferty, Mur. *Six Wakes*
Taylor, Brad. ★*Daughter of War: A Novel*
MILITARY NURSES
Keneally, Thomas. ★*The Daughters of Mars*

MILITARY OCCUPATION
Abulhawa, Susan. *The Blue Between Sky and Water*
Campbell, Rick. *Treason*
Couto, Mia. *The Sword and the Spear*
Escobar, Mario. *The Librarian of Saint-Malo: A Novel*
Feldman, Ellen. *Paris Never Leaves You*
Hahn, Sumi. *The Mermaid from Jeju: A Novel*
Harmel, Kristin. *The Room on Rue Amelie*
Mengiste, Maaza. ★*The Shadow King: A Novel*
Pattison, Eliot. *Bones of the Earth: An Inspector Shan Tao Yun Mystery*
Pike, Signe. *The Forgotten Kingdom: A Novel*
MILITARY PHYSICIANS
Scottoline, Lisa. *Don't Go*
MILITARY PILOTS
Bohjalian, Chris. *Skeletons at the Feast: A Novel*
MILITARY POLICE
Benn, James R. ★*The Red Horse: A Billy Boyle World War II Mystery*
Benn, James R. *Road of Bones: A Billy Boyle World War II Mystery*
Child, Lee. *The Enemy: A Jack Reacher Novel*
DeMille, Nelson. ★*The Deserter: A Novel*
Limon, Martin. *War Women*
MILITARY SCIENCE FICTION
Haldeman, Joe W. ★*The Forever War*
Hurley, Kameron. ★*The Light Brigade*
Lee, Yoon Ha. *Ninefox Gambit*
Lee, Yoon Ha. *Raven Stratagem*
Lee, Yoon Ha. *Revenant Gun*
Lewis, Linden A. *The First Sister: A Novel*
Scalzi, John. ★*Old Man's War*
Wagers, K. B. *Hold Fast Through the Fire*
Wagers, K. B. *A Pale Light in the Black: A Neog Novel*
MILITARY SECRETS
L'Amour, Louis. *The Last of the Breed*
MILITARY SERVICE
De Robertis, Carolina. *Perla*
Stewart, Amy. ★*Dear Miss Kopp*
Stewart, Amy. *Kopp Sisters on the March*
MILITARY SPOUSES
Fallon, Siobhan. *You Know When the Men Are Gone*
Gillham, David R. *City of Women*
MILITARY STRATEGY
Lee, Yoon Ha. *Raven Stratagem*
MILITARY SURGEONS
O'Dell, Claire. *A Study in Honor: A Novel*
MILITARY TACTICS
Clancy, Tom. *Patriot Games*
Novik, Naomi. *His Majesty's Dragon*
MILITARY TRAINING CAMPS
Stewart, Amy. *Kopp Sisters on the March*
MILITIA MOVEMENT
Hiaasen, Carl. *Lucky You: A Novel*
MILITIAS AND IRREGULAR ARMIES
Gabaldon, Diana. ★*The Fiery Cross*
Hage, Rawi. *De Niro's Game*
Milk Blood Heat. Moniz, Dantiel W.
Milk Fed. Broder, Melissa
Milkman: a Novel. Burns, Anna

★The **Mill** on the Floss. Eliot, George
MILL TOWNS
    Luchette, Claire. *Agatha of Little Neon*
MILLENNIALS
    Hamya, Jo. *Three Rooms*
Millennium novels (Stieg Larsson) [Series]. Lagercrantz, David
***Millennium** People*. Ballard, J. G.
***Miller's** Valley*. Quindlen, Anna
Miller, Andrew
    Oxygen
Miller, Derek B.
    ★*American by Day*
    ★*The Girl in Green*
    How to Find Your Way in the Dark
Miller, Henry
    ★*Tropic of Cancer*
    ★*Tropic of Capricorn*
MILLER, HENRY
    Bates, Judy Fong. ★*Midnight at the Dragon Cafe*
    Miller, Henry. ★*Tropic of Cancer*
    Miller, Henry. ★*Tropic of Capricorn*
    Spencer, Sally. *The Ring of Death*
Miller, Holly
    ★*The Sight of You*
Miller, Karen E. Quinones
    An Angry-Ass Black Woman
MILLER, KAREN E. QUINONES
    Miller, Karen E. Quinones. *An Angry-Ass Black Woman*
Miller, Kei
    ★*Augustown*
MILLER, LEE, 1907-1977
    Cole, Alyssa. ★*An Unconditional Freedom*
    Scharer, Whitney. *The Age of Light*
Miller, Madeline
    ★*Circe*
    The Song of Achilles
Miller, Mary
    Biloxi: A Novel
Miller, Rebecca
    ★*Jacob's Folly: A Novel*
Miller, Sue
    The Good Mother
    ★*Monogamy*
    The Senator's Wife
Miller, Walter M.
    ★*A Canticle for Leibowitz*
Miller, Xander
    Zo: A Novel
Millhauser, Steven
    Martin Dressler: The Tale of an American Dreamer
MILLHONE, KINSEY (FICTITIOUS CHARACTER)
    Grafton, Sue. *X*
*A **Million** Aunties*. McKenzie, Alecia
*A **Million** Nightingales*. Straight, Susan
MILLIONAIRES
    Bellow, Saul. ★*Henderson the Rain King: A Novel*
    Christie, Agatha. ★*And Then There Were None*
    Evanovich, Stephanie. *Under the Table*

    Kress, Nancy. *Beggars in Spain*
    Sanders, Lawrence. *The Tenth Commandment: A Novel*
MILLS AND MILLWORK — HISTORY
    Shreve, Anita. *Fortune's Rocks: A Novel*
Milo Milodragovitch mysteries [Series]. Crumley, James
Milo Weaver trilogy [Series]. Steinhauer, Olen
MILWAUKEE, WISCONSIN
    Petrie, Nicholas. *The Breaker*
    Petrie, Nicholas. *The Drifter*
*The **Mime** Order*. Shannon, Samantha
Mina, Denise
    Conviction
    The Less Dead
    ★*Rizzio*
Minato, Kanae
    Confessions
MIND CONTROL
    Asimov, Isaac. *Foundation and Empire*
    Asimov, Isaac. *Second Foundation*
    Glynn, Alan. *Receptor*
    Grant, Mira. *Feed*
★***Mind** Prey*. Sandford, John
MIND TRANSFERS
    Soule, Charles. ★*Anyone*
***Mindsword's** Story*. Saberhagen, Fred
MINERAL INDUSTRY AND TRADE
    Stanley, Michael. *A Death in the Family*
MINERS
    Harvey, John. *Darkness, Darkness*
    Pronzini, Bill. *The Stolen Gold Affair*
MINES AND MINERAL RESOURCES
    Brown, Pierce. *Golden Son*
    Brown, Pierce. *Red Rising*
    Knott, Robert. *Robert B. Parker's Buckskin*
    McDonald, Ian. *New Moon*
    Pronzini, Bill. *The Stolen Gold Affair*
    Spencer, Sally. *Lambs to the Slaughter*
    Stabenow, Dana. *Whisper to the Blood: A Kate Shugak Novel*
Minh, Drew
    Neon Empire
MINIATURE OBJECTS
    Burton, Jessie. *The Miniaturist*
MINIATURE PERSONS (IMAGINARY CHARACTERS)
    Swift, Jonathan. ★*Gulliver's Travels*
*The **Miniaturist***. Burton, Jessie
MINING ENGINEERS
    Buchan, John. *The Thirty-Nine Steps*
    Smith, Martin Cruz. *Rose*
★*The **Ministry** for the Future*. Robinson, Kim Stanley
*The **Ministry** of Special Cases*. Englander, Nathan
★*The **Ministry** of Utmost Happiness: A Novel*. Roy, Arundhati
MINNEAPOLIS, MINNESOTA
    Baxter, Charles. ★*The Sun Collective*
    Baxter, Charles. *There's Something I Want You to Do: Stories*
    Dean, Pamela. *Tam Lin*
    Erdrich, Louise. *Four Souls: A Novel*
    Erdrich, Louise. ★*The Sentence*
    Hunter, Stephen. *Soft Target: A Thriller*

James, Lorelei. *I Want You Back*
Sandford, John. *Broken Prey*
Sandford, John. *Certain Prey*
Sandford, John. *Chosen Prey*
Sandford, John. *Easy Prey*
Sandford, John. *Hidden Prey*
Sandford, John. ★*Invisible Prey*
Sandford, John. ★*Mind Prey*
Sandford, John. *Mortal Prey*
Sandford, John. ★*Naked Prey*
Sandford, John. ★*Phantom Prey*
Sandford, John. *Sudden Prey*

MINNESOTA
Dang, Catherine. *Nice Girls*
Enger, Leif. *Virgil Wander*
Enger, Lin. *Undiscovered Country: A Novel*
Erdrich, Louise. *Future Home of the Living God*
Erdrich, Louise. ★*The Sentence*
Fluke, Joanne. ★*Christmas Cupcake Murder*
Freeman, Brian. *Goodbye to the Dead*
Freeman, Brian. *Marathon*
Freeman, Brian. *Thief River Falls*
Fridlund, Emily. ★*History of Wolves: A Novel*
Goldman, Matt. *The Shallows*
Green, Amy Lynn. *Things We Didn't Say*
Johnston, Tim. *The Current: A Novel*
Krueger, William Kent. ★*Lightning Strike*
Krueger, William Kent. *This Tender Land: A Novel*
Landvik, Lorna. *Chronicles of a Radical Hag: With Recipes*
Lewis, Sinclair. ★*Main Street: The Story of Carol Kennicott*
Lourey, Jess. ★*January Thaw: A Murder-By-Month Mystery*
Reimringer, John. *Vestments*
Sandford, John. *Bloody Genius*
Sandford, John. *Broken Prey*
Sandford, John. *Buried Prey*
Sandford, John. *Certain Prey*
Sandford, John. *Chosen Prey*
Sandford, John. ★*Deadline*
Sandford, John. *Deep Freeze*
Sandford, John. *Easy Prey*
Sandford, John. *Field of Prey*
Sandford, John. *Heat Lightning*
Sandford, John. *Hidden Prey*
Sandford, John. *Holy Ghost*
Sandford, John. ★*Invisible Prey*
Sandford, John. ★*Mind Prey*
Sandford, John. *Mortal Prey*
Sandford, John. ★*Naked Prey*
Sandford, John. ★*Night Prey*
Sandford, John. ★*Phantom Prey*
Sandford, John. ★*Rules of Prey*
Sandford, John. *Shock Wave*
Sandford, John. ★*Silken Prey*
Sandford, John. *Storm Front*
Sandford, John. *Storm Prey*
Sandford, John. *Sudden Prey*
Staples, Dennis E. *This Town Sleeps*
Stradal, J. Ryan. ★*The Lager Queen of Minnesota*

Sundstol, Vidar. *The Land of Dreams*
Tracy, P. J. *Ice Cold Heart*
West, Kathleen. *Minor Dramas & Other Catastrophes*
Minnesota trilogy [Series]. Sundstol, Vidar
Minor Dramas & Other Catastrophes. West, Kathleen
*The **Minority** Report*. Dick, Philip K.
MINOTAUR (GREEK MYTHOLOGY)
Renault, Mary. *The Bull from the Sea*
Renault, Mary. *The King Must Die*
Saint, Jennifer. *Ariadne*
Sherrill, Steven. *The Minotaur Takes His Own Sweet Time: A Novel*
Minotaur novels [Series]. Sherrill, Steven
*The **Minotaur** Takes His Own Sweet Time: A Novel*. Sherrill, Steven
*The **Minotaur**: a Novel*. Vine, Barbara
*A **Minute** to Midnight*. Baldacci, David
Miracle Creek. Kim, Angie
Miracle on 34th Street. Davies, Valentine
MIRACLES
Binchy, Maeve. ★*Whitethorn Woods*
Donoghue, Emma. ★*The Wonder*
Miles, Jonathan. *Anatomy of a Miracle*
Picoult, Jodi. *Keeping Faith: A Novel*
*The **Miracles** of the Namiya General Store*. Higashino, Keigo
Mirrorland. Johnstone, Carole
MIRRORS
Oyeyemi, Helen. *Boy, Snow, Bird: A Novel*
MISADVENTURES
Adams, Douglas. *Dirk Gently's Holistic Detective Agency*
Adams, Douglas. ★*The Hitchhiker's Guide to the Galaxy*
Adams, Douglas. *The Restaurant at the End of the Universe*
Barry, Dave. *Insane City*
Barry, Dave. *Lunatics*
Dickens, Charles. *The Pickwick Papers*
Faulks, Sebastian. *Jeeves and the Wedding Bells*
Russo, Richard. ★*Everybody's Fool*
Russo, Richard. *The Risk Pool*
Smith, Zadie. *The Autograph Man: A Novel*
Spufford, Francis. ★*Golden Hill*
Steinbeck, John. *Tortilla Flat*
Waugh, Evelyn. *Decline and Fall*
Wodehouse, P. G. *My Man Jeeves*
MISANTHROPY
Barnett, David. *Calling Major Tom*
MISCARRIAGE
Davidson, Ash. ★*Damnation Spring*
Endicott, Marina. *The Voyage of the Morning Light*
Hoffmann, R. J. *Other People's Children: A Novel*
Mahmoud, Lena. *Amreekiya: A Novel*
Riley, Lucinda. *The Girl on the Cliff: A Novel*
Mischling: a Novel. Konar, Affinity
MISERLINESS
Dickens, Charles. ★*A Christmas Carol*
★*Misery*. King, Stephen
MISFITS (PERSONS)
Banks, Russell. *Lost Memory of Skin*
Brom. *Slewfoot: A Tale of Bewitchery*
Bruni, Sarah. *The Night Gwen Stacy Died*
Capote, Truman. ★*Breakfast at Tiffany's*

Coetzee, J. M. *Summertime: Scenes from a Provincial Life*
Collins, Ciaran. *The Gamal*
Crummey, Michael. *Sweetland*
Diaz, Junot. ★*The Brief Wondrous Life of Oscar Wao*
Drabble, Margaret. *The Witch of Exmoor*
Dugoni, Robert. ★*The Extraordinary Life of Sam Hell*
Emezi, Akwaeke. ★*The Death of Vivek Oji*
Eugenides, Jeffrey. *Fresh Complaint: Stories*
Extence, Gavin. *The Universe Versus Alex Woods*
Faulkner, William. ★*Light in August*
Fforde, Jasper. ★*Early Riser: A Novel*
Forbes, Curdella. *A Tall History of Sugar*
Hage, Rawi. *Beirut Hellfire Society: A Novel*
Hand, Elizabeth. *Curious Toys*
Headley, Maria Dahvana. *The Mere Wife*
Henderson, Susan. *The Flicker of Old Dreams*
Irving, John. ★*A Prayer for Owen Meany: A Novel*
Layne, Lauren. *Passion on Park Avenue*
Lessing, Doris May. ★*The Fifth Child*
Maaren, Kari. ★*Weave a Circle Round*
Majors, Inman. *Penelope Lemon: Game On!*
Mason, Bobbie Ann. *Dear Ann: A Novel*
McCullers, Carson. ★*The Heart Is a Lonely Hunter*
Murata, Sayaka. *Earthlings: A Novel*
Novik, Naomi. *A Deadly Education: A Novel*
Pearlman, Edith. *Honeydew: Stories*
Phillips, Caryl. *A View of the Empire at Sunset*
Racculia, Kate. ★*Tuesday Mooney Talks to Ghosts: A Novel*
Rash, Ron. ★*The Cove*
Roy, Arundhati. ★*The Ministry of Utmost Happiness: A Novel*
Saunders, George. ★*Tenth of December: Stories*
Schlink, Bernhard. *Olga*
Solomon, Rivers. *An Unkindness of Ghosts*
Spencer, Minerva. *Dangerous*
Steinbeck, John. *Cannery Row*
Stewart, Mary. ★*The Crystal Cave*
Swarthout, Glendon. *Bless the Beasts and Children*
Tartt, Donna. ★*The Goldfinch*
Thorpe, Rufi. ★*The Knockout Queen*
Von Ziegesar, Cecily. *Cobble Hill*
Watson, Brad. *Miss Jane: A Novel*
Whitehead, Colson. *Sag Harbor: A Novel*
Woods, Chavisa. *Things to Do When You're Goth in the Country: And Other Stories*
Young, Heather. *The Distant Dead*
Misfits of Mayfair [Series]. Bennett, Bethany
Mishima, Yukio
   The Sound of Waves
   Spring Snow
   The Temple of Dawn
MISOGYNY
   Cho, Nam-Ju. ★*Kim Jiyoung, Born 1982*
   Dangarembga, Tsitsi. *This Mournable Body*
   Galchen, Rivka. *Everyone Knows Your Mother Is a Witch*
   Holton, India. *The Wisteria Society of Lady Scoundrels*
   Lutz, Lisa. *The Swallows: A Novel*
Miss Austen. Hornby, Gill
Miss Benson's Beetle. Joyce, Rachel

Miss Blaine's Prefect and the Golden Samovar. Wojtas, Olga
Miss Blaine's prefect [Series]. Wojtas, Olga
Miss Burma. Craig, Charmaine
Miss Jane: A Novel. Watson, Brad
Miss Julia Delivers the Goods: A Novel. Ross, Ann B.
★*Miss Julia Happily Ever After*. Ross, Ann B.
Miss Julia Knows a Thing or Two. Ross, Ann B
Miss Julia series [Series]. Ross, Ann B.
Miss Julia Takes the Wheel. Ross, Ann B.
Miss Julia Throws a Wedding. Ross, Ann B.
★*Miss Kopp Investigates*. Stewart, Amy
★*Miss Kopp Just Won't Quit*. Stewart, Amy
Miss Kopp's Midnight Confessions. Stewart, Amy
Miss Lattimore's Letter. Allain, Suzanne
MISS MARTIN'S SCHOOL FOR GIRLS (IMAGINARY PLACE)
   Balogh, Mary. *Simply Love*
Miss Pinkerton. Rinehart, Mary Roberts
Miss Wonderful. Chase, Loretta Lynda
*The **Missing***. Lewis, Beverly
*The **Missing** American*. Quartey, Kwei
MISSING BOYS
   Ahlborn, Ania. *The Devil Crept In*
   Buehlman, Christopher. *The Suicide Motor Club*
   Ellis, Bret Easton. *Lunar Park*
   James, Marlon. ★*Black Leopard, Red Wolf*
   Locke, Attica. ★*Heaven, My Home*
   Porter, Max. ★*Lanny: A Novel*
   Rader-Day, Lori. *The Day I Died*
   Schwarz, Liese O'Halloran. *What Could Be Saved*
MISSING CHILDREN
   Anappara, Deepa. *Djinn Patrol on the Purple Line: A Novel*
   Beck, Haylen. *Here and Gone*
   Bock, Charles. *Beautiful Children: A Novel*
   Candlish, Louise. *Our House*
   Child, Lee. *Worth Dying For: A Reacher Novel*
   Corby, Gary. *The Marathon Conspiracy*
   Corleone, Douglas. *Good as Gone*
   Danticat, Edwidge. *Claire of the Sea Light*
   Dazieri, Sandrone. *Kill the Father*
   DePoy, Phillip. *Sidewalk Saint*
   Englander, Nathan. *The Ministry of Special Cases*
   Fox, Candice. *Gone by Midnight*
   French, Nicci. ★*Blue Monday*
   Greene, Amy. *Long Man*
   Hart, John. *The Last Child*
   Macdonald, Ross. *The Underground Man*
   McCall Smith, Alexander. ★*The No. 1 Ladies' Detective Agency*
   McDermid, Val. *A Place of Execution*
   McEwan, Ian. *The Child in Time*
   McGhee, Alison. *The Opposite of Fate*
   Ohlsson, Kristina. *Unwanted: A Novel*
   Rendell, Ruth. *The Tree of Hands*
   Roy, Lori. ★*Gone Too Long: A Novel*
   Watson, Martine Fournier. *The Dream Peddler*
MISSING GIRLS
   Atkinson, Kate. ★*Case Histories*
   Burdick, Serena. *The Girls with No Names*
   Cohen, Tish. *The Summer We Lost Her: A Novel*

Corey, James S. A. *Caliban's War*
Corey, James S. A. ★*Leviathan Wakes*
Eisler, Barry. *All the Devils*
Franklin, Ariana. ★*Death and the Maiden*
Franklin, Tom. *Crooked Letter, Crooked Letter: A Novel*
Gardner, Lisa. *Love You More: A Detective D.D. Warren Novel*
Griffiths, Elly. *The Crossing Places*
Hamer, Kate. *The Girl in the Red Coat*
Hayder, Mo. *Gone*
Jones, Darynda. *A Bad Day for Sunshine*
Palahniuk, Chuck. *The Invention of Sound*
Phillips, Julia. ★*Disappearing Earth*
Rankin, Ian. *The Falls: An Inspector Rebus Novel*
Reichs, Kathy. *Bones to Ashes*
Robotham, Michael. ★*Say You're Sorry*
Sager, Riley. *The Last Time I Lied: A Novel*
Speller, Elizabeth. *The Strange Fate of Kitty Easton*
*The **Missing** Hours*. Dahl, Julia

MISSING IN ACTION
Cotterill, Colin. *Slash and Burn: A Dr. Siri Mystery Set in Laos*
Dybek, Nick. *The Verdun Affair: A Novel*
Missing Isaac. Luesse, Valerie Fraser

MISSING MEN
Baxter, Charles. ★*The Sun Collective*
Candlish, Louise. *Our House*
Carr, Brian Allen. ★*Opioid, Indiana*
Chavez, Heather. *No Bad Deed*
Corry, Jane. *The Dead Ex*
Coulter, Catherine. *Labyrinth*
Daugherty, Christi. *Revolver Road: A Harper McClain Mystery*
Davidson, Diane Mott. *The Last Suppers*
Dazieri, Sandrone. *Kill the King*
Dimaline, Cherie. *Empire of Wild*
Dimitri, Francesco. *The Book of Hidden Things*
Doiron, Paul. *One Last Lie*
Elliott, Lexie. *The Missing Years*
Feeney, Alice. ★*I Know Who You Are: A Novel*
Glass, Seraphina Nova. *Someone's Listening*
Gosling, Victoria. *Before the Ruins: A Novel*
Hill, Edwin J. *Little Comfort*
Kane, Darby. *Pretty Little Wife*
Limon, Martin. *War Women*
Lippman, Laura. ★*After I'm Gone*
McCall Smith, Alexander. *The Saturday Big Tent Wedding Party*
Miles, Terry. *Rabbits*
Perry, Anne. *A Question of Betrayal*
Rankin, Ian. ★*A Song for the Dark Times*
Saunders, Kate. *The Case of the Wandering Scholar*
Sharp, Zoe. *Fox Hunter*
Thomas, Bev. *A Good Enough Mother: A Novel*

MISSING PERSONS
Abdul-Jabbar, Kareem. *The Empty Birdcage*
Adler-Olsen, Jussi. *The Purity of Vengeance: A Department Q Novel*
Alfon, Dov. *A Long Night in Paris*
Atkinson, Kate. *Human Croquet*
Atkinson, Kate. ★*When Will There Be Good News?: A Novel*
Auster, Paul. ★*In the Country of Last Things*
Auster, Paul. ★*Leviathan*

Banks, Iain. *The Crow Road*
Bannalec, Jean-Luc. *The Granite Coast Murders*
Barr, Nevada. *Destroyer Angel: An Anna Pigeon Novel*
Bartz, Andrea. *The Herd: A Novel*
Bird, Sarah. *The Yokota Officers Club: A Novel*
Bolano, Roberto. ★*2666*
Briscoe, Joanna. *The Seduction*
Carter, Miranda. *The Strangler Vine*
Chandler, Raymond. *The Lady in the Lake*
Child, Lee. *Bad Luck and Trouble*
Child, Lee. *Make Me*
Child, Lee. *The Midnight Line*
Child, Lee. *Night School*
Child, Lee. *Nothing to Lose*
Child, Lee. *Persuader*
Church, James. *A Drop of Chinese Blood*
Cleland, Jane K. *Hidden Treasure*
Crumley, James. *The Last Good Kiss: A Novel*
Currie, Ron. *Flimsy Little Plastic Miracles: A True Story*
Cussler, Clive. *Blue Gold: A Novel from the Numa Files*
Dallas, Sandra. *Tallgrass*
Davys, Tim. *Amberville*
DeMille, Nelson. ★*The Deserter: A Novel*
Dexter, Colin. *The Way Through the Woods*
Didion, Joan. *A Book of Common Prayer*
Doetsch, Richard. *Half-Past Dawn*
Dugoni, Robert. *In Her Tracks*
Eco, Umberto. ★*Foucault's Pendulum*
Eco, Umberto. *The Island of the Day Before*
Englander, Nathan. *The Ministry of Special Cases*
Estleman, Loren D. ★*Indigo: A Valentino Mystery*
Estleman, Loren D. *A Smile on the Face of the Tiger*
Ferraris, Zoe. *Kingdom of Strangers: A Novel*
Finder, Joseph. *Buried Secrets*
Finder, Joseph. *Vanished*
Fox, Candice. *Crimson Lake*
Frear, Caz. *Sweet Little Lies*
French, Tana. *Faithful Place: A Novel*
Gardner, Lisa. *The Neighbor*
Graedon, Alena. *The Word Exchange: A Novel*
Grant, Helen. *The Vanishing of Katharina Linden*
Grebe, Camilla. *The Ice Beneath Her: A Novel*
Greenwood, Kerry. *Death in Daylesford*
Greenwood, Kerry. *Unnatural Habits*
Guskin, Sharon. *The Forgetting Time*
Hall, Tarquin. *The Case of the Love Commandos: From the Files of Vish Puri, India's Most Private Investigator*
Hammett, Dashiell. ★*The Thin Man*
Harris, Sarah J. *The Color of Bee Larkham's Murder: A Novel*
Harrison, Jamie. *The Center of Everything: A Novel*
Harrison, Mette Ivie. *The Bishop's Wife*
Heaberlin, Julia. *We Are All the Same in the Dark: A Novel*
Healey, Emma. ★*Elizabeth Is Missing*
Henderson, Smith. *Fourth of July Creek*
Hosking, Jay. *Three Years with the Rat: A Novel*
Indriðason, Arnaldur. *Strange Shores: An Inspector Erlendur Novel*
Kellerman, Jonathan. ★*Half Moon Bay: A Novel*
Kelman, James. *How Late It Was, How Late*

Kent, Kathleen. *The Pledge*
Kwok, Jean. *Searching for Sylvie Lee*
Larsson, Stieg. *The Girl with the Dragon Tattoo*
Laymon, Kiese. *Long Division*
Lee, Chang-Rae. ★*On Such a Full Sea*
Lutz, Lisa. *The Spellman Files: A Novel*
Macdonald, Ross. *Sleeping Beauty*
Mankell, Henning. *The Troubled Man*
Marske, Freya. *A Marvellous Light*
McLean, Felicity. *The Van Apfel Girls Are Gone*
Meuleman, Sarah. *Find Me Gone*
Mieville, China. ★*The City & The City*
Moriarty, Jaclyn. *Gravity Is the Thing*
Murakami, Haruki. *South of the Border, West of the Sun*
Ogawa, Yoko. ★*The Memory Police: A Novel*
Paretsky, Sara. *Indemnity Only: A Novel*
Penny, Louise. ★*A Better Man: A Chief Inspector Gamache Novel*
Petrie, Nicholas. *The Breaker*
Potenza, Carol. *Hearts of the Missing*
Potzsch, Oliver. *The Poisoned Pilgrim: A Hangman's Daughter Tale*
Preston, Douglas J. *The Obsidian Chamber*
Pronzini, Bill. *Fever*
Quartey, Kwei. *Wife of the Gods: A Novel*
Quinn, Spencer. ★*It's a Wonderful Woof*
Rader-Day, Lori. ★*The Lucky One*
Rankin, Ian. *The Black Book*
Reichs, Kathy. *Bones to Ashes*
Reichs, Kathy. *Break No Bones*
Rendell, Ruth. *Harm Done*
Robinson, Peter. *Close to Home*
Robinson, Peter. *In the Dark Places*
Robinson, Peter. *Strange Affair*
Robotham, Michael. ★*The Wreckage*
Shapiro, Barbara A. *The Muralist*
Shimotakahara, Leslie. *After the Bloom*
Simmons, Dan. *The Abominable: A Novel*
Slaughter, Karin. ★*Fallen: A Novel*
Smith, Julie. *House of Blues*
Smith, Martin Cruz. *Rose*
Spark, Muriel. *Aiding & Abetting*
St. James, Simone. *The Sun Down Motel*
Stanley, Michael. *Deadly Harvest*
Steiner, Susie. *Missing, Presumed: A Novel*
Straub, Peter. *Lost Boy Lost Girl: A Novel*
Sveistrup, Soren. ★*The Chestnut Man: A Novel*
Turnbull, Cadwell. *No Gods, No Monsters*
Turow, Scott. *Testimony*
VanderMeer, Jeff. *Acceptance: A Novel*
Verble, Margaret. ★*Cherokee America*
Ware, Ruth. *The Woman in Cabin Ten*
Woods, Stuart. *Chiefs*
Yu, Charles. *How to Live Safely in a Science Fictional Universe: A Novel*

MISSING PERSONS INVESTIGATION
Abbott, Jeff. *The Three Beths*
Abdul-Jabbar, Kareem. *The Empty Birdcage*
Adler-Olsen, Jussi. *The Keeper of Lost Causes*
Adler-Olsen, Jussi. *The Marco Effect: A Department Q Novel*

Adler-Olsen, Jussi. *The Purity of Vengeance: A Department Q Novel*
Ahlborn, Ania. *The Devil Crept In*
Alfon, Dov. *A Long Night in Paris*
Baldacci, David. *Long Road to Mercy*
Barber, Lizzy. *A Girl Named Anna*
Beukes, Lauren. *Zoo City*
Bohjalian, Chris. *The Sleepwalker*
Box, C. J. *The Highway*
Box, C. J. *Paradise Valley*
Camp, Bryan. *Gather the Fortunes*
Connelly, Michael. *The Wrong Side of Goodbye*
Cook, Thomas H. *The Fate of Katherine Carr*
Corry, Jane. *The Dead Ex*
Cotterill, Colin. *Slash and Burn: A Dr. Siri Mystery Set in Laos*
Crais, Robert. *A Dangerous Man*
Crumley, James. ★*The Wrong Case*
Cussler, Clive. *The Romanov Ransom*
Deaver, Jeffery. ★*The Never Game*
Dexter, Colin. *The Way Through the Woods*
Doiron, Paul. *One Last Lie*
Elliott, Lexie. *The Missing Years*
Evanovich, Janet. *Look Alive Twenty-Five*
Faye, Lyndsay. *Seven for a Secret*
Finch, Charles. *The September Society*
Finlay, Mick. *The Murder Pit*
Fox, Candice. *Crimson Lake*
Fox, Candice. *Gone by Midnight*
Fox, Candice. *Redemption Point*
French, Nicci. ★*Blue Monday*
Gardner, Lisa. *Find Her*
Goddard, Robert. ★*Into the Blue*
Gran, Sara. *Claire Dewitt and the City of the Dead*
Gran, Sara. *The Infinite Blacktop: A Novel*
Hallinan, Timothy. *Fools' River*
Harvey, Michael T. *The Governor's Wife*
Heller, Peter. *Celine: A Novel*
Hill, Susan. *The Shadows in the Street: A Simon Serrailler Mystery*
Hosking, Jay. *Three Years with the Rat: A Novel*
Katzenbach, John. *What Comes Next*
Khan, Ausma Zehanat. *Among the Ruins*
Lansdale, Joe R. *Honky Tonk Samurai*
Lepionka, Kristen. *The Last Place You Look*
Locke, Attica. ★*Heaven, My Home*
Luesse, Valerie Fraser. *Missing Isaac*
Macdonald, Ross. *The Underground Man*
Mankell, Henning. *Before the Frost: A Linda Wallander Mystery*
Miller, Derek B. ★*American by Day*
Moreno-Garcia, Silvia. ★*Velvet Was the Night*
Mosley, Walter. *And Sometimes I Wonder About You: A Leonid McGill Mystery*
Mosley, Walter. ★*Blood Grove*
Moss, Tara. *The War Widow*
Penny, Louise. ★*A Better Man: A Chief Inspector Gamache Novel*
Picoult, Jodi. *Leaving Time: A Novel*
Pochoda, Ivy. *Visitation Street: A Novel*
Porter, Max. ★*Lanny: A Novel*
Preston, Douglas J. *The Obsidian Chamber*
Pronzini, Bill. *Hellbox*

Pronzini, Bill. *Illusions*

Quartey, Kwei. *The Missing American*

Quinn, Spencer. *Dog on It: A Chet and Bernie Mystery*

Quinn, Spencer. ★*It's a Wonderful Woof*

Ragan, Theresa. *Buried Deep*

Rankin, Ian. *Dead Souls: An Inspector Rebus Novel*

Rankin, Ian. *The Falls: An Inspector Rebus Novel*

Rendell, Ruth. *Not in the Flesh*

Robertson, Michael. *The Baker Street Letters*

Robinson, Peter. *Close to Home*

Sandford, John. ★*Phantom Prey*

Schlink, Bernhard. *Self's Deception*

Scott, A. D. ★*The Low Road*

Semple, Maria. *Where'd You Go, Bernadette: A Novel*

Smith, Julie. *82 Desire: A Skip Langdon Novel*

Smith, Martin Cruz. *The Siberian Dilemma*

Solares, Martin. *Don't Send Flowers*

Speller, Elizabeth. *The Strange Fate of Kitty Easton*

Spencer, Sally. *Backlash*

Steiner, Susie. *Missing, Presumed: A Novel*

Swinson, Kiki. *The Safe House*

Wade, Becky. *Falling for You*

Walker, Wendy. *Emma in the Night*

MISSING TEENAGE BOYS

Adam, Claire. *Golden Child: A Novel*

Robinson, Peter. *Close to Home*

MISSING TEENAGE GIRLS

Barton, Fiona. *The Suspect*

Chancellor, Bryn. *Sycamore: A Novel*

Gardner, Lisa. ★*Look for Me: A Novel*

Hambly, Barbara. *House of the Patriarch*

Harper, Jane. *The Survivors*

Harrod-Eagles, Cynthia. *Old Bones*

Lepionka, Kristen. *The Last Place You Look*

McGregor, Jon. *The Reservoir Tapes*

McLain, Paula. ★*When the Stars Go Dark: A Novel*

Overton, Hollie. *The Runaway*

Patterson, James. *Kiss the Girls: A Novel*

Pochoda, Ivy. *Visitation Street: A Novel*

Racculia, Kate. ★*Bellweather Rhapsody*

Spencer, Sally. *The Shivering Turn*

Walker, Wendy. *Emma in the Night*

Watson, S. J. *Final Cut*

MISSING TEENAGERS

Coben, Harlan. ★*The Boy from the Woods*

French, Tana. ★*The Searcher*

Gardner, Lisa. ★*Before She Disappeared: A Novel*

Quinn, Spencer. *Dog on It: A Chet and Bernie Mystery*

*The **Missing** Treasures of Amy Ashton*. Ray, Eleanor

MISSING WOMEN

Abbott, Jeff. *The Three Beths*

Adler-Olsen, Jussi. *The Hanging Girl*

Adler-Olsen, Jussi. *The Keeper of Lost Causes*

Adler-Olsen, Jussi. *The Scarred Woman*

Alexander, Victoria. *The Lady Travelers Guide to Scoundrels and Other Gentlemen*

Belle, Kimberly. *Dear Wife*

Bohjalian, Chris. *The Sleepwalker*

Box, C. J. *The Disappeared*

Box, C. J. *The Highway*

Braffet, Kelly. ★*Last Seen Leaving: A Novel*

Brazier, Eliza Jane. *If I Disappear*

Brown, Karen. *The Clairvoyants: A Novel*

Child, Lee. *Never Go Back*

Cleeves, Ann. *The Long Call*

Cussler, Clive. *The Cutthroat*

Dang, Catherine. *Nice Girls*

Dugoni, Robert. *My Sister's Grave*

Ellis, Bella. *The Vanished Bride*

Eriksson, Kjell. *The Deathwatch Beetle: A Mystery*

Eskens, Allen. *Nothing More Dangerous: A Novel*

Finlay, Mick. *The Murder Pit*

Fleischmann, Raymond. *How Quickly She Disappears*

Flynn, Gillian. ★*Gone Girl: A Novel*

Hajdu, David. *Adrianne Geffel: A Fiction*

Hall, Rachel Howzell. *And Now She's Gone*

Harris, Oliver. *A Shadow Intelligence*

Harrison, Rachel. *The Return*

Harvey, John. *Darkness, Darkness*

Hill, Susan. *The Shadows in the Street: A Simon Serrailler Mystery*

Hoffman, Alice. *The Museum of Extraordinary Things: A Novel*

Johnstone, Carole. *Mirrorland*

Krentz, Jayne Ann. *When All the Girls Have Gone*

Kupersmith, Violet. ★*Build Your House Around My Body*

Lewis, Beverly. *The Missing*

Littlejohn, Emily. *Lost Lake: A Detective Gemma Monroe Mystery*

MacLean, Sarah. *No Good Duke Goes Unpunished*

Mandel, Emily St. John. ★*The Glass Hotel: A Novel*

Minh, Drew. *Neon Empire*

Moreno-Garcia, Silvia. ★*Velvet Was the Night*

Mosley, Walter. *Black Betty: An Easy Rawlins Mystery*

Murakami, Haruki. *The Wind-Up Bird Chronicle*

Paris, B. A. *Bring Me Back: A Novel*

Patrick, Phaedra. ★*The Secrets of Love Story Bridge*

Perry, Thomas. *Death Benefits: A Novel*

Picoult, Jodi. *Leaving Time: A Novel*

Pronzini, Bill. *Hellbox*

Ragan, Theresa. *Buried Deep*

Ragan, Theresa. *Her Last Day*

Raybourn, Deanna. *A Dangerous Collaboration*

Russo, Richard. ★*Chances Are...: A Novel*

Sager, Riley. *Lock Every Door: A Novel*

Schlink, Bernhard. *Self's Deception*

Singh, Nalini. *A Madness of Sunshine*

Smith, Ian. *The Unspoken*

Smith, Martin Cruz. *The Siberian Dilemma*

Spencer, Sally. *Backlash*

Tran, Vu. *Dragonfish: A Novel*

*The **Missing** Years*. Elliott, Lexie

***Missing**, Presumed: A Novel*. Steiner, Susie

*The **Mission** House*. Davies, Carys

★***Mission** to Paris*. Furst, Alan

★***Missionaries***. Klay, Phil

MISSIONARIES

Patterson, Molly. *Rebellion*

MISSISSIPPI
Adlakha, Sarah. *She Wouldn't Change a Thing*
Atkins, Ace. *The Broken Places*
Atkins, Ace. *The Fallen*
Atkins, Ace. *The Forsaken*
Atkins, Ace. *The Innocents*
Atkins, Ace. *The Lost Ones*
Atkins, Ace. *The Ranger*
Atkins, Ace. *The Redeemers*
Atkins, Ace. *The Revelators*
Atkins, Ace. *The Shameless*
Atkins, Ace. *The Sinners*
Barthelme, Frederick. *Elroy Nights*
Benz, Chanelle. ★*The Gone Dead*
Brown, Larry. *Joe: A Novel*
Campbell, Bebe Moore. *Your Blues Ain't Like Mine*
Child, Lee. *The Affair*
Faulkner, William. ★*Absalom, Absalom!*
Faulkner, William. ★*Go Down, Moses*
Faulkner, William. *The Hamlet*
Faulkner, William. *Intruder in the Dust*
Faulkner, William. ★*Light in August*
Faulkner, William. ★*Sanctuary*
Faulkner, William. *Uncollected Stories of William Faulkner*
Franklin, Tom. *Crooked Letter, Crooked Letter: A Novel*
French, Albert. *Billy*
Grisham, John. *The Last Juror*
Grisham, John. *A Time to Kill*
Harris, C. S. *Good Time Coming*
Iles, Greg. *Cemetery Road: A Novel*
Iles, Greg. *Mississippi Blood: A Novel*
Iles, Greg. *Natchez Burning: A Novel*
James, Miranda. *What the Cat Dragged In*
Jones, Robert. ★*The Prophets: A Novel*
Jordan, Hillary. *Mudbound: A Novel*
Kunzru, Hari. *White Tears*
Laymon, Kiese. *Long Division*
Lindsey, Odie. *Some Go Home: A Novel*
Miles, Jonathan. *Anatomy of a Miracle*
Miller, Mary. *Biloxi: A Novel*
Rozan, S. J. ★*Paper Son*
Smith, Michael F. *Blackwood*
Smith, Michael F. *The Fighter: A Novel*
Ward, Jesmyn. ★*Sing, Unburied, Sing*
Watson, Brad. *Miss Jane: A Novel*
Welty, Eudora. ★*Delta Wedding*
Welty, Eudora. *The Optimist's Daughter*
Welty, Eudora. ★*The Robber Bridegroom*
Welty, Eudora. *Stories, Essays & Memoir*
Mississippi Blood: A Novel. Iles, Greg
MISSISSIPPI RIVER
Cheng, Bill. *Southern Cross the Dog*
Clinch, Jon. *Finn: A Novel*
Melville, Herman. *The Confidence-Man: His Masquerade*
Twain, Mark. ★*Adventures of Huckleberry Finn: Tom Sawyer's Comrade ...*
MISSOURI
Berg, Elizabeth. *The Confession Club: A Novel*

Berg, Elizabeth. *Night of Miracles*
Berg, Elizabeth. *The Story of Arthur Truluv: A Novel*
Clinch, Jon. *Finn: A Novel*
Flagg, Fannie. *Standing in the Rainbow: A Novel*
Flynn, Gillian. *Dark Places*
Flynn, Gillian. ★*Sharp Objects: A Novel*
Ganshert, Katie. ★*No One Ever Asked: A Novel*
Gelman, Laurie. *Class Mom: A Novel*
Gelman, Laurie. *Yoga Pant Nation: A Novel*
Gelman, Laurie. *You've Been Volunteered: A Class Mom Novel*
Lovely, Lutishia. *Blind Ambition*
Murr, Naeem. *The Perfect Man: A Novel*
Robinson, Marilynne. ★*Jack*
Twain, Mark. ★*Adventures of Huckleberry Finn: Tom Sawyer's Comrade ...*
Twain, Mark. *Pudd'nhead Wilson ;: And, Those Extraordinary Twins*
Woodrell, Daniel. *The Maid's Version: A Novel*
*The **Mist***. Jónasson, Ragnar
*A **Mist** of Prophecies*. Saylor, Steven
MISTAKEN IDENTITY
Black, Cara. *Murder in the Bastille*
Bowman, Valerie. *The Accidental Countess*
Heyer, Georgette. *These Old Shades*
Hiaasen, Carl. *Star Island*
Twain, Mark. *Pudd'nhead Wilson ;: And, Those Extraordinary Twins*
***Mister** Memory: A Novel*. Sedgwick, Marcus
***Mister** Roberts*. Heggen, Thomas
***Misterioso**: a Crime Novel*. Dahl, Arne
***Mistletoe** in Texas*. Dell, Kari Lynn
***Mistress** novels (Niobia Bryant) [Series]*. Bryant, Niobia
***Mistress** of the Art of Death*. Franklin, Ariana
***Mistress** trilogy (Mary Balogh) [Series]*. Balogh, Mary
MISTRESSES
Balogh, Mary. *More Than a Mistress*
Balogh, Mary. *The Secret Mistress*
Cameron, Peter. *The City of Your Final Destination*
Dreiser, Theodore. ★*Sister Carrie*
Franklin, Ariana. *The Serpent's Tale*
Gregory, Philippa. *The Other Boleyn Girl: A Novel*
Hiaasen, Carl. *Nature Girl*
Hodgson, Antonia. *The Last Confession of Thomas Hawkins*
Ma, Jian. *China Dream*
Medie, Peace A. *His Only Wife: A Novel*
Sagan, Francoise. ★*Bonjour Tristesse*
Sontag, Susan. *The Volcano Lover: A Romance*
Weldon, Fay. *The Life and Loves of a She-Devil*
Wolfe, Paul. *The Lost Diary of M*
MISUNDERSTANDING
Allain, Suzanne. *Miss Lattimore's Letter*
Austen, Jane. *Northanger Abbey*
Henson, Pene. *Into the Blue*
Lansdale, Joe R. ★*Paradise Sky*
Waters, Martha. ★*To Have and to Hoax: A Novel*
Mitchell, David
Black Swan Green: A Novel
The Bone Clocks: A Novel
★*Cloud Atlas: A Novel*
The Thousand Autumns of Jacob De Zoet: A Novel

★*Utopia Avenue: A Novel*
Mitchell, Margaret
   ★*Gone with the Wind*
Mitford, Nancy
   Love in a Cold Climate
   ★*The Pursuit of Love: A Novel*
MIXED-BREED DOGS
   London, Jack. ★*White Fang*
Mizushima, Margaret
   Killing Trail
MOBILE HOME PARKS
   Clement, Jennifer. *Gun Love*
MOBILE, ALABAMA
   Kerley, Jack. ★*The Death Collectors*
MOBY DICK (WHALE)
   Melville, Herman. ★*Moby-Dick; Or, the Whale*
★*Moby-Dick; Or, the Whale*. Melville, Herman
MODERN CLASSICS
   Achebe, Chinua. ★*Things Fall Apart*
   Algren, Nelson. ★*The Man with the Golden Arm: A Novel*
   Amis, Kingsley. ★*Lucky Jim*
   Andric, Ivo. *The Bridge on the Drina*
   Baldwin, James. ★*Go Tell It on the Mountain*
   Baldwin, James. *Just Above My Head*
   Baldwin, James. *Tell Me How Long the Train's Been Gone: A Novel*
   Barnes, Djuna. ★*Nightwood*
   Beckett, Samuel. ★*Murphy*
   Bellow, Saul. ★*Herzog*
   Bellow, Saul. ★*Humboldt's Gift*
   Boll, Heinrich. *Billiards at Half-Past Nine*
   Boll, Heinrich. *The Clown*
   Boschwitz, Ulrich Alexander. *The Passenger: A Novel*
   Bowen, Elizabeth. *The Heat of the Day*
   Burgess, Anthony. ★*A Clockwork Orange*
   Burroughs, William S. ★*Naked Lunch: The Restored Text*
   Caldwell, Erskine. *Tobacco Road*
   Camus, Albert. *The Plague*
   Dos Passos, John. *1919*
   Dos Passos, John. *The 42nd Parallel*
   Durrell, Lawrence. ★*Justine*
   Ellison, Ralph. ★*Invisible Man*
   Ellison, Ralph. ★*Juneteenth*
   Faulkner, William. ★*Go Down, Moses*
   Faulkner, William. *Intruder in the Dust*
   Faulkner, William. ★*Light in August*
   Faulkner, William. *Requiem for a Nun*
   Faulkner, William. ★*Sanctuary*
   Faulkner, William. *Uncollected Stories of William Faulkner*
   Ferber, Edna. *So Big*
   Fitzgerald, F. Scott. ★*The Beautiful and Damned*
   Fitzgerald, F. Scott. ★*The Last Tycoon: An Unfinished Novel*
   Fitzgerald, F. Scott. *Novels and Stories, 1920-1922*
   Fitzgerald, F. Scott. ★*The Short Stories of F. Scott Fitzgerald: A New Collection*
   Fitzgerald, F. Scott. *Six Tales of the Jazz Age and Other Stories*
   Fitzgerald, F. Scott. ★*This Side of Paradise*
   Forster, E. M. ★*Howards End*
   Forster, E. M. ★*A Room with a View*

Fowles, John. *The Magus*
Gaddis, William. ★*The Recognitions*
Galsworthy, John. ★*The Forsyte Saga*
Garcia Marquez, Gabriel. *Chronicle of a Death Foretold*
Garcia Marquez, Gabriel. *The General in His Labyrinth*
Garcia Marquez, Gabriel. *In Evil Hour*
Gide, Andre. ★*The Immoralist*
Graves, Robert. ★*I, Claudius: From the Autobiography of Tiberius Claudius, Born 10 B.C., Murdered and Deified A.D. 54*
Greene, Graham. *The Power and the Glory*
Hemingway, Ernest. *The Nick Adams Stories*
Hemingway, Ernest. *The Snows of Kilimanjaro and Other Stories*
Hemingway, Ernest. ★*The Sun Also Rises*
Hemingway, Ernest. *To Have and Have Not*
Hesse, Hermann. ★*Siddhartha: A New Translation*
Highsmith, Patricia. ★*The Talented Mr. Ripley*
Hughes, Langston. *Not Without Laughter*
Hurston, Zora Neale. ★*Their Eyes Were Watching God*
Irving, John. ★*The Cider House Rules: A Novel*
Irving, John. ★*A Prayer for Owen Meany: A Novel*
Irving, John. ★*The World According to Garp: A Novel*
Jones, James. ★*From Here to Eternity*
Joyce, James. ★*Dubliners*
Joyce, James. ★*Finnegans Wake*
Kafka, Franz. ★*The Metamorphosis*
Kerouac, Jack. *The Dharma Bums*
Kerouac, Jack. ★*On the Road*
Kerouac, Jack. ★*Road Novels 1957-1960*
Kesey, Ken. ★*One Flew Over the Cuckoo's Nest*
Kesey, Ken. *Sometimes a Great Notion: A Novel*
Knowles, John. ★*A Separate Peace*
Lawrence, D. H. ★*Lady Chatterley's Lover*
Lee, Harper. ★*To Kill a Mockingbird*
Lewis, Sinclair. *Babbitt*
Lewis, Sinclair. ★*Elmer Gantry*
Lewis, Sinclair. ★*Main Street: The Story of Carol Kennicott*
Lockridge, Ross Franklin. *Raintree County*
Mailer, Norman. ★*The Naked and the Dead*
Malamud, Bernard. *The Assistant*
Mann, Thomas. *Doctor Faustus*
Maugham, W. Somerset. *The Moon and Sixpence*
McCullers, Carson. ★*The Heart Is a Lonely Hunter*
Miller, Henry. ★*Tropic of Cancer*
Miller, Henry. ★*Tropic of Capricorn*
Mitford, Nancy. *Love in a Cold Climate*
Mitford, Nancy. ★*The Pursuit of Love: A Novel*
Morante, Elsa. *Arturo's Island: A Novel*
Morrison, Toni. *Paradise*
Morrison, Toni. *Sula*
Morrison, Toni. *Tar Baby*
Murdoch, Iris. *The Green Knight*
Musil, Robert. *The Man Without Qualities*
Nabokov, Vladimir Vladimirovich. *King, Queen, Knave: A Novel*
Nabokov, Vladimir Vladimirovich. *Look at the Harlequins!*
Nabokov, Vladimir Vladimirovich. *Novels and Memoirs, 1941-51*
Nabokov, Vladimir Vladimirovich. *Pale Fire*
Nabokov, Vladimir Vladimirovich. *Pnin*
Naipaul, V. S. *A Bend in the River*

Naipaul, V. S. *A House for Mr. Biswas*
O'Connor, Flannery. ★*The Violent Bear It Away*
O'Connor, Flannery. ★*Wise Blood*
O'Hara, John. *Appointment in Samarra*
Percy, Walker. ★*The Moviegoer*
Porter, Katherine Anne. *Pale Horse, Pale Rider: Three Short Novels*
Pynchon, Thomas. ★*The Crying of Lot 49*
Pynchon, Thomas. ★*Gravity's Rainbow*
Pynchon, Thomas. ★*V: A Novel*
Remarque, Erich Maria. ★*All Quiet on the Western Front*
Roth, Henry. ★*Call It Sleep*
Rushdie, Salman. ★*The Satanic Verses*
Sackville-West, V. *All Passion Spent*
Sagan, Francoise. ★*Bonjour Tristesse*
Salinger, J. D. ★*The Catcher in the Rye*
Salinger, J. D. ★*Franny and Zooey*
Saramago, Jose. ★*Blindness*
Smith, Betty. ★*A Tree Grows in Brooklyn*
Solzhenitsyn, Aleksandr Isaevich. *One Day in the Life of Ivan Denisovich*
Spark, Muriel. ★*The Girls of Slender Means*
Spark, Muriel. ★*Memento Mori*
Spark, Muriel. ★*The Prime of Miss Jean Brodie*
Stegner, Wallace. ★*Angle of Repose*
Steinbeck, John. *Cannery Row*
Steinbeck, John. ★*East of Eden*
Steinbeck, John. ★*The Grapes of Wrath*
Steinbeck, John. *The Long Valley*
Steinbeck, John. ★*Of Mice and Men*
Steinbeck, John. *The Pearl*
Steinbeck, John. *Tortilla Flat*
Styron, William. ★*Sophie's Choice*
Svevo, Italo. *Zeno's Conscience*
Tarkington, Booth. ★*Alice Adams*
Tarkington, Booth. ★*The Magnificent Ambersons*
Thompson, Jim. *The Killer Inside Me*
Updike, John. ★*Rabbit Is Rich: A Novel*
Updike, John. ★*Rabbit, Run*
Vonnegut, Kurt. ★*Cat's Cradle*
Vonnegut, Kurt. ★*Slaughterhouse-Five: Or, the Children's Crusade : A Duty-Dance with Death*
Warren, Robert Penn. *All the King's Men*
Waugh, Evelyn. ★*Brideshead Revisited*
Waugh, Evelyn. ★*The Complete Stories of Evelyn Waugh*
Waugh, Evelyn. *Decline and Fall*
Waugh, Evelyn. *The Loved One: An Anglo-American Tragedy*
Waugh, Evelyn. ★*Vile Bodies*
Welty, Eudora. ★*The Collected Stories of Eudora Welty*
Welty, Eudora. ★*Delta Wedding*
Welty, Eudora. *The Optimist's Daughter*
Welty, Eudora. ★*The Ponder Heart*
Welty, Eudora. ★*The Robber Bridegroom*
Welty, Eudora. *Stories, Essays & Memoir*
Wharton, Edith. *The Children*
Wharton, Edith. *Collected Stories, 1891-1910*
Wharton, Edith. ★*Ethan Frome*
Wilson, Sloan. ★*The Man in the Gray Flannel Suit*
Wolfe, Tom. *The Bonfire of the Vanities*

Woolf, Virginia. *Between the Acts*
Woolf, Virginia. *Jacob's Room*
Woolf, Virginia. *Orlando: A Biography*
Woolf, Virginia. ★*To the Lighthouse*
Woolf, Virginia. *The Voyage Out*
Woolf, Virginia. ★*The Years*
Wright, Richard. ★*Native Son*
Yourcenar, Marguerite. ★*Memoirs of Hadrian: And Reflections on the Composition of Memoirs of Hadrian*
Zamyatin, Yevgeny Ivanovich. ★*We*
Modern love [Series]. Rai, Alisha
★***Modern** Lovers*. Straub, Emma
MODERN WESTERNS
    Henderson, Susan. *The Flicker of Old Dreams*
    Johnson, Craig. *Daughter of the Morning Star*
    Johnson, Craig. *Land of Wolves*
    Johnson, Craig. *Next to Last Stand*
    Johnson, Craig. *Spirit of Steamboat: A Walt Longmire Story*
    Kennedy, Randy. *Presidio*
    Rowland, Russell. *Cold Country: A Novel*
    Stansel, Ian. *The Last Cowboys of San Geronimo*
    Sternbergh, Adam. *The Blinds*
MODERNIZATION (SOCIAL SCIENCES)
    Desai, Kiran. *The Inheritance of Loss*
    Dos Passos, John. *Manhattan Transfer*
MOGADISHU, SOMALIA
    Farah, Nuruddin. *Crossbones*
    Farah, Nuruddin. *Knots*
Mohamed, Nadifa
    The Orchard of Lost Souls: A Novel
MOHEGAN INDIANS
    Cooper, James Fenimore. *The Last of the Mohicans: A Narrative of 1757*
MOJAVE DESERT
    Davila, April. *142 Ostriches*
    Lalami, Laila. *The Other Americans: A Novel*
    Watkins, Claire Vaye. *I Love You but I've Chosen Darkness*
MOLECULAR EVOLUTION
    Wilson, Daniel H. *The Andromeda Evolution: A Novel*
MOLES (SPIES)
    Berenson, Alex. *The Prisoner*
    Cumming, Charles. *A Colder War*
    Deighton, Len. *Berlin Game*
    Deighton, Len. *London Match*
★***Moll** Flanders*. Defoe, Daniel
Mollisan Town quartet [Series]. Davys, Tim
Molloy, Aimee
    The Perfect Mother: A Novel
Momaday, N. Scott
    The Ancient Child: A Novel
    House Made of Dawn
*A **Moment** in the Sun*. Sayles, John
MONACO
    Gaynor, Hazel. *Meet Me in Monaco: A Novel*
MONASTERIES
    Pears, Iain. *Death and Restoration*
    Stephenson, Neal. *Anathem*

FICTION CORE COLLECTION
TWENTY-FIRST EDITION

MONASTIC LIBRARIES
    Eco, Umberto. ★*The Name of the Rose*
MONASTICISM AND RELIGIOUS ORDERS
    Davis, Lindsey. *One Virgin Too Many*
MONASTICISM AND RELIGIOUS ORDERS FOR MEN
    Berry, Steve. ★*The Templar Legacy: A Novel of Suspense*
    Hesse, Hermann. *Narcissus and Goldmund*
    Miller, Walter M. ★*A Canticle for Leibowitz*
Monday Mourning. Reichs, Kathy
Monday the Rabbi Took Off. Kemelman, Harry
MONEY
    Bennett, Anna. *First Earl I See Tonight*
    Herrera, Adriana. *American Fairytale*
    Robotham, Michael. *Life or Death*
    Smith, Scott. *A Simple Plan: A Novel*
MONEY LAUNDERING
    Hurwitz, Gregg Andrew. ★*Into the Fire*
    Le Carre, John. ★*Our Kind of Traitor: A Novel*
    Morgan Jones, Chris. *The Silent Oligarch*
    Schlink, Bernhard. *Self's Murder*
    Stephenson, Neal. *Reamde*
MONEY LENDERS
    Dickens, Charles. ★*Nicholas Nickleby*
    Leonard, Elmore. ★*Get Shorty*
    Novik, Naomi. ★*Spinning Silver*
Money Shot. Faust, Christa
The *Money* Shot. Woods, Stuart
MONEY-MAKING PROJECTS
    Ramos, Joanne. *The Farm: A Novel*
★*Mongoose, R.I.P.: A Blackford Oakes Novel*. Buckley, William F.
MONGOOSES
    Oyeyemi, Helen. *Peaces*
Monika Paniatowski mysteries [Series]. Spencer, Sally
Moniz, Dantiel W.
    Milk Blood Heat
Moniz, Tomas
    Big Familia
Monk & robot [Series]. Chambers, Becky
MONK, WILLIAM (FICTITIOUS CHARACTER)
    Perry, Anne. *A Dangerous Mourning*
    Perry, Anne. *The Face of a Stranger*
Monkeewrench [Series]. Tracy, P. J.
MONKS
    Chambers, Becky. ★*A Psalm for the Wild-Built*
    Eco, Umberto. ★*The Name of the Rose*
    Kadare, Ismail. ★*The Three-Arched Bridge*
    Miller, Walter M. ★*A Canticle for Leibowitz*
    Peters, Ellis. *Brother Cadfael's Penance*
    Peters, Ellis. *The Holy Thief*
    Potzsch, Oliver. *The Dark Monk: A Hangman's Daughter Tale*
    Potzsch, Oliver. *The Poisoned Pilgrim: A Hangman's Daughter Tale*
    Rutherfurd, Edward. *The Princes of Ireland: The Dublin Saga*
MONMOUTH'S REBELLION, 1685
    Blackmore, R. D. *Lorna Doone: A Romance of Exmoor*
★*Monogamy*. Miller, Sue
MONROE, MARILYN
    Aciman, Andre. *Find Me*
    Johnson, Charles Richard. ★*Middle Passage*

    Lee, Ji-Min. *The Starlet and the Spy*
    Oates, Joyce Carol. *Blonde: A Novel*
Monroe, Mary
    ★*God Don't Like Ugly*
    God Still Don't Like Ugly
    ★*Mrs. Wiggins*
Monroe, Mary Alice
    Beach House Reunion
    ★*The Summer of Lost and Found*
Monsarrat, Nicholas
    The Cruel Sea
Monsieur Pain. Bolano, Roberto
Monsoon. Smith, Wilbur A.
MONSTER HUNTERS
    Huang, S. L. *Burning Roses*
MONSTERS
    Armfield, Julia. *Salt Slow: Stories*
    Clark, P. Djeli. *Ring Shout*
    Durst, Sarah Beth. *Race the Sands*
    Gallagher, Stephen. *The Bedlam Detective: A Novel*
    Gornichec, Genevieve. ★*The Witch's Heart*
    Goss, Theodora. *The Strange Case of the Alchemist's Daughter*
    Hamill, Shaun. *A Cosmology of Monsters*
    Hill, Joe. ★*Nos4a2*
    Huang, S. L. *Burning Roses*
    Malerman, Josh. *Bird Box: A Novel*
    Malerman, Josh. *Goblin: A Novel in Six Novellas*
    Malerman, Josh. *Malorie: A Bird Box Novel*
    Novik, Naomi. *A Deadly Education: A Novel*
    Novik, Naomi. *The Last Graduate: A Novel*
    Pratchett, Terry. ★*The Color of Magic*
    Priest, Cherie. *The Inexplicables*
    Roanhorse, Rebecca. *Storm of Locusts*
    Roanhorse, Rebecca. ★*Trail of Lightning*
    Shelley, Mary Wollstonecraft. ★*Frankenstein: Or, the Modern Prometheus*
    Turnbull, Cadwell. *No Gods, No Monsters*
    White, Elle Katharine. *Dragonshadow*
    Wolfe, Gene. *The Claw of the Conciliator*
    Yang, JY. *The Descent of Monsters*
    Yang, JY. *The Red Threads of Fortune*
Monstrous Regiment. Pratchett, Terry
Montag, Kassandra
    After the Flood: A Novel
MONTANA
    Adams, Taylor. *Hairpin Bridge*
    Bowen, Peter. *Badlands*
    Box, C. J. ★*The Bitterroots: A Novel*
    Box, C. J. *The Highway*
    Box, C. J. *Paradise Valley*
    Child, Lee. ★*Die Trying*
    Dundas, Chad. *The Blaze*
    Evans, Nicholas. ★*The Horse Whisperer: A Novel*
    Francis-Sharma, Lauren. ★*Book of the Little Axe*
    Harrison, Jamie. *The Center of Everything: A Novel*
    Henderson, Smith. *Fourth of July Creek*
    Henderson, Susan. *The Flicker of Old Dreams*
    Hulse, S. M. ★*Black River*

Hulse, S. M. *Eden Mine*
Johnson, Craig. *Daughter of the Morning Star*
Jones, Stephen Graham. ★*The Only Good Indians: A Novel*
McGuane, Thomas. *Crow Fair: Stories*
Peterson, Tracie. *What Comes My Way*
Roberts, Nora. *Come Sundown*
Rowland, Russell. *Cold Country: A Novel*
Skeslien Charles, Janet. *The Paris Library: A Novel*
Smith, B. J. *The Return of Kid Cooper: A Novel*
Warren, Susan May. *Rescue Me*
Montana rescue [Series]. Warren, Susan May
Montauk. Harrison, Nicola
MONTAUK, NEW YORK
    Harrison, Nicola. *Montauk*
Montclair, Allison
    The Right Sort of Man
    A Rogue's Company
    A Royal Affair
Monte Walsh. Schaefer, Jack
MONTEREY, CALIFORNIA
    Steinbeck, John. *Cannery Row*
    Steinbeck, John. *Tortilla Flat*
MONTERO, BRITT (FICTIONAL CHARACTER)
    Buchanan, Edna. *You Only Die Twice: A Britt Montero Mystery*
Montgomery and Taggert clans series [Series]. Deveraux, Jude
MONTGOMERY, ALABAMA
    Howard, Ravi. *Driving the King: A Novel*
Montgomery, Jess
    The Stills
    The Widows
The **Montgomerys** and Armstrongs [Series]. Banks, Maya
MONTHS
    Gaiman, Neil. *Trigger Warning: Short Fictions and Disturbances*
Montimore, Margarita
    Oona Out of Order
MONTREAL, QUEBEC
    Banks, Russell. *Foregone*
    Ekwuyasi, Francesca. *Butter Honey Pig Bread: A Novel*
    O'Neill, Heather. ★*The Lonely Hearts Hotel: A Novel*
    Reichs, Kathy. *206 Bones*
    Reichs, Kathy. *Bones of the Lost: A Temperance Brennan Novel*
    Reichs, Kathy. *Deadly Decisions*
    Reichs, Kathy. *Death Du Jour*
    Reichs, Kathy. ★*Deja Dead*
    Reichs, Kathy. *Monday Mourning*
    Richler, Mordecai. *Barney's Version: A Novel*
    Richler, Mordecai. *Solomon Gursky Was Here*
MONUMENTS
    McDevitt, Jack. *The Engines of God*
MOODS AND MOODINESS
    Moyes, Jojo. *Me Before You: A Novel*
MOON
    Clarke, Arthur C. ★*2001: A Space Odyssey*
    Heinlein, Robert A. *The Moon Is a Harsh Mistress*
    Kowal, Mary Robinette. *The Relentless Moon*
    McDonald, Ian. *New Moon*
    Michener, James A. *Space*
    Stephenson, Neal. *Seveneves*

Tan, Sue Lynn. ★*Daughter of the Moon Goddess*
Weir, Andy. *Artemis*
*The **Moon** and Sixpence*. Maugham, W. Somerset
Moon and the Mars. Corthron, Kia
Moon Brow. Mandanipour, Shahriar
*The **Moon** Is a Harsh Mistress*. Heinlein, Robert A.
Moon of the Crusted Snow: A Novel. Rice, Waubgeshig
Moon Over Soho. Aaronovitch, Ben
★*Moon Tiger*. Lively, Penelope
Mooney, Chris
    Blood World
★*Moonflower Murders*. Horowitz, Anthony
Moonlight Bay [Series]. Ramsay, Hope
MOONSHINING (ILLEGAL DISTILLING)
    Montgomery, Jess. *The Stills*
★*The **Moonstone***. Collins, Wilkie
★*The **Moor's** Account: A Novel*. Lalami, Laila
*The **Moor's** Last Sigh*. Rushdie, Salman
Moor, Jessica
    The Keeper
Moore, Alan
    Jerusalem: A Novel
Moore, Alison
    The Lighthouse
Moore, Graham
    The Holdout: A Novel
Moore, Liz
    Long Bright River
    The Unseen World
Moore, Lorrie
    A Gate at the Stairs: A Novel
Moore, Meg Mitchell
    The Islanders
MOORS AND HEATHS
    Doyle, Arthur Conan. ★*The Hound of the Baskervilles*
    Hardy, Thomas. ★*The Return of the Native*
Moral Disorder. Atwood, Margaret
Morante, Elsa
    Arturo's Island: A Novel
More Better Deals. Lansdale, Joe R.
More Die of Heartbreak. Bellow, Saul
More Than a Mistress. Balogh, Mary
★*More Than I Love My Life: A Novel*. Grossman, David
Morelli, Laura
    The Stolen Lady
Moreno, Gus
    This Thing Between US: A Novel
Moreno-Garcia, Silvia
    ★*Gods of Jade and Shadow: A Novel*
    Mexican Gothic
    ★*Velvet Was the Night*
Morgan Jones, Chris
    The Silent Oligarch
Morgan, C. E.
    ★*The Sport of Kings*
Morgenstern, Erin
    ★*The Night Circus: A Novel*
    ★*The Starless Sea*

Moriarty Returns a Letter: A Baker Street Mystery. Robertson, Michael

Moriarty, Jaclyn
  Gravity Is the Thing

Moriarty, Liane
  Big Little Lies
  The Husband's Secret
  Nine Perfect Strangers
  Truly Madly Guilty

MORMON FICTION
  Harrison, Mette Ivie. *The Bishop's Wife*
  Harrison, Mette Ivie. *The Prodigal Daughter*

MORMON POLYGAMY
  Vestal, Shawn. *Daredevils*

MORMON WOMEN
  Grey, Zane. ★*Riders of the Purple Sage*

MORMONS
  Ebershoff, David. *The 19th Wife: A Novel*
  Harrison, Mette Ivie. *The Bishop's Wife*
  Harrison, Mette Ivie. *The Prodigal Daughter*
  Vestal, Shawn. *Daredevils*

Morning Star. Brown, Pierce

The Morning Star. Knausgaard, Karl Ove

Morningside Heights. Henkin, Joshua

The Moroccan Girl. Cumming, Charles

MOROCCO
  Bowles, Paul. ★*The Sheltering Sky*
  Cumming, Charles. *The Moroccan Girl*
  Duenas, Maria. *The Time in Between: A Novel*
  Lalami, Laila. ★*The Moor's Account: A Novel*
  Slimani, Leïla. *In the Country of Others*

MORPHINE ADDICTION
  Algren, Nelson. ★*The Man with the Golden Arm: A Novel*

Morrell, David
  Ruler of the Night

Morris, Heather
  Cilka's Journey

Morrison, Toni
  ★*Beloved: A Novel*
  ★*The Bluest Eye: A Novel*
  ★*God Help the Child*
  Home
  Jazz
  Love
  A Mercy: A Novel
  Paradise
  ★*Song of Solomon*
  Sula
  Tar Baby

MORSE, INSPECTOR (FICTITIOUS CHARACTER)
  Dexter, Colin. *The Daughters of Cain*
  Dexter, Colin. *The Remorseful Day*
  Dexter, Colin. *The Way Through the Woods*

Mortal Prey. Sandford, John

MORTALITY
  Banks, Iain. *The Crow Road*
  Ford, Richard. *The Lay of the Land*
  Ford, Richard. *Let Me Be Frank with You*
  Gordimer, Nadine. *Get a Life*

Grodstein, Lauren. *Our Short History*
Helprin, Mark. ★*Winter's Tale*
Johnson, Denis. *The Largesse of the Sea Maiden: Stories*
Moore, Alan. *Jerusalem: A Novel*
Rice, Anne. *Blackwood Farm*
Rice, Anne. *Blood and Gold: Or, the Story of Marius*
Rice, Anne. *Blood Canticle*
Rice, Anne. ★*Interview with the Vampire*
Rice, Anne. *Merrick: A Novel*
Rice, Anne. *Prince Lestat: The Vampire Chronicles*
Rice, Anne. ★*The Queen of the Damned*
Rice, Anne. *The Tale of the Body Thief*
Rice, Anne. ★*The Vampire Lestat*
Roth, Philip. ★*Everyman*
Spark, Muriel. ★*Memento Mori*
Tolkien, J. R. R. *Beren and Luthien*
Updike, John. *The Afterlife and Other Stories*

Morton, Brian
  Florence Gordon

Morton, Kate
  The Distant Hours: A Novel
  The House at Riverton: A Novel

The Moscow Offensive: A Novel. Brown, Dale

MOSCOW, RUSSIA
  Bulgakov, Mikhail. ★*The Master and Margarita*
  Gessen, Keith. *A Terrible Country*
  Grushin, Olga. *The Line*
  Kaminsky, Stuart M. *Murder on the Trans-Siberian Express*
  Morgan Jones, Chris. *The Silent Oligarch*
  Smith, Martin Cruz. ★*Gorky Park*
  Smith, Martin Cruz. *The Siberian Dilemma*
  Smith, Martin Cruz. *Stalin's Ghost*
  Smith, Martin Cruz. ★*Tatiana: An Arkady Renko Novel*
  Smith, Martin Cruz. *Three Stations: An Arkady Renko Novel*
  Smith, Martin Cruz. *Wolves Eat Dogs: A Novel*
  Tolstaya, Tatyana. *The Slynx*
  Towles, Amor. ★*A Gentleman in Moscow*
  Winterson, Jeanette. *The Passion*

MOSCOW, RUSSIA, TRIALS, 1936-1937
  Koestler, Arthur. *Darkness at Noon*

Moshfegh, Ottessa
  ★*Death in Her Hands: A Novel*
  Eileen
  My Year of Rest and Relaxation

Moshi-Moshi. Yoshimoto, Banana

Mosley, Walter
  All I Did Was Shoot My Man: A Leonid McGill Mystery
  And Sometimes I Wonder About You: A Leonid McGill Mystery
  ★*The Awkward Black Man: Stories*
  Black Betty: An Easy Rawlins Mystery
  ★*Blood Grove*
  Charcoal Joe: An Easy Rawlins Mystery
  Devil in a Blue Dress
  Down the River Unto the Sea
  Fortunate Son: A Novel
  ★*John Woman*
  Little Scarlet: An Easy Rawlins Mystery

The Right Mistake: The Further Philosophical Investigations of Socrates Fortlow
Trouble Is What I Do: A Leonid McGill Mystery
★*The Mosquito Coast: A Novel*. Theroux, Paul

Moss, Sarah
  Ghost Wall: A Novel
  Summerwater

Moss, Tara
  The War Widow

Mosse, Kate
  The City of Tears

The Most Beautiful Girl in Cuba. Cleeton, Chanel
The Most Fun We Ever Had: A Novel. Lombardo, Claire
A Most Wanted Man: A Novel. Le Carre, John
Mostly Dead Things. Arnett, Kristen N.

MOTELS
  St. James, Simone. *The Sun Down Motel*
  Wallace, Melanie. *The Girl in the Garden*

The Mother. Edwards, Yvvette

MOTHER AND ADULT CHILD
  Bawden, Nina. *Family Money*
  Enright, Anne. *The Green Road: A Novel*
  Smith, Lee. *Family Linen*
  Straub, Emma. ★*All Adults Here*

MOTHER AND ADULT DAUGHTER
  Coster, Naima. *Halsey Street*
  Delany, Vicki. *Deadly Summer Nights*
  Frank, Dorothea Benton. *Queen Bee*
  Gelman, Laurie. *Yoga Pant Nation: A Novel*
  Gelman, Laurie. *You've Been Volunteered: A Class Mom Novel*
  Gibbons, Kaye. *Charms for the Easy Life*
  Ginzburg, Natalia. *Voices in the Evening*
  Greenidge, Kaitlyn. ★*Libertie: A Novel*
  Macmillan, Gilly. *The Nanny*
  Mallery, Susan. *California Girls*
  Sebold, Alice. *The Almost Moon: A Novel*
  Slaughter, Karin. ★*Fallen: A Novel*
  Vlautin, Willy. ★*The Night Always Comes*
  Wells, Rebecca. *Divine Secrets of the Ya-Ya Sisterhood: A Novel*

MOTHER AND ADULT SON
  Auslander, Shalom. *Hope: A Tragedy*
  Drndic, Dasa. *Trieste*
  Jones, Sandie. *The Other Woman*
  Palahniuk, Chuck. *Choke: A Novel*
  St. Aubyn, Edward. *At Last*
  Tyler, Anne. *A Patchwork Planet*

MOTHER AND CHILD
  Benton, Janet. *Lilli De Jong: A Novel*
  Brown, Sandra. *The Witness*
  Donoghue, Emma. ★*Room: A Novel*
  Duncan, Glen. *Talulla Rising*
  Englander, Nathan. *What We Talk About When We Talk About Anne Frank: Stories*
  Greengrass, Jessie. *Sight: A Novel*
  Hausmann, Romy. ★*Dear Child*
  Malerman, Josh. *Bird Box: A Novel*
  Pinter, Jason. *A Stranger at the Door*
  Rendell, Ruth. *The Tree of Hands*

Saul, John. *Midnight Voices*

MOTHER AND TEENAGER
  Bird, Sarah. *The Gap Year: A Novel*
  Malerman, Josh. *Malorie: A Bird Box Novel*

The Mother Code. Stivers, Carole
Mother Daughter Widow Wife. Wasserman, Robin

MOTHER DESERTED FAMILIES
  James, Wendy. *A Little Bird*

Mother Knows Best. Peikoff, Kira
The Mother Next Door. Laskowski, Tara

MOTHER SEPARATED CHILDREN
  Dimechkie, Karim. *Lifted by the Great Nothing*
  Halls, Stacey. *The Lost Orphan*

A Mother's Lie. Zettel, Sarah

MOTHER-DESERTED CHILDREN
  Bieker, Chelsea Jean. *Godshot: A Novel*
  Coster, Naima. *Halsey Street*
  Packer, Ann. *The Children's Crusade*
  Patchett, Ann. ★*The Dutch House: A Novel*
  Roy, Anuradha. *All the Lives We Never Lived: A Novel*
  Walls, Jeannette. *The Silver Star: A Novel*

MOTHER-SEPARATED BOYS
  Draper, Sharon M. ★*Forged by Fire*
  Hannaham, James. ★*Delicious Foods*

MOTHER-SEPARATED CHILDREN
  Atkinson, Kate. *Human Croquet*

MOTHER-SEPARATED FAMILIES
  Gardner, Lisa. *The Neighbor*
  Russell, Karen. ★*Swamplandia!*

MOTHER-SEPARATED GIRLS
  Foley, Bridget. *Just Get Home*
  Johnson, Daisy. *Everything Under*

MOTHERHOOD
  Arnett, Kristen N. *With Teeth: A Novel*
  Benjamin, Melanie. ★*The Aviator's Wife: A Novel*
  Drabble, Margaret. *The Pure Gold Baby*
  Ferrante, Elena. *The Lost Daughter*
  Freitas, Donna. *The Nine Lives of Rose Napolitano*
  Golding, Melanie. *The Hidden: A Novel*
  Golding, Melanie. *Little Darlings*
  Greengrass, Jessie. *Sight: A Novel*
  Harding, Lisa. *Bright Burning Things*
  Haydon, Elizabeth. *The Merchant Emperor*
  Molloy, Aimee. *The Perfect Mother: A Novel*
  O'Farrell, Maggie. *The Hand That First Held Mine: A Novel*
  Pilcher, Rosamunde. ★*The Shell Seekers*
  Ramqvist, Karolina. *The White City*
  Scottoline, Lisa. ★*Come Home*
  Sekaran, Shanthi. ★*Lucky Boy*
  Stivers, Carole. *The Mother Code*
  Strout, Elizabeth. *My Name Is Lucy Barton*
  Swamy, Shruti. *A House Is a Body: Stories*
  Walbert, Kate. *She Was Like That: New and Selected Stories*
  Yoder, Rachel. *Nightbitch*

MOTHERHOOD — PSYCHOLOGICAL ASPECTS
  Audrain, Ashley. *The Push*
  Stage, Zoje. ★*Baby Teeth: A Novel*

★*Mothering Sunday: A Romance*. Swift, Graham

Motherland Hotel. Atilgan, Yusuf
★*Motherless Brooklyn*. Lethem, Jonathan
The Mothers. Bennett, Brit
MOTHERS
　　Bair, Kristin. *Agatha Arch Is Afraid of Everything*
　　Barclay, Linwood. *Broken Promise*
　　Bock, Charles. *Alice & Oliver: A Novel*
　　Cash, Wiley. *The Last Ballad: A Novel*
　　Clark, Tracy P. *Runner*
　　Cobb, May K. *The Hunting Wives*
　　Coetzee, J. M. *Elizabeth Costello*
　　Dobmeier, Tracy. ★*Girls with Bright Futures: A Novel*
　　Donoghue, Emma. ★*Frog Music*
　　Edwards, Yvvette. *The Mother*
　　Ellmann, Lucy. *Ducks, Newburyport*
　　Enright, Anne. *The Green Road: A Novel*
　　Fisher, Helen. *Space Hopper*
　　Gelman, Laurie. *Class Mom: A Novel*
　　Gornichec, Genevieve. ★*The Witch's Heart*
　　Hamilton, Jane. *A Map of the World*
　　Hankin, Laura. *Happy & You Know It*
　　Hannah, Sophie. *Perfect Little Children*
　　Jemisin, N. K. *The Fifth Season*
　　Jemisin, N. K. *The Obelisk Gate*
　　Jemisin, N. K. *The Stone Sky*
　　Kingsolver, Barbara. ★*Flight Behavior*
　　Laskowski, Tara. *The Mother Next Door*
　　Moriarty, Liane. *The Husband's Secret*
　　Perrotta, Tom. *Little Children*
　　Stuart, Douglas. ★*Shuggie Bain*
MOTHERS — DEATH
　　Barker, Nicola. *Darkmans*
　　Coetzee, J. M. ★*Life & Times of Michael K*
　　Constantine, Liv. *The Last Time I Saw You*
　　Fuller, Claire. *Unsettled Ground*
　　Haywood, Sarah. *The Cactus*
　　Holdstock, Pauline. *Here I Am!*
　　Jin, Meng. *Little Gods*
　　Joukhadar, Zeyn. ★*The Thirty Names of Night: A Novel*
　　Kim, Nancy Jooyoun. *The Last Story of Mina Lee*
　　Kraus, Daniel. *The Autumnal: The Complete Series*
　　Lipman, Elinor. *The Dearly Departed*
　　Lipman, Elinor. *Good Riddance*
　　Macmillan, Gilly. *The Perfect Girl*
　　Masad, Ilana. *All My Mother's Lovers: A Novel*
　　McDonald, Christina. *Behind Every Lie*
　　Sainz Borgo, Karina. ★*It Would Be Night in Caracas*
　　Sapphire. ★*The Kid: A Novel*
　　Schulman, Alex. *The Survivors: A Novel*
　　Scott, Stephanie. *What's Left of Me Is Yours: A Novel*
　　Shafak, Elif. *Honor: A Novel*
　　St. Aubyn, Edward. *At Last*
　　Tartt, Donna. ★*The Goldfinch*
　　Yoshimoto, Banana. *The Lake*
MOTHERS AND DAUGHTERS
　　Abbott, Jeff. *The Three Beths*
　　Abbott, Patricia. *Concrete Angel*
　　Aliu, Xhenet. ★*Brass: A Novel*

Audrain, Ashley. *The Push*
Austen, Jane. ★*Pride and Prejudice*
Austin, Lynn N. *Chasing Shadows*
Bacon, Charlotte. *There Is Room for You*
Bell, Darcey. *Something She's Not Telling Us*
Bennett, Brit. ★*The Vanishing Half*
Bialosky, Jill. *House Under Snow*
Bieker, Chelsea Jean. *Godshot: A Novel*
Braffet, Kelly. ★*Last Seen Leaving: A Novel*
Briscoe, Joanna. *The Seduction*
Campbell, Bonnie Jo. *Once Upon a River*
Carpenter, Emily. *Until the Day I Die*
Chambers, Clare. *Small Pleasures*
Chan, Jessamine. *The School for Good Mothers*
Cho, Zen. *Spirits Abroad and Other Stories*
Clement, Jennifer. *Gun Love*
Cook, Diane. ★*The New Wilderness: A Novel*
Crowell, Jenn. *Etched on Me: A Novel*
Dalcher, Christina. *Femlandia*
Dallas, Sandra. *Westering Women: A Novel*
DeCarlo, Melissa. *The Art of Crash Landing: A Novel*
Deon, Natashia. *Grace*
Dermansky, Marcy. *Very Nice*
Desai, Anita. *Fire on the Mountain*
Diamant, Anita. ★*The Red Tent*
Diehl, Heidi. *Lifelines*
Dodd, Christina. *What Doesn't Kill Her*
Doshi, Avni. *Burnt Sugar: A Novel*
Ekwuyasi, Francesca. *Butter Honey Pig Bread: A Novel*
Enright, Anne. *Actress: A Novel*
Epstein, Jennifer Cody. ★*Wunderland: A Novel*
Erdrich, Louise. *The Beet Queen: A Novel*
Fabry, Chris. *Looking into You*
Fajardo-Anstine, Kali. ★*Sabrina & Corina: Stories*
Ferrante, Elena. *The Lost Daughter*
Fesperman, Dan. *Safe Houses: A Novel*
Ford, Kelli Jo. ★*Crooked Hallelujah*
Frank, Alli. *Tiny Imperfections*
Gabaldon, Diana. ★*Dragonfly in Amber*
Gabaldon, Diana. ★*Drums of Autumn*
Gabaldon, Diana. ★*The Fiery Cross*
Garcia, Gabriela. *Of Women and Salt*
Gerritsen, Tess. *Playing with Fire*
Goldberg, Myla. *Feast Your Eyes*
Golding, Melanie. *The Hidden: A Novel*
Gray, Anissa. *The Care and Feeding of Ravenously Hungry Girls*
Grossman, David. ★*More Than I Love My Life: A Novel*
Harris, Joanne. ★*Chocolat: A Novel*
Hashemzadeh Bonde, Golnaz. *What We Owe*
Hepworth, Sally. *The Secrets of Midwives*
Higgins, Kristan. *Always the Last to Know*
Hoffmann, R. J. *Other People's Children: A Novel*
Hogan, Ruth. *Queenie Malone's Paradise Hotel*
Huisman, Violaine. *The Book of Mother*
Janowitz, Brenda. *The Grace Kelly Dress*
Jin, Meng. *Little Gods*
Johnson, Daisy. *Everything Under*
Johnson, Keith Lee. ★*Little Black Girl Lost*

Jones, Darynda. *A Good Day for Chardonnay*
Kantra, Virginia. ★*Meg and Jo*
Keller, Julia. *A Killing in the Hills*
Kelly, Julia. *The Last Dance of the Debutante*
Kim, Nancy Jooyoun. *The Last Story of Mina Lee*
Kraus, Daniel. *The Autumnal: The Complete Series*
Landau, Alexis. *Those Who Are Saved*
Lethem, Jonathan. *Dissident Gardens*
Levy, Deborah. *Hot Milk: A Novel*
Lewis, Beverly. *The Missing*
Lopez Barrio, Cristina. *The House of the Impossible Loves*
Makkai, Rebecca. ★*The Great Believers*
Makumbi, Jennifer Nansubuga. ★*A Girl Is a Body of Water*
March, William. *The Bad Seed: A Novel*
McDonald, Christina. *Behind Every Lie*
McMurtry, Larry. ★*Terms of Endearment: A Novel : With a New Preface*
Miller, Sue. *The Good Mother*
Mina, Denise. *The Less Dead*
Montag, Kassandra. *After the Flood: A Novel*
Morrison, Toni. ★*Beloved: A Novel*
Morrison, Toni. ★*God Help the Child*
Morton, Kate. *The Distant Hours: A Novel*
Moyes, Jojo. *The Peacock Emporium*
Oates, Joyce Carol. *Blonde: A Novel*
Oyeyemi, Helen. *Boy, Snow, Bird: A Novel*
Oyeyemi, Helen. *Gingerbread: A Novel*
Picoult, Jodi. *Keeping Faith: A Novel*
Picoult, Jodi. *Leaving Time: A Novel*
Pronzini, Bill. *Crazybone*
Rosner, Jennifer. ★*The Yellow Bird Sings*
Rouda, Kaira Sturdivant. *The Favorite Daughter*
Sandford, John. ★*Mind Prey*
Sarton, May. *A Reckoning: A Novel*
Schwarz, Christina. *Drowning Ruth*
Scottoline, Lisa. *After Anna*
See, Lisa. *Dreams of Joy: A Novel*
Semple, Maria. *Where'd You Go, Bernadette: A Novel*
Seth, Vikram. ★*A Suitable Boy: A Novel*
Shafak, Elif. *The Bastard of Istanbul*
Shimotakahara, Leslie. *After the Bloom*
Simpson, Mona. *Anywhere but Here*
Slaughter, Karin. ★*Pieces of Her*
Smith, Lee. ★*Fair and Tender Ladies*
Solomon, Anna. *Leaving Lucy Pear*
Spiotta, Dana. *Wayward*
Stage, Zoje. ★*Baby Teeth: A Novel*
Strout, Elizabeth. *Amy and Isabelle: A Novel*
Strout, Elizabeth. ★*Anything Is Possible: Fiction*
Strout, Elizabeth. *My Name Is Lucy Barton*
Styles, Toy. *Raunchy*
Styles, Toy. *Raunchy 2: Mad's Love*
Sutanto, Jesse Q. *Dial a for Aunties*
Tan, Amy. *The Bonesetter's Daughter*
Tan, Amy. ★*The Joy Luck Club*
Tan, Amy. ★*The Kitchen God's Wife*
Tan, Amy. *The Valley of Amazement*
Tan, Sue Lynn. ★*Daughter of the Moon Goddess*

Tatlock, Ann. *Promises to Keep*
Tepper, Sheri S. *Singer from the Sea*
Tudor, C. J. *The Other People*
Vann, David. *Aquarium*
Waite, Jen. *Survival Instincts*
Walls, Jeannette. *The Silver Star: A Novel*
Weiner, Jennifer. *Little Earthquakes*
Whittall, Zoe. *The Spectacular: A Novel*
Wieland, Liza. *Paris, 7 A.M.*
Woodson, Jacqueline. ★*Red at the Bone*
Wrobel, Stephanie. *Darling Rose Gold*

MOTHERS AND SONS
Arnett, Kristen N. *With Teeth: A Novel*
Barton, Fiona. *The Suspect*
Bear, Elizabeth. *Blood and Iron: A Novel of the Promethean Age*
Beukes, Lauren. *Afterland*
Bourdeaut, Olivier. *Waiting for Bojangles: A Novel*
Boyne, John. *The Heart's Invisible Furies*
Buehlman, Christopher. *The Suicide Motor Club*
Colvin, Jeffrey. ★*Africaville: A Novel*
Cunningham, Michael. ★*The Hours*
Cush, Jean Love. *Endangered*
Cusk, Rachel. *Transit*
Daoud, Kamel. *The Meursault Investigation*
Everett, Percival L. *Erasure: A Novel*
Ferber, Edna. *So Big*
Flagg, Fannie. *Standing in the Rainbow: A Novel*
Flagg, Fannie. ★*The Wonder Boy of Whistle Stop: A Novel*
French, Albert. *Billy*
Gelman, Laurie. *Yoga Pant Nation: A Novel*
Gelman, Laurie. *You've Been Volunteered: A Class Mom Novel*
George, Margaret. *The Confessions of Young Nero*
Gilb, Dagoberto. *The Flowers: A Novel*
Grodstein, Lauren. *Our Short History*
Guskin, Sharon. *The Forgetting Time*
Headley, Maria Dahvana. *The Mere Wife*
Hiaasen, Carl. *Nature Girl*
Hilderbrand, Elin. ★*Troubles in Paradise*
Hill, Nathan. *The Nix: A Novel*
Irving, John. ★*The World According to Garp: A Novel*
Ko, Lisa. *The Leavers*
Lawrence, D. H. *Sons and Lovers*
Lessing, Doris May. ★*The Fifth Child*
Lodato, Victor. *Edgar and Lucy: A Novel*
Miller, Andrew. *Oxygen*
Oates, Joyce Carol. *The Gravedigger's Daughter: A Novel*
Ogawa, Yoko. *The Housekeeper and the Professor*
Persaud, Ingrid. *Love After Love: A Novel*
Phillips, Gin. *Fierce Kingdom: A Novel*
Phillips, Susan Elizabeth. ★*Natural Born Charmer*
Priest, Cherie. *Boneshaker*
Roy, Anuradha. *All the Lives We Never Lived: A Novel*
Rushdie, Salman. *The Moor's Last Sigh*
Schami, Rafik. *Sophia: Or the Beginning of All Tales*
Scottoline, Lisa. *One Perfect Lie*
Speight, Shameek A. ★*A Child of a Crack Head*
Strout, Elizabeth. *Olive Kitteridge*
Strout, Elizabeth. ★*Olive, Again: A Novel*

Styles, Toy. *A Hustler's Son: A Novel*
Tarkington, Booth. ★*The Magnificent Ambersons*
Tenorio, Lysley A. *The Son of Good Fortune: A Novel*
Thomas, Bev. *A Good Enough Mother: A Novel*
Toole, John Kennedy. ★*A Confederacy of Dunces*
Vuong, Ocean. ★*On Earth We're Briefly Gorgeous: A Novel*
Williams, Katie. *Tell the Machine Goodnight*

MOTHERS OF CHILDREN WITH DISABILITIES
Drabble, Margaret. *The Pure Gold Baby*

MOTHERS OF KIDNAPPING VICTIMS
McKinty, Adrian. ★*The Chain*
Montag, Kassandra. *After the Flood: A Novel*

MOTHERS OF MURDER VICTIMS
Bruen, Ken. *The Guards*
Edwards, Yvvette. *The Mother*

MOTHERS WITH TERMINAL ILLNESSES
Grodstein, Lauren. *Our Short History*
Petterson, Per. *I Curse the River of Time*

MOTHERS-IN-LAW
Bellow, Saul. *The Dean's December: A Novel*
Weiner, Jennifer. *Little Earthquakes*

MOTIVE (LAW)
Burnet, Graeme Macrae. *His Bloody Project: Documents Relating to the Case of Roderick Macrae*
Simpson, Dorothy. *Last Seen Alive: A Luke Thanet Mystery*

MOTORCYCLE GANGS
Child, Lee. *The Midnight Line*
Reichs, Kathy. *Deadly Decisions*

Mott, Jason
Hell of a Book

MOUNT ARARAT
Golden, Christopher. *Ararat*

MOUNT EVEREST
Simmons, Dan. *The Abominable: A Novel*

MOUNTAIN LIFE
Brown, Taylor. ★*Gods of Howl Mountain: A Novel*
Carr, Robyn. *The Family Gathering*
Marshall, Catherine. *Christy*
Oe, Kenzaburo. *Nip the Buds, Shoot the Kids*
Panowich, Brian. *Bull Mountain*
Rash, Ron. ★*In the Valley: Stories and a Novella Based on Serena*
Rash, Ron. *Something Rich and Strange: Selected Stories*
Smith, Lee. ★*Fair and Tender Ladies*
Smith, Lee. *Oral History*
Weiss, Leah. *If the Creek Don't Rise: A Novel*

MOUNTAIN MEN
Guthrie, A. B. ★*The Big Sky*

MOUNTAIN SURVIVAL
Nelson, Christina Suzann. *If We Make It Home: A Novel of Faith and Survival in the Oregon Wilderness*

MOUNTAINEERING
Simmons, Dan. *The Abominable: A Novel*

MOUNTAINEERS
Simmons, Dan. *The Abominable: A Novel*

MOUNTAINS
Golden, Christopher. *Ararat*
Kawabata, Yasunari. *The Sound of the Mountain*
★*The Mountains Sing: A Novel*. Nguyen, Phan Que Mai

The *Mountaintop School for Dogs and Other Second Chances*. Cooney, Ellen
Mourners. Pronzini, Bill
Mourning. Halfon, Eduardo

MOURNING CUSTOMS
Rojstaczer, Stuart. *The Mathematician's Shiva: A Novel*
Mouthful of Birds: Stories. Schweblin, Samanta
★*The Moviegoer*. Percy, Walker

MOVING HOUSEHOLD
North, Alex. *The Whisper Man*

MOVING TO A NEW CITY
Copenhaver, John. *The Savage Kind*
Danan, Rosie. *The Roommate*
Dreiser, Theodore. ★*Sister Carrie*
Hirahara, Naomi. ★*Clark and Division*
King, Lily. *Writers & Lovers: A Novel*
Kubica, Mary. ★*The Other Mrs.*
Luchette, Claire. *Agatha of Little Neon*
Macomber, Debbie. *If Not for You: A Novel*
March, William. *The Bad Seed: A Novel*
McQuiston, Casey. ★*One Last Stop*
Mendez, Paul. *Rainbow Milk*
Preston, Caroline. *The Scrapbook of Frankie Pratt*
Simpson, Mona. *Anywhere but Here*
Spencer-Fleming, Julia. *In the Bleak Midwinter*
Swinson, David. *City on the Edge*

MOVING TO A NEW COUNTRY
Bannister, Ilona. *When I Ran Away*
Kantaria, Annabel. *I Know You: A Novel of Suspense*
Quotah, Eman. ★*Bride of the Sea: A Novel*

MOVING TO A NEW STATE
Clark, Wahida. *Thug Lovin'*
Cobb, May K. *The Hunting Wives*
Kimmel, Fran. *No Good Asking: A Novel*
Shelton, Paige. *Thin Ice: A Mystery*
Tyree, Omar. *For the Love of Money: A Novel*

MOVING, HOUSEHOLD
Auslander, Shalom. *Hope: A Tragedy*
Baldwin, Joshua. *The Wilshire Sun*
Chang, Alexandra. ★*Days of Distraction*
Duffy, Brendan. *House of Echoes: A Novel*
Hannah, Kristin. *The Great Alone*
Herrera, Adriana. ★*American Dreamer*
Johnson, Daisy. *Sisters*
Kantaria, Annabel. *I Know You: A Novel of Suspense*
Phillips, Susan Elizabeth. ★*Dance Away with Me*
Ramsay, Hope. *Summer on Moonlight Bay*
Stage, Zoje. *Wonderland*
Vandelly, T. Marie. *Theme Music*

Moyes, Jojo
The Girl You Left Behind
★*The Giver of Stars: A Novel*
Me Before You: A Novel
The Peacock Emporium

MOZAMBIQUE
Couto, Mia. *Rain: And Other Stories*
Couto, Mia. *Sleepwalking Land*
Couto, Mia. *The Sword and the Spear*

Mozley, Fiona
★*Elmet*
Mr Campion's Coven. Ripley, Mike
Mr Campion's Fault. Ripley, Mike
Mr. Campion's War. Ripley, Mike
Mr. Fox. Oyeyemi, Helen
Mr. Mercedes: A Novel. King, Stephen
Mr. Midshipman Hornblower. Forester, C. S.
Mr. Nobody: A Novel. Steadman, Catherine
Mr. Peanut. Ross, Adam
Mr. Penumbra's 24-Hour Bookstore. Sloan, Robin
★*Mr. Sammler's Planet*. Bellow, Saul
Mr. Tall: A Novella and Stories. Earley, Tony
Mr. X. Straub, Peter
Mrs Pargeter's Principle. Brett, Simon
★*Mrs. Dalloway*. Woolf, Virginia
★*Mrs. Everything: A Novel*. Weiner, Jennifer
Mrs. Kimble: A Novel. Haigh, Jennifer
Mrs. Lincoln's Dressmaker: A Novel. Chiaverini, Jennifer
Mrs. Lincoln's Sisters. Chiaverini, Jennifer
Mrs. McGinty's Dead. Christie, Agatha
Mrs. Mike series [Series]. Freedman, Benedict
Mrs. Mike: The Story of Katherine Mary Flannigan. Freedman, Benedict
Mrs. Murphy mysteries [Series]. Brown, Rita Mae
Mrs. Pargeter mysteries [Series]. Brett, Simon
★*Mrs. Wiggins*. Monroe, Mary
Ms. Hempel Chronicles. Bynum, Sarah Shun-Lien
Ms. Ice Sandwich. Kawakami, Mieko
Mudbound: a Novel. Jordan, Hillary
Mueenuddin, Daniyal
In Other Rooms, Other Wonders: Connected Stories
MUGGING
Loren, Roni. *The One You Can't Forget*
MUGHAL EMPIRE
Rushdie, Salman. *The Enchantress of Florence: A Novel*
Muir, Tamsyn
Harrow the Ninth
Mukherjee, Abir
Death in the East
The Shadows of Men
Smoke and Ashes: A Novel
Mukherjee, Neel
The Lives of Others
★*A State of Freedom*
Mullen, Thomas
Darktown: A Novel
Lightning Men: A Novel
Muller, Marcia
Dead Midnight
Ice and Stone
MULTICULTURAL ROMANCES
Billingsley, ReShonda Tate. ★*The Secret She Kept*
Blumberg, Chandra. *Digging up Love*
Bryant, Niobia. *Christmas with the Billionaire*
Cochrun, Alison. *The Charm Offensive*
Cole, Alyssa. ★*A Duke by Default*
Cole, Alyssa. ★*An Extraordinary Union*
Cole, Alyssa. ★*A Hope Divided*

Cole, Alyssa. ★*How to Catch a Queen*
Cole, Alyssa. *How to Find a Princess*
Cole, Alyssa. ★*A Prince on Paper*
Cole, Alyssa. ★*A Princess in Theory*
Cole, Alyssa. ★*An Unconditional Freedom*
Daria, Alexis. ★*A Lot Like Adios*
Daria, Alexis. ★*You Had Me at Hola*
Dev, Sonali. ★*A Bollywood Affair*
Dev, Sonali. *The Bollywood Bride*
Dev, Sonali. *A Distant Heart*
Dev, Sonali. ★*Incense and Sensibility*
Dev, Sonali. ★*Pride, Prejudice, and Other Flavors: A Novel*
Dev, Sonali. ★*Recipe for Persuasion*
Glass, Seressia. ★*The Love Con*
Guillory, Jasmine. *Party of Two*
Guillory, Jasmine. *The Proposal*
Guillory, Jasmine. *Royal Holiday*
Guillory, Jasmine. ★*The Wedding Date*
Guillory, Jasmine. *The Wedding Party*
Guillory, Jasmine. ★*While We Were Dating*
Herrera, Adriana. ★*American Dreamer*
Herrera, Adriana. *American Fairytale*
Herrera, Adriana. *American Love Story*
Hibbert, Talia. ★*Act Your Age, Eve Brown*
Hibbert, Talia. ★*Get a Life, Chloe Brown*
Hibbert, Talia. *A Girl Like Her*
Hibbert, Talia. ★*Take a Hint, Dani Brown*
Hill, Donna. ★*Confessions in B-Flat*
Hoang, Helen. ★*The Bride Test*
Hoang, Helen. ★*The Heart Principle*
Hodges, Cheris F. ★*Rumor Has It*
Jackson, Brenda. *Forged in Desire*
Jackson, K. M. *How to Marry Keanu Reeves in 90 Days*
Jenkins, Beverly. *Forbidden*
Jenkins, Beverly. *Rebel*
Jenkins, Beverly. *Tempest*
Jenkins, Beverly. *Wild Rain*
Lalli, Sonya. *A Holly Jolly Diwali*
Lalli, Sonya. *The Matchmaker's List*
Livesay, Tracey. *Like Lovers Do*
Loren, Roni. *The One You Fight For*
Marsh, Nicola. *The Boy Toy*
Martin, Alexa. *Fumbled*
Martin, Alexa. ★*Intercepted*
Matthews, Mimi. ★*The Siren of Sussex*
Oliveras, Priscilla. *Anchored Hearts*
Pineiro, Caridad. *South Beach Love: A Feel-Good Romance from Hallmark Publishing*
Pope, Jamie. *One Warm Winter*
Quincy, Diana. *Her Night with the Duke*
Quincy, Diana. *The Viscount Made Me Do It*
Rai, Alisha. ★*First Comes Like*
Rai, Alisha. ★*Girl Gone Viral*
Rai, Alisha. ★*The Right Swipe*
Rochon, Farrah. *The Boyfriend Project*
Rogers, Morgan Callan. ★*Honey Girl*
Ryan, Kennedy. ★*Long Shot*
Solomon, Rachel Lynn. ★*The Ex Talk*

Tieu, Julie. *The Donut Trap*
Weatherspoon, Rebekah. *A Cowboy to Remember*
Weatherspoon, Rebekah. *Rafe: A Buff Male Nanny*
Weatherspoon, Rebekah. *A Thorn in the Saddle*
Weatherspoon, Rebekah. ★*Xeni: A Marriage of Inconvenience*
Williams, Denise. *The Fastest Way to Fall*
Williams, Preslaysa. *A Lowcountry Bride*
Williams, Synithia. *Forbidden Promises*

MULTICULTURALISM
Jaswal, Balli Kaur. *Erotic Stories for Punjabi Widows*

MULTINATIONAL CORPORATIONS
Fforde, Jasper. *Lost in a Good Book: A Thursday Next Novel*

MULTIPLE PERSPECTIVES
Abraham, Tola Rotimi. *Black Sunday*
Acker, Jennifer. ★*The Limits of the World*
Adams, Hope. *Dangerous Women*
Adams, Taylor. *Hairpin Bridge*
Adebayo, Ayobami. ★*Stay with Me*
Akinmade-Akerstrom, Lola. *In Every Mirror She's Black*
Akunin, B. *The Coronation: The Further Adventures of Erast Fandorin*
Alvarez, Julia. *How the Garcia Girls Lost Their Accents*
Appanah-Mouriquand, Nathacha. *Tropic of Violence: A Novel*
Atkinson, Kate. ★*Big Sky*
Atkinson, Kate. ★*Case Histories*
Atkinson, Kate. *One Good Turn: A Novel*
Atkinson, Kate. *Started Early, Took My Dog*
Atkinson, Kate. ★*When Will There Be Good News?: A Novel*
Auster, Paul. *Sunset Park*
Banks, Russell. ★*The Sweet Hereafter*
Barber, Lizzy. *A Girl Named Anna*
Barnes, Julian. *The Only Story*
Bartz, Andrea. *The Herd: A Novel*
Bauer, Belinda. *Snap*
Beattie, Ann. *The Doctor's House: A Novel*
Beattie, Ann. ★*Picturing Will*
Beckerman, Hannah. *If Only I Could Tell You*
Belle, Kimberly. *Dear Wife*
Bergstrom, Heather Brittain. *Steal the North: A Novel*
Beukes, Lauren. *The Shining Girls*
Bijan, Donia. *The Last Days of Cafe Leila*
Binchy, Maeve. ★*Whitethorn Woods*
Black, Saul. *Anything for You*
Blakemore, A. K. *The Manningtree Witches*
Block, Stefan Merrill. *Oliver Loving: A Novel*
Blumenfeld, Amy. *The Cast*
Bohjalian, Chris. *The Night Strangers: A Novel*
Box, C. J. *Blue Heaven*
Boyle, T. Coraghessan. *The Terranauts*
Boyle, T. Coraghessan. ★*The Tortilla Curtain*
Brink, Andre P. *Philida: A Novel*
Bronte, Anne. *The Tenant of Wildfell Hall*
Brown, Rosellen. ★*Before and After*
Brundage, Elizabeth. *The Vanishing Point*
Burdick, Serena. *Find Me in Havana*
Burdick, Serena. *The Girls with No Names*
Burke, Sue. *Semiosis*
Butler, Sarah. *Ten Things I've Learnt About Love: A Novel*

Buwalda, Peter. *Bonita Avenue: A Novel*
Campbell, Lisbeth. *The Vanished Queen*
Candlish, Louise. *Our House*
Carter, Michaela. *Leonora in the Morning Light*
Cash, Wiley. *When Ghosts Come Home: A Novel*
Castellani, Christopher. *Leading Men: A Novel*
Castro, V. *Goddess of Filth*
Chancellor, Bryn. *Sycamore: A Novel*
Chancy, Myriam J. A. ★*What Storm, What Thunder*
Chiaverini, Jennifer. *Mrs. Lincoln's Sisters*
Chiaverini, Jennifer. *Resistance Women: A Novel*
Chung, Maxine Mei-Fung. *The Eighth Girl*
Clarke, Susanna. ★*Jonathan Strange & Mr. Norrell*
Clegg, Bill. *Did You Ever Have a Family*
Clegg, Bill. *The End of the Day*
Cobbs Hoffman, Elizabeth. *The Hamilton Affair*
Coben, Harlan. *Hold Tight*
Collins, Wilkie. ★*The Moonstone*
Connelly, Michael. *The Scarecrow: A Novel*
Cook, Diane. ★*The New Wilderness: A Novel*
Cook, Thomas H. *Instruments of Night*
Cooley, Martha. *The Archivist: A Novel*
Cordova, Zoraida. *The Inheritance of Orquidea Divina*
Corry, Jane. *The Dead Ex*
Couto, Mia. *The Sword and the Spear*
Cross-Smith, Leesa. *Whiskey & Ribbons*
Crow, Sarah McCraw. *The Wrong Kind of Woman*
Dahl, Julia. *The Missing Hours*
Daniels, Natalie. *Too Close*
Davidson, Ash. ★*Damnation Spring*
Davies, Carys. *The Mission House*
Davis, Fiona. *The Masterpiece*
De Giovanni, Maurizio. *The Bastards of Pizzofalcone*
De Giovanni, Maurizio. *The Crocodile*
Delaney, J. P. *The Girl Before: A Novel*
Delaney, J. P. *Playing Nice*
DeLillo, Don. *Underworld*
Dennis-Benn, Nicole. ★*Patsy: A Novel*
Dermansky, Marcy. *Very Nice*
Desai, Kiran. *The Inheritance of Loss*
Dickens, Charles. ★*Bleak House*
Dimitri, Francesco. *The Book of Hidden Things*
Diofebi, Dario. *Paradise, Nevada*
Dodd, Christina. *Virtue Falls*
Doerr, Anthony. ★*All the Light We Cannot See: A Novel*
Donohue, Keith. *The Stolen Child*
Ebershoff, David. *The 19th Wife: A Novel*
Elliott, Kate. *Unconquerable Sun*
Ellison, J. T. *Good Girls Lie*
Ellroy, James. *The Cold Six Thousand: A Novel*
Emezi, Akwaeke. ★*The Death of Vivek Oji*
Enright, Anne. *The Green Road: A Novel*
Erdrich, Louise. *The Beet Queen: A Novel*
Erdrich, Louise. *The Last Report on the Miracles at Little No Horse*
Erdrich, Louise. *The Plague of Doves*
Evaristo, Bernardine. ★*Girl, Woman, Other*
Faulkner, William. ★*The Sound and the Fury*
Faulks, Sebastian. *A Week in December*

Faye, Lyndsay. ★*The King of Infinite Space*
Ferrell, Carolyn. *Dear Miss Metropolitan*
ffitch, Madeline. *Stay and Fight*
Fine, Julia. *What Should Be Wild*
Flynn, Gillian. ★*Gone Girl: A Novel*
Foer, Jonathan Safran. *Extremely Loud and Incredibly Close*
Foley, Lucy. *The Hunting Party*
Force, Marie. *Five Years Gone*
Fowler, Karen Joy. *The Jane Austen Book Club*
Fowler, Therese. ★*A Good Neighborhood*
Francis, Patry. *All the Children Are Home*
Francis, Patry. *The Orphans of Race Point: A Novel*
Frankel, Laurie. *One Two Three: A Novel*
Frazier, Charles. ★*Cold Mountain*
Freeman, Anna. *The Fair Fight: A Novel*
Friedland, Elyssa. *The Floating Feldmans*
Friedland, Elyssa. *The Intermission*
Friedland, Elyssa. *Last Summer at the Golden Hotel*
Gabaldon, Diana. ★*Dragonfly in Amber*
Gaige, Amity. *Sea Wife*
Gaines, Ernest J. ★*A Gathering of Old Men*
Gaitskill, Mary. *The Mare: A Novel*
Gala, Marcial. ★*The Black Cathedral*
Garcia, Cristina. *King of Cuba: A Novel*
Garcia, Gabriela. *Of Women and Salt*
Gardner, Lisa. *The Neighbor*
Gaylin, Alison. *Never Look Back*
Geni, Abby. *The Wildlands: A Novel*
Genova, Lisa. *Inside the O'Briens: A Novel*
George, Nina. *The Book of Dreams*
Gerritsen, Tess. *Choose Me*
Gibson, William. ★*Agency*
Glass, Julia. ★*Three Junes*
Godwin, Gail. *Unfinished Desires*
Goodwin, Bobi Gentry. *Revelation*
Gordimer, Nadine. *The Conservationist*
Gordimer, Nadine. *No Time Like the Present: A Novel*
Gray, Anissa. *The Care and Feeding of Ravenously Hungry Girls*
Gregory, Philippa. *The Boleyn Inheritance*
Gregory, Philippa. *The Constant Princess*
Griffiths, Elly. *The Postscript Murders*
Griffiths, Elly. *The Stranger Diaries*
Groff, Lauren. ★*Fates and Furies*
Gunaratne, Guy. *In Our Mad and Furious City*
Gundar-Goshen, Ayelet. *Waking Lions*
Guterson, David. *The Other*
Hall, Araminta. *Imperfect Women: A Novel*
Hall, Louisa. *Speak*
Hallberg, Garth Risk. ★*City on Fire*
Halliday, Lisa. ★*Asymmetry*
Halls, Stacey. *The Lost Orphan*
Hamer, Kate. *The Girl in the Red Coat*
Hand, Elizabeth. *Curious Toys*
Harmel, Kristin. *The Room on Rue Amelie*
Harris, Thomas. *Hannibal*
Harris, Thomas. *Red Dragon*
Harris, Thomas. ★*The Silence of the Lambs*
Hart, Rob. *The Warehouse: A Novel*

Hausmann, Romy. ★*Dear Child*
Hawkins, Paula. ★*The Girl on the Train: A Novel*
Healey, Jane. *The Animals at Lockwood Manor*
Hendricks, Greer. *An Anonymous Girl*
Hepworth, Sally. *The Secrets of Midwives*
Higgins, Kristan. *Always the Last to Know*
Higgins, Kristan. ★*Life and Other Inconveniences*
Hill, Nathan. *The Nix: A Novel*
Hobson, Brandon. ★*The Removed: A Novel*
Holdstock, Pauline. *Here I Am!*
Holmes, J. M. *How Are You Going to Save Yourself*
Holsinger, Bruce W. *The Gifted School: A Novel*
Horrocks, Caitlin. *The Vexations*
Howrey, Meg. *The Wanderers*
Hulme, Keri. ★*The Bone People: A Novel*
Hulse, S. M. *Eden Mine*
Igharo, Jane. *The Sweetest Remedy*
Iweala, Uzodinma. ★*Speak No Evil*
James, Marlon. ★*A Brief History of Seven Killings: A Novel*
James, Wendy. *A Little Bird*
Jemc, Jac. ★*The Grip of It*
Jewell, Lisa. *The Family Upstairs*
Jewell, Lisa. *Then She Was Gone: A Novel*
Jin, Meng. *Little Gods*
Johnson, Daisy. *Sisters*
Jones, Cherie. *How the One-Armed Sister Sweeps Her House*
Jones, Stephen Graham. ★*The Only Good Indians: A Novel*
Jones, Tanen. *The Better Liar: A Novel*
Jordan, Hillary. *Mudbound: A Novel*
Joyce, James. ★*Ulysses*
Katsu, Alma. *The Deep*
Kelly, Erin. *The Burning Air: A Novel*
Kelly, Erin. *Watch Her Fall*
Kennedy, Randy. *Presidio*
Kesey, Ken. *Sometimes a Great Notion: A Novel*
Kidd, Sue Monk. ★*The Invention of Wings: A Novel*
Kim, Crystal Hana. *If You Leave Me*
Kimani, Peter. *Dance of the Jakaranda*
Kimmel, Fran. *No Good Asking: A Novel*
Kingsolver, Barbara. ★*The Poisonwood Bible: A Novel*
Klay, Phil. ★*Missionaries*
Kutsukake, Lynne. *The Translation of Love: A Novel*
Kwok, Jean. *Searching for Sylvie Lee*
Kwon, Yo-Son. *Lemon*
Lalami, Laila. *The Other Americans: A Novel*
Laskowski, Tara. *The Mother Next Door*
Layden, Emily. *All Girls*
Lerner, Ben. ★*The Topeka School*
Levy, Andrea. *Small Island*
Lewis, Linden A. *The First Sister: A Novel*
Lippman, Laura. ★*Lady in the Lake: A Novel*
Logan, T. M. *The Vacation*
Lutz, Lisa. *The Swallows: A Novel*
Mackintosh, Clare. *After the End*
Macmillan, Gilly. *The Nanny*
Majumdar, Megha. *A Burning*
Mandel, Emily St. John. ★*The Glass Hotel: A Novel*
Mapson, Jo-Ann. *Bad Girl Creek: A Novel*

Marcom, Micheline Aharonian. *The New American*
Martin, George R. R. ★*A Clash of Kings*
Martin, George R. R. ★*A Dance with Dragons*
Martin, George R. R. ★*A Feast for Crows*
Martin, George R. R. ★*A Game of Thrones*
Martin, George R. R. ★*A Storm of Swords*
Martine, Arkady. ★*A Desolation Called Peace*
Masad, Ilana. *All My Mother's Lovers: A Novel*
Mason, Jamie. *The Hidden Things*
Maxwell, Everina. *Winter's Orbit*
Mbue, Imbolo. *How Beautiful We Were*
McDonald, Christina. *Behind Every Lie*
McKenzie, Alecia. *A Million Aunties*
Meyerson, Amy. *The Imperfects*
Miller, Holly. ★*The Sight of You*
Minato, Kanae. *Confessions*
Mitchell, David. *The Bone Clocks: A Novel*
Mitchell, David. ★*Cloud Atlas: A Novel*
Molloy, Aimee. *The Perfect Mother: A Novel*
Moore, Graham. *The Holdout: A Novel*
Morgenstern, Erin. ★*The Starless Sea*
Moriarty, Liane. *The Husband's Secret*
Moss, Sarah. *Summerwater*
Moyes, Jojo. *Me Before You: A Novel*
Moyes, Jojo. *The Peacock Emporium*
Ng, Celeste. ★*Little Fires Everywhere: A Novel*
Niffenegger, Audrey. *The Time Traveler's Wife: A Novel*
North, Anna. *The Life and Death of Sophie Stark*
Novik, Naomi. ★*Spinning Silver*
Nussbaum, Susan. *Good Kings, Bad Kings: A Novel*
O'Farrell, Maggie. *This Must Be the Place*
O'Farrell, Maggie. *The Vanishing Act of Esme Lennox*
O'Keefe, Megan E. *Velocity Weapon*
Oates, Joyce Carol. ★*My Life as a Rat*
Obreht, Tea. *Inland: A Novel*
Ohlsson, Kristina. *Unwanted: A Novel*
Orange, Tommy. ★*There There*
Osman, Richard. *The Man Who Died Twice: A Thursday Murder Club Mystery*
Osman, Richard. ★*The Thursday Murder Club*
Otsuka, Julie. *When the Emperor Was Divine: A Novel*
Packer, Ann. *The Children's Crusade*
Panowich, Brian. *Bull Mountain*
Patchett, Ann. ★*Commonwealth*
Paton, Alan. *Ah, but Your Land Is Beautiful*
Pavone, Chris. *The Paris Diversion: A Novel*
Pears, Iain. *An Instance of the Fingerpost*
Peikoff, Kira. *Mother Knows Best*
Percy, Walker. *The Second Coming*
Perry, Thomas. *Fidelity*
Persaud, Ingrid. *Love After Love: A Novel*
Phillips, Jayne Anne. *Lark and Termite: A Novel*
Picoult, Jodi. *Change of Heart: A Novel*
Picoult, Jodi. *Leaving Time: A Novel*
Picoult, Jodi. ★*My Sister's Keeper*
Picoult, Jodi. *Nineteen Minutes: A Novel*
Picoult, Jodi. *Sing You Home: A Novel*
Picoult, Jodi. *A Spark of Light: A Novel*

Picoult, Jodi. *Vanishing Acts: A Novel*
Pinborough, Sarah. ★*Behind Her Eyes: A Novel*
Pinborough, Sarah. ★*Cross Her Heart: A Novel*
Pinborough, Sarah. ★*Dead to Her: A Novel*
Poissant, David James. *Lake Life*
Pride, Christine. ★*We Are Not Like Them*
Pronzini, Bill. *Nightcrawlers*
Pronzini, Bill. *The Violated*
Punke, Michael. *Ridgeline: A Novel*
Pynchon, Thomas. *Vineland*
Rash, Ron. *Above the Waterfall*
Rendell, Ruth. *Road Rage*
Reynolds, Allie. ★*Shiver*
Robinson, Kim Stanley. ★*Red Mars*
Robotham, Michael. ★*When She Was Good*
Romero, George A. *The Living Dead*
Rooney, Kathleen. ★*Cher Ami and Major Whittlesey*
Rooney, Sally. *Normal People: A Novel*
Rossner, Rena. *The Light of the Midnight Stars*
Rous, Emma. *The Perfect Guests*
Roy, Lori. ★*Gone Too Long: A Novel*
Runcie, James. *Canvey Island*
Ruskovich, Emily. *Idaho: A Novel*
Sager, Riley. *Final Girls: A Novel*
Schaitkin, Alexis. *Saint X*
Schmidt, Sarah. *See What I Have Done*
Schwab, Victoria. *The Invisible Life of Addie Larue*
Schwarz, Christina. *Drowning Ruth*
Schwarz, Liese O'Halloran. *What Could Be Saved*
Scott, Stephanie. *What's Left of Me Is Yours: A Novel*
See, Lisa. *The Island of Sea Women*
Sekaran, Shanthi. ★*Lucky Boy*
Shaara, Michael. ★*The Killer Angels: A Novel*
Shaffer, Mary Ann. *The Guernsey Literary and Potato Peel Pie Society*
Shepard, Sara. ★*Reputation*
Shields, Carol. ★*The Stone Diaries*
Shreve, Anita. *Testimony: A Novel*
Shteyngart, Gary. ★*Lake Success: A Novel*
Silber, Joan. *Secrets of Happiness*
Simmons, Dan. *The Fall of Hyperion*
Simmons, Dan. *The Fifth Heart*
Simmons, Dan. ★*Hyperion*
Simmons, Dan. ★*The Terror: A Novel*
Skeslien Charles, Janet. *The Paris Library: A Novel*
Sosa, Mia. ★*The Worst Best Man*
Sparks, Nicholas. *The Guardian*
St. Aubyn, Edward. *Double Blind*
Stage, Zoje. ★*Baby Teeth: A Novel*
Starnone, Domenico. *Ties*
Stegner, Wallace. ★*The Big Rock Candy Mountain*
Steinhauer, Olen. ★*All the Old Knives*
Steinhauer, Olen. *The Middleman*
Stevens, Chevy. *Never Let You Go*
Straub, Peter. ★*A Dark Matter: A Novel*
Straub, Peter. *Lost Boy Lost Girl: A Novel*
Stridsberg, Sara. *Valerie: Or the Faculty of Dreams : Amendment to the Theory of Sexuality*

Sullivan, J. Courtney. *Friends and Strangers*
Suri, Tasha. *The Jasmine Throne*
Sweeney-Baird, Christina. *The End of Men*
Swift, Graham. ★*Last Orders: A Novel*
Tan, Amy. ★*The Joy Luck Club*
Taneja, Preti. *We That Are Young: A Novel*
Thompson, Tade. *The Rosewater Redemption*
Toews, Miriam. *Fight Night*
Tolstoy, Leo. ★*Anna Karenina*
Tudor, C. J. *The Burning Girls: A Novel*
Unger, Lisa. ★*The Stranger Inside*
Valentine, Genevieve. *Mechanique: A Tale of the Circus Tresaulti*
Vargas Llosa, Mario. *The Feast of the Goat*
Vaughan, Sarah. ★*Anatomy of a Scandal: A Novel*
Verble, Margaret. ★*When Two Feathers Fell from the Sky*
Vyleta, Dan. *Smoke: A Novel*
Waldman, Amy. *A Door in the Earth*
Walker, Wendy. *Emma in the Night*
Walton, Jo. ★*Necessity*
Ward, Catriona. *The Last House on Needless Street*
Ward, Jesmyn. ★*Sing, Unburied, Sing*
Washington, Bryan. ★*Memorial*
Wasserman, Robin. *Mother Daughter Widow Wife*
Weiner, Jennifer. *Little Earthquakes*
Wells, Rebecca. *Divine Secrets of the Ya-Ya Sisterhood: A Novel*
Welsh, Irvine. *Dead Men's Trousers*
Welsh, Irvine. *Trainspotting*
Williams, Katie. *Tell the Machine Goodnight*
Willis, Connie. ★*Doomsday Book*
Wilson, Carter. *Dead Girl in 2a*
Winch, Tara June. *The Yield*
Winterson, Jeanette. ★*Frankissstein*
Winthrop, Elizabeth Hartley. *The Mercy Seat: A Novel*
Woolf, Virginia. ★*Mrs. Dalloway*
Wrobel, Stephanie. *Darling Rose Gold*
Yates, Christopher J. *Grist Mill Road: A Novel*
Yocum, Robin. *A Welcome Murder*
Zapata, Mike. *The Lost Book of Adana Moreau*

MULTIRACIAL BOYS
Fowler, Therese. ★*A Good Neighborhood*
Krueger, William Kent. ★*Lightning Strike*
Murr, Naeem. *The Perfect Man: A Novel*
Washington, Bryan. *Lot: Stories*

MULTIRACIAL CHILDREN
Durrow, Heidi W. *The Girl Who Fell from the Sky: A Novel*
Ward, Jesmyn. ★*Sing, Unburied, Sing*

MULTIRACIAL GIRLS
Corthron, Kia. *Moon and the Mars*

MULTIRACIAL MEN
Amis, Martin. *Lionel Asbo: State of England*
Dongala, Emmanuel Boundzeki. *The Bridgetower Sonata: Sonata Mulattica*
Edugyan, Esi. *Half-Blood Blues*
Faulkner, William. ★*Light in August*
Holmes, J. M. *How Are You Going to Save Yourself*
Jenkins, Beverly. *Forbidden*
Jones, Stephen Mack. *Dead of Winter*
Lansdale, Joe R. *More Better Deals*

March, Nev. *Murder in Old Bombay*
Matthews, Mimi. ★*The Siren of Sussex*
Mosley, Walter. ★*John Woman*
Weiden, David L. ★*Winter Counts*

MULTIRACIAL PERSONS
Franck, Julia. *Blindness of the Heart*
Kincaid, Jamaica. *The Autobiography of My Mother*
Orange, Tommy. ★*There There*
Rodriguez, Linda. *Every Last Secret: A Mystery*
Ryan, Kennedy. ★*Long Shot*
Senna, Danzy. *New People*

MULTIRACIAL PERSONS — IDENTITY
Warren, Robert Penn. *Band of Angels*

MULTIRACIAL TEENAGE GIRLS
Jones, Stephen Graham. *My Heart Is a Chainsaw*

MULTIRACIAL TEENAGERS
Straight, Susan. *A Million Nightingales*

MULTIRACIAL WOMEN
Afshar, Tessa. *Jewel of the Nile*
Allen, Jayne. *Black Girls Must Die Exhausted*
Christopher, Andie J. *Not the Girl You Marry*
Clemmons, Zinzi. *What We Lose*
Collins, Sara. *The Confessions of Frannie Langton*
Donati, Sara. *Where the Light Enters*
Erdrich, Louise. *The Painted Drum: A Novel*
Erdrich, Louise. *The Plague of Doves*
Erdrich, Louise. *Tracks: A Novel*
Hoang, Helen. ★*The Bride Test*
Hulme, Keri. ★*The Bone People: A Novel*
Igharo, Jane. *The Sweetest Remedy*
Johnson, Sadeqa. ★*Yellow Wife*
Martin, Alexa. *Fumbled*
McFarland, Jeni. *The House of Deep Water*
Onuzo, Chibundu. *Sankofa: A Novel*
Riley, Vanessa. ★*A Duke, the Lady, and a Baby*
Riley, Vanessa. ★*Island Queen*
Smith, Zadie. ★*Swing Time*
Straight, Susan. *A Million Nightingales*
Warren, Robert Penn. *Band of Angels*
Yun, Jung. *O Beautiful: A Novel*

*A **Multitude** of Sins: Stories.* Ford, Richard

MUMBAI, INDIA
Adiga, Aravind. *Last Man in Tower: A Novel*
Dev, Sonali. *A Distant Heart*
Khan, Vaseem. *The Perplexing Theft of the Jewel in the Crown*
Lalli, Sonya. *A Holly Jolly Diwali*
Linden, Rachel. *The Enlightenment of Bees*
March, Nev. *Murder in Old Bombay*
Massey, Sujata. ★*The Bombay Prince*
Massey, Sujata. *The Satapur Moonstone*
Massey, Sujata. ★*The Widows of Malabar Hill: A Mystery of 1920s Bombay*
Swamy, Shruti. *The Archer*
Umrigar, Thrity N. *The Secrets Between Us*

★***Mumbo** Jumbo.* Reed, Ishmael

MUNCHAUSEN SYNDROME BY PROXY
Wrobel, Stephanie. *Darling Rose Gold*

Munro, Alice
Dear Life: Stories
Family Furnishings: Selected Stories, 1995-2014
Hateship, Friendship, Courtship, Loveship, Marriage: Stories
Lives of Girls and Women
Open Secrets: Stories
Runaway: Stories
Selected Stories
Too Much Happiness: Stories
The View from Castle Rock: Stories

Murakami, Haruki
★*1q84*
After Dark
After the Quake: Stories
Blind Willow, Sleeping Woman: 24 Stories
Colorless Tsukuru Tazaki and His Years of Pilgrimage
★*First Person Singular: Stories*
★*Kafka on the Shore*
Killing Commendatore: A Novel
Men Without Women: Stories
South of the Border, West of the Sun
The Wind-Up Bird Chronicle

Murakami, Ryu
In the Miso Soup

*The **Muralist**. Shapiro, Barbara A.*

MURALISTS
Shapiro, Barbara A. *The Muralist*

Murata, Sayaka
Earthlings: A Novel

MURDER
Abbott, Megan E. *Bury Me Deep*
Abbott, Megan E. *You Will Know Me: A Novel*
Abbott, Patricia. *Concrete Angel*
Adamson, Gil. *The Outlander*
Airth, Rennie. *The Decent Inn of Death*
Andrew, Sally. *The Satanic Mechanic: A Tannie Maria Mystery*
Atkins, Ace. *Wicked City*
Baldacci, David. *Hell's Corner*
Ball, John Dudley. *In the Heat of the Night*
Banville, John. *The Book of Evidence*
Barclay, Linwood. *Far from True: A Novel*
Barclay, Linwood. *Parting Shot*
Barclay, Linwood. *Trust Your Eyes: A Thriller*
Barclay, Linwood. *The Twenty-Three: A Promise Falls Novel*
Barnes, Jonathan. *The Somnambulist*
Barzak, Christopher. *One for Sorrow*
Bayard, Louis. *The Black Tower: A Novel*
Berkowitz, Ira. *Old Flame: A Jackson Steeg Novel*
Beukes, Lauren. *Broken Monsters*
Beukes, Lauren. *The Shining Girls*
Billingham, Mark. ★*Their Little Secret*
Black, Benjamin. *Wolf on a String: A Novel*
Blackstock, Terri. *Smoke Screen*
Bledsoe, Alex. *Gather Her Round: A Novel of the Tufa*
Block, Lawrence. *The Sins of the Fathers*
Bolton, S. J. *A Dark and Twisted Tide*
Box, C. J. *Trophy Hunt: A Joe Pickett Novel*

Bradley, C. Alan. *As Chimney Sweepers Come to Dust: A Flavia De Luce Novel*
Bradley, C. Alan. *Speaking from Among the Bones: A Flavia De Luce Novel*
Bradley, C. Alan. *Thrice the Brinded Cat Hath Mew'd: A Flavia De Luce Novel*
Buchan, John. *The Thirty-Nine Steps*
Burke, Alafair. *The Better Sister: A Novel*
Byrne, Kerrigan. *How to Love a Duke in Ten Days*
Carter, Stephen L. *New England White: A Novel*
Castillo, Linda. *Outsider*
Castro, V. *The Queen of the Cicadas*
Catton, Eleanor. *The Luminaries: A Novel*
Chabon, Michael. *The Yiddish Policemen's Union*
Chandler, Raymond. *The Lady in the Lake*
Chandler, Raymond. *The Long Goodbye*
Cheever, John. *Bullet Park: A Novel*
Child, Lee. *Bad Luck and Trouble*
Child, Lee. *Echo Burning*
Child, Lee. *No Middle Name: The Complete Collected Jack Reacher Short Stories*
Child, Lee. *A Wanted Man*
Childs, Laura. *Lavender Blue Murder*
Christie, Agatha. *Endless Night*
Christie, Agatha. *The Pale Horse*
Clark, Mary Higgins. *Death Wears a Beauty Mask and Other Stories*
Cleave, Paul. *Trust No One: A Thriller*
Cleeves, Ann. ★*The Heron's Cry*
Cleeves, Ann. *The Long Call*
Coben, Harlan. *Don't Let Go*
Connelly, Michael. ★*The Law of Innocence: A Novel*
Cook, Thomas H. *The Fate of Katherine Carr*
Cook, Thomas H. *Instruments of Night*
Cotterill, Colin. *Killed at the Whim of a Hat*
Crais, Robert. *A Dangerous Man*
Crais, Robert. *Demolition Angel: A Novel.*
Cussler, Clive. *Celtic Empire*
Davis, Lindsey. *The Ides of April: A Flavia Albia Mystery*
Davis, Lindsey. *One Virgin Too Many*
De Giovanni, Maurizio. *The Bastards of Pizzofalcone*
Deane, Seamus. *Reading in the Dark*
DeLillo, Don. *The Names*
DeSilva, Bruce. *Rogue Island*
DeSilva, Bruce. *A Scourge of Vipers*
Dexter, Colin. *The Remorseful Day*
Dexter, Pete. *Paris Trout*
Dickens, Charles. *Oliver Twist, or the Parish Boy's Progress*
Dickens, Charles. *Our Mutual Friend*
Didion, Joan. *A Book of Common Prayer*
Diop, David. ★*At Night All Blood Is Black*
Disher, Garry. *Under the Cold Bright Lights*
Doiron, Paul. *The Precipice*
Dostoyevsky, Fyodor. ★*Crime and Punishment*
Dreiser, Theodore. ★*An American Tragedy*
Du Maurier, Daphne. *Jamaica Inn*
Eco, Umberto. ★*The Name of the Rose*
Ellis, Bret Easton. *Lunar Park*
Ellison, J. T. *Good Girls Lie*

Ellroy, James. *This Storm: A Novel*
Fairstein, Linda A. *Entombed*
Farrow, John. *The Storm Murders: A Thriller*
Faulkner, William. ★*Sanctuary*
Faust, Christa. *Choke Hold*
Faust, Christa. *Money Shot*
Finch, Charles. *A Beautiful Blue Death*
Finch, Charles. *The September Society*
Fleming, Ian. *Doctor No*
Flyte, Magnus. *City of Dark Magic: A Novel*
Foley, Lucy. *The Guest List*
Francis, Felix. *Pulse*
Francis, Patry. *The Orphans of Race Point: A Novel*
Franklin, Ariana. *The Serpent's Tale*
French, Albert. *Billy*
French, Nicci. *Thursday's Children*
Friedman, Daniel. *Riot Most Uncouth: A Lord Byron Mystery*
Furst, Alan. *The Foreign Correspondent: A Novel*
Gailey, Sarah. *The Echo Wife*
Galbraith, Robert. *Career of Evil*
Galbraith, Robert. *Lethal White*
Galbraith, Robert. *The Silkworm*
Garcia Marquez, Gabriel. *Chronicle of a Death Foretold*
Garcia Marquez, Gabriel. ★*One Hundred Years of Solitude*
Gardner, Lisa. ★*Never Tell: A Novel*
Gates, Eva. ★*Read and Buried*
Gerritsen, Tess. *The Bone Garden*
Gibson, William. *The Peripheral*
Gleason, Colleen. *Murder at the Capitol*
Goenawan, Clarissa. *Rainbirds*
Goodman, Carol. *The Sea of Lost Girls*
Greene, Graham. ★*Brighton Rock*
Griffiths, Elly. *The Dark Angel*
Grisham, John. ★*The Guardians*
Hall, Araminta. *Imperfect Women: A Novel*
Harrod-Eagles, Cynthia. *Headlong*
Hart, John. *Redemption Road*
Harvey, Michael T. *Brighton*
Herbert, Julian. *Bring Me the Head of Quentin Tarantino: Stories*
Hewson, David. *The Garden of Evil*
Higashino, Keigo. ★*The Devotion of Suspect X*
Hilton, L. S. *Maestra*
Hodgson, Antonia. *The Last Confession of Thomas Hawkins*
Hoffman, Alice. *The River King*
Holt, Victoria. *The Black Opal*
Horowitz, Anthony. *The House of Silk: A Sherlock Holmes Novel*
Hurwitz, Gregg Andrew. ★*Into the Fire*
Indriðason, Arnaldur. *Reykjavik Nights: An Inspector Erlendur Novel*
Indriðason, Arnaldur. *The Shadow District: A Thriller*
Jemisin, N. K. *The Fifth Season*
Jemisin, N. K. *The Obelisk Gate*
Jemisin, N. K. *The Stone Sky*
Jewell, Lisa. *Watching You*
Johnson, Craig. *Next to Last Stand*
Johnson, Micaiah. *The Space Between Worlds*
K'wan. ★*Diamonds and Pearl*
Kaminsky, Stuart M. *Murder on the Trans-Siberian Express*
Kellerman, Jonathan. ★*Half Moon Bay: A Novel*

Kelly, Erin. *Broadchurch: A Novel*
Kemelman, Harry. *Monday the Rabbi Took Off*
Kemelman, Harry. *One Fine Day the Rabbi Bought a Cross*
Kim, Young-Ha. *Diary of a Murderer: And Other Stories*
King, Stephen. ★*Billy Summers*
King, Stephen. *It*
Knopf, Chris. *You're Dead*
Larsson, Stieg. *The Girl Who Played with Fire*
Lehane, Dennis. ★*Mystic River*
Locke, Attica. *The Cutting Season*
Lowe, Kathryn A. *The Furies*
Lundrigan, Nicole. *Glass Boys: A Novel*
MacDonald, John D. *Cinnamon Skin: The Twentieth Adventure of Travis McGee*
MacDonald, John D. *The Green Ripper*
MacDonald, John D. ★*The Lonely Silver Rain*
MacDonald, John D. *The Long Lavender Look*
MacDonald, John D. *A Purple Place for Dying*
Macdonald, Ross. *Sleeping Beauty*
Malerman, Josh. *Unbury Carol*
Malliet, G. M. *Pagan Spring: A Mystery*
Mankell, Henning. *The Man from Beijing*
Marias, Javier. *The Infatuations*
Marsh, Ngaio. *A Man Lay Dead*
May, Peter. *The Blackhouse*
McBride, James. ★*Deacon King Kong: A Novel*
McClure, James. *The Steam Pig*
McCreight, Kimberly. *Friends Like These*
McDermid, Val. *A Place of Execution*
McDowell, Christina. *The Cave Dwellers: A Novel*
McGuire, Seanan. ★*Every Heart a Doorway*
McIlvanney, William. *The Dark Remains: Laidlaw's First Case*
McKevett, G. A. *Murder at Mabel's Motel*
McKinlay, Jenn. *Killer Research*
Meyer, Nicholas. *The Adventure of the Peculiar Protocols: Adapted from the Journals of John H. Watson, M.D.*
Montclair, Allison. *A Rogue's Company*
Moriarty, Liane. *Big Little Lies*
Morrison, Toni. *Jazz*
Mullen, Thomas. *Darktown: A Novel*
Murdoch, Iris. *The Book and the Brotherhood*
Murdoch, Iris. *The Green Knight*
Murdoch, Iris. *The Nice and the Good*
O'Connor, Carlene. *Murder in an Irish Bookshop*
O'Donohue, Clare. *The Lover's Knot: A Someday Quilts Mystery*
Oates, Joyce Carol. *Because It Is Bitter, and Because It Is My Heart*
Panowich, Brian. *Hard Cash Valley*
Paretsky, Sara. *Indemnity Only: A Novel*
Paris, B. A. *The Breakdown*
Patterson, Richard North. *Dark Lady*
Patterson, Richard North. *Eclipse*
Pears, Iain. *An Instance of the Fingerpost*
Perkins, S. C. *Murder Once Removed*
Perry, Anne. *One Fatal Flaw: A Daniel Pitt Novel*
Persson, Leif G. W. *Another Time, Another Life: The Story of a Crime*
Persson, Leif G. W. *Free Falling, as If in a Dream: The Story of a Crime*
Pessl, Marisha. *Night Film: A Novel*

Piccirilli, Tom. *The Last Kind Words*

Pronzini, Bill. *The Violated*

Qiu, Xiaolong. *Death of a Red Heroine*

Qiu, Xiaolong. *Don't Cry Tai Lake: An Inspector Chen Novel*

Qiu, Xiaolong. *Enigma of China*

Qiu, Xiaolong. *Red Mandarin Dress: An Inspector Chen Novel*

Quartey, Kwei. *Gold of Our Fathers*

Quartey, Kwei. *Wife of the Gods: A Novel*

Quincy, D. M. *Murder in Mayfair: An Atlas Catesby Mystery*

Quirk, Matthew. *Dead Man Switch*

Racculia, Kate. ★*Bellweather Rhapsody*

Randisi, Robert J. *Hey There (You with the Gun in Your Hand): A Rat Pack Mystery*

Rankin, Ian. ★*Rather Be the Devil*

Rankin, Ian. *Set in Darkness: An Inspector Rebus Novel*

Redondo, Dolores. *The Invisible Guardian*

Reichs, Kathy. *206 Bones*

Reichs, Kathy. *Bones of the Lost: A Temperance Brennan Novel*

Rendell, Ruth. ★*The Bridesmaid*

Rendell, Ruth. *Collected Stories*

Rendell, Ruth. *The Tree of Hands*

Richmond, Michelle. *No One You Know*

Ridpath, Michael. *Far North*

Rinehart, Mary Roberts. *The Circular Staircase*

Robb, Candace M. ★*A Choir of Crows*

Robb, J. D. *Connections in Death: An Eve Dallas Novel*

Roberts, Nora. *Come Sundown*

Robertson, Imogen. *Instruments of Darkness: A Novel*

Robinson, Peter. *All the Colors of Darkness*

Robinson, Peter. *Close to Home*

Robinson, Peter. *Cold Is the Grave*

Robinson, Peter. *Strange Affair*

Rodriguez, Linda. *Every Broken Trust: A Mystery*

Rodriguez, Linda. *Every Hidden Fear: A Skeet Bannion Mystery*

Rollins, James. *The Eye of God*

Rollins, James. *The Sixth Extinction: A Sigma Force Novel*

Rosen, Renee. *Dollface: A Novel of the Roaring Twenties*

Rowland, Laura Joh. *The Hangman's Secret*

Rowland, Laura Joh. *The Incense Game: A Novel of Feudal Japan*

Rowland, Russell. *Cold Country: A Novel*

Runcie, James. *Sidney Chambers and the Perils of the Night*

Runcie, James. *Sidney Chambers and the Problem of Evil*

Sager, Riley. *Final Girls: A Novel*

Sanders, Lawrence. *McNally's Dilemma*

Sanders, Lawrence. ★*McNally's Gamble*

Sanders, Lawrence. *McNally's Luck*

Sanders, Lawrence. *McNally's Puzzle*

Sanders, Lawrence. *The Second Deadly Sin*

Sandford, John. ★*Deadline*

Sandford, John. *Easy Prey*

Sandford, John. *Heat Lightning*

Sandford, John. *Hidden Prey*

Sandford, John. *Holy Ghost*

Sandford, John. ★*Invisible Prey*

Sandford, John. ★*Naked Prey*

Sandford, John. ★*Night Prey*

Sandford, John. ★*Silent Prey*

Sansom, C. J. ★*Sovereign*

Sansom, C. J. *Tombland*

Sayers, Dorothy L. ★*The Documents in the Case*

Sayers, Dorothy L. ★*The Five Red Herrings*

Sayers, Dorothy L. *Hangman's Holiday*

Sayers, Dorothy L. *In the Teeth of the Evidence*

Sayers, Dorothy L. ★*Lord Peter*

Saylor, Steven. *Rubicon*

Scerbanenco, Giorgio. *A Private Venus*

Schlink, Bernhard. *Self's Punishment*

Schmidt, Sarah. *See What I Have Done*

Scott, A. D. ★*Beneath the Abbey Wall: A Novel*

Scott, A. D. *A Double Death on the Black Isle: A Novel*

Scott, Stephanie. *What's Left of Me Is Yours: A Novel*

Scott, Walter. *The Bride of Lammermoor*

Scottoline, Lisa. *Legal Tender*

Sem-Sandberg, Steve. *The Chosen Ones: A Novel*

Seton, Anya. *Katherine*

Sharp, Zoe. *Second Shot: A Charlie Fox Thriller*

Shaw, M. B. *Murder at the Mill: A Mystery*

Shelton, Paige. *Thin Ice: A Mystery*

Siger, Jeffrey. *Mykonos After Midnight: A Chief Inspector Kaldis Mystery*

Simenon, Georges. *Maigret and the Black Sheep*

Simenon, Georges. *Maigret and the Fortuneteller*

Simenon, Georges. ★*Maigret and the Killer*

Simenon, Georges. *Maigret and the Madwoman*

Simenon, Georges. ★*Maigret and the Saturday Caller*

Simenon, Georges. ★*Maigret and the Toy Village*

Simenon, Georges. *Maigret and the Wine Merchant*

Simenon, Georges. ★*Maigret Bides His Time*

Simenon, Georges. ★*Maigret Goes Home*

Simenon, Georges. *Maigret in Holland*

Simenon, Georges. *My Friend Maigret*

Smith, Julie. *82 Desire: A Skip Langdon Novel*

Smith, Julie. ★*Mean Woman Blues*

Smith, Martin Cruz. ★*Gorky Park*

Smith, Martin Cruz. *Havana Bay*

Smith, Martin Cruz. *Polar Star*

Smith, Tom Rob. *The Secret Speech*

Solares, Martin. *The Black Minutes*

Somer, Mehmet Murat. *The Serenity Murders*

Spain, Jo. *With Our Blessing: An Inspector Tom Reynolds Mystery*

Spann, Susan. *Blade of the Samurai: A Shinobi Mystery*

Spann, Susan. ★*Claws of the Cat: A Shinobi Mystery*

Spencer, Sally. *Death's Dark Shadow*

Spencer, Sally. ★*The Hidden*

Spencer, Scott. *Man in the Woods*

Spencer-Fleming, Julia. *Through the Evil Days: A Clare Fergusson/Russ Van Alstyne Mystery*

Spillane, Mickey. *Kill Me, Darling*

Stabenow, Dana. *A Night Too Dark: A Kate Shugak Novel*

Stark, Richard. *The Jugger: A Parker Novel*

Steiner, Susie. ★*Persons Unknown: A Novel*

Straub, Peter. ★*Mystery*

Stroby, Wallace. *Some Die Nameless*

Swanson, Peter. *Her Every Fear: A Novel*

Unger, Lisa. *Under My Skin*

Vandermeer, Jeff. *Finch*

Vine, Barbara. *The Minotaur: A Novel*
Ware, Ruth. *The Woman in Cabin Ten*
Warren, Robert Penn. *World Enough and Time: A Romantic Novel*
Wiesel, Elie. ★*Dawn*
Wolfe, Paul. *The Lost Diary of M*
Woods, Stuart. *New York Dead*
Woods, Stuart. *Orchid Beach*

MURDER — HISTORY
Atwood, Margaret. *Alias Grace*
Robertson, Imogen. *Anatomy of Murder*
Murder and Magic [Series]. Glover, Nicole
★*Murder and the First Lady*. Roosevelt, Elliott
Murder at Cape Three Points. Quartey, Kwei
Murder at Half Moon Gate. Penrose, Andrea
★*Murder at Kensington Palace*. Penrose, Andrea
Murder at Mabel's Motel. McKevett, G. A.
Murder at Midnight. Roosevelt, Elliott
Murder at the Capitol. Gleason, Colleen
Murder at the Mena House. Neubauer, Erica Ruth
Murder at the Mill: A Mystery. Shaw, M. B.
Murder at the Opera. Quincy, D. M.
★*Murder at the Savoy*. Sjowall, Maj
★*The Murder at the Vicarage*. Christie, Agatha
Murder by Milk Bottle. Truss, Lynne
Murder by month mysteries [Series]. Lourey, Jess

MURDER FOR HIRE
Ashley & JaQuavis. *The Cartel*
Barclay, Linwood. *No Safe House*
Murder in a Teacup. Delany, Vicki
Murder in an Irish Bookshop. O'Connor, Carlene
Murder in Law. Heley, Veronica
Murder in Mayfair: An Atlas Catesby Mystery. Quincy, D. M.
Murder in Old Bombay. March, Nev
Murder in the Bastille. Black, Cara
Murder in the Corn Maze. McKevett, G. A.
Murder in the Map Room: An Eleanor Roosevelt Mystery. Roosevelt, Elliott
Murder in the Marais. Black, Cara
Murder in the Oval Office. Roosevelt, Elliott
Murder in the Rue De Paradis: An Aimee Leduc Investigation. Black, Cara

MURDER INVESTIGATION
Aaronovitch, Ben. *Broken Homes*
Aaronovitch, Ben. *Midnight Riot*
Aaronovitch, Ben. *Whispers Under Ground*
Abdul-Jabbar, Kareem. ★*Mycroft Holmes*
Adler-Olsen, Jussi. *The Absent One*
Airth, Rennie. *The Decent Inn of Death*
Allende, Isabel. *Ripper: A Novel*
Armstrong, Kelley. *Alone in the Wild*
Armstrong, Kelley. *Watcher in the Woods*
Atkins, Ace. ★*The Heathens*
Atkins, Ace. *The Innocents*
Atkins, Ace. *The Ranger*
Atkins, Ace. *Wicked City*
Ayatsuji, Yukito. *The Decagon House Murders*
Baldacci, David. *The Fallen*
Baldacci, David. *Long Road to Mercy*

Bannalec, Jean-Luc. *Death in Brittany*
Bannalec, Jean-Luc. *The Killing Tide: A Brittany Mystery*
Bannister, Jo. *Silent Footsteps*
Barclay, Linwood. *No Safe House*
Barnard, Robert. *Death of a Literary Widow*
Bartz, Andrea. *The Lost Night*
Bauer, Belinda. *Snap*
Bayard, Louis. *The Black Tower: A Novel*
Bayard, Louis. *The Pale Blue Eye: A Novel*
Beaton, M. C. *Agatha Raisin and the Quiche of Death*
Beaton, M. C. *Agatha Raisin and the Witch of Wyckhadden*
Beaton, M. C. *Death of a Macho Man*
Beaton, M. C. *Pushing up Daisies: An Agatha Raisin Mystery*
Black, Benjamin. ★*Christine Falls: A Novel*
Black, Benjamin. *Wolf on a String: A Novel*
Black, Lisa. *That Darkness*
Block, Lawrence. ★*The Burglar in the Library*
Block, Lawrence. *Eight Million Ways to Die*
Block, Lawrence. *The Sins of the Fathers*
Bolton, S. J. *A Dark and Twisted Tide*
Box, C. J. *Badlands*
Box, C. J. ★*Open Season*
Boyle, William. *The Lonely Witness*
Bradley, C. Alan. *I Am Half-Sick of Shadows: A Flavia De Luce Novel*
Bradley, C. Alan. *A Red Herring Without Mustard*
Bradley, C. Alan. *Speaking from Among the Bones: A Flavia De Luce Novel*
Bradley, C. Alan. ★*The Sweetness at the Bottom of the Pie*
Bradley, C. Alan. *The Weed That Strings the Hangman's Bag: A Flavia De Luce Mystery*
Braun, Lilian Jackson. *The Cat Who Ate Danish Modern*
Brett, Simon. *Murder Unprompted*
Brown, Rita Mae. *Wish You Were Here*
Bruen, Ken. *The Guards*
Burdett, John. *Bangkok 8*
Burke, James Lee. *Black Cherry Blues*
Burke, James Lee. ★*The New Iberia Blues*
Burns, V. M. *Killer Words*
Carter, Stephen L. *New England White: A Novel*
Castillo, Linda. *Outsider*
Child, Lee. *The Affair*
Child, Lee. *Echo Burning*
Child, Lee. *The Enemy*
Child, Lee. *Make Me*
Child, Lee. *Never Go Back*
Child, Lee. *Night School*
Child, Lee. *A Wanted Man*
Christie, Agatha. ★*The A B C Murders*
Christie, Agatha. *The Body in the Library*
Christie, Agatha. *Curtain*
Christie, Agatha. *The Hollow*
Christie, Agatha. *Mrs. McGinty's Dead*
Christie, Agatha. ★*The Murder at the Vicarage*
Christie, Agatha. *A Murder Is Announced*
Christie, Agatha. ★*The Murder of Roger Ackroyd*
Christie, Agatha. ★*Murder on the Orient Express*
Christie, Agatha. *The Pale Horse*

Christie, Agatha. *Three Blind Mice, and Other Stories*

Christie, Agatha. *Towards Zero*

Clark, Tracy P. *What You Don't See*

Cleeves, Ann. *The Crow Trap*

Cleeves, Ann. ★*The Heron's Cry*

Cleeves, Ann. *The Long Call*

Cleeves, Ann. *Thin Air*

Cleland, Jane K. *Hidden Treasure*

Coben, Harlan. *Long Lost*

Coleman, Reed Farrel. *Where It Hurts: A Gus Murphy Novel*

Collins, Manda. *A Good Rake Is Hard to Find*

Collins, Manda. *Ready Set Rogue*

Connelly, Michael. *The Black Ice*

Connelly, Michael. *The Brass Verdict: A Novel*

Connelly, Michael. *The Burning Room*

Connelly, Michael. *The Crossing*

Connelly, Michael. *The Late Show*

Connolly, John. *A Book of Bones*

Copperman, E. J. *Judgment at Santa Monica*

Cotterill, Colin. *The Coroner's Lunch*

Cotterill, Colin. *Disco for the Departed*

Cotterill, Colin. *Killed at the Whim of a Hat*

Cotterill, Colin. *Slash and Burn: A Dr. Siri Mystery Set in Laos*

Coulter, Catherine. *The Final Cut*

Coulter, Catherine. *The Lost Key*

Crais, Robert. *Suspect*

Crompton, Richard. *Hell's Gate: A Novel*

Crompton, Richard. *Hour of the Red God*

Crumley, James. *The Last Good Kiss: A Novel*

Crumley, James. ★*The Wrong Case*

Cussler, Clive. *The Cutthroat*

Daugherty, Christi. *A Beautiful Corpse*

Daugherty, Christi. *The Echo Killing*

Davidson, Diane Mott. *Killer Pancake*

Davidson, Diane Mott. *The Last Suppers*

Davis, Lindsey. *The Ides of April: A Flavia Albia Mystery*

Davis, Lindsey. *One Virgin Too Many*

Dazieri, Sandrone. *Kill the Angel*

Dazieri, Sandrone. *Kill the Father*

De Giovanni, Maurizio. *The Bastards of Pizzofalcone*

DeSilva, Bruce. *Providence Rag*

Dexter, Colin. *The Daughters of Cain*

Dexter, Colin. *The Remorseful Day*

Dobyns, Stephen. *Saratoga Payback*

Dodd, Christina. *Dead Girl Running*

Doiron, Paul. *Bad Little Falls: A Novel*

Doiron, Paul. *The Precipice*

Donoghue, Emma. ★*Frog Music*

Dugoni, Robert. *Murder One*

Dundas, Chad. *The Blaze*

Elias, Gerald. *Danse Macabre*

Ellroy, James. *This Storm: A Novel*

Estleman, Loren D. *Frames*

Estleman, Loren D. *Infernal Angels*

Estleman, Loren D. *A Smile on the Face of the Tiger*

Farrow, John. *The Storm Murders: A Thriller*

Ferraris, Zoe. *Finding Nouf*

Ferraris, Zoe. *Kingdom of Strangers: A Novel*

Finch, Charles. *A Beautiful Blue Death*

Finch, Charles. *The Last Passenger*

Flynn, Gillian. ★*Sharp Objects: A Novel*

Flyte, Magnus. *City of Dark Magic: A Novel*

Francis, Felix. *Guilty Not Guilty*

Frear, Caz. *Stone Cold Heart*

Frear, Caz. *Sweet Little Lies*

Fredericks, Mariah. *Death of a Showman*

Freeman, Dianne. *A Lady's Guide to Etiquette and Murder*

French, Nicci. *Dark Saturday*

French, Nicci. ★*The Day of the Dead: A Novel*

French, Nicci. *Sunday Silence*

French, Nicci. *Waiting for Wednesday: A Frieda Klein Mystery*

French, Tana. ★*Broken Harbor*

French, Tana. *In the Woods*

French, Tana. *The Likeness*

Friedman, Daniel. *Riot Most Uncouth: A Lord Byron Mystery*

Galbraith, Robert. *Career of Evil*

Galbraith, Robert. *Lethal White*

Galbraith, Robert. *The Silkworm*

Gallagher, Stephen. *The Bedlam Detective: A Novel*

Garcia Saenz, Eva. *The Silence of the White City*

Gardner, Lisa. *Fear Nothing: A Detective D. D. Warren Novel*

Gardner, Lisa. *Find Her*

Gardner, Lisa. *Love You More: A Detective D.D. Warren Novel*

Gardner, Lisa. *The Neighbor*

Garrett, Kellye. ★*Hollywood Homicide*

Gates, Eva. *Deadly Ever After*

Gaylin, Alison. *Never Look Back*

George, Elizabeth. *Believing the Lie*

George, Elizabeth. *Careless in Red*

George, Elizabeth. *The Punishment She Deserves*

George, Elizabeth. *This Body of Death: An Inspector Lynley Novel*

Gilman, Laura Anne. *Hard Magic*

Giordano, Mario. *Auntie Poldi and the Vineyards of Etna*

Gleason, Colleen. *Murder at the Capitol*

Glover, Nicole. ★*The Conductors*

Glover, Nicole. *The Undertakers*

Goenawan, Clarissa. *Rainbirds*

Goldman, Matt. *Dead West*

Gorman, Edward. *Riders on the Storm : A Sam McCain Mystery*

Grafton, Sue. *X*

Gran, Sara. *Claire DeWitt and the City of the Dead*

Gran, Sara. *The Infinite Blacktop: A Novel*

Grebe, Camilla. *The Ice Beneath Her: A Novel*

Greenwood, Kerry. *Death in Daylesford*

Greer, Robert O. *First of State*

Griffiths, Elly. *The Dark Angel*

Griffiths, Elly. *A Dying Fall: A Ruth Galloway Mystery*

Griffiths, Elly. *The Stone Circle*

Griffiths, Elly. *The Stranger Diaries*

Hall, Tarquin. *The Case of the Deadly Butter Chicken: A Vish Puri Mystery*

Hannah, Sophie. *The Mystery of Three Quarters: The New Hercule Poirot Mystery*

Harkaway, Nick. *Gnomon: A Novel*

Harris, C. S. *What the Devil Knows: A Sebastian St. Cyr Mystery*

Harrison, Cora. *Beyond Absolution: A Mystery Set in 1920s Ireland*

Harrod-Eagles, Cynthia. *Headlong*
Harrod-Eagles, Cynthia. *Old Bones*
Hart, Elsa. *The Cabinets of Barnaby Mayne*
Hart, Erin. *The Book of Killowen*
Hart, John. *The Unwilling*
Harvey, John. *Cold in Hand*
Harvey, Michael T. *Pulse*
Hayder, Mo. *Hanging Hill*
Haywood, Gar Anthony. *Cemetery Road*
Hewson, David. *The Garden of Evil*
Hiaasen, Carl. *Bad Monkey*
Hill, Susan. *The Shadows in the Street: A Simon Serrailler Mystery*
Hillerman, Tony. *The Shape Shifter*
Hoeg, Peter. ★*Smilla's Sense of Snow*
Horowitz, Anthony. ★*Magpie Murders*
Hunter, Stephen. *The 47th Samurai*
Iles, Greg. *Mississippi Blood: A Novel*
Indriðason, Arnaldur. *Outrage*
Indriðason, Arnaldur. *The Shadow District: A Thriller*
James, P. D. *Death of an Expert Witness*
James, P. D. *The Lighthouse*
James, P. D. *Original Sin*
James, P. D. *The Private Patient*
James, P. D. *The Skull Beneath the Skin*
James, P. D. *A Taste for Death*
James, P. D. *An Unsuitable Job for a Woman*
Johnson, Craig. *Next to Last Stand*
Johnston, Tim. *The Current: A Novel*
K'wan. *Lawless*
Kaminsky, Stuart M. *Dancing in the Dark*
Kaminsky, Stuart M. *Murder on the Trans-Siberian Express*
Kaminsky, Stuart M. *To Catch a Spy: A Toby Peters Mystery*
Kemelman, Harry. *Monday the Rabbi Took Off*
Kemelman, Harry. *One Fine Day the Rabbi Bought a Cross*
Kerr, Philip. ★*Metropolis: A Bernie Gunther Novel*
Kerr, Philip. ★*Prussian Blue*
Khan, Ausma Zehanat. *The Unquiet Dead*
Koryta, Michael. ★*How It Happened*
Lafferty, Mur. *Six Wakes*
Lansdale, Joe R. *Edge of Dark Water*
Lansdale, Joe R. *Sunset and Sawdust*
Larsson, Stieg. ★*The Girl Who Kicked the Hornet's Nest*
Larsson, Stieg. *The Girl Who Played with Fire*
Larsson, Stieg. *The Girl with the Dragon Tattoo*
Leon, Donna. *Beastly Things: A Commissario Guido Brunetti Mystery*
Leon, Donna. *Drawing Conclusions: A Commissario Guido Brunetti Mystery*
Leon, Donna. *The Golden Egg*
Leon, Donna. *A Question of Belief: A Commissario Guido Brunetti Mystery*
Leon, Donna. *Trace Elements*
Leon, Donna. *Unto Us a Son Is Given*
Lethem, Jonathan. ★*Motherless Brooklyn*
Limon, Martin. *The Line*
Lin, Jeannie. *The Lotus Palace*
Lippman, Laura. ★*Lady in the Lake: A Novel*
Lippman, Laura. *No Good Deeds*

Lloyd, Catherine. *Death Comes to the Rectory*
Locke, Attica. ★*Bluebird, Bluebird*
Lourey, Jess. ★*January Thaw: A Murder-By-Month Mystery*
Lovesey, Peter. *Beau Death*
Lovesey, Peter. ★*The Last Detective*
Lovesey, Peter. *The Tooth Tattoo*
MacDonald, Philip. *The List of Adrian Messenger*
Mankell, Henning. *Before the Frost: A Linda Wallander Mystery*
Mankell, Henning. *The Dogs of Riga*
Mankell, Henning. *Firewall*
Mankell, Henning. *The Man from Beijing*
Mankell, Henning. *The Man Who Smiled: A Kurt Wallander Mystery*
Mankell, Henning. ★*One Step Behind*
Mankell, Henning. ★*The Return of the Dancing Master*
Mark, David John. *Cruel Mercy*
Maron, Margaret. *Up Jumps the Devil*
Marston, Edward. *The Roaring Boy: A Novel*
Massey, Sujata. ★*The Bombay Prince*
Massey, Sujata. ★*The Widows of Malabar Hill: A Mystery of 1920s Bombay*
May, Peter. *The Blackhouse*
Mayor, Archer. *Red Herring: A Joe Gunther Novel*
Mayor, Archer. *Tag Man: A Joe Gunther Novel*
McCall Smith, Alexander. *The Double Comfort Safari Club*
McClure, James. *The Steam Pig*
McCrumb, Sharyn. ★*If Ever I Return, Pretty Peggy-O*
McDermid, Val. ★*Still Life*
McGuire, Seanan. *Chimes at Midnight: An October Daye Novel*
McHugh, Laura. *The Wolf Wants In: A Novel*
McKevett, G. A. *Murder at Mabel's Motel*
McKevett, G. A. *Murder in the Corn Maze*
McKinlay, Jenn. *Killer Research*
McPherson, Catriona. *Scot & Soda*
Meier, Leslie. *Silver Anniversary Murder*
Meyer, Deon. *Icarus*
Mieville, China. ★*The City & The City*
Mizushima, Margaret. *Killing Trail*
Mosley, Walter. *Little Scarlet: An Easy Rawlins Mystery*
Muller, Marcia. *Ice and Stone*
Nesbo, Jo. *Phantom*
Nesbo, Jo. *The Redeemer*
Nickson, Chris. *Come the Fear*
O'Brien, Perry Edmond. *Fire in the Blood*
O'Connor, Carlene. *Murder in an Irish Bookshop*
O'Mara, Tim. *Crooked Numbers*
Offutt, Chris. ★*The Killing Hills*
Ohlsson, Kristina. *Unwanted: A Novel*
Parker, Robert B. *Death in Paradise*
Parker, Robert B. *Sixkill*
Parris, S. J. *Sacrilege*
Parris, S. J. *Treachery*
Patterson, James. ★*Along Came a Spider: A Novel*
Patterson, James. ★*Private*
Pattison, Eliot. *The Skull Mantra*
Pears, Iain. *The Immaculate Deception*
Pears, Iain. *The Last Judgement*
Penman, Sharon Kay. *The Queen's Man: A Medieval Mystery*
Penny, Louise. *Still Life*

Penrose, Andrea. ★*Murder at Kensington Palace*
Perry, Anne. *A Dangerous Mourning*
Perry, Anne. *The Face of a Stranger*
Perry, Thomas. *Fidelity*
Persson, Leif G. W. *Free Falling, as If in a Dream: The Story of a Crime*
Pessl, Marisha. *Special Topics in Calamity Physics*
Peters, Ellis. *The Holy Thief*
Phillips, Christi. *The Devlin Diary*
Piccirilli, Tom. *The Last Kind Words*
Picoult, Jodi. *House Rules: A Novel*
Pinter, Jason. *Hide Away*
Pobi, Robert. *Under Pressure*
Potzsch, Oliver. *The Beggar King*
Potzsch, Oliver. *The Dark Monk: A Hangman's Daughter Tale*
Potzsch, Oliver. *The Hangman's Daughter: A Historical Novel*
Potzsch, Oliver. *The Play of Death*
Potzsch, Oliver. *The Poisoned Pilgrim: A Hangman's Daughter Tale*
Potzsch, Oliver. *The Werewolf of Bamberg*
Pratchett, Terry. *Thud!: A Novel of Discworld*
Pronzini, Bill. *Spook*
Putnam, Jonathan F. *These Honored Dead*
Qiu, Xiaolong. *Death of a Red Heroine*
Qiu, Xiaolong. *Don't Cry Tai Lake: An Inspector Chen Novel*
Qiu, Xiaolong. *When Red Is Black*
Quartey, Kwei. *Murder at Cape Three Points*
Quick, Amanda. *Garden of Lies*
Raimondo, Lynne. *Dante's Poison: A Mark Angelotti Novel*
Raimondo, Lynne. *Dante's Wood: A Mark Angelotti Novel*
Ramsay, Frederick. *Countdown*
Rankin, Ian. *The Black Book*
Rankin, Ian. *Blood Hunt: A Novel*
Rankin, Ian. *Exit Music*
Rankin, Ian. *The Naming of the Dead: An Inspector Rebus Novel*
Rankin, Ian. *A Question of Blood: An Inspector Rebus Novel*
Raybourn, Deanna. *A Perilous Undertaking: A Veronica Speedwell Mystery*
Raybourn, Deanna. *A Treacherous Curse: A Veronica Speedwell Mystery*
Rees, Matt. *The Fourth Assassin*
Reichs, Kathy. *Bare Bones*
Reichs, Kathy. *Bones of the Lost*
Reichs, Kathy. *Break No Bones*
Reichs, Kathy. *Deadly Decisions*
Reichs, Kathy. *Grave Secrets*
Reichs, Kathy. *Monday Mourning*
Rendell, Ruth. *The Babes in the Wood*
Rendell, Ruth. *End in Tears*
Rendell, Ruth. *Harm Done*
Rendell, Ruth. *Kissing the Gunner's Daughter*
Rendell, Ruth. *Not in the Flesh*
Rendell, Ruth. *Road Rage*
Rendell, Ruth. *A Sleeping Life*
Rendell, Ruth. *Speaker of Mandarin*
Ridpath, Michael. *Far North*
Ripley, Mike. *Mr Campion's Coven*
Robb, Candace M. *A Gift of Sanctuary: An Owen Archer Mystery*
Robb, J. D. *Connections in Death: An Eve Dallas Novel*

Robb, J. D. *Fantasy in Death*
Robb, J. D. *Innocent in Death*
Robb, J. D. *Naked in Death*
Robertson, Imogen. *Anatomy of Murder*
Robertson, Imogen. *Circle of Shadows*
Robertson, Imogen. *Instruments of Darkness: A Novel*
Robertson, Michael. *The Baker Street Letters*
Robertson, Michael. *The Baker Street Translation: A Mystery*
Robertson, Michael. *The Brothers of Baker Street*
Robinson, Peter. *All the Colors of Darkness*
Robinson, Peter. *Close to Home*
Robinson, Peter. *Cold Is the Grave*
Robinson, Peter. *Innocent Graves: An Inspector Banks Mystery*
Robinson, Peter. *Piece of My Heart*
Robinson, Peter. *Strange Affair*
Robotham, Michael. ★*Close Your Eyes*
Robotham, Michael. *The Night Ferry: A Novel*
Robotham, Michael. ★*Say You're Sorry*
Robotham, Michael. ★*When She Was Good*
Rodriguez, Linda. *Every Last Secret: A Mystery*
Roorbach, Bill. *Life Among Giants: A Novel*
Roosevelt, Elliott. ★*Murder and the First Lady*
Roosevelt, Elliott. *Murder at Midnight*
Roosevelt, Elliott. *Murder in the Map Room: An Eleanor Roosevelt Mystery*
Roosevelt, Elliott. *Murder in the Oval Office*
Rosenfelt, David. *Black and Blue: A Doug Brock Thriller*
Ross, Adam. *Mr. Peanut*
Rowland, Laura Joh. *The Incense Game: A Novel of Feudal Japan*
Runcie, James. *Sidney Chambers and the Shadow of Death*
Sanders, Lawrence. *McNally's Luck*
Sanders, Lawrence. *The Second Deadly Sin*
Sandford, John. *Bloody Genius*
Sandford, John. *Chosen Prey*
Sandford, John. *Deep Freeze*
Sandford, John. *Easy Prey*
Sandford, John. *Field of Prey*
Sandford, John. *Heat Lightning*
Sandford, John. *Hidden Prey*
Sandford, John. ★*Invisible Prey*
Sandford, John. *Mad River*
Sandford, John. *Mortal Prey*
Sandford, John. ★*Naked Prey*
Sandford, John. ★*Night Prey*
Sandford, John. ★*Phantom Prey*
Sansom, C. J. *Tombland*
Sayers, Dorothy L. ★*Busman's Honeymoon*
Sayers, Dorothy L. ★*Clouds of Witness*
Sayers, Dorothy L. ★*The Documents in the Case*
Sayers, Dorothy L. ★*The Five Red Herrings*
Sayers, Dorothy L. ★*Gaudy Night*
Sayers, Dorothy L. *Hangman's Holiday*
Sayers, Dorothy L. *Have His Carcase*
Sayers, Dorothy L. *In the Teeth of the Evidence*
Sayers, Dorothy L. ★*Lord Peter*
Sayers, Dorothy L. *Murder Must Advertise*
Sayers, Dorothy L. *The Nine Tailors*
Sayers, Dorothy L. *Thrones, Dominations*

Sayers, Dorothy L. *The Unpleasantness at the Bellona Club*
Sayers, Dorothy L. ★*Whose Body?: A Lord Peter Wimsey Novel*
Saylor, Steven. *A Mist of Prophecies*
Saylor, Steven. *Rubicon*
Scalzi, John. *Head On*
Scalzi, John. ★*Lock In*
Scerbanenco, Giorgio. *A Private Venus*
Schmidt, Sarah. *See What I Have Done*
Scoppettone, Sandra. *Everything You Have Is Mine*
Scoppettone, Sandra. *My Sweet Untraceable You*
Scott, A. D. *A Double Death on the Black Isle: A Novel*
Scott, A. D. ★*The Low Road*
Scottoline, Lisa. ★*Come Home*
Sepetys, Ruta. ★*Out of the Easy*
Shaw, William. *The Birdwatcher*
Shaw, William. *A Song for the Brokenhearted*
Siger, Jeffrey. *Mykonos After Midnight: A Chief Inspector Kaldis Mystery*
Siger, Jeffrey. *Target Tinos: An Inspector Kaldis Mystery*
Silver, Elizabeth L. *The Execution of Noa P. Singleton: A Novel*
Silvis, Randall. *Two Days Gone: A Novel*
Simenon, Georges. *Maigret and the Black Sheep*
Simenon, Georges. *Maigret and the Fortuneteller*
Simenon, Georges. ★*Maigret and the Killer*
Simenon, Georges. *Maigret and the Madwoman*
Simenon, Georges. ★*Maigret and the Toy Village*
Simenon, Georges. *Maigret and the Wine Merchant*
Simenon, Georges. ★*Maigret Bides His Time*
Simenon, Georges. ★*Maigret Goes Home*
Simenon, Georges. *Maigret in Holland*
Simenon, Georges. *My Friend Maigret*
Simmons, Dan. *The Fifth Heart*
Simpson, Dorothy. *Dead and Gone: An Inspector Luke Thanet Novel.*
Simpson, Dorothy. *Dead by Morning*
Simpson, Dorothy. *Doomed to Die*
Simpson, Dorothy. *Last Seen Alive: A Luke Thanet Mystery*
Simpson, Dorothy. *No Laughing Matter*
Simpson, Dorothy. *Once Too Often: An Inspector Luke Thanet Novel*
Simpson, Rosemary. *Let the Dead Keep Their Secrets*
Sjowall, Maj. ★*Cop Killer: The Story of a Crime*
Sjowall, Maj. ★*The Locked Room: The Story of a Crime*
Slaughter, Karin. *Criminal: A Novel*
Smith, Julie. *Crescent City Kill: A Skip Langdon Novel*
Smith, Julie. *House of Blues*
Smith, Julie. *Jazz Funeral*
Smith, Julie. *New Orleans Beat*
Smith, Martin Cruz. *Havana Bay*
Smith, Martin Cruz. *Polar Star*
Smith, Martin Cruz. *Stalin's Ghost*
Smith, Martin Cruz. *Three Stations: An Arkady Renko Novel*
Solares, Martin. *The Black Minutes*
Somer, Mehmet Murat. *The Serenity Murders*
Spann, Susan. *Blade of the Samurai: A Shinobi Mystery*
Spencer, Sally. *Best Served Cold*
Spencer, Sally. *Dead End*
Spencer, Sally. *Death's Dark Shadow*
Spencer, Sally. ★*The Hidden*
Spencer, Sally. *Lambs to the Slaughter*

Spencer, Sally. *Thicker Than Water: A Monika Paniatowski British Police Procedural*
Spencer, Sally. *A Walk with the Dead*
Spencer-Fleming, Julia. *All Mortal Flesh*
St. James, Simone. *The Broken Girls*
Stabenow, Dana. *A Night Too Dark: A Kate Shugak Novel*
Stabenow, Dana. *Restless in the Grave*
Stabenow, Dana. *So Sure of Death: A Liam Campbell Mystery*
Stanley, Michael. *A Carrion Death*
Stanley, Michael. *A Death in the Family*
Stanley, Michael. *Death of the Mantis*
Stanley, Michael. *Dying to Live*
Starr, Melvin R. *Unhallowed Ground*
Steiner, Susie. ★*Persons Unknown: A Novel*
Steinhauer, Olen. *The Bridge of Sighs*
Stout, Rex. *The Doorbell Rang*
Stout, Rex. ★*Gambit*
Straub, Peter. ★*Mystery*
Thomas, Russ. ★*Firewatching*
Thomas, Russ. *Nighthawking*
Tracy, P. J. *Ice Cold Heart*
Truss, Lynne. *The Man That Got Away: A Constable Twitten Mystery*
Turow, Scott. *Presumed Innocent*
Tursten, Helene. *Hunting Game*
Turton, Stuart. *The 7 1/2 Deaths of Evelyn Hardcastle*
Vandelly, T. Marie. *Theme Music*
Vandermeer, Jeff. *Finch*
Walker, Martin. *The Coldest Case*
Welsh, Kaite. *The Wages of Sin*
Willocks, Tim. *Memo from Turner*
Winspear, Jacqueline. ★*The Consequences of Fear: A Maisie Dobbs Novel*
Winthrop, Elizabeth Hartley. ★*The Why of Things*
Wojtas, Olga. *Miss Blaine's Prefect and the Golden Samovar*
Wright, Richard. *The Man Who Lived Underground*
Yocum, Robin. *A Welcome Murder*
A **Murder** Is Announced: A Miss Marple Mystery. Christie, Agatha
Murder Most Fowl: A Meg Langslow Mystery. Andrews, Donna
Murder Must Advertise. Sayers, Dorothy L.
★The **Murder** of Roger Ackroyd: A Hercule Poirot Mystery. Christie, Agatha
Murder on Black Swan Lane. Penrose, Andrea
Murder on the Ile Sordou: A Verlaque and Bonnet Provencal Mystery. Longworth, M. L.
★**Murder** on the Orient Express. Christie, Agatha
Murder on the Trans-Siberian Express. Kaminsky, Stuart M.
Murder on Wall Street. Thompson, Victoria
Murder Once Removed. Perkins, S. C.
Murder One. Dugoni, Robert
MURDER PARTIES
Marsh, Ngaio. *A Man Lay Dead*
Rous, Emma. *The Perfect Guests*
The **Murder** Pit. Finlay, Mick
MURDER SUSPECTS
Abbott, Jeff. *Blame*
Baldacci, David. ★*One Good Deed*
Barnes, Jonathan. *The Somnambulist*
Bayard, Louis. *The Black Tower: A Novel*

Beaton, M. C. *Pushing up Daisies: An Agatha Raisin Mystery*
Buchanan, Cathy Marie. ★*The Painted Girls*
Burke, Alafair. *The Better Sister: A Novel*
Burke, James Lee. *Robicheaux*
Callaghan, Mary Rose. *Billy, Come Home*
Cavanagh, Steve. *Thirteen*
Chaon, Dan. *Ill Will*
Child, Lee. ★*Killing Floor*
Christie, Agatha. *Curtain*
Christie, Agatha. *The Hollow*
Christie, Agatha. *Mrs. McGinty's Dead*
Christie, Agatha. ★*The Murder at the Vicarage*
Christie, Agatha. ★*The Murder of Roger Ackroyd: A Hercule Poirot Mystery*
Christie, Agatha. *The Pale Horse*
Clark, Marcia. *Final Judgment*
Coben, Harlan. *Run Away*
Collins, Sara. *The Confessions of Frannie Langton*
Connelly, Michael. ★*The Law of Innocence: A Novel*
Cotterill, Colin. *Killed at the Whim of a Hat*
Cush, Jean Love. *Endangered*
Davis, Lindsey. *The Ides of April: A Flavia Albia Mystery*
Doiron, Paul. *The Poacher's Son*
Elias, Gerald. *Danse Macabre*
Fitzpatrick, Lydia. *Lights All Night Long: A Novel*
Flynn, Gillian. ★*Gone Girl: A Novel*
Francis, Felix. *Guilty Not Guilty*
French, Nicci. *Dark Saturday*
French, Nicci. ★*The Day of the Dead: A Novel*
French, Nicci. *Friday on My Mind: A Frieda Klein Mystery*
French, Nicci. *Sunday Silence*
George, Elizabeth. *Careless in Red*
George, Elizabeth. *This Body of Death: An Inspector Lynley Novel*
Goldman, Matt. *The Shallows*
Grebe, Camilla. *The Ice Beneath Her: A Novel*
Hannah, Sophie. *The Mystery of Three Quarters: The New Hercule Poirot Mystery*
Hanson, Hart. *The Driver*
Harper, Jane. *The Survivors*
Harrod-Eagles, Cynthia. *Cruel as the Grave*
Hart, John. *Down River*
Hart, John. *The King of Lies*
Harvey, Michael T. *Brighton*
Higashino, Keigo. ★*The Devotion of Suspect X*
Higashino, Keigo. *Newcomer*
Hillerman, Tony. *The Wailing Wind*
Hodgson, Antonia. *The Last Confession of Thomas Hawkins*
Horowitz, Anthony. ★*Moonflower Murders*
Iles, Greg. *Mississippi Blood: A Novel*
Knopf, Chris. *You're Dead*
Koryta, Michael. ★*How It Happened*
Kwon, Yo-Son. *Lemon*
Lovesey, Peter. ★*The Last Detective*
MacDonald, Philip. *The List of Adrian Messenger*
MacLean, Sarah. *No Good Duke Goes Unpunished*
McDermid, Val. *The Distant Echo*
McDonald, Christina. *Behind Every Lie*
Montclair, Allison. *The Right Sort of Man*

Nesbo, Jo. *Phantom*
Peace, David. *Occupied City*
Penrose, Andrea. *Murder at Half Moon Gate*
Penrose, Andrea. *Murder on Black Swan Lane*
Perry, Anne. *One Fatal Flaw: A Daniel Pitt Novel*
Quartey, Kwei. *Wife of the Gods: A Novel*
Rees, Matt. *The Fourth Assassin*
Robb, J. D. *Naked in Death*
Robertson, Michael. *The Brothers of Baker Street*
Robinson, Peter. ★*Careless Love*
Robinson, Peter. *Children of the Revolution*
Robinson, Peter. *In the Dark Places*
Robinson, Peter. *Innocent Graves: An Inspector Banks Mystery*
Robotham, Michael. ★*Say You're Sorry*
Robotham, Michael. ★*Suspect*
Rosenfelt, David. *Black and Blue: A Doug Brock Thriller*
Rosenfelt, David. ★*Dog Eat Dog*
Rowland, Russell. *Cold Country: A Novel*
Rozan, S. J. ★*Paper Son*
Sanders, Lawrence. ★*The Fourth Deadly Sin*
Saums, Mary. *Thistle & Twigg*
Schaitkin, Alexis. *Saint X*
Scottoline, Lisa. ★*Every Fifteen Minutes*
Sedgwick, Marcus. *Mister Memory: A Novel*
Silvis, Randall. *Two Days Gone: A Novel*
Spencer, Sally. *The Dead Hand of History*
Spencer, Sally. ★*The Hidden*
Spencer, Sally. *Thicker Than Water: A Monika Paniatowski British Police Procedural*
Stout, Rex. ★*Gambit*
Swanson, Peter. *Eight Perfect Murders: A Novel*
Thomas, Russ. ★*Firewatching*
Turow, Scott. *The Last Trial*
Tyree, Omar. *Leslie: A Novel*
Verdon, John. *On Harrow Hill*
Welsh, Kaite. *The Unquiet Heart*
Williams, Beatriz. *The Summer Wives*
Yocum, Robin. *A Welcome Murder*
Murder Unprompted. Brett, Simon
MURDER VICTIMS
    Anderson, Kevin J. *Death Warmed Over*
    Andrews, Donna. *The Twelve Jays of Christmas: A Meg Langslow Mystery*
    Barclay, Linwood. ★*Elevator Pitch: A Novel*
    Black, Saul. *Anything for You*
    Brandt, Harry. *The Whites: A Novel*
    Camilleri, Andrea. *Riccardino*
    Cash, Wiley. *The Last Ballad: A Novel*
    Christie, Agatha. ★*And Then There Were None*
    Cooney, Caroline B. *The Grandmother Plot*
    Coulter, Catherine. *Paradox*
    Cross-Smith, Leesa. *Whiskey & Ribbons*
    Daugherty, Christi. *Revolver Road: A Harper McClain Mystery*
    French, Nicci. ★*The Lying Room*
    Galligan, John. *Bad Moon Rising*
    Green, Jocelyn. *Veiled in Smoke*
    Griffiths, Elly. *The Postscript Murders*
    Hand, Elizabeth. *The Book of Lamps and Banners: A Novel*

Hannah, Sophie. *The Mystery of Three Quarters: The New Hercule Poirot Mystery*
Harrod-Eagles, Cynthia. *Cruel as the Grave*
Hawkins, Paula. ★*The Girl on the Train: A Novel*
Hurwitz, Gregg Andrew. ★*Into the Fire*
Jónasson, Ragnar. *The Mist*
Kayode, Femi. ★*Lightseekers*
Kurian, Vera. *Never Saw Me Coming*
Lafferty, Mur. *Six Wakes*
Lansdale, Joe R. *Edge of Dark Water*
Lee, Jonathan. *The Great Mistake*
Matthiessen, Peter. *Shadow Country: A New Rendering of the Watson Legend*
Mukherjee, Abir. *The Shadows of Men*
Nicieza, Fabian. *Suburban Dicks*
Pronzini, Bill. *Spook: A*
Pronzini, Bill. *The Violated*
Rader-Day, Lori. ★*The Lucky One*
Reichs, Kathy. ★*A Conspiracy of Bones*
Schellman, Katharine. *Silence in the Library*
Sebold, Alice. ★*The Lovely Bones*
Shepard, Sara. ★*Reputation*
Simpson, Rosemary. ★*What the Dead Leave Behind*
Sveistrup, Soren. ★*The Chestnut Man: A Novel*
Swanson, Peter. *Eight Perfect Murders: A Novel*
Truss, Lynne. *Murder by Milk Bottle*
Young, Heather. *The Distant Dead*

MURDER WITNESSES
Barclay, Linwood. *A Noise Downstairs: A Novel*
Barclay, Linwood. *Trust Your Eyes: A Thriller*
Boyle, William. *The Lonely Witness*
Dodd, Christina. *Virtue Falls*
Freeman, Brian. *Goodbye to the Dead*
Hawkins, Paula. ★*The Girl on the Train: A Novel*
Keller, Julia. *A Killing in the Hills*
Leonard, Elmore. *Tishomingo Blues: A Novel*
McCammon, Robert R. *Boy's Life*
Oates, Joyce Carol. ★*My Life as a Rat*
Paris, B. A. *The Breakdown*
Parks, Gordon. ★*The Learning Tree*
Sjowall, Maj. *The Man on the Balcony: The Story of a Crime*
Skyhorse, Brando. *Madonnas of Echo Park: A Novel*
Smith, Julie. *New Orleans Beat*
Ware, Ruth. *The Woman in Cabin Ten*

Murderbot diaries [Series]. Wells, Martha
*A **Murdered** Peace*. Robb, Candace M.

MURDERERS
Adiga, Aravind. ★*Amnesty*
Atkins, Ace. *The Broken Places*
Atkins, Ace. *The Forsaken*
Aw, Tash. *We, the Survivors*
Box, C. J. ★*Dark Sky: A Joe Pickett Novel*
Boyle, William. *The Lonely Witness*
Burnet, Graeme Macrae. *His Bloody Project: Documents Relating to the Case of Roderick Macrae*
Camus, Albert. ★*The Stranger*
Cheever, John. *Falconer*
Christie, Agatha. ★*The a B C Murders*

Constantine, Liv. *The Last Time I Saw You*
Cussler, Clive. *The Wrecker*
Daugherty, Christi. *Revolver Road: A Harper McClain Mystery*
Downing, Samantha. *My Lovely Wife*
Dugoni, Robert. *My Sister's Grave*
Faye, Lyndsay. *Jane Steele*
Fielding, Joy. *All the Wrong Places: A Novel*
French, Nicci. *Dark Saturday*
French, Nicci. ★*The Lying Room*
Gardiner, Meg. *Phantom Instinct*
Goldin, Megan. *The Escape Room*
Grisham, John. *The Last Juror*
Highsmith, Patricia. ★*The Talented Mr. Ripley*
Kennedy, William. ★*Ironweed: A Novel*
Kerr, Philip. ★*Greeks Bearing Gifts: A Bernie Gunther Novel*
Lippman, Laura. ★*And When She Was Good*
MacDonald, John D. *The Scarlet Ruse*
Mailer, Norman. ★*The Executioner's Song*
Marias, Javier. *The Infatuations*
Matthiessen, Peter. *Shadow Country: A New Rendering of the Watson Legend*
O'Connor, Joseph. *Star of the Sea*
Picoult, Jodi. *Change of Heart: A Novel*
Quick, Amanda. *Otherwise Engaged*
Roslund, Anders. *Cell 8*
Sandford, John. *Easy Prey*
Sandford, John. *Hidden Prey*
Sandford, John. ★*Naked Prey*
Sandford, John. ★*Night Prey*
Saramago, Jose. *Cain*
Slaughter, Karin. ★*Pretty Girls: A Novel*
Spark, Muriel. *Aiding & Abetting*
Suskind, Patrick. ★*Perfume: The Story of a Murderer*
Swinson, Kiki. *Wifey's Next Sticky Situation*
Thompson, Jim. *The Killer Inside Me*
Winspear, Jacqueline. ★*The Consequences of Fear: A Maisie Dobbs Novel*
Wright, Richard. ★*Native Son*
Zhou, Haohui. *Death Notice: A Novel*

MURDERERS — PSYCHOLOGY
Dostoyevsky, Fyodor. ★*Crime and Punishment*
★*A **Murderous** Relation*. Raybourn, Deanna
Murderville. Ashley & JaQuavis
Murderville trilogy [Series]. Ashley & JaQuavis
Murdoch, Iris
An Accidental Man
The Book and the Brotherhood
The Green Knight
The Nice and the Good
The Philosopher's Pupil
The Sea, the Sea
★***Murphy***. Beckett, Samuel
Murphy Shepherd novels [Series]. Martin, Charles
Murphy, Devin
Tiny Americans
Murphy, Julie
If the Shoe Fits

Murphy, Sara Flannery
The Possessions
Murr, Naeem
The Perfect Man: A Novel
Murray, Paul
Skippy Dies
MUSA DAGH, DEFENSE OF, TURKEY, 1915
Werfel, Franz. ★*The Forty Days of Musa Dagh*
MUSES (PERSONS)
Benjamin, Melanie. *Alice I Have Been*
Oyeyemi, Helen. *Mr. Fox*
MUSEUM CURATORS
Blundell, Judy. *The High Season: A Novel*
Littlejohn, Emily. *Lost Lake: A Detective Gemma Monroe Mystery*
Youngson, Anne. *Meet Me at the Museum*
The **Museum** of Extraordinary Things: A Novel. Hoffman, Alice
The **Museum** of Innocence. Pamuk, Orhan
The **Museum** of Modern Love. Rose, Heather
MUSEUMS
Aridjis, Chloe. *Asunder*
Cotterill, Colin. *The Second Biggest Nothing*
Hummel, Maria. *Lesson in Red*
Pobi, Robert. *Under Pressure*
Ritter, Todd. *Devil's Night*
MUSIC
Baker, Dorothy. ★*Young Man with a Horn*
Bledsoe, Alex. *The Hum and the Shiver*
Bledsoe, Alex. *Long Black Curl*
Cander, Chris. *The Weight of a Piano: A Novel*
Gerritsen, Tess. *Playing with Fire*
Grushin, Olga. *The Line*
Hornby, Nick. *High Fidelity*
Jimenez, Simon. ★*The Vanished Birds*
Mitchell, David. ★*Utopia Avenue: A Novel*
Powers, Richard. *Orfeo: A Novel*
MUSIC — COMPETITIONS
Valente, Catherynne M. *Space Opera*
MUSIC FESTIVALS
Brodie, Emma. *Songs in Ursa Major*
MUSIC INDUSTRY AND TRADE
Beukes, Lauren. *Zoo City*
Egan, Jennifer. ★*A Visit from the Goon Squad*
The **Music** of Bees. Garvin, Eileen
Music of the Ghosts. Ratner, Vaddey
MUSIC STUDENTS
Flyte, Magnus. *City of Dark Magic: A Novel*
Flyte, Magnus. *City of Lost Dreams: A Novel*
MUSIC TEACHERS
Macomber, Debbie. *If Not for You: A Novel*
McClure, James. *The Steam Pig*
MUSIC THERAPISTS
Picoult, Jodi. *Sing You Home: A Novel*
Musical Chairs: A Novel. Poeppel, Amy
MUSICIANS
Beatty, Paul. *Slumberland: A Novel*
Bledsoe, Alex. *Long Black Curl*
Bledsoe, Alex. *Wisp of a Thing*
Brodie, Emma. *Songs in Ursa Major*

Doyle, Roddy. *The Guts*
Gabel, Aja. *The Ensemble: A Novel*
Hambly, Barbara. *Lady of Perdition*
Isaac, Kara. *Then There Was You*
Langan, Sarah. *Good Neighbors*
Lauren, Christina. *Roomies*
Mann, Thomas. *Doctor Faustus*
McEwan, Ian. ★*On Chesil Beach*
McFadden, Bernice L. *The Book of Harlan*
Mitchell, David. ★*Cloud Atlas: A Novel*
Mitchell, David. ★*Utopia Avenue: A Novel*
Poeppel, Amy. *Musical Chairs: A Novel*
Pryor, Mark. *Hollow Man*
Ratner, Vaddey. *Music of the Ghosts*
Romano-Lax, Andromeda. *The Spanish Bow*
Weatherspoon, Rebekah. ★*Xeni: A Marriage of Inconvenience*
MUSICOLOGISTS
Enard, Mathias. *Compass*
Musil, Robert
The Man Without Qualities
MUSKETEERS
Dumas, Alexandre. ★*The Man in the Iron Mask*
Dumas, Alexandre. ★*The Three Musketeers*
Dumas, Alexandre. *Twenty Years After*
MUSLIM AMERICAN FAMILIES
Raheem, Zara. *The Marriage Clock: A Novel*
MUSLIM FAMILIES
Akhtar, Ayad. *American Dervish: A Novel*
Akhtar, Ayad. ★*Homeland Elegies: A Novel*
Jalaluddin, Uzma. ★*Ayesha at Last*
Mahfuz, Najib. ★*Palace Walk*
Masood, Syed M. *The Bad Muslim Discount*
Smith, Zadie. ★*White Teeth: A Novel*
MUSLIM GIRLS
Majumdar, Megha. *A Burning*
Miller, Derek B. ★*The Girl in Green*
MUSLIM MEN
Hibbert, Talia. ★*Take a Hint, Dani Brown*
Khadra, Yasmina. ★*Khalil: A Novel*
Khan, Ausma Zehanat. *Among the Ruins*
Khan, Ausma Zehanat. *The Unquiet Dead*
Rushdie, Salman. *Shalimar the Clown: A Novel*
MUSLIM WOMEN
Aboulela, Leila. *Elsewhere, Home*
Aslam, Nadeem. ★*The Golden Legend: A Novel*
Farah, Nuruddin. *Knots*
Freudenberger, Nell. *The Newlyweds*
Gibb, Camilla. *Sweetness in the Belly*
Hassib, Rajia. *A Pure Heart: A Novel*
Heron, Farah. *Accidentally Engaged*
Massey, Sujata. ★*The Widows of Malabar Hill: A Mystery of 1920s Bombay*
MUSLIMS
Anam, Tahmima. *The Bones of Grace*
Aslam, Nadeem. ★*The Blind Man's Garden*
D'Souza, Tony. *Whiteman*
De Bernieres, Louis. *Birds Without Wings*
Gibb, Camilla. *Sweetness in the Belly*

Houellebecq, Michel. *Submission*
Le Carre, John. *A Most Wanted Man: A Novel*
Shafak, Elif. *Honor: A Novel*
Shamsie, Kamila. *Home Fire: A Novel*
Wilson, G. Willow. ★*The Bird King*

MUTANTS
Gregory, Daryl. *The Devil's Alphabet*
Miller, Walter M. ★*A Canticle for Leibowitz*

MUTATION (BIOLOGY)
Koepp, David. *Cold Storage: A Novel*
Van Vogt, A. E. ★*Slan*

MUTILATION
Box, C. J. *Trophy Hunt: A Joe Pickett Novel*
Gerritsen, Tess. *The Surgeon*
Guinn, Matthew. *The Scribe: A Novel*
Tallis, Frank. *Vienna Blood: A Max Liebermann Mystery*

MUTINY
Johnson, Charles Richard. ★*Middle Passage*
Varley, John. *Dark Lightning*
Wouk, Herman. ★*The Caine Mutiny: A Novel of World War II*
★*My Antonia*. Cather, Willa
My Best Friend's Exorcism. Hendrix, Grady
My Brilliant Career. Franklin, Miles
My Brilliant Friend. Ferrante, Elena
★*My Dark Vanessa*. Russell, Kate Elizabeth
My Education. Choi, Susan
My Father's Tears and Other Stories. Updike, John
My Friend Maigret. Simenon, Georges
★*My Grandmother Asked Me to Tell You She's Sorry: A Novel*.
  Backman, Fredrik
My Heart Is a Chainsaw. Jones, Stephen Graham
My Jim: A Novel. Rawles, Nancy
My Lady Notorious. Beverley, Jo
My Liar: A Novel. Cline, Rachel
★*My Life as a Rat*. Oates, Joyce Carol
★*My Lord and Spymaster*. Bourne, Joanna
My Lovely Wife. Downing, Samantha
My Man Jeeves. Wodehouse, P. G.
★*My Monticello: Fiction*. Johnson, Jocelyn Nicole
My Name Is Anton. Hyde, Catherine Ryan
★*My Name Is Asher Lev*. Potok, Chaim
My Name Is Lucy Barton. Strout, Elizabeth
My Old Home: A Novel of Exile. Schell, Orville
My One and Only Duke. Burrowes, Grace
My Oxford Year. Whelan, Julia
★*My Policeman*. Roberts, Bethan
My Sister's Grave. Dugoni, Robert
★*My Sister's Keeper*. Picoult, Jodi
My Sister, the Serial Killer: A Novel. Braithwaite, Oyinkan
★*My Son's Story*. Gordimer, Nadine
★*My Sweet Girl*. Jayatissa, Amanda
My Sweet Untraceable You. Scoppettone, Sandra
★*My Year Abroad*. Lee, Chang-Rae
My Year of Rest and Relaxation. Moshfegh, Ottessa

MYCENAE (EXTINCT CITY)
George, Margaret. *Helen of Troy*
Toibin, Colm. *House of Names*

MYCOTOXICOSES
Sayers, Dorothy L. ★*The Documents in the Case*
Mycroft and Sherlock. Abdul-Jabbar, Kareem
★*Mycroft Holmes*. Abdul-Jabbar, Kareem
Mycroft Holmes novels [Series]. Abdul-Jabbar, Kareem

MYKONOS (ISLAND)
Siger, Jeffrey. *Mykonos After Midnight: A Chief Inspector Kaldis Mystery*
Mykonos After Midnight: A Chief Inspector Kaldis Mystery. Siger, Jeffrey
Myron Bolitar mysteries [Series]. Coben, Harlan

MYSTERIES
Abdul-Jabbar, Kareem. *The Empty Birdcage*
Abdul-Jabbar, Kareem. *Mycroft and Sherlock*
Abdul-Jabbar, Kareem. ★*Mycroft Holmes*
Abu-Jaber, Diana. *Origin: A Novel*
Akunin, B. *Sister Pelagia and the White Bulldog: A Mystery*
Allende, Isabel. *Ripper: A Novel*
Amis, Martin. *London Fields: A Novel*
Anappara, Deepa. *Djinn Patrol on the Purple Line: A Novel*
Anderson, Kevin J. *Death Warmed Over*
Andrews, Mary Kay. *Sunset Beach*
Armstrong, Kelley. *Alone in the Wild*
Armstrong, Kelley. *Watcher in the Woods*
Atkinson, Kate. ★*Big Sky*
Atkinson, Kate. ★*Case Histories*
Atkinson, Kate. *One Good Turn: A Novel*
Atkinson, Kate. *Started Early, Took My Dog*
Atkinson, Kate. ★*When Will There Be Good News?: A Novel*
Ayatsuji, Yukito. *The Decagon House Murders*
Ball, John Dudley. *In the Heat of the Night*
Bannalec, Jean-Luc. *Death in Brittany*
Bannister, Jo. *Kindred Spirits*
Bannister, Jo. *Silent Footsteps*
Barclay, Linwood. *Broken Promise*
Barclay, Linwood. *Far from True: A Novel*
Barclay, Linwood. *Parting Shot*
Barclay, Linwood. *A Tap on the Window*
Barclay, Linwood. *The Twenty-Three: A Promise Falls Novel*
Barnard, Robert. *Death of a Literary Widow*
Barnes, Jonathan. *The Somnambulist*
Barr, Nevada. *Destroyer Angel: An Anna Pigeon Novel*
Barr, Nevada. *The Rope: An Anna Pigeon Novel*
Barr, Nevada. *Track of the Cat*
Barr, Nevada. *What Rose Forgot*
Bayard, Louis. *The Black Tower: A Novel*
Bayard, Louis. *The Pale Blue Eye: A Novel*
Benn, James R. *Billy Boyle: A World War Two Mystery*
Berkowitz, Ira. *Old Flame: A Jackson Steeg Novel*
Bilal, Parker. *The Burning Gates: A Makana Investigation*
Bilal, Parker. *The Ghost Runner*
Black, Benjamin. ★*Christine Falls: A Novel*
Black, Cara. *Murder in the Bastille*
Black, Cara. *Murder in the Marais*
Black, Cara. *Murder in the Rue De Paradis: An Aimee Leduc Investigation*
Block, Lawrence. *All the Flowers Are Dying*

Block, Lawrence. *A Drop of the Hard Stuff: A Matthew Scudder Novel*

Block, Lawrence. *Eight Million Ways to Die*

Block, Lawrence. *The Sins of the Fathers*

Block, Lawrence. *A Ticket to the Boneyard: A Matthew Scudder Novel*

Block, Lawrence. ★*When the Sacred Ginmill Closes*

Bohjalian, Chris. *Secrets of Eden: A Novel*

Bohjalian, Chris. *The Sleepwalker*

Bolton, S. J. *The Craftsman*

Bowen, Peter. *Badlands*

Box, C. J. *Blue Heaven*

Boyle, William. *The Lonely Witness*

Bradley, C. Alan. *As Chimney Sweepers Come to Dust: A Flavia De Luce Novel*

Bradley, C. Alan. *I Am Half-Sick of Shadows: A Flavia De Luce Novel*

Bradley, C. Alan. *A Red Herring Without Mustard*

Bradley, C. Alan. *Speaking from Among the Bones: A Flavia De Luce Novel*

Bradley, C. Alan. ★*The Sweetness at the Bottom of the Pie*

Bradley, C. Alan. *Thrice the Brinded Cat Hath Mew'd: A Flavia De Luce Novel*

Bradley, C. Alan. *The Weed That Strings the Hangman's Bag: A Flavia De Luce Mystery*

Brandt, Harry. *The Whites: A Novel*

Brett, Simon. *Murder Unprompted*

Bruen, Ken. *Galway Girl: A Jack Taylor Novel*

Bruen, Ken. *The Guards*

Buchanan, Edna. *You Only Die Twice: A Britt Montero Mystery*

Buckley, Fiona. *The Doublet Affair: A Mystery at Queen Elizabeth I's Court*

Buckley, Fiona. *The Siren Queen: An Ursula Blanchard Mystery at Queen Elizabeth I's Court*

Burdett, John. *Bangkok 8*

Butler, Gwendoline. *Death Lives Next Door*

Camilleri, Andrea. *Riccardino*

Carter, Stephen L. *New England White: A Novel*

Cash, Wiley. *When Ghosts Come Home: A Novel*

Chabon, Michael. *The Yiddish Policemen's Union*

Chandler, Raymond. ★*The Big Sleep*

Chandler, Raymond. *The Lady in the Lake*

Chandler, Raymond. *The Long Goodbye*

Christie, Agatha. ★*The A B C Murders*

Christie, Agatha. ★*And Then There Were None*

Christie, Agatha. *The Body in the Library: A Miss Marple Mystery*

Christie, Agatha. *Curtain*

Christie, Agatha. *Endless Night*

Christie, Agatha. *The Hollow*

Christie, Agatha. *Mrs. McGinty's Dead*

Christie, Agatha. ★*The Murder at the Vicarage*

Christie, Agatha. *A Murder Is Announced: A Miss Marple Mystery*

Christie, Agatha. ★*The Murder of Roger Ackroyd: A Hercule Poirot Mystery*

Christie, Agatha. ★*Murder on the Orient Express*

Christie, Agatha. *The Pale Horse*

Christie, Agatha. *Three Blind Mice, and Other Stories*

Christie, Agatha. *Towards Zero*

Church, James. *Bamboo and Blood: An Inspector O Novel*

Church, James. ★*A Corpse in the Koryo*

Church, James. *A Drop of Chinese Blood*

Church, James. *Hidden Moon: An Inspector O Novel*

Clark, Mary Higgins. *Death Wears a Beauty Mask and Other Stories*

Clark, Tracy P. *Runner*

Clark, Tracy P. *What You Don't See*

Cleeves, Ann. *The Crow Trap*

Cleeves, Ann. *The Darkest Evening*

Cleeves, Ann. ★*The Heron's Cry*

Cleeves, Ann. *The Long Call*

Cleeves, Ann. *Raven Black*

Coben, Harlan. *Long Lost*

Coleman, Reed Farrel. *Where It Hurts: A Gus Murphy Novel*

Collins, Wilkie. ★*The Moonstone*

Collins, Wilkie. ★*The Woman in White*

Connelly, Michael. *The Black Ice*

Connelly, Michael. *The Burning Room*

Connelly, Michael. *The Crossing*

Connelly, Michael. ★*The Dark Hours*

Connelly, Michael. *Dark Sacred Night*

Connelly, Michael. *The Late Show*

Connelly, Michael. *The Night Fire*

Connelly, Michael. *The Wrong Side of Goodbye*

Connolly, John. *A Book of Bones*

Connolly, John. *The Dirty South*

Connolly, John. *The Nameless Ones*

Cook, Thomas H. *The Fate of Katherine Carr*

Cook, Thomas H. *Instruments of Night*

Cooney, Caroline B. *The Grandmother Plot*

Corby, Gary. *The Marathon Conspiracy*

Cornwell, Patricia Daniels. *Autopsy*

Cornwell, Patricia Daniels. *Postmortem*

Cotterill, Colin. *The Coroner's Lunch*

Cotterill, Colin. *Disco for the Departed*

Cotterill, Colin. *Don't Eat Me*

Cotterill, Colin. *Killed at the Whim of a Hat*

Cotterill, Colin. *The Second Biggest Nothing*

Cotterill, Colin. *Slash and Burn: A Dr. Siri Mystery Set in Laos*

Crais, Robert. *A Dangerous Man*

Crais, Robert. *The First Rule*

Crombie, Deborah. *A Bitter Feast*

Crompton, Richard. *Hell's Gate: A Novel*

Crompton, Richard. *Hour of the Red God*

Crumley, James. *The Last Good Kiss: A Novel*

Crumley, James. ★*The Wrong Case*

Dahl, Arne. *Bad Blood*

Dahl, Arne. *Misterioso: A Crime Novel*

Dahl, Julia. *Conviction*

Davis, Lindsey. *A Body in the Bathhouse*

Davis, Lindsey. *The Ides of April: A Flavia Albia Mystery*

Davis, Lindsey. *One Virgin Too Many*

Davys, Tim. *Amberville*

De Giovanni, Maurizio. *The Bastards of Pizzofalcone*

Deaver, Jeffery. ★*The Coffin Dancer*

Deaver, Jeffery. *The Empty Chair*

Deaver, Jeffery. *Garden of Beasts: A Novel of Berlin 1936*

Deaver, Jeffery. *The Stone Monkey: A Lincoln Rhyme Novel*

DePoy, Phillip. *Sidewalk Saint*
DeSilva, Bruce. *Providence Rag*
DeSilva, Bruce. *Rogue Island*
DeSilva, Bruce. *A Scourge of Vipers*
Deveraux, Jude. *A Willing Murder*
Dexter, Colin. *The Daughters of Cain*
Dexter, Colin. *The Remorseful Day*
Dexter, Colin. *The Way Through the Woods*
Dibdin, Michael. *Ratking*
Disher, Garry. *Under the Cold Bright Lights*
Dobyns, Stephen. *Saratoga Payback*
Doiron, Paul. *Almost Midnight*
Doiron, Paul. *One Last Lie*
Doiron, Paul. *Stay Hidden*
Doyle, Arthur Conan. ★*The Complete Sherlock Holmes*
Doyle, Arthur Conan. ★*The Hound of the Baskervilles*
Dugoni, Robert. *In Her Tracks*
Dugoni, Robert. *My Sister's Grave*
Elias, Gerald. *Danse Macabre*
Elias, Gerald. ★*Death and Transfiguration: A Daniel Jacobus Novel*
Eriksson, Kjell. *The Deathwatch Beetle: A Mystery*
Eskens, Allen. *Nothing More Dangerous: A Novel*
Estleman, Loren D. ★*Amos Walker: The Complete Story Collection*
Estleman, Loren D. ★*Indigo: A Valentino Mystery*
Estleman, Loren D. *Infernal Angels*
Estleman, Loren D. *A Smile on the Face of the Tiger*
Evanovich, Janet. ★*Game On: Tempting Twenty-Eight*
Evanovich, Janet. *Look Alive Twenty-Five*
Evanovich, Janet. *One for the Money*
Evanovich, Janet. *Turbo Twenty-Three*
Farrow, John. *The Storm Murders: A Thriller*
Faye, Lyndsay. *The Gods of Gotham*
Faye, Lyndsay. *Seven for a Secret*
Ferraris, Zoe. *Finding Nouf*
Ferraris, Zoe. *Kingdom of Strangers: A Novel*
Finch, Charles. *A Beautiful Blue Death*
Finch, Charles. *The September Society*
Florio, Gwen. *Best Laid Plans*
Fowler, Christopher. *Bryant & May: Hall of Mirrors : A Peculiar Crimes Unit Mystery*
Fowler, Christopher. *Bryant & May: Oranges and Lemons*
Fowler, Christopher. *Bryant & May: Strange Tide*
Fowler, Christopher. *Bryant & May: The Lonely Hour*
Fox, Candice. *Gone by Midnight*
Franklin, Ariana. *Mistress of the Art of Death*
Franklin, Ariana. *The Serpent's Tale*
French, Tana. ★*The Searcher*
Friedman, Daniel. ★*Don't Ever Get Old*
Friedman, Daniel. *Running Out of Road*
Galbraith, Robert. *Career of Evil*
Galbraith, Robert. *The Cuckoo's Calling*
Galbraith, Robert. *Lethal White*
Galbraith, Robert. *The Silkworm*
Garcia Saenz, Eva. *The Silence of the White City*
Garcia-Roza, L. A. *Alone in the Crowd: An Inspector Espinosa Mystery*
Garcia-Roza, L. A. *December Heat*
Gardiner, Meg. *The Dirty Secrets Club*

Garrett, Kellye. ★*Hollywood Homicide*
Gaspar de Alba, Alicia. *Desert Blood: The Juarez Murders*
Geni, Abby. *The Lightkeepers: A Novel*
George, Elizabeth. *A Banquet of Consequences*
George, Elizabeth. *Believing the Lie*
George, Elizabeth. *Careless in Red*
George, Elizabeth. *Just One Evil Act*
George, Elizabeth. *The Punishment She Deserves*
George, Elizabeth. *This Body of Death: An Inspector Lynley Novel*
George, Elizabeth. *What Came Before He Shot Her*
Gilman, Laura Anne. *Hard Magic*
Giordano, Mario. ★*Auntie Poldi and the Lost Madonna*
Giordano, Mario. *Auntie Poldi and the Vineyards of Etna*
Glass, Seraphina Nova. *Someone's Listening*
Goddard, Robert. ★*Long Time Coming: A Novel*
Goldman, Matt. *Dead West*
Goldman, Matt. *The Shallows*
Gorman, Edward. *Riders on the Storm : A Sam McCain Mystery*
Grafton, Sue. *X*
Grafton, Sue. *Y Is for Yesterday*
Gran, Sara. *Claire Dewitt and the City of the Dead*
Gran, Sara. *The Infinite Blacktop: A Novel*
Grant, Helen. *The Vanishing of Katharina Linden*
Greaves, Chuck. *Hush Money: A Mystery*
Greenwood, Kerry. *Death in Daylesford*
Greenwood, Kerry. *Unnatural Habits*
Greer, Robert O. *First of State*
Gregory, Daryl. *The Devil's Alphabet*
Griffiths, Elly. *The Crossing Places*
Griffiths, Elly. *The Dark Angel*
Griffiths, Elly. *A Dying Fall: A Ruth Galloway Mystery*
Griffiths, Elly. *The House at Sea's End: A Ruth Galloway Mystery*
Griffiths, Elly. *The Janus Stone*
Griffiths, Elly. *The Night Hawks*
Griffiths, Elly. *The Postscript Murders*
Griffiths, Elly. *The Stranger Diaries*
Grossman, Paul. *Children of Wrath*
Haddam, Jane. *Cheating at Solitaire: A Gregor Demarkian Novel*
Haddam, Jane. *Hardscrabble Road*
Haddon, Mark. ★*The Curious Incident of the Dog in the Night-Time: A Novel*
Hall, Tarquin. *The Case of the Deadly Butter Chicken: A Vish Puri Mystery*
Hall, Tarquin. *The Case of the Love Commandos: From the Files of Vish Puri, India's Most Private Investigator*
Hallinan, Timothy. *Fields Where They Lay*
Hammett, Dashiell. *The Glass Key*
Hammett, Dashiell. ★*The Maltese Falcon*
Hanson, Hart. *The Driver*
Harper, Jane. *The Dry*
Harper, Jane. *The Lost Man*
Harper, Jane. *The Survivors*
Harris, Robert. ★*Fatherland*
Harris, Robert. *The Second Sleep: A Novel*
Harris, Sarah J. *The Color of Bee Larkham's Murder: A Novel*
Harrison, Mette Ivie. *The Bishop's Wife*
Harrison, Mette Ivie. *The Prodigal Daughter*
Harrod-Eagles, Cynthia. *Cruel as the Grave*

Harrod-Eagles, Cynthia. *Headlong*

Hart, Carolyn G. *Letter from Home*

Hart, Erin. *The Book of Killowen*

Hart, Erin. *Haunted Ground: A Crime Novel*

Hart, John. *Down River*

Harvey, John. *A Darker Shade of Blue: Stories*

Harvey, Michael T. *The Chicago Way*

Harvey, Michael T. *The Fifth Floor*

Harvey, Michael T. *The Governor's Wife*

Harvey, Michael T. *Pulse*

Harvey, Michael T. *We All Fall Down*

Hayder, Mo. *Gone*

Hayder, Mo. *Poppet*

Haywood, Gar Anthony. *Cemetery Road*

Heaberlin, Julia. *We Are All the Same in the Dark: A Novel*

Heller, Peter. *Celine: A Novel*

Herron, Mick. *Dolphin Junction: Collected Stories*

Hewson, David. *The Garden of Evil*

Hewson, David. *A Season for the Dead*

Hiaasen, Carl. *Basket Case*

Hiaasen, Carl. *Nature Girl*

Hiaasen, Carl. *Star Island*

Higashino, Keigo. ★*The Devotion of Suspect X*

Higashino, Keigo. *Malice*

Higashino, Keigo. *Newcomer*

Hilderbrand, Elin. *The Perfect Couple*

Hill Gumbao, Toni. *The Good Suicides: A Thriller*

Hill Gumbao, Toni. *The Summer of Dead Toys*

Hill, Edwin J. *Little Comfort*

Hill, Susan. *The Pure in Heart: A Simon Serrailler Crime Novel*

Hill, Susan. *The Shadows in the Street: A Simon Serrailler Mystery*

Hillerman, Tony. *The Shape Shifter*

Hillerman, Tony. *The Wailing Wind*

Horowitz, Anthony. ★*Magpie Murders*

Horowitz, Anthony. ★*Moonflower Murders*

Horowitz, Anthony. ★*The Sentence Is Death*

Horowitz, Anthony. ★*The Word Is Murder*

Hummel, Maria. *Lesson in Red*

Ide, Joe. ★*Hi Five: An IQ Novel*

Iles, Greg. *Cemetery Road: A Novel*

Indriðason, Arnaldur. *Outrage*

Indriðason, Arnaldur. *Reykjavik Nights: An Inspector Erlendur Novel*

Indriðason, Arnaldur. *Strange Shores: An Inspector Erlendur Novel*

Ishiguro, Kazuo. *When We Were Orphans*

James, P. D. *Death of an Expert Witness*

James, P. D. *The Lighthouse*

James, P. D. *Original Sin*

James, P. D. *The Private Patient*

James, P. D. *The Skull Beneath the Skin*

James, P. D. *A Taste for Death*

James, P. D. *An Unsuitable Job for a Woman*

James, Wendy. *A Little Bird*

Johnson, Craig. *Daughter of the Morning Star*

Johnson, Craig. *Land of Wolves*

Johnson, Craig. *Next to Last Stand*

Johnson, Craig. *Spirit of Steamboat: A Walt Longmire Story*

Johnson, D. E. *Detroit Shuffle*

Kaminsky, Stuart M. *Murder on the Trans-Siberian Express*

Kayode, Femi. ★*Lightseekers*

Keller, Julia. ★*Bone on Bone*

Keller, Julia. *A Killing in the Hills*

Kellerman, Jonathan. *Bones: An Alex Delaware Novel*

Kellerman, Jonathan. *Gone*

Kellerman, Jonathan. ★*Half Moon Bay: A Novel*

Kells, Claire. *Vanishing Edge*

Kelly, Erin. *Broadchurch: A Novel*

Kemelman, Harry. *Monday the Rabbi Took Off*

Kemelman, Harry. *One Fine Day the Rabbi Bought a Cross*

Kepler, Lars. *The Sandman*

Kerley, Jack. ★*The Death Collectors*

Khan, Vaseem. *The Perplexing Theft of the Jewel in the Crown*

Knopf, Chris. *You're Dead*

Koryta, Michael. ★*How It Happened*

Krueger, William Kent. ★*Lightning Strike*

Lagercrantz, David. *The Girl Who Lived Twice: A Lisbeth Salander Novel*

Lagercrantz, David. *The Girl Who Takes an Eye for an Eye*

Lalami, Laila. *The Other Americans: A Novel*

Lansdale, Joe R. *The Bottoms*

Lansdale, Joe R. *Devil Red*

Lansdale, Joe R. *Honky Tonk Samurai*

Lansdale, Joe R. *Sunset and Sawdust*

Larsson, Stieg. ★*The Girl Who Kicked the Hornet's Nest*

Larsson, Stieg. *The Girl Who Played with Fire*

Larsson, Stieg. *The Girl with the Dragon Tattoo*

Lawrence, David. *The Dead Sit Round in a Ring*

Leitch, Will. ★*How Lucky*

Leon, Donna. *Beastly Things: A Commissario Guido Brunetti Mystery*

Leon, Donna. *Drawing Conclusions: A Commissario Guido Brunetti Mystery*

Leon, Donna. *Falling in Love: A Commissario Guido Brunetti Mystery*

Leon, Donna. *The Golden Egg*

Leon, Donna. *A Question of Belief: A Commissario Guido Brunetti Mystery*

Leon, Donna. *Uniform Justice*

Leonard, Elmore. *Glitz*

Lepionka, Kristen. *The Last Place You Look*

Lepionka, Kristen. *Once You Go This Far: A Mystery*

Limon, Martin. *The Line*

Limon, Martin. *War Women*

Lippman, Laura. ★*Hush Hush*

Lippman, Laura. *No Good Deeds*

Lippman, Laura. *What the Dead Know*

Littlejohn, Emily. *Inherit the Bones*

Littlejohn, Emily. *Lost Lake: A Detective Gemma Monroe Mystery*

Locke, Attica. ★*Bluebird, Bluebird*

Locke, Attica. *The Cutting Season*

Locke, Attica. ★*Heaven, My Home*

Logan, Kylie. *The Secrets of Bones: A Mystery*

Longworth, M. L. *Murder on the Ile Sordou: A Verlaque and Bonnet Provencal Mystery*

Lourey, Jess. ★*January Thaw: A Murder-By-Month Mystery*

Lovesey, Peter. *Beau Death*

Lovesey, Peter. *Diamond Solitaire*

Lovesey, Peter. ★*The Last Detective*
Lovesey, Peter. *The Tooth Tattoo*
Lovett, Charles C. *The Lost Book of the Grail: Or a Visitor's Guide to Barchester Cathedral*
Lundrigan, Nicole. *Glass Boys: A Novel*
Lutz, Lisa. *The Spellman Files: A Novel*
MacBride, Stuart. *Cold Granite*
MacDonald, John D. *Cinnamon Skin: The Twentieth Adventure of Travis McGee*
MacDonald, John D. *The Green Ripper*
MacDonald, John D. ★*The Lonely Silver Rain*
MacDonald, John D. *The Long Lavender Look*
MacDonald, John D. *A Purple Place for Dying*
MacDonald, John D. *The Scarlet Ruse*
MacDonald, John D. *The Turquoise Lament*
MacDonald, Philip. *The List of Adrian Messenger*
Macdonald, Ross. *The Drowning Pool*
Macdonald, Ross. *The Far Side of the Dollar*
Macdonald, Ross. *The Galton Case*
Macdonald, Ross. *The Goodbye Look*
Macdonald, Ross. *Sleeping Beauty*
Macdonald, Ross. *The Underground Man*
Mankell, Henning. *Before the Frost: A Linda Wallander Mystery*
Mankell, Henning. *The Dogs of Riga*
Mankell, Henning. *Firewall*
Mankell, Henning. *The Man from Beijing*
Mankell, Henning. *The Man Who Smiled: A Kurt Wallander Mystery*
Mankell, Henning. ★*One Step Behind*
Mankell, Henning. ★*The Return of the Dancing Master*
Mark, David John. *Cruel Mercy*
Maron, Margaret. *Bootlegger's Daughter*
Maron, Margaret. *Up Jumps the Devil*
Marsh, Ngaio. *A Man Lay Dead*
Marston, Edward. *The Roaring Boy: A Novel*
Marston, Edward. *The Wanton Angel: A Novel*
May, Peter. *The Blackhouse*
Mayor, Archer. ★*Marked Man*
Mayor, Archer. *Red Herring: A Joe Gunther Novel*
Mayor, Archer. *Tag Man: A Joe Gunther Novel*
McCall Smith, Alexander. ★*The Department of Sensitive Crimes: A Detective Varg Novel*
McCall Smith, Alexander. *The Forgotten Affairs of Youth*
McCall Smith, Alexander. ★*The Geometry of Holding Hands*
McCall Smith, Alexander. *The Lost Art of Gratitude*
McCall Smith, Alexander. ★*The Man with the Silver Saab: A Detective Varg Novel*
McCammon, Robert R. *Boy's Life*
McClure, James. *The Steam Pig*
McCrumb, Sharyn. ★*If Ever I Return, Pretty Peggy-O*
McDermid, Val. *The Distant Echo*
McDermid, Val. *How the Dead Speak: A Tony Hill and Carol Jordan Novel*
McDermid, Val. *A Place of Execution*
McDermid, Val. ★*Still Life*
McIlvanney, William. *The Dark Remains: Laidlaw's First Case*
McLain, Paula. ★*When the Stars Go Dark: A Novel*
McPherson, Catriona. *Quiet Neighbors: A Novel*
McPherson, Catriona. *Scot & Soda*

Meyer, Nicholas. *The Adventure of the Peculiar Protocols: Adapted from the Journals of John H. Watson, M.D.*
Miller, Derek B. ★*American by Day*
Mizushima, Margaret. *Killing Trail*
Moor, Jessica. *The Keeper*
Moshfegh, Ottessa. ★*Death in Her Hands: A Novel*
Mosley, Walter. *All I Did Was Shoot My Man: A Leonid McGill Mystery*
Mosley, Walter. *And Sometimes I Wonder About You: A Leonid McGill Mystery*
Mosley, Walter. *Black Betty: An Easy Rawlins Mystery*
Mosley, Walter. ★*Blood Grove*
Mosley, Walter. *Charcoal Joe: An Easy Rawlins Mystery*
Mosley, Walter. *Down the River Unto the Sea*
Mosley, Walter. *Little Scarlet: An Easy Rawlins Mystery*
Mosley, Walter. *Trouble Is What I Do: A Leonid McGill Mystery*
Muller, Marcia. *Dead Midnight*
Muller, Marcia. *Ice and Stone*
Nava, Michael. ★*Carved in Bone*
Nesbo, Jo. *The Leopard*
Nesbo, Jo. *Phantom*
Nesbo, Jo. *The Redeemer*
Nicieza, Fabian. *Suburban Dicks*
Nickson, Chris. *Come the Fear*
O'Mara, Tim. *Crooked Numbers*
Ohlsson, Kristina. *Unwanted: A Novel*
Orczy, Emmuska Orczy. *The Old Man in the Corner*
Osborne, Lawrence. *Only to Sleep: A Philip Marlowe Novel*
Osman, Richard. *The Man Who Died Twice: A Thursday Murder Club Mystery*
Osman, Richard. ★*The Thursday Murder Club*
Palliser, Charles. *The Quincunx*
Paretsky, Sara. ★*Dead Land*
Paretsky, Sara. *Indemnity Only: A Novel*
Paretsky, Sara. *Love & Other Crimes: Stories*
Paretsky, Sara. *Shell Game*
Parker, Robert B. *Death in Paradise*
Parker, Robert B. *Night Passage*
Parker, Robert B. *Painted Ladies*
Parker, Robert B. *Sixkill*
Parker, Robert B. *Trouble in Paradise*
Parker, T. Jefferson. *The Blue Hour*
Parks, Brad. *The Player: A Mystery*
Parris, S. J. ★*The Dead of Winter*
Parris, S. J. *Sacrilege*
Parris, S. J. *Treachery*
Patterson, James. *1st to Die: A Novel*
Pattison, Eliot. *Bones of the Earth: An Inspector Shan Tao Yun Mystery*
Pattison, Eliot. *The Skull Mantra*
Pava, Sergio de la. *Personae: A Novel*
Pawel, Rebecca. *Death of a Nationalist*
Pearl, Matthew. *The Dante Club: A Novel*
Pearl, Matthew. *The Last Dickens: A Novel*
Pearl, Matthew. *The Poe Shadow: A Novel*
Pearl, Matthew. *The Technologists: A Novel*
Pears, Iain. *Death and Restoration*
Pears, Iain. *The Immaculate Deception*

Pears, Iain. *The Last Judgement*

Pelecanos, George P. *The Big Blowdown*

Pelecanos, George P. *The Cut: A Novel*

Penman, Sharon Kay. *The Queen's Man: A Medieval Mystery*

Penny, Louise. ★*All the Devils Are Here*

Penny, Louise. ★*A Better Man: A Chief Inspector Gamache Novel*

Penny, Louise. *The Cruelest Month: A Three Pines Mystery*

Penny, Louise. *The Madness of Crowds*

Penny, Louise. *Still Life*

Perez-Reverte, Arturo. *The Club Dumas*

Perry, Thomas. *Death Benefits: A Novel*

Perry, Thomas. *Fidelity*

Persson, Leif G. W. *The Dying Detective: A Mystery*

Pessl, Marisha. *Special Topics in Calamity Physics*

Peters, Ellis. *Brother Cadfael's Penance*

Peters, Ellis. *The Holy Thief*

Phillips, Christi. *The Devlin Diary*

Phillips, Christi. *The Rossetti Letter: A Novel*

Pickard, Nancy. *The Scent of Rain and Lightning: A Novel*

Pirie, David. *The Patient's Eyes*

Pobi, Robert. *City of Windows*

Pobi, Robert. *Under Pressure*

Pochoda, Ivy. *Visitation Street: A Novel*

Poole, Sara. *The Borgia Mistress*

Potenza, Carol. *Hearts of the Missing*

Potzsch, Oliver. *The Beggar King*

Potzsch, Oliver. *The Dark Monk: A Hangman's Daughter Tale*

Potzsch, Oliver. *The Hangman's Daughter: A Historical Novel*

Potzsch, Oliver. *The Poisoned Pilgrim: A Hangman's Daughter Tale*

Potzsch, Oliver. *The Werewolf of Bamberg*

Price, Richard. *Clockers*

Pronzini, Bill. *Crazybone*

Pronzini, Bill. *Fever*

Pronzini, Bill. *Hardcase*

Pronzini, Bill. *Hellbox*

Pronzini, Bill. *Illusions*

Pronzini, Bill. *Mourners*

Pronzini, Bill. *Nemesis*

Pronzini, Bill. *Nightcrawlers*

Pronzini, Bill. *Savages*

Pronzini, Bill. *Spook*

Pronzini, Bill. *The Violated*

Pynchon, Thomas. ★*Bleeding Edge*

Qiu, Xiaolong. *Death of a Red Heroine*

Qiu, Xiaolong. *Don't Cry Tai Lake: An Inspector Chen Novel*

Qiu, Xiaolong. *Enigma of China*

Qiu, Xiaolong. *Hold Your Breath, China*

Qiu, Xiaolong. *Red Mandarin Dress: An Inspector Chen Novel*

Qiu, Xiaolong. *Shanghai Redemption: An Inspector Chen Novel*

Qiu, Xiaolong. *When Red Is Black*

Quartey, Kwei. *Children of the Street: A Novel*

Quartey, Kwei. *Gold of Our Fathers*

Quartey, Kwei. *The Missing American*

Quartey, Kwei. *Murder at Cape Three Points*

Quartey, Kwei. ★*Sleep Well, My Lady*

Quartey, Kwei. *Wife of the Gods: A Novel*

Quinn, Spencer. *Dog on It: A Chet and Bernie Mystery*

Quinn, Spencer. ★*It's a Wonderful Woof*

Racculia, Kate. ★*Bellweather Rhapsody*

Rademacher, Cay. *Deadly Camargue: A Provence Mystery*

Rader-Day, Lori. *Little Pretty Things*

Raimondo, Lynne. *Dante's Dilemma: A Mark Angelotti Novel*

Raimondo, Lynne. *Dante's Poison: A Mark Angelotti Novel*

Raimondo, Lynne. *Dante's Wood: A Mark Angelotti Novel*

Randisi, Robert J. *Hey There (You with the Gun in Your Hand): A Rat Pack Mystery*

Rankin, Ian. ★*Black and Blue: An Inspector Rebus Novel*

Rankin, Ian. *The Black Book*

Rankin, Ian. *Blood Hunt: A Novel*

Rankin, Ian. *The Complaints*

Rankin, Ian. *Dead Souls: An Inspector Rebus Novel*

Rankin, Ian. *Exit Music*

Rankin, Ian. *The Falls: An Inspector Rebus Novel*

Rankin, Ian. *The Hanging Garden: An Inspector Rebus Novel*

Rankin, Ian. *The Impossible Dead*

Rankin, Ian. *The Naming of the Dead: An Inspector Rebus Novel*

Rankin, Ian. *A Question of Blood: An Inspector Rebus Novel*

Rankin, Ian. *Resurrection Men: An Inspector Rebus Novel*

Rankin, Ian. *Set in Darkness: An Inspector Rebus Novel*

Redondo, Dolores. *The Invisible Guardian*

Redondo, Dolores. *The North Face of the Heart*

Rees, Matt. *The Fourth Assassin*

Reichs, Kathy. *206 Bones*

Reichs, Kathy. *Bare Bones*

Reichs, Kathy. *Bones of the Lost: A Temperance Brennan Novel*

Reichs, Kathy. *Bones to Ashes*

Reichs, Kathy. *Break No Bones*

Reichs, Kathy. ★*A Conspiracy of Bones*

Reichs, Kathy. *Deadly Decisions*

Reichs, Kathy. *Death Du Jour*

Reichs, Kathy. ★*Deja Dead*

Reichs, Kathy. *Grave Secrets*

Reichs, Kathy. *Monday Mourning*

Rendell, Ruth. *The Babes in the Wood*

Rendell, Ruth. *Collected Stories*

Rendell, Ruth. *End in Tears*

Rendell, Ruth. *Harm Done*

Rendell, Ruth. *Kissing the Gunner's Daughter*

Rendell, Ruth. *Not in the Flesh*

Rendell, Ruth. *Road Rage*

Rendell, Ruth. *Simisola*

Rendell, Ruth. *A Sleeping Life*

Rendell, Ruth. *Speaker of Mandarin*

Rice, Craig. *Home Sweet Homicide*

Richmond, Michelle. *No One You Know*

Ridpath, Michael. *Far North*

Rinehart, Mary Roberts. *The Circular Staircase*

Ripley, Mike. *Mr Campion's Coven*

Ripley, Mike. *Mr Campion's Fault*

Ripley, Mike. *Mr. Campion's War*

Ritter, Todd. *Devil's Night*

Robb, Candace M. *A Gift of Sanctuary: An Owen Archer Mystery*

Robb, Candace M. *The Riddle of St. Leonard's: An Owen Archer Mystery.*

Robertson, Imogen. *Anatomy of Murder*

Robertson, Imogen. *Instruments of Darkness: A Novel*

Robertson, Imogen. *Island of Bones*
Robertson, Michael. *The Baker Street Letters*
Robertson, Michael. *The Baker Street Translation: A Mystery*
Robertson, Michael. *The Brothers of Baker Street*
Robertson, Michael. *Moriarty Returns a Letter: A Baker Street Mystery*
Robinson, Peter. *All the Colors of Darkness*
Robinson, Peter. ★*Careless Love*
Robinson, Peter. *Children of the Revolution*
Robinson, Peter. *Close to Home*
Robinson, Peter. *Cold Is the Grave*
Robinson, Peter. *Friend of the Devil*
Robinson, Peter. *In the Dark Places*
Robinson, Peter. *Innocent Graves: An Inspector Banks Mystery*
Robinson, Peter. *Piece of My Heart*
Robinson, Peter. *Playing with Fire*
Robinson, Peter. *Strange Affair*
Robotham, Michael. *The Night Ferry: A Novel*
Rodriguez, Linda. *Every Broken Trust: A Mystery*
Rodriguez, Linda. *Every Hidden Fear: A Skeet Bannion Mystery*
Rodriguez, Linda. *Every Last Secret: A Mystery*
Roorbach, Bill. *Life Among Giants: A Novel*
Rosenfelt, David. ★*Dog Eat Dog*
Roslund, Anders. *Pen 33*
Ross, Adam. *Mr. Peanut*
Rowland, Laura Joh. *The Incense Game: A Novel of Feudal Japan*
Rowland, Laura Joh. *The Iris Fan: A Novel of Feudal Japan*
Rowland, Laura Joh. *The Shogun's Daughter: A Novel of Feudal Japan*
Rowland, Laura Joh. *The Snow Empress*
Rowland, Russell. *Cold Country: A Novel*
Rozan, S. J. ★*The Art of Violence*
Rozan, S. J. ★*Paper Son*
Rozan, S. J. *The Shanghai Moon: A Lydia Chin/Bill Smith Novel*
Rozan, S. J. *Winter and Night*
Runcie, James. *Sidney Chambers and the Forgiveness of Sins*
Runcie, James. *Sidney Chambers and the Perils of the Night*
Runcie, James. *Sidney Chambers and the Persistence of Love*
Runcie, James. *Sidney Chambers and the Problem of Evil*
Runcie, James. *Sidney Chambers and the Shadow of Death*
Sanders, Lawrence. ★*The First Deadly Sin*
Sanders, Lawrence. ★*The Fourth Deadly Sin*
Sanders, Lawrence. *McNally's Dilemma*
Sanders, Lawrence. ★*McNally's Gamble*
Sanders, Lawrence. *McNally's Luck*
Sanders, Lawrence. *McNally's Puzzle*
Sanders, Lawrence. *McNally's Secret*
Sanders, Lawrence. *McNally's Trial*
Sanders, Lawrence. *The Second Deadly Sin*
Sanders, Lawrence. *The Sixth Commandment: A Novel*
Sanders, Lawrence. *The Tenth Commandment: A Novel*
Sanders, Lawrence. ★*The Third Deadly Sin*
Sanders, Lawrence. *The Timothy Files*
Sanders, Lawrence. *Timothy's Game*
Sansom, C. J. ★*Lamentation*
Sansom, C. J. *Revelation*
Sansom, C. J. ★*Sovereign*
Sansom, C. J. *Tombland*

Sayers, Dorothy L. ★*Busman's Honeymoon*
Sayers, Dorothy L. ★*Clouds of Witness*
Sayers, Dorothy L. ★*The Documents in the Case*
Sayers, Dorothy L. ★*The Five Red Herrings*
Sayers, Dorothy L. ★*Gaudy Night*
Sayers, Dorothy L. *Hangman's Holiday*
Sayers, Dorothy L. *Have His Carcase*
Sayers, Dorothy L. *In the Teeth of the Evidence*
Sayers, Dorothy L. ★*Lord Peter*
Sayers, Dorothy L. *Murder Must Advertise*
Sayers, Dorothy L. *The Nine Tailors*
Sayers, Dorothy L. *Thrones, Dominations*
Sayers, Dorothy L. *The Unpleasantness at the Bellona Club*
Sayers, Dorothy L. ★*Whose Body?: A Lord Peter Wimsey Novel*
Saylor, Steven. *The House of the Vestals: The Investigations of Gordianus the Finder*
Saylor, Steven. *The Judgment of Caesar: A Novel of Ancient Rome*
Saylor, Steven. *A Mist of Prophecies*
Saylor, Steven. *Raiders of the Nile: A Novel of the Ancient World*
Saylor, Steven. *Rubicon*
Saylor, Steven. *The Seven Wonders: A Novel of the Ancient World*
Saylor, Steven. *The Triumph of Caesar: A Novel of Ancient Rome*
Saylor, Steven. *Wrath of the Furies: A Novel of the Ancient World*
Scerbanenco, Giorgio. *A Private Venus*
Scerbanenco, Giorgio. *Traitors to All*
Schlink, Bernhard. *Self's Deception*
Schlink, Bernhard. *Self's Murder*
Schlink, Bernhard. *Self's Punishment*
Scoppettone, Sandra. *Everything You Have Is Mine*
Scoppettone, Sandra. *My Sweet Untraceable You*
Scott, A. D. ★*Beneath the Abbey Wall: A Novel*
Scott, A. D. *A Double Death on the Black Isle: A Novel*
Scott, A. D. *A Kind of Grief: A Novel*
Scott, A. D. ★*The Low Road*
See, Lisa. *Dragon Bones: A Novel*
Sepetys, Ruta. ★*Out of the Easy*
Shames, Terry. ★*An Unsettling Crime for Samuel Craddock*
Shannon, Dell. ★*Chaos of Crime*
Sharp, Zoe. *Second Shot: A Charlie Fox Thriller*
Shaw, William. *The Birdwatcher*
Shelton, Paige. *Thin Ice: A Mystery*
Shoham, Liad. *Asylum City: A Novel*
Siger, Jeffrey. *Mykonos After Midnight: A Chief Inspector Kaldis Mystery*
Siger, Jeffrey. *Target Tinos: An Inspector Kaldis Mystery*
Silvis, Randall. *Two Days Gone: A Novel*
Simenon, Georges. *Maigret and the Black Sheep*
Simenon, Georges. *Maigret and the Fortuneteller*
Simenon, Georges. ★*Maigret and the Killer*
Simenon, Georges. *Maigret and the Madwoman*
Simenon, Georges. ★*Maigret and the Saturday Caller*
Simenon, Georges. ★*Maigret and the Toy Village*
Simenon, Georges. *Maigret and the Wine Merchant*
Simenon, Georges. ★*Maigret Bides His Time*
Simenon, Georges. ★*Maigret Goes Home*
Simenon, Georges. *Maigret in Holland*
Simenon, Georges. *Maigret's Memoirs*
Simenon, Georges. *My Friend Maigret*

Simpson, Dorothy. *Dead and Gone: An Inspector Luke Thanet Novel.*
Simpson, Dorothy. *Dead by Morning*
Simpson, Dorothy. *Doomed to Die*
Simpson, Dorothy. *Last Seen Alive: A Luke Thanet Mystery*
Simpson, Dorothy. *No Laughing Matter*
Simpson, Dorothy. *Once Too Often: An Inspector Luke Thanet Novel*
Sjón. *The Blue Fox*
Sjowall, Maj. ★*Cop Killer: The Story of a Crime*
Sjowall, Maj. ★*The Laughing Policeman*
Sjowall, Maj. ★*The Locked Room: The Story of a Crime*
Sjowall, Maj. *The Man on the Balcony: The Story of a Crime*
Sjowall, Maj. ★*Murder at the Savoy*
Slaughter, Karin. *Cop Town: A Novel*
Smith, B. J. *Crow's Landing: A Novel*
Smith, B. J. *Shoot the Dog: A Virgil Cain Mystery*
Smith, Ian. *Wolf Point*
Smith, Julie. *82 Desire: A Skip Langdon Novel*
Smith, Julie. *Crescent City Kill: A Skip Langdon Novel*
Smith, Julie. *House of Blues*
Smith, Julie. *Jazz Funeral*
Smith, Julie. *The Kindness of Strangers: A Skip Langdon Novel*
Smith, Julie. *Louisiana Hotshot*
Smith, Julie. ★*Mean Woman Blues*
Smith, Julie. *New Orleans Beat*
Smith, Lee. *Family Linen*
Solares, Martin. *The Black Minutes*
Somer, Mehmet Murat. *The Serenity Murders*
Spain, Jo. *With Our Blessing: An Inspector Tom Reynolds Mystery*
Spann, Susan. *Blade of the Samurai: A Shinobi Mystery*
Spann, Susan. ★*Claws of the Cat: A Shinobi Mystery*
Spann, Susan. *Trial on Mount Koya: A Hiro Hattori Novel*
Spark, Muriel. *Aiding & Abetting*
Spark, Muriel. *The Driver's Seat*
Speller, Elizabeth. *The Return of Captain John Emmett*
Speller, Elizabeth. *The Strange Fate of Kitty Easton*
Spencer, Sally. *Backlash*
Spencer, Sally. *Best Served Cold*
Spencer, Sally. *Dead End*
Spencer, Sally. *The Dead Hand of History*
Spencer, Sally. *Death's Dark Shadow*
Spencer, Sally. ★*A Dying Fall*
Spencer, Sally. ★*Echoes of the Dead*
Spencer, Sally. ★*The Hidden*
Spencer, Sally. *Lambs to the Slaughter*
Spencer, Sally. *The Shivering Turn*
Spencer, Sally. *Thicker Than Water: A Monika Paniatowski British Police Procedural*
Spencer, Sally. *A Walk with the Dead*
Spencer-Fleming, Julia. *All Mortal Flesh*
Spencer-Fleming, Julia. *Hid from Our Eyes*
Spencer-Fleming, Julia. *I Shall Not Want: A Clare Fergusson/Russ Van Alstyne Mystery*
Spencer-Fleming, Julia. *In the Bleak Midwinter*
Spencer-Fleming, Julia. *Through the Evil Days: A Clare Fergusson/Russ Van Alstyne Mystery*
Spiegelman, Peter. *Black Maps*
Spillane, Mickey. *The Consummata*
Spillane, Mickey. *The Goliath Bone*

Spillane, Mickey. *Kill Me, Darling*
Spillane, Mickey. *A Long Time Dead: A Mike Hammer Casebook*
St. James, Simone. *The Broken Girls*
Stabenow, Dana. ★*A Deeper Sleep: A Kate Shugak Novel*
Stabenow, Dana. ★*A Fine and Bitter Snow: A Kate Shugak Novel*
Stabenow, Dana. ★*A Grave Denied*
Stabenow, Dana. ★*Hunter's Moon*
Stabenow, Dana. *Killing Grounds: A Kate Shugak Mystery*
Stabenow, Dana. ★*Less Than a Treason*
Stabenow, Dana. *A Night Too Dark: A Kate Shugak Novel*
Stabenow, Dana. *No Fixed Line*
Stabenow, Dana. *Restless in the Grave*
Stabenow, Dana. *The Singing of the Dead*
Stabenow, Dana. *So Sure of Death: A Liam Campbell Mystery*
Stabenow, Dana. *Spoils of the Dead*
Stabenow, Dana. ★*A Taint in the Blood*
Stabenow, Dana. *Though Not Dead: A Kate Shugak Novel*
Stabenow, Dana. *Whisper to the Blood: A Kate Shugak Novel*
Stanley, Michael. *A Carrion Death*
Stanley, Michael. *Deadly Harvest*
Stanley, Michael. *A Death in the Family*
Stanley, Michael. *Death of the Mantis*
Stanley, Michael. *Dying to Live*
Staples, Dennis E. *This Town Sleeps*
Starr, Melvin R. *Unhallowed Ground*
Steiner, Susie. *Missing, Presumed: A Novel*
Steiner, Susie. ★*Persons Unknown: A Novel*
Stout, Rex. *The Doorbell Rang*
Stout, Rex. ★*Gambit*
Straley, John. *The Big Both Ways*
Straub, Peter. ★*Mystery*
Sundstol, Vidar. *The Land of Dreams*
Tallis, Frank. *Vienna Blood: A Max Liebermann Mystery*
Tallo, Katie. *Dark August*
Talton, Jon. *City of Dark Corners*
Thomas, Russ. ★*Firewatching*
Thomas, Russ. *Nighthawking*
Thomas, Will. *Dance with Death*
Tracy, P. J. ★*Deep into the Dark*
Turton, Stuart. *The 7 1/2 Deaths of Evelyn Hardcastle*
Walker, Martin. *The Coldest Case*
Walker, Martin. *The Shooting at Chateau Rock*
Winspear, Jacqueline. *The American Agent*
Winspear, Jacqueline. ★*The Consequences of Fear: A Maisie Dobbs Novel*
Yocum, Robin. *A Welcome Murder*
★*The **Mysteries** of Udolpho*. Radcliffe, Ann Ward
*The **Mysterious** Flame of Queen Loana: An Illustrated Novel*. Eco, Umberto
*The **Mysterious** Island*. Verne, Jules
★***Mystery***. Straub, Peter
Mystery bookshop [Series]. Burns, V. M.
MYSTERY CLASSICS
Christie, Agatha. ★*The A B C Murders*
Christie, Agatha. ★*And Then There Were None*
Christie, Agatha. *Curtain*
Christie, Agatha. *Endless Night*
Christie, Agatha. *A Murder Is Announced: A Miss Marple Mystery*

Christie, Agatha. ★*The Murder of Roger Ackroyd: A Hercule Poirot Mystery*

Christie, Agatha. ★*Murder on the Orient Express*

Hammett, Dashiell. *The Glass Key*

Macdonald, Ross. *The Drowning Pool*

Macdonald, Ross. *The Galton Case*

Macdonald, Ross. *The Underground Man*

Marsh, Ngaio. *A Man Lay Dead*

Rice, Craig. *Home Sweet Homicide*

Rinehart, Mary Roberts. *Miss Pinkerton*

Sayers, Dorothy L. ★*Gaudy Night*

Sayers, Dorothy L. *Have His Carcase*

Sayers, Dorothy L. *Murder Must Advertise*

Sayers, Dorothy L. *The Nine Tailors*

Sayers, Dorothy L. ★*Whose Body?: A Lord Peter Wimsey Novel*

Stout, Rex. *The Doorbell Rang*

Stout, Rex. ★*Gambit*

*The **Mystery** of Three Quarters: The New Hercule Poirot Mystery*. Hannah, Sophie

MYSTERY STORY WRITERS

Burns, V. M. *Killer Words*

Cook, Thomas H. *Instruments of Night*

Griffiths, Elly. *The Postscript Murders*

Horowitz, Anthony. ★*The Sentence Is Death*

Horowitz, Anthony. ★*The Word Is Murder*

Quick, Amanda. *'til Death Do Us Part*

MYSTERY STORY WRITING

Estleman, Loren D. *A Smile on the Face of the Tiger*

★***Mystic** River*. Lehane, Dennis

MYSTICISM

Sharratt, Mary. *Revelations*

MYSTICS

Mitchell, David. *The Bone Clocks: A Novel*

Murakami, Haruki. *The Wind-Up Bird Chronicle*

MYTHICAL CREATURES

Beagle, Peter S. *The Unicorn Sonata*

Gaiman, Neil. ★*Norse Mythology*

Martineau, Maxym M. *Kingdom of Exiles*

Porter, Max. ★*Lanny: A Novel*

Wecker, Helene. ★*The Hidden Palace*

MYTHOLOGICAL FICTION

Arden, Katherine. ★*The Bear and the Nightingale*

Arden, Katherine. ★*The Girl in the Tower*

Arden, Katherine. ★*The Winter of the Witch*

Barker, Pat. ★*The Silence of the Girls: A Novel*

Barker, Pat. *The Women of Troy*

Barth, John. *Chimera*

Bear, Elizabeth. *All the Windwracked Stars*

Bear, Elizabeth. *Blood and Iron: A Novel of the Promethean Age*

Bear, Elizabeth. *Ink and Steel: A Novel of the Promethean Age*

Byatt, A. S. ★*Ragnarok: The End of the Gods*

Gaiman, Neil. ★*American Gods: A Novel*

Gaiman, Neil. ★*Anansi Boys: A Novel*

Gaiman, Neil. ★*Norse Mythology*

Gornichec, Genevieve. ★*The Witch's Heart*

Lewis, C. S. *Till We Have Faces: A Myth Retold*

Marillier, Juliet. *Daughter of the Forest*

Miller, Madeline. ★*Circe*

Momaday, N. Scott. *The Ancient Child: A Novel*

Moreno-Garcia, Silvia. ★*Gods of Jade and Shadow: A Novel*

Oyeyemi, Helen. *The Opposite House*

Power, Susan. *The Grass Dancer*

Saint, Jennifer. *Ariadne*

Sherrill, Steven. *The Minotaur Takes His Own Sweet Time: A Novel*

Tesh, Emily. *Silver in the Wood*

Toibin, Colm. *House of Names*

Walton, Jo. ★*Necessity*

MYTHOLOGY, CELTIC

Golding, Melanie. *The Hidden: A Novel*

MYTHOLOGY, CLASSICAL

MacLaughlin, Nina. *Wake, Siren: Ovid Resung*

MYTHOLOGY, FOLKLORE, AND LEGENDS

Bowles, David. *Feathered Serpent, Dark Heart of Sky: Myths of Mexico*

Gaiman, Neil. ★*Norse Mythology*

MYTHOLOGY, GREEK

Haynes, Natalie. *A Thousand Ships*

MYTHOLOGY, JUDAIC

Reid, Ava. *The Wolf and the Woodsman*

MYTHOLOGY, NORSE

Byatt, A. S. ★*Ragnarok: The End of the Gods*

Gaiman, Neil. ★*Norse Mythology*

Gornichec, Genevieve. ★*The Witch's Heart*

Myths series [Series]. Byatt, A. S.

N

Nabokov, Vladimir Vladimirovich

King, Queen, Knave: A Novel

★*Lolita*

Look at the Harlequins!

Novels and Memoirs, 1941-51

Pale Fire

Pnin

The Stories of Vladimir Nabokov

NABOKOV, VLADIMIR VLADIMIROVICH

Endo, Shusaku. *Silence*

Nabokov, Vladimir Vladimirovich. *Novels and Memoirs, 1941-51*

Nagamatsu, Sequoia

How High We Go in the Dark

Naipaul, V. S.

A Bend in the River

Guerrillas

A House for Mr. Biswas

Magic Seeds

NAIROBI, KENYA

Acker, Jennifer. ★*The Limits of the World*

Crompton, Richard. *Hell's Gate: A Novel*

Crompton, Richard. *Hour of the Red God*

NAISMITH, CORDELIA (FICTITIOUS CHARACTER)

Bujold, Lois McMaster. ★*Shards of Honor*

★*The **Naked** and the Dead*. Mailer, Norman

***Naked** in Death*. Robb, J. D.

★***Naked** Lunch: The Restored Text*. Burroughs, William S.

★*Naked* Prey. Sandford, John
A *Naked Singularity*. Pava, Sergio de la
The *Name* of All Things. Lyons, Jenn
★The *Name* of the Rose. Eco, Umberto
★The *Name* of the Wind. Rothfuss, Patrick
NAME-BRAND PRODUCTS — MARKETING
  Whitehead, Colson. *Apex Hides the Hurt*
NAMELESS DETECTIVE (FICTITIOUS CHARACTER)
  Pronzini, Bill. *Crazybone*
  Pronzini, Bill. *Hardcase*
  Pronzini, Bill. *Hellbox*
  Pronzini, Bill. *Illusions*
  Pronzini, Bill. *Mourners*
  Pronzini, Bill. *Nemesis*
  Pronzini, Bill. *Nightcrawlers*
  Pronzini, Bill. *Savages*
Nameless Detective mysteries [Series]. Pronzini, Bill
The *Nameless Ones*. Connolly, John
The *Names*. DeLillo, Don
★The *Namesake*. Lahiri, Jhumpa
NAMIBIA
  Crouch, Katie. *Embassy Wife*
The *Naming* of the Dead: An Inspector Rebus Novel. Rankin, Ian
★*Nana*. Zola, Emile
NANNIES
  Alam, Rumaan. *That Kind of Mother: A Novel*
  Blau, Jessica Anya. *Mary Jane: A Novel*
  Cargill, C. Robert. *Day Zero*
  Dimberg, Kelsey Rae. *Girl in the Rearview Mirror*
  Foster, Brooke Lea. *Summer Darlings*
  Lewis, Beverly. *The Ebb Tide*
  Macmillan, Gilly. *The Nanny*
  McLaughlin, Emma. *The Nanny Diaries: A Novel*
  Moore, Lorrie. *A Gate at the Stairs: A Novel*
  Stoker, Dacre. *Dracul*
  Ware, Ruth. ★*The Turn of the Key*
  Weatherspoon, Rebekah. *Rafe: A Buff Male Nanny*
The *Nanny*. Macmillan, Gilly
The *Nanny* Diaries: A Novel. McLaughlin, Emma
NANOTECHNOLOGY
  Crichton, Michael. *Prey: A Novel*
  Hossain, Saad Z. *Cyber Mage: A Novel*
  Stephenson, Neal. *The Diamond Age,: Or, a Young Lady's Illustrated Primer*
NANTUCKET, MASSACHUSETTS
  Hilderbrand, Elin. ★*28 Summers*
  Hilderbrand, Elin. *The Perfect Couple*
  Hilderbrand, Elin. ★*Summer of '69*
  Poe, Edgar Allan. *The Narrative of Arthur Gordon Pym of Nantucket*
NAPA VALLEY, CALIFORNIA
  Koontz, Dean R. *Intensity: A Novel*
NAPLES, ITALY
  De Giovanni, Maurizio. *The Bastards of Pizzofalcone*
  De Giovanni, Maurizio. *The Crocodile*
  Ferrante, Elena. *The Lying Life of Adults*
  Ferrante, Elena. *My Brilliant Friend*
  Ferrante, Elena. *The Story of a New Name*
  Ferrante, Elena. *The Story of the Lost Child*

  Ferrante, Elena. *Those Who Leave and Those Who Stay*
  Sontag, Susan. *The Volcano Lover: A Romance*
  Starnone, Domenico. *Ties*
  Starnone, Domenico. *Trick*
NAPOLEONIC WARS VETERANS
  Balogh, Mary. *The Arrangement*
  Balogh, Mary. *The Escape*
  Balogh, Mary. ★*Someone to Cherish*
  Bowman, Valerie. *The Accidental Countess*
  Burrowes, Grace. *The Trouble with Dukes*
  Galen, Shana. *Third Son's a Charm*
NAPOLEONIC WARS, 1800-1815
  Auci, Stefania. *The Florios of Sicily: A Novel*
  Forester, C. S. *Commodore Hornblower*
  Galen, Shana. *Third Son's a Charm*
  Gelernter, J. H. *Hold Fast*
  Novik, Naomi. *His Majesty's Dragon*
  Putney, Mary Jo. *Once a Soldier*
  Tolstoy, Leo. ★*War and Peace*
  Tolstoy, Leo. *War and Peace*
NAPOLEONIC WARS, 1800-1815 — NAVAL OPERATIONS
  O'Brian, Patrick. *Master and Commander*
NAPOLEONIC WARS, 1800-1815 — NAVAL OPERATIONS, BRITISH
  Forester, C. S. *Beat to Quarters*
  Forester, C. S. *Flying Colours*
  Forester, C. S. *Hornblower and the Atropos*
  Forester, C. S. *Hornblower and the Hotspur*
  Forester, C. S. *Lieutenant Hornblower*
  Forester, C. S. *Lord Hornblower*
  Forester, C. S. *Mr. Midshipman Hornblower*
  Forester, C. S. *Ship of the Line*
Napolitano, Ann
  Dear Edward
Narayan, R. K.
  Malgudi Days
NARCISSISM
  Seton, Anya. ★*Dragonwyck*
Narcissus and Goldmund. Hesse, Hermann
NARCOTICS INVESTIGATION
  Kent, Kathleen. *The Burn*
The *Narrative* of Arthur Gordon Pym of Nantucket. Poe, Edgar Allan
★The *Narrow* Road to the Deep North. Flanagan, Richard
NARVAEZ, PANFILO DE
  Dahl, Arne. *Misterioso: A Crime Novel*
  Lalami, Laila. ★*The Moor's Account: A Novel*
NASH, RICHARD
  Lovesey, Peter. *Beau Death*
  Whelan, Julia. *My Oxford Year*
NASHVILLE, TENNESSEE
  Adams, Lyssa Kay. *The Bromance Book Club*
  Alexander, Tamera. ★*A Note yet Unsung*
  Arvin, Reed. *Blood of Angels: A Novel*
  Creech, Sarah. *The Whole Way Home*
  Verble, Margaret. ★*When Two Feathers Fell from the Sky*
NASSAU, BAHAMAS
  Williams, Beatriz. *The Golden Hour*
Natalie Tan's Book of Luck and Fortune. Lim, Roselle

Natchez Burning: A Novel. Iles, Greg

NATCHEZ, MISSISSIPPI
Iles, Greg. *The Bone Tree: A Novel*
Iles, Greg. *Mississippi Blood: A Novel*
Iles, Greg. *Natchez Burning: A Novel*

NATIONAL CHARACTERISTICS
Makumbi, Jennifer Nansubuga. *Kintu*

NATIONAL CHARACTERISTICS, AMERICAN
Gaiman, Neil. ★*American Gods: A Novel*

NATIONAL CHARACTERISTICS, ENGLISH
Barnes, Julian. ★*England, England*

NATIONAL LIBERATION MOVEMENTS
Furst, Alan. ★*A Hero of France*
Slimani, Leïla. *In the Country of Others*

NATIONAL PARKS AND RESERVES
Barr, Nevada. *Track of the Cat*
Kells, Claire. *Vanishing Edge*

NATIONAL SECURITY
Baldacci, David. *Hell's Corner*
Brown, Dale. *Eagle Station: A Novel*
Brown, Dale. *The Moscow Offensive: A Novel*
Cameron, Marc. ★*Code of Honor*
Clements, Oliver. *The Queen's Men*
Coonts, Stephen. ★*The Russia Account*
Eisler, Barry. *The God's Eye View*
Finder, Joseph. *The Switch: A Novel*
Porter, Henry. *Firefly*
Rollins, James. *The Eye of God*
Rollins, James. *The Sixth Extinction: A Sigma Force Novel*
Tata, A. J. *Dark Winter*

NATIONALISM
Davies, Carys. *The Mission House*
Desai, Kiran. *The Inheritance of Loss*
Vargas Llosa, Mario. *The Dream of the Celt*

NATIONALISM AND SOCIAL CLASSES
Vargas Llosa, Mario. *The Dream of the Celt*

NATIONALISTS
Pawel, Rebecca. *Death of a Nationalist*

NATIVE AMERICAN ACTIVISTS
Burke, James Lee. *Black Cherry Blues*

NATIVE AMERICAN CHILDREN
Krueger, William Kent. *This Tender Land: A Novel*

NATIVE AMERICAN FAMILIES
Hobson, Brandon. ★*The Removed: A Novel*
Orange, Tommy. ★*There There*

NATIVE AMERICAN GIRLS
Francis, Patry. *All the Children Are Home*
Silko, Leslie Marmon. *Gardens in the Dunes: A Novel*

NATIVE AMERICAN LAWYERS
Woods, Stuart. *Santa Fe Rules*

NATIVE AMERICAN MEN
Alexie, Sherman. *Blasphemy: New and Selected Stories*
Brown, Dee. *Creek Mary's Blood: A Novel*
Erdrich, Louise. ★*The Night Watchman: A Novel*
Hillerman, Tony. *The Shape Shifter*
Hillerman, Tony. *The Sinister Pig*
Jones, Stephen Graham. ★*The Only Good Indians: A Novel*
L'Amour, Louis. *The Last of the Breed*

Momaday, N. Scott. *House Made of Dawn*
Silko, Leslie Marmon. ★*Ceremony*

NATIVE AMERICAN MYSTICISM
Momaday, N. Scott. *The Ancient Child: A Novel*

NATIVE AMERICAN MYSTICS
L'Amour, Louis. *The Californios*

NATIVE AMERICAN PAINTERS
Momaday, N. Scott. *The Ancient Child: A Novel*

NATIVE AMERICAN RESISTANCE AND REVOLTS
Silko, Leslie Marmon. *Almanac of the Dead*

NATIVE AMERICAN ROCK MUSICIANS
Alexie, Sherman. *Reservation Blues*

NATIVE AMERICAN SOLDIERS
Smith, Martin Cruz. *Stallion Gate*

NATIVE AMERICAN TEENAGE GIRLS
Jones, Stephen Graham. *My Heart Is a Chainsaw*

NATIVE AMERICAN VETERANS
Momaday, N. Scott. *House Made of Dawn*

NATIVE AMERICAN WOMEN
Brown, Dee. *Creek Mary's Blood: A Novel*
Erdrich, Louise. *The Beet Queen: A Novel*
Erdrich, Louise. *Four Souls: A Novel*
Ford, Kelli Jo. ★*Crooked Hallelujah*
Perry, Thomas. ★*The Left-Handed Twin*
Roanhorse, Rebecca. *Storm of Locusts*
Roanhorse, Rebecca. ★*Trail of Lightning*
Rodriguez, Linda. *Every Last Secret: A Mystery*
Schwarz, Christina. *The Edge of the Earth*
Verble, Margaret. ★*Cherokee America*

★*Native Son*. Wright, Richard

Natsukawa, Sosuke
The Cat Who Saved Books

The Natural. Malamud, Bernard

★*Natural Born Charmer*. Phillips, Susan Elizabeth

NATURAL DISASTERS
Anderson, Kevin J. *The Last Days of Krypton*
Chancy, Myriam J. A. ★*What Storm, What Thunder*

NATURAL GAS
Powell, Mark. *Firebird*

NATURAL HISTORY
Brennan, Marie. *Within the Sanctuary of Wings: A Memoir by Lady Trent*
Sjón. *The Blue Fox*

NATURAL HISTORY MUSEUMS
Healey, Jane. *The Animals at Lockwood Manor*

NATURALISTS
Raybourn, Deanna. ★*A Murderous Relation*

NATURE
Adams, Richard. *Watership Down*
Alomar, Osama. *The Teeth of the Comb & Other Stories*
Faulkner, William. ★*Go Down, Moses*
Powers, Richard. ★*The Overstory: A Novel*
Swarup, Shubhangi. *Latitudes of Longing*
Van Meter, Crissy. *Creatures: A Novel*
Woolf, Virginia. ★*To the Lighthouse*

NATURE — EFFECT OF HUMANS ON
Lebbon, Tim. *Eden*

Nature Girl. Hiaasen, Carl

★*Nausea*. Sartre, Jean Paul
Nava, Michael
    ★*Carved in Bone*
NAVAJO INDIAN RESERVATION
    Roanhorse, Rebecca. *Storm of Locusts*
    Roanhorse, Rebecca. ★*Trail of Lightning*
NAVAJO INDIANS
    Hillerman, Tony. *The Shape Shifter*
    Roanhorse, Rebecca. *Storm of Locusts*
    Roanhorse, Rebecca. ★*Trail of Lightning*
NAVAJO SHAMANS
    Hillerman, Tony. *The Wailing Wind*
NAVAL BATTLES
    Beach, Edward L. *Run Silent, Run Deep*
    Forester, C. S. *Beat to Quarters*
    Forester, C. S. *Commodore Hornblower*
    Forester, C. S. *Flying Colours*
    Forester, C. S. *Hornblower and the Atropos*
    Forester, C. S. *Hornblower and the Hotspur*
    Forester, C. S. *Lieutenant Hornblower*
    Forester, C. S. *Lord Hornblower*
    Forester, C. S. *Mr. Midshipman Hornblower*
    Forester, C. S. *Ship of the Line*
    Monsarrat, Nicholas. *The Cruel Sea*
    Poyer, David. *Overthrow: The War with China and North Korea—Fall of an Empire*
NAVAL POWER
    Coonts, Stephen. *The Art of War: A Novel*
NAVAL TACTICS
    O'Brian, Patrick. *Master and Commander*
NAVY SEALS
    Webb, Brandon. ★*Steel Fear*
Naylor, Gloria
    Mama Day
The Nazarene. Asch, Sholem
NAZI COLLABORATORS
    Faulks, Sebastian. *Charlotte Gray: A Novel*
    Pears, Iain. *The Dream of Scipio*
NAZI FUGITIVES
    Cussler, Clive. *The Mediterranean Caper*
    Kerr, Philip. ★*Prussian Blue*
NAZI HUNTERS
    Grecian, Alex. *The Saint of Wolves and Butchers*
    Quinn, Kate. ★*The Huntress*
★*Nazi Literature in the Americas*. Bolano, Roberto
NAZI PHYSICIANS
    Amis, Martin. ★*Time's Arrow, or the Nature of the Offense*
NAZI PLUNDER
    Friedman, Daniel. ★*Don't Ever Get Old*
    Kerr, Philip. ★*Greeks Bearing Gifts: A Bernie Gunther Novel*
NAZIS
    Albahari, David. *Gotz and Meyer*
    Binet, Laurent. ★*HHhH*
    Bolano, Roberto. ★*Nazi Literature in the Americas*
    Clayton, Meg Waite. *The Last Train to London*
    Deaver, Jeffery. *Garden of Beasts: A Novel of Berlin 1936*
    Eliasberg, Jan. ★*Hannah's War*
    Escobar, Mario. *The Librarian of Saint-Malo: A Novel*

    Feldman, Ellen. *Paris Never Leaves You*
    Follett, Ken. *Hornet Flight*
    Furst, Alan. *The Foreign Correspondent: A Novel*
    Furst, Alan. ★*A Hero of France*
    Furst, Alan. *Spies of the Balkans: A Novel*
    Gilbers, Harald. *Germania: A Novel of Nazi Berlin*
    Gillham, David R. *City of Women*
    Grecian, Alex. *The Saint of Wolves and Butchers*
    Hall, Adam. *The Quiller Memorandum*
    Harris, Robert. ★*Fatherland*
    Kaminsky, Stuart M. *To Catch a Spy: A Toby Peters Mystery*
    Kelly, Martha Hall. *Lilac Girls*
    Levin, Ira. *The Boys from Brazil: A Novel*
    McFadden, Bernice L. *The Book of Harlan*
    Morelli, Laura. *The Stolen Lady*
    Rimmer, Kelly. ★*The Warsaw Orphan: A Wwii Novel*
    Russell, Mary Doria. *A Thread of Grace: A Novel*
    Sem-Sandberg, Steve. *The Chosen Ones: A Novel*
    Sundin, Sarah. *When Twilight Breaks*
    Van Booy, Simon. *The Illusion of Separateness*
NAZISM
    Benedict, Marie. *The Only Woman in the Room*
    Bolano, Roberto. ★*Nazi Literature in the Americas*
    Clark, Clare. *In the Full Light of the Sun*
    Fallada, Hans. *Every Man Dies Alone*
    Follett, Ken. *Winter of the World*
    Grecian, Alex. *The Saint of Wolves and Butchers*
    Harris, Robert. ★*Fatherland*
    Hegi, Ursula. *Children and Fire: A Novel*
    Shaara, Jeff. *The Steel Wave: A Novel of World War II*
Neah Bay novels [Series]. Laukkanen, Owen
Neapolitan novels [Series]. Ferrante, Elena
NEAR FUTURE
    Anders, Charlie Jane. *Rock Manning Goes for Broke*
    Atwood, Margaret. ★*The Testaments: A Novel*
    Bacigalupi, Paolo. ★*The Water Knife*
    Beckett, L. X. *Gamechanger*
    Beukes, Lauren. *Afterland*
    Beukes, Lauren. *Slipping: Stories, Essays, & Other Writing*
    Broun, Bill. *Night of the Animals*
    Cantrell, Christian. *Scorpion*
    Cargill, C. Robert. *Day Zero*
    Chen, Qiufan. *Waste Tide*
    Cline, Ernest. *Ready Player One: A Novel*
    Divya, S. B. *Machinehood*
    Doctorow, Cory. *Rapture of the Nerds*
    Eggers, Dave. *The Circle*
    El Akkad, Omar. *American War*
    Gibson, William. ★*Neuromancer*
    Grant, Mira. *Blackout*
    Grant, Mira. *Deadline*
    Grant, Mira. *Feed*
    Grant, Mira. *Feedback*
    Grant, Mira. *Parasite*
    Gregory, Daryl. *Afterparty*
    Hart, Rob. *The Warehouse: A Novel*
    Holroyde, Claire. *The Effort*
    Hossain, Saad Z. *Cyber Mage: A Novel*

Houellebecq, Michel. *Submission*
Jen, Gish. ★*The Resisters*
Kennedy, James. *Dare to Know*
King, Stephen. *Sleeping Beauties: A Novel*
Kroese, Robert. *The Last Iota*
Le Guin, Ursula K. *The Lathe of Heaven*
McKinney, Chris. *Midnight, Water City*
Minh, Drew. *Neon Empire*
Nagamatsu, Sequoia. *How High We Go in the Dark*
O'Dell, Claire. *A Study in Honor: A Novel*
Okorafor, Nnedi. ★*Noor*
Orwell, George. ★*1984: A Novel*
Palmer, Dexter Clarence. *Version Control*
Pressfield, Steven. *36 Righteous Men: A Novel*
Robb, J. D. *Connections in Death: An Eve Dallas Novel*
Robinson, Kim Stanley. ★*The Ministry for the Future*
Robinson, Kim Stanley. *New York 2140*
Russell, Mary Doria. ★*The Sparrow*
Scalzi, John. *Head On*
Scalzi, John. ★*Lock In*
Self, Will. *The Book of Dave: A Revelation of the Recent Past and the Distant Future*
Shepherd, Peng. *The Book of M: A Novel*
Stross, Charles. *Empire Games*
VanderMeer, Jeff. *Dead Astronauts: A Novel*
Vaughn, Carrie. *Bannerless*
Vonnegut, Kurt. *Slapstick: Or, Lonesome No More! a Novel*
Vonnegut, Kurt. *Welcome to the Monkey House*
Watkins, Claire Vaye. ★*Gold Fame Citrus*
Weir, Andy. *Artemis*
Williams, Joy. *Harrow*
Williams, Katie. *Tell the Machine Goodnight*
Willis, Connie. *Crosstalk*
Wong, David. *Futuristic Violence and Fancy Suits*
Yoon, David. *Version Zero*

NEAR-DEATH EXPERIENCE
Higgins, Kristan. *Now That You Mention It*
Pyper, Andrew. *The Damned: A Novel*
The Nearest Exit. Steinhauer, Olen

NEBRASKA
Agee, Jonis. *The Bones of Paradise*
Cather, Willa. *A Lost Lady*
Cather, Willa. ★*My Antonia*
Cather, Willa. *O Pioneers!*
Child, Lee. *Worth Dying For*
Harding Thornton, Christina. *Pickard County Atlas*
Powers, Richard. *The Echo Maker*
Rowell, Rainbow. *Landline*
Stark, Richard. *The Jugger: A Parker Novel*
Necessary People. Pitoniak, Anna
★*Necessity*. Walton, Jo
Necropolis. Gamboa, Santiago
The Need: a Novel. Phillips, Helen

NEEDLEWORK
Chevalier, Tracy. *A Single Thread*

NEFERTITI
Greenwood, Kerry. *Out of the Black Land*
Martin, George R. R. ★*A Feast for Crows*

NEGOTIATION
Cameron, Marc. *Power and Empire*
Singh, Nalini. ★*Silver Silence*
The Neighbor. Gardner, Lisa
The Neighbor's Secret. Heller, L. Alison

NEIGHBORHOOD WATCH PROGRAMS
Chizmar, Richard T. *Chasing the Boogeyman*

NEIGHBORHOODS
Boyle, William. *City of Margins: A Novel*
Dybek, Stuart. *I Sailed with Magellan*
Gala, Marcial. ★*The Black Cathedral*
Jewell, Lisa. *Watching You*
Langan, Sarah. *Good Neighbors*
Pochoda, Ivy. *Visitation Street: A Novel*
Washington, Bryan. *Lot: Stories*

NEIGHBORS
Ajvide Lindqvist, John. *Let the Right One In*
Backman, Fredrik. *A Man Called Ove*
Barker, Nicola. *Darkmans*
Baxter, Charles. *The Feast of Love*
Binchy, Maeve. *Firefly Summer*
Blume, Judy. *In the Unlikely Event*
Cheever, John. *Bullet Park: A Novel*
Chizmar, Richard T. *A Long December*
Finn, A. J. ★*The Woman in the Window*
Franzen, Jonathan. ★*Freedom*
Fuller, Claire. ★*Bitter Orange*
Gala, Marcial. ★*The Black Cathedral*
Haddon, Mark. ★*The Curious Incident of the Dog in the Night-Time: A Novel*
Henry, Emily. *Beach Read*
Heron, Farah. *Accidentally Engaged*
Hibbert, Talia. *A Girl Like Her*
Hyde, Catherine Ryan. *My Name Is Anton*
Kubica, Mary. ★*The Other Mrs.*
Lipman, Elinor. *Good Riddance*
London, Stefanie. *The Aussie Next Door*
Maaren, Kari. ★*Weave a Circle Round*
Masood, Syed M. *The Bad Muslim Discount*
Matthiessen, Peter. *Shadow Country: A New Rendering of the Watson Legend*
O'Donnell, Lisa. *The Death of Bees: A Novel*
Petterson, Per. *Out Stealing Horses: A Novel*
Pineiro, Caridad. *One Summer Night*
Rice, Craig. *Home Sweet Homicide*
Shalvis, Jill. *Sweet Little Lies*
Shaw, William. *The Birdwatcher*
Torre, A. R. *Every Last Secret*
Von Ziegesar, Cecily. *Cobble Hill*
Ward, Catriona. *The Last House on Needless Street*
Wiseman, Ellen Marie. *The Orphan Collector*
★*Neighbors: a Novel*. Berger, Thomas

Nelson, Christina Suzann
If We Make It Home: A Novel of Faith and Survival in the Oregon Wilderness

NELSON, HORATIO NELSON
Sontag, Susan. *The Volcano Lover: A Romance*
Nemesis. Pronzini, Bill

★*Nemesis*. Roth, Philip
Nemesis Games. Corey, James S. A.
NEO-FASCISM
  Ballard, J. G. *Kingdom Come*
NEO-NAZISM
  Black, Cara. *Murder in the Marais*
  Child, Lee. ★*Die Trying*
  Mankell, Henning. ★*The Return of the Dancing Master*
Neog [Series]. Wagers, K. B.
Neon Empire. Minh, Drew
NEPHEWS
  Giordano, Mario. *Auntie Poldi and the Vineyards of Etna*
  Ozick, Cynthia. *Foreign Bodies*
Neptune's Brood. Stross, Charles
NERO
  George, Margaret. *The Confessions of Young Nero*
  George, Margaret. *The Splendor Before the Dark: A Novel of the Emperor Nero*
  Sienkiewicz, Henryk. ★*Quo Vadis: A Story of Faith in the Last Days of the Roman Empire*
Nero novels [Series]. George, Margaret
Nero Wolfe mysteries [Series]. Stout, Rex
NERO, EMPEROR OF ROME, 37-68
  Chakraborty, S. A. *The City of Brass*
  Coulter, Catherine. *The Last Second*
  Somer, Mehmet Murat. *The Serenity Murders*
NERUDA, PABLO
  Allende, Isabel. *A Long Petal of the Sea: A Novel*
  Fowler, Therese. ★*A Good Neighborhood*
NERVOUS BREAKDOWN
  Beyda, Emily. *The Body Double*
  Founds, Kathleen. *When Mystical Creatures Attack!*
  Kirshenbaum, Binnie. *Rabbits for Food*
  Mangan, Christine. *Palace of the Drowned*
  Plath, Sylvia. ★*The Bell Jar*
NERVOUS SYSTEM — DEGENERATION
  Genova, Lisa. *Every Note Played*
Nesbo, Jo
  The Leopard
  Phantom
  The Redeemer
The Nesting Dolls. Adams, Alina
NESTING DOLLS
  Adams, Alina. *The Nesting Dolls*
NETHERLANDS
  Austin, Lynn N. *Chasing Shadows*
  Burton, Jessie. *The Miniaturist*
  Buwalda, Peter. *Bonita Avenue: A Novel*
  Chevalier, Tracy. ★*Girl with a Pearl Earring*
  Groen, Hendrik. *On the Bright Side: The New Secret Diary of Hendrik Groen, 85 Years Old*
  Kitamura, Katie M. *Intimacies*
  Kwok, Jean. *Searching for Sylvie Lee*
  Simenon, Georges. *Maigret in Holland*
  Smith, Dominic. ★*The Last Painting of Sara De Vos*
  Stone, Irving. *Lust for Life: A Novel of Vincent Van Gogh*
  Vreeland, Susan. *Girl in Hyacinth Blue*
Network Effect. Wells, Martha

NETWORKS
  Lu, S. Qiouyi. *In the Watchful City*
Neubauer, Erica Ruth
  Murder at the Mena House
NEUROLOGISTS
  Powers, Richard. *The Echo Maker*
★*Neuromancer*. Gibson, William
NEUROSCIENTISTS
  Afifi, Nadia. *The Sentient*
  Crouch, Blake. *Recursion*
NEUROSES IN MEN
  Moore, Alison. *The Lighthouse*
NEVADA
  Bock, Charles. *Beautiful Children: A Novel*
  Crichton, Michael. *Prey: A Novel*
  Diofebi, Dario. *Paradise, Nevada*
  Jenkins, Beverly. *Forbidden*
  MacDonald, John D. *A Purple Place for Dying*
  Watkins, Claire Vaye. *I Love You but I've Chosen Darkness*
  Young, Heather. *The Distant Dead*
Never a Bride. Frampton, Megan
★*The Never Game*. Deaver, Jeffery
Never Go Back. Goddard, Robert
Never Go Back. Child, Lee
Never Have I Ever. Jackson, Joshilyn
★*Never Let Me Go*. Ishiguro, Kazuo
Never Let You Go. Stevens, Chevy
Never Look Back. Gaylin, Alison
Never Saw Me Coming. Kurian, Vera
Never Seduce a Scot. Banks, Maya
★*Never Tell: A Novel*. Gardner, Lisa
NEW ADULT FICTION
  Henson, Pene. *Into the Blue*
  Hoover, Colleen. *All Your Perfects*
  Hoover, Colleen. *It Ends with Us*
NEW AGE
  Portis, Charles. ★*Gringos: A Novel*
  Redfield, James. *The Celestine Prophecy: An Adventure*
The New American. Marcom, Micheline Aharonian
The New Annotated Dracula. Stoker, Bram
NEW BUSINESSES
  Anam, Tahmima. *The Startup Wife*
  Askaripour, Mateo. ★*Black Buck*
  Nguyen, Kevin. ★*New Waves*
The New Centurions. Wambaugh, Joseph
New Crobuzon series [Series]. Mieville, China
New Directions paperbook [Series]. Erpenbeck, Jenny
NEW ENGLAND
  Amidon, Stephen. *Security: A Novel*
  Awad, Mona. *Bunny*
  Bair, Kristin. *Agatha Arch Is Afraid of Everything*
  Beams, Clare. *The Illness Lesson*
  Block, Lawrence. ★*The Burglar in the Library*
  Brom. *Slewfoot: A Tale of Bewitchery*
  Carter, Stephen L. *New England White: A Novel*
  Clarke, Brock. *An Arsonist's Guide to Writers' Homes in New England: A Novel*
  Dee, Jonathan. *The Locals: A Novel*

Donohue, Keith. *The Stolen Child*
Erdrich, Louise. *The Painted Drum: A Novel*
Harding, Paul. *Tinkers*
Hawthorne, Nathaniel. ★*The House of the Seven Gables*
Hepworth, Sally. *The Secrets of Midwives*
Hoffman, Alice. *The Rules of Magic: A Novel*
Lutz, Lisa. *The Swallows: A Novel*
Maynard, Joyce. *Count the Ways*
Miller, Derek B. *How to Find Your Way in the Dark*
Miller, Sue. *The Senator's Wife*
Olson, Neil. *Before the Devil Fell*
Pearlman, Edith. *Binocular Vision: New & Selected Stories*
Prose, Francine. *Blue Angel: A Novel*
Prose, Francine. *Goldengrove: A Novel*
Rosen, Leonard J. *The Kortelisy Escape*
Roth, Philip. ★*The Human Stain*
Ruff, Matt. *Lovecraft Country: A Novel*
Sharp, Zoe. *Second Shot: A Charlie Fox Thriller*
Shreve, Anita. *Fortune's Rocks: A Novel*
Shreve, Anita. *Testimony: A Novel*
Smith, Zadie. *On Beauty*
Solomon, Anna. *Leaving Lucy Pear*
Strout, Elizabeth. *Amy and Isabelle: A Novel*
Tinti, Hannah. *The Twelve Lives of Samuel Hawley: A Novel*
Urquhart, Rachel. *The Visionist*
Wallace, Melanie. *The Girl in the Garden*
Wharton, Edith. ★*Ethan Frome*
Williams, Beatriz. *The Summer Wives*
Wolff, Tobias. *Old School: A Novel*
New England White: A Novel. Carter, Stephen L.

NEW FRANCE (1534-1763)
Green, Jocelyn. *The Mark of the King*
Proulx, Annie. ★*Barkskins: A Novel*
The New Girl. Silva, Daniel

NEW HAMPSHIRE
Banks, Russell. ★*Affliction*
Beattie, Ann. *A Wonderful Stroke of Luck: A Novel*
Bohjalian, Chris. *The Night Strangers: A Novel*
Brown, Rosellen. ★*Before and After*
Butler, Season. ★*Cygnet*
Costello, Mark. *Big If*
Crow, Sarah McCraw. *The Wrong Kind of Woman*
Delinsky, Barbara. *Lake News: A Novel*
Golden, Christopher. *Red Hands*
Hegi, Ursula. *The Vision of Emma Blau*
Hill, Joe. *The Fireman: A Novel*
Hill, Joe. *Horns*
Irving, John. ★*A Prayer for Owen Meany: A Novel*
King, Stephen. *Doctor Sleep: A Novel*
Knowles, John. ★*A Separate Peace*
Lipman, Elinor. *The Dearly Departed*
Lipman, Elinor. *Good Riddance*
Maynard, Joyce. *Count the Ways*
Merullo, Roland. *The Talk-Funny Girl: A Novel*
Palmer, Daniel. *The New Husband*
Perry, Thomas. *Death Benefits: A Novel*
Picoult, Jodi. *Nineteen Minutes: A Novel*
Picoult, Jodi. *Vanishing Acts: A Novel*

Shreve, Anita. *The Pilot's Wife: A Novel*
Shreve, Anita. *Sea Glass: A Novel*
Shreve, Anita. *The Weight of Water*
Tremblay, Paul. ★*The Cabin at the End of the World: A Novel*
Waite, Jen. *Survival Instincts*

NEW HAVEN, CONNECTICUT
Bardugo, Leigh. ★*Ninth House*
Knopf, Chris. *You're Dead*
New Hercule Poirot mysteries [Series]. Hannah, Sophie
The New Husband. Palmer, Daniel
★*The New Iberia Blues*. Burke, James Lee

NEW IBERIA, LOUISIANA
Burke, James Lee. *Black Cherry Blues*
Burke, James Lee. ★*The New Iberia Blues*
Burke, James Lee. ★*A Private Cathedral*

NEW IDENTITIES
Belle, Kimberly. *Dear Wife*
Card, Maisy. ★*These Ghosts Are Family: A Novel*
Clark, Julie. *Last Flight*
Dimon, HelenKay. *Her Other Secret*
Loren, Roni. *The One You Fight For*
Perry, Thomas. *Vanishing Act*
Steadman, Catherine. *Mr. Nobody: A Novel*

NEW JERSEY
Auster, Paul. *4 3 2 1: A Novel*
Blume, Judy. *In the Unlikely Event*
Cheek, Chip. *Cape May*
Coben, Harlan. *Don't Let Go*
Diaz, Junot. ★*The Brief Wondrous Life of Oscar Wao*
Evanovich, Janet. ★*Game On: Tempting Twenty-Eight*
Evanovich, Janet. *Look Alive Twenty-Five*
Evanovich, Janet. *Turbo Twenty-Three*
Fitzgerald, F. Scott. *Novels and Stories, 1920-1922*
Ford, Richard. ★*Independence Day*
Ford, Richard. *The Lay of the Land*
Ford, Richard. *Let Me Be Frank with You*
Kingsolver, Barbara. ★*Unsheltered*
Larsen, Reif. *I Am Radar: A Novel*
Leilani, Raven. ★*Luster*
Lodato, Victor. *Edgar and Lucy: A Novel*
Nicieza, Fabian. *Suburban Dicks*
Parks, Brad. *The Player: A Mystery*
Perrotta, Tom. *The Leftovers*
Pineiro, Caridad. *One Summer Night*
Pineiro, Caridad. *What Happens in Summer*
Price, Richard. *Clockers*
Rosenfelt, David. *Black and Blue: A Doug Brock Thriller*
Rosenfelt, David. *Blackout*
Rosenfelt, David. ★*Dog Eat Dog*
Roth, Philip. *Indignation*
Roth, Philip. ★*Nemesis*
Rozan, S. J. *Winter and Night*
Stewart, Amy. ★*Girl Waits with Gun*
Stewart, Amy. ★*Miss Kopp Investigates*
Stewart, Amy. ★*Miss Kopp Just Won't Quit*
Swinson, Kiki. *Wifey's Next Sticky Situation*
The New Me: A Novel. Butler, Halle

NEW MEXICO

Allio, Kirstin. *Buddhism for Western Children: A Novel*

Barry, Jessica. ★*Don't Turn Around*

Beagin, Jen. ★*Vacuum in the Dark: A Novel*

Bird, Sarah. ★*The Flamenco Academy: A Novel*

Cather, Willa. ★*Death Comes for the Archbishop*

Glass, Julia. *The Whole World Over*

Hillerman, Tony. *The Shape Shifter*

Hillerman, Tony. *The Sinister Pig*

Hillerman, Tony. *The Wailing Wind*

Jones, Darynda. *A Bad Day for Sunshine*

Jones, Darynda. *A Good Day for Chardonnay*

Leonard, Elmore. *Charlie Martz and Other Stories: The Unpublished Stories*

McCarthy, Cormac. *The Crossing*

McEwan, Ian. *Solar: A Novel*

Oates, Joyce Carol. *Breathe*

Potenza, Carol. *Hearts of the Missing*

Quade, Kirstin Valdez. ★*The Five Wounds: A Novel*

Quade, Kirstin Valdez. *Night at the Fiestas: Stories*

Smith, Martin Cruz. *Stallion Gate*

Valdes, Alisa. *Dirty Girls on Top*

Winslow, Don. *The Border*

New Moon. McDonald, Ian

NEW MOTHERS

Alam, Rumaan. *That Kind of Mother: A Novel*

Evans, Diana. *Ordinary People: A Novel*

Fine, Julia. *The Upstairs House*

Golding, Melanie. *Little Darlings*

Griffiths, Elly. *The House at Sea's End: A Ruth Galloway Mystery*

Molloy, Aimee. *The Perfect Mother: A Novel*

Ramqvist, Karolina. *The White City*

Rimmer, Kelly. *Truths I Never Told You*

Spencer, Sally. *Thicker Than Water: A Monika Paniatowski British Police Procedural*

Sullivan, J. Courtney. *Friends and Strangers*

Watkins, Claire Vaye. *I Love You but I've Chosen Darkness*

NEW NEIGHBORS

Berger, Thomas. ★*Neighbors: A Novel*

Ray, Eleanor. *The Missing Treasures of Amy Ashton*

New Orleans Beat. Smith, Julie

NEW ORLEANS, LOUISIANA

Algren, Nelson. *A Walk on the Wild Side*

Anderson, Kevin J. *Death Warmed Over*

Attenberg, Jami. ★*All This Could Be Yours*

Burke, James Lee. *Black Cherry Blues*

Camp, Bryan. *The City of Lost Fortunes*

Camp, Bryan. *Gather the Fortunes*

Clark, P. Djeli. *The Black God's Drums*

Edwards, Louis. *Ramadan Ramsey: A Novel*

Gran, Sara. *Claire Dewitt and the City of the Dead*

Grisham, John. *The Client*

Hambly, Barbara. *House of the Patriarch*

Jenkins, Beverly. *Rebel*

Johnson, Charles Richard. ★*Middle Passage*

Johnson, Keith Lee. ★*Little Black Girl Lost*

K'wan. *The Diamond Empire*

K'wan. ★*Diamonds and Pearl*

K'wan. *Lawless*

Percy, Walker. ★*The Moviegoer*

Priest, Cherie. *Ganymede*

Redondo, Dolores. *The North Face of the Heart*

Reed, Ishmael. ★*Mumbo Jumbo*

Rhodes, Jewell Parker. *Voodoo Dreams: A Novel of Marie Laveau*

Rhodes, Jewell Parker. *Yellow Moon: A Novel*

Rice, Anne. *Blackwood Farm*

Rice, Anne. *Blood Canticle*

Rice, Anne. *Prince Lestat: The Vampire Chronicles*

Sepetys, Ruta. ★*Out of the Easy*

Sexton, Margaret Wilkerson. *A Kind of Freedom*

Sexton, Margaret Wilkerson. *The Revisioners: A Novel*

Smith, Julie. *82 Desire: A Skip Langdon Novel*

Smith, Julie. *Crescent City Kill: A Skip Langdon Novel*

Smith, Julie. *House of Blues*

Smith, Julie. *Jazz Funeral*

Smith, Julie. *The Kindness of Strangers: A Skip Langdon Novel*

Smith, Julie. *Louisiana Hotshot*

Smith, Julie. ★*Mean Woman Blues*

Smith, Julie. *New Orleans Beat*

Toole, John Kennedy. ★*A Confederacy of Dunces*

Tyree, Omar. *Leslie: A Novel*

Warren, Robert Penn. *Band of Angels*

Woods, Rita. ★*Remembrance*

Zapata, Mike. *The Lost Book of Adana Moreau*

New People. Senna, Danzy

NEW RELIGIOUS MOVEMENTS

Atwood, Margaret. ★*Maddaddam: A Novel*

Oe, Kenzaburo. *Somersault: A Novel*

NEW ROCHELLE, NEW YORK

Doctorow, E. L. ★*Ragtime*

NEW SOUTH WALES

Grenville, Kate. *The Secret River*

Keneally, Thomas. *Shame and the Captives: A Novel*

NEW STUDENTS

Sittenfeld, Curtis. *Prep: A Novel*

★*New Waves*. Nguyen, Kevin

★*The New Wilderness: A Novel*. Cook, Diane

NEW YEAR'S EVE

Connelly, Michael. ★*The Dark Hours*

Montimore, Margarita. *Oona Out of Order*

NEW YORK (STATE)

Abu-Jaber, Diana. *Origin: A Novel*

Banks, Russell. ★*The Sweet Hereafter*

Barbash, Tom. *The Last Good Chance*

Barclay, Linwood. *Broken Promise*

Barclay, Linwood. *Parting Shot*

Barclay, Linwood. *A Tap on the Window*

Barclay, Linwood. *The Twenty-Three: A Promise Falls Novel*

Bayard, Louis. *The Pale Blue Eye: A Novel*

Beattie, Ann. *A Wonderful Stroke of Luck: A Novel*

Benedict, Helen. *Wolf Season*

Berenson, Alex. *The Faithful Spy: A Novel*

Bourland, Barbara. ★*Fake Like Me*

Boyle, T. Coraghessan. *World's End: A Novel*

Brenner, Jamie. *Drawing Home*

Brodesser-Akner, Taffy. *Fleishman Is in Trouble: A Novel*

Brundage, Elizabeth. ★*All Things Cease to Appear*
Bruno, Anna. *Ordinary Hazards: A Novel*
Cohen, Tish. *The Summer We Lost Her: A Novel*
Cook, Thomas H. *Instruments of Night*
Cooper, James Fenimore. *The Last of the Mohicans: A Narrative of 1757*
Delany, Vicki. *Deadly Summer Nights*
Dobyns, Stephen. *Saratoga Payback*
Dolan-Leach, Caite. *We Went to the Woods: A Novel*
Donati, Sara. *Where the Light Enters*
Fowler, Therese. *A Well-Behaved Woman: A Novel of the Vanderbilts*
Freudenberger, Nell. *The Newlyweds*
Friedland, Elyssa. *Last Summer at the Golden Hotel*
Gaitskill, Mary. *The Mare: A Novel*
Groff, Lauren. ★*Arcadia: A Novel*
Grossman, Lev. ★*The Magicians: A Novel*
Hambly, Barbara. *House of the Patriarch*
Hansen, Ron. *Mariette in Ecstasy*
Harrison, Jamie. *The Center of Everything: A Novel*
Herrera, Adriana. *American Love Story*
Higgins, Kristan. ★*The Best Man*
Kane, Darby. *Pretty Little Wife*
Larkin, Allie. *The People We Keep*
McDermott, Alice. *Child of My Heart*
McGhee, Alison. *The Opposite of Fate*
Miller, Derek B. ★*American by Day*
Murphy, Devin. *Tiny Americans*
Nabokov, Vladimir Vladimirovich. *Pnin*
O'Donohue, Clare. *The Lover's Knot: A Someday Quilts Mystery*
Oates, Joyce Carol. *Because It Is Bitter, and Because It Is My Heart*
Oates, Joyce Carol. *The Falls: A Novel*
Oates, Joyce Carol. *The Gravedigger's Daughter: A Novel*
Oates, Joyce Carol. *Night. Sleep. Death. The Stars*
Oates, Joyce Carol. ★*We Were the Mulvaneys*
Perry, Thomas. *Vanishing Act*
Pitoniak, Anna. *Necessary People*
Puzo, Mario. ★*The Godfather*
Ramos, Joanne. *The Farm: A Novel*
Russo, Richard. *Bridge of Sighs*
Russo, Richard. ★*Everybody's Fool*
Russo, Richard. *The Risk Pool*
Schwartz, Lynne Sharon. *Truthtelling: Stories, Fables, Glimpses*
Shreve, Anita. *Eden Close: A Novel*
Shriver, Lionel. *We Need to Talk About Kevin*
Smith, B. J. *Shoot the Dog: A Virgil Cain Mystery*
Spencer, Scott. *Man in the Woods*
Spencer, Scott. *An Ocean Without a Shore*
Spencer-Fleming, Julia. *Hid from Our Eyes*
Spiegelman, Peter. *Black Maps*
Spiotta, Dana. *Wayward*
St. James, Simone. *The Sun Down Motel*
Stage, Zoje. *Wonderland*
Straub, Emma. ★*All Adults Here*
Straub, Peter. ★*Ghost Story*
Verdon, John. *On Harrow Hill*
Walker, Caroline Louise. *Man of the Year*
Walton, Dawnie. ★*The Final Revival of Opal & Nev*
Wood, James. *Upstate*

Yates, Christopher J. *Grist Mill Road: A Novel*
New York 2140. Robinson, Kim Stanley
NEW YORK CITY
Aciman, Andre. *Enigma Variations: A Novel*
Alderson, Kaia. *Sisters in Arms*
Alenyikov, Michael. *Ivan and Misha: Stories*
Allende, Isabel. *In the Midst of Winter: A Novel*
Alvarez, Julia. *How the Garcia Girls Lost Their Accents*
Andreades, Daphne Palasi. *Brown Girls*
Armstrong, Addison. *The Light of Luna Park*
Auster, Paul. *The Brooklyn Follies*
Auster, Paul. *Invisible*
Bacon, Charlotte. *There Is Room for You*
Baldwin, James. ★*Another Country*
Baldwin, James. ★*Go Tell It on the Mountain*
Baldwin, James. ★*If Beale Street Could Talk*
Baldwin, James. *Just Above My Head*
Baldwin, James. *Tell Me How Long the Train's Been Gone: A Novel*
Bambara, Toni Cade. *Gorilla, My Love*
Banasky, Carmiel. *The Suicide of Claire Bishop*
Barclay, Linwood. ★*Elevator Pitch: A Novel*
Barclay, Linwood. *Trust Your Eyes: A Thriller*
Bartz, Andrea. *The Lost Night*
Bauer, Carlene. ★*Frances and Bernard*
Beagle, Peter S. *A Fine and Private Place*
Begley, Louis. *About Schmidt*
Belli, Kate. *Deception by Gaslight: A Gilded Gotham Mystery*
Bellow, Saul. ★*Mr. Sammler's Planet*
Bellow, Saul. ★*Seize the Day*
Berkowitz, Ira. *Old Flame: A Jackson Steeg Novel*
Bisson, Terry. *Any Day Now*
Blake, Sarah. *The Guest Book: A Novel*
Block, Lawrence. *All the Flowers Are Dying*
Block, Lawrence. *The Burglar in the Closet*
Block, Lawrence. ★*The Burglar in the Library*
Block, Lawrence. *A Drop of the Hard Stuff: A Matthew Scudder Novel*
Block, Lawrence. *Eight Million Ways to Die*
Block, Lawrence. *Hit Me: A Keller Novel*
Block, Lawrence. *The Sins of the Fathers*
Block, Lawrence. *A Ticket to the Boneyard: A Matthew Scudder Novel*
Block, Lawrence. ★*When the Sacred Ginmill Closes*
Blum, Jenna. *The Lost Family*
Bock, Charles. *Alice & Oliver: A Novel*
Bourland, Barbara. ★*Fake Like Me*
Boyle, William. *The Lonely Witness*
Bram, Christopher. *Lives of the Circus Animals: A Novel*
Brandt, Harry. *The Whites: A Novel*
Brayden, Melissa. *First Position*
Brinkley, Jamel. *A Lucky Man: Stories*
Browne, S. G. *Less Than Hero: A Novel*
Brunt, Carol Rifka. ★*Tell the Wolves I'm Home: A Novel*
Buntin, Julie. ★*Marlena: A Novel*
Burdick, Serena. *The Girls with No Names*
Burke, Alafair. *The Better Sister: A Novel*
Burton, Tara Isabella. *Social Creature*
Bushnell, Candace. *Is There Still Sex in the City?*

Butler, Marcia. *Pickle's Progress*

Cantero, Edgar. *Meddling Kids: A Novel*

Capri, NeNe. *The Pussy Trap*

Capri, NeNe. *The Pussy Trap.; Part 3,*

Card, Maisy. ★*These Ghosts Are Family: A Novel*

Carr, Caleb. ★*The Alienist*

Carr, Caleb. *The Angel of Darkness*

Carter, Mary Dixie. *The Photographer*

Cassara, Joseph. *The House of Impossible Beauties*

Castellani, Christopher. *Leading Men: A Novel*

Chabon, Michael. *The Amazing Adventures of Kavalier & Clay: A Novel*

Chakrabarti, Jai. *A Play for the End of the World*

Child, Lee. *The Hard Way*

Clark, Mary Higgins. *Death Wears a Beauty Mask and Other Stories*

Clark, Wahida. *Thug Lovin'*

Clark, Wahida. *Thug Matrimony*

Clayborn, Kate. *Love Lettering*

Cleeton, Chanel. *The Most Beautiful Girl in Cuba*

Coben, Harlan. *Run Away*

Cohen, Tish. *The Summer We Lost Her: A Novel*

Cole, Alyssa. ★*A Duke by Default*

Cole, Alyssa. ★*A Prince on Paper*

Cole, Teju. ★*Open City: A Novel*

Conell, Lee. *The Party Upstairs*

Conroy, Pat. *The Prince of Tides*

Corman, Avery. *Prized Possessions*

Corthron, Kia. *Moon and the Mars*

Coulter, Catherine. *The Devil's Triangle*

Coulter, Catherine. *The End Game*

Coulter, Catherine. *The Final Cut*

Coulter, Catherine. *The Last Second*

Coulter, Catherine. *The Lost Key*

Coulter, Catherine. *The Sixth Day*

Crane, Stephen. *Maggie: A Girl of the Streets*

Cruz, Angie. *Dominicana: A Novel*

Cunningham, Michael. *Specimen Days*

Cussler, Clive. *The Cutthroat*

Cussler, Clive. ★*The Titanic Secret*

Dahl, Julia. *Conviction*

Dahl, Julia. *The Missing Hours*

Danler, Stephanie. *Sweetbitter*

Daria, Alexis. ★*A Lot Like Adios*

Daria, Alexis. ★*You Had Me at Hola*

Davies, Valentine. *Miracle on 34th Street*

Davis, Fiona. *The Chelsea Girls*

Davis, Fiona. *The Lions of Fifth Avenue: A Novel*

Davis, Fiona. *The Masterpiece*

De Leon, Aya. *Side Chick Nation*

Deaver, Jeffery. ★*The Coffin Dancer*

Deaver, Jeffery. *The Empty Chair*

Deaver, Jeffery. *The Stone Monkey: A Lincoln Rhyme Novel*

Dee, Jonathan. *The Privileges: A Novel*

Delaney, J. P. *Believe Me: A Novel*

DeLillo, Don. *Falling Man: A Novel*

DeLillo, Don. *The Silence*

DeLillo, Don. *Underworld*

Dennis-Benn, Nicole. ★*Patsy: A Novel*

Desai, Kiran. *The Inheritance of Loss*

Dick, Philip K. *The Minority Report*

Doctorow, E. L. ★*Billy Bathgate: A Novel*

Doctorow, E. L. *Homer and Langley: A Novel*

Doctorow, E. L. *World's Fair*

Dos Passos, John. *Manhattan Transfer*

Dunne, Dominick. *People Like Us: A Novel*

Dunne, Dominick. *Too Much Money*

Egan, Jennifer. ★*Manhattan Beach: A Novel*

Eisenberg, Deborah. *The Twilight of the Superheroes*

Elias, Gerald. *Danse Macabre*

Elias, Gerald. ★*Death and Transfiguration: A Daniel Jacobus Novel*

Ellison, Ralph. ★*Invisible Man*

Evanovich, Stephanie. *Under the Table*

Fairstein, Linda A. *Blood Oath*

Fairstein, Linda A. *Entombed*

Faulks, Sebastian. *On Green Dolphin Street: A Novel*

Faye, Lyndsay. *The Gods of Gotham*

Faye, Lyndsay. ★*The King of Infinite Space*

Faye, Lyndsay. ★*The Paragon Hotel*

Faye, Lyndsay. *Seven for a Secret*

Feldman, Ellen. *Paris Never Leaves You*

Ferrell, Carolyn. *Dear Miss Metropolitan*

Finn, A. J. ★*The Woman in the Window*

Fitzgerald, F. Scott. ★*The Beautiful and Damned*

Flint, Emma. ★*Little Deaths: A Novel*

Foer, Jonathan Safran. *Extremely Loud and Incredibly Close*

Force, Marie. *Five Years Gone*

Fowler, Therese. *A Well-Behaved Woman: A Novel of the Vanderbilts*

Fredericks, Mariah. *Death of a Showman*

Friedland, Elyssa. *The Intermission*

Gaitskill, Mary. *Veronica*

Gilbert, David. *& Sons: A Novel*

Gilbert, Elizabeth. ★*City of Girls*

Goldbloom, Goldie. *On Division*

Goodwin, S. M. *Absence of Mercy*

Gray, Erick S. *Love & a Gangsta: A Novel*

Green, Hank. *An Absolutely Remarkable Thing: A Novel*

Grodstein, Lauren. *Our Short History*

Gross, Andrew. *Button Man*

Gruber, Michael. *The Book of Air and Shadows*

Gruber, Michael. *The Return: A Novel*

Hajdu, David. *Adrianne Geffel: A Fiction*

Hale, Shannon. *Austenland: A Novel*

Hallberg, Garth Risk. ★*City on Fire*

Hammett, Dashiell. ★*The Thin Man*

Hand, Elizabeth. ★*Generation Loss: A Novel*

Hankin, Laura. *Happy & You Know It*

Hart, John. *Iron House*

Hassib, Rajia. *A Pure Heart: A Novel*

Hauck, Rachel. *The Wedding Chapel*

Helprin, Mark. *In Sunlight and in Shadow*

Helprin, Mark. ★*Winter's Tale*

Hendricks, Greer. *An Anonymous Girl*

Herrera, Adriana. ★*American Dreamer*

Herrera, Adriana. *American Fairytale*

Hijuelos, Oscar. *Beautiful Maria of My Soul*

Hijuelos, Oscar. ★*The Mambo Kings Play Songs of Love: A Novel*

Hill, Donna. ★*Confessions in B-Flat*
Hoffman, Alice. *The Museum of Extraordinary Things: A Novel*
Hoffman, Alice. *The Rules of Magic: A Novel*
Horn, Dara. *Eternal Life: A Novel*
Hughes, Langston. ★*Short Stories*
Humphreys, Sara Taney. *Trouble Walks In*
James, Marlon. ★*A Brief History of Seven Killings: A Novel*
Jemisin, N. K. ★*The City We Became*
Jin, Ha. *The Boat Rocker: A Novel*
Joukhadar, Zeyn. ★*The Thirty Names of Night: A Novel*
K'wan. *Animal*
K'wan. *Animal II: The Omen*
K'wan. *The Diamond Empire*
K'wan. ★*Diamonds and Pearl*
K'wan. *The Fix*
K'wan. *Gangsta*
K'wan. *Revelations*
Kaplan, Mitchell James. *Rhapsody*
Katz, Erica. *The Boys' Club*
Kaufman, Bel. *Up the Down Staircase*
Kaufman, Charlie. *Antkind: A Novel*
Kaufman, Sue. *Diary of a Mad Housewife*
Kenney, John. *Talk to Me*
Kirshenbaum, Binnie. *Rabbits for Food*
Ko, Lisa. *The Leavers*
Kotzwinkle, William. *The Bear Went Over the Mountain*
Kress, Nancy. *Tomorrow's Kin*
Kunzru, Hari. *White Tears*
Kwan, Kevin. *Sex and Vanity: A Novel*
Kwok, Jean. *Searching for Sylvie Lee*
Larsen, Nella. *Passing*
Lasdun, James. *Afternoon of a Faun: A Novel*
Lauren, Christina. *Roomies*
Layne, Lauren. *Passion on Park Avenue*
Leavitt, David. ★*Shelter in Place*
Lee, Jonathan. *The Great Mistake*
Leilani, Raven. ★*Luster*
Lethem, Jonathan. *Dissident Gardens*
Lipman, Elinor. *Good Riddance*
Ma, Ling. *Severance*
Mandel, Emily St. John. ★*The Glass Hotel: A Novel*
Mark, David John. *Cruel Mercy*
McCarthy, Jesse. *The Fugitivities*
McDermott, Alice. ★*Charming Billy*
McDermott, Alice. ★*The Ninth Hour*
McKenzie, Alecia. *A Million Aunties*
McQuiston, Casey. ★*One Last Stop*
Meuleman, Sarah. *Find Me Gone*
Miller, Henry. ★*Tropic of Capricorn*
Miller, Karen E. Quinones. *An Angry-Ass Black Woman*
Millhauser, Steven. *Martin Dressler: The Tale of an American Dreamer*
Molloy, Aimee. *The Perfect Mother: A Novel*
Morrison, Toni. *Jazz*
Morton, Brian. *Florence Gordon*
Moshfegh, Ottessa. *My Year of Rest and Relaxation*
Mosley, Walter. *All I Did Was Shoot My Man: A Leonid McGill Mystery*
Mosley, Walter. *And Sometimes I Wonder About You: A Leonid McGill Mystery*
Mosley, Walter. *Down the River Unto the Sea*
Mosley, Walter. *Trouble Is What I Do: A Leonid McGill Mystery*
Naylor, Gloria. *Mama Day*
Newman, Sandra. *The Heavens*
Novic, Sara. *Girl at War*
Nunez, Sigrid. *The Last of Her Kind: A Novel*
O'Brien, Perry Edmond. *Fire in the Blood*
O'Mara, Tim. *Crooked Numbers*
Offill, Jenny. ★*Weather*
Orenstein, Hannah. *Love at First Like*
Ozick, Cynthia. *Heir to the Glimmering World*
Ozick, Cynthia. *The Puttermesser Papers*
Packer, Ann. *The Dive from Clausen's Pier*
Palmer, Dexter Clarence. *Version Control*
Palmer, Lindsey J. *Otherwise Engaged*
Pava, Sergio de la. *A Naked Singularity*
Pellegrino, Amanda. *Smile and Look Pretty*
Persaud, Ingrid. *Love After Love: A Novel*
Pessl, Marisha. *Night Film: A Novel*
Peters, Torrey. ★*Detransition, Baby*
Petry, Ann. ★*The Street*
Picoult, Jodi. ★*Wish You Were Here: A Novel*
Piercy, Marge. *Sex Wars*
Pintoff, Stefanie. *Hostage Taker: A Novel*
Pobi, Robert. *City of Windows*
Pobi, Robert. *Under Pressure*
Pochoda, Ivy. *Visitation Street: A Novel*
Potok, Chaim. ★*The Gift of Asher Lev*
Potok, Chaim. ★*My Name Is Asher Lev*
Price, Reynolds. *The Good Priest's Son*
Price, Richard. *Lush Life*
Pynchon, Thomas. ★*Bleeding Edge*
Pynchon, Thomas. ★*V: A Novel*
Rice, Luanne. *Little Night*
Rivero, Melissa. *The Affairs of the Falcons*
Robb, J. D. *Connections in Death: An Eve Dallas Novel*
Robb, J. D. *Fantasy in Death*
Robb, J. D. *Innocent in Death*
Robb, J. D. *Leverage in Death: An Eve Dallas Novel*
Robb, J. D. *Naked in Death*
Robinson, Kim Stanley. *New York 2140*
Rogers, Morgan Callan. ★*Honey Girl*
Roisin, Fariha. *Like a Bird*
Rooney, Kathleen. ★*Lillian Boxfish Takes a Walk*
Rose, M. J. ★*Cartier's Hope*
Rosen, Renee. *The Social Graces*
Roth, Henry. *From Bondage*
Roth, Henry. *Requiem for Harlem*
Roth, Philip. *Exit Ghost*
Rozan, S. J. ★*The Art of Violence*
Rozan, S. J. *The Shanghai Moon: A Lydia Chin/Bill Smith Novel*
Rushdie, Salman. *Two Years Eight Months and Twenty-Eight Nights: A Novel*
Sager, Riley. *Final Girls: A Novel*
Sager, Riley. *Lock Every Door: A Novel*
Salinger, J. D. ★*The Catcher in the Rye*

Sanders, Lawrence. ★*The First Deadly Sin*
Sanders, Lawrence. ★*The Fourth Deadly Sin*
Sanders, Lawrence. *The Second Deadly Sin*
Sanders, Lawrence. *The Tenth Commandment: A Novel*
Sanders, Lawrence. ★*The Third Deadly Sin*
Sanders, Lawrence. *The Timothy Files*
Sanders, Lawrence. *Timothy's Game*
Sandford, John. ★*Silent Prey*
Sapphire. ★*The Kid: A Novel*
Sapphire. ★*Push: A Novel*
Schaitkin, Alexis. *Saint X*
Schwartz, Lynne Sharon. *Truthtelling: Stories, Fables, Glimpses*
Scoppettone, Sandra. *Everything You Have Is Mine*
Scoppettone, Sandra. *My Sweet Untraceable You*
Sears, Michael. *Tower of Babel*
Senna, Danzy. *New People*
Seton, Anya. ★*Dragonwyck*
Shapiro, Barbara A. *The Muralist*
Shteyngart, Gary. *The Russian Debutante's Handbook*
Shumway, Charity. *Ten Girls to Watch: A Novel*
Shupe, Joanna. *The Prince of Broadway*
Shupe, Joanna. *The Rogue of Fifth Avenue*
Silber, Joan. *Improvement*
Silber, Joan. *Secrets of Happiness*
Simpson, Rosemary. *Let the Dead Keep Their Secrets*
Simpson, Rosemary. ★*What the Dead Leave Behind*
Simsion, Graeme C. *The Rosie Effect*
Simsion, Graeme C. *The Rosie Result*
Singer, Isaac Bashevis. *Enemies, a Love Story*
Sister Souljah. ★*A Deeper Love Inside: The Porsche Santiaga Story*
Sittenfeld, Curtis. *Eligible: A Novel*
Smith, Tom Rob. *Agent 6*
Snyder, Suleikha. *Big Bad Wolf*
Sofer, Dalia. *Man of My Time*
Speight, Shameek A. *The Pleasure of Pain*
Spillane, Mickey. *The Goliath Bone*
Spillane, Mickey. *A Long Time Dead: A Mike Hammer Casebook*
Spufford, Francis. ★*Golden Hill*
Stark, Richard. *The Hunter: A Parker Novel*
Steinke, Rene. *Holy Skirts*
Stewart, Amy. *Lady Cop Makes Trouble*
Stewart, Amy. *Miss Kopp's Midnight Confessions*
Stout, Rex. *The Doorbell Rang*
Stout, Rex. ★*Gambit*
Stringer, Vickie M. ★*Let That Be the Reason*
Strout, Elizabeth. *My Name Is Lucy Barton*
Strout, Elizabeth. ★*Oh William!*
T. I. *Power & Beauty: A Love Story of Life on the Streets*
Tanabe, Karin. ★*A Woman of Intelligence*
Tartt, Donna. ★*The Goldfinch*
Thompson, Victoria. *Murder on Wall Street*
Toro, Guillermo del. *The Hollow Ones*
Towles, Amor. *Rules of Civility: A Novel*
Unger, Lisa. *Under My Skin*
Van der Vliet Oloomi, Azareen. *Call Me Zebra*
Vatner, Jonathan. *Carnegie Hill: A Novel*
Vonnegut, Kurt. *Slapstick: Or, Lonesome No More! a Novel*
Wall, Cara. *The Dearly Beloved: A Novel*

Wallace, Carol. *Our Kind of People*
Walton, Dawnie. ★*The Final Revival of Opal & Nev*
Wayne, Teddy. *Apartment: A Novel*
Wecker, Helene. *The Golem and the Jinni*
Wecker, Helene. ★*The Hidden Palace*
Westlake, Donald E. *Get Real*
Whitehead, Colson. ★*Harlem Shuffle*
Whitehead, Colson. *Zone One: A Novel*
Williams, Tia. ★*Seven Days in June: A Novel*
Wolf, Dick. *The Ultimatum*
Wolfe, Tom. *The Bonfire of the Vanities*
Wood, Tracey Enerson. *The Engineer's Wife: A Novel*
Woods, Stuart. *A Delicate Touch*
Woods, Stuart. *New York Dead*
Woodson, Jacqueline. ★*Another Brooklyn*
Woodson, Jacqueline. ★*Red at the Bone*
Yanagihara, Hanya. *A Little Life: A Novel*
Yates, Christopher J. *Grist Mill Road: A Novel*
Yun, Jung. *O Beautiful: A Novel*
New York Dead. Woods, Stuart
New York Review Books classics [Series]. Ginzburg, Natalia
NEW YORK STATE
Bailey, Tessa. *Fix Her Up*
Duffy, Brendan. *House of Echoes: A Novel*
McCreight, Kimberly. *Friends Like These*
Mehta, Rahul. *No Other World: A Novel*
Prose, Francine. ★*The Vixen*
Unger, Lisa. ★*The Stranger Inside*
NEW ZEALAND
Catton, Eleanor. *The Luminaries: A Novel*
Cleave, Paul. *Trust No One: A Thriller*
Grenville, Kate. *Sarah Thornhill*
Hulme, Keri. ★*The Bone People: A Novel*
Singh, Nalini. *A Madness of Sunshine*
NEW ZEALAND FICTION
Catton, Eleanor. *The Luminaries: A Novel*
Clarke, Diana. *Thin Girls*
Cleave, Paul. *A Killer Harvest: A Thriller*
Cleave, Paul. *Trust No One: A Thriller*
Frame, Janet. *Between My Father and the King: New and Uncollected Stories*
Isaac, Kara. *Then There Was You*
Marsh, Ngaio. *A Man Lay Dead*
Muir, Tamsyn. *Harrow the Ninth*
Parker, Lucy. *The Austen Playbook*
Parker, Lucy. *Battle Royal*
Parry, H. G. *A Declaration of the Rights of Magicians*
Parry, H. G. *The Unlikely Escape of Uriah Heep*
Singh, Nalini. *A Madness of Sunshine*
Singh, Nalini. ★*Silver Silence*
NEWARK, NEW JERSEY
Ca$h. *Thugs Cry: A Novel*
Parks, Brad. *The Player: A Mystery*
Roth, Philip. ★*American Pastoral*
Roth, Philip. ★*Everyman*
Roth, Philip. *I Married a Communist*
Roth, Philip. ★*Nemesis*
Roth, Philip. ★*The Plot Against America*

NEWCASTLE UPON TYNE, ENGLAND
Barker, Pat. *Another World*
Newcomer. Higashino, Keigo
NEWFOUNDLAND AND LABRADOR
Crummey, Michael. *Galore*
Crummey, Michael. *The Innocents*
Crummey, Michael. *Sweetland*
Lundrigan, Nicole. *Glass Boys: A Novel*
Proulx, Annie. ★*The Shipping News*
Newitz, Annalee
Autonomous
Newland, Courttia
A River Called Time
The Newlyweds. Freudenberger, Nell
NEWLYWEDS
Arudpragasam, Anuk. *The Story of a Brief Marriage*
Cheek, Chip. *Cape May*
Freudenberger, Nell. *The Newlyweds*
Huber, Anna Lee. *Penny for Your Secrets*
Hurley, Andrew Michael. *Devil's Day*
Kelly, Cathy. *Secrets of a Happy Marriage*
Leigh, Eva. *Temptations of a Wallflower*
Mahmoud, Lena. *Amreekiya: A Novel*
McCall Smith, Alexander. *The Limpopo Academy of Private Detection*
McEwan, Ian. ★*On Chesil Beach*
Moreno-Garcia, Silvia. *Mexican Gothic*
Oates, Joyce Carol. *Pursuit*
Paris, B. A. *Behind Closed Doors*
Parrish, Christa. *Still Life*
Pinborough, Sarah. ★*Dead to Her: A Novel*
Pufahl, Shannon. *On Swift Horses*
Sayers, Dorothy L. ★*Busman's Honeymoon*
Sayers, Dorothy L. *Thrones, Dominations*
White, Elle Katharine. *Dragonshadow*
Whitfield, Clare. *People of Abandoned Character*
Newman, Sandra
The Heavens
NEWPORT, RHODE ISLAND
Force, Marie. *Deceived by Desire*
Gaynor, Hazel. *The Lighthouse Keeper's Daughter*
Smith, Gregory Blake. ★*The Maze at Windermere: A Novel*
Wilder, Thornton. ★*Theophilus North*
NEWS LEAKS
Taylor, Brad. *Ring of Fire*
News of the World: A Novel. Jiles, Paulette
Newsflesh [Series]. Grant, Mira
NEWSPAPER ADVERTISING
Christie, Agatha. *A Murder Is Announced: A Miss Marple Mystery*
NEWSPAPER EDITORS
Lewis, Sinclair. ★*It Can't Happen Here*
McEwan, Ian. ★*Amsterdam*
Rachman, Tom. *The Imperfectionists: A Novel*
NEWSPAPER EMPLOYEES
Scott, A. D. ★*Beneath the Abbey Wall: A Novel*
Scott, A. D. *A Double Death on the Black Isle: A Novel*
NEWSPAPER PUBLISHERS AND PUBLISHING
Grisham, John. *The Last Juror*

Guhrke, Laura Lee. *The Truth About Love and Dukes*
Hiaasen, Carl. *Basket Case*
Pratchett, Terry. *The Truth: A Novel of Discworld*
Rachman, Tom. *The Imperfectionists: A Novel*
NEWSPAPERS
Barnett, LaShonda K. *Jam on the Vine*
Daugherty, Christi. *A Beautiful Corpse*
Dexter, Colin. *The Way Through the Woods*
Eco, Umberto. *Numero Zero*
Hiaasen, Carl. *Lucky You: A Novel*
Landvik, Lorna. *Chronicles of a Radical Hag: With Recipes*
The Next Person You Meet in Heaven. Albom, Mitch
Next to Last Stand. Johnson, Craig
Next Year in Havana. Cleeton, Chanel
Ng, Celeste
★*Everything I Never Told You: A Novel*
★*Little Fires Everywhere: A Novel*
Nguyen, Kevin
★*New Waves*
Nguyen, Lena
We Have Always Been Here
Nguyen, Phan Que Mai
★*The Mountains Sing: A Novel*
Nguyen, Viet Thanh
★*The Committed*
★*The Refugees*
★*The Sympathizer*
NIAGARA FALLS
Oates, Joyce Carol. *The Falls: A Novel*
Nic Costa mysteries [Series]. Hewson, David
Niccolo Rising. Dunnett, Dorothy
The Nice and the Good. Murdoch, Iris
Nice Girls. Dang, Catherine
NICE, FRANCE
Donoghue, Emma. *Akin*
Levy, Deborah. *Swimming Home: A Novel*
NICHOLAS II, EMPEROR OF RUSSIA, 1868-1918
Akunin, B. *The Coronation: The Further Adventures of Erast Fandorin*
Nicholas Bracewell mysteries [Series]. Marston, Edward
★*Nicholas Nickleby*. Dickens, Charles
Nicholls, David
US: A Novel
Nicholls, Owen
Love, Unscripted: A Novel
Nichols, Peter
The Rocks
Nicieza, Fabian
Suburban Dicks
The Nick Adams Stories. Hemingway, Ernest
Nick Heller novels [Series]. Finder, Joseph
Nick Mason novels [Series]. Hamilton, Steve
★*The Nickel Boys: A Novel*. Whitehead, Colson
Nickson, Chris
Come the Fear
NIECES
Jimenez, Abby. *Life's Too Short*
Rice, Luanne. *Little Night*

Ruiz, Sarah Grunder. *Love, Lists, and Fancy Ships*

NIECES AND NEPHEWS

Trollope, Anthony. *Doctor Thorne*

Niffenegger, Audrey

The Time Traveler's Wife: A Novel

NIGERIA

Abraham, Tola Rotimi. *Black Sunday*

Achebe, Chinua. ★*Things Fall Apart*

Adebayo, Ayobami. ★*Stay with Me*

Adichie, Chimamanda Ngozi. ★*Americanah: A Novel*

Adichie, Chimamanda Ngozi. *Half of a Yellow Sun*

Adichie, Chimamanda Ngozi. *The Thing Around Your Neck*

Adjapon, Bisi. *The Teller of Secrets: A Novel*

Braithwaite, Oyinkan. *My Sister, the Serial Killer: A Novel*

Cole, Teju. *Every Day Is for the Thief*

Cussler, Clive. ★*The Oracle*

Dare, Abi. *The Girl with the Louding Voice*

Ehirim, Nnamdi. *Prince of Monkeys*

Emezi, Akwaeke. ★*The Death of Vivek Oji*

Emezi, Akwaeke. *Freshwater*

Igharo, Jane. *The Sweetest Remedy*

Iweala, Uzodinma. ★*Speak No Evil*

Kayode, Femi. ★*Lightseekers*

O'Brien, Edna. ★*Girl*

Obioma, Chigozie. ★*The Fishermen: A Novel*

Obioma, Chigozie. ★*An Orchestra of Minorities*

Okorafor, Nnedi. ★*Noor*

Okparanta, Chinelo. ★*Under the Udala Trees*

Osondu, E. C. *Voice of America: Stories*

Soyinka, Wole. *Chronicles from the Land of the Happiest People on Earth*

Thompson, Tade. *Rosewater*

Thompson, Tade. *The Rosewater Insurrection*

Thompson, Tade. *The Rosewater Redemption*

NIGERIAN AMERICANS

Iweala, Uzodinma. ★*Speak No Evil*

NIGERIANS IN ENGLAND

Adichie, Chimamanda Ngozi. ★*Americanah: A Novel*

Rendell, Ruth. *Simisola*

NIGERIANS IN THE UNITED STATES

Adichie, Chimamanda Ngozi. ★*Americanah: A Novel*

Adichie, Chimamanda Ngozi. *The Thing Around Your Neck*

Cole, Teju. ★*Open City: A Novel*

Emezi, Akwaeke. *Freshwater*

NIGHT

Fowler, Christopher. *Bryant & May: The Lonely Hour*

Murakami, Haruki. *After Dark*

★*The Night Always Comes*. Vlautin, Willy

Night at the Fiestas: Stories. Quade, Kirstin Valdez

The Night Bird. Freeman, Brian

★*The Night Circus: A Novel*. Morgenstern, Erin

The Night Ferry: A Novel. Robotham, Michael

Night Film: A Novel. Pessl, Marisha

The Night Fire. Connelly, Michael

Night Flight. Saint-Exupery, Antoine de

NIGHT FLYING

Saint-Exupery, Antoine de. *Night Flight*

The Night Gwen Stacy Died. Bruni, Sarah

The Night Hawks. Griffiths, Elly

Night of Miracles. Berg, Elizabeth

Night of the Animals. Broun, Bill

Night of the Jaguar: A Novel. Gruber, Michael

Night Passage. Parker, Robert B.

★*Night Prey*. Sandford, John

Night School. Child, Lee

Night Shift. King, Stephen

Night soldiers [Series]. Furst, Alan

The Night Stages: A Novel. Urquhart, Jane

The Night Strangers: A Novel. Bohjalian, Chris

The Night Swim. Goldin, Megan

★*The Night Tiger: A Novel*. Choo, Yangsze

★*A Night to Surrender*. Dare, Tessa

A Night Too Dark: A Kate Shugak Novel. Stabenow, Dana

The Night Trade. Eisler, Barry

★*The Night Watchman: A Novel*. Erdrich, Louise

Night's edge [Series]. Czerneda, Julie

★*Night, Dawn, the Accident: Three Tales*. Wiesel, Elie

Night. Sleep. Death. The Stars. Oates, Joyce Carol

Nightbitch. Yoder, Rachel

Nightchaser. Bouchet, Amanda

Nightchaser novels [Series]. Bouchet, Amanda

NIGHTCLUB OWNERS

Clark, Wahida. *Thug Lovin'*

NIGHTCLUBS

Connelly, Michael. *The Late Show*

Pelevin, Viktor. *The Hall of Singing Caryatids*

Phillips, Susan Elizabeth. *First Star I See Tonight*

Randall, Alice. ★*Black Bottom Saints*

Siger, Jeffrey. *Mykonos After Midnight: A Chief Inspector Kaldis Mystery*

Nightcrawlers. Pronzini, Bill

Nightfall. Goodis, David

Nighthawk: a Novel from the Numa Files. Cussler, Clive

Nighthawking. Thomas, Russ

The Nightingale. Hannah, Kristin

Nightingale novels [Series]. Copenhaver, John

NIGHTLIFE

Randall, Alice. ★*Black Bottom Saints*

Truss, Lynne. *The Man That Got Away: A Constable Twitten Mystery*

NIGHTMARES

Oates, Joyce Carol. *Pursuit*

Obregon, Nicolas. *Blue Light Yokohama*

Straub, Peter. *Mr. X*

Vandelly, T. Marie. *Theme Music*

★*Nightwood*. Barnes, Djuna

Nightwoods: a Novel. Frazier, Charles

Nikki Griffin novels [Series]. Lelchuk, Saul

Nils Shapiro novels [Series]. Goldman, Matt

Nin, Anais

Cities of the Interior

Nine Coaches Waiting. Stewart, Mary

The Nine Lives of Rose Napolitano. Freitas, Donna

Nine Perfect Strangers. Moriarty, Liane

★*Nine Stories*. Salinger, J. D.

The Nine Tailors. Sayers, Dorothy L.

NINE-YEAR-OLD BOYS

Ammaniti, Niccolo. *I'm Not Scared*

Doctorow, E. L. *World's Fair*

Hill, Susan. *The Pure in Heart: A Simon Serrailler Crime Novel*

Matar, Hisham. *In the Country of Men*

NINE-YEAR-OLD GIRLS

Dunn, Kate. *The Dragonfly*

Gowdy, Barbara. *Helpless: A Novel*

Lansdale, Joe R. *The Bottoms*

Mohamed, Nadifa. *The Orchard of Lost Souls: A Novel*

Stewart, Ann Marie. *Stars in the Grass*

Toews, Miriam. *Fight Night*

Ninefox Gambit. Lee, Yoon Ha

Nineteen Minutes: A Novel. Picoult, Jodi

Ninety-Nine Stories of God. Williams, Joy

NINJA

Spann, Susan. *Blade of the Samurai: A Shinobi Mystery*

Spann, Susan. ★*Claws of the Cat: A Shinobi Mystery*

Spann, Susan. *Trial on Mount Koya: A Hiro Hattori Novel*

★*The Ninth Hour*. McDermott, Alice

★*Ninth House*. Bardugo, Leigh

Ninth House [Series]. Muir, Tamsyn

Nip the Buds, Shoot the Kids. Oe, Kenzaburo

The Nix: a Novel. Hill, Nathan

Niya: Rainbow Dreams. Joseph, Fabiola

No Bad Deed. Chavez, Heather

★*No Country for Old Men*. McCarthy, Cormac

No Fixed Line. Stabenow, Dana

No Gods, No Monsters. Turnbull, Cadwell

No Good Asking: A Novel. Kimmel, Fran

No Good Deeds. Lippman, Laura

No Good Duke Goes Unpunished. MacLean, Sarah

No Heaven for Good Boys: A Novel. Bush, Keisha

No Laughing Matter. Simpson, Dorothy

No Longer a Gentleman. Putney, Mary Jo

No Middle Name: The Complete Collected Jack Reacher Short Stories. Child, Lee

No Ocean Too Wide: A Novel. Turansky, Carrie

No One Can Pronounce My Name: A Novel. Satyal, Rakesh

★*No One Ever Asked: A Novel*. Ganshert, Katie

No One Will Miss Her. Rosenfield, Kat

No One You Know. Richmond, Michelle

No Other Duke but You. Bowman, Valerie

No Other World: A Novel. Mehta, Rahul

No Place for a Dame. Brockway, Connie

No Place for Heroes: A Novel. Restrepo, Laura

No Safe House. Barclay, Linwood

No Safe Place. Patterson, Richard North

No Time Like the Present: A Novel. Gordimer, Nadine

★*The No. 1 Ladies' Detective Agency*. McCall Smith, Alexander

NO. 1 LADIES' DETECTIVE AGENCY (IMAGINARY ORGANIZATION)

McCall Smith, Alexander. *The Good Husband of Zebra Drive*

McCall Smith, Alexander. *The Kalahari Typing School for Men*

McCall Smith, Alexander. *The Limpopo Academy of Private Detection*

No. 1 Ladies' Detective Agency [Series]. McCall Smith, Alexander

NOAH'S ARK

Barnes, Julian. ★*A History of the World in 10 1/2 Chapters*

NOBEL PRIZE WINNERS

McEwan, Ian. *Solar: A Novel*

NOBILITY

Balogh, Mary. *The Secret Mistress*

Balogh, Mary. *Simply Love*

Balogh, Mary. ★*Someone to Love*

Bateman, Kate. *A Reckless Match*

Bennett, Alan. ★*The Uncommon Reader*

Boyle, Elizabeth. *And the Miss Ran Away with the Rake*

Brockway, Connie. *The Golden Season*

Bujold, Lois McMaster. ★*Shards of Honor*

Bujold, Lois McMaster. ★*The Warrior's Apprentice*

Burrowes, Grace. *The Captive*

Burrowes, Grace. *Tremaine's True Love*

Burrowes, Grace. *The Trouble with Dukes*

Byrne, Kerrigan. *How to Love a Duke in Ten Days*

Callihan, Kristen. ★*Firelight*

Chase, Loretta Lynda. *A Duke in Shining Armor*

Cherezinska, Elzbieta. *The Widow Queen*

Cocks, Heather. *The Royal We*

Collins, Wilkie. ★*The Woman in White*

Dumas, Alexandre. ★*Camille*

Dunant, Sarah. *Blood and Beauty: A Novel*

Elliott, Kate. *Unconquerable Sun*

Follett, Ken. ★*The Evening and the Morning*

Frampton, Megan. *The Duke's Guide to Correct Behavior*

Frampton, Megan. *Never a Bride*

Frampton, Megan. *Put up Your Duke*

Garriott, Leah. *Promised*

Garwood, Julie. *The Bride*

Golding, William. *Close Quarters*

Golding, William. *Fire Down Below*

Golding, William. *Rites of Passage*

Gracie, Anne. *Marry in Scandal*

Gregory, Philippa. *The Boleyn Inheritance*

Gregory, Philippa. *The Other Boleyn Girl: A Novel*

Guhrke, Laura Lee. *When the Marquess Met His Match*

Heyer, Georgette. *These Old Shades*

James, Eloisa. *Three Weeks with Lady X*

Jeffries, Sabrina. *Project Duchess*

Laurens, Stephanie. *The Pursuits of Lord Kit Cavanaugh*

Leigh, Eva. *Scandal Takes the Stage*

Lin, Jeannie. *The Lotus Palace*

Long, Julie Anne. *Angel in a Devil's Arms*

Lyons, Jenn. *The Name of All Things*

Lyons, Jenn. *The Ruin of Kings*

Marsh, Ngaio. *A Man Lay Dead*

Martin, George R. R. ★*A Clash of Kings*

Martin, George R. R. ★*A Dance with Dragons*

Martin, George R. R. ★*A Feast for Crows*

Martin, George R. R. ★*A Game of Thrones*

Martin, George R. R. ★*A Storm of Swords*

Milan, Courtney. *The Duchess War*

Morrell, David. *Ruler of the Night*

Parker, Lucy. *Battle Royal*

Pembrooke, Kate. *Not the Kind of Earl You Marry*

Penman, Sharon Kay. *When Christ and His Saints Slept*

Putney, Mary Jo. *Loving a Lost Lord*

Putney, Mary Jo. *The Marriage Spell: A Novel*

Puzo, Mario. *The Family: A Novel*

Quincy, Diana. *Her Night with the Duke*

Quincy, Diana. *The Viscount Made Me Do It*

Raybourn, Deanna. *A Curious Beginning: A Veronica Speedwell Mystery*

Raybourn, Deanna. ★*A Murderous Relation*

Richardson, Samuel. ★*Clarissa, Or, the History of a Young Lady*

Ridley, Erica. ★*The Perks of Loving a Wallflower*

Rutherfurd, Edward. *The Princes of Ireland: The Dublin Saga*

Rutherfurd, Edward. *Russka: The Novel of Russia*

Sansom, C. J. ★*Sovereign*

Sayers, Dorothy L. ★*Clouds of Witness*

Sayers, Dorothy L. *Hangman's Holiday*

Sayers, Dorothy L. *Have His Carcase*

Sayers, Dorothy L. *In the Teeth of the Evidence*

Sayers, Dorothy L. ★*Lord Peter*

Sayers, Dorothy L. *Murder Must Advertise*

Sayers, Dorothy L. ★*Whose Body?: A Lord Peter Wimsey Novel*

Schwartz, John Burnham. *The Commoner: A Novel*

Stewart, Mary. *Nine Coaches Waiting*

Sundaresan, Indu. *The Splendor of Silence: A Novel*

Weir, Alison. *Anna of Kleve: The Princess in the Portrait*

NOBILITY — HISTORY

Du Maurier, Daphne. *Frenchman's Creek*

Putney, Mary Jo. *No Longer a Gentleman*

Woolf, Virginia. *Orlando: A Biography*

★*Nobody's Fool*. Russo, Richard

Nobody's fool [Series]. Russo, Richard

NOIR FICTION

Abbott, Megan E. *Bury Me Deep*

Abbott, Megan E. *Queenpin: A Novel*

Aguilar Camin, Hector. *Death in Veracruz*

Ames, Jonathan. *A Man Named Doll*

Arbol, Victor del. *Breathing Through the Wound*

Atkins, Ace. *Wicked City*

Boyle, William. *City of Margins: A Novel*

Burke, James Lee. *Another Kind of Eden*

Cooper, Tom. *The Marauders*

Ellroy, James. *American Tabloid: A Novel*

Ellroy, James. *Blood's a Rover*

Ellroy, James. *The Cold Six Thousand: A Novel*

Estleman, Loren D. ★*Gas City*

Foster, Fiona King. *The Captive: A Novel*

Hammett, Dashiell. ★*The Thin Man*

Harrison, Jim. *The Great Leader*

Kennedy, William. ★*Ironweed: A Novel*

King, Stephen. ★*Billy Summers*

Lansdale, Joe R. *More Better Deals*

Lehane, Dennis. ★*Mystic River*

Levin, Ira. *A Kiss Before Dying*

Lippman, Laura. ★*Sunburn*

Mandel, Emily St. John. *The Singer's Gun: A Novel*

Moreno-Garcia, Silvia. ★*Velvet Was the Night*

Peace, David. *Occupied City*

Pryor, Mark. *Hollow Man*

Pynchon, Thomas. *Inherent Vice*

Rabe, Peter. ★*Anatomy of a Killer ;: A Shroud for Jesso*

Sallis, James. *Drive*

Solares, Martin. *Don't Send Flowers*

Stark, Richard. *Dirty Money*

Tran, Vu. *Dragonfish: A Novel*

Wolfe, Gene. *The Land Across*

A Noise Downstairs: A Novel. Barclay, Linwood

The Noise of Time. Barnes, Julian

NOMADS

Ahmad, Jamil. *The Wandering Falcon*

NONAGENARIANS

Garcia Marquez, Gabriel. *Memories of My Melancholy Whores*

Gurganus, Allan. *Oldest Living Confederate Widow Tells All*

Ritter, Josh. *The Great Glorious Goddamn of It All*

NONBINARY PEOPLE

Chambers, Becky. ★*A Psalm for the Wild-Built*

Sebastian, Cat. *Unmasked by the Marquess*

NONCONFORMISTS

Austin, Finola. *Bronte's Mistress*

McGuire, Seanan. ★*In an Absent Dream*

Murata, Sayaka. *Earthlings: A Novel*

Ridley, Erica. ★*The Perks of Loving a Wallflower*

Sebastian, Cat. *Unmasked by the Marquess*

Spark, Muriel. ★*The Prime of Miss Jean Brodie*

Walker, Sarai. *Dietland*

None to Accompany Me. Gordimer, Nadine

★*Noor*. Okorafor, Nnedi

Nora Best novels [Series]. Florio, Gwen

Nora Gavin and Cormac Maguire series [Series]. Hart, Erin

Nora Kelly novels (Preston & Child) [Series]. Preston, Douglas J.

Nora Watts novels [Series]. Kamal, Sheena

NORFOLK, ENGLAND

Griffiths, Elly. *The Crossing Places*

Griffiths, Elly. *The House at Sea's End: A Ruth Galloway Mystery*

Griffiths, Elly. *The Janus Stone*

Griffiths, Elly. *The Night Hawks*

Higgins, Jack. *The Eagle Has Flown*

Higgins, Jack. *The Eagle Has Landed*

Rous, Emma. *The Perfect Guests*

Smith, Ali. *The Accidental*

Normal People: A Novel. Rooney, Sally

NORMALITY (PSYCHOLOGY)

Hesse, Hermann. *The Fairy Tales of Hermann Hesse*

NORMAN PERIOD (1066-1154)

Follett, Ken. ★*The Pillars of the Earth*

Franklin, Ariana. *The Siege Winter*

Penman, Sharon Kay. *When Christ and His Saints Slept*

Peters, Ellis. *Brother Cadfael's Penance*

Peters, Ellis. *The Holy Thief*

NORMANDY

Groot, Tracy. *Flame of Resistance*

Wieland, Liza. *Paris, 7 A.M.*

NORMANDY INVASION, JUNE 6, 1944

Shaara, Jeff. *The Steel Wave: A Novel of World War II*

NORMANS IN ENGLAND

Rutherfurd, Edward. *London*

★*Norse Mythology*. Gaiman, Neil

NORTH AFRICA
Cussler, Clive. ★*The Oracle*
Watt, Holly. *To the Lions*

NORTH AMERICA
Atwood, Margaret. ★*The Handmaid's Tale*
Atwood, Margaret. ★*The Testaments: A Novel*
Graedon, Alena. *The Word Exchange: A Novel*
Lalami, Laila. ★*The Moor's Account: A Novel*
★*North and South*. Gaskell, Elizabeth Cleghorn
★*North and South*. Jakes, John
North and South trilogy [Series]. Jakes, John

NORTH ATLANTIC OCEAN
Monsarrat, Nicholas. *The Cruel Sea*

NORTH CAROLINA
Allen, Sarah Addison. *Garden Spells*
Allen, Sarah Addison. *The Girl Who Chased the Moon: A Novel*
Ball, John Dudley. *In the Heat of the Night*
Bambara, Toni Cade. *Gorilla, My Love*
Barr, Nevada. *What Rose Forgot*
Brown, Taylor. ★*Gods of Howl Mountain: A Novel*
Cash, Wiley. *The Last Ballad: A Novel*
Cash, Wiley. *When Ghosts Come Home: A Novel*
Child, Lee. *The Enemy*
Coster, Naima. *What's Mine and Yours: A Novel*
Deaver, Jeffery. *The Empty Chair*
Dektar, Molly. *The Ash Family*
Earley, Tony. *Jim the Boy: A Novel*
Edgerton, Clyde. ★*Walking Across Egypt: A Novel*
Fowler, Therese. ★*A Good Neighborhood*
Frazier, Charles. ★*Cold Mountain*
Frazier, Charles. *Nightwoods: A Novel*
Gabaldon, Diana. ★*A Breath of Snow and Ashes*
Gabaldon, Diana. *An Echo in the Bone*
Gabaldon, Diana. ★*The Fiery Cross*
Gates, Eva. *Deadly Ever After*
Gates, Eva. *A Death Long Overdue*
Gates, Eva. *Read and Buried*
Gibbons, Kaye. *Charms for the Easy Life*
Gibbons, Kaye. ★*Ellen Foster: A Novel*
Gibbons, Kaye. *The Life All Around Me by Ellen Foster*
Godwin, Gail. *Flora: A Novel*
Godwin, Gail. *Unfinished Desires*
Goldin, Megan. *The Night Swim*
Gurganus, Allan. ★*Local Souls: Novellas*
Hart, John. *Down River*
Hart, John. *Iron House*
Hart, John. *The King of Lies*
Hart, John. *The Last Child*
Hodges, Cheris F. *Rumor Has It*
Kantra, Virginia. ★*Meg and Jo*
Maron, Margaret. *Bootlegger's Daughter*
Maron, Margaret. *Up Jumps the Devil*
McCorkle, Jill. ★*Hieroglyphics: A Novel*
McCrumb, Sharyn. ★*The Ballad of Frankie Silver*
McKinlay, Jenn. *The Good Ones*
Owens, Delia. *Where the Crawdads Sing*
Patterson, James. *Kiss the Girls: A Novel*
Pearson, Robin W. *A Long Time Comin'*

Pessl, Marisha. *Special Topics in Calamity Physics*
Poissant, David James. *Lake Life*
Price, Reynolds. *The Good Priest's Son*
Rash, Ron. *Above the Waterfall*
Rash, Ron. ★*The Cove*
Rash, Ron. ★*In the Valley: Stories and a Novella Based on Serena*
Rash, Ron. *Nothing Gold Can Stay: Stories*
Rash, Ron. ★*Serena: A Novel*
Reichs, Kathy. ★*A Conspiracy of Bones*
Reichs, Kathy. *Deadly Decisions*
Roberts, Nora. ★*Under Currents*
Ross, Ann B. *Miss Julia Delivers the Goods: A Novel*
Ross, Ann B. ★*Miss Julia Happily Ever After*
Ross, Ann B. *Miss Julia Knows a Thing or Two*
Ross, Ann B. *Miss Julia Takes the Wheel*
Ross, Ann B. *Miss Julia Throws a Wedding*
Smith, Lee. *On Agate Hill: A Novel*
Sparks, Nicholas. *Every Breath*
Sparks, Nicholas. *The Guardian*
Sparks, Nicholas. ★*The Notebook*
Sparks, Nicholas. *A Walk to Remember*
Weiss, Leah. *If the Creek Don't Rise: A Novel*
Winslow, De'Shawn Charles. ★*In West Mills*
Wolfe, Thomas. ★*Look Homeward, Angel: A Story of a Buried Life*

NORTH DAKOTA
Box, C. J. *Badlands*
Box, C. J. *Paradise Valley*
Erdrich, Louise. *The Beet Queen: A Novel*
Erdrich, Louise. *Four Souls: A Novel*
Erdrich, Louise. ★*Larose*
Erdrich, Louise. *The Last Report on the Miracles at Little No Horse*
Erdrich, Louise. *Love Medicine: A Novel*
Erdrich, Louise. *The Master Butchers Singing Club: A Novel*
Erdrich, Louise. ★*The Night Watchman: A Novel*
Erdrich, Louise. *The Painted Drum: A Novel*
Erdrich, Louise. *The Plague of Doves*
Erdrich, Louise. ★*The Round House: A Novel*
Erdrich, Louise. *Tracks: A Novel*
Power, Susan. *The Grass Dancer*
Sandford, John. ★*Golden Prey*
Yun, Jung. *O Beautiful: A Novel*
*The **North** Face of the Heart*. Redondo, Dolores

NORTH KOREA
Bandi. *The Accusation: Forbidden Stories from Inside North Korea*
Church, James. *Bamboo and Blood: An Inspector O Novel*
Church, James. ★*A Corpse in the Koryo*
Church, James. *A Drop of Chinese Blood*
Church, James. *Hidden Moon: An Inspector O Novel*
Shin, Ann. *The Last Exiles*
Stephens, Alice. *Famous Adopted People*

NORTH MACEDONIA
Porter, Henry. *Firefly*

NORTH SEA
Ware, Ruth. *The Woman in Cabin Ten*

North, Alex
The Shadows
The Whisper Man

North, Anna

   The Life and Death of Sophie Stark

North, Claire

   Notes from the Burning Age

   The Pursuit of William Abbey

NORTHAMPTONSHIRE, ENGLAND

   Moore, Alan. *Jerusalem: A Novel*

Northanger Abbey. Austen, Jane

NORTHERN CALIFORNIA

   Carr, Robyn. ★*Virgin River*

   Davidson, Ash. ★*Damnation Spring*

   Gardiner, Meg. *Unsub: A Novel*

   McLain, Paula. ★*When the Stars Go Dark: A Novel*

   Pynchon, Thomas. *Vineland*

   Rivers, Francine. *Bridge to Haven*

   Sharpe, Tess. *Barbed Wire Heart*

NORTHERN ENGLAND

   Johnson, Daisy. *Sisters*

   Moss, Sarah. *Ghost Wall: A Novel*

   Watson, S. J. *Final Cut*

Northern Heist. O'Rawe, Richard

NORTHERN IRELAND

   Burns, Anna. *Milkman: A Novel*

   Deane, Seamus. *Reading in the Dark*

   Gallen, Michelle. *Big Girl, Small Town: A Novel*

   McKinty, Adrian. *In the Morning I'll Be Gone: A Detective Sean Duffy Novel*

   O'Rawe, Richard. *Northern Heist*

   Shaw, William. *The Birdwatcher*

   Walsh, S. Kirk. *The Elephant of Belfast: A Novel*

NORTHERN MEXICO

   McCarthy, Cormac. ★*All the Pretty Horses*

NORTHUMBERLAND, ENGLAND

   Cleeves, Ann. *The Crow Trap*

   Cleeves, Ann. *The Darkest Evening*

   Gaynor, Hazel. *The Lighthouse Keeper's Daughter*

NORTHUMBRIA (KINGDOM)

   Cornwell, Bernard. *The Last Kingdom: A Novel*

   Cornwell, Bernard. *Sword of Kings*

NORTHWEST PASSAGE

   Macallister, Greer. ★*The Arctic Fury*

   Simmons, Dan. ★*The Terror: A Novel*

NORTHWEST TERRITORIES

   Hay, Elizabeth. *Late Nights on Air*

NORTHWESTERN STATES

   Stegner, Wallace. ★*The Big Rock Candy Mountain*

NORWAY

   Benn, James R. *Billy Boyle: A World War Two Mystery*

   Hargrave, Kiran Millwood. *The Mercies: A Novel*

   Knausgaard, Karl Ove. *The Morning Star*

   Larsen, Reif. *I Am Radar: A Novel*

   Nesbo, Jo. *The Leopard*

   Nesbo, Jo. *Phantom*

   Nesbo, Jo. *The Redeemer*

   Petterson, Per. *Out Stealing Horses: A Novel*

NORWEGIAN AMERICANS

   Shreve, Anita. *The Weight of Water*

Norwegian pioneers trilogy [Series]. Rølvaag, O. E.

NORWEGIANS IN THE UNITED STATES

   Rølvaag, O. E. ★*Giants in the Earth: A Saga of the Prairie*

   Sundstol, Vidar. *The Land of Dreams*

★*Nos4a2*. Hill, Joe

NOSTALGIA

   Bender, Tony. *The Last Ghost Dancer*

   Murakami, Haruki. ★*First Person Singular: Stories*

Nostromo: a Tale of the Seaboard. Conrad, Joseph

Not a Day Goes By: A Novel. Harris, E. Lynn

Not in the Flesh. Rendell, Ruth

Not Like the Movies. Winfrey, Kerry

Not Quite a Wife. Putney, Mary Jo

Not the Duke's Darling. Hoyt, Elizabeth

Not the Girl You Marry. Christopher, Andie J.

Not the Kind of Earl You Marry. Pembrooke, Kate

Not Without Laughter. Hughes, Langston

★*A Note yet Unsung*. Alexander, Tamera

★*The Notebook*. Sparks, Nicholas

Notes from a Black Woman's Diary: Selected Works of Kathleen Collins. Collins, Kathleen

Notes from the Burning Age. North, Claire

Notes from Underground. Dostoyevsky, Fyodor

Nothing but Blackened Teeth. Khaw, Cassandra

Nothing Gold Can Stay: Stories. Rash, Ron

Nothing More Dangerous: A Novel. Eskens, Allen

Nothing to Lose. Child, Lee

Nothing to See Here. Wilson, Kevin

Nothing Ventured. Archer, Jeffrey

NOTTINGHAM, ENGLAND

   Harvey, John. *Cold in Hand*

   Harvey, John. *Darkness, Darkness*

   Lawrence, D. H. *Sons and Lovers*

NOVA SCOTIA

   Endicott, Marina. *The Voyage of the Morning Light*

   Hill, Lawrence. *Someone Knows My Name: A Novel*

Nova Swing. Harrison, M. John

Nova vita protocol [Series]. Merbeth, K. S.

Novels and Memoirs, 1941-51. Nabokov, Vladimir Vladimirovich

Novels and Other Writings. West, Nathanael

Novels and Stories, 1920-1922. Fitzgerald, F. Scott

NOVELS IN VERSE

   Cisneros, Sandra. ★*The House on Mango Street*

   Crossan, Sarah. *Here Is the Beehive*

   Park, Ishle Yi. *Angel & Hannah: A Novel in Verse*

   Robertson, Robin. *The Long Take: A Noir Narrative*

Novels, 1944-1953. Bellow, Saul

NOVELS-WITHIN-NOVELS

   Atwood, Margaret. ★*The Blind Assassin*

   Auster, Paul. *Oracle Night*

   Bulgakov, Mikhail. ★*The Master and Margarita*

   Chabon, Michael. ★*Wonder Boys*

   Crowley, John. *Lord Byron's Novel: The Evening Land*

   Egan, Jennifer. *The Keep*

   Everett, Percival L. *Erasure: A Novel*

   Foer, Jonathan Safran. *Everything Is Illuminated: A Novel*

   Horowitz, Anthony. ★*Moonflower Murders*

   Livesey, Margot. *Criminals: A Novel*

   Means, David. ★*Hystopia: A Novel*

Novic, Sara
  Girl at War
Novik, Naomi
  A Deadly Education: A Novel
  His Majesty's Dragon
  The Last Graduate: A Novel
  ★*Spinning Silver*
  ★*Uprooted*
Now That You Mention It. Higgins, Kristan
Now You See Me. Bolton, S. J.
Nowhere Near Respectable. Putney, Mary Jo
NUCLEAR ACCIDENTS
  Smith, Martin Cruz. *Wolves Eat Dogs: A Novel*
NUCLEAR HOLOCAUST SURVIVORS
  Butler, Octavia E. *Adulthood Rites*
  Butler, Octavia E. ★*Dawn: Xenogenesis*
NUCLEAR PHYSICISTS
  Ignatius, David. *The Increment: A Novel*
NUCLEAR SUBMARINES
  Clancy, Tom. ★*The Hunt for Red October*
  Cussler, Clive. *Pacific Vortex!*
NUCLEAR TERRORISM
  DeMille, Nelson. *Wild Fire*
NUCLEAR WARFARE
  Varley, John. *Demon*
NUCLEAR WEAPONS
  Campbell, Rick. *Treason*
  Coonts, Stephen. *The Art of War: A Novel*
  Cussler, Clive. *Odessa Sea*
  Ignatius, David. *The Increment: A Novel*
  Kiernan, Stephen P. *Universe of Two*
  Parnell, Sean. *Man of War: An Eric Steele Novel*
  Poyer, David. *Overthrow: The War with China and North
    Korea—Fall of an Empire*
  Ricciardi, David. *Warning Light*
NUCLEAR WEAPONS THEFTS
  Parnell, Sean. *Man of War: An Eric Steele Novel*
Nugent, Benjamin
  Fraternity: Stories
*The **Nugget**: a Novel.* Deutermann, Peter T.
NUMA files [Series]. Cussler, Clive
Numero Zero. Eco, Umberto
Nunez, Sigrid
  ★*The Friend*
  The Last of Her Kind: A Novel
  Salvation City
  What Are You Going Through
NUNS
  Akunin, B. *Sister Pelagia and the White Bulldog: A Mystery*
  Dunant, Sarah. *Sacred Hearts: A Novel*
  Godwin, Gail. *Unfinished Desires*
  Haddam, Jane. *Hardscrabble Road*
  Hansen, Ron. *Mariette in Ecstasy*
  Harrison, Cora. *Beyond Absolution: A Mystery Set in 1920s Ireland*
  Luchette, Claire. *Agatha of Little Neon*
  McDermott, Alice. ★*The Ninth Hour*
  Ólafsson, Ólafur Jóhann. *The Sacrament: A Novel*
  Sharratt, Mary. *Illuminations: A Novel of Hildegard Von Bingen*

NURSES
  Abbott, Megan E. *Bury Me Deep*
  Armstrong, Addison. *The Light of Luna Park*
  Balogh, Mary. *More Than a Mistress*
  Carr, Caleb. *The Angel of Darkness*
  Carr, Robyn. ★*Virgin River*
  Colgan, Jenny. *500 Miles from You*
  Deutermann, Peter T. *Pacific Glory: A Novel*
  Faulkner, William. *Requiem for a Nun*
  Fisher, Tarryn. *The Wives*
  Gabaldon, Diana. ★*Outlander*
  Katsu, Alma. *The Deep*
  McCullough, Colleen. *An Indecent Obsession*
  Perry, Anne. *A Dangerous Mourning*
  Priest, Cherie. *Dreadnought*
  Rinehart, Mary Roberts. *Miss Pinkerton*
  Schwarz, Christina. *Drowning Ruth*
  Vine, Barbara. *The Minotaur: A Novel*
  Wood, Shelley. *The Quintland Sisters*
NURSES — HISTORY
  Hemingway, Ernest. ★*A Farewell to Arms*
NURSING HOME PATIENTS
  Cannon, Joanna. *Three Things About Elsie: A Novel*
NURSING HOMES
  Barr, Nevada. *What Rose Forgot*
  Cooney, Caroline B. *The Grandmother Plot*
NURSING STUDENTS
  Miller, Xander. *Zo: A Novel*
Nussbaum, Susan
  Good Kings, Bad Kings: A Novel
★*Nw: a Novel.* Smith, Zadie

O

O Beautiful: A Novel. Yun, Jung
O Pioneers! Cather, Willa
O'Brian, Patrick
  Master and Commander
O'Brien, Edna
  ★*Girl*
O'Brien, Perry Edmond
  Fire in the Blood
O'Brien, Tim
  Going After Cacciato: A Novel
  ★*The Things They Carried: A Work of Fiction*
O'Connor, Carlene
  Murder in an Irish Bookshop
O'Connor, Flannery
  ★*Collected Works*
  The Complete Stories
  ★*The Violent Bear It Away*
  ★*Wise Blood*
O'Connor, Frank
  Collected Stories
O'Connor, Joseph
  Star of the Sea

O'Dell, Claire
A Study in Honor: A Novel
O'Donnell, Lisa
The Death of Bees: A Novel
O'Donnell, Paraic
The House on Vesper Sands: A Novel
O'Donohue, Clare
The Lover's Knot: A Someday Quilts Mystery
O'Farrell, Maggie
Hamnet
The Hand That First Held Mine: A Novel
This Must Be the Place
The Vanishing Act of Esme Lennox
O'Hara, John
Appointment in Samarra
O'HARA, SCARLETT (FICTITIOUS CHARACTER)
Mitchell, Margaret. ★*Gone with the Wind*
O'Keefe, Megan E.
Velocity Weapon
O'Leary, Beth
The Flatshare: A Novel
The Switch
O'LOUGHLIN, JOSEPH (FICTITIOUS CHARACTER)
Robotham, Michael. ★*Close Your Eyes*
Robotham, Michael. ★*The Other Wife*
O'Mara, Tim
Crooked Numbers
O'Nan, Stewart
Henry, Himself
O'Neill, Heather
★*The Lonely Hearts Hotel: A Novel*
O'Rawe, Richard
Northern Heist
O. Henry: 101 Stories. Henry, O.
O. K. CORRAL, ARIZONA
Russell, Mary Doria. *Epitaph: A Novel of the O.K. Corral*
Oak Bluffs [Series]. Hostin, Sunny
OAKES, BLACKFORD (FICTITIOUS CHARACTER)
Buckley, William F. ★*Mongoose, R.I.P.: A Blackford Oakes Novel*
OAKLAND, CALIFORNIA
Anderson, Kent. *Green Sun: A Novel*
Orange, Tommy. ★*There There*
Oakley, Colleen
The Invisible Husband of Frick Island
You Were There Too
Oates, Joyce Carol
The (Other) You: Stories
Because It Is Bitter, and Because It Is My Heart
Blonde: A Novel
Breathe
The Falls: A Novel
A Garden of Earthly Delights
The Gravedigger's Daughter: A Novel
★*My Life as a Rat*
Night. Sleep. Death. The Stars
Pursuit
★*Them*
★*We Were the Mulvaneys*

OATHS
Cornwell, Bernard. *Sword of Kings*
OBEDIENCE
Diachenko, Serhii. *Vita Nostra*
*The **Obelisk** Gate*. Jemisin, N. K.
Obioma, Chigozie
★*The Fishermen: A Novel*
★*An Orchestra of Minorities*
OBITUARY WRITERS
Hiaasen, Carl. *Basket Case*
Oblivion: Stories. Wallace, David Foster
Obregon, Nicolas
Blue Light Yokohama
Obreht, Tea
Inland: A Novel
The Tiger's Wife: A Novel
OBSCENITY (LAW)
Goldberg, Myla. *Feast Your Eyes*
OBSERVING THINGS
Gainza, Maria. *The Optic Nerve*
*The **Obsession***. Roberts, Nora
OBSESSION
Acampora, Lauren. *The Paper Wasp: A Novel*
Austin, Emily. *Everyone in This Room Will Someday Be Dead*
Bannister, Jo. *Silent Footsteps*
Barker, Susan. ★*The Incarnations: A Novel*
Beattie, Ann. *The Doctor's House: A Novel*
Bell, Darcey. *Something She's Not Telling Us*
Bohjalian, Chris. *The Double Bind: A Novel*
Brown, Karen. *The Clairvoyants: A Novel*
Burton, Jessie. *The Miniaturist*
Burton, Tara Isabella. *Social Creature*
Cameron, Lindsay. *Just One Look*
Cander, Chris. *The Weight of a Piano: A Novel*
Cline, Emma. *The Girls: A Novel*
Cooper, Tom. *The Marauders*
Delaney, J. P. *The Girl Before: A Novel*
Dodd, Christina. *Strangers She Knows*
Ellmann, Lucy. *Ducks, Newburyport*
Enard, Mathias. *Compass*
Faulkner, William. *The Hamlet*
Finn, A. J. ★*The Woman in the Window*
Gainza, Maria. *The Optic Nerve*
Gardiner, Meg. *Unsub: A Novel*
Greenwell, Garth. *What Belongs to You: A Novel*
Hamill, Shaun. *A Cosmology of Monsters*
Hendricks, Greer. *An Anonymous Girl*
Horrocks, Caitlin. *The Vexations*
Imamura, Natsuko. *The Woman in the Purple Skirt: A Novel*
Jewell, Lisa. *Watching You*
King, Stephen. *Finders Keepers*
Leon, Donna. *Falling in Love: A Commissario Guido Brunetti Mystery*
Lovett, Charles C. *The Lost Book of the Grail: Or a Visitor's Guide to Barchester Cathedral*
MacDonald, Andrew. *When We Were Vikings*
Marias, Javier. *The Infatuations*
Mason, Bobbie Ann. *Dear Ann: A Novel*

Miles, Terry. *Rabbits*

Moshfegh, Ottessa. ★*Death in Her Hands: A Novel*

Moshfegh, Ottessa. *Eileen*

Pinborough, Sarah. ★*Cross Her Heart: A Novel*

Quick, Amanda. *Otherwise Engaged*

Rendell, Ruth. *Collected Stories*

Russo, Richard. ★*Everybody's Fool*

Shan, Sa. *The Girl Who Played Go*

Spencer, Scott. ★*Endless Love*

Spencer, Scott. *An Ocean Without a Shore*

Swamy, Shruti. *A House Is a Body: Stories*

Tallo, Katie. *Dark August*

Tartt, Donna. ★*The Goldfinch*

Weinberg, Kate. *The Truants*

West, Kathleen. *Minor Dramas & Other Catastrophes*

Winfrey, Kerry. *Waiting for Tom Hanks: A Novel*

Obsession Falls. Dodd, Christina

OBSESSION IN MEN

Atilgan, Yusuf. *Motherland Hotel*

Auster, Paul. ★*Leviathan*

Gowdy, Barbara. *Helpless: A Novel*

Hansen, Ron. ★*The Assassination of Jesse James by the Coward Robert Ford*

Hart, Josephine. *Damage: A Novel*

Mann, Thomas. *Death in Venice and Seven Other Stories*

Melville, Herman. ★*Moby-Dick; Or, the Whale*

Millhauser, Steven. *Martin Dressler: The Tale of an American Dreamer*

Murdoch, Iris. *The Sea, the Sea*

Nabokov, Vladimir Vladimirovich. ★*Lolita*

Nabokov, Vladimir Vladimirovich. *Pale Fire*

Pynchon, Thomas. *Vineland*

Rendell, Ruth. ★*The Bridesmaid*

Rendell, Ruth. *Live Flesh*

Ruiz Zafon, Carlos. *The Angel's Game*

Ruiz Zafon, Carlos. ★*The Shadow of the Wind*

Saramago, Jose. *All the Names*

OBSESSION IN WOMEN

Cain, Chelsea. *One Kick: A Novel*

King, Stephen. ★*Misery*

Messud, Claire. ★*The Woman Upstairs: A Novel*

Rindell, Suzanne. *The Other Typist*

Styles, Toy. *Redbone*

OBSESSIVE-COMPULSIVE DISORDER

Scottoline, Lisa. ★*Every Fifteen Minutes*

The Obsidian Chamber. Preston, Douglas J.

OBSTETRICIANS

Irving, John. ★*The Cider House Rules: A Novel*

OCCULT CENTERS, GROUPS, ETC

Portis, Charles. ★*Masters of Atlantis: A Novel*

OCCULTISM

Bardugo, Leigh. ★*Ninth House*

Campbell, Ramsey. *The Wise Friend*

Fowler, Christopher. *Bryant & May: Oranges and Lemons*

Fowler, Christopher. *Bryant & May: Strange Tide*

Huchu, Tendai. *The Library of the Dead*

OCCUPATIONS

Wallace, David Foster. ★*The Pale King: An Unfinished Novel*

Occupied City. Peace, David

★*The Ocean* at the End of the Lane. Gaiman, Neil

OCEAN BOTTLES

Adler-Olsen, Jussi. *A Conspiracy of Faith*

OCEAN CURRENTS

Bunn, T. Davis. *Outbreak*

OCEAN LINERS

Katsu, Alma. *The Deep*

Porter, Katherine Anne. *Ship of Fools*

OCEAN TRAVEL

Cussler, Clive. *Typhoon Fury*

DeMille, Nelson. ★*The Cuban Affair: A Novel*

Doyle, Brian. *The Plover: A Novel*

Endicott, Marina. *The Voyage of the Morning Light*

Gabaldon, Diana. *An Echo in the Bone*

Grant, Mira. *Into the Drowning Deep*

Holdstock, Pauline. *Here I Am!*

Katsu, Alma. *The Deep*

Laukkanen, Owen. *Gale Force*

Lunde, Maja. *The End of the Ocean: A Novel*

McConaghy, Charlotte. *Migrations*

O'Connor, Joseph. *Star of the Sea*

Porter, Katherine Anne. *Ship of Fools*

Turton, Stuart. ★*The Devil and the Dark Water*

Woolf, Virginia. *The Voyage Out*

OCEAN TRAVEL — HISTORY

Birch, Carol. *Jamrach's Menagerie*

Golding, William. *Close Quarters*

Golding, William. *Fire Down Below*

Golding, William. *Rites of Passage*

An Ocean Without a Shore. Spencer, Scott

OCEANIA

Michener, James A. ★*Tales of the South Pacific*

Smith, Dominic. *Bright and Distant Shores*

Vargas Llosa, Mario. ★*The Way to Paradise*

OCEANS

Lem, Stanislaw. ★*Solaris*

Ogden, Aimee. *Sun-Daughters, Sea-Daughters*

Preston, Douglas J. *Crooked River*

October Daye novels [Series]. McGuire, Seanan

The October List. Deaver, Jeffery

OCTOGENARIANS

Cronin, Marianne. *The One Hundred Years of Lenni and Margot*

Fowler, Christopher. *Bryant & May: Oranges and Lemons*

Fowler, Christopher. *Bryant & May: The Lonely Hour*

Hardiman, Rebecca. *Good Eggs*

Hooper, Emma. *Etta and Otto and Russell and James: A Novel*

Lyons, Annie. *The Brilliant Life of Eudora Honeysett*

Rooney, Kathleen. ★*Lillian Boxfish Takes a Walk*

Turow, Scott. *The Last Trial*

Tursten, Helene. *An Elderly Lady Must Not Be Crossed*

Wilder, Thornton. ★*Theophilus North*

ODESA, UKRAINE

Adams, Alina. *The Nesting Dolls*

Odessa Sea. Cussler, Clive

Odessa, Odessa. Artson, Barbara

Oe, Kenzaburo

The Changeling

★*Death by Water*
Nip the Buds, Shoot the Kids
★*A Quiet Life*
Somersault: A Novel
Of Fire and Lions: A Novel. Andrews, Mesu
★*Of* Human Bondage. Maugham, W. Somerset
Of Love and Shadows. Allende, Isabel
★*Of* Mice and Men. Steinbeck, John
★*Of* Time and the River: A Legend of Man's Hunger in His Youth. Wolfe, Thomas
Of Women and Salt. Garcia, Gabriela
★An **Offer** from a Gentleman. Quinn, Julia
★The **Office** of Historical Corrections: A Novella and Stories. Evans, Danielle

OFFICE POLITICS
Goldin, Megan. *The Escape Room*
Harris, Zakiya Dalila. *The Other Black Girl: A Novel*

OFFICE WORKERS
Pulley, Natasha. *The Watchmaker of Filigree Street*
Saramago, Jose. *All the Names*
Walschots, Natalie Zina. *Hench: A Novel*

An **Officer** and a Spy. Harris, Robert

Offill, Jenny
Dept. Of Speculation
★*Weather*

OFFSHORE OIL
Cussler, Clive. ★*Sea of Greed: A Novel from the Numa Files*

Offutt, Chris
Country Dark
★*The Killing Hills*

Ogawa, Yoko
The Housekeeper and the Professor
★*The Memory Police: A Novel*

Ogden, Aimee
Sun-Daughters, Sea-Daughters

★*Oh* William! Strout, Elizabeth

Ohio. Markley, Stephen

OHIO
Baldacci, David. *One Summer*
Baldacci, David. *Redemption*
Berg, Gretchen. *The Operator*
Bialosky, Jill. *House Under Snow*
Black, Lisa. *Let Justice Descend*
Black, Lisa. *Suffer the Children*
Bloom, Amy. *Lucky Us: A Novel*
Brown, Eleanor. *The Weird Sisters*
Castillo, Linda. ★*Fallen*
Castillo, Linda. *Outsider*
Chevalier, Tracy. *The Last Runaway*
Cole, Alyssa. ★*An Unconditional Freedom*
Cramer, W. Dale. *Levi's Will: A Novel*
Ellmann, Lucy. *Ducks, Newburyport*
ffitch, Madeline. *Stay and Fight*
Lepionka, Kristen. *The Last Place You Look*
Lepionka, Kristen. *Once You Go This Far: A Mystery*
Markley, Stephen. *Ohio*
Monroe, Mary. ★*God Don't Like Ugly*
Monroe, Mary. *God Still Don't Like Ugly*

Montgomery, Jess. *The Stills*
Montgomery, Jess. *The Widows*
Morrison, Toni. ★*Beloved: A Novel*
Morrison, Toni. ★*The Bluest Eye: A Novel*
Morrison, Toni. *Sula*
Ng, Celeste. ★*Everything I Never Told You: A Novel*
Ng, Celeste. ★*Little Fires Everywhere: A Novel*
Pollock, Donald Ray. *The Devil All the Time*
Pollock, Donald Ray. *Knockemstiff*
Roslund, Anders. *Cell 8*
Roth, Philip. *Indignation*
Rouda, Kaira Sturdivant. *Best Day Ever: A Novel*
Satyal, Rakesh. *No One Can Pronounce My Name: A Novel*
Schultz, Connie. *The Daughters of Erietown*
Smith, Scott. *A Simple Plan: A Novel*
Walker, Nico. ★*Cherry: A Novel*
Winfrey, Kerry. *Not Like the Movies*
Winfrey, Kerry. *Waiting for Tom Hanks: A Novel*
Yocum, Robin. *A Welcome Murder*

Ohlsson, Kristina
Unwanted: A Novel

OIL
Patterson, Richard North. *Eclipse*

OIL EXECUTIVES
Stout, Dan. ★*Titanshade*

OIL INDUSTRY AND TRADE
Burke, James Lee. *Black Cherry Blues*
Burke, James Lee. *Wayfaring Stranger: A Novel*
Cussler, Clive. ★*Sea of Greed: A Novel from the Numa Files*
Fuentes, Carlos. *The Eagle's Throne: A Novel*
Furst, Alan. *Blood of Victory: A Novel*
Mbue, Imbolo. *How Beautiful We Were*
Quartey, Kwei. *Murder at Cape Three Points*
Wetmore, Elizabeth. ★*Valentine*
Yun, Jung. *O Beautiful: A Novel*

OIL INDUSTRY AND TRADE — CORRUPT PRACTICES
Aguilar Camin, Hector. *Death in Veracruz*

OIL WELL DRILLING
Stabenow, Dana. ★*A Fine and Bitter Snow: A Kate Shugak Novel*

OIL WELLS
Cussler, Clive. ★*Golden Buddha*

OJIBWA INDIANS
Erdrich, Louise. *Four Souls: A Novel*
Erdrich, Louise. *Future Home of the Living God*
Erdrich, Louise. *The Last Report on the Miracles at Little No Horse*
Erdrich, Louise. ★*The Night Watchman: A Novel*
Erdrich, Louise. ★*The Round House: A Novel*
Erdrich, Louise. ★*The Sentence*
Krueger, William Kent. ★*Lightning Strike*
Staples, Dennis E. *This Town Sleeps*

OJIBWA INDIANS — ANTIQUITIES
Erdrich, Louise. *The Painted Drum: A Novel*

Ok, Mr. Field: A Novel. Kilalea, Katharine

OKINAWA
Bird, Sarah. *The Yokota Officers Club: A Novel*

OKLAHOMA
Belle, Kimberly. *Dear Wife*
DeCarlo, Melissa. *The Art of Crash Landing: A Novel*

Geni, Abby. *The Wildlands: A Novel*
Hart, Carolyn G. *Ghost Blows a Kiss*
Hart, Carolyn G. *Letter from Home*
Hobson, Brandon. ★*The Removed: A Novel*
Leonard, Elmore. *The Hot Kid*
Meadows, Rae. *I Will Send Rain: A Novel*
Momaday, N. Scott. *The Ancient Child: A Novel*
Morrison, Toni. *Paradise*

OKLAHOMA CITY, OKLAHOMA
Harrigan, Stephen. *The Leopard Is Loose: A Novel*

Okorafor, Nnedi
★*Binti*
Binti: Home
Binti: The Night Masquerade
★*Noor*
★*Remote Control*
★*Who Fears Death*

Okparanta, Chinelo
★*Under the Udala Trees*

Okri, Ben
Prayer for the Living

Okuizumi, Hikaru
The Stones Cry Out

Ólafsdóttir, Auður A.
Butterflies in November

Ólafsson, Ólafur Jóhann
The Sacrament: A Novel

OLD AGE HOMES
Leon, Donna. *Drawing Conclusions: A Commissario Guido Brunetti Mystery*

OLD AND NEW THINGS
Bradbury, Ray. ★*Dandelion Wine: A Novel*

Old Bones. Harrod-Eagles, Cynthia
Old Bones. Preston, Douglas J.
The Old Curiosity Shop. Dickens, Charles
★*The Old Drift*. Serpell, Namwali
The Old Enemy. Porter, Henry
Old Filth. Gardam, Jane
Old Filth trilogy [Series]. Gardam, Jane
Old Flame: A Jackson Steeg Novel. Berkowitz, Ira
★*The Old Gringo*. Fuentes, Carlos
Old Lovegood Girls. Godwin, Gail
The Old Man. Perry, Thomas
★*The Old Man and the Sea*. Hemingway, Ernest
The Old Man in the Corner. Orczy, Emmuska Orczy
★*Old Man's War*. Scalzi, John
Old Man's War universe [Series]. Scalzi, John
Old School: A Novel. Wolff, Tobias
Old West series [Series]. Jenkins, Beverly
Oldest Living Confederate Widow Tells All. Gurganus, Allan
Oleander Girl: A Novel. Divakaruni, Chitra Banerjee
Olga. Schlink, Bernhard
Oligarchy. Thomas, Scarlett
Olive Bright, Pigeoneer. Graves, Stephanie
Olive Kitteridge. Strout, Elizabeth
Olive novels [Series]. Strout, Elizabeth
★*Olive, Again: A Novel*. Strout, Elizabeth
Oliver Loving: A Novel. Block, Stefan Merrill

Oliver Twist, or the Parish Boy's Progress. Dickens, Charles
Oliveras, Priscilla
Anchored Hearts
OLMECS — RELIGION
Bowles, David. *Feathered Serpent, Dark Heart of Sky: Myths of Mexico*
Olmstead, Robert
★*Coal Black Horse*
Olson, Neil
Before the Devil Fell
OLYMPIC GAMES
Cleave, Chris. *Gold*
Olympus Texas. Swann, Stacey
OMAN
Alharthi, Jokha. *Celestial Bodies: A Novel*
Omar Yussef mysteries [Series]. Rees, Matt
On Agate Hill: A Novel. Smith, Lee
On Beauty. Smith, Zadie
★*On Chesil Beach*. McEwan, Ian
On Division. Goldbloom, Goldie
★*On Earth We're Briefly Gorgeous: A Novel*. Vuong, Ocean
★*On Fragile Waves*. Yu, E. Lily
On Green Dolphin Street: A Novel. Faulks, Sebastian
On Harrow Hill. Verdon, John
On Her Majesty's Secret Service. Fleming, Ian
★*On Such a Full Sea*. Lee, Chang-Rae
On Swift Horses. Pufahl, Shannon
On the Bright Side: The New Secret Diary of Hendrik Groen, 85 Years Old. Groen, Hendrik
★*On the Road*. Kerouac, Jack
Once a Scoundrel. Putney, Mary Jo
Once a Soldier. Putney, Mary Jo
★*The Once and Future King*. White, T. H.
Once and future king [Series]. White, T. H.
Once There Were Wolves: A Novel. McConaghy, Charlotte
Once Too Often: An Inspector Luke Thanet Novel. Simpson, Dorothy
Once Upon a Prince. Hauck, Rachel
Once Upon a River. Campbell, Bonnie Jo
★*Once Upon a River*. Setterfield, Diane
Once You Go This Far: A Mystery. Lepionka, Kristen
Ondaatje, Michael
★*Warlight*
★*One by One*. Ware, Ruth
One Day in the Life of Ivan Denisovich. Solzhenitsyn, Aleksandr Isaevich
One Fatal Flaw: A Daniel Pitt Novel. Perry, Anne
One Fine Day the Rabbi Bought a Cross. Kemelman, Harry
One Fine Duke. Bell, Lenora
★*One Flew Over the Cuckoo's Nest*. Kesey, Ken
One for Sorrow. Barzak, Christopher
One for the Money. Evanovich, Janet
One for the Rogue. Collins, Manda
★*The One for You*. Loren, Roni
★*One Good Deed*. Baldacci, David
One Good Turn: A Novel. Atkinson, Kate
The One Hundred Years of Lenni and Margot. Cronin, Marianne
★*One Hundred Years of Solitude*. Garcia Marquez, Gabriel
The One Inside. Shepard, Sam

One Kick: A Novel. Cain, Chelsea

One Last Lie. Doiron, Paul

★*One Last Stop.* McQuiston, Casey

The One Man. Gross, Andrew

One More River to Cross. Kirkpatrick, Jane

One Perfect Lie. Scottoline, Lisa

One Shot. Child, Lee

★*One Step Behind.* Mankell, Henning

One Summer. Baldacci, David

One Summer Night. Pineiro, Caridad

★*One Thousand and One Nights: A Sparkling Retelling of the Beloved Classic.* Shaykh, Hanan

One Two Three: A Novel. Frankel, Laurie

One Virgin Too Many. Davis, Lindsey

One Warm Winter. Pope, Jamie

The One You Can't Forget. Loren, Roni

The One You Fight For. Loren, Roni

ONE-NIGHT STANDS (INTERPERSONAL RELATIONS)

Balogh, Mary. ★*Someone to Cherish*

Finder, Joseph. ★*Judgment*

Gaitskill, Mary. *Don't Cry: Stories*

Guillory, Jasmine. *The Wedding Party*

Quincy, Diana. *Her Night with the Duke*

Thomas, Russ. ★*Firewatching*

Van Dyken, Rachel. *Risky Play*

Weatherspoon, Rebekah. *If the Boot Fits*

Ones who got away [Series]. Loren, Roni

ONLINE DATING

Fielding, Joy. *All the Wrong Places: A Novel*

Frankel, Laurie. *Goodbye for Now: A Novel*

Majors, Inman. *Penelope Lemon: Game On!*

Rai, Alisha. ★*The Right Swipe*

Steiner, Susie. *Missing, Presumed: A Novel*

ONLINE IDENTITY THEFT

Ferris, Joshua. *To Rise Again at a Decent Hour: A Novel*

ONLINE ROMANCE

Block, Lawrence. *All the Flowers Are Dying*

ONLINE SHOPPING

Hart, Rob. *The Warehouse: A Novel*

The Only Child. Seo, Mi-Ae

Only Enchanting. Balogh, Mary

★*The Only Good Indians: A Novel.* Jones, Stephen Graham

Only Killers and Thieves: A Novel. Howarth, Paul

Only Revolutions. Danielewski, Mark Z.

The Only Story. Barnes, Julian

Only to Sleep: A Philip Marlowe Novel. Osborne, Lawrence

The Only Woman in the Room. Benedict, Marie

★*Only Yesterday.* Agnon, Shmuel Yosef

Ono, Masatsugu

Echo on the Bay

ONTARIO

Chariandy, David John. *Brother: A Novel*

Lawson, Mary. *Crow Lake*

Munro, Alice. *Family Furnishings: Selected Stories, 1995-2014*

Rice, Waubgeshig. *Moon of the Crusted Snow: A Novel*

Shields, Carol. *Unless*

Wood, Shelley. *The Quintland Sisters*

Onuzo, Chibundu

Sankofa: A Novel

Onyebuchi, Tochi

★*Riot Baby*

Oona Out of Order. Montimore, Margarita

★*Open City: A Novel.* Cole, Teju

OPEN MARRIAGE

Leilani, Raven. ★*Luster*

★*Open Season.* Box, C. J.

Open Secrets: Stories. Munro, Alice

Open Your Eyes. Daly, Paula

OPERA SINGERS

Leon, Donna. *Falling in Love: A Commissario Guido Brunetti Mystery*

OPERAS

Chee, Alexander. *The Queen of the Night*

See, Lisa. *Peony in Love: A Novel*

The Operator. Berg, Gretchen

OPIOID EPIDEMIC

Finder, Joseph. ★*House on Fire: A Novel*

Moore, Liz. *Long Bright River*

★*Opioid, Indiana.* Carr, Brian Allen

OPIUM ADDICTION

Kuang, R. F. ★*The Dragon Republic*

Mukherjee, Abir. *Death in the East*

Nesbo, Jo. *The Leopard*

Robertson, Imogen. *The Paris Winter*

OPIUM INDUSTRY AND TRADE

Ghosh, Amitav. *Flood of Fire*

Ghosh, Amitav. *River of Smoke*

Ghosh, Amitav. *Sea of Poppies*

The Opium Prince. Aimaq, Jasmine

OPIUM SMUGGLING

Abdul-Jabbar, Kareem. *Mycroft and Sherlock*

OPPENHEIMER, J. ROBERT

Smith, Martin Cruz. *Stallion Gate*

The Opposite House. Oyeyemi, Helen

The Opposite of Fate. McGhee, Alison

OPPRESSION (PSYCHOLOGY)

Harris, C. S. *Good Time Coming*

The Optic Nerve. Gainza, Maria

OPTIMISM

Voltaire. *Candide and Other Stories*

The Optimist's Daughter. Welty, Eudora

OPTIONS, ALTERNATIVES, CHOICES

Adiga, Aravind. ★*Amnesty*

Atkinson, Kate. ★*Life After Life: A Novel*

Clark, Wahida. *Blood, Sweat and Payback*

Clark, Wahida. *Payback Ain't Enough*

Clark, Wahida. *Payback with Ya Life*

Cline, Emma. *Daddy: Stories*

Cossette, Connilyn. ★*Shelter of the Most High*

Danielewski, Mark Z. ★*The Familiar.; Volume 4,*

Davies, Peter Ho. *A Lie Someone Told You About Yourself*

Ekwuyasi, Francesca. *Butter Honey Pig Bread: A Novel*

Eliasberg, Jan. ★*Hannah's War*

Finder, Joseph. *Suspicion*

Force, Marie. *Five Years Gone*

Foster, Brooke Lea. *Summer Darlings*
Fridlund, Emily. ★*History of Wolves: A Novel*
Gabaldon, Diana. ★*A Breath of Snow and Ashes*
Greeley, Molly. *The Clergyman's Wife*
Griffin, Anne. *When All Is Said: A Novel*
Haig, Matt. *The Midnight Library*
Harrison, M. John. *Light*
Hempel, Amy. *Sing to It: New Stories*
Itami, Emily. *Fault Lines: A Novel*
Janowitz, Brenda. *The Grace Kelly Dress*
Kawaguchi, Toshikazu. *Before the Coffee Gets Cold*
London, Stefanie. *The Aussie Next Door*
Mackintosh, Anneliese. *Bright and Dangerous Objects*
Mackintosh, Clare. *After the End*
Manning, Max. *The Victim: A Novel*
Mason, Bobbie Ann. *Dear Ann: A Novel*
McGhee, Alison. *The Opposite of Fate*
McPherson, Catriona. *Strangers at the Gate*
Miller, Holly. ★*The Sight of You*
Miller, Mary. *Biloxi: A Novel*
Oates, Joyce Carol. *The (Other) You: Stories*
Picoult, Jodi. ★*The Book of Two Ways*
Pilcher, Rosamunde. *A Place Like Home: Short Stories*
Prose, Francine. ★*The Vixen*
Sainz Borgo, Karina. ★*It Would Be Night in Caracas*
Schulman, Helen. *Come with Me*
Shriver, Lionel. *Should We Stay or Should We Go*
Steadman, Catherine. *Something in the Water*
Or What You Will. Walton, Jo
★*The Oracle*. Cussler, Clive
Oracle Night. Auster, Paul
ORACLES
   Vinge, Joan D. *The Snow Queen*
ORAL HISTORIANS
   Brooks, Max. ★*World War Z: An Oral History of the Zombie War*
ORAL HISTORIES
   Hajdu, David. *Adrianne Geffel: A Fiction*
   Smith, Lee. *Oral History*
Oral History. Smith, Lee
ORANGE COUNTY, CALIFORNIA
   Rouda, Kaira Sturdivant. *The Favorite Daughter*
Orange World and Other Stories. Russell, Karen
Orange, Tommy
   ★*There There*
The Orchard of Lost Souls: A Novel. Mohamed, Nadifa
The Orchardist. Coplin, Amanda
ORCHARDS
   Coplin, Amanda. *The Orchardist*
   Ghaffari, Rabeah. ★*To Keep the Sun Alive*
   Johnson, Caleb. *Treeborne*
★*An Orchestra of Minorities*. Obioma, Chigozie
ORCHESTRAS
   Alexander, Tamera. ★*A Note yet Unsung*
Orchid and the Wasp. Hughes, Caoilinn
Orchid Beach. Woods, Stuart
ORCS
   French, Jonathan. *The Free Bastards*
   French, Jonathan. ★*The Grey Bastards*

French, Jonathan. *The True Bastards*
Orczy, Emmuska Orczy
   The Old Man in the Corner
   ★*The Scarlet Pimpernel*
Ordinary Hazards: A Novel. Bruno, Anna
Ordinary People: A Novel. Evans, Diana
OREGON
   Ahlborn, Ania. *The Devil Crept In*
   Bender, Aimee. *The Butterfly Lampshade*
   Buchman, M. L. *Pure Heat*
   Cantero, Edgar. *Meddling Kids: A Novel*
   Carr, Robyn. ★*The Wanderer*
   Diehl, Heidi. *Lifelines*
   Doyle, Brian. *The Plover: A Novel*
   Garvin, Eileen. *The Music of Bees*
   Keesey, Anna. *Little Century: A Novel*
   Kesey, Ken. ★*One Flew Over the Cuckoo's Nest*
   Kesey, Ken. *Sometimes a Great Notion: A Novel*
   Le Guin, Ursula K. *The Lathe of Heaven*
   Stirling, S. M. *Dies the Fire*
   Stirling, S. M. *A Meeting at Corvallis*
   Stirling, S. M. *The Protector's War*
Oregon files [Series]. Cussler, Clive
OREGON TRAIL
   Guthrie, A. B. ★*The Big Sky*
Orenstein, Hannah
   Love at First Like
Orfeo: a Novel. Powers, Richard
ORGAN AND TISSUE THEFTS
   Soyinka, Wole. *Chronicles from the Land of the Happiest People on Earth*
ORGAN DONORS
   Ishiguro, Kazuo. ★*Never Let Me Go*
   Kerangal, Maylis de. *The Heart: A Novel*
ORGANIZED CRIME
   Abbott, Megan E. *Queenpin: A Novel*
   Ames, Jonathan. *A Man Named Doll*
   Ashley & JaQuavis. *The Cartel*
   Atkins, Ace. *The Redeemers*
   Atkins, Ace. *The Revelators*
   Atkins, Ace. *The Shameless*
   Atkins, Ace. *Wicked City*
   Blake, James Carlos. *The House of Wolfe*
   Bourne, Joanna. ★*My Lord and Spymaster*
   Boyle, William. *City of Margins: A Novel*
   Burke, James Lee. ★*A Private Cathedral*
   Capote, Truman. ★*Breakfast at Tiffany's*
   Child, Lee. *Personal*
   Christie, Agatha. *The Pale Horse*
   Davis, Lindsey. *A Comedy of Terrors: A Flavia Albia Novel*
   Davys, Tim. *Amberville*
   De la Motte, Anders. *Ultimatum: A Thriller*
   Doctorow, E. L. ★*Billy Bathgate: A Novel*
   Ellroy, James. *Blood's a Rover*
   Estleman, Loren D. ★*Indigo: A Valentino Mystery*
   Feehan, Christine. *Shadow Rider*
   Gross, Andrew. *Button Man*
   Hamilton, Steve. *The Second Life of Nick Mason: A Novel*

Hart, John. *Iron House*
Harvey, Michael T. *Brighton*
Horowitz, Anthony. *The House of Silk: A Sherlock Holmes Novel*
K'wan. *Hoodlum*
Kent, Kathleen. *The Burn*
Kent, Kathleen. *The Pledge*
Lagercrantz, David. *The Girl Who Lived Twice: A Lisbeth Salander Novel*
Lagercrantz, David. *The Girl Who Takes an Eye for an Eye*
Laukkanen, Owen. *Gale Force*
Lee, Fonda. ★*Jade City*
Lehane, Dennis. *World Gone By: A Novel*
Mosley, Walter. *Devil in a Blue Dress*
O'Neill, Heather. ★*The Lonely Hearts Hotel: A Novel*
Panowich, Brian. *Like Lions*
Parker, Robert B. *Night Passage*
Parks, Brad. *The Player: A Mystery*
Pelecanos, George P. *The Cut: A Novel*
Puzo, Mario. ★*The Godfather*
Puzo, Mario. *The Sicilian: A Novel*
Rabe, Peter. ★*Anatomy of a Killer ;: A Shroud for Jesso*
Ramqvist, Karolina. *The White City*
Rankin, Ian. *The Hanging Garden: An Inspector Rebus Novel*
Rankin, Ian. *The Naming of the Dead: An Inspector Rebus Novel*
Rankin, Ian. ★*Rather Be the Devil*
Rosen, Renee. *Dollface: A Novel of the Roaring Twenties*
Sharpe, Tess. *Barbed Wire Heart*
Siger, Jeffrey. *Target Tinos: An Inspector Kaldis Mystery*
Sigurðardóttir, Lilja. *Cage*
Smith, Martin Cruz. ★*Tatiana: An Arkady Renko Novel*
Soderberg, Alexander. *The Other Son: A Sophie Brinkmann Novel*
Spillane, Mickey. *Kill Me, Darling*
Stewart, Amy. ★*Girl Waits with Gun*
Swinson, Kiki. *A Gangster and a Gentleman*
Weir, Andy. *Artemis*
Westlake, Donald E. *Get Real*
Winslow, Don. *The Border*
Winspear, Jacqueline. *The American Agent*

ORGANIZED CRIME AND GAMBLING

Pronzini, Bill. *Fever*
*The **Origin** of the Brunists: A Novel*. Coover, Robert
***Origin**: a Novel*. Abu-Jaber, Diana
***Original** Sin*. James, P. D.
***Orlando**: a Biography*. Woolf, Virginia

ORNITHOLOGISTS

Drayson, Nicholas. *A Guide to the Birds of East Africa*
*The **Orphan** Collector*. Wiseman, Ellen Marie

ORPHANAGES

Abdul-Jabbar, Kareem. *Mycroft and Sherlock*
Balogh, Mary. *Someone to Hold*
Irving, John. ★*The Cider House Rules: A Novel*
Jayatissa, Amanda. ★*My Sweet Girl*
Klune, TJ. *The House in the Cerulean Sea*
Obreht, Tea. *The Tiger's Wife: A Novel*
Turansky, Carrie. *No Ocean Too Wide: A Novel*

ORPHANS

Afshar, Tessa. *Jewel of the Nile*
Allain, Suzanne. *Miss Lattimore's Letter*

Andrews, Mesu. *Isaiah's Daughter: A Novel of Prophets and Kings*
Balogh, Mary. ★*Someone to Love*
Barry, Sebastian. ★*A Thousand Moons: A Novel*
Bartlett, Neil. *The Disappearance Boy*
Berne, Lisa. *You May Kiss the Bride*
Blake, Audrey. *The Girl in His Shadow: A Novel*
Bronte, Charlotte. ★*Jane Eyre*
Callender, Kacen. *Queen of the Conquered*
Carey, Edward. *Little: A Novel*
Chen, Da. *Brothers: A Novel*
Childress, Mark. *Crazy in Alabama*
Clark, Cherae. ★*The Unbroken*
Conner, M. Shelly. *Everyman*
Corthron, Kia. *Moon and the Mars*
Crummey, Michael. *The Innocents*
Dickens, Charles. ★*Bleak House*
Dickens, Charles. ★*David Copperfield*
Dickens, Charles. ★*Great Expectations*
Dickens, Charles. ★*Nicholas Nickleby*
Dickens, Charles. *Oliver Twist, or the Parish Boy's Progress*
Everett, Percival L. *I Am Not Sidney Poitier*
Faye, Lyndsay. *Jane Steele*
Fisher, Helen. *Space Hopper*
Francis, Patry. *The Orphans of Race Point: A Novel*
Frazier, Charles. *Nightwoods: A Novel*
Fuentes, Carlos. *Destiny and Desire: A Novel*
Geni, Abby. *The Wildlands: A Novel*
Gnuse, A. J. *Girl in the Walls: A Novel*
Hamill, Pete. *Forever*
Hawkins, Scott. ★*The Library at Mount Char*
Hunt, Laird. *Zorrie*
Irving, John. ★*The Cider House Rules: A Novel*
Ishiguro, Kazuo. *When We Were Orphans*
James, Henry. ★*The Turn of the Screw*
Jewell, Lisa. *The Family Upstairs*
Jiles, Paulette. *News of the World: A Novel*
Keesey, Anna. *Little Century: A Novel*
Krueger, William Kent. *This Tender Land: A Novel*
Kuang, R. F. *The Poppy War*
Lansdale, Joe R. *The Thicket*
Larison, John. *Whiskey When We're Dry*
Lawson, Mary. *Crow Lake*
Lee, Chang-Rae. ★*The Surrendered*
Lethem, Jonathan. ★*Motherless Brooklyn*
Maugham, W. Somerset. ★*Of Human Bondage*
McEwan, Ian. *Black Dogs*
Miller, Derek B. *How to Find Your Way in the Dark*
Moshfegh, Ottessa. *My Year of Rest and Relaxation*
Nunez, Sigrid. *Salvation City*
O'Donnell, Lisa. *The Death of Bees: A Novel*
Priest, Cherie. *The Inexplicables*
Radcliffe, Ann Ward. ★*The Mysteries of Udolpho*
Raybourn, Deanna. *A Curious Beginning: A Veronica Speedwell Mystery*
Roy, Anuradha. *An Atlas of Impossible Longing*
Sapphire. ★*The Kid: A Novel*
Sebald, Winfried Georg. ★*Austerlitz*
Sinha, Indra. *Animal's People*

Smith, Dominic. *Bright and Distant Shores*
Smith, Lee. *On Agate Hill: A Novel*
Tsukiyama, Gail. *The Street of a Thousand Blossoms*
Vlautin, Willy. *Don't Skip Out on Me*
Wells, Benedict. *The End of Loneliness: A Novel*
Welty, Eudora. ★*Delta Wedding*
Wiesel, Elie. *A Mad Desire to Dance: A Novel*
Yoon, Paul. ★*Run Me to Earth: A Novel*
Young, Heather. *The Distant Dead*
The **Orphans** of Race Point: A Novel. Francis, Patry
Orringer, Julie
   ★*The Flight Portfolio: A Novel*
   ★*The Invisible Bridge: A Novel*
Orsinian Tales. Le Guin, Ursula K.
ORTHODOX JEWS
   Henkin, Joshua. *Morningside Heights*
Orwell, George
   ★*1984: A Novel*
   ★*Animal Farm*
★***Oryx*** *and Crake*. Atwood, Margaret
OSAKA, JAPAN
   Washington, Bryan. ★*Memorial*
Osborne, Lawrence
   The Glass Kingdom: A Novel
   Only to Sleep: A Philip Marlowe Novel
OSGOOD, JAMES R.
   Pearl, Matthew. *The Last Dickens: A Novel*
OSLO, NORWAY
   Nesbo, Jo. *The Leopard*
   Nesbo, Jo. *Phantom*
   Nesbo, Jo. *The Redeemer*
Osman, Richard
   The Man Who Died Twice: A Thursday Murder Club Mystery
   ★*The Thursday Murder Club*
Osondu, E. C.
   This House Is Not for Sale: A Novel
   Voice of America: Stories
OSTRACISM
   Hibbert, Talia. *A Girl Like Her*
OSTRICHES
   Davila, April. *142 Ostriches*
OSWALD, LEE HARVEY
   DeLillo, Don. *Libra*
OTASH, FRED
   Ellroy, James. ★*Widespread Panic: A Novel*
The **Other**. Guterson, David
The **Other** Americans: A Novel. Lalami, Laila
The **Other** Black Girl: A Novel. Harris, Zakiya Dalila
The **Other** Boleyn Girl: A Novel. Gregory, Philippa
The **Other** Lady Vanishes. Quick, Amanda
★The **Other** Mrs.. Kubica, Mary
The **Other** People. Tudor, C. J.
Other People's Children. Trollope, Joanna
Other People's Children: A Novel. Hoffmann, R. J.
Other People's Pets. Maizes, R. L.
The **Other** Son: A Sophie Brinkmann Novel. Soderberg, Alexander
The **Other** Typist. Rindell, Suzanne
★The **Other** Wife. Robotham, Michael

The **Other** Wind. Le Guin, Ursula K.
The **Other** Woman. Jones, Sandie
The **Other** Woman. Silva, Daniel
Otherwise Engaged. Palmer, Lindsey J.
Otherwise Engaged. Quick, Amanda
Otsuka, Julie
   The Buddha in the Attic
   When the Emperor Was Divine: A Novel
OTTAWA, ONTARIO
   Cumyn, Alan. *Losing It*
   Shields, Carol. ★*The Stone Diaries*
   Tallo, Katie. *Dark August*
★***Our*** *American Friend*. Pitoniak, Anna
Our *Endless Numbered Days: A Novel*. Fuller, Claire
Our *House*. Candlish, Louise
Our *Kind of People*. Wallace, Carol
★***Our*** *Kind of Traitor: A Novel*. Le Carre, John
Our *Lady of the Forest*. Guterson, David
Our *Man in Havana*. Greene, Graham
Our *Mutual Friend*. Dickens, Charles
Our *Riches*. Adimi, Kaouther
Our *Short History*. Grodstein, Lauren
★***Our*** *Souls at Night*. Haruf, Kent
Our *Story Begins: New and Selected Stories*. Wolff, Tobias
★***Out*** *of Darkness, Shining Light*. Gappah, Petina
Out *of the Black Land*. Greenwood, Kerry
★***Out*** *of the Dark: The Return of Orphan X*. Hurwitz, Gregg Andrew
★***Out*** *of the Easy*. Sepetys, Ruta
Out *Stealing Horses: A Novel*. Petterson, Per
Outbreak. Bunn, T. Davis
Outcasts (Minerva Spencer) [Series]. Spencer, Minerva
OUTER BANKS, NORTH CAROLINA
   Gates, Eva. *Deadly Ever After*
   Gates, Eva. *A Death Long Overdue*
   Gates, Eva. *Read and Buried*
The **Outlander**. Adamson, Gil
★***Outlander***. Gabaldon, Diana
Outlander novels [Series]. Gabaldon, Diana
OUTLAWS
   Blackmore, R. D. *Lorna Doone: A Romance of Exmoor*
   Borges, Jorge Luis. ★*Collected Fictions*
   Brand, Max. *Max Brand's Best Western Stories*
   Brooks, Bill. *Blood Storm*
   Brooks, Bill. *Frontier Justice*
   Brooks, Bill. *Winter Kill*
   Diaz, Hernan. ★*In the Distance*
   Estleman, Loren D. *The Adventures of Johnny Vermillion: A Novel*
   Grey, Zane. ★*Riders of the Purple Sage*
   Groom, Winston. *El Paso: A Novel*
   Hansen, Ron. ★*The Assassination of Jesse James by the Coward Robert Ford*
   Kelton, Elmer. *Hard Ride*
   Lansdale, Joe R. *The Thicket*
   Larison, John. *Whiskey When We're Dry*
   Leonard, Elmore. *Charlie Martz and Other Stories: The Unpublished Stories*
   Locke, Thomas. *Emissary*
   Malerman, Josh. *Unbury Carol*

McCarthy, Cormac. ★*Blood Meridian, Or, the Evening Redness in the West*

McMurtry, Larry. ★*Streets of Laredo: A Novel*

Obreht, Tea. *Inland: A Novel*

Panowich, Brian. *Bull Mountain*

Portis, Charles. ★*True Grit: A Novel*

Outline [Series]. Cusk, Rachel

Outline: a Novel. Cusk, Rachel

Outrage. Indriðason, Arnaldur

Outside Looking In: A Novel. Boyle, T. Coraghessan

Outsider. Castillo, Linda

OVERACHIEVERS

Katz, Erica. *The Boys' Club*

Williams, Denise. *How to Fail at Flirting*

Overkill: an Alex Hawke Novel. Bell, Ted

OVERLAND JOURNEYS TO THE PACIFIC

Dallas, Sandra. *Westering Women: A Novel*

Kirkpatrick, Jane. *One More River to Cross*

Priest, Cherie. *Dreadnought*

OVERLAND TRAILS

Harmon, Amy. *Where the Lost Wander*

OVERPOPULATION

Robinson, Kim Stanley. ★*Blue Mars*

OVERPROTECTIVENESS IN PARENTS

West, Kathleen. *Minor Dramas & Other Catastrophes*

★*The Overstory: a Novel*. Powers, Richard

Overthrow: the War with China and North Korea—Fall of an Empire. Poyer, David

Overton, Hollie

The Runaway

OVERWEIGHT AFRICAN AMERICAN WOMEN

Monroe, Mary. *God Still Don't Like Ugly*

OVERWEIGHT BOYS

Ajvide Lindqvist, John. *Let the Right One In*

OVERWEIGHT GIRLS

Monroe, Mary. ★*God Don't Like Ugly*

OVERWEIGHT MEN

Stanley, Michael. *A Carrion Death*

OVERWEIGHT WOMEN

Christian, Claire. *It's Been a Pleasure, Noni Blake*

McCall Smith, Alexander. *The Double Comfort Safari Club*

McKevett, G. A. *A Few Drops of Bitters*

Murphy, Julie. *If the Shoe Fits*

Walker, Sarai. *Dietland*

Weiner, Jennifer. ★*Big Summer*

OVID, 43 BC-17 OR 18 AD METAMORPHOSES

Lloyd, Catherine. *Death Comes to the Nursery*

MacLaughlin, Nina. *Wake, Siren: Ovid Resung*

Owen Archer mysteries [Series]. Robb, Candace M.

OWEN, WILFRED

Barker, Pat. ★*The Ghost Road*

White, Edmund. *A Boy's Own Story*

Owens, Delia

Where the Crawdads Sing

Owl Be Home for Christmas: A Meg Langslow Mystery. Andrews, Donna

OWLS

Andrews, Donna. *Owl Be Home for Christmas: A Meg Langslow Mystery*

Oxford time travel novels [Series]. Willis, Connie

OXFORD, ENGLAND

Benjamin, Melanie. *Alice I Have Been*

Butler, Gwendoline. *Death Lives Next Door*

Cartwright, Justin. *To Heaven by Water*

Dexter, Colin. *The Daughters of Cain*

Dexter, Colin. *The Remorseful Day*

Dexter, Colin. *The Way Through the Woods*

Dunmore, Evie. ★*Bringing Down the Duke*

Pears, Iain. *An Instance of the Fingerpost*

Sayers, Dorothy L. ★*Gaudy Night*

Shannon, Samantha. *The Bone Season*

Shannon, Samantha. *The Mime Order*

Spencer, Sally. *The Shivering Turn*

Whelan, Julia. *My Oxford Year*

Williams, Pip. *The Dictionary of Lost Words*

OXFORDSHIRE, ENGLAND

Johnson, Daisy. *Everything Under*

Starr, Melvin R. *Unhallowed Ground*

Oxygen. Miller, Andrew

Oyeyemi, Helen

Boy, Snow, Bird: A Novel

Gingerbread: A Novel

Mr. Fox

The Opposite House

Peaces

What Is Not Yours Is Not Yours: Stories

★*The Oysterville Sewing Circle*. Wiggs, Susan

OZ (IMAGINARY PLACE)

Maguire, Gregory. ★*Wicked: The Life and Times of the Wicked Witch of the West : A Novel*

Oz, Amos

Fima

OZARK MOUNTAIN REGION

Eskens, Allen. *Nothing More Dangerous: A Novel*

OZARK MOUNTAINS

McHugh, Laura. *What's Done in Darkness: A Novel*

Ozeki, Ruth L.

The Book of Form and Emptiness: A Novel

★*A Tale for the Time Being*

Ozick, Cynthia

Foreign Bodies

Heir to the Glimmering World

The Puttermesser Papers

P

★*Pachinko*. Lee, Min Jin

PACIFIC AREA

Deutermann, Peter T. *The Iceman*

McCullough, Colleen. *An Indecent Obsession*

Pacific Glory: A Novel. Deutermann, Peter T.

PACIFIC NORTHWEST

Alexie, Sherman. *Blasphemy: New and Selected Stories*

Bauermeister, Erica. *The Scent Keeper*

Brooks, Max. *Devolution: A Firsthand Account of the Rainier Sasquatch Massacre*
Coplin, Amanda. *The Orchardist*
Crumley, James. ★*The Wrong Case*
Dodd, Christina. *Dead Girl Running*
Dodd, Christina. *What Doesn't Kill Her*
Priest, Cherie. *Boneshaker*
Pyper, Andrew. *The Homecoming: A Novel*
Stirling, S. M. *Dies the Fire*
Stirling, S. M. *A Meeting at Corvallis*

PACIFIC OCEAN
Adams, Hope. *Dangerous Women*
Cussler, Clive. ★*The Rising Sea: A Novel from the Numa Files*
Heggen, Thomas. *Mister Roberts*
Martel, Yann. ★*Life of Pi: A Novel*
Wouk, Herman. ★*The Caine Mutiny: A Novel of World War II*
Pacific Vortex! Cussler, Clive
★*Pack up the Moon.* Higgins, Kristan

Packer, Ann
The Children's Crusade
The Dive from Clausen's Pier
Songs Without Words
Paddy Clarke, Ha-Ha-Ha. Doyle, Roddy
Pagan Babies. Leonard, Elmore
Pagan Spring: A Mystery. Malliet, G. M.

PAGANS
Cossette, Connilyn. ★*Shelter of the Most High*

PAGEANTS
Woolf, Virginia. *Between the Acts*

PAIBOUN, SIRI, DOCTOR (FICTITIOUS CHARACTER)
Cotterill, Colin. *Disco for the Departed*

PAIN
Roth, Philip. ★*The Anatomy Lesson*
Paint It Black: A Novel. Fitch, Janet
★*The Painted Bird.* Kosinski, Jerzy
Painted Desert: A Novel. Barthelme, Frederick
The Painted Drum: A Novel. Erdrich, Louise
★*The Painted Girls.* Buchanan, Cathy Marie
Painted Ladies. Parker, Robert B.
The Painter: a Novel. Heller, Peter

PAINTERS
Arbol, Victor del. *Breathing Through the Wound*
Bernhard, Thomas. *Frost: A Novel*
Brown, Dan. *The Da Vinci Code*
Cusset, Catherine. *Life of David Hockney: A Novel*
Dunant, Sarah. *The Birth of Venus: A Novel*
Ebershoff, David. *The Danish Girl: A Novel*
Gaddis, William. ★*The Recognitions*
Gibbon, Maureen. *The Lost Notebook of Edouard Manet: A Novel*
Gilbert, Elizabeth. ★*The Signature of All Things: A Novel*
Gruber, Michael. *The Forgery of Venus: A Novel*
Macneal, Elizabeth. *The Doll Factory*
Maugham, W. Somerset. *The Moon and Sixpence*
McKenzie, Alecia. *A Million Aunties*
Smith, Ali. ★*How to Be Both*
Stone, Irving. *Lust for Life: A Novel of Vincent Van Gogh*
Vargas Llosa, Mario. ★*The Way to Paradise*

PAINTING
Cussler, Clive. *Typhoon Fury*
Murakami, Haruki. *Killing Commendatore: A Novel*
Pilcher, Rosamunde. ★*The Shell Seekers*
Sayers, Dorothy L. ★*The Five Red Herrings*

PAINTING — COLLECTORS AND COLLECTING
Rothschild, Hannah. *The Improbability of Love: A Novel*
Painting the Light. Gunning, Sally

PAINTING, DUTCH
Smith, Dominic. ★*The Last Painting of Sara De Vos*

PAINTING, FLEMISH — FORGERIES
Gaddis, William. ★*The Recognitions*

PAKISTAN
Ahmad, Jamil. *The Wandering Falcon*
Aslam, Nadeem. ★*The Blind Man's Garden*
Aslam, Nadeem. ★*The Golden Legend: A Novel*
Church, James. *Bamboo and Blood: An Inspector O Novel*
Hall, Tarquin. *The Case of the Deadly Butter Chicken: A Vish Puri Mystery*
Hall, Tarquin. *The Case of the Love Commandos: From the Files of Vish Puri, India's Most Private Investigator*
Kamal, Soniah. *Unmarriageable: A Novel*
Mueenuddin, Daniyal. *In Other Rooms, Other Wonders: Connected Stories*

PAKISTANI AMERICANS
Akhtar, Ayad. *American Dervish: A Novel*
Akhtar, Ayad. ★*Homeland Elegies: A Novel*

PAKISTANIS IN AFGHANISTAN
Aslam, Nadeem. ★*The Blind Man's Garden*
Palace insiders [Series]. Parker, Lucy
Palace of rogues [Series]. Long, Julie Anne
Palace of the Drowned. Mangan, Christine
★*Palace Walk.* Mahfuz, Najib

PALACES
Davis, Lindsey. *A Body in the Bathhouse*

Palahniuk, Chuck
Choke: A Novel
Fight Club
The Invention of Sound
Lullaby: A Novel
Pygmy
The Pale Blue Eye: A Novel. Bayard, Louis
Pale Fire. Nabokov, Vladimir Vladimirovich
The Pale Horse. Christie, Agatha
Pale Horse, Pale Rider: Three Short Novels. Porter, Katherine Anne
★*The Pale King: An Unfinished Novel.* Wallace, David Foster
A Pale Light in the Black: A Neog Novel. Wagers, K. B.

PALEONTOLOGISTS
Blumberg, Chandra. *Digging up Love*
Swanwick, Michael. *Bones of the Earth*

PALEONTOLOGY
Collins, Manda. *One for the Rogue*
Michener, James A. ★*Centennial*

PALESTINE
Agnon, Shmuel Yosef. ★*Only Yesterday*
Alyan, Hala. *Salt Houses*
Hammad, Isabella. ★*The Parisian, Or, Al-Barisi: A Novel*
Shalev, Meir. *Two She-Bears: A Novel*

Uris, Leon. ★*Exodus*
Wallace, Lew. ★*Ben-Hur*

PALESTINIAN AMERICAN WOMEN
Mahmoud, Lena. *Amreekiya: A Novel*

PALESTINIANS
Abulhawa, Susan. *The Blue Between Sky and Water*

PALESTINIANS — DIASPORA
Alyan, Hala. *Salt Houses*

PALESTINIANS — IDENTITY
Hammad, Isabella. ★*The Parisian, Or, Al-Barisi: A Novel*

Paley, Grace
★*The Collected Stories*

Palindrome. Woods, Stuart

The **Palliser** novels [Series]. Trollope, Anthony

Palliser, Charles
The Quincunx

PALM BEACH, FLORIDA
Hiaasen, Carl. ★*Squeeze Me: A Novel*
Sanders, Lawrence. *McNally's Dilemma*
Sanders, Lawrence. ★*McNally's Gamble*
Sanders, Lawrence. *McNally's Luck*
Sanders, Lawrence. *McNally's Puzzle*
Sanders, Lawrence. *McNally's Secret*
Sanders, Lawrence. *McNally's Trial*

PALM SPRINGS, CALIFORNIA
Hollis, Lee. *Poppy Harmon Investigates*
Rowley, Steven. ★*The Guncle: A Novel*

★*Palmares*. Jones, Gayl

PALME, OLOF, 1927-1986 ASSASSINATION
Birch, Carol. *Jamrach's Menagerie*
Persson, Leif G. W. *Free Falling, as If in a Dream: The Story of a Crime*

Palmer, Ada
Too Like the Lightning

Palmer, Daniel
The New Husband

Palmer, Dexter Clarence
★*Mary Toft; Or, the Rabbit Queen: A Novel*
Version Control

Palmer, Lindsey J.
Otherwise Engaged

PALO ALTO, CALIFORNIA
Dev, Sonali. ★*Recipe for Persuasion*
McKenzie, Elizabeth. *The Portable Veblen*
Schulman, Helen. *Come with Me*

★*Pamela: Or, Virtue Rewarded*. Richardson, Samuel

PAMPHLETS
Bowman, Valerie. *Secrets of a Wedding Night*

Pamuk, Orhan
The Museum of Innocence
The Red-Haired Woman
Silent House
★*Snow*
★*A Strangeness in My Mind: A Novel*

PANAMA
Le Carre, John. *The Tailor of Panama*

*The **Pandora** Room: A Novel*. Golden, Christopher

Pandora's Star. Hamilton, Peter F.

Pandya, Sameer
Members Only

PANIATOWSKI, MONIKA (FICTITIOUS CHARACTER)
Spencer, Sally. *Dead End*
Spencer, Sally. *The Dead Hand of History*
Spencer, Sally. *The Ring of Death*

PANJABIS (SOUTH ASIAN PEOPLE)
Snyder, Suleikha. *Big Bad Wolf*

Panowich, Brian
Bull Mountain
Hard Cash Valley
Like Lions

PANZA, SANCHO (FICTITIOUS CHARACTER)
Cervantes Saavedra, Miguel de. ★*Don Quixote*

Paolini, Christopher
★*To Sleep in a Sea of Stars*

PAPARAZZI
Gaynor, Hazel. *Meet Me in Monaco: A Novel*
Haddam, Jane. *Cheating at Solitaire: A Gregor Demarkian Novel*
Phillips, Susan Elizabeth. *What I Did for Love*

★*Paper Son*. Rozan, S. J.

*The **Paper** Wasp: A Novel*. Acampora, Lauren

Parable books [Series]. Butler, Octavia E.

★*Parable of the Sower*. Butler, Octavia E.

Parable of the Talents: A Novel. Butler, Octavia E.

PARABLES
Kafka, Franz. ★*Collected Stories*

Paradise. Morrison, Toni

Paradise [Series]. Hilderbrand, Elin

★*Paradise Sky*. Lansdale, Joe R.

Paradise Valley. Box, C. J.

Paradise, Nevada. Diofebi, Dario

Paradox. Coulter, Catherine

PARADOXES
Eco, Umberto. *The Island of the Day Before*
Spufford, Francis. ★*Light Perpetual*

★*The **Paragon** Hotel*. Faye, Lyndsay

PARAGUAY
Greene, Graham. *The Honorary Consul*

PARALLEL NARRATIVES
Aliu, Xhenet. ★*Brass: A Novel*
Anderson, Alison. *The Summer Guest*
Armstrong, Addison. *The Light of Luna Park*
Barry, Sebastian. *The Secret Scripture: A Novel*
Belfer, Lauren. *And After the Fire: A Novel*
Bohjalian, Chris. *The Sandcastle Girls*
Bohjalian, Chris. *Skeletons at the Feast: A Novel*
Boyle, T. Coraghessan. *World's End: A Novel*
Brundage, Elizabeth. ★*All Things Cease to Appear*
Byatt, A. S. ★*Possession: A Romance*
Cander, Chris. *The Weight of a Piano: A Novel*
Chancellor, Bryn. *Sycamore: A Novel*
Cleeton, Chanel. *Next Year in Havana*
Cunningham, Michael. ★*The Hours*
Cussler, Clive. ★*The Titanic Secret*
Davis, Fiona. *The Lions of Fifth Avenue: A Novel*
Delaney, J. P. *The Girl Before: A Novel*
Deon, Natashia. *The Perishing: A Novel*

DeRoux, Margaux. *The Lost Diary of Venice*
Dybek, Nick. *The Verdun Affair: A Novel*
Dykes, Amanda. *Whose Waves These Are*
Ebershoff, David. *The 19th Wife: A Novel*
Enjeti, Anjali. ★*The Parted Earth*
Epstein, Jennifer Cody. ★*Wunderland: A Novel*
Evison, Jonathan. *Legends of the North Cascades: A Novel*
Evison, Jonathan. ★*Small World*
Evison, Jonathan. *West of Here: A Novel*
Flagg, Fannie. ★*Fried Green Tomatoes at the Whistle Stop Cafe*
Flagg, Fannie. ★*The Wonder Boy of Whistle Stop: A Novel*
Garcia Saenz, Eva. *The Silence of the White City*
Gaynor, Hazel. *The Lighthouse Keeper's Daughter*
Gibson, William. ★*Agency*
Gibson, William. *The Peripheral*
Harrison, Jamie. *The Center of Everything: A Novel*
Harvey, John. *Darkness, Darkness*
Hoffman, Alice. *The Museum of Extraordinary Things: A Novel*
Indriðason, Arnaldur. *The Shadow District: A Thriller*
James, Rebecca. *The Woman in the Mirror*
Jhabvala, Ruth Prawer. ★*Heat and Dust*
Jin, Ha. *A Map of Betrayal: A Novel*
Kelly, Julia. *The Light Over London*
Kibler, Julie. *Home for Erring and Outcast Girls*
Kingsolver, Barbara. ★*Unsheltered*
Makkai, Rebecca. ★*The Great Believers*
McCrumb, Sharyn. ★*The Ballad of Frankie Silver*
Miller, Andrew. *Oxygen*
Miller, Kei. ★*Augustown*
Morelli, Laura. *The Stolen Lady*
Morton, Kate. *The Distant Hours: A Novel*
Moyes, Jojo. *The Girl You Left Behind*
Murakami, Haruki. ★*Kafka on the Shore*
Obreht, Tea. *The Tiger's Wife: A Novel*
Paul, Gill. ★*The Lost Daughter*
Pears, Iain. *The Dream of Scipio*
Phillips, Christi. *The Rossetti Letter: A Novel*
Phoenix, Michele. *The Space Between Words*
Picoult, Jodi. *The Storyteller*
Purcell, Laura. *The Silent Companions: A Ghost Story*
Reid, Taylor Jenkins. ★*Malibu Rising*
Restrepo, Laura. *No Place for Heroes: A Novel*
Rosnay, Tatiana de. ★*Sarah's Key*
Roy, Anuradha. *All the Lives We Never Lived: A Novel*
Russell, Kate Elizabeth. ★*My Dark Vanessa*
Scottoline, Lisa. *One Perfect Lie*
Shreve, Anita. *The Weight of Water*
Shriver, Lionel. *The Post-Birthday World*
Silver, Marisa. *Mary Coin: A Novel*
Slaughter, Karin. ★*Pieces of Her*
Smith, Ali. ★*How to Be Both*
Smith, Dominic. ★*The Electric Hotel*
Smith, Dominic. ★*The Last Painting of Sara De Vos*
Smith, Gregory Blake. ★*The Maze at Windermere: A Novel*
Soule, Charles. ★*Anyone*
St. James, Simone. *The Sun Down Motel*
Swyler, Erika. ★*Light from Other Stars: A Novel*
Vargas Llosa, Mario. *Aunt Julia and the Scriptwriter*

Williams, Beatriz. *All the Ways We Said Goodbye: A Novel of the Ritz Paris*
Williams, Beatriz. *The Golden Hour*
Willig, Lauren. *The Summer Country: A Novel*
Wilson, Daniel H. *The Clockwork Dynasty: A Novel*
Wright, Jaime Jo. *The Haunting at Bonaventure Circus*

PARALLEL UNIVERSES
Barker, Clive. ★*Weaveworld*
Chiang, Ted. ★*Exhalation: Stories*
Cipri, Nino. *Defekt*
Crouch, Blake. *Dark Matter: A Novel*
Dekker, Ted. *Black: The Birth of Evil*
Greer, Andrew Sean. *The Impossible Lives of Greta Wells*
Haig, Matt. *The Midnight Library*
Johnson, Micaiah. *The Space Between Worlds*
Kay, Guy Gavriel. *The Summer Tree*
McGuire, Seanan. ★*In an Absent Dream*
Mieville, China. ★*The City & The City*
Murakami, Haruki. ★*1q84*
Roberts, Nora. ★*The Awakening*
Schwab, Victoria. *A Conjuring of Light*
Schwab, Victoria. *A Darker Shade of Magic*
Schwab, Victoria. *A Gathering of Shadows*
Wolfe, Gene. *The Citadel of the Autarch*

PARAMEDICS
Sorenson, Jill. *Aftershock*

PARAMILITARY FORCES
Burns, Anna. *Milkman: A Novel*

PARANOIA
Barker, Pat. ★*The Eye in the Door*
Chavez, Heather. *No Bad Deed*
Gaddis, William. ★*The Recognitions*
Garcia Marquez, Gabriel. *In Evil Hour*
Hendrix, Grady. *The Final Girl Support Group*
Jemc, Jac. ★*The Grip of It*
Nguyen, Lena. *We Have Always Been Here*
Pynchon, Thomas. ★*The Crying of Lot 49*
Starling, Caitlin. *The Death of Jane Lawrence*
Steinhauer, Olen. *The Tourist*

PARANOID SCHIZOPHRENIA
Stridsberg, Sara. *Valerie: Or the Faculty of Dreams : Amendment to the Theory of Sexuality*

PARANORMAL PHENOMENA
Castro, V. *Goddess of Filth*
Flyte, Magnus. *City of Lost Dreams: A Novel*
Griffiths, Elly. *The Lantern Men: A Dr. Ruth Galloway Mystery*
Hill, Joe. *Strange Weather: Four Short Novels*
Hunt, Samantha. *The Dark Dark: Stories*
Katsu, Alma. *The Deep*
King, Stephen. *Night Shift*
Malerman, Josh. *Goblin: A Novel in Six Novellas*
Mitchell, David. *The Bone Clocks: A Novel*
Murakami, Haruki. *Blind Willow, Sleeping Woman: 24 Stories*
Palahniuk, Chuck. *Lullaby: A Novel*
Pearl, Matthew. *The Technologists: A Novel*
Straub, Peter. *Mr. X*
Wong, David. *This Book Is Full of Spiders: Seriously, Dude, Don't Touch It*

PARANORMAL PHENOMENON INVESTIGATION

Jackson, Shirley. ★*The Haunting of Hill House*
Krentz, Jayne Ann. ★*All the Colors of Night*
St. James, Simone. *The Haunting of Maddy Clare*

PARANORMAL ROMANCES

Allen, Susanna. *A Wolf in Duke's Clothing*
Bennett, Jenn. *Bitter Spirits*
Callihan, Kristen. ★*Firelight*
Castle, Jayne. *Illusion Town*
Feehan, Christine. *Dark Illusion*
Feehan, Christine. *Shadow Rider*
Harrison, Thea. *Dragon Bound*
Heger, Amanda. *Crazy Cupid Love*
Putney, Mary Jo. *The Marriage Spell: A Novel*
Roberts, Nora. ★*The Awakening*
Roberts, Nora. ★*The Becoming*
Showalter, Gena. *Shadow and Ice*
Singh, Nalini. ★*Silver Silence*
Snyder, Suleikha. *Big Bad Wolf*
Spear, Terry. *A Billionaire Wolf for Christmas*
Sterling, Erin. *The Ex Hex*

Paranormal scene investigations [Series]. Gilman, Laura Anne

Parasite. Grant, Mira

PARASITES

Grant, Mira. *Parasite*

Parasitology [Series]. Grant, Mira

PARENT AND ADULT CHILD

Escandon, Maria Amparo. ★*L.A. Weather*
Franzen, Jonathan. ★*The Corrections*
Genova, Lisa. *Inside the O'Briens: A Novel*
Gordimer, Nadine. *Get a Life*
Levy, Deborah. *Hot Milk: A Novel*
Poeppel, Amy. *Musical Chairs: A Novel*
Poissant, David James. *Lake Life*
Price, Reynolds. *The Good Priest's Son*
Stross, Charles. *Accelerando*
Woo, Sung J. *Love Love: A Novel*
Zettel, Sarah. *A Mother's Lie*

PARENT AND CHILD

Coben, Harlan. *Hold Tight*
Doctorow, E. L. ★*The Book of Daniel: A Novel*
Ferrante, Elena. *The Lost Daughter*
Grossman, David. *Falling Out of Time*
Lippman, Laura. ★*Hush Hush*
McDermott, Alice. *After This*
McKinty, Adrian. ★*The Chain*
Munro, Alice. *Selected Stories*
Quade, Kirstin Valdez. *Night at the Fiestas: Stories*
Washington, Bryan. ★*Memorial*

PARENT-SEPARATED BOYS

Bailey, Paul. *Uncle Rudolf*
Ballard, J. G. *Empire of the Sun: A Novel*
Ishiguro, Kazuo. *When We Were Orphans*
Ko, Lisa. *The Leavers*

PARENT-SEPARATED CHILDREN

Ausubel, Ramona. *Sons and Daughters of Ease and Plenty*

PARENTAL KIDNAPPING

Fuller, Claire. *Our Endless Numbered Days: A Novel*

Picoult, Jodi. *Vanishing Acts: A Novel*
Quotah, Eman. ★*Bride of the Sea: A Novel*

PARENTHOOD

Davies, Peter Ho. *A Lie Someone Told You About Yourself*
Grodstein, Lauren. *Our Short History*
Mackintosh, Clare. *After the End*
Marcelo, Tif. *In a Book Club Far Away*
McCorkle, Jill. ★*Hieroglyphics: A Novel*
O'Farrell, Maggie. *The Hand That First Held Mine: A Novel*
Straub, Emma. ★*Modern Lovers*

PARENTING

Brodesser-Akner, Taffy. *Fleishman Is in Trouble: A Novel*
Chan, Jessamine. *The School for Good Mothers*
Gelman, Laurie. *Class Mom: A Novel*
Gelman, Laurie. *Yoga Pant Nation: A Novel*
Gelman, Laurie. *You've Been Volunteered: A Class Mom Novel*
Miller, Sue. *The Good Mother*
Phillips, Helen. *The Need: A Novel*

PARENTING — PSYCHOLOGICAL ASPECTS

Bird, Sarah. *The Gap Year: A Novel*

PARENTS

Alderton, Dolly. ★*Ghosts: A Novel*
Moriarty, Liane. *Big Little Lies*

PARENTS — DEATH

Gruen, Sara. ★*Water for Elephants: A Novel*
Jin, Ha. *A Map of Betrayal: A Novel*
Liu, Cixin. *Ball Lightning*
Rowley, Steven. ★*The Guncle: A Novel*
Searles, John. *Help for the Haunted*

PARENTS — PSYCHOLOGY

Holsinger, Bruce W. *The Gifted School: A Novel*

PARENTS OF CHILDREN WITH AUTISM

Sears, Michael. *Black Fridays*

PARENTS OF CHILDREN WITH DEVELOPMENTAL DISABILITIES

Swift, Graham. ★*Last Orders: A Novel*

PARENTS OF CHILDREN WITH DISABILITIES

Offutt, Chris. *Country Dark*

PARENTS OF CHILDREN WITH MENTAL ILLNESSES

Hawley, Noah. *The Good Father*

PARENTS OF CRIMINALS

Brown, Rosellen. ★*Before and After*
Shriver, Lionel. *We Need to Talk About Kevin*

PARENTS OF MISSING CHILDREN

Jewell, Lisa. *Then She Was Gone: A Novel*

PARENTS OF MURDER VICTIMS

Cosby, S. A. ★*Razorblade Tears*

PARENTS WITH TERMINAL ILLNESSES

Brown, Eleanor. *The Weird Sisters*
Miller, Andrew. *Oxygen*

PARENTS' RIGHTS

George, Elizabeth. *Just One Evil Act*

PARENTS-IN-LAW

McEwan, Ian. *Black Dogs*

Paretsky, Sara

★*Dead Land*
Indemnity Only: A Novel
Love & Other Crimes: Stories

Shell Game

PARIAHS

Anderton, Jo. *Debris*

Beckett, L. X. *Gamechanger*

Boyne, John. *The Heart's Invisible Furies*

Hawthorne, Nathaniel. ★*The Scarlet Letter: A Romance*

MacLean, Sarah. *The Rogue Not Taken*

Penelope, L. *Song of Blood and Stone*

Potzsch, Oliver. *The Hangman's Daughter: A Historical Novel*

Rosenfield, Kat. *No One Will Miss Her*

Welsh, Kaite. *The Wages of Sin*

Parini, Jay

The Damascus Road: A Novel of Saint Paul

The Passages of H.M.: A Novel of Herman Melville

Paris. Rutherfurd, Edward

The **Paris** *Architect: A Novel*. Belfoure, Charles

The **Paris** *Diversion: A Novel*. Pavone, Chris

Paris **Echo**: *A Novel*. Faulks, Sebastian

The **Paris** *Hours: A Novel*. George, Alex

Paris **in the Present Tense**. Helprin, Mark

The **Paris** *Library: A Novel*. Skeslien Charles, Janet

Paris **Never Leaves You**. Feldman, Ellen

Paris **Trout**. Dexter, Pete

The **Paris** *Wife: A Novel*. McLain, Paula

The **Paris** *Winter*. Robertson, Imogen

Paris, 7 A.M.. Wieland, Liza

Paris, B. A.

Behind Closed Doors

The Breakdown

Bring Me Back: A Novel

★The Dilemma

PARIS, CHARLES (FICTITIOUS CHARACTER)

Brett, Simon. *Murder Unprompted*

PARIS, FRANCE

Alexander, Victoria. *The Lady Travelers Guide to Scoundrels and Other Gentlemen*

Alfon, Dov. *A Long Night in Paris*

Aridjis, Chloe. *Asunder*

Avery, Ellis. *The Last Nude*

Baldwin, James. ★*Giovanni's Room*

Baldwin, James. *Just Above My Head*

Barbery, Muriel. *The Elegance of the Hedgehog*

Barnes, Djuna. ★*Nightwood*

Beauvoir, Simone de. ★*The Mandarins: A Novel*

Belfoure, Charles. *The Paris Architect: A Novel*

Bellow, Saul. *Ravelstein*

Bernhard, Emilia. *The Books of the Dead*

Black, Cara. *Murder in the Marais*

Black, Cara. *Murder in the Rue De Paradis: An Aimee Leduc Investigation*

Black, Cara. ★*Three Hours in Paris*

Blackwell, Juliet. *Letters from Paris*

Bolano, Roberto. *Monsieur Pain*

Bourdeaut, Olivier. *Waiting for Bojangles: A Novel*

Brown, Dan. *The Da Vinci Code*

Buchanan, Cathy Marie. ★*The Painted Girls*

Camus, Albert. ★*The Fall*

Carey, Edward. *Little: A Novel*

Chee, Alexander. *The Queen of the Night*

Cisneros, Sandra. *Martita, I Remember You: Martita, Te Recuerdo*

Coben, Harlan. *Long Lost*

Corleone, Douglas. *Good as Gone*

Dickens, Charles. ★*A Tale of Two Cities*

Djavadi, Negar. *Disoriental*

Dongala, Emmanuel Boundzeki. *The Bridgetower Sonata: Sonata Mulattica*

Dumas, Alexandre. ★*Camille*

Dumas, Alexandre. *Twenty Years After*

Edugyan, Esi. *Half-Blood Blues*

Faulks, Sebastian. *Paris Echo: A Novel*

Feldman, Ellen. *Paris Never Leaves You*

Flaubert, Gustave. *Sentimental Education*

Furst, Alan. ★*Under Occupation: A Novel*

Gaynor, Hazel. *Three Words for Goodbye*

George, Alex. *The Paris Hours: A Novel*

George, Nina. *The Little Paris Bookshop*

Gibbon, Maureen. *The Lost Notebook of Edouard Manet: A Novel*

Hammad, Isabella. ★*The Parisian, Or, Al-Barisi: A Novel*

Harkness, Deborah E. *Time's Convert*

Harmel, Kristin. *The Room on Rue Amelie*

Helprin, Mark. *Paris in the Present Tense*

Heyer, Georgette. *These Old Shades*

Horrocks, Caitlin. *The Vexations*

Hugo, Victor. ★*The Hunchback of Notre Dame*

Kelly, Martha Hall. *Lilac Girls*

Khoury, Raymond. *Empire of Lies*

Landragin, Alex. ★*Crossings: Consisting of Three Manuscripts : The Education of a Monster : City of Ghosts : Tales Of*

Lim, Roselle. *Vanessa Yu's Magical Paris Tea Shop*

Makkai, Rebecca. ★*The Great Believers*

Mas, Victoria. *The Mad Women's Ball*

Maugham, W. Somerset. *The Moon and Sixpence*

McLain, Paula. *The Paris Wife: A Novel*

Meacham, Leila. *Dragonfly: A Novel*

Miller, Andrew. *Oxygen*

Miller, Henry. ★*Tropic of Cancer*

Mosse, Kate. *The City of Tears*

Nguyen, Viet Thanh. ★*The Committed*

Ozick, Cynthia. *Foreign Bodies*

Pavone, Chris. *The Paris Diversion: A Novel*

Pears, Iain. *The Last Judgement*

Penny, Louise. ★*All the Devils Are Here*

Perez-Reverte, Arturo. *The Club Dumas*

Proust, Marcel. *Within a Budding Grove*

Reich, Christopher. ★*The Take*

Rice, Anne. *The Vampire Armand*

Robertson, Imogen. *The Paris Winter*

Rosnay, Tatiana de. ★*Flowers of Darkness*

Rosnay, Tatiana de. ★*Sarah's Key*

Rutherfurd, Edward. *Paris*

Savas, Aysegul. *Walking on the Ceiling*

Sedgwick, Marcus. *Mister Memory: A Novel*

Shaw, Vivian. ★*Dreadful Company*

Simenon, Georges. *Maigret and the Black Sheep*

Simenon, Georges. *Maigret and the Fortuneteller*

Simenon, Georges. ★*Maigret and the Killer*

Simenon, Georges. *Maigret and the Madwoman*
Simenon, Georges. ★*Maigret and the Saturday Caller*
Simenon, Georges. *Maigret and the Wine Merchant*
Simenon, Georges. ★*Maigret Bides His Time*
Simenon, Georges. ★*Maigret Goes Home*
Simenon, Georges. *Maigret's Memoirs*
Skeslien Charles, Janet. *The Paris Library: A Novel*
Spark, Muriel. *Aiding & Abetting*
Stewart, Mary. *Nine Coaches Waiting*
Tsao, Tiffany. *The Majesties*
Wieland, Liza. *Paris, 7 A.M.*
Williams, Beatriz. *All the Ways We Said Goodbye: A Novel of the Ritz Paris*
Woods, Stuart. *Skin Game*
Zola, Emile. ★*Nana*
★*The **Parisian**, Or, Al-Barisi: A Novel.* Hammad, Isabella

PARK AVENUE, NEW YORK CITY
McLaughlin, Emma. *The Nanny Diaries: A Novel*

PARK RANGERS
Kells, Claire. *Vanishing Edge*
Rash, Ron. *Above the Waterfall*
Stabenow, Dana. ★*A Fine and Bitter Snow: A Kate Shugak Novel*
Stabenow, Dana. ★*Hunter's Moon*
Stabenow, Dana. *A Night Too Dark: A Kate Shugak Novel*
Stabenow, Dana. *The Singing of the Dead*
Stabenow, Dana. *Whisper to the Blood: A Kate Shugak Novel*

Park, Ishle Yi
Angel & Hannah: A Novel in Verse

Park, Sang Young
★*Love in the Big City: A Novel*

PARKER (FICTITIOUS CHARACTER : STARK)
Stark, Richard. *Ask the Parrot: A Parker Novel*
Stark, Richard. *Breakout*
Stark, Richard. *Comeback*
Stark, Richard. *Dirty Money*
Stark, Richard. *The Hunter: A Parker Novel*
Stark, Richard. *The Jugger: A Parker Novel*

Parker thrillers [Series]. Stark, Richard

Parker, Lucy
The Austen Playbook
Battle Royal

Parker, Robert B.
Appaloosa
Blue-Eyed Devil
Death in Paradise
Night Passage
Painted Ladies
Sixkill
Trouble in Paradise

Parker, T. Jefferson
The Blue Hour
L.A. Outlaws: A Novel

Parker-Chan, Shelley
★*She Who Became the Sun*

*The **Parking** Lot Attendant: A Novel.* Tamirat, Nafkote

PARKOUR
Lindsay, Jeffry P. *Just Watch Me*

Parks, Brad
Closer Than You Know
The Player: A Mystery
Say Nothing: A Novel

Parks, Gordon
★*The Learning Tree*

Parmar, Priya
Vanessa and Her Sister

Parnell, Sean
Left for Dead
Man of War: An Eric Steele Novel

PARODIES
Bolano, Roberto. ★*Nazi Literature in the Americas*

PAROLE
DeSilva, Bruce. *Providence Rag*

PAROLEES
Baldacci, David. ★*One Good Deed*
Bell, Shelly. *For His Pleasure*
Rosen, Leonard J. *The Kortelisy Escape*

PARRICIDE
Dostoyevsky, Fyodor. ★*The Brothers Karamazov*
Sebold, Alice. *The Almost Moon: A Novel*

Parris, S. J.
★*The Dead of Winter*
Sacrilege
Treachery

Parrish, Christa
Still Life

Parrish, Roan
Better Than People

PARROTS
Barnes, Julian. ★*Flaubert's Parrot*

Parry, Ambrose
The Way of All Flesh

Parry, H. G.
A Declaration of the Rights of Magicians
The Unlikely Escape of Uriah Heep

★*The **Parted** Earth.* Enjeti, Anjali

PARTIES
Hoyt, Elizabeth. *Not the Duke's Darling*
Reid, Taylor Jenkins. ★*Malibu Rising*
Waugh, Evelyn. ★*Vile Bodies*

Parting Shot. Barclay, Linwood

PARTNER ABUSE
Belle, Kimberly. *Dear Wife*
Clark, Julie. *Last Flight*
Fisher, Tarryn. *The Wives*
Fossey, Brooke. *The Big Finish*
Kandasamy, Meena. *When I Hit You, Or, a Portrait of the Writer as a Young Wife*
Moor, Jessica. *The Keeper*

PARTNERS OF PEOPLE WITH BREAST CANCER
Pronzini, Bill. *Savages*

Party of Two. Guillory, Jasmine
*The **Party** Upstairs.* Conell, Lee
*The **Passage**.* Cronin, Justin
★*A **Passage** to India.* Forster, E. M.
Passage trilogy [Series]. Cronin, Justin

Passage West: A Novel. Reddi, Rishi
The *Passages* of H.M.: A Novel of Herman Melville. Parini, Jay
The *Passenger:* a Novel. Boschwitz, Ulrich Alexander
Passing. Larsen, Nella
PASSING (IDENTITY)
    Bennett, Brit. ★*The Vanishing Half*
    Coster, Naima. *What's Mine and Yours: A Novel*
    Jenkins, Beverly. *Forbidden*
    Lansdale, Joe R. *More Better Deals*
    Oyeyemi, Helen. *Boy, Snow, Bird: A Novel*
    Roth, Philip. ★*The Human Stain*
    Twain, Mark. *Pudd'nhead Wilson ;: And, Those Extraordinary Twins*
The *Passion*. Winterson, Jeanette
Passion Grove [Series]. Bryant, Niobia
Passion on Park Avenue. Layne, Lauren
PASSION-PLAYS
    Potzsch, Oliver. *The Play of Death*
PASSIVE-AGGRESSIVE PERSONALITY
    Schumacher, Julie. *Dear Committee Members*
PASSIVITY (PSYCHOLOGY)
    Garcia Marquez, Gabriel. *Chronicle of a Death Foretold*
    Huxley, Aldous. ★*Brave New World*
The *Past*. Hadley, Tessa
★*Past Tense*. Child, Lee
Pastan, Rachel
    In the Field
Pasternak, Boris Leonidovich
    ★*Doctor Zhivago*
PASTERNAK, BORIS LEONIDOVICH
    Hamya, Jo. *Three Rooms*
    Prescott, Lara. *The Secrets We Kept*
PASTRY CHEFS
    Delany, Vicki. *Tea & Treachery*
Patchett, Ann
    ★*Bel Canto: A Novel*
    ★*Commonwealth*
    ★*The Dutch House: A Novel*
    Run
    ★*State of Wonder: A Novel*
Patchwork. Mason, Bobbie Ann
A *Patchwork* Planet. Tyler, Anne
PATHOGENIC MICROORGANISMS
    Wilson, Daniel H. *The Andromeda Evolution: A Novel*
PATHOLOGISTS
    Black, Benjamin. ★*Christine Falls: A Novel*
The *Patient's* Eyes. Pirie, David
Paton, Alan
    Ah, but Your Land Is Beautiful
    ★*Cry, the Beloved Country*
    Too Late the Phalarope
PATRIARCHS
    Araghi, Alireza Taheri. ★*The Immortals of Tehran*
    Garcia Marquez, Gabriel. ★*The Autumn of the Patriarch*
    Oates, Joyce Carol. *Night. Sleep. Death. The Stars*
PATRIARCHY
    Cho, Nam-Ju. ★*Kim Jiyoung, Born 1982*
    Toews, Miriam. ★*Women Talking: A Novel*
Patrick McLanahan novels [Series]. Brown, Dale

Patrick Melrose novels [Series]. St. Aubyn, Edward
Patrick, Phaedra
    ★*The Secrets of Love Story Bridge*
Patriot Games. Clancy, Tom
PATRIOTISM
    Fountain, Ben. ★*Billy Lynn's Long Halftime Walk*
    Pratchett, Terry. *Monstrous Regiment*
PATRON AND CLIENT
    Hall, Rachel Howzell. *These Toxic Things*
★*Patsy:* a Novel. Dennis-Benn, Nicole
PATTERN PERCEPTION
    Clayborn, Kate. *Love Lettering*
    Gibson, William. *Pattern Recognition*
Pattern Recognition. Gibson, William
Patterson's Bluff [Series]. London, Stefanie
Patterson, James
    1st to Die: A Novel
    ★*Along Came a Spider: A Novel*
    Kiss the Girls: A Novel
    ★*Private*
Patterson, Molly
    Rebellion
Patterson, Richard North
    Balance of Power
    Dark Lady
    Eclipse
    No Safe Place
    Protect and Defend
Pattison, Eliot
    Bones of the Earth: An Inspector Shan Tao Yun Mystery
    The Skull Mantra
Paul Samson novels [Series]. Porter, Henry
Paul, Gill
    ★*The Lost Daughter*
PAUL, THE APOSTLE, SAINT
    Afshar, Tessa. *Thief of Corinth*
    Bennett, Anna. *First Earl I See Tonight*
    Jackson, Joshilyn. *Never Have I Ever*
    Parini, Jay. *The Damascus Road: A Novel of Saint Paul*
Paula Spencer novels [Series]. Doyle, Roddy
Pava, Sergio de la
    Lost Empress: A Novel
    A Naked Singularity
    Personae: A Novel
Pavone, Chris
    ★*The Expats: A Novel*
    The Paris Diversion: A Novel
Pawel, Rebecca
    Death of a Nationalist
Payback Ain't Enough. Clark, Wahida
★*Payback* Is a Mutha. Clark, Wahida
Payback novels [Series]. Clark, Wahida
Payback with Ya Life. Clark, Wahida
PAZ, JIMMY (FICTITIOUS CHARACTER)
    Gruber, Michael. *Night of the Jaguar: A Novel*
    Gruber, Michael. *Valley of Bones: A Novel*
Peace. Bausch, Richard

PEACE
    Adams, Richard. *Watership Down*
    Vonnegut, Kurt. *Armageddon in Retrospect: And Other New and Unpublished Writings on War and Peace*
PEACE ACTIVISTS
    Farah, Nuruddin. *Knots*
    Gorman, Edward. *Riders on the Storm : A Sam McCain Mystery*
PEACE OFFICERS
    Russell, Mary Doria. ★*Doc: A Novel*
Peace, David
    Occupied City
Peaces. Oyeyemi, Helen
The *Peacock* Emporium. Moyes, Jojo
The *Pearl*. Steinbeck, John
PEARL HARBOR, ATTACK ON, 1941
    Smith, Martin Cruz. *December 6*
PEARL HARBOR, HAWAII
    Smith, Martin Cruz. *December 6*
Pearl, Matthew
    The Dante Chamber
    The Dante Club: A Novel
    The Last Dickens: A Novel
    The Poe Shadow: A Novel
    The Technologists: A Novel
Pearlman, Edith
    Binocular Vision: New & Selected Stories
    Honeydew: Stories
PEARLS
    Steinbeck, John. *The Pearl*
Pears, Iain
    Death and Restoration
    The Dream of Scipio
    The Immaculate Deception
    An Instance of the Fingerpost
    The Last Judgement
    Stone's Fall
Pearson, Allison
    ★*How Hard Can It Be?*
Pearson, Ridley
    The Risk Agent
Pearson, Robin W.
    A Long Time Comin'
PEASANT MEN
    Hamill, Pete. *Forever*
PEASANTRY
    Dostoyevsky, Fyodor. ★*The Brothers Karamazov*
★*A Peculiar* Combination. Weaver, Ashley
PEDOPHILES
    Harrison, Jim. *The Great Leader*
    Kane, Darby. *Pretty Little Wife*
    Nabokov, Vladimir Vladimirovich. ★*Lolita*
    Rankin, Ian. *Dead Souls: An Inspector Rebus Novel*
    Robbins, Tom. *Fierce Invalids Home from Hot Climates*
    Roslund, Anders. *Pen 33*
PEDOPHILIA
    Nabokov, Vladimir Vladimirovich. ★*Lolita*
Peebles, Frances de Pontes
    The Air You Breathe

PEGASUS (GREEK MYTHOLOGY)
    Barth, John. *Chimera*
Peikoff, Kira
    Mother Knows Best
Pelecanos, George P.
    The Big Blowdown
    The Cut: A Novel
Pelevin, Viktor
    The Hall of Singing Caryatids
PELHAM, MASSACHUSETTS
    Fay, Juliette. *The Shortest Way Home*
★*The Pelican Brief*. Grisham, John
Pellegrino, Amanda
    Smile and Look Pretty
PELOPONNESIAN WAR, 431-404 B.C.E.
    Renault, Mary. *The Last of the Wine*
Pembrooke, Kate
    Not the Kind of Earl You Marry
Pen 33. Roslund, Anders
PEN PALS
    Lewis, Beverly. *The Preacher's Daughter*
PENAL COLONIES
    Adams, Hope. *Dangerous Women*
    Flanagan, Richard. *Gould's Book of Fish: A Novel in Twelve Fish*
    Grenville, Kate. *The Secret River*
    Schell, Orville. *My Old Home: A Novel of Exile*
Pendergast novels [Series]. Preston, Douglas J.
Penelope Lemon: Game On! Majors, Inman
Penelope, L.
    Cry of Metal & Bone: Earthsinger Chronicles, Book 3
    Song of Blood and Stone
    Whispers of Shadow & Flame
Penhallow dynasty [Series]. Berne, Lisa
Penman, Sharon Kay
    Here Be Dragons
    The Queen's Man: A Medieval Mystery
    The Sunne in Splendour
    When Christ and His Saints Slept
Penn Cage novels [Series]. Iles, Greg
PENNSYLVANIA
    Baldacci, David. *The Fallen*
    Benton, Janet. *Lilli De Jong: A Novel*
    Chabon, Michael. ★*Wonder Boys*
    Clark, Wahida. ★*Thugs and the Women Who Love Them*
    Coover, Robert. *The Origin of the Brunists: A Novel*
    Davies, Carys. *West*
    Glover, Nicole. ★*The Conductors*
    Glover, Nicole. *The Undertakers*
    Haigh, Jennifer. *Baker Towers: A Novel*
    Johnson, Tara. *Engraved on the Heart*
    Krivak, Andrew. *The Signal Flame: A Novel*
    Lewis, Beverly. *The Brethren*
    Lewis, Beverly. *The Missing*
    Lewis, Beverly. *The Preacher's Daughter*
    Machado, Carmen Maria. ★*The Low, Low Woods*
    McAllister, Tom. *How to Be Safe: A Novel*
    McKinney-Whetstone, Diane. *Leaving Cecil Street: A Novel*
    O'Hara, John. *Appointment in Samarra*

Oakley, Colleen. *You Were There Too*
Patchett, Ann. ★*The Dutch House: A Novel*
Powers, Richard. *Orfeo: A Novel*
Quindlen, Anna. *Miller's Valley*
Ritter, Todd. *Devil's Night*
Roberts, Nora. ★*The Awakening*
Russo, Richard. *Straight Man*
Scottoline, Lisa. *Feared*
Shepard, Sara. ★*Reputation*
Sherrill, Steven. *The Minotaur Takes His Own Sweet Time: A Novel*
Silvis, Randall. *Two Days Gone: A Novel*
Stroby, Wallace. *Some Die Nameless*
Thomas, Elisabeth. *Catherine House*
Updike, John. *My Father's Tears and Other Stories*
Updike, John. ★*Rabbit Is Rich: A Novel*
Updike, John. ★*Rabbit, Run*
Weiner, Jennifer. *Little Earthquakes*
Wendig, Chuck. *The Book of Accidents*
Wiseman, Ellen Marie. *The Orphan Collector*
Penny for Your Secrets. Huber, Anna Lee

Penny, Louise
　★*All the Devils Are Here*
　★*A Better Man: A Chief Inspector Gamache Novel*
　The Cruelest Month: A Three Pines Mystery
　★*The Madness of Crowds*
　Still Life

Penrose, Andrea
　Murder at Half Moon Gate
　★*Murder at Kensington Palace*
　Murder on Black Swan Lane

PENZANCE, ENGLAND
　Ware, Ruth. *The Death of Mrs. Westaway*
Peony in Love: A Novel. See, Lisa

PEOPLE IN COMAS
　Abrams, Stacey. *While Justice Sleeps: A Novel*
　Block, Stefan Merrill. *Oliver Loving: A Novel*
　George, Nina. *The Book of Dreams*
　Ma, Jian. *Beijing Coma*
　Mark, David John. *Cruel Mercy*
　Miller, Karen E. Quinones. *An Angry-Ass Black Woman*
　Powers, Richard. *The Echo Maker*
　Rankin, Ian. *The Hanging Garden: An Inspector Rebus Novel*
　Soderberg, Alexander. *The Other Son: A Sophie Brinkmann Novel*
　Winters, Ben H. *The Quiet Boy*
People Like Us: A Novel. Dunne, Dominick
People of Abandoned Character. Whitfield, Clare
The *People* of Forever Are Not Afraid: A Novel. Boianjiu, Shani
The *People* on Privilege Hill and Other Stories. Gardam, Jane
The *People* We Keep. Larkin, Allie
People We Meet on Vacation. Henry, Emily

PEOPLE WHO ARE BLIND
　Doerr, Anthony. ★*All the Light We Cannot See: A Novel*
　Flagg, Fannie. *Standing in the Rainbow: A Novel*
　Mitchell, David. ★*Cloud Atlas: A Novel*
　Raimondo, Lynne. *Dante's Dilemma: A Mark Angelotti Novel*
　Raimondo, Lynne. *Dante's Poison: A Mark Angelotti Novel*
　Saramago, Jose. ★*Blindness*

PEOPLE WHO ARE INTERSEX
　Eugenides, Jeffrey. ★*Middlesex*
　Roy, Arundhati. ★*The Ministry of Utmost Happiness: A Novel*
　Solomon, Rivers. *Sorrowland*

PEOPLE WHO ARE MUTE
　Lacey, Catherine. ★*Pew: A Novel*
　Stage, Zoje. ★*Baby Teeth: A Novel*

PEOPLE WHO HAVE HAD AMPUTATIONS
　Guterson, David. ★*Snow Falling on Cedars*
　Mandanipour, Shahriar. *Moon Brow*
　Pobi, Robert. *City of Windows*

PEOPLE WHO HAVE HAD HEART ATTACKS
　De los Santos, Marisa. *The Precious One*
　Forman, Gayle. *Leave Me: A Novel*

PEOPLE WHO HAVE HAD STROKES
　Higgins, Kristan. *Always the Last to Know*
　Oates, Joyce Carol. *Night. Sleep. Death. The Stars*
　Persson, Leif G. W. *The Dying Detective: A Mystery*

PEOPLE WHO HAVE HAD STROKES — FAMILY RELATIONSHIPS
　Finder, Joseph. *The Fixer*

PEOPLE WITH AIDS
　Bellow, Saul. *Ravelstein*

PEOPLE WITH ALZHEIMER'S DISEASE
　Cleave, Paul. *Trust No One: A Thriller*
　Dean, Debra. *The Madonnas of Leningrad: A Novel*

PEOPLE WITH AMNESIA
　Apostol, Gina. *Gun Dealers' Daughter: A Novel*
　Auster, Paul. *Travels in the Scriptorium: A Novel*
　Brown, Sandra. *The Witness*
　Chen, Mike. *We Could Be Heroes*
　Dybek, Nick. *The Verdun Affair: A Novel*
　Eco, Umberto. *The Mysterious Flame of Queen Loana: An Illustrated Novel*
　Greene, Graham. *The Last Word and Other Stories*
　Perry, Anne. *The Face of a Stranger*
　Putney, Mary Jo. *Loving a Lost Lord*

PEOPLE WITH ASPERGER'S SYNDROME
　Hoang, Helen. ★*The Kiss Quotient*

PEOPLE WITH AUTISM
　Gottlieb, Eli. *Best Boy: A Novel*
　Higgins, Kristan. ★*Pack up the Moon*
　Hoang, Helen. ★*The Bride Test*
　Panowich, Brian. *Hard Cash Valley*
　Vine, Barbara. *The Minotaur: A Novel*

PEOPLE WITH BRAIN INJURIES
　Gardiner, Meg. *Phantom Instinct*
　King, Stephen. *End of Watch: A Novel*

PEOPLE WITH CANCER
　Didion, Joan. *A Book of Common Prayer*
　Doyle, Roddy. *The Guts*
　Haruf, Kent. *Benediction*
　Mankell, Henning. ★*The Return of the Dancing Master*
　Parker, T. Jefferson. *The Blue Hour*
　Saunders, George. ★*Tenth of December: Stories*
　Sparks, Nicholas. *A Walk to Remember*
　Whelan, Julia. *My Oxford Year*

PEOPLE WITH CANCER — FAMILY RELATIONSHIPS
Gordimer, Nadine. *Get a Life*
PEOPLE WITH CHRONIC ILLNESSES
Hibbert, Talia. ★*Get a Life, Chloe Brown*
PEOPLE WITH DEMENTIA
Harding, Paul. *Tinkers*
Healey, Emma. ★*Elizabeth Is Missing*
PEOPLE WITH DEVELOPMENTAL DISABILITIES
Steinbeck, John. ★*Of Mice and Men*
Willink, Jocko. *Final Spin*
PEOPLE WITH DISABILITIES
Dunn, Katherine. *Geek Love*
Gilman, Susan Jane. *The Ice Cream Queen of Orchard Street: A Novel*
Gottlieb, Eli. *Best Boy: A Novel*
Harris, Thomas. *Red Dragon*
Hulse, S. M. *Eden Mine*
Maugham, W. Somerset. ★*Of Human Bondage*
PEOPLE WITH DISFIGUREMENTS
Golding, William. ★*Darkness Visible*
Hugo, Victor. ★*The Hunchback of Notre Dame*
PEOPLE WITH DOWN SYNDROME
Ball, Jesse. *Census*
Sjón. *The Blue Fox*
PEOPLE WITH HIV
Park, Sang Young. ★*Love in the Big City: A Novel*
PEOPLE WITH HUNTINGTON'S DISEASE
Genova, Lisa. *Inside the O'Briens: A Novel*
PEOPLE WITH LEPROSY
Holland, Cecelia. *Jerusalem*
PEOPLE WITH LEUKEMIA
Picoult, Jodi. ★*My Sister's Keeper*
PEOPLE WITH MENTAL ILLNESSES
Banasky, Carmiel. *The Suicide of Claire Bishop*
Bourdeaut, Olivier. *Waiting for Bojangles: A Novel*
Conroy, Pat. *The Prince of Tides*
McCullough, Colleen. *An Indecent Obsession*
Percy, Walker. *The Second Coming*
Spencer, Scott. ★*Endless Love*
Toews, Miriam. *Fight Night*
PEOPLE WITH MENTAL ILLNESSES — CARE AND TREATMENT
Kesey, Ken. ★*One Flew Over the Cuckoo's Nest*
PEOPLE WITH MUSCULAR DYSTROPHY
Evison, Jonathan. *The Revised Fundamentals of Caregiving: A Novel*
PEOPLE WITH PARAPLEGIA
Keller, Julia. ★*Bone on Bone*
Miles, Jonathan. *Anatomy of a Miracle*
PEOPLE WITH PARKINSON'S DISEASE
Franzen, Jonathan. ★*The Corrections*
Robotham, Michael. ★*Suspect*
PEOPLE WITH POLIOMYELITIS
London, Joan. *The Golden Age*
PEOPLE WITH POST-TRAUMATIC STRESS DISORDER
Mandanipour, Shahriar. *Moon Brow*
Tracy, P. J. ★*Deep into the Dark*
PEOPLE WITH QUADRIPLEGIA
Deaver, Jeffery. ★*The Coffin Dancer*

PEOPLE WITH SCHIZOPHRENIA
Banasky, Carmiel. *The Suicide of Claire Bishop*
Boyle, T. Coraghessan. *The Harder They Come*
Vine, Barbara. *The Minotaur: A Novel*
PEOPLE WITH TERMINAL ILLNESSES
Bock, Charles. *Alice & Oliver: A Novel*
Butler, Robert Olen. *Late City*
Cronin, Marianne. *The One Hundred Years of Lenni and Margot*
Giordano, Paolo. *Like Family*
Lewis, Beverly. *The Missing*
Nagamatsu, Sequoia. *How High We Go in the Dark*
PEOPLE WITH TERMINAL ILLNESSES — FAMILY RELATIONSHIPS
Banville, John. *The Infinities*
Genova, Lisa. *Inside the O'Briens: A Novel*
PERCEPTION
Harris, Sarah J. *The Color of Bee Larkham's Murder: A Novel*
Percy, Walker
★*The Moviegoer*
The Second Coming
★*Perdido Street Station*. Mieville, China
★*Perestroika in Paris: A Novel*. Smiley, Jane
Perez-Reverte, Arturo
The Club Dumas
What We Become
The Perfect Couple. Hilderbrand, Elin
A Perfect Explanation. Anstruther, Eleanor
The Perfect Girl. Macmillan, Gilly
The Perfect Guests. Rous, Emma
Perfect Little Children. Hannah, Sophie
The Perfect Man: A Novel. Murr, Naeem
The Perfect Mother: A Novel. Molloy, Aimee
The Perfect Wife: A Novel. Delaney, J. P.
The Perfect World of Miwako Sumida. Goenawan, Clarissa
PERFECTION
Haig, Francesca. *The Fire Sermon: A Novel*
Polansky, Daniel. *The Seventh Perfection*
PERFECTIONISM IN CHILDREN
Kress, Nancy. *Beggars in Spain*
Perfidia. Ellroy, James
PERFORMANCE ARTISTS
Freudenberger, Nell. *The Dissident*
PERFORMING ARTS
Alarcon, Daniel. *At Night We Walk in Circles: A Novel*
PERFORMING ARTS SCHOOLS
Choi, Susan. ★*Trust Exercise: A Novel*
Perfume River. Butler, Robert Olen
★*Perfume: the Story of a Murderer*. Suskind, Patrick
PERFUMES
Robbins, Tom. ★*Jitterbug Perfume*
Suskind, Patrick. ★*Perfume: The Story of a Murderer*
PERFUMES INDUSTRY AND TRADE
Gaynor, Hazel. *Meet Me in Monaco: A Novel*
Perihelion Summer. Egan, Greg
A Perilous Undertaking: A Veronica Speedwell Mystery. Raybourn, Deanna
The Peripheral. Gibson, William
Peripheral [Series]. Gibson, William

The **Perishing**: a Novel. Deon, Natashia
Perkins, S. C.
  Murder Once Removed
★The **Perks** of Loving a Wallflower. Ridley, Erica
Perla. De Robertis, Carolina
Permafrost. Reynolds, Alastair
The **Perplexing** Theft of the Jewel in the Crown. Khan, Vaseem
Perrotta, Tom
  The Abstinence Teacher
  The Leftovers
  Little Children
Perry, Anne
  A Dangerous Mourning
  Dark Tide Rising: A William Monk Novel
  ★A Darker Reality
  ★Death in Focus: An Elena Standish Novel
  ★Death with a Double Edge: A Daniel Pitt Novel
  The Face of a Stranger
  One Fatal Flaw: A Daniel Pitt Novel
  A Question of Betrayal
Perry, Sarah
  The Essex Serpent
  Melmoth: A Novel
Perry, Thomas
  The Bomb Maker
  Death Benefits: A Novel
  Fidelity
  ★The Left-Handed Twin
  The Old Man
  Vanishing Act
Persaud, Ingrid
  Love After Love: A Novel
PERSECUTION
  Werfel, Franz. ★The Forty Days of Musa Dagh
PERSECUTION BY NAZIS
  Boschwitz, Ulrich Alexander. The Passenger: A Novel
  Epstein, Jennifer Cody. ★Wunderland: A Novel
  Hoffman, Alice. ★The World That We Knew
  Konar, Affinity. Mischling: A Novel
  Rosner, Jennifer. ★The Yellow Bird Sings
  Sem-Sandberg, Steve. The Chosen Ones: A Novel
Persepolis Rising. Corey, James S. A.
PERSEUS (GREEK MYTHOLOGY)
  Barth, John. Chimera
The **Persian** Boy. Renault, Mary
PERSIAN EMPIRE
  Amirrezvani, Anita. The Blood of Flowers: A Novel
  Smith, Jill Eileen. Star of Persia: Esther's Story
PERSIAN GULF WAR, 1991
  Al Rawi, Shahad. The Baghdad Clock
PERSISTENCE
  Demirtas, Selahattin. Dawn: Stories
  Diaz, Junot. ★The Brief Wondrous Life of Oscar Wao
Personae: a Novel. Pava, Sergio de la
PERSONAL ADS
  Charles, KJ. Wanted, a Gentleman: Or, Virtue Over-Rated
PERSONAL ASSISTANTS
  Alcott, Kate. A Touch of Stardust

  Alexander, Victoria. The Lady Travelers Guide to Scoundrels and
    Other Gentlemen
  Bram, Christopher. Lives of the Circus Animals: A Novel
  Deaver, Jeffery. The October List
  Guillory, Jasmine. Royal Holiday
  Knight, Renee. The Secretary: A Novel
  Lane, Byron. ★A Star Is Bored
  Marias, Javier. Thus Bad Begins: A Novel
  Pellegrino, Amanda. Smile and Look Pretty
  Rivers, Francine. The Masterpiece
  Thorne, Sally. Second First Impressions
  Van Dyken, Rachel. Risky Play
  Weatherspoon, Rebekah. If the Boot Fits
  Wilsner, Meryl. ★Something to Talk About
PERSONAL CONDUCT
  Alexander, Tamera. With This Pledge
  Amis, Martin. ★The Zone of Interest: A Novel
  Arikawa, Hiro. The Travelling Cat Chronicles
  Bausch, Richard. Peace
  Baxter, Charles. There's Something I Want You to Do: Stories
  Beattie, Ann. A Wonderful Stroke of Luck: A Novel
  Beckett, Samuel. ★Murphy
  Clarke, Susanna. ★Piranesi
  Conrad, Joseph. Complete Short Fiction of Joseph Conrad: The
    Stories: Volume 1
  Doerr, Anthony. ★All the Light We Cannot See: A Novel
  Freeman, Castle. All That I Have: A Novel
  Gaitskill, Mary. Don't Cry: Stories
  Gardam, Jane. Old Filth
  Greene, Graham. ★The Heart of the Matter
  Haslett, Adam. Union Atlantic
  Helprin, Mark. Paris in the Present Tense
  Hession, Ronan. Leonard and Hungry Paul
  Jin, Ha. The Boat Rocker: A Novel
  Pryor, Mark. Hollow Man
  Rawlings, David. The Baggage Handler: A Novel
  Smith, B. J. The Return of Kid Cooper: A Novel
  Smith, Gregory Blake. ★The Maze at Windermere: A Novel
  Twain, Mark. ★Adventures of Huckleberry Finn: Tom Sawyer's
    Comrade ...
  Vargas Llosa, Mario. ★The Discreet Hero
  Warren, Robert Penn. All the King's Men
  Weatherspoon, Rebekah. A Thorn in the Saddle
  Whitehead, Colson. ★Harlem Shuffle
  Wilde, Oscar. ★The Picture of Dorian Gray
  Yourcenar, Marguerite. ★Memoirs of Hadrian: And Reflections on
    the Composition of Memoirs of Hadrian
PERSONAL PROPERTY
  Galsworthy, John. ★The Forsyte Saga
Personal Recollections of Joan of Arc. Twain, Mark
PERSONAL SPACE
  Smith, Ali. There but for The: A Novel
PERSONAL TRAINERS
  Dorn, L. R. The Anatomy of Desire
  Rochon, Farrah. The Dating Playbook
  Sosa, Mia. ★Acting on Impulse
  Williams, Denise. The Fastest Way to Fall
Personal. Child, Lee

PERSONALITY CHANGE
Restrepo, Laura. ★*Delirium: A Novel*
★*Persons* Unknown: A Novel. Steiner, Susie
Persson Giolito, Malin
Beyond All Reasonable Doubt: A Novel
Quicksand
Persson, Leif G. W.
Another Time, Another Life: The Story of a Crime
The Dying Detective: A Mystery
Free Falling, as If in a Dream: The Story of a Crime
Persuader. Child, Lee
★*Persuasion*. Austen, Jane
PERTH, WESTERN AUSTRALIA
London, Joan. *The Golden Age*
PERU
Pulley, Natasha. *The Bedlam Stacks*
Redfield, James. *The Celestine Prophecy: An Adventure*
Rivero, Melissa. *The Affairs of the Falcons*
Robbins, Tom. *Fierce Invalids Home from Hot Climates*
Vargas Llosa, Mario. *The Bad Girl*
Vargas Llosa, Mario. ★*The Discreet Hero*
Vargas Llosa, Mario. *Green House*
Vargas Llosa, Mario. *The Time of the Hero*
PERUGIA, ITALY
Dibdin, Michael. *Ratking*
Perveen Mistry novels [Series]. Massey, Sujata
Pesci, David
Amistad: A Novel
PESSIMISM
Barbery, Muriel. *The Elegance of the Hedgehog*
Pessl, Marisha
Night Film: A Novel
Special Topics in Calamity Physics
PET ADOPTION
Jimenez, Abby. ★*The Happy Ever After Playlist*
PET OWNERS
Parrish, Roan. *Better Than People*
Pet Sematary. King, Stephen
PET SHOPS
Barry, Dave. *Lunatics*
Peter Ash novels [Series]. Petrie, Nicholas
Peter Diamond mysteries [Series]. Lovesey, Peter
Peter Macklin novels [Series]. Estleman, Loren D.
Peters, Ellis
Brother Cadfael's Penance
The Holy Thief
Peters, Torrey
★*Detransition, Baby*
Petersen, Todd Robert
Picnic in the Ruins
Peterson, Tracie
What Comes My Way
Petrie, Nicholas
The Breaker
Burning Bright
The Drifter
Tear It Down
The Wild One

Petry, Ann
★*The Street*
PETS
Maizes, R. L. *Other People's Pets*
PETS — TRAVEL
Arikawa, Hiro. *The Travelling Cat Chronicles*
Petterson, Per
I Curse the River of Time
I Refuse
Out Stealing Horses: A Novel
★*Pew: a Novel*. Lacey, Catherine
Peynado, Brenda
The Rock Eaters: Stories
PHAEDRA (GREEK MYTHOLOGY)
Saint, Jennifer. *Ariadne*
Phantom. Nesbo, Jo
Phantom Instinct. Gardiner, Meg
★*Phantom* Prey. Sandford, John
The Pharaoh's Secret. Cussler, Clive
PHARMACEUTICAL RESEARCH
Patchett, Ann. ★*State of Wonder: A Novel*
Raimondo, Lynne. *Dante's Poison: A Mark Angelotti Novel*
PHARMACEUTICAL RESEARCH — CORRUPT PRACTICES
Le Carre, John. *The Constant Gardener: A Novel*
PHARMACISTS
Flagg, Fannie. *Standing in the Rainbow: A Novel*
Thomson, E. S. *Beloved Poison*
Trigiani, Adriana. *Big Stone Gap: A Novel*
PHARMACOLOGY
Raimondo, Lynne. *Dante's Poison: A Mark Angelotti Novel*
Phase Six. Shepard, Jim
PHELAN FAMILY (FICTITIOUS CHARACTERS)
Kennedy, William. ★*Ironweed: A Novel*
PHILADELPHIA, PENNSYLVANIA
Benton, Janet. *Lilli De Jong: A Novel*
Chan, Jessamine. *The School for Good Mothers*
Clemmons, Zinzi. *What We Lose*
Cush, Jean Love. *Endangered*
Dexter, Pete. *Spooner*
Franzen, Jonathan. ★*The Corrections*
Gilbert, Elizabeth. ★*The Signature of All Things: A Novel*
Glover, Nicole. ★*The Conductors*
Glover, Nicole. *The Undertakers*
Haddam, Jane. *Cheating at Solitaire: A Gregor Demarkian Novel*
Haddam, Jane. *Hardscrabble Road*
Mathis, Ayana. *The Twelve Tribes of Hattie*
McKinney-Whetstone, Diane. *Leaving Cecil Street: A Novel*
Moore, Liz. *Long Bright River*
Patchett, Ann. ★*The Dutch House: A Novel*
Pomerantz, Sharon. *Rich Boy*
Pride, Christine. ★*We Are Not Like Them*
Reid, Kiley. ★*Such a Fun Age*
Roberts, Nora. ★*The Awakening*
Roberts, Nora. ★*The Becoming*
Scottoline, Lisa. ★*Every Fifteen Minutes*
Scottoline, Lisa. *Feared*
Scottoline, Lisa. *Legal Tender*
Solomon, Asali. *Disgruntled: A Novel*

Stevens, Francis. *The Heads of Cerberus*
Tyree, Omar. ★*Flyy Girl*
Tyree, Omar. *For the Love of Money: A Novel*
Weiner, Jennifer. *In Her Shoes: A Novel*
Weiner, Jennifer. *Little Earthquakes*
Wiseman, Ellen Marie. *The Orphan Collector*
Philida: a Novel. Brink, Andre P.

PHILIP

Druon, Maurice. *The Iron King*
Montclair, Allison. *A Royal Affair*
Philip Marlowe mysteries [Series]. Osborne, Lawrence

PHILIPPINE-AMERICAN WAR, 1896-1902

Apostol, Gina. *Insurrecto*

PHILIPPINES

Apostol, Gina. *Bibliolepsy*
Apostol, Gina. *Gun Dealers' Daughter: A Novel*
Apostol, Gina. *Insurrecto*
Castillo, Elaine. *America Is Not the Heart*
Irving, John. *Avenue of Mysteries: A Novel*
Sayles, John. *A Moment in the Sun*

Phillips, Arthur

★*The King at the Edge of the World: Novel*
The Tragedy of Arthur: A Novel

Phillips, Caryl

Dancing in the Dark
A Distant Shore
Foreigners
A View of the Empire at Sunset

Phillips, Christi

The Devlin Diary
The Rossetti Letter: A Novel

Phillips, Gin

Fierce Kingdom: A Novel

Phillips, Helen

The Beautiful Bureaucrat: A Novel
The Need: A Novel

Phillips, Jayne Anne

Lark and Termite: A Novel
Quiet Dell: A Novel

Phillips, Julia

★*Disappearing Earth*

Phillips, Susan Elizabeth

Call Me Irresistible
★*Dance Away with Me*
First Star I See Tonight
The Great Escape
Heroes Are My Weakness
★*Natural Born Charmer*
What I Did for Love
★*When Stars Collide*
The **Philosopher's** Pupil. Murdoch, Iris

PHILOSOPHERS

Beams, Clare. *The Illness Lesson*
Bernhard, Thomas. ★*The Loser*
Bernhard, Thomas. *Wittgenstein's Nephew: A Friendship*
Murdoch, Iris. *The Philosopher's Pupil*
Pipkin, John. *Woodsburner: A Novel*

PHILOSOPHY

Barbery, Muriel. *The Elegance of the Hedgehog*
Saramago, Jose. *Death with Interruptions*

PHILOSOPHY TEACHERS

Sartre, Jean Paul. *The Age of Reason*

PHILOSOPHY, MODERN

Beauvoir, Simone de. ★*The Mandarins: A Novel*

Philyaw, Deesha

The Secret Lives of Church Ladies

PHOBIAS

Semple, Maria. *Where'd You Go, Bernadette: A Novel*
Phoenix Unbound. Draven, Grace

PHOENIX, ARIZONA

Abbott, Megan E. *Bury Me Deep*
Bacigalupi, Paolo. ★*The Water Knife*
Dimberg, Kelsey Rae. *Girl in the Rearview Mirror*
McMillan, Terry. ★*Waiting to Exhale*
Talton, Jon. *City of Dark Corners*

Phoenix, Michele

The Space Between Words
Phoresis. Egan, Greg
The **Photographer**. Carter, Mary Dixie

PHOTOGRAPHERS

Brundage, Elizabeth. *The Vanishing Point*
Hoffman, Alice. *The Museum of Extraordinary Things: A Novel*
Leonard, Elmore. *Labrava*
Oliveras, Priscilla. *Anchored Hearts*
Silver, Marisa. *Mary Coin: A Novel*
Waller, Robert James. ★*The Bridges of Madison County*

PHOTOGRAPHIC MEMORY

Polansky, Daniel. *The Seventh Perfection*
Sedgwick, Marcus. *Mister Memory: A Novel*

PHOTOGRAPHS

Goldberg, Myla. *Feast Your Eyes*
Hand, Elizabeth. *Available Dark: A Thriller*
Hand, Elizabeth. *Hard Light*
Jenoff, Pam. *The Lost Girls of Paris*

PHOTOGRAPHY

Grass, Gunter. *The Box: Tales from the Darkroom*

PHOTOJOURNALISTS

Danielewski, Mark Z. ★*House of Leaves: A Novel*
Phryne Fisher mysteries [Series]. Greenwood, Kerry

PHYSICAL THERAPISTS

Daria, Alexis. ★*A Lot Like Adios*

PHYSICIAN AND PATIENT

Barry, Sebastian. *The Secret Scripture: A Novel*
Steadman, Catherine. *Mr. Nobody: A Novel*

PHYSICIAN DRUG ABUSERS

Irving, John. ★*The Cider House Rules: A Novel*

PHYSICIANS

Allende, Isabel. *A Long Petal of the Sea: A Novel*
Amis, Martin. ★*Time's Arrow, or the Nature of the Offense*
Atkinson, Kate. ★*When Will There Be Good News?: A Novel*
Ballard, J. G. ★*The Day of Creation*
Barry, Sebastian. *The Secret Scripture: A Novel*
Blake, Audrey. *The Girl in His Shadow: A Novel*
Bowen, Kelly. *A Rogue by Night*
Brodesser-Akner, Taffy. *Fleishman Is in Trouble: A Novel*

Camus, Albert. *The Plague*

Christie, Agatha. ★*The Murder of Roger Ackroyd: A Hercule Poirot Mystery*

Cleeves, Ann. ★*The Heron's Cry*

Cook, Robin. *Coma: A Novel*

Cronin, A. J. *Citadel*

Eliot, George. ★*Middlemarch: A Study of Provincial Life*

Forster, E. M. ★*A Passage to India*

Francis, Felix. *Pulse*

Greene, Graham. *The Honorary Consul*

Guillory, Jasmine. *The Proposal*

Guillory, Jasmine. ★*The Wedding Date*

Hawley, Noah. *The Good Father*

Jin, Ha. ★*Waiting*

Johnson, Tara. *Engraved on the Heart*

McCall Smith, Alexander. *The Comforts of a Muddy Saturday: An Isabel Dalhousie Novel*

McCall Smith, Alexander. ★*The No. 1 Ladies' Detective Agency*

North, Claire. *The Pursuit of William Abbey*

Parry, Ambrose. *The Way of All Flesh*

Pasternak, Boris Leonidovich. ★*Doctor Zhivago*

Pears, Iain. *An Instance of the Fingerpost*

Peikoff, Kira. *Mother Knows Best*

Phillips, Arthur. ★*The King at the Edge of the World: Novel*

Pirie, David. *The Patient's Eyes*

Purcell, Laura. *The House of Whispers*

Quirk, Matthew. *Cold Barrel Zero*

Ross, Ann B. *Miss Julia Takes the Wheel*

Sabatini, Rafael. *Captain Blood*

Shaw, Vivian. ★*Dreadful Company*

Shaw, Vivian. ★*Strange Practice*

Shepard, Jim. ★*The Book of Aron*

Snipes, Wesley. *Talon of God*

Spear, Terry. *A Billionaire Wolf for Christmas*

Starling, Caitlin. *The Death of Jane Lawrence*

Steel, Danielle. *First Sight*

Stevenson, Robert Louis. ★*The Strange Case of Dr. Jekyll and Mr. Hyde*

Sthers, Amanda. *Holy Lands: A Novel*

Verghese, A. *Cutting for Stone: A Novel*

Walker, Caroline Louise. *Man of the Year*

Wright, Lawrence. *The End of October*

Yoon, Paul. ★*Run Me to Earth: A Novel*

PHYSICIANS' SPOUSES

Abbott, Megan E. *Bury Me Deep*

Flaubert, Gustave. ★*Madame Bovary: Provincial Ways*

Lewis, Sinclair. ★*Main Street: The Story of Carol Kennicott*

PHYSICISTS

Gross, Andrew. *The One Man*

Harrison, M. John. *Light*

Lightman, Alan P. ★*Einstein's Dreams*

Liu, Cixin. *Ball Lightning*

Liu, Cixin. ★*The Dark Forest*

McEwan, Ian. *Solar: A Novel*

PHYSICS

Lightman, Alan P. ★*Einstein's Dreams*

Liu, Cixin. ★*The Three-Body Problem*

PHYSICS — EXPERIMENTS

Palmer, Dexter Clarence. *Version Control*

PIANISTS

Bernhard, Thomas. ★*The Loser*

Genova, Lisa. *Every Note Played*

Ishiguro, Kazuo. *The Unconsoled*

Kilalea, Katharine. *Ok, Mr. Field: A Novel*

*The **Piano** Tuner*. Mason, Daniel

PIANO TUNERS

Mason, Daniel. *The Piano Tuner*

PIANOS

Cander, Chris. *The Weight of a Piano: A Novel*

PICARESQUE FICTION

Allende, Isabel. ★*Eva Luna*

Auster, Paul. *Timbuktu: A Novel*

Barth, John. ★*The Sot-Weed Factor*

Beatty, Paul. *Slumberland: A Novel*

Bellow, Saul. ★*The Adventures of Augie March*

Boyne, John. *The Heart's Invisible Furies*

Byrne, Trevor. *Ghosts and Lightning*

Cervantes Saavedra, Miguel de. ★*Don Quixote*

Defoe, Daniel. ★*Moll Flanders*

Dickens, Charles. *The Pickwick Papers*

Doyle, Roddy. *A Star Called Henry*

Dunn, Katherine. *Geek Love*

Fielding, Henry. ★*The History of Tom Jones, a Foundling*

Kaufman, Charlie. *Antkind: A Novel*

Lee, Chang-Rae. ★*My Year Abroad*

Ozick, Cynthia. *The Puttermesser Papers*

Portis, Charles. ★*The Dog of the South*

Roth, Philip. *The Great American Novel*

Roth, Philip. ★*Portnoy's Complaint*

Smith, Zadie. *The Autograph Man: A Novel*

Twain, Mark. ★*Adventures of Huckleberry Finn: Tom Sawyer's Comrade ...*

Van der Vliet Oloomi, Azareen. *Call Me Zebra*

Wallace, Daniel. ★*Big Fish: A Novel of Mythic Proportions*

Piccirilli, Tom

The Last Kind Words

The Last Whisper in the Dark: A Novel

Pickard County Atlas. Harding Thornton, Christina

Pickard, Nancy

The Scent of Rain and Lightning: A Novel

Pickle's Progress. Butler, Marcia

PICKPOCKETS

Dickens, Charles. *Oliver Twist, or the Parish Boy's Progress*

*The **Pickup***. Gordimer, Nadine

*The **Pickwick** Papers*. Dickens, Charles

Picnic in the Ruins. Petersen, Todd Robert

Picoult, Jodi

★*The Book of Two Ways*

Change of Heart: A Novel

House Rules: A Novel

Keeping Faith: A Novel

Leaving Time: A Novel

★*My Sister's Keeper*

Nineteen Minutes: A Novel

Sing You Home: A Novel

A Spark of Light: A Novel
The Storyteller
Vanishing Acts: A Novel
  ★*Wish You Were Here: A Novel*
★*The **Picture** of Dorian Gray.* Wilde, Oscar
★*Picturing Will.* Beattie, Ann
Piece of My Heart. Robinson, Peter
★*Pieces of Her.* Slaughter, Karin
PIEGAN INDIANS
  Guthrie, A. B. ★*The Big Sky*
PIERCE, FRANKLIN
  Davies, Carys. *The Mission House*
  Pyper, Andrew. *The Residence: A Novel*
Piercy, Marge
  Gone to Soldiers: A Novel
  Sex Wars
  Vida: A Novel
PIG FARMING
  Del Amo, Jean-Baptiste. *Animalia*
  Sthers, Amanda. *Holy Lands: A Novel*
PIGEON, ANNA (FICTITIOUS CHARACTER)
  Barr, Nevada. *Destroyer Angel: An Anna Pigeon Novel*
  Barr, Nevada. *Track of the Cat*
PIGEONS
  Graves, Stephanie. *Olive Bright, Pigeoneer*
PIGS
  Del Amo, Jean-Baptiste. *Animalia*
  Pigs in Heaven. Kingsolver, Barbara
  Pike Logan thrillers [Series]. Taylor, Brad
Pike, Signe
  The Forgotten Kingdom: A Novel
  The Lost Queen
Pilcher, Rosamunde
  Coming Home
  A Place Like Home: Short Stories
  ★*The Shell Seekers*
PILGRIMS AND PILGRIMAGES
  Crace, Jim. *Quarantine*
  Endo, Shusaku. *Deep River*
  Gunn, James E. *Transcendental*
  Potzsch, Oliver. *The Poisoned Pilgrim: A Hangman's Daughter Tale*
  Sharratt, Mary. *Revelations*
  Simmons, Dan. *The Fall of Hyperion*
  Simmons, Dan. ★*Hyperion*
PILGRIMS AND PILGRIMAGES, CHRISTIAN
  Spark, Muriel. ★*The Mandelbaum Gate*
PILLAGE
  Doctorow, E. L. *The March: A Novel*
★*The **Pillars** of the Earth.* Follett, Ken
Pillars of the Earth [Series]. Follett, Ken
*The **Pilot's** Wife: A Novel.* Shreve, Anita
PILOTS
  Benjamin, Melanie. ★*The Aviator's Wife: A Novel*
  Bolano, Roberto. ★*Distant Star*
  Brown, Sandra. *Tailspin*
  Buchman, M. L. *Pure Heat*
  Clavell, James. *Shogun*
  Deutermann, Peter T. *Pacific Glory: A Novel*

Heller, Peter. ★*The Dog Stars: A Novel*
Priest, Cherie. *Ganymede*
Saint-Exupery, Antoine de. ★*The Little Prince*
Saint-Exupery, Antoine de. *Night Flight*
Pinborough, Sarah
  ★*Behind Her Eyes: A Novel*
  ★*Cross Her Heart: A Novel*
  ★*Dead to Her: A Novel*
Pineiro, Caridad
  One Summer Night
  South Beach Love: A Feel-Good Romance from Hallmark Publishing
  What Happens in Summer
PINOCHET UGARTE, AUGUSTO
  Bolano, Roberto. ★*By Night in Chile*
Pinsker, Sarah
  A Song for a New Day
Pinter, Jason
  Hide Away
  A Stranger at the Door
Pintoff, Stefanie
  Hostage Taker: A Novel
PIONEER MEN
  Durham, David Anthony. ★*Gabriel's Story*
PIONEER WOMEN
  Cather, Willa. ★*My Antonia*
  Cather, Willa. *O Pioneers!*
  McCrumb, Sharyn. ★*The Ballad of Frankie Silver*
  Obreht, Tea. *Inland: A Novel*
  Rivers, Francine. ★*Redeeming Love*
Pipkin, John
  Woodsburner: A Novel
★*Piranesi.* Clarke, Susanna
Pirate Latitudes. Crichton, Michael
Pirate Utopia. Sterling, Bruce
PIRATES
  Barth, John. ★*The Sot-Weed Factor*
  Clark, P. Djeli. *The Black God's Drums*
  Crichton, Michael. *Pirate Latitudes*
  Du Maurier, Daphne. *Frenchman's Creek*
  Michener, James A. *Caribbean*
  Sabatini, Rafael. *Captain Blood*
  Schwab, Victoria. *A Gathering of Shadows*
  Spencer, Minerva. *Barbarous*
  Sterling, Bruce. *Pirate Utopia*
Pirie, David
  The Patient's Eyes
PIRRIP, PHILIP (FICTITIOUS CHARACTER)
  Dickens, Charles. ★*Great Expectations*
*The **Pisces**: a Novel.* Broder, Melissa
PISSARRO, CAMILLE
  Crucet, Jennine Capo. *Make Your Home Among Strangers*
  Hoffman, Alice. *The Marriage of Opposites: A Novel Based on the Life of Rachel Pizzarro*
PITCHERS (BASEBALL)
  Holmes, Linda. ★*Evvie Drake Starts Over: A Novel*
  Malamud, Bernard. *The Natural*
Pitoniak, Anna
  Necessary People

★*Our American Friend*

PITT, DIRK (FICTITIOUS CHARACTER)

Cussler, Clive. *Havana Storm*

Cussler, Clive. *Pacific Vortex!*

Cussler, Clive. ★*Raise the Titanic!*

Pitts, Leonard

Freeman

PITTSBURGH, PENNSYLVANIA

Chabon, Michael. ★*Wonder Boys*

Edwards, Kim. *The Memory Keeper's Daughter*

O'Nan, Stewart. *Henry, Himself*

Wideman, John Edgar. *Look for Me and I'll Be Gone: Stories*

Pizza Girl. Frazier, Jean Kyoung

A Place Like Home: Short Stories. Pilcher, Rosamunde

A Place of Execution. McDermid, Val

PLAGIARISM

McCall Smith, Alexander. *The Lost Art of Gratitude*

The Plague. Camus, Albert

PLAGUE

Brin, David. *Existence*

Bunn, T. Davis. *Outbreak*

Camus, Albert. *The Plague*

Corey, James S. A. *Cibola Burn*

Corey, James S. A. *Nemesis Games*

Golden, Christopher. *The Pandora Room: A Novel*

Hill, Joe. *The Fireman: A Novel*

King, Stephen. ★*The Stand*

Nagamatsu, Sequoia. *How High We Go in the Dark*

O'Farrell, Maggie. *Hamnet*

Oe, Kenzaburo. *Nip the Buds, Shoot the Kids*

Rollins, James. *The Demon Crown: A Sigma Force Novel*

Stewart, George R. *Earth Abides*

Sweeney-Baird, Christina. *The End of Men*

Tepper, Sheri S. ★*Grass*

Walters, Minette. *The Last Hours: A Novel*

PLAGUE — HISTORY

Willis, Connie. ★*Doomsday Book*

The Plague of Doves. Erdrich, Louise

Plain Bad Heroines. Danforth, Emily M.

★*Plainsong*. Haruf, Kent

PLANETS

Chambers, Becky. ★*The Galaxy, and the Ground Within*

Chambers, Becky. *To Be Taught, If Fortunate*

Egan, Greg. *Phoresis*

Starling, Caitlin. *The Luminous Dead*

PLANETS — COLONIZATION

Mackintosh, Anneliese. *Bright and Dangerous Objects*

Robinson, Kim Stanley. ★*Blue Mars*

Robinson, Kim Stanley. ★*Green Mars*

Robinson, Kim Stanley. ★*Red Mars*

PLANETS — EXPLORATION

Cambias, James L. *A Darkling Sea*

Weir, Andy. *The Martian*

PLANNED COMMUNITIES

Heller, L. Alison. *The Neighbor's Secret*

Smith, Zadie. ★*Nw: A Novel*

PLANNERS

Christopher, Andie J. *Not the Girl You Marry*

PLANTAGENET PERIOD (1154-1485)

Cornwell, Bernard. *The Archer's Tale*

Follett, Ken. *World Without End*

Franklin, Ariana. ★*Death and the Maiden*

Franklin, Ariana. *Mistress of the Art of Death*

Franklin, Ariana. *The Serpent's Tale*

Gregory, Philippa. *The Kingmaker's Daughter*

Gregory, Philippa. *The Red Queen: A Novel*

Gregory, Philippa. *The White Princess*

Penman, Sharon Kay. *Here Be Dragons*

Penman, Sharon Kay. *The Queen's Man: A Medieval Mystery*

Penman, Sharon Kay. *The Sunne in Splendour*

Robb, Candace M. ★*A Choir of Crows*

Robb, Candace M. *The Cross-Legged Knight: An Owen Archer Mystery*

Robb, Candace M. *A Gift of Sanctuary: An Owen Archer Mystery*

Robb, Candace M. *A Murdered Peace*

Robb, Candace M. *The Riddle of St. Leonard's: An Owen Archer Mystery.*

Robb, Candace M. *A Twisted Vengeance*

Scott, Walter. ★*Ivanhoe*

Seton, Anya. *Katherine*

Starr, Melvin R. *Unhallowed Ground*

PLANTATION LIFE

Atakora, Afia. ★*Conjure Women*

Faulkner, William. ★*Go Down, Moses*

Johnson, Sadeqa. ★*Yellow Wife*

Jones, Robert. ★*The Prophets: A Novel*

Levy, Andrea. *The Long Song*

Santiago, Esmeralda. *Conquistadora: A Novel*

Smith, Lee. *On Agate Hill: A Novel*

Stowe, Harriet Beecher. ★*Uncle Tom's Cabin*

PLANTATION OWNERS

Hicks, Robert. *The Widow of the South*

PLANTATION OWNERS' SPOUSES

Hicks, Robert. *The Widow of the South*

PLANTATIONS

Crafts, Hannah. *The Bondwoman's Narrative*

Locke, Attica. *The Cutting Season*

Smith, Lee. *On Agate Hill: A Novel*

Straight, Susan. *A Million Nightingales*

PLANTS

Baker, Kage. *In the Garden of Iden: A Novel of the Company*

Burke, Sue. *Semiosis*

PLASTIC SURGERY

Castel-Bloom, Orly. *Textile*

Hiaasen, Carl. *Skin Tight*

James, P. D. *The Private Patient*

Plath, Sylvia

★*The Bell Jar*

A Play for the End of the World. Chakrabarti, Jai

PLAY GROUPS

Hankin, Laura. *Happy & You Know It*

★*Play It as It Lays: A Novel*. Didion, Joan

The Play of Death. Potzsch, Oliver

Playbook (Alexa Martin) [Series]. Martin, Alexa

The Player of Games. Banks, Iain

★*Player Piano*. Vonnegut, Kurt

PLAYER-PIANO
  Gaddis, William. *Agape Agape*
The Player: a Mystery. Parks, Brad
Playful brides [Series]. Bowman, Valerie
PLAYGROUNDS
  Roth, Philip. ★*Nemesis*
Playing Nice. Delaney, J. P.
Playing with Fire. Gerritsen, Tess
Playing with Fire. Meader, Kate
Playing with Fire. Robinson, Peter
PLAYWRITING
  Bausch, Richard. *Hello to the Cannibals: A Novel*
PLEASURE
  Wallace, David Foster. ★*Infinite Jest: A Novel*
PLEASURE CRUISES
  Friedland, Elyssa. *The Floating Feldmans*
  Ware, Ruth. *The Woman in Cabin Ten*
The Pleasure of Pain. Speight, Shameek A.
Pleasure of pain novels [Series]. Speight, Shameek A.
The Pledge. Kent, Kathleen
PLINY, THE ELDER, 23-79
  Harris, Robert. *Pompeii: A Novel*
  Rice, Anne. *Memnoch the Devil*
★*The Plot.* Korelitz, Jean Hanff
★*The Plot Against America.* Roth, Philip
The Plover: a novel. Doyle, Brian
PLUM, STEPHANIE (FICTITIOUS CHARACTER)
  Evanovich, Janet. *Turbo Twenty-Three*
Pnin. Nabokov, Vladimir Vladimirovich
The Poacher's Son. Doiron, Paul
POACHERS
  Box, C. J. ★*Open Season*
  Doiron, Paul. *The Poacher's Son*
  McLaughlin, James A. *Bearskin*
Pobi, Robert
  City of Windows
  Under Pressure
Pochoda, Ivy
  ★*These Women*
  Visitation Street: A Novel
PODCASTERS
  Brazier, Eliza Jane. *If I Disappear*
  Goldin, Megan. *The Night Swim*
  Jalaluddin, Uzma. *Hana Khan Carries On*
PODCASTS
  Gaylin, Alison. *Never Look Back*
  Mina, Denise. *Conviction*
The Poe Shadow: A Novel. Pearl, Matthew
Poe, Edgar Allan
  ★*Complete Stories and Poems of Edgar Allan Poe*
  The Narrative of Arthur Gordon Pym of Nantucket
POE, EDGAR ALLAN
  Aw, Tash. *We, the Survivors*
  Bayard, Louis. *The Pale Blue Eye: A Novel*
  Fairstein, Linda A. *Entombed*
  Morrison, Toni. *Paradise*
  Palahniuk, Chuck. *Fight Club*
  Pearl, Matthew. *The Poe Shadow: A Novel*

  Racculia, Kate. ★*Tuesday Mooney Talks to Ghosts: A Novel*
  Tyler, Anne. *A Patchwork Planet*
Poeppel, Amy
  Musical Chairs: A Novel
POETRY
  Gaiman, Neil. ★*Fragile Things: Short Fictions and Wonders*
  Gilman, Charlotte Perkins. ★*The Yellow Wallpaper and Selected Writings*
  Poe, Edgar Allan. ★*Complete Stories and Poems of Edgar Allan Poe*
  Sapphire. *American Dreams*
  Spencer, Sally. *The Shivering Turn*
POETRY — HISTORY AND CRITICISM
  Nabokov, Vladimir Vladimirovich. *Pale Fire*
POETRY WRITING
  London, Joan. *The Golden Age*
  Martine, Arkady. ★*A Memory Called Empire*
POETS
  Araghi, Alireza Taheri. ★*The Immortals of Tehran*
  Auster, Paul. *Invisible*
  Auster, Paul. *Timbuktu: A Novel*
  Beagle, Peter S. *In Calabria*
  Bolano, Roberto. ★*Distant Star*
  Cooley, Martha. *The Archivist: A Novel*
  Cunningham, Michael. *Specimen Days*
  Darznik, Jasmin. *Song of a Captive Bird: A Novel*
  Dillard, Annie. *The Maytrees: A Novel*
  Levy, Deborah. *Swimming Home: A Novel*
  Littell, Robert. *The Mayakovsky Tapes: A Novel*
  Qiu, Xiaolong. *Death of a Red Heroine*
  Rooney, Sally. ★*Conversations with Friends*
  Senna, Danzy. *New People*
POETS, AMERICAN
  Dos Passos, John. *1919*
POETS, ENGLISH
  Barker, Pat. ★*The Ghost Road*
  Barker, Pat. ★*Regeneration*
  Byatt, A. S. ★*Possession: A Romance*
  Friedman, Daniel. *Riot Most Uncouth: A Lord Byron Mystery*
  Pearl, Matthew. *The Dante Chamber*
  Waugh, Evelyn. *The Loved One: An Anglo-American Tragedy*
POETS, ISRAELI
  Oz, Amos. *Fima*
POETS, MEXICAN
  Bolano, Roberto. *Amulet*
  Bolano, Roberto. ★*The Savage Detectives*
POETS, RUSSIAN
  Pasternak, Boris Leonidovich. ★*Doctor Zhivago*
POETS, TURKISH
  Pamuk, Orhan. ★*Snow*
Pohl, Frederik
  Chernobyl: A Novel
  Gateway
The Point of Return: A Novel. Deb, Siddhartha
POIROT, HERCULE (FICTITIOUS CHARACTER)
  Christie, Agatha. *Mrs. McGinty's Dead*
  Christie, Agatha. ★*Murder on the Orient Express*
The Poisoned Pilgrim: A Hangman's Daughter Tale. Potzsch, Oliver
Poisoner mysteries [Series]. Poole, Sara

POISONING

Barclay, Linwood. *The Twenty-Three: A Promise Falls Novel*
Beaton, M. C. *Agatha Raisin and the Quiche of Death*
Christie, Agatha. *The Hollow*
Hall, Tarquin. *The Case of the Deadly Butter Chicken: A Vish Puri Mystery*
Jackson, Shirley. *We Have Always Lived in the Castle*
McCall Smith, Alexander. *The Saturday Big Tent Wedding Party*
McGuire, Seanan. *Chimes at Midnight: An October Daye Novel*
Potzsch, Oliver. *The Dark Monk: A Hangman's Daughter Tale*
Robb, J. D. *Innocent in Death*
Robertson, Imogen. *Circle of Shadows*
Roosevelt, Elliott. ★*Murder and the First Lady*
Sayers, Dorothy L. *The Unpleasantness at the Bellona Club*
Saylor, Steven. *The Judgment of Caesar: A Novel of Ancient Rome*
Stout, Rex. ★*Gambit*
Tsao, Tiffany. *The Majesties*

POISONOUS GASES

DeLillo, Don. ★*White Noise*
Murakami, Haruki. *After the Quake: Stories*

POISONOUS MUSHROOMS

Sayers, Dorothy L. ★*The Documents in the Case*

POISONS

Bradley, C. Alan. *A Red Herring Without Mustard*
Bradley, C. Alan. *The Weed That Strings the Hangman's Bag: A Flavia De Luce Mystery*
Delany, Vicki. *Murder in a Teacup*
Malliet, G. M. *A Demon Summer: A Max Tudor Mystery*
★*The Poisonwood Bible: A Novel*. Kingsolver, Barbara

Poissant, David James
Lake Life

Poke Rafferty Bangkok thrillers [Series]. Hallinan, Timothy

POLAND

Amis, Martin. ★*The Zone of Interest: A Novel*
Berry, Steve. ★*The Warsaw Protocol*
Cantor, Jillian. *Half Life*
Cherezinska, Elzbieta. *The Widow Queen*
Furst, Alan. *The Spies of Warsaw*
Gross, Andrew. *The One Man*
Gross, Max. *The Lost Shtetl*
Jedrowski, Tomasz. *Swimming in the Dark*
Keneally, Thomas. ★*Schindler's List*
Konar, Affinity. *Mischling: A Novel*
Kosinski, Jerzy. ★*The Painted Bird*
Morris, Heather. *Cilka's Journey*
Rimmer, Kelly. ★*The Warsaw Orphan: A Wwii Novel*
Rosner, Jennifer. ★*The Yellow Bird Sings*
Shepard, Jim. ★*The Book of Aron*
Singer, I. J. *The Brothers Ashkenazi*
Singer, Isaac Bashevis. *The Family Moskat*
Singer, Isaac Bashevis. ★*The Magician of Lublin*
Twardoch, Szczepan. *The King of Warsaw*

Polansky, Daniel
The Seventh Perfection

POLAR EXPEDITIONS

McGregor, Jon. *Lean Fall Stand*
Polar Star. Smith, Martin Cruz

POLICE

Aaronovitch, Ben. *Broken Homes*
Aaronovitch, Ben. *Midnight Riot*
Aaronovitch, Ben. *Moon Over Soho*
Adler-Olsen, Jussi. *The Absent One*
Adler-Olsen, Jussi. *The Keeper of Lost Causes*
Adler-Olsen, Jussi. *The Purity of Vengeance: A Department Q Novel*
Adler-Olsen, Jussi. ★*Victim 2117*
Ahlborn, Ania. *The Devil Crept In*
Anderson, Kent. *Green Sun: A Novel*
Atkinson, Kate. *One Good Turn: A Novel*
Bannalec, Jean-Luc. *Death in Brittany*
Benn, James R. *Billy Boyle: A World War Two Mystery*
Bowen, Peter. *Badlands*
Buchanan, Edna. *You Only Die Twice: A Britt Montero Mystery*
Burdett, John. *Bangkok 8*
Butler, Gwendoline. *Death Lives Next Door*
Butler, Marcia. *Pickle's Progress*
Child, Lee. *Nothing to Lose*
Christie, Agatha. *Towards Zero*
Church, James. ★*A Corpse in the Koryo*
Church, James. *Hidden Moon: An Inspector O Novel*
Cleave, Paul. *A Killer Harvest: A Thriller*
Cleeves, Ann. *Raven Black*
Collins, Wilkie. ★*The Moonstone*
Connelly, Michael. *The Black Ice*
Connelly, Michael. *The Brass Verdict: A Novel*
Connelly, Michael. *The Burning Room*
Connelly, Michael. *The Crossing*
Connelly, Michael. ★*The Dark Hours*
Corleone, Douglas. *Good as Gone*
Corry, Jane. *The Dead Ex*
Crais, Robert. *Suspect*
Cross-Smith, Leesa. *Whiskey & Ribbons*
Dahl, Arne. *Bad Blood*
Dahl, Arne. *Misterioso: A Crime Novel*
De Giovanni, Maurizio. *The Bastards of Pizzofalcone*
De la Motte, Anders. *MemoRandom: A Thriller*
DeSilva, Bruce. *Rogue Island*
Diamond, Elizabeth. *An Accidental Light*
Dibdin, Michael. *Ratking*
Dick, Philip K. *The Minority Report*
Eisler, Barry. *Livia Lone*
Ellroy, James. *The Cold Six Thousand: A Novel*
Ellroy, James. ★*L.A. Confidential*
Ellroy, James. *This Storm: A Novel*
Estleman, Loren D. ★*Gas City*
Evanovich, Janet. *One for the Money*
Faye, Lyndsay. *The Gods of Gotham*
Fowler, Christopher. *Bryant & May: Strange Tide*
Freedman, Benedict. *Mrs. Mike: The Story of Katherine Mary Flannigan*
French, Nicci. *Thursday's Children*
French, Tana. ★*Broken Harbor*
French, Tana. *Faithful Place: A Novel*
French, Tana. ★*The Secret Place*
Furst, Alan. *Spies of the Balkans: A Novel*
Garcia-Roza, L. A. *December Heat*

Gardner, Lisa. *Alone*
George, Elizabeth. *A Banquet of Consequences*
George, Elizabeth. *Careless in Red*
George, Elizabeth. *The Punishment She Deserves*
George, Elizabeth. *This Body of Death: An Inspector Lynley Novel*
Gerritsen, Tess. *The Apprentice: A Novel*
Goodis, David. *Nightfall*
Goodwin, S. M. *Absence of Mercy*
Greene, Graham. ★*The Heart of the Matter*
Gruber, Michael. *Night of the Jaguar: A Novel*
Gruber, Michael. *Valley of Bones: A Novel*
Guinn, Matthew. *The Scribe: A Novel*
Haldane, Sean. *The Devil's Making*
Harris, Robert. ★*Fatherland*
Harrison, M. John. *Nova Swing*
Harvey, John. *Cold in Hand*
Harvey, John. *Darkness, Darkness*
Harvey, Michael T. *The Chicago Way*
Harvey, Michael T. *Pulse*
Hiaasen, Carl. *Bad Monkey*
Higashino, Keigo. *Malice*
Higashino, Keigo. *Newcomer*
Hill, Susan. *The Pure in Heart: A Simon Serrailler Crime Novel*
Hillerman, Tony. *The Wailing Wind*
Humphreys, Sara Taney. *Trouble Walks In*
Indriðason, Arnaldur. *Reykjavik Nights: An Inspector Erlendur Novel*
James, P. D. *Death of an Expert Witness*
James, P. D. *The Lighthouse*
James, P. D. *Original Sin*
James, P. D. *The Private Patient*
James, P. D. *A Taste for Death*
Kaminsky, Stuart M. *Murder on the Trans-Siberian Express*
Kellerman, Jonathan. *Gone*
Kepler, Lars. *The Sandman*
Kerley, Jack. ★*The Death Collectors*
Kerr, Philip. ★*Metropolis: A Bernie Gunther Novel*
Lawrence, David. *The Dead Sit Round in a Ring*
Lehane, Dennis. ★*The Given Day*
Leon, Donna. *Beastly Things: A Commissario Guido Brunetti Mystery*
Leon, Donna. *Drawing Conclusions: A Commissario Guido Brunetti Mystery*
Leon, Donna. *Falling in Love: A Commissario Guido Brunetti Mystery*
Leon, Donna. *The Golden Egg*
Leon, Donna. *A Question of Belief: A Commissario Guido Brunetti Mystery*
Leon, Donna. *Uniform Justice*
Leonard, Elmore. *Glitz*
Lippman, Laura. *What the Dead Know*
Lovesey, Peter. ★*The Last Detective*
MacBride, Stuart. *Cold Granite*
Mankell, Henning. *Before the Frost: A Linda Wallander Mystery*
Mankell, Henning. *The Dogs of Riga*
Mankell, Henning. *Firewall*
Mankell, Henning. *The Man Who Smiled: A Kurt Wallander Mystery*
Mankell, Henning. ★*One Step Behind*
Mankell, Henning. ★*The Return of the Dancing Master*

Mankell, Henning. *The Troubled Man*
Mark, David John. *Cruel Mercy*
Mayor, Archer. *Tag Man: A Joe Gunther Novel*
McCall Smith, Alexander. ★*The Department of Sensitive Crimes: A Detective Varg Novel*
McDermid, Val. *The Distant Echo*
McDermid, Val. *A Place of Execution*
McIlvanney, William. *The Dark Remains: Laidlaw's First Case*
McKinty, Adrian. *In the Morning I'll Be Gone: A Detective Sean Duffy Novel*
Miller, Derek B. ★*American by Day*
Moor, Jessica. *The Keeper*
Mukherjee, Abir. *Smoke and Ashes: A Novel*
Nesbo, Jo. *The Leopard*
Nesbo, Jo. *The Redeemer*
Nickson, Chris. *Come the Fear*
Ono, Masatsugu. *Echo on the Bay*
Parker, T. Jefferson. *L.A. Outlaws: A Novel*
Paton, Alan. *Too Late the Phalarope*
Pawel, Rebecca. *Death of a Nationalist*
Penny, Louise. *The Cruelest Month: A Three Pines Mystery*
Penny, Louise. *Still Life*
Perry, Anne. *A Dangerous Mourning*
Perry, Anne. *Dark Tide Rising: A William Monk Novel*
Perry, Anne. *The Face of a Stranger*
Perry, Thomas. *The Bomb Maker*
Pratchett, Terry. *The Fifth Elephant: A Novel of Discworld*
Pratchett, Terry. *Guards! Guards!*
Pratchett, Terry. *Men at Arms: A Novel of Discworld*
Pratchett, Terry. *Thud!: A Novel of Discworld*
Preston, Douglas J. *City of Endless Night*
Pronzini, Bill. *The Violated*
Qiu, Xiaolong. *Death of a Red Heroine*
Qiu, Xiaolong. *Don't Cry Tai Lake: An Inspector Chen Novel*
Qiu, Xiaolong. *Enigma of China*
Qiu, Xiaolong. *Red Mandarin Dress: An Inspector Chen Novel*
Qiu, Xiaolong. *Shanghai Redemption: An Inspector Chen Novel*
Qiu, Xiaolong. *When Red Is Black*
Quartey, Kwei. *Gold of Our Fathers*
Rankin, Ian. ★*Black and Blue: An Inspector Rebus Novel*
Rankin, Ian. *The Black Book*
Rankin, Ian. *The Complaints*
Rankin, Ian. *Dead Souls: An Inspector Rebus Novel*
Rankin, Ian. *The Falls: An Inspector Rebus Novel*
Rankin, Ian. *The Impossible Dead*
Rankin, Ian. *The Naming of the Dead: An Inspector Rebus Novel*
Rankin, Ian. *A Question of Blood: An Inspector Rebus Novel*
Rendell, Ruth. *The Babes in the Wood: A Chief Inspector Wexford Mystery*
Rendell, Ruth. *Kissing the Gunner's Daughter*
Rendell, Ruth. *Not in the Flesh*
Rendell, Ruth. *A Sleeping Life*
Rendell, Ruth. *Speaker of Mandarin*
Rindell, Suzanne. *The Other Typist*
Robinson, Peter. *All the Colors of Darkness*
Robinson, Peter. ★*Careless Love*
Robinson, Peter. *Children of the Revolution*
Robinson, Peter. *Friend of the Devil*

Robinson, Peter. *In the Dark Places*
Robinson, Peter. *Innocent Graves: An Inspector Banks Mystery*
Robotham, Michael. *The Night Ferry: A Novel*
Rosenfelt, David. *Black and Blue: A Doug Brock Thriller*
Rosenfelt, David. *Blackout*
Roslund, Anders. ★*Knock Knock*
Sanders, Lawrence. ★*The First Deadly Sin*
Sandford, John. *Buried Prey*
Sandford, John. *Certain Prey*
Sandford, John. *Chosen Prey*
Sandford, John. *Easy Prey*
Sandford, John. *Mortal Prey*
Sandford, John. ★*Naked Prey*
Sandford, John. ★*Silken Prey*
Sandford, John. *Sudden Prey*
Sedgwick, Marcus. *Mister Memory: A Novel*
Shannon, Dell. ★*Chaos of Crime*
Shaw, William. *A Song for the Brokenhearted*
Silvis, Randall. *Two Days Gone: A Novel*
Simenon, Georges. *Maigret and the Black Sheep*
Simenon, Georges. *Maigret and the Fortuneteller*
Simenon, Georges. ★*Maigret and the Killer*
Simenon, Georges. *Maigret and the Madwoman*
Simenon, Georges. ★*Maigret and the Saturday Caller*
Simenon, Georges. ★*Maigret and the Toy Village*
Simenon, Georges. ★*Maigret Bides His Time*
Simenon, Georges. ★*Maigret Goes Home*
Simenon, Georges. *Maigret in Holland*
Simenon, Georges. *Maigret's Memoirs*
Simenon, Georges. *My Friend Maigret*
Simpson, Dorothy. *Dead and Gone: An Inspector Luke Thanet Novel.*
Simpson, Dorothy. *Doomed to Die*
Simpson, Dorothy. *No Laughing Matter*
Simpson, Dorothy. *Once Too Often: An Inspector Luke Thanet Novel*
Sjowall, Maj. ★*The Laughing Policeman*
Sjowall, Maj. ★*The Locked Room: The Story of a Crime*
Sjowall, Maj. *The Man on the Balcony: The Story of a Crime*
Smith, Julie. *82 Desire: A Skip Langdon Novel*
Smith, Martin Cruz. *Stalin's Ghost*
Smith, Martin Cruz. ★*Tatiana: An Arkady Renko Novel*
Smith, Martin Cruz. *Three Stations: An Arkady Renko Novel*
Smith, Martin Cruz. *Wolves Eat Dogs: A Novel*
Smith, Tom Rob. *Child 44*
Spencer, Sally. *Death's Dark Shadow*
Spencer, Sally. ★*Echoes of the Dead*
Spencer, Sally. *The Ring of Death*
Spencer, Sally. *A Walk with the Dead*
Stanley, Michael. *Death of the Mantis*
Steinhauer, Olen. *The Bridge of Sighs*
Swinson, Kiki. *Lifestyles of the Rich and Shameless*
Wambaugh, Joseph. *The New Centurions*
Wolfe, Tom. *Back to Blood: A Novel*
Woods, Stuart. *New York Dead*
Zhou, Haohui. *Death Notice: A Novel*

POLICE BRUTALITY
Bump, Gabriel. ★*Everywhere You Don't Belong: A Novel*
Mosley, Walter. *Down the River Unto the Sea*
Whitlow, Robert. *A Time to Stand*

POLICE CHIEFS
Ballard, J. G. ★*The Day of Creation*
Estleman, Loren D. ★*Gas City*
Higgins, Kristan. ★*The Best Man*
Parker, Robert B. *Blue-Eyed Devil*
Parker, Robert B. *Death in Paradise*
Parker, Robert B. *Night Passage*
Parker, Robert B. *Trouble in Paradise*
Russo, Richard. ★*Everybody's Fool*
Shames, Terry. ★*An Unsettling Crime for Samuel Craddock*
Spencer-Fleming, Julia. *Hid from Our Eyes*
Spencer-Fleming, Julia. *In the Bleak Midwinter*
Spencer-Fleming, Julia. *Through the Evil Days: A Clare Fergusson/Russ Van Alstyne Mystery*
Walker, Martin. *The Coldest Case*
Walker, Martin. *The Shooting at Chateau Rock*
Whitaker, Chris. ★*We Begin at the End*

POLICE CORRUPTION
Anappara, Deepa. *Djinn Patrol on the Purple Line: A Novel*
Beck, Haylen. *Here and Gone*
Chandler, Raymond. *The Lady in the Lake*
Coleman, Reed Farrel. *Where It Hurts: A Gus Murphy Novel*
Crompton, Richard. *Hell's Gate: A Novel*
De Giovanni, Maurizio. *The Bastards of Pizzofalcone*
Ellroy, James. ★*L.A. Confidential*
Iles, Greg. *The Bone Tree: A Novel*
Irwin, Stephen M. *The Broken Ones: A Novel*
Laukkanen, Owen. *Deception Cove*
Mosley, Walter. *Down the River Unto the Sea*
Parker, Robert B. *Blue-Eyed Devil*
Rankin, Ian. *The Impossible Dead*
Rankin, Ian. *Resurrection Men: An Inspector Rebus Novel*
Scottoline, Lisa. *Legal Tender*
Slaughter, Karin. ★*Fallen: A Novel*
Smith, Martin Cruz. *Stalin's Ghost*
Smith, Martin Cruz. *Three Stations: An Arkady Renko Novel*
Soderberg, Alexander. *The Other Son: A Sophie Brinkmann Novel*
Solares, Martin. *Don't Send Flowers*
Spencer, Sally. ★*Echoes of the Dead*
Willocks, Tim. *Memo from Turner*

POLICE COVER-UPS
Harvey, Michael T. *The Chicago Way*

POLICE DOGS
Crais, Robert. *Suspect*
Humphreys, Sara Taney. *Trouble Walks In*
Mizushima, Margaret. *Killing Trail*

POLICE INTERNAL AFFAIRS INVESTIGATION
Rankin, Ian. *The Complaints*
Rankin, Ian. *The Impossible Dead*
Rankin, Ian. *Resurrection Men: An Inspector Rebus Novel*

POLICE MISCONDUCT
Aguilar Camin, Hector. *Death in Veracruz*
Box, C. J. *Badlands*
Larsson, Stieg. *The Girl Who Played with Fire*
MacDonald, John D. *The Long Lavender Look*
Mullen, Thomas. *Darktown: A Novel*
Rankin, Ian. *The Complaints*
Rankin, Ian. *Resurrection Men: An Inspector Rebus Novel*

Smith, B. J. *Crow's Landing: A Novel*
Turnbull, Cadwell. *No Gods, No Monsters*

POLICE MURDERS

Atkins, Ace. *The Redeemers*
Bruen, Ken. *Galway Girl: A Jack Taylor Novel*
Slaughter, Karin. *Cop Town: A Novel*

POLICE PROCEDURALS

Alsterdal, Tove. *We Know You Remember*
Anderson, Kent. *Green Sun: A Novel*
Archer, Jeffrey. *Nothing Ventured*
Bannalec, Jean-Luc. *Death in Brittany*
Bannalec, Jean-Luc. *The Granite Coast Murders*
Bannalec, Jean-Luc. *The Killing Tide: A Brittany Mystery*
Bannister, Jo. *Silent Footsteps*
Burke, James Lee. ★*The New Iberia Blues*
Burke, James Lee. ★*A Private Cathedral*
Burke, James Lee. *Robicheaux*
Camilleri, Andrea. *Riccardino*
Castillo, Linda. ★*Fallen*
Church, James. *Bamboo and Blood: An Inspector O Novel*
Church, James. ★*A Corpse in the Koryo*
Church, James. *A Drop of Chinese Blood*
Church, James. *Hidden Moon: An Inspector O Novel*
Cleeves, Ann. *The Crow Trap*
Cleeves, Ann. *The Darkest Evening*
Cleeves, Ann. *Raven Black*
Cleeves, Ann. *Thin Air*
Cleeves, Ann. *Wild Fire*
Connelly, Michael. *The Black Ice*
Connelly, Michael. *The Burning Room*
Connelly, Michael. *The Crossing*
Connelly, Michael. ★*The Dark Hours*
Connelly, Michael. *Dark Sacred Night*
Connelly, Michael. *The Wrong Side of Goodbye*
Crais, Robert. *Demolition Angel: A Novel.*
Crombie, Deborah. *A Bitter Feast*
Dahl, Arne. *Bad Blood*
Dahl, Arne. *Misterioso: A Crime Novel*
De Giovanni, Maurizio. *The Bastards of Pizzofalcone*
De Giovanni, Maurizio. *The Crocodile*
Dexter, Colin. *The Daughters of Cain*
Dexter, Colin. *The Remorseful Day*
Dexter, Colin. *The Way Through the Woods*
Dibdin, Michael. *Ratking*
Dugoni, Robert. *In Her Tracks*
Dugoni, Robert. *My Sister's Grave*
Ellroy, James. *Perfidia*
Ellroy, James. *This Storm: A Novel*
Frear, Caz. *Stone Cold Heart*
Frear, Caz. *Sweet Little Lies*
French, Tana. ★*Broken Harbor*
French, Tana. *Faithful Place: A Novel*
French, Tana. *In the Woods*
French, Tana. *The Likeness*
French, Tana. ★*The Secret Place*
Galligan, John. *Bad Moon Rising*
Gardner, Lisa. ★*Before She Disappeared: A Novel*
George, Elizabeth. *A Banquet of Consequences*

George, Elizabeth. *Believing the Lie*
George, Elizabeth. *Careless in Red*
George, Elizabeth. *Just One Evil Act*
George, Elizabeth. *The Punishment She Deserves*
George, Elizabeth. *This Body of Death: An Inspector Lynley Novel*
George, Elizabeth. *What Came Before He Shot Her*
Gerritsen, Tess. *Choose Me*
Goldberg, Lee. *Bone Canyon*
Griffiths, Elly. *The Lantern Men: A Dr. Ruth Galloway Mystery*
Griffiths, Elly. *The Stone Circle*
Harrod-Eagles, Cynthia. *Cruel as the Grave*
Harrod-Eagles, Cynthia. *Headlong*
Harrod-Eagles, Cynthia. *Old Bones*
Harvey, John. *Cold in Hand*
Harvey, John. *Darkness, Darkness*
Harvey, Michael T. *Pulse*
Hayder, Mo. *Gone*
Hayder, Mo. *Poppet*
Hill, Susan. *The Pure in Heart: A Simon Serrailler Crime Novel*
Hill, Susan. *The Shadows in the Street: A Simon Serrailler Mystery*
Hillerman, Tony. *The Shape Shifter*
Hillerman, Tony. *The Sinister Pig*
Hillerman, Tony. *The Wailing Wind*
James, P. D. *Death of an Expert Witness*
James, P. D. *The Lighthouse*
James, P. D. *Original Sin*
James, P. D. *The Private Patient*
James, P. D. *A Taste for Death*
Jones, Darynda. *A Bad Day for Sunshine*
Jones, Darynda. *A Good Day for Chardonnay*
Kelly, Erin. *Broadchurch: A Novel*
Kent, Kathleen. *The Burn*
Kent, Kathleen. *The Pledge*
Khan, Ausma Zehanat. *Among the Ruins*
Khan, Ausma Zehanat. *The Unquiet Dead*
Leon, Donna. *Beastly Things: A Commissario Guido Brunetti Mystery*
Leon, Donna. *Drawing Conclusions: A Commissario Guido Brunetti Mystery*
Leon, Donna. *Falling in Love: A Commissario Guido Brunetti Mystery*
Leon, Donna. *The Golden Egg*
Leon, Donna. *A Question of Belief: A Commissario Guido Brunetti Mystery*
Leon, Donna. *Trace Elements*
Leon, Donna. ★*Transient Desires*
Leon, Donna. *Uniform Justice*
Leon, Donna. *Unto Us a Son Is Given*
Lovesey, Peter. *Beau Death*
Lovesey, Peter. *Diamond Solitaire*
Lovesey, Peter. ★*The Last Detective*
Lovesey, Peter. *The Tooth Tattoo*
MacBride, Stuart. *Cold Granite*
Mark, David John. *Cruel Mercy*
Mayor, Archer. ★*Marked Man*
Mayor, Archer. *Red Herring: A Joe Gunther Novel*
Mayor, Archer. *Tag Man: A Joe Gunther Novel*
McClure, James. *The Steam Pig*

McDermid, Val. ★*Still Life*

McKinty, Adrian. *In the Morning I'll Be Gone: A Detective Sean Duffy Novel*

Mizushima, Margaret. *Killing Trail*

Moor, Jessica. *The Keeper*

Moore, Liz. *Long Bright River*

Mullen, Thomas. *Darktown: A Novel*

Mullen, Thomas. *Lightning Men: A Novel*

North, Alex. *The Shadows*

North, Alex. *The Whisper Man*

Obregon, Nicolas. *Blue Light Yokohama*

Parker, T. Jefferson. *The Blue Hour*

Pawel, Rebecca. *Death of a Nationalist*

Penny, Louise. ★*All the Devils Are Here*

Penny, Louise. ★*A Better Man: A Chief Inspector Gamache Novel*

Penny, Louise. *The Cruelest Month: A Three Pines Mystery*

Penny, Louise. ★*The Madness of Crowds*

Penny, Louise. *Still Life*

Perry, Anne. *A Dangerous Mourning*

Perry, Anne. *Dark Tide Rising: A William Monk Novel*

Perry, Anne. *The Face of a Stranger*

Qiu, Xiaolong. *Death of a Red Heroine*

Qiu, Xiaolong. *Don't Cry Tai Lake: An Inspector Chen Novel*

Qiu, Xiaolong. *Enigma of China*

Qiu, Xiaolong. *Hold Your Breath, China*

Qiu, Xiaolong. *Red Mandarin Dress: An Inspector Chen Novel*

Qiu, Xiaolong. *Shanghai Redemption: An Inspector Chen Novel*

Qiu, Xiaolong. *When Red Is Black*

Quartey, Kwei. *Children of the Street: A Novel*

Quartey, Kwei. *Gold of Our Fathers*

Quartey, Kwei. *Murder at Cape Three Points*

Quartey, Kwei. *Wife of the Gods: A Novel*

Rankin, Ian. ★*Black and Blue: An Inspector Rebus Novel*

Rankin, Ian. *The Black Book*

Rankin, Ian. *The Complaints*

Rankin, Ian. *Dead Souls: An Inspector Rebus Novel*

Rankin, Ian. *Exit Music*

Rankin, Ian. *The Falls: An Inspector Rebus Novel*

Rankin, Ian. *The Hanging Garden: An Inspector Rebus Novel*

Rankin, Ian. *The Impossible Dead*

Rankin, Ian. *The Naming of the Dead: An Inspector Rebus Novel*

Rankin, Ian. *A Question of Blood: An Inspector Rebus Novel*

Rankin, Ian. ★*Rather Be the Devil*

Rankin, Ian. *Resurrection Men: An Inspector Rebus Novel*

Rankin, Ian. *Set in Darkness: An Inspector Rebus Novel*

Rankin, Ian. ★*A Song for the Dark Times*

Redondo, Dolores. *The Invisible Guardian*

Redondo, Dolores. *The North Face of the Heart*

Rendell, Ruth. *The Babes in the Wood*

Rendell, Ruth. *End in Tears*

Rendell, Ruth. *Harm Done*

Rendell, Ruth. *Kissing the Gunner's Daughter*

Rendell, Ruth. *Not in the Flesh*

Rendell, Ruth. *Road Rage*

Rendell, Ruth. *Simisola*

Rendell, Ruth. *A Sleeping Life*

Rendell, Ruth. *Speaker of Mandarin*

Ridpath, Michael. *Far North*

Robb, J. D. *Fantasy in Death*

Robb, J. D. *Innocent in Death*

Robb, J. D. *Leverage in Death: An Eve Dallas Novel*

Robb, J. D. *Naked in Death*

Robinson, Peter. *All the Colors of Darkness*

Robinson, Peter. ★*Careless Love*

Robinson, Peter. *Children of the Revolution*

Robinson, Peter. *Close to Home*

Robinson, Peter. *Cold Is the Grave*

Robinson, Peter. *Friend of the Devil*

Robinson, Peter. *In the Dark Places*

Robinson, Peter. *Innocent Graves: An Inspector Banks Mystery*

Robinson, Peter. *Piece of My Heart*

Robinson, Peter. *Playing with Fire*

Robinson, Peter. *Strange Affair*

Roslund, Anders. ★*Knock Knock*

Sandford, John. *Bloody Genius*

Sandford, John. *Broken Prey*

Sandford, John. *Buried Prey*

Sandford, John. *Certain Prey*

Sandford, John. *Chosen Prey*

Sandford, John. ★*Deadline*

Sandford, John. *Deep Freeze*

Sandford, John. *Easy Prey*

Sandford, John. *Field of Prey*

Sandford, John. ★*Golden Prey*

Sandford, John. *Hidden Prey*

Sandford, John. *Holy Ghost*

Sandford, John. ★*Invisible Prey*

Sandford, John. *Mad River*

Sandford, John. ★*Mind Prey*

Sandford, John. *Mortal Prey*

Sandford, John. ★*Naked Prey*

Sandford, John. ★*Night Prey*

Sandford, John. ★*Phantom Prey*

Sandford, John. ★*Rules of Prey*

Sandford, John. *Shock Wave*

Sandford, John. ★*Silent Prey*

Sandford, John. ★*Silken Prey*

Sandford, John. *Storm Front*

Sandford, John. *Storm Prey*

Sandford, John. *Sudden Prey*

Sandford, John. ★*Winter Prey*

Schaffhausen, Joanna. *Gone for Good*

Shaw, William. *The Birdwatcher*

Shaw, William. *Salt Lane*

Shaw, William. *A Song for the Brokenhearted*

Silvis, Randall. *Two Days Gone: A Novel*

Simenon, Georges. *Maigret and the Black Sheep*

Simenon, Georges. *Maigret and the Fortuneteller*

Simenon, Georges. ★*Maigret and the Killer*

Simenon, Georges. *Maigret and the Madwoman*

Simenon, Georges. ★*Maigret and the Saturday Caller*

Simenon, Georges. ★*Maigret and the Toy Village*

Simenon, Georges. *Maigret and the Wine Merchant*

Simenon, Georges. ★*Maigret Bides His Time*

Simenon, Georges. ★*Maigret Goes Home*

Simenon, Georges. *Maigret in Holland*

Simenon, Georges. *Maigret's Memoirs*
Simenon, Georges. *My Friend Maigret*
Sjowall, Maj. ★*Cop Killer: The Story of a Crime*
Sjowall, Maj. ★*The Laughing Policeman*
Sjowall, Maj. ★*The Locked Room: The Story of a Crime*
Sjowall, Maj. *The Man on the Balcony: The Story of a Crime*
Sjowall, Maj. ★*Murder at the Savoy*
Slaughter, Karin. ★*Fallen: A Novel*
Slaughter, Karin. ★*Undone: A Novel*
Smith, Martin Cruz. ★*Gorky Park*
Smith, Martin Cruz. *Havana Bay*
Smith, Martin Cruz. *Polar Star*
Smith, Martin Cruz. *The Siberian Dilemma*
Smith, Martin Cruz. *Stalin's Ghost*
Smith, Martin Cruz. ★*Tatiana: An Arkady Renko Novel*
Smith, Martin Cruz. *Three Stations: An Arkady Renko Novel*
Smith, Martin Cruz. *Wolves Eat Dogs: A Novel*
Spain, Jo. *With Our Blessing: An Inspector Tom Reynolds Mystery*
Spencer, Sally. *Best Served Cold*
Spencer, Sally. *Dead End*
Spencer, Sally. ★*The Hidden*
Spencer, Sally. *Thicker Than Water: A Monika Paniatowski British Police Procedural*
Sveistrup, Soren. ★*The Chestnut Man: A Novel*
Thomas, Russ. ★*Firewatching*
Thomas, Russ. *Nighthawking*
Tursten, Helene. *Hunting Game*
Verdon, John. *On Harrow Hill*
Wambaugh, Joseph. *The New Centurions*

POLICE PSYCHOLOGISTS
Patterson, James. *Kiss the Girls: A Novel*

POLICE QUESTIONING
Price, Richard. *Lush Life*

POLICE SPOUSES
Spencer, Sally. *Backlash*

POLICEWOMEN
Bannister, Jo. *Kindred Spirits*
Bannister, Jo. *Silent Footsteps*
Bolton, S. J. *A Dark and Twisted Tide*
Box, C. J. *Paradise Valley*
Crais, Robert. *Demolition Angel: A Novel.*
Gardner, Lisa. ★*Before She Disappeared: A Novel*
George, Elizabeth. *Just One Evil Act*
Hayder, Mo. *Hanging Hill*
Heaberlin, Julia. *We Are All the Same in the Dark: A Novel*
Indriðason, Arnaldur. *Outrage*
James, P. D. *The Lighthouse*
James, P. D. *The Private Patient*
Lansdale, Joe R. *Sunset and Sawdust*
Lawrence, David. *The Dead Sit Round in a Ring*
Mizushima, Margaret. *Killing Trail*
Mooney, Chris. *Blood World*
Moore, Liz. *Long Bright River*
Parker, T. Jefferson. *The Blue Hour*
Ritter, Todd. *Devil's Night*
Robb, J. D. *Connections in Death: An Eve Dallas Novel*
Robb, J. D. *Fantasy in Death*
Robb, J. D. *Innocent in Death*

Robb, J. D. *Leverage in Death: An Eve Dallas Novel*
Robb, J. D. *Naked in Death*
Rodriguez, Linda. *Every Last Secret: A Mystery*
See, Lisa. *Dragon Bones: A Novel*
Shaw, William. *Salt Lane*
Shoham, Liad. *Asylum City: A Novel*
Slaughter, Karin. *Cop Town: A Novel*
Slaughter, Karin. ★*Fallen: A Novel*
Smith, Julie. *House of Blues*
Smith, Julie. *Jazz Funeral*
Spencer, Sally. *Backlash*
Spencer, Sally. *Best Served Cold*
Spencer, Sally. *Dead End*
Spencer, Sally. *Death's Dark Shadow*
Spencer, Sally. ★*Echoes of the Dead*
Spencer, Sally. ★*The Hidden*
Spencer, Sally. *Lambs to the Slaughter*
Spencer, Sally. *The Ring of Death*
Spencer, Sally. *Thicker Than Water: A Monika Paniatowski British Police Procedural*
Spencer, Sally. *A Walk with the Dead*
Stewart, Amy. ★*Girl Waits with Gun*
Stewart, Amy. *Lady Cop Makes Trouble*
Stewart, Amy. *Miss Kopp's Midnight Confessions*

POLIOMYELITIS
Roth, Philip. ★*Nemesis*

POLISH AMERICAN BOYS
Dybek, Stuart. *I Sailed with Magellan*

POLISH AMERICAN FAMILIES
Dybek, Stuart. *I Sailed with Magellan*

POLISH AMERICAN MEN
Dybek, Stuart. *I Sailed with Magellan*

POLISH AMERICANS
Dybek, Stuart. *I Sailed with Magellan*
Sontag, Susan. ★*In America*

Polish boxer novels [Series]. Halfon, Eduardo

POLITICAL ACTIVISTS
Ballard, J. G. *Millennium People*
Forbes, Curdella. *A Tall History of Sugar*
Herrera, Adriana. *American Love Story*
Jedrowski, Tomasz. *Swimming in the Dark*
Ma, Jian. *Beijing Coma*
Piercy, Marge. *Vida: A Novel*
Shoham, Liad. *Asylum City: A Novel*

POLITICAL CAMPAIGNS
Meader, Kate. *Playing with Fire*
Sandford, John. ★*Silken Prey*

POLITICAL CARTOONS
Penrose, Andrea. *Murder at Half Moon Gate*
Penrose, Andrea. *Murder on Black Swan Lane*

POLITICAL CORRUPTION
Ackerman, Elliot. *Red Dress in Black and White*
Adichie, Chimamanda Ngozi. *Half of a Yellow Sun*
Adiga, Aravind. ★*The White Tiger: A Novel*
Atkins, Ace. *The Revelators*
Atwood, Margaret. ★*The Blind Assassin*
Brett, Simon. *Mrs Pargeter's Principle*
Burton, Jeffrey B. *The Keepers: A Mace Reid K-9 Mystery*

Church, James. *Bamboo and Blood: An Inspector O Novel*
Church, James. ★*A Corpse in the Koryo*
Cornwell, Bernard. *The Winter King: A Novel of Arthur*
Crompton, Richard. *Hour of the Red God*
Cumming, Charles. *A Foreign Country*
Dibdin, Michael. *Ratking*
Dowlatabadi, Mahmoud. *The Colonel*
Dumas, Alexandre. ★*The Man in the Iron Mask*
Dumas, Alexandre. *Twenty Years After*
Dunant, Sarah. *Blood and Beauty: A Novel*
Ellroy, James. *American Tabloid: A Novel*
Ellroy, James. *Blood's a Rover*
Ellroy, James. *The Cold Six Thousand: A Novel*
Gogol, Nikolai Vasilievich. ★*Dead Souls*
Harris, Robert. *The Ghost: A Novel*
Harvey, Michael T. *The Fifth Floor*
Harvey, Michael T. *The Governor's Wife*
Hiaasen, Carl. *Skin Tight*
James, Marlon. ★*A Brief History of Seven Killings: A Novel*
Kelton, Elmer. ★*The Way of the Coyote*
Larsson, Stieg. ★*The Girl Who Kicked the Hornet's Nest*
Le Carre, John. ★*A Delicate Truth*
Leon, Donna. *A Question of Belief: A Commissario Guido Brunetti Mystery*
Leon, Donna. *Uniform Justice*
Mantel, Hilary. ★*Wolf Hall*
Martin, George R. R. ★*A Clash of Kings*
Martin, George R. R. ★*A Dance with Dragons*
Martin, George R. R. ★*A Feast for Crows*
Martin, George R. R. ★*A Game of Thrones*
Martin, George R. R. ★*A Storm of Swords*
McCullough, Colleen. *The First Man in Rome*
Meltzer, Brad. *The Zero Game*
Morgan Jones, Chris. *The Silent Oligarch*
Patterson, Richard North. *Dark Lady*
Qiu, Xiaolong. *Hold Your Breath, China*
Qiu, Xiaolong. *Shanghai Redemption: An Inspector Chen Novel*
Ruiz Zafon, Carlos. *The Labyrinth of the Spirits*
Sandford, John. ★*Silken Prey*
Sansom, C. J. ★*Lamentation*
Silko, Leslie Marmon. *Almanac of the Dead*
Smith, Julie. *The Kindness of Strangers: A Skip Langdon Novel*
Steinhauer, Olen. *The Bridge of Sighs*
Vidal, Gore. *Washington, D. C.: A Novel*
Vonnegut, Kurt. *Jailbird: A Novel*
Warren, Robert Penn. *All the King's Men*
Wolfe, Gene. *The Land Across*
Woods, Stuart. *Chiefs*
Yang, JY. *The Descent of Monsters*
POLITICAL CRIMES AND OFFENSES
Smith, Tom Rob. *Child 44*
Smith, Tom Rob. *The Secret Speech*
POLITICAL FICTION
Acevedo, Chantel. *The Distant Marvels*
Adams, Henry. ★*Democracy: An American Novel*
Adichie, Chimamanda Ngozi. ★*Americanah: A Novel*
Adichie, Chimamanda Ngozi. *Half of a Yellow Sun*
Aimaq, Jasmine. *The Opium Prince*

Al-Ramli, Muhsin. *The President's Gardens*
Alarcon, Daniel. *At Night We Walk in Circles: A Novel*
Allende, Isabel. *Of Love and Shadows*
Antopol, Molly. *The Unamericans*
Aslam, Nadeem. ★*The Blind Man's Garden*
Aw, Tash. *We, the Survivors*
Bandi. *The Accusation: Forbidden Stories from Inside North Korea*
Bellow, Saul. *The Dean's December: A Novel*
Benaron, Naomi. *Running the Rift: A Novel*
Benedetti, Mario. *Springtime in a Broken Mirror*
Bolano, Roberto. ★*Distant Star*
Boudjedra, Rachid. *The Barbary Figs*
Boyle, T. Coraghessan. ★*The Tortilla Curtain*
Bulawayo, NoViolet. *We Need New Names: A Novel*
Carter, Stephen L. *Back Channel*
Coe, Jonathan. *The Rotters' Club*
Costello, Mark. *Big If*
Craig, Charmaine. *Miss Burma*
Daoud, Kamel. *The Meursault Investigation*
De Robertis, Carolina. *Cantoras*
Demirtas, Selahattin. *Dawn: Stories*
Dennis-Benn, Nicole. *Here Comes the Sun*
Desai, Kiran. *The Inheritance of Loss*
Didion, Joan. *A Book of Common Prayer*
Dimechkie, Karim. *Lifted by the Great Nothing*
Dowlatabadi, Mahmoud. *The Colonel*
Eco, Umberto. *Numero Zero*
El Akkad, Omar. *American War*
El Akkad, Omar. *What Strange Paradise*
Ellroy, James. *American Tabloid: A Novel*
Ellroy, James. *Blood's a Rover*
Ellroy, James. *The Cold Six Thousand: A Novel*
Englander, Nathan. *The Ministry of Special Cases*
Erpenbeck, Jenny. *The Book of Words*
Farah, Nuruddin. *Crossbones*
Farah, Nuruddin. *Knots*
ffitch, Madeline. *Stay and Fight*
Flanagan, Richard. *The Unknown Terrorist*
Florio, Gwen. *Silent Hearts*
Fuentes, Carlos. *The Eagle's Throne: A Novel*
Fuentes, Carlos. *The Years with Laura Diaz*
Garcia, Cristina. *King of Cuba: A Novel*
Garcia, Cristina. *The Lady Matador's Hotel: A Novel*
Ghaffari, Rabeah. ★*To Keep the Sun Alive*
Gibb, Camilla. *Sweetness in the Belly*
Grass, Gunter. *Too Far Afield*
Greene, Graham. ★*The Quiet American*
Gunaratne, Guy. *In Our Mad and Furious City*
Hage, Rawi. *De Niro's Game*
Han, Kang. ★*Human Acts: A Novel*
Heller, Joseph. *Good as Gold*
Hiaasen, Carl. ★*Squeeze Me: A Novel*
Jin, Ha. *The Boat Rocker: A Novel*
Kingsolver, Barbara. ★*Unsheltered*
Klay, Phil. ★*Missionaries*
Koestler, Arthur. *Darkness at Noon*
Kunzru, Hari. *Red Pill: A Novel*
Lalami, Laila. ★*The Moor's Account: A Novel*

Leavitt, David. ★*Shelter in Place*
Lethem, Jonathan. *Dissident Gardens*
Lewis, Sinclair. ★*It Can't Happen Here*
Limon, Martin. *The Line*
Ma, Jian. *China Dream*
Mabanckou, Alain. ★*Black Moses*
Mahfuz, Najib. ★*Palace Walk*
Mallon, Thomas. *Finale: A Novel*
Mallon, Thomas. *Landfall: A Novel*
Matar, Hisham. *In the Country of Men*
McCann, Colum. ★*Apeirogon: A Novel*
Mengestu, Dinaw. ★*All Our Names*
Mohamed, Nadifa. *The Orchard of Lost Souls: A Novel*
Mosley, Walter. *The Right Mistake: The Further Philosophical Investigations of Socrates Fortlow*
Mueenuddin, Daniyal. *In Other Rooms, Other Wonders: Connected Stories*
Naipaul, V. S. *A Bend in the River*
Naipaul, V. S. *Guerrillas*
Naipaul, V. S. *Magic Seeds*
Obioma, Chigozie. ★*The Fishermen: A Novel*
Okparanta, Chinelo. ★*Under the Udala Trees*
Onyebuchi, Tochi. ★*Riot Baby*
Orwell, George. ★*Animal Farm*
Pamuk, Orhan. ★*Snow*
Pamuk, Orhan. ★*A Strangeness in My Mind: A Novel*
Paton, Alan. *Ah, but Your Land Is Beautiful*
Paton, Alan. ★*Cry, the Beloved Country*
Paton, Alan. *Too Late the Phalarope*
Pitoniak, Anna. ★*Our American Friend*
Restrepo, Laura. ★*Delirium: A Novel*
Restrepo, Laura. *No Place for Heroes: A Novel*
Roth, Philip. ★*The Plot Against America*
Rushdie, Salman. ★*The Golden House*
Russell, Mary Doria. *Dreamers of the Day: A Novel*
Sahota, Sunjeev. *The Year of the Runaways*
Sainz Borgo, Karina. ★*It Would Be Night in Caracas*
Saramago, Jose. *The Manual of Painting and Calligraphy*
Schami, Rafik. *Sophia: Or the Beginning of All Tales*
Schell, Orville. *My Old Home: A Novel of Exile*
Shamsie, Kamila. *Home Fire: A Novel*
Sinclair, Upton. ★*The Jungle*
Sittenfeld, Curtis. *Rodham: A Novel*
Solzhenitsyn, Aleksandr Isaevich. ★*Cancer Ward*
Solzhenitsyn, Aleksandr Isaevich. *In the First Circle: A Novel : The Restored Text*
Soyinka, Wole. *Chronicles from the Land of the Happiest People on Earth*
Steele, Allen M. *Coyote: A Novel of Interstellar Exploration*
Suri, Manil. *The Age of Shiva: A Novel*
Trollope, Anthony. ★*The Prime Minister*
Updike, John. *Memories of the Ford Administration: A Novel*
Vargas Llosa, Mario. *The Feast of the Goat*
Vasquez, Juan Gabriel. ★*The Shape of the Ruins*
Vidal, Gore. ★*Lincoln: A Novel*
Vidal, Gore. *Washington, D. C.: A Novel*
Waldman, Amy. *A Door in the Earth*
Warren, Robert Penn. *All the King's Men*
Zola, Emile. ★*Germinal*

POLITICAL INTRIGUE
Altan, Ahmet. ★*Love in the Days of Rebellion*
Amirrezvani, Anita. *Equal of the Sun*
Andersen, Laura. *The Boleyn Deceit*
Andersen, Laura. ★*The Boleyn King*
Andersen, Laura. *The Boleyn Reckoning*
Arden, Katherine. ★*The Winter of the Witch*
Berry, Steve. ★*The Bishop's Pawn*
Berry, Steve. *The Lost Order*
Black, Benjamin. *Wolf on a String: A Novel*
Campbell, Lisbeth. *The Vanished Queen*
Campisi, Megan. *Sin Eater*
Carrick, M. A. *The Mask of Mirrors*
Cherezinska, Elzbieta. *The Widow Queen*
Cleeton, Chanel. *The Most Beautiful Girl in Cuba*
Edghill, India. *Queenmaker: A Novel of King David's Queen*
Elliott, Kate. *Unconquerable Sun*
Forsyth, Frederick. *The Fox*
Franklin, Ariana. *The Siege Winter*
George, Margaret. *The Confessions of Young Nero*
George, Margaret. *The Splendor Before the Dark: A Novel of the Emperor Nero*
Ghosh, Amitav. *The Glass Palace*
Greenwood, Kerry. *Out of the Black Land*
Harper, Karen. *The Queen's Secret: A Novel of England's World War II Queen*
Hiaasen, Carl. ★*Squeeze Me: A Novel*
Iggulden, Conn. *The Abbot's Tale*
Jin, Yong. *A Hero Born: A Novel*
Lagercrantz, David. *The Girl Who Lived Twice: A Lisbeth Salander Novel*
Lagercrantz, David. *The Girl Who Takes an Eye for an Eye*
Le Carre, John. *Agent Running in the Field*
Leckie, Ann. *Provenance*
Lee, Yoon Ha. *Raven Stratagem*
Lee, Yoon Ha. *Revenant Gun*
London, Julia. *Wild Wicked Scot*
Lyons, Jenn. *The Ruin of Kings*
Martell, Nick. *The Kingdom of Liars*
Martine, Arkady. ★*A Desolation Called Peace*
Massey, Sujata. ★*The Bombay Prince*
Massey, Sujata. *The Satapur Moonstone*
Maxwell, Everina. *Winter's Orbit*
Mina, Denise. ★*Rizzio*
North, Claire. *Notes from the Burning Age*
Polk, C. L. *Soulstar*
Polk, C. L. *Stormsong*
Powell, Mark. *Firebird*
Qiu, Xiaolong. *Enigma of China*
Roanhorse, Rebecca. ★*Black Sun*
Robb, Candace M. ★*A Choir of Crows*
Robb, Candace M. *The Cross-Legged Knight: An Owen Archer Mystery*
Robb, Candace M. *A Murdered Peace*
Robb, Candace M. *A Twisted Vengeance*
Sansom, C. J. *Tombland*
Shannon, Samantha. *The Priory of the Orange Tree*

Sigurðardóttir, Lilja. *Cage*

Spann, Susan. *Blade of the Samurai: A Shinobi Mystery*

Sterling, Bruce. *Pirate Utopia*

Stross, Charles. *Empire Games*

Vyleta, Dan. *Smoke: A Novel*

Wagers, K. B. *There Before the Chaos*

Wolfe, Paul. *The Lost Diary of M*

Wolfe, Suzanne M. *The Course of All Treasons*

POLITICAL LEADERSHIP

Liu, Ken. ★ *The Veiled Throne*

POLITICAL ORATORY

Smith, Tom Rob. *The Secret Speech*

POLITICAL PARTICIPATION

Coe, Jonathan. *The Rotters' Club*

POLITICAL PARTIES — HISTORY

Paton, Alan. *Ah, but Your Land Is Beautiful*

POLITICAL PERSECUTION

Al-Ramli, Muhsin. *The President's Gardens*

Atwood, Margaret. ★ *The Testaments: A Novel*

Barnes, Julian. *The Noise of Time*

Benedetti, Mario. *Springtime in a Broken Mirror*

Craig, Charmaine. *Miss Burma*

Ehirim, Nnamdi. *Prince of Monkeys*

Le Guin, Ursula K. *Orsinian Tales*

Shin, Ann. *The Last Exiles*

Solzhenitsyn, Aleksandr Isaevich. *In the First Circle: A Novel : The Restored Text*

POLITICAL PRISONERS

Benedetti, Mario. *Springtime in a Broken Mirror*

Khan, Ausma Zehanat. *Among the Ruins*

Koestler, Arthur. *Darkness at Noon*

Matar, Hisham. *In the Country of Men*

Pattison, Eliot. *The Skull Mantra*

Richler, Nancy. *Your Mouth Is Lovely: A Novel*

Saramago, Jose. *The Manual of Painting and Calligraphy*

Solzhenitsyn, Aleksandr Isaevich. *In the First Circle: A Novel : The Restored Text*

Solzhenitsyn, Aleksandr Isaevich. *One Day in the Life of Ivan Denisovich*

POLITICAL PRISONS

Richler, Nancy. *Your Mouth Is Lovely: A Novel*

POLITICAL REFUGEES

Allende, Isabel. *Of Love and Shadows*

Farah, Nuruddin. *Crossbones*

Yu, E. Lily. ★ *On Fragile Waves*

POLITICAL RISK INSURANCE

DeLillo, Don. *The Names*

POLITICAL SCIENCE

Fuentes, Carlos. *The Years with Laura Diaz*

Garcia, Cristina. *The Lady Matador's Hotel: A Novel*

Greene, Graham. *The Honorary Consul*

Mallon, Thomas. *Finale: A Novel*

Palmer, Ada. *Too Like the Lightning*

POLITICAL THRILLERS

Abrams, Stacey. *While Justice Sleeps: A Novel*

Baldacci, David. *Hell's Corner*

Berry, Steve. ★ *The Bishop's Pawn*

Berry, Steve. *The Lost Order*

Berry, Steve. ★ *The Malta Exchange: A Novel*

Berry, Steve. ★ *The Warsaw Protocol*

Cameron, Marc. ★ *Code of Honor*

Cameron, Marc. *Power and Empire*

Coes, Ben. *The Russian: A Thriller*

Coonts, Stephen. *The Armageddon File*

Coonts, Stephen. ★ *The Russia Account*

Dimberg, Kelsey Rae. *Girl in the Rearview Mirror*

Eisler, Barry. *The God's Eye View*

Finder, Joseph. *Guilty Minds*

Finder, Joseph. *The Switch: A Novel*

Higgins, Jack. *Eye of the Storm*

Le Carre, John. *The Constant Gardener: A Novel*

Meltzer, Brad. *The Inner Circle*

Meltzer, Brad. *The Tenth Justice*

Meltzer, Brad. *The Zero Game*

Mina, Denise. ★ *Rizzio*

Patterson, Richard North. *Balance of Power*

Patterson, Richard North. *No Safe Place*

Patterson, Richard North. *Protect and Defend*

Persson, Leif G. W. *Another Time, Another Life: The Story of a Crime*

Persson, Leif G. W. *Free Falling, as If in a Dream: The Story of a Crime*

Porter, Henry. *The Bell Ringers*

Powell, Mark. *Firebird*

Reich, Christopher. ★ *The Take*

Sakey, Marcus. *A Better World*

Sakey, Marcus. *Brilliance*

Steinhauer, Olen. *The Bridge of Sighs*

Stross, Charles. *Empire Games*

Tata, A. J. *Dark Winter*

Vachss, Andrew H. *Two Trains Running*

Wiesel, Elie. *Hostage*

POLITICAL VALUES

Smith, Ali. ★ *Spring*

POLITICAL VIOLENCE

Ballard, J. G. *Millennium People*

Bulawayo, NoViolet. *We Need New Names: A Novel*

D'Souza, Tony. *Whiteman*

Erpenbeck, Jenny. *The Book of Words*

Gordimer, Nadine. *None to Accompany Me*

Hamid, Mohsin. ★ *Exit West: A Novel*

Han, Kang. ★ *Human Acts: A Novel*

Kamali, Marjan. ★ *The Stationery Shop*

Osborne, Lawrence. *The Glass Kingdom: A Novel*

Vasquez, Juan Gabriel. ★ *The Shape of the Ruins*

POLITICIANS

Araghi, Alireza Taheri. ★ *The Immortals of Tehran*

Benedict, Marie. ★ *Lady Clementine*

Berry, Steve. ★ *The Bishop's Pawn*

Berry, Steve. *The Lost Order*

Bezmozgis, David. *The Betrayers: A Novel*

Black, Lisa. *Let Justice Descend*

Bradby, Tom. *Double Agent*

Brett, Simon. *Mrs Pargeter's Principle*

Burns, V. M. *Killer Words*

Child, Lee. *Personal*

Cobbs Hoffman, Elizabeth. *The Hamilton Affair*

Dev, Sonali. ★*Incense and Sensibility*
Ellison, Ralph. *Three Days Before the Shooting . . .*
Finder, Joseph. *The Switch: A Novel*
Fowler, Christopher. *Bryant & May: Oranges and Lemons*
Garcia Marquez, Gabriel. *The General in His Labyrinth*
George, Elizabeth. *The Punishment She Deserves*
Grau, Shirley Ann. *The Keepers of the House*
Guillory, Jasmine. *Party of Two*
Hammett, Dashiell. *The Glass Key*
Hart, Josephine. *Damage: A Novel*
Hatcher, Robin Lee. *Who I Am with You*
Hiaasen, Carl. *Strip Tease: A Novel*
Hilton, James. *Random Harvest*
Jedrowski, Tomasz. *Swimming in the Dark*
Kowal, Mary Robinette. *The Relentless Moon*
Ma, Jian. *China Dream*
Mallon, Thomas. *Finale: A Novel*
Mallon, Thomas. *Landfall: A Novel*
Mantel, Hilary. ★*Wolf Hall*
McCall Smith, Alexander. *Tiny Tales: Stories of Romance, Ambition, Kindness, and Happiness*
McCann, Colum. ★*Transatlantic: A Novel*
Pembrooke, Kate. *Not the Kind of Earl You Marry*
Persson, Leif G. W. *Another Time, Another Life: The Story of a Crime*
Rankin, Ian. *The Impossible Dead*
Rodriguez, Linda. *Every Broken Trust: A Mystery*
Roosevelt, Elliott. *Murder in the Oval Office*
Shamsie, Kamila. *Home Fire: A Novel*
Smith, Julie. ★*Mean Woman Blues*
Spencer, Sally. ★*A Dying Fall*
Spencer, Sally. *Thicker Than Water: A Monika Paniatowski British Police Procedural*
Stanley, Michael. *Deadly Harvest*
Trollope, Anthony. ★*The Eustace Diamonds*
Trollope, Anthony. ★*The Prime Minister*
Umrigar, Thrity N. *Everybody's Son*
Vaughan, Sarah. ★*Anatomy of a Scandal: A Novel*
Warren, Robert Penn. *All the King's Men*
Yellin, Jessica. *Savage News*
POLITICIANS' FAMILIES
Dimberg, Kelsey Rae. *Girl in the Rearview Mirror*
POLITICIANS' SPOUSES
Frazier, Charles. *Varina*
Miller, Sue. *The Senator's Wife*
Woolf, Virginia. ★*Mrs. Dalloway*
POLITICS AND CULTURE
Gordimer, Nadine. *Life Times: Stories, 1952-2007*
McCullough, Colleen. *The First Man in Rome*
Suri, Manil. *The Age of Shiva: A Novel*
Thien, Madeleine. *Do Not Say We Have Nothing*
Vidal, Gore. ★*Lincoln: A Novel*
Polk, C. L.
The Midnight Bargain
Soulstar
Stormsong
Witchmark
Pollock, Donald Ray
The Devil All the Time

Knockemstiff
POLLUTION
Harkaway, Nick. *Tigerman*
POLO, MARCO
Calvino, Italo. *Invisible Cities*
POLTERGEISTS
Jackson, Shirley. ★*The Haunting of Hill House*
POLYAMORY
Ripper, Kris. *The Life Revamp*
POLYGAMY
Adebayo, Ayobami. ★*Stay with Me*
Ebershoff, David. *The 19th Wife: A Novel*
Fisher, Tarryn. *The Wives*
Grey, Zane. ★*Riders of the Purple Sage*
Jones, Tayari. *Silver Sparrow: A Novel*
Vestal, Shawn. *Daredevils*
Pomerantz, Sharon
Rich Boy
POMPEII (EXTINCT CITY)
Harris, Robert. *Pompeii: A Novel*
Pompeii: a Novel. Harris, Robert
POMPEY, THE GREAT, 106-48 BC
Allende, Isabel. ★*Eva Luna*
Saylor, Steven. *Rubicon*
★*The Ponder Heart.* Welty, Eudora
Pontoppidan, Henrik
Lucky Per
PONZI SCHEMES
Mandel, Emily St. John. ★*The Glass Hotel: A Novel*
Poole, Sara
The Borgia Mistress
POOR BOYS
Birch, Carol. *Jamrach's Menagerie*
POOR BOYS — EMPLOYMENT
Dickens, Charles. ★*David Copperfield*
POOR CHILDREN
Dreiser, Theodore. ★*An American Tragedy*
POOR FAMILIES
Adam, Claire. *Golden Child: A Novel*
Allison, Dorothy. ★*Bastard Out of Carolina*
Caldwell, Erskine. *Tobacco Road*
Proulx, Annie. *Postcards*
Roberts, Nora. *Chesapeake Blue*
Smith, Betty. ★*A Tree Grows in Brooklyn*
Smith, Dodie. ★*I Capture the Castle*
Stegner, Wallace. ★*The Big Rock Candy Mountain*
Turansky, Carrie. *No Ocean Too Wide: A Novel*
POOR GIRLS
Crane, Stephen. *Maggie: A Girl of the Streets*
POOR MEN
Miller, Xander. *Zo: A Novel*
POOR PEOPLE
Backman, Fredrik. *Britt-Marie Was Here*
Brown, Rita Mae. ★*Rubyfruit Jungle*
Campbell, Bebe Moore. *Your Blues Ain't Like Mine*
Faulkner, William. ★*Absalom, Absalom!*
Macneal, Elizabeth. *The Doll Factory*
Mozley, Fiona. ★*Elmet*

Mukherjee, Neel. ★*A State of Freedom*
Silver, Marisa. *Mary Coin: A Novel*
Steinbeck, John. ★*The Grapes of Wrath*
Steinbeck, John. *The Pearl*
Steinbeck, John. *Tortilla Flat*

POOR WOMEN
Berne, Lisa. *You May Kiss the Bride*
Choo, Yangsze. *The Ghost Bride: A Novel*
Dare, Tessa. *Romancing the Duke*
Freeman, Anna. *The Fair Fight: A Novel*
Garrett, Kellye. ★*Hollywood Homicide*
Milan, Courtney. *The Duchess War*
O'Donnell, Paraic. *The House on Vesper Sands: A Novel*
Oates, Joyce Carol. *A Garden of Earthly Delights*
Oates, Joyce Carol. ★*Them*
Rao, Shobha. ★*Girls Burn Brighter*
Spark, Muriel. ★*The Girls of Slender Means*
Umrigar, Thrity N. *The Secrets Between Us*

Poore, Michael
Reincarnation Blues

POP MUSICIANS
Hiaasen, Carl. *Star Island*

Pope, Jamie
One Warm Winter

POPES — ELECTIONS
Berry, Steve. ★*The Malta Exchange: A Novel*

Poppet. Hayder, Mo

Poppy Harmon Investigates. Hollis, Lee

The *Poppy War*. Kuang, R. F.

Poppy war [Series]. Kuang, R. F.

POPULAR CULTURE
Amis, Martin. *Lionel Asbo: State of England*
Barthelme, Frederick. *Painted Desert: A Novel*
Ellmann, Lucy. *Ducks, Newburyport*
Saunders, George. *In Persuasion Nation: Stories*
Vonnegut, Kurt. *Armageddon in Retrospect: And Other New and Unpublished Writings on War and Peace*

POPULAR MUSIC
Hornby, Nick. *High Fidelity*

POPULARITY
Butler, Nickolas. ★*The Hearts of Men*
Hendricks, Greer. ★*You Are Not Alone*
Penny, Louise. ★*The Madness of Crowds*

PORNOGRAPHIC FILM ACTORS AND ACTRESSES
Faust, Christa. *Money Shot*

PORNOGRAPHIC FILM INDUSTRY AND TRADE
Danan, Rosie. *The Roommate*

PORNOGRAPHY
Banks, Russell. *Lost Memory of Skin*
Hayder, Mo. *Hanging Hill*
Zola, Emile. ★*Nana*

Port William series [Series]. Berry, Wendell

PORT-AU-PRINCE, HAITI
Chancy, Myriam J. A. ★*What Storm, What Thunder*

The *Portable* Veblen. McKenzie, Elizabeth

Porter, Chana
The Seep: A Novel

Porter, Henry
The Bell Ringers
Firefly
The Old Enemy
White Hot Silence

Porter, Katherine Anne
★*The Collected Stories of Katherine Anne Porter*
Pale Horse, Pale Rider: Three Short Novels
Ship of Fools

Porter, Max
★*Grief Is the Thing with Feathers*
★*Lanny: A Novel*

Porter, Regina
The Travelers

Portis, Charles
★*The Dog of the South*
★*Gringos: A Novel*
★*Masters of Atlantis: A Novel*
★*True Grit: A Novel*

PORTLAND, OREGON
Faye, Lyndsay. ★*The Paragon Hotel*
Le Guin, Ursula K. *The Lathe of Heaven*
Macomber, Debbie. *If Not for You: A Novel*
Rogers, Morgan Callan. ★*Honey Girl*
Vlautin, Willy. ★*The Night Always Comes*

★*Portnoy's* Complaint. Roth, Philip

Portrait in Sepia: A Novel. Allende, Isabel

The *Portrait* of a Lady. James, Henry

★*A Portrait* of the Artist as a Young Man. Joyce, James

PORTRAIT PAINTING
Shaw, M. B. *Murder at the Mill: A Mystery*

PORTRAITS
Kawakami, Mieko. *Ms. Ice Sandwich*
Moyes, Jojo. *The Girl You Left Behind*
Wilde, Oscar. ★*The Picture of Dorian Gray*

PORTUGAL
Leavitt, David. *The Two Hotel Francforts: A Novel*
Saramago, Jose. *All the Names*
Saramago, Jose. *The Manual of Painting and Calligraphy*

PORTUGUESE IN JAPAN
Endo, Shusaku. *Silence*

Positive. Wellington, David

Possessing the Secret of Joy. Walker, Alice

★*Possession: a Romance*. Byatt, A. S.

The *Possessions*. Murphy, Sara Flannery

POSSESSIVENESS
Jones, Sandie. *The Other Woman*
Sparks, Nicholas. *The Guardian*

The *Possibilities: a Novel*. Hemmings, Kaui Hart

POST-APARTHEID ERA
Gordimer, Nadine. *No Time Like the Present: A Novel*

POST-APOCALYPSE
Brennan, Marie. *Driftwood*
Delany, Samuel R. *Dhalgren*
Dick, Philip K. ★*Do Androids Dream of Electric Sheep?*
Elison, Meg. *The Book of Etta*
Elison, Meg. *The Book of Flora*
Elison, Meg. *The Book of the Unnamed Midwife*

Fforde, Jasper. *Shades of Grey: A Novel*
Haig, Francesca. *The Fire Sermon: A Novel*
Krivak, Andrew. *The Bear*
Lee, Chang-Rae. ★*On Such a Full Sea*
Mandel, Emily St. John. ★*Station Eleven*
Montag, Kassandra. *After the Flood: A Novel*
North, Claire. *Notes from the Burning Age*
Pinsker, Sarah. *A Song for a New Day*
Poyer, David. *Violent Peace: The War with China - Aftermath of Armageddon*
Tawada, Yoko. ★*The Emissary*
VanderMeer, Jeff. ★*Borne: A Novel*
VanderMeer, Jeff. *Dead Astronauts: A Novel*
Vaughn, Carrie. *Bannerless*
Wellington, David. *Positive*
Wexler, Django. *Ashes of the Sun*
Williams, Joy. *Harrow*
The ***Post-Birthday*** World. Shriver, Lionel

POST-TRAUMATIC STRESS DISORDER
Barclay, Linwood. *A Noise Downstairs: A Novel*
Benedict, Helen. *Wolf Season*
Burke, James Lee. *Robicheaux*
Cain, Chelsea. *One Kick: A Novel*
Colgan, Jenny. *500 Miles from You*
Crais, Robert. *Suspect*
Green, Jocelyn. *Veiled in Smoke*
Hannah, Kristin. *The Great Alone*
Means, David. ★*Hystopia: A Novel*
Petrie, Nicholas. *The Drifter*
Petrie, Nicholas. *Tear It Down*
Petrie, Nicholas. *The Wild One*
Roberts, Nora. *Shelter in Place*
Postcards. Proulx, Annie

POSTCARDS
Pulley, Natasha. ★*The Kingdoms*

POSTCOLONIALISM
Adichie, Chimamanda Ngozi. *Half of a Yellow Sun*
Adjapon, Bisi. *The Teller of Secrets: A Novel*
Appanah-Mouriquand, Nathacha. *Tropic of Violence: A Novel*
Dangarembga, Tsitsi. *This Mournable Body*
Daoud, Kamel. *The Meursault Investigation*
Grenville, Kate. *Sarah Thornhill*

POSTHUMANISM
Winterson, Jeanette. ★*Frankissstein*

POSTMASTERS
Blake, Sarah. *The Postmistress*
Pratchett, Terry. *Going Postal: A Novel of Discworld*
The ***Postmistress***. Blake, Sarah
Postmortem. Cornwell, Patricia Daniels

POSTPARTUM
Fine, Julia. *The Upstairs House*

POSTPARTUM DEPRESSION
Rimmer, Kelly. *Truths I Never Told You*
Watkins, Claire Vaye. *I Love You but I've Chosen Darkness*
The ***Postscript*** Murders. Griffiths, Elly

POSTWAR LIFE
Atkinson, Kate. ★*Transcription*
Baldacci, David. ★*A Gambling Man*

Couto, Mia. *Rain: And Other Stories*
Dybek, Nick. *The Verdun Affair: A Novel*
Gallen, Michelle. *Big Girl, Small Town: A Novel*
Harrigan, Stephen. *The Leopard Is Loose: A Novel*
Huber, Anna Lee. *Penny for Your Secrets*
Jenkins, Beverly. *Rebel*
Jenkins, Beverly. *Wild Rain*
Jenner, Natalie. *The Jane Austen Society*
Jenoff, Pam. *The Lost Girls of Paris*
Joyce, Rachel. *Miss Benson's Beetle*
Kadrey, Richard. *The Grand Dark*
Kerr, Philip. ★*Greeks Bearing Gifts: A Bernie Gunther Novel*
Lee, Ji-Min. *The Starlet and the Spy*
Montclair, Allison. *The Right Sort of Man*
Montclair, Allison. *A Royal Affair*
Moss, Tara. *The War Widow*
Ondaatje, Michael. ★*Warlight*
Pawel, Rebecca. *Death of a Nationalist*
Pufahl, Shannon. *On Swift Horses*
Quinn, Kate. ★*The Huntress*
Rabb, Jonathan. *Among the Living*
Remarque, Erich Maria. *The Road Back*
Robertson, Robin. *The Long Take: A Noir Narrative*
Runcie, James. *The Road to Grantchester*
Stewart, Amy. ★*Miss Kopp Investigates*

Potenza, Carol
Hearts of the Missing

Potok, Chaim
★*The Gift of Asher Lev*
★*My Name Is Asher Lev*

POTTER, FREDERICA (FICTITIOUS CHARACTER)
Byatt, A. S. *A Whistling Woman*

POTTERS
Doctorow, Cory. *Rapture of the Nerds*
Saramago, Jose. ★*The Cave*

Potzsch, Oliver
The Beggar King
The Dark Monk: A Hangman's Daughter Tale
The Hangman's Daughter: A Historical Novel
The Play of Death
The Poisoned Pilgrim: A Hangman's Daughter Tale
The Werewolf of Bamberg

POUGHKEEPSIE, NEW YORK
Armstrong, Addison. *The Light of Luna Park*

POVERTY
Abraham, Tola Rotimi. *Black Sunday*
Appanah-Mouriquand, Nathacha. *Tropic of Violence: A Novel*
Camus, Albert. *The Plague*
Camus, Albert. ★*The Stranger*
Coover, Robert. *The Origin of the Brunists: A Novel*
Dickens, Charles. *Little Dorrit*
Eggers, Dave. *What Is the What: The Autobiography of Valentino Achak Deng*
Fajardo-Anstine, Kali. ★*Sabrina & Corina: Stories*
Ferrante, Elena. *My Brilliant Friend*
Finlay, Mick. *The Murder Pit*
Harman, Patricia. *The Midwife of Hope River: A Novel*
King, Stephen. *Sleeping Beauties: A Novel*

Kingsolver, Barbara. ★*Flight Behavior*
Miller, Karen E. Quinones. *An Angry-Ass Black Woman*
Miller, Kei. ★*Augustown*
Mukherjee, Neel. ★*A State of Freedom*
Petry, Ann. ★*The Street*
Pochoda, Ivy. ★*These Women*
Rash, Ron. *Burning Bright: Stories*
Robertson, Imogen. *The Paris Winter*
Shanbhag, Vivek. *Ghachar Ghochar*
Wideman, John Edgar. *Look for Me and I'll Be Gone: Stories*
Wright, Richard. ★*Native Son*

Powell, Mark
Firebird

Powell, Padgett
★*Edisto: A Novel*

Power & Beauty: A Love Story of Life on the Streets. T. I.

POWER (SOCIAL SCIENCES)
Ackerman, Elliot. *Red Dress in Black and White*
Alderman, Naomi. ★*The Power: A Novel*
Alexis, Andre. *The Hidden Keys*
Anderson, Kevin J. *The Last Days of Krypton*
Bacigalupi, Paolo. ★*The Water Knife*
Beah, Ishmael. *Little Family*
Bennett, Robert Jackson. *Foundryside*
Bennett, Robert Jackson. *Shorefall*
Berry, Steve. ★*The Warsaw Protocol*
Bradford, Barbara Taylor. ★*A Woman of Substance*
Callender, Kacen. *King of the Rising*
Cherezinska, Elzbieta. *The Widow Queen*
Coben, Harlan. ★*The Boy from the Woods*
Coben, Harlan. *Fool Me Once*
Coulter, Catherine. *Labyrinth*
Cussler, Clive. ★*The Rising Sea: A Novel from the Numa Files*
Diofebi, Dario. *Paradise, Nevada*
George, Margaret. *The Splendor Before the Dark: A Novel of the Emperor Nero*
Gilman, Laura Anne. *The Cold Eye*
Gilman, Laura Anne. *Flesh and Fire*
Glynn, Alan. *Receptor*
Gregory, Philippa. *The Kingmaker's Daughter*
Gregory, Philippa. *The Red Queen: A Novel*
Groff, Lauren. ★*Matrix*
Haig, Francesca. *The Fire Sermon: A Novel*
Harkaway, Nick. *The Gone-Away World*
Holland, Cecelia. *Jerusalem*
Kadrey, Richard. *The Grand Dark*
Kincaid, Jamaica. *The Autobiography of My Mother*
Klay, Phil. ★*Missionaries*
Lee, Fonda. ★*Jade City*
Lee, Fonda. *Jade War*
Lee, Yoon Ha. *Raven Stratagem*
Lee, Yoon Ha. *Revenant Gun*
Lyons, Jenn. *The Ruin of Kings*
Martin, George R. R. ★*A Dance with Dragons*
Morrell, David. *Ruler of the Night*
Piercy, Marge. *Sex Wars*
Puzo, Mario. *The Family: A Novel*
Renault, Mary. *Funeral Games*

Rice, Anne. *Blood Communion: A Tale of Prince Lestat*
Schwab, Victoria. *A Conjuring of Light*
Shaykh, Hanan. ★*One Thousand and One Nights: A Sparkling Retelling of the Beloved Classic*
Swinson, Kiki. *Who's Wife Extraordinaire Now*
Taneja, Preti. *We That Are Young: A Novel*
Tata, A. J. *Dark Winter*
Thomas, Elisabeth. *Catherine House*
Umrigar, Thrity N. *Everybody's Son*
Vyleta, Dan. *Smoke: A Novel*
Wecker, Helene. *The Golem and the Jinni*
Woods, Stuart. *Below the Belt*
Woods, Stuart. *Fast & Loose*
Yang, JY. *The Ascent to Godhood*
Yang, JY. *The Black Tides of Heaven*

Power and Empire. Cameron, Marc
The *Power* and the Glory. Greene, Graham

POWER FAILURES
Alam, Rumaan. ★*Leave the World Behind: A Novel*
Hallberg, Garth Risk. ★*City on Fire*
Robinson, Peter. *Piece of My Heart*

Power, Susan
The Grass Dancer

★*The Power: a Novel*. Alderman, Naomi

Powers, Kevin
★*The Yellow Birds: A Novel*

Powers, Richard
★*Bewilderment: A Novel*
The Echo Maker
Generosity: An Enhancement
Orfeo: A Novel
★*The Overstory: A Novel*

Powning, Beth
The Sea Captain's Wife: A Novel

POWWOWS
Orange, Tommy. ★*There There*
Power, Susan. *The Grass Dancer*

Poyer, David
Overthrow: The War with China and North Korea—Fall of an Empire
Violent Peace: The War with China - Aftermath of Armageddon

The *Practical* Heart: Four Novellas. Gurganus, Allan
Practical magic novels [Series]. Hoffman, Alice

PRAGUE, CZECH REPUBLIC
Black, Benjamin. *Wolf on a String: A Novel*
Flyte, Magnus. *City of Dark Magic: A Novel*
Flyte, Magnus. *City of Lost Dreams: A Novel*
Perry, Sarah. *Melmoth: A Novel*

PRAIRIE LIFE
Coldsmith, Don. *Tallgrass: A Novel of the Great Plains*
Rølvaag, O. E. ★*Giants in the Earth: A Saga of the Prairie*

Pratchett, Terry
★*The Color of Magic*
Equal Rites
The Fifth Elephant: A Novel of Discworld
Going Postal: A Novel of Discworld
Guards! Guards!
The Last Hero: A Discworld Fable
Lords and Ladies: A Novel of Discworld

Men at Arms: A Novel of Discworld
Monstrous Regiment
Pyramids: The Book of Going Forth
Reaper Man
Small Gods: A Novel of Discworld
Thief of Time
Thud!: A Novel of Discworld
The Truth: A Novel of Discworld
Witches Abroad
Wyrd Sisters

PRAYER
   Fabry, Chris. *War Room: Prayer Is a Powerful Weapon*
   Salinger, J. D. ★*Franny and Zooey*
★*A **Prayer** for Owen Meany: A Novel*. Irving, John
***Prayer** for the Living*. Okri, Ben

Prcic, Ismet
   Shards: A Novel
*The **Preacher's** Daughter*. Lewis, Beverly
*The **Precious** One*. De los Santos, Marisa
*The **Precipice***. Doiron, Paul
PRECOGNITION
   Auster, Paul. *Oracle Night*
   Dick, Philip K. *The Minority Report*
   Miller, Holly. ★*The Sight of You*
   Pulley, Natasha. *The Lost Future of Pepperharrow*
   Pulley, Natasha. *The Watchmaker of Filigree Street*
PREDATION (BIOLOGY)
   Koepp, David. *Cold Storage: A Novel*
PREGNANCY
   Adlakha, Sarah. *She Wouldn't Change a Thing*
   Billingsley, ReShonda Tate. ★*The Secret She Kept*
   Davies, Peter Ho. *A Lie Someone Told You About Yourself*
   Jordan, Sophie. *This Scot of Mine*
   Lindsey, Odie. *Some Go Home: A Novel*
   McGhee, Alison. *The Opposite of Fate*
   Stringer, Vickie M. *Dirty Red: A Novel*
PREGNANT TEENAGERS
   Bronsky, Alina. *The Hottest Dishes of the Tartar Cuisine*
   Coplin, Amanda. *The Orchardist*
   Frazier, Jean Kyoung. *Pizza Girl*
   Haruf, Kent. ★*Plainsong*
   Quade, Kirstin Valdez. ★*The Five Wounds: A Novel*
★*The **Pregnant** Widow*. Amis, Martin
PREGNANT WOMEN
   Brown, Taylor. *Fallen Land*
   Burrowes, Grace. *My One and Only Duke*
   Clark, Wahida. *Payback with Ya Life*
   Dalcher, Christina. *Femlandia*
   DeCarlo, Melissa. *The Art of Crash Landing: A Novel*
   Dickey, Eric Jerome. ★*Bad Men and Wicked Women*
   Erdrich, Louise. *Future Home of the Living God*
   Faulkner, William. ★*Light in August*
   Goldbloom, Goldie. *On Division*
   Griffiths, Elly. *The Janus Stone*
   Harrod-Eagles, Cynthia. *Cruel as the Grave*
   Hashemzadeh Bonde, Golnaz. *What We Owe*
   Hatcher, Robin Lee. *Who I Am with You*
   Haywood, Sarah. *The Cactus*

   Hepworth, Sally. *The Secrets of Midwives*
   Lansdale, Joe R. *Sunset and Sawdust*
   Littlejohn, Emily. *Inherit the Bones*
   Lloyd, Catherine. *Death Comes to the Nursery*
   Mina, Denise. *The Less Dead*
   Nicieza, Fabian. *Suburban Dicks*
   Parris, S. J. ★*The Dead of Winter*
   Pearson, Robin W. *A Long Time Comin'*
   Picoult, Jodi. *A Spark of Light: A Novel*
   Purcell, Laura. *The Silent Companions: A Ghost Story*
   Putney, Mary Jo. *Not Quite a Wife*
   Rimmer, Kelly. *Before I Let You Go*
   Ross, Ann B. *Miss Julia Delivers the Goods: A Novel*
   Simsion, Graeme C. *The Rosie Effect*
   Steiner, Susie. ★*Persons Unknown: A Novel*
   Thompson, Victoria. *Murder on Wall Street*
   Tremblay, Paul. *Survivor Song*
   van Heemstra, Marjolijn. *In Search of a Name*
   Weiner, Jennifer. *Little Earthquakes*
PREGNANT WOMEN — DEATH
   Cook, Robin. ★*Genesis*
PREHISTORIC HUMANS
   Auel, Jean M. ★*The Clan of the Cave Bear: A Novel*
   Golding, William. *The Inheritors*
PREHISTORIC WOMEN
   Golding, William. *The Inheritors*
PREJUDICE
   Bala, Sharon. *The Boat People: A Novel*
   Brett, Simon. *Guilt at the Garage*
   Brown, Rita Mae. ★*Rubyfruit Jungle*
   Couto, Mia. *The Sword and the Spear*
   Ganshert, Katie. ★*No One Ever Asked: A Novel*
   Gilb, Dagoberto. *The Flowers: A Novel*
   Gilman, Charlotte Perkins. *Herland*
   Harmon, Amy. *Where the Lost Wander*
   Hurston, Zora Neale. *Hitting a Straight Lick with a Crooked Stick: Stories from the Harlem Renaissance*
   Jordan, Hillary. *Mudbound: A Novel*
   King, Stephen. *Elevation*
   Klune, TJ. *The House in the Cerulean Sea*
   Kress, Nancy. *Beggars in Spain*
   Levy, Andrea. *Small Island*
   Morrison, Toni. *A Mercy: A Novel*
   Mukherjee, Abir. *Death in the East*
   Okparanta, Chinelo. ★*Under the Udala Trees*
   Roth, Philip. ★*The Human Stain*
   Seton, Anya. ★*The Winthrop Woman*
   Staples, Dennis E. *This Town Sleeps*
   Wiseman, Ellen Marie. *The Orphan Collector*
PREMATURE BURIAL
   Galligan, John. *Bad Moon Rising*
   Malerman, Josh. *Unbury Carol*
PREMATURE INFANT CARE
   Armstrong, Addison. *The Light of Luna Park*
PREMATURE INFANTS
   Armstrong, Addison. *The Light of Luna Park*
PREP SCHOOL STUDENTS
   Hoffman, Alice. *The River King*

Knowles, John. ★*A Separate Peace*
Sittenfeld, Curtis. *Prep: A Novel*
Wolff, Tobias. *Old School: A Novel*

PREP SCHOOLS
Ellison, J. T. *Good Girls Lie*
Knowles, John. ★*A Separate Peace*
Persson Giolito, Malin. *Quicksand*
Whitehead, Colson. *Sag Harbor: A Novel*
Wolff, Tobias. *Old School: A Novel*

Prep: a Novel. Sittenfeld, Curtis

Prescott, Lara
The Secrets We Kept

PRESCRIPTION DRUG ABUSE
Haddam, Jane. *Hardscrabble Road*
Martin, Steve. *Shopgirl*
Murray, Paul. *Skippy Dies*

The President's Gardens. Al-Ramli, Muhsin

PRESIDENTIAL CANDIDATES
Patterson, Richard North. *No Safe Place*

PRESIDENTIAL CANDIDATES — PROTECTION
Costello, Mark. *Big If*

PRESIDENTIAL ELECTION, 1940
Roth, Philip. ★*The Plot Against America*

PRESIDENTIAL ELECTION, 2016
Butler, Robert Olen. *Late City*
Leavitt, David. ★*Shelter in Place*
Spiotta, Dana. *Wayward*

PRESIDENTIAL ELECTIONS
Coonts, Stephen. *The Armageddon File*

PRESIDENTS
Cameron, Marc. *Power and Empire*
Fuentes, Carlos. *The Eagle's Throne: A Novel*
Gleason, Colleen. *Murder at the Capitol*
Hiaasen, Carl. ★*Squeeze Me: A Novel*
Mallon, Thomas. *Finale: A Novel*
Mallon, Thomas. *Landfall: A Novel*
Patterson, Richard North. *Balance of Power*
Patterson, Richard North. *Protect and Defend*
Pyper, Andrew. *The Residence: A Novel*
Saunders, George. ★*Lincoln in the Bardo: A Novel*
Updike, John. *Memories of the Ford Administration: A Novel*
Vargas Llosa, Mario. *The Feast of the Goat*
Vonnegut, Kurt. *Slapstick: Or, Lonesome No More! a Novel*
Wolfe, Paul. *The Lost Diary of M*

PRESIDENTS — ASSASSINATION
DeLillo, Don. *Libra*
Goldstone, Lawrence. *Assassin of Shadows*

PRESIDENTS — ASSASSINATION PLOTS
Hurwitz, Gregg Andrew. ★*Out of the Dark: The Return of Orphan X*

PRESIDENTS — HISTORY
Vidal, Gore. ★*Lincoln: A Novel*

PRESIDENTS' SPOUSES
Bloom, Amy. ★*White Houses: A Novel*
Chiaverini, Jennifer. *Mrs. Lincoln's Dressmaker: A Novel*
Patterson, Richard North. *Balance of Power*
Pitoniak, Anna. ★*Our American Friend*
Roosevelt, Elliott. ★*Murder and the First Lady*
Roosevelt, Elliott. *Murder at Midnight*

Roosevelt, Elliott. *Murder in the Map Room: An Eleanor Roosevelt Mystery*
Roosevelt, Elliott. *Murder in the Oval Office*

Presidio. Kennedy, Randy

Pressfield, Steven
36 Righteous Men: A Novel

Preston, Caroline
The Scrapbook of Frankie Pratt

Preston, Douglas J.
City of Endless Night
Crooked River
The Obsidian Chamber
Old Bones
Thunderhead
Verses for the Dead

Presumed Innocent. Turow, Scott

PRETENDING
Oakley, Colleen. *The Invisible Husband of Frick Island*
Raybourn, Deanna. *A Dangerous Collaboration*
Smith, Ali. ★*Spring*

★*Pretty Girls: A Novel*. Slaughter, Karin

Pretty Little Wife. Kane, Darby

Prey series [Series]. Sandford, John

Prey: a Novel. Crichton, Michael

PRIAM (GREEK MYTHOLOGY)
Malouf, David. *Ransom*

Price, Reynolds
The Good Priest's Son
Roxanna Slade

Price, Richard
Clockers
Lush Life
Samaritan

★*Pride and Prejudice*. Austen, Jane

PRIDE AND VANITY
Erdrich, Louise. *Tracks: A Novel*
Novik, Naomi. ★*Spinning Silver*
Saint-Exupery, Antoine de. ★*The Little Prince*
Shteyngart, Gary. ★*Super Sad True Love Story: A Novel*

Pride, Christine
★*We Are Not Like Them*

★*Pride, Prejudice, and Other Flavors: A Novel*. Dev, Sonali

Priest, Cherie
Boneshaker
Clementine
Dreadnought
Ganymede
The Inexplicables

PRIESTS
Bolano, Roberto. ★*By Night in Chile*
Cather, Willa. ★*Death Comes for the Archbishop*
Christie, Agatha. *The Pale Horse*
Cronin, A. J. *The Keys of the Kingdom*
Endo, Shusaku. *Silence*
Erdrich, Louise. *The Last Report on the Miracles at Little No Horse*
Francis, Patry. *The Orphans of Race Point: A Novel*
Greene, Graham. *The Power and the Glory*
Gregory, Philippa. *Tidelands*

Harris, Robert. *The Second Sleep: A Novel*
Leonard, Elmore. *Pagan Babies*
Reimringer, John. *Vestments*
Russell, Mary Doria. ★*The Sparrow*
Simmons, Dan. *The Fall of Hyperion*
Simmons, Dan. ★*Hyperion*
Sjón. *The Blue Fox*
Spann, Susan. ★*Claws of the Cat: A Shinobi Mystery*
Spann, Susan. *Trial on Mount Koya: A Hiro Hattori Novel*
Walton, Jo. ★*Lent*

PRIMARIES
Costello, Mark. *Big If*
Primas of power [Series]. Daria, Alexis
★*The* **Prime** *Minister.* Trollope, Anthony
PRIME MINISTERS
Persson, Leif G. W. *Free Falling, as If in a Dream: The Story of a Crime*
Trollope, Anthony. ★*The Prime Minister*
PRIME MINISTERS' SPOUSES
Benedict, Marie. ★*Lady Clementine*
★*The* **Prime** *of Miss Jean Brodie.* Spark, Muriel
Prince *Lestat: The Vampire Chronicles.* Rice, Anne
The **Prince** *of Broadway.* Shupe, Joanna
Prince *of Monkeys.* Ehirim, Nnamdi
The **Prince** *of Tides.* Conroy, Pat
★*A* **Prince** *on Paper.* Cole, Alyssa
PRINCES
Chakraborty, S. A. *The City of Brass*
Cocks, Heather. *The Royal We*
Cole, Alyssa. ★*A Princess in Theory*
Hauck, Rachel. *Once Upon a Prince*
Krueger, Paul. *Steel Crow Saga*
Massey, Sujata. *The Satapur Moonstone*
Maxwell, Everina. *Winter's Orbit*
McQuiston, Casey. ★*Red, White & Royal Blue: A Novel*
Miller, Madeline. *The Song of Achilles*
Reid, Ava. *The Wolf and the Woodsman*
Rutherfurd, Edward. *The Princes of Ireland: The Dublin Saga*
Saberhagen, Fred. *Coinspinner's Story*
Saberhagen, Fred. *Mindsword's Story*
Saberhagen, Fred. *Shieldbreaker's Story*
Saberhagen, Fred. *Woundhealer's Story*
Saint-Exupery, Antoine de. ★*The Little Prince*
Seton, Anya. *Avalon*
Suri, Tasha. ★*Realm of Ash*
The **Princes** *of Ireland: The Dublin Saga.* Rutherfurd, Edward
Princes of Texas [Series]. London, Julia
★*The* **Princess** *Bride: S. Morgenstern's Classic Tale of True Love and High Adventure : The.* Goldman, William
★*A* **Princess** *in Theory.* Cole, Alyssa
PRINCESSES
Amirrezvani, Anita. *Equal of the Sun*
Banks, Iain. *Matter*
Black, Benjamin. ★*The Secret Guests: A Novel*
Carey, Jacqueline. *Starless*
Clark, Cherae. ★*The Unbroken*
Eason, K. *How Rory Thorne Destroyed the Multiverse*
Elliott, Kate. *Unconquerable Sun*

Goldman, William. ★*The Princess Bride: S. Morgenstern's Classic Tale of True Love and High Adventure : The*
Gratton, Tessa. *The Queens of Innis Lear*
Lewis, C. S. *Till We Have Faces: A Myth Retold*
Paul, Gill. ★*The Lost Daughter*
Penman, Sharon Kay. *Here Be Dragons*
Saint, Jennifer. *Ariadne*
Suri, Tasha. *The Jasmine Throne*
The **Priory** *of the Orange Tree.* Shannon, Samantha
Priscilla Hutchins series [Series]. McDevitt, Jack
PRISON GUARDS
Khadra, Yasmina. *The Swallows of Kabul: A Novel*
PRISON RIOTS
Hulse, S. M. ★*Black River*
PRISON SENTENCES
Kushner, Rachel. *The Mars Room*
The **Prisoner.** Berenson, Alex
The **Prisoner** *of Heaven.* Ruiz Zafon, Carlos
PRISONERS
Brooks, Terry. *Child of Light*
Cheever, John. *Falconer*
Coetzee, J. M. ★*Life & Times of Michael K*
Doiron, Paul. *Almost Midnight*
Dumas, Alexandre. ★*The Count of Monte Cristo*
Dumas, Alexandre. ★*The Man in the Iron Mask*
Egan, Jennifer. *The Keep*
Flanagan, Richard. *Gould's Book of Fish: A Novel in Twelve Fish*
Gabaldon, Diana. ★*Dragonfly in Amber*
Grenville, Kate. *The Secret River*
Leckie, Ann. *Provenance*
Lindsey, Odie. *Some Go Home: A Novel*
Lyons, Jenn. *The Ruin of Kings*
McDermid, Val. *How the Dead Speak: A Tony Hill and Carol Jordan Novel*
Putney, Mary Jo. *No Longer a Gentleman*
Ragan, Theresa. *Deranged*
Rajaniemi, Hannu. *The Fractal Prince*
Rajaniemi, Hannu. *The Quantum Thief*
Silber, Joan. *Improvement*
Stewart, Amy. *Miss Kopp's Midnight Confessions*
Turton, Stuart. ★*The Devil and the Dark Water*
Vonnegut, Kurt. *Hocus Pocus*
PRISONERS — HISTORY
Flanagan, Richard. *Gould's Book of Fish: A Novel in Twelve Fish*
PRISONERS OF WAR
Boulle, Pierre. *The Bridge Over the River Kwai: A Novel*
Cotterill, Colin. *The Second Biggest Nothing*
Deutermann, Peter T. *The Nugget: A Novel*
Green, Amy Lynn. *Things We Didn't Say*
McFadden, Bernice L. *The Book of Harlan*
Peters, Ellis. *Brother Cadfael's Penance*
PRISONERS OF WAR, AMERICAN
Vonnegut, Kurt. ★*Slaughterhouse-Five: Or, the Children's Crusade : A Duty-Dance with Death*
Westheimer, David. ★*Von Ryan's Express*
PRISONERS OF WAR, AUSTRALIAN
Keneally, Thomas. *Shame and the Captives: A Novel*

PRISONERS OF WAR, BRITISH

Ballard, J. G. *The Kindness of Women*

Boulle, Pierre. *The Bridge Over the River Kwai: A Novel*

Forester, C. S. *Flying Colours*

PRISONERS OF WAR, CONFEDERATE

Kantor, MacKinlay. ★*Andersonville*

PRISONERS OF WAR, JAPANESE

Keneally, Thomas. *Shame and the Captives: A Novel*

PRISONERS' SPOUSES

Bausch, Richard. ★*Rebel Powers*

Keneally, Thomas. *Shame and the Captives: A Novel*

PRISONS

Bourne, Joanna. ★*The Spymaster's Lady*

Cheever, John. *Falconer*

Doiron, Paul. *Almost Midnight*

Gregory, Daryl. *Afterparty*

Kantor, MacKinlay. ★*Andersonville*

Kushner, Rachel. *The Mars Room*

Persson Giolito, Malin. *Quicksand*

PRISONS — HISTORY

Dickens, Charles. *Little Dorrit*

PRIVACY

Schweblin, Samanta. *Little Eyes*

Styles, Toy. *Redbone*

★*Private*. Patterson, James

PRIVATE BANKS

Schlink, Bernhard. *Self's Murder*

★*A Private Cathedral*. Burke, James Lee

Private Detective Agency novels [Series]. Patterson, James

PRIVATE INVESTIGATORS

Adams, Douglas. *Dirk Gently's Holistic Detective Agency*

Anderson, Kevin J. *Death Warmed Over*

Atkinson, Kate. ★*Big Sky*

Atkinson, Kate. ★*Case Histories*

Atkinson, Kate. *One Good Turn: A Novel*

Atkinson, Kate. *Started Early, Took My Dog*

Atkinson, Kate. ★*When Will There Be Good News?: A Novel*

Baldacci, David. *The Fallen*

Baldacci, David. ★*A Gambling Man*

Baldacci, David. *Redemption*

Barclay, Linwood. *Parting Shot*

Barclay, Linwood. *A Tap on the Window*

Barclay, Linwood. *The Twenty-Three: A Promise Falls Novel*

Bilal, Parker. *The Burning Gates: A Makana Investigation*

Bilal, Parker. *The Ghost Runner*

Block, Lawrence. *A Drop of the Hard Stuff: A Matthew Scudder Novel*

Block, Lawrence. *Eight Million Ways to Die*

Bradley, C. Alan. *The Golden Tresses of the Dead: A Flavia De Luce Novel*

Bruen, Ken. *Galway Girl: A Jack Taylor Novel*

Chandler, Raymond. ★*The Big Sleep*

Chandler, Raymond. *The Lady in the Lake*

Chandler, Raymond. *The Long Goodbye*

Christie, Agatha. *Curtain*

Christie, Agatha. *The Hollow*

Clare, Alys. *The Woman Who Spoke to Spirits*

Coben, Harlan. ★*The Boy from the Woods*

Connelly, Michael. *Dark Sacred Night*

Connelly, Michael. *The Wrong Side of Goodbye*

Connolly, John. *A Book of Bones*

Connolly, John. *The Nameless Ones*

Corby, Gary. *The Marathon Conspiracy*

Corleone, Douglas. *Good as Gone*

Crais, Robert. *A Dangerous Man*

Crumley, James. ★*The Wrong Case*

Cussler, Clive. ★*The Gray Ghost*

Cussler, Clive. ★*The Titanic Secret*

Davis, Lindsey. *The Ides of April: A Flavia Albia Mystery*

Dazieri, Sandrone. *Kill the Angel*

Doyle, Arthur Conan. ★*The Complete Sherlock Holmes*

Doyle, Arthur Conan. ★*The Hound of the Baskervilles*

Ellroy, James. ★*Widespread Panic: A Novel*

Estleman, Loren D. ★*Amos Walker: The Complete Story Collection*

Estleman, Loren D. *Infernal Angels*

Estleman, Loren D. *A Smile on the Face of the Tiger*

Faye, Lyndsay. *The Whole Art of Detection: Lost Mysteries of Sherlock Holmes*

Finch, Charles. *The Last Passenger*

Finlay, Mick. *The Murder Pit*

Fox, Candice. *Crimson Lake*

Friedman, Daniel. ★*Don't Ever Get Old*

Galbraith, Robert. *Career of Evil*

Galbraith, Robert. *The Cuckoo's Calling*

Galbraith, Robert. *Lethal White*

Galbraith, Robert. *The Silkworm*

Gleason, Colleen. *Murder at the Capitol*

Goldman, Matt. *Dead West*

Goldman, Matt. *The Shallows*

Hall, Tarquin. *The Case of the Love Commandos: From the Files of Vish Puri, India's Most Private Investigator*

Hammett, Dashiell. ★*The Maltese Falcon*

Hammett, Dashiell. ★*The Thin Man*

Hannah, Sophie. *The Killings at Kingfisher Hill*

Hannah, Sophie. *The Mystery of Three Quarters: The New Hercule Poirot Mystery*

Harvey, John. *Cold in Hand*

Harvey, John. *A Darker Shade of Blue: Stories*

Harvey, Michael T. *The Chicago Way*

Harvey, Michael T. *The Fifth Floor*

Harvey, Michael T. *The Governor's Wife*

Harvey, Michael T. *We All Fall Down*

Ide, Joe. ★*Hi Five: An IQ Novel*

James, Marlon. ★*Black Leopard, Red Wolf*

Kamal, Sheena. *It All Falls Down*

Kaminsky, Stuart M. *To Catch a Spy: A Toby Peters Mystery*

King, Stephen. *End of Watch: A Novel*

Krentz, Jayne Ann. *When All the Girls Have Gone*

Kroese, Robert. *The Last Iota*

Lawton, John. *Then We Take Berlin*

Lethem, Jonathan. ★*Motherless Brooklyn*

Luna, Louisa. *The Janes*

MacDonald, John D. *Cinnamon Skin: The Twentieth Adventure of Travis McGee*

MacDonald, John D. *The Green Ripper*

MacDonald, John D. ★*The Lonely Silver Rain*

MacDonald, John D. *The Long Lavender Look*
MacDonald, John D. *A Purple Place for Dying*
MacDonald, John D. *The Scarlet Ruse*
MacDonald, John D. *The Turquoise Lament*
Macdonald, Ross. *The Drowning Pool*
Macdonald, Ross. *The Far Side of the Dollar*
Macdonald, Ross. *The Galton Case*
Macdonald, Ross. *The Goodbye Look*
Macdonald, Ross. *Sleeping Beauty*
Macdonald, Ross. *The Underground Man*
Mayor, Archer. ★*Marked Man*
Mosley, Walter. *Black Betty: An Easy Rawlins Mystery*
Mosley, Walter. *Down the River Unto the Sea*
Mosley, Walter. *Trouble Is What I Do: A Leonid McGill Mystery*
Osborne, Lawrence. *Only to Sleep: A Philip Marlowe Novel*
Parker, Robert B. *Painted Ladies*
Parker, Robert B. *Sixkill*
Pelecanos, George P. *The Cut: A Novel*
Pronzini, Bill. *Crazybone*
Pronzini, Bill. *Hardcase*
Pronzini, Bill. *Hellbox*
Pronzini, Bill. *Illusions*
Pronzini, Bill. *Mourners*
Pronzini, Bill. *Nemesis*
Pronzini, Bill. *Nightcrawlers*
Pronzini, Bill. *Savages*
Pronzini, Bill. *The Stolen Gold Affair*
Pynchon, Thomas. *Inherent Vice*
Quartey, Kwei. *The Missing American*
Quick, Amanda. *Close Up*
Quinn, Spencer. *Dog on It: A Chet and Bernie Mystery*
Quinn, Spencer. ★*It's a Wonderful Woof*
Rowland, Laura Joh. *The Hangman's Secret*
Rozan, S. J. ★*The Art of Violence*
Rozan, S. J. *The Shanghai Moon: A Lydia Chin/Bill Smith Novel*
Rozan, S. J. *Winter and Night*
Sanders, Lawrence. *McNally's Dilemma*
Sanders, Lawrence. *McNally's Luck*
Sanders, Lawrence. *McNally's Puzzle*
Sanders, Lawrence. *McNally's Secret*
Sanders, Lawrence. *McNally's Trial*
Sanders, Lawrence. *The Tenth Commandment: A Novel*
Sanders, Lawrence. *The Timothy Files*
Sanders, Lawrence. *Timothy's Game*
Saylor, Steven. *The House of the Vestals: The Investigations of Gordianus the Finder*
Saylor, Steven. *The Judgment of Caesar: A Novel of Ancient Rome*
Saylor, Steven. *A Mist of Prophecies*
Saylor, Steven. *The Triumph of Caesar: A Novel of Ancient Rome*
Schlink, Bernhard. *Self's Deception*
Schlink, Bernhard. *Self's Murder*
Schlink, Bernhard. *Self's Punishment*
Sears, Michael. *Tower of Babel*
Simmons, Dan. *The Fifth Heart*
Smith, Ian. *The Unspoken*
Smith, Ian. *Wolf Point*
Spiegelman, Peter. *Black Maps*
Spillane, Mickey. *Kill Me, Darling*

Spillane, Mickey. *A Long Time Dead: A Mike Hammer Casebook*
Stout, Rex. *The Doorbell Rang*
Stout, Rex. ★*Gambit*
Talton, Jon. *City of Dark Corners*
Woods, Stuart. *A Delicate Touch*
Woods, Stuart. *Hit List*
Woods, Stuart. *Stealth*
The **Private** Patient. James, P. D.
PRIVATE POLICE
    Amidon, Stephen. *Security: A Novel*
PRIVATE SCHOOLS
    Cook, Thomas H. *The Chatham School Affair*
    Frank, Alli. *Tiny Imperfections*
    Hoffman, Alice. *The River King*
    Lutz, Lisa. *The Swallows: A Novel*
PRIVATE SECURITY SERVICES
    Amidon, Stephen. *Security: A Novel*
    Hibbert, Talia. ★*Take a Hint, Dani Brown*
    Hunt, April. *Deadly Obsession*
    Sharp, Zoe. *Fox Hunter*
A **Private** Venus. Scerbanenco, Giorgio
PRIVATEERS
    Spencer, Minerva. *Scandalous*
PRIVILEGE (SOCIAL PSYCHOLOGY)
    Dahl, Julia. *The Missing Hours*
    McDowell, Christina. *The Cave Dwellers: A Novel*
The **Privileges:** a Novel. Dee, Jonathan
The **Prize:** a Novel. Bialosky, Jill
Prized Possessions. Corman, Avery
PRO-LIFE MOVEMENT
    Patterson, Richard North. *No Safe Place*
    Patterson, Richard North. *Protect and Defend*
PROBLEM YOUTH
    Black, Lisa. *Suffer the Children*
    Sister Souljah. ★*A Deeper Love Inside: The Porsche Santiaga Story*
The **Prodigal** Daughter. Harrison, Mette Ivie
PROFESSIONAL ATHLETES
    Henson, Pene. *Into the Blue*
    Rai, Alisha. ★*The Right Swipe*
    Scalzi, John. *Head On*
PROFESSIONAL BASEBALL PLAYERS
    Adams, Lyssa Kay. *The Bromance Book Club*
    King, Stephen. *The Girl Who Loved Tom Gordon*
    Malamud, Bernard. *The Natural*
PROFESSIONAL BASEBALL TEAMS
    DeLillo, Don. *Underworld*
PROFESSIONAL BASKETBALL PLAYERS
    Harris, E. Lynn. *Basketball Jones: A Novel*
    Slaughter, Karin. *The Kept Woman*
PROFESSIONAL CONFERENCES
    Andrews, Donna. *Owl Be Home for Christmas: A Meg Langslow Mystery*
    Gamboa, Santiago. *Necropolis*
PROFESSIONAL FOOTBALL
    Martin, Alexa. *Fumbled*
PROFESSIONAL FOOTBALL PLAYERS
    Martin, Alexa. *Fumbled*
    Martin, Alexa. ★*Intercepted*

PROFESSIONAL SOCCER PLAYERS

Dev, Sonali. ★*Recipe for Persuasion*

Van Dyken, Rachel. *Risky Play*

***Professor** Chandra Follows His Bliss: A Novel*. Balasubramanyam, Rajeev

PROFITEERING

Ellroy, James. *This Storm: A Novel*

PROHIBITION

Brown, Rita Mae. *Six of One*

Lehane, Dennis. *Live by Night*

Montgomery, Jess. *The Widows*

Rindell, Suzanne. *The Other Typist*

***Project** Duchess*. Jeffries, Sabrina

***Project** Hail Mary*. Weir, Andy

Promethean Age [Series]. Bear, Elizabeth

Promise Falls (Linwood Barclay) [Series]. Barclay, Linwood

***Promise** Me This*. Gohlke, Cathy

*The **Promise** of Elsewhere*. Leithauser, Brad

★*A **Promise** of Fire*. Bouchet, Amanda

*The **Promise** of Jesse Woods*. Fabry, Chris

Promised. Garriott, Leah

PROMISES

Bowman, Valerie. *The Unexpected Duchess*

Cameron, W. Bruce. *A Dog's Promise*

Gohlke, Cathy. *Promise Me This*

Hamilton, Karen. *The Last Wife*

Hoover, Colleen. *All Your Perfects*

Pinborough, Sarah. ★*Cross Her Heart: A Novel*

***Promises** to Keep*. Tatlock, Ann

PROMOTIONS

Bowman, Valerie. *A Duke Like No Other*

Pronzini, Bill

Crazybone

Fever

Hardcase

Hellbox

Illusions

Mourners

Nemesis

Nightcrawlers

Savages

Spook

The Stolen Gold Affair

The Violated

PROOFREADING

Saramago, Jose. *The History of the Siege of Lisbon*

*A **Proper** Marriage*. Lessing, Doris May

PROPHECIES

Lyons, Jenn. *The Name of All Things*

McGuire, Seanan. ★*Beneath the Sugar Sky*

Obioma, Chigozie. ★*The Fishermen: A Novel*

Rollins, James. *The Eye of God*

Rollins, James. *The Sixth Extinction: A Sigma Force Novel*

Silko, Leslie Marmon. *Almanac of the Dead*

Stewart, Mary. ★*The Crystal Cave*

PROPHECIES (OCCULTISM)

Kadare, Ismail. ★*The Three-Arched Bridge*

Redfield, James. *The Celestine Prophecy: An Adventure*

PROPHECY

Gratton, Tessa. *The Queens of Innis Lear*

Walton, Jo. ★*Lent*

PROPHETS

Andrews, Mesu. *Isaiah's Daughter: A Novel of Prophets and Kings*

Andrews, Mesu. *Of Fire and Lions: A Novel*

Coover, Robert. *The Origin of the Brunists: A Novel*

Gilman, Carolyn Ives. *Dark Orbit*

O'Connor, Flannery. ★*The Violent Bear It Away*

O'Connor, Flannery. ★*Wise Blood*

Vargas Llosa, Mario. *The War of the End of the World*

★*The **Prophets**: a Novel*. Jones, Robert

*The **Proposal***. Guillory, Jasmine

Prose, Francine

Blue Angel: A Novel

Goldengrove: A Novel

★*The Vixen*

PROSPECTORS

London, Jack. ★*The Call of the Wild*

***Prospero's** Children*. Siegel, Jan

PROSTITUTES

Algren, Nelson. *A Walk on the Wild Side*

Block, Lawrence. *Eight Million Ways to Die*

Block, Lawrence. *The Sins of the Fathers*

Bryant, Niobia. *Madam, May I*

Crane, Stephen. *Maggie: A Girl of the Streets*

Crumley, James. *The Last Good Kiss: A Novel*

Defoe, Daniel. ★*Moll Flanders*

Dennis-Benn, Nicole. *Here Comes the Sun*

Dexter, Colin. *The Daughters of Cain*

Dumas, Alexandre. ★*Camille*

Faber, Michel. *The Crimson Petal and the White*

Garcia-Roza, L. A. *December Heat*

Groot, Tracy. *Flame of Resistance*

Lansdale, Joe R. *Honky Tonk Samurai*

Lawrence, David. *The Dead Sit Round in a Ring*

Murakami, Haruki. *After Dark*

Rowland, Laura Joh. *The Ripper's Shadow*

Tallis, Frank. *Vienna Blood: A Max Liebermann Mystery*

Vargas Llosa, Mario. *Green House*

Zola, Emile. ★*Nana*

PROSTITUTION

Bond, Cynthia. *Ruby: A Novel*

Capote, Truman. ★*Breakfast at Tiffany's*

Johnson, Keith Lee. ★*Little Black Girl Lost*

Stringer, Vickie M. ★*Let That Be the Reason*

Tan, Amy. *The Valley of Amazement*

Vargas Llosa, Mario. *Green House*

***Protect** and Defend*. Patterson, Richard North

PROTECTION RACKET

Parker, Robert B. *Blue-Eyed Devil*

PROTECTIVENESS

Hewson, David. *The Garden of Angels*

Hoffman, Alice. *The Book of Magic*

Hoffman, Alice. ★*The World That We Knew*

Hyde, Catherine Ryan. *My Name Is Anton*

Lu, S. Qiouyi. *In the Watchful City*

Perry, Thomas. *Vanishing Act*

Singh, Nalini. ★*Silver Silence*
Woods, Rita. ★*Remembrance*

PROTECTIVENESS IN CHILDREN
George, Elizabeth. *What Came Before He Shot Her*

PROTECTIVENESS IN MEN
Barclay, Linwood. *No Safe House*
Bell, Lenora. *One Fine Duke*
Bennett, Bethany. *West End Earl*
Box, C. J. *Vicious Circle*
Byrne, Kerrigan. *The Duke with the Dragon Tattoo*
Byrne, Kerrigan. *The Hunter*
Child, Lee. ★*Blue Moon*
Child, Lee. *Echo Burning*
Coben, Harlan. *Run Away*
Dare, Tessa. *A Week to Be Wicked*
Frantz, Laura. *The Lacemaker*
Garwood, Julie. *Wired*
Humphreys, Sara Taney. *Trouble Walks In*
Hunt, April. *Deadly Obsession*
Hurwitz, Gregg Andrew. ★*Into the Fire*
Jackson, Brenda. *Forged in Desire*
Jenkins, Beverly. *Rebel*
Johnson, D. E. *Detroit Shuffle*
K'wan. *Revelations*
Patchett, Ann. *Run*
Phillips, Susan Elizabeth. ★*When Stars Collide*
Showalter, Gena. *Shadow and Ice*
Sister Souljah. *Midnight and the Meaning of Love*
Swinson, Kiki. *A Gangster and a Gentleman*

PROTECTIVENESS IN TEENAGERS
Grames, Juliet. *The Seven or Eight Deaths of Stella Fortuna*

PROTECTIVENESS IN WOMEN
Bouchet, Amanda. *Nightchaser*
Bryant, Niobia. *Madam, May I*
Dodd, Christina. *Strangers She Knows*
Duncan, Glen. *Talulla Rising*
Freeman, Brian. *Thief River Falls*
Gabaldon, Diana. *An Echo in the Bone*
Gabaldon, Diana. *Written in My Own Heart's Blood*
Hendrix, Grady. *The Southern Book Club's Guide to Slaying Vampires*
Phillips, Gin. *Fierce Kingdom: A Novel*

The **Protector's War**. Stirling, S. M.
The **Protectorate** [Series]. O'Keefe, Megan E.
The **Protectors** (Brenda Jackson) [Series]. Jackson, Brenda

PROTEST ART
Larsen, Reif. *I Am Radar: A Novel*

PROTEST MOVEMENTS
Ballard, J. G. *Millennium People*

PROTESTANTS
Barry, Sebastian. *The Secret Scripture: A Novel*

PROTESTS, DEMONSTRATIONS, VIGILS, ETC.
Han, Kang. ★*Human Acts: A Novel*
Jones, Cynan. *Stillicide*
Turnbull, Cadwell. *No Gods, No Monsters*

Proulx, Annie
Bad Dirt: Wyoming Stories 2
★*Barkskins: A Novel*

Fine Just the Way It Is: Wyoming Stories 3
Postcards
★*The Shipping News*

Proust, Marcel
★*Remembrance of Things Past*
Swann's Way
Time Regained
Within a Budding Grove

Provenance. Leckie, Ann
Provence mysteries [Series]. Rademacher, Cay

PROVENCE, FRANCE
Pears, Iain. *The Dream of Scipio*
Rademacher, Cay. *Deadly Camargue: A Provence Mystery*

Providence *Rag*. DeSilva, Bruce

PROVIDENCE, RHODE ISLAND
DeSilva, Bruce. *Providence Rag*
DeSilva, Bruce. *Rogue Island*
DeSilva, Bruce. *A Scourge of Vipers*

PROVINCETOWN, MASSACHUSETTS
Dillard, Annie. *The Maytrees: A Novel*
Francis, Patry. *The Orphans of Race Point: A Novel*

★***Prussian*** *Blue*. Kerr, Philip

Pryor, Mark
Hollow Man

★*A* **Psalm** *for the Wild-Built*. Chambers, Becky
Psy-Changeling trinity [Series]. Singh, Nalini

PSYCHE (GREEK DEITY)
Lewis, C. S. *Till We Have Faces: A Myth Retold*

PSYCHIATRIC HOSPITAL CARE
Kesey, Ken. ★*One Flew Over the Cuckoo's Nest*

PSYCHIATRIC HOSPITAL PATIENTS
Barry, Sebastian. *The Secret Scripture: A Novel*
Collins, Wilkie. ★*The Woman in White*
Greenberg, Joanne. *I Never Promised You a Rose Garden: A Novel*
Hayder, Mo. *Poppet*
Huisman, Violaine. *The Book of Mother*
Kepler, Lars. *The Sandman*
Kesey, Ken. ★*One Flew Over the Cuckoo's Nest*
Sanders, Lawrence. ★*The Fourth Deadly Sin*
Svevo, Italo. *Zeno's Conscience*

PSYCHIATRIC HOSPITALS
Daniels, Natalie. *Too Close*
Deluca, Marjorie. *The Savage Instinct*
Hayder, Mo. *Poppet*
Kagen, Lesley. *Every Now and Then*
Kesey, Ken. ★*One Flew Over the Cuckoo's Nest*
Kirshenbaum, Binnie. *Rabbits for Food*
Lehane, Dennis. *Shutter Island*
Mas, Victoria. *The Mad Women's Ball*
Schlink, Bernhard. *Self's Deception*
Sedgwick, Marcus. *Mister Memory: A Novel*
Stewart, Amy. ★*Miss Kopp Just Won't Quit*

PSYCHIATRIST AND PATIENT
Barker, Pat. ★*Regeneration*
Le Guin, Ursula K. *The Lathe of Heaven*

PSYCHIATRISTS
Barker, Pat. ★*The Ghost Road*
Chung, Maxine Mei-Fung. *The Eighth Girl*

Cole, Teju. ★*Open City: A Novel*
Freudenberger, Nell. *The Dissident*
Glass, Julia. *The Whole World Over*
Harris, Thomas. ★*The Silence of the Lambs*
Miller, Sue. *The Good Mother*
Raimondo, Lynne. *Dante's Dilemma: A Mark Angelotti Novel*
Robotham, Michael. ★*Suspect*

PSYCHIATRISTS WITH MENTAL ILLNESSES
Harris, Thomas. *Hannibal*

PSYCHIC ABILITY
Bennett, Jenn. *Bitter Spirits*
Camp, Bryan. *The City of Lost Fortunes*
Castle, Jayne. *Illusion Town*
Clark, P. Djeli. *Ring Shout*
Feehan, Christine. *Shadow Rider*
Harvey, Michael T. *Pulse*
Herbert, Frank. ★*Dune*
King, Stephen. *Doctor Sleep: A Novel*
King, Stephen. *End of Watch: A Novel*
King, Stephen. *Firestarter*
Krentz, Jayne Ann. ★*All the Colors of Night*
Le Guin, Ursula K. *The Lathe of Heaven*
Miller, Holly. ★*The Sight of You*
Onyebuchi, Tochi. ★*Riot Baby*
Quick, Amanda. ★*The Lady Has a Past*
Reyes, Dolores. *Eartheater*
Sittenfeld, Curtis. *Sisterland: A Novel*
Swarup, Shubhangi. *Latitudes of Longing*
Van Vogt, A. E. ★*Slan*
VanderMeer, Jeff. *Acceptance: A Novel*
VanderMeer, Jeff. ★*Annihilation: A Novel*
VanderMeer, Jeff. *Authority: A Novel*
Yang, JY. *The Ascent to Godhood*
Yang, JY. *The Black Tides of Heaven*
Yang, JY. *The Red Threads of Fortune*

PSYCHIC TRAUMA
Abrams, Melanie. *Meadowlark*
Bannister, Ilona. *When I Ran Away*
Bauer, Belinda. *Snap*
Beattie, Ann. *The Doctor's House: A Novel*
Bender, Aimee. *The Butterfly Lampshade*
Benedict, Helen. *Wolf Season*
Crowell, Jenn. *Etched on Me: A Novel*
Dade, Olivia. *All the Feels*
Doyle, Roddy. *Smile*
Dundas, Chad. *The Blaze*
Erpenbeck, Jenny. *Go, Went, Gone: A Novel*
Ferrell, Carolyn. *Dear Miss Metropolitan*
Gardiner, Meg. *The Dark Corners of the Night*
Grossman, David. ★*More Than I Love My Life: A Novel*
Hendrix, Grady. *The Final Girl Support Group*
Jeffers, Honoree Fanonne. ★*The Love Songs of W. E. B. Du Bois*
Johnson, Daisy. *Sisters*
Jónasson, Ragnar. *The Mist*
Jones, Stephen Graham. *My Heart Is a Chainsaw*
Lehane, Dennis. *Since We Fell*
Loren, Roni. ★*The One for You*
McLain, Paula. ★*When the Stars Go Dark: A Novel*

Morrison, Toni. ★*God Help the Child*
Mott, Jason. *Hell of a Book*
Nguyen, Viet Thanh. ★*The Committed*
Oates, Joyce Carol. *Night. Sleep. Death. The Stars*
Petterson, Per. *I Refuse*
Proulx, Annie. ★*The Shipping News*
Robotham, Michael. ★*When She Was Good*
Schanoes, Veronica L. *Burning Girls and Other Stories*
Shafak, Elif. ★*10 Minutes 38 Seconds in This Strange World*
So, Anthony Veasna. *Afterparties: Stories*
Straub, Peter. ★*A Dark Matter: A Novel*
Toews, Miriam. *Fight Night*
Unger, Lisa. ★*The Stranger Inside*
Yanagihara, Hanya. *A Little Life: A Novel*

PSYCHIC TRAUMA IN MEN
Hamilton, Steve. ★*The Lock Artist*
Morrison, Toni. *Home*

PSYCHICS
Allende, Isabel. ★*The House of the Spirits*
King, Stephen. *Doctor Sleep: A Novel*

PSYCHOANALYSIS
Svevo, Italo. *Zeno's Conscience*

PSYCHOHISTORIANS
Asimov, Isaac. ★*Foundation*
Asimov, Isaac. *Foundation and Empire*

PSYCHOHISTORY
Asimov, Isaac. ★*Foundation*
Asimov, Isaac. *Foundation and Empire*
Asimov, Isaac. *Second Foundation*

PSYCHOKINESIS
Anderton, Jo. *Debris*
King, Stephen. ★*Carrie*
King, Stephen. *Firestarter*
Williams, Drew. *The Stars Now Unclaimed*

PSYCHOLOGICAL FICTION
Abbott, Patricia. *Concrete Angel*
Abu-Jaber, Diana. *Birds of Paradise: A Novel*
Aciman, Andre. *Enigma Variations: A Novel*
Akhtar, Ayad. *American Dervish: A Novel*
Alameddine, Rabih. *An Unnecessary Woman*
Alarcon, Daniel. *At Night We Walk in Circles: A Novel*
Albahari, David. *Gotz and Meyer*
Albom, Mitch. *The Five People You Meet in Heaven*
Albom, Mitch. *The Next Person You Meet in Heaven*
Amdahl, Gary. *I Am Death: Two Novellas*
Amis, Martin. ★*The Zone of Interest: A Novel*
Ammaniti, Niccolo. *I'm Not Scared*
Aridjis, Chloe. *Asunder*
Arnett, Kristen N. *Mostly Dead Things*
Aslam, Nadeem. ★*The Golden Legend: A Novel*
Aswani, Alaa. *Chicago: A Modern Arabic Novel*
Atilgan, Yusuf. *Motherland Hotel*
Atwood, Margaret. *Alias Grace*
Atwood, Margaret. ★*Cat's Eye*
Auster, Paul. ★*The Book of Illusions: A Novel*
Auster, Paul. *The Brooklyn Follies*
Auster, Paul. *Invisible*
Auster, Paul. *Oracle Night*

Bacon, Charlotte. *There Is Room for You*
Bailey, Paul. *Chapman's Odyssey*
Bailey, Paul. *Uncle Rudolf*
Baker, Dorothy. ★*Young Man with a Horn*
Baldwin, James. ★*Giovanni's Room*
Baldwin, Joshua. *The Wilshire Sun*
Ballard, J. G. ★*The Day of Creation*
Banasky, Carmiel. *The Suicide of Claire Bishop*
Banks, Russell. *Lost Memory of Skin*
Banville, John. *Ancient Light*
Banville, John. *The Blue Guitar*
Banville, John. ★*Eclipse: A Novel*
Banville, John. *The Infinities*
Banville, John. ★*The Sea*
Barbash, Tom. *The Last Good Chance*
Barker, Pat. *Another World*
Barnes, Djuna. ★*Nightwood*
Barnes, Julian. *The Only Story*
Barnes, Julian. ★*The Sense of an Ending*
Barry, Brunonia. *The Map of True Places*
Barry, Sebastian. *The Secret Scripture: A Novel*
Barzak, Christopher. *One for Sorrow*
Bausch, Richard. *Hello to the Cannibals: A Novel*
Baxter, Charles. *The Feast of Love*
Baxter, Charles. *Saul and Patsy*
Beattie, Ann. *The Doctor's House: A Novel*
Beattie, Ann. *A Wonderful Stroke of Luck: A Novel*
Beauvoir, Simone de. ★*The Mandarins: A Novel*
Begley, Louis. *About Schmidt*
Bellow, Saul. ★*Herzog*
Bellow, Saul. ★*Mr. Sammler's Planet*
Bellow, Saul. *Novels, 1944-1953*
Bellow, Saul. *Ravelstein*
Bellow, Saul. ★*Seize the Day*
Bennett, Brit. *The Mothers*
Berger, Thomas. ★*Neighbors: A Novel*
Bialosky, Jill. *House Under Snow*
Bialosky, Jill. *The Prize: A Novel*
Bilenchi, Romano. ★*The Chill*
Bird, Sarah. *The Yokota Officers Club: A Novel*
Black, Benjamin. ★*Christine Falls: A Novel*
Bock, Charles. *Beautiful Children: A Novel*
Bohjalian, Chris. *The Buffalo Soldier: A Novel*
Bolano, Roberto. ★*The Savage Detectives*
Boudjedra, Rachid. *The Barbary Figs*
Bowen, Elizabeth. *The Heat of the Day*
Bowles, Paul. ★*The Sheltering Sky*
Boyle, T. Coraghessan. *The Harder They Come*
Boyle, T. Coraghessan. *The Terranauts*
Braffet, Kelly. ★*Last Seen Leaving: A Novel*
Bram, Christopher. *Lives of the Circus Animals: A Novel*
Brautigan, Richard. *An Unfortunate Woman: A Journey*
Breslin, Jimmy. *Table Money*
Brockmeier, Kevin. *The Illumination*
Brown, Rosellen. ★*Before and After*
Brownrigg, Sylvia. ★*The Delivery Room: A Novel*
Buntin, Julie. ★*Marlena: A Novel*
Butler, Marcia. *Pickle's Progress*

Butler, Nickolas. ★*The Hearts of Men*
Byatt, A. S. *Babel Tower*
Byatt, A. S. *A Whistling Woman*
Bynum, Sarah Shun-Lien. *Ms. Hempel Chronicles*
Campbell, Bebe Moore. *Brothers and Sisters*
Camus, Albert. ★*The Fall*
Camus, Albert. ★*The Stranger*
Cannon, Joanna. *Three Things About Elsie: A Novel*
Castel-Bloom, Orly. *Textile*
Cather, Willa. *A Lost Lady*
Cheever, John. *Bullet Park: A Novel*
Cheever, John. *Falconer*
Choi, Susan. *My Education*
Cleage, Pearl. *What Looks Like Crazy on an Ordinary Day: A Novel*
Cleave, Chris. *Gold*
Cline, Emma. *The Girls: A Novel*
Coe, Jonathan. *The Rotters' Club*
Coetzee, J. M. *Disgrace*
Coetzee, J. M. ★*Life & Times of Michael K*
Cole, Teju. *Every Day Is for the Thief*
Cole, Teju. ★*Open City: A Novel*
Collins, Ciaran. *The Gamal*
Conrad, Joseph. ★*Heart of Darkness*
Conrad, Joseph. ★*Lord Jim*
Conrad, Joseph. *Nostromo: A Tale of the Seaboard*
Conrad, Joseph. *Victory: An Island Tale*
Conroy, Pat. *The Prince of Tides*
Cook, Thomas H. *The Chatham School Affair*
Corman, Avery. *Prized Possessions*
Crace, Jim. *Harvest*
Crane, Stephen. *Maggie: A Girl of the Streets*
Cumyn, Alan. *Losing It*
Cusk, Rachel. *Kudos*
Cusk, Rachel. *Outline: A Novel*
Cusk, Rachel. *Transit*
D'Erasmo, Stacey. *The Sky Below*
D'Souza, Tony. *Whiteman*
Danticat, Edwidge. *Claire of the Sea Light*
Danticat, Edwidge. *The Dew Breaker*
Daoud, Kamel. *The Meursault Investigation*
Darnielle, John. *Wolf in White Van: A Novel*
Davidson, Andrew. *The Gargoyle*
De Robertis, Carolina. *Perla*
Dean, Debra. *The Madonnas of Leningrad: A Novel*
DeLillo, Don. *Falling Man: A Novel*
Delinsky, Barbara. *Lake News: A Novel*
Dennis-Benn, Nicole. ★*Patsy: A Novel*
Dexter, Pete. *Spooner*
Didion, Joan. ★*Play It as It Lays: A Novel*
Diffenbaugh, Vanessa. *The Language of Flowers: A Novel*
Diop, David. ★*At Night All Blood Is Black*
Doctorow, E. L. *Andrew's Brain*
Doctorow, E. L. ★*The Book of Daniel: A Novel*
Donoghue, Emma. *Room: A Novel*
Dostoyevsky, Fyodor. *The Best Short Stories of Dostoevsky*
Dostoyevsky, Fyodor. ★*The Brothers Karamazov*
Dostoyevsky, Fyodor. *Notes from Underground*
Dowlatabadi, Mahmoud. *The Colonel*

Doyle, Roddy. *Smile*

Doyle, Roddy. ★*The Woman Who Walked into Doors*

Drabble, Margaret. ★*The Dark Flood Rises*

Drabble, Margaret. *The Pure Gold Baby*

Drabble, Margaret. *The Sea Lady*

Drabble, Margaret. *The Witch of Exmoor*

Dubus, Andre. *Dirty Love*

Durrow, Heidi W. *The Girl Who Fell from the Sky: A Novel*

Ebershoff, David. *The Danish Girl: A Novel*

Eco, Umberto. *The Mysterious Flame of Queen Loana: An Illustrated Novel*

Edwards, Kim. *The Memory Keeper's Daughter*

Edwards, Yvvette. *The Mother*

Egan, Jennifer. ★*A Visit from the Goon Squad*

Eggers, Dave. *How We Are Hungry: Stories*

Eliot, George. ★*Middlemarch: A Study of Provincial Life*

Eliot, George. ★*The Mill on the Floss*

Eliot, George. ★*Silas Marner: The Weaver of Raveloe*

Ellis, Bret Easton. *Imperial Bedrooms*

Ellis, Bret Easton. *Lunar Park*

Enger, Leif. *Virgil Wander*

Enright, Anne. *The Forgotten Waltz*

Enright, Anne. ★*The Gathering*

Erdrich, Louise. *Four Souls: A Novel*

Erdrich, Louise. *The Painted Drum: A Novel*

Erdrich, Louise. ★*Shadow Tag: A Novel*

Essbaum, Jill Alexander. *Hausfrau: A Novel*

Estleman, Loren D. ★*The Master Executioner*

Eugenides, Jeffrey. ★*The Marriage Plot*

Eugenides, Jeffrey. ★*The Virgin Suicides*

Farrell, Henry. ★*What Ever Happened to Baby Jane?*

Faulkner, William. ★*The Sound and the Fury*

Faulks, Sebastian. *Paris Echo: A Novel*

Faulks, Sebastian. *A Week in December*

Ferris, Joshua. *To Rise Again at a Decent Hour: A Novel*

Fitch, Janet. *Paint It Black: A Novel*

Fitch, Janet. *White Oleander: A Novel*

Fitzgerald, F. Scott. ★*The Beautiful and Damned*

Ford, Ford Madox. ★*The Good Soldier: A Tale of Passion*

Ford, Richard. *Canada*

Ford, Richard. ★*Independence Day*

Ford, Richard. *The Lay of the Land*

Ford, Richard. *Let Me Be Frank with You*

Ford, Richard. *A Multitude of Sins: Stories*

Forster, E. M. ★*A Passage to India*

Fowles, John. *The Magus*

Franzen, Jonathan. ★*The Corrections*

Franzen, Jonathan. *Purity*

Freeman, Castle. *All That I Have: A Novel*

Freudenberger, Nell. ★*Lost and Wanted: A Novel*

Fridlund, Emily. ★*History of Wolves: A Novel*

Fuqua, Jonathon Scott. *Gone and Back Again*

Gaddis, William. *Agape Agape*

Gaige, Amity. *Schroder*

Gaige, Amity. *Sea Wife*

Gainza, Maria. *The Optic Nerve*

Gaitskill, Mary. *Don't Cry: Stories*

Gaitskill, Mary. *Veronica*

Galloway, Gregory. *As Simple as Snow*

Gardam, Jane. *Last Friends*

Gardam, Jane. *Old Filth*

Garey, Juliann. *Too Bright to Hear Too Loud to See*

Gentill, Sulari. *Crossing the Lines*

Ghosh, Amitav. *The Hungry Tide*

Gibb, Camilla. *Sweetness in the Belly*

Gilman, Charlotte Perkins. ★*The Yellow Wallpaper and Selected Writings*

Giordano, Paolo. *The Human Body*

Giordano, Paolo. ★*The Solitude of Prime Numbers: A Novel*

Glass, Julia. ★*Three Junes*

Glass, Julia. *The Whole World Over*

Goenawan, Clarissa. *The Perfect World of Miwako Sumida*

Goenawan, Clarissa. *Rainbirds*

Golding, William. ★*Darkness Visible*

Golding, William. ★*Lord of the Flies: A Novel*

Gordimer, Nadine. *Get a Life*

Gordimer, Nadine. *No Time Like the Present: A Novel*

Gottlieb, Eli. *Best Boy: A Novel*

Greenberg, Joanne. *I Never Promised You a Rose Garden: A Novel*

Greene, Graham. *The Captain and the Enemy*

Greene, Graham. ★*The End of the Affair*

Greene, Graham. ★*The Heart of the Matter*

Greene, Graham. ★*The Quiet American*

Greene, Graham. *The Tenth Man*

Greenwell, Garth. *Cleanness*

Greenwell, Garth. *What Belongs to You: A Novel*

Griffin, Anne. *When All Is Said: A Novel*

Grossman, David. ★*A Horse Walks into a Bar*

Grossman, David. ★*To the End of the Land*

Guterson, David. *The Other*

Guterson, David. *Our Lady of the Forest*

Gyasi, Yaa. ★*Transcendent Kingdom*

Haddon, Mark. ★*The Curious Incident of the Dog in the Night-Time: A Novel*

Hannaham, James. ★*Delicious Foods*

Hansen, Ron. *Mariette in Ecstasy*

Harding, Paul. *Tinkers*

Hardy, Thomas. ★*Far from the Madding Crowd*

Hardy, Thomas. ★*The Return of the Native*

Hardy, Thomas. ★*Tess of the D'urbervilles: A Pure Woman Faithfully Presented*

Haruf, Kent. *Benediction*

Haruf, Kent. *Eventide*

Haruf, Kent. ★*Plainsong*

Haslett, Adam. ★*Imagine Me Gone: A Novel*

Heller, Peter. *The Painter: A Novel*

Heller, Peter. *The River: A Novel*

Heller, Zoe. *What Was She Thinking?: Notes on a Scandal*

Hesse, Hermann. ★*Siddhartha: A New Translation*

Hesse, Hermann. ★*Steppenwolf*

Hoffman, Alice. *The Ice Queen: A Novel*

Howrey, Meg. *The Wanderers*

Hulse, S. M. ★*Black River*

Hurston, Zora Neale. ★*Their Eyes Were Watching God*

Irving, John. *Avenue of Mysteries: A Novel*

Irving, John. ★*A Prayer for Owen Meany: A Novel*

Ishiguro, Kazuo. ★*The Remains of the Day*
Ishiguro, Kazuo. *When We Were Orphans*
Jackson, Charles. *The Lost Weekend*
James, Henry. *Complete Stories, 1874-1884*
James, Henry. *Complete Stories, 1884-1891*
James, Henry. *Complete Stories, 1892-1898*
James, Henry. *Complete Stories, 1898-1910*
James, Henry. *Daisy Miller*
James, Henry. *The Golden Bowl*
James, Henry. *The Portrait of a Lady*
James, Henry. ★*The Turn of the Screw*
James, Henry. *The Wings of the Dove*
Jong, Erica. ★*Fear of Flying: A Novel*
Joyce, James. ★*Finnegans Wake*
Joyce, James. ★*Ulysses*
Keneally, Thomas. *Woman of the Inner Sea*
Kerangal, Maylis de. *The Heart: A Novel*
Kitamura, Katie M. *Intimacies*
Kosinski, Jerzy. ★*Being There*
Kwon, Yo-Son. *Lemon*
Lahiri, Jhumpa. *The Lowland: A Novel*
Lahiri, Jhumpa. ★*Whereabouts*
Larsen, Nella. *Passing*
Lasdun, James. *Afternoon of a Faun: A Novel*
Lawson, Mary. *Crow Lake*
Lehane, Dennis. ★*Mystic River*
Lessing, Doris May. ★*The Fifth Child*
Lessing, Doris May. ★*The Golden Notebook*
Lessing, Doris May. *A Proper Marriage*
Lessing, Doris May. *The Sweetest Dream*
Levy, Deborah. *Swimming Home: A Novel*
Lightman, Alan P. *The Diagnosis*
Lively, Penelope. ★*Moon Tiger*
Lodato, Victor. *Mathilda Savitch*
Lurie, Alison. *Foreign Affairs*
Mailer, Norman. ★*The Executioner's Song*
Mann, Thomas. *Buddenbrooks*
Mann, Thomas. *Death in Venice and Seven Other Stories*
Mann, Thomas. *The Magic Mountain*
Martel, Yann. ★*Life of Pi: A Novel*
Martin, Steve. *Shopgirl*
Maugham, W. Somerset. *The Moon and Sixpence*
Maugham, W. Somerset. ★*Of Human Bondage*
McCormack, Mike. ★*Solar Bones*
McCullough, Colleen. *An Indecent Obsession*
McDermott, Alice. *Someone*
McDowell, Christina. *The Cave Dwellers: A Novel*
McEwan, Ian. ★*Amsterdam*
McEwan, Ian. ★*Atonement: A Novel*
McEwan, Ian. *Black Dogs*
McEwan, Ian. *The Child in Time*
McLean, Felicity. *The Van Apfel Girls Are Gone*
Mengestu, Dinaw. ★*All Our Names*
Messud, Claire. ★*The Woman Upstairs: A Novel*
Mihalic, Susan. *Dark Horses*
Miller, Andrew. *Oxygen*
Miller, Sue. *The Good Mother*
Mishima, Yukio. *Spring Snow*

Mishima, Yukio. *The Temple of Dawn*
Moniz, Tomas. *Big Familia*
Moore, Alison. *The Lighthouse*
Morrison, Toni. ★*God Help the Child*
Morrison, Toni. *Home*
Morrison, Toni. *Love*
Moshfegh, Ottessa. *Eileen*
Moshfegh, Ottessa. *My Year of Rest and Relaxation*
Mosley, Walter. ★*John Woman*
Mosley, Walter. *The Right Mistake: The Further Philosophical Investigations of Socrates Fortlow*
Mozley, Fiona. ★*Elmet*
Murakami, Haruki. *South of the Border, West of the Sun*
Murdoch, Iris. *An Accidental Man*
Murdoch, Iris. *The Nice and the Good*
Murdoch, Iris. *The Sea, the Sea*
Musil, Robert. *The Man Without Qualities*
Naipaul, V. S. *A House for Mr. Biswas*
Naipaul, V. S. *Magic Seeds*
Ng, Celeste. ★*Everything I Never Told You: A Novel*
Nguyen, Viet Thanh. ★*The Sympathizer*
Nicholls, David. *US: A Novel*
Nin, Anais. *Cities of the Interior*
Nunez, Sigrid. ★*The Friend*
Nunez, Sigrid. *The Last of Her Kind: A Novel*
O'Brien, Tim. ★*The Things They Carried: A Work of Fiction*
O'Farrell, Maggie. *The Hand That First Held Mine: A Novel*
O'Nan, Stewart. *Henry, Himself*
Oates, Joyce Carol. *Because It Is Bitter, and Because It Is My Heart*
Oates, Joyce Carol. *Breathe*
Oates, Joyce Carol. *The Falls: A Novel*
Oates, Joyce Carol. *A Garden of Earthly Delights*
Oates, Joyce Carol. *The Gravedigger's Daughter: A Novel*
Oates, Joyce Carol. ★*My Life as a Rat*
Oates, Joyce Carol. ★*Them*
Oates, Joyce Carol. ★*We Were the Mulvaneys*
Ogawa, Yoko. *The Housekeeper and the Professor*
Okuizumi, Hikaru. *The Stones Cry Out*
Ólafsson, Ólafur Jóhann. *The Sacrament: A Novel*
Oyeyemi, Helen. *The Opposite House*
Oz, Amos. *Fima*
Ozick, Cynthia. *Foreign Bodies*
Palahniuk, Chuck. *Choke: A Novel*
Palmer, Dexter Clarence. ★*Mary Toft; Or, the Rabbit Queen: A Novel*
Patchett, Ann. ★*Bel Canto: A Novel*
Patchett, Ann. *Run*
Patchett, Ann. ★*State of Wonder: A Novel*
Percy, Walker. ★*The Moviegoer*
Percy, Walker. *The Second Coming*
Perrotta, Tom. *Little Children*
Persson Giolito, Malin. *Quicksand*
Petterson, Per. *I Curse the River of Time*
Petterson, Per. *I Refuse*
Phillips, Caryl. *A Distant Shore*
Phillips, Caryl. *Foreigners*
Picoult, Jodi. *House Rules: A Novel*
Picoult, Jodi. *Sing You Home: A Novel*
Picoult, Jodi. *The Storyteller*

Piercy, Marge. *Vida: A Novel*
Plath, Sylvia. ★*The Bell Jar*
Pomerantz, Sharon. *Rich Boy*
Powers, Richard. *The Echo Maker*
Prcic, Ismet. *Shards: A Novel*
Price, Reynolds. *The Good Priest's Son*
Price, Reynolds. *Roxanna Slade*
Prose, Francine. *Goldengrove: A Novel*
Rachman, Tom. *The Imperfectionists: A Novel*
Rand, Ayn. ★*The Fountainhead*
Restrepo, Laura. ★*Delirium: A Novel*
Rodrigues Fowler, Yara. *Stubborn Archivist*
Rooney, Kathleen. ★*Lillian Boxfish Takes a Walk*
Rooney, Sally. ★*Conversations with Friends*
Rosnay, Tatiana de. ★*Sarah's Key*
Roth, Philip. ★*The Anatomy Lesson*
Roth, Philip. ★*Everyman*
Roth, Philip. *Exit Ghost*
Roth, Philip. ★*The Human Stain*
Roth, Philip. *Zuckerman Bound*
Rushdie, Salman. *Shalimar the Clown: A Novel*
Russell, Kate Elizabeth. ★*My Dark Vanessa*
Sackville-West, V. *All Passion Spent*
Salinger, J. D. ★*The Catcher in the Rye*
Salinger, J. D. ★*Franny and Zooey*
Salinger, J. D. *Raise High the Roof Beam, Carpenters,: And Seymour—An Introduction.*
Sanders, Lawrence. ★*The First Deadly Sin*
Sanders, Lawrence. ★*The Fourth Deadly Sin*
Sanders, Lawrence. *The Second Deadly Sin*
Sanders, Lawrence. ★*The Third Deadly Sin*
Saramago, Jose. *Death with Interruptions*
Sartre, Jean Paul. ★*Nausea*
Savage, Sam. *The Way of the Dog: A Novel*
Schulman, Alex. *The Survivors: A Novel*
Schwarz, Christina. *Drowning Ruth*
Scott, Stephanie. *What's Left of Me Is Yours: A Novel*
Sebald, Winfried Georg. *The Emigrants*
Sebold, Alice. *The Almost Moon: A Novel*
Sebold, Alice. ★*The Lovely Bones*
Shafak, Elif. ★*10 Minutes 38 Seconds in This Strange World*
Sharratt, Mary. *Illuminations: A Novel of Hildegard Von Bingen*
Shriver, Lionel. *The Post-Birthday World*
Shriver, Lionel. *We Need to Talk About Kevin*
Skyhorse, Brando. *Madonnas of Echo Park: A Novel*
Slaughter, Karin. ★*Undone: A Novel*
Smith, Ali. *The Accidental*
Smith, Ali. ★*Autumn*
Smith, Ali. ★*Spring*
Smith, Ali. ★*Winter*
Smith, Zadie. ★*Nw: A Novel*
Sofer, Dalia. *Man of My Time*
Solomon, Asali. *Disgruntled: A Novel*
Spark, Muriel. *The Driver's Seat*
Spark, Muriel. ★*A Far Cry from Kensington*
Spark, Muriel. ★*The Prime of Miss Jean Brodie*
Spencer, Scott. *Man in the Woods*
Spencer, Scott. *An Ocean Without a Shore*

St. Aubyn, Edward. *At Last*
Steinbeck, John. ★*Of Mice and Men*
Styron, William. *Lie Down in Darkness*
Swift, Graham. ★*Last Orders: A Novel*
Swift, Graham. *Wish You Were Here*
Tartt, Donna. ★*The Goldfinch*
Trollope, Anthony. *Doctor Thorne*
Trollope, Anthony. ★*The Eustace Diamonds*
Trollope, Anthony. *Framley Parsonage*
Trollope, Anthony. *The Last Chronicle of Barset*
Trollope, Anthony. ★*The Prime Minister*
Trollope, Anthony. *The Warden*
Trumbo, Dalton. ★*Johnny Got His Gun*
Updike, John. *Seek My Face*
Walser, Robert. *The Assistant*
Watson, Martine Fournier. *The Dream Peddler*
Welty, Eudora. *The Optimist's Daughter*
Westlake, Donald E. *Memory*
Whitehead, Colson. *John Henry Days: A Novel*
Wilson, Sloan. ★*The Man in the Gray Flannel Suit*
Wolff, Tobias. *Old School: A Novel*
Woolf, Virginia. *Between the Acts*
Woolf, Virginia. *Jacob's Room*
Woolf, Virginia. ★*Mrs. Dalloway*
Woolf, Virginia. ★*To the Lighthouse*
Woolf, Virginia. *The Waves*
Yanagihara, Hanya. *A Little Life: A Novel*
Yoshimoto, Banana. *The Lake*
Yourcenar, Marguerite. ★*Memoirs of Hadrian: And Reflections on the Composition of Memoirs of Hadrian*
Psychological profiler novels [Series]. Grebe, Camilla
PSYCHOLOGICAL RESEARCH
Chayefsky, Paddy. *Altered States: A Novel*
PSYCHOLOGICAL SUSPENSE
Abbott, Jeff. *The Three Beths*
Abbott, Megan E. ★*Give Me Your Hand*
Abbott, Megan E. ★*The Turnout: A Novel*
Adler-Olsen, Jussi. *The Absent One*
Alam, Rumaan. ★*Leave the World Behind: A Novel*
Armstrong, Kelley. *Wherever She Goes*
Arvin, Reed. *Blood of Angels: A Novel*
Audrain, Ashley. *The Push*
Baker, Jo. *The Body Lies*
Banville, John. *The Book of Evidence*
Barnett, S. K. *Safe*
Barton, Fiona. *The Child*
Barton, Fiona. *The Suspect*
Bartz, Andrea. *The Herd: A Novel*
Bartz, Andrea. *The Lost Night*
Beck, Haylen. *Lost You*
Bell, Darcey. *Something She's Not Telling Us*
Belle, Kimberly. *Dear Wife*
Beyda, Emily. *The Body Double*
Bezmozgis, David. *The Betrayers: A Novel*
Billingham, Mark. ★*Their Little Secret*
Bolton, S. J. *A Dark and Twisted Tide*
Bolton, S. J. *Now You See Me*
Bolton, S. J. *The Split*

Bourland, Barbara. ★*Fake Like Me*
Brazier, Eliza Jane. *If I Disappear*
Briscoe, Joanna. *The Seduction*
Brundage, Elizabeth. ★*All Things Cease to Appear*
Burke, Alafair. *The Better Sister: A Novel*
Burton, Tara Isabella. *Social Creature*
Cameron, Lindsay. *Just One Look*
Candlish, Louise. *Our House*
Carey, M. R. *Someone Like Me*
Carter, Mary Dixie. *The Photographer*
Chaon, Dan. *Ill Will*
Chavez, Heather. *No Bad Deed*
Chizmar, Richard T. *A Long December*
Chung, Maxine Mei-Fung. *The Eighth Girl*
Cleave, Paul. *Trust No One: A Thriller*
Cook, Thomas H. *The Fate of Katherine Carr*
Cook, Thomas H. *Instruments of Night*
Cornwell, Patricia Daniels. *Postmortem*
Corry, Jane. *The Dead Ex*
Daniels, Natalie. *Too Close*
Delaney, J. P. *Believe Me: A Novel*
Delaney, J. P. *The Girl Before: A Novel*
Delaney, J. P. *The Perfect Wife: A Novel*
Delaney, J. P. *Playing Nice*
Dionne, Karen. *The Wicked Sister*
Downes, Anna. *The Safe Place: A Novel*
Downing, Samantha. *My Lovely Wife*
Du Maurier, Daphne. ★*Rebecca*
Edwards, Rachel. *Darling*
Ellison, J. T. *Good Girls Lie*
Ellison, J. T. *Tear Me Apart*
Feeney, Alice. ★*I Know Who You Are: A Novel*
Feeney, Alice. ★*Sometimes I Lie*
Finn, A. J. ★*The Woman in the Window*
Fisher, Tarryn. *The Wives*
Flynn, Gillian. *Dark Places*
Flynn, Gillian. ★*Gone Girl: A Novel*
Flynn, Gillian. ★*Sharp Objects: A Novel*
Foley, Lucy. *The Hunting Party*
Franklin, Tom. *Crooked Letter, Crooked Letter: A Novel*
Freeman, Brian. *Thief River Falls*
French, Nicci. ★*Blue Monday*
French, Nicci. *Dark Saturday*
French, Nicci. *The Day of the Dead: A Novel*
French, Nicci. *Friday on My Mind: A Frieda Klein Mystery*
French, Nicci. ★*House of Correction*
French, Nicci. ★*The Lying Room*
French, Nicci. *Sunday Silence*
French, Nicci. *Thursday's Children*
French, Nicci. *Tuesday's Gone*
French, Nicci. *Waiting for Wednesday: A Frieda Klein Mystery*
French, Tana. ★*Broken Harbor*
French, Tana. *Faithful Place: A Novel*
French, Tana. *In the Woods*
French, Tana. *The Likeness*
French, Tana. ★*The Secret Place*
Gailey, Sarah. *The Echo Wife*
Gardner, Lisa. *Alone*

Gaylin, Alison. *Never Look Back*
Goddard, Robert. ★*Into the Blue*
Goddard, Robert. *Never Go Back*
Goldin, Megan. *The Night Swim*
Golding, Melanie. *The Hidden: A Novel*
Golding, Melanie. *Little Darlings*
Goodman, Carol. *The Sea of Lost Girls*
Gosling, Victoria. *Before the Ruins: A Novel*
Greene, Graham. ★*Brighton Rock*
Greer, Andrew Sean. *The Impossible Lives of Greta Wells*
Gundar-Goshen, Ayelet. *Waking Lions*
Guterson, David. ★*Snow Falling on Cedars*
Hall, Araminta. *Imperfect Women: A Novel*
Hamilton, Karen. *The Last Wife*
Hannah, Sophie. *Perfect Little Children*
Harris, Thomas. *Hannibal*
Harris, Thomas. *Hannibal Rising*
Harris, Thomas. *Red Dragon*
Harris, Thomas. ★*The Silence of the Lambs*
Hart, John. *The King of Lies*
Hart, John. *The Last Child*
Hart, Josephine. *Damage: A Novel*
Hausmann, Romy. ★*Dear Child*
Hawkins, Paula. ★*The Girl on the Train: A Novel*
Hawley, Noah. *The Good Father*
Healey, Emma. ★*Elizabeth Is Missing*
Heller, L. Alison. *The Neighbor's Secret*
Hendricks, Greer. *An Anonymous Girl*
Hendricks, Greer. ★*You Are Not Alone*
Higashino, Keigo. ★*The Devotion of Suspect X*
Highsmith, Patricia. *The Highsmith Reader: Selected Novels and Short Stories*
Highsmith, Patricia. ★*The Talented Mr. Ripley*
Hill, Reginald. *The Woodcutter: A Novel*
Hill, Susan. *The Shadows in the Street: A Simon Serrailler Mystery*
Hoffmann, R. J. *Other People's Children: A Novel*
Holahan, Cate. *Her Three Lives*
Hunter, Megan. *The Harpy*
Imamura, Natsuko. *The Woman in the Purple Skirt: A Novel*
James, Rebecca. *The Woman in the Mirror*
Jayatissa, Amanda. ★*My Sweet Girl*
Jemc, Jac. ★*The Grip of It*
Jewell, Lisa. *Then She Was Gone: A Novel*
Johnstone, Carole. *Mirrorland*
Jónasson, Ragnar. ★*The Girl Who Died*
Jones, Sandie. *The Other Woman*
Jones, Tanen. *The Better Liar: A Novel*
Kane, Darby. *Pretty Little Wife*
Kantaria, Annabel. *I Know You: A Novel of Suspense*
Katzenbach, John. *What Comes Next*
Kellerman, Jonathan. *Bones: An Alex Delaware Novel*
Kellerman, Jonathan. *Gone*
Kelly, Erin. *The Burning Air: A Novel*
Kelly, Erin. *Watch Her Fall*
King, Stephen. *Dolores Claiborne*
King, Stephen. ★*Misery*
Knight, Renee. *The Secretary: A Novel*
Korelitz, Jean Hanff. ★*The Plot*

Kubica, Mary. ★*The Other Mrs.*
Kurian, Vera. *Never Saw Me Coming*
Lackberg, Camilla. *The Golden Cage*
Lackberg, Camilla. *Silver Tears*
Laskowski, Tara. *The Mother Next Door*
Lattari, Katie. *Dark Things I Adore*
Lawler, Liz. *Don't Wake Up*
Lehane, Dennis. *Shutter Island*
Lippman, Laura. ★*After I'm Gone*
Lippman, Laura. ★*Dream Girl*
Lippman, Laura. *Wilde Lake*
Livesey, Margot. *Criminals: A Novel*
Logan, T. M. *The Vacation*
Macmillan, Gilly. *The Nanny*
Macmillan, Gilly. *The Perfect Girl*
Mangan, Christine. *Palace of the Drowned*
Manning, Max. *The Victim: A Novel*
Marias, Javier. *The Infatuations*
Marias, Javier. *Thus Bad Begins: A Novel*
McCreight, Kimberly. *Friends Like These*
McPherson, Catriona. *Strangers at the Gate*
Merullo, Roland. *The Talk-Funny Girl: A Novel*
Minato, Kanae. *Confessions*
Molloy, Aimee. *The Perfect Mother: A Novel*
Morton, Kate. *The Distant Hours: A Novel*
Mosley, Walter. *Fortunate Son: A Novel*
Murphy, Sara Flannery. *The Possessions*
Nunez, Sigrid. *Salvation City*
O'Farrell, Maggie. *The Vanishing Act of Esme Lennox*
Oates, Joyce Carol. *Pursuit*
Palmer, Daniel. *The New Husband*
Paris, B. A. *Behind Closed Doors*
Paris, B. A. *Bring Me Back: A Novel*
Paris, B. A. ★*The Dilemma*
Pessl, Marisha. *Night Film: A Novel*
Phillips, Helen. *The Need: A Novel*
Pinborough, Sarah. ★*Behind Her Eyes: A Novel*
Pinborough, Sarah. ★*Cross Her Heart: A Novel*
Pinborough, Sarah. ★*Dead to Her: A Novel*
Pitoniak, Anna. *Necessary People*
Price, Richard. *Samaritan*
Pyper, Andrew. *The Homecoming: A Novel*
Rader-Day, Lori. *The Black Hour*
Rader-Day, Lori. *The Day I Died*
Rader-Day, Lori. ★*The Lucky One*
Reid, Iain. *I'm Thinking of Ending Things*
Rendell, Ruth. ★*The Bridesmaid*
Rendell, Ruth. *Collected Stories*
Rendell, Ruth. ★*A Judgement in Stone*
Rendell, Ruth. *Live Flesh*
Rendell, Ruth. *The Tree of Hands*
Reynolds, Allie. ★*Shiver*
Riordan, Kate. *The Heatwave*
Robinson, Peter. *The First Cut*
Robotham, Michael. ★*Close Your Eyes*
Robotham, Michael. ★*The Other Wife*
Robotham, Michael. ★*Say You're Sorry*
Robotham, Michael. ★*Suspect*

Rosenfield, Kat. *No One Will Miss Her*
Rouda, Kaira Sturdivant. *Best Day Ever: A Novel*
Rouda, Kaira Sturdivant. *The Favorite Daughter*
Roy, Lori. *Bent Road*
Sager, Riley. *Final Girls: A Novel*
Sager, Riley. *The Last Time I Lied: A Novel*
Sager, Riley. *Lock Every Door: A Novel*
Schaitkin, Alexis. *Saint X*
Schweblin, Samanta. *Fever Dream: A Novel*
Schweblin, Samanta. *Little Eyes*
Scottoline, Lisa. *After Anna*
Searles, John. *Help for the Haunted*
Shepard, Sara. ★*Reputation*
Silver, Elizabeth L. *The Execution of Noa P. Singleton: A Novel*
Slaughter, Karin. *The Good Daughter*
Stage, Zoje. ★*Baby Teeth: A Novel*
Stage, Zoje. *Getaway*
Stapley, Marissa. *The Last Resort*
Steadman, Catherine. *The Disappearing Act*
Steadman, Catherine. *Mr. Nobody: A Novel*
Steadman, Catherine. *Something in the Water*
Steinhauer, Olen. *The Bridge of Sighs*
Stevens, Chevy. *Never Let You Go*
Stevens, Chevy. *Still Missing*
Straub, Peter. ★*A Dark Matter: A Novel*
Swanson, Peter. *Eight Perfect Murders: A Novel*
Swanson, Peter. *Her Every Fear: A Novel*
Swanson, Peter. *The Kind Worth Killing: A Novel*
Tartt, Donna. ★*The Secret History*
Thomas, Bev. *A Good Enough Mother: A Novel*
Thompson, Jim. *The Killer Inside Me*
Torre, A. R. *Every Last Secret*
Tremblay, Paul. ★*The Cabin at the End of the World: A Novel*
Tudor, C. J. *The Burning Girls: A Novel*
Unger, Lisa. ★*The Stranger Inside*
Unger, Lisa. *Under My Skin*
Vandelly, T. Marie. *Theme Music*
Vernon, P. J. *Bath Haus: A Thriller*
Vine, Barbara. *The Minotaur: A Novel*
Walker, Caroline Louise. *Man of the Year*
Walker, Wendy. *Emma in the Night*
Ward, Catriona. *The Last House on Needless Street*
Ware, Ruth. *The Death of Mrs. Westaway*
Ware, Ruth. *In a Dark, Dark Wood*
Ware, Ruth. *The Lying Game*
Ware, Ruth. ★*The Turn of the Key*
Ware, Ruth. *The Woman in Cabin Ten*
Watson, S. J. *Final Cut*
Wilson, Carter. *Dead Girl in 2a*
Wrobel, Stephanie. *Darling Rose Gold*
Yates, Christopher J. *Grist Mill Road: A Novel*
Youers, Rio. *Lola on Fire*
Young, Heather. *The Distant Dead*
Zettel, Sarah. *A Mother's Lie*

PSYCHOLOGICAL WARFARE
Harris, Oliver. *A Shadow Intelligence*
Kay, Guy Gavriel. *Tigana*

PSYCHOLOGISTS
Ballard, J. G. *Millennium People*
Block, Lawrence. *All the Flowers Are Dying*
Carr, Caleb. ★*The Alienist*
Carr, Caleb. *The Angel of Darkness*
Chaon, Dan. *Ill Will*
Glass, Seraphina Nova. *Someone's Listening*
Kayode, Femi. ★*Lightseekers*
Kellerman, Jonathan. *Bones: An Alex Delaware Novel*
Kellerman, Jonathan. *Gone*
Knopf, Chris. *You're Dead*
Pinborough, Sarah. ★*Behind Her Eyes: A Novel*
Raimondo, Lynne. *Dante's Wood: A Mark Angelotti Novel*
Robotham, Michael. ★*When She Was Good*
Seo, Mi-Ae. *The Only Child*
PSYCHOLOGY
Schweblin, Samanta. *Mouthful of Birds: Stories*
PSYCHOLOGY — EXPERIMENTS
Hendricks, Greer. *An Anonymous Girl*
Thomas, Elisabeth. *Catherine House*
PSYCHOLOGY TEACHERS
Goldstein, Rebecca. *36 Arguments for the Existence of God: A Work of Fiction*
Hendricks, Greer. *An Anonymous Girl*
PSYCHOPATHS
Beukes, Lauren. *Broken Monsters*
Beukes, Lauren. *The Shining Girls*
Black, Saul. ★*The Killing Lessons*
Black, Saul. ★*Lovemurder*
Bruen, Ken. *Galway Girl: A Jack Taylor Novel*
Cooper, Ellison. *Buried*
Coulter, Catherine. *Paradox*
Dexter, Pete. *Paris Trout*
Dionne, Karen. *The Wicked Sister*
French, Nicci. *Sunday Silence*
Grafton, Sue. *X*
Grafton, Sue. *Y Is for Yesterday*
Greene, Graham. ★*Brighton Rock*
Harris, Thomas. *Red Dragon*
Harris, Thomas. ★*The Silence of the Lambs*
Highsmith, Patricia. ★*The Talented Mr. Ripley*
Kerley, Jack. ★*The Death Collectors*
King, Stephen. *End of Watch: A Novel*
King, Stephen. *Mr. Mercedes: A Novel*
Koontz, Dean R. *The Darkest Evening of the Year*
Koontz, Dean R. *The Husband*
Koontz, Dean R. *Intensity: A Novel*
Koontz, Dean R. *Velocity*
Kurian, Vera. *Never Saw Me Coming*
Levin, Ira. *A Kiss Before Dying*
Mason, Timothy. *The Darwin Affair*
Murakami, Ryu. *In the Miso Soup*
Pryor, Mark. *Hollow Man*
Sanders, Lawrence. ★*The Third Deadly Sin*
Sandford, John. ★*Mind Prey*
Sandford, John. ★*Winter Prey*
Thompson, Jim. *The Killer Inside Me*

PSYCHOSES
Freeman, Brian. *The Night Bird*
Jemc, Jac. ★*The Grip of It*
PSYCHOTHERAPIST AND PATIENT
Barry, Brunonia. *The Map of True Places*
Bolton, S. J. *The Split*
Brownrigg, Sylvia. ★*The Delivery Room: A Novel*
French, Nicci. ★*Blue Monday*
Greenberg, Joanne. *I Never Promised You a Rose Garden: A Novel*
Thomas, Bev. *A Good Enough Mother: A Novel*
PSYCHOTHERAPISTS
Briscoe, Joanna. *The Seduction*
French, Nicci. ★*Blue Monday*
Gregory, Daryl. *We Are All Completely Fine*
PUBLIC BATHS
Vernon, P. J. *Bath Haus: A Thriller*
PUBLIC DEFENDERS
Nava, Michael. ★*Carved in Bone*
Pava, Sergio de la. *A Naked Singularity*
Winer, Jeanne. *Her Kind of Case*
PUBLIC HEALTH
Leon, Donna. *Trace Elements*
PUBLIC HOSPITALS
Welsh, Kaite. *The Wages of Sin*
PUBLIC HOUSING
Chariandy, David John. *Brother: A Novel*
Gunaratne, Guy. *In Our Mad and Furious City*
Moore, Alan. *Jerusalem: A Novel*
Price, Richard. *Samaritan*
PUBLIC OFFICIALS
Stanley, Michael. *A Death in the Family*
PUBLIC OPINION
Flint, Emma. ★*Little Deaths: A Novel*
PUBLIC PROSECUTORS
Arvin, Reed. *Blood of Angels: A Novel*
Gran, Sara. *Claire Dewitt and the City of the Dead*
Turow, Scott. *Presumed Innocent*
PUBLIC RELATIONS
Dee, Jonathan. *A Thousand Pardons: A Novel*
PUBLIC RELATIONS CONSULTANTS
Adkins, Mary. *When You Read This*
Manning, Max. *The Victim: A Novel*
PUBLIC RELATIONS PERSONNEL
Kasulke, Calvin. *Several People Are Typing*
PUBLICITY
Guillory, Jasmine. ★*While We Were Dating*
PUBLISHERS AND PUBLISHING
Adimi, Kaouther. *Our Riches*
James, P. D. *Original Sin*
Kotzwinkle, William. *The Bear Went Over the Mountain*
Mott, Jason. *Hell of a Book*
Pearl, Matthew. *The Last Dickens: A Novel*
***Pudd'nhead** Wilson and Those Extraordinary Twins.* Twain, Mark
PUEBLO INDIANS
Silko, Leslie Marmon. ★*Ceremony*
PUERTO RICANS
Quinonez, Ernesto. *Bodega Dreams*

PUERTO RICO
 Santiago, Esmeralda. *Conquistadora: A Novel*
Pufahl, Shannon
 On Swift Horses
PUGET SOUND
 Beagle, Peter S. *Summerlong*
Pulley, Natasha
 The Bedlam Stacks
 ★*The Kingdoms*
 The Lost Future of Pepperharrow
 The Watchmaker of Filigree Street
PULP FICTION
 Faust, Christa. *Choke Hold*
 Faust, Christa. *Money Shot*
 Van Vogt, A. E. ★*Slan*
 Westlake, Donald E. *Forever and a Death*
Pulse. Francis, Felix
Pulse. Harvey, Michael T.
PUMA
 Barr, Nevada. *Track of the Cat*
PUNE, INDIA
 Doshi, Avni. *Burnt Sugar: A Novel*
PUNISHMENT
 Campisi, Megan. *Sin Eater*
 Hunter, Megan. *The Harpy*
The Punishment She Deserves. George, Elizabeth
PUNK CULTURE
 Hallberg, Garth Risk. ★*City on Fire*
PUNK ROCK MUSIC
 Coe, Jonathan. *The Rotters' Club*
 Fitch, Janet. *Paint It Black: A Novel*
PUNK ROCK MUSICIANS
 Egan, Jennifer. ★*A Visit from the Goon Squad*
Punke, Michael
 Ridgeline: A Novel
PUPPETEERS
 Bradley, C. Alan. *The Weed That Strings the Hangman's Bag: A Flavia De Luce Mystery*
 Phillips, Susan Elizabeth. *Heroes Are My Weakness*
PUPPETRY
 Larsen, Reif. *I Am Radar: A Novel*
Purcell, Laura
 The House of Whispers
 The Silent Companions: A Ghost Story
PURDAH
 Massey, Sujata. ★*The Widows of Malabar Hill: A Mystery of 1920s Bombay*
The Pure Gold Baby. Drabble, Margaret
A Pure Heart: A Novel. Hassib, Rajia
Pure Heat. Buchman, M. L.
The Pure in Heart: A Simon Serrailler Crime Novel. Hill, Susan
PURGATORY
 Rice, Anne. *Memnoch the Devil*
PURITAN WOMEN
 Seton, Anya. ★*The Winthrop Woman*
PURITANS
 Brom. *Slewfoot: A Tale of Bewitchery*
 Hawthorne, Nathaniel. ★*The Scarlet Letter: A Romance*

Purity. Franzen, Jonathan
The Purity of Vengeance: A Department Q Novel. Adler-Olsen, Jussi
A Purple Place for Dying. MacDonald, John D.
PURPOSE IN LIFE
 Atkinson, Kate. ★*Life After Life: A Novel*
 Bellow, Saul. ★*The Adventures of Augie March*
 Beverly, William. *Dodgers: A Novel*
 Butler, Halle. *The New Me: A Novel*
 Cameron, W. Bruce. *A Dog's Promise*
 Cartwright, Justin. *To Heaven by Water*
 Hession, Ronan. *Leonard and Hungry Paul*
 Johnson, Denis. *The Largesse of the Sea Maiden: Stories*
 Kafka, Franz. ★*Collected Stories*
 Khadra, Yasmina. ★*Khalil: A Novel*
 Levy, Deborah. *Hot Milk: A Novel*
 Malamud, Bernard. *The Natural*
 Newman, Sandra. *The Heavens*
 Percy, Walker. ★*The Moviegoer*
 Saint-Exupery, Antoine de. ★*The Little Prince*
 Shreve, Anita. *Sea Glass: A Novel*
 Stone, Irving. *Lust for Life: A Novel of Vincent Van Gogh*
 Vonnegut, Kurt. ★*Breakfast of Champions: Or, Goodbye Blue Monday!*
 Vonnegut, Kurt. ★*Galapagos: A Novel*
 Walsh, M. O. ★*The Big Door Prize: A Novel*
 Woolf, Virginia. *The Waves*
Pursuit. Oates, Joyce Carol
The Pursuit of Alice Thrift: A Novel. Lipman, Elinor
★*The Pursuit of Love: A Novel*. Mitford, Nancy
The Pursuit of William Abbey. North, Claire
The Pursuits of Lord Kit Cavanaugh. Laurens, Stephanie
The Push. Audrain, Ashley
★*Push: a Novel*. Sapphire
Pushing up Daisies: An Agatha Raisin Mystery. Beaton, M. C.
Pushkin Hills. Dovlatov, Sergei
The Pussy Trap. Capri, NeNe
Pussy trap [Series]. Capri, NeNe
The Pussy Trap; Part 3. Capri, NeNe
Put up Your Duke. Frampton, Megan
PUTIN, VLADIMIR VLADIMIROVICH
 Matthews, Jason. ★*The Kremlin's Candidate*
 Wideman, John Edgar. ★*American Histories: Stories*
Putnam, Jonathan F.
 These Honored Dead
Putney, Mary Jo
 Loving a Lost Lord
 The Marriage Spell: A Novel
 No Longer a Gentleman
 Not Quite a Wife
 Nowhere Near Respectable
 Once a Scoundrel
 Once a Soldier
The Puttermesser Papers. Ozick, Cynthia
Puzo, Mario
 The Family: A Novel
 ★*The Godfather*
 The Last Don
 The Sicilian: A Novel

Puzzle lady mysteries [Series]. Hall, Parnell
Pygmy. Palahniuk, Chuck
Pym, Barbara
★*Excellent Women*
Pynchon, Thomas
Against the Day: A Novel
★*Bleeding Edge*
★*The Crying of Lot 49*
★*Gravity's Rainbow*
Inherent Vice
Mason & Dixon
★*V: A Novel*
Vineland
Pyper, Andrew
The Damned: A Novel
The Homecoming: A Novel
The Residence: A Novel
Pyramids: *the Book of Going Forth*. Pratchett, Terry
PYTHONS
Hiaasen, Carl. ★*Squeeze Me: A Novel*

Q

Qiu, Xiaolong
Death of a Red Heroine
Don't Cry Tai Lake
Enigma of China
Hold Your Breath, China
Red Mandarin Dress
Shanghai Redemption
When Red Is Black
Quade, Kirstin Valdez
★*The Five Wounds: A Novel*
Night at the Fiestas: Stories
QUAKER FAMILIES
West, Jessamyn. *The Friendly Persuasion*
QUAKER WOMEN
Benton, Janet. *Lilli De Jong: A Novel*
Chevalier, Tracy. *The Last Runaway*
QUAKERS
Chevalier, Tracy. *The Last Runaway*
West, Jessamyn. *The Friendly Persuasion*
Wong, David. *This Book Is Full of Spiders: Seriously, Dude, Don't Touch It*
QUANTUM COMPUTERS
Harrison, M. John. *Light*
QUANTUM THEORY
Labatut, Benjamin. *When We Cease to Understand the World*
*The **Quantum** Thief*. Rajaniemi, Hannu
Quantum thief novels [Series]. Rajaniemi, Hannu
Quarantine. Crace, Jim
QUARANTINE
Gordimer, Nadine. *Get a Life*
Picoult, Jodi. ★*Wish You Were Here: A Novel*
QUARRELING
Haigh, Jennifer. *Mrs. Kimble: A Novel*

Stephens, Alice. *Famous Adopted People*
QUARRIES AND QUARRYING
Shields, Carol. ★*The Stone Diaries*
QUARTERBACKS (FOOTBALL)
Phillips, Susan Elizabeth. ★*Natural Born Charmer*
Phillips, Susan Elizabeth. ★*When Stars Collide*
Wade, Becky. *Falling for You*
Quartey, Kwei
Children of the Street: A Novel
Gold of Our Fathers
The Missing American
Murder at Cape Three Points
★*Sleep Well, My Lady*
Wife of the Gods: A Novel
QUEBEC (PROVINCE)
Dupont, Eric. *The American Fiancee: A Novel*
Farrow, John. *The Storm Murders: A Thriller*
Penny, Louise. ★*A Better Man: A Chief Inspector Gamache Novel*
Penny, Louise. *The Cruelest Month: A Three Pines Mystery*
Penny, Louise. ★*The Madness of Crowds*
Penny, Louise. *Still Life*
Wallace, David Foster. ★*Infinite Jest: A Novel*
Queen Bee. Frank, Dorothea Benton
QUEEN GUINEVERE (LEGENDARY CHARACTER)
Cornwell, Bernard. *The Winter King: A Novel of Arthur*
Queen of America: A Novel. Urrea, Luis Alberto
*The **Queen** of Blood*. Durst, Sarah Beth
*The **Queen** of the Cicadas*. Castro, V.
Queen of the Conquered. Callender, Kacen
★*The **Queen** of the Damned*. Rice, Anne
*The **Queen** of the Night*. Chee, Alexander
*The **Queen's** Man: A Medieval Mystery*. Penman, Sharon Kay
*The **Queen's** Men*. Clements, Oliver
*The **Queen's** Secret: A Novel of England's World War II Queen*. Harper, Karen
★*Queenie*. Carty-Williams, Candice
Queenie Malone's Paradise Hotel. Hogan, Ruth
Queenmaker: a Novel of King David's Queen. Edghill, India
Queenpin: a Novel. Abbott, Megan E.
*The **Queens** of Innis Lear*. Gratton, Tessa
Queens of Innis Lear [Series]. Gratton, Tessa
Queens of Renthia [Series]. Durst, Sarah Beth
QUEENS, NEW YORK CITY
Andreades, Daphne Palasi. *Brown Girls*
Ferrell, Carolyn. *Dear Miss Metropolitan*
Flint, Emma. ★*Little Deaths: A Novel*
Gray, Erick S. *Love & a Gangsta: A Novel*
Sears, Michael. *Tower of Babel*
QUEENSLAND
Harper, Jane. *The Lost Man*
Howarth, Paul. *Dust off the Bones*
Malouf, David. *Remembering Babylon*
QUEST, MARTHA (FICTITIOUS CHARACTER)
Lessing, Doris May. *A Proper Marriage*
*A **Question** of Belief: A Commissario Guido Brunetti Mystery*. Leon, Donna
*A **Question** of Betrayal*. Perry, Anne
*A **Question** of Blood: An Inspector Rebus Novel*. Rankin, Ian

QUESTIONING

Dekker, Ted. *The Girl Behind the Red Rope*

QUESTIONS AND ANSWERS

Rice, Anne. *Christ the Lord: Out of Egypt: A Novel*

QUESTS

Alexis, Andre. *The Hidden Keys*

Bear, Elizabeth. *The Red-Stained Wings*

Bear, Elizabeth. *The Stone in the Skull*

Benioff, David. *City of Thieves: A Novel*

Bolano, Roberto. ★*The Savage Detectives*

Carey, Jacqueline. *Starless*

Cline, Ernest. *Ready Player One: A Novel*

Dalton, Trent. *All Our Shimmering Skies*

Davies, Carys. *West*

Durst, Sarah Beth. *The Queen of Blood*

Foer, Jonathan Safran. *Extremely Loud and Incredibly Close*

Foster, Alan Dean. *Relic*

French, Jonathan. ★*The Grey Bastards*

Gabaldon, Diana. ★*Drums of Autumn*

Gaiman, Neil. ★*Stardust*

Ishiguro, Kazuo. *The Buried Giant: A Novel*

James, Marlon. ★*Black Leopard, Red Wolf*

Johnson, Kij. ★*The Dream-Quest of Vellitt Boe*

Joyce, Rachel. *Miss Benson's Beetle*

Lai, Larissa. *The Tiger Flu*

Le Guin, Ursula K. *The Beginning Place*

Lee, Chang-Rae. ★*On Such a Full Sea*

Liu, Ken. ★*The Veiled Throne*

Locke, Thomas. *Emissary*

Macallister, Greer. ★*The Arctic Fury*

Mason, Daniel. *The Piano Tuner*

Moreno-Garcia, Silvia. ★*Gods of Jade and Shadow: A Novel*

Natsukawa, Sosuke. *The Cat Who Saved Books*

Novik, Naomi. ★*Uprooted*

Ogden, Aimee. *Sun-Daughters, Sea-Daughters*

Olmstead, Robert. ★*Coal Black Horse*

Poore, Michael. *Reincarnation Blues*

Preston, Douglas J. *Thunderhead*

Redfield, James. *The Celestine Prophecy: An Adventure*

Rothfuss, Patrick. ★*The Name of the Wind*

Rothfuss, Patrick. ★*The Wise Man's Fear*

Roy, Anuradha. *All the Lives We Never Lived: A Novel*

Rushdie, Salman. ★*Quichotte: A Novel*

Russell, Karen. ★*Swamplandia!*

Saberhagen, Fred. *Coinspinner's Story*

Saberhagen, Fred. *Farslayer's Story*

Saberhagen, Fred. *Mindsword's Story*

Saberhagen, Fred. *Shieldbreaker's Story*

Saberhagen, Fred. *Stonecutter's Story*

Saberhagen, Fred. *Wayfinder's Story*

Saberhagen, Fred. *Woundhealer's Story*

Smith, Mark Haskell. *Baked*

Tolkien, J. R. R. *The Fellowship of the Ring: Being the First Part of the Lord of the Rings*

Tolkien, J. R. R. ★*The Hobbit, Or, There and Back Again*

Tolkien, J. R. R. ★*The Lord of the Rings*

Tolkien, J. R. R. *The Return of the King: Being the Third Part of the Lord of the Rings*

Tolkien, J. R. R. *The Two Towers: Being the Second Part of the Lord of the Rings*

White, Elle Katharine. *Dragonshadow*

★*Quichotte: a Novel*. Rushdie, Salman

Quick, Amanda

'til Death Do Us Part

Close Up

Garden of Lies

The Girl Who Knew Too Much

★*The Lady Has a Past*

The Other Lady Vanishes

Otherwise Engaged

Quicksand. Persson Giolito, Malin

★*The Quiet American*. Greene, Graham

The Quiet Boy. Winters, Ben H.

Quiet Dell: A Novel. Phillips, Jayne Anne

★*A Quiet Life*. Oe, Kenzaburo

Quiet Neighbors: A Novel. McPherson, Catriona

QUILLER (FICTITIOUS CHARACTER)

Hall, Adam. *The Quiller Memorandum*

Quiller adventures [Series]. Hall, Adam

The Quiller Memorandum. Hall, Adam

QUILTING

O'Donohue, Clare. *The Lover's Knot: A Someday Quilts Mystery*

QUINCEANERA

Pineiro, Caridad. *South Beach Love: A Feel-Good Romance from Hallmark Publishing*

The Quincunx. Palliser, Charles

Quincunx cycle [Series]. Alexis, Andre

Quincy, D. M.

Murder at the Opera

Murder in Mayfair: An Atlas Catesby Mystery

Quincy, Diana

Her Night with the Duke

The Viscount Made Me Do It

Quindlen, Anna

Miller's Valley

Quinn Colson novels [Series]. Atkins, Ace

Quinn, Julia

★*An Offer from a Gentleman*

Quinn, Kate

★*The Huntress*

Quinn, Spencer

Dog on It: A Chet and Bernie Mystery

★*It's a Wonderful Woof*

Quinonez, Ernesto

Bodega Dreams

The Quintland Sisters. Wood, Shelley

QUINTUPLETS

Wood, Shelley. *The Quintland Sisters*

Quirk, Matthew

Cold Barrel Zero

Dead Man Switch

Quirke mysteries [Series]. Black, Benjamin

★*Quo Vadis: A Story of Faith in the Last Days of the Roman Empire*. Sienkiewicz, Henryk

Quotah, Eman

★*Bride of the Sea: A Novel*

R

Rabb, Jonathan
  Among the Living
Rabbi David Small mysteries [Series]. Kemelman, Harry
RABBIS
  Danan, Rosie. *The Intimacy Experiment*
  Goldberg, Tod. *Gangsterland: A Novel*
  Kemelman, Harry. *Monday the Rabbi Took Off*
  Rossner, Rena. *The Light of the Midnight Stars*
Rabbit Angstrom novels [Series]. Updike, John
★*Rabbit Is Rich: A Novel*. Updike, John
Rabbit tales [Series]. Adams, Richard
★*Rabbit, Run*. Updike, John
Rabbits. Miles, Terry
RABBITS
  Adams, Richard. *Watership Down*
  Palmer, Dexter Clarence. ★*Mary Toft; Or, the Rabbit Queen: A Novel*
Rabbits for Food. Kirshenbaum, Binnie
Rabe, Peter
  ★*Anatomy of a Killer ;: A Shroud for Jesso*
RABIES
  Tremblay, Paul. *Survivor Song*
RABIES IN ANIMALS
  King, Stephen. *Cujo*
Racculia, Kate
  ★*Bellweather Rhapsody*
  ★*Tuesday Mooney Talks to Ghosts: A Novel*
RACE (SOCIAL SCIENCES)
  Callender, Kacen. *King of the Rising*
  Edugyan, Esi. *Half-Blood Blues*
  Gordimer, Nadine. *Life Times: Stories, 1952-2007*
  Moniz, Dantiel W. *Milk Blood Heat*
  Whitehead, Colson. ★*The Underground Railroad: A Novel*
RACE HORSES
  Francis, Felix. *Crisis*
  Gordon, Jaimy. ★*Lord of Misrule: A Novel*
  Smiley, Jane. *Horse Heaven*
  Smiley, Jane. ★*Perestroika in Paris: A Novel*
RACE RELATIONS
  Abdul-Jabbar, Kareem. *Mycroft and Sherlock*
  Abdul-Jabbar, Kareem. ★*Mycroft Holmes*
  Adjei-Brenyah, Nana Kwame. *Friday Black: Stories*
  Agee, Jonis. *The Bones of Paradise*
  Alam, Rumaan. *That Kind of Mother: A Novel*
  Allende, Isabel. *The Japanese Lover*
  Atkins, Ace. *The Forsaken*
  Baldwin, James. ★*Another Country*
  Baldwin, James. ★*Going to Meet the Man*
  Baldwin, James. ★*If Beale Street Could Talk*
  Baldwin, James. *Just Above My Head*
  Baldwin, James. *Tell Me How Long the Train's Been Gone: A Novel*
  Bambara, Toni Cade. *Gorilla, My Love*
  Banks, Russell. *Cloudsplitter: A Novel*
  Beatty, Paul. ★*The Sellout: A Novel*
  Beatty, Paul. *Slumberland: A Novel*
  Benz, Chanelle. ★*The Gone Dead*
  Boyle, T. Coraghessan. ★*The Tortilla Curtain*

Carey, Peter. *A Long Way from Home*
Carty-Williams, Candice. ★*Queenie*
Clarke, Maxine Beneba. ★*Foreign Soil*
Coetzee, J. M. *Age of Iron*
Coetzee, J. M. *Disgrace*
Cole, Teju. ★*Open City: A Novel*
Collins, Kathleen. ★*Whatever Happened to Interracial Love?: Stories*
Corthron, Kia. *Moon and the Mars*
D'Souza, Tony. *Whiteman*
Depestre, Rene. *Hadriana in All My Dreams*
Dexter, Pete. *Paris Trout*
Ellison, Ralph. ★*Invisible Man*
Ellison, Ralph. ★*Juneteenth*
Ellison, Ralph. *Three Days Before the Shooting . . .*
Eskens, Allen. *Nothing More Dangerous: A Novel*
Evans, Danielle. ★*The Office of Historical Corrections: A Novella and Stories*
Everett, Percival L. *God's Country*
Everett, Percival L. *I Am Not Sidney Poitier*
Faulkner, William. ★*Go Down, Moses*
Faulkner, William. *Intruder in the Dust*
Gaines, Ernest J. ★*The Autobiography of Miss Jane Pittman*
Gaines, Ernest J. ★*A Gathering of Old Men*
Gala, Marcial. ★*The Black Cathedral*
Gordimer, Nadine. ★*July's People*
Gordimer, Nadine. *No Time Like the Present: A Novel*
Grau, Shirley Ann. *The Keepers of the House*
Grisham, John. *A Time to Kill*
Gyasi, Yaa. ★*Homegoing: A Novel*
Haldane, Sean. *The Devil's Making*
Hughes, Langston. ★*Short Stories*
Hunt, Laird. *The Evening Road*
Hurston, Zora Neale. *Hitting a Straight Lick with a Crooked Stick: Stories from the Harlem Renaissance*
Iles, Greg. *The Bone Tree: A Novel*
Iles, Greg. *Natchez Burning: A Novel*
Jemisin, N. K. ★*The City We Became*
Jhabvala, Ruth Prawer. ★*Heat and Dust*
Johnson, Keith Lee. ★*Little Black Girl Lost*
Krueger, William Kent. ★*Lightning Strike*
Lansdale, Joe R. ★*Paradise Sky*
Larsen, Nella. *Passing*
Lee, Harper. ★*Go Set a Watchman*
Lee, Harper. ★*To Kill a Mockingbird*
Lehane, Dennis. ★*The Given Day*
Leilani, Raven. ★*Luster*
Levy, Andrea. *The Long Song*
Levy, Andrea. *Small Island*
Lippman, Laura. ★*Lady in the Lake: A Novel*
Locke, Attica. ★*Bluebird, Bluebird*
Locke, Attica. ★*Heaven, My Home*
Luesse, Valerie Fraser. *Missing Isaac*
McBride, James. *Five-Carat Soul*
Moore, Graham. *The Holdout: A Novel*
Mosley, Walter. *Black Betty: An Easy Rawlins Mystery*
Mosley, Walter. ★*Blood Grove*
Mosley, Walter. *Fortunate Son: A Novel*

Mullen, Thomas. *Darktown: A Novel*
Mullen, Thomas. *Lightning Men: A Novel*
Oates, Joyce Carol. ★*Them*
Paton, Alan. *Ah, but Your Land Is Beautiful*
Paton, Alan. ★*Cry, the Beloved Country*
Paton, Alan. *Too Late the Phalarope*
Phillips, Caryl. *A View of the Empire at Sunset*
Rhys, Jean. ★*Wide Sargasso Sea*
Row, Jess. *Your Face in Mine: A Novel*
Sayles, John. *A Moment in the Sun*
Scott, Paul. ★*Staying On: A Novel*
Scott, Rion Amilcar. ★*The World Doesn't Require You: Stories*
Senna, Danzy. *New People*
Serpell, Namwali. ★*The Old Drift*
Sexton, Margaret Wilkerson. *The Revisioners: A Novel*
Silko, Leslie Marmon. *Almanac of the Dead*
Silko, Leslie Marmon. *Gardens in the Dunes: A Novel*
Slaughter, Karin. *Cop Town: A Novel*
Smith, Ian. *Wolf Point*
Smith, Zadie. ★*Swing Time*
Solomon, Rivers. *An Unkindness of Ghosts*
Styron, William. *The Confessions of Nat Turner*
Tademy, Lalita. *Cane River*
Thompson-Spires, Nafissa. *Heads of the Colored People: Stories*
Twain, Mark. *Pudd'nhead Wilson ;: And, Those Extraordinary Twins*
Umrigar, Thrity N. *Everybody's Son*
Warren, Robert Penn. *All the King's Men*
Whitehead, Colson. *The Intuitionist*
Whitlow, Robert. *A Time to Stand*
Wideman, John Edgar. ★*American Histories: Stories*
Williams, Beatriz. *The Golden Hour*
Willig, Lauren. *The Summer Country: A Novel*
Winch, Tara June. *The Yield*
Winthrop, Elizabeth Hartley. *The Mercy Seat: A Novel*
Race the Sands. Durst, Sarah Beth

RACE TRACKS

Gordon, Jaimy. ★*Lord of Misrule: A Novel*
Stark, Richard. *Ask the Parrot: A Parker Novel*

Rachel Getty and Esa Khattak novels [Series]. Khan, Ausma Zehanat

Rachel Marin novels [Series]. Pinter, Jason

Rachman, Tom

The Imperfectionists: A Novel
The Italian Teacher

RACISM

Adiga, Aravind. ★*The White Tiger: A Novel*
Adjei-Brenyah, Nana Kwame. *Friday Black: Stories*
Alexie, Sherman. *Blasphemy: New and Selected Stories*
Baldwin, James. ★*Another Country*
Baldwin, James. ★*Go Tell It on the Mountain*
Baldwin, James. ★*Going to Meet the Man*
Baldwin, James. *Tell Me How Long the Train's Been Gone: A Novel*
Ball, John Dudley. *In the Heat of the Night*
Banks, Russell. *Cloudsplitter: A Novel*
Banks, Russell. *Continental Drift*
Bartels, Erin. *We Hope for Better Things*
Beatty, Paul. ★*The Sellout: A Novel*
Blake, Sarah. *The Guest Book: A Novel*
Campbell, Bebe Moore. *Brothers and Sisters*

Campbell, Bebe Moore. *Your Blues Ain't Like Mine*
Cash, Wiley. *When Ghosts Come Home: A Novel*
Childress, Mark. *Crazy in Alabama*
Cho, Zen. *Sorcerer to the Crown*
Cisneros, Sandra. *Martita, I Remember You: Martita, Te Recuerdo*
Clarke, Maxine Beneba. ★*Foreign Soil*
Collins, Kathleen. *Notes from a Black Woman's Diary: Selected Works of Kathleen Collins*
Colvin, Jeffrey. ★*Africaville: A Novel*
Cush, Jean Love. *Endangered*
Dev, Sonali. ★*Pride, Prejudice, and Other Flavors: A Novel*
Dexter, Pete. *Paris Trout*
Dickey, Eric Jerome. ★*The Son of Mr. Suleman*
Ellroy, James. *Blood's a Rover*
Eskens, Allen. *Nothing More Dangerous: A Novel*
Evans, Danielle. ★*The Office of Historical Corrections: A Novella and Stories*
Fajardo-Anstine, Kali. ★*Sabrina & Corina: Stories*
Faulkner, William. *Intruder in the Dust*
Faulkner, William. ★*Light in August*
Faye, Lyndsay. ★*The Paragon Hotel*
Fowler, Therese. ★*A Good Neighborhood*
French, Albert. *Billy*
Guinn, Matthew. *The Scribe: A Novel*
Guterson, David. ★*Snow Falling on Cedars*
Herrera, Adriana. *American Love Story*
Howard, Ravi. *Driving the King: A Novel*
Howarth, Paul. *Only Killers and Thieves: A Novel*
Hurston, Zora Neale. *Hitting a Straight Lick with a Crooked Stick: Stories from the Harlem Renaissance*
Jackson-Brown, Angela. ★*When Stars Rain Down: A Novel*
Johnson, Jocelyn Nicole. ★*My Monticello: Fiction*
Johnson, Nancy. *The Kindest Lie*
Jordan, Hillary. *Mudbound: A Novel*
Kimani, Peter. *Dance of the Jakaranda*
Kunzru, Hari. *White Tears*
Lee, Harper. ★*Go Set a Watchman*
Lee, Harper. ★*To Kill a Mockingbird*
Levin, Ira. *The Boys from Brazil: A Novel*
Levy, Andrea. *Small Island*
Limon, Martin. *The Line*
Lindsey, Odie. *Some Go Home: A Novel*
Lippman, Laura. ★*Lady in the Lake: A Novel*
Malouf, David. *Remembering Babylon*
Matthews, Mimi. ★*The Siren of Sussex*
McCullers, Carson. ★*The Heart Is a Lonely Hunter*
Mendez, Paul. *Rainbow Milk*
Michener, James A. *Chesapeake*
Monroe, Mary. ★*Mrs. Wiggins*
Moore, Lorrie. *A Gate at the Stairs: A Novel*
Morrison, Toni. *Home*
Morrison, Toni. *A Mercy: A Novel*
Mullen, Thomas. *Darktown: A Novel*
Mullen, Thomas. *Lightning Men: A Novel*
Muller, Marcia. *Ice and Stone*
Nguyen, Kevin. ★*New Waves*
Oates, Joyce Carol. *Because It Is Bitter, and Because It Is My Heart*
Oates, Joyce Carol. ★*My Life as a Rat*

Onyebuchi, Tochi. ★*Riot Baby*
Pandya, Sameer. *Members Only*
Parks, Gordon. ★*The Learning Tree*
Paton, Alan. *Too Late the Phalarope*
Phillips, Caryl. *Foreigners*
Reid, Kiley. ★*Such a Fun Age*
Rendell, Ruth. *Simisola*
Roy, Lucinda. *The Freedom Race*
Ruff, Matt. *Lovecraft Country: A Novel*
Sexton, Margaret Wilkerson. *A Kind of Freedom*
Shames, Terry. ★*An Unsettling Crime for Samuel Craddock*
Shocklee, Michelle. *Under the Tulip Tree*
Solomon, Asali. *Disgruntled: A Novel*
Solomon, Rivers. *An Unkindness of Ghosts*
Updike, John. *Brazil: A Novel*
Vachss, Andrew H. *Two Trains Running*
Vo, Nghi. ★*The Chosen and the Beautiful*
Welty, Eudora. *Stories, Essays & Memoir*
Whitehead, Colson. ★*The Nickel Boys: A Novel*
Whitehead, Colson. ★*The Underground Railroad: A Novel*
Winthrop, Elizabeth Hartley. *The Mercy Seat: A Novel*
Woods, Rita. ★*Remembrance*
Wright, Richard. *The Man Who Lived Underground*
Wright, Richard. ★*Native Son*

RACISM — HISTORY
Doctorow, E. L. ★*Ragtime*
RACISM IN EMPLOYMENT
Harris, Zakiya Dalila. *The Other Black Girl: A Novel*
RACISM IN TEENAGERS
Edwards, Rachel. *Darling*
RACISM IN THE JUDICIAL SYSTEM
Howard, Ravi. *Driving the King: A Novel*
RACISM IN THE MILITARY
Limon, Martin. *The Line*
RADAR — HISTORY
Follett, Ken. *Hornet Flight*
Radcliffe, Ann Ward
★*The Mysteries of Udolpho*
Rademacher, Cay
Deadly Camargue: A Provence Mystery
Rader-Day, Lori
The Black Hour
The Day I Died
Little Pretty Things
★*The Lucky One*
Radiance. Valente, Catherynne M.
Radiant emperor [Series]. Parker-Chan, Shelley
RADIATION VICTIMS
Smith, Martin Cruz. *Wolves Eat Dogs: A Novel*
RADICALISM
Bisson, Terry. *Any Day Now*
Khadivi, Laleh. ★*A Good Country: A Novel*
Radicalized. Doctorow, Cory
RADIO
Blake, Sarah. *The Postmistress*
RADIO NEWSCASTERS AND COMMENTATORS
Hay, Elizabeth. *Late Nights on Air*

RADIO PERSONALITIES
Billingsley, ReShonda Tate. *A Little Bit of Karma: A Novel*
Solomon, Rachel Lynn. ★*The Ex Talk*
Wendig, Chuck. ★*Wanderers: A Novel*
RADIO PLAYWRITING
Vargas Llosa, Mario. *Aunt Julia and the Scriptwriter*
RADIO PRODUCERS AND DIRECTORS
Solomon, Rachel Lynn. ★*The Ex Talk*
RADIO PROGRAMS
Atkinson, Kate. ★*Transcription*
Billingsley, ReShonda Tate. *A Little Bit of Karma: A Novel*
Solomon, Rachel Lynn. ★*The Ex Talk*
RADIO STATIONS
Hay, Elizabeth. *Late Nights on Air*
Solomon, Rachel Lynn. ★*The Ex Talk*
RADIO TALK SHOW HOSTS AND GUESTS
Haddam, Jane. *Hardscrabble Road*
Shields, Carol. *The Republic of Love*
Rafe: a Buff Male Nanny. Weatherspoon, Rebekah
Raft of Stars. Graff, Andrew J.
RAFTS
Graff, Andrew J. *Raft of Stars*
Ragan, Theresa
Buried Deep
Deadly Recall
Deranged
Her Last Day
★*The Rage of Dragons*. Winter, Evan
★*Ragnarok: the End of the Gods*. Byatt, A. S.
★*Ragtime*. Doctorow, E. L.
Raheem, Zara
The Marriage Clock: A Novel
Rai, Alisha
★*First Comes Like*
★*Girl Gone Viral*
★*The Right Swipe*
Raiders of the Nile: A Novel of the Ancient World. Saylor, Steven
RAIDS (MILITARY SCIENCE)
Crichton, Michael. *Pirate Latitudes*
RAILROAD ACCIDENTS
Cussler, Clive. *The Wrecker*
Pyper, Andrew. *The Residence: A Novel*
RAILROAD ACCIDENTS — PSYCHOLOGICAL ASPECTS
Simmons, Dan. *Drood: A Novel*
RAILROAD ENGINEERS
Goodman, Jo. *A Touch of Forever*
RAILROAD TRAVEL
Boschwitz, Ulrich Alexander. *The Passenger: A Novel*
Christie, Agatha. ★*Murder on the Orient Express*
Kaminsky, Stuart M. *Murder on the Trans-Siberian Express*
Oyeyemi, Helen. *Peaces*
Simmons, Dan. *Drood: A Novel*
RAILROADS
Cussler, Clive. *The Wrecker*
Evison, Jonathan. ★*Small World*
Groom, Winston. *El Paso: A Novel*
Kimani, Peter. *Dance of the Jakaranda*

RAILROADS — HISTORY
    Cather, Willa. *A Lost Lady*
Raimondo, Lynne
    Dante's Dilemma: A Mark Angelotti Novel
    Dante's Poison: A Mark Angelotti Novel
    Dante's Wood: A Mark Angelotti Novel
RAIN AND RAINFALL
    Moss, Sarah. *Summerwater*
RAIN MAKERS
    Bellow, Saul. ★*Henderson the Rain King: A Novel*
Rain: and Other Stories. Couto, Mia
Rainbirds. Goenawan, Clarissa
Rainbow Milk. Mendez, Paul
Raintree County. Lockridge, Ross Franklin
Raise High the Roof Beam, Carpenters,: And Seymour—An Introduction.. Salinger, J. D.
★*Raise the Titanic!* Cussler, Clive
RAISIN, AGATHA (FICTITIOUS CHARACTER)
    Beaton, M. C. *Agatha Raisin and the Witch of Wyckhadden*
Rajaniemi, Hannu
    The Fractal Prince
    The Quantum Thief
The **Rajes** [Series]. Dev, Sonali
RAMA (IMAGINARY SPACE VEHICLE)
    Clarke, Arthur C. *Rendezvous with Rama*
Rama series [Series]. Clarke, Arthur C.
Ramadan Ramsey: A Novel. Edwards, Louis
Ramadan, Ahmad Danny
    The Clothesline Swing
Ramos, Joanne
    The Farm: A Novel
Ramqvist, Karolina
    The White City
Ramsay, Frederick
    Countdown
Ramsay, Hope
    Summer on Moonlight Bay
Ramzipoor, E. R.
    The Ventriloquists
RANCH LIFE
    Proulx, Annie. *Bad Dirt: Wyoming Stories 2*
    Proulx, Annie. *Fine Just the Way It Is: Wyoming Stories 3*
    Steinbeck, John. ★*Of Mice and Men*
RANCHERS
    Box, C. J. *Blue Heaven*
    Evans, Nicholas. ★*The Horse Whisperer: A Novel*
    Haruf, Kent. *Eventide*
    Haruf, Kent. ★*Plainsong*
    Johnson, Julia Claiborne. *Better Luck Next Time: A Novel*
    Kelton, Elmer. *Hard Ride*
    Meyer, Philipp. ★*The Son: A Novel*
    Parker, Robert B. *Appaloosa*
    Roberts, Nora. *Come Sundown*
    Rowland, Russell. *Cold Country: A Novel*
    Schaefer, Jack. ★*Shane*
    Smith, B. J. *Crow's Landing: A Novel*
    Urrea, Luis Alberto. *The Hummingbird's Daughter: A Novel*
    Weatherspoon, Rebekah. *A Thorn in the Saddle*

RANCHES
    Box, C. J. *The Disappeared*
    Box, C. J. ★*Wolf Pack*
    Davila, April. *142 Ostriches*
    Fields, Hilary. *Last Chance Llama Ranch*
    Goodman, Jo. *In Want of a Wife*
    Harper, Jane. *The Lost Man*
    Howarth, Paul. *Dust off the Bones*
    Johnson, Julia Claiborne. *Better Luck Next Time: A Novel*
    L'Amour, Louis. *The Californios*
    March, Emily. *Jackson*
    Roberts, Nora. *Come Sundown*
    Schaefer, Jack. ★*Shane*
    Vlautin, Willy. *Don't Skip Out on Me*
    Weatherspoon, Rebekah. *If the Boot Fits*
Rand, Ayn
    ★*The Fountainhead*
Randall, Alice
    ★*Black Bottom Saints*
RANDALL, CLAIRE (FICTITIOUS CHARACTER)
    Gabaldon, Diana. ★*Voyager*
Randisi, Robert J.
    Hey There (You with the Gun in Your Hand): A Rat Pack Mystery
Random Harvest. Hilton, James
Range of Ghosts. Bear, Elizabeth
RANGE WARS
    Keesey, Anna. *Little Century: A Novel*
The *Ranger*. Atkins, Ace
Rankin, Ian
    ★*Black and Blue: An Inspector Rebus Novel*
    The Black Book
    Blood Hunt: A Novel
    The Complaints
    Dead Souls: An Inspector Rebus Novel
    Exit Music
    The Falls: An Inspector Rebus Novel
    The Hanging Garden: An Inspector Rebus Novel
    The Impossible Dead
    The Naming of the Dead: An Inspector Rebus Novel
    A Question of Blood: An Inspector Rebus Novel
    ★*Rather Be the Devil*
    Resurrection Men: An Inspector Rebus Novel
    Set in Darkness: An Inspector Rebus Novel
    ★*A Song for the Dark Times*
Ransom. Malouf, David
RANSOM
    Akunin, B. *The Coronation: The Further Adventures of Erast Fandorin*
    Blake, James Carlos. *The House of Wolfe*
    Deaver, Jeffery. *The October List*
    Gay, Roxane. ★*An Untamed State*
    McBain, Ed. *Alice in Jeopardy*
    Mosley, Walter. *Charcoal Joe: An Easy Rawlins Mystery*
    Parker, Robert B. *Painted Ladies*
    Perry, Anne. *Dark Tide Rising: A William Monk Novel*
Rao, Shobha
    ★*Girls Burn Brighter*

RAPE

Box, C. J. ★*The Bitterroots: A Novel*

Campbell, Bonnie Jo. *Once Upon a River*

Faulkner, William. ★*Sanctuary*

Gay, Roxane. ★*An Untamed State*

Grisham, John. *The Last Juror*

Lasdun, James. *Afternoon of a Faun: A Novel*

Layden, Emily. *All Girls*

Levin, Ira. ★*Rosemary's Baby: A Novel*

Smith, Julie. *Louisiana Hotshot*

RAPE INVESTIGATION

Box, C. J. ★*The Bitterroots: A Novel*

Connelly, Michael. *The Wrong Side of Goodbye*

French, Nicci. *Thursday's Children*

Scoppettone, Sandra. *Everything You Have Is Mine*

RAPE SUSPECTS

Layden, Emily. *All Girls*

RAPE VICTIMS

Brink, Andre P. *Philida: A Novel*

Byrne, Kerrigan. *How to Love a Duke in Ten Days*

Corman, Avery. *Prized Possessions*

Dahl, Julia. *The Missing Hours*

Faulkner, William. *Requiem for a Nun*

Gardner, Lisa. *Find Her*

Gerritsen, Tess. *The Surgeon*

Hardy, Thomas. ★*Tess of the D'urbervilles: A Pure Woman Faithfully Presented*

Lawler, Liz. *Don't Wake Up*

McGhee, Alison. *The Opposite of Fate*

O'Brien, Edna. ★*Girl*

Parks, Brad. *Closer Than You Know*

Sebold, Alice. ★*The Lovely Bones*

Sharp, Zoe. *Fox Hunter*

Shreve, Anita. *Eden Close: A Novel*

Toews, Miriam. ★*Women Talking: A Novel*

Welsh, Kaite. *The Wages of Sin*

RAPISTS

Grafton, Sue. *Y Is for Yesterday*

Pronzini, Bill. *The Violated*

Rendell, Ruth. *Live Flesh*

Sharp, Zoe. *Fox Hunter*

Rapture of the Nerds. Doctorow, Cory

RARE AND ENDANGERED ANIMALS

Box, C. J. ★*Open Season*

McConaghy, Charlotte. *Once There Were Wolves: A Novel*

Woods, Stuart. *Skin Game*

RARE AND ENDANGERED BIRDS

Joukhadar, Zeyn. ★*The Thirty Names of Night: A Novel*

RARE AND ENDANGERED PLANTS

Baker, Kage. *In the Garden of Iden: A Novel of the Company*

RARE BOOKS

Davis, Fiona. *The Lions of Fifth Avenue: A Novel*

DeRoux, Margaux. *The Lost Diary of Venice*

Goodman, Allegra. *The Cookbook Collector: A Novel*

Gruber, Michael. *The Book of Air and Shadows*

Hand, Elizabeth. *The Book of Lamps and Banners: A Novel*

Perez-Reverte, Arturo. *The Club Dumas*

Reay, Katherine. *The Bronte Plot*

Rollins, James. *Crucible*

Ruiz Zafon, Carlos. *The Labyrinth of the Spirits*

Ruiz Zafon, Carlos. *The Prisoner of Heaven*

Ruiz Zafon, Carlos. ★*The Shadow of the Wind*

Runcie, James. *Sidney Chambers and the Persistence of Love*

RARE BOOKS — COLLECTORS AND COLLECTING

Grossman, David. *Be My Knife*

Rash, Ron

Above the Waterfall

Burning Bright: Stories

★*The Cove*

★*In the Valley: Stories and a Novella Based on Serena*

Nothing Gold Can Stay: Stories

★*Serena: A Novel*

Something Rich and Strange: Selected Stories

RASTAFARI MOVEMENT

Miller, Kei. ★*Augustown*

RASTAFARIANS

Michener, James A. *Caribbean*

Rat pack mysteries [Series]. Randisi, Robert J.

★*Rather* Be the Devil. Rankin, Ian

RATIONALISM

Voltaire. *Candide and Other Stories*

Ratking. Dibdin, Michael

Ratner, Vaddey

Music of the Ghosts

RATS

Hosking, Jay. *Three Years with the Rat: A Novel*

Savage, Sam. *Firmin: Adventures of a Metropolitan Lowlife*

RATTLESNAKES

Crews, Harry. *A Feast of Snakes: A Novel*

Raunchy. Styles, Toy

Raunchy 2: Mad's Love. Styles, Toy

Ravelstein. Bellow, Saul

Raven Black. Cleeves, Ann

Raven Stratagem. Lee, Yoon Ha

★*The Raven Tower*. Leckie, Ann

The **Ravenels** [Series]. Kleypas, Lisa

Ravenswood [Series]. Hibbert, Talia

Rawles, Nancy

My Jim: A Novel

Rawlings, David

The Baggage Handler: A Novel

RAWLINS, EASY (FICTITIOUS CHARACTER)

Mosley, Walter. *Black Betty: An Easy Rawlins Mystery*

Mosley, Walter. *Devil in a Blue Dress*

Mosley, Walter. *Little Scarlet: An Easy Rawlins Mystery*

Ray Cruz novels [Series]. Hunter, Stephen

Ray, Eleanor

The Missing Treasures of Amy Ashton

Raybourn, Deanna

A Curious Beginning: A Veronica Speedwell Mystery

A Dangerous Collaboration

★*A Murderous Relation*

A Perilous Undertaking: A Veronica Speedwell Mystery

A Treacherous Curse: A Veronica Speedwell Mystery

★*Raylan*. Leonard, Elmore

Raylan Givens thrillers [Series]. Leonard, Elmore

Raymond Donne novels [Series]. O'Mara, Tim

★*Razorblade Tears*. Cosby, S. A.

REACHER, JACK (FICTITIOUS CHARACTER)

Child, Lee. *No Middle Name: The Complete Collected Jack Reacher Short Stories*

Read and Buried. Gates, Eva

The Reader: a Novel. Schlink, Bernhard

The Readers of Broken Wheel Recommend. Bivald, Katarina

Reading in the Dark. Deane, Seamus

★*The Reading List*. Adams, Sara Nisha

Ready player novels [Series]. Cline, Ernest

Ready Player One: A Novel. Cline, Ernest

Ready Set Rogue. Collins, Manda

REAGAN, RONALD

Mallon, Thomas. *Finale: A Novel*

REAL ESTATE AGENTS

Ford, Richard. ★*Independence Day*

Hiaasen, Carl. *Nature Girl*

Lewis, Sinclair. *Babbitt*

Stevens, Chevy. *Still Missing*

REAL ESTATE DEVELOPERS

Adiga, Aravind. *Last Man in Tower: A Novel*

Pineiro, Caridad. *One Summer Night*

Qiu, Xiaolong. *When Red Is Black*

Wood, James. *Upstate*

REAL ESTATE DEVELOPMENT

Hiaasen, Carl. *Bad Monkey*

Maron, Margaret. *Up Jumps the Devil*

Paretsky, Sara. ★*Dead Land*

Pearson, Ridley. *The Risk Agent*

Quartey, Kwei. *Murder at Cape Three Points*

Sandford, John. *Shock Wave*

★*Real Life*. Taylor, Brandon

REALISTIC FICTION

Booth, Coe. ★*Bronxwood*

Draper, Sharon M. ★*Forged by Fire*

REALITY

Faulks, Sebastian. *A Week in December*

Montimore, Margarita. *Oona Out of Order*

Okri, Ben. *Prayer for the Living*

Vonnegut, Kurt. ★*Breakfast of Champions: Or, Goodbye Blue Monday!*

REALITY TELEVISION PROGRAMS

Cochrun, Alison. *The Charm Offensive*

Dell'Antonia, K. J. *The Chicken Sisters*

Dev, Sonali. ★*Recipe for Persuasion*

Hall, Alexis. *Rosaline Palmer Takes the Cake*

Parker, Lucy. *Battle Royal*

Westlake, Donald E. *Get Real*

★*Realm of Ash*. Suri, Tasha

Reamde. Stephenson, Neal

Reaper Man. Pratchett, Terry

Reasons to Be Cheerful. Stibbe, Nina

Reay, Katherine

The Bronte Plot

★*Rebecca*. Du Maurier, Daphne

Rebekah Roberts novels [Series]. Dahl, Julia

Rebel. Jenkins, Beverly

The Rebel and the Rake. Sullivan, Emily

★*Rebel Powers*. Bausch, Richard

Rebellion. Patterson, Molly

REBELS

Acevedo, Chantel. *The Distant Marvels*

Baker, Kage. *The House of the Stag*

Banks, Russell. *Cloudsplitter: A Novel*

Beckett, L. X. *Gamechanger*

Elliott, Kate. *Servant Mage*

Kay, Guy Gavriel. ★*A Brightness Long Ago*

Liu, Ken. ★*The Grace of Kings*

Penelope, L. *Cry of Metal & Bone: Earthsinger Chronicles, Book 3*

Penelope, L. *Whispers of Shadow & Flame*

Scott, Walter. ★*Rob Roy*

Vonnegut, Kurt. ★*Player Piano*

REBELS — HISTORY

Doyle, Roddy. *A Star Called Henry*

The Rebels of Ireland: The Dublin Saga. Rutherfurd, Edward

REBUS, INSPECTOR (FICTITIOUS CHARACTER)

Rankin, Ian. *Exit Music*

Rankin, Ian. *The Naming of the Dead: An Inspector Rebus Novel*

Rankin, Ian. *A Question of Blood: An Inspector Rebus Novel*

Rankin, Ian. *Resurrection Men: An Inspector Rebus Novel*

Rankin, Ian. *Set in Darkness: An Inspector Rebus Novel*

RECEPTIONISTS

Austin, Emily. *Everyone in This Room Will Someday Be Dead*

Receptor. Glynn, Alan

RECESSION (ECONOMICS)

Eggers, Dave. *A Hologram for the King: A Novel*

Markley, Stephen. *Ohio*

★*Recipe for Persuasion*. Dev, Sonali

RECIPES

Haratischvili, Nino. *The Eighth Life: (For Brilka)*

Harbison, Beth. *The Cookbook Club*

Reckless in Texas. Dell, Kari Lynn

A Reckless Match. Bateman, Kate

A Reckoning: a Novel. Sarton, May

RECLUSES

Allen, Sarah Addison. *The Girl Who Chased the Moon: A Novel*

Beagle, Peter S. *A Fine and Private Place*

Brunkhorst, Alex. *The Gilded Life of Matilda Duplaine*

Clarke, Susanna. ★*Jonathan Strange & Mr. Norrell*

Doctorow, E. L. *Homer and Langley: A Novel*

Eliot, George. ★*Silas Marner: The Weaver of Raveloe*

Fleming, Ian. *You Only Live Twice*

Godwin, Gail. *Grief Cottage: A Novel*

Guterson, David. *The Other*

King, Stephen. *Finders Keepers*

Murdoch, Iris. *The Sea, the Sea*

Phillips, Susan Elizabeth. ★*Dance Away with Me*

Ward, Catriona. *The Last House on Needless Street*

Ware, Ruth. *In a Dark, Dark Wood*

★*The Recognitions*. Gaddis, William

RECONCILIATION

Cole, Teju. *Every Day Is for the Thief*

Genova, Lisa. *Every Note Played*

Higgins, Kristan. ★*Life and Other Inconveniences*

Higgins, Kristan. *Now That You Mention It*

Murphy, Devin. *Tiny Americans*

RECONCILIATION IN MEN
Franklin, Tom. *Crooked Letter, Crooked Letter: A Novel*

RECONSTRUCTION (UNITED STATES HISTORY)
Greenidge, Kaitlyn. ★*Libertie: A Novel*
Mitchell, Margaret. ★*Gone with the Wind*

RECORD INDUSTRY AND TRADE
Leonard, Elmore. ★*Be Cool: Everyone Is Looking for the Next Big Hit*

Record of a Spaceborn Few. Chambers, Becky

RECOVERED MEMORY
Picoult, Jodi. *Vanishing Acts: A Novel*
Stross, Charles. *Glasshouse*
Unger, Lisa. ★*The Stranger Inside*

RECOVERING ADDICTS
Burroughs, William S. ★*Naked Lunch: The Restored Text*

RECOVERING ALCOHOLICS
Block, Lawrence. *A Ticket to the Boneyard: A Matthew Scudder Novel*
Gilman, Susan Jane. *Donna Has Left the Building*
Hatcher, Robin Lee. *Cross My Heart*
Parker, Robert B. *Trouble in Paradise*

RECOVERING DRUG ABUSERS
George, Elizabeth. *Believing the Lie*

RECOVERING WOMEN DRUG ABUSERS
Cleage, Pearl. *Some Things I Never Thought I'd Do*

RECREATIONAL VEHICLES
Florio, Gwen. *Best Laid Plans*

Recursion. Crouch, Blake

RECYCLING (WASTE, ETC.)
Chen, Qiufan. *Waste Tide*

★*Red at the Bone*. Woodson, Jacqueline
★*The Red Badge of Courage: An Episode of the American Civil War*. Crane, Stephen
Red card [Series]. Van Dyken, Rachel
The Red Convertible: Selected and New Stories, 1978-2008. Erdrich, Louise
Red Dragon. Harris, Thomas
Red Dress in Black and White. Ackerman, Elliot
Red Hands. Golden, Christopher
A Red Herring Without Mustard. Bradley, C. Alan
Red Herring: A Joe Gunther Novel. Mayor, Archer
★*The Red Horse: A Billy Boyle World War II Mystery*. Benn, James R.
Red Island House. Lee, Andrea
Red Letter Days. Stratford, Sarah-Jane
★*The Red Lotus*. Bohjalian, Chris
Red Mandarin Dress: An Inspector Chen Novel. Qiu, Xiaolong
★*Red Mars*. Robinson, Kim Stanley
Red Pill: A Novel. Kunzru, Hari
Red princess mysteries [Series]. See, Lisa
The Red Queen: A Novel. Gregory, Philippa
Red Rising. Brown, Pierce
Red rising novels [Series]. Brown, Pierce
Red Sparrow: A Novel. Matthews, Jason
★*The Red Tent*. Diamant, Anita
The Red Threads of Fortune. Yang, JY
★*Red, White & Royal Blue: A Novel*. McQuiston, Casey
The Red-Haired Woman. Pamuk, Orhan

The Red-Stained Wings. Bear, Elizabeth
Red: the Heroic Rescue. Dekker, Ted
Redbone. Styles, Toy
Redbone novels [Series]. Styles, Toy

Reddi, Rishi
Passage West: A Novel

The Redeemer. Nesbo, Jo
The Redeemers. Atkins, Ace
★*Redeeming Love*. Rivers, Francine
Redemption. Baldacci, David

REDEMPTION
Afshar, Tessa. *Thief of Corinth*
Ashley & JaQuavis. *Murderville*
Bowman, Conor. ★*Horace Winter Says Goodbye*
Brown, Larry. *Joe: A Novel*
Danticat, Edwidge. *The Dew Breaker*
Hand, Elizabeth. ★*Generation Loss: A Novel*
Hulse, S. M. ★*Black River*
Mosley, Walter. *All I Did Was Shoot My Man: A Leonid McGill Mystery*
O'Connor, Flannery. ★*The Violent Bear It Away*
Percy, Walker. ★*The Moviegoer*
Proulx, Annie. ★*The Shipping News*
Rice, Anne. ★*Interview with the Vampire*
Rivers, Francine. ★*Redeeming Love*
Seton, Anya. *Katherine*
Sylvester, Natalia. *Everyone Knows You Go Home*
Winslow, Don. *The Border*

REDEMPTION (CHRISTIANITY)
Rivers, Francine. *Bridge to Haven*

Redemption Point. Fox, Candice
Redemption Road. Hart, John
Redemption: a Novel. Uris, Leon

Redfield, James
The Celestine Prophecy: An Adventure

★*Redhead by the Side of the Road*. Tyler, Anne

REDHEADS
Burrowes, Grace. *The Trouble with Dukes*

Redondo, Dolores
The Invisible Guardian
The North Face of the Heart

Redshirts: a Novel with Three Codas. Scalzi, John

REDWOOD INDUSTRY AND TRADE
Davidson, Ash. ★*Damnation Spring*

Reed, Ishmael
Flight to Canada
★*Mumbo Jumbo*

Rees, Matt
The Fourth Assassin

REEVES, KEANU
Adjapon, Bisi. *The Teller of Secrets: A Novel*
Jackson, K. M. *How to Marry Keanu Reeves in 90 Days*

Reflections in a Golden Eye. McCullers, Carson

REFUGEE CAMPS
Alameddine, Rabih. *The Wrong End of the Telescope*
Arudpragasam, Anuk. *The Story of a Brief Marriage*
El Akkad, Omar. *American War*
Turow, Scott. *Testimony*

★*The **Refugees**. Nguyen, Viet Thanh
REFUGEES
  Abulhawa, Susan. *The Blue Between Sky and Water*
  Ackerman, Elliot. *Dark at the Crossing*
  Adichie, Chimamanda Ngozi. ★*Americanah: A Novel*
  Adler-Olsen, Jussi. ★*Victim 2117*
  Ahmad, Jamil. *The Wandering Falcon*
  Akinmade-Akerstrom, Lola. *In Every Mirror She's Black*
  Alameddine, Rabih. *The Wrong End of the Telescope*
  Allende, Isabel. *A Long Petal of the Sea: A Novel*
  Alyan, Hala. *Salt Houses*
  Appanah-Mouriquand, Nathacha. *Tropic of Violence: A Novel*
  Aswani, Alaa. *Chicago: A Modern Arabic Novel*
  Bala, Sharon. *The Boat People: A Novel*
  Bohjalian, Chris. *Skeletons at the Feast: A Novel*
  Clarke, Maxine Beneba. ★*Foreign Soil*
  Couto, Mia. *Sleepwalking Land*
  Edwards, Louis. *Ramadan Ramsey: A Novel*
  El Akkad, Omar. *What Strange Paradise*
  Erpenbeck, Jenny. *Go, Went, Gone: A Novel*
  Fowler, Christopher. *Bryant & May: Strange Tide*
  Furst, Alan. *Dark Voyage: A Novel*
  George, Alex. *The Paris Hours: A Novel*
  Gundar-Goshen, Ayelet. *Waking Lions*
  Hamid, Mohsin. ★*Exit West: A Novel*
  Kim, Crystal Hana. *If You Leave Me*
  Lebrecht, Norman. *The Song of Names*
  Lefteri, Christy. *The Beekeeper of Aleppo: A Novel*
  Lunde, Maja. *The End of the Ocean: A Novel*
  Nguyen, Viet Thanh. ★*The Committed*
  Phillips, Caryl. *A Distant Shore*
  Rabb, Jonathan. *Among the Living*
  Ratner, Vaddey. *Music of the Ghosts*
  Smith, Ali. ★*Summer*
  So, Anthony Veasna. *Afterparties: Stories*
  Turow, Scott. *Testimony*
  Van der Vliet Oloomi, Azareen. *Call Me Zebra*
  Vinge, Vernor. *A Fire Upon the Deep*
  Yu, E. Lily. ★*On Fragile Waves*
REFUGEES' RIGHTS
  Bala, Sharon. *The Boat People: A Novel*
REFUGEES, HUNGARIAN
  London, Joan. *The Golden Age*
REFUGEES, JEWISH
  Bellow, Saul. *The Bellarosa Connection*
  Hoffman, Alice. *The Marriage of Opposites: A Novel Based on the Life of Rachel Pizzarro*
  Ozick, Cynthia. *Heir to the Glimmering World*
  Sebald, Winfried Georg. ★*Austerlitz*
REFUGEES, RUSSIAN
  Nabokov, Vladimir Vladimirovich. *Novels and Memoirs, 1941-51*
REFUGEES, SUDANESE
  Eggers, Dave. *What Is the What: The Autobiography of Valentino Achak Deng*
REFUGEES, SYRIAN
  Hosseini, Khaled. ★*Sea Prayer*
Regency impostors [Series]. Sebastian, Cat

REGENCY PERIOD (1811-1820)
  Allain, Suzanne. *Miss Lattimore's Letter*
  Allen, Susanna. *A Wolf in Duke's Clothing*
  Baker, Jo. *Longbourn*
  Balogh, Mary. *The Arrangement*
  Balogh, Mary. *The Escape*
  Balogh, Mary. *More Than a Mistress*
  Balogh, Mary. *Only Enchanting*
  Balogh, Mary. *The Secret Mistress*
  Balogh, Mary. *Simply Love*
  Balogh, Mary. ★*Someone to Care*
  Balogh, Mary. ★*Someone to Cherish*
  Balogh, Mary. *Someone to Hold*
  Balogh, Mary. ★*Someone to Love*
  Balogh, Mary. ★*Someone to Remember: A Westcott Story*
  Balogh, Mary. *Someone to Trust*
  Balogh, Mary. *Someone to Wed*
  Bateman, Kate. *A Reckless Match*
  Bateman, Kate. *This Earl of Mine*
  Bell, Lenora. *For the Duke's Eyes Only*
  Bell, Lenora. ★*How the Duke Was Won*
  Bell, Lenora. *One Fine Duke*
  Bell, Lenora. ★*What a Difference a Duke Makes*
  Bennett, Anna. *First Earl I See Tonight*
  Bennett, Bethany. *West End Earl*
  Berne, Lisa. *You May Kiss the Bride*
  Bourne, Joanna. *The Black Hawk*
  Bourne, Joanna. ★*The Spymaster's Lady*
  Bowen, Kelly. ★*Between the Devil and the Duke*
  Bowen, Kelly. *A Rogue by Night*
  Bowman, Valerie. *The Accidental Countess*
  Bowman, Valerie. *A Duke Like No Other*
  Bowman, Valerie. *No Other Duke but You*
  Bowman, Valerie. *Secrets of a Wedding Night*
  Bowman, Valerie. *The Unexpected Duchess*
  Boyle, Elizabeth. *Along Came a Duke*
  Boyle, Elizabeth. *And the Miss Ran Away with the Rake*
  Bradley, Anna. *A Season of Ruin*
  Bradley, Anna. *A Wicked Way to Win an Earl*
  Brockway, Connie. *The Golden Season*
  Brockway, Connie. *No Place for a Dame*
  Burrowes, Grace. *The Captive*
  Burrowes, Grace. *My One and Only Duke*
  Burrowes, Grace. ★*A Rogue of Her Own*
  Chase, Loretta Lynda. *Don't Tempt Me*
  Chase, Loretta Lynda. *Miss Wonderful*
  Collins, Manda. *A Good Rake Is Hard to Find*
  Collins, Manda. *One for the Rogue*
  Collins, Manda. *Ready Set Rogue*
  Crowley, John. *Lord Byron's Novel: The Evening Land*
  Dare, Tessa. *Do You Want to Start a Scandal*
  Dare, Tessa. ★*The Duchess Deal*
  Dare, Tessa. ★*The Governess Game*
  Dare, Tessa. ★*A Night to Surrender*
  Dare, Tessa. *Romancing the Duke*
  Dare, Tessa. ★*Say Yes to the Marquess*
  Dare, Tessa. ★*The Wallflower Wager*
  Dare, Tessa. *A Week to Be Wicked*

Dare, Tessa. *When a Scot Ties the Knot*
Drake, Olivia. *When a Duke Loves a Governess*
Force, Marie. *Deceived by Desire*
Galen, Shana. *Third Son's a Charm*
Garriott, Leah. *Promised*
Gracie, Anne. *Marry in Scandal*
Greeley, Molly. *The Clergyman's Wife*
Harrington, Anna. *An Extraordinary Lord*
Harrington, Anna. *An Inconvenient Duke*
Harris, C. S. *What the Devil Knows: A Sebastian St. Cyr Mystery*
Hawks, Arlem. *Georgana's Secret*
Heyer, Georgette. *Black Sheep*
Heyer, Georgette. *The Grand Sophy*
James, Eloisa. *The Ugly Duchess*
Leigh, Eva. *Forever Your Earl*
Leigh, Eva. *Scandal Takes the Stage*
Leigh, Eva. *Temptations of a Wallflower*
Lloyd, Catherine. *Death Comes to the Nursery*
Lloyd, Catherine. *Death Comes to the Rectory*
Long, Julie Anne. *Angel in a Devil's Arms*
Long, Julie Anne. ★*Lady Derring Takes a Lover*
MacLean, Sarah. *No Good Duke Goes Unpunished*
MacLean, Sarah. *The Rogue Not Taken*
Pembrooke, Kate. *Not the Kind of Earl You Marry*
Penrose, Andrea. ★*Murder at Kensington Palace*
Penrose, Andrea. *Murder on Black Swan Lane*
Polk, C. L. *The Midnight Bargain*
Putney, Mary Jo. *Loving a Lost Lord*
Putney, Mary Jo. *No Longer a Gentleman*
Putney, Mary Jo. *Not Quite a Wife*
Quincy, D. M. *Murder at the Opera*
Quincy, D. M. *Murder in Mayfair: An Atlas Catesby Mystery*
Quincy, Diana. *Her Night with the Duke*
Quincy, Diana. *The Viscount Made Me Do It*
Quinn, Julia. ★*An Offer from a Gentleman*
Ridley, Erica. *The Duke Heist*
Ridley, Erica. ★*The Perks of Loving a Wallflower*
Riley, Vanessa. ★*A Duke, the Lady, and a Baby*
Riley, Vanessa. ★*An Earl, the Girl, and a Toddler*
Romain, Theresa. *Fortune Favors the Wicked*
Schellman, Katharine. *Silence in the Library*
Sebastian, Cat. *It Takes Two to Tumble*
Sebastian, Cat. *The Lawrence Browne Affair*
Sebastian, Cat. *Unmasked by the Marquess*
Spencer, Minerva. *Scandalous*
Vayden, Kristin. *Fortune Favors the Duke*
Waite, Olivia. *The Care and Feeding of Waspish Widows*
Waite, Olivia. ★*The Lady's Guide to Celestial Mechanics*
Waters, Martha. ★*To Have and to Hoax: A Novel*
Waters, Martha. *To Love and to Loathe: A Novel*
Willig, Lauren. *The Summer Country: A Novel*

REGENCY ROMANCES
Allain, Suzanne. *Miss Lattimore's Letter*
Allen, Susanna. *A Wolf in Duke's Clothing*
Balogh, Mary. *The Arrangement*
Balogh, Mary. *The Escape*
Balogh, Mary. *More Than a Mistress*
Balogh, Mary. *Only Enchanting*

Balogh, Mary. *The Secret Mistress*
Balogh, Mary. *Simply Love*
Balogh, Mary. ★*Someone to Care*
Balogh, Mary. ★*Someone to Cherish*
Balogh, Mary. *Someone to Hold*
Balogh, Mary. ★*Someone to Love*
Balogh, Mary. ★*Someone to Remember: A Westcott Story*
Balogh, Mary. *Someone to Trust*
Balogh, Mary. *Someone to Wed*
Bateman, Kate. *A Reckless Match*
Bateman, Kate. *This Earl of Mine*
Bell, Lenora. *For the Duke's Eyes Only*
Bell, Lenora. ★*How the Duke Was Won*
Bell, Lenora. *One Fine Duke*
Bell, Lenora. ★*What a Difference a Duke Makes*
Bennett, Anna. *First Earl I See Tonight*
Bennett, Bethany. *West End Earl*
Berne, Lisa. *You May Kiss the Bride*
Bourne, Joanna. *The Black Hawk*
Bourne, Joanna. ★*The Spymaster's Lady*
Bowen, Kelly. ★*Between the Devil and the Duke*
Bowen, Kelly. *A Rogue by Night*
Bowman, Valerie. *The Accidental Countess*
Bowman, Valerie. *A Duke Like No Other*
Bowman, Valerie. *No Other Duke but You*
Bowman, Valerie. *Secrets of a Wedding Night*
Bowman, Valerie. *The Unexpected Duchess*
Boyle, Elizabeth. *Along Came a Duke*
Boyle, Elizabeth. *And the Miss Ran Away with the Rake*
Bradley, Anna. *A Season of Ruin*
Bradley, Anna. *A Wicked Way to Win an Earl*
Brockway, Connie. *The Golden Season*
Brockway, Connie. *No Place for a Dame*
Burrowes, Grace. *The Captive*
Burrowes, Grace. *My One and Only Duke*
Burrowes, Grace. ★*A Rogue of Her Own*
Burrowes, Grace. *Tremaine's True Love*
Burrowes, Grace. *The Trouble with Dukes*
Chase, Loretta Lynda. *Don't Tempt Me*
Chase, Loretta Lynda. *Miss Wonderful*
Collins, Manda. *A Good Rake Is Hard to Find*
Collins, Manda. *One for the Rogue*
Collins, Manda. *Ready Set Rogue*
Dare, Tessa. *Do You Want to Start a Scandal*
Dare, Tessa. ★*The Duchess Deal*
Dare, Tessa. ★*The Governess Game*
Dare, Tessa. ★*A Night to Surrender*
Dare, Tessa. *Romancing the Duke*
Dare, Tessa. ★*Say Yes to the Marquess*
Dare, Tessa. ★*The Wallflower Wager*
Dare, Tessa. *A Week to Be Wicked*
Dare, Tessa. *When a Scot Ties the Knot*
Drake, Olivia. *When a Duke Loves a Governess*
Force, Marie. *Deceived by Desire*
Galen, Shana. *Third Son's a Charm*
Garriott, Leah. *Promised*
Gracie, Anne. *Marry in Scandal*
Harrington, Anna. *An Extraordinary Lord*

Harrington, Anna. *An Inconvenient Duke*
Heyer, Georgette. *Black Sheep*
Heyer, Georgette. *The Grand Sophy*
James, Eloisa. *The Ugly Duchess*
Leigh, Eva. *Forever Your Earl*
Leigh, Eva. *Scandal Takes the Stage*
Leigh, Eva. *Temptations of a Wallflower*
Long, Julie Anne. *Angel in a Devil's Arms*
Long, Julie Anne. ★*Lady Derring Takes a Lover*
MacLean, Sarah. *No Good Duke Goes Unpunished*
MacLean, Sarah. *The Rogue Not Taken*
Pembrooke, Kate. *Not the Kind of Earl You Marry*
Putney, Mary Jo. *Loving a Lost Lord*
Putney, Mary Jo. *No Longer a Gentleman*
Putney, Mary Jo. *Not Quite a Wife*
Quincy, Diana. *Her Night with the Duke*
Quincy, Diana. *The Viscount Made Me Do It*
Quinn, Julia. ★*An Offer from a Gentleman*
Ridley, Erica. *The Duke Heist*
Ridley, Erica. ★*The Perks of Loving a Wallflower*
Riley, Vanessa. ★*A Duke, the Lady, and a Baby*
Riley, Vanessa. ★*An Earl, the Girl, and a Toddler*
Romain, Theresa. *Fortune Favors the Wicked*
Sebastian, Cat. *It Takes Two to Tumble*
Sebastian, Cat. *The Lawrence Browne Affair*
Sebastian, Cat. *Unmasked by the Marquess*
Vayden, Kristin. *Fortune Favors the Duke*
Waite, Olivia. *The Care and Feeding of Waspish Widows*
Waite, Olivia. ★*The Lady's Guide to Celestial Mechanics*
Waters, Martha. ★*To Have and to Hoax: A Novel*
Waters, Martha. *To Love and to Loathe: A Novel*
Regency vows [Series]. Waters, Martha
★***Regeneration***. Barker, Pat
REGENERATION (BIOLOGY)
Shelley, Mary Wollstonecraft. ★*Frankenstein: Or, the Modern Prometheus*
Regeneration trilogy (Pat Barker) [Series]. Barker, Pat
REGGAE MUSICIANS
James, Marlon. ★*A Brief History of Seven Killings: A Novel*
REGICIDE
Martell, Nick. *The Kingdom of Liars*
*A **Registry** of My Passage Upon the Earth: Stories*. Mason, Daniel
REGRESSION (CIVILIZATION)
Atwood, Margaret. ★*Maddaddam: A Novel*
Atwood, Margaret. ★*The Year of the Flood: A Novel*
Stirling, S. M. *Dies the Fire*
Stirling, S. M. *A Meeting at Corvallis*
Stirling, S. M. *The Protector's War*
REGRET
Aciman, Andre. *Find Me*
Diop, David. ★*At Night All Blood Is Black*
Means, David. ★*Instructions for a Funeral: Stories*
Oates, Joyce Carol. ★*My Life as a Rat*
Updike, John. *Licks of Love: Short Stories and a Sequel*
REGRET IN MEN
Barnes, Julian. ★*The Sense of an Ending*
Savage, Sam. *The Way of the Dog: A Novel*

REGRET IN WOMEN
Fabry, Chris. *Looking into You*
*The **Regrets***. Bonnaffons, Amy
REHABILITATION
Tanen, Sloane. *There's a Word for That*
REHABILITATION CENTERS
Tanen, Sloane. *There's a Word for That*
Reich, Christopher
★*The Take*
Reichs, Kathy
206 Bones
Bare Bones
Bones of the Lost: A Temperance Brennan Novel
Bones to Ashes
Break No Bones
★*A Conspiracy of Bones*
Deadly Decisions
Death Du Jour
★*Deja Dead*
Grave Secrets
Monday Mourning
Reid, Ava
The Wolf and the Woodsman
Reid, Iain
I'm Thinking of Ending Things
Reid, Kiley
★*Such a Fun Age*
Reid, Taylor Jenkins
★*Daisy Jones & The Six: A Novel*
Forever, Interrupted: A Novel
★*Malibu Rising*
*The **Reign** of the Kingfisher: A Novel*. Martinson, T. J.
Reimringer, John
Vestments
REINCARNATION
Atkinson, Kate. ★*Life After Life: A Novel*
Barker, Susan. ★*The Incarnations: A Novel*
Cameron, W. Bruce. *A Dog's Promise*
Davidson, Andrew. *The Gargoyle*
Durst, Sarah Beth. *Race the Sands*
Miller, Rebecca. ★*Jacob's Folly: A Novel*
Mishima, Yukio. *The Temple of Dawn*
Mitchell, David. ★*Cloud Atlas: A Novel*
Poore, Michael. *Reincarnation Blues*
Seton, Anya. *Green Darkness*
Turton, Stuart. *The 7 1/2 Deaths of Evelyn Hardcastle*
***Reincarnation** Blues*. Poore, Michael
*The **Reivers**: a Reminiscence*. Faulkner, William
REJECTION (PSYCHOLOGY)
Kafka, Franz. ★*The Metamorphosis*
Swarthout, Glendon. *Bless the Beasts and Children*
RELATIONSHIP FICTION
Adams, Sara Nisha. ★*The Reading List*
Allen, Jayne. *Black Girls Must Die Exhausted*
Allen, Sarah Addison. *Garden Spells*
Alvarez, Julia. *How the Garcia Girls Lost Their Accents*
Anam, Tahmima. *The Startup Wife*
Andrews, Mary Kay. *Sunset Beach*

Awad, Mona. ★*13 Ways of Looking at a Fat Girl*
Backman, Fredrik. ★*Anxious People: A Novel*
Backman, Fredrik. ★*Beartown: A Novel*
Backman, Fredrik. *Britt-Marie Was Here*
Backman, Fredrik. *A Man Called Ove*
Backman, Fredrik. ★*My Grandmother Asked Me to Tell You She's Sorry: A Novel*
Backman, Fredrik. *Us Against You: A Novel*
Bair, Kristin. *Agatha Arch Is Afraid of Everything*
Balasubramanyam, Rajeev. *Professor Chandra Follows His Bliss: A Novel*
Bannister, Ilona. *When I Ran Away*
Barnett, David. *Calling Major Tom*
Bauermeister, Erica. *The Scent Keeper*
Berg, Elizabeth. *The Confession Club: A Novel*
Berg, Elizabeth. *Night of Miracles*
Berg, Elizabeth. *The Story of Arthur Truluv: A Novel*
Binchy, Maeve. *Circle of Friends*
Binchy, Maeve. *Firefly Summer*
Binchy, Maeve. ★*Whitethorn Woods*
Bivald, Katarina. *The Readers of Broken Wheel Recommend*
Blundell, Judy. *The High Season: A Novel*
Brenner, Jamie. *Blush: A Novel*
Brenner, Jamie. *Drawing Home*
Broder, Melissa. *The Pisces: A Novel*
Brown, Eleanor. *The Weird Sisters*
Brown, Rita Mae. *Six of One*
Butland, Stephanie. *The Lost for Words Bookshop: A Novel*
Carr, Robyn. *The View from Alameda Island: A Novel*
Carter, Michaela. *Leonora in the Morning Light*
Center, Katherine. *How to Walk Away: A Novel*
Center, Katherine. *Things You Save in a Fire*
Center, Katherine. *What You Wish For*
Cisneros, Sandra. *Martita, I Remember You: Martita, Te Recuerdo*
Cleage, Pearl. *What Looks Like Crazy on an Ordinary Day: A Novel*
Cocks, Heather. *The Heir Affair*
Cocks, Heather. *The Royal We*
Colgan, Jenny. *500 Miles from You*
Colgan, Jenny. ★*The Endless Beach*
Colgan, Jenny. *Sunrise by the Sea*
Cronin, Marianne. *The One Hundred Years of Lenni and Margot*
Cullen, Helen. *The Dazzling Truth*
De los Santos, Marisa. *The Precious One*
Delinsky, Barbara. *A Week at the Shore*
Dell'Antonia, K. J. *The Chicken Sisters*
Doan, Amy Mason. *The Summer List*
Ekwuyasi, Francesca. *Butter Honey Pig Bread: A Novel*
Fisher, Helen. *Space Hopper*
Flagg, Fannie. ★*Fried Green Tomatoes at the Whistle Stop Cafe*
Forman, Gayle. *Leave Me: A Novel*
Fossey, Brooke. *The Big Finish*
Fowler, Karen Joy. *The Jane Austen Book Club*
Fowler, Therese. ★*A Good Neighborhood*
Frank, Alli. *Tiny Imperfections*
Frank, Dorothea Benton. *Queen Bee*
Freitas, Donna. *The Nine Lives of Rose Napolitano*
Ganshert, Katie. *Life After*
Garcia, Cristina. *Dreaming in Cuban*

Garvin, Eileen. *The Music of Bees*
Gelman, Laurie. *Class Mom: A Novel*
Gelman, Laurie. *Yoga Pant Nation: A Novel*
Gelman, Laurie. *You've Been Volunteered: A Class Mom Novel*
George, Nina. *The Little Paris Bookshop*
Gibson, Claire. *Beyond the Point: A Novel*
Gideon, Melanie. *Wife 22*
Gilman, Susan Jane. *Donna Has Left the Building*
Hannah, Kristin. *Home Front*
Harbison, Beth. *The Cookbook Club*
Haywood, Sarah. *The Cactus*
Heiny, Katherine. ★*Early Morning Riser*
Hepworth, Sally. *The Secrets of Midwives*
Higgins, Kristan. *Always the Last to Know*
Higgins, Kristan. ★*Life and Other Inconveniences*
Higgins, Kristan. *Now That You Mention It*
Higgins, Kristan. ★*Pack up the Moon*
Hilderbrand, Elin. ★*28 Summers*
Hilderbrand, Elin. *The Perfect Couple*
Hilderbrand, Elin. ★*Summer of '69*
Hilderbrand, Elin. ★*Troubles in Paradise*
Hilderbrand, Elin. ★*What Happens in Paradise: A Novel*
Hilderbrand, Elin. ★*Winter in Paradise: A Novel*
Ho, Lauren. *Last Tang Standing*
Holmes, Linda. ★*Evvie Drake Starts Over: A Novel*
Hornby, Nick. *High Fidelity*
Hornby, Nick. *Just Like You*
Hostin, Sunny. ★*Summer on the Bluffs*
Hyde, Catherine Ryan. *My Name Is Anton*
Igharo, Jane. *The Sweetest Remedy*
Jackson, Joshilyn. *Never Have I Ever*
Janowitz, Brenda. *The Grace Kelly Dress*
Johnson, Nancy. *The Kindest Lie*
Joyce, Rachel. *Miss Benson's Beetle*
Kagen, Lesley. *Every Now and Then*
Kane, Jessica Francis. *Rules for Visiting*
Kantra, Virginia. *Beth & Amy*
Kelly, Cathy. *Secrets of a Happy Marriage*
Kingsolver, Barbara. ★*The Bean Trees: A Novel*
Kingsolver, Barbara. *Pigs in Heaven*
Kwan, Kevin. *China Rich Girlfriend*
Kwan, Kevin. *Crazy Rich Asians*
Kwan, Kevin. *Rich People Problems*
Kwan, Kevin. *Sex and Vanity: A Novel*
Lalli, Sonya. *Serena Singh Flips the Script*
Landvik, Lorna. *Chronicles of a Radical Hag: With Recipes*
Lane, Byron. ★*A Star Is Bored*
Lim, Roselle. *Natalie Tan's Book of Luck and Fortune*
Linden, Rachel. *Ascension of Larks*
Lipman, Elinor. *The Dearly Departed*
Lipman, Elinor. *Good Riddance*
Lipman, Elinor. *The Pursuit of Alice Thrift: A Novel*
Lovely, Lutishia. *Blind Ambition*
Luchette, Claire. *Agatha of Little Neon*
Lyons, Annie. *The Brilliant Life of Eudora Honeysett*
Majors, Inman. *Penelope Lemon: Game On!*
Mallery, Susan. *California Girls*
Mallery, Susan. *The Summer of Sunshine and Margot*

Mapson, Jo-Ann. *Bad Girl Creek: A Novel*
Marcelo, Tif. *In a Book Club Far Away*
Mason, Meg. *Sorrow and Bliss*
Masood, Syed M. *The Bad Muslim Discount*
McFarlane, Mhairi. *Don't You Forget About Me*
McGhee, Alison. *The Opposite of Fate*
McMillan, Terry. ★*How Stella Got Her Groove Back*
McMillan, Terry. ★*It's Not All Downhill from Here: A Novel*
McMillan, Terry. ★*Waiting to Exhale*
Medie, Peace A. *His Only Wife: A Novel*
Miller, Sue. *The Good Mother*
Miller, Sue. *The Senator's Wife*
Monroe, Mary Alice. *Beach House Reunion*
Monroe, Mary Alice. ★*The Summer of Lost and Found*
Montimore, Margarita. *Oona Out of Order*
Moriarty, Jaclyn. *Gravity Is the Thing*
Moyes, Jojo. *The Girl You Left Behind*
Moyes, Jojo. ★*The Giver of Stars: A Novel*
Moyes, Jojo. *The Peacock Emporium*
O'Leary, Beth. *The Switch*
Oakley, Colleen. *The Invisible Husband of Frick Island*
Oakley, Colleen. *You Were There Too*
Parrish, Christa. *Still Life*
Pastan, Rachel. *In the Field*
Patrick, Phaedra. ★*The Secrets of Love Story Bridge*
Peters, Torrey. ★*Detransition, Baby*
Picoult, Jodi. ★*The Book of Two Ways*
Picoult, Jodi. *Change of Heart: A Novel*
Picoult, Jodi. *A Spark of Light: A Novel*
Picoult, Jodi. ★*Wish You Were Here: A Novel*
Poeppel, Amy. *Musical Chairs: A Novel*
Ray, Eleanor. *The Missing Treasures of Amy Ashton*
Reid, Taylor Jenkins. ★*Daisy Jones & The Six: A Novel*
Reid, Taylor Jenkins. *Forever, Interrupted: A Novel*
Rice, Luanne. *Little Night*
Rimmer, Kelly. *Before I Let You Go*
Rimmer, Kelly. *Truths I Never Told You*
Rowell, Rainbow. *Landline*
Sampson, Freya. *The Last Chance Library*
Schine, Cathleen. *The Grammarians*
Semple, Maria. *Where'd You Go, Bernadette: A Novel*
Serle, Rebecca. *In Five Years: A Novel*
Shin, Ann. *The Last Exiles*
Shipman, Viola. *The Clover Girls*
Shipman, Viola. *The Heirloom Garden*
Silver, Marisa. *Mary Coin: A Novel*
Simonson, Helen. *Major Pettigrew's Last Stand: A Novel*
Sittenfeld, Curtis. *Eligible: A Novel*
Slimani, Leïla. *In the Country of Others*
Sparks, Nicholas. *Every Breath*
Sparks, Nicholas. *The Guardian*
Sparks, Nicholas. ★*The Notebook*
Sparks, Nicholas. *A Walk to Remember*
Stockett, Kathryn. ★*The Help*
Stradal, J. Ryan. ★*The Lager Queen of Minnesota*
Straub, Emma. ★*Modern Lovers*
Sutanto, Jesse Q. *Dial a for Aunties*
Sweeney, Cynthia D'Aprix. ★*Good Company: A Novel*

Tan, Amy. *The Bonesetter's Daughter*
Tan, Amy. ★*The Joy Luck Club*
Tan, Amy. ★*The Kitchen God's Wife*
Thayne, RaeAnne. *The Cliff House*
Trollope, Joanna. *Other People's Children*
Tyler, Anne. ★*Redhead by the Side of the Road*
Umrigar, Thrity N. *Everybody's Son*
Umrigar, Thrity N. ★*Honor*
Umrigar, Thrity N. *The Secrets Between Us*
Valdes, Alisa. *Dirty Girls on Top*
Von Ziegesar, Cecily. *Cobble Hill*
Walsh, M. O. ★*The Big Door Prize: A Novel*
Waxman, Abbi. *The Bookish Life of Nina Hill*
Weiner, Jennifer. *In Her Shoes: A Novel*
Weiner, Jennifer. *Little Earthquakes*
Weiner, Jennifer. ★*Mrs. Everything: A Novel*
Weiss, Leah. *If the Creek Don't Rise: A Novel*
Wells, Rebecca. *Divine Secrets of the Ya-Ya Sisterhood: A Novel*
Wiggs, Susan. ★*The Oysterville Sewing Circle*

*The **Relentless** Moon.* Kowal, Mary Robinette
Relic. Foster, Alan Dean

RELICS

Brown, Dan. *The Da Vinci Code*
Grant, Helen. *The Glass Demon*
Mosse, Kate. *The City of Tears*
Sandford, John. *Storm Front*
Spillane, Mickey. *The Goliath Bone*

RELIGION

Akhtar, Ayad. *American Dervish: A Novel*
Butler, Octavia E. ★*Parable of the Sower*
Dick, Philip K. ★*The Man in the High Castle*
Hambly, Barbara. *House of the Patriarch*
Heinlein, Robert A. ★*Stranger in a Strange Land*
Miller, Kei. ★*Augustown*
Oe, Kenzaburo. *Somersault: A Novel*
Phillips, Arthur. ★*The King at the Edge of the World: Novel*
Russell, Mary Doria. ★*Children of God: A Novel*
Scott, Walter. ★*Rob Roy*
Simmons, Dan. *The Rise of Endymion*
Vonnegut, Kurt. *Welcome to the Monkey House*

RELIGION — SOCIAL ASPECTS

Waugh, Evelyn. ★*Brideshead Revisited*

RELIGION AND SCIENCE

Atwood, Margaret. ★*Maddaddam: A Novel*
Atwood, Margaret. ★*The Year of the Flood: A Novel*
Miles, Jonathan. *Anatomy of a Miracle*

RELIGIOUS COMMUNITIES

Bennett, Brit. *The Mothers*
Dekker, Ted. *The Girl Behind the Red Rope*
Mendez, Paul. *Rainbow Milk*

RELIGIOUS CORRUPTION

Hewson, David. *A Season for the Dead*

RELIGIOUS COVER-UPS

Black, Benjamin. ★*Christine Falls: A Novel*

RELIGIOUS FANATICISM

De Bernieres, Louis. *Birds Without Wings*
Golding, William. ★*Darkness Visible*
Holbert, Bruce. *Whiskey*

O'Connor, Flannery. ★*The Violent Bear It Away*
Pollock, Donald Ray. *The Devil All the Time*
Vargas Llosa, Mario. *The War of the End of the World*

RELIGIOUS FANATICS
Gala, Marcial. ★*The Black Cathedral*
Hamilton, Peter F. *The Dreaming Void*
Harrison, Jim. *The Great Leader*
Hewson, David. *A Season for the Dead*
Sansom, C. J. *Revelation*
Tepper, Sheri S. *The Visitor*

RELIGIOUS FICTION
Goldbloom, Goldie. *On Division*

RELIGIOUS PERSECUTION
Artson, Barbara. *Odessa, Odessa*
Banks, Iain. *Consider Phlebas*
Barker, Pat. ★*The Eye in the Door*
Endo, Shusaku. *Silence*
Enjeti, Anjali. ★*The Parted Earth*
Greene, Graham. *The Power and the Glory*
Gregory, Philippa. *The Last Tudor*
Phoenix, Michele. *The Space Between Words*
Sofer, Dalia. *The Septembers of Shiraz*
Twain, Mark. *Personal Recollections of Joan of Arc*

RELIGIOUS RADICALS
Butler, Nickolas. *Little Faith: A Novel*
*The **Relive** Box: And Other Stories.* Boyle, T. Coraghessan
Reluctant royals [Series]. Cole, Alyssa
★*The **Remains** of the Day.* Ishiguro, Kazuo
Remarque, Erich Maria
  ★*All Quiet on the Western Front*
  The Road Back
  A Time to Love and a Time to Die

REMARRIAGE
Du Maurier, Daphne. ★*Rebecca*
Ford, Richard. *The Lay of the Land*
Miller, Sue. ★*Monogamy*
Phillips, Susan Elizabeth. *What I Did for Love*
Rindell, Suzanne. ★*The Two Mrs. Carlyles*
Trollope, Joanna. *Other People's Children*
Updike, John. *Gertrude and Claudius*

REMBRANDT HARMENSZOON VAN RIJN
Garcia, Cristina. *The Aguero Sisters*
Smith, Zadie. *On Beauty*
Remembering Babylon. Malouf, David
★*Remembrance.* Woods, Rita
Remembrance of Earth's past [Series]. Liu, Cixin
★*Remembrance* of Things Past. Proust, Marcel

REMINISCING IN OLD AGE
Alameddine, Rabih. *An Unnecessary Woman*
Banks, Russell. *Foregone*
Banville, John. *Ancient Light*
Barnes, Julian. *The Only Story*
Boudjedra, Rachid. *The Barbary Figs*
Butler, Robert Olen. *Late City*
Cannon, Joanna. *Three Things About Elsie: A Novel*
Cartwright, Justin. *To Heaven by Water*
Dean, Debra. *The Madonnas of Leningrad: A Novel*
Diamant, Anita. *The Boston Girl: A Novel*

Flagg, Fannie. ★*Fried Green Tomatoes at the Whistle Stop Cafe*
Flagg, Fannie. ★*The Wonder Boy of Whistle Stop: A Novel*
Garcia Marquez, Gabriel. *Memories of My Melancholy Whores*
Gardam, Jane. *Last Friends*
Gardam, Jane. *Old Filth*
Gilbert, Elizabeth. ★*City of Girls*
Griffin, Anne. *When All Is Said: A Novel*
Gruen, Sara. ★*Water for Elephants: A Novel*
Harding, Paul. *Tinkers*
Hijuelos, Oscar. *Beautiful Maria of My Soul*
Hijuelos, Oscar. ★*The Mambo Kings Play Songs of Love: A Novel*
Mason, Bobbie Ann. *Dear Ann: A Novel*
Morton, Kate. *The House at Riverton: A Novel*
Murdoch, Iris. *The Sea, the Sea*
Nabokov, Vladimir Vladimirovich. *Look at the Harlequins!*
O'Nan, Stewart. *Henry, Himself*
Randall, Alice. ★*Black Bottom Saints*
Rawles, Nancy. *My Jim: A Novel*
Ritter, Josh. *The Great Glorious Goddamn of It All*
Robinson, Marilynne. ★*Gilead*
Robinson, Marilynne. *Home*
Roth, Philip. *Sabbath's Theater*
Smith, Dominic. ★*The Electric Hotel*
Spark, Muriel. ★*A Far Cry from Kensington*
Updike, John. *Seek My Face*
Williams, Niall. *This Is Happiness*

REMORSE
Danticat, Edwidge. *The Dew Breaker*
Oates, Joyce Carol. *The (Other) You: Stories*
*The **Remorseful** Day.* Dexter, Colin
★*Remote* Control. Okorafor, Nnedi
★*The **Removed**: a Novel.* Hobson, Brandon

RENAISSANCE (1300-1600)
Brandreth, Benet. *The Spy of Venice*
Dunant, Sarah. *Blood and Beauty: A Novel*
Dunant, Sarah. *In the Company of the Courtesan: A Novel*
Dunnett, Dorothy. *Niccolo Rising*
Mantel, Hilary. ★*Bring up the Bodies: A Novel*
Morelli, Laura. *The Stolen Lady*
Mosse, Kate. *The City of Tears*
Poole, Sara. *The Borgia Mistress*
Stone, Irving. ★*The Agony and the Ecstasy: A Biographical Novel of Michelangelo*
Walton, Jo. ★*Lent*

RENAISSANCE FAIRS
DeLuca, Jen. *Well Matched*
DeLuca, Jen. ★*Well Met*

Renault, Mary
  The Bull from the Sea
  Funeral Games
  The King Must Die
  The Last of the Wine
  The Persian Boy

Rendell, Ruth
  The Babes in the Wood
  ★*The Bridesmaid*
  Collected Stories
  End in Tears

Harm Done
★*A Judgement in Stone*
Kissing the Gunner's Daughter
Live Flesh
Not in the Flesh
Road Rage
Simisola
A Sleeping Life
Speaker of Mandarin
The Tree of Hands
Rendezvous with Rama. Clarke, Arthur C.
Renee Ballard novels [Series]. Connelly, Michael

RENKO, ARKADY (FICTITIOUS CHARACTER)
    Smith, Martin Cruz. *Havana Bay*
    Smith, Martin Cruz. *Stalin's Ghost*
    Smith, Martin Cruz. *Three Stations: An Arkady Renko Novel*
    Smith, Martin Cruz. *Wolves Eat Dogs: A Novel*

RENNES-LE-CHATEAU, FRANCE
    Berry, Steve. ★*The Templar Legacy: A Novel of Suspense*

RENO, NEVADA
    Johnson, Julia Claiborne. *Better Luck Next Time: A Novel*

RENOVATION (ARCHITECTURE)
    Deveraux, Jude. *A Willing Murder*
    McKinlay, Jenn. *The Good Ones*

REPAIRERS
    Dimon, HelenKay. *Her Other Secret*
    Haywood, Gar Anthony. *Cemetery Road*
    Hibbert, Talia. ★*Get a Life, Chloe Brown*

REPENTANCE
    Picoult, Jodi. *Change of Heart: A Novel*
Repo Madness. Cameron, W. Bruce.

REPOSSESSORS
    Cameron, W. Bruce. *Repo Madness*

REPRODUCTIVE RIGHTS
    Glass, Jenna. *The Women's War*

REPRODUCTIVE TECHNOLOGY
    Picoult, Jodi. *Sing You Home: A Novel*
*The **Republic** of Love.* Shields, Carol
★***Reputation***. Shepard, Sara

REPUTATION
    Alexander, V. S. *The Magdalen Girls*
    Bell, Lenora. ★*How the Duke Was Won*
    Bradley, Anna. *A Season of Ruin*
    Ciotta, Beth. *Her Sky Cowboy*
    Dare, Tessa. *Do You Want to Start a Scandal*
    Jordan, Sophie. *This Scot of Mine*
    Kenney, John. *Talk to Me*
    Laureano, C. E. ★*The Saturday Night Supper Club*
    MacLean, Sarah. ★*Bombshell*
    MacLean, Sarah. *The Rogue Not Taken*
    Martin, Alexa. ★*Intercepted*
    McElroy, Alex. *The Atmospherians*
    Qiu, Xiaolong. *Shanghai Redemption: An Inspector Chen Novel*
Requiem for a Nun. Faulkner, William
Requiem for Harlem. Roth, Henry

RESCUE DOGS
    Jimenez, Abby. ★*The Happy Ever After Playlist*
Rescue Me. Warren, Susan May

RESCUES
    Box, C. J. ★*Dark Sky: A Joe Pickett Novel*
    Box, C. J. ★*Long Range*
    Burdick, Serena. *The Girls with No Names*
    Butler, Octavia E. ★*Kindred*
    Corleone, Douglas. *Good as Gone*
    El Akkad, Omar. *What Strange Paradise*
    Hannah, Kristin. *The Nightingale*
    King, Stephen. *11/22/63*
    Laukkanen, Owen. *Deception Cove*
    Meader, Kate. *Playing with Fire*
    Olmstead, Robert. ★*Coal Black Horse*
    Orczy, Emmuska Orczy. ★*The Scarlet Pimpernel*
    Peters, Ellis. *Brother Cadfael's Penance*
    Priest, Cherie. *Boneshaker*
    Putney, Mary Jo. *No Longer a Gentleman*
    Putney, Mary Jo. *Nowhere Near Respectable*
    Putney, Mary Jo. *Once a Scoundrel*
    Quincy, D. M. *Murder in Mayfair: An Atlas Catesby Mystery*
    Quinn, Julia. ★*An Offer from a Gentleman*
    Saylor, Steven. *Wrath of the Furies: A Novel of the Ancient World*
    Sorenson, Jill. *Aftershock*
    Spencer, Minerva. *Scandalous*
    Spillane, Mickey. *The Consummata*
    Tan, Sue Lynn. ★*Daughter of the Moon Goddess*
    Warren, Susan May. *Rescue Me*

RESEARCH
    Abbott, Megan E. ★*Give Me Your Hand*
    Egan, Greg. *Schild's Ladder*
    Flynn, Michael. *Eifelheim*
    Liu, Cixin. ★*The Dark Forest*
    Turnbull, Cadwell. ★*The Lesson*

RESEARCH INSTITUTES
    Child, Lincoln. *Deep Storm: A Novel*

RESENTFULNESS
    Cleeves, Ann. *Wild Fire*
    Davies, Carys. *The Mission House*
    Edwards, Rachel. *Darling*
    Enright, Anne. ★*The Gathering*
    Goldin, Megan. *The Escape Room*
    Kelly, Cathy. *Secrets of a Happy Marriage*
    Williams, Tennessee. ★*The Roman Spring of Mrs. Stone*

RESENTFULNESS IN MEN
    Moyes, Jojo. *Me Before You: A Novel*
Reservation Blues. Alexie, Sherman
Reservoir novels [Series]. McGregor, Jon
*The **Reservoir** Tapes.* McGregor, Jon
*The **Residence**: a Novel.* Pyper, Andrew

RESILIENCE (PERSONAL QUALITY)
    Morris, Heather. *Cilka's Journey*

RESISTANCE (PSYCHOLOGY)
    Orwell, George. ★*1984: A Novel*

RESISTANCE TO GOVERNMENT
    Atwood, Margaret. ★*The Testaments: A Novel*
    Binet, Laurent. ★*HHhH*
    Brown, Pierce. *Red Rising*
    Buckley, Fiona. *The Siren Queen: An Ursula Blanchard Mystery at Queen Elizabeth I's Court*

Chiaverini, Jennifer. *Resistance Women: A Novel*
Fallada, Hans. *Every Man Dies Alone*
Furst, Alan. *Blood of Victory: A Novel*
Furst, Alan. ★*A Hero of France*
Mbue, Imbolo. *How Beautiful We Were*
Restrepo, Laura. *No Place for Heroes: A Novel*
Robb, Candace M. *A Murdered Peace*
Stross, Charles. *Glasshouse*
Yang, JY. *The Ascent to Godhood*
Yang, JY. *The Black Tides of Heaven*

RESISTANCE TO MILITARY OCCUPATION
Belfoure, Charles. *The Paris Architect: A Novel*
Benn, James R. *Billy Boyle: A World War Two Mystery*
Binet, Laurent. ★*HHhH*
Faulks, Sebastian. *Charlotte Gray: A Novel*
Furst, Alan. *Spies of the Balkans: A Novel*
Hannah, Kristin. *The Nightingale*
Mengiste, Maaza. ★*The Shadow King: A Novel*
Ramzipoor, E. R. *The Ventriloquists*
Russell, Mary Doria. *A Thread of Grace: A Novel*

RESISTANCE TO ROAD CONSTRUCTION, POWERLINES, ETC.
Rendell, Ruth. *Road Rage*
Resistance Women: A Novel. Chiaverini, Jennifer
★*The Resisters*. Jen, Gish

RESNICK, CHARLIE (FICTITIOUS CHARACTER)
Harvey, John. *A Darker Shade of Blue: Stories*

RESORTS
Bannalec, Jean-Luc. *The Granite Coast Murders*
Beaton, M. C. *Agatha Raisin and the Witch of Wyckhadden*
Delany, Vicki. *Deadly Summer Nights*
Dodd, Christina. *Dead Girl Running*
Harrison, Nicola. *Montauk*
James, P. D. *The Lighthouse*
Ko-Eun, Yun. *The Disaster Tourist*
Simpson, Dorothy. *Last Seen Alive: A Luke Thanet Mystery*
Stapley, Marissa. *The Last Resort*
Williams, Joy. *Harrow*

RESOURCEFULNESS IN WOMEN
McCall Smith, Alexander. *The Good Husband of Zebra Drive*

RESOURCEFULNESS IN YOUNG MEN
Forester, C. S. *Lieutenant Hornblower*

RESPONSIBILITY
Bolano, Roberto. ★*By Night in Chile*
Esquivel, Laura. ★*Like Water for Chocolate: A Novel in Monthly Installments, with Recipes, Romances, and Home Remedies*
Ishiguro, Kazuo. *An Artist of the Floating World*
Winfrey, Kerry. *Not Like the Movies*
The Restaurant at the End of the Universe. Adams, Douglas

RESTAURANTS
Adams, Douglas. *The Restaurant at the End of the Universe*
Bijan, Donia. *The Last Days of Cafe Leila*
Childs, Laura. *Egg Shooters*
Danler, Stephanie. *Sweetbitter*
Dell'Antonia, K. J. *The Chicken Sisters*
Jalaluddin, Uzma. *Hana Khan Carries On*
Manansala, Mia P. ★*Arsenic and Adobo*

RESTAURATEURS
Dev, Sonali. ★*Recipe for Persuasion*
Itami, Emily. *Fault Lines: A Novel*
Pineiro, Caridad. *South Beach Love: A Feel-Good Romance from Hallmark Publishing*
Smith, Julie. *House of Blues*
Restless in the Grave. Stabenow, Dana

RESTORATION ENGLAND (1660-1688)
Du Maurier, Daphne. *Frenchman's Creek*
Pears, Iain. *An Instance of the Fingerpost*
Phillips, Christi. *The Devlin Diary*
Restrepo, Laura
★*Delirium: A Novel*
No Place for Heroes: A Novel

RESURRECTION
Setterfield, Diane. ★*Once Upon a River*
Resurrection Men: An Inspector Rebus Novel. Rankin, Ian

RETAIL STORES
Higashino, Keigo. *The Miracles of the Namiya General Store*

RETIRED MILITARY PERSONNEL
Lee, Patrick. *Runner*

RETIRED TEACHERS
Phillips, Caryl. *A Distant Shore*
Picoult, Jodi. *The Storyteller*

RETIREES
Bear, Elizabeth. *Stone Mad*
Connelly, Michael. ★*The Dark Hours*
Donoghue, Emma. *Akin*
Eriksson, Kjell. *The Deathwatch Beetle: A Mystery*
Erpenbeck, Jenny. *Go, Went, Gone: A Novel*
Friedman, Daniel. *Running Out of Road*
Hauck, Rachel. *The Wedding Chapel*
Hiaasen, Carl. *Skin Tight*
Horowitz, Anthony. ★*Moonflower Murders*
Indriðason, Arnaldur. *The Darkness Knows*
King, Stephen. *Mr. Mercedes: A Novel*
Krauss, Nicole. *Forest Dark*
McCorkle, Jill. ★*Hieroglyphics: A Novel*
Osborne, Lawrence. *Only to Sleep: A Philip Marlowe Novel*
Osman, Richard. ★*The Thursday Murder Club*
Persson, Leif G. W. *The Dying Detective: A Mystery*
Powers, Richard. *Orfeo: A Novel*
Simonson, Helen. *Major Pettigrew's Last Stand: A Novel*
Verdon, John. *On Harrow Hill*

RETIREMENT
Dobyns, Stephen. *Saratoga Payback*
Rankin, Ian. *Exit Music*
Shriver, Lionel. *So Much for That*

RETIREMENT COMMUNITIES
Groen, Hendrik. *On the Bright Side: The New Secret Diary of Hendrik Groen, 85 Years Old*
Hollis, Lee. *Poppy Harmon Investigates*
Osman, Richard. *The Man Who Died Twice: A Thursday Murder Club Mystery*
Osman, Richard. ★*The Thursday Murder Club*
Thorne, Sally. *Second First Impressions*
Weiner, Jennifer. *In Her Shoes: A Novel*
The Return. Harrison, Rachel

RETURN MIGRATION

Urrea, Luis Alberto. *Into the Beautiful North: A Novel*

*The **Return** of Captain John Emmett*. Speller, Elizabeth

*The **Return** of Kid Cooper: A Novel*. Smith, B. J.

★*The **Return** of the Dancing Master*. Mankell, Henning

*The **Return** of the King: Being the Third Part of the Lord of the Rings*. Tolkien, J. R. R.

★*The **Return** of the Native*. Hardy, Thomas

*The **Return**: a Novel*. Gruber, Michael

REUNIONS

Abrams, Melanie. *Meadowlark*

Anders, Charlie Jane. ★*All the Birds in the Sky*

Blumenfeld, Amy. *The Cast*

Cantero, Edgar. *Meddling Kids: A Novel*

Dodd, Christina. *Virtue Falls*

Drabble, Margaret. *The Sea Lady*

Fabry, Chris. *The Promise of Jesse Woods*

Gates, Eva. *A Death Long Overdue*

Harrison, Rachel. *The Return*

Johnson, Craig. *Spirit of Steamboat: A Walt Longmire Story*

Jónasson, Ragnar. *The Island*

McCreight, Kimberly. *Friends Like These*

McFarlane, Mhairi. *Don't You Forget About Me*

Monroe, Mary Alice. *Beach House Reunion*

O'Farrell, Maggie. *The Vanishing Act of Esme Lennox*

Reynolds, Allie. ★*Shiver*

Shipman, Viola. *The Clover Girls*

Welty, Eudora. *The Optimist's Daughter*

Revelation. Goodwin, Bobi Gentry

Revelation. Sansom, C. J.

Revelation Space. Reynolds, Alastair

Revelation space universe [Series]. Reynolds, Alastair

Revelations. K'wan

Revelations. Sharratt, Mary

*The **Revelators***. Atkins, Ace

Revenant Gun. Lee, Yoon Ha

REVENGE

Arbol, Victor del. *Breathing Through the Wound*

Atkins, Ace. *The Broken Places*

Atkins, Ace. *The Sinners*

Atwood, Margaret. ★*Stone Mattress: Nine Tales*

Auci, Stefania. *The Florios of Sicily: A Novel*

Baker, Kage. *The House of the Stag*

Balogh, Mary. *Only Enchanting*

Bear, Greg. *Anvil of Stars*

Bittner, Rosanne. *Logan's Lady*

Block, Lawrence. *A Ticket to the Boneyard: A Matthew Scudder Novel*

Box, C. J. *Vicious Circle*

Boyle, William. *City of Margins: A Novel*

Brom. *Slewfoot: A Tale of Bewitchery*

Bronte, Emily. ★*Wuthering Heights*

Brooks, Bill. *Frontier Justice*

Burrowes, Grace. *The Captive*

Burrowes, Grace. *My One and Only Duke*

Buwalda, Peter. *Bonita Avenue: A Novel*

Callender, Kacen. *King of the Rising*

Callender, Kacen. *Queen of the Conquered*

Capri, NeNe. *The Pussy Trap*

Castro, V. *The Queen of the Cicadas*

Child, Lee. ★*Killing Floor*

Christy, Bryan. *In the Company of Killers*

Cole, Alyssa. ★*An Unconditional Freedom*

Corey, James S. A. *Abaddon's Gate*

Cosby, S. A. ★*Razorblade Tears*

Coughlin, Jack. *In the Crosshairs: A Sniper Novel*

Coulter, Catherine. *Paradox*

Crais, Robert. *The First Rule*

Cronin, Justin. *The City of Mirrors*

Dahl, Julia. *The Missing Hours*

Deaver, Jeffery. *Edge: A Novel*

deWitt, Patrick. *The Sisters Brothers: A Novel*

Dickens, Charles. ★*Great Expectations*

Dickey, Eric Jerome. *Finding Gideon*

Doctorow, E. L. ★*Billy Bathgate: A Novel*

Dumas, Alexandre. ★*The Count of Monte Cristo*

Dumas, Alexandre. ★*The Three Musketeers*

Egan, Jennifer. *The Keep*

Eisler, Barry. *Livia Lone*

Ellis, Helen. *American Housewife: Stories*

Enger, Lin. *Undiscovered Country: A Novel*

Erdrich, Louise. ★*The Round House: A Novel*

Faust, Christa. *Money Shot*

Faye, Lyndsay. ★*The King of Infinite Space*

Follett, Ken. ★*The Pillars of the Earth*

Fox, Candice. *Redemption Point*

Fuentes, Carlos. *Destiny and Desire: A Novel*

Fuentes, Carlos. *The Eagle's Throne: A Novel*

Gaines, Ernest J. ★*A Gathering of Old Men*

Garcia, Cristina. *King of Cuba: A Novel*

Garcia, Cristina. *The Lady Matador's Hotel: A Novel*

George, Elizabeth. *What Came Before He Shot Her*

Grisham, John. *A Time to Kill*

Gruber, Michael. *The Return: A Novel*

Hagberg, David. *Gambit*

Hamill, Pete. *Forever*

Harper, Jane. *The Dry*

Harris, Thomas. *Hannibal Rising*

Hart, John. *Iron House*

Hart, John. *Redemption Road*

Hawthorne, Nathaniel. ★*The House of the Seven Gables*

Hawthorne, Nathaniel. ★*The Scarlet Letter: A Romance*

Haywood, Gar Anthony. *Cemetery Road*

Hill, Joe. *Horns*

Hill, Reginald. *The Woodcutter: A Novel*

Hodges, Cheris F. *Rumor Has It*

Hoyt, Elizabeth. *Not the Duke's Darling*

Hunter, Megan. *The Harpy*

Hunter, Stephen. *The 47th Samurai*

Jakes, John. *Love and War*

Jakes, John. ★*North and South*

James, P. D. *Original Sin*

Jordan, Sophie. *The Duke Goes Down*

K'wan. *Animal*

K'wan. *Animal II: The Omen*

Kay, Guy Gavriel. ★*Children of Earth and Sky*

Kelly, Erin. *The Burning Air: A Novel*
Kent, Kathleen. *The Pledge*
Lackberg, Camilla. *The Golden Cage*
Larsson, Stieg. ★*The Girl Who Kicked the Hornet's Nest*
Leckie, Ann. *Ancillary Justice*
Leckie, Ann. *Ancillary Mercy*
Leckie, Ann. *Ancillary Sword*
Leonard, Elmore. *Glitz*
Long, Julie Anne. *Angel in a Devil's Arms*
Lowe, Kathryn A. *The Furies*
Mamet, David. *Chicago: A Novel*
Marston, Edward. *The Wanton Angel: A Novel*
McFarlane, Mhairi. *If I Never Met You: A Novel*
McGuire, Ian. *The Abstainer: A Novel*
McKinty, Adrian. *In the Morning I'll Be Gone: A Detective Sean Duffy Novel*
Minato, Kanae. *Confessions*
Palliser, Charles. *The Quincunx*
Patterson, James. ★*Private*
Pinborough, Sarah. ★*Dead to Her: A Novel*
Portis, Charles. ★*True Grit: A Novel*
Ragan, Theresa. *Deadly Recall*
Rankin, Ian. *Blood Hunt: A Novel*
Rash, Ron. ★*In the Valley: Stories and a Novella Based on Serena*
Reynolds, Allie. ★*Shiver*
Robertson, Imogen. *The Paris Winter*
Rushdie, Salman. *Shalimar the Clown: A Novel*
Sanders, Lawrence. *The Tenth Commandment: A Novel*
Sandford, John. *Mortal Prey*
Sandford, John. *Sudden Prey*
Schanoes, Veronica L. *Burning Girls and Other Stories*
Schwab, Victoria. *Vengeful*
Schwab, Victoria. *Vicious*
Sigurðardóttir, Lilja. *Cage*
Silva, Daniel. *The Other Woman*
Skarmeta, Antonio. *The Dancer and the Thief: A Novel*
Smith, Julie. *82 Desire: A Skip Langdon Novel*
Smith, Tom Rob. *The Secret Speech*
Smith, Wilbur A. *Birds of Prey*
Spain, Jo. *With Our Blessing: An Inspector Tom Reynolds Mystery*
Spencer, Sally. *Best Served Cold*
St. James, Simone. *The Haunting of Maddy Clare*
Stark, Richard. *The Hunter: A Parker Novel*
Straley, John. *The Big Both Ways*
Styles, Toy. *Raunchy 2: Mad's Love*
Swinson, Kiki. *Wifey's Next Sticky Situation*
Walker, Alice. *Possessing the Secret of Joy*
Walker, Sarai. *Dietland*
Wallace, Lew. ★*Ben-Hur*
Weldon, Fay. *The Life and Loves of a She-Devil*
Winslow, Don. *Broken: Six Short Novels*
Winter, Evan. ★*The Rage of Dragons*
Woods, Stuart. *Palindrome*
Yoon, David. *Version Zero*
Youers, Rio. *Lola on Fire*
Zhou, Haohui. *Death Notice: A Novel*

REVENGE IN MEN
Bourne, Joanna. *The Forbidden Rose*

Ca$h. *Thugs Cry: A Novel*
Clancy, Tom. *Patriot Games*
Westlake, Donald E. *Forever and a Death*

REVENGE IN WOMEN
Buehlman, Christopher. *The Suicide Motor Club*
Dodd, Christina. *The Woman Who Couldn't Scream*
Erdrich, Louise. *Four Souls: A Novel*
Gardiner, Meg. *Unsub: A Novel*
Gentry, Amy. *Last Woman Standing*
Reynolds, Alastair. ★*Revenger*
Scottoline, Lisa. *Feared*
Toibin, Colm. *House of Names*
★*Revenger*. Reynolds, Alastair
Revenger novels [Series]. Reynolds, Alastair
Reverend Clare Fergusson mysteries [Series]. Spencer-Fleming, Julia
Reverend Mother mysteries [Series]. Harrison, Cora
The **Revised** Fundamentals of Caregiving: A Novel. Evison, Jonathan
The **Revisioners**: a Novel. Sexton, Margaret Wilkerson
Revival Season: A Novel. West, Monica

REVIVALS
Dimaline, Cherie. *Empire of Wild*
Lewis, Sinclair. ★*Elmer Gantry*

REVOLUTIONARIES
Bolano, Roberto. *Amulet*
Brown, Pierce. *Morning Star*
Cleeton, Chanel. *The Most Beautiful Girl in Cuba*
Cleeton, Chanel. *Next Year in Havana*
Cumming, Charles. *The Moroccan Girl*
Frantz, Laura. *The Lacemaker*
Fuentes, Carlos. ★*The Old Gringo*
Hugo, Victor. ★*LES Miserables*
Koestler, Arthur. *Darkness at Noon*
Mengestu, Dinaw. ★*All Our Names*
Naipaul, V. S. *Magic Seeds*
Restrepo, Laura. *No Place for Heroes: A Novel*
Robinson, Kim Stanley. ★*Green Mars*
Robinson, Kim Stanley. ★*Red Mars*
Sainz Borgo, Karina. ★*It Would Be Night in Caracas*
Shaara, Jeff. *Gone for Soldiers*
Steinhauer, Olen. *The Middleman*
Sterling, Bruce. *Pirate Utopia*
Vargas Llosa, Mario. *The War of the End of the World*
Zola, Emile. ★*Germinal*

REVOLUTIONARY AMERICA (1775-1783)
Frantz, Laura. *The Lacemaker*
Gabaldon, Diana. ★*A Breath of Snow and Ashes*
Gabaldon, Diana. *An Echo in the Bone*
Gabaldon, Diana. *Written in My Own Heart's Blood*
Harkness, Deborah E. *Time's Convert*
Hill, Lawrence. *Someone Knows My Name: A Novel*

REVOLUTIONARY FRANCE (1789-1799)
Carey, Edward. *Little: A Novel*
Dickens, Charles. ★*A Tale of Two Cities*
Dongala, Emmanuel Boundzeki. *The Bridgetower Sonata: Sonata Mulattica*
Orczy, Emmuska Orczy. ★*The Scarlet Pimpernel*
Sabatini, Rafael. *Scaramouche: A Romance of the French Revolution*

REVOLUTIONS

Apostol, Gina. *Gun Dealers' Daughter: A Novel*
Boudjedra, Rachid. *The Barbary Figs*
Campbell, Lisbeth. *The Vanished Queen*
Carey, Edward. *Little: A Novel*
Conrad, Joseph. *Nostromo: A Tale of the Seaboard*
Didion, Joan. *A Book of Common Prayer*
Fuentes, Carlos. ★*The Old Gringo*
Gao, XIngjian. *Soul Mountain*
Garcia, Cristina. *King of Cuba: A Novel*
Ghaffari, Rabeah. ★*To Keep the Sun Alive*
Heinlein, Robert A. *The Moon Is a Harsh Mistress*
Herbert, Frank. ★*Dune*
Hozar, Nazanine. *Aria*
Hugo, Victor. ★*Les Miserables*
Kelly, Martha Hall. *Lost Roses: A Novel*
Liu, Cixin. ★*The Three-Body Problem*
Polk, C. L. *Stormsong*
Robinson, Kim Stanley. *The Martians*
Russell, Mary Doria. ★*Children of God: A Novel*
Rutherfurd, Edward. *Paris*
Shaara, Jeff. *Gone for Soldiers*
Sofer, Dalia. *The Septembers of Shiraz*
Werfel, Franz. ★*The Forty Days of Musa Dagh*
Wilson, Daniel H. *Robogenesis: A Novel*

REVOLUTIONS — HISTORY

Bourne, Joanna. *The Forbidden Rose*
Revolver Road: A Harper McClain Mystery. Daugherty, Christi

Reyes, Dolores

Eartheater

Reykjavik Nights: An Inspector Erlendur Novel. Indriðason, Arnaldur

Reykjavik noir novels [Series]. Sigurðardóttir, Lilja

Reykjavik wartime mysteries [Series]. Indriðason, Arnaldur

REYKJAVIK, ICELAND

Indriðason, Arnaldur. *Outrage*
Indriðason, Arnaldur. *Reykjavik Nights: An Inspector Erlendur Novel*
Indriðason, Arnaldur. *The Shadow District: A Thriller*
Indriðason, Arnaldur. *Strange Shores: An Inspector Erlendur Novel*
Sigurðardóttir, Lilja. *Cage*

Reynolds, Alastair

Permafrost
Revelation Space
★*Revenger*

Reynolds, Allie

★*Shiver*

Rhapsody. Kaplan, Mitchell James

RHODE ISLAND

Danforth, Emily M. *Plain Bad Heroines*
Delinsky, Barbara. *A Week at the Shore*
DeSilva, Bruce. *Providence Rag*
DeSilva, Bruce. *Rogue Island*
DeSilva, Bruce. *A Scourge of Vipers*
Holmes, J. M. *How Are You Going to Save Yourself*
Mayor, Archer. ★*Marked Man*
Moore, Meg Mitchell. *The Islanders*
Smith, Gregory Blake. ★*The Maze at Windermere: A Novel*
Updike, John. *The Widows of Eastwick*
Updike, John. ★*The Witches of Eastwick*

Wilder, Thornton. ★*Theophilus North*

Rhodes, Jewell Parker

Voodoo Dreams: A Novel of Marie Laveau
Yellow Moon: A Novel

RHYME, LINCOLN (FICTITIOUS CHARACTER)

Deaver, Jeffery. ★*The Coffin Dancer*
Deaver, Jeffery. *The Empty Chair*

Rhymes with love [Series]. Boyle, Elizabeth

Rhys, Jean

★*Wide Sargasso Sea*

RHYS, JEAN

Phillips, Caryl. *A View of the Empire at Sunset*

Rhys, Rachel

Fatal Inheritance

Riccardino. Camilleri, Andrea

Ricciardi, David

Warning Light

RICCIO, DAVID

Gendry-Kim, Keum Suk. ★*The Waiting*
Mina, Denise. ★*Rizzio*

Rice, Anne

Blackwood Farm
Blood and Gold: Or, the Story of Marius
Blood Canticle
Blood Communion: A Tale of Prince Lestat
Christ the Lord: Out of Egypt: A Novel
Christ the Lord: The Road to Cana: A Novel
★*Interview with the Vampire*
Memnoch the Devil
Merrick: A Novel
Prince Lestat: The Vampire Chronicles
★*The Queen of the Damned*
The Tale of the Body Thief
The Vampire Armand
★*The Vampire Lestat*

Rice, Christopher

Blood Victory

Rice, Craig

Home Sweet Homicide

Rice, Luanne

★*Last Day*
The Lemon Orchard
Little Night

Rice, Waubgeshig

Moon of the Crusted Snow: A Novel

Rice-Gonzalez, Charles

Chulito

RICH AFRICAN AMERICAN FAMILIES

Morrison, Toni. ★*Song of Solomon*

Rich Boy. Pomerantz, Sharon

RICH BOYS

Hosseini, Khaled. ★*The Kite Runner*
Mosley, Walter. *Fortunate Son: A Novel*

RICH FAMILIES

Austen, Jane. ★*Sense and Sensibility*
Ausubel, Ramona. *Sons and Daughters of Ease and Plenty*
Bateman, Kate. *A Reckless Match*
Blake, Sarah. *The Guest Book: A Novel*

Bryant, Niobia. *Christmas with the Billionaire*
Carter, Mary Dixie. *The Photographer*
Clark, Mary Higgins. *The Melody Lingers On*
Crombie, Deborah. *A Bitter Feast*
Dahl, Julia. *The Missing Hours*
Feehan, Christine. *Shadow Rider*
Finch, Charles. *The Vanishing Man*
Finder, Joseph. ★*House on Fire: A Novel*
Foster, Brooke Lea. *Summer Darlings*
Ginzburg, Natalia. *Voices in the Evening*
Hamilton, Peter F. *Great North Road*
Harrington, Anna. *An Extraordinary Lord*
Heller, L. Alison. *The Neighbor's Secret*
Hilderbrand, Elin. *The Perfect Couple*
Kelly, Erin. *The Burning Air: A Novel*
Kunzru, Hari. *White Tears*
Kwan, Kevin. *Crazy Rich Asians*
Lackberg, Camilla. *The Golden Cage*
Lackberg, Camilla. *Silver Tears*
Macmillan, Gilly. *The Nanny*
McEwan, Ian. ★*Atonement: A Novel*
Michener, James A. *Chesapeake*
Mitford, Nancy. *Love in a Cold Climate*
Mitford, Nancy. ★*The Pursuit of Love: A Novel*
Moore, Lorrie. *A Gate at the Stairs: A Novel*
Mukherjee, Neel. *The Lives of Others*
Pamuk, Orhan. *The Museum of Innocence*
Patchett, Ann. *Run*
Rendell, Ruth. ★*A Judgement in Stone*
Rosen, Renee. *The Social Graces*
Rushdie, Salman. ★*The Golden House*
Sanders, Lawrence. *McNally's Trial*
Seth, Vikram. ★*A Suitable Boy: A Novel*
Shupe, Joanna. *The Rogue of Fifth Avenue*
Silber, Joan. *Secrets of Happiness*
Smith, Ian. *The Unspoken*
Solomons, Natasha. *House of Gold*
St. George, Harper. *The Heiress Gets a Duke*
Tan, Lucy. *What We Were Promised*
Tarkington, Booth. ★*The Magnificent Ambersons*
Tsao, Tiffany. *The Majesties*
Veletzos, Roxanne. *The Girl They Left Behind*
Wang, Kathy. *Family Trust: A Novel*
Woolf, Virginia. ★*The Years*
★*Rich Man, Poor Man*. Shaw, Irwin

RICH MEN
Akinmade-Akerstrom, Lola. *In Every Mirror She's Black*
Amis, Martin. *London Fields: A Novel*
Antoinette, Ashley. *Butterfly*
Berne, Lisa. *You May Kiss the Bride*
Binchy, Maeve. *Firefly Summer*
Brockway, Connie. *No Place for a Dame*
Bronte, Charlotte. ★*Jane Eyre*
Burrowes, Grace. ★*A Rogue of Her Own*
Burrowes, Grace. *Tremaine's True Love*
Clark, Mary Higgins. ★*Kiss the Girls and Make Them Cry*
Cohen, Joshua. *Book of Numbers: A Novel*
Dare, Tessa. ★*The Wallflower Wager*

De Leon, Aya. *Side Chick Nation*
Dunmore, Evie. ★*Bringing Down the Duke*
Eliot, George. ★*Adam Bede*
Faber, Michel. *The Crimson Petal and the White*
Force, Marie. *Deceived by Desire*
Fuentes, Carlos. *The Death of Artemio Cruz*
Greene, Graham. *The Tenth Man*
Heinlein, Robert A. ★*Stranger in a Strange Land*
James, Eloisa. *Three Weeks with Lady X*
Layne, Lauren. *Passion on Park Avenue*
Lewis, Sinclair. *Dodsworth*
London, Julia. *The Charmer in Chaps*
Nickson, Chris. *Come the Fear*
Pynchon, Thomas. ★*Bleeding Edge*
Pynchon, Thomas. *Inherent Vice*
Robb, J. D. *Fantasy in Death*
Shteyngart, Gary. ★*Lake Success: A Novel*
Thorne, Sally. *Second First Impressions*
Vonnegut, Kurt. ★*The Sirens of Titan*
Welty, Eudora. ★*The Ponder Heart*
Westlake, Donald E. *Get Real*
Rich novels (Kevin Kwan) [Series]. Kwan, Kevin
RICH PEOPLE
Bainbridge, Beryl. *Every Man for Himself*
Billingsley, ReShonda Tate. *A Little Bit of Karma: A Novel*
Blundell, Judy. *The High Season: A Novel*
Boyle, T. Coraghessan. ★*The Tortilla Curtain*
Brunkhorst, Alex. *The Gilded Life of Matilda Duplaine*
Butler, Nickolas. *Godspeed*
Chandler, Raymond. ★*The Big Sleep*
Chandler, Raymond. *The Long Goodbye*
Constantine, Liv. *The Last Time I Saw You*
Dee, Jonathan. *The Privileges: A Novel*
Dermansky, Marcy. *Very Nice*
Divya, S. B. *Machinehood*
Du Maurier, Daphne. ★*Rebecca*
Dunne, Dominick. *People Like Us: A Novel*
Dunne, Dominick. *Too Much Money*
Faulks, Sebastian. *Jeeves and the Wedding Bells*
Faulks, Sebastian. *A Week in December*
Fitzgerald, F. Scott. ★*The Beautiful and Damned*
Fitzgerald, F. Scott. *Novels and Stories, 1920-1922*
Galbraith, Robert. *The Cuckoo's Calling*
Gallagher, Stephen. *The Bedlam Detective: A Novel*
Gilbert, David. *& Sons: A Novel*
Hankin, Laura. *Happy & You Know It*
Hawley, Noah. *Before the Fall*
Hill, Edwin J. *Little Comfort*
Hostin, Sunny. ★*Summer on the Bluffs*
Iles, Greg. *Cemetery Road: A Novel*
Kosinski, Jerzy. *The Devil Tree*
Kwan, Kevin. *China Rich Girlfriend*
Kwan, Kevin. *Rich People Problems*
Kwan, Kevin. *Sex and Vanity: A Novel*
Landau, Alexis. *Those Who Are Saved*
Leavitt, David. ★*Shelter in Place*
Macdonald, Ross. *The Goodbye Look*
Macdonald, Ross. *Sleeping Beauty*

McLaughlin, Emma. *The Nanny Diaries: A Novel*

Medie, Peace A. *His Only Wife: A Novel*

Murdoch, Iris. *An Accidental Man*

Osborne, Lawrence. *The Glass Kingdom: A Novel*

Osborne, Lawrence. *Only to Sleep: A Philip Marlowe Novel*

Penny, Louise. ★*All the Devils Are Here*

Pomerantz, Sharon. *Rich Boy*

Quartey, Kwei. ★*Sleep Well, My Lady*

Rindell, Suzanne. ★*The Two Mrs. Carlyles*

Siger, Jeffrey. *Mykonos After Midnight: A Chief Inspector Kaldis Mystery*

Slaughter, Karin. *The Kept Woman*

Torre, A. R. *Every Last Secret*

Vatner, Jonathan. *Carnegie Hill: A Novel*

Waugh, Evelyn. ★*Vile Bodies*

Wodehouse, P. G. *My Man Jeeves*

RICH PEOPLE — RELATIONS WITH POOR PEOPLE

Forster, E. M. ★*Howards End*

Rich People Problems. Kwan, Kevin

Rich Richardson series [Series]. Beach, Edward L.

RICH WOMEN

Bourne, Joanna. ★*My Lord and Spymaster*

Bradford, Barbara Taylor. ★*A Woman of Substance*

Fowler, Therese. *A Well-Behaved Woman: A Novel of the Vanderbilts*

James, Henry. *Daisy Miller*

Knight, Renee. *The Secretary: A Novel*

Landragin, Alex. ★*Crossings: Consisting of Three Manuscripts : The Education of a Monster : City of Ghosts : Tales Of*

Malerman, Josh. *Unbury Carol*

Pitoniak, Anna. *Necessary People*

Sanders, Lawrence. *McNally's Dilemma*

Stout, Rex. *The Doorbell Rang*

RICHARD III, KING OF ENGLAND, 1452-1485

Penman, Sharon Kay. *The Sunne in Splendour*

Scott, Walter. ★*Ivanhoe*

Richard Hannay adventures [Series]. Buchan, John

Richard Nottingham mysteries [Series]. Nickson, Chris

Richard Oppenheimer novels [Series]. Gilbers, Harald

Richardson, C. S.

The End of the Alphabet

RICHARDSON, RICH (FICTITIOUS CHARACTER)

Beach, Edward L. *Run Silent, Run Deep*

Richardson, Samuel

★*Clarissa, Or, the History of a Young Lady*

★*Pamela: Or, Virtue Rewarded*

Richler, Mordecai

Barney's Version: A Novel

Solomon Gursky Was Here

Richler, Nancy

Your Mouth Is Lovely: A Novel

Richman, Alyson

The Secret of Clouds

Richmond, Michelle

No One You Know

RICHMOND, VIRGINIA

Cornwell, Patricia Daniels. *Postmortem*

★*Ricochet*. Brown, Sandra

The **Riddle** of St. Leonard's: An Owen Archer Mystery.. Robb, Candace M.

★*Riders* of the Purple Sage. Grey, Zane

Riders on the Storm : A Sam McCain Mystery. Gorman, Edward

Ridgeline: a Novel. Punke, Michael

Ridley, Erica

The Duke Heist

★*The Perks of Loving a Wallflower*

Ridpath, Michael

Far North

The **Right** Mistake: The Further Philosophical Investigations of Socrates Fortlow. Mosley, Walter

The **Right** Sort of Man. Montclair, Allison

★The **Right** Swipe. Rai, Alisha

RIGHT-WING EXTREMISTS

Bolano, Roberto. ★*Nazi Literature in the Americas*

Haddam, Jane. *Hardscrabble Road*

Spillane, Mickey. *The Goliath Bone*

RIGHTEOUS GENTILES IN THE HOLOCAUST

Bellow, Saul. *The Bellarosa Connection*

Keneally, Thomas. ★*Schindler's List*

Orringer, Julie. ★*The Flight Portfolio: A Novel*

Riley Wolfe novels [Series]. Lindsay, Jeffry P.

Riley, Lucinda

The Girl on the Cliff: A Novel

Riley, Vanessa

★*A Duke, the Lady, and a Baby*

★*An Earl, the Girl, and a Toddler*

★*Island Queen*

Rimmer, Kelly

Before I Let You Go

Truths I Never Told You

★*The Warsaw Orphan: A Wwii Novel*

Rindell, Suzanne

The Other Typist

★*The Two Mrs. Carlyles*

Rinehart, Mary Roberts

The Circular Staircase

Miss Pinkerton

The **Ring** of Death. Spencer, Sally

Ring of Fire. Taylor, Brad

Ring Shout. Clark, P. Djeli

RINGS

Child, Lee. *The Midnight Line*

RIO DE JANEIRO, BRAZIL

Garcia-Roza, L. A. *Alone in the Crowd: An Inspector Espinosa Mystery*

Garcia-Roza, L. A. *December Heat*

RIO GRANDE

Fuentes, Carlos. *The Crystal Frontier: A Novel in Nine Stories*

RIO GRANDE VALLEY

MacDonald, John D. *Cinnamon Skin: The Twentieth Adventure of Travis McGee*

Riordan, Kate

The Heatwave

★*Riot* Baby. Onyebuchi, Tochi

Riot Most Uncouth: A Lord Byron Mystery. Friedman, Daniel

RIOTS

Barthelme, Frederick. *Painted Desert: A Novel*
Bump, Gabriel. ★*Everywhere You Don't Belong: A Novel*
Gunaratne, Guy. *In Our Mad and Furious City*
Marston, Edward. *The Roaring Boy: A Novel*

Ripley novels [Series]. Highsmith, Patricia

Ripley, Mike

Mr Campion's Coven
Mr Campion's Fault
Mr. Campion's War

RIPLEY, TOM (FICTITIOUS CHARACTER)

Highsmith, Patricia. ★*The Talented Mr. Ripley*

*The **Ripper's** Shadow*. Rowland, Laura Joh

Ripper, Kris

The Hate Project
The Life Revamp
The Love Study

Ripper: a Novel. Allende, Isabel

*The **Rise** and Fall of D.O.D.O.: A Novel*. Stephenson, Neal

*The **Rise** of Endymion*. Simmons, Dan

★*The **Rising** Sea: A Novel from the Numa Files*. Cussler, Clive

*The **Rising** Tide: A Novel of World War II*. Shaara, Jeff

RISK

Deutermann, Peter T. *The Iceman*
Heller, Peter. ★*The Dog Stars: A Novel*

*The **Risk** Agent*. Pearson, Ridley

*The **Risk** Pool*. Russo, Richard

Risky Play. Van Dyken, Rachel

RITES AND CEREMONIES

Awad, Mona. *Bunny*
Gilligan, Ruth. *The Butchers' Blessing*
Straub, Peter. ★*A Dark Matter: A Novel*

Rites of Passage. Golding, William

Ritter, Josh

The Great Glorious Goddamn of It All

Ritter, Todd

Devil's Night

RIVER BOAT PILOTS

Forester, C. S. *The African Queen*

RIVER BOATS

Melville, Herman. *The Confidence-Man: His Masquerade*

*A **River** Called Time*. Newland, Courttia

*The **River** King*. Hoffman, Alice

RIVER LIFE

Campbell, Bonnie Jo. *Once Upon a River*

River of Porcupines. Aalborg, Gordon

River of Smoke. Ghosh, Amitav

RIVER TRAVEL

Melville, Herman. *The Confidence-Man: His Masquerade*

*The **River**: a Novel*. Heller, Peter

Rivero, Melissa

The Affairs of the Falcons

RIVERS

Bacigalupi, Paolo. ★*The Water Knife*
Baker, Kage. *The Bird of the River*
Ballard, J. G. ★*The Day of Creation*
Bolton, S. J. *A Dark and Twisted Tide*
George, Nina. *The Little Paris Bookshop*

Greene, Amy. *Long Man*

Rivers of London [Series]. Aaronovitch, Ben

Rivers, Francine

Bridge to Haven
The Masterpiece
★*Redeeming Love*

RIVERS, WILLIAM, 1864-1922

Barker, Pat. ★*The Eye in the Door*
King, Stephen. *Salem's Lot*

Riyria revelations [Series]. Sullivan, Michael J.

★*Rizzio*. Mina, Denise

RIZZOLI, JANE, DETECTIVE (FICTITIOUS CHARACTER)

Gerritsen, Tess. *The Apprentice: A Novel*

Rizzuto, Rahna R.

Shadow Child

★*The **Road***. McCarthy, Cormac

*The **Road** Back*. Remarque, Erich Maria

★*Road Novels 1957-1960*. Kerouac, Jack

Road of Bones: A Billy Boyle World War II Mystery. Benn, James R.

Road Rage. Rendell, Ruth

*The **Road** to Grantchester*. Runcie, James

Road to Nowhere [Series]. Elison, Meg

*The **Road** to Ruin*. Westlake, Donald E.

ROADS

Dixon, Stephen. *Interstate: A Novel*

Roads to freedom [Series]. Sartre, Jean Paul

Roanhorse, Rebecca

★*Black Sun*
Storm of Locusts
★*Trail of Lightning*

Roar. Ahern, Cecelia

*The **Roaring** Boy: A Novel*. Marston, Edward

Roaring twenties [Series]. Bennett, Jenn

★*Rob Roy*. Scott, Walter

ROB ROY, 1671-1734

Scott, Walter. ★*Rob Roy*
Uris, Leon. ★*Trinity*

Rob Tacoma novels [Series]. Coes, Ben

Robards, Karen

The Ultimatum

Robb, Candace M.

★*A Choir of Crows*
The Cross-Legged Knight: An Owen Archer Mystery
A Gift of Sanctuary: An Owen Archer Mystery
A Murdered Peace
The Riddle of St. Leonard's: An Owen Archer Mystery.
A Twisted Vengeance

Robb, J. D.

Connections in Death: An Eve Dallas Novel
Fantasy in Death
Innocent in Death
Leverage in Death: An Eve Dallas Novel
Naked in Death

★*The **Robber** Bridegroom*. Welty, Eudora

ROBBERY

Atkins, Ace. *The Fallen*
Barclay, Linwood. *Far from True: A Novel*
Block, Lawrence. ★*When the Sacred Ginmill Closes*

Fleming, Ian. ★*Goldfinger*
Piccirilli, Tom. *The Last Whisper in the Dark: A Novel*
Price, Richard. *Lush Life*
Ross, Ann B. *Miss Julia Delivers the Goods: A Novel*
Sanders, Lawrence. *McNally's Secret*
Sandford, John. ★*Golden Prey*
Sandford, John. *Storm Prey*
Shannon, Dell. ★*Chaos of Crime*
Stabenow, Dana. *Whisper to the Blood: A Kate Shugak Novel*
Stark, Richard. *Breakout*
Stark, Richard. *Comeback*
Willink, Jocko. *Final Spin*
Youers, Rio. *Lola on Fire*

ROBBERY INVESTIGATION
Mosley, Walter. *All I Did Was Shoot My Man: A Leonid McGill Mystery*
Sandford, John. ★*Golden Prey*
Sandford, John. *Storm Prey*

Robbins, David L.
Last Citadel: A Novel of the Battle of Kursk
War of the Rats: A Novel

Robbins, Tom
Fierce Invalids Home from Hot Climates
★*Jitterbug Perfume*

***Robert* B. Parker's Buckskin**. Knott, Robert
Robert Langdon novels [Series]. Brown, Dan

Roberts, Bethan
★*My Policeman*

Roberts, Nora
★*The Awakening*
★*The Becoming*
Chesapeake Blue
Come Sundown
The Obsession
Sea Swept
Shelter in Place
★*Under Currents*

Robertson, Imogen
Anatomy of Murder
Circle of Shadows
Instruments of Darkness: A Novel
Island of Bones
The Paris Winter

Robertson, Michael
The Baker Street Letters
The Baker Street Translation: A Mystery
The Brothers of Baker Street
Moriarty Returns a Letter: A Baker Street Mystery

Robertson, Robin
The Long Take: A Noir Narrative

***Robicheaux*. Burke, James Lee
★*Robinson* Crusoe**. Defoe, Daniel

ROBINSON, BETTY
Hooper, Elise. *Fast Girls: A Novel of the 1936 Women's Olympic Team*
Tudor, C. J. *The Burning Girls: A Novel*

Robinson, Kim Stanley
Antarctica

Aurora
★*Blue Mars*
★*Green Mars*
The Martians
★*The Ministry for the Future*
New York 2140
★*Red Mars*
The Years of Rice and Salt

Robinson, Marilynne
★*Gilead*
Home
★*Jack*
★*Lila*

Robinson, Peter
All the Colors of Darkness
★*Careless Love*
Children of the Revolution
Close to Home
Cold Is the Grave
The First Cut
Friend of the Devil
In the Dark Places
Innocent Graves: An Inspector Banks Mystery
Piece of My Heart
Playing with Fire
Strange Affair

***Robogenesis*: a Novel**. Wilson, Daniel H.
Robopocalypse novels [Series]. Wilson, Daniel H.

Robotham, Michael
★*Close Your Eyes*
★*Good Girl, Bad Girl: A Novel*
Life or Death
The Night Ferry: A Novel
★*The Other Wife*
★*Say You're Sorry*
★*Suspect*
★*When She Was Good*
★*The Wreckage*

ROBOTICS
Asimov, Isaac. ★*I, Robot*

ROBOTS
Asimov, Isaac. ★*I, Robot*
Banks, Iain. *Use of Weapons*
Bear, Greg. *Anvil of Stars*
Bear, Greg. *The Forge of God*
Cargill, C. Robert. *Day Zero*
Chambers, Becky. ★*A Psalm for the Wild-Built*
Green, Hank. *An Absolutely Remarkable Thing: A Novel*
Hall, Louisa. *Speak*
Ishiguro, Kazuo. ★*Klara and the Sun*
Levin, Adam. *Bubblegum*
Levin, Ira. ★*The Stepford Wives: A Novel*
Stivers, Carole. *The Mother Code*
Stross, Charles. *Neptune's Brood*
Stross, Charles. *Saturn's Children: A Space Opera*
Weinstein, Alexander. *Children of the New World: Stories*
Wells, Martha. *All Systems Red*
Wilson, Daniel H. *The Clockwork Dynasty: A Novel*

Wilson, Daniel H. *Robogenesis: A Novel*

ROBOTS — BEHAVIOR
Asimov, Isaac. ★*I, Robot*

ROCHESTER, NEW YORK
Freudenberger, Nell. *The Newlyweds*

Rochon, Farrah
The Boyfriend Project
The Dating Playbook

ROCK CONCERT TOURS
Brodie, Emma. *Songs in Ursa Major*

ROCK CONCERTS
Robinson, Peter. *Piece of My Heart*
The Rock Eaters: Stories. Peynado, Brenda

ROCK GROUPS
Reid, Taylor Jenkins. ★*Daisy Jones & The Six: A Novel*
Rock Manning Goes for Broke. Anders, Charlie Jane

ROCK MUSIC
Bauman, Bruce. ★*Broken Sleep: An American Dream*
Brodie, Emma. *Songs in Ursa Major*

ROCK MUSICIANS
Blau, Jessica Anya. *Mary Jane: A Novel*
Hill, Joe. *Heart-Shaped Box*
Jimenez, Abby. ★*The Happy Ever After Playlist*
Walton, Dawnie. ★*The Final Revival of Opal & Nev*
Wendig, Chuck. ★*Wanderers: A Novel*

ROCK MUSICIANS — DEATH
Hiaasen, Carl. *Basket Case*
Rock the Boat: A Novel. Dorey-Stein, Beck

Rockaway, Kristin
How to Hack a Heartbreak

ROCKETRY — HISTORY
Michener, James A. *Space*

ROCKETS (ORDNANCE)
Pynchon, Thomas. ★*Gravity's Rainbow*
The Rocks. Nichols, Peter

ROCKY MOUNTAIN REGION
Carr, Robyn. *The Family Gathering*
Carr, Robyn. *What We Find*

RODEOS
Dell, Kari Lynn. *Mistletoe in Texas*
Dell, Kari Lynn. *Reckless in Texas*
Kelton, Elmer. *Hard Ride*
Roderick Alleyn mysteries [Series]. Marsh, Ngaio
Rodham: a Novel. Sittenfeld, Curtis

Rodrigues Fowler, Yara
Stubborn Archivist

RODRIGUEZ, ESTELITA
Barry, Ava. *Windhall*
Burdick, Serena. *Find Me in Havana*

Rodriguez, Linda
Every Broken Trust: A Mystery
Every Hidden Fear: A Skeet Bannion Mystery
Every Last Secret: A Mystery

Rodriques, Elias
All the Water I've Seen Is Running: A Novel

ROEBLING, EMILY WARREN, 1843-1903
Mukherjee, Abir. *Death in the East*
Wood, Tracey Enerson. *The Engineer's Wife: A Novel*

Rogers, Morgan Callan
★*Honey Girl*
A Rogue by Night. Bowen, Kelly
Rogue files [Series]. Jordan, Sophie
Rogue Island. DeSilva, Bruce
The Rogue Not Taken. MacLean, Sarah
The Rogue of Fifth Avenue. Shupe, Joanna
★*A Rogue of Her Own*. Burrowes, Grace
Rogue Spy. Bourne, Joanna
A Rogue's Company. Montclair, Allison

ROGUES
Beverley, Jo. *Tempting Fortune*
Dean, Michael. *I, Hogarth*
Gracie, Anne. *Marry in Scandal*
Steinbeck, John. *Tortilla Flat*
Rogues and remarkable women [Series]. Riley, Vanessa
Rogues redeemed [Series]. Putney, Mary Jo
Rogues to riches [Series]. Burrowes, Grace

Roisin, Fariha
Like a Bird

Rojas Contreras, Ingrid
★*Fruit of the Drunken Tree: A Novel*

Rojstaczer, Stuart
The Mathematician's Shiva: A Novel

ROLE MODELS
Roth, Philip. *The Ghost Writer*

ROLE PLAYING
DeLuca, Jen. ★*Well Met*

ROLE PLAYING GAMES
Darnielle, John. *Wolf in White Van: A Novel*
Ruff, Matt. ★*88 Names*

Rollins, James
Crucible
The Demon Crown: A Sigma Force Novel
The Devil Colony
The Eye of God
★*The Last Odyssey*
The Sixth Extinction: A Sigma Force Novel

Rølvaag, O. E.
★*Giants in the Earth: A Saga of the Prairie*
Roma Sub Rosa series [Series]. Saylor, Steven
Roma: the Novel of Ancient Rome. Saylor, Steven

Romain, Theresa
Fortune Favors the Wicked

ROMAN BRITAIN (55 BCE-449 CE)
Davis, Lindsey. *A Body in the Bathhouse*
Rutherfurd, Edward. *London*

ROMAN EMPERORS
George, Margaret. *The Splendor Before the Dark: A Novel of the Emperor Nero*
Graves, Robert. *Claudius the God and His Wife Messalina: The Troublesome Reign of Tiberius Claudius Caesar, Emperor*
Graves, Robert. ★*I, Claudius: From the Autobiography of Tiberius Claudius, Born 10 B.C., Murdered and Deified A.D. 54*
Yourcenar, Marguerite. ★*Memoirs of Hadrian: And Reflections on the Composition of Memoirs of Hadrian*

ROMAN EMPIRE (27 BCE-476 CE)
Afshar, Tessa. *Jewel of the Nile*

Afshar, Tessa. *Thief of Corinth*
Davis, Lindsey. *A Comedy of Terrors: A Flavia Albia Novel*
Davis, Lindsey. *The Ides of April: A Flavia Albia Mystery*
Davis, Lindsey. *One Virgin Too Many*
George, Margaret. *The Confessions of Young Nero*
George, Margaret. *The Splendor Before the Dark: A Novel of the Emperor Nero*
Graves, Robert. *Claudius the God and His Wife Messalina: The Troublesome Reign of Tiberius Claudius Caesar, Emperor*
Graves, Robert. ★*I, Claudius: From the Autobiography of Tiberius Claudius, Born 10 B.C., Murdered and Deified A.D. 54*
Kane, Ben. *Spartacus: The Gladiator*
Kidd, Sue Monk. ★*The Book of Longings*
Pears, Iain. *The Dream of Scipio*
Saylor, Steven. *Roma: The Novel of Ancient Rome*
Sienkiewicz, Henryk. ★*Quo Vadis: A Story of Faith in the Last Days of the Roman Empire*
Wallace, Lew. ★*Ben-Hur*
Yourcenar, Marguerite. ★*Memoirs of Hadrian: And Reflections on the Composition of Memoirs of Hadrian*

ROMAN REPUBLIC (509-27 BCE)
McCullough, Colleen. *The First Man in Rome*
Saylor, Steven. *The Judgment of Caesar: A Novel of Ancient Rome*
Saylor, Steven. *A Mist of Prophecies*
Saylor, Steven. *Raiders of the Nile: A Novel of the Ancient World*
Saylor, Steven. *Roma: The Novel of Ancient Rome*
Saylor, Steven. *Rubicon*
Saylor, Steven. *The Seven Wonders: A Novel of the Ancient World*
Saylor, Steven. *The Triumph of Caesar: A Novel of Ancient Rome*
Saylor, Steven. *Wrath of the Furies: A Novel of the Ancient World*
★*The Roman Spring of Mrs. Stone*. Williams, Tennessee

ROMANCE WRITERS
Brookner, Anita. *Hotel Du Lac*
Turner, Bethany. *The Secret Life of Sarah Hollenbeck*

ROMANCE WRITING
Williams, Tia. ★*Seven Days in June: A Novel*
Romancing the Duke. Dare, Tessa

ROMANI WOMEN
Bradley, C. Alan. *A Red Herring Without Mustard*
Hugo, Victor. ★*The Hunchback of Notre Dame*

ROMANIA
Bellow, Saul. *The Dean's December: A Novel*
Furst, Alan. *Blood of Victory: A Novel*
King, Laurie R. *Castle Shade*
Veletzos, Roxanne. *The Girl They Left Behind*

ROMANIANS IN FOREIGN COUNTRIES
Bailey, Paul. *Uncle Rudolf*

ROMANIES
Adler-Olsen, Jussi. *The Marco Effect: A Department Q Novel*
Siger, Jeffrey. *Target Tinos: An Inspector Kaldis Mystery*

Romano-Lax, Andromeda
The Spanish Bow

ROMANOV DYNASTY (1613-1917)
Akunin, B. *The Coronation: The Further Adventures of Erast Fandorin*
Akunin, B. *Sister Pelagia and the White Bulldog: A Mystery*
Alpsten, Ellen. *Tsarina*
Dostoyevsky, Fyodor. ★*The Brothers Karamazov*

Dostoyevsky, Fyodor. *Notes from Underground*
Gogol, Nikolai Vasilievich. ★*Dead Souls*
Richler, Nancy. *Your Mouth Is Lovely: A Novel*
Stachniak, Eva. *The Winter Palace: A Novel of Catherine the Great*
Tolstoy, Leo. ★*Anna Karenina*
Tolstoy, Leo. ★*War and Peace*
Turgenev, Ivan Sergeevich. ★*Fathers and Sons*
The Romanov Ransom. Cussler, Clive

ROMANS
Saylor, Steven. *Raiders of the Nile: A Novel of the Ancient World*
Saylor, Steven. *Roma: The Novel of Ancient Rome*
Saylor, Steven. *Wrath of the Furies: A Novel of the Ancient World*

ROMANS IN GREAT BRITAIN
Davis, Lindsey. *A Body in the Bathhouse*

ROMANTIC COMEDIES
Adams, Lyssa Kay. *The Bromance Book Club*
Alexander, Jennet. *I Kissed a Girl*
Allain, Suzanne. *Miss Lattimore's Letter*
Bailey, Tessa. *Fix Her Up*
Bellefleur, Alexandria. *Hang the Moon*
Bellefleur, Alexandria. *Written in the Stars*
Christopher, Andie J. *Not the Girl You Marry*
Clayborn, Kate. *Love Lettering*
Cochrun, Alison. *The Charm Offensive*
Cocks, Heather. *The Heir Affair*
Cocks, Heather. *The Royal We*
Dade, Olivia. *All the Feels*
Dade, Olivia. *Spoiler Alert*
Danan, Rosie. *The Roommate*
Daria, Alexis. ★*A Lot Like Adios*
Daria, Alexis. ★*You Had Me at Hola*
Davidson, MaryJanice. *Truth, Lies, and Second Dates*
DeLuca, Jen. *Well Matched*
DeLuca, Jen. ★*Well Met*
Dev, Sonali. ★*Incense and Sensibility*
Dev, Sonali. ★*Recipe for Persuasion*
Fields, Hilary. *Last Chance Llama Ranch*
Glass, Seressia. ★*The Love Con*
Greer, Andrew Sean. ★*Less*
Hall, Alexis. ★*Boyfriend Material*
Hall, Alexis. *Rosaline Palmer Takes the Cake*
Harris, E. Lynn. *Not a Day Goes By: A Novel*
Hazelwood, Ali. *The Love Hypothesis*
Heger, Amanda. *Crazy Cupid Love*
Henry, Emily. *People We Meet on Vacation*
Heron, Farah. *Accidentally Engaged*
Hibbert, Talia. ★*Act Your Age, Eve Brown*
Hibbert, Talia. ★*Get a Life, Chloe Brown*
Hibbert, Talia. ★*Take a Hint, Dani Brown*
Hockman, Angie. *Shipped*
Isaac, Kara. *Then There Was You*
Jackson, K. M. *How to Marry Keanu Reeves in 90 Days*
Jalaluddin, Uzma. ★*Ayesha at Last*
Jimenez, Abby. ★*The Happy Ever After Playlist*
Jimenez, Abby. *Life's Too Short*
Kamal, Soniah. *Unmarriageable: A Novel*
Lalli, Sonya. *A Holly Jolly Diwali*
Lalli, Sonya. *The Matchmaker's List*

Lau, Jackie. *Donut Fall in Love*
Lauren, Christina. *Dating You / Hating You*
Lauren, Christina. *In a Holidaze*
Lauren, Christina. *The Soulmate Equation*
Lim, Roselle. *Vanessa Yu's Magical Paris Tea Shop*
Lipman, Elinor. *Good Riddance*
Marsh, Nicola. *The Boy Toy*
McFarlane, Mhairi. *Don't You Forget About Me*
McFarlane, Mhairi. *If I Never Met You: A Novel*
McQuiston, Casey. ★*One Last Stop*
McQuiston, Casey. ★*Red, White & Royal Blue: A Novel*
Meltzer, Jean. ★*The Matzah Ball*
Menon, Lily. *Make up Break Up: A Novel*
Murphy, Julie. *If the Shoe Fits*
O'Leary, Beth. *The Flatshare: A Novel*
O'Leary, Beth. *The Switch*
Orenstein, Hannah. *Love at First Like*
Parker, Lucy. *The Austen Playbook*
Parker, Lucy. *Battle Royal*
Ripper, Kris. *The Hate Project*
Ripper, Kris. *The Life Revamp*
Ripper, Kris. *The Love Study*
Rochon, Farrah. *The Dating Playbook*
Rogers, Morgan Callan. ★*Honey Girl*
Ruiz, Sarah Grunder. *Love, Lists, and Fancy Ships*
Simsion, Graeme C. *The Rosie Effect*
Simsion, Graeme C. ★*The Rosie Project*
Simsion, Graeme C. *The Rosie Result*
Sittenfeld, Curtis. *Eligible: A Novel*
Solomon, Rachel Lynn. *Weather Girl*
Sosa, Mia. ★*The Worst Best Man*
Sterling, Erin. *The Ex Hex*
Thorne, Sally. *Second First Impressions*
Tieu, Julie. *The Donut Trap*
Trigiani, Adriana. *Big Stone Gap: A Novel*
Waters, Martha. ★*To Have and to Hoax: A Novel*
Waters, Martha. *To Love and to Loathe: A Novel*
Williams, Denise. *The Fastest Way to Fall*
Williams, Denise. *How to Fail at Flirting*
Winfrey, Kerry. *Not Like the Movies*
Winfrey, Kerry. *Waiting for Tom Hanks: A Novel*

ROMANTIC COMEDY FILMS
Turner, Bethany. *Wooing Cadie McCaffrey*

ROMANTIC LOVE
Adams, Lyssa Kay. *The Bromance Book Club*
Beagle, Peter S. *A Fine and Private Place*
Bellefleur, Alexandria. *Hang the Moon*
Benedict, Marie. ★*Lady Clementine*
Bloom, Amy. ★*White Houses: A Novel*
Dare, Tessa. *Romancing the Duke*
Dev, Sonali. *A Distant Heart*
El-Mohtar, Amal. ★*This Is How You Lose the Time War*
Follett, Ken. ★*The Evening and the Morning*
Garcia Marquez, Gabriel. ★*Love in the Time of Cholera*
George, Nina. *The Book of Dreams*
Greeley, Molly. *The Clergyman's Wife*
Hale, Shannon. *Austenland: A Novel*

Hall, Tarquin. *The Case of the Love Commandos: From the Files of Vish Puri, India's Most Private Investigator*
Hazzard, Shirley. ★*The Transit of Venus*
Henry, Emily. *People We Meet on Vacation*
Hoang, Helen. ★*The Bride Test*
Hoang, Helen. ★*The Heart Principle*
James, Eloisa. *The Ugly Duchess*
Kincaid, Jamaica. *See Now Then*
Miller, Holly. ★*The Sight of You*
Richardson, C. S. *The End of the Alphabet*
Robinson, Marilynne. ★*Jack*
Saramago, Jose. *Death with Interruptions*
Schlink, Bernhard. *Olga*
Scott, Walter. ★*Ivanhoe*
Shreve, Anita. *The Last Time They Met: A Novel*
Smith, Ali. ★*How to Be Both*
Sundaresan, Indu. *The Splendor of Silence: A Novel*
Thayne, RaeAnne. *The Cliff House*
Turner, Bethany. *Wooing Cadie McCaffrey*
Waller, Robert James. ★*The Bridges of Madison County*
Williams, Beatriz. *All the Ways We Said Goodbye: A Novel of the Ritz Paris*

ROMANTIC SUSPENSE
Ashley & JaQuavis. *The Cartel*
Bell, Shelly. *At His Mercy*
Bell, Shelly. *For His Pleasure*
Billingsley, ReShonda Tate. *A Little Bit of Karma: A Novel*
Brown, Sandra. ★*Blind Tiger*
Brown, Sandra. ★*Ricochet*
Brown, Sandra. *Tailspin*
Brown, Sandra. *The Witness*
Buchman, M. L. *Pure Heat*
De Leon, Aya. ★*A Spy in the Struggle*
Dimon, HelenKay. *Her Other Secret*
Dodd, Christina. *Because I'm Watching*
Dodd, Christina. *Obsession Falls*
Dodd, Christina. *The Woman Who Couldn't Scream*
Du Maurier, Daphne. *Jamaica Inn*
Garwood, Julie. *Wired*
Holt, Victoria. *The Black Opal*
Hunt, April. *Deadly Obsession*
Jackson, Brenda. *Forged in Desire*
Krentz, Jayne Ann. ★*All the Colors of Night*
Krentz, Jayne Ann. *Secret Sisters*
Krentz, Jayne Ann. *When All the Girls Have Gone*
Malpas, Jodi Ellen. *Leave Me Breathless*
Quick, Amanda. *'til Death Do Us Part*
Quick, Amanda. *Close Up*
Quick, Amanda. *The Girl Who Knew Too Much*
Quick, Amanda. ★*The Lady Has a Past*
Quick, Amanda. *The Other Lady Vanishes*
Quick, Amanda. *Otherwise Engaged*
Robards, Karen. *The Ultimatum*
Robb, J. D. *Connections in Death: An Eve Dallas Novel*
Robb, J. D. *Fantasy in Death*
Robb, J. D. *Innocent in Death*
Robb, J. D. *Leverage in Death: An Eve Dallas Novel*
Robb, J. D. *Naked in Death*

Roberts, Nora. *Come Sundown*
Roberts, Nora. *The Obsession*
Roberts, Nora. ★*Under Currents*
Snyder, Suleikha. *Big Bad Wolf*
Sorenson, Jill. *Aftershock*
Sparks, Nicholas. *The Guardian*

ROME

Afshar, Tessa. *Jewel of the Nile*
Davis, Lindsey. *A Body in the Bathhouse*
Davis, Lindsey. *A Comedy of Terrors: A Flavia Albia Novel*
Davis, Lindsey. *The Ides of April: A Flavia Albia Mystery*
Davis, Lindsey. *One Virgin Too Many*
George, Margaret. *The Confessions of Young Nero*
George, Margaret. *The Splendor Before the Dark: A Novel of the Emperor Nero*
Graves, Robert. *Claudius the God and His Wife Messalina: The Troublesome Reign of Tiberius Claudius Caesar, Emperor*
Graves, Robert. ★*I, Claudius: From the Autobiography of Tiberius Claudius, Born 10 B.C., Murdered and Deified A.D. 54*
Kane, Ben. *Spartacus: The Gladiator*
McCullough, Colleen. *The First Man in Rome*
Pears, Iain. *The Dream of Scipio*
Saylor, Steven. *The House of the Vestals: The Investigations of Gordianus the Finder*
Saylor, Steven. *The Judgment of Caesar: A Novel of Ancient Rome*
Saylor, Steven. *A Mist of Prophecies*
Saylor, Steven. *Raiders of the Nile: A Novel of the Ancient World*
Saylor, Steven. *Roma: The Novel of Ancient Rome*
Saylor, Steven. *Rubicon*
Saylor, Steven. *The Seven Wonders: A Novel of the Ancient World*
Saylor, Steven. *The Triumph of Caesar: A Novel of Ancient Rome*
Saylor, Steven. *Wrath of the Furies: A Novel of the Ancient World*
Sienkiewicz, Henryk. ★*Quo Vadis: A Story of Faith in the Last Days of the Roman Empire*
Yourcenar, Marguerite. ★*Memoirs of Hadrian: And Reflections on the Composition of Memoirs of Hadrian*

ROME, ITALY

Dazieri, Sandrone. *Kill the Angel*
Dazieri, Sandrone. *Kill the Father*
Dazieri, Sandrone. *Kill the King*
Hewson, David. *The Garden of Evil*
Hewson, David. *A Season for the Dead*
Leithauser, Brad. *The Promise of Elsewhere*
Pears, Iain. *Death and Restoration*
Pears, Iain. *The Immaculate Deception*
Pears, Iain. *The Last Judgement*
Poole, Sara. *The Borgia Mistress*
Schami, Rafik. *Sophia: Or the Beginning of All Tales*
Williams, Tennessee. ★*The Roman Spring of Mrs. Stone*

Romero, George A.

The Living Dead

ROMULUS (ROMAN MYTHOLOGY)

Saylor, Steven. *Roma: The Novel of Ancient Rome*

Rook & **Rose** [Series]. Carrick, M. A.

ROOKIE POLICE

Steinhauer, Olen. *The Bridge of Sighs*

*The **Room** on Rue Amelie*. Harmel, Kristin

★*A **Room** with a View*. Forster, E. M.

★***Room:*** *a Novel*. Donoghue, Emma

Roomies. Lauren, Christina

*The **Roommate***. Danan, Rosie

ROOMMATES

Aridjis, Chloe. *Asunder*
Danan, Rosie. *The Roommate*
Dean, Pamela. *Tam Lin*
Gottlieb, Eli. *Best Boy: A Novel*
Henson, Pene. *Into the Blue*
Murray, Paul. *Skippy Dies*
O'Leary, Beth. *The Flatshare: A Novel*
Styles, Toy. *Redbone*

Rooney, Kathleen

★*Cher Ami and Major Whittlesey*
★*Lillian Boxfish Takes a Walk*

Rooney, Sally

★*Beautiful World, Where Are You*
★*Conversations with Friends*
Normal People: A Novel

Roorbach, Bill

Life Among Giants: A Novel

ROOSEVELT, ELEANOR, 1884-1962

Bloom, Amy. ★*White Houses: A Novel*
Cleary, Jon. *The Sundowners*
Dexter, Pete. ★*Deadwood*
Faulks, Sebastian. *Jeeves and the Wedding Bells*
Marsh, Ngaio. *A Man Lay Dead*
Roosevelt, Elliott. ★*Murder and the First Lady*
Roosevelt, Elliott. *Murder at Midnight*
Roosevelt, Elliott. *Murder in the Map Room: An Eleanor Roosevelt Mystery*
Roosevelt, Elliott. *Murder in the Oval Office*
Rose, Heather. *The Museum of Modern Love*

Roosevelt, Elliott

★*Murder and the First Lady*
Murder at Midnight
Murder in the Map Room: An Eleanor Roosevelt Mystery
Murder in the Oval Office

ROOSEVELT, THEODORE, 1858-1919

Carr, Caleb. ★*The Alienist*

*The **Rope**: an Anna Pigeon Novel*. Barr, Nevada

***Rosaline** Palmer Takes the Cake*. Hall, Alexis

Rosato and Associates novels [Series]. Scottoline, Lisa

Rose. Smith, Martin Cruz

ROSE, BILLY, 1899-1966

Bellow, Saul. *The Bellarosa Connection*

Rose, Heather

The Museum of Modern Love

Rose, M. J.

★*Cartier's Hope*
Tiffany Blues: A Novel

★***Rosemary's** Baby: A Novel*. Levin, Ira

Rosen, Leonard J.

The Kortelisy Escape

Rosen, Renee

Dollface: A Novel of the Roaring Twenties
The Social Graces

ROSENBERG, ETHEL, 1915-1953
  Doctorow, E. L. ★*The Book of Daniel: A Novel*
  Schanbacher, Gary Lester. *Crossing Purgatory*
Rosenfelt, David
  Black and Blue: A Doug Brock Thriller
  Blackout
  ★*Dog Eat Dog*
Rosenfield, Kat
  No One Will Miss Her
***Rosewater*.** Thompson, Tade
The *Rosewater* Insurrection. Thompson, Tade
The *Rosewater* Redemption. Thompson, Tade
The *Rosie* Effect. Simsion, Graeme C.
Rosie novels (Graeme Simsion) [Series]. Simsion, Graeme C.
★*The **Rosie** Project*. Simsion, Graeme C.
The *Rosie* Result. Simsion, Graeme C.
Roslund, Anders
  Cell 8
  ★*Knock Knock*
  Pen 33
Rosnay, Tatiana de
  ★*Flowers of Darkness*
  ★*Sarah's Key*
Rosner, Jennifer
  ★*The Yellow Bird Sings*
Ross, Adam
  Mr. Peanut
Ross, Ann B.
  Miss Julia Delivers the Goods: A Novel
  ★*Miss Julia Happily Ever After*
  Miss Julia Knows a Thing or Two
  Miss Julia Takes the Wheel
  Miss Julia Throws a Wedding
ROSS, CARTER (FICTITIOUS CHARACTER)
  Parks, Brad. *The Player: A Mystery*
The *Rossetti* Letter: A Novel. Phillips, Christi
Rossner, Rena
  The Light of the Midnight Stars
Roth, Henry
  ★*Call It Sleep*
  A Diving Rock on the Hudson
  From Bondage
  Requiem for Harlem
  A Star Shines Over Mt. Morris Park
Roth, Joseph
  The Collected Stories of Joseph Roth
Roth, Philip
  ★*American Pastoral*
  ★*The Anatomy Lesson*
  ★*Everyman*
  Exit Ghost
  The Ghost Writer
  ★*Goodbye, Columbus, and Five Short Stories*
  The Great American Novel
  ★*The Human Stain*
  I Married a Communist
  Indignation
  ★*Nemesis*
  ★*The Plot Against America*
  ★*Portnoy's Complaint*
  Sabbath's Theater
  Zuckerman Bound
  Zuckerman Unbound
ROTH, PHILIP, 1933-
  Roth, Philip. ★*American Pastoral*
  Roth, Philip. ★*The Anatomy Lesson*
  Roth, Philip. ★*Everyman*
  Roth, Philip. *Exit Ghost*
  Roth, Philip. *The Ghost Writer*
  Roth, Philip. *I Married a Communist*
  Roth, Philip. *Zuckerman Bound*
  Roth, Philip. *Zuckerman Unbound*
Rothfuss, Patrick
  ★*The Name of the Wind*
  ★*The Wise Man's Fear*
Rothschild, Hannah
  The Improbability of Love: A Novel
The *Rotters'* Club. Coe, Jonathan
Rotters' Club [Series]. Coe, Jonathan
Rouda, Kaira Sturdivant
  Best Day Ever: A Novel
  The Favorite Daughter
Rougon-Macquart [Series]. Zola, Emile
★*The **Round** House: A Novel*. Erdrich, Louise
Rous, Emma
  The Perfect Guests
Row, Jess
  Your Face in Mine: A Novel
Rowell, Rainbow
  Landline
Rowland, Laura Joh
  The Hangman's Secret
  The Incense Game: A Novel of Feudal Japan
  The Iris Fan: A Novel of Feudal Japan
  The Ripper's Shadow
  The Shogun's Daughter: A Novel of Feudal Japan
  The Snow Empress
Rowland, Russell
  Cold Country: A Novel
Rowley, Steven
  ★*The Guncle: A Novel*
Rowling, J. K.
  The Casual Vacancy
Roxane Weary novels [Series]. Lepionka, Kristen
Roxanna Slade. Price, Reynolds
Roy, Anuradha
  All the Lives We Never Lived: A Novel
  An Atlas of Impossible Longing
Roy, Arundhati
  ★*The God of Small Things*
  ★*The Ministry of Utmost Happiness: A Novel*
Roy, Lori
  Bent Road
  ★*Gone Too Long: A Novel*
Roy, Lucinda
  The Freedom Race

*A **Royal** Affair.* Montclair, Allison

ROYAL AIR FORCE VETERANS

    Lawton, John. *Then We Take Berlin*

***Royal** Holiday.* Guillory, Jasmine

ROYAL HOUSES

    Callender, Kacen. *King of the Rising*

    Callender, Kacen. *Queen of the Conquered*

    Cocks, Heather. *The Heir Affair*

    Cole, Alyssa. ★*How to Catch a Queen*

    Gregory, Philippa. *The Kingmaker's Daughter*

    Gregory, Philippa. *The Taming of the Queen*

    Harper, Karen. *The Queen's Secret: A Novel of England's World War II Queen*

    Hurley, Kameron. *The Stars Are Legion*

    Martin, George R. R. *Fire & Blood: 300 Years Before a Game of Thrones (A Targaryen History)*

    Montclair, Allison. *A Royal Affair*

    Penman, Sharon Kay. *Here Be Dragons*

    Penman, Sharon Kay. *The Queen's Man: A Medieval Mystery*

    Penman, Sharon Kay. *When Christ and His Saints Slept*

    Raybourn, Deanna. ★*A Murderous Relation*

    Shannon, Samantha. *The Priory of the Orange Tree*

    Weir, Alison. *Katharine Parr, the Sixth Wife*

ROYAL PRETENDERS

    Eason, K. *How Rory Thorne Destroyed the Multiverse*

    Penman, Sharon Kay. *The Queen's Man: A Medieval Mystery*

***Royal** rewards* [Series]. Romain, Theresa

*The **Royal** We.* Cocks, Heather

***Royal** wedding novels* [Series]. Hauck, Rachel

ROYAL WEDDINGS

    Hauck, Rachel. *Once Upon a Prince*

Rozan, S. J.

    ★*The Art of Violence*

    ★*Paper Son*

    The Shanghai Moon: A Lydia Chin/Bill Smith Novel

    Winter and Night

Rubart, James L.

    ★*The Man He Never Was*

RUBBER PLANTATIONS

    Tanabe, Karin. *A Hundred Suns*

Rubicon. Saylor, Steven

***Ruby:** a Novel.* Bond, Cynthia

★***Rubyfruit** Jungle.* Brown, Rita Mae

***Ruddy** McCann novels* [Series]. Cameron, W. Bruce

RUDENESS

    Berger, Thomas. ★*Neighbors: A Novel*

Ruff, Matt

    ★*88 Names*

    Lovecraft Country: A Novel

RUGBY FOOTBALL

    Hibbert, Talia. ★*Take a Hint, Dani Brown*

RUGS

    Barker, Clive. ★*Weaveworld*

*The **Ruin** of Kings.* Lyons, Jenn

*The **Ruins:** a Novel.* Smith, Scott

Ruiz Zafon, Carlos

    The Angel's Game

    The Labyrinth of the Spirits

    The Prisoner of Heaven

    ★*The Shadow of the Wind*

Ruiz, Sarah Grunder

    Love, Lists, and Fancy Ships

***Ruler** of the Night.* Morrell, David

RULERS

    Alpsten, Ellen. *Tsarina*

    Andersen, Laura. *The Boleyn Deceit*

    Andersen, Laura. ★*The Boleyn King*

    Andersen, Laura. *The Boleyn Reckoning*

    Andrews, Mesu. *Isaiah's Daughter: A Novel of Prophets and Kings*

    Beagle, Peter S. ★*The Last Unicorn*

    Bear, Elizabeth. *The Red-Stained Wings*

    Bear, Elizabeth. *The Stone in the Skull*

    Binet, Laurent. *Civilizations*

    Black, Benjamin. *Wolf on a String: A Novel*

    Calvino, Italo. *Invisible Cities*

    Campbell, Lisbeth. *The Vanished Queen*

    Chakraborty, S. A. *The Empire of Gold*

    Chakraborty, S. A. *The Kingdom of Copper: A Novel*

    Cole, Alyssa. ★*How to Catch a Queen*

    Cornwell, Bernard. *The Winter King: A Novel of Arthur*

    Druon, Maurice. *The Iron King*

    Dumas, Alexandre. ★*The Man in the Iron Mask*

    Edghill, India. *Queenmaker: A Novel of King David's Queen*

    Franklin, Ariana. *Mistress of the Art of Death*

    Franklin, Ariana. *The Siege Winter*

    George, Margaret. *The Confessions of Young Nero*

    Greenwood, Kerry. *Out of the Black Land*

    Gregory, Philippa. *The White Princess*

    Grossman, Lev. *The Magician King: A Novel*

    Grossman, Lev. *The Magician's Land: A Novel*

    Herbert, Frank. ★*Dune*

    Hodgson, Antonia. *The Last Confession of Thomas Hawkins*

    Iggulden, Conn. *The Abbot's Tale*

    Kuang, R. F. ★*The Dragon Republic*

    Le Guin, Ursula K. *The Other Wind*

    Leckie, Ann. *Ancillary Justice*

    Leckie, Ann. *Ancillary Mercy*

    Leckie, Ann. *Ancillary Sword*

    Leckie, Ann. ★*The Raven Tower*

    Liu, Ken. *The Wall of Storms*

    Martin, George R. R. *Fire & Blood: 300 Years Before a Game of Thrones (A Targaryen History)*

    Parris, S. J. *Treachery*

    Penman, Sharon Kay. *Here Be Dragons*

    Penman, Sharon Kay. *The Sunne in Splendour*

    Pike, Signe. *The Forgotten Kingdom: A Novel*

    Pratchett, Terry. *Pyramids: The Book of Going Forth*

    Renault, Mary. *Funeral Games*

    Renault, Mary. *The Persian Boy*

    Rowland, Laura Joh. *The Iris Fan: A Novel of Feudal Japan*

    Sansom, C. J. ★*Lamentation*

    Sansom, C. J. ★*Sovereign*

    Self, Will. *The Book of Dave: A Revelation of the Recent Past and the Distant Future*

    Shaykh, Hanan. ★*One Thousand and One Nights: A Sparkling Retelling of the Beloved Classic*

Stewart, Mary. ★*The Hollow Hills*
Sullivan, Michael J. *Theft of Swords*
Suri, Tasha. ★*Empire of Sand*
Sutcliff, Rosemary. *Sword at Sunset*
Tolkien, J. R. R. *The Fall of Gondolin*
Tolstaya, Tatyana. *The Slynx*
Updike, John. *Gertrude and Claudius*
Wagers, K. B. *There Before the Chaos*
Yourcenar, Marguerite. ★*Memoirs of Hadrian: And Reflections on the Composition of Memoirs of Hadrian*

RULERS — SUCCESSION
Addison, Katherine. ★*The Goblin Emperor*
Gratton, Tessa. *The Queens of Innis Lear*
Massey, Sujata. *The Satapur Moonstone*

RULES
Center, Katherine. *What You Wish For*
Rowley, Steven. ★*The Guncle: A Novel*
Sager, Riley. *Lock Every Door: A Novel*
Rules for Visiting. Kane, Jessica Francis
Rules of Civility: A Novel. Towles, Amor
The *Rules of Magic: A Novel*. Hoffman, Alice
★*Rules of Prey*. Sandford, John
Rules of scoundrels [Series]. MacLean, Sarah
Rum Punch. Leonard, Elmore

RUMOR
Abbott, Megan E. *The Fever*
Ashley, Jennifer. *The Madness of Lord Ian Mackenzie*
Bilenchi, Romano. ★*The Chill*
Dare, Tessa. *Do You Want to Start a Scandal*
Delinsky, Barbara. *Lake News: A Novel*
Grushin, Olga. *The Line*
King, Laurie R. *Castle Shade*
Long, Julie Anne. *Angel in a Devil's Arms*
Marias, Javier. *Thus Bad Begins: A Novel*
Wilsner, Meryl. ★*Something to Talk About*
Rumor Has It. Hodges, Cheris F.
Rumor novels [Series]. Hodges, Cheris F.
Run. Patchett, Ann
Run Away. Coben, Harlan
★*Run Me to Earth: A Novel*. Yoon, Paul
Run Silent, Run Deep. Beach, Edward L.
The *Runaway*. Overton, Hollie

RUNAWAY BOYS
Freeman, Brian. *Thief River Falls*
Graff, Andrew J. *Raft of Stars*

RUNAWAY CHILDREN
Barclay, Linwood. *A Tap on the Window*
Clinch, Jon. *Finn: A Novel*
Runaway royals (Alyssa Cole) [Series]. Cole, Alyssa

RUNAWAY TEENAGE BOYS
Murakami, Haruki. ★*Kafka on the Shore*

RUNAWAY TEENAGE GIRLS
Robinson, Peter. *Cold Is the Grave*

RUNAWAY TEENAGERS
Abu-Jaber, Diana. *Birds of Paradise: A Novel*
Aoki, Ryka. *Light from Uncommon Stars*
Clark, Tracy P. *Runner*
Ferencik, Erica. *Into the Jungle*

Guterson, David. *Our Lady of the Forest*
Rozan, S. J. *Winter and Night*
Salinger, J. D. ★*The Catcher in the Rye*
Tyler, Anne. *The Amateur Marriage: A Novel*

RUNAWAY WIVES, HUSBANDS, ETC.
Ashley, Jennifer. *Lady Isabella's Scandalous Marriage*
Dodd, Christina. *Dead Girl Running*
Joshi, Alka. *The Henna Artist*
Keneally, Thomas. *Woman of the Inner Sea*
Lessing, Doris May. *The Sweetest Dream*
McMurtry, Larry. *Boone's Lick: A Novel*
Murakami, Haruki. *The Wind-Up Bird Chronicle*
Phillips, Susan Elizabeth. *The Great Escape*
Portis, Charles. ★*The Dog of the South*
Updike, John. ★*Rabbit, Run*
Vestal, Shawn. *Daredevils*
Runaway: Stories. Munro, Alice

RUNAWAYS
Burke, James Lee. ★*A Private Cathedral*
Cassara, Joseph. *The House of Impossible Beauties*
Coben, Harlan. *Run Away*
Connelly, Michael. *Dark Sacred Night*
Freeman, Brian. *Thief River Falls*
Gibbons, Kaye. ★*Ellen Foster: A Novel*
Hegi, Ursula. *The Vision of Emma Blau*
Holbert, Bruce. *Whiskey*
Kingsolver, Barbara. *Pigs in Heaven*
McPherson, Catriona. *Quiet Neighbors: A Novel*
Overton, Hollie. *The Runaway*
Smith, Julie. *Jazz Funeral*

Runcie, James
Canvey Island
The Road to Grantchester
Sidney Chambers and the Forgiveness of Sins
Sidney Chambers and the Perils of the Night
Sidney Chambers and the Persistence of Love
Sidney Chambers and the Problem of Evil
Sidney Chambers and the Shadow of Death
Runner. Clark, Tracy P.
Runner. Lee, Patrick

RUNNERS
Benaron, Naomi. *Running the Rift: A Novel*
Running Out of Road. Friedman, Daniel
Running the Rift: A Novel. Benaron, Naomi

RURAL AFRICAN AMERICANS
Gaines, Ernest J. ★*A Gathering of Old Men*

RURAL FAMILIES
Berry, Wendell. *Jayber Crow: A Novel*
Berry, Wendell. ★*That Distant Land: The Collected Stories of Wendell Berry*
Crummey, Michael. *Sweetland*
Del Amo, Jean-Baptiste. *Animalia*
Lawson, Mary. *Crow Lake*
Meadows, Rae. *I Will Send Rain: A Novel*
Roy, Lori. *Bent Road*
Smiley, Jane. *Some Luck*
Steinbeck, John. ★*The Grapes of Wrath*

RURAL LIFE

Adam, Claire. *Golden Child: A Novel*
Baker, Jo. *The Body Lies*
Beagle, Peter S. *In Calabria*
Berry, Wendell. ★*That Distant Land: The Collected Stories of Wendell Berry*
Bledsoe, Alex. *Gather Her Round: A Novel of the Tufa*
Butler, Nickolas. *Little Faith: A Novel*
Caldwell, Erskine. *Tobacco Road*
Carr, Robyn. *The Family Gathering*
Christie, Agatha. *Endless Night*
Connolly, Sheila. *The Lost Traveller*
Eliot, George. ★*Adam Bede*
Eliot, George. ★*Silas Marner: The Weaver of Raveloe*
Eriksson, Kjell. *The Deathwatch Beetle: A Mystery*
Faulkner, William. *Uncollected Stories of William Faulkner*
Fuller, Claire. *Unsettled Ground*
Gaskell, Elizabeth Cleghorn. ★*Cranford*
Graley, Lisa. *The Current That Carries: Stories*
Hardy, Thomas. ★*Far from the Madding Crowd*
Hardy, Thomas. ★*The Return of the Native*
Harper, Jane. *The Lost Man*
Healey, Jane. *The Animals at Lockwood Manor*
Hunt, Laird. *Zorrie*
Irving, John. ★*The Cider House Rules: A Novel*
Kim, Angie. *Miracle Creek*
Lockridge, Ross Franklin. *Raintree County*
Lucashenko, Melissa. *Too Much Lip*
Luesse, Valerie Fraser. *Under the Bayou Moon: A Novel*
Mason, Bobbie Ann. *Shiloh and Other Stories*
Mitford, Nancy. ★*The Pursuit of Love: A Novel*
Oates, Joyce Carol. ★*We Were the Mulvaneys*
Rademacher, Cay. *Deadly Camargue: A Provence Mystery*
Rash, Ron. ★*In the Valley: Stories and a Novella Based on Serena*
Roy, Lori. *Bent Road*
Schweblin, Samanta. *Fever Dream: A Novel*
Shalev, Meir. *Two She-Bears: A Novel*
Shaw, William. *Salt Lane*
Simonson, Helen. *Major Pettigrew's Last Stand: A Novel*
Simonson, Helen. *The Summer Before the War: A Novel*
Smith, Lee. *Oral History*
Smith, Michael F. *Blackwood*
Stage, Zoje. *Wonderland*
Sternbergh, Adam. *The Blinds*
Trollope, Anthony. ★*Barchester Towers*
Trollope, Anthony. *Doctor Thorne*
Trollope, Anthony. *Framley Parsonage*
Trollope, Anthony. *The Last Chronicle of Barset*
Walker, Martin. *The Coldest Case*
Walker, Martin. *The Shooting at Chateau Rock*
Weiss, Leah. *If the Creek Don't Rise: A Novel*

RURAL NOIR

Brown, Larry. *Joe: A Novel*
Brown, Taylor. ★*Gods of Howl Mountain: A Novel*
Campbell, Bonnie Jo. *Once Upon a River*
Darnielle, John. *Universal Harvester*
Frazier, Charles. *Nightwoods: A Novel*
Harding Thornton, Christina. *Pickard County Atlas*

Panowich, Brian. *Bull Mountain*
Panowich, Brian. *Like Lions*
Pollock, Donald Ray. *The Devil All the Time*
Pollock, Donald Ray. *Knockemstiff*
Rash, Ron. *Above the Waterfall*
Rash, Ron. *Burning Bright: Stories*
Rash, Ron. ★*The Cove*
Rash, Ron. *Nothing Gold Can Stay: Stories*
Rash, Ron. *Something Rich and Strange: Selected Stories*
Sharpe, Tess. *Barbed Wire Heart*

RURAL PHYSICIANS

Trollope, Anthony. *Doctor Thorne*

RURAL POOR PEOPLE

Caldwell, Erskine. *Tobacco Road*

RURAL WOMEN

Frazier, Charles. *Nightwoods: A Novel*

Rush, Norman

★*Mating*

Rushdie, Salman

The Enchantress of Florence: A Novel
★*The Golden House*
Haroun and the Sea of Stories
★*Midnight's Children: A Novel*
The Moor's Last Sigh
★*Quichotte: A Novel*
★*The Satanic Verses*
Shalimar the Clown: A Novel
Two Years Eight Months and Twenty-Eight Nights: A Novel

Ruskovich, Emily

Idaho: A Novel

Russell, Karen

Orange World and Other Stories
★*Swamplandia!*
Vampires in the Lemon Grove: Stories

Russell, Kate Elizabeth

★*My Dark Vanessa*

Russell, Mary Doria

★*Children of God: A Novel*
★*Doc: A Novel*
Dreamers of the Day: A Novel
Epitaph: A Novel of the O.K. Corral
★*The Sparrow*
A Thread of Grace: A Novel
The Women of the Copper Country: A Novel

RUSSIA

Akunin, B. *The Coronation: The Further Adventures of Erast Fandorin*
Akunin, B. *Sister Pelagia and the White Bulldog: A Mystery*
Alpsten, Ellen. *Tsarina*
Arden, Katherine. ★*The Bear and the Nightingale*
Arden, Katherine. ★*The Girl in the Tower*
Arden, Katherine. ★*The Winter of the Witch*
Bell, Ted. *Overkill: An Alex Hawke Novel*
Brown, Dale. *Eagle Station: A Novel*
Campbell, Rick. *Treason*
Coughlin, Jack. *Long Shot: A Sniper Novel*
Dostoyevsky, Fyodor. *The Best Short Stories of Dostoevsky*
Dostoyevsky, Fyodor. ★*The Brothers Karamazov*

Dostoyevsky, Fyodor. ★*Crime and Punishment*
Dostoyevsky, Fyodor. *Notes from Underground*
Dugoni, Robert. *The Eighth Sister: A Thriller*
Fitzpatrick, Lydia. *Lights All Night Long: A Novel*
Gessen, Keith. *A Terrible Country*
Gogol, Nikolai Vasilievich. *The Collected Tales of Nikolai Gogol*
Gogol, Nikolai Vasilievich. ★*Dead Souls*
Haratischvili, Nino. *The Eighth Life: (For Brilka)*
Harris, Robert. *Archangel: A Novel*
Kelly, Martha Hall. *Lost Roses: A Novel*
Malamud, Bernard. ★*The Fixer*
Marra, Anthony. ★*A Constellation of Vital Phenomena: A Novel*
Marra, Anthony. *The Tsar of Love and Techno: Stories*
Matthews, Jason. ★*The Kremlin's Candidate*
Matthews, Jason. *Red Sparrow: A Novel*
Meyer, Nicholas. *The Adventure of the Peculiar Protocols: Adapted from the Journals of John H. Watson, M.D.*
Pasternak, Boris Leonidovich. ★*Doctor Zhivago*
Pelevin, Viktor. *The Hall of Singing Caryatids*
Phillips, Julia. ★*Disappearing Earth*
Richler, Nancy. *Your Mouth Is Lovely: A Novel*
Rutherfurd, Edward. *Russka: The Novel of Russia*
Sebastian, Tim. *Fatal Ally*
Stachniak, Eva. *The Winter Palace: A Novel of Catherine the Great*
Tolstoy, Leo. ★*Anna Karenina*
Tolstoy, Leo. ★*War and Peace*
Towles, Amor. ★*A Gentleman in Moscow*
Turgenev, Ivan Sergeevich. ★*Fathers and Sons*
Wilson, Daniel H. *The Clockwork Dynasty: A Novel*
Wojtas, Olga. *Miss Blaine's Prefect and the Golden Samovar*
★*The **Russia** Account*. Coonts, Stephen

RUSSIAN AMERICAN WOMEN
Dean, Debra. *The Madonnas of Leningrad: A Novel*
RUSSIAN AMERICANS
Dean, Debra. *The Madonnas of Leningrad: A Novel*
Nabokov, Vladimir Vladimirovich. *Novels and Memoirs, 1941-51*
Nabokov, Vladimir Vladimirovich. *Pnin*
Shteyngart, Gary. *The Russian Debutante's Handbook*
*The **Russian** Debutante's Handbook*. Shteyngart, Gary
RUSSIAN REVOLUTION AND CIVIL WAR (1917-1921)
Kelly, Martha Hall. *Lost Roses: A Novel*
Pasternak, Boris Leonidovich. ★*Doctor Zhivago*
Stachniak, Eva. *The Chosen Maiden: A Novel*
*The **Russian**: a Thriller*. Coes, Ben
RUSSIANS IN THE UNITED STATES
Alenyikov, Michael. *Ivan and Misha: Stories*
Coes, Ben. *The Russian: A Thriller*
Fitzpatrick, Lydia. *Lights All Night Long: A Novel*
Sandford, John. *Hidden Prey*
***Russka**: the Novel of Russia*. Rutherfurd, Edward
Russo, Richard
Bridge of Sighs
★*Chances Are...: A Novel*
★*Empire Falls*
★*Everybody's Fool*
★*Nobody's Fool*
The Risk Pool
Straight Man

Rust & Stardust. Greenwood, T.
Ruth Galloway mysteries [Series]. Griffiths, Elly
Rutherfurd, Edward
London
Paris
The Princes of Ireland: The Dublin Saga
The Rebels of Ireland: The Dublin Saga
Russka: The Novel of Russia
Sarum: The Novel of England
Ruthless rivals [Series]. Bateman, Kate
RUTHLESSNESS IN MEN
Stegner, Wallace. ★*The Big Rock Candy Mountain*
RUTHLESSNESS IN WOMEN
Patterson, Richard North. *Dark Lady*
RWANDA
Benaron, Naomi. *Running the Rift: A Novel*
Faye, Gael. ★*Small Country: A Novel*
Leonard, Elmore. *Pagan Babies*
Ryan DeMarco novels [Series]. Silvis, Randall
Ryan, Anthony
The Waking Fire
RYAN, JACK, SR. (FICTITIOUS CHARACTER)
Clancy, Tom. ★*The Hunt for Red October*
Ryan, Jennifer
The Spies of Shilling Lane: A Novel
Ryan, Kennedy
★*Long Shot*

S

Sabatini, Rafael
Captain Blood
Scaramouche: A Romance of the French Revolution
***Sabbath's** Theater*. Roth, Philip
Saberhagen, Fred
Coinspinner's Story
Farslayer's Story
Mindsword's Story
Shieldbreaker's Story
Sightblinder's Story
Stonecutter's Story
Wayfinder's Story
Woundhealer's Story
SABOTAGE
Barclay, Linwood. ★*Elevator Pitch: A Novel*
Brown, Sandra. *Tailspin*
Coonts, Stephen. *The Armageddon File*
Cumming, Charles. *A Colder War*
Cussler, Clive. *The Mediterranean Caper*
Cussler, Clive. *The Wrecker*
Deaver, Jeffery. *The Stone Monkey: A Lincoln Rhyme Novel*
French, Nicci. *Waiting for Wednesday: A Frieda Klein Mystery*
Herbert, Frank. ★*Dune*
Laurens, Stephanie. *The Pursuits of Lord Kit Cavanaugh*
Michener, James A. ★*The Bridges at Toko-Ri*

Reichs, Kathy. *206 Bones*
Robinson, Kim Stanley. *Antarctica*
Stabenow, Dana. *Restless in the Grave*
Sundin, Sarah. *Through Waters Deep: A Novel*
Woods, Stuart. *Stealth*
SABOTAGE — HISTORY
Benn, James R. *Billy Boyle: A World War Two Mystery*
★*Sabrina & Corina: Stories*. Fajardo-Antine, Kali
SACKETT FAMILY (FICTITIOUS CHARACTERS)
L'Amour, Louis. *To the Far Blue Mountains*
The **Sacketts** [Series]. L'Amour, Louis
Sackville-West, V.
All Passion Spent
The Edwardians
The **Sacrament**: *a Novel*. Ólafsson, Ólafur Jóhann
SACRAMENTO, CALIFORNIA
Ragan, Theresa. *Buried Deep*
Ragan, Theresa. *Deadly Recall*
Ragan, Theresa. *Deranged*
Ragan, Theresa. *Her Last Day*
Sacred Hearts: A Novel. Dunant, Sarah
SACRED SPACE
Binchy, Maeve. ★*Whitethorn Woods*
Spann, Susan. *Trial on Mount Koya: A Hiro Hattori Novel*
Sacred Stone. Cussler, Clive
Sacrilege. Parris, S. J.
SADISM
Gallagher, Stephen. *The Kingdom of Bones: A Novel*
Katzenbach, John. *What Comes Next*
Roosevelt, Elliott. *Murder at Midnight*
SADISTS
Fleming, Ian. *Doctor No*
Roosevelt, Elliott. *Murder at Midnight*
SAFARI GUIDES
Sparks, Nicholas. *Every Breath*
SAFARIS
Hemingway, Ernest. *The Snows of Kilimanjaro and Other Stories*
Safe. Barnett, S. K.
The *Safe* House. Swinson, Kiki
Safe Houses: *A Novel*. Fesperman, Dan
The *Safe* Place: *A Novel*. Downes, Anna
SAFECRACKERS
Hamilton, Steve. ★*The Lock Artist*
SAFETY
Adams, Richard. *Watership Down*
Dalcher, Christina. *Femlandia*
SAG HARBOR, NEW YORK
Brenner, Jamie. *Drawing Home*
Walker, Caroline Louise. *Man of the Year*
Whitehead, Colson. *Sag Harbor: A Novel*
Sag Harbor: A Novel. Whitehead, Colson
Sagan, Carl
Contact: A Novel
Sagan, Francoise
★*Bonjour Tristesse*
Sager, Riley
Final Girls: A Novel
The Last Time I Lied: A Novel

Lock Every Door: A Novel
SAHARA
Ballard, J. G. ★*The Day of Creation*
Bowles, Paul. ★*The Sheltering Sky*
Cussler, Clive. *Sahara: A Novel*
Saint-Exupery, Antoine de. ★*The Little Prince*
Sahara: a Novel. Cussler, Clive
Sahota, Sunjeev
The Year of the Runaways
SAILBOATS
Gaige, Amity. *Sea Wife*
Lunde, Maja. *The End of the Ocean: A Novel*
SAILING
Doller, Trish. *Float Plan*
Putney, Mary Jo. *Once a Scoundrel*
Swift, Jonathan. ★*Gulliver's Travels*
SAILING SHIPS
Forester, C. S. *Admiral Hornblower in the West Indies*
Forester, C. S. *Beat to Quarters*
Forester, C. S. *Commodore Hornblower*
Forester, C. S. *Flying Colours*
Forester, C. S. *Hornblower and the Atropos*
Forester, C. S. *Hornblower and the Hotspur*
Forester, C. S. *Lieutenant Hornblower*
Forester, C. S. *Lord Hornblower*
Forester, C. S. *Mr. Midshipman Hornblower*
Forester, C. S. *Ship of the Line*
O'Brian, Patrick. *Master and Commander*
Sabatini, Rafael. *Captain Blood*
SAILORS
Conrad, Joseph. ★*Lord Jim*
Conrad, Joseph. *Nostromo: A Tale of the Seaboard*
Deutermann, Peter T. *The Iceman*
Doller, Trish. *Float Plan*
Dos Passos, John. *1919*
Dumas, Alexandre. ★*The Count of Monte Cristo*
Frampton, Megan. *Never a Bride*
Ghosh, Amitav. *Flood of Fire*
Ghosh, Amitav. *River of Smoke*
Ghosh, Amitav. *Sea of Poppies*
Golding, William. *Fire Down Below*
Hawks, Arlem. *Georgana's Secret*
London, Jack. *Martin Eden*
Poe, Edgar Allan. *The Narrative of Arthur Gordon Pym of Nantucket*
Romain, Theresa. *Fortune Favors the Wicked*
Simenon, Georges. ★*Maigret and the Toy Village*
Smith, Wilbur A. *Monsoon*
Thomson, E. S. *The Blood*
Wouk, Herman. ★*The Caine Mutiny: A Novel of World War II*
SAINT BARTHOLOMEW'S DAY, MASSACRE OF, FRANCE, 1572
Mosse, Kate. *The City of Tears*
★*Saint Maybe*. Tyler, Anne
The *Saint* of Wolves and Butchers. Grecian, Alex
Saint X. Schaitkin, Alexis
Saint, Jennifer
Ariadne

Saint-Exupery, Antoine de
  ★*The Little Prince*
  Night Flight
Sainz Borgo, Karina
  ★*It Would Be Night in Caracas*
Sakey, Marcus
  A Better World
  Brilliance
Salem's Lot. King, Stephen
SALEM, MASSACHUSETTS
  Conde, Maryse. *I, Tituba, Black Witch of Salem*
  Hawthorne, Nathaniel. ★*The House of the Seven Gables*
SALES
  Askaripour, Mateo. ★*Black Buck*
SALES PERSONNEL
  Kennedy, James. *Dare to Know*
  Watson, Martine Fournier. *The Dream Peddler*
SALINAS VALLEY, CALIFORNIA
  Steinbeck, John. ★*East of Eden*
  Steinbeck, John. *The Long Valley*
  Steinbeck, John. ★*Of Mice and Men*
Salinger, J. D.
  ★*The Catcher in the Rye*
  ★*Franny and Zooey*
  ★*Nine Stories*
  Raise High the Roof Beam, Carpenters,: And Seymour—An Introduction.
Sallis, James
  Drive
★*The Salt Eaters.* Bambara, Toni Cade
Salt Houses. Alyan, Hala
SALT LAKE CITY, UTAH
  Harrison, Mette Ivie. *The Prodigal Daughter*
Salt Lane. Shaw, William
SALT MINES AND MINING
  Camilleri, Andrea. *Riccardino*
Salt River. White, Randy Wayne
Salt Slow: Stories. Armfield, Julia
Salter, James
  Last Night
SALVAGE
  Cussler, Clive. ★*Raise the Titanic!*
  Forester, C. S. *Hornblower and the Atropos*
  Laukkanen, Owen. *Gale Force*
SALVATION
  Nunez, Sigrid. *Salvation City*
Salvation City. Nunez, Sigrid
Salvo Montalbano mysteries [Series]. Camilleri, Andrea
Sam Dryden novels [Series]. Lee, Patrick
Sam McCain mysteries [Series]. Gorman, Edward
Sam Wyndham novels [Series]. Mukherjee, Abir
Samantha Brinkman novels [Series]. Clark, Marcia
Samaritan. Price, Richard
SAMBA MUSIC
  Peebles, Frances de Pontes. *The Air You Breathe*
Sampson, Freya
  The Last Chance Library
Samuel Craddock mysteries [Series]. Shames, Terry

SAMURAI
  Clavell, James. *Shogun*
  Rowland, Laura Joh. *The Iris Fan: A Novel of Feudal Japan*
  Rowland, Laura Joh. *The Snow Empress*
  Spann, Susan. ★*Claws of the Cat: A Shinobi Mystery*
  Spann, Susan. *Trial on Mount Koya: A Hiro Hattori Novel*
SAN (AFRICAN PEOPLE)
  Stanley, Michael. *Dying to Live*
SAN ANTONIO, TEXAS
  Estleman, Loren D. ★*Something Borrowed, Something Black*
  Irvin, Kelly. *Tell Her No Lies*
  Jiles, Paulette. *News of the World: A Novel*
SAN DIEGO, CALIFORNIA
  Lauren, Christina. *The Soulmate Equation*
  Luna, Louisa. *The Janes*
  Pufahl, Shannon. *On Swift Horses*
  Rankin, Ian. *Blood Hunt: A Novel*
  Sorenson, Jill. *Aftershock*
  Urrea, Luis Alberto. ★*The House of Broken Angels*
SAN FRANCISCO BAY AREA
  Carr, Robyn. *The View from Alameda Island: A Novel*
  Gardiner, Meg. *Unsub: A Novel*
  Lelchuk, Saul. *Save Me from Dangerous Men: A Novel*
  Packer, Ann. *The Children's Crusade*
SAN FRANCISCO EARTHQUAKE AND FIRE, CALIF., 1906
  Rindell, Suzanne. ★*The Two Mrs. Carlyles*
SAN FRANCISCO, CALIFORNIA
  Allende, Isabel. *The Japanese Lover*
  Allende, Isabel. *Ripper: A Novel*
  Anders, Charlie Jane. ★*All the Birds in the Sky*
  Bennett, Jenn. *Bitter Spirits*
  Black, Saul. *Anything for You*
  Black, Saul. ★*The Killing Lessons*
  Black, Saul. ★*Lovemurder*
  Chen, Mike. *Here and Now and Then*
  Crumley, James. *The Last Good Kiss: A Novel*
  Darznik, Jasmin. *The Bohemians*
  Dev, Sonali. ★*Pride, Prejudice, and Other Flavors: A Novel*
  Diffenbaugh, Vanessa. *The Language of Flowers: A Novel*
  Donoghue, Emma. ★*Frog Music*
  Frank, Alli. *Tiny Imperfections*
  Freeman, Brian. *The Night Bird*
  Gabel, Aja. *The Ensemble: A Novel*
  Gardiner, Meg. *The Dirty Secrets Club*
  Goodwin, Bobi Gentry. *Revelation*
  Greer, Andrew Sean. *The Impossible Lives of Greta Wells*
  Hammett, Dashiell. ★*The Maltese Falcon*
  Jayatissa, Amanda. ★*My Sweet Girl*
  Kerouac, Jack. *The Dharma Bums*
  Kushner, Rachel. *The Mars Room*
  Lescroart, John T. *Guilt*
  Lim, Roselle. *Natalie Tan's Book of Luck and Fortune*
  Lutz, Lisa. *The Spellman Files: A Novel*
  Masood, Syed M. *The Bad Muslim Discount*
  McGuire, Seanan. *Chimes at Midnight: An October Daye Novel*
  Muller, Marcia. *Dead Midnight*
  Otsuka, Julie. *The Buddha in the Attic*
  Patterson, James. *1st to Die: A Novel*

Patterson, Richard North. *Eclipse*
Perry, Thomas. *Death Benefits: A Novel*
Pronzini, Bill. *Crazybone*
Pronzini, Bill. *Fever*
Pronzini, Bill. *Hardcase*
Pronzini, Bill. *Hellbox*
Pronzini, Bill. *Illusions*
Pronzini, Bill. *Mourners*
Pronzini, Bill. *Nightcrawlers*
Pronzini, Bill. *Savages*
Pronzini, Bill. *Spook*
Pronzini, Bill. *The Stolen Gold Affair*
Richmond, Michelle. *No One You Know*
Rindell, Suzanne. ★*The Two Mrs. Carlyles*
Rivers, Francine. ★*Redeeming Love*
Shafak, Elif. *The Bastard of Istanbul*
Shalvis, Jill. *Sweet Little Lies*
Sloan, Robin. *Mr. Penumbra's 24-Hour Bookstore*
Tan, Amy. *The Bonesetter's Daughter*
Tan, Amy. ★*The Joy Luck Club*
Tan, Amy. *The Valley of Amazement*
Title, Sarah. *The Undateable*
Tyler, Anne. *The Amateur Marriage: A Novel*

SANATORIUMS
　Mann, Thomas. *The Magic Mountain*
★***Sanctuary***. Faulkner, William
Sand, George
　Marianne
*The **Sandcastle** Girls*. Bohjalian, Chris
Sanders, Lawrence
　★*The First Deadly Sin*
　★*The Fourth Deadly Sin*
　McNally's Dilemma
　★*McNally's Gamble*
　McNally's Luck
　McNally's Puzzle
　McNally's Secret
　McNally's Trial
　The Second Deadly Sin
　The Sixth Commandment: A Novel
　The Tenth Commandment: A Novel
　★*The Third Deadly Sin*
　The Timothy Files
　Timothy's Game
SANDERSON, JOE
　Tobar, Hector. *The Last Great Road Bum*
Sandford, John
　Bloody Genius
　Broken Prey
　Buried Prey
　Certain Prey
　Chosen Prey
　★*Deadline*
　Deep Freeze
　Easy Prey
　Field of Prey
　★*Golden Prey*
　Heat Lightning

　Hidden Prey
　Holy Ghost
　★*Invisible Prey*
　Mad River
　★*Mind Prey*
　Mortal Prey
　★*Naked Prey*
　★*Night Prey*
　★*Phantom Prey*
　★*Rules of Prey*
　Shock Wave
　★*Silent Prey*
　★*Silken Prey*
　Storm Front
　Storm Prey
　Sudden Prey
　★*Winter Prey*
*The **Sandman***. Kepler, Lars
***Sandrine's** Case*. Cook, Thomas H.
Sands of the emperor [Series]. Couto, Mia
SANKARA, THOMAS, 1949-1987
　Anders, Charlie Jane. ★*The City in the Middle of the Night*
　Wilkinson, Lauren. ★*American Spy: A Novel*
***Sankofa**: a Novel*. Onuzo, Chibundu
Sano Ichiro mysteries [Series]. Rowland, Laura Joh
SANO, ICHIRO (FICTITIOUS CHARACTER)
　Rowland, Laura Joh. *The Iris Fan: A Novel of Feudal Japan*
Sansom, C. J.
　★*Lamentation*
　Revelation
　★*Sovereign*
　Tombland
SANTA CRUZ ISLAND, CALIFORNIA
　Boyle, T. Coraghessan. *When the Killing's Done: A Novel*
***Santa** Fe Rules*. Woods, Stuart
SANTA FE, NEW MEXICO
　Cather, Willa. ★*Death Comes for the Archbishop*
　Woods, Stuart. *Below the Belt*
　Woods, Stuart. *Santa Fe Rules*
Santiago, Danny
　Famous All Over Town
Santiago, Esmeralda
　Conquistadora: A Novel
Sapphire
　American Dreams
　★*The Kid: A Novel*
　★*Push: A Novel*
Sarah Gilchrist series [Series]. Welsh, Kaite
***Sarah** Thornhill*. Grenville, Kate
★***Sarah's** Key*. Rosnay, Tatiana de
Saramago, Jose
　All the Names
　★*Blindness*
　Cain
　★*The Cave*
　Death with Interruptions
　★*The Elephant's Journey*
　The History of the Siege of Lisbon

The Manual of Painting and Calligraphy
Saratoga Payback. Dobyns, Stephen
SARATOGA SPRINGS, NEW YORK
    Dobyns, Stephen. *Saratoga Payback*
    Wood, James. *Upstate*
Saroyan, William
    ★*The Human Comedy*
Sarton, May
    A Reckoning: A Novel
Sartre, Jean Paul
    The Age of Reason
    ★*Nausea*
    Troubled Sleep
Sarum: the Novel of England. Rutherfurd, Edward
SASKATCHEWAN
    Ford, Richard. *Canada*
SASQUATCH
    Brooks, Max. *Devolution: A Firsthand Account of the Rainier Sasquatch Massacre*
SASSOON, SIEGFRIED, 1886-1967
    Barker, Pat. ★*Regeneration*
    Steinbeck, John. *Tortilla Flat*
The Satanic Mechanic: A Tannie Maria Mystery. Andrew, Sally
★*The Satanic Verses.* Rushdie, Salman
The Satapur Moonstone. Massey, Sujata
Sathian, Sanjena
    Gold Diggers
SATIE, ERIK
    French, Nicci. ★*The Day of the Dead: A Novel*
    Horrocks, Caitlin. *The Vexations*
SATIRICAL FICTION
    Abrams, David. *Fobbit*
    Adiga, Aravind. ★*The White Tiger: A Novel*
    Adjei-Brenyah, Nana Kwame. *Friday Black: Stories*
    Allen, Jane. *I Lost My Girlish Laughter*
    Amidon, Stephen. *Security: A Novel*
    Amis, Kingsley. ★*Lucky Jim*
    Amis, Martin. *Lionel Asbo: State of England*
    Askaripour, Mateo. ★*Black Buck*
    Auslander, Shalom. *Hope: A Tragedy*
    Austen, Jane. ★*Northanger Abbey*
    Ballard, J. G. *Kingdom Come*
    Ballard, J. G. *Millennium People*
    Barnes, Julian. ★*England, England*
    Barth, John. ★*Giles Goat-Boy ;: Or, the Revised New Syllabus*
    Beatty, Paul. ★*The Sellout: A Novel*
    Bellow, Saul. ★*Henderson the Rain King: A Novel*
    Berger, Thomas. *Being Invisible: A Novel*
    Bernhard, Thomas. ★*Woodcutters*
    Bourland, Barbara. ★*Fake Like Me*
    Braithwaite, Oyinkan. *My Sister, the Serial Killer: A Novel*
    Brooks, Max. ★*World War Z: An Oral History of the Zombie War*
    Brown, Rita Mae. ★*Rubyfruit Jungle*
    Browne, S. G. *Less Than Hero: A Novel*
    Butler, Halle. *The New Me: A Novel*
    Butler, Robert Olen. *Hell: A Novel*
    Crouch, Katie. *Embassy Wife*
    Currie, Ron. *Flimsy Little Plastic Miracles: A True Story*

Dee, Jonathan. *A Thousand Pardons: A Novel*
DeLillo, Don. ★*White Noise*
Dickens, Charles. ★*Bleak House*
Dickens, Charles. *Little Dorrit*
Dickens, Charles. *Martin Chuzzlewit*
Dickens, Charles. *Our Mutual Friend*
Dickens, Charles. *The Pickwick Papers*
Dovlatov, Sergei. *Pushkin Hills*
Drabble, Margaret. *The Witch of Exmoor*
Dunne, Dominick. *People Like Us: A Novel*
Dunne, Dominick. *Too Much Money*
Eco, Umberto. *Numero Zero*
Eggers, Dave. *The Circle*
Ellis, Helen. *American Housewife: Stories*
Everett, Percival L. *Erasure: A Novel*
Everett, Percival L. *God's Country*
Everett, Percival L. *I Am Not Sidney Poitier*
Ferris, Joshua. *To Rise Again at a Decent Hour: A Novel*
Fielding, Henry. ★*The History of Tom Jones, a Foundling*
Fitzgerald, F. Scott. ★*The Beautiful and Damned*
Fountain, Ben. ★*Billy Lynn's Long Halftime Walk*
Frankel, Laurie. *Goodbye for Now: A Novel*
Fuentes, Carlos. *The Eagle's Throne: A Novel*
Gaddis, William. *A Frolic of His Own: A Novel*
Gaddis, William. ★*J R: A Novel*
Gessen, Keith. *A Terrible Country*
Greene, Graham. *Our Man in Havana*
Hajdu, David. *Adrianne Geffel: A Fiction*
Hankin, Laura. *Happy & You Know It*
Heller, Joseph. ★*Catch-22*
Heller, Joseph. *Good as Gold*
Heller, Zoe. *What Was She Thinking?: Notes on a Scandal*
Hiaasen, Carl. *Skinny Dip: A Novel*
Hiaasen, Carl. ★*Squeeze Me: A Novel*
Houellebecq, Michel. *Submission*
Kasulke, Calvin. *Several People Are Typing*
Kaufman, Charlie. *Antkind: A Novel*
Kesey, Ken. ★*One Flew Over the Cuckoo's Nest*
Ko-Eun, Yun. *The Disaster Tourist*
Kotzwinkle, William. *The Bear Went Over the Mountain*
Lee, Chang-Rae. ★*My Year Abroad*
Lewis, Sinclair. *Babbitt*
Lewis, Sinclair. *Dodsworth*
Lewis, Sinclair. ★*Elmer Gantry*
Lewis, Sinclair. ★*Main Street: The Story of Carol Kennicott*
Lipsyte, Sam. *The Ask*
Ma, Jian. *China Dream*
Ma, Ling. *Severance*
Mabanckou, Alain. ★*Black Moses*
McAllister, Tom. *How to Be Safe: A Novel*
McDowell, Christina. *The Cave Dwellers: A Novel*
McElroy, Alex. *The Atmospherians*
McEwan, Ian. ★*Amsterdam*
McEwan, Ian. *Solar: A Novel*
McKenzie, Elizabeth. *The Portable Veblen*
McLaughlin, Emma. *The Nanny Diaries: A Novel*
Melville, Herman. *The Confidence-Man: His Masquerade*
Miles, Jonathan. *Anatomy of a Miracle*

Mitford, Nancy. *Love in a Cold Climate*

Mitford, Nancy. ★*The Pursuit of Love: A Novel*

Nabokov, Vladimir Vladimirovich. *King, Queen, Knave: A Novel*

Nabokov, Vladimir Vladimirovich. *Pale Fire*

Nabokov, Vladimir Vladimirovich. *Pnin*

Nguyen, Kevin. ★*New Waves*

Nicieza, Fabian. *Suburban Dicks*

Nugent, Benjamin. *Fraternity: Stories*

Orwell, George. ★*Animal Farm*

Palahniuk, Chuck. *Pygmy*

Pava, Sergio de la. *Lost Empress: A Novel*

Pava, Sergio de la. *A Naked Singularity*

Pelevin, Viktor. *The Hall of Singing Caryatids*

Perrotta, Tom. *The Leftovers*

Phillips, Arthur. *The Tragedy of Arthur: A Novel*

Phillips, Helen. *The Beautiful Bureaucrat: A Novel*

Prose, Francine. *Blue Angel: A Novel*

Pym, Barbara. ★*Excellent Women*

Pynchon, Thomas. *Against the Day: A Novel*

Pynchon, Thomas. ★*The Crying of Lot 49*

Pynchon, Thomas. *Vineland*

Reed, Ishmael. *Flight to Canada*

Reed, Ishmael. ★*Mumbo Jumbo*

Richler, Mordecai. *Barney's Version: A Novel*

Rothschild, Hannah. *The Improbability of Love: A Novel*

Rushdie, Salman. ★*The Golden House*

Rushdie, Salman. *The Moor's Last Sigh*

Rushdie, Salman. *Two Years Eight Months and Twenty-Eight Nights: A Novel*

Saramago, Jose. *Death with Interruptions*

Saunders, George. *In Persuasion Nation: Stories*

Schumacher, Julie. *Dear Committee Members*

Self, Will. *The Book of Dave: A Revelation of the Recent Past and the Distant Future*

Shafak, Elif. *The Bastard of Istanbul*

Shriver, Lionel. *Should We Stay or Should We Go*

Shteyngart, Gary. ★*Lake Success: A Novel*

Shteyngart, Gary. *The Russian Debutante's Handbook*

Shteyngart, Gary. ★*Super Sad True Love Story: A Novel*

Smiley, Jane. *Horse Heaven*

Smith, Zadie. ★*White Teeth: A Novel*

Spark, Muriel. ★*The Girls of Slender Means*

Spark, Muriel. ★*Memento Mori*

Sterling, Bruce. *Pirate Utopia*

Stibbe, Nina. *Reasons to Be Cheerful*

Swift, Jonathan. ★*Gulliver's Travels*

Thackeray, William Makepeace. ★*Vanity Fair: A Novel Without a Hero*

Toole, John Kennedy. ★*A Confederacy of Dunces*

Twain, Mark. ★*A Connecticut Yankee in King Arthur's Court*

Twain, Mark. *Pudd'nhead Wilson and Those Extraordinary Twins*

Unsworth, Emma Jane. *Grown Ups*

Updike, John. *Memories of the Ford Administration: A Novel*

Updike, John. *The Widows of Eastwick*

Updike, John. ★*The Witches of Eastwick*

Vargas Llosa, Mario. *The Time of the Hero*

Voltaire. *Candide and Other Stories*

Vonnegut, Kurt. ★*Breakfast of Champions: Or, Goodbye Blue Monday!*

Vonnegut, Kurt. ★*Cat's Cradle*

Vonnegut, Kurt. ★*Galapagos: A Novel*

Vonnegut, Kurt. *Hocus Pocus*

Vonnegut, Kurt. *Jailbird: A Novel*

Vonnegut, Kurt. ★*Player Piano*

Vonnegut, Kurt. ★*The Sirens of Titan*

Vonnegut, Kurt. *Timequake*

Vonnegut, Kurt. *Welcome to the Monkey House*

Walker, Sarai. *Dietland*

Wallace, David Foster. ★*Infinite Jest: A Novel*

Wallace, David Foster. ★*The Pale King: An Unfinished Novel*

Wang, Kathy. *Impostor Syndrome: A Novel*

Waugh, Evelyn. *Decline and Fall*

Waugh, Evelyn. *The Loved One: An Anglo-American Tragedy*

Waugh, Evelyn. ★*Vile Bodies*

Wayne, Teddy. *Apartment: A Novel*

West, Nathanael. *Novels and Other Writings*

Whitehead, Colson. *Apex Hides the Hurt*

Whitehead, Colson. *Zone One: A Novel*

Willis, Connie. *Crosstalk*

Wolfe, Tom. *Back to Blood: A Novel*

Wolfe, Tom. *The Bonfire of the Vanities*

Wong, David. *Futuristic Violence and Fancy Suits*

Woolf, Virginia. *Orlando: A Biography*

Yellin, Jessica. *Savage News*

Yoder, Rachel. *Nightbitch*

The **Saturday** Big Tent Wedding Party. McCall Smith, Alexander

★The **Saturday** Night Supper Club. Laureano, C. E.

Saturday Night Supper Club novels [Series]. Laureano, C. E.

SATURN (PLANET)

Clarke, Arthur C. ★*2001: A Space Odyssey*

Saturn's Children: A Space Opera. Stross, Charles

Satyal, Rakesh

No One Can Pronounce My Name: A Novel

SAUDI ARABIA

Eggers, Dave. *A Hologram for the King: A Novel*

Ferraris, Zoe. *Finding Nouf*

Ferraris, Zoe. *Kingdom of Strangers: A Novel*

Saul and Patsy. Baxter, Charles

Saul, John

Midnight Voices

Saums, Mary

Thistle & Twigg

Saunders, George

In Persuasion Nation: Stories

★*Lincoln in the Bardo: A Novel*

★*Tenth of December: Stories*

Saunders, Kate

The Case of the Wandering Scholar

The Secrets of Wishtide

SAUNDERS, MARY, DIED 1764

Donoghue, Emma. *Slammerkin*

Lawrence, D. H. *Women in Love*

★The **Savage** Detectives. Bolano, Roberto

The **Savage** Instinct. Deluca, Marjorie

The **Savage** Kind. Copenhaver, John

Savage News. Yellin, Jessica
Savage Run. Box, C. J.
Savage, Sam
    Firmin: Adventures of a Metropolitan Lowlife
    The Way of the Dog: A Novel
Savages. Pronzini, Bill
Savannah Reid mysteries [Series]. McKevett, G. A.
SAVANNAH, GEORGIA
    Brown, Sandra. ★*Ricochet*
    Daugherty, Christi. *A Beautiful Corpse*
    Daugherty, Christi. *The Echo Killing*
    Johnson, Tara. *Engraved on the Heart*
    Pinborough, Sarah. ★*Dead to Her: A Novel*
    Rabb, Jonathan. *Among the Living*
SAVANT SYNDROME
    Haddon, Mark. ★*The Curious Incident of the Dog in the Night-Time: A Novel*
    Oe, Kenzaburo. ★*A Quiet Life*
Savas, Aysegul
    Walking on the Ceiling
Save Me from Dangerous Men: A Novel. Lelchuk, Saul
SAVONAROLA, GIROLAMO, 1452-1498
    Dunant, Sarah. *The Birth of Venus: A Novel*
    Ellroy, James. *American Tabloid: A Novel*
    Quartey, Kwei. *The Missing American*
    Walton, Jo. ★*Lent*
Saxon stories [Series]. Cornwell, Bernard
SAXONS
    Cornwell, Bernard. *Sword of Kings*
SAXOPHONISTS
    Goonan, Kathleen Ann. *In War Times*
Say Nothing: A Novel. Parks, Brad
★*Say* Yes to the Marquess. Dare, Tessa
Say You're One of Them. Akpan, Uwem
★*Say* You're Sorry. Robotham, Michael
Sayers, Constance
    The Ladies of the Secret Circus
Sayers, Dorothy L.
    ★*Busman's Honeymoon*
    ★*Clouds of Witness*
    ★*The Documents in the Case*
    ★*The Five Red Herrings*
    ★*Gaudy Night*
    Hangman's Holiday
    Have His Carcase
    In the Teeth of the Evidence
    ★*Lord Peter*
    Murder Must Advertise
    The Nine Tailors
    Thrones, Dominations
    The Unpleasantness at the Bellona Club
    ★*Whose Body?: A Lord Peter Wimsey Novel*
Sayles, John
    A Moment in the Sun
Saylor, Steven
    The House of the Vestals: The Investigations of Gordianus the Finder
    The Judgment of Caesar: A Novel of Ancient Rome
    A Mist of Prophecies
    Raiders of the Nile: A Novel of the Ancient World
    Roma: The Novel of Ancient Rome
    Rubicon
    The Seven Wonders: A Novel of the Ancient World
    The Triumph of Caesar: A Novel of Ancient Rome
    Wrath of the Furies: A Novel of the Ancient World
Scalzi, John
    The Collapsing Empire
    Head On
    ★*Lock In*
    ★*Old Man's War*
    Redshirts: A Novel with Three Codas
Scandal & scoundrel [Series]. MacLean, Sarah
Scandal in Babylon. Hambly, Barbara
Scandal Takes the Stage. Leigh, Eva
Scandalous. Spencer, Minerva
SCANDALS
    Alcott, Kate. *A Touch of Stardust*
    Ashley, Jennifer. *Lady Isabella's Scandalous Marriage*
    Backman, Fredrik. ★*Beartown: A Novel*
    Baldacci, David. ★*A Gambling Man*
    Balogh, Mary. *More Than a Mistress*
    Balogh, Mary. ★*Someone to Care*
    Balogh, Mary. *Someone to Hold*
    Benton, Janet. *Lilli De Jong: A Novel*
    Bowen, Kelly. ★*Between the Devil and the Duke*
    Bowman, Valerie. *Secrets of a Wedding Night*
    Bradley, Anna. *A Season of Ruin*
    Burrowes, Grace. ★*A Rogue of Her Own*
    Chase, Loretta Lynda. *Don't Tempt Me*
    Dare, Tessa. *Do You Want to Start a Scandal*
    Dimberg, Kelsey Rae. *Girl in the Rearview Mirror*
    Dunne, Dominick. *People Like US: A Novel*
    Finch, Charles. *The Vanishing Man*
    Freeman, Dianne. *A Fiancee's Guide to First Wives and Murder*
    Gilbert, Elizabeth. ★*City of Girls*
    Godwin, Gail. *Unfinished Desires*
    Groff, Lauren. *Delicate Edible Birds and Other Stories*
    Guhrke, Laura Lee. *The Truth About Love and Dukes*
    Hatcher, Robin Lee. *Who I Am with You*
    Hoffman, Alice. *The Marriage of Opposites: A Novel Based on the Life of Rachel Pizzarro*
    Holt, Victoria. *The Black Opal*
    Horan, Nancy. *Loving Frank: A Novel*
    Hurston, Zora Neale. ★*Their Eyes Were Watching God*
    James, Henry. *Daisy Miller*
    Layden, Emily. *All Girls*
    Leon, Donna. *The Golden Egg*
    MacLean, Sarah. ★*Bombshell*
    MacLean, Sarah. *No Good Duke Goes Unpunished*
    MacLean, Sarah. *The Rogue Not Taken*
    Mangan, Christine. *Palace of the Drowned*
    Patterson, James. ★*Private*
    Patterson, Richard North. *No Safe Place*
    Pope, Jamie. *One Warm Winter*
    Prose, Francine. *Blue Angel: A Novel*
    Robinson, Peter. *Children of the Revolution*
    Roth, Philip. *The Great American Novel*

Roth, Philip. ★*The Human Stain*
Sanders, Lawrence. *Timothy's Game*
Saunders, Kate. *The Secrets of Wishtide*
Shepard, Sara. ★*Reputation*
Shreve, Anita. *Testimony: A Novel*
Vargas Llosa, Mario. *Aunt Julia and the Scriptwriter*
Wilsner, Meryl. ★*Something to Talk About*
Woods, Stuart. *A Delicate Touch*

SCANDINAVIAN CRIME FICTION
Adler-Olsen, Jussi. *A Conspiracy of Faith*
Adler-Olsen, Jussi. *The Hanging Girl*
Adler-Olsen, Jussi. *The Marco Effect: A Department Q Novel*
Adler-Olsen, Jussi. *The Purity of Vengeance: A Department Q Novel*
Adler-Olsen, Jussi. *The Scarred Woman*
Adler-Olsen, Jussi. ★*Victim 2117*
Alsterdal, Tove. *We Know You Remember*
De la Motte, Anders. *MemoRandom: A Thriller*
De la Motte, Anders. *Ultimatum: A Thriller*
Eriksson, Kjell. *The Deathwatch Beetle: A Mystery*
Grebe, Camilla. *After She's Gone: A Novel*
Grebe, Camilla. *The Ice Beneath Her: A Novel*
Hand, Elizabeth. *Available Dark: A Thriller*
Indriðason, Arnaldur. *The Darkness Knows*
Indriðason, Arnaldur. *Outrage*
Indriðason, Arnaldur. *Reykjavik Nights: An Inspector Erlendur Novel*
Indriðason, Arnaldur. *The Shadow District: A Thriller*
Indriðason, Arnaldur. *Strange Shores: An Inspector Erlendur Novel*
Jónasson, Ragnar. *The Island*
Jónasson, Ragnar. *The Mist*
Kepler, Lars. *The Sandman*
Lagercrantz, David. *The Girl Who Lived Twice: A Lisbeth Salander Novel*
Lagercrantz, David. *The Girl Who Takes an Eye for an Eye*
Larsson, Stieg. *The Girl with the Dragon Tattoo*
Mankell, Henning. *Before the Frost: A Linda Wallander Mystery*
Mankell, Henning. *The Dogs of Riga*
Mankell, Henning. *Firewall*
Mankell, Henning. *The Man from Beijing*
Mankell, Henning. *The Man Who Smiled: A Kurt Wallander Mystery*
Mankell, Henning. ★*One Step Behind*
Mankell, Henning. ★*The Return of the Dancing Master*
Mankell, Henning. *The Troubled Man*
Nesbo, Jo. *The Leopard*
Nesbo, Jo. *Phantom*
Nesbo, Jo. *The Redeemer*
Persson Giolito, Malin. *Beyond All Reasonable Doubt: A Novel*
Persson Giolito, Malin. *Quicksand*
Persson, Leif G. W. *Free Falling, as If in a Dream: The Story of a Crime*
Ramqvist, Karolina. *The White City*
Ridpath, Michael. *Far North*
Roslund, Anders. *Cell 8*
Roslund, Anders. ★*Knock Knock*
Roslund, Anders. *Pen 33*
Sigurðardóttir, Lilja. *Cage*
Soderberg, Alexander. *The Other Son: A Sophie Brinkmann Novel*
Sundstol, Vidar. *The Land of Dreams*
Sveistrup, Soren. ★*The Chestnut Man: A Novel*

Tursten, Helene. *Hunting Game*
SCAPEGOATS (PERSONS)
Barker, Pat. ★*The Eye in the Door*
Hamilton, Jane. *A Map of the World*
Limon, Martin. *The Line*
Scaramouche: a Romance of the French Revolution. Sabatini, Rafael
SCARBOROUGH, ONTARIO
Chariandy, David John. *Brother: A Novel*
The Scarecrow: a Novel. Connelly, Michael
★*The Scarlet Letter: A Romance.* Hawthorne, Nathaniel
★*The Scarlet Pimpernel.* Orczy, Emmuska Orczy
Scarlet Pimpernel [Series]. Orczy, Emmuska Orczy
The Scarlet Ruse. MacDonald, John D.
The Scarred Woman. Adler-Olsen, Jussi
SCARS
Pressfield, Steven. *36 Righteous Men: A Novel*
SCAVENGING
Griffiths, Elly. *The Night Hawks*
Scenes from Early Life: A Novel. Hensher, Philip
The Scent Keeper. Bauermeister, Erica
The Scent of Rain and Lightning: A Novel. Pickard, Nancy
Scerbanenco, Giorgio
A Private Venus
Traitors to All
Schaefer, Jack
Monte Walsh
★*Shane*
Schaffhausen, Joanna
Gone for Good
Schaitkin, Alexis
Saint X
Schami, Rafik
Sophia: Or the Beginning of All Tales
Schanbacher, Gary Lester
Crossing Purgatory
Schanoes, Veronica L.
Burning Girls and Other Stories
Scharer, Whitney
The Age of Light
SCHEHERAZADE
Barth, John. *Chimera*
Schell, Orville
My Old Home: A Novel of Exile
Schellman, Katharine
Silence in the Library
Schild's Ladder. Egan, Greg
★*Schindler's List.* Keneally, Thomas
SCHINDLER, OSKAR, 1908-1974
Keneally, Thomas. ★*Schindler's List*
Schine, Cathleen
The Grammarians
SCHIZOPHRENIA
Billingsley, ReShonda Tate. ★*The Secret She Kept*
Schlink, Bernhard
Olga
The Reader: A Novel
Self's Deception
Self's Murder

Self's Punishment
Schmidt, Sarah
  See What I Have Done
SCHOLARS AND ACADEMICS
  Barnes, Julian. ★*Flaubert's Parrot*
  Bolano, Roberto. ★*2666*
  Eliot, George. ★*Middlemarch: A Study of Provincial Life*
  Pearl, Matthew. *The Technologists: A Novel*
  Sandford, John. *Bloody Genius*
  Taseer, Aatish. *The Way Things Were: A Novel*
Scholomance [Series]. Novik, Naomi
SCHOOL CHILDREN
  Hegi, Ursula. *Children and Fire: A Novel*
School for dukes [Series]. Bell, Lenora
The ***School*** *for Good Mothers*. Chan, Jessamine
SCHOOL INTEGRATION
  Coster, Naima. *What's Mine and Yours: A Novel*
SCHOOL LIBRARIANS
  Center, Katherine. *What You Wish For*
SCHOOL PRINCIPALS
  Center, Katherine. *What You Wish For*
SCHOOL SHOOTINGS
  Block, Stefan Merrill. *Oliver Loving: A Novel*
  Loren, Roni. ★*The One for You*
  McAllister, Tom. *How to Be Safe: A Novel*
  Persson Giolito, Malin. *Quicksand*
  Picoult, Jodi. *Nineteen Minutes: A Novel*
  Rankin, Ian. *A Question of Blood: An Inspector Rebus Novel*
  Shriver, Lionel. *We Need to Talk About Kevin*
SCHOOL YEARBOOKS
  Lipman, Elinor. *Good Riddance*
SCHOOLS
  Corby, Gary. *The Marathon Conspiracy*
  Cussler, Clive. ★*The Oracle*
  Diachenko, Serhii. *Vita Nostra*
  Gailey, Sarah. *Magic for Liars*
  Ganshert, Katie. ★*No One Ever Asked: A Novel*
  Grossman, Lev. ★*The Magicians: A Novel*
  Holsinger, Bruce W. *The Gifted School: A Novel*
  Krueger, William Kent. *This Tender Land: A Novel*
  Laurens, Stephanie. *The Pursuits of Lord Kit Cavanaugh*
  March, William. *The Bad Seed: A Novel*
  McCall Smith, Alexander. *The Limpopo Academy of Private Detection*
  Moriarty, Liane. *Big Little Lies*
  Moriarty, Liane. *The Husband's Secret*
SCHOONERS
  Ghosh, Amitav. *Flood of Fire*
  Ghosh, Amitav. *River of Smoke*
  Ghosh, Amitav. *Sea of Poppies*
Schroder. Gaige, Amity
Schulman, Alex
  The Survivors: A Novel
Schulman, Helen
  Come with Me
Schultz, Connie
  The Daughters of Erietown

SCHULTZ, DUTCH, 1900?-1935
  Doctorow, E. L. ★*Billy Bathgate: A Novel*
Schumacher, Julie
  Dear Committee Members
Schwab, Victoria
  A Conjuring of Light
  A Darker Shade of Magic
  A Gathering of Shadows
  The Invisible Life of Addie Larue
  Vengeful
  Vicious
Schwartz, John Burnham
  The Commoner: A Novel
Schwartz, Lynne Sharon
  Truthtelling: Stories, Fables, Glimpses
Schwarz, Christina
  Drowning Ruth
  The Edge of the Earth
Schwarz, Liese O'Halloran
  What Could Be Saved
Schwarz-Bart, Andre
  The Last of the Just: A Novel
Schweblin, Samanta
  Fever Dream: A Novel
  Little Eyes
  Mouthful of Birds: Stories
SCIENCE
  Edugyan, Esi. ★*Washington Black: A Novel*
  Mann, Thomas. *The Magic Mountain*
SCIENCE — EXPERIMENTS
  Pynchon, Thomas. ★*Gravity's Rainbow*
SCIENCE — MORAL AND ETHICAL ASPECTS
  Labatut, Benjamin. *When We Cease to Understand the World*
SCIENCE — PUBLIC OPINION
  Egan, Greg. *Perihelion Summer*
SCIENCE FANTASY
  Anders, Charlie Jane. ★*All the Birds in the Sky*
  Aoki, Ryka. *Light from Uncommon Stars*
  Davis, Kathryn. *Duplex*
  Hossain, Saad Z. *Cyber Mage: A Novel*
  Kadrey, Richard. *The Grand Dark*
  McCaffrey, Anne. ★*Acorna: The Unicorn Girl*
  McCaffrey, Anne. *Dragonflight*
  Mieville, China. ★*Perdido Street Station*
  Muir, Tamsyn. *Harrow the Ninth*
  Okorafor, Nnedi. ★*Who Fears Death*
  Shannon, Samantha. *The Bone Season*
  Shannon, Samantha. *The Mime Order*
  Tepper, Sheri S. *The Visitor*
  Wolfe, Gene. *The Citadel of the Autarch*
  Wolfe, Gene. *The Claw of the Conciliator*
SCIENCE FICTION
  Adams, Douglas. *Dirk Gently's Holistic Detective Agency*
  Adams, Douglas. *The Restaurant at the End of the Universe*
  Adlakha, Sarah. *She Wouldn't Change a Thing*
  Afifi, Nadia. *The Sentient*
  Alderman, Naomi. ★*The Power: A Novel*
  Alexie, Sherman. *Flight*

Anders, Charlie Jane. ★*The City in the Middle of the Night*

Anderton, Jo. *Debris*

Aoki, Ryka. *Light from Uncommon Stars*

Atwood, Margaret. ★*Oryx and Crake*

Bacigalupi, Paolo. ★*The Water Knife*

Bacigalupi, Paolo. ★*The Windup Girl*

Baker, Kage. *In the Garden of Iden: A Novel of the Company*

Ballard, J. G. ★*The Complete Stories of J.G. Ballard.*

Ballard, J. G. *Kingdom Come*

Bear, Greg. *Anvil of Stars*

Bear, Greg. *The Collected Stories of Greg Bear*

Bear, Greg. *The Forge of God*

Beukes, Lauren. *Slipping: Stories, Essays, & Other Writing*

Bradbury, Ray. *Bradbury Stories: 100 of His Most Celebrated Tales*

Bradbury, Ray. ★*The Martian Chronicles: The Fortieth Anniversary Edition*

Brennan, Marie. *Driftwood*

Brin, David. *Existence*

Brown, Pierce. *Golden Son*

Brown, Pierce. *Morning Star*

Brown, Pierce. *Red Rising*

Bujold, Lois McMaster. ★*Shards of Honor*

Bujold, Lois McMaster. ★*The Warrior's Apprentice*

Burke, Sue. *Semiosis*

Butler, Octavia E. *Bloodchild: And Other Stories*

Butler, Octavia E. ★*Kindred*

Butler, Octavia E. *Parable of the Talents: A Novel*

Cambias, James L. *A Darkling Sea*

Card, Orson Scott. ★*Ender's Game*

Cargill, C. Robert. *Day Zero*

Chambers, Becky. *A Closed and Common Orbit*

Chambers, Becky. ★*The Galaxy, and the Ground Within*

Chambers, Becky. ★*The Long Way to a Small, Angry Planet*

Chambers, Becky. ★*A Psalm for the Wild-Built*

Chambers, Becky. *Record of a Spaceborn Few*

Chen, Mike. *Here and Now and Then*

Chen, Qiufan. *Waste Tide*

Cherryh, C. J. *Foreigner: A Novel of First Contact*

Chiang, Ted. ★*Exhalation: Stories*

Chiang, Ted. ★*Stories of Your Life and Others*

Cipri, Nino. *Defekt*

Clarke, Arthur C. ★*Childhood's End*

Clarke, Arthur C. ★*The Collected Stories of Arthur C. Clarke*

Clarke, Arthur C. *Rendezvous with Rama*

Cline, Ernest. *Ready Player One: A Novel*

Corey, James S. A. *Abaddon's Gate*

Corey, James S. A. *Babylon's Ashes*

Corey, James S. A. *Caliban's War*

Corey, James S. A. *Cibola Burn*

Corey, James S. A. ★*Leviathan Wakes*

Corey, James S. A. *Nemesis Games*

Corey, James S. A. *Persepolis Rising*

Corey, James S. A. *Tiamat's Wrath*

Davis, Kathryn. *Duplex*

Delaney, J. P. *The Perfect Wife: A Novel*

Delany, Samuel R. *Aye, and Gomorrah: Stories*

Delany, Samuel R. *Stars in My Pocket Like Grains of Sand*

Deon, Natashia. *The Perishing: A Novel*

Dewes, J. S. *The Last Watch*

Dick, Philip K. ★*Do Androids Dream of Electric Sheep?*

Dick, Philip K. ★*The Man in the High Castle*

Dick, Philip K. *The Minority Report*

Divya, S. B. *Machinehood*

Doctorow, Cory. *Radicalized*

Doctorow, Cory. *Rapture of the Nerds*

Doctorow, Cory. *Walkaway*

Due, Tananarive. *Ghost Summer: Stories*

Eason, K. *How Rory Thorne Destroyed the Multiverse*

Egan, Greg. *Perihelion Summer*

Egan, Greg. *Schild's Ladder*

Eggers, Dave. *A Hologram for the King: A Novel*

El-Mohtar, Amal. ★*This Is How You Lose the Time War*

Elison, Meg. *The Book of Etta*

Elison, Meg. *The Book of Flora*

Elison, Meg. *The Book of the Unnamed Midwife*

Elliott, Kate. *Unconquerable Sun*

Faber, Michel. *The Book of Strange New Things*

Flynn, Michael. *Eifelheim*

Flynn, Michael. *The January Dancer*

Foster, Alan Dean. *Relic*

Gibson, William. *Pattern Recognition*

Gibson, William. *The Peripheral*

Gilman, Carolyn Ives. *Dark Orbit*

Gilman, Charlotte Perkins. *Herland*

Gladstone, Max. ★*Empress of Forever*

Goonan, Kathleen Ann. *In War Times*

Graedon, Alena. *The Word Exchange: A Novel*

Grant, Mira. *Parasite*

Green, Hank. *An Absolutely Remarkable Thing: A Novel*

Gregory, Daryl. *Afterparty*

Gunn, James E. *Transcendental*

Haig, Francesca. *The Fire Sermon: A Novel*

Haig, Matt. *The Humans: A Novel*

Haig, Matt. *The Midnight Library*

Hall, Louisa. *Speak*

Hamilton, Peter F. *The Dreaming Void*

Hamilton, Peter F. *Great North Road*

Hamilton, Peter F. *Pandora's Star*

Hao, Jingfang. *Vagabonds: A Novel*

Harkaway, Nick. *Angelmaker*

Harkaway, Nick. *Gnomon: A Novel*

Harkaway, Nick. *The Gone-Away World*

Harrison, M. John. *Light*

Harrison, M. John. *Nova Swing*

Heinlein, Robert A. ★*Starship Troopers*

Heinlein, Robert A. ★*Stranger in a Strange Land*

Higgins, C. A. *Lightless*

Hosking, Jay. *Three Years with the Rat: A Novel*

Huang, S. L. *Zero Sum Game*

Hurley, Kameron. ★*The Light Brigade*

Hurley, Kameron. *The Stars Are Legion*

Huxley, Aldous. ★*Brave New World*

Ishiguro, Kazuo. ★*Klara and the Sun*

Ishiguro, Kazuo. ★*Never Let Me Go*

Jemisin, N. K. *How Long 'Til Black Future Month?*

Jen, Gish. ★*The Resisters*

Jimenez, Simon. ★*The Vanished Birds*

Kadrey, Richard. *The Grand Dark*

Khoury, Raymond. *Empire of Lies*

Kim, Bo Young. ★*I'm Waiting for You: And Other Stories*

Kowal, Mary Robinette. *The Calculating Stars: A Lady Astronaut Novel*

Kowal, Mary Robinette. *The Fated Sky: A Lady Astronaut Novel*

Kowal, Mary Robinette. *The Relentless Moon*

Kress, Nancy. *Beggars in Spain*

Kress, Nancy. *If Tomorrow Comes*

Kress, Nancy. *Tomorrow's Kin*

Lafferty, Mur. *Six Wakes*

Lai, Larissa. *The Tiger Flu*

Le Guin, Ursula K. *The Birthday of the World: And Other Stories*

Le Guin, Ursula K. *Four Ways to Forgiveness*

Le Guin, Ursula K. *The Lathe of Heaven*

Le Guin, Ursula K. ★*The Left Hand of Darkness*

Le Guin, Ursula K. *The Telling*

Leckie, Ann. *Ancillary Justice*

Leckie, Ann. *Ancillary Mercy*

Leckie, Ann. *Provenance*

Lee, Yoon Ha. *Ninefox Gambit*

Lee, Yoon Ha. *Raven Stratagem*

Lee, Yoon Ha. *Revenant Gun*

Levine, David D. *Arabella of Mars*

Lewis, Linden A. *The First Sister: A Novel*

Liu, Cixin. *Ball Lightning*

Liu, Cixin. ★*The Dark Forest*

Liu, Cixin. ★*Death's End*

Liu, Cixin. ★*The Three-Body Problem*

Liu, Ken. *Invisible Planets: Contemporary Chinese Science Fiction in Translation*

Lu, S. Qiouyi. *In the Watchful City*

Mackintosh, Anneliese. *Bright and Dangerous Objects*

Mandel, Emily St. John. ★*Station Eleven*

McCaffrey, Anne. ★*Acorna: The Unicorn Girl*

McDonald, Ian. *New Moon*

McKinney, Chris. *Midnight, Water City*

Merbeth, K. S. ★*Fortuna*

Mieville, China. *Embassytown*

Mieville, China. ★*Perdido Street Station*

Miles, Terry. *Rabbits*

Minh, Drew. *Neon Empire*

Montag, Kassandra. *After the Flood: A Novel*

Montimore, Margarita. *Oona Out of Order*

Newitz, Annalee. *Autonomous*

Newland, Courttia. *A River Called Time*

Nguyen, Lena. *We Have Always Been Here*

North, Claire. *Notes from the Burning Age*

O'Keefe, Megan E. *Velocity Weapon*

Ogden, Aimee. *Sun-Daughters, Sea-Daughters*

Okorafor, Nnedi. ★*Binti*

Okorafor, Nnedi. *Binti: Home*

Okorafor, Nnedi. *Binti: The Night Masquerade*

Okorafor, Nnedi. ★*Noor*

Okorafor, Nnedi. ★*Remote Control*

Orwell, George. ★*1984: A Novel*

Palmer, Ada. *Too Like the Lightning*

Palmer, Dexter Clarence. *Version Control*

Paolini, Christopher. ★*To Sleep in a Sea of Stars*

Pohl, Frederik. *Gateway*

Porter, Chana. *The Seep: A Novel*

Rajaniemi, Hannu. *The Fractal Prince*

Rajaniemi, Hannu. *The Quantum Thief*

Reynolds, Alastair. *Permafrost*

Reynolds, Alastair. *Revelation Space*

Reynolds, Alastair. ★*Revenger*

Robinson, Kim Stanley. *Antarctica*

Robinson, Kim Stanley. *Aurora*

Robinson, Kim Stanley. ★*Blue Mars*

Robinson, Kim Stanley. ★*Green Mars*

Robinson, Kim Stanley. *The Martians*

Robinson, Kim Stanley. *New York 2140*

Ruff, Matt. *Lovecraft Country: A Novel*

Russell, Mary Doria. ★*Children of God: A Novel*

Russell, Mary Doria. ★*The Sparrow*

Sakey, Marcus. *A Better World*

Sakey, Marcus. *Brilliance*

Scalzi, John. *The Collapsing Empire*

Scalzi, John. *Head On*

Scalzi, John. ★*Lock In*

Scalzi, John. ★*Old Man's War*

Scalzi, John. *Redshirts: A Novel with Three Codas*

Simmons, Dan. *Endymion*

Simmons, Dan. *The Rise of Endymion*

Sloan, Robin. *Mr. Penumbra's 24-Hour Bookstore*

Starling, Caitlin. *The Luminous Dead*

Steele, Allen M. *Coyote: A Novel of Interstellar Exploration*

Stephenson, Neal. *Anathem*

Stephenson, Neal. ★*Cryptonomicon*

Stephenson, Neal. *The Diamond Age,: Or, a Young Lady's Illustrated Primer*

Stephenson, Neal. ★*Fall Or, Dodge in Hell: A Novel*

Stephenson, Neal. *Reamde*

Stephenson, Neal. *Seveneves*

Stephenson, Neal. ★*Snow Crash*

Sterling, Bruce. *Pirate Utopia*

Stewart, George R. *Earth Abides*

Stirling, S. M. *Dies the Fire*

Stirling, S. M. *A Meeting at Corvallis*

Stirling, S. M. *The Protector's War*

Stross, Charles. *Accelerando*

Stross, Charles. *Empire Games*

Stross, Charles. *Glasshouse*

Stross, Charles. *Neptune's Brood*

Stross, Charles. *Saturn's Children: A Space Opera*

Suarez, Daniel. *Change Agent: A Novel*

Swanwick, Michael. *Bones of the Earth*

Sweeney-Baird, Christina. *The End of Men*

Swyler, Erika. ★*Light from Other Stars: A Novel*

Tepper, Sheri S. *The Gate to Women's Country*

Tepper, Sheri S. ★*Grass*

Tepper, Sheri S. *Singer from the Sea*

Tepper, Sheri S. *The Visitor*

Thompson, Tade. *Rosewater*

Thompson, Tade. *The Rosewater Insurrection*

Thompson, Tade. *The Rosewater Redemption*
Turnbull, Cadwell. ★*The Lesson*
Valente, Catherynne M. *Radiance*
Valente, Catherynne M. *Space Opera*
VanderMeer, Jeff. *Acceptance: A Novel*
Vandermeer, Jeff. ★*Annihilation: A Novel*
VanderMeer, Jeff. *Authority: A Novel*
VanderMeer, Jeff. ★*Borne: A Novel*
VanderMeer, Jeff. *Dead Astronauts: A Novel*
Varley, John. *Dark Lightning*
Varley, John. *Demon*
Varley, John. ★*Titan*
Verne, Jules. ★*Journey to the Centre of the Earth*
Vinge, Joan D. *The Snow Queen*
Vinge, Vernor. *The Children of the Sky*
Vonnegut, Kurt. ★*Galapagos: A Novel*
Vonnegut, Kurt. ★*The Sirens of Titan*
Vonnegut, Kurt. *Welcome to the Monkey House*
Wagers, K. B. *After the Crown*
Wagers, K. B. *There Before the Chaos*
Walker, Karen Thompson. *The Age of Miracles: A Novel*
Walton, Jo. ★*Necessity*
Weinstein, Alexander. *Children of the New World: Stories*
Weir, Andy. *Artemis*
Weir, Andy. *The Martian*
Wells, H. G. *The Complete Short Stories of H. G. Wells*
Wells, Martha. *All Systems Red*
Wells, Martha. *Network Effect*
Wendig, Chuck. ★*Wanderers: A Novel*
Whiteley, Aliya. *From the Neck up and Other Stories*
Wilhelm, Kate. *Where Late the Sweet Birds Sang*
Williams, Drew. *The Stars Now Unclaimed*
Willis, Connie. *Crosstalk*
Willis, Connie. ★*Doomsday Book*
Wilson, Daniel H. *The Andromeda Evolution: A Novel*
Wilson, Daniel H. *The Clockwork Dynasty: A Novel*
Wilson, Daniel H. *Robogenesis: A Novel*
Winters, Ben H. *The Quiet Boy*
Winterson, Jeanette. ★*Frankissstein*
Wolfe, Gene. ★*The Best of Gene Wolfe: A Definitive Retrospective of His Finest Short Fiction*
Wong, David. *Futuristic Violence and Fancy Suits*
Yu, Charles. *How to Live Safely in a Science Fictional Universe: A Novel*

SCIENCE FICTION AUTHORS
Savage, Sam. *Firmin: Adventures of a Metropolitan Lowlife*

SCIENCE FICTION CLASSICS
Adams, Douglas. ★*The Hitchhiker's Guide to the Galaxy*
Asimov, Isaac. ★*Foundation*
Asimov, Isaac. *Foundation and Empire*
Asimov, Isaac. *Second Foundation*
Atwood, Margaret. ★*The Handmaid's Tale*
Banks, Iain. *Consider Phlebas*
Banks, Iain. *The Hydrogen Sonata*
Banks, Iain. *Matter*
Banks, Iain. *The Player of Games*
Banks, Iain. *Use of Weapons*
Bear, Greg. *The Forge of God*

Bradbury, Ray. ★*Fahrenheit 451*
Bradbury, Ray. ★*The Martian Chronicles: The Fortieth Anniversary Edition*
Card, Orson Scott. ★*Ender's Game*
Clarke, Arthur C. ★*2001: A Space Odyssey*
Clarke, Arthur C. ★*Childhood's End*
Clarke, Arthur C. *Rendezvous with Rama*
Dick, Philip K. ★*Do Androids Dream of Electric Sheep?*
Dick, Philip K. ★*The Man in the High Castle*
Gibson, William. ★*Neuromancer*
Gilman, Charlotte Perkins. *Herland*
Haldeman, Joe W. ★*The Forever War*
Heinlein, Robert A. *The Moon Is a Harsh Mistress*
Heinlein, Robert A. ★*Stranger in a Strange Land*
Herbert, Frank. ★*Dune*
Huxley, Aldous. ★*Brave New World*
Kress, Nancy. *Beggars in Spain*
Le Guin, Ursula K. ★*The Dispossessed: An Ambiguous Utopia*
Le Guin, Ursula K. *The Lathe of Heaven*
Le Guin, Ursula K. ★*The Left Hand of Darkness*
Miller, Walter M. ★*A Canticle for Leibowitz*
Orwell, George. ★*1984: A Novel*
Pohl, Frederik. *Gateway*
Pynchon, Thomas. ★*Gravity's Rainbow*
Robinson, Kim Stanley. ★*Blue Mars*
Robinson, Kim Stanley. ★*Green Mars*
Robinson, Kim Stanley. ★*Red Mars*
Sagan, Carl. *Contact: A Novel*
Simmons, Dan. *The Fall of Hyperion*
Simmons, Dan. ★*Hyperion*
Stephenson, Neal. ★*Snow Crash*
Stewart, George R. *Earth Abides*
Tepper, Sheri S. ★*Grass*
Van Vogt, A. E. ★*Slan*
Vinge, Joan D. *The Snow Queen*
Vinge, Vernor. *A Fire Upon the Deep*
Vonnegut, Kurt. ★*Player Piano*
Vonnegut, Kurt. ★*The Sirens of Titan*
Wells, H. G. ★*The Invisible Man*
Wilhelm, Kate. *Where Late the Sweet Birds Sang*
Willis, Connie. ★*Doomsday Book*
Wolfe, Gene. *The Citadel of the Autarch*
Wolfe, Gene. *The Claw of the Conciliator*

SCIENCE FICTION MYSTERIES
Adams, Douglas. *Dirk Gently's Holistic Detective Agency*
Deon, Natashia. *The Perishing: A Novel*
Gibson, William. *Pattern Recognition*
Hamilton, Peter F. *Great North Road*
Harkaway, Nick. *Angelmaker*
Kroese, Robert. *The Last Iota*
Martine, Arkady. ★*A Desolation Called Peace*
Martine, Arkady. ★*A Memory Called Empire*
McKinney, Chris. *Midnight, Water City*
O'Dell, Claire. *A Study in Honor: A Novel*
Rajaniemi, Hannu. *The Fractal Prince*
Rajaniemi, Hannu. *The Quantum Thief*
Vaughn, Carrie. *Bannerless*

SCIENCE FICTION THRILLERS
Cantrell, Christian. *Scorpion*
Crouch, Blake. *Dark Matter: A Novel*
Crouch, Blake. *Recursion*
Gailey, Sarah. *The Echo Wife*
Grant, Mira. *Parasite*
Johnson, Micaiah. *The Space Between Worlds*
Lafferty, Mur. *Six Wakes*
McDevitt, Jack. *The Engines of God*
Nguyen, Lena. *We Have Always Been Here*
Stephenson, Neal. *Reamde*
Weir, Andy. *Project Hail Mary*
Wilson, Daniel H. *The Andromeda Evolution: A Novel*
Wilson, Daniel H. *Robogenesis: A Novel*
SCIENTIFIC DISCOVERIES
Labatut, Benjamin. *When We Cease to Understand the World*
Liu, Cixin. *Ball Lightning*
SCIENTIFIC EXPEDITIONS
McGregor, Jon. *Lean Fall Stand*
Verne, Jules. ★*Journey to the Centre of the Earth*
SCIENTISTS
Abbott, Megan E. ★*Give Me Your Hand*
Abe, Kobo. *The Woman in the Dunes*
Boyle, T. Coraghessan. *The Terranauts*
Bunn, T. Davis. *Outbreak*
Chayefsky, Paddy. *Altered States: A Novel*
Collins, Manda. *One for the Rogue*
Crouch, Blake. *Dark Matter: A Novel*
Cussler, Clive. *Ghost Ship*
DeLillo, Don. *Zero K: A Novel*
Doctorow, E. L. *Andrew's Brain*
Egan, Greg. *Schild's Ladder*
Fowles, John. ★*The French Lieutenant's Woman*
Giordano, Paolo. *Like Family*
Grant, Mira. *Into the Drowning Deep*
Holroyde, Claire. *The Effort*
Jones, Cynan. *Stillicide*
Kress, Nancy. *If Tomorrow Comes*
Kress, Nancy. *Tomorrow's Kin*
Labatut, Benjamin. *When We Cease to Understand the World*
Lem, Stanislaw. *His Master's Voice*
Lem, Stanislaw. ★*Solaris*
Liu, Cixin. ★*Death's End*
Mieville, China. ★*Perdido Street Station*
Newitz, Annalee. *Autonomous*
Penrose, Andrea. *Murder at Half Moon Gate*
Penrose, Andrea. ★*Murder at Kensington Palace*
Penrose, Andrea. *Murder on Black Swan Lane*
Perry, Anne. ★*A Darker Reality*
Persson Giolito, Malin. *Beyond All Reasonable Doubt: A Novel*
Sanders, Lawrence. *The Sixth Commandment: A Novel*
Sebastian, Cat. *The Lawrence Browne Affair*
Shelley, Mary Wollstonecraft. ★*Frankenstein: Or, the Modern Prometheus*
Stevenson, Robert Louis. ★*The Strange Case of Dr. Jekyll and Mr. Hyde*
Tyler, Anne. *Vinegar Girl: The Taming of the Shrew Retold*
VanderMeer, Jeff. *Acceptance: A Novel*

Vandermeer, Jeff. ★*Annihilation: A Novel*
VanderMeer, Jeff. *Authority: A Novel*
Vonnegut, Kurt. ★*Cat's Cradle*
Wells, H. G. ★*The Invisible Man*
Wells, H. G. ★*The Time Machine*
Wells, Martha. *All Systems Red*
Williams, Beatriz. *The Golden Hour*
Scoppettone, Sandra
Everything You Have Is Mine
My Sweet Untraceable You
Scorpion. Cantrell, Christian
Scot & Soda. McPherson, Catriona
SCOTLAND
Anstruther, Eleanor. *A Perfect Explanation*
Atkinson, Kate. *One Good Turn: A Novel*
Banks, Iain. *The Crow Road*
Banks, Maya. *Never Seduce a Scot*
Beaton, M. C. *Death of a Macho Man*
Brockway, Connie. *So Enchanting*
Buchan, John. *The Thirty-Nine Steps*
Cleeves, Ann. *Raven Black*
Cleeves, Ann. *Thin Air*
Cleeves, Ann. *Wild Fire*
Cole, Alyssa. ★*A Duke by Default*
Colgan, Jenny. ★*The Endless Beach*
Cronin, Marianne. *The One Hundred Years of Lenni and Margot*
Dare, Tessa. *When a Scot Ties the Knot*
Elliott, Lexie. *The Missing Years*
Foley, Lucy. *The Hunting Party*
Follett, Ken. *Eye of the Needle*
Follett, Ken. ★*Whiteout*
Gabaldon, Diana. ★*Dragonfly in Amber*
Gabaldon, Diana. ★*Outlander*
Gabaldon, Diana. ★*Voyager*
Glass, Julia. ★*Three Junes*
Goddard, Robert. *Never Go Back*
Griffiths, Elly. *The Postscript Murders*
Hill, Susan. *The Shadows in the Street: A Simon Serrailler Mystery*
Jordan, Sophie. *This Scot of Mine*
Livesey, Margot. *Criminals: A Novel*
London, Julia. *Wild Wicked Scot*
MacBride, Stuart. *Cold Granite*
May, Peter. *The Blackhouse*
McCall Smith, Alexander. *The Comforts of a Muddy Saturday: An Isabel Dalhousie Novel*
McCall Smith, Alexander. *The Forgotten Affairs of Youth*
McCall Smith, Alexander. *The Lost Art of Gratitude*
McConaghy, Charlotte. *Once There Were Wolves: A Novel*
McDermid, Val. *The Distant Echo*
McDermid, Val. ★*Still Life*
McPherson, Catriona. *Quiet Neighbors: A Novel*
McPherson, Catriona. ★*A Step so Grave*
McPherson, Catriona. *Strangers at the Gate*
Mina, Denise. *Conviction*
Mina, Denise. *The Less Dead*
Mina, Denise. ★*Rizzio*
Moss, Sarah. *Summerwater*
O'Farrell, Maggie. *The Vanishing Act of Esme Lennox*

Parry, Ambrose. *The Way of All Flesh*
Pike, Signe. *The Forgotten Kingdom: A Novel*
Pike, Signe. *The Lost Queen*
Pirie, David. *The Patient's Eyes*
Pulley, Natasha. ★*The Kingdoms*
Rankin, Ian. *Blood Hunt: A Novel*
Rankin, Ian. *Exit Music*
Rankin, Ian. *The Naming of the Dead: An Inspector Rebus Novel*
Rankin, Ian. ★*Rather Be the Devil*
Rankin, Ian. *Set in Darkness: An Inspector Rebus Novel*
Rankin, Ian. ★*A Song for the Dark Times*
Sayers, Dorothy L. ★*The Five Red Herrings*
Scott, A. D. ★*Beneath the Abbey Wall: A Novel*
Scott, A. D. *A Double Death on the Black Isle: A Novel*
Scott, A. D. *A Kind of Grief: A Novel*
Scott, A. D. ★*The Low Road*
Scott, Walter. *The Bride of Lammermoor*
Scott, Walter. ★*Rob Roy*
Spark, Muriel. ★*The Prime of Miss Jean Brodie*
Sullivan, Emily. *The Rebel and the Rake*
Ware, Ruth. ★*The Turn of the Key*
Welsh, Kaite. *The Unquiet Heart*
Welsh, Kaite. *The Wages of Sin*
Woods, Stuart. *Stealth*
Wynne, Phoebe. *Madam*

SCOTS
Burrowes, Grace. *The Trouble with Dukes*

SCOTS IN AMERICA
Gabaldon, Diana. ★*A Breath of Snow and Ashes*
Gabaldon, Diana. ★*Drums of Autumn*
Gabaldon, Diana. *An Echo in the Bone*
Gabaldon, Diana. ★*The Fiery Cross*
Gabaldon, Diana. *Written in My Own Heart's Blood*

SCOTS IN THE UNITED STATES
Glass, Julia. ★*Three Junes*
Mark, David John. *Cruel Mercy*
McPherson, Catriona. *Scot & Soda*

Scott, A. D.
★*Beneath the Abbey Wall: A Novel*
A Double Death on the Black Isle: A Novel
A Kind of Grief: A Novel
★*The Low Road*

Scott, Paul
★*Staying On: A Novel*

Scott, Rion Amilcar
★*The World Doesn't Require You: Stories*

Scott, Stephanie
What's Left of Me Is Yours: A Novel

Scott, Walter
The Bride of Lammermoor
★*Ivanhoe*
★*Rob Roy*

SCOTTISH STEWART PERIOD (1371-1603)
Mina, Denise. ★*Rizzio*

Scottoline, Lisa
After Anna
★*Come Home*
Don't Go

★*Every Fifteen Minutes*
Feared
Legal Tender
One Perfect Lie
A Scourge of Vipers. DeSilva, Bruce

SCOUTING (RECONNAISSANCE)
Cobbs Hoffman, Elizabeth. *The Tubman Command: A Novel*
The Scrapbook of Frankie Pratt. Preston, Caroline

SCRAPBOOKS
Preston, Caroline. *The Scrapbook of Frankie Pratt*

SCREENPLAY WRITING
Kleeman, Alexandra. *Something New Under the Sun*
Winfrey, Kerry. *Waiting for Tom Hanks: A Novel*

SCREENWRITERS
Baldwin, Joshua. *The Wilshire Sun*
The Scribe: a Novel. Guinn, Matthew

SCRIBES
Greenwood, Kerry. *Out of the Black Land*

SCUBA DIVING
Steadman, Catherine. *Something in the Water*

SCUDDER, MATT (FICTITIOUS CHARACTER)
Block, Lawrence. *A Drop of the Hard Stuff: A Matthew Scudder Novel*

SCULPTORS
Carey, Edward. *Little: A Novel*
McLaughlin, Danielle. *The Art of Falling*

SCULPTURE
Blackwell, Juliet. *Letters from Paris*
★*The Sea*. Banville, John
The Sea Captain's Wife: A Novel. Powning, Beth
Sea Glass: A Novel. Shreve, Anita
The Sea Lady. Drabble, Margaret

SEA LEVEL
Cussler, Clive. ★*The Rising Sea: A Novel from the Numa Files*
Robinson, Kim Stanley. *New York 2140*

SEA MONSTERS
Alten, Steve. *Meg: Generations*
Grant, Mira. *Into the Drowning Deep*
Simmons, Dan. ★*The Terror: A Novel*
Sea of fertility [Series]. Mishima, Yukio
★*Sea of Greed: A Novel from the Numa Files*. Cussler, Clive
The Sea of Lost Girls. Goodman, Carol
Sea of Poppies. Ghosh, Amitav
★*Sea Prayer*. Hosseini, Khaled

SEA STORIES
Alten, Steve. *Meg: Generations*
Beach, Edward L. *Run Silent, Run Deep*
Clancy, Tom. ★*The Hunt for Red October*
Conrad, Joseph. ★*Lord Jim*
Cussler, Clive. ★*Golden Buddha*
Cussler, Clive. *Pacific Vortex!*
Cussler, Clive. ★*Raise the Titanic!*
Cussler, Clive. *Sacred Stone*
Doyle, Brian. *The Plover: A Novel*
Endicott, Marina. *The Voyage of the Morning Light*
Forester, C. S. *Admiral Hornblower in the West Indies*
Forester, C. S. *Beat to Quarters*
Forester, C. S. *Commodore Hornblower*

Forester, C. S. *Flying Colours*
Forester, C. S. *Hornblower and the Atropos*
Forester, C. S. *Hornblower and the Hotspur*
Forester, C. S. *Lieutenant Hornblower*
Forester, C. S. *Lord Hornblower*
Forester, C. S. *Mr. Midshipman Hornblower*
Forester, C. S. *Ship of the Line*
Furst, Alan. *Dark Voyage: A Novel*
Gelernter, J. H. *Hold Fast*
Golding, William. *Close Quarters*
Golding, William. *Fire Down Below*
Golding, William. *Rites of Passage*
Hawks, Arlem. *Georgana's Secret*
Heggen, Thomas. *Mister Roberts*
Johnson, Charles Richard. ★*Middle Passage*
Melville, Herman. ★*Moby-Dick; Or, the Whale*
Monsarrat, Nicholas. *The Cruel Sea*
O'Brian, Patrick. *Master and Commander*
Poe, Edgar Allan. *The Narrative of Arthur Gordon Pym of Nantucket*
Poyer, David. *Overthrow: The War with China and North Korea—Fall of an Empire*
Poyer, David. *Violent Peace: The War with China - Aftermath of Armageddon*
Sabatini, Rafael. *Captain Blood*
Simmons, Dan. ★*The Terror: A Novel*
Smith, Wilbur A. *Birds of Prey*
Smith, Wilbur A. *Monsoon*
Verne, Jules. *The Mysterious Island*
Wouk, Herman. ★*The Caine Mutiny: A Novel of World War II*
Sea Swept. Roberts, Nora
Sea trilogy [Series]. Golding, William
Sea Wife. Gaige, Amity
The Sea, the Sea. Murdoch, Iris
SEAFARING LIFE
Adams, Hope. *Dangerous Women*
Birch, Carol. *Jamrach's Menagerie*
Conrad, Joseph. *Complete Short Fiction of Joseph Conrad: The Stories: Volume 1*
Gaige, Amity. *Sea Wife*
Ghosh, Amitav. *Flood of Fire*
Heggen, Thomas. *Mister Roberts*
O'Brian, Patrick. *Master and Commander*
Powning, Beth. *The Sea Captain's Wife: A Novel*
Sabatini, Rafael. *Captain Blood*
SEAMSTRESSES
Duenas, Maria. *The Time in Between: A Novel*
Medie, Peace A. *His Only Wife: A Novel*
Sean Dillon thrillers [Series]. Higgins, Jack
Sean Duffy novels [Series]. McKinty, Adrian
SEANCES
Clare, Alys. *The Woman Who Spoke to Spirits*
Pyper, Andrew. *The Residence: A Novel*
SEARCH AND RESCUE OPERATIONS
Deutermann, Peter T. *The Nugget: A Novel*
Gaynor, Hazel. *The Lighthouse Keeper's Daughter*
Higgins, Jack. *The Eagle Has Flown*
Shalvis, Jill. *Second Chance Summer*
Snow, Jennifer. *An Alaskan Christmas*

Warren, Susan May. *Rescue Me*
★*The Searcher*. French, Tana
SEARCHING
Baxter, Charles. ★*The Sun Collective*
Lovett, Charles C. *The Lost Book of the Grail: Or a Visitor's Guide to Barchester Cathedral*
Luesse, Valerie Fraser. *Missing Isaac*
Pitts, Leonard. *Freeman*
Quotah, Eman. ★*Bride of the Sea: A Novel*
Searching for Sylvie Lee. Kwok, Jean
Searles, John
Help for the Haunted
Sears, Michael
Black Fridays
Tower of Babel
SEASIDE RESORTS
James, P. D. *The Lighthouse*
Season for scandal [Series]. Bowen, Kelly
A Season for the Dead. Hewson, David
A Season of Ruin. Bradley, Anna
Seasonal [Series]. Smith, Ali
Seasons of grace (Beverly Lewis) [Series]. Lewis, Beverly
SEATTLE, WASHINGTON
Bellefleur, Alexandria. *Hang the Moon*
Bellefleur, Alexandria. *Written in the Stars*
Burns, Charles. ★*Black Hole*
Buxton, Kira Jane. ★*Hollow Kingdom*
Cain, Chelsea. *One Kick: A Novel*
Dugoni, Robert. *The Conviction*
Dugoni, Robert. *Murder One*
Dugoni, Robert. *My Sister's Grave*
Eisler, Barry. *Livia Lone*
Fisher, Tarryn. *The Wives*
Hockman, Angie. *Shipped*
Kohnstamm, Thomas B. *Lake City*
Krentz, Jayne Ann. *When All the Girls Have Gone*
Lalli, Sonya. *A Holly Jolly Diwali*
McDonald, Christina. *Behind Every Lie*
Priest, Cherie. *Boneshaker*
Priest, Cherie. *The Inexplicables*
Rimmer, Kelly. *Truths I Never Told You*
Robbins, Tom. ★*Jitterbug Perfume*
Semple, Maria. *Where'd You Go, Bernadette: A Novel*
Solomon, Rachel Lynn. ★*The Ex Talk*
Van Dyken, Rachel. *Risky Play*
Vann, David. *Aquarium*
Sebald, Winfried Georg
★*Austerlitz*
The Emigrants
Vertigo
Sebastian Becker mysteries [Series]. Gallagher, Stephen
Sebastian St. Cyr mysteries [Series]. Harris, C. S.
Sebastian, Cat
It Takes Two to Tumble
The Lawrence Browne Affair
Unmasked by the Marquess
Sebastian, Tim
Fatal Ally

Sebold, Alice

The Almost Moon: A Novel

★*The Lovely Bones*

The **Second** Biggest Nothing. Cotterill, Colin

Second Chance Summer. Shalvis, Jill

SECOND CHANCES

Anders, Adriana. *Under Her Skin*

Ashley, Jennifer. *Lady Isabella's Scandalous Marriage*

Balogh, Mary. ★*Someone to Remember: A Westcott Story*

Dev, Sonali. *The Bollywood Bride*

Dimon, HelenKay. *Her Other Secret*

Drake, Laura. *The Sweet Spot*

Gaynor, Hazel. *Meet Me in Monaco: A Novel*

Hart, John. *Iron House*

Hiaasen, Carl. *Star Island*

Patrick, Phaedra. ★*The Secrets of Love Story Bridge*

Pineiro, Caridad. *What Happens in Summer*

Putney, Mary Jo. *Not Quite a Wife*

Rai, Alisha. ★*The Right Swipe*

Shalvis, Jill. *Second Chance Summer*

Shalvis, Jill. *The Sweetest Thing*

The **Second** Coming. Percy, Walker

SECOND COMING OF CHRIST

Percy, Walker. *The Second Coming*

The **Second** Deadly Sin. Sanders, Lawrence

Second First Impressions. Thorne, Sally

Second Foundation. Asimov, Isaac

Second L. A. quartet [Series]. Ellroy, James

The **Second** Life of Nick Mason: A Novel. Hamilton, Steve

SECOND PERSON NARRATIVES

Acampora, Lauren. *The Paper Wasp: A Novel*

Audrain, Ashley. *The Push*

Dangarembga, Tsitsi. *This Mournable Body*

Hendricks, Greer. *An Anonymous Girl*

Jedrowski, Tomasz. *Swimming in the Dark*

Leckie, Ann. ★*The Raven Tower*

Polansky, Daniel. *The Seventh Perfection*

Second Place. Cusk, Rachel

Second Shot: A Charlie Fox Thriller. Sharp, Zoe

The **Second** Sleep: A Novel. Harris, Robert

SECOND WIVES

Blum, Jenna. *The Lost Family*

SECOND WORLD WAR ERA (1939-1945)

Adimi, Kaouther. *Our Riches*

Alderson, Kaia. *Sisters in Arms*

Amis, Martin. ★*The Zone of Interest: A Novel*

Austin, Lynn N. *Chasing Shadows*

Ballard, J. G. *Empire of the Sun: A Novel*

Balzano, Marco. *I'm Staying Here*

Bausch, Richard. *Peace*

Beach, Edward L. *Run Silent, Run Deep*

Belfoure, Charles. *The Paris Architect: A Novel*

Benioff, David. *City of Thieves: A Novel*

Benn, James R. *Billy Boyle: A World War Two Mystery*

Benn, James R. ★*The Red Horse: A Billy Boyle World War II Mystery*

Benn, James R. *Road of Bones: A Billy Boyle World War II Mystery*

Binder, L. Annette. *The Vanishing Sky*

Binet, Laurent. ★*HHhH*

Black, Benjamin. ★*The Secret Guests: A Novel*

Black, Cara. ★*Three Hours in Paris*

Blake, Sarah. *The Postmistress*

Bohjalian, Chris. *Skeletons at the Feast: A Novel*

Boulle, Pierre. *The Bridge Over the River Kwai: A Novel*

Bowen, Elizabeth. *The Heat of the Day*

Byatt, A. S. ★*Ragnarok: The End of the Gods*

Carter, Michaela. *Leonora in the Morning Light*

Dallas, Sandra. *Tallgrass*

Dalton, Trent. *All Our Shimmering Skies*

Deutermann, Peter T. *The Iceman*

Deutermann, Peter T. *The Nugget: A Novel*

Deutermann, Peter T. *Pacific Glory: A Novel*

Doerr, Anthony. ★*All the Light We Cannot See: A Novel*

Downing, David. *Diary of a Dead Man on Leave*

Egan, Jennifer. ★*Manhattan Beach: A Novel*

Eliasberg, Jan. ★*Hannah's War*

Ellroy, James. *Perfidia*

Ellroy, James. *This Storm: A Novel*

Escobar, Mario. *The Librarian of Saint-Malo: A Novel*

Faulks, Sebastian. *Charlotte Gray: A Novel*

Feldman, Ellen. *Paris Never Leaves You*

Fleischmann, Raymond. *How Quickly She Disappears*

Follett, Ken. *Eye of the Needle*

Follett, Ken. *Hornet Flight*

Follett, Ken. *Jackdaws*

Furst, Alan. *Blood of Victory: A Novel*

Furst, Alan. ★*A Hero of France*

Furst, Alan. ★*Under Occupation: A Novel*

Gilbers, Harald. *Germania: A Novel of Nazi Berlin*

Gillham, David R. *City of Women*

Graves, Stephanie. *Olive Bright, Pigeoneer*

Green, Amy Lynn. *Things We Didn't Say*

Gross, Andrew. *The One Man*

Hannah, Kristin. *The Nightingale*

Harmel, Kristin. *The Room on Rue Amelie*

Harper, Karen. *The Queen's Secret: A Novel of England's World War II Queen*

Healey, Jane. *The Animals at Lockwood Manor*

Hewson, David. *The Garden of Angels*

Hirahara, Naomi. ★*Clark and Division*

Hoffman, Alice. ★*The World That We Knew*

Indriðason, Arnaldur. *The Shadow District: A Thriller*

Jensen, Nancy. *In Our Midst*

Johnson, Alaya Dawn. *Trouble the Saints*

Kelly, Julia. *The Light Over London*

Kelly, Martha Hall. *Lilac Girls*

Kelly, Stephen. *The Wages of Desire: A World War II Mystery*

Kerr, Philip. ★*Greeks Bearing Gifts: A Bernie Gunther Novel*

Kerr, Philip. ★*Prussian Blue*

Kiernan, Stephen P. *Universe of Two*

Knowles, John. ★*A Separate Peace*

Konar, Affinity. *Mischling: A Novel*

Landau, Alexis. *Those Who Are Saved*

Lehane, Dennis. *World Gone By: A Novel*

Loigman, Lynda Cohen. *The Wartime Sisters: A Novel*

MacNeal, Susan Elia. *The King's Justice*

Mailer, Norman. ★*The Naked and the Dead*

McFadden, Bernice L. *The Book of Harlan*
Meacham, Leila. *Dragonfly: A Novel*
Mengiste, Maaza. ★*The Shadow King: A Novel*
Michener, James A. ★*Tales of the South Pacific*
Monsarrat, Nicholas. *The Cruel Sea*
Morelli, Laura. *The Stolen Lady*
Orringer, Julie. ★*The Flight Portfolio: A Novel*
Orringer, Julie. ★*The Invisible Bridge: A Novel*
Otsuka, Julie. *The Buddha in the Attic*
Otsuka, Julie. *When the Emperor Was Divine: A Novel*
Piercy, Marge. *Gone to Soldiers: A Novel*
Pilcher, Rosamunde. *Coming Home*
Pynchon, Thomas. ★*Gravity's Rainbow*
Ramzipoor, E. R. *The Ventriloquists*
Remarque, Erich Maria. *A Time to Love and a Time to Die*
Rimmer, Kelly. ★*The Warsaw Orphan: A Wwii Novel*
Ripley, Mike. *Mr. Campion's War*
Rizzuto, Rahna R. *Shadow Child*
Robbins, David L. *Last Citadel: A Novel of the Battle of Kursk*
Robbins, David L. *War of the Rats: A Novel*
Roosevelt, Elliott. *Murder in the Map Room: An Eleanor Roosevelt Mystery*
Rosner, Jennifer. ★*The Yellow Bird Sings*
Russell, Mary Doria. *A Thread of Grace: A Novel*
Ryan, Jennifer. *The Spies of Shilling Lane: A Novel*
Sartre, Jean Paul. *Troubled Sleep*
Sem-Sandberg, Steve. *The Chosen Ones: A Novel*
Shaara, Jeff. *The Rising Tide: A Novel of World War II*
Shaara, Jeff. *The Steel Wave: A Novel of World War II*
Shaffer, Mary Ann. *The Guernsey Literary and Potato Peel Pie Society*
Skeslien Charles, Janet. *The Paris Library: A Novel*
Slimani, Leïla. *In the Country of Others*
Smith, Martin Cruz. *December 6*
Steinhauer, Olen. *The Bridge of Sighs*
Sundaresan, Indu. *The Splendor of Silence: A Novel*
Sundin, Sarah. *Through Waters Deep: A Novel*
Szabo, Magda. *Abigail*
Van Booy, Simon. *The Illusion of Separateness*
Vonnegut, Kurt. ★*Slaughterhouse-Five: Or, the Children's Crusade : A Duty-Dance with Death*
Walsh, S. Kirk. *The Elephant of Belfast: A Novel*
Weaver, Ashley. ★*A Peculiar Combination*
Williams, Beatriz. *All the Ways We Said Goodbye: A Novel of the Ritz Paris*
Williams, Beatriz. *The Golden Hour*
Winspear, Jacqueline. *The American Agent*
Winspear, Jacqueline. ★*The Consequences of Fear: A Maisie Dobbs Novel*
Wouk, Herman. ★*The Caine Mutiny: A Novel of World War II*
Wouk, Herman. ★*War and Remembrance: A Novel*
Wouk, Herman. ★*The Winds of War: A Novel*

SECRECY
Black, Benjamin. ★*The Secret Guests: A Novel*
Butland, Stephanie. *The Lost for Words Bookshop: A Novel*
Catton, Eleanor. *The Luminaries: A Novel*
Cussler, Clive. ★*Final Option*
Cussler, Clive. *Shadow Tyrants*

Deaver, Jeffery. ★*The Goodbye Man*
Parris, S. J. ★*The Dead of Winter*
Parris, S. J. *Treachery*
Steinhauer, Olen. *An American Spy*
Steinhauer, Olen. *The Nearest Exit*
Stephenson, Neal. ★*Cryptonomicon*
Tenorio, Lysley A. *The Son of Good Fortune: A Novel*
Tudor, C. J. *The Burning Girls: A Novel*
Williams, Beatriz. *The Summer Wives*

SECRECY IN GOVERNMENT
Amirrezvani, Anita. *Equal of the Sun*
Benn, James R. ★*The Red Horse: A Billy Boyle World War II Mystery*
Berry, Steve. ★*The Malta Exchange: A Novel*
Church, James. *Hidden Moon: An Inspector O Novel*
Eisler, Barry. *The God's Eye View*
Golden, Christopher. *Red Hands*
Hurwitz, Gregg Andrew. ★*Out of the Dark: The Return of Orphan X*
Meltzer, Brad. *The Escape Artist*
Mukherjee, Abir. *The Shadows of Men*
Pattison, Eliot. *Bones of the Earth: An Inspector Shan Tao Yun Mystery*
Schlink, Bernhard. *Self's Deception*
Stout, Rex. *The Doorbell Rang*
Thompson, Tade. *Rosewater*
Thompson, Tade. *The Rosewater Insurrection*
VanderMeer, Jeff. *Authority: A Novel*
Vasquez, Juan Gabriel. ★*The Shape of the Ruins*
Secret brides [Series]. Bowman, Valerie
Secret diary of Hendrik Groen [Series]. Groen, Hendrik
★*The **Secret** Guests: A Novel*. Black, Benjamin
★*The **Secret** History*. Tartt, Donna

SECRET IDENTITY
Bouchet, Amanda. ★*A Promise of Fire*
Boyle, Elizabeth. *And the Miss Ran Away with the Rake*
Bronte, Charlotte. ★*Emma*
Buchanan, Edna. *You Only Die Twice: A Britt Montero Mystery*
Dodd, Christina. *Obsession Falls*
Harrington, Anna. *An Extraordinary Lord*
Hawks, Arlem. *Georgana's Secret*
Heath, Lorraine. *Falling into Bed with a Duke*
Jenkins, Beverly. *Forbidden*
Le Carre, John. *The Tailor of Panama*
Leigh, Eva. *Temptations of a Wallflower*
Littlejohn, Emily. *Inherit the Bones*
Malpas, Jodi Ellen. *Leave Me Breathless*
Orczy, Emmuska Orczy. ★*The Scarlet Pimpernel*
Parker, T. Jefferson. *L.A. Outlaws: A Novel*
Penrose, Andrea. ★*Murder at Kensington Palace*
Quick, Amanda. *The Other Lady Vanishes*
Rader-Day, Lori. ★*The Lucky One*
Rendell, Ruth. *A Sleeping Life*
Riley, Vanessa. ★*A Duke, the Lady, and a Baby*
Robinson, Peter. *Friend of the Devil*
Robotham, Michael. ★*Good Girl, Bad Girl: A Novel*
Shupe, Joanna. *The Courtesan Duchess*
Stewart, Amy. ★*Dear Miss Kopp*
★*The **Secret** Life of Bees*. Kidd, Sue Monk
*The **Secret** Life of Sarah Hollenbeck*. Turner, Bethany

The **Secret** Lives of Church Ladies. Philyaw, Deesha
The **Secret** Mistress. Balogh, Mary
The **Secret** of Clouds. Richman, Alyson
★The **Secret** Place. French, Tana
SECRET PLACES
   Hill, Joe. ★Nos4a2
The **Secret** River. Grenville, Kate
Secret scientists of London [Series]. Everett, Elizabeth
The **Secret** Scripture: A Novel. Barry, Sebastian
SECRET SERVICE
   Child, Lee. Without Fail
   Deighton, Len. Berlin Game
   Fleming, Ian. ★Casino Royale: A James Bond Novel
   Fleming, Ian. The Man with the Golden Gun
   Follett, Ken. Jackdaws
   Harris, Robert. Enigma
   Higgins, Jack. The Eagle Has Flown
   Higgins, Jack. The Eagle Has Landed
   Higgins, Jack. Eye of the Storm
   Higgins, Jack. Touch the Devil
   Persson, Leif G. W. Another Time, Another Life: The Story of a Crime
   Silva, Daniel. ★The Kill Artist: A Novel
   Smith, Tom Rob. Agent 6
   Smith, Tom Rob. Child 44
   Smith, Tom Rob. The Secret Speech
★The **Secret** She Kept. Billingsley, ReShonda Tate
Secret Sisters. Krentz, Jayne Ann
SECRET SOCIETIES
   Baldacci, David. Hell's Corner
   Bardugo, Leigh. ★Ninth House
   Bear, Elizabeth. Ink and Steel: A Novel of the Promethean Age
   Berry, Steve. ★The Bishop's Pawn
   Berry, Steve. The Lost Order
   Berry, Steve. ★The Malta Exchange: A Novel
   Brown, Dan. The Da Vinci Code
   Finch, Charles. The September Society
   Flynn, Gillian. Dark Places
   Goss, Theodora. The Sinister Mystery of the Mesmerizing Girl
   Goss, Theodora. The Strange Case of the Alchemist's Daughter
   Hoyt, Elizabeth. Not the Duke's Darling
   Huchu, Tendai. The Library of the Dead
   Hummel, Maria. Lesson in Red
   Iles, Greg. Cemetery Road: A Novel
   Krentz, Jayne Ann. ★All the Colors of Night
   Larsen, Reif. I Am Radar: A Novel
   MacLean, Sarah. ★Bombshell
   McGuire, Ian. The Abstainer: A Novel
   Meyer, Nicholas. The Adventure of the Peculiar Protocols: Adapted from the Journals of John H. Watson, M.D.
   Morgenstern, Erin. ★The Starless Sea
   Murakami, Haruki. ★1q84
   Palahniuk, Chuck. Fight Club
   Pearl, Matthew. The Technologists: A Novel
   Portis, Charles. ★Masters of Atlantis: A Novel
   Robertson, Imogen. Circle of Shadows
   Rollins, James. The Demon Crown: A Sigma Force Novel
   Siger, Jeffrey. Target Tinos: An Inspector Kaldis Mystery
   Sloan, Robin. Mr. Penumbra's 24-Hour Bookstore

   Spencer, Sally. ★The Hidden
   Spencer, Sally. The Shivering Turn
   Straub, Peter. ★Ghost Story
   Tallis, Frank. Vienna Blood: A Max Liebermann Mystery
   Williams, Lara. Supper Club: A Novel
   Wilson, Daniel H. The Clockwork Dynasty: A Novel
The **Secret** Speech. Smith, Tom Rob
SECRETARIES
   Allen, Jane. I Lost My Girlish Laughter
   McCall Smith, Alexander. The Full Cupboard of Life
   McCall Smith, Alexander. The Kalahari Typing School for Men
   Moreno-Garcia, Silvia. ★Velvet Was the Night
   Quick, Amanda. Garden of Lies
   Sundin, Sarah. Through Waters Deep: A Novel
The **Secretary**: a Novel. Knight, Renee
SECRETS
   Abbott, Megan E. ★Give Me Your Hand
   Abdul-Jabbar, Kareem. ★Mycroft Holmes
   Abrams, Melanie. Meadowlark
   Adams, Taylor. Hairpin Bridge
   Adjapon, Bisi. The Teller of Secrets: A Novel
   Adler-Olsen, Jussi. ★Victim 2117
   Albom, Mitch. The Five People You Meet in Heaven
   Antoinette, Ashley. Butterfly; Vol 2
   Antoinette, Ashley. Butterfly; Vol 3
   Armstrong, Kelley. Wherever She Goes
   Aslam, Nadeem. ★The Golden Legend: A Novel
   Atkins, Ace. The Innocents
   Balogh, Mary. The Secret Mistress
   Banks, Maya. Never Seduce a Scot
   Barclay, Linwood. A Tap on the Window
   Barry, Jessica. ★Don't Turn Around
   Barton, Fiona. The Child
   Beams, Clare. The Illness Lesson
   Beckerman, Hannah. If Only I Could Tell You
   Bell, Darcey. Something She's Not Telling Us
   Berg, Elizabeth. The Confession Club: A Novel
   Berg, Gretchen. The Operator
   Berry, Steve. ★The Templar Legacy: A Novel of Suspense
   Black, Saul. Anything for You
   Blake, Sarah. The Postmistress
   Bolano, Roberto. ★By Night in Chile
   Bourne, Joanna. ★The Spymaster's Lady
   Boyd, William. Trio
   Brown, Sandra. Tailspin
   Buchan, John. The Thirty-Nine Steps
   Butler, Nickolas. Godspeed
   Byrne, Kerrigan. The Hunter
   Capri, NeNe. The Pussy Trap; Part 3
   Castillo, Linda. ★Fallen
   Charles, KJ. Wanted, a Gentleman: Or, Virtue Over-Rated
   Chee, Alexander. The Queen of the Night
   Child, Lee. Worth Dying For
   Chizmar, Richard T. A Long December
   Christie, Agatha. ★And Then There Were None
   Clark, Marcia. Final Judgment
   Clark, Tracy P. Runner
   Cleave, Paul. A Killer Harvest: A Thriller

Cleeves, Ann. *Raven Black*
Cleeves, Ann. *Thin Air*
Clegg, Bill. *The End of the Day*
Cline, Emma. *Daddy: Stories*
Coben, Harlan. *Don't Let Go*
Coben, Harlan. *The Stranger*
Cogman, Genevieve. *The Invisible Library*
Cogman, Genevieve. *The Masked City*
Cook, Thomas H. *Sandrine's Case*
Creech, Sarah. *The Whole Way Home*
Dallas, Sandra. *The Last Midwife*
Daly, Paula. *Open Your Eyes*
Dang, Catherine. *Nice Girls*
Danticat, Edwidge. *Claire of the Sea Light*
Dare, Tessa. *When a Scot Ties the Knot*
De la Motte, Anders. *Ultimatum: A Thriller*
Deaver, Jeffery. *The October List*
Dell, Kari Lynn. *Fearless in Texas*
Dickey, Eric Jerome. *The Blackbirds*
Dimitri, Francesco. *The Book of Hidden Things*
Dodd, Christina. *Virtue Falls*
Du Maurier, Daphne. *Jamaica Inn*
Dunmore, Helen. *Exposure*
Edugyan, Esi. *Half-Blood Blues*
Ellison, Ralph. ★*Juneteenth*
Ellroy, James. ★*Widespread Panic: A Novel*
Everett, Elizabeth. ★*A Lady's Formula for Love*
Evison, Jonathan. *Legends of the North Cascades: A Novel*
Feehan, Christine. *Shadow Rider*
Feeney, Alice. ★*I Know Who You Are: A Novel*
Feeney, Alice. ★*Sometimes I Lie*
Finder, Joseph. *Buried Secrets*
Franzen, Jonathan. ★*Crossroads*
Frayn, Michael. *Spies: A Novel*
French, Jonathan. ★*The Grey Bastards*
French, Nicci. *Waiting for Wednesday: A Frieda Klein Mystery*
French, Tana. ★*The Witch Elm: A Novel*
Furst, Alan. *The Foreign Correspondent: A Novel*
Galbraith, Robert. *Career of Evil*
Galbraith, Robert. *Lethal White*
Galbraith, Robert. *The Silkworm*
Gardiner, Meg. *The Dirty Secrets Club*
Gardner, Lisa. ★*Never Tell: A Novel*
Gardner, Lisa. ★*When You See Me: A Novel*
George, Alex. *The Paris Hours: A Novel*
Gillham, David R. *City of Women*
Gnuse, A. J. *Girl in the Walls: A Novel*
Goddard, Robert. *Beyond Recall: A Novel*
Goddard, Robert. *Never Go Back*
Goldin, Megan. *The Escape Room*
Goldin, Megan. *The Night Swim*
Grant, Helen. *The Vanishing of Katharina Linden*
Grebe, Camilla. *After She's Gone: A Novel*
Gregory, Daryl. *The Devil's Alphabet*
Grisham, John. *The Client*
Guterson, David. *The Other*
Hall, Araminta. *Imperfect Women: A Novel*

Hall, Tarquin. *The Case of the Deadly Butter Chicken: A Vish Puri Mystery*
Hand, Elizabeth. ★*Generation Loss: A Novel*
Harding Thornton, Christina. *Pickard County Atlas*
Harman, Patricia. *The Midwife of Hope River: A Novel*
Harrod-Eagles, Cynthia. *Headlong*
Hart, John. *Iron House*
Harvey, Michael T. *The Governor's Wife*
Hawkins, Paula. ★*The Girl on the Train: A Novel*
Hawkins, Scott. ★*The Library at Mount Char*
Healey, Jane. *The Animals at Lockwood Manor*
Hegi, Ursula. *Stones from the River*
Herbert, Julian. *Bring Me the Head of Quentin Tarantino: Stories*
Higashino, Keigo. *Newcomer*
Higgins, Kristan. *Always the Last to Know*
Hilderbrand, Elin. ★*What Happens in Paradise: A Novel*
Hilderbrand, Elin. ★*Winter in Paradise: A Novel*
Hill, Joe. *Heart-Shaped Box*
Hoffman, Alice. *The Ice Queen: A Novel*
Hornby, Gill. *Miss Austen*
Horowitz, Anthony. ★*The Sentence Is Death*
Horowitz, Anthony. ★*The Word Is Murder*
Indriðason, Arnaldur. *Outrage*
Jackson, Joshilyn. *Never Have I Ever*
James, Rebecca. *The Woman in the Mirror*
Jayatissa, Amanda. ★*My Sweet Girl*
Jewell, Lisa. *Watching You*
Jimenez, Abby. *The Friend Zone*
Jónasson, Ragnar. ★*The Girl Who Died*
K'wan. *Animal*
Kagen, Lesley. *Every Now and Then*
Kelly, Erin. *Broadchurch: A Novel*
Kelly, Martha Hall. *Lilac Girls*
Kim, Angie. *Miracle Creek*
Knight, Renee. *The Secretary: A Novel*
Krentz, Jayne Ann. *Secret Sisters*
Kubica, Mary. ★*The Other Mrs.*
Kuhn, M. J. *Among Thieves*
Kunsken, Derek. *The House of Styx*
Landvik, Lorna. *Chronicles of a Radical Hag: With Recipes*
Langan, Sarah. *Good Neighbors*
Lasdun, James. *Afternoon of a Faun: A Novel*
Lattari, Katie. *Dark Things I Adore*
Leckie, Ann. ★*The Raven Tower*
Lee, Chang-Rae. ★*The Surrendered*
Lee, Jonathan. *The Great Mistake*
Lepionka, Kristen. *Once You Go This Far: A Mystery*
Loren, Roni. *The One You Can't Forget*
MacDonald, John D. *The Long Lavender Look*
Macdonald, Ross. *The Underground Man*
Machado, Carmen Maria. ★*The Low, Low Woods*
MacLean, Sarah. ★*Brazen and the Beast*
Malerman, Josh. *Goblin: A Novel in Six Novellas*
Markley, Stephen. *Ohio*
Martell, Nick. *The Kingdom of Liars*
McCreight, Kimberly. *Friends Like These*
McGuire, Ian. *The Abstainer: A Novel*
McPherson, Catriona. *Quiet Neighbors: A Novel*

McPherson, Catriona. *Strangers at the Gate*
Meltzer, Brad. *The Inner Circle*
Meltzer, Jean. ★*The Matzah Ball*
Meuleman, Sarah. *Find Me Gone*
Milan, Courtney. *The Duchess War*
Miller, Sue. ★*Monogamy*
Molloy, Aimee. *The Perfect Mother: A Novel*
Moore, Meg Mitchell. *The Islanders*
Morelli, Laura. *The Stolen Lady*
Moriarty, Liane. *The Husband's Secret*
Moriarty, Liane. *Nine Perfect Strangers*
Morton, Kate. *The House at Riverton: A Novel*
Murakami, Haruki. *Killing Commendatore: A Novel*
Murr, Naeem. *The Perfect Man: A Novel*
Ng, Celeste. ★*Little Fires Everywhere: A Novel*
Novic, Sara. *Girl at War*
Oates, Joyce Carol. *Pursuit*
Olson, Neil. *Before the Devil Fell*
Parker, Robert B. *Painted Ladies*
Pavone, Chris. ★*The Expats: A Novel*
Penman, Sharon Kay. *The Queen's Man: A Medieval Mystery*
Penny, Louise. ★*All the Devils Are Here*
Perry, Thomas. *Fidelity*
Persson, Leif G. W. *Another Time, Another Life: The Story of a Crime*
Phillips, Susan Elizabeth. ★*When Stars Collide*
Pinborough, Sarah. ★*Behind Her Eyes: A Novel*
Pochoda, Ivy. *Visitation Street: A Novel*
Polk, C. L. *Soulstar*
Polk, C. L. *Witchmark*
Poole, Sara. *The Borgia Mistress*
Putney, Mary Jo. *Nowhere Near Respectable*
Quartey, Kwei. ★*Sleep Well, My Lady*
Rader-Day, Lori. *Little Pretty Things*
Raybourn, Deanna. *A Perilous Undertaking: A Veronica Speedwell Mystery*
Redondo, Dolores. *The Invisible Guardian*
Richmond, Michelle. *No One You Know*
Robb, Candace M. ★*A Choir of Crows*
Robotham, Michael. ★*When She Was Good*
Rollins, James. *The Demon Crown: A Sigma Force Novel*
Rollins, James. *The Devil Colony*
Rose, M. J. *Tiffany Blues: A Novel*
Rouda, Kaira Sturdivant. *Best Day Ever: A Novel*
Rous, Emma. *The Perfect Guests*
Roy, Lori. *Bent Road*
Rozan, S. J. *Winter and Night*
Ruiz Zafon, Carlos. *The Angel's Game*
Russo, Richard. ★*Chances Are...: A Novel*
Sager, Riley. *Lock Every Door: A Novel*
Sanders, Lawrence. ★*The First Deadly Sin*
Saul, John. *Midnight Voices*
Schellman, Katharine. *Silence in the Library*
Shalvis, Jill. *Sweet Little Lies*
Shannon, Samantha. *The Mime Order*
Sharp, Zoe. *Second Shot: A Charlie Fox Thriller*
Shaw, William. *The Birdwatcher*
Shreve, Anita. *Eden Close: A Novel*
Shreve, Anita. *The Pilot's Wife: A Novel*

Shupe, Joanna. *The Heiress Hunt*
Simmons, Dan. *The Abominable: A Novel*
Simmons, Dan. *Drood: A Novel*
Slaughter, Karin. *Criminal: A Novel*
Slaughter, Karin. *The Good Daughter*
Slaughter, Karin. ★*Pieces of Her*
Sorenson, Jill. *Aftershock*
Spark, Muriel. ★*Memento Mori*
Spencer, Sally. *Best Served Cold*
Stage, Zoje. *Getaway*
Statovci, Pajtim. *Bolla*
Steadman, Catherine. *Mr. Nobody: A Novel*
Stoker, Dacre. *Dracul*
Styles, Toy. *Redbone*
Sullivan, Emily. *The Rebel and the Rake*
Sweeney, Cynthia D'Aprix. ★*Good Company: A Novel*
Swift, Graham. ★*Here We Are*
Swinson, Kiki. *Who's Wife Extraordinaire Now*
Talton, Jon. *City of Dark Corners*
Tan, Amy. ★*The Kitchen God's Wife*
Tan, Lucy. *What We Were Promised*
Tatlock, Ann. *Promises to Keep*
Taylor, Brad. *Ring of Fire*
Thomas, Elisabeth. *Catherine House*
Thomson, E. S. *Beloved Poison*
Urquhart, Rachel. *The Visionist*
Von Ziegesar, Cecily. *Cobble Hill*
Walton, Dawnie. ★*The Final Revival of Opal & Nev*
Watson, S. J. *Final Cut*
Whitfield, Clare. *People of Abandoned Character*
Willocks, Tim. *Memo from Turner*
Wilson, Daniel H. *The Clockwork Dynasty: A Novel*
Wong, David. *Futuristic Violence and Fancy Suits*
Woods, Stuart. *Chiefs*
Woods, Stuart. *A Delicate Touch*
Woods, Stuart. *Santa Fe Rules*
Wynne, Phoebe. *Madam*
Yang, JY. *The Black Tides of Heaven*
Yang, JY. *The Descent of Monsters*
Young, Heather. *The Distant Dead*
The Secrets Between Us. Umrigar, Thrity N.
Secrets of a Happy Marriage. Kelly, Cathy
Secrets of a Wedding Night. Bowman, Valerie
The Secrets of Bones: A Mystery. Logan, Kylie
Secrets of Eden: A Novel. Bohjalian, Chris
Secrets of Happiness. Silber, Joan
★*The Secrets of Love Story Bridge.* Patrick, Phaedra
The Secrets of Midwives. Hepworth, Sally
The Secrets of Wishtide. Saunders, Kate
The Secrets We Kept. Prescott, Lara
SECTS
Giordano, Paolo. *Heaven and Earth*
Whitehead, Colson. *The Intuitionist*
SECURITIES
Rinehart, Mary Roberts. *The Circular Staircase*
SECURITY CLASSIFICATION (GOVERNMENT DOCUMENTS)
Finder, Joseph. *The Switch: A Novel*
Limon, Martin. *War Women*

SECURITY CONSULTANTS
    Atkinson, Kate. *Started Early, Took My Dog*
    Finder, Joseph. *Guilty Minds*
    Finder, Joseph. *Vanished*
    Pearson, Ridley. *The Risk Agent*
    Wells, Martha. *Network Effect*
Security: a Novel. Amidon, Stephen
Sedaris, David
    Holidays on Ice
Sedgwick, Marcus
    Mister Memory: A Novel
Seducing the Sedgwicks [Series]. Sebastian, Cat
The Seduction. Briscoe, Joanna
SEDUCTION
    Ashley, Jennifer. *Lady Isabella's Scandalous Marriage*
    Bowman, Valerie. *Secrets of a Wedding Night*
    Boyle, Elizabeth. *And the Miss Ran Away with the Rake*
    Bradley, Anna. *A Wicked Way to Win an Earl*
    Frampton, Megan. *Put up Your Duke*
    Gerritsen, Tess. ★*The Shape of Night: A Novel*
    Guhrke, Laura Lee. *Governess Gone Rogue*
    Handke, Peter. *Don Juan: His Own Version*
    London, Julia. *Wild Wicked Scot*
    Matthews, Jason. *Red Sparrow: A Novel*
    Richardson, Samuel. ★*Pamela: Or, Virtue Rewarded*
    Shupe, Joanna. *The Courtesan Duchess*
See Now Then. Kincaid, Jamaica
See What I Have Done. Schmidt, Sarah
See, Lisa
    Dragon Bones: A Novel
    Dreams of Joy: A Novel
    The Island of Sea Women
    Peony in Love: A Novel
    Shanghai Girls: A Novel
    The Tea Girl of Hummingbird Lane
Seek My Face. Updike, John
The Seep: a Novel. Porter, Chana
Segal, Erich
    ★*Love Story*
SEGREGATION
    Beatty, Paul. ★*The Sellout: A Novel*
    Mullen, Thomas. *Lightning Men: A Novel*
★*Seize the Day.* Bellow, Saul
Sekaran, Shanthi
    ★*Lucky Boy*
SELDON, HARI (FICTITIOUS CHARACTER)
    Asimov, Isaac. *Second Foundation*
Selected Stories. Munro, Alice
Selection Day. Adiga, Aravind
SELF
    Emezi, Akwaeke. *Freshwater*
SELF MEDICATION
    Stevenson, Robert Louis. ★*The Strange Case of Dr. Jekyll and Mr. Hyde*
Self's Deception. Schlink, Bernhard
Self's Murder. Schlink, Bernhard
Self's Punishment. Schlink, Bernhard

Self, Will
    The Book of Dave: A Revelation of the Recent Past and the Distant Future
SELF-ACCEPTANCE
    Ahern, Cecelia. *Roar*
    Shumway, Charity. *Ten Girls to Watch: A Novel*
SELF-ACCEPTANCE IN GAY MEN
    Louis, Edouard. *The End of Eddy: A Novel*
SELF-ACCEPTANCE IN GIRLS
    Morrison, Toni. ★*The Bluest Eye: A Novel*
SELF-ACCEPTANCE IN MEN
    Morrison, Toni. ★*Song of Solomon*
SELF-ACCEPTANCE IN WOMEN
    Hoffman, Alice. *The Ice Queen: A Novel*
    Kingsolver, Barbara. *Pigs in Heaven*
    Valdes, Alisa. *Dirty Girls on Top*
SELF-AWARENESS
    Aciman, Andre. *Enigma Variations: A Novel*
    Mailer, Norman. ★*The Naked and the Dead*
    Sartre, Jean Paul. ★*Nausea*
SELF-AWARENESS IN WOMEN
    French, Marilyn. ★*The Women's Room*
SELF-CONFIDENCE IN WOMEN
    Ali, Monica. ★*Brick Lane: A Novel*
SELF-CONSCIOUSNESS
    Wallace, David Foster. *Oblivion: Stories*
SELF-DECEPTION
    Barnes, Julian. ★*The Sense of an Ending*
    Cusk, Rachel. *Outline: A Novel*
SELF-DEFENSE
    Mason, Jamie. *The Hidden Things*
SELF-DEFENSE (LAW)
    Murdoch, Iris. *The Green Knight*
SELF-DESTRUCTIVE BEHAVIOR
    Baker, Dorothy. ★*Young Man with a Horn*
    Byrne, Trevor. *Ghosts and Lightning*
    Greenwell, Garth. *What Belongs to You: A Novel*
    O'Hara, John. *Appointment in Samarra*
    Spark, Muriel. *The Driver's Seat*
    Yanagihara, Hanya. *A Little Life: A Novel*
SELF-DESTRUCTIVE BEHAVIOR IN MEN
    Chabon, Michael. ★*Wonder Boys*
    Duncan, Glen. *The Last Werewolf*
SELF-DESTRUCTIVE BEHAVIOR IN WOMEN
    Hand, Elizabeth. ★*Generation Loss: A Novel*
SELF-DISCLOSURE
    Cusk, Rachel. *Outline: A Novel*
SELF-DISCOVERY
    Ahern, Cecelia. *Roar*
    Beverly, William. *Dodgers: A Novel*
    Broder, Melissa. *Milk Fed*
    Brown, Eleanor. *The Weird Sisters*
    Christian, Claire. *It's Been a Pleasure, Noni Blake*
    Coelho, Paulo. ★*The Alchemist*
    Doyle, Brian. *The Plover: A Novel*
    Evanovich, Stephanie. *Under the Table*
    Green, Hank. *An Absolutely Remarkable Thing: A Novel*
    Joseph, Fabiola. *Niya: Rainbow Dreams*

Krauss, Nicole. *Forest Dark*

Lebrecht, Norman. *The Song of Names*

Lipman, Elinor. *The Dearly Departed*

Lipman, Elinor. *The Pursuit of Alice Thrift: A Novel*

Livesey, Margot. ★*The Boy in the Field*

London, Julia. *The Charmer in Chaps*

Mabanckou, Alain. ★*Black Moses*

Malamud, Bernard. ★*The Fixer*

Mason, Meg. *Sorrow and Bliss*

Monroe, Mary. *God Still Don't Like Ugly*

Murakami, Haruki. ★*1q84*

Onuzo, Chibundu. *Sankofa: A Novel*

Packer, Ann. *The Dive from Clausen's Pier*

Rose, Heather. *The Museum of Modern Love*

Walker, Alice. *The Temple of My Familiar*

SELF-DISCOVERY IN MEN

Aciman, Andre. *Find Me*

Bellow, Saul. ★*Henderson the Rain King: A Novel*

Bellow, Saul. ★*Seize the Day*

Flagg, Fannie. ★*The Wonder Boy of Whistle Stop: A Novel*

Foer, Jonathan Safran. *Here I Am: A Novel*

Fountain, Ben. ★*Billy Lynn's Long Halftime Walk*

Garey, Juliann. *Too Bright to Hear Too Loud to See*

Hesse, Hermann. ★*Steppenwolf*

Morrison, Toni. ★*Song of Solomon*

Murakami, Haruki. *Colorless Tsukuru Tazaki and His Years of Pilgrimage*

Percy, Walker. ★*The Moviegoer*

Roth, Philip. ★*The Anatomy Lesson*

Roth, Philip. *The Ghost Writer*

Roth, Philip. ★*Goodbye, Columbus, and Five Short Stories*

Roth, Philip. *Zuckerman Bound*

Roth, Philip. *Zuckerman Unbound*

Saramago, Jose. *The Manual of Painting and Calligraphy*

Shields, Carol. *The Republic of Love*

Shteyngart, Gary. ★*Lake Success: A Novel*

Tyler, Anne. ★*Redhead by the Side of the Road*

SELF-DISCOVERY IN TEENAGE BOYS

Aciman, Andre. *Call Me by Your Name*

SELF-DISCOVERY IN TEENAGE GIRLS

Blau, Jessica Anya. *Mary Jane: A Novel*

Kincaid, Jamaica. ★*Annie John*

SELF-DISCOVERY IN TEENAGERS

Walls, Jeannette. *The Silver Star: A Novel*

SELF-DISCOVERY IN WOMEN

Abraham, Tola Rotimi. *Black Sunday*

Adams, Alina. *The Nesting Dolls*

Ali, Monica. ★*Brick Lane: A Novel*

Atwood, Margaret. ★*Cat's Eye*

Backman, Fredrik. *Britt-Marie Was Here*

Batuman, Elif. ★*The Idiot*

Benjamin, Melanie. ★*The Aviator's Wife: A Novel*

Bruni, Sarah. *The Night Gwen Stacy Died*

Carty-Williams, Candice. ★*Queenie*

Cather, Willa. *The Song of the Lark*

Cusk, Rachel. *Transit*

Ferrante, Elena. *The Story of a New Name*

Flagg, Fannie. ★*Fried Green Tomatoes at the Whistle Stop Cafe*

Frank, Dorothea Benton. *Folly Beach: A Lowcountry Tale*

Gideon, Melanie. *Wife 22*

Haywood, Sarah. *The Cactus*

Linden, Rachel. *Ascension of Larks*

McDermott, Alice. *Someone*

McMillan, Terry. ★*Waiting to Exhale*

Munro, Alice. *Lives of Girls and Women*

Nin, Anais. *Cities of the Interior*

Shumway, Charity. *Ten Girls to Watch: A Novel*

Swift, Graham. ★*Mothering Sunday: A Romance*

Van der Vliet Oloomi, Azareen. *Call Me Zebra*

Woolf, Virginia. *The Voyage Out*

SELF-ESTEEM

Bellow, Saul. ★*Seize the Day*

Hall, Alexis. ★*Boyfriend Material*

SELF-ESTEEM IN GIRLS

Morrison, Toni. ★*The Bluest Eye: A Novel*

SELF-ESTEEM IN WOMEN

Awad, Mona. ★*13 Ways of Looking at a Fat Girl*

Dangarembga, Tsitsi. *This Mournable Body*

Styles, Toy. *Black and Ugly*

Walker, Sarai. *Dietland*

SELF-EVALUATION IN MEN

Auster, Paul. *The Brooklyn Follies*

SELF-FULFILLMENT

De Kretser, Michelle. *The Life to Come*

Hesse, Hermann. ★*Siddhartha: A New Translation*

Hill, Nathan. *The Nix: A Novel*

Kosinski, Jerzy. *The Devil Tree*

Lipman, Elinor. *The Pursuit of Alice Thrift: A Novel*

Macomber, Debbie. *If Not for You: A Novel*

Nguyen, Viet Thanh. ★*The Refugees*

Packer, Ann. *The Dive from Clausen's Pier*

Pomerantz, Sharon. *Rich Boy*

Roy, Arundhati. ★*The Ministry of Utmost Happiness: A Novel*

Sears, Michael. *Black Fridays*

Smith, Gregory Blake. ★*The Maze at Windermere: A Novel*

Walsh, M. O. ★*The Big Door Prize: A Novel*

SELF-FULFILLMENT — RELIGIOUS ASPECTS

Reimringer, John. *Vestments*

SELF-FULFILLMENT IN AFRICAN AMERICAN WOMEN

Hurston, Zora Neale. ★*Their Eyes Were Watching God*

SELF-FULFILLMENT IN MEN

Conrad, Joseph. ★*Lord Jim*

Hornby, Nick. *High Fidelity*

Joyce, James. ★*A Portrait of the Artist as a Young Man*

Pamuk, Orhan. ★*A Strangeness in My Mind: A Novel*

Potok, Chaim. ★*My Name Is Asher Lev*

Roth, Philip. *Exit Ghost*

Roth, Philip. *Indignation*

Toole, John Kennedy. ★*A Confederacy of Dunces*

SELF-FULFILLMENT IN TEENAGE BOYS

Ford, Richard. *Canada*

SELF-FULFILLMENT IN TEENAGE GIRLS

Gibbons, Kaye. *The Life All Around Me by Ellen Foster*

SELF-FULFILLMENT IN WOMEN

Adams, Alina. *The Nesting Dolls*

Buntin, Julie. ★*Marlena: A Novel*

Clark, Georgia. *The Bucket List*
Colwin, Laurie. *Goodbye Without Leaving*
Danler, Stephanie. *Sweetbitter*
Dennis-Benn, Nicole. *Here Comes the Sun*
Dorn, L. R. *The Anatomy of Desire*
Eliot, George. ★*The Mill on the Floss*
Essbaum, Jill Alexander. *Hausfrau: A Novel*
Ferrante, Elena. *Those Who Leave and Those Who Stay*
Forman, Gayle. *Leave Me: A Novel*
Genova, Lisa. *Left Neglected: A Novel*
Goodman, Allegra. *The Cookbook Collector: A Novel*
Hall, Alexis. *Rosaline Palmer Takes the Cake*
Harrison, Nicola. *Montauk*
Jong, Erica. ★*Fear of Flying: A Novel*
Levy, Deborah. *Hot Milk: A Novel*
Linden, Rachel. *The Enlightenment of Bees*
Mallery, Susan. *The Summer of Sunshine and Margot*
Monroe, Mary Alice. *Beach House Reunion*
Ólafsdóttir, Auður A. *Butterflies in November*
Phillips, Susan Elizabeth. *The Great Escape*
Picoult, Jodi. ★*Wish You Were Here: A Novel*
Rockaway, Kristin. *How to Hack a Heartbreak*
Stevens, Chevy. *Still Missing*
Weiner, Jennifer. *In Her Shoes: A Novel*
Williams, Denise. *How to Fail at Flirting*
Wolitzer, Meg. *The Female Persuasion*

SELF-FULFILLMENT IN YOUNG WOMEN
Merullo, Roland. *The Talk-Funny Girl: A Novel*

SELF-HARM
Crowell, Jenn. *Etched on Me: A Novel*
Flynn, Gillian. ★*Sharp Objects: A Novel*
Hayder, Mo. *Poppet*

SELF-HATE (PSYCHOLOGY)
Roth, Henry. *A Diving Rock on the Hudson*

SELF-HATE IN MEN
Robinson, Marilynne. ★*Jack*

SELF-HATE IN WOMEN
Moshfegh, Ottessa. *Eileen*

SELF-HELP PSYCHOLOGY
Moriarty, Jaclyn. *Gravity Is the Thing*

SELF-INTEREST
Rand, Ayn. ★*The Fountainhead*

SELF-PERCEPTION
Butler, Marcia. *Pickle's Progress*
Clarke, Diana. *Thin Girls*
Cusk, Rachel. *Transit*
Mailer, Norman. ★*The Naked and the Dead*
Packer, Ann. *Songs Without Words*

SELF-PERCEPTION IN MEN
McBride, James. ★*The Good Lord Bird*
Updike, John. ★*Rabbit, Run*

SELF-PERCEPTION IN WOMEN
Ahern, Cecelia. *Roar*
Colwin, Laurie. *Goodbye Without Leaving*

SELF-RELIANCE
Cleary, Jon. *The Sundowners*

SELF-SACRIFICE
George, Margaret. *Helen of Troy*

Marra, Anthony. *The Tsar of Love and Techno: Stories*
Saylor, Steven. *Rubicon*

SELF-SACRIFICE IN WOMEN
Lessing, Doris May. *The Sweetest Dream*
A Selfie as Big as the Ritz: Stories. Williams, Lara

SELFISHNESS
Dickens, Charles. *Martin Chuzzlewit*
Thorne, Sally. *Second First Impressions*
Vonnegut, Kurt. *Jailbird: A Novel*

SELFISHNESS IN MEN
McEwan, Ian. *Solar: A Novel*
Schwarz, Christina. *The Edge of the Earth*
★*The Sellout: a Novel*. Beatty, Paul

Sem-Sandberg, Steve
The Chosen Ones: A Novel

SEMANTICS (PHILOSOPHY)
Gao, XIngjian. *Soul Mountain*

Semiosis. Burke, Sue
Semiosis duology [Series]. Burke, Sue

SEMIOTICS
Eugenides, Jeffrey. ★*The Marriage Plot*

Semple, Maria
Where'd You Go, Bernadette: A Novel

The Senator's Wife. Miller, Sue

SENATORIAL CANDIDATES
Stabenow, Dana. *The Singing of the Dead*

SENECA INDIANS
Perry, Thomas. ★*The Left-Handed Twin*

SENECA WOMEN
Perry, Thomas. ★*The Left-Handed Twin*

SENEGAL
Bush, Keisha. *No Heaven for Good Boys: A Novel*
Diop, David. ★*At Night All Blood Is Black*

SENEGALESE IN FRANCE
Diop, David. ★*At Night All Blood Is Black*

SENIOR COUPLES
Hooper, Emma. *Etta and Otto and Russell and James: A Novel*
Scott, Paul. ★*Staying On: A Novel*

SENIOR MEN
Auster, Paul. *Travels in the Scriptorium: A Novel*
Backman, Fredrik. *A Man Called Ove*
Balasubramanyam, Rajeev. *Professor Chandra Follows His Bliss: A Novel*
Banville, John. *Ancient Light*
Bellow, Saul. ★*Mr. Sammler's Planet*
Berg, Elizabeth. *The Story of Arthur Truluv: A Novel*
Bernhard, Thomas. *Frost: A Novel*
Bowman, Conor. ★*Horace Winter Says Goodbye*
Burns, Olive Ann. ★*Cold Sassy Tree*
Cartwright, Justin. *To Heaven by Water*
Christie, Agatha. ★*The A B C Murders*
Christie, Agatha. *Curtain*
Christie, Agatha. *The Hollow*
Cleave, Paul. *Trust No One: A Thriller*
Cotterill, Colin. *The Coroner's Lunch*
Cotterill, Colin. *Disco for the Departed*
Couto, Mia. *Sleepwalking Land*
Dunne, Dominick. *Too Much Money*

Egan, Jennifer. ★*A Visit from the Goon Squad*

Flagg, Fannie. ★*The Wonder Boy of Whistle Stop: A Novel*

Fossey, Brooke. *The Big Finish*

Friedman, Daniel. ★*Don't Ever Get Old*

Friedman, Daniel. *Running Out of Road*

Gaines, Ernest J. ★*A Gathering of Old Men*

Garcia Marquez, Gabriel. ★*The Autumn of the Patriarch*

Garcia, Cristina. *King of Cuba: A Novel*

Glass, Julia. *The Widower's Tale*

Goddard, Robert. *Never Go Back*

Grass, Gunter. *Too Far Afield*

Greene, Graham. *The Last Word and Other Stories*

Griffin, Anne. *When All Is Said: A Novel*

Groen, Hendrik. *On the Bright Side: The New Secret Diary of Hendrik Groen, 85 Years Old*

Hemingway, Ernest. ★*The Old Man and the Sea*

Ishiguro, Kazuo. *An Artist of the Floating World*

Joyce, James. ★*Finnegans Wake*

Kawabata, Yasunari. *The Sound of the Mountain*

MacDonald, John D. *The Scarlet Ruse*

Mann, Thomas. *Death in Venice and Seven Other Stories*

McDermott, Alice. *Child of My Heart*

Mishima, Yukio. *The Temple of Dawn*

Murakami, Haruki. ★*Kafka on the Shore*

Murdoch, Iris. *The Sea, the Sea*

O'Nan, Stewart. *Henry, Himself*

Oe, Kenzaburo. ★*Death by Water*

Osborne, Lawrence. *Only to Sleep: A Philip Marlowe Novel*

Petterson, Per. *Out Stealing Horses: A Novel*

Ripley, Mike. *Mr. Campion's War*

Roth, Philip. ★*Everyman*

Russo, Richard. *Bridge of Sighs*

Saramago, Jose. ★*The Cave*

Savage, Sam. *The Way of the Dog: A Novel*

Scalzi, John. ★*Old Man's War*

Updike, John. *My Father's Tears and Other Stories*

Vann, David. *Aquarium*

SENIOR MEN — FRIENDSHIP

Swift, Graham. ★*Last Orders: A Novel*

SENIOR MEN — SEXUALITY

Garcia Marquez, Gabriel. *Memories of My Melancholy Whores*

Roth, Philip. *Exit Ghost*

Roth, Philip. *Sabbath's Theater*

SENIOR MURDER VICTIMS

Sandford, John. ★*Invisible Prey*

Stanley, Michael. *Dying to Live*

SENIOR ROMANCE

Sparks, Nicholas. ★*The Notebook*

SENIOR WOMEN

Alameddine, Rabih. *An Unnecessary Woman*

Backman, Fredrik. *Britt-Marie Was Here*

Barry, Sebastian. *The Secret Scripture: A Novel*

Berg, Elizabeth. *Night of Miracles*

Cannon, Joanna. *Three Things About Elsie: A Novel*

Christie, Agatha. *The Body in the Library: A Miss Marple Mystery*

Christie, Agatha. ★*The Murder at the Vicarage*

Christie, Agatha. *A Murder Is Announced: A Miss Marple Mystery*

Christie, Agatha. *Three Blind Mice, and Other Stories*

Dean, Debra. *The Madonnas of Leningrad: A Novel*

Deveraux, Jude. *A Willing Murder*

Drabble, Margaret. ★*The Dark Flood Rises*

Drndic, Dasa. *Trieste*

Edgerton, Clyde. ★*Walking Across Egypt: A Novel*

Flanagan, Richard. *The Living Sea of Waking Dreams*

Friedland, Elyssa. *The Floating Feldmans*

Gaiman, Neil. ★*The Ocean at the End of the Lane*

Gendry-Kim, Keum Suk. ★*The Waiting*

Gessen, Keith. *A Terrible Country*

Giordano, Mario. ★*Auntie Poldi and the Lost Madonna*

Giordano, Mario. *Auntie Poldi and the Vineyards of Etna*

Gurganus, Allan. *Oldest Living Confederate Widow Tells All*

Heller, Peter. *Celine: A Novel*

Heller, Zoe. *What Was She Thinking?: Notes on a Scandal*

Lyons, Annie. *The Brilliant Life of Eudora Honeysett*

McKevett, G. A. *Murder at Mabel's Motel*

McKevett, G. A. *Murder in the Corn Maze*

McMillan, Terry. ★*It's Not All Downhill from Here: A Novel*

McMurtry, Larry. *The Evening Star: A Novel*

Morton, Brian. *Florence Gordon*

Moshfegh, Ottessa. ★*Death in Her Hands: A Novel*

Munro, Alice. *Runaway: Stories*

O'Farrell, Maggie. *The Vanishing Act of Esme Lennox*

Phillips, Caryl. *A Distant Shore*

Sackville-West, V. *All Passion Spent*

Shocklee, Michelle. *Under the Tulip Tree*

Tursten, Helene. *An Elderly Lady Must Not Be Crossed*

Tyler, Anne. ★*Clock Dance: A Novel*

Umrigar, Thrity N. *The Secrets Between Us*

SENIOR WOMEN — FRIENDSHIP

Tatlock, Ann. *Promises to Keep*

SENIOR WOMEN AUTHORS

Lively, Penelope. ★*Moon Tiger*

SENIORS

Atwood, Margaret. ★*Stone Mattress: Nine Tales*

Bannalec, Jean-Luc. *Death in Brittany*

Butler, Robert Olen. *Perfume River*

Butler, Season. ★*Cygnet*

Cotterill, Colin. *Don't Eat Me*

Gardam, Jane. *Old Filth*

Groen, Hendrik. *On the Bright Side: The New Secret Diary of Hendrik Groen, 85 Years Old*

Helprin, Mark. *Paris in the Present Tense*

Osman, Richard. *The Man Who Died Twice: A Thursday Murder Club Mystery*

Osman, Richard. ★*The Thursday Murder Club*

Perry, Thomas. *The Old Man*

Pronzini, Bill. *Nightcrawlers*

Spark, Muriel. ★*Memento Mori*

Straub, Peter. ★*Ghost Story*

Youngson, Anne. *Meet Me at the Museum*

SENIORS — CARE

Gessen, Keith. *A Terrible Country*

SENIORS — IDENTITY

Harding, Paul. *Tinkers*

SENIORS — SEXUALITY

McMurtry, Larry. *The Evening Star: A Novel*

Senna, Danzy
New People
★*Sense* and Sensibility. Austen, Jane
★The *Sense* of an Ending. Barnes, Julian
SENSES AND SENSATION
Bauermeister, Erica. *The Scent Keeper*
Harris, Sarah J. *The Color of Bee Larkham's Murder: A Novel*
Tan, Amy. *The Hundred Secret Senses*
SENSITIVITY IN TEENAGERS
Salinger, J. D. ★*The Catcher in the Rye*
SENSORY DEPRIVATION
Malerman, Josh. *Bird Box: A Novel*
Malerman, Josh. *Malorie: A Bird Box Novel*
★The *Sentence*. Erdrich, Louise
★The *Sentence* Is Death. Horowitz, Anthony
The *Sentient*. Afifi, Nadia
Sentimental Education. Flaubert, Gustave
★The *Sentinel*. Child, Lee
Seo, Mi-Ae
The Only Child
SEOUL, KOREA
Lee, Ji-Min. *The Starlet and the Spy*
Park, Sang Young. ★*Love in the Big City: A Novel*
★A *Separate* Peace. Knowles, John
SEPARATED BROTHERS
Howarth, Paul. *Dust off the Bones*
SEPARATED COUPLES
Benedetti, Mario. *Springtime in a Broken Mirror*
Bowman, Valerie. *A Duke Like No Other*
DeLillo, Don. *Falling Man: A Novel*
Guhrke, Laura Lee. *How to Lose a Duke in Ten Days*
James, Eloisa. *The Ugly Duchess*
McPherson, Catriona. *Quiet Neighbors: A Novel*
O'Neill, Heather. ★*The Lonely Hearts Hotel: A Novel*
Peters, Torrey. ★*Detransition, Baby*
Shupe, Joanna. *The Courtesan Duchess*
Spencer-Fleming, Julia. *I Shall Not Want: A Clare Fergusson/Russ Van Alstyne Mystery*
SEPARATED FRIENDS, RELATIVES, ETC.
Abraham, Tola Rotimi. *Black Sunday*
Alameddine, Rabih. *The Wrong End of the Telescope*
Bulgakov, Mikhail. ★*The Master and Margarita*
Engel, Patricia. ★*Infinite Country*
Feng, Linda Rui. *Swimming Back to Trout River*
Gendry-Kim, Keum Suk. ★*The Waiting*
Gyasi, Yaa. ★*Homegoing: A Novel*
Krueger, William Kent. *This Tender Land: A Novel*
Landau, Alexis. *Those Who Are Saved*
Lange, Tracey. ★*We Are the Brennans*
Rawles, Nancy. *My Jim: A Novel*
Schulman, Alex. *The Survivors: A Novel*
Walker, Alice. ★*The Color Purple: A Novel*
SEPARATED MEN (MARITAL RELATIONS)
Barthelme, Frederick. *Elroy Nights*
Tracy, P. J. ★*Deep into the Dark*
Tyler, Anne. ★*The Accidental Tourist: A Novel*
Updike, John. *Memories of the Ford Administration: A Novel*

SEPARATED SISTERS
Kim, Eugenia. *The Kinship of Secrets*
Lovely, Lutishia. *Blind Ambition*
SEPARATED TWIN SISTERS
Rizzuto, Rahna R. *Shadow Child*
SEPARATED WOMEN (MARITAL RELATIONS)
Carr, Robyn. *The View from Alameda Island: A Novel*
Florio, Gwen. *Best Laid Plans*
Hornby, Nick. *Just Like You*
Shaw, M. B. *Murder at the Mill: A Mystery*
Spiotta, Dana. *Wayward*
Tyler, Anne. ★*The Accidental Tourist: A Novel*
SEPARATION (MARITAL RELATIONS)
Bellow, Saul. ★*Seize the Day*
Carr, Robyn. *The View from Alameda Island: A Novel*
Evanovich, Stephanie. *Under the Table*
Friedland, Elyssa. *The Intermission*
Spencer-Fleming, Julia. *All Mortal Flesh*
Waters, Martha. ★*To Have and to Hoax: A Novel*
SEPARATION (PSYCHOLOGY)
Harris, E. Lynn. *Not a Day Goes By: A Novel*
Sepetys, Ruta
★*Out of the Easy*
SEPTEMBER 11 TERRORIST ATTACKS, 2001
Akhtar, Ayad. ★*Homeland Elegies: A Novel*
Aslam, Nadeem. ★*The Blind Man's Garden*
Bannister, Ilona. *When I Ran Away*
DeLillo, Don. *Falling Man: A Novel*
Gibson, Claire. *Beyond the Point: A Novel*
Price, Reynolds. *The Good Priest's Son*
The *September* Society. Finch, Charles
The *Septembers* of Shiraz. Sofer, Dalia
SEPTUAGENARIANS
Banks, Russell. *Foregone*
Edgerton, Clyde. ★*Walking Across Egypt: A Novel*
O'Nan, Stewart. *Henry, Himself*
Richler, Mordecai. *Barney's Version: A Novel*
Saramago, Jose. ★*The Cave*
Scalzi, John. ★*Old Man's War*
SEQUOIA NATIONAL PARK
Kells, Claire. *Vanishing Edge*
SERBS IN ENGLAND
Brownrigg, Sylvia. ★*The Delivery Room: A Novel*
Lawrence, David. *The Dead Sit Round in a Ring*
Serena Singh Flips the Script. Lalli, Sonya
★*Serena: a Novel*. Rash, Ron
The *Serenity* Murders. Somer, Mehmet Murat
SERFDOM
Gogol, Nikolai Vasilievich. ★*Dead Souls*
Grenville, Kate. *The Secret River*
SERIAL MURDER INVESTIGATION
Abdul-Jabbar, Kareem. *The Empty Birdcage*
Abdul-Jabbar, Kareem. *Mycroft and Sherlock*
Baldacci, David. *A Minute to Midnight*
Black, Saul. ★*The Killing Lessons*
Bolton, S. J. *Now You See Me*
Bowen, Peter. *Badlands*
Box, C. J. *The Highway*

Box, C. J. *Paradise Valley*
Cameron, W. Bruce. *Repo Madness*
Connelly, Michael. ★*Fair Warning*
Connelly, Michael. *The Scarecrow: A Novel*
Cussler, Clive. *The Cutthroat*
Dahl, Arne. *Bad Blood*
Dahl, Arne. *Misterioso: A Crime Novel*
Daniel, Ray. *Hacked: A Tucker Mystery*
Daugherty, Christi. *The Echo Killing*
Fowler, Christopher. *Bryant & May: The Lonely Hour*
Franklin, Ariana. *Mistress of the Art of Death*
Freeman, Brian. *The Night Bird*
Gardiner, Meg. *Into the Black Nowhere*
Gardiner, Meg. *Unsub: A Novel*
Gerritsen, Tess. *I Know a Secret*
Gilbers, Harald. *Germania: A Novel of Nazi Berlin*
Grossman, Paul. *Children of Wrath*
Guinn, Matthew. *The Scribe: A Novel*
Hamilton, Peter F. *Great North Road*
Irwin, Stephen M. *The Broken Ones: A Novel*
Jones, Darynda. *A Good Day for Chardonnay*
Kerley, Jack. ★*The Death Collectors*
Kerr, Philip. ★*Metropolis: A Bernie Gunther Novel*
MacNeal, Susan Elia. *The King's Justice*
Mukherjee, Abir. *Smoke and Ashes: A Novel*
Nesbo, Jo. *The Leopard*
Pearl, Matthew. *The Dante Chamber*
Pearl, Matthew. *The Dante Club: A Novel*
Pressfield, Steven. *36 Righteous Men: A Novel*
Preston, Douglas J. *City of Endless Night*
Preston, Douglas J. *Verses for the Dead*
Quartey, Kwei. *Children of the Street: A Novel*
Rankin, Ian. ★*Black and Blue: An Inspector Rebus Novel*
Redondo, Dolores. *The Invisible Guardian*
Redondo, Dolores. *The North Face of the Heart*
Reichs, Kathy. ★*Deja Dead*
Rozan, S. J. ★*The Art of Violence*
Sanders, Lawrence. ★*The First Deadly Sin*
Sandford, John. *Broken Prey*
Sandford, John. *Buried Prey*
Sandford, John. *Field of Prey*
Sandford, John. ★*Rules of Prey*
Sandford, John. ★*Silent Prey*
Sandford, John. ★*Winter Prey*
Schaffhausen, Joanna. *Gone for Good*
Sjowall, Maj. *The Man on the Balcony: The Story of a Crime*
Slaughter, Karin. *Cop Town: A Novel*
Smith, Tom Rob. *Child 44*
Spencer, Sally. *The Ring of Death*
Stanley, Michael. *Deadly Harvest*
Stroud, Carsten. *The Shimmer*
Sveistrup, Soren. ★*The Chestnut Man: A Novel*

SERIAL MURDERERS
Allende, Isabel. *Ripper: A Novel*
Bauer, Belinda. *The Beautiful Dead*
Beukes, Lauren. *The Shining Girls*
Black, Saul. ★*The Killing Lessons*
Black, Saul. ★*Lovemurder*

Box, C. J. *Paradise Valley*
Burton, Jeffrey B. ★*The Finders: A Mace Reid K-9 Mystery*
Carr, Caleb. ★*The Alienist*
Chizmar, Richard T. *Chasing the Boogeyman*
Chizmar, Richard T. *A Long December*
Connelly, Michael. ★*Fair Warning*
Deaver, Jeffery. ★*The Coffin Dancer*
Deaver, Jeffery. *The Stone Monkey: A Lincoln Rhyme Novel*
Dodd, Christina. *Strangers She Knows*
Donati, Sara. *Where the Light Enters*
Faye, Lyndsay. *The Gods of Gotham*
Gallagher, Stephen. *The Kingdom of Bones: A Novel*
Garcia Saenz, Eva. *The Silence of the White City*
Gardiner, Meg. *Into the Black Nowhere*
Gardiner, Meg. *Unsub: A Novel*
Gardner, Lisa. ★*When You See Me: A Novel*
Grafton, Sue. *X*
Grossman, Paul. *Children of Wrath*
Harris, C. S. *What the Devil Knows: A Sebastian St. Cyr Mystery*
Harris, Thomas. *Hannibal*
Harris, Thomas. *Red Dragon*
Harrison, M. John. *Light*
Knott, Robert. *Robert B. Parker's Buckskin*
Koontz, Dean R. *Velocity*
Lansdale, Joe R. *The Bottoms*
Nesbo, Jo. *The Redeemer*
North, Alex. *The Whisper Man*
Ohlsson, Kristina. *Unwanted: A Novel*
Parker, T. Jefferson. *The Blue Hour*
Patterson, James. *1st to Die: A Novel*
Patterson, James. *Kiss the Girls: A Novel*
Phillips, Jayne Anne. *Quiet Dell: A Novel*
Pochoda, Ivy. ★*These Women*
Pollock, Donald Ray. *The Devil All the Time*
Qiu, Xiaolong. *Red Mandarin Dress: An Inspector Chen Novel*
Rankin, Ian. *Dead Souls: An Inspector Rebus Novel*
Redondo, Dolores. *The North Face of the Heart*
Reichs, Kathy. ★*Deja Dead*
Rendell, Ruth. *End in Tears*
Rice, Christopher. *Blood Victory*
Sandford, John. *Broken Prey*
Sandford, John. *Chosen Prey*
Sandford, John. *Deep Freeze*
Sandford, John. ★*Rules of Prey*
Sandford, John. ★*Silent Prey*
Sandford, John. ★*Winter Prey*
Sansom, C. J. *Revelation*
Schaffhausen, Joanna. *Gone for Good*
Seo, Mi-Ae. *The Only Child*
Smith, Tom Rob. *Child 44*
Spencer, Sally. *The Ring of Death*
Spencer-Fleming, Julia. *I Shall Not Want: A Clare Fergusson/Russ Van Alstyne Mystery*
Straub, Peter. *Mr. X*
Stroud, Carsten. *The Shimmer*
Swanson, Peter. *Eight Perfect Murders: A Novel*
Webb, Brandon. ★*Steel Fear*

SERIAL MURDERS

Abdul-Jabbar, Kareem. *The Empty Birdcage*

Abdul-Jabbar, Kareem. *Mycroft and Sherlock*

Abu-Jaber, Diana. *Origin: A Novel*

Baldacci, David. *A Minute to Midnight*

Block, Lawrence. *A Ticket to the Boneyard: A Matthew Scudder Novel*

Box, C. J. *The Highway*

Braithwaite, Oyinkan. *My Sister, the Serial Killer: A Novel*

Child, Lee. *One Shot*

Christie, Agatha. ★*The A B C Murders*

Connolly, John. *A Book of Bones*

Cornwell, Patricia Daniels. *Postmortem*

Dahl, Arne. *Bad Blood*

Dahl, Arne. *Misterioso: A Crime Novel*

De Giovanni, Maurizio. *The Crocodile*

Deluca, Marjorie. *The Savage Instinct*

Estleman, Loren D. ★*Gas City*

Ferraris, Zoe. *Kingdom of Strangers: A Novel*

Fowler, Christopher. *Bryant & May: The Lonely Hour*

Freeman, Brian. *The Night Bird*

Garcia Saenz, Eva. *The Silence of the White City*

Gaspar de Alba, Alicia. *Desert Blood: The Juarez Murders*

Gerritsen, Tess. *The Apprentice: A Novel*

Gerritsen, Tess. *The Bone Garden*

Gerritsen, Tess. *The Surgeon*

Goodwin, S. M. *Absence of Mercy*

Hand, Elizabeth. *Available Dark: A Thriller*

Harris, C. S. *What the Devil Knows: A Sebastian St. Cyr Mystery*

Hewson, David. *A Season for the Dead*

Kepler, Lars. *The Sandman*

Lansdale, Joe R. *The Bottoms*

Lansdale, Joe R. *Devil Red*

MacBride, Stuart. *Cold Granite*

MacNeal, Susan Elia. *The King's Justice*

Mankell, Henning. ★*One Step Behind*

Mayor, Archer. *Red Herring: A Joe Gunther Novel*

Patterson, James. *1st to Die: A Novel*

Phillips, Christi. *The Devlin Diary*

Preston, Douglas J. *Verses for the Dead*

Qiu, Xiaolong. *Hold Your Breath, China*

Rendell, Ruth. *Simisola*

Roberts, Nora. *Shelter in Place*

Robinson, Peter. *The First Cut*

Robotham, Michael. ★*Close Your Eyes*

Sandford, John. *Buried Prey*

Sandford, John. *Certain Prey*

Sandford, John. *Field of Prey*

Sandford, John. *Heat Lightning*

St. James, Simone. *The Sun Down Motel*

Suskind, Patrick. ★*Perfume: The Story of a Murderer*

Tallis, Frank. *Vienna Blood: A Max Liebermann Mystery*

SERIAL RAPE

Fairstein, Linda A. *Entombed*

SERIAL RAPISTS

Connolly, Michael. *The Wrong Side of Goodbye*

Eisler, Barry. *All the Devils*

Serle, Rebecca

In Five Years: A Novel

Serpell, Namwali

★*The Old Drift*

Serpent Gates [Series]. Larkwood, A. K.

*The **Serpent's** Tale*. Franklin, Ariana

***Serpent:** a Novel from the Numa Files*. Cussler, Clive

***Servant** Mage*. Elliott, Kate

***Set** in Darkness: An Inspector Rebus Novel*. Rankin, Ian

Seth, Vikram

★*A Suitable Boy: A Novel*

Seton, Anya

Avalon

★*Dragonwyck*

Green Darkness

Katherine

★*The Winthrop Woman*

Setterfield, Diane

★*Once Upon a River*

The Thirteenth Tale: A Novel

★***Seven** Days in June: A Novel*. Williams, Tia

***Seven** for a Secret*. Faye, Lyndsay

★***Seven** Minutes in Heaven*. James, Eloisa

*The **Seven** or Eight Deaths of Stella Fortuna*. Grames, Juliet

*The **Seven** Wonders: A Novel of the Ancient World*. Saylor, Steven

SEVEN-YEAR-OLD GIRLS

Backman, Fredrik. ★*My Grandmother Asked Me to Tell You She's Sorry: A Novel*

King, Stephen. *Firestarter*

Stage, Zoje. ★*Baby Teeth: A Novel*

Seveneves. Stephenson, Neal

SEVENTEEN-YEAR-OLD BOYS

Benioff, David. *City of Thieves: A Novel*

Picoult, Jodi. *Nineteen Minutes: A Novel*

Power, Susan. *The Grass Dancer*

Tyler, Anne. ★*Saint Maybe*

SEVENTEEN-YEAR-OLD GIRLS

Bird, Sarah. ★*The Flamenco Academy: A Novel*

Sagan, Francoise. ★*Bonjour Tristesse*

Sepetys, Ruta. ★*Out of the Easy*

Welty, Eudora. ★*The Ponder Heart*

*The **Seventh** Perfection*. Polansky, Daniel

Sevenwaters fantasies [Series]. Marillier, Juliet

***Several** People Are Typing*. Kasulke, Calvin

Severance. Ma, Ling

SEWER WORKERS

Pynchon, Thomas. ★*V: A Novel*

SEWING

Wiggs, Susan. ★*The Oysterville Sewing Circle*

SEX (PSYCHOLOGY)

Woolf, Virginia. *Orlando: A Biography*

SEX ADDICTION IN MEN

Palahniuk, Chuck. *Choke: A Novel*

SEX ADDICTS

Banks, Russell. *Lost Memory of Skin*

***Sex** and Vanity: A Novel*. Kwan, Kevin

SEX CRIMES

Amidon, Stephen. *Security: A Novel*

Clark, Mary Higgins. ★*Kiss the Girls and Make Them Cry*
Eisler, Barry. *The Killer Collective*
Fairstein, Linda A. *Blood Oath*
Gaitskill, Mary. *Don't Cry: Stories*
Luna, Louisa. *The Janes*
Rowland, Laura Joh. *The Ripper's Shadow*
Russell, Kate Elizabeth. ★*My Dark Vanessa*
Sandford, John. ★*Invisible Prey*
Toews, Miriam. ★*Women Talking: A Novel*

SEX CUSTOMS
Bushnell, Candace. *Is There Still Sex in the City?*
Miller, Henry. ★*Tropic of Capricorn*

SEX DISCRIMINATION
Elison, Meg. *The Book of the Unnamed Midwife*

SEX EDUCATION FOR ADULTS
Danan, Rosie. *The Intimacy Experiment*

SEX EDUCATION FOR TEENAGERS
Perrotta, Tom. *The Abstinence Teacher*

SEX INDUSTRY AND TRADE
Faust, Christa. *Choke Hold*
Faust, Christa. *Money Shot*
Larsson, Stieg. *The Girl Who Played with Fire*

SEX OFFENDERS
Banks, Russell. *Lost Memory of Skin*
Harrison, Jim. *The Great Leader*
Sandford, John. *Broken Prey*

SEX SCANDALS
Jhabvala, Ruth Prawer. ★*Heat and Dust*
McEwan, Ian. ★*Amsterdam*

SEX SCANDALS — HISTORY
Shreve, Anita. *Fortune's Rocks: A Novel*
Sex Wars. Piercy, Marge

SEX WORKERS
Mendez, Paul. *Rainbow Milk*
Shafak, Elif. ★*10 Minutes 38 Seconds in This Strange World*

SEXISM
Alexander, Tamera. ★*A Note yet Unsung*
Blake, Audrey. *The Girl in His Shadow: A Novel*
Cho, Nam-Ju. ★*Kim Jiyoung, Born 1982*
Collins, Kathleen. *Notes from a Black Woman's Diary: Selected Works of Kathleen Collins*
Darznik, Jasmin. *Song of a Captive Bird: A Novel*
Davis, Fiona. *The Masterpiece*
French, Marilyn. ★*The Women's Room*
Gibson, Claire. *Beyond the Point: A Novel*
Gilman, Charlotte Perkins. *Herland*
Goldberg, Lee. *Bone Canyon*
Hooper, Elise. *Fast Girls: A Novel of the 1936 Women's Olympic Team*
Le Guin, Ursula K. *Four Ways to Forgiveness*
McCall Smith, Alexander. *The Kalahari Typing School for Men*
Stewart, Amy. *Lady Cop Makes Trouble*
Stewart, Amy. *Miss Kopp's Midnight Confessions*
Yellin, Jessica. *Savage News*

SEXISM IN EMPLOYMENT
Gentry, Amy. *Last Woman Standing*
Katz, Erica. *The Boys' Club*
Rockaway, Kristin. *How to Hack a Heartbreak*

SEXPLOITATION
Pelevin, Viktor. *The Hall of Singing Caryatids*

Sexton, Margaret Wilkerson
A Kind of Freedom
The Revisioners: A Novel

SEXUAL ATTRACTION
Apostol, Gina. *Bibliolepsy*
Bailey, Tessa. *Fix Her Up*
Brayden, Melissa. *First Position*
Ca$h. ★*Trust No Bitch*
Clark, Wahida. *Thugs*
Dickey, Eric Jerome. *Before We Were Wicked*
Greenwell, Garth. *Cleanness*
Harrison, Thea. *Dragon Bound*
Malone, Minx. *Bad Blood*
O'Leary, Beth. *The Flatshare: A Novel*
Putney, Mary Jo. *Once a Scoundrel*
Rooney, Sally. ★*Beautiful World, Where Are You*
Sosa, Mia. ★*Acting on Impulse*

SEXUAL DOMINANCE AND SUBMISSION
Bell, Shelly. *At His Mercy*
Bell, Shelly. *For His Pleasure*
Hall, Alexis. *For Real*

SEXUAL ETHICS
Lawrence, D. H. ★*Lady Chatterley's Lover*

SEXUAL FREEDOM
Heinlein, Robert A. ★*Stranger in a Strange Land*

SEXUAL HARASSMENT
Baker, Chandler. *Whisper Network: A Novel*
Campbell, Bebe Moore. *Brothers and Sisters*
Connelly, Michael. *The Late Show*
Dickey, Eric Jerome. ★*The Son of Mr. Suleman*
Gentry, Amy. *Last Woman Standing*
Pellegrino, Amanda. *Smile and Look Pretty*

SEXUAL SLAVERY
Larsson, Stieg. *The Girl Who Played with Fire*

SEXUAL VIOLENCE
Dare, Abi. *The Girl with the Louding Voice*
Rendell, Ruth. *Simisola*
Woodson, Jacqueline. ★*Another Brooklyn*

SEXUAL VIOLENCE VICTIMS
Clark, Mary Higgins. ★*Kiss the Girls and Make Them Cry*
Shafak, Elif. ★*10 Minutes 38 Seconds in This Strange World*

SEXUALITY
Babalola, Bolu. *Love in Color: Mythical Tales from Around the World, Retold*
Bagshawe, Tilly. *Adored*
Ballard, J. G. *The Kindness of Women*
Barth, John. ★*The Floating Opera*
Barth, John. ★*The Sot-Weed Factor*
Bellow, Saul. *More Die of Heartbreak*
Broder, Melissa. *The Pisces: A Novel*
Burton, Jessie. *The Miniaturist*
Capri, NeNe. *The Pussy Trap*
Carter, Angela. ★*Burning Your Boats: The Collected Short Stories*
Clark, Wahida. *Honor Thy Thug*
Clark, Wahida. *Justify My Thug: A Novel*
Coetzee, J. M. *Disgrace*

Dickey, Eric Jerome. *The Blackbirds*
Dickey, Eric Jerome. *The Business of Lovers*
Dubus, Andre. *Dirty Love*
Fowles, John. *The Magus*
Gamboa, Santiago. *Necropolis*
Garwood, Julie. *The Bride*
Gordimer, Nadine. *Life Times: Stories, 1952-2007*
Hamill, Shaun. *A Cosmology of Monsters*
Harris, E. Lynn. *Invisible Life: A Novel*
Hilton, L. S. *Maestra*
Kim, Young-Ha. *Diary of a Murderer: And Other Stories*
Kundera, Milan. ★*Immortality*
Kundera, Milan. ★*The Unbearable Lightness of Being*
Lawrence, D. H. ★*Lady Chatterley's Lover*
Lawrence, D. H. *Sons and Lovers*
Lawrence, D. H. *Women in Love*
Machado, Carmen Maria. *Her Body and Other Parties: Stories*
MacLeod, Alison. *Tenderness*
Miller, Henry. ★*Tropic of Capricorn*
Murakami, Haruki. *Colorless Tsukuru Tazaki and His Years of Pilgrimage*
Nabokov, Vladimir Vladimirovich. ★*Lolita*
Oates, Joyce Carol. *Blonde: A Novel*
Philyaw, Deesha. *The Secret Lives of Church Ladies*
Piercy, Marge. *Vida: A Novel*
Prose, Francine. *Goldengrove: A Novel*
Pynchon, Thomas. *Against the Day: A Novel*
Rice, Anne. *The Vampire Armand*
Shreve, Anita. *Testimony: A Novel*
Spark, Muriel. *The Driver's Seat*
Stone, Irving. ★*The Agony and the Ecstasy: A Biographical Novel of Michelangelo*
Stringer, Vickie M. *Dirty Red: A Novel*
Stross, Charles. *Saturn's Children: A Space Opera*
Styles, Toy. *Raunchy*
Swinson, Kiki. *Wifey*
Taylor, Brandon. ★*Filthy Animals*
Varley, John. *Demon*
Varley, John. ★*Titan*
Vollmann, William T. *Last Stories and Other Stories*
Wallace, David Foster. ★*Brief Interviews with Hideous Men*
Welsh, Irvine. *Dead Men's Trousers*
Winterson, Jeanette. ★*Frankissstein*
Woods, Stuart. *New York Dead*

SEXUALITY — SPIRITUAL ASPECTS
Momaday, N. Scott. *The Ancient Child: A Novel*

SEXUALLY ABUSED BOYS
Sapphire. ★*The Kid: A Novel*

SEXUALLY ABUSED CHILDREN
Allison, Dorothy. ★*Bastard Out of Carolina*
Draper, Sharon M. ★*Forged by Fire*

SEXUALLY ABUSED TEENAGERS
Mihalic, Susan. *Dark Horses*

SEXUALLY ABUSED WOMEN
Fairstein, Linda A. *Blood Oath*

SEXUALLY TRANSMITTED DISEASES
Burns, Charles. ★*Black Hole*

Shaara, Jeff
  Gods and Generals: A Novel of the Civil War
  Gone for Soldiers
  The Last Full Measure
  The Rising Tide: A Novel of World War II
  The Steel Wave: A Novel of World War II

Shaara, Michael
  ★*The Killer Angels: A Novel*

Shades of Grey: A Novel. Fforde, Jasper
Shadow and Ice. Showalter, Gena
Shadow Child. Rizzuto, Rahna R.
Shadow Country: A New Rendering of the Watson Legend. Matthiessen, Peter
The *Shadow* District: A Thriller. Indriðason, Arnaldur
Shadow histories [Series]. Parry, H. G.
A *Shadow* Intelligence. Harris, Oliver
★*The Shadow* King: A Novel. Mengiste, Maaza
Shadow of Night. Harkness, Deborah E.
★*The Shadow* of the Wind. Ruiz Zafon, Carlos
Shadow Rider. Feehan, Christine
Shadow riders novels [Series]. Feehan, Christine
★*Shadow* Tag: A Novel. Erdrich, Louise
Shadow Tyrants. Cussler, Clive
The *Shadows*. North, Alex

SHADOWS
  North, Claire. *The Pursuit of William Abbey*
The *Shadows* in the Street: A Simon Serrailler Mystery. Hill, Susan
The *Shadows* of Men. Mukherjee, Abir

Shafak, Elif
  ★*10 Minutes 38 Seconds in This Strange World*
  The Bastard of Istanbul
  Honor: A Novel

Shaffer, Mary Ann
  The Guernsey Literary and Potato Peel Pie Society

SHAKESPEARE, WILLIAM
  Akhtar, Ayad. ★*Homeland Elegies: A Novel*
  Bear, Elizabeth. *Ink and Steel: A Novel of the Promethean Age*
  Brandreth, Benet. *The Spy of Venice*
  Calvi, Mary. *Dear George, Dear Mary: A Novel of George Washington's First Love*
  Gibson, William. *The Peripheral*
  Gruber, Michael. *The Book of Air and Shadows*
  Mankell, Henning. *The Dogs of Riga*
  Munro, Alice. *The View from Castle Rock: Stories*
  O'Farrell, Maggie. *Hamnet*
  Phillips, Arthur. *The Tragedy of Arthur: A Novel*
  Roth, Philip. ★*The Human Stain*
  Rutherfurd, Edward. *London*

Shalev, Meir
  Two She-Bears: A Novel

Shalimar the Clown: A Novel. Rushdie, Salman
The *Shallows*. Goldman, Matt

Shalvis, Jill
  Second Chance Summer
  Simply Irresistible
  Sweet Little Lies
  The Sweetest Thing

SHAMANISM

Gruber, Michael. *Night of the Jaguar: A Novel*

SHAMANS

Gruber, Michael. *Night of the Jaguar: A Novel*

Kuang, R. F. ★*The Dragon Republic*

Kuang, R. F. *The Poppy War*

McCall Smith, Alexander. ★*The No. 1 Ladies' Detective Agency*

Roanhorse, Rebecca. ★*Trail of Lightning*

Shamble & Die Investigations [Series]. Anderson, Kevin J.

SHAME

McEwan, Ian. ★*Atonement: A Novel*

Roth, Henry. *A Diving Rock on the Hudson*

Roth, Henry. *From Bondage*

Shame and the Captives: A Novel. Keneally, Thomas

SHAME IN MEN

Banks, Russell. *Continental Drift*

Crane, Stephen. ★*The Red Badge of Courage: An Episode of the American Civil War*

Greene, Graham. *The Tenth Man*

The *Shameless*. Atkins, Ace

Shames, Terry

★*An Unsettling Crime for Samuel Craddock*

Shamsie, Kamila

Home Fire: A Novel

Shan Tao Yun mysteries [Series]. Pattison, Eliot

Shan, Sa

The Girl Who Played Go

Shanbhag, Vivek

Ghachar Ghochar

★*Shane*. Schaefer, Jack

Shanghai Girls: A Novel. See, Lisa

The *Shanghai* Moon: A Lydia Chin/Bill Smith Novel. Rozan, S. J.

Shanghai Redemption: An Inspector Chen Novel. Qiu, Xiaolong

SHANGHAI, CHINA

Ballard, J. G. *Empire of the Sun: A Novel*

Ballard, J. G. *The Kindness of Women*

Ishiguro, Kazuo. *When We Were Orphans*

Pearson, Ridley. *The Risk Agent*

Qiu, Xiaolong. *Death of a Red Heroine*

Qiu, Xiaolong. *Don't Cry Tai Lake: An Inspector Chen Novel*

Qiu, Xiaolong. *Enigma of China*

Qiu, Xiaolong. *Hold Your Breath, China*

Qiu, Xiaolong. *Red Mandarin Dress: An Inspector Chen Novel*

Qiu, Xiaolong. *Shanghai Redemption: An Inspector Chen Novel*

Qiu, Xiaolong. *When Red Is Black*

Rozan, S. J. *The Shanghai Moon: A Lydia Chin/Bill Smith Novel*

Stephenson, Neal. *The Diamond Age,: Or, a Young Lady's Illustrated Primer*

Tan, Amy. *The Valley of Amazement*

Tan, Lucy. *What We Were Promised*

Thien, Madeleine. *Do Not Say We Have Nothing*

SHANGRI-LA (IMAGINARY PLACE)

Hilton, James. ★*Lost Horizon: A Novel*

Shannon, Dell

★*Chaos of Crime*

Shannon, Samantha

The Bone Season

The Mime Order

The Priory of the Orange Tree

★The *Shape* of Night: A Novel. Gerritsen, Tess

★The *Shape* of the Ruins. Vasquez, Juan Gabriel

The *Shape* Shifter. Hillerman, Tony

SHAPESHIFTERS

Allen, Susanna. *A Wolf in Duke's Clothing*

James, Marlon. ★*Black Leopard, Red Wolf*

Singh, Nalini. ★*Silver Silence*

Snyder, Suleikha. *Big Bad Wolf*

Wong, David. *This Book Is Full of Spiders: Seriously, Dude, Don't Touch It*

Shapeshifters of the Beau Monde [Series]. Allen, Susanna

SHAPESHIFTING

Choo, Yangsze. ★*The Night Tiger: A Novel*

Shapiro, Barbara A.

The Muralist

SHARDLAKE, MATTHEW (FICTITIOUS CHARACTER)

Sansom, C. J. ★*Sovereign*

★*Shards* of Honor. Bujold, Lois McMaster

Shards: a Novel. Prcic, Ismet

SHARECROPPERS

Caldwell, Erskine. *Tobacco Road*

Faulkner, William. *The Hamlet*

Reddi, Rishi. *Passage West: A Novel*

SHARED HOUSING

O'Leary, Beth. *The Flatshare: A Novel*

SHARKS

Alten, Steve. *Meg: Generations*

Sharon McCone mysteries [Series]. Muller, Marcia

★*Sharp* Objects: A Novel. Flynn, Gillian

Sharp, Zoe

Fox Hunter

Second Shot: A Charlie Fox Thriller

Sharpe, Tess

Barbed Wire Heart

Sharratt, Mary

Daughters of the Witching Hill

Illuminations: A Novel of Hildegard Von Bingen

Revelations

Shattered Pillars. Bear, Elizabeth

Shaw, Irwin

Beggarman, Thief

★*Rich Man, Poor Man*

Shaw, M. B.

Murder at the Mill: A Mystery

Shaw, Vivian

★*Dreadful Company*

★*Strange Practice*

Shaw, William

The Birdwatcher

Salt Lane

A Song for the Brokenhearted

Shaykh, Hanan

★*One Thousand and One Nights: A Sparkling Retelling of the Beloved Classic*

She Was Like That: New and Selected Stories. Walbert, Kate

★*She* Who Became the Sun. Parker-Chan, Shelley

She Wouldn't Change a Thing. Adlakha, Sarah

SHEEP
Hurley, Andrew Michael. *Devil's Day*

SHEFFIELD, ENGLAND
Sahota, Sunjeev. *The Year of the Runaways*

Sheldon Horowitz novels [Series]. Miller, Derek B.

Shell Game. Paretsky, Sara

★*The Shell Seekers*. Pilcher, Rosamunde

Shelley, Mary Wollstonecraft
★*Frankenstein: Or, the Modern Prometheus*

SHELLEY, MARY WOLLSTONECRAFT
Alharthi, Jokha. *Celestial Bodies: A Novel*
Winterson, Jeanette. ★*Frankissstein*

★*Shelter* in Place. Leavitt, David

Shelter in Place. Roberts, Nora

★*Shelter* of the Most High. Cossette, Connilyn

★*The Sheltering Sky*. Bowles, Paul

SHELTERS FOR THE HOMELESS
Bohjalian, Chris. *The Double Bind: A Novel*

Shelton, Paige
Thin Ice: A Mystery

Shepard, Jim
★*The Book of Aron*
Phase Six
The World to Come: Stories

Shepard, Sam
The One Inside

Shepard, Sara
★*Reputation*

*The **Shepherd's** Hut*. Winton, Tim

Shepherd, Peng
The Book of M: A Novel

SHEPHERDS
Hardy, Thomas. ★*Far from the Madding Crowd*
Johnson, Craig. *Land of Wolves*

SHEPPERTON, LONDON, ENGLAND
Ballard, J. G. *The Kindness of Women*

SHERIFFS
Armstrong, Kelley. *Alone in the Wild*
Armstrong, Kelley. *Watcher in the Woods*
Atkins, Ace. *The Broken Places*
Atkins, Ace. *The Fallen*
Atkins, Ace. *The Forsaken*
Atkins, Ace. ★*The Heathens*
Atkins, Ace. *The Innocents*
Atkins, Ace. *The Lost Ones*
Atkins, Ace. *The Revelators*
Atkins, Ace. *The Shameless*
Atkins, Ace. *The Sinners*
Bowen, Peter. *Badlands*
Cash, Wiley. *When Ghosts Come Home: A Novel*
Dodd, Christina. *The Woman Who Couldn't Scream*
Freeman, Castle. *All That I Have: A Novel*
Harding Thornton, Christina. *Pickard County Atlas*
Hulse, S. M. *Eden Mine*
Johnson, Craig. *Daughter of the Morning Star*
Johnson, Craig. *Land of Wolves*
Johnson, Craig. *Next to Last Stand*
Johnson, Craig. *Spirit of Steamboat: A Walt Longmire Story*

Laukkanen, Owen. *Deception Cove*
McCarthy, Cormac. ★*No Country for Old Men*
McCrumb, Sharyn. ★*The Ballad of Frankie Silver*
McCrumb, Sharyn. ★*If Ever I Return, Pretty Peggy-O*
Panowich, Brian. *Bull Mountain*
Panowich, Brian. *Like Lions*
Ramsay, Frederick. *Countdown*
Rash, Ron. *Above the Waterfall*
Ross, Ann B. *Miss Julia Throws a Wedding*
Sternbergh, Adam. *The Blinds*
Stewart, Amy. *Miss Kopp's Midnight Confessions*
Thompson, Jim. *The Killer Inside Me*

Sherlock Holmes mysteries [Series]. Doyle, Arthur Conan

Sherlock Holmes novels [Series]. Horowitz, Anthony

SHERMAN'S MARCH TO THE SEA
Doctorow, E. L. *The March: A Novel*

SHERMAN, WILLIAM TECUMSEH, 1820-1891
Doctorow, E. L. *The March: A Novel*
Richler, Mordecai. *Barney's Version: A Novel*

Sherrill, Steven
The Minotaur Takes His Own Sweet Time: A Novel

SHETLAND ISLANDS
Cleeves, Ann. *Raven Black*
Cleeves, Ann. *Thin Air*
Cleeves, Ann. *Wild Fire*

Shetland mysteries [Series]. Cleeves, Ann

Shieldbreaker's Story. Saberhagen, Fred

Shields, Carol
The Republic of Love
★*The Stone Diaries*
Unless

Shiloh and Other Stories. Mason, Bobbie Ann

*The **Shimmer***. Stroud, Carsten

Shimotakahara, Leslie
After the Bloom

Shin, Ann
The Last Exiles

★*The **Shining***. King, Stephen

*The **Shining** Girls*. Beukes, Lauren

Shinobi mysteries [Series]. Spann, Susan

SHIP CAPTAINS
Bujold, Lois McMaster. ★*Shards of Honor*
Bujold, Lois McMaster. ★*The Warrior's Apprentice*
Conrad, Joseph. ★*Heart of Darkness*
Cussler, Clive. *Sacred Stone*
Doyle, Brian. *The Plover: A Novel*
Forester, C. S. *Admiral Hornblower in the West Indies*
Forester, C. S. *Commodore Hornblower*
Forester, C. S. *Hornblower and the Atropos*
Forester, C. S. *Hornblower and the Hotspur*
Forester, C. S. *Lord Hornblower*
Forester, C. S. *Mr. Midshipman Hornblower*
Furst, Alan. *Dark Voyage: A Novel*
Long, Julie Anne. ★*Lady Derring Takes a Lover*
Novik, Naomi. *His Majesty's Dragon*
O'Brian, Patrick. *Master and Commander*
Powning, Beth. *The Sea Captain's Wife: A Novel*
Ripley, Mike. *Mr Campion's Coven*

Sebastian, Cat. *It Takes Two to Tumble*
Simmons, Dan. ★*The Terror: A Novel*
Smith, Dominic. *Bright and Distant Shores*
Spencer, Minerva. *Scandalous*
SHIP CAPTAINS' SPOUSES
    Powning, Beth. *The Sea Captain's Wife: A Novel*
Ship of Fools. Porter, Katherine Anne
Ship of the Line. Forester, C. S.
Shipman, Viola
    The Clover Girls
    The Heirloom Garden
Shipped. Hockman, Angie
SHIPPING
    Furst, Alan. *Dark Voyage: A Novel*
SHIPPING INDUSTRY AND TRADE
    Kleypas, Lisa. ★*Devil in Disguise*
★*The Shipping News*. Proulx, Annie
SHIPS
    Cussler, Clive. *Odessa Sea*
    O'Connor, Joseph. *Star of the Sea*
    Turton, Stuart. ★*The Devil and the Dark Water*
SHIPWRECK SURVIVORS
    El Akkad, Omar. *What Strange Paradise*
    Katsu, Alma. *The Deep*
    Riley, Vanessa. ★*An Earl, the Girl, and a Toddler*
    Seton, Anya. *Avalon*
SHIPWRECKS
    Albom, Mitch. *The Stranger in the Lifeboat*
    Barnes, Julian. ★*A History of the World in 10 1/2 Chapters*
    Barth, John. *The Last Voyage of Somebody the Sailor*
    Coetzee, J. M. ★*Foe*
    Conrad, Joseph. ★*Lord Jim*
    Cussler, Clive. *Serpent: A Novel from the Numa Files*
    Defoe, Daniel. ★*Robinson Crusoe*
    Du Maurier, Daphne. *Jamaica Inn*
    Eco, Umberto. *The Island of the Day Before*
    El Akkad, Omar. *What Strange Paradise*
    Gabaldon, Diana. ★*Voyager*
    Golding, William. *Close Quarters*
    Grant, Mira. *Into the Drowning Deep*
    Grass, Gunter. *Crabwalk*
    Simmons, Dan. ★*The Terror: A Novel*
    Wells, H. G. ★*The Island of Dr. Moreau*
SHIPWRECKS — HISTORY
    Bainbridge, Beryl. *Every Man for Himself*
★*Shiver*. Reynolds, Allie
The Shivering Turn. Spencer, Sally
Shock Wave. Sandford, John
Shocklee, Michelle
    Under the Tulip Tree
SHOE SELLERS
    Roosevelt, Elliott. *Murder in the Map Room: An Eleanor Roosevelt Mystery*
SHOES
    McCall Smith, Alexander. *Blue Shoes and Happiness*
    Murphy, Julie. *If the Shoe Fits*
Shogun. Clavell, James
The Shogun's Daughter: A Novel of Feudal Japan. Rowland, Laura Joh

SHOGUNS
    Rowland, Laura Joh. *The Incense Game: A Novel of Feudal Japan*
    Rowland, Laura Joh. *The Iris Fan: A Novel of Feudal Japan*
    Rowland, Laura Joh. *The Shogun's Daughter: A Novel of Feudal Japan*
Shoham, Liad
    Asylum City: A Novel
Shoot the Dog: A Virgil Cain Mystery. Smith, B. J.
SHOOTING
    Black, Cara. ★*Three Hours in Paris*
    Brett, Simon. *Murder Unprompted*
    Graff, Andrew J. *Raft of Stars*
    Sjowall, Maj. ★*Murder at the Savoy*
    Stabenow, Dana. ★*A Deeper Sleep: A Kate Shugak Novel*
The Shooting at Chateau Rock. Walker, Martin
★*The Shootist*. Swarthout, Glendon
Shootist [Series]. Swarthout, Glendon
Shopgirl. Martin, Steve
SHOPKEEPERS
    Higashino, Keigo. *The Miracles of the Namiya General Store*
SHOPLIFTING
    Hallinan, Timothy. *Fields Where They Lay*
SHOPPING MALLS
    Ballard, J. G. *Kingdom Come*
    Hallinan, Timothy. *Fields Where They Lay*
Shorefall. Bennett, Robert Jackson
The Short Stories. Hemingway, Ernest
★*Short Stories*. Hughes, Langston
SHORT STORIES
    Aboulela, Leila. *Elsewhere, Home*
    Acampora, Lauren. *The Wonder Garden*
    Adichie, Chimamanda Ngozi. *The Thing Around Your Neck*
    Adjei-Brenyah, Nana Kwame. *Friday Black: Stories*
    Ahern, Cecelia. *Roar*
    Akpan, Uwem. *Say You're One of Them*
    Alarcon, Daniel. *The King Is Always Above the People: Stories*
    Aleichem, Sholem. *Tevye the Dairyman and the Railroad Stories*
    Alenyikov, Michael. *Ivan and Misha: Stories*
    Alexie, Sherman. *Blasphemy: New and Selected Stories*
    Allende, Isabel. *The Stories of Eva Luna*
    Alomar, Osama. *The Teeth of the Comb & Other Stories*
    Alvar, Mia. *In the Country: Stories*
    Anaya, Rudolfo A. *The Man Who Could Fly and Other Stories*
    Antopol, Molly. *The Unamericans*
    Arimah, Lesley Nneka. ★*What It Means When a Man Falls from the Sky: Stories*
    Armfield, Julia. *Salt Slow: Stories*
    Asimov, Isaac. ★*I, Robot*
    Atwood, Margaret. *Bluebeard's Egg and Other Stories*
    Atwood, Margaret. *Moral Disorder*
    Atwood, Margaret. ★*Stone Mattress: Nine Tales*
    Babalola, Bolu. *Love in Color: Mythical Tales from Around the World, Retold*
    Balaskovits, A. A. *Magic for Unlucky Girls: Stories*
    Baldwin, James. ★*Going to Meet the Man*
    Ballard, J. G. ★*The Complete Stories of J.G. Ballard.*
    Bambara, Toni Cade. *Gorilla, My Love*
    Bandi. *The Accusation: Forbidden Stories from Inside North Korea*

Barnhill, Kelly Regan. *Dreadful Young Ladies and Other Stories*

Barthelme, Donald. *Sixty Stories*

Bausch, Richard. *The Stories of Richard Bausch*

Baxter, Charles. *There's Something I Want You to Do: Stories*

Bear, Greg. *The Collected Stories of Greg Bear*

Beattie, Ann. *The State We're In: Maine Stories*

Beauvoir, Simone de. *The Woman Destroyed*

Bergman, Megan Mayhew. *Almost Famous Women: Stories*

Berlin, Lucia. ★*Evening in Paradise: More Stories*

Berlin, Lucia. ★*A Manual for Cleaning Women: Selected Stories*

Berry, Wendell. ★*That Distant Land: The Collected Stories of Wendell Berry*

Beukes, Lauren. *Slipping: Stories, Essays, & Other Writing*

Bhuvaneswar, Chaya. *White Dancing Elephants: Stories*

Bolano, Roberto. *Last Evenings on Earth*

Bonnaffons, Amy. *The Wrong Heaven: Stories*

Borges, Jorge Luis. ★*Collected Fictions*

Borges, Jorge Luis. *Ficciones*

Boyle, T. Coraghessan. *The Relive Box: And Other Stories*

Bradbury, Ray. *Bradbury Stories: 100 of His Most Celebrated Tales*

Bradbury, Ray. *The Illustrated Man*

Brand, Max. ★*The Collected Stories of Max Brand*

Brand, Max. *Max Brand's Best Western Stories*

Brinkley, Jamel. *A Lucky Man: Stories*

Brown, Larry. ★*Tiny Love: The Complete Stories of Larry Brown*

Butler, Octavia E. *Bloodchild: And Other Stories*

Butler, Robert Olen. *A Good Scent from a Strange Mountain: Stories*

Byatt, A. S. *Medusa's Ankles: Selected Stories*

Capote, Truman. ★*Breakfast at Tiffany's*

Capote, Truman. ★*The Complete Stories of Truman Capote*

Carter, Angela. ★*Burning Your Boats: The Collected Short Stories*

Carver, Raymond. *What We Talk About When We Talk About Love: Stories*

Chai, May-Lee. *Useful Phrases for Immigrants: Stories*

Chekhov, Anton Pavlovich. *Early Short Stories, 1883-1888*

Chekhov, Anton Pavlovich. *Later Short Stories, 1888-1903*

Chiang, Ted. ★*Exhalation: Stories*

Chiang, Ted. ★*Stories of Your Life and Others*

Child, Lee. *No Middle Name: The Complete Collected Jack Reacher Short Stories*

Chizmar, Richard T. *A Long December*

Cho, Zen. *Spirits Abroad and Other Stories*

Choi, Yoon. *Skinship: Stories*

Christie, Agatha. *Three Blind Mice, and Other Stories*

Clarke, Arthur C. ★*The Collected Stories of Arthur C. Clarke*

Clarke, Maxine Beneba. ★*Foreign Soil*

Cline, Emma. *Daddy: Stories*

Colette. *The Collected Stories of Colette*

Collins, Kathleen. ★*Whatever Happened to Interracial Love?: Stories*

Conrad, Joseph. *Complete Short Fiction of Joseph Conrad: The Stories: Volume 1*

Coover, Robert. *Going for a Beer: Selected Short Fictions*

Couto, Mia. *Rain: And Other Stories*

Dahl, Roald. *Collected Stories*

Danticat, Edwidge. ★*Everything Inside: Stories*

Danticat, Edwidge. ★*Krik? Krak!*

Davis, Lydia. *The Collected Stories of Lydia Davis*

Delany, Samuel R. *Aye, and Gomorrah: Stories*

Demirtas, Selahattin. *Dawn: Stories*

Diaz, Junot. ★*This Is How You Lose Her*

Doctorow, E. L. *All the Time in the World: New and Selected Stories*

Doctorow, E. L. *Doctorow: Collected Stories*

Dostoyevsky, Fyodor. *The Best Short Stories of Dostoevsky*

Doyle, Arthur Conan. ★*The Complete Sherlock Holmes*

Drabble, Margaret. *A Day in the Life of a Smiling Woman: Complete Short Stories*

Dubus, Andre. *Dirty Love*

Due, Tananarive. *Ghost Summer: Stories*

Dumas, Henry. *Echo Tree: The Collected Short Fiction of Henry Dumas*

Dybek, Stuart. *I Sailed with Magellan*

Earley, Tony. *Mr. Tall: A Novella and Stories*

Eggers, Dave. *How We Are Hungry: Stories*

Eisenberg, Deborah. *The Twilight of the Superheroes*

Ellis, Helen. *American Housewife: Stories*

Englander, Nathan. *What We Talk About When We Talk About Anne Frank: Stories*

Enright, Anne. *Yesterday's Weather: Stories*

Epstein, Joseph. *The Love Song of A. Jerome Minkoff, and Other Stories*

Erdrich, Louise. *The Red Convertible: Selected and New Stories, 1978-2008*

Eugenides, Jeffrey. *Fresh Complaint: Stories*

Evans, Danielle. ★*The Office of Historical Corrections: A Novella and Stories*

Fajardo-Anstine, Kali. ★*Sabrina & Corina: Stories*

Fallon, Siobhan. *You Know When the Men Are Gone*

Faulkner, William. ★*Go Down, Moses*

Faulkner, William. *Uncollected Stories of William Faulkner*

Faye, Lyndsay. *The Whole Art of Detection: Lost Mysteries of Sherlock Holmes*

Fitzgerald, F. Scott. *Novels and Stories, 1920-1922*

Fitzgerald, F. Scott. ★*The Short Stories of F. Scott Fitzgerald: A New Collection*

Fitzgerald, F. Scott. *Six Tales of the Jazz Age and Other Stories*

Fitzgerald, Penelope. *The Means of Escape: Stories*

Ford, Kelli Jo. ★*Crooked Hallelujah*

Ford, Richard. *A Multitude of Sins: Stories*

Ford, Richard. *Sorry for Your Trouble: Stories*

Founds, Kathleen. *When Mystical Creatures Attack!*

Frame, Janet. *Between My Father and the King: New and Uncollected Stories*

Fuentes, Carlos. *The Crystal Frontier: A Novel in Nine Stories*

Gaiman, Neil. ★*Fragile Things: Short Fictions and Wonders*

Gaiman, Neil. *Trigger Warning: Short Fictions and Disturbances*

Gaitskill, Mary. *Don't Cry: Stories*

Gaitskill, Mary. *Veronica*

Galchen, Rivka. *American Innovations: Stories*

Garcia Marquez, Gabriel. *Leaf Storm, and Other Stories*

Garcia Marquez, Gabriel. ★*Strange Pilgrims: Twelve Stories*

Gardam, Jane. *The People on Privilege Hill and Other Stories*

Gay, Roxane. ★*Ayiti*

Gay, Roxane. ★*Difficult Women*

Gilchrist, Ellen. ★*Collected Stories*

Gilman, Charlotte Perkins. ★*The Yellow Wallpaper and Selected Writings*

Gogol, Nikolai Vasilievich. *The Collected Tales of Nikolai Gogol*

Gonzalez, Christopher. *I'm Not Hungry but I Could Eat*

Gordimer, Nadine. *Life Times: Stories, 1952-2007*

Graley, Lisa. *The Current That Carries: Stories*

Greene, Graham. *Collected Stories: Including May We Borrow Your Husband? a Sense of Reality, Twenty-One Stories*

Greene, Graham. *The Last Word and Other Stories*

Groff, Lauren. *Delicate Edible Birds and Other Stories*

Groff, Lauren. ★*Florida*

Gurganus, Allan. ★*Local Souls: Novellas*

Gurganus, Allan. *The Practical Heart: Four Novellas*

Gurganus, Allan. *White People: Stories and Novellas*

Gustine, Amy. *You Should Pity Us Instead: Stories*

Hadley, Tessa. *Bad Dreams and Other Stories*

Harte, Bret. ★*The Best Short Stories of Bret Harte*

Harvey, John. *A Darker Shade of Blue: Stories*

Hemingway, Ernest. *The Nick Adams Stories*

Hemingway, Ernest. *The Short Stories*

Hemingway, Ernest. *The Snows of Kilimanjaro and Other Stories*

Hempel, Amy. *Sing to It: New Stories*

Henry, O. ★*The Complete Works of O. Henry*

Henry, O. *O. Henry: 101 Stories*

Herbert, Julian. *Bring Me the Head of Quentin Tarantino: Stories*

Herron, Mick. *Dolphin Junction: Collected Stories*

Highsmith, Patricia. *The Highsmith Reader: Selected Novels and Short Stories*

Hill, Joe. ★*Full Throttle: Stories*

Hill, Joe. *Strange Weather: Four Short Novels*

Horrocks, Caitlin. *Life Among the Terranauts*

Howland, Bette. *Calm Sea and Prosperous Voyage*

Hughes, Langston. ★*Short Stories*

Hurston, Zora Neale. *Hitting a Straight Lick with a Crooked Stick: Stories from the Harlem Renaissance*

Jackson, Shirley. ★*The Lottery: And Other Stories*

James, Henry. *Complete Stories, 1864-1874*

James, Henry. *Complete Stories, 1874-1884*

James, Henry. *Complete Stories, 1884-1891*

James, Henry. *Complete Stories, 1892-1898*

James, Henry. *Complete Stories, 1898-1910*

Jemisin, N. K. *How Long 'Til Black Future Month?*

Jen, Gish. ★*Thank You, Mr. Nixon: Stories*

Jhabvala, Ruth Prawer. *At the End of the Century: The Stories of Ruth Prawer Jhabvala.*

Johnson, Denis. *The Largesse of the Sea Maiden: Stories*

Johnson, Jocelyn Nicole. ★*My Monticello: Fiction*

Joyce, James. ★*Dubliners*

Kafka, Franz. ★*Collected Stories*

Kelton, Elmer. *Hard Ride*

Kim, Bo Young. ★*I'm Waiting for You: And Other Stories*

Kim, Young-Ha. *Diary of a Murderer: And Other Stories*

Krauss, Nicole. ★*To Be a Man: Stories*

Le Guin, Ursula K. *The Birthday of the World: And Other Stories*

Le Guin, Ursula K. *Orsinian Tales*

Leonard, Elmore. *Charlie Martz and Other Stories: The Unpublished Stories*

Leonard, Elmore. ★*The Complete Western Stories of Elmore Leonard.*

Leonard, Elmore. *When the Women Come Out to Dance: Stories*

Lovecraft, H. P. ★*Tales*

Machado, Carmen Maria. *Her Body and Other Parties: Stories*

MacLaughlin, Nina. *Wake, Siren: Ovid Resung*

MacLaverty, Bernard. ★*Blank Pages: And Other Stories*

Malamud, Bernard. ★*The Complete Stories*

Malerman, Josh. *Goblin: A Novel in Six Novellas*

Mann, Thomas. *Death in Venice and Seven Other Stories*

Manning, Corinne. *We Had No Rules: Stories*

Marra, Anthony. *The Tsar of Love and Techno: Stories*

Mason, Bobbie Ann. *Patchwork*

Mason, Bobbie Ann. *Shiloh and Other Stories*

Mason, Daniel. *A Registry of My Passage Upon the Earth: Stories*

Mayer, Mark. *Aerialists: Stories*

McBride, James. *Five-Carat Soul*

McCall Smith, Alexander. *Tiny Tales: Stories of Romance, Ambition, Kindness, and Happiness*

McCracken, Elizabeth. *The Souvenir Museum: Stories*

McGuane, Thomas. ★*Cloudbursts: Collected and New Stories*

McGuane, Thomas. *Crow Fair: Stories*

Means, David. ★*Instructions for a Funeral: Stories*

Melville, Herman. *The Complete Shorter Fiction*

Moniz, Dantiel W. *Milk Blood Heat*

Mosley, Walter. ★*The Awkward Black Man: Stories*

Mueenuddin, Daniyal. *In Other Rooms, Other Wonders: Connected Stories*

Munro, Alice. *Dear Life: Stories*

Munro, Alice. *Family Furnishings: Selected Stories, 1995-2014*

Munro, Alice. *Hateship, Friendship, Courtship, Loveship, Marriage: Stories*

Munro, Alice. *Open Secrets: Stories*

Munro, Alice. *Runaway: Stories*

Munro, Alice. *Selected Stories*

Munro, Alice. *Too Much Happiness: Stories*

Munro, Alice. *The View from Castle Rock: Stories*

Murakami, Haruki. *After the Quake: Stories*

Murakami, Haruki. *Blind Willow, Sleeping Woman: 24 Stories*

Murakami, Haruki. *Men Without Women: Stories*

Nabokov, Vladimir Vladimirovich. *The Stories of Vladimir Nabokov*

Narayan, R. K. *Malgudi Days*

Nguyen, Viet Thanh. ★*The Refugees*

Nugent, Benjamin. *Fraternity: Stories*

O'Brien, Tim. ★*The Things They Carried: A Work of Fiction*

O'Connor, Flannery. ★*Collected Works*

O'Connor, Flannery. *The Complete Stories*

O'Connor, Frank. *Collected Stories*

Oates, Joyce Carol. *The (Other) You: Stories*

Okri, Ben. *Prayer for the Living*

Orczy, Emmuska Orczy. *The Old Man in the Corner*

Osondu, E. C. *Voice of America: Stories*

Oyeyemi, Helen. *What Is Not Yours Is Not Yours: Stories*

Paley, Grace. ★*The Collected Stories*

Paretsky, Sara. *Love & Other Crimes: Stories*

Pearlman, Edith. *Binocular Vision: New & Selected Stories*

Pearlman, Edith. *Honeydew: Stories*

Peynado, Brenda. *The Rock Eaters: Stories*

Philyaw, Deesha. *The Secret Lives of Church Ladies*

Pilcher, Rosamunde. *A Place Like Home: Short Stories*

Poe, Edgar Allan. ★*Complete Stories and Poems of Edgar Allan Poe*
Pollock, Donald Ray. *Knockemstiff*
Porter, Katherine Anne. ★*The Collected Stories of Katherine Anne Porter*
Porter, Katherine Anne. *Pale Horse, Pale Rider: Three Short Novels*
Proulx, Annie. *Bad Dirt: Wyoming Stories 2*
Proulx, Annie. *Fine Just the Way It Is: Wyoming Stories 3*
Quade, Kirstin Valdez. *Night at the Fiestas: Stories*
Rash, Ron. *Burning Bright: Stories*
Rash, Ron. ★*In the Valley: Stories and a Novella Based on Serena*
Rash, Ron. *Nothing Gold Can Stay: Stories*
Rash, Ron. *Something Rich and Strange: Selected Stories*
Rendell, Ruth. *Collected Stories*
Robinson, Kim Stanley. *The Martians*
Roth, Joseph. *The Collected Stories of Joseph Roth*
Roth, Philip. ★*Goodbye, Columbus, and Five Short Stories*
Runcie, James. *Sidney Chambers and the Perils of the Night*
Runcie, James. *Sidney Chambers and the Problem of Evil*
Russell, Karen. *Orange World and Other Stories*
Russell, Karen. *Vampires in the Lemon Grove: Stories*
Salinger, J. D. ★*Nine Stories*
Salter, James. *Last Night*
Saunders, George. *In Persuasion Nation: Stories*
Saunders, George. ★*Tenth of December: Stories*
Sayers, Dorothy L. *Hangman's Holiday*
Sayers, Dorothy L. *In the Teeth of the Evidence*
Sayers, Dorothy L. ★*Lord Peter*
Saylor, Steven. *The House of the Vestals: The Investigations of Gordianus the Finder*
Schanoes, Veronica L. *Burning Girls and Other Stories*
Schwartz, Lynne Sharon. *Truthtelling: Stories, Fables, Glimpses*
Schweblin, Samanta. *Mouthful of Birds: Stories*
Scott, Rion Amilcar. ★*The World Doesn't Require You: Stories*
Sedaris, David. *Holidays on Ice*
Shepard, Jim. *The World to Come: Stories*
Singer, Isaac Bashevis. *Collected Stories: A Friend of Kafka to Passions*
Singer, Isaac Bashevis. *Collected Stories: Gimpel the Fool to the Letter Writer*
Sittenfeld, Curtis. ★*You Think It, I'll Say It: Stories*
Smith, Zadie. ★*Grand Union: Stories*
So, Anthony Veasna. *Afterparties: Stories*
Spencer, Elizabeth. *The Southern Woman: New and Selected Fiction*
Spencer, Elizabeth. *The Stories of Elizabeth Spencer*
Stein, Gertrude. ★*Three Lives*
Steinbeck, John. *The Long Valley*
Strout, Elizabeth. *Olive Kitteridge*
Strout, Elizabeth. ★*Olive, Again: A Novel*
Swamy, Shruti. *A House Is a Body: Stories*
Taylor, Brandon. ★*Filthy Animals*
Thammavongsa, Souvankham. *How to Pronounce Knife: Stories*
Thomas, Dylan. *The Collected Stories*
Thompson-Spires, Nafissa. *Heads of the Colored People: Stories*
Tolstaya, Tatyana. *Aetherial Worlds: Stories*
Tolstoy, Leo. *Divine and Human and Other Stories*
Tremblay, Paul. *Growing Things and Other Stories*
Trevor, William. *Last Stories*
Tursten, Helene. *An Elderly Lady Must Not Be Crossed*

Twain, Mark. ★*The Complete Short Stories of Mark Twain*
Updike, John. *The Afterlife and Other Stories*
Updike, John. *Licks of Love: Short Stories and a Sequel*
Updike, John. *My Father's Tears and Other Stories*
Urrea, Luis Alberto. *The Water Museum: Stories*
Vandermeer, Jeff. *The Third Bear*
Vollmann, William T. *Last Stories and Other Stories*
Voltaire. *Candide and Other Stories*
Vonnegut, Kurt. *Bagombo Snuff Box: Uncollected Short Fiction*
Vonnegut, Kurt. *Complete Stories*
Vonnegut, Kurt. *Welcome to the Monkey House*
Vonnegut, Kurt. *While Mortals Sleep: Unpublished Short Fiction*
Walbert, Kate. *She Was Like That: New and Selected Stories*
Walker, Alice. *You Can't Keep a Good Woman Down: Stories*
Wallace, David Foster. ★*Brief Interviews with Hideous Men*
Wallace, David Foster. *Oblivion: Stories*
Washington, Bryan. *Lot: Stories*
Waugh, Evelyn. ★*The Complete Stories of Evelyn Waugh*
Weinstein, Alexander. *Children of the New World: Stories*
Wells, H. G. *The Complete Short Stories of H. G. Wells*
Welty, Eudora. ★*The Collected Stories of Eudora Welty*
Welty, Eudora. *Stories, Essays & Memoir*
West, Nathanael. *Novels and Other Writings*
Wharton, Edith. *Collected Stories, 1891-1910*
Whiteley, Aliya. *From the Neck up and Other Stories*
Wideman, John Edgar. ★*American Histories: Stories*
Wideman, John Edgar. *Look for Me and I'll Be Gone: Stories*
Williams, Joy. *Ninety-Nine Stories of God*
Williams, Lara. *A Selfie as Big as the Ritz: Stories*
Williams, Tennessee. ★*Collected Stories*
Winslow, Don. *Broken: Six Short Novels*
Wodehouse, P. G. ★*The Inimitable Jeeves*
Wodehouse, P. G. *My Man Jeeves*
Wolfe, Gene. ★*The Best of Gene Wolfe: A Definitive Retrospective of His Finest Short Fiction*
Wolff, Tobias. *Our Story Begins: New and Selected Stories*
Woods, Chavisa. *Things to Do When You're Goth in the Country: And Other Stories*
Yates, Richard. ★*The Collected Stories of Richard Yates*
Zaman, Nadeem. *Up in the Main House & Other Stories*
★*The **Short** Stories of F. Scott Fitzgerald: A New Collection*. Fitzgerald, F. Scott

SHORT-TERM MEMORY
Ogawa, Yoko. *The Housekeeper and the Professor*
*The **Shortest** Way Home*. Fay, Juliette
SHOSHONI INDIANS
McMurtry, Larry. *Boone's Lick: A Novel*
SHOSTAKOVICH, DMITRI DMITRIEVICH, 1906-1975
Barnes, Julian. *The Noise of Time*
Shames, Terry. ★*An Unsettling Crime for Samuel Craddock*
***Should** We Stay or Should We Go*. Shriver, Lionel
SHOW JUMPING
Greaves, Chuck. *Hush Money: A Mystery*
Showalter, Gena
Shadow and Ice
Shreve, Anita
Eden Close: A Novel
Fortune's Rocks: A Novel

The Last Time They Met: A Novel
The Pilot's Wife: A Novel
Sea Glass: A Novel
Testimony: A Novel
The Weight of Water

SHREWSBURY, ENGLAND

Peters, Ellis. *The Holy Thief*

Shriver, Lionel

The Post-Birthday World
Should We Stay or Should We Go
So Much for That
We Need to Talk About Kevin

SHTETL

Aleichem, Sholem. *Tevye the Dairyman and the Railroad Stories*
Aleichem, Sholem. *Tevye's Daughters*
Gross, Max. *The Lost Shtetl*
Singer, Isaac Bashevis. ★*The Magician of Lublin*

Shteyngart, Gary

★*Lake Success: A Novel*
The Russian Debutante's Handbook
★*Super Sad True Love Story: A Novel*

SHUGAK, KATE (FICTITIOUS CHARACTER)

Stabenow, Dana. ★*A Deeper Sleep: A Kate Shugak Novel*
Stabenow, Dana. ★*A Fine and Bitter Snow: A Kate Shugak Novel*
Stabenow, Dana. ★*A Grave Denied*
Stabenow, Dana. ★*Hunter's Moon*
Stabenow, Dana. *Killing Grounds: A Kate Shugak Mystery*
Stabenow, Dana. ★*A Taint in the Blood*

★*Shuggie* Bain. Stuart, Douglas

Shumway, Charity

Ten Girls to Watch: A Novel

Shupe, Joanna

The Courtesan Duchess
The Heiress Hunt
The Prince of Broadway
The Rogue of Fifth Avenue

Shutter Island. Lehane, Dennis

SHYNESS IN WOMEN

Gracie, Anne. *Marry in Scandal*
Sampson, Freya. *The Last Chance Library*

SIBERIA

Adams, Alina. *The Nesting Dolls*
Kaminsky, Stuart M. *Murder on the Trans-Siberian Express*
L'Amour, Louis. *The Last of the Breed*
Morris, Heather. *Cilka's Journey*

The Siberian Dilemma. Smith, Martin Cruz

SIBLING RIVALRY

Atwood, Margaret. ★*The Blind Assassin*
Dostoyevsky, Fyodor. ★*The Brothers Karamazov*
Farrell, Henry. ★*What Ever Happened to Baby Jane?*
Gaynor, Hazel. *Three Words for Goodbye*
Gregory, Philippa. *The Other Boleyn Girl: A Novel*
Lombardo, Claire. *The Most Fun We Ever Had: A Novel*
Schine, Cathleen. *The Grammarians*
Smith, Wilbur A. *Monsoon*
Stachniak, Eva. *The Chosen Maiden: A Novel*
Stansel, Ian. *The Last Cowboys of San Geronimo*
Steinbeck, John. ★*East of Eden*

Weiner, Jennifer. *In Her Shoes: A Novel*

SIBLINGS

Auster, Paul. ★*In the Country of Last Things*
Bayard, Louis. *The Pale Blue Eye: A Novel*
Benjamin, Chloe. ★*The Immortalists: A Novel*
Bordas, Camille. *How to Behave in a Crowd*
Callaghan, Mary Rose. *Billy, Come Home*
Card, Orson Scott. ★*Ender's Game*
Cather, Willa. *O Pioneers!*
Crumley, James. ★*The Wrong Case*
Dann, Patty. *The Wright Sister*
Downing, Samantha. *He Started It*
Dunant, Sarah. *Blood and Beauty: A Novel*
Eliot, George. ★*The Mill on the Floss*
Fay, Juliette. *The Shortest Way Home*
Ferraris, Zoe. *Finding Nouf*
Flynn, Gillian. *Dark Places*
Fu, Kim. *For Today I Am a Boy*
Garcia Marquez, Gabriel. *Chronicle of a Death Foretold*
Garwood, Julie. *Wired*
Geni, Abby. *The Wildlands: A Novel*
Gibson, William. *The Peripheral*
Goenawan, Clarissa. *Rainbirds*
Gohlke, Cathy. *Promise Me This*
Gregory, Philippa. *The Other Boleyn Girl: A Novel*
Hadley, Tessa. *The Past*
Hazzard, Shirley. ★*The Great Fire*
Hilderbrand, Elin. ★*Summer of '69*
Hoffman, Alice. *The Rules of Magic: A Novel*
Horrocks, Caitlin. *The Vexations*
Hosking, Jay. *Three Years with the Rat: A Novel*
Hulse, S. M. *Eden Mine*
Khalfah, Khlid. *Death Is Hard Work: A Novel*
Lansdale, Joe R. *The Thicket*
Lawson, Mary. *Crow Lake*
Lee, Fonda. *Jade War*
Lipman, Elinor. *The Dearly Departed*
Lippman, Laura. *Wilde Lake*
Livesey, Margot. ★*The Boy in the Field*
Livesey, Margot. *Criminals: A Novel*
Loren, Roni. *The One You Fight For*
MacDonald, Andrew. *When We Were Vikings*
Makkai, Rebecca. ★*The Great Believers*
Mallery, Susan. ★*When We Found Home*
Marillier, Juliet. *Daughter of the Forest*
Marlantes, Karl. *Deep River*
Maynard, Joyce. *Count the Ways*
McCullers, Carson. *The Member of the Wedding*
McDermott, Alice. *After This*
McDermott, Alice. *At Weddings and Wakes*
McDermott, Alice. *Someone*
McDonald, Ian. *New Moon*
Meyerson, Amy. *The Imperfects*
Miller, Derek B. ★*American by Day*
Millhauser, Steven. *Martin Dressler: The Tale of an American Dreamer*
Morrison, Toni. *Home*
Murphy, Devin. *Tiny Americans*

Naipaul, V. S. *Magic Seeds*
O'Keefe, Megan E. *Velocity Weapon*
Offutt, Chris. ★*The Killing Hills*
Ondaatje, Michael. ★*Warlight*
Onyebuchi, Tochi. ★*Riot Baby*
Ozick, Cynthia. *Foreign Bodies*
Packer, Ann. *The Children's Crusade*
Parker-Chan, Shelley. ★*She Who Became the Sun*
Patchett, Ann. ★*The Dutch House: A Novel*
Phillips, Jayne Anne. *Lark and Termite: A Novel*
Powers, Richard. *The Echo Maker*
Robertson, Imogen. *The Paris Winter*
Salinger, J. D. ★*Franny and Zooey*
Sayers, Dorothy L. ★*Clouds of Witness*
Schwarz, Liese O'Halloran. *What Could Be Saved*
Shamsie, Kamila. *Home Fire: A Novel*
Smith, Lee. *Family Linen*
Stachniak, Eva. *The Chosen Maiden: A Novel*
Stoker, Dacre. *Dracul*
Strout, Elizabeth. ★*Anything Is Possible: Fiction*
Swinson, Kiki. *I'm New York's Finest*
Turansky, Carrie. *No Ocean Too Wide: A Novel*
Wells, Benedict. *The End of Loneliness: A Novel*
Wexler, Django. *Ashes of the Sun*
Williams, Synithia. *Forbidden Promises*
Woo, Sung J. *Love Love: A Novel*
Youers, Rio. *Lola on Fire*

SIBLINGS — DEATH
Adler-Olsen, Jussi. *The Absent One*
The Sicilian: a Novel. Puzo, Mario
SICILY, ITALY
Auci, Stefania. *The Florios of Sicily: A Novel*
Camilleri, Andrea. *Riccardino*
Giordano, Mario. ★*Auntie Poldi and the Lost Madonna*
Giordano, Mario. *Auntie Poldi and the Vineyards of Etna*
Hersey, John. ★*A Bell for Adano*
Puzo, Mario. *The Sicilian: A Novel*
Shaara, Jeff. *The Rising Tide: A Novel of World War II*
SICK CHILDREN
Mackintosh, Clare. *After the End*
Richman, Alyson. *The Secret of Clouds*
SICK FATHERS
Ball, Jesse. *Census*
Coster, Naima. *Halsey Street*
Sparks, Nicholas. *Every Breath*
SICK MEN
Wang, Kathy. *Family Trust: A Novel*
SICK MOTHERS
Hilderbrand, Elin. ★*28 Summers*
SICK PERSONS
Child, Lincoln. *Deep Storm: A Novel*
Cook, Diane. ★*The New Wilderness: A Novel*
Dev, Sonali. *A Distant Heart*
Rose, Heather. *The Museum of Modern Love*
Ross, Ann B. *Miss Julia Knows a Thing or Two*
SICK WOMEN
Muir, Tamsyn. *Harrow the Ninth*
Walton, Jo. *Or What You Will*

★*Siddhartha: a New Translation*. Hesse, Hermann
Side Chick Nation. De Leon, Aya
SIDESHOWS
Dunn, Katherine. *Geek Love*
Sidewalk Saint. DePoy, Phillip
Sidney Chambers and the Forgiveness of Sins. Runcie, James
Sidney Chambers and the Perils of the Night. Runcie, James
Sidney Chambers and the Persistence of Love. Runcie, James
Sidney Chambers and the Problem of Evil. Runcie, James
Sidney Chambers and the Shadow of Death. Runcie, James
The Siege Winter. Franklin, Ariana
Siegel, Jan
    Prospero's Children
Sienkiewicz, Henryk
    ★*Quo Vadis: A Story of Faith in the Last Days of the Roman Empire*
SIERRA NEVADA MOUNTAINS
Kerouac, Jack. *The Dharma Bums*
Kirkpatrick, Jane. *One More River to Cross*
Pronzini, Bill. *Hellbox*
Siger, Jeffrey
    Mykonos After Midnight: A Chief Inspector Kaldis Mystery
    Target Tinos: An Inspector Kaldis Mystery
★*The Sight of You*. Miller, Holly
Sight: a Novel. Greengrass, Jessie
Sightblinder's Story. Saberhagen, Fred
Sigma Force novels [Series]. Rollins, James
SIGN LANGUAGE
Greenidge, Kaitlyn. *We Love You, Charlie Freeman: A Novel*
The Signal Flame: A Novel. Krivak, Andrew
★*The Signature of All Things: A Novel*. Gilbert, Elizabeth
SIGNS AND SYMBOLS
Clayborn, Kate. *Love Lettering*
Obregon, Nicolas. *Blue Light Yokohama*
Sigurðardóttir, Lilja
    Cage
SIKH WOMEN
Robotham, Michael. *The Night Ferry: A Novel*
Snyder, Suleikha. *Big Bad Wolf*
SIKSIKA INDIANS
Jones, Stephen Graham. ★*The Only Good Indians: A Novel*
★*Silas Marner: The Weaver of Raveloe*. Eliot, George
Silber, Joan
    Improvement
    Secrets of Happiness
The Silence. DeLillo, Don
Silence. Endo, Shusaku
Silence in the Library. Schellman, Katharine
★*The Silence of the Girls: A Novel*. Barker, Pat
★*The Silence of the Lambs*. Harris, Thomas
The Silence of the White City. Garcia Saenz, Eva
The Silent Companions: A Ghost Story. Purcell, Laura
SILENT FILMS
Smith, Dominic. ★*The Electric Hotel*
Silent Footsteps. Bannister, Jo
Silent Hearts. Florio, Gwen
Silent House. Pamuk, Orhan
The Silent Oligarch. Morgan Jones, Chris
★*Silent Prey*. Sandford, John

★*The **Silent** Wife*. Slaughter, Karin
SILICON VALLEY, CALIFORNIA
  Chang, Alexandra. ★*Days of Distraction*
  Deaver, Jeffery. ★*The Never Game*
  Wang, Kathy. *Family Trust: A Novel*
  Wang, Kathy. *Impostor Syndrome: A Novel*
SILK WORKERS' STRIKE, PATERSON, NEW JERSEY, 1913
  Stewart, Amy. ★*Girl Waits with Gun*
★*Silken Prey*. Sandford, John
Silko, Leslie Marmon
  Almanac of the Dead
  ★*Ceremony*
  Gardens in the Dunes: A Novel
*The **Silkworm***. Galbraith, Robert
*The **Silmarillion***. Tolkien, J. R. R.
Silva, Daniel
  ★*The Black Widow*
  ★*The Kill Artist: A Novel*
  The New Girl
  The Other Woman
Silver Anniversary Murder. Meier, Leslie
Silver in the Wood. Tesh, Emily
SILVER MINES AND MINING — HISTORY
  Conrad, Joseph. *Nostromo: A Tale of the Seaboard*
Silver on the Road. Gilman, Laura Anne
Silver screen historical novels [Series]. Hambly, Barbara
★*Silver Silence*. Singh, Nalini
Silver Sparrow: A Novel. Jones, Tayari
*The **Silver** Star: A Novel*. Walls, Jeannette
Silver Tears. Lackberg, Camilla
Silver, Elizabeth L.
  The Execution of Noa P. Singleton: A Novel
Silver, Marisa
  Mary Coin: A Novel
Silvis, Randall
  Two Days Gone: A Novel
Simenon, Georges
  Maigret and the Black Sheep
  Maigret and the Fortuneteller
  ★*Maigret and the Killer*
  Maigret and the Madwoman
  ★*Maigret and the Saturday Caller*
  ★*Maigret and the Toy Village*
  Maigret and the Wine Merchant
  ★*Maigret Bides His Time*
  ★*Maigret Goes Home*
  Maigret in Holland
  Maigret's Memoirs
  My Friend Maigret
Simisola. Rendell, Ruth
Simmons, Dan
  The Abominable: A Novel
  Drood: A Novel
  Endymion
  The Fall of Hyperion
  The Fifth Heart
  ★*Hyperion*
  The Rise of Endymion

★*The Terror: A Novel*
Simon Fisk novels [Series]. Corleone, Douglas
Simon Riske novels [Series]. Reich, Christopher
Simon Serrailler crime novels [Series]. Hill, Susan
Simonson, Helen
  Major Pettigrew's Last Stand: A Novel
  The Summer Before the War: A Novel
*A **Simple** Plan: A Novel*. Smith, Scott
Simply Irresistible. Shalvis, Jill
Simply Love. Balogh, Mary
Simply quartet (Mary Balogh) [Series]. Balogh, Mary
Simpson, Dorothy
  Dead and Gone: An Inspector Luke Thanet Novel.
  Dead by Morning
  Doomed to Die
  Last Seen Alive: A Luke Thanet Mystery
  No Laughing Matter
  Once Too Often: An Inspector Luke Thanet Novel
Simpson, Mona
  Anywhere but Here
Simpson, Rosemary
  Let the Dead Keep Their Secrets
  ★*What the Dead Leave Behind*
Simsion, Graeme C.
  The Rosie Effect
  ★*The Rosie Project*
  The Rosie Result
SIN
  Campisi, Megan. *Sin Eater*
Sin Eater. Campisi, Megan
SINATRA, FRANK
  Dean, Debra. *The Madonnas of Leningrad: A Novel*
  Randisi, Robert J. *Hey There (You with the Gun in Your Hand): A Rat Pack Mystery*
Since We Fell. Lehane, Dennis
Sinclair, Upton
  ★*The Jungle*
Sing to It: New Stories. Hempel, Amy
Sing You Home: A Novel. Picoult, Jodi
★*Sing, Unburied, Sing*. Ward, Jesmyn
SINGAPORE
  Ho, Lauren. *Last Tang Standing*
  Kwan, Kevin. *Crazy Rich Asians*
  Kwan, Kevin. *Rich People Problems*
  Suarez, Daniel. *Change Agent: A Novel*
Singer from the Sea. Tepper, Sheri S.
*The **Singer's** Gun: A Novel*. Mandel, Emily St. John
Singer, I. J.
  The Brothers Ashkenazi
Singer, Isaac Bashevis
  Collected Stories: A Friend of Kafka to Passions
  Collected Stories: Gimpel the Fool to the Letter Writer
  Enemies, a Love Story
  The Family Moskat
  ★*The Magician of Lublin*
SINGERS
  Burdick, Serena. *Find Me in Havana*
  Creech, Sarah. *The Whole Way Home*

Heller, Peter. *The Guide*
Kay, Guy Gavriel. *Tigana*
Penelope, L. *Cry of Metal & Bone: Earthsinger Chronicles, Book 3*
Penelope, L. *Whispers of Shadow & Flame*
Singh, Nalini
    A Madness of Sunshine
    ★*Silver Silence*
SINGING
    Patchett, Ann. ★*Bel Canto: A Novel*
SINGING CONTESTS
    Valente, Catherynne M. *Space Opera*
*The **Singing** of the Dead*. Stabenow, Dana
SINGLE FATHERS
    Barclay, Linwood. *Broken Promise*
    Bell, Lenora. ★*What a Difference a Duke Makes*
    Burrowes, Grace. *The Captive*
    Finder, Joseph. *Suspicion*
    Greene, Graham. *Our Man in Havana*
    Jenkins, Beverly. *Tempest*
    Jewell, Lisa. *Then She Was Gone: A Novel*
    Kerr, Laurel. *Wild on My Mind*
    Landon, Sydney. *Wishing for Us*
    Lehane, Dennis. *World Gone By: A Novel*
    McKinlay, Jenn. *The Good Ones*
    Patrick, Phaedra. ★*The Secrets of Love Story Bridge*
    Scottoline, Lisa. ★*Every Fifteen Minutes*
    Sebastian, Cat. *It Takes Two to Tumble*
    Tyler, Anne. ★*Saint Maybe*
    Williams, Preslaysa. *A Lowcountry Bride*
SINGLE MEN
    Berger, Thomas. *Being Invisible: A Novel*
    Cameron, W. Bruce. *The Dogs of Christmas*
    Chase, Loretta Lynda. *Miss Wonderful*
    Haruf, Kent. *Eventide*
    Haruf, Kent. ★*Plainsong*
    Hession, Ronan. *Leonard and Hungry Paul*
    Jackson, K. M. *How to Marry Keanu Reeves in 90 Days*
    Lurie, Alison. *Foreign Affairs*
    Mallery, Susan. *Best of My Love*
    Murdoch, Iris. *The Sea, the Sea*
    Pembrooke, Kate. *Not the Kind of Earl You Marry*
    Phillips, Susan Elizabeth. ★*Natural Born Charmer*
    Rai, Alisha. ★*First Comes Like*
    Ripper, Kris. *The Life Revamp*
    Rowland, Russell. *Cold Country: A Novel*
    Saramago, Jose. *The History of the Siege of Lisbon*
    Sparks, Nicholas. ★*The Notebook*
    White, Randy Wayne. *Salt River*
    Wodehouse, P. G. ★*The Inimitable Jeeves*
    Wodehouse, P. G. *My Man Jeeves*
SINGLE MEN AND CHILDREN
    Wharton, Edith. *The Children*
SINGLE MOTHERS
    Armstrong, Kelley. *Wherever She Goes*
    Balogh, Mary. *Simply Love*
    Beck, Haylen. *Lost You*
    Benton, Janet. *Lilli De Jong: A Novel*
    Box, C. J. ★*The Bitterroots: A Novel*

Box, C. J. *Blue Heaven*
Boyne, John. *The Heart's Invisible Furies*
Butler, Nickolas. *Little Faith: A Novel*
Byatt, A. S. *Babel Tower*
Carey, M. R. *Someone Like Me*
Connelly, Michael. *The Fifth Witness*
Cosimano, Elle. *Finlay Donovan Is Killing It*
Delinsky, Barbara. *A Week at the Shore*
Dell, Kari Lynn. *Reckless in Texas*
DeLuca, Jen. *Well Matched*
Duncan, Glen. *Talulla Rising*
Feldman, Ellen. *Paris Never Leaves You*
Fitch, Janet. *White Oleander: A Novel*
Flint, Emma. ★*Little Deaths: A Novel*
Foley, Bridget. *Just Get Home*
Foster, Lori. *Sisters of Summer's End*
Gortner, C. W. *The First Actress: A Novel of Sarah Bernhardt*
Gowdy, Barbara. *Helpless: A Novel*
Guskin, Sharon. *The Forgetting Time*
Haigh, Jennifer. *Baker Towers: A Novel*
Hall, Alexis. *Rosaline Palmer Takes the Cake*
Hamer, Kate. *The Girl in the Red Coat*
Harding, Lisa. *Bright Burning Things*
Harris, Joanne. ★*Chocolat: A Novel*
Haruf, Kent. *Eventide*
Higgins, Kristan. ★*Life and Other Inconveniences*
James, Lorelei. *I Want You Back*
K'wan. *Revelations*
Kingsolver, Barbara. ★*The Bean Trees: A Novel*
Kingsolver, Barbara. *Pigs in Heaven*
Kushner, Rachel. *The Mars Room*
Lauren, Christina. *The Soulmate Equation*
Majors, Inman. *Penelope Lemon: Game On!*
Martin, Alexa. *Fumbled*
Palmer, Daniel. *The New Husband*
Perry, Sarah. *The Essex Serpent*
Pinborough, Sarah. ★*Cross Her Heart: A Novel*
Pinter, Jason. *Hide Away*
Pinter, Jason. *A Stranger at the Door*
Poeppel, Amy. *Musical Chairs: A Novel*
Richler, Nancy. *Your Mouth Is Lovely: A Novel*
Rivers, Francine. *The Masterpiece*
Scott, A. D. ★*Beneath the Abbey Wall: A Novel*
Scottoline, Lisa. *One Perfect Lie*
Sekaran, Shanthi. ★*Lucky Boy*
Sexton, Margaret Wilkerson. *A Kind of Freedom*
Shafak, Elif. *The Bastard of Istanbul*
Shaw, William. *Salt Lane*
Silber, Joan. *Improvement*
Soderberg, Alexander. *The Other Son: A Sophie Brinkmann Novel*
Solomon, Rivers. *Sorrowland*
Spencer, Sally. *The Dead Hand of History*
Tyler, Anne. ★*Clock Dance: A Novel*
Vuong, Ocean. ★*On Earth We're Briefly Gorgeous: A Novel*
Walbert, Kate. *She Was Like That: New and Selected Stories*
Weatherspoon, Rebekah. *Rafe: A Buff Male Nanny*
Whitaker, Chris. ★*We Begin at the End*
Zettel, Sarah. *A Mother's Lie*

SINGLE PARENTS

Tudor, C. J. *The Burning Girls: A Novel*

SINGLE PEOPLE

Fielding, Helen. ★*Bridget Jones's Diary: A Novel*

*A **Single** Thread.* Chevalier, Tracy

SINGLE WOMEN

Alderton, Dolly. ★*Ghosts: A Novel*

Barnett, Karen. *Ever Faithful*

Beverley, Jo. *Tempting Fortune*

Blakemore, A. K. *The Manningtree Witches*

Boyle, Elizabeth. *Along Came a Duke*

Chase, Loretta Lynda. *Miss Wonderful*

Christian, Claire. *It's Been a Pleasure, Noni Blake*

Colgan, Jenny. *Sunrise by the Sea*

Dare, Tessa. *Romancing the Duke*

Dare, Tessa. ★*The Wallflower Wager*

Daria, Alexis. ★*You Had Me at Hola*

Drake, Olivia. *When a Duke Loves a Governess*

Fielding, Helen. ★*Bridget Jones's Diary: A Novel*

Frampton, Megan. *Never a Bride*

Gerritsen, Tess. ★*The Shape of Night: A Novel*

Ginzburg, Natalia. *Voices in the Evening*

Hale, Shannon. *Austenland: A Novel*

Heyer, Georgette. *Black Sheep*

Hibbert, Talia. *A Girl Like Her*

Ho, Lauren. *Last Tang Standing*

Imamura, Natsuko. *The Woman in the Purple Skirt: A Novel*

Joyce, Rachel. *Miss Benson's Beetle*

Lahiri, Jhumpa. ★*Whereabouts*

Lalli, Sonya. *Serena Singh Flips the Script*

Landon, Sydney. *Wishing for Us*

Lange, Tracey. ★*We Are the Brennans*

Lauren, Christina. *In a Holidaze*

Lim, Roselle. *Vanessa Yu's Magical Paris Tea Shop*

London, Stefanie. *The Aussie Next Door*

Loren, Roni. ★*The One for You*

MacLean, Sarah. ★*Brazen and the Beast*

MacLean, Sarah. ★*Wicked and the Wallflower*

Mapson, Jo-Ann. *Bad Girl Creek: A Novel*

Milan, Courtney. *The Duchess War*

Mina, Denise. *The Less Dead*

O'Leary, Beth. *The Switch*

Pembrooke, Kate. *Not the Kind of Earl You Marry*

Phillips, Susan Elizabeth. ★*Natural Born Charmer*

Pym, Barbara. ★*Excellent Women*

Rai, Alisha. ★*First Comes Like*

Rothschild, Hannah. *The Improbability of Love: A Novel*

Ruiz, Sarah Grunder. *Love, Lists, and Fancy Ships*

Schmidt, Sarah. *See What I Have Done*

Shumway, Charity. *Ten Girls to Watch: A Novel*

Sittenfeld, Curtis. *Eligible: A Novel*

Sittenfeld, Curtis. *Rodham: A Novel*

Spark, Muriel. ★*The Girls of Slender Means*

St. George, Harper. *The Heiress Gets a Duke*

Title, Sarah. *The Undateable*

Trigiani, Adriana. *Big Stone Gap: A Novel*

Wade, Becky. ★*True to You*

Wharton, Edith. ★*Ethan Frome*

Williams, Denise. *The Fastest Way to Fall*

Winfrey, Kerry. *Waiting for Tom Hanks: A Novel*

SINGLE-PARENT FAMILIES

Beattie, Ann. ★*Picturing Will*

Bergstrom, Heather Brittain. *Steal the North: A Novel*

Lee, Harper. ★*To Kill a Mockingbird*

Petry, Ann. ★*The Street*

SINGLETON, HUGH DE (FICTITIOUS CHARACTER)

Starr, Melvin R. *Unhallowed Ground*

Sinha, Indra

Animal's People

*The **Sinister** Mystery of the Mesmerizing Girl.* Goss, Theodora

*The **Sinister** Pig.* Hillerman, Tony

SINKHOLES

Cooper, Tom. *Florida Man*

*The **Sinners**.* Atkins, Ace

*The **Sins** of the Fathers.* Block, Lawrence

★*The **Siren** of Sussex.* Matthews, Mimi

*The **Siren** Queen: An Ursula Blanchard Mystery at Queen Elizabeth I's Court.* Buckley, Fiona

★*The **Sirens** of Titan.* Vonnegut, Kurt

★***Sister** Carrie.* Dreiser, Theodore

***Sister** Pelagia and the White Bulldog: A Mystery.* Akunin, B.

Sister Pelagia mysteries [Series]. Akunin, B.

Sister Souljah

★*The Coldest Winter Ever: A Novel*

★*A Deeper Love Inside: The Porsche Santiaga Story*

Midnight and the Meaning of Love

SISTERHOOD

Braithwaite, Oyinkan. *My Sister, the Serial Killer: A Novel*

***Sisterland:** a Novel.* Sittenfeld, Curtis

***Sisters**.* Johnson, Daisy

SISTERS

Abbott, Megan E. ★*The Turnout: A Novel*

Alharthi, Jokha. *Celestial Bodies: A Novel*

Allen, Sarah Addison. *Garden Spells*

Alvarez, Julia. ★*Afterlife: A Novel*

Alvarez, Julia. *How the Garcia Girls Lost Their Accents*

Austen, Jane. *Mansfield Park*

Austen, Jane. ★*Persuasion*

Austen, Jane. ★*Pride and Prejudice*

Austen, Jane. ★*Sense and Sensibility*

Barber, Lizzy. *A Girl Named Anna*

Bartz, Andrea. *The Herd: A Novel*

Beckerman, Hannah. *If Only I Could Tell You*

Bird, Sarah. *The Yokota Officers Club: A Novel*

Box, C. J. *The Highway*

Bradley, C. Alan. *The Grave's a Fine and Private Place: A Flavia De Luce Novel*

Braithwaite, Oyinkan. *My Sister, the Serial Killer: A Novel*

Brown, Eleanor. *The Weird Sisters*

Brown, Karen. *The Clairvoyants: A Novel*

Brown, Rita Mae. *Six of One*

Buchanan, Cathy Marie. ★*The Painted Girls*

Burdick, Serena. *The Girls with No Names*

Burke, Alafair. *The Better Sister: A Novel*

Burns, Anna. *Milkman: A Novel*

Butler, Sarah. *Ten Things I've Learnt About Love: A Novel*

Carrick, M. A. *The Mask of Mirrors*
Chiaverini, Jennifer. *Mrs. Lincoln's Sisters*
Clarke, Diana. *Thin Girls*
Cocks, Heather. *The Royal We*
Coplin, Amanda. *The Orchardist*
De los Santos, Marisa. *The Precious One*
Dell'Antonia, K. J. *The Chicken Sisters*
Dennis-Benn, Nicole. *Here Comes the Sun*
Desai, Anita. *Clear Light of Day*
Dionne, Karen. *The Wicked Sister*
Doiron, Paul. *Stay Hidden*
Dugoni, Robert. *My Sister's Grave*
Eisler, Barry. *Livia Lone*
Ellis, Bella. *The Vanished Bride*
Endicott, Marina. *The Voyage of the Morning Light*
Eugenides, Jeffrey. ★*The Virgin Suicides*
Farrell, Henry. ★*What Ever Happened to Baby Jane?*
Feeney, Alice. ★*Sometimes I Lie*
Fowler, Karen Joy. ★*We Are All Completely Beside Ourselves*
Gaskell, Elizabeth Cleghorn. ★*Cranford*
Gaynor, Hazel. *Three Words for Goodbye*
Golden, Arthur. ★*Memoirs of a Geisha: A Novel*
Grames, Juliet. *The Seven or Eight Deaths of Stella Fortuna*
Gray, Anissa. *The Care and Feeding of Ravenously Hungry Girls*
Green, Jocelyn. *Veiled in Smoke*
Hannah, Kristin. *The Nightingale*
Hassib, Rajia. *A Pure Heart: A Novel*
Hayder, Mo. *Hanging Hill*
Hazzard, Shirley. ★*The Transit of Venus*
Hendricks, Greer. ★*You Are Not Alone*
Higgins, Kristan. *Always the Last to Know*
Hoffman, Alice. *The Book of Magic*
Hoffman, Alice. *The Rules of Magic: A Novel*
Hornby, Gill. *Miss Austen*
Hurley, Kameron. *The Stars Are Legion*
Johnson, Daisy. *Sisters*
Johnstone, Carole. *Mirrorland*
Jones, Sherry. *Four Sisters, All Queens*
Jones, Tanen. *The Better Liar: A Novel*
Kantra, Virginia. *Beth & Amy*
Kantra, Virginia. ★*Meg and Jo*
Keneally, Thomas. ★*The Daughters of Mars*
Kidd, Sue Monk. ★*The Secret Life of Bees*
Kim, Eugenia. *The Kinship of Secrets*
Kwok, Jean. *Searching for Sylvie Lee*
Kwon, Yo-Son. *Lemon*
Lawrence, D. H. *Women in Love*
Loigman, Lynda Cohen. *The Wartime Sisters: A Novel*
Lombardo, Claire. *The Most Fun We Ever Had: A Novel*
Lutz, Lisa. *The Spellman Files: A Novel*
Mallery, Susan. *California Girls*
McEwan, Ian. ★*Atonement: A Novel*
McHugh, Laura. *The Wolf Wants In: A Novel*
Moore, Liz. *Long Bright River*
Morton, Kate. *The House at Riverton: A Novel*
Murakami, Haruki. *After Dark*
O'Donnell, Lisa. *The Death of Bees: A Novel*
Orenstein, Hannah. *Love at First Like*

Paris, B. A. *Bring Me Back: A Novel*
Parmar, Priya. *Vanessa and Her Sister*
Patterson, Molly. *Rebellion*
Picoult, Jodi. ★*My Sister's Keeper*
Pronzini, Bill. *Savages*
Ragan, Theresa. *Her Last Day*
Rice, Luanne. ★*Last Day*
Rice, Luanne. *Little Night*
Rimmer, Kelly. *Before I Let You Go*
Rojas Contreras, Ingrid. ★*Fruit of the Drunken Tree: A Novel*
Rossner, Rena. *The Light of the Midnight Stars*
Schine, Cathleen. *The Grammarians*
Schmidt, Sarah. *See What I Have Done*
Searles, John. *Help for the Haunted*
See, Lisa. *Shanghai Girls: A Novel*
Shalvis, Jill. *The Sweetest Thing*
Simpson, Dorothy. *Dead by Morning*
Sittenfeld, Curtis. *Eligible: A Novel*
Sittenfeld, Curtis. *Sisterland: A Novel*
Slaughter, Karin. ★*Pretty Girls: A Novel*
Smiley, Jane. ★*A Thousand Acres*
Smith, Ali. ★*Winter*
Smith, Lee. ★*Fair and Tender Ladies*
St. James, Simone. *The Broken Girls*
Stage, Zoje. *Getaway*
Stewart, Amy. ★*Dear Miss Kopp*
Stewart, Amy. *Kopp Sisters on the March*
Stewart, Amy. *Lady Cop Makes Trouble*
Stewart, Amy. ★*Miss Kopp Investigates*
Stewart, Amy. *Miss Kopp's Midnight Confessions*
Stradal, J. Ryan. ★*The Lager Queen of Minnesota*
Tan, Amy. *The Hundred Secret Senses*
Thayne, RaeAnne. *The Cliff House*
Walker, Alice. ★*The Color Purple: A Novel*
Walker, Wendy. *Emma in the Night*
Walls, Jeannette. *The Silver Star: A Novel*
Warren, Susan May. *Rescue Me*
Weiner, Jennifer. *In Her Shoes: A Novel*
Weiner, Jennifer. ★*Mrs. Everything: A Novel*
Weiss, Elizabeth. *The Sisters Sweet*
Wood, James. *Upstate*
SISTERS — DEATH
Atwood, Margaret. ★*The Blind Assassin*
Goenawan, Clarissa. *Rainbirds*
Harrington, Anna. *An Inconvenient Duke*
Harris, Thomas. *Hannibal Rising*
Hirahara, Naomi. ★*Clark and Division*
O'Leary, Beth. *The Switch*
Potzsch, Oliver. *The Beggar King*
Quincy, D. M. *Murder at the Opera*
Richmond, Michelle. *No One You Know*
Roisin, Fariha. *Like a Bird*
Schaitkin, Alexis. *Saint X*
Shaw, William. *A Song for the Brokenhearted*
The **Sisters** *Brothers: A Novel.* deWitt, Patrick
Sisters *in Arms.* Alderson, Kaia
SISTERS OF MURDER VICTIMS
Pronzini, Bill. *Mourners*

Whitaker, Chris. ★*We Begin at the End*

Sisters of Summer's End. Foster, Lori

The Sisters Sweet. Weiss, Elizabeth

SISTERS-IN-LAW

Hambly, Barbara. *Scandal in Babylon*

Sittenfeld, Curtis

Eligible: A Novel

Prep: A Novel

Rodham: A Novel

Sisterland: A Novel

★*You Think It, I'll Say It: Stories*

Six of One. Brown, Rita Mae

Six Tales of the Jazz Age and Other Stories. Fitzgerald, F. Scott

Six Tudor queens [Series]. Weir, Alison

Six Wakes. Lafferty, Mur

SIX-YEAR-OLD BOYS

Grodstein, Lauren. *Our Short History*

Sixkill. Parker, Robert B.

SIXTEEN-YEAR-OLD BOYS

Booth, Coe. ★*Bronxwood*

Connelly, Michael. *The Scarecrow: A Novel*

Danielewski, Mark Z. *Only Revolutions*

McCarthy, Cormac. ★*All the Pretty Horses*

McCarthy, Cormac. *The Crossing*

Pratchett, Terry. *Thief of Time*

Salinger, J. D. ★*The Catcher in the Rye*

SIXTEEN-YEAR-OLD GIRLS

Chevalier, Tracy. ★*Girl with a Pearl Earring*

Danielewski, Mark Z. *Only Revolutions*

Ferraris, Zoe. *Finding Nouf*

Sapphire. ★*Push: A Novel*

The Sixth Commandment: A Novel. Sanders, Lawrence

The Sixth Day. Coulter, Catherine

The Sixth Extinction: A Sigma Force Novel. Rollins, James

Sixth world [Series]. Roanhorse, Rebecca

SIXTH-GRADERS

Fuqua, Jonathon Scott. *Gone and Back Again*

SIXTIES (AGE)

Ford, Richard. *Let Me Be Frank with You*

Miller, Mary. *Biloxi: A Novel*

Russo, Richard. ★*Chances Are...: A Novel*

Sixty Stories. Barthelme, Donald

Sjón

The Blue Fox

Sjowall, Maj

★*Cop Killer: The Story of a Crime*

★*The Laughing Policeman*

★*The Locked Room: The Story of a Crime*

The Man on the Balcony: The Story of a Crime

★*Murder at the Savoy*

Skarmeta, Antonio

The Dancer and the Thief: A Novel

SKELETON

Griffiths, Elly. *A Dying Fall: A Ruth Galloway Mystery*

Griffiths, Elly. *The House at Sea's End: A Ruth Galloway Mystery*

Skeletons at the Feast: A Novel. Bohjalian, Chris

SKEPTICISM

Armstrong, Kelley. *Wherever She Goes*

Lawler, Liz. *Don't Wake Up*

Skeslien Charles, Janet

The Paris Library: A Novel

SKI RESORTS

Reynolds, Allie. ★*Shiver*

Ware, Ruth. ★*One by One*

SKIERS

Ellison, J. T. *Tear Me Apart*

Skin Game. Woods, Stuart

Skin Tight. Hiaasen, Carl

Skink novels (Carl Hiaasen) [Series]. Hiaasen, Carl

Skinny Dip: A Novel. Hiaasen, Carl

Skinship: Stories. Choi, Yoon

Skip Langdon mysteries [Series]. Smith, Julie

Skippy Dies. Murray, Paul

SKULL

Walker, Martin. *The Coldest Case*

The Skull Beneath the Skin. James, P. D.

The Skull Mantra. Pattison, Eliot

The Sky Below. D'Erasmo, Stacey

Skyhorse, Brando

Madonnas of Echo Park: A Novel

SLACKERS

Barry, Dave. *Insane City*

Wong, David. *This Book Is Full of Spiders: Seriously, Dude, Don't Touch It*

Slammerkin. Donoghue, Emma

★*Slan*. Van Vogt, A. E.

SLAPSTICK

Anders, Charlie Jane. *Rock Manning Goes for Broke*

Slapstick: Or, Lonesome No More! a Novel. Vonnegut, Kurt

Slash and Burn: A Dr. Siri Mystery Set in Laos. Cotterill, Colin

Slaughter, Karin

Cop Town: A Novel

Criminal: A Novel

★*Fallen: A Novel*

The Good Daughter

The Kept Woman

★*The Last Widow*

★*Pieces of Her*

★*Pretty Girls: A Novel*

★*The Silent Wife*

★*Undone: A Novel*

★*Slaughterhouse-Five: Or, the Children's Crusade : A Duty-Dance with Death*. Vonnegut, Kurt

SLAVE TRADE

Clinch, Jon. *Marley: A Novel*

Faye, Lyndsay. *Seven for a Secret*

Johnson, Charles Richard. ★*Middle Passage*

Pesci, David. *Amistad: A Novel*

Roy, Lucinda. *The Freedom Race*

Solomon, Rivers. *The Deep*

SLAVEHOLDERS

Doctorow, E. L. *The March: A Novel*

SLAVERY

Asim, Jabari. ★*Yonder*

Atakora, Afia. ★*Conjure Women*

Brink, Andre P. *Philida: A Novel*

Butler, Octavia E. ★*Kindred*
Callender, Kacen. *King of the Rising*
Deon, Natashia. *Grace*
Faulkner, William. ★*Go Down, Moses*
Gappah, Petina. ★*Out of Darkness, Shining Light*
Gyasi, Yaa. ★*Homegoing: A Novel*
Hill, Lawrence. *Someone Knows My Name: A Novel*
Jakes, John. *Love and War*
Jakes, John. ★*North and South*
Johnson, Sadeqa. ★*Yellow Wife*
Kidd, Sue Monk. ★*The Invention of Wings: A Novel*
Lalami, Laila. ★*The Moor's Account: A Novel*
Levy, Andrea. *The Long Song*
Morrison, Toni. *A Mercy: A Novel*
Parry, H. G. *A Declaration of the Rights of Magicians*
Pesci, David. *Amistad: A Novel*
Pitts, Leonard. *Freeman*
Reed, Ishmael. *Flight to Canada*
Rhodes, Jewell Parker. *Voodoo Dreams: A Novel of Marie Laveau*
Santiago, Esmeralda. *Conquistadora: A Novel*
Shocklee, Michelle. *Under the Tulip Tree*
Stowe, Harriet Beecher. ★*Uncle Tom's Cabin*
Straight, Susan. *A Million Nightingales*
Styron, William. *The Confessions of Nat Turner*
Twain, Mark. ★*Adventures of Huckleberry Finn: Tom Sawyer's Comrade ...*
Vidal, Gore. ★*Lincoln: A Novel*
Warren, Robert Penn. *Band of Angels*
Woods, Rita. ★*Remembrance*

SLAVERY — HISTORY
Jones, Gayl. ★*Palmares*
Riley, Vanessa. ★*Island Queen*
Robinson, Marilynne. ★*Gilead*

SLED DOGS
London, Jack. ★*The Call of the Wild*

SLEEP
Fforde, Jasper. ★*Early Riser: A Novel*

SLEEP DISORDERS
Walker, Karen Thompson. *The Dreamers*
★*Sleep Well, My Lady*. Quartey, Kwei

SLEEP-WALKERS
Barnes, Jonathan. *The Somnambulist*
Wendig, Chuck. ★*Wanderers: A Novel*

SLEEP-WALKING
Barnes, Jonathan. *The Somnambulist*
Bohjalian, Chris. *The Sleepwalker*
Sleeping Beauties: A Novel. King, Stephen
Sleeping Beauty. Macdonald, Ross
A *Sleeping* Life. Rendell, Ruth
The *Sleepwalker*. Bohjalian, Chris
Sleepwalking Land. Couto, Mia
Slewfoot: a Tale of Bewitchery. Brom

SLIGO, IRELAND
Barry, Sebastian. *The Secret Scripture: A Novel*

Slimani, Leïla
In the Country of Others
Slipping: Stories, Essays, & Other Writing. Beukes, Lauren

Sloan, Robin
Mr. Penumbra's 24-Hour Bookstore
Slumberland: a Novel. Beatty, Paul

SLUMS
Beukes, Lauren. *Zoo City*
Moore, Alan. *Jerusalem: A Novel*
Reyes, Dolores. *Eartheater*
Roth, Henry. ★*Call It Sleep*
The *Slynx*. Tolstaya, Tatyana
★*Small* Country: A Novel. Faye, Gael
Small Gods: A Novel of Discworld. Pratchett, Terry
Small Island. Levy, Andrea
Small Pleasures. Chambers, Clare

SMALL TOWN FAMILIES
Wolfe, Thomas. ★*Look Homeward, Angel: A Story of a Buried Life*

SMALL TOWN LIFE
Alsterdal, Tove. *We Know You Remember*
Andric, Ivo. *The Bridge on the Drina*
Backman, Fredrik. *Britt-Marie Was Here*
Backman, Fredrik. *Us Against You: A Novel*
Berg, Elizabeth. *Night of Miracles*
Berry, Wendell. *Jayber Crow: A Novel*
Berry, Wendell. ★*That Distant Land: The Collected Stories of Wendell Berry*
Binchy, Maeve. *Firefly Summer*
Binchy, Maeve. ★*Whitethorn Woods*
Bivald, Katarina. *The Readers of Broken Wheel Recommend*
Bond, Cynthia. *Ruby: A Novel*
Brown, Larry. *Joe: A Novel*
Brown, Rita Mae. *Six of One*
Brown, Rosellen. ★*Before and After*
Bruni, Sarah. *The Night Gwen Stacy Died*
Burns, Olive Ann. ★*Cold Sassy Tree*
Carr, Brian Allen. ★*Opioid, Indiana*
Carr, Robyn. ★*The Wanderer*
Cleeves, Ann. *Thin Air*
Collins, Ciaran. *The Gamal*
Crummey, Michael. *Galore*
Darnielle, John. *Universal Harvester*
Duffy, Brendan. *House of Echoes: A Novel*
Dugoni, Robert. ★*The Extraordinary Life of Sam Hell*
Earley, Tony. *Jim the Boy: A Novel*
Erdrich, Louise. *The Plague of Doves*
Eskens, Allen. *Nothing More Dangerous: A Novel*
Evison, Jonathan. *West of Here: A Novel*
Faulkner, William. *The Hamlet*
Fay, Juliette. *The Shortest Way Home*
Franklin, Tom. *Crooked Letter, Crooked Letter: A Novel*
Freeman, Castle. *All That I Have: A Novel*
Gallen, Michelle. *Big Girl, Small Town: A Novel*
Grau, Shirley Ann. *The Keepers of the House*
Greene, Amy. *Long Man*
Gregory, Daryl. *The Devil's Alphabet*
Gurganus, Allan. ★*Local Souls: Novellas*
Haigh, Jennifer. *Baker Towers: A Novel*
Harris, Joanne. ★*Chocolat: A Novel*
Hart, Carolyn G. *Letter from Home*
Hart, John. *Down River*

Hart, John. *The Last Child*
Haruf, Kent. ★*Our Souls at Night*
Haruf, Kent. ★*Plainsong*
Hegi, Ursula. *Stones from the River*
Heiny, Katherine. ★*Early Morning Riser*
Henderson, Susan. *The Flicker of Old Dreams*
Hoffman, Alice. *The River King*
Hughes, Langston. *Not Without Laughter*
Iles, Greg. *Cemetery Road: A Novel*
Jackson, Shirley. ★*The Lottery: And Other Stories*
Keller, Julia. *A Killing in the Hills*
Kelly, Erin. *Broadchurch: A Novel*
Keneally, Thomas. *Woman of the Inner Sea*
Kesey, Ken. *Sometimes a Great Notion: A Novel*
Landvik, Lorna. *Chronicles of a Radical Hag: With Recipes*
Lewis, Sinclair. ★*Main Street: The Story of Carol Kennicott*
Lourey, Jess. ★*January Thaw: A Murder-By-Month Mystery*
Mann, Thomas. *Buddenbrooks*
Maron, Margaret. *Bootlegger's Daughter*
McCrumb, Sharyn. ★*If Ever I Return, Pretty Peggy-O*
McDermid, Val. *A Place of Execution*
McGregor, Jon. *The Reservoir Tapes*
McPherson, Catriona. *Quiet Neighbors: A Novel*
Mitchell, David. *Black Swan Green: A Novel*
Mizushima, Margaret. *Killing Trail*
Morrison, Toni. *Sula*
Munro, Alice. *Dear Life: Stories*
Munro, Alice. *Family Furnishings: Selected Stories, 1995-2014*
Munro, Alice. *Lives of Girls and Women*
Munro, Alice. *Open Secrets: Stories*
Munro, Alice. *Selected Stories*
Munro, Alice. *Too Much Happiness: Stories*
Munro, Alice. *The View from Castle Rock: Stories*
O'Donohue, Clare. *The Lover's Knot: A Someday Quilts Mystery*
Ono, Masatsugu. *Echo on the Bay*
Packer, Ann. *The Dive from Clausen's Pier*
Parker, Robert B. *Death in Paradise*
Parker, Robert B. *Night Passage*
Parker, Robert B. *Trouble in Paradise*
Penny, Louise. ★*A Better Man: A Chief Inspector Gamache Novel*
Penny, Louise. *The Cruelest Month: A Three Pines Mystery*
Penny, Louise. *Still Life*
Phillips, Susan Elizabeth. *Call Me Irresistible*
Pollock, Donald Ray. *Knockemstiff*
Price, Reynolds. *Roxanna Slade*
Proulx, Annie. *Bad Dirt: Wyoming Stories 2*
Proulx, Annie. ★*The Shipping News*
Putnam, Jonathan F. *These Honored Dead*
Quincy, D. M. *Murder in Mayfair: An Atlas Catesby Mystery*
Rash, Ron. *Above the Waterfall*
Rash, Ron. *Burning Bright: Stories*
Rash, Ron. ★*The Cove*
Riordan, Kate. *The Heatwave*
Ripley, Mike. *Mr Campion's Fault*
Ritter, Todd. *Devil's Night*
Ross, Ann B. *Miss Julia Takes the Wheel*
Ross, Ann B. *Miss Julia Throws a Wedding*
Rowland, Russell. *Cold Country: A Novel*

Russo, Richard. *Bridge of Sighs*
Russo, Richard. ★*Empire Falls*
Russo, Richard. ★*Everybody's Fool*
Russo, Richard. ★*Nobody's Fool*
Russo, Richard. *The Risk Pool*
Russo, Richard. *Straight Man*
Sandford, John. *Shock Wave*
Scott, A. D. *A Kind of Grief: A Novel*
Scott, A. D. ★*The Low Road*
Shames, Terry. ★*An Unsettling Crime for Samuel Craddock*
Slaughter, Karin. *The Good Daughter*
Smith, Lee. *Family Linen*
Staples, Dennis E. *This Town Sleeps*
Strout, Elizabeth. ★*Anything Is Possible: Fiction*
Strout, Elizabeth. *Olive Kitteridge*
Strout, Elizabeth. ★*Olive, Again: A Novel*
Trollope, Anthony. ★*Barchester Towers*
Trollope, Anthony. *Framley Parsonage*
Trollope, Anthony. *The Last Chronicle of Barset*
Trollope, Anthony. *The Warden*
Updike, John. *My Father's Tears and Other Stories*
Updike, John. ★*Rabbit Is Rich: A Novel*
Updike, John. ★*Rabbit, Run*
Wallace, Melanie. *The Girl in the Garden*
Wells, Rebecca. *Divine Secrets of the Ya-Ya Sisterhood: A Novel*
Welty, Eudora. ★*The Ponder Heart*
Winslow, De'Shawn Charles. ★*In West Mills*
Winthrop, Elizabeth Hartley. *The Mercy Seat: A Novel*
Wolfe, Thomas. ★*Look Homeward, Angel: A Story of a Buried Life*
Woods, Stuart. *Orchid Beach*

SMALL TOWNS
Ahlborn, Ania. *The Devil Crept In*
Allen, Sarah Addison. *Garden Spells*
Anders, Adriana. *Under Her Skin*
Andric, Ivo. *The Bridge on the Drina*
Atkins, Ace. ★*The Heathens*
Baldacci, David. *The Fallen*
Bannalec, Jean-Luc. *Death in Brittany*
Bannister, Jo. *Kindred Spirits*
Barclay, Linwood. *Broken Promise*
Barclay, Linwood. *Far from True: A Novel*
Baxter, Charles. *Saul and Patsy*
Binchy, Maeve. ★*Whitethorn Woods*
Bledsoe, Alex. *The Hum and the Shiver*
Bobotis, Andrea. *The Last List of Miss Judith Kratt*
Bolton, S. J. *The Craftsman*
Bordas, Camille. *How to Behave in a Crowd*
Bowen, Peter. *Badlands*
Chancellor, Bryn. *Sycamore: A Novel*
Child, Lee. ★*Past Tense*
Chizmar, Richard T. *Chasing the Boogeyman*
Cobb, May K. *The Hunting Wives*
Cooper, Tom. *The Marauders*
Coover, Robert. *The Origin of the Brunists: A Novel*
Crews, Harry. *A Feast of Snakes: A Novel*
Darnielle, John. *Universal Harvester*
Dee, Jonathan. *The Locals: A Novel*
Dubus, Andre. *Dirty Love*

Dugoni, Robert. ★*The Extraordinary Life of Sam Hell*
Earley, Tony. *Mr. Tall: A Novella and Stories*
Faulkner, William. *Uncollected Stories of William Faulkner*
Gates, Eva. *Deadly Ever After*
Gross, Max. *The Lost Shtetl*
Hersey, John. ★*A Bell for Adano*
Horrocks, Caitlin. *Life Among the Terranauts*
Hunt, Laird. *The Evening Road*
Johnson, Caleb. *Treeborne*
Jones, Darynda. *A Bad Day for Sunshine*
Jones, Darynda. *A Good Day for Chardonnay*
Kagen, Lesley. *Every Now and Then*
Kim, Angie. *Miracle Creek*
King, Stephen. *Salem's Lot*
King, Stephen. *Sleeping Beauties: A Novel*
Kingsolver, Barbara. ★*Flight Behavior*
Kraus, Daniel. *The Autumnal: The Complete Series*
Krivak, Andrew. *The Signal Flame: A Novel*
Lansdale, Joe R. *Edge of Dark Water*
Laymon, Kiese. *Long Division*
Littlejohn, Emily. *Inherit the Bones*
Locke, Attica. ★*Bluebird, Bluebird*
Luesse, Valerie Fraser. *Missing Isaac*
Malerman, Josh. *Goblin: A Novel in Six Novellas*
Mallery, Susan. *Best of My Love*
McFarland, Jeni. *The House of Deep Water*
McHugh, Laura. *The Wolf Wants In: A Novel*
Meier, Leslie. *Silver Anniversary Murder*
Murdoch, Iris. *The Philosopher's Pupil*
O'Hara, John. *Appointment in Samarra*
Pronzini, Bill. *The Violated*
Ritter, Josh. *The Great Glorious Goddamn of It All*
Rosenfield, Kat. *No One Will Miss Her*
Russo, Richard. *Bridge of Sighs*
Sanders, Lawrence. *The Sixth Commandment: A Novel*
Saroyan, William. ★*The Human Comedy*
Schultz, Connie. *The Daughters of Erietown*
Smith, Michael F. *Blackwood*
Spencer, Sally. *Lambs to the Slaughter*
Swann, Stacey. *Olympus Texas*
Urrea, Luis Alberto. *The Water Museum: Stories*
Vargas Llosa, Mario. *Green House*
Walls, Jeannette. *The Silver Star: A Novel*
Warren, Susan May. *Rescue Me*
West, Monica. *Revival Season: A Novel*
Wetmore, Elizabeth. ★*Valentine*
Woods, Stuart. *Chiefs*
Yocum, Robin. *A Welcome Murder*
★***Small** World*. Evison, Jonathan
SMALLPOX
    Rowland, Laura Joh. *The Shogun's Daughter: A Novel of Feudal Japan*
SMART, HENRY (FICTITIOUS CHARACTER)
    Doyle, Roddy. *A Star Called Henry*
*The **Smash-Up:** a Novel*. Benjamin, Ali
SMELL
    Suskind, Patrick. ★*Perfume: The Story of a Murderer*
Smile. Doyle, Roddy

***Smile** and Look Pretty*. Pellegrino, Amanda
*A **Smile** on the Face of the Tiger*. Estleman, Loren D.
***Smiley's** People*. Le Carre, John
SMILEY, GEORGE (FICTITIOUS CHARACTER)
    Le Carre, John. ★*The Honourable Schoolboy*
    Le Carre, John. *Smiley's People*
    Le Carre, John. *The Spy Who Came in from the Cold*
Smiley, Jane
    Early Warning
    Golden Age
    Horse Heaven
    ★*Perestroika in Paris: A Novel*
    Some Luck
    ★*A Thousand Acres*
★***Smilla's** Sense of Snow*. Hoeg, Peter
Smith, Ali
    The Accidental
    ★*Autumn*
    ★*How to Be Both*
    ★*Spring*
    ★*Summer*
    There but for The: A Novel
    ★*Winter*
Smith, B. J.
    All Hat: A Novel
    Crow's Landing: A Novel
    The Return of Kid Cooper: A Novel
    Shoot the Dog: A Virgil Cain Mystery
Smith, Betty
    ★*A Tree Grows in Brooklyn*
Smith, Dodie
    ★*I Capture the Castle*
Smith, Dominic
    Bright and Distant Shores
    ★*The Electric Hotel*
    ★*The Last Painting of Sara De Vos*
Smith, Gregory Blake
    ★*The Maze at Windermere: A Novel*
Smith, Ian
    The Unspoken
    Wolf Point
Smith, Jill Eileen
    Star of Persia: Esther's Story
Smith, Julie
    82 Desire: A Skip Langdon Novel
    Crescent City Kill: A Skip Langdon Novel
    House of Blues
    Jazz Funeral
    The Kindness of Strangers: A Skip Langdon Novel
    Louisiana Hotshot
    ★*Mean Woman Blues*
    New Orleans Beat
Smith, Lee
    ★*Fair and Tender Ladies*
    Family Linen
    On Agate Hill: A Novel
    Oral History

Smith, Mark Haskell
Baked
Smith, Martin Cruz
December 6
★*Gorky Park*
Havana Bay
Polar Star
Rose
The Siberian Dilemma
Stalin's Ghost
Stallion Gate
★*Tatiana: An Arkady Renko Novel*
Three Stations: An Arkady Renko Novel
Wolves Eat Dogs: A Novel
Smith, Michael F.
Blackwood
The Fighter: A Novel
Smith, Scott
The Ruins: A Novel
A Simple Plan: A Novel
Smith, Tom Rob
Agent 6
Child 44
The Secret Speech
Smith, Wilbur A.
Birds of Prey
Monsoon
Smith, Zadie
The Autograph Man: A Novel
★*Grand Union: Stories*
★*Nw: A Novel*
On Beauty
★*Swing Time*
★*White Teeth: A Novel*
Smoke and *Ashes: A Novel.* Mukherjee, Abir
Smoke Screen. Blackstock, Terri
Smoke [Series]. Vyleta, Dan
Smoke: a Novel. Vyleta, Dan
Smokescreen. Francis, Dick
Smooth Operator. Woods, Stuart
SMUGGLERS
Bowen, Kelly. *A Rogue by Night*
Cussler, Clive. *Odessa Sea*
Merbeth, K. S. ★*Fortuna*
Newitz, Annalee. *Autonomous*
Pulley, Natasha. *The Bedlam Stacks*
Wagers, K. B. *After the Crown*
Weir, Andy. *Artemis*
SMUGGLING
Bannalec, Jean-Luc. *The Killing Tide: A Brittany Mystery*
Bilal, Parker. *The Burning Gates: A Makana Investigation*
Bowen, Kelly. *A Rogue by Night*
Davidson, Andy. *The Boatman's Daughter: A Novel*
Du Maurier, Daphne. *Jamaica Inn*
Hand, Elizabeth. *Hard Light*
Hemingway, Ernest. *To Have and Have Not*
Hillerman, Tony. *The Sinister Pig*
Lawton, John. *Hammer to Fall*

Lawton, John. *Then We Take Berlin*
Priest, Cherie. *Ganymede*
Silber, Joan. *Improvement*
SNAKES
Crews, Harry. *A Feast of Snakes: A Novel*
Snap. Bauer, Belinda
Sniper thrillers [Series]. Coughlin, Jack
SNIPERS
Child, Lee. *One Shot*
Child, Lee. *Personal*
Coughlin, Jack. *In the Crosshairs*
Coughlin, Jack. *Long Shot*
Gardner, Lisa. *Alone*
Hunter, Stephen. *Game of Snipers*
Hunter, Stephen. *Soft Target: A Thriller*
King, Stephen. ★*Billy Summers*
MacDonald, John D. *A Purple Place for Dying*
Robbins, David L. *War of the Rats: A Novel*
Webb, Brandon. ★*Steel Fear*
Wolf, Dick. *The Ultimatum*
Woods, Stuart. *Smooth Operator*
Snipes, Wesley
Talon of God
SNOOPING
Bair, Kristin. *Agatha Arch Is Afraid of Everything*
Hannah, Sophie. *Perfect Little Children*
SNOPES FAMILY (FICTITIOUS CHARACTERS)
Faulkner, William. *The Hamlet*
Snopes Family [Series]. Faulkner, William
★*Snow.* Pamuk, Orhan
SNOW
O'Donnell, Paraic. *The House on Vesper Sands: A Novel*
★*Snow Crash.* Stephenson, Neal
The Snow Empress. Rowland, Laura Joh
★*Snow Falling on Cedars.* Guterson, David
The Snow Queen. Vinge, Joan D.
Snow, C. P.
★*Strangers and Brothers*
Snow, Jennifer
An Alaskan Christmas
The Snows of Kilimanjaro and Other Stories. Hemingway, Ernest
Snyder, Suleikha
Big Bad Wolf
So Big. Ferber, Edna
So Enchanting. Brockway, Connie
So Much for That. Shriver, Lionel
So Sure of Death: A Liam Campbell Mystery. Stabenow, Dana
So, Anthony Veasna
Afterparties: Stories
SOAP OPERA ACTORS AND ACTRESSES
Daria, Alexis. ★*You Had Me at Hola*
SOBRIETY
Block, Lawrence. *A Drop of the Hard Stuff: A Matthew Scudder Novel*
SOCIAL ACCEPTANCE
Cline, Emma. *The Girls: A Novel*
Drabble, Margaret. *The Sea Lady*
Eggers, Dave. *How We Are Hungry: Stories*

Frankel, Laurie. *This Is How It Always Is*
Fridlund, Emily. ★*History of Wolves: A Novel*
Hesse, Hermann. *The Fairy Tales of Hermann Hesse*
Maguire, Gregory. ★*Wicked: The Life and Times of the Wicked Witch of the West : A Novel*
Morrison, Toni. ★*The Bluest Eye: A Novel*

SOCIAL ADVOCACY
Shields, Carol. *Unless*

SOCIAL ADVOCATES
Walton, Dawnie. ★*The Final Revival of Opal & Nev*

SOCIAL BEHAVIOR
Diaz, Junot. ★*This Is How You Lose Her*

SOCIAL CHANGE
Adjapon, Bisi. *The Teller of Secrets: A Novel*
Alderman, Naomi. ★*The Power: A Novel*
Alharthi, Jokha. *Celestial Bodies: A Novel*
Aw, Tash. *We, the Survivors*
Bowman, David. *Big Bang: A Nonfiction Novel*
Chen, Da. *Brothers: A Novel*
Dos Passos, John. *Manhattan Transfer*
Feng, Linda Rui. *Swimming Back to Trout River*
Follett, Ken. *Edge of Eternity*
Ghaffari, Rabeah. ★*To Keep the Sun Alive*
Gilligan, Ruth. *The Butchers' Blessing*
Groff, Lauren. ★*Matrix*
Hilderbrand, Elin. ★*Summer of '69*
Houellebecq, Michel. *Submission*
Jedrowski, Tomasz. *Swimming in the Dark*
Kimani, Peter. *Dance of the Jakaranda*
Kingsolver, Barbara. ★*Unsheltered*
Ma, Jian. *Beijing Coma*
Ma, Jian. *China Dream*
Pontoppidan, Henrik. *Lucky Per*
Robertson, Robin. *The Long Take: A Noir Narrative*
Robinson, Kim Stanley. *New York 2140*
Rooney, Kathleen. ★*Lillian Boxfish Takes a Walk*
Schami, Rafik. *Sophia: Or the Beginning of All Tales*
Serpell, Namwali. ★*The Old Drift*
Smith, Ali. ★*Autumn*
Smith, Ali. ★*Spring*
Smith, Ali. ★*Summer*
Smith, Ali. ★*Winter*
Thien, Madeleine. *Do Not Say We Have Nothing*
Wall, Cara. *The Dearly Beloved: A Novel*

SOCIAL CLASSES
Adiga, Aravind. *Selection Day*
Adiga, Aravind. ★*The White Tiger: A Novel*
Aliu, Xhenet. ★*Brass: A Novel*
Anderton, Jo. *Debris*
Austen, Jane. *Mansfield Park*
Aw, Tash. *We, the Survivors*
Bainbridge, Beryl. *Every Man for Himself*
Baker, Jo. *Longbourn*
Bambara, Toni Cade. *Gorilla, My Love*
Bambara, Toni Cade. ★*The Salt Eaters*
Barbery, Muriel. *The Elegance of the Hedgehog*
Brockway, Connie. *No Place for a Dame*
Buck, Pearl S. *The Good Earth*

Choo, Yangsze. ★*The Night Tiger: A Novel*
Collins, Sara. *The Confessions of Frannie Langton*
Cosby, S. A. ★*Blacktop Wasteland*
Dangarembga, Tsitsi. *This Mournable Body*
Dev, Sonali. *A Distant Heart*
Dickens, Charles. ★*Bleak House*
Dickens, Charles. *Our Mutual Friend*
Doctorow, Cory. *Radicalized*
Doctorow, Cory. *Walkaway*
Ferrante, Elena. *The Lying Life of Adults*
Fforde, Jasper. *Shades of Grey: A Novel*
Fielding, Henry. ★*The History of Tom Jones, a Foundling*
Fitzgerald, Penelope. *The Means of Escape: Stories*
Forster, E. M. ★*Howards End*
Freeman, Anna. *The Fair Fight: A Novel*
Gardam, Jane. *Last Friends*
Gogol, Nikolai Vasilievich. ★*Dead Souls*
Hall, Tarquin. *The Case of the Love Commandos: From the Files of Vish Puri, India's Most Private Investigator*
Harrison, Nicola. *Montauk*
Haslett, Adam. *Union Atlantic*
Holmes, J. M. *How Are You Going to Save Yourself*
Hosseini, Khaled. ★*The Kite Runner*
Hughes, Langston. ★*Short Stories*
Hurston, Zora Neale. *Hitting a Straight Lick with a Crooked Stick: Stories from the Harlem Renaissance*
Ishiguro, Kazuo. ★*The Remains of the Day*
James, P. D. *A Taste for Death*
Jen, Gish. ★*The Resisters*
Jhabvala, Ruth Prawer. *At the End of the Century: The Stories of Ruth Prawer Jhabvala.*
Jones, Stephen Graham. *My Heart Is a Chainsaw*
Kay, Guy Gavriel. ★*A Brightness Long Ago*
Lee, Chang-Rae. ★*On Such a Full Sea*
Lehane, Dennis. ★*The Given Day*
Logan, T. M. *The Vacation*
McCullough, Colleen. *The First Man in Rome*
Mueenuddin, Daniyal. *In Other Rooms, Other Wonders: Connected Stories*
Mukherjee, Neel. *The Lives of Others*
Parry, Ambrose. *The Way of All Flesh*
Perry, Anne. *The Face of a Stranger*
Perry, Sarah. *The Essex Serpent*
Peynado, Brenda. *The Rock Eaters: Stories*
Pilcher, Rosamunde. *Coming Home*
Ridley, Erica. ★*The Perks of Loving a Wallflower*
Ripley, Mike. *Mr Campion's Fault*
Rooney, Sally. *Normal People: A Novel*
Roth, Philip. ★*Goodbye, Columbus, and Five Short Stories*
Rowling, J. K. *The Casual Vacancy*
Roy, Arundhati. ★*The God of Small Things*
Schaitkin, Alexis. *Saint X*
Schlink, Bernhard. *Olga*
Schwartz, John Burnham. *The Commoner: A Novel*
Singer, I. J. *The Brothers Ashkenazi*
Smith, Gregory Blake. ★*The Maze at Windermere: A Novel*
Solomon, Rivers. *An Unkindness of Ghosts*

Stephenson, Neal. *The Diamond Age,: Or, a Young Lady's Illustrated Primer*
Sullivan, J. Courtney. *Friends and Strangers*
Swamy, Shruti. *The Archer*
Swift, Graham. ★*Mothering Sunday: A Romance*
Tarkington, Booth. ★*Alice Adams*
Tarkington, Booth. ★*The Magnificent Ambersons*
Tepper, Sheri S. *Singer from the Sea*
Umrigar, Thrity N. *Everybody's Son*
Vyleta, Dan. *Smoke: A Novel*
Williams, Beatriz. *The Golden Hour*
Winter, Evan. ★*The Rage of Dragons*
Wolfe, Tom. *The Bonfire of the Vanities*
Wolff, Tobias. *Old School: A Novel*
Woodson, Jacqueline. ★*Red at the Bone*
Woolf, Virginia. *Jacob's Room*
Woolf, Virginia. ★*Mrs. Dalloway*
Zaman, Nadeem. *Up in the Main House & Other Stories*

SOCIAL CONFLICT
Adiga, Aravind. *Last Man in Tower: A Novel*
Beauvoir, Simone de. ★*The Mandarins: A Novel*
Boyle, T. Coraghessan. *When the Killing's Done: A Novel*
Boyle, T. Coraghessan. *World's End: A Novel*
Frazier, Charles. *Varina*
Hammad, Isabella. ★*The Parisian, Or, Al-Barisi: A Novel*
Hensher, Philip. *Scenes from Early Life: A Novel*
Holsinger, Bruce W. *The Gifted School: A Novel*
Kwan, Kevin. *Crazy Rich Asians*
Mozley, Fiona. ★*Elmet*
Mukherjee, Neel. *The Lives of Others*
Thien, Madeleine. *Do Not Say We Have Nothing*
Walton, Jo. ★*Necessity*
Woolf, Virginia. ★*Mrs. Dalloway*

SOCIAL CONTROL
Burgess, Anthony. ★*A Clockwork Orange*
Social Creature. Burton, Tara Isabella

SOCIAL CRITICISM
Lethem, Jonathan. *Chronic City*
The Social Graces. Rosen, Renee

SOCIAL HISTORY
Akpan, Uwem. *Say You're One of Them*

SOCIAL INTERACTION
Smith, Ali. *There but for The: A Novel*

SOCIAL ISOLATION
Beckett, Samuel. ★*Murphy*
Brooks, Max. *Devolution: A Firsthand Account of the Rainier Sasquatch Massacre*
Butler, Season. ★*Cygnet*
Camus, Albert. *The Plague*
Conrad, Joseph. *Victory: An Island Tale*
Crummey, Michael. *The Innocents*
Darnielle, John. *Wolf in White Van: A Novel*
DeLillo, Don. *The Silence*
Dev, Sonali. *A Distant Heart*
Dolan-Leach, Caite. *We Went to the Woods: A Novel*
Dostoyevsky, Fyodor. *Notes from Underground*
Fine, Julia. *What Should Be Wild*
Fuller, Claire. *Unsettled Ground*

Geni, Abby. *The Lightkeepers: A Novel*
Gross, Max. *The Lost Shtetl*
Jackson, Shirley. *We Have Always Lived in the Castle*
Johnson, Daisy. *Sisters*
McCullers, Carson. ★*The Heart Is a Lonely Hunter*
McCullers, Carson. *The Member of the Wedding*
Moshfegh, Ottessa. *My Year of Rest and Relaxation*
Pinsker, Sarah. *A Song for a New Day*
Pyper, Andrew. *The Homecoming: A Novel*
Ray, Eleanor. *The Missing Treasures of Amy Ashton*
Smith, Zadie. ★*Nw: A Novel*
Stedman, M. L. ★*The Light Between Oceans: A Novel*
Vonnegut, Kurt. *While Mortals Sleep: Unpublished Short Fiction*
Wayne, Teddy. *Apartment: A Novel*

SOCIAL JUSTICE
Paretsky, Sara. *Love & Other Crimes: Stories*

SOCIAL MARGINALITY
Fajardo-Anstine, Kali. ★*Sabrina & Corina: Stories*
Peynado, Brenda. *The Rock Eaters: Stories*
Schanoes, Veronica L. *Burning Girls and Other Stories*

SOCIAL MEDIA
Angelo, Megan. *Followers*
Bellefleur, Alexandria. *Written in the Stars*
Eggers, Dave. *The Circle*
Green, Hank. *An Absolutely Remarkable Thing: A Novel*
Guillory, Jasmine. *The Proposal*
Hankin, Laura. *Happy & You Know It*
Kantaria, Annabel. *I Know You: A Novel of Suspense*
Majumdar, Megha. *A Burning*
Mason, Jamie. *The Hidden Things*
Minh, Drew. *Neon Empire*
Orenstein, Hannah. *Love at First Like*
Sullivan, J. Courtney. *Friends and Strangers*
Unsworth, Emma Jane. *Grown Ups*
Weiner, Jennifer. ★*Big Summer*
Weinstein, Alexander. *Children of the New World: Stories*
Yoon, David. *Version Zero*

SOCIAL MOBILITY
Ehirim, Nnamdi. *Prince of Monkeys*

SOCIAL NETWORKS
Frankel, Laurie. *Goodbye for Now: A Novel*

SOCIAL OBLIGATIONS
Offill, Jenny. ★*Weather*
Rosen, Renee. *The Social Graces*

SOCIAL PHOBIA
Rai, Alisha. ★*Girl Gone Viral*

SOCIAL PROBLEMS
Bellow, Saul. *The Dean's December: A Novel*
Dos Passos, John. *1919*
Liu, Ken. *Invisible Planets: Contemporary Chinese Science Fiction in Translation*

SOCIAL REFORMERS
Toole, John Kennedy. ★*A Confederacy of Dunces*
Trollope, Anthony. *The Warden*

SOCIAL SCIENCE FICTION
Alderman, Naomi. ★*The Power: A Novel*
Alexie, Sherman. *Flight*
Anders, Charlie Jane. ★*The City in the Middle of the Night*

Aoki, Ryka. *Light from Uncommon Stars*
Atwood, Margaret. ★*Maddaddam: A Novel*
Atwood, Margaret. ★*Oryx and Crake*
Atwood, Margaret. ★*The Year of the Flood: A Novel*
Ballard, J. G. ★*The Complete Stories of J.G. Ballard.*
Beckett, L. X. *Gamechanger*
Bradbury, Ray. ★*Fahrenheit 451*
Bradbury, Ray. ★*The Martian Chronicles: The Fortieth Anniversary Edition*
Butler, Octavia E. *Adulthood Rites*
Butler, Octavia E. ★*Dawn: Xenogenesis*
Butler, Octavia E. ★*Kindred*
Butler, Octavia E. *Parable of the Talents: A Novel*
Cambias, James L. *A Darkling Sea*
DeLillo, Don. *Zero K: A Novel*
Doctorow, Cory. *Radicalized*
Eggers, Dave. *A Hologram for the King: A Novel*
Elison, Meg. *The Book of Etta*
Elison, Meg. *The Book of Flora*
Elison, Meg. *The Book of the Unnamed Midwife*
Gilman, Charlotte Perkins. *Herland*
Haig, Matt. *The Humans: A Novel*
Hall, Louisa. *Speak*
Hao, Jingfang. *Vagabonds: A Novel*
Heinlein, Robert A. ★*Stranger in a Strange Land*
Holroyde, Claire. *The Effort*
Jemisin, N. K. *The Fifth Season*
Jemisin, N. K. *The Obelisk Gate*
Jemisin, N. K. *The Stone Sky*
King, Stephen. *Sleeping Beauties: A Novel*
Kowal, Mary Robinette. *The Calculating Stars: A Lady Astronaut Novel*
Kowal, Mary Robinette. *The Fated Sky: A Lady Astronaut Novel*
Kowal, Mary Robinette. *The Relentless Moon*
Le Guin, Ursula K. *The Birthday of the World: And Other Stories*
Le Guin, Ursula K. ★*The Dispossessed: An Ambiguous Utopia*
Le Guin, Ursula K. *Four Ways to Forgiveness*
Le Guin, Ursula K. ★*The Left Hand of Darkness*
Le Guin, Ursula K. *The Telling*
Liu, Ken. *Invisible Planets: Contemporary Chinese Science Fiction in Translation*
Maxwell, Everina. *Winter's Orbit*
Mieville, China. *Embassytown*
Miller, Walter M. ★*A Canticle for Leibowitz*
Nagamatsu, Sequoia. *How High We Go in the Dark*
O'Dell, Claire. *A Study in Honor: A Novel*
Pinsker, Sarah. *A Song for a New Day*
Russell, Mary Doria. ★*Children of God: A Novel*
Russell, Mary Doria. ★*The Sparrow*
Solomon, Rivers. *An Unkindness of Ghosts*
Stross, Charles. *Glasshouse*
Tepper, Sheri S. *The Gate to Women's Country*
Tepper, Sheri S. ★*Grass*
Tepper, Sheri S. *Singer from the Sea*
Tepper, Sheri S. *The Visitor*
Zamyatin, Yevgeny Ivanovich. ★*We*
SOCIAL STATUS
Balogh, Mary. *Someone to Hold*

Faber, Michel. *The Crimson Petal and the White*
Fitzgerald, F. Scott. ★*This Side of Paradise*
James, Eloisa. *Three Weeks with Lady X*
London, Jack. *Martin Eden*
Thackeray, William Makepeace. ★*Vanity Fair: A Novel Without a Hero*
Wallace, Carol. *Our Kind of People*
SOCIAL STRUCTURE
Achebe, Chinua. ★*Things Fall Apart*
Doctorow, Cory. *Walkaway*
SOCIAL VALUES
Smith, Ali. ★*Spring*
SOCIAL WORKERS
DePoy, Phillip. *Sidewalk Saint*
Goodwin, Bobi Gentry. *Revelation*
Henderson, Smith. *Fourth of July Creek*
Herrera, Adriana. *American Fairytale*
Klune, TJ. *The House in the Cerulean Sea*
Offutt, Chris. *Country Dark*
Roberts, Nora. *Sea Swept*
SOCIALISM
Solzhenitsyn, Aleksandr Isaevich. ★*Cancer Ward*
SOCIALITES
Bergman, Megan Mayhew. *Almost Famous Women: Stories*
Carter, Michaela. *Leonora in the Morning Light*
Danan, Rosie. *The Roommate*
Fitzgerald, F. Scott. ★*The Beautiful and Damned*
Fowler, Therese. *A Well-Behaved Woman: A Novel of the Vanderbilts*
Fowler, Therese. ★*Z: A Novel of Zelda Fitzgerald*
Hall, Araminta. *Imperfect Women: A Novel*
Kelly, Julia. *The Last Dance of the Debutante*
Lethem, Jonathan. *Chronic City*
McDowell, Christina. *The Cave Dwellers: A Novel*
Moreno-Garcia, Silvia. *Mexican Gothic*
Moyes, Jojo. *The Peacock Emporium*
Rosen, Renee. *The Social Graces*
Wallace, Carol. *Our Kind of People*
Waugh, Evelyn. ★*Vile Bodies*
SOCIOLOGY
Rader-Day, Lori. *The Black Hour*
SOCRATES
Renault, Mary. *The Last of the Wine*
Socrates Fortlow novels [Series]. Mosley, Walter
Soderberg, Alexander
The Other Son: A Sophie Brinkmann Novel
Sofer, Dalia
Man of My Time
The Septembers of Shiraz
Soft Target: A Thriller. Hunter, Stephen
Sojourn novels (Andrew Krivak) [Series]. Krivak, Andrew
SOLANAS, VALERIE
Stridsberg, Sara. *Valerie: Or the Faculty of Dreams : Amendment to the Theory of Sexuality*
★*Solar Bones.* McCormack, Mike
SOLAR ENERGY
Ishiguro, Kazuo. ★*Klara and the Sun*
SOLAR SYSTEM
Reynolds, Alastair. ★*Revenger*

Solar: a Novel. McEwan, Ian
Solares, Martin
   The Black Minutes
   Don't Send Flowers
★*Solaris*. Lem, Stanislaw
SOLDIERS
   Antopol, Molly. *The Unamericans*
   Balogh, Mary. *The Escape*
   Barker, Pat. ★*The Ghost Road*
   Barker, Pat. ★*Regeneration*
   Barry, Sebastian. *Days Without End: A Novel*
   Bausch, Richard. *Peace*
   Benn, James R. *Billy Boyle: A World War Two Mystery*
   Binder, L. Annette. *The Vanishing Sky*
   Calvi, Mary. *Dear George, Dear Mary: A Novel of George Washington's First Love*
   Carter, Miranda. *The Strangler Vine*
   Cornwell, Bernard. *The Last Kingdom: A Novel*
   Dallas, Sandra. *Tallgrass*
   Dare, Tessa. ★*A Night to Surrender*
   Dare, Tessa. *When a Scot Ties the Knot*
   Deutermann, Peter T. *Pacific Glory: A Novel*
   Dewes, J. S. *The Last Watch*
   Dowlatabadi, Mahmoud. *The Colonel*
   Downing, David. *Diary of a Dead Man on Leave*
   Dumas, Alexandre. ★*The Three Musketeers*
   Dumas, Alexandre. *Twenty Years After*
   Force, Marie. *Five Years Gone*
   Fountain, Ben. ★*Billy Lynn's Long Halftime Walk*
   Frazier, Charles. ★*Cold Mountain*
   Fuentes, Carlos. ★*The Old Gringo*
   Furst, Alan. *The Spies of Warsaw*
   Giordano, Paolo. *The Human Body*
   Harmel, Kristin. *The Room on Rue Amelie*
   Hazzard, Shirley. ★*The Great Fire*
   Heller, Joseph. ★*Catch-22*
   Hemingway, Ernest. *For Whom the Bell Tolls*
   Hersey, John. ★*A Bell for Adano*
   Jones, James. ★*From Here to Eternity*
   Jones, James. ★*The Thin Red Line*
   Kane, Ben. *Spartacus: The Gladiator*
   Krivak, Andrew. *The Signal Flame: A Novel*
   Lee, Chang-Rae. ★*The Surrendered*
   Lewis, Linden A. *The First Sister: A Novel*
   Liu, Cixin. *Ball Lightning*
   Mailer, Norman. ★*The Naked and the Dead*
   Mandanipour, Shahriar. *Moon Brow*
   Mann, Thomas. *The Magic Mountain*
   Marlantes, Karl. ★*Matterhorn: A Novel of the Vietnam War*
   Moyes, Jojo. *The Girl You Left Behind*
   O'Brien, Perry Edmond. *Fire in the Blood*
   O'Brien, Tim. *Going After Cacciato: A Novel*
   Penelope, L. *Song of Blood and Stone*
   Powers, Kevin. ★*The Yellow Birds: A Novel*
   Putney, Mary Jo. *Once a Soldier*
   Pynchon, Thomas. ★*Gravity's Rainbow*
   Remarque, Erich Maria. ★*All Quiet on the Western Front*
   Remarque, Erich Maria. *A Time to Love and a Time to Die*

   Robbins, David L. *Last Citadel: A Novel of the Battle of Kursk*
   Rooney, Kathleen. ★*Cher Ami and Major Whittlesey*
   Rutherfurd, Edward. *The Princes of Ireland: The Dublin Saga*
   Saunders, George. ★*Tenth of December: Stories*
   Shaara, Jeff. *Gone for Soldiers*
   Shaara, Jeff. *The Rising Tide: A Novel of World War II*
   Shaara, Jeff. *The Steel Wave: A Novel of World War II*
   Simmons, Dan. ★*Hyperion*
   Slimani, Leïla. *In the Country of Others*
   Speller, Elizabeth. *The Return of Captain John Emmett*
   Swift, Graham. *Wish You Were Here*
   Todd, Charles. ★*A Hanging at Dawn*
   Winterson, Jeanette. *The Passion*
   Woolf, Virginia. *Jacob's Room*
SOLDIERS — HISTORY
   Faulks, Sebastian. ★*Birdsong*
SOLDIERS — PSYCHOLOGY
   O'Brien, Tim. ★*The Things They Carried: A Work of Fiction*
Soli, Tatjana
   The Lotus Eaters
SOLITUDE
   Coetzee, J. M. ★*Foe*
   Defoe, Daniel. ★*Robinson Crusoe*
   Frazier, Charles. *Nightwoods: A Novel*
   Giordano, Paolo. ★*The Solitude of Prime Numbers: A Novel*
   Morante, Elsa. *Arturo's Island: A Novel*
   Reid, Iain. *I'm Thinking of Ending Things*
   Starnone, Domenico. *Trick*
   Weir, Andy. *Project Hail Mary*
   Woods, Stuart. *Palindrome*
★*The **Solitude** of Prime Numbers: A Novel*. Giordano, Paolo
Solomon Gursky Was Here. Richler, Mordecai
Solomon, Anna
   Leaving Lucy Pear
Solomon, Asali
   The Days of Afrekete
   Disgruntled: A Novel
Solomon, Rachel Lynn
   ★*The Ex Talk*
   Weather Girl
Solomon, Rivers
   The Deep
   Sorrowland
   An Unkindness of Ghosts
Solomons, Natasha
   House of Gold
Solzhenitsyn, Aleksandr Isaevich
   ★*Cancer Ward*
   In the First Circle: A Novel : The Restored Text
   One Day in the Life of Ivan Denisovich
SOMALI AMERICANS
   Farah, Nuruddin. *Crossbones*
SOMALIA
   Farah, Nuruddin. *Crossbones*
   Mohamed, Nadifa. *The Orchard of Lost Souls: A Novel*
Some Die Nameless. Stroby, Wallace
Some Go Home: A Novel. Lindsey, Odie
Some Luck. Smiley, Jane

Some Things I Never Thought I'd Do. Cleage, Pearl
Someday Quilts mysteries [Series]. O'Donohue, Clare
Someone. McDermott, Alice
Someone Knows My Name: A Novel. Hill, Lawrence
Someone Like Me. Carey, M. R.
★*Someone to Care*. Balogh, Mary
★*Someone to Cherish*. Balogh, Mary
Someone to Hold. Balogh, Mary
★*Someone to Love*. Balogh, Mary
Someone to Love. Deveraux, Jude
★*Someone to Remember: A Westcott Story*. Balogh, Mary
Someone to Trust. Balogh, Mary
Someone to Wed. Balogh, Mary
Someone's Listening. Glass, Seraphina Nova
Somer, Mehmet Murat
    The Serenity Murders
Somersault: a Novel. Oe, Kenzaburo
★*Something Borrowed, Something Black*. Estleman, Loren D.
Something in the Water. Steadman, Catherine
Something New Under the Sun. Kleeman, Alexandra
Something Rich and Strange: Selected Stories. Rash, Ron
Something She's Not Telling Us. Bell, Darcey
★*Something to Talk About*. Wilsner, Meryl
★*Something Wicked This Way Comes*. Bradbury, Ray
Sometimes a Great Notion: A Novel. Kesey, Ken
★*Sometimes I Lie*. Feeney, Alice
The Somnambulist. Barnes, Jonathan
Son of a Witch: A Novel. Maguire, Gregory
The Son of Good Fortune: A Novel. Tenorio, Lysley A.
★*The Son of Mr. Suleman*. Dickey, Eric Jerome
★*The Son: a Novel*. Meyer, Philipp
Sonchai Jitpleecheep mysteries [Series]. Burdett, John
A Song for a New Day. Pinsker, Sarah
A Song for the Brokenhearted. Shaw, William
★*A Song for the Dark Times*. Rankin, Ian
Song of a Captive Bird: A Novel. Darznik, Jasmin
The Song of Achilles. Miller, Madeline
Song of Blood and Stone. Penelope, L.
Song of ice and fire [Series]. Martin, George R. R.
Song of ice and fire prequel stories [Series]. Martin, George R.R.
The Song of Names. Lebrecht, Norman
★*Song of Solomon*. Morrison, Toni
The Song of the Lark. Cather, Willa
Songs in Ursa Major. Brodie, Emma
Songs Without Words. Packer, Ann
SONGWRITERS
    March, Emily. *Jackson*
SONS
    Erdrich, Louise. ★*Larose*
    Goodman, Carol. *The Sea of Lost Girls*
    Obreht, Tea. *Inland: A Novel*
    Wendig, Chuck. *The Book of Accidents*
SONS — DEATH
    Hemmings, Kaui Hart. *The Possibilities: A Novel*
    King, Stephen. *Pet Sematary*
    May, Peter. *The Blackhouse*
    Peikoff, Kira. *Mother Knows Best*
    Trigiani, Adriana. *Big Cherry Holler: A Big Stone Gap Novel*

Sons and Daughters of Ease and Plenty. Ausubel, Ramona
Sons and Lovers. Lawrence, D. H.
Sontag, Susan
    ★*In America*
    The Volcano Lover: A Romance
Sophia: or the Beginning of All Tales. Schami, Rafik
Sophie Brinkman trilogy [Series]. Soderberg, Alexander
★*Sophie's Choice*. Styron, William
SOPRANOS (SINGERS)
    Chee, Alexander. *The Queen of the Night*
Sorcerer royal [Series]. Cho, Zen
Sorcerer to the Crown. Cho, Zen
Sorenson, Jill
    Aftershock
Sorrow and Bliss. Mason, Meg
The Sorrow of War: A Novel of North Vietnam. Bao, Ninh
Sorrowland. Solomon, Rivers
Sorry for Your Trouble: Stories. Ford, Richard
Sosa, Mia
    ★*Acting on Impulse*
    ★*The Worst Best Man*
★*The Sot-Weed Factor*. Barth, John
SOUL
    Camp, Bryan. *Gather the Fortunes*
    Klune, TJ. ★*Under the Whispering Door*
    Mann, Thomas. *Doctor Faustus*
    Newland, Courttia. *A River Called Time*
    Stephenson, Neal. ★*Fall Or, Dodge in Hell: A Novel*
SOUL MATES
    Barker, Susan. ★*The Incarnations: A Novel*
    Frankel, Laurie. *Goodbye for Now: A Novel*
    O'Neill, Heather. ★*The Lonely Hearts Hotel: A Novel*
Soul Mountain. Gao, XIngjian
Soule, Charles
    ★*Anyone*
The Soulmate Equation. Lauren, Christina
Souls Raised from the Dead: A Novel. Betts, Doris
Soulstar. Polk, C. L.
★*The Sound and the Fury*. Faulkner, William
The Sound of the Mountain. Kawabata, Yasunari
The Sound of Waves. Mishima, Yukio
SOUND RECORDING EXECUTIVES AND PRODUCERS
    Egan, Jennifer. ★*A Visit from the Goon Squad*
SOUTH AFRICA
    Andrew, Sally. *The Satanic Mechanic: A Tannie Maria Mystery*
    Brink, Andre P. *Philida: A Novel*
    Coetzee, J. M. *Age of Iron*
    Coetzee, J. M. *Disgrace*
    Coetzee, J. M. ★*Life & Times of Michael K*
    Coetzee, J. M. *Summertime: Scenes from a Provincial Life*
    Flanery, Patrick. *Absolution: A Novel*
    Francis, Dick. *Smokescreen*
    Gordimer, Nadine. *The Conservationist*
    Gordimer, Nadine. *Get a Life*
    Gordimer, Nadine. ★*July's People*
    Gordimer, Nadine. *Life Times: Stories, 1952-2007*
    Gordimer, Nadine. ★*My Son's Story*
    Gordimer, Nadine. *No Time Like the Present: A Novel*

Gordimer, Nadine. *None to Accompany Me*
McClure, James. *The Steam Pig*
Meyer, Deon. *Icarus*
Paton, Alan. *Ah, but Your Land Is Beautiful*
Paton, Alan. ★*Cry, the Beloved Country*
Paton, Alan. *Too Late the Phalarope*
Tursten, Helene. *An Elderly Lady Must Not Be Crossed*
Willocks, Tim. *Memo from Turner*
SOUTH AFRICANS
Paton, Alan. ★*Cry, the Beloved Country*
SOUTH AMERICA
Alarcon, Daniel. *At Night We Walk in Circles: A Novel*
Allende, Isabel. ★*Eva Luna*
Allende, Isabel. ★*The House of the Spirits*
Allende, Isabel. *The Stories of Eva Luna*
Conrad, Joseph. *Nostromò: A Tale of the Seaboard*
Cussler, Clive. *Blue Gold: A Novel from the Numa Files*
Garcia Marquez, Gabriel. ★*The Autumn of the Patriarch*
Garcia Marquez, Gabriel. *The General in His Labyrinth*
Patchett, Ann. ★*Bel Canto: A Novel*
Skarmeta, Antonio. *The Dancer and the Thief: A Novel*
Toews, Miriam. ★*Women Talking: A Novel*
SOUTH ASIA
Swarup, Shubhangi. *Latitudes of Longing*
SOUTH ASIANS
Bhuvaneswar, Chaya. *White Dancing Elephants: Stories*
South Beach Love: A Feel-Good Romance from Hallmark Publishing.
    Pineiro, Caridad
SOUTH CAROLINA
Allison, Dorothy. ★*Bastard Out of Carolina*
Baldacci, David. *One Summer*
Bobotis, Andrea. *The Last List of Miss Judith Kratt*
Brown, Sandra. *The Witness*
Childs, Laura. *Haunted Hibiscus*
Childs, Laura. *Lavender Blue Murder*
Childs, Laura. *Twisted Tea Christmas*
Cobbs Hoffman, Elizabeth. *The Tubman Command: A Novel*
Conroy, Pat. *The Prince of Tides*
Doctorow, E. L. *The March: A Novel*
Dunn, Mark. *Ella Minnow Pea: A Progressively Lipogrammatic
    Epistolary Fable*
Frank, Dorothea Benton. *Folly Beach: A Lowcountry Tale*
Godwin, Gail. *Grief Cottage: A Novel*
Hendrix, Grady. *My Best Friend's Exorcism*
Hendrix, Grady. *The Southern Book Club's Guide to Slaying
    Vampires*
Kidd, Sue Monk. ★*The Invention of Wings: A Novel*
Kidd, Sue Monk. ★*The Secret Life of Bees*
Monroe, Mary Alice. *Beach House Reunion*
Monroe, Mary Alice. ★*The Summer of Lost and Found*
Naylor, Gloria. *Mama Day*
Ramsay, Hope. *Summer on Moonlight Bay*
Williams, Preslaysa. *A Lowcountry Bride*
SOUTH DAKOTA
Child, Lee. *61 Hours*
Lansdale, Joe R. ★*Paradise Sky*
Rølvaag, O. E. ★*Giants in the Earth: A Saga of the Prairie*
Weiden, David L. ★*Winter Counts*

SOUTH GEORGIA ISLAND
Bolton, S. J. *The Split*
SOUTH KOREA
Cho, Nam-Ju. ★*Kim Jiyoung, Born 1982*
Han, Kang. ★*Human Acts: A Novel*
Kim, Eugenia. *The Kinship of Secrets*
Kwon, Yo-Son. *Lemon*
Lee, Ji-Min. *The Starlet and the Spy*
Park, Sang Young. ★*Love in the Big City: A Novel*
See, Lisa. *The Island of Sea Women*
Stephens, Alice. *Famous Adopted People*
SOUTH MIAMI BEACH, FLORIDA
Leonard, Elmore. *Labrava*
South of the Border, West of the Sun. Murakami, Haruki
SOUTH PACIFIC OCEAN
Michener, James A. ★*Tales of the South Pacific*
SOUTH SIDE, CHICAGO, ILLINOIS
Dybek, Stuart. *I Sailed with Magellan*
SOUTHEASTERN STATES
Atkins, Ace. *Wicked City*
SOUTHERN AFRICA
Crouch, Katie. *Embassy Wife*
The Southern Book Club's Guide to Slaying Vampires. Hendrix, Grady
SOUTHERN CALIFORNIA
Bennett, Brit. *The Mothers*
Danan, Rosie. *The Intimacy Experiment*
Escandon, Maria Amparo. ★*L.A. Weather*
Hendrix, Grady. *The Final Girl Support Group*
Hummel, Maria. *Lesson in Red*
Koontz, Dean R. *The Husband*
Lee, Patrick. *Runner*
Macdonald, Ross. *The Underground Man*
McMillan, Terry. ★*It's Not All Downhill from Here: A Novel*
McPherson, Catriona. *Scot & Soda*
Parker, T. Jefferson. *The Blue Hour*
Pynchon, Thomas. ★*The Crying of Lot 49*
Rice, Luanne. *The Lemon Orchard*
Thorpe, Rufi. ★*The Knockout Queen*
Van Meter, Crissy. *Creatures: A Novel*
Walker, Karen Thompson. *The Dreamers*
Watkins, Claire Vaye. ★*Gold Fame Citrus*
Waxman, Abbi. *The Bookish Life of Nina Hill*
Southern Cross the Dog. Cheng, Bill
SOUTHERN FICTION
Agee, James. ★*A Death in the Family*
Allen, Sarah Addison. *Garden Spells*
Allen, Sarah Addison. *The Girl Who Chased the Moon: A Novel*
Benz, Chanelle. ★*The Gone Dead*
Bobotis, Andrea. *The Last List of Miss Judith Kratt*
Brown, Larry. *Joe: A Novel*
Brown, Larry. ★*Tiny Love: The Complete Stories of Larry Brown*
Brown, Taylor. ★*Gods of Howl Mountain: A Novel*
Burke, James Lee. ★*The New Iberia Blues*
Burke, James Lee. ★*A Private Cathedral*
Burke, James Lee. *Robicheaux*
Cash, Wiley. *The Last Ballad: A Novel*
Conroy, Pat. *The Prince of Tides*
Cooper, Tom. *Florida Man*

Cooper, Tom. *The Marauders*
Cosby, S. A. ★*Blacktop Wasteland*
Cosby, S. A. ★*Razorblade Tears*
Earley, Tony. *Jim the Boy: A Novel*
Edgerton, Clyde. ★*Walking Across Egypt: A Novel*
Edwards, Louis. *Ramadan Ramsey: A Novel*
Faulkner, William. ★*As I Lay Dying: The Corrected Text*
Faulkner, William. *Requiem for a Nun*
Faulkner, William. ★*Sanctuary*
Flagg, Fannie. *Standing in the Rainbow: A Novel*
Flagg, Fannie. ★*The Wonder Boy of Whistle Stop: A Novel*
Frank, Dorothea Benton. *Folly Beach: A Lowcountry Tale*
Frank, Dorothea Benton. *Queen Bee*
Franklin, Tom. *Crooked Letter, Crooked Letter: A Novel*
Frazier, Charles. *Nightwoods: A Novel*
Frazier, Charles. *Thirteen Moons: A Novel*
Gibbons, Kaye. *Charms for the Easy Life*
Gibbons, Kaye. ★*Ellen Foster: A Novel*
Gibbons, Kaye. *The Life All Around Me by Ellen Foster*
Graley, Lisa. *The Current That Carries: Stories*
Grau, Shirley Ann. *The Keepers of the House*
Greene, Amy. *Long Man*
Gurganus, Allan. *Oldest Living Confederate Widow Tells All*
Hart, John. *Down River*
Hendrix, Grady. *The Southern Book Club's Guide to Slaying Vampires*
Jackson, Joshilyn. *Never Have I Ever*
Johnson, Caleb. *Treeborne*
Jones, Tayari. ★*An American Marriage: A Novel*
Keller, Julia. ★*Bone on Bone*
Keller, Julia. *A Killing in the Hills*
Lansdale, Joe R. *The Bottoms*
Laymon, Kiese. *Long Division*
Lee, Harper. ★*Go Set a Watchman*
Leitch, Will. ★*How Lucky*
Lindsey, Odie. *Some Go Home: A Novel*
Luesse, Valerie Fraser. *Under the Bayou Moon: A Novel*
Maron, Margaret. *Bootlegger's Daughter*
Maron, Margaret. *Up Jumps the Devil*
McCrumb, Sharyn. ★*The Ballad of Frankie Silver*
McCrumb, Sharyn. ★*If Ever I Return, Pretty Peggy-O*
McCullers, Carson. *Reflections in a Golden Eye*
Miller, Mary. *Biloxi: A Novel*
Monroe, Mary. ★*Mrs. Wiggins*
Monroe, Mary Alice. *Beach House Reunion*
Monroe, Mary Alice. ★*The Summer of Lost and Found*
Panowich, Brian. *Like Lions*
Pearson, Robin W. *A Long Time Comin'*
Percy, Walker. *The Second Coming*
Rash, Ron. ★*In the Valley: Stories and a Novella Based on Serena*
Rash, Ron. ★*Serena: A Novel*
Smith, Julie. *82 Desire: A Skip Langdon Novel*
Smith, Julie. *Crescent City Kill: A Skip Langdon Novel*
Smith, Julie. *House of Blues*
Smith, Julie. *Jazz Funeral*
Smith, Julie. *The Kindness of Strangers: A Skip Langdon Novel*
Smith, Julie. *Louisiana Hotshot*
Smith, Julie. ★*Mean Woman Blues*

Smith, Julie. *New Orleans Beat*
Smith, Lee. ★*Fair and Tender Ladies*
Smith, Lee. *Family Linen*
Smith, Lee. *On Agate Hill: A Novel*
Smith, Lee. *Oral History*
Smith, Michael F. *Blackwood*
Smith, Michael F. *The Fighter: A Novel*
Toole, John Kennedy. ★*A Confederacy of Dunces*
Trigiani, Adriana. *Big Cherry Holler: A Big Stone Gap Novel*
Walsh, M. O. ★*The Big Door Prize: A Novel*
Ward, Jesmyn. ★*Sing, Unburied, Sing*
Warren, Robert Penn. *Band of Angels*
Warren, Robert Penn. *World Enough and Time: A Romantic Novel*
Watson, Brad. *Miss Jane: A Novel*
Weiss, Leah. *If the Creek Don't Rise: A Novel*
Welty, Eudora. ★*The Collected Stories of Eudora Welty*
Welty, Eudora. ★*Delta Wedding*
Welty, Eudora. ★*The Ponder Heart*
Woodrell, Daniel. *The Maid's Version: A Novel*

SOUTHERN FRANCE
Riordan, Kate. *The Heatwave*
Walker, Martin. *The Coldest Case*
Walker, Martin. *The Shooting at Chateau Rock*

SOUTHERN GOTHIC
Allison, Dorothy. ★*Bastard Out of Carolina*
Bond, Cynthia. *Ruby: A Novel*
Caldwell, Erskine. *Tobacco Road*
Crews, Harry. *A Feast of Snakes: A Novel*
Davidson, Andy. *The Boatman's Daughter: A Novel*
Faulkner, William. ★*As I Lay Dying: The Corrected Text*
Faulkner, William. ★*Light in August*
Franklin, Tom. *Crooked Letter, Crooked Letter: A Novel*
Godwin, Gail. *Grief Cottage: A Novel*
McCarthy, Cormac. ★*Blood Meridian, Or, the Evening Redness in the West*
McCullers, Carson. *The Member of the Wedding*
McCullers, Carson. *Reflections in a Golden Eye*
McHugh, Laura. *What's Done in Darkness: A Novel*
O'Connor, Flannery. *The Complete Stories*
O'Connor, Flannery. ★*The Violent Bear It Away*
Offutt, Chris. *Country Dark*
Smith, Michael F. *Blackwood*
Smith, Michael F. *The Fighter: A Novel*
Styron, William. *Lie Down in Darkness*
Watson, Brad. *Miss Jane: A Novel*
Weiss, Leah. *If the Creek Don't Rise: A Novel*
Welty, Eudora. ★*The Robber Bridegroom*

SOUTHERN ITALY
Beagle, Peter S. *In Calabria*

Southern Reach novels [Series]. VanderMeer, Jeff

SOUTHERN STATES
Alexander, Tamera. ★*A Note yet Unsung*
Asim, Jabari. ★*Yonder*
Atakora, Afia. ★*Conjure Women*
Ball, John Dudley. *In the Heat of the Night*
Bambara, Toni Cade. ★*The Salt Eaters*
Barr, Mark. *Watershed*
Benz, Chanelle. ★*The Gone Dead*

Betts, Doris. *Souls Raised from the Dead: A Novel*
Brown, Larry. ★*Tiny Love: The Complete Stories of Larry Brown*
Brown, Rita Mae. ★*Rubyfruit Jungle*
Cheng, Bill. *Southern Cross the Dog*
Choi, Susan. ★*Trust Exercise: A Novel*
Clark, Martin. *The Substitution Order*
Coates, Ta-Nehisi. ★*The Water Dancer: A Novel*
Cole, Alyssa. ★*A Hope Divided*
Deon, Natashia. *Grace*
Dumas, Henry. *Echo Tree: The Collected Short Fiction of Henry Dumas*
Earley, Tony. *Mr. Tall: A Novella and Stories*
Edgerton, Clyde. ★*Walking Across Egypt: A Novel*
Ellison, Ralph. ★*Juneteenth*
Gibbons, Kaye. ★*Ellen Foster: A Novel*
Gilchrist, Ellen. ★*Collected Stories*
Grau, Shirley Ann. *The Keepers of the House*
Gurganus, Allan. ★*Local Souls: Novellas*
Gurganus, Allan. *Oldest Living Confederate Widow Tells All*
Jackson, Joshilyn. *Never Have I Ever*
Johnson, Caleb. *Treeborne*
Jones, Robert. ★*The Prophets: A Novel*
Lacey, Catherine. ★*Pew: A Novel*
Lee, Harper. ★*Go Set a Watchman*
Lee, Harper. ★*To Kill a Mockingbird*
Leonard, Elmore. *Tishomingo Blues: A Novel*
Locke, Attica. *The Cutting Season*
Locke, Attica. ★*Heaven, My Home*
McCullers, Carson. ★*The Heart Is a Lonely Hunter*
McCullers, Carson. *The Member of the Wedding*
McCullers, Carson. *Reflections in a Golden Eye*
O'Connor, Flannery. *The Complete Stories*
O'Connor, Flannery. ★*The Violent Bear It Away*
O'Connor, Flannery. ★*Wise Blood*
Price, Reynolds. *Roxanna Slade*
Rash, Ron. *Something Rich and Strange: Selected Stories*
Rawles, Nancy. *My Jim: A Novel*
Reed, Ishmael. *Flight to Canada*
Rice, Anne. *Blackwood Farm*
Smith, Lee. *On Agate Hill: A Novel*
Spencer, Elizabeth. *The Southern Woman: New and Selected Fiction*
Stowe, Harriet Beecher. ★*Uncle Tom's Cabin*
Styron, William. *Lie Down in Darkness*
Vachss, Andrew H. *Two Trains Running*
Walker, Alice. ★*The Color Purple: A Novel*
Warren, Robert Penn. *All the King's Men*
Welty, Eudora. ★*The Collected Stories of Eudora Welty*
Welty, Eudora. ★*Delta Wedding*
Welty, Eudora. *Stories, Essays & Memoir*
Whitehead, Colson. ★*The Nickel Boys: A Novel*
Whitehead, Colson. ★*The Underground Railroad: A Novel*
The **Southern** Woman: New and Selected Fiction. Spencer, Elizabeth

SOUTHWEST (UNITED STATES)

Anaya, Rudolfo A. *The Man Who Could Fly and Other Stories*
Bacigalupi, Paolo. ★*The Water Knife*
Berlin, Lucia. ★*A Manual for Cleaning Women: Selected Stories*
Leonard, Elmore. ★*The Complete Western Stories of Elmore Leonard.*
Obreht, Tea. *Inland: A Novel*

Quinn, Spencer. ★*It's a Wonderful Woof*
Silko, Leslie Marmon. *Almanac of the Dead*
Silko, Leslie Marmon. *Gardens in the Dunes: A Novel*
Swarthout, Glendon. *Bless the Beasts and Children*
The **Souvenir** Museum: Stories. McCracken, Elizabeth

SOUVENIRS (KEEPSAKES)

Hall, Rachel Howzell. *These Toxic Things*
★*Sovereign*. Sansom, C. J.

SOVIET UNION

Barnes, Julian. *The Noise of Time*
Benn, James R. *Road of Bones: A Billy Boyle World War II Mystery*
Bezmozgis, David. *The Betrayers: A Novel*
Bronsky, Alina. *The Hottest Dishes of the Tartar Cuisine*
Bulgakov, Mikhail. ★*The Master and Margarita*
Dean, Debra. *The Madonnas of Leningrad: A Novel*
Haratischvili, Nino. *The Eighth Life: (For Brilka)*
Harris, Robert. *Archangel: A Novel*
Koestler, Arthur. *Darkness at Noon*
Kuznetsov, Anatolii Petrovich. *Babi Yar: A Document in the Form of a Novel*
Littell, Robert. *The Mayakovsky Tapes: A Novel*
Mankell, Henning. *The Dogs of Riga*
Pasternak, Boris Leonidovich. ★*Doctor Zhivago*
Paul, Gill. ★*The Lost Daughter*
Prescott, Lara. *The Secrets We Kept*
Remarque, Erich Maria. *A Time to Love and a Time to Die*
Robbins, David L. *Last Citadel: A Novel of the Battle of Kursk*
Robbins, David L. *War of the Rats: A Novel*
Rutherfurd, Edward. *Russka: The Novel of Russia*
Smith, Martin Cruz. *Polar Star*
Smith, Tom Rob. *Agent 6*
Smith, Tom Rob. *Child 44*
Smith, Tom Rob. *The Secret Speech*
Solzhenitsyn, Aleksandr Isaevich. ★*Cancer Ward*
Solzhenitsyn, Aleksandr Isaevich. *In the First Circle: A Novel : The Restored Text*
Solzhenitsyn, Aleksandr Isaevich. *One Day in the Life of Ivan Denisovich*

SOVIETOLOGISTS

Harris, Robert. *Archangel: A Novel*

SOVIETS IN ENGLAND

Sayers, Dorothy L. *Have His Carcase*

Soyinka, Wole

Chronicles from the Land of the Happiest People on Earth
Space. Michener, James A.

SPACE

Barnett, David. *Calling Major Tom*
Bujold, Lois McMaster. ★*The Warrior's Apprentice*
Chambers, Becky. *To Be Taught, If Fortunate*
Egan, Greg. *Schild's Ladder*
Foster, Alan Dean. *Relic*
Gilman, Carolyn Ives. *Dark Orbit*
Hurley, Kameron. *The Stars Are Legion*
Jimenez, Simon. ★*The Vanished Birds*
Lee, Yoon Ha. *Ninefox Gambit*
Lee, Yoon Ha. *Raven Stratagem*
Lee, Yoon Ha. *Revenant Gun*
Merbeth, K. S. ★*Fortuna*

Rajaniemi, Hannu. *The Fractal Prince*
Rajaniemi, Hannu. *The Quantum Thief*
Reynolds, Alastair. ★*Revenger*
Robinson, Kim Stanley. *Aurora*
Stross, Charles. *Accelerando*
Swyler, Erika. ★*Light from Other Stars: A Novel*
Weir, Andy. *Project Hail Mary*

SPACE AND TIME
Doerr, Anthony. ★*Cloud Cuckoo Land: A Novel*
El-Mohtar, Amal. ★*This Is How You Lose the Time War*
Gibson, William. ★*Agency*
Jimenez, Simon. ★*The Vanished Birds*
Moore, Alan. *Jerusalem: A Novel*
Swyler, Erika. ★*Light from Other Stars: A Novel*
*The **Space** Between Words*. Phoenix, Michele
*The **Space** Between Worlds*. Johnson, Micaiah

SPACE COLONIES
Asimov, Isaac. *Foundation and Empire*
Bradbury, Ray. ★*The Martian Chronicles: The Fortieth Anniversary Edition*
Burke, Sue. *Semiosis*
Cherryh, C. J. *Foreigner: A Novel of First Contact*
Corey, James S. A. *Babylon's Ashes*
Corey, James S. A. *Cibola Burn*
Corey, James S. A. *Nemesis Games*
Corey, James S. A. *Persepolis Rising*
Egan, Greg. *Phoresis*
Kowal, Mary Robinette. *The Fated Sky: A Lady Astronaut Novel*
Kowal, Mary Robinette. *The Relentless Moon*
Kunsken, Derek. *The House of Styx*
Reynolds, Alastair. *Revelation Space*
Robinson, Kim Stanley. *The Martians*
Scalzi, John. ★*Old Man's War*
Steele, Allen M. *Coyote: A Novel of Interstellar Exploration*
Stephenson, Neal. *Seveneves*
Wagers, K. B. *Hold Fast Through the Fire*
Weir, Andy. *Artemis*

SPACE EXPLORATION
Bradbury, Ray. *Bradbury Stories: 100 of His Most Celebrated Tales*
Bradbury, Ray. ★*The Martian Chronicles: The Fortieth Anniversary Edition*
Chambers, Becky. *To Be Taught, If Fortunate*
Clarke, Arthur C. ★*2001: A Space Odyssey*
Clarke, Arthur C. *Rendezvous with Rama*
Dewes, J. S. *The Last Watch*
Hamilton, Peter F. *Pandora's Star*
Kowal, Mary Robinette. *The Fated Sky: A Lady Astronaut Novel*
Kowal, Mary Robinette. *The Relentless Moon*
Michener, James A. *Space*
Nguyen, Lena. *We Have Always Been Here*
Paolini, Christopher. ★*To Sleep in a Sea of Stars*
Stephenson, Neal. *Seveneves*
Wagers, K. B. *A Pale Light in the Black: A Neog Novel*

SPACE FLIGHT
Adams, Douglas. ★*The Hitchhiker's Guide to the Galaxy*
Anderson, Kevin J. *The Last Days of Krypton*
Banks, Iain. *The Hydrogen Sonata*
Bear, Greg. *Anvil of Stars*

Bouchet, Amanda. *Nightchaser*
Bradbury, Ray. *Bradbury Stories: 100 of His Most Celebrated Tales*
Cambias, James L. *A Darkling Sea*
Chambers, Becky. ★*The Galaxy, and the Ground Within*
Chambers, Becky. *Record of a Spaceborn Few*
Corey, James S. A. *Abaddon's Gate*
Corey, James S. A. *Babylon's Ashes*
Corey, James S. A. *Caliban's War*
Corey, James S. A. *Cibola Burn*
Corey, James S. A. ★*Leviathan Wakes*
Corey, James S. A. *Nemesis Games*
Egan, Greg. *Schild's Ladder*
Elliott, Kate. *Unconquerable Sun*
Flynn, Michael. *The January Dancer*
Gunn, James E. *Transcendental*
Haldeman, Joe W. ★*The Forever War*
Hamilton, Peter F. *Pandora's Star*
Jimenez, Simon. ★*The Vanished Birds*
Leckie, Ann. *Ancillary Justice*
Leckie, Ann. *Ancillary Mercy*
Leckie, Ann. *Ancillary Sword*
Levine, David D. *Arabella of Mars*
Lewis, Linden A. *The First Sister: A Novel*
Liu, Cixin. ★*Death's End*
McDevitt, Jack. *The Engines of God*
O'Keefe, Megan E. *Velocity Weapon*
Ogden, Aimee. *Sun-Daughters, Sea-Daughters*
Okorafor, Nnedi. ★*Binti*
Pohl, Frederik. *Gateway*
Robinson, Kim Stanley. *The Martians*
Russell, Mary Doria. ★*Children of God: A Novel*
Simmons, Dan. *Endymion*
Simmons, Dan. *The Rise of Endymion*
Steele, Allen M. *Coyote: A Novel of Interstellar Exploration*
Stross, Charles. *Neptune's Brood*
Stross, Charles. *Saturn's Children: A Space Opera*
Tepper, Sheri S. ★*Grass*
Valente, Catherynne M. *Radiance*
Varley, John. ★*Titan*
Vinge, Vernor. *A Fire Upon the Deep*
Vonnegut, Kurt. ★*Slaughterhouse-Five: Or, the Children's Crusade : A Duty-Dance with Death*
Wagers, K. B. *A Pale Light in the Black: A Neog Novel*
Weir, Andy. *Project Hail Mary*

SPACE FLIGHT TO MARS
Howrey, Meg. *The Wanderers*
Vonnegut, Kurt. ★*The Sirens of Titan*
Weir, Andy. *The Martian*
Space Hopper. Fisher, Helen
Space Odyssey series [Series]. Clarke, Arthur C.
Space Opera. Valente, Catherynne M.

SPACE OPERA
Asimov, Isaac. ★*Foundation*
Asimov, Isaac. *Foundation and Empire*
Asimov, Isaac. *Second Foundation*
Banks, Iain. *Consider Phlebas*
Banks, Iain. *The Hydrogen Sonata*
Banks, Iain. *Matter*

Banks, Iain. *The Player of Games*
Banks, Iain. *Use of Weapons*
Bujold, Lois McMaster. ★*Shards of Honor*
Bujold, Lois McMaster. ★*The Warrior's Apprentice*
Chambers, Becky. *A Closed and Common Orbit*
Chambers, Becky. ★*The Galaxy, and the Ground Within*
Chambers, Becky. ★*The Long Way to a Small, Angry Planet*
Chambers, Becky. *Record of a Spaceborn Few*
Corey, James S. A. *Abaddon's Gate*
Corey, James S. A. *Babylon's Ashes*
Corey, James S. A. *Caliban's War*
Corey, James S. A. *Cibola Burn*
Corey, James S. A. ★*Leviathan Wakes*
Corey, James S. A. *Nemesis Games*
Corey, James S. A. *Persepolis Rising*
Corey, James S. A. *Tiamat's Wrath*
Dewes, J. S. *The Last Watch*
Eason, K. *How Rory Thorne Destroyed the Multiverse*
Elliott, Kate. *Unconquerable Sun*
Flynn, Michael. *The January Dancer*
Gladstone, Max. ★*Empress of Forever*
Gunn, James E. *Transcendental*
Hamilton, Peter F. *The Dreaming Void*
Hamilton, Peter F. *Pandora's Star*
Harrison, M. John. *Light*
Herbert, Frank. ★*Dune*
Higgins, C. A. *Lightless*
Hurley, Kameron. *The Stars Are Legion*
Jimenez, Simon. ★*The Vanished Birds*
Leckie, Ann. *Ancillary Justice*
Leckie, Ann. *Ancillary Mercy*
Leckie, Ann. *Ancillary Sword*
Leckie, Ann. *Provenance*
Lee, Yoon Ha. *Ninefox Gambit*
Lee, Yoon Ha. *Raven Stratagem*
Lee, Yoon Ha. *Revenant Gun*
Martine, Arkady. ★*A Desolation Called Peace*
Martine, Arkady. ★*A Memory Called Empire*
Merbeth, K. S. ★*Fortuna*
Muir, Tamsyn. *Harrow the Ninth*
O'Keefe, Megan E. *Velocity Weapon*
Okorafor, Nnedi. ★*Binti*
Okorafor, Nnedi. *Binti: Home*
Okorafor, Nnedi. *Binti: The Night Masquerade*
Paolini, Christopher. ★*To Sleep in a Sea of Stars*
Pohl, Frederik. *Gateway*
Reynolds, Alastair. *Revelation Space*
Reynolds, Alastair. ★*Revenger*
Scalzi, John. *The Collapsing Empire*
Simmons, Dan. *Endymion*
Simmons, Dan. *The Fall of Hyperion*
Simmons, Dan. ★*Hyperion*
Simmons, Dan. *The Rise of Endymion*
Steele, Allen M. *Coyote: A Novel of Interstellar Exploration*
Stross, Charles. *Neptune's Brood*
Stross, Charles. *Saturn's Children: A Space Opera*
Valente, Catherynne M. *Radiance*
Valente, Catherynne M. *Space Opera*

Varley, John. *Dark Lightning*
Vinge, Vernor. *The Children of the Sky*
Vinge, Vernor. *A Fire Upon the Deep*
Wagers, K. B. *After the Crown*
Wagers, K. B. *There Before the Chaos*
Williams, Drew. *The Stars Now Unclaimed*

SPACE PROGRAMS
Michener, James A. *Space*

SPACE STATIONS
Brown, Dale. *Eagle Station: A Novel*
Eason, K. *How Rory Thorne Destroyed the Multiverse*
Wagers, K. B. *Hold Fast Through the Fire*
Wagers, K. B. *A Pale Light in the Black: A Neog Novel*

SPACE TRAVELERS
Higgins, C. A. *Lightless*
Robinson, Kim Stanley. *Aurora*

SPACE VEHICLES
Chambers, Becky. *A Closed and Common Orbit*
Chambers, Becky. ★*The Galaxy, and the Ground Within*
Chambers, Becky. ★*The Long Way to a Small, Angry Planet*
Chambers, Becky. *Record of a Spaceborn Few*
Clarke, Arthur C. ★*2001: A Space Odyssey*
Clarke, Arthur C. ★*Childhood's End*
Clarke, Arthur C. *Rendezvous with Rama*
Corey, James S. A. *Persepolis Rising*
Corey, James S. A. *Tiamat's Wrath*
Coulter, Catherine. *The Last Second*
Flynn, Michael. *Eifelheim*
Hamilton, Peter F. *The Dreaming Void*
Higgins, C. A. *Lightless*
Lafferty, Mur. *Six Wakes*
Levine, David D. *Arabella of Mars*
Lewis, Linden A. *The First Sister: A Novel*
Merbeth, K. S. ★*Fortuna*
Nguyen, Lena. *We Have Always Been Here*
Robinson, Kim Stanley. *Aurora*
Solomon, Rivers. *An Unkindness of Ghosts*
Tepper, Sheri S. ★*Grass*
Varley, John. *Dark Lightning*
Vonnegut, Kurt. ★*The Sirens of Titan*
Wagers, K. B. *After the Crown*
Wells, H. G. ★*The War of the Worlds*

SPACE WARFARE
Bear, Greg. *Anvil of Stars*
Bear, Greg. *The Forge of God*
Bujold, Lois McMaster. ★*Shards of Honor*
Bujold, Lois McMaster. ★*The Warrior's Apprentice*
Card, Orson Scott. ★*Ender's Game*
Corey, James S. A. *Abaddon's Gate*
Corey, James S. A. *Babylon's Ashes*
Corey, James S. A. *Caliban's War*
Corey, James S. A. *Cibola Burn*
Corey, James S. A. ★*Leviathan Wakes*
Corey, James S. A. *Nemesis Games*
Corey, James S. A. *Persepolis Rising*
Corey, James S. A. *Tiamat's Wrath*
Haldeman, Joe W. ★*The Forever War*
Heinlein, Robert A. *The Moon Is a Harsh Mistress*

Heinlein, Robert A. ★*Starship Troopers*
Lee, Yoon Ha. *Ninefox Gambit*
Lee, Yoon Ha. *Raven Stratagem*
Lee, Yoon Ha. *Revenant Gun*
Mieville, China. *Embassytown*
O'Keefe, Megan E. *Velocity Weapon*
Okorafor, Nnedi. ★*Binti*
Okorafor, Nnedi. *Binti: Home*
Scalzi, John. ★*Old Man's War*
Scalzi, John. *Redshirts: A Novel with Three Codas*
Simmons, Dan. *The Fall of Hyperion*
Simmons, Dan. ★*Hyperion*
Vinge, Vernor. *A Fire Upon the Deep*

SPACE WEAPONS
Brown, Dale. *Eagle Station: A Novel*

SPACESHIP CAPTAINS
Reynolds, Alastair. ★*Revenger*
Scalzi, John. *The Collapsing Empire*

SPADE, SAM (FICTITIOUS CHARACTER)
Hammett, Dashiell. ★*The Maltese Falcon*

SPAIN
Allende, Isabel. *A Long Petal of the Sea: A Novel*
Arbol, Victor del. *Breathing Through the Wound*
Bourdeaut, Olivier. *Waiting for Bojangles: A Novel*
Cervantes Saavedra, Miguel de. ★*Don Quixote*
Duenas, Maria. *The Time in Between: A Novel*
Follett, Ken. *Winter of the World*
Forester, C. S. *Commodore Hornblower*
Garcia Saenz, Eva. *The Silence of the White City*
Hemingway, Ernest. *For Whom the Bell Tolls*
Hill Gumbao, Toni. *The Good Suicides: A Thriller*
Hill Gumbao, Toni. *The Summer of Dead Toys*
Levy, Deborah. *Hot Milk: A Novel*
Lopez Barrio, Cristina. *The House of the Impossible Loves*
Marias, Javier. *The Infatuations*
McLain, Paula. *Love and Ruin*
Nichols, Peter. *The Rocks*
Pawel, Rebecca. *Death of a Nationalist*
Redondo, Dolores. *The Invisible Guardian*
Romano-Lax, Andromeda. *The Spanish Bow*
Ruiz Zafon, Carlos. *The Angel's Game*
Ruiz Zafon, Carlos. *The Labyrinth of the Spirits*
Straub, Emma. *The Vacationers*
Thelen, Albert Vigoleis. *The Island of Second Sight: From the Applied Recollections of Vigoleis*
Van der Vliet Oloomi, Azareen. *Call Me Zebra*
Wilson, G. Willow. ★*The Bird King*

Spain, Jo
With Our Blessing: An Inspector Tom Reynolds Mystery

SPANIARDS IN MOROCCO
Duenas, Maria. *The Time in Between: A Novel*
The *Spanish* Bow. Romano-Lax, Andromeda

SPANISH HARLEM, NEW YORK CITY
Quinonez, Ernesto. *Bodega Dreams*

Spann, Susan
Blade of the Samurai: A Shinobi Mystery
★*Claws of the Cat: A Shinobi Mystery*
Trial on Mount Koya: A Hiro Hattori Novel

The *Spare* Room. Garner, Helen
A *Spark* of Light: A Novel. Picoult, Jodi

Spark, Muriel
Aiding & Abetting
The Driver's Seat
★*A Far Cry from Kensington*
★*The Girls of Slender Means*
★*The Mandelbaum Gate*
★*Memento Mori*
★*The Prime of Miss Jean Brodie*

SPARK, MURIEL
Wojtas, Olga. *Miss Blaine's Prefect and the Golden Samovar*
Sparks & Bainbridge mysteries [Series]. Montclair, Allison

Sparks, Nicholas
Every Breath
The Guardian
★*The Notebook*
A Walk to Remember

★The *Sparrow*. Russell, Mary Doria
Sparrow novels [Series]. Russell, Mary Doria

SPARTACUS
Coben, Harlan. *Hold Tight*
Kane, Ben. *Spartacus: The Gladiator*
Spartacus: the Gladiator. Kane, Ben
Speak. Hall, Louisa
★*Speak No Evil*. Iweala, Uzodinma
Speaker of Mandarin. Rendell, Ruth
Speaking from Among the Bones: A Flavia De Luce Novel. Bradley, C. Alan

Spear, Terry
A Billionaire Wolf for Christmas

SPECIAL FORCES
Brown, Dale. *The Moscow Offensive: A Novel*
DeMille, Nelson. ★*The Deserter: A Novel*
Hanson, Hart. *The Driver*
Lee, Patrick. *Runner*
Parnell, Sean. *Man of War: An Eric Steele Novel*
Taylor, Brad. ★*Daughter of War: A Novel*
Taylor, Brad. *Ring of Fire*

SPECIAL OPERATIONS (MILITARY SCIENCE)
Brown, Dale. *The Moscow Offensive: A Novel*
Coes, Ben. *The Russian: A Thriller*
Cussler, Clive. ★*Golden Buddha*
Taylor, Brad. *Ring of Fire*
Special Topics in Calamity Physics. Pessl, Marisha
Specimen Days. Cunningham, Michael
The *Spectacular: a Novel*. Whittall, Zoe

SPEECHES, ADDRESSES, ETC.
Coetzee, J. M. *Elizabeth Costello*

Speight, Shameek A.
★*A Child of a Crack Head*
The Pleasure of Pain

Speller, Elizabeth
The Return of Captain John Emmett
The Strange Fate of Kitty Easton
Spellman files [Series]. Lutz, Lisa
The *Spellman* Files: A Novel. Lutz, Lisa

SPELLS (MAGIC)

Gilman, Laura Anne. *Hard Magic*
Glass, Jenna. *The Women's War*
Hairston, Andrea. *Master of Poisons*
Hoffman, Alice. *The Book of Magic*
Hoffman, Alice. *The Rules of Magic: A Novel*
Pratchett, Terry. *Wyrd Sisters*

SPELUNKERS

Starling, Caitlin. *The Luminous Dead*

Spencer, Elizabeth

The Southern Woman: New and Selected Fiction
The Stories of Elizabeth Spencer

Spencer, Minerva

Barbarous
Dangerous
Scandalous

Spencer, Sally

Backlash
Best Served Cold
Dead End
The Dead Hand of History
Death's Dark Shadow
★*A Dying Fall*
★*Echoes of the Dead*
★*The Hidden*
Lambs to the Slaughter
The Ring of Death
The Shivering Turn
Thicker Than Water: A Monika Paniatowski British Police Procedural
A Walk with the Dead

Spencer, Scott

★*Endless Love*
Man in the Woods
An Ocean Without a Shore

Spencer-Fleming, Julia

All Mortal Flesh
Hid from Our Eyes
I Shall Not Want: A Clare Ferguson/Russ Van Alstyne Mystery
In the Bleak Midwinter
Through the Evil Days: A Clare Ferguson/Russ Van Alstyne Mystery

Spenser novels [Series]. Parker, Robert B.

SPERM DONORS

White, Randy Wayne. *Salt River*

Spero Lucas mysteries [Series]. Pelecanos, George P.

SPICE INDUSTRY AND TRADE

Rushdie, Salman. *The Moor's Last Sigh*
Shanbhag, Vivek. *Ghachar Ghochar*

Spiegelman, Peter

Black Maps

SPIES

Banks, Iain. *Matter*
Banks, Iain. *Use of Weapons*
Bell, Ted. *Overkill: An Alex Hawke Novel*
Black, Cara. ★*Three Hours in Paris*
Bourne, Joanna. *The Black Hawk*
Bourne, Joanna. *The Forbidden Rose*
Bourne, Joanna. *Rogue Spy*

Bourne, Joanna. ★*The Spymaster's Lady*
Brandreth, Benet. *The Spy of Venice*
Buchan, John. *The Thirty-Nine Steps*
Buckley, William F. ★*Mongoose, R.I.P.: A Blackford Oakes Novel*
Cameron, Marc. *Power and Empire*
Chen, Mike. *Here and Now and Then*
Christy, Bryan. *In the Company of Killers*
Church, James. ★*A Corpse in the Koryo*
Clancy, Tom. ★*The Hunt for Red October*
Cole, Alyssa. ★*An Extraordinary Union*
Cole, Alyssa. ★*A Hope Divided*
Cole, Alyssa. ★*An Unconditional Freedom*
Cumming, Charles. *A Colder War*
Cumming, Charles. ★*The Trinity Six*
Cussler, Clive. *Sacred Stone*
Deighton, Len. *London Match*
Dick, Philip K. ★*The Man in the High Castle*
Doctorow, E. L. ★*The Book of Daniel: A Novel*
Downing, David. *Diary of a Dead Man on Leave*
Dunmore, Helen. *Exposure*
Eisler, Barry. *The God's Eye View*
Fleming, Ian. ★*Casino Royale: A James Bond Novel*
Fleming, Ian. *Doctor No*
Fleming, Ian. *From Russia with Love*
Fleming, Ian. ★*Goldfinger*
Fleming, Ian. *The Man with the Golden Gun*
Fleming, Ian. *On Her Majesty's Secret Service*
Fleming, Ian. *You Only Live Twice*
Follett, Ken. *Eye of the Needle*
Follett, Ken. *Hornet Flight*
Forsyth, Frederick. *The Fox*
Furst, Alan. *Blood of Victory: A Novel*
Furst, Alan. ★*Mission to Paris*
Furst, Alan. *Spies of the Balkans: A Novel*
Furst, Alan. *The Spies of Warsaw*
Furst, Alan. ★*Under Occupation: A Novel*
Greene, Graham. *The Human Factor*
Greene, Graham. *The Last Word and Other Stories*
Greene, Graham. *Our Man in Havana*
Groot, Tracy. *Flame of Resistance*
Hall, Adam. *The Quiller Memorandum*
Harris, Oliver. *A Shadow Intelligence*
Harris, Robert. *Archangel: A Novel*
Harris, Robert. *The Ghost: A Novel*
Harris, Robert. *An Officer and a Spy*
Higgins, Jack. *Confessional*
Higgins, Jack. *Eye of the Storm*
Higgins, Jack. *Touch the Devil*
Ignatius, David. *The Increment: A Novel*
Kaminsky, Stuart M. *To Catch a Spy: A Toby Peters Mystery*
Le Carre, John. *Agent Running in the Field*
Le Carre, John. ★*The Honourable Schoolboy*
Le Carre, John. *A Most Wanted Man: A Novel*
Le Carre, John. ★*Our Kind of Traitor: A Novel*
Le Carre, John. *Smiley's People*
Le Carre, John. *The Spy Who Came in from the Cold*
Le Carre, John. *The Tailor of Panama*
Le Carre, John. ★*Tinker, Tailor, Soldier, Spy*

Lehane, Dennis. *World Gone By: A Novel*
Ludlum, Robert. ★*The Bourne Identity*
Ludlum, Robert. *The Bourne Ultimatum*
Mankell, Henning. *The Troubled Man*
Matthews, Jason. ★*The Kremlin's Candidate*
Matthews, Jason. *Red Sparrow: A Novel*
Meacham, Leila. *Dragonfly: A Novel*
Meyer, Nicholas. *The Adventure of the Peculiar Protocols: Adapted from the Journals of John H. Watson, M.D.*
Murdoch, Iris. *The Nice and the Good*
Nguyen, Viet Thanh. ★*The Committed*
Nguyen, Viet Thanh. ★*The Sympathizer*
Parris, S. J. *Treachery*
Penelope, L. *Song of Blood and Stone*
Perry, Anne. ★*Death in Focus: An Elena Standish Novel*
Phillips, Arthur. ★*The King at the Edge of the World: Novel*
Quick, Amanda. *Otherwise Engaged*
Rabe, Peter. ★*Anatomy of a Killer ;: A Shroud for Jesso*
Reich, Christopher. ★*The Take*
Robinson, Peter. *All the Colors of Darkness*
Ruff, Matt. ★*88 Names*
Russell, Mary Doria. *Dreamers of the Day: A Novel*
Silva, Daniel. ★*The Black Widow*
Silva, Daniel. *The New Girl*
Silva, Daniel. *The Other Woman*
Steinhauer, Olen. *The Tourist*
Stewart, Amy. ★*Dear Miss Kopp*
Stross, Charles. *Empire Games*
Sullivan, Emily. *The Rebel and the Rake*
Wang, Kathy. *Impostor Syndrome: A Novel*
Wilkinson, Lauren. ★*American Spy: A Novel*
Wolfe, Gene. *The Land Across*
Wolfe, Suzanne M. *The Course of All Treasons*

SPIES — HISTORY
Parris, S. J. *Sacrilege*
*The **Spies** of Shilling Lane: A Novel*. Ryan, Jennifer
***Spies** of the Balkans: A Novel*. Furst, Alan
*The **Spies** of Warsaw*. Furst, Alan
***Spies**: a Novel*. Frayn, Michael
Spillane, Mickey
  The Consummata
  The Goliath Bone
  Kill Me, Darling
  A Long Time Dead: A Mike Hammer Casebook

SPIN CONTROL (PUBLIC RELATIONS)
Abrams, David. *Fobbit*

SPINAL MUSCULAR ATROPHY
Leitch, Will. ★*How Lucky*

Spindle Cove [Series]. Dare, Tessa
★***Spinning** Silver*. Novik, Naomi
Spiotta, Dana
  Wayward
Spires novels [Series]. Hall, Alexis

SPIRIT GUIDES
Camp, Bryan. *Gather the Fortunes*
***Spirit** of Steamboat: A Walt Longmire Story*. Johnson, Craig

SPIRIT POSSESSION
Castro, V. *Goddess of Filth*

Toro, Guillermo del. *The Hollow Ones*

SPIRITS
Arden, Katherine. ★*The Bear and the Nightingale*
Arden, Katherine. ★*The Girl in the Tower*
Arden, Katherine. ★*The Winter of the Witch*
Bonnaffons, Amy. *The Regrets*
Clark, P. Djeli. *The Black God's Drums*
Durst, Sarah Beth. *The Queen of Blood*
Ekwuyasi, Francesca. *Butter Honey Pig Bread: A Novel*
Hart, Carolyn G. *Ghost Blows a Kiss*
Murphy, Sara Flannery. *The Possessions*
Olson, Neil. *Before the Devil Fell*
Polk, C. L. *The Midnight Bargain*
Power, Susan. *The Grass Dancer*
Yoshimoto, Banana. *Moshi-Moshi*
***Spirits** Abroad and Other Stories*. Cho, Zen

SPIRITUAL FICTION
Coelho, Paulo. ★*The Alchemist*
Redfield, James. *The Celestine Prophecy: An Adventure*

SPIRITUAL JOURNEYS
Gao, XIngjian. *Soul Mountain*
Heacox, Kim. *Jimmy Bluefeather: A Novel*
Saunders, George. ★*Lincoln in the Bardo: A Novel*

SPIRITUAL LIFE
Redfield, James. *The Celestine Prophecy: An Adventure*

SPIRITUAL LIFE — BUDDHISM
Hesse, Hermann. ★*Siddhartha: A New Translation*

SPIRITUAL RETREATS
Temple, Emily. *The Lightness*

SPIRITUAL WARFARE
Gaiman, Neil. ★*American Gods: A Novel*

SPIRITUALISM
Murphy, Sara Flannery. *The Possessions*
Penny, Louise. *The Cruelest Month: A Three Pines Mystery*

SPIRITUALISTS
Bear, Elizabeth. *Stone Mad*

SPIRITUALITY
Allio, Kirstin. *Buddhism for Western Children: A Novel*
Bender, Tony. *The Last Ghost Dancer*
Cather, Willa. ★*Death Comes for the Archbishop*
Oe, Kenzaburo. *Somersault: A Novel*
Palmer, Ada. *Too Like the Lightning*
Walton, Jo. ★*Lent*
Williams, Joy. *Ninety-Nine Stories of God*
*The **Splendor** Before the Dark: A Novel of the Emperor Nero*. George, Margaret
*The **Splendor** of Silence: A Novel*. Sundaresan, Indu
*The **Split***. Bolton, S. J.

SPOILED CHILDREN
Szabo, Magda. *Abigail*
***Spoiler** Alert*. Dade, Olivia
***Spoils** of the Dead*. Stabenow, Dana

SPOKANE INDIAN RESERVATION
Alexie, Sherman. *Reservation Blues*

SPOKANE INDIANS
Alexie, Sherman. *Reservation Blues*

SPONTANEOUS COMBUSTION
Hill, Joe. *The Fireman: A Novel*

SPONTANEOUS HUMAN COMBUSTION

Wilson, Kevin. *Nothing to See Here*

Spook. Pronzini, Bill

Spooner. Dexter, Pete

SPORES

Hill, Joe. *The Fireman: A Novel*

★*The **Sport** of Kings*. Morgan, C. E.

SPORTS

Adiga, Aravind. *Selection Day*

Backman, Fredrik. ★*Beartown: A Novel*

Backman, Fredrik. *Us Against You: A Novel*

SPORTS BETTING — CORRUPT PRACTICES

DeSilva, Bruce. *A Scourge of Vipers*

SPORTS RIVALRY

Backman, Fredrik. *Us Against You: A Novel*

SPORTS ROMANCES

Adams, Lyssa Kay. *The Bromance Book Club*

James, Lorelei. *I Want You Back*

Martin, Alexa. *Fumbled*

Martin, Alexa. ★*Intercepted*

Phillips, Susan Elizabeth. *First Star I See Tonight*

Phillips, Susan Elizabeth. ★*Natural Born Charmer*

Phillips, Susan Elizabeth. ★*When Stars Collide*

Ryan, Kennedy. ★*Long Shot*

Van Dyken, Rachel. *Risky Play*

SPORTS TEAMS

Backman, Fredrik. ★*Beartown: A Novel*

SPORTS-AGENTS

Coben, Harlan. *Long Lost*

SPORTSWRITERS

Solomon, Rachel Lynn. *Weather Girl*

SPOUSES OF CLERGY

Greeley, Molly. *The Clergyman's Wife*

SPOUSES OF MURDER VICTIMS

Coben, Harlan. *Long Lost*

Sprawl trilogy [Series]. Gibson, William

★*Spring*. Smith, Ali

SPRING

Smith, Ali. ★*Spring*

Spring Snow. Mishima, Yukio

SPRINGER, JULIA (FICTITIOUS CHARACTER)

Ross, Ann B. *Miss Julia Delivers the Goods: A Novel*

Springtime in a Broken Mirror. Benedetti, Mario

Spufford, Francis

★*Golden Hill*

★*Light Perpetual*

SPY FICTION

Alfon, Dov. *A Long Night in Paris*

Bell, Ted. *Overkill: An Alex Hawke Novel*

Berenson, Alex. *The Deceivers*

Berenson, Alex. *The Faithful Spy: A Novel*

Berenson, Alex. *The Prisoner*

Black, Cara. ★*Three Hours in Paris*

Bradby, Tom. *Double Agent*

Buchan, John. *The Thirty-Nine Steps*

Buckley, William F. ★*Mongoose, R.I.P.: A Blackford Oakes Novel*

Cantrell, Christian. *Scorpion*

Christy, Bryan. *In the Company of Killers*

Clancy, Tom. *Clear and Present Danger*

Clements, Oliver. *The Eyes of the Queen*

Clements, Oliver. *The Queen's Men*

Coonts, Stephen. *The Armageddon File*

Coonts, Stephen. *The Art of War: A Novel*

Coonts, Stephen. ★*The Russia Account*

Cumming, Charles. *A Colder War*

Cumming, Charles. *A Divided Spy*

Cumming, Charles. *A Foreign Country*

Cumming, Charles. *The Moroccan Girl*

Cumming, Charles. ★*The Trinity Six*

Cussler, Clive. ★*Golden Buddha*

Cussler, Clive. *Sacred Stone*

Deighton, Len. *Berlin Game*

Downing, David. *Diary of a Dead Man on Leave*

Dugoni, Robert. *The Eighth Sister: A Thriller*

Dunmore, Helen. *Exposure*

Eisler, Barry. *The God's Eye View*

Eisler, Barry. *The Killer Collective*

Eliasberg, Jan. ★*Hannah's War*

Fesperman, Dan. *Safe Houses: A Novel*

Fleming, Ian. ★*Casino Royale: A James Bond Novel*

Fleming, Ian. *Doctor No*

Fleming, Ian. *From Russia with Love*

Fleming, Ian. ★*Goldfinger*

Fleming, Ian. *The Man with the Golden Gun*

Fleming, Ian. *On Her Majesty's Secret Service*

Fleming, Ian. *You Only Live Twice*

Follett, Ken. *Eye of the Needle*

Follett, Ken. *Hornet Flight*

Follett, Ken. *Jackdaws*

Forsyth, Frederick. *The Kill List*

Furst, Alan. *Blood of Victory: A Novel*

Furst, Alan. *Dark Voyage: A Novel*

Furst, Alan. *The Foreign Correspondent: A Novel*

Furst, Alan. ★*A Hero of France*

Furst, Alan. ★*Mission to Paris*

Furst, Alan. *Spies of the Balkans: A Novel*

Furst, Alan. *The Spies of Warsaw*

Furst, Alan. ★*Under Occupation: A Novel*

Gelernter, J. H. *Hold Fast*

Goldberg, Lee. *Fake Truth*

Greene, Graham. *The Human Factor*

Greene, Graham. *Our Man in Havana*

Hagberg, David. *Gambit*

Hall, Adam. *The Quiller Memorandum*

Harkaway, Nick. *Angelmaker*

Harris, Oliver. *A Shadow Intelligence*

Harris, Robert. *Enigma*

Hayes, Terry. *I Am Pilgrim*

Higgins, Jack. *Confessional*

Higgins, Jack. *Eye of the Storm*

Higgins, Jack. *Touch the Devil*

Ignatius, David. *The Increment: A Novel*

Jin, Ha. *A Map of Betrayal: A Novel*

Lawton, John. *Hammer to Fall*

Le Carre, John. *Agent Running in the Field*

Le Carre, John. ★*A Delicate Truth*

Le Carre, John. ★*The Honourable Schoolboy*
Le Carre, John. *A Most Wanted Man: A Novel*
Le Carre, John. ★*Our Kind of Traitor: A Novel*
Le Carre, John. *Smiley's People*
Le Carre, John. *The Spy Who Came in from the Cold*
Le Carre, John. *The Tailor of Panama*
Le Carre, John. ★*Tinker, Tailor, Soldier, Spy*
Littell, Robert. *The Company: A Novel of the Cia*
Matthews, Jason. ★*The Kremlin's Candidate*
Matthews, Jason. *Red Sparrow: A Novel*
Pavone, Chris. ★*The Expats: A Novel*
Pavone, Chris. *The Paris Diversion: A Novel*
Pearson, Ridley. *The Risk Agent*
Perry, Anne. ★*A Darker Reality*
Perry, Anne. *A Question of Betrayal*
Phillips, Arthur. ★*The King at the Edge of the World: Novel*
Pitoniak, Anna. ★*Our American Friend*
Porter, Henry. *The Bell Ringers*
Porter, Henry. *Firefly*
Porter, Henry. *The Old Enemy*
Porter, Henry. *White Hot Silence*
Priest, Cherie. *Clementine*
Quick, Amanda. *Otherwise Engaged*
Reich, Christopher. ★*The Take*
Sebastian, Tim. *Fatal Ally*
Silva, Daniel. ★*The Black Widow*
Silva, Daniel. ★*The Kill Artist: A Novel*
Silva, Daniel. *The New Girl*
Silva, Daniel. *The Other Woman*
Steinhauer, Olen. ★*All the Old Knives*
Steinhauer, Olen. *An American Spy*
Steinhauer, Olen. *The Cairo Affair*
Steinhauer, Olen. *The Last Tourist*
Steinhauer, Olen. *The Nearest Exit*
Steinhauer, Olen. *The Tourist*
Stross, Charles. *Empire Games*
Tanabe, Karin. ★*A Woman of Intelligence*
Wilkinson, Lauren. ★*American Spy: A Novel*
★*A **Spy** in the Struggle*. De Leon, Aya
*The **Spy** of Venice*. Brandreth, Benet
*The **Spy** Who Came in from the Cold*. Le Carre, John
Spymaster series [Series]. Bourne, Joanna
★*The **Spymaster's** Lady*. Bourne, Joanna
SQUATTERS
Auster, Paul. *Sunset Park*
Watkins, Claire Vaye. ★*Gold Fame Citrus*
★***Squeeze** Me: A Novel*. Hiaasen, Carl
SRI LANKA
Arudpragasam, Anuk. *The Story of a Brief Marriage*
Bala, Sharon. *The Boat People: A Novel*
Gunesekera, Romesh. ★*Suncatcher: A Novel*
Jayatissa, Amanda. ★*My Sweet Girl*
ST. ANDREWS, SCOTLAND
McDermid, Val. *The Distant Echo*
St. Aubyn, Edward
At Last
Double Blind

St. George, Harper
The Heiress Gets a Duke
St. James, Simone
The Broken Girls
The Haunting of Maddy Clare
The Sun Down Motel
ST. LOUIS, MISSOURI
Robinson, Marilynne. ★*Jack*
ST. PAUL, MINNESOTA
Franzen, Jonathan. ★*Freedom*
Sandford, John. *Buried Prey*
Sandford, John. *Field of Prey*
Sandford, John. ★*Silken Prey*
Sandford, John. *Storm Prey*
ST. PETERSBURG, RUSSIA
Benioff, David. *City of Thieves: A Novel*
Dean, Debra. *The Madonnas of Leningrad: A Novel*
Dostoyevsky, Fyodor. ★*Crime and Punishment*
Gogol, Nikolai Vasilievich. *The Collected Tales of Nikolai Gogol*
Stachniak, Eva. *The Chosen Maiden: A Novel*
ST. SIMON'S ISLAND, GEORGIA
Hauck, Rachel. *Once Upon a Prince*
STABBING VICTIMS
Child, Lee. *A Wanted Man*
Scott, Walter. *The Bride of Lammermoor*
Stabenow, Dana
★*A Deeper Sleep: A Kate Shugak Novel*
★*A Fine and Bitter Snow: A Kate Shugak Novel*
★*A Grave Denied*
★*Hunter's Moon*
Killing Grounds: A Kate Shugak Mystery
★*Less Than a Treason*
A Night Too Dark: A Kate Shugak Novel
No Fixed Line
Restless in the Grave
The Singing of the Dead
So Sure of Death: A Liam Campbell Mystery
Spoils of the Dead
★*A Taint in the Blood*
Though Not Dead: A Kate Shugak Novel
Whisper to the Blood: A Kate Shugak Novel
STABLES
Francis, Felix. *Crisis*
Stachniak, Eva
The Chosen Maiden: A Novel
The Winter Palace: A Novel of Catherine the Great
Stage, Zoje
★*Baby Teeth: A Novel*
Getaway
Wonderland
STAGED DEATHS
Clark, Mary Higgins. *The Melody Lingers On*
Currie, Ron. *Flimsy Little Plastic Miracles: A True Story*
Hannah, Sophie. *Keep Her Safe*
Martinson, T. J. *The Reign of the Kingfisher: A Novel*
Stalin's Ghost. Smith, Martin Cruz
STALIN, JOSEPH
Harris, Robert. *Archangel: A Novel*

Winterson, Jeanette. *The Passion*

STALINISM

Harris, Robert. *Archangel: A Novel*

Koestler, Arthur. *Darkness at Noon*

Stalker. Hampton, Brenda

STALKERS

Bannister, Jo. *Silent Footsteps*

Bolton, S. J. *Now You See Me*

Burns, Anna. *Milkman: A Novel*

Chavez, Heather. *No Bad Deed*

Feeney, Alice. ★*I Know Who You Are: A Novel*

Gerritsen, Tess. *The Surgeon*

Gowdy, Barbara. *Helpless: A Novel*

Hampton, Brenda. *Stalker*

Kantaria, Annabel. *I Know You: A Novel of Suspense*

Kelly, Erin. *Watch Her Fall*

Rankin, Ian. *Set in Darkness: An Inspector Rebus Novel*

Slaughter, Karin. ★*Pretty Girls: A Novel*

Stevens, Chevy. *Never Let You Go*

STALKING

Barker, Susan. ★*The Incarnations: A Novel*

Coben, Harlan. *Hold Tight*

French, Nicci. ★*The Day of the Dead: A Novel*

French, Nicci. *Sunday Silence*

Hill, Susan. *The Pure in Heart: A Simon Serrailler Crime Novel*

Koontz, Dean R. *The Darkest Evening of the Year*

Koontz, Dean R. *Intensity: A Novel*

Leon, Donna. *Falling in Love: A Commissario Guido Brunetti Mystery*

Paris, B. A. *The Breakdown*

Preston, Douglas J. *Thunderhead*

Quick, Amanda. *'til Death Do Us Part*

Rendell, Ruth. *End in Tears*

Schweblin, Samanta. *Little Eyes*

Stage, Zoje. *Getaway*

STALKING VICTIMS

Sparks, Nicholas. *The Guardian*

Stallion Gate. Smith, Martin Cruz

STAMP COLLECTING

Block, Lawrence. *Hit Me: A Keller Novel*

STAMP THEFTS

MacDonald, John D. *The Scarlet Ruse*

★*The Stand*. King, Stephen

STAND-UP COMEDY

Grossman, David. ★*A Horse Walks into a Bar*

Standing in the Rainbow: A Novel. Flagg, Fannie

Stanley, Michael

A Carrion Death

Deadly Harvest

A Death in the Family

Death of the Mantis

Dying to Live

Stansel, Ian

The Last Cowboys of San Geronimo

STANTON, ELIZABETH CADY

Piercy, Marge. *Sex Wars*

Sanders, Lawrence. ★*McNally's Gamble*

Staples, Dennis E.

This Town Sleeps

Stapley, Marissa

The Last Resort

A Star Called Henry. Doyle, Roddy

★*A Star Is Bored*. Lane, Byron

Star Island. Hiaasen, Carl

Star of Persia: Esther's Story. Smith, Jill Eileen

Star of the Sea. O'Connor, Joseph

A Star Shines Over Mt. Morris Park. Roth, Henry

★*Stardust*. Gaiman, Neil

Stark, Richard

Ask the Parrot: A Parker Novel

Breakout

Comeback

Dirty Money

The Hunter: A Parker Novel

The Jugger: A Parker Novel

Starless. Carey, Jacqueline

★*The Starless Sea*. Morgenstern, Erin

The Starlet and the Spy. Lee, Ji-Min

Starling, Caitlin

The Death of Jane Lawrence

The Luminous Dead

Starnone, Domenico

Ties

Trick

Starr, Melvin R.

Unhallowed Ground

STARS

Knausgaard, Karl Ove. *The Morning Star*

The Stars Are Legion. Hurley, Kameron

Stars in My Pocket Like Grains of Sand. Delany, Samuel R.

Stars in the Grass. Stewart, Ann Marie

The Stars Now Unclaimed. Williams, Drew

★*Starship Troopers*. Heinlein, Robert A.

Started Early, Took My Dog. Atkinson, Kate

The Startup Wife. Anam, Tahmima

★*A State of Freedom*. Mukherjee, Neel

★*State of Wonder: A Novel*. Patchett, Ann

STATE PARKS

Stabenow, Dana. *A Night Too Dark: A Kate Shugak Novel*

STATE POLICE

Adams, Taylor. *Hairpin Bridge*

Gardner, Lisa. *Alone*

Rosenfield, Kat. *No One Will Miss Her*

Stabenow, Dana. ★*A Fine and Bitter Snow: A Kate Shugak Novel*

Stabenow, Dana. *Restless in the Grave*

Stabenow, Dana. *So Sure of Death: A Liam Campbell Mystery*

Stabenow, Dana. *Spoils of the Dead*

Stabenow, Dana. ★*A Taint in the Blood*

The State We're In: Maine Stories. Beattie, Ann

STATE-SPONSORED TERRORISM

Erpenbeck, Jenny. *The Book of Words*

Fernandez, Nona. *The Twilight Zone*

Hugo, Victor. ★*Les Miserables*

Khadra, Yasmina. *The Swallows of Kabul: A Novel*

Le Guin, Ursula K. *Orsinian Tales*

Lewis, Sinclair. ★*It Can't Happen Here*
Moreno-Garcia, Silvia. ★*Velvet Was the Night*
Ruiz Zafon, Carlos. *The Labyrinth of the Spirits*
★*Station Eleven*. Mandel, Emily St. John
★*The Stationery Shop*. Kamali, Marjan
STATISTICS
    Penny, Louise. ★*The Madness of Crowds*
Statovci, Pajtim
    Bolla
STATUES
    Szabo, Magda. *Abigail*
Stay and Fight. ffitch, Madeline
Stay Hidden. Doiron, Paul
★*Stay with Me*. Adebayo, Ayobami
STAY-AT-HOME MOTHERS
    Daughters, Amy Weinland. *You Cannot Mess This Up: A True Story That Never Happened*
    Headley, Maria Dahvana. *The Mere Wife*
    Mina, Denise. *Conviction*
    Nicieza, Fabian. *Suburban Dicks*
    Tanabe, Karin. ★*A Woman of Intelligence*
    Yoder, Rachel. *Nightbitch*
★*Staying On: A Novel*. Scott, Paul
Stead, Christina
    ★*The Man Who Loved Children*
Steadman, Catherine
    The Disappearing Act
    Mr. Nobody: A Novel
    Something in the Water
Steal the North: A Novel. Bergstrom, Heather Brittain
STEALING
    Atkins, Ace. *The Redeemers*
    Beah, Ishmael. *Little Family*
    Benioff, David. *City of Thieves: A Novel*
    Berry, Steve. ★*The Warsaw Protocol*
    Blau, Jessica Anya. *The Wonder Bread Summer*
    Cussler, Clive. ★*The Chase*
    Eliot, George. ★*Silas Marner: The Weaver of Raveloe*
    Greer, Robert O. *First of State*
    Harrison, Thea. *Dragon Bound*
    Pryor, Mark. *Hollow Man*
    Skarmeta, Antonio. *The Dancer and the Thief: A Novel*
Stealth. Woods, Stuart
The Steam Pig. McClure, James
STEAMBOATS
    Conrad, Joseph. ★*Heart of Darkness*
STEAMPUNK
    Addison, Katherine. ★*The Goblin Emperor*
    Bear, Elizabeth. *Stone Mad*
    Ciotta, Beth. *Her Sky Cowboy*
    Clark, P. Djeli. *The Black God's Drums*
    Cogman, Genevieve. *The Invisible Library*
    Cogman, Genevieve. *The Masked City*
    Gilman, Felix. *The Half-Made World*
    Kadrey, Richard. *The Grand Dark*
    Levine, David D. *Arabella of Mars*
    Mieville, China. ★*Perdido Street Station*
    Polk, C. L. *Soulstar*

Polk, C. L. *Stormsong*
Polk, C. L. *Witchmark*
Priest, Cherie. *Boneshaker*
Priest, Cherie. *Clementine*
Priest, Cherie. *Dreadnought*
Priest, Cherie. *Ganymede*
Priest, Cherie. *The Inexplicables*
Pulley, Natasha. *The Bedlam Stacks*
Pulley, Natasha. *The Lost Future of Pepperharrow*
Pulley, Natasha. *The Watchmaker of Filigree Street*
Ryan, Anthony. *The Waking Fire*
Valentine, Genevieve. *Mechanique: A Tale of the Circus Tresaulti*
Wilson, Daniel H. *The Clockwork Dynasty: A Novel*
Yang, JY. *The Ascent to Godhood*
Yang, JY. *The Black Tides of Heaven*
Yang, JY. *The Descent of Monsters*
Yang, JY. *The Red Threads of Fortune*
Stedman, M. L.
    ★*The Light Between Oceans: A Novel*
Steel Crow Saga. Krueger, Paul
★*Steel Fear*. Webb, Brandon
The Steel Wave: A Novel of World War II. Shaara, Jeff
Steel, Danielle
    First Sight
Steele ops [Series]. Hunt, April
Steele, Allen M.
    Coyote: A Novel of Interstellar Exploration
STEEPLECHASING
    Francis, Dick. *Smokescreen*
Stegner, Wallace
    ★*Angle of Repose*
    ★*The Big Rock Candy Mountain*
    Crossing to Safety
Stein, Garth
    The Art of Racing in the Rain: A Novel
Stein, Gertrude
    ★*Three Lives*
Steinbeck, John
    Cannery Row
    ★*East of Eden*
    ★*The Grapes of Wrath*
    The Long Valley
    ★*Of Mice and Men*
    The Pearl
    Tortilla Flat
Steiner, Susie
    Missing, Presumed: A Novel
    ★*Persons Unknown: A Novel*
Steinhauer, Olen
    ★*All the Old Knives*
    An American Spy
    The Bridge of Sighs
    The Cairo Affair
    The Last Tourist
    The Middleman
    The Nearest Exit
    The Tourist

Steinke, Rene
 Holy Skirts
Steles of the Sky. Bear, Elizabeth
Stella Mooney mysteries [Series]. Lawrence, David
★*A Step* so Grave. McPherson, Catriona
STEPCHILDREN
 Barker, Pat. *Another World*
 Seo, Mi-Ae. *The Only Child*
 Trollope, Joanna. *Other People's Children*
STEPDAUGHTERS
 Edwards, Rachel. *Darling*
 Kelly, Cathy. *Secrets of a Happy Marriage*
 Quincy, Diana. *Her Night with the Duke*
 Scottoline, Lisa. ★*Come Home*
STEPFATHERS
 Allison, Dorothy. ★*Bastard Out of Carolina*
 Beattie, Ann. ★*Picturing Will*
 Dexter, Pete. *Spooner*
 Dickens, Charles. ★*David Copperfield*
 Lundrigan, Nicole. *Glass Boys: A Novel*
★*The Stepford* Wives: A Novel. Levin, Ira
Stephanie Plum mysteries [Series]. Evanovich, Janet
Stephens, Alice
 Famous Adopted People
Stephenson, Neal
 Anathem
 ★*Cryptonomicon*
 The Diamond Age,: Or, a Young Lady's Illustrated Primer
 ★*Fall Or, Dodge in Hell: A Novel*
 Reamde
 The Rise and Fall of D.O.D.O.: A Novel
 Seveneves
 ★*Snow Crash*
STEPMOTHERS
 Edwards, Rachel. *Darling*
 Morante, Elsa. *Arturo's Island: A Novel*
 Murphy, Julie. *If the Shoe Fits*
 Patchett, Ann. ★*The Dutch House: A Novel*
 Quinn, Julia. ★*An Offer from a Gentleman*
 Trollope, Joanna. *Other People's Children*
★*Steppenwolf*. Hesse, Hermann
STEPSIBLINGS
 Chen, Da. *Brothers: A Novel*
 Draper, Sharon M. ★*Forged by Fire*
 Mosley, Walter. *Fortunate Son: A Novel*
 Patchett, Ann. ★*Commonwealth*
 Wharton, Edith. *The Children*
STEPSISTERS
 Evison, Jonathan. *All About Lulu: A Novel*
 Krentz, Jayne Ann. *When All the Girls Have Gone*
STEREOTYPES (SOCIAL PSYCHOLOGY)
 Aboulela, Leila. *Elsewhere, Home*
 Yu, Charles. ★*Interior Chinatown*
Sterling, Bruce
 Pirate Utopia
Sterling, Erin
 The Ex Hex

Sternbergh, Adam
 The Blinds
Stevens, Chevy
 Never Let You Go
 Still Missing
Stevens, Francis
 The Heads of Cerberus
Stevenson, Robert Louis
 ★*The Strange Case of Dr. Jekyll and Mr. Hyde*
Stewart, Amy
 ★*Dear Miss Kopp*
 ★*Girl Waits with Gun*
 Kopp Sisters on the March
 Lady Cop Makes Trouble
 ★*Miss Kopp Investigates*
 ★*Miss Kopp Just Won't Quit*
 Miss Kopp's Midnight Confessions
Stewart, Ann Marie
 Stars in the Grass
Stewart, George R.
 Earth Abides
Stewart, Mary
 ★*The Crystal Cave*
 ★*The Hollow Hills*
 The Last Enchantment
 Nine Coaches Waiting
 The Wicked Day
Sthers, Amanda
 Holy Lands: A Novel
Stibbe, Nina
 Reasons to Be Cheerful
STIGMATIZATION
 Hansen, Ron. *Mariette in Ecstasy*
 Picoult, Jodi. *Keeping Faith: A Novel*
Still Dirty: A Novel. Stringer, Vickie M.
★*Still Life*. McDermid, Val
Still Life. Parrish, Christa
Still Life. Penny, Louise
Still Missing. Stevens, Chevy
Stillicide. Jones, Cynan
The Stills. Montgomery, Jess
The Stingaree. Brand, Max
Stirling, S. M.
 Dies the Fire
 A Meeting at Corvallis
 The Protector's War
Stivers, Carole
 The Mother Code
STOCK MARKET
 Sanders, Lawrence. *The Timothy Files*
 Sanders, Lawrence. *Timothy's Game*
Stockett, Kathryn
 ★*The Help*
STOCKHOLM, SWEDEN
 Akinmade-Akerstrom, Lola. *In Every Mirror She's Black*
 Dahl, Arne. *Bad Blood*
 Dahl, Arne. *Misterioso: A Crime Novel*
 De la Motte, Anders. *MemoRandom: A Thriller*

De la Motte, Anders. *Ultimatum: A Thriller*
Kepler, Lars. *The Sandman*
Persson Giolito, Malin. *Quicksand*
Sjowall, Maj. ★*Cop Killer: The Story of a Crime*
Sjowall, Maj. ★*The Laughing Policeman*
Sjowall, Maj. ★*The Locked Room: The Story of a Crime*
Sjowall, Maj. *The Man on the Balcony: The Story of a Crime*
Sjowall, Maj. ★*Murder at the Savoy*

Stoker, Bram
  ★*Dracula*
  The New Annotated Dracula
STOKER, BRAM
  Collins, Kathleen. *Notes from a Black Woman's Diary: Selected Works of Kathleen Collins*
  Robbins, David L. *Last Citadel: A Novel of the Battle of Kursk*
  Stoker, Bram. *The New Annotated Dracula*
  Stoker, Dacre. *Dracul*
Stoker, Dacre
  Dracul
*The **Stolen** Child*. Donohue, Keith
*The **Stolen** Gold Affair*. Pronzini, Bill
*The **Stolen** Lady*. Morelli, Laura
STOLEN MONEY
  Kennedy, Randy. *Presidio*
  Mosley, Walter. ★*Blood Grove*
STOLEN PROPERTY RECOVERY
  Aaronovitch, Ben. *Broken Homes*
  Hiaasen, Carl. *Lucky You: A Novel*
  Pelecanos, George P. *The Cut: A Novel*
  Peters, Ellis. *The Holy Thief*
  Ramsay, Frederick. *Countdown*
  Reich, Christopher. ★*The Take*
  Ridley, Erica. *The Duke Heist*
  Rozan, S. J. *The Shanghai Moon: A Lydia Chin/Bill Smith Novel*
  Spillane, Mickey. *The Consummata*
STONE AGE
  Auel, Jean M. ★*The Clan of the Cave Bear: A Novel*
  Golding, William. *The Inheritors*
Stone Barrington novels [Series]. Woods, Stuart
STONE BUILDING
  Follett, Ken. ★*The Pillars of the Earth*
*The **Stone** Circle*. Griffiths, Elly
Stone Cold Heart. Frear, Caz
★*The **Stone** Diaries*. Shields, Carol
*The **Stone** in the Skull*. Bear, Elizabeth
Stone Mad. Bear, Elizabeth
★*Stone Mattress: Nine Tales*. Atwood, Margaret
*The **Stone** Monkey: A Lincoln Rhyme Novel*. Deaver, Jeffery
*The **Stone** Sky*. Jemisin, N. K.
Stone's Fall. Pears, Iain
Stone, Irving
  ★*The Agony and the Ecstasy: A Biographical Novel of Michelangelo*
  Lust for Life: A Novel of Vincent Van Gogh
Stone, Nick
  The Verdict
STONE, OLIVER (FICTITIOUS CHARACTER)
  Baldacci, David. *Hell's Corner*
Stonecutter's Story. Saberhagen, Fred

STONEHENGE, ENGLAND
  Rutherfurd, Edward. *Sarum: The Novel of England*
STONEMASONS
  Hardy, Thomas. ★*Jude the Obscure*
*The **Stones** Cry Out*. Okuizumi, Hikaru
★*Stones for Ibarra*. Doerr, Harriet
Stones from the River. Hegi, Ursula
STONING
  Jackson, Shirley. ★*The Lottery: And Other Stories*
*The **Stories** of Elizabeth Spencer*. Spencer, Elizabeth
*The **Stories** of Eva Luna*. Allende, Isabel
*The **Stories** of Richard Bausch*. Bausch, Richard
*The **Stories** of Vladimir Nabokov*. Nabokov, Vladimir Vladimirovich
★*Stories of Your Life and Others*. Chiang, Ted
STORIES TOLD BY ANIMALS
  Auster, Paul. *Timbuktu: A Novel*
  Buxton, Kira Jane. ★*Hollow Kingdom*
  Cameron, W. Bruce. *A Dog's Promise*
  Quinn, Spencer. *Dog on It: A Chet and Bernie Mystery*
  Quinn, Spencer. ★*It's a Wonderful Woof*
  Rooney, Kathleen. ★*Cher Ami and Major Whittlesey*
  Savage, Sam. *Firmin: Adventures of a Metropolitan Lowlife*
  Smiley, Jane. *Horse Heaven*
  Stein, Garth. *The Art of Racing in the Rain: A Novel*
Stories, Essays & Memoir. Welty, Eudora
Storm Front. Sandford, John
*The **Storm** Murders: A Thriller*. Farrow, John
Storm of Locusts. Roanhorse, Rebecca
★*A **Storm** of Swords*. Martin, George R. R.
Storm Prey. Sandford, John
STORMS
  Foley, Lucy. *The Guest List*
  Hargrave, Kiran Millwood. *The Mercies: A Novel*
  Longworth, M. L. *Murder on the Ile Sordou: A Verlaque and Bonnet Provencal Mystery*
Stormsong. Polk, C. L.
*The **Story** of a Brief Marriage*. Arudpragasam, Anuk
Story of a crime trilogy [Series]. Persson, Leif G. W.
*The **Story** of a New Name*. Ferrante, Elena
*The **Story** of Arthur Truluv: A Novel*. Berg, Elizabeth
*The **Story** of the Lost Child*. Ferrante, Elena
*The **Storyteller***. Picoult, Jodi
STORYTELLERS
  Rushdie, Salman. *The Enchantress of Florence: A Novel*
  Rushdie, Salman. *Haroun and the Sea of Stories*
STORYTELLING
  Acevedo, Chantel. *The Distant Marvels*
  Allende, Isabel. ★*Eva Luna*
  Barth, John. *Chimera*
  Barth, John. *The Last Voyage of Somebody the Sailor*
  Bradbury, Ray. *The Illustrated Man*
  Calvino, Italo. *Invisible Cities*
  Coetzee, J. M. *Elizabeth Costello*
  Eco, Umberto. *Baudolino*
  Ferris, Joshua. *A Calling for Charlie Barnes*
  Ghosh, Amitav. ★*Gun Island*
  Martel, Yann. ★*Life of Pi: A Novel*
  Ramadan, Ahmad Danny. *The Clothesline Swing*

Rushdie, Salman. *Haroun and the Sea of Stories*
Setterfield, Diane. ★*Once Upon a River*
Shalev, Meir. *Two She-Bears: A Novel*
Shaykh, Hanan. ★*One Thousand and One Nights: A Sparkling Retelling of the Beloved Classic*
Ugresic, Dubravka. *Fox*
Wiesel, Elie. *Hostage*
Yu, E. Lily. ★*On Fragile Waves*

Stout, Dan
  ★*Titanshade*

Stout, Rex
  The Doorbell Rang
  ★*Gambit*

STOWAWAYS
  Afshar, Tessa. *Jewel of the Nile*
  Holdstock, Pauline. *Here I Am!*
  Phillips, Caryl. *Foreigners*
  Poe, Edgar Allan. *The Narrative of Arthur Gordon Pym of Nantucket*

Stowe, Harriet Beecher
  ★*Uncle Tom's Cabin*

Stradal, J. Ryan
  ★*The Lager Queen of Minnesota*

Straight Man. Russo, Richard

Straight, Susan
  A Million Nightingales

Straley, John
  The Big Both Ways

Strange Affair. Robinson, Peter
★*The Strange Case of Dr. Jekyll and Mr. Hyde*. Stevenson, Robert Louis
The Strange Case of the Alchemist's Daughter. Goss, Theodora
The Strange Fate of Kitty Easton. Speller, Elizabeth
★*Strange Pilgrims: Twelve Stories*. Garcia Marquez, Gabriel
★*Strange Practice*. Shaw, Vivian
Strange Shores: An Inspector Erlendur Novel. Indriðason, Arnaldur
Strange Weather: Four Short Novels. Hill, Joe
★*A Strangeness in My Mind: A Novel*. Pamuk, Orhan
★*The Stranger*. Camus, Albert
The Stranger. Coben, Harlan
A Stranger at the Door. Pinter, Jason
The Stranger Diaries. Griffiths, Elly
★*Stranger in a Strange Land*. Heinlein, Robert A.
The Stranger in the Lifeboat. Albom, Mitch
★*The Stranger Inside*. Unger, Lisa

STRANGERS
  Alam, Rumaan. ★*Leave the World Behind: A Novel*
  Barry, Jessica. ★*Don't Turn Around*
  Bradbury, Jamey. *The Wild Inside: A Novel*
  Camus, Albert. ★*The Fall*
  Chambers, Becky. ★*The Galaxy, and the Ground Within*
  Christie, Agatha. *And Then There Were None*
  Coben, Harlan. *The Stranger*
  Colgan, Jenny. *500 Miles from You*
  Cossette, Connilyn. ★*Shelter of the Most High*
  Danan, Rosie. *The Roommate*
  Finder, Joseph. ★*Judgment*
  Fleischmann, Raymond. *How Quickly She Disappears*
  Garvin, Eileen. *The Music of Bees*
  Gosling, Victoria. *Before the Ruins: A Novel*

Hendrix, Grady. *The Southern Book Club's Guide to Slaying Vampires*
Kawakami, Mieko. *Ms. Ice Sandwich*
Lacey, Catherine. ★*Pew: A Novel*
Levy, Deborah. *Swimming Home: A Novel*
Lippman, Laura. ★*Sunburn*
Lu, S. Qiouyi. *In the Watchful City*
Malouf, David. *Remembering Babylon*
Moriarty, Liane. *Nine Perfect Strangers*
Moss, Sarah. *Summerwater*
Murdoch, Iris. *The Green Knight*
Oakley, Colleen. *You Were There Too*
Ross, Ann B. *Miss Julia Knows a Thing or Two*
Smith, Ali. *The Accidental*
Sparks, Nicholas. *Every Breath*
Swanson, Peter. *The Kind Worth Killing: A Novel*
Tremblay, Paul. ★*The Cabin at the End of the World: A Novel*

★*Strangers and Brothers*. Snow, C. P.
Strangers and brothers [Series]. Snow, C. P.
Strangers at the Gate. McPherson, Catriona
Strangers She Knows. Dodd, Christina
The Strangler Vine. Carter, Miranda

STRANGLING
  Higashino, Keigo. *Malice*
  Higashino, Keigo. *Newcomer*

STRASBOURG, FRANCE
  Rushdie, Salman. *Shalimar the Clown: A Novel*

STRATEGIC ALLIANCES (MILITARY)
  Poyer, David. *Overthrow: The War with China and North Korea—Fall of an Empire*
  Poyer, David. *Violent Peace: The War with China - Aftermath of Armageddon*
  Priest, Cherie. *Clementine*
  Vachss, Andrew H. *Two Trains Running*

Stratford, Sarah-Jane
  Red Letter Days

STRATFORD-UPON-AVON, ENGLAND
  O'Farrell, Maggie. *Hamnet*

Straub, Emma
  ★*All Adults Here*
  ★*Modern Lovers*
  The Vacationers

Straub, Peter
  ★*A Dark Matter: A Novel*
  ★*Ghost Story*
  Lost Boy Lost Girl: A Novel
  Mr. X
  ★*Mystery*

★*The Street*. Petry, Ann
Street Dreams. K'wan

STREET LIFE
  Ashley & JaQuavis. *The Cartel*
  Bush, Keisha. *No Heaven for Good Boys: A Novel*
  Capri, NeNe. *The Pussy Trap*
  Capri, NeNe. *The Pussy Trap; Part 3*
  Clark, Wahida. *Blood, Sweat and Payback*
  Clark, Wahida. *Payback Ain't Enough*
  Clark, Wahida. ★*Payback Is a Mutha*

Holmes, Shannon. ★*B-More Careful: A Novel*
K'wan. *Animal*
K'wan. *Animal II: The Omen*
K'wan. *The Diamond Empire*
K'wan. ★*Diamonds and Pearl*
K'wan. *The Fix*
K'wan. *Gutter*
K'wan. *Hoodlum*
K'wan. *Revelations*
Pochoda, Ivy. ★*These Women*
Quartey, Kwei. *Children of the Street: A Novel*
Santiago, Danny. *Famous All Over Town*
Sapphire. *American Dreams*
Sister Souljah. ★*The Coldest Winter Ever: A Novel*
Sister Souljah. ★*A Deeper Love Inside: The Porsche Santiaga Story*
Speight, Shameek A. *The Pleasure of Pain*
Stringer, Vickie M. ★*Let That Be the Reason*
Stringer, Vickie M. *Still Dirty: A Novel*
Styles, Toy. *Black and Ugly*
Styles, Toy. *A Hustler's Son: A Novel*
Swinson, Kiki. *Lifestyles of the Rich and Shameless*
Swinson, Kiki. *Wifey*
Swinson, Kiki. *Wifey's Next Sticky Situation*
T. I. *Power & Beauty: A Love Story of Life on the Streets*
T. I. *Trouble & Triumph: A Novel of Power & Beauty*
Tyree, Omar. ★*Flyy Girl*

STREET MUSICIANS
Petrie, Nicholas. *Tear It Down*
Smith, Julie. *Jazz Funeral*
*The **Street** of a Thousand Blossoms*. Tsukiyama, Gail
STREET VENDORS
Gilman, Susan Jane. *The Ice Cream Queen of Orchard Street: A Novel*
Pamuk, Orhan. ★*A Strangeness in My Mind: A Novel*
★*Streets of Laredo: A Novel*. McMurtry, Larry
STRENGTH AND WEAKNESS
Haigh, Jennifer. *Mrs. Kimble: A Novel*
STRESS
Cosimano, Elle. *Finlay Donovan Is Killing It*
STRESS IN MEN
Powers, Kevin. ★*The Yellow Birds: A Novel*
STRESS MANAGEMENT
Dev, Sonali. ★*Incense and Sensibility*
Stridsberg, Sara
Valerie: Or the Faculty of Dreams : Amendment to the Theory of Sexuality
STRIKEBREAKERS
Kesey, Ken. *Sometimes a Great Notion: A Novel*
STRIKES
Harvey, John. *Darkness, Darkness*
Kesey, Ken. *Sometimes a Great Notion: A Novel*
Lehane, Dennis. ★*The Given Day*
Spencer, Sally. *Lambs to the Slaughter*
STRIKES — COAL MINERS
Zola, Emile. ★*Germinal*
STRING QUARTETS (GROUPS)
Gabel, Aja. *The Ensemble: A Novel*
STRINGED INSTRUMENTS
Gabel, Aja. *The Ensemble: A Novel*

Stringer, Vickie M.
Dirty Red: A Novel
★*Let That Be the Reason*
Still Dirty: A Novel
Strip Tease: A Novel. Hiaasen, Carl
STRIPTEASERS
Barry, Dave. *Insane City*
Flanagan, Richard. *The Unknown Terrorist*
Hiaasen, Carl. *Strip Tease: A Novel*
Stroby, Wallace
Some Die Nameless
Stross, Charles
Accelerando
Empire Games
Glasshouse
Neptune's Brood
Saturn's Children: A Space Opera
Stroud, Carsten
The Shimmer
Strout, Elizabeth
Amy and Isabelle: A Novel
★*Anything Is Possible: Fiction*
★*The Burgess Boys: A Novel*
My Name Is Lucy Barton
★*Oh William!*
Olive Kitteridge
★*Olive, Again: A Novel*
STUART PERIOD (1603-1714)
Blackmore, R. D. *Lorna Doone: A Romance of Exmoor*
Blakemore, A. K. *The Manningtree Witches*
Du Maurier, Daphne. *Frenchman's Creek*
Gregory, Philippa. *Tidelands*
Hart, Elsa. *The Cabinets of Barnaby Mayne*
London, Julia. *Wild Wicked Scot*
Phillips, Christi. *The Devlin Diary*
Stuart, Douglas
★*Shuggie Bain*
Stubborn Archivist. Rodrigues Fowler, Yara
STUDENT EXCHANGE PROGRAMS
Hao, Jingfang. *Vagabonds: A Novel*
STUDENT ORGANIZATIONS
Ayatsuji, Yukito. *The Decagon House Murders*
STUDENT SUSPENSION
Carr, Brian Allen. ★*Opioid, Indiana*
STUDENTS
Blau, Jessica Anya. *The Wonder Bread Summer*
Orringer, Julie. ★*The Invisible Bridge: A Novel*
Pears, Iain. *An Instance of the Fingerpost*
Shreve, Anita. *Testimony: A Novel*
STUDENTS — PERSONAL CONDUCT
Vargas Llosa, Mario. *The Time of the Hero*
Studies in scandal novels [Series]. Collins, Manda
*A **Study** in Honor: A Novel*. O'Dell, Claire
STUDYING ABROAD
Lee, Chang-Rae. ★*My Year Abroad*
Whelan, Julia. *My Oxford Year*
STUFFED ANIMALS (TOYS)
Davys, Tim. *Amberville*

Schweblin, Samanta. *Little Eyes*

STUFFED TIGERS (TOYS)
Cargill, C. Robert. *Day Zero*

STUNT PERFORMERS
Marsh, Nicola. *The Boy Toy*
Sallis, James. *Drive*
Woods, Stuart. *The Money Shot*

STUNTS
Anders, Charlie Jane. *Rock Manning Goes for Broke*

STURGIS, MILO (FICTITIOUS CHARACTER)
Kellerman, Jonathan. *Bones: An Alex Delaware Novel*

STUTTERERS
Mitchell, David. *Black Swan Green: A Novel*

Styles, Toy
Black and Ugly
A Hustler's Son: A Novel
Raunchy
Raunchy 2: Mad's Love
Redbone
★*War*
War 2: All Hell Breaks Loose

Styron, William
The Confessions of Nat Turner
Lie Down in Darkness
★*Sophie's Choice*

Suarez, Daniel
Change Agent: A Novel

SUB-SAHARAN AFRICA
Akpan, Uwem. *Say You're One of Them*
Naipaul, V. S. *A Bend in the River*

SUBCULTURES
Pessl, Marisha. *Night Film: A Novel*

SUBMARINE WARFARE
Beach, Edward L. *Run Silent, Run Deep*

SUBMARINES
Cussler, Clive. ★*Sea of Greed: A Novel from the Numa Files*
Deutermann, Peter T. *The Iceman*
Priest, Cherie. *Ganymede*

SUBMARINES, AMERICAN
Beach, Edward L. *Run Silent, Run Deep*

SUBMARINES, SOVIET
Clancy, Tom. ★*The Hunt for Red October*

Submission. Houellebecq, Michel

The Substitution Order. Clark, Martin

Suburban Dicks. Nicieza, Fabian

SUBURBAN FAMILIES
Cheever, John. *Falconer*
Eugenides, Jeffrey. ★*The Virgin Suicides*

SUBURBAN LIFE
Acampora, Lauren. *The Wonder Garden*
Ajvide Lindqvist, John. *Let the Right One In*
Boyle, T. Coraghessan. ★*The Tortilla Curtain*
Cheever, John. *Bullet Park: A Novel*
Ellis, Bret Easton. *Lunar Park*
Eugenides, Jeffrey. ★*Middlesex*
Fabry, Chris. *War Room: Prayer Is a Powerful Weapon*
Langan, Sarah. *Good Neighbors*
Laskowski, Tara. *The Mother Next Door*

Levin, Ira. ★*The Stepford Wives: A Novel*
McDermott, Alice. ★*That Night*
McLean, Felicity. *The Van Apfel Girls Are Gone*
Moriarty, Liane. *Big Little Lies*
Nicieza, Fabian. *Suburban Dicks*
Paris, B. A. *Behind Closed Doors*
Perrotta, Tom. *Little Children*
Satyal, Rakesh. *No One Can Pronounce My Name: A Novel*
Unger, Lisa. ★*The Stranger Inside*
Updike, John. ★*The Witches of Eastwick*
Wilson, Sloan. ★*The Man in the Gray Flannel Suit*

SUBURBS
Cosimano, Elle. *Finlay Donovan Is Killing It*
Fowler, Therese. ★*A Good Neighborhood*
Laskowski, Tara. *The Mother Next Door*
McLean, Felicity. *The Van Apfel Girls Are Gone*
Sathian, Sanjena. *Gold Diggers*

SUBVERSIVE ACTIVITIES
Harkaway, Nick. *Gnomon: A Novel*

SUBWAY PASSENGERS
McQuiston, Casey. ★*One Last Stop*

SUCCESS (CONCEPT)
Balasubramanyam, Rajeev. *Professor Chandra Follows His Bliss: A Novel*
Baldwin, Joshua. *The Wilshire Sun*
Cusset, Catherine. *Life of David Hockney: A Novel*
Dee, Jonathan. *The Privileges: A Novel*
Dorn, L. R. *The Anatomy of Desire*
Dreiser, Theodore. ★*An American Tragedy*
Dreiser, Theodore. ★*Sister Carrie*
Lalli, Sonya. *Serena Singh Flips the Script*
Riley, Vanessa. ★*Island Queen*
Shanbhag, Vivek. *Ghachar Ghochar*
Wolitzer, Meg. *The Interestings*

★*Such a Fun Age*. Reid, Kiley

SUDAN
Eggers, Dave. *What Is the What: The Autobiography of Valentino Achak Deng*

SUDDEN INFANT DEATH SYNDROME
Palahniuk, Chuck. *Lullaby: A Novel*

Sudden Prey. Sandford, John

Suffer the Children. Black, Lisa

SUFFERING
Brockmeier, Kevin. *The Illumination*
Gyasi, Yaa. ★*Transcendent Kingdom*
Palahniuk, Chuck. *The Invention of Sound*
Perry, Sarah. *Melmoth: A Novel*

SUFFERING IN MEN
Dostoyevsky, Fyodor. *Notes from Underground*

SUFFOLK, ENGLAND
French, Nicci. *Friday on My Mind: A Frieda Klein Mystery*
French, Nicci. *Thursday's Children*

SUFFRAGE
Follett, Ken. *Fall of Giants*

SUFFRAGIST MOVEMENT
Dunmore, Evie. ★*Bringing Down the Duke*
Fowler, Therese. *A Well-Behaved Woman: A Novel of the Vanderbilts*

SUFFRAGISTS
Dann, Patty. *The Wright Sister*
Johnson, D. E. *Detroit Shuffle*
Piercy, Marge. *Sex Wars*

SUGAR INDUSTRY AND TRADE
Hiaasen, Carl. *Strip Tease: A Novel*

SUGAR INDUSTRY AND TRADE — CORRUPT PRACTICES
Hiaasen, Carl. *Strip Tease: A Novel*

SUGAR PLANTATIONS
Willig, Lauren. *The Summer Country: A Novel*

SUICIDAL BEHAVIOR
Altan, Ahmet. ★*Love in the Days of Rebellion*
Backman, Fredrik. *A Man Called Ove*
Chiaverini, Jennifer. *Mrs. Lincoln's Sisters*

SUICIDE
Banasky, Carmiel. *The Suicide of Claire Bishop*
Barry, Brunonia. *The Map of True Places*
Barth, John. ★*The Floating Opera*
Baxter, Charles. *Saul and Patsy*
Chandler, Raymond. *The Long Goodbye*
Christie, Agatha. ★*The Murder of Roger Ackroyd: A Hercule Poirot Mystery*
Christie, Agatha. *Towards Zero*
Cullen, Helen. *The Dazzling Truth*
Deaver, Jeffery. ★*The Goodbye Man*
Dodd, Christina. *Because I'm Watching*
Enger, Lin. *Undiscovered Country: A Novel*
Eugenides, Jeffrey. ★*The Virgin Suicides*
Faulkner, William. ★*The Sound and the Fury*
Fitch, Janet. *Paint It Black: A Novel*
Gardiner, Meg. *The Dirty Secrets Club*
Hummel, Maria. *Lesson in Red*
James, P. D. *An Unsuitable Job for a Woman*
King, Stephen. *End of Watch: A Novel*
Muller, Marcia. *Dead Midnight*
Oe, Kenzaburo. *The Changeling*
Pamuk, Orhan. ★*Snow*
Pessl, Marisha. *Night Film: A Novel*
Potenza, Carol. *Hearts of the Missing*
Preston, Douglas J. *Verses for the Dead*
Pronzini, Bill. *Illusions*
Rankin, Ian. *The Impossible Dead*
Sanders, Lawrence. *The Tenth Commandment: A Novel*
Styron, William. *Lie Down in Darkness*

SUICIDE BOMBERS
Khadra, Yasmina. ★*Khalil: A Novel*
Pavone, Chris. *The Paris Diversion: A Novel*
Robb, J. D. *Leverage in Death: An Eve Dallas Novel*

SUICIDE BOMBINGS
McCann, Colum. ★*Apeirogon: A Novel*

SUICIDE INVESTIGATION
Adams, Taylor. *Hairpin Bridge*
Atkins, Ace. *The Shameless*
Billingham, Mark. ★*Their Little Secret*
Elias, Gerald. ★*Death and Transfiguration: A Daniel Jacobus Novel*
Galbraith, Robert. *The Cuckoo's Calling*
George, Elizabeth. *The Punishment She Deserves*
Gerritsen, Tess. *Choose Me*

Hill Gumbao, Toni. *The Good Suicides: A Thriller*
Johnson, Craig. *Land of Wolves*
Pronzini, Bill. *Illusions*
Qiu, Xiaolong. *Enigma of China*
Robinson, Peter. ★*Careless Love*
Smith, Ian. *Wolf Point*
Speller, Elizabeth. *The Return of Captain John Emmett*
Starr, Melvin R. *Unhallowed Ground*

The Suicide Motor Club. Buehlman, Christopher

SUICIDE NOTES
Abbott, Jeff. *Blame*

The Suicide of Claire Bishop. Banasky, Carmiel

SUICIDE PACTS
Shriver, Lionel. *Should We Stay or Should We Go*

SUICIDE VICTIMS
Bartz, Andrea. *The Lost Night*
Goenawan, Clarissa. *The Perfect World of Miwako Sumida*
Hill Gumbao, Toni. *The Good Suicides: A Thriller*
Littell, Robert. *The Mayakovsky Tapes: A Novel*
St. James, Simone. *The Haunting of Maddy Clare*
Straub, Peter. *Lost Boy Lost Girl: A Novel*

SUING (LAW)
Delaney, J. P. *Playing Nice*
Picoult, Jodi. ★*My Sister's Keeper*
Richler, Mordecai. *Solomon Gursky Was Here*
Scottoline, Lisa. *Feared*

★*A Suitable Boy: A Novel*. Seth, Vikram

Sula. Morrison, Toni

Sullivan's Crossing [Series]. Carr, Robyn

Sullivan, Emily
The Rebel and the Rake

Sullivan, J. Courtney
Friends and Strangers

Sullivan, Michael J.
Theft of Swords

SULTANS
Altan, Ahmet. ★*Love in the Days of Rebellion*

★*Summer*. Smith, Ali

SUMMER
Aciman, Andre. *Call Me by Your Name*
Andrews, Donna. *Murder Most Fowl: A Meg Langslow Mystery*
Bender, Tony. *The Last Ghost Dancer*
Boyd, William. *Trio*
Foster, Brooke Lea. *Summer Darlings*
Giordano, Paolo. *Heaven and Earth*
Henry, Emily. *People We Meet on Vacation*
Hilderbrand, Elin. ★*28 Summers*
Hilderbrand, Elin. *The Perfect Couple*
Hostin, Sunny. ★*Summer on the Bluffs*
Knausgaard, Karl Ove. *The Morning Star*
Mallery, Susan. *The Summer of Sunshine and Margot*
Moss, Sarah. *Summerwater*
Poeppel, Amy. *Musical Chairs: A Novel*
Reid, Taylor Jenkins. ★*Malibu Rising*
Temple, Emily. *The Lightness*

The Summer Before the War: A Novel. Simonson, Helen

SUMMER CAMPS
Butler, Nickolas. ★*The Hearts of Men*

Sager, Riley. *The Last Time I Lied: A Novel*

Shipman, Viola. *The Clover Girls*

Swarthout, Glendon. *Bless the Beasts and Children*

The **Summer** *Country: A Novel*. Willig, Lauren

Summer *Darlings*. Foster, Brooke Lea

The **Summer** *Guest*. Anderson, Alison

The **Summer** *List*. Doan, Amy Mason

★**Summer** *of '69*. Hilderbrand, Elin

The **Summer** *of Dead Toys*. Hill Gumbao, Toni

★The **Summer** *of Lost and Found*. Monroe, Mary Alice

The **Summer** *of Sunshine and Margot*. Mallery, Susan

Summer *on Moonlight Bay*. Ramsay, Hope

★**Summer** *on the Bluffs*. Hostin, Sunny

The **Summer** *Tree*. Kay, Guy Gavriel

The **Summer** *We Lost Her: A Novel*. Cohen, Tish

The **Summer** *Wives*. Williams, Beatriz

Summerlong. Beagle, Peter S.

Summertime: *Scenes from a Provincial Life*. Coetzee, J. M.

Summerwater. Moss, Sarah

SUMO WRESTLING

Tsukiyama, Gail. *The Street of a Thousand Blossoms*

★The **Sun** *Also Rises*. Hemingway, Ernest

Sun chronicles [Series]. Elliott, Kate

★The **Sun** *Collective*. Baxter, Charles

The **Sun** *Down Motel*. St. James, Simone

Sun-Daughters, *Sea-Daughters*. Ogden, Aimee

★**Sunburn**. Lippman, Laura

★**Suncatcher:** *a Novel*. Gunesekera, Romesh

SUNDARBANS (BANGLADESH AND INDIA)

Ghosh, Amitav. *The Hungry Tide*

Sundaresan, Indu

The Splendor of Silence: A Novel

Sunday *Silence*. French, Nicci

Sundin, Sarah

Through Waters Deep: A Novel

When Twilight Breaks

The **Sundowners**. Cleary, Jon

Sundstol, Vidar

The Land of Dreams

The **Sunne** *in Splendour*. Penman, Sharon Kay

Sunny and warm [Series]. Pope, Jamie

SUNRISE AND SUNSET

Czerneda, Julie. *A Turn of Light*

Sunrise *by the Sea*. Colgan, Jenny

Sunset *and Sawdust*. Lansdale, Joe R.

Sunset *Beach*. Andrews, Mary Kay

Sunset *Park*. Auster, Paul

SUNSET PARK (NEW YORK, N.Y.)

Auster, Paul. *Sunset Park*

Sunshine Vicram [Series]. Jones, Darynda

★**Super** *Sad True Love Story: A Novel*. Shteyngart, Gary

SUPERCOMPUTERS

Heinlein, Robert A. *The Moon Is a Harsh Mistress*

SUPERHERO STORIES

Anderson, Kevin J. *The Last Days of Krypton*

Chen, Mike. *We Could Be Heroes*

Harkaway, Nick. *Tigerman*

Martinson, T. J. *The Reign of the Kingfisher: A Novel*

Schwab, Victoria. *Vengeful*

Schwab, Victoria. *Vicious*

Walschots, Natalie Zina. *Hench: A Novel*

Wong, David. *Futuristic Violence and Fancy Suits*

SUPERHEROES

Chabon, Michael. *The Amazing Adventures of Kavalier & Clay: A Novel*

Chen, Mike. *We Could Be Heroes*

Martinson, T. J. *The Reign of the Kingfisher: A Novel*

Schwab, Victoria. *Vengeful*

Walschots, Natalie Zina. *Hench: A Novel*

Wong, David. *Futuristic Violence and Fancy Suits*

SUPERHUMAN ABILITIES

Alderman, Naomi. ★*The Power: A Novel*

Callihan, Kristen. ★*Firelight*

Fine, Julia. *What Should Be Wild*

Jemisin, N. K. *The Fifth Season*

Jemisin, N. K. *The Obelisk Gate*

Jemisin, N. K. *The Stone Sky*

King, Stephen. *The Institute*

Lu, S. Qiouyi. *In the Watchful City*

Parry, H. G. *The Unlikely Escape of Uriah Heep*

Rice, Christopher. *Blood Victory*

Rushdie, Salman. *Two Years Eight Months and Twenty-Eight Nights: A Novel*

Sakey, Marcus. *A Better World*

Sakey, Marcus. *Brilliance*

Schwab, Victoria. *Vengeful*

Schwab, Victoria. *Vicious*

Superintendent Battle mysteries [Series]. Christie, Agatha

SUPERIORITY AND INFERIORITY (PSYCHOLOGY)

Gordimer, Nadine. *The Conservationist*

SUPERNATURAL

Aaronovitch, Ben. *Moon Over Soho*

Anderson, Kevin J. *Death Warmed Over*

Baker, Kage. *The Bird of the River*

Bear, Elizabeth. *Stone Mad*

Camp, Bryan. *The City of Lost Fortunes*

Castro, V. *Goddess of Filth*

Cotterill, Colin. *Disco for the Departed*

Davidson, Andy. *The Boatman's Daughter: A Novel*

Duncan, Glen. *By Blood We Live*

Grant, Helen. *The Glass Demon*

Gregory, Daryl. *We Are All Completely Fine*

Gruber, Michael. *Night of the Jaguar: A Novel*

Gruber, Michael. *Valley of Bones: A Novel*

Hamill, Shaun. *A Cosmology of Monsters*

Hill, Joe. *Heart-Shaped Box*

Hill, Joe. *Strange Weather: Four Short Novels*

James, Henry. ★*The Turn of the Screw*

Katsu, Alma. *The Hunger: A Novel*

Kidd, Jess. ★*Things in Jars*

King, Stephen. *Doctor Sleep: A Novel*

King, Stephen. *Firestarter*

King, Stephen. *Night Shift*

King, Stephen. *Pet Sematary*

King, Stephen. *Salem's Lot*

King, Stephen. ★*The Shining*

McGuire, Seanan. *Chimes at Midnight: An October Daye Novel*
Miller, Madeline. ★*Circe*
Murakami, Haruki. *After Dark*
Murakami, Haruki. *Blind Willow, Sleeping Woman: 24 Stories*
Newland, Courttia. *A River Called Time*
Okri, Ben. *Prayer for the Living*
Rice, Anne. *Blood Communion: A Tale of Prince Lestat*
Rushdie, Salman. ★*Midnight's Children: A Novel*
Shaw, Vivian. ★*Dreadful Company*
Shaw, Vivian. ★*Strange Practice*
Stage, Zoje. *Wonderland*
Straub, Peter. ★*A Dark Matter: A Novel*
Updike, John. *The Widows of Eastwick*
Wolfe, Gene. *The Land Across*
Woods, Rita. ★*Remembrance*
SUPERNATURAL MYSTERIES
Cameron, W. Bruce. *Repo Madness*
Cantero, Edgar. *Meddling Kids: A Novel*
Connolly, John. *A Book of Bones*
Gailey, Sarah. *Magic for Liars*
Gallagher, Stephen. *The Bedlam Detective: A Novel*
Gallagher, Stephen. *The Kingdom of Bones: A Novel*
Hart, Carolyn G. *Ghost Blows a Kiss*
Harvey, Michael T. *Pulse*
Huchu, Tendai. *The Library of the Dead*
Irwin, Stephen M. *The Broken Ones: A Novel*
Olson, Neil. *Before the Devil Fell*
Racculia, Kate. ★*Bellweather Rhapsody*
Rhodes, Jewell Parker. *Yellow Moon: A Novel*
Shaw, Vivian. ★*Dreadful Company*
Shaw, Vivian. ★*Strange Practice*
SUPERSTITION
Campisi, Megan. *Sin Eater*
Choo, Yangsze. ★*The Night Tiger: A Novel*
Colgan, Jenny. ★*The Endless Beach*
Hoffman, Alice. *The River King*
Hurley, Andrew Michael. *Devil's Day*
Jackson, Shirley. *We Have Always Lived in the Castle*
McPherson, Catriona. ★*A Step so Grave*
Perry, Sarah. *Melmoth: A Novel*
Purcell, Laura. *The House of Whispers*
Scott, A. D. *A Kind of Grief: A Novel*
Sutanto, Jesse Q. *Dial a for Aunties*
SUPERVILLAINS
Chen, Mike. *We Could Be Heroes*
Walschots, Natalie Zina. *Hench: A Novel*
Wong, David. *Futuristic Violence and Fancy Suits*
SUPERVISORS
Baker, Chandler. *Whisper Network: A Novel*
Reichs, Kathy. ★*A Conspiracy of Bones*
Supper Club: A Novel. Williams, Lara
SUPPORT GROUPS
Chen, Mike. *We Could Be Heroes*
Hendrix, Grady. *The Final Girl Support Group*
SURFERS
Henson, Pene. *Into the Blue*
Watkins, Claire Vaye. ★*Gold Fame Citrus*

SURFING
Monroe, Mary Alice. *Beach House Reunion*
Reid, Taylor Jenkins. ★*Malibu Rising*
*The **Surgeon**. Gerritsen, Tess
SURGEONS
Blake, Audrey. *The Girl in His Shadow: A Novel*
Cook, Robin. *Charlatans*
Cook, Robin. *Coma: A Novel*
Gundar-Goshen, Ayelet. *Waking Lions*
Harkness, Deborah E. *Time's Convert*
Hoover, Colleen. *It Ends with Us*
Starr, Melvin R. *Unhallowed Ground*
Whitfield, Clare. *People of Abandoned Character*
SURGERY PATIENTS
Cook, Robin. *Coma: A Novel*
Row, Jess. *Your Face in Mine: A Novel*
Suri, Manil
The Age of Shiva: A Novel
Suri, Tasha
★*Empire of Sand*
The Jasmine Throne
★*Realm of Ash*
SURREALISM (ART)
Carter, Michaela. *Leonora in the Morning Light*
SURREALIST COMICS
Burns, Charles. ★*Black Hole*
SURREALIST FICTION
Bonnaffons, Amy. *The Regrets*
Burroughs, William S. ★*Naked Lunch: The Restored Text*
Founds, Kathleen. *When Mystical Creatures Attack!*
Gamboa, Santiago. *Necropolis*
Horrocks, Caitlin. *Life Among the Terranauts*
Ishiguro, Kazuo. *The Unconsoled*
Kafka, Franz. ★*The Trial*
Murakami, Haruki. ★*1q84*
Murakami, Haruki. *After the Quake: Stories*
Murakami, Haruki. *Blind Willow, Sleeping Woman: 24 Stories*
Murakami, Haruki. *Colorless Tsukuru Tazaki and His Years of Pilgrimage*
Murakami, Haruki. ★*Kafka on the Shore*
Murakami, Haruki. *Killing Commendatore: A Novel*
Murakami, Haruki. *Men Without Women: Stories*
Murakami, Haruki. *The Wind-Up Bird Chronicle*
Pelevin, Viktor. *The Hall of Singing Caryatids*
Scott, Rion Amilcar. ★*The World Doesn't Require You: Stories*
★*The **Surrendered**. Lee, Chang-Rae
SURROGATE MOTHERHOOD — PSYCHOLOGICAL ASPECTS
Beck, Haylen. *Lost You*
SURROGATE MOTHERS
Beck, Haylen. *Lost You*
Ramos, Joanne. *The Farm: A Novel*
SURVEILLANCE
Angelo, Megan. *Followers*
Eggers, Dave. *The Circle*
Finn, A. J. ★*The Woman in the Window*
Ragan, Theresa. *Deranged*
Wilson, G. Willow. *Alif the Unseen*

SURVEYING — HISTORY

Pynchon, Thomas. *Mason & Dixon*

SURVEYORS

Pynchon, Thomas. *Mason & Dixon*

SURVIVAL

Adams, Richard. *Watership Down*

Anders, Charlie Jane. ★*The City in the Middle of the Night*

Auster, Paul. ★*In the Country of Last Things*

Austin, Lynn N. *Chasing Shadows*

Barclay, Linwood. *No Safe House*

Beah, Ishmael. *Little Family*

Bear, Elizabeth. *All the Windwracked Stars*

Bear, Greg. *Anvil of Stars*

Box, C. J. ★*Dark Sky: A Joe Pickett Novel*

Brown, Pierce. *Golden Son*

Brown, Pierce. *Red Rising*

Brown, Taylor. *Fallen Land*

Bush, Keisha. *No Heaven for Good Boys: A Novel*

Calvino, Italo. *Invisible Cities*

Cook, Diane. ★*The New Wilderness: A Novel*

Cronin, Justin. *The City of Mirrors*

Cronin, Justin. *The Passage*

Cronin, Justin. *The Twelve*

Crummey, Michael. *The Innocents*

Darnielle, John. *Wolf in White Van: A Novel*

Eggers, Dave. *What Is the What: The Autobiography of Valentino Achak Deng*

Faye, Gael. ★*Small Country: A Novel*

Golding, William. *The Inheritors*

Gregory, Daryl. *We Are All Completely Fine*

Hargrave, Kiran Millwood. *The Mercies: A Novel*

Harmel, Kristin. *The Room on Rue Amelie*

Heller, Joseph. ★*Catch-22*

Heller, Peter. ★*The Dog Stars: A Novel*

Heller, Peter. *The River: A Novel*

Hughes, Langston. ★*Short Stories*

Johnson, Micaiah. *The Space Between Worlds*

K'wan. ★*Diamonds and Pearl*

Kirkpatrick, Jane. *One More River to Cross*

Kunsken, Derek. *The House of Styx*

Lai, Larissa. *The Tiger Flu*

Lalami, Laila. ★*The Moor's Account: A Novel*

Mabanckou, Alain. ★*Black Moses*

Malerman, Josh. *Bird Box: A Novel*

Malerman, Josh. *Malorie: A Bird Box Novel*

Matheson, Richard. ★*I Am Legend*

McCaffrey, Anne. *Dragonflight*

Mitchell, Margaret. ★*Gone with the Wind*

Newland, Courttia. *A River Called Time*

Phillips, Gin. *Fierce Kingdom: A Novel*

Rice, Waubgeshig. *Moon of the Crusted Snow: A Novel*

Sainz Borgo, Karina. ★*It Would Be Night in Caracas*

Saramago, Jose. ★*Blindness*

Shepard, Jim. *Phase Six*

Stabenow, Dana. ★*Less Than a Treason*

Stephenson, Neal. *Seveneves*

Stevens, Chevy. *Still Missing*

Straley, John. *The Big Both Ways*

Stroby, Wallace. *Some Die Nameless*

Turow, Scott. *Testimony*

Vandermeer, Jeff. ★*Annihilation: A Novel*

VanderMeer, Jeff. ★*Borne: A Novel*

Verne, Jules. *The Mysterious Island*

Weir, Andy. *The Martian*

Winton, Tim. *The Shepherd's Hut*

SURVIVAL (AFTER AIRPLANE ACCIDENTS, SHIPWRECKS, ETC.)

Barnes, Julian. ★*A History of the World in 10 1/2 Chapters*

Coetzee, J. M. ★*Foe*

Defoe, Daniel. ★*Robinson Crusoe*

Golding, William. ★*Lord of the Flies: A Novel*

Hilton, James. ★*Lost Horizon: A Novel*

Martel, Yann. ★*Life of Pi: A Novel*

Napolitano, Ann. *Dear Edward*

Picoult, Jodi. ★*The Book of Two Ways*

Poe, Edgar Allan. *The Narrative of Arthur Gordon Pym of Nantucket*

Rushdie, Salman. ★*The Satanic Verses*

Simmons, Dan. ★*The Terror: A Novel*

Wells, H. G. ★*The Island of Dr. Moreau*

SURVIVAL (AFTER AUTOMOBILE, TRUCK, TRAIN ACCIDENTS, ETC.)

Banks, Russell. ★*The Sweet Hereafter*

Enger, Leif. *Virgil Wander*

SURVIVAL (AFTER DISASTER)

Brooks, Max. *Devolution: A Firsthand Account of the Rainier Sasquatch Massacre*

Delany, Samuel R. *Dhalgren*

Golden, Christopher. *Ararat*

Stirling, S. M. *Dies the Fire*

Tolstaya, Tatyana. *The Slynx*

Vinge, Vernor. *The Children of the Sky*

SURVIVAL (AFTER ENVIRONMENTAL CATASTROPHE)

Montag, Kassandra. *After the Flood: A Novel*

Stewart, George R. *Earth Abides*

Vaughn, Carrie. *Bannerless*

SURVIVAL (AFTER EPIDEMICS)

Elison, Meg. *The Book of Etta*

Elison, Meg. *The Book of Flora*

Elison, Meg. *The Book of the Unnamed Midwife*

King, Stephen. ★*The Stand*

Ma, Ling. *Severance*

Matheson, Richard. ★*I Am Legend*

SURVIVAL (AFTER FLOODS)

Cheng, Bill. *Southern Cross the Dog*

SURVIVAL (AFTER NUCLEAR WARFARE)

McCarthy, Cormac. ★*The Road*

Miller, Walter M. ★*A Canticle for Leibowitz*

Okorafor, Nnedi. ★*Who Fears Death*

Poyer, David. *Violent Peace: The War with China - Aftermath of Armageddon*

Tepper, Sheri S. *The Gate to Women's Country*

SURVIVAL (IN CONCENTRATION CAMPS, PRISONS, ETC.)

Alexander, V. S. *The Magdalen Girls*

Brouwer, Sigmund. *Thief of Glory: A Novel*

Morris, Heather. *Cilka's Journey*

Tan, Twan Eng. *The Garden of Evening Mists*

SURVIVAL — PSYCHOLOGICAL ASPECTS
  Ganshert, Katie. *Life After*
  Remarque, Erich Maria. *The Road Back*
Survival Instincts. Waite, Jen
SURVIVAL STORIES
  Defoe, Daniel. ★*Robinson Crusoe*
  Ferencik, Erica. *Into the Jungle*
  Heller, Peter. *The River: A Novel*
  Martel, Yann. ★*Life of Pi: A Novel*
SURVIVALISM
  Wilhelm, Kate. *Where Late the Sweet Birds Sang*
SURVIVALISTS
  Box, C. J. *Winterkill: A Novel*
  Fuller, Claire. *Our Endless Numbered Days: A Novel*
  Henderson, Smith. *Fourth of July Creek*
  Rankin, Ian. *Blood Hunt: A Novel*
SURVIVOR GUILT
  Chakrabarti, Jai. *A Play for the End of the World*
Survivor Song. Tremblay, Paul
The Survivors. Harper, Jane
Survivors [Series]. Galen, Shana
SURVIVORS OF SUICIDE VICTIMS
  Bartz, Andrea. *The Lost Night*
  Bennett, Brit. *The Mothers*
  Doller, Trish. *Float Plan*
  Lodato, Victor. *Edgar and Lucy: A Novel*
  Nunez, Sigrid. ★*The Friend*
  Oates, Joyce Carol. *The Falls: A Novel*
  Roisin, Fariha. *Like a Bird*
  Yoshimoto, Banana. *Moshi-Moshi*
Survivors' Club septet [Series]. Balogh, Mary
The Survivors: a Novel. Schulman, Alex
Suskind, Patrick
  ★*Perfume: The Story of a Murderer*
The Suspect. Barton, Fiona
Suspect. Crais, Robert
★*Suspect*. Robotham, Michael
SUSPECTS (CRIMINAL INVESTIGATION)
  Heaberlin, Julia. *We Are All the Same in the Dark: A Novel*
  Majumdar, Megha. *A Burning*
SUSPENDED ANIMATION
  Varley, John. *Dark Lightning*
Suspicion. Finder, Joseph
SUSPICION
  Abbott, Jeff. *The Three Beths*
  Abbott, Megan E. *You Will Know Me: A Novel*
  Adams, Taylor. *Hairpin Bridge*
  Alsterdal, Tove. *We Know You Remember*
  Barton, Fiona. *The Suspect*
  Blakemore, A. K. *The Manningtree Witches*
  Bolton, S. J. *The Craftsman*
  Brundage, Elizabeth. ★*All Things Cease to Appear*
  Chanter, Catherine. *The Well*
  Clark, Mary Higgins. *Death Wears a Beauty Mask and Other Stories*
  Clark, Mary Higgins. *The Melody Lingers On*
  Constantine, Liv. *The Last Time I Saw You*
  Deighton, Len. *London Match*
  Faye, Lyndsay. ★*The King of Infinite Space*

French, Nicci. *Friday on My Mind: A Frieda Klein Mystery*
Goddard, Robert. *Never Go Back*
Goldman, Matt. *Dead West*
Goldman, Matt. *The Shallows*
Jemc, Jac. ★*The Grip of It*
Jensen, Nancy. *In Our Midst*
Klune, TJ. *The House in the Cerulean Sea*
Kwon, Yo-Son. *Lemon*
MacDonald, John D. *The Turquoise Lament*
March, Nev. *Murder in Old Bombay*
Owens, Delia. *Where the Crawdads Sing*
Perry, Anne. *Dark Tide Rising: A William Monk Novel*
Perry, Anne. ★*Death with a Double Edge: A Daniel Pitt Novel*
Powers, Richard. *Orfeo: A Novel*
Simpson, Dorothy. *Dead by Morning*
Steinhauer, Olen. *The Bridge of Sighs*
Swinson, Kiki. *I'm New York's Finest*
Tursten, Helene. *An Elderly Lady Must Not Be Crossed*
Urquhart, Rachel. *The Visionist*
Walker, Caroline Louise. *Man of the Year*
Whitfield, Clare. *People of Abandoned Character*
SUSSEX, ENGLAND
  Gaiman, Neil. ★*The Ocean at the End of the Lane*
  Robertson, Imogen. *Instruments of Darkness: A Novel*
SUSTAINABILITY
  Vaughn, Carrie. *Bannerless*
SUSTAINABLE COMMUNITIES
  Boyle, T. Coraghessan. *The Terranauts*
SUSTAINABLE LIVING
  ffitch, Madeline. *Stay and Fight*
Sutanto, Jesse Q.
  Dial a for Aunties
Sutcliff, Rosemary
  Sword at Sunset
Sutherland scandals [Series]. Bradley, Anna
SUTPEN FAMILY (FICTITIOUS CHARACTERS)
  Faulkner, William. ★*Absalom, Absalom!*
Sveistrup, Soren
  ★*The Chestnut Man: A Novel*
Svevo, Italo
  Zeno's Conscience
The Swallows of Kabul: A Novel. Khadra, Yasmina
The Swallows: a Novel. Lutz, Lisa
★*Swamplandia!*. Russell, Karen
SWAMPS
  Davidson, Andy. *The Boatman's Daughter: A Novel*
  Russell, Karen. ★*Swamplandia!*
Swamy, Shruti
  The Archer
  A House Is a Body: Stories
Swann's Way. Proust, Marcel
Swann, Stacey
  Olympus Texas
Swanson, Peter
  Eight Perfect Murders: A Novel
  Her Every Fear: A Novel
  The Kind Worth Killing: A Novel

Swanwick, Michael
Bones of the Earth
Swarthout, Glendon
Bless the Beasts and Children
★*The Shootist*
Swarup, Shubhangi
Latitudes of Longing
SWASHBUCKLING TALES
Dumas, Alexandre. ★*The Man in the Iron Mask*
Dumas, Alexandre. ★*The Three Musketeers*
Dumas, Alexandre. *Twenty Years After*
Holton, India. *The Wisteria Society of Lady Scoundrels*
Sabatini, Rafael. *Captain Blood*
SWEDEN
Ajvide Lindqvist, John. *Let the Right One In*
Alsterdal, Tove. *We Know You Remember*
Backman, Fredrik. ★*Anxious People: A Novel*
Backman, Fredrik. ★*Beartown: A Novel*
Backman, Fredrik. ★*My Grandmother Asked Me to Tell You She's Sorry: A Novel*
Backman, Fredrik. *Us Against You: A Novel*
Dahl, Arne. *Bad Blood*
Dahl, Arne. *Misterioso: A Crime Novel*
Eriksson, Kjell. *The Deathwatch Beetle: A Mystery*
Furst, Alan. *Dark Voyage: A Novel*
Grebe, Camilla. *After She's Gone: A Novel*
Hand, Elizabeth. *The Book of Lamps and Banners: A Novel*
Hashemzadeh Bonde, Golnaz. *What We Owe*
Kepler, Lars. *The Sandman*
Lagercrantz, David. *The Girl Who Lived Twice: A Lisbeth Salander Novel*
Lagercrantz, David. *The Girl Who Takes an Eye for an Eye*
Larsson, Stieg. ★*The Girl Who Kicked the Hornet's Nest*
Larsson, Stieg. *The Girl Who Played with Fire*
Larsson, Stieg. *The Girl with the Dragon Tattoo*
Mankell, Henning. *Before the Frost: A Linda Wallander Mystery*
Mankell, Henning. *Firewall*
Mankell, Henning. *The Man from Beijing*
Mankell, Henning. *The Man Who Smiled: A Kurt Wallander Mystery*
Mankell, Henning. ★*One Step Behind*
Mankell, Henning. ★*The Return of the Dancing Master*
Mankell, Henning. *The Troubled Man*
McCall Smith, Alexander. ★*The Department of Sensitive Crimes: A Detective Varg Novel*
McCall Smith, Alexander. ★*The Man with the Silver Saab: A Detective Varg Novel*
Ohlsson, Kristina. *Unwanted: A Novel*
Persson Giolito, Malin. *Beyond All Reasonable Doubt: A Novel*
Persson, Leif G. W. *Another Time, Another Life: The Story of a Crime*
Persson, Leif G. W. *The Dying Detective: A Mystery*
Persson, Leif G. W. *Free Falling, as If in a Dream: The Story of a Crime*
Ramqvist, Karolina. *The White City*
Roslund, Anders. *Cell 8*
Roslund, Anders. ★*Knock Knock*
Roslund, Anders. *Pen 33*
Tursten, Helene. *An Elderly Lady Must Not Be Crossed*
Tursten, Helene. *Hunting Game*

SWEDES IN THE UNITED STATES
Diaz, Hernan. ★*In the Distance*
SWEDISH AMERICAN FAMILIES
Cather, Willa. *O Pioneers!*
Cather, Willa. *The Song of the Lark*
Sweeney, Cynthia D'Aprix
★*Good Company: A Novel*
Sweeney-Baird, Christina
The End of Men
★*The Sweet Hereafter*. Banks, Russell
Sweet Little Lies. Frear, Caz
Sweet Little Lies. Shalvis, Jill
Sweet on a cowboy novels [Series]. Drake, Laura
The Sweet Spot. Drake, Laura
Sweetbitter. Danler, Stephanie
The Sweetest Dream. Lessing, Doris May
The Sweetest Fruits. Truong, Monique T. D.
The Sweetest Remedy. Igharo, Jane
The Sweetest Thing. Shalvis, Jill
Sweetland. Crummey, Michael
★*The Sweetness at the Bottom of the Pie*. Bradley, C. Alan
Sweetness in the Belly. Gibb, Camilla
The Sweetness of Water. Harris, Nathan
Swift, Graham
★*Here We Are*
★*Last Orders: A Novel*
★*Mothering Sunday: A Romance*
Wish You Were Here
Swift, Jonathan
★*Gulliver's Travels*
SWIFT, KAY
Jackson, K. M. *How to Marry Keanu Reeves in 90 Days*
Kaplan, Mitchell James. *Rhapsody*
Swimming Back to Trout River. Feng, Linda Rui
Swimming Home: A Novel. Levy, Deborah
Swimming in the Dark. Jedrowski, Tomasz
SWINDLERS AND SWINDLING
Billingham, Mark. ★*Their Little Secret*
Clark, Martin. *The Substitution Order*
Clark, Wahida. ★*Payback Is a Mutha*
Estleman, Loren D. *The Adventures of Johnny Vermillion: A Novel*
French, Nicci. *Tuesday's Gone*
Gogol, Nikolai Vasilievich. ★*Dead Souls*
Higgins, George V. *The Friends of Eddie Coyle*
Hill, Edwin J. *Little Comfort*
Hughes, Caoilinn. *Orchid and the Wasp*
Jones, Tanen. *The Better Liar: A Novel*
Lawton, John. *Then We Take Berlin*
Leonard, Elmore. *Pagan Babies*
Lipman, Elinor. *The Pursuit of Alice Thrift: A Novel*
MacLean, Sarah. ★*Brazen and the Beast*
MacLean, Sarah. ★*Wicked and the Wallflower*
Melville, Herman. *The Confidence-Man: His Masquerade*
Michener, James A. *Space*
Palahniuk, Chuck. *Choke: A Novel*
Phillips, Jayne Anne. *Quiet Dell: A Novel*
Piccirilli, Tom. *The Last Whisper in the Dark: A Novel*
Portis, Charles. ★*Gringos: A Novel*

Pratchett, Terry. *Going Postal: A Novel of Discworld*
Quick, Amanda. *The Other Lady Vanishes*
Robards, Karen. *The Ultimatum*
Robotham, Michael. ★*The Wreckage*
Sears, Michael. *Tower of Babel*
Smith, B. J. *All Hat: A Novel*
Smith, Julie. *Crescent City Kill: A Skip Langdon Novel*
Smith, Martin Cruz. *December 6*
Spufford, Francis. ★*Golden Hill*
Stewart, Amy. *Lady Cop Makes Trouble*
Stringer, Vickie M. *Dirty Red: A Novel*
Tamirat, Nafkote. *The Parking Lot Attendant: A Novel*
Westlake, Donald E. ★*Bank Shot*
Westlake, Donald E. *The Road to Ruin*
Zettel, Sarah. *A Mother's Lie*
★*Swing Time*. Smith, Zadie

Swinson, David
   City on the Edge

Swinson, Kiki
   A Gangster and a Gentleman
   I'm New York's Finest
   Lifestyles of the Rich and Shameless
   The Safe House
   Who's Wife Extraordinaire Now
   Wifey
   Wifey's Next Sticky Situation
*The **Switch***. O'Leary, Beth
*The **Switch**: a Novel*. Finder, Joseph

SWITZERLAND
   Brookner, Anita. *Hotel Du Lac*
   Essbaum, Jill Alexander. *Hausfrau: A Novel*

SWORD AND SORCERY
   French, Jonathan. *The Free Bastards*
   French, Jonathan. ★*The Grey Bastards*
   French, Jonathan. *The True Bastards*
   Saberhagen, Fred. *Coinspinner's Story*
   Saberhagen, Fred. *Farslayer's Story*
   Saberhagen, Fred. *Mindsword's Story*
   Saberhagen, Fred. *Shieldbreaker's Story*
   Saberhagen, Fred. *Sightblinder's Story*
   Saberhagen, Fred. *Stonecutter's Story*
   Saberhagen, Fred. *Wayfinder's Story*
   Saberhagen, Fred. *Woundhealer's Story*
   Sullivan, Michael J. *Theft of Swords*
   Winter, Evan. *The Fires of Vengeance*
   Winter, Evan. ★*The Rage of Dragons*
*The **Sword** and the Spear*. Couto, Mia
Sword at Sunset. Sutcliff, Rosemary
Sword of Kings. Cornwell, Bernard

SWORDFIGHTERS
   Goldman, William. ★*The Princess Bride: S. Morgenstern's Classic Tale of True Love and High Adventure : The*
   Sabatini, Rafael. *Scaramouche: A Romance of the French Revolution*

SWORDMAKING
   Cole, Alyssa. ★*A Duke by Default*

SWORDPLAY
   Dumas, Alexandre. ★*The Three Musketeers*
   Dumas, Alexandre. *Twenty Years After*

Sullivan, Michael J. *Theft of Swords*
SWORDS
   Saberhagen, Fred. *Coinspinner's Story*
   Saberhagen, Fred. *Farslayer's Story*
   Saberhagen, Fred. *Sightblinder's Story*
   Saberhagen, Fred. *Stonecutter's Story*
   Saberhagen, Fred. *Wayfinder's Story*
   Stewart, Mary. ★*The Hollow Hills*

Swyler, Erika
   ★*Light from Other Stars: A Novel*
Sycamore: a Novel. Chancellor, Bryn

SYDNEY, NEW SOUTH WALES
   Adiga, Aravind. ★*Amnesty*
   Clarke, Maxine Beneba. ★*Foreign Soil*
   Flanagan, Richard. *The Unknown Terrorist*
   Isaac, Kara. *Then There Was You*
   Moriarty, Liane. *The Husband's Secret*
   Moriarty, Liane. *Truly Madly Guilty*
   Moss, Tara. *The War Widow*

Sylvester, Natalia
   Everyone Knows You Go Home
★*The **Sympathizer***. Nguyen, Viet Thanh
***Symphony** of Ages* [Series]. Haydon, Elizabeth

SYNAGOGUES
   Lukas, Michael David. *The Last Watchman of Old Cairo: A Novel*

SYNDROMES
   Gregory, Daryl. *The Devil's Alphabet*

SYNESTHESIA
   Harris, Sarah J. *The Color of Bee Larkham's Murder: A Novel*

SYPHILIS
   Gibbon, Maureen. *The Lost Notebook of Edouard Manet: A Novel*

SYRACUSE, NEW YORK
   Abu-Jaber, Diana. *Origin: A Novel*
   Spiotta, Dana. *Wayward*

SYRIA
   Edwards, Louis. *Ramadan Ramsey: A Novel*
   Hosseini, Khaled. ★*Sea Prayer*
   Joukhadar, Zeyn. ★*The Thirty Names of Night: A Novel*
   Khalfah, Khlid. *Death Is Hard Work: A Novel*
   Lefteri, Christy. *The Beekeeper of Aleppo: A Novel*
   Miller, Derek B. ★*The Girl in Green*
   Porter, Henry. *Firefly*
   Ramadan, Ahmad Danny. *The Clothesline Swing*
   Sebastian, Tim. *Fatal Ally*

SYRIAN AMERICANS
   Joukhadar, Zeyn. ★*The Thirty Names of Night: A Novel*

Szabo, Magda
   Abigail

T

T. I.
   Power & Beauty: A Love Story of Life on the Streets
   Trouble & Triumph: A Novel of Power & Beauty
***Table** Money*. Breslin, Jimmy

TABLOID NEWSPAPERS
    Daria, Alexis. ★*You Had Me at Hola*
TADEMY FAMILY
    Tademy, Lalita. *Cane River*
Tademy family chronicles [Series]. Tademy, Lalita
Tademy, Lalita
    Cane River
Tag Man: A Joe Gunther Novel. Mayor, Archer
The *Tailor* of Panama. Le Carre, John
TAILORS
    Le Carre, John. *The Tailor of Panama*
    Matthews, Mimi. ★*The Siren of Sussex*
Tailspin. Brown, Sandra
★*A Taint in the Blood.* Stabenow, Dana
Takamura, Kaoru
    ★*Lady Joker*
★The *Take.* Reich, Christopher
★*Take a Hint, Dani Brown.* Hibbert, Talia
★*A Tale for the Time Being.* Ozeki, Ruth L.
The *Tale* of the Body Thief. Rice, Anne
★*A Tale of Two Cities.* Dickens, Charles
TALENT AGENTS
    Lauren, Christina. *Dating You / Hating You*
★The *Talented* Mr. Ripley. Highsmith, Patricia
★*Tales.* Lovecraft, H. P.
Tales of the Modern Navy [Series]. Poyer, David
★*Tales* of the South Pacific. Michener, James A.
Talk to Me. Kenney, John
The *Talk-Funny* Girl: A Novel. Merullo, Roland
TALKING ANIMALS
    Orwell, George. ★*Animal Farm*
TALKING CATS
    Natsukawa, Sosuke. *The Cat Who Saved Books*
A *Tall* History of Sugar. Forbes, Curdella
Tallgrass. Dallas, Sandra
Tallgrass: a Novel of the Great Plains. Coldsmith, Don
Tallis, Frank
    Vienna Blood: A Max Liebermann Mystery
TALLNESS AND SHORTNESS
    Irving, John. ★*A Prayer for Owen Meany: A Novel*
Tallo, Katie
    Dark August
Talon of God. Snipes, Wesley
Talton, Jon
    City of Dark Corners
Talulla Rising. Duncan, Glen
Tam Lin. Dean, Pamela
Tambudzai novels [Series]. Dangarembga, Tsitsi
The *Taming* of the Queen. Gregory, Philippa
Tamirat, Nafkote
    The Parking Lot Attendant: A Novel
TAMPA, FLORIDA
    Lehane, Dennis. *World Gone By: A Novel*
Tan, Amy
    The Bonesetter's Daughter
    The Hundred Secret Senses
    ★*The Joy Luck Club*
    ★*The Kitchen God's Wife*

    The Valley of Amazement
Tan, Lucy
    What We Were Promised
Tan, Sue Lynn
    ★*Daughter of the Moon Goddess*
Tan, Twan Eng
    The Garden of Evening Mists
Tanabe, Karin
    A Hundred Suns
    ★*A Woman of Intelligence*
Taneja, Preti
    We That Are Young: A Novel
Tanen, Sloane
    There's a Word for That
TANG DYNASTY (618-907)
    Lin, Jeannie. *The Lotus Palace*
TANGO (DANCE)
    Perez-Reverte, Arturo. *What We Become*
TANGO MUSIC
    De Robertis, Carolina. *The Gods of Tango*
TANKS (MILITARY SCIENCE)
    Shaara, Jeff. *The Rising Tide: A Novel of World War II*
Tannie Maria novels [Series]. Andrew, Sally
A *Tap* on the Window. Barclay, Linwood
Tar Baby. Morrison, Toni
Target Tinos: An Inspector Kaldis Mystery. Siger, Jeffrey
Tarkington, Booth
    ★*Alice Adams*
    ★*The Magnificent Ambersons*
TAROT
    Burke, James Lee. ★*The New Iberia Blues*
    Ware, Ruth. *The Death of Mrs. Westaway*
Tartt, Donna
    ★*The Goldfinch*
    ★*The Secret History*
Taseer, Aatish
    The Way Things Were: A Novel
TASMANIA
    Flanagan, Richard. *The Living Sea of Waking Dreams*
    Harper, Jane. *The Survivors*
A *Taste* for Death. James, P. D.
Tata, A. J.
    Dark Winter
★*Tatiana:* an Arkady Renko Novel. Smith, Martin Cruz
Tatlock, Ann
    Promises to Keep
TATTOO ARTISTS
    Danielewski, Mark Z. ★*House of Leaves: A Novel*
TATTOOING
    Anders, Adriana. *Under Her Skin*
    Bradbury, Ray. *The Illustrated Man*
    Byrne, Kerrigan. *The Duke with the Dragon Tattoo*
    Shafak, Elif. *The Bastard of Istanbul*
Tawada, Yoko
    ★*The Emissary*
TAXICAB DRIVERS
    Aciman, Andre. *Harvard Square*
    Blackstock, Terri. *Catching Christmas*

Rivero, Melissa. *The Affairs of the Falcons*
Self, Will. *The Book of Dave: A Revelation of the Recent Past and the Distant Future*

TAXIDERMY
Arnett, Kristen N. *Mostly Dead Things*

Taylor, Brad
★*Daughter of War: A Novel*
Ring of Fire

Taylor, Brandon
★*Filthy Animals*
★*Real Life*

TEA
Avon, Joy. *In Peppermint Peril: A Book Tea Shop Mystery*
See, Lisa. *The Tea Girl of Hummingbird Lane*
Tea & Treachery. Delany, Vicki
Tea by the Sea mysteries [Series]. Delany, Vicki
The Tea Girl of Hummingbird Lane. See, Lisa

TEA PLANTATIONS
Tan, Twan Eng. *The Garden of Evening Mists*
Tea Shop mysteries (Laura Childs) [Series]. Childs, Laura

TEACHER-STUDENT RELATIONSHIPS
Beattie, Ann. *A Wonderful Stroke of Luck: A Novel*
Bell, Shelly. *At His Mercy*
Choi, Susan. ★*Trust Exercise: A Novel*
Cumyn, Alan. *Losing It*
Founds, Kathleen. *When Mystical Creatures Attack!*
Heller, Zoe. *What Was She Thinking?: Notes on a Scandal*
McCarthy, Jesse. *The Fugitivities*
Messud, Claire. ★*The Woman Upstairs: A Novel*
Murdoch, Iris. *The Philosopher's Pupil*
Murray, Paul. *Skippy Dies*
Prose, Francine. *Blue Angel: A Novel*
Richman, Alyson. *The Secret of Clouds*
Russell, Kate Elizabeth. ★*My Dark Vanessa*
Sapphire. ★*Push: A Novel*
Schumacher, Julie. *Dear Committee Members*
Spark, Muriel. ★*The Prime of Miss Jean Brodie*
Strout, Elizabeth. *Amy and Isabelle: A Novel*

TEACHERS
Adiga, Aravind. *Last Man in Tower: A Novel*
Albahari, David. *Gotz and Meyer*
DeLuca, Jen. ★*Well Met*
Gailey, Sarah. *Magic for Liars*
Goenawan, Clarissa. *Rainbirds*
Greenwell, Garth. *Cleanness*
Heiny, Katherine. ★*Early Morning Riser*
Hilton, James. ★*Good-Bye, Mr. Chips*
Jónasson, Ragnarn. ★*The Girl Who Died*
Kamal, Soniah. *Unmarriageable: A Novel*
O'Mara, Tim. *Crooked Numbers*
Parker, T. Jefferson. *L.A. Outlaws: A Novel*
Roberts, Nora. ★*The Becoming*
Sandford, John. *Deep Freeze*
Scottoline, Lisa. *One Perfect Lie*
Strout, Elizabeth. *Olive Kitteridge*
Thompson, Jim. *The Killer Inside Me*
Weiss, Leah. *If the Creek Don't Rise: A Novel*
Wynne, Phoebe. *Madam*

Young, Heather. *The Distant Dead*

TEACHERS — DEATH
Pessl, Marisha. *Special Topics in Calamity Physics*

TEACHING — PHILOSOPHY
Kaufman, Bel. *Up the Down Staircase*
Team Seven. Burke, Marcus
Tear It Down. Petrie, Nicholas
Tear Me Apart. Ellison, J. T.

TEAROOMS
Childs, Laura. *Haunted Hibiscus*
Childs, Laura. *Lavender Blue Murder*
Childs, Laura. *Twisted Tea Christmas*
Delany, Vicki. *Murder in a Teacup*
Delany, Vicki. *Tea & Treachery*
Lim, Roselle. *Vanessa Yu's Magical Paris Tea Shop*
Orczy, Emmuska Orczy. *The Old Man in the Corner*
Tears of the Trufflepig. Flores, Fernando A.

TECHNO-THRILLERS
Brown, Dale. *Eagle Station: A Novel*
Brown, Dale. *The Moscow Offensive: A Novel*
Campbell, Rick. *Treason*
Clancy, Tom. *Clear and Present Danger*
Clancy, Tom. ★*The Hunt for Red October*
Clancy, Tom. *Patriot Games*
Coonts, Stephen. *The Art of War: A Novel*
Coonts, Stephen. ★*Flight of the Intruder*
Crichton, Michael. *Prey: A Novel*
Doctorow, Cory. *Walkaway*
Glynn, Alan. *Receptor*
Lee, Patrick. *Runner*
Miles, Terry. *Rabbits*
Parnell, Sean. *Left for Dead*
Parnell, Sean. *Man of War: An Eric Steele Novel*
Poyer, David. *Overthrow: The War with China and North Korea—Fall of an Empire*
Poyer, David. *Violent Peace: The War with China - Aftermath of Armageddon*
Quirk, Matthew. *Cold Barrel Zero*
Quirk, Matthew. *Dead Man Switch*
Soule, Charles. ★*Anyone*
Webb, Brandon. ★*Steel Fear*
The Technologists: a Novel. Pearl, Matthew

TECHNOLOGY
Banks, Iain. *Matter*
Bennett, Robert Jackson. *Foundryside*
Bennett, Robert Jackson. *Shorefall*
Cussler, Clive. ★*Final Option*
Cussler, Clive. *Shadow Tyrants*
Eggers, Dave. *The Circle*
Garwood, Julie. *Wired*
Goonan, Kathleen Ann. *In War Times*
Petrie, Nicholas. *The Breaker*
Robinson, Kim Stanley. ★*The Ministry for the Future*
Stephenson, Neal. *Reamde*
Stephenson, Neal. ★*Snow Crash*
Vonnegut, Kurt. *While Mortals Sleep: Unpublished Short Fiction*
Ware, Ruth. ★*The Turn of the Key*
Yoon, David. *Version Zero*

TECHNOLOGY — SOCIAL ASPECTS

Fforde, Jasper. *Shades of Grey: A Novel*
Gaddis, William. *Agape Agape*
Graedon, Alena. *The Word Exchange: A Novel*
Lightman, Alan P. *The Diagnosis*
Liu, Ken. *Invisible Planets: Contemporary Chinese Science Fiction in Translation*
Schulman, Helen. *Come with Me*

TECHNOLOGY AND CIVILIZATION

Bradbury, Ray. *The Illustrated Man*
Cather, Willa. *A Lost Lady*
Chiang, Ted. ★*Exhalation: Stories*
Crichton, Michael. *Prey: A Novel*
Hall, Louisa. *Speak*
Rutherfurd, Edward. *Sarum: The Novel of England*
Stirling, S. M. *Dies the Fire*
Stirling, S. M. *A Meeting at Corvallis*
Wilson, Daniel H. *Robogenesis: A Novel*
Teddy Fay novels [Series]. Woods, Stuart

TEENAGE ABUSE VICTIMS

Guterson, David. *Our Lady of the Forest*
Whitehead, Colson. ★*The Nickel Boys: A Novel*

TEENAGE ARSONISTS

Clarke, Brock. *An Arsonist's Guide to Writers' Homes in New England: A Novel*

TEENAGE BOY/BOY RELATIONS

Vuong, Ocean. ★*On Earth We're Briefly Gorgeous: A Novel*

TEENAGE BOY/GIRL RELATIONS

Booth, Coe. ★*Bronxwood*
Galloway, Gregory. *As Simple as Snow*
Mishima, Yukio. *The Sound of Waves*
Sparks, Nicholas. *A Walk to Remember*
Walker, Karen Thompson. *The Age of Miracles: A Novel*

TEENAGE BOYS

Adler-Olsen, Jussi. *The Marco Effect: A Department Q Novel*
Alexie, Sherman. *Flight*
Atkinson, Kate. ★*Big Sky*
Barzak, Christopher. *One for Sorrow*
Beverly, William. *Dodgers: A Novel*
Bilenchi, Romano. ★*The Chill*
Binder, L. Annette. *The Vanishing Sky*
Campbell, Ramsey. *The Wise Friend*
Cline, Ernest. *Ready Player One: A Novel*
Coben, Harlan. *Hold Tight*
Coe, Jonathan. *The Rotters' Club*
Dazieri, Sandrone. *Kill the King*
Deb, Siddhartha. *The Point of Return: A Novel*
Erdrich, Louise. ★*The Round House: A Novel*
Eugenides, Jeffrey. ★*The Virgin Suicides*
Evison, Jonathan. *All About Lulu: A Novel*
Extence, Gavin. *The Universe Versus Alex Woods*
Ford, Richard. ★*Independence Day*
Galloway, Gregory. *As Simple as Snow*
Golding, William. ★*Lord of the Flies: A Novel*
Gunesekera, Romesh. ★*Suncatcher: A Novel*
Knowles, John. ★*A Separate Peace*
Maguire, Gregory. *Son of a Witch: A Novel*
Martel, Yann. ★*Life of Pi: A Novel*

McCarthy, Cormac. ★*Blood Meridian, Or, the Evening Redness in the West*
Mishima, Yukio. *The Sound of Waves*
Morante, Elsa. *Arturo's Island: A Novel*
Nunez, Sigrid. *Salvation City*
Oe, Kenzaburo. *Nip the Buds, Shoot the Kids*
Park, Ishle Yi. *Angel & Hannah: A Novel in Verse*
Parks, Gordon. ★*The Learning Tree*
Price, Richard. *Lush Life*
Remarque, Erich Maria. ★*All Quiet on the Western Front*
Restrepo, Laura. *No Place for Heroes: A Novel*
Saroyan, William. ★*The Human Comedy*
Schlink, Bernhard. *The Reader: A Novel*
Scottoline, Lisa. *One Perfect Lie*
Smith, Ali. *The Accidental*
Swinson, David. *City on the Edge*
Tenorio, Lysley A. *The Son of Good Fortune: A Novel*
Williams, Katie. *Tell the Machine Goodnight*
Winters, Ben H. *The Quiet Boy*
Winton, Tim. *The Shepherd's Hut*
Wolff, Tobias. *Old School: A Novel*

TEENAGE BOYS — DEATH

Murray, Paul. *Skippy Dies*

TEENAGE BOYS — FRIENDSHIP

Barzak, Christopher. *One for Sorrow*

TEENAGE BOYS — PSYCHOLOGY

Mitchell, David. *Black Swan Green: A Novel*
Roth, Henry. *A Diving Rock on the Hudson*

TEENAGE BOYS AND HORSES

Olmstead, Robert. ★*Coal Black Horse*

TEENAGE COUPLES

Baldwin, James. ★*If Beale Street Could Talk*

TEENAGE DETECTIVES

Cantero, Edgar. *Meddling Kids: A Novel*
Copenhaver, John. *The Savage Kind*

TEENAGE DRUG ABUSERS

Pearlman, Edith. *Honeydew: Stories*

TEENAGE EQUESTRIANS

Mihalic, Susan. *Dark Horses*

TEENAGE FATHERS

Tyler, Anne. ★*Saint Maybe*

TEENAGE GIRL ABUSE VICTIMS

Merullo, Roland. *The Talk-Funny Girl: A Novel*

TEENAGE GIRL BASKETBALL PLAYERS

Johnson, Craig. *Daughter of the Morning Star*

TEENAGE GIRL DRUG ABUSERS

Buntin, Julie. ★*Marlena: A Novel*

TEENAGE GIRL JOURNALISTS

Hart, Carolyn G. *Letter from Home*
Shocklee, Michelle. *Under the Tulip Tree*

TEENAGE GIRL KIDNAPPING VICTIMS

Silva, Daniel. *The New Girl*

TEENAGE GIRL MURDER VICTIMS

Atkins, Ace. *The Innocents*
Ferraris, Zoe. *Finding Nouf*
Hannah, Sophie. *Keep Her Safe*
Kwon, Yo-Son. *Lemon*
Luna, Louisa. *The Janes*

Parker, Robert B. *Death in Paradise*
Persson Giolito, Malin. *Beyond All Reasonable Doubt: A Novel*
Reichs, Kathy. *Monday Mourning*
Sebold, Alice. ★*The Lovely Bones*

TEENAGE GIRL MUSICIANS
Larkin, Allie. *The People We Keep*

TEENAGE GIRLS
Abbott, Jeff. *Blame*
Abbott, Jeff. *The Three Beths*
Abu-Jaber, Diana. *Birds of Paradise: A Novel*
Amirrezvani, Anita. *The Blood of Flowers: A Novel*
Atkinson, Kate. ★*When Will There Be Good News?: A Novel*
Austen, Jane. *Northanger Abbey*
Beagle, Peter S. *The Unicorn Sonata*
Berg, Elizabeth. *The Story of Arthur Truluv: A Novel*
Blau, Jessica Anya. *Mary Jane: A Novel*
Brunt, Carol Rifka. ★*Tell the Wolves I'm Home: A Novel*
Burdick, Serena. *The Girls with No Names*
Burns, Anna. *Milkman: A Novel*
Campbell, Bonnie Jo. *Once Upon a River*
Campisi, Megan. *Sin Eater*
Clement, Jennifer. *Gun Love*
Cline, Emma. *The Girls: A Novel*
Copenhaver, John. *The Savage Kind*
Coster, Naima. *What's Mine and Yours: A Novel*
Cronin, Marianne. *The One Hundred Years of Lenni and Margot*
Cruz, Angie. *Dominicana: A Novel*
D'Eramo, Luce. *Deviation*
Dare, Abi. *The Girl with the Louding Voice*
Diachenko, Serhii. *Vita Nostra*
Doan, Amy Mason. *The Summer List*
Dunant, Sarah. *The Birth of Venus: A Novel*
Edwards, Rachel. *Darling*
Ellison, J. T. *Good Girls Lie*
Ellison, J. T. *Tear Me Apart*
Erpenbeck, Jenny. *The Book of Words*
Eugenides, Jeffrey. ★*The Virgin Suicides*
Ferrante, Elena. *The Lying Life of Adults*
Foley, Bridget. *Just Get Home*
Franklin, Miles. *My Brilliant Career*
French, Tana. ★*The Secret Place*
Fridlund, Emily. ★*History of Wolves: A Novel*
Galloway, Gregory. *As Simple as Snow*
Gaynor, Hazel. *The Lighthouse Keeper's Daughter*
Gibbons, Kaye. *The Life All Around Me by Ellen Foster*
Grames, Juliet. *The Seven or Eight Deaths of Stella Fortuna*
Grant, Helen. *The Glass Demon*
Hansen, Ron. *Mariette in Ecstasy*
Hart, Carolyn G. *Letter from Home*
Hayder, Mo. *Hanging Hill*
Johnson, Craig. *Daughter of the Morning Star*
Keller, Julia. *A Killing in the Hills*
Kelly, Martha Hall. *Lilac Girls*
Kidd, Sue Monk. ★*The Secret Life of Bees*
Kincaid, Jamaica. ★*Annie John*
King, Stephen. ★*Carrie*
Larison, John. *Whiskey When We're Dry*
Layden, Emily. *All Girls*

Machado, Carmen Maria. ★*The Low, Low Woods*
Macmillan, Gilly. *The Perfect Girl*
Makumbi, Jennifer Nansubuga. ★*A Girl Is a Body of Water*
McDermott, Alice. *Child of My Heart*
McGuire, Seanan. ★*Down Among the Sticks and Bones*
McHugh, Laura. *The Wolf Wants In: A Novel*
McLean, Felicity. *The Van Apfel Girls Are Gone*
Murakami, Ryu. *In the Miso Soup*
O'Donnell, Lisa. *The Death of Bees: A Novel*
Overton, Hollie. *The Runaway*
Palmer, Daniel. *The New Husband*
Pessl, Marisha. *Special Topics in Calamity Physics*
Picoult, Jodi. *Leaving Time: A Novel*
Pinborough, Sarah. ★*Cross Her Heart: A Novel*
Prose, Francine. *Goldengrove: A Novel*
Roisin, Fariha. *Like a Bird*
Rojas Contreras, Ingrid. ★*Fruit of the Drunken Tree: A Novel*
Rous, Emma. *The Perfect Guests*
Sepetys, Ruta. ★*Out of the Easy*
Shan, Sa. *The Girl Who Played Go*
Smith, Ali. ★*How to Be Both*
Smith, Dodie. ★*I Capture the Castle*
Spark, Muriel. ★*The Prime of Miss Jean Brodie*
Strout, Elizabeth. *Amy and Isabelle: A Novel*
Szabo, Magda. *Abigail*
Temple, Emily. *The Lightness*
Thomas, Scarlett. *Oligarchy*
Tudor, C. J. *The Burning Girls: A Novel*
Urquhart, Rachel. *The Visionist*
Urrea, Luis Alberto. *The Hummingbird's Daughter: A Novel*
Vestal, Shawn. *Daredevils*
Walker, Karen Thompson. *The Age of Miracles: A Novel*

TEENAGE GIRLS — DEATH
Adler-Olsen, Jussi. *The Hanging Girl*

TEENAGE GIRLS — FRIENDSHIP
Buntin, Julie. ★*Marlena: A Novel*
Ferrante, Elena. *My Brilliant Friend*

TEENAGE GIRLS — IDENTITY
De Robertis, Carolina. *Perla*

TEENAGE GIRLS — INTERPERSONAL RELATIONS
Bird, Sarah. *The Gap Year: A Novel*

TEENAGE GIRLS — PSYCHOLOGY
Bieker, Chelsea Jean. *Godshot: A Novel*
Greenberg, Joanne. *I Never Promised You a Rose Garden: A Novel*

TEENAGE GIRLS — RELATIONS WITH OLDER MEN
Russell, Kate Elizabeth. ★*My Dark Vanessa*
Tamirat, Nafkote. *The Parking Lot Attendant: A Novel*

TEENAGE GIRLS — SEXUALITY
Abbott, Megan E. *The Fever*
DeWoskin, Rachel. *Big Girl Small: A Novel*

TEENAGE GIRLS WHO ARE MUTE
Heaberlin, Julia. *We Are All the Same in the Dark: A Novel*

TEENAGE GIRLS WITH MENTAL ILLNESSES
Greenberg, Joanne. *I Never Promised You a Rose Garden: A Novel*
Shields, Carol. *Unless*

TEENAGE KIDNAPPING VICTIMS
McHugh, Laura. *What's Done in Darkness: A Novel*

TEENAGE MOTHERS
Hadley, Tessa. *Clever Girl*
Sapphire. ★*Push: A Novel*
Tyler, Anne. *The Amateur Marriage: A Novel*

TEENAGE MURDER SUSPECTS
Brown, Rosellen. ★*Before and After*
Winer, Jeanne. *Her Kind of Case*

TEENAGE MURDER VICTIMS
Ajvide Lindqvist, John. *Let the Right One In*
Cleeves, Ann. *Raven Black*
Harvey, John. *Cold in Hand*
Quartey, Kwei. *Children of the Street: A Novel*
Robinson, Peter. *Friend of the Devil*

TEENAGE MURDERERS
Flynn, Gillian. *Dark Places*
Gaylin, Alison. *Never Look Back*
Greene, Graham. ★*Brighton Rock*
North, Alex. *The Shadows*
Sandford, John. *Mad River*
Shriver, Lionel. *We Need to Talk About Kevin*

TEENAGE MUSICIANS
Macmillan, Gilly. *The Perfect Girl*

TEENAGE NONCONFORMISTS
Franklin, Miles. *My Brilliant Career*

TEENAGE NUNS
Hansen, Ron. *Mariette in Ecstasy*

TEENAGE PREGNANCY
Bennett, Brit. *The Mothers*
Bronsky, Alina. *The Hottest Dishes of the Tartar Cuisine*
Greenwood, Kerry. *Unnatural Habits*
Hoffmann, R. J. *Other People's Children: A Novel*
McKinney-Whetstone, Diane. *Leaving Cecil Street: A Novel*
Moniz, Tomas. *Big Familia*

TEENAGE PRISONERS
Ballard, J. G. *Empire of the Sun: A Novel*
Persson Giolito, Malin. *Quicksand*

TEENAGE PROSTITUTES
Donoghue, Emma. *Slammerkin*
Garcia Marquez, Gabriel. *Memories of My Melancholy Whores*

TEENAGE PSYCHICS
King, Stephen. ★*Carrie*

TEENAGE REBELS
Ferrante, Elena. *The Lying Life of Adults*

TEENAGE REFUGEES
Porter, Henry. *Firefly*

TEENAGE ROMANCE
Choi, Susan. ★*Trust Exercise: A Novel*
Fowler, Therese. ★*A Good Neighborhood*
Kamali, Marjan. ★*The Stationery Shop*
Mishima, Yukio. *The Sound of Waves*
Park, Ishle Yi. *Angel & Hannah: A Novel in Verse*
Sagan, Francoise. ★*Bonjour Tristesse*
Sepetys, Ruta. ★*Out of the Easy*

TEENAGE SERIAL MURDERERS
DeSilva, Bruce. *Providence Rag*

TEENAGE WIZARDS
Grossman, Lev. ★*The Magicians: A Novel*

TEENAGERS
Allende, Isabel. *Ripper: A Novel*
Backman, Fredrik. *Us Against You: A Novel*
Baker, Kage. *The Bird of the River*
Baxter, Charles. *Saul and Patsy*
Bruen, Ken. *The Guards*
Dallas, Sandra. *Tallgrass*
Danielewski, Mark Z. *Only Revolutions*
Freudenberger, Nell. *The Dissident*
Galloway, Gregory. *As Simple as Snow*
Hao, Jingfang. *Vagabonds: A Novel*
McDermott, Alice. ★*That Night*
Meltzer, Brad. *The Zero Game*
Price, Richard. *Lush Life*
Sparks, Nicholas. *A Walk to Remember*
Straub, Peter. ★*A Dark Matter: A Novel*
Vinge, Vernor. *The Children of the Sky*
Whitehead, Colson. *Sag Harbor: A Novel*

TEENAGERS — CAREER ASPIRATIONS
Franklin, Miles. *My Brilliant Career*

TEENAGERS — DEATH
Pessl, Marisha. *Special Topics in Calamity Physics*

TEENAGERS — RELIGIOUS LIFE
Salinger, J. D. ★*Franny and Zooey*

TEENAGERS — SEXUALITY
Burns, Charles. ★*Black Hole*

TEENAGERS AND WAR
Olmstead, Robert. ★*Coal Black Horse*

TEENAGERS WITH DEVELOPMENTAL DISABILITIES
Raimondo, Lynne. *Dante's Wood: A Mark Angelotti Novel*

TEENAGERS WITH DISABILITIES
Frankel, Laurie. *One Two Three: A Novel*
Nussbaum, Susan. *Good Kings, Bad Kings: A Novel*

TEENAGERS WITH DISFIGUREMENTS
Burns, Charles. ★*Black Hole*

TEENAGERS WITH MENTAL ILLNESSES
Brenner, Jamie. *Drawing Home*

TEENAGERS WITH MUSCULAR DYSTROPHY
Evison, Jonathan. *The Revised Fundamentals of Caregiving: A Novel*

TEENAGERS WITH SCHIZOPHRENIA
Greenberg, Joanne. *I Never Promised You a Rose Garden: A Novel*
*The **Teeth** of the Comb & Other Stories*. Alomar, Osama

TEHRAN, IRAN
Araghi, Alireza Taheri. ★*The Immortals of Tehran*
Bijan, Donia. *The Last Days of Cafe Leila*
Hozar, Nazanine. *Aria*
Ignatius, David. *The Increment: A Novel*
Kamali, Marjan. ★*The Stationery Shop*
Mandanipour, Shahriar. *Moon Brow*
Sofer, Dalia. *The Septembers of Shiraz*

Teixcalaan novels [Series]. Martine, Arkady

TEJADA ALONSO Y LEON, CARLOS (FICTITIOUS CHARACTER)
Pawel, Rebecca. *Death of a Nationalist*

TEL AVIV, ISRAEL
Castel-Bloom, Orly. *Textile*
Krauss, Nicole. *Forest Dark*
Shoham, Liad. *Asylum City: A Novel*

TELEPATHY
Bear, Elizabeth. *Steles of the Sky*
Hamilton, Peter F. *The Dreaming Void*
Huang, S. L. *Zero Sum Game*
King, Stephen. *Doctor Sleep: A Novel*
King, Stephen. ★*The Shining*

TELEPHONE CALLS
Berg, Gretchen. *The Operator*
Lippman, Laura. ★*Dream Girl*

TELEPHONE OPERATORS
Berg, Gretchen. *The Operator*

TELEPHONES
Follett, Ken. *Jackdaws*

TELEPORTATION
Hurley, Kameron. ★*The Light Brigade*
Scalzi, John. *The Collapsing Empire*

TELEVISION — SOCIAL ASPECTS
Kosinski, Jerzy. ★*Being There*

TELEVISION ACTORS AND ACTRESSES
Dade, Olivia. *All the Feels*
Dade, Olivia. *Spoiler Alert*
Rai, Alisha. ★*First Comes Like*

TELEVISION INDUSTRY AND TRADE
Pitoniak, Anna. *Necessary People*
Yellin, Jessica. *Savage News*

TELEVISION JOURNALISTS
Butler, Robert Olen. *Hell: A Novel*

TELEVISION NEWS
Barthelme, Frederick. *Painted Desert: A Novel*

TELEVISION NEWSCASTERS AND COMMENTATORS
Kenney, John. *Talk to Me*

TELEVISION PERSONALITIES
Hart, Erin. *The Book of Killowen*

TELEVISION PRODUCERS AND DIRECTORS
Cochrun, Alison. *The Charm Offensive*

TELEVISION PROGRAMS
Byatt, A. S. *A Whistling Woman*
Kunzru, Hari. *Red Pill: A Novel*
Rushdie, Salman. ★*Quichotte: A Novel*
Somer, Mehmet Murat. *The Serenity Murders*

TELEVISION TALK SHOW HOSTS AND GUESTS
Smith, Julie. ★*Mean Woman Blues*
Tell Her No Lies. Irvin, Kelly
Tell Me How Long the Train's Been Gone: A Novel. Baldwin, James
Tell the Machine Goodnight. Williams, Katie
★*Tell the Wolves I'm Home: A Novel*. Brunt, Carol Rifka
The Teller of Secrets: A Novel. Adjapon, Bisi
The Telling. Le Guin, Ursula K.
Temeraire [Series]. Novik, Naomi
Temperance Brennan mysteries [Series]. Reichs, Kathy
Tempest. Jenkins, Beverly
★*The Templar Legacy: A Novel of Suspense*. Berry, Steve
The Temple of Dawn. Mishima, Yukio
The Temple of My Familiar. Walker, Alice
Temple, Emily
The Lightness

TEMPORARY EMPLOYEES
Butler, Halle. *The New Me: A Novel*

Cameron, Lindsay. *Just One Look*
TEMPTATION
Clark, Wahida. *Thug Lovin'*
Reimringer, John. *Vestments*
Temptations of a Wallflower. Leigh, Eva
Tempting Fortune. Beverley, Jo
Ten Girls to Watch: A Novel. Shumway, Charity
Ten Things I've Learnt About Love: A Novel. Butler, Sarah
TEN THOUSAND ISLANDS, FLORIDA
Russell, Karen. ★*Swamplandia!*
TEN-YEAR-OLD BOYS
Bohjalian, Chris. *The Buffalo Soldier: A Novel*
Earley, Tony. *Jim the Boy: A Novel*
French, Albert. *Billy*
TEN-YEAR-OLD GIRLS
Grant, Helen. *The Vanishing of Katharina Linden*
Pronzini, Bill. *Crazybone*
The Tenant of Wildfell Hall. Bronte, Anne
Tender Mercies. Brown, Rosellen
Tenderness. MacLeod, Alison
TENNESSEE
Alexander, Tamera. *With This Pledge*
Barr, Mark. *Watershed*
Barry, Sebastian. ★*A Thousand Moons: A Novel*
Bledsoe, Alex. *Gather Her Round: A Novel of the Tufa*
Bledsoe, Alex. *The Hum and the Shiver*
Bledsoe, Alex. *Long Black Curl*
Bledsoe, Alex. *Wisp of a Thing*
Child, Lee. ★*The Sentinel*
Dekker, Ted. *The Girl Behind the Red Rope*
Greene, Amy. *Long Man*
Gregory, Daryl. *The Devil's Alphabet*
Grisham, John. ★*The Firm*
Hauck, Rachel. *The Wedding Chapel*
Hicks, Robert. *The Widow of the South*
Kingsolver, Barbara. ★*Flight Behavior*
Mason, Bobbie Ann. *Patchwork*
McCrumb, Sharyn. ★*The Ballad of Frankie Silver*
McCrumb, Sharyn. ★*If Ever I Return, Pretty Peggy-O*
Petrie, Nicholas. *Tear It Down*
Petrie, Nicholas. *The Wild One*
Phillips, Susan Elizabeth. ★*Dance Away with Me*
Phillips, Susan Elizabeth. ★*Natural Born Charmer*
Verble, Margaret. ★*When Two Feathers Fell from the Sky*
Tenorio, Lysley A.
The Son of Good Fortune: A Novel
TENOS, GREECE
Siger, Jeffrey. *Target Tinos: An Inspector Kaldis Mystery*
Tensorate novellas [Series]. Yang, JY
The Tenth Commandment: A Novel. Sanders, Lawrence
The Tenth Justice. Meltzer, Brad
The Tenth Man. Greene, Graham
The Tenth Muse: A Novel. Chung, Catherine
★*Tenth of December: Stories*. Saunders, George
Tepper, Sheri S.
The Gate to Women's Country
★*Grass*
Singer from the Sea

The Visitor

TERMINAL ILLNESS

Higgins, Kristan. ★*Life and Other Inconveniences*

James, Henry. *The Wings of the Dove*

Sarton, May. *A Reckoning: A Novel*

★*Terms* of Endearment: A Novel : With a New Preface. McMurtry, Larry

Terra Ignota [Series]. Palmer, Ada

TERRAFORMING

McDevitt, Jack. *The Engines of God*

Robinson, Kim Stanley. ★*Blue Mars*

*The **Terranauts**. Boyle, T. Coraghessan*

*A **Terrible** Country. Gessen, Keith*

★*The **Terror**: a Novel. Simmons, Dan*

TERRORISM

Aramburu, Fernando. *Homeland*

Buchman, M. L. *Pure Heat*

Clancy, Tom. *Patriot Games*

Coulter, Catherine. *The Devil's Triangle*

Coulter, Catherine. *The End Game*

Coulter, Catherine. *The Sixth Day*

Cumming, Charles. *A Divided Spy*

Cussler, Clive. *Blue Gold: A Novel from the Numa Files*

Flanagan, Richard. *The Unknown Terrorist*

Freeman, Brian. *Marathon*

Gilman, Felix. *The Half-Made World*

Higgins, Jack. *Touch the Devil*

Khadra, Yasmina. ★*Khalil: A Novel*

Le Carre, John. *A Most Wanted Man: A Novel*

Leonard, Elmore. ★*Killshot*

Majumdar, Megha. *A Burning*

Murakami, Haruki. *After the Quake: Stories*

Palahniuk, Chuck. *Pygmy*

Pavone, Chris. *The Paris Diversion: A Novel*

Perry, Thomas. *The Bomb Maker*

Pinsker, Sarah. *A Song for a New Day*

Porter, Henry. *The Bell Ringers*

Quirk, Matthew. *Cold Barrel Zero*

Sakey, Marcus. *A Better World*

Sakey, Marcus. *Brilliance*

Silva, Daniel. *The Other Woman*

TERRORISM — PREVENTION

Berenson, Alex. *The Deceivers*

Brown, Dale. *The Moscow Offensive: A Novel*

Cameron, Marc. *Power and Empire*

Harvey, Michael T. *We All Fall Down*

Hunter, Stephen. *Soft Target: A Thriller*

Le Carre, John. ★*A Delicate Truth*

Rosenfelt, David. *Blackout*

Tata, A. J. *Dark Winter*

Taylor, Brad. *Ring of Fire*

TERRORISM — PSYCHOLOGICAL ASPECTS

DeLillo, Don. *Falling Man: A Novel*

TERRORISTS

Adler-Olsen, Jussi. ★*Victim 2117*

Bilal, Parker. *The Ghost Runner*

Coulter, Catherine. *The Devil's Triangle*

Coulter, Catherine. *The End Game*

Crais, Robert. *Demolition Angel: A Novel.*

Cussler, Clive. *Sacred Stone*

Hayes, Terry. *I Am Pilgrim*

Higgins, C. A. *Lightless*

MacDonald, John D. *Cinnamon Skin: The Twentieth Adventure of Travis McGee*

MacDonald, John D. *The Green Ripper*

Palahniuk, Chuck. *Pygmy*

Porter, Henry. *Firefly*

Rosenfelt, David. *Blackout*

Spillane, Mickey. *The Goliath Bone*

Steinhauer, Olen. ★*All the Old Knives*

Steinhauer, Olen. *The Last Tourist*

Steinhauer, Olen. *The Middleman*

Tesh, Emily

Silver in the Wood

Tess Monaghan mysteries [Series]. Lippman, Laura

★*Tess* of the D'urbervilles: A Pure Woman Faithfully Presented. Hardy, Thomas

TEST PILOTS

L'Amour, Louis. *The Last of the Breed*

★*The **Testaments**: a Novel. Atwood, Margaret*

***Testimony**. Turow, Scott*

***Testimony**: a Novel. Shreve, Anita*

TEVYE (FICTITIOUS CHARACTER : SHOLEM ALEICHEM)

Aleichem, Sholem. *Tevye the Dairyman and the Railroad Stories*

Aleichem, Sholem. *Tevye's Daughters*

***Tevye** the Dairyman and the Railroad Stories. Aleichem, Sholem*

***Tevye's** Daughters. Aleichem, Sholem*

TEXAS

Abbott, Jeff. *Blame*

Barnett, LaShonda K. *Jam on the Vine*

Barr, Nevada. *Track of the Cat*

Berlin, Lucia. ★*Evening in Paradise: More Stories*

Block, Stefan Merrill. *Oliver Loving: A Novel*

Bond, Cynthia. *Ruby: A Novel*

Brown, Sandra. ★*Blind Tiger*

Burke, James Lee. *House of the Rising Sun: A Novel*

Burke, James Lee. *Wayfaring Stranger: A Novel*

Castro, V. *Goddess of Filth*

Center, Katherine. *What You Wish For*

Child, Lee. *Echo Burning*

Cobb, May K. *The Hunting Wives*

Dell, Kari Lynn. *Fearless in Texas*

Dell, Kari Lynn. *Mistletoe in Texas*

Dell, Kari Lynn. *Reckless in Texas*

Dow, David R. *Confessions of an Innocent Man*

Drake, Laura. *The Sweet Spot*

Fallon, Siobhan. *You Know When the Men Are Gone*

Flores, Fernando A. *Tears of the Trufflepig*

Founds, Kathleen. *When Mystical Creatures Attack!*

Fountain, Ben. ★*Billy Lynn's Long Halftime Walk*

Gardiner, Meg. *Into the Black Nowhere*

Groom, Winston. *El Paso: A Novel*

Hambly, Barbara. *Lady of Perdition*

Hamill, Shaun. *A Cosmology of Monsters*

Heaberlin, Julia. *We Are All the Same in the Dark: A Novel*

Irvin, Kelly. *Tell Her No Lies*

Jiles, Paulette. *News of the World: A Novel*

Kelton, Elmer. ★*The Way of the Coyote*
Kennedy, Randy. *Presidio*
Kibler, Julie. *Home for Erring and Outcast Girls*
Lansdale, Joe R. *The Bottoms*
Lansdale, Joe R. *Devil Red*
Lansdale, Joe R. *Honky Tonk Samurai*
Lansdale, Joe R. *More Better Deals*
Lansdale, Joe R. ★*Paradise Sky*
Locke, Attica. ★*Bluebird, Bluebird*
Locke, Attica. ★*Heaven, My Home*
London, Julia. *The Charmer in Chaps*
March, Emily. *Jackson*
McCarthy, Cormac. ★*Blood Meridian, Or, the Evening Redness in the West*
McCarthy, Cormac. ★*No Country for Old Men*
McMurtry, Larry. *Comanche Moon: A Novel*
McMurtry, Larry. *The Evening Star: A Novel*
McMurtry, Larry. ★*Lonesome Dove: A Novel*
McMurtry, Larry. ★*Streets of Laredo: A Novel*
McMurtry, Larry. ★*Terms of Endearment: A Novel : With a New Preface*
Meyer, Philipp. ★*The Son: A Novel*
Perkins, S. C. *Murder Once Removed*
Phillips, Susan Elizabeth. *Call Me Irresistible*
Phillips, Susan Elizabeth. *The Great Escape*
Phillips, Susan Elizabeth. *What I Did for Love*
Pryor, Mark. *Hollow Man*
Reichs, Kathy. *Death Du Jour*
Rice, Christopher. *Blood Victory*
Robotham, Michael. *Life or Death*
Rochon, Farrah. *The Boyfriend Project*
Shames, Terry. ★*An Unsettling Crime for Samuel Craddock*
Sternbergh, Adam. *The Blinds*
Swann, Stacey. *Olympus Texas*
Sylvester, Natalia. *Everyone Knows You Go Home*
Thompson, Jim. *The Killer Inside Me*
Wetmore, Elizabeth. ★*Valentine*
TEXAS PANHANDLE
Kennedy, Randy. *Presidio*
Texas Rangers (Elmer Kelton) [Series]. Kelton, Elmer
Texas rodeo [Series]. Dell, Kari Lynn
Textile. Castel-Bloom, Orly
Thackeray, William Makepeace
★*Vanity Fair: A Novel Without a Hero*
THAI AMERICANS
Eisler, Barry. *All the Devils*
THAILAND
Barton, Fiona. *The Suspect*
Boulle, Pierre. *The Bridge Over the River Kwai: A Novel*
Burdett, John. *Bangkok 8*
Cotterill, Colin. *Killed at the Whim of a Hat*
Eisler, Barry. *The Night Trade*
Flanagan, Richard. ★*The Narrow Road to the Deep North*
Hallinan, Timothy. *Fools' River*
Osborne, Lawrence. *The Glass Kingdom: A Novel*
Schwarz, Liese O'Halloran. *What Could Be Saved*
THAMES RIVER
Bolton, S. J. *A Dark and Twisted Tide*

James, P. D. *Original Sin*
Setterfield, Diane. ★*Once Upon a River*
Thammavongsa, Souvankham
How to Pronounce Knife: Stories
THANET, LUKE (FICTITIOUS CHARACTER)
Simpson, Dorothy. *Dead and Gone: An Inspector Luke Thanet Novel.*
Simpson, Dorothy. *Dead by Morning*
Simpson, Dorothy. *Doomed to Die*
Simpson, Dorothy. *Last Seen Alive: A Luke Thanet Mystery*
Simpson, Dorothy. *No Laughing Matter*
Simpson, Dorothy. *Once Too Often: An Inspector Luke Thanet Novel*
★*Thank You, Mr. Nixon: Stories.* Jen, Gish
That Darkness. Black, Lisa
★*That Distant Land: The Collected Stories of Wendell Berry.* Berry, Wendell
That Kind of Mother: A Novel. Alam, Rumaan
★*That Night*. McDermott, Alice
Thayne, RaeAnne
The Cliff House
THE HAGUE, NETHERLANDS
Kitamura, Katie M. *Intimacies*
THE SIXTIES GENERATION
Pynchon, Thomas. *Vineland*
THE WEST (CANADA)
Brand, Max. *The Stingaree*
THE WEST (UNITED STATES)
Bear, Elizabeth. *Stone Mad*
Bittner, Rosanne. *Logan's Lady*
Brand, Max. *Max Brand's Best Western Stories*
Brooks, Bill. *Blood Storm*
Brooks, Bill. *Frontier Justice*
Brooks, Bill. *Winter Kill*
Burke, James Lee. *Another Kind of Eden*
Cussler, Clive. *The Wrecker*
Dallas, Sandra. *Tallgrass*
Dallas, Sandra. *Westering Women: A Novel*
Davies, Carys. *West*
deWitt, Patrick. *The Sisters Brothers: A Novel*
Dexter, Pete. ★*Deadwood*
Diaz, Hernan. ★*In the Distance*
Donoghue, Emma. ★*Frog Music*
Enger, Lin. *The High Divide: A Novel*
Erdrich, Louise. *The Master Butchers Singing Club: A Novel*
Estleman, Loren D. ★*The Master Executioner*
Everett, Percival L. *God's Country*
Fajardo-Anstine, Kali. ★*Sabrina & Corina: Stories*
Gilman, Laura Anne. *The Cold Eye*
Gilman, Laura Anne. *Silver on the Road*
Goodman, Jo. *A Touch of Forever*
Guthrie, A. B. ★*The Big Sky*
Harmon, Amy. *Where the Lost Wander*
Harte, Bret. ★*The Best Short Stories of Bret Harte*
Holbert, Bruce. *Whiskey*
Jenkins, Beverly. *Forbidden*
Jenkins, Beverly. *Tempest*
Katsu, Alma. *The Hunger: A Novel*
Kelton, Elmer. *Hard Ride*
Kirkpatrick, Jane. *One More River to Cross*

Knott, Robert. *Robert B. Parker's Buckskin*
L'Amour, Louis. ★*Bendigo Shafter*
L'Amour, Louis. *The Californios*
L'Amour, Louis. *End of the Drive*
Larison, John. *Whiskey When We're Dry*
Malerman, Josh. *Unbury Carol*
McMurtry, Larry. *Boone's Lick: A Novel*
McMurtry, Larry. *Comanche Moon: A Novel*
McMurtry, Larry. ★*Lonesome Dove: A Novel*
McMurtry, Larry. ★*Streets of Laredo: A Novel*
Meyer, Philipp. ★*The Son: A Novel*
Michener, James A. ★*Centennial*
Parker, Robert B. *Appaloosa*
Parker, Robert B. *Blue-Eyed Devil*
Petersen, Todd Robert. *Picnic in the Ruins*
Peterson, Tracie. *What Comes My Way*
Portis, Charles. ★*True Grit: A Novel*
Punke, Michael. *Ridgeline: A Novel*
Schanbacher, Gary Lester. *Crossing Purgatory*
Stegner, Wallace. ★*Angle of Repose*
Stegner, Wallace. ★*The Big Rock Candy Mountain*
Swarthout, Glendon. ★*The Shootist*
Williams, Joy. *Harrow*

THEATER
Andrews, Donna. *Murder Most Fowl: A Meg Langslow Mystery*
Choi, Susan. ★*Trust Exercise: A Novel*
Hawke, Ethan. *A Bright Ray of Darkness*
Quincy, D. M. *Murder at the Opera*
Sontag, Susan. ★*In America*

THEATER — HISTORY
Gallagher, Stephen. *The Kingdom of Bones: A Novel*

THEATER ACTORS AND ACTRESSES
Enright, Anne. *Actress: A Novel*

THEATER AND TEENAGERS
Choi, Susan. ★*Trust Exercise: A Novel*

THEATER COMPANIES
Gilbert, Elizabeth. ★*City of Girls*

THEATER CRITICS
Bram, Christopher. *Lives of the Circus Animals: A Novel*
Parker, Lucy. *The Austen Playbook*

THEATRICAL PRODUCERS AND DIRECTORS
Fredericks, Mariah. *Death of a Showman*
Theft of Swords. Sullivan, Michael J.
★*Their Eyes Were Watching God*. Hurston, Zora Neale
★*Their Little Secret*. Billingham, Mark

Thelen, Albert Vigoleis
The Island of Second Sight: From the Applied Recollections of Vigoleis
★*Them*. Oates, Joyce Carol
Theme Music. Vandelly, T. Marie
Then She Was Gone: A Novel. Jewell, Lisa
Then There Was You. Isaac, Kara
Then We Take Berlin. Lawton, John

THEOCRACY
Seton, Anya. ★*The Winthrop Woman*

THEOLOGIANS
Mukherjee, Abir. *The Shadows of Men*
★*Theophilus North*. Wilder, Thornton

THERA (ISLANDS)
Walton, Jo. ★*Necessity*
There Before the Chaos. Wagers, K. B.
There but for The: A Novel. Smith, Ali
There Is Room for You. Bacon, Charlotte
★*There There*. Orange, Tommy
There's a Word for That. Tanen, Sloane
There's Something I Want You to Do: Stories. Baxter, Charles

Theroux, Paul
★*The Mosquito Coast: A Novel*
★*These Ghosts Are Family: A Novel*. Card, Maisy
These Honored Dead. Putnam, Jonathan F.
These Old Shades. Heyer, Georgette
These Toxic Things. Hall, Rachel Howzell
★*These Women*. Pochoda, Ivy

THESEUS (GREEK MYTHOLOGY)
Renault, Mary. *The Bull from the Sea*
Renault, Mary. *The King Must Die*
Saint, Jennifer. *Ariadne*
Thicker Than Water: A Monika Paniatowski British Police Procedural. Spencer, Sally
The Thicket. Lansdale, Joe R.
Thief of Corinth. Afshar, Tessa
Thief of Glory: A Novel. Brouwer, Sigmund
Thief of Time. Pratchett, Terry
Thief River Falls. Freeman, Brian

Thien, Madeleine
Do Not Say We Have Nothing

THIEVES
Adler-Olsen, Jussi. *The Marco Effect: A Department Q Novel*
Afshar, Tessa. *Thief of Corinth*
Alexis, Andre. *The Hidden Keys*
Atkins, Ace. *The Redeemers*
Banville, John. *The Blue Guitar*
Block, Lawrence. *The Burglar in the Closet*
Brown, Taylor. *Fallen Land*
Dickens, Charles. *Oliver Twist, or the Parish Boy's Progress*
Hallinan, Timothy. *Fields Where They Lay*
Hallinan, Timothy. *Fools' River*
Hamilton, Steve. *The Second Life of Nick Mason: A Novel*
Harrison, Thea. *Dragon Bound*
Helprin, Mark. ★*Winter's Tale*
Higashino, Keigo. *The Miracles of the Namiya General Store*
Kennedy, Randy. *Presidio*
Krueger, Paul. *Steel Crow Saga*
Leckie, Ann. *Provenance*
Lindsay, Jeffry P. *Just Watch Me*
Maizes, R. L. *Other People's Pets*
Mayor, Archer. *Tag Man: A Joe Gunther Novel*
McMurtry, Larry. ★*Streets of Laredo: A Novel*
Parker, T. Jefferson. *L.A. Outlaws: A Novel*
Perez-Reverte, Arturo. *What We Become*
Pratchett, Terry. *Thief of Time*
Rajaniemi, Hannu. *The Fractal Prince*
Rajaniemi, Hannu. *The Quantum Thief*
Sandford, John. *Storm Front*
Schwab, Victoria. *A Darker Shade of Magic*
Skarmeta, Antonio. *The Dancer and the Thief: A Novel*

Stark, Richard. *Breakout*
Stark, Richard. *Comeback*
Stark, Richard. *The Hunter: A Parker Novel*
Sullivan, Michael J. *Theft of Swords*
Urrea, Luis Alberto. *Into the Beautiful North: A Novel*
Welty, Eudora. ★*The Robber Bridegroom*
Westlake, Donald E. *Get Real*
Thin Air. Cleeves, Ann
Thin Girls. Clarke, Diana
Thin Ice: A Mystery. Shelton, Paige
★*The Thin Man*. Hammett, Dashiell
★*The Thin Red Line*. Jones, James
The Thing Around Your Neck. Adichie, Chimamanda Ngozi
★*Things Fall Apart*. Achebe, Chinua
★*Things in Jars*. Kidd, Jess
★*The Things They Carried: A Work of Fiction*. O'Brien, Tim
Things to Do When You're Goth in the Country; And Other Stories. Woods, Chavisa
Things We Didn't Say. Green, Amy Lynn
Things You Save in a Fire. Center, Katherine
The Third Bear. Vandermeer, Jeff
★*The Third Deadly Sin*. Sanders, Lawrence
THIRD GRADERS
Gelman, Laurie. *You've Been Volunteered: A Class Mom Novel*
The Third Life of Grange Copeland. Walker, Alice
★*The Third Reich*. Bolano, Roberto
Third Shift [Series]. Snyder, Suleikha
Third Son's a Charm. Galen, Shana
Thirteen. Cavanagh, Steve
Thirteen Moons: A Novel. Frazier, Charles
THIRTEEN-YEAR-OLD BOYS
Adichie, Chimamanda Ngozi. *Half of a Yellow Sun*
Bradbury, Ray. ★*Something Wicked This Way Comes*
Carr, Caleb. *The Angel of Darkness*
Mitchell, David. *Black Swan Green: A Novel*
THIRTEEN-YEAR-OLD GIRLS
Beagle, Peter S. *The Unicorn Sonata*
McEwan, Ian. ★*Atonement: A Novel*
Picoult, Jodi. ★*My Sister's Keeper*
The Thirteenth Tale: A Novel. Setterfield, Diane
THIRTIES (AGE)
Allen, Jayne. *Black Girls Must Die Exhausted*
Christian, Claire. *It's Been a Pleasure, Noni Blake*
Egan, Jennifer. *The Keep*
Foley, Lucy. *The Hunting Party*
Hale, Shannon. *Austenland: A Novel*
Hession, Ronan. *Leonard and Hungry Paul*
Ho, Lauren. *Last Tang Standing*
Lalli, Sonya. *Serena Singh Flips the Script*
Ólafsdóttir, Auður A. *Butterflies in November*
Spencer, Minerva. *Barbarous*
Unsworth, Emma Jane. *Grown Ups*
Valdes, Alisa. *Dirty Girls on Top*
★*The Thirty Names of Night: A Novel*. Joukhadar, Zeyn
The Thirty-Nine Steps. Buchan, John
This Body of Death: An Inspector Lynley Novel. George, Elizabeth
This Book Is Full of Spiders: Seriously, Dude, Don't Touch It. Wong, David

This Earl of Mine. Bateman, Kate
This House Is Not for Sale: A Novel. Osondu, E. C.
This Is Happiness. Williams, Niall
This Is How It Always Is. Frankel, Laurie
★*This Is How You Lose Her*. Diaz, Junot
★*This Is How You Lose the Time War*. El-Mohtar, Amal
This Mournable Body. Dangarembga, Tsitsi
This Must Be the Place. O'Farrell, Maggie
This Scot of Mine. Jordan, Sophie
★*This Side of Paradise*. Fitzgerald, F. Scott
This Storm: A Novel. Ellroy, James
This Tender Land: A Novel. Krueger, William Kent
This Thing Between US: A Novel. Moreno, Gus
This Town Sleeps. Staples, Dennis E.
Thistle & Twigg. Saums, Mary
Thistle & Twigg [Series]. Saums, Mary
Thomas De Quincey mysteries [Series]. Morrell, David
Thomas Kell novels [Series]. Cumming, Charles
Thomas Lynley mysteries [Series]. George, Elizabeth
THOMAS OF HOOKTON (FICTITIOUS CHARACTER)
Cornwell, Bernard. *The Archer's Tale*
Thomas, Bev
A Good Enough Mother: A Novel
THOMAS, DOROTHY KIRWAN
Jónasson, Ragnar. ★*The Girl Who Died*
Riley, Vanessa. ★*Island Queen*
Thomas, Dylan
The Collected Stories
Thomas, Elisabeth
Catherine House
Thomas, Russ
★*Firewatching*
Nighthawking
Thomas, Scarlett
Oligarchy
Thomas, Will
Dance with Death
Thompson, Jim
The Killer Inside Me
Thompson, Tade
Rosewater
The Rosewater Insurrection
The Rosewater Redemption
Thompson, Victoria
Murder on Wall Street
Thompson-Spires, Nafissa
Heads of the Colored People: Stories
Thomson, E. S.
Beloved Poison
The Blood
THOREAU, HENRY DAVID
Pipkin, John. *Woodsburner: A Novel*
Rutherfurd, Edward. *The Princes of Ireland: The Dublin Saga*
A Thorn in the Saddle. Weatherspoon, Rebekah
Thorne chronicles [Series]. Eason, K.
Thorne, Sally
Second First Impressions

THOROUGHBRED HORSES
   Morgan, C. E. ★*The Sport of Kings*
Thorpe, Rufi
   ★*The Knockout Queen*
Those Bones Are Not My Child. Bambara, Toni Cade
Those Who Are Saved. Landau, Alexis
Those Who Leave and Those Who Stay. Ferrante, Elena
Though Not Dead: A Kate Shugak Novel. Stabenow, Dana
THOUGHT AND THINKING
   Brookner, Anita. *Hotel Du Lac*
★*A Thousand Acres*. Smiley, Jane
The *Thousand* Autumns of Jacob De Zoet: A Novel. Mitchell, David
★*A Thousand Moons: A Novel*. Barry, Sebastian
A Thousand Pardons: A Novel. Dee, Jonathan
A Thousand Ships. Haynes, Natalie
A Thread of Grace: A Novel. Russell, Mary Doria
THREAT (PSYCHOLOGY)
   Aimaq, Jasmine. *The Opium Prince*
   Ashley, Jennifer. *Death at the Crystal Palace*
   Barr, Nevada. *What Rose Forgot*
   Burns, Anna. *Milkman: A Novel*
   Clare, Alys. *The Woman Who Spoke to Spirits*
   Clark, Mary Higgins. *Death Wears a Beauty Mask and Other Stories*
   Cleeves, Ann. *Wild Fire*
   Cussler, Clive. *Nighthawk: A Novel from the Numa Files*
   Cussler, Clive. *The Pharaoh's Secret*
   Daugherty, Christi. *Revolver Road: A Harper McClain Mystery*
   Davis, Lindsey. *A Comedy of Terrors: A Flavia Albia Novel*
   Glass, Seraphina Nova. *Someone's Listening*
   Hampton, Brenda. *Stalker*
   Humphreys, Sara Taney. *Trouble Walks In*
   Jackson, Brenda. *Forged in Desire*
   Lepionka, Kristen. *Once You Go This Far: A Mystery*
   Pinter, Jason. *A Stranger at the Door*
   Reid, Iain. *I'm Thinking of Ending Things*
   Rice, Waubgeshig. *Moon of the Crusted Snow: A Novel*
   Roberts, Nora. *The Obsession*
   Roberts, Nora. *Shelter in Place*
   Tudor, C. J. *The Other People*
   VanderMeer, Jeff. *Acceptance: A Novel*
   VanderMeer, Jeff. *Authority: A Novel*
   Woods, Stuart. *Hit List*
The *Three* Beths. Abbott, Jeff
Three Blind Mice, and Other Stories. Christie, Agatha
Three Days Before the Shooting . . . . Ellison, Ralph
★*Three Hours in Paris*. Black, Cara
★*Three Junes*. Glass, Julia
★*Three Lives*. Stein, Gertrude
★*The Three Musketeers*. Dumas, Alexandre
Three musketeers [Series]. Dumas, Alexandre
Three Rooms. Hamya, Jo
Three Stations: An Arkady Renko Novel. Smith, Martin Cruz
Three Things About Elsie: A Novel. Cannon, Joanna
Three Weeks with Lady X. James, Eloisa
Three Words for Goodbye. Gaynor, Hazel
Three Years with the Rat: A Novel. Hosking, Jay
★*The Three-Arched Bridge*. Kadare, Ismail
★*The Three-Body Problem*. Liu, Cixin

Threshold. Doyle, Rob
Thrice the Brinded Cat Hath Mew'd: A Flavia De Luce Novel. Bradley, C. Alan
THRILLERS AND SUSPENSE
   Abbott, Jeff. *Blame*
   Abbott, Megan E. *The Fever*
   Abbott, Megan E. *You Will Know Me: A Novel*
   Abrams, Melanie. *Meadowlark*
   Adams, Taylor. *Hairpin Bridge*
   Adler-Olsen, Jussi. *The Absent One*
   Adler-Olsen, Jussi. *A Conspiracy of Faith*
   Adler-Olsen, Jussi. *The Hanging Girl*
   Adler-Olsen, Jussi. *The Keeper of Lost Causes*
   Adler-Olsen, Jussi. *The Marco Effect: A Department Q Novel*
   Adler-Olsen, Jussi. *The Purity of Vengeance: A Department Q Novel*
   Adler-Olsen, Jussi. *The Scarred Woman*
   Adler-Olsen, Jussi. ★*Victim 2117*
   Aimaq, Jasmine. *The Opium Prince*
   Alfon, Dov. *A Long Night in Paris*
   Atkins, Ace. *The Broken Places*
   Atkins, Ace. *The Fallen*
   Atkins, Ace. *The Forsaken*
   Atkins, Ace. ★*The Heathens*
   Atkins, Ace. *The Innocents*
   Atkins, Ace. *The Lost Ones*
   Atkins, Ace. *The Ranger*
   Atkins, Ace. *The Redeemers*
   Atkins, Ace. *The Revelators*
   Atkins, Ace. *The Shameless*
   Atkins, Ace. *The Sinners*
   Atkins, Ace. *Wicked City*
   Baker, Chandler. *Whisper Network: A Novel*
   Baldacci, David. *The Fallen*
   Baldacci, David. *Hell's Corner*
   Baldacci, David. *Long Road to Mercy*
   Baldacci, David. *A Minute to Midnight*
   Baldacci, David. *Redemption*
   Barber, Lizzy. *A Girl Named Anna*
   Barclay, Linwood. ★*Elevator Pitch: A Novel*
   Barclay, Linwood. *No Safe House*
   Barclay, Linwood. *A Noise Downstairs: A Novel*
   Barclay, Linwood. *Trust Your Eyes: A Thriller*
   Barry, Ava. *Windhall*
   Barry, Jessica. ★*Don't Turn Around*
   Bauer, Belinda. *The Beautiful Dead*
   Bauer, Belinda. *Snap*
   Beck, Haylen. *Here and Gone*
   Berenson, Alex. *The Deceivers*
   Berenson, Alex. *The Faithful Spy: A Novel*
   Berenson, Alex. *The Prisoner*
   Berry, Steve. ★*The Templar Legacy: A Novel of Suspense*
   Beukes, Lauren. *Afterland*
   Beukes, Lauren. *Broken Monsters*
   Billingham, Mark. ★*Their Little Secret*
   Black, Lisa. *Let Justice Descend*
   Black, Lisa. *Suffer the Children*
   Black, Lisa. *That Darkness*
   Black, Saul. *Anything for You*

Black, Saul. ★*The Killing Lessons*
Black, Saul. ★*Lovemurder*
Blake, James Carlos. *The House of Wolfe*
Block, Lawrence. *Killing Castro*
Bohjalian, Chris. *The Flight Attendant: A Novel*
Bohjalian, Chris. ★*The Red Lotus*
Box, C. J. *Badlands*
Box, C. J. ★*The Bitterroots*
Box, C. J. ★*Dark Sky*
Box, C. J. *The Disappeared*
Box, C. J. *The Highway*
Box, C. J. ★*Long Range*
Box, C. J. ★*Open Season*
Box, C. J. *Paradise Valley*
Box, C. J. *Savage Run*
Box, C. J. *Trophy Hunt*
Box, C. J. *Vicious Circle*
Box, C. J. *Winterkill*
Box, C. J. ★*Wolf Pack*
Bradby, Tom. *Double Agent*
Brown, Dan. *The Da Vinci Code*
Burton, Jeffrey B. ★*The Finders: A Mace Reid K-9 Mystery*
Burton, Jeffrey B. *The Keepers: A Mace Reid K-9 Mystery*
Cain, Chelsea. *One Kick: A Novel*
Cameron, Marc. ★*Code of Honor*
Cameron, Marc. *Power and Empire*
Carpenter, Emily. *Until the Day I Die*
Castillo, Linda. ★*Fallen*
Castillo, Linda. *Outsider*
Chavez, Heather. *No Bad Deed*
Child, Lee. *61 Hours*
Child, Lee. *The Affair*
Child, Lee. *Bad Luck and Trouble*
Child, Lee. ★*Blue Moon*
Child, Lee. ★*Die Trying*
Child, Lee. *Echo Burning*
Child, Lee. *The Hard Way*
Child, Lee. ★*Killing Floor*
Child, Lee. *Make Me*
Child, Lee. *The Midnight Line*
Child, Lee. *Never Go Back*
Child, Lee. *Night School*
Child, Lee. *No Middle Name: The Complete Collected Jack Reacher Short Stories*
Child, Lee. *Nothing to Lose*
Child, Lee. *One Shot*
Child, Lee. ★*Past Tense*
Child, Lee. *Personal*
Child, Lee. *Persuader*
Child, Lee. ★*The Sentinel*
Child, Lee. *A Wanted Man*
Child, Lee. *Without Fail*
Child, Lee. *Worth Dying For*
Child, Lincoln. *Deep Storm: A Novel*
Chizmar, Richard T. *Chasing the Boogeyman*
Christy, Bryan. *In the Company of Killers*
Clancy, Tom. *Clear and Present Danger*
Clancy, Tom. ★*The Hunt for Red October*

Clancy, Tom. *Patriot Games*
Clark, Julie. *Last Flight*
Clark, Mary Higgins. *Death Wears a Beauty Mask and Other Stories*
Clark, Mary Higgins. ★*Kiss the Girls and Make Them Cry*
Clark, Mary Higgins. *The Melody Lingers On*
Cleave, Paul. *A Killer Harvest: A Thriller*
Cobb, May K. *The Hunting Wives*
Coben, Harlan. ★*The Boy from the Woods*
Coben, Harlan. *Don't Let Go*
Coben, Harlan. *Fool Me Once*
Coben, Harlan. *Hold Tight*
Coben, Harlan. *Run Away*
Coben, Harlan. *The Stranger*
Connelly, Michael. ★*Fair Warning*
Connelly, Michael. *The Scarecrow: A Novel*
Constantine, Liv. *The Last Time I Saw You*
Cook, Robin. *Coma: A Novel*
Cooper, Ellison. *Buried*
Corleone, Douglas. *Good as Gone*
Coughlin, Jack. *In the Crosshairs: A Sniper Novel*
Coughlin, Jack. *Long Shot: A Sniper Novel*
Coulter, Catherine. *The Devil's Triangle*
Coulter, Catherine. *The End Game*
Coulter, Catherine. *The Final Cut*
Coulter, Catherine. *Labyrinth*
Coulter, Catherine. *The Last Second*
Coulter, Catherine. *The Lost Key*
Coulter, Catherine. *Paradox*
Coulter, Catherine. *The Sixth Day*
Crais, Robert. *Demolition Angel: A Novel.*
Crais, Robert. *Suspect*
Crichton, Michael. *Pirate Latitudes*
Cumming, Charles. *A Colder War*
Cumming, Charles. *A Divided Spy*
Cumming, Charles. *A Foreign Country*
Cussler, Clive. *Blue Gold: A Novel from the Numa Files*
Cussler, Clive. *Celtic Empire*
Cussler, Clive. ★*Final Option*
Cussler, Clive. *Ghost Ship*
Cussler, Clive. ★*The Gray Ghost*
Cussler, Clive. *Havana Storm*
Cussler, Clive. *Nighthawk: A Novel from the Numa Files*
Cussler, Clive. *Odessa Sea*
Cussler, Clive. ★*The Oracle*
Cussler, Clive. *Pacific Vortex!*
Cussler, Clive. *The Pharaoh's Secret*
Cussler, Clive. ★*Raise the Titanic!*
Cussler, Clive. ★*The Rising Sea: A Novel from the Numa Files*
Cussler, Clive. *The Romanov Ransom*
Cussler, Clive. *Sahara: A Novel*
Cussler, Clive. ★*Sea of Greed: A Novel from the Numa Files*
Cussler, Clive. *Serpent: A Novel from the Numa Files*
Cussler, Clive. *Shadow Tyrants*
Cussler, Clive. *Typhoon Fury*
Dahl, Julia. *The Missing Hours*
Daly, Paula. *Clear My Name*
Daly, Paula. *Open Your Eyes*
Dang, Catherine. *Nice Girls*

Daniel, Ray. *Hacked: A Tucker Mystery*
Daugherty, Christi. *A Beautiful Corpse*
Daugherty, Christi. *The Echo Killing*
Daugherty, Christi. *Revolver Road: A Harper McClain Mystery*
Dazieri, Sandrone. *Kill the Angel*
Dazieri, Sandrone. *Kill the Father*
Dazieri, Sandrone. *Kill the King*
De la Motte, Anders. *MemoRandom: A Thriller*
De la Motte, Anders. *Ultimatum: A Thriller*
Deaver, Jeffery. *Edge: A Novel*
Deaver, Jeffery. ★*The Goodbye Man*
Deaver, Jeffery. ★*The Never Game*
Deaver, Jeffery. *The October List*
Delaney, J. P. *Playing Nice*
DeMille, Nelson. ★*The Deserter: A Novel*
DeMille, Nelson. *Wild Fire*
Dickey, Eric Jerome. *Finding Gideon*
Dimberg, Kelsey Rae. *Girl in the Rearview Mirror*
Dobmeier, Tracy. ★*Girls with Bright Futures: A Novel*
Dodd, Christina. *Dead Girl Running*
Dodd, Christina. *Strangers She Knows*
Dodd, Christina. *Virtue Falls*
Dodd, Christina. *What Doesn't Kill Her*
Doetsch, Richard. *Half-Past Dawn*
Doiron, Paul. *Bad Little Falls: A Novel*
Doiron, Paul. *The Poacher's Son*
Doiron, Paul. *The Precipice*
Dorn, L. R. *The Anatomy of Desire*
Dow, David R. *Confessions of an Innocent Man*
Downing, Samantha. *He Started It*
Dugoni, Robert. *The Conviction*
Dugoni, Robert. *The Eighth Sister: A Thriller*
Dugoni, Robert. *Murder One*
Dundas, Chad. *The Blaze*
Egan, Jennifer. *The Keep*
Eisler, Barry. *All the Devils*
Eisler, Barry. *The God's Eye View*
Eisler, Barry. *The Killer Collective*
Eisler, Barry. *Livia Lone*
Eisler, Barry. *The Night Trade*
Ellis, David. *In the Company of Liars*
Estleman, Loren D. ★*Something Borrowed, Something Black*
Fairstein, Linda A. *Blood Oath*
Fairstein, Linda A. *Entombed*
Ferencik, Erica. *Into the Jungle*
Fesperman, Dan. *Safe Houses: A Novel*
Fielding, Joy. *All the Wrong Places: A Novel*
Fielding, Joy. *The Bad Daughter: A Novel*
Finder, Joseph. *Guilty Minds*
Finder, Joseph. ★*House on Fire: A Novel*
Finder, Joseph. ★*Judgment*
Finder, Joseph. *The Switch: A Novel*
Flyte, Magnus. *City of Dark Magic: A Novel*
Flyte, Magnus. *City of Lost Dreams: A Novel*
Foley, Lucy. *The Guest List*
Follett, Ken. *Hornet Flight*
Follett, Ken. ★*Whiteout*
Forsyth, Frederick. *The Fox*

Forsyth, Frederick. *The Kill List*
Fox, Candice. *Crimson Lake*
Fox, Candice. *Gone by Midnight*
Fox, Candice. *Redemption Point*
Francis, Dick. *Smokescreen*
Francis, Felix. *Crisis*
Francis, Felix. *Guilty Not Guilty*
Francis, Felix. *Pulse*
Frayn, Michael. *Spies: A Novel*
Frear, Caz. *Stone Cold Heart*
Frear, Caz. *Sweet Little Lies*
Freeman, Brian. *Goodbye to the Dead*
Freeman, Brian. *Marathon*
Freeman, Brian. *The Night Bird*
French, Nicci. *Tuesday's Gone*
French, Tana. ★*The Witch Elm: A Novel*
Galligan, John. *Bad Moon Rising*
Gardiner, Meg. *The Dark Corners of the Night*
Gardiner, Meg. *Into the Black Nowhere*
Gardiner, Meg. *Phantom Instinct*
Gardiner, Meg. *Unsub: A Novel*
Gardner, Lisa. *Alone*
Gardner, Lisa. *Fear Nothing: A Detective D. D. Warren Novel*
Gardner, Lisa. *Find Her*
Gardner, Lisa. ★*Look for Me: A Novel*
Gardner, Lisa. *Love You More: A Detective D.D. Warren Novel*
Gardner, Lisa. *The Neighbor*
Gardner, Lisa. ★*Never Tell: A Novel*
Gardner, Lisa. ★*When You See Me: A Novel*
Gentry, Amy. *Last Woman Standing*
Gerritsen, Tess. *The Bone Garden*
Gerritsen, Tess. *Playing with Fire*
Gnuse, A. J. *Girl in the Walls: A Novel*
Goddard, Robert. *Beyond Recall: A Novel*
Goddard, Robert. ★*Into the Blue*
Goddard, Robert. *Never Go Back*
Goldberg, Lee. *Fake Truth*
Golden, Christopher. *Red Hands*
Goldin, Megan. *The Escape Room*
Gowdy, Barbara. *Helpless: A Novel*
Grebe, Camilla. *The Ice Beneath Her: A Novel*
Grecian, Alex. *The Saint of Wolves and Butchers*
Greene, Graham. *The Honorary Consul*
Grippando, James. *The Girl in the Glass Box*
Grisham, John. *The Client*
Grisham, John. ★*The Firm*
Grisham, John. *The Last Juror*
Grisham, John. ★*The Pelican Brief*
Gruber, Michael. *The Book of Air and Shadows*
Gruber, Michael. *The Forgery of Venus: A Novel*
Gruber, Michael. *Night of the Jaguar: A Novel*
Gruber, Michael. *The Return: A Novel*
Gruber, Michael. *Valley of Bones: A Novel*
Hagberg, David. *Gambit*
Hall, Rachel Howzell. *And Now She's Gone*
Hall, Rachel Howzell. *These Toxic Things*
Hallinan, Timothy. *Fools' River*
Hampton, Brenda. *Stalker*

Hand, Elizabeth. *Available Dark: A Thriller*
Hand, Elizabeth. *The Book of Lamps and Banners: A Novel*
Hand, Elizabeth. ★*Generation Loss: A Novel*
Hand, Elizabeth. *Hard Light*
Hannah, Sophie. *Keep Her Safe*
Harris, Oliver. *A Shadow Intelligence*
Harris, Robert. *Archangel: A Novel*
Harris, Robert. *The Ghost: A Novel*
Harris, Zakiya Dalila. *The Other Black Girl: A Novel*
Hart, John. *Iron House*
Hart, John. *Redemption Road*
Hart, John. *The Unwilling*
Hart, Rob. *The Warehouse: A Novel*
Harvey, Michael T. *Brighton*
Hawley, Noah. *Before the Fall*
Hayder, Mo. *Hanging Hill*
Hayes, Terry. *I Am Pilgrim*
Heller, Peter. *The Guide*
Herron, Mick. *Dolphin Junction: Collected Stories*
Hiaasen, Carl. *Skin Tight*
Hiaasen, Carl. *Skinny Dip: A Novel*
Higgins, George V. *The Friends of Eddie Coyle*
Higgins, Jack. *Confessional*
Higgins, Jack. *Eye of the Storm*
Higgins, Jack. *Touch the Devil*
Highsmith, Patricia. ★*The Talented Mr. Ripley*
Hill, Reginald. *The Woodcutter: A Novel*
Hunter, Stephen. *The 47th Samurai*
Hunter, Stephen. *Game of Snipers: A Bob Lee Swagger Novel*
Hunter, Stephen. *Soft Target: A Thriller*
Hurwitz, Gregg Andrew. ★*Into the Fire*
Hurwitz, Gregg Andrew. ★*Out of the Dark: The Return of Orphan X*
Iles, Greg. *The Bone Tree: A Novel*
Iles, Greg. *Mississippi Blood: A Novel*
Iles, Greg. *Natchez Burning: A Novel*
Jackson, Joshilyn. *Never Have I Ever*
Jewell, Lisa. *The Family Upstairs*
Jewell, Lisa. *Watching You*
Johnson, Keith Lee. ★*Little Black Girl Lost*
Johnston, Tim. *The Current: A Novel*
Kamal, Sheena. *It All Falls Down*
Kennedy, James. *Dare to Know*
Kent, Kathleen. *The Burn*
Kent, Kathleen. *The Pledge*
King, Stephen. *11/22/63*
King, Stephen. *End of Watch: A Novel*
King, Stephen. *Finders Keepers*
King, Stephen. *The Girl Who Loved Tom Gordon*
King, Stephen. *The Institute*
King, Stephen. *Mr. Mercedes: A Novel*
Koepp, David. *Cold Storage: A Novel*
Koontz, Dean R. *The Darkest Evening of the Year*
Koontz, Dean R. *The Husband*
Koontz, Dean R. *Intensity: A Novel*
Koontz, Dean R. *Velocity*
Koryta, Michael. *If She Wakes*
Laukkanen, Owen. *Deception Cove*
Laukkanen, Owen. *Gale Force*

Laukkanen, Owen. *Lone Jack Trail*
Lawton, John. *Hammer to Fall*
Le Carre, John. *The Constant Gardener: A Novel*
Le Carre, John. *A Most Wanted Man: A Novel*
Le Carre, John. ★*Our Kind of Traitor: A Novel*
Lee, Patrick. *Runner*
Lehane, Dennis. ★*Mystic River*
Lehane, Dennis. *Since We Fell*
Lelchuk, Saul. *Save Me from Dangerous Men: A Novel*
Leonard, Elmore. *Charlie Martz and Other Stories: The Unpublished Stories*
Leonard, Elmore. *Labrava*
Leonard, Elmore. *Rum Punch*
Lescroart, John T. *Guilt*
Levin, Ira. *The Boys from Brazil: A Novel*
Levin, Ira. *A Kiss Before Dying*
Lippman, Laura. ★*And When She Was Good*
Lowe, Kathryn A. *The Furies*
Ludlum, Robert. ★*The Bourne Identity*
Ludlum, Robert. *The Bourne Supremacy*
Ludlum, Robert. *The Bourne Ultimatum*
Luna, Louisa. *The Janes*
Lutz, Lisa. *The Swallows: A Novel*
Majumdar, Megha. *A Burning*
Mankell, Henning. *The Troubled Man*
March, William. *The Bad Seed: A Novel*
Mason, Jamie. *The Hidden Things*
Matthews, Jason. ★*The Kremlin's Candidate*
Matthews, Jason. *Red Sparrow: A Novel*
McBain, Ed. *Alice in Jeopardy*
McDonald, Christina. *Behind Every Lie*
McHugh, Laura. *What's Done in Darkness: A Novel*
McHugh, Laura. *The Wolf Wants In: A Novel*
McKinty, Adrian. ★*The Chain*
McLaughlin, James A. *Bearskin*
McMahon, Jennifer. *The Invited: A Novel*
Meltzer, Brad. *The Escape Artist*
Meltzer, Brad. *The Inner Circle*
Meltzer, Brad. *The Tenth Justice*
Meltzer, Brad. *The Zero Game*
Meuleman, Sarah. *Find Me Gone*
Meyer, Deon. *Icarus*
Mina, Denise. *Conviction*
Mina, Denise. *The Less Dead*
Mooney, Chris. *Blood World*
Morgan Jones, Chris. *The Silent Oligarch*
Murakami, Ryu. *In the Miso Soup*
North, Alex. *The Shadows*
North, Alex. *The Whisper Man*
O'Brien, Perry Edmond. *Fire in the Blood*
Offutt, Chris. ★*The Killing Hills*
Osborne, Lawrence. *The Glass Kingdom: A Novel*
Overton, Hollie. *The Runaway*
Palahniuk, Chuck. *Pygmy*
Paris, B. A. *The Breakdown*
Parker, T. Jefferson. *L.A. Outlaws: A Novel*
Parks, Brad. *Closer Than You Know*
Parks, Brad. *Say Nothing: A Novel*

Parnell, Sean. *Left for Dead*
Patterson, James. ★*Along Came a Spider: A Novel*
Patterson, James. *Kiss the Girls: A Novel*
Patterson, James. ★*Private*
Patterson, Richard North. *Balance of Power*
Patterson, Richard North. *Dark Lady*
Patterson, Richard North. *Eclipse*
Patterson, Richard North. *No Safe Place*
Patterson, Richard North. *Protect and Defend*
Pavone, Chris. ★*The Expats: A Novel*
Pavone, Chris. *The Paris Diversion: A Novel*
Pearson, Ridley. *The Risk Agent*
Perry, Thomas. *The Bomb Maker*
Perry, Thomas. ★*The Left-Handed Twin*
Perry, Thomas. *The Old Man*
Perry, Thomas. *Vanishing Act*
Persson, Leif G. W. *Another Time, Another Life: The Story of a Crime*
Persson, Leif G. W. *Free Falling, as If in a Dream: The Story of a Crime*
Petrie, Nicholas. *The Breaker*
Petrie, Nicholas. *Burning Bright*
Petrie, Nicholas. *The Drifter*
Petrie, Nicholas. *Tear It Down*
Petrie, Nicholas. *The Wild One*
Phillips, Gin. *Fierce Kingdom: A Novel*
Phillips, Julia. ★*Disappearing Earth*
Piccirilli, Tom. *The Last Kind Words*
Piccirilli, Tom. *The Last Whisper in the Dark: A Novel*
Pinborough, Sarah. ★*Dead to Her: A Novel*
Pinter, Jason. *Hide Away*
Pinter, Jason. *A Stranger at the Door*
Pintoff, Stefanie. *Hostage Taker: A Novel*
Pochoda, Ivy. ★*These Women*
Porter, Henry. *The Bell Ringers*
Porter, Henry. *Firefly*
Porter, Henry. *The Old Enemy*
Porter, Henry. *White Hot Silence*
Powers, Richard. *Orfeo: A Novel*
Pressfield, Steven. *36 Righteous Men: A Novel*
Preston, Douglas J. *City of Endless Night*
Preston, Douglas J. *Crooked River*
Preston, Douglas J. *The Obsidian Chamber*
Preston, Douglas J. *Old Bones*
Preston, Douglas J. *Thunderhead*
Preston, Douglas J. *Verses for the Dead*
Pyper, Andrew. *The Homecoming: A Novel*
Rader-Day, Lori. ★*The Lucky One*
Ragan, Theresa. *Buried Deep*
Ragan, Theresa. *Deadly Recall*
Ragan, Theresa. *Deranged*
Ragan, Theresa. *Her Last Day*
Rendell, Ruth. ★*A Judgement in Stone*
Ricciardi, David. *Warning Light*
Rice, Christopher. *Blood Victory*
Rice, Luanne. ★*Last Day*
Roberts, Nora. *Shelter in Place*
Robotham, Michael. ★*Close Your Eyes*
Robotham, Michael. ★*Good Girl, Bad Girl: A Novel*

Robotham, Michael. ★*The Other Wife*
Robotham, Michael. ★*Say You're Sorry*
Robotham, Michael. ★*Suspect*
Robotham, Michael. ★*When She Was Good*
Robotham, Michael. ★*The Wreckage*
Rollins, James. ★*The Last Odyssey*
Rosenfelt, David. *Black and Blue: A Doug Brock Thriller*
Rosenfelt, David. *Blackout*
Roslund, Anders. *Cell 8*
Roslund, Anders. ★*Knock Knock*
Rouda, Kaira Sturdivant. *Best Day Ever: A Novel*
Rous, Emma. *The Perfect Guests*
Roy, Lori. ★*Gone Too Long: A Novel*
Sandford, John. *Broken Prey*
Sandford, John. *Buried Prey*
Sandford, John. *Certain Prey*
Sandford, John. *Chosen Prey*
Sandford, John. *Easy Prey*
Sandford, John. *Field of Prey*
Sandford, John. ★*Golden Prey*
Sandford, John. *Hidden Prey*
Sandford, John. ★*Invisible Prey*
Sandford, John. ★*Mind Prey*
Sandford, John. *Mortal Prey*
Sandford, John. ★*Naked Prey*
Sandford, John. ★*Night Prey*
Sandford, John. ★*Phantom Prey*
Sandford, John. ★*Rules of Prey*
Sandford, John. ★*Silent Prey*
Sandford, John. ★*Silken Prey*
Sandford, John. *Storm Prey*
Sandford, John. *Sudden Prey*
Sandford, John. ★*Winter Prey*
Saul, John. *Midnight Voices*
Scottoline, Lisa. ★*Come Home*
Scottoline, Lisa. *Don't Go*
Scottoline, Lisa. ★*Every Fifteen Minutes*
Scottoline, Lisa. *Legal Tender*
Scottoline, Lisa. *One Perfect Lie*
Sebastian, Tim. *Fatal Ally*
Seo, Mi-Ae. *The Only Child*
Sharp, Zoe. *Fox Hunter*
Silva, Daniel. ★*The Black Widow*
Silva, Daniel. ★*The Kill Artist: A Novel*
Silva, Daniel. *The New Girl*
Silva, Daniel. *The Other Woman*
Singh, Nalini. *A Madness of Sunshine*
Slaughter, Karin. *Criminal: A Novel*
Slaughter, Karin. ★*Fallen: A Novel*
Slaughter, Karin. *The Kept Woman*
Slaughter, Karin. ★*The Last Widow*
Slaughter, Karin. ★*Pieces of Her*
Slaughter, Karin. ★*Pretty Girls: A Novel*
Slaughter, Karin. ★*The Silent Wife*
Slaughter, Karin. ★*Undone: A Novel*
Smith, Ian. *The Unspoken*
Smith, Martin Cruz. ★*Gorky Park*
Smith, Martin Cruz. *Havana Bay*

Smith, Martin Cruz. *Polar Star*
Smith, Martin Cruz. *The Siberian Dilemma*
Smith, Martin Cruz. *Stalin's Ghost*
Smith, Martin Cruz. ★*Tatiana: An Arkady Renko Novel*
Smith, Martin Cruz. *Three Stations: An Arkady Renko Novel*
Smith, Martin Cruz. *Wolves Eat Dogs: A Novel*
Smith, Scott. *A Simple Plan: A Novel*
Steinhauer, Olen. *An American Spy*
Steinhauer, Olen. *The Cairo Affair*
Steinhauer, Olen. *The Last Tourist*
Steinhauer, Olen. *The Middleman*
Steinhauer, Olen. *The Nearest Exit*
Steinhauer, Olen. *The Tourist*
Stroby, Wallace. *Some Die Nameless*
Stroud, Carsten. *The Shimmer*
Swinson, David. *City on the Edge*
Takamura, Kaoru. ★*Lady Joker*
Tata, A. J. *Dark Winter*
Taylor, Brad. ★*Daughter of War: A Novel*
Taylor, Brad. *Ring of Fire*
Tracy, P. J. *Ice Cold Heart*
Tudor, C. J. *The Burning Girls: A Novel*
Tudor, C. J. *The Chalk Man: A Novel*
Tudor, C. J. *The Other People*
Tyree, Omar. *Leslie: A Novel*
Verdon, John. *On Harrow Hill*
Vernon, P. J. *Bath Haus: A Thriller*
Vidich, Paul. *The Coldest Warrior*
Waite, Jen. *Survival Instincts*
Wambaugh, Joseph. *The New Centurions*
Wang, Kathy. *Impostor Syndrome: A Novel*
Ware, Ruth. ★*One by One*
Watt, Holly. *To the Lions*
Westlake, Donald E. *Forever and a Death*
Whitaker, Chris. ★*We Begin at the End*
White, Randy Wayne. *Salt River*
Wiesel, Elie. *Hostage*
Willocks, Tim. *Memo from Turner*
Wolf, Dick. *The Ultimatum*
Woods, Stuart. *Below the Belt*
Woods, Stuart. ★*Bombshell*
Woods, Stuart. *Chiefs*
Woods, Stuart. *A Delicate Touch*
Woods, Stuart. *Fast & Loose*
Woods, Stuart. *Hit List*
Woods, Stuart. *The Money Shot*
Woods, Stuart. *New York Dead*
Woods, Stuart. *Orchid Beach*
Woods, Stuart. *Palindrome*
Woods, Stuart. *Santa Fe Rules*
Woods, Stuart. *Skin Game*
Woods, Stuart. *Smooth Operator*
Woods, Stuart. *Stealth*
Youers, Rio. *Lola on Fire*
Zhou, Haohui. *Death Notice: A Novel*
Thrones, *Dominations*. Sayers, Dorothy L.
Through the Evil Days: A Clare Fergusson/Russ Van Alstyne Mystery.
    Spencer-Fleming, Julia

Through *Waters Deep: A Novel*. Sundin, Sarah
Thud!: *a Novel of Discworld*. Pratchett, Terry
Thug *Lovin'*. Clark, Wahida
Thug *Matrimony*. Clark, Wahida
Thug novels [Series]. Clark, Wahida
Thugs. Clark, Wahida
★**Thugs** *and the Women Who Love Them*. Clark, Wahida
Thugs cry novels (Ca$h) [Series]. Ca$h
Thugs *Cry: A Novel*. Ca$h
Thunder and lightning [Series]. Varley, John
Thunder Point novels [Series]. Carr, Robyn
Thunderhead. Preston, Douglas J.
★*The* **Thursday** *Murder Club*. Osman, Richard
Thursday Murder Club novels [Series]. Osman, Richard
Thursday Next novels [Series]. Fforde, Jasper
Thursday's *Children*. French, Nicci
Thus *Bad Begins: A Novel*. Marias, Javier
Tiamat's *Wrath*. Corey, James S. A.
TIBBS, VIRGIL (FICTITIOUS CHARACTER)
    Ball, John Dudley. *In the Heat of the Night*
TIBET
    Cussler, Clive. ★*Golden Buddha*
    Pattison, Eliot. *Bones of the Earth: An Inspector Shan Tao Yun
        Mystery*
    Pattison, Eliot. *The Skull Mantra*
A **Ticket** *to the Boneyard: A Matthew Scudder Novel*. Block, Lawrence
Tidelands. Gregory, Philippa
Ties. Starnone, Domenico
Tieu, Julie
    The Donut Trap
Tiffany *Blues: A Novel*. Rose, M. J.
TIFFANY, LOUIS COMFORT, 1848-1933
    Holahan, Cate. *Her Three Lives*
    Rose, M. J. *Tiffany Blues: A Novel*
Tigana. Kay, Guy Gavriel
The **Tiger** *Flu*. Lai, Larissa
The **Tiger's** *Wife: A Novel*. Obreht, Tea
Tigerman. Harkaway, Nick
TIGERS
    Martel, Yann. ★*Life of Pi: A Novel*
Till *We Have Faces: A Myth Retold*. Lewis, C. S.
Timber Creek K-9 novels [Series]. Mizushima, Margaret
Timbuktu: *a Novel*. Auster, Paul
TIME
    Lightman, Alan P. ★*Einstein's Dreams*
    Mitchell, David. *The Bone Clocks: A Novel*
    Pratchett, Terry. *Thief of Time*
    Smith, Ali. ★*Autumn*
    Vonnegut, Kurt. *Timequake*
    Winters, Ben H. *The Quiet Boy*
The **Time** *in Between: A Novel*. Duenas, Maria
The **Time** *It Takes to Fall*. Dean, Margaret Lazarus
★*The* **Time** *Machine*. Wells, H. G.
TIME MACHINES
    Palmer, Dexter Clarence. *Version Control*
    Yu, Charles. *How to Live Safely in a Science Fictional Universe: A
        Novel*
The **Time** *of the Hero*. Vargas Llosa, Mario

Time Regained. Proust, Marcel

A Time to Kill. Grisham, John

A Time to Love and a Time to Die. Remarque, Erich Maria

A Time to Stand. Whitlow, Robert

TIME TRAVEL

    Adams, Douglas. *Dirk Gently's Holistic Detective Agency*

    Beukes, Lauren. *The Shining Girls*

    Chen, Mike. *Here and Now and Then*

    Davis, Kathryn. *Duplex*

    Deon, Natashia. *The Perishing: A Novel*

    Fforde, Jasper. *The Eyre Affair: A Novel*

    Fforde, Jasper. *Lost in a Good Book: A Thursday Next Novel*

    Hurley, Kameron. ★*The Light Brigade*

    Kawaguchi, Toshikazu. *Before the Coffee Gets Cold*

    Khoury, Raymond. *Empire of Lies*

    Kim, Bo Young. ★*I'm Waiting for You: And Other Stories*

    McGuire, Seanan. ★*Middlegame*

    Montimore, Margarita. *Oona Out of Order*

    Niffenegger, Audrey. *The Time Traveler's Wife: A Novel*

    Powers, Richard. *Orfeo: A Novel*

    Steele, Allen M. *Coyote: A Novel of Interstellar Exploration*

    Stroud, Carsten. *The Shimmer*

    Swanwick, Michael. *Bones of the Earth*

    Vonnegut, Kurt. ★*Slaughterhouse-Five: Or, the Children's Crusade : A Duty-Dance with Death*

    Wells, H. G. ★*The Time Machine*

    Wolfe, Gene. *The Citadel of the Autarch*

    Yu, Charles. *How to Live Safely in a Science Fictional Universe: A Novel*

TIME TRAVEL (FUTURE)

    Gladstone, Max. ★*Empress of Forever*

    Goonan, Kathleen Ann. *In War Times*

    Simmons, Dan. *Endymion*

    Stevens, Francis. *The Heads of Cerberus*

TIME TRAVEL (PAST)

    Adlakha, Sarah. *She Wouldn't Change a Thing*

    Alexie, Sherman. *Flight*

    Baker, Kage. *In the Garden of Iden: A Novel of the Company*

    Barth, John. *The Last Voyage of Somebody the Sailor*

    Butler, Octavia E. ★*Kindred*

    Daughters, Amy Weinland. *You Cannot Mess This Up: A True Story That Never Happened*

    Fisher, Helen. *Space Hopper*

    Gabaldon, Diana. ★*Dragonfly in Amber*

    Gabaldon, Diana. ★*Drums of Autumn*

    Gabaldon, Diana. ★*Outlander*

    Greer, Andrew Sean. *The Impossible Lives of Greta Wells*

    Harkness, Deborah E. *Shadow of Night*

    King, Stephen. *11/22/63*

    Maaren, Kari. ★*Weave a Circle Round*

    Newman, Sandra. *The Heavens*

    Reynolds, Alastair. *Permafrost*

    Seton, Anya. *Green Darkness*

    Stephenson, Neal. *The Rise and Fall of D.O.D.O.: A Novel*

    Twain, Mark. ★*A Connecticut Yankee in King Arthur's Court*

    Willis, Connie. ★*Doomsday Book*

    Wojtas, Olga. *Miss Blaine's Prefect and the Golden Samovar*

TIME TRAVEL ROMANCES

    Gabaldon, Diana. ★*A Breath of Snow and Ashes*

    Gabaldon, Diana. ★*Dragonfly in Amber*

    Gabaldon, Diana. ★*Drums of Autumn*

    Gabaldon, Diana. *An Echo in the Bone*

    Gabaldon, Diana. ★*The Fiery Cross*

    Gabaldon, Diana. ★*Outlander*

    Gabaldon, Diana. ★*Voyager*

The Time Traveler's Wife: A Novel. Niffenegger, Audrey

★*Time's Arrow, or the Nature of the Offense.* Amis, Martin

Time's Convert. Harkness, Deborah E.

Timequake. Vonnegut, Kurt

Timothy Cone mysteries [Series]. Sanders, Lawrence

The Timothy Files. Sanders, Lawrence

Timothy's Game. Sanders, Lawrence

★*Tinker, Tailor, Soldier, Spy.* Le Carre, John

Tinkers. Harding, Paul

Tinti, Hannah

    The Twelve Lives of Samuel Hawley: A Novel

Tiny Americans. Murphy, Devin

Tiny Imperfections. Frank, Alli

★*Tiny Love: The Complete Stories of Larry Brown.* Brown, Larry

Tiny Tales: Stories of Romance, Ambition, Kindness, and Happiness. McCall Smith, Alexander

Tishomingo Blues: A Novel. Leonard, Elmore

Tita Rosie's kitchen [Series]. Manansala, Mia P.

★*Titan.* Varley, John

★*The Titanic Secret.* Cussler, Clive

TITANS (MYTHOLOGY)

    Miller, Madeline. ★*Circe*

★*Titanshade.* Stout, Dan

Title, Sarah

    The Undateable

TITUBA

    Conde, Maryse. *I, Tituba, Black Witch of Salem*

★*To Be a Man: Stories.* Krauss, Nicole

To Be Taught, If Fortunate. Chambers, Becky

To Catch a Spy: A Toby Peters Mystery. Kaminsky, Stuart M.

To Have and Have Not. Hemingway, Ernest

★*To Have and to Hoax: A Novel.* Waters, Martha

To Heaven by Water. Cartwright, Justin

★*To Keep the Sun Alive.* Ghaffari, Rabeah

★*To Kill a Mockingbird.* Lee, Harper

To kill a mockingbird [Series]. Lee, Harper

To Love and to Loathe: A Novel. Waters, Martha

To Rise Again at a Decent Hour: A Novel. Ferris, Joshua

★*To Sleep in a Sea of Stars.* Paolini, Christopher

★*To the End of the Land.* Grossman, David

To the Far Blue Mountains. L'Amour, Louis

★*To the Lighthouse.* Woolf, Virginia

To the Lions. Watt, Holly

Tobacco Road. Caldwell, Erskine

Tobar, Hector

    The Last Great Road Bum

Toby Peters mysteries [Series]. Kaminsky, Stuart M.

Todd, Charles

    ★*A Hanging at Dawn*

Toews, Miriam
Fight Night
★Women Talking: A Novel
Toibin, Colm
House of Names
★The Magician: A Novel
Tokyo trilogy [Series]. Peace, David
Tokyo Ueno Station. Yu, Miri
TOKYO, JAPAN
Gibson, William. *Pattern Recognition*
Higashino, Keigo. *Newcomer*
Hunter, Stephen. *The 47th Samurai*
Kutsukake, Lynne. *The Translation of Love: A Novel*
Murakami, Haruki. ★*1q84*
Murakami, Haruki. *After Dark*
Murakami, Ryu. *In the Miso Soup*
Obregon, Nicolas. *Blue Light Yokohama*
Ozeki, Ruth L. ★*A Tale for the Time Being*
Peace, David. *Occupied City*
Smith, Martin Cruz. *December 6*
Yoshimoto, Banana. *The Lake*
Yoshimoto, Banana. *Moshi-Moshi*
Tolkien, J. R. R.
Beren and Luthien
The Children of Hurin
The Fall of Gondolin
The Fellowship of the Ring: Being the First Part of the Lord of the Rings
★The Hobbit, Or, There and Back Again
★The Lord of the Rings
The Return of the King: Being the Third Part of the Lord of the Rings
The Silmarillion
The Two Towers: Being the Second Part of the Lord of the Rings
Tolstaya, Tatyana
Aetherial Worlds: Stories
The Slynx
Tolstoy, Leo
★Anna Karenina
Divine and Human and Other Stories
★War and Peace
TOLTECS — RELIGION
Bowles, David. *Feathered Serpent, Dark Heart of Sky: Myths of Mexico*
Tom Hawkins novels [Series]. Hodgson, Antonia
Tom Thorne novels [Series]. Billingham, Mark
Tombland. Sansom, C. J.
TOMBS
Cussler, Clive. *Celtic Empire*
Robertson, Imogen. *Island of Bones*
Saylor, Steven. *Raiders of the Nile: A Novel of the Ancient World*
Tommy Carmellini novels [Series]. Coonts, Stephen
Tomorrow's Kin. Kress, Nancy
Tony Hill and Carol Jordan mysteries [Series]. McDermid, Val
Too Bright to Hear Too Loud to See. Garey, Juliann
Too Close. Daniels, Natalie
Too Far Afield. Grass, Gunter
Too Late the Phalarope. Paton, Alan
Too Like the Lightning. Palmer, Ada

Too Much Happiness: Stories. Munro, Alice
Too Much Lip. Lucashenko, Melissa
Too Much Money. Dunne, Dominick
Toole, John Kennedy
★A Confederacy of Dunces
The *Tooth* Tattoo. Lovesey, Peter
★The *Topeka* School. Lerner, Ben
TORAH SCROLLS
Lukas, Michael David. *The Last Watchman of Old Cairo: A Novel*
Toro, Guillermo del
The Hollow Ones
TORONTO, ONTARIO
Alexis, Andre. *Fifteen Dogs*
Atwood, Margaret. ★*The Blind Assassin*
Atwood, Margaret. ★*Cat's Eye*
Atwood, Margaret. *Moral Disorder*
Choi, Ann Y. K. *Kay's Lucky Coin Variety*
Heron, Farah. *Accidentally Engaged*
Hosking, Jay. *Three Years with the Rat: A Novel*
Jalaluddin, Uzma. ★*Ayesha at Last*
Jalaluddin, Uzma. *Hana Khan Carries On*
Khan, Ausma Zehanat. *Among the Ruins*
Khan, Ausma Zehanat. *The Unquiet Dead*
Lalli, Sonya. *The Matchmaker's List*
Lau, Jackie. *Donut Fall in Love*
Mandel, Emily St. John. ★*Station Eleven*
Shimotakahara, Leslie. *After the Bloom*
Toews, Miriam. *Fight Night*
Torre, A. R.
Every Last Secret
★The *Tortilla* Curtain. Boyle, T. Coraghessan
Tortilla Flat. Steinbeck, John
TORTURE
Dahl, Arne. *Bad Blood*
Deaver, Jeffery. *Edge: A Novel*
Ferrell, Carolyn. *Dear Miss Metropolitan*
Katzenbach, John. *What Comes Next*
King, Stephen. *The Institute*
Ricciardi, David. *Warning Light*
Slaughter, Karin. ★*Undone: A Novel*
TORTURE VICTIMS
Kayode, Femi. ★*Lightseekers*
TORTURERS
Danticat, Edwidge. *The Dew Breaker*
Fernandez, Nona. *The Twilight Zone*
Wolfe, Gene. *The Citadel of the Autarch*
Wolfe, Gene. *The Claw of the Conciliator*
TOTALITARIANISM
Bandi. *The Accusation: Forbidden Stories from Inside North Korea*
Bradbury, Ray. ★*Fahrenheit 451*
Church, James. ★*A Corpse in the Koryo*
Erpenbeck, Jenny. *The Book of Words*
Huxley, Aldous. ★*Brave New World*
Jen, Gish. ★*The Resisters*
Kafka, Franz. ★*The Trial*
Kundera, Milan. ★*The Unbearable Lightness of Being*
Lewis, Sinclair. ★*It Can't Happen Here*

Liu, Ken. *Invisible Planets: Contemporary Chinese Science Fiction in Translation*
Ma, Jian. *China Dream*
Orwell, George. ★*1984: A Novel*
Orwell, George. ★*Animal Farm*
Zamyatin, Yevgeny Ivanovich. ★*We*

TOTALITARIANISM — PSYCHOLOGICAL ASPECTS
Saramago, Jose. *The Manual of Painting and Calligraphy*

TOUCH
Okorafor, Nnedi. ★*Remote Control*
*A **Touch** of Forever*. Goodman, Jo
*A **Touch** of Stardust*. Alcott, Kate
***Touch** the Devil*. Higgins, Jack

TOUR GUIDES (PERSONS)
Dovlatov, Sergei. *Pushkin Hills*
Hiaasen, Carl. *Nature Girl*

TOURETTE SYNDROME
Lethem, Jonathan. ★*Motherless Brooklyn*

TOURISM
Harrison, M. John. *Nova Swing*
*The **Tourist***. Steinhauer, Olen

TOURISTS
Sandford, John. *Holy Ghost*
Smith, Scott. *The Ruins: A Novel*

TOURNAMENTS
Bouchet, Amanda. *Breath of Fire*
***Towards** Zero*. Christie, Agatha
***Tower** of Babel*. Sears, Michael

Towles, Amor
★*A Gentleman in Moscow*
Rules of Civility: A Novel

TOXINS
Sayers, Dorothy L. ★*The Documents in the Case*
***Trace** Elements*. Leon, Donna

TRACK AND FIELD ATHLETES
Hooper, Elise. *Fast Girls: A Novel of the 1936 Women's Olympic Team*
***Track** of the Cat*. Barr, Nevada

TRACKERS
Deaver, Jeffery. ★*The Goodbye Man*
Deaver, Jeffery. ★*The Never Game*
McMurtry, Larry. *Comanche Moon: A Novel*

TRACKING AND TRAILING
Hunter, Stephen. *Game of Snipers: A Bob Lee Swagger Novel*
***Tracks**: a Novel*. Erdrich, Louise
***Tracy** Crosswhite novels* [Series]. Dugoni, Robert
***Tracy** Ellison novels* [Series]. Tyree, Omar

Tracy, P. J.
★*Deep into the Dark*
Ice Cold Heart

TRADING POSTS
Mitchell, David. *The Thousand Autumns of Jacob De Zoet: A Novel*

TRADITION (PHILOSOPHY)
Alharthi, Jokha. *Celestial Bodies: A Novel*
Wynne, Phoebe. *Madam*

TRAFFIC ACCIDENT VICTIMS
Agee, James. ★*A Death in the Family*
Brown, Sandra. *The Witness*

Davidson, Andrew. *The Gargoyle*
De la Motte, Anders. *MemoRandom: A Thriller*

TRAFFIC ACCIDENTS
Abbott, Jeff. *Blame*
Barclay, Linwood. *Parting Shot*
Coulter, Catherine. *Labyrinth*
Johnston, Tim. *The Current: A Novel*
Kerangal, Maylis de. *The Heart: A Novel*
Willocks, Tim. *Memo from Turner*
Wolfe, Tom. *The Bonfire of the Vanities*

TRAGEDY
Anshaw, Carol. *Carry the One*
Cantrell, Christian. *Scorpion*
Diamond, Elizabeth. *An Accidental Light*
Grossman, David. *Falling Out of Time*
Obioma, Chigozie. ★*The Fishermen: A Novel*
Runcie, James. *Canvey Island*
Spufford, Francis. ★*Light Perpetual*
Uris, Leon. *Redemption: A Novel*
Uris, Leon. ★*Trinity*
*The **Tragedy** of Arthur: A Novel*. Phillips, Arthur
★***Trail** of Lightning*. Roanhorse, Rebecca

TRAIN ROBBERIES
Horowitz, Anthony. *The House of Silk: A Sherlock Holmes Novel*

TRAINING
Durst, Sarah Beth. *Race the Sands*
Muir, Tamsyn. *Harrow the Ninth*

TRAINS
Dazieri, Sandrone. *Kill the Angel*
Finch, Charles. *The Last Passenger*
Morrell, David. *Ruler of the Night*
Oyeyemi, Helen. *Peaces*
Trainspotting. Welsh, Irvine
Trainspotting [Series]. Welsh, Irvine

TRAITORS
Bourne, Joanna. ★*My Lord and Spymaster*
Bradby, Tom. *Double Agent*
Coughlin, Jack. *Long Shot: A Sniper Novel*
Cumming, Charles. ★*The Trinity Six*
Lee, Yoon Ha. *Ninefox Gambit*
Penny, Louise. *The Cruelest Month: A Three Pines Mystery*
***Traitors** to All*. Scerbanenco, Giorgio

Tran, Vu
Dragonfish: A Novel

TRANS MEN
Joukhadar, Zeyn. ★*The Thirty Names of Night: A Novel*
Winterson, Jeanette. ★*Frankissstein*

TRANS WOMEN
Alameddine, Rabih. *The Wrong End of the Telescope*
Ebershoff, David. *The Danish Girl: A Novel*
Peters, Torrey. ★*Detransition, Baby*
Porter, Chana. *The Seep: A Novel*

TRANSATLANTIC VOYAGES
Gelernter, J. H. *Hold Fast*
McCann, Colum. ★*Transatlantic: A Novel*
★***Transatlantic**: a Novel*. McCann, Colum
★***Transcendent** Kingdom*. Gyasi, Yaa
Transcendental. Gunn, James E.

Transcendental novels [Series]. Gunn, James E.
TRANSCONTINENTAL JOURNEYS
  Shteyngart, Gary. ★*Lake Success: A Novel*
★*Transcription*. Atkinson, Kate
TRANSFER STUDENTS
  Ellison, J. T. *Good Girls Lie*
TRANSFORMATIONS (MAGIC)
  Armfield, Julia. *Salt Slow: Stories*
  Czerneda, Julie. *A Turn of Light*
  Harkness, Deborah E. *Time's Convert*
  Hill, Joe. *Horns*
  Hill, Joe. ★*Nos4a2*
  Kafka, Franz. ★*The Metamorphosis*
TRANSFORMATIONS, PERSONAL
  Bailey, Tessa. *Fix Her Up*
  Cusk, Rachel. *Transit*
  Dickens, Charles. ★*A Christmas Carol*
  Gilman, Susan Jane. *Donna Has Left the Building*
  Miller, Rebecca. ★*Jacob's Folly: A Novel*
  Patchett, Ann. ★*State of Wonder: A Novel*
  Rubart, James L. ★*The Man He Never Was*
  Sittenfeld, Curtis. *Rodham: A Novel*
TRANSGENDER CHILDREN
  Frankel, Laurie. *This Is How It Always Is*
TRANSGENDER PERSONS
  Cassara, Joseph. *The House of Impossible Beauties*
  Fu, Kim. *For Today I Am a Boy*
  Manning, Corinne. *We Had No Rules: Stories*
  Woolf, Virginia. *Orlando: A Biography*
TRANSGENDER TEENAGE GIRLS
  Aoki, Ryka. *Light from Uncommon Stars*
  Cassara, Joseph. *The House of Impossible Beauties*
TRANSGRESSIVE FICTION
  Burgess, Anthony. ★*A Clockwork Orange*
  Burroughs, William S. ★*Naked Lunch: The Restored Text*
  Dunn, Katherine. *Geek Love*
  Miller, Henry. ★*Tropic of Cancer*
  Miller, Henry. ★*Tropic of Capricorn*
  Murakami, Ryu. *In the Miso Soup*
  Palahniuk, Chuck. *Fight Club*
  Palahniuk, Chuck. *The Invention of Sound*
  Palahniuk, Chuck. *Lullaby: A Novel*
★*Transient* Desires. Leon, Donna
Transit. Cusk, Rachel
★*The Transit* of Venus. Hazzard, Shirley
TRANSITIONING (GENDER IDENTITY)
  Ebershoff, David. *The Danish Girl: A Novel*
  Peters, Torrey. ★*Detransition, Baby*
The Translation of Love: A Novel. Kutsukake, Lynne
TRANSLATIONS
  Abe, Kobo. *The Woman in the Dunes*
  Adimi, Kaouther. *Our Riches*
  Adler-Olsen, Jussi. *The Absent One*
  Adler-Olsen, Jussi. *A Conspiracy of Faith*
  Adler-Olsen, Jussi. *The Hanging Girl*
  Adler-Olsen, Jussi. *The Keeper of Lost Causes*
  Adler-Olsen, Jussi. *The Marco Effect: A Department Q Novel*
  Adler-Olsen, Jussi. *The Purity of Vengeance: A Department Q Novel*

  Adler-Olsen, Jussi. *The Scarred Woman*
  Adler-Olsen, Jussi. ★*Victim 2117*
  Agnon, Shmuel Yosef. ★*Only Yesterday*
  Aguilar Camin, Hector. *Death in Veracruz*
  Ajvide Lindqvist, John. *Let the Right One In*
  Akunin, B. *The Coronation: The Further Adventures of Erast Fandorin*
  Akunin, B. *Sister Pelagia and the White Bulldog: A Mystery*
  Al Rawi, Shahad. *The Baghdad Clock*
  Al-Ramli, Muhsin. *The President's Gardens*
  Aleichem, Sholem. *Tevye the Dairyman and the Railroad Stories*
  Aleichem, Sholem. *Tevye's Daughters*
  Alfon, Dov. *A Long Night in Paris*
  Alharthi, Jokha. *Celestial Bodies: A Novel*
  Allende, Isabel. *Daughter of Fortune: A Novel*
  Allende, Isabel. *A Long Petal of the Sea: A Novel*
  Allende, Isabel. *Portrait in Sepia: A Novel*
  Allende, Isabel. *Ripper: A Novel*
  Alomar, Osama. *The Teeth of the Comb & Other Stories*
  Alsterdal, Tove. *We Know You Remember*
  Altan, Ahmet. ★*Love in the Days of Rebellion*
  Amado, Jorge. ★*Dona Flor and Her Two Husbands: A Moral and Amorous Tale*
  Amado, Jorge. *Gabriela, Clove and Cinnamon*
  Ammaniti, Niccolo. *I'm Not Scared*
  Andric, Ivo. *The Bridge on the Drina*
  Appanah-Mouriquand, Nathacha. *Tropic of Violence: A Novel*
  Aramburu, Fernando. *Homeland*
  Arbol, Victor del. *Breathing Through the Wound*
  Arikawa, Hiro. *The Travelling Cat Chronicles*
  Aswani, Alaa. *Chicago: A Modern Arabic Novel*
  Atilgan, Yusuf. *Motherland Hotel*
  Ayatsuji, Yukito. *The Decagon House Murders*
  Backman, Fredrik. ★*Anxious People: A Novel*
  Backman, Fredrik. ★*Beartown: A Novel*
  Backman, Fredrik. *Britt-Marie Was Here*
  Backman, Fredrik. *A Man Called Ove*
  Backman, Fredrik. ★*My Grandmother Asked Me to Tell You She's Sorry: A Novel*
  Backman, Fredrik. *Us Against You: A Novel*
  Balzac, Honore de. *Eugenie Grandet*
  Balzano, Marco. *I'm Staying Here*
  Bannalec, Jean-Luc. *Death in Brittany*
  Bannalec, Jean-Luc. *The Granite Coast Murders*
  Bannalec, Jean-Luc. *The Killing Tide: A Brittany Mystery*
  Bao, Ninh. *The Sorrow of War: A Novel of North Vietnam*
  Barbery, Muriel. *The Elegance of the Hedgehog*
  Beauvoir, Simone de. ★*The Mandarins: A Novel*
  Beauvoir, Simone de. *The Woman Destroyed*
  Benedetti, Mario. *Springtime in a Broken Mirror*
  Bernhard, Thomas. *Frost: A Novel*
  Bernhard, Thomas. ★*The Loser*
  Bernhard, Thomas. ★*Woodcutters*
  Bilenchi, Romano. ★*The Chill*
  Binet, Laurent. ★*HHhH*
  Bivald, Katarina. *The Readers of Broken Wheel Recommend*
  Bolano, Roberto. ★*2666*
  Bolano, Roberto. *Amulet*

Bolano, Roberto. ★*By Night in Chile*
Bolano, Roberto. *Last Evenings on Earth*
Bolano, Roberto. *Monsieur Pain*
Bolano, Roberto. ★*Nazi Literature in the Americas*
Bolano, Roberto. ★*The Savage Detectives*
Bolano, Roberto. ★*The Third Reich*
Boll, Heinrich. *Billiards at Half-Past Nine*
Boll, Heinrich. *The Clown*
Boschwitz, Ulrich Alexander. *The Passenger: A Novel*
Boudjedra, Rachid. *The Barbary Figs*
Bourdeaut, Olivier. *Waiting for Bojangles: A Novel*
Bronsky, Alina. *The Hottest Dishes of the Tartar Cuisine*
Buwalda, Peter. *Bonita Avenue: A Novel*
Calvino, Italo. *Invisible Cities*
Camilleri, Andrea. *Riccardino*
Camus, Albert. *The Plague*
Camus, Albert. ★*The Stranger*
Cervantes Saavedra, Miguel de. ★*Don Quixote*
Chekhov, Anton Pavlovich. *Early Short Stories, 1883-1888*
Chekhov, Anton Pavlovich. *Later Short Stories, 1888-1903*
Chen, Qiufan. *Waste Tide*
Cherezinska, Elzbieta. *The Widow Queen*
Cho, Nam-Ju. ★*Kim Jiyoung, Born 1982*
Colette. *The Collected Stories of Colette*
Conde, Maryse. *I, Tituba, Black Witch of Salem*
Couto, Mia. *Rain: And Other Stories*
Couto, Mia. *Sleepwalking Land*
Cusset, Catherine. *Life of David Hockney: A Novel*
D'Eramo, Luce. *Deviation*
Dahl, Arne. *Bad Blood*
Dahl, Arne. *Misterioso: A Crime Novel*
Davys, Tim. *Amberville*
Dazieri, Sandrone. *Kill the Angel*
Dazieri, Sandrone. *Kill the Father*
Dazieri, Sandrone. *Kill the King*
De la Motte, Anders. *MemoRandom: A Thriller*
De la Motte, Anders. *Ultimatum: A Thriller*
Del Amo, Jean-Baptiste. *Animalia*
Demirtas, Selahattin. *Dawn: Stories*
Depestre, Rene. *Hadriana in All My Dreams*
Diachenko, Serhii. *Vita Nostra*
Djavadi, Negar. *Disoriental*
Dongala, Emmanuel Boundzeki. *The Bridgetower Sonata: Sonata Mulattica*
Dostoyevsky, Fyodor. ★*The Brothers Karamazov*
Dostoyevsky, Fyodor. ★*Crime and Punishment*
Dowlatabadi, Mahmoud. *The Colonel*
Drndic, Dasa. *Trieste*
Dumas, Alexandre. ★*Camille*
Dumas, Alexandre. ★*The Count of Monte Cristo*
Dupont, Eric. *The American Fiancee: A Novel*
Eco, Umberto. *Baudolino*
Eco, Umberto. ★*Foucault's Pendulum*
Eco, Umberto. *The Island of the Day Before*
Eco, Umberto. *The Mysterious Flame of Queen Loana: An Illustrated Novel*
Enard, Mathias. *Compass*
Endo, Shusaku. *Deep River*

Endo, Shusaku. *Silence*
Eriksson, Kjell. *The Deathwatch Beetle: A Mystery*
Erpenbeck, Jenny. *Go, Went, Gone: A Novel*
Escobar, Mario. *The Librarian of Saint-Malo: A Novel*
Esquivel, Laura. ★*Like Water for Chocolate: A Novel in Monthly Installments, with Recipes, Romances, and Home Remedies*
Faye, Gael. ★*Small Country: A Novel*
Fernandez, Nona. *The Twilight Zone*
Ferrante, Elena. *The Lying Life of Adults*
Ferrante, Elena. *My Brilliant Friend*
Ferrante, Elena. *The Story of a New Name*
Ferrante, Elena. *The Story of the Lost Child*
Ferrante, Elena. *Those Who Leave and Those Who Stay*
Flaubert, Gustave. ★*Madame Bovary: Provincial Ways*
Flaubert, Gustave. *Sentimental Education*
Fuentes, Carlos. *The Crystal Frontier: A Novel in Nine Stories*
Fuentes, Carlos. *The Death of Artemio Cruz*
Fuentes, Carlos. *Destiny and Desire: A Novel*
Fuentes, Carlos. ★*The Old Gringo*
Fuentes, Carlos. *The Years with Laura Diaz*
Gainza, Maria. *The Optic Nerve*
Gala, Marcial. ★*The Black Cathedral*
Gamboa, Santiago. *Necropolis*
Gao, XIngjian. *Soul Mountain*
Garcia Marquez, Gabriel. ★*The Autumn of the Patriarch*
Garcia Marquez, Gabriel. *Chronicle of a Death Foretold*
Garcia Marquez, Gabriel. *Collected Novellas*
Garcia Marquez, Gabriel. *In Evil Hour*
Garcia Marquez, Gabriel. *Leaf Storm, and Other Stories*
Garcia Marquez, Gabriel. ★*Love in the Time of Cholera*
Garcia Marquez, Gabriel. *Memories of My Melancholy Whores*
Garcia Saenz, Eva. *The Silence of the White City*
Garcia-Roza, L. A. *Alone in the Crowd: An Inspector Espinosa Mystery*
Garcia-Roza, L. A. *December Heat*
Gendry-Kim, Keum Suk. ★*The Waiting*
George, Nina. *The Book of Dreams*
George, Nina. *The Little Paris Bookshop*
Gide, Andre. ★*The Immoralist*
Gilbers, Harald. *Germania: A Novel of Nazi Berlin*
Ginzburg, Natalia. *Voices in the Evening*
Giordano, Mario. ★*Auntie Poldi and the Lost Madonna*
Giordano, Mario. *Auntie Poldi and the Vineyards of Etna*
Giordano, Paolo. *Heaven and Earth*
Giordano, Paolo. *Like Family*
Gogol, Nikolai Vasilievich. *The Collected Tales of Nikolai Gogol*
Gogol, Nikolai Vasilievich. ★*Dead Souls*
Grass, Gunter. *Crabwalk*
Grass, Gunter. *Too Far Afield*
Grebe, Camilla. *After She's Gone: A Novel*
Grebe, Camilla. *The Ice Beneath Her: A Novel*
Groen, Hendrik. *On the Bright Side: The New Secret Diary of Hendrik Groen, 85 Years Old*
Grossman, David. *Be My Knife*
Grossman, David. *Falling Out of Time*
Grossman, David. ★*A Horse Walks into a Bar*
Grossman, David. ★*More Than I Love My Life: A Novel*
Grossman, David. ★*To the End of the Land*

Gunday, Hakan. *The Few*
Halfon, Eduardo. *Mourning*
Han, Kang. ★*Human Acts: A Novel*
Haratischvili, Nino. *The Eighth Life: (For Brilka)*
Hashemzadeh Bonde, Golnaz. *What We Owe*
Hausmann, Romy. ★*Dear Child*
Hertmans, Stefan. ★*The Convert: A Novel*
Hesse, Hermann. *The Fairy Tales of Hermann Hesse*
Hesse, Hermann. ★*Siddhartha: A New Translation*
Hesse, Hermann. ★*Steppenwolf*
Higashino, Keigo. *Malice*
Higashino, Keigo. *The Miracles of the Namiya General Store*
Higashino, Keigo. *Newcomer*
Hill Gumbao, Toni. *The Good Suicides: A Thriller*
Hill Gumbao, Toni. *The Summer of Dead Toys*
Hoeg, Peter. ★*Smilla's Sense of Snow*
Houellebecq, Michel. *Submission*
Hugo, Victor. ★*The Hunchback of Notre Dame*
Hugo, Victor. ★*Les Miserables*
Huisman, Violaine. *The Book of Mother*
Indriðason, Arnaldur. *The Darkness Knows*
Indriðason, Arnaldur. *Outrage*
Indriðason, Arnaldur. *Reykjavik Nights: An Inspector Erlendur Novel*
Indriðason, Arnaldur. *Strange Shores: An Inspector Erlendur Novel*
Jin, Yong. *A Hero Born: A Novel*
Jónasson, Ragnar. ★*The Girl Who Died*
Jónasson, Ragnar. *The Island*
Jónasson, Ragnar. *The Mist*
Kawabata, Yasunari. *The Sound of the Mountain*
Kawaguchi, Toshikazu. *Before the Coffee Gets Cold*
Kawakami, Mieko. *Ms. Ice Sandwich*
Kazantzakis, Nikos. *The Last Temptation of Christ*
Kepler, Lars. *The Sandman*
Kerangal, Maylis de. *The Heart: A Novel*
Khadra, Yasmina. ★*Khalil: A Novel*
Khadra, Yasmina. *The Swallows of Kabul: A Novel*
Khalfah, Khlid. *Death Is Hard Work: A Novel*
Kim, Young-Ha. *Diary of a Murderer: And Other Stories*
Knausgaard, Karl Ove. *The Morning Star*
Ko-Eun, Yun. *The Disaster Tourist*
Koestler, Arthur. *Darkness at Noon*
Kundera, Milan. ★*Immortality*
Kundera, Milan. ★*The Unbearable Lightness of Being*
Kuznetsov, Anatolii Petrovich. *Babi Yar: A Document in the Form of a Novel*
Kwon, Yo-Son. *Lemon*
Labatut, Benjamin. *When We Cease to Understand the World*
Lackberg, Camilla. *The Golden Cage*
Lackberg, Camilla. *Silver Tears*
Lagercrantz, David. *The Girl Who Lived Twice: A Lisbeth Salander Novel*
Lagercrantz, David. *The Girl Who Takes an Eye for an Eye*
Lahiri, Jhumpa. ★*Whereabouts*
Larsson, Stieg. ★*The Girl Who Kicked the Hornet's Nest*
Larsson, Stieg. *The Girl Who Played with Fire*
Larsson, Stieg. *The Girl with the Dragon Tattoo*
Lee, Ji-Min. *The Starlet and the Spy*
Lem, Stanislaw. *His Master's Voice*

Liu, Cixin. *Ball Lightning*
Liu, Cixin. ★*The Dark Forest*
Liu, Cixin. ★*Death's End*
Liu, Cixin. ★*The Three-Body Problem*
Liu, Ken. *Invisible Planets: Contemporary Chinese Science Fiction in Translation*
Lunde, Maja. *The End of the Ocean: A Novel*
Ma, Jian. *Beijing Coma*
Mahfuz, Najib. ★*Palace Walk*
Mankell, Henning. *Before the Frost: A Linda Wallander Mystery*
Mankell, Henning. *The Dogs of Riga*
Mankell, Henning. *Firewall*
Mankell, Henning. *The Man from Beijing*
Mankell, Henning. *The Man Who Smiled: A Kurt Wallander Mystery*
Mankell, Henning. ★*One Step Behind*
Mankell, Henning. ★*The Return of the Dancing Master*
Mankell, Henning. *The Troubled Man*
Mann, Thomas. *Doctor Faustus*
Marias, Javier. *Thus Bad Begins: A Novel*
Mas, Victoria. *The Mad Women's Ball*
Meyer, Deon. *Icarus*
Mishima, Yukio. *The Sound of Waves*
Mishima, Yukio. *Spring Snow*
Mishima, Yukio. *The Temple of Dawn*
Murakami, Haruki. ★*1q84*
Murakami, Haruki. *After Dark*
Murakami, Haruki. *After the Quake: Stories*
Murakami, Haruki. *Blind Willow, Sleeping Woman: 24 Stories*
Murakami, Haruki. *Colorless Tsukuru Tazaki and His Years of Pilgrimage*
Murakami, Haruki. ★*First Person Singular: Stories*
Murakami, Haruki. ★*Kafka on the Shore*
Murakami, Haruki. *Killing Commendatore: A Novel*
Murakami, Haruki. *South of the Border, West of the Sun*
Murakami, Haruki. *The Wind-Up Bird Chronicle*
Murakami, Ryu. *In the Miso Soup*
Murata, Sayaka. *Earthlings: A Novel*
Musil, Robert. *The Man Without Qualities*
Nabokov, Vladimir Vladimirovich. *The Stories of Vladimir Nabokov*
Natsukawa, Sosuke. *The Cat Who Saved Books*
Nesbo, Jo. *The Leopard*
Nesbo, Jo. *Phantom*
Nesbo, Jo. *The Redeemer*
Nguyen, Phan Que Mai. ★*The Mountains Sing: A Novel*
Oe, Kenzaburo. *The Changeling*
Oe, Kenzaburo. ★*Death by Water*
Oe, Kenzaburo. *Nip the Buds, Shoot the Kids*
Oe, Kenzaburo. ★*A Quiet Life*
Oe, Kenzaburo. *Somersault: A Novel*
Ogawa, Yoko. *The Housekeeper and the Professor*
Ogawa, Yoko. ★*The Memory Police: A Novel*
Ohlsson, Kristina. *Unwanted: A Novel*
Okuizumi, Hikaru. *The Stones Cry Out*
Ólafsdóttir, Auður A. *Butterflies in November*
Ólafsson, Ólafur Jóhann. *The Sacrament: A Novel*
Ono, Masatsugu. *Echo on the Bay*
Oz, Amos. *Fima*
Pamuk, Orhan. *The Museum of Innocence*

Pamuk, Orhan. *The Red-Haired Woman*

Pamuk, Orhan. *Silent House*

Pamuk, Orhan. ★*Snow*

Park, Sang Young. ★*Love in the Big City: A Novel*

Pasternak, Boris Leonidovich. ★*Doctor Zhivago*

Perez-Reverte, Arturo. *What We Become*

Persson Giolito, Malin. *Beyond All Reasonable Doubt: A Novel*

Persson, Leif G. W. *Another Time, Another Life: The Story of a Crime*

Persson, Leif G. W. *The Dying Detective: A Mystery*

Petterson, Per. *I Curse the River of Time*

Petterson, Per. *I Refuse*

Petterson, Per. *Out Stealing Horses: A Novel*

Pontoppidan, Henrik. *Lucky Per*

Potzsch, Oliver. *The Beggar King*

Potzsch, Oliver. *The Dark Monk: A Hangman's Daughter Tale*

Potzsch, Oliver. *The Hangman's Daughter: A Historical Novel*

Potzsch, Oliver. *The Play of Death*

Potzsch, Oliver. *The Poisoned Pilgrim: A Hangman's Daughter Tale*

Potzsch, Oliver. *The Werewolf of Bamberg*

Proust, Marcel. ★*Remembrance of Things Past*

Proust, Marcel. *Swann's Way*

Proust, Marcel. *Time Regained*

Proust, Marcel. *Within a Budding Grove*

Rademacher, Cay. *Deadly Camargue: A Provence Mystery*

Ramqvist, Karolina. *The White City*

Redondo, Dolores. *The Invisible Guardian*

Redondo, Dolores. *The North Face of the Heart*

Remarque, Erich Maria. *The Road Back*

Roslund, Anders. *Cell 8*

Roslund, Anders. *Pen 33*

Roth, Joseph. *The Collected Stories of Joseph Roth*

Ruiz Zafon, Carlos. *The Prisoner of Heaven*

Ruiz Zafon, Carlos. ★*The Shadow of the Wind*

Rølvaag, O. E. ★*Giants in the Earth: A Saga of the Prairie*

Sagan, Francoise. ★*Bonjour Tristesse*

Saint-Exupery, Antoine de. ★*The Little Prince*

Sainz Borgo, Karina. ★*It Would Be Night in Caracas*

Sand, George. *Marianne*

Saramago, Jose. *All the Names*

Saramago, Jose. ★*Blindness*

Saramago, Jose. *Cain*

Saramago, Jose. ★*The Cave*

Saramago, Jose. *Death with Interruptions*

Saramago, Jose. ★*The Elephant's Journey*

Saramago, Jose. *The History of the Siege of Lisbon*

Saramago, Jose. *The Manual of Painting and Calligraphy*

Sartre, Jean Paul. *The Age of Reason*

Sartre, Jean Paul. ★*Nausea*

Sartre, Jean Paul. *Troubled Sleep*

Scerbanenco, Giorgio. *A Private Venus*

Scerbanenco, Giorgio. *Traitors to All*

Schami, Rafik. *Sophia: Or the Beginning of All Tales*

Schlink, Bernhard. *The Reader: A Novel*

Schlink, Bernhard. *Self's Deception*

Schlink, Bernhard. *Self's Murder*

Schlink, Bernhard. *Self's Punishment*

Schulman, Alex. *The Survivors: A Novel*

Schwarz-Bart, Andre. *The Last of the Just: A Novel*

Schweblin, Samanta. *Fever Dream: A Novel*

Schweblin, Samanta. *Little Eyes*

Sebald, Winfried Georg. ★*Austerlitz*

Sebald, Winfried Georg. *The Emigrants*

Sebald, Winfried Georg. *Vertigo*

Sem-Sandberg, Steve. *The Chosen Ones: A Novel*

Shalev, Meir. *Two She-Bears: A Novel*

Shan, Sa. *The Girl Who Played Go*

Shanbhag, Vivek. *Ghachar Ghochar*

Shoham, Liad. *Asylum City: A Novel*

Sienkiewicz, Henryk. ★*Quo Vadis: A Story of Faith in the Last Days of the Roman Empire*

Sigurðardóttir, Lilja. *Cage*

Simenon, Georges. *Maigret and the Black Sheep*

Simenon, Georges. *Maigret and the Fortuneteller*

Simenon, Georges. ★*Maigret and the Killer*

Simenon, Georges. *Maigret and the Madwoman*

Simenon, Georges. ★*Maigret and the Saturday Caller*

Simenon, Georges. ★*Maigret and the Toy Village*

Simenon, Georges. *Maigret and the Wine Merchant*

Simenon, Georges. ★*Maigret Bides His Time*

Simenon, Georges. ★*Maigret Goes Home*

Simenon, Georges. *Maigret in Holland*

Simenon, Georges. *Maigret's Memoirs*

Simenon, Georges. *My Friend Maigret*

Singer, I. J. *The Brothers Ashkenazi*

Singer, Isaac Bashevis. *Collected Stories: A Friend of Kafka to Passions*

Singer, Isaac Bashevis. *Collected Stories: Gimpel the Fool to the Letter Writer*

Singer, Isaac Bashevis. *Enemies, a Love Story*

Singer, Isaac Bashevis. *The Family Moskat*

Singer, Isaac Bashevis. ★*The Magician of Lublin*

Sjón. *The Blue Fox*

Sjowall, Maj. ★*Cop Killer: The Story of a Crime*

Sjowall, Maj. ★*The Laughing Policeman*

Sjowall, Maj. ★*The Locked Room: The Story of a Crime*

Sjowall, Maj. *The Man on the Balcony: The Story of a Crime*

Sjowall, Maj. ★*Murder at the Savoy*

Skarmeta, Antonio. *The Dancer and the Thief: A Novel*

Slimani, Leïla. *In the Country of Others*

Soderberg, Alexander. *The Other Son: A Sophie Brinkmann Novel*

Solares, Martin. *The Black Minutes*

Solares, Martin. *Don't Send Flowers*

Solzhenitsyn, Aleksandr Isaevich. ★*Cancer Ward*

Solzhenitsyn, Aleksandr Isaevich. *In the First Circle: A Novel : The Restored Text*

Solzhenitsyn, Aleksandr Isaevich. *One Day in the Life of Ivan Denisovich*

Somer, Mehmet Murat. *The Serenity Murders*

Starnone, Domenico. *Ties*

Starnone, Domenico. *Trick*

Sthers, Amanda. *Holy Lands: A Novel*

Suskind, Patrick. ★*Perfume: The Story of a Murderer*

Sveistrup, Soren. ★*The Chestnut Man: A Novel*

Svevo, Italo. *Zeno's Conscience*

Szabo, Magda. *Abigail*

Thelen, Albert Vigoleis. *The Island of Second Sight: From the Applied Recollections of Vigoleis*
Tolstaya, Tatyana. *Aetherial Worlds: Stories*
Tolstaya, Tatyana. *The Slynx*
Tolstoy, Leo. *Divine and Human and Other Stories*
Tolstoy, Leo. ★*War and Peace*
Traven, B. ★*The Treasure of the Sierra Madre*
Turgenev, Ivan Sergeevich. ★*Fathers and Sons*
Tursten, Helene. *An Elderly Lady Must Not Be Crossed*
Tursten, Helene. *Hunting Game*
Twardoch, Szczepan. *The King of Warsaw*
Ugresic, Dubravka. *Fox*
Ullmann, Linn. *Unquiet: A Novel*
Vargas Llosa, Mario. *The Bad Girl*
Vargas Llosa, Mario. ★*The Discreet Hero*
Vargas Llosa, Mario. *Green House*
Vargas Llosa, Mario. *The Time of the Hero*
Verne, Jules. ★*Around the World in Eighty Days*
Verne, Jules. ★*Journey to the Centre of the Earth*
Verne, Jules. *The Mysterious Island*
Voltaire. *Candide and Other Stories*
Walser, Robert. *The Assistant*
Wells, Benedict. *The End of Loneliness: A Novel*
Werfel, Franz. ★*The Forty Days of Musa Dagh*
Wiesel, Elie. ★*Dawn*
Wiesel, Elie. *Hostage*
Wiesel, Elie. *A Mad Desire to Dance: A Novel*
Wiesel, Elie. ★*Night, Dawn, the Accident: Three Tales*
Yoshimoto, Banana. *The Lake*
Yoshimoto, Banana. *Moshi-Moshi*
Yu, Miri. *Tokyo Ueno Station*
Zhou, Haohui. *Death Notice: A Novel*
Zola, Emile. ★*Germinal*
Zola, Emile. ★*Nana*

TRANSLATORS
Apostol, Gina. *Insurrecto*
Foer, Jonathan Safran. *Everything Is Illuminated: A Novel*
Miller, Andrew. *Oxygen*
Qiu, Xiaolong. *When Red Is Black*

TRANSPLANTATION OF ORGANS, TISSUES, ETC.
Kerangal, Maylis de. *The Heart: A Novel*
Picoult, Jodi. *Change of Heart: A Novel*

TRANSYLVANIA, ROMANIA
Stoker, Bram. ★*Dracula*
Stoker, Bram. *The New Annotated Dracula*

TRAUMATIC BRAIN-INJURY
McGregor, Jon. *Lean Fall Stand*

TRAVEL AGENCIES
Ko-Eun, Yun. *The Disaster Tourist*

TRAVEL WRITERS
Cook, Thomas H. *The Fate of Katherine Carr*
Hallinan, Timothy. *Fools' River*
Wolfe, Gene. *The Land Across*
The Travelers. Porter, Regina

TRAVELERS
Bowles, Paul. ★*The Sheltering Sky*
Doyle, Rob. *Threshold*
Eugenides, Jeffrey. *Fresh Complaint: Stories*

Evison, Jonathan. ★*Small World*
Ghosh, Amitav. *Sea of Poppies*
Kerouac, Jack. ★*On the Road*
Leithauser, Brad. *The Promise of Elsewhere*
Sebald, Winfried Georg. *Vertigo*
Vargas Llosa, Mario. ★*The Way to Paradise*
Verne, Jules. ★*Around the World in Eighty Days*

TRAVELING LIBRARIES
Bennett, Alan. ★*The Uncommon Reader*
Moyes, Jojo. ★*The Giver of Stars: A Novel*

TRAVELING SALES PERSONNEL
Rushdie, Salman. ★*Quichotte: A Novel*

TRAVELING THEATER
Sabatini, Rafael. *Scaramouche: A Romance of the French Revolution*
The Travelling Cat Chronicles. Arikawa, Hiro
Travels in the Scriptorium: A Novel. Auster, Paul
Traven, B.
 ★*The Treasure of the Sierra Madre*
Travis McGee novels [Series]. MacDonald, John D.
A Treacherous Curse: A Veronica Speedwell Mystery. Raybourn, Deanna
Treachery. Parris, S. J.
Treason. Campbell, Rick

TREASON
Bourne, Joanna. *Rogue Spy*
Buckley, Fiona. *The Doublet Affair: A Mystery at Queen Elizabeth I's Court*
Buckley, Fiona. *The Siren Queen: An Ursula Blanchard Mystery at Queen Elizabeth I's Court*
Dumas, Alexandre. ★*The Count of Monte Cristo*
Mantel, Hilary. ★*Bring up the Bodies: A Novel*
Vargas Llosa, Mario. *The Dream of the Celt*
Wolfe, Suzanne M. *The Course of All Treasons*
Woods, Stuart. *Skin Game*

TREASURE HUNTERS
Berry, Steve. *The Lost Order*
Cooper, Tom. *The Marauders*
Coulter, Catherine. *The Last Second*
Coulter, Catherine. *The Lost Key*
Cussler, Clive. ★*The Oracle*
Cussler, Clive. *The Romanov Ransom*
Cussler, Clive. *Sahara: A Novel*
Reynolds, Alastair. ★*Revenger*

TREASURE HUNTING
Alexis, Andre. *The Hidden Keys*
Berry, Steve. ★*The Templar Legacy: A Novel of Suspense*
Crichton, Michael. *Pirate Latitudes*
Cussler, Clive. *Havana Storm*
DeMille, Nelson. ★*The Cuban Affair: A Novel*
Gates, Eva. *Read and Buried*
Potzsch, Oliver. *The Dark Monk: A Hangman's Daughter Tale*
Romain, Theresa. *Fortune Favors the Wicked*

TREASURE HUNTS (GAMES)
Racculia, Kate. ★*Tuesday Mooney Talks to Ghosts: A Novel*
★*The Treasure of the Sierra Madre*. Traven, B.

TREASURE TROVES
Berry, Steve. *The Lost Order*
Coulter, Catherine. *The Lost Key*
Cussler, Clive. ★*The Oracle*

Cussler, Clive. *The Romanov Ransom*
Romain, Theresa. *Fortune Favors the Wicked*

TREAT, MARY

Hoang, Helen. ★*The Bride Test*
Kingsolver, Barbara. ★*Unsheltered*

★*A **Tree** Grows in Brooklyn*. Smith, Betty
*The **Tree** of Hands*. Rendell, Ruth
Treeborne. Johnson, Caleb

TREES

Christie, Michael. ★*Greenwood: A Novel*
Powers, Richard. ★*The Overstory: A Novel*
Stage, Zoje. *Wonderland*

***Tremaine's** True Love*. Burrowes, Grace

Tremblay, Paul

★*The Cabin at the End of the World: A Novel*
Growing Things and Other Stories
Survivor Song

TRENCH WARFARE

Faulks, Sebastian. ★*Birdsong*
Remarque, Erich Maria. ★*All Quiet on the Western Front*

TRENTON, NEW JERSEY

Evanovich, Janet. ★*Game On: Tempting Twenty-Eight*
Evanovich, Janet. *Look Alive Twenty-Five*
Evanovich, Janet. *One for the Money*
Evanovich, Janet. *Turbo Twenty-Three*

Trevor, William

Last Stories

★*The **Trial***. Kafka, Franz
***Trial** on Mount Koya: A Hiro Hattori Novel*. Spann, Susan

TRIALS

Gardam, Jane. *Last Friends*
Kafka, Franz. ★*The Trial*
Koestler, Arthur. *Darkness at Noon*
Parks, Brad. *Say Nothing: A Novel*
Phillips, Jayne Anne. *Quiet Dell: A Novel*
Umrigar, Thrity N. ★*Honor*

TRIALS (ASSAULT AND BATTERY)

Connelly, Michael. *The Lincoln Lawyer: A Novel*

TRIALS (CHILD CUSTODY)

Miller, Sue. *The Good Mother*

TRIALS (CHILD CUSTODY) — HISTORY

Shreve, Anita. *Fortune's Rocks: A Novel*

TRIALS (ESPIONAGE)

Doctorow, E. L. ★*The Book of Daniel: A Novel*

TRIALS (MURDER)

Arvin, Reed. *Blood of Angels: A Novel*
Atwood, Margaret. *Alias Grace*
Burnet, Graeme Macrae. *His Bloody Project: Documents Relating to the Case of Roderick Macrae*
Camus, Albert. ★*The Stranger*
Cavanagh, Steve. *Thirteen*
Connelly, Michael. *The Brass Verdict: A Novel*
Connelly, Michael. *The Fifth Witness*
Connelly, Michael. *The Gods of Guilt*
Cook, Thomas H. *Sandrine's Case*
Copperman, E. J. *Judgment at Santa Monica*
Cush, Jean Love. *Endangered*
Edwards, Yvvette. *The Mother*

Faulkner, William. *Intruder in the Dust*
Grisham, John. *The Client*
Grisham, John. *A Time to Kill*
Guterson, David. ★*Snow Falling on Cedars*
Kim, Angie. *Miracle Creek*
Lescroart, John T. *Guilt*
Lindsey, Odie. *Some Go Home: A Novel*
Lippman, Laura. *Wilde Lake*
Moore, Graham. *The Holdout: A Novel*
Picoult, Jodi. *Nineteen Minutes: A Novel*
Scottoline, Lisa. *After Anna*
Stone, Nick. *The Verdict*
Turow, Scott. *The Last Trial*
Twain, Mark. *Pudd'nhead Wilson ;: And, Those Extraordinary Twins*
Whitlow, Robert. *A Time to Stand*

TRIALS (MUTINY) — HISTORY

Pesci, David. *Amistad: A Novel*

TRIALS (RAPE)

Forster, E. M. ★*A Passage to India*
Goldin, Megan. *The Night Swim*
Lee, Harper. ★*To Kill a Mockingbird*
Vaughan, Sarah. ★*Anatomy of a Scandal: A Novel*
Winthrop, Elizabeth Hartley. *The Mercy Seat: A Novel*

TRIALS (WITCHCRAFT)

Conde, Maryse. *I, Tituba, Black Witch of Salem*
Galchen, Rivka. *Everyone Knows Your Mother Is a Witch*
Scott, A. D. *A Kind of Grief: A Novel*
Sharratt, Mary. *Daughters of the Witching Hill*

TRIBAL POLICE

Hillerman, Tony. *The Sinister Pig*
Hillerman, Tony. *The Wailing Wind*
Potenza, Carol. *Hearts of the Missing*

Trick. Starnone, Domenico

TRICK RIDING

Peterson, Tracie. *What Comes My Way*

TRICKSTERS

Estleman, Loren D. *The Adventures of Johnny Vermillion: A Novel*
Gaiman, Neil. ★*Anansi Boys: A Novel*

***Trident** deception* [Series]. Campbell, Rick
Trieste. Drndic, Dasa

TRIESTE, ITALY

Drndic, Dasa. *Trieste*

***Trigger** Warning: Short Fictions and Disturbances*. Gaiman, Neil

Trigiani, Adriana

Big Cherry Holler: A Big Stone Gap Novel
Big Stone Gap: A Novel

TRINIDAD AND TOBAGO

Abdul-Jabbar, Kareem. *Mycroft and Sherlock*
Abdul-Jabbar, Kareem. ★*Mycroft Holmes*
Adam, Claire. *Golden Child: A Novel*
Francis-Sharma, Lauren. ★*Book of the Little Axe*
Naipaul, V. S. *A House for Mr. Biswas*
Persaud, Ingrid. *Love After Love: A Novel*

TRINIDADIANS IN CANADA

Chariandy, David John. *Brother: A Novel*

★***Trinity***. Uris, Leon
★*The **Trinity** Six*. Cumming, Charles
Trio. Boyd, William

TRIPLETS
    Frankel, Laurie. *One Two Three: A Novel*
TRIPS AROUND THE WORLD
    Verne, Jules. ★*Around the World in Eighty Days*
TRISTAN, FLORA
    Balogh, Mary. *The Arrangement*
    Vargas Llosa, Mario. ★*The Way to Paradise*
*The **Triumph** of Caesar: A Novel of Ancient Rome*. Saylor, Steven
TROJAN WAR
    Barker, Pat. ★*The Silence of the Girls: A Novel*
    Barker, Pat. *The Women of Troy*
    George, Margaret. *Helen of Troy*
    Haynes, Natalie. *A Thousand Ships*
    Miller, Madeline. *The Song of Achilles*
Trollope, Anthony
    ★*Barchester Towers*
    Doctor Thorne
    ★*The Eustace Diamonds*
    Framley Parsonage
    The Last Chronicle of Barset
    ★*The Prime Minister*
    The Warden
Trollope, Joanna
    Other People's Children
*Trophy** Hunt: A Joe Pickett Novel*. Box, C. J.
TROPHY WIVES
    Brown, Sandra. ★*Ricochet*
    Dodd, Christina. *The Woman Who Couldn't Scream*
★*Tropic** of Cancer*. Miller, Henry
★*Tropic** of Capricorn*. Miller, Henry
*Tropic** of Violence: A Novel*. Appanah-Mouriquand, Nathacha
TROPICS
    Erpenbeck, Jenny. *The Book of Words*
*Trouble** & Triumph: A Novel of Power & Beauty*. T. I.
*Trouble** in Paradise*. Parker, Robert B.
*Trouble** Is What I Do: A Leonid McGill Mystery*. Mosley, Walter
*Trouble** the Saints*. Johnson, Alaya Dawn
*Trouble** Walks In*. Humphreys, Sara Taney
*The **Trouble** with Dukes*. Burrowes, Grace
*The **Trouble** with True Love*. Guhrke, Laura Lee
*The **Troubled** Man*. Mankell, Henning
*Troubled** Sleep*. Sartre, Jean Paul
★*Troubles** in Paradise*. Hilderbrand, Elin
TROUT, KILGORE (FICTITIOUS CHARACTER)
    Vonnegut, Kurt. *Jailbird: A Novel*
    Vonnegut, Kurt. *Timequake*
TROY (EXTINCT CITY)
    Barker, Pat. ★*The Silence of the Girls: A Novel*
    Barker, Pat. *The Women of Troy*
    George, Margaret. *Helen of Troy*
    Haynes, Natalie. *A Thousand Ships*
    Malouf, David. *Ransom*
    Miller, Madeline. *The Song of Achilles*
*The **Truants***. Weinberg, Kate
TRUCK DRIVERS
    Albahari, David. *Gotz and Meyer*
    Rice, Christopher. *Blood Victory*
*The **True** Bastards*. French, Jonathan

*True** gentlemen novels [Series]. Burrowes, Grace
★*True** Grit: A Novel*. Portis, Charles
★*True** to You*. Wade, Becky
TRUJILLO MOLINA, RAFAEL LEONIDAS, 1891-1961
    ASSASSINATION
    Vargas Llosa, Mario. *The Feast of the Goat*
*Truly** Madly Guilty*. Moriarty, Liane
Trumbo, Dalton
    ★*Johnny Got His Gun*
TRUMPETERS
    Baker, Dorothy. ★*Young Man with a Horn*
Truong, Monique T. D.
    The Sweetest Fruits
Truss, Lynne
    The Man That Got Away: A Constable Twitten Mystery
    Murder by Milk Bottle
TRUST
    Butland, Stephanie. *The Lost for Words Bookshop: A Novel*
    Center, Katherine. *Things You Save in a Fire*
    Cook, Thomas H. *Instruments of Night*
    Dallas, Sandra. *The Last Midwife*
    Frear, Caz. *Sweet Little Lies*
    Goodman, Allegra. *The Cookbook Collector: A Novel*
    Hatcher, Robin Lee. *Cross My Heart*
    Krentz, Jayne Ann. *Secret Sisters*
    Lee, Yoon Ha. *Ninefox Gambit*
    Meltzer, Brad. *The Tenth Justice*
    Mosley, Walter. *Fortunate Son: A Novel*
    Wagers, K. B. *A Pale Light in the Black: A Neog Novel*
★*Trust** Exercise: A Novel*. Choi, Susan
TRUST IN GOD
    Andrews, Mesu. *Isaiah's Daughter: A Novel of Prophets and Kings*
TRUST IN WOMEN
    Mallery, Susan. *Best of My Love*
    Shalvis, Jill. *Simply Irresistible*
★*Trust** No Bitch*. Ca$h
*Trust** No One: A Thriller*. Cleave, Paul
*Trust** Your Eyes: A Thriller*. Barclay, Linwood
TRUTH
    Ashley, Jennifer. *The Madness of Lord Ian Mackenzie*
    Cusk, Rachel. *Outline: A Novel*
    Dionne, Karen. *The Wicked Sister*
    Flanery, Patrick. *Absolution: A Novel*
    Hilderbrand, Elin. ★*What Happens in Paradise: A Novel*
    Lasdun, James. *Afternoon of a Faun: A Novel*
    Polansky, Daniel. *The Seventh Perfection*
    Rice, Anne. *Christ the Lord: The Road to Cana: A Novel*
    Schwartz, Lynne Sharon. *Truthtelling: Stories, Fables, Glimpses*
*The **Truth** About Love and Dukes*. Guhrke, Laura Lee
Truth, Lies, and Second Dates. Davidson, MaryJanice
*The **Truth**: a Novel of Discworld*. Pratchett, Terry
*Truths** I Never Told You*. Rimmer, Kelly
Truthtelling: Stories, Fables, Glimpses. Schwartz, Lynne Sharon
Tsao, Tiffany
    The Majesties
*The **Tsar** of Love and Techno: Stories*. Marra, Anthony
Tsarina. Alpsten, Ellen

Tsukiyama, Gail
The Street of a Thousand Blossoms
TSUNAMIS
Ozeki, Ruth L. ★*A Tale for the Time Being*
TUBERCULOSIS
Purcell, Laura. *The House of Whispers*
The **Tubman** Command: A Novel. Cobbs Hoffman, Elizabeth
TUBMAN, HARRIET
Cobbs Hoffman, Elizabeth. *The Tubman Command: A Novel*
Goodman, Jo. *A Touch of Forever*
Tucker mysteries [Series]. Daniel, Ray
TUCSON, ARIZONA
Kingsolver, Barbara. ★*The Bean Trees: A Novel*
Silko, Leslie Marmon. *Almanac of the Dead*
Tudor novels (Philippa Gregory) [Series]. Gregory, Philippa
TUDOR PERIOD (1485-1603)
Andersen, Laura. ★*The Boleyn King*
Bear, Elizabeth. *Ink and Steel: A Novel of the Promethean Age*
Buckley, Fiona. *The Doublet Affair: A Mystery at Queen Elizabeth I's Court*
Clements, Oliver. *The Eyes of the Queen*
Clements, Oliver. *The Queen's Men*
Follett, Ken. *A Column of Fire*
Gregory, Philippa. *The Boleyn Inheritance*
Gregory, Philippa. *The Constant Princess*
Gregory, Philippa. *The Last Tudor*
Gregory, Philippa. *The Other Boleyn Girl: A Novel*
Gregory, Philippa. *The Taming of the Queen*
Mantel, Hilary. ★*Bring up the Bodies: A Novel*
Mantel, Hilary. ★*Wolf Hall*
Phillips, Arthur. ★*The King at the Edge of the World: Novel*
Sansom, C. J. ★*Lamentation*
Sansom, C. J. *Revelation*
Sansom, C. J. ★*Sovereign*
Sansom, C. J. *Tombland*
Weir, Alison. *Anna of Kleve: The Princess in the Portrait*
Wolfe, Suzanne M. *The Course of All Treasons*
Tudor, C. J.
The Burning Girls: A Novel
The Chalk Man: A Novel
The Other People
★**Tuesday** Mooney Talks to Ghosts: A Novel. Racculia, Kate
Tuesday's Gone. French, Nicci
Tufa novels [Series]. Bledsoe, Alex
TUNISIA
Cumming, Charles. *A Foreign Country*
Turansky, Carrie
No Ocean Too Wide: A Novel
Turbo Twenty-Three. Evanovich, Janet
Turgenev, Ivan Sergeevich
★*Fathers and Sons*
TURKEY
Ackerman, Elliot. *Dark at the Crossing*
Ackerman, Elliot. *Red Dress in Black and White*
Altan, Ahmet. ★*Love in the Days of Rebellion*
Cumming, Charles. *A Colder War*
De Bernieres, Louis. *Birds Without Wings*
Demirtas, Selahattin. *Dawn: Stories*

Golden, Christopher. *Ararat*
Gunday, Hakan. *The Few*
Hayes, Terry. *I Am Pilgrim*
Pamuk, Orhan. *Silent House*
Pamuk, Orhan. ★*Snow*
Pamuk, Orhan. ★*A Strangeness in My Mind: A Novel*
Shafak, Elif. ★*10 Minutes 38 Seconds in This Strange World*
Somer, Mehmet Murat. *The Serenity Murders*
Werfel, Franz. ★*The Forty Days of Musa Dagh*
TURKISH AMERICANS
Batuman, Elif. ★*The Idiot*
A **Turn** of Light. Czerneda, Julie
★The **Turn** of the Key. Ware, Ruth
★The **Turn** of the Screw. James, Henry
Turnbull, Cadwell
★*The Lesson*
No Gods, No Monsters
The **Turner** House. Flournoy, Angela
Turner series (Cat Sebastian) [Series]. Sebastian, Cat
TURNER'S SLAVE REVOLT, SOUTHAMPTON, VIRGINIA, 1831
Styron, William. *The Confessions of Nat Turner*
Turner, Bethany
The Secret Life of Sarah Hollenbeck
Wooing Cadie McCaffrey
TURNER, NAT, 1800?-1831
Styron, William. *The Confessions of Nat Turner*
★The **Turnout**: a Novel. Abbott, Megan E.
Turow, Scott
The Last Trial
Presumed Innocent
Testimony
The **Turquoise** Lament. MacDonald, John D.
Tursten, Helene
An Elderly Lady Must Not Be Crossed
Hunting Game
Turton, Stuart
The 7 1/2 Deaths of Evelyn Hardcastle
★*The Devil and the Dark Water*
TUSCANY, ITALY
Bilenchi, Romano. ★*The Chill*
TUSSAUD, MARIE
Carey, Edward. *Little: A Novel*
Eisler, Barry. *The Killer Collective*
TUTORING
Richman, Alyson. *The Secret of Clouds*
TUTORS
Guhrke, Laura Lee. *Governess Gone Rogue*
Saylor, Steven. *The Seven Wonders: A Novel of the Ancient World*
Sebastian, Cat. *It Takes Two to Tumble*
Wilder, Thornton. ★*Theophilus North*
Twain & Stanley Enter Paradise. Hijuelos, Oscar
Twain, Mark
★*Adventures of Huckleberry Finn: Tom Sawyer's Comrade ...*
★*The Complete Short Stories of Mark Twain*
★*A Connecticut Yankee in King Arthur's Court*
Personal Recollections of Joan of Arc
Pudd'nhead Wilson and Those Extraordinary Twins

TWAIN, MARK
Burrowes, Grace. *Tremaine's True Love*
Heller, Peter. *The Painter: A Novel*
Hijuelos, Oscar. *Twain & Stanley Enter Paradise*
Twain, Mark. ★*Adventures of Huckleberry Finn: Tom Sawyer's Comrade ...*
Twardoch, Szczepan
The King of Warsaw
The **Twelve**. Cronin, Justin
The **Twelve** Jays of Christmas: A Meg Langslow Mystery. Andrews, Donna
The **Twelve** Lives of Samuel Hawley: A Novel. Tinti, Hannah
The **Twelve** Tribes of Hattie. Mathis, Ayana
TWELVE-YEAR-OLD BOYS
Ajvide Lindqvist, John. *Let the Right One In*
Bock, Charles. *Beautiful Children: A Novel*
Bradbury, Ray. ★*Dandelion Wine: A Novel*
Childress, Mark. *Crazy in Alabama*
Hiaasen, Carl. *Nature Girl*
Krueger, William Kent. ★*Lightning Strike*
McCammon, Robert R. *Boy's Life*
TWELVE-YEAR-OLD GIRLS
Allison, Dorothy. ★*Bastard Out of Carolina*
Dean, Margaret Lazarus. *The Time It Takes to Fall*
McCullers, Carson. *The Member of the Wedding*
Smith, Ali. *The Accidental*
Tinti, Hannah. *The Twelve Lives of Samuel Hawley: A Novel*
Vann, David. *Aquarium*
TWENTIES (AGE)
Bartlett, Neil. *The Disappearance Boy*
Dolan-Leach, Caite. *We Went to the Woods: A Novel*
Gallen, Michelle. *Big Girl, Small Town: A Novel*
MacDonald, Andrew. *When We Were Vikings*
Nguyen, Kevin. ★*New Waves*
Tallo, Katie. *Dark August*
Twenty Years After. Dumas, Alexandre
The **Twenty-Three**: a Promise Falls Novel. Barclay, Linwood
The **Twilight** of the Superheroes. Eisenberg, Deborah
The **Twilight** Zone. Fernandez, Nona
TWIN BROTHERS
Alenyikov, Michael. *Ivan and Misha: Stories*
Dumas, Alexandre. ★*The Man in the Iron Mask*
Santiago, Esmeralda. *Conquistadora: A Novel*
TWIN CITIES METROPOLITAN AREA
Sandford, John. ★*Rules of Prey*
TWIN SISTERS
Abraham, Tola Rotimi. *Black Sunday*
Adams, Taylor. *Hairpin Bridge*
Baldacci, David. *Long Road to Mercy*
Baldacci, David. *A Minute to Midnight*
Bennett, Brit. ★*The Vanishing Half*
Ekwuyasi, Francesca. *Butter Honey Pig Bread: A Novel*
Fleischmann, Raymond. *How Quickly She Disappears*
Gailey, Sarah. *Magic for Liars*
Konar, Affinity. *Mischling: A Novel*
Levin, Ira. *A Kiss Before Dying*
Mallery, Susan. *The Summer of Sunshine and Margot*
McGuire, Seanan. ★*Down Among the Sticks and Bones*

Rizzuto, Rahna R. *Shadow Child*
Sittenfeld, Curtis. *Sisterland: A Novel*
TWINS
Adam, Claire. *Golden Child: A Novel*
Bell, Lenora. ★*What a Difference a Duke Makes*
Clarke, Diana. *Thin Girls*
Coben, Harlan. *Don't Let Go*
Dexter, Pete. *Spooner*
Fuller, Claire. *Unsettled Ground*
Golding, Melanie. *Little Darlings*
Haig, Francesca. *The Fire Sermon: A Novel*
Hart, John. *The Last Child*
McGuire, Seanan. ★*Middlegame*
Pike, Signe. *The Lost Queen*
Pyper, Andrew. *The Damned: A Novel*
Roy, Arundhati. ★*The God of Small Things*
Setterfield, Diane. *The Thirteenth Tale: A Novel*
Varley, John. *Dark Lightning*
Whitten, Hannah. *For the Wolf*
Wilson, Kevin. *Nothing to See Here*
Yang, JY. *The Black Tides of Heaven*
Twisted Tea Christmas. Childs, Laura
A **Twisted** Vengeance. Robb, Candace M.
Two Days Gone: A Novel. Silvis, Randall
The **Two** Hotel Francforts: A Novel. Leavitt, David
★The **Two** Mrs. Carlyles. Rindell, Suzanne
Two rivers [Series]. Cleeves, Ann
Two She-Bears: A Novel. Shalev, Meir
The **Two** Towers: Being the Second Part of the Lord of the Rings. Tolkien, J. R. R.
Two Trains Running. Vachss, Andrew H.
Two Years Eight Months and Twenty-Eight Nights: A Novel. Rushdie, Salman
Tyler, Anne
★*The Accidental Tourist: A Novel*
The Amateur Marriage: A Novel
★*Clock Dance: A Novel*
A Patchwork Planet
★*Redhead by the Side of the Road*
★*Saint Maybe*
Vinegar Girl: The Taming of the Shrew Retold
TYPE A PERSONALITY
Serle, Rebecca. *In Five Years: A Novel*
Typhoon Fury. Cussler, Clive
TYPISTS
Rindell, Suzanne. *The Other Typist*
Tyree, Omar
★*Flyy Girl*
For the Love of Money: A Novel
Leslie: A Novel

U

U.S.A. [Series]. Dos Passos, John
UFO ABDUCTIONS
Evanovich, Janet. *Look Alive Twenty-Five*

UGANDA

Makumbi, Jennifer Nansubuga. ★*A Girl Is a Body of Water*

Makumbi, Jennifer Nansubuga. *Kintu*

*The **Ugly** Duchess*. James, Eloisa

Ugresic, Dubravka

Fox

UHTRED (FICTITIOUS CHARACTER)

Cornwell, Bernard. *The Last Kingdom: A Novel*

UKRAINE

Anderson, Alison. *The Summer Guest*

Artson, Barbara. *Odessa, Odessa*

Benn, James R. *Road of Bones: A Billy Boyle World War II Mystery*

Campbell, Rick. *Treason*

Foer, Jonathan Safran. *Everything Is Illuminated: A Novel*

Higgins, Jack. *Confessional*

Powell, Mark. *Firebird*

Smith, Martin Cruz. *Wolves Eat Dogs: A Novel*

Ullmann, Linn

Unquiet: A Novel

*The **Ultimatum***. Robards, Karen

*The **Ultimatum***. Wolf, Dick

***Ultimatum**: a Thriller*. De la Motte, Anders

★*Ulysses*. Joyce, James

Umrigar, Thrity N.

Everybody's Son

★*Honor*

The Secrets Between Us

*The **Unamericans***. Antopol, Molly

★*The **Unbearable** Lightness of Being*. Kundera, Milan

★*The **Unbroken***. Clark, Cherae

***Unbury** Carol*. Malerman, Josh

UNCERTAINTY

Levy, Deborah. *Hot Milk: A Novel*

Monroe, Mary Alice. ★*The Summer of Lost and Found*

Pynchon, Thomas. *Against the Day: A Novel*

UNCLE AND NEPHEW

Bellow, Saul. *More Die of Heartbreak*

Church, James. *A Drop of Chinese Blood*

Dickens, Charles. ★*Nicholas Nickleby*

Harris, Thomas. *Hannibal Rising*

Luesse, Valerie Fraser. *Under the Bayou Moon: A Novel*

Nabokov, Vladimir Vladimirovich. *King, Queen, Knave: A Novel*

Scott, Walter. ★*Rob Roy*

UNCLE AND NIECE

Belfer, Lauren. *And After the Fire: A Novel*

Hoyt, Elizabeth. *When a Rogue Meets His Match*

Weaver, Ashley. ★*A Peculiar Combination*

Uncle Rudolf. Bailey, Paul

★*Uncle Tom's Cabin*. Stowe, Harriet Beecher

UNCLES

Cornwell, Bernard. *The Last Kingdom: A Novel*

Erdrich, Louise. ★*The Night Watchman: A Novel*

French, Tana. ★*The Witch Elm: A Novel*

Maturin, Charles Robert. *Melmoth the Wanderer: A Tale*

Rowley, Steven. ★*The Guncle: A Novel*

Smith, Lee. *On Agate Hill: A Novel*

Stewart, Mary. *Nine Coaches Waiting*

UNCLES — DEATH

Atkins, Ace. *The Ranger*

Brunt, Carol Rifka. ★*Tell the Wolves I'm Home: A Novel*

Irvin, Kelly. *Tell Her No Lies*

***Uncollected** Stories of William Faulkner*. Faulkner, William

★*The **Uncommon** Reader*. Bennett, Alan

★*An **Unconditional** Freedom*. Cole, Alyssa

***Unconquerable** Sun*. Elliott, Kate

*The **Unconsoled***. Ishiguro, Kazuo

***Unconventional** ladies of Mayfair [Series]*. Pembrooke, Kate

*The **Undateable***. Title, Sarah

UNDEAD

Anderson, Kevin J. *Death Warmed Over*

Brooks, Max. ★*World War Z: An Oral History of the Zombie War*

King, Stephen. *Pet Sematary*

Muir, Tamsyn. *Harrow the Ninth*

Shaw, Vivian. ★*Dreadful Company*

Shaw, Vivian. ★*Strange Practice*

Thompson, Tade. *The Rosewater Redemption*

Verdon, John. *On Harrow Hill*

★*Under Currents*. Roberts, Nora

Under Her Skin. Anders, Adriana

Under My Skin. Unger, Lisa

★*Under Occupation: A Novel*. Furst, Alan

Under Pressure. Pobi, Robert

Under the Bayou Moon: A Novel. Luesse, Valerie Fraser

Under the Cold Bright Lights. Disher, Garry

Under the Table. Evanovich, Stephanie

Under the Tulip Tree. Shocklee, Michelle

★*Under the Udala Trees*. Okparanta, Chinelo

★*Under the Whispering Door*. Klune, TJ

UNDERCLASS

Choo, Yangsze. ★*The Night Tiger: A Novel*

Kohnstamm, Thomas B. *Lake City*

UNDERCOVER OPERATIONS

Bateman, Kate. *This Earl of Mine*

Berenson, Alex. *The Faithful Spy: A Novel*

Berenson, Alex. *The Prisoner*

Bernhard, Emilia. *The Books of the Dead*

Bourne, Joanna. ★*My Lord and Spymaster*

Buckley, Fiona. *The Doublet Affair: A Mystery at Queen Elizabeth I's Court*

Child, Lee. *The Affair*

Child, Lee. *The Hard Way*

Child, Lincoln. *Deep Storm: A Novel*

Cole, Alyssa. ★*An Extraordinary Union*

Collins, Manda. *A Good Rake Is Hard to Find*

Coulter, Catherine. *The Devil's Triangle*

Coulter, Catherine. *The End Game*

De Leon, Aya. ★*A Spy in the Struggle*

Delaney, J. P. *Believe Me: A Novel*

Downing, David. *Diary of a Dead Man on Leave*

Finder, Joseph. *Suspicion*

Fleming, Ian. *The Man with the Golden Gun*

Fleming, Ian. *On Her Majesty's Secret Service*

Forsyth, Frederick. *The Kill List*

French, Tana. *The Likeness*

George, Elizabeth. *Believing the Lie*

Groot, Tracy. *Flame of Resistance*
Gross, Andrew. *The One Man*
Hart, Rob. *The Warehouse: A Novel*
Higgins, Jack. *Confessional*
Higgins, Jack. *The Eagle Has Landed*
Higgins, Jack. *Eye of the Storm*
Mooney, Chris. *Blood World*
Muller, Marcia. *Ice and Stone*
Pavone, Chris. *The Paris Diversion: A Novel*
Phillips, Arthur. ★*The King at the Edge of the World: Novel*
Pronzini, Bill. *The Stolen Gold Affair*
Quartey, Kwei. ★*Sleep Well, My Lady*
Quick, Amanda. ★*The Lady Has a Past*
Quick, Amanda. *The Other Lady Vanishes*
Raybourn, Deanna. ★*A Murderous Relation*
Ricciardi, David. *Warning Light*
Robbins, David L. *War of the Rats: A Novel*
Simpson, Rosemary. *Let the Dead Keep Their Secrets*
Smith, Martin Cruz. *The Siberian Dilemma*
Stabenow, Dana. *Killing Grounds: A Kate Shugak Mystery*
Stabenow, Dana. *Restless in the Grave*
Steinhauer, Olen. *The Middleman*
Steinhauer, Olen. *The Nearest Exit*
Steinhauer, Olen. *The Tourist*
Watt, Holly. *To the Lions*
Wilkinson, Lauren. ★*American Spy: A Novel*
Wolfe, Suzanne M. *The Course of All Treasons*
Woods, Stuart. ★*Bombshell*
Woods, Stuart. *Skin Game*
The **Underground** Man. Macdonald, Ross
UNDERGROUND MOVEMENTS
Naipaul, V. S. *Magic Seeds*
UNDERGROUND RAILROAD
Chevalier, Tracy. *The Last Runaway*
Coates, Ta-Nehisi. ★*The Water Dancer: A Novel*
Cole, Alyssa. ★*A Hope Divided*
Faye, Lyndsay. *Seven for a Secret*
Johnson, Tara. *Engraved on the Heart*
Whitehead, Colson. ★*The Underground Railroad: A Novel*
★The **Underground** Railroad: A Novel. Whitehead, Colson
UNDERHILL, TIM (FICTITIOUS CHARACTER)
Straub, Peter. *Lost Boy Lost Girl: A Novel*
Undermajordomo Minor. deWitt, Patrick
The **Undertakers**. Glover, Nicole
UNDERTAKERS
Hage, Rawi. *Beirut Hellfire Society: A Novel*
Henderson, Susan. *The Flicker of Old Dreams*
Waugh, Evelyn. *The Loved One: An Anglo-American Tragedy*
UNDERWATER ARCHAEOLOGY
Cussler, Clive. *Serpent: A Novel from the Numa Files*
UNDERWATER CITIES
Cambias, James L. *A Darkling Sea*
McKinney, Chris. *Midnight, Water City*
Solomon, Rivers. *The Deep*
UNDERWATER RESCUE OPERATIONS
Cussler, Clive. *Pacific Vortex!*
UNDERWATER WARFARE
Cussler, Clive. *Havana Storm*

Underworld. DeLillo, Don
Underworld U.S.A. trilogy [Series]. Ellroy, James
Undiscovered Country: A Novel. Enger, Lin
UNDOCUMENTED IMMIGRANTS
Adiga, Aravind. ★*Amnesty*
Allende, Isabel. *In the Midst of Winter: A Novel*
Atkins, Ace. *The Revelators*
Boyle, T. Coraghessan. ★*The Tortilla Curtain*
Deaver, Jeffery. *The Stone Monkey: A Lincoln Rhyme Novel*
Dennis-Benn, Nicole. ★*Patsy: A Novel*
Engel, Patricia. ★*Infinite Country*
Gordimer, Nadine. *The Pickup*
Grippando, James. *The Girl in the Glass Box*
Ko, Lisa. *The Leavers*
Luiselli, Valeria. ★*Lost Children Archive: A Novel*
Marcom, Micheline Aharonian. *The New American*
Persaud, Ingrid. *Love After Love: A Novel*
Phillips, Caryl. *A Distant Shore*
Rivero, Melissa. *The Affairs of the Falcons*
Sahota, Sunjeev. *The Year of the Runaways*
Sekaran, Shanthi. ★*Lucky Boy*
Skyhorse, Brando. *Madonnas of Echo Park: A Novel*
Tenorio, Lysley A. *The Son of Good Fortune: A Novel*
Urrea, Luis Alberto. *Into the Beautiful North: A Novel*
Wiggs, Susan. ★*The Oysterville Sewing Circle*
UNDOCUMENTED WORKERS
Boyle, T. Coraghessan. ★*The Tortilla Curtain*
Phillips, Caryl. *A Distant Shore*
★**Undone**: a Novel. Slaughter, Karin
UNEMPLOYED PERSONS
Ballard, J. G. *Kingdom Come*
Russo, Richard. ★*Nobody's Fool*
Stockett, Kathryn. ★*The Help*
UNEMPLOYED PERSONS — FAMILY RELATIONSHIPS
Dean, Margaret Lazarus. *The Time It Takes to Fall*
UNEMPLOYED WOMEN
Dade, Olivia. *All the Feels*
Harding, Lisa. *Bright Burning Things*
Hibbert, Talia. ★*Act Your Age, Eve Brown*
The **Unexpected** Duchess. Bowman, Valerie
Unfinished Desires. Godwin, Gail
An **Unfortunate** Woman: A Journey. Brautigan, Richard
Unger, Lisa
    ★*The Stranger Inside*
    Under My Skin
Unhallowed Ground. Starr, Melvin R.
UNHAPPINESS
Garcia, Cristina. *The Lady Matador's Hotel: A Novel*
UNHAPPINESS IN MEN
Berger, Thomas. *Being Invisible: A Novel*
Garcia Marquez, Gabriel. *The General in His Labyrinth*
Gide, Andre. ★*The Immoralist*
UNHAPPINESS IN WOMEN
Enright, Anne. ★*The Gathering*
Ferrante, Elena. *The Story of a New Name*
Gowar, Imogen Hermes. *The Mermaid and Mrs. Hancock*
The **Unicorn** Sonata. Beagle, Peter S.

UNICORNS
Beagle, Peter S. *In Calabria*
Beagle, Peter S. ★*The Last Unicorn*
Beagle, Peter S. *The Unicorn Sonata*
Uniform Justice. Leon, Donna
Union Atlantic. Haslett, Adam

UNION SOLDIERS
Cole, Alyssa. ★*A Hope Divided*
Crane, Stephen. ★*The Red Badge of Courage: An Episode of the American Civil War*

UNITED STATES
Acker, Jennifer. ★*The Limits of the World*
Adjei-Brenyah, Nana Kwame. *Friday Black: Stories*
Akhtar, Ayad. ★*Homeland Elegies: A Novel*
Alam, Rumaan. *That Kind of Mother: A Novel*
Anders, Charlie Jane. *Rock Manning Goes for Broke*
Angelo, Megan. *Followers*
Artson, Barbara. *Odessa, Odessa*
Baker, Dorothy. ★*Young Man with a Horn*
Balasubramanyam, Rajeev. *Professor Chandra Follows His Bliss: A Novel*
Baldwin, James. ★*Going to Meet the Man*
Banks, Russell. *Cloudsplitter: A Novel*
Barry, Sebastian. *Days Without End: A Novel*
Barry, Sebastian. ★*A Thousand Moons: A Novel*
Barth, John. ★*Giles Goat-Boy ;: Or, the Revised New Syllabus*
Bausch, Richard. *The Stories of Richard Bausch*
Benjamin, Melanie. ★*The Aviator's Wife: A Novel*
Beukes, Lauren. *Afterland*
Bird, Sarah. *Daughter of a Daughter of a Queen*
Bohjalian, Chris. ★*The Red Lotus*
Boyne, John. *The Heart's Invisible Furies*
Brown, Dale. *Eagle Station: A Novel*
Bulawayo, NoViolet. *We Need New Names: A Novel*
Burdick, Serena. *Find Me in Havana*
Butler, Robert Olen. *Late City*
Calvi, Mary. *Dear George, Dear Mary: A Novel of George Washington's First Love*
Cameron, Marc. ★*Code of Honor*
Cameron, Marc. *Power and Empire*
Carver, Raymond. *What We Talk About When We Talk About Love: Stories*
Chai, May-Lee. *Useful Phrases for Immigrants: Stories*
Chiaverini, Jennifer. *Mrs. Lincoln's Dressmaker: A Novel*
Chiaverini, Jennifer. *Mrs. Lincoln's Sisters*
Clancy, Tom. *Clear and Present Danger*
Clark, Julie. *Last Flight*
Cobbs Hoffman, Elizabeth. *The Hamilton Affair*
Cobbs Hoffman, Elizabeth. *The Tubman Command: A Novel*
Coben, Harlan. *Long Lost*
Coes, Ben. *The Russian: A Thriller*
Collins, Kathleen. *Notes from a Black Woman's Diary: Selected Works of Kathleen Collins*
Connelly, Michael. ★*Fair Warning*
Coonts, Stephen. *The Armageddon File*
Coonts, Stephen. *The Art of War: A Novel*
Cooper, James Fenimore. *The Last of the Mohicans: A Narrative of 1757*

Coughlin, Jack. *In the Crosshairs: A Sniper Novel*
Coughlin, Jack. *Long Shot: A Sniper Novel*
Crafts, Hannah. *The Bondwoman's Narrative*
Crane, Stephen. ★*The Red Badge of Courage: An Episode of the American Civil War*
Cruse, Howard. *The Complete Wendel*
Cusset, Catherine. *Life of David Hockney: A Novel*
Davies, Peter Ho. *The Fortunes*
Delany, Samuel R. *Dhalgren*
DeLillo, Don. *Libra*
DeLillo, Don. *Underworld*
Diaz, Junot. ★*This Is How You Lose Her*
Dickens, Charles. *Martin Chuzzlewit*
Doctorow, E. L. ★*The Book of Daniel: A Novel*
Doctorow, E. L. ★*Ragtime*
Dos Passos, John. *1919*
Dos Passos, John. *The 42nd Parallel*
Dugoni, Robert. *The Eighth Sister: A Thriller*
Dumas, Henry. *Echo Tree: The Collected Short Fiction of Henry Dumas*
El Akkad, Omar. *American War*
Ellison, J. T. *Good Girls Lie*
Ellroy, James. *American Tabloid: A Novel*
Ellroy, James. *Blood's a Rover*
Ellroy, James. *The Cold Six Thousand: A Novel*
Evans, Danielle. ★*The Office of Historical Corrections: A Novella and Stories*
Evison, Jonathan. *All About Lulu: A Novel*
Feng, Linda Rui. *Swimming Back to Trout River*
Fine, Julia. *The Upstairs House*
Fitzgerald, F. Scott. *Novels and Stories, 1920-1922*
Fitzgerald, F. Scott. ★*The Short Stories of F. Scott Fitzgerald: A New Collection*
Fitzgerald, F. Scott. *Six Tales of the Jazz Age and Other Stories*
Ford, Kelli Jo. ★*Crooked Hallelujah*
Fowler, Therese. ★*Z: A Novel of Zelda Fitzgerald*
Frantz, Laura. *The Lacemaker*
Frazier, Charles. *Varina*
Fuentes, Carlos. *The Eagle's Throne: A Novel*
Fuentes, Carlos. ★*The Old Gringo*
Gabaldon, Diana. ★*A Breath of Snow and Ashes*
Gabaldon, Diana. *An Echo in the Bone*
Gabaldon, Diana. *Written in My Own Heart's Blood*
Gaitskill, Mary. *Don't Cry: Stories*
Gay, Roxane. ★*Ayiti*
Gibson, Claire. *Beyond the Point: A Novel*
Gilman, Susan Jane. *The Ice Cream Queen of Orchard Street: A Novel*
Gleason, Colleen. *Murder at the Capitol*
Goldberg, Lee. *Fake Truth*
Goodman, Carol. *The Sea of Lost Girls*
Greenidge, Kaitlyn. ★*Libertie: A Novel*
Gross, Andrew. *The One Man*
Gurganus, Allan. *The Practical Heart: Four Novellas*
Hannah, Kristin. *Home Front*
Harris, E. Lynn. *Basketball Jones: A Novel*
Heller, Joseph. *Good as Gold*
Hijuelos, Oscar. *Twain & Stanley Enter Paradise*
Hill, Lawrence. *Someone Knows My Name: A Novel*

Hooper, Elise. *Fast Girls: A Novel of the 1936 Women's Olympic Team*
Howard, Ravi. *Driving the King: A Novel*
Jakes, John. *Love and War*
James, Henry. *Complete Stories, 1864-1874*
Jeffers, Honoree Fanonne. ★*The Love Songs of W. E. B. Du Bois*
Jen, Gish. ★*The Resisters*
Jen, Gish. ★*Thank You, Mr. Nixon: Stories*
Jensen, Nancy. *In Our Midst*
Jimenez, Abby. ★*The Happy Ever After Playlist*
Jin, Ha. *A Map of Betrayal: A Novel*
Kantor, MacKinlay. ★*Andersonville*
Kate, Jessica. *A Girl's Guide to the Outback: A Novel*
Kelly, Martha Hall. *Lost Roses: A Novel*
Kiernan, Stephen P. *Universe of Two*
Kim, Eugenia. *The Kinship of Secrets*
Kosinski, Jerzy. ★*Being There*
Kowal, Mary Robinette. *The Relentless Moon*
Landau, Alexis. *Those Who Are Saved*
Leavitt, David. ★*Shelter in Place*
Lee, Chang-Rae. ★*On Such a Full Sea*
Lehane, Dennis. *Live by Night*
Leonard, Elmore. *Tishomingo Blues: A Novel*
Lewis, Sinclair. *Dodsworth*
Lewis, Sinclair. ★*It Can't Happen Here*
Lockridge, Ross Franklin. *Raintree County*
Luiselli, Valeria. ★*Lost Children Archive: A Novel*
MacLeod, Alison. *Tenderness*
Malerman, Josh. *Malorie: A Bird Box Novel*
Mallon, Thomas. *Finale: A Novel*
Mallon, Thomas. *Landfall: A Novel*
Marcom, Micheline Aharonian. *The New American*
Masad, Ilana. *All My Mother's Lovers: A Novel*
Matthews, Jason. ★*The Kremlin's Candidate*
Matthews, Jason. *Red Sparrow: A Novel*
McCann, Colum. ★*Transatlantic: A Novel*
McCarthy, Cormac. ★*The Road*
McDermott, Alice. *After This*
McDonald, Christina. *Behind Every Lie*
Means, David. ★*Hystopia: A Novel*
Mengestu, Dinaw. ★*All Our Names*
Michener, James A. *Space*
Mitchell, Margaret. ★*Gone with the Wind*
Mosley, Walter. ★*The Awkward Black Man: Stories*
Mott, Jason. *Hell of a Book*
Olmstead, Robert. ★*Coal Black Horse*
Onyebuchi, Tochi. ★*Riot Baby*
Osborne, Lawrence. *Only to Sleep: A Philip Marlowe Novel*
Osondu, E. C. *Voice of America: Stories*
Parini, Jay. *The Passages of H.M.: A Novel of Herman Melville*
Patterson, Molly. *Rebellion*
Patterson, Richard North. *Balance of Power*
Patterson, Richard North. *Protect and Defend*
Perry, Thomas. *The Old Man*
Pesci, David. *Amistad: A Novel*
Piercy, Marge. *Sex Wars*
Pitts, Leonard. *Freeman*
Porter, Regina. *The Travelers*

Powell, Mark. *Firebird*
Powers, Kevin. ★*The Yellow Birds: A Novel*
Poyer, David. *Overthrow: The War with China and North Korea—Fall of an Empire*
Poyer, David. *Violent Peace: The War with China - Aftermath of Armageddon*
Priest, Cherie. *Dreadnought*
Prose, Francine. ★*The Vixen*
Proulx, Annie. *Postcards*
Pynchon, Thomas. *Against the Day: A Novel*
Pynchon, Thomas. *Mason & Dixon*
Rao, Shobha. ★*Girls Burn Brighter*
Rawles, Nancy. *My Jim: A Novel*
Reed, Ishmael. *Flight to Canada*
Rollins, James. *The Devil Colony*
Rooney, Kathleen. ★*Cher Ami and Major Whittlesey*
Roth, Philip. ★*Goodbye, Columbus, and Five Short Stories*
Roth, Philip. ★*The Human Stain*
Rushdie, Salman. ★*Quichotte: A Novel*
Russell, Mary Doria. *The Women of the Copper Country: A Novel*
Sayles, John. *A Moment in the Sun*
Schmidt, Sarah. *See What I Have Done*
See, Lisa. *Shanghai Girls: A Novel*
Shaara, Jeff. *Gods and Generals: A Novel of the Civil War*
Shaara, Jeff. *Gone for Soldiers*
Shaara, Jeff. *The Last Full Measure*
Shaara, Jeff. *The Steel Wave: A Novel of World War II*
Shaara, Michael. ★*The Killer Angels: A Novel*
Sinclair, Upton. ★*The Jungle*
Sittenfeld, Curtis. *Rodham: A Novel*
Smiley, Jane. *Early Warning*
Smiley, Jane. *Golden Age*
Smiley, Jane. *Some Luck*
Solomon, Rivers. *Sorrowland*
Spufford, Francis. ★*Light Perpetual*
St. Aubyn, Edward. *Double Blind*
St. James, Simone. *The Sun Down Motel*
Steinhauer, Olen. *The Middleman*
Stephenson, Neal. ★*Cryptonomicon*
Stewart, Amy. *Kopp Sisters on the March*
Stewart, Amy. ★*Miss Kopp Just Won't Quit*
Stewart, Amy. *Miss Kopp's Midnight Confessions*
Stivers, Carole. *The Mother Code*
Stowe, Harriet Beecher. ★*Uncle Tom's Cabin*
Stridsberg, Sara. *Valerie: Or the Faculty of Dreams : Amendment to the Theory of Sexuality*
Stross, Charles. *Empire Games*
Swamy, Shruti. *A House Is a Body: Stories*
Updike, John. *In the Beauty of the Lilies*
Updike, John. *Licks of Love: Short Stories and a Sequel*
Updike, John. *Memories of the Ford Administration: A Novel*
Urrea, Luis Alberto. *Queen of America: A Novel*
Vidal, Gore. ★*Lincoln: A Novel*
Vidal, Gore. *Washington, D. C.: A Novel*
Vonnegut, Kurt. *Armageddon in Retrospect: And Other New and Unpublished Writings on War and Peace*
Vonnegut, Kurt. *Bagombo Snuff Box: Uncollected Short Fiction*
West, Jessamyn. *The Friendly Persuasion*

Wharton, Edith. *Collected Stories, 1891-1910*

Whitehead, Colson. ★*The Underground Railroad: A Novel*

Wideman, John Edgar. ★*American Histories: Stories*

Williams, Joy. *Harrow*

Woods, Chavisa. *Things to Do When You're Goth in the Country: And Other Stories*

Yates, Richard. ★*The Collected Stories of Richard Yates*

Yoon, David. *Version Zero*

UNITED STATES CIVIL WAR, 1861-1865

Cobbs Hoffman, Elizabeth. *The Tubman Command: A Novel*

Kantor, MacKinlay. ★*Andersonville*

Lockridge, Ross Franklin. *Raintree County*

Shaara, Jeff. *The Last Full Measure*

Shaara, Michael. ★*The Killer Angels: A Novel*

West, Jessamyn. *The Friendly Persuasion*

UNITED STATES DEPUTY MARSHALS

Leonard, Elmore. *The Hot Kid*

Parker, Robert B. *Appaloosa*

UNITED STATES MARSHALS

Armstrong, Kelley. *Watcher in the Woods*

Knott, Robert. *Robert B. Parker's Buckskin*

Lehane, Dennis. *Shutter Island*

Leonard, Elmore. *Charlie Martz and Other Stories: The Unpublished Stories*

Leonard, Elmore. ★*Raylan*

Sandford, John. ★*Golden Prey*

Universal Harvester. Darnielle, John

Universe after [Series]. Williams, Drew

Universe of Two. Kiernan, Stephen P.

The *Universe* Versus Alex Woods. Extence, Gavin

UNIVERSITIES AND COLLEGES

Amis, Kingsley. ★*Lucky Jim*

Baker, Jo. *The Body Lies*

Bardugo, Leigh. ★*Ninth House*

Barth, John. ★*Giles Goat-Boy ;: Or, the Revised New Syllabus*

Bolano, Roberto. ★*Distant Star*

Cho, Zen. *Sorcerer to the Crown*

Crow, Sarah McCraw. *The Wrong Kind of Woman*

Dean, Pamela. *Tam Lin*

DeLillo, Don. ★*White Noise*

Dunmore, Evie. ★*Bringing Down the Duke*

Griffiths, Elly. *A Dying Fall: A Ruth Galloway Mystery*

Hazelwood, Ali. *The Love Hypothesis*

Kurian, Vera. *Never Saw Me Coming*

Murdoch, Iris. *The Book and the Brotherhood*

Nugent, Benjamin. *Fraternity: Stories*

Prose, Francine. *Blue Angel: A Novel*

Rodriguez, Linda. *Every Broken Trust: A Mystery*

Rodriguez, Linda. *Every Hidden Fear: A Skeet Bannion Mystery*

Rodriguez, Linda. *Every Last Secret: A Mystery*

Rooney, Sally. *Normal People: A Novel*

Sandford, John. *Bloody Genius*

Sayers, Dorothy L. ★*Gaudy Night*

Shepard, Sara. ★*Reputation*

Stegner, Wallace. *Crossing to Safety*

Thomas, Elisabeth. *Catherine House*

Walker, Karen Thompson. *The Dreamers*

Williams, Denise. *How to Fail at Flirting*

UNIVERSITIES AND COLLEGES — ADMISSION

Dobmeier, Tracy. ★*Girls with Bright Futures: A Novel*

UNIVERSITIES AND COLLEGES — FACULTY

Russo, Richard. *Straight Man*

An *Unkindness* of Ghosts. Solomon, Rivers

The *Unknown* Terrorist. Flanagan, Richard

Unless. Shields, Carol

Unlikely duchesses [Series]. Drake, Olivia

The *Unlikely* Escape of Uriah Heep. Parry, H. G.

Unmarriageable: a Novel. Kamal, Soniah

UNMARRIED COUPLES

Shriver, Lionel. *The Post-Birthday World*

Unmasked by the Marquess. Sebastian, Cat

The *Unnamed.* Ferris, Joshua

Unnatural Habits. Greenwood, Kerry

An *Unnecessary* Woman. Alameddine, Rabih

UNPLANNED PREGNANCY

Dickey, Eric Jerome. *Before We Were Wicked*

Hardy, Thomas. ★*Tess of the D'urbervilles: A Pure Woman Faithfully Presented*

Lee, Min Jin. ★*Pachinko*

Levin, Ira. ★*Rosemary's Baby: A Novel*

Schultz, Connie. *The Daughters of Erietown*

Woodson, Jacqueline. ★*Red at the Bone*

The *Unpleasantness* at the Bellona Club. Sayers, Dorothy L.

The *Unquiet* Dead. Khan, Ausma Zehanat

The *Unquiet* Heart. Welsh, Kaite

Unquiet: a Novel. Ullmann, Linn

UNREQUITED LOVE

Berry, Wendell. *Jayber Crow: A Novel*

Bolano, Roberto. *Monsieur Pain*

Calvi, Mary. *Dear George, Dear Mary: A Novel of George Washington's First Love*

Dennis-Benn, Nicole. ★*Patsy: A Novel*

Evison, Jonathan. *All About Lulu: A Novel*

Garcia Marquez, Gabriel. ★*Love in the Time of Cholera*

Maugham, W. Somerset. ★*Of Human Bondage*

McDermott, Alice. ★*Charming Billy*

Roy, Arundhati. ★*The Ministry of Utmost Happiness: A Novel*

Smith, Dodie. ★*I Capture the Castle*

The *Unseen* World. Moore, Liz

Unsettled Ground. Fuller, Claire

★An *Unsettling* Crime for Samuel Craddock. Shames, Terry

★*Unsheltered.* Kingsolver, Barbara

The *Unspoken.* Smith, Ian

The *Unspoken* Name. Larkwood, A. K.

Unsub novels [Series]. Gardiner, Meg

Unsub: a Novel. Gardiner, Meg

An *Unsuitable* Job for a Woman. James, P. D.

Unsworth, Emma Jane

Grown Ups

★An *Untamed* State. Gay, Roxane

Until the Day I Die. Carpenter, Emily

Unto Us a Son Is Given. Leon, Donna

UNWANTED GUESTS

Clark, Wahida. *Thug Matrimony*

Unwanted: a Novel. Ohlsson, Kristina

The *Unwilling.* Hart, John

Up in the Main House & Other Stories. Zaman, Nadeem
Up Jumps the Devil. Maron, Margaret
Up the Down Staircase. Kaufman, Bel
Updike, John
    The Afterlife and Other Stories
    Brazil: A Novel
    Gertrude and Claudius
    In the Beauty of the Lilies
    Licks of Love: Short Stories and a Sequel
    Memories of the Ford Administration: A Novel
    My Father's Tears and Other Stories
    ★*Rabbit Is Rich: A Novel*
    ★*Rabbit, Run*
    Seek My Face
    The Widows of Eastwick
    ★*The Witches of Eastwick*
UPPER CLASS
    Black, Benjamin. ★*Christine Falls: A Novel*
    Corman, Avery. *Prized Possessions*
    Dunne, Dominick. *People Like Us: A Novel*
    Dunne, Dominick. *Too Much Money*
    Dunnett, Dorothy. *Niccolo Rising*
    Forster, E. M. ★*A Room with a View*
    Fredericks, Mariah. *Death of a New American: A Mystery*
    Hannah, Sophie. *The Killings at Kingfisher Hill*
    James, Henry. *The Wings of the Dove*
    McDowell, Christina. *The Cave Dwellers: A Novel*
    McLaughlin, Emma. *The Nanny Diaries: A Novel*
    Mishima, Yukio. *Spring Snow*
    Morgan Jones, Chris. *The Silent Oligarch*
    Pelevin, Viktor. *The Hall of Singing Caryatids*
    Perez-Reverte, Arturo. *What We Become*
    Pinborough, Sarah. ★*Dead to Her: A Novel*
    Raybourn, Deanna. *A Dangerous Collaboration*
    Raybourn, Deanna. *A Perilous Undertaking: A Veronica Speedwell Mystery*
    Raybourn, Deanna. *A Treacherous Curse: A Veronica Speedwell Mystery*
    Rosen, Renee. *The Social Graces*
    Sackville-West, V. *The Edwardians*
    Sanders, Lawrence. ★*The First Deadly Sin*
    Schellman, Katharine. *Silence in the Library*
    Seth, Vikram. ★*A Suitable Boy: A Novel*
    Shupe, Joanna. *The Prince of Broadway*
    Soyinka, Wole. *Chronicles from the Land of the Happiest People on Earth*
    Spencer, Sally. *The Shivering Turn*
    Straub, Peter. ★*Mystery*
    Towles, Amor. *Rules of Civility: A Novel*
    Vatner, Jonathan. *Carnegie Hill: A Novel*
    Waugh, Evelyn. *Decline and Fall*
    Williams, Beatriz. *The Summer Wives*
    Wodehouse, P. G. ★*The Inimitable Jeeves*
    Woods, Stuart. *A Delicate Touch*
    Yang, Susie. *White Ivy: A Novel*
UPPER EAST SIDE, NEW YORK CITY
    Fairstein, Linda A. *Entombed*
    Gilbert, David. *& Sons: A Novel*

    Layne, Lauren. *Passion on Park Avenue*
    Moshfegh, Ottessa. *My Year of Rest and Relaxation*
    Vatner, Jonathan. *Carnegie Hill: A Novel*
UPPER WEST SIDE, NEW YORK CITY
    Helprin, Mark. ★*Winter's Tale*
    Morton, Brian. *Florence Gordon*
★*Uprooted*. Novik, Naomi
*The **Upstairs** House*. Fine, Julia
Upstate. Wood, James
Uptown girls [Series]. Shupe, Joanna
UPWARD MOBILITY
    Thackeray, William Makepeace. ★*Vanity Fair: A Novel Without a Hero*
    Towles, Amor. *Rules of Civility: A Novel*
URBAN EROTICA
    Swinson, Kiki. *Lifestyles of the Rich and Shameless*
URBAN FANTASY
    Aaronovitch, Ben. *Broken Homes*
    Aaronovitch, Ben. *Midnight Riot*
    Aaronovitch, Ben. *Moon Over Soho*
    Aaronovitch, Ben. *Whispers Under Ground*
    Bardugo, Leigh. ★*Ninth House*
    Beukes, Lauren. *Zoo City*
    Bledsoe, Alex. *Gather Her Round: A Novel of the Tufa*
    Bledsoe, Alex. *The Hum and the Shiver*
    Bledsoe, Alex. *Long Black Curl*
    Bledsoe, Alex. *Wisp of a Thing*
    Camp, Bryan. *The City of Lost Fortunes*
    Camp, Bryan. *Gather the Fortunes*
    Dimaline, Cherie. *Empire of Wild*
    Flyte, Magnus. *City of Dark Magic: A Novel*
    Flyte, Magnus. *City of Lost Dreams: A Novel*
    Gailey, Sarah. *Magic for Liars*
    Gilman, Laura Anne. *Hard Magic*
    Hamill, Pete. *Forever*
    Huchu, Tendai. *The Library of the Dead*
    Jemisin, N. K. ★*The City We Became*
    McGuire, Seanan. *Chimes at Midnight: An October Daye Novel*
    Shaw, Vivian. ★*Dreadful Company*
    Shaw, Vivian. ★*Strange Practice*
    Snipes, Wesley. *Talon of God*
    Stout, Dan. ★*Titanshade*
    Turnbull, Cadwell. *No Gods, No Monsters*
    Wilson, G. Willow. *Alif the Unseen*
URBAN FICTION
    Ashley & JaQuavis. *Murderville*
    Ca$h. *Thugs Cry: A Novel*
    Ca$h. ★*Trust No Bitch*
    Capri, NeNe. *The Pussy Trap*
    Capri, NeNe. *The Pussy Trap; Part 3*
    Chariandy, David John. *Brother: A Novel*
    Clark, Wahida. *Blood, Sweat and Payback*
    Clark, Wahida. *Honor Thy Thug*
    Clark, Wahida. *Justify My Thug: A Novel*
    Clark, Wahida. *Payback Ain't Enough*
    Clark, Wahida. ★*Payback Is a Mutha*
    Clark, Wahida. *Payback with Ya Life*
    Clark, Wahida. *Thug Lovin'*

Clark, Wahida. *Thug Matrimony*
Clark, Wahida. *Thugs*
Clark, Wahida. ★*Thugs and the Women Who Love Them*
De Leon, Aya. *Side Chick Nation*
Gray, Erick S. *Love & a Gangsta: A Novel*
Holmes, Shannon. ★*B-More Careful: A Novel*
Johnson, Keith Lee. ★*Little Black Girl Lost*
Joseph, Fabiola. *Niya: Rainbow Dreams*
K'wan. *Animal*
K'wan. *Animal II: The Omen*
K'wan. *The Diamond Empire*
K'wan. ★*Diamonds and Pearl*
K'wan. *The Fix*
K'wan. *Gangsta*
K'wan. *Gutter*
K'wan. *Hoodlum*
K'wan. *Lawless*
K'wan. *Revelations*
K'wan. *Street Dreams*
Petry, Ann. ★*The Street*
Quinonez, Ernesto. *Bodega Dreams*
Santiago, Danny. *Famous All Over Town*
Sister Souljah. ★*The Coldest Winter Ever: A Novel*
Sister Souljah. ★*A Deeper Love Inside: The Porsche Santiaga Story*
Sister Souljah. *Midnight and the Meaning of Love*
Speight, Shameek A. ★*A Child of a Crack Head*
Speight, Shameek A. *The Pleasure of Pain*
Styles, Toy. *A Hustler's Son: A Novel*
Styles, Toy. *Raunchy*
Styles, Toy. *Raunchy 2: Mad's Love*
Styles, Toy. *Redbone*
Styles, Toy. ★*War*
Styles, Toy. *War 2: All Hell Breaks Loose*
Swinson, Kiki. *I'm New York's Finest*
Swinson, Kiki. *The Safe House*
Swinson, Kiki. *Wifey*
Swinson, Kiki. *Wifey's Next Sticky Situation*
T. I. *Power & Beauty: A Love Story of Life on the Streets*
T. I. *Trouble & Triumph: A Novel of Power & Beauty*
Tyree, Omar. ★*Flyy Girl*
Tyree, Omar. *For the Love of Money: A Novel*
Tyree, Omar. *Leslie: A Novel*

URBAN LEGENDS
Childs, Laura. *Haunted Hibiscus*
Staples, Dennis E. *This Town Sleeps*

URBAN PLANNERS
Lee, Jonathan. *The Great Mistake*

URBAN PLANNING
Lee, Jonathan. *The Great Mistake*

URBAN PROBLEMS
Anderson, Kent. *Green Sun: A Novel*

URBAN RENEWAL
Barbash, Tom. *The Last Good Chance*

Uris, Leon
Armageddon: A Novel of Berlin
★*Exodus*
Redemption: A Novel
★*Trinity*

Urquhart, Jane
The Night Stages: A Novel
Urquhart, Rachel
The Visionist
Urrea, Luis Alberto
★*The House of Broken Angels*
The Hummingbird's Daughter: A Novel
Into the Beautiful North: A Novel
Queen of America: A Novel
The Water Museum: Stories
Ursula Blanchard mysteries [Series]. Buckley, Fiona
URUGUAY
Benedetti, Mario. *Springtime in a Broken Mirror*
Cameron, Peter. *The City of Your Final Destination*
De Robertis, Carolina. *Cantoras*
Us Against You: A Novel. Backman, Fredrik
Us: a Novel. Nicholls, David
Use of Weapons. Banks, Iain
USED CAR SELLING
Lansdale, Joe R. *More Better Deals*
Useful Phrases for Immigrants: Stories. Chai, May-Lee
UTAH
Ebershoff, David. *The 19th Wife: A Novel*
Grey, Zane. ★*Riders of the Purple Sage*
Harrison, Mette Ivie. *The Bishop's Wife*
Harrison, Mette Ivie. *The Prodigal Daughter*
Howrey, Meg. *The Wanderers*
Lauren, Christina. *In a Holidaze*
Mailer, Norman. ★*The Executioner's Song*
Miller, Walter M. ★*A Canticle for Leibowitz*
Petersen, Todd Robert. *Picnic in the Ruins*
★*Utopia* Avenue: A Novel. Mitchell, David
UTOPIANS
Theroux, Paul. ★*The Mosquito Coast: A Novel*
UTOPIAS
Gilman, Charlotte Perkins. *Herland*
Hilton, James. ★*Lost Horizon: A Novel*
Kingsolver, Barbara. ★*Unsheltered*
Le Guin, Ursula K. ★*The Dispossessed: An Ambiguous Utopia*
Palmer, Ada. *Too Like the Lightning*
Porter, Chana. *The Seep: A Novel*
Sontag, Susan. ★*In America*
Vargas Llosa, Mario. *The War of the End of the World*
Whiteley, Aliya. *From the Neck up and Other Stories*
UZBEKISTAN
Solzhenitsyn, Aleksandr Isaevich. ★*Cancer Ward*

V

V. I. Warshawski mysteries [Series]. Paretsky, Sara
★*V: a Novel*. Pynchon, Thomas
The Vacation. Logan, T. M.
VACATION HOMES
Alam, Rumaan. ★*Leave the World Behind: A Novel*
Cohen, Tish. *The Summer We Lost Her: A Novel*
Downes, Anna. *The Safe Place: A Novel*

Hilderbrand, Elin. *The Perfect Couple*
Lee, Andrea. *Red Island House*
Monroe, Mary Alice. *Beach House Reunion*
Pineiro, Caridad. *One Summer Night*
Poeppel, Amy. *Musical Chairs: A Novel*
Poissant, David James. *Lake Life*
The **Vacationers**. Straub, Emma
VACATIONS
Alam, Rumaan. ★*Leave the World Behind: A Novel*
Cusk, Rachel. *Second Place*
Dexter, Colin. *The Way Through the Woods*
Ferrante, Elena. *The Lost Daughter*
Force, Marie. *Deceived by Desire*
Friedland, Elyssa. *Last Summer at the Golden Hotel*
Henry, Emily. *People We Meet on Vacation*
Kane, Jessica Francis. *Rules for Visiting*
Kemelman, Harry. *One Fine Day the Rabbi Bought a Cross*
Lalli, Sonya. *A Holly Jolly Diwali*
Le Carre, John. ★*Our Kind of Traitor: A Novel*
Logan, T. M. *The Vacation*
Longworth, M. L. *Murder on the Ile Sordou: A Verlaque and Bonnet Provencal Mystery*
Moss, Sarah. *Summerwater*
Picoult, Jodi. ★*Wish You Were Here: A Novel*
Potzsch, Oliver. *The Werewolf of Bamberg*
Rouda, Kaira Sturdivant. *Best Day Ever: A Novel*
Russo, Richard. ★*Chances Are...: A Novel*
Snow, Jennifer. *An Alaskan Christmas*
Sosa, Mia. ★*Acting on Impulse*
Tursten, Helene. *Hunting Game*
Vachss, Andrew H.
Two Trains Running
VACUUM
Egan, Greg. *Schild's Ladder*
★**Vacuum** in the Dark: A Novel*. Beagin, Jen
Vagabonds: a Novel*. Hao, Jingfang
The **Vagrants**: a Novel*. Li, Yiyun
Valdes, Alisa
Dirty Girls on Top
Valente, Catherynne M.
Radiance
Space Opera
★**Valentine**. Wetmore, Elizabeth
Valentine, Genevieve
Mechanique: A Tale of the Circus Tresaulti
Valentino mysteries [Series]. Estleman, Loren D.
Valerie Hart novels [Series]. Black, Saul
Valerie: or the Faculty of Dreams : Amendment to the Theory of Sexuality*. Stridsberg, Sara
VALETS
Wodehouse, P. G. *My Man Jeeves*
VALKYRIES (NORSE MYTHOLOGY)
Bear, Elizabeth. *All the Windwracked Stars*
VALLEJO, CESAR
Bolano, Roberto. *Monsieur Pain*
The **Valley** of Amazement*. Tan, Amy
Valley of Bones: A Novel*. Gruber, Michael

VALUES
McKenzie, Elizabeth. *The Portable Veblen*
Santiago, Danny. *Famous All Over Town*
Smith, B. J. *The Return of Kid Cooper: A Novel*
The **Vampire** Armand*. Rice, Anne
Vampire chronicles [Series]. Rice, Anne
★The **Vampire** Lestat*. Rice, Anne
VAMPIRE SLAYERS
Buehlman, Christopher. *The Suicide Motor Club*
Matheson, Richard. ★*I Am Legend*
VAMPIRES
Buehlman, Christopher. *The Suicide Motor Club*
Cho, Zen. *Spirits Abroad and Other Stories*
Cronin, Justin. *The City of Mirrors*
Cronin, Justin. *The Passage*
Cronin, Justin. *The Twelve*
Duncan, Glen. *By Blood We Live*
Feehan, Christine. *Dark Illusion*
Gallagher, Stephen. *The Kingdom of Bones: A Novel*
Harkness, Deborah E. *The Book of Life*
Harkness, Deborah E. *A Discovery of Witches: A Novel*
Harkness, Deborah E. *Shadow of Night*
Harkness, Deborah E. *Time's Convert*
Harkness, Deborah E. *The World of All Souls: The Complete Guide to a Discovery of Witches, Shadow of Night, and the Book*
Hendrix, Grady. *The Southern Book Club's Guide to Slaying Vampires*
King, Stephen. *Salem's Lot*
Lansdale, Joe R. *Devil Red*
Matheson, Richard. ★*I Am Legend*
Rhodes, Jewell Parker. *Yellow Moon: A Novel*
Rice, Anne. *Blackwood Farm*
Rice, Anne. *Blood and Gold: Or, the Story of Marius*
Rice, Anne. *Blood Canticle*
Rice, Anne. *Blood Communion: A Tale of Prince Lestat*
Rice, Anne. ★*Interview with the Vampire*
Rice, Anne. *Memnoch the Devil*
Rice, Anne. *Merrick: A Novel*
Rice, Anne. *Prince Lestat: The Vampire Chronicles*
Rice, Anne. ★*The Queen of the Damned*
Rice, Anne. *The Tale of the Body Thief*
Rice, Anne. *The Vampire Armand*
Rice, Anne. ★*The Vampire Lestat*
Stoker, Bram. ★*Dracula*
Stoker, Bram. *The New Annotated Dracula*
Stoker, Dacre. *Dracul*
Vampires in the Lemon Grove: Stories*. Russell, Karen
The **Van** Apfel Girls Are Gone*. McLean, Felicity
Van Booy, Simon
The Illusion of Separateness
Van der Vliet Oloomi, Azareen
Call Me Zebra
Van Dyken, Rachel
Risky Play
van Heemstra, Marjolijn
In Search of a Name
Van Meter, Crissy
Creatures: A Novel

Van Vogt, A. E.
  ★*Slan*
VANCOUVER ISLAND
  Ozeki, Ruth L. ★*A Tale for the Time Being*
VANCOUVER, BRITISH COLUMBIA
  Bala, Sharon. *The Boat People: A Novel*
  Mandel, Emily St. John. ★*The Glass Hotel: A Novel*
VANDALISM
  Brett, Simon. *Guilt at the Garage*
  Greene, Graham. *Collected Stories: Including May We Borrow Your Husband? a Sense of Reality, Twenty-One Stories*
Vandelly, T. Marie
  Theme Music
VanderMeer, Jeff
  Acceptance: A Novel
  ★*Annihilation: A Novel*
  Authority: A Novel
  ★*Borne: A Novel*
  Dead Astronauts: A Novel
  Finch
  The Third Bear
VANE, HARRIET (FICTITIOUS CHARACTER)
  Sayers, Dorothy L. ★*Busman's Honeymoon*
  Sayers, Dorothy L. *Have His Carcase*
Vanessa and Her Sister. Parmar, Priya
Vanessa Yu's Magical Paris Tea Shop. Lim, Roselle
Vanished. Finder, Joseph
★*The Vanished Birds*. Jimenez, Simon
The Vanished Bride. Ellis, Bella
The Vanished Queen. Campbell, Lisbeth
VANISHED SHIPS
  Grant, Mira. *Into the Drowning Deep*
Vanishing Act. Perry, Thomas
The Vanishing Act of Esme Lennox. O'Farrell, Maggie
Vanishing Acts: A Novel. Picoult, Jodi
Vanishing Edge. Kells, Claire
★*The Vanishing Half*. Bennett, Brit
The Vanishing Man. Finch, Charles
The Vanishing of Katharina Linden. Grant, Helen
The Vanishing Point. Brundage, Elizabeth
The Vanishing Sky. Binder, L. Annette
★*Vanity Fair: A Novel Without a Hero*. Thackeray, William Makepeace
Vann, David
  Aquarium
Vargas Llosa, Mario
  Aunt Julia and the Scriptwriter
  The Bad Girl
  ★*The Discreet Hero*
  The Dream of the Celt
  The Feast of the Goat
  Green House
  The Time of the Hero
  The War of the End of the World
  ★*The Way to Paradise*
Varina. Frazier, Charles
Varley, John
  Dark Lightning
  Demon

★*Titan*
Vasquez, Juan Gabriel
  ★*The Shape of the Ruins*
VATICAN
  Hewson, David. *A Season for the Dead*
VATICAN CITY
  Berry, Steve. ★*The Malta Exchange: A Novel*
Vatner, Jonathan
  Carnegie Hill: A Novel
VAUDEVILLE
  Weiss, Elizabeth. *The Sisters Sweet*
VAUDEVILLE PERFORMERS
  Swift, Graham. ★*Here We Are*
  Weiss, Elizabeth. *The Sisters Sweet*
Vaughan, Sarah
  ★*Anatomy of a Scandal: A Novel*
Vaughn, Carrie
  Bannerless
Vayden, Kristin
  Fortune Favors the Duke
Veiled in Smoke. Green, Jocelyn
★*The Veiled Throne*. Liu, Ken
Veiled worlds trilogy [Series]. Anderton, Jo
Veletzos, Roxanne
  The Girl They Left Behind
Velocity. Koontz, Dean R.
Velocity Weapon. O'Keefe, Megan E.
★*Velvet Was the Night*. Moreno-Garcia, Silvia
VENEZUELA
  Cussler, Clive. *Blue Gold: A Novel from the Numa Files*
  Sainz Borgo, Karina. ★*It Would Be Night in Caracas*
Vengeful. Schwab, Victoria
VENICE, ITALY
  Alexander, Victoria. *The Lady Travelers Guide to Larceny with a Dashing Stranger*
  Brandreth, Benet. *The Spy of Venice*
  DeRoux, Margaux. *The Lost Diary of Venice*
  Dunant, Sarah. *In the Company of the Courtesan: A Novel*
  Dyer, Geoff. *Jeff in Venice, Death in Varanasi*
  Hewson, David. *The Garden of Angels*
  James, Henry. *The Wings of the Dove*
  Leon, Donna. *Beastly Things: A Commissario Guido Brunetti Mystery*
  Leon, Donna. *Drawing Conclusions: A Commissario Guido Brunetti Mystery*
  Leon, Donna. *Falling in Love: A Commissario Guido Brunetti Mystery*
  Leon, Donna. *The Golden Egg*
  Leon, Donna. *A Question of Belief: A Commissario Guido Brunetti Mystery*
  Leon, Donna. *Trace Elements*
  Leon, Donna. ★*Transient Desires*
  Leon, Donna. *Uniform Justice*
  Leon, Donna. *Unto Us a Son Is Given*
  Mangan, Christine. *Palace of the Drowned*
  Mann, Thomas. *Death in Venice and Seven Other Stories*
  Phillips, Christi. *The Rossetti Letter: A Novel*
  Sebald, Winfried Georg. *Vertigo*

Shupe, Joanna. *The Courtesan Duchess*
Winterson, Jeanette. *The Passion*
The **Ventriloquists**. Ramzipoor, E. R.
VENTURE CAPITALISTS
    Barnes, Julian. ★*England, England*
    Deaver, Jeffery. *The October List*
    St. Aubyn, Edward. *Double Blind*
VENUS (PLANET)
    Kunsken, Derek. *The House of Styx*
    Valente, Catherynne M. *Radiance*
Venus ascendant [Series]. Kunsken, Derek
Vera Stanhope novels [Series]. Cleeves, Ann
Verble, Margaret
    ★*Cherokee America*
    ★*When Two Feathers Fell from the Sky*
The **Verdict**. Stone, Nick
Verdon, John
    On Harrow Hill
The **Verdun** *Affair: A Novel*. Dybek, Nick
VERDUN, FRANCE
    Dybek, Nick. *The Verdun Affair: A Novel*
Verghese, A.
    Cutting for Stone: A Novel
Verity Kent novels [Series]. Huber, Anna Lee
Verlaque and Bonnet mysteries [Series]. Longworth, M. L.
VERMEER, JOHANNES, 1632-1675
    Chevalier, Tracy. ★*Girl with a Pearl Earring*
    Faulkner, William. ★*Absalom, Absalom!*
    Leonard, Elmore. ★*Killshot*
    Vreeland, Susan. *Girl in Hyacinth Blue*
VERMONT
    Auster, Paul. ★*The Book of Illusions: A Novel*
    Bohjalian, Chris. *The Buffalo Soldier: A Novel*
    Bohjalian, Chris. *The Double Bind: A Novel*
    Bohjalian, Chris. *Secrets of Eden: A Novel*
    Bohjalian, Chris. *The Sleepwalker*
    Freeman, Castle. *All That I Have: A Novel*
    Mayor, Archer. ★*Marked Man*
    Mayor, Archer. *Red Herring: A Joe Gunther Novel*
    Mayor, Archer. *Tag Man: A Joe Gunther Novel*
    McMahon, Jennifer. *The Invited: A Novel*
    Perry, Thomas. *The Old Man*
    Shreve, Anita. *Testimony: A Novel*
    St. James, Simone. *The Broken Girls*
    Stegner, Wallace. *Crossing to Safety*
    Tartt, Donna. ★*The Secret History*
    Updike, John. *Seek My Face*
    Waite, Jen. *Survival Instincts*
Verne, Jules
    ★*Around the World in Eighty Days*
    ★*Journey to the Centre of the Earth*
    The Mysterious Island
Vernon, P. J.
    Bath Haus: A Thriller
Veronica. Gaitskill, Mary
Veronica Speedwell novels [Series]. Raybourn, Deanna
Verses *for the Dead*. Preston, Douglas J.
Version *Control*. Palmer, Dexter Clarence

Version *Zero*. Yoon, David
Vertigo. Sebald, Winfried Georg
The **Very** *Best of Caitlin R. Kiernan*. Kiernan, Caitlin R.
Very *Nice*. Dermansky, Marcy
Vestal, Shawn
    Daredevils
Vestments. Reimringer, John
VESUVIUS
    Sontag, Susan. *The Volcano Lover: A Romance*
VETERANS
    Ackerman, Elliot. ★*Waiting for Eden: A Novel*
    Ames, Jonathan. *A Man Named Doll*
    Atkins, Ace. *The Fallen*
    Child, Lee. ★*Blue Moon: A Jack Reacher Novel*
    Colgan, Jenny. *500 Miles from You*
    DeMille, Nelson. ★*The Cuban Affair: A Novel*
    DeMille, Nelson. ★*The Deserter: A Novel*
    Dodd, Christina. *Because I'm Watching*
    Dundas, Chad. *The Blaze*
    Dunmore, Helen. *The Lie*
    Evison, Jonathan. *Legends of the North Cascades: A Novel*
    Finder, Joseph. ★*House on Fire: A Novel*
    Galen, Shana. *Third Son's a Charm*
    Gunn, James E. *Transcendental*
    Hanson, Hart. *The Driver*
    Harkaway, Nick. *Tigerman*
    Harrington, Anna. *An Extraordinary Lord*
    Harrington, Anna. *An Inconvenient Duke*
    Harris, Nathan. *The Sweetness of Water*
    Hart, John. *The Unwilling*
    Helprin, Mark. *In Sunlight and in Shadow*
    Hibbert, Talia. *A Girl Like Her*
    Krivak, Andrew. *The Signal Flame: A Novel*
    March, Nev. *Murder in Old Bombay*
    McKinty, Adrian. *In the Morning I'll Be Gone: A Detective Sean Duffy Novel*
    Miles, Jonathan. *Anatomy of a Miracle*
    O'Connor, Flannery. ★*Wise Blood*
    O'Dell, Claire. *A Study in Honor: A Novel*
    Offutt, Chris. *Country Dark*
    Offutt, Chris. ★*The Killing Hills*
    Perry, Thomas. *The Old Man*
    Petrie, Nicholas. *Burning Bright*
    Polk, C. L. *Witchmark*
    Pollock, Donald Ray. *The Devil All the Time*
    Remarque, Erich Maria. *The Road Back*
    Ruff, Matt. *Lovecraft Country: A Novel*
    Sayers, Dorothy L. ★*Whose Body?: A Lord Peter Wimsey Novel*
    Sorenson, Jill. *Aftershock*
    Talton, Jon. *City of Dark Corners*
    Vonnegut, Kurt. *Hocus Pocus*
    Wade, Becky. ★*True to You*
    Walker, Nico. ★*Cherry: A Novel*
VETERANS WITH DISABILITIES
    Trumbo, Dalton. ★*Johnny Got His Gun*
VETERINARIANS
    Deb, Siddhartha. *The Point of Return: A Novel*
    Ramsay, Hope. *Summer on Moonlight Bay*

The *Vexations*. Horrocks, Caitlin
VICARS
    Malliet, G. M. *A Demon Summer: A Max Tudor Mystery*
    Malliet, G. M. *Pagan Spring: A Mystery*
    Runcie, James. *Sidney Chambers and the Shadow of Death*
    Tudor, C. J. *The Burning Girls: A Novel*
VICE-PRESIDENTS
    Costello, Mark. *Big If*
VICES
    Baxter, Charles. *There's Something I Want You to Do: Stories*
VICHY (FRANCE)
    Orringer, Julie. ★*The Flight Portfolio: A Novel*
Vicious. Schwab, Victoria
Vicious Circle. Box, C. J.
★*Victim 2117*. Adler-Olsen, Jussi
The *Victim: a Novel*. Manning, Max
VICTIMS
    Gregory, Daryl. *We Are All Completely Fine*
VICTIMS OF TERRORISM
    DeLillo, Don. *Falling Man: A Novel*
    Patchett, Ann. ★*Bel Canto: A Novel*
    Phoenix, Michele. *The Space Between Words*
VICTIMS OF VIOLENT CRIMES
    Bell, Shelly. *At His Mercy*
    Daly, Paula. *Open Your Eyes*
    Mason, Jamie. *The Hidden Things*
    Penny, Louise. *Still Life*
    Price, Richard. *Samaritan*
    Robinson, Peter. *The First Cut*
    Sager, Riley. *Final Girls: A Novel*
VICTORIA, BRITISH COLUMBIA
    Haldane, Sean. *The Devil's Making*
VICTORIAN ERA (1837-1901)
    Alexander, Victoria. *The Lady Travelers Guide to Larceny with a Dashing Stranger*
    Alexander, Victoria. *The Lady Travelers Guide to Scoundrels and Other Gentlemen*
    Ashley, Jennifer. *Death at the Crystal Palace*
    Ashley, Jennifer. *Lady Isabella's Scandalous Marriage*
    Ashley, Jennifer. *The Madness of Lord Ian Mackenzie*
    Austin, Finola. *Bronte's Mistress*
    Birch, Carol. *Jamrach's Menagerie*
    Blake, Audrey. *The Girl in His Shadow: A Novel*
    Bronte, Anne. *The Tenant of Wildfell Hall*
    Byrne, Kerrigan. *The Duke with the Dragon Tattoo*
    Byrne, Kerrigan. *How to Love a Duke in Ten Days*
    Byrne, Kerrigan. *The Hunter*
    Callihan, Kristen. ★*Firelight*
    Carlyle, Christy. *Duke Gone Rogue*
    Clare, Alys. *The Woman Who Spoke to Spirits*
    Collins, Manda. ★*A Lady's Guide to Mischief and Mayhem*
    Collins, Wilkie. ★*The Moonstone*
    Collins, Wilkie. ★*The Woman in White*
    Deluca, Marjorie. *The Savage Instinct*
    Dunmore, Evie. ★*Bringing Down the Duke*
    Ellis, Bella. *The Vanished Bride*
    Faber, Michel. *The Crimson Petal and the White*

Faye, Lyndsay. *The Whole Art of Detection: Lost Mysteries of Sherlock Holmes*
Finch, Charles. *A Beautiful Blue Death*
Finch, Charles. *The September Society*
Finlay, Mick. *The Murder Pit*
Fowles, John. ★*The French Lieutenant's Woman*
Frampton, Megan. *Never a Bride*
Frampton, Megan. *Put up Your Duke*
Freeman, Dianne. *A Fiancee's Guide to First Wives and Murder*
Freeman, Dianne. *A Lady's Guide to Etiquette and Murder*
Gaiman, Neil. ★*Stardust*
Gallagher, Stephen. *The Kingdom of Bones: A Novel*
Galsworthy, John. ★*The Forsyte Saga*
Goss, Theodora. *The Sinister Mystery of the Mesmerizing Girl*
Goss, Theodora. *The Strange Case of the Alchemist's Daughter*
Guhrke, Laura Lee. *Governess Gone Rogue*
Guhrke, Laura Lee. *The Trouble with True Love*
Guhrke, Laura Lee. *The Truth About Love and Dukes*
Hardy, Thomas. ★*Far from the Madding Crowd*
Heath, Lorraine. *Falling into Bed with a Duke*
Holton, India. *The Wisteria Society of Lady Scoundrels*
Jordan, Sophie. *The Duke Goes Down*
Kidd, Jess. ★*Things in Jars*
Kleypas, Lisa. *Cold-Hearted Rake*
Kleypas, Lisa. ★*Devil in Disguise*
Laurens, Stephanie. *The Pursuits of Lord Kit Cavanaugh*
Macallister, Greer. ★*The Arctic Fury*
MacLean, Sarah. ★*Bombshell*
Macneal, Elizabeth. *The Doll Factory*
Mason, Timothy. *The Darwin Affair*
Matthews, Mimi. ★*The Siren of Sussex*
McGuire, Ian. *The Abstainer: A Novel*
Milan, Courtney. *The Duchess War*
Morrell, David. *Ruler of the Night*
O'Donnell, Paraic. *The House on Vesper Sands: A Novel*
Parry, Ambrose. *The Way of All Flesh*
Perry, Anne. *A Dangerous Mourning*
Perry, Anne. *Dark Tide Rising: A William Monk Novel*
Perry, Anne. *The Face of a Stranger*
Perry, Sarah. *The Essex Serpent*
Pulley, Natasha. *The Bedlam Stacks*
Pulley, Natasha. *The Lost Future of Pepperharrow*
Pulley, Natasha. *The Watchmaker of Filigree Street*
Quick, Amanda. *'til Death Do Us Part*
Quick, Amanda. *Garden of Lies*
Raybourn, Deanna. *A Curious Beginning: A Veronica Speedwell Mystery*
Raybourn, Deanna. *A Dangerous Collaboration*
Raybourn, Deanna. ★*A Murderous Relation*
Raybourn, Deanna. *A Perilous Undertaking: A Veronica Speedwell Mystery*
Raybourn, Deanna. *A Treacherous Curse: A Veronica Speedwell Mystery*
Rowland, Laura Joh. *The Hangman's Secret*
Rowland, Laura Joh. *The Ripper's Shadow*
Saunders, Kate. *The Case of the Wandering Scholar*
Saunders, Kate. *The Secrets of Wishtide*
Setterfield, Diane. ★*Once Upon a River*

St. George, Harper. *The Heiress Gets a Duke*
Sullivan, Emily. *The Rebel and the Rake*
Tesh, Emily. *Silver in the Wood*
Thomas, Will. *Dance with Death*
Thomson, E. S. *Beloved Poison*
Thomson, E. S. *The Blood*
Vyleta, Dan. *Smoke: A Novel*
Welsh, Kaite. *The Unquiet Heart*
Welsh, Kaite. *The Wages of Sin*
Wilde, Oscar. ★*The Picture of Dorian Gray*
Willig, Lauren. *The Summer Country: A Novel*

VICTORIAN HOUSES
Bohjalian, Chris. *The Night Strangers: A Novel*
Heley, Veronica. *Murder in Law*

VICTORIAN MYSTERIES
Ashley, Jennifer. *Death at the Crystal Palace*
Clare, Alys. *The Woman Who Spoke to Spirits*
Collins, Manda. ★*A Lady's Guide to Mischief and Mayhem*
Collins, Wilkie. ★*The Moonstone*
Collins, Wilkie. ★*The Woman in White*
Faye, Lyndsay. *The Whole Art of Detection: Lost Mysteries of Sherlock Holmes*
Finch, Charles. *A Beautiful Blue Death*
Finch, Charles. *The September Society*
Finch, Charles. *The Vanishing Man*
Finlay, Mick. *The Murder Pit*
Freeman, Dianne. *A Fiancee's Guide to First Wives and Murder*
Freeman, Dianne. *A Lady's Guide to Etiquette and Murder*
Mason, Timothy. *The Darwin Affair*
Morrell, David. *Ruler of the Night*
O'Donnell, Paraic. *The House on Vesper Sands: A Novel*
Parry, Ambrose. *The Way of All Flesh*
Perry, Anne. *A Dangerous Mourning*
Perry, Anne. *Dark Tide Rising: A William Monk Novel*
Perry, Anne. *The Face of a Stranger*
Quick, Amanda. *Garden of Lies*
Rowland, Laura Joh. *The Hangman's Secret*
Rowland, Laura Joh. *The Ripper's Shadow*
Saunders, Kate. *The Case of the Wandering Scholar*
Saunders, Kate. *The Secrets of Wishtide*
Thomas, Will. *Dance with Death*
Thomson, E. S. *Beloved Poison*
Thomson, E. S. *The Blood*
Victorian mysteries [Series]. Rowland, Laura Joh
Victorian rebels [Series]. Byrne, Kerrigan

VICTORIAN ROMANCES
Alexander, Victoria. *The Lady Travelers Guide to Larceny with a Dashing Stranger*
Alexander, Victoria. *The Lady Travelers Guide to Scoundrels and Other Gentlemen*
Ashley, Jennifer. *Lady Isabella's Scandalous Marriage*
Ashley, Jennifer. *The Madness of Lord Ian Mackenzie*
Byrne, Kerrigan. *The Duke with the Dragon Tattoo*
Byrne, Kerrigan. *How to Love a Duke in Ten Days*
Byrne, Kerrigan. *The Hunter*
Callihan, Kristen. ★*Firelight*
Carlyle, Christy. *Duke Gone Rogue*
Collins, Manda. ★*A Lady's Guide to Mischief and Mayhem*

Dunmore, Evie. ★*Bringing Down the Duke*
Everett, Elizabeth. ★*A Lady's Formula for Love*
Frampton, Megan. *Never a Bride*
Frampton, Megan. *Put up Your Duke*
Guhrke, Laura Lee. *Governess Gone Rogue*
Guhrke, Laura Lee. *The Trouble with True Love*
Guhrke, Laura Lee. *The Truth About Love and Dukes*
Heath, Lorraine. *Falling into Bed with a Duke*
Holton, India. *The Wisteria Society of Lady Scoundrels*
Jordan, Sophie. *The Duke Goes Down*
Kleypas, Lisa. *Cold-Hearted Rake*
Kleypas, Lisa. ★*Devil in Disguise*
Laurens, Stephanie. *The Pursuits of Lord Kit Cavanaugh*
MacLean, Sarah. ★*Bombshell*
Matthews, Mimi. ★*The Siren of Sussex*
Milan, Courtney. *The Duchess War*
Quick, Amanda. *'til Death Do Us Part*
Shupe, Joanna. *The Heiress Hunt*
St. George, Harper. *The Heiress Gets a Duke*
Sullivan, Emily. *The Rebel and the Rake*

VICTORIANA
Dickens, Charles. ★*Great Expectations*
Trollope, Anthony. ★*Barchester Towers*
Trollope, Anthony. ★*The Prime Minister*
*The **Victory** Garden*. Bowen, Rhys
***Victory**: an Island Tale*. Conrad, Joseph
***Vida**: a Novel*. Piercy, Marge
Vidal, Gore
  ★*Lincoln: A Novel*
  Washington, D. C.: A Novel

VIDEO GAMES
Deaver, Jeffery. ★*The Never Game*

VIDEO GAMES INDUSTRY AND TRADE
Deaver, Jeffery. ★*The Never Game*

VIDEO STORES
Darnielle, John. *Universal Harvester*

VIDEOS
Blumenfeld, Amy. *The Cast*
Danielewski, Mark Z. ★*The Familiar.; Volume 4,*

Vidich, Paul
  The Coldest Warrior

VIDOCQ, FRANCOIS EUGENE, 1775-1857
Bayard, Louis. *The Black Tower: A Novel*
Hosseini, Khaled. ★*The Kite Runner*

***Vienna** Blood: A Max Liebermann Mystery*. Tallis, Frank

VIENNA, AUSTRIA
Benedict, Marie. *The Only Woman in the Room*
Bernhard, Thomas. ★*Woodcutters*
Clayton, Meg Waite. *The Last Train to London*
Musil, Robert. *The Man Without Qualities*
Sem-Sandberg, Steve. *The Chosen Ones: A Novel*
Tallis, Frank. *Vienna Blood: A Max Liebermann Mystery*

VIETNAM
Bao, Ninh. *The Sorrow of War: A Novel of North Vietnam*
Bohjalian, Chris. ★*The Red Lotus*
Butler, Robert Olen. *A Good Scent from a Strange Mountain: Stories*
Greene, Graham. ★*The Quiet American*
Kupersmith, Violet. ★*Build Your House Around My Body*

Marlantes, Karl. ★*Matterhorn: A Novel of the Vietnam War*
Nguyen, Phan Que Mai. ★*The Mountains Sing: A Novel*
Nguyen, Viet Thanh. ★*The Sympathizer*
O'Brien, Tim. *Going After Cacciato: A Novel*
Soli, Tatjana. *The Lotus Eaters*
Tanabe, Karin. *A Hundred Suns*
Tran, Vu. *Dragonfish: A Novel*

VIETNAM VETERANS
Anderson, Kent. *Green Sun: A Novel*
Bausch, Richard. ★*Rebel Powers*
Boyle, T. Coraghessan. *The Harder They Come*
Breslin, Jimmy. *Table Money*
Burke, James Lee. *Robicheaux*
Butler, Nickolas. ★*The Hearts of Men*
Butler, Robert Olen. *Perfume River*
Connelly, Michael. *The Black Ice*
Gorman, Edward. *Riders on the Storm : A Sam McCain Mystery*
Greer, Robert O. *First of State*
Hannah, Kristin. *The Great Alone*
Hunter, Stephen. *The 47th Samurai*
Johnson, Craig. *Land of Wolves*
McCarthy, Cormac. ★*No Country for Old Men*
Means, David. ★*Hystopia: A Novel*
Mosley, Walter. ★*Blood Grove*
O'Brien, Tim. ★*The Things They Carried: A Work of Fiction*
Sanders, Lawrence. *The Timothy Files*
Sanders, Lawrence. *Timothy's Game*
Straub, Peter. *Lost Boy Lost Girl: A Novel*
Vonnegut, Kurt. *Hocus Pocus*

VIETNAM VETERANS — FAMILY RELATIONSHIPS
Bausch, Richard. ★*Rebel Powers*

VIETNAM VETERANS' SPOUSES
Bausch, Richard. ★*Rebel Powers*

VIETNAM WAR PROTESTERS
Auster, Paul. ★*Leviathan*

VIETNAM WAR, 1961-1975
Bao, Ninh. *The Sorrow of War: A Novel of North Vietnam*
Del Vecchio, John M. *The 13th Valley: A Novel*
Follett, Ken. *Edge of Eternity*
Hart, John. *The Unwilling*
Hilderbrand, Elin. ★*Summer of '69*
Marlantes, Karl. ★*Matterhorn: A Novel of the Vietnam War*
McDermott, Alice. *After This*
Murdoch, Iris. *An Accidental Man*
Nguyen, Phan Que Mai. ★*The Mountains Sing: A Novel*
Nguyen, Viet Thanh. ★*The Sympathizer*
O'Brien, Tim. *Going After Cacciato: A Novel*
Sandford, John. *Heat Lightning*
Soli, Tatjana. *The Lotus Eaters*

VIETNAM WAR, 1961-1975 — AERIAL OPERATIONS, AMERICAN
Coonts, Stephen. ★*Flight of the Intruder*

VIETNAM WAR, 1961-1975 — CASUALTIES
O'Brien, Tim. ★*The Things They Carried: A Work of Fiction*

VIETNAM WAR, 1961-1975 — PSYCHOLOGICAL ASPECTS
Butler, Robert Olen. *Perfume River*
Means, David. ★*Hystopia: A Novel*

VIETNAMESE AMERICAN WOMEN
Kupersmith, Violet. ★*Build Your House Around My Body*

VIETNAMESE AMERICANS
Butler, Robert Olen. *A Good Scent from a Strange Mountain: Stories*
Hoang, Helen. ★*The Bride Test*
Nguyen, Viet Thanh. ★*The Refugees*
Tran, Vu. *Dragonfish: A Novel*
Vuong, Ocean. ★*On Earth We're Briefly Gorgeous: A Novel*

VIETNAMESE IN FRANCE
Nguyen, Viet Thanh. ★*The Committed*

VIETNAMESE IN THE UNITED STATES
Nguyen, Viet Thanh. ★*The Sympathizer*

The View from Alameda Island: A Novel. Carr, Robyn
The View from Castle Rock: Stories. Munro, Alice
A View of the Empire at Sunset. Phillips, Caryl

VIGILANTES
Black, Lisa. *Let Justice Descend*
Black, Lisa. *Suffer the Children*
Browne, S. G. *Less Than Hero: A Novel*
Gardner, Lisa. *Fear Nothing: A Detective D. D. Warren Novel*
Gardner, Lisa. *Find Her*
Harkaway, Nick. *Tigerman*
Martinson, T. J. *The Reign of the Kingfisher: A Novel*
Roslund, Anders. *Pen 33*
Sandford, John. ★*Silent Prey*
Smith, Julie. *Crescent City Kill: A Skip Langdon Novel*
Snyder, Suleikha. *Big Bad Wolf*
Solomon, Asali. *Disgruntled: A Novel*
Unger, Lisa. ★*The Stranger Inside*
Zhou, Haohui. *Death Notice: A Novel*

VIKINGS
Binet, Laurent. *Civilizations*
Cornwell, Bernard. *The Last Kingdom: A Novel*
Cornwell, Bernard. *Sword of Kings*
Follett, Ken. ★*The Evening and the Morning*
MacDonald, Andrew. *When We Were Vikings*

★*Vile Bodies*. Waugh, Evelyn

VILLA, PANCHO
Groom, Winston. *El Paso: A Novel*
Roy, Arundhati. ★*The Ministry of Utmost Happiness: A Novel*

VILLAGES
Aguilar Camin, Hector. *Death in Veracruz*
Alharthi, Jokha. *Celestial Bodies: A Novel*
Arden, Katherine. ★*The Bear and the Nightingale*
Beaton, M. C. *Agatha Raisin and the Quiche of Death*
Beaton, M. C. *Death of a Macho Man*
Binchy, Maeve. *Circle of Friends*
Brett, Simon. *Guilt at the Garage*
Connolly, Sheila. *The Lost Traveller*
Crace, Jim. *Harvest*
Crombie, Deborah. *A Bitter Feast*
De Bernieres, Louis. *Birds Without Wings*
Dev, Sonali. ★*A Bollywood Affair*
Doerr, Harriet. ★*Stones for Ibarra*
Donoghue, Emma. ★*The Wonder*
Dunmore, Helen. *The Lie*
Flynn, Michael. *Eifelheim*
French, Nicci. ★*House of Correction*

French, Tana. ★*The Searcher*
Gao, XIngjian. *Soul Mountain*
Garcia Marquez, Gabriel. *Chronicle of a Death Foretold*
Garcia Marquez, Gabriel. *In Evil Hour*
Garcia Marquez, Gabriel. ★*One Hundred Years of Solitude*
Ginzburg, Natalia. *Voices in the Evening*
Goenawan, Clarissa. *The Perfect World of Miwako Sumida*
Gordimer, Nadine. ★*July's People*
Grant, Helen. *The Vanishing of Katharina Linden*
Graves, Stephanie. *Olive Bright, Pigeoneer*
Gurganus, Allan. *The Practical Heart: Four Novellas*
Harris, Joanne. ★*Chocolat: A Novel*
Heacox, Kim. *Jimmy Bluefeather: A Novel*
Hibbert, Talia. *A Girl Like Her*
Jackson, Shirley. ★*The Lottery: And Other Stories*
Jenner, Natalie. *The Jane Austen Society*
Jónasson, Ragnar. ★*The Girl Who Died*
Kadare, Ismail. ★*The Three-Arched Bridge*
Kelly, Stephen. *The Wages of Desire: A World War II Mystery*
Lai, Larissa. *The Tiger Flu*
Liardet, Frances. *We Must Be Brave*
Makumbi, Jennifer Nansubuga. ★*A Girl Is a Body of Water*
Mankell, Henning. ★*The Return of the Dancing Master*
Mbue, Imbolo. *How Beautiful We Were*
McGregor, Jon. *The Reservoir Tapes*
Naipaul, V. S. *A Bend in the River*
Porter, Max. ★*Lanny: A Novel*
Potzsch, Oliver. *The Dark Monk: A Hangman's Daughter Tale*
Potzsch, Oliver. *The Hangman's Daughter: A Historical Novel*
Potzsch, Oliver. *The Play of Death*
Proust, Marcel. *Swann's Way*
Quartey, Kwei. *Wife of the Gods: A Novel*
Robinson, Peter. *Cold Is the Grave*
Simonson, Helen. *The Summer Before the War: A Novel*
Tinti, Hannah. *The Twelve Lives of Samuel Hawley: A Novel*
Watson, S. J. *Final Cut*
Williams, Niall. *This Is Happiness*
Woolf, Virginia. *Between the Acts*

VILLAINS
Martinson, T. J. *The Reign of the Kingfisher: A Novel*
Schwab, Victoria. *Vicious*
Villains [Series]. Schwab, Victoria
Vine, Barbara
The Minotaur: A Novel
Vineart war trilogy [Series]. Gilman, Laura Anne
Vinegar Girl: The Taming of the Shrew Retold. Tyler, Anne
Vineland. Pynchon, Thomas
VINEYARDS
Gilman, Laura Anne. *Flesh and Fire*
Giordano, Mario. *Auntie Poldi and the Vineyards of Etna*
Vinge, Joan D.
The Snow Queen
Vinge, Vernor
The Children of the Sky
A Fire Upon the Deep
Vintage national parks novels [Series]. Barnett, Karen
VINTAGE RECORD STORE OWNERS
Hornby, Nick. *High Fidelity*

*The **Violated**.* Pronzini, Bill
VIOLENCE
Akpan, Uwem. *Say You're One of Them*
Appanah-Mouriquand, Nathacha. *Tropic of Violence: A Novel*
Berkowitz, Ira. *Old Flame: A Jackson Steeg Novel*
Bilal, Parker. *The Burning Gates: A Makana Investigation*
Bilal, Parker. *The Ghost Runner*
Boyle, T. Coraghessan. *The Harder They Come*
Burgess, Anthony. ★*A Clockwork Orange*
Butler, Octavia E. *Parable of the Talents: A Novel*
Carver, Raymond. *What We Talk About When We Talk About Love: Stories*
Connolly, John. *The Nameless Ones*
Conrad, Joseph. ★*Heart of Darkness*
Crichton, Michael. *Pirate Latitudes*
Deaver, Jeffery. ★*The Coffin Dancer*
Doctorow, E. L. ★*Ragtime*
Enjeti, Anjali. ★*The Parted Earth*
Faust, Christa. *Choke Hold*
Ferrante, Elena. *My Brilliant Friend*
Flanagan, Richard. ★*The Narrow Road to the Deep North*
Gerritsen, Tess. *Playing with Fire*
Greene, Graham. *Collected Stories: Including May We Borrow Your Husband? a Sense of Reality, Twenty-One Stories*
Hand, Elizabeth. *Available Dark: A Thriller*
Hand, Elizabeth. *Hard Light*
Heinlein, Robert A. ★*Starship Troopers*
King, Stephen. *Sleeping Beauties: A Novel*
Lehane, Dennis. *Live by Night*
Leon, Donna. *A Question of Belief: A Commissario Guido Brunetti Mystery*
Li, Yiyun. *The Vagrants: A Novel*
McCann, Colum. ★*Apeirogon: A Novel*
McCarthy, Cormac. ★*No Country for Old Men*
McDermott, Alice. ★*That Night*
Mosley, Walter. *The Right Mistake: The Further Philosophical Investigations of Socrates Fortlow*
Palahniuk, Chuck. *Fight Club*
Pollock, Donald Ray. *The Devil All the Time*
Preston, Douglas J. *Crooked River*
Punke, Michael. *Ridgeline: A Novel*
Puzo, Mario. ★*The Godfather*
Puzo, Mario. *The Last Don*
Puzo, Mario. *The Sicilian: A Novel*
Rash, Ron. *Nothing Gold Can Stay: Stories*
Sanders, Lawrence. ★*The Third Deadly Sin*
Sanders, Lawrence. *The Timothy Files*
Sanders, Lawrence. *Timothy's Game*
Sapphire. *American Dreams*
Seton, Anya. ★*Dragonwyck*
Sharpe, Tess. *Barbed Wire Heart*
Slaughter, Karin. *Cop Town: A Novel*
Stringer, Vickie M. *Dirty Red: A Novel*
Styles, Toy. *A Hustler's Son: A Novel*
Swinson, David. *City on the Edge*
Tremblay, Paul. ★*The Cabin at the End of the World: A Novel*
Trumbo, Dalton. ★*Johnny Got His Gun*

Vonnegut, Kurt. *Armageddon in Retrospect: And Other New and Unpublished Writings on War and Peace*

Welty, Eudora. *Stories, Essays & Memoir*

VIOLENCE — PSYCHOLOGICAL ASPECTS

Al-Ramli, Muhsin. *The President's Gardens*

Cha, Steph. ★*Your House Will Pay*

Fernandez, Nona. *The Twilight Zone*

Klay, Phil. ★*Missionaries*

Lerner, Ben. ★*The Topeka School*

Livesey, Margot. ★*The Boy in the Field*

Nguyen, Phan Que Mai. ★*The Mountains Sing: A Novel*

Sofer, Dalia. *Man of My Time*

Turnbull, Cadwell. ★*The Lesson*

VIOLENCE AGAINST AFRICAN AMERICANS

Onyebuchi, Tochi. ★*Riot Baby*

VIOLENCE AGAINST GAY MEN AND LESBIANS

De Robertis, Carolina. *Cantoras*

VIOLENCE AGAINST MARGINALIZED PEOPLE

Ellroy, James. *Perfidia*

Howard, Ravi. *Driving the King: A Novel*

Johnson, Jocelyn Nicole. ★*My Monticello: Fiction*

VIOLENCE AGAINST MARGINALIZED WOMEN

Muller, Marcia. *Ice and Stone*

VIOLENCE AGAINST MEN

Alderman, Naomi. ★*The Power: A Novel*

Rankin, Ian. ★*Rather Be the Devil*

Sanders, Lawrence. ★*The Third Deadly Sin*

VIOLENCE AGAINST PROSTITUTES

Hewson, David. *The Garden of Evil*

VIOLENCE AGAINST RADICALS

Gorman, Edward. *Riders on the Storm : A Sam McCain Mystery*

VIOLENCE AGAINST TEENAGE GIRLS

Yates, Christopher J. *Grist Mill Road: A Novel*

VIOLENCE AGAINST TEENAGERS

Livesey, Margot. ★*The Boy in the Field*

VIOLENCE AGAINST WOMEN

Adler-Olsen, Jussi. *The Scarred Woman*

Baker, Jo. *The Body Lies*

Barry, Jessica. ★*Don't Turn Around*

Bradbury, Jamey. *The Wild Inside: A Novel*

Castillo, Elaine. *America Is Not the Heart*

Connelly, Michael. ★*Fair Warning*

Copenhaver, John. *The Savage Kind*

Cornwell, Patricia Daniels. *Postmortem*

Deon, Natashia. *Grace*

Dodd, Christina. *The Woman Who Couldn't Scream*

Donati, Sara. *Where the Light Enters*

Ferrell, Carolyn. *Dear Miss Metropolitan*

Hambly, Barbara. *Lady of Perdition*

Harris, Thomas. *Hannibal*

Harris, Thomas. ★*The Silence of the Lambs*

Hendrix, Grady. *The Final Girl Support Group*

Lagercrantz, David. *The Girl Who Lived Twice: A Lisbeth Salander Novel*

Lagercrantz, David. *The Girl Who Takes an Eye for an Eye*

Larsson, Stieg. *The Girl with the Dragon Tattoo*

Lawler, Liz. *Don't Wake Up*

Lelchuk, Saul. *Save Me from Dangerous Men: A Novel*

O'Brien, Edna. ★*Girl*

Pochoda, Ivy. ★*These Women*

Rendell, Ruth. *Harm Done*

Rollins, James. *Crucible*

Sager, Riley. *Final Girls: A Novel*

Shoham, Liad. *Asylum City: A Novel*

Slaughter, Karin. ★*Undone: A Novel*

Spillane, Mickey. *The Consummata*

Waite, Jen. *Survival Instincts*

Wetmore, Elizabeth. ★*Valentine*

VIOLENCE IN BOYS

Lessing, Doris May. ★*The Fifth Child*

VIOLENCE IN GANGS

Child, Lee. ★*Blue Moon*

O'Mara, Tim. *Crooked Numbers*

VIOLENCE IN MEN

Banks, Russell. ★*Affliction*

Barry, Jessica. ★*Don't Turn Around*

Bolano, Roberto. ★*The Third Reich*

Burke, James Lee. *The Jealous Kind*

Clark, Mary Higgins. ★*Kiss the Girls and Make Them Cry*

Ferrell, Carolyn. *Dear Miss Metropolitan*

Ford, Richard. *Canada*

Gruber, Michael. *The Return: A Novel*

Hand, Elizabeth. *Curious Toys*

Heller, Peter. *The Painter: A Novel*

K'wan. *Gutter*

Mailer, Norman. ★*The Executioner's Song*

Matthiessen, Peter. *Shadow Country: A New Rendering of the Watson Legend*

Morrison, Toni. *Jazz*

Mozley, Fiona. ★*Elmet*

Pelecanos, George P. *The Cut: A Novel*

Rollins, James. ★*The Last Odyssey*

Stegner, Wallace. ★*The Big Rock Candy Mountain*

Stevens, Chevy. *Never Let You Go*

Toro, Guillermo del. *The Hollow Ones*

Tran, Vu. *Dragonfish: A Novel*

Whitfield, Clare. *People of Abandoned Character*

Woodson, Jacqueline. ★*Another Brooklyn*

VIOLENCE IN SCHOOLS

Shriver, Lionel. *We Need to Talk About Kevin*

VIOLENCE IN WOMEN

Adler-Olsen, Jussi. *The Scarred Woman*

Rice, Christopher. *Blood Victory*

Slaughter, Karin. ★*Pieces of Her*

★*The **Violent** Bear It Away.* O'Connor, Flannery

VIOLENT CRIMES

Davis, Lindsey. *A Comedy of Terrors: A Flavia Albia Novel*

Fleischmann, Raymond. *How Quickly She Disappears*

O'Rawe, Richard. *Northern Heist*

***Violent** Peace: The War with China - Aftermath of Armageddon.* Poyer, David

VIOLIN

Elias, Gerald. *Danse Macabre*

VIOLIN TEACHERS

Elias, Gerald. *Danse Macabre*

Elias, Gerald. ★*Death and Transfiguration: A Daniel Jacobus Novel*

VIOLINISTS
Alexander, Tamera. ★*A Note yet Unsung*
Aoki, Ryka. *Light from Uncommon Stars*
De Robertis, Carolina. *The Gods of Tango*
Dongala, Emmanuel Boundzeki. *The Bridgetower Sonata: Sonata Mulattica*
Elias, Gerald. *Danse Macabre*
Elias, Gerald. ★*Death and Transfiguration: A Daniel Jacobus Novel*
Lebrecht, Norman. *The Song of Names*
Lovesey, Peter. *The Tooth Tattoo*
Virgil Cain mysteries [Series]. Smith, B. J.
Virgil Cole and Everett Hitch [Series]. Knott, Robert
Virgil Flowers mysteries [Series]. Sandford, John
Virgil Tibbs mystery novels [Series]. Ball, John Dudley
Virgil Wander. Enger, Leif
VIRGIN BIRTH (CHRISTIAN DOCTRINE)
Chambers, Clare. *Small Pleasures*
VIRGIN ISLANDS OF THE UNITED STATES
Hilderbrand, Elin. ★*Troubles in Paradise*
Hilderbrand, Elin. ★*What Happens in Paradise: A Novel*
Hilderbrand, Elin. ★*Winter in Paradise: A Novel*
Turnbull, Cadwell. ★*The Lesson*
★*Virgin River*. Carr, Robyn
Virgin River [Series]. Carr, Robyn
★*The Virgin Suicides*. Eugenides, Jeffrey
VIRGINIA
Anders, Adriana. *Under Her Skin*
Andrews, Donna. *Murder Most Fowl: A Meg Langslow Mystery*
Andrews, Donna. *Owl Be Home for Christmas: A Meg Langslow Mystery*
Andrews, Donna. *The Twelve Jays of Christmas: A Meg Langslow Mystery*
Baldacci, David. *Hell's Corner*
Bausch, Richard. *Hello to the Cannibals: A Novel*
Brown, Rita Mae. *Wish You Were Here*
Child, Lee. *Never Go Back*
Clark, Martin. *The Substitution Order*
Coates, Ta-Nehisi. ★*The Water Dancer: A Novel*
Cole, Alyssa. ★*An Extraordinary Union*
Cooper, Ellison. *Buried*
Cosby, S. A. ★*Blacktop Wasteland*
Cosby, S. A. ★*Razorblade Tears*
Cosimano, Elle. *Finlay Donovan Is Killing It*
Coulter, Catherine. *Labyrinth*
Crane, Stephen. ★*The Red Badge of Courage: An Episode of the American Civil War*
Ellison, J. T. *Good Girls Lie*
Emezi, Akwaeke. *Freshwater*
Fuqua, Jonathon Scott. *Gone and Back Again*
Johnson, Sadeqa. ★*Yellow Wife*
Kim, Angie. *Miracle Creek*
L'Amour, Louis. *To the Far Blue Mountains*
Majors, Inman. *Penelope Lemon: Game On!*
McLaughlin, James A. *Bearskin*
Parks, Brad. *Closer Than You Know*
Patchett, Ann. ★*Commonwealth*
Pearl, Matthew. *The Poe Shadow: A Novel*
Ramsay, Frederick. *Countdown*

Redondo, Dolores. *The North Face of the Heart*
Smith, Lee. ★*Fair and Tender Ladies*
Smith, Lee. *Family Linen*
Smith, Lee. *Oral History*
Styron, William. *The Confessions of Nat Turner*
Swinson, Kiki. *The Safe House*
Trigiani, Adriana. *Big Cherry Holler: A Big Stone Gap Novel*
Trigiani, Adriana. *Big Stone Gap: A Novel*
Vandelly, T. Marie. *Theme Music*
Walls, Jeannette. *The Silver Star: A Novel*
Wilhelm, Kate. *Where Late the Sweet Birds Sang*
VIRGINS
Spencer, Minerva. *Scandalous*
Van Dyken, Rachel. *Risky Play*
VIRTUAL COMMUNITY
Dade, Olivia. *Spoiler Alert*
VIRTUAL REALITY
Cline, Ernest. *Ready Player One: A Novel*
Robb, J. D. *Fantasy in Death*
Ruff, Matt. ★*88 Names*
Stephenson, Neal. *Reamde*
Stephenson, Neal. ★*Snow Crash*
Weinstein, Alexander. *Children of the New World: Stories*
Virtue Falls. Dodd, Christina
Virtue Falls [Series]. Dodd, Christina
VIRTUES
Baxter, Charles. *There's Something I Want You to Do: Stories*
VIRUS DISEASES
Dekker, Ted. *Red: The Heroic Rescue*
Dekker, Ted. *White: The Great Pursuit*
Scalzi, John. *Head On*
Scalzi, John. ★*Lock In*
Stewart, George R. *Earth Abides*
Whitehead, Colson. *Zone One: A Novel*
VIRUSES
Cronin, Justin. *The City of Mirrors*
Cronin, Justin. *The Passage*
Cronin, Justin. *The Twelve*
Grant, Mira. *Blackout*
Grant, Mira. *Deadline*
Grant, Mira. *Feed*
Grant, Mira. *Feedback*
Shepard, Jim. *Phase Six*
Tremblay, Paul. *Survivor Song*
Wright, Lawrence. *The End of October*
VISAS
Lauren, Christina. *Roomies*
The Viscount Made Me Do It. Quincy, Diana
VISCOUNTS AND VISCOUNTESSES
Leigh, Eva. *Scandal Takes the Stage*
Quincy, Diana. *The Viscount Made Me Do It*
VISEGRAD (BOSNIA AND HERCEGOVINA : EAST)
Andric, Ivo. *The Bridge on the Drina*
Vish Puri mysteries [Series]. Hall, Tarquin
The Vision of Emma Blau. Hegi, Ursula
The Visionist. Urquhart, Rachel
VISIONS
Groff, Lauren. ★*Matrix*

Guterson, David. *Our Lady of the Forest*
Hamilton, Peter F. *The Dreaming Void*
Harvey, Michael T. *Pulse*
Millhauser, Steven. *Martin Dressler: The Tale of an American Dreamer*
Reyes, Dolores. *Eartheater*
Seton, Anya. *Green Darkness*
Sharratt, Mary. *Revelations*
Shepard, Sam. *The One Inside*
★*A Visit* from the Goon Squad. Egan, Jennifer
Visitation Street: A Novel. Pochoda, Ivy
The *Visitor*. Tepper, Sheri S.
Vita Nostra. Diachenko, Serhii

VITAL STATISTICS
Saramago, Jose. *All the Names*
★The *Vixen*. Prose, Francine

Vlautin, Willy
Don't Skip Out on Me
★*The Night Always Comes*

Vo, Nghi
★*The Chosen and the Beautiful*
Voice of America: Stories. Osondu, E. C.
Voices in the Evening. Ginzburg, Natalia
Void trilogy [Series]. Hamilton, Peter F.

VOLCANIC ERUPTIONS
Brooks, Max. *Devolution: A Firsthand Account of the Rainier Sasquatch Massacre*
The *Volcano* Lover: A Romance. Sontag, Susan

VOLCANOES
Verne, Jules. ★*Journey to the Centre of the Earth*

Vollmann, William T.
Last Stories and Other Stories

Voltaire
Candide and Other Stories

VOLUNTEERS
Boyle, William. *The Lonely Witness*
Linden, Rachel. *The Enlightenment of Bees*
Moyes, Jojo. ★*The Giver of Stars: A Novel*
Stross, Charles. *Glasshouse*
★*Von Ryan's Express*. Westheimer, David

Von Ziegesar, Cecily
Cobble Hill

Vonnegut, Kurt
Armageddon in Retrospect: And Other New and Unpublished Writings on War and Peace
Bagombo Snuff Box: Uncollected Short Fiction
★*Breakfast of Champions: Or, Goodbye Blue Monday!*
★*Cat's Cradle*
Complete Stories
★*Galapagos: A Novel*
Hocus Pocus
Jailbird: A Novel
★*Player Piano*
★*The Sirens of Titan*
Slapstick: Or, Lonesome No More! a Novel
★*Slaughterhouse-Five: Or, the Children's Crusade : A Duty-Dance with Death*
Timequake

Welcome to the Monkey House
While Mortals Sleep: Unpublished Short Fiction

VOODOO
Depestre, Rene. *Hadriana in All My Dreams*
Garcia, Cristina. *Dreaming in Cuban*
Rhodes, Jewell Parker. *Voodoo Dreams: A Novel of Marie Laveau*
Rhodes, Jewell Parker. *Yellow Moon: A Novel*
Tyree, Omar. *Leslie: A Novel*
Voodoo Dreams: A Novel of Marie Laveau. Rhodes, Jewell Parker
Voodoo trilogy [Series]. Rhodes, Jewell Parker
Vorkosigan saga [Series]. Bujold, Lois McMaster
The *Voyage* of the Morning Light. Endicott, Marina
The *Voyage* Out. Woolf, Virginia
★*Voyager*. Gabaldon, Diana

VOYAGES AND TRAVELS
Aalborg, Gordon. *River of Porcupines*
Adamson, Gil. *The Outlander*
Afshar, Tessa. *Jewel of the Nile*
Alexander, Victoria. *The Lady Travelers Guide to Larceny with a Dashing Stranger*
Alvar, Mia. *In the Country: Stories*
Arikawa, Hiro. *The Travelling Cat Chronicles*
Ball, Jesse. *Census*
Barry, Dave. *Lunatics*
Barth, John. ★*The Sot-Weed Factor*
Blackwell, Juliet. *Letters from Paris*
Bloom, Amy. *Lucky Us: A Novel*
Bohjalian, Chris. ★*The Red Lotus*
Bowles, Paul. ★*The Sheltering Sky*
Brennan, Marie. *Within the Sanctuary of Wings: A Memoir by Lady Trent*
Brooks, Bill. *Winter Kill*
Burke, James Lee. *House of the Rising Sun: A Novel*
Carey, Peter. *A Long Way from Home*
Carter, Michaela. *Leonora in the Morning Light*
Cheng, Bill. *Southern Cross the Dog*
Coelho, Paulo. ★*The Alchemist*
Conrad, Joseph. ★*Heart of Darkness*
Cook, Diane. ★*The New Wilderness: A Novel*
Dare, Tessa. *A Week to Be Wicked*
Dickens, Charles. *The Old Curiosity Shop*
Dickens, Charles. *The Pickwick Papers*
Doyle, Brian. *The Plover: A Novel*
Doyle, Rob. *Threshold*
Edwards, Louis. *Ramadan Ramsey: A Novel*
Enard, Mathias. *Compass*
Enger, Lin. *The High Divide: A Novel*
Enright, Anne. *The Green Road: A Novel*
Florio, Gwen. *Best Laid Plans*
Ford, Richard. *Let Me Be Frank with You*
Franklin, Ariana. ★*Death and the Maiden*
Gabaldon, Diana. ★*Voyager*
Gappah, Petina. ★*Out of Darkness, Shining Light*
Gaynor, Hazel. *Three Words for Goodbye*
George, Nina. *The Little Paris Bookshop*
Ghosh, Amitav. *Flood of Fire*
Ghosh, Amitav. ★*Gun Island*
Ghosh, Amitav. *River of Smoke*

Ghosh, Amitav. *Sea of Poppies*
Gilman, Laura Anne. *The Cold Eye*
Green, Jocelyn. *The Mark of the King*
Grossman, Lev. *The Magician King: A Novel*
Grossman, Lev. *The Magician's Land: A Novel*
Hambly, Barbara. *House of the Patriarch*
Harmon, Amy. *Where the Lost Wander*
Hertmans, Stefan. ★*The Convert: A Novel*
Hijuelos, Oscar. *Twain & Stanley Enter Paradise*
Hooper, Emma. *Etta and Otto and Russell and James: A Novel*
Hunter, Stephen. *The 47th Samurai*
Irving, John. *Avenue of Mysteries: A Novel*
James, Henry. *Daisy Miller*
Jiles, Paulette. *News of the World: A Novel*
Jimenez, Abby. *Life's Too Short*
Kay, Guy Gavriel. ★*Children of Earth and Sky*
Kelly, Martha Hall. *Lost Roses: A Novel*
Ko-Eun, Yun. *The Disaster Tourist*
Krivak, Andrew. *The Bear*
Krueger, William Kent. *This Tender Land: A Novel*
Lalami, Laila. ★*The Moor's Account: A Novel*
Larkin, Allie. *The People We Keep*
Lefteri, Christy. *The Beekeeper of Aleppo: A Novel*
Leithauser, Brad. *The Promise of Elsewhere*
Livesey, Margot. *Criminals: A Novel*
Marcom, Micheline Aharonian. *The New American*
McCarthy, Jesse. *The Fugitivities*
McMurtry, Larry. *Boone's Lick: A Novel*
Mitchell, David. *The Bone Clocks: A Novel*
Mott, Jason. *Hell of a Book*
Murakami, Haruki. *Colorless Tsukuru Tazaki and His Years of Pilgrimage*
O'Farrell, Maggie. *This Must Be the Place*
Parini, Jay. *The Damascus Road: A Novel of Saint Paul*
Phillips, Susan Elizabeth. *The Great Escape*
Pohl, Frederik. *Gateway*
Porter, Katherine Anne. *Ship of Fools*
Potzsch, Oliver. *The Werewolf of Bamberg*
Pratchett, Terry. ★*The Color of Magic*
Quick, Amanda. *Otherwise Engaged*
Rendell, Ruth. *Speaker of Mandarin*
Robertson, Michael. *Moriarty Returns a Letter: A Baker Street Mystery*
Ryan, Anthony. *The Waking Fire*
Saramago, Jose. *Cain*
Saramago, Jose. ★*The Elephant's Journey*
Saylor, Steven. *The Seven Wonders: A Novel of the Ancient World*
Sebald, Winfried Georg. *Vertigo*
Seton, Anya. *Avalon*
Smith, Dominic. *Bright and Distant Shores*
Swift, Jonathan. ★*Gulliver's Travels*
Taseer, Aatish. *The Way Things Were: A Novel*
Truong, Monique T. D. *The Sweetest Fruits*
Updike, John. *My Father's Tears and Other Stories*
Updike, John. *The Widows of Eastwick*
Verne, Jules. ★*Around the World in Eighty Days*
Vonnegut, Kurt. ★*Galapagos: A Novel*
Waldman, Amy. *A Door in the Earth*

Walton, Jo. ★*Necessity*
Zapata, Mike. *The Lost Book of Adana Moreau*
VOYEURISM
Fuller, Claire. ★*Bitter Orange*
Mishima, Yukio. *The Temple of Dawn*
Vreeland, Susan
Girl in Hyacinth Blue
VULNERABILITY
Schwartz, Lynne Sharon. *Truthtelling: Stories, Fables, Glimpses*
Vuong, Ocean
★*On Earth We're Briefly Gorgeous: A Novel*
Vyleta, Dan
Smoke: A Novel

W

Wade, Becky
Falling for You
★*True to You*
Wagers, K. B.
After the Crown
Hold Fast Through the Fire
A Pale Light in the Black: A Neog Novel
There Before the Chaos
The **Wages** of Desire: A World War II Mystery. Kelly, Stephen
The **Wages** of Sin. Welsh, Kaite
WAGON TRAINS
Dallas, Sandra. *Westering Women: A Novel*
Katsu, Alma. *The Hunger: A Novel*
Kirkpatrick, Jane. *One More River to Cross*
The **Wailing** Wind. Hillerman, Tony
Waite, Jen
Survival Instincts
Waite, Olivia
The Care and Feeding of Waspish Widows
★*The Lady's Guide to Celestial Mechanics*
★The **Waiting**. Gendry-Kim, Keum Suk
★**Waiting**. Jin, Ha
WAITING
Jin, Ha. ★*Waiting*
Waiting for Bojangles: A Novel. Bourdeaut, Olivier
★**Waiting** for Eden: A Novel. Ackerman, Elliot
Waiting for Tom Hanks [Series]. Winfrey, Kerry
Waiting for Tom Hanks: A Novel. Winfrey, Kerry
Waiting for Wednesday: A Frieda Klein Mystery. French, Nicci
★**Waiting** to Exhale. McMillan, Terry
WAITRESSES
Beagle, Peter S. *Summerlong*
Danler, Stephanie. *Sweetbitter*
Jalaluddin, Uzma. *Hana Khan Carries On*
King, Lily. *Writers & Lovers: A Novel*
Majors, Inman. *Penelope Lemon: Game On!*
Vlautin, Willy. ★*The Night Always Comes*
Wake, Siren: Ovid Resung. MacLaughlin, Nina
The **Waking** Fire. Ryan, Anthony
Waking Lions. Gundar-Goshen, Ayelet

Walbert, Kate
   She Was Like That: New and Selected Stories
WALDEN POND REGION, MASSACHUSETTS
   Pipkin, John. *Woodsburner: A Novel*
Waldman, Amy
   A Door in the Earth
WALES
   Balogh, Mary. *Simply Love*
   Bateman, Kate. *A Reckless Match*
   Cronin, A. J. *Citadel*
   Fforde, Jasper. ★*Early Riser: A Novel*
   Fforde, Jasper. *The Eyre Affair: A Novel*
   Llewellyn, Richard. ★*How Green Was My Valley*
   Penman, Sharon Kay. *Here Be Dragons*
   Robb, Candace M. *A Gift of Sanctuary: An Owen Archer Mystery*
   Thomas, Dylan. *The Collected Stories*
*A **Walk** on the Wild Side*. Algren, Nelson
*A **Walk** to Remember*. Sparks, Nicholas
*A **Walk** with the Dead*. Spencer, Sally
Walkaway. Doctorow, Cory
Walker, Alice
   ★*The Color Purple: A Novel*
   Possessing the Secret of Joy
   The Temple of My Familiar
   The Third Life of Grange Copeland
   You Can't Keep a Good Woman Down: Stories
WALKER, AMOS (FICTITIOUS CHARACTER)
   Estleman, Loren D. *Infernal Angels*
   Estleman, Loren D. *A Smile on the Face of the Tiger*
Walker, Caroline Louise
   Man of the Year
Walker, Karen Thompson
   The Age of Miracles: A Novel
   The Dreamers
Walker, Martin
   The Coldest Case
   The Shooting at Chateau Rock
Walker, Nico
   ★*Cherry: A Novel*
Walker, Sarai
   Dietland
Walker, Wendy
   Emma in the Night
WALKING
   Hooper, Emma. *Etta and Otto and Russell and James: A Novel*
★***Walking** Across Egypt: A Novel*. Edgerton, Clyde
***Walking** on the Ceiling*. Savas, Aysegul
*The **Wall** of Storms*. Liu, Ken
WALL STREET, NEW YORK CITY
   Goldin, Megan. *The Escape Room*
   Sanders, Lawrence. *The Timothy Files*
   Sanders, Lawrence. *Timothy's Game*
   Sears, Michael. *Black Fridays*
   Towles, Amor. *Rules of Civility: A Novel*
Wall, Cara
   The Dearly Beloved: A Novel
Wallace, Carol
   Our Kind of People

Wallace, Daniel
   ★*Big Fish: A Novel of Mythic Proportions*
Wallace, David Foster
   ★*Brief Interviews with Hideous Men*
   ★*Infinite Jest: A Novel*
   Oblivion: Stories
   ★*The Pale King: An Unfinished Novel*
Wallace, Lew
   ★*Ben-Hur*
Wallace, Melanie
   The Girl in the Garden
WALLANDER, KURT (FICTITIOUS CHARACTER)
   Mankell, Henning. *Before the Frost: A Linda Wallander Mystery*
   Mankell, Henning. *The Dogs of Riga*
   Mankell, Henning. *Firewall*
   Mankell, Henning. *The Man Who Smiled: A Kurt Wallander Mystery*
   Mankell, Henning. ★*One Step Behind*
Waller, Robert James
   ★*The Bridges of Madison County*
★*The **Wallflower** Wager*. Dare, Tessa
WALLS
   Gaiman, Neil. ★*Stardust*
Walls, Jeannette
   The Silver Star: A Novel
Walschots, Natalie Zina
   Hench: A Novel
Walser, Robert
   The Assistant
Walsh, M. O.
   ★*The Big Door Prize: A Novel*
Walsh, S. Kirk
   The Elephant of Belfast: A Novel
Walt Longmire mysteries [Series]. Johnson, Craig
Walters, Minette
   The Last Hours: A Novel
Walton, Dawnie
   ★*The Final Revival of Opal & Nev*
Walton, Jo
   ★*Lent*
   ★*Necessity*
   Or What You Will
Wambaugh, Joseph
   The New Centurions
★*The **Wanderer***. Carr, Robyn
*The **Wanderers***. Howrey, Meg
WANDERERS AND WANDERING
   Child, Lee. *No Middle Name: The Complete Collected Jack Reacher Short Stories*
   French, Jonathan. *The True Bastards*
   Gao, XIngjian. *Soul Mountain*
   Kerouac, Jack. ★*Road Novels 1957-1960*
   Lippman, Laura. ★*Sunburn*
   Maturin, Charles Robert. *Melmoth the Wanderer: A Tale*
   Parker, Robert B. *Appaloosa*
   Proulx, Annie. *Postcards*
   Richler, Mordecai. *Solomon Gursky Was Here*
   Tobar, Hector. *The Last Great Road Bum*
   Wendig, Chuck. ★*Wanderers: A Novel*

★*Wanderers: a Novel*. Wendig, Chuck
The *Wandering* Falcon. Ahmad, Jamil
Wang, Kathy
    Family Trust: A Novel
    Impostor Syndrome: A Novel
Want you series [Series]. James, Lorelei
A *Wanted* Man. Child, Lee
Wanted, a Gentleman: Or, Virtue Over-Rated. Charles, KJ
The *Wanton* Angel: A Novel. Marston, Edward
★*War*. Styles, Toy
WAR
    Adimi, Kaouther. *Our Riches*
    Blake, Sarah. *The Postmistress*
    Brooks, Max. ★*World War Z: An Oral History of the Zombie War*
    Coetzee, J. M. ★*Life & Times of Michael K*
    Dupont, Eric. *The American Fiancee: A Novel*
    Follett, Ken. *Winter of the World*
    Frazier, Charles. *Varina*
    George, Margaret. *Helen of Troy*
    Harmel, Kristin. *The Room on Rue Amelie*
    Hurley, Kameron. ★*The Light Brigade*
    Jakes, John. *Love and War*
    Jones, James. ★*From Here to Eternity*
    Mailer, Norman. ★*The Naked and the Dead*
    Mandanipour, Shahriar. *Moon Brow*
    Marlantes, Karl. ★*Matterhorn: A Novel of the Vietnam War*
    Mitchell, Margaret. ★*Gone with the Wind*
    Poyer, David. *Overthrow: The War with China and North Korea—Fall of an Empire*
    Robinson, Kim Stanley. *The Years of Rice and Salt*
    Statovci, Pajtim. *Bolla*
    Thompson, Tade. *The Rosewater Redemption*
    Vonnegut, Kurt. *Armageddon in Retrospect: And Other New and Unpublished Writings on War and Peace*
WAR — HISTORY
    Follett, Ken. *Fall of Giants*
WAR — MORAL AND ETHICAL ASPECTS
    Bellow, Saul. *Dangling Man*
    Franck, Julia. *Blindness of the Heart*
    Haldeman, Joe W. ★*The Forever War*
WAR — PREVENTION
    Cussler, Clive. *Odessa Sea*
WAR — PSYCHOLOGICAL ASPECTS
    Ackerman, Elliot. ★*Waiting for Eden: A Novel*
    Alyan, Hala. *Salt Houses*
    Arudpragasam, Anuk. *The Story of a Brief Marriage*
    Butler, Robert Olen. *Perfume River*
    Connolly, John. *The Nameless Ones*
    Giordano, Paolo. *The Human Body*
    Jenner, Natalie. *The Jane Austen Society*
    Jensen, Nancy. *In Our Midst*
    Klay, Phil. ★*Missionaries*
    Malouf, David. *Ransom*
    McCullough, Colleen. *An Indecent Obsession*
    Miller, Derek B. ★*The Girl in Green*
    Nguyen, Phan Que Mai. ★*The Mountains Sing: A Novel*
    Novic, Sara. *Girl at War*
    Powers, Kevin. ★*The Yellow Birds: A Novel*

Remarque, Erich Maria. ★*All Quiet on the Western Front*
Rooney, Kathleen. ★*Cher Ami and Major Whittlesey*
Soli, Tatjana. *The Lotus Eaters*
Speller, Elizabeth. *The Return of Captain John Emmett*
Speller, Elizabeth. *The Strange Fate of Kitty Easton*
Trumbo, Dalton. ★*Johnny Got His Gun*
Yoon, Paul. ★*Run Me to Earth: A Novel*
War 2: All Hell Breaks Loose. Styles, Toy
★*War* and Peace. Tolstoy, Leo
★*War* and Remembrance: A Novel. Wouk, Herman
WAR AND SOCIETY
    Al-Ramli, Muhsin. *The President's Gardens*
    Atkinson, Kate. ★*Transcription*
    Demirtas, Selahattin. *Dawn: Stories*
    Doerr, Anthony. ★*All the Light We Cannot See: A Novel*
    Franklin, Ariana. *The Siege Winter*
    Gendry-Kim, Keum Suk. ★*The Waiting*
    Grossman, David. ★*To the End of the Land*
    Hage, Rawi. *De Niro's Game*
    Hannah, Kristin. *The Nightingale*
    Harper, Karen. *The Queen's Secret: A Novel of England's World War II Queen*
    Kim, Crystal Hana. *If You Leave Me*
    Marra, Anthony. *The Tsar of Love and Techno: Stories*
    Mohamed, Nadifa. *The Orchard of Lost Souls: A Novel*
    O'Brien, Tim. *Going After Cacciato: A Novel*
    Remarque, Erich Maria. ★*All Quiet on the Western Front*
    Sayles, John. *A Moment in the Sun*
    Simonson, Helen. *The Summer Before the War: A Novel*
    Solomons, Natasha. *House of Gold*
    Spark, Muriel. ★*The Girls of Slender Means*
    Speller, Elizabeth. *The Return of Captain John Emmett*
    Speller, Elizabeth. *The Strange Fate of Kitty Easton*
    Waldman, Amy. *A Door in the Earth*
    Walsh, S. Kirk. *The Elephant of Belfast: A Novel*
WAR CASUALTIES
    Dybek, Nick. *The Verdun Affair: A Novel*
WAR CORRESPONDENTS
    Abrams, David. *Fobbit*
    Greene, Graham. ★*The Quiet American*
    McLain, Paula. *Love and Ruin*
    Quinn, Kate. ★*The Huntress*
WAR CRIME TRIALS
    Kitamura, Katie M. *Intimacies*
    Schlink, Bernhard. *The Reader: A Novel*
WAR CRIMES — HISTORY
    Goddard, Robert. ★*Long Time Coming: A Novel*
WAR CRIMINALS
    Bilal, Parker. *The Burning Gates: A Makana Investigation*
    Connolly, John. *The Nameless Ones*
    Grecian, Alex. *The Saint of Wolves and Butchers*
    Khan, Ausma Zehanat. *The Unquiet Dead*
    Kitamura, Katie M. *Intimacies*
    Rankin, Ian. *The Hanging Garden: An Inspector Rebus Novel*
WAR GAMES
    Bolano, Roberto. ★*The Third Reich*
WAR MEMORIALS
    Dykes, Amanda. *Whose Waves These Are*

*The **War** of the End of the World*. Vargas Llosa, Mario
War of the Rats: A Novel. Robbins, David L.
★*The **War** of the Worlds*. Wells, H. G.
WAR ON TERRORISM, 2001-2009
 Le Carre, John. *A Most Wanted Man: A Novel*
War Room: Prayer Is a Powerful Weapon. Fabry, Chris
WAR STORIES
 Abrams, David. *Fobbit*
 Albahari, David. *Gotz and Meyer*
 Alderson, Kaia. *Sisters in Arms*
 Aramburu, Fernando. *Homeland*
 Arudpragasam, Anuk. *The Story of a Brief Marriage*
 Ballard, J. G. *Empire of the Sun: A Novel*
 Bao, Ninh. *The Sorrow of War: A Novel of North Vietnam*
 Barker, Pat. ★*The Eye in the Door*
 Barker, Pat. ★*The Ghost Road*
 Barker, Pat. ★*Regeneration*
 Barker, Pat. ★*The Silence of the Girls: A Novel*
 Barker, Pat. *The Women of Troy*
 Bausch, Richard. *Peace*
 Bausch, Richard. ★*Rebel Powers*
 Beach, Edward L. *Run Silent, Run Deep*
 Benaron, Naomi. *Running the Rift: A Novel*
 Bird, Sarah. *Daughter of a Daughter of a Queen*
 Bohjalian, Chris. *Skeletons at the Feast: A Novel*
 Boianjiu, Shani. *The People of Forever Are Not Afraid: A Novel*
 Boulle, Pierre. *The Bridge Over the River Kwai: A Novel*
 Brouwer, Sigmund. *Thief of Glory: A Novel*
 Cobbs Hoffman, Elizabeth. *The Tubman Command: A Novel*
 Cooper, James Fenimore. *The Last of the Mohicans: A Narrative of 1757*
 Couto, Mia. *Sleepwalking Land*
 Crane, Stephen. ★*The Red Badge of Courage: An Episode of the American Civil War*
 De Bernieres, Louis. *Birds Without Wings*
 Del Vecchio, John M. *The 13th Valley: A Novel*
 Deutermann, Peter T. *Pacific Glory: A Novel*
 Doctorow, E. L. *The March: A Novel*
 El Akkad, Omar. *American War*
 Faulks, Sebastian. ★*Birdsong*
 Faulks, Sebastian. *Charlotte Gray: A Novel*
 Follett, Ken. *Hornet Flight*
 Follett, Ken. *Jackdaws*
 Franck, Julia. *Blindness of the Heart*
 Furst, Alan. *Blood of Victory: A Novel*
 Furst, Alan. *Dark Voyage: A Novel*
 Furst, Alan. ★*A Hero of France*
 Furst, Alan. ★*Mission to Paris*
 Furst, Alan. ★*Under Occupation: A Novel*
 Giordano, Paolo. *The Human Body*
 Greene, Graham. ★*The Quiet American*
 Groot, Tracy. *Flame of Resistance*
 Hage, Rawi. *De Niro's Game*
 Hamid, Mohsin. ★*Exit West: A Novel*
 Harmel, Kristin. *The Room on Rue Amelie*
 Harris, C. S. *Good Time Coming*
 Harris, Robert. *Enigma*
 Heggen, Thomas. *Mister Roberts*

 Heller, Joseph. ★*Catch-22*
 Hemingway, Ernest. ★*A Farewell to Arms*
 Hemingway, Ernest. *For Whom the Bell Tolls*
 Hersey, John. ★*A Bell for Adano*
 Hicks, Robert. *The Widow of the South*
 Higgins, Jack. *Confessional*
 Higgins, Jack. *The Eagle Has Flown*
 Higgins, Jack. *The Eagle Has Landed*
 Higgins, Jack. *Touch the Devil*
 Hosseini, Khaled. ★*Sea Prayer*
 Jakes, John. *Love and War*
 Jakes, John. ★*North and South*
 Jones, James. ★*From Here to Eternity*
 Jones, James. ★*The Thin Red Line*
 Kane, Ben. *Spartacus: The Gladiator*
 Kantor, MacKinlay. ★*Andersonville*
 Keneally, Thomas. ★*The Daughters of Mars*
 Khalfah, Khlid. *Death Is Hard Work: A Novel*
 Mailer, Norman. ★*The Naked and the Dead*
 Mandanipour, Shahriar. *Moon Brow*
 Marlantes, Karl. ★*Matterhorn: A Novel of the Vietnam War*
 Marra, Anthony. ★*A Constellation of Vital Phenomena: A Novel*
 Michener, James A. ★*The Bridges at Toko-Ri*
 Michener, James A. ★*Tales of the South Pacific*
 Miller, Derek B. ★*The Girl in Green*
 Miller, Madeline. *The Song of Achilles*
 Mitchell, Margaret. ★*Gone with the Wind*
 Monsarrat, Nicholas. *The Cruel Sea*
 O'Brien, Tim. *Going After Cacciato: A Novel*
 O'Brien, Tim. ★*The Things They Carried: A Work of Fiction*
 Otsuka, Julie. *When the Emperor Was Divine: A Novel*
 Piercy, Marge. *Gone to Soldiers: A Novel*
 Pilcher, Rosamunde. *Coming Home*
 Pitts, Leonard. *Freeman*
 Powers, Kevin. ★*The Yellow Birds: A Novel*
 Remarque, Erich Maria. ★*All Quiet on the Western Front*
 Remarque, Erich Maria. *The Road Back*
 Remarque, Erich Maria. *A Time to Love and a Time to Die*
 Robbins, David L. *Last Citadel: A Novel of the Battle of Kursk*
 Robbins, David L. *War of the Rats: A Novel*
 Russell, Mary Doria. *A Thread of Grace: A Novel*
 Sartre, Jean Paul. *Troubled Sleep*
 Shaara, Jeff. *Gods and Generals: A Novel of the Civil War*
 Shaara, Jeff. *Gone for Soldiers*
 Shaara, Jeff. *The Last Full Measure*
 Shaara, Jeff. *The Rising Tide: A Novel of World War II*
 Shaara, Jeff. *The Steel Wave: A Novel of World War II*
 Shaara, Michael. ★*The Killer Angels: A Novel*
 Soli, Tatjana. *The Lotus Eaters*
 Tolstoy, Leo. *War and Peace*
 Uris, Leon. *Armageddon: A Novel of Berlin*
 West, Jessamyn. *The Friendly Persuasion*
 Westheimer, David. ★*Von Ryan's Express*
 Wouk, Herman. ★*The Caine Mutiny: A Novel of World War II*
 Wouk, Herman. ★*War and Remembrance: A Novel*
 Wouk, Herman. ★*The Winds of War: A Novel*
WAR VICTIMS
 Akpan, Uwem. *Say You're One of Them*

The **War** Widow. Moss, Tara
War Women. Limon, Martin
WAR WOUNDS
  March, Nev. *Murder in Old Bombay*
  Van Booy, Simon. *The Illusion of Separateness*
Ward, Catriona
  The Last House on Needless Street
Ward, Jesmyn
  ★*Sing, Unburied, Sing*
The **Warden**. Trollope, Anthony
Ware, Ruth
  The Death of Mrs. Westaway
  In a Dark, Dark Wood
  The Lying Game
  ★*One by One*
  ★*The Turn of the Key*
  The Woman in Cabin Ten
The **Warehouse:** a Novel. Hart, Rob
★*Warlight*. Ondaatje, Michael
Warlord chronicles [Series]. Cornwell, Bernard
WARLORDS
  Bouchet, Amanda. *Breath of Fire*
  Bouchet, Amanda. ★*A Promise of Fire*
  Clavell, James. *Shogun*
  Farah, Nuruddin. *Knots*
  Rowland, Laura Joh. *The Snow Empress*
Warning Light. Ricciardi, David
WARNINGS
  Turton, Stuart. ★*The Devil and the Dark Water*
Warren, Robert Penn
  All the King's Men
  Band of Angels
  World Enough and Time: A Romantic Novel
Warren, Susan May
  Rescue Me
Warrior witch duology [Series]. Kelly, Greta
★*The Warrior's* Apprentice. Bujold, Lois McMaster
WARRIORS
  Banks, Maya. *Never Seduce a Scot*
  Barker, Pat. ★*The Silence of the Girls: A Novel*
  Bear, Elizabeth. *All the Windwracked Stars*
  Bear, Elizabeth. *Steles of the Sky*
  Binet, Laurent. *Civilizations*
  Carey, Jacqueline. *Starless*
  Chakraborty, S. A. *The City of Brass*
  Chakraborty, S. A. *The Empire of Gold*
  Cornwell, Bernard. *The Last Kingdom: A Novel*
  Cornwell, Bernard. *Sword of Kings*
  Durst, Sarah Beth. *The Queen of Blood*
  Jin, Yong. *A Hero Born: A Novel*
  Leckie, Ann. ★*The Raven Tower*
  Miller, Madeline. *The Song of Achilles*
  Showalter, Gena. *Shadow and Ice*
  Snipes, Wesley. *Talon of God*
  Tepper, Sheri S. *The Gate to Women's Country*
  Winter, Evan. *The Fires of Vengeance*
  Winter, Evan. ★*The Rage of Dragons*

WARS OF THE ROSES, 1455-1485
  Gregory, Philippa. *The Lady of the Rivers*
  Penman, Sharon Kay. *The Sunne in Splendour*
  ★*The Warsaw Orphan: A Wwii Novel*. Rimmer, Kelly
  ★*The Warsaw Protocol*. Berry, Steve
WARSAW, POLAND
  Berry, Steve. ★*The Warsaw Protocol*
  Furst, Alan. *The Spies of Warsaw*
  Twardoch, Szczepan. *The King of Warsaw*
WARSHIPS
  Hawks, Arlem. *Georgana's Secret*
The **Wartime** Sisters: A Novel. Loigman, Lynda Cohen
WASHINGTON (STATE)
  Alexie, Sherman. *Reservation Blues*
  Beagle, Peter S. *Summerlong*
  Bellefleur, Alexandria. *Hang the Moon*
  Bellefleur, Alexandria. *Written in the Stars*
  Brooks, Max. *Devolution: A Firsthand Account of the Rainier Sasquatch Massacre*
  Deaver, Jeffery. ★*The Goodbye Man*
  Dexter, Pete. *Spooner*
  Dimon, HelenKay. *Her Other Secret*
  Dodd, Christina. *Dead Girl Running*
  Dodd, Christina. *Obsession Falls*
  Dodd, Christina. *Virtue Falls*
  Dodd, Christina. *What Doesn't Kill Her*
  Dugoni, Robert. *The Conviction*
  Dugoni, Robert. *In Her Tracks*
  Dugoni, Robert. *Murder One*
  Dugoni, Robert. *My Sister's Grave*
  Evison, Jonathan. ★*Lawn Boy: A Novel*
  Evison, Jonathan. *The Revised Fundamentals of Caregiving: A Novel*
  Evison, Jonathan. *West of Here: A Novel*
  Grodstein, Lauren. *Our Short History*
  Guterson, David. *The Other*
  Guterson, David. *Our Lady of the Forest*
  Guterson, David. ★*Snow Falling on Cedars*
  Hannah, Kristin. *Home Front*
  Holbert, Bruce. *Whiskey*
  Laukkanen, Owen. *Lone Jack Trail*
  Mallery, Susan. ★*When We Found Home*
  Marlantes, Karl. *Deep River*
  Robbins, Tom. ★*Jitterbug Perfume*
  Roberts, Nora. *The Obsession*
  Shalvis, Jill. *Simply Irresistible*
  Shalvis, Jill. *The Sweetest Thing*
  Stein, Garth. *The Art of Racing in the Rain: A Novel*
  Van Dyken, Rachel. *Risky Play*
  Wiggs, Susan. ★*The Oysterville Sewing Circle*
  Wilson, Daniel H. *The Andromeda Evolution: A Novel*
★*Washington* Black: A Novel. Edugyan, Esi
Washington, Bryan
  Lot: Stories
  ★*Memorial*
Washington, D. C.: A Novel. Vidal, Gore
WASHINGTON, D.C.
  Abrams, Stacey. *While Justice Sleeps: A Novel*
  Blatty, William Peter. ★*The Exorcist*

Chiaverini, Jennifer. *Mrs. Lincoln's Dressmaker: A Novel*
Child, Lee. *Without Fail*
Cleage, Pearl. *Some Things I Never Thought I'd Do*
Copenhaver, John. *The Savage Kind*
Cornwell, Patricia Daniels. *Autopsy*
Coulter, Catherine. *Labyrinth*
Deaver, Jeffery. *Edge: A Novel*
Everett, Percival L. *Erasure: A Novel*
Faulks, Sebastian. *On Green Dolphin Street: A Novel*
Finder, Joseph. *Vanished*
Foer, Jonathan Safran. *Here I Am: A Novel*
Gleason, Colleen. *Murder at the Capitol*
Grisham, John. ★*The Pelican Brief*
Harbison, Beth. *The Cookbook Club*
Iweala, Uzodinma. ★*Speak No Evil*
Kurian, Vera. *Never Saw Me Coming*
Lalli, Sonya. *Serena Singh Flips the Script*
Laskowski, Tara. *The Mother Next Door*
McDowell, Christina. ★*The Cave Dwellers: A Novel*
McQuiston, Casey. ★*Red, White & Royal Blue: A Novel*
Meltzer, Brad. *The Inner Circle*
Meltzer, Brad. *The Tenth Justice*
Meltzer, Brad. *The Zero Game*
O'Dell, Claire. *A Study in Honor: A Novel*
Patterson, James. ★*Along Came a Spider: A Novel*
Patterson, James. *Kiss the Girls: A Novel*
Patterson, Richard North. *Balance of Power*
Patterson, Richard North. *Protect and Defend*
Pelecanos, George P. *The Big Blowdown*
Pelecanos, George P. *The Cut: A Novel*
Perry, Anne. ★*A Darker Reality*
Prescott, Lara. *The Secrets We Kept*
Pyper, Andrew. *The Residence: A Novel*
Roosevelt, Elliott. ★*Murder and the First Lady*
Roosevelt, Elliott. *Murder at Midnight*
Roosevelt, Elliott. *Murder in the Map Room: An Eleanor Roosevelt Mystery*
Stead, Christina. ★*The Man Who Loved Children*
Styles, Toy. *Redbone*
Swinson, Kiki. *Wifey*
Swinson, Kiki. *Wifey's Next Sticky Situation*
Vernon, P. J. *Bath Haus: A Thriller*
Vidal, Gore. *Washington, D. C.: A Novel*
Woods, Stuart. *Smooth Operator*
Yellin, Jessica. *Savage News*

WASHINGTON, GEORGE, 1732-1799
Baker, Jo. *The Body Lies*
Calvi, Mary. *Dear George, Dear Mary: A Novel of George Washington's First Love*

Wasserman, Robin
Mother Daughter Widow Wife

Waste Tide. Chen, Qiufan
Watch Her Fall. Kelly, Erin
Watcher in the Woods. Armstrong, Kelley
Watching You. Jewell, Lisa
The *Watchmaker* of Filigree Street. Pulley, Natasha
Watchmaker of Filigree Street series [Series]. Pulley, Natasha

WATER
Bacigalupi, Paolo. ★*The Water Knife*
Jones, Cynan. *Stillicide*
Water City novels [Series]. McKinney, Chris
★*The Water Dancer: A Novel*. Coates, Ta-Nehisi
★*Water for Elephants: A Novel*. Gruen, Sara
The *Water Keeper*. Martin, Charles
★*The Water Knife*. Bacigalupi, Paolo
The *Water Museum: Stories*. Urrea, Luis Alberto
WATER SUPPLY
Ballard, J. G. ★*The Day of Creation*
Cussler, Clive. *Blue Gold: A Novel from the Numa Files*
Watkins, Claire Vaye. ★*Gold Fame Citrus*
WATERGATE SCANDAL
Vonnegut, Kurt. *Jailbird: A Novel*
Waters, Martha
★*To Have and to Hoax: A Novel*
To Love and to Loathe: A Novel
Watershed. Barr, Mark
Watership Down. Adams, Richard
Watkins, Claire Vaye
★*Gold Fame Citrus*
I Love You but I've Chosen Darkness
WATKINS, CLAIRE VAYE
Watkins, Claire Vaye. *I Love You but I've Chosen Darkness*
Watson, Brad
Miss Jane: A Novel
WATSON, EDGAR J, 1855-1910
Egan, Greg. *Schild's Ladder*
Matthiessen, Peter. *Shadow Country: A New Rendering of the Watson Legend*
WATSON, JOHN H. (FICTITIOUS CHARACTER)
Doyle, Arthur Conan. ★*The Complete Sherlock Holmes*
Faye, Lyndsay. *The Whole Art of Detection: Lost Mysteries of Sherlock Holmes*
Watson, Martine Fournier
The Dream Peddler
Watson, S. J.
Final Cut
Watt, Holly
To the Lions
WATTS RIOT, LOS ANGELES, CALIFORNIA, 1965
Mosley, Walter. *Little Scarlet: An Easy Rawlins Mystery*
WATTS, LOS ANGELES, CALIFORNIA
Mosley, Walter. *Devil in a Blue Dress*
Mosley, Walter. *Little Scarlet: An Easy Rawlins Mystery*
Waugh, Evelyn
★*Brideshead Revisited*
★*The Complete Stories of Evelyn Waugh*
Decline and Fall
The Loved One: An Anglo-American Tragedy
★*Vile Bodies*
Waverley family novels [Series]. Allen, Sarah Addison
Waverley novels [Series]. Scott, Walter
Waverley novels
/Tales of my landlord [Series]. Scott, Walter
The Waves. Woolf, Virginia
Waves of freedom [Series]. Sundin, Sarah

WAX MODELLERS
Carey, Edward. *Little: A Novel*
Waxman, Abbi
The Bookish Life of Nina Hill
WAXWORKS
Carey, Edward. *Little: A Novel*
The Way of All Flesh. Parry, Ambrose
Way of all flesh [Series]. Parry, Ambrose
★*The Way of the Coyote*. Kelton, Elmer
The Way of the Dog: A Novel. Savage, Sam
The Way Things Were: A Novel. Taseer, Aatish
The Way Through the Woods. Dexter, Colin
★*The Way to Paradise*. Vargas Llosa, Mario
Wayfarers (Becky Chambers) [Series]. Chambers, Becky
Wayfaring Stranger: A Novel. Burke, James Lee
Wayfinder's Story. Saberhagen, Fred
Wayne, Teddy
Apartment: A Novel
Wayward. Spiotta, Dana
Wayward children [Series]. McGuire, Seanan
★*We*. Zamyatin, Yevgeny Ivanovich
We All Fall Down. Harvey, Michael T.
★*We Are All Completely Beside Ourselves*. Fowler, Karen Joy
We Are All Completely Fine. Gregory, Daryl
We Are All the Same in the Dark: A Novel. Heaberlin, Julia
★*We Are Not Like Them*. Pride, Christine
★*We Are the Brennans*. Lange, Tracey
★*We Begin at the End*. Whitaker, Chris
We Could Be Heroes. Chen, Mike
We Had No Rules: Stories. Manning, Corinne
We Have Always Been Here. Nguyen, Lena
We Have Always Lived in the Castle. Jackson, Shirley
We Hope for Better Things. Bartels, Erin
We Know You Remember. Alsterdal, Tove
We Love You, Charlie Freeman: A Novel. Greenidge, Kaitlyn
We Must Be Brave. Liardet, Frances
We Need New Names: A Novel. Bulawayo, NoViolet
We Need to Talk About Kevin. Shriver, Lionel
We That Are Young: A Novel. Taneja, Preti
We Went to the Woods: A Novel. Dolan-Leach, Caite
★*We Were the Mulvaneys*. Oates, Joyce Carol
We, the Survivors. Aw, Tash
WEALTH
Brockway, Connie. *The Golden Season*
Gaddis, William. ★*J R: A Novel*
Mallery, Susan. ★*When We Found Home*
Shanbhag, Vivek. *Ghachar Ghochar*
Swinson, Kiki. *Lifestyles of the Rich and Shameless*
Wallace, Carol. *Our Kind of People*
WEAPONS
Clark, P. Djeli. *The Black God's Drums*
Cussler, Clive. *Nighthawk: A Novel from the Numa Files*
Cussler, Clive. *The Pharaoh's Secret*
Cussler, Clive. ★*The Rising Sea: A Novel from the Numa Files*
Liu, Cixin. *Ball Lightning*
Rollins, James. ★*The Last Odyssey*
WEAPONS OF MASS DESTRUCTION
Taylor, Brad. ★*Daughter of War: A Novel*

★*Weather*. Offill, Jenny
WEATHER
Coulter, Catherine. *The Devil's Triangle*
Farrow, John. *The Storm Murders: A Thriller*
Weather Girl. Solomon, Rachel Lynn
Weatherspoon, Rebekah
A Cowboy to Remember
If the Boot Fits
Rafe: A Buff Male Nanny
A Thorn in the Saddle
★*Xeni: A Marriage of Inconvenience*
WEATHERWAX, GRANNY (FICTITIOUS CHARACTER)
Pratchett, Terry. *Lords and Ladies: A Novel of Discworld*
Pratchett, Terry. *Witches Abroad*
Pratchett, Terry. *Wyrd Sisters*
★*Weave a Circle Round*. Maaren, Kari
Weaver, Ashley
★*A Peculiar Combination*
★*Weaveworld*. Barker, Clive
Webb, Brandon
★*Steel Fear*
WEBCAMS
Schweblin, Samanta. *Little Eyes*
WEBSITE DESIGNERS
Sloan, Robin. *Mr. Penumbra's 24-Hour Bookstore*
Wecker, Helene
The Golem and the Jinni
★*The Hidden Palace*
The Wedding. West, Dorothy
WEDDING CAKES
Bradley, C. Alan. *The Golden Tresses of the Dead: A Flavia De Luce Novel*
The Wedding Chapel. Hauck, Rachel
WEDDING CONSULTANTS
Sosa, Mia. ★*The Worst Best Man*
★*The Wedding Date*. Guillory, Jasmine
Wedding dates [Series]. Guillory, Jasmine
WEDDING DRESS
Janowitz, Brenda. *The Grace Kelly Dress*
The Wedding Party. Guillory, Jasmine
WEDDING PLANNING
Guillory, Jasmine. *The Wedding Party*
Palmer, Lindsey J. *Otherwise Engaged*
Ross, Ann B. ★*Miss Julia Happily Ever After*
WEDDING PRESENTS
Saramago, Jose. ★*The Elephant's Journey*
WEDDINGS
Beaton, M. C. ★*Hot to Trot*
Bradley, C. Alan. *The Golden Tresses of the Dead: A Flavia De Luce Novel*
Castro, V. *The Queen of the Cicadas*
Clark, Wahida. *Thug Matrimony*
Cocks, Heather. *The Royal We*
Davidson, Diane Mott. *The Last Suppers*
Depestre, Rene. *Hadriana in All My Dreams*
Faulks, Sebastian. *Jeeves and the Wedding Bells*
Foley, Lucy. *The Guest List*
Fredericks, Mariah. *Death of a New American: A Mystery*

Hilderbrand, Elin. *The Perfect Couple*
Jimenez, Abby. *The Friend Zone*
Kantra, Virginia. *Beth & Amy*
Khaw, Cassandra. *Nothing but Blackened Teeth*
Kwan, Kevin. *China Rich Girlfriend*
McCall Smith, Alexander. *The Saturday Big Tent Wedding Party*
Meier, Leslie. *Silver Anniversary Murder*
Phillips, Susan Elizabeth. *Call Me Irresistible*
Pineiro, Caridad. *What Happens in Summer*
Ross, Ann B. ★*Miss Julia Happily Ever After*
Ross, Ann B. *Miss Julia Throws a Wedding*
Salinger, J. D. *Raise High the Roof Beam, Carpenters,: And Seymour—An Introduction.*
Thomas, Will. *Dance with Death*
Weiner, Jennifer. ★*Big Summer*
Welty, Eudora. ★*Delta Wedding*
West, Dorothy. *The Wedding*
*The **Weed** That Strings the Hangman's Bag: A Flavia De Luce Mystery.* Bradley, C. Alan
*A **Week** at the Shore.* Delinsky, Barbara
*A **Week** in December.* Faulks, Sebastian
*A **Week** to Be Wicked.* Dare, Tessa
WEEKENDS
Hilderbrand, Elin. ★*28 Summers*
Poissant, David James. *Lake Life*
Urrea, Luis Alberto. ★*The House of Broken Angels*
Weiden, David L.
★*Winter Counts*
WEIGHT CONTROL
Thomas, Scarlett. *Oligarchy*
*The **Weight** of a Piano: A Novel.* Cander, Chris
*The **Weight** of Water.* Shreve, Anita
WEIGHTLESSNESS
King, Stephen. *Elevation*
Weinberg, Kate
The Truants
Weiner, Jennifer
★*Big Summer*
In Her Shoes: A Novel
Little Earthquakes
★*Mrs. Everything: A Novel*
Weinstein, Alexander
Children of the New World: Stories
Weir, Alison
Anna of Kleve: The Princess in the Portrait
Katharine Parr, the Sixth Wife
Weir, Andy
Artemis
The Martian
Project Hail Mary
*The **Weird** Sisters.* Brown, Eleanor
WEIRD WESTERNS
Bear, Elizabeth. *Stone Mad*
Gilman, Felix. *The Half-Made World*
Gilman, Laura Anne. *The Cold Eye*
Gilman, Laura Anne. *Silver on the Road*
Katsu, Alma. *The Hunger: A Novel*
Malerman, Josh. *Unbury Carol*

Weiss, Elizabeth
The Sisters Sweet
Weiss, Leah
If the Creek Don't Rise: A Novel
*A **Welcome** Murder.* Yocum, Robin
***Welcome** to the Monkey House.* Vonnegut, Kurt
Weldon, Fay
The Life and Loves of a She-Devil
*The **Well**.* Chanter, Catherine
***Well** Matched.* DeLuca, Jen
★***Well** Met.* DeLuca, Jen
***Well** met novels* [Series]. DeLuca, Jen
*A **Well-Behaved** Woman: A Novel of the Vanderbilts.* Fowler, Therese
Wellington, David
Positive
WELLNESS LIFESTYLE
Moriarty, Liane. *Nine Perfect Strangers*
Wells, Benedict
The End of Loneliness: A Novel
Wells, H. G.
The Complete Short Stories of H. G. Wells
★*The Invisible Man*
★*The Island of Dr. Moreau*
★*The Time Machine*
★*The War of the Worlds*
Wells, Martha
All Systems Red
Network Effect
Wells, Rebecca
Divine Secrets of the Ya-Ya Sisterhood: A Novel
***Welsh** trilogy* [Series]. Penman, Sharon Kay
Welsh, Irvine
Dead Men's Trousers
Trainspotting
Welsh, Kaite
The Unquiet Heart
The Wages of Sin
Welty, Eudora
★*The Collected Stories of Eudora Welty*
★*Delta Wedding*
The Optimist's Daughter
★*The Ponder Heart*
★*The Robber Bridegroom*
Stories, Essays & Memoir
WELTY, EUDORA
Burns, Olive Ann. ★*Cold Sassy Tree*
Welty, Eudora. *Stories, Essays & Memoir*
Wendig, Chuck
The Book of Accidents
★*Wanderers: A Novel*
*The **Werewolf** of Bamberg.* Potzsch, Oliver
WEREWOLVES
Dimaline, Cherie. *Empire of Wild*
Duncan, Glen. *By Blood We Live*
Duncan, Glen. *The Last Werewolf*
Duncan, Glen. *Talulla Rising*
Potzsch, Oliver. *The Werewolf of Bamberg*
Pratchett, Terry. *The Fifth Elephant: A Novel of Discworld*

Spear, Terry. *A Billionaire Wolf for Christmas*
Turnbull, Cadwell. *No Gods, No Monsters*
Werfel, Franz
  ★*The Forty Days of Musa Dagh*
WESSEX, ENGLAND
  Hardy, Thomas. ★*Tess of the D'urbervilles: A Pure Woman Faithfully Presented*
West. Davies, Carys
WEST AFRICA
  D'Souza, Tony. *Whiteman*
  Greene, Graham. ★*The Heart of the Matter*
  Onuzo, Chibundu. *Sankofa: A Novel*
  Patterson, Richard North. *Eclipse*
  Smith, Zadie. ★*Swing Time*
  Thompson, Tade. *Rosewater*
  Thompson, Tade. *The Rosewater Insurrection*
  Thompson, Tade. *The Rosewater Redemption*
WEST BANK (JORDAN RIVER)
  Spark, Muriel. ★*The Mandelbaum Gate*
WEST BERLIN, GERMANY
  Boyne, John. ★*A Ladder to the Sky*
West End Earl. Bennett, Bethany
WEST GERMANY
  Fesperman, Dan. *Safe Houses: A Novel*
  Hegi, Ursula. *Stones from the River*
WEST INDIAN AMERICANS
  De Leon, Aya. *Side Chick Nation*
WEST INDIAN WOMEN
  Francis-Sharma, Lauren. ★*Book of the Little Axe*
  Kincaid, Jamaica. *The Autobiography of My Mother*
  Kincaid, Jamaica. ★*Lucy*
WEST INDIANS
  Kincaid, Jamaica. ★*Annie John*
WEST INDIES
  Gabaldon, Diana. ★*Voyager*
  Hilderbrand, Elin. ★*Troubles in Paradise*
  Hilderbrand, Elin. ★*What Happens in Paradise: A Novel*
  Hilderbrand, Elin. ★*Winter in Paradise: A Novel*
  Hoffman, Alice. *The Marriage of Opposites: A Novel Based on the Life of Rachel Pizzarro*
  Naipaul, V. S. *Guerrillas*
  Phillips, Caryl. *A View of the Empire at Sunset*
  Rhys, Jean. ★*Wide Sargasso Sea*
  Riley, Vanessa. ★*Island Queen*
  Willig, Lauren. *The Summer Country: A Novel*
West of Here: A Novel. Evison, Jonathan
WEST POINT, NEW YORK
  Bayard, Louis. *The Pale Blue Eye: A Novel*
  Jakes, John. ★*North and South*
WEST SUSSEX, ENGLAND
  Griffiths, Elly. *The Stranger Diaries*
WEST TEXAS
  Heaberlin, Julia. *We Are All the Same in the Dark: A Novel*
  McCarthy, Cormac. ★*All the Pretty Horses*
WEST VIRGINIA
  Fabry, Chris. *The Promise of Jesse Woods*
  Gordon, Jaimy. ★*Lord of Misrule: A Novel*
  Harman, Patricia. *The Midwife of Hope River: A Novel*

Keller, Julia. ★*Bone on Bone*
Keller, Julia. *A Killing in the Hills*
Phillips, Jayne Anne. *Lark and Termite: A Novel*
Pollock, Donald Ray. *The Devil All the Time*
Whitehead, Colson. *John Henry Days: A Novel*
West, Dorothy
  The Wedding
West, Jessamyn
  The Friendly Persuasion
West, Kathleen
  Minor Dramas & Other Catastrophes
West, Monica
  Revival Season: A Novel
West, Nathanael
  Novels and Other Writings
WESTCHESTER COUNTY, NEW YORK
  Lange, Tracey. ★*We Are the Brennans*
Westcott novels [Series]. Balogh, Mary
Westering Women: A Novel. Dallas, Sandra
WESTERN AUSTRALIA
  Winton, Tim. *The Shepherd's Hut*
WESTERN ROMANCES
  Bittner, Rosanne. *Logan's Lady*
  Dell, Kari Lynn. *Fearless in Texas*
  Dell, Kari Lynn. *Mistletoe in Texas*
  Dell, Kari Lynn. *Reckless in Texas*
  Drake, Laura. *The Sweet Spot*
  Goodman, Jo. *In Want of a Wife*
  Goodman, Jo. *A Touch of Forever*
  Jenkins, Beverly. *Forbidden*
  Jenkins, Beverly. *Tempest*
  London, Julia. *The Charmer in Chaps*
  Phillips, Susan Elizabeth. *Call Me Irresistible*
  Phillips, Susan Elizabeth. *What I Did for Love*
  Weatherspoon, Rebekah. *A Cowboy to Remember*
  Weatherspoon, Rebekah. *If the Boot Fits*
  Weatherspoon, Rebekah. *A Thorn in the Saddle*
Western saga [Series]. Guthrie, A. B.
WESTERNS
  Brand, Max. ★*The Collected Stories of Max Brand*
  Brand, Max. *Max Brand's Best Western Stories*
  Brand, Max. *The Stingaree*
  Brooks, Bill. *Blood Storm*
  Brooks, Bill. *Frontier Justice*
  Brooks, Bill. *Winter Kill*
  Coldsmith, Don. *Tallgrass: A Novel of the Great Plains*
  deWitt, Patrick. *The Sisters Brothers: A Novel*
  Dexter, Pete. ★*Deadwood*
  Diaz, Hernan. ★*In the Distance*
  Durham, David Anthony. ★*Gabriel's Story*
  Enger, Lin. *The High Divide: A Novel*
  Estleman, Loren D. *The Adventures of Johnny Vermillion: A Novel*
  Estleman, Loren D. ★*The Master Executioner*
  Everett, Percival L. *God's Country*
  Grey, Zane. ★*Riders of the Purple Sage*
  Grey, Zane. *Woman of the Frontier: A Western Story*
  Groom, Winston. *El Paso: A Novel*
  Guthrie, A. B. ★*The Big Sky*

Hansen, Ron. ★*The Assassination of Jesse James by the Coward Robert Ford*

Harmon, Amy. *Where the Lost Wander*

Harte, Bret. ★*The Best Short Stories of Bret Harte*

Hulse, S. M. *Eden Mine*

Jones, Douglas C. *The Court-Martial of George Armstrong Custer*

Keesey, Anna. *Little Century: A Novel*

Kelton, Elmer. *Hard Ride*

Kelton, Elmer. ★*The Way of the Coyote*

Knott, Robert. *Robert B. Parker's Buckskin*

L'Amour, Louis. ★*Bendigo Shafter*

L'Amour, Louis. *The Californios*

L'Amour, Louis. *End of the Drive*

L'Amour, Louis. *To the Far Blue Mountains*

Lansdale, Joe R. ★*Paradise Sky*

Larison, John. *Whiskey When We're Dry*

Leonard, Elmore. *Charlie Martz and Other Stories: The Unpublished Stories*

Leonard, Elmore. ★*The Complete Western Stories of Elmore Leonard.*

Leonard, Elmore. *The Hot Kid*

Leonard, Elmore. *When the Women Come Out to Dance: Stories*

McCarthy, Cormac. ★*Blood Meridian, Or, the Evening Redness in the West*

McMurtry, Larry. *Boone's Lick: A Novel*

McMurtry, Larry. *Comanche Moon: A Novel*

McMurtry, Larry. ★*Lonesome Dove: A Novel*

McMurtry, Larry. ★*Streets of Laredo: A Novel*

Meyer, Philipp. ★*The Son: A Novel*

Michener, James A. ★*Centennial*

Parker, Robert B. *Appaloosa*

Parker, Robert B. *Blue-Eyed Devil*

Portis, Charles. ★*True Grit: A Novel*

Proulx, Annie. *Bad Dirt: Wyoming Stories 2*

Proulx, Annie. *Fine Just the Way It Is: Wyoming Stories 3*

Russell, Mary Doria. ★*Doc: A Novel*

Russell, Mary Doria. *Epitaph: A Novel of the O.K. Corral*

Schaefer, Jack. *Monte Walsh*

Schaefer, Jack. ★*Shane*

Smith, B. J. *The Return of Kid Cooper: A Novel*

Swarthout, Glendon. ★*The Shootist*

Traven, B. ★*The Treasure of the Sierra Madre*

Westheimer, David
  ★*Von Ryan's Express*

Westlake, Donald E.
  ★*Bank Shot*
  Forever and a Death
  Get Real
  The Hot Rock
  Memory
  The Road to Ruin

Wetmore, Elizabeth
  ★*Valentine*

WEXFORD, CHIEF INSPECTOR (FICTITIOUS CHARACTER)
  Rendell, Ruth. *The Babes in the Wood*
  Rendell, Ruth. *End in Tears*
  Rendell, Ruth. *Harm Done*
  Rendell, Ruth. *Kissing the Gunner's Daughter*
  Rendell, Ruth. *Not in the Flesh*

Rendell, Ruth. *Road Rage*

Rendell, Ruth. *Simisola*

Rendell, Ruth. *A Sleeping Life*

Rendell, Ruth. *Speaker of Mandarin*

Wexler, Django
  Ashes of the Sun

WHALES
  Crummey, Michael. *Galore*

WHALING
  Melville, Herman. ★*Moby-Dick; Or, the Whale*

WHALING SHIPS
  Poe, Edgar Allan. *The Narrative of Arthur Gordon Pym of Nantucket*

Wharton, Edith
  The Children
  Collected Stories, 1891-1910
  ★*Ethan Frome*

★*What a Difference a Duke Makes*. Bell, Lenora

What Are You Going Through. Nunez, Sigrid

What belongs to you [Series]. Greenwell, Garth

What Belongs to You: A Novel. Greenwell, Garth

What Came Before He Shot Her. George, Elizabeth

What Comes My Way. Peterson, Tracie

What Comes Next. Katzenbach, John

What Could Be Saved. Schwarz, Liese O'Halloran

What Doesn't Kill Her. Dodd, Christina

★*What Ever Happened to Baby Jane?*. Farrell, Henry

★*What Happens in Paradise: A Novel*. Hilderbrand, Elin

What Happens in Summer. Pineiro, Caridad

What I Did for Love. Phillips, Susan Elizabeth

What Is Not Yours Is Not Yours: Stories. Oyeyemi, Helen

What Is the What: The Autobiography of Valentino Achak Deng. Eggers, Dave

★*What It Means When a Man Falls from the Sky: Stories*. Arimah, Lesley Nneka

What Looks Like Crazy on an Ordinary Day: A Novel. Cleage, Pearl

What Rose Forgot. Barr, Nevada

What Should Be Wild. Fine, Julia

★*What Storm, What Thunder*. Chancy, Myriam J. A.

What Strange Paradise. El Akkad, Omar

What the Cat Dragged In. James, Miranda

What the Dead Know. Lippman, Laura

★*What the Dead Leave Behind*. Simpson, Rosemary

What the Devil Knows: A Sebastian St. Cyr Mystery. Harris, C. S.

What Was She Thinking?: Notes on a Scandal. Heller, Zoe

What We Become. Perez-Reverte, Arturo

What We Find. Carr, Robyn

What We Lose. Clemmons, Zinzi

What We Owe. Hashemzadeh Bonde, Golnaz

What We Talk About When We Talk About Anne Frank: Stories. Englander, Nathan

What We Talk About When We Talk About Love: Stories. Carver, Raymond

What We Were Promised. Tan, Lucy

What You Don't See. Clark, Tracy P.

What You Wish For. Center, Katherine

What's Done in Darkness: A Novel. McHugh, Laura

What's Left of Me Is Yours: A Novel. Scott, Stephanie

What's Mine and Yours: A Novel. Coster, Naima

★*Whatever Happened to Interracial Love?: Stories*. Collins, Kathleen
WHEELCHAIR USERS
    Leitch, Will. ★*How Lucky*
    Moyes, Jojo. *Me Before You: A Novel*
    Nussbaum, Susan. *Good Kings, Bad Kings: A Novel*
Whelan, Julia
    My Oxford Year
When a Duke Loves a Governess. Drake, Olivia
When a Rogue Meets His Match. Hoyt, Elizabeth
When a Scot Ties the Knot. Dare, Tessa
When All Is Said: A Novel. Griffin, Anne
When All the Girls Have Gone. Krentz, Jayne Ann
When Christ and His Saints Slept. Penman, Sharon Kay
When Ghosts Come Home: A Novel. Cash, Wiley
When I Hit You, Or, a Portrait of the Writer as a Young Wife. Kandasamy, Meena
When I Ran Away. Bannister, Ilona
When Mystical Creatures Attack! Founds, Kathleen
When Red Is Black. Qiu, Xiaolong
★*When She Was Good*. Robotham, Michael
★*When Stars Collide*. Phillips, Susan Elizabeth
★*When Stars Rain Down: A Novel*. Jackson-Brown, Angela
When the Emperor Was Divine: A Novel. Otsuka, Julie
When the Killing's Done: A Novel. Boyle, T. Coraghessan
When the Marquess Met His Match. Guhrke, Laura Lee
★*When the Sacred Ginmill Closes*. Block, Lawrence
★*When the Stars Go Dark: A Novel*. McLain, Paula
When the Women Come Out to Dance: Stories. Leonard, Elmore
When Twilight Breaks. Sundin, Sarah
★*When Two Feathers Fell from the Sky*. Verble, Margaret
When We Cease to Understand the World. Labatut, Benjamin
★*When We Found Home*. Mallery, Susan
When We Were Orphans. Ishiguro, Kazuo
When We Were Vikings. MacDonald, Andrew
★*When Will There Be Good News?: A Novel*. Atkinson, Kate
When You Read This. Adkins, Mary
★*When You See Me: A Novel*. Gardner, Lisa
Where It Hurts: A Gus Murphy Novel. Coleman, Reed Farrel
Where Late the Sweet Birds Sang. Wilhelm, Kate
Where the Crawdads Sing. Owens, Delia
Where the Light Enters. Donati, Sara
Where the Lost Wander. Harmon, Amy
Where the wild hearts are [Series]. Kerr, Laurel
Where'd You Go, Bernadette: A Novel. Semple, Maria
★*Whereabouts*. Lahiri, Jhumpa
Wherever She Goes. Armstrong, Kelley
While Justice Sleeps: A Novel. Abrams, Stacey
While Mortals Sleep: Unpublished Short Fiction. Vonnegut, Kurt
★*While We Were Dating*. Guillory, Jasmine
Whiskey. Holbert, Bruce
Whiskey & Ribbons. Cross-Smith, Leesa
Whiskey When We're Dry. Larison, John
The Whisper Man. North, Alex
Whisper Network: A Novel. Baker, Chandler
Whisper to the Blood: A Kate Shugak Novel. Stabenow, Dana
Whispers of Shadow & Flame. Penelope, L.
Whispers Under Ground. Aaronovitch, Ben

WHISTLE BLOWERS
    Crais, Robert. *A Dangerous Man*
    Finder, Joseph. ★*House on Fire: A Novel*
    Fowler, Christopher. *Bryant & May: Hall of Mirrors : A Peculiar Crimes Unit Mystery*
WHISTLE BLOWING
    Franzen, Jonathan. *Purity*
A Whistling Woman. Byatt, A. S.
Whitaker Island [Series]. Dimon, HelenKay
Whitaker, Chris
    ★*We Begin at the End*
WHITBY, ENGLAND
    Byatt, A. S. ★*Possession: A Romance*
    Robinson, Peter. *The First Cut*
WHITE (COLOR)
    Han, Kang. *The White Book*
The White Book. Han, Kang
The White City. Ramqvist, Karolina
White city trilogy [Series]. Garcia Saenz, Eva
WHITE COLLAR CRIME
    Paretsky, Sara. *Shell Game*
    Spiegelman, Peter. *Black Maps*
White Dancing Elephants: Stories. Bhuvaneswar, Chaya
★*White Fang*. London, Jack
White Hot Silence. Porter, Henry
★*White Houses: A Novel*. Bloom, Amy
White Ivy: A Novel. Yang, Susie
★*White Noise*. DeLillo, Don
White Oleander: A Novel. Fitch, Janet
White People: Stories and Novellas. Gurganus, Allan
WHITE PLAINS, NEW YORK
    Block, Lawrence. *Hit Me: A Keller Novel*
The White Princess. Gregory, Philippa
WHITE PRIVILEGE
    Reid, Kiley. ★*Such a Fun Age*
WHITE SUPREMACISTS
    Atkins, Ace. *The Ranger*
    Child, Lee. ★*Die Trying*
    Clark, P. Djeli. *Ring Shout*
White Tears. Kunzru, Hari
★*White Teeth: A Novel*. Smith, Zadie
★*The White Tiger: A Novel*. Adiga, Aravind
White, Edmund
    A Boy's Own Story
White, Elle Katharine
    Dragonshadow
White, Randy Wayne
    Salt River
White, T. H.
    ★*The Once and Future King*
White: the Great Pursuit. Dekker, Ted
WHITEFIELD, JANE (FICTITIOUS CHARACTER)
    Perry, Thomas. ★*The Left-Handed Twin*
    Perry, Thomas. *Vanishing Act*
Whitehead, Colson
    Apex Hides the Hurt
    ★*Harlem Shuffle*
    The Intuitionist

John Henry Days: A Novel

★*The Nickel Boys: A Novel*

Sag Harbor: A Novel

★*The Underground Railroad: A Novel*

Zone One: A Novel

Whiteley, Aliya

From the Neck up and Other Stories

Whiteman. D'Souza, Tony

★*Whiteout*. Follett, Ken

The Whites: a Novel. Brandt, Harry

★*Whitethorn Woods*. Binchy, Maeve

Whitfield, Clare

People of Abandoned Character

Whitlow, Robert

A Time to Stand

WHITMAN, WALT

Cunningham, Michael. *Specimen Days*

Robinson, Kim Stanley. ★*Blue Mars*

Whittall, Zoe

The Spectacular: A Novel

Whitten, Hannah

For the Wolf

★*Who Fears Death*. Okorafor, Nnedi

Who I Am with You. Hatcher, Robin Lee

Who's Wife Extraordinaire Now. Swinson, Kiki

The Whole Art of Detection: Lost Mysteries of Sherlock Holmes. Faye, Lyndsay

The Whole Way Home. Creech, Sarah

The Whole World Over. Glass, Julia

★*Whose Body?: A Lord Peter Wimsey Novel*. Sayers, Dorothy L.

Whose Waves These Are. Dykes, Amanda

★*The Why of Things*. Winthrop, Elizabeth Hartley

★*Wicked and the Wallflower*. MacLean, Sarah

Wicked City. Atkins, Ace

The Wicked Day. Stewart, Mary

Wicked deceptions [Series]. Shupe, Joanna

Wicked quills of London [Series]. Leigh, Eva

The Wicked Sister. Dionne, Karen

A Wicked Way to Win an Earl. Bradley, Anna

WICKED WITCH OF THE WEST (FICTITIOUS CHARACTER)

Maguire, Gregory. ★*Wicked: The Life and Times of the Wicked Witch of the West : A Novel*

Wicked years [Series]. Maguire, Gregory

★*Wicked: the Life and Times of the Wicked Witch of the West : A Novel*. Maguire, Gregory

WICKEDNESS

Maguire, Gregory. *Son of a Witch: A Novel*

Maguire, Gregory. ★*Wicked: The Life and Times of the Wicked Witch of the West : A Novel*

★*Wide Sargasso Sea*. Rhys, Jean

Wideman, John Edgar

★*American Histories: Stories*

Look for Me and I'll Be Gone: Stories

★*Widespread Panic: A Novel*. Ellroy, James

The Widow of the South. Hicks, Robert

The Widow Queen. Cherezinska, Elzbieta

The Widower's Tale. Glass, Julia

WIDOWERS

Adams, Sara Nisha. ★*The Reading List*

Alexander, Tamera. *With This Pledge*

Arbol, Victor del. *Breathing Through the Wound*

Baldacci, David. *One Summer*

Baldacci, David. *Redemption*

Banville, John. ★*The Sea*

Barclay, Linwood. *Broken Promise*

Bayard, Louis. *The Pale Blue Eye: A Novel*

Begley, Louis. *About Schmidt*

Berg, Elizabeth. *The Story of Arthur Truluv: A Novel*

Brockmeier, Kevin. *The Illumination*

Burke, James Lee. *Robicheaux*

Connolly, John. *The Dirty South*

Daniel, Ray. *Hacked: A Tucker Mystery*

Davies, Carys. *West*

Delaney, J. P. *The Girl Before: A Novel*

Donoghue, Emma. *Akin*

Du Maurier, Daphne. ★*Rebecca*

Dugoni, Robert. *The Conviction*

Dugoni, Robert. *Murder One*

Dunn, Kate. *The Dragonfly*

Erdrich, Louise. *Tracks: A Novel*

Extence, Gavin. *The Universe Versus Alex Woods*

Flores, Fernando A. *Tears of the Trufflepig*

Freeman, Brian. *Goodbye to the Dead*

Ganshert, Katie. *Life After*

Garcia Saenz, Eva. *The Silence of the White City*

Garwood, Julie. *The Bride*

Gelernter, J. H. *Hold Fast*

Glass, Julia. *The Widower's Tale*

Haruf, Kent. ★*Our Souls at Night*

Helprin, Mark. *Paris in the Present Tense*

Hulse, S. M. ★*Black River*

Jenkins, Beverly. *Tempest*

Jiles, Paulette. *News of the World: A Novel*

McKenzie, Alecia. *A Million Aunties*

Moreno, Gus. *This Thing Between US: A Novel*

North, Alex. *The Whisper Man*

O'Brien, Perry Edmond. *Fire in the Blood*

Palahniuk, Chuck. *Lullaby: A Novel*

Palmer, Daniel. *The New Husband*

Percy, Walker. *The Second Coming*

Powers, Richard. ★*Bewilderment: A Novel*

Proulx, Annie. ★*The Shipping News*

Quartey, Kwei. *The Missing American*

Reid, Taylor Jenkins. *Forever, Interrupted: A Novel*

Ross, Adam. *Mr. Peanut*

Schanbacher, Gary Lester. *Crossing Purgatory*

Scottoline, Lisa. *After Anna*

Simonson, Helen. *Major Pettigrew's Last Stand: A Novel*

Spencer, Minerva. *Dangerous*

Stroud, Carsten. *The Shimmer*

Williams, Preslaysa. *A Lowcountry Bride*

Wood, James. *Upstate*

Youngson, Anne. *Meet Me at the Museum*

The Widows. Montgomery, Jess

WIDOWS

Abe, Kobo. *The Woman in the Dunes*

Adamson, Gil. *The Outlander*

Alexander, Victoria. *The Lady Travelers Guide to Larceny with a Dashing Stranger*

Ashley, Jennifer. *Death at the Crystal Palace*

Ashley, Jennifer. *The Madness of Lord Ian Mackenzie*

Aslam, Nadeem. ★*The Golden Legend: A Novel*

Atwood, Margaret. ★*The Blind Assassin*

Balogh, Mary. *The Escape*

Balogh, Mary. ★*Someone to Care*

Balogh, Mary. *Someone to Trust*

Barnard, Robert. *Death of a Literary Widow*

Beaton, M. C. *Pushing up Daisies: An Agatha Raisin Mystery*

Berry, Connie. *A Legacy of Murder*

Bowman, Valerie. *Secrets of a Wedding Night*

Brett, Simon. *Mrs Pargeter's Principle*

Brown, Sandra. ★*Blind Tiger*

Burrowes, Grace. *My One and Only Duke*

Carpenter, Emily. *Until the Day I Die*

Carr, Robyn. ★*Virgin River*

Chiaverini, Jennifer. *Mrs. Lincoln's Sisters*

Christie, Agatha. *Towards Zero*

Coetzee, J. M. ★*Foe*

Collins, Manda. ★*A Lady's Guide to Mischief and Mayhem*

Coughlin, Jack. *In the Crosshairs: A Sniper Novel*

Crow, Sarah McCraw. *The Wrong Kind of Woman*

Delany, Vicki. *Deadly Summer Nights*

Deutermann, Peter T. *Pacific Glory: A Novel*

Dunnett, Dorothy. *Niccolo Rising*

Dybek, Nick. *The Verdun Affair: A Novel*

Edgerton, Clyde. ★*Walking Across Egypt: A Novel*

Erdrich, Louise. *The Master Butchers Singing Club: A Novel*

Frank, Dorothea Benton. *Folly Beach: A Lowcountry Tale*

Giordano, Mario. ★*Auntie Poldi and the Lost Madonna*

Giordano, Paolo. *Like Family*

Gregory, Philippa. *The Constant Princess*

Gregory, Philippa. *The Red Queen: A Novel*

Gregory, Philippa. *The Taming of the Queen*

Gunning, Sally. *Painting the Light*

Gurganus, Allan. *Oldest Living Confederate Widow Tells All*

Halls, Stacey. *The Lost Orphan*

Hammett, Dashiell. ★*The Maltese Falcon*

Hannaham, James. ★*Delicious Foods*

Harmon, Amy. *Where the Lost Wander*

Hatcher, Robin Lee. *Who I Am with You*

Hiaasen, Carl. *Bad Monkey*

Hilderbrand, Elin. ★*Troubles in Paradise*

Hilderbrand, Elin. ★*What Happens in Paradise: A Novel*

Hoffman, Alice. *The Marriage of Opposites: A Novel Based on the Life of Rachel Pizzarro*

Hollis, Lee. *Poppy Harmon Investigates*

Holmes, Linda. ★*Evvie Drake Starts Over: A Novel*

James, Eloisa. ★*Seven Minutes in Heaven*

Jones, Sandie. *The Other Woman*

Kleypas, Lisa. *Cold-Hearted Rake*

L'Amour, Louis. ★*Bendigo Shafter*

L'Amour, Louis. *The Californios*

Lahiri, Jhumpa. *The Lowland: A Novel*

Laukkanen, Owen. *Deception Cove*

Leon, Donna. *Drawing Conclusions: A Commissario Guido Brunetti Mystery*

Lessing, Doris May. *The Sweetest Dream*

Linden, Rachel. *Ascension of Larks*

Long, Julie Anne. ★*Lady Derring Takes a Lover*

Marias, Javier. *The Infatuations*

McBain, Ed. *Alice in Jeopardy*

McMurtry, Larry. ★*Terms of Endearment: A Novel : With a New Preface*

Miller, Sue. ★*Monogamy*

Montgomery, Jess. *The Stills*

Montgomery, Jess. *The Widows*

Moshfegh, Ottessa. ★*Death in Her Hands: A Novel*

Moss, Tara. *The War Widow*

Moyes, Jojo. *The Girl You Left Behind*

Oakley, Colleen. *The Invisible Husband of Frick Island*

Oates, Joyce Carol. *Breathe*

Oates, Joyce Carol. *The Falls: A Novel*

Osborne, Lawrence. *Only to Sleep: A Philip Marlowe Novel*

Pamuk, Orhan. *Silent House*

Patterson, Molly. *Rebellion*

Perry, Sarah. *The Essex Serpent*

Petrie, Nicholas. *The Drifter*

Phillips, Jayne Anne. *Quiet Dell: A Novel*

Phillips, Susan Elizabeth. ★*Dance Away with Me*

Pinter, Jason. *Hide Away*

Priest, Cherie. *Dreadnought*

Quick, Amanda. *Garden of Lies*

Quincy, Diana. *Her Night with the Duke*

Robb, Candace M. *A Twisted Vengeance*

Robertson, Imogen. *Circle of Shadows*

Ross, Ann B. *Miss Julia Throws a Wedding*

Sanders, Lawrence. ★*McNally's Gamble*

Saul, John. *Midnight Voices*

Saums, Mary. *Thistle & Twigg*

Saunders, Kate. *The Case of the Wandering Scholar*

Saunders, Kate. *The Secrets of Wishtide*

Schellman, Katharine. *Silence in the Library*

Sharratt, Mary. *Daughters of the Witching Hill*

Shipman, Viola. *The Heirloom Garden*

Shreve, Anita. *The Last Time They Met: A Novel*

Shreve, Anita. *The Pilot's Wife: A Novel*

Simonson, Helen. *Major Pettigrew's Last Stand: A Novel*

Smith, Lee. *On Agate Hill: A Novel*

Spark, Muriel. ★*A Far Cry from Kensington*

Spencer, Minerva. *Barbarous*

Stansel, Ian. *The Last Cowboys of San Geronimo*

Stewart, Amy. ★*Miss Kopp Investigates*

Straub, Emma. ★*All Adults Here*

Strout, Elizabeth. ★*Oh William!*

Trollope, Anthony. ★*The Eustace Diamonds*

Unger, Lisa. *Under My Skin*

Updike, John. *The Widows of Eastwick*

Waite, Olivia. *The Care and Feeding of Waspish Widows*

Waite, Olivia. ★*The Lady's Guide to Celestial Mechanics*

Waters, Martha. *To Love and to Loathe: A Novel*

Weir, Alison. *Katharine Parr, the Sixth Wife*

The Widows of Eastwick. Updike, John

★*The Widows of Malabar Hill: A Mystery of 1920s Bombay*. Massey, Sujata

Wieland, Liza
  Paris, 7 A.M.

Wiesel, Elie
  ★*Dawn*
  Hostage
  A Mad Desire to Dance: A Novel
  ★*Night, Dawn, the Accident: Three Tales*

WIESEL, ELIE
  Stanley, Michael. *Deadly Harvest*
  Wiesel, Elie. ★*Night, Dawn, the Accident: Three Tales*

Wife 22. Gideon, Melanie

Wife extraordinaire [Series]. Swinson, Kiki

Wife of the Gods: A Novel. Quartey, Kwei

WIFE-KILLING
  Brundage, Elizabeth. ★*All Things Cease to Appear*
  Cook, Thomas H. *Sandrine's Case*
  MacDonald, John D. *The Turquoise Lament*
  Swanson, Peter. *The Kind Worth Killing: A Novel*

Wifey. Swinson, Kiki

Wifey's Next Sticky Situation. Swinson, Kiki

Wifey [Series]. Swinson, Kiki

WIGGIN, ENDER (FICTITIOUS CHARACTER)
  Card, Orson Scott. ★*Ender's Game*

Wiggins novels [Series]. Monroe, Mary

Wiggs, Susan
  ★*The Oysterville Sewing Circle*

WIJSMULLER-MEIJER, TRUUS
  Clayton, Meg Waite. *The Last Train to London*

WILD ANIMALS AS PETS
  London, Jack. ★*White Fang*

WILD CHILDREN
  Bledsoe, Alex. *Wisp of a Thing*

Wild Fire. Cleeves, Ann

Wild Fire. DeMille, Nelson

The Wild Inside: A Novel. Bradbury, Jamey

Wild on My Mind. Kerr, Laurel

The Wild One. Petrie, Nicholas

Wild Rain. Jenkins, Beverly

Wild River [Series]. Snow, Jennifer

WILD WEST SHOWS
  Peterson, Tracie. *What Comes My Way*

Wild Wicked Scot. London, Julia

Wild Wynchesters [Series]. Ridley, Erica

Wilde [Series]. Coben, Harlan

Wilde in Love. James, Eloisa

Wilde Lake. Lippman, Laura

Wilde, Oscar
  ★*The Picture of Dorian Gray*

Wilder, Thornton
  ★*Theophilus North*

WILDERNESS AREAS
  Armstrong, Kelley. *Alone in the Wild*
  Armstrong, Kelley. *Watcher in the Woods*
  Barnett, Karen. *Ever Faithful*

Box, C. J. *The Disappeared*

Box, C. J. *Vicious Circle*

Bradbury, Jamey. *The Wild Inside: A Novel*

Doiron, Paul. *Bad Little Falls: A Novel*

Doiron, Paul. *The Precipice*

Enger, Lin. *The High Divide: A Novel*

ffitch, Madeline. *Stay and Fight*

Henderson, Smith. *Fourth of July Creek*

Howarth, Paul. *Only Killers and Thieves: A Novel*

Jónasson, Ragnar. *The Island*

Keneally, Thomas. *Woman of the Inner Sea*

Lebbon, Tim. *Eden*

Macallister, Greer. ★*The Arctic Fury*

McGuane, Thomas. ★*Cloudbursts: Collected and New Stories*

McLaughlin, James A. *Bearskin*

Proulx, Annie. ★*Barkskins: A Novel*

Stabenow, Dana. ★*Hunter's Moon*

Stabenow, Dana. *No Fixed Line*

WILDERNESS SURVIVAL
  Boyle, T. Coraghessan. *The Terranauts*
  Crace, Jim. *Quarantine*
  Dodd, Christina. *What Doesn't Kill Her*
  Evison, Jonathan. *Legends of the North Cascades: A Novel*
  Fuller, Claire. *Our Endless Numbered Days: A Novel*
  Graff, Andrew J. *Raft of Stars*
  Hannah, Kristin. *The Great Alone*
  Heller, Peter. *The River: A Novel*
  King, Stephen. *The Girl Who Loved Tom Gordon*
  Krivak, Andrew. *The Bear*
  L'Amour, Louis. *The Last of the Breed*
  Nelson, Christina Suzann. *If We Make It Home: A Novel of Faith and Survival in the Oregon Wilderness*

Wilderwood novels [Series]. Whitten, Hannah

Wildes of Lindow Castle [Series]. James, Eloisa

WILDFIRE FIGHTERS
  Buchman, M. L. *Pure Heat*
  Shalvis, Jill. *Second Chance Summer*

WILDFIRES
  Buchman, M. L. *Pure Heat*
  Flanagan, Richard. *The Living Sea of Waking Dreams*
  Goldberg, Lee. *Bone Canyon*

The Wildlands: a Novel. Geni, Abby

WILDLIFE
  Lebbon, Tim. *Eden*

WILDLIFE CONSERVATION
  Ghosh, Amitav. *The Hungry Tide*

WILDLIFE REFUGES
  Drayson, Nicholas. *A Guide to the Birds of East Africa*
  Geni, Abby. *The Lightkeepers: A Novel*

WILDLIFE REINTRODUCTION
  McConaghy, Charlotte. *Once There Were Wolves: A Novel*

WILDLIFE WATCHING
  Drayson, Nicholas. *A Guide to the Birds of East Africa*

Wilhelm, Kate
  Where Late the Sweet Birds Sang

Wilkinson, Lauren
  ★*American Spy: A Novel*

Will Anderson novels [Series]. Johnson, D. E.

Will Trent series [Series]. Slaughter, Karin
Willett, Marcia
  The Garden House
Willi Kraus novels [Series]. Grossman, Paul
William Monk and Hester Latterly mysteries [Series]. Perry, Anne
William Shakespeare novels (Benet Brandreth) [Series]. Brandreth, Benet
William Warwick novels [Series]. Archer, Jeffrey
WILLIAM, OF WYKEHAM, BISHOP OF WINCHESTER, 1324-1404
  Cherryh, C. J. *Foreigner: A Novel of First Contact*
  Robb, Candace M. *The Cross-Legged Knight: An Owen Archer Mystery*
Williams, Beatriz
  All the Ways We Said Goodbye: A Novel of the Ritz Paris
  The Golden Hour
  The Summer Wives
WILLIAMS, BERT, 1874-1922
  Carr, Caleb. *The Angel of Darkness*
  Phillips, Caryl. *Dancing in the Dark*
WILLIAMS, CATHY, B 1844
  Bird, Sarah. *Daughter of a Daughter of a Queen*
  Robb, J. D. *Connections in Death: An Eve Dallas Novel*
Williams, Denise
  The Fastest Way to Fall
  How to Fail at Flirting
Williams, Drew
  The Stars Now Unclaimed
Williams, Eley
  The Liar's Dictionary
Williams, Joy
  Harrow
  Ninety-Nine Stories of God
Williams, Katie
  Tell the Machine Goodnight
Williams, Lara
  A Selfie as Big as the Ritz: Stories
  Supper Club: A Novel
Williams, Niall
  This Is Happiness
Williams, Pip
  The Dictionary of Lost Words
Williams, Preslaysa
  A Lowcountry Bride
Williams, Synithia
  Forbidden Promises
Williams, Tennessee
  ★*Collected Stories*
  ★*The Roman Spring of Mrs. Stone*
WILLIAMS, TENNESSEE
  Castellani, Christopher. *Leading Men: A Novel*
  Hall, Parnell. *Lights! Camera! Puzzles!*
Williams, Tia
  ★*Seven Days in June: A Novel*
WILLIAMSBURG, VIRGINIA
  Frantz, Laura. *The Lacemaker*
WILLIAMSON COUNTY (TENN.)
  Hicks, Robert. *The Widow of the South*

Willig, Lauren
  The Summer Country: A Novel
*A **Willing** Murder*. Deveraux, Jude
Willink, Jocko
  Final Spin
Willis, Connie
  Crosstalk
  ★*Doomsday Book*
Willocks, Tim
  Memo from Turner
WILLS
  Jones, Tanen. *The Better Liar: A Novel*
  Massey, Sujata. ★*The Widows of Malabar Hill: A Mystery of 1920s Bombay*
  Pyper, Andrew. *The Homecoming: A Novel*
  Rhys, Rachel. *Fatal Inheritance*
  Robertson, Michael. *The Baker Street Translation: A Mystery*
  Stabenow, Dana. *Though Not Dead: A Kate Shugak Novel*
  Ware, Ruth. *The Death of Mrs. Westaway*
*The **Wilshire** Sun*. Baldwin, Joshua
Wilsner, Meryl
  ★*Something to Talk About*
Wilson, Carter
  Dead Girl in 2a
Wilson, Daniel H.
  The Andromeda Evolution: A Novel
  The Clockwork Dynasty: A Novel
  Robogenesis: A Novel
Wilson, G. Willow
  Alif the Unseen
  ★*The Bird King*
Wilson, Kevin
  Nothing to See Here
Wilson, Sloan
  ★*The Man in the Gray Flannel Suit*
WILTSHIRE, ENGLAND
  Speller, Elizabeth. *The Strange Fate of Kitty Easton*
WIMSEY, PETER, LORD (FICTITIOUS CHARACTER)
  Sayers, Dorothy L. ★*Busman's Honeymoon*
  Sayers, Dorothy L. ★*Clouds of Witness*
  Sayers, Dorothy L. ★*Gaudy Night*
  Sayers, Dorothy L. *Hangman's Holiday*
  Sayers, Dorothy L. *Have His Carcase*
  Sayers, Dorothy L. *In the Teeth of the Evidence*
  Sayers, Dorothy L. ★*Lord Peter*
  Sayers, Dorothy L. *The Nine Tailors*
  Sayers, Dorothy L. *The Unpleasantness at the Bellona Club*
  Sayers, Dorothy L. ★*Whose Body?: A Lord Peter Wimsey Novel*
Winch, Tara June
  The Yield
*The **Wind-Up** Bird Chronicle*. Murakami, Haruki
Windhall. Barry, Ava
Windham brides [Series]. Burrowes, Grace
★*The **Winds** of War: A Novel*. Wouk, Herman
WINDSOR, EDWARD, DUKE OF, 1894-1972
  Paretsky, Sara. ★*Dead Land*
  Williams, Beatriz. *The Golden Hour*
★*The **Windup** Girl*. Bacigalupi, Paolo

Windy City saga [Series]. Green, Jocelyn
WINE AND WINE MAKING
    Gilman, Laura Anne. *Flesh and Fire*
    Longworth, M. L. *Murder on the Ile Sordou: A Verlaque and Bonnet Provencal Mystery*
    Simenon, Georges. *Maigret and the Wine Merchant*
Winer, Jeanne
    Her Kind of Case
WINERIES
    Brenner, Jamie. *Blush: A Novel*
    Higgins, Kristan. ★*The Best Man*
Winfrey, Kerry
    Not Like the Movies
    Waiting for Tom Hanks: A Novel
The **Wings** of the Dove. James, Henry
Winner bakes all [Series]. Hall, Alexis
WINNIPEG, MANITOBA
    Shields, Carol. ★*The Stone Diaries*
Winslow, De'Shawn Charles
    ★*In West Mills*
Winslow, Don
    The Border
    Broken: Six Short Novels
Winspear, Jacqueline
    The American Agent
    ★*The Consequences of Fear: A Maisie Dobbs Novel*
★**Winter**. Smith, Ali
WINTER
    Fforde, Jasper. ★*Early Riser: A Novel*
    Foley, Lucy. *The Hunting Party*
    Foster, Fiona King. *The Captive: A Novel*
    Rice, Waubgeshig. *Moon of the Crusted Snow: A Novel*
    Sandford, John. ★*Winter Prey*
    Smith, Ali. ★*Winter*
Winter and Night. Rozan, S. J.
★**Winter** Counts. Weiden, David L.
★**Winter** in Paradise: A Novel. Hilderbrand, Elin
Winter Kill. Brooks, Bill
The **Winter** King: A Novel of Arthur. Cornwell, Bernard
★The **Winter** of the Witch. Arden, Katherine
Winter of the World. Follett, Ken
The **Winter** Palace: A Novel of Catherine the Great. Stachniak, Eva
★**Winter** Prey. Sandford, John
WINTER SOLSTICE
    Roanhorse, Rebecca. ★*Black Sun*
WINTER STORMS
    Airth, Rennie. *The Decent Inn of Death*
    Child, Lee. *61 Hours: A Reacher Novel*
    Kirkpatrick, Jane. *One More River to Cross*
Winter's Orbit. Maxwell, Everina
★**Winter's** Tale. Helprin, Mark
Winter, Evan
    The Fires of Vengeance
    ★*The Rage of Dragons*
Winterkill: a Novel. Box, C. J.
Winternight trilogy [Series]. Arden, Katherine
Winters, Ben H.
    The Quiet Boy

Winterson, Jeanette
    ★*Frankissstein*
    The Passion
★The **Winthrop** Woman. Seton, Anya
WINTHROP, ELIZABETH, CA 1610-CA 1668
    Grenville, Kate. *Sarah Thornhill*
    Seton, Anya. ★*The Winthrop Woman*
Winthrop, Elizabeth Hartley
    The Mercy Seat: A Novel
    ★*The Why of Things*
Winton, Tim
    The Shepherd's Hut
Wired. Garwood, Julie
WISCONSIN
    Beverly, William. *Dodgers: A Novel*
    Butler, Nickolas. ★*The Hearts of Men*
    Butler, Nickolas. *Little Faith: A Novel*
    Child, Lee. *The Midnight Line*
    Galligan, John. *Bad Moon Rising*
    Graff, Andrew J. *Raft of Stars*
    Hamilton, Jane. *A Map of the World*
    Horan, Nancy. *Loving Frank: A Novel*
    Packer, Ann. *The Dive from Clausen's Pier*
    Rojstaczer, Stuart. *The Mathematician's Shiva: A Novel*
    Sandford, John. ★*Winter Prey*
    Schwarz, Christina. *Drowning Ruth*
    Straub, Peter. ★*Mystery*
    Wright, Jaime Jo. *The Haunting at Bonaventure Circus*
WISDOM
    Coelho, Paulo. ★*The Alchemist*
    Saberhagen, Fred. *Wayfinder's Story*
★**Wise** Blood. O'Connor, Flannery
The **Wise** Friend. Campbell, Ramsey
★The **Wise** Man's Fear. Rothfuss, Patrick
Wiseman, Beth
    Listening to Love
Wiseman, Ellen Marie
    The Orphan Collector
Wish You Were Here. Brown, Rita Mae
Wish You Were Here. Swift, Graham
★**Wish** You Were Here: A Novel. Picoult, Jodi
WISHING AND WISHES
    Binchy, Maeve. ★*Whitethorn Woods*
    Hoffman, Alice. *The Ice Queen: A Novel*
    Lauren, Christina. *In a Holidaze*
    Shalvis, Jill. *Sweet Little Lies*
    Stein, Garth. *The Art of Racing in the Rain: A Novel*
Wishing for Us. Landon, Sydney
Wisp of a Thing. Bledsoe, Alex
The **Wisteria** Society of Lady Scoundrels. Holton, India
★The **Witch** Elm: A Novel. French, Tana
WITCH HUNTING
    Conde, Maryse. *I, Tituba, Black Witch of Salem*
The **Witch** of Exmoor. Drabble, Margaret
★The **Witch's** Heart. Gornichec, Genevieve
WITCHCRAFT
    Blakemore, A. K. *The Manningtree Witches*
    Brom. *Slewfoot: A Tale of Bewitchery*

Hoffman, Alice. *The Book of Magic*
Hoffman, Alice. *The Rules of Magic: A Novel*
Lackberg, Camilla. *The Golden Cage*
Lowe, Kathryn A. *The Furies*
McCall Smith, Alexander. *Blue Shoes and Happiness*
Olson, Neil. *Before the Devil Fell*
Potzsch, Oliver. *The Hangman's Daughter: A Historical Novel*
Scott, A. D. *A Kind of Grief: A Novel*
Sharratt, Mary. *Daughters of the Witching Hill*
Sterling, Erin. *The Ex Hex*

WITCHCRAFT — HISTORY
Conde, Maryse. *I, Tituba, Black Witch of Salem*
Sharratt, Mary. *Daughters of the Witching Hill*

WITCHES
Barnhill, Kelly Regan. *Dreadful Young Ladies and Other Stories*
Beaton, M. C. *Agatha Raisin and the Witch of Wyckhadden*
Brockway, Connie. *So Enchanting*
Gornichec, Genevieve. ★*The Witch's Heart*
Harkness, Deborah E. *The Book of Life*
Harkness, Deborah E. *A Discovery of Witches: A Novel*
Harkness, Deborah E. *Shadow of Night*
Harkness, Deborah E. *The World of All Souls: The Complete Guide to a Discovery of Witches, Shadow of Night, and the Book*
Hoffman, Alice. *The Book of Magic*
Hoffman, Alice. *The Rules of Magic: A Novel*
Maguire, Gregory. *The Brides of Maracoor*
Maguire, Gregory. *Son of a Witch: A Novel*
Maguire, Gregory. ★*Wicked: The Life and Times of the Wicked Witch of the West : A Novel*
Makumbi, Jennifer Nansubuga. ★*A Girl Is a Body of Water*
Marillier, Juliet. *Daughter of the Forest*
Miller, Madeline. ★*Circe*
Novik, Naomi. *A Deadly Education: A Novel*
Novik, Naomi. *The Last Graduate: A Novel*
Novik, Naomi. ★*Uprooted*
Polk, C. L. *The Midnight Bargain*
Polk, C. L. *Soulstar*
Polk, C. L. *Stormsong*
Power, Susan. *The Grass Dancer*
Pratchett, Terry. *Lords and Ladies: A Novel of Discworld*
Pratchett, Terry. *Witches Abroad*
Pratchett, Terry. *Wyrd Sisters*
Rice, Anne. *Merrick: A Novel*
Stewart, Mary. *The Last Enchantment*
Stirling, S. M. *The Protector's War*
Updike, John. ★*The Witches of Eastwick*
Witches Abroad. Pratchett, Terry
★*The Witches of Eastwick*. Updike, John
Witchmark. Polk, C. L.
With Our Blessing: An Inspector Tom Reynolds Mystery. Spain, Jo
With Teeth: A Novel. Arnett, Kristen N.
With This Pledge. Alexander, Tamera
Within a Budding Grove. Proust, Marcel
Within the Sanctuary of Wings: A Memoir by Lady Trent. Brennan, Marie
Without Fail. Child, Lee
The Witness. Brown, Sandra

WITNESSES
Aaronovitch, Ben. *Midnight Riot*

Adiga, Aravind. ★*Amnesty*
Beverly, William. *Dodgers: A Novel*
Box, C. J. ★*Wolf Pack*
Connelly, Michael. *The Fifth Witness*
Grisham, John. *The Client*
Grisham, John. ★*The Pelican Brief*
Hannah, Sophie. *Keep Her Safe*
Hill Gumbao, Toni. *The Summer of Dead Toys*
Leitch, Will. ★*How Lucky*
Leonard, Elmore. ★*Killshot*
Lippman, Laura. *No Good Deeds*
Perry, Thomas. *Vanishing Act*
Sager, Riley. *The Last Time I Lied: A Novel*
Truss, Lynne. *The Man That Got Away: A Constable Twitten Mystery*
Yates, Christopher J. *Grist Mill Road: A Novel*

WITNESSES — PROTECTION
Child, Lee. *61 Hours: A Reacher Novel*
Roslund, Anders. ★*Knock Knock*
Wittgenstein's Nephew: A Friendship. Bernhard, Thomas
The Wives. Fisher, Tarryn

WIZARDS
Aaronovitch, Ben. *Broken Homes*
Aaronovitch, Ben. *Midnight Riot*
Aaronovitch, Ben. *Whispers Under Ground*
Baker, Kage. *The House of the Stag*
Bear, Elizabeth. *Range of Ghosts*
Bear, Elizabeth. *The Red-Stained Wings*
Bear, Elizabeth. *Shattered Pillars*
Bear, Elizabeth. *The Stone in the Skull*
Cho, Zen. *Sorcerer to the Crown*
Cornwell, Bernard. *The Winter King: A Novel of Arthur*
Davis, Kathryn. *Duplex*
Gilman, Laura Anne. *Flesh and Fire*
Grossman, Lev. *The Magician King: A Novel*
Grossman, Lev. *The Magician's Land: A Novel*
Kay, Guy Gavriel. *Tigana*
Larkwood, A. K. *The Unspoken Name*
Le Guin, Ursula K. *The Other Wind*
Lyons, Jenn. *The Name of All Things*
Novik, Naomi. ★*Uprooted*
Pratchett, Terry. *Equal Rites*
Pratchett, Terry. *The Last Hero: A Discworld Fable*
Pratchett, Terry. *Reaper Man*
Pratchett, Terry. *Thief of Time*
Putney, Mary Jo. *The Marriage Spell: A Novel*
Rothfuss, Patrick. ★*The Name of the Wind*
Saberhagen, Fred. *Sightblinder's Story*
Saberhagen, Fred. *Wayfinder's Story*
Stewart, Mary. ★*The Crystal Cave*
Stewart, Mary. ★*The Hollow Hills*
Stewart, Mary. *The Last Enchantment*
Tolkien, J. R. R. *The Children of Hurin*
Tolkien, J. R. R. *The Fall of Gondolin*
Tolkien, J. R. R. ★*The Hobbit, Or, There and Back Again*
White, T. H. ★*The Once and Future King*

Wodehouse, P. G.
★*The Inimitable Jeeves*
My Man Jeeves

Wojtas, Olga
   Miss Blaine's Prefect and the Golden Samovar
*The **Wolf** and the Woodsman*. Reid, Ava
★***Wolf** Hall*. Mantel, Hilary
Wolf Hall trilogy [Series]. Mantel, Hilary
*A **Wolf** in Duke's Clothing*. Allen, Susanna
***Wolf** in White Van: A Novel*. Darnielle, John
***Wolf** on a String: A Novel*. Black, Benjamin
★***Wolf** Pack*. Box, C. J.
WOLF PACKS
   Spear, Terry. *A Billionaire Wolf for Christmas*
***Wolf** Point*. Smith, Ian
***Wolf** Season*. Benedict, Helen
*The **Wolf** Wants In: A Novel*. McHugh, Laura
Wolf, Dick
   The Ultimatum
WOLFDOGS
   Stabenow, Dana. ★*Less Than a Treason*
Wolfe family novels [Series]. Blake, James Carlos
Wolfe, Gene
   ★*The Best of Gene Wolfe: A Definitive Retrospective of His Finest Short Fiction*
   The Citadel of the Autarch
   The Claw of the Conciliator
   The Land Across
Wolfe, Paul
   The Lost Diary of M
Wolfe, Suzanne M.
   The Course of All Treasons
Wolfe, Thomas
   ★*Look Homeward, Angel: A Story of a Buried Life*
   ★*Of Time and the River: A Legend of Man's Hunger in His Youth*
Wolfe, Tom
   Back to Blood: A Novel
   The Bonfire of the Vanities
Wolff, Tobias
   Old School: A Novel
   Our Story Begins: New and Selected Stories
Wolitzer, Meg
   The Female Persuasion
   The Interestings
WOLVES
   Allen, Susanna. *A Wolf in Duke's Clothing*
   Bear, Elizabeth. *Steles of the Sky*
   Doiron, Paul. *Almost Midnight*
   Johnson, Craig. *Land of Wolves*
   London, Jack. ★*The Call of the Wild*
   McCarthy, Cormac. *The Crossing*
   McConaghy, Charlotte. *Once There Were Wolves: A Novel*
   Whitten, Hannah. *For the Wolf*
***Wolves** Eat Dogs: A Novel*. Smith, Martin Cruz
*The **Woman** Destroyed*. Beauvoir, Simone de
*The **Woman** in Cabin Ten*. Ware, Ruth
*The **Woman** in the Dunes*. Abe, Kobo
*The **Woman** in the Mirror*. James, Rebecca
*The **Woman** in the Purple Skirt: A Novel*. Imamura, Natsuko
★*The **Woman** in the Window*. Finn, A. J.
★*The **Woman** in White*. Collins, Wilkie

★*A **Woman** of Intelligence*. Tanabe, Karin
★*A **Woman** of Substance*. Bradford, Barbara Taylor
***Woman** of the Frontier: A Western Story*. Grey, Zane
***Woman** of the Inner Sea*. Keneally, Thomas
★*The **Woman** Upstairs: A Novel*. Messud, Claire
*The **Woman** Who Couldn't Scream*. Dodd, Christina
*The **Woman** Who Spoke to Spirits*. Clare, Alys
★*The **Woman** Who Walked into Doors*. Doyle, Roddy
WOMANIZERS
   Alexander, Victoria. *The Lady Travelers Guide to Scoundrels and Other Gentlemen*
   Armstrong, Richard. *The Don Con*
   Balogh, Mary. ★*Someone to Care*
   Bell, Lenora. *One Fine Duke*
   Bradley, Anna. *A Season of Ruin*
   Bradley, Anna. *A Wicked Way to Win an Earl*
   Cole, Alyssa. ★*A Prince on Paper*
   Dare, Tessa. ★*The Governess Game*
   Dare, Tessa. ★*Say Yes to the Marquess*
   Dare, Tessa. ★*The Wallflower Wager*
   Dupont, Eric. *The American Fiancee: A Novel*
   Guhrke, Laura Lee. *The Trouble with True Love*
   Guhrke, Laura Lee. *When the Marquess Met His Match*
   Heiny, Katherine. ★*Early Morning Riser*
   Kleypas, Lisa. *Cold-Hearted Rake*
   Leigh, Eva. *Forever Your Earl*
   London, Julia. *The Charmer in Chaps*
   MacLean, Sarah. *The Rogue Not Taken*
WOMEN
   Ahern, Cecelia. *Roar*
   Allende, Isabel. ★*Eva Luna*
   Amado, Jorge. ★*Dona Flor and Her Two Husbands: A Moral and Amorous Tale*
   Babalola, Bolu. *Love in Color: Mythical Tales from Around the World, Retold*
   Balaskovits, A. A. *Magic for Unlucky Girls: Stories*
   Beattie, Ann. *The State We're In: Maine Stories*
   Bergman, Megan Mayhew. *Almost Famous Women: Stories*
   Bhuvaneswar, Chaya. *White Dancing Elephants: Stories*
   Binchy, Maeve. *Circle of Friends*
   Bronte, Anne. *The Tenant of Wildfell Hall*
   Butler, Octavia E. *Bloodchild: And Other Stories*
   Cameron, Lindsay. *Just One Look*
   Castro, V. *The Queen of the Cicadas*
   Cole, Alyssa. ★*A Prince on Paper*
   Conroy, Pat. *The Prince of Tides*
   D'Eramo, Luce. *Deviation*
   Dalcher, Christina. *Femlandia*
   Desai, Anita. *Clear Light of Day*
   Desai, Anita. *Fire on the Mountain*
   Egan, Greg. *Phoresis*
   Ellis, Helen. *American Housewife: Stories*
   Flagg, Fannie. ★*Fried Green Tomatoes at the Whistle Stop Cafe*
   Forster, E. M. ★*Howards End*
   Fowles, John. ★*The French Lieutenant's Woman*
   Fuentes, Carlos. *The Years with Laura Diaz*
   Gainza, Maria. *The Optic Nerve*
   Gilchrist, Ellen. ★*Collected Stories*

Gordimer, Nadine. *The Pickup*
Griffiths, Elly. *The Stranger Diaries*
Hardy, Thomas. ★*The Return of the Native*
Hashemzadeh Bonde, Golnaz. *What We Owe*
Hassib, Rajia. *A Pure Heart: A Novel*
Howland, Bette. *Calm Sea and Prosperous Voyage*
Ishiguro, Kazuo. ★*Never Let Me Go*
Johnson, Caleb. *Treeborne*
Kelly, Martha Hall. *Lilac Girls*
Keneally, Thomas. *Woman of the Inner Sea*
Kincaid, Jamaica. *The Autobiography of My Mother*
Leon, Donna. ★*Transient Desires*
Machado, Carmen Maria. *Her Body and Other Parties: Stories*
Miller, Kei. ★*Augustown*
Mohamed, Nadifa. *The Orchard of Lost Souls: A Novel*
Montimore, Margarita. *Oona Out of Order*
Munro, Alice. *Hateship, Friendship, Courtship, Loveship, Marriage: Stories*
Munro, Alice. *Open Secrets: Stories*
Munro, Alice. *Runaway: Stories*
Munro, Alice. *Selected Stories*
Munro, Alice. *Too Much Happiness: Stories*
Munro, Alice. *The View from Castle Rock: Stories*
Nin, Anais. *Cities of the Interior*
Peters, Torrey. ★*Detransition, Baby*
Phillips, Julia. ★*Disappearing Earth*
Polansky, Daniel. *The Seventh Perfection*
Price, Reynolds. *Roxanna Slade*
Rader-Day, Lori. ★*The Lucky One*
Rhys, Jean. ★*Wide Sargasso Sea*
Richardson, C. S. *The End of the Alphabet*
Rush, Norman. ★*Mating*
Rushdie, Salman. *The Enchantress of Florence: A Novel*
Schanoes, Veronica L. *Burning Girls and Other Stories*
Schwartz, John Burnham. *The Commoner: A Novel*
See, Lisa. *Peony in Love: A Novel*
Sexton, Margaret Wilkerson. *The Revisioners: A Novel*
Shields, Carol. ★*The Stone Diaries*
Solomon, Rivers. *The Deep*
Spencer, Elizabeth. *The Southern Woman: New and Selected Fiction*
Starling, Caitlin. *The Death of Jane Lawrence*
Stein, Gertrude. ★*Three Lives*
Swamy, Shruti. *A House Is a Body: Stories*
Sweeney-Baird, Christina. *The End of Men*
Ugresic, Dubravka. *Fox*
Unsworth, Emma Jane. *Grown Ups*
Walker, Alice. *You Can't Keep a Good Woman Down: Stories*
Woolf, Virginia. ★*To the Lighthouse*
WOMEN — BOOKS AND READING
Heller, L. Alison. *The Neighbor's Secret*
WOMEN — DEATH
Cullen, Helen. *The Dazzling Truth*
O'Donnell, Paraic. *The House on Vesper Sands: A Novel*
WOMEN — FAMILY RELATIONSHIPS
Lim, Roselle. *Natalie Tan's Book of Luck and Fortune*
Ryan, Jennifer. *The Spies of Shilling Lane: A Novel*
Sarton, May. *A Reckoning: A Novel*
Waxman, Abbi. *The Bookish Life of Nina Hill*

WOMEN — HISTORY
Gaskell, Elizabeth Cleghorn. ★*Cranford*
WOMEN — IDENTITY
Ali, Monica. ★*Brick Lane: A Novel*
Kaufman, Sue. *Diary of a Mad Housewife*
Medie, Peace A. *His Only Wife: A Novel*
Munro, Alice. *Lives of Girls and Women*
Pynchon, Thomas. ★*V: A Novel*
Savas, Aysegul. *Walking on the Ceiling*
Wasserman, Robin. *Mother Daughter Widow Wife*
WOMEN — INTERPERSONAL RELATIONS
Allende, Isabel. ★*Eva Luna*
Atwood, Margaret. ★*The Testaments: A Novel*
Center, Katherine. *How to Walk Away: A Novel*
Fielding, Joy. *All the Wrong Places: A Novel*
Frank, Dorothea Benton. *Queen Bee*
Gay, Roxane. ★*Difficult Women*
McFarlane, Mhairi. *Don't You Forget About Me*
WOMEN — MENTAL HEALTH
Audrain, Ashley. *The Push*
WOMEN — MYTHOLOGY
MacLaughlin, Nina. *Wake, Siren: Ovid Resung*
WOMEN — PERSONAL CONDUCT
Carey, M. R. *Someone Like Me*
WOMEN — PSYCHOLOGY
Blundell, Judy. *The High Season: A Novel*
Butland, Stephanie. *The Lost for Words Bookshop: A Novel*
Center, Katherine. *Things You Save in a Fire*
Gay, Roxane. ★*Difficult Women*
Pochoda, Ivy. ★*These Women*
Spark, Muriel. *The Driver's Seat*
Stridsberg, Sara. *Valerie: Or the Faculty of Dreams : Amendment to the Theory of Sexuality*
Wasserman, Robin. *Mother Daughter Widow Wife*
WOMEN — RELIGIOUS LIFE
Turner, Bethany. *The Secret Life of Sarah Hollenbeck*
WOMEN — SEXUALITY
Amado, Jorge. ★*Dona Flor and Her Two Husbands: A Moral and Amorous Tale*
Broder, Melissa. *Milk Fed*
Lawrence, D. H. *Women in Love*
Whittall, Zoe. *The Spectacular: A Novel*
WOMEN — SOCIAL CONDITIONS
Alexander, V. S. *The Magdalen Girls*
Bronte, Anne. *The Tenant of Wildfell Hall*
Dangarembga, Tsitsi. *This Mournable Body*
Dunant, Sarah. *Sacred Hearts: A Novel*
Galsworthy, John. ★*The Forsyte Saga*
Kibler, Julie. *Home for Erring and Outcast Girls*
Shafak, Elif. ★*10 Minutes 38 Seconds in This Strange World*
Zola, Emile. ★*Nana*
WOMEN — SOCIAL LIFE AND CUSTOMS
Evaristo, Bernardine. ★*Girl, Woman, Other*
WOMEN — SPIRITUAL LIFE
Gilbert, Elizabeth. ★*The Signature of All Things: A Novel*
Twain, Mark. *Personal Recollections of Joan of Arc*
WOMEN — SUFFRAGE
Davis, Fiona. *The Lions of Fifth Avenue: A Novel*

WOMEN ABOLITIONISTS
Kidd, Sue Monk. ★*The Invention of Wings: A Novel*

WOMEN ACTUARIES
Bellefleur, Alexandria. *Written in the Stars*

WOMEN ADMINISTRATIVE ASSISTANTS
McCall Smith, Alexander. *Blue Shoes and Happiness*
McCall Smith, Alexander. *The Full Cupboard of Life*
McCall Smith, Alexander. *The Good Husband of Zebra Drive*
McCall Smith, Alexander. *In the Company of Cheerful Ladies*

WOMEN ADOPTEES
Pope, Jamie. *One Warm Winter*

WOMEN ADVENTURERS
Macallister, Greer. ★*The Arctic Fury*

WOMEN AMATEUR DETECTIVES
Akunin, B. *Sister Pelagia and the White Bulldog: A Mystery*
Andrew, Sally. *The Satanic Mechanic: A Tannie Maria Mystery*
Andrews, Donna. *Murder Most Fowl: A Meg Langslow Mystery*
Andrews, Donna. *Owl Be Home for Christmas: A Meg Langslow Mystery*
Andrews, Donna. *The Twelve Jays of Christmas: A Meg Langslow Mystery*
Barr, Nevada. *Track of the Cat*
Belli, Kate. *Deception by Gaslight: A Gilded Gotham Mystery*
Bernhard, Emilia. *The Books of the Dead*
Berry, Connie. *A Legacy of Murder*
Boyle, William. *The Lonely Witness*
Brett, Simon. *Guilt at the Garage*
Burns, V. M. *Killer Words*
Childs, Laura. *Egg Shooters*
Childs, Laura. *Haunted Hibiscus*
Childs, Laura. *Lavender Blue Murder*
Childs, Laura. *Twisted Tea Christmas*
Christie, Agatha. *The Body in the Library: A Miss Marple Mystery*
Christie, Agatha. ★*The Murder at the Vicarage*
Christie, Agatha. *A Murder Is Announced: A Miss Marple Mystery*
Christie, Agatha. *Three Blind Mice, and Other Stories*
Cleland, Jane K. *Hidden Treasure*
Connolly, Sheila. *The Lost Traveller*
Dahl, Julia. *Conviction*
Davidson, Diane Mott. *Killer Pancake*
Delany, Vicki. *Murder in a Teacup*
Ellis, Bella. *The Vanished Bride*
Fredericks, Mariah. *Death of a New American: A Mystery*
Freeman, Dianne. *A Fiancee's Guide to First Wives and Murder*
Freeman, Dianne. *A Lady's Guide to Etiquette and Murder*
Garrett, Kellye. ★*Hollywood Homicide*
Gaspar de Alba, Alicia. *Desert Blood: The Juarez Murders*
Gates, Eva. *Read and Buried*
Giordano, Mario. ★*Auntie Poldi and the Lost Madonna*
Giordano, Mario. *Auntie Poldi and the Vineyards of Etna*
Graves, Stephanie. *Olive Bright, Pigeoneer*
Greenwood, Kerry. *Unnatural Habits*
Griffiths, Elly. *The Stranger Diaries*
Hall, Parnell. *Lights! Camera! Puzzles!*
Hambly, Barbara. *Scandal in Babylon*
Harrison, Cora. *Beyond Absolution: A Mystery Set in 1920s Ireland*
Hart, Carolyn G. *Ghost Blows a Kiss*
Hart, Elsa. *The Cabinets of Barnaby Mayne*

Heley, Veronica. *Murder in Law*
Hollis, Lee. *Poppy Harmon Investigates*
Logan, Kylie. *The Secrets of Bones: A Mystery*
Lourey, Jess. ★*January Thaw: A Murder-By-Month Mystery*
Manansala, Mia P. ★*Arsenic and Adobo*
McCall Smith, Alexander. ★*The Geometry of Holding Hands*
McKevett, G. A. *Murder at Mabel's Motel*
McKevett, G. A. *Murder in the Corn Maze*
McKinlay, Jenn. *Killer Research*
McPherson, Catriona. *Scot & Soda*
Meier, Leslie. *Silver Anniversary Murder*
Montclair, Allison. *The Right Sort of Man*
Montclair, Allison. *A Royal Affair*
Moshfegh, Ottessa. ★*Death in Her Hands: A Novel*
O'Connor, Carlene. *Murder in an Irish Bookshop*
O'Donohue, Clare. *The Lover's Knot: A Someday Quilts Mystery*
Perkins, S. C. *Murder Once Removed*
Rader-Day, Lori. *Little Pretty Things*
Raybourn, Deanna. *A Dangerous Collaboration*
Raybourn, Deanna. ★*A Murderous Relation*
Raybourn, Deanna. *A Perilous Undertaking: A Veronica Speedwell Mystery*
Raybourn, Deanna. *A Treacherous Curse: A Veronica Speedwell Mystery*
Robb, Candace M. *A Murdered Peace*
Robb, Candace M. *A Twisted Vengeance*
Robertson, Imogen. *Anatomy of Murder*
Robertson, Imogen. *Instruments of Darkness: A Novel*
Ross, Ann B. *Miss Julia Takes the Wheel*
Saums, Mary. *Thistle & Twigg*
Schaffhausen, Joanna. *Gone for Good*
Schellman, Katharine. *Silence in the Library*
Shaw, M. B. *Murder at the Mill: A Mystery*
Simpson, Rosemary. *Let the Dead Keep Their Secrets*
Simpson, Rosemary. ★*What the Dead Leave Behind*
Stewart, Amy. ★*Miss Kopp Investigates*

WOMEN AND DOGS
Hogan, Ruth. *Queenie Malone's Paradise Hotel*
Koontz, Dean R. *The Darkest Evening of the Year*
Laukkanen, Owen. *Lone Jack Trail*

WOMEN AND NATURE
Powers, Richard. ★*The Overstory: A Novel*
Watson, Brad. *Miss Jane: A Novel*

WOMEN AND POLITICS
Didion, Joan. *A Book of Common Prayer*

WOMEN AND SUCCESS
Avery, Ellis. *The Last Nude*
Loigman, Lynda Cohen. *The Wartime Sisters: A Novel*

WOMEN AND WAR
Alderson, Kaia. *Sisters in Arms*
Barker, Pat. ★*The Silence of the Girls: A Novel*
Barker, Pat. *The Women of Troy*
Bowen, Rhys. *The Victory Garden*
Demirtas, Selahattin. *Dawn: Stories*
Epstein, Jennifer Cody. ★*Wunderland: A Novel*
Harris, C. S. *Good Time Coming*
Haynes, Natalie. *A Thousand Ships*
Jenoff, Pam. *The Lost Girls of Paris*

Lee, Ji-Min. *The Starlet and the Spy*
Mengiste, Maaza. ★*The Shadow King: A Novel*
Piercy, Marge. *Gone to Soldiers: A Novel*
Ryan, Jennifer. *The Spies of Shilling Lane: A Novel*
Williams, Beatriz. *All the Ways We Said Goodbye: A Novel of the Ritz Paris*

WOMEN ANTHROPOLOGISTS
Butler, Gwendoline. *Death Lives Next Door*
Drabble, Margaret. *The Pure Gold Baby*
Dykes, Amanda. *Whose Waves These Are*
Petersen, Todd Robert. *Picnic in the Ruins*
Rush, Norman. ★*Mating*

WOMEN ANTIQUE DEALERS
Cleland, Jane K. *Hidden Treasure*

WOMEN ARCHAEOLOGISTS
Bell, Lenora. *For the Duke's Eyes Only*
Byrne, Kerrigan. *How to Love a Duke in Ten Days*
Griffiths, Elly. *The Crossing Places*
Griffiths, Elly. *The Dark Angel*
Griffiths, Elly. *A Dying Fall: A Ruth Galloway Mystery*
Griffiths, Elly. *The House at Sea's End: A Ruth Galloway Mystery*
Griffiths, Elly. *The Janus Stone*
Griffiths, Elly. *The Lantern Men: A Dr. Ruth Galloway Mystery*
Griffiths, Elly. *The Night Hawks*
Griffiths, Elly. *The Stone Circle*
Hassib, Rajia. *A Pure Heart: A Novel*
Preston, Douglas J. *Old Bones*
Preston, Douglas J. *Thunderhead*

WOMEN ARCHITECTS
Semple, Maria. *Where'd You Go, Bernadette: A Novel*

WOMEN ARCHIVISTS
Hall, Rachel Howzell. *These Toxic Things*
Morelli, Laura. *The Stolen Lady*

WOMEN ART CURATORS
McLaughlin, Danielle. *The Art of Falling*

WOMEN ART TEACHERS
Lewis, Beverly. *The Preacher's Daughter*

WOMEN ARTISTS
Acampora, Lauren. *The Paper Wasp: A Novel*
Bergman, Megan Mayhew. *Almost Famous Women: Stories*
Bourland, Barbara. ★*Fake Like Me*
Briscoe, Joanna. *The Seduction*
Coster, Naima. *Halsey Street*
Davis, Fiona. *The Masterpiece*
Fuentes, Carlos. *The Years with Laura Diaz*
Gunning, Sally. *Painting the Light*
Hijuelos, Oscar. *Twain & Stanley Enter Paradise*
Jackson, K. M. *How to Marry Keanu Reeves in 90 Days*
Joshi, Alka. *The Henna Artist*
Leilani, Raven. ★*Luster*
Lewis, Beverly. *The Brethren*
Lewis, Beverly. *The Preacher's Daughter*
Malpas, Jodi Ellen. *Leave Me Breathless*
Meltzer, Brad. *The Escape Artist*
Messud, Claire. ★*The Woman Upstairs: A Novel*
Oakley, Colleen. *You Were There Too*
Packer, Ann. *The Children's Crusade*
Penrose, Andrea. *Murder at Half Moon Gate*

Penrose, Andrea. ★*Murder at Kensington Palace*
Penrose, Andrea. *Murder on Black Swan Lane*
Rose, M. J. *Tiffany Blues: A Novel*
Simpson, Dorothy. *Doomed to Die*
Smith, Dominic. ★*The Last Painting of Sara De Vos*
Steinke, Rene. *Holy Skirts*
Wendig, Chuck. *The Book of Accidents*
Yoder, Rachel. *Nightbitch*

WOMEN ASSASSINS
Black, Cara. ★*Three Hours in Paris*
Johnson, Alaya Dawn. *Trouble the Saints*
Kay, Guy Gavriel. ★*A Brightness Long Ago*
Robbins, David L. *War of the Rats: A Novel*
Sandford, John. *Certain Prey*
Sandford, John. *Mortal Prey*
Shannon, Samantha. *The Priory of the Orange Tree*

WOMEN ASSISTANT DISTRICT ATTORNEYS
Fairstein, Linda A. *Blood Oath*

WOMEN ASTROLOGERS
Bellefleur, Alexandria. *Written in the Stars*

WOMEN ASTRONAUTS
Chambers, Becky. *To Be Taught, If Fortunate*
Kowal, Mary Robinette. *The Calculating Stars: A Lady Astronaut Novel*
Kowal, Mary Robinette. *The Fated Sky: A Lady Astronaut Novel*
Kowal, Mary Robinette. *The Relentless Moon*
Lethem, Jonathan. *Chronic City*
Swyler, Erika. ★*Light from Other Stars: A Novel*

WOMEN AUTHORS
Alderton, Dolly. ★*Ghosts: A Novel*
Alvarez, Julia. ★*Afterlife: A Novel*
Baker, Jo. *The Body Lies*
Bohjalian, Chris. *Secrets of Eden: A Novel*
Brookner, Anita. *Hotel Du Lac*
Brown, Amy Belding. *Emily's House*
Coetzee, J. M. *Elizabeth Costello*
Cosimano, Elle. *Finlay Donovan Is Killing It*
Cusk, Rachel. *Kudos*
Dodd, Christina. *Because I'm Watching*
Drabble, Margaret. *The Witch of Exmoor*
Ellis, David. *In the Company of Liars*
Ferrante, Elena. *The Story of the Lost Child*
Ferrante, Elena. *Those Who Leave and Those Who Stay*
Flanery, Patrick. *Absolution: A Novel*
Florio, Gwen. *Best Laid Plans*
Freeman, Brian. *Thief River Falls*
Gendry-Kim, Keum Suk. ★*The Waiting*
Gentill, Sulari. *Crossing the Lines*
Glass, Seraphina Nova. *Someone's Listening*
Godwin, Gail. *Old Lovegood Girls*
Guillory, Jasmine. *The Proposal*
Henry, Emily. *Beach Read*
Hornby, Gill. *Miss Austen*
Kagen, Lesley. *Every Now and Then*
Kandasamy, Meena. *When I Hit You, Or, a Portrait of the Writer as a Young Wife*
Kidd, Sue Monk. ★*The Book of Longings*
King, Lily. *Writers & Lovers: A Novel*

Kirshenbaum, Binnie. *Rabbits for Food*
Lauren, Christina. *Roomies*
Lessing, Doris May. ★*The Golden Notebook*
Mangan, Christine. *Palace of the Drowned*
Meltzer, Jean. ★*The Matzah Ball*
Moriarty, Liane. *Nine Perfect Strangers*
Ozeki, Ruth L. ★*A Tale for the Time Being*
Phillips, Caryl. *A View of the Empire at Sunset*
Preston, Caroline. *The Scrapbook of Frankie Pratt*
Prose, Francine. ★*The Vixen*
Rosnay, Tatiana de. ★*Flowers of Darkness*
Setterfield, Diane. *The Thirteenth Tale: A Novel*
Shaffer, Mary Ann. *The Guernsey Literary and Potato Peel Pie Society*
Shelton, Paige. *Thin Ice: A Mystery*
Shields, Carol. *Unless*
Shumway, Charity. *Ten Girls to Watch: A Novel*
Spencer, Scott. *Man in the Woods*
Strout, Elizabeth. ★*Oh William!*
Turner, Bethany. *The Secret Life of Sarah Hollenbeck*
Walton, Jo. *Or What You Will*
Ware, Ruth. *In a Dark, Dark Wood*
Watkins, Claire Vaye. *I Love You but I've Chosen Darkness*
Zapata, Mike. *The Lost Book of Adana Moreau*

WOMEN AUTHORS, AMERICAN
Plath, Sylvia. ★*The Bell Jar*

WOMEN AUTHORS, ENGLISH
Cunningham, Michael. ★*The Hours*
Ellis, Bella. *The Vanished Bride*

WOMEN BAIL BOND AGENTS
Evanovich, Janet. *Look Alive Twenty-Five*
Evanovich, Janet. *Turbo Twenty-Three*

WOMEN BAKERS
Blumberg, Chandra. *Digging up Love*
Fluke, Joanne. ★*Christmas Cupcake Murder*
Glass, Julia. *The Whole World Over*
Hall, Alexis. *Rosaline Palmer Takes the Cake*
Heron, Farah. *Accidentally Engaged*
Lau, Jackie. *Donut Fall in Love*
Mallery, Susan. *Best of My Love*

WOMEN BALLET DANCERS
Roorbach, Bill. *Life Among Giants: A Novel*

WOMEN BANKERS
Campbell, Bebe Moore. *Brothers and Sisters*

WOMEN BAR OWNERS
Connolly, Sheila. *The Lost Traveller*

WOMEN BEEKEEPERS
Waite, Olivia. *The Care and Feeding of Waspish Widows*

WOMEN BICYCLISTS
Cleave, Chris. *Gold*

WOMEN BIOCHEMISTS
Cussler, Clive. *Sahara: A Novel*

WOMEN BIOGRAPHERS
Pitoniak, Anna. ★*Our American Friend*
Smith, Ali. *The Accidental*

WOMEN BIOLOGISTS
Boyle, T. Coraghessan. *When the Killing's Done: A Novel*
McConaghy, Charlotte. *Once There Were Wolves: A Novel*

WOMEN BODYGUARDS
Divya, S. B. *Machinehood*
Larkwood, A. K. *The Unspoken Name*
Sharp, Zoe. *Second Shot: A Charlie Fox Thriller*

WOMEN BOOKKEEPERS
Delany, Vicki. *Deadly Summer Nights*

WOMEN BOOKSELLERS
Bivald, Katarina. *The Readers of Broken Wheel Recommend*
Burns, V. M. *Killer Words*
Erdrich, Louise. ★*The Sentence*
March, Emily. *Jackson*

WOMEN BOTANISTS
Baker, Kage. *In the Garden of Iden: A Novel of the Company*
Gilbert, Elizabeth. ★*The Signature of All Things: A Novel*

WOMEN BOUNTY HUNTERS
Evanovich, Janet. *Look Alive Twenty-Five*
Evanovich, Janet. *One for the Money*
Evanovich, Janet. *Turbo Twenty-Three*
Foster, Fiona King. *The Captive: A Novel*

WOMEN BOXERS
Freeman, Anna. *The Fair Fight: A Novel*

WOMEN BUSINESS OWNERS
Bartz, Andrea. *The Herd: A Novel*
Castel-Bloom, Orly. *Textile*
Childs, Laura. *Egg Shooters*
Clayborn, Kate. *Love Lettering*
Delany, Vicki. *Murder in a Teacup*
Delany, Vicki. *Tea & Treachery*
Jimenez, Abby. *The Friend Zone*
McCall Smith, Alexander. *The Joy and Light Bus Company*
Moyes, Jojo. *The Peacock Emporium*
Orenstein, Hannah. *Love at First Like*
Pava, Sergio de la. *Lost Empress: A Novel*
Umrigar, Thrity N. *The Secrets Between Us*
Waite, Olivia. *The Care and Feeding of Waspish Widows*

WOMEN BUSINESS PARTNERS
Brenner, Jamie. *Drawing Home*

WOMEN CANCER SURVIVORS
Blumenfeld, Amy. *The Cast*

WOMEN CAREGIVERS
Garner, Helen. *The Spare Room*
Hardiman, Rebecca. *Good Eggs*
Hicks, Robert. *The Widow of the South*
Wilson, Kevin. *Nothing to See Here*
Winfrey, Kerry. *Not Like the Movies*

WOMEN CATERERS
Davidson, Diane Mott. *Killer Pancake*
Davidson, Diane Mott. *The Last Suppers*
Evanovich, Stephanie. *Under the Table*

WOMEN CELEBRITIES
Bergman, Megan Mayhew. *Almost Famous Women: Stories*
Burdick, Serena. *Find Me in Havana*
Clark, Tracy P. *What You Don't See*

WOMEN CHIEF EXECUTIVE OFFICERS
Akinmade-Akerstrom, Lola. *In Every Mirror She's Black*
Lackberg, Camilla. *Silver Tears*

WOMEN CHRISTIAN MISSIONARIES
Forester, C. S. *The African Queen*

WOMEN CIA AGENTS
Goldberg, Lee. *Fake Truth*
Prescott, Lara. *The Secrets We Kept*

WOMEN CIRCUS PERFORMERS
Wright, Jaime Jo. *The Haunting at Bonaventure Circus*

WOMEN COLLEGE FRIENDS
Godwin, Gail. *Old Lovegood Girls*
Nelson, Christina Suzann. *If We Make It Home: A Novel of Faith and Survival in the Oregon Wilderness*

WOMEN COLLEGE GRADUATES
Robinson, Peter. *The First Cut*
Shumway, Charity. *Ten Girls to Watch: A Novel*
Tieu, Julie. *The Donut Trap*
Waldman, Amy. *A Door in the Earth*

WOMEN COLLEGE STUDENTS
Bardugo, Leigh. ★*Ninth House*
Batuman, Elif. ★*The Idiot*
Bell, Shelly. *At His Mercy*
Bohjalian, Chris. *The Double Bind: A Novel*
Bolano, Roberto. *Amulet*
Braffet, Kelly. ★*Last Seen Leaving: A Novel*
Dahl, Julia. *The Missing Hours*
Dean, Pamela. *Tam Lin*
Foster, Brooke Lea. *Summer Darlings*
Gerritsen, Tess. *Choose Me*
Kurian, Vera. *Never Saw Me Coming*
McLaughlin, Emma. *The Nanny Diaries: A Novel*
Nunez, Sigrid. *The Last of Her Kind: A Novel*
Rooney, Sally. ★*Conversations with Friends*
Steiner, Susie. *Missing, Presumed: A Novel*
Weinberg, Kate. *The Truants*
Willis, Connie. ★*Doomsday Book*

WOMEN COLLEGE TEACHERS
Allende, Isabel. *In the Midst of Winter: A Novel*
Bear, Elizabeth. *Blood and Iron: A Novel of the Promethean Age*
Byatt, A. S. ★*Possession: A Romance*
Gaspar de Alba, Alicia. *Desert Blood: The Juarez Murders*
Hewson, David. *A Season for the Dead*
Johnson, Kij. ★*The Dream-Quest of Vellitt Boe*
Loren, Roni. *The One You Fight For*
McKinlay, Jenn. *The Good Ones*
Penny, Louise. ★*The Madness of Crowds*
Rader-Day, Lori. *The Black Hour*
Weinberg, Kate. *The Truants*

WOMEN COLUMNISTS
Guhrke, Laura Lee. *The Truth About Love and Dukes*
O'Donnell, Paraic. *The House on Vesper Sands: A Novel*

WOMEN COMPOSERS
Bledsoe, Lucy Jane. *The Big Bang Symphony: A Novel of Antarctica*

WOMEN COMPUTER PROGRAMMERS
Menon, Lily. *Make up Break Up: A Novel*
Rochon, Farrah. *The Boyfriend Project*
Rockaway, Kristin. *How to Hack a Heartbreak*

WOMEN COMPUTER SCIENTISTS
Gladstone, Max. ★*Empress of Forever*

WOMEN CONSULTANTS
Weatherspoon, Rebekah. *A Thorn in the Saddle*

WOMEN COOKS
Abu-Jaber, Diana. *Crescent*
Amado, Jorge. *Gabriela, Clove and Cinnamon*
Ashley, Jennifer. *Death at the Crystal Palace*
Bledsoe, Lucy Jane. *The Big Bang Symphony: A Novel of Antarctica*
Davidson, Diane Mott. *Killer Pancake*
Dev, Sonali. ★*Recipe for Persuasion*
Esquivel, Laura. ★*Like Water for Chocolate: A Novel in Monthly Installments, with Recipes, Romances, and Home Remedies*
Glass, Julia. *The Whole World Over*
Hibbert, Talia. ★*Act Your Age, Eve Brown*
Jenkins, Beverly. *Forbidden*
Laureano, C. E. ★*The Saturday Night Supper Club*
Lim, Roselle. *Natalie Tan's Book of Luck and Fortune*
Weatherspoon, Rebekah. *A Cowboy to Remember*

WOMEN CORONERS
Cornwell, Patricia Daniels. *Postmortem*
Patterson, James. *1st to Die: A Novel*

WOMEN COURIERS
Cleeton, Chanel. *The Most Beautiful Girl in Cuba*

WOMEN CRIMINALS
Abbott, Megan E. *Queenpin: A Novel*
Hill, Nathan. *The Nix: A Novel*
Speight, Shameek A. *The Pleasure of Pain*

WOMEN CULT LEADERS
Reichs, Kathy. *Death Du Jour*

WOMEN DANCERS
Brayden, Melissa. *First Position*

WOMEN DEFENSE ATTORNEYS
Beckett, L. X. *Gamechanger*
Child, Lee. *One Shot*
Sandford, John. *Certain Prey*

WOMEN DEPUTY POLICE CHIEFS
Atkins, Ace. *The Broken Places*
Atkins, Ace. *The Ranger*
Woods, Stuart. *Orchid Beach*

WOMEN DESIGNERS
Clayborn, Kate. *Love Lettering*

WOMEN DETECTIVES
Alsterdal, Tove. *We Know You Remember*
Armstrong, Kelley. *Alone in the Wild*
Armstrong, Kelley. *Watcher in the Woods*
Atkinson, Kate. ★*When Will There Be Good News?: A Novel*
Beaton, M. C. *Agatha Raisin and the Quiche of Death*
Beukes, Lauren. *Broken Monsters*
Billingham, Mark. ★*Their Little Secret*
Black, Saul. *Anything for You*
Black, Saul. ★*The Killing Lessons*
Black, Saul. ★*Lovemurder*
Bolton, S. J. *The Craftsman*
Bolton, S. J. *Now You See Me*
Buckley, Fiona. *The Siren Queen: An Ursula Blanchard Mystery at Queen Elizabeth I's Court*
Castillo, Linda. *Outsider*
Cleeves, Ann. *The Crow Trap*
Cleeves, Ann. *The Darkest Evening*
Connelly, Michael. ★*The Dark Hours*
Connelly, Michael. *Dark Sacred Night*

Connelly, Michael. *The Late Show*
Connelly, Michael. *The Night Fire*
Dazieri, Sandrone. *Kill the Angel*
Dazieri, Sandrone. *Kill the Father*
Dazieri, Sandrone. *Kill the King*
Dugoni, Robert. *In Her Tracks*
Dugoni, Robert. *My Sister's Grave*
Eisler, Barry. *All the Devils*
Eisler, Barry. *The Killer Collective*
Eisler, Barry. *The Night Trade*
Fforde, Jasper. *The Eyre Affair: A Novel*
Fforde, Jasper. *Lost in a Good Book: A Thursday Next Novel*
Frear, Caz. *Stone Cold Heart*
Frear, Caz. *Sweet Little Lies*
French, Tana. *The Likeness*
Gardiner, Meg. *Unsub: A Novel*
Gardner, Lisa. *Fear Nothing: A Detective D. D. Warren Novel*
Gardner, Lisa. *Find Her*
Gardner, Lisa. ★*Look for Me: A Novel*
Gardner, Lisa. *Love You More: A Detective D.D. Warren Novel*
Gardner, Lisa. ★*Never Tell: A Novel*
Gardner, Lisa. ★*When You See Me: A Novel*
George, Elizabeth. *Careless in Red*
George, Elizabeth. *The Punishment She Deserves*
George, Elizabeth. *This Body of Death: An Inspector Lynley Novel*
Gerritsen, Tess. *The Bone Garden*
Gerritsen, Tess. *Choose Me*
Gerritsen, Tess. *I Know a Secret*
Goldberg, Lee. *Bone Canyon*
Golding, Melanie. *The Hidden: A Novel*
Griffiths, Elly. *The Postscript Murders*
Hart, John. *Redemption Road*
Hoeg, Peter. ★*Smilla's Sense of Snow*
Hunt, April. *Deadly Obsession*
Jónasson, Ragnar. *The Island*
Jónasson, Ragnar. *The Mist*
Kelly, Erin. *Broadchurch: A Novel*
Kent, Kathleen. *The Burn*
Kent, Kathleen. *The Pledge*
Laukkanen, Owen. *Lone Jack Trail*
Littlejohn, Emily. *Inherit the Bones*
Littlejohn, Emily. *Lost Lake: A Detective Gemma Monroe Mystery*
McDermid, Val. ★*Still Life*
McLain, Paula. ★*When the Stars Go Dark: A Novel*
Miller, Derek B. ★*American by Day*
Parker, T. Jefferson. *The Blue Hour*
Patterson, James. *1st to Die: A Novel*
Pava, Sergio de la. *Personae: A Novel*
Potenza, Carol. *Hearts of the Missing*
Rankin, Ian. ★*A Song for the Dark Times*
Redondo, Dolores. *The Invisible Guardian*
Redondo, Dolores. *The North Face of the Heart*
Ritter, Todd. *Devil's Night*
Robb, J. D. *Fantasy in Death*
Robb, J. D. *Innocent in Death*
Robb, J. D. *Naked in Death*
Rodriguez, Linda. *Every Broken Trust: A Mystery*
Rodriguez, Linda. *Every Hidden Fear: A Skeet Bannion Mystery*

Roosevelt, Elliott. ★*Murder and the First Lady*
Roosevelt, Elliott. *Murder at Midnight*
Roosevelt, Elliott. *Murder in the Map Room: An Eleanor Roosevelt Mystery*
Roosevelt, Elliott. *Murder in the Oval Office*
Ruiz Zafon, Carlos. *The Labyrinth of the Spirits*
Schaffhausen, Joanna. *Gone for Good*
Smith, Julie. *The Kindness of Strangers: A Skip Langdon Novel*
Smith, Julie. *New Orleans Beat*
Spencer, Sally. ★*A Dying Fall*
Steiner, Susie. *Missing, Presumed: A Novel*
Steiner, Susie. ★*Persons Unknown: A Novel*
Tracy, P. J. ★*Deep into the Dark*
Tursten, Helene. *Hunting Game*

WOMEN DIPLOMATS
Martine, Arkady. ★*A Desolation Called Peace*
WOMEN DISTRICT ATTORNEYS
Lippman, Laura. *Wilde Lake*
WOMEN DIVERS
See, Lisa. *The Island of Sea Women*
WOMEN DOG TRAINERS
Tyler, Anne. ★*The Accidental Tourist: A Novel*
WOMEN DOMESTICS
Chevalier, Tracy. ★*Girl with a Pearl Earring*
WOMEN DRAMATISTS
Bausch, Richard. *Hello to the Cannibals: A Novel*
Leigh, Eva. *Scandal Takes the Stage*
Woolf, Virginia. *Between the Acts*
WOMEN DRUG ABUSERS
Coben, Harlan. *Run Away*
Moore, Liz. *Long Bright River*
Ward, Jesmyn. ★*Sing, Unburied, Sing*
WOMEN DRUG DEALERS
Stringer, Vickie M. ★*Let That Be the Reason*
WOMEN EDITORS
Horowitz, Anthony. ★*Moonflower Murders*
McCall Smith, Alexander. *The Comforts of a Muddy Saturday: An Isabel Dalhousie Novel*
McCall Smith, Alexander. *The Lost Art of Gratitude*
WOMEN EDUCATORS
Danan, Rosie. *The Intimacy Experiment*
WOMEN EMPLOYEES
Baker, Chandler. *Whisper Network: A Novel*
Ferrante, Elena. *Those Who Leave and Those Who Stay*
Pearson, Allison. ★*How Hard Can It Be?*
WOMEN ENGINEERS
Elliott, Kate. *Unconquerable Sun*
Higgins, C. A. *Lightless*
WOMEN ENTERTAINERS
Golden, Arthur. ★*Memoirs of a Geisha: A Novel*
WOMEN ENTREPRENEURS
Dorn, L. R. *The Anatomy of Desire*
Kate, Jessica. *A Girl's Guide to the Outback: A Novel*
McElroy, Alex. *The Atmospherians*
Rai, Alisha. ★*The Right Swipe*
Riley, Vanessa. ★*Island Queen*
WOMEN ENVIRONMENTALISTS
McConaghy, Charlotte. *Migrations*

Porter, Henry. *The Old Enemy*

WOMEN EQUESTRIANS
Matthews, Mimi. ★*The Siren of Sussex*

WOMEN EROTICA WRITERS
Leigh, Eva. *Temptations of a Wallflower*

WOMEN EXECUTIVES
Layne, Lauren. *Passion on Park Avenue*
Steel, Danielle. *First Sight*

WOMEN EXILES
Glass, Jenna. *The Women's War*
Lai, Larissa. *The Tiger Flu*
Martineau, Maxym M. *Kingdom of Exiles*

WOMEN FARMERS
Hunt, Laird. *Zorrie*
Kingsolver, Barbara. ★*Flight Behavior*

WOMEN FASHION DESIGNERS
Guillory, Jasmine. *Royal Holiday*
Williams, Preslaysa. *A Lowcountry Bride*

WOMEN FBI AGENTS
Baldacci, David. *Long Road to Mercy*
Baldacci, David. *A Minute to Midnight*
Cooper, Ellison. *Buried*
Gardiner, Meg. *The Dark Corners of the Night*
Gardiner, Meg. *Into the Black Nowhere*
Gardner, Lisa. ★*When You See Me: A Novel*
Harris, Thomas. ★*The Silence of the Lambs*
Panowich, Brian. *Hard Cash Valley*
Pintoff, Stefanie. *Hostage Taker: A Novel*
Preston, Douglas J. *Old Bones*
Swanson, Peter. *Eight Perfect Murders: A Novel*
Toro, Guillermo del. *The Hollow Ones*

WOMEN FILM EDITORS
Cline, Rachel. *My Liar: A Novel*

WOMEN FILM PRODUCERS AND DIRECTORS
Cline, Rachel. *My Liar: A Novel*

WOMEN FILMMAKERS
Apostol, Gina. *Insurrecto*

WOMEN FIRE FIGHTERS
Center, Katherine. *Things You Save in a Fire*
Meader, Kate. *Playing with Fire*
Oliveras, Priscilla. *Anchored Hearts*

WOMEN FLORISTS
Hoover, Colleen. *It Ends with Us*

WOMEN FOLK SINGERS
McCrumb, Sharyn. ★*If Ever I Return, Pretty Peggy-O*

WOMEN FOLKLORISTS
Shields, Carol. *The Republic of Love*

WOMEN FORENSIC ANTHROPOLOGISTS
Reichs, Kathy. *206 Bones*
Reichs, Kathy. *Bare Bones*
Reichs, Kathy. *Bones of the Lost: A Temperance Brennan Novel*
Reichs, Kathy. *Bones to Ashes*
Reichs, Kathy. *Break No Bones*
Reichs, Kathy. ★*A Conspiracy of Bones*
Reichs, Kathy. *Deadly Decisions*
Reichs, Kathy. *Death Du Jour*
Reichs, Kathy. ★*Deja Dead*
Reichs, Kathy. *Grave Secrets*

Reichs, Kathy. *Monday Mourning*

WOMEN FORENSIC PATHOLOGISTS
Cornwell, Patricia Daniels. *Autopsy*
Cornwell, Patricia Daniels. *Postmortem*

WOMEN FORENSIC PSYCHIATRISTS
Daniels, Natalie. *Too Close*
Gardiner, Meg. *The Dirty Secrets Club*

WOMEN FORENSIC PSYCHOLOGISTS
Black, Lisa. *Let Justice Descend*
Black, Lisa. *Suffer the Children*

WOMEN FORENSIC SCIENTISTS
Abu-Jaber, Diana. *Origin: A Novel*
Black, Lisa. *That Darkness*

WOMEN FUGITIVES
Faye, Lyndsay. ★*The Paragon Hotel*
Roth, Philip. ★*American Pastoral*
Shannon, Samantha. *The Mime Order*

WOMEN GAMBLERS
Bowen, Kelly. ★*Between the Devil and the Duke*

WOMEN GARDENERS
Kane, Jessica Francis. *Rules for Visiting*
Mapson, Jo-Ann. *Bad Girl Creek: A Novel*

WOMEN GENEALOGISTS
Perkins, S. C. *Murder Once Removed*

WOMEN GEOLOGISTS
Dade, Olivia. *Spoiler Alert*

WOMEN GLASS-WORKERS
Cleeves, Ann. ★*The Heron's Cry*

WOMEN GRADUATE STUDENTS
Awad, Mona. *Bunny*
Cole, Alyssa. ★*A Princess in Theory*
Fine, Julia. *The Upstairs House*
French, Marilyn. ★*The Women's Room*
Gyasi, Yaa. ★*Transcendent Kingdom*
Hibbert, Talia. ★*Take a Hint, Dani Brown*
Shamsie, Kamila. *Home Fire: A Novel*
Whelan, Julia. *My Oxford Year*

WOMEN HEALERS
Atakora, Afia. ★*Conjure Women*
Brown, Taylor. ★*Gods of Howl Mountain: A Novel*
Franklin, Ariana. ★*Death and the Maiden*
Gregory, Philippa. *Tidelands*
Johnson, Sadeqa. ★*Yellow Wife*
Putney, Mary Jo. *The Marriage Spell: A Novel*
Quincy, Diana. *The Viscount Made Me Do It*
Urrea, Luis Alberto. *The Hummingbird's Daughter: A Novel*
Urrea, Luis Alberto. *Queen of America: A Novel*

WOMEN HEART SURGEONS
Gerritsen, Tess. *The Surgeon*

WOMEN HEROIN ADDICTS
Robinson, Peter. *Playing with Fire*

WOMEN HIGH SCHOOL TEACHERS
Shalev, Meir. *Two She-Bears: A Novel*
Shreve, Anita. *The Pilot's Wife: A Novel*

WOMEN HISTORIANS
Faulks, Sebastian. *Paris Echo: A Novel*
Lively, Penelope. ★*Moon Tiger*

WOMEN HOLOCAUST SURVIVORS

Drndic, Dasa. *Trieste*

Styron, William. ★*Sophie's Choice*

WOMEN HOSTAGES

Picoult, Jodi. *A Spark of Light: A Novel*

Slaughter, Karin. ★*Fallen: A Novel*

WOMEN HOUSE CLEANERS

Beagin, Jen. ★*Vacuum in the Dark: A Novel*

WOMEN HUNTERS

Yang, JY. *The Red Threads of Fortune*

WOMEN IMMIGRANTS

Ali, Monica. ★*Brick Lane: A Novel*

Djavadi, Negar. *Disoriental*

Grippando, James. *The Girl in the Glass Box*

Gurganus, Allan. *The Practical Heart: Four Novellas*

Kincaid, Jamaica. ★*Lucy*

Ramos, Joanne. *The Farm: A Novel*

Tan, Amy. *The Bonesetter's Daughter*

WOMEN IMPOSTORS

Beverley, Jo. *My Lady Notorious*

Hawks, Arlem. *Georgana's Secret*

Robinson, Peter. *The First Cut*

WOMEN IN LITERATURE

Lippman, Laura. ★*Dream Girl*

Women in Love. Lawrence, D. H.

WOMEN IN THE BIBLE

Diamant, Anita. ★*The Red Tent*

Edghill, India. *Queenmaker: A Novel of King David's Queen*

WOMEN IN THE OLD TESTAMENT

Smith, Jill Eileen. *Star of Persia: Esther's Story*

WOMEN INTELLECTUALS

Horan, Nancy. *Loving Frank: A Novel*

WOMEN INTELLIGENCE OFFICERS

Bradby, Tom. *Double Agent*

Porter, Henry. *The Bell Ringers*

WOMEN INTERPRETERS

Florio, Gwen. *Silent Hearts*

Kitamura, Katie M. *Intimacies*

WOMEN INVENTORS

Benedict, Marie. *The Only Woman in the Room*

WOMEN INVESTIGATIVE JOURNALISTS

Watt, Holly. *To the Lions*

WOMEN JOURNALISTS

Barnett, LaShonda K. *Jam on the Vine*

Bartels, Erin. *We Hope for Better Things*

Barton, Fiona. *The Child*

Barton, Fiona. *The Suspect*

Bartz, Andrea. *The Herd: A Novel*

Belli, Kate. *Deception by Gaslight: A Gilded Gotham Mystery*

Bloom, Amy. ★*White Houses: A Novel*

Buchanan, Edna. *You Only Die Twice: A Britt Montero Mystery*

Chambers, Clare. *Small Pleasures*

Clark, Mary Higgins. ★*Kiss the Girls and Make Them Cry*

Cleeton, Chanel. *The Most Beautiful Girl in Cuba*

Cobb, May K. *The Hunting Wives*

Collins, Manda. ★*A Lady's Guide to Mischief and Mayhem*

Cotterill, Colin. *Killed at the Whim of a Hat*

Dahl, Julia. *Conviction*

Daugherty, Christi. *A Beautiful Corpse*

Daugherty, Christi. *The Echo Killing*

Daugherty, Christi. *Revolver Road: A Harper McClain Mystery*

Dundas, Chad. *The Blaze*

Fields, Hilary. *Last Chance Llama Ranch*

Flynn, Gillian. ★*Sharp Objects: A Novel*

Greenwood, Kerry. *Unnatural Habits*

Hart, Carolyn G. *Letter from Home*

Irvin, Kelly. *Tell Her No Lies*

James, P. D. *The Private Patient*

Laskowski, Tara. *The Mother Next Door*

Lourey, Jess. ★*January Thaw: A Murder-By-Month Mystery*

McDermid, Val. *A Place of Execution*

McLain, Paula. *Love and Ruin*

Meuleman, Sarah. *Find Me Gone*

Phillips, Jayne Anne. *Quiet Dell: A Novel*

Pitoniak, Anna. ★*Our American Friend*

Quick, Amanda. *The Girl Who Knew Too Much*

Rooney, Sally. ★*Conversations with Friends*

Rose, M. J. ★*Cartier's Hope*

Rosnay, Tatiana de. ★*Sarah's Key*

Smith, Martin Cruz. *The Siberian Dilemma*

Smith, Martin Cruz. ★*Tatiana: An Arkady Renko Novel*

Spencer, Sally. ★*A Dying Fall*

St. James, Simone. *The Broken Girls*

Sullivan, J. Courtney. *Friends and Strangers*

Umrigar, Thrity N. ★*Honor*

Unger, Lisa. ★*The Stranger Inside*

Williams, Beatriz. *The Golden Hour*

Winspear, Jacqueline. *The American Agent*

Yellin, Jessica. *Savage News*

WOMEN JUDGES

Finder, Joseph. ★*Judgment*

Mankell, Henning. *The Man from Beijing*

Maron, Margaret. *Bootlegger's Daughter*

Maron, Margaret. *Up Jumps the Devil*

WOMEN JURORS

Jackson, Brenda. *Forged in Desire*

WOMEN KIDNAPPING VICTIMS

Cumming, Charles. *A Foreign Country*

Everett, Percival L. *God's Country*

Gay, Roxane. ★*An Untamed State*

Katzenbach, John. *What Comes Next*

Koontz, Dean R. *The Husband*

O'Brien, Edna. ★*Girl*

Pronzini, Bill. *Nightcrawlers*

Putney, Mary Jo. *Once a Scoundrel*

Rollins, James. *Crucible*

Sandford, John. ★*Mind Prey*

Shelton, Paige. *Thin Ice: A Mystery*

WOMEN LABOR LEADERS

Russell, Mary Doria. *The Women of the Copper Country: A Novel*

WOMEN LABOR ORGANIZERS

Straley, John. *The Big Both Ways*

Vargas Llosa, Mario. ★*The Way to Paradise*

WOMEN LAW STUDENTS

Estleman, Loren D. *Frames*

Grisham, John. ★*The Pelican Brief*

WOMEN LAWYERS
Baker, Chandler. *Whisper Network: A Novel*
Blackstock, Terri. *Catching Christmas*
Brown, Sandra. *The Witness*
Clark, Marcia. *Final Judgment*
Coben, Harlan. ★*The Boy from the Woods*
Copperman, E. J. *Judgment at Santa Monica*
Crossan, Sarah. *Here Is the Beehive*
De Giovanni, Maurizio. *The Crocodile*
Fairstein, Linda A. *Entombed*
Gordimer, Nadine. *None to Accompany Me*
Guillory, Jasmine. *Party of Two*
Ho, Lauren. *Last Tang Standing*
Hodges, Cheris F. *Rumor Has It*
Katz, Erica. *The Boys' Club*
Maron, Margaret. *Bootlegger's Daughter*
Massey, Sujata. ★*The Bombay Prince*
Massey, Sujata. *The Satapur Moonstone*
Massey, Sujata. ★*The Widows of Malabar Hill: A Mystery of 1920s Bombay*
McFarlane, Mhairi. *If I Never Met You: A Novel*
Patterson, Richard North. *Protect and Defend*
Persson Giolito, Malin. *Beyond All Reasonable Doubt: A Novel*
Ross, Ann B. *Miss Julia Throws a Wedding*
Scottoline, Lisa. *Feared*
Scottoline, Lisa. *Legal Tender*
Serle, Rebecca. *In Five Years: A Novel*
Silver, Elizabeth L. *The Execution of Noa P. Singleton: A Novel*
Slaughter, Karin. *The Good Daughter*
Vargas Llosa, Mario. *The Feast of the Goat*
Vaughan, Sarah. ★*Anatomy of a Scandal: A Novel*
WOMEN LIBRARIANS
Hegi, Ursula. *Stones from the River*
Hoffman, Alice. *The Ice Queen: A Novel*
Lourey, Jess. ★*January Thaw: A Murder-By-Month Mystery*
McKinlay, Jenn. *Killer Research*
Moyes, Jojo. ★*The Giver of Stars: A Novel*
Title, Sarah. *The Undateable*
WOMEN LOTTERY WINNERS
Hiaasen, Carl. *Lucky You: A Novel*
WOMEN MAGICIANS
Hairston, Andrea. *Master of Poisons*
Kelly, Greta. *The Frozen Crown*
WOMEN MARINE BIOLOGISTS
Ghosh, Amitav. *The Hungry Tide*
WOMEN MARRIAGE RESISTERS
Berne, Lisa. *You May Kiss the Bride*
Dare, Tessa. *Do You Want to Start a Scandal*
Franklin, Miles. *My Brilliant Career*
WOMEN MARTIAL ARTISTS
Cain, Chelsea. *One Kick: A Novel*
WOMEN MATHEMATICIANS
Chung, Catherine. *The Tenth Muse: A Novel*
Crowley, John. *Lord Byron's Novel: The Evening Land*
Hoang, Helen. ★*The Kiss Quotient*
Munro, Alice. *Too Much Happiness: Stories*
Smith, Martin Cruz. *Stallion Gate*

WOMEN MAYORS
Ozick, Cynthia. *The Puttermesser Papers*
WOMEN MECHANICS
Ciotta, Beth. *Her Sky Cowboy*
WOMEN MEDICAL STUDENTS
Welsh, Kaite. *The Unquiet Heart*
Welsh, Kaite. *The Wages of Sin*
WOMEN MEDIUMS
Huchu, Tendai. *The Library of the Dead*
WOMEN MENTORS
James, Eloisa. *Three Weeks with Lady X*
WOMEN MERCHANTS
Kawakami, Mieko. *Ms. Ice Sandwich*
WOMEN MIGRANT WORKERS
Silver, Marisa. *Mary Coin: A Novel*
WOMEN MISSIONARIES
Lee, Chang-Rae. ★*The Surrendered*
Spencer, Minerva. *Scandalous*
WOMEN MURDER SUSPECTS
Brooks, Bill. *Winter Kill*
Dionne, Karen. *The Wicked Sister*
Ellis, David. *In the Company of Liars*
Freeman, Brian. *Goodbye to the Dead*
French, Nicci. ★*House of Correction*
Gardner, Lisa. ★*Never Tell: A Novel*
Hannah, Sophie. *The Killings at Kingfisher Hill*
Hart, Carolyn G. *Ghost Blows a Kiss*
Hurston, Zora Neale. ★*Their Eyes Were Watching God*
Ide, Joe. ★*Hi Five: An IQ Novel*
Logan, Kylie. *The Secrets of Bones: A Mystery*
Neubauer, Erica Ruth. *Murder at the Mena House*
Putnam, Jonathan F. *These Honored Dead*
Scottoline, Lisa. *Legal Tender*
Stewart, Amy. *Kopp Sisters on the March*
Ware, Ruth. ★*The Turn of the Key*
WOMEN MURDER VICTIMS
Barry, Ava. *Windhall*
Bauer, Belinda. *The Beautiful Dead*
Beaton, M. C. ★*Hot to Trot*
Black, Lisa. *That Darkness*
Block, Lawrence. *The Burglar in the Closet*
Block, Lawrence. *Eight Million Ways to Die*
Block, Lawrence. ★*When the Sacred Ginmill Closes*
Braun, Lilian Jackson. *The Cat Who Ate Danish Modern*
Brundage, Elizabeth. ★*All Things Cease to Appear*
Burke, James Lee. *Another Kind of Eden*
Cameron, W. Bruce. *Repo Madness*
Castillo, Linda. ★*Fallen*
Child, Lee. *The Affair: A Reacher Novel*
Childs, Laura. *Twisted Tea Christmas*
Cleeves, Ann. *The Crow Trap*
Cleeves, Ann. *The Darkest Evening*
Connelly, Michael. ★*Fair Warning*
Connolly, John. *A Book of Bones*
Cussler, Clive. *The Cutthroat*
Daugherty, Christi. *A Beautiful Corpse*
Delaney, J. P. *Believe Me: A Novel*
Deon, Natashia. *Grace*

Dexter, Colin. *The Remorseful Day*
Doiron, Paul. *Stay Hidden*
Dow, David R. *Confessions of an Innocent Man*
Fleming, Ian. ★*Goldfinger*
Frear, Caz. *Stone Cold Heart*
French, Tana. *The Likeness*
Gardiner, Meg. *Into the Black Nowhere*
Gates, Eva. *A Death Long Overdue*
Harris, Thomas. *Hannibal*
Harris, Thomas. ★*The Silence of the Lambs*
Hiaasen, Carl. ★*Squeeze Me: A Novel*
Hill, Susan. *The Shadows in the Street: A Simon Serrailler Mystery*
Kaminsky, Stuart M. *Dancing in the Dark*
Khan, Ausma Zehanat. *Among the Ruins*
Lepionka, Kristen. *Once You Go This Far: A Mystery*
Lippman, Laura. ★*After I'm Gone*
Mamet, David. *Chicago: A Novel*
March, Nev. *Murder in Old Bombay*
McPherson, Catriona. ★*A Step so Grave*
Moor, Jessica. *The Keeper*
Neubauer, Erica Ruth. *Murder at the Mena House*
Nickson, Chris. *Come the Fear*
Parker, Robert B. *Sixkill*
Parry, Ambrose. *The Way of All Flesh*
Putnam, Jonathan F. *These Honored Dead*
Quartey, Kwei. ★*Sleep Well, My Lady*
Quick, Amanda. *Close Up*
Raimondo, Lynne. *Dante's Wood: A Mark Angelotti Novel*
Rankin, Ian. ★*Rather Be the Devil*
Reichs, Kathy. ★*Deja Dead*
Rice, Luanne. ★*Last Day*
Robinson, Peter. *Friend of the Devil*
Rosenfield, Kat. *No One Will Miss Her*
Rowland, Laura Joh. *The Incense Game: A Novel of Feudal Japan*
Rowland, Laura Joh. *The Ripper's Shadow*
Scerbanenco, Giorgio. *A Private Venus*
Shreve, Anita. *The Weight of Water*
Sjowall, Maj. *The Man on the Balcony: The Story of a Crime*
Slaughter, Karin. ★*The Silent Wife*
Spain, Jo. *With Our Blessing: An Inspector Tom Reynolds Mystery*
Spencer, Sally. *Backlash*
Spencer-Fleming, Julia. *Hid from Our Eyes*
Spencer-Fleming, Julia. *In the Bleak Midwinter*
Stabenow, Dana. ★*A Deeper Sleep: A Kate Shugak Novel*
Suskind, Patrick. ★*Perfume: The Story of a Murderer*
Talton, Jon. *City of Dark Corners*
Turton, Stuart. *The 7 1/2 Deaths of Evelyn Hardcastle*

WOMEN MURDER WITNESSES
Koontz, Dean R. *Intensity: A Novel*

WOMEN MURDERERS
Adler-Olsen, Jussi. *The Scarred Woman*
Atwood, Margaret. *Alias Grace*
Donoghue, Emma. *Slammerkin*
Faye, Lyndsay. *Jane Steele*
Fitch, Janet. *White Oleander: A Novel*
Kane, Darby. *Pretty Little Wife*
King, Stephen. *Dolores Claiborne*
Kushner, Rachel. *The Mars Room*

McCrumb, Sharyn. ★*The Ballad of Frankie Silver*
Purcell, Laura. *The Silent Companions: A Ghost Story*
Raimondo, Lynne. *Dante's Dilemma: A Mark Angelotti Novel*
Richler, Nancy. *Your Mouth Is Lovely: A Novel*
Ruskovich, Emily. *Idaho: A Novel*
Sanders, Lawrence. ★*The Third Deadly Sin*
Swanson, Peter. *The Kind Worth Killing: A Novel*
Toibin, Colm. *House of Names*

WOMEN MUSICIANS
Alexander, Tamera. ★*A Note yet Unsung*
Creech, Sarah. *The Whole Way Home*
Hajdu, David. *Adrianne Geffel: A Fiction*
Hankin, Laura. *Happy & You Know It*
McEwan, Ian. ★*On Chesil Beach*
Pinsker, Sarah. *A Song for a New Day*

WOMEN MYSTERY STORY WRITERS
Rice, Craig. *Home Sweet Homicide*

WOMEN NEUROSCIENTISTS
Cooper, Ellison. *Buried*

WOMEN NEWSPAPER EDITORS
Hiaasen, Carl. *Basket Case*

WOMEN NONCONFORMISTS
Jhabvala, Ruth Prawer. ★*Heat and Dust*
*The **Women** of the Copper Country: A Novel*. Russell, Mary Doria
*The **Women** of Troy*. Barker, Pat

WOMEN OLYMPIC ATHLETES
Hooper, Elise. *Fast Girls: A Novel of the 1936 Women's Olympic Team*

WOMEN OPERA SINGERS
Cather, Willa. *The Song of the Lark*
Patchett, Ann. ★*Bel Canto: A Novel*
Phillips, Susan Elizabeth. ★*When Stars Collide*

WOMEN OWNED BUSINESSES
McCall Smith, Alexander. *The Joy and Light Bus Company*

WOMEN PAINTERS
Atwood, Margaret. ★*Cat's Eye*
Avery, Ellis. *The Last Nude*
Dunant, Sarah. *The Birth of Venus: A Novel*
Lattari, Katie. *Dark Things I Adore*
O'Farrell, Maggie. *The Hand That First Held Mine: A Novel*
Robertson, Imogen. *The Paris Winter*
Updike, John. *Seek My Face*

WOMEN PARAMEDICS
Oliveras, Priscilla. *Anchored Hearts*

WOMEN PARK RANGERS
Barr, Nevada. *Destroyer Angel: An Anna Pigeon Novel*
Barr, Nevada. *Track of the Cat*

WOMEN PAROLE OFFICERS
Bell, Shelly. *For His Pleasure*

WOMEN PATHOLOGISTS
Hart, Erin. *The Book of Killowen*
Hart, Erin. *Haunted Ground: A Crime Novel*

WOMEN PEDIATRICIANS
Tremblay, Paul. *Survivor Song*

WOMEN PERFORMANCE ARTISTS
Steinke, Rene. *Holy Skirts*

WOMEN PERIODICAL EDITORS
Clark, Tracy P. *What You Don't See*

WOMEN PHARMACISTS
Trigiani, Adriana. *Big Cherry Holler: A Big Stone Gap Novel*
Trigiani, Adriana. *Big Stone Gap: A Novel*
WOMEN PHILOSOPHERS
McCall Smith, Alexander. ★*The Geometry of Holding Hands*
WOMEN PHOTOGRAPHERS
Beattie, Ann. ★*Picturing Will*
Carter, Mary Dixie. *The Photographer*
Darznik, Jasmin. *The Bohemians*
Delinsky, Barbara. *A Week at the Shore*
Geni, Abby. *The Lightkeepers: A Novel*
Goldberg, Myla. *Feast Your Eyes*
Hand, Elizabeth. *Available Dark: A Thriller*
Hand, Elizabeth. *The Book of Lamps and Banners: A Novel*
Hand, Elizabeth. ★*Generation Loss: A Novel*
Hand, Elizabeth. *Hard Light*
Hauck, Rachel. *The Wedding Chapel*
Linden, Rachel. *Ascension of Larks*
Miller, Sue. ★*Monogamy*
Perry, Anne. ★*A Darker Reality*
Perry, Anne. ★*Death in Focus: An Elena Standish Novel*
Perry, Anne. *A Question of Betrayal*
Quick, Amanda. *Close Up*
Roberts, Nora. *The Obsession*
Rowland, Laura Joh. *The Hangman's Secret*
Rowland, Laura Joh. *The Ripper's Shadow*
Scharer, Whitney. *The Age of Light*
Shreve, Anita. *The Weight of Water*
Silver, Marisa. *Mary Coin: A Novel*
Woods, Stuart. *Palindrome*
WOMEN PHOTOJOURNALISTS
Chung, Maxine Mei-Fung. *The Eighth Girl*
Petrie, Nicholas. *Tear It Down*
Polk, C. L. *Stormsong*
WOMEN PHYSICIANS
Alameddine, Rabih. *The Wrong End of the Telescope*
Anderson, Alison. *The Summer Guest*
Blake, Audrey. *The Girl in His Shadow: A Novel*
Bohjalian, Chris. ★*The Red Lotus*
Brown, Sandra. *Tailspin*
Donati, Sara. *Where the Light Enters*
Franklin, Ariana. *Mistress of the Art of Death*
Franklin, Ariana. *The Serpent's Tale*
Gabaldon, Diana. ★*Voyager*
Lawler, Liz. *Don't Wake Up*
Lipman, Elinor. *The Pursuit of Alice Thrift: A Novel*
Marra, Anthony. ★*A Constellation of Vital Phenomena: A Novel*
Mina, Denise. *The Less Dead*
Obreht, Tea. *The Tiger's Wife: A Novel*
Phillips, Christi. *The Devlin Diary*
Shaw, Vivian. ★*Dreadful Company*
Shaw, Vivian. ★*Strange Practice*
Slaughter, Karin. ★*Undone: A Novel*
Sweeney-Baird, Christina. *The End of Men*
Weatherspoon, Rebekah. *Rafe: A Buff Male Nanny*
WOMEN PHYSICISTS
Eliasberg, Jan. ★*Hannah's War*
Flynn, Michael. *Eifelheim*

WOMEN PIANISTS
Kaplan, Mitchell James. *Rhapsody*
Singh, Nalini. *A Madness of Sunshine*
WOMEN PILOTS
Davidson, MaryJanice. *Truth, Lies, and Second Dates*
Johnson, Julia Claiborne. *Better Luck Next Time: A Novel*
Kowal, Mary Robinette. *The Calculating Stars: A Lady Astronaut Novel*
McLain, Paula. *Circling the Sun*
Quinn, Kate. ★*The Huntress*
Urquhart, Jane. *The Night Stages: A Novel*
WOMEN POETS
Brown, Amy Belding. *Emily's House*
Byatt, A. S. ★*Possession: A Romance*
Conroy, Pat. *The Prince of Tides*
Cumyn, Alan. *Losing It*
Darznik, Jasmin. *Song of a Captive Bird: A Novel*
Fitch, Janet. *White Oleander: A Novel*
Groff, Lauren. ★*Matrix*
Hill, Donna. ★*Confessions in B-Flat*
Jalaluddin, Uzma. ★*Ayesha at Last*
Jong, Erica. ★*Fear of Flying: A Novel*
Pearl, Matthew. *The Dante Chamber*
Steinke, Rene. *Holy Skirts*
Wieland, Liza. *Paris, 7 A.M.*
WOMEN POISONERS
Poole, Sara. *The Borgia Mistress*
WOMEN POLICE CHIEFS
Castillo, Linda. ★*Fallen*
Sandford, John. ★*Night Prey*
WOMEN POLITICIANS
Guillory, Jasmine. ★*The Wedding Date*
Mallon, Thomas. *Landfall: A Novel*
Sittenfeld, Curtis. *Rodham: A Novel*
Stabenow, Dana. *The Singing of the Dead*
WOMEN PRESIDENTS
McQuiston, Casey. ★*Red, White & Royal Blue: A Novel*
WOMEN PRIESTS
Greenwood, Kerry. *Out of the Black Land*
Kane, Ben. *Spartacus: The Gladiator*
Lewis, Linden A. *The First Sister: A Novel*
WOMEN PRISON GUARDS
Schlink, Bernhard. *The Reader: A Novel*
WOMEN PRISONERS
Cleeton, Chanel. *The Most Beautiful Girl in Cuba*
Collins, Sara. *The Confessions of Frannie Langton*
Deluca, Marjorie. *The Savage Instinct*
Gray, Anissa. *The Care and Feeding of Ravenously Hungry Girls*
Hamilton, Jane. *A Map of the World*
Khadra, Yasmina. *The Swallows of Kabul: A Novel*
Kushner, Rachel. *The Mars Room*
Radcliffe, Ann Ward. ★*The Mysteries of Udolpho*
Richler, Nancy. *Your Mouth Is Lovely: A Novel*
Ruskovich, Emily. *Idaho: A Novel*
Shannon, Samantha. *The Bone Season*
Silver, Elizabeth L. *The Execution of Noa P. Singleton: A Novel*
Ware, Ruth. ★*The Turn of the Key*

WOMEN PRISONERS — TRANSPORTATION

Adams, Hope. *Dangerous Women*

WOMEN PRIVATE INVESTIGATORS

Beaton, M. C. ★*Hot to Trot*

Beaton, M. C. *Pushing up Daisies: An Agatha Raisin Mystery*

Black, Cara. *Murder in the Bastille*

Black, Cara. *Murder in the Marais*

Black, Cara. *Murder in the Rue De Paradis: An Aimee Leduc Investigation*

Box, C. J. ★*The Bitterroots: A Novel*

Clare, Alys. *The Woman Who Spoke to Spirits*

Clark, Tracy P. *Runner*

Clark, Tracy P. *What You Don't See*

Davis, Lindsey. *A Comedy of Terrors: A Flavia Albia Novel*

Davis, Lindsey. *The Ides of April: A Flavia Albia Mystery*

Gailey, Sarah. *Magic for Liars*

Grafton, Sue. *X*

Grafton, Sue. *Y Is for Yesterday*

Gran, Sara. *Claire Dewitt and the City of the Dead*

Gran, Sara. *The Infinite Blacktop: A Novel*

Hall, Rachel Howzell. *And Now She's Gone*

Heller, Peter. *Celine: A Novel*

Hill, Edwin J. *Little Comfort*

James, P. D. *The Skull Beneath the Skin*

James, P. D. *An Unsuitable Job for a Woman*

King, Laurie R. *Castle Shade*

Lelchuk, Saul. *Save Me from Dangerous Men: A Novel*

Lepionka, Kristen. *The Last Place You Look*

Lepionka, Kristen. *Once You Go This Far: A Mystery*

Lippman, Laura. *No Good Deeds*

Luna, Louisa. *The Janes*

Lutz, Lisa. *The Spellman Files: A Novel*

McCall Smith, Alexander. *Blue Shoes and Happiness*

McCall Smith, Alexander. *The Double Comfort Safari Club*

McCall Smith, Alexander. *The Full Cupboard of Life*

McCall Smith, Alexander. *The Good Husband of Zebra Drive*

McCall Smith, Alexander. *In the Company of Cheerful Ladies*

McCall Smith, Alexander. *The Joy and Light Bus Company*

McCall Smith, Alexander. *The Kalahari Typing School for Men*

McCall Smith, Alexander. *The Limpopo Academy of Private Detection*

McCall Smith, Alexander. ★*The No. 1 Ladies' Detective Agency*

McCall Smith, Alexander. *The Saturday Big Tent Wedding Party*

McKevett, G. A. *A Few Drops of Bitters*

McPherson, Catriona. ★*A Step so Grave*

Moss, Tara. *The War Widow*

Muller, Marcia. *Dead Midnight*

Paretsky, Sara. ★*Dead Land*

Paretsky, Sara. *Indemnity Only: A Novel*

Paretsky, Sara. *Shell Game*

Phillips, Susan Elizabeth. *First Star I See Tonight*

Quartey, Kwei. ★*Sleep Well, My Lady*

Quick, Amanda. ★*The Lady Has a Past*

Ragan, Theresa. *Buried Deep*

Ragan, Theresa. *Deadly Recall*

Ragan, Theresa. *Deranged*

Ragan, Theresa. *Her Last Day*

Rowland, Laura Joh. *The Hangman's Secret*

Rozan, S. J. ★*The Art of Violence*

Rozan, S. J. ★*Paper Son*

Rozan, S. J. *The Shanghai Moon: A Lydia Chin/Bill Smith Novel*

Rozan, S. J. *Winter and Night*

Saunders, Kate. *The Case of the Wandering Scholar*

Saunders, Kate. *The Secrets of Wishtide*

Scoppettone, Sandra. *Everything You Have Is Mine*

Smith, Julie. *Louisiana Hotshot*

Spencer, Sally. *The Shivering Turn*

Stabenow, Dana. ★*A Fine and Bitter Snow: A Kate Shugak Novel*

Stabenow, Dana. ★*Less Than a Treason*

Stabenow, Dana. *No Fixed Line*

Winspear, Jacqueline. *The American Agent*

Winspear, Jacqueline. ★*The Consequences of Fear: A Maisie Dobbs Novel*

WOMEN PROFESSIONAL EMPLOYEES

Bartz, Andrea. *The Herd: A Novel*

Hall, Rachel Howzell. *These Toxic Things*

Hockman, Angie. *Shipped*

Williams, Katie. *Tell the Machine Goodnight*

WOMEN PSYCHIATRIC HOSPITAL PATIENTS

Gruber, Michael. *Valley of Bones: A Novel*

Mas, Victoria. *The Mad Women's Ball*

WOMEN PSYCHIATRISTS

Adlakha, Sarah. *She Wouldn't Change a Thing*

Sandford, John. ★*Mind Prey*

Steadman, Catherine. *Mr. Nobody: A Novel*

WOMEN PSYCHICS

Amis, Martin. *London Fields: A Novel*

Bouchet, Amanda. *Breath of Fire*

Bouchet, Amanda. ★*A Promise of Fire*

Brown, Karen. *The Clairvoyants: A Novel*

Butler, Octavia E. ★*Parable of the Sower*

Butler, Octavia E. *Parable of the Talents: A Novel*

Castle, Jayne. *Illusion Town*

Clare, Alys. *The Woman Who Spoke to Spirits*

Gregory, Philippa. *The Lady of the Rivers*

Lim, Roselle. *Vanessa Yu's Magical Paris Tea Shop*

Sanders, Lawrence. *McNally's Luck*

Shannon, Samantha. *The Bone Season*

Shannon, Samantha. *The Mime Order*

Yang, JY. *The Red Threads of Fortune*

WOMEN PSYCHOLOGISTS

Nguyen, Lena. *We Have Always Been Here*

WOMEN PSYCHOTHERAPISTS

Barry, Brunonia. *The Map of True Places*

Brownrigg, Sylvia. ★*The Delivery Room: A Novel*

Dade, Olivia. *All the Feels*

Fielding, Joy. *The Bad Daughter: A Novel*

French, Nicci. *Dark Saturday*

French, Nicci. ★*The Day of the Dead: A Novel*

French, Nicci. *Friday on My Mind: A Frieda Klein Mystery*

French, Nicci. *Sunday Silence*

French, Nicci. *Thursday's Children*

French, Nicci. *Tuesday's Gone*

French, Nicci. *Waiting for Wednesday: A Frieda Klein Mystery*

Thomas, Bev. *A Good Enough Mother: A Novel*

WOMEN PUBLIC PROSECUTORS
Fairstein, Linda A. *Entombed*
WOMEN PUBLIC RELATIONS CONSULTANTS
Hunting, Helena. *Handle with Care*
WOMEN RADICALS
Morton, Brian. *Florence Gordon*
Nunez, Sigrid. *The Last of Her Kind: A Novel*
Piercy, Marge. *Vida: A Novel*
Stridsberg, Sara. *Valerie: Or the Faculty of Dreams : Amendment to the Theory of Sexuality*
Walker, Sarai. *Dietland*
WOMEN RADIO BROADCASTERS
Flagg, Fannie. *Standing in the Rainbow: A Novel*
WOMEN RADIO NEWSCASTERS AND COMMENTATORS
Hay, Elizabeth. *Late Nights on Air*
WOMEN RANCHERS
Grey, Zane. ★*Riders of the Purple Sage*
Jenkins, Beverly. *Wild Rain*
WOMEN REAL ESTATE AGENTS
Humphreys, Sara Taney. *Trouble Walks In*
WOMEN RECLUSES
Finn, A. J. ★*The Woman in the Window*
Ray, Eleanor. *The Missing Treasures of Amy Ashton*
Setterfield, Diane. *The Thirteenth Tale: A Novel*
WOMEN RESTAURATEURS
Colgan, Jenny. ★*The Endless Beach*
WOMEN RETIREES
Hollis, Lee. *Poppy Harmon Investigates*
WOMEN REVOLUTIONARIES
Apostol, Gina. *Gun Dealers' Daughter: A Novel*
Loedel, Daniel. *Hades, Argentina*
Mbue, Imbolo. *How Beautiful We Were*
WOMEN ROCK MUSICIANS
Walton, Dawnie. ★*The Final Revival of Opal & Nev*
WOMEN ROOMMATES
Nunez, Sigrid. *The Last of Her Kind: A Novel*
WOMEN RULERS
Alpsten, Ellen. *Tsarina*
Bear, Elizabeth. *Blood and Iron: A Novel of the Promethean Age*
Cherezinska, Elzbieta. *The Widow Queen*
Clements, Oliver. *The Eyes of the Queen*
Clements, Oliver. *The Queen's Men*
Durst, Sarah Beth. *The Queen of Blood*
Edghill, India. *Queenmaker: A Novel of King David's Queen*
George, Margaret. *Elizabeth I: A Novel*
Gladstone, Max. ★*Empress of Forever*
Glass, Jenna. *The Women's War*
Gregory, Philippa. *The Last Tudor*
Gregory, Philippa. *The Taming of the Queen*
Haydon, Elizabeth. *The Merchant Emperor*
Jones, Sherry. *Four Sisters, All Queens*
King, Laurie R. *Castle Shade*
McCaffrey, Anne. *Dragonflight*
Mina, Denise. ★*Rizzio*
Pike, Signe. *The Forgotten Kingdom: A Novel*
Pike, Signe. *The Lost Queen*
Rushdie, Salman. *The Enchantress of Florence: A Novel*
Shannon, Samantha. *The Priory of the Orange Tree*

Smith, Jill Eileen. *Star of Persia: Esther's Story*
Stachniak, Eva. *The Winter Palace: A Novel of Catherine the Great*
Stevens, Francis. *The Heads of Cerberus*
Vinge, Joan D. *The Snow Queen*
Wagers, K. B. *There Before the Chaos*
Walters, Minette. *The Last Hours: A Novel*
Weir, Alison. *Katharine Parr, the Sixth Wife*
Winter, Evan. *The Fires of Vengeance*
Yang, JY. *The Ascent to Godhood*
WOMEN SAINTS
Griffith, Nicola. *Hild: A Novel*
Twain, Mark. *Personal Recollections of Joan of Arc*
Urrea, Luis Alberto. *The Hummingbird's Daughter: A Novel*
Urrea, Luis Alberto. *Queen of America: A Novel*
WOMEN SCHOLARS AND ACADEMICS
Collins, Manda. *Ready Set Rogue*
Drabble, Margaret. *The Sea Lady*
Harkness, Deborah E. *The Book of Life*
Harkness, Deborah E. *A Discovery of Witches: A Novel*
Harkness, Deborah E. *Shadow of Night*
Phillips, Christi. *The Rossetti Letter: A Novel*
St. Aubyn, Edward. *Double Blind*
WOMEN SCIENTISTS
Afifi, Nadia. *The Sentient*
Benedict, Marie. *The Only Woman in the Room*
Bolton, S. J. *The Split*
Brennan, Marie. *Within the Sanctuary of Wings: A Memoir by Lady Trent*
Cantor, Jillian. *Half Life*
Cole, Alyssa. ★*A Princess in Theory*
Collins, Manda. *One for the Rogue*
Cussler, Clive. *Blue Gold: A Novel from the Numa Files*
Dare, Tessa. *A Week to Be Wicked*
Everett, Elizabeth. ★*A Lady's Formula for Love*
Freudenberger, Nell. ★*Lost and Wanted: A Novel*
Gailey, Sarah. *The Echo Wife*
Gilman, Carolyn Ives. *Dark Orbit*
Gyasi, Yaa. ★*Transcendent Kingdom*
Hart, Elsa. *The Cabinets of Barnaby Mayne*
Newitz, Annalee. *Autonomous*
Paolini, Christopher. ★*To Sleep in a Sea of Stars*
Parnell, Sean. *Left for Dead*
Pastan, Rachel. *In the Field*
Peikoff, Kira. *Mother Knows Best*
Perry, Anne. *One Fatal Flaw: A Daniel Pitt Novel*
Phillips, Helen. *The Need: A Novel*
Sagan, Carl. *Contact: A Novel*
Soule, Charles. ★*Anyone*
Vandermeer, Jeff. ★*Annihilation: A Novel*
Waite, Olivia. ★*The Lady's Guide to Celestial Mechanics*
WOMEN SCREENWRITERS
Davis, Fiona. *The Chelsea Girls*
Stratford, Sarah-Jane. *Red Letter Days*
WOMEN SERIAL MURDERERS
Braithwaite, Oyinkan. *My Sister, the Serial Killer: A Novel*
Deluca, Marjorie. *The Savage Instinct*
Sandford, John. *Certain Prey*

WOMEN SHAMANS
Okorafor, Nnedi. ★*Who Fears Death*
WOMEN SHARPSHOOTERS
Larison, John. *Whiskey When We're Dry*
WOMEN SHERIFFS
Galligan, John. *Bad Moon Rising*
Jones, Darynda. *A Bad Day for Sunshine*
Jones, Darynda. *A Good Day for Chardonnay*
Lansdale, Joe R. *Sunset and Sawdust*
Montgomery, Jess. *The Stills*
Montgomery, Jess. *The Widows*
Offutt, Chris. ★*The Killing Hills*
Stewart, Amy. ★*Miss Kopp Just Won't Quit*
WOMEN SHIP CAPTAINS
Laukkanen, Owen. *Gale Force*
Poyer, David. *Violent Peace: The War with China - Aftermath of Armageddon*
Shalvis, Jill. *Sweet Little Lies*
WOMEN SHOPKEEPERS
Childs, Laura. *Haunted Hibiscus*
Childs, Laura. *Lavender Blue Murder*
Childs, Laura. *Twisted Tea Christmas*
Tieu, Julie. *The Donut Trap*
WOMEN SINGERS
Delinsky, Barbara. *Lake News: A Novel*
Penelope, L. *Cry of Metal & Bone: Earthsinger Chronicles, Book 3*
Penelope, L. *Whispers of Shadow & Flame*
Reid, Taylor Jenkins. ★*Daisy Jones & The Six: A Novel*
WOMEN SOCIAL ADVOCATES
Benjamin, Ali. *The Smash-Up: A Novel*
WOMEN SOCIAL WORKERS
Mengestu, Dinaw. ★*All Our Names*
WOMEN SOLDIERS
Bird, Sarah. *Daughter of a Daughter of a Queen*
Boianjiu, Shani. *The People of Forever Are Not Afraid: A Novel*
Gibson, Claire. *Beyond the Point: A Novel*
Hurley, Kameron. ★*The Light Brigade*
Krueger, Paul. *Steel Crow Saga*
Lee, Yoon Ha. *Ninefox Gambit*
Meltzer, Brad. *The Escape Artist*
Mohamed, Nadifa. *The Orchard of Lost Souls: A Novel*
O'Keefe, Megan E. *Velocity Weapon*
Pratchett, Terry. *Monstrous Regiment*
WOMEN SPACESHIP CAPTAINS
Bouchet, Amanda. *Nightchaser*
McDevitt, Jack. *The Engines of God*
Wagers, K. B. *Hold Fast Through the Fire*
WOMEN SPIES
Bourne, Joanna. *The Black Hawk*
Bourne, Joanna. *Rogue Spy*
Bourne, Joanna. ★*The Spymaster's Lady*
Buckley, Fiona. *The Siren Queen: An Ursula Blanchard Mystery at Queen Elizabeth I's Court*
Cantrell, Christian. *Scorpion*
Chiaverini, Jennifer. *Resistance Women: A Novel*
Follett, Ken. *Jackdaws*
Frayn, Michael. *Spies: A Novel*
Harkaway, Nick. *Angelmaker*

Huber, Anna Lee. *Penny for Your Secrets*
Jenoff, Pam. *The Lost Girls of Paris*
Matthews, Jason. ★*The Kremlin's Candidate*
Matthews, Jason. *Red Sparrow: A Novel*
Meacham, Leila. *Dragonfly: A Novel*
Perry, Anne. ★*A Darker Reality*
Perry, Anne. *A Question of Betrayal*
Priest, Cherie. *Clementine*
Putney, Mary Jo. *No Longer a Gentleman*
Sebastian, Tim. *Fatal Ally*
WOMEN SPIRITUALISTS
Mas, Victoria. *The Mad Women's Ball*
WOMEN STALKING VICTIMS
Bannister, Jo. *Silent Footsteps*
Pirie, David. *The Patient's Eyes*
Quick, Amanda. *'til Death Do Us Part*
WOMEN STAND-UP COMEDIANS
Leonard, Elmore. *Pagan Babies*
WOMEN STATISTICIANS
Lauren, Christina. *The Soulmate Equation*
WOMEN STUDENTS
Durst, Sarah Beth. *The Queen of Blood*
Johnson, Kij. ★*The Dream-Quest of Vellitt Boe*
WOMEN SURGEONS
Carr, Robyn. *What We Find*
Livesay, Tracey. *Like Lovers Do*
Snow, Jennifer. *An Alaskan Christmas*
WOMEN SWINDLERS
Carrick, M. A. *The Mask of Mirrors*
Chakraborty, S. A. *The City of Brass*
Chakraborty, S. A. *The Empire of Gold*
Chakraborty, S. A. *The Kingdom of Copper: A Novel*
Hilton, L. S. *Maestra*
Robards, Karen. *The Ultimatum*
★*Women Talking: A Novel*. Toews, Miriam
WOMEN TEACHERS
Abe, Kobo. *The Woman in the Dunes*
Balogh, Mary. *Simply Love*
Balzano, Marco. *I'm Staying Here*
Crow, Sarah McCraw. *The Wrong Kind of Woman*
Goodman, Carol. *The Sea of Lost Girls*
Hegi, Ursula. *Children and Fire: A Novel*
Heller, Zoe. *What Was She Thinking?: Notes on a Scandal*
Jalaluddin, Uzma. ★*Ayesha at Last*
Luesse, Valerie Fraser. *Under the Bayou Moon: A Novel*
Marshall, Catherine. *Christy*
Reynolds, Alastair. *Permafrost*
Richman, Alyson. *The Secret of Clouds*
Simonson, Helen. *The Summer Before the War: A Novel*
Spark, Muriel. ★*The Prime of Miss Jean Brodie*
West, Kathleen. *Minor Dramas & Other Catastrophes*
WOMEN TELEVISION JOURNALISTS
Bauer, Belinda. *The Beautiful Dead*
WOMEN TELEVISION NEWSCASTERS AND COMMENTATORS
Pride, Christine. ★*We Are Not Like Them*
Woods, Stuart. *New York Dead*

WOMEN TELEVISION PERSONALITIES
Byatt, A. S. *A Whistling Woman*
WOMEN TELEVISION PRODUCERS AND DIRECTORS
Elliott, Lexie. *The Missing Years*
Stratford, Sarah-Jane. *Red Letter Days*
Wilsner, Meryl. ★*Something to Talk About*
WOMEN TELEVISION WRITERS
Rowell, Rainbow. *Landline*
WOMEN TEXTILE WORKERS
Cash, Wiley. *The Last Ballad: A Novel*
WOMEN THIEVES
Bennett, Robert Jackson. *Foundryside*
Bennett, Robert Jackson. *Shorefall*
Bouchet, Amanda. *Nightchaser*
De Leon, Aya. *Side Chick Nation*
Hardiman, Rebecca. *Good Eggs*
Harrington, Anna. *An Extraordinary Lord*
Holton, India. *The Wisteria Society of Lady Scoundrels*
McCall Smith, Alexander. *Blue Shoes and Happiness*
Ridley, Erica. *The Duke Heist*
Robards, Karen. *The Ultimatum*
Yang, Susie. *White Ivy: A Novel*
WOMEN TRACK AND FIELD ATHLETES
Hooper, Elise. *Fast Girls: A Novel of the 1936 Women's Olympic Team*
WOMEN TRACKERS
Bradbury, Jamey. *The Wild Inside: A Novel*
WOMEN TRANSLATORS
Alameddine, Rabih. *An Unnecessary Woman*
Green, Amy Lynn. *Things We Didn't Say*
Perry, Sarah. *Melmoth: A Novel*
WOMEN TRAVEL AGENTS
Ko-Eun, Yun. *The Disaster Tourist*
WOMEN TRAVELERS
Alexander, Victoria. *The Lady Travelers Guide to Larceny with a Dashing Stranger*
Alexander, Victoria. *The Lady Travelers Guide to Scoundrels and Other Gentlemen*
Atilgan, Yusuf. *Motherland Hotel*
Bacon, Charlotte. *There Is Room for You*
Erdrich, Louise. *The Painted Drum: A Novel*
Jimenez, Abby. *Life's Too Short*
Spark, Muriel. *The Driver's Seat*
Woolf, Virginia. *The Voyage Out*
WOMEN UNDERWATER ARCHAEOLOGISTS
Cussler, Clive. *Serpent: A Novel from the Numa Files*
WOMEN VETERANS
Bledsoe, Alex. *The Hum and the Shiver*
Child, Lee. *The Midnight Line*
Coben, Harlan. *Fool Me Once*
Headley, Maria Dahvana. *The Mere Wife*
Laukkanen, Owen. *Lone Jack Trail*
Lindsey, Odie. *Some Go Home: A Novel*
Ramsay, Hope. *Summer on Moonlight Bay*
Sharp, Zoe. *Fox Hunter*
WOMEN VETERINARIANS
Chavez, Heather. *No Bad Deed*

WOMEN VICE-PRESIDENTS
Child, Lee. *Without Fail*
WOMEN VIGILANTES
Gardner, Lisa. ★*Look for Me: A Novel*
Gardner, Lisa. ★*Never Tell: A Novel*
Lelchuk, Saul. *Save Me from Dangerous Men: A Novel*
MacLean, Sarah. ★*Bombshell*
Pinter, Jason. *Hide Away*
WOMEN VIOLINISTS
Austin, Lynn N. *Chasing Shadows*
Gerritsen, Tess. *Playing with Fire*
Hoang, Helen. ★*The Heart Principle*
Williams, Synithia. *Forbidden Promises*
WOMEN VOLUNTEERS
DeLuca, Jen. ★*Well Met*
Racculia, Kate. ★*Tuesday Mooney Talks to Ghosts: A Novel*
WOMEN WAR CORRESPONDENTS
Deveraux, Jude. *Someone to Love*
WOMEN WAR PHOTOGRAPHERS
Soli, Tatjana. *The Lotus Eaters*
WOMEN WARRIORS
Clark, Cherae. ★*The Unbroken*
French, Jonathan. *The True Bastards*
Larkwood, A. K. *The Unspoken Name*
WOMEN WEREWOLVES
Spear, Terry. *A Billionaire Wolf for Christmas*
WOMEN WHEELCHAIR USERS
Brown, Rosellen. *Tender Mercies*
WOMEN WHO ARE BLIND
Black, Cara. *Murder in the Bastille*
Dunant, Sarah. *In the Company of the Courtesan: A Novel*
Lefteri, Christy. *The Beekeeper of Aleppo: A Novel*
Miller, Kei. ★*Augustown*
Shreve, Anita. *Eden Close: A Novel*
WOMEN WHO ARE DEAF
Banks, Maya. *Never Seduce a Scot*
Women who dare [Series]. Jenkins, Beverly
WOMEN WITH ALZHEIMER'S DISEASE
Palahniuk, Chuck. *Choke: A Novel*
WOMEN WITH AMNESIA
Bawden, Nina. *Family Money*
Daniels, Natalie. *Too Close*
Dodd, Christina. *What Doesn't Kill Her*
Grebe, Camilla. *After She's Gone: A Novel*
Harrison, Rachel. *The Return*
Riley, Vanessa. ★*An Earl, the Girl, and a Toddler*
Robinson, Peter. *The First Cut*
Wasserman, Robin. *Mother Daughter Widow Wife*
WOMEN WITH AUTISM
Gallen, Michelle. *Big Girl, Small Town: A Novel*
WOMEN WITH BIPOLAR DISORDER
Huisman, Violaine. *The Book of Mother*
WOMEN WITH BRAIN INJURIES
Genova, Lisa. *Left Neglected: A Novel*
WOMEN WITH CANCER
Bock, Charles. *Alice & Oliver: A Novel*
Coetzee, J. M. *Age of Iron*
Garner, Helen. *The Spare Room*

Hashemzadeh Bonde, Golnaz. *What We Owe*
McMurtry, Larry. ★*Terms of Endearment: A Novel : With a New Preface*
Nunez, Sigrid. *What Are You Going Through*
Shriver, Lionel. *So Much for That*
Stabenow, Dana. ★*A Taint in the Blood*

WOMEN WITH DEPRESSION
Bambara, Toni Cade. ★*The Salt Eaters*
Cullen, Helen. *The Dazzling Truth*
French, Nicci. ★*House of Correction*
Kimmel, Fran. *No Good Asking: A Novel*
Kirshenbaum, Binnie. *Rabbits for Food*
Mason, Meg. *Sorrow and Bliss*
Plath, Sylvia. ★*The Bell Jar*
Price, Reynolds. *Roxanna Slade*

WOMEN WITH DIABETES
McMillan, Terry. ★*It's Not All Downhill from Here: A Novel*

WOMEN WITH DISABILITIES
Binchy, Maeve. *Firefly Summer*
Mapson, Jo-Ann. *Bad Girl Creek: A Novel*

WOMEN WITH EPILEPSY
Johnson, Tara. *Engraved on the Heart*

WOMEN WITH MENTAL ILLNESSES
Billingsley, ReShonda Tate. ★*The Secret She Kept*
Cunningham, Michael. ★*The Hours*
Emezi, Akwaeke. *Freshwater*
Founds, Kathleen. *When Mystical Creatures Attack!*
Fowler, Therese. ★*Z: A Novel of Zelda Fitzgerald*
Gilman, Charlotte Perkins. ★*The Yellow Wallpaper and Selected Writings*
Kirshenbaum, Binnie. *Rabbits for Food*
Livesey, Margot. *Criminals: A Novel*
Plath, Sylvia. ★*The Bell Jar*
Purcell, Laura. *The Silent Companions: A Ghost Story*
Rendell, Ruth. ★*The Bridesmaid*
Rhys, Jean. ★*Wide Sargasso Sea*
Roy, Anuradha. *An Atlas of Impossible Longing*
Sebold, Alice. *The Almost Moon: A Novel*
Stridsberg, Sara. *Valerie: Or the Faculty of Dreams : Amendment to the Theory of Sexuality*

WOMEN WITH POLIOMYELITIS
Stegner, Wallace. *Crossing to Safety*

WOMEN WITH SCHIZOPHRENIA
Butler, Gwendoline. *Death Lives Next Door*

WOMEN WITH TERMINAL ILLNESSES
Adkins, Mary. *When You Read This*
Ashley & JaQuavis. *Murderville*
Coetzee, J. M. *Age of Iron*
Garner, Helen. *The Spare Room*
Higgins, Kristan. ★*Pack up the Moon*
Lively, Penelope. ★*Moon Tiger*
Pearson, Robin W. *A Long Time Comin'*
Schweblin, Samanta. *Fever Dream: A Novel*
Segal, Erich. ★*Love Story*

WOMEN WITNESSES
Collins, Manda. ★*A Lady's Guide to Mischief and Mayhem*
Dodd, Christina. *Obsession Falls*
Garrett, Kellye. ★*Hollywood Homicide*

Ide, Joe. ★*Hi Five: An IQ Novel*
Sandford, John. *Storm Prey*

WOMEN WIZARDS
Elliott, Kate. *Servant Mage*
Feehan, Christine. *Dark Illusion*
Gailey, Sarah. *Magic for Liars*
Muir, Tamsyn. *Harrow the Ninth*
Putney, Mary Jo. *The Marriage Spell: A Novel*

WOMEN ZOOLOGISTS
Lawson, Mary. *Crow Lake*

WOMEN'S FANTASIES
Shriver, Lionel. *The Post-Birthday World*

WOMEN'S HEALTH CENTERS AND CLINICS
Picoult, Jodi. *A Spark of Light: A Novel*

Women's Murder Club [Series]. Patterson, James

WOMEN'S ORGANIZATIONS
Holton, India. *The Wisteria Society of Lady Scoundrels*
Williams, Lara. *Supper Club: A Novel*

WOMEN'S POWER
Schanoes, Veronica L. *Burning Girls and Other Stories*

WOMEN'S RIGHTS
Dare, Abi. *The Girl with the Louding Voice*
Kidd, Sue Monk. ★*The Invention of Wings: A Novel*
Piercy, Marge. *Sex Wars*

WOMEN'S ROLE
Anam, Tahmima. *The Bones of Grace*
Atwood, Margaret. ★*The Handmaid's Tale*
Atwood, Margaret. *Moral Disorder*
Beams, Clare. *The Illness Lesson*
Chung, Catherine. *The Tenth Muse: A Novel*
Darznik, Jasmin. *Song of a Captive Bird: A Novel*
Davis, Fiona. *The Lions of Fifth Avenue: A Novel*
Eliot, George. ★*Middlemarch: A Study of Provincial Life*
Eliot, George. ★*The Mill on the Floss*
Fowler, Therese. *A Well-Behaved Woman: A Novel of the Vanderbilts*
Gibson, Claire. *Beyond the Point: A Novel*
Kowal, Mary Robinette. *The Calculating Stars: A Lady Astronaut Novel*
Le Guin, Ursula K. *The Birthday of the World: And Other Stories*
Macneal, Elizabeth. *The Doll Factory*
Mahmoud, Lena. *Amreekiya: A Novel*
Oates, Joyce Carol. *A Garden of Earthly Delights*
Perry, Anne. *A Dangerous Mourning*
Rose, M. J. ★*Cartier's Hope*
Tyler, Anne. *Vinegar Girl: The Taming of the Shrew Retold*
Weiner, Jennifer. ★*Mrs. Everything: A Novel*
Williams, Pip. *The Dictionary of Lost Words*
★*The **Women's** Room*. French, Marilyn

WOMEN'S SHELTERS
Kibler, Julie. *Home for Erring and Outcast Girls*
Moor, Jessica. *The Keeper*
Morrison, Toni. *Paradise*
*The **Women's** War*. Glass, Jenna
Women's war [Series]. Glass, Jenna

WOMEN-OWNED BUSINESSES
Montclair, Allison. *A Rogue's Company*
Montclair, Allison. *A Royal Affair*
Stradal, J. Ryan. ★*The Lager Queen of Minnesota*

WOMEN/WOMEN RELATIONS
Bloom, Amy. ★*White Houses: A Novel*
Brayden, Melissa. *First Position*
Kent, Kathleen. *The Burn*
Wieland, Liza. *Paris, 7 A.M.*
The Women: a Novel. Boyle, T. Coraghessan
★*The Wonder*. Donoghue, Emma
★*The Wonder Boy of Whistle Stop: A Novel*. Flagg, Fannie
★*Wonder Boys*. Chabon, Michael
The Wonder Bread Summer. Blau, Jessica Anya
The Wonder Garden. Acampora, Lauren
A Wonderful Stroke of Luck: A Novel. Beattie, Ann
Wonderland. Stage, Zoje
Wong, David
Futuristic Violence and Fancy Suits
This Book Is Full of Spiders: Seriously, Dude, Don't Touch It
Woo, Sung J.
Love Love: A Novel
Wood, James
Upstate
Wood, Shelley
The Quintland Sisters
Wood, Tracey Enerson
The Engineer's Wife: A Novel
The Woodcutter: a Novel. Hill, Reginald
★*Woodcutters*. Bernhard, Thomas
WOODEND, CHARLIE (FICTITIOUS CHARACTER)
Spencer, Sally. ★*A Dying Fall*
Woodrell, Daniel
The Maid's Version: A Novel
Woods, Chavisa
Things to Do When You're Goth in the Country: And Other Stories
Woods, Rita
★*Remembrance*
Woods, Stuart
Below the Belt
★*Bombshell*
Chiefs
A Delicate Touch
Fast & Loose
Hit List
The Money Shot
New York Dead
Orchid Beach
Palindrome
Santa Fe Rules
Skin Game
Smooth Operator
Stealth
Woodsburner: a Novel. Pipkin, John
Woodson, Jacqueline
★*Another Brooklyn*
★*Red at the Bone*
Wooing Cadie McCaffrey. Turner, Bethany
Woolf, Virginia
Between the Acts
Jacob's Room
★*Mrs. Dalloway*

Orlando: A Biography
★*To the Lighthouse*
The Voyage Out
The Waves
★*The Years*
WOOLF, VIRGINIA
Cunningham, Michael. ★*The Hours*
Furst, Alan. ★*Mission to Paris*
WORCESTERSHIRE, ENGLAND
Mitchell, David. *Black Swan Green: A Novel*
The Word Exchange: A Novel. Graedon, Alena
★*The Word Is Murder*. Horowitz, Anthony
WORDS
Williams, Eley. *The Liar's Dictionary*
Williams, Pip. *The Dictionary of Lost Words*
WORKAHOLICS
Forman, Gayle. *Leave Me: A Novel*
Hockman, Angie. *Shipped*
Lauren, Christina. *Dating You / Hating You*
Livesay, Tracey. *Like Lovers Do*
Obregon, Nicolas. *Blue Light Yokohama*
WORKAHOLISM
Fitzgerald, F. Scott. ★*The Last Tycoon: An Unfinished Novel*
WORKING CLASS
Davidson, Ash. ★*Damnation Spring*
Evison, Jonathan. ★*Lawn Boy: A Novel*
Finlay, Mick. *The Murder Pit*
Holmes, J. M. *How Are You Going to Save Yourself*
Russo, Richard. ★*Empire Falls*
Sherrill, Steven. *The Minotaur Takes His Own Sweet Time: A Novel*
Washington, Bryan. *Lot: Stories*
Welsh, Irvine. *Trainspotting*
Zaman, Nadeem. *Up in the Main House & Other Stories*
Zola, Emile. ★*Germinal*
WORKING CLASS AFRICAN AMERICANS
Mosley, Walter. *Devil in a Blue Dress*
WORKING CLASS BOYS
Stuart, Douglas. ★*Shuggie Bain*
WORKING CLASS FAMILIES
Barnett, David. *Calling Major Tom*
Conell, Lee. *The Party Upstairs*
Dee, Jonathan. *The Locals: A Novel*
Doyle, Roddy. *Paddy Clarke, Ha-Ha-Ha*
Haigh, Jennifer. *Baker Towers: A Novel*
Louis, Edouard. *The End of Eddy: A Novel*
McDermott, Alice. *Child of My Heart*
Moss, Sarah. *Ghost Wall: A Novel*
Oates, Joyce Carol. ★*Them*
Schultz, Connie. *The Daughters of Erietown*
Stuart, Douglas. ★*Shuggie Bain*
WORKING CLASS MEN
Barker, Pat. ★*The Ghost Road*
Kelman, James. *How Late It Was, How Late*
London, Jack. *Martin Eden*
WORKING CLASS NEIGHBORHOODS
Lehane, Dennis. ★*Mystic River*
WORKING CLASS WOMEN
Breslin, Jimmy. *Table Money*

Doyle, Roddy. ★*The Woman Who Walked into Doors*
Quincy, Diana. *The Viscount Made Me Do It*

WORKING DOGS
Burton, Jeffrey B. ★*The Finders: A Mace Reid K-9 Mystery*
Burton, Jeffrey B. *The Keepers: A Mace Reid K-9 Mystery*
Logan, Kylie. *The Secrets of Bones: A Mystery*

WORKING MOTHERS
Fabry, Chris. *War Room: Prayer Is a Powerful Weapon*
Forman, Gayle. *Leave Me: A Novel*
Pearson, Allison. ★*How Hard Can It Be?*
Phillips, Helen. *The Need: A Novel*

WORKING POOR PEOPLE
Louis, Edouard. *The End of Eddy: A Novel*
★*The World According to Garp: A Novel.* Irving, John
★*The World Doesn't Require You: Stories.* Scott, Rion Amilcar
World Enough and Time: A Romantic Novel. Warren, Robert Penn
World Gone By: A Novel. Lehane, Dennis
The World of All Souls: The Complete Guide to a Discovery of Witches, Shadow of Night, and the Book. Harkness, Deborah E.

WORLD POLITICS
Carter, Stephen L. *Back Channel*
Follett, Ken. *Edge of Eternity*
Follett, Ken. *Fall of Giants*
★*The World That We Knew.* Hoffman, Alice
The World to Come: Stories. Shepard, Jim

WORLD WAR I
Barker, Pat. ★*The Eye in the Door*
Barker, Pat. ★*The Ghost Road*
Diop, David. ★*At Night All Blood Is Black*
Dunmore, Helen. *The Lie*
Faulks, Sebastian. ★*Birdsong*
Follett, Ken. *Fall of Giants*
Forester, C. S. *The African Queen*
Hemingway, Ernest. ★*A Farewell to Arms*
Keneally, Thomas. ★*The Daughters of Mars*
Mann, Thomas. *The Magic Mountain*
Rash, Ron. ★*The Cove*
Russell, Mary Doria. *Dreamers of the Day: A Novel*
Steinbeck, John. ★*East of Eden*
Trumbo, Dalton. ★*Johnny Got His Gun*

WORLD WAR I — WOMEN
Bowen, Rhys. *The Victory Garden*

WORLD WAR I HOME FRONT
Stewart, Amy. ★*Dear Miss Kopp*
Stewart, Amy. *Kopp Sisters on the March*

WORLD WAR I VETERANS
Barker, Pat. *Another World*
Boschwitz, Ulrich Alexander. *The Passenger: A Novel*
Brown, Sandra. ★*Blind Tiger*
Hilton, James. *Random Harvest*
Kerr, Philip. ★*Metropolis: A Bernie Gunther Novel*
Mamet, David. *Chicago: A Novel*
Mukherjee, Abir. *Death in the East*
Mukherjee, Abir. *The Shadows of Men*
Mukherjee, Abir. *Smoke and Ashes: A Novel*
Smiley, Jane. *Some Luck*
Speller, Elizabeth. *The Return of Captain John Emmett*
Speller, Elizabeth. *The Strange Fate of Kitty Easton*

Trumbo, Dalton. ★*Johnny Got His Gun*

WORLD WAR II
Alderson, Kaia. *Sisters in Arms*
Allende, Isabel. *The Japanese Lover*
Atkinson, Kate. ★*Life After Life: A Novel*
Ballard, J. G. *Empire of the Sun: A Novel*
Balzano, Marco. *I'm Staying Here*
Beach, Edward L. *Run Silent, Run Deep*
Belfoure, Charles. *The Paris Architect: A Novel*
Benn, James R. *Billy Boyle: A World War Two Mystery*
Benn, James R. ★*The Red Horse: A Billy Boyle World War II Mystery*
Binder, L. Annette. *The Vanishing Sky*
Binet, Laurent. ★*HHhH*
Blake, Sarah. *The Postmistress*
Bohjalian, Chris. *Skeletons at the Feast: A Novel*
Bowen, Elizabeth. *The Heat of the Day*
Boulle, Pierre. *The Bridge Over the River Kwai: A Novel*
Brouwer, Sigmund. *Thief of Glory: A Novel*
D'Eramo, Luce. *Deviation*
Deutermann, Peter T. *The Nugget: A Novel*
Dick, Philip K. ★*The Man in the High Castle*
Doerr, Anthony. ★*All the Light We Cannot See: A Novel*
Downing, David. *Diary of a Dead Man on Leave*
Drndic, Dasa. *Trieste*
Duenas, Maria. *The Time in Between: A Novel*
Egan, Jennifer. ★*Manhattan Beach: A Novel*
Ellroy, James. *Perfidia*
Epstein, Jennifer Cody. ★*Wunderland: A Novel*
Escobar, Mario. *The Librarian of Saint-Malo: A Novel*
Fallada, Hans. *Every Man Dies Alone*
Faulks, Sebastian. *Charlotte Gray: A Novel*
Foer, Jonathan Safran. *Everything Is Illuminated: A Novel*
Follett, Ken. *Eye of the Needle*
Follett, Ken. *Jackdaws*
Follett, Ken. *Winter of the World*
Franck, Julia. *Blindness of the Heart*
Furst, Alan. *Spies of the Balkans: A Novel*
Furst, Alan. ★*Under Occupation: A Novel*
Gilbers, Harald. *Germania: A Novel of Nazi Berlin*
Gillham, David R. *City of Women*
Goddard, Robert. ★*Long Time Coming: A Novel*
Godwin, Gail. *Flora: A Novel*
Goonan, Kathleen Ann. *In War Times*
Hannah, Kristin. *The Nightingale*
Harmel, Kristin. *The Room on Rue Amelie*
Harris, Robert. *Enigma*
Hegi, Ursula. *Stones from the River*
Heller, Joseph. ★*Catch-22*
Hersey, John. ★*A Bell for Adano*
Higgins, Jack. *The Eagle Has Flown*
Higgins, Jack. *The Eagle Has Landed*
Indriðason, Arnaldur. *The Shadow District: A Thriller*
Jenoff, Pam. *The Lost Girls of Paris*
Jones, James. ★*From Here to Eternity*
Jones, James. ★*The Thin Red Line*
Kelly, Julia. *The Light Over London*
Kelly, Martha Hall. *Lilac Girls*
Kelly, Stephen. *The Wages of Desire: A World War II Mystery*

Keneally, Thomas. *Shame and the Captives: A Novel*
Kiernan, Stephen P. *Universe of Two*
Kosinski, Jerzy. ★*The Painted Bird*
Landragin, Alex. ★*Crossings: Consisting of Three Manuscripts : The Education of a Monster : City of Ghosts : Tales Of*
Mailer, Norman. ★*The Naked and the Dead*
Michener, James A. ★*Tales of the South Pacific*
Monsarrat, Nicholas. *The Cruel Sea*
Morelli, Laura. *The Stolen Lady*
Morton, Kate. *The Distant Hours: A Novel*
Orringer, Julie. ★*The Invisible Bridge: A Novel*
Otsuka, Julie. *The Buddha in the Attic*
Otsuka, Julie. *When the Emperor Was Divine: A Novel*
Pears, Iain. *The Dream of Scipio*
Pilcher, Rosamunde. *Coming Home*
Ramzipoor, E. R. *The Ventriloquists*
Remarque, Erich Maria. *A Time to Love and a Time to Die*
Rizzuto, Rahna R. *Shadow Child*
Robbins, David L. *War of the Rats: A Novel*
Rosnay, Tatiana de. ★*Sarah's Key*
Roy, Anuradha. *All the Lives We Never Lived: A Novel*
Runcie, James. *The Road to Grantchester*
Ryan, Jennifer. *The Spies of Shilling Lane: A Novel*
Saroyan, William. ★*The Human Comedy*
Sartre, Jean Paul. *Troubled Sleep*
Sebald, Winfried Georg. ★*Austerlitz*
Sebald, Winfried Georg. *The Emigrants*
Shaara, Jeff. *The Rising Tide: A Novel of World War II*
Shaara, Jeff. *The Steel Wave: A Novel of World War II*
Shimotakahara, Leslie. *After the Bloom*
Slimani, Leïla. *In the Country of Others*
Smith, Martin Cruz. *December 6*
Sundin, Sarah. *When Twilight Breaks*
Szabo, Magda. *Abigail*
Tan, Twan Eng. *The Garden of Evening Mists*
Van Booy, Simon. *The Illusion of Separateness*
Vonnegut, Kurt. *Armageddon in Retrospect: And Other New and Unpublished Writings on War and Peace*
Vonnegut, Kurt. ★*Slaughterhouse-Five: Or, the Children's Crusade : A Duty-Dance with Death*
Weaver, Ashley. ★*A Peculiar Combination*
Westheimer, David. ★*Von Ryan's Express*
Winspear, Jacqueline. *The American Agent*
Winspear, Jacqueline. ★*The Consequences of Fear: A Maisie Dobbs Novel*
Wouk, Herman. ★*War and Remembrance: A Novel*
Wouk, Herman. ★*The Winds of War: A Novel*
World War II [Series]. Robbins, David L.
WORLD WAR II — ART AND THE WAR
Ishiguro, Kazuo. *An Artist of the Floating World*
WORLD WAR II — CHILDREN
Frayn, Michael. *Spies: A Novel*
WORLD WAR II — INFLUENCE
Tsukiyama, Gail. *The Street of a Thousand Blossoms*
Uris, Leon. *Armageddon: A Novel of Berlin*
WORLD WAR II — JEWS
Bellow, Saul. *The Bellarosa Connection*
Keneally, Thomas. ★*Schindler's List*

Orringer, Julie. ★*The Flight Portfolio: A Novel*
Russell, Mary Doria. *A Thread of Grace: A Novel*
WORLD WAR II — NAVAL OPERATIONS
Deutermann, Peter T. *The Iceman*
Heggen, Thomas. *Mister Roberts*
WORLD WAR II — NAVAL OPERATIONS, AMERICAN
Heggen, Thomas. *Mister Roberts*
Wouk, Herman. ★*The Caine Mutiny: A Novel of World War II*
WORLD WAR II — PRISONERS AND PRISONS, GERMAN
Furst, Alan. ★*Under Occupation: A Novel*
Greene, Graham. *The Tenth Man*
WORLD WAR II — PRISONERS AND PRISONS, JAPANESE
Ballard, J. G. *Empire of the Sun: A Novel*
Flanagan, Richard. ★*The Narrow Road to the Deep North*
WORLD WAR II — RADAR
Follett, Ken. *Hornet Flight*
WORLD WAR II — REFUGEES
Orringer, Julie. ★*The Flight Portfolio: A Novel*
WORLD WAR II — UNDERGROUND MOVEMENTS
Hewson, David. *The Garden of Angels*
WORLD WAR II — WOMEN
Loigman, Lynda Cohen. *The Wartime Sisters: A Novel*
Mengiste, Maaza. ★*The Shadow King: A Novel*
WORLD WAR II — WOMEN'S PARTICIPATION
Piercy, Marge. *Gone to Soldiers: A Novel*
WORLD WAR II HOME FRONT
Bowen, Elizabeth. *The Heat of the Day*
Graves, Stephanie. *Olive Bright, Pigeoneer*
Green, Amy Lynn. *Things We Didn't Say*
Healey, Jane. *The Animals at Lockwood Manor*
Jensen, Nancy. *In Our Midst*
MacNeal, Susan Elia. *The King's Justice*
Ryan, Jennifer. *The Spies of Shilling Lane: A Novel*
Walsh, S. Kirk. *The Elephant of Belfast: A Novel*
World War II novels [Series]. Deutermann, Peter T.
World War II novels [Series]. Shaara, Jeff
WORLD WAR II VETERANS
Baldacci, David. ★*A Gambling Man*
Baldacci, David. ★*One Good Deed*
Binder, L. Annette. *The Vanishing Sky*
Dillard, Annie. *The Maytrees: A Novel*
Hazzard, Shirley. ★*The Great Fire*
Johnson, Craig. *Spirit of Steamboat: A Walt Longmire Story*
Jordan, Hillary. *Mudbound: A Novel*
McCarthy, Cormac. ★*No Country for Old Men*
Okuizumi, Hikaru. *The Stones Cry Out*
Robertson, Robin. *The Long Take: A Noir Narrative*
Runcie, James. *The Road to Grantchester*
Silko, Leslie Marmon. ★*Ceremony*
Sparks, Nicholas. ★*The Notebook*
Swift, Graham. ★*Last Orders: A Novel*
van Heemstra, Marjolijn. *In Search of a Name*
Wilson, Sloan. ★*The Man in the Gray Flannel Suit*
★***World** War Z: An Oral History of the Zombie War*. Brooks, Max
***World** Without End*. Follett, Ken
***World's** End Bureau* [Series]. Clare, Alys
***World's** End: A Novel*. Boyle, T. Coraghessan
***World's** Fair*. Doctorow, E. L.

WORMHOLES (ASTROPHYSICS)

Hamilton, Peter F. *Pandora's Star*

Wormwood trilogy [Series]. Thompson, Tade

WORRY IN GIRLS

Lodato, Victor. *Mathilda Savitch*

★*The* **Worst** *Best Man*. Sosa, Mia

Worth *Dying For: A Reacher Novel*. Child, Lee

Wouk, Herman

★*The Caine Mutiny: A Novel of World War II*

★*War and Remembrance: A Novel*

★*The Winds of War: A Novel*

WOUNDED KNEE, SOUTH DAKOTA

Brown, Dee. *Creek Mary's Blood: A Novel*

Woundhealer's *Story*. Saberhagen, Fred

WOUNDS AND INJURIES

Dell, Kari Lynn. *Mistletoe in Texas*

Kelly, Erin. *Watch Her Fall*

Kilalea, Katharine. *Ok, Mr. Field: A Novel*

Walschots, Natalie Zina. *Hench: A Novel*

Wrath *of the Furies: A Novel of the Ancient World*. Saylor, Steven

★*The* **Wreckage**. Robotham, Michael

The **Wrecker**. Cussler, Clive

WRECKERS (PLUNDERERS OF SHIPS)

Du Maurier, Daphne. *Jamaica Inn*

Wrexford and Sloane historical mysteries [Series]. Penrose, Andrea

The **Wright** *Sister*. Dann, Patty

WRIGHT, FRANK LLOYD, 1867-1959

Boyle, T. Coraghessan. *The Women: A Novel*

Smith, B. J. *All Hat: A Novel*

Wright, Jaime Jo

The Haunting at Bonaventure Circus

Wright, Lawrence

The End of October

Wright, Richard

The Man Who Lived Underground

★*Native Son*

WRITER'S BLOCK

Henry, Emily. *Beach Read*

Leigh, Eva. *Scandal Takes the Stage*

Oe, Kenzaburo. ★*Death by Water*

Writers *& Lovers: A Novel*. King, Lily

WRITING

Amis, Martin. ★*Inside Story*

Barclay, Linwood. *A Noise Downstairs: A Novel*

Boyd, William. *Trio*

Boyne, John. ★*A Ladder to the Sky*

Calvino, Italo. ★*If on a Winter's Night a Traveler*

Coetzee, J. M. *Elizabeth Costello*

Coetzee, J. M. *Summertime: Scenes from a Provincial Life*

Collins, Ciaran. *The Gamal*

Doyle, Rob. *Threshold*

Halliday, Lisa. ★*Asymmetry*

Henry, Emily. *Beach Read*

Kidd, Sue Monk. ★*The Book of Longings*

Kim, Young-Ha. *Diary of a Murderer: And Other Stories*

Miller, Henry. ★*Tropic of Cancer*

Miller, Henry. ★*Tropic of Capricorn*

Moore, Meg Mitchell. *The Islanders*

O'Brien, Tim. ★*The Things They Carried: A Work of Fiction*

Oyeyemi, Helen. *Mr. Fox*

Phillips, Arthur. *The Tragedy of Arthur: A Novel*

Powers, Richard. *Generosity: An Enhancement*

Roth, Philip. *The Ghost Writer*

Roth, Philip. *Zuckerman Bound*

Roth, Philip. *Zuckerman Unbound*

Saramago, Jose. *The History of the Siege of Lisbon*

Tobar, Hector. *The Last Great Road Bum*

Ugresic, Dubravka. *Fox*

Walton, Jo. *Or What You Will*

WRITING — PSYCHOLOGICAL ASPECTS

Prcic, Ismet. *Shards: A Novel*

Written *in My Own Heart's Blood*. Gabaldon, Diana

Written *in the Stars*. Bellefleur, Alexandria

Wrobel, Stephanie

Darling Rose Gold

★*The* **Wrong** *Case*. Crumley, James

The **Wrong** *End of the Telescope*. Alameddine, Rabih

The **Wrong** *Heaven: Stories*. Bonnaffons, Amy

The **Wrong** *Kind of Woman*. Crow, Sarah McCraw

The **Wrong** *Side of Goodbye*. Connelly, Michael

WRONGFUL DEATH

Dugoni, Robert. *Murder One*

★**Wunderland**: *a Novel*. Epstein, Jennifer Cody

★**Wuthering** *Heights*. Bronte, Emily

Wynette [Series]. Phillips, Susan Elizabeth

Wynne, Phoebe

Madam

WYOMING

Box, C. J. *The Disappeared*

Box, C. J. ★*Open Season*

Box, C. J. *Savage Run*

Box, C. J. *Trophy Hunt: A Joe Pickett Novel*

Box, C. J. *Vicious Circle*

Box, C. J. *Winterkill: A Novel*

Box, C. J. ★*Wolf Pack*

Brooks, Bill. *Frontier Justice*

Brooks, Bill. *Winter Kill*

Florio, Gwen. *Best Laid Plans*

Goodman, Jo. *In Want of a Wife*

Heller, Peter. *Celine: A Novel*

Jenkins, Beverly. *Tempest*

Jenkins, Beverly. *Wild Rain*

Johnson, Craig. *Land of Wolves*

Johnson, Craig. *Next to Last Stand*

L'Amour, Louis. ★*Bendigo Shafter*

Parrish, Roan. *Better Than People*

Proulx, Annie. *Bad Dirt: Wyoming Stories 2*

Proulx, Annie. *Fine Just the Way It Is: Wyoming Stories 3*

Schaefer, Jack. ★*Shane*

Wyoming stories [Series]. Proulx, Annie

Wyrd *Sisters*. Pratchett, Terry

X

X. Grafton, Sue
★*Xeni: a Marriage of Inconvenience*. Weatherspoon, Rebekah
Xenogenesis series [Series]. Butler, Octavia E.
XENOPHOBIA
Crace, Jim. *Harvest*
Kress, Nancy. *Tomorrow's Kin*
Okorafor, Nnedi. *Binti: Home*
Okorafor, Nnedi. *Binti: The Night Masquerade*

Y

Y Is for Yesterday. Grafton, Sue
Ya-Yas [Series]. Wells, Rebecca
YACHTS
Laurens, Stephanie. *The Pursuits of Lord Kit Cavanaugh*
MacDonald, John D. ★*The Lonely Silver Rain*
Yanagihara, Hanya
A Little Life: A Novel
Yang, JY
The Ascent to Godhood
The Black Tides of Heaven
The Descent of Monsters
The Red Threads of Fortune
Yang, Susie
White Ivy: A Novel
YANGTZE RIVER
See, Lisa. *Dragon Bones: A Novel*
Yates, Christopher J.
Grist Mill Road: A Novel
Yates, Richard
★*The Collected Stories of Richard Yates*
★*The Year of the Flood: A Novel*. Atwood, Margaret
The Year of the Runaways. Sahota, Sunjeev
Year's best science fiction (Gardner Dozois) [Series].
★*The Years*. Woolf, Virginia
The Years of Rice and Salt. Robinson, Kim Stanley
The Years with Laura Diaz. Fuentes, Carlos
Yellin, Jessica
Savage News
★*The Yellow Bird Sings*. Rosner, Jennifer
★*The Yellow Birds: A Novel*. Powers, Kevin
Yellow Moon: A Novel. Rhodes, Jewell Parker
★*The Yellow Wallpaper and Selected Writings*. Gilman, Charlotte Perkins
★*Yellow Wife*. Johnson, Sadeqa
YELLOWKNIFE, NORTHWEST TERRITORIES
Hay, Elizabeth. *Late Nights on Air*
YELLOWSTONE NATIONAL PARK
Barnett, Karen. *Ever Faithful*
Heller, Peter. *Celine: A Novel*
Yesterday's kin [Series]. Kress, Nancy
***Yesterday's** Weather: Stories*. Enright, Anne
*The **Yiddish** Policemen's Union*. Chabon, Michael
*The **Yield***. Winch, Tara June

Yocum, Robin
A Welcome Murder
Yoder, Rachel
Nightbitch
YOGA
Dev, Sonali. ★*Incense and Sensibility*
Yoga Pant Nation: A Novel. Gelman, Laurie
YOKNAPATAWPHA COUNTY (MISS. : IMAGINARY PLACE)
Faulkner, William. ★*Absalom, Absalom!*
Faulkner, William. ★*As I Lay Dying: The Corrected Text*
Faulkner, William. ★*Go Down, Moses*
Faulkner, William. *Uncollected Stories of William Faulkner*
*The **Yokota** Officers Club: A Novel*. Bird, Sarah
★*Yonder*. Asim, Jabari
Yoon, David
Version Zero
Yoon, Paul
★*Run Me to Earth: A Novel*
YORK, ENGLAND
Butland, Stephanie. *The Lost for Words Bookshop: A Novel*
Robb, Candace M. *The Cross-Legged Knight: An Owen Archer Mystery*
Robb, Candace M. *A Murdered Peace*
Robb, Candace M. *A Twisted Vengeance*
YORKSHIRE, ENGLAND
Atkinson, Kate. ★*Big Sky*
Austin, Finola. *Bronte's Mistress*
Ellis, Bella. *The Vanished Bride*
Gardam, Jane. *The Flight of the Maidens*
Mozley, Fiona. ★*Elmet*
O'Leary, Beth. *The Switch*
Ripley, Mike. *Mr Campion's Fault*
Robinson, Peter. *All the Colors of Darkness*
Robinson, Peter. *Close to Home*
Robinson, Peter. *Cold Is the Grave*
Robinson, Peter. *Friend of the Devil*
Robinson, Peter. *Innocent Graves: An Inspector Banks Mystery*
Robinson, Peter. *Piece of My Heart*
Robinson, Peter. *Playing with Fire*
Robinson, Peter. *Strange Affair*
Yoshimoto, Banana
The Lake
Moshi-Moshi
★*You Are Not Alone*. Hendricks, Greer
You Can't Keep a Good Woman Down: Stories. Walker, Alice
You Cannot Mess This Up: A True Story That Never Happened. Daughters, Amy Weinland
★*You Had Me at Hola*. Daria, Alexis
You Know When the Men Are Gone. Fallon, Siobhan
You May Kiss the Bride. Berne, Lisa
You Only Die Twice: A Britt Montero Mystery. Buchanan, Edna
You Only Live Twice. Fleming, Ian
You Should Pity Us Instead: Stories. Gustine, Amy
★*You Think It, I'll Say It: Stories*. Sittenfeld, Curtis
You Were There Too. Oakley, Colleen
You Will Know Me: A Novel. Abbott, Megan E.
You're Dead. Knopf, Chris
You've Been Volunteered: A Class Mom Novel. Gelman, Laurie

Youers, Rio
  Lola on Fire
YOUNG ADULTS
  Auster, Paul. *Sunset Park*
  Palahniuk, Chuck. *Pygmy*
  Smith, Zadie. ★*Nw: A Novel*
YOUNG GAY MEN
  Rice-Gonzalez, Charles. *Chulito*
  Silber, Joan. *Secrets of Happiness*
★*Young* Man with a Horn. Baker, Dorothy
YOUNG MEN
  Abdul-Jabbar, Kareem. ★*Mycroft Holmes*
  Bainbridge, Beryl. *Every Man for Himself*
  Bayard, Louis. *The Pale Blue Eye: A Novel*
  Bellow, Saul. *Dangling Man*
  Bernhard, Thomas. *Frost: A Novel*
  Chabon, Michael. ★*Wonder Boys*
  Chatterjee, Upamanyu. *English, August: An Indian Story*
  Darnielle, John. *Universal Harvester*
  Deb, Siddhartha. *The Point of Return: A Novel*
  Dickens, Charles. ★*David Copperfield*
  Durham, David Anthony. ★*Gabriel's Story*
  Ehirim, Nnamdi. *Prince of Monkeys*
  Fitzgerald, F. Scott. ★*This Side of Paradise*
  Flaubert, Gustave. *Sentimental Education*
  Ginzburg, Natalia. *Voices in the Evening*
  Giordano, Paolo. *The Human Body*
  Golding, William. *Close Quarters*
  Golding, William. *Fire Down Below*
  Golding, William. *Rites of Passage*
  Grossman, Lev. *The Magician King: A Novel*
  Grossman, Lev. *The Magician's Land: A Novel*
  Grossman, Lev. ★*The Magicians: A Novel*
  Hage, Rawi. *De Niro's Game*
  Harris, Robert. *The Second Sleep: A Novel*
  Heller, Peter. *The Guide*
  Hemingway, Ernest. *The Nick Adams Stories*
  Hesse, Hermann. *Narcissus and Goldmund*
  Indriðason, Arnaldur. *Reykjavik Nights: An Inspector Erlendur Novel*
  Joyce, James. ★*A Portrait of the Artist as a Young Man*
  K'wan. *Hoodlum*
  K'wan. *Street Dreams*
  Kerouac, Jack. *The Dharma Bums*
  Kerr, Philip. ★*Metropolis: A Bernie Gunther Novel*
  Lahiri, Jhumpa. ★*The Namesake*
  Larsen, Reif. *I Am Radar: A Novel*
  Lawrence, D. H. *Sons and Lovers*
  Le Carre, John. *Agent Running in the Field*
  Llewellyn, Richard. ★*How Green Was My Valley*
  Locke, Thomas. *Emissary*
  Louis, Edouard. *The End of Eddy: A Novel*
  Maguire, Gregory. *Son of a Witch: A Novel*
  Nugent, Benjamin. *Fraternity: Stories*
  Oe, Kenzaburo. ★*A Quiet Life*
  Palahniuk, Chuck. *Fight Club*
  Pamuk, Orhan. *The Red-Haired Woman*
  Percy, Walker. ★*The Moviegoer*
  Poe, Edgar Allan. *The Narrative of Arthur Gordon Pym of Nantucket*

  Prcic, Ismet. *Shards: A Novel*
  Roberts, Nora. *Chesapeake Blue*
  Saylor, Steven. *Raiders of the Nile: A Novel of the Ancient World*
  Shteyngart, Gary. *The Russian Debutante's Handbook*
  Veletzos, Roxanne. *The Girl They Left Behind*
  Waugh, Evelyn. *Decline and Fall*
  Waugh, Evelyn. ★*Vile Bodies*
  Welsh, Irvine. *Trainspotting*
  Woolf, Virginia. *Jacob's Room*
  Woolf, Virginia. *Orlando: A Biography*
YOUNG MEN — FAMILY RELATIONSHIPS
  Roth, Henry. *Requiem for Harlem*
YOUNG MEN — IDENTITY
  Conrad, Joseph. ★*Lord Jim*
YOUNG MEN — INTERPERSONAL RELATIONS
  Miller, Madeline. *The Song of Achilles*
YOUNG MEN — PERSONAL CONDUCT
  Fountain, Ben. ★*Billy Lynn's Long Halftime Walk*
  Roth, Philip. ★*Nemesis*
YOUNG MEN — RELATIONS WITH OLDER WOMEN
  Austin, Finola. *Bronte's Mistress*
  Balogh, Mary. *Someone to Trust*
  Barnes, Julian. *The Only Story*
  McMillan, Terry. ★*How Stella Got Her Groove Back*
  Roth, Henry. *Requiem for Harlem*
  Sackville-West, V. *The Edwardians*
  Williams, Tennessee. ★*The Roman Spring of Mrs. Stone*
YOUNG WIDOWS
  Allende, Isabel. *A Long Petal of the Sea: A Novel*
  Balogh, Mary. ★*Someone to Cherish*
  Bateman, Kate. *This Earl of Mine*
  Goodman, Jo. *A Touch of Forever*
  Hambly, Barbara. *Scandal in Babylon*
  Kleypas, Lisa. ★*Devil in Disguise*
  March, Emily. *Jackson*
  Neubauer, Erica Ruth. *Murder at the Mena House*
  Suri, Tasha. ★*Realm of Ash*
YOUNG WOMEN
  Abbott, Megan E. *Queenpin: A Novel*
  Arden, Katherine. ★*The Bear and the Nightingale*
  Arden, Katherine. ★*The Girl in the Tower*
  Arden, Katherine. ★*The Winter of the Witch*
  Atwood, Margaret. ★*The Handmaid's Tale*
  Atwood, Margaret. ★*The Year of the Flood: A Novel*
  Austen, Jane. ★*Pride and Prejudice*
  Austen, Jane. ★*Sense and Sensibility*
  Banasky, Carmiel. *The Suicide of Claire Bishop*
  Barnett, S. K. *Safe*
  Barry, Jessica. ★*Don't Turn Around*
  Bausch, Richard. *Hello to the Cannibals: A Novel*
  Beams, Clare. *The Illness Lesson*
  Bergstrom, Heather Brittain. *Steal the North: A Novel*
  Beukes, Lauren. *The Shining Girls*
  Bird, Sarah. ★*The Flamenco Academy: A Novel*
  Blau, Jessica Anya. *The Wonder Bread Summer*
  Brenner, Jamie. *Blush: A Novel*
  Bronte, Charlotte. ★*Jane Eyre*
  Bruni, Sarah. *The Night Gwen Stacy Died*

Burton, Jessie. *The Miniaturist*
Burton, Tara Isabella. *Social Creature*
Butler, Halle. *The New Me: A Novel*
Bynum, Sarah Shun-Lien. *Ms. Hempel Chronicles*
Chase, Loretta Lynda. *Don't Tempt Me*
Chevalier, Tracy. *A Single Thread*
Clark, Georgia. *The Bucket List*
Colette. *The Complete Claudine*
Conner, M. Shelly. *Everyman*
Crucet, Jennine Capo. *Make Your Home Among Strangers*
Cunningham, Michael. *Specimen Days*
Danler, Stephanie. *Sweetbitter*
Dare, Tessa. *A Week to Be Wicked*
Dektar, Molly. *The Ash Family*
Dickens, Charles. *Little Dorrit*
Diffenbaugh, Vanessa. *The Language of Flowers: A Novel*
Dimberg, Kelsey Rae. *Girl in the Rearview Mirror*
Divakaruni, Chitra Banerjee. *Oleander Girl: A Novel*
Donoghue, Emma. *Slammerkin*
Egan, Jennifer. ★*Manhattan Beach: A Novel*
Fitch, Janet. *Paint It Black: A Novel*
Forster, E. M. ★*A Room with a View*
Franzen, Jonathan. *Purity*
Gaitskill, Mary. *Veronica*
Gardam, Jane. *The Flight of the Maidens*
Gardner, Lisa. *The Neighbor*
Garriott, Leah. *Promised*
Gaskell, Elizabeth Cleghorn. ★*North and South*
Gilman, Laura Anne. *The Cold Eye*
Gilman, Laura Anne. *Silver on the Road*
Graves, Stephanie. *Olive Bright, Pigeoneer*
Green, Hank. *An Absolutely Remarkable Thing: A Novel*
Grenville, Kate. *Sarah Thornhill*
Haig, Matt. *The Midnight Library*
Hamya, Jo. *Three Rooms*
Harrington, Anna. *An Inconvenient Duke*
Harrison, M. John. *Nova Swing*
Hausmann, Romy. ★*Dear Child*
Hegi, Ursula. *The Vision of Emma Blau*
Hertmans, Stefan. ★*The Convert: A Novel*
Hirahara, Naomi. ★*Clark and Division*
Hoffman, Alice. *The Museum of Extraordinary Things: A Novel*
Holmes, Linda. ★*Evvie Drake Starts Over: A Novel*
Ishiguro, Kazuo. ★*Never Let Me Go*
James, Henry. *Daisy Miller*
James, Henry. *The Portrait of a Lady*
James, Rebecca. *The Woman in the Mirror*
Jewell, Lisa. *The Family Upstairs*
Joshi, Alka. *The Henna Artist*
Kantra, Virginia. ★*Meg and Jo*
Kincaid, Jamaica. ★*Lucy*
Levine, David D. *Arabella of Mars*
Marias, Javier. *The Infatuations*
Marillier, Juliet. *Daughter of the Forest*
Martin, Steve. *Shopgirl*
Mitford, Nancy. *Love in a Cold Climate*
Mitford, Nancy. ★*The Pursuit of Love: A Novel*
Moreno-Garcia, Silvia. ★*Gods of Jade and Shadow: A Novel*

Moshfegh, Ottessa. *My Year of Rest and Relaxation*
Moyes, Jojo. *Me Before You: A Novel*
Munro, Alice. *Lives of Girls and Women*
Munro, Alice. *Runaway: Stories*
Oates, Joyce Carol. ★*Them*
Oe, Kenzaburo. ★*A Quiet Life*
Okorafor, Nnedi. ★*Binti*
Okorafor, Nnedi. *Binti: Home*
Okorafor, Nnedi. *Binti: The Night Masquerade*
Oyeyemi, Helen. *The Opposite House*
Ozick, Cynthia. *Heir to the Glimmering World*
Packer, Ann. *The Dive from Clausen's Pier*
Qiu, Xiaolong. *Red Mandarin Dress: An Inspector Chen Novel*
Raheem, Zara. *The Marriage Clock: A Novel*
Raybourn, Deanna. *A Curious Beginning: A Veronica Speedwell Mystery*
Redondo, Dolores. *The North Face of the Heart*
Reid, Ava. *The Wolf and the Woodsman*
Reyes, Dolores. *Eartheater*
Richardson, Samuel. ★*Clarissa, Or, the History of a Young Lady*
Rimmer, Kelly. ★*The Warsaw Orphan: A Wwii Novel*
Roberts, Nora. ★*The Awakening*
Roberts, Nora. ★*The Becoming*
Rosen, Renee. *Dollface: A Novel of the Roaring Twenties*
Rous, Emma. *The Perfect Guests*
Russell, Mary Doria. *The Women of the Copper Country: A Novel*
Sager, Riley. *Final Girls: A Novel*
Sager, Riley. *The Last Time I Lied: A Novel*
Sayers, Constance. *The Ladies of the Secret Circus*
Schwartz, John Burnham. *The Commoner: A Novel*
Sharpe, Tess. *Barbed Wire Heart*
Shaykh, Hanan. ★*One Thousand and One Nights: A Sparkling Retelling of the Beloved Classic*
Shupe, Joanna. *The Prince of Broadway*
Spark, Muriel. ★*The Girls of Slender Means*
Spark, Muriel. ★*The Mandelbaum Gate*
St. James, Simone. *The Sun Down Motel*
Sterling, Erin. *The Ex Hex*
Suri, Tasha. ★*Empire of Sand*
Tarkington, Booth. ★*Alice Adams*
Towles, Amor. *Rules of Civility: A Novel*
Tyree, Omar. *For the Love of Money: A Novel*
Urrea, Luis Alberto. *The Hummingbird's Daughter: A Novel*
Van der Vliet Oloomi, Azareen. *Call Me Zebra*
Ware, Ruth. *The Death of Mrs. Westaway*
Weaver, Ashley. ★*A Peculiar Combination*
Welsh, Irvine. *Trainspotting*
Welty, Eudora. *The Optimist's Daughter*
Whitten, Hannah. *For the Wolf*
Williams, Lara. *Supper Club: A Novel*
Willis, Connie. *Crosstalk*
Wong, David. *Futuristic Violence and Fancy Suits*
Woolf, Virginia. *The Voyage Out*
YOUNG WOMEN — HISTORY
Austen, Jane. ★*Emma*
Faber, Michel. *The Crimson Petal and the White*
Thackeray, William Makepeace. ★*Vanity Fair: A Novel Without a Hero*

YOUNG WOMEN — PSYCHOLOGY
Center, Katherine. *How to Walk Away: A Novel*

YOUNG WOMEN — RELATIONS WITH OLDER MEN
Aciman, Andre. *Find Me*
Cruz, Angie. *Dominicana: A Novel*
Eliot, George. ★*Middlemarch: A Study of Provincial Life*
Hardy, Thomas. ★*Tess of the D'urbervilles: A Pure Woman Faithfully
Presented*
Marston, Edward. *The Wanton Angel: A Novel*
Sand, George. *Marianne*

YOUNG WOMEN — SEXUALITY
Shreve, Anita. *Fortune's Rocks: A Novel*

YOUNG, ANN ELIZA, B 1844
Ebershoff, David. *The 19th Wife: A Novel*
Faulks, Sebastian. *On Green Dolphin Street: A Novel*

Young, Heather
The Distant Dead

Youngson, Anne
Meet Me at the Museum

Your Blues Ain't Like Mine. Campbell, Bebe Moore
Your Face in Mine: A Novel. Row, Jess
★*Your* House Will Pay. Cha, Steph
Your Mouth Is Lovely: A Novel. Richler, Nancy

Yourcenar, Marguerite
★*Memoirs of Hadrian: And Reflections on the Composition of
Memoirs of Hadrian*

YOUTUBERS
Ripper, Kris. *The Love Study*

Yu, Charles
How to Live Safely in a Science Fictional Universe: A Novel
★*Interior Chinatown*

Yu, E. Lily
★*On Fragile Waves*

Yu, Miri
Tokyo Ueno Station

YUCATAN PENINSULA
Portis, Charles. ★*Gringos: A Novel*

YUGOSLAV WAR, 1991-1995
Novic, Sara. *Girl at War*

YUGOSLAVIA
Albahari, David. *Gotz and Meyer*
Grossman, David. ★*More Than I Love My Life: A Novel*

Yugoslavian trilogy [Series]. Andric, Ivo

YUKON TERRITORY
Armstrong, Kelley. *Alone in the Wild*
Armstrong, Kelley. *Watcher in the Woods*
London, Jack. ★*White Fang*

Yun, Jung
O Beautiful: A Novel

YUSSEF, OMAR (FICTITIOUS CHARACTER)
Rees, Matt. *The Fourth Assassin*

Z

★*Z*: a Novel of Zelda Fitzgerald. Fowler, Therese

Zaman, Nadeem
Up in the Main House & Other Stories

ZAMBIA
Serpell, Namwali. ★*The Old Drift*

Zamyatin, Yevgeny Ivanovich
★*We*

Zapata, Mike
The Lost Book of Adana Moreau

ZAVALA, JOE (FICTITIOUS CHARACTER)
Cussler, Clive. *Nighthawk: A Novel from the Numa Files*
Cussler, Clive. *The Pharaoh's Secret*

ZEN BUDDHISM
Kerouac, Jack. *The Dharma Bums*
Ozeki, Ruth L. *The Book of Form and Emptiness: A Novel*

Zeno's Conscience. Svevo, Italo
The Zero Game. Meltzer, Brad
Zero K: A Novel. DeLillo, Don
Zero Sum Game. Huang, S. L.

Zettel, Sarah
A Mother's Lie

Zhou, Haohui
Death Notice: A Novel

Zig and Nola novels [Series]. Meltzer, Brad

ZIMBABWE
Bulawayo, NoViolet. *We Need New Names: A Novel*
Dangarembga, Tsitsi. *This Mournable Body*

ZIONISM
Uris, Leon. ★*Exodus*

ZIONISTS
Agnon, Shmuel Yosef. ★*Only Yesterday*

Zo: a Novel. Miller, Xander
Zoey Ashe novels [Series]. Wong, David

Zola, Emile
★*Germinal*
★*Nana*

ZOMBIES
Anderson, Kevin J. *Death Warmed Over*
Brooks, Max. ★*World War Z: An Oral History of the Zombie War*
Buxton, Kira Jane. ★*Hollow Kingdom*
Depestre, Rene. *Hadriana in All My Dreams*
Grant, Mira. *Blackout*
Grant, Mira. *Deadline*
Grant, Mira. *Feed*
Grant, Mira. *Feedback*
Priest, Cherie. *Boneshaker*
Priest, Cherie. *Dreadnought*
Priest, Cherie. *Ganymede*
Priest, Cherie. *The Inexplicables*
Romero, George A. *The Living Dead*
Wellington, David. *Positive*
Whitehead, Colson. *Zone One: A Novel*
Wong, David. *This Book Is Full of Spiders: Seriously, Dude, Don't
Touch It*

★*The* Zone of Interest: A Novel. Amis, Martin
Zone One: A Novel. Whitehead, Colson
Zones of thought [Series]. Vinge, Vernor

ZOO ANIMALS
Broun, Bill. *Night of the Animals*

Zoo City. Beukes, Lauren
ZOO KEEPERS
    Walsh, S. Kirk. *The Elephant of Belfast: A Novel*
ZOOS
    Kerr, Laurel. *Wild on My Mind*

    Phillips, Gin. *Fierce Kingdom: A Novel*
Zorrie. Hunt, Laird
Zuckerman Bound. Roth, Philip
Zuckerman novels [Series]. Roth, Philip
Zuckerman Unbound. Roth, Philip